# Is it in Fo[...]
# Winter 2022–2023

A guide to the commencement of statutes
passed since 1st January 1960

**Compiled by the editorial staff of Halsbury's Statutes**

---

**Halsbury's Statutes Is it in Force? Summer 2022 should now be discarded.**

Is it in Force? Winter 2022–2023 includes the effect of commencement orders published up to 20 October 2022.

---

**LexisNexis® UK & Worldwide**

| | |
|---|---|
| United Kingdom | RELX (UK) Limited trading as LexisNexis®, 1–3 Strand, London WC2N 5JR |
| LNUK Global Partners | LexisNexis® encompasses authoritative legal publishing brands dating back to the 19th century including: Butterworths® in the United Kingdom, Canada and the Asia-Pacific region; Les Editions du Juris Classeur® in France; and Matthew Bender® worldwide. Details of LexisNexis® locations worldwide can be found at www.lexisnexis.com |

A CIP Catalogue record for this book is available from the British Library

ISBN: 978 1 4743 2104 4

Typeset by Letterpart Ltd, Caterham on the Hill, Surrey CR5 3XL

Printed and bound in Great Britain by CPI Group (UK) Ltd, Croydon, CR0 4YY

**Visit LexisNexis® UK at www.lexisnexis.co.uk**

# Contents

*Preface* .................................................................................................... iii
**Pre 1960 Acts** ...................................................................................... 1
**1960** ....................................................................................................... 3
**1961** ....................................................................................................... 17
**1962** ....................................................................................................... 29
**1963** ....................................................................................................... 41
**1964** ....................................................................................................... 57
**1965** ....................................................................................................... 79
**1966** ....................................................................................................... 93
**1967** ....................................................................................................... 105
**1968** ....................................................................................................... 125
**1969** ....................................................................................................... 157
**1970** ....................................................................................................... 179
**1971** ....................................................................................................... 195
**1972** ....................................................................................................... 217
**1973** ....................................................................................................... 239
**1974** ....................................................................................................... 263
**1975** ....................................................................................................... 291
**1976** ....................................................................................................... 327
**1977** ....................................................................................................... 349
**1978** ....................................................................................................... 365
**1979** ....................................................................................................... 383
**1980** ....................................................................................................... 401
**1981** ....................................................................................................... 431
**1982** ....................................................................................................... 453
**1983** ....................................................................................................... 475
**1984** ....................................................................................................... 493
**1985** ....................................................................................................... 515
**1986** ....................................................................................................... 541
**1987** ....................................................................................................... 585
**1988** ....................................................................................................... 601
**1989** ....................................................................................................... 637

| | | |
|---|---|---|
| **1990** | ........................................................................... | 673 |
| **1991** | ........................................................................... | 717 |
| **1992** | ........................................................................... | 753 |
| **1993** | ........................................................................... | 785 |
| **1994** | ........................................................................... | 821 |
| **1995** | ........................................................................... | 863 |
| **1996** | ........................................................................... | 909 |
| **1997** | ........................................................................... | 937 |
| **1998** | ........................................................................... | 977 |
| **1999** | ........................................................................... | 1063 |
| **2000** | ........................................................................... | 1129 |
| **2001** | ........................................................................... | 1257 |
| **2002** | ........................................................................... | 1293 |
| **2003** | ........................................................................... | 1383 |
| **2004** | ........................................................................... | 1513 |
| **2005** | ........................................................................... | 1621 |
| **2006** | ........................................................................... | 1689 |
| **2007** | ........................................................................... | 1847 |
| **2008** | ........................................................................... | 1935 |
| **2009** | ........................................................................... | 2019 |
| **2010** | ........................................................................... | 2071 |
| **2011** | ........................................................................... | 2127 |
| **2012** | ........................................................................... | 2175 |
| **2013** | ........................................................................... | 2269 |
| **2014** | ........................................................................... | 2317 |
| **2015** | ........................................................................... | 2395 |
| **2016** | ........................................................................... | 2441 |
| **2017** | ........................................................................... | 2495 |
| **2018** | ........................................................................... | 2537 |
| **2019** | ........................................................................... | 2577 |
| **2020** | ........................................................................... | 2597 |
| **2021** | ........................................................................... | 2627 |
| **2022** | ........................................................................... | 2699 |

# Pre 1960 Acts

## Easter Act 1928 (c 35)

*RA:* 3 Aug 1928

*Not yet in force*

---

# 1960 Acts

## Abandonment of Animals Act 1960 (8 & 9 Eliz 2 c 43)

*RA:* 2 Jun 1960

Whole Act in force 2 Jun 1960 (RA)

---

## Administration of Justice Act 1960 (8 & 9 Eliz 2 c 65)

*RA:* 27 Oct 1960

Whole Act in force 27 Oct 1960 (RA)

---

## Administration of Justice (Judges and Pensions) Act 1960 (9 & 10 Eliz 2 c 3)

*RA:* 20 Dec 1960

Whole Act in force 20 Dec 1960 (RA)

---

## Adoption Act 1960 (8 & 9 Eliz 2 c 59)

*RA:* 29 Jul 1960

Whole Act in force 29 Jul 1960 (RA)

---

## Air Corporations Act 1960 (8 & 9 Eliz 2 c 13)

*RA:* 22 Mar 1960

Whole Act in force 22 Mar 1960 (RA)

---

## Appropriation Act 1960 (8 & 9 Eliz 2 c 45)

*RA:* 29 Jul 1960

Whole Act in force 29 Jul 1960 (RA)

---

## Betting and Gaming Act 1960 (8 & 9 Eliz 2 c 60)

*RA:* 26 Jul 1960

*Commencement provisions:* s 31(1); Betting and Gaming Act 1960 (Commencement No 1) Order 1960, SI 1960/1556; Betting and Gaming Act 1960 (Commencement No 2) Order 1961, SI 1961/2092

| | | |
|---|---|---|
| 1 | | 1 May 1961 (SI 1960/1556) |
| 2 | (1) | 1 May 1961 (SI 1960/1556) |
| | (2) | 30 Sep 1960 (SI 1960/1556) |

**Betting and Gaming Act 1960 (8 & 9 Eliz 2 c 60)**—*contd*

| | | |
|---|---|---|
| 3 | | 1 Jun 1961 (SI 1960/1556) |
| 4 | (1) | 1 May 1961 (SI 1960/1556) |
| | (2)–(4) | 30 Sep 1960 (SI 1960/1556) |
| 5 | | 1 May 1961 (SI 1960/1556) |
| 6 | | 1 Dec 1961 (SI 1961/2092) |
| 7 | | 1 May 1961 (SI 1960/1556) |
| 8 | | 30 Sep 1960 (SI 1960/1556) |
| 9 | | 1 May 1961 (SI 1960/1556) |
| 10 | | 30 Sep 1960 (SI 1960/1556) |
| 11, 12 | | 1 May 1961 (SI 1960/1556) |
| 13, 14 | | 1 Aug 1961 (SI 1960/1556) |
| 15–18 | | 1 Jan 1961 (SI 1960/1556) |
| 19 | (1)–(4) | 1 Jan 1961 (SI 1960/1556) |
| | (5) | 30 Sep 1960 (SI 1960/1556) |
| 20–26 | | 1 Jan 1961 (SI 1960/1556) |
| 27, 28 | | 30 Sep 1960 (SI 1960/1556) |
| 29 | (1) | See Sch 4 below |
| | (2) | See Sch 5 below |
| | (3) | See Sch 6, Pt II below |
| | (4) | 30 Sep 1960 (SI 1960/1556) |
| 30 | | 30 Sep 1960 (SI 1960/1556) |
| 31 | (1), (2) | 30 Sep 1960 (SI 1960/1556) |
| | (3) | 26 Jul 1960 (RA) |
| Sch 1 | | 30 Sep 1960 (SI 1960/1556) |
| Sch 2 | | 1 May 1961 (SI 1960/1556) |
| Sch 3 | | 30 Sep 1960 (SI 1960/1556) |
| Sch 4 | | 1 Jan 1961 (amendments of Gaming Act 1845, s 11) (SI 1960/1556) |
| | | 1 May 1961 (otherwise) (SI 1960/1556) |
| Sch 5 | paras 1–3 | 1 May 1961 (SI 1960/1556) |
| | para 4 | 1 Jan 1961 (SI 1960/1556) amendments of— Betting and Lotteries Act 1934, ss 23(1), 24(3); Small Lotteries and Gaming Act 1956, s 1(3) |
| | | 1 May 1961 (otherwise) (SI 1960/1556) |
| | paras 5–16 | 1 May 1961 (SI 1960/1556) |
| Sch 6 | Pt I | 1 Jan 1961 (SI 1960/1556) |
| | Pt II | 1 Jan 1961 (SI 1960/1556), repeals of or in— Gaming Act 1845; Small Lotteries and Gaming Act 1956 (Amendment) Act 1959 |
| | | 1 May 1961 (except repeal of or in Street Betting Act 1906, s 1(3)) (SI 1960/1556) |
| | | 1 Dec 1961 (exception noted above) (SI 1961/2092) |

---

**British North America Act 1960 (9 & 10 Eliz 2 c 2)**

*RA:* 20 Dec 1960

*Commencement provisions:* s 3

Whole Act in force 1 Mar 1961 (s 3)

---

**Building Societies Act 1960 (8 & 9 Eliz 2 c 64)**

*RA:* 29 Jul 1960

*Commencement provisions:* s 77(4)

Whole Act in force 1 Oct 1960 (s 77(4))

---

## Caravan Sites and Control of Development Act 1960 (8 & 9 Eliz 2 c 62)

*RA:* 29 Jul 1960

*Commencement provisions:* s 50(4)

Whole Act in force 29 Aug 1960 (s 50(4))

---

## Charities Act 1960 (8 & 9 Eliz 2 c 58)

*RA:* 29 Jul 1960

*Commencement provisions:* s 49(3)

| | | |
|---|---|---|
| 1 | | 26 Jul 1960 (s 49(3)) |
| 2–37 | | 1 Jan 1961 (s 49(3)) |
| 38 | | 26 Jul 1960 (s 49(3)) |
| 39–46 | | 1 Jan 1961 (s 49(3)) |
| 47 | | 26 Jul 1960 (s 49(3)) |
| 48, 49 | | 1 Jan 1961 (s 49(3)) |
| Sch 1 | | 26 Jul 1960 (s 49(3)) |
| Schs 2–6 | | 1 Jan 1961 (s 49(3)) |
| Sch 7 | Pt I | 1 Jan 1961 (s 49(3)) |
| | Pt II | 26 Jul 1960 (s 49(3)) |

---

## Church Property (Miscellaneous Provisions) Measure 1960 (8 & 9 Eliz 2 No 1)

*RA:* 13 Apr 1960

Whole Act in force 13 Apr 1960 (RA)

---

## Cinematograph Films Act 1960 (8 & 9 Eliz 2 c 14)

*RA:* 22 Mar 1960

*Commencement provisions:* s 17(5)

| | | |
|---|---|---|
| 1–5 | | 24 Apr 1960 (s 17(5)) |
| 6–8 | | 1 Jan 1961 (s 17(5)(b)) |
| 9 | | 24 Apr 1960 (s 17(5)) |
| 10 | | 1 Jan 1961 (s 17(5)(b)) |
| 11–15 | | 1 Oct 1960 (s 17(5)(a)) |
| 16, 17 | | 24 Apr 1960 (s 17(5)) |
| Sch 1 | | 1 Oct 1960 (s 17(5)(a)) |
| Sch 2 | paras 1–5 | 1 Oct 1960 (s 17(5)(a)) |
| | paras 6, 7 | 24 Apr 1960 (s 17(5)) |
| | para 8 | 1 Jan 1961 (s 17(5)(b)) |
| | para 9 | 24 Apr 1960 (s 17(5)) |
| | paras 10, 11 | 1 Oct 1960 (s 17(5)(a)) |
| | paras 12, 13 | 24 Apr 1960 (s 17(5)) |
| | paras 14, 15 | 1 Jan 1961 (s 17(5)(b)) |
| | paras 16–21 | 24 Apr 1960 (s 17(5)) |
| Sch 3 | | 24 Apr 1960 (except repeals of or in Cinematograph Films Act 1938, s 44) (s 17(5)) |
| | | 1 Jan 1961 (exception noted above) (s 17(5)(b)) |

---

## Civil Aviation (Licensing) Act 1960 (8 & 9 Eliz 2 c 38)

*RA:* 2 Jun 1960

*Commencement provisions:* s 12(3); Civil Aviation (Licensing) Act (Commencement) Order 1960, SI 1960/1287; Civil Aviation (Licensing) Act (Commencement) (No 2) Order 1960, SI 1960/2093; Civil Aviation (Licensing) Act (Commencement) (No 3) Order 1961, SI 1961/304

| | | |
|---|---|---|
| 1 | (1) | 26 Jul 1960 (SI 1960/1287) |
| | (2) | 30 Mar 1961 (SI 1961/304) |
| | (3), (4) | 1 Dec 1960 (SI 1960/2093) |
| 2, 3 | | 1 Dec 1960 (SI 1960/2093) |
| 4 | | 1 Jan 1961 (SI 1960/2093) |
| 5 | | 26 Jul 1960 (SI 1960/1287) |
| 6 | | 30 Mar 1961 (SI 1961/304) |
| 7 | | 1 Jan 1962 (SI 1960/2093) |
| 8 | | 26 Jul 1960 (SI 1960/1287) |
| 9 | (a) | 30 Mar 1961 (SI 1961/304) |
| | (b) | 30 Mar 1961 (except in so far as it repeals Civil Aviation Act 1949, s 12) (SI 1961/304) |
| | | 31 Jul 1961 (exception noted above) (SI 1961/304) |
| | (c) | 31 Jul 1961 (SI 1961/304) |
| 10–12 | | 26 Jul 1960 (SI 1960/1287) |
| Schedule | | 26 Jul 1960 (SI 1960/1287) |

## Clean Rivers (Estuaries and Tidal Waters) Act 1960 (8 & 9 Eliz 2 c 54)

*RA:* 29 Jul 1960

*Commencement provisions:* s 2(4)

Whole Act in force 29 Sep 1960 (s 2(4))

## Coal Industry Act 1960 (8 & 9 Eliz 2 c 17)

*RA:* 22 Mar 1960

Whole Act in force 22 Mar 1960 (RA)

## Commonwealth Teachers Act 1960 (8 & 9 Eliz 2 c 40)

*RA:* 2 Jun 1960

Whole Act in force 2 Jun 1960 (RA)

## Consolidated Fund Act 1960 (8 & 9 Eliz 2 c 10)

*RA:* 22 Mar 1960

Whole Act in force 22 Mar 1960 (RA)

## Corporate Bodies' Contracts Act 1960 (8 & 9 Eliz 2 c 46)

*RA:* 29 Jul 1960

Whole Act in force 29 Jul 1960 (RA)

### Cyprus Act 1960 (8 & 9 Eliz 2 c 52)

*RA:* 29 Jul 1960

This Act generally had effect from 16 Aug 1960 (the "appointed day")

---

### Distress for Rates Act 1960 (8 & 9 Eliz 2 c 12)

*RA:* 22 Mar 1960

*Commencement provisions:* s 16(3)

Whole Act in force 1 Apr 1960 (s 16(3))

---

### Dock Workers (Pensions) Act 1960 (8 & 9 Eliz 2 c 39)

*RA:* 2 Jun 1960

2 Jun 1960 (RA)

---

### European Free Trade Association Act 1960 (8 & 9 Eliz 2 c 19)

*RA:* 22 Mar 1960

Whole Act in force 22 Mar 1960 (RA)

---

### Expiring Laws Continuance Act 1960 (9 & 10 Eliz 2 c 4)

*RA:* 20 Dec 1960

Whole Act in force 20 Dec 1960 (RA)

---

### Films Act 1960 (8 & 9 Eliz 2 c 57)

*RA:* 29 Jul 1960

*Commencement provisions:* s 52(2)

Whole Act in force 1 Jan 1961 (s 52(2))

---

### Finance Act 1960 (8 & 9 Eliz 2 c 44)

*RA:* 29 Jul 1960

The commencement details of Finance Acts are not set out, as the dates from which their provisions take effect are usually stated clearly and unambiguously in the text of the Act, and charging provisions will normally state for which year or years of assessment they are to have effect.

---

### First Offenders (Scotland) Act 1960 (8 & 9 Eliz 2 c 23)

*RA:* 13 Apr 1960

*Commencement provisions:* s 2(2)

Whole Act in force 13 May 1960 (s 2(2))

---

**Foreign Service Act 1960 (8 & 9 Eliz 2 c 11)**

*RA:* 22 Mar 1960

Whole Act in force 22 Mar 1960 (RA)

---

**Game Laws (Amendment) Act 1960 (8 & 9 Eliz 2 c 36)**

*RA:* 2 Jun 1960

*Commencement provisions:* s 6(4)

Whole Act in force 2 Aug 1960 (s 6(4))

---

**Gas Act 1960 (8 & 9 Eliz 2 c 27)**

*RA:* 13 Apr 1960

Whole Act in force 13 Apr 1960 (RA)

---

**Ghana (Consequential Provisions) Act 1960 (8 & 9 Eliz 2 c 41)**

*RA:* 2 Jun 1960

Whole Act in force 2 Jun 1960 (RA)

---

**Highland and Islands Shipping Services Act 1960 (8 & 9 Eliz 2 c 31)**

*RA:* 2 Jun 1960

Whole Act in force 2 Jun 1960 (RA)

---

**Horticulture Act 1960 (8 & 9 Eliz 2 c 22)**

*RA:* 22 Mar 1960

*Commencement provisions:* s 19; Horticulture Act 1960 (Commencement) Order 1961, SI 1960/804

| | |
|---|---|
| 1–8 | 22 Mar 1960 (RA) |
| 9–19 | 9 May 1960 (SI 1960/804) |
| 20–22 | 22 Mar 1960 (RA) |
| Schs 1, 2 | 22 Mar 1960 (RA) |

---

**House of Commons Members' Fund Act 1960 (8 & 9 Eliz 2 c 50)**

*RA:* 29 Jul 1960

Whole Act in force 29 Jul 1960 (RA)

---

**Indecency with Children Act 1960 (8 & 9 Eliz 2 c 33)**

*RA:* 2 Jun 1960

*Commencement provisions:* s 3(3)

Whole Act in force 1 Jul 1960 (s 3(3))

---

**Indus Basin Development Fund Act 1960 (9 & 10 Eliz 2 c 1)**

*RA:* 20 Dec 1960

Whole Act in force 20 Dec 1960 (RA)

---

**International Development Association Act 1960 (8 & 9 Eliz 2 c 35)**

*RA:* 2 Jun 1960

Whole Act in force 2 Jun 1960 (RA)

---

**Iron and Steel (Financial Provisions) Act 1960 (8 & 9 Eliz 2 c 26)**

*RA:* 13 Apr 1960

Whole Act in force 13 Apr 1960 (RA)

---

**Legal Aid Act 1960 (8 & 9 Eliz 2 c 28)**

*RA:* 13 Apr 1960

Whole Act in force 13 Apr 1960 (RA)

---

**Local Employment Act 1960 (8 & 9 Eliz 2 c 18)**

*RA:* 22 Mar 1960

*Commencement provisions:* s 29(2); Local Employment Act 1960 (Commencement) Order 1960, SI 1960/562

Whole Act in force 1 Apr 1960 (SI 1960/562)

---

**Marriage (Enabling) Act 1960 (8 & 9 Eliz 2 c 29)**

*RA:* 13 Apr 1960

Whole Act in force 13 Apr 1960 (RA)

---

**Matrimonial Proceedings (Magistrates' Courts) Act 1960 (8 & 9 Eliz 2 c 48)**

*RA:* 29 Jul 1960

*Commencement provisions:* s 19(3); Matrimonial Proceedings (Magistrates' Courts) Act 1960 (Commencement) Order 1960, SI 1960/2223

Whole Act in force 1 Jan 1961 (SI 1960/2223)

---

**Mental Health (Scotland) Act 1960 (8 & 9 Eliz 2 c 61)**

*RA:* 29 Jul 1960

*Commencement provisions:* s 117(1), (2); Mental Health (Scotland) Act 1960 (Appointed Day) Order 1960, SI 1960/2296; Mental Health (Scotland) Act 1960 (Appointed Day No 2) Order 1961, SI 1961/668; Mental Health (Scotland) Act 1960 (Appointed Day No 3) Order 1962, SI 1962/516

**Mental Health (Scotland) Act 1960 (8 & 9 Eliz 2 c 61)**—*contd*

| | | |
|---|---|---|
| 1 | | 1 Jan 1961 (so far as it causes to cease to have effect any provision of the Lunacy (Scotland) Acts 1857–1913 which prevents a patient who requires treatment for mental disorder from being admitted to any hospital for that treatment in pursuance of arrangements made in that behalf without any application or without any certificate or order rendering him liable to be detained) (SI 1960/2296) |
| | | 15 May 1961 (so far as it repeals Mental Deficiency and Lunacy (Scotland) Act 1913, s 26) (SI 1961/668) |
| | | 1 Jun 1962 (otherwise) (SI 1962/516) |
| 2–5 | | 1 Jun 1962 (SI 1962/516) |
| 6–14 | | 15 May 1961 (SI 1961/668) |
| 15–107 | | 1 Jun 1962 (SI 1962/516) |
| 108–110 | | 15 May 1961 (SI 1961/668) |
| 111 | | 1 Jun 1962 (SI 1962/516) |
| 112 | | See Sch 3 below |
| 113 | (1), (2) | See Schs 4, 5 below |
| | (3) | 15 May 1961 (so far as it repeals Mental Deficiency and Lunacy (Scotland) Act 1913, s 26) (SI 1961/668) |
| | | 1 Jun 1962 (otherwise) (SI 1962/516) |
| 114–118 | | 1 Jun 1962 (SI 1962/516) |
| Schs 1, 2 | | 1 Jun 1962 (SI 1962/516) |
| Sch 3 | paras 1, 2 | 15 May 1961 (SI 1961/668) |
| | paras 3–16 | 1 Jun 1962 (SI 1962/516) |
| Sch 4 | | 15 May 1961 (SI 1961/668), amendments of— |
| | | National Health Service (Scotland) Act 1947, ss 63, 80; |
| | | National Assistance Act 1948, ss 29(1), 41(1); |
| | | Children Act 1948, s 39; |
| | | Local Government Superannuation, Act 1953, s 15 |
| | | 1 Jun 1962 (otherwise) (SI 1962/516) |
| Sch 5 | | 15 May 1961 (SI 1961/668), repeals of or in— |
| | | Education (Scotland) Act 1946, s 58; |
| | | National Health Service (Scotland) Act 1947, ss 16, 17, 27, 28, 51, 80; |
| | | Local Government Superannuation Act 1953, s 15 |
| | | 1 Jun 1962 (otherwise) (SI 1962/516) |

---

**Merchant Shipping (Minicoy Lighthouse) Act 1960 (8 & 9 Eliz 2 c 42)**

*RA:* 2 Jun 1960

Whole Act in force 2 Jun 1960 (RA)

---

**Ministers of the Crown (Parliamentary Secretaries) Act 1960 (9 & 10 Eliz 2 c 6)**

*RA:* 20 Dec 1960

Whole Act in force 20 Dec 1960 (RA)

---

**National Insurance Act 1960 (9 & 10 Eliz 2 c 5)**

*RA:* 20 Dec 1960

*Commencement provisions:* s 6(3); National Insurance Act 1960 (Commencement) Order 1960, SI 1960/2421[1]

| | | |
|---|---|---|
| 1 | (1) | 20 Dec 1960 (RA) |
| | (2) | See Sch 1, Pt II below |
| | (3) | See Sch 1, Pt III below |

**National Insurance Act 1960 (9 & 10 Eliz 2 c 5)**—*contd*

| | | |
|---|---|---|
| 2 | (1) | 20 Dec 1960 (RA) |
| | (2) | See Sch 3 below |
| | (3) | 3 Apr 1961 (SI 1960/2421) |
| | (4), (5) | 20 Dec 1960 (RA) |
| 3 | | 30 Dec 1960 (SI 1960/2421) |
| 4, 5 | | 20 Dec 1960 (RA) |
| 6 | (1)–(3) | 20 Dec 1960 (RA) |
| | (4) | See Sch 6 below |
| | (5) | 20 Dec 1960 (RA) |
| Sch 1 | Pt I | 20 Dec 1960 (RA) |
| | Pt II | 3 Apr 1961 (so far as relates to higher rates and amounts of benefit under National Insurance (Industrial Injuries) Act 1946, in the case of death benefit) (SI 1960/2421) |
| | | 5 Apr 1961 (so far as relates to higher rates and amounts of benefit under National Insurance (Industrial Injuries) Act 1946, in the case of any benefit, other than death benefit) (SI 1960/2421) |
| | Pt III | 3 Apr 1961 (so far as relates to amendments of National Insurance (Industrial Injuries) Act 1946, ss 21, 30, Sch 4) (SI 1960/2421) |
| | | 5 Apr 1961 (so far as relates to amendments of National Insurance (Industrial Injuries) Act 1946, ss 14, 29) (SI 1960/2421) |
| Sch 2 | | 20 Dec 1960 (RA) |
| Sch 3 | | 3 Apr 1961 (so far as relates to higher rates of benefit under the National Insurance Act 1946, in the case of maternity allowance, widow's benefit, guardian's allowance, retirement pension and child's special allowance) (SI 1960/2421) |
| | | 6 Apr 1961 (so far as relates to higher rates of benefit under the National Insurance Act 1946, in the case of unemployment benefit and sickness benefit) (SI 1960/2421) |
| Sch 4 | para 1 | 20 Dec 1960 (RA) |
| | paras 2–5 | 3 Apr 1961 (SI 1960/2421) |
| | paras 6, 7 | 20 Dec 1960 (RA) |
| Sch 5 | | 20 Dec 1960 (RA) |
| Sch 6 | | 6 Apr 1961 (SI 1960/2421), repeals of or in— National Insurance Act 1951, Schedule, para 4; National Insurance (No 2) Act 1957, ss 1, 2(1), (3), (4), Schs 1–3, Sch 4, Pts I, III, Sch 5 (except so far as relates to the National Insurance Act 1946, s 72); National Insurance Act 1959, Sch 1 |
| | | 30 Dec 1960 (otherwise) (SI 1960/2421) |

[1]   For transitional provisions and savings, see SI 1960/2421, arts 2, 3

---

**Nigeria Independence Act 1960 (8 & 9 Eliz 2 c 55)**

*RA:* 29 Jul 1960

This Act generally had effect from 1 Oct 1960 (the "appointed day")

---

**Noise Abatement Act 1960 (8 & 9 Eliz 2 c 68)**

*RA:* 27 Oct 1960

*Commencement provisions:* s 5(3)

Whole Act in force 27 Nov 1960 (s 5(3))

---

## Occupiers Liability (Scotland) Act 1960 (8 & 9 Eliz 2 c 30)

*RA:* 2 Jun 1960

*Commencement provisions:* s 5(2)

Whole Act in force 2 Sep 1960 (s 5(2))

---

## Offices Act 1960 (8 & 9 Eliz 2 c 47)

*RA:* 29 Jul 1960

*Commencement provisions:* s 15(1)

Whole Act in force 1 Jan 1962 (s 15(1))

---

## Oil Burners (Standards) Act 1960 (8 & 9 Eliz 2 c 53)

*RA:* 29 Jul 1960

*Commencement provisions:* s 9(2)

Whole Act in force 1 Jan 1961 (s 9(2))

---

## Pawnbrokers Act 1960 (8 & 9 Eliz 2 c 24)

*RA:* 13 Apr 1960

*Commencement provisions:* s 7(1)

Whole Act in force 13 May 1960 (s 7(1))

---

## Payment of Wages Act 1960 (8 & 9 Eliz 2 c 37)

*RA:* 2 Jun 1960

*Commencement provisions:* s 9(2), (3); Payment of Wages Act 1960 (Appointed Day) Order 1963, SI 1963/19

| | | |
|---|---|---|
| 1 | (1), (2) | 2 Dec 1960 (s 9(3)) |
| | (3)(a)–(c) | 2 Dec 1960 (s 9(3)) |
| | (3)(d) | 1 Mar 1963 (SI 1963/19) |
| 2 | | 2 Jul 1960 (for the purposes of s 4) (s 9(2)) |
| | | 2 Dec 1960 (otherwise) (s 9(3)) |
| 3 | | 2 Dec 1960 (s 9(3)) |
| 4 | | 2 Jul 1960 (s 9(2)) |
| 5–7 | | 2 Jul 1960 (for the purposes of s 4) (s 9(2)) |
| | | 2 Dec 1960 (otherwise) (s 9(3)) |
| 8 | | 2 Jun 1960 (RA) |
| 9 | | 2 Dec 1960 (s 9(3)) |
| Schedule | | 2 Jul 1960 (for the purposes of s 4) (s 9(2)) |
| | | 2 Dec 1960 (otherwise) (s 9(3)) |

---

## Population (Statistics) Act 1960 (8 & 9 Eliz 2 c 32)

*RA:* 2 Jun 1960

*Commencement provisions:* s 5(3)

| | |
|---|---|
| 1 | 1 Jan 1961 (s 5(3)) |
| 2–4 | 1 Oct 1960 (s 5(3)) |
| 5 | 2 Jan 1960 (RA) |

**Population (Statistics) Act 1960 (8 & 9 Eliz 2 c 32)**—*contd*
Schedule                                 1 Jan 1961 (s 5(3))

---

**Professions Supplementary to Medicine Act 1960 (8 & 9 Eliz 2 c 66)**

*RA:* 27 Oct 1960

*Commencement provisions:* s 14(3); Professions Supplementary to Medicine Act 1960 (Commencement No 1) Order 1961, SI 1961/1201; Professions Supplementary to Medicine Act 1960 (Commencement No 2) Order 1962, SI 1962/828; Professions Supplementary to Medicine Act 1960 (Commencement No 3) Order 1962, SI 1962/1651; Professions Supplementary to Medicine Act 1960 (Commencement No 4) Order 1963, SI 1963/1044; Professions Supplementary to Medicine Act 1960 (Commencement No 5) Order 1964, SI 1964/927

| | | |
|---|---|---|
| 1 | | 1 Jul 1961 (SI 1961/1201) |
| 2 | | 1 May 1962 (SI 1962/828) |
| 3, 4 | | 17 Sep 1962 (SI 1962/1651) |
| 5 | | 30 Jun 1963 (SI 1963/1044) |
| 6 | (1) | 17 Sep 1962 (SI 1962/1651) |
| | (2) | 31 Dec 1963 (SI 1963/1044) |
| 7 | | 17 Sep 1962 (SI 1962/1651) |
| 8, 9 | | 1 Jul 1964 (SI 1964/927) |
| 10 | | 1 May 1962 (SI 1962/828) |
| 11–14 | | 1 Jul 1961 (SI 1961/1201) |
| Sch 1 | | 1 Jul 1961 (SI 1961/1201) |
| Sch 2 | | 1 Jul 1964 (SI 1964/927) |

---

**Public Bodies (Admission to Meetings) Act 1960 (8 & 9 Eliz 2 c 67)**

*RA:* 27 Oct 1960

*Commencement provisions:* s 3(4)

Whole Act in force 1 Jan 1961 (s 3(4))

---

**Public Health Laboratory Service Act 1960 (8 & 9 Eliz 2 c 49)**

*RA:* 29 Jul 1960

*Commencement provisions:* s 5(3); Public Health Laboratory Service (Appointed Day) Order 1961, SI 1961/1408

Whole Act in force 1 Aug 1961 (SI 1961/1408)

---

**Radioactive Substances Act 1960 (8 & 9 Eliz 2 c 34)**

*RA:* 2 Jun 1960

*Commencement provisions:* s 19(1); Radioactive Substances Act 1960 (Appointed Day) Order 1962, SI 1962/2604

Whole Act in force 1 Dec 1962 (SI 1962/2604)

---

**Requisitioned Houses Act 1960 (8 & 9 Eliz 2 c 20)**

*RA:* 22 Mar 1960

Whole Act in force 22 Mar 1960 (RA)

---

## Road Traffic Act 1960 (8 & 9 Eliz 2 c 16)

*RA:* 22 Mar 1960

*Commencement provisions:* s 270, Sch 20

| | | |
|---|---|---|
| 1–18 | | 1 Sep 1960 (s 270(1)) |
| 19 | (1) | 1 Sep 1960 (s 270(1)) |
| | (2) | *Never in force* (repealed) |
| | (3) | 1 Sep 1960 (s 270(1)) |
| 20–40 | | 1 Sep 1960 (s 270(1)) |
| 41 | | *Never in force* (repealed) |
| 42–65 | | 1 Sep 1960 (s 270(1)) |
| 66, 67 | | *Never in force* (repealed) |
| 68–101 | | 1 Sep 1960 (s 270(1)) |
| 102 | (1)–(3) | 1 Sep 1960 (s 270(1)) |
| | (4) | *Never in force* (repealed) |
| 103–265 | | 1 Sep 1960 (s 270(1)) |
| 266 | | *Never in force* (repealed) |
| 267–270 | | 1 Sep 1960 (s 270(1)) |
| Schs 1–7 | | 1 Sep 1960 (s 270(1)) |
| Sch 8 | | *Never in force* (repealed) |
| Schs 9–17 | | 1 Sep 1960 (s 270(1)) |
| Sch 18 | | 1 Sep 1960 (except repeals of or in Road Traffic Act 1956, ss 2, 3, 4(3), (4), 18(1), Sch 1) (s 270(1)) |
| | | *Never in force* (exception noted above) (repealed) |
| Schs 19, 20 | | 1 Sep 1960 (s 270(1)) |

## Road Traffic and Roads Improvement Act 1960 (8 & 9 Eliz 2 c 63)

*RA:* 29 Jul 1960

*Commencement provisions:* s 25(2)

Whole Act in force 1 Sep 1960 (s 25(2))

## Road Traffic (Amendment) Act 1960 (8 & 9 Eliz 2 c 51)

*RA:* 29 Jul 1960

Whole Act in force 29 Jul 1960 (RA)

## Road Traffic (Driving of Motor Cycles) Act 1960 (8 & 9 Eliz 2 c 69)

*RA:* 27 Oct 1960

Whole Act in force 27 Oct 1960 (RA)

## Statute Law Revision Act 1960 (8 & 9 Eliz 2 c 56)

*RA:* 29 Jul 1960

Whole Act in force 29 Jul 1960 (RA)

## Wages Arrestment Limitation (Amendment) (Scotland) Act 1960 (8 & 9 Eliz 2 c 21)

*RA:* 22 Mar 1960

*Commencement provisions:* s 2(2)

**Wages Arrestment Limitation (Amendment) (Scotland) Act 1960 (8 & 9 Eliz 2 c 21)**—*contd*
Whole Act in force 22 Apr 1960 (s 2(2))

**War Damage (Clearance Payments) Act 1960 (8 & 9 Eliz 2 c 25)**

*RA:* 13 Apr 1960

Whole Act in force 13 Apr 1960 (RA)

**Water Officers Compensation Act 1960 (8 & 9 Eliz 2 c 15)**

*RA:* 22 Mar 1960

*Commencement provisions:* s 2(2); Water Officers Compensation Act 1960 (Commencement) Order 1964, SI 1964/352

Whole Act in force 1 Apr 1964 (SI 1964/352)

# 1961 Acts

## Agricultural Research etc (Pensions) Act 1961 (9 & 10 Eliz 2 c 9)

*RA:* 2 Mar 1961

Whole Act in force 2 Mar 1961 (RA)

---

## Appropriation Act 1961 (9 & 10 Eliz 2 c 59)

*RA:* 3 Aug 1961

Whole Act in force 3 Aug 1961 (RA)

---

## Army and Air Force Act 1961 (9 & 10 Eliz 2 c 52)

*RA:* 27 Jul 1961

*Commencement provisions:* s 39(3)

| | |
|---|---|
| 1 | 27 Jul 1961 (RA) |
| 2–16 | 1 Jan 1962 (s 39(3)) |
| 17 | 27 Jul 1961 (RA) |
| 18–35 | 1 Jan 1962 (s 39(3)) |
| 36, 37 | 27 Jul 1961 (RA) |
| 38 | 1 Jan 1962 (s 39(3)) |
| 39 | 27 Jul 1961 (RA) |
| Schs 1–3 | 1 Jan 1962 (s 39(3)) |

---

## Baptismal Registers Measure 1961 (9 & 10 Eliz 2 No 2)

*RA:* 3 Aug 1961

Whole Measure in force 3 Aug 1961 (RA)

---

## Barristers (Qualification for Office) Act 1961 (9 & 10 Eliz 2 c 44)

*RA:* 19 Jul 1961

Whole Act in force 19 Jul 1961 (RA)

---

## Betting Levy Act 1961 (9 & 10 Eliz 2 c 17)

*RA:* 28 Mar 1961

*Commencement provisions:* s 10(2); Betting Levy Act 1961 (Commencement) Order 1961, SI 1961/1545

| | |
|---|---|
| 1 | 1 Sep 1961 (except for the purposes of assessing and collecting monetary contributions from bookmakers and the Totalisator Board) (1961/1545) |

**Betting Levy Act 1961 (9 & 10 Eliz 2 c 17)**—*contd*

|  |  |  |
|---|---|---|
|  |  | 1 Apr 1962 (exception noted above) (SI 1961/1545) |
| 2 | (1)(a) | 1 Jan 1962 (SI 1961/1545) |
|  | (1)(b), (c) | 1 Sep 1961 (except for the purposes of assessing and collecting monetary contributions from bookmakers and the Totalisator Board) (1961/1545) |
|  |  | 1 Apr 1962 (exception noted above) (SI 1961/1545) |
|  | (1)(d) | 1 Sep 1961 (except in so far as it relates to activities in which under para (a) the Levy Board are empowered to engage) (SI 1961/1545) |
|  |  | 1 Jan 1962 (exception noted above) (SI 1961/1545) |
|  | (1)(e) | 1 Sep 1961 (except for the purposes of assessing and collecting monetary contributions from bookmakers and the Totalisator Board) (1961/1545) |
|  |  | 1 Apr 1962 (exception noted above) (SI 1961/1545) |
|  | (2)(a), (b) | 1 Sep 1961 (except for the purposes of assessing and collecting monetary contributions from bookmakers and the Totalisator Board) (1961/1545) |
|  |  | 1 Apr 1962 (exception noted above) (SI 1961/1545) |
|  | (2)(c), (d) | 1 Jan 1962 (SI 1961/1545) |
| 3–6 |  | 1 Sep 1961 (except for the purposes of assessing and collecting monetary contributions from bookmakers and the Totalisator Board) (1961/1545) |
|  |  | 1 Apr 1962 (exception noted above) (SI 1961/1545) |
| 7 | (1)–(5) | 1 Sep 1961 (except for the purposes of assessing and collecting monetary contributions from bookmakers and the Totalisator Board) (1961/1545) |
|  |  | 1 Apr 1962 (exception noted above) (SI 1961/1545) |
|  | (6), (7) | 1 Jan 1962 (SI 1961/1545) |
|  | (8) | 1 Sep 1961 (except for the purposes of assessing and collecting monetary contributions from bookmakers and the Totalisator Board) (1961/1545) |
|  |  | 1 Apr 1962 (exception noted above) (SI 1961/1545) |
| 8 |  | 1 Jan 1962 (SI 1961/1545) |
| 9, 10 |  | 1 Sep 1961 (except for the purposes of assessing and collecting monetary contributions from bookmakers and the Totalisator Board) (1961/1545) |
|  |  | 1 Apr 1962 (exception noted above) (SI 1961/1545) |
| Schs 1, 2 |  | 1 Sep 1961 (except for the purposes of assessing and collecting monetary contributions from bookmakers and the Totalisator Board) (1961/1545) |
|  |  | 1 Apr 1962 (exception noted above) (SI 1961/1545) |

---

**Carriage by Air Act 1961 (9 & 10 Eliz 2 c 27)**

*RA:* 22 Jun 1961

*Commencement provisions:* ss 1(3), 14(3); Carriage by Air (Convention) Order 1967, SI 1967/479

|  |  |
|---|---|
| 1 | 1 Jun 1967 (SI 1967/479) |
| 2–14 | 22 Jun 1961 (RA) (note that although many provisions of this Act came technically into force on 22 Jun 1961 on receiving royal assent, those provisions which relate to the Convention set out in Sch 1 did not come into full force and effect until the Convention came into force in the United Kingdom on 1 Jun 1967 by virtue of SI 1967/479) |
| Schs 1, 2 | 1 Jun 1967 (SI 1967/479) |

---

**Clergy Pensions Measure 1961 (9 & 10 Eliz 2 No 3)**

*RA:* 3 Aug 1961

Whole Measure in force 3 Aug 1961 (RA)

---

**Coal Industry Act 1961 (10 & 11 Eliz 2 c 5)**

*RA:* 20 Dec 1961

Whole Act in force 20 Dec 1961 (RA)

**Companies (Floating Charges) (Scotland) Act 1961 (9 & 10 Eliz 2 c 46)**

*RA:* 27 Jul 1961

*Commencement provisions:* s 9(3)

Whole Act in force 27 Oct 1961 (s 9(3))

**Consolidated Fund Act 1961 (9 & 10 Eliz 2 c 7)**

*RA:* 2 Mar 1961

Whole Act in force 2 Mar 1961 (RA)

**Consolidated Fund (No 2) Act 1961 (9 & 10 Eliz 2 c 12)**

*RA:* 28 Mar 1961

Whole Act in force 28 Mar 1961 (RA)

**Consumer Protection Act 1961 (9 & 10 Eliz 2 c 40)**

*RA:* 19 Jul 1961

*Commencement provisions:* s 7(2)

Whole Act in force 19 Aug 1961 (s 7(2))

**Court of Chancery of Lancaster (Amendment) Act 1961 (9 & 10 Eliz 2 c 38)**

*RA:* 19 Jul 1961

Whole Act in force 19 Jul 1961 (RA)

**Covent Garden Market Act 1961 (9 & 10 Eliz 2 c 49)**

*RA:* 27 Jul 1961

Whole Act in force 27 Jul 1961 (RA)

**Credit-Sale Agreements (Scotland) Act 1961 (9 & 10 Eliz 2 c 56)**

*RA:* 27 Jul 1961

*Commencement provisions:* s 2(2)

Whole Act in force 27 Aug 1961 (s 2(2))

## Criminal Justice Act 1961 (9 & 10 Eliz 2 c 39)

*RA:* 19 Jul 1961

*Commencement provisions*: s 44(1); Criminal Justice Act 1961 (Commencement No 1) Order 1961, SI 1961/1672; Criminal Justice Act 1961 (Commencement No 2) Order 1963, SI 1963/755; Criminal Justice Act 1961 (Commencement No 3) Order 1963, SI 1963/2070

| | | |
|---|---|---|
| 1–7 | | 1 Aug 1963 (SI 1963/755) |
| 8–12 | | 2 Oct 1961 (SI 1961/1672) |
| 13 | | 1 Jan 1963 (SI 1963/2070) |
| 14–19 | | 2 Oct 1961 (SI 1961/1672) |
| 20 | | *Never in force* (repealed) |
| 21–24 | | 2 Oct 1961 (SI 1961/1672) |
| 25 | | 1 Aug 1963 (SI 1963/755) |
| 26–31 | | 2 Oct 1961 (SI 1961/1672) |
| 32 | (1) | 2 Oct 1961 (SI 1961/1672) |
| | (2)(a)–(c) | 2 Oct 1961 (SI 1961/1672) |
| | (2)(d) | *Never in force* (repealed) |
| | (3) | *Never in force* (repealed) |
| 33 | | 2 Oct 1961 (SI 1961/1672) |
| 34 | | 1 Aug 1963 (SI 1963/755) |
| 35–40 | | 2 Oct 1961 (SI 1961/1672) |
| 41 | (1)–(3) | 2 Oct 1961 (SI 1961/1672) |
| | (4) | 1 Aug 1963 (SI 1963/755) |
| 42, 43 | | 2 Oct 1961 (SI 1961/1672) |
| 44, 45 | | 19 Jul 1961 (RA) |
| Sch 1 | | 1 Jan 1963 (SI 1963/2070) |
| Sch 2 | | 2 Oct 1961 (SI 1961/1672) |
| Sch 3 | | *Never in force* (repealed) |
| Sch 4 | | 2 Oct 1961 (SI 1961/1672), amendments of— |

Sch 4 (continued):

2 Oct 1961 (SI 1961/1672), amendments of—
Children and Young Persons Act 1933, ss 72, 78, 82, 83, 88, Sch 4;
Children and Young Persons Act 1938;
Family Allowances Act 1945;
Children Act 1948;
Criminal Justice Act 1948, ss 19(1) (substitution of word "twelve"), 38, 39, 48, 52, 72;
Prison Act 1952, ss 13, 25(3), (7), 39, 43–45, 47, 49, 55;
Magistrates' Courts Act 1952, ss 20, 32, 54, 126;
Prisons (Scotland) Act 1952;
Criminal Justice Act (Northern Ireland) 1953;
Prison Act (Northern Ireland) 1953;
Naval Discipline Act 1957;
Mental Health Act 1959

1 Aug 1963 (SI 1963/755), amendments of—
Children and Young Persons Act 1933, ss 53, 54;
Criminal Justice Act 1948, ss 18, 19(1) (substitution of words from "section 17"), 20, 80;
Magistrates' Courts Act 1952, s 28

Sch 5 — 2 Oct 1961 (SI 1961/1672), repeals of or in—
Children and Young Persons Act 1933;
Children Act 1948;
Criminal Justice Act 1948, ss 19, 22, 23, 38, 52, 72;
Prison Act 1952;
Prisons (Scotland) Act 1952;
Administration of Justice Act 1960

1 Aug 1963 (SI 1963/755), repeals of or in—
Criminal Justice Act 1948, ss 18, 20(7), (8);
Magistrates' Courts Act 1952

Sch 6 — 1 Aug 1963 (SI 1963/755)

**Crofters (Scotland) Act 1961 (9 & 10 Eliz 2 c 58)**

*RA:* 27 Jul 1961

*Commencement provisions:* s 19(2)

Whole Act in force 27 Aug 1961, except s 12 (never in force (repealed)) (s 19(2))

---

**Crown Estate Act 1961 (9 & 10 Eliz 2 c 55)**

*RA:* 27 Jul 1961

Whole Act in force 27 Jul 1961 (RA)

---

**Department of Technical Co-operation Act 1961 (9 & 10 Eliz 2 c 30)**

*RA:* 22 Jun 1961

Whole Act in force 22 Jun 1961 (RA)

---

**Diplomatic Immunities (Conferences with Commonwealth Countries and Republic of Ireland) Act 1961 (9 & 10 Eliz 2 c 11)**

*RA:* 2 Mar 1961

Whole Act in force 2 Mar 1961 (RA)

---

**Electricity (Amendment) Act 1961 (9 & 10 Eliz 2 c 8)**

*RA:* 2 Mar 1961

Whole Act in force 2 Mar 1961 (RA)

---

**Expiring Laws Continuance Act 1961 (10 & 11 Eliz 2 c 4)**

*RA:* 20 Dec 1961

Whole Act in force 20 Dec 1961 (RA)

---

**Export Guarantees Act 1961 (10 & 11 Eliz 2 c 3)**

*RA:* 20 Dec 1961

Whole Act in force 20 Dec 1961 (RA)

---

**Factories Act 1961 (9 & 10 Eliz 2 c 34)**

*RA:* 22 Jun 1961

*Commencement provisions:* s 185(2)

Whole Act in force 1 Apr 1962 (s 185(2))

---

**Family Allowances and National Insurance Act 1961 (10 & 11 Eliz 2 c 6)**

*RA:* 20 Dec 1961

*Commencement provisions:* s 14(3), Sch 3, para 1; Family Allowances and National Insurance Act 1961 (Commencement) Order 1961, SI 1961/2449; Family Allowances and National Insurance Act 1961 (Commencement No 2) Order 1962, SI 1962/7

| | | |
|---|---|---|
| 1 | (1) | 17 Jan 1962 (SI 1962/7) |
| | (2)–(4) | 28 Feb 1962 (SI 1962/7) |
| 2 | | 20 Dec 1961 (RA) |
| 3 | (1), (2) | 20 Dec 1961 (RA) |
| | (3) | 26 Feb 1962 (SI 1962/7) |
| | (4) | 20 Dec 1961 (except so far as it relates to sub-s (3)) (RA) |
| | | 26 Feb 1962 (exception noted above) (SI 1962/7) |
| 4 | (1) | 20 Dec 1961 (RA) |
| | (2), (3) | 26 Feb 1962 (SI 1962/7) |
| 5 | | 25 Dec 1961 (SI 1961/2449) |
| 6 | | 20 Dec 1961 (RA) |
| 7 | (1) | 12 Feb 1962 (SI 1962/7) |
| | (2) | 20 Dec 1961 (RA) |
| | (3), (4) | 15 Jan 1962 (SI 1962/7) |
| 8 | (a) | 20 Dec 1961 (RA) |
| | (b) | 3 Apr 1962 (SI 1962/7) |
| 9 | | 26 Feb 1962 (SI 1962/7) |
| 10–14 | | 20 Dec 1961 (RA) |
| Schs 1–4 | | 20 Dec 1961 (RA) |

**Farnham Castle Measure 1961 (9 & 10 Eliz 2 No 1)**

*RA:* 2 Mar 1961

Whole Measure in force 2 Mar 1961 (RA)

**Finance Act 1961 (9 & 10 Eliz 2 c 36)**

*RA:* 19 Jul 1961

The commencement details of Finance Acts are not set out, as the dates from which their provisions take effect are usually stated clearly and unambiguously in the text of the Act, and charging provisions will normally state for which year or years of assessment they are to have effect.

**Flood Prevention (Scotland) Act 1961 (9 & 10 Eliz 2 c 41)**

*RA:* 19 Jul 1961

*Commencement provisions*: s 16(2)

Whole Act in force 19 Aug 1961 (s 16(2))

**Highways (Miscellaneous Provisions) Act 1961 (9 & 10 Eliz 2 c 63)**

*RA:* 3 Aug 1961

*Commencement provisions*: s 17(2)

Whole Act in force 3 Sep 1961, except s 1, which came into force on 3 Aug 1961 (s 17(2))

# Preface

*Is it in Force?* contains the information you need to establish the exact commencement dates of Acts of general application in England, Wales and Scotland and General Synod Measures passed between 1 January 1960 and 20 October 2022 (also incorporating the Easter Act 1928, the only Act from before this period which is not yet in force).

## 1 What's in Is it in Force?

The short title and chapter number of every Public General Act is given, and unless an Act is of limited application only, the following details are provided:

    (a)  the date on which the Act received royal assent;

    (b)  a list of provisions which deal with the commencement of an Act or any part of an Act (including any commencement orders which have been made);

    (c)  any date or dates which have been appointed for the provisions of the Act to come into force; and

    (d)  an indication where any provision is not in force.

Provisions which have been repealed or otherwise amended are not indicated in *Is it in Force?*, and subscribers should make reference to the latest edition of **Halsbury's Statutes Citator** where the current status of all statutes in England and Wales is recorded.

## 2 How to use Is it in Force?

Acts passed during each calendar year are arranged alphabetically, and the years are dealt with in chronological order.

Each Act is dealt with according to its commencement provisions. Thus, an Act is treated as a single unit if the whole Act was brought into force on one date. An Act will only be treated on a section by section or subsection by subsection basis where the complexity of its commencement provisions demands this.

It should also be noted that saving and transitional provisions are not in general noted to any Act in this book.

Where a provision of an Act applying both to England and Wales and to Scotland is brought into force on the same date by different provisions, it is noted thus:

    11 Apr 1983 (SI 1982/1857; SI 1983/24)

Where such a provision is brought into force on different dates, it is noted thus:

    1 Jul 1978 (E) (W) (SI 1977/2164)
    1 Sep 1978 (S) (1978/816)

## 3 Finance Acts

Finance Acts are not dealt with in detail, as the dates from which their provisions take effect are usually stated clearly and unambiguously in the text of the Act, and charging provisions will normally state for which year or years of assessment they are to have effect.

The following information may be of use to readers when considering the effect of taxing provisions in Finance Acts which are expressed to have effect from a date prior to that on which the Act received royal assent:

(a) Income tax and corporation tax are annual taxes which have to be reimposed by Parliament for each year of assessment (Income and Corporation Taxes Act 1988, ss 1, 6).

(b) Under the rules of procedure of the House of Commons a ways and means resolution is a necessary preliminary to the imposition, increase or extension of income tax (but not for its alleviation).

(c) From 1998, the Chancellor of the Exchequer will normally open his budget in March (usually on a Tuesday) and at the conclusion of his speech move a set of ways and means resolutions which embody his proposals.

(d) The Provisional Collection of Taxes Act 1968, s 1, makes provision, subject to certain conditions, for statutory effect to be given to those resolutions in so far as they relate to income tax for a period ending on 5 May in the next calendar year (in the case of a resolution passed in November or December) and for a period ending with 5 August in the same calendar year in the case of a resolution passed in February or March in any year (or at the end of 4 months after the date on which the resolution takes effect if the resolution is passed at any other time).

(e) If statutory effect is lost, or expires without an Act coming into operation to renew or vary the tax, or the provisions in the resolution are modified by the Act renewing or varying the tax, any money paid or overpaid must be repaid or made good (Provisional Collection of Taxes Act 1968, s 1(6), (7)).

(f) It may be desirable that some motions should have immediate effect without waiting for the conclusion of the Budget debate. The House of Commons may therefore resolve that *provisional* statutory effect shall be given to one or more motions which, if passed, would be resolutions to which statutory effect could be given under s 1 of the 1968 Act. Upon the House so resolving, the motions have statutory effect immediately, subject to that motion or a similar motion being agreed to by a confirmatory resolution of the House within the next 10 sitting days; the provisions of s 1 then apply. If not confirmed, the motion is of no effect and any money paid or overpaid must be repaid or made good; there is similar adjustment if the confirmatory resolution differs from the original motion (Provisional Collection of Taxes Act 1968, s 5).

## 4 General principles governing commencement of statutes

(a) 'Commencement' means the time when the Act comes into force (Interpretation Act 1978, s 5, Sch 1).

(b) Where no provision is made for the coming into force of an Act, it comes into force at the beginning of the day on which it receives royal assent (Interpretation Act 1978, s 4(b)).

(c) Where provision is made for an Act to come into force on a particular day, it comes into force at the beginning of that day (Interpretation Act 1978, s 4(a)).

(d) Where an Act does not come into force immediately on its passing, and it confers power to make subordinate legislation, or to make appointments, give notices, prescribe forms or do any other thing for the purposes of the Act, then, unless the contrary intention appears, the power may be exercised, and any instrument made under it may be made so as to come into force, at any time after the passing of the Act so far as may be necessary or expedient for the purpose of (i) bringing the Act or any provision of the Act into force, or (ii) giving full effect to the Act or any such provision at or after the time when it comes into force (Interpretation Act 1978, s 13).

(e) There is a general presumption that an enactment is not intended to have retrospective effect. Parliament undoubtedly has power to enact with retrospective effect, so the general presumption applies unless the contrary is clearly stated.

## Updating and the Is it in Force? Inbox

*Is it in Force?* is a biannual publication. Each subsequent edition incorporates the most recent year's statutes and in addition deals with new commencement orders affecting material already published.

Interim updating is provided for subscribers to Halsbury's Statutes as part of their Service in the form of looseleaf pages filed following the guide card 'Is it in Force?' in the Noter-up Service binder.

Where a provision has not been noted as having been brought into force in either this volume or the current service issue, subscribers to Halsbury's Statutes are invited to email **legislation.direct@lexisnexis.co.uk** for the latest available information.

*Is it in Force?* is updated daily on Lexis®Library at **www.lexisnexis.com/uk/legal**, in both the "Is it in Force?" and "Status Snapshots" sources.

Queries on the content or scope of this work should be directed to the Head of Legislation, LexisNexis® UK, Lexis House, 30 Farringdon Street, London EC4A 4HH.

LEXISNEXIS®
*OCTOBER 2022*

LexisNexis
October 2022

### Home Safety Act 1961 (9 & 10 Eliz 2 c 20)

*RA:* 18 May 1961

Whole Act in force 18 May 1961 (RA)

---

### Housing Act 1961 (9 & 10 Eliz 2 c 65)

*RA:* 24 Oct 1961

*Commencement provisions:* s 36(3)

Whole Act in force 24 Nov 1961 (s 36(3))

---

### Human Tissue Act 1961 (9 & 10 Eliz 2 c 54)

*RA:* 27 Jul 1961

*Commencement provisions:* s 4(3)

Whole Act in force 27 Sep 1961 (s 4(3))

---

### Hyde Park (Underground Parking) Act 1961 (9 & 10 Eliz 2 c 26)

*RA:* 22 Jun 1961

Whole Act in force 22 Jun 1961 (RA)

---

### Industrial and Provident Societies Act 1961 (9 & 10 Eliz 2 c 28)

*RA:* 22 Jun 1961

*Commencement provisions:* s 4(3)

Whole Act in force 22 Jul 1961 (s 4(3))

---

### Land Compensation Act 1961 (9 & 10 Eliz 2 c 33)

*RA:* 22 Jun 1961

*Commencement provisions:* s 42(2)

Whole Act in force 1 Aug 1961 (s 42(2))

---

### Land Drainage Act 1961 (9 & 10 Eliz 2 c 48)

*RA:* 27 Jul 1961

Whole Act in force 27 Jul 1961 (RA)

---

### Licensing Act 1961 (9 & 10 Eliz 2 c 61)

*RA:* 3 Aug 1961

*Commencement provisions:* ss 6(1), 35(7), 38(5), Sch 8, paras 3, 4; Licensing Act 1961 (Commencement) Order 1961, SI 1961/1670

1–4                              1 Nov 1961 (SI 1961/1670)

**Licensing Act 1961 (9 & 10 Eliz 2 c 61)**—*contd*

| | | |
|---|---|---|
| 5 | (1)–(6) | 1 Jan 1962 (for the purpose of enabling licensing justices to make orders under the said section having effect on or after the 1 Mar 1962) (SI 1961/1670) |
| | | 1 Mar 1962 (otherwise) (SI 1961/1670) |
| | (7) | 1 Nov 1961 (SI 1961/1670) |
| | (8)–(12) | 1 Jan 1962 (for the purpose of enabling licensing justices to make orders under the said section having effect on or after the 1 Mar 1962) (SI 1961/1670) |
| | | 1 Mar 1962 (otherwise) (SI 1961/1670) |
| 6 | (1)–(4) | 3 Aug 1961 (s 6(11)) |
| | (5) | See Sch 2 below |
| | (6)–(11) | 3 Aug 1961 (s 6(11)) |
| 7 | (1)–(3) | 1 Nov 1961 (SI 1961/1670) |
| | (4) | 1 Mar 1962 (SI 1961/1670) |
| | (5)–(7) | 1 Nov 1961 (SI 1961/1670) |
| 8 | (1) | 1 Mar 1962 (SI 1961/1670) |
| | (2)–(9) | 1 Nov 1961 (SI 1961/1670) |
| 9 | | 1 Jan 1962 (for the purpose of enabling licensing justices to make orders under the said section having effect on or after the 1 Mar 1962) (SI 1961/1670) |
| | | 1 Mar 1962 (otherwise) (SI 1961/1670) |
| 10–24 | | 1 Nov 1961 (SI 1961/1670) |
| 25–34 | | 1 Mar 1962 (SI 1961/1670) |
| 35 | | 3 Aug 1961 (s 35(7)) |
| 36 | | 1 Mar 1962 (SI 1961/1670) |
| 37 | (1)–(3) | 1 Nov 1961 (SI 1961/1670) |
| | (4), (5) | 1 Mar 1962 (SI 1961/1670) |
| | (6), (7) | 1 Nov 1961 (SI 1961/1670) |
| 38 | | 1 Nov 1961 (SI 1961/1670) |
| Sch 1 | | 1 Nov 1961 (SI 1961/1670) |
| Sch 2 | | 3 Aug 1961 (s 6(11)) |
| Sch 3 | | 1 Mar 1962 (SI 1961/1670) |
| Sch 4 | | 1 Nov 1961 (SI 1961/1670) |
| Schs 5–7 | | 1 Mar 1962 (SI 1961/1670) |
| Sch 8 | paras 1, 2 | 1 Mar 1962 (SI 1961/1670) |
| | paras 3, 4 | 3 Aug 1961 (Sch 8, paras 3(4), 4(4)) |
| | paras 5, 6 | 1 Mar 1962 (SI 1961/1670) |
| Sch 9 | Pt I | 1 Nov 1961 (SI 1961/1670) |
| | Pt II | 1 Nov 1961 (SI 1961/1670), repeals of or in— |

Pt II cont:
Civic Restaurants Act 1947;
Licensing Act 1949;
Customs and Excise Act 1952 s 151, para (a) to the proviso to sub-s (1);
Licensing Act 1953, ss 3–6, 8–11, 18, 20–26, 29, 32, 33, 35, 41, 44, 45, 48–52, 59, 61, 62, 71, 74, 75, 83, 84, 91, 94, 99, 100, 104(7), (8) (in so far as that sub-s relates to sub-s (7)), 105–107, 109, 113(5), 117, 120, 127–129, 134, 148, 157(1) (definitions "new justices' licence" and "old off-licence"), (5), 167, Schs 1–3, 5, 6;
Licensing (Seamen's Canteens) Act 1954, s 7, proviso to sub-s (1), (6);
Occasional Licences and Young Persons Act 1956;
Street Offences Act 1959
1 Mar 1962 (SI 1961/1670), repeals of or in—
Customs and Excise Act 1952, s 307;
Licensing Act 1953, ss 77, 101–103, 104(2)–(4), (8), 112, 113(1), 114, 115, 119, 123, 125, Part IX, 149, 165 (definitions "registered club" and "unregistered club");
Licensing (Seamen's Canteens) Act 1954, s 7(2)–(4);
Finance Act 1959

## Local Authorities (Expenditure on Special Purposes) (Scotland) Act 1961 (9 & 10 Eliz 2 c 32)

*RA:* 22 Jun 1961

Whole Act in force 22 Jun 1961 (RA)

## Mock Auctions Act 1961 (9 & 10 Eliz 2 c 47)

*RA:* 27 Jul 1961

*Commencement provisions:* s 4(2)

Whole Act in force 27 Aug 1961 (s 4(2))

## National Health Service Act 1961 (9 & 10 Eliz 2 c 19)

*RA:* 9 May 1961

*Commencement provisions:* s 5(3)

Whole Act in force 16 May 1961 (s 5(3))

## National Health Service Contributions Act 1961 (9 & 10 Eliz 2 c 13)

*RA:* 28 Mar 1961

Whole Act in force 28 Mar 1961 (RA)

## North Atlantic Shipping Act 1961 (9 & 10 Eliz 2 c 53)

*RA:* 27 Jul 1961

Whole Act in force 27 Jul 1961 (RA)

## Nurses (Amendment) Act 1961 (9 & 10 Eliz 2 c 14)

*RA:* 28 Mar 1961

*Commencement provisions:* s 15(2)

Whole Act in force 28 Jun 1961 (s 15(2))

## Oaths Act 1961 (9 & 10 Eliz 2 c 21)

*RA:* 18 May 1961

Whole Act in force 18 May 1961 (RA)

## Overseas Service Act 1961 (9 & 10 Eliz 2 c 10)

*RA:* 2 Mar 1961

Whole Act in force 2 Mar 1961 (RA)

**Patents and Designs (Renewals, Extensions and Fees) Act 1961 (9 & 10 Eliz 2 c 25)**

*RA:* 22 Jun 1961

Whole Act in force 22 Jun 1961 (RA)

---

**Police Federation Act 1961 (9 & 10 Eliz 2 c 51)**

*RA:* 27 Jul 1961

*Commencement provisions*: s 3(2); Police Federation Act 1961 (Commencement No 1) Order 1961, SI 1961/1976

Whole Act in force 1 Nov 1961 (SI 1961/1976)

---

**Police Pensions Act 1961 (9 & 10 Eliz 2 c 35)**

*RA:* 22 Jun 1961

Whole Act in force 22 Jun 1961 (RA)

---

**Post Office Act 1961 (9 & 10 Eliz 2 c 15)**

*RA:* 28 Mar 1961

*Commencement provisions*: s 30(3)

Whole Act in force 1 Apr 1961 (s 30(3))

---

**Printer's Imprint Act 1961 (9 & 10 Eliz 2 c 31)**

*RA:* 22 Jun 1961

Whole Act in force 22 Jun 1961 (RA)

---

**Private Street Works Act 1961 (9 & 10 Eliz 2 c 24)**

*RA:* 18 May 1961

*Commencement provisions*: s 3(4)

Whole Act in force 18 Jun 1961 (s 3(4))

---

**Public Authorities (Allowances) Act 1961 (9 & 10 Eliz 2 c 43)**

*RA:* 19 Jul 1961

*Commencement provisions*: s 9(3); Public Authorities (Allowances) Act 1961 (Commencement) Order 1961, SI 1961/1822

| | |
|---|---|
| 1–3 | 19 Aug 1961 (s 9(3)) |
| 4–6 | 1 Oct 1961 (SI 1961/1822) |
| 7–9 | 19 Aug 1961 (s 9(3)) |

---

**Public Health Act 1961 (9 & 10 Eliz 2 c 64)**

*RA:* 3 Aug 1961

*Commencement provisions*: s 86(2)(b)

**Public Health Act 1961 (9 & 10 Eliz 2 c 64)**—*contd*
Whole Act in force 3 Oct 1961 (s 86(2)(b))

---

**Rating and Valuation Act 1961 (9 & 10 Eliz 2 c 45)**

*RA:* 27 Jul 1961

Whole Act in force 27 Jul 1961 (RA)

---

**Republic of South Africa (Temporary Provisions) Act 1961 (9 & 10 Eliz 2 c 23)**

*RA:* 18 May 1961

Whole Act in force 18 May 1961 (RA)

---

**Restriction of Offensive Weapons Act 1961 (9 & 10 Eliz 2 c 22)**

*RA:* 18 May 1961

*Commencement provisions:* s 3(3)

Whole Act in force 18 Jun 1961 (s 3(3))

---

**Rivers (Prevention of Pollution) Act 1961 (9 & 10 Eliz 2 c 50)**

*RA:* 27 Jul 1961

*Commencement provisions:* ss 1(11), 15(5); Rivers (Prevention of Pollution) Act 1961 (Appointed Day) Order 1963, SI 1963/320; Port of London Act 1968, s 95(g)

| | |
|---|---|
| 1 | 1 Jun 1963 (generally) (SI 1963/320) |
| | 1 Jul 1968 (Thames area) (Port of London Act 1968, s 95(g)) |
| 2–15 | 27 Sep 1961 (s 15(5)) |
| Schs 1, 2 | 27 Sep 1961 (s 15(5)) |

---

**Rural Water Supplies and Sewerage Act 1961 (9 & 10 Eliz 2 c 29)**

*RA:* 22 Jun 1961

Whole Act in force 22 Jun 1961 (RA)

---

**Sheriffs' Pensions (Scotland) Act 1961 (9 & 10 Eliz 2 c 42)**

*RA:* 19 Jul 1961

Whole Act in force 19 Jul 1961 (RA)

---

**Sierra Leone Independence Act 1961 (9 & 10 Eliz 2 c 16)**

*RA:* 28 Mar 1961

This Act generally had effect from 27 Apr 1961 (the "appointed day")

---

**Small Estates (Representation) Act 1961 (9 & 10 Eliz 2 c 37)**

*RA:* 19 Jul 1961

*Commencement provisions*: s 3(2); Small Estates Representation Act 1961 (Commencement) Order 1961 (SI 1961/2147)

Whole Act in force 1 Jan 1962 (SI 1961/2147)

**Southern Rhodesia (Constitution) Act 1961 (10 & 11 Eliz 2 c 2)**

*RA:* 22 Nov 1961

Whole Act in force 22 Nov 1961 (RA)

**Suicide Act 1961 (9 & 10 Eliz 2 c 60)**

*RA:* 3 Aug 1961

Whole Act in force 3 Aug 1961 (RA)

**Tanganyika Independence Act 1961 (10 & 11 Eliz 2 c 1)**

*RA:* 22 Nov 1961

This Act generally had effect from 9 Dec 1961 (s 1(1))

**Trustee Investments Act 1961 (9 & 10 Eliz 2 c 62)**

*RA:* 3 Aug 1961

Whole Act in force 3 Aug 1961 (RA)

**Trusts (Scotland) Act 1961 (9 & 10 Eliz 2 c 57)**

*RA:* 27 Jul 1961

*Commencement provisions*: s 7(3)

Whole Act in force 27 Aug 1961 (s 7(3))

**White Fish and Herring Industries Act 1961 (9 & 10 Eliz 2 c 18)**

*RA:* 9 May 1961

Whole Act in force 9 May 1961 (RA)

# 1962 Acts

### Acts of Parliament Numbering and Citation Act 1962 (10 & 11 Eliz 2 c 34)

*RA:* 19 Jul 1962

Whole Act in force 19 Jul 1962 (RA)

---

### Agricultural and Forestry Associations Act 1962 (10 & 11 Eliz 2 c 29)

*RA:* 3 Jul 1962

*Commencement provisions:* s 2(4)

Whole Act in force 3 Oct 1963 (s 2(4))

---

### Air Corporations Act 1962 (11 & 12 Eliz 2 c 5)

*RA:* 20 Dec 1962

Whole Act in force 20 Dec 1962 (RA)

---

### Air Guns and Shot Guns, etc Act 1962 (10 & 11 Eliz 2 c 49)

*RA:* 1 Aug 1962

Whole Act in force 1 Aug 1962 (RA)

---

### Animals (Cruel Poisons) Act 1962 (10 & 11 Eliz 2 c 26)

*RA:* 3 Jul 1962

*Commencement provisions:* s 4(4)

Whole Act in force 1 Jan 1963 (s 4(4))

---

### Appropriation Act 1962 (10 & 11 Eliz 2 c 45)

*RA:* 1 Aug 1962

Whole Act in force 1 Aug 1962 (RA)

---

### Army Reserve Act 1962 (10 & 11 Eliz 2 c 10)

*RA:* 15 Mar 1962

Whole Act in force 15 Mar 1962 (RA)

---

**See Halsbury's Statutes Citator for amendments to these Acts**    29

### British Museum Act 1962 (10 & 11 Eliz 2 c 18)

*RA:* 18 Apr 1962

Whole Act in force 18 Apr 1962 (RA)

---

### Building Societies Act 1962 (10 & 11 Eliz 2 c 37)

*RA:* 19 Jul 1962

*Commencement provisions:* s 135(2)

Whole Act in force 1 Oct 1962 (s 135(2))

---

### Carriage by Air (Supplementary Provisions) Act 1962 (10 & 11 Eliz 2 c 43)

*RA:* 19 Jul 1962

*Commencement provisions:* ss 5(4), 6(2), 7(2); Carriage by Air (Supplementary Provisions) Act 1962
    (Commencement) Order 1964, SI 1964/486

| | |
|---|---|
| 1–4 | 1 May 1964 (SI 1964/486) |
| 5 | 19 Jul 1962 (RA) |
| 6 | 1 Jun 1967 (s 6(2)) |
| 7 | 19 Jul 1962 (RA) |
| Schedule | 1 May 1964 (SI 1964/486) |

---

### Civil Aviation (Eurocontrol) Act 1962 (10 & 11 Eliz 2 c 8)

*RA:* 21 Feb 1962

*Commencement provisions:* s 10(2); Civil Aviation (Eurocontrol) Act 1962 (Commencement) Order 1963,
    SI 1963/458

Whole Act in force 16 Mar 1963 (SI 1963/458) except s 10, which came into force on 21 Feb 1962 (RA)

---

### Coal Consumers' Councils (Northern Irish Interests) Act 1962 (10 & 11 Eliz 2 c 22)

*RA:* 24 May 1962

Whole Act in force 24 May 1962 (RA)

---

### Coal Industry Act 1962 (11 & 12 Eliz 2 c 6)

*RA:* 20 Dec 1962

Whole Act in force 20 Dec 1962 (RA)

---

### Colonial Loans Act 1962 (10 & 11 Eliz 2 c 41)

*RA:* 19 Jul 1962

Whole Act in force 19 Jul 1962 (RA)

---

## Commonwealth Immigrants Act 1962 (10 & 11 Eliz 2 c 21)

*RA:* 18 Apr 1962

*Commencement provisions:* s 21(5); Commonwealth Immigrants Act 1962 (Commencement) Order 1962, SI 1962/863

| | |
|---|---|
| 1–5 | 1 Jul 1962 (SI 1962/863) |
| 6–21 | 31 May 1962 (SI 1962/863) |
| Sch 1 | 1 Jul 1962 (SI 1962/863) |
| Schs 2, 3 | 31 May 1962 (SI 1962/863) |

## Commonwealth Settlement Act 1962 (10 & 11 Eliz 2 c 17)

*RA:* 29 Mar 1962

Whole Act in force 29 Mar 1962 (RA)

## Consolidated Fund Act 1962 (10 & 11 Eliz 2 c 7)

*RA:* 21 Feb 1962

Whole Act in force 21 Feb 1962 (RA)

## Consolidated Fund (No 2) Act 1962 (10 & 11 Eliz 2 c 11)

*RA:* 29 Mar 1962

Whole Act in force 29 Mar 1962 (RA)

## Criminal Justice Administration Act 1962 (10 & 11 Eliz 2 c 15)

*RA:* 29 Mar 1962

*Commencement provisions:* ss 3(6), 21(3); Criminal Justice Administration Act (Commencement) Order 1962, SI 1962/791; Criminal Justice Administration Act (Commencement No 2) Order 1962, SI 1962/1120; Criminal Justice Administration Act (Commencement No 3) Order 1963, SI 1963/416

| | | |
|---|---|---|
| 1–3 | | 29 Mar 1962 (RA) |
| 4 | | 30 Apr 1962 (SI 1962/791) |
| 5–11 | | 29 Mar 1962 (RA) |
| 12–14 | | 18 Jun 1962 (SI 1962/1120) |
| 15, 16 | | 1 Apr 1963 (SI 1963/416) |
| 17 | | 18 Jun 1962 (SI 1962/1120) |
| 18 | | 1 Apr 1963 (SI 1963/416) |
| 19–21 | | 29 Mar 1962 (RA) |
| Sch 1 | | 29 Mar 1962 (RA) |
| Schs 2, 3 | | 18 Jun 1962 (SI 1962/1120) |
| Sch 4 | Pt I | 29 Mar 1962 (RA) |
| | Pt II | 30 Apr 1962 (SI 1962/791), amendments of— |
| | | County of Hertford Act 1878; |
| | | Municipal Corporations Act 1882; |
| | | Criminal Justice Act 1925 |
| | | 18 Jun 1962 (otherwise) (SI 1962/1120) |
| Sch 5 | Pt I | 29 Mar 1962 (RA) |
| | Pt II | 30 Apr 1962 (SI 1962/791), repeals of or in— |
| | | Chapter 12 Ric. 2. c.10; |
| | | Laws in Wales Act 1542; |
| | | Middlesex Sessions Act 1859; |
| | | Municipal Corporations Act 1882; |

**Criminal Justice Administration Act 1962 (10 & 11 Eliz 2 c 15)**—*contd*

        Summary Jurisdiction (Appeals) Act 1933;
        Firearms Act 1937;
        Administration of Justice (Miscellaneous Provisions) Act 1938, s 11;
        Criminal Justice Act 1948;
        Justices of the Peace Act 1949;
        Costs in Criminal Cases Act 1952;
        Magistrates' Courts Act 1952;
        Pool Betting Act 1954;
        Criminal Justice Administration Act 1956;
        Highways Act 1959;
        Betting and Gaming Act 1960;
        Criminal Justice Act 1961
      18 Jun 1962 (SI 1962/1120), repeals of or in—
        Night Poaching Act 1828;
        Quarter Sessions Act 1842;
        Magistrates' Courts Act 1952, Sch 1
      1 Apr 1963 (otherwise) (SI 1963/416)

---

**Drainage Rates Act 1962 (10 & 11 Eliz 2 c 39)**

*RA:* 19 Jul 1962

Whole Act in force 19 Jul 1962 (RA)

---

**Education Act 1962 (10 & 11 Eliz 2 c 12)**

*RA:* 29 Mar 1962

Whole Act in force 29 Mar 1962 (RA)

---

**Electricity (Borrowing Powers) (Scotland) Act 1962 (11 & 12 Eliz 2 c 7)**

*RA:* 20 Dec 1962

Whole Act in force 20 Dec 1962 (RA)

---

**Expiring Laws Continuance Act 1962 (11 & 12 Eliz 2 c 3)**

*RA:* 20 Dec 1962

Whole Act in force 20 Dec 1962 (RA)

---

**Finance Act 1962 (10 & 11 Eliz 2 c 44)**

*RA:* 1 Aug 1962

The commencement details of Finance Acts are not set out, as the dates from which their provisions take effect are usually stated clearly and unambiguously in the text of the Act, and charging provisions will normally state for which year or years of assessment they are to have effect.

---

**Foreign Compensation Act 1962 (11 & 12 Eliz 2 c 4)**

*RA:* 20 Dec 1962

Whole Act in force 20 Dec 1962 (RA)

---

**Forth and Clyde Canal (Extinguishment of Rights of Navigation) Act 1962 (10 & 11 Eliz 2 c 16)**

*RA*: 29 Mar 1962

Whole Act in force 29 Mar 1962 (RA)

---

**Health Visiting and Social Work (Training) Act 1962 (10 & 11 Eliz 2 c 33)**

*RA*: 3 Jul 1962

*Commencement provisions*: s 7(3); Health Visiting and Social Work (Training) Act 1962 (Commencement) Order 1962, SI 1962/1957

Whole Act in force 1 Oct 1962 (SI 1962/1957)

---

**House of Commons Members' Fund Act 1962 (10 & 11 Eliz 2 c 53)**

*RA*: 1 Aug 1962

Whole Act in force 1 Aug 1962 (RA)

---

**Housing (Scotland) Act 1962 (10 & 11 Eliz 2 c 28)**

*RA*: 3 Jul 1962

Whole Act in force 3 Jul 1962 (RA)

---

**International Monetary Fund Act 1962 (10 & 11 Eliz 2 c 20)**

*RA*: 18 Apr 1962

Whole Act in force 18 Apr 1962 (RA)

---

**Jamaica Independence Act 1962 (10 & 11 Eliz 2 c 40)**

*RA*: 19 Jul 1962

This Act generally had effect from 6 Aug 1962 (the "appointed day")

---

**Landlord and Tenant Act 1962 (10 & 11 Eliz 2 c 50)**

*RA*: 1 Aug 1962

*Commencement provisions*: s 7(2)

Whole Act in force 1 Nov 1962 (s 7(2))

---

**Law Reform (Damages and Solatium) (Scotland) Act 1962 (10 & 11 Eliz 2 c 42)**

*RA*: 19 Jul 1962

Whole Act in force 19 Jul 1962 (RA)

---

**See Halsbury's Statutes Citator for amendments to these Acts**

**Law Reform (Husband and Wife) Act 1962 (10 & 11 Eliz 2 c 48)**

*RA:* 1 Aug 1962

Whole Act in force 1 Aug 1962 (RA)

---

**Licensing (Scotland) Act 1962 (10 & 11 Eliz 2 c 51)**

*RA:* 1 Aug 1962

*Commencement provisions:* s 27(3); Licensing (Scotland) Act 1962 (Commencement) Order 1962, SI 1962/1818

| | | |
|---|---|---|
| 1, 2 | | 3 Sep 1962 (SI 1962/1818) |
| 3 | (1) | 1 Oct 1962 (SI 1962/1818) |
| | (2) | 3 Sep 1962 (SI 1962/1818) |
| | (3), (4) | 1 Oct 1962 (SI 1962/1818) |
| 4 | | 1 Oct 1962 (SI 1962/1818) |
| 5 | | 3 Sep 1962 (SI 1962/1818) |
| 6–8 | | 1 Oct 1962 (SI 1962/1818) |
| 9, 10 | | 3 Sep 1962 (SI 1962/1818) |
| 11 | | 1 Oct 1962 (SI 1962/1818) |
| 12 | | 3 Sep 1962 (SI 1962/1818) |
| 13–24 | | 1 Oct 1962 (SI 1962/1818) |
| 25 | (1)–(3) | 3 Sep 1962 (SI 1962/1818) |
| | (4) | 3 Sep 1962 (so far as it applies Licensing (Scotland) Act 1959, ss 29, 195, 196, 199 for the purposes of this Act) (SI 1962/1818) |
| | | 1 Oct 1962 (otherwise) (SI 1962/1818) |
| 26 | (1), (2) | 3 Sep 1962 (SI 1962/1818) |
| | (3) | 1 Oct 1962 (SI 1962/1818) |
| 27 | | 3 Sep 1962 (SI 1962/1818) |
| Sch 1 | | 3 Sep 1962 (SI 1962/1818) |
| Sch 2 | paras 1, 2 | 1 Oct 1962 (SI 1962/1818) |
| | para 3 | 3 Sep 1962 (SI 1962/1818) |
| | para 4 | 1 Oct 1962 (SI 1962/1818) |
| | paras 5–10 | 3 Sep 1962 (SI 1962/1818) |
| | para 11(a), (b) | 3 Sep 1962 (SI 1962/1818) |
| | para 11(c) | 1 Oct 1962 (SI 1962/1818) |
| | paras 12–15 | 1 Oct 1962 (SI 1962/1818) |
| | para 16 | 3 Sep 1962 (SI 1962/1818) |
| | paras 17, 18 | 1 Oct 1962 (SI 1962/1818) |
| | para 19 | 3 Sep 1962 (SI 1962/1818) |
| | paras 20–31 | 1 Oct 1962 (SI 1962/1818) |
| | paras 32, 33 | 3 Sep 1962 (SI 1962/1818) |
| | para 34 | 1 Oct 1962 (SI 1962/1818) |
| | para 35(a) | 3 Sep 1962 (except the words from "the definitions" onwards) (SI 1962/1818) |
| | | 1 Oct 1962 (exception noted above) (SI 1962/1818) |
| | para 35(b)–(e) | 3 Sep 1962 (SI 1962/1818) |
| | para 36 | 1 Oct 1962 (SI 1962/1818) |
| | paras 37, 38 | 3 Sep 1962 (SI 1962/1818) |
| Sch 3 | | 3 Sep 1962 (repeal of or in Licensing (Scotland) Act 1959, s 111(2)–(5)) (SI 1962/1818) |
| | | 1 Oct 1962 (otherwise) (SI 1962/1818) |

---

**Local Authorities (Historic Buildings) Act 1962 (10 & 11 Eliz 2 c 36)**

*RA:* 19 Jul 1962

Whole Act in force 19 Jul 1962 (RA)

---

**Local Government (Financial Provisions etc) (Scotland) Act 1962 (10 & 11 Eliz 2 c 9)**

*RA:* 21 Feb 1962

Whole Act in force 21 Feb 1962 (RA)

---

**Local Government (Records) Act 1962 (10 & 11 Eliz 2 c 56)**

*RA:* 1 Aug 1962

*Commencement provisions:* s 9(3)

Whole Act in force 1 Oct 1962 (s 9(3))

---

**Lotteries and Gaming Act 1962 (10 & 11 Eliz 2 c 55)**

*RA:* 1 Aug 1962

Whole Act in force 1 Aug 1962 (RA)

---

**Marriage (Wales and Monmouthshire) Act 1962 (10 & 11 Eliz 2 c 32)**

*RA:* 3 Jul 1962

Whole Act in force 3 Jul 1962 (RA)

---

**National Assistance Act 1948 (Amendment) Act 1962 (10 & 11 Eliz 2 c 24)**

*RA:* 24 May 1962

Whole Act in force 24 May 1962 (RA)

---

**Northern Ireland Act 1962 (10 & 11 Eliz 2 c 30)**

*RA:* 3 Jul 1962

*Commencement provisions:* ss 1(1), 2(6), 10(6); Northern Ireland Act 1962 (Commencement No 1) Order 1965, SI 1965/1308; Northern Ireland Act 1962 (Commencement No 2) Order 1966, SI 1966/86

Whole Act in force 3 Jul 1963 (RA), except s 10(1)–(4), which came into force on 15 Sep 1965 (SI 1965/1308), and s 2(1), which came into force on 14 Feb 1966 (the appointed day for purposes of s 1) (SI 1966/86)

---

**Penalties for Drunkenness Act 1962 (10 & 11 Eliz 2 c 52)**

*RA:* 1 Aug 1962

*Commencement provisions:* s 2(2)

Whole Act in force 1 Sep 1962 (s 2(2))

---

**Pensions (Increase) Act 1962 (11 & 12 Eliz 2 c 2)**

*RA:* 20 Dec 1962

Whole Act in force 20 Dec 1962 (RA)

---

**Pipe-lines Act 1962 (10 & 11 Eliz 2 c 58)**

*RA:* 1 Aug 1962

*Commencement provisions:* s 70(3); Pipe-lines Act 1962 (Commencement) Order 1962, SI 1962/2790

Whole Act in force 1 Jan 1963 (SI 1962/2790) except s 41, which came into force on 1 Aug 1962 (RA)

---

**Police Federations Act 1962 (10 & 11 Eliz 2 c 25)**

*RA:* 24 May 1962

*Commencement provisions:* s 2(2); Police Federation Regulations 1965, SI 1965/619

Whole Act in force 24 May 1962 (RA) except the Schedule, which came into force, in relation to England and Wales on 1 Apr 1965 (s 2(2); SI 1965/619)

---

**Recorded Delivery Service Act 1962 (10 & 11 Eliz 2 c 27)**

*RA:* 3 Jul 1962

Whole Act in force 3 Jul 1962 (RA)

---

**Road Traffic Act 1962 (10 & 11 Eliz 2 c 59)**

*RA:* 1 Aug 1962

*Commencement provisions:* s 52(3); Road Traffic Act 1962 (Commencement No 1) Order 1962, SI 1962/2088; Road Traffic Act 1962 (Commencement No 2) Order 1962, SI 1962/2697; Road Traffic Act 1962 (Commencement No 3) Order 1963, SI 1963/539; Road Traffic Act 1962 (Commencement No 4) Order 1963, SI 1963/828; Road Traffic Act 1962 (Commencement No 5) Order 1963, SI 1963/1028; Road Traffic Act 1962 (Commencement No 6) Order 1964, SI 1964/183; Road Traffic Act 1962 (Commencement No 7) Order 1971, SI 1971/1335

| | | |
|---|---|---|
| 1 | | 20 Dec 1962 (SI 1962/2697) |
| 2 | (1)–(5) | 20 Dec 1962 (SI 1962/2697) |
| | (6) | *Never in force* (repealed) |
| | (7) | 20 Dec 1962 (SI 1962/2697) |
| 3 | | 20 Dec 1962 (SI 1962/2697) |
| 4 | | 1 Nov 1962 (SI 1962/2088) |
| 5–9 | | 29 May 1963 (SI 1963/828) |
| 10–13 | | 1 Nov 1962 (SI 1962/2088) |
| 14–19 | | 28 Sep 1962 (SI 1962/2088) |
| 20, 21 | | 1 Nov 1962 (SI 1962/2088) |
| 22 | | 28 Sep 1962 (SI 1962/2088) |
| 23 | | 15 Feb 1964 (SI 1964/183) |
| 24–28 | | 28 Sep 1962 (SI 1962/2088) |
| 29 | | 1 Jan 1963 (SI 1962/2088) |
| 30–35 | | 28 Sep 1962 (SI 1962/2088) |
| 36 | | 15 Feb 1964 (SI 1964/183) |
| 37 | | 1 Nov 1962 (SI 1962/2088) |
| 38–40 | | 29 May 1963 (SI 1963/828) |
| 41 | | 1 Oct 1971 (SI 1971/1335) |
| 42 | | 1 Nov 1962 (SI 1962/2088) |
| 43 | | 28 Sep 1962 (SI 1962/2088) |
| 44, 45 | | 1 Nov 1962 (SI 1962/2088) |
| 46–50 | | 28 Sep 1962 (SI 1962/2088) |
| 51 | | See Sch 4 below |
| 52 | | See Sch 5 below |
| Sch 1 | | 29 May 1963 (SI 1963/828) |
| Sch 2 | | 1 Jan 1963 (SI 1962/2088) |

**Road Traffic Act 1962 (10 & 11 Eliz 2 c 59)**—*contd*

Sch 3      29 May 1963 (SI 1963/828)

Sch 4      28 Sep 1962 (SI 1962/2088), amendments of—
Road Transport Lighting Act 1957;
Highways Act 1959;
Road Traffic Act 1960, ss 22(6), 27, 36(1), (4), 52, 64, 66(8), 67, 81, 97, 99(2), 113, 130, 135, 136, 142, 247, 250;
Road Traffic and Roads Improvement Act 1960, s 9
1 Nov 1962 (amendments of Road Traffic Act 1960, ss 4, 22(4), 36(3), 48, 99(1), 226, 231, 241, 242, 259) (SI 1962/2088)
1 Jan 1963 (SI 1962/2088), amendments of—
Road Traffic Act 1960, ss 88, 233(1)(h);
Road Traffic and Roads Improvement Act 1960, ss 5, 6, 11, 15, 16
1 Apr 1963 (amendments of Road Traffic Act 1960, ss 36(11), 66(9), (9A)) (SI 1963/539)
29 May 1963 (amendments of Road Traffic Act 1960, ss 68, 106, 109, 112, 116) (SI 1963/828)
1 Jul 1963 (amendments of Road Traffic (Driving of Motor Cycles) Act 1960) (SI 1963/1028)
15 Feb 1964 (amendments of Road Traffic Act 1960, s 233(1)(g), 235(1)) (SI 1964/183)

Sch 5      28 Sep 1962 (SI 1962/2088), repeals of or in—
Road Transport Lighting Act 1957, s 5(1);
Road Traffic Act 1960, ss 26(5), 36, 64(1), 113, Sch 20
1 Nov 1962 (repeals of or in Road Traffic Act 1960, ss 19, 21, 26(3), 220, 241) (SI 1962/2088)
20 Dec 1962 (repeals of or in Road Traffic Act 1960, s 6(6)) (SI 1962/2697)
1 Jan 1963 (repeals of or in Road Traffic and Roads Improvement Act 1960, ss 6, 15, Schedule, entries relating to Road Traffic Act 1960, ss 86–88) (SI 1962/2088)
29 May 1963 (SI 1963/828), repeals of or in—
Road Transport Lighting Act 1957, s 18(2);
Road Traffic Act 1960, ss 4, 6(5), 64(2), 104, 110, 111, 218, 219, 226(3), 238, 245, Schs 11, 19;
Road Traffic and Roads Improvement Act 1960, Schedule, entry relating to Road Traffic Act 1960, s 245

---

**Sea Fish Industry Act 1962 (10 & 11 Eliz 2 c 31)**

*RA:* 3 Jul 1962

Whole Act in force 3 Jul 1962 (RA)

---

**Shops (Airports) Act 1962 (10 & 11 Eliz 2 c 35)**

*RA:* 19 Jul 1962

Whole Act in force 19 Jul 1962 (RA)

---

**South Africa Act 1962 (10 & 11 Eliz 2 c 23)**

*RA:* 24 May 1962

*Commencement provisions:* s 4(2)

Whole Act in force 31 May 1962 (s 4(2))

---

## Tanganyika Republic Act 1962 (11 & 12 Eliz 2 c 1)

*RA:* 6 Dec 1962

This Act generally had effect from 9 Dec 1962 (the "appointed day")

---

## Telegraph Act 1962 (10 & 11 Eliz 2 c 14)

*RA:* 29 Mar 1962

*Commencement provisions:* s 2(6)

Whole Act in force 29 Apr 1962 (s 2(6))

---

## Town and Country Planning Act 1962 (10 & 11 Eliz 2 c 38)

*RA:* 19 Jul 1962

*Commencement provisions:* s 225

Whole Act in force 1 Apr 1963 (s 225)

---

## Transport Act 1962 (10 & 11 Eliz 2 c 46)

*RA:* 1 Aug 1962

*Commencement provisions:* ss 31(1), 96(2); Transport Act 1962 (Commencement No 1) Order 1962, SI 1962/1788; Transport Act 1962 (Vesting Date) Order 1962, SI 1962/2634; Transport Act 1962 (Commencement No 2) Order 1964, SI 1964/2025

| | | |
|---|---|---|
| 1–64 | | 1 Sep 1962 (SI 1962/1788) |
| 65 | (1)–(3) | 1 Sep 1962 (SI 1962/1788) |
| | (4)–(6) | 1 Jan 1963 (s 31(1); SI 1962/2634) |
| 66 | | 1 Sep 1962 (SI 1962/1788) |
| 67 | | 1 Jan 1963 (s 31(1); SI 1962/2634) |
| 68–70 | | 1 Sep 1963 (SI 1962/1788) |
| 71 | | 1 Jan 1965 (SI 1964/2025) |
| 72–96 | | 1 Sep 1962 (SI 1962/1788) |
| Schs 1–11 | | 1 Sep 1962 (SI 1962/1788) |

---

## Trinidad and Tobago Independence Act 1962 (10 & 11 Eliz 2 c 54)

*RA:* 1 Aug 1962

This Act generally had effect from 31 Aug 1962 (the "appointed day")

---

## Uganda Independence Act 1962 (10 & 11 Eliz 2 c 57)

*RA:* 1 Aug 1962

This Act generally had effect from 9 Oct 1962 (the "appointed day")

---

## Vehicles (Excise) Act 1962 (10 & 11 Eliz 2 c 13)

*RA:* 29 Mar 1962

*Commencement provisions:* s 26(3)

Whole Act in force 1 Apr 1962 (s 26(3))

---

**West Indies Act 1962 (10 & 11 Eliz 2 c 19)**

*RA:* 18 Apr 1962

Whole Act in force 18 Apr 1962 (RA)

# 1963 Acts

**Agriculture (Miscellaneous Provisions) Act 1963 (c 11)**

*RA:* 15 May 1963

Whole Act in force 15 May 1963 (RA)

---

**Animal Boarding Establishments Act 1963 (c 43)**

*RA:* 31 Jul 1963

*Commencement provisions:* s 7(4)

Whole Act in force 1 Jan 1969 (s 7(4))

---

**Appropriation Act 1963 (c 26)**

*RA:* 31 Jul 1963

Whole Act in force 31 Jul 1963 (RA)

---

**Bahama Islands (Constitution) Act 1963 (c 56)**

*RA:* 3 Dec 1963

Whole Act in force 3 Dec 1963 (RA)

---

**Betting Duties Act 1963 (c 3)**

*RA:* 28 Feb 1963

*Commencement provisions:* s 7(4)

Whole Act in force 28 Mar 1963 (s 7(4); being the same day as the Betting, Gaming and Lotteries Act 1963 comes into force)

---

**Betting, Gaming and Lotteries Act 1963 (c 2)**

*RA:* 28 Feb 1963

*Commencement provisions:* s 58(3)

Whole Act in force 28 Mar 1963 (s 58(3))

---

## British Museum Act 1963 (c 24)

*RA:* 10 Jul 1963

*Commencement provisions*: s 13(2); British Museum Act 1963 (Commencement) Order 1963, SI 1963/1546

Whole Act in force 30 Sep 1963 (SI 1963/1546)

---

## Cathedrals Measure 1963 (No 2)

*RA:* 31 Jul 1963

Whole Measure in force 31 Jul 1963 (RA)

---

## Children and Young Persons Act 1963 (c 37)

*RA:* 31 Jul 1963

*Commencement provisions*: s 65(6); Children and Young Persons Act 1963 (Commencement No 1) Order 1963, SI 1963/1561; Children and Young Persons Act 1963 (Commencement No 2) Order 1963, SI 1963/2056; Children and Young Persons Act 1963 (Commencement No 3) Order 1968, SI 1968/1727

| | | |
|---|---|---|
| 1 | | 1 Oct 1963 (SI 1963/1561) |
| 2–13 | | 1 Feb 1964 (SI 1963/2056) |
| 14, 15 | | 1 Oct 1963 (SI 1963/1561) |
| 16–33 | | 1 Feb 1964 (SI 1963/2056) |
| 34–44 | | 2 Dec 1968 (for the purposes of applying for licences under s 37, and granting such licences to have effect on and after that date) (SI 1968/1727) |
| | | 3 Mar 1969 (otherwise) (SI 1968/1727) |
| 45–49 | | 1 Oct 1963 (SI 1963/1561) |
| 50–53 | | 1 Feb 1964 (SI 1963/2056) |
| 54 | | 1 Oct 1963 (SI 1963/1561) |
| 55 | | *Never in force* (repealed) |
| 56 | | 1 Oct 1963 (SI 1963/1561) |
| 57 | | 1 Feb 1964 (SI 1963/2056) |
| 58–63 | | 1 Oct 1963 (SI 1963/1561) |
| 64 | (1) | 1 Oct 1963 (SI 1963/1561) |
| | (2) | 1 Feb 1964 (SI 1963/2056) |
| | (3) | 1 Oct 1963 (SI 1963/1561) |
| 65 | | 1 Oct 1963 (SI 1963/1561) |
| Schs 1, 2 | | 1 Feb 1964 (SI 1963/2056) |
| Sch 3 | paras 1–3 | 1 Oct 1963 (SI 1963/1561) |
| | paras 4–10 | 2 Dec 1968 (for the purposes of applying for licences under s 37, and granting such licences to have effect on and after that date) (SI 1968/1727) |
| | | 3 Mar 1969 (otherwise) (SI 1968/1727) |
| | paras 11–28 | 1 Feb 1964 (SI 1963/2056) |
| | paras 29–32 | 2 Dec 1968 (for the purposes of applying for licences under s 37, and granting such licences to have effect on and after that date) (SI 1968/1727) |
| | | 3 Mar 1969 (otherwise) (SI 1968/1727) |
| | paras 33–37 | 1 Feb 1964 (SI 1963/2056) |
| | paras 38–43 | 1 Oct 1963 (SI 1963/1561) |
| | para 44 | 1 Feb 1964 (SI 1963/2056) |
| | para 45 | 1 Oct 1963 (SI 1963/1561) |
| | paras 46–51 | 1 Feb 1964 (SI 1963/2056) |
| Sch 4 | paras 1, 2 | 1 Feb 1964 (SI 1963/2056) |

**Children and Young Persons Act 1963 (c 37)**—*contd*

|  | paras 3, 4 | 2 Dec 1968 (for the purposes of applying for licences under s 37, and granting such licences to have effect on and after that date) (SI 1968/1727) |
|---|---|---|

paras 3, 4 — 2 Dec 1968 (for the purposes of applying for licences under s 37, and granting such licences to have effect on and after that date) (SI 1968/1727)

3 Mar 1969 (otherwise) (SI 1968/1727)

paras 5–9 — 1 Feb 1964 (SI 1963/2056)

Sch 5 — 1 Oct 1963 (SI 1963/1561), repeals of or in—
Children and Young Persons Act 1933, ss 1(1), 3(1), 4(1), 87(5);
Children Act 1948

1 Feb 1964 (SI 1963/2056), repeals of or in—
Children and Young Persons Act 1933, ss 14(3), 35(2), 39(1), 48, 53(4), 61, 63(1), 64, 66–70, 72, 73, 84, 107(1), Sch 2, Sch 4, para 10;
Children and Young Persons (Scotland) Act 1937, s 46(1);
Children and Young Persons Act 1938;
Education Act 1944;
Family Allowance Act 1945;
Criminal Justice Act 1948;
Justices of the Peace Act 1949;
Children and Young Persons (Amendment) Act 1952;
Children and Young Persons Act 1956;
Sexual Offences Act 1956;
Mental Health Act 1959;
Criminal Justice Act 1961

2 Dec 1968 (SI 1968/1727) (for the purposes of applying for licences under s 37, and granting such licences to have effect on and after that date) repeals of or in—
Children and Young Persons Act 1933, ss 22, 24–26, 29;
Children and Young Persons (Scotland) Act 1937, ss 32, 34, 37, 38

3 Mar 1969 (otherwise) (SI 1968/1727), repeals of or in—
Children and Young Persons Act 1933, ss 22, 24–26, 29;
Children and Young Persons (Scotland) Act 1937, ss 32, 34, 37, 38

---

**Commonwealth Development Act 1963 (c 40)**

*RA:* 31 Jul 1963

Whole Act in force 31 Jul 1963 (RA)

---

**Commonwealth Scholarships (Amendment) Act 1963 (c 6)**

*RA:* 28 Feb 1963

Whole Act in force 28 Feb 1963 (RA)

---

**Consolidated Fund Act 1963 (c 1)**

*RA:* 28 Feb 1963

Whole Act in force 28 Feb 1963 (RA)

---

**Consolidated Fund (No 2) Act 1963 (c 8)**

*RA:* 28 Mar 1963

Whole Act in force 28 Mar 1963 (RA)

---

## Contracts of Employment Act 1963 (c 49)

*RA:* 31 Jul 1963

*Commencement provisions:* s 10(3); Contracts of Employment Act 1963 (Commencement) Order 1963, SI 1963/1916

Whole Act in force 6 Jul 1964 (SI 1963/1916)

## Corn Rents Act 1963 (c 14)

*RA:* 15 May 1963

Whole Act in force 15 May 1963 (RA) (but note that repeals (s 3(4), Schedule) and the amendments of Law of Property Act 1925 s 191(12) made by s 3(5) do not take effect until the coming into operation of the first scheme under s 1. No such scheme has yet been made)

## County Courts (Jurisdiction) Act 1963 (c 5)

*RA:* 28 Feb 1963

*Commencement provisions:* s 5(2)

Whole Act in force 1 Apr 1963 (s 5(2))

## Criminal Justice (Scotland) Act 1963 (c 39)

*RA:* 31 Jul 1963

*Commencement provisions:* s 55; Criminal Justice (Scotland) Act 1963 (Commencement No 1) Order 1963, SI 1963/1681; Criminal Justice (Scotland) Act 1963 (Commencement No 2) Order 1964, SI 1964/187; Criminal Justice (Scotland) Act 1963 (Commencement No 3) Order 1964, SI 1964/2102; Criminal Justice (Scotland) Act 1963 (Commencement No 4) Order 1965, SI 1965/1317

| | |
|---|---|
| 1, 2 | 18 Jan 1965 (SI 1964/2102) |
| 3, 4 | 1 Nov 1963 (SI 1963/1681) |
| 5 | 18 Jan 1965 (SI 1964/2102) |
| 6, 7 | 1 Nov 1963 (SI 1963/1681) |
| 8–13 | 18 Jan 1965 (SI 1964/2102) |
| 14, 15 | 1 Jul 1965 (SI 1965/1317) |
| 16–22 | 1 Nov 1963 (SI 1963/1681) |
| 23–26 | 2 Mar 1964 (SI 1964/187) |
| 27–42 | 1 Nov 1963 (SI 1963/1681) |
| 43 | 2 Mar 1964 (SI 1964/187) |
| 44–51 | 1 Nov 1963 (SI 1963/1681) |
| 52 | See Schs 5 and 6 below |
| 53 | 1 Nov 1963 (to the extent that it extends furth of Scotland the application of provisions of the Act brought into force by this order) (SI 1963/1681) |
| | 2 Mar 1964 (to the extent that it extends furth of Scotland the application of provisions of the Act brought into force by this order) (SI 1964/187) |
| | 18 Jan 1965 (to the extent that it extends furth of Scotland the application of provisions of the Act brought into force by this order) (SI 1964/2102) |
| | 1 Jul 1965 (to the extent that it extends furth of Scotland the application of provisions of the Act brought into force by this order) (SI 1965/1317) |
| 54 | 1 Nov 1963 (SI 1963/1681) |
| 55 | 31 Jul 1963 (RA) |
| Sch 1 | 1 Jul 1965 (SI 1965/1317) |

**Criminal Justice (Scotland) Act 1963 (c 39)**—*contd*

| | |
|---|---|
| Sch 2 | 1 Nov 1963 (SI 1963/1681) |
| Sch 3 | 2 Mar 1964 (SI 1964/187) |
| Sch 4 | 1 Nov 1963 (SI 1963/1681) |
| Sch 5 | 1 Nov 1963 (SI 1963/1681), amendments of— |

                Criminal Appeal (Scotland) Act 1926;

                Children and Young Persons (Scotland) Act 1937;

                Family Allowances Act 1945;

                Children Act 1948;

                Criminal Justice (Scotland) Act 1949;

                Prisons (Scotland) Act 1952, ss 9, 16(1), 33(2), (3), 33(4) (except substitution of words "borstal institution");

                Summary Jurisdiction (Scotland) Act 1952, ss 4, 20(1), 21, 31(1), 45(2), 76(1)(a), 77;

                First Offenders Act 1958;

                First Offenders (Scotland) Act 1960, s 1(3);

                Mental Health (Scotland) Act 1960

            2 Mar 1964 (amendments of Summary Jurisdiction (Scotland) Act 1954, ss 3, 7, 33, 40, 48, 50) (SI 1964/187)

            18 Jan 1965 (SI 1964/2102), amendments of—

                Prisons (Scotland) Act 1952, ss 28(2), 31, 33(4) (substitution of words "borstal institution"), 33(5), 34, 35, 37;

                Summary Jurisdiction (Scotland) Act 1954, s 26(4);

                First Offenders (Scotland) Act 1960, s 1(1), (2);

                Criminal Justice Act 1961, ss 32(2), 34(6), 38(5)(a), 39(1)

| | |
|---|---|
| Sch 6 | 1 Nov 1963 (SI 1963/1681), except repeals of or in— |

                Summary Jurisdiction (Scotland) Act 1954, ss 18(3), 49(2);

                Criminal Justice (Scotland) Act 1949, s 18(2)–(5)

            2 Mar 1964 (repeals of or in Summary Jurisdiction (Scotland) Act 1954, ss 18(3), 49(2)) (SI 1964/187)

            18 Jan 1965 (repeals of or in Criminal Justice (Scotland) Act 1949, s 18(2)–(5)) (SI 1964/2102)

---

**Deer Act 1963 (c 36)**

*RA:* 31 Jul 1963

*Commencement provisions:* ss 1(5), 13(3)

| | |
|---|---|
| 1 | 1 Nov 1963 (s 1(5)) |
| 2–13 | 31 Aug 1963 (s 13(3)) |
| Sch 1 | 1 Nov 1963 (s 1(5)) |
| Sch 2 | 31 Aug 1963 (s 13(3)) |

---

**Dog Racing (Betting Days) Act 1963 (c 42)**

*RA:* 31 Jul 1963

Whole Act in force 31 Jul 1963 (RA)

---

**Drainage Rates Act 1963 (c 10)**

*RA:* 28 Mar 1963

Whole Act in force 28 Mar 1963 (RA)

---

**Ecclesiastical Jurisdiction Measure 1963 (No 1)**

*RA:* 31 Jul 1963

*Commencement provisions:* s 88

Whole Measure in force 1 Mar 1965 (s 88, see *London Gazette*, 22 Feb 1965)

---

**Education (Scotland) Act 1963 (c 21)**

*RA:* 10 Jul 1963

Whole Act in force 10 Jul 1963 (RA)

---

**Electricity and Gas Act 1963 (c 59)**

*RA:* 18 Dec 1963

Whole Act in force 18 Dec 1963 (RA)

---

**Expiring Laws Continuance Act 1963 (c 58)**

*RA:* 18 Dec 1963

Whole Act in force 18 Dec 1963 (RA)

---

**Finance Act 1963 (c 25)**

*RA:* 31 Jul 1963

The commencement details of Finance Acts are not set out, as the dates from which their provisions take effect are usually stated clearly and unambiguously in the text of the Act, and charging provisions will normally state for which year or years of assessment they are to have effect.

---

**Forestry (Sale of Land) (Scotland) Act 1963 (c 23)**

*RA:* 10 Jul 1963

Whole Act in force 10 Jul 1963 (RA)

---

**Fort William Pulp and Paper Mills Act 1963 (c 15)**

*RA:* 15 May 1963

Whole Act in force 15 May 1963 (RA)

---

**Kenya Independence Act 1963 (c 54)**

*RA:* 3 Dec 1963

This Act generally had effect from 12 Dec 1963 (the "appointed day")

---

**Land Compensation (Scotland) Act 1963 (c 51)**

*RA:* 31 Jul 1963

*Commencement provisions:* s 49(2)

**Land Compensation (Scotland) Act 1963 (c 51)**—*contd*
Whole Act in force 1 Jan 1964, except Part II (ss 8–12) which comes into force on 1 Mar 1971, (the appointed day under Lands Tribunal Act 1949, s 10(2)) (s 49(2))

**Limitation Act 1963 (c 47)**

*RA:* 31 Jul 1963

Whole Act in force 31 Jul 1963 (RA)

**Local Authorities (Land) Act 1963 (c 29)**

*RA:* 31 Jul 1963

Whole Act in force 31 Jul 1963 (RA)

**Local Employment Act 1963 (c 19)**

*RA:* 10 Jul 1963

Whole Act in force 10 Jul 1963 (RA)

**Local Government (Financial Provisions) Act 1963 (c 46)**

*RA:* 31 Jul 1963
Whole Act in force 31 Jul 1963 (RA)

**Local Government (Financial Provisions) (Scotland) Act 1963 (c 12)**

*RA:* 15 May 1963

Whole Act in force 15 May 1963 (RA)

**London Government Act 1963 (c 33)**

*RA:* 31 Jul 1963

*Commencement provisions*: s 94(2)

| | | |
|---|---|---|
| 1–8 | | 31 Jul 1963 (RA) |
| 9–29 | | 1 Apr 1965 (s 94(2)) |
| 30–34 | | 31 Jul 1963 (RA) |
| 35–47 | | 1 Apr 1965 (s 94(2)) |
| 48 | (1) | 1 Apr 1965 (s 94(2)) |
| | (2) | 31 Jul 1963 (RA) |
| | (3) | 1 Apr 1965 (s 94(2)) |
| 49–61 | | 1 Apr 1965 (s 94(2)) |
| 62 | (1)–(3) | 1 Apr 1965 (s 94(2)) |
| | (4) | 31 Jul 1963 (RA) |
| | (5) | 1 Apr 1965 (s 94(2)) |
| 63–65 | | 1 Apr 1965 (s 94(2)) |
| 66 | | 31 Jul 1963 (RA) |
| 67–69 | | 1 Apr 1965 (s 94(2)) |
| 70–94 | | 31 Jul 1963 (RA) |
| Schs 1–4 | | 31 Jul 1963 (RA) |
| Schs 5–15 | | 1 Apr 1965 (s 94(2)) |
| Sch 16 | | 31 Jul 1963 (RA) |

**London Government Act 1963 (c 33)**—*contd*
Sch 17                 1 Apr 1965 (s 94(2))
Sch 18                 31 Jul 1963 (RA)

**Malaysia Act 1963 (c 35)**

*RA:* 31 Jul 1963

This Act generally had effect from 16 Sep 1963 (the "appointed day")

**Matrimonial Causes Act 1963 (c 45)**

*RA:* 31 Jul 1963

Whole Act in force 31 Jul 1963 (RA)

**National Insurance Act 1963 (c 7)**

*RA:* 28 Feb 1963

*Commencement provisions*: s 8, Sch 4, para 1(1); National Insurance Act 1963 (Commencement) Order 1963, SI 1963/393[1]

| | | |
|---|---|---|
| 1 | (1), (2) | 3 Jun 1963 (SI 1963/393) |
| | (3) | See Sch 2 below |
| | (4) | 11 Mar 1963 (SI 1963/393) |
| | (5) | 7 Mar 1963 (so far as it relates to higher rates and amounts of benefit under National Insurance (Industrial Injuries) Act 1946, in the case of unemployment and sickness benefit) (SI 1963/393) |
| | | 11 Mar 1963 (so far as it relates to higher rates and amounts of benefit under National Insurance (Industrial Injuries) Act 1946, in the case of maternity allowance) (SI 1963/393) |
| | | 27 May 1963 (so far as it relates to higher rates and amounts of benefit under National Insurance (Industrial Injuries) Act 1946, in the case of widow's benefit, guardian's allowance, retirement pension and child's special allowance) (SI 1963/393) |
| 2 | (1)–(3) | 27 May 1963 (SI 1963/393) |
| | (4) | 7 Mar 1963 (so far as it relates to the amendment of the National Insurance Act 1946, s 24(1), in its application to unemployment and sickness benefits) (SI 1963/393) |
| | | 27 May 1963 (so far as it relates to the amendment of the National Insurance Act 1946, s 24(1), in its application to retirement pensions) (SI 1963/393) |
| 3 | (1) | 1 Jun 1963 (SI 1963/393) |
| | (2) | 5 Jan 1964 (SI 1963/393) |
| | (3) | 28 Feb 1963 (RA) |
| | (4) | 7 Apr 1963 (so far as it amends National Insurance Act 1959, s 7(5)) (SI 1963/393) |
| | | 5 Jan 1964 (so far as it amends National Insurance Act 1959, s 7(3)) (SI 1963/393) |
| | (5), (6) | 28 Feb 1963 (RA) |
| 4 | | See Sch 3 below |
| 5 | | 27 May 1963 (SI 1963/393) |
| 6–8 | | 28 Feb 1963 (RA) |
| Sch 1 | | 3 Jun 1963 (SI 1963/393) |
| Sch 2 | | 7 Mar 1963 (so far as it relates to higher rates and amounts of benefit under National Insurance (Industrial Injuries) Act 1946, in the case of unemployment and sickness benefit) (SI 1963/393) |

**National Insurance Act 1963 (c 7)**—*contd*

|   |   |   |
|---|---|---|
|   |   | 11 Mar 1963 (so far as it relates to higher rates and amounts of benefit under National Insurance (Industrial Injuries) Act 1946, in the case of maternity allowance) (SI 1963/393) |
|   |   | 27 May 1963 (so far as it relates to higher rates and amounts of benefit under National Insurance (Industrial Injuries) Act 1946, in the case of widow's benefit, guardian's allowance, retirement pension and child's special allowance) (SI 1963/393) |
| Sch 3 | Pt I | 3 Jun 1963 (SI 1963/393) |
|   | Pt II | 7 Mar 1963 (so far as it relates to higher rates and amounts of benefit under National Insurance (Industrial Injuries) Act 1946, in the case of injury benefit (including increases thereof), and increases of disablement pension on account of unemployability and in respect of children and adult dependants) (SI 1963/393) |
|   |   | 27 May 1963 (otherwise) (SI 1963/393) |
|   | Pt III | 7 Mar 1963 (so far as it relates to the amendments of the National Insurance (Industrial Injuries) Act 1946, s 29, in relation to an aggregate weekly rate of benefit by way of injury benefit and a disablement pension or pensions) (SI 1963/393) |
|   |   | 27 May 1963 (so far as it relates to the amendments of the National Insurance (Industrial Injuries) Act 1946, ss 14, 21, 29, in relation to an aggregate weekly rate of benefit by way of two or more disablement pensions) (SI 1963/393) |
| Sch 4 |   | 28 Feb 1963 (RA) |
| Sch 5 |   | 27 May 1963 (repeal of or in National Insurance Act 1946, s 17(3)) (SI 1963/393) |
|   |   | 3 Jun 1963 (otherwise) (SI 1963/393) |

[1]   For transitional provisions, see SI 1963/393, arts 2, 3(2)

---

**Nigeria Republic Act 1963 (c 57)**

*RA:* 18 Dec 1963

Whole Act in force 18 Dec 1963 (RA; but note that s 1 is deemed to have had effect from 1 Oct 1963 (s 1(4))

---

**Nursing Homes Act 1963 (c 13)**

*RA:* 15 May 1963

Whole Act in force 15 May 1963 (RA)

---

**Oaths and Evidence (Overseas Authorities and Countries) Act 1963 (c 27)**

*RA:* 31 Jul 1963

Whole Act in force 31 Jul 1963 (RA)

---

**Offices, Shops and Railway Premises Act 1963 (c 41)**

*RA:* 31 Jul 1963

*Commencement provisions*: s 91(2); Offices, Shops and Railway Premises Act 1963 (Commencement No 1) Order 1964, SI 1964/191; Offices, Shops and Railway Premises Act 1963 (Commencement No 2) Order 1964, SI 1964/1045

| | |
|---|---|
| 1–3 | 1 May 1964 (SI 1964/191) |
| 4–22 | 1 Aug 1964 (except in relation to premises which are in a covered market place to which s 51 relates) (SI 1964/191) |

**Offices, Shops and Railway Premises Act 1963 (c 41)**—*contd*

|       |          | |
|-------|----------|--|
| | | *Never in force* (exception noted above) (repealed) |
| 23 | | 1 Aug 1964 (except in relation to premises which are in a covered market place to which s 51 relates) (SI 1964/191) |
| | | *Never in force* (exception noted above) (repealed) |
| 24 | (1)–(3) | 1 Dec 1964 (except in relation to covered market places) (SI 1964/1045) |
| | | *Never in force* (exception noted above) (repealed) |
| | (4)–(6) | 1 Sep 1965 (except in relation to covered market places) (SI 1964/1045) |
| | | *Never in force* (exception noted above) (repealed) |
| | (7) | 1 Dec 1964 (except in relation to covered market places) (SI 1964/1045) |
| | | *Never in force* (exception noted above) (repealed) |
| | (8) | 1 Sep 1965 (except in relation to covered market places) (SI 1964/1045) |
| | | *Never in force* (exception noted above) (repealed) |
| | (9) | 1 Dec 1964 (except in relation to covered market places) (SI 1964/1045) |
| | | *Never in force* (exception noted above) (repealed) |
| 25, 26 | | 1 Dec 1964 (except in relation to covered market places) (SI 1964/1045) |
| | | *Never in force* (exception noted above) (repealed) |
| 27, 28 | | 1 Aug 1964 (except in relation to premises which are in a covered market place to which s 51 relates) (SI 1964/191) |
| | | *Never in force* (exception noted above) (repealed) |
| 29 | (1) | 1 Aug 1964 (except in relation to premises which are in a covered market place to which s 51 relates) (SI 1964/191) |
| | | *Never in force* (exception noted above) (repealed) |
| | (2) | 1 May 1964 (except in relation to premises which are in a covered market place to which s 51 relates) (SI 1964/191) |
| | | *Never in force* (exception noted above) (repealed) |
| | (3)–(11) | 1 Aug 1964 (except in relation to premises which are in a covered market place to which s 51 relates) (SI 1964/191) |
| | | *Never in force* (exception noted above) (repealed) |
| 30–38 | | 1 Aug 1964 (except in relation to premises which are in a covered market place to which s 51 relates) (SI 1964/191) |
| | | *Never in force* (exception noted above) (repealed) |
| 39, 40 | | 1 May 1964 (except in relation to premises which are in a covered market place to which s 51 relates) (SI 1964/191) |
| | | *Never in force* (exception noted above) (repealed) |
| 41 | | 1 Aug 1964 (except in relation to premises which are in a covered market place to which s 51 relates) (SI 1964/191) |
| | | *Never in force* (exception noted above) (repealed) |
| 42 | (1) | 1 May 1964 (except in relation to premises which are in a covered market place to which s 51 relates) (SI 1964/191) |
| | | *Never in force* (exception noted above) (repealed) |
| | (2)–(10) | 1 Aug 1964 (except in relation to premises which are in a covered market place to which s 51 relates) (SI 1964/191) |
| | | *Never in force* (exception noted above) (repealed) |
| | (11) | 1 May 1964 (except in relation to premises which are in a covered market place to which s 51 relates) (SI 1964/191) |
| | | *Never in force* (exception noted above) (repealed) |
| | (12)–(16) | 1 Aug 1964 (except in relation to premises which are in a covered market place to which s 51 relates) (SI 1964/191) |
| | | *Never in force* (exception noted above) (repealed) |
| 43 | (1) | 1 May 1964 (except in relation to premises which are in a covered market place to which s 51 relates) (SI 1964/191) |
| | | *Never in force* (exception noted above) (repealed) |
| | (2)–(5) | 1 Aug 1964 (except in relation to premises which are in a covered market place to which s 51 relates) (SI 1964/191) |

## Offices, Shops and Railway Premises Act 1963 (c 41)—*contd*

|  |  |  |
|---|---|---|
| | | *Never in force* (exception noted above) (repealed) |
| | (6)–(8) | 1 Aug 1964 (except in relation to premises which are in a covered market place to which s 51 relates) (SI 1964/191) |
| | | *Never in force* (exception noted above) (repealed) |
| | (9)(a) | 1 May 1964 (except in relation to premises which are in a covered market place to which s 51 relates) (SI 1964/191) |
| | | *Never in force* (exception noted above) (repealed) |
| | (9)(b), (c) | 1 Aug 1964 (except in relation to premises which are in a covered market place to which s 51 relates) (SI 1964/191) |
| | | *Never in force* (exception noted above) |
| | (10)–(14) | 1 Aug 1964 (except in relation to premises which are in a covered market place to which s 51 relates) (SI 1964/191) |
| | | *Never in force* (exception noted above) (repealed) |
| 44, 45 | | 1 Aug 1964 (except in relation to premises which are in a covered market place to which s 51 relates) (SI 1964/191) |
| | | *Never in force* (exception noted above) (repealed) |
| 46 | | 1 May 1964 (except in relation to premises which are in a covered market place to which s 51 relates) (SI 1964/191) |
| | | *Never in force* (exception noted above) (repealed) |
| 47, 48 | | 1 Aug 1964 (except in relation to premises which are in a covered market place to which s 51 relates) (SI 1964/191) |
| | | *Never in force* (exception noted above) (repealed) |
| 49 | | 1 May 1964 (SI 1964/191) |
| 50 | | 1 Aug 1964 (except in relation to premises which are in a covered market place to which s 51 relates) (SI 1964/191) |
| | | *Never in force* (exception noted above) (repealed) |
| 51 | | *Never in force* (repealed) |
| 52–56 | | 1 May 1964 (SI 1964/191) |
| 57 | (1) | 18 Feb 1964 (except in relation to premises which are in a covered market place to which s 51 relates) (SI 1964/191) |
| | | 1 May 1964 (exception noted above) (SI 1964/191) |
| | (2)–(5) | 1 May 1964 (SI 1964/191) |
| 58–62 | | 1 May 1964 (SI 1964/191) |
| 63 | | 1 May 1964 (except in relation to premises which are in a covered market place to which s 51 relates) (SI 1964/191) |
| | | *Never in force* (exception noted above) (repealed) |
| 64 | | 1 May 1964 (except in relation to premises which are in a covered market place to which s 51 relates) (SI 1964/191) |
| | | *Never in force* (exception noted above) (repealed) |
| 65–68 | | 1 May 1964 (SI 1964/191) |
| 69 | | 1 May 1964 (except in relation to premises which are in a covered market place to which s 51 relates) (SI 1964/191) |
| | | *Never in force* (exception noted above) (repealed) |
| 70–73 | | 1 May 1964 (except in relation to premises which are in a covered market place to which s 51 relates) (SI 1964/191) |
| | | *Never in force* (exception noted above) (repealed) |
| 74, 75 | | 1 May 1964 (except in relation to premises which are in a covered market place to which s 51 relates) (SI 1964/191) |
| | | *Not yet in force* (exception noted above) |
| 76 | (1) | 1 May 1964 (except in relation to premises which are in a covered market place to which s 51 relates) (SI 1964/191) |
| | | *Never in force* (exception noted above) (repealed) |
| | (2), (3) | 1 Aug 1964 (except in relation to premises which are in a covered market place to which s 51 relates) (SI 1964/191) |
| | | *Never in force* (exception noted above) (repealed) |
| 77 | | 1 Aug 1964 (except in relation to premises which are in a covered market place to which s 51 relates) (SI 1964/191) |
| | | *Never in force* (exception noted above) (repealed) |
| 78 | | 1 May 1964 (except in relation to premises which are in a covered market place to which s 51 relates) (SI 1964/191) |

**Offices, Shops and Railway Premises Act 1963 (c 41)**—*contd*

|   |   |   |
|---|---|---|
|   |   | *Never in force* (exception noted above) (repealed) |
| 79 |   | 1 Jan 1965 (except in relation to premises which are in a covered market place to which s 51 relates) (SI 1964/191) |
|   |   | *Never in force* (exception noted above) (repealed) |
| 80 |   | 18 Feb 1964 (except in relation to premises which are in a covered market place to which s 51 relates) (SI 1964/191) |
|   |   | 1 May 1964 (exception noted above) (SI 1964/191) |
| 81 |   | 1 May 1964 (SI 1964/191) |
| 82 |   | 18 Feb 1964 (except in relation to premises which are in a covered market place to which s 51 relates) (SI 1964/191) |
|   |   | 1 May 1964 (exceptions noted above) (SI 1964/191) |
| 83 | (1) | 1 Aug 1964 (except so far as it relates to s 24 and in relation to covered market places) (SI 1964/191) |
|   |   | 1 Dec 1964 (so far as relates to s 24(1), (3)) (SI 1964/1045) |
|   |   | 1 Sep 1965 (otherwise, except in relation to covered market places) (SI 1964/1045) |
|   |   | *Never in force* (exception noted above) (repealed) |
|   | (2) | 1 Dec 1964 (except in relation to covered market places) (SI 1964/1045) |
|   |   | *Never in force* (exception noted above) (repealed) |
|   | (3) | 1 May 1964 (so far as it relates to s 29(2) and except in relation to covered market places) (SI 1964/191) |
|   |   | 1 Aug 1964 (so far as it relates to s 29(2)) (SI 1964/191) |
|   |   | *Never in force* (in relation to covered market places) (repealed) |
|   | (4) | 1 May 1964 (except in relation to covered market places) (SI 1964/191) |
|   |   | *Never in force* (exception noted above) (repealed) |
|   | (5) | 1 May 1964 (except in relation to covered market places) (SI 1964/191) |
|   |   | *Never in force* (exception noted above) (repealed) |
|   | (6), (7) | 1 Aug 1964 (except in relation to covered market places) (SI 1964/191) |
|   |   | *Never in force* (exception noted above) (repealed) |
| 84 |   | 1 Aug 1964 (except in relation to premises which are in a covered market place to which s 51 relates) (SI 1964/191) |
|   |   | *Never in force* (exception noted above) (repealed) |
| 85, 86 |   | 1 May 1964 (SI 1964/191) |
| 87 |   | 1 May 1964 (except in relation to premises which are in a covered market place to which s 51 relates) (SI 1964/191) |
|   |   | *Never in force* (exception noted above) (repealed) |
| 88 |   | 1 May 1964 (SI 1964/191) |
| 89 |   | 1 May 1964 (except in relation to premises which are in a covered market place to which s 51 relates) (SI 1964/191) |
|   |   | *Never in force* (exception noted above) (repealed) |
| 90 |   | 18 Feb 1964 (except in relation to premises which are in a covered market place to which s 51 relates) (SI 1964/191) |
|   |   | 1 May 1964 (exception noted above) (SI 1964/191) |
| 91 | (1)–(3) | 18 Feb 1964 (except in relation to premises which are in a covered market place to which s 51 relates) (SI 1964/191) |
|   |   | 1 May 1964 (exception noted above) (SI 1964/191) |
|   | (4) | See Sch 2 below |
| Sch 1 |   | 18 Feb 1964 (except in relation to premises which are in a covered market place to which s 51 relates) (SI 1964/191) |
|   |   | 1 May 1964 (in relation to covered market places, except so far as they relate to repeals of or in Shops Act 1950, s 37) (SI 1964/191) |
|   |   | *Never in force* (exception noted above) (repealed) |
| Sch 2 |   | 1 Aug 1964 (SI 1964/191) |

## Oil in Navigable Waters Act 1963 (c 28)

*RA:* 31 Jul 1963

*Commencement provisions:* s 4(3); Oil in Navigable Waters Act 1963 (Commencement) Order 1967, SI 1967/708

Whole Act in force 18 May 1967 (SI 1967/708)

---

## Peerage Act 1963 (c 48)

*RA:* 31 Jul 1963

Whole Act in force 31 Jul 1963 (RA)

---

## Performers' Protection Act 1963 (c 53)

*RA:* 31 Jul 1963

*Commencement provisions:* s 5(3)

Whole Act in force 31 Aug 1963 (s 5(3); note that the Act applies only in relation to performances taking place after 30 Aug 1963)

---

## Protection of Depositors Act 1963 (c 16)

*RA:* 10 Jul 1963

*Commencement provisions:* s 28(2)

Whole Act in force 10 Oct 1963 (s 28(2))

---

## Public Lavatories (Turnstiles) Act 1963 (c 32)

*RA:* 31 Jul 1963

Whole Act in force 31 Jul 1963 (RA)

---

## Public Order Act 1963 (c 52)

*RA:* 31 Jul 1963

Whole Act in force 31 Jul 1963 (RA)

---

## Purchase Tax Act 1963 (c 9)

*RA:* 28 Mar 1963

*Commencement provisions:* s 42(2)

Whole Act in force 1 Apr 1963 (s 42(2))

---

## Remuneration of Teachers Act 1963 (c 20)

*RA:* 10 Jul 1963

Whole Act in force 10 Jul 1963 (RA)

---

## Rhodesia and Nyasaland Act 1963 (c 34)

*RA:* 31 Jul 1963

Whole Act in force 31 Jul 1963 (RA; note that the Federation of Rhodesia and Nyasaland was dissolved as
  from 1 Jan 1964 by Federation of Rhodesia and Nyasaland (Dissolution) Order in Council 1963,
  SI 1963/2085, made under s 1)

## Sheriff Courts (Civil Jurisdiction and Procedure) (Scotland) Act 1963 (c 22)

*RA:* 10 Jul 1963

*Commencement provisions*: s 4(3)

Whole Act in force 1 Oct 1963 (s 4(3))

## Statute Law Revision Act 1963 (c 30)

*RA:* 31 Jul 1963

Whole Act in force 31 Jul 1963 (RA)

## Stock Transfer Act 1963 (c 18)

*RA:* 10 Jul 1963

*Commencement provisions*: s 6(2); Stock Transfer Act 1963 (Commencement) Order 1963 (SI 1963/1592)

| | | |
|---|---|---|
| 1–4 | | 26 Oct 1963 (SI 1963/1592) |
| 5 | (1), (2) | 26 Oct 1963 (SI 1963/1592) |
| | (3) | 10 Jul 1963 (s 6(2)) |
| | (4) | 26 Oct 1963 (SI 1963/1592) |
| 6 | | 26 Oct 1963 (SI 1963/1592) |
| Schs 1, 2 | | 26 Oct 1963 (SI 1963/1592) |

## Television Act 1963 (c 50)

*RA:* 31 Jul 1963

*Commencement provisions*: s 24

Whole Act in force 31 Aug 1964 (s 24(3); subject to sub-ss (1), (2))

## Town and Country Planning Act 1963 (c 17)

*RA:* 10 Jul 1963

*Commencement provisions*: s 4(2)

Whole Act in force 25 Feb 1963 (s 4(2); subject to transitional provisions and savings)

## Towyn Trewan Common Act 1963 (c 4)

*RA:* 28 Feb 1963

Whole Act in force 28 Feb 1963 (RA)

**Water Resources Act 1963 (c 38)**

*RA:* 31 Jul 1963

Whole Act in force 31 Jul 1963 (RA) (note that the Act provides for the establishment of river authorities, to come into existence on "the appointed day" and to perform certain functions on and after "the second appointed day" under s 3(4). The "appointed day" was 15 Oct 1964 (River Authorities (First Appointed Day) Order 1964, SI 1964/1267) and "the second appointed day" was 1 Apr 1965 (River Authorities (Second Appointed Day) Order 1964, SI 1964/1268))

**Weights and Measures Act 1963 (c 31)**

*RA:* 31 Jul 1963

*Commencement provisions:* ss 63(1)(b), (2), 66(2)

| | | |
|---|---|---|
| 1–17 | | 31 Jan 1964 (s 66(2)) |
| 18–33 | | 31 Jul 1965 (s 66(2)) |
| 34–60 | | 31 Jan 1964 (s 66(2)) |
| 61 | (1)–(3) | 31 Jan 1964 (s 66(2)) |
| | (4) | 31 Jul 1963 (s 66(2)) |
| | (5) | 31 Jan 1964 (s 66(2)) |
| 62–66 | | 31 Jan 1964 (s 66(2)) |
| Schs 1–3 | | 31 Jan 1964 (s 66(2)) |
| Schs 4–8 | | 31 Jul 1965 (s 66(2)) |
| Schs 9, 10 | | 31 Jan 1964 (s 66(2)) |

**Wills Act 1963 (c 44)**

*RA:* 31 Jul 1963

*Commencement provisions:* s 7(2)

Whole Act in force 1 Jan 1964 (s 7(2)) (note that the Act applies to wills of testators who died on or after 1 Jan 1964 regardless of when the will was executed (s 7(4)))

**Zanzibar Act 1963 (c 55)**

*RA:* 3 Dec 1963

This Act generally had effect from 10 Dec 1963 (the "appointed day")

# 1964 Acts

## Administration of Justice Act 1964 (c 42)

*RA:* 10 Jun 1964

*Commencement provisions:* s 41(2)–(4); Administration of Justice Act 1964 (Commencement No 1) Order 1964, SI 1964/864; Administration of Justice Act 1964 (Commencement No 2) Order 1964, SI 1964/1435

| | | |
|---|---|---|
| 1 | (1) | 1 Apr 1965 (s 41(2)) |
| | (2) | 1 Jan 1965 (SI 1964/1435) |
| | (3) | See Sch 1 below |
| | (4) | 1 Apr 1965 (s 41(2)) |
| 2–4 | | 1 Apr 1965 (s 41(2)) |
| 5 | (1) | 1 Apr 1965 (s 41(2)) |
| | (2) | 1 Jul 1964 (SI 1964/864) |
| | (3)–(5) | 1 Apr 1965 (s 41(2)) |
| 6, 7 | | 1 Apr 1965 (s 41(2)) |
| 8 | (1)–(7) | 1 Apr 1965 (s 41(2)) |
| | (8), (9) | 1 Oct 1964 (SI 1964/1435) |
| | (10), (11) | 1 Apr 1965 (s 41(2)) |
| 9 | | 1 Apr 1965 (s 41(2)) |
| 10 | (1) | 1 Jul 1964 (so far as it relates to the maximum number of metropolitan stipendiary magistrates) (SI 1964/864) |
| | | 1 Apr 1965 (otherwise) (s 41(2)) |
| | (2)–(8) | 1 Apr 1965 (s 41(2)) |
| 11 | | 1 Apr 1965 (s 41(2)) |
| 12 | (1), (2) | 1 Apr 1965 (s 41(2)) |
| | (3) | 1 Jul 1964 (SI 1964/864) |
| 13–18 | | 1 Apr 1965 (s 41(2)) |
| 19 | (1) | 1 Jan 1965 (SI 1964/1435) |
| | (2)(a), (b) | 1 Jan 1965 (SI 1964/1435) |
| | (2)(c) | 1 Apr 1965 (s 41(2)) |
| | (3), (4) | 1 Jan 1965 (SI 1964/1435) |
| 20–23 | | 1 Apr 1965 (s 41(2)) |
| 24 | | 1 Jul 1964 (SI 1964/864) |
| 25 | | 1 Apr 1965 (s 41(2)) |
| 26 | | 1 Jul 1964 (SI 1964/864) |
| 27 | | 1 Oct 1964 (except in so far as it relates to a metropolitan stipendiary magistrate or a clerk or other officer of a metropolitan stipendiary court) (SI 1964/1435) |
| | | 1 Apr 1965 (otherwise) (SI 1964/1435) |
| 28 | | 1 Oct 1964 (SI 1964/1435) |
| 29 | (1)–(10) | 1 Apr 1965 (SI 1964/1435) |
| | (11) | 1 Jul 1964 (SI 1964/864) |
| | (12), (13) | 1 Apr 1965 (SI 1964/1435) |
| 30 | | 1 Jul 1964 (SI 1964/864) |
| 31 | | 1 Apr 1965 (SI 1964/1435) |
| 32–34 | | 1 Jul 1964 (SI 1964/864) |
| 35–38 | | 10 Jun 1964 (RA) |

## Administration of Justice Act 1964 (c 42)—*contd*

| | | |
|---|---|---|
| 39 | | See Sch 3 below |
| 40 | | 10 Jun 1964 (RA) |
| 41 | (1)–(7) | 10 Jun 1964 (RA) |
| | (8) | See Sch 5 below |
| Sch 1 | paras 1–8 | 10 Jun 1964 (RA) |
| | paras 9–14 | 1 Jan 1965 (SI 1964/1435) |
| | paras 15–18 | 10 Jun 1964 (RA) |
| Sch 2 | | 10 Jun 1964 (RA) |
| Sch 3 | paras 1–10 | 1 Apr 1965 (SI 1964/1435) |
| | para 11 | 1 Jul 1964 (SI 1964/864) |
| | paras 12–14 | 1 Apr 1965 (SI 1964/1435) |
| | para 15(1) | 1 Jul 1964 (SI 1964/864) |
| | para 15(2) | 1 Apr 1965 (SI 1964/1435) |
| | para 16 | 1 Oct 1964 (SI 1964/1435) |
| | para 17(1) | 1 Jul 1964 (SI 1964/864) |
| | para 17(2) | 1 Apr 1965 (SI 1964/1435) |
| | para 18 | 1 Apr 1965 (SI 1964/1435) |
| | para 19(1), (2) | 1 Apr 1965 (SI 1964/1435) |
| | para 19(3), (4) | 1 Oct 1964 (SI 1964/1435) |
| | para 20(1) | 1 Jul 1964 (SI 1964/864) |
| | para 20(2)–(8) | 1 Apr 1965 (SI 1964/1435) |
| | para 21 | 1 Apr 1965 (SI 1964/1435) |
| | para 22(1) | 1 Jan 1965 (SI 1964/1435) |
| | para 22(2) | 1 Apr 1965 (SI 1964/1435) |
| | para 22(3) | 1 Jan 1965 (SI 1964/1435) |
| | para 22(4), (5) | 1 Apr 1965 (SI 1964/1435) |
| | para 23(1)(a), (b) | 1 Jul 1964 (SI 1964/864) |
| | para 23(1)(c) | 1 Apr 1965 (SI 1964/1435) |
| | para 24 | 1 Apr 1965 (SI 1964/1435) |
| | para 25 | 1 Jul 1964 (SI 1964/864) |
| | paras 26–31 | 1 Apr 1965 (SI 1964/1435) |
| Sch 4 | | 10 Jun 1964 (RA) |
| Sch 5 | | 1 Jul 1964 (SI 1964/864), repeals of or in— |

Sch 5 (1 Jul 1964):
- Metropolitan Police Courts Act 1839, s 2, the proviso;
- Metropolitan Police Courts Act 1840, s 2, the second proviso;
- An Act to provide for the more effectual execution of the office of a justice of the peace within the parish of Merthyr Tidvil and certain adjoining parishes;
- Manchester Division and Borough of Salford (Stipendiary Justices) Act 1878;
- Municipal Corporations Act 1882;
- London County Council (General Powers) Act 1926;
- Local Government (Clerks) Act 1931, s 12;
- Local Government Act 1933;
- Administration of Justice (Miscellaneous Provisions) Act 1938, s 1(3);
- Criminal Justice Administration Act 1956, s 4(2);
- House of Commons Disqualification Act 1957;
- Metropolitan Magistrates' Courts Act 1959;
- London Government Act 1963, Sch 2, para 1(2)(a)

1 Oct 1964 (SI 1964/1435), repeals of or in—
- Local Government Act 1888, s 66;
- Justices of the Peace Act 1949, ss 25(2), 26(3)

1 Jan 1965 (SI 1964/1435), repeals of or in—
- Central Criminal Court Act 1834, s 15;
- Supreme Court of Judicature (Consolidation) Act 1925, s 74

1 Apr 1965 (otherwise) (SI 1964/1435)

### Adoption Act 1964 (c 57)

*RA:* 16 Jul 1964

Whole Act in force 16 Jul 1964 (RA)

### Agriculture and Horticulture Act 1964 (c 28)

*RA:* 15 Apr 1964

Whole Act in force 15 Apr 1964 (RA)

### Air Corporations Act 1964 (c 2)

*RA:* 6 Feb 1964

Whole Act in force 6 Feb 1964 (RA)

### Animals (Restriction of Importation) Act 1964 (c 61)

*RA:* 16 Jul 1964

*Commencement provisions:* s 5(2)

Whole Act in force 16 Jan 1965 (s 5(2))

### Appropriation Act 1964 (c 62)

*RA:* 31 Jul 1964

Whole Act in force 31 Jul 1964 (RA)

### Betting, Gaming and Lotteries Act 1964 (c 78)

*RA:* 31 Jul 1964

*Commencement provisions:* s 4(3)

Whole Act in force 31 Jul 1964, except s 2, which came into force on 31 Oct 1965 (s 4(3))

### British Nationality Act 1964 (c 22)

*RA:* 25 Mar 1964

*Commencement provisions:* s 3(3)

Whole Act in force 25 May 1964 (s 3(3))

### British Nationality (No 2) Act 1964 (c 54)

*RA:* 16 Jul 1964

*Commencement provisions:* s 6(3)

Whole Act in force 16 Sep 1964 (s 6(3))

**British North America Act 1964 (c 73)**

*RA:* 31 Jul 1964

Whole Act in force 31 Jul 1964 (RA)

---

**Burgh Police (Amendment) (Scotland) Act 1964 (c 33)**

*RA:* 10 Jun 1964

Whole Act in force 10 Jun 1964 (RA)

---

**Church Commissioners Measure 1964 (No 8)**

*RA:* 31 Jul 1964

Whole Act in force 31 Jul 1964 (RA)

---

**Church Commissioners (Loans for Theological Colleges and Training Houses) Measure 1964 (No 1)**

*RA:* 27 Feb 1964

Whole Act in force 27 Feb 1964 (RA)

---

**Churchwardens (Appointment and Resignation) Measure 1964 (No 3)**

*RA:* 27 Feb 1964

*Commencement provisions:* s 15(3)

Whole Act in force 1 Jan 1965 (s 15(3))

---

**Clergy (Ordination and Miscellaneous Provisions) Measure 1964 (No 6)**

*RA:* 10 Jun 1964

Whole Act in force 10 Jun 1964 (RA)

---

**Consolidated Fund Act 1964 (c 1)**

*RA:* 6 Feb 1964

Whole Act in force 6 Feb 1964 (RA)

---

**Consolidated Fund (No 2) Act 1964 (c 17)**

*RA:* 25 Mar 1964

Whole Act in force 25 Mar 1964 (RA)

---

**Continental Shelf Act 1964 (c 29)**

*RA:* 15 Apr 1964

Whole Act in force 15 Apr 1964 (RA)

---

## Criminal Appeal Act 1964 (c 43)

*RA:* 10 Jun 1964

Whole Act in force 10 Jun 1964 (RA)

---

## Criminal Procedure (Insanity) Act 1964 (c 84)

*RA:* 31 Jul 1964

*Commencement provisions:* s 8(3)

Whole Act in force 31 Aug 1964 (s 8(3))

---

## Criminal Procedure (Right of Reply) Act 1964 (c 34)

*RA:* 10 Jun 1964

*Commencement provisions:* s 2(2)

Whole Act in force 10 Jul 1964 (s 2(2))

---

## Dangerous Drugs Act 1964 (c 36)

*RA:* 10 Jun 1964

Whole Act in force 10 Jun 1964 (RA)

---

## Defence (Transfer of Functions) Act 1964 (c 15)

*RA:* 12 Mar 1964

*Commencement provisions:* s 1(1); Defence (Transfer of Functions) (Appointed Day) Order 1964, SI 1964/487

Whole Act in force 1 Apr 1964 (SI 1964/487)

---

## Diplomatic Privileges Act 1964 (c 81)

*RA:* 31 Jul 1964

*Commencement provisions:* s 8(3); Diplomatic Privileges Act 1964 (Commencement) Order 1964, SI 1964/1400

Whole Act in force 1 Oct 1964 (SI 1964/1400)

---

## Divorce (Scotland) Act 1964 (c 91)

*RA:* 31 Jul 1964

Whole Act in force 31 Jul 1964 (RA)

---

## Drugs (Prevention of Misuse) Act 1964 (c 64)

*RA:* 31 Jul 1964

*Commencement provisions:* s 11(2)

**Drugs (Prevention of Misuse) Act 1964 (c 64)**—*contd*
Whole Act in force 31 Jul 1964 (in so far as relates to the registration of persons for the purposes of s 1(1)(c) and to the licensing of the importation of substances), otherwise the whole Act comes into force on 31 Oct 1964 (s 11(2))

**Education Act 1964 (c 82)**

*RA:* 31 Jul 1964

Whole Act in force 31 Jul 1964 (RA)

**Elections (Welsh Forms) Act 1964 (c 31)**

*RA:* 10 Jun 1964

Whole Act in force 10 Jun 1964 (RA)

**Emergency Laws (Re-enactments and Repeals) Act 1964 (c 60)**

*RA:* 16 Jul 1964

Whole Act in force 16 Jul 1964 (RA)

**Emergency Powers Act 1964 (c 38)**

*RA:* 10 Jun 1964

Whole Act in force 10 Jun 1964 (RA)

**Episcopal Church (Scotland) Act 1964 (c 12)**

*RA:* 27 Feb 1964

Whole Act in force 27 Feb 1964 (RA)

**Expiring Laws Continuance Act 1964 (c 94)**

*RA:* 17 Dec 1964

Whole Act in force 17 Dec 1964 (RA)

**Export Guarantees Act 1964 (c 6)**

*RA:* 27 Feb 1964

Whole Act in force 27 Feb 1964 (RA)

**Faculty Jurisdiction Measure 1964 (No 5)**

*RA:* 15 Apr 1964

Whole Act in force 15 Apr 1964 (RA)

## Family Allowances and National Insurance Act 1964 (c 10)

*RA:* 27 Feb 1964

*Commencement provisions:* s 6(3), Sch 3; Family Allowances and National Insurance Act 1964
(Commencement) Order 1964, SI 1964/296

| | |
|---|---|
| 1, 2 | 30 Mar 1964 (SI 1964/296) |
| 3 | 27 Feb 1964 (RA) |
| 4 | 30 Mar 1964 (SI 1964/296) |
| 5, 6 | 27 Feb 1964 (RA) |
| Schs 1, 2 | 30 Mar 1964 (SI 1964/296) |
| Sch 3 | 27 Feb 1964 (RA) |
| Sch 4 | 30 Mar 1964 (SI 1964/296) |

## Films Act 1964 (c 52)

*RA:* 16 Jul 1964

Whole Act in force 16 Jul 1964 (RA)

## Finance Act 1964 (c 49)

*RA:* 16 Jul 1964

The commencement details of Finance Acts are not set out, as the dates from which their provisions take
effect are usually stated clearly and unambiguously in the text of the Act, and charging provisions will
normally state for which year or years of assessment they are to have effect.

## Finance (No 2) Act 1964 (c 92)

*RA:* 17 Dec 1964

The commencement details of Finance Acts are not set out, as the dates from which their provisions take
effect are usually stated clearly and unambiguously in the text of the Act, and charging provisions will
normally state for which year or years of assessment they are to have effect.

## Fireworks Act 1964 (c 23)

*RA:* 25 Mar 1964

Whole Act in force 25 Mar 1964 (RA)

## Fishery Limits Act 1964 (c 72)

*RA:* 31 Jul 1964

*Commencement provisions:* s 5(2); Fishery Limits Act 1964 (Commencement) Order 1964, SI 1964/1553

Whole Act in force 30 Sep 1964 (SI 1964/1553)

## Gambia Independence Act 1964 (c 93)

*RA:* 17 Dec 1964

This Act generally had effect from 18 Feb 1965 (the "appointed day")

## Hairdressers (Registration) Act 1964 (c 89)

*RA:* 31 Jul 1964

Whole Act in force 31 Jul 1964 (RA)

## Harbours Act 1964 (c 40)

*RA:* 10 Jun 1964

*Commencement provisions:* s 63(4); Harbours Act 1964 (Commencement) Order 1964, SI 1964/1424

| | | |
|---|---|---|
| 1–25 | | 10 Jun 1964 (RA) |
| 26–40 | | 1 Oct 1964 (SI 1964/1424) |
| 41–62 | | 10 Jun 1964 (RA) |
| 63 | (1), (2) | 10 Jun 1964 (RA) |
| | (3) | 1 Oct 1964 (SI 1964/1424) |
| | (4) | 10 Jun 1964 (RA) |
| Schs 1–6 | | 10 Jun 1964 (RA) |

## Hire–Purchase Act 1964 (c 53)

*RA:* 16 Jul 1964

*Commencement provisions:* s 36

Whole Act in force 1 Jan 1965 (except s 36 and in relation to any provisions of this Act which confer any power to make regulations and any provisions relating to the exercise of any such power, which came into force on 16 Jul 1964) (s 36(1), (2))

## Holy Table Measure 1964 (No 4)

*RA:* 15 Apr 1964

Whole Act in force 15 Apr 1964 (RA)

## Housing Act 1964 (c 56)

*RA:* 16 Jul 1964

*Commencement provisions:* s 108(4), (5)

| | | |
|---|---|---|
| 1–12 | | 16 Jul 1964 (s 108(5)) |
| 13–98 | | 16 Aug 1964 (s 108(4)) |
| 99 | | 16 Jul 1964 (s 108(5)) |
| 100–103 | | 16 Aug 1964 (s 108(4)) |
| 104, 105 | | 16 Jul 1964 (s 108(5)) |
| 106 | (1)–(4) | 16 Jul 1964 (s 108(5)) |
| | (5) | 1 Apr 1965 (s 108(5) |
| 107 | | 16 Jul 1964 (s 108(5)) |
| 108 | | 16 Aug 1964 (s 108(4)) |
| Schs 1–5 | | 16 Aug 1964 (s 108(4)) |

## Income Tax Management Act 1964 (c 37)

*RA:* 10 Jun 1964

*Commencement provisions:* ss 1(9), 2(7), 3(4), 4(6), 17(4)

**Income Tax Management Act 1964 (c 37)**—*contd*
Whole Act in force 6 Apr 1965, except ss 1–4 and Sch 1, which came into force on 10 Jul 1964 (ss 1(9), 2(7), 3(4), 4(6), 17(4))

---

**Incumbents and Churchwardens (Trusts) Measure 1964 (No 2)**

*RA:* 27 Feb 1964

*Commencement provisions:* s 6(2)

Whole Act in force 1 Jan 1965 (s 6(2))

---

**Industrial Training Act 1964 (c 16)**

*RA:* 12 Mar 1964

Whole Act in force 12 Mar 1964 (RA)

---

**International Development Association Act 1964 (c 13)**

*RA:* 12 Mar 1964

Whole Act in force 12 Mar 1964 (RA)

---

**International Headquarters and Defence Organisations Act 1964 (c 5)**

*RA:* 27 Feb 1964

Whole Act in force 27 Feb 1964 (RA)

---

**John F Kennedy Memorial Act 1964 (c 85)**

*RA:* 31 Jul 1964

*Commencement provisions:* s 3(2); John F. Kennedy Memorial Act 1964 (Commencement) Order 1964, dated 14 Aug 1964

Whole Act in force 18 Aug 1964 (1964 Order)

---

**Law of Property (Joint Tenants) Act 1964 (c 63)**

*RA:* 31 Jul 1964

*Commencement provisions:* s 2

| | |
|---|---|
| 1 | 1 Jan 1926 (retrospectively; s 2) |
| 2–4 | 31 Jul 1964 (RA) |

---

**Legal Aid Act 1964 (c 30)**

*RA:* 15 Apr 1964

*Commencement provisions:* s 6(2); Legal Aid Act 1964 (Commencement) Order 1964, SI 1964/1275; Legal Aid Act 1964 (Commencement) (Scotland) Order 1964, SI 1964/1605

Whole Act in force 1 Oct 1964 (SI 1964/1275; SI 1964/1605), except s 4 which came into force on 15 Apr 1964 (s 6(2))

---

**Licensing Act 1964 (c 26)**

*RA:* 25 Mar 1964

*Commencement provisions:* s 204(2)

Whole Act in force 1 Jan 1965 (s 204(2))

_____

**Local Government (Development and Finance) (Scotland) Act 1964 (c 67)**

*RA:* 31 Jul 1964

Whole Act in force 31 Jul 1964 (RA)

_____

**Local Government (Pecuniary Interests) Act 1964 (c 77)**

*RA:* 31 Jul 1964

Whole Act in force 31 Jul 1964 (RA)

_____

**Malawi Independence Act 1964 (c 46)**

*RA:* 10 Jun 1964

This Act generally had effect from 6 Jul 1964 (the "appointed day")

_____

**Malicious Damage Act 1964 (c 76)**

*RA:* 31 Jul 1964

Whole Act in force 31 Jul 1964 (RA)

_____

**Malta Independence Act 1964 (c 86)**

*RA:* 31 Jul 1964

This Act generally had effect from 21 Sep 1964 (the "appointed day")

_____

**Married Women's Property Act 1964 (c 19)**

*RA:* 25 Mar 1964

Whole Act in force 25 Mar 1964 (RA)

_____

**Merchant Shipping Act 1964 (c 47)**

*RA:* 10 Jun 1964

*Commencement provisions:* s 19(1); Merchant Shipping Act 1964 (Commencement) Order 1965, SI 1965/317

Whole Act in force 26 May 1965 (SI 1965/317)

_____

## Ministers of the Crown Act 1964 (c 98)

*RA:* 23 Dec 1964

Whole Act in force 23 Dec 1964 (RA)

## National Health Service (Hospital Boards) Act 1964 (c 32)

*RA:* 10 Jun 1964

*Commencement provisions:* s 2(3)

Whole Act in force 10 Jul 1964 (s 2(3))

## National Insurance &c Act 1964 (c 96)

*RA:* 17 Dec 1964

*Commencement provisions:* s 6(3), Sch 7, para 1; National Insurance &c Act 1964 (Commencement) Order 1964, SI 1964/2000[1]

| | | |
|---|---|---|
| 1 | (1) | 29 Mar 1965 (SI 1964/2000) |
| | (2) | 21 Dec 1964 (SI 1964/2000) |
| | (3) | See Sch 2 below |
| | (4) | 25 Jan 1965 (SI 1964/2000) |
| | (5) | 21 Dec 1964 (SI 1964/2000) |
| | (6) | 25 Jan 1965 (SI 1964/2000) |
| | (7) | See Sch 5 below |
| | (8) | 25 Jan 1965 (in relation to higher rates of benefit under the National Insurance Act 1946, in the case of maternity allowance) (SI 1964/2000) |
| | | 28 Jan 1965 (in relation to higher rates of benefit under the National Insurance Act 1946, in the case of unemployment benefit and sickness benefit) (SI 1964/2000) |
| | | 29 Mar 1965 (in relation to higher rates of benefit under the National Insurance Act 1946, in the case of widow's benefit, guardian's allowance, retirement pension and child's special) (SI 1964/2000) |
| 2 | (1) | See Sch 3 below |
| | (2) | See Sch 4 below |
| 3 | | 31 Mar 1965 (SI 1964/2000) |
| 4 | | See Sch 6 below |
| 5 | | 21 Dec 1964 (SI 1964/2000) |
| 6 | (1)–(3) | 21 Dec 1964 (SI 1964/2000) |
| | (4) | 31 Mar 1965 (SI 1964/2000) |
| | (5)–(7) | 21 Dec 1964 (SI 1964/2000) |
| Sch 1 | | 29 Mar 1965 (SI 1964/2000) |
| Sch 2 | | 25 Jan 1965 (in relation to higher rates of benefit under the National Insurance Act 1946, in the case of maternity allowance) (SI 1964/2000) |
| | | 28 Jan 1965 (in relation to higher rates of benefit under the National Insurance Act 1946, in the case of unemployment benefit and sickness benefit) (SI 1964/2000) |
| | | 29 Mar 1965 (in relation to higher rates of benefit under the National Insurance Act 1946, in the case of widow's benefit, guardian's allowance, retirement pension and child's special) (SI 1964/2000) |
| Sch 3 | | 29 Mar 1965 (SI 1964/2000) |

**National Insurance &c Act 1964 (c 96)**—*contd*

Sch 4

27 Jan 1965 (in relation to higher rates and amounts of benefit under the National Insurance (Industrial Injuries) Act 1946, in the case of injury benefit (including increases thereof), and increases of disablement pension on account of unemployability and in respect of children and adult dependants and maximum aggregate of weekly benefit payable for successive accidents, where the payments are by way of injury benefit and disablement pensions or pensions) (SI 1964/2000)

29 Mar 1965 (in relation to higher rates and amounts of benefit under the National Insurance (Industrial Injuries) Act 1946, in the case of death benefit) (SI 1964/2000)

31 Mar 1965 (in relation to higher rates and amounts of benefit under the National Insurance (Industrial Injuries) Act 1946, in the case of disablement benefit (including increases of disablement pensions other than those referred to above and the maximum aggregate of weekly benefit payable for successive accidents, where the payments are by way of two or more disablement pensions)) (SI 1964/2000)

Sch 5     paras 1–13

27 Jan 1965 (in relation to higher rates and amounts of benefit under the National Insurance (Industrial Injuries) Act 1946, in the case of injury benefit (including increases thereof), and increases of disablement pension on account of unemployability and in respect of children and adult dependants and the maximum aggregate of weekly benefit payable for successive accidents, where the payments are by way of injury benefit and disablement pensions or pensions) (SI 1964/2000)

29 Mar 1965 (in relation to higher rates and amounts of benefit under the National Insurance (Industrial Injuries) Act 1946, in the case of death benefit) (SI 1964/2000)

31 Mar 1965 (in relation to higher rates and amounts of benefit under the National Insurance (Industrial Injuries) Act 1946, in the case of disablement benefit (including increases of disablement pensions other than those referred to above and the maximum aggregate of weekly benefit payable for successive accidents, where the payments are by way of 2 or more disablement pensions)) (SI 1964/2000)

paras 14–17

25 Jan 1965 (in relation to higher rates of benefit under the National Insurance Act 1946, in the case of maternity allowance) (SI 1964/2000)

28 Jan 1965 (in relation to higher rates of benefit under the National Insurance Act 1946, in the case of unemployment benefit and sickness benefit) (SI 1964/2000)

29 Mar 1965 (in relation to higher rates of benefit under the National Insurance Act 1946, in the case of widow's benefit, guardian's allowance, retirement pension and child's special) (SI 1964/2000)

para 18(a)

25 Jan 1965 (in relation to higher rates of benefit under the National Insurance Act 1946, in the case of maternity allowance) (SI 1964/2000)

28 Jan 1965 (in relation to higher rates of benefit under the National Insurance Act 1946, in the case of unemployment benefit and sickness benefit) (SI 1964/2000)

29 Mar 1965 (in relation to higher rates of benefit under the National Insurance Act 1946, in the case of widow's benefit, guardian's allowance, retirement pension and child's special) (SI 1964/2000)

**National Insurance &c Act 1964 (c 96)**—*contd*

| | | |
|---|---|---|
| | para 18(b), (c) | 27 Jan 1965 (in relation to higher rates and amounts of benefit under the National Insurance (Industrial Injuries) Act 1946, in the case of injury benefit (including increases thereof), and increases of disablement pension on account of unemployability and in respect of children and adult dependants and the maximum aggregate of weekly benefit payable for successive accidents, where the payments are by way of injury benefit and disablement pensions or pensions) (SI 1964/2000) |
| | | 29 Mar 1965 (in relation to higher rates and amounts of benefit under the National Insurance (Industrial Injuries) Act 1946, in the case of death benefit) (SI 1964/2000) |
| | | 31 Mar 1965 (in relation to higher rates and amounts of benefit under the National Insurance (Industrial Injuries) Act 1946, in the case of disablement benefit (including increases of disablement pensions other than those referred to above and the maximum aggregate of weekly benefit payable for successive accidents, where the payments are by way of 2 or more disablement pensions)) (SI 1964/2000) |
| | paras 19, 20 | 25 Jan 1965 (in relation to higher rates of benefit under the National Insurance Act 1946, in the case of maternity allowance) (SI 1964/2000) |
| | | 28 Jan 1965 (in relation to higher rates of benefit under the National Insurance Act 1946, in the case of unemployment benefit and sickness benefit) (SI 1964/2000) |
| | | 29 Mar 1965 (in relation to higher rates of benefit under the National Insurance Act 1946, in the case of widow's benefit, guardian's allowance, retirement pension and child's special) (SI 1964/2000) |
| | para 21 | 29 Mar 1965 (SI 1964/2000) |
| | para 22 | 27 Jan 1965 (in relation to higher rates and amounts of benefit under the National Insurance (Industrial Injuries) Act 1946, in the case of injury benefit (including increases thereof), and increases of disablement pension on account of unemployability and in respect of children and adult dependants and the maximum aggregate of weekly benefit payable for successive accidents, where the payments are by way of injury benefit and disablement pensions or pensions) (SI 1964/2000) |
| | | 29 Mar 1965 (in relation to higher rates and amounts of benefit under the National Insurance (Industrial Injuries) Act 1946, in the case of death benefit) (SI 1964/2000) |
| | | 31 Mar 1965 (in relation to higher rates and amounts of benefit under the National Insurance (Industrial Injuries) Act 1946, in the case of disablement benefit (including increases of disablement pensions other than those referred to above and the maximum aggregate of weekly benefit payable for successive accidents, where the payments are by way of 2 or more disablement pensions)) (SI 1964/2000) |
| Sch 6 | paras 1–4 | 21 Dec 1964 (SI 1964/2000) |
| | para 5 | 25 Jan 1965 (SI 1964/2000) |
| | paras 6, 7 | 30 Mar 1965 (SI 1964/2000) |
| | para 8 | 21 Dec 1964 (SI 1964/2000) |
| | para 9 | 30 Mar 1965 (SI 1964/2000) |
| | para 10 | 21 Dec 1964 (SI 1964/2000) |
| | para 11 | 29 Mar 1965 (SI 1964/2000) |
| | paras 12–14 | 21 Dec 1964 (SI 1964/2000) |
| | para 15 | 29 Mar 1965 (SI 1964/2000) |
| | paras 16–26 | 21 Dec 1964 (SI 1964/2000) |
| | para 27 | 29 Mar 1965 (SI 1964/2000) |
| | paras 28, 29 | 21 Dec 1964 (SI 1964/2000) |
| Sch 7 | | 21 Dec 1964 (SI 1964/2000) |

**National Insurance &c Act 1964 (c 96)**—*contd*
Sch 8                                   31 Mar 1965 (SI 1964/2000)

1    For transitional provisions and savings, see SI 1964/2000, arts 1(2), 2, 3

---

**Navy, Army and Air Force Reserves Act 1964 (c 11)**

*RA:* 27 Feb 1964

Whole Act in force 27 Feb 1964 (RA)

---

**New Forest Act 1964 (c 83)**

*RA:* 31 Jul 1964

Whole Act in force 31 Jul 1964 (RA)

---

**New Towns Act 1964 (c 8)**

*RA:* 27 Feb 1964

Whole Act in force 27 Feb 1964 (RA)

---

**New Towns (No 2) Act 1964 (c 68)**

*RA:* 31 Jul 1964

Whole Act in force 31 Jul 1964 (RA)

---

**Nurses Act 1964 (c 44)**

*RA:* 10 Jun 1964

Whole Act in force 10 Jun 1964 (RA)

---

**Obscene Publications Act 1964 (c 74)**

*RA:* 31 Jul 1964
*Commencement provisions*: s 3(2)

Whole Act in force 31 Aug 1964 (s 3(2))

---

**Perpetuities and Accumulations Act 1964 (c 55)**

*RA:* 16 Jul 1964

Whole Act in force 16 Jul 1964 (RA)

---

**Pharmacy and Poisons (Amendment) Act 1964 (c 35)**

*RA:* 10 Jun 1964

Whole Act in force 10 Jun 1964 (RA)

---

### Plant Varieties and Seeds Act 1964 (c 14)

*RA:* 12 Mar 1964

*Commencement provisions:* s 41(2); Plant Varieties and Seeds Act 1964 (Commencement No 1) Order 1966, SI 1966/276; Plant Varieties and Seeds Act 1964 (Commencement No 2) Order 1968, SI 1968/206; Plant Varieties and Seeds Act 1964 (Commencement No 3) Order 1973, SI 1973/928; Plant Varieties and Seeds Act 1964 (Commencement No 4) Order 1978, SI 1978/1002

| | |
|---|---|
| 1–15 | 12 Mar 1964 (RA) |
| 16–19 | 1 Jul 1973 (SI 1973/928) |
| 20–23 | 8 Mar 1966 (SI 1966/276) |
| 24–30 | 1 Jul 1973 (SI 1973/928) |
| 31 | 1 Jul 1979 (SI 1978/1002) |
| 32 | 1 Jul 1973 (SI 1973/928) |
| 33 | 17 Feb 1968 (SI 1968/206) |
| 34–41 | 12 Mar 1964 (RA) |
| Schs 1–4 | 12 Mar 1964 (RA) |
| Sch 5 | 8 Mar 1966 (SI 1966/276) |
| Sch 6 | 1 Jul 1979 (SI 1978/1002) |
| Sch 7 | 17 Feb 1968 (SI 1968/206) |

### Police Act 1964 (c 48)

*RA:* 10 Jun 1964

*Commencement provisions:* s 65(2)–(4); Police Act 1964 (Commencement No 1) Order 1964, SI 1964/873[1]

| | | |
|---|---|---|
| 1 | | 1 Jul 1964 (SI 1964/873) |
| 2 | | 1 Jun 1965 (but note that sub-ss (6) and (7), as applied by Sch 1, brought into force on 1 Jul 1964) (SI 1964/873) |
| 3 | (1) | 1 Jul 1964 (SI 1964/873) |
| | (2) | 1 Jun 1965 (SI 1964/873) |
| | (3), (4) | 1 Jul 1964 (SI 1964/873) |
| 4 | | 1 Aug 1964 (SI 1964/873) |
| 5 | (1)–(3) | 1 Aug 1964 (SI 1964/873) |
| | (4)–(6) | 1 Apr 1965 (SI 1964/873) |
| 6, 7 | | 1 Aug 1964 (SI 1964/873) |
| 8 | (1), (2) | 1 Aug 1964 (SI 1964/873) |
| | (3), (4) | 1 Apr 1965 (SI 1964/873) |
| | (5) | 1 Aug 1964 (SI 1964/873) |
| 9–15 | | 1 Aug 1964 (SI 1964/873) |
| 16, 17 | | 1 Apr 1965 (SI 1964/873) |
| 18 | | 1 Aug 1964 (SI 1964/873) |
| 19 | (1) | 1 Aug 1964 (SI 1964/873) |
| | (2)–(5) | 1 Apr 1965 (SI 1964/873) |
| | (6) | 1 Aug 1964 (SI 1964/873) |
| 20 | | 1 Aug 1964 (SI 1964/873) |
| 21–24 | | 1 Jul 1964 (SI 1964/873) |
| 25 | | 1 Apr 1965 (SI 1964/873) |
| 26, 27 | | 1 Jul 1964 (SI 1964/873) |
| 28 | | 1 Aug 1964 (SI 1964/873) |
| 29 | | 1 Apr 1965 (SI 1964/873) |
| 30–32 | | 1 Aug 1964 (SI 1964/873) |
| 33–35 | | 1 Apr 1965 (SI 1964/873) |
| 36 | | 1 Aug 1964 (SI 1964/873) |
| 37 | | 1 Apr 1965 (SI 1964/873) |
| 38–43 | | 1 Aug 1964 (SI 1964/873) |
| 44–47 | | 1 Apr 1965 (SI 1964/873) |
| 48–50 | | 1 Aug 1964 (SI 1964/873) |
| 51–58 | | 1 Jul 1964 (SI 1964/873) |
| 59 | | *Never in force* (repealed) |

**Police Act 1964 (c 48)**—*contd*

| | | |
|---|---|---|
| 60, 61 | | 1 Jul 1964 (SI 1964/873) |
| 62 | | 1 Jul 1964 (as it relates to the interpretation of this Act) (SI 1964/873) |
| | | 1 Aug 1964 (as it relates to the interpretation of other enactments) (SI 1964/873) |
| 63 | | See Sch 9 below |
| 64 | (1), (2) | 1 Jul 1964 (SI 1964/873) |
| | (3) | See Sch 10 below |
| | (4) | 1 Aug 1964 (SI 1964/873) |
| | (5) | 1 Jul 1964 (SI 1964/873) |
| | (6) | 1 Aug 1964 (SI 1964/873) |
| 65 | | 1 Jul 1964 (SI 1964/873) |
| Sch 1 | | 1 Jul 1964 (SI 1964/873) |
| Sch 2 | | 1 Aug 1964 (SI 1964/873) |
| Schs 3, 4 | | 1 Jul 1964 (SI 1964/873) |
| Sch 5 | | 1 Apr 1965 (SI 1964/873) |
| Sch 6 | | 1 Aug 1964 (SI 1964/873) |
| Sch 7 | | *Never in force* (repealed) |
| Sch 8 | | 1 Jul 1964 (SI 1964/873) |
| Sch 9 | | 1 Jul 1964 (as it relates to amendment of Local Government Act 1958, s 60(2)) (SI 1964/873) |

1 Aug 1964 (SI 1964/873), amendments of—
City of London Police Act 1839, s 44;
Metropolitan Police Act 1839, s 63;
Town Police Clauses Act 1847;
Juries Act 1870;
Metropolitan Police Staff (Superannuation) Act 1875;
Metropolitan Police Act 1886;
Riot (Damages) Act 1886;
Metropolitan Police (Receiver) Act 1895;
Children and Young Persons Act 1933;
Local Government Act 1933;
Firearms Act 1937;
Police (Overseas Service) Act 1945;
National Insurance (Industrial Injuries) Act 1946;
Police Pensions Act 1948;
Local Government (Miscellaneous Provisions) Act 1953;
Homicide Act 1957

1 Apr 1965 (amendment of Betting, Gaming and Lotteries Act 1963, Sch 2, para 1(5)) (SI 1964/873)

1 Jun 1965 (amendment of Road Traffic and Roads Improvement Act 1960, s 2(8)) (SI 1964/873)

| | | |
|---|---|---|
| Sch 10 | Pt I | 1 Aug 1964 (SI 1964/873), repeals of or in— |

Constables Expenses Act 1801;
Metropolitan Police Act 1829, ss 4, 12;
City of London Police Act 1839;
County Police Act 1839 (except in so far as it relates to the dismissal of chief constables, s 4);
Metropolitan Police Act 1839;
County Police Act 1840;
Parish Constables Act 1842;
Town Police Clauses Act 1847;
Tyne Improvement Act 1852;
County and Borough Police Act 1856;
County Police Act 1857;
County and Borough Police Act 1859 (except in so far as it relates to the suspension of constables, s 26);
Metropolitan Police Act 1860;
Metropolitan Police Act 1861;

**Police Act 1964 (c 48)**—*contd*

> Offences Against the Person Act 1861;
> Sunday Observation Prosecution Act 1871;
> Pedlars Act 1871;
> Prevention of Crimes Act 1871;
> Parish Constables Act 1872;
> Explosives Act 1875;
> Metropolitan Police Staff (Superannuation) Act 1875;
> Municipal Corporation Act 1882, Part IX (except ss 190, 191(4), 193, 196), Sch 5;
> Cheap Trains Act 1883;
> Prosecution of Offences Act 1884;
> Prevention of Crimes Amendment Act 1885;
> Riot (Damages) Act 1886;
> Local Government Act 1888, ss 3, 9(2), (3), 66 (words "police officer or constable" in both places they appear);
> Police Act 1890;
> Public Health Acts Amendment Act 1890;
> Police Returns Act 1892;
> Dogs Act 1906;
> Cinematograph Act 1909;
> Police Reservists (Allowances) Act 1914;
> Larceny Act 1916;
> County and Borough Police Act 1919;
> Port of London (Consolidation) Act 1920;
> Thames Conservancy Act 1932;
> Children and Young Persons Act 1933;
> Public Order Act 1936;
> Firearms Act 1937;
> House to House Collections Act 1939;
> Police and Firemen (War Service) Act 1939;
> Police (His Majesty's Inspectors of Constabulary) Act 1945;
> Police Act 1946; whole Act (except ss 3(3), 5(5), 9(1), 16, Sch 2, paras 2, 4, 8, 9, Sch 3, para 4, Sch 4);
> Acquisition of Land (Authorisation Procedure) Act 1946;
> National Insurance (Industrial Injuries) Act 1946;
> Fire Services Act 1947;
> Civil Defence Act 1948;
> Civil Aviation Act 1949;
> Representation of the People Act 1949;
> Miscellaneous Financial Provisions Act 1950;
> Diseases of Animals Act 1950;
> Reserve and Auxiliary Forces (Protection of Civil Interests) Act 1951;
> Magistrates' Courts Act 1952;
> Local Government Act 1958;
> Road Traffic Act 1960;
> Road Traffic and Roads Improvement Act 1960, s 2(10)

1 Apr 1965 (SI 1964/873), repeals of or in—
> Metropolitan Police Act 1829, s 5;
> Special Constables Act 1831;
> Special Constables Act 1835;
> Special Constables Act 1838;
> City of London Police Act 1839;
> County Police Act 1839;
> Cambridge Award Act 1856;
> County and Borough Police Act 1859;
> Municipal Corporations Act 1882, ss 191(4), 196;

**Police Act 1964 (c 48)**—*contd*

|  |  |  |
|---|---|---|

Local Government Act 1888, ss 9(1), 30(3), 66 (except words "police officer or constable" in both places they appear), 78(1), 93;
Police (Weekly Rest-Day) Act 1910;
Special Constables Act 1914;
Police Act 1919;
Local Government Act 1933;
Police Act 1946, ss 3(3), 5(5), 16, Sch 2, paras 2, 4, 8, Sch 4;
Police, Fire and Probation Officers' Remuneration Act 1956;
Betting, Gaming and Lotteries Act 1963
1 Jun 1965 (SI 1964/873), repeals of or in—
Municipal Corporations Act 1882, s 190;
Local Government Act 1888, ss 30(1), (2), 34(3)(c), 81(7), (8);
Local Government (Clerks) Act 1931;
Police Act 1946, ss 3(3), 5(5), 9(1), 16, Sch 2, paras 2, 4, 8, 9, Sch 3, para 4, Sch 4;
Road Traffic and Roads Improvement Act 1960, s 2(8)
*Never in force* (repeals of or in Borough Constables Act 1883) (repealed)

Pt II — 1 Aug 1964 (SI 1964/873), repeals of or in—
Police Act 1919;
Police Pensions Act 1921, Whole Act, except s 10
1 Apr 1965 (SI 1964/873), repeals of or in—
Special Constables Act 1923;
Police (Appeals) Act 1927;
Police (Appeals) Act 1943;
Police Federation Act 1959;
Police Federation Act 1961;
Police Federation Act 1962
*Never in force* (otherwise) (repealed)

| Sch 11 | paras 1–4 | 1 Jun 1965 (SI 1964/873) |
|---|---|---|
|  | paras 5–7 | 1 Aug 1964 (SI 1964/873) |
|  | paras 8, 9 | 1 Jul 1964 (SI 1964/873) |
|  | para 10 | 1 Aug 1964 (SI 1964/873) |
|  | paras 11–13 | 1 Jun 1965 (SI 1964/873) |

[1] For transitional provisions, see SI 1964/873, art 2, Sch 5

---

**Post Office (Borrowing Powers) Act 1964 (c 3)**

*RA:* 6 Feb 1964

Whole Act in force 6 Feb 1964 (RA)

---

**Protection from Eviction Act 1964 (c 97)**

*RA:* 17 Dec 1964

Whole Act in force 17 Dec 1964 (RA)

---

**Protection of Animals (Anaesthetics) Act 1964 (c 39)**

*RA:* 10 Jun 1964

*Commencement provisions:* s 2(3)

Whole Act in force 10 Aug 1964 (s 2(3))

---

### Protection of Birds Act 1954 (Amendment) Act 1964 (c 59)

*RA:* 16 Jul 1964

Whole Act in force 16 Jul 1964 (RA)

---

### Public Libraries and Museums Act 1964 (c 75)

*RA:* 31 Jul 1964

*Commencement provisions:* s 26(7)

Whole Act in force 1 Apr 1965 (s 26(7))

---

### Public Works Loans Act 1964 (c 9)

*RA:* 27 Feb 1964

Whole Act in force 27 Feb 1964 (RA)

---

### Rating (Interim Relief) Act 1964 (c 18)

*RA:* 25 Mar 1964

Whole Act in force 25 Mar 1964 (RA)

---

### Refreshment Houses Act 1964 (c 88)

*RA:* 31 Jul 1964

*Commencement provisions:* s 4(4)

Whole Act in force 1 Apr 1965 (s 4(4))

---

### Resale Prices Act 1964 (c 58)

*RA:* 16 Jul 1964

*Commencement provisions:* s 14(2), (3); Resale Prices Act (Commencement) Order 1965, SI 1965/228

| | | |
|---|---|---|
| 1–4 | | 30 Apr 1965 (SI 1965/228) |
| 5–7 | | 16 Aug 1964 (s 14(2)(b)) |
| 8 | (1) | 16 Jul 1964 (s 14(2)(a)) |
| | (2), (3) | 16 Aug 1964 (s 14(2)(b)) |
| | (4) | 16 Jul 1964 (s 14(2)(a)) |
| 9–14 | | 16 Jul 1964 (s 14(2)(a)) |
| Schedule | | 30 Apr 1965 (SI 1965/228) |

---

### Riding Establishments Act 1964 (c 70)

*RA:* 31 Jul 1964

*Commencement provisions:* s 9(3)

Whole Act in force 1 Apr 1965 (s 9(3))

---

## Road Traffic Act 1964 (c 45)

*RA:* 10 Jun 1964

*Commencement provisions*: s 2(2)

Whole Act in force 10 Jul 1965 (s 2(2))

## Salmon and Freshwater Fisheries Act 1923 (Amendment) Act 1964 (c 27)

*RA:* 25 Mar 1964

*Commencement provisions*: s 2(2)

Whole Act in force 1 Apr 1965 (s 2(2))

## Scrap Metal Dealers Act 1964 (c 69)

*RA:* 31 Jul 1964

*Commencement provisions*: s 11(2)

Whole Act in force 1 Apr 1965 (s 11(2))

## Shipbuilding Credit Act 1964 (c 7)

*RA:* 27 Feb 1964

Whole Act in force 27 Feb 1964 (RA)

## Shipping Contracts and Commercial Documents Act 1964 (c 87)

*RA:* 31 Jul 1964

Whole Act in force 31 Jul 1964 (RA)

## Spray Irrigation (Scotland) Act 1964 (c 90)

*RA:* 31 Jul 1964

*Commencement provisions*: s 9(3)

Whole Act in force 31 Aug 1964 (s 9(3))

## Statute Law Revision Act 1964 (c 79)

*RA:* 31 Jul 1964

Whole Act in force 31 Jul 1964 (RA)

## Statute Law Revision (Scotland) Act 1964 (c 80)

*RA:* 31 Jul 1964

Whole Act in force 31 Jul 1964 (RA)

### Succession (Scotland) Act 1964 (c 41)

*RA:* 10 Jun 1964

*Commencement provisions*: s 38(3)

Whole Act in force 10 Sep 1964 (s 38(3))

---

### Television Act 1964 (c 21)

*RA:* 25 Mar 1964

*Commencement provisions*: s 30(4)

Whole Act in force 31 Jul 1964 (s 30(4))

---

### Tenancy of Shops (Scotland) Act 1964 (c 50)

*RA:* 16 Jul 1964

Whole Act in force 16 Jul 1964 (RA)

---

### Trade Union (Amalgamations, etc) Act 1964 (c 24)

*RA:* 25 Mar 1964

*Commencement provisions*: s 11(4); Trade Union (Amalgamations, etc) Act 1964 (Commencement) Order 1964, SI 1964/878

Whole Act in force 1 Jul 1964 (SI 1964/878)

---

### Trading Stamps Act 1964 (c 71)

*RA:* 31 Jul 1964

*Commencement provisions*: s 11(3)

| | |
|---|---|
| 1 | 31 Jan 1965 (s 11(3)) |
| 2–7 | 31 Jul 1965 (s 11(3)) |
| 8–11 | 31 Jul 1964 (RA) |

---

### Travel Concessions Act 1964 (c 95)

*RA:* 17 Dec 1964

Whole Act in force 17 Dec 1964 (RA)

---

### Trustee Savings Banks Act 1964 (c 4)

*RA:* 27 Feb 1964

Whole Act in force 27 Feb 1964 (RA)

---

### Uganda Act 1964 (c 20)

*RA:* 25 Mar 1964

*Commencement provisions*: s 1(3)

| | |
|---|---|
| 1 | 9 Oct 1963 (retrospective; s 1(3)) |

**Uganda Act 1964 (c 20)**—*contd*
2–4                                                 25 Mar 1964 (RA)

---

**Universities and College Estates Act 1964 (c 51)**

*RA:* 16 Jul 1964

*Commencement provisions*: s 5(4)

Whole Act in force 16 Aug 1964 (s 5(4))

---

**Vestures of Ministers Measure 1964 (No 7)**

*RA:* 31 Jul 1964

Whole Measure in force 31 Jul 1964 (RA)

---

**War Damage Act 1964 (c 25)**

*RA:* 25 Mar 1964

*Commencement provisions*: s 14(3)

Whole Act in force 1 Oct 1964 (s 14(3))

---

**Young Persons (Employment) Act 1964 (c 66)**

*RA:* 31 Jul 1964

*Commencement provisions*: s 4(2)

Whole Act in force 3 Jan 1965 (s 4(2))

---

**Zambia Independence Act 1964 (c 65)**

*RA:* 31 Jul 1964

This Act generally had effect from 24 Oct 1964 (the "appointed day")

---

# 1965 Acts

### Administration of Estates (Small Payments) Act 1965 (c 32)

*RA:* 5 Aug 1965

*Commencement provisions:* ss 2(2), 6(2), 7(5)

Whole Act applied in relation to deaths occurring after 5 Sep 1965 (s 7(5)) (but see ss 2(2), 6(2), in relation to the effect of s 2 by virtue of any order made under s 6(2))

### Administration of Justice Act 1965 (c 2)

*RA:* 23 Mar 1965

*Commencement provisions:* s 36(2), (3); Administration of Justice Act 1965 (Commencement No 1) Order 1965, SI 1965/706; Administration of Justice Act 1965 (Commencement No 2) Order 1965, SI 1965/1466

| | |
|---|---|
| 1–18 | 1 Oct 1965 (SI 1965/1466) |
| 19–29 | 27 Apr 1965 (SI 1965/706) |
| 30 | 1 Oct 1965 (SI 1965/1466) |
| 31–35 | 27 Apr 1965 (SI 1965/706) |
| 36 | 27 Apr 1965 (except so far as it relates to Part I or the repeals consequential thereon) (SI 1965/706) |
| | 1 Oct 1965 (otherwise) (SI 1965/1466) |
| Sch 1 | 1 Oct 1965 (SI 1965/1466) |
| Sch 2 | 27 Apr 1965 (SI 1965/706) |
| Sch 3 | 27 Apr 1965 (repeals of or in Prosecution of Offences Act 1879) (SI 1965/706) |
| | 1 Oct 1965 (otherwise) (SI 1965/1466) |

### Airports Authority Act 1965 (c 16)

*RA:* 2 Jun 1965

Whole Act in force 2 Jun 1965 (RA)

### Appropriation Act 1965 (c 23)

*RA:* 5 Aug 1965

Whole Act in force 5 Aug 1965 (RA)

### Armed Forces (Housing Loans) Act 1965 (c 9)

*RA:* 29 Mar 1965

Whole Act in force 29 Mar 1965 (RA)

**Backing of Warrants (Republic of Ireland) Act 1965 (c 45)**

*RA:* 5 Aug 1965

*Commencement provisions*: s 13(2); Backing of Warrants (Republic of Ireland) Act 1965 (Commencement) Order 1965, SI 1965/1850

Whole Act in force 15 Nov 1965 (SI 1965/1850), except ss 9(3) and 13, which came into force on 5 Aug 1965 (s 13(2))

---

**Benefices (Suspension of Presentation) (Continuance) Measure 1965 (No 2)**

*RA:* 2 Jun 1965

Whole Measure in force 2 Jun 1965 (RA)

---

**British Nationality Act 1965 (c 34)**

*RA:* 5 Aug 1965

*Commencement provisions*: s 5(4)

Whole Act in force 5 Oct 1965 (s 5(4))

---

**Carriage of Goods by Road Act 1965 (c 37)**

*RA:* 5 Aug 1965

*Commencement provisions*: s 14(4); Carriage of Goods by Road Act 1965 (Commencement) Order 1967, SI 1967/819

Whole Act in force 5 Jun 1967 (SI 1967/819)

---

**Cereals Marketing Act 1965 (c 14)**

*RA:* 2 Jun 1965

Whole Act in force 2 Jun 1965 (RA)

---

**Coal Industry Act 1965 (c 82)**

*RA:* 22 Dec 1965

Whole Act in force 22 Dec 1965 (RA)

---

**Commons Registration Act 1965 (c 64)**

*RA:* 5 Aug 1965

*Commencement provisions*: s 25(2); Commons Registration Act 1965 (Commencement No 1) Order 1965, SI 1965/2000; Commons Registration Act 1965 (Commencement No 2) Order 1966, SI 1966/971

| | | |
|---|---|---|
| 1 | | 2 Jan 1967 (SI 1966/971) |
| 2 | (1) | 2 Jan 1967 (SI 1966/971) |
| | (2) | 1 Jan 1966 (SI 1965/2000) |
| 3 | | 2 Jan 1967 (SI 1966/971) |
| 4 | (1)–(6) | 2 Jan 1967 (SI 1966/971) |
| | (7) | 1 Oct 1966 (SI 1966/971) |
| 5–10 | | 2 Jan 1967 (SI 1966/971) |
| 11 | | 1 Jan 1966 (SI 1965/2000) |

## Commons Registration Act 1965 (c 64)—*contd*

| | |
|---|---|
| 12–16 | 2 Jan 1967 (SI 1966/971) |
| 17, 18 | 1 Jan 1970 (SI 1966/971) |
| 19–21 | 2 Jan 1967 (SI 1966/971) |
| 22–25 | 5 Aug 1965 (RA) |

## Compulsory Purchase Act 1965 (c 56)

*RA:* 5 Aug 1965

*Commencement provisions:* s 40(2)

Whole Act in force 1 Jan 1966 (s 40(2))

## Consolidated Fund Act 1965 (c 1)

*RA:* 4 Feb 1965

Whole Act in force 4 Feb 1965 (RA)

## Consolidated Fund (No 2) Act 1965 (c 8)

*RA:* 29 Mar 1965

Whole Act in force 29 Mar 1965 (RA)

## Control of Office and Industrial Development Act 1965 (c 33)

*RA:* 5 Aug 1965

Whole Act in force 5 Aug 1965 (RA)

## Criminal Evidence Act 1965 (c 20)

*RA:* 2 Jun 1965

Whole Act in force 2 Jun 1965 (RA)

## Criminal Justice Act 1965 (c 26)

*RA:* 5 Aug 1965

*Commencement provisions:* s 2(2)

Whole Act in force 5 Sep 1965 (s 2(2))

## Criminal Procedure (Attendance of Witnesses) Act 1965 (c 69)

*RA:* 5 Aug 1965

*Commencement provisions:* s 10(4)

Whole Act in force 5 Oct 1965 (s 10(4))

## Criminal Procedure (Scotland) Act 1965 (c 39)

*RA*: 5 Aug 1965

Whole Act in force 5 Aug 1965 (RA)

---

## Dangerous Drugs Act 1965 (c 15)

*RA*: 2 Jun 1965

Whole Act in force 2 Jun 1965 (RA)

---

## Development of Inventions Act 1965 (c 21)

*RA*: 2 Jun 1965

*Commencement provisions*: s 10(3)

Whole Act in force 2 Jul 1965 (s 10(3))

---

## Education (Scotland) Act 1965 (c 7)

*RA*: 23 Mar 1965

Whole Act in force 23 Mar 1965 (RA)

---

## Expiring Laws Continuance Act 1965 (c 77)

*RA*: 22 Dec 1965

Whole Act in force 22 Dec 1965 (RA)

---

## Family Allowances Act 1965 (c 53)

*RA*: 5 Aug 1965

*Commencement provisions*: s 25(3); National Insurance Act 1965 (Commencement) Order 1965, SI 1965/1650

Whole Act in force 6 Sep 1965 (s 25(3); see SI 1965/1650)

---

## Finance Act 1965 (c 25)

*RA*: 5 Aug 1965

The commencement details of Finance Acts are not set out, as the dates from which their provisions take effect are usually stated clearly and unambiguously in the text of the Act, and charging provisions will normally state for which year or years of assessment they are to have effect.

---

## Firearms Act 1965 (c 44)

*RA*: 5 Aug 1965

*Commencement provisions*: s 11(5); Firearms Act 1965 (Commencement No 1) Order 1965, SI 1965/1577

| | |
|---|---|
| 1–6 | 5 Sep 1965 (s 11(5)) |
| 7–9 | 1 Nov 1965 (SI 1965/1577) |
| 10, 11 | 5 Aug 1965 (RA) |
| Schs 1, 2 | 5 Aug 1965 (RA) |

---

## Gas Act 1965 (c 36)

*RA:* 5 Aug 1965

*Commencement provisions:* s 32(5); Gas Act 1965 (Commencement) Order 1965, SI 1965/1983

| | |
|---|---|
| 1–3 | 5 Aug 1965 (RA) |
| 4–28 | 1 Dec 1965 (SI 1965/1983) |
| 29–32 | 5 Aug 1965 (RA) |
| Sch 1 | 5 Aug 1965 (RA) |
| Schs 2–6 | 1 Dec 1965 (SI 1965/1983) |

## Gas (Borrowing Powers) Act 1965 (c 60)

*RA:* 5 Aug 1965

Whole Act in force 5 Aug 1965 (RA)

## Highlands and Islands Development (Scotland) Act 1965 (c 46)

*RA:* 5 Aug 1965

Whole Act in force 5 Aug 1965 (RA)

## Highways (Amendment) Act 1965 (c 30)

*RA:* 5 Aug 1965

Whole Act in force 5 Aug 1965 (RA)

## Hire-Purchase Act 1965 (c 66)

*RA:* 5 Aug 1965

*Commencement provisions:* s 61

Whole Act in force 1 Oct 1965 (s 61)

## Hire-Purchase (Scotland) Act 1965 (c 67)

*RA:* 5 Aug 1965

*Commencement provisions:* s 57

Whole Act in force 5 Aug 1965 (in relation to s 57 and in so far as any provision confers any power to make regulations, or revoke or vary any regulations (s 57(2), (3)) and 1 Oct 1965 (otherwise) (s 57(1))

## Honourable Lady Hylton-Foster's Annuity Act 1965 (c 70)

*RA:* 8 Nov 1965

Whole Act in force 8 Nov 1965 (RA)

## Housing (Amendment) (Scotland) Act 1965 (c 40)

*RA:* 5 Aug 1965

Whole Act in force 5 Aug 1965 (RA)

**Housing (Slum Clearance Compensation) Act 1965 (c 81)**

*RA:* 22 Dec 1965

Whole Act in force 22 Dec 1965 (RA)

---

**Industrial and Provident Societies Act 1965 (c 12)**

*RA:* 2 Jun 1965

*Commencement provisions*: s 78(3); Industrial and Provident Societies Act 1965 (Commencement) Order 1965, SI 1965/2051

Whole Act in force 1 Jan 1966 (SI 1965/2051)

---

**International Monetary Fund Act 1965 (c 65)**

*RA:* 5 Aug 1965

Whole Act in force 5 Aug 1965 (RA)

---

**Judges' Remuneration Act 1965 (c 61)**

*RA:* 5 Aug 1965

Whole Act in force 5 Aug 1965 (RA)

---

**Justices of the Peace Act 1965 (c 28)**

*RA:* 5 Aug 1965

Whole Act in force 5 Aug 1965 (RA)

---

**Kenya Republic Act 1965 (c 5)**

*RA:* 23 Mar 1965

Whole Act in force 23 Mar 1965 (RA); but note that s 1 is deemed to have had effect from 12 Dec 1964, by virtue of s 1(3)

---

**Law Commissions Act 1965 (c 22)**

*RA:* 15 Jun 1965

Whole Act in force 15 Jun 1965 (RA)

---

**Local Government (Scotland) Act 1947 (Amendment) Act 1965 (c 41)**

*RA:* 5 Aug 1965

Whole Act in force 5 Aug 1965 (RA)

---

**Lost Property (Scotland) Act 1965 (c 27)**

*RA:* 5 Aug 1965

Whole Act in force 5 Aug 1965 (RA)

---

## Matrimonial Causes Act 1965 (c 72)

*RA:* 8 Nov 1965

*Commencement provisions:* s 46(3); Matrimonial Causes Act 1965 (Commencement) Order 1965, SI 1965/1974

Whole Act in force 1 Jan 1966 (SI 1965/1974)

## Merchant Shipping Act 1965 (c 47)

*RA:* 5 Aug 1965

*Commencement provisions:* s 8(4); Merchant Shipping Act 1965 (Commencement) Order 1967, SI 1967/157

Whole Act in force 1 Mar 1967 (SI 1967/157)

## Ministerial Salaries and Members' Pensions Act 1965 (c 11)

*RA:* 29 Mar 1965

*Commencement provisions:* s 21(3)

Whole Act in force 16 Oct 1964 (s 21(3)(a)), except ss 1, 2, 15–17, 20, 21, which came into force on 1 Apr 1965 (s 21(3)(b))

## Ministerial Salaries Consolidation Act 1965 (c 58)

*RA:* 5 Aug 1965

Whole Act in force 5 Aug 1965 (RA)

## Monopolies and Mergers Act 1965 (c 50)

*RA:* 5 Aug 1965

Whole Act in force 5 Aug 1965 (RA)

## Murder (Abolition of Death Penalty) Act 1965 (c 71)

*RA:* 8 Nov 1965

*Commencement provisions:* s 3(4)

Whole Act in force 9 Nov 1965 (s 3(4))

## Museum of London Act 1965 (c 17)

*RA:* 2 Jun 1965

Whole Act in force 2 Jun 1965 (RA)

## National Health Service Contributions Act 1965 (c 54)

*RA:* 5 Aug 1965

*Commencement provisions:* s 9(3); National Insurance Act 1965 (Commencement) Order 1965, SI 1965/1650

**National Health Service Contributions Act 1965 (c 54)**—*contd*
Whole Act in force 6 Sep 1965 (s 9(3); see SI 1965/1650)

**National Insurance Act 1965 (c 51)**

*RA:* 5 Aug 1965

*Commencement provisions:* s 118(3); National Insurance Act 1965 (Commencement) Order 1965, SI 1965/1650

Whole Act in force 6 Sep 1965 (SI 1965/1650)

**National Insurance (Industrial Injuries) Act 1965 (c 52)**

*RA:* 5 Aug 1965

*Commencement provisions:* s 88(3); National Insurance Act 1965 (Commencement) Order 1965, SI 1965/1650

Whole Act in force 6 Sep 1965 (s 88(3); see SI 1965/1650)

**New Towns Act 1965 (c 59)**

*RA:* 5 Aug 1965

*Commencement provisions:* s 57(2)

Whole Act in force 5 Sep 1965 (s 57(2))

**Nuclear Installations Act 1965 (c 57)**

*RA:* 5 Aug 1965

*Commencement provisions:* s 30(2); Nuclear Installations Act 1965 (Commencement No 1) Order 1965, SI 1965/1880; Energy Act 1983, s 37(3); Energy Act 1983 (Commencement No 1) Order 1983, SI 1983/790 (made under s 37(1) of the 1983 Act)

Whole Act in force 1 Dec 1965 (SI 1965/1880), except s 17(5), which came into force on 1 Sep 1983 (by the combined effect of Energy Act 1983, s 37(3), and SI 1983/790)

**Nuclear Installations (Amendment) Act 1965 (c 6)**

*RA:* 23 Mar 1965

*Commencement provisions:* s 18(3); Nuclear Installations (Amendment) Act 1965 (Commencement No 1) Order 1965, SI 1965/1131; Nuclear Installations (Amendment) Act 1965 (Commencement No 2) Order 1965, SI 1965/1879

| | | |
|---|---|---|
| 1–10 | | *Never in force* (repealed) |
| 11 | | 1 Jun 1965 (SI 1965/1131) |
| 12 | | *Never in force* (repealed) |
| 13 | | 1 Jun 1965 (SI 1965/1131) |
| 14–16 | | *Never in force* (repealed) |
| 17 | (1) | *Never in force* (repealed) |
| | (2) | 1 Dec 1965 (SI 1965/1879) |
| 18 | | *Never in force* (repealed) |
| Sch 1 | | *Never in force* (repealed) |

## Overseas Development and Service Act 1965 (c 38)

*RA:* 5 Aug 1965

Whole Act in force 5 Aug 1965 (RA)

---

## Pensions (Increase) Act 1965 (c 78)

*RA:* 22 Dec 1965

Whole Act in force 22 Dec 1965 (RA)

---

## Prayer Book (Alternative and Other Services) Measure 1965 (No 1)

*RA:* 23 Mar 1965

*Commencement provisions:* s 11(1)

Whole Measure in force 1 May 1966 (see *London Gazette*, 29 Apr 1966)

---

## Prayer Book (Miscellaneous Provisions) Measure 1965 (No 3)

*RA:* 5 Aug 1965

Whole Measure in force 5 Aug 1965 (RA)

---

## Prayer Book (Versions of the Bible) Measure 1965 (No 4)

*RA:* 22 Dec 1965

Whole Measure in force 22 Dec 1965 (RA)

---

## Public Health (Notification of Births) Act 1965 (c 42)

*RA:* 5 Aug 1965

*Commencement provisions:* s 2(2)

Whole Act in force 5 Sep 1965 (s 2(2))

---

## Public Works Loans Act 1965 (c 63)

*RA:* 5 Aug 1965

*Commencement provisions:* s 4(4)

Whole Act in force 5 Nov 1965 (s 4(4))

---

## Race Relations Act 1965 (c 73)

*RA:* 8 Nov 1965

*Commencement provisions:* s 8(2)

Whole Act in force 8 Dec 1965 (s 8(2))

---

**Redundancy Payments Act 1965 (c 62)**

*RA:* 5 Aug 1965

*Commencement provisions:* s 56(2); Redundancy Payments Act 1965 (Appointed Day) Order 1965, SI 1965/1757

Whole Act in force 6 Dec 1965 (SI 1965/1757)

---

**Registration of Births, Deaths and Marriages (Scotland) Act 1965 (c 49)**

*RA:* 5 Aug 1965

*Commencement provisions:* s 59(3)

Whole Act in force 1 Jan 1966 (s 59(3))

---

**Remuneration of Teachers Act 1965 (c 3)**

*RA:* 23 Mar 1965

Whole Act in force 23 Mar 1965 (RA)

---

**Rent Act 1965 (c 75)**

*RA:* 8 Nov 1965

*Commencement provisions:* ss 21(1), 53(1); Rent Regulation (Greater London) Appointed Day Order 1965, SI 1965/2081; Rent Regulation (West Midland) Appointed Day Order 1966, SI 1966/122; Rent Regulation (Wales) Appointed Day Order 1966, SI 1966/161; Rent Regulation Appointed Day (Scotland) (No 1) Order 1966, SI 1966/176; Rent Regulation (Northern Area) Appointed Day Order 1966, SI 1966/180; Rent Regulation (Yorkshire) Appointed Day Order 1966, SI 1966/181; Rent Regulation (Bristol Area) Appointed Day Order 1966, SI 1966/264; Rent Regulation (East Midlands) Appointed Day Order 1966, SI 1966/265; Rent Regulation (Surrey and Sussex) Appointed Day Order 1966, SI 1966/293; Rent Regulation (Liverpool Area) Appointed Day Order 1966, SI 1966/313; Rent Regulation (Manchester Area) Appointed Day Order 1966, SI 1966/314; Rent Regulation Appointed Day (Scotland) (No 2) Order 1966, SI 1966/345; Rent Regulation (Devon and Cornwall) Appointed Day Order 1966, SI 1966/404; Rent Regulation (Kent) Appointed Day Order 1966, SI 1966/405; Rent Regulation (Southern Area) Appointed Day Order 1966, SI 1966/406; Rent Regulation (Thames Valley) Appointed Day Order 1966, SI 1966/537; Rent Regulation Appointed Day (Scotland) (No 3) Order 1966, SI 1966/555; Rent Regulation (Eastern Area) Appointed Day Order 1966, SI 1966/631; Rent Regulation (Luton Area) Appointed Day Order 1966, SI 1966/632; Rent Regulation Appointed Day (Scotland) (No 4) Order 1966, SI 1966/934; Rent Regulation Appointed Day (Scotland) (No 5) Order 1966, SI 1966/1580; Rent Regulation Appointed Day (Scotland) (No 1) Order 1967, SI 1967/764

| | |
|---|---|
| 1–20 | 8 Dec 1965 (s 53(1)) |
| 21–29 | 3 Jan 1966 (in relation to registration areas in Greater London) (SI 1966/122) |
| | 14 Feb 1966 (in relation to registration areas in the West Midlands) (SI 1966/122) |
| | 1 Mar 1966 (in relation to the cities of Aberdeen, Dundee, Edinburgh and Glasgow) (SI 1966/176) |
| | 1 Mar 1966 (in relation to registration areas in the North of England) (SI 1966/180) |
| | 1 Mar 1966 (in relation to registration areas in Yorkshire) (SI 1966/181) |
| | 14 Mar 1966 (in relation to Wales and Monmouthshire) (SI 1966/161) |
| | 16 Mar 1966 (in relation to registration areas in the area of Bristol) (SI 1966/264) |

**Rent Act 1965 (c 75)**—*contd*

|  |  |
|---|---|
|  | 16 Mar 1966 (in relation to registration areas in the East Midlands) (SI 1966/265) |
|  | 28 Mar 1966 (in relation to registration areas in Surrey and Sussex) (SI 1966/293) |
|  | 1 Apr 1966 (in relation to the counties and Dunbarton, Fife, Lanark and Renfrew and the large burghs of Airdrie, Clydebank, Coatbridge, Dumbarton, Dunfermline, Greenock, Hamilton, Kirkcaldy, Motherwell and Wishaw, Paisley, Port Glasgow and Rutherglen in Scotland) (SI 1966/345) |
|  | 4 Apr 1966 (in relation to registration areas in the Liverpool area) (SI 1966/313) |
|  | 4 Apr 1966 (in relation to registration areas in the Manchester area) (SI 1966/314) |
|  | 18 Apr 1966 (in relation to registration areas in Devon and Cornwall) (SI 1966/404) |
|  | 18 Apr 1966 (in relation to registration areas in Kent and Canterbury) (SI 1966/405) |
|  | 18 Apr 1966 (in relation to registration areas in the South of England) (SI 1966/406) |
|  | 16 May 1966 (in relation to registration areas in the Thames Valley) (SI 1966/537) |
|  | 16 May 1966 (in relation to the counties of Aberdeen, Ayr, Clackmannan, East Lothian, Kincardine, Kinross, Midlothian, Peebles, Perth, Stirling, West Lothian and the large burghs of Ayr, Falkirk, Kilmarnock, Perth and Stirling in Scotland) (SI 1966/555) |
|  | 20 Jun 1966 (in relation to registration areas in the East of England) (SI 1966/631) |
|  | 20 Jun 1966 (in relation to registration areas in the Luton area) (SI 1966/632) |
|  | 25 Jul 1966 (in relation to the counties of Angus, Argyll, Banff, Bute, Caithness, Inverness, Moray, Nairn, Ross and Cromarty, Sutherland and the large burghs of Arbroath and Inverness in Scotland) (SI 1966/934) |
|  | 19 Dec 1966 (in relation to the counties of Berwick, Dumfries, Kirkcudbright, Roxburgh, Selkirk, Wigtown and the large burgh of Dumfries in Scotland) (SI 1966/1580) |
|  | 23 May 1967 (in relation to registration areas of the counties of Orkney and Zetland) (SI 1967/764) |
| 30–53 | 8 Dec 1965 (s 53(1)) |
| Schs 1–6 | 8 Dec 1965 (s 53(1)) |

---

**Rivers (Prevention of Pollution) (Scotland) Act 1965 (c 13)**

*RA:* 2 Jun 1965

*Commencement provisions:* s 17(7)

Whole Act in force 2 Aug 1965 (s 17(7))

---

**Rural Water Supplies and Sewerage Act 1965 (c 80)**

*RA:* 22 Dec 1965

Whole Act in force 22 Dec 1965 (RA)

---

## Salmon and Fisheries Act 1965 (c 68)

*RA:* 5 Aug 1965

*Commencement provisions*: s 2(5)

Whole Act in force 5 Nov 1965 (s 2(5))

---

## Science and Technology Act 1965 (c 4)

*RA:* 23 Mar 1965

*Commencement provisions*: ss 3(8), 6(3); Science and Technology Act 1965 (Commencement No 1) Order 1965, SI 1965/597; Science and Technology Act 1965 (Commencement No 2) Order 1965, SI 1965/1127

| | | |
|---|---|---|
| 1, 2 | | 23 Mar 1965 (RA) |
| 3 | (1), (2) | 1 Apr 1965 (SI 1965/597) |
| | (3), (4) | 1 Jun 1965 (SI 1965/1127) |
| | (5) | See Schs 2, 3 below |
| | (6)–(8) | 23 Mar 1965 (RA) |
| 4, 5 | | 23 Mar 1965 (RA) |
| 6 | (1), (2) | 23 Mar 1965 (RA) |
| | (3) | See Sch 4 below |
| Sch 1 | | 23 Mar 1965 (RA) |
| Sch 2 | | 1 Apr 1965 (amendments of the Income Tax Act 1952) (SI 1965/597) |
| | | 1 Jun 1965 (otherwise) (SI 1965/1127) |
| Sch 3 | | 1 Apr 1965 (SI 1965/597) |
| Sch 4 | | 23 Mar 1965 (repeal of Atomic Energy Authority Act 1959, s 2) (RA) |
| | | 1 Jun 1965 (otherwise) (SI 1965/1127) |

---

## Severn Bridge Tolls Act 1965 (c 24)

*RA:* 5 Aug 1965

*Commencement provisions*: s 23(2)

Whole Act in force 5 Sep 1965 (s 23(2))

---

## Shops (Early Closing Days) Act 1965 (c 35)

*RA:* 5 Aug 1965

Whole Act in force 5 Aug 1965 (RA)

---

## Solicitors Act 1965 (c 31)

*RA:* 5 Aug 1965

*Commencement provisions*: s 30(2); Solicitors Act 1965 (Commencement No 1) Order 1965, SI 1965/1573; Solicitors Act 1965 (Commencement No 2) Order 1966, SI 1966/862; Solicitors Act 1965 (Commencement No 3) Order 1967, SI 1967/831; Solicitors Act 1965 (Commencement No 4) Order 1972, SI 1972/642

| | |
|---|---|
| 1, 2 | 1 Jun 1972 (SI 1972/642) |
| 3 | 17 Aug 1965 (SI 1965/1573) |
| 4 | 28 Jul 1966 (SI 1966/862) |
| 5–8 | 17 Aug 1965 (SI 1965/1573) |
| 9 | 26 Jun 1967 (SI 1967/831) |

**Solicitors Act 1965 (c 31)**—*contd*

| | |
|---|---|
| 10–13 | 1 Dec 1966 (SI 1966/862) |
| 14 | *Never in force* (repealed) |
| 15 | 1 Sep 1966 (SI 1966/862) |
| 16 | 1 Nov 1966 (SI 1966/862) |
| 17 | 17 Aug 1965 (SI 1965/1573) |
| 18–23 | 1 Sep 1966 (SI 1966/862) |
| 24 | 1 Nov 1966 (SI 1966/862) |
| 25–30 | 17 Aug 1965 (SI 1965/1573) |
| Sch 1 | 1 Dec 1966 (SI 1966/862) |
| Sch 2 | 17 Aug 1965 (SI 1965/1573) |
| Sch 3 | 17 Aug 1965 (so far as it relates to Solicitors Act 1957, s 15) (SI 1965/1573) |
| | 1 Sep 1966 (so far as it relates to Solicitors Act 1957, ss 39, 84) (SI 1966/862) |
| | 1 Jun 1972 (so far as it relates to Solicitors Act 1957, s 54) (SI 1972/642) |
| Sch 4 | 17 Aug 1965 (so far as it relates to Solicitors Act 1957, ss 4(4), 11(1), 86(1)) (SI 1965/1573) |
| | 1 Sep 1966 (so far as it relates to Solicitors Act 1957, ss 8, 49(2)) (SI 1966/862) |
| | 1 Nov 1966 (so far as it relates to Solicitors Act 1957, s 75(2)) (SI 1966/862) |
| | 1 Jun 1972 (so far as it relates to Solicitors Act 1957, ss 3(2), 40–45) (SI 1972/642) |

**Solicitors (Scotland) Act 1965 (c 29)**

*RA:* 5 Aug 1965

*Commencement provisions*: s 5(3)

Whole Act in force 1 Jan 1966 (s 5(3))

**Southern Rhodesia Act 1965 (c 76)**

*RA:* 16 Nov 1965

Whole Act in force 16 Nov 1965 (RA)

**Statute Law Revision (Consequential Repeals) Act 1965 (c 55)**

*RA:* 5 Aug 1965

*Commencement provisions*: s 2(3); National Insurance Act 1965 (Commencement) Order 1965, SI 1965/1650 (made under National Insurance Act 1965, s 118(3))

Whole Act in force 6 Sep 1965 (SI 1965/1650)

**Statutory Orders (Special Procedure) Act 1965 (c 43)**

*RA:* 5 Aug 1965

*Commencement provisions*: s 2(3)

Whole Act in force 5 Sep 1965 (s 2(3))

### Superannuation Act 1965 (c 74)

*RA:* 8 Nov 1965

*Commencement provisions:* s 106

Whole Act in force 8 Dec 1965 (s 106)

---

### Superannuation (Amendment) Act 1965 (c 10)

*RA:* 29 Mar 1965

*Commencement provisions:* ss 4(6), 9(6)

Whole Act in force 29 Apr 1965 (s 9(6)), apart from s 4, which had effect from 1 Jan 1965 (s 4(6))

---

### Teachers' Superannuation Act 1965 (c 83)

*RA:* 22 Dec 1965

*Commencement provisions:* s 1; Teachers' Superannuation Regulations 1967, SI 1967/489

Whole Act in force 22 Dec 1965 (RA), but note that for the purposes of s 2 the appointed day is 1 Apr 1967 (SI 1967/489)

---

### Teaching Council (Scotland) Act 1965 (c 19)

*RA:* 2 Jun 1965

*Commencement provisions:* s 18(3); Teaching Council (Scotland) Act 1965 (Commencement No 1) Order 1965, SI 1965/1852; Teaching Council (Scotland) Act 1965 (Commencement No 2) Order 1968, SI 1968/1794

Whole Act in force 1 Nov 1965 (SI 1965/1852), except s 16 which came into force on 15 Nov 1968 (SI 1968/1794)

---

### Trade Disputes Act 1965 (c 48)

*RA:* 5 Aug 1965

Whole Act in force 5 Aug 1965 (RA)

---

### War Damage Act 1965 (c 18)

*RA:* 2 Jun 1965

Whole Act in force 2 Jun 1965 (RA)

---

### Workmen's Compensation and Benefit (Amendment) Act 1965 (c 79)

*RA:* 22 Dec 1965

*Commencement provisions:* s 6(2); Workmen's Compensation and Benefit (Amendment) Act 1965 (Commencement) Order 1966, SI 1966/18

Whole Act in force 1 Mar 1966 (SI 1966/18)

---

# 1966 Acts

### Air Corporations Act 1966 (c 11)

*RA:* 10 Mar 1966

Whole Act in force 10 Mar 1966 (RA)

---

### Appropriation Act 1966 (c 3)

*RA:* 10 Mar 1966

Whole Act in force 10 Mar 1966 (RA)

---

### Appropriation (No 2) Act 1966 (c 26)

*RA:* 9 Aug 1966

Whole Act in force 9 Aug 1966 (RA)

---

### Arbitration (International Investment Disputes) Act 1966 (c 41)

*RA:* 13 Dec 1966

*Commencement provisions:* s 9(2)

Whole Act in force 18 Jan 1967 (s 9(2))

---

### Armed Forces Act 1966 (c 45)

*RA:* 21 Dec 1966

*Commencement provisions:* s 38(5); Armed Forces Act 1966 (Commencement) Order 1967, SI 1967/45

| | | |
|---|---|---|
| 1 | | 21 Dec 1966 (RA) |
| 2 | | 1 Feb 1967 (SI 1967/45) |
| 3–16 | | 1 Apr 1967 (SI 1967/45) |
| 17 | | 1 Feb 1967 (SI 1967/45) |
| 18–20 | | 1 Apr 1967 (SI 1967/45) |
| 21, 22 | | 1 Feb 1967 (SI 1967/45) |
| 23–31 | | 1 Apr 1967 (SI 1967/45) |
| 32 | | 1 Feb 1967 (SI 1967/45) |
| 33–36 | | 1 Apr 1967 (SI 1967/45) |
| 37 | | 1 Feb 1967 (SI 1967/45) |
| 38 | | 21 Dec 1966 (RA) |
| Sch 1 | | 1 Feb 1967 (SI 1967/45) |
| Schs 2, 3 | | 1 Apr 1967 (SI 1967/45) |
| Sch 4 | | 1 Feb 1967 (SI 1967/45) |
| Sch 5 | | 1 Apr 1967 (SI 1967/45) |
| Sch 6 | para 1 | 1 Feb 1967 (SI 1967/45) |

**Armed Forces Act 1966 (c 45)**—*contd*

| | | |
|---|---|---|
| para 2 | 1 Apr 1967 (SI 1967/45) | |
| paras 3–5 | 1 Feb 1967 (SI 1967/45) | |
| paras 6–9 | 1 Apr 1967 (SI 1967/45) | |

**Barbados Independence Act 1966 (c 37)**

*RA:* 17 Nov 1966

This Act generally had effect from 30 Nov 1966 (the "appointed day")

**Botswana Independence Act 1966 (c 23)**

*RA:* 3 Aug 1966

This Act generally had effect from 30 Sep 1966 (the "appointed day")

**Building Control Act 1966 (c 27)**

*RA:* 9 Aug 1966

Whole Act in force 9 Aug 1966 (RA)

**Bus Fuel Grants Act 1966 (c 46)**

*RA:* 21 Dec 1966

Whole Act in force 21 Dec 1966 (RA)

**Church of England Convocations Act 1966 (c 2)**

*RA:* 24 Feb 1966

Whole Act in force 24 Feb 1966 (RA)

**Commonwealth Secretariat Act 1966 (c 10)**

*RA:* 10 Mar 1966

*Commencement provisions:* s 2(2)

Whole Act in force 1 Jul 1965 (s 2(2)); this is the date on which this Act is deemed to have come into force, but not to affect any cause of action arising, or liability to criminal proceedings incurred, before 10 Mar 1966

**Consolidated Fund Act 1966 (c 1)**

*RA:* 24 Feb 1966

Whole Act in force 24 Feb 1966 (RA)

**Criminal Appeal Act 1966 (c 31)**

*RA:* 9 Aug 1966

*Commencement provisions:* s 12(8); Criminal Appeal Act 1966 (Commencement No 1) Order 1966, SI 1966/1018; Criminal Appeal Act 1966 (Commencement No 2) Order 1967, SI 1967/1676

**Criminal Appeal Act 1966 (c 31)**—*contd*

| | |
|---|---|
| 1–6 | 1 Oct 1966 (SI 1966/1018) |
| 7 | 1 Jan 1968 (SI 1967/1676) |
| 8–10 | 1 Oct 1966 (SI 1966/1018) |
| 11 | 1 Oct 1966 (except so far as it applies s 7 to Northern Ireland) (SI 1966/1018) |
| | 1 Jan 1968 (exception noted above) (SI 1967/1676) |
| 12 | 1 Oct 1966 (SI 1966/1018) |
| Schs 1, 2 | 1 Oct 1966 (SI 1966/1018) |
| Sch 3 | 1 Oct 1966 (SI 1966/1018), except entries relating to— |
| | Criminal Appeal Act 1907, s 16; |
| | Criminal Appeal (Northern Ireland) Act 1930, s 15; |
| | Northern Ireland Act 1962 |
| | 1 Jan 1968 (exceptions noted above) (SI 1967/1676) |

---

**Docks and Harbours Act 1966 (c 28)**

*RA:* 9 Aug 1966

*Commencement provisions:* s 60(2); Docks and Harbours Act 1966 (Commencement No 1) Order 1966, SI 1966/1072; Docks and Harbours Act 1966 (Commencement No 2) Order 1967, SI 1967/312; Docks and Harbours Act 1966 (Commencement No 3) Order 1967, SI 1967/1253; Docks and Harbours Act 1966 (Commencement No 4) Order 1967, SI 1967/1617; Docks and Harbours Act 1966 (Commencement No 5) Order 1967, SI 1967/1777; Docks and Harbours Act 1966 (Commencement No 6) Order 1967, SI 1967/1849; Docks and Harbours Act 1966 (Commencement No 7) Order 1967, SI 1967/1972; Docks and Harbours Act 1966 (Commencement No 8) Order 1968, SI 1968/261; Docks and Harbours Act 1966 (Commencement No 9) Order 1968, SI 1968/436; Docks and Harbours Act 1966 (Commencement No 10) Order 1968, SI 1968/1046; Docks and Harbours Act 1966 (Commencement No 11) Order 1968, SI 1968/1538; Docks and Harbours Act 1966 (Amendment and Commencement) (Hunterston) Order 1981, SI 1981/918

| | |
|---|---|
| 1 | 18 Sep 1967 (in relation to the following ports: Middlesborough, The Hartlepools, Ipswich, Faversham Navigation, Milton Creek, Queenborough Corporation, Plymouth, Fowey, Penryn, Bristol, Sharpness, Gloucester, Newport, Barry, Port Talbot, Swansea, Birkenhead, Bromborough, Liverpool, Garston, Widnes, Ellesmere Port, Manchester, Partington, Runcorn, Weston Point, Preston, Fleetwood, Barrow-in-Furness, Whitehaven, Workington, Troon, Glasgow, Kirkcaldy, Methil, Burntisland, Grangemouth) (SI 1967/1253) |
| | 11 Dec 1967 (in relation to the following ports: Boston, Lowestoft, River Medway, Hayle, Newlyn, Truro, Ayr, Greenock, Dundee, Tayport, Granton, Leith) (SI 1967/1617) |
| | 1 Jan 1968 (in relation to the following ports: London, Southampton, Weymouth, Charlestown, Par, Porthleven, Portreath, Silloth, Irvine, Ardrossan) (SI 1967/1777) |
| | 22 Jan 1968 (in relation to the following ports: Wisbech, Poole and Hamworthy) (SI 1967/1849) |
| | 12 Feb 1968 (in relation to the following ports: Dunston, Sunderland, Hull, Goole, Grimsby, Immingham) (SI 1967/1972) |
| | 1 Apr 1968 (in relation to the following ports: Blyth, Gateshead, Newcastle, Seaham, Kings Lynn, Great Yarmouth, Whitstable, Penzance, Cardiff and Penarth) (SI 1968/261) |
| | 5 Aug 1968 (in relation to the following port: Falmouth) (SI 1968/1046) |
| | 21 Oct 1968 (in relation to the following ports: South Shields, North Shields) (SI 1968/1538) |
| | 1 Aug 1981 (in relation to the following port: Hunterston (inserted in Sch 1 to Act by SI 1981/918)) (SI 1981/918) |
| | *Never in force* (in relation to the port of Aberdeen) (repealed) |
| 2–24 | 1 Sep 1966 (SI 1966/1072) |

**Docks and Harbours Act 1966 (c 28)**—*contd*

| | |
|---|---|
| 25–35 | 1 Apr 1966 (SI 1968/436) |
| 36–50 | 9 Aug 1966 (RA) |
| 51 | 15 Mar 1967 (SI 1967/312) |
| 52–60 | 9 Aug 1966 (RA) |
| Sch 1 | See ss 1, 2, 25 above |
| Sch 2 | 9 Aug 1966 (RA) |

**Expiring Laws Continuance Act 1966 (c 40)**

*RA:* 13 Dec 1966

Whole Act in force 13 Dec 1966 (RA)

**Family Provision Act 1966 (c 35)**

*RA:* 17 Nov 1966

*Commencement provisions*: s 10(4); Family Provision Act 1966 (Commencement No 1) Order 1966, SI 1966/1453

Whole Act in force 1 Jan 1967 (SI 1966/1453)

**Films Act 1966 (c 48)**

*RA:* 21 Dec 1966

Whole Act in force 21 Dec 1966 (RA)

**Finance Act 1966 (c 18)**

*RA:* 3 Aug 1966

The commencement details of Finance Acts are not set out, as the dates from which their provisions take effect are usually stated clearly and unambiguously in the text of the Act, and charging provisions will normally state for which year or years of assessment they are to have effect.

**Guyana Independence Act 1966 (c 14)**

*RA:* 12 May 1966

This Act generally had effect from 26 May 1966 (the "appointed day")

**Housing (Scotland) Act 1966 (c 49)**

*RA:* 21 Dec 1966

*Commencement provisions*: s 213(2)

Whole Act in force 1 Apr 1967 (s 213(2))

**Industrial Development Act 1966 (c 34)**

*RA:* 12 Aug 1966

*Commencement provisions*: s 31(6)

Whole Act in force 19 Aug 1966 (s 31(6))

**Industrial Reorganisation Corporation Act 1966 (c 50)**

*RA:* 21 Dec 1966

Whole Act in force 21 Dec 1966 (RA)

---

**Land Registration Act 1966 (c 39)**

*RA:* 13 Dec 1966

*Commencement provisions:* s 2(4)

Whole Act in force 13 Jan 1967 (s 2(4))

---

**Law Reform (Miscellaneous Provisions) (Scotland) Act 1966 (c 19)**

*RA:* 3 Aug 1966

Whole Act in force 3 Aug 1966 (RA)

---

**Lesotho Independence Act 1966 (c 24)**

*RA:* 3 Aug 1966

This Act generally had effect from 4 Oct 1966 (the "appointed day")

---

**Local Government Act 1966 (c 42)**

*RA:* 13 Dec 1966

Whole Act in force 13 Dec 1966 (RA)

---

**Local Government (Pecuniary Interests) (Scotland) Act 1966 (c 7)**

*RA:* 10 Mar 1966

Whole Act in force 10 Mar 1966 (RA)

---

**Local Government (Scotland) Act 1966 (c 51)**

*RA:* 21 Dec 1966

Whole Act in force 21 Dec 1966 (RA)

---

**Malawi Republic Act 1966 (c 22)**

*RA:* 3 Aug 1966

Malawi became a Republic on 6 Jul 1966

---

**Military Aircraft (Loans) Act 1966 (c 15)**

*RA:* 26 May 1966

Whole Act in force 26 May 1966 (RA)

---

## Mines (Working Facilities and Support) Act 1966 (c 4)

*RA*: 10 Mar 1966

*Commencement provisions*: s 16(3)

Whole Act in force 10 Apr 1966 (s 16(3))

---

## Ministry of Social Security Act 1966 (c 20)

*RA*: 3 Aug 1966

*Commencement provisions*: s 40(2); Ministry of Social Security Act 1966 (Commencement) Order 1966, SI 1966/986

| | | |
|---|---|---|
| 1–3 | | 6 Aug 1966 (s 40(2)(b)) |
| 4 | | 28 Nov 1966 (SI 1966/986) |
| 5 | | See Sch 2 below |
| 6–16 | | 28 Nov 1966 (SI 1966/986) |
| 17–20 | | 11 Aug 1966 (SI 1966/986) |
| 21 | | 2 Dec 1966 (SI 1966/986) |
| 22–26 | | 28 Nov 1966 (SI 1966/986) |
| 27 | | 11 Aug 1966 (SI 1966/986) |
| 28 | | See Sch 3 below |
| 29 | | 11 Aug 1966 (SI 1966/986) |
| 30 | | 28 Nov 1966 (SI 1966/986) |
| 31–33 | | 11 Aug 1966 (SI 1966/986) |
| 34 | | See Sch 4 below |
| 35, 36 | | 11 Aug 1966 (SI 1966/986) |
| 37 | | See Sch 5 below |
| 38 | | 3 Aug 1966 (s 40(2)(a)) |
| 39 | (1) | See Sch 6 below |
| | (2) | See Sch 7 below |
| | (3) | See Sch 8 below |
| 40 | | 3 Aug 1966 (s 40(2)(a)) |
| Sch 1 | | 6 Aug 1966 (s 40(2)(b)) |
| Schs 2, 3 | | 11 Aug 1966 (SI 1966/986) |
| Schs 4, 5 | | 28 Nov 1966 (SI 1966/986) |
| Sch 6 | paras 1–8 | 28 Nov 1966 (SI 1966/986) |
| | para 9 | 11 Aug 1966 (SI 1966/986) |
| | paras 10–14 | 28 Nov 1966 (SI 1966/986) |
| | para 15 | 6 Aug 1966 (s 40(2)(b)) |
| | para 16 | 11 Aug 1966 (SI 1966/986) |
| | para 17 | 28 Nov 1966 (SI 1966/986) |
| | para 18 | 6 Aug 1966 (s 40(2)(b)) |
| Sch 7 | | 11 Aug 1966 (SI 1966/986) |
| Sch 8 | | 6 Aug 1966 (so far as it relates to House of Commons Disqualification Act 1957, Sch 2, Ministers of the Crown Act 1964, Ministerial Salaries Consolidation Act 1965) (s 40(2)(b)) |
| | | 11 Aug 1966 (repeals of or in Ministry of National Insurance Act 1944) (SI 1966/986) |
| | | 28 Nov 1966 (otherwise, exceptions noted below) (SI 1966/986) |
| | | 2 Dec 1966 (SI 1966/986), repeals of or in— |
| | | Old Age Pensions Act 1936; |
| | | Blind Persons Act 1938; |
| | | Pensions and Determination of Needs Act 1943; |
| | | National Insurance Act 1946; |
| | | National Assistance Act 1948, ss 46, 61, Sch 4; |
| | | Pensions (Increase) Act 1956; |
| | | National Insurance (No 2) Act 1957; |

**Ministry of Social Security Act 1966 (c 20)**—*contd*

Pensions (Increase) Act 1959;
South Africa Act 1965
1 Jul 1967 (repeals of or in National Insurance Act 1965, s 89)
(SI 1966/986)

---

**National Coal Board (Additional Powers) Act 1966 (c 47)**

*RA:* 21 Dec 1966

Whole Act in force 21 Dec 1966 (RA)

---

**National Health Service Act 1966 (c 8)**

*RA:* 10 Mar 1966

*Commencement provisions:* s 12(3); National Health Service Act 1966 (Commencement No 1) Order 1966, SI 1966/1431

| | |
|---|---|
| 1–9 | 21 Nov 1966 (SI 1966/1431) |
| 10 | *Never in force* (repealed) |
| 11, 12 | 21 Nov 1966 (SI 1966/1431) |
| Schedule | 21 Nov 1966 (SI 1966/1431) |

---

**National Insurance Act 1966 (c 6)**

*RA:* 10 Mar 1966

*Commencement provisions:* s 14(4); National Insurance Act 1966 (Commencement) Order 1966, SI 1966/327; National Insurance Act 1966 (Commencement) (No 2) Order 1966, SI 1966/633[1]

| | | |
|---|---|---|
| 1 | | 5 Oct 1966 (SI 1966/633) |
| 2 | (1)–(7) | 6 Oct 1966 (SI 1966/633) |
| | (8), (9) | 5 Oct 1966 (SI 1966/633) |
| 3 | | 6 Oct 1966 (SI 1966/633) |
| 4 | (1)–(3) | 5 Oct 1966 (SI 1966/633) |
| | (4) | 6 Apr 1966 (SI 1966/327) |
| 5 | (1)–(4) | 6 Oct 1966 (SI 1966/633) |
| | (5) | 5 Oct 1966 (SI 1966/633) |
| 6, 7 | | 6 Apr 1966 (SI 1966/327) |
| 8 | | 6 Oct 1966 (SI 1966/633) |
| 9 | | 1 Jul 1966 (SI 1966/633) |
| 10, 11 | | 6 Apr 1966 (SI 1966/327) |
| 12 | (1) | 26 Mar 1966 (SI 1966/327) |
| | (2) | 6 Oct 1966 (SI 1966/633) |
| | (3) | 6 Apr 1966 (SI 1966/327) |
| 13 | (1) | See Sch 3 below |
| | (2) | 1 Jul 1966 (SI 1966/633) |
| | (3) | 1 Jul 1966 (in relation only to entry 11(c)) (SI 1966/633) |
| | | 6 Oct 1966 (otherwise) (SI 1966/633) |
| 14 | | 26 Mar 1966 (SI 1966/327) |
| Sch 1 | | 5 Oct 1966 (SI 1966/633) |
| Sch 2 | | 6 Oct 1966 (SI 1966/633) |
| Sch 3 | para 1 | 5 Oct 1966 (SI 1966/633) |
| | paras 2–4 | 6 Oct 1966 (SI 1966/633) |
| | para 5(a)–(g) | 6 Oct 1966 (SI 1966/633) |
| | para 5(h) | 1 Jul 1966 (only in relation to National Insurance (Industrial Injuries) Act 1965, s 52) (SI 1966/633) |
| | | 6 Oct 1966 (otherwise) (SI 1966/633) |

**National Insurance Act 1966 (c 6)**—*contd*

|  |  |
|---|---|
| para 5(i) | 1 Jul 1966 (only in relation to National Insurance (Industrial Injuries) Act 1965, s 53(1)) (SI 1966/633) |
|  | 6 Oct 1966 (otherwise) (SI 1966/633) |
| para 5(k) | 1 Jul 1966 (only in relation to National Insurance (Industrial Injuries) Act 1965, s 61(1)(d), figures "52(5)") (SI 1966/633) |
|  | 6 Oct 1966 (otherwise) (SI 1966/633) |
| para 5(l), (m) | 1 Jul 1966 (SI 1966/633) |
| para 5(n) | 6 Oct 1966 (SI 1966/633) |
| para 6 | 6 Oct 1966 (SI 1966/633) |
| para 7 | 1 Jul 1966 (SI 1966/633) |
| para 8 | 6 Apr 1966 (SI 1966/327) |
| para 9 | 5 Oct 1966 (SI 1966/633) |

[1]   For transitional provisions, see SI 1966/633, arts 3, 4

---

**New Towns Act 1966 (c 44)**

*RA:* 13 Dec 1966

Whole Act in force 13 Dec 1966 (RA)

---

**Overseas Aid Act 1966 (c 21)**

*RA:* 3 Aug 1966

Whole Act in force 3 Aug 1966 (RA)

---

**Police (Scotland) Act 1966 (c 52)**

*RA:* 21 Dec 1966

Whole Act in force 21 Dec 1966 (RA)

---

**Post Office Savings Bank Act 1966 (c 12)**

*RA:* 10 Mar 1966

*Commencement provisions:* s 9(5)

Whole Act in force 10 May 1966 (s 9(5))

---

**Post Office (Subway) Act 1966 (c 25)**

*RA:* 3 Aug 1966

Whole Act in force 3 Aug 1966 (RA)

---

**Prices and Incomes Act 1966 (c 33)**

*RA:* 12 Aug 1966

*Commencement provisions:* ss 6(1), 25(1); Prices and Incomes Act 1966 (Commencement of Part IV) Order 1966, SI 1966/1262; Prices and Incomes Act 1966 (Commencement of Part II) Order 1967, SI 1967/1142

| | |
|---|---|
| 1–6 | 12 Aug 1966 (RA) |
| 7–22 | 12 Aug 1966 (SI 1967/1142)[1] |

## Prices and Incomes Act 1966 (c 33)—*contd*

| | |
|---|---|
| 23, 24 | 12 Aug 1966 (RA) |
| 25–33 | 6 Oct 1966 (SI 1966/1262) |
| 34–37 | 12 Aug 1966 (RA) |
| Schs 1–3 | 12 Aug 1966 (RA) |

¹ Ss 7–22 come into force for a period of 12 months beginning with 12 Aug 1967, see SI 1967/1142, art 1

## Public Works Loans Act 1966 (c 16)

*RA:* 26 May 1966

Whole Act in force 26 May 1966 (RA)

## Rating Act 1966 (c 9)

*RA:* 10 Mar 1966

*Commencement provisions:* s 13(3)

Whole Act in force 1 Apr 1966 (s 13(3)), in application to England and Wales, as respects rates for any period beginning on or after that date

## Reserve Forces Act 1966 (c 30)

*RA:* 9 Aug 1966

*Commencement provisions:* s 25(2); Reserve Forces Act 1966 (Commencement) Order 1966, SI 1966/1204

| | | |
|---|---|---|
| 1 | | 1 Apr 1967 (in so far as relates to the territorial army) (SI 1966/1204) |
| | | 1 Oct 1966 (otherwise) (SI 1966/1204) |
| 2 | | 1 Oct 1966 (SI 1966/1204)¹ |
| 3–5 | | 1 Apr 1967 (SI 1966/1204) |
| 6 | | 1 Oct 1966 (SI 1966/1204)¹ |
| 7, 8 | | 1 Oct 1966 (SI 1966/1204) |
| 9–13 | | 1 Apr 1967 (SI 1966/1204) |
| 14 | | 1 Oct 1966 (SI 1966/1204) |
| 15, 16 | | 1 Oct 1966 (SI 1966/1204)¹ |
| 17–22 | | 1 Oct 1966 (SI 1966/1204) |
| 23 | (1)–(4) | 1 Apr 1967 (SI 1966/1204) |
| | (5)–(7) | 1 Oct 1966 (SI 1966/1204) |
| 24 | | 1 Oct 1966 (SI 1966/1204) |
| 25 | | 9 Aug 1966 (RA) |
| Sch 1 | paras 1, 2 | 1 Apr 1967 (SI 1966/1204) |
| | para 3 | 1 Nov 1966 (SI 1966/1204) |
| | paras 4–9 | 1 Apr 1967 (SI 1966/1204) |
| | para 10 | 1 Oct 1966 (SI 1966/1204) |
| | para 11 | 1 Apr 1967 (SI 1966/1204) |
| | para 12 | 1 Oct 1966 (SI 1966/1204) |
| | paras 13, 14 | 1 Apr 1967 (SI 1966/1204) |
| | para 15 | 1 Oct 1966 (SI 1966/1204) |
| | para 16 | 1 Apr 1967 (SI 1966/1204) |
| | para 17 | 1 Oct 1966 (SI 1966/1204) |
| | para 18 | 1 Apr 1967 (SI 1966/1204) |
| | paras 19, 20 | 1 Oct 1966 (SI 1966/1204) |
| | paras 21, 22 | 1 Apr 1967 (SI 1966/1204) |
| | para 23 | 1 Oct 1966 (SI 1966/1204) |
| | paras 24–26 | 1 Apr 1967 (SI 1966/1204) |

**Reserve Forces Act 1966 (c 30)**—*contd*

|  |  |  |
|---|---|---|
|  | paras 27–30 | 1 Oct 1966 (SI 1966/1204) |
|  | paras 31, 32 | 1 Apr 1967 (SI 1966/1204) |
|  | para 33 | 1 Oct 1966 (SI 1966/1204) |
|  | paras 34–37 | 1 Apr 1967 (SI 1966/1204) |
|  | paras 38, 39 | 1 Oct 1966 (SI 1966/1204) |
| Sch 2 |  | 1 Oct 1966 (otherwise, exceptions noted below) (SI 1966/1204) |

1 Nov 1966 (SI 1966/1204), repeals of or in—
Militia Act 1882;
Deputy Lieutenants Act 1918;
Administration of Justice Act 1964
1 Apr 1967 (SI 1966/1204), repeals of or in—
Royal Naval Reserve (Volunteer) Act 1859;
Naval Reserve (Mobilisation) Act 1900;
Naval Forces Act 1903;
Royal Marines Act 1948;
Auxiliary & Reserves Forces Act 1949;
Air Force Reserve Act 1950 (except ss 6(7), 12(1), 13(4), 14(2), 20(2), 25, 27(2), 30(2), Sch 1);
Army Reserve Act 1950 (except ss 6(7), 12(1), 13(4), 14(2), 20(2), 26, Sch 1);
Auxiliary Forces Act 1953 (except ss 2(3), 41(2)–(4), 42(1), 46(1), Sch 4);
Army Reserve Act 1962, ss 3(6), 4(4)(a)

[1] As to appointed days for the purposes of certain provisions of ss 2, 6, 15, 16, see further the Reserve Forces Act 1966 (Appointed Days) Order 1966, SI 1966/1205

---

**Sea Fisheries Regulation Act 1966 (c 38)**

*RA:* 17 Nov 1966

*Commencement provisions:* s 22(1)

Whole Act in force 17 Dec 1966 (s 22(1))

---

**Selective Employment Payments Act 1966 (c 32)**

*RA:* 9 Aug 1966

Whole Act in force 9 Aug 1966 (RA)

---

**Singapore Act 1966 (c 29)**

*RA:* 9 Aug 1966

Singapore became an independent sovereign state on 9 Aug 1966

---

**Statute Law Revision Act 1966 (c 5)**

*RA:* 10 Mar 1966

Whole Act in force 10 Mar 1966 (RA)

**Transport Finances Act 1966 (c 17)**

*RA:* 26 May 1966

Whole Act in force 26 May 1966 (RA)

---

**Tribunals and Inquiries Act 1966 (c 43)**

*RA:* 13 Dec 1966

Whole Act in force 13 Dec 1966 (RA)

---

**Veterinary Surgeons Act 1966 (c 36)**

*RA:* 17 Nov 1966

*Commencement provisions:* s 29(3); Veterinary Surgeons Act 1966 (Commencement No 1) Order 1967, SI 1967/251

Whole Act in force 15 Mar 1967 (SI 1967/251), except s 28(1) which came into force on 15 Nov 1967 (SI 1967/251)

---

# 1967 Acts

### Abortion Act 1967 (c 87)

*RA:* 27 Oct 1967

*Commencement provisions*: s 7(2)

Whole Act in force 27 Apr 1968 (s 7(2))

---

### Aden, Perim and Kuria Muria Islands Act 1967 (c 71)

*RA:* 27 Jul 1967

This Act generally had effect from 30 Nov 1967 (the "appointed day")

---

### Advertisements (Hire-Purchase) Act 1967 (c 42)

*RA:* 14 Jul 1967

*Commencement provisions*: s 8(4)

Whole Act in force 14 Aug 1967 (s 8(4))

---

### Agriculture Act 1967 (c 22)

*RA:* 10 May 1967

*Commencement provisions*: s 75(8); Agriculture Act 1967 (Commencement No 1) Order 1967, SI 1967/733; Agriculture Act 1967 (Commencement No 2) Order 1968, SI 1968/1539

Whole Act in force 15 May 1967 (SI 1967/733), except s 22, which came into force on 1 Oct 1968 (SI 1968/1539)

---

### Air Corporations Act 1967 (c 33)

*RA:* 10 May 1967

Whole Act in force 10 May 1967 (RA)

---

### Anchors and Chain Cables Act 1967 (c 64)

*RA:* 27 Jul 1967

*Commencement provisions*: s 2(4); Anchors and Chain Cables Act 1967 (Commencement) Order 1970, SI 1970/1443

Whole Act in force 19 Oct 1970 (SI 1970/1443)

---

## Antarctic Treaty Act 1967 (c 65)

*RA:* 27 Jul 1967

Whole Act in force 27 Jul 1967 (RA); but note that most of the Act was not effective until 1 Jul 1968, the day appointed by Antarctic Treaty Act 1967 (Appointed Day) Order 1968, SI 1968/886, made under s 10(5)

## Appropriation Act 1967 (c 59)

*RA:* 27 Jul 1967

Whole Act in force 27 Jul 1967 (RA)

## Bermuda Constitution Act 1967 (c 63)

*RA:* 27 Jul 1967

Whole Act in force 27 Jul 1967 (RA)

## Civic Amenities Act 1967 (c 69)

*RA:* 27 Jul 1967

*Commencement provisions:* ss 18(7), (8); 20(9); 32(2)

| | | |
|---|---|---|
| 1 | | 27 Aug 1967 (s 32(2)) |
| 2 | (1) | 27 Jul 1967 (RA) |
| | (2), (3) | 27 Aug 1967 (s 32(2)) |
| 3–17 | | 27 Aug 1967 (s 32(2)) |
| 18 | (1) | 27 Aug 1968 (s 32(2)) |
| | (2)–(9) | 27 Aug 1967 (s 32(2)) |
| 19 | | 27 Aug 1967 (s 32(2)) |
| 20 | (1)–(8) | 27 Aug 1967 (s 32(2)) |
| | (9) | 27 Jan 1968 (s 32(2)) |
| 21, 22 | | 27 Jan 1968 (s 32(2)) |
| 23–27 | | 27 Aug 1967 (s 32(2)) |
| 28–32 | | 27 Jul 1967 (RA) |

## Clergy Pensions (Amendment) Measure 1967 (No 1)

*RA:* 22 Mar 1967

Whole Measure in force 22 Mar 1967 (RA)

## Coal Industry Act 1967 (c 91)

*RA:* 20 Dec 1967

Whole Act in force 20 Dec 1967 (RA)

## Commonwealth Settlement Act 1967 (c 31)

*RA:* 10 May 1967

Whole Act in force 10 May 1967 (RA)

## Companies Act 1967 (c 81)

*RA:* 27 Jul 1967

Whole Act in force 27 Jul 1967 (RA)

---

## Consolidated Fund Act 1967 (c 2)

*RA:* 16 Feb 1967

Whole Act in force 16 Feb 1967 (RA)

---

## Consolidated Fund (No 2) Act 1967 (c 6)

*RA:* 22 Mar 1967

Whole Act in force 22 Mar 1967 (RA)

---

## Control of Liquid Fuel Act 1967 (c 57)

*RA:* 21 Jul 1967

Whole Act in force 21 Jul 1967 (RA)

---

## Countryside (Scotland) Act 1967 (c 86)

*RA:* 27 Oct 1967

Whole Act in force 27 Oct 1967 (RA)

---

## Criminal Justice Act 1967 (c 80)

*RA:* 27 Jul 1967

*Commencement provisions:* s 106(5); Criminal Justice Act 1967 (Commencement No 1) Order 1967, SI 1967/1234, as amended by SI 1967/1380, SI 1968/325; Criminal Justice Act 1967 (Commencement No 2) Order 1967, SI 1967/1380; Criminal Justice Act 1967 (Commencement No 3) Order 1968, SI 1968/325; Criminal Justice Act 1967 (Commencement No 4) Order 1977, SI 1977/2139

| | | |
|---|---|---|
| 1–6 | | 1 Jan 1968 (SI 1967/1234) |
| 7, 8 | | 1 Oct 1967 (SI 1967/1234) |
| 9–12 | | 1 Jan 1968 (SI 1967/1234) |
| 13–17 | | 1 Oct 1967 (SI 1967/1234) |
| 18–24 | | 1 Jan 1968 (SI 1967/1234) |
| 25–30 | | 1 Oct 1967 (SI 1967/1234) |
| 31, 32 | | 1 Jan 1968 (SI 1967/1234) |
| 33–37 | | 1 Oct 1967 (SI 1967/1234) |
| 38 | (1)–(5) | 1 Oct 1967 (SI 1967/1234) |
| | (6) | 1 Apr 1968 (SI 1967/1234) |
| | (7) | 1 Oct 1967 (SI 1967/1234) |
| 39–50 | | 1 Jan 1968 (SI 1967/1234) |
| 51, 52 | | 1 Oct 1967 (SI 1967/1234) |
| 53 | | 1 Jan 1968 (SI 1967/1234) |
| 54, 55 | | 1 Oct 1967 (SI 1967/1234) |
| 56 | | 1 Jan 1968 (SI 1967/1234) |
| 57 | | *Never in force* (repealed) |
| 58, 59 | | 1 Oct 1967 (SI 1967/1234) |
| 60–64 | | 1 Apr 1968 (SI 1967/1234) |

**Criminal Justice Act 1967 (c 80)**—*contd*

| | | |
|---|---|---|
| 65 | | 1 Oct 1967 (SI 1967/1234) |
| 66 | (1), (2) | 1 Apr 1968 (SI 1967/1234) |
| | (3), (4) | 1 Oct 1967 (SI 1967/1234) |
| | (5) | 1 Apr 1968 (SI 1967/1234) |
| 67–72 | | 1 Oct 1967 (SI 1967/1234) |
| 73–84 | | 1 Oct 1968 (SI 1967/1234) |
| 85–88 | | 1 May 1968 (SI 1967/1234) |
| 89, 90 | | 1 Jan 1968 (SI 1967/1234) |
| 91 | | 1 Feb 1978 (SI 1977/2139) |
| 92, 93 | | 1 Jan 1968 (SI 1967/1234) |
| 94–97 | | 1 Oct 1967 (SI 1967/1234) |
| 98 | | 1 Sep 1968 (SI 1967/1234) |
| 99–106 | | 1 Oct 1967 (SI 1967/1234) |
| Sch 1 | | 1 Jan 1968 (SI 1967/1234) |
| Sch 2 | | 1 Oct 1967 (SI 1967/1234) |
| Sch 3 | | 1 Jan 1968 (SI 1967/1234) |
| Sch 4 | | 1 Sep 1968 (except para 20(3)) (SI 1967/1234) |
| | | 1 Oct 1968 (para 20(3)) (SI 1967/1234) |
| Sch 5 | | 1 Oct 1967 (SI 1967/1234) |
| Sch 6 | para 1 | 1 Jan 1968 (SI 1967/1234) |
| | para 2 | 1 Sep 1968 (SI 1968/325) |
| | para 3 | 1 Jan 1968 (SI 1967/1234) |
| | para 4 | 1 Oct 1967 (SI 1967/1234) |
| | para 5 | 1 Jan 1968 (SI 1967/1234) |
| | para 6 | 1 Apr 1968 (SI 1967/1234) |
| | para 7 | 1 Oct 1968 (SI 1967/1234) |
| | para 8 | 1 Apr 1968 (SI 1967/1234) |
| | paras 9, 10 | 1 Oct 1967 (SI 1967/1234) |
| | paras 11–20 | 1 Jan 1968 (SI 1967/1234) |
| | para 21 | *Never in force* (repealed) |
| | paras 22, 23 | 1 Sep 1968 (SI 1968/325) |
| | paras 24, 25 | 1 Apr 1968 (SI 1967/1234) |
| | para 26 | *Never in force* (spent) |
| | paras 27, 28 | 1 Jan 1968 (SI 1967/1234) |
| Sch 7 | | 1 Oct 1967 (SI 1967/1234), repeals of or in— |

Sch 7 (contd):

1 Oct 1967 (SI 1967/1234), repeals of or in—
Criminal Appeal Act 1907, s 4(3);
Criminal Justice Administration Act 1914, s 27;
Criminal Justice Act 1948, ss 5(2), (3), 9(3), (4), 20(5)(d), 21, 23, 29(3)(d), (5), 38(3), Sch 5, para 4(2), proviso to para 5(1);
Magistrates' Courts Act 1952, s 113(2), various entries in Sch 4;
Prison Act 1952, ss 5(2)(c), 18, 43(3)(b), 52(2);
Magistrates' Courts Act 1957, in s 1, proviso (iii) to sub-s (1);
Mental Health Act 1959, s 69;
Criminal Justice Administration Act 1962, s 17(2), Sch 3, para 3;
Children and Young Persons Act 1963, Sch 1, para 13;
Administration of Justice Act 1964, s 20;
Criminal Law Act 1967, Sch 1, Div II of List A, para 5(c)(ii), (iii)

1 Jan 1968 (SI 1967/1234), repeals of or in—
Levy of Fines Act 1822;
Levy of Fines Act 1823;
Vagrancy Act 1824, s 10;
Juries Act 1825, s 53;
Fines Act 1833, ss 34–40, 47;
Quarter Sessions Act 1849, s 17;
Criminal Procedure Act 1853, s 2;
Queen's Remembrancer Act 1859, ss 30–39;
Municipal Corporations Act 1882, s 222;
Coroners Act 1887, s 19(4);

## Criminal Justice Act 1967 (c 80)—*contd*

Summary Jurisdiction (Appeals) Act 1933, s 6;
Criminal Justice Act 1948, ss 8(4), (5), 14(2), 15, 37(1), (6);
Magistrates' Courts Act 1952, ss 4(2), 15(2), proviso (a), 69, 70(1), 114(1)(c)–(e), (2);
Air Force Act 1955, s 99(2);
Army Act 1955, s 99(2);
Metropolitan Police Act 1839 (Amendment) Act 1958
1 Apr 1968 (SI 1967/1234), repeals of or in—
Prison Act 1952, ss 15, 25(2)–(6), 26, 27, 43(4)(b), 47(4), 49;
Children and Young Persons Act 1953, s 53(4);
Criminal Justice Act 1961, s 20, Sch 3;
Murder (Abolition of Death Penalty) Act 1965, s 2
1 May 1968 (SI 1967/1234), repeals of or in—
Firearms Act 1937, s 12(3);
Firearms Act 1965, s 9(2)
1 Sep 1968 (SI 1968/325), repeals of or in—
Criminal Appeal Act 1907, ss 4(2), 8, 9, 11(1), 12, 15(1), 18;
Supreme Court of Judicature (Consolidation) Act 1925, s 29;
Criminal Appeal (Northern Ireland) Act 1930, s 7(1);
Criminal Justice Act 1948, s 38(4);
Costs in Criminal Cases Act 1952, ss 16(3), 17(6);
Criminal Justice Administration Act 1956, s 19(1);
Administration of Justice Act 1960, ss 5(2), 6(2), 9(1), Sch 2, Pt I;
Criminal Appeal Act 1964, Sch 1, para 6;
Criminal Procedure (Insanity) Act 1964, ss 2(4)(a), 3;
Criminal Appeal Act 1966, s 57(1);
Criminal Justice Act (Northern Ireland) 1966, s 16(3)
1 Oct 1968 (SI 1967/1234), repeals of or in—
Poor Prisoners' Defence Act 1930;
Summary Jurisdiction (Appeals) Act 1933, s 2;
Legal Aid and Advice Act 1949, Pt II;
Courts-Martial (Appeals) Act 1951, ss 10, 21(c);
Costs in Criminal Cases Act 1952, s 16(1);
Magistrates' Courts (Appeals from Binding Over Orders) Act 1956, s 1(2)(b);
Mental Health Act 1959, s 67(3);
Administration of Justice Act 1960, ss 8(1), (2), 9(4)(c), Sch 1, para 3(2);
Criminal Appeal Act 1964, s 2(4);
Criminal Appeal Act 1967, ss 10, 15(5), 17
1 Feb 1978 (SI 1977/2139), repeals of or in—
City of London Police Act 1839, s 37;
Metropolitan Police Act 1839, s 58;
Town Police Clauses Act 1847, s 29;
Licensing Act 1872, s 12

## Criminal Law Act 1967 (c 58)

*RA:* 21 Jul 1967

*Commencement provisions:* s 12(1)

Whole Act in force 1 Jan 1968 (s 12(1)), except ss 13–15, Schs 1–4, which came into force on 21 Jul 1967 (RA)

**Dangerous Drugs Act 1967 (c 82)**

*RA:* 27 Oct 1967

Whole Act in force 27 Oct 1967 (RA)

---

**Decimal Currency Act 1967 (c 47)**

*RA:* 14 Jul 1967

Whole Act in force 14 Jul 1967 (RA); but note that the Act was partly effective as from 15 Feb 1971, the day appointed by Decimal Currency (Appointed Day) Order 1968, SI 1968/195, made under s 1(1)

---

**Deer (Amendment) (Scotland) Act 1967 (c 37)**

*RA:* 28 Jun 1967

Whole Act in force 28 Jun 1967 (RA)

---

**Development of Inventions Act 1967 (c 32)**

*RA:* 10 May 1967

*Commencement provisions:* s 15(8)

Whole Act in force 10 Jun 1967 (s 15(8))

---

**Education Act 1967 (c 3)**

*RA:* 16 Feb 1967

Whole Act in force 16 Feb 1967 (RA)

---

**Expiring Laws Continuance Act 1967 (c 89)**

*RA:* 20 Dec 1967

Whole Act in force 20 Dec 1967 (RA)

---

**Export Guarantees Act 1967 (c 11)**

*RA:* 22 Mar 1967

Whole Act in force 22 Mar 1967 (RA)

---

**Extra-Parochial Ministry Measure 1967 (No 2)**

*RA:* 14 Jul 1967

Whole Act in force 14 Jul 1967 (RA)

---

**Family Allowances and National Insurance Act 1967 (c 90)**

*RA:* 20 Dec 1967

Whole Act in force 20 Dec 1967 (RA)

---

## Farm and Garden Chemicals Act 1967 (c 50)

*RA:* 14 Jul 1967

Whole Act in force 14 Jul 1967 (RA)

## Finance Act 1967 (c 54)

*RA:* 21 Jul 1967

The commencement details of Finance Acts are not set out, as the dates from which their provisions take effect are usually stated clearly and unambiguously in the text of the Act, and charging provisions will normally state for which year or years of assessment they are to have effect.

## Fishing Vessel Grants Act 1967 (c 35)

*RA:* 28 Jun 1967

Whole Act in force 28 Jun 1967 (RA)

## Forestry Act 1967 (c 10)

*RA:* 22 Mar 1967

Whole Act in force 22 Mar 1967 (RA)

## Fugitive Offenders Act 1967 (c 68)

*RA:* 27 Jul 1967

*Commencement provisions:* s 22; Fugitive Offenders Act 1967 (Commencement No 1) Order 1967, SI 1967/1256; Fugitive Offenders Act 1967 (Commencement No 2) Order 1968, SI 1968/1988; Fugitive Offenders Act 1967 (Commencement No 3) Order 1981, SI 1981/1745

Whole Act in force as follows—

25 Aug 1967 (for the purposes of any provision conferring power to make an Order in Council, except in relation to Zimbabwe) (SI 1967/1256)

1 Sep 1967 (except in relation to Zimbabwe and, as regards most provisions, in relation to any country falling within s 2(2)(c)) (SI 1967/1256)

1 Jan 1969 (in relation to any country falling within s 2(2)(c)) (SI 1968/1988)

2 Feb 1982 (in relation to Zimbabwe) (SI 1981/1745)

## General Rate Act 1967 (c 9)

*RA:* 22 Mar 1967

*Commencement provisions:* s 119(4); General Rate Act 1967 (Commencement) Order 1967, SI 1967/499

Whole Act in force 1 Apr 1967 (SI 1967/499)

## Greenwich Hospital Act 1967 (c 74)

*RA:* 27 Jul 1967

Whole Act in force 27 Jul 1967 (RA)

**Housing (Financial Provisions, &c.) (Scotland) Act 1967 (c 20)**

*RA:* 10 May 1967

Whole Act in force 10 May 1967 (RA)

---

**Housing Subsidies Act 1967 (c 29)**

*RA:* 10 May 1967

Whole Act in force 10 May 1967 (RA)

---

**Industrial and Provident Societies Act 1967 (c 48)**

*RA:* 14 Jul 1967

*Commencement provisions:* s 8(2)

Whole Act in force 14 Sep 1967 (s 8(2))

---

**Industrial Injuries and Diseases (Old Cases) Act 1967 (c 34)**

*RA:* 12 Jun 1967

*Commencement provisions:* s 16(3); Industrial Injuries and Diseases (Old Cases) Act 1967 (Commencement) Order 1967, SI 1967/921

Whole Act in force 22 Jun 1967 (SI 1967/921)

---

**Irish Sailors and Soldiers Land Trust Act 1967 (c 67)**

*RA:* 27 Jul 1967

Whole Act in force 27 Jul 1967 (RA)

---

**Iron and Steel Act 1967 (c 17)**

*RA:* 22 Mar 1967

Whole Act in force 22 Mar 1967 (RA)

---

**Land Commission Act 1967 (c 1)**

*RA:* 1 Feb 1967

Whole Act in force 1 Feb 1967 (RA)

---

**Leasehold Reform Act 1967 (c 88)**

*RA:* 27 Oct 1967

*Commencement provisions:* s 41(4), (5); Leasehold Reform Act 1967 Commencement Order 1967, SI 1967/1836

| | |
|---|---|
| 1–33 | 1 Jan 1968 (SI 1967/1836) |
| 34–36 | 27 Oct 1967 (s 41(4)) |
| 37 | 1 Jan 1968 (SI 1967/1836) |
| 38–41 | 27 Nov 1967 (s 41(5)) |
| Schs 1–4 | 1 Jan 1968 (SI 1967/1836) |

**Leasehold Reform Act 1967 (c 88)**—*contd*
Schs 5–7                                27 Nov 1967 (s 41(5))

---

**Legal Aid (Scotland) Act 1967 (c 43)**

*RA:* 14 Jul 1967

*Commencement provisions*: s 22(2), (3); Legal Aid (Scotland) Act 1967 (Commencement No 1) Order 1971, SI 1971/190; Legal Aid (Scotland) Act 1967 (Commencement No 2) Order 1975, SI 1975/716

| | | |
|---|---|---|
| 1 | (1)–(5) | 14 Jul 1967 (exceptions noted below) (s 22(2), (3)) |
| | | 1 Mar 1971 (so far as they provide for and relate to legal aid in connection with civil proceedings in the Scottish Land Court or by any person to whom a case is referred in whole or in part by that Court) (SI 1971/190) |
| | | 16 May 1975 (so far as they provide for and relate to legal aid in connection with proceedings in the District Court) (SI 1975/716) |
| | (6) | 14 Jul 1967 (exception noted below) (s 22(2), (3)) |
| | | 1 Mar 1971 (so far as they provide for and relate to legal aid in connection with civil proceedings in the Scottish Land Court or by any person to whom a case is referred in whole or in part by that Court) (SI 1971/190) |
| | (7) | 14 Jul 1967 (exception noted below) (s 22(2), (3)) |
| | | 16 May 1975 (so far as they provide for and relate to legal aid in connection with proceedings in the District Court) (SI 1975/716) |
| | (8) | 14 Jul 1967 (exceptions noted below) (s 22(2), (3)) |
| | | 1 Mar 1971 (so far as they provide for and relate to legal aid in connection with civil proceedings in the Scottish Land Court or by any person to whom a case is referred in whole or in part by that Court) (SI 1971/190) |
| | | 16 May 1975 (so far as they provide for and relate to legal aid in connection with proceedings in the District Court) (SI 1975/716) |
| 2 | (1) | 14 Jul 1967 (exception noted below) (s 22(2), (3)) |
| | | 1 Mar 1971 (so far as they provide for and relate to legal aid in connection with civil proceedings in the Scottish Land Court or by any person to whom a case is referred in whole or in part by that Court) (SI 1971/190) |
| | (2) | 14 Jul 1967 (exception noted below) (s 22(2), (3)) |
| | | 16 May 1975 (so far as they provide for and relate to legal aid in connection with proceedings in the District Court) (SI 1975/716) |
| | (3)(a) | 14 Jul 1967 (exception noted below) (s 22(2), (3)) |
| | | 16 May 1975 (so far as they provide for and relate to legal aid in connection with proceedings in the District Court) (SI 1975/716) |
| | (3)(b) | 14 Jul 1967 (s 22(2)) |
| | (3)(c) | 14 Jul 1967 (exception noted below) (s 22(2), (3)) |
| | | 16 May 1975 (so far as they provide for and relate to legal aid in connection with proceedings in the District Court) (SI 1975/716) |
| | (3)(d) | 14 Jul 1967 (s 22(2)) |
| | (4) | 14 Jul 1967 (exception noted below) (s 22(2), (3)) |
| | | 16 May 1975 (so far as they provide for and relate to legal aid in connection with proceedings in the District Court) (SI 1975/716) |
| | (5) | 14 Jul 1967 (exception noted below) (s 22(2), (3)) |
| | | 16 May 1975 (so far as they provide for and relate to legal aid in connection with proceedings in the District Court) (SI 1975/716) |

**Legal Aid (Scotland) Act 1967 (c 43)**—*contd*

|  |  |  |
|---|---|---|
| | (6)–(8) | 14 Jul 1967 (exceptions noted below) (s 22(2), (3)) |
| | | 1 Mar 1971 (so far as they provide for and relate to legal aid in connection with civil proceedings in the Scottish Land Court or by any person to whom a case is referred in whole or in part by that Court) (SI 1971/190) |
| | | 16 May 1975 (so far as they provide for and relate to legal aid in connection with proceedings in the District Court) (SI 1975/716) |
| 3, 4 | | 14 Jul 1967 (exception noted below) (s 22(2), (3)) |
| | | 1 Mar 1971 (so far as they provide for and relate to legal aid in connection with civil proceedings in the Scottish Land Court or by any person to whom a case is referred in whole or in part by that Court) (SI 1971/190) |
| 5 | | 14 Jul 1967 (s 22(2)) |
| 6 | | 14 Jul 1967 (exceptions noted below) (s 22(2), (3)) |
| | | 1 Mar 1971 (so far as they provide for and relate to legal aid in connection with civil proceedings in the Scottish Land Court or by any person to whom a case is referred in whole or in part by that Court) (SI 1971/190) |
| | | 16 May 1975 (so far as they provide for and relate to legal aid in connection with proceedings in the District Court) (SI 1975/716) |
| 7 | (1)–(3) | 14 Jul 1967 (s 22(2)) |
| | (4)–(7) | *Never in force* (repealed) |
| | (8)–(12) | 14 Jul 1967 (s 22(2)) |
| 8–11 | | 14 Jul 1967 (exceptions noted below) (s 22(2), (3)) |
| | | 1 Mar 1971 (so far as they provide for and relate to legal aid in connection with civil proceedings in the Scottish Land Court or by any person to whom a case is referred in whole or in part by that Court) (SI 1971/190) |
| | | 16 May 1975 (so far as they provide for and relate to legal aid in connection with proceedings in the District Court) (SI 1975/716) |
| 12 | | 14 Jul 1967 (s 22(2)) |
| 13, 14 | | 14 Jul 1967 (exception noted below) (s 22(2), (3)) |
| | | 1 Mar 1971 (so far as they provide for and relate to legal aid in connection with civil proceedings in the Scottish Land Court or by any person to whom a case is referred in whole or in part by that Court) (SI 1971/190) |
| 15, 16 | | 14 Jul 1967 (exceptions noted below) (s 22(2), (3)) |
| | | 1 Mar 1971 (so far as they provide for and relate to legal aid in connection with civil proceedings in the Scottish Land Court or by any person to whom a case is referred in whole or in part by that Court) (SI 1971/190) |
| | | 16 May 1975 (so far as they provide for and relate to legal aid in connection with proceedings in the District Court) (SI 1975/716) |
| 17 | (1)–(5) | 14 Jul 1967 (exceptions noted below) (s 22(2), (3)) |
| | | 1 Mar 1971 (so far as they provide for and relate to legal aid in connection with civil proceedings in the Scottish Land Court or by any person to whom a case is referred in whole or in part by that Court) (SI 1971/190) |
| | | 16 May 1975 (so far as they provide for and relate to legal aid in connection with proceedings in the District Court) (SI 1975/716) |
| | (6) | 14 Jul 1967 (exception noted below) (s 22(2), (3)) |
| | | 16 May 1975 (so far as they provide for and relate to legal aid in connection with proceedings in the District Court) (SI 1975/716) |
| 18–20 | | 14 Jul 1967 (exceptions noted below) (s 22(2), (3)) |

**Legal Aid (Scotland) Act 1967 (c 43)**—*contd*

|  |  |  |
|---|---|---|
|  |  | 1 Mar 1971 (so far as they provide for and relate to legal aid in connection with civil proceedings in the Scottish Land Court or by any person to whom a case is referred in whole or in part by that Court) (SI 1971/190) |
|  |  | 16 May 1975 (so far as they provide for and relate to legal aid in connection with proceedings in the District Court) (SI 1975/716) |
| 21 | (1) | 14 Jul 1967 (s 22(2)) |
|  | (2)–(4) | 14 Jul 1967 (exception noted below) (s 22(2), (3)) |
|  |  | 16 May 1975 (so far as they provide for and relate to legal aid in connection with proceedings in the District Court) (SI 1975/716) |
| 22 |  | 14 Jul 1967 (s 22(2)) |
| Sch 1 | Pt I, paras 1, 2 | 14 Jul 1967 (exception noted below) (s 22(2), (3)) |
|  |  | 1 Mar 1971 (so far as they provide for and relate to legal aid in connection with civil proceedings in the Scottish Land Court or by any person to whom a case is referred in whole or in part by that Court) (SI 1971/190) |
|  | Pt I, para 3 | 14 Jul 1967 (exceptions noted below) (s 22(2), (3)) |
|  |  | 1 Mar 1971 (so far as they provide for and relate to legal aid in connection with civil proceedings in the Scottish Land Court or by any person to whom a case is referred in whole or in part by that Court) (SI 1971/190) |
|  |  | 16 May 1975 (so far as they provide for and relate to legal aid in connection with proceedings in the District Court) (SI 1975/716) |
|  | Pt II | 14 Jul 1967 (exception noted below) (s 22(2), (3)) |
|  |  | 1 Mar 1971 (so far as they provide for and relate to legal aid in connection with civil proceedings in the Scottish Land Court or by any person to whom a case is referred in whole or in part by that Court) (SI 1971/190) |
| Sch 2 | para 1(1), (2) | 14 Jul 1967 (exception noted below) (s 22(2), (3)) |
|  |  | 1 Mar 1971 (so far as they provide for and relate to legal aid in connection with civil proceedings in the Scottish Land Court or by any person to whom a case is referred in whole or in part by that Court) (SI 1971/190) |
|  | para 1(3) | 14 Jul 1967 (exceptions noted below) (s 22(2), (3)) |
|  |  | 1 Mar 1971 (so far as they provide for and relate to legal aid in connection with civil proceedings in the Scottish Land Court or by any person to whom a case is referred in whole or in part by that Court) (SI 1971/190) |
|  |  | 16 May 1975 (so far as they provide for and relate to legal aid in connection with proceedings in the District Court) (SI 1975/716) |
|  | para 2(1), (2) | 14 Jul 1967 (exception noted below) (s 22(2), (3)) |
|  |  | 1 Mar 1971 (so far as they provide for and relate to legal aid in connection with civil proceedings in the Scottish Land Court or by any person to whom a case is referred in whole or in part by that Court) (SI 1971/190) |
|  | para 2(3), (4) | 14 Jul 1967 (exceptions noted below) (s 22(2), (3)) |
|  |  | 1 Mar 1971 (so far as they provide for and relate to legal aid in connection with civil proceedings in the Scottish Land Court or by any person to whom a case is referred in whole or in part by that Court) (SI 1971/190) |
|  |  | 16 May 1975 (so far as they provide for and relate to legal aid in connection with proceedings in the District Court) (SI 1975/716) |
|  | para 3 | 14 Jul 1967 (exceptions noted below) (s 22(2), (3)) |

**See Halsbury's Statutes Citator for amendments to these Acts**    115

**Legal Aid (Scotland) Act 1967 (c 43)**—*contd*

|  |  |
|---|---|
|  | 1 Mar 1971 (so far as they provide for and relate to legal aid in connection with civil proceedings in the Scottish Land Court or by any person to whom a case is referred in whole or in part by that Court) (SI 1971/190) |
|  | 16 May 1975 (so far as they provide for and relate to legal aid in connection with proceedings in the District Court) (SI 1975/716) |
| para 4 | 14 Jul 1967 (exception noted below) (s 22(2), (3)) |
|  | 1 Mar 1971 (so far as they provide for and relate to legal aid in connection with civil proceedings in the Scottish Land Court or by any person to whom a case is referred in whole or in part by that Court) (SI 1971/190) |
| paras 5, 6 | 14 Jul 1967 (exceptions noted below) (s 22(2), (3)) |
|  | 1 Mar 1971 (so far as they provide for and relate to legal aid in connection with civil proceedings in the Scottish Land Court or by any person to whom a case is referred in whole or in part by that Court) (SI 1971/190) |
|  | 16 May 1975 (so far as they provide for and relate to legal aid in connection with proceedings in the District Court) (SI 1975/716) |
| Sch 3 | 14 Jul 1967 (s 22(2)) |

**Licensing (Amendment) Act 1967 (c 51)**

*RA:* 14 Jul 1967

*Commencement provisions:* s 2(2)

Whole Act in force 14 Aug 1967 (s 2(2))

**Licensing (Certificates in Suspense) (Scotland) Act 1967 (c 14)**

*RA:* 22 Mar 1967

Whole Act in force 22 Mar 1967 (RA)

**Llangollen International Musical Eisteddfod Act 1967 (c 49)**

*RA:* 14 Jul 1967

Whole Act in force 14 Jul 1967 (RA)

**Local Government (Termination of Reviews) Act 1967 (c 18)**

*RA:* 10 May 1967

Whole Act in force 10 May 1967 (RA)

**London Government Act 1967 (c 5)**

*RA:* 16 Feb 1967

Whole Act in force 16 Feb 1967 (RA)

## Marine, &c, Broadcasting (Offences) Act 1967 (c 41)

*RA:* 14 Jul 1967

*Commencement provisions*: s 11(2); Marine &c Broadcasting (Offences) Act 1967 (Commencement) Order 1967, SI 1967/1149

Whole Act in force 15 Aug 1967 (SI 1967/1149)

## Matrimonial Causes Act 1967 (c 56)

*RA:* 21 Jul 1967

*Commencement provisions*: s 11(2); Matrimonial Causes Act 1967 (Commencement) Order 1968, SI 1968/228

Whole Act in force 11 Apr 1968 (SI 1968/228)

## Matrimonial Homes Act 1967 (c 75)

*RA:* 27 Jul 1967

*Commencement provisions*: s 8(1); Matrimonial Homes Act 1967 (Commencement) Order 1967, SI 1967/1790

Whole Act in force 1 Jan 1968 (SI 1967/1790)

## Merchant Shipping Act 1967 (c 26)

*RA:* 10 May 1967

Whole Act in force 10 May 1967 (RA)

## Merchant Shipping (Load Lines) Act 1967 (c 27)

*RA:* 10 May 1967

*Commencement provisions*: s 34(3); Merchant Shipping (Load Lines) Act 1967 (Commencement) Order 1968, SI 1968/1108

Whole Act in force 21 Jul 1968 (SI 1968/1108), except s 25 and Sch 1, which came into force on 10 May 1967 (s 34(3))

## Misrepresentation Act 1967 (c 7)

*RA:* 22 Mar 1967

*Commencement provisions*: s 6(2)

Whole Act in force 22 Apr 1967 (s 6(2))

## National Health Service (Family Planning) Act 1967 (c 39)

*RA:* 28 Jun 1967

Whole Act in force 28 Jun 1967 (RA)

## National Insurance Act 1967 (c 73)

*RA:* 27 Jul 1967

*Commencement provisions:* s 7(3), Sch 7, para 1(1); National Insurance Act 1967 (Commencement) Order 1967, SI 1967/1174[1]

| | | |
|---|---|---|
| 1 | (1)(a) | See Sch 1 below |
| | (1)(b) | See Sch 2 below |
| | (1)(c) | See Sch 3 below |
| | (1)(d), (e) | 30 Oct 1967 (SI 1967/1174) |
| | (2) | See Sch 4 below |
| 2 | (1)(a) | See Sch 5 below |
| | (1)(b), (c) | See Sch 6 below |
| | (2) | 7 Aug 1967 (SI 1967/1174) |
| 3 | (1) | 31 Oct 1967 (SI 1967/1174) |
| | (2) | 31 Aug 1967 (SI 1967/1174) |
| | (3) | 3 Aug 1967 (SI 1967/1174) |
| 4 | | 3 Aug 1967 (SI 1967/1174) |
| 5 | | 27 Jul 1967 (s 7(3), Sch 7, para 1(1)) |
| 6, 7 | | 3 Aug 1967 (SI 1967/1174) |
| Sch 1 | | 30 Oct 1967 (SI 1967/1174) |
| Sch 2 | | 26 Oct 1967 (in so far as it relates to higher rates of benefit under the National Insurance Act 1965 in the case of unemployment and sickness benefit) (SI 1967/1174) |
| | | 30 Oct 1967 (in so far as it relates to higher rates of benefit under the National Insurance Act 1965 in the case of maternity allowance, widow's benefit, guardian's allowance, retirement pension and child's special allowance) (SI 1967/1174) |
| Sch 3 | | 30 Oct 1967 (SI 1967/1174) |
| Sch 4 | para 1 | 3 Aug 1967 (SI 1967/1174) |
| | para 2 | 30 Oct 1967 (SI 1967/1174) |
| | para 3 | 3 Aug 1967 (SI 1967/1174) |
| | para 4 | 31 Oct 1967 (SI 1967/1174) |
| Sch 5 | | 30 Oct 1967 (SI 1967/1174) |
| Sch 6 | | 26 Oct 1967 (in so far as it relates to higher rates and amounts of benefit under the National Insurance (Industrial Injuries) Act 1965, in the case of injury benefit (including increases thereof) and increases of disablement pension in respect of children and adult dependants in the case of a beneficiary receiving, as an in-patient in a hospital or similar institution, medical treatment for the relevant injury of loss of faculty and maximum under s 29(1)(a), of aggregate of weekly benefits payable for successive accidents) (SI 1967/1174) |
| | | 30 Oct 1967 (in so far as it relates to higher rates and amounts of benefit under the National Insurance (Industrial Injuries) Act 1965, in the case of death benefit) (SI 1967/1174) |
| | | 1 Nov 1967 (in so far as it relates to higher rates and amounts of benefit under the National Insurance (Industrial Injuries) Act 1965, in the case of disablement benefit (including increases of disablement pension other than those already in force) (SI 1967/1174) |
| Sch 7 | | 3 Aug 1967 (SI 1967/1174) |

[1]   For transitional provisions, see SI 1967/1174, art 2

---

## National Insurance (Industrial Injuries) (Amendment) Act 1967 (c 25)

*RA:* 10 May 1967

Whole Act in force 10 May 1967 (RA)

---

### Overseas and Other Clergy (Ministry and Ordination) Measure 1967 (No 3)

*RA*: 14 Jul 1967

Whole Act in force 14 Jul 1967 (RA)

---

### Parliamentary Commissioner Act 1967 (c 13)

*RA*: 22 Mar 1967

*Commencement provisions*: s 14(2); Parliamentary Commissioner Act 1967 (Commencement) Order 1967, SI 1967/485

Whole Act in force 1 Apr 1967 (SI 1967/485)

---

### Plant Health Act 1967 (c 8)

*RA*: 22 Mar 1967

Whole Act in force 22 Mar 1967 (RA)

---

### Police (Scotland) Act 1967 (c 77)

*RA*: 27 Jul 1967

*Commencement provisions*: s 53(3)

Whole Act in force 27 Oct 1967 (so far as this Act extends to the whole of Great Britain) (s 53(3))

---

### Post Office (Borrowing Powers) Act 1967 (c 15)

*RA*: 22 Mar 1967

Whole Act in force 22 Mar 1967 (RA)

---

### Post Office (Data Processing Service) Act 1967 (c 62)

*RA*: 27 Jul 1967

Whole Act in force 27 Jul 1967 (RA)

---

### Prices and Incomes Act 1967 (c 53)

*RA*: 14 Jul 1967

Whole Act in force 14 Jul 1967 (RA)

---

### Private Places of Entertainment (Licensing) Act 1967 (c 19)

*RA*: 10 May 1967

Whole Act in force 10 May 1967 (RA)

---

### Protection of Birds Act 1967 (c 46)

*RA*: 14 Jul 1967

*Commencement provisions*: s 12(4)

**Protection of Birds Act 1967 (c 46)**—*contd*

Whole Act in force 14 Jan 1968 (s 12(4))

---

**Public Records Act 1967 (c 44)**

*RA:* 14 Jul 1967

*Commencement provisions:* s 2(2)

Whole Act in force 1 Jan 1968 (s 2(2))

---

**Public Works Loans Act 1967 (c 61)**

*RA:* 27 Jul 1967

Whole Act in force 27 Jul 1967 (RA)

---

**Refreshment Houses Act 1967 (c 38)**

*RA:* 28 Jun 1967

*Commencement provisions:* s 5(4)

Whole Act in force 28 Jul 1967 (s 5(4))

---

**Remuneration of Teachers (Scotland) Act 1967 (c 36)**

*RA:* 28 Jun 1967

Whole Act in force 28 Jun 1967 (RA)

---

**Road Safety Act 1967 (c 30)**

*RA:* 10 May 1967

*Commencement provisions:* s 33(3); Road Safety Act 1967 (Commencement No 1) Order 1967,
SI 1967/904; Road Safety Act 1967 (Commencement No 2) Order 1967, SI 1967/1307; Road Safety
Act 1967 (Commencement No 3) Order 1969, SI 1969/826; Road Safety Act 1967 (Commencement
No 4) Order 1971, SI 1971/1805

| | | |
|---|---|---|
| 1–6 | | 9 Oct 1967 (SI 1967/1307) |
| 7 | | 15 Jun 1967 (SI 1967/904) |
| 8–15 | | 10 May 1967 (RA) |
| 16 | | 1 Jan 1972 (SI 1971/1805) |
| 17 | (1) | 8 Jul 1969 (SI 1969/826) |
| | (2) | 1 Jan 1972 (SI 1971/1805) |
| 18–33 | | 10 May 1967 (RA) |
| Sch 1 | paras 1, 2 | 9 Oct 1967 (SI 1967/1307) |
| | para 3 | 1 Jan 1972 (SI 1971/1805) |
| | paras 4–8 | 10 May 1967 (RA) |
| | para 9 | 9 Oct 1967 (in so far as it provides that in the Road Traffic Act 1960, s 232(1)(a) the reference to Part 1 of the principal Act shall include a reference to Road Safety Act 1967, Part I) (SI 1967/1307) |
| | | 8 Jul 1969 (in so far as it provides that in the Road Traffic Act 1960, s 232(1)(a) the reference to Part 1 of the principal Act shall include a reference to Road Safety Act 1967, s 17(1)) (SI 1969/826) |

## Road Safety Act 1967 (c 30)—*contd*

|  |  |  |
|---|---|---|
|  |  | 1 Jan 1972 (in so far as it provides that in the Road Traffic Act 1960, s 232(1)(a) the reference to Part 1 of the principal Act shall include a reference to Road Safety Act 1967, ss 14, 16(9)) (SI 1971/1805) |
|  | paras 10–20 | 10 May 1967 (RA) |
| Sch 2 |  | 10 May 1967 (except repeals of or in Road Traffic Act 1960, ss 6, 184, 185, 232, or Sch 15, para 2) (RA) |
|  |  | 9 Oct 1967 (repeal in Road Traffic Act 1960, s 6(2)) (SI 1967/1307) |
|  |  | 1 Jan 1972 (repeals of or in Road Traffic Act 1960, ss 184, 185(1), 232(1)(b)) (SI 1971/1805) |

## Road Traffic Act 1967 (c 21)

*RA:* 10 May 1967

Whole Act in force 10 May 1967 (RA)

## Road Traffic (Amendment) Act 1967 (c 70)

*RA:* 27 Jul 1967

*Commencement provisions*: s 10(3); Road Traffic (Amendment) Act 1967 (Commencement No 1) Order 1967, SI 1967/1474; Road Traffic (Amendment) Act 1967 (Commencement No 2) Order 1969, SI 1969/434

| | |
|---|---|
| 1, 2 | *Never in force* (repealed) |
| 3 | 8 Nov 1967 (SI 1967/1474) |
| 4 | 1 May 1969 (SI 1969/434) |
| 5–10 | 8 Nov 1967 (SI 1967/1474) |

## Road Traffic (Driving Instruction) Act 1967 (c 79)

*RA:* 27 Jul 1967

*Commencement provisions*: s 22(2); Road Traffic (Driving Instruction) Act 1967 (Commencement No 1) Order 1969, SI 1969/84; Road Traffic (Driving Instruction) Act 1967 (Commencement No 2) Order 1970, SI 1970/965

| | |
|---|---|
| 1, 2 | 1 Oct 1970 (SI 1970/965) |
| 3–5 | 17 Mar 1969 (SI 1969/84) |
| 6 | 1 Oct 1970 (SI 1970/965) |
| 7 | 17 Mar 1969 (except so far as they relate to licences granted under s 6) (SI 1969/84) |
| | 1 Oct 1970 (otherwise) (SI 1970/965) |
| 8 | 17 Mar 1969 (SI 1969/84) |
| 9 | 17 Mar 1969 (except so far as they relate to licences granted under s 6) (SI 1969/84) |
| | 1 Oct 1970 (otherwise) (SI 1970/965) |
| 10 | 17 Mar 1969 (SI 1969/84) |
| 11–14 | 17 Mar 1969 (except so far as they relate to licences granted under s 6) (SI 1969/84) |
| | 1 Oct 1970 (otherwise) (SI 1970/965) |
| 15–22 | 17 Mar 1969 (SI 1969/84) |
| Schs 1, 2 | 17 Mar 1969 (except so far as they relate to licences granted under s 6) (SI 1969/84) |
| | 1 Oct 1970 (otherwise) (SI 1970/965) |

**Road Traffic Regulation Act 1967 (c 76)**

*RA:* 27 Jul 1967

*Commencement provisions:* s 113(2)

Whole Act in force 27 Oct 1967 (s 113(2))

**Road Transport Lighting Act 1967 (c 55)**

*RA:* 21 Jul 1967

Whole Act in force 21 Jul 1967 (RA)

**Royal Assent Act 1967 (c 23)**

*RA:* 10 May 1967

Whole Act in force 10 May 1967 (RA)

**Sea Fish (Conservation) Act 1967 (c 84)**

*RA:* 27 Oct 1967

*Commencement provisions:* s 26

Whole Act in force 27 Nov 1967 (s 26)

**Sea Fisheries (Shellfish) Act 1967 (c 83)**

*RA:* 27 Oct 1967

*Commencement provisions:* s 25(1)

Whole Act in force 27 Nov 1967 (s 25(1))

**Sexual Offences Act 1967 (c 60)**

*RA:* 27 Jul 1967

Whole Act in force 27 Jul 1967 (RA)

**Shipbuilding Industry Act 1967 (c 40)**

*RA:* 28 Jul 1967

Whole Act in force 28 Jul 1967 (RA)

**Slaughter of Poultry Act 1967 (c 24)**

*RA:* 10 May 1967

*Commencement provisions:* s 9(3); Slaughter of Poultry Act 1967 (Commencement) Order 1969, SI 1969/1096

Whole Act in force 1 Jan 1970 (SI 1969/1096)

## Superannuation (Miscellaneous Provisions) Act 1967 (c 28)

*RA:* 10 May 1967

Whole Act in force 10 May 1967 (RA)

---

## Teachers of Nursing Act 1967 (c 16)

*RA:* 22 Mar 1967

*Commencement provisions:* s 3(3)

Whole Act in force 22 Sep 1967 (s 5(4))

---

## Teachers' Superannuation Act 1967 (c 12)

*RA:* 22 Mar 1967

*Commencement provisions:* s 18(2); Teachers' Superannuation Regulations 1967, SI 1967/489

| | | |
|---|---|---|
| 1–17 | | 1 Apr 1967 (SI 1967/489) |
| 18 | | 22 Mar 1967 (RA) |
| Schs 1, 2 | | 1 Apr 1967 (SI 1967/489) |
| Sch 3 | paras 1–6 | 1 Apr 1967 (SI 1967/489) |
| | para 7 | 22 Mar 1967 (RA) |

---

## Tokyo Convention Act 1967 (c 52)

*RA:* 14 Jul 1967

*Commencement provisions:* s 9(3); Tokyo Convention Act 1967 (Commencement) Order 1968, SI 1968/469; Tokyo Convention Act 1967 (Commencement No 2) Order 1969, SI 1969/1688

Whole Act in force 1 Apr 1968 (SI 1968/469) except s 2, which came into force on 4 Dec 1969 (SI 1969/1688)

---

## Uniform Laws on International Sales Act 1967 (c 45)

*RA:* 14 Jul 1967

Whole Act in force 14 Jul 1967 (RA)

---

## Vessels Protection Act 1967 (c 85)

*RA:* 27 Oct 1967

Whole Act in force 27 Oct 1967 (RA)

---

## Water (Scotland) Act 1967 (c 78)

*RA:* 27 Jul 1967

Whole Act in force 27 Jul 1967 (RA)

---

### Welsh Language Act 1967 (c 66)

*RA:* 27 Jul 1967

Whole Act in force 27 Jul 1967 (RA)

### West Indies Act 1967 (c 4)

*RA:* 16 Feb 1967

This Act generally had effect as follows—

27 Feb 1967 (in relation to Antigua, St Christopher, Nevis and Anguilla)

1 Mar 1967 (in relation to Dominica and St Lucia)

3 Mar 1967 (in relation to Grenada)

27 Oct 1969 (in relation to Saint Vincent)

### Wireless Telegraphy Act 1967 (c 72)

*RA:* 27 Jul 1967

Whole Act in force 27 Jul 1967 (RA); but note that ss 1–3 were effective from 1 Jan 1968, the day
appointed by Wireless Telegraphy Act 1967 (Appointed Day) Order 1967, SI 1967/1691, made under
s 6(1); s 9(2), (3) were effective from 27 Aug 1967, by virtue of s 9(5)

# 1968 Acts

## Administration of Justice Act 1968 (c 5)

*RA:* 15 Feb 1968

Whole Act in force 15 Feb 1968 (RA)

---

## Adoption Act 1968 (c 53)

*RA:* 26 Jul 1968

*Commencement provisions:* s 14(2); Adoption Act 1968 (Commencement No 1) Order 1973, SI 1973/18; Adoption Act 1968 (Commencement No 2) Order 1978, SI 1978/1430

| | | |
|---|---|---|
| 1–3 | | 1 Feb 1973 (SI 1973/18) |
| 4 | (1) | 1 Feb 1973 (SI 1973/18) |
| | (2) | 1 Feb 1973 (except the figure "19(1)") (SI 1973/18) |
| | | 23 Oct 1978 (otherwise) (SI 1978/1430) |
| | (3) | 1 Feb 1973 (SI 1973/18) |
| 5–7 | | 23 Oct 1978 (SI 1978/1430) |
| 8 | (1) | 23 Oct 1978 (SI 1978/1430) |
| | (2)–(5) | 1 Feb 1973 (SI 1973/18) |
| 9 | | 23 Oct 1978 (SI 1978/1430) |
| 10–14 | | 1 Feb 1973 (SI 1973/18) |

---

## Agriculture (Miscellaneous Provisions) Act 1968 (c 34)

*RA:* 3 Jul 1968

*Commencement provisions:* s 54(2)

| | |
|---|---|
| 1–8 | 3 Sep 1968 (s 54(2)) |
| 9–54 | 3 Jul 1968 (RA) |
| Schs 1–8 | 3 Jul 1968 (RA) |

---

## Air Corporations Act 1968 (c 30)

*RA:* 30 May 1968

Whole Act in force 30 May 1968 (RA)

---

## Appropriation Act 1968 (c 43)

*RA:* 26 Jul 1968

Whole Act in force 26 Jul 1968 (RA)

---

## British Standard Time Act 1968 (c 45)

*RA:* 26 Jul 1968

*Commencement provisions:* s 4(1)

Whole Act in force 27 Oct 1968 (s 4(1))

## Capital Allowances Act 1968 (c 3)

*RA:* 1 Feb 1968

*Commencement provisions:* ss 26(7), 81(3), 83(5), 96

Whole Act in force 6 Apr 1968 (ss 26(7), 81(3), 83(5), 96)

## Caravan Sites Act 1968 (c 52)

*RA:* 26 Jul 1968

*Commencement provisions:* s 17(2); Caravan Sites Act 1968 (Part II) (Commencement) Order 1970, SI 1970/199

| | |
|---|---|
| 1–5 | 26 Aug 1968 (s 17(2)) |
| 6–12 | 1 Apr 1970 (SI 1970/199) |
| 13–17 | 26 Aug 1968 (s 17(2)) |

## Civil Aviation Act 1968 (c 61)

*RA:* 25 Oct 1968

*Commencement provisions:* ss 13(2), 14(13); Civil Aviation Act 1968 (Commencement) Order 1971, SI 1971/1133

Whole Act in force 25 Oct 1968 (RA); except ss 13(2), 14(1)–(12), which came into force on 13 Jul 1971 (SI 1971/1133)

## Civil Evidence Act 1968 (c 64)

*RA:* 25 Oct 1968

*Commencement provisions:* s 20(4); Civil Evidence Act 1968 (Commencement No 1) Order 1968, SI 1968/1734; Civil Evidence Act 1968 (Commencement No 2) Order 1969, SI 1969/1104; Civil Evidence Act 1968 (Commencement No 3) Order 1970, SI 1970/18

| | | |
|---|---|---|
| 1–10 | | 1 Oct 1969 (except as regards bankruptcy proceedings and proceedings in county courts, magistrates' courts and other inferior courts) (SI 1969/1104) |
| | | 16 Feb 1970 (except as regards bankruptcy proceedings) (SI 1970/18) |
| | | *Never in force* (as regards bankruptcy proceedings) (repealed) |
| 11, 12 | | 2 Dec 1968 (SI 1968/1734) |
| 13–19 | | 25 Oct 1968 (s 20(4)) |
| 20 | (1) | 25 Oct 1968 (s 20(4)) |
| | (2) | See ss 1–10 above |
| | (3), (4) | 25 Oct 1968 (s 20(4)) |
| Schedule | | 25 Oct 1968 (s 20(4)) |

## Clean Air Act 1968 (c 62)

*RA:* 25 Oct 1968

*Commencement provisions:* s 15(3); Clean Air Act 1968 (Commencement No 1) Order 1968, SI 1968/1922; Clean Air Act 1968 (Commencement No 2) Order 1969, SI 1969/995

| | | |
|---|---|---|
| 1 | | 1 Oct 1969 (SI 1969/995) |
| 2 | | 1 Apr 1969 (SI 1968/1922) |
| 3–5 | | 1 Oct 1969 (SI 1969/995) |
| 6 | | 1 Apr 1969 (SI 1968/1922) |
| 7 | | 1 Oct 1969 (SI 1969/995) |
| 8–15 | | 1 Apr 1969 (SI 1968/1922) |
| Sch 1 | para 1 | 1 Apr 1969 (except so far as it refers to ss 1, 3–5) (SI 1968/1922) |
| | | 1 Oct 1969 (exception noted above) (SI 1969/995) |
| | para 2 | 1 Oct 1969 (SI 1969/995) |
| | paras 3, 4 | 1 Apr 1969 (except so far as it refers to ss 1, 3–5) (SI 1968/1922) |
| | | 1 Oct 1969 (exception noted above) (SI 1969/995) |
| | para 5 | 1 Oct 1969 (SI 1969/995) |
| | paras 6, 7 | 1 Apr 1969 (except so far as it refers to ss 1, 3–5) (SI 1968/1922) |
| | | 1 Oct 1969 (exception noted above) (SI 1969/995) |
| | paras 8, 9 | 1 Oct 1969 (SI 1969/995) |
| | para 10 | 1 Apr 1969 (except so far as it refers to ss 1, 3–5) (SI 1968/1922) |
| | | 1 Oct 1969 (exception noted above) (SI 1969/995) |
| | para 11 | 1 Oct 1969 (SI 1969/995) |
| | para 12 | 1 Apr 1969 (except so far as it refers to ss 1, 3–5) (SI 1968/1922) |
| | | 1 Oct 1969 (exception noted above) (SI 1969/995) |
| Sch 2 | | 1 Apr 1969 (SI 1968/1922) |

## Commonwealth Immigrants Act 1968 (c 9)

*RA:* 1 Mar 1968

*Commencement provisions:* s 7(2)

Whole Act in force 2 Mar 1968 (except ss 3, 5, which came into force on 9 Mar 1968) (s 7(2))

## Commonwealth Telecommunications Act 1968 (c 24)

*RA:* 8 May 1968

Whole Act in force 8 May 1968 (RA)

## Consolidated Fund Act 1968 (c 1)

*RA:* 1 Feb 1968

Whole Act in force 1 Feb 1968 (RA)

## Consolidated Fund (No 2) Act 1968 (c 15)

*RA:* 28 Mar 1968

Whole Act in force 28 Mar 1968 (RA)

## Consular Relations Act 1968 (c 18)

*RA:* 10 Apr 1968

*Commencement provisions:* s 16(3); Consular Relations Act 1968 (Commencement) Order 1970, SI 1970/1684

| | |
|---|---|
| 1–6 | 1 Jan 1971 (SI 1970/1684) |
| 7–11 | 10 Apr 1968 (RA) |
| 12–16 | 1 Jan 1971 (SI 1970/1684) |
| Schs 1, 2 | 1 Jan 1971 (SI 1970/1684) |

## Countryside Act 1968 (c 41)

*RA:* 3 Jul 1968

*Commencement provisions:* s 50(3)

Whole Act in force 3 Aug 1968 (s 50(3))

## Court Martial Appeals Act 1968 (c 20)

*RA:* 8 May 1968

*Commencement provisions:* s 61(2); Criminal Justice Act 1967 (Commencement No 3) Order 1968, SI 1968/325

Whole Act in force 1 Sep 1968 (SI 1968/325)

As from 31 Oct 2009, this Act is renamed the Court Martial Appeals Act 1968 by virtue of the amendments made to s 61(1) by the Armed Forces Act 2006, s 272(2), Sch 8, paras 1, 53

## Courts-Martial (Appeals) Act 1968 (c 20)

See the Court Martial (Appeals) Act 1968

## Criminal Appeal Act 1968 (c 19)

*RA:* 8 May 1968

*Commencement provisions:* s 55(2); Criminal Justice Act 1967 (Commencement No 3) Order 1968, SI 1968/325

Whole Act in force 1 Sep 1968 (SI 1968/325)

## Criminal Appeal (Northern Ireland) Act 1968 (c 21)

*RA:* 8 May 1968

*Commencement provisions:* s 55(2); Criminal Justice Act 1967 (Commencement No 3) Order 1968, SI 1968/325

Whole Act in force 1 Sep 1968 (SI 1968/325)

## Customs Duties (Dumping and Subsidies) Amendment Act 1968 (c 33)

*RA:* 3 Jul 1968

Whole Act in force 3 Jul 1968 (RA)

### Customs (Import Deposits) Act 1968 (c 74)

*RA:* 5 Dec 1968

Whole Act in force 5 Dec 1968 (RA)

---

### Design Copyright Act 1968 (c 68)

*RA:* 25 Oct 1968

Whole Act in force 25 Oct 1968 (RA)

---

### Domestic and Appellate Proceedings (Restriction of Publicity) Act 1968 (c 63)

*RA:* 25 Oct 1968

Whole Act in force 25 Oct 1968 (RA)

---

### Education Act 1968 (c 17)

*RA:* 10 Apr 1968

Whole Act in force 10 Apr 1968 (RA)

---

### Education (No 2) Act 1968 (c 37)

*RA:* 3 Jul 1968

*Commencement provisions*: s 4(1); Education (No 2) Act 1968 (Commencement No 1) Order 1969, SI 1969/709; Education (No 2) Act 1968 (Commencement No 2) Order 1969, SI 1969/1106; Education (No 2) Act 1968 (Commencement No 3) Order 1972, SI 1972/212

Whole Act in force as follows—

1 Jul 1969 (for the purposes of colleges of education) (SI 1969/709)

1 Oct 1969 (for the purposes of special schools) (SI 1969/1106)

1 Sep 1972 (for the purposes of establishments of further education) (SI 1972/212)

---

### Erskine Bridge Tolls Act 1968 (c 4)

*RA:* 15 Feb 1968

Whole Act in force 15 Feb 1968 (RA)

---

### Expiring Laws Continuance Act 1968 (c 76)

*RA:* 18 Dec 1968

Whole Act in force 18 Dec 1968 (RA)

---

### Export Guarantees Act 1968 (c 26)

*RA:* 30 May 1968

Whole Act in force 30 May 1968 (RA)

---

## Family Allowances and National Insurance Act 1968 (c 40)

*RA:* 3 Jul 1968

*Commencement provisions*: s 3(3), Sch 3; Family Allowances and National Insurance Act 1968 (Commencement) Order 1968, SI 1968/1060

| | | |
|---|---|---|
| 1 | (1) | 7 Oct 1968 (so far as it relates to the altered rates of minimum weekly contributions in relation to benefit under the National Insurance Act 1965 or National Insurance (Industrial Injuries) Act 1965 in any case in which the appointed day under this Schedule is 7 Oct 1968) (SI 1968/1060) |
| | | 8 Oct 1968 (so far as it relates to the altered rate of allowances and minimum weekly contributions in relation to allowances under the Family Allowances Act 1965 and the altered rates of minimum weekly contributions in relation to benefit under the National Insurance Act 1965 or National Insurance (Industrial Injuries) Act 1965 in any case in which the appointed day under this Schedule is 8 Oct 1968) (SI 1968/1060) |
| | | 10 Oct 1968 (so far as it relates to the altered rates of minimum weekly contributions in relation to benefit under the National Insurance Act 1965 or National Insurance (Industrial Injuries) Act 1965 in any case in which the appointed day under this Schedule is 10 Oct 1968) (SI 1968/1060) |
| | (2) | 7 Oct 1968 (so far as it relates to the altered rates of benefit for children under the National Insurance Act 1965 in the case of maternity allowance) (SI 1968/1060) |
| | | 8 Oct 1968 (so far as it relates to the altered rates of benefit for children under the National Insurance Act 1965 in the case of widow's benefit, guardian's allowance, retirement pension and child's special allowance) (SI 1968/1060) |
| | | 10 Oct 1968 (so far as it relates to the altered rates of benefit for children under the National Insurance Act 1965, in the case of unemployment and sickness benefit) (SI 1968/1060) |
| | (3) | 8 Oct 1968 (so far as it relates to the altered rates of benefit for children under the National Insurance (Industrial Injuries) Act 1965, in the case of increases of disablement pension in respect of children in the case of a beneficiary entitled to an unemployability supplement or death benefit) (SI 1968/1060) |
| | | 10 Oct 1968 (so far as it relates to the altered rates of benefit for children under the National Insurance (Industrial Injuries) Act 1965, in the case of increases of injury benefit in respect of children and increases of disablement pension in respect of children in the case of a beneficiary receiving, as an in-patient in a hospital or similar institution, medical treatment for the relevant injury or loss of faculty) (SI 1968/1060) |
| | (4) | 7 Oct 1968 (so far as it relates to the construction of the National Insurance Act 1965, s 114(2)(c), and the National Insurance (Industrial Injuries) Act 1965, s 86(2)(c), in relation to any subject matter in relation to which the appointed day under the foregoing provisions of this Schedule is 7 Oct 1968) (SI 1968/1060) |
| | | 8 Oct 1968 (otherwise) (SI 1968/1060) |
| 2, 3 | | 3 Jul 1968 (RA) |
| Schs 1–3 | | 3 Jul 1968 (RA) |

## Finance Act 1968 (c 44)

*RA:* 26 Jul 1968

The commencement details of Finance Acts are not set out, as the dates from which their provisions take effect are usually stated clearly and unambiguously in the text of the Act, and charging provisions will normally state for which year or years of assessment they are to have effect.

## Firearms Act 1968 (c 27)

*RA:* 30 May 1968

*Commencement provisions:* s 60(2)

Whole Act in force 1 Aug 1968 (s 60(2))

---

## Friendly and Industrial and Provident Societies Act 1968 (c 55)

*RA:* 26 Jul 1968

Whole Act in force 26 Jul 1968 (RA)

---

## Gaming Act 1968 (c 65)

*RA:* 25 Oct 1968

*Commencement provisions:* s 54(3), (4); Gaming Act 1968 (Commencement No 1) Order 1968, SI 1968/1784; Gaming Act 1968 (Commencement No 2) Order 1969, SI 1969/488, as amended by SI 1970/427; Gaming Act 1968 (Commencement No 3) Order 1969, SI 1969/549; Gaming Act 1968 (Commencement No 4) Order 1969, SI 1969/1108; Gaming Act 1968 (Commencement No 5) Order 1970, SI 1970/427; Gaming Act 1968 (Commencement No 6) Order 1971, SI 1971/1755

| | | |
|---|---|---|
| 1–9 | | 1 Jul 1970 (SI 1969/1108) |
| 10 | | 25 Oct 1968 (s 54(3)) |
| 11 | (1) | 29 Nov 1968 (SI 1968/1784) |
| | (2) | 1 May 1969 (SI 1969/594) |
| 12–18 | | 1 Jul 1970 (SI 1969/1108) |
| 19 | (1)–(4) | 1 Jun 1971 (SI 1971/755) |
| | (5), (6) | 10 May 1971 (SI 1971/755) |
| | (7) | 1 Jun 1971 (SI 1971/755) |
| 20 | (1)–(6) | 1 Jul 1970 (SI 1969/1108) |
| | (7) | 1 Jun 1971 (SI 1971/755) |
| | (8), (9) | 1 Jul 1970 (SI 1969/1108) |
| 21 | | 1 Jul 1970 (SI 1969/1108) |
| 22 | | 1 Oct 1969 (SI 1969/1108) |
| 23 | (1)–(5) | 1 Jul 1970 (SI 1969/1108) |
| | (6) | 10 May 1971 (SI 1971/755) |
| 24, 25 | | 1 Jul 1970 (SI 1969/1108) |
| 26 | | 1 Apr 1970 (SI 1969/488) |
| 27 | (1)–(5) | 1 Oct 1970 (SI 1969/488) |
| | (6) | 1 May 1969 (SI 1969/488) |
| | (7) | 1 Oct 1970 (SI 1969/488) |
| 28, 29 | | 1 Apr 1970 (SI 1969/488) |
| 30 | | 1 Oct 1969 (SI 1969/408) |
| 31 | | 1 Jul 1970 (SI 1969/1108) |
| 32 | (1) | 1 Oct 1969 (SI 1969/1108) |
| | (2) | 1 Jul 1970 (SI 1969/1108) |
| 33 | | 1 Jul 1970 (SI 1969/1108) |
| 34 | (1)–(5) | 1 Jul 1970 (SI 1969/1108) |
| | (6) | 1 Oct 1969 (SI 1969/1108) |
| | (7)–(9) | 1 Jul 1970 (SI 1969/1108) |
| 35–37 | | 1 Jul 1970 (SI 1969/1108) |
| 38 | (1) | 1 Oct 1970 (SI 1969/488) |
| | (2) | 1 Apr 1970 (SI 1969/488) |
| | (3)–(11) | 1 Jul 1970 (SI 1969/1108) |
| | (12) | 1 Apr 1970 (SI 1969/488) |
| 39 | (1) | 1 Apr 1970 (SI 1969/488) |
| | (2)–(4) | 1 Jul 1970 (SI 1969/1108) |
| 40–42 | | 1 Jul 1970 (SI 1969/1108) |

**Gaming Act 1968 (c 65)**—*contd*

| | | |
|---|---|---|
| 43 | (1) | 25 Oct 1968 (s 54(3)) |
| | (2)–(10) | 1 Jul 1970 (SI 1969/1108) |
| 44–46 | | 1 Jul 1970 (SI 1969/1108) |
| 47 | | 1 Oct 1969 (SI 1969/1108) |
| 48 | | 25 Oct 1968 (s 54(3)) |
| 49 | | 1 May 1969 (SI 1969/549) |
| 50 | | 1 Apr 1970 (SI 1969/488) |
| 51, 52 | | 25 Oct 1968 (s 54(3)) |
| 53 | | 1 Jul 1970 (SI 1969/1108) |
| 54 | | 25 Oct 1968 (s 54(3)) |
| Sch 1 | | 25 Oct 1968 (s 54(3)) |
| Sch 2 | | 1 May 1969 (for the purposes of Schs 3, 4) (SI 1969/549) |
| | para 1 | 1 Oct 1969 (SI 1969/1108) |
| | para 2(1) | 1 Oct 1969 (SI 1969/1108) |
| | para 2(2) | 29 Nov 1968 (SI 1968/1784) |
| | para 3 | 1 Oct 1969 (SI 1969/1108) |
| | para 4 | 29 Nov 1968 (SI 1968/1784) |
| | paras 5–34 | 1 Oct 1969 (SI 1969/1108) |
| | para 35 | 29 Nov 1968 (SI 1968/1784) |
| | paras 36–65 | 1 Oct 1969 (SI 1969/1108) |
| Schs 3, 4 | | 1 May 1969 (SI 1969/549) |
| Sch 5 | | 10 May 1971 (SI 1971/755) |
| Sch 6 | | 1 May 1969 (SI 1969/488) |
| Schs 7–9 | | 1 Oct 1969 (SI 1969/1108) |
| Sch 10 | para 1 | 1 Oct 1969 (SI 1969/1108) |
| | para 2 | 1 May 1969 (SI 1969/549) |
| | paras 3–7 | 1 Oct 1969 (SI 1969/1108) |
| Schs 11, 12 | | 1 Jul 1970 (SI 1969/1105) |

---

**Gas and Electricity Act 1968 (c 39)**

*RA:* 3 Jul 1968

Whole Act in force 3 Jul 1968 (RA)

---

**Health Services and Public Health Act 1968 (c 46)**

*RA:* 26 Jul 1968

*Commencement provisions*: s 79; Health Services and Public Health Act 1968 (Commencement No 1) Order 1968, SI 1968/1362; Health Services and Public Health Act 1968 (Commencement No 1) (Scotland) Order 1968, SI 1968/1387; Health Services and Public Health Act 1968 (Commencement No 2) Order 1968, SI 1968/1662; Health Services and Public Health Act 1968 (Commencement No 3) Order 1969, SI 1969/158; Health Services and Public Health Act 1968 (Commencement No 4) Order 1969, SI 1969/296; Health Services and Public Health Act 1968 (Commencement No 5) Order 1971, SI 1971/423; Health Services and Public Health Act 1968 (Commencement No 6) Order 1973, SI 1973/1187; Health Services and Public Health Act 1968 (Commencement No 7) Order 1974, SI 1974/286

| | |
|---|---|
| 1–4 | 31 Mar 1969 (E) (W) (SI 1969/158) |
| | *Never in force* (S) (repealed) |
| 5, 6 | 9 Sep 1968 (SI 1968/1362) |
| 7 | 1 Apr 1969 (E) (W) (SI 1969/158) |
| | *Never in force* (S) (repealed) |
| 8 | 9 Sep 1968 (SI 1968/1362; SI 1968/1387) |
| 9 | 1 Apr 1969 (E) (W) (SI 1969/158) |
| | *Never in force* (S) (repealed) |
| 10, 11 | 9 Sep 1968 (SI 1968/1362; SI 1968/1387) |
| 12 | 9 Sep 1968 (SI 1968/1362) |

**Health Services and Public Health Act 1968 (c 46)**—*contd*

| | | |
|---|---|---|
| 13 | (1)–(3) | 1 Apr 1971 (E) (W) (SI 1971/423) |
| | | *Never in force* (S) (repealed) |
| | (4) | *Never in force* (repealed) |
| 14 | (1) | 1 Nov 1968 (E) (W) (SI 1968/1662) |
| | | *Never in force* (S) (repealed) |
| | (2) | *Never in force* (repealed) |
| 15, 16 | | 1 Apr 1969 (E) (W) (SI 1969/158) |
| | | *Never in force* (S) (repealed) |
| 17 | | 9 Sep 1968 (SI 1968/1362) |
| 18 | (1), (2) | 1 Apr 1969 (E) (W) (SI 1969/158) |
| | | *Never in force* (S) (repealed) |
| | (3) | 9 Sep 1968 (SI 1968/1362) |
| 19, 20 | | 9 Sep 1968 (SI 1968/1362; SI 1968/1387) |
| 21 | (1) | 1 Nov 1968 (E) (W) (SI 1968/1662) |
| | | 9 Sep 1968 (S) (SI 1968/1387) |
| | (2), (3) | 9 Sep 1968 (SI 1968/1362; SI 1968/1387) |
| 22 | | 9 Sep 1968 (SI 1968/1362) |
| 23 | | 3 Mar 1969 (E) (W) (SI 1969/158) |
| | | *Never in force* (S) (repealed) |
| 24, 25 | | 9 Sep 1968 (SI 1968/1362; SI 1968/1387) |
| 26 | | 1 Sep 1973 (SI 1973/1187) |
| 27–29 | | 1 Apr 1969 (E) (W) (SI 1969/158) |
| | | *Never in force* (S) (repealed) |
| 30–33 | | 9 Sep 1968 (SI 1968/1362; SI 1968/1387) |
| 34 | | 9 Sep 1968 (SI 1968/1362) |
| 35 | | 9 Sep 1968 (SI 1968/1362; SI 1968/1387) |
| 36 | | 9 Sep 1968 (SI 1968/1362) |
| 37 | | 9 Sep 1968 (SI 1968/1362; SI 1968/1387) |
| 38 | | 1 Apr 1974 (SI 1974/286) |
| 39–44 | | 9 Sep 1968 (SI 1968/1362; SI 1968/1387) |
| 45 | | 1 Apr 1971 (E) (W) (SI 1971/423) |
| | | *Never in force* (S) (repealed) |
| 46 | | 9 Sep 1968 (SI 1968/1362) |
| 47–58 | | 1 Oct 1968 (SI 1968/1362) |
| | | *Never in force* (S) (repealed) |
| 59 | | 9 Sep 1968 (SI 1968/1362; SI 1968/1387) |
| 60 | | 1 Nov 1968 (E) (W) (SI 1968/1662) |
| | | *Never in force* (S) (repealed) |
| 61–67 | | 9 Sep 1968 (SI 1968/1362; SI 1968/1387) |
| 68 | | 9 Sep 1968 (SI 1968/1362) |
| 69, 70 | | 1 Oct 1968 (E) (W) (SI 1968/1362) |
| | | *Never in force* (S) (repealed) |
| 71–76 | | 9 Sep 1968 (SI 1968/1387) |
| 77 | | 9 Sep 1968 (SI 1968/1362; SI 1968/1387) |
| 78 | (1) | 9 Sep 1968 (SI 1968/1362; SI 1968/1387) |
| | (2) | See Schs 3, 4 below |
| 79 | | 9 Sep 1968 (SI 1968/1362; SI 1968/1387) |
| Sch 1 | | 1 Apr 1969 (E) (W) (SI 1969/158) |
| | | *Never in force* (S) (repealed) |
| Sch 2 | | 9 Sep 1968 (SI 1968/1362; SI 1968/1387) |
| Sch 3 | | 9 Sep 1968 (except so far as the amendments refer to ss 13 and 45 of this Act) (SI 1968/1362; SI 1968/1387) |
| | | 1 Apr 1971 (so far as the amendments relate specifically to ss 13 and 45 of this Act) (SI 1971/423) |
| Sch 4 | | 9 Sep 1968 (SI 1968/1362; SI 1968/1387), repeals of or in— |
| | | Infectious Disease (Notification) Act 1889; |
| | | Public Health (Scotland) Act 1897; |

**Health Services and Public Health Act 1968 (c 46)**—*contd*

National Health Service Act 1946, ss 11, 22(5), 23, 28, 31, 40(2), 48, 54(5), 63, Sch 1, para 2, Sch 3, Pt IV, Sch 6, para 3(b), Sch 7, para 6(b);

National Health Service (Scotland) Act 1947;

National Assistance Act 1948, ss 26(6), 30(2), 31(1), (3), 33(3);

National Health Service (Amendment) Act 1949, in s 21, the words "or ophthalmic or dispensing optician" and the words "or optician", s 22, in the Schedule, Pt I, the words from "In subsection (5) of section 54" to "(including travelling, and subsistence expenses)", the words from "In paragraph 2 of the First Schedule" to "usual place of residence" and the words from "At the end of the said Part IV" onwards (except so far as those words relate to the constitution of Executive Councils the term of office of chairmen and the duties of medical officers of health), Pt II;

Midwives Act 1951, s 11(2);

Emergency Laws (Miscellaneous Provisions) Act 1953, s 6(4);

Mental Health Act 1959, ss 6, 7, 153(3), Sch 6, para 1, Sch 7;

Mental Health (Scotland) Act 1960;

Public Authorities (Allowances) Act 1961, ss 4–6;

National Assistance Act 1948 (Amendment) Act 1962, s 1(1), sub-s (3) of the section substituted for s 31 of the National Assistance Act 1948, except in relation to councils of county districts;

London Government Act 1963, ss 45(4), 46(3);

Newcastle upon Tyne Corporation Act 1964, s 29;

National Health Service (Family Planning) Act 1967, ss 2, 3(1)

1 Oct 1968 (SI 1968/1362), repeals of or in—

Public Health Act 1936, ss 144 to 146, 172;

National Health Service Act 1946, Sch 10;

National Health Service (Amendment) Act 1949 in the Schedule, Pt I, the words from "At the end of the said Part IV" onwards so far as the relate to the duties of medical officers of health;

Food and Drugs Act 1955, s 26

1 Nov 1968 (repeal of or in Nurseries and Child-Minders Regulation Act 1948, ss 4(4), 7(2), 12) (SI 1968/1662)

31 Mar 1969 (repeal of National Health Service Act 1946, s 5) (SI 1969/296)

1 Apr 1969 (SI 1969/158), repeals of or in—

National Health Service Act 1946, ss 7(5)(c), (d), 11(9)(ii), 41(2), (4), in s 54(3) the words "or by an Ophthalmic Services Committee on behalf of the Council", s 57(1);

National Health Service (Amendment) Act 1949, in the Schedule, the words from "At the end of the said Part IV" onwards

1 Apr 1971 (SI 1971/423), repeals of or in—

National Health Service Act 1946, s 29(1), (2);

National Assistance Act 1948, s 31(1), (2), (4);

National Assistance Act 1948 (Amendment) Act 1962, subsections (1), (2), (4) of the section substituted for s 31 of the National Assistance Act 1948

**Hearing Aid Council Act 1968 (c 50)**

*RA:* 26 Jul 1968

*Commencement provisions:* s 15; Hearing Aid Council Act (Commencement) Order 1969, SI 1969/1598

Whole Act in force 29 Dec 1969 (SI 1969/1598)

## Highlands and Islands Development (Scotland) Act 1968 (c 51)

*RA:* 26 Jul 1968

Whole Act in force 26 Jul 1968 (RA)

## Housing (Financial Provisions) (Scotland) Act 1968 (c 31)

*RA:* 30 May 1968

*Commencement provisions:* s 71(2)

Whole Act in force 30 Aug 1969 (s 71(2))

## Hovercraft Act 1968 (c 59)

*RA:* 26 Jul 1968

*Commencement provisions:* s 7(2); Hovercraft Act 1968 (Commencement) Order 1972, SI 1972/979

| | | |
|---|---|---|
| 1–3 | | 26 Aug 1968 (s 7(2)) |
| 4 | (1), (2) | 26 Aug 1968 (s 7(2)) |
| | (3) | 29 Jun 1972 (SI 1972/979) |
| 5–7 | | 26 Aug 1968 (s 7(2)) |
| Schedule | | 26 Aug 1968 (s 7(2)) |

## Industrial Expansion Act 1968 (c 32)

*RA:* 30 May 1968

Whole Act in force 30 May 1968 (RA)

## International Monetary Fund Act 1968 (c 58)

*RA:* 26 Jul 1968

Whole Act in force 26 Jul 1968 (RA)

## International Organisations Act 1968 (c 48)

*RA:* 26 Jul 1968

Whole Act in force 26 Jul 1968 (RA)

## Justices of the Peace Act 1968 (c 69)

*RA:* 25 Oct 1968

*Commencement provisions:* s 7; Justices of the Peace Act 1968 (Commencement No 1) Order 1968, SI 1968/2035; Justices of the Peace Act 1968 (Commencement No 2) Order 1969, SI 1969/376; Justices of the Peace Act 1968 (Commencement No 3) Order 1969, SI 1969/1373; Justices of the Peace Act 1968 (Commencement No 4) Order 1971, SI 1971/412

| | | |
|---|---|---|
| 1 | (1)–(4) | 1 Feb 1969 (SI 1968/2035) |
| | (5) | 1 Feb 1969 (except words from "but" to the end) (SI 1968/2035) |
| | | *Never in force* (exception noted above) (repealed) |
| | (6), (7) | 1 Feb 1969 (SI 1968/2035) |
| | (8) | 1 Oct 1969 (SI 1969/376) |
| 2–8 | | 25 Oct 1968 (RA) |
| Schs 1, 2 | | 25 Oct 1968 (RA) |

**Justices of the Peace Act 1968 (c 69)**—*contd*

| | | |
|---|---|---|
| Sch 3 | Pt I | 10 Nov 1969 (SI 1969/1373) |
| | Pts II, III | 1 Oct 1969 (SI 1969/376) |
| Schs 4, 5 | | 25 Oct 1968 (RA) |

---

**Law Reform (Miscellaneous Provisions) (Scotland) Act 1968 (c 70)**

*RA:* 25 Oct 1968

*Commencement provisions:* s 22(5)

Whole Act in force 25 Nov 1968 (except ss 10–15, never in force (repealed)) (s 22(5))

---

**Legitimation (Scotland) Act 1968 (c 22)**

*RA:* 8 May 1968

*Commencement provisions:* s 9(3)

Whole Act in force 8 Jun 1968 (s 9(3))

---

**Local Authorities' Mutual Investment Trust Act 1968 (c 25)**

*RA:* 30 May 1968

Whole Act in force 30 May 1968 (RA)

---

**London Cab Act 1968 (c 7)**

*RA:* 15 Feb 1968

*Commencement provisions:* s 4(6); London Cab Act 1968 (Commencement) Order 1968, SI 1968/597

| | |
|---|---|
| 1–3 | 15 Feb 1968 (RA) |
| 4 | 15 Jul 1968 (SI 1968/597) |
| 5 | 15 Feb 1968 (RA) |

---

**Maintenance Orders Act 1968 (c 36)**

*RA:* 3 Jul 1968

*Commencement provisions:* s 3(3)

Whole Act in force 3 Aug 1968 (s 3(3))

---

**Mauritius Independence Act 1968 (c 8)**

*RA:* 29 Feb 1968

This Act generally had effect from 12 Mar 1968 (the "appointed day")

---

**Medicines Act 1968 (c 67)**

*RA:* 25 Oct 1968

*Commencement provisions:* s 136(3); Medicines Act 1968 (Commencement No 1) Order 1972, SI 1972/788; Medicines Act 1968 (Commencement No 2) Order 1972, SI 1972/1225; Medicines Act 1968 (Commencement No 3) Order 1973, SI 1973/1529; Medicines Act 1968 (Commencement No 4) Order 1973, SI 1973/1851[1]; Medicines Act 1968 (Commencement No 5) Order 1976, SI 1976/74;

**Medicines Act 1968 (c 67)**—*contd*

Medicines Act 1968 (Commencement No 6) Order 1977, SI 1977/1068; Medicines Act 1968 (Commencement No 7) Order 1977, SI 1977/2128; Medicines Act 1968 (Commencement No 8) Order 1989, SI 1989/192

| | | |
|---|---|---|
| 1–62 | | 25 Oct 1968 (RA) |
| 63, 64 | | 1 Feb 1978 (SI 1977/2128) |
| 65 | | 1 Jun 1972 (SI 1972/788) |
| 66–76 | | 25 Oct 1968 (RA) |
| 77 | | 1 Jan 1974 (SI 1973/1851) |
| 78–84 | | 25 Oct 1968 (RA) |
| 85 | (1)–(4) | 25 Oct 1968 (RA) |
| | (5) | 1 Sep 1972 (SI 1972/1225) |
| 86 | (1), (2) | 25 Oct 1968 (RA) |
| | (3) | 1 Sep 1972 (SI 1972/1225) |
| 87–89 | | 25 Oct 1968 (RA) |
| 90 | (1) | 25 Oct 1968 (RA) |
| | (2) | 1 Jan 1974 (SI 1973/1529) |
| | (3), (4) | 25 Oct 1968 (RA) |
| 91, 92 | | 25 Oct 1968 (RA) |
| 93 | | 1 Sep 1972 (SI 1972/1225) |
| 94–96 | | 25 Oct 1968 (RA) |
| 97 | | 1 Sep 1972 (SI 1972/1225) |
| 98–134 | | 25 Oct 1968 (RA) |
| 135 | | See Schs below |
| Schs 1–4 | | 25 Oct 1968 (RA) |
| Sch 5 | paras 1–10 | 1 Feb 1978 (SI 1977/2128) |
| | para 11 | 18 Jul 1977 (SI 1977/1068) |
| | para 12 | *Never in force* (repealed) |
| | para 13 | 1 Feb 1978 (SI 1977/2128) |
| | paras 14, 15 | *Never in force* (repealed) |
| | paras 16, 17 | 14 Feb 1989 (SI 1989/192) |

Sch 6 — 1 Jan 1974 (repeals in Pharmacy and Poisons Act 1933, s 12(1), (2) (except the words "it shall be the duty of the registrar to keep, in accordance with the provisions of the byelaws, a register for the purposes of this section (in this Act referred to as "the register of premises")") and (3)) (SI 1973/1851)

20 Feb 1976 (repeals in Therapeutic Substances Act 1956, s 1, in respect of (a) the substances specified in Sch 1, paras 2 and 4, (b) the substances specified in Sch 1, paras 1 and 3 in so far as those substances are substances to which the restrictions imposed by ss 7(3), 31(4) of the Act apply, or in the case of s 7(3) would apply but for any exemption from that subsection conferred under or by any provision of the 1956 Act, (c) all the substances added to Sch 1 by regulations made under s 5(1)(d) of the 1956 Act except the following in so far as they are not substances to which the restrictions imposed by ss 7(3), 31(4) of the Act apply or, in the case of s 7(3) would apply but for any exemption from that subsection conferred under or by any provision of the Act:
  (i) preparations of the pituitary (posterior lobe) or the active principles thereof (whether obtained by fractionation of the gland or by synthesis) or of derivatives of those principles with the same specific biological action, which are intended for use by parenteral injection,
  (ii) corticotrophin and preparations thereof,
  (iii) heparin and preparations thereof intended for use by parenteral injection,
  (iv) hyaluronidase and preparations thereof intended for use by parenteral injection; s 2) (SI 1976/74)
1 Feb 1978 (SI 1977/2128), repeals of or in—
Venereal Disease Act 1917;

**Medicines Act 1968 (c 67)**—*contd*

|  |  |  |
|---|---|---|
|  |  | Pharmacy and Poisons Act 1933; |
|  |  | Cancer Act 1939; |
|  |  | Pharmacy and Medicines Act 1941; |
|  |  | Radioactive Substances Act 1948; |
|  |  | Pharmacy Act 1954; |
|  |  | Food and Drugs Act 1955; |
|  |  | Therapeutic Substances Act 1956, Pt II; |
|  |  | Food and Drugs (Scotland) Act 1956; |
|  |  | Medical Act 1956; |
|  |  | Purchase Tax Act 1963; |
|  |  | Drugs (Prevention of Misuse) Act 1964; |
|  |  | Dangerous Drugs Act 1965 |
|  |  | *Never in force* (repeal of Therapeutic Substances Act 1956, ss 1 (part), 3–7, Pt III) (spent) |
| Sch 7 | paras 1–5 | 1 Feb 1978 (SI 1977/2128) |
|  | para 6 | *Never in force* (repealed) |
|  | paras 7–26 | 1 Feb 1978 (SI 1977/2128) |
|  | para 27 | 1 Jan 1974 (SI 1973/1851) |
|  | paras 28–30 | 1 Feb 1978 (SI 1977/2128) |
| Sch 8 |  | 1 Jan 1974 (SI 1973/1851), repeals of or in— |
|  |  | Pharmacy and Poisons Act (Northern Ireland) 1925, s 17(1)–(3), Sch 3; |
|  |  | Pharmacy and Poisons Act (Northern Ireland) 1955, s 14 |
|  |  | 1 Feb 1978 (SI 1977/2128), repeals of or in— |
|  |  | Pharmacy and Poisons Act (Northern Ireland) 1925, ss 17(4), (5), 18; |
|  |  | Medicines, Pharmacy and Poisons Act (Northern Ireland) 1945, Pt I, ss 14, 15–19, 28, 32, 35–38, Sch 2; |
|  |  | Pharmacy and Poisons Act (Northern Ireland) (Northern Ireland) 1955, s 2; |
|  |  | Food and Drugs Act (Northern Ireland) 1958; |
|  |  | Pharmacy Act (Northern Ireland) 1967; |
|  |  | Increase of Fines Act (Northern Ireland) 1967, Schedule, entry relating to Medicines, Pharmacy and Poisons Act (Northern Ireland) 1945 |
|  |  | *Not yet in force* (otherwise) |

[1]    For transitional provisions, see SI 1973/1851, art 3

---

**Miscellaneous Financial Provisions Act 1968 (c 75)**

*RA:* 18 Dec 1968

Whole Act in force 18 Dec 1968 (RA)

---

**National Loans Act 1968 (c 13)**

*RA:* 13 Mar 1968

*Commencement provisions:* s 24

Whole Act in force 1 Apr 1968 (s 24)

---

**New Towns (Scotland) Act 1968 (c 16)**

*RA:* 28 Mar 1968

*Commencement provisions:* s 49(2)

### New Towns (Scotland) Act 1968 (c 16)—*contd*

Whole Act in force 1 Apr 1968 (s 49(2))

### Overseas Aid Act 1968 (c 57)

*RA:* 26 Jul 1968

Whole Act in force 26 Jul 1968 (RA)

### Pastoral Measure 1968 (No 1)

*RA:* 30 May 1968

*Commencement provisions:* s 96(3)

Whole Measure in force 1 Apr 1969 (see *London Gazette*, 7 Feb 1969)

### Prayer Book (Further Provisions) Measure 1968 (No 2)

*RA:* 18 Dec 1968

Whole Measure in force 18 Dec 1968 (RA)

### Prices and Incomes Act 1968 (c 42)

*RA:* 10 Jul 1968

Whole Act in force 10 Jul 1968 (RA)

### Provisional Collection of Taxes Act 1968 (c 2)

*RA:* 1 Feb 1968

Whole Act in force 1 Feb 1968 (RA)

### Public Expenditure and Receipts Act 1968 (c 14)

*RA:* 20 Mar 1968

*Commencement provisions:* s 1(4); Public Expenditure and Receipts Act 1968 (Commencement) Order 1968, SI 1968/598

Whole Act in force 20 Mar 1968 (RA)

### Race Relations Act 1968 (c 71)

*RA:* 25 Oct 1968

*Commencement provisions:* s 29(3)

Whole Act in force 25 Nov 1968 (s 29(3))

### Rent Act 1968 (c 23)

*RA:* 8 May 1968

*Commencement provisions:* s 118(2)

### Rent Act 1968 (c 23)—*contd*

Whole Act in force 8 Jun 1968 (s 118(2))

---

### Restrictive Trade Practices Act 1968 (c 66)

*RA:* 25 Oct 1968

*Commencement provisions:* s 17(2)

Whole Act in force 25 Nov 1968 (s 17(2))

---

### Revenue Act 1968 (c 11)

*RA:* 13 Mar 1968

*Commencement provisions:* Schedule, para 8; Export Rebates (Appointed Date) Order 1972, SI 1972/202

| | | |
|---|---|---|
| 1–4 | | 13 Mar 1968 (RA) |
| Schedule | paras 1–7 | 13 Mar 1968 (RA) |
| | paras 8, 9 | 16 Mar 1972 (SI 1972/202) |

---

### Sale of Venison (Scotland) Act 1968 (c 38)

*RA:* 3 Jul 1968

Whole Act in force 3 Jul 1968 (RA)

---

### Sea Fisheries Act 1968 (c 77)

*RA:* 18 Dec 1968

*Commencement provisions:* s 23; Sea Fisheries Act 1968 (Commencement No 1) Order 1968, SI 1969/1551

| | | |
|---|---|---|
| 1–4 | | 18 Dec 1968 (RA) |
| 5–14 | | 24 Nov 1969 (SI 1969/1551) |
| 15–23 | | 18 Dec 1968 (RA) |
| Sch 1 | Pt I | 18 Dec 1968 (RA) |
| | Pt II | 24 Nov 1969 (SI 1969/1551) |
| Sch 2 | Pt I | 18 Dec 1968 (RA) |
| | Pt II | 24 Nov 1969 (except as mentioned below) (SI 1969/1551) |
| | | *Never in force* (spent), so far as it relates to the repeals— |
| | | Sea Fisheries Act 1883, ss 1–5, 11, 12, 14–22, in s 25 the words "this Act shall apply to the whole of the British Islands as defined by this Act and to the seas surrounding the same whether within or without the fishery limits of the British Islands", ss 26, 28, 31, Sch 1, Arts XIII–XXIII, XXX, XXXI and XXXIII (repealed); |
| | | Sea Fisheries (Scotland) Amendment Act 1885, s 5; |
| | | Illegal Trawling (Scotland) Act 1934, s 3; |
| | | Sea Fish Industry Act 1951, s 25; |
| | | Sea Fish Industry Act 1962, s 18; |
| | | Fishery Limits Act 1964, s 3(2) (repealed) |

---

### Sewerage (Scotland) Act 1968 (c 47)

*RA:* 26 Jul 1968

*Commencement provisions:* s 61(2); Sewerage (Scotland) Act 1968 (Commencement) Order 1972, SI 1972/363

**Sewerage (Scotland) Act 1968 (c 47)**—*contd*
Whole Act in force 16 May 1973, except ss 18 (in so far as it provides for an appointed day on which all
special drainage districts and drainage districts shall be dissolved), 59(1), which come into force on
16 May 1972 (SI 1972/363)

---

**Social Work (Scotland) Act 1968 (c 49)**

*RA:* 26 Jul 1968

*Commencement provisions:* s 98; Social Work (Scotland) Act 1968 (Commencement No 1) Order 1969,
SI 1969/430; Social Work (Scotland) Act 1968 (Commencement No 2) Order 1969, SI 1969/1274;
Social Work (Scotland) Act 1968 (Commencement No 3) Order 1970, SI 1970/196; Social Work
(Scotland) Act 1968 (Commencement No 4) Order 1970, SI 1970/846; Social Work (Scotland)
Act 1968 (Commencement No 5) Order 1971, SI 1971/184[1]

| | | |
|---|---|---|
| 1 | (1)–(3) | 1 Apr 1969 (SI 1969/430) |
| | (4) | 17 Nov 1969 (SI 1969/1274) |
| | (5) | 15 Apr 1971 (SI 1971/184) |
| | (6) | 1 Apr 1969 (SI 1969/430) |
| 2 | (1) | 1 Apr 1969 (SI 1969/430) |
| | (2) | 17 Nov 1969 (SI 1969/1274) |
| | (3) | 1 Apr 1969 (SI 1969/430) |
| | (4) | 17 Nov 1969 (SI 1969/1274) |
| 3 | (1)–(8) | 1 Jul 1969 (SI 1969/430) |
| | (9) | 17 Nov 1969 (SI 1969/1274) |
| 4 | | 17 Nov 1969 (SI 1969/1274) |
| 5 | | 1 Apr 1969 (SI 1969/430) |
| 6 | | 17 Nov 1969 (SI 1969/1274) |
| 7–10 | | 1 Jul 1969 (SI 1969/430) |
| 11–13 | | 17 Nov 1969 (SI 1969/1274) |
| 14 | (1)–(3) | *Not yet in force* |
| | (4) | 17 Nov 1969 (so far as it provides for Health Services and Public Health Act 1968, ss 44, 45 to cease to have effect) (SI 1969/1274) |
| | | *Not yet in force* (otherwise) |
| 15–18 | | 17 Nov 1969 (SI 1969/1274) |
| 19 | | 1 Apr 1969 (SI 1969/430) |
| 20–26 | | 17 Nov 1969 (SI 1969/1274) |
| 27 | (1) | 17 Nov 1969 (SI 1969/1274) |
| | (2)–(5) | 1 Apr 1969 (SI 1969/430) |
| | (6), (7) | 17 Nov 1969 (SI 1969/1274) |
| 28, 29 | | 17 Nov 1969 (SI 1969/1274) |
| 30–32 | | 15 Apr 1971 (SI 1971/184) |
| 33 | | 17 Nov 1969 (SI 1969/1274) |
| 34 | (1), (2) | 15 Apr 1971 (SI 1971/184) |
| | (3) | 1 Jul 1970 (SI 1970/846) |
| 35 | (1)–(3) | 15 Apr 1971 (SI 1971/184) |
| | (4), (5) | 17 Nov 1969 (SI 1969/1274) |
| 36 | (1)–(7) | 1 Jul 1970 (SI 1970/846) |
| | (8) | 17 Nov 1969 (SI 1969/1274) |
| 37–44 | | 15 Apr 1971 (SI 1971/184) |
| 45 | | 17 Nov 1969 (SI 1969/1274) |
| 46–58 | | 15 Apr 1971 (SI 1971/184) |
| 59 | | 17 Nov 1969 (SI 1969/1274) |
| 60 | | 1 Jul 1969 (SI 1969/430) |
| 61 | | 17 Nov 1969 (SI 1969/1274) |
| 62 | (1) | 17 Nov 1969 (SI 1969/1274) |
| | (2) | 1 Jul 1969 (SI 1969/430) |
| | (3)–(10) | 17 Nov 1969 (SI 1969/1274) |
| 63 | | 1 Jul 1969 (SI 1969/430) |

**Social Work (Scotland) Act 1968 (c 49)**—*contd*

| | | |
|---|---|---|
| 64–68 | | 17 Nov 1969 (SI 1969/1274) |
| 69–83 | | 15 Apr 1971 (SI 1971/184) |
| 84, 85 | | 1 Apr 1969 (SI 1969/430) |
| 86 | | 17 Nov 1969 (SI 1969/1274) |
| 87 | (1)–(4) | 17 Nov 1969 (SI 1969/1274) |
| | (5) | 1 Jul 1969 (SI 1969/430) |
| | (6) | 17 Nov 1969 (SI 1969/1274) |
| 88, 89 | | 17 Nov 1969 (SI 1969/1274) |
| 90 | | 1 Apr 1969 (SI 1969/430) |
| 91 | | 1 Jul 1969 (SI 1969/430) |
| 92 | | 9 Feb 1970 (SI 1970/196) |
| 93 | | 17 Nov 1969 (SI 1969/1274) |
| 94 | | 1 Apr 1969 (SI 1969/430) |
| 95 | (1) | 17 Nov 1969 (SI 1969/1274) |
| | (2) | 1 Apr 1969 (SI 1969/430) |
| | (3) | 17 Nov 1969 (SI 1969/1274) |
| 96 | | 1 Apr 1969 (SI 1969/430) |
| 97 | (1) | 17 Nov 1969 (so far as it extends the application of ss 86, 87, Sch 8, 9, Pt II to England and Wales) (SI 1969/1274) |
| | | 15 Apr 1971 (otherwise) (SI 1971/184) |
| | (2) | 1 Apr 1969 (so far as it extends the application of s 96 to Northern Ireland) (SI 1969/430) |
| | | 15 Apr 1971 (otherwise) (SI 1971/184) |
| | (3) | 15 Apr 1971 (SI 1971/184) |
| | (4) | 17 Nov 1969 (SI 1969/1274) |
| 98 | | 15 Apr 1971 (SI 1971/184) |
| 99 | | 1 Apr 1969 (SI 1969/430) |
| Sch 1 | | 1 Apr 1969 (SI 1969/430) |
| Sch 2 | | 15 Apr 1971 (SI 1971/184) |
| Sch 3 | | 17 Nov 1969 (SI 1969/1274) |
| Sch 4 | | 15 Apr 1971 (SI 1971/184) |
| Sch 5 | | 17 Nov 1969 (SI 1969/1274) |
| Sch 6 | | 1 Apr 1969 (SI 1969/430) |
| Sch 7 | para 1 | 17 Nov 1969 (SI 1969/1274) |
| | para 2 | 15 Apr 1971 (SI 1971/184) |
| | para 3 | 17 Nov 1969 (SI 1969/1274) |
| | para 4 | 1 Mar 1971 (SI 1971/184) |
| | paras 5–7 | 15 Apr 1971 (SI 1971/184) |
| | paras 8, 9 | 17 Nov 1969 (SI 1969/1274) |
| Sch 8 | para 1 | 15 Apr 1971 (SI 1971/184) |
| | paras 2–4 | 17 Nov 1969 (SI 1969/1247) |
| | para 5 | *Never in force* (repealed) |
| | paras 6, 7 | 15 Apr 1971 (SI 1971/184) |
| | para 8 | 17 Nov 1969 (SI 1969/1274) |
| | paras 9, 10 | 15 Apr 1971 (SI 1971/184) |
| | paras 11–20 | 17 Nov 1969 (SI 1969/1247) |
| | para 21 | *Never in force* (repealed) |
| | paras 22–24 | 17 Nov 1969 (SI 1969/1274) |
| | paras 25, 26 | 15 Apr 1971 (SI 1971/184) |
| | para 27 | 17 Nov 1969 (in so far as it substitutes words "an officer of a local authority" for words a "probation officer") (SI 1969/1274) |
| | | 15 Apr 1971 (otherwise) (SI 1971/184) |
| | paras 28, 29 | 15 Apr 1971 (SI 1971/184) |
| | para 30 | 17 Nov 1969 (in so far as it adds definition "local authority") (SI 1969/1274) |
| | | 15 Apr 1971 (otherwise) (SI 1971/184) |
| | para 31 | 17 Nov 1969 (SI 1969/1274) |
| | paras 32–34 | 15 Apr 1971 (SI 1971/184) |
| | para 35 | *Never in force* (repealed) |

**Social Work (Scotland) Act 1968 (c 49)**—*contd*

|  |  |  |
|--|--|--|
| | para 36 | 17 Nov 1969 (SI 1969/1274) |
| | para 37 | 17 Nov 1969 (so far as it inserts para (d) in Adoption Act 1958, s 4(3)) (SI 1969/1274) |
| | | 15 Apr 1971 (otherwise) (SI 1971/184) |
| | para 38 | 17 Nov 1969 (SI 1969/1274) |
| | para 39 | 15 Apr 1971 (SI 1971/184) |
| | paras 40–54 | 17 Nov 1969 (SI 1969/1247) |
| | para 55 | 15 Apr 1971 (SI 1971/184) |
| | para 56 | 17 Nov 1969 (SI 1969/1247) |
| | para 57 | 15 Apr 1971 (SI 1971/184) |
| | para 58 | 17 Nov 1969 (so far as it inserted a definition of "residential establishment") (SI 1969/1247) |
| | | 15 Apr 1971 (otherwise) (SI 1971/184) |
| | para 59 | 17 Nov 1969 (SI 1969/1274) |
| | para 59A | 15 Apr 1971 (SI 1971/184) |
| | para 60 | 17 Nov 1969 (SI 1969/1274) |
| | paras 61, 62 | 15 Apr 1971 (SI 1971/184) |
| | paras 63, 64 | *Never in force* (repealed) |
| | paras 65–67 | 15 Apr 1971 (SI 1971/184) |
| | para 68 | 17 Nov 1969 (so far as it inserts a reference to Social Work (Scotland) Act 1968, s 23) (SI 1969/1274) |
| | | 15 Apr 1971 (otherwise) (SI 1971/184) |
| | para 69(1) | 15 Apr 1971 (SI 1971/184) |
| | para 69(2) | *Never in force* (repealed) |
| | paras 70–72 | 15 Apr 1971 (SI 1971/184) |
| | para 73 | 17 Nov 1969 (SI 1969/1274) |
| | para 74(1) | 15 Apr 1971 (SI 1971/184) |
| | para 74(2) | 17 Nov 1969 (SI 1969/1274) |
| | para 74(3) | 15 Apr 1971 (SI 1971/184) |
| Sch 9 | Pt I | 1 Apr 1969 (SI 1969/430), repeals of or in— |

Criminal Justice (Scotland) Act 1949, s 4(2), (3);
Children Act 1958, ss 1, 2(6), (7)

1 Jul 1969 (SI 1969/430), repeals of or in—
Children Act 1948, s 44;
Prisons (Scotland) Act 1952, s 18(1)–(3A);
Criminal Justice (Scotland) Act 1963, s 15(2)

17 Nov 1969 (SI 1969/1274), repeals of or in—
Children and Young Persons (Scotland) Act 1937, ss 96–98, 106;
National Assistance Act 1948;
Children Act 1948, Whole Act (so far as not already in force, except ss 5, 6(3), (9), Pt III);
Criminal Justice (Scotland) Act 1949, ss 2, 7, 11–13, 75(1)(a), (3)(d), (4)(a), (c) (in so far as it refers to the training of probation officers or of officers or servants serving in approved probation hostels or homes or of persons for appointment as probation officers or as such officers or servants), 75(3)(a)–(c), (4)(b), (5), 78(1) (definitions "Approved probation hostel", "Approved probation home", "Salaried probation officer", "Voluntary probation officer" and "Whole-time probation officer"), Schs 1–3;
Police, Fire and Probation Officers Remuneration Act 1956;
Matrimonial Proceedings (Children) Act 1958;
Mental Health (Scotland) Act 1960, ss 8, 9, 12, 19–21, 111;
Children and Young Persons Act 1963, ss 1, 45–50, 58;
Criminal Justice (Scotland) Act 1963, s 15(1);
Health Services and Public Health Act 1968, ss 44, 45

15 Apr 1971 (SI 1971/184), repeals of or in—
Children and Young Persons (Scotland) Act 1937, ss 21, 42, 47, 49, 51, 53, 59–61, 63, 65, 66, 68–86, 88–95, 101, 107, 109–112, Schs 2, 3;

**Social Work (Scotland) Act 1968 (c 49)**—*contd*

|                | |
|----------------|-----------------------------------------------------|
|                | Children Act 1948, ss 5, 6(3), (4), Pt III; |
|                | Criminal Justice (Scotland) Act 1949, ss 5, 28, 50, 51, 69–73, 75, 78(1) (so far as not already in force above); |
|                | Maintenance Orders Act 1950; |
|                | Prisons (Scotland) Act 1952, s 32; |
|                | Children and Young Persons Act 1956; |
|                | Family Allowances and National Insurance Act 1956; |
|                | Adoption Act 1958; |
|                | Mental Health (Scotland) Act 1960, ss 10, 46, 55–57, 69, 71, 72; |
|                | Education (Scotland) Act 1962, ss 36, 44; |
|                | Criminal Justice (Scotland) Act 1963, s 11, Pt II, Sch 2 |
|                | *Not yet in force* (otherwise) |
| Pt II          | 17 Nov 1969 (repeal of or in Children and Young Persons Act 1963, s 45(1)) (SI 1969/1274) |
|                | 15 Apr 1971 (SI 1971/184), repeals of or in— |
|                | Children Act 1958, s 2(4); |
|                | Mental Health Act 1959, ss 10(1), 50(b); |
|                | Children and Young Persons Act 1963, ss 51, 52; |
|                | Family Allowances Act 1965, s 11(2) |
|                | *Not yet in force* (otherwise) |

1   For transitional provisions, see SI 1971/184, art 3, Sch 3

---

**Swaziland Independence Act 1968 (c 56)**

*RA:* 26 Jul 1968

This Act generally had effect from 6 Sep 1968 (the "appointed day")

---

**Teachers' Superannuation (Scotland) Act 1968 (c 12)**

*RA:* 13 Mar 1968

Whole Act in force 13 Mar 1968 (RA)

---

**Theatres Act 1968 (c 54)**

*RA:* 26 Jul 1968

*Commencement provisions:* s 20(2), (3)

| | | |
|-----|--------|-----------------------------------------------------|
| 1   | (1)    | 26 Sep 1968 (s 20(2)) |
|     | (2)    | 26 Jul 1968 (s 20(2), (3)) |
| 2–11|        | 26 Sep 1968 (s 20(2)) |
| 12  | (1)–(3)| 26 Sep 1968 (s 20(2)) |
|     | (4)    | 26 Jul 1968 (s 20(2), (3)) |
| 13  |        | 26 Sep 1968 (s 20(2)) |
| 14  |        | 26 Jul 1968 (s 20(2), (3)) |
| 15, 16 |     | 26 Sep 1968 (s 20(2)) |
| 17  | (1)    | 26 Sep 1968 (s 20(2)) |
|     | (2)    | 26 Jul 1968 (s 20(2), (3)) |
|     | (3)    | 26 Jul 1968 (so far as it relates to s 14 or Sch 1, para 7) (s 20(2), (3)) |
|     |        | 26 Sep 1968 (otherwise) (s 20(2)) |
| 18  | (1)    | 26 Jul 1968 (s 20(2)) |
|     | (2)    | 26 Sep 1968 (s 20(2)) |
| 19  |        | 26 Sep 1968 (s 20(2)) |
| 20  |        | 26 Jul 1968 (s 20(2)) |

## Theatres Act 1968 (c 54)—*contd*

Sch 1                                26 Jul 1968 (s 20(2), (3))
Schs 2, 3                            26 Sep 1968 (s 20(2))

---

## Theft Act 1968 (c 60)

*RA:* 26 Jul 1968

*Commencement provisions:* s 35(1)

Whole Act in force 1 Jan 1969 (s 35(1))

---

## Town and Country Planning Act 1968 (c 72)

*RA:* 25 Oct 1968

*Commencement provisions:* s 105; Town and Country Planning Act 1968 (Commencement No 1) Order 1968, SI 1968/1908; Town and Country Planning Act 1968 (Commencement No 2) Order 1968, SI 1968/1909; Town and Country Planning Act 1968 (Commencement No 3) Order 1969, SI 1969/16; Town and Country Planning Act 1968 (Commencement No 4) Order 1969, SI 1969/275; Town and Country Planning Act 1968 (Commencement No 5) Order 1971, SI 1971/842; Town and Country Planning Act 1968 (Commencement No 6) (Teesside etc) Order 1971, SI 1971/1108; Town and Country Planning Act 1968 (Commencement No 7) (South Hampshire) Order 1971, SI 1971/2079; Town and Country Planning Act 1968 (Commencement No 8) (Leicester–Leicestershire) Order 1971, SI 1971/2080

| | |
|---|---|
| 1–12 | 1 Jun 1971 (so far as it enables any matter of thing to be prescribed) (SI 1971/842) |
| | 6 Aug 1971 (except so far as it enables any matter or thing to be prescribed, and for the county borough of Teesside and administrative counties of Durham and the North Riding of Yorkshire) (SI 1971/1108) |
| | 31 Dec 1971 (except so far as it enables any matter or thing to be prescribed, and for the county boroughs of Portsmouth and Southampton and certain areas of the administrative county of Hampshire) (SI 1971/2079) |
| | 31 Dec 1971 (for the county borough of Leicester and the administrative county of Leicestershire) (SI 1971/2079) |
| | *Never in force* (otherwise) (repealed) |
| 13 | 1 Apr 1969 (SI 1969/275) |
| 14 | *Never in force* (repealed) |
| 15–20 | 1 Apr 1969 (SI 1969/275) |
| 21–26 | 1 Jan 1969 (SI 1968/1909) |
| 27–38 | 1 Apr 1969 (SI 1969/275) |
| 39 | 6 Dec 1968 (SI 1968/1908) |
| 40–60 | 1 Jan 1969 (SI 1968/1909) |
| 61–63 | 6 Dec 1968 (SI 1968/1908) |
| 64–68 | 1 Apr 1969 (SI 1969/275) |
| 69–75 | 6 Dec 1968 (SI 1968/1908) |
| 76–78 | 1 Apr 1969 (SI 1969/275) |
| 79 | 6 Dec 1968 (SI 1968/1908) |
| 80 | 1 Apr 1969 (SI 1969/275) |
| 81 | 10 Feb 1969 (SI 1969/16) |
| 82 | 6 Dec 1968 (SI 1968/1908) |
| 83–88 | 1 Apr 1969 (SI 1969/275) |
| 89–91 | 1 May 1969 (SI 1969/275) |
| 92, 93 | 1 Apr 1969 (SI 1969/275) |
| 94–96 | 1 May 1969 (SI 1969/275) |
| 97 | 1 Apr 1969 (so far as it applies to orders under s 92 of the Act) (SI 1969/275) |
| | 1 May 1969 (otherwise) (SI 1969/275) |

**Town and Country Planning Act 1968 (c 72)**—*contd*

| | | |
|---|---|---|
| 98–108 | | 6 Dec 1968 (SI 1968/1908) |
| 109 | | 6 Dec 1968 (except so far as it relates to amendments to Industrial Development Act 1966, s 24(9), and Civic Amenities Act 1967, s 8(3)) (SI 1968/1908) |
| | | 1 Apr 1969 (otherwise) (SI 1969/275) |
| Sch 1 | | *Never in force* (repealed) |
| Schs 2–4 | | 1 Apr 1969 (SI 1969/275) |
| Sch 5 | | 1 Jan 1969 (SI 1968/1909) |
| Sch 6 | | 6 Dec 1968 (SI 1968/1908) |
| Sch 7 | | 1 May 1969 (SI 1969/275) |
| Sch 8 | | 6 Dec 1968 (SI 1968/1908) |
| Sch 9 | Pt I | *Never in force* (repealed) |
| | Pt II, paras 1–4 | *Never in force* (repealed) |
| | Pt II, para 5 | 6 Aug 1971 (for the county borough of Teesside and administrative counties of Durham and the North Riding of Yorkshire) (SI 1971/1108)[4] |
| | | 31 Dec 1971 (for the county boroughs of Portsmouth and Southampton and certain areas of the administrative county of Hampshire) (SI 1971/2079)[5] |
| | | 31 Dec 1971 (for the county borough of Leicester and the administrative county of Leicestershire) (SI 1971/2079) |
| | | *Never in force* (otherwise) (repealed) |
| | Pt II, para 6 | 1 Apr 1969 (SI 1969/275) |
| | Pt II, para 7 | *Never in force* (repealed) |
| | Pt II, para 8 | 1 Apr 1969 (SI 1969/275) |
| | Pt II, para 9 | 1 May 1969 (SI 1969/275) |
| | Pt II, para 10 | 1 Jan 1969 (SI 1968/1909) |
| | Pt II, para 11 | 1 Apr 1969 (SI 1969/275) |
| | Pt II, para 12 | 1 Jan 1969 (so far as it relates to functions under Part V of the Act) (SI 1968/1909) |
| | | 1 Apr 1969 (otherwise) (SI 1969/275) |
| | Pt II, paras 13–16 | 1 Apr 1969 (SI 1969/275) |
| | Pt II, para 17 | 1 Jan 1969 (SI 1968/1909) |
| | Pt II, paras 18, 19 | 6 Dec 1968 (SI 1968/1908) |
| | Pt II, paras 20, 21 | 1 Apr 1969 (SI 1969/275) |
| | Pt II, paras 22, 23 | 1 Jan 1969 (so far as it relates to Sch 5, Part IV of the Act) (SI 1968/1909) |
| | | 1 Apr 1969 (so far as it relates to Part II of the Act) (SI 1969/275) |
| | | *Never in force* (otherwise) (repealed) |
| | Pt II, para 24 | 1 Apr 1969 (SI 1969/275) |
| | Pt II, para 25 | 1 Jan 1969 (SI 1968/1909) |
| | Pt II, paras 26–29 | 1 Apr 1969 (SI 1969/275) |
| | Pt II, para 30 | 6 Dec 1968 (SI 1968/1908) |
| | Pt II, paras 31, 32 | 1 Jan 1969 (so far as it relates to Part V of the Act) (SI 1968/1909) |
| | | 1 Apr 1969 (otherwise) (SI 1969/275) |
| | Pt II, para 33 | 1 Apr 1969 (SI 1969/275) |
| | Pt II, para 34 | 6 Dec 1968 (SI 1968/1908) |
| | Pt II, para 35(a) | *Never in force* (repealed) |
| | Pt II, para 35(b) | 1 Apr 1969 (so far as it relates to orders under s 92 of the Act) (SI 1969/275) |
| | | 1 May 1969 (otherwise) (SI 1969/275) |
| | Pt II, para 35(c) | 1 Jan 1969 (SI 1968/1909) |
| | Pt II, para 35(d) | 1 Jan 1969 (so far as it relates to listed building purchase notices and to certain decisions) (SI 1968/1909) |
| | | 1 Apr 1969 (so far as it relates to listed building purchase notices and certain decisions) (SI 1969/275) |
| | | *Never in force* (otherwise) (repealed) |
| | Pt II, para 36 | 1 Jan 1969 (so far as it relates to listed building enforcement notices) (SI 1968/1909)[2] |

**Town and Country Planning Act 1968 (c 72)**—*contd*

|  |  |
|---|---|
|  | 1 Apr 1969 (so far as relates to enforcement notices other than listed building enforcement notices) (SI 1969/275) |
| Pt II, para 37 | 1 Apr 1969 (SI 1969/275)[2] |
| Pt II, para 38 | 1 Apr 1969 (SI 1969/275) |
| Pt II, para 39 | 1 Jan 1969 (so far as it relates to appeals under Sch 5, Part IV to the Act) (SI 1968/1909)[2] |
|  | 1 Apr 1969 (so far as it relates to appeals under Part II of the Act against enforcement notices) (SI 1969/275) |
|  | *Never in force* (otherwise) (repealed) |
| Pt II, para 40 | 1 Apr 1969 (so far as relates to s 92 of the Act) (SI 1969/275) |
|  | 1 May 1969 (otherwise) (SI 1969/275) |
| Pt II, para 41 | 1 Jan 1969 (so far as it relates to Part III or V of the Act) (SI 1968/1909) |
|  | 1 Apr 1969 (so far as it relates to Part II of the Act) (SI 1969/275) |
| Pt II, para 42 | 1 Jan 1969 (so far as it relates to Part V of, or Sch 5 to the Act) (SI 1968/1909) |
|  | 1 Apr 1969 (so far as it relates to Part II of the Act) (SI 1969/275) |
| Pt II, paras 43, 44 | 6 Dec 1968 (SI 1968/1908) |
| Pt II, para 45(a) | 6 Dec 1968 (SI 1968/1908) |
| Pt II, para 45(b) | 1 Jan 1969 (in relation to the references to the Town and Country Planning Act 1962, ss 30, 31 and s 44 of the Act) (SI 1968/1909) |
|  | 1 Apr 1969 (in relation to the references to the Town and Country Planning Act 1962, ss 28, 29, 36, and s 15 of the Act) (SI 1969/275) |
| Pt II, para 45(c) | 1 Jan 1969 (so far as it relates to enforcement notices under s 44 of the Act) (SI 1968/1909) |
|  | 1 Apr 1969 (so far as it relates to enforcement notices under s 15 of the Act) (SI 1969/275) |
| Pt II, para 45(d) | 1 Jan 1969 (SI 1968/1909) |
| Pt II, paras 46, 47 | 6 Dec 1968 (SI 1968/1908) |
| Pt II, para 48(a) | 6 Dec 1968 (SI 1968/1908) |
| Pt II, para 48(b) | 1 Jan 1969 (so far as it relates to s 49 of the Act) (SI 1968/1909) |
|  | 1 Apr 1969 (so far as it relates to ss 20, 92 of the Act) (SI 1969/275) |
| Pt II, para 49(a) | 10 Feb 1969 (SI 1969/16) |
| Pt II, para 49(b) | 1 Jan 1969 (so far as it relates to enforcement notices under s 44 of the Act) (SI 1968/1909) |
|  | 1 Apr 1969 (otherwise) (SI 1969/275) |
| Pt II, para 49(c) | 1 Apr 1969 (SI 1969/275) |
| Pt II, para 50 | 1 Jan 1969 (so far as it relates to listed buildings and buildings proposed to be listed) (SI 1968/1909) |
|  | 1 Apr 1969 (otherwise) (SI 1969/275) |
| Pt II, para 51 | 6 Dec 1968 (SI 1968/1908) |
| Pt II, para 52(a), (b) | 6 Dec 1968 (SI 1968/1908) |
| Pt II, para 52(c) | 1 May 1969 (SI 1969/275) |
| Pt II, para 53(a) | 6 Dec 1968 (SI 1968/1908) |
| Pt II, para 53(b), (c) | 1 Apr 1969 (SI 1969/275) |
| Pt II, para 54 | 6 Aug 1971 (for the county borough of Teesside and administrative counties of Durham and the North Riding of Yorkshire) (SI 1971/1108) |
|  | 31 Dec 1971 (for the county boroughs of Portsmouth and Southampton and certain areas of the administrative county of Hampshire) (SI 1971/2079) |
|  | 31 Dec 1971 (for the county borough of Leicester and the administrative county of Leicestershire) (SI 1971/2079) |
|  | *Never in force* (otherwise) (repealed) |

**Town and Country Planning Act 1968 (c 72)**—*contd*

| | | |
|---|---|---|
| | Pt II, para 55 | 1 Apr 1969 (except so far as it relates to the Town and Country Planning Act 1962, ss 1–12) (SI 1969/275) |
| | | *Never in force* (otherwise) (repealed) |
| | Pt II, para 56 | 1 Apr 1969 (SI 1969/275) |
| | Pt II, para 57 | *Never in force* (repealed) |
| | Pt II, para 58 | 6 Dec 1968 (except so far as it relates to applications under Part V of this Act listed for building consent) (SI 1968/1908)[1] |
| | | 1 Jan 1969 (exception noted above) (SI 1968/1909) |
| | Pt II, para 59 | 6 Dec 1968 (except so far as it relates to Part II of this Act) (SI 1968/1908) |
| | | 1 Apr 1969 (exception noted above) (SI 1969/275) |
| | Pt II, para 60 | 1 Jan 1969 (SI 1968/1909) |
| | Pt II, para 61 | *Never in force* (repealed) |
| | Pt II, paras 62–66 | 1 Apr 1969 (SI 1969/275) |
| | Pt II, para 67 | *Never in force* (repealed) |
| | Pt II, paras 68–71 | 1 Jan 1969 (SI 1968/1909) |
| | Pt II, para 72 | 1 Apr 1969 (SI 1969/275) |
| | Pt II, para 73 | 10 Feb 1969 (SI 1969/16) |
| | Pt II, para 74 | 1 Jan 1969 (SI 1968/1909) |
| | Pt II, para 75 | 1 Apr 1969 (SI 1969/275) |
| Sch 10 | para 1 | 6 Dec 1968 (SI 1968/1908) |
| | paras 2–7 | 1 Apr 1969 (SI 1969/275) |
| | para 8 | 6 Dec 1968 (SI 1968/1908) |
| | para 9 | 6 Dec 1968 (SI 1968/1908)[2] |
| | paras 10–17 | 1 Apr 1969 (SI 1969/275) |
| | paras 18–20 | 1 Jan 1969 (SI 1968/1909) |
| | para 21 | 6 Dec 1968 (SI 1968/1908) |
| Sch 11 | | 6 Dec 1968 (SI 1968/1908), repeals of or in— |
| | | Town and Country Planning Act 1959, s 26(5)(b); |
| | | Town and Country Planning Act 1962, ss 13(6), (10), 34(4), 37(1), 159(2), 160(1), 161(2), 162(2), 163(3)(b), 165(3), 200(2), 203(1) |
| | | 1 Jan 1969 (SI 1968/1909), repeals of or in— |
| | | Housing Act 1957; |
| | | Local Authorities (Historic Buildings) Act 1962; |
| | | Town and Country Planning Act 1962, ss 23(3), 30, 31, 33, 52–55, 62(2), (4), 64(2)(b), 125(1), (2), 199(2)(b); |
| | | Local Government Act 1963, s 28(2), (3); |
| | | Civic Amenities Act 1967, ss 1(6), 2, 6(2), 7, 9, 10 |
| | | 10 Feb 1969 (SI 1969/16), repeals of or in— |
| | | Town and Country Planning Act 1962, s 29(5); |
| | | Civic Amenities Act 1967, s 16(1) |
| | | 1 Apr 1969 (SI 1969/275)[2], otherwise, except repeals of or in— |
| | | Town and Country Planning Act 1962, Part II (except s 9), 210, 221, definition "development plan"; |
| | | Local Government Act, ss 25–27, 29(6) |
| | | 1 Jun 1971 (repeals of or in Town and Country Planning Act 1962, ss 4(3)(b), (c), 4(4), 5(1)–(5), 6(3), (4), 10(5), 11(3)) (SI 1971/842)[3] |
| | | 6 Aug 1971 (repeal of or in the Town and Country Planning Act 1962, s 210, in relation to the county borough of Teesside and administrative counties of Durham and the North Riding of Yorkshire) (SI 1971/1108) |
| | | 31 Dec 1971 (repeal of or in the Town and Country Planning Act 1962, s 210, in relation to the county boroughs of Portsmouth and Southampton and certain areas of the administrative county of Hampshire) (SI 1971/2079) |
| | | 31 Dec 1971 (repeal of or in the Town and Country Planning Act 1962, s 210, in relation to the county borough of Leicester and the administrative county of Leicestershire) (SI 1971/2079) |

## Town and Country Planning Act 1968 (c 72)—*contd*

*Never in force* (otherwise) (repealed)

¹   For transitional provisions, see SI 1968/1908, art 2, Sch 2

²   For transitional provisions, see SI 1968/1909, art 2, Sch 2

³   For transitional provisions, see SI 1971/842, art 2, Sch 2

⁴   For transitional provisions, see SI 1971/1108, art 3

⁵   For transitional provisions, see SI 1971/2079, art 3

## Trade Descriptions Act 1968 (c 29)

*RA:* 30 May 1968

*Commencement provisions:* s 43(2)

Whole Act in force 30 Nov 1968 (s 43(2))

## Transport Act 1968 (c 73)

*RA:* 25 Oct 1968

*Commencement provisions:* s 166(2); Transport Act 1968 (Commencement No 1) Order 1968, SI 1968/1822; Transport Act 1968 (Commencement No 2) Order 1969, SI 1969/507; Transport Act 1968 (Commencement No 3) Order 1969, SI 1969/1613; Transport Act 1968 (Commencement No 4) Order 1970, SI 1970/41; Transport Act 1968 (Commencement No 5) Order 1970, SI 1970/188; Transport Act 1968 (Commencement No 6) Order 1970, SI 1970/259; Transport Act 1968 (Commencement No 7) Order 1970, SI 1970/385; Transport Act 1968 (Commencement No 8) Order 1970, SI 1970/1151; Transport Act 1968 (Commencement No 9) Order 1970, SI 1970/1631; Transport Act 1968 (Commencement No 10) Order 1970, SI 1970/1767; Transport Act 1968 (Commencement No 11) Order 2003, SI 2003/1985

| | | |
|---|---|---|
| 1, 2 | | 18 Nov 1968 (SI 1968/1822) |
| 3 | (1)(a) | 1 Jan 1969 (SI 1968/1822) |
| | (1)(b)–(d) | 18 Nov 1968 (SI 1968/1822) |
| | (1)(e) | 1 Jan 1969 (SI 1968/1822) |
| | (2), (3) | 1 Jan 1969 (SI 1968/1822) |
| 4 | (1) | 1 Jan 1969 (SI 1968/1822) |
| | (2) | 18 Nov 1968 (SI 1968/1822) |
| | (3) | 1 Jan 1969 (SI 1968/1822) |
| | (4), (5) | 18 Nov 1968 (SI 1968/1822) |
| 5 | (1), (2) | 18 Nov 1968 (SI 1968/1822) |
| | (3)(a) | 18 Nov 1968 (SI 1968/1822) |
| | (3)(b) | 1 Jan 1969 (SI 1968/1822) |
| | (4), (5) | 18 Nov 1968 (SI 1968/1822) |
| 6–26 | | 18 Nov 1968 (SI 1968/1822) |
| 27 | (1)(a) | 1 Jan 1969 (SI 1968/1822) |
| | (1)(b)–(d) | 18 Nov 1968 (SI 1968/1822) |
| | (1)(e) | 1 Jan 1969 (SI 1968/1822) |
| | (2), (3) | 1 Jan 1969 (SI 1968/1822) |
| 28 | (1)–(3) | 1 Jan 1969 (SI 1968/1822) |
| | (4)–(6) | 18 Nov 1968 (SI 1968/1822) |
| 29 | (1) | 18 Nov 1968 (SI 1968/1822) |
| | (2)–(4) | 1 Jan 1969 (SI 1968/1822) |
| | (5), (6) | 18 Nov 1968 (SI 1968/1822) |
| 30–33 | | 18 Nov 1968 (SI 1968/1822) |
| 34–36 | | 1 Jan 1969 (SI 1968/1822) |
| 37 | | 18 Nov 1968 (SI 1968/1822) |
| 38 | | 1 Jan 1969 (SI 1968/1822) |
| 39, 40 | | 18 Nov 1968 (SI 1968/1822) |

**Transport Act 1968 (c 73)**—*contd*

| | |
|---|---|
| 41–44 | 1 Jan 1969 (SI 1968/1822) |
| 45–52 | 18 Nov 1968 (SI 1968/1822) |
| 53–55 | 1 Jan 1969 (SI 1968/1822) |
| 56–58 | 18 Nov 1968 (SI 1968/1822) |
| 59 | 20 Nov 1969 (SI 1969/1613) |
| 60 | 20 Nov 1969 (for the purpose of enabling regulations to be made) (SI 1969/1613) |

Different dates for different descriptions of persons as follows:

1 Mar 1970 (Any person (other than the Post Office) who—

(1) proposes to use a goods vehicle (other than a farmer's goods vehicle) on a road for the carriage of goods for hire or reward or for or in connection with any trade or business carried on by him, not being a use for which an operator's licence is not required by virtue of s 60(2) of the Act, and does not hold a carrier's licence or holds a carrier's licence of Class A or B in relation to any vehicle, and

(2) Any person who holds a carrier's licence of any Class which has been granted or has effect as if granted to him under Regulation 13 (simplified procedure for the grant, etc of carriers' licences in respect of Northern Ireland or foreign goods vehicles temporarily in Great Britain) of the Goods Vehicles (Carriers' Licences) (Temporary Use in Great Britain) Regulations 1969) (SI 1969/1613)

1 Jun 1970 (Any person (except the Post Office) who holds a carrier's licence of Class C, the number whereof ends with figures between 000 and 333 inclusive, in relation to any vehicles) (SI 1969/1613)

1 Sep 1970 (Any person (except the Post Office) who holds a carrier's licence of Class C, the number whereof ends with figures between 334 and 666 inclusive, in relation to any vehicles) (SI 1969/1613)

30 Nov 1970 (in relation to the use of vehicles by the Post Office) (SI 1970/1631)

1 Dec 1970 (Any person (except the Post Office) who holds a carrier's licence of Class C, the number whereof ends with figures between 667 and 999 inclusive, in relation to any vehicles) (SI 1969/1613)

1 Mar 1971 (in relation to the use of farmers' goods vehicles) (SI 1970/1631)

| | |
|---|---|
| 61 | 20 Nov 1969 (SI 1969/1613) |
| 62 | Different dates for different descriptions of persons as follows: |

1 Dec 1969 (Any person (other than the Post Office) who—

(1) proposes to use a goods vehicle (other than a farmer's goods vehicle) on a road for carriage of goods for hire or reward or for or in connection with any trade or business carried on by him, not being a use for which an operator's licence is not required by virtue of s 60(2) of the Act, and does not hold a carrier's licence or holds a carrier's licence of Class A or B in relation to any vehicle, and

(2) Any person who holds a carrier's licence of any Class which has been granted or has effect as if granted to him under Regulation 13 (simplified procedure for the grant, etc. of carrier's licences in respect of Northern Ireland or foreign goods vehicles temporarily in Great Britain) of the Goods Vehicles (Carrier's Licences) (Temporary Use in Great Britain) Regulations 1969) (SI 1969/1613)

1 Mar 1970 (Any person (except the Post Office) who holds a carrier's licence of Class C, the number whereof ends with figures between 000 and 333 inclusive in relation to any vehicles) (SI 1969/1613)

**Transport Act 1968 (c 73)**—*contd*

|  |  |  |
|---|---|---|
|  |  | 1 Jun 1970 (Any person (except the Post Office) who holds a carrier's licence of Class C, the number whereof ends with figures between 334 and 666 inclusive, in relation to any vehicles) (SI 1969/1613) |
|  |  | 1 Sep 1970 (Any person (except the Post Office) who holds a carrier's licence of Class C, the number whereof ends with figures between 667 and 999 inclusive, in relation to any vehicles) (SI 1969/1613) |
|  |  | 30 Nov 1970 (in relation to the use of vehicles by the Post Office) (SI 1970/1631) |
|  |  | 1 Mar 1971 (in relation to the use of farmers' goods vehicles) (SI 1970/1631) |
| 63 |  | 20 Nov 1969 (for the purpose of enabling regulations to be made) (SI 1969/1613) |
|  |  | 1 Dec 1969; 1 Mar 1970; 1 Jun 1970; 1 Sep 1970. See the note to s 62 |
|  |  | 30 Nov 1970 (in relation to the use of vehicles by the Post Office) (SI 1970/1631) |
|  |  | 1 Mar 1971 (in relation to the use of farmers' goods vehicles) (SI 1970/1631) |
| 64 | (1)–(4) | 1 Dec 1969; 1 Mar 1970; 1 Jun 1970; 1 Sep 1970. See the note to s 62 |
|  |  | 30 Nov 1970 (in relation to the use of vehicles by the Post Office) (SI 1970/1631) |
|  |  | 1 Mar 1971 (in relation to the use of farmers' goods vehicles) (SI 1970/1631) |
|  | (5) | 1 Mar 1970 (SI 1970/259) |
| 65 |  | *Never in force* (repealed) |
| 66 |  | 1 Dec 1969; 1 Mar 1970; 1 Jun 1970; 1 Sep 1970. See the note to s 62 |
|  |  | 30 Nov 1970 (in relation to the use of vehicles by the Post Office) (SI 1970/1631) |
|  |  | 1 Mar 1971 (in relation to the use of farmers' goods vehicles) (SI 1970/1631) |
| 67 |  | 20 Nov 1969 (for the purpose only of enabling regulations to be made) (SI 1969/1613) |
|  |  | 1 Dec 1969; 1 Mar 1970; 1 Jun 1970; 1 Sep 1970. See the note to s 62 |
|  |  | 30 Nov 1970 (in relation to the use of vehicles by the Post Office) (SI 1970/1631) |
|  |  | 1 Mar 1971 (in relation to the use of farmers' goods vehicles) (SI 1970/1631) |
| 68 |  | 1 Dec 1969; 1 Mar 1970; 1 Jun 1970; 1 Sep 1970. See the note to s 62 |
|  |  | 30 Nov 1970 (in relation to the use of vehicles by the Post Office) (SI 1970/1631) |
|  |  | 1 Mar 1971 (in relation to the use of farmers' goods vehicles) (SI 1970/1631) |
| 69 |  | 20 Nov 1969 (SI 1969/1613) |
|  |  | 1 Dec 1969; 1 Mar 1970; 1 Jun 1970; 1 Sep 1970. See the note to s 62 |
| 70 |  | 1 Dec 1969; 1 Mar 1970; 1 Jun 1970; 1 Sep 1970. See the note to s 62 |
|  |  | 30 Nov 1970 (in relation to the use of vehicles by the Post Office) (SI 1970/1631) |
|  |  | 1 Mar 1971 (in relation to the use of farmers' goods vehicles) (SI 1970/1631) |
| 71 | (1)–(5) | *Never in force* (repealed) |
|  | (6) | 20 Nov 1969 (for the purpose only of enabling regulations relating to operators licensing to be made) (SI 1969/1613) |

**Transport Act 1968 (c 73)**—*contd*

|  |  |  |
|---|---|---|
|  |  | 1 Mar 1970; 1 Jun 1970; 1 Sep 1970; 1 Dec 1970 (so far as it relates to operators' licensing. See the note to s 60 |
|  | (7) | *Never in force* (repealed) |
|  | (8) | 1 Mar 1970 (except the definition of "pallet") (SI 1970/259) |
|  |  | *Never in force (otherwise)* (repealed) |
|  | (9), (10) | *Never in force* (repealed) |
| 72–81 |  | *Never in force* (repealed) |
| 82 | (1)–(3) | *Never in force* (repealed) |
|  | (4), (5) | 1 Dec 1969; 1 Mar 1970; 1 Jun 1970; 1 Sep 1970. See the note to s 62 |
|  |  | 30 Nov 1970 (in relation to the use of vehicles by the Post Office) (SI 1970/1631) |
|  |  | 1 Mar 1971 (in relation to the use of farmers' goods vehicles) |
|  | (6) | 1 Mar 1970 (except in so far as it relates to any special authorisation under Pt V of this Act, any record or other document required to be made under ss 76, 81, or any means of identification required to be carried on, or by the driver of, a vehicle in pursuance of the provisions of Pt V of this Act relating to special authorisations) (SI 1970/259) |
|  |  | *Never in force (above-mentioned exceptions)* (repealed) |
|  | (7)–(9) | 1 Mar 1970 (SI 1970/259) |
| 83 |  | *Never in force* (repealed) |
| 84 |  | 1 Mar 1970; 1 Jun 1970; 1 Sep 1970; 1 Dec 1970 (so far as it relates to operators' licensing. See the note to s 60 |
|  |  | 30 Nov 1970 (in relation to the use of vehicles by the Post Office) (SI 1970/1631) |
|  |  | 1 Mar 1971 (in relation to the use of farmers' goods vehicles) (SI 1970/1631) |
| 85 |  | 20 Nov 1969 (SI 1969/1613) |
| 86, 87 |  | 20 Nov 1969 (for the purpose only of enabling regulations to be made) (SI 1969/1613) |
|  |  | 1 Mar 1970; 1 Jun 1970; 1 Sep 1970; 1 Dec 1970 (so far as it relates to operators' licensing. See the note to s 60 |
|  |  | 30 Nov 1969 (in relation to the use of vehicles by the Post Office) (SI 1970/1631) |
|  |  | 1 Mar 1971 (in relation to the use of farmers' goods vehicles) (SI 1970/1631) |
| 88 |  | 20 Nov 1969 (so far as it relates to operators' licensing) (SI 1969/1613) |
|  |  | *Never in force (otherwise)* (repealed) |
| 89 |  | 20 Nov 1969 (for the purpose only of enabling regulations to be made) (SI 1969/1613) |
|  |  | 1 Mar 1970; 1 Jun 1970; 1 Sep 1970; 1 Dec 1970 (so far as it relates to operators' licensing. See the note to s 60 |
|  |  | 30 Nov 1970 (in relation to the use of vehicles by the Post Office) (SI 1970/1631) |
|  |  | 1 Mar 1971 (in relation to the use of farmers' goods vehicles) (SI 1970/1631) |
| 90–92 |  | 20 Nov 1969 (so far as it relates to operators' licensing) (SI 1969/1613) |
|  |  | *Never in force (otherwise)* (repealed) |
| 93 |  | 25 Oct 1968 (RA) |
| 94 | (1), (2) | 1 Dec 1969; 1 Mar 1970; 1 Jun 1970; 1 Sep 1970. See the note to s 62 |
|  |  | 30 Nov 1970 (in relation to the use of vehicles by the Post Office) (SI 1970/1631) |
|  |  | 1 Mar 1971 (in relation to the use of farmers' goods vehicles) (SI 1970/1631) |
|  | (3)–(6) | *Never in force* (repealed) |

**Transport Act 1968 (c 73)**—*contd*

| | | |
|---|---|---|
| | (7) | 1 Dec 1969; 1 Mar 1970; 1 Jun 1970; 1 Sep 1970. See the note to s 62 |
| | (8)–(10) | 1 Dec 1970 (SI 1970/1631) |
| 95 | | 20 Nov 1969 (SI 1969/1613) |
| 96 | (1)–(9) | 1 Mar 1970 (except so far as they relate to passenger vehicles) (SI 1970/259) |
| | | 15 Mar 1970 (in relation to passenger vehicles) (SI 1970/385) |
| | (10) | 22 Jan 1970 (SI 1970/41) |
| | (11) | 1 Mar 1970 (except so far as they relate to passenger vehicles) (SI 1970/259) |
| | | 15 Mar 1970 (in relation to passenger vehicles) (SI 1970/385) |
| | (12) | 22 Jan 1970 (SI 1970/41) |
| 97 | | *Never in force* (substituted) |
| 98 | | 20 Nov 1969 (SI 1969/1613) |
| 99 | (1)–(9) | 1 Mar 1970 (except in so far as they relate to the entry and inspection of any vehicle or to any equipment installed on any vehicle for the purposes of s 97) (SI 1970/259) |
| | | 1 Sep 2003 (otherwise) (SI 2003/1985) |
| | (10) | 1 Sep 2003 (SI 2003/1985) |
| 100 | | 1 Mar 1970 (SI 1970/259) |
| 101, 102 | | 20 Nov 1969 (SI 1969/1613) |
| 103 | (1)–(7) | 20 Nov 1969 (SI 1969/1013) |
| | (8) | 1 Mar 1970 (SI 1970/259) |
| | (9) | 20 Nov 1969 (SI 1969/1013) |
| 104–111 | | 18 Nov 1968 (SI 1968/1822) |
| 112 | (1)–(6) | 18 Nov 1968 (SI 1968/1822) |
| | (7) | 1 Jan 1969 (SI 1968/1822) |
| 113–115 | | 18 Nov 1968 (SI 1968/1822) |
| 116, 117 | | 1 Jan 1969 (except so far as they apply to any highway carried by a bridge over an inland waterway of the British Waterways Board or any other installation on land used by that Board in connection with an inland waterway) (SI 1968/1822) |
| | | 1 Jan 1971 (for other purposes) (SI 1970/1151) |
| 118 | | 1 Jan 1969 (SI 1968/1822) |
| 119–125 | | 18 Nov 1968 (SI 1968/1822) |
| 126–129 | | 21 Apr 1969 (SI 1969/507) |
| 130 | (1)–(4) | 21 Apr 1969 (SI 1969/507) |
| | (5)(a), (b) | 21 Apr 1969 (SI 1969/507) |
| | (5)(c) | 18 Nov 1968 (for the purpose only of enabling procedure regulations to be made under Road Traffic Regulation Act 1967, s 84C) (SI 1968/1822) |
| | | 21 Apr 1969 (otherwise) (SI 1969/507) |
| | (5)(d), (e) | 21 Apr 1969 (SI 1969/507) |
| | (6) | 21 Apr 1969 (SI 1969/507) |
| 131 | (1) | 1 Sep 1970 (SI 1970/188) |
| | (2)–(6) | 1 Mar 1970 (SI 1970/188) |
| 132–149 | | 18 Nov 1968 (SI 1968/1822) |
| 150 | | 1 Jan 1969 (SI 1968/1822) |
| 151–164 | | 18 Nov 1968 (SI 1968/1822) |
| 165 | | See Sch 18 below |
| 166 | | 18 Nov 1968 (SI 1968/1822) |
| Sch 1 | | 18 Nov 1968 (SI 1968/1822) |
| Sch 2 | | 1 Jan 1969 (SI 1968/1822) |
| Schs 3–8 | | 18 Nov 1968 (SI 1968/1822) |
| Sch 9 | | *Never in force* (repealed) |
| Sch 10 | Pt I | 1 Dec 1969; 1 Mar 1970; 1 Jun 1970; 1 Sep 1970. See the note to s 62 |
| | | 30 Nov 1970 (in relation to the use of vehicles by the Post Office) (SI 1970/1631) |

**Transport Act 1968 (c 73)**—*contd*

|  |  |  |
|---|---|---|
|  |  | 1 Mar 1971 (in relation to the use of farmers' goods vehicles) (SI 1970/1631) |
|  | Pt II | 1 Dec 1970 (SI 1970/1767) |
| Sch 11 |  | 1 Mar 1970 (SI 1970/259) |
| Schs 12, 13 |  | 18 Nov 1968 (SI 1968/1822) |
| Sch 14 | Pts I–IV | 21 Apr 1969 (SI 1969/507) |
|  | Pt V | 18 Nov 1968 (for the purpose only of enabling procedure regulations to be made under the inserted Road Traffic Regulation Act 1967, s 84C) (SI 1968/1822) |
|  |  | 21 Apr 1969 (otherwise) (SI 1969/507) |
|  | Pt VI | 21 Apr 1969 (SI 1969/507) |
| Schs 15–17 |  | 18 Nov 1968 (SI 1968/1822) |
| Sch 18 | Pt I | 18 Nov 1968 (repeals of or in Transport Act 1962, ss 6, 10(2), (4), 11(4), 13(2), (4), (5)–(8), 22(2), (3), (6), 25(3), 55, 61(1), (3), 64, 72(4), 85(1)–(3), 87) (SI 1968/1822) |
|  |  | 1 Jan 1969 (otherwise) (SI 1968/1822) |
|  | Pt II | 21 Apr 1969 (except repeal in Road Traffic Regulation Act 1967, s 80(1)(a)) (SI 1969/507) |
|  |  | 1 Sep 1970 (exception noted above) (SI 1970/188) |
|  | Pt III | 18 Nov 1968 (SI 1968/1822), repeals of or in— |

Road Traffic Act 1930, s 102;

Transport Act 1947, s 37;

Harbours, Piers and Ferries (Scotland) Act 1953;

Public Service Vehicles (Travel Concessions) Act 1955, s 1(4), (6);

House of Commons Disqualification Act 1957, Sch 1, Pt II entry "The Nationalised Transport Advisory Council", Sch 1, Pt III, Sch 3;

Local Government Act 1958, s 38(6);

Road Traffic Act 1960, ss 154(1), 188(1);

Harbours Act 1964, s 30(4);

Redundancy Payments Act 1965, s 48(5), (6);

Transport Finances Act 1966, ss 1(2), (3), 3(3);

Bus Fuel Grants Act 1966;

Capital Allowances Act 1968, s 83(4);

Finance Act 1968, s 2(1)(b)

1 Jan 1969 (SI 1968/1822), repeals of or in—

Railway and Canal Traffic Act 1888, s 45;

House of Commons Disqualification Act, Sch 1, Pt II entry "A Regional Railways Board"

21 Apr 1969 (repeal of or in Greater London Council (General Powers) Act 1967, s 26) (SI 1969/507)

1 Mar 1970 (SI 1970/259), repeals of or in—

Road Traffic Act 1960, ss 73, 186, 234;

Road Traffic Act 1962, ss 20, 21

15 Mar 1970 (SI 1970/385), repeals of or in—

Road Traffic Act 1960, ss 73, 250(3);

Road Traffic Act 1962, Sch 4

*Never in force* (repeals of or in Road Traffic Act 1960, ss 227(1), (2), 237(1), (2) (repealed)

|  |  |  |
|---|---|---|
|  | Pt IV | 1 Dec 1970 (SI 1970/1767) |

**Transport Holding Company Act 1968 (c 10)**

*RA:* 6 Mar 1968

Whole Act in force 6 Mar 1968 (RA)

**Trustee Savings Banks Act 1968 (c 6)**

*RA:* 15 Feb 1968

Whole Act in force 15 Feb 1968 (RA)

---

**Water Resources Act 1968 (c 35)**

*RA:* 3 Jul 1968

Whole Act in force 3 Jul 1968 (RA)

---

**Wills Act 1968 (c 28)**

*RA:* 30 May 1968

Whole Act in force 30 May 1968 (RA)

---

# 1969 Acts

## Administration of Justice Act 1969 (c 58)

*RA*: 22 Oct 1969

*Commencement provisions:* s 36(5); Administration of Justice Act 1969 (Commencement No 1) Order 1969, SI 1969/1607; Administration of Justice Act 1969 (Commencement No 2) Order 1970, SI 1970/672[1]

| | | |
|---|---|---|
| 1–5 | | 26 May 1970 (SI 1970/672) |
| 6–8 | | 1 Dec 1969 (SI 1969/1607) |
| 9 | (1) | 26 May 1970 (SI 1970/672) |
| | (2) | 1 Dec 1969 (SI 1969/1607) |
| 10 | | 26 May 1970 (SI 1970/672) |
| 11 | | 1 Dec 1969 (SI 1969/1607) |
| 12–16 | | 1 Jan 1970 (SI 1969/1607) |
| 17–19 | | 1 Dec 1969 (SI 1969/1607) |
| 20–22 | | 1 Jan 1970 (SI 1969/1607) |
| 23–26 | | 1 Dec 1969 (SI 1969/1607) |
| 27, 28 | | 1 Jan 1970 (SI 1969/1607) |
| 29 | | 1 Dec 1969 (SI 1969/1607) |
| 30 | | 1 Jan 1970 (SI 1969/1607) |
| 31–36 | | 1 Dec 1969 (SI 1969/1607) |
| Sch 1 | | 1 Dec 1969 (except so far as it relates to Settled Land Act 1925; Solicitors Act 1957; County Courts Act 1959; Northern Ireland Act 1962) (SI 1969/1607) |
| | | 1 Jan 1970 (so far as it relates to Northern Ireland Act 1962) (SI 1969/1607) |
| | | 26 May 1970 (otherwise) (SI 1970/672) |
| Sch 2 | | 1 Dec 1969 (SI 1969/1607), repeals of or in— |
| | | Supreme Court of Judicature (Consolidation) Act 1925, ss 106, 117, 126, 128; |
| | | Administration of Justice (Pensions) Act 1950; |
| | | Public Records Act 1958; |
| | | County Courts Act 1959, ss 36, 46, 74, 89; |
| | | Mental Health Act 1959; |
| | | Superannuation (Miscellaneous Provisions) Act 1967 |
| | | 1 Jan 1970 (SI 1969/1607), repeals of or in— |
| | | Probates and Letters of Administration (Ireland) Act 1857; |
| | | Supreme Court of Judicature (Consolidation) Act 1925, s 153; |
| | | Northern Ireland Act 1962 |
| | | 26 May 1970 (SI 1970/672), repeals of or in— |
| | | County Courts Act 1959, s 47; |
| | | County Courts Jurisdiction Order 1965 |

[1]  For transitional provisions, see SI 1970/672, art 3, Schedule

## Age of Majority (Scotland) Act 1969 (c 39)

*RA*: 25 Jul 1969

*Commencement provisions:* s 2(3); Age of Majority (Scotland) Act 1969 (Commencement) Order 1969, SI 1969/1243

**Age of Majority (Scotland) Act 1969 (c 39)**—*contd*
Whole Act in force 1 Jan 1970 (SI 1969/1243)

**Agriculture (Spring Traps) (Scotland) Act 1969 (c 26)**

*RA:* 25 Jun 1969

Whole Act in force 25 Jun 1969 (RA)

**Air Corporations Act 1969 (c 43)**

*RA:* 25 Jul 1969

Whole Act in force 25 Jul 1969 (RA)

**Appropriation Act 1969 (c 31)**

*RA:* 25 Jul 1969

Whole Act in force 25 Jul 1969 (RA)

**Architects Registration (Amendment) Act 1969 (c 42)**

*RA:* 25 Jul 1969

Whole Act in force 25 Jul 1969 (RA)

**Army Reserve Act 1969 (c 23)**

*RA:* 16 May 1969

Whole Act in force 16 May 1969 (RA)

**Auctions (Bidding Agreements) Act 1969 (c 56)**

*RA:* 22 Oct 1969

*Commencement provisions:* s 5(2)

Whole Act in force 22 Nov 1969 (s 5(2))

**Betting, Gaming and Lotteries (Amendment) Act 1969 (c 17)**

*RA:* 16 May 1969

Whole Act in force 16 May 1969 (RA)

**Children and Young Persons Act 1969 (c 54)**

*RA:* 22 Oct 1969

*Commencement provisions:* ss 69(4), 73(2), (3); Children and Young Persons Act 1969 (Commencement No 1) Order 1969, SI 1969/1552; Children and Young Persons Act 1969 (Commencement No 2) Order 1969, SI 1969/1565; Children and Young Persons Act 1969 (Commencement No 3) Order 1970, SI 1970/1498[2], as amended by SI 1970/1883; Children and Young Persons Act 1969 (Commencement No 4) Order 1971, SI 1971/588

1–3                1 Jan 1971 (SI 1970/1498)

**Children and Young Persons Act 1969 (c 54)**—*contd*

| | | |
|---|---|---|
| 4 | | *Never in force* (repealed) |
| 5 | (1)–(7) | *Never in force* (repealed) |
| | (8) | 1 Jan 1971 (SI 1970/1498) |
| | (9) | 1 Jan 1971 (so far as it relates to the definition of "the appropriate local authority") (SI 1970/1498) |
| | | *Never in force* (otherwise) (repealed) |
| 6 | | 1 Jan 1971 (SI 1970/1498) |
| 7 | (1) | *Never in force* (repealed) |
| | (2) | 1 Jan 1971 (SI 1970/1498) |
| | (3) | *Never in force* (repealed) |
| | (4)–(9) | 1 Jan 1971 (SI 1970/1498) |
| 8 | | *Never in force* (repealed) |
| 9–23 | | 1 Jan 1971 (SI 1970/1498) |
| 24 | (1)–(4) | 1 Jan 1971 (SI 1970/1498) |
| | (5), (6) | 1 Apr 1971 (SI 1970/1498) |
| | (7), (8) | 1 Jan 1971 (SI 1970/1498) |
| 25–28 | | 1 Jan 1971 (SI 1970/1498) |
| 29 | (1)–(3) | 1 Jan 1971 (SI 1970/1498) |
| | (4) | *Never in force* (substituted) |
| | (5), (6) | 1 Jan 1971 (SI 1970/1498) |
| 30–32 | | 1 Jan 1971 (SI 1970/1498) |
| 33 | (1) | 1 Dec 1969 (so far as it relates to Sch 1, para 6) (SI 1969/1565) |
| | | 1 Jan 1971 (otherwise) (SI 1970/1498) |
| | (2) | 1 Jan 1971 (SI 1970/1498) |
| 34 | | 1 Jan 1971 (SI 1970/1498) |
| 35–45 | | 1 Dec 1969 (SI 1969/1565) |
| 46 | (1) | 1 Dec 1969 (SI 1969/1565) |
| | (2) | See Sch 3 below |
| 47–50 | | 1 Dec 1969 (SI 1969/1565) |
| 51–55 | | 1 Jan 1970 (SI 1969/1565) |
| 56 | (1)(a) | 1 Jan 1971 (SI 1970/1498) |
| | (1)(b)–(d) | 1 Jan 1970 (SI 1969/1565) |
| | (2) | 1 Jan 1970 (SI 1969/1565) |
| 57 | | 1 Jan 1970 (SI 1969/1565) |
| 58–60 | | 1 Dec 1969 (SI 1969/1565) |
| 61 | | 1 Jan 1971 (SI 1970/1498) |
| 62 | (1) | 1 Jan 1971 (SI 1970/1498) |
| | (2) | 1 Dec 1969 (SI 1969/1565) |
| | (3)–(8) | 1 Jan 1971 (SI 1970/1498) |
| 63–68 | | 1 Dec 1969 (SI 1969/1565) |
| 69, 70 | | 16 Nov 1969 (SI 1969/1552) |
| 71 | | 1 Dec 1969 (SI 1969/1565) |
| 72 | | See Schs 4–7 below |
| 73 | | 16 Nov 1969 (SI 1969/1552) |
| Sch 1 | paras 1–5 | 1 Jan 1971 (SI 1970/1498) |
| | para 6 | 1 Dec 1969 (SI 1969/1565) |
| | paras 7, 8 | 1 Jan 1971 (SI 1970/1498) |
| Sch 2 | | 1 Dec 1969 (SI 1969/1565) |
| Sch 3 | paras 1, 2 | 1 Dec 1969 (SI 1969/1565) |
| | paras 3, 4 | 1 Jan 1971 (SI 1970/1498) |
| | paras 5–7 | 1 Dec 1969 (SI 1969/1565) |
| | para 8 | 1 Jan 1971 (SI 1970/1498) |
| | paras 9–11 | 1 Dec 1969 (SI 1969/1565) |
| Sch 4 | paras 1, 1A | 1 Jan 1971 (SI 1970/1498) |
| | paras 2, 3 | *Never in force* (repealed) |
| | para 4 | 1 Jan 1971 (SI 1970/1498) |
| | para 5(1) | *Not yet in force* |
| | para 5(2) | 1 Jan 1971 (SI 1970/1498) |
| | paras 6–12 | 1 Jan 1971 (SI 1970/1498) |

**Children and Young Persons Act 1969 (c 54)**—*contd*

|  |  |  |
|---|---|---|
|  | paras 13, 14 | 1 Dec 1969 (SI 1969/1565) |
|  | paras 15–24 | 1 Jan 1971 (SI 1970/1498) |
| Sch 5 | paras 1–3 | 1 Jan 1971 (SI 1970/1498) |
|  | para 4 | 1 Dec 1969 (SI 1969/1565) |
|  | paras 5–10 | 1 Jan 1971 (SI 1970/1498) |
|  | para 11 | *Never in force* (repealed) |
|  | paras 12, 13 | 1 Jan 1971 (SI 1970/1498) |
|  | paras 14, 15 | 1 Dec 1969 (SI 1969/1565) |
|  | paras 16, 17 | 1 Jan 1971 (SI 1970/1498) |
|  | paras 18, 19 | 1 Dec 1969 (SI 1969/1565) |
|  | para 20(1) | 1 Dec 1969 (so far as it substitutes words in Children Act 1948, s 51(1)) (SI 1969/1565)[1] |
|  |  | 1 Jan 1971 (otherwise) (SI 1970/1498) |
|  | para 20(2) | 1 Dec 1969 (SI 1969/1565) |
|  | para 21(1) | 1 Dec 1969 (SI 1969/1565) |
|  | para 21(2) | 1 Jan 1971 (SI 1970/1498) |
|  | para 21(3) | 1 Dec 1969 (SI 1969/1565) |
|  | para 22 | 1 Jan 1971 (SI 1970/1498) |
|  | para 23 | *Never in force* (repealed) |
|  | paras 24–29 | 1 Jan 1971 (SI 1970/1498) |
|  | paras 30, 31 | 1 Jan 1970 (SI 1969/1565) |
|  | paras 32–34 | 1 Jan 1971 (SI 1970/1498) |
|  | para 35 | 1 Jan 1970 (SI 1969/1565) |
|  | para 36 | 1 Jan 1971 (SI 1970/1498) |
|  | para 37 | 1 Dec 1969 (SI 1969/1565)[1] |
|  | paras 38–50 | 1 Jan 1971 (SI 1970/1498) |
|  | paras 51, 52 | 1 Dec 1969 (SI 1969/1565) |
|  | para 53 | 1 Jan 1971 (SI 1970/1498) |
|  | para 54(1) | 1 Jan 1971 (SI 1970/1498) |
|  | para 54(2) | 1 Dec 1969 (so far as the words from "5(1)" to "1956" are substituted) (E) (W) (SI 1969/1565) |
|  |  | 1 Jan 1971 (otherwise, except so far as the substitution relates to Scotland) (SI 1970/1498) |
|  |  | 15 Apr 1971 (so far as the words from "5(1)" to "1956" are substituted) (S) (SI 1971/588) |
|  | para 54(3) | 1 Dec 1969 (E) (W) (SI 1969/1565) |
|  |  | 15 Apr 1971 (S) (SI 1971/588) |
|  | para 55 | *Not yet in force* |
|  | paras 56–62 | 1 Jan 1971 (SI 1970/1498) |
|  | para 63 | 16 Nov 1969 (SI 1969/1552) |
|  | para 64(1) | 16 Nov 1969 (SI 1969/1552) |
|  | para 64(2) | 1 Jan 1971 (SI 1970/1498) |
|  | para 65(1) | 1 Jan 1971 (SI 1970/1498) |
|  | para 65(2) | 1 Dec 1969 (SI 1969/1565) |
|  | para 66 | 1 Dec 1969 (SI 1969/1565) |
|  | paras 67, 68 | 1 Jan 1971 (SI 1970/1498) |
|  | para 69 | 16 Nov 1969 (SI 1969/1552) |
|  | paras 70–72 | 1 Jan 1971 (SI 1970/1498) |
|  | para 73 | 16 Nov 1969 (SI 1969/1552) |
|  | para 74 | 1 Jan 1971 (SI 1970/1498) |
|  | paras 75, 76 | 16 Nov 1969 (SI 1969/1552) |
|  | paras 77–83 | 1 Jan 1971 (SI 1970/1498) |
| Sch 6 |  | 16 Nov 1969 (repeal of or in Social Work (Scotland) Act 1968, s 90(1)) (SI 1969/1552) |
|  |  | 1 Dec 1969 (SI 1969/1565), repeals of or in— |
|  |  | Merchant Shipping Act 1894; |
|  |  | War Pensions (Administrative Provisions) Act 1918; |
|  |  | War Pensions Act 1920; |
|  |  | Children and Young Persons Act 1933, ss 76(2), 77(1), 94; |

**Children and Young Persons Act 1969 (c 54)**—*contd*

Children Act 1948, ss 3(3)–(5), 4(3) (the proviso), 7, 15, 16, 39(1)(e), 51(2), 54(1), (2);

Family Allowances and National Insurance Act 1956;

Children Act 1958, Sch 2, entry relating to Children Act 1948, s 54;

Children and Young Persons Act 1963, s 1(4);

Social Work (Scotland) Act 1968

1 Jan 1970 (SI 1969/1565), repeals of or in—

Children Act 1958, ss 2(1), (6), (7), 3(4)–(6);

Adoption Act 1958, s 37(1), (2)

1 Jan 1971 (SI 1970/1498), repeals of or in—

Children and Young Persons Act 1933, ss 10(2), 26(6), 29(3), 32, 34(2), 35, 44, 48(2), 54, 55, 57, 62–75, 76(1), 1A, 1B, 77(3), (4), 78, 79(4), 81(2), 82–85, 86, 89–91, 102, 107(1) (so far as it relates to definitions "approved school order" and "special reception centre"), 107(2), 108, Sch 4, paras 4, 5, 7–9, 11–13;

Children and Young Persons (Scotland) Act 1937, ss 82, 86, 87, 89;

Children and Young Persons Act 1938;

Education Act 1944;

Education (Miscellaneous Provisions) Act 1948;

Children Act 1948, ss 5, 6(3), (4), 23, 25, 26, 59(1), Sch 3;

Criminal Justice Act 1948, ss 3(5), 11(1), 46(1), 47(1), 48(4), 49(5), 71, 72, 75, 80(1) (definitions "supervision order" and "sentence"), Sch 9, entries relating to Criminal Justice Act 1933, ss 48(2), 54, 70, 78, 82, 90 and Children and Young Persons Act 1938;

Justices of the Peace Act 1949;

Maintenance Orders Act 1950;

Children and Young Persons (Amendment) Act 1952;

Prison Act 1952;

Magistrates' Courts Act 1952, ss 20, 21, 26(2), 38(1);

Education (Miscellaneous Provisions) Act 1953;

Children and Young Persons Act 1956;

Affiliation Proceedings Act 1957;

Adoption Act 1958, ss 15(3), 37;

Children Act 1958, ss 2(4), 17;

Local Government Act 1958;

Mental Health Act 1959;

Criminal Justice Act 1961, ss 5(2), (3), 6, 7(3), 8(2), 9, 14–17, 22(4), 25, 29(1), (3), Sch 2, Sch 4;

Children and Young Persons Act 1963, ss 2, 4–15, 22–24, 25(1), 29, 33, 53(1), (2), 55, 59–61, 65(5), Schs 1, 3;

Criminal Justice (Scotland) Act 1963;

Local Government Act 1963, Sch 17, para 18(c);

Family Allowances Act 1965;

Criminal Justice Act 1967;

Social Work (Scotland) Act 1968

*Not yet in force,* repeals in—

Children and Young Persons Act 1933, ss 58, 77(2), (2A), 79(1)–(3), (5), 80, 81(1), (3), 103, 104, 106(3)–(5), 107(1) (so far as it relates to the definitions of "approved school" and "managers") and Sch 4, paras 1–3, 14;

Superannuation (Miscellaneous Provisions) Act 1948, s 14;

Children Act 1948, ss 49(1), 59(2);

Criminal Justice Act 1948, ss 49(1)–(4), (6), 77, 80(1) (so far as it relates to the definitions of "approved school" and "remand house"), Sch 9 (so far as it relates to Children and Young Persons Act 1933, ss 58, 77);

**Children and Young Persons Act 1969 (c 54)**—*contd*

|  |  |
|---|---|
|  | Magistrates' Courts Act 1952, s 32; |
|  | Criminal Justice Act 1961, ss 1, 4, 7(2), 8(1), 10(2), 18, 19; |
|  | Children and Young Persons Act 1963, Sch 3, para 15; |
|  | London Government Act 1963, s 47; |
|  | *Never in force,* repeals in— |
|  | Children and Young Persons Act 1933, ss 55 (except repeals in sub-ss (2) and (4) thereof), 56(1), 59(1) |
| Sch 7 | 1 Jan 1970 (except amendments of Children Act 1958, s 2(4), 6(1)(b)) (SI 1969/1565) |
|  | 1 Jan 1971 (exception noted above) (SI 1970/1498) |

[1] For transitional provisions, see SI 1969/1565, art 4, Sch 3
[2] For transitional provisions, see SI 1970/1498, art 4, Sch 3

---

**Clergy Pensions (Amendment) Measure 1969 (No 1)**

*RA:* 25 Jul 1969

Whole Measure in force 25 Jul 1969 (RA)

---

**Consolidated Fund Act 1969 (c 3)**

*RA:* 12 Feb 1969

Whole Act in force 12 Feb 1969 (RA)

---

**Consolidated Fund (No 2) Act 1969 (c 9)**

*RA:* 27 Mar 1969

Whole Act in force 27 Mar 1969 (RA)

---

**Customs Duties (Dumping and Subsidies) Act 1969 (c 16)**

*RA:* 24 Apr 1969

*Commencement provisions:* s 19(3)

Whole Act in force 1 May 1969 (s 19(3))

---

**Customs (Import Deposits) Act 1969 (c 64)**

*RA:* 11 Dec 1969

Whole Act in force 11 Dec 1969 (RA)

---

**Decimal Currency Act 1969 (c 19)**

*RA:* 16 May 1969

*Commencement provisions:* s 19(2)

|  |  |  |
|---|---|---|
| 1 |  | *Never in force* (repealed) |
| 2–14 |  | 16 May 1969 (RA) |
| 15 | (1)–(3) | *Never in force* (repealed) |
|  | (4), (5) | 16 May 1969 (RA) |
|  | (6) | *Never in force* (repealed) |

**Decimal Currency Act 1969 (c 19)**—*contd*

|          | (7)      | 16 May 1969 (RA) |
| 16–19    |          | 16 May 1969 (RA) |
| Schs 1–4 |          | 16 May 1969 (RA) |

---

**Development of Tourism Act 1969 (c 51)**

*RA:* 25 Jul 1969

*Commencement provisions:* s 21(2)

Whole Act in force 25 Aug 1969 (s 21(2))

---

**Divorce Reform Act 1969 (c 55)**

*RA:* 22 Oct 1969

*Commencement provisions:* s 11(3)

Whole Act in force 1 Jan 1971 (s 11(3))

---

**Education (Scotland) Act 1969 (c 49)**

*RA:* 25 Jul 1969

*Commencement provisions:* ss 16(4), 29(2); Education (Scotland) Act 1969 (Commencement) Order 1970, SI 1970/540

Whole Act in force 25 Aug 1971 (except s 16 (which comes into force on 1 Aug 1970 (SI 1970/540)) (s 29(2)))

---

**Electricity (Scotland) Act 1969 (c 1)**

*RA:* 30 Jan 1969

Whole Act in force 30 Jan 1969 (RA)

---

**Employers' Liability (Compulsory Insurance) Act 1969 (c 57)**

*RA:* 22 Oct 1969

*Commencement provisions:* s 7(3); Employers' Liability (Compulsory Insurance) Act 1969 (Commencement) Order 1971, SI 1971/1116

Whole Act in force 1 Jan 1972 (SI 1971/1116)

---

**Employer's Liability (Defective Equipment) Act 1969 (c 37)**

*RA:* 25 Jul 1969

*Commencement provisions:* s 2(2)

Whole Act in force 25 Oct 1969 (s 2(2))

---

**Expiring Laws Act 1969 (c 61)**

*RA:* 11 Dec 1969

Whole Act in force 11 Dec 1969 (RA)

---

**Family Law Reform Act 1969 (c 46)**

*RA:* 25 Jul 1969

*Commencement provisions:* s 28(3); Family Law Reform Act 1969 (Commencement No 1) Order 1969, SI 1969/1140; Family Law Reform Act 1969 (Commencement No 2) Order 1971, SI 1971/1857

| | |
|---|---|
| 1–19 | 1 Jan 1970 (SI 1969/1140) |
| 20–25 | 1 Mar 1972 (SI 1971/1857) |
| 26–28 | 1 Jan 1970 (SI 1969/1140) |
| Schs 1–3 | 1 Jan 1970 (SI 1969/1140) |

**Finance Act 1969 (c 32)**

*RA:* 25 Jul 1969

The commencement details of Finance Acts are not set out, as the dates from which their provisions take effect are usually stated clearly and unambiguously in the text of the Act, and charging provisions will normally state for which year or years of assessment they are to have effect.

**Foreign Compensation Act 1969 (c 20)**

*RA:* 16 May 1969

Whole Act in force 16 May 1969 (RA)

**Genocide Act 1969 (c 12)**

*RA:* 27 Mar 1969

Whole Act in force 27 Mar 1969 (RA)

**Horserace Betting Levy Act 1969 (c 14)**

*RA:* 27 Mar 1969

Whole Act in force 27 Mar 1969 (RA)

**Housing Act 1969 (c 33)**

*RA:* 25 Jul 1969

*Commencement provisions:* s 91(4)

Whole Act in force 25 Aug 1969 (except ss 80–82, which came into force on 25 Jul 1969 (RA)) (s 91(4))

**Housing (Scotland) Act 1969 (c 34)**

*RA:* 25 Jul 1969

*Commencement provisions:* s 70(3)

Whole Act in force 25 Aug 1969 (s 70(3))

**Immigration Appeals Act 1969 (c 21)**

*RA:* 16 May 1969

*Commencement provisions:* s 24(5); Immigration Appeals Act 1969 (Commencement No 1) Order 1970, SI 1970/118; Immigration Appeals Act 1969 (Commencement No 2) Order 1970, SI 1970/791

## Immigration Appeals Act 1969 (c 21)—*contd*

| | | |
|---|---|---|
| 1 | | 1 Jul 1970 (SI 1970/791) |
| 2 | (1), (2) | 1 Jul 1970 (in so far as they relate to an appeal to an adjudicator under sub-s (1)(c) against a refusal of an application for the grant of an entry certificate) (SI 1970/791) |
| | | *Never in force* (otherwise) (repealed) |
| | (3) | *Never in force* (repealed) |
| 3 | (1) | 1 Jul 1970 (in so far as they relate to an appeal to an adjudicator under sub-s (1)(b) against the variation of a condition of admission or under sub-s (1)(c) against a refusal to revoke or vary such a condition) (SI 1970/791) |
| | | *Never in force* (otherwise) (repealed) |
| | (2) | *Never in force* (repealed) |
| | (3), (4) | 1 Jul 1970 (in so far as they relate to an appeal to an adjudicator under sub-s (1)(b) against the variation of a condition of admission or under sub-s (1)(c) against a refusal to revoke or vary such a condition) (SI 1970/791) |
| | | *Never in force* (otherwise) (repealed) |
| 4–6 | | 1 Jul 1970 (SI 1970/791) |
| 7 | | *Never in force* (repealed) |
| 8–12 | | 1 Jul 1970 (SI 1970/791) |
| 13 | | *Never in force* (repealed) |
| 14 | | 1 Feb 1970 (SI 1970/118) |
| 15–19 | | 1 Jul 1970 (SI 1970/791) |
| 20, 21 | | 16 May 1969 (RA) |
| 22–24 | | 1 Jul 1970 (SI 1970/791) |
| Sch 1 | | 1 Jul 1970 (SI 1970/791) |
| Sch 2 | | *Never in force* (repealed) |
| Sch 3 | | 1 Jul 1970 (SI 1970/791) |

## Iron and Steel Act 1969 (c 45)

*RA:* 25 Jul 1969

Whole Act in force 25 Jul 1969 (RA)

## Late Night Refreshment Houses Act 1969 (c 53)

*RA:* 22 Oct 1969

*Commencement provisions:* s 15(2)

Whole Act in force 1 Jan 1970 (s 15(2))

## Law of Property Act 1969 (c 59)

*RA:* 22 Oct 1969

*Commencement provisions:* s 31(2)

Whole Act in force 1 Jan 1970 (s 31(2)), except s 28(6), which came into force on 22 Oct 1969 (RA)

## Licensing (Scotland) Act 1969 (c 13)

*RA:* 27 Mar 1969

Whole Act in force 27 Mar 1969 (RA)

## Local Government Grants (Social Need) Act 1969 (c 2)

*RA:* 30 Jan 1969

Whole Act in force 30 Jan 1969 (RA) (note that grants under s 1 of the Act are authorised for the year 1968–69 or any later year)

## Medical Act 1969 (c 40)

*RA:* 25 Jul 1969

*Commencement provisions:* s 24(2); Medical Act 1969 (Commencement) Order 1969, SI 1969/1492

| | | |
|---|---|---|
| 1 | | 26 Jan 1970 (SI 1969/1492) |
| 2 | | 26 Jan 1970 (except so far as it replaces Medical Act 1956, s 45) (SI 1969/1492) |
| | | 1 May 1970 (exception noted above) (SI 1969/1492) |
| 3, 4 | | 26 Jan 1970 (SI 1969/1492) |
| 5, 6 | | 1 May 1970 (SI 1969/1492) |
| 7, 8 | | 26 Jan 1970 (SI 1969/1492) |
| 9 | | 26 Jan 1970 (except for the words "in the principal list" in sub-s (1)) (SI 1969/1492) |
| | | 1 Jan 1971 (otherwise) (SI 1969/1492) |
| 10 | | 1 Jan 1970 (SI 1969/1492) |
| 11 | | 27 Oct 1969 (SI 1969/1492) |
| 12 | (1)–(5) | 27 Oct 1969 (SI 1969/1492) |
| | (6) | 26 Jan 1970 (SI 1969/1492) |
| 13–16 | | 1 Apr 1970 (SI 1969/1492) |
| 17 | | 1 May 1970 (SI 1969/1492) |
| 18, 19 | | 26 Jan 1970 (SI 1969/1492) |
| 20 | | 27 Oct 1969 (SI 1969/1492) |
| 21 | | 27 Oct 1969 (except for definitions of "the register" and "registered") (SI 1969/1492) |
| | | 26 Jan 1970 (otherwise) (SI 1969/1492) |
| 22 | | 27 Oct 1969 (SI 1969/1492) |
| 23 | (1) | See Sch 2 below |
| | (2) | See Sch 3 below |
| 24 | | 27 Oct 1969 (SI 1969/1492) |
| Sch 1 | | 27 Oct 1969 (SI 1969/1492) |
| Sch 2 | | 27 Oct 1969 (repeals of or in Medical Act 1956, ss 9(5), 10(7), 11(4)(a), 12(1), 13(1), 18, 24(1)(b), 28(3), 38(4), 54(1), Sch 1, paras 7(1), 9, 11, Sch 3) (SI 1969/1492) |
| | | 1 Jan 1970 (repeals of or in Medical Act 1956, s 6(4), Sch 1, paras 12, 13) (SI 1969/1492) |
| | | 26 Jan 1970 (repeals of or in Medical Act 1956, ss 41–44, 46, 48(2) (in so far as it applies to s 44 of that Act), 49(1) (proviso, words "subsection (2) of section 46"), 51, 54(1), 57(7), (8)) (SI 1969/1492) |
| | | 1 May 1970 (repeals of or in Medical Act 1956, ss 4(8), 45, 48(2) (to the extent that it applies to s 45 of that Act), 49(1) (proviso, words "or forty-five"), Sch 2) (SI 1969/1492) |
| Sch 3 | paras 1–3 | 27 Oct 1969 (SI 1969/1492) |
| | paras 4–7 | 26 Jan 1970 (SI 1969/1492) |
| | paras 8–11 | 27 Oct 1969 (SI 1969/1492) |

## Mines and Quarries (Tips) Act 1969 (c 10)

*RA:* 27 Mar 1969

*Commencement provisions:* s 38(3); Mines and Quarries (Tips) Act 1969 (Commencement No 1) Order 1969, SI 1969/804; Mines and Quarries (Tips) Act 1969 (Commencement No 2) Order 1969, SI 1969/805

**Mines and Quarries (Tips) Act 1969 (c 10)**—*contd*

| | |
|---|---|
| 1–10 | 30 Jun 1969 (SI 1969/804) |
| 11–36 | 30 Jun 1969 (E) (W) (SI 1969/805) |
| 37, 38 | 27 Mar 1969 (RA) |
| Sch 1 | 30 Jun 1969 (SI 1969/804) |
| Schs 2–4 | 30 Jun 1969 (E) (W) (SI 1969/805) |

**National Insurance Act 1969 (c 44)**

*RA:* 25 Jul 1969

*Commencement provisions:* s 11(2), Sch 6; National Insurance Act 1969 (Commencement) Order 1969, SI 1969/1018[1]; National Insurance Act 1969 (Commencement No 2) Order 1970, SI 1970/1550

| | | |
|---|---|---|
| 1 | | 3 Nov 1969 (SI 1969/1018) |
| 2 | (1) | 3 Nov 1969 (higher rates and amounts of benefit under National Insurance Act 1965, in the case of maternity allowance, widow's benefit, guardian's allowance, retirement pension and child's special allowance) (SI 1969/1018) |
| | | 6 Nov 1969 (higher rates and amounts of benefit under National Insurance Act 1965, in the case of unemployment and sickness benefit) (SI 1969/1018) |
| | (2) | 3 Nov 1969 (SI 1969/1018) |
| 3 | | 3 Nov 1969 (SI 1969/1018) |
| 4 | | 1 Aug 1969 (SI 1969/1018) |
| 5 | | 3 Nov 1969 (SI 1969/1018) |
| 6 | (1) | See Sch 5 below |
| | (2) | 3 Nov 1969 (SI 1969/1018) |
| 7, 8 | | 28 Oct 1970 (SI 1970/1550) |
| 9, 10 | | 1 Aug 1969 (SI 1969/1018) |
| 11 | | See Schs 6, 7 below |
| Sch 1 | | 3 Nov 1969 (SI 1969/1018) |
| Sch 2 | | 3 Nov 1969 (higher rates and amounts of benefit under National Insurance Act 1965, in the case of maternity allowance, widow's benefit, guardian's allowance, retirement pension and child's special allowance) (SI 1969/1018) |
| | | 6 Nov 1969 (higher rates and amounts of benefit under National Insurance Act 1965, in the case of unemployment and sickness benefit) (SI 1969/1018) |
| Schs 3, 4 | | 3 Nov 1969 (SI 1969/1018) |
| Sch 5 | | 3 Nov 1969 (higher rates and amounts of benefit under the National Insurance (Industrial Injuries) Act 1965, in the case of widow's pension under s 19 and widower's pension under s 20 and allowance in respect of children of deceased's family under s 21 of the 1965 Act) (SI 1969/1018) |
| | | 5 Nov 1969 (higher rates and amounts of benefit under the National Insurance (Industrial Injuries) Act 1965, in the case of disablement benefit (including increase of disablement pension other than those coming into force on 6 Nov 1969 below, maximum under s 29(1)(a), of aggregate of weekly benefits payable for successive accidents and maximum disablement gratuity under s 12(3) of the 1965 Act)) (SI 1969/1018) |
| | | 6 Nov 1969 (higher rates and amounts of benefit under the National Insurance (Industrial Injuries) Act 1965, in the case of injury benefit (including increases thereof) and increases of disablement pension in respect of children and adult dependants in the case of a beneficiary receiving, as an in-patient in a hospital or similar institution, medical treatment for the relevant injury of loss of faculty) (SI 1969/1018) |
| Sch 6 | | 1 Aug 1969 (SI 1969/1018) |
| Sch 7 | | 3 Nov 1969 (except repeal of National Insurance (Industrial Injuries) Act 1965, Sch 4, para 1(b)) (SI 1969/1018) |

**National Insurance Act 1969 (c 44)**—*contd*

28 Oct 1970 (exception noted above) (SI 1970/1550)

[1]    For transitional provisions and savings, see SI 1969/1018, art 2

---

**National Insurance &c Act 1969 (c 4)**

*RA:* 6 Mar 1969

Whole Act in force 6 Mar 1969 (RA)

---

**National Mod (Scotland) Act 1969 (c 41)**

*RA:* 25 Jul 1969

Whole Act in force 25 Jul 1969 (RA)

---

**National Theatre Act 1969 (c 11)**

*RA:* 27 Mar 1969

Whole Act in force 27 Mar 1969 (RA)

---

**New Towns Act 1969 (c 5)**

*RA:* 6 Mar 1969

Whole Act in force 6 Mar 1969 (RA)

---

**Nuclear Installations Act 1969 (c 18)**

*RA:* 16 May 1969

Whole Act in force 16 May 1969 (RA)

---

**Nurses Act 1969 (c 47)**

*RA:* 25 Jul 1969

*Commencement provisions:* s 11(1)

Whole Act in force 25 Aug 1969 (except ss 2–4 (Never in force, repealed)) (s 11(1))

---

**Overseas Resources Development Act 1969 (c 36)**

*RA:* 25 Jul 1969

Whole Act in force 25 Jul 1969 (RA)

---

**Pensions (Increase) Act 1969 (c 7)**

*RA:* 6 Mar 1969

Whole Act in force 6 Mar 1969 (RA)

## Police Act 1969 (c 63)

*RA:* 11 Dec 1969

*Commencement provisions:* s 7(2); Police Act 1969 (Commencement No 1) Order 1969, SI 1969/1775; Police Act 1969 (Commencement No 2) Order 1970, SI 1970/1028; Police Act 1969 (Commencement No 3) Order 1971, SI 1971/408

| | |
|---|---|
| 1 | 13 Mar 1971 (SI 1971/408) |
| 2 | 17 Dec 1969 (SI 1969/1775) |
| 3 | *Never in force* (repealed) |
| 4 | 29 Jul 1970 (SI 1970/1028) |
| 5 | *Never in force* (repealed) |
| 6, 7 | 17 Dec 1969 (SI 1969/1775) |

## Ponies Act 1969 (c 28)

*RA:* 25 Jun 1969

*Commencement provisions:* s 4(2)

Whole Act in force 1 Jan 1970 (s 4(2))

## Post Office Act 1969 (c 48)

*RA:* 25 Jul 1969

Whole Act in force 25 Jul 1969 (RA); but note that by Post Office Act 1969 (Appointed Day) Order 1969, SI 1969/1066, made under s 1(1), the day appointed for the abolition of the office of master of the Post Office was 1 Oct 1969

## Public Health (Recurring Nuisances) Act 1969 (c 25)

*RA:* 25 Jun 1969

*Commencement provisions:* s 4(7)

Whole Act in force 25 Jul 1969 (s 4(7))

## Redundancy Rebates Act 1969 (c 8)

*RA:* 6 Mar 1969

Whole Act in force 6 Mar 1969 (RA)

## Redundant Churches and Other Religious Buildings Act 1969 (c 22)

*RA:* 16 May 1969

Whole Act in force 16 May 1969 (RA)

## Rent (Control of Increases) Act 1969 (c 62)

*RA:* 11 Dec 1969

*Commencement provisions:* s 7(2)

Whole Act in force 1 Jan 1970 (s 7(2))

## Representation of the People Act 1969 (c 15)

*RA:* 17 Apr 1969

*Commencement provisions:* s 27; Representation of the People Act 1969 (Commencement) Order 1969, SI 1969/630[1]; Representation of the People Act 1969 (Commencement No 2) Order 1971, SI 1971/544; Representation of the People Act 1969 (Commencement No 3) Order 1976, SI 1976/2064

| | | |
|---|---|---|
| 1–3 | | 1 Feb 1977 (SI 1976/2064) |
| 4–6 | | 16 Feb 1970 (SI 1969/630) |
| 7 | (1) | 12 May 1969 (SI 1969/630) |
| | (2) | 16 Feb 1970 (SI 1969/630) |
| | (3) | 12 May 1969 (SI 1969/630) |
| 8 | (1)–(3) | 1 Aug 1969 (SI 1969/630) |
| | (4)–(6) | 16 Feb 1970 (SI 1969/630) |
| 9, 10 | | 1 Aug 1969 (SI 1969/630) |
| 11–17 | | 16 Feb 1969 (SI 1969/630) |
| 18 | (1) | 1 Jul 1971 (SI 1971/544) |
| | (2)–(5) | 16 Feb 1970 (SI 1969/630) |
| 19–22 | | 12 May 1969 (SI 1969/630) |
| 23 | (1), (2) | 1 Feb 1977 (SI 1976/2064) |
| | (3) | 16 Feb 1970 (SI 1969/630) |
| | (4) | 12 May 1969 (SI 1969/630) |
| 24 | (1) | 12 May 1969 (SI 1969/630) |
| | (2), (3) | 16 Feb 1970 (SI 1969/630) |
| | (4) | 12 May 1969 (SI 1969/630) |
| | (5) | 16 Feb 1970 (SI 1969/630) |
| 25–28 | | 12 May 1969 (SI 1969/630) |
| Sch 1 | Pt I | 16 Feb 1970 (SI 1969/630) |
| | Pt II, paras 1–3 | 16 Feb 1970 (SI 1969/630) |
| | Pt II, para 4 | 1 Feb 1977 (SI 1976/2064) |
| | Pt II, paras 5–13 | 16 Feb 1970 (SI 1969/630) |
| Sch 2 | para 1 | 1 Feb 1977 (SI 1976/2064) |
| | para 2(1) | 1 Feb 1977 (SI 1976/2064) |
| | para 2(2) | 12 May 1969 (SI 1969/630) |
| | paras 3, 4 | 1 Feb 1977 (SI 1976/2064) |
| | para 5 | 16 Feb 1970 (SI 1969/630) |
| | para 6 | 1 Feb 1977 (SI 1976/2064) |
| | paras 7–9 | 16 Feb 1970 (SI 1969/630) |
| | paras 10, 11 | 1 Feb 1977 (SI 1976/2064) |
| | para 12 | 12 May 1969 (SI 1969/630) |
| | para 13(1) | 1 Feb 1977 (SI 1976/2064) |
| | para 13(2) | 16 Feb 1970 (SI 1969/630) |
| | paras 14, 15 | 16 Feb 1970 (SI 1969/630) |
| | para 16 | 1 Aug 1969 (SI 1969/630) |
| | para 17 | 1 Feb 1977 (SI 1976/2064) |
| | paras 18, 19 | 16 Feb 1970 (SI 1969/630) |
| | para 20 | 1 Aug 1969 (SI 1969/630) |
| | para 21 | 1 Feb 1977 (SI 1976/2064) |
| | para 22 | 16 Feb 1970 (SI 1969/630) |
| | para 23(1) | 1 Feb 1977 (SI 1976/2064) |
| | para 23(2) | 16 Feb 1970 (SI 1969/630) |
| | paras 24–27 | 16 Feb 1970 (SI 1969/630) |
| | para 28 | 1 Feb 1977 (SI 1976/2064) |
| | paras 29–32 | 16 Feb 1970 (SI 1969/630) |
| | para 33 | 1 Feb 1977 (SI 1976/2064) |
| | paras 34, 35 | 16 Feb 1970 (SI 1969/630) |
| | paras 36, 37 | 1 Feb 1977 (SI 1976/2064) |
| | para 38 | 12 May 1969 (SI 1969/630) |
| | para 39 | 16 Feb 1970 (SI 1969/630) |

**Representation of the People Act 1969 (c 15)**—*contd*

|        | para 40  | 1 Feb 1977 (SI 1976/2064)                                                   |
|--------|----------|-----------------------------------------------------------------------------|
| Sch 3  | Pt I     | 12 May 1969 (SI 1969/630)                                                   |
|        | Pt II    | 12 May 1969 (repeals of or in Representation of the People Act 1949, ss 38, 46(4), 115(2), 159(5), 165(3), Sch 4, para 5(2)) (SI 1969/630) |

1 Aug 1969 (repeals of or in Representation of the People Act 1949, ss 65(2), 97) (SI 1969/630)

16 Feb 1970 (SI 1969/630), repeals of or in—
Local Government Act 1933, ss 57(b), 67(5)(b);
Representation of the People Act 1949, ss 12, 23, 25, 57(2), 70, Sch 2 (in the parliamentary elections rules, rules 1, 7(4), 24, 55(2) and in the local election rules, rules 7(1), 19(2)(e), 20), Sch 3, rules 7, 18, 46(2)

1 Feb 1977 (otherwise) (SI 1976/2064)

| Sch 4 | 12 May 1969 (SI 1969/630) |
|-------|----------------------------|

[1]   For transitional provisions, see SI 1969/630, art 2

---

**Sharing of Church Buildings Act 1969 (c 38)**

*RA:* 25 Jul 1969

Whole Act in force 25 Jul 1969 (RA)

---

**Shipbuilding Industry Act 1969 (c 6)**

*RA:* 6 Mar 1969

Whole Act in force 6 Mar 1969 (RA)

---

**Statute Law (Repeals) Act 1969 (c 52)**

*RA:* 22 Oct 1969

*Commencement provisions:* s 7(2)

Whole Act in force 1 Jan 1970 (s 7(2))

---

**Synodical Government Measure 1969 (No 2)**

*RA:* 25 Jul 1969

Whole Measure in force 25 Jul 1969; but note that the Church Assembly was renamed and reconstituted as the General Synod as from 4 Nov 1970; see the *London Gazette*, 16 Jun 1970

---

**Tanzania Act 1969 (c 29)**

*RA:* 25 Jun 1969

Whole Act in force 25 Jun 1969 (RA), except for s 3, which is deemed to have come into operation on 26 Apr 1964 by virtue of s 3(3)

---

**Tattooing of Minors Act 1969 (c 24)**

*RA:* 16 May 1969

*Commencement provisions:* s 4(2)

**Tattooing of Minors Act 1969 (c 24)**—*contd*
Whole Act in force 16 Jun 1969 (s 4(2))

---

**Town and Country Planning (Scotland) Act 1969 (c 30)**

*RA:* 25 Jun 1969

*Commencement provisions:* s 104; Town and Country Planning (Scotland) Act 1969 (Commencement No 1)
    Order 1969, SI 1969/1569¹; Town and Country Planning (Scotland) Act 1969 (Commencement
    No 2) Order 1970, SI 1970/594; Town and Country Planning (Scotland) Act 1969 (Commencement
    No 3) Order 1970, SI 1970/1034

| | | |
|---|---|---|
| 1–12 | | *Never in force* (repealed) |
| 13–17 | | 8 Dec 1969 (SI 1969/1569) |
| 18–21 | | 18 May 1970 (SI 1970/594) |
| 22–27 | | *Never in force* (repealed) |
| 28–34 | | 8 Dec 1969 (SI 1969/1569) |
| 35 | | 18 May 1970 (SI 1970/594) |
| 36 | | 8 Dec 1969 (except in so far as it relates to s 35) (SI 1969/1569) |
| | | 18 May 1970 (otherwise) (SI 1970/594) |
| 37–39 | | 8 Dec 1969 (SI 1969/1569) |
| 40–60 | | 3 Aug 1970 (SI 1970/1034) |
| 61–76 | | 8 Dec 1969 (SI 1969/1569) |
| 77 | | 18 May 1970 (SI 1970/594) |
| 78–80 | | 8 Dec 1969 (SI 1969/1569) |
| 81 | | 18 May 1970 (SI 1970/594) |
| 82 | | *Never in force* (repealed) |
| 83–90 | | 8 Dec 1969 (SI 1969/1569) |
| 91, 92 | | 18 May 1970 (SI 1970/594) |
| 93–104 | | 8 Dec 1969 (SI 1969/1569) |
| 105 | | See Sch 9 below |
| 106 | | See Sch 10 below |
| 107 | | See Sch 11 below |
| 108 | | 8 Dec 1969 (SI 1969/1569) |
| Sch 1 | | 18 May 1970 (SI 1970/594) |
| Sch 2 | | 8 Dec 1969 (SI 1969/1569) |
| Sch 3 | | 18 May 1970 (SI 1970/594) |
| Sch 4 | | 3 Aug 1970 (SI 1970/1034) |
| Schs 5–8 | | 8 Dec 1969 (SI 1969/1569) |
| Sch 9 | paras 1–4 | *Never in force* (repealed) |
| | para 5 | 8 Dec 1969 (SI 1969/1569) |
| | para 6 | *Never in force* (repealed) |
| | paras 7–14 | 8 Dec 1969 (SI 1969/1569) |
| | para 15 | 3 Aug 1970 (SI 1970/1034) |
| | paras 16–19 | 8 Dec 1969 (SI 1969/1569) |
| | para 20 | 3 Aug 1970 (SI 1970/1034) |
| | paras 21–24 | 8 Dec 1969 (SI 1969/1569) |
| | para 25(a) | 8 Dec 1969 (in relation to the references to the Town and Country Planning Act 1947, ss 24, 26, 31 and s 15 of this Act) (SI 1969/1569) |
| | | 3 Aug 1970 (otherwise) (SI 1970/1034) |
| | para 25(b) | 3 Aug 1970 (SI 1970/1034) |
| | para 25(c) | 8 Dec 1969 (so far as it relates to enforcement notices under s 15 of this Act) (SI 1969/1569) |
| | | 3 Aug 1970 (so far as it relates to enforcement notices under s 44 of this Act) (SI 1970/1034) |
| | para 26 | 8 Dec 1969 (SI 1969/1569) |
| | para 27 | 8 Dec 1969 (so far as it relates to Part II of the Act of 1969) (SI 1969/1569) |

**Town and Country Planning (Scotland) Act 1969 (c 30)**—*contd*

|  |  |  |
|---|---|---|
|  |  | 3 Aug 1970 (so far as it relates to Part V of the Act of 1969) (SI 1970/1034) |
|  |  | *Never in force* (so far as it relates to Part III of the Act of 1969) (repealed) |
|  | para 28 | 8 Dec 1969 (so far as it relates to Part II) (SI 1969/1569) |
|  |  | 3 Aug 1970 (so far as it relates to Part V and Sch 4) (SI 1970/1034) |
|  | para 29 | 8 Dec 1969 (SI 1969/1569) |
|  | para 30 | 8 Dec 1969 (except so far as it relates to enforcement notices under s 44 of this Act) (SI 1969/1569) |
|  |  | 3 Aug 1970 (otherwise) (SI 1970/1034) |
|  | para 31 | 8 Dec 1969 (except so far as it relates to listed buildings and buildings proposed to be listed) (SI 1969/1569) |
|  |  | 3 Aug 1970 (otherwise) (SI 1970/1034) |
|  | para 32 | 8 Dec 1969 (except so far as it relates to Part V) (SI 1969/1569) |
|  |  | 3 Aug 1970 (otherwise) (SI 1970/1034) |
|  | para 33 | 8 Dec 1969 (SI 1969/1569) |
|  | para 34 | *Never in force* (repealed) |
|  | para 35 | 8 Dec 1969 (except so far as it relates to Part V) (SI 1969/1569) |
|  |  | 3 Aug 1970 (otherwise) (SI 1970/1034) |
|  | para 36 | 8 Dec 1969 (SI 1969/1569) |
|  | para 37 | 3 Aug 1970 (SI 1970/1034) |
|  | para 38(a) | 8 Dec 1969 (so far as it relates to the inserted Town and Country Planning (Scotland) Act 1959 s 31(3)(f)–(k)) (SI 1969/1569) |
|  |  | 3 Aug 1970 (so far as it relates to the inserted Town and Country Planning (Scotland) Act 1959 s 31(3)(l)) (SI 1970/1034) |
|  | para 38(b) | 8 Dec 1969 (so far as it relates to the inserted Town and Country Planning (Scotland) Act 1959 s 31(4)(f)–(i), (k)) (SI 1969/1569) |
|  |  | 3 Aug 1970 (so far as it relates to the inserted Town and Country Planning (Scotland) Act 1959 s 31(4)(j), (l)–(n)) (SI 1970/1034) |
|  | para 38(c) | 8 Dec 1969 (SI 1969/1569) |
|  | paras 39–42 | 8 Dec 1969 (SI 1969/1569) |
|  | paras 43, 44 | 3 Aug 1970 (SI 1970/1034) |
|  | para 45 | *Never in force* (repealed) |
|  | para 46 | 8 Dec 1969 (SI 1969/1569) |
|  | paras 47–49 | 3 Aug 1970 (SI 1970/1034) |
|  | para 50 | 8 Dec 1969 (SI 1969/1569) |
|  | para 51 | *Never in force* (repealed) |
|  | para 52 | 8 Dec 1969 (SI 1969/1569) |
| Sch 10 | paras 1–15 | 8 Dec 1969 (SI 1969/1569) |
|  | paras 16–18 | 3 Aug 1970 (SI 1970/1034) |
|  | para 19 | 8 Dec 1969 (SI 1969/1569) |
| Sch 11 |  | 8 Dec 1969 (SI 1969/1569), repeals of or in— |
|  |  | Town and Country Planning (Scotland) Act 1945; |
|  |  | Town and Country Planning (Scotland) Act 1947, ss 7, 21, 23, 29, 34–37, 39, 42, 83(2)(a), 84, 107(4), Schs 5, 6, 10; |
|  |  | Post Office Act 1953; |
|  |  | Electricity Act 1957; |
|  |  | Land Powers (Defence) Act 1958; |
|  |  | Town and Country Planning (Scotland) Act 1959, ss 31(9) (proviso), 38, 42(5), Sch 5; |
|  |  | Post Office Act 1961; |
|  |  | Land Compensation (Scotland) Act 1963; |
|  |  | Housing (Scotland) Act 1966; |
|  |  | Land Commission Act 1967; |
|  |  | New Towns (Scotland) Act 1968; |
|  |  | Town and Country Planning Act 1968, Sch 9, para 66(b) |
|  |  | 18 May 1970 (repeals of or in Town and Country Planning (Scotland) Act 1947, ss 10, 16, 17, 30, 72) (SI 1970/594) |
|  |  | 3 Aug 1970 (SI 1970/1034), repeals of or in— |

**Town and Country Planning (Scotland) Act 1969 (c 30)**—*contd*

Town and Country Planning (Scotland) Act 1947, ss 27, 28, 38, 83(3)(b), 96, 113 (definition building preservation order);

Town and Country Planning (Scotland) Act 1959, ss 31(3)(d), (4)(d), (5), (10);

Civic Amenities Act 1967, ss 1, 2, 6, 7, 9, 10;

Town and Country Planning Act 1968, Sch 9, para 71(c)

*Never in force* (repealed) repeals of or in—

Town and Country Planning (Scotland) Act 1947, ss 3–6, 8, 9, 26, 33, 38(1), (2), (3)(a), (4), 113 (definition development plan);

Town and Country Planning (Scotland) Act 1959, s 42(6);

Civic Amenities Act 1967, s 16

¹   For transitional provisions, see SI 1969/1569, art 3, Sch 2

---

**Transport (London) Act 1969 (c 35)**

*RA:* 25 Jul 1969

*Commencement provisions:* s 47(5); Transport (London) Act 1969 (Commencement No 1) Order 1969, SI 1969/1130; Transport (London) Act 1969 (Commencement No 2) Order 1969, SI 1969/1510; Transport (London) Act 1969 (Commencement No 3) Order 1969, SI 1969/1588; Transport (London) Act 1969 (Commencement No 4) Order 1972, SI 1972/1097; Transport (London) Act 1969 (Commencement No 5) Order 1974, SI 1974/407

| | | |
|---|---|---|
| 1–15 | | 30 Oct 1969 (SI 1969/1510) |
| 16, 17 | | 1 Jan 1970 (SI 1969/1510) |
| 18 | | 30 Oct 1969 (SI 1969/1510) |
| 19 | (1)(a) | 19 Nov 1969 (SI 1969/1588) |
| | (1)(b)–(d) | *Never in force* (repealed) |
| | (2)–(7) | *Never in force* (repealed) |
| | (8) | 8 Aug 1969 (SI 1969/1130) |
| 20–22 | | 30 Oct 1969 (SI 1969/1510) |
| 23 | (1)–(5) | 30 Oct 1969 (SI 1969/1510) |
| | (6) | 1 Jan 1970 (SI 1969/1510) |
| | (7) | 30 Oct 1969 (SI 1969/1510) |
| 24 | | 1 Jan 1970 (SI 1969/1510) |
| 25, 26 | | 30 Oct 1969 (SI 1969/1510) |
| 27, 28 | | 8 Aug 1969 (SI 1969/1130) |
| 29 | (1)–(3) | 1 Apr 1974 (SI 1974/407) |
| | (4) | 8 Aug 1969 (SI 1969/1130) |
| | (5), (6) | 1 Apr 1974 (SI 1974/407) |
| 30 | | 1 Apr 1974 (SI 1974/407) |
| 31 | | 1 Jan 1970 (SI 1969/1510) |
| 32 | | 1 Oct 1972 (SI 1972/1097) |
| 33–36 | | 1 Jan 1970 (SI 1969/1510) |
| 37–40 | | 30 Oct 1969 (SI 1969/1510) |
| 41 | (1) | 30 Oct 1969 (SI 1969/1510) |
| | (2), (3) | 8 Aug 1969 (so far as applicable for the purposes of s 27) (SI 1969/1130) |
| | | 30 Oct 1969 (otherwise) (SI 1969/1510) |
| 42 | | 30 Oct 1969 (SI 1969/1510) |
| 43 | | 8 Aug 1969 (SI 1969/1130) |
| 44 | | 30 Oct 1969 (SI 1969/1510) |
| 45, 46 | | 8 Aug 1969 (SI 1969/1130) |
| 47 | (1) | 8 Aug 1969 (SI 1969/1130) |
| | (2) | See Sch 6 below |
| | (3)–(5) | 8 Aug 1969 (SI 1969/1130) |
| Schs 1, 2 | | 30 Oct 1969 (SI 1969/1510) |

**Transport (London) Act 1969 (c 35)**—*contd*

| | |
|---|---|
| Sch 3 | 1 Jan 1970 (SI 1969/1510) |
| Sch 4 | 30 Oct 1969 (SI 1969/1510) |
| Sch 5 | 1 Jan 1970 (SI 1969/1510) |
| Sch 6 | 8 Aug 1969 (SI 1969/1130), repeals of or in— |

Transport Act 1962, ss 44–49, 57(3)(a), Sch 7, Pt II, in Sch 10, para 9, the words from "but" onwards;

London Government Act 1963, Sch 17, para 26(a);

Prices and Incomes Act 1966, Sch 3, para 2(1)(g)

1 Jan 1970 (remaining repeals, except those specified below) (SI 1969/1510)

1 Apr 1974 (SI 1974/407), repeals of or in—

Highways Act 1959, in s 295(1), the definition of "metropolitan road";

London Government Act 1963, s 17(1)–(3), in sub-s (4) the words from "otherwise" to "section)", sub-s (6), in s 89(1), the definition of "metropolitan road", Sch 6, para 68(d), Sch 7;

Road Traffic Regulation Act 1967, in s 104(1), the definition of "metropolitan road"

**Transport (London) Amendment Act 1969 (c 60)**

*RA:* 11 Dec 1969

Whole Act in force 11 Dec 1969 (RA)

**Trustee Savings Banks Act 1969 (c 50)**

*RA:* 25 Jul 1969

*Commencement provisions:* s 100(2); Trustee Savings Banks Act 1969 (Commencement) Order 1969, SI 1969/1285

Whole Act in force 1 Oct 1969 (SI 1969/1285)

**Ulster Defence Regiment Act 1969 (c 65)**

*RA:* 18 Dec 1969

*Commencement provisions:* s 6(2); Ulster Defence Regiment Act 1969 (Commencement) Order 1969, SI 1969/1860

Whole Act in force 1 Jan 1970 (SI 1969/1860)

**Vehicle and Driving Licences Act 1969 (c 27)**

*RA:* 25 Jun 1969

*Commencement provisions:* s 38(2); Vehicle and Driving Licences Act 1969 (Commencement No 1) Order 1969, SI 1969/866; Vehicle and Driving Licences Act 1969 (Commencement No 2) Order 1969, SI 1969/913; Vehicles and Driving Licences Act 1969 (Commencement No 3) Order 1969, SI 1969/1579; Vehicle and Driving Licences Act 1969 (Commencement No 4) Order 1969, SI 1969/1637; Vehicles and Driving Licences Act 1969 (Commencement No 5) Order 1970, SI 1970/169; Vehicles and Driving Licences Act 1969 (Commencement No 6) Order 1970, SI 1970/757; Vehicles and Driving Licences Act 1969 (Commencement No 7) Order 1971, SI 1971/244; Vehicles and Driving Licences Act 1969 (Commencement No 8) Order 1971, SI 1971/376; Vehicles and Driving Licences Act 1969 (Commencement No 9) Order 1971, SI 1971/1477

| | | |
|---|---|---|
| 1 | | 22 Feb 1971 (SI 1971/244) |
| 2 | (1), (2) | 22 Feb 1971 (SI 1971/244) |

**Vehicle and Driving Licences Act 1969 (c 27)**—*contd*

| | | |
|---|---|---|
| | (3), (4) | 19 Nov 1969 (SI 1969/1579) |
| | (5)–(7) | 22 Feb 1971 (SI 1971/244) |
| | (8) | 1 Apr 1971 (in so far as it relates to Sch 1, paras 2–12) (SI 1971/376) |
| | | *Never in force* (otherwise) (repealed) |
| 3 | | 22 Feb 1971 (SI 1971/244) |
| 4–8 | | *Never in force* (repealed) |
| 9, 10 | | 1 Feb 1970 (SI 1969/1637) |
| 11, 12 | | *Never in force* (repealed) |
| 13–15 | | 1 Jun 1970 (SI 1970/169) |
| 16 | (1) | 1 Jun 1970 (SI 1970/169) |
| | (2) | See Sch 2 below |
| | (3), (4) | 1 Jun 1970 (SI 1970/169) |
| | (5) | 30 Jun 1969 (SI 1969/866) |
| | (6) | 1 Feb 1970 (SI 1969/1637) |
| | (7) | 27 Sep 1971 (SI 1971/1477) |
| 17 | | *Never in force* (repealed) |
| 18 | (1) | 27 Sep 1971 (SI 1971/1477) |
| | (2) | 14 Jul 1969 (SI 1969/913) |
| 19, 20 | | *Never in force* (repealed) |
| 21 | (1)(a), (b) | *Never in force* (repealed) |
| | (1)(c) | 1 Apr 1971 (SI 1971/376) |
| | (2) | *Never in force* (repealed) |
| | (3) | 1 Apr 1971 (SI 1971/376) |
| 22 | | 1 Feb 1970 (SI 1969/1637) |
| 23 | (1)(a)–(e) | 1 Jun 1970 (SI 1970/169) |
| | (1)(f) | *Never in force* (repealed) |
| | (2) | 1 Jun 1970 (SI 1970/169) |
| 24 | | *Never in force* (repealed) |
| 25, 26 | | 1 Feb 1970 (SI 1969/1637) |
| 27 | | 1 Apr 1970 (SI 1970/169) |
| 28 | (1) | 1 Feb 1970 (SI 1969/1637) |
| | (2)(a) | 1 Feb 1970 (SI 1969/1637) |
| | (2)(b) | *Never in force* (repealed) |
| | (2)(c) | 1 Feb 1970 (SI 1969/1637) |
| | (3) | *Never in force* (repealed) |
| | (4)–(6) | 1 Feb 1970 (SI 1969/1637) |
| 29 | | *Never in force* (repealed) |
| 30, 31 | | 1 Feb 1970 (SI 1969/1637) |
| 32 | | 1 Feb 1970 (in so far as it relates to s 22) (SI 1969/1637) |
| | | *Never in force* (otherwise) (repealed) |
| 33, 34 | | 30 Jun 1969 (SI 1969/866) |
| 35 | | 1 Feb 1970 (in so far as it relates to s 22) (SI 1969/1637) |
| | | 1 Jun 1970 (in so far as it relates to notices authorised to be served on any person by Road Traffic Act 1960, ss 100, 102(2)) (SI 1970/169) |
| | | *Never in force* (otherwise) (repealed) |
| 36 | | 1 Apr 1971 (SI 1971/376) |
| 37 | | See Sch 3 below |
| 38 | | 30 Jun 1969 (SI 1969/866) |
| Sch 1 | Pt I, para 1 | 1 Jun 1970 (SI 1970/757) |
| | Pt I, paras 2–12 | 1 Apr 1971 (SI 1971/376) |
| | Pt II | *Never in force* (repealed) |
| Sch 2 | paras 1–3 | 1 Jun 1970 (SI 1970/169) |
| | para 4 | *Never in force* (repealed) |
| | para 5 | 1 Jun 1970 (SI 1970/169) |
| | para 6 | 1 Feb 1970 (SI 1969/1637) |
| | para 7 | 1 Jun 1970 (SI 1970/169) |
| | paras 8–12 | 1 Feb 1970 (SI 1969/1637) |

**Vehicle and Driving Licences Act 1969 (c 27)**—*contd*

| | |
|---|---|
| para 13 | 30 Jun 1969 (SI 1969/866) |
| Sch 3 | 1 Feb 1970 (in so far as it relates to repeals of or in Vehicles (Excise) Act 1962, s 19(1), (3)) (SI 1969/1637) |
| | 1 Jun 1970 (in so far as it relates to repeals of or in Road Traffic Act 1960, ss 99(4), 109(3), 100(a), 113(g), 115, 225, 226(2)) (SI 1970/169) |
| | 1 Apr 1971 (remainder, except in so far as it relates to Road Traffic Act 1960, s 112(3), and to Vehicles (Excise) Act 1962, ss 2, 3, 9, 12(4)) (SI 1971/376) |
| | *Never in force* (exceptions noted above) (repealed) |

# 1970 Acts

## Administration of Justice Act 1970 (c 31)

*RA:* 29 May 1970

*Commencement provisions:* s 54(4); Administration of Justice Act 1970 (Commencement No 1) Order 1970, SI 1970/886; Administration of Justice Act 1970 (Commencement No 2) Order 1970, SI 1970/1207; Administration of Justice Act 1970 (Commencement No 3) Order 1970, SI 1970/1962; Administration of Justice Act 1970 (Commencement No 4) Order 1971, SI 1971/834; Administration of Justice Act 1970 (Commencement No 5) Order 1971, SI 1971/1244

| | | |
|---|---|---|
| 1–4 | | 1 Oct 1971 (SI 1971/1244) |
| 5–10 | | 1 Jul 1970 (SI 1970/886) |
| 11–27 | | 2 Aug 1971 (SI 1971/834) |
| 28 | | 1 Sep 1970 (definition of "maintenance order" for purposes of s 48 below) (SI 1970/1207) |
| | | 2 Aug 1971 (otherwise) (SI 1971/834) |
| 29–35 | | 2 Aug 1971 (SI 1971/834) |
| 36–39 | | 1 Feb 1971 (SI 1970/1962) |
| 40 | | 1 Jul 1970 (SI 1970/886) |
| 41–43 | | 2 Aug 1971 (SI 1971/834) |
| 44–47 | | 1 Jul 1970 (SI 1970/886) |
| 48 | | 1 Sep 1970 (SI 1970/1207) |
| 49 | | 1 Jul 1970 (SI 1970/886) |
| 50 | | 1 Oct 1971 (SI 1971/1244) |
| 51 | | 1 Jan 1971 (SI 1970/1962) |
| 52 | | 1 Jul 1970 (SI 1970/886) |
| 53 | | 1 Feb 1971 (SI 1970/1962) |
| 54 | (1), (2) | 1 Jul 1970 (SI 1970/886) |
| | (3) | See Sch 11 below |
| | (4), (5) | 1 Jul 1970 (SI 1970/886) |
| | (6) | 1 Feb 1971 (SI 1970/1962) |
| Schs 1–3 | | 1 Oct 1971 (SI 1971/1244) |
| Schs 4–10 | | 2 Aug 1971 (SI 1971/834) |
| Sch 11 | | 1 Jul 1970 (SI 1970/886), repeals of or in— |
| | | Guardianship of Infants Act 1886, ss 5, 11; |
| | | Supreme Court of Judicature (Consolidation) Act 1925; |
| | | Patents Act 1949; |
| | | Registered Designs Act 1949; |
| | | Administration of Justice Act 1964; |
| | | Criminal Appeal Act 1966; |
| | | Criminal Appeal Act 1968, s 45(2) |
| | | 1 Sep 1970 (SI 1970/1207), repeals of or in— |
| | | Maintenance Orders Act 1958, s 4(3); |
| | | Maintenance Orders Act 1968 |
| | | 2 Aug 1971 (SI 1971/834), repeals of or in— |
| | | Forfeiture Act 1870; |
| | | Bankruptcy Act 1914; |
| | | Children and Young Persons Act 1933; |
| | | Summary Jurisdiction (Appeals) Act 1933; |

**Administration of Justice Act 1970 (c 31)**—*contd*

> Criminal Justice Act 1948;
> Costs in Criminal Cases Act 1952;
> Magistrates' Courts Act 1952;
> Maintenance Orders Act 1958 (except s 4(3), repealed as noted above);
> County Courts Act 1959;
> Matrimonial Causes Act 1965;
> Ministry of Social Security Act 1966;
> Criminal Justice Act 1967;
> Criminal Appeal Act 1968, Sch 5;
> Children and Young Persons Act 1969;
> Family Law Reform Act 1969
> 1 Oct 1971 (SI 1971/1244), repeals of or in—
> Administration of Estates Act 1925;
> Supreme Court of Judicature (Consolidation) Act 1925, ss 5(1), 58, 225

---

**Agriculture Act 1970 (c 40)**

*RA:* 29 May 1970

*Commencement provisions:* ss 65(1), 87(1); Agriculture Act 1970 (Commencement No 1) Order 1970, SI 1970/1045; Agriculture Act 1970 (Commencement No 2) Order 1970, SI 1970/1048; Agriculture Act 1970 (Commencement No 3) Order 1970, SI 1970/1098 (relating to Scotland only); Agriculture Act 1970 (Commencement No 4) Order 1970, SI 1970/1755; Agriculture Act 1970 (Commencement No 5) Order 1973, SI 1973/1520

| | | |
|---|---|---|
| 1–28 | | 29 May 1970 (RA) |
| 29 | | 29 May 1970 (RA; note that Farm Capital Grant (Repeal of Enactments) Order 1970, SI 1970/1867, made under sub-s (6), appointed 1 Jan 1971 for the purposes of that subsection; note also that Farm Capital Grant (Repeal of Enactments) (Savings) Order 1970, SI 1970/1758, made under sub-s (7), continued the enactments specified in Sch 5, Pt I, and instruments made thereunder, in force for 4 years after 1 Jan 1971 for certain purposes) |
| 30 | | 29 May 1970 (RA) |
| 31 | (1) | 1 Jan 1971 (SI 1970/1755) |
| | (2), (3) | 29 May 1970 (RA) |
| 32 | | 1 Jan 1971 (sub-s (8) and Farm Capital Grant (Repeal of Enactments) Order 1970, SI 1970/1867, made under s 29(6) above) |
| 33, 34 | | 29 May 1970 (RA) |
| 35 | | 5 Nov 1975 (sub-s (1) and Livestock Rearing Land Improvement Schemes (Terminal Date) Order 1971, SI 1971/832) |
| 36 | | 29 May 1970 (RA) |
| 37–65 | | 1 Aug 1970 (SI 1970/1048) |
| 66–87 | | 1 Jan 1974 (SI 1973/1520) |
| 88–107 | | 29 May 1970 (RA) |
| 108 | (1), (2) | 29 May 1970 (RA) |
| | (3) | 31 Jul 1970 (SI 1970/1045; SI 1970/1098) |
| | (4), (5) | 29 May 1970 (RA) |
| 109–113 | | 29 May 1970 (RA) |
| Schs 1, 2 | | 29 May 1970 (RA) |
| Schs 3, 4 | | 1 Aug 1970 (SI 1970/1048) |
| Sch 5 | Pt I | 1 Jan 1971 (ie the date appointed by the Farm Capital Grant (Repeal of Enactments) Order 1970, SI 1970/1867, for the purposes of s 29(6)) |
| | Pt II | *Never in force* (repealed) |
| | Pt III | 1 Aug 1970 (SI 1970/1048) |

**Agriculture Act 1970 (c 40)**—*contd*

|  |  |  |
|---|---|---|
| | Pt IV | 31 Jul 1970 (SI 1970/1045) |
| | Pt V | 29 May 1970 (RA), repeals of or in— |
| | | Diseases of Animals Act 1950; |
| | | Trade Descriptions Act 1968 |
| | | 1 Jan 1971 (repeals in Horticulture Act 1960) (SI 1970/1755) |
| | | 1 Jan 1974 (repeal of Fertilisers and Feeding Stuffs Act 1926) (SI 1973/1520) |
| | | *Never in force* (repeal of Agricultural Improvement Grants Act 1959) (repealed) |

---

**Appropriation Act 1970 (c 25)**

*RA:* 29 May 1970

Whole Act in force 29 May 1970 (RA)

---

**Appropriation (No 2) Act 1970 (c 48)**

*RA:* 23 Jul 1970

Whole Act in force 23 Jul 1970 (RA)

---

**Building (Scotland) Act 1970 (c 38)**

*RA:* 29 May 1970

*Commencement provisions:* s 8(3); Building (Scotland) Act 1970 (Commencement) Order 1971, SI 1971/744

| | | |
|---|---|---|
| 1 | | 29 Jun 1970 (s 8(3)(b)) |
| 2 | | 15 Jun 1971 (SI 1971/744) |
| 3 | | 29 Jun 1970 (s 8(3)(b)) |
| 4 | | 15 Jun 1971 (SI 1971/744) |
| 5–8 | | 29 Jun 1970 (s 8(3)(b)) |
| Sch 1 | Pt I, para 1(a), (b) | 15 Jun 1971 (SI 1971/744) |
| | Pt I, para 1(c) | 29 Jun 1970 (s 8(3)(b)) |
| | Pt I, paras 2–5 | 15 Jun 1971 (SI 1971/744) |
| | Pt I, para 6 | 29 Jun 1970 (s 8(3)(b)) |
| | Pt I, para 7(a) | 15 Jun 1971 (SI 1971/744) |
| | Pt I, para 7(b) | 29 Jun 1970 (s 8(3)(b)) |
| | Pt I, para 8 | 15 Jun 1971 (SI 1971/744) |
| | Pt I, para 9 | 29 Jun 1970 (s 8(3)(b)) |
| | Pt II, paras 1–5 | 29 Jun 1970 (s 8(3)(b)) |
| | Pt II, para 6 | 15 Jun 1971 (SI 1971/744) |
| | Pt II, para 7 | 29 Jun 1970 (s 8(3)(b)) |
| Sch 2 | | 29 Jun 1970 (except repeals of or in Building (Scotland) Act 1959, s 10, Sch 5) (s 8(3)(b)) |
| | | 15 Jun 1971 (exception noted above) (SI 1971/744) |

---

**Chronically Sick and Disabled Persons Act 1970 (c 44)**

*RA:* 29 May 1970

*Commencement provisions:* s 29(4); Chronically Sick and Disabled Persons Act 1970 (Commencement No 1) Order 1971, SI 1971/698; Chronically Sick and Disabled Persons Act 1970 (Commencement No 2) Order 1971, SI 1971/1491

| | |
|---|---|
| 1 | 1 Oct 1971 (SI 1971/698) |
| 2, 3 | 29 Aug 1970 (s 29(4)(c)) |
| 4–8 | 29 Nov 1970 (s 29(4)(b)) |

**Chronically Sick and Disabled Persons Act 1970 (c 44)**—*contd*

| | |
|---|---|
| 9–20 | 29 Aug 1970 (s 29(4)(c)) |
| 21 | 1 Dec 1971 (SI 1971/1491) |
| 22–29 | 29 Aug 1970 (s 29(4)(c)) |

**Church Commissioners Measure 1970 (No 3)**

*RA:* 17 Dec 1970

Whole Measure in force 17 Dec 1970 (RA)

**Collegiate Churches (Capital Endowments) Measure 1970 (No 1)**

*RA:* 24 Mar 1970

Whole Measure in force 24 Mar 1970 (RA)

**Conservation of Seals Act 1970 (c 30)**

*RA:* 29 May 1970

*Commencement provisions:* s 17(4)

Whole Act in force 29 Aug 1970 (s 17(4))

**Consolidated Fund Act 1970 (c 1)**

*RA:* 29 Jan 1970

Whole Act in force 29 Jan 1970 (RA)

**Consolidated Fund (No 2) Act 1970 (c 12)**

*RA:* 24 Mar 1970

Whole Act in force 24 Mar 1970 (RA)

**Contingencies Fund Act 1970 (c 56)**

*RA:* 17 Dec 1970

*Commencement provisions:* s 3(2)

Whole Act in force 17 Jan 1971 (s 3(2))

**Conveyancing and Feudal Reform (Scotland) Act 1970 (c 35)**

*RA:* 29 May 1970

*Commencement provisions:* s 54(2); Conveyancing and Feudal Reform (Scotland) Act 1970 (Commencement) Order 1971, SI 1971/199

| | |
|---|---|
| 1–6 | 1 Mar 1971 (SI 1971/199) |
| 7–49 | 29 Nov 1970 (s 54(2)(a)) |
| 50 | 29 May 1970 (s 54(2)(c)) |
| 51–53 | 29 May 1970 (so far as they relate s 50) (s 54(2)(c)) |
| | 1 Mar 1971 (so far as they relate to ss 1–6) (SI 1971/199) |
| 54 | 29 May 1970 (s 54(2)(c)) |
| Schs 1–11 | 29 Nov 1970 (s 54(2)(a)) |

## Education (Handicapped Children) Act 1970 (c 52)

*RA:* 23 Jul 1970

Whole Act in force 23 Jul 1970 (RA); but note that this Act mainly took effect from 1 Apr 1971, the day appointed by Education (Handicapped Children) Act 1970 (Appointed Day) Order 1971, SI 1971/187, made under s 1(1)

## Education (School Milk) Act 1970 (c 14)

*RA:* 26 Mar 1970

Whole Act in force 26 Mar 1970 (RA)

## Equal Pay Act 1970 (c 41)

*RA:* 29 May 1970

*Commencement provisions:* s 9

Whole Act in force 29 Dec 1975 (s 9(1))

## Expiring Laws Continuance Act 1970 (c 58)

*RA:* 17 Dec 1970

Whole Act in force 17 Dec 1970 (RA)

## Export Guarantees and Payments Act 1970 (c 15)

*RA:* 16 Apr 1970

Whole Act in force 16 Apr 1970 (RA)

## Family Income Supplements Act 1970 (c 55)

*RA:* 17 Dec 1970

Whole Act in force 17 Dec 1970 (RA); but note no supplement was payable until 3 Aug 1971; see the Family Income Supplements (General) Regulations 1971, SI 1971/226, reg 9, made under s 16(1)

## Fiji Independence Act 1970 (c 50)

*RA:* 23 Jul 1970

This Act generally has effect from 10 Oct 1970 (the "appointed day" s 1(1))

## Films Act 1970 (c 26)

*RA:* 29 May 1970

*Commencement provisions:* s 22(2)

Whole Act in force 29 May 1970 (RA), except ss 11–13, which came into force on 1 Jan 1971 (s 22(2))

## Finance Act 1970 (c 24)

*RA:* 29 May 1970

The commencement details of Finance Acts are not set out, as the dates from which their provisions take
effect are usually stated clearly and unambiguously in the text of the Act, and charging provisions will
normally state for which year or years of assessment they are to have effect.

## Fishing Vessels (Safety Provisions) Act 1970 (c 27)

*RA:* 29 May 1970

*Commencement provisions:* s 11(2); Fishing Vessels (Safety Provisions) Act 1970 (Commencement)
Order 1975, SI 1975/337

Whole Act in force 30 Apr 1975 (SI 1975/337)

## Food and Drugs (Milk) Act 1970 (c 3)

*RA:* 29 Jan 1970

Whole Act in force 29 Jan 1970 (RA)

## Game Act 1970 (c 13)

*RA:* 26 Mar 1970

*Commencement provisions:* s 2(1)

Whole Act in force 2 Feb 1971 (s 2(1))

## General Rate Act 1970 (c 19)

*RA:* 15 May 1970

*Commencement provisions:* s 2(4)

Whole Act in force 15 Jun 1970 (s 2(4))

## Guyana Republic Act 1970 (c 18)

*RA:* 15 May 1970

Whole Act in force 15 May 1970 (RA); but note that the Act has retrospective effect as Guyana became a
republic on 23 Feb 1970

## Harbours (Amendment) Act 1970 (c 53)

*RA:* 23 Jul 1970

Whole Act in force 23 Jul 1970 (RA)

## Housing (Amendment) (Scotland) Act 1970 (c 5)

*RA:* 26 Feb 1970

Whole Act in force 26 Feb 1970 (RA)

### Income and Corporation Taxes Act 1970 (c 10)

*RA:* 12 Mar 1970

*Commencement provisions:* s 536

Whole Act in force 6 Apr 1970 (s 536(1)–(3))

### Income and Corporation Taxes (No 2) Act 1970 (c 54)

*RA:* 17 Dec 1970

Whole Act in force 17 Dec 1970 (RA)

### Indecent Advertisements (Amendment) Act 1970 (c 47)

*RA:* 29 May 1970

Whole Act in force 29 May 1970 (RA)

### Industrial Development (Ships) Act 1970 (c 2)

*RA:* 29 Jan 1970

Whole Act in force 29 Jan 1970 (RA)

### Insolvency Services (Accounting and Investment) Act 1970 (c 8)

*RA:* 26 Feb 1970

*Commencement provisions:* s 9(2); Insolvency Services (Accounting and Investment) Act 1970 (Commencement) Order 1970, SI 1970/465

Whole Act in force 1 Apr 1970 (SI 1970/465)

### International Monetary Fund Act 1970 (c 49)

*RA:* 23 Jul 1970

Whole Act in force 23 Jul 1970 (RA)

### Law Reform (Miscellaneous Provisions) Act 1970 (c 33)

*RA:* 29 May 1970

*Commencement provisions:* s 7(3)

Whole Act in force 1 Jan 1971 (s 7(3))

### Local Authorities (Goods and Services) Act 1970 (c 39)

*RA:* 29 May 1970

Whole Act in force 29 May 1970 (RA)

## Local Authority Social Services Act 1970 (c 42)

*RA:* 29 May 1970

*Commencement provisions:* s 15(4); Local Authority Social Services Act 1970 (Commencement No 1) Order 1970, SI 1970/1143; Local Authority Social Services Act 1970 (Commencement No 2) Order 1970, SI 1970/1813; Local Authority Social Services Act 1970 (Commencement No 3) Order 1971, SI 1971/1221

| | | |
|---|---|---|
| 1 | | 1 Sep 1970 (SI 1970/1143) |
| 2–5 | | 1 Jan 1971 (in relation to all local authorities except Hertfordshire and Manchester) (SI 1970/1813) |
| | | 1 Apr 1971 (in relation to Hertfordshire) (SI 1970/1813) |
| | | 26 May 1971 (in relation to Manchester) (SI 1970/1813) |
| 6 | | 1 Jan 1971 (in relation to all local authorities except Hertfordshire, Manchester and Lancashire) (SI 1970/1813) |
| | | 1 Apr 1971 (in relation to Hertfordshire) (SI 1970/1813) |
| | | 26 May 1971 (in relation to Manchester) (SI 1970/1813) |
| | | 1 Oct 1971 (in relation to Lancashire) (SI 1970/1813) |
| 7, 8 | | 1 Jan 1971 (in relation to all local authorities except Hertfordshire and Manchester) (SI 1970/1813) |
| | | 1 Apr 1971 (in relation to Hertfordshire) (SI 1970/1813) |
| | | 26 May 1971 (in relation to Manchester) (SI 1970/1813) |
| 9, 10 | | 1 Sep 1970 (SI 1970/1143) |
| 11 | | 1 Oct 1971 (SI 1971/1221) |
| 12, 13 | | 1 Sep 1970 (SI 1970/1143) |
| 14 | (1) | See Sch 2 below |
| | (2) | See Sch 3 below |
| | (3), (4) | 1 Sep 1970 (SI 1970/1143) |
| 15 | | 1 Sep 1970 (SI 1970/1143) |
| Sch 1 | | 1 Jan 1971 (in relation to all local authorities except Hertfordshire and Manchester) (SI 1970/1813) |
| | | 1 Apr 1971 (in relation to Hertfordshire) (SI 1970/1813) |
| | | 26 May 1971 (in relation to Manchester) (SI 1970/1813) |
| Sch 2 | paras 1–6 | 1 Jan 1971 (in relation to all local authorities except Hertfordshire and Manchester) (SI 1970/1813) |
| | | 1 Apr 1971 (in relation to Hertfordshire) (SI 1970/1813) |
| | | 26 May 1971 (in relation to Manchester) (SI 1970/1813) |
| | paras 7, 8 | 1 Sep 1970 (SI 1970/1143) |
| | paras 9–12 | 1 Jan 1971 (in relation to all local authorities except Hertfordshire and Manchester) (SI 1970/1813) |
| | | 1 Apr 1971 (in relation to Hertfordshire) (SI 1970/1813) |
| | | 26 May 1971 (in relation to Manchester) (SI 1970/1813) |
| Sch 3 | | 1 Sep 1970 (SI 1970/1143), repeals of or in— Local Government Act 1958; London Government Act 1963; Health Services and Public Health Act 1968 |
| | | 1 Jan 1971 (all remaining repeals in relation to all local authorities except Hertfordshire, Lancashire and Manchester) (SI 1970/1813) |
| | | 1 Jan 1971 (all remaining repeals (except repeal of Children Act 1948, s 41)) (SI 1970/1813) |
| | | 1 Apr 1971 (all remaining repeals in relation to Hertfordshire) (SI 1970/1813) |
| | | 26 May 1971 (all remaining repeals in relation to Manchester) (SI 1970/1813) |
| | | 1 Oct 1971 (repeal of Children Act 1948, s 41 (in relation to Lancashire local authority) (SI 1970/1813) |

## Local Employment Act 1970 (c 7)

*RA:* 26 Feb 1970

*Commencement provisions:* s 9(3)

## Local Employment Act 1970 (c 7)—*contd*
Whole Act in force 5 Mar 1970 (s 9(3))

---

## Local Government (Footpaths and Open Spaces) (Scotland) Act 1970 (c 28)

*RA:* 29 May 1970

Whole Act in force 29 May 1970 (RA)

---

## Marriage (Registrar General's Licence) Act 1970 (c 34)

*RA:* 29 May 1970

*Commencement provisions:* s 20(3)

Whole Act in force 1 Jan 1971 (s 20(3))

---

## Matrimonial Proceedings and Property Act 1970 (c 45)

*RA:* 29 May 1970

*Commencement provisions:* s 43(2)

| | | |
|---|---|---|
| 1–32 | | 1 Jan 1971 (s 43(2)) |
| 33 | | 1 Aug 1970 (s 43(2)) |
| 34, 35 | | 1 Jan 1971 (s 43(2)) |
| 36–41 | | 1 Aug 1970 (s 43(2)) |
| 42 | (1) | See Sch 2 below |
| | (2) | See Sch 3 below |
| 43 | | 1 Aug 1970 (s 43(2)) |
| Schs 1, 2 | | 1 Jan 1971 (s 43(2)) |
| Sch 3 | | 1 Aug 1970 (repeals of or in Matrimonial Causes Act 1965, s 20(3), (4)) (s 43(2)) |
| | | 1 Jan 1971 (otherwise) (s 43(2)) |

---

## Merchant Shipping Act 1970 (c 36)

*RA:* 29 May 1970

*Commencement provisions:* s 101(4); Merchant Shipping Act 1970 (Commencement No 1) Order 1972, SI 1972/1977; Merchant Shipping Act 1970 (Commencement No 2) Order 1974, SI 1974/1194; Merchant Shipping Act 1970 (Commencement No 3) Order 1974, SI 1974/1908; Merchant Shipping Act 1970 (Commencement No 4) Order 1975, SI 1975/2156; Merchant Shipping Act 1970 (Commencement No 5) Order 1978, SI 1978/797; Merchant Shipping Act 1970 (Commencement No 6) Order 1979, SI 1979/809; Merchant Shipping Act 1970 (Commencement No 7) Order 1981, SI 1981/1186; Merchant Shipping Act 1970 (Commencement No 8) Order 1982, SI 1982/840; Merchant Shipping Act 1970 (Commencement No 9) Order 1982, SI 1982/1617; Merchant Shipping Act 1970 (Commencement No 10) Order 1986, SI 1986/2066; Merchant Shipping Act 1970 (Commencement No 11) Order 1995, SI 1995/965; Merchant Shipping Act 1970 (Commencement No 12) Order 1995, SI 1995/1426

| | |
|---|---|
| 1–5 | 1 Jan 1973 (SI 1972/1977) |
| 6 | *Never in force* (repealed) |
| 7–14 | 1 Jan 1973 (SI 1972/1977) |
| 15 | 1 Aug 1979 (SI 1979/809) |
| 16–18 | 1 Jan 1973 (SI 1972/1977) |
| 19 | 1 Aug 1979 (SI 1979/809) |
| 20 | 19 Dec 1975 (SI 1975/2156) |
| 21–23 | 1 Jan 1973 (SI 1972/1977) |
| 24 | 1 Oct 1974 (SI 1974/1194) |

**Merchant Shipping Act 1970 (c 36)**—*contd*

| | | |
|---|---|---|
| 25–35 | | 1 Jan 1973 (SI 1972/1977) |
| 36 | | *Never in force* (repealed) |
| 37–42 | | 1 Jan 1973 (SI 1972/1977) |
| 43–47 | | 19 Dec 1975 (SI 1975/2156) |
| 48 | | 1 Jan 1973 (SI 1972/1977) |
| 49 | | 19 Dec 1975 (SI 1975/2156) |
| 50 | | 1 Sep 1981 (SI 1981/1186) |
| 51 | | 1 May 1995 (SI 1995/965) |
| 52–54 | | 1 Jan 1983 (SI 1972/1977) |
| 55, 56 | | 1 Jul 1983 (SI 1972/1977) |
| 57 | | 1 Jan 1983 (to the extent it applies to an inquiry under ss 52, 54) (SI 1982/1617) |
| | | 1 Jul 1983 (otherwise) (SI 1982/1617) |
| 58 | | 1 Dec 1982 (SI 1982/1617) |
| 59 | | 1 Jan 1983 (to the extent it applies to an inquiry under ss 52, 54) (SI 1982/1617) |
| | | 1 Jul 1983 (otherwise) (SI 1982/1617) |
| 60 | | 1 Sep 1981 (SI 1981/1186) |
| 61–84 | | 1 Jan 1973 (SI 1972/1977) |
| 85, 86 | | 18 Nov 1974 (SI 1974/1908) |
| 87 | | *Never in force* (repealed) |
| 88–90 | | 1 Jan 1973 (SI 1972/1977) |
| 91 | | 16 Jul 1982 (SI 1982/840) |
| 92–94 | | 1 Jan 1973 (SI 1972/1977) |
| 95 | (1) | 1 Jan 1973 (SI 1972/1977) |
| | (2) | 1 Aug 1979 (SI 1979/809) |
| | (3) | *Never in force* (repealed) |
| | (4)–(6) | 1 Jan 1973 (SI 1972/1977) |
| 96–99 | | 1 Jan 1973 (SI 1972/1977) |
| 100 | | See Schs 3–5 below |
| 101 | | 1 Jan 1973 (SI 1972/1977) |
| Sch 1 | | 18 Nov 1974 (SI 1974/1908) |
| Sch 2 | Pt I, para 1 | 1 Jan 1973 (SI 1972/1977) |
| | Pt I, paras 2–5 | *Never in force* (repealed) |
| | Pt II | 1 Jan 1973 (SI 1972/1977) |
| Sch 3 | paras 1–4 | 1 Jan 1973 (SI 1972/1977) |
| | paras 5–7 | 1 Sep 1981 (SI 1981/1186) |
| | paras 8, 9 | 1 Jan 1973 (SI 1972/1977) |
| | para 10 | 18 Nov 1974 (SI 1974/1908) |
| | paras 11–13 | 1 Jan 1973 (SI 1972/1977) |
| | para 14 | 6 Apr 1974 (SI 1972/1977) |
| Sch 4 | paras 1–4 | 1 Jan 1973 (SI 1972/1977) |
| | paras 5–7 | *Never in force* (repealed) |
| | para 8 | 1 Jan 1983 (to the extent it applies to an inquiry) (SI 1982/1617) |
| | | 1 Jul 1983 (otherwise) (SI 1982/1617) |
| | para 9 | 1 Sep 1981 (SI 1981/1186) |
| | para 10 | *Never in force* (repealed) |
| Sch 5 | | 1 Jan 1973 (SI 1972/1977), so far as it relates to the following repeals— |

**Merchant Shipping Act 1970 (c 36)**—*contd*

Merchant Shipping Act 1894, in Pt I, s 85(3), the words "in the ship's official log book, and also", in Pt II, ss 105–109, 113–125, 127–156, 159–199, 201–206, 211–255, 257–266, in Pt III, ss 268–270, 271(3), 289–355, 356, para (a), 357, 358, 359(2), 360(1), (2), 361, 362, in s 363, the words "or emigrant ship", ss 364, 365 in Pt IV, in s 370 in the definition of "fishing boat", the words from "but" to "profit", ss 376–384, 387, 388, 391–412, Pt V, ss 423, 425, 426, 436(3), in s 458(1), the words from "and in every" to "on board any ship", in s 463, the words "or apprentice" wherever they occur, in Pt VI, s 477, in s 487(3) the words from "by the local marine board" to "board", and s 491, in Pt VIII, s 507, in Pt XIII, s 690, in Pt XIV, in s 714 the words "local marine boards and", s 725, in s 745(1)(b), the words "savings bank or", and Schs 7, 8;

Merchant Shipping Act 1906, ss 9, 12, 14, in s 16(1) the words "whether cabin or steerage passengers", ss 17–20, 23–26, 28–43, in s 44, in para (a) of sub-s (1), the words "in the case of a foreign-going ship" and the words from "before whom the offender is discharged" to "at which the crew are discharged", in para (b) of sub-s (1), the words "by whose sanction he is discharged" and in para (b) of sub-s (2), the words from "before whom the crew is discharged" to "the port at which the crew is discharged", ss 45–48, 57, 59–63, 65, 74, 82(1) and Sch 1;

Merchant Shipping (Seamen's Allotment) Act 1911;

Fees (Increase) Act 1923, s 2(1)(c);

Merchant Shipping Acts (Amendment) Act 1923;

Illegal Trawling (Scotland) Act 1934, in s 6 the words "mercantile marine office";

Merchant Shipping (Superannuation Contributions) Act 1937;

Sea Fish Industry Act 1938, Pt IV;

Emergency Laws (Transitional Provisions) Act 1946, in Sch 2, the entry relating to the Merchant Shipping Act 1894;

Emergency Laws (Miscellaneous Provisions) Act 1947, s 2(2);

Merchant Shipping Act 1948, s 7;

Consular Conventions Act 1949, s 5(1);

Merchant Shipping (Safety Conventions) Act 1949, ss 2(3), 18(5), 19(1)(d), 22(6), (7);

Merchant Shipping Act 1950, s 2, Sch 2;

Births and Deaths Registration Act 1953, s 13(3);

Emergency Laws (Miscellaneous Provisions) Act 1953, s 4;

Contracts of Employment Act 1963, s 6(2)(b);

Contracts of Employment and Redundancy Payments Act (Northern Ireland) 1965, s 6(1)(b);

Administration of Estates (Small Payments) Act 1965, in Sch 1, Pt I, the entry relating to the Merchant Shipping Act 1894;

Ministry of Social Security Act 1966, ss 37, 38(c) and the word "and" preceding that paragraph, Sch 5 and Sch 6, paras 1, 2;

Supplementary Benefits &c. Act (Northern Ireland) 1966, s 41 and Sch 4;

Births and Deaths Registration Act (Northern Ireland) 1967, s 28(5);

Merchant Shipping (Load Lines) Act 1967, in s 10(1), para (b) and the word "and" immediately preceding that paragraph, and in sub-s (2), para (a);

Children and Young Persons Act (Northern Ireland) 1968, Sch 7, paras 1, 2;

Post Office Act 1969, in Sch 6, Pt III the entry relating to the Merchant Shipping Act 1894, s 141;

6 Apr 1974 (repeal of Income and Corporation Taxes Act 1970, s 414(1)(c) and the word "or" before it, and the definition of "seamen's savings bank" in s 414(7)) (SI 1972/1977)

**Merchant Shipping Act 1970 (c 36)**—*contd*

1 Oct 1974 (repeal of Merchant Shipping Act 1894, s 200)
(SI 1974/1194)

18 Nov 1974 (repeal in Merchant Shipping (Safety Convention)
Act 1949, s 5(2)) (SI 1974/1908)

1 Jul 1979 (SI 1978/797), repeals of or in—
Merchant Shipping Act 1948, ss 1–4;
Merchant Shipping Act 1950, s 1, Sch 1;
Merchant Shipping Act 1952

1 Aug 1979 (SI 1979/809), repeals of or in—
Merchant Shipping Act 1894, ss 157, 158;
Merchant Shipping (International Labour Conventions)
Act 1925, s 1, Sch 1, Pt I

1 Sep 1981 (SI 1981/1186), so far as it relates to the following
repeals—
Merchant Shipping Act 1894, in Pt II, ss 92, 93, 96–104, 209,
except to the extent that those sections apply in relation to: (a)
fishing vessels by virtue of s 414 of that Act, or (b) British ships
registered outside the United Kingdom;
Merchant Shipping Act 1906, in Pt III, s 27 and in Pt V, ss 56,
64, except to the extent that ss 27, 56 apply in relation to
British ships registered outside the United Kingdom;
Merchant Shipping (Certificates) Act 1914;
Merchant Shipping Act 1948, ss 6, 8–12;
Merchant Shipping Act 1950, s 6;
Merchant Shipping Act 1967, the whole Act, except to the
extent that s 92(2) of the 1894 Act, as amended, applies in
relation to British ships registered outside the United Kingdom

16 Jul 1982 (repeal of Merchant Shipping Act 1894, ss 92, 93,
96–104, 209—all to the extent they apply in relation to British
ships registered in the Channel Islands or the Isle of Man)
(SI 1982/840)

1 Jan 1983 (SI 1982/1617), so far as it relates to the following
repeals except in relation to fishing vessels:
Merchant Shipping Act 1894, in Pt VI, ss 470 (to the extent that
it applies in relation to an inquiry), 471–474 (to the extent that
the said ss 473 and 474 apply in relation to a certificate
cancelled or suspended under the said 470 (to the extent that it
is now repealed)), 475 and 479 (to the extent that the said
ss 475 and 479 apply in relation to an inquiry into the conduct
of a master, mate or engineer under Pt VI of the Act of 1894);
Merchant Shipping Act 1906, in Pt V, ss 66 (to the extent that it
applies in relation to an inquiry under Part VI of the Merchant
Shipping Act 1894), 67 and 68;
Merchant Shipping Act 1950, s 3

1 Jul 1983 (SI 1982/1617), so far as it relates to the following
repeals except in relation to fishing vessels:
Merchant Shipping Act 1894, in Pt VI, ss 464–467, 470 (to the
extent that it applies in relation to a formal investigation) 473,
474 (to the extent that the said ss 473 and 474 apply in relation
to a certificate cancelled or suspended under the said s 470 so
far as it related to formal investigations) 475, 479 (to the extent
that the said ss 475 and 479 apply in relation to a formal
investigation into the conduct of a master, mate or engineer
under Pt VI of the Act of 1894) and 476;
Merchant Shipping Act 1906, in Pt V, s 66 (to the extent that it
applies in relation to a formal investigation under Pt VI of the
Merchant Shipping Act 1894)

1 Jan 1987 (repeals of Merchant Shipping Act 1894, ss 369, 385,
386, 390, 413, 415–417, 469) (SI 1986/2066)

1 Sep 1987 (SI 1986/2066), repeals of or in—

**Merchant Shipping Act 1970 (c 36)**—*contd*

> Merchant Shipping Act 1894, ss 92, 93, 96–104 (to the extent that those sections apply in relation to fishing vessels by virtue of s 414 of that Act), ss 209, 370 (definitions "second hand" and "voyage"), 371, 414, and ss 464–468, 470–476, 479 (so far as not already repealed);
>
> Merchant Shipping Act 1906, ss 66–68 (so far as not already repealed), and s 81
>
> 1 May 1995 (SI 1995/965), repeals of or in—
>
> Merchant Shipping Act 1894, Pt II (so far as unrepealed), ss 369, 413, 415–417, 676, 677, 721, 722, Schs 5, 6;
>
> Merchant Shipping Act 1906, s 56;
>
> Employment of Women, Young Persons and Children Act 1920, s 1;
>
> Merchant Shipping (International Labour Conventions) Act 1925;
>
> Merchant Shipping Act 1950, s 3 (so far as not already repealed);
> Merchant Shipping Act 1967
>
> 1 Aug 1995 (repeal of Aliens Restriction (Amendment) Act 1919, s 5) (SI 1995/1426)
>
> *Never in force* (remaining repeals or purposes) (repealed)

---

**National Health Service Contributions Act 1970 (c 16)**

*RA:* 15 May 1970

*Commencement provisions:* s 2(2); National Health Service Contributions Act 1970 (Commencement) Order 1970, SI 1970/808

Whole Act in force 6 Jul 1970 (SI 1970/808)

---

**National Insurance (Old persons' and widows' pensions and attendance allowance) Act 1970 (c 51)**

*RA:* 23 Jul 1970

*Commencement provisions:* s 10(2); National Insurance (Old persons' and widows' pensions and attendance allowance) Act 1970 (Commencement) Order 1970, SI 1970/1189

| | | |
|---|---|---|
| 1 | | 2 Nov 1970 (SI 1970/1189) |
| 2, 3 | | 5 Apr 1971 (SI 1970/1189) |
| 4 | | *Never in force* (repealed) |
| 5 | | 17 Aug 1970 (SI 1970/1189) |
| 6 | | *Never in force* (repealed) |
| 7 | | 17 Aug 1970 (SI 1970/1189) |
| 8 | (1)–(7) | 17 Aug 1970 (SI 1970/1189) |
| | (8) | 2 Nov 1970 (in the case of any benefit payable under or by virtue of s 1) (SI 1970/1189) |
| | | 5 Apr 1971 (in the case of any benefit payable by virtue of ss 2 or 9(2)(a)) |
| 9 | (1) | See Sch 2, Part I below |
| | (2) | 17 Aug 1970 (SI 1970/1189) |
| | (3) | See Sch 2, Part II below |
| 10 | | 17 Aug 1970 (SI 1970/1189) |
| Sch 1 | | *Never in force* (repealed) |
| Sch 2 | Pt I, paras 1, 2 | 17 Aug 1970 (SI 1970/1189) |
| | Pt I, para 3 | 5 Apr 1971 (SI 1970/1189) |
| | Pt I, para 4 | 2 Nov 1970 (SI 1970/1189) |
| | Pt I, paras 5–7 | *Never in force* (repealed) |
| | Pt I, para 8 | 2 Nov 1970 (SI 1970/1189) |
| | Pt I, para 9 | *Never in force* (repealed) |

**National Insurance (Old persons' and widows' pensions and attendance allowance) Act 1970 (c 51)**—*contd*

| | |
|---|---|
| Pt I, para 10 | 2 Nov 1970 (SI 1970/1189) |
| Pt I, paras 11–13 | *Never in force* (repealed) |
| Pt II | 5 Apr 1971 (SI 1970/1189) repeals of or in National Insurance Act 1965, ss 28, 32 |
| | 17 Aug 1970 (otherwise) (SI 1970/1189) |

**New Forest Act 1970 (c 21)**

*RA:* 15 May 1970

Whole Act in force 15 May 1970 (RA)

**Parish Councils and Burial Authorities (Miscellaneous Provisions) Act 1970 (c 29)**

*RA:* 29 May 1970

Whole Act in force 29 May 1970 (RA)

**Proceedings Against Estates Act 1970 (c 17)**

*RA:* 15 May 1970

*Commencement provisions:* s 3(2); Proceedings Against Estates Act 1970 (Commencement) Order 1970, SI 1970/1860

Whole Act in force 1 Jan 1971 (SI 1970/1860)

**Radiological Protection Act 1970 (c 46)**

*RA:* 29 May 1970

*Commencement provisions:* s 7(2)

Whole Act in force 1 Oct 1970 (s 7(2))

**Republic of The Gambia Act 1970 (c 37)**

*RA:* 29 May 1970

Whole Act in force 29 May 1970 (RA); note that by s 1(3), s 1 was deemed to have effect from 24 Apr 1970, the day The Gambia became a republic

**Riding Establishments Act 1970 (c 32)**

*RA:* 29 May 1970

*Commencement provisions:* s 8(3)

Whole Act in force 1 Jan 1971 (s 8(3))

**Road Traffic (Disqualification) Act 1970 (c 23)**

*RA:* 15 May 1970

*Commencement provisions:* s 3(2)

**Road Traffic (Disqualification) Act 1970 (c 23)**—*contd*
Whole Act in force 15 Jul 1970 (s 3(2))

**Roads (Scotland) Act 1970 (c 20)**

*RA:* 15 May 1970

*Commencement provisions:* s 52(2)

Whole Act in force 15 Jun 1970 (s 52(2))

**Rural Water Supplies and Sewerage (Scotland) Act 1970 (c 6)**

*RA:* 26 Feb 1970

Whole Act in force 26 Feb 1970 (RA)

**Sea Fish Industry Act 1970 (c 11)**

*RA:* 12 Mar 1970

*Commencement provisions:* s 62(2), (3)

Whole Act in force 12 May 1970 (s 62(2)), except Sch 6, Pt I, repeals of or in Sea Fish Industry Act 1962, s 33(b), (c) (never in force, repealed) (s 62(3))

**Sharing of Church Buildings Measure 1970 (No 2)**

*RA:* 24 Mar 1970

Whole Measure in force 24 Mar 1970 (RA)

**Taxes Management Act 1970 (c 9)**

*RA:* 12 Mar 1970

*Commencement provisions:* s 119(1)

Whole Act in force 6 Apr 1970 (s 119(1))

**Tonga Act 1970 (c 22)**

*RA:* 15 May 1970

Whole Act in force 15 May 1970 (RA); but note that s 1(2)–(4) had effect from 4 Jun 1970 (Independence Day (s 1(1)))

**Town and Country Planning Regulations (London) (Indemnity) Act 1970 (c 57)**

*RA:* 17 Dec 1970

Whole Act in force 17 Dec 1970 (RA)

**Trees Act 1970 (c 43)**

*RA:* 29 May 1970

Whole Act in force 29 May 1970 (RA)

---

**Valuation for Rating (Scotland) Act 1970 (c 4)**

*RA:* 26 Feb 1970

Whole Act in force 26 Feb 1970 (RA)

---

# 1971 Acts

## Administration of Estates Act 1971 (c 25)

*RA:* 12 May 1971

*Commencement provisions:* s 14(2)

| | |
|---|---|
| 1–12 | 1 Jan 1972 (s 14(2)) |
| 13, 14 | 12 May 1971 (s 14(2)) |
| Schs 1, 2 | 1 Jan 1972 (s 14(2)) |

## Air Corporations Act 1971 (c 5)

*RA:* 17 Feb 1971

Whole Act in force 17 Feb 1971 (RA)

## Anguilla Act 1971 (c 63)

*RA:* 27 Jul 1971

Whole Act in force 27 Jul 1971 (RA)

## Animals Act 1971 (c 22)

*RA:* 12 May 1971

*Commencement provisions:* s 13(3)

Whole Act in force 1 Oct 1971 (s 13(3))

## Appropriation Act 1971 (c 67)

*RA:* 5 Aug 1971

Whole Act in force 5 Aug 1971 (RA)

## Armed Forces Act 1971 (c 33)

*RA:* 27 May 1971

*Commencement provisions:* s 78(3); Armed Forces Act 1971 (Commencement) Order 1972, SI 1972/359

| | |
|---|---|
| 1 | 27 May 1971 (RA) |
| 2–77 | 1 Jul 1972 (SI 1972/359) |
| 78 | 27 May 1971 (RA) |
| Schs 1–4 | 1 Jul 1972 (SI 1972/359) |

### Atomic Energy Authority Act 1971 (c 11)

*RA:* 16 Mar 1971

Whole Act in force 16 Mar 1971 (RA)

---

### Attachment of Earnings Act 1971 (c 32)

*RA:* 12 May 1971

*Commencement provisions:* s 29(4) (which provides that the Act is to come into force on the day appointed under Administration of Justice Act 1970, s 54, for the coming into force of Pt II of that Act); Administration of Justice Act 1970 (Commencement No 4) Order 1971, SI 1971/834 (made under Administration of Justice Act 1970, s 54)

Whole Act in force 2 Aug 1971 (SI 1971/834)

---

### Banking and Financial Dealings Act 1971 (c 80)

*RA:* 16 Dec 1971

*Commencement provisions:* s 3(3)

| | |
|---|---|
| 1, 2 | 16 Dec 1971 (RA) |
| 3 | 16 Jan 1972 (s 3(3)) |
| 4, 5 | 16 Dec 1971 (RA) |
| Schs 1, 2 | 16 Dec 1971 (RA) |

---

### Betting, Gaming and Lotteries (Amendment) Act 1971 (c 26)

*RA:* 12 May 1971

*Commencement provisions:* s 5(2)

Whole Act in force 1 Jul 1972 (s 5(2))

---

### Carriage of Goods by Sea Act 1971 (c 19)

*RA:* 8 Apr 1971

*Commencement provisions:* s 6(5); Carriage of Goods by Sea Act 1971 (Commencement) Order 1977, SI 1977/981

Whole Act in force 23 Jun 1977 (SI 1977/981)

---

### Civil Aviation Act 1971 (c 75)

*RA:* 5 Aug 1971

*Commencement provisions:* s 70(2); Civil Aviation Act 1971 (Commencement No 1) Order 1971, SI 1971/1573; Civil Aviation Act 1971 (Commencement No 2) Order 1971, SI 1971/1636; Civil Aviation Act 1971 (Commencement No 3) Order 1971, SI 1971/1992; Civil Aviation Act 1971 (Commencement No 4) Order 1972, SI 1972/138; Civil Aviation Act 1971 (Commencement No 5) Order 1976, SI 1976/1593

| | | |
|---|---|---|
| 1–20 | | 20 Dec 1971 (SI 1971/1992) |
| 21 | (1) | 1 Apr 1972 (SI 1972/138) |
| | (2) | 20 Dec 1971 (for the purpose of making instruments) (SI 1971/1992) |
| | | 1 Apr 1972 (otherwise) (SI 1972/138) |
| | (3) | 20 Dec 1971 (SI 1971/1992) |
| | (4)–(8) | 1 Apr 1972 (SI 1972/138) |

**Civil Aviation Act 1971 (c 75)**—*contd*

| | | |
|---|---|---|
| 22 | (1) | 20 Dec 1971 (for the purpose of publishing notices and making regulations) (SI 1971/1992) |
| | | 1 Apr 1972 (otherwise) (SI 1972/138) |
| | (2)–(5) | 1 Apr 1972 (SI 1972/138) |
| | (6) | 20 Dec 1971 (for the purpose of publishing notices and making regulations) (SI 1971/1992) |
| | | 1 Apr 1972 (otherwise) (SI 1972/138) |
| | (7) | 20 Dec 1971 (SI 1971/1992) |
| 23 | (1) | 20 Dec 1971 (for the purpose of making regulations) (SI 1971/1992) |
| | | 1 Apr 1972 (otherwise) (SI 1972/138) |
| | (2), (3) | 1 Apr 1972 (SI 1972/138) |
| | (4) | 20 Dec 1971 (for the purpose of making regulations) (SI 1971/1992) |
| | | 1 Apr 1972 (otherwise) (SI 1972/138) |
| | (5) | 1 Apr 1972 (SI 1972/138) |
| 24 | (1) | 20 Dec 1971 (for the purpose of making regulations) (SI 1971/1992) |
| | | 1 Apr 1972 (otherwise) (SI 1972/138) |
| | (2) | 1 Apr 1972 (SI 1972/138) |
| | (3) | 20 Dec 1971 (for the purpose of making regulations) (SI 1971/1992) |
| | | 1 Apr 1972 (otherwise) (SI 1972/138) |
| | (4), (5) | 1 Apr 1972 (SI 1972/138) |
| | (6) | 20 Dec 1971 (for the purpose of making regulations) (SI 1971/1992) |
| | | 1 Apr 1972 (otherwise) (SI 1972/138) |
| | (7) | 1 Apr 1972 (SI 1972/138) |
| 25 | | 1 Apr 1972 (SI 1972/138) |
| 26 | | 20 Dec 1971 (SI 1971/1992) |
| 27 | (1) | 1 Apr 1972 (SI 1972/138) |
| | (2) | 20 Dec 1971 (for the purpose of making regulations) (SI 1971/1992) |
| | | 1 Apr 1972 (otherwise) (SI 1972/138) |
| | (3)–(5) | 20 Dec 1971 (SI 1971/1992) |
| 28 | (1) | 1 Apr 1972 (SI 1972/138) |
| | (2) | 20 Dec 1971 (for the purpose of giving a direction) (SI 1971/1992) |
| | | 1 Apr 1972 (otherwise) (SI 1972/138) |
| | (3) | 1 Apr 1972 (SI 1972/138) |
| 29 | | 1 Nov 1971 (SI 1971/1573) |
| 30 | | 1 Apr 1972 (SI 1972/138) |
| 31–36 | | 20 Dec 1971 (SI 1971/1992) |
| 37 | | 7 Oct 1971 (SI 1971/1636) |
| 38 | (1)(a)–(e) | 1 Apr 1972 (SI 1972/138) |
| | (1)(f) | 7 Oct 1971 (SI 1971/1636) |
| | (2) | 1 Apr 1972 (SI 1972/138) |
| 39, 40 | | 1 Apr 1972 (SI 1972/138) |
| 41 | (1) | 7 Oct 1971 (SI 1971/1636) |
| | (2), (3) | 1 Apr 1972 (SI 1972/138) |
| | (4), (5) | 7 Oct 1971 (SI 1971/1636) |
| 42–52 | | 1 Apr 1972 (SI 1972/138) |
| 53 | (1)(a) | 7 Oct 1971 (SI 1971/1636) |
| | (1)(b) | 1 Apr 1972 (SI 1972/138) |
| | (2), (3) | 1 Apr 1972 (SI 1972/138) |
| 54–60 | | 1 Apr 1972 (SI 1972/138) |
| 61 | | 20 Dec 1971 (SI 1971/1992) |
| 62 | (1) | 1 Apr 1972 (SI 1972/138) |
| | (2)–(5) | 20 Dec 1971 (SI 1971/1992) |

**Civil Aviation Act 1971 (c 75)**—*contd*

| | | |
|---|---|---|
| 63–68 | | 20 Dec 1971 (SI 1971/1992) |
| 69 | (1) | See Sch 10 below |
| | (2) | See Sch 11 below |
| 70 | | 5 Aug 1971 (RA) |
| Schs 1–3 | | 20 Dec 1971 (SI 1971/1992) |
| Sch 4 | | 1 Apr 1972 (SI 1972/138) |
| Schs 5–7 | | 20 Dec 1971 (SI 1971/1992) |
| Sch 8 | | 7 Oct 1971 (SI 1971/1636) |
| Sch 9 | | 20 Dec 1971 (SI 1971/1992) |
| Sch 10 | para 1 | 20 Dec 1971 (SI 1971/1992) |
| | para 2 | 1 Apr 1972 (SI 1972/138) |
| | para 3 | 1 Oct 1971 (SI 1971/1573) |
| | para 4 | 20 Dec 1971 (SI 1971/1992) |
| | para 5 | 1 Apr 1972 (SI 1972/138) |
| | paras 6, 7 | 1 Oct 1971 (except so far as they relate to the Civil Aviation Authority) (SI 1971/1573) |
| | | 20 Dec 1971 (exception noted above) (SI 1971/1992) |
| | paras 8–10 | 1 Oct 1971 (SI 1971/1573) |
| | para 11 | 1 Nov 1971 (SI 1971/1573) |
| | para 12 | 1 Oct 1971 (SI 1971/1573) |
| | paras 13–15 | 20 Dec 1971 (SI 1971/1992) |
| | para 16 | 1 Apr 1972 (except so far as it amends Air Corporations Act 1967, s 8(6)) (SI 1972/138) |
| | | *Never in force* (otherwise) (repealed) |
| | paras 17–24 | 1 Apr 1972 (SI 1972/138) |
| | paras 25–27 | 1 Oct 1971 (SI 1971/1573) |
| Sch 11 | | 1 Apr 1972 (except repeal of or in the Air Corporations Act 1967, s 8(6)) (SI 1972/138) |
| | | 26 Oct 1976 (exception noted above) (SI 1976/1593) |

---

**Civil Aviation (Declaratory Provisions) Act 1971 (c 6)**

*RA:* 17 Feb 1971

Whole Act in force 17 Feb 1971 (RA)

---

**Coal Industry Act 1971 (c 16)**

*RA:* 30 Mar 1971

Whole Act in force 30 Mar 1971 (RA)

---

**Coinage Act 1971 (c 24)**

*RA:* 12 May 1971

*Commencement provisions:* s 14(2)

Whole Act in force 1 Sep 1971 (s 14(2))

---

**Consolidated Fund Act 1971 (c 1)**

*RA:* 17 Feb 1971

Whole Act in force 17 Feb 1971 (RA)

---

## Consolidated Fund (No 2) Act 1971 (c 14)

*RA:* 30 Mar 1971

Whole Act in force 30 Mar 1971 (RA)

---

## Consolidated Fund (No 3) Act 1971 (c 79)

*RA:* 16 Dec 1971

Whole Act in force 16 Dec 1971 (RA)

---

## Consumer Protection Act 1971 (c 15)

*RA:* 30 Mar 1971

*Commencement provisions:* s 2(2)

Whole Act in force 30 Apr 1971 (s 2(2))

---

## Copyright (Amendment) Act 1971 (c 4)

*RA:* 17 Feb 1971

Whole Act in force 17 Feb 1971 (RA)

---

## Courts Act 1971 (c 23)

*RA:* 12 May 1971

*Commencement provisions:* s 59(2); Courts Act 1971 (Commencement) Order 1971, SI 1971/1151

| | | |
|---|---|---|
| 1–19 | | 1 Jan 1972 (SI 1971/1151) |
| 20 | (1), (2) | 1 Jan 1972 (SI 1971/1151) |
| | (3) | 1 Oct 1971 (in so far as it relates to judges of the Court of Appeal and of the High Court) (SI 1971/1151) |
| | | 1 Jan 1972 (otherwise) (SI 1971/1151) |
| | (4)–(7) | 1 Jan 1972 (SI 1971/1151) |
| 21–38 | | 1 Jan 1972 (SI 1971/1151) |
| 39 | | 1 Oct 1971 (SI 1971/1151) |
| 40–45 | | 1 Jan 1972 (SI 1971/1151) |
| 46 | | 1 Oct 1971 (SI 1971/1151) |
| 47–55 | | 1 Jan 1972 (SI 1971/1151) |
| 56 | (1) | See Sch 8 below |
| | (2), (3) | 1 Jan 1972 (SI 1972/1151) |
| | (4) | See Sch 11 below |
| 57 | | 1 Jan 1972 (SI 1971/1151) |
| 58, 59 | | 1 Oct 1971 (SI 1971/1151) |
| Schs 1–7 | | 1 Jan 1972 (SI 1971/1151) |
| Sch 8 | paras 1–17 | 1 Jan 1972 (SI 1971/1151) |
| | para 18(1), (2) | 1 Jan 1972 (SI 1971/1151) |
| | para 18(3) | 1 Oct 1971 (SI 1971/1151) |
| | para 18(4)–(6) | 1 Jan 1972 (SI 1971/1151) |
| | paras 19–33 | 1 Jan 1972 (SI 1971/1151) |
| | para 34(1) | 1 Jan 1972 (SI 1971/1151) |
| | para 34(2) | 1 Oct 1971 (SI 1971/1151) |
| | para 34(3), (4) | 1 Jan 1972 (SI 1971/1151) |
| | paras 35–45 | 1 Jan 1972 (SI 1971/1151) |
| | para 46 | 1 Oct 1971 (SI 1971/1151) |
| | paras 47–60 | 1 Jan 1972 (SI 1971/1151) |

**Courts Act 1971 (c 23)**—*contd*

| | | |
|---|---|---|
| Schs 9, 10 | | 1 Jan 1972 (SI 1971/1151) |
| Sch 11 | Pt I | 1 Oct 1971 (repeal of County Courts Act 1959, s 96(3)) (SI 1971/1151) |
| | | 1 Jan 1972 (otherwise) (SI 1971/1151) |
| | Pts II, III | 1 Jan 1972 (SI 1971/1151) |
| | Pt IV | 1 Oct 1971 (SI 1971/1151), repeals of or in— Magistrates' Courts Act 1952, s 1(4); Criminal Appeal Act 1966, s 1(3) |
| | | 1 Jan 1972 (otherwise) (SI 1971/1151) |

**Criminal Damage Act 1971 (c 48)**

*RA:* 14 Jul 1971

*Commencement provisions:* s 12(1)

Whole Act in force 14 Oct 1971 (s 12(1))

**Dangerous Litter Act 1971 (c 35)**

*RA:* 27 May 1971

*Commencement provisions:* s 3(3)

Whole Act in force 27 Jun 1971 (s 3(3))

**Diplomatic and other Privileges Act 1971 (c 64)**

*RA:* 27 Jul 1971

*Commencement provisions:* s 4(2)★; Commonwealth Countries and Republic of Ireland (Immunities and Privileges) Order 1971, SI 1971/1237

| | | |
|---|---|---|
| 1–3 | | 27 Jul 1971 (RA) |
| 4 | (1) | 27 Jul 1971 (RA) |
| | (2)★ | 1 Sep 1971 (SI 1971/1237) |
| Schedule | | 27 Jul 1971 (RA) |

★ SI 1971/1237 was made under Consular Relations Act 1968, s 12, as inserted by the Schedule to this Act

**Education (Milk) Act 1971 (c 74)**

*RA:* 5 Aug 1971

Whole Act in force 5 Aug 1971 (RA)

**Education (Scotland) Act 1971 (c 42)**

*RA:* 1 Jul 1971

*Commencement provisions:* s 4(5)

Whole Act in force 1 Aug 1971 (s 4(5); except s 4(1), (2), (4), which came into force on 1 Jul 1971)

**Finance Act 1971 (c 68)**

*RA:* 5 Aug 1971

The commencement details of Finance Acts are not set out, as the dates from which their provisions take effect are usually stated clearly and unambiguously in the text of the Act, and charging provisions will normally state for which year or years of assessment they are to have effect.

---

**Fire Precautions Act 1971 (c 40)**

*RA:* 27 May 1971

*Commencement provisions:* s 44(3); Fire Precautions Act 1971 (Commencement No 1) Order 1972, SI 1972/236; Fire Precautions Act 1971 (Commencement No 2) Order 1976, SI 1976/2006

| | | |
|---|---|---|
| 1, 2 | | 20 Mar 1972 (SI 1972/236) |
| 3, 4 | | *Never in force* (repealed) |
| 5–11 | | 20 Mar 1972 (SI 1972/236) |
| 12 | (1) | 1 Jan 1977 (SI 1976/2006) |
| | (2) | *Never in force* (repealed) |
| | (3)–(8) | 1 Jan 1977 (SI 1976/2006) |
| | (9) | *Never in force* (repealed) |
| | (10) | 1 Jan 1977 (SI 1976/2006) |
| | (11), (12) | *Never in force* (repealed) |
| 13, 14 | | 20 Mar 1972 (SI 1972/236) |
| 15 | | 9 Sep 1971 (SI 1971/1423) |
| 16 | (1)(a) | 20 Mar 1972 (SI 1972/236) |
| | (1)(b) | *Never in force* (repealed) |
| | (2)(a) | 20 Mar 1972 (SI 1972/236) |
| | (2)(b) | *Never in force* (repealed) |
| | (3) | 20 Mar 1972 (SI 1972/236) |
| 17, 18 | | 20 Mar 1972 (SI 1972/236) |
| 19 | (1), (2) | 20 Mar 1972 (SI 1972/236) |
| | (3)(a), (b) | 20 Mar 1972 (SI 1972/236) |
| | (3)(c) | *Never in force* (repealed) |
| | (3)(d) | 20 Mar 1972 (SI 1972/236) |
| | (4)–(6) | 20 Mar 1972 (SI 1972/236) |
| 20–27 | | 20 Mar 1972 (SI 1972/236) |
| 28 | | 1 Jan 1977 (SI 1976/2006) |
| 29–33 | | 20 Mar 1972 (SI 1972/236) |
| 34 | | *Never in force* (repealed) |
| 35 | | 20 Mar 1972 (SI 1972/236) |
| 36 | | *Never in force* (repealed) |
| 37–39 | | 20 Mar 1972 (SI 1972/236) |
| 40 | | 20 Mar 1972 (except so far as it relates to ss 3, 4, 12 of this Act) (SI 1972/236) |
| | | 1 Jan 1977 (otherwise, except so far as it relates to ss 3, 4, 12(2), (9)) (SI 1976/2006) |
| | | *Never in force* (exception noted above) (repealed) |
| 41–44 | | 20 Mar 1972 (SI 1972/236) |
| Schedule | | *Never in force* (repealed) |

---

**Friendly Societies Act 1971 (c 66)**

*RA:* 27 Jul 1971

*Commencement provisions:* s 15(6); Friendly Societies Act 1971 (Commencement) Order 1971, SI 1971/1899

Whole Act in force 31 Dec 1971 (SI 1971/1899)

---

## Guardianship of Minors Act 1971 (c 3)

*RA:* 17 Feb 1971

*Commencement provisions:* s 20(5)

Whole Act in force 17 Mar 1971 (s 20(5))

---

## Highways Act 1971 (c 41)

*RA:* 1 Jul 1971

*Commencement provisions*: s 87(3), Highways Act 1971 (Commencement No 1) Order 1971, SI 1971/1705; Highways Act 1971 (Commencement No 2) Order 1971, SI 1971/2003; Highways Act 1971 (Commencement No 3) Order 1973, SI 1973/685; Highways Act 1971 (Commencement No 4) Order 1977, SI 1977/2003

| | | |
|---|---|---|
| 1–13 | | 1 Nov 1971 (SI 1971/1705) |
| 14 | (1)–(9) | 1 Nov 1971 (SI 1971/1705) |
| | (10) | 4 Jan 1978 (SI 1977/2003) |
| 15–17 | | 1 Nov 1971 (SI 1971/1705) |
| 18 | | 7 May 1973 (SI 1973/685) |
| 19–30 | | 1 Nov 1971 (SI 1971/1705) |
| 31, 32 | | 17 Jan 1972 (SI 1971/2003) |
| 33–39 | | 1 Nov 1971 (SI 1971/1705) |
| 40–43 | | 17 Jan 1972 (SI 1971/2003) |
| 44–52 | | 1 Nov 1971 (SI 1971/1705) |
| 53 | (1)–(3) | 1 Nov 1971 (SI 1971/1705) |
| | (4) | 4 Jan 1978 (SI 1977/2003) |
| 54–85 | | 1 Nov 1971 (SI 1971/1705) |
| 86 | (1) | See Sch 11 below |
| | (2) | See Sch 12 below |
| | (3) | 1 Nov 1971 (SI 1971/1705) |
| Schs 1, 2 | | 1 Nov 1971 (SI 1971/1705) |
| Sch 3 | | 17 Jan 1972 (SI 1971/2003) |
| Schs 4–10 | | 1 Nov 1971 (SI 1971/1705) |
| Sch 11 | paras 1–4 | 1 Nov 1971 (SI 1971/1705) |
| | para 5 | 17 Jan 1972 (SI 1971/2003) |
| | paras 6–8 | 1 Nov 1971 (SI 1971/1705) |
| Sch 12 | | 1 Nov 1971 (SI 1971/1705), repeals of or in— |
| | | Highways Act 1959, ss 13, 76, 100, 103, 104, 137, 139, 214, 215, 235, 254, 266, 284(5), 292, 300, 308, Schs 1, 3; |
| | | Criminal Justice Act 1967; |
| | | Countryside Act 1968; |
| | | Post Office Act 1969 |
| | | 17 Jan 1972 (SI 1971/2003), repeals of or in— |
| | | Highways Act 1959, s 155, Schs 6, 18; |
| | | Local Government Act 1963 |
| | | 4 Jan 1978 (repeals of or in the Highways Act 1959, s 284(2), (3)(a), (b), (4)(a), (b)) (SI 1977/2003) |
| Sch 13 | | 1 Nov 1971 (SI 1971/1705) |

---

## Hijacking Act 1971 (c 70)

*RA:* 5 Aug 1971

*Commencement provisions:* s 7(2); Hijacking Act 1971 (Commencement) Order 1971, SI 1971/1734

Whole Act in force 27 Oct 1971 (SI 1971/1734)

---

## Hospital Endowments (Scotland) Act 1971 (c 8)

*RA:* 17 Feb 1971

Whole Act in force 17 Feb 1971 (RA)

---

## Housing Act 1971 (c 76)

*RA:* 5 Aug 1971

Whole Act in force 5 Aug 1971 (RA)

---

## Hydrocarbon Oil (Customs and Excise) Act 1971 (c 12)

*RA:* 16 Mar 1971

*Commencement provisions:* s 25(2)

Whole Act in force 12 Apr 1971 (s 25(2))

---

## Immigration Act 1971 (c 77)

*RA:* 28 Oct 1971

*Commencement provisions:* ss 34(1), 35(1)–(3); Immigration Act 1971 (Commencement) Order 1972, SI 1972/1514

| | | |
|---|---|---|
| 1–24 | | 1 Jan 1973 (SI 1972/1514) |
| 25 | (1) | 28 Nov 1971 (s 35(2)) |
| | (2) | 1 Jan 1973 (SI 1972/1514) |
| | (3)–(8) | 28 Nov 1971 (s 35(2)) |
| 26, 27 | | 1 Jan 1973 (SI 1972/1514) |
| 28 | (1), (2) | 28 Oct 1971 (as it relates to Commonwealth Immigrants Act 1962, s 4A) (s 35(3)) |
| | | 28 Nov 1971 (as it relates to s 25(1) of this Act) (s 35(2)) |
| | | 1 Jan 1973 (otherwise) (SI 1972/1514) |
| 29–37 | | 28 Oct 1971 (RA) |
| Schs 1–5 | | 1 Jan 1973 (SI 1972/1514) |
| Sch 6 | | 28 Oct 1971 (s 34(1)) |

---

## Industrial Relations Act 1971 (c 72)

*RA:* 5 Aug 1971

*Commencement provisions:* s 170(2); Industrial Relations Act 1971 (Commencement No 1) Order 1971, SI 1971/1522[1]; Industrial Relations Act 1971 (Commencement No 2) Order 1971, SI 1971/1682; Industrial Relations Act 1971 (Commencement No 3) Order 1971, SI 1971/1761[3]; Industrial Relations Act 1971 (Commencement No 4) Order 1972, SI 1972/36[4]

| | | |
|---|---|---|
| 1–4 | | 1 Oct 1971 (SI 1971/1522) |
| 5–7 | | 28 Feb 1972 (SI 1972/36) |
| 8, 9 | | 1 Dec 1971 (SI 1971/1761) |
| 10 | | 28 Feb 1972 (SI 1972/36) |
| 11–18 | | 1 Dec 1971 (SI 1971/1761) |
| 19–30 | | 28 Feb 1972 (SI 1972/36) |
| 31, 32 | | 1 Dec 1971 (SI 1971/1761) |
| 33 | (1) | 28 Feb 1972 (SI 1972/36) |
| | (2) | 1 Dec 1971 (SI 1971/1761) |
| | (3)(a)–(c) | 28 Feb 1972 (SI 1972/36) |
| | (3)(d) | 1 Dec 1971 (SI 1971/1761) |
| | (4) | 1 Oct 1971 (SI 1971/1522) |

**Industrial Relations Act 1971 (c 72)**—*contd*

| | | |
|---|---|---|
| 34 | | 1 Dec 1971 (SI 1971/1761) |
| 35 | (1) | 1 Oct 1971 (so far as necessary for the purposes of s 135) (SI 1971/1522) |
| | | 1 Dec 1971 (otherwise) (SI 1971/1761) |
| | (2)–(5) | 1 Dec 1971 (SI 1971/1761) |
| 36–55 | | 1 Dec 1971 (SI 1971/1761) |
| 56–57 | | *Never in force* (repealed) |
| 58–60 | | 1 Dec 1971 (SI 1971/1761) |
| 61–65 | | 1 Oct 1971 (SI 1971/1522) |
| 66 | | 28 Feb 1972 (SI 1972/36) |
| 67–69 | | 1 Oct 1971 (SI 1971/1522) |
| 70 | | 28 Feb 1972 (SI 1972/36) |
| 71–75 | | 1 Oct 1971 (SI 1971/1522) |
| 76, 77 | | 1 Dec 1971 (SI 1971/1761) |
| 78–80 | | 1 Oct 1971 (SI 1971/1522) |
| 81–83 | | 28 Feb 1972 (SI 1972/36) |
| 84–95 | | 1 Oct 1971 (SI 1971/1522) |
| 96–98 | | 28 Feb 1972 (SI 1972/36) |
| 99 | | 1 Oct 1971 (SI 1971/1522) |
| 100 | (1) | 28 Feb 1972 (SI 1972/36) |
| | (2), (3) | 1 Dec 1971 (SI 1971/1761) |
| 101 | | 1 Dec 1971 (SI 1971/1761) |
| 102 | (1)(a) | 1 Dec 1971 (SI 1971/1761) |
| | (1)(b) | *Never in force* (repealed) |
| | (2)(a), (b) | 1 Dec 1971 (SI 1971/1761) |
| | (2)(c) | *Never in force* (repealed) |
| 103, 104 | | 28 Feb 1972 (SI 1972/36) |
| 105 | | 1 Dec 1971 (SI 1971/1761) |
| 106–109 | | 28 Feb 1972 (SI 1972/36) |
| 110 | | *Never in force* (repealed) |
| 111 | | 28 Feb 1972 (SI 1972/36) |
| 112 | | 1 Dec 1971 (SI 1971/1761) |
| 113 | | *Never in force* (repealed) |
| 114 | | 1 Oct 1971 (SI 1971/1522) |
| 115–117 | | 1 Dec 1971 (SI 1971/1761) |
| 118, 119 | | 28 Feb 1972 (SI 1972/36) |
| 120 | | 1 Nov 1971 (SI 1971/1682) |
| 121 | (1) | 1 Nov 1971 (SI 1971/1682)[2] |
| | (2), (3) | 1 Nov 1971 (SI 1971/1682) |
| 122 | | 1 Nov 1971 (SI 1971/1682) |
| 123 | | 28 Feb 1972 (SI 1972/36) |
| 124, 125 | | 1 Dec 1971 (SI 1971/1761) |
| 126 | | *Never in force* (repealed) |
| 127 | | 1 Dec 1971 (so far as relates to s 125) (SI 1971/1761) |
| | | *Never in force* (otherwise) (repealed) |
| 128 | | 28 Feb 1972 (SI 1972/36) |
| 129 | | 1 Dec 1971 (SI 1971/1761) |
| 130 | (1), (2) | *Never in force* (repealed) |
| | (3) | 28 Feb 1972 (SI 1972/36) |
| 131–134 | | 28 Feb 1972 (SI 1972/36) |
| 135 | | 1 Oct 1971 (SI 1971/1522) |
| 136 | (a) | 28 Feb 1972 (SI 1972/36) |
| | (b) | 1 Dec 1971 (SI 1971/1761) |
| 137 | | 28 Feb 1972 (SI 1972/36) |
| 138–145 | | 1 Dec 1971 (SI 1971/1761) |
| 146–149 | | 28 Feb 1972 (SI 1972/36) |
| 150 | | 1 Nov 1971 (SI 1971/1682) |
| 151, 152 | | 28 Feb 1972 (SI 1972/36) |
| 153, 154 | | 1 Oct 1971 (SI 1971/1522) |

**Industrial Relations Act 1971 (c 72)**—*contd*

| | | |
|---|---|---|
| 155 | | 1 Nov 1971 (SI 1971/1682) |
| 156, 157 | | 1 Oct 1971 (SI 1971/1522) |
| 158 | (1) | 1 Oct 1971 (so far as necessary for the purposes of Pt I) (SI 1971/1522) |
| | | 1 Dec 1971 (otherwise) (SI 1971/1761) |
| | (2) | 1 Oct 1971 (SI 1971/1522) |
| | (3), (4) | 1 Dec 1971 (SI 1971/1761) |
| 159–162 | | 1 Dec 1971 (SI 1971/1761) |
| 163, 164 | | 1 Oct 1971 (SI 1971/1522) |
| 165 | | 1 Nov 1971 (SI 1971/1682) |
| 166 | | 1 Oct 1971 (SI 1971/1522) |
| 167 | | 1 Oct 1971 (except for the definitions "agency shop agreement", "bargaining unit", "the Commission", "conciliation officer", "dismiss", "dismissal", "industrial tribunal regulations", "joint negotiating panel", "joint negotiating panel of trade unions", "negotiating rights" and "sole bargaining agent") (SI 1971/1522) |
| | | 1 Nov 1971 (in so far as it refers to "the Commission") (SI 1971/1682) |
| | | 1 Dec 1971 (otherwise) (SI 1971/1761) |
| 168–170 | | 1 Oct 1971 (SI 1971/1522) |
| Sch 1 | | 1 Dec 1971 (SI 1971/1761) |
| Sch 2 | | 28 Feb 1972 (SI 1972/36) |
| Sch 3 | Pts I, II | 1 Oct 1971 (SI 1971/1522) |
| | Pt III | 1 Nov 1971 (SI 1971/1682) |
| | Pt IV | 1 Nov 1971 (in so far as its provisions relate to the Commission and to members, officers and servants of the Commission) (SI 1971/1682) |
| | | 1 Dec 1971 (in so far as para 43 is not already in force) (SI 1971/1761) |
| | | 28 Feb 1972 (otherwise) (SI 1972/36) |
| | Pt V | 1 Oct 1971 (in so far as its provisions relate to the Chief Registrar, assistant registrars and other officers and servants of the Chief Registrar, and to the Industrial Court and officers and servants of the Industrial Court) (SI 1971/1522) |
| | | 1 Nov 1971 (in so far as its provisions relate to the Commission and to members, officers and servants of the Commission) (SI 1971/1682) |
| | | 1 Dec 1971 (in so far as para 53 is not already in force) (SI 1971/1761) |
| | | 28 Feb 1972 (otherwise) (SI 1972/36) |
| Schs 4, 5 | | 1 Oct 1971 (SI 1971/1522) |
| Sch 6 | | 1 Dec 1971 (except for the purposes of regulations with respect to proceedings in pursuance of appeals under Industrial Training Act 1964, s 12 and with respect to proceedings to determine any question in pursuance of Selective Employment Payments Act 1966, s 7(5)) (SI 1971/1761) |
| | | *Never in force* (otherwise) (repealed) |
| Sch 7 | | 28 Feb 1972 (SI 1972/36) |
| Sch 8 | | 1 Oct 1971 (SI 1971/1522), amendments of— |
| | | Trade Union Act 1913 (except so far as they relate to s 3(2) and except for the purposes of Trade Union Act 1871, ss 4, 7–10, 17, Trade Union Act Amendment Act 1876, s 10, and Trade Disputes Act 1906); |
| | | Road Haulage Wages Act 1938; |
| | | Industrial Assurance and Friendly Societies Act 1948; |
| | | Insurance Companies Act 1958; |
| | | Trade Union (Amalgamations, etc) Act 1964; |
| | | Companies Act 1967 |

**See Halsbury's Statutes Citator for amendments to these Acts**

**Industrial Relations Act 1971 (c 72)**—*contd*

        1 Nov 1971 (amendments of Wages Councils Act 1959)
           (SI 1971/1682)
        1 Dec 1971 (SI 1971/1761), amendments of—
        Conspiracy, and Protection of Property Act 1875;
        Industrial Courts Act 1919;
        Trade Union Act 1931 (so far as it relates to the Trade Union
           Act 1871, s 4);
        Merchant Shipping Act 1970
        28 Feb 1972 (otherwise, except entry relating to Trade Union
           Act 1913 for the purposes of the Trade Union Act 1871,
           ss 7–10) (SI 1972/36)
        *Never in force* (exception noted above) (repealed)

Sch 9       1 Oct 1971 (SI 1971/1522), repeals of or in—
        Trade Union Act 1871, whole Act (except ss 4, 17 and in
           respect of any organisation which immediately before the
           coming into force of this Order was registered as a trade union
           under the Trade Union Acts 1871 to 1964 and which is on the
           provisional register instituted under the Industrial Relations
           Act 1971, ss 7–10);
        Trade Union Act Amendment Act 1876, whole Act except s 10;
        Friendly Societies Act 1896, ss 2(1), 4(1);
        Trade Union Act 1913, s 1(1) (except for the purposes of Trade
           Union Act 1871, s 4, 7–10, 17, Trade Union Act Amendment
           Act 1876, s 10 and Trade Disputes Act 1906), and (2) "words
           the objects mentioned in section sixteen of the Trade Union
           Act Amendment Act 1876, namely", s 2(2)–(4);
        Industrial Assurance and Friendly Societies Act 1948, s 23(1)(d);
        Insurance Companies Act 1958, s 1(5);
        Trade Union (Amalgamations, etc) Act 1964, ss 4, 7;
        Companies Act 1967
        1 Nov 1971 (SI 1971/1682), repeals of or in—
        Wages Councils Act 1959;
        Trade Union (Amalgamations, etc) Act 1964, s 8
        28 Feb 1972 (SI 1972/36), otherwise, except entries relating to—
        Trade Union Act 1871, ss 7–10, in respect of any organisation
           which immediately before 1 Oct 1971 was registered as a trade
           union under the Trade Union Acts 1871 to 1964 and which is
           on the provisional register instituted under Industrial Relations
           Act 1971;
        Trade Union Act 1913, ss 1(1), 2(5), for the purposes of Trade
           Union Act 1871, ss 7–10;
        Redundancy Payments Act 1965, s 46(1)–(4) for the purposes of
           regulations with respect to proceedings in pursuance of appeals
           under Industrial Training Act 1964, s 12, and with respect to
           proceedings to determine any question in pursuance of
           Selective Employment Payments Act 1966, s 78(5)
        *Never in force* (exceptions noted above) (repealed)

[1]   For transitional provisions, see SI 1971/1522, art 3

[2]   For transitional provisions, see SI 1971/1682, art 3

[3]   For transitional provisions, see SI 1971/1761, art 3

[4]   For transitional provisions, see SI 1972/36, art 3

---

**Industry Act 1971 (c 17)**

*RA:* 8 Apr 1971

Whole Act in force 8 Apr 1971 (RA)

---

### Interest on Damages (Scotland) Act 1971 (c 31)

*RA*: 12 May 1971

Whole Act in force 12 May 1971 (RA)

---

### Investment and Building Grants Act 1971 (c 51)

*RA*: 27 Jul 1971

Whole Act in force 27 Jul 1971 (RA)

---

### Land Commission (Dissolution) Act 1971 (c 18)

*RA*: 8 Apr 1971

*Commencement provisions*: s 1(2); Land Commission (Dissolution) (Appointed Day) Order 1971, SI 1971/670

| | | |
|---|---|---|
| 1–7 | | 8 Apr 1971 (RA) |
| Sch 1 | Pts I, II | 8 Apr 1971 (RA) |
| | Pt III | 1 May 1971 (SI 1971/670) |
| Sch 2 | | 8 Apr 1971 (RA) |
| Sch 3 | Pt I | 8 Apr 1971 (RA) |
| | Pt II | 1 May 1971 (SI 1971/670) |

---

### Land Registration and Land Charges Act 1971 (c 54)

*RA*: 27 Jul 1971

*Commencement provisions*: s 15(5); Land Registration and Land Charges Act 1971 (Commencement No 1) Order 1971, SI 1971/1489

| | | |
|---|---|---|
| 1, 2 | | 1 Oct 1971 (SI 1971/1489) |
| 3, 4 | | 27 Jul 1971 (s 15(5)) |
| 5 | (1) | 27 Jul 1971 (s 15(5)) |
| | (2)–(7) | *Never in force* (repealed) |
| 6–13 | | 27 Jul 1971 (s 15(5)) |
| 14 | (1) | 27 Jul 1971 (s 15(5)) |
| | (2)(a) | 27 Jul 1971 (s 15(5)) |
| | (2)(b) | See Sch 2, Pt II below |
| 15 | | 27 Jul 1971 (s 15(5)) |
| Sch 1 | | 27 Jul 1971 (s 15(5)) |
| Sch 2 | Pt I | 27 Jul 1971 (s 15(5)) |
| | Pt II | 1 Oct 1971 (exceptions noted below) (SI 1971/1489) |
| | | 2 Oct 1972 (so far as it relates to Land Registration Act 1925, s 85(5)) (SI 1971/1489) |
| | | *Never in force* (so far as it relates to Land Charges Act 1925, ss 16, 17(4)) (repealed) |

---

### Law Reform (Jurisdiction in Delict) (Scotland) Act 1971 (c 55)

*RA*: 27 Jul 1971

Whole Act in force 27 Jul 1971 (RA)

---

## Law Reform (Miscellaneous Provisions) Act 1971 (c 43)

*RA:* 1 Jul 1971

*Commencement provisions:* s 6(2)

Whole Act in force 1 Aug 1971 (s 6(2))

---

## Licensing (Abolition of State Management) Act 1971 (c 65)

*RA:* 27 Jul 1971

Whole Act in force 27 Jul 1971 (RA)

---

## Local Authorities (Qualification of Members) Act 1971 (c 7)

*RA:* 17 Feb 1971

Whole Act in force 17 Feb 1971 (RA)

---

## Medicines Act 1971 (c 69)

*RA:* 5 Aug 1971

Whole Act in force 5 Aug 1971 (RA)

---

## Merchant Shipping (Oil Pollution) Act 1971 (c 59)

*RA:* 27 Jul 1971

*Commencement provisions:* s 21(3); Merchant Shipping (Oil Pollution) Act 1971 (Commencement) Order 1971, SI 1971/1423; Merchant Shipping (Oil Pollution) Act 1971 (Commencement No 2) Order 1975, SI 1975/867

| | | |
|---|---|---|
| 1 | (1) | 9 Sep 1971 (SI 1971/1423) |
| | (2) | 19 Jun 1975 (SI 1975/867) |
| | (3)–(5) | 9 Sep 1971 (SI 1971/1423) |
| 2, 3 | | 9 Sep 1971 (SI 1971/1423) |
| 4–8 | | 19 Jun 1975 (SI 1975/867) |
| 9 | | 9 Sep 1971 (SI 1971/1423) |
| 10–12 | | 19 Jun 1975 (SI 1975/867) |
| 13 | (1) | 9 Sep 1971 (SI 1971/1423) |
| | (2), (3) | 19 Jun 1975 (SI 1975/867) |
| 14 | (1) | 9 Sep 1971 (SI 1971/1423) |
| | (2), (3) | 19 Jun 1975 (SI 1975/867) |
| 15–18 | | 9 Sep 1971 (SI 1971/1423) |
| 19 | | 19 Jun 1975 (SI 1975/867) |
| 20, 21 | | 9 Sep 1971 (SI 1971/1423) |

---

## Mineral Workings Act 1971 (c 71)

*RA:* 5 Aug 1971

Whole Act in force 5 Aug 1971 (RA)

---

## Mineral Workings (Offshore Installations) Act 1971 (c 61)

*RA*: 27 Jul 1971

*Commencement provisions*: s 14(2); Mineral Workings (Offshore Installations) Act 1971 (Commencement)
    Order 1972, SI 1972/644

| | |
|---|---|
| 1–3 | 1 May 1972 (SI 1972/644) |
| 4, 5 | 31 Aug 1972 (SI 1972/644) |
| 6–14 | 1 May 1972 (SI 1972/644) |
| Schedule | 1 May 1972 (SI 1972/644) |

## Mines Management Act 1971 (c 20)

*RA*: 8 Apr 1971

Whole Act in force 8 Apr 1971 (RA)

## Misuse of Drugs Act 1971 (c 38)

*RA*: 27 May 1971

*Commencement provisions*: s 40(3); Misuse of Drugs Act 1971 (Commencement No 1) Order 1971,
    SI 1971/2120; Misuse of Drugs Act 1971 (Commencement No 2) Order 1973, SI 1973/795

| | |
|---|---|
| 1 | 1 Feb 1972 (SI 1971/2120) |
| 2–31 | 1 Jul 1973 (SI 1973/795) |
| 32 | 1 Feb 1972 (SI 1971/2120) |
| 33, 34 | 1 Jul 1973 (SI 1973/795) |
| 35 | 1 Feb 1972 (SI 1971/2120) |
| 36 | 1 Jul 1973 (SI 1973/795) |
| 37, 38 | 1 Feb 1972 (SI 1971/2120) |
| 39 | 1 Jul 1973 (SI 1973/795) |
| 40 | 1 Feb 1972 (SI 1971/2120) |
| Sch 1 | 1 Feb 1972 (SI 1971/2120) |
| Schs 2–5 | 1 Jul 1973 (SI 1973/795) |

## Motor Vehicles (Passenger Insurance) Act 1971 (c 36)

*RA*: 27 May 1971

*Commencement provisions*: s 2(2); Motor Vehicles (Passenger Insurance) Act 1971 (Commencement)
    Order 1971, SI 1971/964

Whole Act in force 1 Dec 1971 (SI 1971/964)

## Mr Speaker King's Retirement Act 1971 (c 13)

*RA*: 30 Mar 1971

Whole Act in force 30 Mar 1971 (RA)

## National Insurance Act 1971 (c 50)

*RA*: 14 Jul 1971

*Commencement provisions*: s 16(3), Sch 6, para 1; National Insurance Act 1971 (Commencement No 1)
    Order 1971, SI 1971/1149[1]; National Insurance Act 1971 (Commencement No 2) Order 1971,
    SI 1971/1332; National Insurance Act 1971 (Commencement No 3) Order 1972, SI 1972/1149

| | | |
|---|---|---|
| 1 | (1), (2) | 20 Sep 1971 (SI 1971/1149) |

**National Insurance Act 1971 (c 50)**—*contd*

|  |  |  |
|---|---|---|
|  | (3) | 21 Sep 1971 (SI 1971/1149) |
|  | (4) | 6 Sep 1971 (in relation to relaxation of restrictions on crediting of contributions to persons excepted from liability on grounds of small income) (SI 1971/1149) |
|  |  | 20 Sep 1971 (in relation to higher income limit for exception from liability on grounds of small income) (SI 1971/1149) |
|  | (5) | 20 Sep 1971 (SI 1971/1149) |
| 2 | (1) | See Sch 2 below |
|  | (2), (3) | 20 Sep 1971 (SI 1971/1149) |
| 3 |  | 20 Sep 1971 (SI 1971/1149) |
| 4 |  | 20 Sep 1971 (in relation to increase for adult dependants in the case of retirement pension) (SI 1971/1149) |
|  |  | 23 Sep 1971 (in relation to increase for adult dependants in the case of invalidity pension) (SI 1971/1149) |
| 5 |  | 20 Sep 1971 (SI 1971/1149) |
| 6 | (1) | 20 Sep 1971 (SI 1971/1149) |
|  | (2) | 23 Sep 1971 (SI 1971/1149) |
|  | (3) | 20 Sep 1971 (SI 1971/1149) |
| 7 |  | 20 Sep 1971 (SI 1971/1149) |
| 8 | (1) | See Sch 4 below |
|  | (2) | 26 Jul 1971 (SI 1971/1149) |
|  | (3) | 22 Sep 1971 (SI 1971/1149) |
|  | (4) | 20 Sep 1971 (SI 1971/1149) |
| 9 |  | 22 Sep 1971 (SI 1971/1149) |
| 10 | (1) | 26 Jul 1971 (SI 1971/1149) |
|  | (2) | 8 Dec 1971 (SI 1971/1149) |
| 11 |  | 22 Sep 1971 (SI 1971/1149) |
| 12 |  | 28 Aug 1971 (SI 1972/1149) |
| 13 |  | 20 Sep 1971 (SI 1971/1149) |
| 14 |  | See Sch 5 below |
| 15 |  | 26 Jul 1971 (SI 1971/1149) |
| 16 | (1)(a), (b) | 23 Aug 1971 (SI 1971/1332) |
|  | (1)(c) | 26 Jul 1971 (SI 1971/1149) |
|  | (2) | 26 Jul 1971 (SI 1971/1149) |
|  | (3) | See Schs 6, 7 below |
|  | (4) | 26 Jul 1971 (SI 1971/1149) |
| Sch 1 |  | 20 Sep 1971 (SI 1971/1149) |
| Sch 2 |  | 20 Sep 1971 (in relation to rates of benefit under National Insurance Act 1965 in the case of maternity allowance, widow's benefit, guardian's allowance, retirement pension, age addition and child's special allowance) (SI 1971/1149) |
|  |  | 23 Sep 1971 (in relation to rates of benefit under National Insurance Act 1965 in the case of unemployment, sickness and invalidity benefit) (SI 1971/1149) |
|  |  | 6 Dec 1971 (in relation to rates of benefit under National Insurance Act 1965 in the case of attendance allowance) (SI 1971/1149) |
| Sch 3 |  | 20 Sep 1971 (SI 1971/1149) |
| Sch 4 |  | 20 Sep 1971 (in relation to higher rates and amount of benefit under the National Insurance (Industrial Injuries) Act 1965 in the case of widow's pension under s 19, widower's pension under s 20, and allowance in respect of children of deceased's family under s 21) (SI 1971/1149) |
|  |  | 22 Sep 1971 (in relation to higher rates and amount of benefit under the National Insurance (Industrial Injuries) Act 1965 in the case of disablement benefit (including increase of disablement pension other than those coming into force on 23 Sep 1971 below, maximum under s 29(1)(a) of aggregate of weekly benefits payable for successive accidents and maximum disablement gratuity under s 12(3)) (SI 1971/1149) |

**National Insurance Act 1971 (c 50)**—*contd*

|  | 23 Sep 1971 (in relation to higher rates and amount of benefit under the National Insurance (Industrial Injuries) Act 1965 in the case of injury benefit (including increases thereof) and increases of disablement pension in respect of children and adult dependants in the case of a beneficiary receiving, as an in-patient in a hospital or similar institution, medical treatment for the relevant injury of loss of faculty) (SI 1971/1149) |
|---|---|
| Sch 5 | 26 Jul 1971 (amendments of Industrial Injuries and Diseases (Old Cases) Act 1967 and in relation to payment of benefit to third party) (SI 1971/1149) |
|  | 20 Sep 1971 (SI 1971/1149), amendments to— |
|  | Law Reform (Personal Injuries) Act 1948, in the case of maternity allowance, widow's benefit, guardian's allowance retirement pension, age addition and child's special allowance; |
|  | National Insurance Act 1965, in the case of maternity allowance, widow's benefit, guardian's allowance retirement pension, age addition and child's special allowance; |
|  | Ministry of Social Security Act 1966, in the case of maternity allowance, widow's benefit, guardian's allowance retirement pension, age addition and child's special allowance; |
|  | National Insurance Act 1969, in the case of maternity allowance, widow's benefit, guardian's allowance retirement pension, age addition and child's special allowance; |
|  | National Insurance (Old persons' and attendance allowance) Act 1970, in the case of maternity allowance, widow's benefit, guardian's allowance retirement pension, age addition and child's special allowance |
|  | 22 Sep 1971 (SI 1971/1149), amendments to— |
|  | National Insurance (Industrial Injuries) Act 1965, in the case of disablement benefit (including increases of disablement pension other than those coming into force on 23 Sep 1971 and adjustments for successive accidents under s 29(2); |
|  | National Insurance Act 1966, s 6(1) (substitution of words "by three pounds") |
|  | 23 Sep 1971 (SI 1971/1149), amendments to— |
|  | Law Reform (Personal Injuries) Act 1948, in the case of unemployment, sickness and invalidity benefit; |
|  | National Insurance Act 1965, in the case of unemployment, sickness and invalidity benefit; |
|  | National Insurance (Industrial Injuries) Act 1965, in the case of injury benefit (including increases thereof) and increases of disablement pension in respect of children and adult dependants in the case of a beneficiary receiving as an in-patient in a hospital or similar institution, medical treatment for the relevant injury or loss of faculty; |
|  | Ministry of Social Security Act 1966, in the case of unemployment, sickness and invalidity benefit; |
|  | National Insurance Act 1969, in the case of unemployment, sickness and invalidity benefit; |
|  | National Insurance (Old persons' and attendance allowance) Act 1970, in the case of unemployment, sickness and invalidity benefit |
|  | 8 Dec 1971 (amendments to National Insurance Act 1966, s 6(1)(a)) (SI 1971/1149) |
| Sch 6 | 26 Jul 1971 (in so far as relates to s 8(2)) (SI 1971/1149) |
|  | 20 Sep 1971 (in so far as relates to s 2(3)) (SI 1971/1149) |
|  | 22 Sep 1971 (in so far as relates to s 9) (SI 1971/1149) |
|  | 23 Sep 1971 (in so far as relates to s 6(2)) (SI 1971/1149) |
| Sch 7 | 20 Sep 1971 (SI 1971/1149), repeals of or in— |
|  | National Insurance Act 1965, s 43(1), (4), (5); |
|  | National Insurance Act 1967, s 1(1)(d); |

**National Insurance Act 1971 (c 50)**—*contd*

National Insurance Act 1969, ss 1(1), (4), 3(1), (2), 5, Schs 1, 4 and s 2(1), Sch 2 (in the case of maternity allowance, widows benefit, guardians allowance, retirement pension and child's special allowance) and s 6, Sch 5 (in the case of widow's and widower's pension and allowance in respect of children of deceased's family);

National Insurance (Old persons' and widows' pensions and attendance allowance) Act 1970, ss 1(2)(b), 7(1)

22 Sep 1971 (SI 1971/1149), repeals of or in—

National Insurance Act 1969, s 6, Sch 5 (in the case of disablement benefit (including increases of disablement pension other than those coming into force on 23 Sep 1971))

23 Sep 1971 (SI 1971/1149), repeals of or in—

National Insurance Act 1969, s 2(1), Sch 2 (in the case of unemployment, and sickness benefit) and s 6, Sch 5 (in the case of injury benefit (including increases) and increases of disablement pension in respect of children and adult dependants in the case of a beneficiary receiving as an in-patient in a hospital or similar institution, medical treatment for the relevant injury or loss of faculty)

8 Dec 1971 (SI 1971/1149), repeals of or in—

National Insurance (Industrial Injuries) Act 1965, s 15(2);

National Insurance (Old persons' and widows' pensions and attendance allowance) Act 1970, Sch 2, para 11

28 Aug 1972 (SI 1972/1149), repeals of or in—

National Insurance Act 1965, s 113(1);

National Insurance (Industrial Injuries) Act 1965, s 86(5);

Family Allowances Act 1965, s 17(9);

National Insurance Act 1969, s 6(1), Sch 5 (in the case of maximum under s 29(1)(a) of aggregate of weekly benefits payable for successive accidents and maximum disablement gratuity under s 12(3)) and ss 6(2), 10(1)

[1]    For transitional provisions and savings, see SI 1971/1149, art 2(2), (3)

---

**National Savings Bank Act 1971 (c 29)**

*RA:* 12 May 1971

*Commencement provisions:* s 29(2)

Whole Act in force 12 Jun 1971 (s 29(2))

---

**New Towns Act 1971 (c 81)**

*RA:* 16 Dec 1971

Whole Act in force 16 Dec 1971 (RA)

---

**Nullity of Marriage Act 1971 (c 44)**

*RA:* 1 Jul 1971

*Commencement provisions:* s 7(5)

Whole Act in force 1 Aug 1971 (s 7(5))

---

## Oil in Navigable Waters Act 1971 (c 21)

*RA:* 8 Apr 1971

*Commencement provisions*: s 12(3); Oil in Navigable Waters Act 1971 (Commencement No 1) Order 1971, SI 1971/932; Oil in Navigable Waters Act 1971 (Commencement No 2) Order 1972, SI 1972/1927

| | | |
|---|---|---|
| 1 | | 5 Jan 1973 (SI 1972/1927) |
| 2, 3 | | 21 Jun 1971 (SI 1971/932) |
| 4 | | 5 Jan 1973 (SI 1972/1927) |
| 5 | | 21 Jun 1971 (SI 1971/932) |
| 6 | | 5 Jan 1973 (SI 1972/1927) |
| 7–10 | | 21 Jun 1971 (SI 1971/932) |
| 11 | (1) | See Sch 1 below |
| | (2) | See Sch 3 below |
| 12 | | 21 Jun 1971 (SI 1971/932) |
| Sch 1 | paras 1–5 | 5 Jan 1973 (SI 1972/1927) |
| | para 6 | 21 Jun 1971 (SI 1971/932) |
| Sch 2 | | 21 Jun 1971 (SI 1971/932) |
| Sch 3 | | 21 Jun 1971 (repeals of or in Navigable Waters Act 1955, ss 4, 23) (SI 1971/932) |
| | | 5 Jan 1973 (otherwise) (SI 1972/1927) |

## Pensions (Increase) Act 1971 (c 56)

*RA:* 27 Jul 1971

Whole Act in force 27 Jul 1971 (RA)

## Pool Competitions Act 1971 (c 57)

*RA:* 27 Jul 1971

Whole Act in force 27 Jul 1971 (RA)

## Powers of Attorney Act 1971 (c 27)

*RA:* 12 May 1971

*Commencement provisions*: s 11(4)

Whole Act in force 1 Oct 1971 (s 11(4))

## Prevention of Oil Pollution Act 1971 (c 60)

*RA:* 27 Jul 1971

*Commencement provisions*: s 34(2); Prevention of Oil Pollution Act 1971 (Commencement) Order 1973, SI 1973/203

Whole Act in force 1 Mar 1973 (SI 1973/203)

## Rating Act 1971 (c 39)

*RA:* 27 May 1971

Whole Act in force 27 May 1971 (RA)

## Recognition of Divorces and Legal Separations Act 1971 (c 53)

*RA:* 27 Jul 1971

*Commencement provisions:* s 10(5)

Whole Act in force 1 Jan 1972 (s 10(5))

---

## Redemption of Standard Securities (Scotland) Act 1971 (c 45)

*RA:* 1 Jul 1971

Whole Act in force 1 Jul 1971 (RA)

---

## Rent (Scotland) Act 1971 (c 28)

*RA:* 12 May 1971

*Commencement provisions:* s 136(2)

Whole Act in force 12 Aug 1971 (s 136(2))

---

## Rolls-Royce (Purchase) Act 1971 (c 9)

*RA:* 17 Feb 1971

Whole Act in force 17 Feb 1971 (RA)

---

## Rural Water Supplies and Sewerage Act 1971 (c 49)

*RA:* 14 Jul 1971

Whole Act in force 14 Jul 1971 (RA)

---

## Sheriff Courts (Scotland) Act 1971 (c 58)

*RA:* 27 Jul 1971

*Commencement provisions:* s 47(2); Sheriff Courts (Scotland) Act 1971 (Commencement No 1) Order 1971/1582; Sheriff Courts (Scotland) Act 1971 (Commencement No 2) Order 1973, SI 1973/276; Sheriff Courts (Scotland) Act 1971 (Commencement No 3) Order 1976, SI 1976/236

| | | |
|---|---|---|
| 1–22 | | 1 Nov 1971 (SI 1971/1582) |
| 23–30 | | 1 Apr 1973 (SI 1973/276) |
| 31 | | 1 Sep 1976 (SI 1976/236) |
| 32–34 | | 1 Nov 1971 (SI 1971/1582) |
| 35–42 | | 1 Sep 1976 (SI 1976/236) |
| 43 | | 1 Nov 1971 (SI 1971/1582) |
| 44 | (1), (2) | 1 Nov 1971 (SI 1971/1582) |
| | (3) | 1 Apr 1973 (SI 1973/276) |
| 45–47 | | 1 Nov 1971 (SI 1971/1582) |
| Sch 1 | para 1 | 1 Nov 1971 (SI 1971/1582) |
| | paras 2–4 | 1 Sep 1976 (SI 1976/236) |
| Sch 2 | Pt I | 1 Nov 1971 (SI 1971/1582), repeals of or in— |
| | | Sheriffs of Edinburgh and Lancashire Act 1822; |
| | | Sheriff Courts (Scotland) Act 1907; |
| | | Sheriff Courts and Legal Officers (Scotland) Act 1927; |
| | | Administration of Justice (Scotland) Act 1933; |
| | | Sheriff Courts (Scotland) Act 1939; |
| | | Administration of Justice (Scotland) Act 1948 |

**Sheriff Courts (Scotland) Act 1971 (c 58)**—*contd*

|  |  |  |
|---|---|---|
|  | 1 Apr 1973 (SI 1973/276), repeals of or in— |  |
|  | Sheriff Court Houses Act 1860; |  |
|  | Sheriff Court Houses (Scotland) Act 1866; |  |
|  | Sheriff Court Houses (Scotland) Amendment Act 1884; |  |
|  | Local Government (Scotland) Act 1889 |  |
| Pt II | 1 Sep 1976 (SI 1976/236) |  |

---

**Shipbuilding Industry Act 1971 (c 46)**

*RA:* 1 Jul 1971

Whole Act in force 1 Jul 1971 (RA)

---

**Social Security Act 1971 (c 73)**

*RA:* 5 Aug 1971

*Commencement provisions*: s 11(4); Social Security (Commencement No 1) Order 1971, SI 1971/1291; Social Security (Commencement No 2) Order 1971, SI 1971/1683

| 1 | (1) | 5 Nov 1971 (so far as it relates to sub-s (2)) (s 11(4)(b)) |
|---|---|---|
|  |  | 3 Nov 1971 (so far as it relates to sub-ss (3), (4)) (SI 1971/1683) |
|  | (2) | 5 Nov 1971 (s 11(4)(b)) |
|  | (3), (4) | 3 Nov 1971 (SI 1971/1683) |
|  | (5) | 5 Nov 1971 (s 11(4)(b)) |
| 2 |  | 3 Apr 1971 (SI 1971/1683) |
| 3–6 |  | 5 Aug 1971 (s 11(4)(a)) |
| 7 |  | 16 Aug 1971 (SI 1971/1291) |
| 8 |  | 6 Sep 1971 (SI 1971/1291) |
| 9, 10 |  | 5 Aug 1971 (s 11(4)(a)) |
| 11 | (1)–(5) | 5 Aug 1971 (s 11(4)(a)) |
|  | (6) | See Sch 2 below |
|  | (7) | 5 Aug 1971 (s 11(4)(a)) |
| Sch 1 |  | 3 Nov 1971 (SI 1971/1683) |
| Sch 2 | Pt I | 5 Aug 1971 (s 11(4)(a)) |
|  | Pt II | 16 Aug 1971 (SI 1971/1291) |

---

**Statute Law (Repeals) Act 1971 (c 52)**

*RA:* 27 Jul 1971

Whole Act in force 27 Jul 1971 (RA)

---

**Teaching Council (Scotland) Act 1971 (c 2)**

*RA:* 17 Feb 1971

*Commencement provisions*: s 5(2)

Whole Act in force 17 Feb 1971 (s 5(2)), except Schedule, para 2, which came into force on 15 Apr 1971 (the same day as Social Work (Scotland) Act 1968, Pt III

---

**Town and Country Planning Act 1971 (c 78)**

*RA:* 28 Oct 1971

*Commencement provisions*: ss 21, 294

**Town and Country Planning Act 1971 (c 78)**—*contd*
This Act mainly came into force on 1 Apr 1972 (s 294(1)) but provision was made for Pt II (dealing with
development plans), with certain exceptions, to come into force on days appointed by the Secretary of
State, with different days appointed for the commencement of the same provisions in different areas.
In addition, by virtue of s 292(1) of, and Sch 24, para 1(2) to, the Act, certain provisions of Pt II came
into force in certain areas on the passing of the Act.

**Tribunals and Inquiries Act 1971 (c 62)**

*RA:* 27 Jul 1971

*Commencement provisions:* s 20(2)

Whole Act in force 27 Aug 1971 (s 20(2))

**Unsolicited Goods and Services Act 1971 (c 30)**

*RA:* 12 May 1971

*Commencement provisions:* s 7(2)

Whole Act in force 12 Aug 1971 (s 7(2))

**Vehicles (Excise) Act 1971 (c 10)**

*RA:* 16 Mar 1971

*Commencement provisions:* s 40(2); Vehicle and Driving Licences (Transfer of Functions) (Appointed Date)
Order 1971, SI 1971/377

| | | |
|---|---|---|
| 1–38 | | 1 Apr 1971 (SI 1971/377) |
| 39 | (1) | 1 Apr 1971 (SI 1971/377) |
| | (2), (3) | 16 Mar 1971 (RA) |
| | (4)–(6) | 1 Apr 1971 (SI 1971/377) |
| 40 | | 16 Mar 1971 (RA) |
| Schs 1–8 | | 1 Apr 1971 (SI 1971/377) |

**Water Resources Act 1971 (c 34)**

*RA:* 27 May 1971

Whole Act in force 27 May 1971 (RA)

**Welsh National Opera Company Act 1971 (c 37)**

*RA:* 27 May 1971

Whole Act in force 27 May 1971 (RA)

**Wild Creatures and Forest Laws Act 1971 (c 47)**

*RA:* 1 Jul 1971

Whole Act in force 1 Jul 1971 (RA)

# 1972 Acts

## Administration of Justice (Scotland) Act 1972 (c 59)

*RA:* 9 Aug 1972

*Commencement provisions:* s 5(3); Administration of Justice (Scotland) Act 1972 (Commencement) Order 1973, SI 1973/339

| | |
|---|---|
| 1 | 2 Apr 1973 (SI 1973/339) |
| 2 | 9 Aug 1972 (RA) |
| 3 | 2 Apr 1973 (SI 1973/339) |
| 4, 5 | 9 Aug 1972 (RA) |

## Admission to Holy Communion Measure 1972 (No 1)

*RA:* 10 Feb 1972

Whole Measure in force 10 Feb 1972 (RA)

## Affiliation Proceedings (Amendment) Act 1972 (c 49)

*RA:* 27 Jul 1972

*Commencement provisions:* s 4(3)

Whole Act in force 27 Oct 1972 (s 4(3))

## Agriculture (Miscellaneous Provisions) Act 1972 (c 62)

*RA:* 9 Aug 1972

*Commencement provisions:* s 27(2), (3); Agriculture (Miscellaneous Provisions) Act 1972 (Commencement) Order 1972, SI 1972/1260

| | | |
|---|---|---|
| 1–4 | | 9 Aug 1972 (RA) |
| 5 | (1)(a) | 1 Jan 1974 (s 27(2)(a)) |
| | (1)(b) | 9 Aug 1972 (RA) |
| | (1)(c)–(e) | 1 Jan 1974 (s 27(2)(a)) |
| | (2), (3) | 1 Jan 1974 (s 27(2)(a)) |
| | (4) | 9 Aug 1972 (RA) |
| 6 | | 1 Jan 1974 (s 27(2)(a)) |
| 7–17 | | 9 Aug 1972 (RA) |
| 18 | | 15 Aug 1972 (SI 1972/1260) |
| 19–25 | | 9 Aug 1972 (RA) |
| 26 | (1), (2) | 9 Aug 1972 (RA) |
| | (3) | See Sch 6 below |
| | (4) | 9 Aug 1972 (RA) |
| 27 | | 9 Aug 1972 (RA) |
| Sch 1 | | 1 Jan 1974 (s 27(2)(a)) |
| Schs 2–5 | | 9 Aug 1972 (RA) |

**Agriculture (Miscellaneous Provisions) Act 1972 (c 62)**—*contd*
Sch 6                          9 Aug 1972 (except repeals of or in Agriculture Act 1947, ss 77,
                                   78) (RA)
                              15 Aug 1972 (exception noted above) (SI 1972/1260)
                              1 Jan 1974 (s 27(2)), repeals of or in—
                                   Slaughterhouses Act 1954;
                                   Food and Drugs Act 1955, ss 65, 70(1), 75–78;
                                   Slaughterhouses Act 1958;
                                   London Government Act 1963, s 54(2)

**Airports Authority Act 1972 (c 8)**

*RA:* 24 Feb 1972

Whole Act in force 24 Feb 1972 (RA)

**Appropriation Act 1972 (c 56)**

*RA:* 9 Aug 1972

Whole Act in force 9 Aug 1972 (RA)

**Benefices Measure 1972 (No 3)**

*RA:* 10 Feb 1972

Whole Measure in force 10 Feb 1972 (RA)

**Betting and Gaming Duties Act 1972 (c 25)**

*RA:* 11 May 1972

*Commencement provisions:* s 30(3)

Whole Act in force 11 Jun 1972 (s 30(3))

**British Library Act 1972 (c 54)**

*RA:* 27 Jul 1972

Whole Act in force 27 Jul 1972 (RA)

**Carriage by Railway Act 1972 (c 33)**

*RA:* 29 Jun 1972

*Commencement provisions:* s 13(3), (4); Carriage by Railway Act 1972 (Commencement) Order 1972,
   SI 1972/1579

1                            29 Jun 1972 (RA)
2–8                          1 Jan 1973 (SI 1972/1579)
9–13                         29 Jun 1972 (RA)
Schedule                     29 Jun 1972 (RA)

## Children Act 1972 (c 44)

*RA:* 27 Jul 1972

Whole Act in force 27 Jul 1972 (RA)

---

## Chronically Sick and Disabled Persons (Scotland) Act 1972 (c 51)

*RA:* 27 Jul 1972

Whole Act in force 27 Jul 1972 (RA)

---

## Civil Evidence Act 1972 (c 30)

*RA:* 12 Jun 1972

*Commencement provisions:* s 6(3); Civil Evidence Act 1972 (Commencement No 1) Order 1974, SI 1974/280; Civil Evidence Act 1972 (Commencement No 2) Order 1974, SI 1974/1137

| | | |
|---|---|---|
| 1 | | 1 Jun 1974 (for purpose of proceedings other than in bankruptcy in the Supreme Court; proceedings before tribunals to which strict rules of evidence apply; arbitrations and references (other than references under County Courts Act 1959, s 92 (now County Courts Act 1984, s 64)) to which strict rules of evidence apply; applications and appeals arising from the above) (SI 1974/280) |
| | | 1 Sep 1974 (proceedings, other than in bankruptcy, in county courts) (SI 1974/1137) |
| | | *Never in force* (otherwise) (repealed) |
| 2, 3 | | 1 Jan 1973 (s 6(3)) |
| 4 | (1) | 1 Jan 1973 (s 6(3)) |
| | (2)–(5) | 1 Jun 1974 (for purpose of proceedings other than in bankruptcy in the Supreme Court; proceedings before tribunals to which strict rules of evidence apply; arbitrations and references (other than references under County Courts Act 1959, s 92 (now County Courts Act 1984, s 64)) to which strict rules of evidence apply; applications and appeals arising from the above) (SI 1974/280) |
| | | 1 Sep 1974 (proceedings, other than in bankruptcy, in county courts) (SI 1974/1137) |
| | | *Never in force* (otherwise) |
| 5, 6 | | 1 Jan 1973 (s 6(3)) |

---

## Civil List Act 1972 (c 7)

*RA:* 24 Feb 1972

*Commencement provisions:* s 8(5), (6)

| | | |
|---|---|---|
| 1–3 | | Effective as respects payments for 1972 onwards (s 8(5)) |
| 4 | (1) | 1 Apr 1972 (s 8(6)) |
| | (2) | 24 Feb 1972 (RA) |
| 5–7 | | 24 Feb 1972 (RA) |
| 8 | (1)–(3) | 24 Feb 1972 (RA) |
| | (4) | See Schedule below |
| | (5), (6) | 24 Feb 1972 (RA) |
| Schedule | | 24 Feb 1972 (except repeals of or in Civil List Act 1952, s 13(1)) (RA) |
| | | 1 Apr 1972 (otherwise) (s 8(6)) |

---

## Clergy Pensions (Amendment) Measure 1972 (No 5)

*RA:* 9 Aug 1972

Whole Measure in force 9 Aug 1972 (RA)

---

## Companies (Floating Charges and Receivers) (Scotland) Act 1972 (c 67)

*RA:* 17 Oct 1972

*Commencement provisions:* s 32(3)

Whole Act in force 17 Nov 1972 (s 32(3))

---

## Consolidated Fund Act 1972 (c 13)

*RA:* 23 Mar 1972

Whole Act in force 23 Mar 1972 (RA)

---

## Consolidated Fund (No 2) Act 1972 (c 23)

*RA:* 11 May 1972

Whole Act in force 11 May 1972 (RA)

---

## Consolidated Fund (No 3) Act 1972 (c 78)

*RA:* 12 Dec 1972

Whole Act in force 12 Dec 1972 (RA)

---

## Contracts of Employment Act 1972 (c 53)

*RA:* 27 Jul 1972

Whole Act in force 27 Jul 1972 (RA)

---

## Counter-Inflation (Temporary Provisions) Act 1972 (c 74)

*RA:* 30 Nov 1972

Whole Act in force 30 Nov 1972 (RA); note that s 2 expired by 29 Apr 1973

---

## Criminal Justice Act 1972 (c 71)

*RA:* 26 Oct 1972

*Commencement provisions:* s 66(6); Criminal Justice Act 1972 (Commencement No 1) Order 1972, SI 1972/1763; Criminal Justice Act 1972 (Commencement No 2) Order 1973, SI 1973/272; Criminal Justice Act 1972 (Commencement No 3) Order 1973, SI 1973/1472; Criminal Justice Act 1972 (Commencement No 4) Order 1973, SI 1973/1995; Criminal Justice Act 1972 (Commencement No 5) Order 1976, SI 1976/299

| | | |
|---|---|---|
| 1–6 | | 1 Jan 1973 (SI 1972/1763) |
| 7–10 | | 1 Apr 1973 (SI 1973/272) |
| 11–20 | | 1 Jan 1973 (SI 1972/1763) |
| 21 | (1) | 1 Jan 1973 (SI 1972/1763) |
| | (2), (3) | *Never in force* (repealed) |

**Criminal Justice Act 1972 (c 71)**—*contd*

| | | |
|---|---|---|
| 22, 23 | | 1 Jan 1973 (SI 1972/1763) |
| 24 | | 1 Apr 1973 (SI 1973/272) |
| 25 | | 30 Mar 1974 (SI 1973/1472) |
| 26 | (1) | 1 Jan 1973 (SI 1972/1763) |
| | (2), (3) | 1 Apr 1973 (SI 1973/272) |
| 27–33 | | 1 Jan 1973 (SI 1972/1763) |
| 34 | | 1 Apr 1976 (SI 1976/299) |
| 35 | | 1 Jan 1973 (SI 1972/1763) |
| 36 | | 1 Oct 1973 (SI 1973/1472) |
| 37–40 | | 1 Jan 1973 (SI 1972/1763) |
| 41 | | 1 Apr 1973 (SI 1973/272) |
| 42–44 | | 1 Jan 1973 (SI 1972/1763) |
| 45 | | 1 May 1973 (SI 1973/272) |
| 46–48 | | 1 Jan 1973 (SI 1972/1763) |
| 49 | | *Never in force* (repealed) |
| 50 | | 1 Apr 1973 (SI 1973/272) |
| 51–60 | | 1 Jan 1973 (SI 1972/1763) |
| 61, 62 | | 1 Apr 1973 (SI 1973/272) |
| 63 | (1), (2) | 1 Jan 1973 (SI 1972/1763) |
| | (3) | 1 Jan 1974 (SI 1973/1995) |
| 64 | | See Schs 5, 6 below |
| 65, 66 | | 1 Jan 1973 (SI 1972/1763) |
| Sch 1 | | 1 Apr 1973 (SI 1973/272) |
| Sch 2 | | 30 Mar 1974 (SI 1973/1472) |
| Sch 3 | | 1 Jan 1973 (SI 1972/1763) |
| Sch 4 | | 1 Jan 1974 (SI 1973/1995) |
| Sch 5 | | 1 Jan 1973 (SI 1972/1763), amendments of— |

> Petty Sessions (Ireland) Act 1851;
> Theatrical Employers Registration Act 1925;
> Children and Young Persons Act 1933;
> Incitement to Disaffection Act 1934;
> Dogs Amendment Act 1938;
> Criminal Justice Act 1948;
> Reserve and Auxiliary Forces (Training) Act 1951;
> Costs in Criminal Cases Act 1952;
> Magistrates' Courts Act 1952;
> Prevention of Fraud (Investment) Act 1958;
> Criminal Justice Act 1961;
> Criminal Justice Act 1967, ss 18(7), 53, 67(1), 73(8), 74(12), 84(1);
> Criminal Appeal Act 1968;
> Theft Act 1968;
> Children and Young Persons Act 1969, s 7(8);
> Administration of Justice Act 1970;
> Immigration Act 1971
>
> 1 Mar 1973 (amendment of Criminal Justice Act 1967, s 60(2)) (SI 1973/272)
> 1 Apr 1973 (amendment of Road Traffic Act 1972, s 105(2)) (SI 1973/272)
> 30 Mar 1974 (amendment of Courts Act 1971) (SI 1973/1472)

| | | |
|---|---|---|
| Sch 6 | Pt I | 1 Apr 1973 (SI 1973/272), repeals of or in— |

> Juries Act 1922, ss 1, 2(2), 6, 7;
> Representation of the People Act 1948;
> Electoral Registers Act 1949;
> Courts Act 1971, Sch 4, paras 1(1)–(6), 2(1), (2)
>
> 30 Mar 1974 (except repeal of Aliens Restriction (Amendment) Act 1919, s 8) (SI 1973/1472)
> *Not yet in force* (exception noted above)

| | | |
|---|---|---|
| | Pt II | 1 Jan 1973 (SI 1972/1763), repeals of or in— |

**Criminal Justice Act 1972 (c 71)**—*contd*
>>Forfeiture Act 1870;
>>Summary Jurisdiction (Scotland) Act 1908;
>>Protection of Animals Act 1911;
>>Criminal Justice Act 1948;
>>Costs in Criminal Cases Act 1952;
>>Prison Act 1952;
>>Magistrates' Courts Act 1952;
>>First Offenders Act 1958;
>>Criminal Justice Act 1961;
>>Criminal Justice (Scotland) Act 1963;
>>Administration of Justice Act 1964;
>>Criminal Law Act 1967;
>>Criminal Justice Act 1967, ss 39, 54;
>>Firearms Act 1968;
>>Theft Act 1968;
>>Children and Young Persons Act 1969;
>>Administration of Justice Act 1970;
>>Courts Act 1971;
>>Criminal Damage Act 1971
>1 Mar 1973 (repeals of or in Criminal Justice Act 1967, s 60(2))
>>(SI 1973/272)
>1 Apr 1973 (SI 1973/272), repeals of or in—
>>Legitimacy Act 1926;
>>Justices of the Peace Act 1949;
>>Births and Deaths Registration Act 1953;
>>Mines and Quarries Act 1954;
>>Air Force Act 1955;
>>Army Act 1955;
>>Naval Discipline Act 1957;
>>County Courts Act 1959;
>>Road Traffic Act 1960;
>>Post Office Act 1961;
>>Factories Act 1961;
>>Severn Bridge Tolls Act 1965;
>>Criminal Justice Act 1967, ss 47, 60;
>>Forestry Act 1967;
>>Road Traffic Regulation Act 1967;
>>Sea Fisheries (Shellfish) Act 1967;
>>Immigration Act 1971;
>>Vehicles (Excise) Act 1971;
>>Road Traffic Act 1972

---

**Deaconesses and Lay Ministry Measure 1972 (No 4)**

*RA:* 9 Aug 1972

Whole Measure in force 9 Aug 1972 (RA)

---

**Defective Premises Act 1972 (c 35)**

*RA:* 29 Jun 1972

*Commencement provisions:* s 7(2)

Whole Act in force 1 Jan 1974 (s 7(2))

---

## Deposit of Poisonous Waste Act 1972 (c 21)

*RA:* 30 Mar 1972

*Commencement provisions:* s 8(2); Deposit of Poisonous Waste Act 1972 (Commencement) Order 1972, SI 1972/1016

| | | |
|---|---|---|
| 1, 2 | | 30 Mar 1972 (RA) |
| 3, 4 | | 3 Aug 1972 (SI 1972/1016) |
| 5 | (1), (2) | 30 Mar 1972 (RA) |
| | (3), (4) | 3 Aug 1972 (SI 1972/1016) |
| 6–8 | | 30 Mar 1972 (RA) |

## Electricity Act 1972 (c 17)

*RA:* 23 Mar 1972

Whole Act in force 23 Mar 1972 (RA)

## Employment Medical Advisory Service Act 1972 (c 28)

*RA:* 22 May 1972

*Commencement provisions:* s 9(2); Employment Medical Advisory Service Act 1972 (Commencement) Order 1973, SI 1973/28

Whole Act in force 1 Feb 1973 (SI 1973/28)

## European Communities Act 1972 (c 68)

*RA:* 17 Oct 1972

*Commencement provisions:* s 4, Schs 3, 4; Sugar Act 1956 (Repeals) (Appointed Day) (No 1) Order 1973, SI 1973/135; Sugar Act 1956 (Repeals) (Appointed Day) (No 2) Order 1973, SI 1973/1019; Import Duties Act 1958 (Repeals) (Appointed Day) Order 1973, SI 1973/2176; Sugar Act 1956 (Repeals) (Appointed Day) (No 3) Order 1975, SI 1975/1164; Sugar Act 1956 (Repeals) (Appointed Day) (No 4) Order 1976, SI 1976/548; Customs Duties (Repeals) (Appointed Day) Order 1976, SI 1976/1304; Sugar Act 1956 (Repeals) (Appointed Day) (No 5) Order 1976, SI 1976/2016; Customs Duties (Repeals) (Appointed Day) Order 1977, SI 1977/2028, as amended by SI 1987/2106; Plant Varieties and Seeds Act 1964 (Repeals) (Appointed Day) Order 1978, SI 1978/1003; Sugar Act 1956 (Repeals) (Appointed Day) (No 6) Order 1981, SI 1981/1192; Plant Varieties and Seeds Act 1964 (Repeals) (Appointed Day) Order 1982, SI 1982/1048

| | | |
|---|---|---|
| 1–12 | | 17 Oct 1972 (RA) (generally with practical effect from 1 Jan 1973) |
| Schs 1, 2 | | 17 Oct 1972 (RA) (generally with practical effect from 1 Jan 1973) |
| Sch 3 | Pt I | 1 Jan 1974 (repeal of Import Duties Act 1958, ss 5(2), (3), (6), 9(4), (5) (words from "and" onwards)) (Import Duties Act 1958 (Repeals) (Appointed Day) Order 1973, SI 1973/2176) |
| | | 1 Sep 1976 (repeals of Import Duties Act 1958, ss 5(5), 7(1)(c), 16(3), Schs 2, 6; European Free Trade Association Act 1960; Finance Act 1965, s 2 (except sub-s (5)); Finance Act 1966, ss 1(6), 9) (Customs Duties (Repeals) (Appointed Day) Order 1976, SI 1976/1304) |
| | | 1 Jan 1978 (repeals of Import Duties Act 1958, ss 1–3, 11, 12 (except part of sub-s (4)), Sch 1, Sch 4, para 1; Finance Act 1971, s 1(1)–(3)) (Customs Duties (Repeals) (Appointed Day) Order 1977, SI 1977/2028, as amended by SI 1987/2106) |

**European Communities Act 1972 (c 68)**—*contd*

| | |
|---|---|
| Pt II | 1 Feb 1973 (repeals of Sugar Act 1956, ss 3(2)(b), 4(2), (3), 17(1) (from the beginning to words "this section"), (3)–(5), 18(3), (4), 21, 22, 24–32, 33(2) (words "except" to "subsection"), (3), (5), Sch 4; South Africa Act 1962, Sch 2, para 5; Finance Act 1968, s 58) (Sugar Act 1956 (Repeals) (Appointed Day) (No 1) Order 1973, SI 1973/135) |
| | 1 Jul 1973 (repeals of Sugar Act 1956, ss 7–16, 20(6), 33(1) (words "regulations or"), (2) (words "Every instrument containing any such regulations, and,"), 34 (words "or the Commissioners"), 35(2) (definitions of "Commissioners," "composite sugar products", "distribution payments", "distribution repayments", "manufacture", "refiner", "surcharge" and "surcharge repayment"), (4)–(6), 36(2); Finance Act 1962, s 3(6) (words from "the Sugar Act 1956" onwards), Sch 5, Pt II; Finance Act 1964, s 22; Finance Act 1966, s 52) (Sugar Act 1956 (Repeals) (Appointed Day) (No 2) Order 1973, SI 1973/1019) |
| | 1 Aug 1975 (repeals of Sugar Act 1956, s 17(2), (6), (7), Sch 3, paras 2, 3; Agriculture Act 1957, ss 4, 36(2) (words "and to sugar beet"); Agriculture (Miscellaneous Provisions) Act 1963, s 25) (Sugar Act 1956 (Repeals) (Appointed Day) (No 3) Order 1975, SI 1975/1164) |
| | 5 May 1976 (repeals of Sugar Act 1956, ss 3(1) (words from "including" onwards), 19, 20(1)–(5), (7), (8), 35(2) (definitions of "the Consolidated Fund" and "refined sugar"), Sch 3, para 4) (Sugar Act 1956 (Repeals) (Appointed Day) (No 4) Order 1976, SI 1976/548) |
| | 1 Dec 1976 (repeals of Sugar Act 1956, ss 5, 23(5), 35(2) (definition of "the Minister"); National Loans Act 1968, Sch 1, the entry for the Sugar Act 1956) (Sugar Act 1956 (Repeals) (Appointed Day) (No 5) Order 1976, SI 1976/2016) |
| | 1 Sep 1981 (repeal of Sugar Act 1956, s 23(1)–(3), but without prejudice to the modification made by s 23(2) in the articles of the British Sugar Corporation) (Sugar Act 1956 (Repeals) (Appointed Day) (No 6) Order 1981, SI 1981/1192) |
| | *Never in force* (otherwise) (spent) |
| Pt III | 1 Sep 1978 (repeals of Plant Varieties and Seeds Act 1964, s 32; Trade Descriptions Act 1968, s 2(4)(a)) (Plant Varieties and Seeds Act 1964 (Repeals) (Appointed Day) Order 1978, SI 1978/1003) |
| | 16 Aug 1982 (all repeals in 1964 Act save s 32 mentioned above; repeal of Agriculture (Miscellaneous Provisions) Act 1968, Sch 7) (Plant Varieties and Seeds Act 1964 (Repeals) (Appointed Day) Order 1982, SI 1982/1048) |
| Pt IV | 1 Jan 1973 (s 4(1)) |
| Sch 4    para 1 | 17 Oct 1972 (RA) (generally with practical effect from 1 Jan 1973) |
| para 2 | 1 Jan 1973 (Sch 4, para 2(2)) |
| para 3 | 17 Oct 1972 (RA) (para 3(1), (2) generally with practical effect from 1 Jan 1973; and para 3(3) from the end of the year 1975) |
| paras 4–6 | 17 Oct 1972 (RA) (generally with practical effect from 1 Jan 1973) |
| para 7 | 1 Jan 1973 (Sch 4, para 7(1)) |
| para 8 | 1 Jan 1973 (Sch 4, para 8(1)) |
| paras 9, 10 | 17 Oct 1972 (RA) (generally with practical effect from 1 Jan 1973) |

**Field Monuments Act 1972 (c 43)**

*RA:* 27 Jul 1972

Whole Act in force 27 Jul 1972 (RA)

## Finance Act 1972 (c 41)

*Budget Day:* 21 Mar 1972

*RA:* 27 Jul 1972

The commencement details of Finance Acts are not set out, as the dates from which their provisions take effect are usually stated clearly and unambiguously in the text of the Act, and charging provisions will normally state for which year or years of assessment they are to have effect.

## Gas Act 1972 (c 60)

*RA:* 9 Aug 1972

Whole Act in force 9 Aug 1972 (RA); but note that this Act was effective from 1 Jan 1973, the day appointed for the creation of the British Gas Corporation by Gas Act 1972 (Appointed Day) Order 1972, SI 1972/1440, made under s 1(1)

## Harbours Development (Scotland) Act 1972 (c 64)

*RA:* 9 Aug 1972

Whole Act in force 9 Aug 1972 (RA)

## Harbours (Loans) Act 1972 (c 16)

*RA:* 23 Mar 1972

Whole Act in force 23 Mar 1972 (RA)

## Harbours, Piers and Ferries (Scotland) Act 1972 (c 29)

*RA:* 12 Jun 1972

Whole Act in force 12 Jun 1972 (RA)

## Horserace Totalisator and Betting Levy Boards Act 1972 (c 69)

*RA:* 17 Oct 1972

*Commencement provisions:* s 3(3)

| | |
|---|---|
| 1–8 | 17 Oct 1972 (RA) |

## Housing Finance Act 1972 (c 47)

*RA:* 27 Jul 1972

*Commencement provisions:* ss 34(6), 39(3), 47(3), 108(5)

| | | |
|---|---|---|
| 1–26 | | 10 Aug 1972 (s 108(5)) |
| 27–34 | | 27 Aug 1972 (s 34(6)) |
| 35–38 | | 10 Aug 1972 (s 108(5)) |
| 39 | | 27 Aug 1972 (s 39(3)) |
| 40–46 | | 10 Aug 1972 (s 108(5)) |
| 47 | | 27 Aug 1972 (s 47(3)) |
| 48–108 | | 10 Aug 1972 (s 108(5)) |
| Schs 1–10 | | 10 Aug 1972 (s 108(5)) |
| Sch 11 | Pt I | 10 Aug 1972 (s 108(5)) |
| | Pt II | 1 Jan 1973 (Sch 11, Pt II) |

**Housing Finance Act 1972 (c 47)**—*contd*

| | | |
|---|---|---|
| | Pts III–V | 10 Aug 1972 (s 108(5)) |
| | Pt VI | 10 Aug 1972 (s 108(5)), repeals of or in— |

Housing Act 1957, ss 113(4), 120, 123, 125, 134;
Housing (Financial Provisions) Act 1958, s 57;
House Purchase and Housing Act 1959;
Town and Country Planning Act 1959;
Landlord and Tenant Act 1962;
Housing Act 1964;
Prices and Incomes Act 1968;
Rent Act 1968;
Housing Act 1969, ss 85(3), 87

27 Aug 1972 (repeals of or in Housing Act 1969, Pt III, Schs 2, 3 (subject to Sch 6, para 10 of this Act)) (Sch 11, Pt VI)

1 Oct 1972 (repeals of or in Housing Act 1957, s 113(3)) (Sch 11, Pt VI)

1 Jan 1973 (repeals of or in Housing Act 1957, s 121(2)) (Sch 11, Pt VI)

---

**Housing (Financial Provisions) (Scotland) Act 1972 (c 46)**

*RA:* 27 Jul 1972

*Commencement provisions:* s 81(3); Housing (Financial Provisions) (Scotland) Act 1972 (Commencement) Order 1972, SI 1972/1130

| | | |
|---|---|---|
| 1–33 | | 3 Aug 1972 (SI 1972/1130) |
| 34–50 | | 27 Aug 1972 (s 81(3)) |
| 51–59 | | 3 Aug 1972 (SI 1972/1130) |
| 60–67 | | 27 Aug 1972 (s 81(3)) |
| 68–81 | | 3 Aug 1972 (SI 1972/1130) |
| Schs 1–8 | | 3 Aug 1972 (SI 1972/1130) |
| Sch 9 | paras 1–22 | 3 Aug 1972 (SI 1972/1130) |
| | para 23 | 27 Aug 1972 (s 81(3)) |
| | para 24 | 3 Aug 1972 (SI 1972/1130) |
| | para 25 | 27 Aug 1972 (s 81(3)) |
| | para 26 | 3 Aug 1972 (SI 1972/1130) |
| | paras 27–31 | 27 Aug 1972 (s 81(3)) |
| | para 32 | 3 Aug 1972 (SI 1972/1130) |
| Sch 10 | paras 1–3 | 3 Aug 1972 (SI 1972/1130) |
| | para 4 | 27 Aug 1972 (s 81(3)) |
| Sch 11 | Pt I | 3 Aug 1972 (SI 1972/1130) |
| | Pt II | 1 Jan 1973 (Sch 11, Pt II) |
| | Pts III, IV | 3 Aug 1972 (SI 1972/1130) |
| | Pt V | 3 Aug 1972 (SI 1972/1130), repeals of or in— |

Housing and Town Development (Scotland) Act 1957;
Housing (Scotland) Act 1966;
Housing (Financial Provisions) (Scotland) Act 1968;
Town and Country Planning (Scotland) Act 1969

27 Aug 1972 (s 81(3)), repeals of or in—
Fire Precautions Act 1971;
Rent (Scotland) Act 1971

---

**Industry Act 1972 (c 63)**

*RA:* 9 Aug 1972

Whole Act in force 9 Aug 1972 (RA)

---

## Iron and Steel Act 1972 (c 12)

*RA:* 1 Mar 1972

Whole Act in force 1 Mar 1972 (RA)

---

## Island of Rockall Act 1972 (c 2)

*RA:* 10 Feb 1972

Whole Act in force 10 Feb 1972 (RA)

---

## Land Charges Act 1972 (c 61)

*RA:* 9 Aug 1972

*Commencement provisions*: s 19(2); Land Charges Act 1972 (Commencement) Order 1972, SI 1972/2058

Whole Act in force 29 Jan 1973 (SI 1972/2058)

---

## Legal Advice and Assistance Act 1972 (c 50)

*RA:* 27 Jul 1972

*Commencement provisions*: s 14(4); Legal Advice and Assistance Act 1972 (Commencement No 1) Order 1973, SI 1973/299; Legal Advice and Assistance Act 1972 (Scotland) (Commencement No 1) Order 1973, SI 1973/320

| | |
|---|---|
| 1–6 | 2 Apr 1973 (SI 1973/299; SI 1973/320) |
| 7–10 | *Never in force* (repealed) |
| 11–14 | 2 Apr 1973 (SI 1973/299; SI 1973/320) |
| Schs 1–3 | 2 Apr 1973 (SI 1973/299; SI 1973/320) |

---

## Local Employment Act 1972 (c 5)

*RA:* 10 Feb 1972

*Commencement provisions*: s 23(2)

Whole Act in force 10 Mar 1972 (s 23(2))

---

## Local Government Act 1972 (c 70)

*RA:* 26 Oct 1972

*Commencement provisions*: ss 1(1), 20(1), 273; Local Government Act 1972 (Commencement No 1) (England) Order 1973, SI 1973/373; Local Government Act 1972 (Commencement No 2) (Wales) Order 1973, SI 1973/375

This Act largely came into force on receiving royal assent, and the whole Act was effective from 1 Apr 1974. The details of its commencement (whereby for administrative reasons slightly earlier dates were prescribed for the coming into force of certain provisions) are of only historical interest; consequently the section by section commencement dates are omitted here.

---

## Maintenance Orders (Reciprocal Enforcement) Act 1972 (c 18)

*RA:* 23 Mar 1972

*Commencement provisions*: s 49(2); Maintenance Orders (Reciprocal Enforcement) Act 1972 (Commencement No 1) Order 1974, SI 1974/517; Maintenance Orders (Reciprocal Enforcement) Act 1972 (Commencement No 2) Order 1975, SI 1975/377

**Maintenance Orders (Reciprocal Enforcement) Act 1972 (c 18)**—*contd*

| | | |
|---|---|---|
| 1–21 | | 1 Apr 1974 (SI 1974/517) |
| 22 | (1) | 1 Apr 1974 (SI 1974/517) |
| | (2)(a) | *Not yet in force* |
| | (2)(b) | *Never in force* (repealed) |
| | (2)(c) | *Not yet in force* |
| | (2)(d) | *Never in force* (repealed) |
| 23, 24 | | 1 Apr 1974 (SI 1974/517) |
| 25–39 | | 12 Apr 1975 (SI 1975/377) |
| 40–49 | | 1 Apr 1974 (SI 1974/517) |
| Schedule | | 1 Apr 1974 (SI 1974/517) |

**Matrimonial Proceedings (Polygamous Marriages) Act 1972 (c 38)**

*RA:* 29 Jun 1972

Whole Act in force 29 Jun 1972 (RA)

**Mineral Exploration and Investment Grants Act 1972 (c 9)**

*RA:* 24 Feb 1972

Whole Act in force 24 Feb 1972 (RA)

**Ministerial and other Salaries Act 1972 (c 3)**

*RA:* 10 Feb 1972

*Commencement provisions:* s 1(7)

| | |
|---|---|
| 1 | 1 Apr 1972 (s 1(7)) |
| 2 | 10 Feb 1972 (RA) |

**Museums and Galleries Admission Charges Act 1972 (c 73)**

*RA:* 26 Oct 1972

Whole Act in force 26 Oct 1972 (RA)

**National Debt Act 1972 (c 65)**

*RA:* 9 Aug 1972

Whole Act in force 9 Aug 1972 (RA)

**National Health Service (Family Planning) Amendment Act 1972 (c 72)**

*RA:* 26 Oct 1972

Whole Act in force 26 Oct 1972 (RA)

**National Health Service (Scotland) Act 1972 (c 58)**

*RA:* 9 Aug 1972

*Commencement provisions:* s 65(1); National Health Service (Scotland) Act 1972 (Commencement No 1) Order 1972, SI 1972/1256; National Health Service (Scotland) Act 1972 (Commencement No 2)

### National Health Service (Scotland) Act 1972 (c 58)—*contd*

Order 1973, SI 1973/372; National Health Service (Scotland) Act 1972 (Commencement No 3) Order 1973, SI 1973/1421; National Health Service (Scotland) Act 1972 (Commencement No 4) Order 1974, SI 1974/145

| | | |
|---|---|---|
| 1 | | 1 Mar 1973 (SI 1973/372) |
| 2–12 | | 1 Apr 1974 (SI 1974/145) |
| 13 | | 1 Mar 1973 (SI 1973/372) |
| 14–16 | | 1 Sep 1973 (SI 1973/1421) |
| 17–19 | | 1 Apr 1974 (SI 1974/145) |
| 20–23 | | 1 Sep 1973 (SI 1973/1421) |
| 24–27 | | 1 Apr 1974 (SI 1974/145) |
| 28 | | 21 Aug 1972 (SI 1972/1256) |
| 29–41 | | 1 Apr 1974 (SI 1974/145) |
| 42–50 | | 1 Oct 1973 (SI 1973/1421) |
| 51 | | 1 Apr 1974 (SI 1974/145) |
| 52 | | 1 Mar 1973 (SI 1973/372) |
| 53–57 | | 1 Apr 1974 (SI 1974/145) |
| 58, 59 | | 1 Sep 1973 (SI 1973/1421) |
| 60–63 | | 1 Mar 1973 (SI 1973/372) |
| 64 | (1) | See Sch 6 below |
| | (2) | See Sch 7 below |
| 65 | | 9 Aug 1972 (s 65(1)) |
| Schs 1–5 | | 1 Apr 1974 (SI 1974/145) |
| Sch 6 | para 1 | 1 Mar 1973 (amendments of National Health Service (Scotland) Act 1947, s 1) (SI 1973/372) |
| | paras 2–113 | 1 Apr 1974 (SI 1974/145) |
| | para 114 | 1 Mar 1973 (amendment of Mental Health (Scotland) Act 1960, s 92(2)) (SI 1973/372) |
| | paras 115–157 | 1 Apr 1974 (SI 1974/145) |
| Sch 7 | | 1 Apr 1974 (SI 1974/145) |

---

### National Insurance Act 1972 (c 57)

*RA:* 9 Aug 1972

*Commencement provisions:* s 6(5), Sch 4, Pt 1, para 1; National Insurance Act 1972 (Commencement No 1) Order 1972, SI 1972/1229[1]; National Insurance Act 1972 (Commencement No 2) Order 1972, SI 1972/1230; National Insurance Act 1972 (Commencement No 3) Order 1972, SI 1972/1665; National Insurance (Commencement) Order (Northern Ireland) 1973, SR 1973/154; National Insurance (Commencement No 2) Order (Northern Ireland) 1973, SR 1973/269; National Insurance Act 1972 (Commencement No 4) Order 1973, SI 1973/833; National Insurance Act 1972 (Commencement No 5) Order 1973, SI 1973/1335

| | | |
|---|---|---|
| 1 | (1) | See Sch 1 below |
| | (2)–(5) | 2 Oct 1972 (rates of benefit under the National Insurance Act 1965, in the case of maternity allowance, widow's benefit, guardian's allowance, retirement pension, age addition and child's special allowance and the calculation of earnings-related supplement and widow's supplementary allowance) (SI 1972/1229) |
| | | 5 Oct 1972 (rates of benefit under the National Insurance Act 1965, in the case of unemployment, sickness and invalidity benefit) (SI 1972/1229) |
| 2 | | See Sch 2 below |
| 3 | | 2 Oct 1972 (SI 1972/1229) |
| 4 | (1) | See Sch 3 below |
| | (2) | 2 Oct 1972 (SI 1972/1229) |
| | (3), (4) | 4 Oct 1972 (SI 1972/1229) |
| | (5) | 2 Oct 1972 (SI 1972/1229) |
| 5 | | 9 Aug 1972 (Sch 4, Pt 1, para 1) |
| 6 | (1)–(4) | 2 Oct 1972 (SI 1972/1229) |

**National Insurance Act 1972 (c 57)**—*contd*

| | | |
|---|---|---|
| | (5) | 11 Aug 1972 (SI 1972/1229) |
| 7 | | *Never in force* (repealed) |
| 8 | (1), (2) | 11 Aug 1972 (SI 1972/1229) |
| | (3) | *Never in force* (repealed) |
| | (4) | 11 Aug 1972 (SI 1972/1229) |
| | (5) | See Sch 6 below |

Sch 1 — 2 Oct 1972 (rates of benefit under the National Insurance Act 1965, in the case of maternity allowance, widow's benefit, guardian's allowance, retirement pension, age addition and child's special allowance and the calculation of earnings-related supplement and widow's supplementary allowance) (SI 1972/1229)

2 Oct 1972 (higher weekly rate of attendance allowance) (SI 1972/1230)

5 Oct 1972 (rates of benefit under the National Insurance Act 1965, in the case of unemployment, sickness and invalidity benefit) (SI 1972/1229)

4 Jun 1973 (lower weekly rate of attendance allowance for persons who, under Sch 4, para 4(3) of this Act are of category I, or who, under para 6 of that Sch are treated as belonging to that Category) (SI 1972/1665)[2]

1 Oct 1973 (in the case of lower weekly rate of attendance allowance for persons who, under Sch 4, para 4(3) of this Act are of category 2) (SI 1973/833; SR 1973/154)

1 Dec 1973 (in the case of lower weekly rate of attendance allowance for persons who, under Sch 4, para 4(3) of this Act are of category 3) (SI 1973/1335; SR 1973/269)

3 Dec 1973 (in the case of lower weekly rate of attendance allowance for persons who, under Sch 4, para 4(3) of this Act are of category 4) (SI 1973/1335; SR 1973/269)

Sch 2 — 2 Oct 1972 (SI 1972/1229)

Sch 3 — 2 Oct 1972 (rates and amounts of benefit under the National Insurance (Industrial Injuries) Act 1965, in the case of widows pension under s 19, widower's pensions under s 20 and allowance in respect of children of deceased's family under s 21) (SI 1972/1229)

4 Oct 1972 (rates and amounts of benefit under the National Insurance (Industrial Injuries) Act 1965, in the case of disablement benefit (including increases thereof), other than those under this Schedule coming into force on 5 Oct 1972, increase of unemployability supplement under s 13A, maximum under s 29(1)(a) of aggregate of weekly benefits payable for successive accidents and maximum disablement gratuity under s 12(3)) (SI 1972/1229)

5 Oct 1972 (rates and amounts of benefit under the National Insurance (Industrial Injuries) Act 1965, in the case of injury benefit (including increases thereof) and increase of disablement pension in respect of children and adult dependants in the case of a beneficiary receiving, as an in-patient in a hospital or similar institution, medical treatment for the relevant injury or loss of faculty) (SI 1972/1229)

Sch 4 — Pt I — 11 Aug 1972 (SI 1972/1229)

Pt II — 10 Aug 1973 (in the case of lower weekly rate of attendance allowance for persons who, under Sch 4, para 4(3) of this Act are of category 3) (SI 1973/1355; SR 1973/269)

11 Aug 1973 (in the case of lower weekly rate of attendance allowance for persons who, under Sch 4, para 4(3) of this Act are of category 4) (SI 1973/1355; SR 1973/269)

21 Aug 1972 (in relation to attendance allowance except as they relate to the lower weekly rate) (SI 1972/1230)

**National Insurance Act 1972 (c 57)**—*contd*

|  |  |  |
|---|---|---|
|  |  | 10 May 1973 (in the case of lower weekly rate of attendance allowance for persons who, under Sch 4, para 4(3) of this Act are of category 2) (SI 1973/833) |
|  |  | 16 May 1973 (in the case of lower weekly rate of attendance allowance for persons who, under Sch 4, para 4(3) of this Act are of category 2) (SR 1973/154) |
|  |  | 15 Nov 1973 (lower weekly rate of attendance allowance for persons who, under Sch 4, para 4(3) of this Act are of category I, or who, under para 6 of that Sch are treated as belonging to that Category) (SI 1972/1665)[2] |
| Sch 5 |  | *Never in force* (repealed) |
| Sch 6 | Pt I | 21 Aug 1972 (SI 1972/1230), repeals of or in— |

National Insurance Act 1970, ss 4(2), (5), 6(1);
National Insurance Act 1971, Sch 5, para 12(2)

2 Oct 1972 (SI 1972/1229), repeals of or in—
National Insurance (Industrial Injuries) Act 1965, s 19;
National Insurance Act 1966, s 5(5);
National Insurance Act 1970, s 7(3);
National Insurance Act 1971, ss 1(1)–(3), (5), 2(1), 8(1), Sch 1, Sch 2 (in the case of maternity allowance, widow's benefit, guardian's allowance, retirement pension, age addition and child's special allowance) and Sch 4 (in the case of widow's pension, widower's pension and allowance in respect of children of deceased's family)

2 Oct 1972 (repeals of or in National Insurance Act 1971, s 2(1), Sch 2 (as far as they relate to attendance allowance)) (SI 1972/1230)

4 Oct 1972 (SI 1972/1229), repeals of or in—
National Insurance Act 1971, s 8(1), Sch 4 (in the case of disablement pensions (including increases thereof), other than those under this Part of this Schedule coming into force on 5 Oct 1972, and increase of unemployability supplement, maximum of aggregate of weekly benefits payable for successive accidents and maximum disablement gratuity)

5 Oct 1972 (SI 1972/1229), repeals of or in—
National Insurance Act 1971, ss 2(1), 8(1), Sch 2 (in the case of unemployment, sickness and invalidity benefit) and Sch 4 (in the case of injury benefit (including increases thereof) and increase of disablement pension in respect of children and adult dependants in the case of a beneficiary receiving as an in-patient in a hospital or similar institution, medical treatment for the relevant injury or loss of faculty)

|  |  |  |
|---|---|---|
|  | Pt II | *Never in force* (repealed) |

[1]   For transitional provisions, see SI 1972/1229, art 2

[2]   For transitional provisions, see SI 1972/1665, art 3

---

**National Insurance (Amendment) Act 1972 (c 36)**

*RA:* 29 Jun 1972

*Commencement provisions:* s 3(2), (3); National Insurance (Amendment) Act 1972 Commencement Order 1972, SI 1972/1176

Whole Act in force 2 Oct 1972 (SI 1972/1176)

---

**National Insurance Regulations (Validation) Act 1972 (c 4)**

*RA:* 10 Feb 1972

Whole Act in force 10 Feb 1972 (RA)

**Northern Ireland Act 1972 (c 10)**

*RA:* 24 Feb 1972

Whole Act in force 24 Feb 1972 (RA)

**Northern Ireland (Border Poll) Act 1972 (c 77)**

*RA:* 7 Dec 1972

Whole Act in force 7 Dec 1972 (RA)

**Northern Ireland (Financial Provisions) Act 1972 (c 76)**

*RA:* 7 Dec 1972

Whole Act in force 7 Dec 1972 (RA)

**Northern Ireland (Temporary Provisions) Act 1972 (c 22)**

*RA:* 30 Mar 1972

Whole Act in force 30 Mar 1972 (RA); note that s 1 expired on 1 Jan 1974, the commencement date for the Northern Ireland Constitution Act 1973, Pt II

**Overseas Investment and Export Guarantees Act 1972 (c 40)**

*RA:* 29 Jun 1972

Whole Act in force 29 Jun 1972 (RA)

**Parliamentary and other Pensions Act 1972 (c 48)**

*RA:* 27 Jul 1972

Whole Act in force 27 Jul 1972 (RA)

**Pensioners and Family Income Supplement Payments Act 1972 (c 75)**

*RA:* 30 Nov 1972

*Commencement provisions:* s 3(3)

Whole Act in force 30 Nov 1972 (RA), with the exception of s 3(1), (2), which were brought into force on 3 Apr 1973 by s 3(3)

**Pensioners' Payments and National Insurance Contributions Act 1972 (c 80)**

*RA:* 21 Dec 1972

Whole Act in force 21 Dec 1972 (RA)

## Performers' Protection Act 1972 (c 32)

*RA:* 29 Jun 1972

*Commencement provisions:* s 4(2)

Whole Act in force 29 Jul 1972 (s 4(2))

---

## Poisons Act 1972 (c 66)

*RA:* 9 Aug 1972

*Commencement provisions:* s 13(1); Medicines Act 1968 (Commencement No 7) Order 1977, SI 1977/2128

Whole Act in force 1 Feb 1978 (SI 1977/2128)

---

## Police Act 1972 (c 39)

*RA:* 29 Jun 1972

Whole Act in force 29 Jun 1972 (RA)

---

## Post Office (Borrowing) Act 1972 (c 79)

*RA:* 21 Dec 1972

Whole Act in force 21 Dec 1972 (RA)

---

## Repair of Benefice Buildings Measure 1972 (No 2)

*RA:* 10 Feb 1972

This Measure came into force in different dioceses on different dates, as shown below, in accordance with orders of the Church Commissioners (and is in force for every diocese):

Bath and Wells:—1 Jan 1973

Birmingham:—1 Jan 1974

Blackburn:—1 Jan 1974

Bradford:—1 Apr 1973

Bristol:—1 Jan 1973

Canterbury:—1 Jul 1973

Carlisle:—1 Jan 1974

Chelmsford:—1 Jan 1974

Chester:—1 Jan 1974

Chichester:—1 Jan 1974

Coventry:—1 Apr 1973

Derby:—1 Jan 1974

Durham:—1 Jan 1974

Ely:—1 Jan 1973

Exeter:—1 Jan 1973

Gloucester:—1 Jan 1974

**Repair of Benefice Buildings Measure 1972 (No 2)**—*contd*

Guildford:—1 Jan 1974

Hereford:—1 Apr 1973

Leicester:—1 Apr 1974

Lichfield:—1 Apr 1974

Lincoln:—1 Jan 1974

Liverpool:—1 Jan 1973

London:—1 Jan 1974

Manchester:—1 Jan 1974

Newcastle:—1 Jan 1973

Norwich:—1 Jan 1974

Oxford:—1 Jan 1974

Peterborough:—1 Apr 1974

Portsmouth:—1 Jan 1974

Ripon:—1 Jan 1974

Rochester:—1 Jan 1973

St Albans:—1 Jan 1973

St Edmundsbury and Ipswich:—1 Jan 1974

Salisbury:—1 Apr 1973

Sheffield:—1 Jan 1974

Southwark:—1 Jan 1974

Southwell:—1 Jan 1974

Truro:—1 Jan 1973

Wakefield:—1 Jan 1974

Winchester:—1 Apr 1973

Worcester:—1 Jan 1974

York:—1 Jan 1974

**Road Traffic Act 1972 (c 20)**

*RA:* 30 Mar 1972

*Commencement provisions:* s 208

Whole Act in force 1 Jul 1972 (s 208)

**Road Traffic (Foreign Vehicles) Act 1972 (c 27)**

*RA:* 11 May 1972

*Commencement provisions:* s 8(2); Road Traffic (Foreign Vehicles) Act 1972 Commencement Order 1972, SI 1972/1018

Whole Act in force 31 Jul 1972 (SI 1972/1018)

### Salmon and Freshwater Fisheries Act 1972 (c 37)

*RA:* 29 Jun 1972

Whole Act in force 29 Jun 1972 (RA)

___

### Sierra Leone Republic Act 1972 (c 1)

*RA:* 10 Feb 1972

Whole Act in force 10 Feb 1972 (RA); but as Sierra Leone became a Republic before this date, this Act is deemed to have come into force on 19 Apr 1971 (s 1(4))

___

### Social Work (Scotland) Act 1972 (c 24)

*RA:* 11 May 1972

Whole Act in force 11 May 1972 (RA)

___

### Sound Broadcasting Act 1972 (c 31)

*RA:* 12 Jun 1972

*Commencement provisions:* s 13(6)

Whole Act in force 12 Jul 1972 (s 13(6))

___

### Sri Lanka Republic Act 1972 (c 55)

*RA:* 27 Jul 1972

Whole Act in force 27 Jul 1972 (RA); but as Ceylon became a Republic before this date, this Act is deemed to have come into force on 22 May 1972 (s 1(6))

___

### Summer Time Act 1972 (c 6)

*RA:* 10 Feb 1972

*Commencement provisions:* s 6(2)

Whole Act in force 10 Mar 1972 (s 6(2))

___

### Sunday Cinema Act 1972 (c 19)

*RA:* 30 Mar 1972

*Commencement provisions:* s 6(1)

Whole Act in force 1 Jul 1972 (s 6(1))

___

### Sunday Theatre Act 1972 (c 26)

*RA:* 11 Apr 1972

*Commencement provisions:* s 6(3)

Whole Act in force 11 May 1972 (s 6(3))

___

**Superannuation Act 1972 (c 11)**

*RA:* 1 Mar 1972

*Commencement provisions:* s 30(4); Superannuation Act 1972 (Commencement No 1) Order 1972, SI 1972/325; Superannuation Act 1972 (Commencement No 2) Order 1972, SI 1972/384

Whole Act in force 25 Mar 1972 (SI 1972/325)

---

**Town and Country Planning (Amendment) Act 1972 (c 42)**

*RA:* 27 Jul 1972

*Commencement provisions:* s 12(2)

Whole Act in force 27 Jul 1972 (RA), except ss 8, 9, which came into force on 27 Aug 1972 (s 12(2))

---

**Town and Country Planning (Scotland) Act 1972 (c 52)**

*RA:* 27 Jul 1972

*Commencement provisions:* ss 18, 279, 280; Town and Country Planning (Scotland) Act 1972 (Commencement No 1) (Orkney Islands Area) Order 1975, SI 1975/379; Town and Country Planning (Scotland) Act 1972 (Commencement No 2) Order 1975, SI 1975/380; Town and Country Planning (Scotland) Act 1972 (Commencement No 3) Order 1975, SI 1975/1203; Town and Country Planning (Scotland) Act 1972 (Commencement No 4) Order 1976, SI 1976/464

The Act mainly came into force on 27 Aug 1972 (s 280(1)), except for s 280, Sch 23 (so far as it relates to the repeal of Pt I of the Control of Office and Industrial Development Act 1965). Provision was made in s 18 for Pt II (dealing with development plans), with certain exceptions, to come into force on days appointed by the Secretary of State, with different days appointed for the commencement of the same provisions in different areas; see SI 1975/379, appointing 1 Apr 1975 for the Orkney Islands Area and SI 1975/ 380 appointing 16 May 1975 for the remainder of Scotland. In addition, ss 58(5), 59(1)–(3) came into force on 17 Jul 1975 by virtue of SI 1975/1203 and Sch 7 came into force on 1 Apr 1976 by virtue of SI 1976/464.

---

**Trade Descriptions Act 1972 (c 34)**

*RA:* 29 Jun 1972

*Commencement provisions:* s 4(2)

Whole Act in force 29 Dec 1972 (s 4(2)), except s 1(5) which came into force on 29 Jun 1972 (RA)

---

**Trading Representations (Disabled Persons) Amendment Act 1972 (c 45)**

*RA:* 27 Jul 1972

*Commencement provisions:* s 3(2)

Whole Act in force 1 Jan 1973 (s 3(2))

---

**Transport (Grants) Act 1972 (c 15)**

*RA:* 23 Mar 1972

Whole Act in force 23 Mar 1972 (RA)

---

**Transport Holding Company Act 1972 (c 14)**

*RA:* 23 Mar 1972

Whole Act in force 23 Mar 1972 (RA)

# 1973 Acts

## Administration of Justice Act 1973 (c 15)

*RA:* 18 Apr 1973

*Commencement provisions:* s 20; Administration of Justice Act 1973 (Commencement) Order 1974, SI 1974/43

| | | |
|---|---|---|
| 1–5 | | 1 Apr 1974 (s 20(1)(a)) |
| 6, 7 | | 18 Apr 1973 (RA) |
| 8 | | 18 May 1973 (s 20(1)(b)) |
| 9 | | 18 Apr 1973 (RA) |
| 10 | | 1 Feb 1974 (SI 1974/43) |
| 11–16 | | 18 Apr 1973 (RA) |
| 17, 18 | | 18 May 1973 (s 20(1)(b)) |
| 19–21 | | 18 Apr 1973 (RA) |
| Sch 1 | | 1 Apr 1974 (s 20(1)) |
| Schs 2–4 | | 18 Apr 1973 (RA) |
| Sch 5 | Pt I | 18 Apr 1973 (RA) |
| | Pt II | 1 Apr 1974 (s 20(1)(a)) |
| | Pts III–VI | 18 Apr 1973 (RA) |

## Atomic Energy Authority (Weapons Group) Act 1973 (c 4)

*RA:* 6 Mar 1973

Whole Act in force 6 Mar 1973 (RA); but note that ss 1–5 had no effect: until 1 Apr 1973, the day appointed for the purposes of s 1(1) by SI 1973/463

## Badgers Act 1973 (c 57)

*RA:* 25 Jul 1973

*Commencement provisions:* s 12(3)

Whole Act in force 25 Jan 1974 (s 12(3))

## Bahamas Independence Act 1973 (c 27)

*RA:* 14 Jun 1973

Whole Act in force 14 Jun 1973 (RA); but did not generally have effect until 10 Jul 1973 (the "appointed day" (s 1(1))

### Bangladesh Act 1973 (c 49)

*RA:* 25 Jul 1973

25 Jul 1973 (RA); but note that Bangladesh was recognised as an independent sovereign state on 4 Feb 1972, and most provisions of this Act are deemed to have had effect from that date

### Breeding of Dogs Act 1973 (c 60)

*RA:* 25 Oct 1973

*Commencement provisions:* s 7

Whole Act in force 1 Apr 1974 (s 7(3))

### Channel Tunnel (Initial Finance) Act 1973 (c 66)

*RA:* 13 Nov 1973

Whole Act in force 13 Nov 1973 (RA)

### Coal Industry Act 1973 (c 8)

*RA:* 22 Mar 1973

*Commencement provisions:* s 14(3)

Whole Act in force 22 Mar 1973 (RA) except for s 2(1), and the provisions in Sch 2 which relate to the Coal Industry Acts 1965, 1967 and 1971, which came into force on 1 Apr 1973 (s 14(3))

### Concorde Aircraft Act 1973 (c 7)

*RA:* 22 Mar 1973

Whole Act in force 22 Mar 1973 (RA)

### Costs in Criminal Cases Act 1973 (c 14)

*RA:* 18 Apr 1973

*Commencement provisions:* s 22(2)

Whole Act in force 18 Jul 1973 (s 22(2))

### Counter-Inflation Act 1973 (c 9)

*RA:* 22 Mar 1973

Whole Act in force 22 Mar 1973 (RA)

### Dentists (Amendment) Act 1973 (c 31)

*RA:* 5 Jul 1973

Whole Act in force 5 Jul 1973 (RA)

## Domicile and Matrimonial Proceedings Act 1973 (c 45)

*RA:* 25 Jul 1973

*Commencement provisions:* s 17(5)

Whole Act in force 1 Jan 1974 (s 17(5))

## Education Act 1973 (c 16)

*RA:* 18 Apr 1973

*Commencement provisions:* s 1(5); Education Act 1973 (Commencement) Order 1973, SI 1973/1661

| | | |
|---|---|---|
| 1 | (1)(a) | 1 Feb 1974 (SI 1973/1661) |
| | (1)(b) | 18 Apr 1973 (RA) |
| | (2)–(5) | 18 Apr 1973 (RA) |
| 2–5 | | 18 Apr 1973 (RA) |
| Sch 1 | | 18 Apr 1973 (RA) |
| Sch 2 | Pts I, II | 18 Apr 1973 (RA) |
| | Pt III | 1 Feb 1974 (SI 1973/1661) |

## Education (Work Experience) Act 1973 (c 23)

*RA:* 23 May 1973

Whole Act in force 23 May 1973 (RA)

## Employment Agencies Act 1973 (c 35)

*RA:* 18 Jul 1973

*Commencement provisions:* s 14; Employment Agencies Act 1973 (Commencement) Order 1976, SI 1976/709

| | |
|---|---|
| 1 | 30 Jun 1976 (purposes of s 1(3)) (SI 1976/709) |
| | 1 Nov 1976 (all other purposes) (SI 1976/709) |
| 2–14 | 1 Jul 1976 (SI 1976/709) |
| Schedule | 1 Jul 1976 (SI 1976/709) |

## Employment and Training Act 1973 (c 50)

*RA:* 25 Jul 1973

*Commencement provisions:* s 15(2); Employment and Training Act 1973 (Commencement No 1) Order 1973, SI 1973/2063, as amended by SI 1974/398; Employment and Training Act 1973 (Commencement No 2) Order 1974, SI 1974/398; Employment and Training Act 1973 (Commencement No 3) Order 1974, SI 1974/1463; Employment and Training Act 1973 (Commencement No 4) Order 1975, SI 1975/689

| | | |
|---|---|---|
| 1 | (1) | 1 Jan 1974 (in relation to the Commission) (SI 1973/2063) |
| | | 1 Apr 1974 (in relation to Training Services Agency) (SI 1974/398) |
| | | 1 Oct 1974 (otherwise) (SI 1974/1463) |
| | (2), (3) | 1 Jan 1974 (SI 1973/2063) |
| | (4) | 1 Apr 1974 (in relation to Training Services Agency) (SI 1974/398) |
| | | 1 Oct 1974 (otherwise) (SI 1974/1463) |
| | (5) | 1 Jan 1974 (in relation to Sch 1, para 21 of this Act) (SI 1973/2063) |
| | | 1 Apr 1974 (in relation to Training Services Agency) (SI 1974/398) |
| | | 1 Oct 1974 (otherwise) (SI 1974/1463) |
| | (6), (7) | 1 Jan 1974 (in relation to the Commission) (SI 1973/2063) |
| | | 1 Apr 1974 (in relation to Training Services Agency) (SI 1974/398) |

**Employment and Training Act 1973 (c 50)**—*contd*

| | | |
|---|---|---|
| | | 1 Oct 1974 (otherwise) (SI 1974/1463) |
| 2 | (1)–(3) | 1 Jan 1974 (SI 1973/2063) |
| | (4) | 1 Apr 1974 (in relation to Training Services Agency) (SI 1974/398) |
| | | 1 Oct 1974 (otherwise) (SI 1974/1463) |
| | (5) | 1 Jan 1974 (in relation to the Commission) (SI 1973/2063) |
| | | 1 Apr 1974 (in relation to Training Services Agency) (SI 1974/398) |
| | | 1 Oct 1974 (otherwise) (SI 1974/1463) |
| 3–5 | | 1 Jan 1974 (SI 1973/2063) |
| 6 | (1) | See Sch 2, Pt I |
| | (2) | 16 May 1975 (SI 1973/2063) |
| | (3)(a) | See Sch 2, Pt III |
| | (3)(b) | 1 Apr 1974 (SI 1973/2063) |
| | (4) | 1 Apr 1975 (SI 1973/2063) |
| | (5) | 1 Jan 1974 (SI 1973/2063) |
| 7 | (1)–(4) | 1 Jan 1974 (in relation to the Commission) (SI 1973/2063) |
| | | 1 Apr 1974 (in relation to Training Services Agency) (SI 1974/398) |
| | | 1 Oct 1974 (otherwise) (SI 1974/1463) |
| | (5) | 1 Jan 1974 (SI 1973/2063) |
| 8 | | 1 Apr 1974 (E) (W) (SI 1974/398) |
| | | 16 May 1975 (S) (SI 1975/689) |
| 9 | (1), (2) | 1 Apr 1974 (E) (W) (SI 1974/398) |
| | | 16 May 1975 (S) (SI 1975/689) |
| | (3), (4) | *Never in force* (substituted) |
| | (5), (6) | 1 Apr 1974 (E) (W) (SI 1974/398) |
| | | 16 May 1975 (S) (SI 1975/689) |
| 10 | (1) | 1 Apr 1974 (E) (W) (SI 1974/398) |
| | | 16 May 1975 (S) (SI 1975/689) |
| | (2) | 1 Apr 1974 (SI 1974/398) |
| 11 | (1) | 1 Jan 1974 (in relation to the Commission) (SI 1973/2063) |
| | | 1 Apr 1974 (in relation to Training Services Agency) (SI 1974/398) |
| | | 1 Oct 1974 (otherwise) (SI 1974/1463) |
| | (2), (3) | 1 Jan 1974 (SI 1973/2063) |
| 12 | (1) | 1 Jan 1974 (SI 1973/2063) |
| | (2) | 1 Jan 1974 (in relation to the Commission) (SI 1973/2063) |
| | | 1 Apr 1974 (in relation to local education authorities) (SI 1974/398) |
| | | 16 May 1975 (otherwise) (SI 1975/689) |
| | (3) | 1 Apr 1974 (E) (W) (SI 1974/398) |
| | | 16 May 1975 (S) (SI 1975/689) |
| | (4)–(6) | 1 Jan 1974 (SI 1973/2063) |
| 13 | | 1 Jan 1974 (SI 1973/2063) |
| 14 | | See Schs 3, 4 below |
| 15 | | 1 Jan 1974 (SI 1973/2063) |
| Sch 1 | paras 1–20 | 1 Jan 1974 (SI 1973/2063) |
| | para 21 | 1 Oct 1974 (SI 1974/1463) |
| Sch 2 | Pt I, para 1 | 1 Jan 1974 (except so far as it amends Industrial Training Act 1964, ss 5(1), (2), (5), 8(3)) (SI 1973/2063)[1] |
| | | 1 Apr 1974 (exception noted above) (SI 1973/2063) |
| | Pt I, paras 2, 3 | 1 Jan 1974 (SI 1973/2063) |
| | Pt I, para 4(1) | 1 Jan 1974 (SI 1973/2063) |
| | Pt I, para 4(2) | 1 Jan 1974 (except so far as it relates to the determination by Ministers of travelling, subsistence and other allowances (other than allowances for loss of remunerative time) (SI 1973/2063) |
| | | 1 Apr 1975 (exception noted above) (SI 1973/2063) |
| | Pt I, para 4(3) | 1 Jan 1974 (SI 1973/2063) |

**Employment and Training Act 1973 (c 50)**—*contd*

| | |
|---|---|
| Pt I, para 5 | 1 Aug 1974 (in relation to Carpet, Ceramics, Glass and Mineral Products, Clothing and Allied Products, Construction, Food, Drink and Tobacco, Footwear, Leather and Fur Skin, Furniture and Timber, Iron and Steel, Knitting, Lace and Net and Road Transport Industrial Training Boards) (SI 1973/2063) |
| | 1 Sept 1974 (in relation to Engineering[1], Paper and Paper Products, and Petroleum Industrial Training Boards) (SI 1973/2063) |
| | 1 Apr 1975 (in relation to Air Transport and Travel, Cotton and Allied Textiles, Hotel and Catering, Man-made Fibres Producing, Printing and Publishing, Rubber and Plastics Processing, Shipbuilding and Wool, Jute and Flax) (SI 1973/2063) |
| | 1 Aug 1975 (in relation to Chemical and Allied Products and Distributive Industrial Training Boards) (SI 1973/2063) |
| Pt I, para 6 | 1 Jan 1974 (SI 1973/2063)[1] |
| Pt I, para 7(1) | 1 Apr 1974 (SI 1973/2063) |
| Pt I, para 7(2) | 1 Apr 1975 (SI 1973/2063) |
| Pt I, paras 8, 9 | 1 Jan 1974 (SI 1973/2063) |
| Pt I, para 10 | 1 Jan 1974 (SI 1973/2063)[1] |
| Pt I, para 11 | 1 Apr 1974 (SI 1973/2063)[1] |
| Pt I, paras 12–16 | 1 Jan 1974 (SI 1973/2063) |
| Pt I, para 17(a)–(d) | 1 Jan 1974 (SI 1973/2063) |
| Pt I, para 17(e) | 1 Apr 1975 (SI 1973/2063) |
| Pt I, para 17(f) | 1 Jan 1974 (except so far as it relates to the determination by Ministers of travelling, subsistence and other allowances (other than allowances for loss of remunerative time) (SI 1973/2063) |
| | 1 Apr 1975 (exception noted above) (SI 1973/2063) |
| Pt I, para 18(a) | 1 Apr 1974 (so far as it relates to arrangements made by local education authorities in England and Wales) (SI 1973/2063) |
| | 16 May 1975 (otherwise) (SI 1973/2063) |
| Pt I, para 18(b) | 1 Jan 1974 (SI 1973/2063) |
| Pt I, para 18(c) | 1 Apr 1974 (SI 1973/2063) |
| Pt I, para 18(d) | 1 Jan 1974 (SI 1973/2063) |
| Pt I, para 18(e) | 1 Jan 1974 (except so far as it repeals Industrial Training Act 1964, s 17) (SI 1973/2063) |
| | 1 Apr 1974 (exception noted above) (SI 1973/2063) |
| Pt I, para 18(f) | 1 Jan 1974 (SI 1973/2063) |
| Pt II | 16 May 1975 (SI 1973/2063) |
| Pt III, para 1(a)–(e) | 1 Apr 1974 (SI 1973/2063) |
| Pt III, para 1(f) | 1 Jan 1974 (in so far as it refers to the Industrial Training Act 1964, s 11) (SI 1973/2063) |
| | 1 Apr 1974 (otherwise) (SI 1973/2063) |
| Pt III, para 1(g) | 1 Apr 1974 (SI 1973/2063) |
| Pt III, para 2 | 1 Jan 1974 (except so far as it relates to the definition "the Minister") (SI 1973/2063)[1] |
| | 1 Apr 1974 (otherwise) (SI 1973/2063) |
| Pt III, para 3 | 1 Jan 1974 (except so far as it relates to the Industrial Training Act 1964, s 2(1)(f)) (SI 1973/2063) |
| | 1 Apr 1974 (otherwise) (SI 1973/2063) |
| Pt III, para 4 | 1 Apr 1974 (SI 1973/2063) |
| Pt III, para 5(1) | 1 Apr 1974 (SI 1973/2063) |
| Pt III, para 5(2) | 1 Jan 1974 (except so far as it relates to the determination by Ministers of travelling, subsistence and other allowances (other than allowances for loss of remunerative time) (SI 1973/2063) |
| | 1 Apr 1975 (otherwise) (SI 1973/2063) |
| Pt III, para 5(3) | 1 Jan 1974 (SI 1973/2063) |
| Pt III, paras 6, 7 | 1 Apr 1974 (SI 1973/2063) |
| Pt III, para 8 | 1 Jan 1974 (SI 1973/2063) |
| Pt III, para 9(a)–(c) | 1 Jan 1974 (SI 1973/2063) |

**Employment and Training Act 1973 (c 50)**—*contd*

|          | Pt III, para 9(d) | 1 Apr 1975 (SI 1973/2063) |
|----------|-------------------|---------------------------|
|          | Pt III, para 9(e) | 1 Jan 1974 (except so far as it relates to the determination by Ministers of travelling, subsistence and other allowances (other than allowances for loss of remunerative time) (SI 1973/2063) |
|          |                   | 1 Apr 1975 (otherwise) (SI 1973/2063) |
|          | Pt IV             | 1 Apr 1975 (SI 1973/2063) |
| Sch 3    | para 1            | 1 Apr 1974 (SI 1974/398) |
|          | para 2            | 1 Oct 1974 (SI 1974/463) |
|          | paras 3–5         | 1 Jan 1974 (SI 1973/2063) |
|          | para 6            | 1 Apr 1974 (E) (W) (SI 1974/398) |
|          |                   | 16 May 1975 (S) (SI 1975/689) |
|          | para 7(1)         | 1 Oct 1974 (SI 1974/463) |
|          | para 7(2)         | 1 Apr 1974 (SI 1974/398) |
|          | para 7(3)         | 1 Jan 1974 (SI 1973/2063) |
|          | para 8            | 1 Apr 1974 (SI 1974/398) |
|          | paras 9, 10       | 1 Jan 1974 (SI 1973/2063) |
|          | para 11(1)        | 1 Apr 1974 (SI 1974/398) |
|          | para 11(2)        | 1 Jan 1974 (SI 1973/2063) |
|          | para 12           | 1 Oct 1974 (SI 1974/1463) |
|          | para 13           | 1 Jan 1974 (SI 1973/2063) |
|          | paras 14, 15      | 1 Oct 1974 (SI 1974/1463) |
| Sch 4    |                   | 1 Jan 1974 (SI 1973/2063), repeals of or in— |
|          |                   | Employment and Training Act 1948, ss 4, 20(2); |
|          |                   | Industrial Training Act 1964, ss 3(1), 6, 11, 13, Schedule, para 6(2); |
|          |                   | Chronically Sick and Disabled Persons Act 1970, s 13(2) |
|          |                   | 1 Apr 1974 (repeal of Industrial Training Act 1964, ss 2(1)(f) (so far as it relates to arrangements made by local education authorities in England and Wales) 5, 17) (SI 1973/2063) |
|          |                   | 1 Apr 1974 (SI 1974/398), repeals of or in— |
|          |                   | Unemployment Insurance Act 1935, s 80; |
|          |                   | Employment and Training Act 1948, ss 3, 8–13, 14(2), 15, Sch 1; |
|          |                   | Agriculture (Miscellaneous Provisions) Act 1949, s 8(5); |
|          |                   | London Government Act 1963, s 34; |
|          |                   | National Insurance (Industrial Injuries) Act 1965, s 72; |
|          |                   | Agriculture Act 1970, s 104; |
|          |                   | Local Government Act 1972, s 209 |
|          |                   | 1 Oct 1974 (SI 1974/1463), repeals of or in— |
|          |                   | Disabled Persons (Employment) Act 1944, ss 2–4, 16 (in part); |
|          |                   | Employment and Training Act 1948, s 2(5), (8); |
|          |                   | National Insurance (Industrial Injuries) Act 1965, s 25(2)(c); |
|          |                   | Local Employment Act 1972, s 6 |
|          |                   | 16 May 1975 (repeal of Industrial Training Act 1964, s 2(1)(f) (otherwise)) (SI 1973/2063) |
|          |                   | 16 May 1975 (SI 1975/689), repeals of or in— |
|          |                   | Employment and Training Act 1948 (so far as unrepealed); |
|          |                   | Criminal Justice Act 1967, in Sch 3, the entry relating to Employment and Training Act 1948; |
|          |                   | Employment Medical Advisory Service Act 1972, s 5(2) (SI 1975/689) |

[1]   For transitional provisions, see SI 1973/2063, arts 4, 5A

---

**Employment of Children Act 1973 (c 24)**

*RA:* 23 May 1973

*Commencement provisions*: s 3(4)

**Employment of Children Act 1973 (c 24)**—*contd*
*Never in force* (repealed)

---

**Fair Trading Act 1973 (c 41)**

*RA*: 25 Jul 1973

*Commencement provisions*: s 140(3); Fair Trading Act 1973 (Commencement No 1) Order 1973, SI 1973/1545; Fair Trading Act 1973 (Commencement No 2) Order 1973, SI 1973/1652

| | | |
|---|---|---|
| 1–28 | | 1 Nov 1973 (SI 1973/1652) |
| 29–32 | | 14 Sep 1973 (SI 1973/1545) |
| 33 | (1) | 1 Nov 1973 (SI 1973/1652) |
| | (2)(a), (b) | 1 Nov 1973 (SI 1973/1652) |
| | (2)(c), (d) | 14 Sep 1973 (SI 1973/1545) |
| 34–117 | | 1 Nov 1973 (SI 1973/1652) |
| 118–123 | | 14 Sep 1973 (SI 1973/1545) |
| 124–128 | | 1 Nov 1973 (SI 1973/1652) |
| 129 | | 14 Sep 1973 (SI 1973/1545) |
| 130, 131 | | 1 Nov 1973 (SI 1973/1652) |
| 132 | | 14 Sep 1973 (SI 1973/1545) |
| 133 | | 1 Nov 1973 (SI 1973/1652) |
| 134 | | 14 Sep 1973 (SI 1973/1545) |
| 135 | (1) | 1 Nov 1973 (SI 1973/1652) |
| | (2)(a), (b) | 14 Sep 1973 (SI 1973/1545) |
| | (2)(c), (d) | 1 Nov 1973 (SI 1973/1652) |
| 136 | | 1 Nov 1973 (SI 1973/1652) |
| 137 | | 14 Sep 1973 (SI 1973/1545) |
| 138, 139 | | 1 Nov 1973 (SI 1973/1652) |
| 140 | | 14 Sep 1973 (SI 1973/1545) |
| Schs 1–13 | | 1 Nov 1973 (SI 1973/1652) |

---

**Finance Act 1973 (c 51)**

*Budget Day:* 6 Mar 1973

*RA*: 25 Jul 1973

The commencement details of Finance Acts are not set out, as the dates from which their provisions take effect are usually stated clearly and unambiguously in the text of the Act, and charging provisions will normally state for which year or years of assessment they are to have effect.

---

**Fire Precautions (Loans) Act 1973 (c 11)**

*RA*: 29 Mar 1973

Whole Act in force 29 Mar 1973 (RA)

---

**Fuel and Electricity (Control) Act 1973 (c 67)**

*RA*: 6 Dec 1973

Whole Act in force 6 Dec 1973 (RA)

---

## Furnished Lettings (Rent Allowances) Act 1973 (c 6)

*RA:* 22 Mar 1973

Whole Act in force 22 Mar 1973 (RA)

## Gaming (Amendment) Act 1973 (c 12)

*RA:* 18 Apr 1973

Whole Act in force 18 Apr 1973 (RA)

## Government Trading Funds Act 1973 (c 63)

*RA:* 25 Oct 1973

Whole Act in force 25 Oct 1973 (RA)

## Guardianship Act 1973 (c 29)

*RA:* 5 Jul 1973

*Commencement provisions*: s 15(3); Guardianship Act 1973 (Commencement No 1) Order 1974, SI 1974/695; Guardianship Act 1973 (Commencement No 2) Order 1974, SI 1974/836

Whole Act in force 8 May 1974 (SI 1974/695; SI 1974/836)

## Hallmarking Act 1973 (c 43)

*RA:* 25 Jul 1973

*Commencement provisions*: s 24(2)

| | |
|---|---|
| 1–12 | 1 Jan 1975 (s 24(2)) |
| 13 | 1 Jan 1974 (s 24(2)) |
| 14–24 | 1 Jan 1975 (s 24(2)) |
| Schs 1–3 | 1 Jan 1975 (s 24(2)) |
| Sch 4 | 1 Jan 1974 (s 24(2)) |
| Schs 5–7 | 1 Jan 1975 (s 24(2)) |

## Heavy Commercial Vehicles (Controls and Regulations) Act 1973 (c 44)

*RA:* 25 Jul 1973

Whole Act in force 25 Jul 1973 (RA)

## Housing (Amendment) Act 1973 (c 5)

*RA:* 6 Mar 1973

Whole Act in force 6 Mar 1973 (RA)

## Independent Broadcasting Authority Act 1973 (c 19)

*RA:* 23 May 1973

*Commencement provisions*: s 40(4)

**Independent Broadcasting Authority Act 1973 (c 19)**—*contd*
Whole Act in force 31 Jul 1973 (s 40(4))

---

**Insurance Companies Amendment Act 1973 (c 58)**

*RA:* 25 Jul 1973

*Commencement provisions:* s 57(3)–(8)

Whole Act in force 25 Jul 1973 (RA)

---

**International Cocoa Agreement Act 1973 (c 46)**

*RA:* 25 Jul 1973

*Commencement provisions:* s 2(2); International Cocoa Agreement Act 1973 (Commencement) Order 1973, SI 1973/1617

Whole Act in force 1 Oct 1973 (SI 1973/1617)

---

**International Sugar Organisation Act 1973 (c 68)**

*RA:* 19 Dec 1973

Whole Act in force 19 Dec 1973 (RA)

---

**Land Compensation Act 1973 (c 26)**

*RA:* 23 May 1973

*Commencement provisions:* s 89(2)

| | |
|---|---|
| 1–19 | 23 Jun 1973 (s 89(2)) |
| 20–89 | 23 May 1973 (RA) |
| Schs 1–3 | 23 May 1973 (RA) |

---

**Local Government (Scotland) Act 1973 (c 65)**

*RA:* 25 Oct 1973

*Commencement provisions:* s 238(2); Local Government (Scotland) Act 1973 (Commencement No 1) Order 1973, SI 1973/1886; Local Government (Scotland) Act 1973 (Commencement No 2) Order 1973, SI 1973/2181

| | | |
|---|---|---|
| 1, 2 | | 20 Dec 1973 (SI 1973/2181) |
| 3 | (1)–(5) | 20 Dec 1973 (SI 1973/2181) |
| | (6) | 16 May 1975 (SI 1973/2181) |
| | (7) | 20 Dec 1973 (SI 1973/2181) |
| 4–6 | | 20 Dec 1973 (SI 1973/2181) |
| 7 | (1) | 12 Nov 1973 (except words from "and accordingly" to the end) (SI 1973/1886) |
| | | 1 Apr 1974 (otherwise) (SI 1973/2181) |
| | (2)–(7) | 12 Nov 1973 (SI 1973/1886) |
| 8–10 | | 20 Dec 1973 (SI 1973/2181) |
| 11 | (1), (2) | 12 Nov 1973 (SI 1973/1886) |
| | (3) | See Sch 3 below |
| | (4) | 12 Nov 1973 (SI 1973/1886) |
| 12–43 | | 20 Dec 1973 (SI 1973/2181) |
| 44–50 | | 16 May 1975 (SI 1973/2181) |
| 51–55 | | 20 Dec 1973 (SI 1973/2181) |

**Local Government (Scotland) Act 1973 (c 65)**—*contd*

| | | |
|---|---|---|
| 56 | (1)–(7) | 20 Dec 1973 (SI 1973/2181) |
| | (8)–(10) | 16 May 1975 (SI 1973/2181) |
| | (11)–(15) | 20 Dec 1973 (SI 1973/2181) |
| 57–63 | | 20 Dec 1973 (SI 1973/2181) |
| 64 | (1)–(3) | 20 Dec 1973 (SI 1973/2181) |
| | (4), (5) | 16 May 1975 (SI 1973/2181) |
| | (6), (7) | 20 Dec 1973 (SI 1973/2181) |
| 65–68 | | 20 Dec 1973 (SI 1973/2181) |
| 69 | | 16 May 1975 (SI 1973/2181) |
| 70–74 | | 20 Dec 1973 (SI 1973/2181) |
| 75 | | 16 May 1975 (SI 1973/2181) |
| 76, 77 | | 20 Dec 1973 (SI 1973/2181) |
| 78 | | 16 May 1975 (SI 1973/2181) |
| 79–81 | | 20 Dec 1973 (SI 1973/2181) |
| 82, 83 | | 16 May 1975 (SI 1973/2181) |
| 84 | | 20 Dec 1973 (SI 1973/2181) |
| 85 | | 16 May 1975 (SI 1973/2181) |
| 86–89 | | 20 Dec 1973 (SI 1973/2181) |
| 90–92 | | 16 May 1975 (SI 1973/2181) |
| 93–107 | | 20 Dec 1973 (SI 1973/2181) |
| 108, 109 | | 16 May 1975 (SI 1973/2181) |
| 110–117 | | 20 Dec 1973 (SI 1973/2181) |
| 118 | | 16 May 1975 (SI 1973/2181) |
| 119, 120 | | 20 Dec 1973 (SI 1973/2181) |
| 121 | | 16 May 1974 (SI 1973/2181) |
| 122 | | See Sch 9 below |
| 123–134 | | 16 May 1975 (SI 1973/2181) |
| 135 | (1) | 16 May 1975 (SI 1973/2181) |
| | (2)–(7) | 20 Dec 1973 (SI 1973/2181) |
| | (8)–(10) | 16 May 1975 (SI 1973/2181) |
| 136–145 | | 16 May 1975 (SI 1973/2181) |
| 146 | (1)–(6) | 16 May 1975 (SI 1973/2181) |
| | (7) | 20 Dec 1973 (SI 1973/2181) |
| | (8) | 16 May 1973 (SI 1973/2181) |
| | (9) | 20 Dec 1973 (SI 1973/2181) |
| | (10) | 16 May 1975 (SI 1973/2181) |
| 147 | (1) | 16 May 1975 (SI 1973/2181) |
| | (2)–(6) | 20 Dec 1973 (SI 1973/2181) |
| | (7), (8) | 16 May 1975 (SI 1973/2181) |
| 148 | (1)–(7) | 16 May 1975 (SI 1973/2181) |
| | (8) | 16 May 1975 (SI 1973/2181) |
| 149 | | 16 May 1975 (SI 1973/2181) |
| 150 | (1), (2) | 16 May 1975 (SI 1973/2181) |
| | (3) | 20 Dec 1973 (SI 1973/2181) |
| | (4), (5) | 16 May 1975 (SI 1973/2181) |
| 151–164 | | 16 May 1975 (SI 1973/2181) |
| 165 | | 20 Dec 1973 (SI 1973/2181) |
| 166–171 | | 16 May 1975 (SI 1973/2181) |
| 172 | (1) | 16 May 1975 (SI 1973/2181) |
| | (2) | 20 Dec 1973 (SI 1973/2181) |
| | (3), (4) | 16 May 1975 (SI 1973/2181) |
| 173, 174 | | 16 May 1975 (SI 1973/2181) |
| 175 | | 20 Dec 1973 (SI 1973/2181) |
| 176–184 | | 16 May 1975 (SI 1973/2181) |
| 185 | | 20 Dec 1973 (so far as necessary to bring into operation the new Licensing (Scotland) Act 1959, ss 1(2), 5(2), (3)) (SI 1973/2181) |
| | | 16 May 1975 (otherwise) (SI 1973/2181) |
| 186 | (1) | 20 Dec 1973 (SI 1973/2181) |
| | (2) | See Sch 24, Pt I below |

**Local Government (Scotland) Act 1973 (c 65)**—*contd*

| | | |
|---|---|---|
| 187–189 | | 16 May 1975 (SI 1973/2181) |
| 190–197 | | 20 Dec 1973 (SI 1973/2181) |
| 198–207 | | 16 May 1975 (SI 1973/2181) |
| 208 | | 20 Dec 1973 (SI 1973/2181) |
| 209–213 | | 16 May 1975 (SI 1973/2181) |
| 214 | (1) | See Sch 27, Pt I below |
| | (2) | See Sch 27, Pt II below |
| 215–217 | | 20 Dec 1973 (SI 1973/2181) |
| 218 | | 12 Nov 1973 (SI 1973/1886) |
| 219–223 | | 20 Dec 1973 (SI 1973/2181) |
| 224 | | 12 Nov 1973 (SI 1973/1886) |
| 225 | (1)–(7) | 20 Dec 1973 (SI 1973/2181) |
| | (8) | 16 May 1975 (SI 1973/2181) |
| | (9), (10) | 20 Dec 1973 (SI 1973/2181) |
| 226 | | 20 Dec 1973 (SI 1973/2181) |
| 227–229 | | 16 May 1975 (SI 1973/2181) |
| 230–232 | | 20 Dec 1973 (SI 1973/2181) |
| 233 | | 12 Nov 1973 (SI 1973/1886) |
| 234–236 | | 20 Dec 1973 (SI 1973/2181) |
| 237 | (1) | See Sch 29 below |
| | (2) | 20 Dec 1973 (SI 1973/2181) |
| 238 | | 20 Dec 1973 (SI 1973/2181) |
| Sch 1 | | 20 Dec 1973 (SI 1973/2181) |
| Sch 2 | | 12 Nov 1973 (SI 1973/1886) |
| Sch 3 | paras 1, 2 | 16 May 1975 (SI 1973/2181) |
| | para 3(1) | 20 Dec 1973 (SI 1973/2181) |
| | para 3(2) | 7 May 1974 (SI 1973/2181) |
| | para 4 | 20 Dec 1973 (SI 1973/2181) |
| | paras 5–8 | 16 May 1975 (SI 1973/2181) |
| | para 9 | 20 Dec 1973 (SI 1973/2181) |
| | paras 10, 11 | 16 May 1975 (SI 1973/2181) |
| | paras 12–14 | 20 Dec 1973 (SI 1973/2181) |
| | para 15 | 7 May 1974 (SI 1973/2181) |
| | para 16(a) | 16 May 1975 (SI 1973/2181) |
| | para 16(b) | 1 Apr 1974 (SI 1973/2181) |
| | para 16(c) | 15 Feb 1974 (so far as it relates to the definition "local government area") (SI 1973/2181) |
| | | 1 Apr 1974 (so far as it relates to the definitions "elected district councillor", "local elections rules" and "local government Act") (SI 1973/2181) |
| | | 16 May 1975 (otherwise) (SI 1973/2181) |
| | paras 17–23 | 1 Apr 1974 (SI 1973/2181) |
| Schs 4–8 | | 20 Dec 1973 (SI 1973/2181) |
| Sch 9 | paras 1–43 | 16 May 1975 (SI 1973/2181) |
| | para 44 | 20 Dec 1973 (in relation to regional and islands councils) (SI 1973/2181) |
| | | 16 May 1975 (otherwise) (SI 1973/2181) |
| | paras 45–51 | 16 May 1975 (SI 1973/2181) |
| | para 52 | 16 May 1974 (SI 1973/2181) |
| | para 53 | 16 May 1975 (SI 1973/2181) |
| | para 54 | 20 Dec 1973 (in relation to any financial year commencing on or after 16 May 1975) (SI 1973/2181) |
| | | 16 May 1975 (otherwise) (SI 1973/2181) |
| | paras 55–57 | 16 May 1975 (SI 1973/2181) |
| | para 58 | 20 Dec 1973 (in relation to any financial year commencing on or after 16 May 1975) (SI 1973/2181) |
| | | 16 May 1975 (otherwise) (SI 1973/2181) |
| | paras 59–61 | 16 May 1975 (SI 1973/2181) |
| | para 62(a) | 16 May 1974 (SI 1973/2181) |

**Local Government (Scotland) Act 1973 (c 65)**—*contd*

| | | |
|---|---|---|
| | para 62(b) | 16 May 1975 (SI 1973/2181) |
| | para 63 | 16 May 1975 (SI 1973/2181) |
| | para 64 | 16 May 1974 (SI 1973/2181) |
| | para 65 | 20 Dec 1973 (SI 1973/2181) |
| | paras 66–72 | 20 Dec 1973 (in relation to any financial year commencing on or after 16 May 1975) (SI 1973/2181)<br>16 May 1975 (otherwise) (SI 1973/2181) |
| | para 73 | 16 May 1974 (SI 1973/2181) |
| | para 74 | 20 Dec 1973 (SI 1973/2181) |
| Schs 10–16 | | 16 May 1975 (SI 1973/2181) |
| Sch 17 | paras 1–51 | 16 May 1975 (SI 1973/2181) |
| | para 52 | 16 May 1974 (SI 1973/2181) |
| | paras 53–64 | 16 May 1975 (SI 1973/2181) |
| Schs 18–23 | | 16 May 1975 (SI 1973/2181) |
| Sch 24 | paras 1–11 | 16 May 1975 (SI 1973/2181) |
| | para 12 | 20 Dec 1973 (to the extent required for the operation of the new Licensing (Scotland) Ac 1959, s 5(2), (3), which is brought into force by s 185 above) (SI 1973/2181)<br>16 May 1975 (otherwise) (SI 1973/2181) |
| | paras 13–21 | 16 May 1975 (SI 1973/2181) |
| | para 22 | 20 Dec 1973 (to the extent required for the operation of the new Licensing (Scotland) Act 1959, s 5(2), (3), which is brought into force by s 185 above) (SI 1973/2181)<br>16 May 1975 (otherwise) (SI 1973/2181) |
| | paras 23–47 | 16 May 1975 (SI 1973/2181) |
| Schs 25, 26 | | 16 May 1975 (SI 1973/2181) |
| Sch 27 | paras 1–186 | 16 May 1975 (SI 1973/2181) |
| | para 187 | 20 Dec 1973 (SI 1973/2181) |
| | paras 188–211 | 16 May 1975 (SI 1973/2181) |
| Sch 28 | | 16 May 1975 (SI 1973/2181) |
| Sch 29 | | 20 Dec 1973 (SI 1973/2181), repeals of or in—<br>Representation Act 1949, s 55(6);<br>Valuation and Rating (Scotland) Act 1956, s 1 (in relation to regional and islands councils);<br>Local Government (Scotland) Act 1966, s 2(2)(b)<br>1 Apr 1974 (SI 1973/2181), repeals of or in—<br>Representation of the People Act 1949, s 173(3), (8) (definition "elected district councillor"), Sch 3;<br>Representation of the People Act 1969, ss 12(2), 13(5), 14, Schs 1, 2<br>16 May 1974 (SI 1973/2181), repeals of or in—<br>Rating Act 1966, ss 5–8;<br>Rate Rebate Act 1973<br>16 May 1975 (otherwise) (SI 1973/2181)[1] |

[1] In so far as the provisions of the Local Government (Scotland) Act 1947 repealed in Sch 29 relate to accounts and audit the repeal shall be effective only in relation to any financial year commencing on or after 16 May 1975, see SI 1973/2181, art 9

**London Cab Act 1973 (c 20)**

*RA:* 23 May 1973

Whole Act in force 23 May 1973 (RA)

**Maplin Development Act 1973 (c 64)**

*RA:* 25 Oct 1973

Whole Act in force 25 Oct 1973 (RA)

## Matrimonial Causes Act 1973 (c 18)

*RA*: 23 May 1973

*Commencement provisions*: s 55(2); Matrimonial Causes Act 1973 (Commencement) Order 1973, SI 1973/1972

Whole Act in force 1 Jan 1974 (SI 1973/1972)

---

## National Health Service Reorganisation Act 1973 (c 32)

*RA*: 5 Jul 1973

*Commencement provisions*: ss 55(1), 58(2), (3); National Health Service Reorganisation Act 1973 (Appointed Day) Order 1973, SI 1973/1956; National Health Service Reorganisation Act 1973 (Commencement No 1) (Scotland) Order 1973, SI 1973/1185; National Health Service Reorganisation Act 1973 (Commencement No 2) Order 1973, SI 1973/1523; Isles of Scilly (National Health Service) Order 1973, SI 1973/1935; National Health Service Reorganisation Act 1973 (Commencement No 3) Order 1974, SI 1974/188; National Health Service Reorganisation Act 1973 (Commencement No 4) Order 1974, SI 1974/1191

| | | |
|---|---|---|
| 1 | | 5 Jul 1973 (s 58(2)) |
| 2–4 | | 1 Apr 1974 (SI 1974/188) |
| 5–10 | | 5 Jul 1973 (s 58(2)) |
| 11–13 | | 1 Apr 1974 (SI 1974/188) |
| 14 | | 5 Jul 1973 (s 58(2); but note that appointed day for purposes of s 14 is 1 Apr 1974) (SI 1973/1956) |
| 15 | | 5 Jul 1973 (s 58(2); but note that appointed day for purposes of s 15(2) is 1 Apr 1974) (SI 1973/1956) |
| 16–20 | | 5 Jul 1973 (s 58(2); but note that appointed day for purposes of ss 16(1), (2), (4), 17(1), 18(1)–(3) is 1 Apr 1974) (SI 1974/1956) |
| 21 | | 5 Jul 1973 (s 58(2)) |
| 22 | | 1 Apr 1974 (SI 1974/188) |
| 23–26 | | 5 Jul 1973 (s 58(2); but note that appointed day for purposes of ss 24, 25(1)–(3) is 1 Apr 1974) (SI 1973/1956) |
| 27 | | 1 Apr 1974 (SI 1974/188; note that 1 Apr is also appointed day for purposes of s 27(1)) (SI 1973/1956) |
| 28 | | 1 Apr 1974 (SI 1974/188) |
| 29, 30 | | 5 Jul 1973 (s 58(2); but note that appointed day for purposes of s 29(1) is 1 Apr 1974) (SI 1973/1956) |
| 31–33 | | 1 Oct 1973 (SI 1973/1523) |
| 34 | (1) | 1 Apr 1974 (SI 1973/1956) |
| | (2)–(7) | 1 Oct 1973 (SI 1973/1523) |
| 35–39 | | 1 Oct 1973 (SI 1973/1523) |
| 40 | | 1 Apr 1974 (SI 1974/188) |
| 41 | | 5 Jul 1973 (so far as it is applied by ss 16, 18) (s 58(2)) 1 Apr 1974 (otherwise) (SI 1974/188) |
| 42, 43 | | 1 Apr 1974 (SI 1974/188) |
| 44 | | 5 Jul 1973 (s 58(2)) |
| 45, 46 | | 1 Apr 1974 (SI 1974/188) |
| 47–49 | | 5 Jul 1973 (s 58(2)) |
| 50 | | 1 Nov 1974 (1974/1191) |
| 51–58 | | 5 Jul 1973 (s 58(2); but note that 1 Apr is also appointed day for purposes of s 54(5)[1]) (SI 1973/1956) |
| Schs 1, 2 | | 5 Jul 1973 (s 58(2); but note that 1 Apr is also appointed day for purposes of Sch 1, paras 1(3), 2(2), 4, 6(4)) (SI 1973/1956) |
| Sch 3 | | 1 Oct 1973 (SI 1973/1523) |
| Sch 4 | paras 1–21 | 1 Apr 1974 (SI 1974/188) |
| | para 22 | 5 Jul 1973 (s 58(2)) |
| | paras 23–40 | 1 Apr 1974 (SI 1974/188) |
| | para 41 | 5 Jul 1973 (SI 1973/1185) |

**National Health Service Reorganisation Act 1973 (c 32)**—*contd*

| | |
|---|---|
| paras 42–58 | 1 Apr 1974 (SI 1974/188) |
| para 59(1) | 1 Oct 1973 (SI 1973/1523) |
| para 59(2) | 1 Apr 1974 (SI 1974/188) |
| paras 60–78 | 1 Apr 1974 (SI 1974/188) |
| para 79 | 5 Jul 1973 (s 58(2)) |
| paras 80–129 | 5 Jul 1973 (SI 1973/1185) |
| para 130 | 1 Mar 1974 (in so far as relates to Post Office Act 1969, s 86(1)(c) definition "national health service authority") (SI 1974/188) |
| | 1 Apr 1974 (in so far as relates to Post Office Act 1969, s 86(1)(a) definition "national health service authority") (SI 1974/188) |
| para 131 | *Never in force* (repealed) |
| para 132 | 1 Apr 1974 (SI 1974/188) |
| para 133 | 5 Jul 1973 (s 58(2)) |
| paras 134–137 | 1 Apr 1974 (SI 1974/188) |
| paras 138–140 | 5 Jul 1973 (SI 1973/1185) |
| para 141 | 5 Jul 1973 (s 58(2)) |
| paras 142–150 | 5 Jul 1973 (SI 1973/1185) |
| paras 151, 152 | 5 Jul 1973 (s 58(2)) |
| Sch 5 | 5 Jul 1973 (entry relating to National Health Service Act 1946, s 36(3)(c)) (s 58(2)) |
| | 5 Jul 1973 (SI 1973/1185), entries relating to— |
| | National Health Service (Scotland) Act 1947; |
| | National Health Service (Scotland) Act 1972 |
| | 1 Apr 1974 (remainder, save entries relating to Ministry of Social Security Act 1966) (SI 1974/188)[1] |
| | 1 Nov 1974 (entries relating to Ministry of Social Security Act 1966, subject to transitional provisions) (SI 1974/1191) |
| | 1 Apr 1975 (entries relating to National Health Service Act 1946, ss 7(5)(a), (b), (7), 52(2)) (SI 1973/118)[1] |
| | 1 Apr 1976 (entry relating to National Health Service 1946, s 56) (SI 1974/188) |

[1]   For savings and transitional provisions, see SI 1974/188, arts 4–6, Sch 2

---

**National Insurance and Supplementary Benefit Act 1973 (c 42)**

*RA:* 25 Jul 1973

*Commencement provisions*: s 9(5), Sch 6, para 1; National Insurance and Supplementary Benefit Act 1973 (Commencement) Order 1973, SI 1973/1349[1]; National Insurance, Industrial Injuries and Supplementary Benefit Commencement Order (Northern Ireland) 1973, SR 1973/271[2]

| | | |
|---|---|---|
| 1 | (1) | See Sch 1 below |
| | (2) | 1 Oct 1973 (SR 1973/271) |
| 2 | | 1 Oct 1973 (SI 1973/1349; SR 1973/271) |
| 3 | (1) | See Sch 3 below |
| | (2), (3) | 3 Oct 1973 (SI 1973/1349; SR 1973/271) |
| | (4) | 1 Oct 1973 (SI 1973/1349; SR 1973/271) |
| 4, 5 | | 25 Jul 1973 (Sch 6, para 1(1)(a)) |
| 6 | | 1 Oct 1973 (SI 1973/1349; SR 1973/271) |
| 7 | | 1 Oct 1973 (SI 1973/1349) |
| 8 | | 6 Aug 1973 (SR 1973/271) |
| 9 | (1) | 6 Aug 1973 (SI 1973/1349; SR 1973/271) |
| | (2), (3) | 6 Aug 1973 (SI 1973/1349) |
| | (4) | 6 Aug 1973 (SR 1973/271) |
| | (5) | 6 Aug 1973 (SI 1973/1349; SR 1973/271) |
| | (6) | See Sch 7 below |

**National Insurance and Supplementary Benefit Act 1973 (c 42)**—*contd*

| | | |
|---|---|---|
| Sch 1 | | 1 Oct 1973 (rates of benefit under the National Insurance Act 1965 in the case of attendance allowance, maternity allowance, widow's benefit, guardians' allowance, retirement pension, age addition, child's special allowance and the calculation of earnings-related supplement and widow's supplementary allowance) (SI 1973/1349) |
| | | 1 Oct 1973 (rates of benefit under the National Insurance Act (Northern Ireland) 1966 in the case of attendance allowance, maternity allowance, widow's benefit, guardians' allowance, retirement pension, age addition, child's special allowance) (SR 1973/271) |
| | | 4 Oct 1973 (rates of benefit under the National Insurance Act 1965 in the case of unemployment, sickness and invalidity benefit) (SR 1973/271) |
| | | 4 Oct 1973 (rates of benefit under the National Insurance Act (Northern Ireland) 1966 rates of benefit under the National Insurance Act 1965 in the case of unemployment, sickness and invalidity benefit) (SI 1973/1349) |
| Sch 2 | | 1 Oct 1973 (SI 1973/1349; SR 1973/271) |
| Sch 3 | | 1 Oct 1973 (rates and amounts of benefit under the National Insurance (Industrial Injuries) Act 1965, in the case of widow's pension (s 19), widower's pension (s 20) and allowance in respect of children of deceased's family (s 21)) (SI 1973/1349) |
| | | 1 Oct 1973 (rates and amounts of benefit under the National Insurance (Industrial Injuries) (Northern Ireland) Act 1966, in the case of widow's pension (s 19), widower's pension (s 20) and allowance in respect of children of deceased's family (s 21)) (SR 1973/271) |
| | | 3 Oct 1973 (rates and amounts of benefit under the National Insurance (Industrial Injuries) Act 1965, in the case of disablement benefit (including increases of disablement pension other than those coming into force on 4 Oct 1972 under this Sch), increase of unemployability supplement under s 13A, maximum, under s 29(1)(a), of aggregate of weekly benefits payable for successive accidents and maximum disablement gratuity under s 12(4)) (SI 1973/1349) |
| | | 3 Oct 1973 (rates and amounts of benefit under the National Insurance (Industrial Injuries) (Northern Ireland) Act 1966, in the case of disablement benefit (including increases of disablement pension other than those coming into force on 4 Oct 1972 under this Sch), increase of unemployability supplement under s 13A, maximum, under s 29(1)(a), of aggregate of weekly benefits payable for successive accidents and maximum disablement gratuity under s 12(4)) (SR 1973/271) |
| | | 4 Oct 1973 (rates and amounts of benefit under the National Insurance (Industrial Injuries) Act 1965 in the case of injury benefit (including increases thereof) and increases of disablement pension in respect of children and adult dependants in the case of a beneficiary receiving as an in-patient in a hospital or similar institution, medical treatment for the relevant injury or loss of faculty) (SI 1973/1349) |
| | | 4 Oct 1973 (rates and amounts of benefit under the National Insurance (Industrial Injuries) Act 1965 in the case of injury benefit (including increases thereof) and increases of disablement pension in respect of children and adult dependants in the case of a beneficiary receiving as an in-patient in a hospital or similar institution, medical treatment for the relevant injury or loss of faculty) (SR 1973/271) |
| Sch 4 | paras 1–7 | 1 Oct 1973 (SI 1973/1349; SR 1973/271) |
| | para 8 | 25 Jul 1973 (Sch 6, para 1(1)(b)) |

**National Insurance and Supplementary Benefit Act 1973 (c 42)**—*contd*

| | |
|---|---|
| Sch 5 | 6 Aug 1973 (SR 1973/271) |
| Sch 6 | 6 Aug 1973 (SI 1973/1349; SR 1973/271) |
| Sch 7 | 1 Oct 1973 (SI 1973/1349; SR 1973/271), repeals of or in— |

Ministry of Social Security Act 1966;
National Insurance Act 1972, ss 1(1), 3 (except sub-s (3) as it applies to the year 1973–1974 or earlier years), 4(1), (5), Sch 1 (in the case of attendance allowance, maternity allowance, widow's benefit, guardian's allowance, retirement pension, age addition and child's special allowance), Sch 2, Sch 3 (in the case of widow's pension, widower's pension and allowance in respect of children of deceased's family)

1 Oct 1973 (SR 1973/271), repeals of or in—
Supplementary Benefits &c Act (Northern Ireland) Act 1966;
National Insurance Act 1972, Sch 5, paras 2(1) (entry relating to National Insurance Act 1969), 2(2) (entry relating to National Insurance Act 1971, s 1(3)), 3(a), 5

3 Oct 1973 (SI 1973/1349), repeals of or in—
National Insurance Act 1972, s 4(1), (4), Sch 3 (in the case of disablement benefit (including increases of disablement pension other than those coming into force on 4 Oct 1972 under this Sch), increase of unemployability supplement, maximum of aggregate of weekly benefits payable for successive accidents and maximum disablement gratuity)

3 Oct 1973 (SR 1973/271), repeals of or in—
National Insurance Act 1972, Sch 5, paras 2(1) (entry relating to Industrial Injuries and Diseases (Old Cases) Act 1967), 2(2) (entry relating to National Insurance (Industrial Injuries) Act 1965, s 12(3)(5)), 3(b)

4 Oct 1973 (SI 1973/1349), repeals of or in—
National Insurance Act 1972, ss 1(1), 4(1), Sch 1 (in the case of unemployment, sickness and invalidity benefit), Sch 3 (in the case of injury benefit (including increases thereof) and increases of disablement pension in respect of children and adult dependants in the case of a beneficiary receiving as an in-patient in a hospital or similar institution, medical treatment for the relevant injury or loss of faculty)

4 Oct 1973 (repeals of or in National Insurance Act 1972, Sch 5, paras 2(2) (entry relating to National Insurance Act 1965, ss 19(3), 43(3)(b), 43A(8)(b))) (SR 1973/271)

3 Dec 1973 (repeals of or in Post Office Act 1969, s 51) (SI 1973/1349)

[1]  For transitional provisions and savings, see SI 1973/1349, art 2
[2]  For transitional provisions and savings, see SR 1973/271, art 2

---

**National Theatre and Museum of London Act 1973 (c 2)**

*RA:* 13 Feb 1973

Whole Act in force 13 Feb 1973 (RA)

---

**Nature Conservancy Council Act 1973 (c 54)**

*RA:* 25 Jul 1973

*Commencement provisions*: s 1(7); Nature Conservancy Council (Appointed Day) Order 1973, SI 1973/1721

**Nature Conservancy Council Act 1973 (c 54)**—*contd*
Whole Act in force 25 Jul 1973 (RA); but note that this Act for the most part took effect from 1 Nov
    1973, the day appointed on and after which the Council was to discharge its functions under the Act

---

**Northern Ireland Assembly Act 1973 (c 17)**

*RA:* 3 May 1973

Whole Act in force 3 May 1973 (RA); but note that the Assembly had no legislative powers until 11 Jan
    1974, when the Northern Ireland Constitution Act 1973, Pt II, came into force

---

**Northern Ireland Constitution Act 1973 (c 36)**

*RA:* 18 Jul 1973

*Commencement provisions*: ss 2, 41(1), 43(5), (6); Northern Ireland Constitution (Devolution) Order 1973,
    SI 1973/2162; Northern Ireland Constitution Act 1973 (Commencement No 1) Order 1973,
    SI 1973/1418

| | | |
|---|---|---|
| 1–3 | | 18 Jul 1973 (s 43(5)) |
| 4–16 | | 1 Jan 1974 (SI 1973/2162) |
| 17–23 | | 1 Sep 1973 (SI 1973/1418) |
| 24–43 | | 18 Jul 1973 (s 43(5)) |
| Schs 1–3 | | 18 Jul 1973 (s 43(5)) |
| Sch 4 | | 1 Jan 1974 (SI 1973/2162) |
| Sch 5 | | 18 Jul 1973 (s 43(5)) |
| Sch 6 | Pt I | 18 Jul 1973 (s 41(1)(a)) |
| | Pt II | 1 Jan 1974 (s 41(1)(b); SI 1973/2162) |

---

**Northern Ireland Constitution (Amendment) Act 1973 (c 69)**

*RA:* 19 Dec 1973

Whole Act in force 19 Dec 1973 (RA)

---

**Northern Ireland (Emergency Provisions) Act 1973 (c 53)**

*RA:* 25 Jul 1973

*Commencement provisions*: s 30(1)–(3)

Whole Act in force 8 Aug 1973 (s 30(1))

---

**Overseas Pensions Act 1973 (c 21)**

*RA:* 23 May 1973

Whole Act in force 23 May 1973 (RA)

---

**Pakistan Act 1973 (c 48)**

*RA:* 25 Jul 1973

*Commencement provisions*: s 6(4)

Whole Act in force 1 Sep 1973 (s 6(4))

---

## Pensioners' Payments and National Insurance Act 1973 (c 61)

*RA:* 25 Oct 1973

*Commencement provisions*: s 8(1); Pensioners' Payments and National Insurance Act 1973 (Commencement) Order 1973, SI 1973/1969

Whole Act in force 25 Oct 1973 (RA)

---

## Powers of Criminal Courts Act 1973 (c 62)

*RA:* 25 Oct 1973

*Commencement provisions*: s 60(2); Powers of Criminal Courts Act 1973 (Commencement No 1) Order 1974, SI 1974/941

Whole Act in force 1 Jul 1974 (SI 1974/941) (except s 6(3)(b), (6)(b), (10) (never in force (repealed))

---

## Protection of Aircraft Act 1973 (c 47)

*RA:* 25 Jul 1973

*Commencement provisions*: s 28(2), (3); Protection of Aircraft Act 1973 (Commencement) Order 1973, SI 1973/1753

| | | |
|---|---|---|
| 1–5 | | 24 Nov 1973 (SI 1973/1753) |
| 6 | (1) | 24 Nov 1973 (SI 1973/1753) |
| | (2) | 25 Jul 1973 (s 28(2)) |
| | (3) | 24 Nov 1973 (SI 1973/1753) |
| 7–28 | | 25 Jul 1973 (s 28(2)) |
| Schedule | | 25 Jul 1973 (s 28(2)) |

---

## Protection of Wrecks Act 1973 (c 33)

*RA:* 18 Jul 1973

Whole Act in force 18 Jul 1973 (RA)

---

## Rate Rebate Act 1973 (c 28)

*RA:* 14 Jun 1973

Whole Act in force 14 Jun 1973 (RA)

---

## Sea Fish Industry Act 1973 (c 3)

*RA:* 13 Feb 1973

Whole Act in force 13 Feb 1973 (RA)

---

## Sea Fisheries (Shellfish) Act 1973 (c 30)

*RA:* 5 Jul 1973

*Commencement provisions*: s 2(2)

Whole Act in force 1 May 1974 (s 2(2))

---

## Social Security Act 1973 (c 38)

*RA:* 18 Jul 1973

*Commencement provisions:* s 101(2); Social Security Act 1973 (Commencement) Order 1973, SI 1973/1249; Social Security Act 1973 (Commencement No 2) Order 1973, SI 1973/1433, as amended by SI 1974/823; Social Security Act 1973 (Commencement No 3) Order 1974, SI 1974/164, as amended by SI 1974/823; Social Security Act 1973 (Commencement No 4) Order 1974, SI 1974/823; Social Security Act 1973 (Commencement No 5) Order 1975, SI 1975/124

| | | |
|---|---|---|
| 1–6 | | 6 Apr 1975 (SI 1973/1249) |
| 7, 8 | | 6 Apr 1974 (SI 1974/164) |
| 9 | | 6 Apr 1975 (SI 1973/1249) |
| 10, 11 | | 6 Apr 1975 (SI 1974/164) |
| 12 | (1), (2) | 6 Apr 1975 (SI 1974/164) |
| | (3) | 6 Apr 1975 (for the purposes of earnings-related supplement under s 10(8) of this Act) |
| | | *Never in force* (otherwise) (repealed) |
| 13–35 | | 6 Apr 1975 (SI 1974/164) |
| 36 | | 19 Jul 1973 (SI 1973/1249) |
| 37, 38 | | 6 Apr 1975 (SI 1974/164) |
| 39 | | 6 Apr 1974 (SI 1974/164) |
| 40, 41 | | 6 Apr 1975 (SI 1974/164) |
| 42 | | 6 Apr 1975 (SI 1973/1249) |
| 43 | | 6 Apr 1975 (SI 1974/164) |
| 44 | (1) | 6 Apr 1975 (SI 1974/164) |
| | (2)–(5) | 1 Apr 1975 (SI 1974/164) |
| | (6) | 6 Apr 1975 (SI 1974/164) |
| 45 | | 6 Apr 1975 (SI 1974/164) |
| 46 | (1) | 6 Apr 1975 (SI 1974/164) |
| | (2) | 28 Feb 1974 (in relation to expenses of carrying the Act into operation) (SI 1974/164) |
| | | 6 Apr 1975 (otherwise) (SI 1974/164) |
| | (3) | 6 Apr 1975 (SI 1974/164) |
| | (4) | 28 Feb 1974 (SI 1974/164) |
| 47 | | 6 Apr 1975 (SI 1974/164) |
| 48 | | 19 Jul 1973 (SI 1973/1249) |
| 49 | (1) | 28 Feb 1974 (SI 1974/164) |
| | (2) | 6 Apr 1974 (SI 1974/164) |
| | (3)–(6) | 28 Feb 1974 (SI 1974/164) |
| | (7), (8) | 6 Apr 1975 (SI 1974/164) |
| 50 | | 6 Apr 1975 (SI 1974/164) |
| 51 | | 5 Sep 1973 (for the purposes of the issue, cancellation, variation or surrender before, but with effect from dates not earlier than, 6 Apr 1975 of recognition certificates and for connected purposes) (SI 1973/1433)[1] |
| | | 6 Apr 1975 (all other purposes) (SI 1973/1433) |
| 52 | | 5 Sep 1973 (SI 1973/1433) |
| 53–60 | | 5 Sep 1973 (for the purposes of the issue, cancellation, variation or surrender before, but with effect from dates not earlier than, 6 Apr 1975 of recognition certificates and for connected purposes) (SI 1973/1433)[1] |
| | | 6 Apr 1975 (all other purposes) (SI 1973/1433) |
| 61, 62 | | 6 Apr 1975 (SI 1973/1433) |
| 63 | | 5 Sep 1973 (for purpose of enabling steps to be taken to ensure that on and after 6 Apr 1975 schemes conform with the preservation requirements and for connected purposes) (SI 1973/1433)[1] |
| | | 6 Apr 1975 (for all other purposes) (SI 1973/1433) |
| 64, 65 | | 5 Sep 1973 (SI 1973/1433) |
| 66 | (1)–(5) | 5 Sep 1973 (SI 1973/1433) |
| | (6) | 5 Mar 1975 (SI 1975/124) |

**Social Security Act 1973 (c 38)**—*contd*

| | | |
|---|---|---|
| | (7)–(9) | 5 Sep 1973 (SI 1973/1433) |
| 67 | | 5 Sep 1973 (SI 1973/1433) |
| 68 | | 18 Jan 1974 (SI 1973/1433) |
| 69 | (1)–(6) | 5 Sep 1973 (SI 1973/1433) |
| | (7) | *Not yet in force* |
| | (8) | 5 Sep 1973 (SI 1973/1433) |
| 70–72 | | 5 Sep 1973 (SI 1973/1433) |
| 73, 74 | | See Sch 18 below |
| 75 | (1)–(5) | 5 Sep 1973 (SI 1973/1433) |
| | (6) | 6 Apr 1975 (SI 1973/1433) |
| 76 | | *Never in force* (repealed) |
| 77, 78 | | 6 Apr 1975 (SI 1973/1249) |
| 79–83 | | 6 Apr 1975 (SI 1973/1433) |
| 84 | | 6 Apr 1975 (SI 1974/164) |
| 85 | | 6 Apr 1975 (SI 1973/1433) |
| 86 | | 5 Sep 1973 (in relation to Occupational Pensions Board) (SI 1973/1433; 1974/164) |
| | | 6 Apr 1975 (in relation to Reserve Pensions Board) (SI 1973/1433) |
| 87, 88 | | 6 Apr 1975 (SI 1974/164) |
| 89 | (1) | 6 Apr 1975 (SI 1974/164) |
| | (2) | 5 Sep 1973 (SI 1974/1433) |
| | (3) | 5 Sep 1973 (in relation to sub-s (2)) (SI 1973/1433) |
| | | 6 Apr 1975 (otherwise) (SI 1974/164) |
| | (4) | 6 Apr 1975 (SI 1974/164) |
| 90 | | 6 Apr 1975 (SI 1974/164) |
| 91 | (1), (2) | 6 Apr 1975 (SI 1973/1433) |
| | (3) | 5 Sep 1973 (SI 1973/1433) |
| | (4) | 6 Apr 1975 (SI 1973/1433) |
| | (5) | 5 Sep 1973 (SI 1973/1433) |
| 92 | (1), (2) | 6 Apr 1975 (SI 1974/164) |
| | (3), (4) | 5 Sep 1973 (SI 1973/1433) |
| | (5)–(8) | 6 Apr 1975 (SI 1974/164) |
| 93 | | 6 Apr 1975 (SI 1974/164) |
| 94 | (1)–(6) | 6 Apr 1975 (SI 1974/164) |
| | (7) | 1 Apr 1975 (SI 1974/164)[2] |
| | (8) | 6 Apr 1975 (SI 1974/164) |
| | (9) | 28 Feb 1974 (SI 1974/164) |
| | (10), (11) | 6 Apr 1975 (SI 1974/164) |
| 95 | (1) | 19 Jul 1973 (in relation to s 96) (SI 1973/1249) |
| | | 28 Feb 1974 (otherwise) (SI 1974/164) |
| | (2)–(4) | 28 Feb 1974 (SI 1974/164) |
| | (5) | 6 Apr 1975 (SI 1974/164) |
| 96, 97 | | 19 Jul 1973 (SI 1973/1249) |
| 98 | | 5 Sep 1973 (SI 1973/1433) |
| 99 | | 19 Jul 1973 (SI 1973/1249) |
| 100 | | See Schs 26–28 below |
| 101 | | 19 Jul 1973 (SI 1973/1249) |
| Schs 1–3 | | 6 Apr 1975 (SI 1973/1249) |
| Schs 4–11 | | 6 Apr 1975 (SI 1974/164) |
| Sch 12 | | 19 Jul 1975 (SI 1973/1249) |
| Schs 13, 14 | | 28 Feb 1974 (SI 1974/164) |
| Sch 15 | | 6 Apr 1975 (SI 1974/164) |
| Sch 16 | | 5 Sep 1973 (for purpose of enabling steps to be taken to ensure that on and after 6 Apr 1975 schemes conform with the preservation requirements and for connected purposes) (SI 1973/1433)[1] |
| | | 6 Apr 1975 (otherwise) (SI 1973/1433) |
| Schs 17, 18 | | 5 Sep 1973 (SI 1973/1433) |
| Sch 19 | | 6 Apr 1975 (SI 1973/1249) |

**Social Security Act 1973 (c 38)**—*contd*

| | | |
|---|---|---|
| Schs 20–22 | | 6 Apr 1975 (SI 1974/164) |
| Sch 23 | paras 1–6 | 5 Sep 1973 (SI 1973/1433) |
| | paras 7–15 | 6 Apr 1975 (SI 1974/164) |
| Sch 24 | | 6 Apr 1975 (SI 1974/164) |
| Sch 25 | paras 1–11 | 28 Feb 1974 (SI 1974/164) |
| | paras 12, 13 | 6 Apr 1975 (SI 1974/164) |
| | para 14(1), (2) | 6 Apr 1975 (SI 1973/1433) |
| | para 14(3) | 5 Sep 1973 (SI 1973/1433) |
| | para 14(4) | 6 Apr 1975 (SI 1973/1433) |
| | para 14(5) | 5 Sep 1973 (SI 1973/1433) |
| | paras 15, 16 | 28 Feb 1974 (SI 1974/164) |
| | paras 17–80 | 6 Apr 1975 (SI 1974/164) |
| Sch 26 | para 1 | 6 Apr 1975 (SI 1974/164) |
| | para 2(1) | 6 Apr 1975 (SI 1974/164) |
| | para 2(2), (3) | 28 Feb 1974 (SI 1974/164) |
| | paras 3–7 | 28 Feb 1974 (SI 1974/164) |
| | para 8 | 6 Apr 1975 (SI 1974/164) |
| Sch 27 | paras 1–23 | 6 Apr 1975 (SI 1974/164) |
| | para 24 | 6 Apr 1975 (except words "or premiums" and "or premium") (SI 1974/164) |
| | | *Not yet in force* (exception noted above) |
| | paras 25–63 | 6 Apr 1975 (SI 1974/164) |
| | para 64 | 6 Apr 1975 (except words "or premiums" and "or premium") (SI 1974/164) |
| | | *Not yet in force* (exception noted above) |
| | paras 65–77 | 6 Apr 1975 (SI 1974/164) |
| | para 78 | 6 Apr 1975 (except words "or premiums" and "or premium") (SI 1974/164) |
| | | *Not yet in force* (exception noted above) |
| | para 79 | 6 Apr 1975 (SI 1974/164) |
| | para 80 | 6 Apr 1975 (except words "or premiums" in sub-para (a) and sub-para (b)) (SI 1974/164) |
| | | *Not yet in force* (exception noted above) |
| | paras 81–176 | 6 Apr 1975 (SI 1974/164) |
| Sch 28 | | 28 Feb 1974 (repeals of or in National Insurance Act 1965, s 104(3), Sch 10) (SI 1974/164) |
| | | 1 Apr 1974 (SI 1974/164), repeals of or in— National Insurance Act 1965, ss 86, 87; National Insurance (Industrial Injuries) Act 1965, s 60; National Insurance Act (Northern Ireland) 1966, s 84; National Insurance (Industrial Injuries) Act (Northern Ireland) 1966, s 58 |
| | | 1 Apr 1975 (SI 1974/164)², repeals of or in— National Insurance Act 1965, ss 83(1)(c), (2)–(6), 84(1), (2) (in so far as it applies s 83(3), (5)), 84(3), (5); National Insurance (Industrial Injuries) Act 1965, s 59(3); National Insurance Act (Northern Ireland) 1966, ss 81(1)(c), (2)–(6), 82; National Insurance (Industrial Injuries) Act (Northern Ireland) 1966, s 57(3) |
| | | 6 Apr 1975 (otherwise, except those specified below) (SI 1974/164) |
| | | 1 Apr 1976 (SI 1974/164), repeals of or in— National Insurance Act 1965, s 84(2) (in so far as it applies s 83(4), (6)); National Insurance (Industrial Injuries) Act 1965, s 59(2), (4); National Insurance Act (Northern Ireland) 1966, s 82(2) (in so far as it applies s 81(4), (6)); National Insurance (Industrial Injuries) Act (Northern Ireland) 1966, s 57(2), (4) |

**Social Security Act 1973 (c 38)**—*contd*

*Not yet in force,* repeals of or in—

Superannuation and other Trust Funds (Validation) Act 1927, ss 1–8, 10, 11(2) from "but save as aforesaid" onwards;
Superannuation and other Trust Funds (Validation) Act (Northern Ireland) 1928

[1]   For transitional provisions, see SI 1973/1433, art 4

[2]   For transitional provisions, see SI 1974/164, art 5

---

**Statute Law (Repeals) Act 1973 (c 39)**

*RA:* 18 Jul 1973

Whole Act in force 18 Jul 1973 (RA)

---

**Statute Law Revision (Northern Ireland) Act 1973 (c 55)**

*RA:* 25 Jul 1973

Whole Act in force 25 Jul 1973 (RA)

---

**Supply of Goods (Implied Terms) Act 1973 (c 13)**

*RA:* 18 Apr 1973

*Commencement provisions:* s 181(3)

Whole Act in force 18 May 1973 (s 181(3))

---

**Ulster Defence Regiment Act (c 34)**

*RA:* 18 Jul 1973

Whole Act in force 18 Jul 1973 (RA)

---

**Water Act 1973 (c 37)**

*RA:* 18 Jul 1973

*Commencement provisions:* s 39(1)

| | | |
|---|---|---|
| 1–8 | | 18 Jul 1973 (RA) |
| 9 | | 1 Apr 1974 (s 39(1); except so far as relating to Land Drainage Act 1930, ss 21, 22; Local Government Act 1948, Pt VI; Land Drainage Act 1961, s 21; Water Resources Act 1963, s 82) |
| | | 18 Jul 1973 (exceptions noted above) (RA) |
| 10 | | 1 Apr 1974 (s 39(1)) |
| 11 | | 18 Jul 1973 (sub-s (6) so far as relating to Water Act 1945, s 12) (RA) |
| | | 1 Apr 1974 (s 39(1); exception noted above) |
| 12 | (1) | 1 Apr 1974 (s 39(1)) |
| | (2)–(5) | 18 Jul 1973 (RA) |
| | (6)–(11) | 1 Apr 1974 (s 39(1); except sub-ss (9) and (11) so far as relating to Water Act 1945, s 12) |
| | | 18 Jul 1973 (exceptions noted above) (RA) |
| 13 | (1), (2) | 18 Jul 1973 (RA) |
| | (3), (4) | 1 Apr 1974 (s 39(1)) |
| 14 | | 1 Apr 1974 (s 39(1)) |

**Water Act 1973 (c 37)**—*contd*

| | | |
|---|---|---|
| 15 | | 18 Jul 1973 (RA) |
| 16–18 | | 1 Apr 1974 (s 39(1)) |
| 19 | (1)–(5) | 18 Jul 1973 (RA) |
| | (6)–(11) | 1 Apr 1974 (s 39(1)) |
| 20 | | 1 Apr 1974 (s 39(1)) |
| 21 | (1), (2) | 18 Jul 1973 (RA) |
| | (3)–(6) | 1 Apr 1974 (s 39(1)) |
| 22, 23 | | 18 Jul 1973 (RA) |
| 24 | | 1 Apr 1974 (s 39(1)) |
| 25–27 | | 18 Jul 1973 (RA) |
| 28 | | 1 Apr 1974 (s 39(1)) |
| 29 | (1) | 1 Apr 1974 (s 39(1)) |
| | (2)–(5) | 18 Jul 1973 (RA) |
| 30–32 | | 18 Jul 1973 (RA) |
| 33 | | 1 Apr 1974 (s 39(1)) |
| 34–39 | | 18 Jul 1973 (RA) |
| 40 | (1) | 18 Jul 1973 (RA) |
| | (2), (3) | 1 Apr 1974 (s 39(1)) |
| | (4)–(6) | 18 Jul 1973 (RA) |
| Schs 1–3 | | 18 Jul 1973 (RA) |
| Sch 4 | | 18 Jul 1973 (so far as it relates to Water Act 1945, s 12) (RA) |
| | | 1 Apr 1974 (otherwise) (s 39(1)) |
| Schs 5–7 | | 18 Jul 1973 (RA) |
| Schs 8, 9 | | 1 Apr 1974 (s 39(1)) |

# 1974 Acts

## Appropriation Act 1974 (c 2)

*RA:* 8 Feb 1974

Whole Act in force 8 Feb 1974 (RA)

## Appropriation (No 2) Act 1974 (c 31)

*RA:* 31 Jul 1974

Whole Act in force 31 Jul 1974 (RA)

## Biological Weapons Act 1974 (c 6)

*RA:* 8 Feb 1974

Whole Act in force 8 Feb 1974 (RA)

## Carriage of Passengers by Road Act 1974 (c 35)

*RA:* 31 Jul 1974

*Commencement provisions:* s 14(5)

| | |
|---|---|
| 1–6 | *Never in force* (repealed) |
| 7–14 | 31 Jul 1974 (RA) |

## Charlwood and Horley Act 1974 (c 11)

*RA:* 8 Feb 1974

Whole Act in force 8 Feb 1974 (RA)

## Church of England (Worship and Doctrine) Measure 1974 (No 3)

*RA:* 12 Dec 1974

*Commencement provisions:* s 7(2); Instrument of the Archbishops of 22 Jul 1975

Whole Measure in force 1 Sep 1975 (Instrument of the Archbishops of 22 Jul 1975)

## Consolidated Fund Act 1974 (c 1)

*RA:* 22 Jan 1974

Whole Act in force 22 Jan 1974 (RA)

**Consolidated Fund (No 2) Act 1974 (c 12)**

*RA:* 21 Mar 1974

Whole Act in force 21 Mar 1974 (RA)

---

**Consolidated Fund (No 3) Act 1974 (c 15)**

*RA:* 23 May 1974

Whole Act in force 23 Mar 1974 (RA)

---

**Consolidated Fund (No 4) Act 1974 (c 57)**

*RA:* 12 Dec 1974

Whole Act in force 12 Dec 1974 (RA)

---

**Consumer Credit Act 1974 (c 39)**

*RA:* 31 Jul 1974

*Commencement provisions*: s 192(2), (4); Consumer Credit Act 1974 (Commencement No 1) Order 1975, SI 1975/2123; Consumer Credit Act 1974 (Commencement No 2) Order 1977, SI 1977/325; Consumer Credit Act 1974 (Commencement No 3) Order 1977, SI 1977/802; Consumer Credit Act 1974 (Commencement No 4) Order 1977, SI 1977/2163; Consumer Credit Act 1974 (Commencement No 5) Order 1979, SI 1979/1685[1]; Consumer Credit Act 1974 (Commencement No 6) Order 1980, SI 1980/50; Consumer Credit Act 1974 (Commencement No 7) Order 1981, SI 1981/280; Consumer Credit Act 1974 (Commencement No 8) Order 1983, SI 1983/1551; Consumer Credit Act 1974 (Commencement No 9) Order 1984, SI 1984/436; Consumer Credit Act 1974 (Commencement No 10) Order 1989, SI 1989/1128

| | | |
|---|---|---|
| 1–193 | | 31 Jul 1974 (RA) |
| Schs 1, 2 | | 31 Jul 1974 (RA) |
| Sch 3 | para 1 | 1 Apr 1977 (SI 1977/325) |
| | para 2 | 31 Jul 1974 (RA) |
| | para 3 | 19 May 1985 (SI 1983/1551) |
| | para 4 | 31 Jul 1974 (RA) |
| | para 5 | 1 Oct 1977 (SI 1977/325) only for the following purposes— in the case of any consumer credit business, not being a consumer credit business which is carried on by an individual and in the course of which only the following regulated consumer credit agreements (excluding agreements made before that date) are made, namely: agreements for fixed-sum credit not exceeding £30, and agreements for running-account credit where the credit limit does not exceed that amount, and in the case of any consumer-hire business 31 Jul 1989 (otherwise) (SI 1989/1128) |
| | para 6 | 2 Feb 1976 (SI 1975/2123) |
| | para 7 | 28 Feb 1977 (SI 1977/325) |
| | para 8 | 6 Oct 1980 (SI 1980/50) |
| | para 9 | 1 Oct 1977 (SI 1977/802) |
| | paras 10, 11 | 1 Jul 1977 (SI 1977/802) |
| | para 12 | 16 May 1977 (SI 1977/325) |
| | paras 13, 14 | 19 May 1985 (SI 1983/1551) |
| | para 15 | 1 Jul 1977 (SI 1977/802) |
| | paras 16–18 | 19 May 1985 (SI 1983/1551) |
| | para 19 | 1 Apr 1977 (SI 1977/325) |
| | paras 20–39 | 19 May 1985 (SI 1983/1551) |
| | para 40 | 19 May 1985 (SI 1984/436) |
| | para 41 | 19 May 1985 (SI 1983/1551) |

**Consumer Credit Act 1974 (c 39)**—*contd*

| | | |
|---|---|---|
| para 42 | 16 May 1977 (SI 1977/325) | |
| para 43 | 19 May 1985 (SI 1983/1551) | |

paras 44, 45    3 Aug 1976 (in the case of any ancillary credit business so far as it comprises or relates to debt-adjusting, debt-counselling, debt-collecting or the operation of a credit reference agency) (SI 1975/2123)

1 Jul 1978 (SI 1977/2163) (in the case of any ancillary credit business so far as it comprises or relates to credit brokerage, not being a business which is carried on by an individual and in the course of which introductions are effected only of individuals desiring to obtain credit:

(a) under debtor-creditor-supplier agreements which fall under s 12(a) of the Act and where, in the case of any such agreement—

(i) the person carrying on the business would be willing to sell the goods which are the subject of the agreement to the debtor under a transaction not financed through credit, and

(ii) the amount of credit does not exceed £30; and

(b) under debtor-creditor-supplier agreements which fall within section 12(b) or (c) of the Act and where, in the case of any such agreement—

(i) the person carrying on the business is the supplier,

(ii) the creditor is a person referred to in s 145(2)(a)(i) of the Act, and

(iii) the amount of credit or, in the case of an agreement for running-account credit, the credit limit does not exceed £30)

para 46    1 Jul 1978 (SI 1977/2163) (in the case of any ancillary credit business so far as it comprises or relates to credit brokerage, not being a business which is carried on by an individual and in the course of which introductions are effected only of individuals desiring to obtain credit:

(a) under debtor-creditor-supplier agreements which fall under s 12(a) of the Act and where, in the case of any such agreement—

(i) the person carrying on the business would be willing to sell the goods which are the subject of the agreement to the debtor under a transaction not financed through credit, and

(ii) the amount of credit does not exceed £30; and

(b) under debtor-creditor-supplier agreements which fall within section 12(b) or (c) of the Act and where, in the case of any such agreement—

(i) the person carrying on the business is the supplier,

(ii) the creditor is a person referred to in s 145(2)(a)(i) of the Act, and

(iii) the amount of credit or, in the case of an agreement for running-account credit, the credit limit does not exceed £30)

| | | |
|---|---|---|
| | para 47 | 6 Oct 1980 (SI 1980/50) |
| | para 48 | 16 May 1977 (SI 1977/325) |
| | paras 49, 50 | 31 Jul 1974 (RA) |
| Sch 4 | paras 1, 2 | 19 May 1985 (SI 1983/1551) |
| | paras 3, 4 | *Never in force* (repealed) |
| | paras 5–18 | 19 May 1985 (SI 1983/1551) |
| | para 19 | 30 Mar 1977 (SI 1977/325) |
| | paras 20–23 | 19 May 1985 (SI 1983/1551) |
| | paras 24–26 | 6 Oct 1980 (SI 1980/50) |
| | para 27 | 19 May 1985 (SI 1983/1551) |
| | para 28 | 1 Apr 1977 (SI 1977/325) |
| | paras 29–33 | 19 May 1985 (SI 1983/1551) |
| | para 34 | *Never in force* (superseded) |
| | paras 35–40 | 19 May 1985 (SI 1983/1551) |
| | paras 41, 42 | *Never in force* (repealed) |

**Consumer Credit Act 1974 (c 39)**—*contd*

| | | |
|---|---|---|
| | paras 43–45 | 6 Oct 1980 (SI 1980/50) |
| | paras 46, 47 | 19 May 1985 (SI 1983/1551) |
| | para 48 | *Never in force* (repealed) |
| | paras 49, 50 | 19 May 1985 (SI 1983/1551) |
| | para 51 | 1 Oct 1977 (SI 1977/325) |

Sch 5                    16 May 1977 (SI 1977/325), repeals of or in—

Moneylenders Act 1900, s 1 (in relation to agreements made before 16 May 1977 which are not personal credit agreements);

Moneylenders Act 1927, ss 10, 13(2) (both in relation to agreements made before 16 May 1977 which are not personal credit agreements);

Moneylenders Act (Northern Ireland) 1933, ss 10, 11, 13(2) (all in relation to agreements made before 16 May 1977 which are not personal credit agreements)

1 Jul 1977 (SI 1977/802), repeals of or in—

Betting and Loans (Infants) Act 1892, ss 2–4, 6 (except as far as it extends to Northern Ireland), 7;

Moneylenders Act 1900, s 5

1 Aug 1977 (SI 1977/325), repeals of or in—

Pawnbrokers Act 1872, ss 37–44, 52, Sch 6;

Local Government Act 1894;

Moneylenders Act 1927, ss 1–3, 4(1), (2), 18;

Companies Act 1948;

Finance Act 1949;

Customs and Excise Act 1952;

Finance Act 1961;

Administration of Justice Act 1964;

Local Government Act 1966, Sch 3, Pt II;

Local Government (Scotland) Act 1966, Sch 4, Pt II;

Theft Act 1968, Sch 2, Pt III;

Courts Act 1971, Sch 9, Pt I, the entry relating to the Moneylenders Act 1927;

Local Government Act 1972;

Local Government (Scotland) Act 1973

1 Aug 1977 (NI) (SI 1977/325), repeals of or in—

Moneylenders Act (Northern Ireland) 1933, ss 1–3, 4(1), (2);

Pawnbrokers Act (Northern Ireland) 1954, ss 5–9;

Betting and Lotteries Act (Northern Ireland) 1957;

Companies Act (Northern Ireland) 1960;

Theft Act (Northern Ireland) 1969;

Licensing Act (Northern Ireland) 1971;

Miscellaneous Transferred Duties Act (Northern Ireland) 1972, Pt VII, Sch 4

1 Oct 1977 (SI 1977/802), repeals of or in—

Moneylenders Act 1927, s 5(3) (in relation to moneylending transactions made before 1 Oct 1977);

Moneylenders Act (Northern Ireland) 1933, s 5(3) (in relation to moneylending transactions made before 1 Oct 1977)

1 Oct 1977 (NI) (SI 1977/325), repeals of or in—

Charitable Pawn Offices (Ireland) Act 1842;

Miscellaneous Transferred Duties Act (Northern Ireland) 1972, Pt VI

27 Jan 1980 (repeals of or in Moneylenders Act 1927, ss 4(2), 5(1), (2), (4)–(6) (all in relation to moneylending transactions made before 27 Jan 1980 which are not consumer credit agreements) 6–8, 9 (in relation to moneylending transactions made before 27 Jan 1980 which are not consumer credit agreements) 11–14, 15(2), 16, Sch 1) (SI 1979/1685)

**Consumer Credit Act 1974 (c 39)**—*contd*

27 Jan 1980 (NI) (repeals of or in Moneylenders Act (Northern Ireland) 1933, ss 4(2), 5(1), (2), (4)–(6) (all in relation to moneylending transactions made before 27 Jan 1980 which are not consumer credit agreements) 6–8, 9 (in relation to moneylending transactions made before 27 Jan 1980 which are not consumer credit agreements) 12–16, Sch 1) (SI 1979/1685)

6 Oct 1980 (SI 1980/50), repeals of or in—
Pawnbrokers Act 1872, s 13;
Moneylenders Act 1900, s 4;
Moneylenders Act 1927, s 4;
Trading Stamps Act 1964;
Advertisements (Hire-Purchase) Act 1967

6 Oct 1980 (NI) (SI 1980/50), repeals of or in—
Moneylenders Act (Northern Ireland) 1933, s 4(3);
Pawnbrokers Act (Northern Ireland) 1954, s 11;
Trading Stamps Act (Northern Ireland) 1965;
Hire-Purchase Act (Northern Ireland) 1966, Pt V, Sch 4;
Increase of Fines Act (Northern Ireland) 1967;
Criminal Justice (Miscellaneous Provisions) Act (Northern Ireland) 1968

30 Mar 1981 (SI 1981/280), repeals of or in (in relation to consumer agreements made on or after that day)—
Moneylenders Act 1927, s 14(1)(a);
Moneylenders Act (Northern Ireland) 1933

19 May 1985 (SI 1983/1551), repeals of or in—
Statutory Declarations Act 1835;
Metropolitan Police Act 1839;
Police Courts (Metropolis) Act 1839;
Pawnbrokers Act 1872 (so far as unrepealed);
Commissioners for Oaths Act 1891;
Burgh Police (Scotland) Act 1892;
Police (Property) Act 1897;
Moneylenders Act 1900 (so far as unrepealed);
Law of Distress Amendment Act 1908;
Moneylenders Act 1927 (so far as unrepealed);
Children and Young Persons Act 1933;
Moneylenders Act (Northern Ireland) 1933 (so far as unrepealed);
Children and Young Persons (Scotland) Act 1937;
Compensation (Defence) Act 1939;
Liability for War Damage (Miscellaneous Provisions) Act 1939;
Liability for War Damage (Miscellaneous Provisions) Act (Northern Ireland) 1939;
Law Reform (Miscellaneous Provisions) (Scotland) Act 1940;
Limitation (Enemies and War Prisoners) Act 1945;
Agriculture Act (Northern Ireland) 1949;
Pawnbrokers Act (Northern Ireland) 1954 (so far as unrepealed);
Pawnbrokers Act 1960;
Hire-Purchase Act 1964;
Emergency Laws (Re-enactments and Repeals) Act 1964;
Hire-Purchase Act 1965;
Hire-Purchase (Scotland) Act 1965;
Hire-Purchase Act (Northern Ireland) 1966 (so far as unrepealed, except Pt VI, s 68);
Companies Act 1967;
Increase of Fines Act (Northern Ireland) 1967, Schedule, Pt I;
Criminal Justice (Miscellaneous Provisions) Act (Northern Ireland) 1968, Sch 2;
Decimal Currency Act 1969;
Industrial and Provident Societies Act (Northern Ireland) 1969;

**Consumer Credit Act 1974 (c 39)**—*contd*

> Judgments (Enforcement) Act (Northern Ireland) 1969;
> Moneylenders (Amendment) Act (Northern Ireland) 1969;
> Post Office Act 1969;
> Courts Act 1971, Sch 9, Pt I, entry relating to Pawnbrokers Act 1872
> *Not yet in force,* repeals of or in—
> Restrictive Trade Practices Act 1956

[1]  For transitional provisions, see SI 1979/1685, art 3

---

**Contingencies Fund Act 1974 (c 18)**

*RA:* 23 May 1974

Whole Act in force 23 May 1974 (RA)

---

**Control of Pollution Act 1974 (c 40)**

*RA:* 31 Jul 1974

*Commencement provisions:* s 109(2); Control of Pollution Act 1974 (Commencement No 1) Order 1974, SI 1974/2039; Control of Pollution Act 1974 (Commencement No 2) Order 1974, SI 1974/2169; Control of Pollution Act 1974 (Commencement No 3) Order 1975, SI 1975/230; Control of Pollution Act 1974 (Commencement No 4) Order 1975, SI 1975/2118; Control of Pollution Act 1974 (Commencement No 5) Order 1976, SI 1976/731; Control of Pollution Act 1974 (Commencement No 6) Order 1976, SI 1976/956; Control of Pollution Act 1974 (Commencement No 7) Order 1976, SI 1976/1080; Control of Pollution Act 1974 (Commencement No 8) Order 1977, SI 1977/336; Control of Pollution Act 1974 (Commencement No 9) Order 1977, SI 1977/476; Control of Pollution Act 1974 (Commencement No 10) Order 1977, SI 1977/1587; Control of Pollution Act 1974 (Commencement No 11) Order 1977, SI 1977/2164; Control of Pollution Act 1974 (Commencement No 12) Order 1978, SI 1978/816; Control of Pollution Act 1974 (Commencement No 13) Order 1978, SI 1978/954; Control of Pollution Act 1974 (Commencement No 14) Order 1981, SI 1981/196; Control of Pollution Act 1974 (Commencement No 15) Order 1988, SI 1982/624; Control of Pollution Act 1974 (Commencement No 15 (renumbered 16 by Order No 17 below)) Order 1983, SI 1983/1175; Control of Pollution Act 1974 (Commencement No 17) Order 1984, SI 1984/853; Control of Pollution Act 1974 (Commencement No 18) Order 1985, SI 1985/70; Control of Pollution Act 1974 (Commencement No 19) Order 1988, SI 1988/818; Control of Pollution Act 1974 (Commencement No 20) (Scotland) Order 1991, SI 1991/1173

| | | |
|---|---|---|
| 1 | | *Never in force* (repealed) |
| 2 | | 1 Jul 1978 (E) (W) (SI 1977/2164) |
| | | 1 Sep 1978 (S) (SI 1978/816) |
| 3–11 | | 14 Jun 1976 (SI 1976/731) |
| 12 | (1)–(4) | 6 Jun 1988 (SI 1988/818) |
| | (5) | 1 Jan 1976 (so far as it defines "privy" for the purpose of s 30(4)) (SI 1975/2118) |
| | | 1 Apr 1977 (as respects inner London boroughs) (SI 1977/336) |
| | | 6 Jun 1988 (otherwise) (SI 1988/818) |
| | (6) | 1 Jan 1976 (in its application to s 21) (SI 1975/2118) |
| | | 6 Jun 1988 (otherwise) (SI 1988/818) |
| | (7) | 1 Jan 1976 (in its application to ss 21, 26) (SI 1975/2118) |
| | | 6 Jun 1988 (otherwise) (SI 1988/818) |
| | (8), (9) | 6 Jun 1988 (SI 1988/818) |
| | (10) | *Never in force* (repealed) |
| | (11) | 6 Jun 1988 (SI 1988/818) |
| 13 | (1), (2) | 6 Jun 1988 (SI 1988/818) |
| | (3) | 1 Aug 1978 (in relation to appeals under sub-s (6) against a notice under sub-s (5)) (SI 1978/954) |
| | | 6 Jun 1988 (otherwise) (SI 1988/818) |

**Control of Pollution Act 1974 (c 40)**—*contd*

| | | |
|---|---|---|
| | (4) | 6 Jun 1988 (SI 1988/818) |
| | (5)–(7) | 1 Aug 1978 (SI 1978/954) |
| | (8) | 1 Aug 1978 (so far as it relates to sub-ss (3), (5)–(7)) (SI 1978/954) |
| | | 6 Jun 1988 (otherwise) (SI 1988/818) |
| 14 | (1)–(8) | 6 Jun 1988 (SI 1988/818) |
| | (9)–(11) | 1 Apr 1977 (in relation to inner London boroughs) (SI 1977/336) |
| | | 6 Jun 1988 (otherwise) (SI 1988/818) |
| | (12) | 6 Jun 1988 (SI 1988/818) |
| 15 | | *Never in force* (repealed) |
| 16 | | 14 Jun 1976 (SI 1976/731) |
| 17 | | 1 Jan 1976 (SI 1975/2118) |
| 18 | (1), (2) | 14 Jun 1976 (SI 1976/731) |
| | (3) | 6 Jun 1988 (SI 1988/818) |
| 19–21 | | 1 Jan 1976 (SI 1975/2118) |
| 22, 23 | | 14 Jun 1976 (SI 1976/731) |
| 24 | (1)–(3) | *Not yet in force* |
| | (4) | 1 Apr 1977 (SI 1977/476) |
| 25, 26 | | 1 Jan 1976 (SI 1975/2118) |
| 27 | (1)(a) | 1 Jan 1976 (SI 1975/2118) |
| | (1)(b) | 6 Jun 1988 (SI 1988/818) |
| | (2) | 1 Jan 1976 (SI 1975/2118) |
| 28 | | 1 Jan 1976 (in its application to ss 12(6), 21(4), 26) (SI 1975/2118) |
| | | 6 Jun 1988 (otherwise) (SI 1988/818) |
| 29, 30 | | 1 Jan 1976 (SI 1975/2118) |
| 31 | (1) | 4 Jul 1984 (so far as it defines "relevant waters" for the purposes of Pt II) (SI 1984/853) |
| | | 31 Jan 1985 (otherwise) (SI 1985/70) |
| | (2)–(9) | 31 Jan 1985 (SI 1985/70) |
| 32 | (1), (2) | 31 Jan 1985 (SI 1985/70) |
| | (3) | 1 Aug 1983 (SI 1983/1175) |
| | (4)–(7) | 31 Jan 1985 (SI 1985/70) |
| 33 | | *Never in force* (repealed) |
| 34 | (1), (2) | 4 Jul 1984 (SI 1984/853) |
| | (3) | *Never in force* (repealed) |
| | (4), (5) | 4 Jul 1984 (SI 1984/853) |
| 35–37 | | 4 Jul 1984 (SI 1984/853) |
| 38 | (1), (2) | 4 Jul 1984 (SI 1984/853) |
| | (3)–(5) | *Never in force* (repealed) |
| 39 | (1) | 4 Jul 1984 (SI 1984/853) |
| | (2) | 31 Jan 1985 (SI 1985/70) |
| | (3) | *Never in force* (repealed) |
| | (4), (5) | 4 Jul 1984 (SI 1984/853) |
| | (6)–(8) | 4 Jul 1984 (for purposes of sub-s (1)) (SI 1984/853) |
| | | *Never in force* (otherwise) (repealed) |
| 40 | | 4 Jul 1984 (SI 1984/853) |
| 41 | | 31 Jan 1985 (SI 1985/70) |
| 42 | | 4 Jul 1984 (SI 1984/853) |
| 43, 44 | | 12 Dec 1974 (SI 1974/2039) |
| 45 | | *Never in force* (repealed) |
| 46 | (1)–(3) | *Never in force* (repealed) |
| | (4)–(7) | 31 Jan 1985 (SI 1985/70) |
| | (8) | *Never in force* (repealed) |
| 47, 48 | | *Never in force* (repealed) |
| 49, 50 | | 1 Jan 1976 (SI 1975/2118) |
| 51 | | 31 Jan 1985 (SI 1985/70) |
| 52, 53 | | *Never in force* (repealed) |
| 54, 55 | | 4 Jul 1984 (SI 1984/853) |
| 56 | | 1 Jan 1976 (SI 1975/2118) |
| 57 | (a) | 1 Jan 1976 (SI 1975/2118) |

**See Halsbury's Statutes Citator for amendments to these Acts**

**Control of Pollution Act 1974 (c 40)**—*contd*

| | | |
|---|---|---|
| | (b) | 1 Jan 1976 (E) (W) (SI 1975/2118) |
| | | 1 Aug 1982 (S) (SI 1982/624) |
| 58 | (1)–(5) | 1 Jan 1976 (SI 1975/2118) |
| | (6) | 1 Jan 1976 (E) (W) (SI 1975/2118) |
| | | 1 Aug 1982 (S) (SI 1982/624) |
| | (7) | 1 Jan 1976 (SI 1975/2118) |
| | (8) | 1 Jan 1976 (E) (W) (SI 1975/2118) |
| | | 1 Aug 1982 (S) (in relation to references to ss 60, 61) (SI 1982/624) |
| | | *Never in force* (S) (otherwise) (repealed) |
| | (9) | 1 Jan 1976 (SI 1975/2118) |
| 59 | | 1 Jan 1976 (SI 1975/2118) |
| 60, 61 | | 1 Jan 1976 (E) (W) (SI 1975/2118) |
| | | 1 Aug 1982 (S) (SI 1982/624) |
| 62 | | 1 Jan 1976 (SI 1975/2118) |
| 63–67 | | 1 Jan 1976 (E) (W) (SI 1975/2118) |
| | | 1 Aug 1982 (S) (SI 1982/624) |
| 68 | | 1 Jan 1976 (SI 1975/2118) |
| 69 | | 1 Jan 1976 (E) (W) (SI 1975/2118) |
| | | 1 Aug 1982 (S) (so far as applying or referring to a "noise reduction notice" or to s 65) (SI 1982/624) |
| | | *Never in force* (S) (otherwise) |
| 70 | | 1 Jan 1976 (SI 1975/2118) |
| 71 | (1) | 1 Jan 1976 (SI 1975/2118) |
| | (2) | 1 Jan 1976 (E) (W) (SI 1975/2118) |
| | | 1 Aug 1982 (S) (SI 1982/624) |
| | (3) | 1 Jan 1976 (SI 1975/2118) |
| 72 | | 1 Jan 1976 (SI 1975/2118) |
| 73 | | 1 Jan 1976 (E) (W) (SI 1975/2118) |
| | | 18 Jul 1976 (S) (except definitions "noise abatement order", "noise abatement zone", "noise level register" and "noise reduction notice") (SI 1976/1080) |
| | | 1 Aug 1982 (S) (otherwise) (SI 1982/624) |
| 79–83 | | 1 Jan 1976 (E) (W) (SI 1975/2118) |
| | | 1 Aug 1982 (S) (SI 1982/624) |
| 84–87 | | 1 Jan 1976 (SI 1975/2118) |
| 88 | | 14 Jun 1976 (SI 1976/731) |
| 89–94 | | 1 Jan 1976 (SI 1975/2118) |
| 95 | | 12 Dec 1974 (SI 1974/2039) |
| 96–103 | | 1 Jan 1976 (SI 1975/2118) |
| 104, 105 | | 12 Dec 1974 (SI 1974/2039) |
| 106 | | 1 Jan 1976 (SI 1975/2118) |
| 107 | | 12 Dec 1974 (SI 1974/2039) |
| 108 | (1), (2) | See Schs 3, 4 below |
| | (3) | 1 Jan 1976 (SI 1975/2118) |
| 109 | | 12 Dec 1974 (SI 1974/2039) |
| Schs 1, 2 | | 1 Jan 1976 (SI 1975/2118) |
| Sch 3 | paras 1–4 | 1 Jan 1975 (SI 1974/2169) |
| | para 5 | *Never in force* (repealed) |
| | para 6 | 1 Jan 1976 (SI 1975/2118) |
| | para 7 | *Not yet in force* |
| | para 8 | 1 Jan 1976 (SI 1975/2118) |
| | para 9 | 20 Jul 1976 (SI 1976/956) |
| | para 10 | 1 Jan 1976 (SI 1975/2118) |
| | paras 11, 12 | 31 Jan 1985 (SI 1985/70) |
| | paras 13–15 | 4 Jul 1984 (SI 1984/853) |
| | para 16 | 1 Jan 1976 (SI 1975/2118) |
| | para 17 | 4 Jul 1984 (SI 1984/853) |
| | para 18 | 14 Jun 1976 (SI 1976/731) |

**Control of Pollution Act 1974 (c 40)**—*contd*

| | | |
|---|---|---|
| | para 19 | 1 Jan 1976 (SI 1975/2118) |
| | paras 20, 21 | 31 Jan 1985 (SI 1985/70) |
| | para 22 | 1 Jan 1976 (SI 1975/2118) |
| | paras 23, 24 | 31 Jan 1985 (SI 1985/70) |
| | para 25 | *Never in force* (repealed) |
| | para 26 | 1 Jan 1976 (SI 1975/2118) |
| | para 27 | 12 Dec 1974 (SI 1974/2039) |
| | paras 28, 29 | 1 Jan 1976 (SI 1975/2118) |
| | paras 30, 31 | *Never in force* (repealed) |
| Sch 4 | | 1 Jan 1975 (repeals in Alkali and Works Regulations Act 1906) (SI 1974/2169) |

3 Mar 1975 (repeal in Local Government (Scotland) Act 1973, s 135(3)) (SI 1975/230)

1 Jan 1976 (SI 1975/2118), repeals of or in—
Administration of Justice (Appeals) Act 1934;
Public Health (Drainage of Trade Premises) Act 1937, ss 2(4), 3(2), 7(1) proviso, 11, definition of "interested body" in s 14(1);
Rivers (Prevention of Pollution) Act 1951, s 4;
Clean Air Act 1956, ss 16(1) proviso, para 1, 25(a), (b), the words "manufacturing process or" in s 26, Sch 2, the amendments of the Alkali Act 1936, ss 3, 8, 18;
Noise Abatement Act 1960;
Public Health Act 1961, ss 55(4), 57(3);
London Government Act 1963, s 40(4)(g), Sch 11, Pt I, para 32;
Criminal Justice Act 1967

14 Jun 1976 (SI 1976/731), repeals of or in—
Public Health Act 1875;
Trunk Roads Act 1936;
Highways Act 1959;
London Government Act 1963, Sch 11, Pt I, so far as it repeals para 14(1)(c)

18 Jul 1976 (S) (SI 1976/1080), repeals of or in—
Clean Air Act 1956, Sch 2;
Noise Abatement Act 1960;
Criminal Justice Act 1967, entry relating to Public Health (Scotland) Act 1897, s 22

20 Jul 1976 (SI 1976/956), repeals of or in—
Public Health (Drainage of Trade Premises) Act 1937;
Public Health Act 1961, ss 55(1)–(3), (5)–(9), 56, 57(1), (2), (4)–(8), 58, 63(5)

1 Apr 1977 (as respects inner London boroughs) (SI 1977/336) repeals of or in—
Public Health Act 1936, s 72(1)(b), (2) (in relation to cleansing of earthclosets, privys, ashpits or cesspools;
London Government Act 1963, Sch 11, Pt I, para 14(1), to the extent that the Public Health Act 1936, s 72(1)(b), (2) relate to the cleansing of the above items)

1 Apr 1977 (as respects inner London boroughs) (repeals of or in Public Health Act 1936, s 77) (SI 1977/476)

16 Mar 1981 (repeal of Deposit of Poisonous Waste Act 1972) (SI 1981/196)

31 Jan 1985 (SI 1985/70), repeals of or in—
Salmon Fisheries (Scotland) Act 1862;
Sea Fisheries Regulation (Scotland) Act 1895;
Public Health Act 1936, s 259(2);
Rivers (Prevention of Pollution) Act 1951, save s 5(1)(c), (6) and (7), s 11(1) so far as it defines "stream", s 11(6), s 12(1) and (3);

## Control of Pollution Act 1974 (c 40)—*contd*

Rivers Prevention of Pollution (Scotland) Act 1951, save (in
addition to provisions saved in col 3 of Sch 4) ss 18(6),
25(1)(c), (4), 26(2), (4), (7)–(9) and certain definitions in
s 35(1);

Clean Rivers (Estuaries and Tidal Waters) Act 1960;

Rivers (Prevention of Pollution) Act 1961;

Water Resources Act 1963, except s 79;

Rivers Prevention of Pollution (Scotland) Act 1965;

Water Act 1973

6 Jun 1988 (SI 1988/818), repeals of or in—

Public Health Act 1936, ss 72(1)–(5), 73–76;

London Government Act 1963, Sch 11, Pt I, paras 14, 16, 32;

Local Government Act 1972, Sch 14, paras 5–8

31 May 1991 (repeals of or in Rivers (Prevention of Pollution)
(Scotland) Act 1951, ss 25(1)(c), (4), 26(2), (4), (7)–(9))
(SI 1991/1173)

*Not yet in force,* repeals of or in—

Burgh Police (Scotland) Act 1892 (repealed);

Burgh Police (Scotland) Act 1903 (repealed);

Salmon and Freshwater Fisheries Act 1923 (repealed);

Public Health Act 1936, ss 79, 80;

Water Act 1945, s 18 (repealed);

Rivers (Prevention of Pollution) Act 1951, ss 5(1)(c), (6), (7), 11,
12 (part) (repealed);

Local Government (Miscellaneous Provisions) Act 1953, s 8;

Radioactive Substances Act 1960, Sch 1, paras 3, 6, 7, 8A, 15
(repealed);

London Government Act 1963, s 40(4)(d);

Water Resources Act 1963, s 79;

Gas Act 1965, s 4(5);

Sea Fisheries Regulation Act 1966, s 5(1)(c);

Civic Amenities Act 1967, s 23 (repealed);

Criminal Justice Act 1967, Sch 3, entries (now spent) relating to
Burgh Police (Scotland) Act 1892, s 114 and Public Health
Act 1936, s 76(3);

Countryside Act 1968, s 22 (repealed);

Local Government Act 1972, ss 180, 236, Sch 14, paras 4, 49;

Local Government (Scotland) Act 1973, s 136, Sch 16,
paras 7–9, Sch 28, para 69 (repealed)

*Never in force,* repeals of or in—

Public Health (Scotland) Act 1897, s 39 (repealed)

## Dumping at Sea Act 1974 (c 20)

*RA:* 27 Jun 1974

Whole Act in force 27 Jun 1974 (RA)

## Ecclesiastical Jurisdiction (Amendment) Measure 1974 (No 2)

*RA:* 9 Jul 1974

Whole Measure in force 9 Jul 1974 (RA)

## Education (Mentally Handicapped Children) (Scotland) Act 1974 (c 27)

*RA:* 17 Jul 1974

Whole Act in force 17 Jul 1974 (RA)

---

## Finance Act 1974 (c 30)

*Budget Day:* 26 Mar 1974

*RA:* 31 Jul 1974

The commencement details of Finance Acts are not set out, as the dates from which their provisions take effect are usually stated clearly and unambiguously in the text of the Act, and charging provisions will normally state for which year or years of assessment they are to have effect.

---

## Friendly Societies Act 1974 (c 46)

*RA:* 31 Jul 1974

*Commencement provisions:* s 117(2); Friendly Societies Act 1974 (Commencement) Order 1975, SI 1975/204

| | |
|---|---|
| 1–108 | 1 Apr 1975 (SI 1975/204) |
| 109 | 31 Jul 1974 (so far as it relates to regulations under s 115) (RA) |
| | 1 Apr 1975 (otherwise) (SI 1975/204) |
| 110, 111 | 1 Apr 1975 (SI 1975/204) |
| 112, 113 | 31 Jul 1974 (RA) |
| 114 | 1 Apr 1975 (SI 1975/204) |
| 115 | 31 Jul 1974 (RA) |
| 116 | 1 Apr 1975 (SI 1975/204) |
| 117 | 31 Jul 1974 (RA) |
| Schs 1–11 | 1 Apr 1975 (SI 1975/204) |

---

## Health and Safety at Work etc Act 1974 (c 37)

*RA:* 31 Jul 1974

*Commencement provisions:* s 85(2); Health and Safety at Work etc. Act 1974 (Commencement No 1) Order 1974, SI 1974/1439; Health and Safety at Work etc. Act 1974 (Commencement No 2) Order 1975, SI 1975/344; Health and Safety at Work etc. Act 1974 (Commencement No 3) Order 1975, SI 1975/1364; Health and Safety at Work etc. Act 1974 (Commencement No 4) Order 1977, SI 1977/294; Health and Safety at Work etc Act 1974 (Commencement No 5) Order 1980, SI 1980/208; Health and Safety at Work etc. Act 1974 (Commencement No 6) Order 1980, SI 1980/269

| | | |
|---|---|---|
| 1 | | 1 Oct 1974 (SI 1974/1439) |
| 2–9 | | 1 Apr 1975 (SI 1974/1439) |
| 10 | (1) | 1 Oct 1974 (in relation to the Commission) (SI 1974/1439) |
| | | 1 Jan 1975 (in relation to the Executive) (SI 1974/1439) |
| | (2)–(4) | 1 Oct 1974 (SI 1974/1439) |
| | (5) | 1 Jan 1975 (SI 1974/1439) |
| | (6), (7) | 1 Oct 1974 (in relation to the Commission) (SI 1974/1439) |
| | | 1 Jan 1975 (in relation to the Executive) (SI 1974/1439) |
| | (8) | 1 Jan 1976 (SI 1975/1938) |
| 11 | (1)–(3) | 1 Oct 1974 (in relation to the Commission) (SI 1974/1439) |
| | | 1 Jan 1975 (in relation to the Executive) (SI 1974/1439) |
| | (4), (5) | 1 Jan 1975 (SI 1974/1439) |
| | (6) | 1 Oct 1974 (in relation to the Commission) (SI 1974/1439) |
| | | 1 Jan 1975 (in relation to the Executive) (SI 1974/1439) |
| 12, 13 | | 1 Oct 1974 (SI 1974/1439) |
| 14 | | 1 Jan 1975 (SI 1974/1439) |

**Health and Safety at Work etc Act 1974 (c 37)**—*contd*

| | | |
|---|---|---|
| 15, 16 | | 1 Oct 1974 (SI 1974/1439) |
| 17–28 | | 1 Jan 1975 (SI 1974/1439) |
| 29, 30 | | 1 Oct 1974 (SI 1974/1439) |
| 31 | | 1 Jan 1975 (SI 1974/1439) |
| 32 | | 1 Oct 1974 (so far as it relates to ss 13, 16, Sch 4, paras 1, 3) (SI 1974/1439) |
| | | 1 Jan 1975 (otherwise) (SI 1974/1439) |
| 33 | (1)(a), (b) | 1 Apr 1975 (SI 1974/1439) |
| | (1)(c)–(o) | 1 Jan 1975 (SI 1974/1439) |
| | (2)–(6) | 1 Jan 1975 (SI 1974/1439) |
| 34–42 | | 1 Jan 1975 (SI 1974/1439) |
| 43 | | 1 Oct 1974 (in relation to payments to the Commission) (SI 1974/1439) |
| | | 1 Jan 1975 (other purposes) (SI 1974/1439) |
| 44–46 | | 1 Jan 1975 (SI 1974/1439) |
| 47 | | 1 Jan 1975 (except in relation to ss 2–8 above) (SI 1974/1439) |
| | | 1 Apr 1975 (the remainder) (SI 1974/1439) |
| 48 | | 1 Jan 1975 (except in relation to ss 2–9 above) (SI 1974/1439) |
| | | 1 Apr 1975 (the remainder) (SI 1974/1439) |
| 49 | | 1 Jan 1975 (SI 1974/1439) |
| 50–52 | | 1 Oct 1974 (SI 1974/1439) |
| 53 | | 1 Oct 1974, 1 Jan 1975 (in relation to other provisions in force on those dates) (SI 1974/1439) |
| | | 1 Apr 1975 (other purposes) (SI 1974/1439) |
| 54–60 | | 1 Jan 1975 (SI 1974/1439) |
| 61 | | 17 Mar 1977 (except for sub-ss (4), (5), (7), (8) which were never brought into force) (SI 1977/294) |
| 62 | | 17 Mar 1977 (SI 1977/294) |
| 63 | | 17 Mar 1977 (except for sub-ss (2), (6), (7) which were never brought into force) (SI 1977/294) |
| 64 | | *Never in force* (repealed) |
| 65 | | 17 Mar 1977 (SI 1977/294) |
| 66 | | 3 Sep 1975 (SI 1975/1364) |
| 67 | | 17 Mar 1977 (except for sub-ss (3)–(6), (8)–(11) which were never brought into force) (SI 1977/294) |
| 68 | | *Never in force* (repealed) |
| 69 | | 17 Mar 1977 (except for sub-ss (1)–(4) which were never brought into force) (SI 1977/294) |
| 70 | | 17 Mar 1977 (SI 1977/294) |
| 71 | | 17 Mar 1977 (except for sub-ss (2), (3) which were never brought into force) (SI 1977/294) |
| 72, 73 | | *Never in force* (repealed) |
| 74 | (1), (2) | 17 Mar 1977 (SI 1977/294) |
| | (3) | 3 Sep 1975 (SI 1975/1364) |
| 75 | | See Sch 7 below |
| 76 | (1)–(3) | 3 Sep 1975 (SI 1975/1364) |
| | (4) | 3 Sep 1975 (so far as it relates to s 66) (SI 1975/1364) |
| | | 17 Mar 1977 (otherwise) (SI 1977/294) |
| 77 | (1) | 1 Oct 1974 (SI 1974/1439) |
| | (2) | 1 Jan 1975 (SI 1974/1439) |
| 78, 79 | | 1 Apr 1974 (SI 1974/1439) |
| 80–82 | | 1 Oct 1974 (SI 1974/1439) |
| 83 | | See Schs 9, 10 below |
| 84, 85 | | 1 Oct 1974 (SI 1974/1439) |
| Sch 1 | | 1 Oct 1974 (SI 1974/1439) |
| Sch 2 | paras 1–9 | 1 Oct 1974 (SI 1974/1439) |
| | paras 10–12 | 1 Jan 1975 (SI 1974/1439) |
| | paras 13–19 | 1 Oct 1974 (SI 1974/1439) |
| | para 20 | 1 Jan 1975 (SI 1974/1439) |

**Health and Safety at Work etc Act 1974 (c 37)**—*contd*

| | | |
|---|---|---|
| Sch 3 | | 1 Oct 1974 (SI 1974/1439) |
| Sch 4 | para 1 | 1 Oct 1974 (SI 1974/1439) |
| | para 2 | 1 Jan 1975 (SI 1974/1439) |
| | para 3 | 1 Oct 1974 (SI 1974/1439) |
| | paras 4, 5 | 1 Jan 1975 (SI 1974/1439) |
| Sch 5 | | 17 Mar 1977 (SI 1977/294) |
| Sch 6 | Pt I, para 1(a) | *Never in force* (repealed) |
| | Pt I, para 1(b) | 17 Mar 1977 (SI 1977/294) |
| | Pt I, para 2 | *Never in force* (repealed) |
| | Pt I, para 3 | 17 Mar 1977 (SI 1977/294) |
| | Pt I, para 4(a) | 17 Mar 1977 (SI 1977/294) |
| | Pt I, para 4(b) | 17 Mar 1977 (for the purposes of enabling regulations to be made for the purposes of Public Health Act 1961, s 4(6) as amended) (SI 1977/294) |
| | | 17 Mar 1977 (otherwise) (SI 1977/294) |
| | Pt I, para 5(a) | *Never in force* (repealed) |
| | Pt I, para 5(b), (c) | 17 Mar 1980 (SI 1980/208) |
| | Pt I, para 5(d) | *Never in force* (repealed) |
| | Pt I, para 5(e) | 17 Mar 1977 (SI 1977/294) |
| | Pt I, para 6(a), (b) | 17 Mar 1977 (for the purposes of enabling regulations to be made for the purposes of the Public Health Act 1961, s 7(1), (2)) (SI 1977/294) |
| | | *Never in force* (otherwise) (repealed) |
| | Pt I, para 6(c), (d) | *Never in force* (repealed) |
| | Pt I, para 7 | 17 Mar 1977 (for the purpose of enabling regulations to be made for the purposes of the new s 8) (SI 1977/294) |
| | | *Never in force* (otherwise) (repealed) |
| | Pt I, para 8 | 17 Mar 1977 (SI 1977/294) |
| | Pt II | *Never in force* (repealed) |
| Sch 7 | para 1 | 27 Mar 1975 (SI 1975/344) |
| | para 2(a), (b) | 27 Mar 1975 (SI 1975/344) |
| | paras 2(c), 3 | *Never in force* (repealed) |
| | paras 4–6 | 27 Mar 1975 (SI 1975/344) |
| | para 7 | 17 Mar 1980 (SI 1980/269) |
| | paras 8, 9 | *Never in force* (repealed) |
| Sch 8 | | 1 Apr 1975 (SI 1974/1439) |
| Sch 9 | para 1 | 1 Jan 1975 (SI 1974/1439) |
| | para 2 | 1 Oct 1974 (as it relates to the Commission) (SI 1974/1439) |
| | | *Never in force* (otherwise) (repealed) |
| | para 3 | 1 Oct 1974 (as it relates to the Commission) (SI 1974/1439) |
| | | 1 Jan 1975 (as it relates to the Executive) (SI 1974/1439) |
| Sch 10 | | 1 Jan 1975 (SI 1974/1439), repeals of or in— |

Employment Medical Advisory Service Act 1972;
National Health Service (Scotland) Act 1972;
Employment and Training Act 1973;
National Health Service Reorganisation Act 1973

17 Mar 1977 (SI 1977/294), repeals of or in—
Public Health Act 1936, ss 64(4), (5), 343(1) (definition "building regulations");
Clean Air Act 1956, s 24;
Public Health Act 1961, ss 4, 6;
Fire Precautions Act 1971, ss 11, 43(1) (definition "building regulations")

*Never in force* (remaining repeals) (repealed)

## Horticulture (Special Payments) Act 1974 (c 5)

*RA:* 8 Feb 1974

Whole Act in force 8 Feb 1974 (RA)

## Housing Act 1974 (c 44)

*RA:* 31 Jul 1974

*Commencement provisions:* s 131(3); Housing Act 1974 (Commencement No 1) Order 1974, SI 1974/1406; Housing Act 1974 (Commencement No 2) Order 1974, SI 1974/1562; Housing Act 1974 (Commencement No 3) Order 1974, SI 1974/1791[1]; Housing Act 1974 (Commencement No 4) Order 1975, SI 1975/374; Housing Act 1974 (Commencement No 5) Order 1975, SI 1975/1113; Housing Act 1974 (Commencement No 6) Order 1979, SI 1979/1214

| | | |
|---|---|---|
| 1 | | 18 Sep 1974 (SI 1974/1562) |
| 2 | | 20 Aug 1974 (SI 1974/1406) |
| 3 | (1), (2) | 18 Sep 1974 (SI 1974/1562) |
| | (3)–(5) | 2 Dec 1974 (SI 1974/1791) |
| | (6) | 18 Sep 1974 (SI 1974/1562) |
| 4–8 | | 18 Sep 1974 (SI 1974/1562) |
| 9 | (1)–(4) | 18 Sep 1974 (except so far as it relates to sub-s (1)(a), (b)) (SI 1974/1562) |
| | | 1 Apr 1975 (otherwise) (SI 1975/374) |
| | (5), (6) | 1 Apr 1975 (SI 1975/374) |
| 10–12 | | 18 Sep 1974 (SI 1974/1562) |
| 13, 14 | | 20 Aug 1974 (SI 1974/1406) |
| 15–17 | | 2 Dec 1974 (SI 1974/1791) |
| 18 | | 1 Apr 1975 ("the operative date" defined in s 129(1)) |
| | | 2 Dec 1974 (otherwise) (SI 1974/1791) |
| 19–28 | | 2 Dec 1974 (SI 1974/1791) |
| 29–33 | | 18 Sep 1974 (SI 1974/1562) |
| 34 | | 1 Apr 1975 (SI 1975/374) |
| 35 | | 18 Sep 1974 (SI 1974/1562; but note references to the "operative date" (1 Apr 1975) defined by s 129(1)) |
| 36–104 | | 2 Dec 1974 (SI 1974/1791) |
| 105 | | 1 Apr 1975 (SI 1975/374) |
| 106 | | 2 Dec 1974 (SI 1974/1791) |
| 107 | | 18 Sep 1974 (SI 1974/1562) |
| 108 | | 31 Aug 1974 (sub-s (3)) |
| 109–112 | | 2 Dec 1974 (SI 1974/1791) |
| 113 | | *Never in force* (repealed) |
| 114–116 | | 2 Dec 1974 (SI 1974/1791) |
| 117 | | 20 Aug 1974 (SI 1974/1406) |
| 118 | | 31 Jul 1974 (sub-s (5)) |
| 119 | (1) | 2 Dec 1974 (so far as it relates to Sch 11, paras 3(2), 4) (SI 1974/1791) |
| | | 1 Sep 1975 (otherwise) (SI 1975/1113) |
| | (2)–(6) | 1 Sep 1975 (SI 1975/1113) |
| 120 | | 2 Dec 1974 (SI 1974/1791) |
| 121, 122 | | 31 Aug 1974 (sub-s (10)) |
| 123 | | 2 Dec 1974 (SI 1974/1791) |
| 124 | | *Never in force* (repealed) |
| 125 | | 31 Jul 1974 (sub-s (10)) |
| 126 | | 2 Dec 1974 (SI 1974/1791) |
| 127–129 | | 20 Aug 1974 (SI 1974/1406) |
| 130 | | See Schs 13, 15 below |
| 131 | | 20 Aug 1974 (SI 1974/1406) |
| Sch 1 | | 18 Sep 1974 (SI 1974/1562) |
| Sch 2 | | 20 Aug 1974 (SI 1974/1406) |

**Housing Act 1974 (c 44)**—*contd*

| | | |
|---|---|---|
| Sch 3 | Pt I | 31 Jul 1974 (s 18(6)) |
| | Pts II, III | 2 Dec 1974 (SI 1974/1791) |
| Schs 4–7 | | 2 Dec 1974 (SI 1974/1791) |
| Sch 8 | | 31 Jul 1974 (s 118(5)) |
| Sch 9 | | 31 Aug 1974 (s 108(3); SI 1974/1406) |
| Sch 10 | | 2 Dec 1974 (SI 1974/1791) |
| Sch 11 | para 1(1) | 1 Apr 1975 (SI 1975/374) |
| | para 1(2) | 1 Sep 1975 (SI 1975/1113) |
| | para 1(3) | 1 Apr 1975 (so far as it relates to insertion of Housing Subsidies Act 1967, s 24(3)(viii)) (SI 1975/374) |
| | | 1 Sep 1975 (otherwise) (SI 1975/1113) |
| | para 1(4) | 1 Apr 1975 (SI 1975/374) |
| | para 1(5), (6) | 1 Sep 1975 (SI 1975/1113) |
| | para 2 | 1 Sep 1975 (SI 1975/1113) |
| | para 3(1) | 1 Sep 1975 (SI 1975/1113) |
| | para 3(2) | 2 Dec 1974 (SI 1974/1791) |
| | para 4 | 2 Dec 1974 (so far as it relates to the insertion of Housing Subsidies Act 1967, s 27(1)) (SI 1974/1791) |
| | | 1 Sep 1975 (otherwise) (SI 1975/1113) |
| | para 5 | 1 Apr 1975 (SI 1975/374) |
| | paras 6, 7 | 1 Sep 1975 (SI 1975/1113) |
| Sch 12 | | 31 Aug 1974 (s 124(3)) |
| Sch 13 | para 1 | 18 Sep 1974 (SI 1974/1562) |
| | para 2 | 1 Sep 1975 (SI 1975/1113) |
| | para 3 | 9 Oct 1979 (SI 1979/1214) |
| | para 4 | 2 Dec 1974 (SI 1974/1791) |
| | para 5 | 1 Apr 1975 (SI 1975/374) |
| | para 6 | 18 Sep 1974 (SI 1974/1562) |
| | para 7 | 9 Oct 1979 (SI 1979/1214) |
| | para 8 | 20 Aug 1974 (SI 1974/1406) |
| | para 9 | 2 Dec 1974 (SI 1974/1791) |
| | para 10(1) | *Never in force* (repealed) |
| | para 10(2)–(4) | 18 Sep 1974 (SI 1974/1562) |
| | para 10(5) | 2 Dec 1974 (SI 1974/1791) |
| | para 11 | 9 Oct 1979 (SI 1979/1214) |
| | para 12 | 2 Dec 1974 (SI 1974/1791) |
| | para 13 | 1 Apr 1975 (SI 1975/374) |
| | para 14 | 2 Dec 1974 (SI 1974/1791) |
| | paras 15, 16 | 18 Sep 1974 (SI 1974/1562) |
| | para 17 | 2 Dec 1974 (SI 1974/1791) |
| | para 18 | 1 Apr 1975 (SI 1975/374) |
| | para 19 | 9 Oct 1979 (SI 1979/1214) |
| | para 20 | 2 Dec 1974 (SI 1974/1791) |
| | para 21 | 9 Oct 1979 (SI 1979/1214) |
| | para 22 | 18 Sep 1974 (SI 1974/1562) |
| | para 23(1)–(4) | 18 Sep 1974 (SI 1974/1562) |
| | para 23(5), (6) | 2 Dec 1974 (SI 1974/1791) |
| | paras 24–29 | 2 Dec 1974 (SI 1974/1791) |
| | paras 30–32 | 18 Sep 1974 (SI 1974/1562) |
| | paras 33, 34 | 2 Dec 1974 (SI 1974/1791) |
| | para 35 | 1 Apr 1975 (sub-para (2)) |
| | paras 36, 37 | 2 Dec 1974 (SI 1974/1791) |
| | paras 38–45 | 20 Aug 1974 (SI 1974/1406) |
| | para 46 | *Not yet in force* |
| Sch 14 | paras 1, 2 | *Never in force* (repealed) |
| | paras 3–7 | 2 Dec 1974 (SI 1974/1791) |
| Sch 15 | | 20 Aug 1974 (SI 1974/1406) repeals in— |
| | | Land Compensation Act 1973; |
| | | Land Compensation (Scotland) Act 1973 |

**Housing Act 1974 (c 44)**—*contd*

        18 Sep 1974 (SI 1974/1562), repeals of or in—
           Housing Act 1964, ss 1, 3, 4, 6, 8, 9, 11, 12;
           National Loans Act 1968;
           Housing Finance Act 1972, s 77(1), (3)
        2 Dec 1974 (SI 1974/1791), repeals of or in—
           Housing Act 1964, Pt II, ss 57, 59, 72;
           Housing Act 1969, Pt I (including Sch 1, but excluding s 21),
              ss 30, 36, 37, 40, 41, 70, 75–77, 88, Sch 8;
           Housing Finance Act 1972, Sch 1;
           Local Government Act 1972, s 171
        1 Apr 1975 (SI 1975/374), repeals of or in—
           Housing Act 1957, s 121;
           Housing (Scotland) Act 1966, ss 153–155, 159;
           Housing (Financial Provisions) (Scotland) Act 1968, ss 16–18;
           Housing Act 1969, s 21;
           Local Government (Scotland) Act 1973, s 131, Sch 12
        9 Oct 1979 (SI 1999/1214), repeals of or in—
           Housing Act 1957, ss 43(1), 44–46, 50, 51, 53, 54, 60(1), 67(1),
              70(2), 159(b)(iv), 162(1), 163(1), 166(1), Sch 2, paras 4(1)(c),
              6(1), 7(2), Sch 4, paras 1, 5;
           Public Health Act 1961, s 29(4)(b);
           Housing Act 1961, s 24, Sch 3;
           Housing (Slum Clearance Compensation) Act 1965, s 1(1);
           Housing Act 1969, ss 29(2), 69(c), Sch 5, paras 3(1), 5(2);
           Housing Finance Act 1972, s 11(7)

[1]   For savings, see SI 1974/1791, art 3, Sch 2

---

**Housing (Scotland) Act 1974 (c 45)**

*RA:* 31 Jul 1974

*Commencement provisions:* s 51(3); Housing (Scotland) Act 1974 (Commencement) Order 1974, SI 1974/1755

Whole Act in force 27 Nov 1974 (SI 1974/1755)

---

**Independent Broadcasting Authority Act 1974 (c 16)**

*RA:* 23 May 1974

*Commencement provisions:* s 4(4)

Whole Act in force 23 Jun 1974 (s 4(4))

---

**Independent Broadcasting Authority (No 2) Act 1974 (c 42)**

*RA:* 31 Jul 1974

Whole Act in force 31 Jul 1974 (RA)

---

**Insurance Companies Act 1974 (c 49)**

*RA:* 31 Jul 1974

*Commencement provisions:* s 90(2)

Whole Act in force 31 Aug 1974 (s 90(2))

---

## Juries Act 1974 (c 23)

*RA:* 9 Jul 1974

*Commencement provisions:* s 23(3)

Whole Act in force 9 Aug 1974 (s 23(3))

---

## Land Tenure Reform (Scotland) Act 1974 (c 38)

*RA:* 31 Jul 1974

Whole Act in force 1 Sep 1974 (s 24(2))

---

## Legal Aid Act 1974 (c 4)

*RA:* 8 Feb 1974

*Commencement provisions:* s 43(3), (4); Legal Aid Act 1974 (Commencement No 1) Order 1974, SI 1974/709

| | | |
|---|---|---|
| 1–15 | | 8 May 1974 (s 43(3)) |
| 16 | | *Never in force* (repealed) |
| 17–25 | | 8 May 1974 (s 43(3)) |
| 26 | | *Never in force* (repealed) |
| 28–43 | | 8 May 1974 (s 43(3)) |
| Sch 1 | Pt I, para 1(a) | 8 May 1974 (s 43(3)) |
| | Pt I, para 1(b), (c) | *Never in force* (repealed) |
| | Pt I, para 1(d)–(f) | 8 May 1974 (s 43(3)) |
| | Pt I, para 2 | 8 May 1974 (s 43(3)) |
| | Pt I, para 3(a)–(d) | 8 May 1974 (s 43(3)) |
| | Pt I, para 3(e) | 8 May 1974 (SI 1974/709) |
| | Pt I, para 4 | *Never in force* (repealed) |
| | Pt I, paras 5–8 | 8 May 1974 (s 43(3)) |
| | Pt II | 8 May 1974 (s 43(3)) |
| Schs 2–5 | | 8 May 1974 (s 43(3)) |

---

## Local Government Act 1974 (c 7)

*RA:* 8 Feb 1974

*Commencement provisions:* s 42(2), (3); Local Government Act 1974 (Commencement No 1) Order 1974, SI 1974/335; Local Government Act 1974 (Commencement No 2) Order 1977, SI 1977/943; Local Government Act 1974 (Commencement No 3) Order 1978, SI 1978/1583

| | |
|---|---|
| 1–10 | 8 Feb 1974 (RA) |
| 11–14 | 1 Apr 1974 (SI 1974/335) |
| 15 | 14 Mar 1974 (SI 1974/335) |
| 16 | 8 Feb 1974 (RA) |
| 17 | 4 Mar 1974 (SI 1974/335) |
| 18–21 | 1 Apr 1974 (SI 1974/335) |
| 22–34 | 8 Feb 1974 (RA) |
| 35 | 1 Apr 1974 (SI 1974/335) |
| 36 | 8 Feb 1974 (RA) |
| 37 | 1 Apr 1974 (SI 1974/335) |
| 38–41 | 8 Feb 1974 (RA) |
| 42 | 4 Mar 1974 (SI 1974/335; see also Schs 7, 8 below) |
| 43 | 8 Feb 1974 (RA) |
| Schs 1, 2 | 8 Feb 1974 (RA) |
| Sch 3 | 1 Apr 1974 (SI 1974/335) |
| Schs 4, 5 | 8 Feb 1974 (RA) |

**Local Government Act 1974 (c 7)**—*contd*

| | | |
|---|---|---|
| Sch 6 | paras 1–14 | 1 Apr 1974 (SI 1974/335) |
| | para 15 | 1 Oct 1974 (SI 1974/335) |
| | paras 16–22 | 1 Apr 1974 (SI 1974/335) |
| | para 23(1) | 1 Apr 1974 (SI 1974/335) |
| | para 23(2) | 1 Apr 1975 (SI 1974/335) |
| | paras 24–26 | 1 Apr 1974 (SI 1974/335) |
| Sch 7 | para 1 | 1 Apr 1974 (SI 1974/335) |
| | para 2 | 1 Apr 1975 (SI 1974/335) |
| | paras 3–7 | 1 Apr 1974 (SI 1974/335) |
| | para 8 | 4 Mar 1974 (SI 1974/335) |
| | paras 9–12 | 1 Apr 1974 (SI 1974/335) |
| | para 13 | 4 Mar 1974 (SI 1974/335) |
| | paras 14, 15 | 1 Apr 1974 (SI 1974/335) |
| Sch 8 | | 1 Apr 1974 (except as below) (SI 1974/335) |

1 Oct 1974 (repeals in Weights and Measures Act 1963) (SI 1974/335)

1 Apr 1975 (SI 1974/335), repeals of or in—
Local Government Act 1966, s 27(2);
Road Traffic Regulation Act 1967, ss 72(6)(a), 84B(8)(a);
Transport Act 1968, s 34(2), (3);
Transport (London) Act 1969, ss 7(5), (6), 29(1)(a);
Highways Act 1971;
Town and Country Planning Act 1971, s 212(1)

1 Jun 1977 (SI 1977/943), repeals of or in—
National Parks and Access to the Countryside Act 1949, s 98;
Local Government Act 1966, ss 1–5, 10, Sch 1;
General Rate Act 1967, s 49, Sch 9;
Transport Act 1968, ss 13(7), 138(6);
Transport (London) Act 1969, s 3(1);
Housing Finance Act 1972;
Local Government Act 1972, s 203(5), Sch 24, para 12;
Rate Rebate Act 1973

1 Apr 1979 (SI 1978/1583), repeals of or in—
National Parks and Access to the Countryside Act 1949, s 97;
Local Government Act 1966, s 8;
Rating Act 1966, ss 9, 12(a);
Countryside Act 1968, ss 33–36

**Lord Chancellor (Tenure of Office and Discharge of Ecclesiastical Functions) Act 1974 (c 25)**

*RA:* 9 Jul 1974

Whole Act in force 9 Jul 1974 (RA)

**Lord High Commissioner (Church of Scotland) Act 1974 (c 19)**

*RA:* 27 Jun 1974

Whole Act in force 27 Jun 1974 (RA)

**Merchant Shipping Act 1974 (c 43)**

*RA:* 31 Jul 1974

*Commencement provisions*: s 24(2); Merchant Shipping Act 1974 (Commencement No 1) Order 1974, SI 1974/1792; Merchant Shipping Act 1974 (Commencement No 2) Order 1975, SI 1975/866;

## Merchant Shipping Act 1974 (c 43)—*contd*

Merchant Shipping Act 1974 (Commencement No 3) Order 1978, SI 1978/1466; Merchant Shipping Act 1974 (Commencement No 4) Order 1979, SI 1979/808

| | | |
|---|---|---|
| 1, 2 | | 16 Oct 1978 (SI 1978/1466) |
| 3 | | 1 Nov 1974 (SI 1974/1792) |
| 4–8 | | 16 Oct 1978 (SI 1978/1466) |
| 9 | | 19 Jun 1975 (SI 1975/866) |
| 10, 11 | | 1 Nov 1974 (SI 1974/1792) |
| 12, 13 | | *Never in force* (repealed) |
| 14, 15 | | 1 Aug 1979 (SI 1979/808) |
| 16–23 | | 1 Nov 1974 (SI 1974/1792) |
| 24 | (1)–(3) | 1 Nov 1974 (SI 1974/1792) |
| | (4) | *Never in force* (repealed) |
| | (5) | 1 Nov 1974 (SI 1974/1792) |
| Sch 1 | | 16 Oct 1978 (SI 1978/1466) |
| Sch 2 | paras 1, 2 | 1 Nov 1974 (SI 1974/1792) |
| | paras 3, 4 | *Never in force* (repealed) |
| | paras 5, 6 | 1 Nov 1974 (SI 1974/1792) |
| Sch 3 | | *Never in force* (repealed) |
| Sch 4 | | 1 Aug 1979 (SI 1979/808) |
| Sch 5 | | 1 Nov 1974 (SI 1974/1792) |

## Mines (Working Facilities and Support) Act 1974 (c 36)

*RA*: 31 Jul 1974

Whole Act in force 31 Jul 1974 (RA)

## Ministers of the Crown Act 1974 (c 21)

*RA*: 27 Jun 1974

Whole Act in force 27 Jun 1974 (RA)

## National Insurance Act 1974 (c 14)

*RA*: 13 May 1974

*Commencement provisions*: s 8(4), Sch 5; National Insurance Act 1974 (Commencement) Order 1974, SI 1974/841[1]

| | | |
|---|---|---|
| 1 | | 22 Jul 1974 (rates of benefit under the National Insurance Act 1965 in the case of, attendance allowance, maternity allowance, widow's benefit, guardian's allowance, retirement pension, age addition, child's special allowance and the calculation of earnings-related supplement and widow's supplementary allowance) (SI 1974/841) |
| | | 25 Jul 1974 (rates of benefit under the National Insurance Act 1965 in the case of, unemployment, sickness and invalidity benefit) (SI 1974/841) |
| 2 | | 5 Aug 1974 (SI 1974/841) |
| 3 | (1) | See Sch 3 below |
| | (2) | 24 Jul 1974 (SI 1974/841) |
| | (3) | 5 Aug 1974 (SI 1974/841) |
| 4 | | 22 Jul 1974 (so far as relates to relaxation of the earnings rule in the case of retirement pensioners under the National Insurance Act 1965 and certain of their wives) (SI 1974/841) |

**National Insurance Act 1974 (c 14)**—*contd*

|  |  |  |
|---|---|---|
|  |  | 24 Jul 1974 (so far as relates to relaxation of the earnings rule in the case of certain wives entitled to an increase of disablement pension by way of unemployability supplement under the National Insurance (Industrial Injuries) Act 1965) (SI 1974/841) |
|  |  | 25 Jul 1974 (so far as relates to relaxation of the earnings rule in the case of certain wives of persons entitled to invalidity pension under the National Insurance Act 1965) (SI 1974/841) |
| 5 |  | 17 May 1974 (SI 1974/841) |
| 6 | (1)–(4) | 13 Jun 1974 (SI 1974/841) |
|  | (5) | See Sch 4 below |
| 7 |  | 17 May 1974 (SI 1974/841) |
| 8 | (1), (2) | 13 May 1974 (Sch 5, para 1(1)) |
|  | (3) | 17 May 1974 (SI 1974/841) |
|  | (4) | 13 May 1974 (Sch 5, para 1(1)) |
|  | (5) | See Sch 6 below |
|  | (6) | 17 May 1974 (SI 1974/841) |
| Sch 1 |  | 22 Jul 1974 (rates of benefit under the National Insurance Act 1965 in the case of, attendance allowance, maternity allowance, widow's benefit, guardian's allowance, retirement pension, age addition, child's special allowance and the calculation of earnings-related supplement and widow's supplementary allowance) (SI 1974/841) |
|  |  | 25 Jul 1974 (rates of benefit under the National Insurance Act 1965 in the case of, unemployment, sickness and invalidity benefit) (SI 1974/841) |
| Sch 2 |  | 5 Aug 1974 (SI 1974/841) |
| Sch 3 |  | 22 Jul 1974 (in relation to rates and amounts of benefit under the National Insurance (Industrial Injuries) Act 1965, in the case of widow's pension under s 19, widower's pension under s 20 and allowance in respect of children of deceased's family under s 21) (SI 1974/841) |
|  |  | 24 Jul 1974 (in relation to rates and amounts of benefit under the National Insurance (Industrial Injuries) Act 1965, in the case of disablement benefit (including increases of disablement pension other than those brought into force on 25 Jul 1974 below), increases of unemployability supplement under s 13A, maximum under s 29(1)(a) of aggregate of weekly benefits payable for successive accidents and maximum disablement gratuity under s 12(3)) (SI 1974/841) |
|  |  | 25 Jul 1974 (in relation to rates and amounts of benefit under the National Insurance (Industrial Injuries) Act 1965, in the case of injury benefit (including increases thereof), and increases of disablement pension in respect of children and adult dependants in the case of a beneficiary receiving, as an in-patient in a hospital or similar institution, medical treatment for the relevant injury of loss of faculty) (SI 1974/841) |
| Sch 4 | paras 1–12 | 6 Apr 1975 (SI 1974/841) |
|  | paras 13, 14 | 17 May 1974 (SI 1974/841) |
|  | paras 15, 16 | 6 Apr 1975 (SI 1974/841) |
|  | para 17 | 22 Jul 1974 (SI 1974/841) |
|  | para 18 | 17 May 1974 (SI 1974/841) |
|  | paras 19–24 | 6 Apr 1975 (SI 1974/841) |
|  | para 25 | 17 May 1974 (SI 1974/841) |
|  | paras 26, 27 | 6 Apr 1975 (SI 1974/841) |
|  | para 28 | 17 May 1974 (SI 1974/841) |
|  | paras 29–32 | 6 Apr 1975 (SI 1974/841) |
|  | para 33 | 17 May 1974 (SI 1974/841) |
|  | paras 34, 35 | 6 Apr 1975 (SI 1974/841) |
|  | paras 36, 37 | 17 May 1974 (SI 1974/841) |
|  | paras 38, 39 | 6 Apr 1975 (SI 1974/841) |

## National Insurance Act 1974 (c 14)—*contd*

|        | para 40(a), (b) | 6 Apr 1975 (SI 1974/841) |
|--------|-----------------|--------------------------|
|        | para 40(c), (d) | 1 Apr 1975 (SI 1974/841) |
|        | paras 41–54     | 6 Apr 1975 (SI 1974/841) |
|        | paras 55, 56    | 17 May 1974 (SI 1974/841) |
| Sch 5  | para 1          | 13 May 1974 (Sch 5, para 1(1)) |
|        | para 2          | 17 May 1974 (SI 1974/841) |
| Sch 6  |                 | 17 May 1974 (repeals of or in National Insurance and Supplementary Benefit Act 1973, ss 7, 8(1)) (SI 1974/841) |

13 Jun 1974 (repeals of or in National Insurance Regulations (Validation) Act 1972) (SI 1974/841)

22 Jul 1974 (SI 1974/841), repeals of or in—
National Insurance Act 1972, s 4(2);
National Insurance and Supplementary Benefit Act 1973, s 1(1), Sch 1 (in relation to attendance allowance, maternity allowance, widow's benefit, guardian's allowance, retirement pension, age addition and child's special allowance), s 3(1), Sch 3 (in relation to widow's pension under s 19, widower's pension under s 20 and allowance in respect of children of deceased's family under s 21)

24 Jul 1974 (repeals of or in National Insurance and Supplementary Benefit Act 1973, s 3(1), Sch 3 (in relation to disablement benefit (including increases of disablement pension other than those brought into force on 25 Jul 1974), increase of unemployability supplement under s 13A, maximum under s 29(1)(a) of aggregate of weekly benefits payable for successive accidents and maximum disablement gratuity under s 12(3)), s 3(3)) (SI 1974/841)

25 Jul 1974 (repeals of or in National Insurance and Supplementary Benefit Act 1973, s 1(1), Sch 1 (in relation to unemployment, sickness and invalidity benefit), s 3(1), Sch 3 (in relation to injury benefit (including increases thereof) and increases disablement pension in respect of children and adult dependants in the case of a beneficiary receiving as an in-patient in a hospital or similar institution, medical treatment for the relevant injury or loss of faculty) (SI 1974/841)

5 Aug 1974 (repeals of or in National Insurance and Supplementary Benefit Act 1973, ss 2, 3(4), Sch 2) (SI 1974/841)

1 Apr 1975 (repeals of or in National Insurance and Supplementary Benefit Act 1973, s 4(3)) (SI 1974/841)

6 Apr 1975 (SI 1974/841), repeals of or in—
National Insurance (Industrial Injuries) Act 1965;
National Insurance (Industrial Injuries) Act 1966;
Social Security Act 1973

[1]   For transitional provisions and savings, see SI 1974/841, art 2(2)–(4)

---

## National Theatre Act 1974 (c 55)

*RA:* 29 Nov 1974

Whole Act in force 29 Nov 1974 (RA)

---

## Northern Ireland Act 1974 (c 28)

*RA:* 17 Jul 1974

Whole Act in force 17 Jul 1974 (RA)

---

**Northern Ireland (Young Persons) Act 1974 (c 33)**

*RA:* 31 Jul 1974

Whole Act in force 31 Jul 1974 (RA)

---

**Pakistan Act 1974 (c 34)**

*RA:* 31 Jul 1974

Whole Act in force 31 Jul 1974 (RA); note, however, that s 1 applies to the years 1975 onwards, and that s 2(1) amended the Pakistan Act 1973, as from 1 Apr 1974

---

**Parks Regulation (Amendment) Act 1974 (c 29)**

*RA:* 17 Jul 1974

Whole Act in force 17 Jul 1974 (RA)

---

**Pensioners' Payments Act 1974 (c 54)**

*RA:* 14 Nov 1974

Whole Act in force 14 Nov 1974 (RA)

---

**Pensions (Increase) Act 1974 (c 9)**

*RA:* 8 Feb 1974

Whole Act in force 8 Feb 1974 (RA)

---

**Policing of Airports Act 1974 (c 41)**

*RA:* 31 Jul 1974

Whole Act in force 31 Jul 1974 (RA)

---

**Prevention of Terrorism (Temporary Provisions) Act 1974 (c 56)**

*RA:* 29 Nov 1974

Whole Act in force 29 Nov 1974 (RA)

---

**Prices Act 1974 (c 24)**

*RA:* 9 Jul 1974

Whole Act in force 9 Jul 1974 (RA)

---

**Rabies Act 1974 (c 17)**

*RA:* 23 May 1974

Whole Act in force 23 May 1974 (RA)

---

## Railways Act 1974 (c 48)

*RA:* 31 Jul 1974

*Commencement provisions:* s 10(4)

| | | |
|---|---|---|
| 1, 2 | | 1 Jan 1975 (s 10(4)) |
| 3 | (1)–(6) | 31 Jul 1974 (RA) |
| | (7) | 1 Jan 1975 (s 10(4)) |
| 4–10 | | 31 Jul 1974 (RA) |

## Rehabilitation of Offenders Act 1974 (c 53)

*RA:* 31 Jul 1974

*Commencement provisions:* s 11(2)

Whole Act in force 1 Jul 1975 (s 11(2))

## Rent Act 1974 (c 51)

*RA:* 31 Jul 1974

*Commencement provisions:* s 17(5)

Whole Act in force 14 Aug 1974 (s 17(5))

## Representation of the People Act 1974 (c 10)

*RA:* 8 Feb 1974

Whole Act in force 8 Feb 1974 (RA)

## Road Traffic Act 1974 (c 50)

*RA:* 31 Jul 1974

*Commencement provisions:* s 24(4); Road Traffic Act 1974 (Commencement No 1) Order 1974, SI 1974/2075; Road Traffic Act 1974 (Commencement No 2) (Section 20: Northern Ireland) Order 1975, SI 1975/264; Road Traffic Act 1974 (Commencement No 3) Order 1975, SI 1975/489; Road Traffic Act 1974 (Commencement No 4) Order 1975, SI 1975/756; Road Traffic Act 1974 (Commencement No 5) Order 1975, SI 1975/1154[1]; Road Traffic Act 1974 (Commencement No 6) Order 1975, SI 1975/1479; Road Traffic Act 1974 (Commencement No 7) Order 1975, SI 1975/1653; Road Traffic Act 1974 (Commencement No 1) (Scotland) Order 1979, SI 1979/85; Road Traffic Act 1974 (Commencement No 8) Order 1984, SI 1984/811

| | | |
|---|---|---|
| 1–5 | | 1 Sep 1975 (SI 1975/1154) |
| 6 | | 1 Jan 1975 (SI 1974/2075) |
| 7 | (1) | 31 Oct 1975 (bringing Road Traffic Act 1972, s 36B(5)–(8) only into force) (SI 1975/1653) |
| | | *Never in force* (otherwise) (repealed) |
| | (2) | *Never in force* (repealed) |
| 8 | | 1 Mar 1975 (SI 1974/2075) |
| 9 | (1), (2) | 1 Jan 1975 (SI 1974/2075) |
| | (3)–(6) | 1 Aug 1984 (SI 1984/811) |
| 10 | (1)–(6) | 1 Jan 1975 (SI 1974/2075) |
| | (7) | See Sch 2 below |
| 11, 12 | | 1 Jan 1975 (SI 1974/2075) |
| 13 | (1) | See Sch 3 below |
| | (2) | 1 Jan 1976 (SI 1975/1479) |
| | (3) | 1 Mar 1975 (SI 1974/2075) |

## Road Traffic Act 1974 (c 50)—*contd*

| | | |
|---|---|---|
| | (4) | 1 Jan 1976 (SI 1975/1479) |
| 14–19 | | 1 Jan 1975 (SI 1974/2075) |
| 20 | (1) | 1 Mar 1975 (SI 1974/2075) |
| | (2), (3) | 1 Mar 1975 (in its application to Great Britain) (SI 1974/2075) |
| | | 1 Apr 1975 (in its application to Northern Ireland) (SI 1975/264) |
| 21–23 | | 1 Jan 1975 (SI 1974/2075) |
| 24 | (1) | 1 Jan 1975 (SI 1974/2075) |
| | (2) | See Sch 6 below |
| | (3) | See Sch 7 below |
| | (4), (5) | 1 Jan 1975 (SI 1974/2075) |
| Sch 1 | | 1 Sep 1975 (SI 1975/1154) |
| Sch 2 | Pt I, para 1(1), (2) | 1 Jan 1975 (SI 1974/2075) |
| | Pt I, para 1(3) | *Never in force* (repealed) |
| | Pt I, para 1(4), (5) | 1 Jan 1975 (SI 1974/2075) |
| | Pt I, paras 2, 3 | *Never in force* (repealed) |
| | Pt I, para 4 | 1 Jan 1975 (SI 1974/2075) |
| | Pt I, para 5 | *Never in force* (repealed) |
| | Pt II | 1 Jan 1975 (SI 1974/2075) |
| Sch 3 | para 1 | 1 Jan 1976 (SI 1975/1479) |
| | para 2(1) | 1 Oct 1975 (SI 1975/1479) |
| | para 2(2), (3) | 1 Jun 1975 (SI 1975/756) |
| | para 2(4) | 1 Jan 1975 (SI 1974/2075) |
| | para 2(5) | 1 Jan 1976 (SI 1975/1479) |
| | para 2(6) | 1 Apr 1975 (SI 1975/489) |
| | para 3 | 1 Apr 1975 (for the purposes of inserting Road Traffic Act 1972, s 87A(2)–(7), except in relation to prospective disabilities) (SI 1975/489) |
| | | 1 Oct 1975 (for the purposes of inserting Road Traffic Act 1972, s 87A(2)–(7) in relation to prospective disabilities, but only in relation to applicants for the grant of licences to take effect on or after 1 Jan 1976) (SI 1975/1479) |
| | | 1 Jan 1976 (bringing s 87A(1), (7) into force) (SI 1975/1479) |
| | para 4(1) | 1 Jan 1975 (SI 1974/2075) |
| | para 4(2) | 1 Apr 1975 (except in relation to prospective disabilities) (SI 1975/489) |
| | | 1 Oct 1975 (in relation to prospective disabilities, but only in relation to applicants for the grant of licences to take effect on or after 1 Jan 1976) (SI 1975/1479) |
| | para 4(3), (4) | 1 Jan 1975 (SI 1974/2075) |
| | para 5(1) | 1 Oct 1975 (so far as it amends Road Traffic Act 1972, s 89(1)(a), but only in relation to applicants for the grant of licences to take effect on or after 1 Jan 1976) (SI 1975/1479) |
| | | 1 Jan 1976 (amendment of s 84(1)(c)) (SI 1975/1479) |
| | para 5(2) | 1 Jan 1975 (SI 1974/2075) |
| | para 5(3) | 1 Jan 1976 (SI 1975/1479) |
| | para 6 | 1 Oct 1975 (so far as it inserts Road Traffic Act 1972, s 90(1), but only in relation to applicants for the grant of licences to take effect on or after 1 Jan 1976) (SI 1975/1479) |
| | | 1 Jan 1976 (otherwise) (SI 1975/1479) |
| | para 7 | 1 Jan 1976 (SI 1975/1479) |
| | para 8 | 1 Jan 1975 (SI 1974/2075) |
| | para 9 | 1 Jan 1976 (SI 1975/1479) |
| | para 10(1) | 1 Mar 1975 (SI 1974/2075) |
| | para 10(2), (3) | 1 Oct 1975 (SI 1975/1479) |
| | para 10(4) | 1 Mar 1975 (SI 1974/2075) |
| | para 11 | 1 Mar 1975 (SI 1974/2075) |
| | para 12 | 1 Jan 1976 (SI 1975/1479) |
| Schs 4, 5 | | 1 Jan 1975 (SI 1974/2075) |
| Sch 6 | para 1 | *Never in force* (repealed) |
| | para 2 | 1 Jan 1975 (SI 1974/2075) |

## Road Traffic Act 1974 (c 50)—*contd*

| | | |
|---|---|---|
| | para 3 | 1 Mar 1975 (SI 1974/2075) |
| | paras 4–12 | 1 Jan 1975 (SI 1974/2075) |
| | para 13 | *Never in force* (repealed) |
| | paras 14, 15 | 1 Jan 1975 (SI 1974/2075) |
| | para 16 | 1 Apr 1975 (SI 1975/489) |
| | paras 17–20 | 1 Jan 1975 (SI 1974/2075) |
| | para 21 | *Never in force* (repealed) |
| | para 22 | 1 Jan 1975 (SI 1974/2075) |
| | para 23 | 1 Apr 1975 (SI 1975/489) |
| | para 24 | 1 Jan 1975 (SI 1974/2075) |
| Sch 7 | | 1 Jan 1975 (SI 1974/2075), repeals of or in— |

Road Traffic Act 1960, s 133(4);
Road Traffic Act 1962, Schs 1, 4;
Road Traffic Regulation Act 1967, ss 9(10), 31(3), 42(4), 85(1);
Criminal Justice Act 1967, Sch 3;
Road Traffic Act 1972, ss 47, 48(3), 50, 51, 53(2), 62(2)(c), 64, 88(5) (without affecting regulations made under it), 162(1)(iii), 188;
Road Traffic (Foreign Vehicles) Act 1972

1 Apr 1975 (repeals of or in Road Traffic Act 1972, s 65, Sch 4, Pt I) (SI 1975/489)

1 Sep 1975 (repeal of Road Traffic Regulation Act 1967, s 80(10) and s 24(3) thereof so far as it relates to s 80(10)) (SI 1975/1154)

1 Jan 1976 (repeal of Road Traffic Act 1972, ss 104(1)–(3), (6)(a), 105(2)) (SI 1975/1479)

1 Aug 1984 (repeals of or in Road Traffic Act 1972, ss 68–80, 81(1), 82) (SI 1984/811)

*Not yet in force,* repeals of or in—
Road Traffic Act 1960, s 130;
Road Traffic Act 1972, s 40(7)

*Never in force* (repealed) repeals of or in—
Road Traffic Act 1960, s 131

[1] For transitional provisions, see SI 1975/1154, art 3

---

## Slaughterhouses Act 1974 (c 3)

*RA*: 8 Feb 1974

*Commencement provisions*: s 48(3)

Whole Act in force 1 Apr 1974 (s 48(3))

---

## Social Security Amendment Act 1974 (c 58)

*RA*: 12 Dec 1974

*Commencement provisions*: s 6(4); Social Security Amendment Act 1974 (Commencement) Order 1975, SI 1975/3

| | | |
|---|---|---|
| 1–4 | | 12 Dec 1974 (RA) |
| 5 | (1)–(5) | 12 Dec 1974 (RA) |
| | (6) | 17 Jan 1975 (SI 1975/3) |
| 6 | | 12 Dec 1974 (RA) |
| Sch 1 | | 17 Jan 1975 (in so far as it relates to the amendment of the Social Security Act 1973, s 45) (SI 1975/3) |
| | | 6 Apr 1975 (otherwise) (SI 1975/3) |
| Sch 2 | | 12 Dec 1974 (RA), repeals of or in— |

**Social Security Amendment Act 1974 (c 58)**—*contd*
> Social Security Act 1973, ss 2(7)(c), 3(2)(c), 42(4), 48(4), 49,
> 71(1), 96(6), 97(3), Sch 25, para 7;
> Statutory Rules Act (Northern Ireland) 1958
> 6 Apr 1975 (otherwise) (SI 1975/3)

**Solicitors Act 1974 (c 47)**

*RA:* 31 Jul 1974

*Commencement provisions:* s 90(2); Solicitors Act 1974 (Commencement) Order 1975, SI 1975/534

Whole Act in force 1 May 1975 (SI 1975/534)

**Solicitors (Amendment) Act 1974 (c 26)**

*RA:* 17 Jul 1974

*Commencement provisions:* s 19(6), (7); Solicitors Acts 1974 (Commencement) Order 1975, SI 1975/534[1]

| | | |
|---|---|---|
| 1–4 | | 17 Jul 1974 (s 19(6)) |
| 5 | | 1 May 1975 (SI 1975/534) |
| 6, 7 | | 17 Jul 1974 (s 19(6)) |
| 8 | | See Sch 1 below |
| 9 | (1) | 1 May 1975 (SI 1975/534) |
| | (2) | 17 Jul 1974 (s 19(6)) |
| 10 | | 17 Jul 1974 (s 19(6)) |
| 11, 12 | | 1 May 1975 (SI 1975/534) |
| 13–15 | | 17 Jul 1974 (s 19(6)) |
| 16 | | 1 May 1975 (SI 1975/534) |
| 17, 18 | | 17 Jul 1974 (s 19(6)) |
| 19 | (1)–(4) | 17 Jul 1974 (s 19(6)) |
| | (5) | See Sch 2 below |
| | (6)–(11) | 17 Jul 1974 (s 19(6)) |
| Sch 1 | | 1 May 1975 (SI 1975/534) |
| Sch 2 | para 1 | 1 May 1975 (SI 1975/534) |
| | paras 2–14 | 17 Jul 1974 (s 19(6)) |
| | para 15 | 1 May 1975 (SI 1975/534) |
| | para 16(1), (2) | 17 Jul 1974 (s 19(6)) |
| | para 16(3) | 1 May 1975 (SI 1975/534) |
| | para 17 | 17 Jul 1974 (s 19(6)) |
| | paras 18, 19 | 1 May 1975 (SI 1975/534) |
| | paras 20–31 | 17 Jul 1974 (s 19(6)) |
| | para 32 | 1 May 1975 (SI 1975/534) |
| | para 33(1) | 1 May 1975 (SI 1975/534) |
| | para 33(2) | 17 Jul 1974 (s 19(6)) |
| | para 34(1), (2) | 17 Jul 1974 (s 19(6)) |
| | para 34(3) | 1 May 1975 (SI 1975/534) |
| Sch 3 | Pt I | 17 Jul 1974 (s 19(6)) |
| | Pt II | 1 May 1975 (SI 1975/534) |

[1]  For savings, see SI 1975/534, art 2, Schedule

**Statute Law (Repeals) Act 1974 (c 22)**

*RA:* 27 Jun 1974

Whole Act in force 27 Jun 1974 (RA)

### Statutory Corporations (Financial Provisions) Act 1974 (c 8)

*RA*: 8 Feb 1974

Whole Act in force 8 Feb 1974 (RA)

---

### Synodical Government (Amendment) Measure 1974 (No 1)

*RA*: 9 Jul 1974

Whole Measure in force 9 Jul 1974 (RA)

---

### Town and Country Amenities Act 1974 (c 32)

*RA*: 31 Jul 1974

*Commencement provisions*: s 13(3), (4); Town and Country Amenities Act 1974 (Commencement) Order 1975, SI 1975, SI 1975/147

| | |
|---|---|
| 1–7 | 31 Aug 1974 (s 13(3)) |
| 8, 9 | 12 Mar 1975 (SI 1975/147) |
| 10–13 | 31 Aug 1974 (s 13(3)) |
| Schedule | 31 Aug 1974 (s 13(3)) |

---

### Trade Union and Labour Relations Act 1974 (c 52)

*RA*: 31 Jul 1974

*Commencement provisions*: s 31(2); Trade Union and Labour Relations Act 1974 (Commencement) Order 1974, SI 1974/1385[1]

| | |
|---|---|
| 1 | 16 Sep 1974 (SI 1974/1385; but see sub-s (3) in relation to repeals) |
| 2–20 | 16 Sep 1974 (SI 1974/1385) |
| 21–23 | 31 Jul 1974 (RA) |
| 24–30 | 16 Sept 1974 (SI 1974/1385) |
| 31 | 31 Jul 1974 (RA) |
| Schs 1–5 | 16 Sept 1974 (SI 1974/1385) |

[1]  For transitional provisions, see SI 1974/1385, art 3

---

**Statutory Corporations (Financial Provisions) Act 1974 (c.8)**

13.3 Feb 1974

Whole Act in force 8 Feb 1974 (RA)

---

**Synodical Government (Amendment) Measure 1974 (No.1)**

RA 8 Jul 1974

Whole Measure in force 9 Jul 1974 (RA)

---

**Town and Country Amenities Act 1974 (c.32)**

RA 31 Jul 1974

Commencement provisions: s 13(3), (4). Town and Country Amenities Act 1974 (Commencement)
Order 1975, SI 1975/1458:

| | |
|---|---|
| 1–7 | 31 Aug 1974 (s 13(5)) |
| 8–9 | 12 Mar 1975, SI 1975/1458 |
| 10–13 | 31 Aug 1974 (s 13(4)) |
| Schedule | 31 Aug 1974, s 13(3) |

---

**Trade Union and Labour Relations Act 1974 (c.52)**

RA 31 Jul 1974

Commencement provisions: s 31(2). Trade Union and Labour Relations Act 1974 (Commencement)
Order 1974, SI 1974/1385:

| | |
|---|---|
| 1–20 | 16 Sep 1974 (SI 1974/1385, but see sub-s (3) in relation to repeals) |
| 21–25 | 16 Sep 1974 (SI 1974/1385) |
| 26–30 | 31 Jul 1974 (RA) |
| 31 | 16 Sep 1974 (SI 1974/1385) |
| Sch 1–5 | 31 Jul 1974 (RA) |

For transitional provisions see SI 1974/1385, art 3.

# 1975 Acts

### Air Travel Reserve Fund Act 1975 (c 36)

*RA:* 22 May 1975

Whole Act in force 22 May 1975 (RA)

---

### Airports Authority Act 1975 (c 78)

*RA:* 12 Nov 1975

*Commencement provisions:* s 26(2)

Whole Act in force 12 Dec 1975 (s 26(2))

---

### Appropriation Act 1975 (c 44)

*RA:* 1 Aug 1975

Whole Act in force 1 Aug 1975 (RA)

---

### Arbitration Act 1975 (c 3)

*RA:* 25 Feb 1975

*Commencement provisions:* s 8; Arbitration Act 1975 (Commencement) Order 1975, SI 1975/1682

Whole Act in force 23 Dec 1975 (SI 1975/1682)

---

### Biological Standards Act 1975 (c 4)

*RA:* 25 Feb 1975

*Commencement provisions:* s 9; Biological Standards Act 1975 (Commencement) Order 1976, SI 1976/885

Whole Act in force 1 Jul 1976 (SI 1976/885)

---

### British Leyland Act 1975 (c 43)

*RA:* 3 Jul 1975

Whole Act in force 3 Jul 1975 (RA)

---

## Child Benefit Act 1975 (c 61)

*RA:* 7 Aug 1975

Whole Act in force 7 Aug 1975 (RA)

---

## Children Act 1975 (c 72)

*RA:* 12 Nov 1975

*Commencement provisions*: s 108(2)–(4); Children Act 1975 (Commencement No 1) Order 1976, SI 1976/1744[1]; Children Act 1975 (Scotland) (Commencement No 1) Order 1977, SI 1977/227[2]; Children Act 1975 (Commencement No 2) Order 1977, SI 1977/1036; Children Act 1975 (Commencement No 3) Order 1978, SI 1978/1433[3]; Children Act 1975 (Scotland) (Commencement No 2) Order 1978, SI 1978/1440[4]; Children Act 1975 (Commencement No 4) Order 1980, SI 1980/1475; Children Act 1975 (Commencement No 5) Order 1981, SI 1981/1792[5], as amended by SI 1983/86; Children Act 1975 (Scotland) (Commencement No 3) Order 1982, SI 1982/33[6], as amended by SI 1983/107; Children Act 1975 and the Adoption Act 1976 (Commencement) Order 1983, SI 1983/1946[7]; Children Act 1975 (Scotland) (Commencement No 4) Order 1984, SI 1984/554[8]; Children Act 1975 (Scotland) (Commencement No 5) Order 1984, SI 1984/1702[9]; Children Act 1975 and the Domestic Proceedings and Magistrates' Courts Act 1978 (Commencement) Order 1985, SI 1985/449; Children Act 1975 and the Adoption Act 1976 (Commencement No 2) Order 1987, SI 1987/1242

| | | |
|---|---|---|
| 1, 2 | | 1 Jan 1988 (SI 1987/1242) |
| 3 | | 1 Jan 1976 (s 108(4)) |
| 4–7 | | 15 Feb 1982 (SI 1981/1792; SI 1982/33) |
| 8 | (1)–(5) | 26 Nov 1976 (E) (W) (SI 1976/1744) |
| | | 7 Mar 1977 (S) (SI 1977/227) |
| | (6) | 7 Mar 1977 (SI 1977/227) |
| | (7), (8) | 26 Nov 1976 (E) (W) (SI 1976/1744) |
| | | 7 Mar 1977 (S) (SI 1977/227) |
| | (9), (10) | 1 Jan 1976 (s 108(4)) |
| 9 | | 27 May 1984 (E) (W) (SI 1983/1946) |
| | | 1 Sep 1984 (S) (SI 1984/554) |
| 10 | (1), (2) | 26 Nov 1976 (E) (W) (SI 1976/1744) |
| | | 7 Mar 1977 (S) (SI 1977/227) |
| | (3) | 26 Nov 1976 (SI 1976/1744) |
| 11 | (1)–(3) | 26 Nov 1976 (E) (W) (SI 1976/1744) |
| | | 7 Mar 1977 (S) (SI 1977/227) |
| | (4) | 26 Nov 1976 (SI 1976/1744) |
| 12 | | 26 Nov 1976 (E) (W) (SI 1976/1744) |
| | | 7 Mar 1977 (S) (SI 1977/227) |
| 13 | | 1 Jan 1976 (s 108(4)) |
| 14 | (1)–(4) | 27 May 1984 (E) (W) (SI 1983/1946) |
| | | 1 Sep 1984 (S) (SI 1984/554) |
| | (5) | 1 Sep 1984 (SI 1984/554) |
| | (6)–(8) | 27 May 1984 (E) (W) (SI 1983/1946) |
| | | 1 Sep 1984 (S) (SI 1984/554) |
| 15, 16 | | 27 May 1984 (E) (W) (SI 1983/1946) |
| | | 1 Sep 1984 (S) (SI 1984/554) |
| 17 | (1), (2) | 26 Nov 1976 (E) (W) (SI 1976/1744) |
| | | 7 Mar 1977 (S) (SI 1977/227) |
| | (3) | 26 Nov 1976 (SI 1976/1744) |
| | (4) | 7 Mar 1977 (SI 1977/227) |
| 18–20 | | 27 May 1984 (E) (W) (SI 1983/1946) |
| | | 1 Sep 1984 (S) (SI 1984/554) |
| 21 | (1), (2) | 26 Nov 1976 (SI 1976/1744) |
| | (3) | *Never in force* (repealed) |
| | (4) | 7 Mar 1977 (SI 1977/227) |
| 22 | (1)–(3) | 27 May 1984 (E) (W) (SI 1983/1946) |

**Children Act 1975 (c 72)**—*contd*

|  |  |  |
|---|---|---|
|  |  | 1 Sep 1984 (S) (SI 1984/554) |
|  | (4), (5) | 26 Nov 1976 (E) (W) (SI 1976/1744) |
|  |  | 7 Mar 1977 (S) (SI 1977/227) |
|  | (6) | 7 Mar 1977 (SI 1977/227) |
| 23 |  | 27 May 1984 (E) (W) (SI 1983/1946) |
|  |  | 1 Sep 1984 (S) (SI 1984/554) |
| 24 |  | 23 Oct 1978 (SI 1978/1433; SI 1978/1440[4]) |
| 25 |  | 27 May 1984 (E) (W) (SI 1983/1946) |
|  |  | 1 Sep 1984 (S) (SI 1984/554) |
| 26 |  | 26 Nov 1976 (SI 1976/1744) |
| 27 |  | 7 Mar 1977 (SI 1977/227) |
| 28 | (a), (b) | 15 Feb 1982 (SI 1981/1792; SI 1982/33) |
|  | (c)(i) | 15 Feb 1982 (SI 1981/1792; SI 1982/33) |
|  | (c)(ii) | 26 Nov 1976 (E) (W) (SI 1976/1744) |
|  |  | 7 Mar 1977 (S) (SI 1977/227) |
|  | (d) | 15 Feb 1982 (SI 1981/1792; SI 1982/33) |
| 29 |  | 26 Nov 1976 (E) (W) (SI 1976/1744) |
|  |  | 7 Mar 1977 (S) (SI 1977/227) |
| 30 | (1), (2) | 26 Nov 1976 (E) (W) (SI 1976/1744) |
|  |  | 7 Mar 1977 (S) (SI 1977/227) |
|  | (3)–(5) | 26 Nov 1976 (SI 1976/1744) |
|  | (6) | 26 Nov 1976 (E) (W) (SI 1976/1744) |
|  |  | 7 Mar 1977 (S) (SI 1977/227) |
| 31 |  | 26 Nov 1976 (E) (W) (SI 1976/1744) |
|  |  | 7 Mar 1977 (S) (SI 1977/227) |
| 32 |  | 15 Feb 1982 (SI 1981/1792; SI 1982/33) |
| 33–46 |  | 1 Dec 1985 (SI 1985/779) |
| 47 |  | *Never in force* (repealed) |
| 48 | (1), (2) | *Never in force* (repealed) |
|  | (3), (4) | 1 Sep 1984 (SI 1984/554) |
| 49–55 |  | *Never in force* (repealed) |
| 56, 57 |  | 26 Nov 1976 (SI 1976/1744) |
| 58 |  | 26 Nov 1976 (only in so far as it provides for the insertion of Children Act 1948, s 4A) (SI 1976/1744) |
|  |  | 27 May 1984 (only in so far as it provides for the insertion of Children Act 1948, s 4B) (SI 1983/1946) |
| 59 |  | 1 Jan 1976 (s 108(4)) |
| 60–63 |  | 15 Feb 1982 (SI 1981/1792) |
| 64 |  | 26 Nov 1976 (as respects insertion of Children and Young Persons Act 1969, ss 32A(2)–(5), 32B(1), (3)) (SI 1976/1744) |
|  |  | 27 May 1984 (as respects insertion of Children and Young Persons Act 1969, ss 32A(1), 32B(2)) (SI 1983/1946) |
| 65 |  | 26 Nov 1976 (SI 1976/1744) |
| 66 |  | 30 Jun 1985 (SI 1984/1702) |
| 67, 68 |  | 26 Nov 1976 (SI 1976/1744) |
| 69 |  | 1 Aug 1977 (SI 1977/1036) |
| 70 |  | *Never in force* (repealed) |
| 71, 72 |  | 12 Nov 1975 (s 108(3)) |
| 73, 74 |  | 7 Mar 1977 (SI 1977/227) |
| 74 |  | 7 Mar 1977 (except the amendments of Social Work (Scotland) Act 1968, s 16(1)(b), (4), (5), (11)(d)) (SI 1977/227) |
|  |  | 15 Feb 1982 (exception noted above) (SI 1982/33) |
| 75 |  | 15 Feb 1982 (SI 1982/33) |
| 76 |  | 7 Mar 1977 (SI 1977/227) |
| 77 |  | 7 Mar 1977 (in so far as it inserts Social Work (Scotland) Act 1968, s 18(4A)(a)) (SI 1977/227) |
|  |  | 1 Sep 1984 (otherwise) (SI 1984/554) |
| 78 |  | 30 Jun 1985 (SI 1984/1702) |
| 79 |  | 7 Mar 1977 (SI 1977/227) |

**Children Act 1975 (c 72)**—*contd*

| | | |
|---|---|---|
| 80 | | 1 Sep 1984 (SI 1984/554) |
| 81 | | 7 Mar 1977 (SI 1977/227) |
| 82 | | 12 Nov 1975 (s 108(3)) |
| 83–91 | | 1 Jan 1976 (s 108(4)) |
| 92, 93 | | 1 Jan 1977 (SI 1976/1744) |
| 94 | | 1 Jan 1976 (s 108(4)) |
| 95–97 | | *Never in force* (repealed) |
| 98–100 | | 1 Jan 1976 (s 108(4)) |
| 101 | | 26 Nov 1976 (SI 1976/1744) |
| 102 | | 27 May 1984 (E) (W) (SI 1983/1946) |
| | | 1 Sep 1984 (S) (SI 1984/554) |
| 103–107 | | 1 Jan 1976 (s 108(4)) |
| 108, 109 | | 12 Nov 1975 (s 108(3)) |
| Schs 1, 2 | | 1 Jan 1976 (s 108(4)) |
| Sch 3 | paras 1–4 | 1 Jan 1976 (s 108(4)) |
| | para 5(a) | *Never in force* (repealed) |
| | para 5(b) | 26 Nov 1976 (SI 1976/1744) |
| | para 6 | 1 Jan 1976 (s 108(4)) |
| | para 7 | 1 Dec 1985 (SI 1985/779) |
| | paras 8, 9 | 1 Jan 1976 (s 108(4)) |
| | paras 10, 11 | 1 Dec 1985 (SI 1985/779) |
| | para 12 | *Never in force* (repealed) |
| | para 13(1)–(5) | 1 Jan 1977 (SI 1976/1744) |
| | para 13(6) | 1 Jan 1976 (s 108(4)) |
| | para 14 | 1 Dec 1985 (SI 1985/779) |
| | para 15 | 1 Jan 1976 (s 108(4)) |
| | para 16 | *Never in force* (repealed) |
| | paras 17–20 | 1 Jan 1976 (s 108(4)) |
| | para 21(1), (2) | 1 Jan 1976 (s 108(4)) |
| | para 21(3) | 15 Feb 1982 (SI 1981/1792; SI 1982/33) |
| | para 21(4) | 1 Jan 1976 (s 108(4)) |
| | paras 22–25 | 1 Jan 1976 (s 108(4)) |
| | para 26 | *Never in force* (repealed) |
| | para 27(a) | 15 Feb 1982 (SI 1981/1792; SI 1982/33) |
| | para 27(b) | 1 Jan 1976 (s 108(4)) |
| | para 27(c) | 15 Feb 1982 (SI 1981/1792; SI 1982/33) |
| | para 28 | 15 Feb 1982 (SI 1981/1792; SI 1982/33) |
| | para 29 | 1 Jan 1976 (s 108(4)) |
| | para 30(a) | 27 May 1984 (E) (W) (SI 1983/1946) |
| | | 1 Sep 1984 (S) (SI 1984/554) |
| | para 30(b) | 26 Nov 1976 (E) (W) (SI 1976/1744) |
| | | 7 Mar 1977 (S) (SI 1977/227) |
| | para 31(a) | 27 May 1984 (E) (W) (SI 1983/1946) |
| | | 1 Sep 1984 (S) (SI 1984/554) |
| | para 31(b) | 26 Nov 1976 (E) (W) (only in so far as it provides for the substitution of Children Act 1958, s 37(4)) (SI 1976/1744) |
| | | 7 Mar 1977 (S) (only in so far as it provides for the substitution of Children Act 1958, s 37(4)) (SI 1977/227) |
| | | *Never in force* (otherwise) (repealed) |
| | para 32 | 27 May 1984 (E) (W) (SI 1983/1946) |
| | | 1 Sep 1984 (S) (SI 1984/554) |
| | para 33 | 1 Jan 1976 (s 108(4)) |
| | para 34(a) | 26 Nov 1976 (E) (W) (SI 1976/1744) |
| | | 7 Mar 1977 (S) (SI 1977/227) |
| | para 34(b) | 1 Jan 1976 (s 108(4)) |
| | para 34(c) | 15 Feb 1982 (SI 1981/1792; SI 1982/33) |
| | para 35 | 1 Jan 1976 (s 108(4)) |
| | para 36(a) | 27 May 1984 (E) (W) (SI 1983/1946) |
| | | 1 Sep 1984 (S) (SI 1984/554) |

**Children Act 1975 (c 72)**—*contd*

| | |
|---|---|
| para 36(b) | 1 Jan 1976 (s 108(4)) |
| para 37 | 26 Nov 1976 (E) (W) (SI 1976/1744) |
| | 7 Mar 1977 (S) (SI 1977/227) |
| para 38 | 1 Jan 1976 (s 108(4)) |
| para 39(a) | 26 Nov 1976 (E) (W) (SI 1976/1744) |
| | 7 Mar 1977 (S) (SI 1977/227) |
| para 39(b) | 15 Feb 1982 (SI 1981/1792; SI 1982/33) |
| para 39(c)–(e) | 1 Jan 1976 (s 108(4)) |
| para 40 | 1 Jan 1976 (s 108(4)) |
| paras 41, 42 | 26 Nov 1976 (SI 1976/1744) |
| para 43 | 1 Jan 1976 (s 108(4)) |
| paras 44, 45 | 27 May 1984 (E) (W) (SI 1983/1946) |
| | 1 Sep 1984 (S) (SI 1984/554) |
| paras 46, 47 | 26 Nov 1976 (SI 1976/1744) |
| paras 48, 49 | 1 Jan 1976 (s 108(4)) |
| para 50 | 15 Feb 1982 (SI 1982/33) |
| para 51(a) | 1 Jan 1976 (s 108(4)) |
| para 51(b) | 15 Feb 1982 (SI 1982/33) |
| para 52(a) | 7 Mar 1977 (SI 1977/227) |
| para 52(b) | 15 Feb 1982 (SI 1982/33) |
| para 52(c), (d) | 7 Mar 1977 (SI 1977/227) |
| para 52(e) | 15 Feb 1982 (SI 1982/33) |
| para 52(f)(i) | 7 Mar 1977 (SI 1977/227) |
| para 52(f)(ii) | 1 Jan 1976 (s 108(4)) |
| para 52(g)(i) | 15 Feb 1982 (SI 1982/33) |
| para 52(g)(ii) | 1 Jan 1976 (s 108(4)) |
| para 53(a) | 7 Mar 1977 (SI 1977/227) |
| para 53(b)(i), (ii) | 7 Mar 1977 (SI 1977/227) |
| para 53(b)(iii) | 15 Feb 1982 (SI 1982/33) |
| para 53(c) | 15 Feb 1982 (SI 1982/33) |
| paras 54, 55 | 1 Jan 1976 (s 108(4)) |
| para 56 | *Never in force* (repealed) |
| para 57 | 12 Nov 1975 (s 108(3)) |
| paras 58–63 | 1 Jan 1976 (s 108(4)) |
| para 64 | 26 Nov 1976 (E) (W) (SI 1976/1744) |
| | 7 Mar 1977 (S) (SI 1977/227) |
| paras 65–68 | 1 Jan 1976 (s 108(4)) |
| para 69 | 1 Aug 1977 (SI 1977/1036) |
| para 70 | 1 Jan 1976 (s 108(4)) |
| para 71 | *Never in force* (but see as to repeal of this paragraph and commencement: Child Care Act 1980, ss 89(3), 90(3), Sch 6) (repealed) |
| para 72 | *Never in force* (repealed) |
| para 73(1) | 26 Nov 1976 (SI 1976/1744) |
| para 73(2) | 1 Dec 1985 (SI 1985/779) |
| para 74(a) | 26 Nov 1976 (1976/1744) |
| para 74(b) | 27 May 1984 (except in so far as it relates to the words from "Maintenance of Adoption Service" to "adoption agency" in the entry relating to Children Act 1975, Pt I) (SI 1983/1946) |
| | 1 Dec 1985 (in so far as it inserts the entry relating to Pt II of this Act into the Local Authority Social Services Act 1970, Sch 1) (SI 1985/779) |
| | 1 Jan 1988 (otherwise) (SI 1987/1242) |
| para 75(1)(a)–(c) | 1 Dec 1985 (SI 1985/779) |
| para 75(1)(d) | 1 Dec 1985 (as respects insertion of Guardianship of Minors Act 1971, s 9(5)) (SI 1985/779) |
| | 27 May 1984 (as respects insertion of Guardianship of Minors Act 1971, s 9(6)) (SI 1983/1946) |
| para 75(2) | 27 May 1984 (SI 1983/1946) |

**Children Act 1975 (c 72)**—*contd*

| | | |
|---|---|---|
| | para 75(3) | 1 Jan 1976 (s 108(4)) |
| | para 76 | 1 Dec 1985 (SI 1985/779) |
| | paras 77, 78 | 1 Jan 1976 (s 108(4)) |
| | para 79 | 1 Dec 1985 (SI 1985/779) |
| | para 80 | 1 Feb 1981 (SI 1980/1475) |
| | para 81 | 1 Jan 1976 (s 108(4)) |
| | para 82(a) | 26 Nov 1976 (SI 1976/1744) |
| | para 82(b) | 1 Dec 1985 (as respects insertion of Legal Aid Act 1974, Sch 1, para 3(f)) (SI 1985/779) |
| | | *Never in force* (otherwise) (repealed) |
| | para 83 | 1 Jan 1976 (s 108(4)) |
| Sch 4 | Pts I–III | 1 Jan 1976 (s 108(4)) |
| | Pt IV | 26 Nov 1976 (E) (W) (except in relation to provisions of ss 4(3) (but not paras (c), (d)), 9(5), 12(3) of Adoption Act 1958) (SI 1976/1744) |
| | | 7 Mar 1977 (S) (except repeal of or in Adoption Act 1958, s 12(3)) (SI 1977/227) |
| | | 27 May 1984 (E) (W) (otherwise) (SI 1983/1946) |
| | | 1 Sep 1984 (S) (otherwise) (SI 1984/554) |
| | Pt V | 26 Nov 1976 (E) (W) (SI 1976/1744) |
| | | 7 Mar 1977 (S) (SI 1977/227) |
| | Pt VI | 1 Jan 1977 (SI 1976/1744) |
| | Pt VII | 15 Feb 1982 (except in relation to provisions of Adoption Act 1958, s 28(2), and to the words "Making etc arrangements for the adoption of children;" in Sch 2, col 2, to the Local Authority Social Services Act 1970) (SI 1981/1792; SI 1982/33) |
| | | *Never in force* (otherwise) (repealed) |
| | Pts VIII, IX | 27 May 1984 (E) (W) (SI 1983/1946) |
| | | 1 Sep 1984 (S) (SI 1984/554) |
| | Pt X | 26 Nov 1976 (SI 1976/1744) |
| | Pt XI | 27 May 1984 (E) (W) (in effect; this Pt of the Sch was to take effect on commencement of Sch 3, para 31, to this Act (qv)) (SI 1983/1946) |
| | | 1 Sep 1984 (S) (SI 1984/554) |
| | Pt XII | 1 Dec 1985 (SI 1985/779) |

[1] For transitional provisions, see SI 1976/1744, art 4, Sch 3

[2] For transitional provisions, see SI 1977/227, art 4, Sch 2

[3] For transitional provisions, see SI 1978/1433, art 3

[4] For transitional provisions, see SI 1978/1440, art 4

[5] For transitional provisions, see SI 1981/1792, art 3, Sch 2

[6] For transitional provisions, see SI 1982/33, art 4, Sch 2

[7] For transitional provisions, see SI 1983/1946, art 3, Sch 2

[8] For transitional provisions, see SI 1984/554, art 4, Sch 2

[9] For transitional provisions, see SI 1984/1702, art 4, Sch 2

## Church Commissioners (Miscellaneous Provisions) Measure 1975 (No 1)

*RA:* 1 Aug 1975

Whole Measure in force 1 Aug 1975 (RA)

**Cinematograph Films Act 1975 (c 73)**

*RA:* 12 Nov 1975

Whole Act in force 12 Nov 1975 (RA)

---

**Civil List Act 1975 (c 82)**

*RA:* 19 Dec 1975

Whole Act in force 19 Dec 1975 (RA)

---

**Coal Industry Act 1975 (c 56)**

*RA:* 1 Aug 1975

*Commencement provisions:* s 8(2)

Whole Act in force 1 Sep 1975 (s 8(2))

---

**Community Land Act 1975 (c 77)**

*RA:* 12 Nov 1975

Whole Act in force 12 Nov 1975 (RA)

---

**Conservation of Wild Creatures and Wild Plants Act 1975 (c 48)**

*RA:* 1 Aug 1975

Whole Act in force 1 Aug 1975 (RA)

---

**Consolidated Fund Act 1975 (c 1)**

*RA:* 30 Jan 1975

Whole Act in force 30 Jan 1975 (RA)

---

**Consolidated Fund (No 2) Act 1975 (c 12)**

*RA:* 20 Mar 1975

Whole Act in force 20 Mar 1975 (RA)

---

**Consolidated Fund (No 3) Act 1975 (c 79)**

*RA:* 19 Dec 1975

Whole Act in force 19 Dec 1975 (RA)

---

**Criminal Jurisdiction Act 1975 (c 59)**

*RA:* 7 Aug 1975

*Commencement provisions:* s 14(2), (3); Criminal Jurisdiction Act 1975 (Commencement No 1) Order 1975, SI 1975/1347; Criminal Jurisdiction Act 1975 (Commencement No 2) Order 1976, SI 1976/813

1        1 Jun 1976 (SI 1976/813)

**Criminal Jurisdiction Act 1975 (c 59)**—*contd*

| | | |
|---|---|---|
| 2 | | 21 Aug 1975 (only as respects an act done in Northern Ireland) (SI 1975/1347) |
| | | 1 Jun 1976 (otherwise) (SI 1976/813) |
| 3 | | 1 Jun 1976 (SI 1976/813) |
| 4 | | 21 Aug 1975 (so far as it relates to Sch 2, para 2(2), (3)) (SI 1975/1347) |
| | | 1 Jun 1976 (otherwise) (SI 1976/813) |
| 5–11 | | 1 Jun 1976 (SI 1976/813) |
| 12, 13 | | 7 Aug 1975 (s 14(2)) |
| 14 | | 7 Aug 1975 (all but specified below) (s 14(2)) |
| | | 1 Jun 1976 (so far as sub-s (5) relates to Sch 6, Pts III, IV) (SI 1976/813) |
| Sch 1 | | 1 Jun 1976 (SI 1976/813) |
| Sch 2 | para 1 | 21 Aug 1975 (SI 1975/1347) |
| | para 2(1) | 1 Jun 1976 (SI 1976/813) |
| | para 2(2), (3) | 21 Aug 1975 (SI 1975/1347) |
| | para 3 | 1 Jun 1976 (SI 1976/813) |
| Schs 3, 4 | | 1 Jun 1976 (SI 1976/813) |
| Sch 5 | | 7 Aug 1975 (s 14(2)) |
| Sch 6 | Pts I, II | 7 Aug 1975 (s 14(2)) |
| | Pts III, IV | 1 Jun 1976 (SI 1976/813) |

**Criminal Procedure (Scotland) Act 1975 (c 21)**

*RA:* 8 May 1975

*Commencement provisions*: s 464(2)

Whole Act in force 16 May 1975 (s 464(2)) (in so far as Act extends to England and Wales)

**Diseases of Animals Act 1975 (c 40)**

*RA:* 3 Jul 1975

*Commencement provisions*: s 5(2); Diseases of Animals Act 1975 (Commencement No 1) Order 1976, SI 1976/159; Diseases of Animals Act 1975 (Commencement No 2) Order 1976, SI 1976/596; Diseases of Animals Act 1975 (Commencement No 3) Order 1976, SI 1976/775; Diseases of Animals Act 1975 (Commencement No 4) Order 1977, SI 1977/1124

| | | |
|---|---|---|
| 1–3 | | 5 Feb 1976 (SI 1976/159) |
| 4 | (1), (2) | 5 Feb 1976 (SI 1976/159) |
| | (3) | See Sch 2 below |
| 5 | | 3 Jul 1975 (RA) |
| Sch 1 | | 5 Feb 1976 (SI 1976/159) |
| Sch 2 | | 12 Apr 1976 (repeals of or in Diseases of Animals Act 1950, ss 29, 30) (SI 1976/596) |
| | | 19 May 1976 (repeals of or in Diseases of Animals Act 1950, s 31) (SI 1976/775) |
| | | 1 Jul 1977 (otherwise, except repeals of or in Diseases of Animals Act 1950, s 19(6)) (SI 1977/1124) |
| | | *Never in force* (exception noted above) (repealed) |

**District Courts (Scotland) Act 1975 (c 20)**

*RA:* 27 Mar 1975

*Commencement provisions*: s 27(2)

| | |
|---|---|
| 1–7 | 16 May 1975 (s 27(2)) |
| 8 | 27 Mar 1975 (RA) |

**District Courts (Scotland) Act 1975 (c 20)**—*contd*

| | |
|---|---|
| 9 | 16 May 1975 (s 27(2)) |
| 10, 11 | 27 Mar 1975 (RA) |
| 12, 13 | 16 May 1975 (s 27(2)) |
| 14 | 27 Mar 1975 (RA) |
| 15 | 16 May 1975 (s 27(2)) |
| 16, 17 | 27 Mar 1975 (RA) |
| 18, 19 | 16 May 1975 (s 27(2)) |
| 20 | 27 Mar 1975 (RA) |
| 21, 22 | 16 May 1975 (s 27(2)) |
| 23 | 27 Mar 1975 (RA) |
| 24, 25 | 16 May 1975 (s 27(2)) |
| 26, 27 | 27 Mar 1975 (RA) |
| Schs 1, 2 | 16 May 1975 (s 27(2)) |

**Ecclesiastical Offices (Age Limit) Measure 1975 (No 2)**

*RA:* 1 Aug 1975

*Commencement provisions*: s 7(4)

Whole Measure in force 1 Jan 1976 (day appointed by Archbishops of Canterbury and York under s 7(4))

**Education Act 1975 (c 2)**

*RA:* 25 Feb 1975

*Commencement provisions*: s 5(4), (5)

| | | |
|---|---|---|
| 1 | (1) | 25 Feb 1975 (RA) |
| | (2), (3) | 1 Sep 1975 (s 5(4)) |
| | (4) | 25 Feb 1975 (RA) |
| 2, 3 | | 25 Feb 1975 (RA) |
| 4 | | See Schedule below |
| 5 | | 25 Feb 1975 (RA) |
| Schedule | Pt I | 1 Sep 1975 (s 5(4)) |
| | Pt II | 25 Feb 1975 (RA; but the repeals here do not affect contributions or grants in respect of expenditure on work begun before 6 Nov 1974; see s 5(5)) |

**Employment Protection Act 1975 (c 71)**

*RA:* 12 Nov 1975

*Commencement provisions*: s 129(3); Employment Protection Act 1975 (Commencement No 1) Order 1975, SI 1975/1938[1]; Employment Protection Act 1975 (Commencement No 2) Order 1976, SI 1976/144[2]; Employment Protection Act 1975 (Commencement No 3) Order 1976, SI 1976/321[3]; Employment Protection Act 1975 (Commencement No 4) Order 1976, SI 1976/530, as amended by SI 1976/1379, SI 1977/82; Employment Protection Act 1975 (Commencement No 5) Order 1976, SI 1976/1379; Employment Protection Act 1975 (Commencement No 6) Order 1976, SI 1976/1996; Employment Protection Act 1975 (Commencement No 7) Order 1977, SI 1977/433; Employment Protection Act 1975 (Commencement No 8) Order 1977, SI 1977/936; Employment Protection Act 1975 (Commencement No 9) Order 1977, SI 1977/2075

| | |
|---|---|
| 1, 2 | 1 Jan 1976 (SI 1975/1938) |
| 3 | 1 Jan 1976 (so far as it relates to the Central Arbitration Committee) (SI 1975/1938) |
| | 1 Feb 1976 (otherwise) (SI 1975/1938) |
| 4–6 | 1 Jan 1976 (SI 1975/1938) |
| 7–16 | 1 Feb 1976 (SI 1975/1938) |
| 17–21 | 22 Aug 1977 (SI 1977/936) |

**See Halsbury's Statutes Citator for amendments to these Acts**

**Employment Protection Act 1975 (c 71)**—*contd*

| | | |
|---|---|---|
| 22–24 | | 1 Feb 1977 (SI 1976/1996) |
| 25 | (1)–(4) | 1 Feb 1977 (SI 1976/1996) |
| | (5) | 1 Jun 1976 (SI 1976/530) |
| 26, 27 | | 1 Feb 1977 (SI 1976/1996) |
| 28 | | 1 Jan 1977 (SI 1976/1996) |
| 29 | (1), (2) | 1 Jun 1976 (SI 1976/530) |
| | (3) | 20 Apr 1976 (SI 1976/530) |
| | (4) | 1 Jun 1976 (SI 1976/530) |
| 30–34 | | 1 Jun 1976 (SI 1976/530) |
| 35 | (1)(a) | 6 Apr 1977 (SI 1976/530) |
| | (1)(b) | 1 Jun 1976 (SI 1976/530) |
| | (2)–(5) | 1 Jun 1976 (SI 1976/530) |
| 36–41 | | 6 Apr 1977 (SI 1976/530) |
| 42 | (1)–(3) | 6 Apr 1977 (SI 1976/530) |
| | (4) | 1 Jun 1976 (SI 1976/530) |
| 43–47 | | 6 Apr 1977 (SI 1976/530) |
| 48–56 | | 1 Jun 1976 (SI 1976/530) |
| 57, 58 | | 1 Apr 1978 (SI 1977/2075) |
| 59 | (1)–(3) | 6 Apr 1977 (SI 1977/433) |
| | (4)(a) | 6 Apr 1977 (SI 1977/433) |
| | (4)(b) | 6 Apr 1977 (apart from the words "or sections 57 and 58 above") (SI 1977/433) |
| | | 1 Apr 1978 (otherwise) (SI 1977/2075) |
| | (4)(c) | 6 Apr 1977 (SI 1977/433) |
| | (5), (6) | 6 Apr 1977 (SI 1977/433) |
| 60 | | 6 Apr 1977 (so far as it relates to s 59) (SI 1977/433) |
| | | 1 Apr 1978 (otherwise) (SI 1977/2075) |
| 61 | | 1 Jun 1976 (SI 1976/530) |
| 62 | | 1 Jun 1976 (so far as it relates to the purposes of s 61) (SI 1976/530) |
| | | 6 Apr 1977 (so far as it relates to s 59) (SI 1977/433) |
| | | 1 Apr 1978 (otherwise) (SI 1977/2075) |
| 63 | (1) | 20 Apr 1976 (SI 1976/144) |
| | (2)(a) | 1 Feb 1977 (SI 1976/1996) |
| | (2)(b) | 1 Jun 1976 (SI 1976/530) |
| | (2)(c) | 1 Jun 1976 (so far as it relates to any payment under s 61(3)) (SI 1976/530) |
| | | 1 Apr 1978 (otherwise) (SI 1977/2075) |
| | (2)(d) | 20 Apr 1976 (SI 1976/144) |
| 64 | (1), (2) | 20 Apr 1976 (SI 1976/144) |
| | (3)(a)–(c) | 20 Apr 1976 (SI 1976/144) |
| | (3)(d) | 1 Jun 1976 (SI 1976/530) |
| | (3)(e) | 20 Apr 1976 (SI 1976/144) |
| | (4), (5) | 20 Apr 1976 (SI 1976/144) |
| | (6) | 1 Jun 1976 (SI 1976/530) |
| | (7)–(11) | 20 Apr 1976 (SI 1976/144) |
| 65–69 | | 20 Apr 1976 (SI 1976/144) |
| 70–80 | | 1 Jun 1976 (SI 1976/530) |
| 81–84 | | 6 Apr 1977 (SI 1976/1379) |
| 85 | | 8 Mar 1976 (so far as it relates to the purposes of s 102) (SI 1976/144) |
| | | 1 Jun 1976 (otherwise) (SI 1976/530) |
| 86 | | 1 Jun 1976 (SI 1976/530) |
| 87, 88 | | 30 Mar 1976 (SI 1976/321) |
| 89–91 | | 1 Jan 1976 (SI 1975/1938) |
| 92 | | 1 Jan 1976 (except so far as it relates to the Central Arbitration Committee) (SI 1975/1938) |
| | | 1 Feb 1976 (otherwise) (SI 1975/1938) |
| 93–97 | | 1 Jan 1976 (SI 1975/1938) |

**Employment Protection Act 1975 (c 71)**—*contd*

| | | |
|---|---|---|
| 98 | | 1 Jan 1977 (SI 1976/1996) |
| 99–108 | | 8 Mar 1976 (SI 1976/144) |
| 109 | | 1 Jan 1976 (SI 1975/1938) |
| 110 | | See Sch 12 below |
| 111 | | 1 Feb 1977 (SI 1976/1996) |
| 112 | | 1 Jan 1976 (SI 1975/1938) |
| 113 | | 8 Mar 1976 (so far as it relates to remuneration paid under a protective award under s 101) (SI 1976/144) |
| | | 1 Jun 1976 (otherwise) (SI 1976/530) |
| 114, 115 | | 1 Jan 1976 (SI 1975/1938) |
| 116 | | 1 Jan 1976 (so far as it relates to Sch 15, paras 2, 3, 9 below) (SI 1975/1938) |
| | | 1 Mar 1976 (otherwise) (SI 1975/1938) |
| 117 | | 8 Mar 1976 (so far as it relates to any offence under s 105 of the Act) (SI 1976/144) |
| | | 20 Apr 1976 (otherwise) (SI 1976/530) |
| 118 | | 1 Jan 1976 (SI 1975/1938) |
| 119 | | 8 Mar 1976 (so far as it relates to ss 99, 100 of the Act) (SI 1976/144) |
| | | 20 Apr 1976 (so far as relates to ss 64, 65) (SI 1976/530) |
| | | 1 Jun 1976 (otherwise) (SI 1976/530) |
| 120 | | 1 Jun 1976 (SI 1976/530) |
| 121–123 | | 1 Jan 1976 (SI 1975/1938) |
| 124 | (1) | 1 Jan 1976 (SI 1975/1938) |
| | (2)(a) | 20 Apr 1976 (SI 1976/530) |
| | (2)(b) | 1 Jan 1976 (SI 1975/1938) |
| | (3) | 6 Apr 1977 (SI 1976/530) |
| | (4)(a) | 6 Apr 1977 (SI 1976/530) |
| | (4)(b) | 1 Jun 1976 (SI 1976/530) |
| | (5), (6) | 1 Jan 1976 (SI 1975/1938) |
| 125 | | See Schs 16–18 below |
| 126 | (1) | 1 Jan 1976 (so far as it relates to the definitions of "associated employer", "collective agreement", "employee", "employer", "official", "trade union", "worker", "collective bargaining", "the 1974 Act", "recognition" and "Service") (SI 1975/1938) |
| | | 1 Feb 1976 (so far as it relates to the definitions of "independent trade union", "independence", "independent", "successor", "union membership agreement" and "Committee") (SI 1975/1938) |
| | | 8 Mar 1976 (so far as it relates to the definitions of "business", "dismiss", "dismissal" and "effective date of termination") (SI 1976/144) |
| | | 1 Jun 1976 (otherwise, except definitions of "guarantee payment" and "maternity pay") (SI 1976/530) |
| | | 1 Feb 1977 (so far as it relates to the definition of "guarantee payment") (SI 1976/1996) |
| | | 6 Apr 1977 (so far as it relates to the definition of "maternity pay") (SI 1976/530) |
| | (2) | 1 Jan 1976 (SI 1975/1938) |
| | (3) | 20 Apr 1977 (SI 1976/530) |
| | (4) | 1 Feb 1976 (SI 1975/1938) |
| | (5)–(7) | 8 Mar 1976 (SI 1976/144) |
| | (8), (9) | 1 Jan 1976 (SI 1975/1938) |
| 127 | | 1 Jan 1976 (SI 1975/1938) |
| 128 | | 1 Feb 1976 (SI 1975/1938) |
| 129 | | 1 Jan 1976 (SI 1975/1938) |
| Sch 1 | Pt I | 1 Jan 1976 (so far as it relates to the Advisory, Conciliation and Arbitration Service and its Council) (SI 1975/1938) |
| | | 1 Feb 1976 (otherwise) (SI 1975/1938) |
| | Pt II | 1 Feb 1976 (SI 1975/1938) |

**Employment Protection Act 1975 (c 71)**—*contd*

| | | |
|---|---|---|
| | Pt III | 1 Jan 1976 (so far as it relates to the Advisory, Conciliation and Arbitration Service and its Council) (SI 1975/1938) |
| | | 1 Feb 1976 (otherwise) (SI 1975/1938) |
| Schs 2, 3 | | 1 Jun 1976 (SI 1976/530) |
| Sch 4 | | 8 Mar 1976 (so far as it relates to the purposes of s 102) (SI 1976/144) |
| | | 1 Jun 1976 (otherwise) (SI 1976/530) |
| Sch 5 | | 1 Jun 1976 (SI 1976/530) |
| Sch 6 | | 30 Mar 1976 (SI 1976/321) |
| Schs 7–10 | | 1 Jan 1976 (SI 1975/1938) |
| Sch 11 | | 1 Jan 1977 (SI 1976/1996) |
| Sch 12 | | 8 Mar 1976 (so far as it relates to ss 99–107 of the Act) (SI 1976/144) |
| | | 20 Apr 1976 (otherwise) (SI 1976/530) |
| Schs 13, 14 | | 1 Jan 1976 (SI 1975/1938) |
| Sch 15 | para 1 | 1 Mar 1976 (SI 1975/1938) |
| | paras 2, 3 | 1 Jan 1976 (SI 1975/1938) |
| | paras 4–8 | 1 Mar 1976 (SI 1975/1938) |
| | para 9 | 1 Jan 1976 (SI 1975/1938) |
| | paras 10–21 | 1 Mar 1976 (SI 1975/1938) |
| Sch 16 | Pt I, paras 1–5 | 1 Jun 1976 (SI 1976/530) |
| | Pt I, para 6 | 1 Jan 1977 (SI 1976/1996) |
| | Pt I, paras 7–16 | 1 Jun 1976 (SI 1976/530) |
| | Pt I, para 17 | 1 Jan 1976 (SI 1975/1938) |
| | Pt I, paras 18–34 | 1 Jun 1976 (SI 1976/530) |
| | Pt II, paras 1–6 | 1 Jun 1976 (SI 1976/530) |
| | Pt II, paras 7, 8 | 1 Feb 1977 (SI 1976/1996) |
| | Pt II, paras 9, 10 | 1 Jun 1976 (SI 1976/530) |
| | Pt II, para 11 | 1 Feb 1977 (SI 1976/1996) |
| | Pt II, para 12 | 1 Jun 1976 (SI 1976/530) |
| | Pt II, paras 13, 14 | 1 Feb 1977 (SI 1976/1996) |
| | Pt II, paras 15–19 | 1 Jun 1976 (SI 1976/530) |
| | Pt III, paras 1–4 | 1 Feb 1976 (SI 1975/1938) |
| | Pt III, paras 5, 6 | 1 Jan 1976 (SI 1975/1938) |
| | Pt III, para 7(1) | 1 Feb 1976 (SI 1975/1938) |
| | Pt III, para 7(2) | 1 Jan 1976 (SI 1975/1938) |
| | Pt III, para 7(3) | 1 Feb 1976 (SI 1975/1938) |
| | Pt III, para 7(4) | 1 Jun 1976 (SI 1976/530) |
| | Pt III, para 7(5) | 1 Jan 1976 (SI 1975/1938) |
| | Pt III, paras 8–10 | 1 Jun 1976 (SI 1976/530) |
| | Pt III, para 11 | 1 Jan 1976 (SI 1975/1938) |
| | Pt III, para 12 | 1 Feb 1976 (SI 1975/1938) |
| | Pt III, para 13 | 1 Jun 1976 (SI 1976/530) |
| | Pt III, para 14(1)(a) | 1 Oct 1976 (SI 1976/1379) |
| | Pt III, para 14(1)(b), (c) | 1 Jun 1976 (SI 1976/530) |
| | Pt III, para 14(2) | 1 Jun 1976 (SI 1976/530) |
| | Pt III, para 15 | 1 Oct 1976 (SI 1976/1379) |
| | Pt III, paras 16, 17 | 1 Jun 1976 (SI 1976/530) |
| | Pt III, para 18 | 1 Jan 1976 (SI 1975/1938) |
| | Pt III, para 19 | 20 Apr 1976 (SI 1976/530) |
| | Pt III, paras 20, 21 | 1 Jun 1976 (SI 1976/530) |
| | Pt III, para 22 | 20 Apr 1976 (SI 1976/530) |
| | Pt III, para 23 | 1 Jan 1976 (SI 1975/1938) |
| | Pt III, para 24 | 1 Jun 1976 (SI 1976/530) |
| | Pt III, para 25 | 1 Jan 1976 (SI 1975/1938) |
| | Pt III, paras 26–29 | 1 Jun 1976 (SI 1976/530) |
| | Pt III, para 30 | 20 Apr 1976 (SI 1976/530) |
| | Pt III, paras 31–33 | 1 Jan 1976 (SI 1975/1938) |

**Employment Protection Act 1975 (c 71)**—*contd*

| | | |
|---|---|---|
| | Pt III, para 34 | 1 Jun 1976 (SI 1976/530) |
| | Pt III, para 35 | 1 Feb 1976 (SI 1975/1938) |
| | Pt IV, para 1 | 1 Jan 1976 (SI 1975/1938) |
| | Pt IV, paras 2–5 | 1 Feb 1976 (SI 1975/1938) |
| | Pt IV, para 6 | 1 Jan 1976 (SI 1975/1938) |
| | Pt IV, paras 7, 8 | 1 Feb 1976 (SI 1975/1938) |
| | Pt IV, para 9 | 1 Jun 1976 (SI 1976/530) |
| | Pt IV, paras 10–12 | 1 Feb 1976 (SI 1975/1938) |
| | Pt IV, para 13(1)–(5) | 1 Feb 1976 (SI 1975/1938) |
| | Pt IV, para 13(6) | 1 Jan 1976 (SI 1975/1938) |
| | Pt IV, para 13(7)–(9) | 1 Feb 1976 (SI 1975/1938) |
| | Pt IV, para 13(10), (11) | 1 Jan 1976 (SI 1975/1938) |
| | Pt IV, paras 14, 15 | 1 Feb 1976 (SI 1975/1938) |
| | Pt IV, para 16 | 1 Jan 1976 (so far as it relates to the Council of the Advisory, Conciliation and Arbitration Service, the Employment Service Agency and the Training Services Agency) (SI 1975/1938) |
| | | 1 Feb 1976 (exception noted above) (SI 1975/1938) |
| | Pt IV, para 17 | 1 Feb 1976 (SI 1975/1938) |
| | Pt IV, para 18(1) | 1 Jan 1976 (SI 1975/1938) |
| | Pt IV, para 18(2) | 1 Jun 1976 (SI 1976/530) |
| | Pt IV, para 18(3) | 1 Jan 1976 (as far as it relates to para 13(6), (10), (11)) (SI 1975/1938) |
| | | 1 Feb 1976 (otherwise) (SI 1975/1938) |
| Sch 17 | paras 1, 2 | 1 Jan 1976 (SI 1975/1938) |
| | para 3 | 1 Feb 1976 (SI 1975/1938) |
| | para 4 | 1 Jan 1976 (SI 1975/1938) |
| | paras 5, 6 | 1 Feb 1976 (SI 1975/1938) |
| | para 7 | 1 Jun 1976 (SI 1976/530) |
| | para 8 | 20 Apr 1976 (SI 1976/144) |
| | paras 9, 10 | 1 Feb 1976 (SI 1975/1938) |
| | paras 11, 12 | 1 Jan 1976 (SI 1975/1938) |
| | para 13 | 1 Jan 1977 (SI 1976/1996) |
| | paras 14, 15 | 1 Jan 1976 (SI 1975/1938) |
| | paras 16, 17 | 1 Jun 1976 (SI 1976/530) |
| | paras 18, 19 | 1 Jan 1976 (SI 1975/1938) |
| Sch 18 | | 1 Jan 1976 (SI 1975/1938), so far as it relates to— |

Conciliation Act 1896;
Agricultural Wages (Scotland) Act 1949;
Public Records Act 1958;
Wages Councils Act 1959;
Equal Pay Act 1970;
Superannuation Act 1972;
Employment Agencies Act 1973;
Employment and Training Act 1973;
Health and Safety at Work etc Act 1974, s 2(5);
Trade Union and Labour Relations Act 1974, s 8(10), Sch 1, para 26(1), Sch 3, para 9(4), (6), (7);
House of Commons Disqualification Act 1975, Sch 1, Pt III;
Northern Ireland Assembly Disqualification Act 1975, Sch 1, Pt III;
Sex Discrimination Act 1975
1 Feb 1976 (SI 1975/1938), so far as it relates to—
Trade Union Act 1913;
Industrial Courts Act 1919;
Road Haulage Wages Act 1938;
National Health Service (Amendment) Act 1949;

**Employment Protection Act 1975 (c 71)**—*contd*

Trade Union (Amalgamations, etc) Act 1964;
Remuneration of Teachers Act 1965;
Remuneration of Teachers (Scotland) Act 1967;
Transport Act 1968;
Consumer Credit Act 1974;
Trade Union and Labour Relations Act 1974, ss 8(1), (8), 30(1), Sch 3, paras 2(6), 3, 10(4), (6), 15;
House of Commons Disqualification Act 1975, Sch 1, Pt II;
Northern Ireland Assembly Disqualification Act 1975, Sch 1, Pt II

1 Mar 1976 (remaining repeals in Health and Safety at Work etc Act 1974) (SI 1975/1938)

1 Jun 1976 (SI 1976/530), so far as it relates to—
Education (Scotland) Act 1962;
Redundancy Payments Act 1965;
Social Security Act 1973;
remaining provisions relating to Trade Union and Labour Relations Act 1974, except Sch 1, para 9(1)(a)

1 Oct 1976 (so far as it relates to Trade Union and Labour Relations Act 1974) (SI 1976/1379)

1 Jan 1977 (so far as it relates to Terms and Conditions of Employment Act 1959) (SI 1976/1996)

1 Feb 1977 (except so far as it relates to the Payment of Wages Act 1960) (SI 1976/1996)

6 Apr 1977 (so far as relates to the Payment of Wages Act 1960) (SI 1976/1379)

[1]   For transitional provisions, see SI 1975/1938, art 3

[2]   For transitional provisions and savings, see SI 1976/144, art 3

[3]   For transitional provisions and savings, see SI 1976/321, arts 4, 5

**Evidence (Proceedings in Other Jurisdictions) Act 1975 (c 34)**

*RA:* 22 May 1975

*Commencement provisions:* s 10(2); Evidence (Proceedings in other Jurisdictions) Act 1975 (Commencement) Order 1976, SI 1976/429

Whole Act in force 4 May 1976 (SI 1976/429)

**Export Guarantees Act 1975 (c 38)**

*RA:* 3 Jul 1975

*Commencement provisions:* s 12(2)

Whole Act in force 3 Aug 1975 (s 12(2))

**Export Guarantees Amendment Act 1975 (c 19)**

*RA:* 27 Mar 1975

Whole Act in force 27 Mar 1975 (RA)

## Farriers (Registration) Act 1975 (c 35)

*RA:* 22 May 1975

*Commencement provisions:* s 19(2), (3); Farriers (Registration) Act 1975 (Commencement No 1) Order 1975, SI 1975/2018; Farriers (Registration) Act 1975 (Commencement No 2) Order 1978, SI 1978/1928; Farriers (Registration) Act 1975 (Commencement No 3) Order 1981, SI 1981/767; Farriers (Registration) Act 1975 (Commencement No 4) (Scotland) Order 2006, SI 2006/581

| | |
|---|---|
| 1–15 | 1 Jan 1976 (SI 1975/2018) |
| 16 | 1 Jun 1979 (E) (W) (SI 1978/1928) |
| | 1 Nov 1981 (S) (except in relation to the Highland Region, Western Isles Islands Area, Orkney Islands Area, Shetland Islands Area and all other islands) (SI 1981/767) |
| | 30 Mar 2007 (S) (exception noted above) (SI 2006/581) |
| 17–19 | 1 Jan 1976 (SI 1975/2018) |
| Schs 1–3 | 1 Jan 1976 (SI 1975/2018) |

## Finance Act 1975 (c 7)

*RA:* 13 Mar 1975

The commencement details of Finance Acts are not set out, as the dates from which their provisions take effect are usually stated clearly and unambiguously in the text of the Act, and charging provisions will normally state for which year or years of assessment they are to have effect.

## Finance (No 2) Act 1975 (c 45)

*Budget Day:* 15 Apr 1975

*RA:* 1 Aug 1975

The commencement details of Finance Acts are not set out, as the dates from which their provisions take effect are usually stated clearly and unambiguously in the text of the Act, and charging provisions will normally state for which year or years of assessment they are to have effect.

## General Rate Act 1975 (c 5)

*RA:* 25 Feb 1975

Whole Act in force 25 Feb 1975 (RA)

## Guard Dogs Act 1975 (c 50)

*RA:* 1 Aug 1975

*Commencement provisions:* s 8(2); Guard Dogs Act 1975 (Commencement No 1) Order 1975, SI 1975/1767

| | |
|---|---|
| 1 | 1 Feb 1976 (SI 1975/1767) |
| 2–4 | *Not yet in force* |
| 5 | 1 Feb 1976 (except in relation to ss 2–4, 6) (SI 1975/1767) |
| | *Not yet in force* (otherwise) |
| 6 | *Not yet in force* |
| 7, 8 | 1 Feb 1976 (SI 1975/1767) |

## Hearing Aid Council (Extension) Act 1975 (c 39)

*RA:* 3 Jul 1975

*Commencement provisions:* s 2(2); Hearing Aid Council (Extension) Act 1975 (Commencement) Order 1975, SI 1975/1882

**Hearing Aid Council (Extension) Act 1975 (c 39)**—*contd*
Whole Act in force 29 Dec 1975 (SI 1975/1882)

---

**House of Commons Disqualification Act 1975 (c 24)**

*RA:* 8 May 1975

Whole Act in force 8 May 1975 (RA)

---

**Housing Finance (Special Provisions) Act 1975 (c 67)**

*RA:* 12 Nov 1975

Whole Act in force 12 Nov 1975 (RA)

---

**Housing Rents and Subsidies Act 1975 (c 6)**
*RA:* 25 Feb 1975

*Commencement provisions:* s 17(7), (9)

| | | |
|---|---|---|
| 1 | | 25 Feb 1975 (s 17(7)) |
| 2–10 | | 11 Mar 1975 (s 17(9)) |
| 11 | (1)–(4) | 25 Feb 1975 (s 17(7)) |
| | (5)–(9) | 11 Mar 1975 (s 17(9)) |
| | (10), (11) | 25 Feb 1975 (s 17(7)) |
| 12–16 | | 11 Mar 1975 (s 17(9)) |
| 17 | (1)–(7) | 11 Mar 1975 (s 17(9)) |
| | (8) | 25 Feb 1975 (s 17(7)) |
| | (9), (10) | 11 Mar 1975 (s 17(9)) |
| | (11) | 25 Feb 1975 (s 17(7)) |
| Sch 1 | Pt I, paras 1–12 | 11 Mar 1975 (s 17(9)) |
| | Pt I, para 13 | 25 Feb 1975 (s 17(7)) |
| | Pts II, III | 25 Feb 1975 (s 17(7)) |
| Schs 2–4 | | 11 Mar 1975 (s 17(9)) |
| Sch 5 | paras 1–3 | 11 Mar 1975 (s 17(9)) |
| | para 4 | 25 Feb 1975 (s 17(7)) |
| | paras 5, 6 | 11 Mar 1975 (s 17(9)) |
| | para 7 | 25 Feb 1975 (s 17(7)) |
| | paras 8–26 | 11 Mar 1975 (s 17(9)) |
| Sch 6 | Pt I | 25 Feb 1975 (s 17(7)) |
| | Pt II | 11 Mar 1975 (s 17(9); only has effect in relation to the year 1975–79 and later years) |
| | Pt III | 11 Mar 1975 (s 17(9)) |
| | Pt IV | 25 Feb 1975 (in relation to the Housing Finance Act 1972, ss 25(2)(c), 80) (s 17(7)) |
| | Pt V | 11 Mar 1975 (otherwise) (s 17(9)) |

---

**Housing Rents and Subsidies (Scotland) Act 1975 (c 28)**

*RA:* 8 May 1975

*Commencement provisions:* s 17(4)

Whole Act in force 16 May 1975 (s 17(4))

---

## Industrial and Provident Societies Act 1975 (c 41)

*RA:* 3 Jul 1975

*Commencement provisions:* s 3(4)

Whole Act in force 3 Aug 1975 (s 3(4))

---

## Industrial Injuries and Diseases (Northern Ireland Old Cases) Act 1975 (c 17)

*RA:* 20 Mar 1975

*Commencement provisions:* s 10(3)

Whole Act in force 6 Apr 1975 (s 10(3); subject to Social Security (Consequential Provisions) Act 1975, s 3)

---

## Industrial Injuries and Diseases (Old Cases) Act 1975 (c 16)

*RA:* 20 Mar 1975

*Commencement provisions:* s 15(3) (subject to Social Security (Consequential Provisions) Act 1975, s 3)

Whole Act in force 6 Apr 1975 (s 15(3)). Note, however, that in so far as ss 2(6)(c), 7(2)(b) of this Act re-enact amendments made by the Social Security Benefits Act 1975, s 2(5), they came into force on 9 Apr 1975, by virtue of the Social Security Benefits Act 1975 (Commencement No 1) Order 1975, SI 1975/400

---

## Industry Act 1975 (c 68)

*RA:* 12 Nov 1975

*Commencement provisions:* s 39(6), (7); Industry Act 1975 (Commencement) Order 1975, SI 1975/1881

Whole Act in force 20 Nov 1975 (SI 1975/1881)

---

## Inheritance (Provision for Family and Dependants) Act 1975 (c 63)

*RA:* 12 Nov 1975

*Commencement provisions:* s 27(3)

Whole Act in force 1 Apr 1976 (s 27(3); note that Act only applies to persons dying on or after this date)

---

## International Road Haulage Permits Act 1975 (c 46)

*RA:* 1 Aug 1975

*Commencement provisions:* s 5(2)

Whole Act in force 1 Sep 1975 (s 5(2))

---

## Iron and Steel Act 1975 (c 64)

*RA:* 12 Nov 1975

*Commencement provisions:* s 39(3)

Whole Act in force 12 Dec 1975 (s 39(3))

---

## Limitation Act 1975 (c 54)

*RA:* 1 Aug 1975

*Commencement provisions*: s 4(6)

Whole Act in force 1 Sep 1975 (s 4(6))

---

## Litigants in Person (Costs and Expenses) Act 1975 (c 47)

*RA:* 1 Aug 1975

*Commencement provisions*: s 2(2); Litigants in Person (Costs and Expenses) Act 1975 (Commencement) Order 1976, SI 1976/364; Litigants in Person (Costs and Expenses) Act 1975 (Commencement) (Northern Ireland) Order 1977, SI 1977/509; Litigants in Person (Costs and Expenses) Act 1975 (Commencement No 2) Order 1980, SI 1980/1158

Whole Act in force as follows—

1 Apr 1976 (as respects civil proceedings in a county court, the Supreme Court and the Lands Tribunal in relation to England and Wales) (SI 1976/364)

1 May 1977 (as respects civil proceedings in a county court, the Supreme Court and the Lands Tribunal in relation to Northern Ireland) (SI 1977/509)

1 Sep 1980 (otherwise, in relation to England and Wales) (SI 1980/1158)

## Local Government (Scotland) Act 1975 (c 30)

*RA:* 8 May 1975

*Commencement provisions*: s 39(2); Local Government (Scotland) Act 1975 (Commencement) Order 1975, SI 1975/824

| | | |
|---|---|---|
| 1 | | 16 May 1975 (SI 1975/824) |
| 2 | (1)(a)–(c) | 16 Sep 1975 (SI 1975/824) |
| | (1)(d) | 1 Apr 1976 (SI 1975/824) |
| | (1)(e)–(h) | 16 Sep 1975 (SI 1975/824) |
| | (2)(a), (b) | 16 Sep 1975 (SI 1975/824) |
| | (2)(c) | 1 Apr 1976 (SI 1975/824) |
| | (2)(d) | 16 Sep 1975 (SI 1975/824) |
| | (3), (4) | 16 Sep 1975 (SI 1975/824) |
| 3 | | 16 Sep 1975 (SI 1975/824) |
| 4 | | 15 Aug 1975 (SI 1975/824) |
| 5 | | 1 Apr 1976 (SI 1975/824) |
| 6, 7 | | 16 May 1975 (SI 1975/824) |
| 8 | | 1 Apr 1976 (SI 1975/824) |
| 9–38 | | 16 May 1975 (SI 1975/824) |
| 39 | | 8 May 1975 (s 39(2)) |
| Sch 1 | | 16 May 1975 (SI 1975/824) |
| Sch 2 | para 1 | 16 May 1975 (SI 1975/824) |
| | para 2 | 16 May 1975 (as respects rate support grants for the year 1976–77 and any subsequent year) (SI 1975/824) |
| | para 3 | 16 May 1975 (as respects rate support grants for the year 1975–76 and any subsequent year and so far as relates to the new s 4(1)–(3), (6), (7)) (SI 1975/824) |
| | | 16 May 1975 (as respects rate support grants for the year 1976–77 and any subsequent year and so far as relates to the new s 4(4), (5)) (SI 1975/824) |
| | para 4 | 16 May 1975 (as respects rate support grants for the year 1976–77 and any subsequent year) (SI 1975/824) |
| | para 5 | 16 May 1975 (as respects rate support grants for the year 1975–76 and any subsequent year) (SI 1975/824) |

**Local Government (Scotland) Act 1975 (c 30)**—*contd*

| | | |
|---|---|---|
| | paras 6, 7 | 16 May 1975 (as respects rate support grants for the year 1976–77 and any subsequent year) (SI 1975/824) |
| Schs 3–5 | | 16 May 1975 (SI 1975/824) |
| Sch 6 | Pt I, para 1 | 1 Apr 1976 (SI 1975/824) |
| | Pt I, para 2 | 16 May 1975 (SI 1975/824) |
| | Pt II, para 1 | 16 May 1975 (SI 1975/824) |
| | Pt II, paras 2, 3 | 1 Apr 1976 (SI 1975/824) |
| | Pt II, paras 4–6 | 16 May 1975 (SI 1975/824) |
| | Pt II, para 7 | 1 Apr 1976 (SI 1975/824) |
| | Pt II, para 8 | 16 May 1975 (SI 1975/824) |
| | Pt II, para 9 | 1 Apr 1976 (SI 1975/824) |
| | Pt II, paras 10–13 | 16 May 1975 (SI 1975/824) |
| | Pt II, para 14 | 1 Apr 1976 (SI 1975/824) |
| | Pt II, paras 15, 16 | 16 May 1975 (SI 1975/824) |
| | Pt II, paras 17, 18 | 1 Apr 1976 (SI 1975/824) |
| | Pt II, paras 19–21 | 16 May 1975 (SI 1975/824) |
| | Pt II, para 22 | 1 Apr 1976 (SI 1975/824) |
| | Pt II, para 23 | 16 May 1975 (SI 1975/824) |
| | Pt II, para 24 | 16 May 1975 (as respects rate support grants for the year 1976–77 and any subsequent year) (SI 1975/824) |
| | Pt II, paras 25–31 | 16 May 1975 (SI 1975/824) |
| | Pt II, para 32 | 16 Sep 1975 (SI 1975/824) |
| | Pt II, paras 33–36 | 16 May 1975 (SI 1975/824) |
| | Pt II, para 37 | 1 Apr 1976 (SI 1975/824) |
| | Pt II, paras 38–42 | 16 May 1975 (SI 1975/824) |
| | Pt II, para 43 | 1 Apr 1976 (SI 1975/824) |
| | Pt II, paras 44–62 | 16 May 1975 (SI 1975/824) |
| Sch 7 | | 16 May 1975 (all repeals, except those stated below) (SI 1975/824) |

15 Aug 1975 (repeals of or in Valuation and Rating (Scotland) Act 1956, s 5) (SI 1975/824)

16 Sep 1975 (SI 1975/824), repeals of or in—

Lands Valuation (Scotland) Act 1854, ss 1, 5;

Valuation and Rating (Scotland) Act 1956, ss 9(1), (2), (4), (7), 13(2), Sch 2;

Local Government (Financial Provisions etc) (Scotland) Act 1962, s 9, Sch 2, para 4

1 Apr 1976 (SI 1975/824), repeals of or in—

Lands Valuation (Scotland) Act 1854, ss 23, 24, 27;

Valuation of Lands (Scotland) Acts Amendment Act 1894;

Local Government (Scotland) Act 1947, ss 231, 232;

Local Government Act 1948;

Rating and Valuation (Scotland) Act 1952;

Valuation and Rating (Scotland) Act 1956, ss 9(6), 10;

Local Government (Financial Provisions) (Scotland) Act 1963, s 21;

Local Government (Development and Finance) (Scotland) Act 1964, s 12;

Rating Act 1966;

Local Government (Scotland) Act 1966, Sch 2;

Local Government (Scotland) Act 1973, Sch 9, para 57

1 Apr 1977 (repeals of or in Lands Valuation (Scotland) Act 1854, s 9) (SI 1975/824)

1 Apr 1978 (SI 1975/824), repeals of or in—

Lands Valuation (Scotland) Act 1854, s 42;

Registration Amendment (Scotland) Act 1885;

Local Government (Financial Provisions) (Scotland) Act 1963, s 13(1), (2)(b), (e), (3), (4), (6)–(8)

## Local Land Charges Act 1975 (c 76)

*RA:* 12 Nov 1975

*Commencement provisions:* s 20(3); Local Land Charges Act 1975 (Commencement) Order 1977, SI 1977/984

Whole Act in force 1 Aug 1977 (SI 1977/984)

## Lotteries Act 1975 (c 58)

*RA:* 7 Aug 1975

*Commencement provisions:* s 20(6); Lotteries Act 1975 (Commencement No 1) Order 1975, SI 1975/1413; Lotteries Act 1975 (Commencement No 2) Order 1977, SI 1977/409

| | |
|---|---|
| 1–12 | 1 May 1977 (SI 1977/409) |
| 13, 14 | 5 Sep 1975 (SI 1975/1413) |
| 15 | 1 May 1977 (SI 1977/409) |
| 16–20 | 5 Sep 1975 (SI 1975/1413) |
| Schs 1–3 | 1 May 1977 (SI 1977/409) |
| Sch 4 | 5 Sep 1975 (SI 1975/1413) |
| Sch 5 | 5 Sep 1975 (entry relating to the Gaming Act 1968) (SI 1975/1413) |
| | 1 May 1977 (otherwise) (SI 1977/409) |

## Malta Republic Act 1975 (c 31)

*RA:* 8 May 1975

This Act generally had retrospective effect from 13 Dec 1974 (Independence Day)

## Mental Health (Amendment) Act 1975 (c 29)

*RA:* 8 May 1975

*Commencement provisions:* s 2(3); Mental Health (Amendment) Act 1975 (Commencement) Order 1975, SI 1975/1218

Whole Act in force 1 Sep 1975 (SI 1975/1218)

## Ministerial and other Salaries Act 1975 (c 27)

*RA:* 8 May 1975

Whole Act in force 8 May 1975 (RA)

## Ministers of the Crown Act 1975 (c 26)

*RA:* 8 May 1975

Whole Act in force 8 May 1975 (RA)

## Mobile Homes Act 1975 (c 49)

*RA:* 1 Aug 1975

*Commencement provisions:* s 10(2)

**Mobile Homes Act 1975 (c 49)**—*contd*
Whole Act in force 1 Oct 1975 (s 10(2))

---

**Moneylenders (Crown Agents) Act 1975 (c 81)**

*RA:* 19 Dec 1975

Whole Act in force 19 Dec 1975 (RA)

---

**New Towns Act 1975 (c 42)**

*RA:* 3 Jul 1975

Whole Act in force 3 Jul 1975 (RA)

---

**Northern Ireland Assembly Disqualification Act 1975 (c 25)**

*RA:* 8 May 1975

Whole Act in force 8 May 1975 (RA)

---

**Northern Ireland (Emergency Provisions) (Amendment) Act 1975 (c 62)**

*RA:* 7 Aug 1975

*Commencement provisions:* s 21(1)

Whole Act in force 21 Aug 1975 (s 21(1))

---

**Northern Ireland (Loans) Act 1975 (c 83)**

*RA:* 19 Dec 1975

Whole Act in force 19 Dec 1975 (RA)

---

**Nursing Homes Act 1975 (c 37)**

*RA:* 3 Jul 1975

*Commencement provisions:* s 24(2); Nursing Homes Act 1975 Commencement Order 1975, SI 1975/1281

Whole Act in force 18 Aug 1975 (SI 1975/1281)

---

**OECD Support Fund Act 1975 (c 80)**

*RA:* 19 Dec 1975

Whole Act in force 19 Dec 1975 (RA)

---

**Offshore Petroleum Development (Scotland) Act 1975 (c 8)**

*RA:* 13 Mar 1975

Whole Act in force 13 Mar 1975 (RA)

---

## Oil Taxation Act 1975 (c 22)

*RA:* 8 May 1975

Whole Act in force 8 May 1975 (RA)

---

## Petroleum and Submarine Pipe-lines Act 1975 (c 74)

*RA:* 12 Nov 1975

*Commencement provisions:* s 49(2); Petroleum and Submarine Pipe-lines Act 1975 (Commencement) Order 1975, SI 1975/2120

Whole Act in force 1 Jan 1976 (SI 1975/2120)

---

## Policyholders Protection Act 1975 (c 75)

*RA:* 12 Nov 1975

Whole Act in force 12 Nov 1975 (RA)

---

## Prices Act 1975 (c 32)

*RA:* 8 May 1975

Whole Act in force 8 May 1975 (RA)

---

## Public Service Vehicles (Arrest of Offenders) Act 1975 (c 53)

*RA:* 1 Aug 1975

Whole Act in force 1 Aug 1975 (RA); although note s 1, in part, never in force, in pursuance of s 2(3) (repealed)

---

## Recess Elections Act 1975 (c 66)

*RA:* 12 Nov 1975

*Commencement provisions:* s 5(7)

Whole Act in force 12 Dec 1975 (s 5(7))

---

## Referendum Act 1975 (c 33)

*RA:* 8 May 1975

Whole Act in force 8 May 1975 (RA)

---

## Remuneration, Charges and Grants Act 1975 (c 57)

*RA:* 1 Aug 1975

Whole Act in force 1 Aug 1975 (RA)

---

## Reservoirs Act 1975 (c 23)

*RA:* 8 May 1975

*Commencement provisions*: s 29; Reservoirs Act 1975 (Commencement No 1) Order 1983, SI 1983/1666; Reservoirs Act 1975 (Commencement No 2) Order 1985, SI 1985/176[1], as amended by SI 1986/2202; Reservoirs Act 1975 (Commencement No 3) Order 1986, SI 1986/466[2], as amended by SI 1986/2202; Reservoirs Act 1975 (Commencement No 4) Order 1986, SI 1986/2202

| | | |
|---|---|---|
| 1 | | 30 Nov 1983 (SI 1983/1666) |
| 2, 3 | | 1 Apr 1985 (except in relation to Greater London and the metropolitan counties) (SI 1985/176) |
| | | 1 Apr 1986 (exception noted above) (SI 1986/466) |
| 4, 5 | | 30 Nov 1983 (SI 1983/1666) |
| 6–10 | | 1 Apr 1986 (except in relation to Greater London and the metropolitan counties) (SI 1986/466) |
| | | 1 Apr 1987 (exception noted above) (SI 1986/2202) |
| 11 | | 1 Apr 1985 (except in relation to Greater London and the metropolitan counties) (SI 1985/176) |
| | | 1 Apr 1986 (exception noted above) (SI 1986/466) |
| 12–14 | | 1 Apr 1986 (except in relation to Greater London and the metropolitan counties) (SI 1986/466) |
| | | 1 Apr 1987 (exception noted above) (SI 1986/2202) |
| 15 | (1)–(3) | 1 Apr 1986 (except in relation to Greater London and the metropolitan counties) (SI 1986/466) |
| | | 1 Apr 1987 (exception noted above) (SI 1986/2202) |
| | (4) | 1 Apr 1985 (so far as applied by s 16(5), except in relation to Greater London and the metropolitan counties) (SI 1985/176) |
| | | 1 Apr 1986 (otherwise, except in relation to Greater London and the metropolitan counties and in force in relation to Greater London and the metropolitan counties so far as applied by s 16(5)) (SI 1986/466) |
| | | 1 Apr 1987 (otherwise, in relation to Greater London and the metropolitan counties) (SI 1986/2202) |
| | (5) | 1 Apr 1986 (except in relation to Greater London and the metropolitan counties) (SI 1986/466) |
| | | 1 Apr 1987 (exception noted above) (SI 1986/2202) |
| 16 | | 1 Apr 1985 (except in relation to Greater London and the metropolitan counties) (SI 1985/176) |
| | | 1 Apr 1986 (exception noted above) (SI 1986/466) |
| 17 | (1)(a) | 1 Apr 1985 (except in relation to Greater London and the metropolitan counties) (SI 1985/176) |
| | | 1 Apr 1986 (exception noted above) (SI 1986/466) |
| | (1)(b)–(d) | 1 Apr 1986 (except in relation to Greater London and the metropolitan counties) (SI 1986/466) |
| | | 1 Apr 1987 (exception noted above) (SI 1986/2202) |
| | (1)(e) | 1 Apr 1985 (except in relation to Greater London and the metropolitan counties) (SI 1985/176) |
| | | 1 Apr 1986 (exception noted above) (SI 1986/466) |
| | (2) | 1 Apr 1985 (except in relation to Greater London and the metropolitan counties) (SI 1985/176) |
| | | 1 Apr 1986 (exception noted above) (SI 1986/466) |
| | (3) | 1 Apr 1986 (except in relation to Greater London and the metropolitan counties) (SI 1986/466) |
| | | 1 Apr 1987 (exception noted above) (SI 1986/2202) |
| | (4)–(9) | 1 Apr 1985 (except in relation to Greater London and the metropolitan counties) (SI 1985/176) |
| | | 1 Apr 1986 (exception noted above) (SI 1986/466) |
| 18 | | 1 Apr 1985 (except in relation to Greater London and the metropolitan counties) (SI 1985/176) |
| | | 1 Apr 1986 (exception noted above) (SI 1986/466) |
| 19, 20 | | 1 Apr 1986 (except in relation to Greater London and the metropolitan counties) (SI 1986/466) |

**Reservoirs Act 1975 (c 23)**—*contd*

|  |  |  |
|---|---|---|
|  |  | 1 Apr 1987 (exception noted above) (SI 1986/2202) |
| 21 | (1)–(4) | 1 Apr 1986 (except in relation to Greater London and the metropolitan counties) (SI 1986/466) |
|  |  | 1 Apr 1987 (exception noted above) (SI 1986/2202) |
|  | (5), (6) | 1 Apr 1985 (so far they relate to the provision of information to persons appointed under s 16(3), except in relation to Greater London and the metropolitan counties) (SI 1985/176) |
|  |  | 1 Apr 1986 (otherwise, except in relation to Greater London and the metropolitan counties) (SI 1986/466) |
|  |  | 1 Apr 1987 (otherwise, in relation to Greater London and the metropolitan counties) (SI 1986/2202) |
| 22 |  | 1 Apr 1985 (so far as it relates to provisions brought into force by SI 1983/1666 or SI 1985/176) (SI 1985/176) |
|  |  | 1 Apr 1986 (otherwise, except in relation to Greater London and the metropolitan counties) (SI 1986/466) |
|  |  | 1 Apr 1987 (exception noted above) (SI 1986/2202) |
| 23 |  | 1 Apr 1986 (except in relation to Greater London and the metropolitan counties) (SI 1986/466) |
|  |  | 1 Apr 1987 (exception noted above) (SI 1986/2202) |
| 24 |  | 1 Apr 1985 (SI 1985/176) |
|  |  | 1 Apr 1986 (exception noted above) (SI 1986/466) |
| 25–28 |  | 1 Apr 1986 (except in relation to Greater London and the metropolitan counties) (SI 1986/466) |
|  |  | 1 Apr 1987 (exception noted above) (SI 1986/2202) |
| 29, 30 |  | 30 Nov 1983 (SI 1983/1666) |
| Sch 1 |  | 30 Nov 1983 (SI 1983/1666) |
| Sch 2 |  | 1 Apr 1986 (except in relation to Greater London and the metropolitan counties) (SI 1986/466) |
|  |  | 1 Apr 1987 (exception noted above) (SI 1986/2202) |

[1]  Note that any references in these provisions to a reservoir shall apply in the case of a reservoir situated partly in Greater London or one or more of the metropolitan counties as if it were wholly situated in the adjacent non-metropolitan county or counties in which it is partly situated, see SI 1985/176, art 2

[2]  Note that any references in these provisions to a reservoir shall apply in the case of a reservoir situated partly in Greater London or one or more of the metropolitan counties as if it were wholly situated in the adjacent non-metropolitan county or counties in which it is partly situated, see SI 1986/466, art 2

---

**Safety of Sports Grounds Act 1975 (c 52)**

*RA:* 1 Aug 1975

*Commencement provisions:* s 19(6); Safety of Sports Grounds Act 1975 (Commencement) Order 1975, SI 1975/1375

Whole Act in force 1 Sep 1975 (SI 1975/1375)

---

**Salmon and Freshwater Fisheries Act 1975 (c 51)**

*RA:* 1 Aug 1975

*Commencement provisions:* s 43(4)

Whole Act in force 1 Aug 1975 (s 43(4))

---

**Scottish Development Agency Act 1975 (c 69)**

*RA:* 12 Nov 1975

*Commencement provisions:* s 28(2); Scottish Development Agency Act 1975 (Commencement) Order 1975, SI 1975/1898

**Scottish Development Agency Act 1975 (c 69)**—*contd*
Whole Act in force 15 Dec 1975 (SI 1975/1898) (except s 28, which comes into force on 12 Nov 1975
   (s 28(2))

---

## Sex Discrimination Act 1975 (c 65)

*RA:* 12 Nov 1975

*Commencement provisions:* s 83(2), (4), (5); Sex Discrimination Act 1975 (Commencement) Order 1975,
   SI 1975/1845, as amended by SI 1975/2112

| | | |
|---|---|---|
| 1–5 | | 12 Nov 1975 (RA) |
| 6, 7 | | 29 Dec 1975 (SI 1975/1845) |
| 8 | (1)–(5) | 29 Dec 1975 (SI 1975/1845) |
| | (6) | See Sch 1 below |
| 9–21 | | 29 Dec 1975 (SI 1975/1845) |
| 22 | | 29 Dec 1975 (SI 1975/1845; note however that this section and s 25, so far as relate to admission of pupils to educational establishments for certain purposes, do not apply to offers of, or applications for, admission on date before 1 Sep 1976) |
| 23, 24 | | 29 Dec 1975 (SI 1975/1845) |
| 25 | | 29 Dec 1975 (SI 1975/1845; see note to s 22 above) |
| 26–37 | | 29 Dec 1975 (SI 1975/1845) |
| 38 | | 29 Dec 1975 (SI 1975/1845 as amended by SI 1975/2112; but note it is not unlawful to publish or cause to be published printed advertisement before 1 Apr 1976 if printed or made up for publication before 15 Dec 1975) |
| 39–52 | | 29 Dec 1975 (SI 1975/1845) |
| 53 | | 12 Nov 1975 (SI 1975/1845) |
| 54, 55 | | 29 Dec 1975 (SI 1975/1845) |
| 56 | | 1 Jan 1976 (SI 1975/1845) |
| 57–76 | | 29 Dec 1975 (SI 1975/1845) |
| 77–87 | | 12 Nov 1975 (RA) |
| Sch 1 | | 29 Dec 1975 (SI 1975/1845; but note that so far as Schedule amends Equal Pay Act 1970, s 6, and as regards that Act as set out in Pt II of this Schedule, it comes into force on 6 Apr 1978 (SI 1975/1845). In interim period SI 1975/1845 provided for substituted para 3 of this Schedule for the purposes of s 8(6) of this Act) |
| Schs 2, 3 | | 29 Dec 1975 (SI 1975/1845) |
| Sch 4 | | 12 Nov 1975 (RA) |
| Schs 5, 6 | | 29 Dec 1975 (SI 1975/1845) |

---

## Social Security Act 1975 (c 14)

*RA:* 20 Mar 1975

*Commencement provisions:* s 169(3) (subject to Social Security (Consequential Provisions) Act 1975, s 3(5))

| | |
|---|---|
| 1–12 | 6 Apr 1975 (s 169(3)) |
| 13 | 6 Apr 1975 (s 169(3); but note in so far as sub-s (5) re-enacts minor amendments made by Social Security Benefits Act 1975, s 8(1), it came into force on that date by virtue of Social Security Benefits Act 1975 (Commencement) (No 1) Order 1975, SI 1975/400) |
| 14–19 | 6 Apr 1975 (s 169(3)) |
| 20 | 6 Apr 1975 (s 169(3); but note in so far as sub-s (5) re-enacts minor amendments made by Social Security Benefits Act 1975, s 8(2), it came into force on 16 May 1975 by virtue of Social Security Benefits Act 1975 (Commencement) (No 1) Order 1975, SI 1975/400) |

**Social Security Act 1975 (c 14)**—*contd*

| | |
|---|---|
| 21–29 | 6 Apr 1975 (s 169(3)) |
| 30 | 6 Apr 1975 (s 169(3)); but note in so far as section re-enacts amendments made by Social Security Benefits Act 1975, s 1(3), it came into force on 7 Apr 1975 by virtue of Social Security Benefits Act 1975 (Commencement) (No 1) Order 1975, SI 1975/400) |
| 31–33 | 6 Apr 1975 (s 169(3)) |
| 34 | 6 Apr 1975[1, 2] |
| 35, 36 | 6 Apr 1975 (s 169(3)) |
| 37 | See note 2 below |
| 38–40 | 6 Apr 1975 (s 169(3)) |
| 41 | See note 3 below |
| 42, 43 | 6 Apr 1975 (s 169(3)) |
| 44 | 6 Apr 1975 (s 169(3))[3] |
| 45 | 6 Apr 1975 (s 169(3)); but note in so far as section re-enacts amendments made by Social Security Benefits Act 1975, s 1(3), (4), it came into force on 7 Apr 1975 (as respects wives of retirement pensioners) and 10 Apr 1975 (as respects wives of persons entitled to invalidity pension) by virtue of Social Security Benefits Act 1975 (Commencement) (No 1) Order 1975, SI 1975/400)[3] |
| 46–48 | 6 Apr 1975 (s 169(3))[3] |
| 49 | See notes 1, 2 below |
| 50–65 | 6 Apr 1975 (s 169(3)) |
| 66 | 6 Apr 1975 (s 169(3)); but note in so far as section re-enacts amendments made by Social Security Benefits Act 1975, s 2(2), it came into force on 9 Apr 1975 by virtue of Social Security Benefits Act (Commencement) (No 1) Order 1975, SI 1975/400) |
| 67 | 6 Apr 1975 (s 169(3)) |
| 68 | 6 Apr 1975 (s 169(3)); but note in so far as sub-s (2) re-enacts amendments made by Social Security Benefits Act 1975, s 2(3), it came into force on that date by virtue of Social Security Benefits Act 1975 (Commencement) (No 1) Order 1975, SI 1975/400) |
| 69–105 | 6 Apr 1975 (s 169(3)) |
| 106 | 6 Apr 1975 (s 169(3)); but note in so far as sub-s (1)(a) re-enacts a minor amendment made by Social Security Benefits Act 1975, s 8(3), it came into force on that date by virtue of the Social Security Benefits Act 1975 (Commencement) (No 1) Order 1975, SI 1975/400) |
| 107–125 | 6 Apr 1975 (s 169(3)) |
| 126 | 6 Apr 1975 (s 169(3)); but note in so far as sub-s (6) re-enacts minor amendments made by Social Security Benefits Act 1975, s 8(7), it came into force on that date by virtue of the Social Security Benefits Act 1975 (Commencement) (No 1) Order 1975, SI 1975/400) |
| 127–134 | 6 Apr 1975 (s 169(3)) |
| 135 | 6 Apr 1975 (s 169(3))[1, 3] |
| 136–169 | 6 Apr 1975 (s 169(3)) |
| Schs 1–3 | 6 Apr 1975 (s 169(3)) |
| Sch 4 | Schedule set out in SI 1984/1104 (specified dates in week beginning 26 Nov 1984) |
| Schs 5–13 | 6 Apr 1975 (s 169(3)) |
| Sch 14 | 6 Apr 1975 (s 169(3)); but note in so far as schedule re-enacts amendments made by Social Security Benefits Act 1975, s 8(7), it came into force on that date by virtue of Social Security Benefits Act 1975 (Commencement) (No 1) Order 1975, SI 1975/400) |
| Sch 15 | 6 Apr 1975 (s 169(3)) |

## Social Security Act 1975 (c 14)—*contd*

Sch 16
6 Apr 1975 (s 169(3); but note in so far as Pt II of this Schedule re-enacts amendment made by Social Security Benefits Act 1975, s 8(10) it came into force on that date by virtue of Social Security Benefits Act 1975 (Commencement) (No 1) Order 1975, SI 1975/400)

Schs 17–20
6 Apr 1975 (s 169(3))

[1] Under the Social Security Act 1975 (Commencement No 1) Order 1975, SI 1975/1013 (made under Social Security Benefits Act 1975, Sch 5, para 1, and continued by Social Security (Consequential Provisions) Act 1975, Sch 3, para 27(3)) provisions of this Act relating to non-contributory invalidity pension came into force on 20 Jul 1975, but not so as to confer entitlement to pension in respect of period before 20 Nov 1975

[2] Under the Social Security Act 1975 (Commencement No 2) Order 1976, SI 1976/408 (made under Social Security Benefits Act 1975, Sch 5, para 1, and continued by Social Security (Consequential Provisions) Act 1975, Sch 3, para 27(3)) provisions of this Act relating to invalid care allowance came into force on 12 Apr 1976, but not so as to confer entitlement to that allowance in respect of period before 5 Jul 1976

[3] As far as ss 41, 44–48 re-enact consequential amendments made by Social Security Benefits Act 1975, s 1(2), they came into force (*a*) as respects unemployment benefit, sickness benefit and invalidity pension on 10 Apr 1975 and (*b*) as respects maternity allowance, widows' benefit, retirement pensions and child's special allowance on 7 Apr 1975, by virtue of Social Security Benefits Act 1975 (Commencement) (No 1) Order 1975, SI 1975/400

## Social Security Benefits Act 1975 (c 11)

*RA:* 13 Mar 1975

*Commencement provisions*: s 14(5), Sch 5; Social Security Benefits Act 1975 (Commencement) (No 1) Order 1975, SI 1975/400[1]; Social Security Benefits (1975 Act) (Commencement No 1) (Northern Ireland) Order 1975, SR 1975/60; Social Security Benefits Act 1975 (Commencement) (No 2) Order 1975, SI 1975/1336; Social Security Benefits (1975 Act) (Commencement No 2) (Northern Ireland) Order 1975, SR 1975/243

| | | |
|---|---|---|
| 1 | (1), (2) | See Sch 1 below |
| | (3), (4) | 7 Apr 1975 (in the case of retirement pensioners and certain of their wives under the Social Security Act 1973) (SI 1975/400) |
| | | 9 Apr 1975 (in the case of certain wives of persons entitled to an increase of disablement pension by way of unemployability supplement under the National Insurance (Industrial Injuries) Act 1965) (SI 1975/400) |
| | | 10 Apr 1975 (in the case of certain wives of persons entitled to invalidity pension under the Social Security Act 1973) (SI 1975/400) |
| 2 | (1) | See Sch 2 below |
| | (2) | 7 Apr 1975 (in the case of retirement pensioners and certain of their wives under the Social Security Act 1973) (SI 1975/400) |
| | | 9 Apr 1975 (in the case of certain wives of persons entitled to an increase of disablement pension by way of unemployability supplement under the National Insurance (Industrial Injuries) Act 1965) (SI 1975/400) |
| | | 10 Apr 1975 (in the case of certain wives of persons entitled to invalidity pension under the Social Security Act 1973) (SI 1975/400) |
| | (3), (4) | 6 Apr 1975 (SI 1975/400) |
| | (5) | 9 Apr 1975 (SI 1975/400) |
| 3, 4 | | 24 Mar 1975 (SI 1975/400) |
| 5–7 | | *Never in force* (repealed) |
| 8 | (1) | 6 Apr 1975 (SI 1975/400) |
| | (2) | 16 May 1975 (SI 1975/400) |
| | (3), (4) | 6 Apr 1975 (SI 1975/400) |

**Social Security Benefits Act 1975 (c 11)**—*contd*

| | | |
|---|---|---|
| | (5), (6) | *Never in force* (repealed) |
| | (7) | 6 Apr 1975 (SI 1975/400) |
| | (8) | *Never in force* (repealed) |
| | (9), (10) | 6 Apr 1975 (SI 1975/400) |
| 9 | | 8 Apr 1975 (SI 1975/400) |
| 10 | | 6 Apr 1975 (SI 1975/400) |
| 11 | | See Sch 3 below |
| 12 | | 24 Mar 1975 (SI 1975/400) |
| 13 | | 24 Mar 1975 (NI) (SR 1975/60) |
| 14 | (1)–(5) | 24 Mar 1975 (NI) (SI 1975/400, SR 1975/60) |
| | (6) | See Sch 6 below |
| Sch 1 | | 7 Apr 1975 (so far as relates to rates of basic scheme benefits under the Social Security Act 1973, in the case of attendance allowance, maternity allowance, widow's benefit, guardian's allowance, retirement pensions, age addition and child's special allowance (including increases for dependants where appropriate)) (SI 1975/400) |
| | | 10 Apr 1975 (so far as relates to rates of basic scheme benefits under the Social Security Act 1973, in the case of unemployment, sickness and invalidity benefit (including increases for dependants)) (SI 1975/400) |
| Sch 2 | | 7 Apr 1975 (so far as relates to rates and amounts of benefit under the National Insurance (Industrial Injuries) Act 1965, in the case of widow's pension under s 19, widower's pension under s 20 and allowances in respect of children of deceased's family under s 21) (SI 1975/400) |
| | | 9 Apr 1975 (so far as relates to rates and amounts of benefit under the National Insurance (Industrial Injuries) Act 1965, in the case of disablement benefit (including increases of disablement pension), increase of unemployability supplement under s 13A, maximum under s 29(1)(a) of aggregate of weekly benefits payable for successive accidents and maximum disablement gratuity under s 12(3)) (SI 1975/400) |
| | | 10 Apr 1975 (so far as relates to rates and amounts of benefit under the National Insurance (Industrial Injuries) Act 1965, in the case of injury benefit (including increases for dependants)) (SI 1975/400) |
| Sch 3 | para 1 | 24 Mar 1975 (SI 1975/400) (so far as relates to the cessation of rounding of amounts of benefit under the Supplementary Benefit Act 1966 in the case of any award of supplementary pension or allowance made on or after 7 Apr 1975 in respect of a period beginning in the preceding 14 days and made— |
| | | (i) on a fresh claim, that is to say, where not preceded by an award of such pension or allowance for an earlier period continuous with the first mentioned period, or |
| | | (ii) by way of review of an earlier award on account of a change of circumstances occurring within or immediately before those 14 days (SI 1975/400) |
| | | 7 Apr 1975 (so far as relates to the cessation of rounding of amounts of benefit under the Supplementary Benefit Act 1966 in the case of any other award of supplementary pension or allowance) (SI 1975/1336) |
| | paras 2–6 | 17 Nov 1975 (SI 1975/1336) |
| Schs 4, 5 | | 24 Mar 1975 (NI) (SI 1975/400, SR 1975/60) |
| Sch 6 | Pt I | 24 Mar 1975 (SI 1975/400), so far as relates to— |
| | | Social Security Act 1973, ss 9(3) (part), 24(8) (part), 25(11) (part), 39, Sch 11, Sch 13, paras 4, 9 (part); |
| | | National Insurance Act 1974, s 5, Sch 4, para 22 |
| | | 6 Apr 1975 (SI 1975/400), repeals relating to— |
| | | National Insurance (Industrial Injuries) Act 1965, ss 19(3)(d), 21(4) (part); |

**Social Security Benefits Act 1975 (c 11)**—*contd*

> National Insurance Act 1969;
> National Insurance Act 1971;
> Social Security Act 1973, Sch 28, Pt I, so much as relates to the National Insurance Act 1967, s 4(4);
> National Insurance Act 1974, ss 1(1), 7(a), Sch 1
>
> 6 Apr 1975 (NI) (SR 1975/60), so far as relates to—
> Social Security Act, Sch 28, Pt II;
> National Insurance Act (Northern Ireland) 1967, s 5(4)
>
> 7 Apr 1975 (SI 1975/400), repeals relating to—
> National Insurance (Industrial Injuries) Act 1965, Sch 5, para 1 (parts);
> Supplementary Benefit Act 1966, Sch 2, para 2(2);
> Social Security Act 1973, s 32(4)(a) (parts);
> National Insurance Act 1974, s 3(1), (2), Sch 3 in the case of widow's pension under s 19, widower's pension under s 20 and allowances in respect of children of deceased's family under s 21
>
> 7 Apr 1975 (NI) (so far as relates to the Social Security Act 1973, s 32(4)(a) (parts)) (SR 1975/60)
>
> 8 Apr 1975 (so far as relates to the Family Allowances and National Insurance Act 1968) (SI 1975/400)
>
> 9 Apr 1975 (SI 1975/400), so far as relates to—
> National Insurance Act 1974, s 3(1), (2), Sch 3 in the case of disablement benefit (including increases of disablement pension), increase of unemployability supplement under s 13A, maximum under s 29(1)(a) of aggregate of weekly benefits payable for successive accidents and maximum disablement gratuity under s 12(3);
> National Insurance Act 1974, s 3(1), (2), Sch 3 in the case of benefit under the Industrial Injuries and Diseases (Old Cases) Act 1967)
>
> 10 Apr 1975 (so far as relates to the National Insurance Act 1974, s 3(1), (2), Sch 3, in the case of injury benefit (including increase for dependants)) (SI 1975/400)
>
> 6 May 1975 (NI) (so far as relates to the Social Security Act 1973, s 14(6)(c) (part)) (SR 1975/60)
>
> 16 May 1975 (so far as relates to the Social Security Act 1973, s 14(6)(c) (part)) (SI 1975/400)
>
> 17 Nov 1975 (SI 1975/1336), repeals relating to—
> Supplementary Benefit Act 1966, Sch 2, para 23(1);
> Family Income Supplements Act 1970, s 13(3);
> National Insurance and Supplementary Benefit Act 1973, Sch 4, para 8;
> Social Security Act 1973, Sch 27, para 70(d), (e);
> National Insurance Act 1974, Sch 4, para 14
>
> 17 Nov 1975 (NI) (SR 1975/243), repeals relating to—
> National Insurance and Supplementary Benefit Act 1973, Sch 4, para 8;
> Social Security Act 1973, Sch 7, para 161(d), (e);
> National Insurance Act 1974, Sch 4, para 56

Pt II

> 6 Apr 1975 (NI) (SR 1975/60), repeals relating to—
> National Insurance (Industrial Injuries) Act (Northern Ireland) 1966, ss 19(3)(d), 21(4) (part);
> National Insurance &c (No 2) Act (Northern Ireland) 1969;
> Social Services (Parity) Order (Northern Ireland) 1971;
> National Insurance Measure (Northern Ireland) 1974, s 1(1), Sch 1
>
> 7 Apr 1975 (NI) (SR 1975/60), repeals relating to—
> National Insurance (Industrial Injuries) Act (Northern Ireland) 1966, Sch 5, para 1 (parts);

**Social Security Benefits Act 1975 (c 11)**—*contd*

> Supplementary Benefits &c (Northern Ireland) 1966, Sch 2, para 2(2);
>
> National Insurance Measure (Northern Ireland) 1974, s 3(1), (2) and Sch 3, in the case of widow's pension under s 19, widower's pension under s 20 and allowances in respect of children of deceased's family under s 21
>
> 8 Apr 1975 (NI) (SR 1975/60), repeals relating to—
>
> Family Allowances and National Insurance (No 2) Act (Northern Ireland) 1968
>
> 9 Apr 1975 (NI) (SR 1975/60), repeals relating to—
>
> National Insurance Measure (Northern Ireland) 1974, s 3(1), (2) and Sch 3, in the case of disablement benefit (including increases of disablement pension), increases of unemployability supplement under s 13A, maximum under s 29(1)(a) of aggregate of weekly benefits payable for successive accidents and maximum disablement gratuity under s 12(4);
>
> National Insurance Measure (Northern Ireland) 1974, s 3(1), (2) and Sch 3, in the case of benefit under the Workmen's Compensation (Supplementation) Act (Northern Ireland) 1966
>
> 10 Apr 1975 (NI) (repeals relating to National Insurance Measure (Northern Ireland) 1974, s 3(1), (2) and Sch 3, in the case of injury benefit (including increases for dependants)) (SR 1975/60)
>
> 16 May 1975 (NI) (repeals relating to National Insurance Measure (Northern Ireland) 1974, Sch 4, para 2(b) so far as it relates to the Social Security Act 1973, Sch 13, para 5(2)) (SR 1975/60)
>
> 17 Nov 1975 (NI) (SR 1975/243), repeals relating to—
>
> Supplementary Benefits Act (Northern Ireland) 1966, Sch 2, para 23(1);
>
> Family Income Supplements Act (Northern Ireland) 1971, s 13(3)

[1]  For transitional provisions, see SI 1975/400, arts 2–4

---

**Social Security (Consequential Provisions) Act 1975 (c 18)**

*RA:* 20 Mar 1975

*Commencement provisions:* s 3(2)

This Act came into force, subject to s 3(3)–(5) as soon as all the provisions mentioned in s 3(1) of this Act came into force, which for most purposes was 6 Apr 1975

---

**Social Security (Northern Ireland) Act 1975 (c 15)**

*RA:* 20 Mar 1975

*Commencement provisions:* s 158(3)

Whole Act in force 6 Apr 1975 (s 158(3); subject to Social Security (Consequential Provisions) Act 1975, s 3)

---

**Social Security Pensions Act 1975 (c 60)**

*RA:* 7 Aug 1975

*Commencement provisions:* s 67(1)–(3); Social Security Pensions Act 1975 (Commencement No 1) Order 1975, SI 1975/1318; Social Security Pensions Act 1975 (Commencement No 2) Order 1975, SI 1975/1572; Social Security Pensions Act 1975 (Commencement No 3) Order 1975, SI 1975/1689[1], as amended by SI 1977/2038; Social Security Pensions Act 1975 (Commencement No 4) Order 1975, SI 1975/2079[2]; Social Security Pensions Act 1975 (Commencement No 5)

**Social Security Pensions Act 1975 (c 60)**—*contd*
Order 1976, SI 1976/141; Social Security Pensions Act 1975 (Commencement No 6) Order 1976, SI 1976/1173; Social Security Pensions Act 1975 (Commencement No 7) Order 1976, SI 1976/2129; Social Security Pensions Act 1975 (Commencement No 8) Order 1977, SI 1977/778; Social Security Pensions Act 1975 (Commencement No 9) Order 1977, SI 1977/1403; Social Security Pensions Act 1975 (Commencement No 10) Order 1977, SI 1977/1617; Social Security Pensions Act 1975 (Commencement No 11) Order 1977, SI 1977/2038; Social Security Pensions Act 1975 (Commencement No 12) Order 1978, SI 1978/367; Social Security Pensions Act 1975 (Commencement No 13) Order 1979, SI 1979/171; Social Security Pensions Act 1975 (Commencement No 14) Order 1979, SI 1979/367 (revoked); Social Security Pensions Act 1975 (Commencement No 15) Order 1979, SI 1979/394; Social Security Pensions Act 1975 (Commencement No 16) Order 1979, SI 1979/1030

| | |
|---|---|
| 1, 2 | 6 Apr 1978 (SI 1975/1689) |
| 3 | 6 Apr 1977 (SI 1975/1689) |
| 4, 5 | 6 Apr 1978 (SI 1975/1689) |
| 6–17 | 6 Apr 1979 (SI 1975/1689) |
| 18 | 6 Apr 1978 (SI 1975/1689) |
| 19–21 | 6 Apr 1979 (SI 1975/1689) |
| 22 | 1 Oct 1975 (in relation to persons born on or after 2 Jan 1950 but before 2 Jan 1961, for the purposes of making claims for, and the determination of claims and questions relating to, mobility allowance) (SI 1975/1572) |
| | 1 Jan 1976 (in relation to persons born on or after 2 Jan 1950 but before 2 Jan 1961, for all other purposes) (SI 1975/1572) |
| | 1 Jan 1976 (in relation to persons born on or after 2 Apr 1925 but before 2 Jan 1950 and to persons born on or after 2 Jan 1961 but before 2 Apr 1961, for the purposes of making claims for, and the determination of claims and questions relating to, mobility allowance) (SI 1975/2079) |
| | 1 Apr 1976 (in relation to persons born on or after 2 Apr 1925 but before 2 Jan 1950 and to persons born on or after 2 Jan 1961 but before 2 Apr 1961, for all other purposes) (SI 1975/2079) |
| | 25 May 1977 (in relation to persons born on or after 25 Aug 1923 but before 2 Apr 1925, for the purposes of making claims for, and the determination of claims and questions relating to, mobility allowance) (SI 1977/778) |
| | 24 Aug 1977 (in relation to persons born on or after 25 Aug 1925 but before 2 Apr 1925, for all other purposes) (SI 1977/778) |
| | 2 Nov 1977 (in relation to persons born on or after 2 Feb 1922 but before 25 Aug 1923, for the purposes of making claims for, and the determination of claims and questions relating to, mobility allowance) (SI 1977/1617) |
| | 1 Feb 1978 (in relation to persons born on or after 2 Feb 1922 but before 25 Aug 1923, for all other purposes) (SI 1977/1617) |
| | 5 Apr 1978 (in relation to persons born before 25 Aug 1923 who is a vehicle scheme beneficiary as defined in Mobility Allowance (Vehicle Scheme Beneficiaries) Regulations 1977, SI 1977/1229, reg 1(2), and if on or after 1 Aug 1977 that person is receiving payments in pursuance of Health Services and Public Health Act 1968, s 33, for the purposes of making claims for, and the determination of claims and questions relating to, mobility allowance) (SI 1977/1403)[3] |
| | 7 Jun 1978 (in relation to persons born on or after 14 Jan 1921 but before 2 Feb 1922, for the purposes of making claims for, and the determination of claims and questions relating to, mobility allowance) (SI 1978/367) |

**Social Security Pensions Act 1975 (c 60)**—*contd*

5 Jul 1978 (in relation to persons born before 25 Aug 1923 who is a vehicle scheme beneficiary as defined in Mobility Allowance (Vehicle Scheme Beneficiaries) Regulations 1977, SI 1977/1229, reg 1(2), and if on or after 1 Aug 1977 that person is receiving payments in pursuance of Health Services and Public Health Act 1968, s 33, for all other purposes) (SI 1977/1403)[4]

6 Sep 1978 (in relation to persons born on or after 14 Jan 1921 but before 2 Feb 1922, for all other purposes) (SI 1978/367)

20 Sep 1978 (in relation to persons born on or after 21 Dec 1919 but before 14 Jan 1921, for the purposes of making claims for, and the determination of claims and questions relating to, mobility allowance) (SI 1978/367)

20 Dec 1978 (in relation to persons born on or after 21 Dec 1919 but before 14 Jan 1921, for all other purposes) (SI 1978/367)

7 Mar 1979 (in relation to men born on or after 7 Jun 1918 but before 21 Dec 1919, for the purposes of making claims for, and the determination of claims and questions relating to, mobility allowance) (SI 1977/171)

29 Mar 1979 (in relation to women born on or after 23 Mar 1919 but before 21 Dec 1919, for the purposes of making claims for, and the determination of claims and questions relating to, mobility allowance) (SI 1979/367)

6 Jun 1979 (in relation to men born on or after 7 Jun 1918 but before 21 Dec 1919, for all other purposes and women born on or after 23 Mar 1919 but before 21 Dec 1919, for all other purposes) (SI 1977/171; SI 1979/367)

5 Sep 1979 (in relation to persons born on or after 29 Nov 1914 but before 7 Jun 1918, for the purposes of making claims for, and the determination of claims and questions relating to, mobility allowance) (SI 1979/1030)

28 Nov 1979 (in relation to persons born on or after 29 Nov 1914 but before 7 Jun 1918, for all other purposes) (SI 1979/1030)

| | | |
|---|---|---|
| 23 | (1) | 6 Apr 1976 (so far as sub-s (1) relates to sum specified in s 6(1)(a) and as far as sub-s (4) relates to sub-s (1)(a) of this section) (SI 1975/1689) |
| | (2), (3) | 6 Apr 1979 (SI 1975/1689) |
| | (4) | 6 Apr 1976 (so far as sub-s (1) relates to sum specified in s 6(1)(a) and as far as sub-s (4) relates to sub-s (1)(a) of this section) (SI 1975/1689) |
| | (5) | 6 Apr 1979 (SI 1975/1689) |
| 24 | | 6 Apr 1978 (SI 1975/1689) |
| 25 | | 7 Aug 1975 (SI 1975/1318) |
| 26 | | 21 Nov 1975 (for purpose of issue, cancellation, variation or surrender before, but with effect from dates not earlier than, 6 Apr 1978, of contracted-out certificates and for purposes connected therewith) (SI 1975/1689) |
| | | 6 Apr 1978 (all other purposes) (SI 1975/1689) |
| 27, 28 | | 6 Apr 1978 (SI 1975/1689) |
| 29 | | 6 Apr 1979 (SI 1975/1689) |
| 30 | (1)(a) | 21 Nov 1975 (SI 1975/1689; see note to s 26 above) |
| | | 6 Apr 1978 (all other purposes) (SI 1975/1689) |
| | (1)(b), (c) | 21 Nov 1975 (SI 1975/1689) |
| | (2), (3) | 21 Nov 1975 (SI 1975/1689; see note to s 26 above) |
| | | 6 Apr 1978 (all other purposes) (SI 1975/1689) |
| | (4) | 21 Nov 1975 (SI 1975/1689) |
| | (5) | 6 Apr 1978 (SI 1976/141) |
| 31 | | 21 Nov 1975 (SI 1975/1689) |
| 32–41 | | 21 Nov 1975 (SI 1975/1689; see the note to s 26 above) |
| 42–47 | | 6 Apr 1978 (SI 1976/141) |
| 48, 49 | | 6 Apr 1978 (SI 1975/1689) |

**Social Security Pensions Act 1975 (c 60)**—*contd*

| | | |
|---|---|---|
| 50–52 | | 21 Nov 1975 (SI 1975/1689) |
| 53–55 | | 21 Nov 1975 (for purpose of enabling steps to be taken before 6 Apr 1978 to secure compliance of occupational pension scheme with equal access requirements and connected purposes) (SI 1975/1689) |
| | | 6 Apr 1978 (all other purposes) (SI 1975/1689) |
| 56 | (1)–(4) | 21 Nov 1975 (see note to ss 53–55 above) (SI 1975/1689) |
| | | 6 Apr 1978 (all other purposes) (SI 1975/1689) |
| | (5) | 21 Nov 1975 (SI 1975/1689) |
| 57 | | 21 Nov 1975 (SI 1975/1689) |
| 58 | | See Sch 3 below |
| 59 | | 6 Apr 1979 (SI 1975/1689) |
| 60 | | 21 Nov 1975 (SI 1975/1689) |
| 61–64 | | 7 Aug 1975 (SI 1975/1318) |
| 65 | (1) | See Sch 4 below |
| | (2) | 7 Aug 1975 (SI 1975/1318) |
| | (3) | See Sch 5 below |
| | (4), (5) | 7 Aug 1975 (SI 1975/1318) |
| 66–68 | | 7 Aug 1975 (SI 1975/1318) |
| Sch 1 | | 6 Apr 1979 (SI 1975/1689) |
| Sch 2 | | 21 Nov 1975 (SI 1975/1689) |
| Sch 3 | paras 1, 2 | 6 Apr 1978 (SI 1975/1689) |
| | para 3 | 6 Apr 1978 (SI 1976/141) |
| | para 4 | 6 Apr 1978 (SI 1975/1689) |
| Sch 4 | para 1 | 6 Apr 1978 (SI 1975/1689) |
| | para 2(a) | 6 Apr 1978 (SI 1975/1689) |
| | para 2(b) | 7 Aug 1975 (SI 1975/1318) |
| | para 3 | 6 Apr 1978 (SI 1975/1689) |
| | para 4 | 6 Apr 1979 (SI 1975/1689) |
| | para 5 | 6 Apr 1978 (SI 1975/1689) |
| | paras 6–8 | 6 Apr 1979 (SI 1975/1689) |
| | para 9(a) | 6 Apr 1978 (SI 1975/1689) |
| | para 9(b), (c) | 6 Apr 1979 (SI 1975/1689) |
| | para 10 | 6 Apr 1979 (SI 1975/1689) |
| | para 11 | 7 Aug 1975 (SI 1975/1318) |
| | para 12 | 6 Apr 1979 (SI 1975/1689) |
| | para 13 | 7 Aug 1975 (SI 1975/1318) |
| | para 14 | 6 Apr 1979 (SI 1975/1689) |
| | para 15 | 6 Apr 1978 (SI 1975/1689) |
| | para 16 | 7 Aug 1975 (SI 1975/1318) |
| | paras 17–22 | 6 Apr 1979 (SI 1975/1689) |
| | paras 23–28 | 21 Nov 1975 (SI 1975/1689) |
| | paras 29, 30 | 7 Aug 1975 (SI 1975/1318) |
| | paras 31–33 | 21 Nov 1975 (SI 1975/1689) |
| | para 34 | 6 Apr 1979 (SI 1975/1689) |
| | paras 35, 36 | 6 Apr 1978 (SI 1975/1689) |
| | para 37 | 6 Apr 1979 (SI 1975/1689) |
| | para 38(a) | 6 Apr 1978 (SI 1975/1689) |
| | para 38(b) | 6 Apr 1977 (SI 1975/1689) |
| | paras 39–46 | 6 Apr 1979 (SI 1975/1689) |
| | para 47 | See note to s 22 above |
| | para 48 | 6 Apr 1979 (SI 1975/1689) |
| | para 49 | See note to s 22 above |
| | para 50 | 6 Apr 1978 (SI 1975/1689) |
| | paras 51–53 | See note to s 22 above |
| | paras 54–57 | 6 Apr 1978 (SI 1976/141) |
| | paras 58–60 | 7 Aug 1975 (SI 1975/1318) |
| | para 61 | 21 Nov 1975 (SI 1975/1689) |
| | paras 62, 63 | 6 Apr 1979 (SI 1975/1689) |

**Social Security Pensions Act 1975 (c 60)**—*contd*

|  | paras 64–70 | 7 Aug 1975 (SI 1975/1318) |
|--|--|--|
|  | para 71 | 1 Oct 1975 (SI 1975/1572) |

Sch 5             7 Aug 1975 (SI 1975/1318), entries relating to—
                                         Public Records Act 1958;
                                         Income and Corporation Taxes Act 1970;
                                         Attachment of Earnings Act 1971;
                                         Social Security Act 1973, Pt III, ss 85, 86, 89(4), 98, Schs 18–20;
                                         Social Security Act 1975, ss 27(6), 133(6), Sch 20;
                                         Social Security (Consequential Provisions) Act 1975, Sch 2, paras 53–59, 63, 64(a), Sch 3;
                                         House of Commons Disqualification Act 1975

                                  21 Nov 1975 (SI 1975/1689), entries relating to—
                                         Contracts of Employment Act 1972;
                                         Social Security Act 1973, ss 1, 23, 51–62, 88, 89(3), 91, 92, 99, Schs 15, 22, 23;
                                         National Insurance Act 1974;
                                         Social Security (Consequential Provisions) Act 1975, Sch 2, paras 51, 62, 64(b), 65

                                  6 Apr 1977 (entries relating to Social Security Act 1975, ss 4, 5, 7(2)(c), 130, 167) (SI 1975/1689)

                                  6 Apr 1978 (SI 1975/1689), entries relating to—
                                         Social Security Act 1973, s 93, Sch 24;
                                         Social Security Act 1975, ss 6, 7(2)(a), (b), (3), 8, 9, 120;
                                         Social Security (Consequential Provisions) Act 1975, Sch 2, paras 1(b), 2(b), 7(a)

                                  6 Apr 1979 (SI 1975/1689), entries relating to—
                                         Pensions (Increase) Act 1971;
                                         Parliamentary and other Pensions Act 1972;
                                         Superannuation Act 1972;
                                         Pensions (Increase) Act 1974;
                                         Social Security Act 1975, ss 28, 29, Schs 4, 7;
                                         Social Security (Consequential Provisions) Act 1975, Sch 2, para 47

                                  *Not yet in force* (otherwise)

[1]     For a saving, see SI 1975/1689, art 3

[2]     For a saving, see SI 1975/2079, art 3

[3]     Note that if a person does not fall into this category and their surname begins with any letter from A to K in the alphabet, the relevant date for the coming into force of this section, for those purposes is 6 Sep 1977, and if their surname begins with any letter from L to Z, the date shall be 16 Nov 1977, see SI 1977/1403, art 2(b)

[4]     Note that if a person does not fall into this category and their surname begins with any letter from A to K in the alphabet, the relevant date for the coming into force of this section, for those purposes is 16 Nov 1977, and if their surname begins with any letter from L to Z, the date shall be 15 Feb 1978, see SI 1977/1403, art 2(c)

---

**Statute Law (Repeals) Act 1975 (c 10)**

*RA:* 13 Mar 1975

Whole Act in force 13 Mar 1975 (RA)

---

**Statutory Corporations (Financial Provisions) Act 1975 (c 55)**

*RA:* 1 Aug 1975

Whole Act in force 1 Aug 1975 (RA)

---

**Supply Powers Act 1975 (c 9)**

*RA:* 13 Mar 1975

*Commencement provisions:* s 9(2)

Whole Act in force 13 Apr 1975 (s 9(2))

---

**Unsolicited Goods and Services (Amendment) Act 1975 (c 13)**

*RA:* 20 Mar 1975

*Commencement provisions:* s 4(2), (3); Unsolicited Goods and Services (Amendment) Act 1975 (Commencement No 1) Order 1975, SI 1975/731

| | | |
|---|---|---|
| 1 | | 20 Mar 1975 (s 4(2)) |
| 2 | (1) | *Never in force* (repealed) |
| | (2) | 30 May 1975 (SI 1975/731) |
| 3, 4 | | 20 Mar 1975 (s 4(2)) |

---

**Welsh Development Agency Act 1975 (c 70)**

*RA:* 12 Nov 1975

*Commencement provisions:* s 29(2); Welsh Development Agency Act 1975 (Commencement) Order 1975, SI 1975/2028

Whole Act in force 1 Jan 1976 (SI 1975/2028)

---

**Supply Powers Act 1975 (c. 9)**

R.A. 13 May 1975

(general statute provisions, s.6(2))

Whole Act in force 13 Apr 1975 (s.9(2))

---

**Unsolicited Goods and Services (Amendment) Act 1975 (c. 13)**

R.A. 20 May 1975

Commencement Provisions — s(?) (The Unsolicited Goods and Services (Amendment) Act 1975 (Commencement No. 1) Order 1975, SI 1975/721)

| 1 | ... | ... | 20 Mar 1976 (s.4(2)) |
| 2 | (1) | | Never in force (repealed) |
| | (2) | | 20 Mar 1976 (s.4(2)(?)(?)) |
| 3, 4 | | | 20 Mar 1976 (s.4(2)) |

---

**Welsh Development Agency Act 1975 (c. 70)**

R.A. 6 Nov 1975

Commencement Provisions — s.29(1) (Welsh Development Agency Act 1975 (Commencement) Order 1975, SI 1975/2028

Whole Act in force 1 Jan 1976 (SI 1975/2028)

# 1976 Acts

## Adoption Act 1976 (c 36)

*RA*: 22 Jul 1976

*Commencement provisions*: s 74(2); Children Act 1975 and the Adoption Act 1976 (Commencement) Order 1983, SI 1983/1946; Children Act 1975 and the Adoption Act 1976 (Commencement No 2) Order 1987, SI 1987/1242

| | | |
|---|---|---|
| 1–72 | | 1 Jan 1988 (SI 1987/1242) |
| 73 | (1) | 1 Jan 1988 (SI 1987/1242) |
| | (2) | See Sch 3 below |
| | (3) | See Sch 4 below |
| 74 | | 27 May 1984 (SI 1983/1946) |
| Schs 1–3 | | 1 Jan 1988 (SI 1987/1242) |
| Sch 4 | | 15 Aug 1983 (repeal of Adoption Act 1958, s 33; see Health and Social Services and Social Security Adjudications Act 1983, s 9, Sch 2, para 1 and SI 1983/974, noted to s 58A above) |
| | | 1 Jan 1988 (otherwise, except repeal of Children Act 1975, Sch 3, paras 6, 26, 63) (SI 1987/1242) |
| | | *Never in force* (exception noted above) (repealed) |

## Agriculture (Miscellaneous Provisions) Act 1976 (c 55)

*RA*: 15 Nov 1976

*Commencement provisions*: s 27(2), (3); Agriculture (Miscellaneous Provisions) Act 1976 (Commencement No 1) Order 1977, SI 1977/39; Agriculture (Miscellaneous Provisions) Act 1976 (Commencement No 2) Order 1978, SI 1978/402

| | | |
|---|---|---|
| 1, 2 | | 15 Nov 1976 (RA) |
| 3 | | 1 Feb 1977 (SI 1977/39) |
| 4–11 | | 15 Nov 1976 (RA) |
| 12 | (1)–(4) | *Never in force* (repealed) |
| | (5)–(8) | 15 Nov 1976 (RA) |
| 13, 14 | | 7 Apr 1978 (SI 1978/402) |
| 15–27 | | 15 Nov 1976 (RA) |
| Sch 1 | | 1 Feb 1977 (SI 1977/39) |
| Schs 2, 3 | | 15 Nov 1976 (RA) |
| Sch 4 | Pt I | 15 Nov 1976 (RA) |
| | Pt II | 15 Nov 1976 (except repeals in Agriculture Act 1967) (RA) |
| | | 1 Feb 1977 (exception noted above) (SI 1977/39) |

## Appropriation Act 1976 (c 43)

*RA*: 6 Aug 1976

Whole Act in force 6 Aug 1976 (RA)

## Armed Forces Act 1976 (c 52)

*RA:* 26 Oct 1976

*Commencement provisions:* s 22(7)–(9); Armed Forces Act 1976 (Commencement) Order 1977, SI 1977/897

| | | |
|---|---|---|
| 1 | | 26 Oct 1976 (s 22(7)) |
| 2–9 | | 1 Jul 1977 (SI 1977/897) |
| 10 | | 26 Oct 1976 (s 22(7)) |
| 11–16 | | 1 Jul 1977 (SI 1977/897) |
| 17 | (1) | 26 Oct 1976 (s 22(7)) |
| | (2) | 1 Jul 1977 (SI 1977/897) |
| 18, 19 | | 1 Jul 1977 (SI 1977/897) |
| 20 | (a) | 26 Oct 1976 (s 22(7)) |
| | (b) | 1 Jul 1977 (SI 1977/897) |
| 21 | | 26 Oct 1976 (s 22(7)) |
| 22 | (1)–(4) | 26 Oct 1976 (s 22(7)) |
| | (5) | See Sch 9 below |
| | (6) | See Sch 10 below |
| | (7)–(9) | 26 Oct 1976 (s 22(7)) |
| Schs 1–8 | | 1 Jul 1977 (SI 1977/897) |
| Sch 9 | paras 1–3 | 1 Jul 1977 (SI 1977/897) |
| | para 4 | 26 Oct 1976 (s 22(7)) |
| | paras 5–10 | 1 Jul 1977 (SI 1977/897) |
| | para 11 | 26 Oct 1976 (s 22(7)) |
| | paras 12–19 | 1 Jul 1977 (SI 1977/897) |
| | para 20(1) | 1 Jul 1977 (SI 1977/897) |
| | para 20(2) | 26 Oct 1976 (s 22(7)) |
| | para 20(3) | 1 Jul 1977 (SI 1977/897) |
| | para 20(4), (5) | 26 Oct 1976 (s 22(7)) |
| | paras 21, 22 | 1 Jul 1977 (SI 1977/897) |
| Sch 10 | | 26 Oct 1976 (s 22(7)), repeals of or in— |
| | | Naval Knights of Windsor (Dissolution) Act 1892; |
| | | Armed Forces Act 1971, s 1; |
| | | House of Commons Disqualification Act 1975, s 10(4); |
| | | Northern Ireland Assembly Disqualification Act 1975, s 5(3) |
| | | 1 Jul 1977 (otherwise) (SI 1977/897) |

## Atomic Energy Authority (Special Constables) Act 1976 (c 23)

*RA:* 10 Jun 1976

Whole Act in force 10 Jun 1976 (RA)

## Bail Act 1976 (c 63)

*RA:* 15 Nov 1976

*Commencement provisions:* s 13(2); Bail Act 1976 (Commencement) Order 1978, SI 1978/132

| | |
|---|---|
| 1–12 | 17 Apr 1978 (SI 1978/132) |
| 13 | 15 Nov 1976 (RA) |
| Schs 1–4 | 17 Apr 1978 (SI 1978/132) |

## Cathedrals Measure 1976 (No 1)

*RA:* 25 Mar 1976

Whole Measure in force 25 Mar 1976 (RA)

## Chronically Sick and Disabled Persons (Amendment) Act 1976 (c 49)

*RA:* 26 Oct 1976

Whole Act in force 26 Oct 1976 (RA)

---

## Church of England (Miscellaneous Provisions) Measure 1976 (No 3)

*RA:* 15 Nov 1976

*Commencement provisions:* s 8(3)

Whole Measure in force 15 Dec 1976 (s 8(3))

---

## Companies Act 1976 (c 69)

*RA:* 15 Nov 1976

*Commencement provisions:* s 45(3); Companies Act 1976 (Commencement) Order 1976, SI 1976/2188; Companies Act 1976 (Commencement No 2) Order 1977, SI 1977/165; Companies Act 1976 (Commencement No 3) Order 1977, SI 1977/529; Companies Act 1976 (Commencement No 4) Order 1977, SI 1977/774; Companies Act 1976 (Commencement No 5) Order 1977, SI 1977/1348; Companies Act 1976 (Commencement No 6) Order 1979, SI 1979/1544; Companies Act 1976 (Commencement No 7) Order 1980, SI 1980/1748; Companies Act 1976 (Commencement No 8) Order 1982, SI 1982/671; Companies Act 1976 (Commencement No 9) Order 1984, SI 1984/683

| | | |
|---|---|---|
| 1 | | 1 Oct 1977 (SI 1977/1348) |
| 2 | (1) | 1 Mar 1977 (SI 1977/165) |
| | (2)–(6) | 1 Oct 1977 (SI 1977/1348) |
| 3 | | 1 Oct 1977 (SI 1977/1348) |
| 4 | (1), (2) | 1 Oct 1977 (SI 1977/1348) |
| | (3), (4) | *Never in force* (repealed) |
| | (5) | 1 Oct 1977 (SI 1977/1348) |
| 5, 6 | | 1 Oct 1977 (SI 1977/1348) |
| 7 | (1)–(6) | 1 Oct 1977 (SI 1977/1348) |
| | (7) | 1 Oct 1977 (except in relation to proceedings for an offence under Companies Act 1948, s 148, against an unregistered company to which the said s 148 is applied by virtue of s 435 of that Act) (SI 1977/1348) |
| | | 1 Jan 1985 (otherwise) (SI 1984/683) |
| | (8) | 1 Oct 1977 (SI 1977/1348) |
| 8, 9 | | 1 Oct 1977 (SI 1977/1348) |
| 10 | (1) | 1 Mar 1977 (so far as it applies s 2(1) in relation to overseas companies) (SI 1977/165) |
| | | 1 Oct 1977 (otherwise) (SI 1977/1348) |
| | (2) | 1 Mar 1977 (SI 1977/165) |
| | (4)–(7) | 1 Oct 1977 (SI 1977/1348) |
| 11, 12 | | 1 Oct 1977 (SI 1977/1348) |
| 13 | | 18 Apr 1977 (SI 1977/529) |
| 14 | (1)–(10) | 18 Apr 1977 (SI 1977/529) |
| | (11) | 18 Apr 1977 (except in so far as it relates to the repeal of Companies Act 1948, s 159, as that section is applied to unregistered companies by virtue of s 435 of that Act) (SI 1977/529) |
| | | 1 Jan 1985 (otherwise) (SI 1984/683) |
| | (12) | 18 Apr 1977 (SI 1977/529) |
| 15 | (1)–(6) | 18 Apr 1977 (SI 1977/529) |
| | (7) | 18 Apr 1977 (except in so far as it relates to the repeal of Companies Act 1948, s 160, as that section is applied to unregistered companies by virtue of s 435 of that Act) (SI 1977/529) |
| | | 1 Jan 1985 (otherwise) (SI 1984/683) |

**Companies Act 1976 (c 69)**—*contd*

| | | |
|---|---|---|
| 16–22 | | 18 Apr 1977 (SI 1977/529) |
| 23 | (1)–(4) | 18 Apr 1977 (SI 1977/529) |
| | (5) | 18 Apr 1977 (except in so far as it relates to the repeal of Companies Act 1948, s 107, as that section is applied to unregistered companies by virtue of s 435 of that Act) (SI 1977/529) |
| | | 1 Jan 1985 (otherwise) (SI 1984/683) |
| | (6) | 18 Apr 1977 (except in so far as it amends European Communities Act 1972, s 9(3)(e), as that section is applied to unregistered companies by virtue of Companies Act 1948, s 435) (SI 1977/529) |
| | | 1 Jan 1985 (otherwise) (SI 1984/683) |
| | (7) | 18 Apr 1977 (SI 1977/529) |
| 24–27 | | 18 Apr 1977 (SI 1977/529) |
| 28, 29 | | 1 Jun 1977 (SI 1977/774) |
| 30–32 | | 18 Apr 1977 (SI 1977/529) |
| 33 | | 24 Jan 1977 (SI 1976/2188) |
| 34 | (1) | See Sch 1 below |
| | (2) | 18 Apr 1977 (except in so far as it relates to the form provided for the purposes of Companies Act 1948, s 52(1)(a)) (SI 1977/529) |
| | | 1 Jan 1985 (otherwise) (SI 1984/683) |
| 35, 36 | | 18 Apr 1977 (SI 1977/529) |
| 37 | (1)–(3) | 18 Apr 1977 (SI 1977/529) |
| | (4) | 22 Dec 1980 (SI 1980/1748) |
| | (5), (6) | 18 Apr 1977 (SI 1977/529) |
| 38 | (1) | 18 Apr 1977 (SI 1977/529) |
| | (2), (3) | 15 Jun 1982 (SI 1982/671) |
| | (4) | 1 Mar 1977 (SI 1977/165) |
| 39 | | 18 Apr 1977 (SI 1977/529) |
| 40 | | 24 Jan 1977 (SI 1976/2188) |
| 41 | | 18 Apr 1977 (SI 1977/529) |
| 42 | (1) | See Sch 2 below |
| | (2) | See Sch 3 below |
| | (3) | 18 Apr 1977 (SI 1977/529) |
| 43 | | 1 Mar 1977 (SI 1977/165) |
| 44, 45 | | 24 Jan 1977 (SI 1976/2188) |
| Sch 1 | | 18 Apr 1977 (except in so far as it relates to the amendments of Companies Act 1948, s 52(1)(a), and Companies Act 1967, ss 26(3), 29(8)) (SI 1977/529) |
| | | 1 Oct 1977 (otherwise, except in so far as it relates to amendment of Companies Act 1948, s 52(1)(a)) (SI 1977/1348) |
| | | 28 Nov 1979 (otherwise) (SI 1979/1544) |
| Sch 2 | | 24 Jan 1977 (so far as amends Companies Act 1948, s 52(1)(a)) (SI 1976/2188) |
| | | 1 Mar 1977 (so far as amends Insurance Companies Act 1974, s 75(2)) (SI 1977/165) |
| | | 18 Apr 1977 (SI 1977/529), amendments of— |
| | | Companies Act 1948, ss 12, 15(2) (except to the extent that that sub-s has effect in relation to a statutory declaration in a case where the memorandum of a company has been delivered to the registrar before 18 Apr 1977), 38(5)(b), 39(1)(b), 51(1), 409, 417(5)(b), 418(1)(b), 439, Sch 1, regs 110, 130, Sch 8; |
| | | Companies Act 1967, ss 25(2)(a), (b), 27(9), 33(10); |
| | | Insurance Companies Act 1974, s 17(1); |
| | | Stock Exchange (Completion of Bargains) Act 1976, s 3(3), (4) |
| | | 1 Jun 1977 (amendments of Companies Act 1948, Sch 1, Pt 1, Table A, reg 88, Table C, art 38) (SI 1977/774) |
| | | 1 Oct 1977 (SI 1977/1348), amendments of— |
| | | Companies Act 1948, ss 149(6), 151(1), 152(1), 155, 156(1), 157(1), 158(1), 415, 436, Sch 1, regs 123, 124, 126, 127; |

**Companies Act 1976 (c 69)**—*contd*

                Betting Gaming and Lotteries Act 1963, Sch 2, para 24(1)
                    (except in relation to unregistered companies to which
                    Companies Act 1948, s 148 is applied by virtue of s 435 of that
                    Act);
                Protection of Depositors Act 1963, ss 13(3) (except in relation to
                    unregistered companies to which any provision in Part IV of
                    Companies Act 1948 is applied by virtue of s 435 of that Act),
                    16(1)(d) (except in relation to unregistered companies to which
                    Companies Act 1948, s 147 is applied by virtue of s 435 of hat
                    Act);
                Companies Act 1967, ss 14, 15(1), 23, Sch 3;
                Insurance Companies Act 1974, s 46(1)(c) (except in relation to
                    unregistered companies to which Companies Act 1948, s 147 is
                    applied by virtue of s 435 of that Act)
                1 Jan 1985 (otherwise) (SI 1984/683)

Sch 3          1 Mar 1977 (repeals of or in Companies Act 1948, s 424(6))
                (SI 1977/165)
                18 Apr 1977 (SI 1977/529), repeals of or in—
                Companies Act 1948, ss 107, 159, 160, 161(5) (except in so far
                    as those provisions are applied to unregistered companies by
                    virtue of s 435 of that Act), 181(1), (4), 185(4), 453;
                Protection of Depositors Act 1963, ss 18, 19;
                Companies Act 1967, ss 13(2), (3), 14(8)(c), 35(1), 112, Sch 4,
                    entry relating to s 451
                1 Oct 1977 (SI 1977/1348), repeals of or in—
                Companies Act 1948, ss 127, 147, 148, 153(2), 331, 410,
                    Sch 15, entry relating to s 410;
                Protection of Depositors Act 1963, s 13(7) (except in relation to
                    unregistered companies to which Companies Act 1948, s 127 is
                    applied by virtue of s 435 of that Act);
                Companies Act 1967, ss 21, 47, 56(2), (3), Sch 4, entry relating
                    to s 410;
                Iron and Steel Act 1975, s 24(5) (except in so far as that sub-s
                    relates to the report of the directors of unregistered companies
                    to which Companies Act 1948, s 157, is applied by virtue of
                    s 435 of that Act)
                22 Dec 1980 (SI 1980/1748), repeals of or in—
                Companies Act 1948, ss 98, 102, 106D, 425(1), 426;
                Companies Act 1967, s 48, Sch 3
                15 Jun 1982 (repeals of or in Companies Act 1948, ss 390, 459(4),
                  Sch 14) (SI 1982/671)
                1 Jan 1985 (otherwise) (SI 1984/683)

---

**Congenital Disabilities (Civil Liability) Act 1976 (c 28)**

*RA:* 22 Jul 1976

Whole Act in force 22 Jul 1976 (RA)

---

**Consolidated Fund Act 1976 (c 2)**

*RA:* 25 Mar 1976

Whole Act in force 25 Mar 1976 (RA)

---

**Consolidated Fund (No 2) Act 1976 (c 84)**

*RA:* 22 Dec 1976

Whole Act in force 22 Dec 1976 (RA)

---

**Crofting Reform (Scotland) Act 1976 (c 21)**

*RA:* 10 Jun 1976

Whole Act in force 10 Jun 1976 (RA)

---

**Damages (Scotland) Act 1976 (c 13)**

*RA:* 13 Apr 1976

*Commencement provisions:* s 12(3)

Whole Act in force 13 May 1976 (s 12(3))

---

**Dangerous Wild Animals Act 1976 (c 38)**

*RA:* 22 Jul 1976

*Commencement provisions:* s 10(2)

Whole Act in force 22 Oct 1976 (s 10(2))

---

**Development Land Tax Act 1976 (c 24)**

*RA:* 22 Jul 1976

*Commencement provisions:* s 47(1); Development Land Tax (Appointed Day) Order 1976, SI 1976/1148

Whole Act in force 1 Aug 1976 (1976/1148)

---

**Development of Rural Wales Act 1976 (c 75)**

*RA:* 22 Nov 1976

*Commencement provisions:* s 35(2); Development of Rural Wales (Commencement No 1) Order 1976, SI 1976/2038; Development of Rural Wales (Commencement No 2) Order 1977, SI 1977/116

| | | |
|---|---|---|
| 1 | | 1 Jan 1977 (SI 1976/2038) |
| 2 | | 1 Apr 1977 (SI 1977/116) |
| 3 | (1) | 1 Apr 1977 (SI 1977/116) |
| | (2)(a) | 11 Feb 1977 (SI 1977/116) |
| | (2)(b) | 1 Apr 1977 (SI 1977/116) |
| | (3), (4) | 11 Feb 1977 (SI 1977/116) |
| | (5)–(8) | 1 Apr 1977 (SI 1977/116) |
| 4–10 | | 1 Apr 1977 (SI 1977/116) |
| 11 | | 1 Jan 1977 (SI 1976/2038) |
| 12, 13 | | 1 Apr 1977 (SI 1977/116) |
| 14 | (1)(a) | 1 Jan 1977 (SI 1976/2038) |
| | (1)(b) | 1 Apr 1977 (SI 1977/116) |
| | (2)–(6) | 1 Apr 1977 (SI 1977/116) |
| 15–22 | | 1 Apr 1977 (SI 1977/116) |
| 23 | (1)–(3) | 1 Jan 1977 (SI 1976/2038) |
| | (4) | 1 Apr 1977 (SI 1977/116) |
| 24 | | 11 Feb 1977 (SI 1977/116) |

## Development of Rural Wales Act 1976 (c 75)—*contd*

| | | |
|---|---|---|
| 25–28 | | 1 Apr 1977 (SI 1977/116) |
| 29 | (1), (2) | 1 Jan 1977 (SI 1976/2038) |
| | (3) | 11 Feb 1977 (SI 1977/116) |
| | (4)–(6) | 1 Apr 1977 (SI 1977/116) |
| 30–34 | | 1 Apr 1977 (SI 1977/116) |
| 35 | | 22 Nov 1976 (RA) |
| Sch 1 | | 1 Jan 1977 (SI 1976/2038) |
| Sch 2 | paras 1, 2 | 1 Apr 1977 (SI 1977/116) |
| | paras 3–5 | 11 Feb 1977 (SI 1977/116) |
| | para 6 | 1 Apr 1977 (SI 1977/116) |
| Sch 3 | para 1(1) | 1 Apr 1977 (SI 1977/116) |
| | para 1(2) | 11 Feb 1977 (SI 1977/116) |
| | paras 2–56 | 1 Apr 1977 (SI 1977/116) |
| Schs 4, 5 | | 1 Apr 1977 (SI 1977/116) |
| Sch 6 | para 1 | 11 Feb 1977 (SI 1977/116) |
| | para 2 | 1 Apr 1977 (SI 1977/116) |
| | paras 3–5 | 11 Feb 1977 (SI 1977/116) |
| | para 6 | 1 Apr 1977 (SI 1977/116) |
| Sch 7 | | 1 Apr 1977 (SI 1977/116) |

## Divorce (Scotland) Act 1976 (c 39)

*RA:* 22 Jul 1976

*Commencement provisions*: s 14(2)

Whole Act in force 1 Jan 1977 (s 14(2)) (except s 8 (never in force) (repealed))

## Dock Work Regulation Act 1976 (c 79)

*RA:* 22 Nov 1976

*Commencement provisions*: s 17(1); Dock Work Regulation Act 1976 (Commencement No 1) Order 1977, SI 1977/1122; Dock Work Regulation Act 1976 (Commencement No 2) Order 1977, SI 1977/1775

| | | |
|---|---|---|
| 1 | | 1 Aug 1977 (SI 1977/1122) |
| 2 | | *Never in force* (repealed) |
| 3 | | 1 Aug 1977 (SI 1977/1122) |
| 4 | (1)–(4) | 1 Aug 1977 (SI 1977/1122) |
| | (5) | 1 Dec 1977 (SI 1977/1775) |
| | (6)–(8) | *Never in force* (repealed) |
| 5 | (1)–(3) | 1 Aug 1977 (SI 1977/1122) |
| | (4) | 1 Dec 1977 (so far as it relates to s 6) (SI 1977/1775) |
| | | *Never in force* (otherwise) (repealed) |
| | (5)–(11) | 1 Aug 1977 (SI 1977/1122) |
| 6 | | 1 Dec 1977 (SI 1977/1775) |
| 7–10 | | *Never in force* (repealed) |
| 11 | (1) | 1 Dec 1977 (SI 1977/1775) |
| | (2)(a) | 1 Dec 1977 (SI 1977/1775) |
| | (2)(b) | *Never in force* (repealed) |
| | (3)–(15) | *Never in force* (repealed) |
| 12 | | 1 Dec 1977 (SI 1977/1775) |
| 13 | | 1 Aug 1977 (SI 1977/1122) |
| 14 | | *Never in force* (repealed) |
| 15 | | 1 Aug 1977 (SI 1977/1122) |
| 16 | (1) | 1 Aug 1977 (SI 1977/1122) |
| | (2) | 1 Dec 1977 (so far as it relates to orders in pursuance of s 11(2)) (SI 1977/1775) |
| | | *Never in force* (otherwise) (repealed) |

**Dock Work Regulation Act 1976 (c 79)**—*contd*

|  |  |  |
|---|---|---|
|  | (3) | *Never in force* (repealed) |
| 17 | (1), (2) | 1 Aug 1977 (SI 1977/1122) |
|  | (3) | 1 Dec 1977 (SI 1977/1775) |
|  | (4) | *Never in force* (repealed) |
| 18 |  | 1 Aug 1977 (SI 1977/1122) |
| Sch 1 |  | 1 Aug 1977 (SI 1977/1122) |
| Sch 2 |  | *Never in force* (repealed) |
| Sch 3 |  | 1 Aug 1977 (SI 1977/1122) |
| Schs 4–6 |  | *Never in force* (repealed) |

**Domestic Violence and Matrimonial Proceedings Act 1976 (c 50)**

*RA:* 26 Oct 1976

*Commencement provisions*: s 5(2); Domestic Violence and Matrimonial Proceedings Act 1976 (Commencement) Order 1977, SI 1977/559

Whole Act in force 1 Jun 1977 (SI 1977/559)

**Drought Act 1976 (c 44)**

*RA:* 6 Aug 1976

Whole Act in force 6 Aug 1976 (RA)

**Ecclesiastical Judges and Legal Officers Measure 1976 (No 2)**

*RA:* 25 Mar 1976

*Commencement provisions*: s 9(2)

Whole Measure in force 25 Apr 1976 (s 9(2))

**Education Act 1976 (c 81)**

*RA:* 22 Nov 1976

Commencement provisions: s 10(3)

Whole Act in force 22 Nov 1976 (s 10(3)) (except s 10 (never in force (repealed))

**Education (School-leaving Dates) Act 1976 (c 5)**

*RA:* 25 Mar 1976

*Commencement provisions*: s 3(5)

|  |  |  |
|---|---|---|
| 1 |  | 25 Mar 1976 (RA) |
| 2 | (1)–(3) | 25 Mar 1976 (RA) |
|  | (4) | 6 Apr 1976 (s 3(5)) |
| 3 |  | 25 Mar 1976 (RA) |
| Schedule |  | 25 Mar 1976 (except repeal in Social Security Act 1975, Sch 20) (RA) |
|  |  | 6 Apr 1976 (exception noted above) (s 3(4)) |

## Education (Scotland) Act 1976 (c 20)

*RA:* 10 Jun 1976

*Commencement provisions:* s 7(2); Education (Scotland) Act 1976 (Commencement No 1) Order 1976, SI 1976/925; Education (Scotland) Act 1976 (Commencement No 2) Order 1978, SI 1978/970

| | | |
|---|---|---|
| 1, 2 | | 30 Jun 1976 (SI 1976/925) |
| 3 | | 16 Aug 1978 (SI 1978/970) |
| 4, 5 | | 30 Jun 1976 (SI 1976/925) |
| 6 | (1) | See Sch 1 below |
| | (2) | See Sch 2 below |
| 7 | | 10 Jun 1976 (RA) |
| Sch 1 | | 30 Jun 1976 (SI 1976/925) |
| Sch 2 | | 30 Jun 1976 (except repeals of or in Education (Milk) Act 1971, s 2(3)) (SI 1976/925) |
| | | 16 Aug 1978 (exception noted above) (SI 1978/970) |

## Electricity (Financial Provisions) (Scotland) Act 1976 (c 61)

*RA:* 15 Nov 1976

Whole Act in force 15 Nov 1976 (RA)

## Endangered Species (Import and Export) Act 1976 (c 72)

*RA:* 22 Nov 1976

*Commencement provisions:* s 13(3)

Whole Act in force 3 Feb 1977 (s 13(3))

## Endowments and Glebe Measure 1976 (No 4)

*RA:* 22 Nov 1976

*Commencement provisions:* s 49(2); Order of the Church Commissioners dated 11 Aug 1977

| | | |
|---|---|---|
| 1–8 | | 1 Apr 1978 (order dated 11 Aug 1977) |
| 9 | | 22 Nov 1976 (s 49(2)) |
| 10–15 | | 1 Apr 1978 (order dated 11 Aug 1977) |
| 16 | | 22 Nov 1976 (s 49(2)) |
| 17, 18 | | 1 Apr 1978 (order dated 11 Aug 1977) |
| 19 | (1) | 1 Apr 1978 (order dated 11 Aug 1977) |
| | (2)–(4) | 22 Nov 1976 (s 49(2)) |
| 20 | | 1 Apr 1978 (order dated 11 Aug 1977) |
| 21 | | 22 Nov 1976 (s 49(2)) |
| 22–27 | | 1 Apr 1978 (order dated 11 Aug 1977) |
| 28 | | 22 Nov 1976 (s 49(2)) |
| 29, 30 | | 1 Apr 1978 (order dated 11 Aug 1977) |
| 31, 32 | | 22 Nov 1976 (s 49(2)) |
| 33 | | 1 Apr 1978 (order dated 11 Aug 1977) |
| 34 | | 22 Nov 1976 (s 49(2)) |
| 35, 36 | | 1 Apr 1978 (order dated 11 Aug 1977) |
| 37 | | 22 Nov 1976 (s 49(2)) |
| 38–41 | | 1 Apr 1978 (order dated 11 Aug 1977) |
| 42–44 | | 22 Nov 1976 (s 49(2)) |
| 45–49 | | 1 Apr 1978 (order dated 11 Aug 1977) |
| Schs 1–8 | | 1 Apr 1978 (order dated 11 Aug 1977) |

## Energy Act 1976 (c 76)

*RA:* 22 Nov 1976

*Commencement provisions:* s 23(2); Energy Act 1976 (Commencement No 1) Order 1976, SI 1976/1964; Energy Act 1976 (Commencement No 2) Order 1976, SI 1976/2127; Energy Act 1976 (Commencement No 3) Order 1977, SI 1977/652

| | |
|---|---|
| 1–6 | 30 Nov 1976 (SI 1976/1964) |
| 7 | 1 Jan 1977 (SI 1976/2127) |
| 8–12 | 1 May 1977 (SI 1977/652) |
| 13 | 30 Nov 1976 (SI 1976/1964) |
| 14–16 | 1 Jan 1977 (SI 1976/2127) |
| 17–21 | 30 Nov 1976 (so far as relate to ss 1–6, 13, Sch 1 or provisions made under them) (SI 1976/1964) |
| | 1 Jan 1977 (so far as relate to ss 7, 14–16 or provisions made under them or to obligations specified in Sch 3) (SI 1976/2127) |
| | 1 May 1977 (otherwise) (SI 1977/652) |
| 22 | See Sch 4 below |
| 23 | 30 Nov 1976 (SI 1976/1964) |
| Sch 1 | 30 Nov 1976 (SI 1976/1964) |
| Schs 2, 3 | See ss 17–21 above |
| Sch 4 | 30 Nov 1976 (repeal of Fuel and Electricity (Control) Act 1973) (SI 1976/1964) |
| | 1 May 1977 (otherwise) (SI 1977/652) |

## Explosives (Age of Purchase etc) Act 1976 (c 26)

*RA:* 22 Jul 1976

*Commencement provisions:* s 2(3)

Whole Act in force 22 Aug 1976 (s 2(3))

## Fair Employment (Northern Ireland) Act 1976 (c 25)

*RA:* 22 Jul 1976

*Commencement provisions:* s 59(5), (6); Fair Employment (Northern Ireland) Act 1976 (Commencement) Order 1976, SI 1976/1182

| | | |
|---|---|---|
| 1–3 | | 1 Sep 1976 (SI 1976/1182) |
| 4 | | 1 Dec 1976 (SI 1976/1182) |
| 5 | | 1 Sep 1976 (SI 1976/1182) |
| 6–36 | | 1 Dec 1976 (SI 1976/1182) |
| 37 | (1), (2) | 1 Sep 1976 (SI 1976/1182) |
| | (3) | 1 Dec 1976 (SI 1976/1182) |
| | (4), (5) | 1 Sep 1976 (SI 1976/1182) |
| 38–55 | | 1 Dec 1976 (SI 1976/1182) |
| 56 | (1) | 1 Sep 1976 (SI 1976/1182) |
| | (2), (3) | 1 Dec 1976 (SI 1976/1182) |
| 57 | (1)–(3) | 1 Sep 1976 (SI 1976/1182) |
| | (4) | 1 Dec 1976 (SI 1976/1182) |
| | (5), (6) | 1 Sep 1976 (SI 1976/1182) |
| | (7) | 1 Dec 1976 (SI 1976/1182) |
| | (8) | 1 Sep 1976 (SI 1976/1182) |
| | (9), (10) | 1 Dec 1976 (SI 1976/1182) |
| 58 | (1) | See Sch 6 below |
| | (2), (3) | 1 Dec 1976 (SI 1976/1182) |
| 59 | (1)–(3) | 1 Sep 1976 (SI 1976/1182) |
| | (4) | 1 Dec 1976 (SI 1976/1182) |
| | (5), (6) | 1 Sep 1976 (SI 1976/1182) |

**Fair Employment (Northern Ireland) Act 1976 (c 25)**—*contd*

| | | |
|---|---|---|
| Sch 1 | | 1 Sep 1976 (SI 1976/1182) |
| Schs 2–5 | | 1 Dec 1976 (SI 1976/1182) |
| Sch 6 | para 1 | 1 Dec 1976 (SI 1976/1182) |
| | paras 2–4 | 1 Sep 1976 (SI 1976/1182) |

**Fatal Accidents Act 1976 (c 30)**

*RA:* 22 Jul 1976

*Commencement provisions:* s 7(2)

Whole Act in force 1 Sep 1976 (s 7(2); note the Act does not apply to any cause of action arising on a death before that date)

**Fatal Accidents and Sudden Deaths Inquiry (Scotland) Act 1976 (c 14)**

*RA:* 13 Apr 1976

*Commencement provisions:* s 10(5); Fatal Accidents and Sudden Deaths Inquiry (Scotland) Act 1976 Commencement Order 1977, SI 1977/190

Whole Act in force 1 Mar 1977 (SI 1977/190)

**Finance Act 1976 (c 40)**

*Budget Day:* 6 Apr 1976

*RA:* 29 Jul 1976

The commencement details of Finance Acts are not set out, as the dates from which their provisions take effect are usually stated clearly and unambiguously in the text of the Act, and charging provisions will normally state for which year or years of assessment they are to have effect.

**Fishery Limits Act 1976 (c 86)**

*RA:* 22 Dec 1976

*Commencement provisions:* s 12(2)

Whole Act in force 1 Jan 1977 (s 12(2))

**Food and Drugs (Control of Food Premises) Act 1976 (c 37)**

*RA:* 22 Jul 1976

*Commencement provisions:* s 8(2)

Whole Act in force 22 Sep 1976 (s 8(2))

**Freshwater and Salmon Fisheries (Scotland) Act 1976 (c 22)**

*RA:* 10 Jun 1976

Whole Act in force 10 Jun 1976 (RA)

## Health Services Act 1976 (c 83)

*RA*: 22 Nov 1976

*Commencement provisions*: s 24(2)

| | |
|---|---|
| 1–11 | 22 Nov 1976 (RA) |
| 12–20 | 22 Jan 1977 (s 24(2)) |
| 21–24 | 22 Nov 1976 (RA) |
| Schs 1–5 | 22 Nov 1976 (RA) |

## Housing (Amendment) (Scotland) Act 1976 (c 11)

*RA*: 13 Apr 1976

Whole Act in force 13 Apr 1976 (RA)

## Industrial Common Ownership Act 1976 (c 78)

*RA*: 22 Nov 1976

Whole Act in force 22 Nov 1976 (RA)

## Industry (Amendment) Act 1976 (c 73)

*RA*: 22 Nov 1976

Whole Act in force 22 Nov 1976 (RA)

## Insolvency Act 1976 (c 60)

*RA*: 15 Nov 1976

*Commencement provisions*: s 14(5); Insolvency Act 1976 (Commencement No 1) Order 1976, SI 1976/1960; Insolvency Act 1976 (Commencement No 2) Order 1977, SI 1977/363; Insolvency Act 1976 (Commencement No 3) Order 1977, SI 1977/1375; Insolvency Act 1976 (Commencement No 4) Order 1978, SI 1978/139

| | |
|---|---|
| 1 | 20 Dec 1976 (SI 1976/1960) |
| 2 | 1 Oct 1977 (SI 1977/1375) |
| 3, 4 | 1 Apr 1977 (SI 1977/363) |
| 5–9 | 1 Oct 1977 (SI 1977/1375) |
| 10 | 20 Dec 1976 (SI 1976/1960) |
| 11 | *Never in force* (repealed) |
| 12 | 1 Mar 1978 (SI 1978/139) |
| 13 | 20 Dec 1976 (SI 1976/1960) |
| 14 | See Sch 3 below |
| Sch 1 | 20 Dec 1976 (SI 1976/1960) |
| Sch 2 | 1 Apr 1977 (SI 1977/363) |
| Sch 3 | 1 Oct 1977 (SI 1977/1375), repeals of or in— |
| | Bankruptcy Act 1914, s 92(3); |
| | Companies Act 1948, s 249(3) |
| | 1 Mar 1978 (otherwise) (SI 1978/139) |

## International Carriage of Perishable Foodstuffs Act 1976 (c 58)

*RA*: 15 Nov 1976

*Commencement provisions*: s 21(2); International Carriage of Perishable Foodstuffs Act 1976 (Commencement) Order 1979, SI 1979/413

**International Carriage of Perishable Foodstuffs Act 1976 (c 58)**—*contd*

Whole Act in force 1 Oct 1979 (SI 1979/413)

---

**Iron and Steel (Amendment) Act 1976 (c 41)**

*RA:* 29 Jul 1976

Whole Act in force 29 Jul 1976 (RA)

---

**Land Drainage Act 1976 (c 70)**

*RA:* 15 Nov 1976

*Commencement provisions:* s 118(2)

Whole Act in force 17 Jan 1977 (s 118(2)); 17 Jan 1977 was the day appointed for the coming into force of the Land Drainage (Amendment) Act 1976

---

**Land Drainage (Amendment) Act 1976 (c 17)**

*RA:* 27 May 1976

*Commencement provisions:* s 10(5); Land Drainage (Amendment) Act 1976 (Commencement) Order 1976, SI 1976/2244

Whole Act in force 17 Jan 1977 (SI 1976/2244)

---

**Legitimacy Act 1976 (c 31)**

*RA:* 22 Jul 1976

*Commencement provisions:* s 12(2)

Whole Act in force 22 Aug 1976 (s 12(2))

---

**Licensing (Amendment) Act 1976 (c 18)**

*RA:* 27 May 1976

Whole Act in force 27 May 1976 (RA)

---

**Licensing (Scotland) Act 1976 (c 66)**

*RA:* 15 Nov 1976

*Commencement provisions:* s 141(2); Licensing (Scotland) Act 1976 (Commencement No 1) Order 1976, SI 1976/2068; Licensing (Scotland) Act 1976 (Commencement No 2) Order 1977, SI 1977/212; Licensing (Scotland) Act 1976 (Commencement No 3) Order 1977, SI 1977/718

| | | |
|---|---|---|
| 1, 2 | | 1 Mar 1977 (SI 1977/212) |
| 3–7 | | 1 Jul 1977 (SI 1977/718) |
| 8 | | 1 Mar 1977 (SI 1977/212) |
| 9–52 | | 1 Jul 1977 (SI 1977/718) |
| 53 | (1) | 13 Dec 1976 (SI 1976/2068) |
| | (2) | 13 Dec 1976 (only in so far as applies to permitted hours for days except Sundays) (SI 1976/2068) |
| | | 1 Jul 1977 (otherwise) (SI 1977/718) |
| | (3), (4) | 13 Dec 1976 (SI 1976/2068) |
| 54 | (1) | 13 Dec 1976 (SI 1976/2068) |

**Licensing (Scotland) Act 1976 (c 66)**—*contd*

|  |  |  |
|---|---|---|
|  | (2) | 1 Jul 1977 (SI 1977/718) |
|  | (3)–(5) | 13 Dec 1976 (SI 1976/2068) |
| 55 |  | 1 Jul 1977 (SI 1977/718) |
| 56–59 |  | 13 Dec 1976 (SI 1976/2068) |
| 60 |  | 1 Mar 1977 (SI 1977/212) |
| 61, 62 |  | 1 Jul 1977 (SI 1977/718) |
| 63 |  | 1 May 1977 (SI 1977/718) |
| 64–66 |  | 1 Jul 1977 (SI 1977/718) |
| 67 |  | 13 Dec 1976 (SI 1976/2068) |
| 68–118 |  | 1 Jul 1977 (SI 1977/718) |
| 119 |  | 1 May 1977 (SI 1977/718) |
| 120–131 |  | 1 Jul 1977 (SI 1977/718) |
| 132 |  | 1 Mar 1977 (SI 1977/212) |
| 133 | (1)–(3) | 1 Jul 1977 (SI 1977/718) |
|  | (4) | 1 Oct 1977 (SI 1977/718) |
| 134, 135 |  | 1 Jul 1977 (SI 1977/718) |
| 136 | (1) | 1 Jul 1977 (SI 1977/718) |
|  | (2) | See Sch 8 below |
| 137, 138 |  | 1 Jul 1977 (SI 1977/718) |
| 139 |  | 13 Dec 1976 (so far as necessary for purposes of SI 1976/2068) (SI 1976/2068) |
|  |  | 1 Mar 1977 (so far as necessary for purposes of SI 1977/212) (SI 1977/212) |
|  |  | 1 Jul 1977 (otherwise) (SI 1977/718) |
| 140 | (1) | 1 Jul 1977 (SI 1977/718) |
|  | (2)–(8) | 13 Dec 1976 (SI 1976/2068) |
| 141 |  | 15 Nov 1976 (s 141(2)) |
| Schs 1–4 |  | 1 Jul 1977 (SI 1977/718) |
| Sch 5 |  | 13 Dec 1976 (entries relating to ss 54(1)(a), (b), 57(7), (8), 58(7), (8), 59(7)) (SI 1976/2068) |
|  |  | 1 Mar 1977 (entry relating to s 2) (SI 1977/212) |
|  |  | 1 May 1977 (entry relating to s 119) (SI 1977/718) |
|  |  | 1 Jul 1977 (otherwise) (SI 1977/718) |
| Schs 6, 7 |  | 1 Jul 1977 (SI 1977/718) |
| Sch 8 |  | 13 Dec 1976 (SI 1976/2068), repeals of or in— Licensing (Scotland) Act 1959, ss 121, 126; Licensing (Scotland) Act 1962, ss 3(3), 4–8 |
|  |  | 1 Mar 1977 (repeal of Licensing (Scotland) Act 1959, s 29) (SI 1977/212) |
|  |  | 1 May 1977 (SI 1977/718), repeals of or in— Licensing (Scotland) Act 1959, s 130; Licensing (Scotland) Act 1962, s 20 |
|  |  | 1 Jul 1977 (otherwise, except repeals noted below) (SI 1977/718) |
|  |  | 1 Oct 1977 (SI 1977/718), repeals of or in— Betting, Gaming and Lotteries Act 1963, Sch 1, para 24(2); Gaming Act 1968, Sch 2, paras 33(2), (3), 34(2) |

**Local Government (Miscellaneous Provisions) Act 1976 (c 57)**

*RA:* 15 Nov 1976

*Commencement provisions:* ss 45, 83(2); Local Government (Miscellaneous Provisions) Act 1976 (Commencement) Order 1977, SI 1977/68

|  |  |
|---|---|
| 1–44 | 14 Feb 1977 (SI 1977/68) |
| 45–80 | Came into force for different areas on different dates in accordance with resolutions of district councils (see s 45) |
| 81–83 | 14 Feb 1977 (SI 1977/68) |
| Schs 1, 2 | 14 Feb 1977 (SI 1977/68) |

## Lotteries and Amusements Act 1976 (c 32)

*RA:* 22 Jul 1976

*Commencement provisions:* s 25(9)

Whole Act in force 1 May 1977 (s 25(9))

---

## Maplin Development Authority (Dissolution) Act 1976 (c 51)

*RA:* 26 Oct 1976

Whole Act in force 26 Oct 1976 (RA)

---

## Motor-Cycle Crash-Helmets (Religious Exemption) Act 1976 (c 62)

*RA:* 15 Nov 1976

Whole Act in force 15 Nov 1976 (RA)

---

## National Coal Board (Finance) Act 1976 (c 1)

*RA:* 4 Mar 1976

Whole Act in force 4 Mar 1976 (RA)

---

## National Health Service (Vocational Training) Act 1976 (c 59)

*RA:* 15 Nov 1976

Whole Act in force 15 Nov 1976 (RA)

---

## National Insurance Surcharge Act 1976 (c 85)

*RA:* 22 Dec 1976

Whole Act in force 22 Dec 1976 (RA)

---

## New Towns (Amendment) Act 1976 (c 68)

*RA:* 15 Nov 1976

Whole Act in force 15 Nov 1976 (RA)

---

## Parliamentary and other Pensions and Salaries Act 1976 (c 48)

*RA:* 12 Oct 1976

Whole Act came into force generally on 12 Oct 1976, but certain provisions were retrospective in effect

| | |
|---|---|
| 1 | 13 Jun 1975 (s 1(4)) |
| 3 | 2 May 1974 (s 3(2)) |
| 4 | Effective from date of commencement of Parliamentary and other Pensions Act 1972, Pt I (s 4(1)) |
| 6 | 1 Jan 1975 (s 6(5)) |

---

**See Halsbury's Statutes Citator for amendments to these Acts**

**Police Act 1976 (c 46)**

*RA:* 6 Aug 1976

*Commencement provisions*: s 13(1); Police Act 1976 (Commencement No 1) Order 1976, SI 1976/1998; Police Act 1976 (Commencement No 2) Order 1977, SI 1977/576

| | |
|---|---|
| 1 | 8 Dec 1976 (SI 1976/1998) |
| 2 | 1 Jun 1977 (SI 1977/576)[1] |
| 3–6 | 1 Jun 1977 (SI 1977/576) |
| 7 | 1 Sep 1977 (SI 1977/576) |
| 8 | 1 Jun 1977 (SI 1977/576) |
| 9 | 8 Dec 1976 (SI 1976/1998) |
| 10–12 | 1 Jun 1977 (SI 1977/576) |
| 13, 14 | 8 Dec 1976 (SI 1976/1998) |
| Schedule | 8 Dec 1976 (SI 1976/1998) |

[1]   For transitional provisions, see SI 1977/576, art 4, Sch 2

**Police Pensions Act 1976 (c 35)**

*RA:* 22 Jul 1976

Whole Act in force 22 Jul 1976 *(RA)*

**Post Office (Banking Services) Act 1976 (c 10)**

*RA:* 25 Mar 1976

Whole Act in force 25 Mar 1976 *(RA)*

**Prevention of Terrorism (Temporary Provisions) Act 1976 (c 8)**

*RA:* 25 Mar 1976

Whole Act in force 25 Mar 1976 (RA)

**Protection of Birds (Amendment) Act 1976 (c 42)**

*RA:* 29 Jul 1976

Whole Act in force 29 Jul 1976 (RA)

**Race Relations Act 1976 (c 74)**

*RA:* 22 Nov 1976

*Commencement provisions*: s 79(2); Race Relations Act 1976 (Commencement No 1) Order 1977, SI 1977/680; Race Relations Act 1976 (Commencement No 2) Order 1977, SI 1977/840

| | | |
|---|---|---|
| 1–72 | | 13 Jun 1977 (SI 1977/840) |
| 73–75 | | 28 Apr 1977 (SI 1977/680) |
| 76 | | 13 Jun 1977 (SI 1977/840) |
| 77, 78 | | 28 Apr 1977 (SI 1977/680) |
| 79 | (1) | 13 Jun 1977 (SI 1977/840) |
| | (2) | 22 Nov 1976 (RA) |
| | (3)–(6) | 13 Jun 1977 (SI 1977/840) |
| | (7) | 22 Nov 1976 (RA) |
| 80 | | 28 Apr 1977 (SI 1977/680) |

**Race Relations Act 1976 (c 74)**—*contd*
Schs 1–5                                        13 Jun 1977 (SI 1977/840)

Note: s 43(1)–(4), Sch 1 of this Act came into force for transitional purposes on 28 Apr 1977 (SI 1977/680)

---

**Rating (Caravan Sites) Act 1976 (c 15)**

*RA:* 13 Apr 1976

Whole Act in force 13 Apr 1976 (RA); but mainly effective for rate periods beginning after Mar 1976, see
  s 1(9)

---

**Rating (Charity Shops) Act 1976 (c 45)**

*RA:* 6 Aug 1976

Whole Act in force 6 Aug 1976 (RA)

---

**Rent (Agriculture) Act 1976 (c 80)**

*RA:* 22 Nov 1976

*Commencement provisions:* s 1(5), (6); Rent (Agriculture) Act 1976 (Commencement No 1) Order 1976,
  SI 1976/2124; Rent (Agriculture) Act 1976 (Commencement No 2) Order 1977, SI 1977/1268

Whole Act in force 1 Jan 1977 (SI 1976/2124); but note that in relation to forestry workers the Act came
  into force on 1 Oct 1976, by virtue of s 1(5)(b), Sch 3, Pt II, SI 1977/1268

---

**Representation of the People (Armed Forces) Act 1976 (c 29)**

*RA:* 22 Jul 1976

*Commencement provisions:* s 4(2); Representation of the People (Armed Forces) Act 1976 (Commencement)
  Order 1976, SI 1976/2044

Whole Act in force 1 Feb 1977 (SI 1976/2044)

---

**Resale Prices Act 1976 (c 53)**

*RA:* 26 Oct 1976

*Commencement provisions:* s 30(3); Resale Prices Act 1976 (Commencement) Order 1976, SI 1976/1876

Whole Act in force 15 Dec 1976 (SI 1976/1876)

---

**Restrictive Practices Court Act 1976 (c 33)**

*RA:* 22 Jul 1976

*Commencement provisions:* s 12(3); Restrictive Practices Court Act 1976 (Commencement) Order 1976,
  SI 1976/1896

Whole Act in force 15 Dec 1976 (SI 1976/1896)

---

## Restrictive Trade Practices Act 1976 (c 34)

*RA:* 22 Jul 1976

*Commencement provisions:* s 45(3); Restrictive Trade Practices Act 1976 (Commencement) Order 1976, SI 1976/1877

Whole Act in force 15 Dec 1976 (SI 1976/1877)

---

## Retirement of Teachers (Scotland) Act 1976 (c 65)

*RA:* 15 Nov 1976

*Commencement provisions:* s 2(2)

Whole Act in force 15 Nov 1976 (RA) (except s 1, which came into force on 1 Mar 1976 (s 2(2))

---

## Road Traffic (Drivers' Ages and Hours of Work) Act 1976 (c 3)

*RA:* 25 Mar 1976

*Commencement provisions:* s 4(2)–(4); Road Traffic (Drivers' Ages and Hours of Work) Act 1976 (Commencement No 1) Order 1976, SI 1976/471; Road Traffic (Drivers' Ages and Hours of Work) Act 1976 (Commencement No 2) Order 1978, SI 1978/6

| | | |
|---|---|---|
| 1 | | 25 Mar 1976 (s 4(2)) |
| 2 | | 4 Jan 1978 (SI 1978/6) |
| 3, 4 | | 25 Mar 1976 (s 4(2)) |
| Sch 1 | paras 1–7 | 25 Mar 1976 (s 4(2)) |
| | para 8 | 15 Apr 1976 (SI 1976/471) |
| | paras 9, 10 | 25 Mar 1976 (s 4(2)) |
| | para 11 | 25 Mar 1976 (except for purposes of Road Traffic Act 1972, s 119) (s 4(2)) |
| | | 15 Apr 1976 (otherwise) (SI 1976/471) |
| | paras 12–16 | 25 Mar 1976 (s 4(2)) |
| Sch 2 | paras 1, 2 | 25 Mar 1976 (s 4(2)) |
| | para 3(1)–(3) | 15 Apr 1976 (SI 1976/471) |
| | para 3(4)–(6) | 25 Mar 1976 (s 4(2)) |
| | para 3(7) | 15 Apr 1976 (SI 1976/471) |
| | para 4 | 25 Mar 1976 (s 4(2)) |
| Sch 3 | Pt I | 25 Mar 1976 (s 4(2)) |
| | Pt II | 4 Jan 1978 (SI 1978/6) |

---

## Sexual Offences (Amendment) Act 1976 (c 82)

*RA:* 22 Nov 1976

*Commencement provisions:* s 7(4); Sexual Offences (Amendment) Act 1976 (Commencement) Order 1978, SI 1978/485

| | | |
|---|---|---|
| 1–4 | | 22 Dec 1976 (s 7(4)) |
| 5 | (1)(a) | 22 Dec 1976 (s 7(4)) |
| | (1)(b) | 22 Apr 1978 (SI 1978/485) |
| | (1)(c)–(e) | 22 Dec 1976 (s 7(4)) |
| | (2)–(6) | 22 Dec 1976 (s 7(4)) |
| 6, 7 | | 22 Dec 1976 (s 7(4)) |

---

## Sexual Offences (Scotland) Act 1976 (c 67)

*RA:* 15 Nov 1976

*Commencement provisions:* s 22(2)

**Sexual Offences (Scotland) Act 1976 (c 67)**—*contd*
Whole Act in force 15 Dec 1976 (s 22(2))

---

**Seychelles Act 1976 (c 19)**

*RA:* 27 May 1976

Whole Act in force 27 May 1976 (RA), but did not generally have effect until 29 Jun 1976 (the "appointed day" (s 1(1)))

---

**Solicitors (Scotland) Act 1976 (c 6)**

*RA:* 25 Mar 1976

Whole Act in force 25 Mar 1976 (RA)

---

**Statute Law (Repeals) Act 1976 (c 16)**

*RA:* 27 May 1976

Whole Act in force 27 May 1976 (RA)

---

**Statute Law Revision (Northern Ireland) Act 1976 (c 12)**

*RA:* 13 Apr 1976

Whole Act in force 13 Apr 1976 (RA)

---

**Stock Exchange (Completion of Bargains) Act 1976 (c 47)**

*RA:* 12 Oct 1976

*Commencement provisions*: s 7(4); Stock Exchange (Completion of Bargains) Act 1976 (Commencement Order) 1979, SI 1979/55

Whole Act in force 12 Feb 1979 (SI 1979/55)

---

**Supplementary Benefit (Amendment) Act 1976 (c 56)**

*RA:* 15 Nov 1976

Whole Act in force 15 Nov 1976 (RA)

---

**Supplementary Benefits Act 1976 (c 71)**

*RA:* 15 Nov 1976

*Commencement provisions*: s 36(3)

Whole Act in force 15 Nov 1976 (s 36(3))

---

**Theatres Trust Act 1976 (c 27)**

*RA:* 22 Jul 1976

*Commencement provisions*: s 6(2); Theatres Trust Act (Appointed Day) Order 1976, SI 1976/2236

**Theatres Trust Act 1976 (c 27)**—*contd*
Whole Act in force 21 Jan 1977 (SI 1976/2236)

---

**Trade Union and Labour Relations (Amendment) Act 1976 (c 7)**

*RA:* 25 Mar 1976

Whole Act in force 25 Mar 1976 (RA)

---

**Trinidad and Tobago Republic Act 1976 (c 54)**

*RA:* 26 Oct 1976

Whole Act in force 26 Oct 1976 (RA); but s 1 had retrospective effect from 1 Aug 1976 (SI 1976/1914)

---

**Trustee Savings Banks Act 1976 (c 4)**

*RA:* 25 Mar 1976

*Commencement provisions:* s 38(3); Trustee Savings Banks Act 1976 (Commencement No 1) Order 1976, SI 1976/642; Trustee Savings Banks Act 1976 (Commencement No 2) Order 1976, SI 1976/1054; Trustee Savings Banks Act 1976 (Commencement No 3) Order 1976, SI 1976/1829; Trustee Savings Banks Act 1976 (Commencement No 4) Order 1977, SI 1977/1740; Trustee Savings Banks Act 1976 (Commencement No 5) Order 1978, SI 1978/533; Trustee Savings Banks Act 1976 (Commencement No 6) Order 1978, SI 1978/1079; Trustee Savings Banks Act 1976 (Commencement No 7) Order 1979, SI 1979/1475; Trustee Savings Banks Act 1976 (Commencement No 8) Order 1981, SI 1981/848; Trustee Savings Banks Act 1976 (Commencement No 9) Order 1986, SI 1986/1221

| | | |
|---|---|---|
| 1 | (1)–(3) | 21 May 1976 (SI 1976/642) |
| | (4) | 21 Nov 1976 (SI 1976/1829) |
| | (5)–(7) | 21 May 1976 (SI 1976/642) |
| 2, 3 | | 21 May 1976 (SI 1976/642) |
| 4–6 | | 21 Nov 1976 (SI 1976/1829) |
| 7 | | 21 May 1976 (SI 1976/642) |
| 8, 9 | | 21 Nov 1976 (SI 1976/1829) |
| 10 | (1) | 28 Apr 1978 (SI 1978/533) |
| | (2) | 21 Nov 1976 (SI 1976/1829) |
| | (3) | 28 Apr 1978 (SI 1978/533) |
| 11 | | 21 Nov 1976 (SI 1976/1829) |
| 12 | (1) | 21 Nov 1976 (SI 1976/1829) |
| | (2) | *Never in force* (repealed) |
| | (3) | 18 Aug 1978 (SI 1978/1079) |
| | (4) | 21 Nov 1976 (SI 1976/1829) |
| 13–15 | | 21 Nov 1976 (SI 1976/1829) |
| 16 | (1) | *Never in force* (repealed) |
| | (2)–(7) | 21 Nov 1976 (SI 1976/1829) |
| 17–23 | | 21 Nov 1976 (SI 1976/1829) |
| 24 | (1)–(3) | 21 Nov 1976 (SI 1976/1829) |
| | (4) | *Never in force* (repealed) |
| | (5) | 21 Nov 1976 (SI 1976/1829) |
| 25–32 | | 21 Nov 1976 (SI 1976/1829) |
| 33 | | 2 Aug 1976 (SI 1976/1054) |
| 34 | | 21 Nov 1976 (SI 1976/1829) |
| 35 | | 21 May 1976 (SI 1976/642) |
| 36 | (1) | See Sch 5 below |
| | (2) | See Sch 6 below |
| 37, 38 | | 21 May 1976 (SI 1976/642) |
| Sch 1 | | 21 May 1976 (SI 1976/642) |
| Schs 2–4 | | 21 Nov 1976 (SI 1976/1829) |

**Trustee Savings Banks Act 1976 (c 4)**—*contd*

| | | |
|---|---|---|
| Sch 5 | paras 1–7 | 21 Nov 1976 (SI 1976/1829) |
| | para 8(1)(a) | 21 Nov 1976 (except in so far as it relates to the words in brackets being omitted) (SI 1976/1829) |
| | | 21 Nov 1979 (exception noted above) (SI 1979/1475) |
| | para 8(1)(b)–(d) | 21 Nov 1976 (SI 1976/1829) |
| | para 8(2) | 21 Nov 1976 (SI 1976/1829) |
| | paras 9–14 | 21 Nov 1976 (SI 1976/1829) |
| | para 15(a) | 21 Nov 1976 (except in so far as relates to the definitions "the Fund", "ordinary deposit" and "savings account deposit") (SI 1976/1829) |
| | | 18 Aug 1978 (in so far as relates to the definition "savings account deposit") (SI 1978/1079) |
| | | 21 Nov 1979 (in so far as relates to the definition "ordinary deposit") (SI 1979/1475) |
| | | *Never in force* (in so far as relates to the definition "the Fund") (repealed) |
| | para 15(b), (c) | *Never in force* (repealed) |
| | paras 16–18 | 21 Nov 1976 (SI 1976/1829) |
| | paras 19, 20 | 20 Jul 1986 (SI 1986/1221) |
| Sch 6 | | 21 Nov 1976 (SI 1976/1829)[1], repeals of or in— |

Pensions Commutation Act 1871, s 6;

Trustee Investments Act 1961, Sch 1, Part II, para 11, Part IV, para 4, definition "special investment";

Trustee Savings Bank Act 1969, ss 2(2), 4, 7(1), 8, 12(2), (3) (in relation only to the words from "and the investment" onwards), 13(1)–(3), 14(2), 16(3), 17–26, 27(1), 30(7), 33(3), 34(3), (5), 41(2), 43–54, 57, 58, 60, 61(1), 62, 63, 66, 67, 68(1), 69, 71, 73–82, 94, 95(1) (except for the definitions "the Fund", "ordinary deposit" and "Savings account deposit"), 96(3), (5), (6), Sch 2;

Pensions (Increase) Act 1971, s 19(2)(b), Sch 2, Pt III, para 65;

Superannuation Act 1972, Sch 6, paras 75, 76

18 Nov 1977 (repeals of or in Trustee Savings Bank Act 1969, ss 2(5), 13(4) (in relation to definition "current account service"), 56) (SI 1977/1740)

28 Apr 1978 (repeals of or in Trustee Savings Bank Act 1969, s 11(1), (3), (4)) (SI 1978/533)

18 Aug 1978 (repeals of or in Trustee Savings Bank Act 1969, ss 13(4), 93(3), 95(1) (in relation to definition "savings account deposit")) (SI 1978/1079)

21 Nov 1979 (SI 1979/1475), repeals of or in—

Trustee Investments Act 1961, Sch 1, Part I, para 2, Part IV, para 4 (in relation to definition "ordinary deposits");

Trustee Savings Bank Act 1969, ss 1(1), 12(1), (3), 14(1), (3)–(5), 15, 16(1), (2), 28(1), 30(1)–(6), 40(1)(a), (b) (in relation only to words "(b) in the second place,", 95(1) (in relation to definition "ordinary deposit");

Trustee Savings Bank Act 1976, Sch 5, para 11(a)

11 Jun 1981 (SI 1981/848)[2], repeals of or in—

Trustee Savings Bank Act 1969, ss 32, 33(2), 34(1), (2) (in relation to words "Subject to subsections (3) and (5) below,"), (7);

Trustee Savings Bank Act 1976, s 12(4)

20 Jul 1986 (repeals of or in National Debt Act 1972) (SI 1986/1221)

---

[1]   For transitional provisions, see SI 1976/1829, art 4, Sch 2

[2]   For consequential modifications, see SI 1981/848, art 4, Sch 2

## Valuation and Rating (Exempted Classes) (Scotland) Act 1976 (c 64)

*RA:* 15 Nov 1976

Whole Act in force 15 Nov 1976 (RA)

---

## Water Charges Act 1976 (c 9)

*RA:* 25 Mar 1976

Whole Act in force 25 Mar 1976 (RA)

---

## Weights and Measures &c Act 1976 (c 77)

*RA:* 22 Nov 1976

*Commencement provisions:* s 15(2)

Whole Act in force 22 Dec 1976 (s 15(2))

---

# 1977 Acts

## Administration of Justice Act 1977 (c 38)

*RA:* 29 Jul 1977

*Commencement provisions:* s 32(5)–(7); Administration of Justice Act 1977 (Commencement No 1) Order 1977, SI 1977/1405; Administration of Justice Act 1977 (Commencement No 2) Order 1977, SI 1977/1490; Administration of Justice Act 1977 (Commencement No 3) Order 1977, SI 1977/1589; Administration of Justice Act 1977 (Commencement No 4) Order 1977, SI 1977/2202; Administration of Justice Act 1977 (Commencement No 5) Order 1978, SI 1978/810; Administration of Justice Act 1977 (Commencement No 6) Order 1979, SI 1979/972; Administration of Justice Act 1977 (Commencement No 7) Order 1980, SI 1980/1981

| | | |
|---|---|---|
| 1, 2 | | 29 Aug 1977 (s 32(5)) |
| 3 | | See Sch 3 below |
| 4–13 | | 29 Aug 1977 (s 32(5)) |
| 14 | | 1 Feb 1978 (1977/2202) |
| 15 | | 17 Oct 1977 (1977/1589) |
| 16 | | 29 Aug 1977 (s 32(5)) |
| 17 | (1) | 1 Feb 1978 (1977/2202) |
| | (2) | 29 Aug 1977 (s 32(5)) |
| 18 | | 17 Oct 1977 (1977/1589) |
| 19 | (1) | 1 Feb 1978 (1977/2202) |
| | (2), (3) | 3 Jul 1978 (1978/810) |
| | (4) | 29 Aug 1977 (s 32(5)) |
| | (5) | 3 Jul 1978 (SI 1978/810) |
| 20 | | 3 Sep 1979 (1979/972) |
| 21, 22 | | 29 Aug 1977 (s 32(5)) |
| 23 | | 17 Oct 1977 (SI 1977/1589) |
| 24–26 | | 29 Aug 1977 (s 32(5)) |
| 27 | | 1 Feb 1978 (1977/2202) |
| 28 | | 15 Sep 1977 (SI 1977/1490) |
| 29, 30 | | 29 Aug 1977 (s 32(5)) |
| 31, 32 | | 29 Jul 1977 (RA) |
| Schs 1, 2 | | 29 Aug 1977 (s 32(5)) |
| Sch 3 | paras 1–10 | 1 Jan 1981 (SI 1980/1981) |
| | paras 11, 12 | 1 Sep 1977 (SI 1977/1405) |
| Sch 4 | | 17 Oct 1977 (SI 1977/1589) |
| Sch 5 | Pts I–IV | 29 Aug 1977 (s 32(5)) |
| | Pt V | 17 Oct 1977 (SI 1977/1589) |
| | Pt VI | 29 Jul 1977 (s 32(6)) |

## Agricultural Holdings (Notices to Quit) Act 1977 (c 12)

*RA:* 30 Mar 1977

*Commencement provisions:* s 15(2); Agricultural Holdings (Notices to Quit) Act 1977 (Commencement) Order 1978, SI 1978/256

Whole Act in force 7 Apr 1978 (SI 1978/256)

**Aircraft and Shipbuilding Industries Act 1977 (c 3)**

*RA:* 17 Mar 1977

Whole Act in force 17 Mar 1977 (RA). Note that under ss 19, 56, the vesting date for the aircraft industry was 29 Apr 1977 (under Aircraft and Shipbuilding Industries (Aircraft Industry Vesting Date) Order 1977, SI 1977/539) and for the shipbuilding industry was 1 Jul 1977 (under Aircraft and Shipbuilding Industries (Shipbuilding Industry Vesting Date) Order 1977, SI 1977/540)

**Appropriation Act 1977 (c 35)**

*RA:* 29 Jul 1977

Whole Act in force 29 Jul 1977 (RA)

**British Airways Board Act 1977 (c 13)**

*RA:* 30 Mar 1977

*Commencement provisions:* s 25(2)

Whole Act in force 30 Apr 1977 (s 25(2))

**Coal Industry Act 1977 (c 39)**

*RA:* 29 Jul 1977

*Commencement provisions:* s 16(2)

Whole Act in force 29 Aug 1977 (s 16(2))

**Consolidated Fund Act 1977 (c 1)**

*RA:* 17 Mar 1977

Whole Act in force 17 Mar 1977 (RA)

**Consolidated Fund (No 2) Act 1977 (c 52)**

*RA:* 15 Dec 1977

Whole Act in force 15 Dec 1977 (RA)

**Control of Food Premises (Scotland) Act 1977 (c 28)**

*RA:* 22 Jul 1977

*Commencement provisions:* s 9(2); Control of Food Premises (Scotland) Act 1977 (Commencement) Order 1978, SI 1978/172

Whole Act in force 16 Mar 1978 (SI 1978/172)

**Control of Office Development Act 1977 (c 40)**

*RA:* 29 Jul 1977

Whole Act in force 29 Jul 1977 (RA)

## Criminal Law Act 1977 (c 45)

*RA*: 29 Jul 1977

*Commencement provisions:* s 65(7); Criminal Law Act 1977 (Commencement No 1) Order 1977, SI 1977/1365; Criminal Law Act 1977 (Commencement No 2) Order 1977, SI 1977/1426; Criminal Law Act 1977 (Commencement No 3) Order 1977, SI 1977/1682; Criminal Law Act 1977 (Commencement No 4) (Scotland) Order 1977, SI 1977/1744; Criminal Law Act 1977 (Commencement No 5) Order 1978, SI 1978/712; Criminal Law Act 1977 (Commencement No 6) (Scotland) Order 1978, SI 1978/900; Criminal Law Act 1977 (Commencement No 7) Order 1980, SI 1980/487; Criminal Law Act 1977 (Commencement No 8) (Scotland) Order 1980, SI 1980/587; Criminal Law Act 1977 (Commencement No 9) Order 1980, SI 1980/1632; Criminal Law Act 1977 (Commencement No 10) (Scotland) Order 1980, SI 1980/1701; Criminal Law Act 1977 (Commencement No 11) Order 1982, SI 1982/243; Criminal Law Act 1977 (Commencement No 12) Order 1985, SI 1985/579

| | | |
|---|---|---|
| 1–4 | | 1 Dec 1977 (SI 1977/1682) |
| 5 | (1)–(9) | 1 Dec 1977 (SI 1977/1682) |
| | (10)(a) | 1 Dec 1977 (SI 1977/1682) |
| | (10)(b) | 8 Sep 1977 (SI 1977/1365) |
| | (11) | 1 Dec 1977 (SI 1977/1682) |
| 6–13 | | 1 Dec 1977 (SI 1977/1682) |
| 14 | | 17 Jul 1978 (SI 1978/712) |
| 15 | (1) | 17 Jul 1978 (SI 1978/712) |
| | (2)–(4) | 17 Jul 1978 (SI 1978/712; SI 1978/900) |
| | (5) | 17 Jul 1978 (SI 1978/712) |
| 16–29 | | 17 Jul 1978 (SI 1978/712) |
| 30 | (1), (2) | 17 Jul 1978 (SI 1978/712) |
| | (3) | 17 Jul 1978 (SI 1978/712; SI 1978/900) |
| | (4) | 17 Jul 1978 (SI 1978/712) |
| 31 | (1) | 8 Sep 1977 (SI 1977/1365) |
| | (2)–(9) | 17 Jul 1978 (SI 1978/712) |
| | (10) | 17 Jul 1978 (SI 1978/712; SI 1978/900) |
| | (11) | 17 Jul 1978 (SI 1978/712) |
| 32 | (1), (2) | 17 Jul 1978 (SI 1978/712) |
| | (3) | 17 Jul 1978 (SI 1978/712; SI 1978/900) |
| 33 | | 8 Sep 1977 (SI 1977/1365) |
| 34–37 | | 17 Jul 1978 (SI 1978/712) |
| 38, 39 | | 12 May 1980 (SI 1980/487; SI 1980/587) |
| 40 | | 1 Dec 1980 (SI 1980/1632; SI 1980/1701) |
| 41, 42 | | 17 Jul 1978 (SI 1978/712) |
| 43 | | 8 Sep 1977 (SI 1977/1365) |
| 44 | | 1 Dec 1977 (SI 1977/1682) |
| 45, 46 | | 17 Jul 1978 (SI 1978/712) |
| 47 | | 29 Mar 1982 (SI 1982/243) |
| 48 | | 20 May 1985 (SI 1985/579) |
| 49, 50 | | 1 Dec 1977 (SI 1977/1682; SI 1977/1744) |
| 51, 52 | | 8 Sep 1977 (SI 1977/1365) |
| 53 | | 1 Dec 1977 (SI 1977/1682) |
| 54, 55 | | 8 Sep 1977 (SI 1977/1365) |
| 56 | | 1 Jan 1978 (SI 1977/1682) |
| 57 | | 8 Sep 1977 (SI 1977/1365) |
| 58 | | 17 Jul 1978 (SI 1978/712) |
| 59 | | 8 Sep 1977 (SI 1977/1426) |
| 60 | | 1 Dec 1977 (SI 1977/1682) |
| 61 | | 17 Jul 1978 (SI 1978/712) |
| 62 | | 19 Jun 1978 (SI 1978/712) |
| 63 | (1) | 8 Sep 1977 (SI 1977/1365) |
| | (2) | 8 Sep 1977 (so far as relates to ss 33, 51, 52, 55, 65, Schs 12 (part), 13 (part), 14) (SI 1977/1365) |
| | | 1 Dec 1977 (so far as relates to s 50, Schs 12 (part), 13 (part)) (SI 1977/1744) |

**Criminal Law Act 1977 (c 45)**—*contd*

| | | |
|---|---|---|
| | | 17 Jul 1978 (so far as relates to ss 15(2)–(4), 30(3), 31(10), 32(3), Sch 9, para 3(3), Schs 12 (part), 13 (part)) (SI 1978/900) |
| | | 12 May 1980 (so far as relates to ss 38, 39, Sch 13 (part)) (SI 1980/587) |
| | | 1 Dec 1980 (so far as relates to s 40, Schs 7, 12 (part), 13 (part)) (SI 1980/1701) |
| 64 | | 17 Jul 1978 (SI 1978/712) |
| 65 | | 8 Sep 1977 (SI 1977/1365) |
| Schs 1–5 | | 17 Jul 1978 (SI 1978/712) |
| Sch 6 | | 8 Sep 1977 (SI 1977/1365) |
| Sch 7 | | 1 Dec 1980 (SI 1980/1632) |
| Sch 8 | | 17 Jul 1978 (SI 1978/712) |
| Sch 9 | paras 1, 2 | 29 Mar 1982 (SI 1982/243) |
| | para 3(1), (2) | 29 Mar 1982 (SI 1982/243) |
| | para 3(3) | 17 Jul 1978 (SI 1978/712; SI 1978/900) |
| | paras 4–11 | 29 Mar 1982 (SI 1982/243) |
| Sch 10 | | 1 Jan 1978 (SI 1977/1682) |
| Sch 11 | paras 1, 2 | 17 Jul 1978 (SI 1978/900) |
| | paras 3, 4 | 1 Dec 1977 (SI 1977/1744) |
| | para 5 | 8 Sep 1977 (so far as relates to Criminal Procedure (Scotland) Act 1975, s 289C(1)) (SI 1977/1365) |
| | | 1 Dec 1977 (so far as relates to Criminal Procedure (Scotland) Act 1975, s 289B(6), definition "the prescribed sum") (SI 1977/1744) |
| | | 17 Jul 1978 (otherwise) (SI 1978/900) |
| | para 6 | 1 Dec 1977 (SI 1977/1744) |
| | para 7 | 17 Jul 1978 (SI 1978/900) |
| | para 8 | 1 Dec 1980 (SI 1980/1701) |
| | paras 9, 10 | 1 Dec 1977 (SI 1977/1744) |
| | paras 11, 12 | 17 Jul 1978 (SI 1978/900) |
| | para 13 | 8 Sep 1977 (SI 1977/1365) |
| Sch 12 | | 8 Sep 1977 (SI 1977/1365), so far as relates to— |

Offences Against the Person Act 1861;
Explosive Substances Act 1883;
Criminal Justice Act 1948;
Sexual Offences Act 1956, Sch 2, Pt II, paras 14, 15;
Adoption Act 1958;
Licensing Act 1964, s 169;
Housing Act 1964;
Housing (Scotland) Act 1966;
Gaming Act 1968, s 8(7);
Children and Young Persons Act 1969, s 13(3);
Powers of Criminal Courts Act 1973, ss 15(2), 17(3);
Adoption Act 1976;
Bail Act 1976, ss 3(8), 5
1 Dec 1977 (SI 1977/1682) (E) (W), so far as relates to—
Metropolitan Police Courts Act 1839;
Public Stores Act 1875;
Prison Act 1952;
Magistrates' Courts Act 1952, ss 87(2), 130;
Obscene Publications Act 1959;
Criminal Justice Act 1961;
Licensing Act 1964, s 30(5);
Road Traffic Regulation Act 1967, ss 43(2), 78A, 80(5);
Criminal Justice Act 1967, ss 23(2), 24, 44(5), 60, 63, 91;
Companies Act 1967;
Theft Act 1968;
Criminal Justice Act 1972;
Finance Act 1972;

**Criminal Law Act 1977 (c 45)**—*contd*

> Road Traffic Act 1972;
> Administration of Justice Act 1973;
> Powers of Criminal Courts Act 1973, ss 1, 2(5), 49–51, 57(1),
>  Schs 1, 3;
> Juries Act 1974;
> Legal Aid Act 1974;
> Bail Act 1976, s 7(4)
> 1 Dec 1977 (SI 1977/1744) (S), so far as relates to—
> Public Stores Act 1875;
> Prison Act 1952 (in its application to persons for the time being
>  in Scotland);
> Criminal Justice Act 1961, ss 26, 28, 29, 39(1);
> Companies Act 1967;
> Criminal Justice Act 1967, s 60;
> Road Traffic Regulations 1967;
> Road Traffic Act 1972, s 179
> 1 Jan 1978 (SI 1977/1682), so far as relates to—
> Coroners Act 1887;
> Births and Deaths Registration Act 1953;
> Bail Act 1976, s 2(2);
> Criminal Justice Act 1967, s 22
> 17 Jul 1978 (SI 1978/712) (E) (W), so far as relates to—
> Night Poaching Act 1828;
> Accessories and Abettors Act 1861;
> Sexual Offences Act 1956, Sch 2, Pt II, paras 17, 18;
> Criminal Law Act 1967;
> Firearms Act 1968;
> Children and Young Persons Act 1969, ss 15, 16;
> Powers of Criminal Courts Act 1973, s 9(1);
> Health and Safety at Work etc Act 1974;
> Rehabilitation of Offenders Act 1974
> 17 Jul 1978 (SI 1978/900) (S), so far as relates to—
> Night Poaching Act 1828;
> Criminal Justice Act 1967;
> Health and Safety at Work etc Act 1974;
> Rehabilitation of Offenders Act 1974

Sch 13
> 8 Sep 1977 (SI 1977/1365), repeals of or in—
> Criminal Justice Act 1848, s 19(3);
> Children Act 1948;
> Criminal Justice Act 1967, Sch 3, Pt I;
> Children and Young Persons Act 1969, s 13(3);
> Powers of Criminal Courts Act 1973, Sch 3, para 9;
> Bail Act 1976, Sch 2, para 38
> 8 Sep 1977 (SI 1977/1426), repeals of or in—
> Exchange Control Act 1947, Sch 5, Pt II, para 3(1);
> Customs and Excise Act 1952, s 285(1);
> Magistrates' Courts Act 1952, Sch 3, para 3;
> Criminal Justice Act 1967, s 93;
> Land Commission Act 1967, s 82(5)
> 1 Dec 1977 (SI 1977/1682; SI 1977/1744), repeals of or in—
> Forcible Entry Act 1381;
> Statutes concerning forcible entries and riots confirmed;
> Forcible Entry Act 1429;
> Forcible Entry Act 1623;
> Metropolitan Police Courts Act 1839, s 24;
> Offences against the Person Act 1861, s 4;
> Public Stores Act 1875, ss 7, 9, 10;
> Conspiracy and Protection of Property Act 1875, s 3;
> Justices of the Peace Act 1949, s 43(3);

**Criminal Law Act 1977 (c 45)**—*contd*

Obscene Publications Act 1959, s 1(3);
Criminal Justice Act 1961, ss 26(6), 28(2);
Licensing Act 1964, s 30(5);
Criminal Justice Act 1967, ss 60(6)(a), (8)(d), 91(5);
Road Traffic Regulation Act 1967, ss 43(2), 80(5), (11);
Transport Act 1968, s 131(2);
Criminal Justice Act 1972, s 34(1);
Road Traffic Act 1972, Sch 4, Pt I;
Powers of Criminal Courts Act 1973, ss 2(8)(a), 49(1)–(3), 50(1)–(3), 51, 57(1), Sch 1, para 3(2)(b), Sch 3, paras 11, 12, 18(1)(b);
Road Traffic Act 1974, Sch 5, Pts II, III

1 Jan 1978 (SI 1977/1682), repeals of or in—
Prosecution of Offences Act 1879, s 5;
Coroners Act 1887, ss 4(2), (3), 5, 9, 10, 16, 18(4), (5), 20;
City of London Fire Inquests Act 1888;
Interpretation Act 1889, s 27;
Indictments Act 1915, s 8(3);
Coroners (Amendment) Act 1926, ss 13(2)(a), (d), 25;
Suicide Act 1961, Sch 1;
Criminal Justice Act 1967, s 22(4);
Administration of Justice Act 1970, Sch 9, Pt I, para 4;
Courts Act 1971, s 57(2);
Bail Act 1976, ss 2(2), 10, Sch 2, paras 4, 37(4)

17 Jul 1978 (SI 1978/712; SI 1978/900), repeals of or in—
Night Poaching Act 1828, ss 4, 11;
Truck Act 1831, s 10;
Conspiracy and Protection of Property Act 1875, ss 5, 7, 9, 19(1), (2);
Cruelty to Animals Act 1876, ss 15, 17;
Newspaper Libel and Registration Act 1881, s 5;
Truck Amendment Act 1887, s 13(1), (3);
Witnesses (Public Inquiries) Protection Act 1892, ss 3, 6(2);
Criminal Justice Act 1925, s 28(3);
Water Act 1945, Sch 3, s 71(1);
Exchange Control Act 1947, Sch 5, Pt II, para 2(3);
Children Act 1948, s 29(5);
Customs and Excise Act 1952, s 283(2)(a);
Magistrates' Courts Act 1952, ss 18, 19, 24, 25, 32, 104, 125, 127(2), Sch 1, Sch 2, para 8;
Protection of Animals (Amendment) Act 1954, s 3;
Police, Fire and Probation Officers Remuneration Act 1956;
Sexual Offences Act 1956, Sch 2, Pt II, Sch 3;
Magistrates' Courts Act 1957, s 1(1)(a);
Prevention of Fraud (Investments) Act 1958, s 13(2);
Obscene Publications Act 1959, s 2(2), (3);
Films Act 1960, s 45(3);
Criminal Justice Act 1961, ss 8(1), 11(2);
Criminal Justice Administration Act 1962, ss 12(3), 13, Sch 3, Sch 4, Pt II;
Penalties for Drunkenness Act 1962, s 1(2)(a), (b);
Public Order Act 1963, s 1(1);
Building Control Act 1966, s 1(8);
Industrial Development Act 1966, s 8(10);
Veterinary Surgeons Act 1966, ss 19(2), 20(6);
Criminal Law Act 1967, ss 4(5), 5(4);
Finance Act 1967, Sch 7, para 4;
Road Traffic Regulation Act 1967, s 91;
Sexual Offences Act 1967, ss 4(2), 5(2), 7(2)(b), 9;

**Criminal Law Act 1977 (c 45)**—*contd*

Criminal Justice Act 1967, ss 27, 35, 43, 92(8), 106(2)(f), Sch 3, Pt II;

Firearms Act 1968, s 57(4);

Theft Act 1968, s 29(2), Sch 2, Pt III;

Transport Act 1968, Sch 8, para 8;

Auctions (Bidding Agreements) Act 1969, s 1(2), (4);

Children and Young Persons Act 1969, ss 3(1)(b), (6), 6(1), (2), 12(2)(a), (3)(b)–(e), 15(1), 34(5), Sch 5, para 56;

Decimal Currency Act 1969, Sch 2, para 21;

Development of Tourism Act 1969, Sch 2, para 3(2), (4);

Administration of Justice Act 1970, s 51(1);

Courts Act 1971, Sch 8, paras 15(1), 16, 20, 34(1);

Misuse of Drugs Act 1971, s 26(4);

Criminal Justice Act 1972, s 47;

Gas Act 1972, s 43(2)(b);

Road Traffic Act 1972, Sch 5, Pt IV, para 3;

Industry Act 1972, Sch 1, para 4(2), (5);

Costs in Criminal Cases Act 1973, s 20(3);

Hallmarking Act 1973, Sch 3, para 2(2), (5);

Powers of Criminal Courts Act 1973, s 30(1), (2);

Control of Pollution Act 1974, s 87(3);

Housing Act 1974, Sch 13, para 2;

Road Traffic Act 1974, Sch 5, Pt IV, para 4(1)–(3), (4)(a);

Trade Union and Labour Relations Act 1974, s 29(7);

Criminal Procedure (Scotland) Act 1975, s 403(4);

District Courts (Scotland) Act 1975, ss 3(3), 27(1), Sch 1, para 26;

Protection of Birds (Amendment) Act 1976

12 May 1980 (SI 1980/487; SI 1980/587), repeals of or in—

Magistrates' Courts Act 1952, s 102(3);

Criminal Procedure (Scotland) Act 1975, ss 17, 325, 463(1)(a), (b)

1 Dec 1980 (SI 1980/1632; SI 1980/1701), repeals of or in—

Criminal Justice (Scotland) Act 1963, ss 26, 53(1), Sch 3, Pt II;

Criminal Justice Act 1967, s 106(2)(f), Sch 6, paras 14–16, 21;

Administration of Justice Act 1970, s 41(6)(a);

Courts Act 1971, s 59(5)(e), Sch 8, paras 34(3), 48(a);

Powers of Criminal Courts Act 1973, ss 33, 58(a), Sch 5, paras 6, 8;

Criminal Procedure (Scotland) Act 1975, ss 403(1), (5), 463(1);

District Courts (Scotland) Act 1975, Sch 1, para 26

29 Mar 1982 (repeals of or in Criminal Procedure (Scotland) Act 1975, Sch 9, paras 15, 35) (SI 1982/243)

Sch 14        8 Sep 1977 (SI 1977/1365)

**Farriers (Registration) (Amendment) Act 1977 (c 31)**

*RA:* 22 Jul 1977

*Commencement provisions:* s 2(2), (3)

| | | |
|---|---|---|
| 1, 2 | | 22 Oct 1977 (s 2(2)) |
| Schedule | paras 1–4 | 22 Oct 1977 (s 2(2)) |
| | para 5 | 22 Jan 1978 (s 2(3)) |
| | paras 6, 7 | 22 Oct 1977 (s 2(2)) |

## Finance Act 1977 (c 36)

*Budget Day:* 29 Mar 1977

*RA:* 29 Jul 1977

The commencement details of Finance Acts are not set out, as the dates from which their provisions take effect are usually stated clearly and unambiguously in the text of the Act, and charging provisions will normally state for which year or years of assessment they are to have effect.

## Finance (Income Tax Reliefs) Act 1977 (c 53)

*RA:* 15 Dec 1977

The commencement details of Finance Acts are not set out, as the dates from which their provisions take effect are usually stated clearly and unambiguously in the text of the Act, and charging provisions will normally state for which year or years of assessment they are to have effect.

## General Rate (Public Utilities) Act 1977 (c 11)

*RA:* 30 Mar 1977

Whole Act in force 30 Mar 1977 (RA)

## Housing (Homeless Persons) Act 1977 (c 48)

*RA:* 29 Jul 1977

*Commencement provisions:* s 21(3)(a)

Whole Act in force 1 Dec 1977 (s 21(3)(a))

## Incumbents (Vacation of Benefices) Measure 1977 (No 1)

*RA:* 30 Jun 1977

*Commencement provisions:* s 21(3)

Whole Measure in force 30 Dec 1977 (s 21(3)), except Sch 2, para 2(1), (2) which came into force on 30 Jun 1977 (s 21(3))

## Insurance Brokers (Registration) Act 1977 (c 46)

*RA:* 29 Jul 1977

*Commencement provisions:* s 30(3), (4); Insurance Brokers (Registration) Act 1977 (Commencement No 1) Order 1977, SI 1977/1782; Insurance Brokers (Registration) Act 1977 (Commencement No 2) Order 1978, SI 1978/1393; Insurance Brokers (Registration) Act 1977 (Commencement No 3) Order 1980, SI 1980/1824

| | | |
|---|---|---|
| 1 | | 1 Dec 1977 (SI 1977/1782) |
| 2–5 | | 20 Oct 1978 (SI 1978/1393) |
| 6–8 | | 1 Dec 1977 (SI 1977/1782) |
| 9 | | 20 Oct 1978 (SI 1978/1393) |
| 10–12 | | 1 Dec 1977 (SI 1977/1782) |
| 13–18 | | 20 Oct 1978 (SI 1978/1393) |
| 19 | (1)–(3) | 20 Oct 1978 (SI 1978/1393) |
| | (4)–(6) | 1 Dec 1977 (SI 1977/1782) |
| 20 | | 20 Oct 1978 (SI 1978/1393) |
| 21 | | 1 Dec 1977 (SI 1977/1782) |
| 22–24 | | 1 Dec 1981 (SI 1980/1824) |

**Insurance Brokers (Registration) Act 1977 (c 46)**—*contd*

| | |
|---|---|
| 25–30 | 1 Dec 1977 (SI 1977/1782) |
| Schedule | 1 Dec 1977 (SI 1977/1782) |

**International Finance, Trade and Aid Act 1977 (c 6)**

*RA:* 30 Mar 1977

Whole Act in force 30 Mar 1977 (RA)

**Job Release Act 1977 (c 8)**

*RA:* 30 Mar 1977

Whole Act in force 30 Mar 1977 (RA); s 1(4) of the Act stated that it would have effect for a period of eighteen months from royal assent unless further extended by order made by the Secretary of State; the last such order extended the Act to 29 Sep 1988 (SI 1987/1339)

**Licensing (Amendment) Act 1977 (c 26)**

*RA:* 22 Jul 1977

*Commencement provisions:* s 2(2)

Whole Act in force 22 Aug 1977 (s 2(2))

**Local Authorities (Restoration of Works Powers) Act 1977 (c 47)**

*RA:* 29 Jul 1977

Whole Act in force 29 Jul 1977 (RA)

**Marriage (Scotland) Act 1977 (c 15)**

*RA:* 26 May 1977

*Commencement provisions:* s 29(2)

| | |
|---|---|
| 1–28 | 1 Jan 1978 (s 29(2)) |
| 29 | 26 May 1977 (RA) |
| Schs 1–3 | 1 Jan 1978 (s 29(2)) |

**Merchant Shipping (Safety Convention) Act 1977 (c 24)**

*RA:* 22 Jul 1977

*Commencement provisions:* s 4(1); Merchant Shipping (Safety Convention) Act 1977 (Commencement) Order 1980, SI 1980/528

Whole Act in force 25 May 1980 (SI 1980/528)

**Minibus Act 1977 (c 25)**

*RA:* 22 Jul 1977

*Commencement provisions:* s 4(3)

Whole Act in force 22 Oct 1977 (s 4(3))

**National Health Service Act 1977 (c 49)**

*RA:* 29 Jul 1977

*Commencement provisions:* s 130(5)

Whole Act in force 29 Aug 1977 (s 130(5))

---

**New Towns Act 1977 (c 23)**

*RA:* 22 Jul 1977

Whole Act in force 22 Jul 1977 (RA)

---

**New Towns (Scotland) Act 1977 (c 16)**

*RA:* 26 May 1977

Whole Act in force 26 May 1977 (RA)

---

**Northern Ireland (Emergency Provisions) (Amendment) Act 1977 (c 34)**

*RA:* 22 Jul 1977

*Commencement provisions:* s 2(2)

Whole Act in force 5 Aug 1977 (s 2(2))

---

**Nuclear Industry (Finance) Act 1977 (c 7)**

*RA:* 30 Mar 1977

Whole Act in force 30 Mar 1977 (RA)

---

**Passenger Vehicles (Experimental Areas) Act 1977 (c 21)**

*RA:* 22 Jul 1977

Whole Act in force 22 Jul 1977 (RA)

---

**Patents Act 1977 (c 37)**

*RA:* 29 Jul 1977

*Commencement provisions:* s 132(5); Patents Act 1977 (Commencement No 1) Order 1977, SI 1977/2090; Patents Act 1977 (Commencement No 2) Order 1978, SI 1978/586; Patents (Amendment) Rules 1987, SI 1987/288, r 4 (made for the purposes of ss 77(9), 78(8))

| | | |
|---|---|---|
| 1–52 | | 1 Jun 1978 (SI 1978/586) |
| 53 | (1) | *Never in force* (repealed) |
| | (2)–(5) | 1 Jun 1978 (SI 1978/586) |
| 54–59 | | 1 Jun 1978 (SI 1978/586) |
| 60 | (1)–(3) | 1 Jun 1978 (SI 1978/586) |
| | (4) | *Never in force* (repealed) |
| | (5), (7) | 1 Jun 1978 (SI 1978/586) |
| 61–76 | | 1 Jun 1978 (SI 1978/586) |
| 77 | (1)–(5) | 1 Jun 1978 (SI 1978/586) |
| | (6), (7) | 29 Jul 1977 (RA) |
| | (8) | 1 Jun 1978 (SI 1978/586) |
| | (9) | 1 Sep 1987 (SI 1987/288) |

**Patents Act 1977 (c 37)**—*contd*

| | | |
|---|---|---|
| 78 | (1)–(6) | 1 Jun 1978 (SI 1978/586) |
| | (7) | 29 Jul 1977 (RA) |
| | (8) | 1 Sep 1987 (SI 1987/288) |
| 79–83 | | 1 Jun 1978 (SI 1978/586) |
| 84, 85 | | 31 Dec 1977 (SI 1977/2090) |
| 86–88 | | *Never in force* (repealed) |
| 89–113 | | 1 Jun 1978 (SI 1978/586) |
| 114 | | 31 Dec 1977 (SI 1977/2090) |
| 115–126 | | 1 Jun 1978 (SI 1978/586) |
| 127 | (1)–(4) | 1 Jun 1978 (SI 1978/586) |
| | (5) | See Sch 3 below |
| | (6), (7) | 1 Jun 1978 (SI 1978/586) |
| 128, 129 | | 1 Jun 1978 (SI 1978/586) |
| 130 | | 31 Dec 1977 (SI 1977/2090) |
| 131 | | 1 Jun 1978 (SI 1978/586) |
| 132 | (1)–(4) | 1 Jun 1978 (SI 1978/586) |
| | (5) | 29 Jul 1977 (RA) |
| | (6) | 1 Jun 1978 (SI 1978/586) |
| | (7) | See Sch 6 below |
| Schs 1, 2 | | 1 Jun 1978 (SI 1978/586) |
| Sch 3 | | 29 Jul 1977 (repeals of or in Patents Act 1949, s 41) (RA) |
| | | 1 Jun 1978 (otherwise) (SI 1978/586) |
| Schs 4, 5 | | 1 Jun 1978 (SI 1978/586) |
| Sch 6 | | 29 Jul 1977 (repeals of or in Patents Act 1949, s 41) (RA) |
| | | 31 Dec 1977 (repeals of or in Patents Act 1949, s 88) (SI 1977/2090) |
| | | 1 Jun 1978 (otherwise) (SI 1978/586) |

**Pensioners Payments Act 1977 (c 51)**

*RA:* 24 Nov 1977

Whole Act in force 24 Nov 1977 (RA)

**Post Office Act 1977 (c 44)**

*RA:* 29 Jul 1977

Whole Act in force 29 Jul 1977 (RA)

**Presumption of Death (Scotland) Act 1977 (c 27)**

*RA:* 22 Jul 1977

*Commencement provisions:* s 20(2); Presumption of Death (Scotland) Act 1977 (Commencement) Order 1978, SI 1978/159

| | | |
|---|---|---|
| 1–19 | | 1 Mar 1978 (SI 1978/159) |
| 20 | | 22 Jul 1977 (RA) |
| Schs 1, 2 | | 1 Mar 1978 (SI 1978/159) |

**Price Commission Act 1977 (c 33)**

*RA:* 22 Jul 1977

*Commencement provisions:* s 24(2)

| | | |
|---|---|---|
| 1–16 | | 1 Aug 1977 (s 24(2)) |
| 17 | (1), (2) | 22 Jul 1977 (RA) |

**Price Commission Act 1977 (c 33)**—*contd*

|        |                |                           |
|--------|----------------|---------------------------|
|        | (3)            | 1 Aug 1977 (s 24(2))      |
| 18–23  |                | 1 Aug 1977 (s 24(2))      |
| 24     |                | 22 Jul 1977 (RA)          |
| Sch 1  |                | 1 Aug 1977 (s 24(2))      |
| Sch 2  | para 1         | 22 Jul 1977 (RA)          |
|        | para 2         | 1 Aug 1977 (s 24(2))      |
|        | para 3(1)      | 1 Aug 1977 (s 24(2))      |
|        | para 3(2), (3) | 22 Jul 1977 (RA)          |
|        | para 4(a)      | 1 Aug 1977 (s 24(2))      |
|        | para 4(b)      | 22 Jul 1977 (RA)          |
|        | para 4(c)      | 1 Aug 1977 (s 24(2))      |
|        | para 4(d)      | 22 Jul 1977 (RA)          |
|        | paras 5–10     | 1 Aug 1977 (s 24(2))      |
| Sch 3  |                | 1 Aug 1977 (s 24(2))      |

---

**Protection from Eviction Act 1977 (c 43)**

*RA:* 29 Jul 1977

*Commencement provisions:* s 13(2)

Whole Act in force 29 Aug 1977 (s 13(2))

---

**Redundancy Rebates Act 1977 (c 22)**

*RA:* 22 Jul 1977

Whole Act in force 22 Jul 1977 (RA)

---

**Rent Act 1977 (c 42)**

*RA:* 29 Jul 1977

*Commencement provisions:* s 156(2)

Whole Act in force 29 Aug 1977 (s 156(2))

---

**Rent (Agriculture) Amendment Act 1977 (c 17)**

*RA:* 26 May 1977

*Commencement provisions:* s 2(2)

Whole Act in force 9 Jun 1977 (s 2(2))

---

**Rentcharges Act 1977 (c 30)**

*RA:* 22 Jul 1977

*Commencement provisions:* s 18(2); Rentcharges Act 1977 (Commencement) Order 1978, SI 1978/15

|        |     |                                                        |
|--------|-----|--------------------------------------------------------|
| 1–3    |     | 22 Aug 1977 (s 18(2))                                  |
| 4–11   |     | 1 Feb 1978 (SI 1978/15)                                |
| 12–15  |     | 22 Aug 1977 (s 18(2))                                  |
| 16     |     | 1 Feb 1978 (SI 1978/15)                                |
| 17     | (1) | 22 Aug 1977 (in relation to Sch 1, para 2) (s 18(2))   |
|        |     | 1 Feb 1978 (otherwise) (SI 1978/15)                    |
|        | (2) | See Sch 2 below                                        |
|        | (3) | 22 Aug 1977 (s 18(2))                                  |

**Rentcharges Act 1977 (c 30)**—*contd*

|  |  |  |
|---|---|---|
|  | (4), (5) | 1 Feb 1978 (SI 1978/15) |
|  | (6) | 22 Aug 1977 (s 18(2)) |
| 18 |  | 22 Aug 1977 (s 18(2)) |
| Sch 1 | para 1 | 1 Feb 1978 (SI 1978/15) |
|  | para 2 | 22 Aug 1977 (s 18(2)) |
|  | paras 3, 4 | 1 Feb 1978 (SI 1978/15) |
| Sch 2 |  | 22 Aug 1977 (s 18(2)), except repeals of or in— |
|  |  | Inclosure Act 1854, s 10; |
|  |  | Law of Property Act 1925, s 191 |
|  |  | 1 Feb 1978 (exceptions noted above) (SI 1978/15) |

---

**Representation of the People Act 1977 (c 9)**

*RA:* 30 Mar 1977

Whole Act in force 30 Mar 1977 (RA)

---

**Restrictive Trade Practices Act 1977 (c 19)**

*RA:* 30 Jun 1977

Whole Act in force 30 Jun 1977 (RA)

---

**Returning Officers (Scotland) Act 1977 (c 14)**

*RA:* 26 May 1977

*Commencement provisions:* s 4(1); Returning Officers (Scotland) Act 1977 (Commencement) Order 1977, SI 1977/1162

Whole Act in force 1 Aug 1977 (SI 1977/1162)

---

**Roe Deer (Close Seasons) Act 1977 (c 4)**

*RA:* 17 Mar 1977

*Commencement provisions:* s 2(2)

Whole Act in force 1 Nov 1977 (s 2(2))

---

**Social Security (Miscellaneous Provisions) Act 1977 (c 5)**

*RA:* 30 Mar 1977

*Commencement provisions:* s 25(2)–(4); Social Security (Miscellaneous Provisions) Act 1977 (Commencement No 1) Order 1977, SI 1977/617; Social Security (Miscellaneous Provisions) Act 1977 (Commencement No 2) Order 1977, SI 1977/618

|  |  |  |
|---|---|---|
| 1 | (1), (2) | 25 Apr 1977 (SI 1977/618) |
|  | (3) | 6 Apr 1975 (s 25(2)) |
|  | (4) | 6 Apr 1978 (SI 1977/618) |
|  | (5) | 30 Mar 1977 (RA) |
|  | (6), (7) | 25 Apr 1977 (SI 1977/618) |
| 2 |  | 30 Mar 1977 (RA) |
| 3 |  | 25 Apr 1977 (SI 1977/618) |
| 4 | (1), (2) | 6 Apr 1975 (s 25(2)) |
|  | (3), (4) | 25 Apr 1977 (SI 1977/618) |
| 5 |  | 30 Mar 1977 (RA) |
| 6 |  | 25 Apr 1977 (SI 1977/618) |

**Social Security (Miscellaneous Provisions) Act 1977 (c 5)**—*contd*

| | | |
|---|---|---|
| 7 | | 6 Apr 1977 (s 25(3)) |
| 8 | (1), (2) | 6 Apr 1979 (SI 1977/618) |
| | (3) | 25 Apr 1977 (SI 1977/618) |
| 9 | | 30 Mar 1977 (RA) |
| 10, 11 | | 1 Jul 1977 (SI 1977/618) |
| 12, 13 | | 25 Apr 1977 (SI 1977/618) |
| 14 | (1)–(3) | 30 Mar 1977 (RA) |
| | (4)–(7) | 25 Apr 1977 (SI 1977/618) |
| | (8) | 30 Mar 1977 (RA) |
| | (9) | 25 Apr 1977 (SI 1977/618) |
| | (10) | 30 Mar 1977 (RA) |
| 15, 16 | | 30 Mar 1977 (RA) |
| 17 | (1) | 3 Apr 1978 (SI 1977/618) |
| | (2) | 25 Apr 1977 (SI 1977/618) |
| | (3) | 30 Mar 1977 (RA) |
| | (4), (5) | 25 Apr 1977 (SI 1977/618) |
| | (6) | 6 Apr 1979 (SI 1977/618) |
| 18 | | 30 Mar 1977 (RA) |
| 19, 20 | | 25 Apr 1977 (SI 1977/618) |
| 21 | | 6 Apr 1978 (SI 1977/618) |
| 22 | (1) | 27 Jun 1977 (SI 1977/618) |
| | (2) | 25 Apr 1977 (SI 1977/618) |
| | (3) | 4 Apr 1977(s 25(3)) |
| | (4)–(8) | 25 Apr 1977 (SI 1977/618) |
| | (9), (10) | 6 Apr 1978 (SI 1977/618) |
| | (11), (12) | 25 Apr 1977 (SI 1977/618) |
| | (13) | 6 Apr 1978 (SI 1977/618) |
| | (14)–(16) | 25 Apr 1977 (SI 1977/618) |
| | (17) | 6 Apr 1975 (s 25(2)) |
| 23 | | 25 Apr 1977 (SI 1977/618) |
| 24 | (1)–(5) | 30 Mar 1977 (RA) |
| | (6) | See Sch 2 below |
| 25 | | 30 Mar 1977 (RA) |
| Sch 1 | | 1 Jul 1977 (SI 1977/618) |
| Sch 2 | | 30 Mar 1977 (repeals of or in Social Security Act 1975, ss 30(2), 45(4), 66(5), 124(1)(d)) (RA) |
| | | 6 Apr 1977 (SI 1977/617), repeals of or in— Employment Protection Act 1975, s 113; Supplementary Benefits Act 1976, Sch 7, para 41 |
| | | 25 Apr 1977 (SI 1977/618), repeals of or in— Tribunals and Inquiries Act 1971; Social Security Act 1975, ss 1(5), 129(3); Employment Protection Act 1975, s 40(3); Social Security (Northern Ireland) Act 1975; Social Security Pensions Act 1975; Supplementary Benefits Act 1976, s 29 |
| | | 27 Jun 1977 (repeals of or in Social Security Act 1975, Sch 20) (SI 1977/618) |
| | | 1 Jul 1977 (repeals of or in Industrial Injuries and Diseases (Old Cases) Act 1975) (SI 1977/618) |

**Statute Law (Repeals) Act 1977 (c 18)**

*RA:* 16 Jun 1977

Whole Act in force 16 Jun 1977 (RA)

## Torts (Interference with Goods) Act 1977 (c 32)

*RA:* 22 Jul 1977

*Commencement provisions:* s 17(2); Torts (Interference with Goods) Act 1977 (Commencement No 1) Order 1977, SI 1977/1910; Torts (Interference with Goods) Act 1977 (Commencement No 2) Order 1978, SI 1978/627; Torts (Interference with Goods) Act 1977 (Commencement No 3) Order 1980, SI 1980/2024[1]

| | | |
|---|---|---|
| 1–11 | | 1 Jun 1978 (SI 1978/627) |
| 12–16 | | 1 Jan 1978 (SI 1977/1910) |
| 17 | (1), (2) | 1 Jan 1978 (SI 1977/1910) |
| | (3) | 1 Jun 1978 (SI 1978/627) |
| Sch 1 | | 1 Jan 1978 (SI 1977/1910) |
| Sch 2 | | 1 Jun 1978 (SI 1978/627) |

[1]   Note that Torts (Interference with Goods) Act 1977 (Commencement No 3) Order 1980, SI 1980/2024, brought this Act into force, so far as not already in force by virtue of SI 1977/1910, in Northern Ireland on 1 Jan 1981 (SI 1978/627 applied to England and Wales only)

## Town and Country Planning (Amendment) Act 1977 (c 29)

*RA:* 22 Jul 1977

*Commencement provisions:* s 4(2)

Whole Act in force 22 Aug 1977 (s 4(2))

## Town and Country Planning (Scotland) Act 1977 (c 10)

*RA:* 30 Mar 1977

Whole Act in force 30 Mar 1977 (RA)

## Transport (Financial Provisions) Act 1977 (c 20)

*RA:* 30 Jun 1977

Whole Act in force 30 Jun 1977 (RA)

## Unfair Contract Terms Act 1977 (c 50)

*RA:* 26 Oct 1977

*Commencement provisions:* s 31(1)

Whole Act in force 1 Feb 1978 (s 31(1); note that this Act does not apply to contracts before this date but applies to liability for loss or damage suffered on or after that date (s 31(2)))

## Water Charges Equalisation Act 1977 (c 41)

*RA:* 29 Jul 1977

*Commencement provisions:* s 6(3)

Whole Act in force 29 Oct 1977 (s 6(3))

# 1978 Acts

## Adoption (Scotland) Act 1978 (c 28)

*RA:* 20 Jul 1978

*Commencement provisions:* s 67(2); Adoption (Scotland) Act 1978 Commencement Order 1984, SI 1984/1050

| | |
|---|---|
| 1, 2 | 1 Feb 1985 (SI 1984/1050) |
| 3–67 | 1 Sep 1984 (SI 1984/1050) |
| Schs 1–4 | 1 Sep 1984 (SI 1984/1050) |

## Appropriation Act 1978 (c 57)

*RA:* 2 Aug 1978

Whole Act in force 2 Aug 1978 (RA)

## Chronically Sick and Disabled Persons (Northern Ireland) Act 1978 (c 53)

*RA:* 31 Jul 1978

*Commencement provisions:* s 21(2); Chronically Sick and Disabled Persons (1978 Act) (Commencement No 1) Order (Northern Ireland) 1978, SR 1978/365; Chronically Sick and Disabled Persons (1978 Act) (Commencement No 2) Order (Northern Ireland) 1979, SR 1979/364

Whole Act in force 29 Dec 1978 (SR 1978/365) except s 14, which came into force on 31 Oct 1979 (SI 1979/364)

## Church of England (Miscellaneous Provisions) Measure 1978 (No 3)

*RA:* 30 Jun 1978

*Commencement provisions:* s 13(4)

Whole Measure in force 30 Jul 1978 (s 13(4))

## Civil Aviation Act 1978 (c 8)

*RA:* 23 Mar 1978

*Commencement provisions:* s 16(2); Civil Aviation Act 1978 (Commencement) Order 1978, SI 1978/486

| 1 | (1) | 23 Mar 1978 (SI 1978/486) |
|---|---|---|
| | (2) | 1 Apr 1978 (for the defraying of expenses incurred on or after that date) (SI 1978/486) |
| | | 1 May 1978 (otherwise) (SI 1978/486) |
| | (3)–(5) | 23 Mar 1978 (SI 1978/486) |
| 2, 3 | | 23 Mar 1978 (SI 1978/486) |
| 4–12 | | 1 May 1978 (SI 1978/486) |

**Civil Aviation Act 1978 (c 8)**—*contd*

| | |
|---|---|
| 13 | 23 Mar 1978 (SI 1978/486) |
| 14, 15 | 1 May 1978 (SI 1978/486) |
| 16 | 23 Mar 1978 (SI 1978/486) |
| Schs 1, 2 | 1 May 1978 (SI 1978/486) |

**Civil Liability (Contribution) Act 1978 (c 47)**

*RA:* 31 Jul 1978

*Commencement provisions:* s 10(2)

Whole Act in force 1 Jan 1979 (s 10(2))

**Commonwealth Development Corporation Act 1978 (c 2)**

*RA:* 23 Mar 1978

*Commencement provisions:* s 19(2)

Whole Act in force 23 Mar 1978 (s 19(2))

**Community Service by Offenders (Scotland) Act 1978 (c 49)**

*RA:* 31 Jul 1978

*Commencement provisions:* s 15(2); Community Service by Offenders (Scotland) Act 1978 (Commencement No 1) Order 1978, SI 1978/1944; Community Service by Offenders (Scotland) Act 1978 (Commencement No 2) Order 1980, SI 1980/268

| | | |
|---|---|---|
| 1–5 | | 1 Feb 1979 (SI 1978/1944) |
| 6 | | 1 Apr 1980 (SI 1980/268) |
| 7–14 | | 1 Feb 1979 (SI 1978/1944) |
| 15 | (1)–(4) | 1 Feb 1979 (SI 1978/1944) |
| | (5) | 1 Apr 1980 (SI 1980/268) |
| Sch 1 | | 1 Apr 1980 (SI 1980/268) |
| Sch 2 | | 1 Feb 1979 (SI 1978/1944) |

**Consolidated Fund Act 1978 (c 7)**

*RA:* 23 Mar 1978

Whole Act in force 23 Mar 1978 (RA)

**Consolidated Fund (No 2) Act 1978 (c 59)**

*RA:* 14 Dec 1978

Whole Act in force 14 Dec 1978 (RA)

**Consumer Safety Act 1978 (c 38)**

*RA:* 20 Jul 1978

*Commencement provisions:* s 12(2); Consumer Safety Act 1978 (Commencement No 1) Order 1978, SI 1978/1445; Consumer Safety Act 1978 (Commencement No 2) Order 1986, SI 1986/1297; Consumer Safety Act 1978 (Commencement No 3) Order 1987, SI 1987/1681

| | | |
|---|---|---|
| 1–9 | | 1 Nov 1978 (SI 1978/1445) |
| 10 | (1) | See Sch 3 below |

## Consumer Safety Act 1978 (c 38)—*contd*

| | |
|---|---|
| (2)–(6) | 1 Nov 1978 (SI 1978/1445) |
| 11, 12 | 1 Nov 1978 (SI 1978/1445) |
| Schs 1, 2 | 1 Nov 1978 (SI 1978/1445) |
| Sch 3 | 8 Aug 1986 (SI 1986/1297), repeals of or in— |
| |     Consumer Protection Act 1961, s 3(2A), (2B); |
| |     Consumer Protection Act (Northern Ireland) 1965, s 3(3), (4); |
| |     Consumer Protection Act 1971; |
| |     Consumer Protection and Advice (Northern Ireland) Order 1977, |
| |       art 3 |
| | 1 Oct 1987 (otherwise) (SI 1987/1681) |

## Co-operative Development Agency Act 1978 (c 21)

*RA:* 30 Jun 1978

Whole Act in force 30 Jun 1978 (RA)

## Dioceses Measure 1978 (No 1)

*RA:* 2 Feb 1978

*Commencement provisions:* s 25(2)

Whole Act in force 2 May 1978 (s 25(2))

## Dividends Act 1978 (c 54)

*RA:* 31 Jul 1978

Whole Act in force 31 Jul 1978 (RA)

## Domestic Proceedings and Magistrates' Courts Act 1978 (c 22)

*RA:* 30 Jun 1978

*Commencement provisions:* s 89(3); Domestic Proceedings and Magistrates' Courts Act 1978 (Commencement No 1) Order 1978, SI 1978/997; Domestic Proceedings and Magistrates' Courts Act 1978 (Commencement No 2) Order 1978, SI 1978/1489; Domestic Proceedings and Magistrates' Courts Act 1978 (Commencement No 1) (Scotland) Order 1978, SI 1978/1490; Domestic Proceedings and Magistrates' Courts Act 1978 (Commencement No 3) Order 1979, SI 1979/731; Domestic Proceedings and Magistrates' Courts Act 1978 (Commencement No 4) Order 1980, SI 1980/1478; Domestic Proceedings and Magistrates' Courts Act 1978 (Commencement No 2) (Scotland) Order 1980, SI 1980/2036; Children Act 1975 and the Domestic Proceedings and Magistrates' Courts Act 1978 (Commencement) Order 1985, SI 1985/779

| | |
|---|---|
| 1 | 1 Feb 1981 (SI 1980/1478) |
| 2 | 1 Feb 1981 (SI 1980/1478)[2] |
| 3–5 | 1 Feb 1981 (SI 1980/1478) |
| 6–11 | 1 Feb 1981 (SI 1980/1478)[2] |
| 12, 13 | 1 Feb 1981 (SI 1980/1478) |
| 14 | 1 Feb 1981 (SI 1980/1478)[2] |
| 15 | 1 Feb 1981 (SI 1980/1478) |
| 16, 17 | 1 Nov 1979 (SI 1979/731)[1] |
| 18 | 1 Nov 1979 (SI 1979/731) |
| 19–21 | 1 Feb 1981 (SI 1980/1478)[2] |
| 22–24 | 1 Feb 1981 (SI 1980/1478) |
| 25 | 1 Feb 1981 (SI 1980/1478)[2] |
| 26, 27 | 1 Feb 1981 (SI 1980/1478) |
| 28 | 1 Nov 1979 (SI 1979/731) |

**Domestic Proceedings and Magistrates' Courts Act 1978 (c 22)**—*contd*

| 29 | (1), (2) | 1 Nov 1979 (SI 1979/731) |
|---|---|---|
|  | (3), (4) | 1 Feb 1981 (SI 1980/1478) |
|  | (5) | 1 Nov 1979 (SI 1979/731) |
| 30 |  | 1 Nov 1979 (SI 1979/731)[1] |
| 31–33 |  | 1 Feb 1981 (SI 1980/1478) |
| 34 |  | 1 Feb 1981 (SI 1980/1478)[2] |
| 35–39 |  | 1 Feb 1981 (SI 1980/1478) |
| 40 |  | 17 Sep 1979 (SI 1979/731) |
| 41 |  | 1 Feb 1981 (SI 1980/1478)[2] |
| 42–44 |  | 1 Feb 1981 (SI 1980/1478) |
| 45, 46 |  | 1 Feb 1981 (SI 1980/1478)[2] |
| 47–54 |  | 1 Feb 1981 (SI 1980/1478) |
| 55 |  | 23 Oct 1978 (S) (SI 1978/1490) |
|  |  | 1 Feb 1981 (E) (W) (SI 1980/1478) |
| 56–60 |  | 1 Feb 1981 (SI 1980/1478) |
| 61 |  | 23 Oct 1978 (S) (SI 1978/1490) |
|  |  | 1 Feb 1981 (E) (W) (SI 1980/1478) |
| 62, 63 |  | 1 Feb 1981 (SI 1980/1478) |
| 64–71 |  | 1 Dec 1985 (SI 1985/779) |
| 72 |  | 1 Feb 1981 (SI 1980/1478) |
| 73 |  | 20 Nov 1978 (SI 1978/1489) |
| 74 | (1) | 23 Oct 1978 (S) (SI 1978/1490) |
|  |  | 20 Nov 1978 (E) (W) (SI 1978/1489) |
|  | (2) | 20 Nov 1978 (SI 1978/1489) |
|  | (3) | 23 Oct 1978 (S) (SI 1978/1490) |
|  |  | 20 Nov 1978 (E) (W) (SI 1978/1489) |
|  | (4), (5) | 20 Nov 1978 (SI 1978/1489) |
| 75–85 |  | 1 Nov 1979 (SI 1979/731) |
| 86 |  | 18 Jul 1978 (SI 1978/997) |
| 87 |  | 23 Oct 1978 (S) (SI 1978/1490) |
|  |  | 20 Nov 1978 (E) (W) (SI 1978/1489) |
| 88 | (1)–(4) | 1 Nov 1979 (SI 1979/731) |
|  | (5) | 18 Jul 1978 (SI 1978/997) |
| 89 | (1) | 18 Jul 1978 (SI 1978/997) |
|  | (2)(a) | 23 Oct 1978 (S) (so far as it brings Sch 2, paras 17, 18 into force) (SI 1978/1490) |
|  |  | 29 Nov 1978 (E) (W) (SI 1978/1489) |
|  |  | 1 Feb 1981 (S) (otherwise) (SI 1980/2036) |
|  | (2)(b) | 18 Jul 1978 (SI 1978/997) |
|  | (3)–(6) | 18 Jul 1978 (SI 1978/997) |
| 90 |  | 18 Jul 1978 (SI 1978/997) |
| Sch 1 |  | 18 Jul 1978 (SI 1978/997) |
| Sch 2 | paras 1–9 | 1 Feb 1981 (SI 1980/1478) |
|  | para 10 | 1 Nov 1979 (SI 1979/731) |
|  | para 11 | 1 Feb 1981 (SI 1980/1478) |
|  | para 12 | 1 Nov 1979 (SI 1979/731)[1] |
|  | paras 13–16 | 1 Feb 1981 (SI 1980/1478) |
|  | paras 17, 18 | 23 Oct 1978 (S) (SI 1978/1490) |
|  |  | 20 Nov 1978 (E) (W) (SI 1978/1489) |
|  | para 19(a) | 1 Feb 1981 (SI 1980/1478) |
|  | para 19(b), (c) | 20 Nov 1978 (SI 1978/1489) |
|  | para 20 | 1 Feb 1981 (SI 1980/1478) |
|  | para 21 | 1 Nov 1979 (SI 1979/731) |
|  | paras 22–24 | 1 Feb 1981 (SI 1980/1478) |
|  | para 25 | 1 Nov 1979 (SI 1979/731)[1] |
|  | paras 26–29 | 1 Feb 1981 (SI 1980/1478) |
|  | paras 30, 31 | 17 Sep 1979 (SI 1979/731) |
|  | paras 32–37 | 1 Feb 1981 (SI 1980/1478) |
|  | para 38 | 1 Nov 1979 (SI 1979/731) |

**Domestic Proceedings and Magistrates' Courts Act 1978 (c 22)**—*contd*

|  | paras 39, 40 | 1 Nov 1979 (SI 1979/731)[1] |
|---|---|---|
|  | paras 41–44 | 1 Feb 1981 (SI 1980/1478) |
|  | para 45(a) | 1 Feb 1981 (SI 1980/1478) |
|  | para 45(b) | 20 Nov 1978 (SI 1978/1489) |
|  | para 45(c) | 1 Nov 1979 (SI 1979/731) |
|  | paras 46–48 | 1 Dec 1985 (SI 1985/779) |
|  | paras 49–53 | 20 Nov 1978 (SI 1978/1489) |
|  | para 54 | 1 Feb 1981 (SI 1980/1478) |

Sch 3       18 Jul 1978 (repeal in Administration of Justice Act 1964, s 2) (SI 1978/997)

20 Nov 1978 (SI 1978/1489), repeals of or in—
Adoption (Hague Convention) Act (Northern Ireland) 1969, s 7(2);
Children Act 1975, Sch 3, para 26;
Adoption Act 1976, Sch 1, para 6

1 Nov 1979 (SI 1979/731), repeals of or in—
National Assistance Act 1948, s 43(7);
Magistrates' Courts Act 1952, ss 57(4), 60(1), (2)(a), 61, 62, 121(2);
Matrimonial Proceedings (Magistrates' Courts) Act 1960, s 8(3);
Criminal Justice Act 1961, Sch 4;
Affiliation Proceedings (Amendment) Act 1972, s 3(1), (2);
Maintenance Orders (Reciprocal Enforcement) Act 1972, s 17(1)–(3), Schedule, para 1;
Children Act 1975, s 21(3), Sch 3, para 12;
Adoption Act 1976, s 64(c), Sch 3, para 4;
Supplementary Benefits Act 1976, s 18(7), Sch 7

1 Feb 1981 (SI 1980/1478), repeals of or in—
Maintenance Orders Act 1950, s 2(3);
Magistrates' Courts Act 1952, s 59;
Affiliation Proceedings Act 1957, s 7(1)–(3);
Matrimonial Proceedings (Magistrates' Courts) Act 1960, except s 8(3) (repealed as above);
Administration of Justice Act 1964, Sch 3, para 27;
Matrimonial Causes Act 1965, s 42;
Criminal Justice Act 1967, Sch 3 (entry relating to Matrimonial Proceedings (Magistrates' Courts) Act 1960);
Maintenance Orders Act 1968, Sch (entry relating to Matrimonial Proceedings (Magistrates' Courts) Act 1960);
Family Law Reform Act 1969, s 5(2);
Local Authority Social Services Act 1970, Sch 1 (entry relating to Matrimonial Proceedings (Magistrates' Courts) Act 1960);
Matrimonial Proceedings and Property Act 1970, ss 30(1), 31–33;
Guardianship of Minors Act 1971, ss 9(3), 14(4);
Misuse of Drugs Act 1971, s 34;
Local Government Act 1972, Sch 23, para 10;
Maintenance Orders (Reciprocal Enforcement) Act 1972, s 27(3);
Guardianship Act 1973, ss 2(5), 3(2), 8, Sch 2, para 1(2);
Matrimonial Causes Act 1973, s 27(8);
Legal Aid Act 1974, Sch 1, para 3(a);
Children Act 1975, ss 17(1), 91;
Adoption Act 1976, s 26(1)

[1]  For transitional provisions, see SI 1979/731, Sch 2

[2]  For transitional provisions, see SI 1980/1478, Sch 2

## Education (Northern Ireland) Act 1978 (c 13)

*RA:* 25 May 1978

Whole Act in force 25 May 1978 (RA)

## Employment (Continental Shelf) Act 1978 (c 46)

*RA:* 31 Jul 1978

Whole Act in force 31 Jul 1978 (RA)

## Employment Protection (Consolidation) Act 1978 (c 44)

*RA:* 31 Jul 1978

*Commencement provisions:* s 160(2)

Whole Act in force 1 Nov 1978 (except s 139(2)–(9), Sch 17, repeal of or in Employment Protection Act 1975, s 122, which came into force on 1 Jan 1979 (s 160(2)))

## Employment Subsidies Act 1978 (c 6)

*RA:* 23 Mar 1978

Whole Act in force 23 Mar 1978 (RA)

## European Parliamentary Elections Act 1978 (c 10)

*RA:* 5 May 1980

Whole Act in force 5 May 1980 (RA)

## Export Guarantees and Overseas Investment Act 1978 (c 18)

*RA:* 30 Jun 1978

*Commencement provisions:* s 16(4)

Whole Act in force 30 Jul 1978 (s 16(4))

## Finance Act 1978 (c 42)

*Budget Day:* 11 Apr 1978

*RA:* 31 Jul 1978

The commencement details of Finance Acts are not set out, as the dates from which their provisions take effect are usually stated clearly and unambiguously in the text of the Act, and charging provisions will normally state for which year or years of assessment they are to have effect.

## Gun Barrel Proof Act 1978 (c 9)

*RA:* 5 May 1978

*Commencement provisions:* s 9(3); Gun Barrel Proof Act 1978 (Commencement No 1) Order 1978, SI 1978/1587; Gun Barrel Proof Act 1978 (Commencement No 2) Order 1980, SI 1980/640

| | |
|---|---|
| 1 | 5 Jun 1980 (SI 1980/640) |
| 2–7 | 1 Dec 1978 (SI 1978/1587) |

**Gun Barrel Proof Act 1978 (c 9)**—*contd*

| | | |
|---|---|---|
| 8 | (1) | 1 Dec 1978 (so far as relates to Sch 3) (SI 1978/1587) |
| | | 5 Jun 1980 (otherwise) (SI 1980/640) |
| | (2) | 1 Dec 1978 (SI 1978/1587) |
| | (3) | 5 Jun 1980 (SI 1980/640) |
| 9 | | 1 Dec 1978 (SI 1978/1587) |
| Schs 1, 2 | | 5 Jun 1980 (SI 1980/640) |
| Sch 3 | para 1(a) | 5 Jun 1980 (SI 1980/640) |
| | para 1(b) | 1 Dec 1978 (except definition "convention proof mark") (SI 1978/1587) |
| | | 5 Jun 1980 (exception noted above) (SI 1980/640) |
| | paras 2–9 | 1 Dec 1978 (SI 1978/1587) |
| | para 10(1) | 1 Dec 1978 (SI 1978/1587) |
| | para 10(2) | 5 Jun 1980 (SI 1980/640) |
| | paras 11–14 | 1 Dec 1978 (SI 1978/1587) |
| | para 15(1), (2) | 1 Dec 1978 (SI 1978/1587) |
| | para 15(3) | 5 Jun 1980 (SI 1980/640) |
| | para 16 | 1 Dec 1978 (except words "or which is or at any time was a convention proof mark") (SI 1978/1587) |
| | | 5 Jun 1980 (exception noted above) (SI 1980/640) |
| | paras 17–20 | 1 Dec 1978 (SI 1978/1587) |
| Sch 4 | | 1 Dec 1978 (SI 1978/1587) |

**Home Purchase Assistance and Housing Corporation Guarantee Act 1978 (c 27)**

*RA:* 30 Jun 1978

*Commencement provisions:* s 6(2); Home Purchase Assistance and Housing Corporation Guarantee Act 1978 (Appointed Day) Order 1978, SI 1978/1412

| | |
|---|---|
| 1–3 | 1 Dec 1978 (SI 1978/1412) |
| 4–6 | 30 Jun 1978 (RA) |
| Schedule | 1 Dec 1978 (SI 1978/1412) |

**Homes Insulation Act 1978 (c 48)**

*RA:* 31 Jul 1978

Whole Act in force 31 Jul 1978 (RA)

**House of Commons (Administration) Act 1978 (c 36)**

*RA:* 20 Jul 1978

*Commencement provisions:* s 5(5)

| | | |
|---|---|---|
| 1 | | 20 Jul 1978 (RA) |
| 2 | | 1 Jan 1979 (s 5(5)) |
| 3–5 | | 20 Jul 1978 (RA) |
| Sch 1 | | 20 Jul 1978 (RA) |
| Sch 2 | paras 1, 2 | 20 Jul 1978 (RA) |
| | paras 3–5 | 1 Jan 1979 (s 5(5)) |
| Sch 3 | | 1 Jan 1979 (s 5(5)) |

**Housing (Financial Provisions) (Scotland) Act 1978 (c 14)**

*RA:* 25 May 1978

*Commencement provisions:* s 19(2), (3)

| | |
|---|---|
| 1–10 | 25 Jun 1978 (s 19(2)) |

**Housing (Financial Provisions) (Scotland) Act 1978 (c 14)**—*contd*

| | | |
|---|---|---|
| 11 | | 1 Apr 1979 (s 19(3)) |
| 12–18 | | 25 Jun 1978 (s 19(2)) |
| 19 | | 25 May 1978 (RA) |
| Sch 1 | | 25 Jun 1978 (s 19(2)) |
| Sch 2 | paras 1–32 | 25 Jun 1978 (s 19(2)) |
| | para 33 | 1 Apr 1979 (s 19(3)) |
| | paras 34–36 | 25 Jun 1978 (s 19(2)) |
| | paras 37, 38 | 1 Apr 1979 (s 19(3)) |
| | paras 39–43 | 25 Jun 1978 (s 19(2)) |
| Sch 3 | | 25 Jun 1978 (repeals of or in Housing (Financial Provisions) (Scotland) Act 1972, Sch 2, Pt II, Sch 3, Pt II) (s 19(2)) |
| | | 1 Apr 1979 (s 19(3)) 25 Jun 1978 (s 19(2)), repeals of or in— |
| | | Housing (Scotland) Act 1949; |
| | | Housing (Scotland) Act 1950; |
| | | Housing (Financial Provisions) (Scotland) Act 1968; |
| | | Housing (Scotland) Act 1969; |
| | | Housing (Financial Provisions) (Scotland) Act 1972, ss 1–4, 8–10, 12; |
| | | Housing Act 1974; |
| | | Housing (Scotland) Act 1974 |

**Import of Live Fish (Scotland) Act 1978 (c 35)**

*RA:* 20 Jul 1978

Whole Act in force 20 Jul 1978 (RA)

**Independent Broadcasting Authority Act 1978 (c 43)**

*RA:* 31 Jul 1978

Whole Act in force 31 Jul 1978 (RA)

**Industrial and Provident Societies Act 1978 (c 34)**

*RA:* 20 Jul 1978

*Commencement provisions:* s 3(3)

Whole Act in force 20 Aug 1978 (s 3(3))

**Inner Urban Areas Act 1978 (c 50)**

*RA:* 31 Jul 1978

Whole Act in force 31 Jul 1978 (RA)

**Internationally Protected Persons Act 1978 (c 17)**

*RA:* 30 Jun 1978

*Commencement provisions:* s 5(5); Internationally Protected Persons Act 1978 (Commencement) Order 1979, SI 1979/455

Whole Act in force 24 May 1979 (SI 1979/455)

## Interpretation Act 1978 (c 30)

*RA:* 20 Jul 1978

*Commencement provisions:* s 26

Whole Act in force 1 Jan 1979 (s 26)

---

## Iron and Steel (Amendment) Act 1978 (c 41)

*RA:* 20 Jul 1978

Whole Act in force 20 Jul 1978 (RA)

---

## Judicature (Northern Ireland) Act 1978 (c 23)

*RA:* 30 Jun 1978

*Commencement provisions:* s 123(2); Judicature (Northern Ireland) Act 1978 (Commencement No 1) Order 1978, SI 1978/1101; Judicature (Northern Ireland) Act 1978 (Commencement No 2) Order 1978, SI 1978/1829; Judicature (Northern Ireland) Act 1978 (Commencement No 3) Order 1979, SI 1979/124; Judicature (Northern Ireland) Act 1978 (Commencement No 4) Order 1979, SI 1979/422

| | | |
|---|---|---|
| 1–51 | | 18 Apr 1979 (SI 1979/422) |
| 52, 53 | | 21 Aug 1978 (SI 1978/1101) |
| 54 | (1) | 2 Jan 1979 (SI 1978/1829) |
| | (2)–(4) | 21 Aug 1978 (so far as they apply to the Crown Court Rules Committee and Crown Court Rules) (SI 1978/1101) |
| | | 2 Jan 1979 (otherwise) (SI 1978/1829) |
| | (5) | 2 Jan 1979 (SI 1978/1829) |
| | (6) | 21 Aug 1978 (so far as they apply to the Crown Court Rules Committee and Crown Court Rules) (SI 1978/1101) |
| | | 2 Jan 1979 (otherwise) (SI 1978/1829) |
| 55 | (1), (2) | 2 Jan 1979 (SI 1978/1829) |
| | (3) | 21 Aug 1978 (so far as they apply to the Crown Court Rules Committee and Crown Court Rules) (SI 1978/1101) |
| | | 2 Jan 1979 (otherwise) (SI 1978/1829) |
| 56 | (1)–(3) | 21 Aug 1978 (so far as they apply to the Crown Court Rules Committee and Crown Court Rules) (SI 1978/1101) |
| | | 2 Jan 1979 (otherwise) (SI 1978/1829) |
| | (4) | 2 Jan 1979 (SI 1978/1829) |
| 57–98 | | 18 Apr 1979 (SI 1979/422) |
| 99 | | 21 Aug 1978 (SI 1978/1101) |
| 100–106 | | 18 Apr 1979 (SI 1979/422) |
| 107 | | 21 Aug 1978 (SI 1978/1101) |
| 108–115 | | 18 Apr 1979 (SI 1979/422) |
| 116 | | 21 Aug 1978 (SI 1978/1101) |
| 117 | | 18 Apr 1979 (SI 1979/422) |
| 118–121 | | 21 Aug 1978 (SI 1978/1101) |
| 122 | | See Schs 5–7 below |
| 123 | | 21 Aug 1978 (SI 1978/1101) |
| Schs 1–4 | | 18 Apr 1979 (SI 1979/422) |
| Sch 5 | Pt I, paras 1, 2 | 18 Apr 1979 (SI 1979/422) |
| | Pt I, paras 3, 4 | 2 Jan 1979 (SI 1978/1829) |
| | Pt II | 21 Aug 1978 (SI 1978/1101), amendments of or in— |
| | | Bills of Sale (Ireland) Act 1879; |
| | | Deeds of Arrangement Act 1887; |
| | | Deeds of Arrangement Amendment Act 1890; |
| | | Coroners Act (Northern Ireland) 1959, s 2(3); |
| | | County Courts Act (Northern Ireland) 1959, ss 105, 134; |

**Judicature (Northern Ireland) Act 1978 (c 23)**—*contd*

Lands Tribunal and Compensation Act (Northern Ireland) 1964;
Magistrates' Courts Act (Northern Ireland) 1964, ss 10, 11;
Judgments (Enforcement) Act (Northern Ireland) 1969, except ss 3, 129;
Payments for Debt (Emergency Provisions) Act (Northern Ireland) 1971, s 3

2 Jan 1979 (SI 1978/1829), amendments of or in—
Probates and Letters of Administration Act (Ireland) 1857;
Juries Act (Ireland) 1871, s 18;
Bankruptcy (Ireland) Amendment Act 1872, ss 57, 124;
Bills of Sale (Ireland) Act 1879, s 4;
Land Law (Ireland) Act 1887;
Bankruptcy Amendment Act (Northern Ireland) 1929, ss 21(1), 28(1) (definition "Prescribed");
Foreign Judgments (Reciprocal Enforcement) Act 1933;
Trade Marks Act 1938;
Evidence Act (Northern Ireland) 1939;
Landlord and Tenant (War Damage) Act (Northern Ireland) 1941, s 38(1);
Exchange Control Act 1947;
Representation of the People Act 1949, s 163;
Arbitration Act 1950;
Interpretation Act (Northern Ireland) 1954, s 21;
County Courts Act (Northern Ireland) 1959, ss 146, 147 (except (b)(ii));
County Courts Appeals Act (Northern Ireland) 1964, s 8(2);
Magistrates' Courts Act (Northern Ireland) 1964, ss 23–25;
Arbitration (International Investment Disputes) Act 1966;
Criminal Appeal (Northern Ireland) Act 1968, ss 49, 50 (definition "rules of court");
Criminal Cases Act (Northern Ireland) 1968, s 7;
Administration of Justice Act 1970;
Social Security (Northern Ireland) Act 1975;
Northern Ireland (Crown Proceedings) Order 1949, SI 1949/1836;
Solicitors (Northern Ireland) Order 1976, SI 1976/582 (NI 12), art 75(3)

18 Apr 1979 (otherwise) (SI 1979/422)

| | | |
|---|---|---|
| Sch 6 | paras 1, 2 | 18 Apr 1979 (SI 1979/422) |
| | para 3 | 2 Jan 1979 (SI 1978/1829) |
| | paras 4–6 | 18 Apr 1979 (SI 1979/422) |
| | para 7 | 21 Aug 1978 (SI 1978/1101) |
| | paras 8, 9 | 18 Apr 1979 (SI 1979/422) |
| | para 10 | 21 Aug 1978 (in so far as it relates to para 7) (SI 1978/1101) |
| | | 2 Jan 1979 (in so far as it relates to para 3) (SI 1978/1829) |
| | paras 11–18 | 18 Apr 1979 (SI 1979/422) |
| Sch 7 | | 21 Aug 1978 (SI 1978/1101), repeals of or in— |

Supreme Court of Judicature Act (Ireland) 1877, s 84;
Interpretation Act (Northern Ireland) 1954, s 21(1), (2);
County Courts Act (Northern Ireland) 1959, ss 116, 147(e)(ii), Sch 3;
Magistrates' Courts Act (Northern Ireland) 1964, ss 23(7) (except para (a)), (9), 24, 26;
Judgments (Enforcement) Act (Northern Ireland) 1969, ss 5(4), 7(3), (4), 18, 19, 30, 40, 114(1), 118, 119, 133(2);
Payments for Debt (Emergency Provisions) Act (Northern Ireland) 1971, ss 13, 14;
Solicitors (Northern Ireland) Order 1976, SI 1976/582 (NI 12), art 79

2 Jan 1979 (SI 1978/1829), repeals of or in—

**Judicature (Northern Ireland) Act 1978 (c 23)**—*contd*

> Law of Property Amendment Act 1860;
> Settled Estates Act 1877;
> Bills of Sale (Ireland) Act 1879, s 21;
> Conveyancing Act 1881, ss 48, 72(5);
> Deeds of Arrangement Act 1887;
> Deeds of Arrangement Amendment Act 1890;
> Administration of Justice Act 1920;
> Probates and Letters of Administration Act (Northern Ireland) 1933;
> Law Reform (Miscellaneous Provisions) Act (Northern Ireland) 1937;
> Evidence Act (Northern Ireland) 1939;
> Representation of the People Act 1949, s 160;
> Arbitration Act 1950;
> County Courts Act (Northern Ireland) 1959, ss 138, 146;
> Administration of Justice Act 1960, s 9(2);
> Northern Ireland Act 1962, ss 7–9, Sch 1;
> Criminal Appeal (Northern Ireland) Act 1968;
> Magistrates' Courts Act (Northern Ireland) 1964, ss 23–25, 28(3)
> 18 Apr 1979 (otherwise) (SI 1979/422)

**Local Government Act 1978 (c 39)**

*RA:* 20 Jul 1978

Whole Act in force 20 Jul 1978 (RA)

**Local Government (Scotland) Act 1978 (c 4)**

*RA:* 23 Mar 1978

*Commencement provisions:* s 8(3)

Whole Act in force 23 Mar 1978 (RA) (except Schedule, para 2 which came into force on 1 Jan 1979 (s 8(3)))

**Medical Act 1978 (c 12)**

*RA:* 5 May 1978

*Commencement provisions:* s 32(2); Medical Act 1978 (Commencement No 1) Order 1978, SI 1978/1035; Medical Act 1978 (Commencement No 2) Order 1979, SI 1979/920; Medical Act 1978 (Commencement No 3) Order 1980, SI 1980/868; Medical Act 1978 (Commencement No 4) Order 1980, SI 1980/1524

| | | |
|---|---|---|
| 1 | (1)–(12) | 23 Aug 1978 (SI 1978/1035) |
| | (13), (14) | 27 Sep 1979 (SI 1979/920) |
| | (15), (16) | 23 Aug 1978 (SI 1978/1035) |
| 2 | | 23 Aug 1978 (SI 1978/1035) |
| 3 | | 27 Sep 1979 (SI 1979/920) |
| 4 | | 5 May 1978 (RA) |
| 5 | | 27 Sep 1979 (SI 1979/920) |
| 6–14 | | 1 Aug 1980 (SI 1980/868) |
| 15, 16 | | 27 Sep 1979 (SI 1979/920) |
| 17 | | 5 May 1978 (RA) |
| 18–21 | | 1 Dec 1980 (SI 1980/1524) |
| 22–28 | | 15 Feb 1979 (SI 1978/1035) |
| 29 | | 1 Dec 1978 (SI 1978/1035) |
| 30 | | 23 Aug 1978 (SI 1978/1035) |

**Medical Act 1978 (c 12)**—*contd*

| | | |
|---|---|---|
| 31 | (1) | See Sch 6 below |
| | (2) | See Sch 7 below |
| | (3) | 27 Sep 1979 (SI 1979/920) |
| | (4) | 23 Aug 1978 (SI 1978/1035) |
| 32 | | 5 May 1978 (RA) |
| Sch 1 | | 27 Sep 1979 (SI 1979/920) |
| Sch 2 | | *Never in force* (repealed) |
| Schs 3, 4 | | 1 Aug 1980 (SI 1980/868) |
| Sch 5 | | *Never in force* (repealed) |
| Sch 6 | paras 1–3 | 27 Sep 1979 (SI 1979/920) |
| | para 4 | *Never in force* (repealed) |
| | paras 5–12 | 27 Sep 1979 (SI 1979/920) |
| | para 13 | 1 Dec 1980 (SI 1980/1524) |
| | para 14 | 27 Sep 1979 (SI 1979/920) |
| | paras 15–17 | 15 Feb 1979 (SI 1978/1035) |
| | para 18(1), (2) | 15 Feb 1979 (SI 1978/1035) |
| | para 18(3) | 1 Aug 1980 (SI 1980/868) |
| | para 19 | 27 Sep 1979 (SI 1979/920) |
| | para 20 | 15 Feb 1979 (SI 1978/1035) |
| | para 21(1)–(3) | 15 Feb 1979 (SI 1978/1035) |
| | para 21(4) | 23 Aug 1978 (SI 1978/1035) |
| | para 21(5) | 15 Feb 1979 (SI 1978/1035) |
| | para 21(6) | 23 Aug 1978 (SI 1978/1035) |
| | para 21(7) | 15 Feb 1979 (SI 1978/1035) |
| | para 22 | 15 Feb 1979 (SI 1978/1035) |
| | para 23(1), (2) | 1 Dec 1980 (SI 1980/1524) |
| | para 23(3), (4) | 1 Aug 1980 (SI 1980/868) |
| | paras 24–26 | 15 Feb 1979 (SI 1978/1035) |
| | para 27 | 1 Dec 1980 (SI 1980/1524) |
| | para 28 | 15 Feb 1979 (SI 1978/1035) |
| | para 29 | 23 Aug 1978 (SI 1978/1035) |
| | para 30 | *Never in force* (repealed) |
| | paras 31–36 | 23 Aug 1978 (SI 1978/1035) |
| | para 37 | 27 Sep 1979 (SI 1979/920) |
| | paras 38–40 | *Never in force* (repealed) |
| | para 41 | 23 Aug 1978 (SI 1978/1035) |
| | para 42 | *Never in force* (repealed) |
| | paras 43–46 | 23 Aug 1978 (SI 1978/1035) |
| | para 47 | 1 Aug 1980 (SI 1980/868) |
| | para 48(a) | 27 Sep 1979 (SI 1979/920) |
| | para 48(b) | *Never in force* (repealed) |
| | para 49 | 23 Aug 1978 (in so far as it relates to the definition "primary United Kingdom qualification") (SI 1978/1035) |
| | | 15 Feb 1979 (in so far as it relates to the definition "fully registered person") (SI 1978/1035) |
| | | 27 Sep 1979 (in so far as it relates to the definitions "appointed member", "elected member" and "the General Council") (SI 1979/920) |
| | | *Never in force* (in so far as it relates to the definition "primary Irish qualification") (repealed) |
| | paras 50–53 | 23 Aug 1978 (SI 1978/1035) |
| | para 54 | 1 Aug 1980 (SI 1980/868) |
| | para 55 | 23 Aug 1978 (SI 1978/1035) |
| | para 56 | 27 Sep 1979 (SI 1979/920) |
| | para 57 | 1 Aug 1980 (SI 1980/868) |
| | para 58 | 23 Aug 1978 (SI 1978/1035) |
| | para 59 | 27 Sep 1979 (SI 1979/920) |
| | paras 60, 61 | 1 Aug 1980 (SI 1980/868) |
| | paras 62–66 | 23 Aug 1978 (SI 1978/1035) |

**Medical Act 1978 (c 12)**—*contd*

| | |
|---|---|
| Sch 7 | 23 Aug 1978 (SI 1978/1035), repeals of or in—<br>Medical Act 1950;<br>Medical Act 1956, ss 7A(1), 11(4), 12(2), 14, 17(3), 48, 56(3),<br>Sch 3, Pt I, column 2<br>27 Sep 1979 (SI 1979/920), repeals of or in—<br>Medical Act 1956, ss 1–6, 9(1), (5), 10(1), (7), 15(4), (5),<br>28(1)(b), (3), 30, 40, 49(1), 54(1), 57(6), (11), (12), Sch 1;<br>Universities (Scotland) Act 1966, Sch 6, paras 18, 19;<br>Medical Act 1969, ss 8(3)(b), 10(7), 17, 18(1), (3), Sch 1,<br>paras 9–12, Sch 3, paras 1, 4, 9<br>1 Dec 1980 (SI 1980/1524), repeals of or in—<br>Medical Practitioners and Pharmacists Act 1947;<br>Medical Act 1956, ss 13(3), 18–26, 32–38, 51, 54(3), 57(2), (5),<br>Sch 4;<br>Medical Act 1969, ss 1(2)(b), 3(3), (7), 4(7), 7(7), 9(4),<br>11(2), (3), 12–16, 19, Sch 1, paras 1, 3–5, Sch 3, paras 2, 3, 6,<br>7, 10, 11 |

## National Health Service (Scotland) Act 1978 (c 29)

*RA:* 20 Jul 1978

*Commencement provisions:* s 110(4)

Whole Act in force 1 Jan 1979 (s 110(4))

## Northern Ireland (Emergency Provisions) Act 1978 (c 5)

*RA:* 23 Mar 1978

*Commencement provisions:* s 33(1)

| | |
|---|---|
| 1–31 | 1 Jun 1978 (s 33(1)) |
| 32, 33 | 23 Mar 1978 (s 33(1)) |

## Nuclear Safeguards and Electricity (Finance) Act 1978 (c 25)

*RA:* 30 Jun 1978

Whole Act in force 30 Jun 1978 (RA)

## Oaths Act 1978 (c 19)

*RA:* 30 Jun 1978

*Commencement provisions:* s 8(5)

Whole Act in force 1 Aug 1978 (s 8(5))

## Parliamentary Pensions Act 1978 (c 56)

*RA:* 2 Aug 1978

Whole Act in force 2 Aug 1978 (RA)

**Parochial Registers and Records Measure 1978 (No 2)**

*RA*: 2 Feb 1978

*Commencement provisions*: s 27(2)

Whole Measure in force 1 Jan 1979 (the day appointed by the Archbishops of Canterbury and York under s 27(2))

---

**Participation Agreements Act 1978 (c 1)**

*RA*: 23 Feb 1978

Whole Act in force 23 Feb 1978 (RA)

---

**Pensioners Payments Act 1978 (c 58)**

*RA*: 23 Nov 1978

Whole Act in force 23 Nov 1978 (RA)

---

**Protection of Children Act 1978 (c 37)**

*RA*: 20 Jul 1978

*Commencement provisions*: s 9(3)

| | |
|---|---|
| 1–7 | 20 Aug 1978 (s 9(3)) |
| 8, 9 | 20 Jul 1978 (s 9(3)) |

---

**Rating (Disabled Persons) Act 1978 (c 40)**

*RA*: 20 Jul 1978

*Commencement provisions*: s 9(4)

Whole Act in force 1 Apr 1979 (s 9(4))

---

**Refuse Disposal (Amenity) Act 1978 (c 3)**

*RA*: 23 Mar 1978

*Commencement provisions*: s 13(2)

Whole Act in force 23 Apr 1978 (s 13(2)), except ss 1(8), 4(2) (never in force (repealed)), 6(8)

---

**Representation of the People Act 1978 (c 32)**

*RA*: 20 Jul 1978

Whole Act in force 20 Jul 1978 (RA)

---

**Scotland Act 1978 (c 51)**

*RA*: 31 Jul 1978

*Commencement provisions*: s 83(1)

Never in force (repealed) (this Act was not to come into force until a date to be appointed by order made by the Secretary of State, and approved by a resolution of each House of Parliament. Before such an

**Scotland Act 1978 (c 51)**—*contd*

order could be made, a referendum was to be held. As a result of the referendum held on 1 Mar 1979 an order for repeal of the Act was passed: SI 1979/928)

**Shipbuilding (Redundancy Payments) Act 1978 (c 11)**

*RA:* 5 May 1978

Whole Act in force 5 May 1978 (RA)

**Solomon Islands Act 1978 (c 15)**

*RA:* 25 May 1978

Whole Act in force 25 May 1978 (RA) (but note that the Act did not generally have effect until 7 Jul 1978 (Independence Day))

**State Immunity Act 1978 (c 33)**

*RA:* 20 Jul 1978

*Commencement provisions:* s 23(5); State Immunity Act 1978 (Commencement) Order 1978, SI 1978/1572

Whole Act in force 22 Nov 1978 (SI 1978/1572) (note that Pts I, II of this Act do not apply to proceedings in respect of matters that occurred before 22 Nov 1978 (s 23(3), (4)))

**Statute Law (Repeals) Act 1978 (c 45)**

*RA:* 31 Jul 1978

Whole Act in force 31 Jul 1978 (RA)

**Suppression of Terrorism Act 1978 (c 26)**

*RA:* 30 Jun 1978

*Commencement provisions:* s 9(3); Suppression of Terrorism Act 1978 (Commencement) Order 1978, SI 1978/1063

Whole Act in force 21 Aug 1978 (SI 1978/1063)

**Theatres Trust (Scotland) Act 1978 (c 24)**

*RA:* 30 Jun 1978

Whole Act in force 30 Jun 1978 (RA)

**Theft Act 1978 (c 31)**

*RA:* 20 Jul 1978

*Commencement provisions:* s 7(2)

Whole Act in force 20 Oct 1978 (s 7(2))

**Transport Act 1978 (c 55)**

*RA:* 2 Aug 1978

*Commencement provisions:* s 24(1); Transport Act 1978 (Commencement No 1) Order 1978, SI 1978/1150; Transport Act 1978 (Commencement No 2) Order 1978, SI 1978/1187; Transport Act 1978 (Commencement No 3) Order 1978, SI 1978/1289

| | | |
|---|---|---|
| 1–4 | | 1 Sep 1978 (SI 1978/1187) |
| 5, 6 | | 1 Nov 1978 (SI 1978/1187) |
| 7 | | 1 Sep 1978 (SI 1978/1187) |
| 8 | | See Sch 2 below |
| 9 | | 1 Nov 1978 (SI 1978/1187) |
| 10–14 | | 1 Sep 1978 (SI 1978/1187) |
| 15 | | 4 Aug 1978 (SI 1978/1150) |
| 16 | | 1 Sep 1978 (SI 1978/1187) |
| 17, 18 | | 4 Aug 1978 (SI 1978/1150) |
| 19, 20 | | 1 Oct 1978 (SI 1978/1289) |
| 21 | | 4 Aug 1978 (SI 1978/1150) |
| 22 | | 1 Sep 1978 (SI 1978/1187) |
| 23 | | 4 Aug 1978 (SI 1978/1150) |
| 24 | (1)–(3) | 4 Aug 1978 (SI 1978/1150) |
| | (4) | See Sch 4 below |
| 25 | | 2 Aug 1978 (RA) |
| Sch 1 | | 1 Sep 1978 (SI 1978/1187) |
| Sch 2 | paras 1, 2 | 1 Sep 1978 (SI 1978/1187) |
| | paras 3–5 | 1 Nov 1978 (SI 1978/1187) |
| | paras 6, 7 | 1 Sep 1978 (SI 1978/1187) |
| Sch 3 | | 1 Nov 1978 (SI 1978/1187) |
| Sch 4 | | 4 Aug 1978 (repeals of or in Transport Act 1968, Sch 2, para 3) (SI 1978/1150) |
| | | 1 Sep 1978 (SI 1978/1187), repeals of or in— |
| | | Road Traffic Regulation Act 1967, s 6; |
| | | Transport Act 1968, s 30; |
| | | Transport (London) Act 1969, s 24(4); |
| | | Local Government Act 1972, s 203; |
| | | Local Government (Scotland) Act 1973, Sch 18; |
| | | Local Government Act 1974, s 6; |
| | | Minibus Act 1977, s 6 |
| | | 1 Nov 1978 (repeals of or in Road Traffic Act 1972, s 57(7)) (SI 1978/1187) |

---

**Trustee Savings Banks Act 1978 (c 16)**

*RA:* 30 Jun 1978

Whole Act in force 30 Jun 1978 (RA)

---

**Tuvalu Act 1978 (c 20)**

*RA:* 30 Jun 1978

Whole Act in force 30 Jun 1978 (but note that the Act did not generally have effect until 1 Oct 1978 (Independence Day))

---

**Wales Act 1978 (c 52)**

*RA:* 31 Jul 1978

*Commencement provisions:* s 79(1)

**Wales Act 1978 (c 52)**—*contd*

Never in force (repealed) (this Act was not to come into force until a date to be appointed by order made by the Secretary of State, and approved by a resolution of each House of Parliament. Before such an order could be made, a referendum was to be held. As a result of the referendum held on 1 Mar 1979 an order for repeal of the Act was passed: SI 1979/928)

# 1979 Acts

## Administration of Justice (Emergency Provisions) (Scotland) Act 1979 (c 19)

*RA:* 22 Mar 1979

*Commencement provisions:* s 1

Whole Act in force 23 Feb 1979 (s 1); note that this Act is deemed to have effect during the "emergency period" from 23 Feb 1979 until one month after the date prescribed by order by the Secretary of State

## Agricultural Statistics Act 1979 (c 13)

*RA:* 4 Apr 1979

*Commencement provisions:* s 8(2)

Whole Act in force 22 Apr 1979 (s 8(2))

## Alcoholic Liquor Duties Act 1979 (c 4)

*RA:* 22 Feb 1979

*Commencement provisions:* s 93(2)

Whole Act in force 1 Apr 1979 (s 93(2))

## Ancient Monuments and Archaeological Areas Act 1979 (c 46)

*RA:* 4 Apr 1979

*Commencement provisions:* s 65(2); Ancient Monuments and Archaeological Areas Act 1979 (Commencement No 1) Order 1979, SI 1979/786; Ancient Monuments and Archaeological Areas Act 1979 (Commencement No 2) Order 1981, SI 1981/1300; Ancient Monuments and Archaeological Areas Act 1979 (Commencement No 3) Order 1981, SI 1981/1466; Ancient Monuments and Archaeological Areas Act 1979 (Commencement No 4) Order 1982, SI 1982/362

| | |
|---|---|
| 1–32 | 9 Oct 1981 (E) (W) (SI 1981/1300) |
| | 30 Nov 1981 (S) (SI 1981/1466) |
| 33–41 | 14 Apr 1982 (E) (W) (SI 1982/362) |
| | *Not yet in force* (S) |
| 42–47 | 9 Oct 1981 (except so far as it relates to Pt II) (E) (W) (SI 1981/1300) |
| | 30 Nov 1981 (S) (SI 1981/1466) |
| | 14 Apr 1982 (so far as it relates to Pt II) (E) (W) (SI 1982/362) |
| 48, 49 | 16 Jul 1979 (E) (W) (SI 1979/786) |
| | 30 Nov 1981 (S) (SI 1981/1466) |
| 50–64 | 9 Oct 1981 (except so far as it relates to Pt II) (E) (W) (SI 1981/1300) |
| | 30 Nov 1981 (S) (SI 1981/1466) |
| | 14 Apr 1982 (so far as relates to Pt II) (E) (W) (SI 1982/362) |

**Ancient Monuments and Archaeological Areas Act 1979 (c 46)**—*contd*

| | | |
|---|---|---|
| 65 | | 4 Apr 1979 (RA) |
| Sch 1 | | 9 Oct 1981 (E) (W) (SI 1981/1300) |
| | | 30 Nov 1981 (S) (SI 1981/1466) |
| Sch 2 | | 14 Apr 1982 (E) (W) (SI 1982/362) |
| | | *Never in force* (S) (repealed) |
| Schs 3–5 | | 9 Oct 1981 (except so far as it relates to Pt II) (E) (W) (SI 1981/1300) |
| | | 30 Nov 1981 (S) (SI 1981/1466) |
| | | 14 Apr 1982 (so far as it relates to Pt II) (E) (W) (SI 1982/362) |

---

**Appropriation Act 1979 (c 24)**

*RA:* 4 Mar 1979

Whole Act in force 4 Mar 1979 (RA)

---

**Appropriation (No 2) Act 1979 (c 51)**

*RA:* 27 Jul 1979

Whole Act in force 27 Jul 1979 (RA)

---

**Arbitration Act 1979 (c 42)**

*RA:* 4 Apr 1979

*Commencement provisions:* s 8(2); Arbitration Act 1979 (Commencement) Order 1979, SI 1979/750

Whole Act in force 1 Aug 1979 (except in relation to arbitrations commenced before that date. If all the parties to a reference to arbitration which commenced before that date agree in writing that the Act should apply to that arbitration, the Act applies from 1 Aug 1979 or the date of the agreement whichever is the later) (SI 1979/750)

---

**Banking Act 1979 (c 37)**

*RA:* 4 Apr 1979

*Commencement provisions:* s 52(3), (4); Banking Act 1979 (Commencement No 1) Order 1979, SI 1979/938; Banking Act 1979 (Commencement No 2) Order 1982, SI 1982/188; Banking Act 1979 (Commencement No 3) Order 1985, SI 1985/797

| | | |
|---|---|---|
| 1–20 | | 1 Oct 1979 (SI 1979/938) |
| 21–33 | | 19 Feb 1982 (SI 1982/188) |
| 34–38 | | 1 Oct 1979 (SI 1979/938) |
| 39 | | 1 Jul 1985 (SI 1985/797) |
| 40–45 | | 1 Oct 1979 (SI 1979/938) |
| 46 | | 19 Feb 1982 (SI 1982/188) |
| 47 | | 1 Oct 1979 (SI 1979/938) |
| 48 | (1)–(6) | 1 Oct 1979 (SI 1979/938) |
| | (7) | *Never in force* (repealed) |
| 49, 50 | | 1 Oct 1979 (SI 1979/938) |
| 51 | (1) | See Sch 6 below |
| | (2) | See Sch 7 below |
| 52 | | 1 Oct 1979 (SI 1979/938) |
| Schs 1–4 | | 1 Oct 1979 (SI 1979/938) |
| Sch 5 | | 19 Feb 1982 (SI 1982/188) |
| Sch 6 | paras 1–3 | 19 Feb 1982 (SI 1982/188) |
| | paras 4, 5 | 1 Jul 1985 (SI 1985/797) |
| | paras 6, 7 | 19 Feb 1982 (SI 1982/188) |

**Banking Act 1979 (c 37)**—*contd*

|  | para 8 | *Never in force* (repealed) |
| | para 9 | 1 Jul 1985 (SI 1985/797) |
| | para 10 | *Never in force* (repealed) |
| | para 11 | 1 Jul 1985 (SI 1985/797) |
| | para 12 | *Never in force* (repealed) |
| | paras 13–17 | 19 Feb 1982 (SI 1982/188) |
| | para 18 | *Never in force* (repealed) |
| | para 19 | 19 Feb 1982 (SI 1982/188) |

Sch 7                                     19 Feb 1982 (SI 1982/188), repeals of or in—

Bank Charter Act 1844;

Bank Notes (Scotland) Act 1845;

Inland Revenue Act 1880;

Limited Partnerships Act 1907;

Companies Act 1948;

Companies Act (Northern Ireland) 1960;

Companies Act 1967, ss 119–121;

Post Office Act 1969;

Companies Act 1976;

Companies (Northern Ireland) Order 1978, arts 133–135

1 Jul 1985 (SI 1985/797), repeals of or in—

Protection of Depositors Act 1963;

Protection of Depositors Act (Northern Ireland) 1964;

Financial Provisions Act (Northern Ireland) 1968;

Post Office (Banking Services) Act 1976;

Trustee Savings Bank Act 1976;

Companies (Northern Ireland) Order 1978, Sch 6, Pt II

---

**Capital Gains Tax Act 1979 (c 14)**

*RA:* 22 Mar 1979

*Commencement provisions:* s 156

This Act generally came into force in relation to tax for the year 1979/1980 and thereafter, and in relation to tax for other chargeable periods beginning after 5 Apr 1979 (s 156(1))

So much of any provision as authorises the making of orders or other instruments, or which confers any powers or imposes any duty the exercise or performance of which operates or may operate in relation to tax for more than one chargeable period (except where the tax is all for chargeable periods to which this Act does not apply), came into operation on 6 Apr 1979 (s 156(2))

---

**Carriage by Air and Road Act 1979 (c 28)**

*RA:* 4 Apr 1979

*Commencement provisions:* ss 2(2), 7(2); Carriage by Air and Road Act 1979 (Commencement No 1) Order 1980, SI 1980/1966; Carriage by Air and Road Act 1979 (Commencement No 2) Order 1997, SI 1997/2565; Carriage by Air and Road Act 1979 (Commencement No 3) Order 1998, SI 1998/2562; Carriage by Air and Road Act 1979 (Commencement No 4) Order 2000, SI 2000/2768

| 1 | | *Not yet in force* |
| 2 | | 4 Apr 1979 (does not apply to loss which occurred before that date) (s 2(2)) |
| 3 | (1) | 22 Oct 1998 (SI 1998/2562) |
| | (2) | 12 Oct 2000 (SI 2000/2768) |
| | (3) | 28 Dec 1980 (SI 1980/1966) |
| | (4) | *Never in force* (repealed) |
| 4 | (1) | 1 Dec 1997 (SI 1997/2565) |
| | (2) | 28 Dec 1980 (SI 1980/1966) |

**Carriage by Air and Road Act 1979 (c 28)**—*contd*

|         |         |                                                                                               |
|---------|---------|-----------------------------------------------------------------------------------------------|
| (3)     |         | *Never in force* (repealed)                                                                   |
| (4)     |         | 28 Dec 1980 (so far as it relates to amendment of Carriage of Goods by Road Act 1965 by s 4(2)) (SI 1980/1966) |
|         |         | 1 Dec 1997 (so far as it relates to amendment of Carriage by Air Act 1961 by s 4(1)) (SI 1997/2565) |
|         |         | *Never in force* (otherwise) (repealed)                                                       |
| 5       |         | 28 Dec 1980 (so far as it relates to amendment of Carriage of Goods by Road Act 1965 by s 4(2)) (SI 1980/1966) |
|         |         | 1 Dec 1997 (so far as it relates to amendment of Carriage by Air Act 1961 by s 4(1)) (SI 1997/2565) |
|         |         | *Never in force* (otherwise) (repealed)                                                       |
| 6       | (1)(a)  | 1 Dec 1997 (so far as it relates to Carriage by Air Act 1961, ss 9, 10) (SI 1997/2565)        |
|         |         | 12 Oct 2000 (otherwise) (SI 2000/2768)                                                        |
|         | (1)(b)  | 28 Dec 1980 (SI 1980/1966)                                                                    |
|         | (1)(c)  | *Never in force* (repealed)                                                                   |
|         | (2)     | *Not yet in force*                                                                            |
|         | (3)     | 1 Dec 1997 (so far as it relates to the provisions specified in SI 1997/2565, Schedule) (SI 1997/2565) |
|         |         | 12 Oct 2000 (so far as it relates to the provisions specified in SI 2000/2768, Schedule) (SI 2000/2768) |
|         | (4)     | *Not yet in force* (sub-s (4)(b) repealed)                                                    |
| 7       |         | 4 Apr 1979 (RA)                                                                               |
| Schs 1, 2 |       | *Not yet in force* (Sch 2, para 5 repealed)                                                   |

---

**Charging Orders Act 1979 (c 53)**

*RA:* 6 Dec 1979

*Commencement provisions:* s 8(2); Charging Orders Act 1979 (Commencement) Order 1980, SI 1980/627

Whole Act in force 3 Jun 1980 (SI 1980/627)

---

**Confirmation to Small Estates (Scotland) Act 1979 (c 22)**

*RA:* 29 Mar 1979

*Commencement provisions:* s 3(2); Confirmation to Small Estates (Scotland) Act 1979 (Commencement) Order 1980, SI 1980/734

|          |                             |
|----------|-----------------------------|
| 1, 2     | 1 Jul 1980 (SI 1980/734)    |
| 3        | 29 Mar 1979 (RA)            |
| Schedule | 1 Jul 1980 (SI 1980/734)    |

---

**Consolidated Fund Act 1979 (c 20)**

*RA:* 22 Mar 1979

Whole Act in force 22 Mar 1979 (RA)

---

**Consolidated Fund (No 2) Act 1979 (c 56)**

*RA:* 20 Dec 1979

Whole Act in force 20 Dec 1979 (RA)

---

## Credit Unions Act 1979 (c 34)

*RA:* 4 Apr 1979

*Commencement provisions:* s 33(2); Credit Unions Act 1979 (Commencement No 1) Order 1979, SI 1979/936; Credit Unions Act 1979 (Commencement No 2) Order 1980, SI 1980/481; Credit Unions Act 1979 (Commencement No 3) Order 2003, SI 2003/306

| | | |
|---|---|---|
| 1, 2 | | 20 Aug 1979 (SI 1979/936) |
| 3 | (1) | 20 Aug 1979 (SI 1979/936) |
| | (2), (3) | 1 Sep 2003 (SI 2003/306) |
| | (4) | 20 Aug 1979 (SI 1979/936) |
| 4–14 | | 20 Aug 1979 (SI 1979/936) |
| 15 | | 1 Oct 1980 (SI 1980/481) |
| 16–31 | | 20 Aug 1979 (SI 1979/936) |
| 32, 33 | | 4 Apr 1979 (s 33(2)) |
| Schs 1–3 | | 20 Aug 1979 (SI 1979/936) |

## Criminal Evidence Act 1979 (c 16)

*RA:* 22 Mar 1979

*Commencement provisions:* s 2(2)

Whole Act in force 22 Apr 1979 (s 2(2))

## Crown Agents Act 1979 (c 43)

*RA:* 4 Apr 1979

4 Apr 1979 (RA); but note that most of the provisions of the Act became effective from 1 Jan 1980, the day appointed by the Crown Agents Act 1979 (Appointed Day) Order 1979, SI 1979/1672, made under s 1(1)

## Customs and Excise Duties (General Reliefs) Act 1979 (c 3)

*RA:* 22 Feb 1979

*Commencement provisions:* ss 20(2), 59(7), 62(2)

Whole Act in force 1 Apr 1979 (s 20(2))

## Customs and Excise Management Act 1979 (c 2)

*RA:* 22 Feb 1979

*Commencement provisions:* ss 59(7), 62(2), 178(3)

Whole Act in force 1 Apr 1979 (s 178(3)); except ss 59, 62(2) (these sections shall not come into force until such day as the Commissioners may appoint by statutory instrument)

## Education Act 1979 (c 49)

*RA:* 26 Jul 1979

Whole Act in force 26 Jul 1979 (RA)

## Electricity (Scotland) Act 1979 (c 11)

*RA:* 22 Mar 1979

*Commencement provisions:* s 47(4)

Whole Act in force 22 Apr 1979 (s 47(4))

## Estate Agents Act 1979 (c 38)

*RA:* 4 Apr 1979

*Commencement provisions:* s 36(2); Estate Agents Act 1979 (Commencement No 1) Order 1981, SI 1981/1517

| | |
|---|---|
| 1–15 | 3 May 1982 (SI 1981/1517) |
| 16, 17 | *Not yet in force* |
| 18 | 3 May 1982 (SI 1981/1517) |
| 19 | *Not yet in force* |
| 20, 21 | 3 May 1982 (SI 1981/1517) |
| 22 | *Not yet in force* |
| 23–34 | 3 May 1982 (SI 1981/1517) |
| 35 | *Never in force* (repealed) |
| 36 | 3 May 1982 (SI 1981/1517) |
| Schs 1, 2 | 3 May 1982 (SI 1981/1517) |

## European Communities (Greek Accession) Act 1979 (c 57)

*RA:* 20 Dec 1979

Whole Act in force 20 Dec 1979 (RA); but note that the accession of Greece to the European Communities did not take effect until 1 Jan 1981

## European Parliament (Pay and Pensions) Act 1979 (c 50)

*RA:* 26 Jul 1979

Whole Act in force 26 Jul 1979 (RA)

## Exchange Equalisation Account Act 1979 (c 30)

*RA:* 4 Apr 1979

*Commencement provisions:* s 5(3)

Whole Act in force 5 May 1979 (s 5(3))

## Excise Duties (Surcharges or Rebates) Act 1979 (c 8)

*RA:* 22 Feb 1979

*Commencement provisions:* s 5(2)

Whole Act in force 1 Apr 1979 (s 5(2))

## Films Act 1979 (c 9)

*RA:* 22 Feb 1979

Whole Act in force 22 Feb 1979 (RA)

---

## Finance Act 1979 (c 25)

*RA:* 4 Apr 1979

The commencement details of Finance Acts are not set out, as the dates from which their provisions take effect are usually stated clearly and unambiguously in the text of the Act, and charging provisions will normally state for which year or years of assessment they are to have effect.

---

## Finance (No 2) Act 1979 (c 47)

*Budget Day:* 12 Jun 1979

*RA:* 26 Jul 1979

The commencement details of Finance Acts are not set out, as the dates from which their provisions take effect are usually stated clearly and unambiguously in the text of the Act, and charging provisions will normally state for which year or years of assessment they are to have effect.

---

## Forestry Act 1979 (c 21)

*RA:* 29 Mar 1979

*Commencement provisions:* s 3(3)

Whole Act in force 30 May 1979 (s 3(3))

---

## House of Commons (Redistribution of Seats) Act 1979 (c 15)

*RA:* 22 Mar 1979

Whole Act in force 22 Mar 1979 (RA)

---

## Hydrocarbon Oil Duties Act 1979 (c 5)

*RA:* 22 Feb 1979

*Commencement provisions:* s 29(2)

Whole Act in force 1 Apr 1979 (s 29(2))

---

## Independent Broadcasting Authority Act 1979 (c 35)

*RA:* 4 Apr 1979

Whole Act in force 4 Apr 1979 (RA)

---

## Industry Act 1979 (c 32)

*RA:* 4 Apr 1979

Whole Act in force 4 Apr 1979 (RA)

---

## International Monetary Fund Act 1979 (c 29)

*RA:* 4 Apr 1979

*Commencement provisions:* s 7(2)

Whole Act in force 5 May 1979 (s 7(2))

---

## Isle of Man Act 1979 (c 58)

*RA:* 20 Dec 1979

*Commencement provisions:* s 14(6), (7)

| | |
|---|---|
| 1–5 | 1 Apr 1980 (s 14(6)) |
| 6, 7 | 20 Dec 1979 (subject to the provision that no Order in Council and no provision by virtue of s 6(5) or 7(5) be made by or under an Act of Tynwald so as to come into force before 1 Apr 1980) (s 14(7)) |
| 8, 9 | 1 Apr 1980 (s 14(6)) |
| 10 | 20 Dec 1979 (s 14(7)) |
| 11 | 20 Dec 1979 (subject to the provision that no Order in Council be made under this section so as to come into force before 1 Apr 1980) (s 14(7)) |
| 12–14 | 1 Apr 1980 (s 14(6)) |
| Schs 1, 2 | 1 Apr 1980 (s 14(6)) |

---

## Justices of the Peace Act 1979 (c 55)

*RA:* 6 Dec 1979

*Commencement provisions:* s 72(2)

Whole Act in force 6 Mar 1979 (s 72(2))

---

## Kiribati Act 1979 (c 27)

*RA:* 19 Jun 1979

Whole Act in force 19 Jun 1979 (RA); note that most provisions of this Act did not take effect until 12 Jul 1979 (that is, "Independence Day" (s 1(1))

---

## Land Registration (Scotland) Act 1979 (c 33)

*RA:* 4 Apr 1979

*Commencement provisions:* s 30(2); Land Registration (Scotland) Act 1979 (Commencement No 1) Order 1980, SI 1980/1412; Land Registration (Scotland) Act 1979 (Commencement No 2) Order 1982, SI 1982/520; Land Registration (Scotland) Act 1979 (Commencement No 3) Order 1983, SI 1983/745; Land Registration (Scotland) Act 1979 (Commencement No 4) Order 1985, SI 1985/501; Land Registration (Scotland) Act 1979 (Commencement No 5) Order 1992, SI 1992/815; Land Registration (Scotland) Act 1979 (Commencement No 6) Order 1992, SI 1992/2060; Land Registration (Scotland) Act 1979 (Commencement No 7) Order 1993, SI 1993/922; Land Registration (Scotland) Act 1979 (Commencement No 8) Order 1994, SI 1994/2588; Land Registration (Scotland) Act 1979 (Commencement No 9) Order 1995, SI 1995/2547; Land Registration (Scotland) Act 1979 (Commencement No 10) Order 1996, SI 1996/2490; Land Registration (Scotland) Act 1979 (Commencement No 11) Order 1998, SI 1998/1810; Land Registration (Scotland) Act 1979 (Commencement No 12) Order 1998, SI 1998/2980; Land Registration (Scotland) Act 1979 (Commencement No 13) Order 1999, SSI 1999/111; Land Registration (Scotland) Act 1979 (Commencement No 14)

**Land Registration (Scotland) Act 1979 (c 33)**—*contd*

Order 2000, SSI 2000/338; Land Registration (Scotland) Act 1979 (Commencement No 15) Order 2001, SSI 2001/309; Land Registration (Scotland) Act 1979 (Commencement No 16) Order 2002, SSI 2002/432

| | | |
|---|---|---|
| 1 | | 4 Apr 1979 (s 30(2)) |
| 2 | (1), (2) | 6 Apr 1981 (in the area, for the purpose of registration of writs, of the County of Renfrew) (SI 1980/1412) |
| | | 4 Oct 1982 (in the area, for the purpose of registration of writs, of the County of Dunbarton) (SI 1982/520) |
| | | 3 Jan 1984 (in the area, for the purpose of registration of writs, of the County of Lanark) (SI 1983/745) |
| | | 30 Sep 1985 (in the area, for the purpose of registration of writs, of the Barony and Regality of Glasgow) (SI 1985/501) |
| | | 1 Oct 1992 (in the area, for the purpose of registration of writs, of the County of Clackmannan) (SI 1992/815) |
| | | 1 Apr 1993 (in the area, for the purpose of registration of writs, of the County of Stirling) (SI 1992/2060) |
| | | 1 Oct 1993 (in the area, for the purpose of registration of writs, of the County of West Lothian) (SI 1993/922) |
| | | 1 Apr 1995 (in the area, for the purpose of registration of writs, of the County of Fife) (SI 1994/2588) |
| | | 1 Apr 1996 (in the areas, for the purpose of registration of writs, of the Counties of Aberdeen and Kincardine) (SI 1995/2547) |
| | | 1 Apr 1997 (in the areas, for the purpose of registration of writs, of the Counties of Ayr, Dumfries, Stewartry of Kirkcudbright and Wigtown) (SI 1996/2490) |
| | | 1 Apr 1999 (in the areas, for the purpose of registration of writs, of the Counties of Perth, Angus and Kinross) (SI 1998/1810) |
| | | 1 Oct 1999 (in the areas, for the purpose of registration of writs, of the Counties of Berwick, East Lothian, Roxburgh, Selkirk and Peebles) (SI 1998/2980) |
| | | 1 Apr 2000 (in the areas, for the purpose of registration of writs, of the Counties of Argyll and Bute) (SSI 1999/111) |
| | | 1 Apr 2001 (in the area, for the purpose of registration of writs, of the County of Midlothian) (SSI 2000/338) |
| | | 1 Apr 2002 (in the areas, for the purpose of registration of writs, of the Counties of Inverness and Nairn) (SSI 2001/309) |
| | | 1 Apr 2003 (in the areas, for the purpose of registration of writs, of the Counties of Banff, Moray, Ross and Cromarty, Caithness, Sutherland, Orkney and Zetland) (SSI 2002/432) |
| | (3)–(6) | 6 Apr 1981 (SI 1980/1412) |
| 3 | (1), (2) | 6 Apr 1981 (SI 1980/1412) |
| | (3) | 6 Apr 1981 (in the area, for the purpose of registration of writs, of the County of Renfrew) (SI 1980/1412) |
| | | 4 Oct 1982 (in the area for the purpose of registration of writs, of the County of Dunbarton) (SI 1982/520) |
| | | 3 Jan 1984 (in the area, for the purpose of registration of writs, of the County of Lanark) (SI 1983/745) |
| | | 30 Sep 1985 (in the area, for the purpose of registration of writs, of the Barony and Regality of Glasgow) (SI 1985/501) |
| | | 1 Oct 1992 (in the area, for the purpose of registration of writs, of the County of Clackmannan) (SI 1992/815) |
| | | 1 Apr 1993 (in the area, for the purpose of registration of writs, of the County of Stirling) (SI 1992/2060) |
| | | 1 Oct 1993 (in the area, for the purpose of registration of writs, of the County of West Lothian) (SI 1993/922) |
| | | 1 Apr 1995 (in the area, for the purpose of registration of writs, of the County of Fife) (SI 1994/2588) |
| | | 1 Apr 1996 (in the areas, for the purpose of registration of writs, of the Counties of Aberdeen and Kincardine) (SI 1995/2547) |

## Land Registration (Scotland) Act 1979 (c 33)—*contd*

|  |  |
|---|---|
| | 1 Apr 1997 (in the areas, for the purpose of registration of writs, of the Counties of Ayr, Dumfries, Stewartry of Kirkcudbright and Wigtown) (SI 1996/2490) |
| | 1 Apr 1999 (in the areas, for the purpose of registration of writs, of the Counties of Perth, Angus and Kinross) (SI 1998/1810) |
| | 1 Oct 1999 (in the areas, for the purpose of registration of writs, of the Counties of Berwick, East Lothian, Roxburgh, Selkirk and Peebles) (SI 1998/2980) |
| | 1 Apr 2000 (in the areas, for the purpose of registration of writs, of the Counties of Argyll and Bute) (SSI 1999/111) |
| | 1 Apr 2001 (in the area, for the purpose of registration of writs, of the County of Midlothian) (SSI 2000/338) |
| | 1 Apr 2002 (in the areas, for the purpose of registration of writs, of the Counties of Inverness and Nairn) (SSI 2001/309) |
| | 1 Apr 2003 (in the areas, for the purpose of registration of writs, of the Counties of Banff, Moray, Ross and Cromarty, Caithness, Sutherland, Orkney and Zetland) (SSI 2002/432) |
| (4)–(7) | 6 Apr 1981 (SI 1980/1412) |
| 4–15 | 6 Apr 1981 (SI 1980/1412) |
| 16–23 | 4 Apr 1979 (s 30(2)) |
| 24–29 | 4 Apr 1979 (so far as relate to ss 1, 16–23, 30) (s 30(2)) |
| | 6 Apr 1981 (otherwise) (SI 1980/1412) |
| 30 | 4 Apr 1979 (s 30(2)) |
| Sch 1 | 4 Apr 1979 (s 30(2)) |
| Schs 2–4 | 4 Apr 1979 (so far as it relates to ss 1, 16–23, 30) (s 30(2)) |
| | 6 Apr 1981 (otherwise) (SI 1980/1412) |

## Leasehold Reform Act 1979 (c 44)

*RA:* 4 Apr 1979

Whole Act in force 4 Apr 1979 (RA)

## Legal Aid Act 1979 (c 26)

*RA:* 4 Apr 1979

*Commencement provisions:* s 14(3); Legal Aid Act 1979 (Commencement No 1) Order 1979, SI 1979/756; Legal Aid Act 1979 (Commencement No 1) (Scotland) Order 1979, SI 1979/826; Legal Aid Act 1979 (Commencement No 2) Order 1980, SI 1980/476

| | | |
|---|---|---|
| 1–3 | | 28 Apr 1980 (SI 1980/476) |
| 4 | | 20 Jul 1979 (SI 1979/756) |
| 5 | | 28 Apr 1980 (SI 1980/476) |
| 6–8 | | *Never in force* (repealed) |
| 9 | | 20 Jul 1979 (SI 1979/826) |
| 10 | | *Never in force* (repealed) |
| 11, 12 | | 28 Apr 1980 (SI 1980/476) |
| 13 | (1) | See Sch 1 below |
| | (2) | See Sch 2 below |
| 14 | | No specified date |
| Sch 1 | paras 1–12 | 28 Apr 1980 (SI 1980/476) |
| | para 13 | 20 Jul 1979 (SI 1979/756) |
| | paras 14–20 | 28 Apr 1980 (SI 1980/476) |
| Sch 2 | | 20 Jul 1979 (for the purposes of the repeal in the Legal Aid Act 1974, s 9(2)(qv)) (SI 1979/756) |
| | | 28 Apr 1980 (otherwise) (SI 1980/476) |

## Matches and Mechanical Lighters Duties Act 1979 (c 6)

*RA:* 22 Feb 1979

*Commencement provisions:* s 10(2)

Whole Act in force 1 Apr 1979 (s 10(2))

## Merchant Shipping Act 1979 (c 39)

*RA:* 4 Apr 1979

*Commencement provisions:* s 52(2); Merchant Shipping Act 1979 (Commencement No 1) Order 1979, SI 1979/807; Merchant Shipping Act 1979 (Commencement No 2) Order 1979, SI 1979/1578; Merchant Shipping Act 1979 (Commencement No 3) Order 1980, SI 1980/354; Merchant Shipping Act 1979 (Commencement No 4) Order 1980, SI 1980/923; Carriage of Passengers and their Luggage by Sea (Interim Provisions) Order 1980, SI 1980/1092, as amended by SI 1987/670; Merchant Shipping Act 1979 (Commencement No 5) Order 1981, SI 1981/405; Merchant Shipping Act 1979 (Commencement No 6) Order 1982, SI 1982/1616; Merchant Shipping Act 1979 (Commencement No 7) Order 1983, SI 1983/440; Merchant Shipping Act 1979 (Commencement No 8) Order 1983, SI 1983/1312; Merchant Shipping Act 1979 (Commencement No 9) Order 1985, SI 1985/1827; Merchant Shipping Act 1979 (Commencement No 10) Order 1986, SI 1986/1052; Merchant Shipping Act 1979 (Commencement No 11) Order 1987, SI 1987/635; Merchant Shipping Act 1979 (Commencement No 12) Order 1987, SI 1987/719; Merchant Shipping Act 1979 (Commencement No 13) Order 1987, SI 1989/1881

| | | |
|---|---|---|
| 1–6 | | 1 Aug 1979 (SI 1979/807) |
| 7 | | 1 Sep 1980 (SI 1980/923) |
| 8 | (1), (2) | 4 Jul 1980 (SI 1980/923) |
| | (3) | *Never in force* (repealed) |
| | (4) | 4 Jul 1980 (SI 1980/923) |
| | (5) | *Never in force* (repealed) |
| | (6) | 4 Jul 1980 (in so far as it relates to the repeal of Pilotage Act 1913, s 13) (SI 1980/923) |
| | | *Never in force* (in so far as it relates to the repeal of Pilotage Act 1913, s 14) (repealed) |
| 9 | | 1 Sep 1980 (SI 1980/923) |
| 10 | | 4 Jul 1980 (SI 1980/923) |
| 11 | | 1 Sep 1980 (SI 1980/923) |
| 12 | | 1 Aug 1979 (SI 1979/807) |
| 13 | (1) | See Sch 2 below |
| | (2)–(4) | 1 Jan 1980 (SI 1979/807) |
| | (5) | 1 Aug 1979 (SI 1979/807) |
| 14 | (1), (2) | 30 Apr 1987 (SI 1987/635) |
| | (3) | 10 Nov 1989 (SI 1989/1881) |
| | (4), (5) | 30 Apr 1987 (SI 1987/635) |
| | (6) | 30 Apr 1987 (except in its application to sub-s (3) of this section) (SI 1987/635) |
| | | 10 Nov 1989 (otherwise) (SI 1989/1881) |
| | (7) | 30 Apr 1987 (SI 1987/635) |
| 15 | (1) | 17 Dec 1979 (SI 1979/1578) |
| | (2) | 17 Dec 1979 (from words "and any" to the end) (SI 1979/1578) |
| | | 30 Apr 1987 (otherwise) (SI 1987/635) |
| | (3) | *Never in force* (repealed) |
| 16 | | 1 Aug 1979 (SI 1979/807) |
| 17, 18 | | 1 Dec 1986 (SI 1986/1052) |
| 19 | (1) | 1 Dec 1986 (SI 1986/1052) |
| | (2), (3) | 17 Dec 1979 (SI 1979/1578) |
| | (4) | 1 Dec 1986 (SI 1986/1052) |
| 20–22 | | 1 Aug 1979 (SI 1979/807) |
| 23 | (1)–(6) | *Never in force* (repealed) |
| | (7) | 31 Dec 1985 (SI 1985/1827) |

**Merchant Shipping Act 1979 (c 39)**—*contd*

| | | |
|---|---|---|
| 24, 25 | | *Never in force* (repealed) |
| 26 | | 1 Aug 1979 (SI 1979/807) |
| 27, 28 | | 1 Oct 1979 (SI 1979/807) |
| 29, 30 | | 1 Jan 1980 (SI 1979/807) |
| 31 | | 3 May 1983 (SI 1983/440) |
| 32 | (1) | 1 Aug 1979 (SI 1979/807) |
| | (2), (3) | 1 Jul 1983 (SI 1982/1616) |
| 33, 34 | | 1 Aug 1979 (SI 1979/807) |
| 35 | (1) | 1 Aug 1979 (except in so far as it applies to fishing vessels) (SI 1979/807) |
| | | *Never in force* (exception noted above) (repealed) |
| | (2) | 30 Apr 1987 (except in so far as it applies to fishing vessels) (SI 1987/719) |
| | | 10 Nov 1989 (otherwise) (SI 1989/1881) |
| 36 | (1) | 1 Aug 1979 (SI 1979/807) |
| | (2) | 1 Apr 1980 (SI 1980/354) |
| | (3) | 1 Aug 1979 (SI 1979/807) |
| 37 | (1)–(3) | 1 Aug 1979 (SI 1979/807) |
| | (4) | 1 Jan 1983 (SI 1982/1616) |
| | (5) | 1 Aug 1979 (SI 1979/807) |
| | (6) | *Never in force* (repealed) |
| | (7), (8) | 1 Aug 1979 (SI 1979/807) |
| 38 | (1)–(3) | 8 Apr 1981 (SI 1981/405) |
| | (4) | *Never in force* (repealed) |
| | (5) | 17 Dec 1979 (SI 1979/1578) |
| | (6) | 8 Apr 1981 (SI 1981/405) |
| 39–41 | | 1 Aug 1979 (SI 1979/807) |
| 42–45 | | 1 Jan 1980 (SI 1979/807) |
| 46 | | 1 Oct 1979 (except in sub-s (1) the words and figures "23(6)" and "or 44(1)") (SI 1979/807) |
| | | 4 Jul 1980 (otherwise) (SI 1980/923) |
| 47 | (1) | 1 Aug 1979 (SI 1979/807) (this subsection was also purportedly brought into force on 17 Dec 1979 by SI 1979/1578) |
| | (2) | 1 Aug 1979 (so far as it relates to ss 21, 22, 26, 32(1), 35(1) except in so far as it applies to fishing vessels, 37(2), (3), (5), (7), (8), 39, 41, 49, 50(1), (2), (4), so far as it relates to those provisions of Sch 7, Pt II, which came into force on 1 Aug 1979, and s 52) (SI 1979/807) |
| | | 1 Oct 1979 (so far as it relates to ss 27, 28, 46 and 50(4) so far as the last relates to those provisions of Sch 7, Pt II which came into force on 1 Oct 1979) (SI 1979/807) |
| | | 17 Dec 1979 (so far as it relates to ss 48–52 and Sch 7, Pt I) (SI 1979/1578) |
| | | 1 Jan 1980 (so far as it relates to ss 45, 50(4) so far as the latter relate to those provisions of Sch 7, Pt II which came into force on 1 Jan 1980) (SI 1979/807) |
| | | 14 Sep 1983 (otherwise) (SI 1983/1312) |
| | (3) | 1 Aug 1979 (SI 1979/807) (this subsection was also purportedly brought into force on 17 Dec 1979 by SI 1979/1578) |
| 48, 49 | | 1 Aug 1979 (SI 1979/807) |
| 50 | (1), (2) | 1 Aug 1979 (SI 1979/807) |
| | (3) | 4 Jul 1980 (SI 1980/923) |
| | (4) | See Sch 7 below |
| 51 | (1) | 1 Aug 1979 (SI 1979/807) |
| | (2) | 1 Jan 1983 (so far as it relates to s 38(2)) (SI 1982/1616) |
| | | *Never in force* (otherwise) (repealed) |
| | (3) | 1 Aug 1979 (SI 1979/807) |
| 52 | | 1 Aug 1979 (SI 1979/807) |
| Sch 1 | | 1 Aug 1979 (SI 1979/807) |
| Sch 2 | paras 1–4 | 1 Aug 1979 (SI 1979/807) |

**Merchant Shipping Act 1979 (c 39)**—*contd*

|  |  |  |
|---|---|---|
| | para 5(1) | 4 Jul 1980 (SI 1980/923) |
| | para 5(2) | 1 Aug 1979 (SI 1979/807) |
| | paras 6, 7 | 1 Aug 1979 (SI 1979/807) |
| | paras 8, 9 | 4 Jul 1980 (SI 1980/923) |
| | para 10(1) | 4 Jul 1980 (SI 1980/923) |
| | para 10(2) | 1 Aug 1979 (SI 1979/807) |
| | para 11 | 1 Aug 1979 (SI 1979/807) |
| | para 12 | 1 Jan 1980 (SI 1979/807) |
| | para 13(1), (2) | *Never in force* (repealed) |
| | para 13(3) | 4 Jul 1980 (SI 1980/923) |
| | paras 14–19 | 1 Aug 1979 (SI 1979/807) |
| | para 20(1) | 1 Aug 1979 (SI 1979/807) |
| | para 20(2) | 1 Aug 1979 (words from "In section 44(3)" to "on summary conviction") (SI 1979/807) |
| | | 4 Jul 1980 (words from "and the words" to the end) (SI 1980/923) |
| | | *Never in force* (otherwise) (repealed) |
| | para 21 | 1 Aug 1979 (SI 1979/807) |
| | para 22 | 1 Jan 1980 (SI 1979/807) |
| | paras 23–27 | 1 Aug 1979 (SI 1979/807) |
| Sch 3 | Pts I, II | 1 Jan 1981 (brought into force for some purposes, with modifications, by the Carriage of Passengers and their Luggage by Sea (Interim Provisions) Order 1980) (SI 1980/1092) |
| | | 30 Apr 1987 (otherwise) (SI 1987/635) |
| | Pt III | 1 Jan 1981 (brought into force for some purposes, with modifications, by the Carriage of Passengers and their Luggage by Sea (Interim Provisions) Order 1980) (SI 1980/1092) |
| | | 10 Nov 1989 (otherwise) (SI 1989/1881) |
| Schs 4, 5 | | 1 Dec 1986 (SI 1986/1052) |
| Sch 6 | | 1 Jan 1980 (SI 1979/807) |
| Sch 7 | Pt I | 1 Dec 1986 (SI 1986/1052) |
| | Pt II | 1 Aug 1979 (SI 1979/807), repeals of or in— |
| | | Merchant Shipping Act 1894, ss 637, 638, 640, 641, 670–672, 675, 677; |
| | | Merchant Shipping (Mercantile Marine Fund) Act 1898, ss 2(1), (2), 7, Sch 3, para II; |
| | | Pilotage Act 1913, ss 1, 2, 6, 7(4), 8, 9, 17(1)(i), 22, 30, 33, 35, 39, 48, 56, 58, 59; |
| | | Merchant Shipping (Load Lines) Act 1967, s 27; |
| | | Merchant Shipping Act 1970, s 15 |
| | | 1 Oct 1979 (SI 1979/807), repeals of or in— |
| | | Merchant Shipping Act 1894, ss 369, 420, 431, 729, 730; |
| | | Merchant Shipping Act 1964; |
| | | Merchant Shipping (Load Lines) Act 1967, ss 11, 17, 24; |
| | | Fishing Vessels (Safety Provisions) Act 1970; |
| | | Prevention of Oil Pollution Act 1971 |
| | | 1 Jan 1980 (SI 1979//807), repeals of or in— |
| | | Merchant Shipping Act 1894, ss 73, 360, 446, 457, 724; |
| | | Merchant Shipping Act 1906; |
| | | Merchant Shipping (Safety Convention) Act 1949; |
| | | Merchant Shipping (Load Lines) Act 1967, s 4, Sch 1; |
| | | Merchant Shipping Act 1970, s 6, Schs 2, 5; |
| | | Merchant Shipping Act 1974, s 19(2); |
| | | Criminal Procedure (Scotland) Act 1975; |
| | | Criminal Law Act 1977 |
| | | 1 Apr 1980 (repeal of or in Merchant Shipping (Mercantile Marine Fund) Act 1898, s 5, Sch 2) (SI 1980/354) |
| | | 4 Jul 1980 (SI 1980/923), repeals of or in— |
| | | Pilotage Act 1913, ss 11, 14, 24; |
| | | Aliens Restriction (Amendment) Act 1919 |

**Merchant Shipping Act 1979 (c 39)**—*contd*

                1 Sep 1980 (repeals of or in Pilotage Act 1913, ss 7(5), (6), 17(1)(f), (h), 34, Sch 1) (SI 1980/923)

                8 Apr 1981 (repeals of or in Merchant Shipping (Oil Pollution) Act 1971) (SI 1981/405)

                3 May 1983 (repeals of or in Merchant Shipping Act 1965) (SI 1983/440)

                31 Dec 1985 (SI 1985/1827), repeals of or in—
                Merchant Shipping Act 1970, ss 34–38, 95(1)(a);
                Merchant Shipping Act 1974, s 19(5)

                *Never in force* (repealed), repeals of or in—
                Pilotage Act 1913, ss 7(1), 10, 13, 32(2);
                Merchant Shipping Act 1970, s 99(1);
                Merchant Shipping Act 1974, ss 1, 19(6)

**Nurses, Midwives and Health Visitors Act 1979 (c 36)**

*RA:* 4 Apr 1979

*Commencement provisions:* s 24(2); Nurses, Midwives and Health Visitors Act 1979 (Commencement No 1) Order 1980, SI 1980/893; Nurses, Midwives and Health Visitors Act 1979 (Commencement No 2) Order 1982, SI 1982/963; Nurses, Midwives and Health Visitors Act 1979 (Commencement No 3) Order 1982, SI 1982/1565; Nurses, Midwives and Health Visitors Act 1979 (Commencement No 4) Order 1983, SI 1983/668

| | | |
|---|---|---|
| 1 | | 1 Nov 1980 (SI 1980/893) |
| 2 | | 1 Jul 1983 (SI 1983/668) |
| 3 | (1) | 1 Nov 1980 (in so far as it relates to the Finance Committee and s 3(2)) (SI 1980/893) |
| | | 1 Dec 1982 (otherwise) (SI 1982/1565) |
| | (2) | 1 Nov 1980 (SI 1980/893) |
| | (3) | 1 Dec 1982 (SI 1982/1565) |
| | (4)(a) | 1 Nov 1980 (in so far as it relates to the Finance Committee and s 3(2)) (SI 1980/893) |
| | | 1 Dec 1982 (otherwise) (SI 1982/1565) |
| | (4)(b) | 1 Dec 1982 (SI 1982/1565) |
| 4 | | 1 Jul 1983 (SI 1983/668) |
| 5 | | 15 Sep 1980 (SI 1980/893) |
| 6 | | 1 Jul 1983 (SI 1983/668) |
| 7 | (1) | 15 Sep 1980 (in so far as it relates to the Finance Committee and s 7(5)) (SI 1980/893) |
| | | 1 Dec 1982 (otherwise) (SI 1982/1565) |
| | (2)–(4) | 1 Dec 1982 (SI 1982/1565) |
| | (5) | 15 Sep 1980 (SI 1980/893) |
| | (6) | 1 Dec 1982 (SI 1982/1565) |
| | (7)(a) | 15 Sep 1980 (in so far as it relates to the Finance Committee and s 7(5)) (SI 1980/893) |
| | | 1 Dec 1982 (otherwise) (SI 1982/1565) |
| | (7)(b) | 1 Dec 1982 (SI 1982/1565) |
| 8 | | 1 Dec 1982 (SI 1982/1565) |
| 9–17 | | 1 Jul 1983 (SI 1983/668) |
| 18 | | *Never in force* (repealed) |
| 19 | (1), (2) | 1 Jul 1983 (SI 1983/668) |
| | (3)(a) | 15 Sep 1980 (in so far as they relate to National Boards) (SI 1980/893) |
| | | 1 Nov 1980 (otherwise) (SI 1980/893) |
| | (3)(b) | 1 Jul 1983 (SI 1983/668) |
| | (4), (5) | 15 Sep 1980 (in so far as they relate to National Boards) (SI 1980/893) |
| | | 1 Nov 1980 (otherwise) (SI 1980/893) |

**Nurses, Midwives and Health Visitors Act 1979 (c 36)**—*contd*

| | | |
|---|---|---|
| 20 | | 15 Sep 1980 (in so far as they relate to National Boards) (SI 1980/893) |
| | | 1 Nov 1980 (otherwise) (SI 1980/893) |
| 21 | (1) | 1 Jul 1983 (SI 1983/668) |
| | (2) | 4 Apr 1979 (s 24(2)) |
| | (3), (4) | 1 Jul 1983 (SI 1983/668) |
| 22 | | 1 Jul 1983 (SI 1983/668) |
| 23 | (1)–(3) | 15 Sep 1980 (SI 1980/893) |
| | (4), (5) | 1 Jul 1983 (SI 1983/668) |
| 24 | | 4 Apr 1979 (s 24(2)) |
| Sch 1 | paras 1–5 | 1 Nov 1980 (SI 1980/893) |
| | para 6(1) | 1 Nov 1980 (SI 1980/893) |
| | para 6(2) | 1 Nov 1983 (SI 1982/963) |
| | para 6(3)–(7) | 1 Nov 1980 (SI 1980/893) |
| | paras 7, 8 | 1 Nov 1980 (SI 1980/893) |
| Sch 2 | Pt I | 1 Nov 1980 (SI 1980/893) |
| | Pt II | 15 Sep 1980 (SI 1980/893) |
| Sch 3 | | 1 Jul 1983 (SI 1983/668) |
| Sch 4 | | 15 Sep 1980 (in so far as it relates to National Boards) (SI 1980/893) |
| | | 1 Nov 1980 (otherwise) (SI 1980/893) |
| Sch 5 | | 1 Jul 1983 (SI 1983/668) |
| Sch 6 | | 15 Sep 1980 (SI 1980/893) |
| Schs 7, 8 | | 1 Jul 1983 (SI 1983/668) |

**Pensioners' Payments and Social Security Act 1979 (c 48)**

*RA:* 26 Jul 1979

Whole Act in force 26 Jul 1979 (RA)

**Pneumoconiosis etc (Workers' Compensation) Act 1979 (c 41)**

*RA:* 4 Apr 1979

*Commencement provisions:* s 10(3)

Whole Act in force 4 Jul 1979 (s 10(3))

**Price Commission (Amendment) Act 1979 (c 1)**

*RA:* 12 Feb 1979

Whole Act in force 12 Feb 1979 (RA)

**Prosecution of Offences Act 1979 (c 31)**

*RA:* 4 Apr 1979

*Commencement provisions:* s 12(2)

Whole Act in force 4 May 1979 (s 12(2))

## Public Health Laboratory Service Act 1979 (c 23)

*RA:* 29 Mar 1979

Whole Act in force 29 Mar 1979 (RA)

## Public Lending Right Act 1979 (c 10)

*RA:* 22 Mar 1979

*Commencement provisions:* s 5(3); Public Lending Right Act 1979 (Commencement) Order 1980, SI 1980/83

Whole Act in force 1 Mar 1980 (SI 1980/83)

## Representation of the People Act 1979 (c 40)

*RA:* 4 Apr 1979

Whole Act in force 4 Apr 1979 (RA)

## Sale of Goods Act 1979 (c 54)

*RA:* 6 Dec 1979

*Commencement provisions:* s 64(2)

Whole Act in force 1 Jan 1980 (s 64(2))

## Shipbuilding Act 1979 (c 59)

*RA:* 20 Dec 1979

Whole Act in force 20 Dec 1979 (RA)

## Social Security Act 1979 (c 18)

*RA:* 22 Mar 1979

*Commencement provisions:* s 21(2), (3); Social Security Act 1979 (Commencement No 1) Order 1979, SI 1979/369; Social Security Act 1979 (Commencement No 2) Order 1979, SI 1979/1031

| | | |
|---|---|---|
| 1, 2 | | 22 Mar 1979 (RA) |
| 3 | (1), (2) | 22 Mar 1979 (RA) |
| | (3) | 22 Mar 1979 (in relation to beneficiaries other than those mentioned below) (RA) |
| | | 29 Mar 1979 (in relation to women born on or after 7 Jun 1918 but before 23 Mar 1919, for purposes of the making and determination of claims) (SI 1979/369) |
| | | 6 Jun 1979 (in relation to women born between dates specified above, for all other purposes) (SI 1979/369) |
| | | 5 Sep 1979 (in relation to women born on or after 29 Nov 1914 but before 7 Jun 1918, for purposes of the making and determination of claims) (SI 1979/1031) |
| | | 28 Nov 1979 (in relation to women born between dates specified immediately above, for all other purposes) (SI 1979/1031) |
| | (4), (5) | 22 Mar 1979 (RA) |
| 4–10 | | 22 Mar 1979 (RA) |
| 11, 12 | | 6 Apr 1979 (s 21(3)) |
| 13–21 | | 22 Mar 1979 (RA) |

## Social Security Act 1979 (c 18)—*contd*

| | | |
|---|---|---|
| Sch 1 | para 1 | 22 Mar 1979 (RA) |
| | paras 2–22 | 6 Apr 1979 (s 21(3)) |
| Sch 2 | | 22 Mar 1979 (RA) |
| Sch 3 | paras 1–4 | 22 Mar 1979 (RA) |
| | paras 5–7 | 6 Apr 1979 (s 21(3)) |
| | paras 8–10 | 22 Mar 1979 (RA) |
| | para 11 | 6 Apr 1979 (s 21(3)) |
| | paras 12, 13 | 22 Mar 1979 (RA) |
| | paras 14–20 | 6 Apr 1979 (s 21(3)) |
| | para 21 | 22 Mar 1979 (RA) |
| | paras 22, 23 | 6 Apr 1979 (s 21(3)) |
| | paras 24–28 | 22 Mar 1979 (RA) |
| | para 29(a), (b) | 6 Apr 1979 (s 21(3)) |
| | para 29(c) | 22 Mar 1979 (RA) |
| | paras 30–32 | 22 Mar 1979 (RA) |

## Southern Rhodesia Act 1979 (c 52)

*RA:* 14 Nov 1979

Whole Act in force 14 Nov 1979 (RA); but note that this Act did not generally take effect until 18 Apr 1980 (the date appointed under the Zimbabwe Act 1979, s 1(1))

## Tobacco Products Duty Act 1979 (c 7)

*RA:* 22 Feb 1979

*Commencement provisions:* s 12(2)

Whole Act in force 1 Apr 1979 (s 12(2))

## Vaccine Damage Payments Act 1979 (c 17)

*RA:* 22 Feb 1979

Whole Act in force 22 Feb 1979 (RA)

## Wages Councils Act 1979 (c 12)

*RA:* 22 Mar 1979

*Commencement provisions:* s 32(2)

Whole Act in force 22 Apr 1979 (s 32(2))

## Weights and Measures Act 1979 (c 45)

*RA:* 4 Apr 1979

*Commencement provisions:* s 24(3); Weights and Measures Act 1979 (Commencement No 1) Order 1979, SI 1979/1228

| | |
|---|---|
| 1–5 | 1 Jan 1980 (s 24(3)(a)) |
| 6, 7 | 2 Oct 1979 (SI 1979/1228) |
| 8–13 | 1 Jan 1980 (s 24(3)(a)) |
| 14 | 4 Apr 1979 (s 24(3)) |
| 15 | 1 Jan 1980 (s 24(3)(a)) |
| 16–18 | 4 Apr 1979 (s 24(3)) |

**Weights and Measures Act 1979 (c 45)**—*contd*

| | | |
|---|---|---|
| 19 | | *Never in force* (repealed) |
| 20 | | See Sch 5 below |
| 21, 22 | | 4 Apr 1979 (s 24(3)) |
| 23 | | See Sch 7 below |
| 24 | | 4 Apr 1979 (s 24(3)) |
| Schs 1, 2 | | 1 Jan 1980 (s 24(3)(a)) |
| Sch 3 | | 2 Oct 1979 (SI 1979/1228) |
| Sch 4 | | 4 Apr 1979 (s 24(3)) |
| Sch 5 | para 1 | 4 Oct 1979 (s 24(3)(c)) |
| | paras 2–15 | 4 Apr 1979 (s 24(3)) |
| | para 16 | 1 Jan 1980 (s 24(3)(a)) |
| | paras 17–21 | 4 Apr 1979 (s 24(3)) |
| Sch 6 | | 4 Apr 1979 (s 24(3)) |
| Sch 7 | | 1 Jan 1980 (so far as it relates to Weights and Measures Act 1963 (other than s 60 and the figures "60(3)" in s 54(4)(c)) and 1976) (s 24(3)(a)) |
| | | 4 Apr 1979 (otherwise) (s 24(3)) |

---

**Zimbabwe Act 1979 (c 60)**

*RA:* 20 Dec 1979

Whole Act in force 20 Dec 1979 (RA) (but note that this Act did not generally take effect until 18 Apr 1980 (the date appointed as Independence Day under s 1(1)))

---

# 1980 Acts

## Anguilla Act 1980 (c 67)

*RA:* 16 Dec 1980

Whole Act in force 16 Dec 1980 (RA; but note the Anguilla (Appointed Day) Order 1980, SI 1980/1953, appointing 19 Dec 1980 for the purposes of s 1(1) (repealed))

---

## Appropriation Act 1980 (c 54)

*RA:* 8 Aug 1980

Whole Act in force 8 Aug 1980 (RA)

---

## Bail etc (Scotland) Act 1980 (c 4)

*RA:* 31 Jan 1980

*Commencement provisions:* s 13(2); Bail etc (Scotland) Act 1980 (Commencement) Order 1980, SI 1980/315

| | |
|---|---|
| 1–12 | 31 Mar 1980 (SI 1980/315) |
| 13 | 31 Jan 1980 (RA) |
| Schs 1, 2 | 31 Mar 1980 (SI 1980/315) |

---

## Bees Act 1980 (c 12)

*RA:* 20 Mar 1980

*Commencement provisions:* s 5(2); Bees Act 1980 (Commencement) Order 1980, SI 1980/791

Whole Act in force 10 Jun 1980 (SI 1980/791)

---

## Betting, Gaming and Lotteries (Amendment) Act 1980 (c 18)

*RA:* 31 Mar 1980

Whole Act in force 31 Mar 1980 (RA)

---

## British Aerospace Act 1980 (c 26)

*RA:* 1 May 1980

Whole Act in force 1 May 1980 (RA); but Act largely took effect on 1 Jan 1981, the day appointed under s 14(1)

---

## Broadcasting Act 1980 (c 64)

*RA:* 13 Nov 1980

*Commencement provisions:* s 41(4), (5); Broadcasting Act 1980 (Commencement No 1) Order 1980, SI 1980/1907; Broadcasting Act 1980 (Commencement No 2) Order 1981, SI 1981/759; Broadcasting Act 1980 (Commencement No 3) Order 1981, SI 1981/1262

| | | |
|---|---|---|
| 1 | | 13 Nov 1980 (s 41(4)(a)) |
| 2–16 | | 1 Jan 1981 (SI 1980/1907) |
| 17 | | 1 Feb 1981 (SI 1980/1907) |
| 18–23 | | 1 Jun 1981 (SI 1981/759) |
| 24 | | 1 Feb 1981 (SI 1980/1907) |
| 25 | | 1 Jun 1981 (SI 1981/759) |
| 26, 27 | | 1 Oct 1981 (SI 1981/1262) |
| 28, 29 | | 1 Feb 1981 (SI 1980/1907) |
| 30 | | 1 Jan 1981 (SI 1980/1907) |
| 31, 32 | | 13 Nov 1980 (s 41(4)(a)) |
| 33 | | 1 Jan 1981 (SI 1980/1907) |
| 34 | | 13 Nov 1980 (s 41(4)(a)) |
| 35 | | 1 Jan 1982 (SI 1981/1262) |
| 36–39 | | 13 Nov 1980 (s 41(4)(a)) |
| 40 | (1)–(3) | 13 Nov 1980 (s 41(4)(a)) |
| | (4) | See Sch 6 below |
| | (5) | 1 Oct 1981 (SI 1981/1262) |
| | (6) | See Sch 7 below |
| 41 | | 13 Nov 1980 (s 41(4)(a)) |
| Schs 1, 2 | | 1 Jan 1981 (SI 1980/1907) |
| Sch 3 | | 1 Feb 1981 (SI 1980/1907) |
| Sch 4 | | 1 Oct 1981 (SI 1981/1262) |
| Sch 5 | | 1 Feb 1981 (SI 1980/1907) |
| Sch 6 | para 1 | 1 Feb 1981 (so far as applies to s 24) (SI 1980/1907) |
| | | 1 Jun 1981 (so far as applies to s 20) (SI 1981/759) |
| | | 1 Oct 1981 (so far as applies to s 26) (SI 1981/1262) |
| | | 1 Jan 1982 (so far as applies to s 35) (SI 1981/1262) |
| | para 2 | 1 Oct 1981 (SI 1981/1262) |
| | paras 3, 4 | 1 Jan 1981 (SI 1980/1907) |
| Sch 7 | | 13 Nov 1980 (s 41(4)(a)), repeals of or in— |
| | | Independent Broadcasting Authority Act 1973, ss 18, 19; |
| | | Independent Broadcasting Authority (No 2) Act 1974; |
| | | Independent Broadcasting Authority Act 1978 |
| | | 1 Jan 1981 (repeal of Independent Broadcasting Authority Act 1973, s 34) (SI 1980/1907) |
| | | 1 Oct 1981 (otherwise) (SI 1981/1262) |

## Child Care Act 1980 (c 5)

*RA:* 31 Jan 1980

*Commencement provisions:* s 90; Child Care Act 1980 (Commencement) Order 1980, SI 1980/1935

| | | |
|---|---|---|
| 1–6 | | 1 Apr 1981 (SI 1980/1935) |
| 7 | | 27 May 1984 (SI 1983/1946) |
| 8–19 | | 1 Apr 1981 (SI 1980/1935) |
| 20 | | *Never in force* (repealed) |
| 21–30 | | 1 Apr 1981 (SI 1980/1935) |
| 31 | (1)–(3) | 1 Apr 1981 (SI 1980/1935) |
| | (4) | See Sch 1 below |
| | (5) | 1 Apr 1981 (SI 1980/1935) |
| 32–54 | | 1 Apr 1981 (SI 1980/1935) |
| 55 | (1)–(3) | 1 Apr 1981 (SI 1980/1935) |
| | (4) | See Sch 2 below |

## Child Care Act 1980 (c 5)—*contd*

| | | |
|---|---|---|
| | (5) | 1 Apr 1981 (SI 1980/1935) |
| 56, 57 | | 1 Apr 1981 (SI 1980/1935) |
| 58 | (1) | 1 Apr 1981 (SI 1980/1935) |
| | (2) | See Sch 3 below |
| | (3)–(6) | 1 Apr 1981 (SI 1980/1935) |
| 59 | | See Schs 4–6 below |
| 60–63 | | 1 Apr 1981 (SI 1980/1935) |
| 64–67 | | 15 Feb 1982 (SI 1981/1792) |
| 68–91 | | 1 Apr 1981 (SI 1980/1935) |
| Schs 1–6 | | 1 Apr 1981 (SI 1980/1935) |

## Civil Aviation Act 1980 (c 60)

*RA:* 13 Nov 1980

*Commencement provisions:* ss 10(1), 12; Civil Aviation Act 1980 (Commencement) Order 1981, SI 1981/671; Civil Aviation Act 1980 (Appointed Day) Order 1983, SI 1983/1940

| | |
|---|---|
| 1–10 | 13 Nov 1980 (RA), but not effective until 1 Apr 1984, the day appointed under s 10(1) by SI 1983/1940 |
| 11 | 13 Nov 1980 (RA) |
| 12 | 22 May 1981 (SI 1981/671) |
| 13–27 | 13 Nov 1980 (RA) |
| 28 | See Sch 3 below |
| 29–31 | 13 Nov 1980 (RA) |
| Schs 1, 2 | 13 Nov 1980 (RA) |
| Sch 3 | 13 Nov 1980 (except repeal of Civil Aviation Act 1971, s 24(2)) (RA) |
| | 22 May 1981 (exception noted above) (SI 1981/671) |

## Coal Industry Act 1980 (c 50)

*RA:* 8 Aug 1980

Whole Act in force 8 Aug 1980 (RA)

## Companies Act 1980 (c 22)

*RA:* 1 May 1980

*Commencement provisions:* Companies Act 1980 (Commencement) Order 1980, SI 1980/745; Companies Act 1980 (Commencement No 2) Order 1980, SI 1980/1785; Companies Act 1980 (Commencement No 3) Order 1981, SI 1981/1683; Companies Act 1980 (Commencement No 4) Order 1983, SI 1983/1022

| | | |
|---|---|---|
| 1–45 | | 22 Dec 1980 (SI 1980/1785) |
| 46 | | 23 Jun 1980 (SI 1980/745) |
| 47–64 | | 22 Dec 1980 (SI 1980/1785) |
| 65 | | 22 Dec 1980 (except words "either" and "or has another subsidiary which is not a private company; or" in para (b) of definition "relevant company", and para (c) of that definition) (SI 1980/1785) |
| | | 22 Dec 1981 (exceptions noted above) (SI 1981/1683) |
| 66, 67 | | 22 Dec 1980 (SI 1980/1785) |
| 68–73 | | 23 Jun 1980 (SI 1980/745) |
| 74–79 | | 22 Dec 1980 (SI 1980/1785) |
| 80, 81 | | 23 Jun 1980 (SI 1980/745) |
| 82 | (a)–(e) | 22 Dec 1980 (SI 1980/1785) |
| | (f) | 1 Oct 1983 (SI 1983/1022) |
| 83 | | 23 Jun 1980 (SI 1980/745) |

**Companies Act 1980 (c 22)**—*contd*

| | | |
|---|---|---|
| 84 | (1)(a), (b) | 22 Dec 1980 (SI 1980/1785) |
| | (1)(c) | 23 Jun 1980 (SI 1980/745) |
| | (1)(d) | 22 Dec 1980 (SI 1980/1785) |
| | (2), (3) | 23 Jun 1980 (SI 1980/745) |
| 85 | | 22 Dec 1980 (SI 1980/1785) |
| 86 | | 23 Jun 1980 (in so far as it applies for the purposes of the provisions brought into operation by SI 1980/745) (SI 1980/745) |
| | | 22 Dec 1980 (otherwise) (SI 1980/1785) |
| 87 | (1) | 23 Jun 1980 (SI 1980/745) |
| | (2)–(4) | 22 Dec 1980 (SI 1980/1785) |
| | (5)–(7) | 23 Jun 1980 (SI 1980/745) |
| 88 | | See Schs 3, 4 below |
| 89, 90 | | 23 Jun 1980 (SI 1980/745) |
| Sch 1 | | 22 Dec 1980 (SI 1980/1785) |
| Sch 2 | | 23 Jun 1980 (SI 1980/745) |
| Sch 3 | paras 1–9 | 22 Dec 1980 (SI 1980/1785) |
| | para 10(a) | 23 Jun 1980 (SI 1980/745) |
| | para 10(b) | 22 Dec 1980 (SI 1980/1785) |
| | paras 11–17 | 22 Dec 1980 (SI 1980/1785) |
| | para 18(a) | 22 Dec 1980 (SI 1980/1785) |
| | para 18(b) | 23 Jun 1980 (SI 1980/745) |
| | paras 19, 20(a) | 22 Dec 1980 (SI 1980/1785) |
| | para 20(b) | 23 Jun 1980 (SI 1980/745) |
| | paras 21–23 | 22 Dec 1980 (SI 1980/1785) |
| | para 24 | 23 Jun 1980 (SI 1980/745) |
| | paras 25–32 | 22 Dec 1980 (SI 1980/1785) |
| | para 33 | 23 Jun 1980 (SI 1980/745) |
| | paras 34–40 | 22 Dec 1980 (SI 1980/1785) |
| | para 41(1), (2) | 23 Jun 1980 (SI 1980/745) |
| | para 41(3) | 22 Dec 1980 (SI 1980/1785) |
| | para 42 | 23 Jun 1980 (SI 1980/745) |
| | paras 43–49 | 22 Dec 1980 (SI 1980/1785) |
| | paras 50, 51 | 23 Jun 1980 (SI 1980/745) |
| | para 52 | 22 Dec 1980 (SI 1980/1785) |
| Sch 4 | | 23 Jun 1980 (SI 1980/745), repeals of or in— |
| | | Companies Act 1948, ss 13, 440; |
| | | Companies Act 1967, s 49; |
| | | Companies Act 1976, s 30; |
| | | Criminal Law Act 1977 |
| | | 22 Dec 1980 (otherwise, except repeals of Companies Act 1948, s 438, Sch 15) (SI 1980/1785) |
| | | 1 Oct 1983 (exceptions noted above) (SI 1983/1022) |

---

**Competition Act 1980 (c 21)**

*RA:* 3 Apr 1980

*Commencement provisions:* s 33(5); Competition Act 1980 (Commencement No 1) Order 1980, SI 1980/497; Competition Act 1980 (Commencement No 2) Order 1980, SI 1980/978

| | | |
|---|---|---|
| 1 | | 4 Apr 1980 (SI 1980/497) |
| 2 | | 12 Aug 1980 (SI 1980/978) |
| 3 | (1)–(6) | 12 Aug 1980 (SI 1980/978) |
| | (7), (8) | 1 May 1980 (as applied by s 13(7)) (SI 1980/497) |
| | | 12 Aug 1980 (otherwise) (SI 1980/978) |
| 4–10 | | 12 Aug 1980 (SI 1980/978) |
| 11 | (1), (2) | 4 Apr 1980 (SI 1980/497) |
| | (3)(a) | 4 Apr 1980 (SI 1980/497) |

**Competition Act 1980 (c 21)**—*contd*

| | | |
|---|---|---|
| | (3)(b) | 12 Aug 1980 (SI 1980/978) |
| | (3)(c)–(e) | 4 Apr 1980 (SI 1980/497) |
| | (3)(f) | 4 Apr 1980 (except so far as relates to s 11(3)(b)) (SI 1980/497) |
| | | 12 Aug 1980 (exception noted above) (SI 1980/978) |
| | (4), (5) | 12 Aug 1980 (SI 1980/978) |
| | (6)–(11) | 4 Apr 1980 (SI 1980/497) |
| 12–14 | | 1 May 1980 (SI 1980/497) |
| 15 | (1) | 1 May 1980 (SI 1980/497) |
| | (2)(a), (b) | 12 Aug 1980 (SI 1980/978) |
| | (2)(c) | 4 Apr 1980 (for purposes of s 11) (SI 1980/497) |
| | | 12 Aug 1980 (otherwise) (SI 1980/978) |
| | (3), (4) | 12 Aug 1980 (SI 1980/978) |
| | (5) | 4 Apr 1980 (for purposes of s 11) (SI 1980/497) |
| | | 12 Aug (otherwise) (SI 1980/978) |
| 16 | | 4 Apr 1980 (for purposes of reports under s 11) (SI 1980/497) |
| | | 12 Aug 1980 (otherwise) (SI 1980/978) |
| 17 | (1) | 4 Apr 1980 (for purposes of reports under s 11) (SI 1980/497) |
| | | 1 May 1980 (for purposes of reports under s 13) (SI 1980/497) |
| | | 12 Aug 1980 (otherwise) (SI 1980/978) |
| | (2) | 4 Apr 1980 (for purposes of reports under s 11) (SI 1980/497) |
| | | 12 Aug 1980 (otherwise) (SI 1980/978) |
| | (3)–(5) | 4 Apr 1980 (for purposes of reports under s 11) (SI 1980/497) |
| | | 1 May 1980 (for purposes of reports under s 13) (SI 1980/497) |
| | | 12 Aug 1980 (otherwise) (SI 1980/978) |
| | (6) | 1 May 1980 (for purposes of reports under s 12) (SI 1980/497) |
| | | 12 Aug 1980 (otherwise) (SI 1980/978) |
| 18 | | 1 May 1980 (SI 1980/497) |
| 19 | | 4 Apr 1980 (SI 1980/497) |
| 20–22 | | 1 May 1980 (SI 1980/497) |
| 23 | | 4 Apr 1980 (SI 1980/497) |
| 24–30 | | 1 May 1980 (SI 1980/497) |
| 31 | (1) | 4 Apr 1980 (SI 1980/497) |
| | (2) | 12 Aug 1980 (SI 1980/978) |
| | (3) | 1 May 1980 (for purposes of s 12) (SI 1980/497) |
| | | 12 Aug 1980 (otherwise) (SI 1980/978) |
| | (4) | 1 May 1980 (SI 1980/497) |
| 32 | | 4 Apr 1980 (SI 1980/497) |
| 33 | (1), (2) | 4 Apr 1980 (SI 1980/497) |
| | (3) | 1 May 1980 (SI 1980/497) |
| | (4) | See Sch 2 below |
| | (5)–(8) | 4 Apr 1980 (SI 1980/497) |
| Sch 1 | | 4 Apr 1980 (SI 1980/457) |
| Sch 2 | | 4 Apr 1980 (except as noted below) (SI 1980/457) |
| | | 1 Jan 2011 (SI 1980/497), repeals of or in— |
| | | Counter-Inflation Act 1973, ss 17(6), (8), (9), 18(4), (5), 19, 20(4), (5)(i), (iii), (7), 23(2), Sch 4, para 4 (except sub-para (2)(b)); |
| | | Price Commission Act 1977, s 15(4), Sch 2, para 4(b), (d) |

## Concessionary Travel for Handicapped Persons (Scotland) Act 1980 (c 29)

*RA:* 23 May 1980

Whole Act in force 23 May 1980 (RA)

## Consolidated Fund Act 1980 (c 14)

*RA:* 20 Mar 1980

Whole Act in force 20 Mar 1980 (RA)

## Consolidated Fund (No 2) Act 1980 (c 68)

*RA:* 18 Dec 1980

Whole Act in force 18 Dec 1980 (RA)

---

## Consular Fees Act 1980 (c 23)

*RA:* 1 May 1980

Whole Act in force 1 May 1980 (RA)

---

## Coroners Act 1980 (c 38)

*RA:* 17 Jul 1980

Whole Act in force 17 Jul 1980 (RA)

---

## Criminal Appeal (Northern Ireland) Act 1980 (c 47)

*RA:* 1 Aug 1980

*Commencement provisions:* s 52(2)

Whole Act in force 1 Sep 1980 (s 52(2))

---

## Criminal Justice (Scotland) Act 1980 (c 62)

*RA:* 13 Mar 1980

*Commencement provisions:* s 84(2); Criminal Justice (Scotland) Act 1980 (Commencement No 1) Order 1981, SI 1981/50; Criminal Justice (Scotland) Act 1980 (Commencement No 2) Order 1981, SI 1981/444; Criminal Justice (Scotland) Act 1980 (Commencement No 3) Order 1981, SI 1981/766; Criminal Justice (Scotland) Act 1980 (Commencement No 4) Order 1981, SI 1981/1751; Criminal Justice (Scotland) Act 1980 (Commencement No 5) Order 1983, SI 1983/1580

| | |
|---|---|
| 1 | 1 Feb 1981 (SI 1981/50) |
| 2, 3 | 1 Jun 1981 (SI 1981/766) |
| 4 | 1 Feb 1981 (SI 1981/50) |
| 5 | 1 Jun 1981 (SI 1981/766) |
| 6 | 1 Jan 1982 (SI 1982/1751) |
| 7–9 | 1 Feb 1981 (SI 1981/50) |
| 10 | 1 Apr 1981 (SI 1981/444) |
| 11 | 1 Feb 1981 (SI 1981/50) |
| 12, 13 | 1 Jan 1982 (SI 1982/1751) |
| 14, 15 | 1 Feb 1981 (SI 1981/50) |
| 16 | 1 Jan 1982 (SI 1982/1751) |
| 17–30 | 1 Feb 1981 (SI 1981/50) |
| 31 | *Never in force* (repealed) |
| 32 | 1 Feb 1981 (SI 1981/50) |
| 33–35 | 1 Apr 1981 (SI 1981/444) |
| 36 | 1 Jan 1982 (SI 1982/1751) |
| 37–42 | 1 Feb 1981 (SI 1981/50) |
| 43, 44 | 1 Apr 1981 (SI 1981/444) |
| 45 | 15 Nov 1983 (SI 1983/1580) |
| 46–50 | 1 Feb 1981 (SI 1981/50) |
| 51 | 1 Jun 1981 (SI 1981/766) |
| 52–57 | 1 Feb 1981 (SI 1981/50) |
| 58–67 | 1 Apr 1981 (SI 1981/444) |
| 68–82 | 1 Feb 1981 (SI 1981/50) |

**Criminal Justice (Scotland) Act 1980 (c 62)**—*contd*

| | | |
|---|---|---|
| 83 | | See Schs 6–8 below |
| 84 | (1)–(4) | 1 Feb 1981 (SI 1981/50) |
| | (5) | 1 Feb 1981 (for purposes of extending to England and Wales ss 22, 84(1)–(5), Sch 6, paras 2, 8, Sch 7, paras 8, 9, 11(a), 24(c), 58, 79, Sch 8 (so far as repeals Criminal Procedure (Scotland) Act 1975, s 365)) (SI 1981/50) |
| | | 1 Apr 1981 (for purposes of extending to England and Wales s 66, Sch 6, para 9) (SI 1981/444) |
| | | 1 Jun 1981 (for purposes of extending to England and Wales s 51, Sch 6, para 10) (SI 1981/766) |
| | | 15 Nov 1983 (for purposes of extending to England and Wales Sch 7, paras 6(a), 10, 24(a), (b)(i), (ii), (d)(i), (ii), Sch 8 (so far as repeals Criminal Justice Act 1961, s 32(2)(b) and words in ss 32(2)(f), 38(3)(a))) (SI 1983/1580) |
| | (6) | 1 Feb 1981 (for purposes of extending to Northern Ireland ss 22, 84(1)–(4), (6), Sch 6, paras 2, 8, Sch 7, paras 8, 9, 11(a), 77) (SI 1981/50) |
| | | 1 Apr 1981 (for purposes of extending to Northern Ireland s 66, Sch 6, para 9) (SI 1981/444) |
| | | 1 Jun 1981 (for purposes of extending to Northern Ireland s 51, Sch 6, para 10) (SI 1981/766) |
| | | 15 Nov 1983 (for purposes of extending to Northern Ireland Sch 7, paras 6(a), 10, Sch 8 (so far as repeals Criminal Justice Act 1961, s 32(2)(b) and words in ss 32(2)(f), 38(3)(a))) (SI 1983/1580) |
| | (7) | 15 Nov 1983 (for purposes of extending to Channel Islands and Isle of Man s 84(1)–(4), (7), Sch 7, paras 6(a), 10(a), Sch 8 (so far as repeals Criminal Justice Act 1961, s 32(2)(b))) (SI 1983/1580) |
| Sch 1 | | 1 Feb 1981 (SI 1981/50) |
| Schs 2, 3 | | 1 Apr 1981 (SI 1981/444) |
| Sch 4 | | 1 Jan 1982 (SI 1981/1751) |
| Sch 5 | | *Never in force* (repealed) |
| Sch 6 | paras 1–8 | 1 Feb 1981 (SI 1981/50) |
| | para 9 | 1 Apr 1981 (SI 1981/444) |
| | para 10 | 1 Jun 1981 (SI 1981/766) |
| Sch 7 | para 1 | 1 Feb 1981 (SI 1981/50) |
| | paras 2–4 | 15 Nov 1983 (SI 1983/1580) |
| | para 5(a) | 15 Nov 1983 (SI 1983/1580) |
| | para 5(b) | 1 Feb 1981 (SI 1981/50) |
| | para 5(c) | *Never in force* (repealed) |
| | para 6(a), (b) | 15 Nov 1983 (SI 1983/1580) |
| | para 6(c) | 1 Apr 1981 (SI 1981/444) |
| | paras 7–9 | 1 Feb 1981 (SI 1981/50) |
| | para 10 | 15 Nov 1983 (SI 1983/1580) |
| | para 11(a) | 1 Feb 1981 (SI 1981/50) |
| | para 11(b) | *Never in force* (repealed) |
| | para 12 | *Never in force* (repealed) |
| | para 13 | 1 Feb 1981 (SI 1981/50) |
| | para 14 | 15 Nov 1983 (SI 1983/1580) |
| | para 15(a) | *Never in force* (repealed) |
| | para 15(b) | 15 Nov 1983 (SI 1983/1580) |
| | para 16 | 1 Feb 1981 (SI 1981/50) |
| | para 17 | 15 Nov 1983 (SI 1983/1580) |
| | para 18 | 1 Apr 1981 (SI 1981/444) |
| | para 19(a) | 1 Apr 1981 (SI 1981/444) |
| | para 19(b) | 1 Apr 1981 (for the purpose of bringing Criminal Justice Act 1967, s 62(12) into force and in so far as relating to the Criminal Procedure (Scotland) Act 1975, s 205(3)) (SI 1981/444) |
| | | *Never in force* (otherwise) (repealed) |

**Criminal Justice (Scotland) Act 1980 (c 62)**—*contd*

| | |
|---|---|
| paras 20–22 | 1 Feb 1981 (SI 1981/50) |
| para 23 | 1 Apr 1981 (SI 1981/444) |
| para 24(a) | 1 Apr 1981 (SI 1981/444) |
| para 24(b)(i) | 1 Apr 1981 (SI 1981/444) |
| para 24(b)(ii) | 15 Nov 1983 (SI 1983/1580) |
| para 24(c) | 1 Feb 1981 (SI 1981/50) |
| para 24(d)(i) | 15 Nov 1983 (SI 1983/1580) |
| para 24(d)(ii) | 1 Apr 1981 (SI 1981/444) |
| para 25 | 1 Jun 1981 (SI 1981/766) |
| paras 26–30 | 1 Feb 1981 (SI 1981/50) |
| para 31 | 1 Jan 1982 (SI 1981/1751) |
| para 32 | 1 Apr 1981 (SI 1981/444) |
| paras 33–37 | 1 Feb 1981 (SI 1981/50) |
| para 38 | 15 Nov 1983 (SI 1983/1580) |
| para 39 | 1 Feb 1981 (SI 1981/50) |
| para 40 | 15 Nov 1983 (SI 1983/1580) |
| paras 41–45 | 1 Apr 1981 (SI 1981/444) |
| para 46 | 15 Nov 1983 (SI 1983/1580) |
| paras 47–51 | 1 Feb 1981 (SI 1981/50) |
| para 52 | 1 Jun 1981 (SI 1981/766) |
| paras 53–59 | 1 Feb 1981 (SI 1981/50) |
| para 60 | 15 Nov 1983 (SI 1983/1580) |
| paras 61–66 | 1 Feb 1981 (SI 1981/50) |
| paras 67, 68 | 15 Nov 1983 (SI 1983/1580) |
| para 69 | 1 Feb 1981 (SI 1981/50) |
| para 70 | 15 Nov 1983 (SI 1983/1580) |
| paras 71, 72 | 1 Feb 1981 (SI 1981/50) |
| paras 73, 74 | 15 Nov 1983 (SI 1983/1580) |
| paras 75–77 | 1 Feb 1981 (SI 1981/50) |
| para 78 | 1 Jan 1982 (SI 1981/1751) |
| para 79 | 1 Feb 1981 (SI 1981/50) |
| Sch 8 | 1 Feb 1981 (SI 1980/50), repeals of or in— |

Treason Act 1708, s 7;
Treason Act 1800;
Conspiracy and Protection of Property Act 1875, s 11;
Burgh Police (Scotland) Act 1892, s 382;
Children and Young Persons Act 1933, s 26(5);
Treason Act 1945;
Criminal Justice (Scotland) Act 1949, ss 21, 75(3)(e);
Prisons (Scotland) Act 1952, ss 7(4), 19, 31(4), 35(5)(a);
Road Traffic Act 1960, s 246;
Criminal Justice Act 1961, s 70(1);
Penalties for Drunkenness Act 1962, s 1(2)(a), (b);
Road Traffic Regulation Act 1967, s 93;
Firearms Act 1968, Sch 6, Pt II, para 1;
Road Traffic Act 1972, Sch 4, Pt IV, para 3;
Child Benefit Act 1975, s 11(8);
Criminal Procedure (Scotland) Act 1975, ss 141, 191(1), 193(2), 195, 197–202, 228, 285, 289D(3)(c), 296(5), 310, 314(3), 337(e), 346, 365, 392(1), 399(1), 405, 410, 411(2), 417, 434(3), 460(5), (6), Schs 4, 7B, para 1;
Social Security Act 1975, s 147(6);
Licensing (Scotland) Act 1976, s 128(2);
Sexual Offences (Scotland) Act 1976, ss 7, 16;
Supplementary Benefits Act 1976, s 26(5);
Criminal Law Act 1977, Sch 11, paras 11–13;
Customs and Excise Management Act 1979, s 149(2)

1 Apr 1981 (SI 1981/444), repeals of or in—
Railways Clauses Consolidation (Scotland) Act 1845, s 144;

**Criminal Justice (Scotland) Act 1980 (c 62)**—*contd*

Protection of Animals (Scotland) Act 1912, s 4;

Criminal Justice Act 1967, s 60(6), (8);

Immigration Act 1971, s 6(5);

Criminal Procedure (Scotland) Act 1975, ss 229, 232, 234(1), (3), 236, 240, 245(3), 247, 253(2), 257, 263(1), 265(3), 272, 274(1), 277, 444(6), 445, 447(2), 448(9), 454(2), Sch 9, para 40

1 Jan 1982 (repeals of or in Criminal Procedure (Scotland) Act 1887, ss 68(3), 74(3), 105–107, 120–122, Schs F, G) (SI 1981/1751)

15 Nov 1983 (SI 1983/1580), repeals of or in—

Prisons (Scotland) Act 1952, ss 32, 33, 37(2);

Criminal Justice Act 1961, ss 32(2)(b), (f), 38(3)(a);

Criminal Justice (Scotland) Act 1963, ss 2, 4, 5, 9(1), (2), 11, 50(1);

Criminal Procedure (Scotland) Act 1975, ss 204, 208–11, 218, 414, 416, 418–420;

Rehabilitation of Offenders Act 1975, s 5(2)

**Deaconesses and Lay Workers (Pensions) Measure 1980 (No 1)**

*RA:* 20 Mar 1980

Whole Measure in force 20 Mar 1980 (RA)

**Deer Act 1980 (c 49)**

*RA:* 8 Aug 1980

*Commencement provisions:* s 9(4)

| | |
|---|---|
| 1 | 8 Nov 1980 (s 9(4)) |
| 2, 3 | 1 Nov 1980 (s 9(4)) |
| 4–9 | 8 Nov 1980 (s 9(4)) |
| Sch 1 | 1 Nov 1980 (s 9(4)) |
| Sch 2 | 8 Nov 1980 (s 9(4)) |

**Diocese in Europe Measure 1980 (No 2)**

*RA:* 30 Jun 1980

*Commencement provisions:* s 7(2)

Whole Measure in force 2 Jul 1980 (s 7(2) (following establishment of Diocese in Europe))

**Education Act 1980 (c 20)**

*RA:* 3 Apr 1980

*Commencement provisions:* s 37(2); Education Act 1980 (Commencement No 1) Order 1980, SI 1980/489; Education Act 1980 (Commencement No 2) Order 1980, SI 1980/959; Education Act 1980 (Commencement No 3) Order 1981, SI 1981/789; Education Act 1980 (Commencement No 4) Order 1981, SI 1981/1064

| | | |
|---|---|---|
| 1 | | 5 May 1980 (SI 1980/489) |
| 2, 3 | | 1 Jul 1981 (SI 1981/789) |
| 4 | (1)–(3) | 1 Aug 1981 (SI 1981/789 (and note transitional provisions in Sch 3 to the Order)) |
| | (4), (5) | 1 Jul 1981 (SI 1981/789) |
| 5 | | 1 Jul 1981 (SI 1981/789) |

**Education Act 1980 (c 20)**—*contd*

| | | |
|---|---|---|
| 6–9 | | 1 Oct 1980 (SI 1980/959) |
| 10 | (1)–(4) | 1 Jul 1982 (SI 1980/959) |
| | (5)–(7) | 5 May 1980 (SI 1980/489) |
| 11 | | 1 Jul 1982 (SI 1980/959) |
| 12 | (1)(a)–(d) | 1 Aug 1980 (SI 1980/489) |
| | (1)(e) | 5 May 1980 (SI 1980/489) |
| | (2), (3) | 5 May 1980 (SI 1980/489) |
| | (4) | 1 Aug 1980 (SI 1980/489) |
| | (5)–(9) | 5 May 1980 (SI 1980/489) |
| 13 | | 1 Aug 1980 (SI 1980/489) |
| 14 | (1), (2) | 5 May 1980 (SI 1980/489) |
| | (3) | 1 Aug 1980 (SI 1980/489) |
| | (4) | 5 May 1980 (SI 1980/489) |
| 15 | | 1 Aug 1980 (SI 1980/489) |
| 16 | (1) | 5 May 1980 (SI 1980/489) |
| | (2)–(5) | 1 Aug 1980 (SI 1980/489) |
| | (6), (7) | 5 May 1980 (SI 1980/489) |
| 17, 18 | | 1 Oct 1980 (SI 1980/959) |
| 19–21 | | 5 May 1980 (SI 1980/489) |
| 22, 23 | | 14 Apr 1980 (SI 1980/489) |
| 24–26 | | 5 May 1980 (SI 1980/489) |
| 27 | | 1 Sep 1981 (SI 1981/1064) |
| 28–30 | | 5 May 1980 (SI 1980/489) |
| 31 | | 1 Aug 1980 (SI 1980/489) |
| 32 | | 5 May 1980 (SI 1980/489) |
| 33 | (1), (2) | 5 May 1980 (SI 1980/489) |
| | (3) | 1 Sep 1981 (SI 1981/1064) |
| 34 | | 1 Oct 1980 (SI 1980/959) |
| 35–37 | | 14 Apr 1980 (SI 1980/489) |
| 38 | (1)–(3) | 14 Apr 1980 (SI 1980/489) |
| | (4) | 1 Oct 1980 (SI 1980/959) |
| | (5) | 1 Aug 1980 (SI 1980/489) |
| | (6) | See Sch 7 below |
| | (7) | 14 Apr 1980 (SI 1980/489) |
| Sch 1 | | 5 May 1980 (SI 1980/489) |
| Sch 2 | | 1 Oct 1980 (SI 1980/959) |
| Sch 3 | | 1 Aug 1980 (SI 1980/489) |
| Sch 4 | | 1 Oct 1980 (SI 1980/959) |
| Schs 5, 6 | | 1 Aug 1980 (SI 1980/489) |
| Sch 7 | | 14 Apr 1980 (SI 1980/489), repeals of or in— |

      Education Act 1944, s 49;
      Education (Scotland) Act 1962, ss 53, 55;
      Education (Milk) Act 1971;
      Education Act 1976, s 9;
      Education (Scotland) Act 1976, s 3
   5 May 1980 (SI 1980/489), repeals of or in—
      Education Act 1944, ss 8(2)(b), 9(1), 11, 12, 31(1), 32, 53(1),
        61(2), 66, 82–84, 90, 97, 100(1), 114, Sch 1, Pt I, para 3,
        Sch 3, para 3;
      Education (Miscellaneous Provisions) Act 1953, s 6(1);
      Local Government Act 1958, Sch 8, para 16(2);
      London Government Act 1963, ss 31(1)–(3), 33;
      Local Government Act 1966, s 14;
      Education Act 1973, s 4;
      Education Act 1975, ss 1, 2, 5(4);
      Education Act 1976, ss 5, 7, 8
   1 Aug 1980 (SI 1980/489), repeals of or in—
      Education Act 1944, s 13;
      Education Act 1946, Sch 2, Pt II;

**Education Act 1980 (c 20)**—*contd*

Education (Miscellaneous Provisions) Act 1948, ss 6, 7;
Education (Miscellaneous Provisions) Act 1953, ss 7, 9, 16, Sch 1;
London Government Act 1963, s 31(9);
Education Act 1968, ss 1(2), 3, 5, Sch 1, para 7, Sch 3, Pt A;
Education Act 1976, s 4
1 Aug 1981 (repeals of Education Act 1944, s 21(2), Sch 4) (SI 1981/789)
1 Sep 1981 (repeal of Sex Discrimination Act 1975, Sch 2, para 2) (SI 1981/1064)

**Education (Scotland) Act 1980 (c 44)**

*RA:* 1 Aug 1980

*Commencement provisions:* s 137(2)–(4); Education (Scotland) Act 1980 (Commencement) Order 1980, SI 1980/1287

| | | |
|---|---|---|
| 1 | (1), (2) | 1 Sep 1980 (s 137(2)) |
| | (3) | 1 Sep 1980 (s 137(2), (3))[1] |
| | (4), (5) | 1 Sep 1980 (s 137(2)) |
| 2–9 | | 1 Sep 1980 (s 137(2)) |
| 10, 11 | | 1 Sep 1980 (s 137(2), (3))[1] |
| 12–22 | | 1 Sep 1980 (s 137(2)) |
| 23 | (1)–(4) | 1 Sep 1980 (s 137(2), (3))[1] |
| | (5)–(7) | 1 Sep 1980 (SI 1980/1287) |
| 24–44 | | 1 Sep 1980 (s 137(2)) |
| 45–48 | | *Never in force* (repealed) |
| 49 | | 1 Sep 1980 (s 137(2)) |
| 50 | (1)(a), (b) | 1 Sep 1980 (s 137(2), (3))[1] |
| | (1)(c) | *Never in force* (repealed) |
| | (2) | 1 Sep 1980 (s 137(2), (3))[1] |
| 51 | | 1 Sep 1980 (s 137(2)) |
| 52 | | 1 Sep 1980 (s 137(2), (3))[1] |
| 53–56 | | 1 Sep 1980 (s 137(2)) |
| 57–59 | | 1 Sep 1980 (s 137(2), (3))[1] |
| 60–65 | | 1 Sep 1980 (s 137(2)) |
| 66 | | 1 Sep 1980 (s 137(2), (3))[1] |
| 67 | | 1 Sep 1980 (s 137(2)) |
| 68 | | 1 Sep 1980 (s 137(2), (3))[1] |
| 69–71 | | 1 Sep 1980 (s 137(2)) |
| 72 | (1) | 1 Sep 1980 (s 137(2)) |
| | (2) | 1 Sep 1980 (s 137(2), (3))[1] |
| 73–85 | | 1 Sep 1980 (s 137(2)) |
| 86, 87 | | 1 Sep 1980 (s 137(2), (3))[1] |
| 88–123 | | 1 Sep 1980 (s 137(2)) |
| 124 | | *Never in force* (repealed) |
| 125, 126 | | 1 Sep 1980 (s 137(2)) |
| 127 | (1), (2) | 1 Sep 1980 (s 137(2)) |
| | (3), (4) | *Never in force* (repealed) |
| | (5), (6) | 1 Sep 1980 (s 137(2)) |
| 128–137 | | 1 Sep 1980 (s 137(2)) |
| Schs 1–6 | | 1 Sep 1980 (s 137(2)) |

[1] So far as relating to junior colleges (or, in the case of s 1(3), as originally enacted, so far as relating to compulsory further education and junior colleges), the commencement of the provision(s) was postponed under paras 1–15 (now repealed) of Sch 6, until a day appointed under s 137(3); no day was appointed before the Self-Governing Schools etc (Scotland) Act 1989 removed references to junior colleges in the provision(s)

## Employment Act 1980 (c 42)

*RA:* 1 Aug 1980

*Commencement provisions:* s 21(2); Employment Act 1980 (Commencement No 1) Order 1980, SI 1980/1170[1]; Employment Act 1980 (Commencement No 2) Order 1980, SI 1980/1926

| | | |
|---|---|---|
| 1 | | 1 Aug 1980 (RA) |
| 2 | | 1 Oct 1980 (SI 1980/1170) |
| 3 | | 1 Aug 1980 (RA) |
| 4, 5 | | 8 Sep 1980 (SI 1980/1170) |
| 6 | | 1 Oct 1980 (SI 1980/1170) |
| 7 | | 15 Aug 1980 (SI 1980/1170) |
| 8, 9 | | 1 Oct 1980 (SI 1980/1170) |
| 10 | | 8 Sep 1980 (SI 1980/1170) |
| 11–14 | | 1 Oct 1980 (SI 1980/1170) |
| 15–18 | | 8 Sep 1980 (SI 1980/1170) |
| 19 | (a) | 22 Dec 1980 (SI 1980/1926) |
| | (b), (c) | 15 Aug 1980 (SI 1980/1170) |
| 20 | (1) | 1 Aug 1980 (RA) |
| | (2) | See Sch 1 below |
| | (3) | See Sch 2 below |
| 21 | | 1 Aug 1980 (RA) |
| Sch 1 | paras 1, 2 | 15 Aug 1980 (SI 1980/1170) |
| | paras 3, 4 | 1 Oct 1980 (SI 1980/1170) |
| | paras 5, 6 | 15 Aug 1980 (SI 1980/1170) |
| | paras 7–11 | 1 Oct 1980 (SI 1980/1170) |
| | para 12 | 15 Aug 1980 (SI 1980/1170) |
| | para 13 | 1 Oct 1980 (SI 1980/1170) |
| | para 14 | 15 Aug 1980 (SI 1980/1170) |
| | para 15 | 1 Oct 1980 (SI 1980/1170) |
| | para 16 | 8 Sep 1980 (SI 1980/1170) |
| | para 17 | 8 Sep 1980 (so far as it relates to s 4) (SI 1980/1170) |
| | | 1 Oct 1980 (otherwise) (SI 1980/1170) |
| | para 18 | 1 Oct 1980 (SI 1980/1170) |
| | para 19 | 8 Sep 1980 (so far as it relates to ss 4, 5) (SI 1980/1170) |
| | | 1 Oct 1980 (otherwise) (SI 1980/1170) |
| | para 20 | 15 Aug 1980 (SI 1980/1170) |
| | para 21(a) | 1 Oct 1980 (SI 1980/1170) |
| | para 21(b) | 15 Aug 1980 (SI 1980/1170) |
| | paras 22, 23 | 1 Oct 1980 (SI 1980/1170) |
| | para 24 | 15 Aug 1980 (SI 1980/1170) |
| | para 25 | 1 Oct 1980 (SI 1980/1170) |
| | para 26 | 8 Sep 1980 (SI 1980/1170) |
| | para 27 | 1 Oct 1980 (SI 1980/1170) |
| | paras 28, 29 | 8 Sep 1980 (SI 1980/1170) |
| | paras 30–33 | 1 Oct 1980 (SI 1980/1170) |
| Sch 2 | | 15 Aug 1980 (SI 1980/1170), all repeals except that of— |

Sch 2 (continued):

15 Aug 1980 (SI 1980/1170), all repeals except that of—
Trade Union and Labour Relations Act 1974;
Employment Protection Act 1975, s 127(1)(g);
Trade Union and Labour Relations (Amendment) Act 1976, s 2;
Employment Protection (Consolidation) Act 1978, ss 23, 25(1), 33(3), 66(1), 73(1)(c), (8), 135(1), 154(1)

8 Sep 1980 (SI 1980/1770), repeals of or in—
Trade Union and Labour Relations Act 1974, s 13(3);
Employment Protection (Consolidation) Act 1978, ss 23, 25(1), 135(1)

1 Oct 1980 (SI 1980/1170), all remaining repeals except that of—
Trade Union and Labour Relations Act 1974;
Trade Union and Labour Relations (Amendment) Act 1976, s 2

22 Dec 1980 (SI 1980/1926), repeals of or in—

**Employment Act 1980 (c 42)**—*contd*

> Trade Union and Labour Relations Act 1974;
> Trade Union and Labour Relations (Amendment) Act 1976, s 2

[1]   See the transitional provisions in Employment Act 1980 (Commencement No 1) Order 1980, SI 1980/1170, art 4, Sch 3

---

**Films Act 1980 (c 41)**

*RA:* 17 Jul 1980

*Commencement provisions:* s 9(2); Films Act 1980 (Commencement) Order 1982, SI 1982/1020

| | |
|---|---|
| 1–7 | 20 Jul 1980 (s 9(2)) |
| 8 | 22 Jul 1982 (SI 1982/1020) |
| 9 | 20 Jul 1980 (s 9(2)) |
| Schedule | 20 Jul 1980 (s 9(2)) |

---

**Finance Act 1980 (c 48)**

*Budget Day:* 26 Mar 1980

*RA:* 1 Aug 1980

The commencement details of Finance Acts are not set out, as the dates from which their provisions take effect are usually stated clearly and unambiguously in the text of the Act, and charging provisions will normally state for which year or years of assessment they are to have effect.

---

**Foster Children Act 1980 (c 6)**

*RA:* 31 Jan 1980

*Commencement provisions:* s 24(2); Child Care Act 1980 (Commencement) Order 1980, SI 1980/1935

Whole Act in force 1 Apr 1981 (SI 1980/1935) (s 24(2) provided for the commencement of this Act on the date appointed under the Child Care Act 1980, s 90(1) for the coming into force of that Act)

---

**Gaming (Amendment) Act 1980 (c 8)**

*RA:* 20 Mar 1980

Whole Act in force 20 Mar 1980 (RA)

---

**Gas Act 1980 (c 37)**

*RA:* 30 Jun 1980

Whole Act in force 30 Jun 1980 (RA)

---

**Health Services Act 1980 (c 53)**

*RA:* 8 Aug 1980

*Commencement provisions:* s 26(2), (3); Health Services Act 1980 (Commencement) Order 1980, SI 1980/1257; Health Services Act 1980 (Commencement No 2) Order 1981, SI 1981/306; Health Services Act 1980 (Commencement No 3) Order 1981, SI 1981/884; Health Services Act 1980 (Commencement No 4) Order 1983, SI 1983/303

| | |
|---|---|
| 1–13 | 8 Aug 1980 (RA) |
| 14 | 8 Sep 1980 (SI 1980/1257) |

**Health Services Act 1980 (c 53)**—*contd*

| | | |
|---|---|---|
| 15 | | 8 Aug 1980 (RA) |
| 16 | | 1 Aug 1981 (SI 1981/884) |
| 17–20 | | 8 Aug 1980 (RA) |
| 21 | | 1 Apr 1983 (SI 1983/303) |
| 22–24 | | 8 Aug 1980 (RA) |
| 25 | (1) | 8 Aug 1980 (RA) |
| | (2) | 1 Apr 1981 (SI 1981/306) |
| | (3) | 8 Aug 1980 (RA) |
| | (4) | See Sch 7 below |
| 26 | | 8 Aug 1980 (RA) |
| Schs 1–3 | | 8 Aug 1980 (RA) |
| Sch 4 | | 1 Aug 1981 (SI 1981/884) |
| Sch 5 | | 1 Apr 1981 (SI 1981/306) |
| Sch 6 | | 8 Aug 1980 (RA) |
| Sch 7 | | 8 Aug 1980 (RA), except repeals in— |
| | | Nursing Homes Registration (Scotland) Act 1938; |
| | | Nursing Homes Act 1975; |
| | | Nurses, Midwives and Health Visitors Act 1979 |
| | | 1 Aug 1981 (exceptions noted above) (SI 1981/884) |

**Highlands and Islands Air Services (Scotland) Act 1980 (c 19)**

*RA:* 3 Apr 1980

*Commencement provisions:* s 5(2)

Whole Act in force 15 Dec 1980 (s 5(2))

**Highways Act 1980 (c 66)**

*RA:* 13 Nov 1980

*Commencement provisions:* s 345(2)

Whole Act in force 1 Jan 1981 (s 345(2))

**Housing Act 1980 (c 51)**

*RA:* 8 Aug 1980

*Commencement provisions:* s 153; Housing Act 1980 (Commencement No 1) Order 1980, SI 1980/1406; Housing Act 1980 (Commencement No 2) Order 1980, SI 1980/1466; Housing Act 1980 (Commencement No 3) Order 1980, SI 1980/1557; Housing Act 1980 (Commencement No 4) Order 1980, SI 1980/1693; Housing Act 1980 (Commencement No 5) Order 1980, SI 1980/1706; Housing Act 1980 (Commencement No 6) Order 1980, SI 1980/1781; Housing Act 1980 (Commencement No 7) Order 1981, SI 1981/119; Housing Act 1980 (Commencement No 8) Order 1981, SI 1981/296; Rent Rebates and Rent Allowances (England and Wales) (Appointed Day) Order 1981, SI 1981/297

| | | |
|---|---|---|
| 1–27 | | 3 Oct 1980 (s 153(1)) |
| 28–50 | | 3 Oct 1980 (s 153(2)) |
| 51–55 | | 28 Nov 1980 (SI 1980/1706) |
| 56–58 | | 6 Oct 1980 (SI 1980/1706) |
| 59 | (1), (2) | 28 Nov 1980 (SI 1980/1706) |
| | (3) | See Sch 6 below |
| 60–77 | | 28 Nov 1980 (SI 1980/1706) |
| 78, 79 | | 20 Oct 1980 (SI 1980/1557) |
| 80–89 | | 3 Oct 1980 (SI 1980/1406) |
| 90–105 | | 8 Aug 1980 (s 153(3)) |
| 106 | | 15 Dec 1980 (SI 1980/1781) |

**Housing Act 1980 (c 51)**—*contd*

| | | |
|---|---|---|
| 107 | | See Sch 12 below |
| 108 | | 8 Aug 1980 (s 153(3)) |
| 109 | | 15 Dec 1980 (SI 1980/1781) |
| 110, 111 | | 3 Oct 1980 (SI 1980/1406) |
| 112, 113 | | 8 Aug 1980 (s 153(3)) |
| 114 | | 3 Oct 1980 (SI 1980/1406) |
| 115 | | 11 Nov 1980 (SI 1980/1693) |
| 116 | (1) | See Sch 14 below |
| | (2) | 3 Oct 1980 (SI 1980/1406) |
| 117 | | 1 Apr 1981 (SI 1981/296) |
| 118 | | 20 Oct 1980 (SI 1980/1557) |
| 119 | | 1 Apr 1981 (SI 1981/296) |
| 120 | | 8 Aug 1980 (s 153(3)) |
| 121 | | 1 Oct 1980 (SI 1980/1406) |
| 122–127 | | 8 Aug 1980 (s 153(3)) |
| 128, 129 | | 3 Oct 1980 (SI 1980/1406) |
| 130, 131 | | 8 Aug 1980 (s 153(3)) |
| 132 | | 3 Oct 1980 (SI 1980/1406) |
| 133–135 | | 8 Aug 1980 (s 153(3)) |
| 136 | | 3 Oct 1980 (SI 1980/1406) |
| 137–140 | | 8 Aug 1980 (s 153(3)) |
| 141 | | 3 Oct 1980 (except in relation to Sch 21, para 7) (SI 1980/1406) |
| | | *Not yet in force* (exception noted above) |
| 142 | | 31 Mar 1981 (SI 1981/119) |
| 143–146 | | 3 Oct 1980 (SI 1980/1406) |
| 147 | | 27 Oct 1980 (SI 1980/1557) |
| 148 | | 3 Oct 1980 (SI 1980/1406) |
| 149 | | 28 Nov 1980 (SI 1980/1706) |
| 150, 151 | | 8 Aug 1980 (s 153(3)) |
| 152 | (1) | See Sch 25 below |
| | (2) | 8 Aug 1980 (s 153(3)) |
| | (3) | See Sch 26 below |
| 153 | | 8 Aug 1980 (RA) |
| 154, 155 | | 8 Aug 1980 (s 153(3)) |
| Schs 1, 2 | | 3 Oct 1980 (s 153(1)) |
| Schs 3, 4 | | 3 Oct 1980 (s 153(2)) |
| Sch 5 | | 6 Oct 1980 (SI 1980/1466) |
| Sch 6 | | *Not yet in force* (it has been stated that amendments made by this Schedule will not be brought into operation: Regulated Tenancies (Procedure) Regulations 1980, made under Rent Act 1977, s 74) (SI 1980/1696) |
| Schs 7–10 | | 28 Nov 1980 (SI 1980/1706) |
| Sch 11 | | 8 Aug 1980 (s 153(3)) |
| Sch 12 | paras 1–3 | 27 Oct 1980 (SI 1980/1557) |
| | para 4 | 15 Dec 1980 (SI 1980/1781) |
| | paras 5–11 | 27 Oct 1980 (SI 1980/1557) |
| | para 12 | 15 Dec 1980 (SI 1980/1781) |
| | paras 13–27 | 27 Oct 1980 (SI 1980/1557) |
| | paras 28–32 | 15 Dec 1980 (SI 1980/1781) |
| Sch 13 | | 15 Dec 1980 (SI 1980/1781) |
| Sch 14 | paras 1–5 | *Never in force* (repealed) |
| | para 6(1), (2) | 3 Oct 1980 (SI 1980/1406) |
| | para 6(3) | *Never in force* (repealed) |
| Sch 15 | | 20 Oct 1980 (SI 1980/1557) |
| Sch 16 | | 8 Aug 1980 (s 153(3)) |
| Sch 17 | | 3 Oct 1980 (SI 1980/1406) |
| Sch 18 | | 8 Aug 1980 (s 153(3)) |
| Sch 19 | | 3 Oct 1980 (SI 1980/1406) |
| Sch 20 | | 8 Aug 1980 (s 153(3)) |

**Housing Act 1980 (c 51)**—*contd*

| | | |
|---|---|---|
| Sch 21 | paras 1–6 | 3 Oct 1980 (SI 1980/1406) |
| | para 7 | *Not yet in force* |
| | para 8 | 3 Oct 1980 (SI 1980/1406) |
| Sch 22 | | 31 Mar 1981 (SI 1981/119) |
| Sch 23 | | 3 Oct 1980 (SI 1980/1406) |
| Sch 24 | | 27 Oct 1980 (SI 1980/1557) |
| Sch 25 | paras 1–3 | 28 Nov 1980 (SI 1980/1706) |
| | para 4 | 3 Oct 1980 (SI 1980/1406) |
| | para 5 | 15 Dec 1980 (SI 1980/1781) |
| | para 6 | 3 Oct 1980 (SI 1980/1406) |
| | para 7 | 15 Dec 1980 (SI 1980/1781) |
| | paras 8–16 | 3 Oct 1980 (SI 1980/1406) |
| | para 17 | 28 Nov 1980 (SI 1980/1706) |
| | paras 18–20 | 3 Oct 1980 (SI 1980/1406) |
| | para 21 | 27 Oct 1980 (SI 1980/1557) |
| | paras 22, 23 | 15 Dec 1980 (SI 1980/1781) |
| | paras 24–29 | 3 Oct 1980 (SI 1980/1406) |
| | para 30 | 27 Oct 1980 (SI 1980/1557) |
| | para 31 | 3 Oct 1980 (SI 1980/1406) |
| | paras 32, 33 | 28 Nov 1980 (SI 1980/1706) |
| | para 34 | 3 Oct 1980 (SI 1980/1406) |
| | para 35 | 28 Nov 1980 (SI 1980/1706) |
| | para 36 | 3 Oct 1980 (SI 1980/1406) |
| | paras 37–60 | 28 Nov 1980 (SI 1980/1706) |
| | para 61 | 3 Oct 1980 (SI 1980/1406) |
| | paras 62–78 | 8 Aug 1980 (s 153(3)) |
| Sch 26 | | 28 Mar 1980 (SI 1980/1706), repeals of or in— |

Housing Act 1957, ss 5, 43(4), 113(5), 119(3);
Housing (Financial Provisions) Act 1958, s 43(1);
Housing Act 1961, s 20;
Housing Act 1964, ss 65(1A), 66;
Housing Subsidies Act 1967, ss 24(5), 26A;
Leasehold Reform Act 1967, Sch 1;
Housing Act 1969, s 61(6);
Housing Finance Act 1972, ss 90–91A;
Local Government Act 1972;
Housing Act 1974, ss 5(3), 13(4), (5)(a), 14, 19(1), 30(5), 31, 32(1), (4), (8), 33(6), 104, 114;
Criminal Law Act 1977, Schs 6, 12

27 Oct 1980 (SI 1980/1557), repeals of or in—
Housing Act 1961 (so far as not already repealed);
Housing Act 1969, s 60;
Housing Act 1974, ss 56(1)(d), 57(6), 62(3), 64(7), 67, 84

15 Dec 1980 (SI 1980/1781), repeals of or in—
Housing Act 1957, s 96(e);
Housing (Financial Provisions) Act 1958, ss 14, 15;
Housing Act 1969 (so far as not already repealed);
Chronically Sick and Disabled Persons Act 1970;
Local Employment Act 1972;
Housing (Amendment) Act 1973;
Housing Act 1974, ss 38(2)(a), 42, 50, 52–55, 56(2)(d), 71(3)(a), Sch 5, Pt I, Pt II, para 4;
Housing Rents and Subsidies Act 1975, Schs 1, 5;
Local Land Charges Act 1975;
Remuneration, Charges and Grants Act 1975

31 Mar 1981 (repeal of Leasehold Reform Act 1967 (so far as not already repealed)) (SI 1981/119)

**Housing Act 1980 (c 51)**—*contd*

> 1 Apr 1981 (repeals of Housing Finance Act 1972, ss 8, 20(5), (7), 24(5), 26(1), Sch 3, Pt II, Sch 4, paras 1(3)(a), 16, 17) (SI 1981/296)
>
> *Not yet in force,* repeals of or in—
> Housing Act 1957, ss 91, 105, 106;
> Housing (Financial Provisions) Act 1958, s 45;
> New Towns Act 1959, s 4;
> Housing Subsidies Act 1967, ss 24(2)–(4), (5A), 24B, 26, 28A;
> Town and Country Planning Act 1968, s 39;
> Housing Finance Act 1972, Sch 4, para 14;
> Housing Act 1974, s 79, Schs 8, 11;
> Housing Rents and Subsidies Act 1975, ss 1, 2, 4;
> Development of Rural Wales Act 1976, ss 18, 22, Sch 5;
> New Towns (Amendment) Act 1976, s 9;
> Supplementary Benefits Act 1976, Sch 7, para 28;
> Rent Act 1977, Sch 12, paras 4, 9

**Import of Live Fish (England and Wales) Act 1980 (c 27)**

*RA:* 15 May 1980

Whole Act in force 15 May 1980 (RA)

**Imprisonment (Temporary Provisions) Act 1980 (c 57)**

*RA:* 29 Oct 1980

Whole Act in force 29 Oct 1980 (RA)

**Industry Act 1980 (c 33)**

*RA:* 30 Jun 1980

Whole Act in force 30 Jun 1980 (RA)

**Insurance Companies Act 1980 (c 25)**

*RA:* 1 May 1980

*Commencement provisions:* s 5(2); Insurance Companies Act 1980 (Commencement) Order 1980, SI 1980/678

Whole Act in force 1 Jun 1980 (SI 1980/678)

**Iran (Temporary Powers) Act 1980 (c 28)**

*RA:* 15 May 1980

*Commencement provisions:* s 2(2)

Whole Act in force 17 May 1980 (s 2(2))

**Law Reform (Miscellaneous Provisions) (Scotland) Act 1980 (c 55)**

*RA:* 29 Oct 1980

*Commencement provisions:* s 29(2); Law Reform (Miscellaneous Provisions) (Scotland) Act 1980 (Commencement) Order 1980, SI 1980/1726

**Law Reform (Miscellaneous Provisions) (Scotland) Act 1980 (c 55)**—*contd*
Whole Act in force 22 Dec 1980 (SI 1980/1726)

---

**Licensed Premises (Exclusion of Certain Persons) Act 1980 (c 32)**

*RA:* 30 Jun 1980

Whole Act in force 30 Jun 1980 (RA)

---

**Licensing (Amendment) Act 1980 (c 40)**

*RA:* 17 Jul 1980

*Commencement provisions:* s 4(2); Licensing (Amendment) Act 1980 (Commencement) Order 1982, SI 1982/1383

| | |
|---|---|
| 1 | 17 Jul 1980 (RA) |
| 2, 3 | 1 Oct 1982 (SI 1982/1383) |
| 4 | 17 Jul 1980 (RA) |

---

**Limitation Act 1980 (c 58)**

*RA:* 13 Nov 1980

*Commencement provisions:* s 41(2), (3); Limitation Act 1980 (Commencement) Order 1981, SI 1981/588

Whole Act in force 1 May 1981 (s 41(2); note that s 35 also came into force on that date by virtue of SI 1981/588)

---

**Limitation Amendment Act 1980 (c 24)**

*RA:* 1 May 1980

Whole Act in force 1 Aug 1980 (s 14(3))

---

**Local Government, Planning and Land Act 1980 (c 65)**

*RA:* 13 Nov 1980

*Commencement provisions:* ss 23(3), 47, 68(8), 85, 86(8)–(11), 178; Local Government, Planning and Land Act 1980 (Commencement No 1) Order 1980, SI 1980/1871; Local Government, Planning and Land Act 1980 (Commencement No 2) Order 1980, SI 1980/1893; Local Government, Planning and Land Act 1980 (Commencement No 3) Order 1980, SI 1980/2014; Local Government, Planning and Land Act 1980 (Commencement No 4) Order 1981, SI 1981/194; Local Government, Planning and Land Act 1980 (Commencement No 5) Order 1981, SI 1981/341; Local Government, Planning and Land Act 1980 (Commencement No 6) Order 1981, SI 1981/1251; Local Government, Planning and Land Act 1980 (Commencement No 7) Order 1981, SI 1981/1618; Local Government, Planning and Land Act 1980 (Commencement No 8) (Scotland) Order 1982, SI 1982/317[1]; Local Government, Planning and Land Act 1980 (Commencement No 8) Order 1983, SI 1983/94; Community Land Act 1975 (Appointed Day for Repeal) Order 1983, SI 1983/673; Local Government, Planning and Land Act 1980 (Commencement No 9) Order 1984, SI 1984/1493

| | | |
|---|---|---|
| 1–4 | | 13 Nov 1980 (RA) |
| 5–15 | | 1 Apr 1981 (SI 1981/341) |
| 16 | (1) | 1 Apr 1981 (except in so far as it applies to relevant work) (SI 1981/341) |
| | | 1 Apr 1982 (so far as it applies to relevant work) (SI 1981/341) |
| | (2)–(6) | 1 Apr 1981 (SI 1981/341) |
| 17–22 | | 1 Apr 1981 (SI 1981/341) |
| 23–27 | | 13 Nov 1980 (RA) |

**Local Government, Planning and Land Act 1980 (c 65)**—*contd*

| | | |
|---|---|---|
| 28–32 | | 13 Nov 1980 (s 47(7)) |
| 33, 34 | | 13 Nov 1980, but only to have effect for any rate passed beginning after 31 Mar 1981 (s 47(1), (7); SI 1980/2014) |
| 35, 36 | | 13 Nov 1980 (s 47(7)) |
| 37 | | 13 Nov 1980, but only to have effect for any rate period beginning after 31 Mar 1981 (s 47(1), (7); SI 1980/2014) |
| 38–40 | | 13 Dec 1980 (s 47(3)) |
| 41–43 | | 13 Nov 1980 (s 47(7)) |
| 44 | | 13 Nov 1980, but only to have effect for rate periods beginning after 31 Mar 1981 (s 47(1), (7); SI 1980/2014) |
| 45 | | 13 Nov 1980 (s 47(7)), but note sub-ss (1)–(4) have effect for rebate periods beginning after 31 Mar 1981 (SI 1980/2014) |
| 46 | | Applies to Scotland only |
| 47 | | 13 Nov 1980 (RA) |
| 48–67 | | 13 Nov 1980 (RA); but the commencing year for purposes of Pt VI of this Act was that beginning 1 Apr 1981 (SI 1980/1893) |
| 68 | (1) | 13 Nov 1980 (RA); but the commencing year for purposes of Pt VI of this Act was that beginning 1 Apr 1981 (SI 1980/1893) |
| | (2)–(6) | 11 Dec 1980 (s 68(8); SI 1980/1893) |
| | (7)–(9) | 13 Nov 1980 (RA) |
| 69, 70 | | 13 Nov 1980 (RA) |
| 71 | | 11 Dec 1980 (SI 1980/1893) |
| 72 | (1), (2) | 11 Dec 1980 (for purpose of enabling the Secretary of State to make or withdraw specifications of amounts of prescribed expenditure, or to give directions for years commencing 1 Apr 1981 onwards) (SI 1980/1893) |
| | | 1 Apr 1981 (otherwise) (SI 1980/1893) |
| | (3)–(10) | 1 Apr 1981 (SI 1980/1893) |
| 73, 74 | | 11 Dec 1980 (for purpose of enabling the Secretary of State to make or withdraw specifications of amounts of prescribed expenditure, or to give directions for years commencing 1 Apr 1981 onwards) (SI 1980/1893) |
| | | 1 Apr 1981 (otherwise) (SI 1980/1893) |
| 75 | (1)–(4) | 1 Apr 1981 (SI 1980/1893) |
| | (5) | 11 Dec 1980 (SI 1980/1893) |
| 76 | | 11 Dec 1980 (SI 1980/1893) |
| 77–83 | | 1 Apr 1981 (SI 1980/1893) |
| 84 | | 11 Dec 1980 (SI 1980/1893) |
| 85 | | 13 Nov 1980 (RA) |
| 86 | (1)–(4) | 12 Jan 1981 (sub-ss (8)–(11)) |
| | (5), (6) | 13 Nov 1980 (RA) |
| | (7) | 12 Jan 1981 (sub-ss (8)–(11)) |
| | (8)–(11) | 13 Jan 1981 (s 86(8), (11)) |
| 87–92 | | 13 Nov 1980 (RA) |
| 93–100 | | Brought into force, together with ss 98–100 of this Act, area by area on different dates as follows: |
| | | 31 Dec 1980 (Birmingham, Bradford, Bristol, Coventry, Dudley, Ealing, Gateshead, Leeds, Liverpool, Manchester, Middlesbrough, Newcastle-under-Lyme, Newcastle-upon-Tyne, Preston, Salford, Sefton, Stockport, Stoke, Trafford, Wandsworth, Wirral) (SI 1980/1871) |
| | | 19 Mar 1981 (Derby, Leicester, Newham, North Bedfordshire, Nottingham, Portsmouth, Sandwell, Sheffield, South Staffordshire, Southwark, Tower Hamlets, Walsall) (SI 1981/194) |
| | | 2 Oct 1981 (Knowsley, St Helens) (SI 1981/1251) |
| | | 11 Dec 1981 (areas of all other councils of districts in England, all other London boroughs and the City of London) (SI 1981/1618) |

**See Halsbury's Statutes Citator for amendments to these Acts** 419

**Local Government, Planning and Land Act 1980 (c 65)**—*contd*

|  |  |  |
|---|---|---|
|  |  | 3 Mar 1983 (Alyn and Deeside, Cardiff, Newport, Swansea, Vale of Glamorgan, Wrexham, Maelor) (SI 1983/94) |
|  |  | 24 Oct 1984 (areas of all other district councils in Wales) (SI 1984/1493) |
| 101 |  | See Sch 17 below |
| 102–116 |  | 13 Nov 1980 (RA) |
| 117 |  | *Never in force* (repealed) |
| 118–120 |  | 13 Nov 1980 (RA) |
| 121 |  | 13 Nov 1980 (RA) but effective from 12 Dec 1975 (s 121(1)) |
| 122 |  | 13 Nov 1980 (RA) |
| 123 |  | 13 Nov 1980 (RA) but effective from 12 Dec 1975 (s 123(1)) |
| 124, 125 |  | 13 Nov 1980 (RA) |
| 126–130 |  | *Never in force* (repealed) |
| 131–172 |  | 13 Nov 1980 (RA) |
| 173 | (a) | 13 Dec 1980 (s 178(3)) |
|  | (b) | 13 Dec 1981 (s 178(2)) |
| 174 |  | 13 Feb 1981 (s 178(1)) |
| 175–178 |  | 13 Dec 1980 (s 178(3)) |
| 179–197 |  | 13 Nov 1980 (RA) |
| Schs 1–10 |  | 13 Nov 1980 (RA) |
| Sch 11 |  | *Never in force* (repealed) |
| Sch 12 |  | 11 Dec 1980 (SI 1980/1893) |
| Sch 13 |  | 1 Apr 1981 (SI 1980/1893) |
| Sch 14 |  | 13 Nov 1980 (RA) |
| Sch 15 | paras 1–3 | 13 Nov 1980 (RA) |
|  | para 4 | 12 Jan 1981 (s 86(8)–(11)) |
|  | paras 5–11 | 13 Nov 1980 (RA) |
|  | paras 12, 13 | 12 Jan 1981 (s 86(8)–(11)) |
|  | para 14 | 13 Nov 1980 (RA) |
|  | paras 15, 16 | 12 Jan 1981 (s 86(8)–(11)) |
|  | paras 17–19 | 13 Nov 1980 (RA) |
|  | para 20 | 12 Jan 1981 (s 86(8)–(11)) |
|  | paras 21–23 | 13 Nov 1980 (RA) |
|  | para 24 | 12 Jan 1980 (s 86(8)–(11)) |
|  | paras 25–28 | 13 Nov 1980 (RA) |
| Sch 16 |  | 13 Nov 1980 (RA) |
| Sch 17 | Pt I | 13 Nov 1980 (RA) |
|  | Pt II | 13 Nov 1980 (repeals of Community Land Act 1975, except as noted below) (RA) |
|  |  | 1 Jun 1983 (repeals of Community Land Act 1975, ss 1, 2, 6(1) (part), (6), 7, 26, 40, 43, 44 (except part of sub-s (3)), 51–58, Sch 2) (SI 1983/673) |
|  | Pts III, IV | 13 Nov 1980 (RA) |
| Schs 18–24 |  | 13 Nov 1980 (RA) |
| Sch 25 | Pt I | *Never in force* (repealed) |
|  | Pts II–IV | 13 Nov 1980 (RA) |
| Schs 26–32 |  | 13 Nov 1980 (RA) |
| Sch 33 | paras 1–3 | 13 Nov 1980 (RA) |
|  | para 4 | Effective from 25 Mar 1981 when power to prescribe appropriate multiplier first exercised (s 47(5), (6)); Landlord and Tenant Act 1954 (Appropriate Multiplier) Regulations 1981, SI 1981/69 |
|  | para 5 | 13 Nov 1980 (RA) |
|  | para 6 | *Never in force* (repealed) |
|  | para 7 | 13 Nov 1980 (RA) |
|  | para 8 | *Never in force* (repealed) |
|  | para 9 | 13 Nov 1980 (RA) |

## Local Government, Planning and Land Act 1980 (c 65)—*contd*

|  |  |  |
|---|---|---|
| | para 10 | 13 Nov 1980, but not to have effect for rate periods beginning before first date after 13 Nov 1980, on which new valuation lists were to come into force[2] (s 47(4), (7)) |
| | paras 11, 12 | 13 Nov 1980 (RA) |
| | para 13 | 13 Nov 1980 (RA; but note para 13(2) only effective for applications after 12 Dec 1975) |
| | para 14 | Effective when power to prescribe multipliers is exercised (s 47(5), (6)) (it is thought that the coming into force of Landlord and Tenant Act 1954 (Appropriate Multiplier) Regulations 1981, SI 1981/69, brought this paragraph into effect on 25 Mar 1981) |
| Sch 34 | Pts I–VIII | 13 Nov 1980 (RA) |
| | Pt IX | Rate periods beginning after 31 Mar 1981 (SI 1980/2014) repeals of or in— |
| | | General Rate Act 1967, ss 4(2), 5(1)(g), 48(4), 50(2), Sch 10; |
| | | Decimal Currency Act 1969; |
| | | GLC (General Powers) Act 1973; |
| | | Local Government Act 1974, s 47(1) |
| | | Rate periods beginning after first date after 13 Nov 1980 on which new valuation lists in force (repeals of General Rate Act 1967, ss 19, 30) (s 47(4)(d)) |
| | | 13 Nov 1980 (RA), repeals of or in— |
| | | General Rate Act 1967, s 20, Schs 1, 2; |
| | | General Rate Act 1975; |
| | | Rating (Caravan Sites) Act 1976 |
| | Pt X | 13 Nov 1980 (RA) |
| | Pt XI | 13 Nov 1980 (RA; but note Sch 17 above in relation to repeal of Community Land Act 1975) |
| | Pts XII–XVI | 13 Nov 1980 (RA) |

[1]   No commencement orders under this Act, which affect Scotland, were made prior to this order; certain provisions of this Act, not subject to commencement order, were already in force in Scotland

[2]   The New Valuation Lists Order 1987, SI 1987/921 (made under General Rate Act 1967, s 68(1) (repealed), as substituted by s 28 of this Act), specified 1 Apr 1990 as the date on which new valuation lists were to come into force; that Order was revoked by SI 1988/2146, made under Local Government Finance Act 1988; SI 1988/2146 was itself revoked and replaced by SI 1992/1643, made under Sch 6, para 2(3)(b) to 1988 Act. Accordingly, SI 1987/921 was ineffective to bring s 29(1)–(3) of, and Sch 33, para 10(1) to, this Act into force

## Magistrates' Courts Act 1980 (c 43)

*RA:* 1 Aug 1980

*Commencement provisions:* s 155(7)

Whole Act in force 6 Jul 1981 (s 155(7))

## Married Women's Policies of Assurance (Scotland) (Amendment) Act 1980 (c 56)

*RA:* 29 Oct 1980

Whole Act in force 29 Oct 1980 (RA)

## National Health Service (Invalid Direction) Act 1980 (c 15)

*RA:* 20 Mar 1980

Whole Act in force 20 Mar 1980 (RA)

## National Heritage Act 1980 (c 17)

*RA:* 31 Mar 1980

Whole Act in force 31 Mar 1980 (RA)

## New Hebrides Act 1980 (c 16)

*RA:* 20 Mar 1980

*Commencement provisions:* s 4(2); New Hebrides Order 1980, SI 1980/1079

| | |
|---|---|
| 1, 2 | 30 Jul 1980 (SI 1980/1079) |
| 3, 4 | 20 Mar 1980 (RA) |
| Schs 1, 2 | 30 Jul 1980 (SI 1980/1079) |

## New Towns Act 1980 (c 36)

*RA:* 30 Jun 1980

Whole Act in force 30 Jun 1980 (RA)

## Overseas Development and Co-operation Act 1980 (c 63)

*RA:* 13 Nov 1980

Commencement provisions: s 19(2)

Whole Act in force 14 Dec 1980 (s 19(2))

## Papua New Guinea, Western Samoa and Nauru (Miscellaneous Provisions) Act 1980 (c 2)

*RA:* 31 Jan 1980

*Commencement provisions:* s 3(3)

| | | |
|---|---|---|
| 1, 2 | | 31 Jan 1980 (RA) |
| 3 | (1) | See Schedule below |
| | (2) | 31 Jan 1980 (RA) |
| | (3) | See Schedule below |
| 4 | | 31 Jan 1980 (RA) |
| Schedule | para 1 | 16 Sep 1975 (retrospective; s 3(3)) |
| | para 2 | 31 Jan 1980 (RA) |
| | para 3 | 16 Sep 1975 (retrospective; s 3(3)) |
| | para 4 | 31 Jan 1980 (RA) |
| | para 5 | 16 Sep 1975 (retrospective; s 3(3)) |
| | paras 6–14 | 31 Jan 1980 (RA) |

## Petroleum Revenue Tax Act 1980 (c 1)

*RA:* 31 Jan 1980

*Commencement provisions:* s 3(3)

| | | |
|---|---|---|
| 1 | | Effective for chargeable periods ending on or after 31 Dec 1979 (s 3(3)) |
| 2 | (1), (2) | Effective for chargeable periods ending on or after 31 Dec 1979 (s 3(3)) |
| | (3) | 1 Jan 1980 (s 3(3)) |
| 3 | | 31 Jan 1980 (RA) |
| Schedule | | Effective for chargeable periods ending on or after 31 Dec 1979 (s 3(3)) |

## Police Negotiating Board Act 1980 (c 10)

*RA:* 20 Mar 1980

*Commencement provisions:* s 3(2)

Whole Act in force 20 May 1980 (s 3(2))

## Port of London (Financial Assistance) Act 1980 (c 31)

*RA:* 30 Jun 1980

Whole Act in force 30 Jun 1980 (RA)

## Protection of Trading Interests Act 1980 (c 11)

*RA:* 20 Mar 1980

Whole Act in force 20 Mar 1980 (RA)

## Representation of the People Act 1980 (c 3)

*RA:* 31 Jan 1980

*Commencement provisions:* s 3(3); Representation of the People Act 1980 (Commencement) Order 1980, SI 1980/1030

| | | |
|---|---|---|
| 1 | | 15 Aug 1980 (SI 1980/1030) |
| 2 | | 16 Feb 1981 (SI 1980/1030) |
| 3 | (1) | 15 Aug 1980 (SI 1980/1030) |
| | (2) | See Schedule below |
| | (3) | 15 Aug 1980 (SI 1980/1030) |
| Schedule | | 15 Aug 1980 (except repeals in Representation of the People Act 1969) (SI 1980/1030) |
| | | 16 Feb 1981 (exceptions noted above) (SI 1980/1030) |

## Reserve Forces Act 1980 (c 9)

*RA:* 20 Mar 1980

*Commencement provisions:* s 158(4)

Whole Act in force 20 Apr 1980 (s 158(4))

### Residential Homes Act 1980 (c 7)

*RA:* 20 Mar 1980

*Commencement provisions:* s 12(2); Residential Homes Act 1980 (Commencement) Order 1980, SI 1980/947

Whole Act in force 20 Aug 1980 (SI 1980/947)

---

### Sea Fish Industry Act 1980 (c 35)

*RA:* 30 Jun 1980

Whole Act in force 30 Jun 1980 (RA)

---

### Slaughter of Animals (Scotland) Act 1980 (c 13)

*RA:* 20 Mar 1980

Whole Act in force 20 Mar 1980 (RA)

---

### Social Security Act 1980 (c 30)

*RA:* 23 May 1980

*Commencement provisions:* s 21(5); Social Security Act 1980 (Commencement No 1) Order 1980, SI 1980/729; Social Security Act 1980 (Commencement No 2) Order 1981, SI 1981/1438; Social Security Act 1980 (Commencement No 3) Order 1983, SI 1983/1002; Social Security Act 1980 (Commencement No 4) Order 1984, SI 1984/1492

| | | |
|---|---|---|
| 1–4 | | 23 May 1980 (s 21(5)) |
| 5 | | 23 May 1980 (s 21(5), but note the section only applies from 4 Jul 1982, the date appointed by SI 1981/1156) |
| 6 | (1)–(3) | 24 Nov 1980 (SI 1980/729) |
| | (4) | 23 May 1980 (s 21(5)) |
| 7 | (1)(a), (b) | 21 Nov 1983 (SI 1983/1002) |
| | (1)(c) | 24 Nov 1980 (SI 1980/729) |
| | (2)–(5) | 24 Nov 1980 (SI 1980/729) |
| | (6) | 24 Nov 1980 (so far as it relates to definition of "supplement officer") (SI 1980/729) |
| | | 21 Nov 1983 (otherwise) (SI 1983/1002) |
| 8 | | 23 May 1980 (SI 1980/729) |
| 9, 10 | | 24 Nov 1980 (SI 1980/729) |
| 11–13 | | 23 May 1980 (s 21(5)) |
| 14, 15 | | 24 Nov 1980 (SI 1980/729) |
| 16–21 | | 23 May 1980 (s 21(5)) |
| Sch 1 | para 1(1) | 21 Nov 1983 (SI 1983/1002) |
| | para 1(2) | 26 Nov 1984 (SI 1984/1492) |
| | para 2 | 21 Nov 1983 (SI 1983/1002) |
| | para 3 | 23 Nov 1981 (SI 1981/1438) |
| | para 4 | 26 Nov 1984 (SI 1984/1492) |
| | para 5 | 14 Jul 1980 (repeal of Social Security Act 1975, ss 44(5)(b), 47(2)(b) and insertion of s 47A) (SI 1980/729) |
| | | *Never in force* (for other purposes) (repealed) |
| | paras 6, 7 | 21 Nov 1983 (SI 1983/1002) |
| | paras 8, 9 | 23 May 1980 (s 21(5)) |
| | para 10 | 24 Nov 1980 (SI 1980/729) |
| | paras 11–13 | 23 May 1980 (s 21(5)) |
| | para 14 | 26 Nov 1984 (SI 1984/1492) |
| | paras 15, 16 | 23 May 1980 (s 21(5)) |
| Schs 2, 3 | | 24 Nov 1980 (SI 1980/729) |

## Social Security Act 1980 (c 30)—*contd*

| | | |
|---|---|---|
| Sch 4 | paras 1–11 | 24 Nov 1980 (SI 1980/729) |
| | para 12 | 23 May 1980 (s 21(5)) |
| | paras 13, 14 | 24 Nov 1980 (SI 1980/729) |
| Sch 5 | Pt I | 23 May 1980 (s 21(5)) |
| | Pt II | 14 Jul 1980 (SI 1980/729), repeals of or in— |

    Social Security Act 1975, ss 44(5)(b), 47(2)(b), Sch 4, Pt IV;
    Social Security (Miscellaneous Provisions) Act 1977, s 8(3)

24 Nov 1980 (SI 1980/729), repeals of or in—
    Polish Resettlement Act 1947;
    National Assistance Act 1948;
    Legal Aid (Scotland) Act 1967;
    Social Work (Scotland) Act 1968;
    Merchant Shipping Act 1970;
    Family Income Supplements Act 1970, ss 7(2), 10(2)(h);
    Housing Finance Act 1972;
    Housing (Financial Provisions) (Scotland) Act 1972;
    Legal Aid Act 1974;
    Child Benefit Act 1975;
    House of Commons Disqualification Act 1975;
    Northern Ireland Assembly Disqualification Act 1975;
    Social Security Act 1975, ss 138, 139, 142(5), 168(4), Sch 15;
    Social Security (Consequential Provisions) Act 1975;
    Social Security Pensions Act 1975;
    National Insurance Surcharge Act 1976;
    Supplementary Benefits Act 1976;
    Social Security (Miscellaneous Provisions) Act 1977,
    ss 14(1)–(4), (7)–(10), 15, 24(4);
    Employment Protection (Consolidation) Act 1978;
    Legal Aid Act 1979;
    Social Security Act 1979;
    Reserve Forces Act 1980

23 Nov 1981 (repeals of or in Social Security Act 1975, ss 44(3)(b),
    (6), 47 (so far as not already repealed), 66(1)(c), (8))
    (SI 1981/1438)

21 Nov 1983 (SI 1983/1002), repeals of or in—
    Family Income Supplements Act 1970, s 17(1);
    Social Security Act 1975, ss 44(5) (so far as not already repealed),
    66(1)(b), Sch 20

26 Nov 1984 (repeal of Social Security Act 1975, ss 41(1), 65(4),
    158, Sch 19) (SI 1984/1492)

---

## Social Security (No 2) Act 1980 (c 39)

*RA:* 17 Jul 1980

*Commencement provisions:* s 8(2); Social Security (No 2) Act 1980 (Commencement) Order 1980,
    SI 1980/1025

| | | |
|---|---|---|
| 1, 2 | | 17 Jul 1980 (s 8(2)) |
| 3 | | 14 Sep 1980 (SI 1980/1025) |
| 4 | para (1) | 4 Jan 1981 (SI 1980/1025) |
| | para (2) | 3 Jan 1982 (SI 1980/1025) |
| 5 | | 6 Apr 1981 (SI 1980/1025) |
| 6 | | 24 Nov 1980 (SI 1980/1025) |
| 7 | paras (1)–(6) | 17 Jul 1980 (s 8(2); but note Sch below in relation to repeals) |
| | para (7) | 3 Jan 1982 (SI 1980/1025) |
| 8 | | 17 Jul 1980 (s 8(2)) |
| Schedule | | 17 Jul 1980 (s 8(2)), repeals of or in— |

    Social Security Act 1975, ss 125, 126;
    Social Security (Miscellaneous Provisions) Act 1977;

**Social Security (No 2) Act 1980 (c 39)**—*contd*

Social Security Act 1980

14 Sep 1980 (repeal of Social Security Act 1975, s 56(6))
(SI 1980/1025)

3 Jan 1982 (repeal of Social Security Act 1975, ss 12(1), 13(2)(b),
(3), (4), 14(7), 17(3), 22(4), 24(3), 79(4), 92(2), 124(1)(b),
Sch 6) (SI 1980/1025)

**Solicitors (Scotland) Act 1980 (c 46)**

*RA:* 1 Aug 1980

*Commencement provisions:* s 67(3)

Whole Act in force 1 Sep 1980 (s 67(3))

**Statute Law Revision (Northern Ireland) Act 1980 (c 59)**

*RA:* 13 Nov 1980

Whole Act in force 13 Nov 1980 (RA)

**Tenants' Rights, Etc (Scotland) Act 1980 (c 52)**

*RA:* 8 Aug 1980

*Commencement provisions:* s 86(4); Tenants' Rights, etc (Scotland) Act 1980 (Commencement) Order 1980,
SI 1980/1387

| | |
|---|---|
| 1–32 | 3 Oct 1980 (SI 1980/1387) |
| 33–42 | 1 Dec 1980 (SI 1980/1387) |
| 43 | 3 Oct 1980 (SI 1980/1387) |
| 44–52 | 1 Dec 1980 (SI 1980/1387) |
| 53 | 3 Oct 1980 (SI 1980/1387) |
| 54–65 | 1 Dec 1980 (SI 1980/1387) |
| 66–77 | 3 Oct 1980 (SI 1980/1387) |
| 78 (a) | 3 Oct 1980 (SI 1980/1387) |
| (b), (c) | 1 Apr 1981 (SI 1980/1387) |
| 79 | 3 Oct 1980 (SI 1980/1387) |
| 80 | 1 Apr 1981 (SI 1980/1387) |
| 81–83 | 3 Oct 1980 (SI 1980/1387) |
| 84 | See Sch 5 below |
| 85, 86 | 3 Oct 1980 (SI 1980/1387) |
| Schs 1–4 | 3 Oct 1980 (SI 1980/1387) |
| Sch 5 | 3 Oct 1980 (SI 1980/1387), except repeals of or in— |

Reserve and Auxiliary Forces (Protection of Civil Interests)
Act 1951, ss 16(1), (2)(c), (4)(b), 17(2)(a), (b), 18(2)(a), (b),
19(5);

Fire Precautions Act 1971, Schedule, Pt III, paras 1(1), (2)(a),
(6), (7), 4;

Rent (Scotland) Act 1971, ss 4(1), 5(4), (5), 7(1), (2), 9(1), 24,
25(1), 29, 30, 36, Pt V, ss 70–76, 80(2), 81, 82, 84, 85, 97(2),
100, 106(8), 110(1)(b), (2), 111(1), 113–115, 122(1)(b),
123(2), (3), 125(2), 129(2), 133, 135(1), Sch 2, Sch 3, Cases 5,
6, 9, Schs 8, 10–12, 14, 16, 17, 19, paras 9, 10, 14(1) (c),
19(1);

Housing (Financial Provisions) (Scotland) Act 1972, ss 61(3),
62(2), (4), 64, 65, Sch 7, paras 1–7;

Local Government (Scotland) Act 1973, Sch 13, paras 4, 5, 7;
Housing Act 1974, s 18(2), (5);

**Tenants' Rights, Etc (Scotland) Act 1980 (c 52)**—*contd*

> Rent Act 1974, s 1(3);
> Criminal Procedure (Scotland) Act 1975, Sch 7C;
> Housing Rents and Subsidies (Scotland) Act 1975, ss 7–11, Schs 2, 3, para 5
> 1 Dec 1980 (exceptions noted above) (SI 1980/1387)

---

**Tenants' Rights, Etc (Scotland) (Amendment) Act 1980 (c 61)**

*RA:* 13 Nov 1980

Whole Act in force 13 Nov 1980 (RA)

---

**Transport Act 1980 (c 34)**

*RA:* 30 Jun 1980

*Commencement provisions:* s 70; Transport Act 1980 (Commencement No 1) Order 1980, SI 1980/913, as amended by SI 1980/1353; Transport Act 1980 (Commencement No 2) Order 1980, SI 1980/1353; Transport Act 1980 (Commencement No 3) Order 1980, SI 1980/1424; Transport Act 1980 (Commencement No 4) Order 1981, SI 1981/256

| | | |
|---|---|---|
| 1 | (1), (2) | *Never in force* (repealed) |
| | (3), (4) | 31 Jul 1980 (so far as relates to the provisions brought into force by SI 1980/913, Schedule, Pt I) (SI 1980/913) |
| | | 6 Oct 1980 (so far as relates to the provisions brought into force by SI 1980/1353, Schedule, Pt I) (SI 1980/1353) |
| | | 1 Apr 1981 (so far as relates to the provisions brought into force by SI 1981/256, Schedule, Pt I) (SI 1981/256) |
| | | *Never in force* (remaining purposes) (repealed) |
| 2–15 | | 6 Oct 1980 (SI 1980/1353) |
| 16–26 | | 1 Apr 1981 (SI 1981/256) |
| 27 | | 31 Jul 1980 (SI 1980/913) |
| 28 | (1)–(5) | 6 Oct 1980 (so far as relates to road service licences) (SI 1980/1353) |
| | | 1 Apr 1981 (so far as it relates to PSV operators' licences) (SI 1981/256) |
| | | *Never in force* (remaining purposes) (repealed) |
| | (6) | 1 Apr 1981 (SI 1981/256) |
| | (7), (8) | 6 Oct 1980 (so far as relates to road service licences) (SI 1980/1353) |
| | | *Never in force* (remaining purposes) (repealed) |
| | (9), (10) | 6 Oct 1980 (so far as relates to road service licences) (SI 1980/1353) |
| | | 1 Apr 1981 (so far as it relates to PSV operators' licences) (SI 1981/256) |
| | | *Never in force* (remaining purposes) (repealed) |
| 29 | | 6 Oct 1980 (so far as relates to road service licences) (SI 1980/1353) |
| | | 1 Apr 1981 (otherwise) (SI 1981/256) |
| 30, 31 | | 1 Apr 1981 (SI 1981/256) |
| 32, 33 | | 6 Oct 1980 (SI 1980/1353) |
| 34 | | 1 Apr 1981 (SI 1981/256) |
| 35 | | 6 Oct 1980 (SI 1980/1353) |
| 36 | | 31 Jul 1980 (SI 1980/913) |
| 37 | | 6 Oct 1980 (SI 1980/1353) |
| 38 | | 6 Oct 1980 (so far as it amends Road Traffic Act 1960, s 159) (SI 1980/1353) |
| | | 1 Apr 1981 (otherwise) (SI 1981/256) |
| 39 | | 31 Jul 1980 (SI 1980/913) |
| 40 | | 6 Oct 1980 (SI 1980/1353) |

**Transport Act 1980 (c 34)**—*contd*

| | | |
|---|---|---|
| 41 | | 6 Oct 1980 (so far as relates to road service licences) (SI 1980/1353) |
| | | 1 Apr 1981 (otherwise) (SI 1981/256) |
| 42 | (1) | 6 Oct 1980 (so far as relates to the provisions specified in s 42(2), except ss 25(5), 26(4)) (SI 1980/1353) |
| | | 1 Apr 1981 (otherwise) (SI 1981/256) |
| | (2)(a) | 6 Oct 1980 (except so far as it specifies ss 25(5), 26(4)) (SI 1980/1353) |
| | | 1 Apr 1981 (otherwise) (SI 1981/256) |
| | (2)(b) | 6 Oct 1980 (SI 1980/1353) |
| | (3) | 6 Oct 1980 (so far as relates to the provisions specified in s 42(4), except ss 17(3), 18(9)(b), 19(5), 22(7), 24(4)) (SI 1980/1353) |
| | | 1 Apr 1981 (otherwise) (SI 1981/256) |
| | (4) | 6 Oct 1980 (except in so far as specifies ss 17(3), 18(9)(b), 19(5), 22(7), 24(4)) (SI 1980/1353) |
| | | 1 Apr 1981 (otherwise) (SI 1981/256) |
| 43 | (1) | See Sch 5, Pt II below |
| | (2) | 6 Oct 1980 (SI 1980/1353) |
| 44 | | 6 Oct 1980 (in so far as relates to any provision specified in SI 1980/1353) (SI 1980/1353) |
| | | 1 Apr 1981 (otherwise) (SI 1981/256) |
| 45–50 | | 30 Jun 1980 (s 70(3), but generally of no effect until 1 Oct 1980, the day appointed under s 45(2) by SI 1980/1380) |
| 51 | (1) | 30 Jun 1980 (s 70(3)) |
| | (2) | 1 Oct 1980 (appointed day under SI 1980/1380) |
| 52–60 | | 30 Jun 1980 (s 70(3)) |
| 61, 62 | | 6 Oct 1980 (SI 1980/1353) |
| 63 | | 1 Apr 1981 (SI 1981/256) |
| 64 | | 31 Jul 1980 (SI 1980/913) |
| 65 | | 6 Oct 1980 (SI 1980/913) |
| 66–68 | | 30 Jun 1980 (s 70(3)) |
| 69 | | See Sch 9 below |
| 70 | | 30 Jun 1980 (s 70(3)) |
| Sch 1 | Pts I–III | 6 Oct 1980 (SI 1980/1353) |
| | Pt IV | 6 Oct 1980 (SI 1980/1424) |
| Sch 2 | | 6 Oct 1980 (SI 1980/1424) |
| Sch 3 | | 1 Apr 1981 (SI 1981/256) |
| Sch 4 | | 6 Oct 1980 (SI 1980/913) |
| Sch 5 | Pt I, paras 1–3 | 1 Apr 1981 (SI 1981/256) |
| | Pt I, para 4(a) | 31 Jul 1980 (SI 1980/913) |
| | Pt I, para 4(b) | 1 Apr 1981 (SI 1981/256) |
| | Pt I, para 4(c) | 6 Oct 1980 (SI 1980/1353) |
| | Pt I, paras 5, 6 | 31 Jul 1980 (SI 1980/913) |
| | Pt I, para 7 | 6 Oct 1980 (SI 1980/1353) |
| | Pt I, para 8 | 1 Apr 1981 (SI 1981/256) |
| | Pt I, para 9 | 6 Oct 1980 (SI 1980/1353) |
| | Pt I, para 10 | 1 Apr 1981 (SI 1981/256) |
| | Pt I, para 11(a) | 1 Apr 1981 (SI 1981/256) |
| | Pt I, para 11(b)–(d) | 6 Oct 1980 (SI 1980/1353) |
| | Pt I, para 11(e) | *Never in force* (repealed) |
| | Pt I, para 12(a), (b) | 1 Apr 1981 (SI 1981/256) |
| | Pt I, para 12(c)–(e) | 31 Jul 1980 (SI 1980/913) |
| | Pt I, para 13 | 6 Oct 1980 (SI 1980/1353) |
| | Pt I, paras 14, 15 | 31 Jul 1980 (SI 1980/913) |
| | Pt II | 6 Oct 1980 (SI 1980/913), amendments of— |
| | | Local Government (Miscellaneous Provisions) Act 1953; |
| | | Transport Act 1962; |
| | | Road Traffic Act 1972; |
| | | Road Traffic (Foreign Vehicles) Act 1972 (paras 1(b), 2 only); |

**Transport Act 1980 (c 34)**—*contd*

Local Government (Miscellaneous Provisions) Act 1976 (para 2 only);

Energy Act 1976 (sub-paras (a), (c) only)

1 Apr 1981 (SI 1981/256) amendments of—

Road Traffic (Foreign Vehicles) Act 1972 (paras 1(a), 3);

Road Traffic Act 1974;

Energy Act 1976 (sub-para (b));

Local Government (Miscellaneous Provisions) Act 1976 (para 1)

*Never in force* (remaining purposes) (repealed)

| | | |
|---|---|---|
| Sch 6 | | 30 Jun 1980 (s 70(3); but not generally effective until 1 Oct 1980, the date appointed under s 45(2) by SI 1980/1380) |
| Sch 7 | | 1 Oct 1980 (appointed day under SI 1980/1380) |
| Sch 8 | | 30 Jun 1980 (s 70(3)) |
| Sch 9 | Pt I | 31 Jul 1980 (SI 1980/913), repeals of or in— |

Road Traffic Act 1960, ss 144, 145(1), 147(1)(d), 154, 155, 158, 160(1)(f), 163(1);

Transport (London) Act 1969, s 24(2), (3);

Local Government (Scotland) Act 1973, Sch 18, para 30;

Road Traffic Act 1974, Sch 6, para 2;

Energy Act 1976, Sch 1, para 2

6 Oct 1980 (SI 1980/1353), repeals of or in—

Education (Miscellaneous Provisions) Act 1953, s 12;

Transport Charges &c (Miscellaneous Provisions) Act 1954, s 2, Sch 1;

Public Service Vehicles (Travel Concessions) Act 1955, s 1(7);

Local Government (Omnibus Shelters and Queue Barriers) (Scotland) Act 1958, s 7(1);

Road Traffic Act 1960, ss 117, 118, 119(3)(a), 128(2), 134–139, 139A, 140, 143(1)–(4), (9) (in so far as relate to road service licences), 149, 156(1), 160 (repeals in heads (a) and (c)), 234, 240, 247(2), 257(1) (definition "road service licence"), 258, Schs 12, 17;

Transport Act 1962, Sch 2, Pt I;

London Government Act 1963, ss 9(6)(b), 14(6)(d), Sch 5, Pt I, para 25;

Finance Act 1965, s 92(8);

Road Traffic Regulation Act 1967, s 1(3), Sch 6;

Transport Act 1968, ss 21(1), 30, 138(1)(a), (3)(a), 145(1), 159(1);

Transport (London) Act 1969, ss 23(6), (7), 24(4)(b), (d), Sch 3, paras 8, 11;

Tribunals and Inquiries Act 1971, s 13(5), (6)(a), Sch 1, para 30(a) (in so far as relate to road service licences);

European Communities Act 1972, Sch 4, para 10;

Local Government Act 1972, s 186(3);

Local Government (Scotland) Act 1973, Sch 18, paras 26, 31–35;

Road Traffic Act 1974, Sch 5, Pt I (except entries relating to Road Traffic Act 1960, ss 127, 128(3), 132(3), 148(2), 239), Sch 6, para 1, Sch 7;

Transport Act 1978, ss 6, 7(1), (2), 8, Schs 1, 2

1 Apr 1981 (SI 1981/256), repeals of or in—

Road Traffic Act 1960, ss 127, 129, 130(2), 132, 133, 133A, 143 (so far as unrepealed), 153(2), 257(1) (definition "owner");

Transport Act 1968, s 35(1), (2), (3)(a);

Tribunals and Inquiries Act 1971, s 13(5), (6)(a), Sch 1, para 30(a) (so far as unrepealed);

Road Traffic Act 1972, s 44(4);

Road Traffic Act 1974, Sch 2, paras 1, 3–5, Sch 5, Pt I (entries relating to Road Traffic Act 1960, ss 127, 128(3), 132(2));

Transport Act 1978, s 5(10)

**Transport Act 1980 (c 34)**—*contd*

| | |
|---|---|
| Pt II | 30 Jun 1980 (s 70(3)) |
| Pt III | 1 Oct 1980 (date appointed by SI 1980/1380) |
| Pt IV | 1 Apr 1981 (SI 1981/256) |

---

**Water (Scotland) Act 1980 (c 45)**

*RA:* 1 Aug 1980

Whole Act in force 1 Aug 1980 (RA)

---

# 1981 Acts

## Acquisition of Land Act 1981 (c 67)

*RA:* 30 Oct 1981

*Commencement provisions:* s 35(2)

Whole Act in force 30 Jan 1982 (s 35(2))

---

## Animal Health Act 1981 (c 22)

*RA:* 11 Jun 1981

*Commencement provisions:* s 97(3)

Whole Act in force 11 Jul 1981 (s 97(3))

---

## Appropriation Act 1981 (c 51)

*RA:* 28 Jul 1981

Whole Act in force 28 Jul 1981 (RA)

---

## Armed Forces Act 1981 (c 55)

*RA:* 28 Jul 1981

*Commencement provisions:* ss 1(5), 29(1)–(3), (5), Sch 5, Pt II, para 1; Armed Forces Act 1981 (Commencement No 1) Order 1981, SI 1981/1503; Armed Forces Act 1981 (Commencement No 2) Order 1982, SI 1982/497

| | | |
|---|---|---|
| 1 | | 28 Jul 1981 (s 29(4)) |
| 2–5 | | 1 May 1982 (SI 1982/497) |
| 6 | | 1 Nov 1981 (SI 1981/1503) |
| 7 | | 28 Jul 1981 (s 29(4)) |
| 8–14 | | 1 May 1982 (SI 1982/497) |
| 15–17 | | 28 Jul 1981 (s 29(4)) |
| 18 | | 1 May 1982 (SI 1982/497) |
| 19–22 | | 28 Jul 1981 (s 29(4)) |
| 23, 24 | | 1 May 1982 (SI 1982/497) |
| 25–27 | | 28 Jul 1981 (s 29(4)) |
| 28 | (1) | 1 May 1982 (SI 1982/497) |
| | (2) | 28 Jul 1981 (s 29(4)) |
| 29, 30 | | 28 Jul 1981 (s 29(4)) |
| Schs 1, 2 | | 1 May 1982 (SI 1982/497) |
| Sch 3 | | 28 Jul 1981 (s 29(4)) |
| Sch 4 | | 1 May 1982 (SI 1982/497) |
| Sch 5 | Pt I | 28 Jul 1982 (s 29(5), Sch 5, para 2) |
| | Pt II | 28 Jul 1982 (s 29(5), Sch 5, para 1), repeals of or in— Naval Agency and Distribution Act 1864, s 17; |

---

**Armed Forces Act 1981 (c 55)**—*contd*

> Naval and Marine Pay and Pensions Act 1865, s 12;
> Army Pensions Act 1914;
> Naval Discipline Act 1957, s 93;
> Armed Forces Act 1976, Sch 9
>
> 1 Sep 1981 (repeal of Armed Forces Act 1976, s 1) (s 29(5), Sch 5, para 2)
>
> 1 May 1982 (s 29(1); SI 1982/497), repeals of or in—
> Greenwich Hospital Act 1885, s 4;
> Colonial Naval Defence Act 1931, s 2(1);
> Colonial Naval Defence Act 1949, s 1(4);
> Army Act 1955, ss 82(2)(b), 99(2), 131(2), 153(3), 209(3), Sch 7, para 6;
> Air Force Act 1955, ss 82(2)(b), 99(2), 131(2), 153(3), 209(3);
> Naval Discipline Act 1957, ss 51(1), (2), 101(2);
> Army and Air Force Act 1961, s 26(3);
> Criminal Justice (Scotland) Act 1963, s 9(3), (4);
> Armed Forces Act 1976, Sch 9, para 12

**Atomic Energy (Miscellaneous Provisions) Act 1981 (c 48)**

*RA:* 27 Jul 1981

Whole Act in force 27 Jul 1981 (RA)

**Belize Act 1981 (c 52)**

*RA:* 28 Jul 1981

*Commencement provisions:* s 6(2); Belize Independence Order 1981, SI 1981/1107

Whole Act in force 28 Jul 1981 (RA); note, however, that most provisions of this Act did not take effect until 21 Sep 1981 (the day appointed by SI 1981/1107 as "Independence Day")

**Betting and Gaming Duties Act 1981 (c 63)**

*RA:* 30 Oct 1981

Whole Act in force 30 Oct 1981 (RA)

**British Nationality Act 1981 (c 61)**

*RA:* 30 Oct 1981

*Commencement provisions:* s 53(2), (3); British Nationality Act 1981 (Commencement) Order 1982, SI 1982/933

| | |
|---|---|
| 1–48 | 1 Jan 1983 (SI 1982/933) |
| 49 | 30 Oct 1981 (s 53(3)) |
| 50–52 | 1 Jan 1983 (SI 1982/933) |
| 53 | 30 Oct 1981 (s 53(3)) |
| Schs 1–9 | 1 Jan 1983 (SI 1982/933) |

## British Telecommunications Act 1981 (c 38)

*RA:* 27 Jul 1981

Whole Act in force 27 Jul 1981 (RA); note, however, that many provisions of the Act did not come into force until 1 Oct 1981, the date appointed by British Telecommunications Act 1981 (Appointed Day) Order 1981, SI 1981/1274, made under s 1(2) (repealed)

## Broadcasting Act 1981 (c 68)

*RA:* 30 Oct 1981

*Commencement provisions:* s 66(4)

Whole Act in force 1 Jan 1982 (s 66(4))

## Companies Act 1981 (c 62)

*RA:* 30 Oct 1981

*Commencement Provisions:* s 119(3); Companies Act 1981 (Commencement No 1) Order 1981, SI 1981/1621; Companies Act 1981 (Commencement No 2) Order 1981, SI 1981/1684; Companies Act 1981 (Commencement No 3) Order 1982, SI 1982/103; Companies Act 1981 (Commencement No 4) Order 1982, SI 1982/672; Companies Act 1981 (Commencement No 5) Order 1983, SI 1983/1024; Companies Act 1981 (Commencement No 6) Order 1984, SI 1984/684

| | | |
|---|---|---|
| 1–15 | | 15 Jun 1982 (except so far as amends or repeals any provision of the Companies Act 1948 or the Companies Act 1967 as that provision applies to unregistered companies by virtue of s 435 of the 1948 Act) (SI 1982/672) |
| | | 1 Jan 1985 (exceptions noted above) (SI 1984/684) |
| 16 | (1), (2)(a), (b) | 15 Jun 1982 (except so far as amends or repeals any provision of the Companies Act 1948 or the Companies Act 1967 as that provision applies to unregistered companies by virtue of s 435 of the 1948 Act) (SI 1982/672) |
| | | 1 Jan 1985 (exceptions noted above) (SI 1984/684) |
| | (2)(c) | 24 Nov 1981 (SI 1981/1684) |
| | (2)(d), (e) | 15 Jun 1982 (except so far as amends or repeals any provision of the Companies Act 1948 or the Companies Act 1967 as that provision applies to unregistered companies by virtue of s 435 of the 1948 Act) (SI 1982/672) |
| | | 1 Jan 1985 (exceptions noted above) (SI 1984/684) |
| 17 | (1) | See Sch 2 below |
| | (2) | 15 Jun 1982 (except so far as amends or repeals any provision of the Companies Act 1948 or the Companies Act 1967 as that provision applies to unregistered companies by virtue of s 435 of the 1948 Act) (SI 1982/672) |
| | | 1 Jan 1985 (exceptions noted above) (SI 1984/684) |
| 18 | | 15 Jun 1982 (except so far as amends or repeals any provision of the Companies Act 1948 or the Companies Act 1967 as that provision applies to unregistered companies by virtue of s 435 of the 1948 Act) (SI 1982/672) |
| | | 1 Jan 1985 (exceptions noted above) (SI 1984/684) |
| 19 | | 10 May 1982 (SI 1982/672) |
| 20 | | 1 Jul 1984 (SI 1984/684) |
| 21 | | 15 Jun 1982 (except so far as amends or repeals any provision of the Companies Act 1948 or the Companies Act 1967 as that provision applies to unregistered companies by virtue of s 435 of the 1948 Act) (SI 1982/672) |
| | | 1 Jan 1985 (exceptions noted above) (SI 1984/684) |
| 22–30 | | 26 Feb 1982 (SI 1982/103) |
| 31 | | 24 Nov 1981 (SI 1981/1684) |

**Companies Act 1981 (c 62)**—*contd*

| | | |
|---|---|---|
| 32 | (1)(a), (b)(i) | 24 Nov 1981 (SI 1981/1684) |
| | (1)(b)(ii) | 26 Feb 1982 (SI 1982/103) |
| | (2) | 24 Nov 1981 (SI 1981/1684) |
| 33 | | 30 Oct 1981 (s 119(3)) |
| 34 | | 24 Nov 1981 (in so far as relates to the definition "business" for the purposes of Pt II of this Act) (SI 1981/1684) |
| | | 26 Feb 1982 (otherwise) (SI 1982/103) |
| 35 | | 26 Feb 1982 (SI 1982/103) |
| 36–41 | | 30 Oct 1981 (s 119(3)) |
| 42–44 | | 3 Dec 1981 (SI 1981/1621) |
| 45–59 | | 15 Jun 1982 (SI 1982/672) |
| 60 | | 3 Dec 1981 (in so far as applies to financial assistance given by a company) (SI 1981/1621) |
| | | 15 Jun 1982 (otherwise) (SI 1982/672) |
| 61 | | 1 Jan 1985 (SI 1984/684) |
| 62 | (1) | 3 Dec 1981 (in so far as provides for the definition of "distributable profits" and "distribution" for the purposes of Pt III of this Act in relation to the giving of financial assistance by a company) (SI 1981/1621) |
| | | 15 Jun 1982 (otherwise) (SI 1982/672) |
| | (2)–(4) | 15 Jun 1982 (SI 1982/672) |
| 63–84 | | 15 Jun 1982 (SI 1982/672) |
| 85 | | 24 Nov 1981 (except so far as inserts Companies Act 1980, s 43A(b)) (SI 1981/1684) |
| | | 15 Jun 1982 (exception noted above) (SI 1982/672) |
| 86–92 | | 24 Nov 1981 (SI 1981/1684) |
| 93, 94 | | 15 Jun 1982 (SI 1982/672) |
| 95 | | 1 Jan 1984 (SI 1983/1024) |
| 96–100 | | 24 Nov 1981 (SI 1981/1684) |
| 101, 102 | | 1 Jan 1985 (SI 1984/684) |
| 103–106 | | 24 Nov 1981 (SI 1981/1684) |
| 107 | | 30 Oct 1981 (s 119(3)) |
| 108 | | 24 Nov 1981 (SI 1981/1684) |
| 109 | | 26 Feb 1982 (SI 1982/103) |
| 110–112 | | 24 Nov 1981 (SI 1981/1684) |
| 113–115 | | 3 Dec 1981 (SI 1981/1621) |
| 116 | | 24 Nov 1981 (SI 1981/1684) |
| 117, 118 | | 3 Dec 1981 (SI 1981/1621) |
| 119 | (1)–(3) | 3 Dec 1981 (SI 1981/1621) |
| | (4) | See Sch 3 below |
| | (5) | See Sch 4 below |
| | (6) | 1 Jan 1985 (SI 1984/684) |
| Schs 1, 2 | | 1 Jan 1985 (SI 1984/684) |
| Sch 3 | para 1 | 3 Dec 1981 (SI 1981/1621) |
| | para 2 | 3 Dec 1981 (in so far as relates to Companies Act 1948, Sch 1, Table A, regs 73A, 80) (SI 1981/1621) |
| | | 26 Feb 1982 (in so far as relates to ss 1, 4, 5, and 10 of the 1948 Act) (SI 1982/103) |
| | | 15 Jun 1982 (otherwise, except so far as amends any provision of the Companies Act 1948, as that provision applies to unregistered companies by virtue of s 435 of the 1948 Act) (SI 1982/672) |
| | | 1 Jan 1985 (exceptions noted above) (SI 1984/684) |
| | paras 3, 4 | 24 Nov 1981 (SI 1981/1684) |
| | paras 5, 6 | 15 Jun 1982 (except so far as amends any provision of the Companies Act 1948, as that provision applies to unregistered companies by virtue of s 435 of the 1948 Act) (SI 1982/672) |
| | | 1 Jan 1985 (exceptions noted above) (SI 1984/684) |
| | paras 7, 8 | 24 Nov 1981 (SI 1981/1684) |
| | para 9 | 15 Jun 1982 (SI 1982/672) |

**Companies Act 1981 (c 62)**—*contd*

|  |  |  |
|---|---|---|
| | para 10 | 15 Jun 1982 (except so far as amends any provision of the Companies Act 1948, as that provision applies to unregistered companies by virtue of s 435 of the 1948 Act) (SI 1982/672) |
| | | 1 Jan 1985 (exceptions noted above) (SI 1984/684) |
| | paras 11, 12 | 24 Nov 1981 (SI 1981/1684) |
| | para 13(a) | 26 Feb 1982 (SI 1982/103) |
| | para 13(b) | 1 Jan 1984 (SI 1983/1024) |
| | para 14 | 26 Feb 1982 (SI 1982/103) |
| | para 15 | 15 Jun 1982 (SI 1982/672) |
| | paras 16–19 | 3 Dec 1981 (SI 1981/1621) |
| | paras 20, 21 | 15 Jun 1982 (SI 1982/672) |
| | para 22 | 1 Jul 1984 (SI 1984/684) |
| | para 23 | 15 Jun 1982 (except so far as amends any provision of the Companies Act 1967, as that provision applies to unregistered companies by virtue of s 435 of the 1948 Act) (SI 1982/672) |
| | | 1 Jan 1985 (exceptions noted above) (SI 1984/684) |
| | para 24 | 15 Jun 1982 (SI 1982/672) |
| | paras 25, 26 | 15 Jun 1982 (except so far as amends any provision of the Companies Act 1967, as that provision applies to unregistered companies by virtue of s 435 of the 1948 Act) (SI 1982/672) |
| | | 1 Jan 1985 (exceptions noted above) (SI 1984/684) |
| | para 27 | 3 Dec 1981 (SI 1981/1621) |
| | para 28 | 24 Nov 1981 (SI 1981/1684) |
| | para 29 | 15 Jun 1982 (SI 1982/672) |
| | paras 30, 31 | 26 Feb 1982 (SI 1982/103) |
| | para 32 | 24 Nov 1981 (SI 1981/1684) |
| | para 33 | 15 Jun 1982 (except so far as amends any provision of the Companies Act 1967, as that provision applies to unregistered companies by virtue of s 435 of the 1948 Act) (SI 1982/672) |
| | | 1 Jan 1985 (exceptions noted above) (SI 1984/684) |
| | para 34 | 24 Nov 1981 (SI 1981/1684) |
| | para 35 | 3 Dec 1981 (SI 1981/1621) |
| | para 36 | 15 Jun 1982 (SI 1982/672) |
| | paras 37, 38 | 24 Nov 1981 (SI 1981/1684) |
| | para 39 | 3 Dec 1981 (SI 1981/1621) |
| | paras 40–42 | 24 Nov 1981 (SI 1981/1684) |
| | paras 43, 44 | 15 Jun 1982 (SI 1982/672) |
| | para 45(1)(a) | 15 Jun 1982 (SI 1982/672) |
| | para 45(1)(b), (2) | 24 Nov 1981 (SI 1981/1684) |
| | para 46 | 15 Jun 1982 (SI 1982/672) |
| | para 47(a)(i) | 15 Jun 1982 (SI 1982/672) |
| | para 47(a)(ii) | 24 Nov 1981 (SI 1981/1684) |
| | para 47(b) | 15 Jun 1982 (SI 1982/672) |
| | para 47(c) | 24 Nov 1981 (SI 1981/1684) |
| | paras 47(d), 48(a) | 15 Jun 1982 (SI 1982/672) |
| | paras 48(b), 49–54 | 24 Nov 1981 (SI 1981/1684) |
| | para 55 | 15 Jun 1982 (SI 1982/672) |
| | paras 56–60 | 24 Nov 1981 (SI 1981/1684) |
| | para 61 | 3 Dec 1981 (SI 1981/1621) |
| | para 62 | 15 Jun 1982 (except so far as amends any provision of the Companies Act 1980, as that provision applies to unregistered companies by virtue of s 435 of the 1948 Act) (SI 1982/672) |
| | | 1 Jan 1985 (exceptions noted above) (SI 1984/684) |
| | para 63 | 3 Dec 1981 (SI 1981/1621) |
| Sch 4 | | 3 Dec 1981 (SI 1981/1621), repeals of or in— Companies Act 1948, s 54, Sch 1, Table A, reg 10; Companies Act 1980, Sch 3, paras 10, 36, 46 |
| | | 24 Nov 1981 (SI 1981/1684), repeals of or in— Companies Act 1948, ss 165, 167, 174, 201, 283, 354; |

**Companies Act 1981 (c 62)**—*contd*

Companies Act 1967, s 20;

Companies Act 1976, ss 34, 36, 38, Sch 2 (entries relating to ss 13, 69, 98, 106E, 390 and 426 of the 1948 Act);

Companies Act 1980, Sch 2 (entries relating to ss 124, 125 of the 1948 Act)

26 Feb 1982 (SI 1982/103), repeals of or in—

Registration of Business Names Act 1916;

Fees (Increase) Act 1923;

Companies Act 1947;

Companies Act 1948, ss 5, 17–19, 388, 389, 456, Sch 16;

Companies Act 1976, ss 30, 32;

Banking Act 1979;

Companies Act 1980, Sch 2 (entries relating to ss 18, 19 of the 1948 Act), Sch 3, paras 2, 5, 30

10 May 1982 (repeal in Companies Act 1976, s 9) (SI 1982/672)

15 Jun 1982 (SI 1982/672), repeals of or in—

Companies Act 1948, ss 56, 58, 62, 188, Sch 1 (otherwise);

Companies Act 1948, ss 156, 157, 163, 196 except so far as they apply to unregistered companies by virtue of s 435 of that Act;

Companies Act 1967, ss 12, 33, 34, 54;

Companies Act 1967, ss 9, 16(1)(b), (d), (2), 22 except so far as they apply to unregistered companies by virtue of s 435 of the 1948 Act;

European Communities Act 1972;

Companies Act 1976, ss 26–29, Sch 2 (entries relating to Sch 1, Tables A and C of the 1948 Act);

Companies Act 1980, ss 39–41, 43, 45, 81, Sch 3, paras 13, 14;

Companies Act 1980, Sch 3, paras 19, 20, 24 except so far as they amend any provision of the Companies Act 1948 in its application to unregistered companies by virtue of s 435 of the 1948 Act

1 Jan 1984 (SI 1983/1024), repeals of or in—

Companies Act 1967, s 16(3);

Companies Act 1980, Sch 2 (entry relating to s 200 of the 1948 Act)

1 Jul 1984 (repeal of Companies Act 1976, Sch 2 (otherwise)) (SI 1984/684)

1 Jan 1985 (otherwise) (SI 1984/684)

**Compulsory Purchase (Vesting Declarations) Act 1981 (c 66)**

*RA:* 30 Oct 1981

*Commencement provisions:* s 17(2)

Whole Act in force 30 Jan 1982 (s 17(2))

**Consolidated Fund Act 1981 (c 4)**

*RA:* 19 Mar 1981

Whole Act in force 19 Mar 1981 (RA)

**Consolidated Fund (No 2) Act 1981 (c 70)**

*RA:* 22 Dec 1981

Whole Act in force 22 Dec 1981 (RA)

## Contempt of Court Act 1981 (c 49)

*RA:* 27 Jul 1981

*Commencement provisions:* s 21(2), (3)

Whole Act in force 27 Aug 1981 (s 21(3)) with the exception of the provisions relating to legal aid (namely, s 13, Sch 2, Pts I, II) which, in relation to (E) (W) (S), were never brought in force and are now repealed

## Countryside (Scotland) Act 1981 (c 44)

*RA:* 27 Jul 1981

*Commencement provisions:* s 18(2); Countryside (Scotland) Act 1981 (Commencement) Order 1981, SI 1981/1614

| | |
|---|---|
| 1 | 1 Apr 1982 (SI 1981/1614) |
| 2–14 | 5 Nov 1981 (SI 1981/1614) |
| 15 | See Sch 2 below |
| 16–18 | 5 Nov 1981 (SI 1981/1614) |
| Sch 1 | 5 Nov 1981 (SI 1981/1614) |
| Sch 2 | 5 Nov 1981 (except repeal of Countryside (Scotland) Act 1967, ss 67, 68) (SI 1981/1614) |
| | 1 Apr 1982 (exception noted above) (SI 1981/1614) |

## Criminal Attempts Act 1981 (c 47)

*RA:* 27 Jul 1981

*Commencement provisions:* s 11(1)

Whole Act in force 27 Aug 1981 (s 11(1))

## Criminal Justice (Amendment) Act 1981 (c 27)

*RA:* 2 Jul 1981

*Commencement provisions:* s 2(2)

Whole Act in force 2 Oct 1981 (s 2(2))

## Deep Sea Mining (Temporary Provisions) Act 1981 (c 53)

*RA:* 28 Jul 1981

*Commencement provisions:* s 18(2); Deep Sea Mining (Temporary Provisions) Act 1981 (Appointed Day) Order 1982, SI 1982/52

Whole Act in force 25 Jan 1982 (SI 1982/52)

## Disabled Persons Act 1981 (c 43)

*RA:* 27 Jul 1981

*Commencement provisions:* ss 6(6), 9(2) (both repealed)

| | |
|---|---|
| 1–5 | 27 Oct 1981 (s 9(2)) |
| 6 | *Never in force* (repealed) |
| 7–9 | 27 Oct 1981 (s 9(2)) |

## Disused Burial Grounds (Amendment) Act 1981 (c 18)

*RA:* 21 May 1981

Whole Act in force 21 May 1981 (RA)

## Education Act 1981 (c 60)

*RA:* 31 Jul 1981

*Commencement provisions:* s 20(2); Education Act 1981 (Commencement No 1) Order 1981, SI 1981/1711; Education Act 1981 (Commencement No 2) Order 1983, SI 1983/7

| | | |
|---|---|---|
| 1–13 | | 1 Apr 1983 (SI 1983/7) |
| 14 | | 5 Jan 1982 (SI 1981/1711) |
| 15–19 | | 1 Apr 1983 (SI 1983/7) |
| 20 | | 5 Jan 1982 (SI 1981/1711) |
| 21 | (1), (2) | 5 Jan 1982 (SI 1981/1711) |
| | (3), (4) | 1 Apr 1983 (SI 1983/7) |
| | (5) | 5 Jan 1982 (SI 1981/1711) |
| Schs 1–4 | | 1 Apr 1983 (SI 1983/7) |

## Education (Scotland) Act 1981 (c 58)

*RA:* 30 Oct 1981

*Commencement provisions:* s 22(2), (3); Education (Scotland) Act 1981 (Commencement No 1) Order 1981, SI 1981/1557; Education (Scotland) Act 1981 (Commencement No 2) Order 1982, SI 1982/951; Education (Scotland) Act 1981 (Commencement No 3) Order 1982, SI 1982/1737; Education (Scotland) Act 1981 (Commencement No 4) Order 1983, SI 1983/371

| | | |
|---|---|---|
| 1 | (1) | 15 Feb 1982 (so far as inserts Education (Scotland) Act 1980, ss 28A, 28B (except s 28B(1)(d)), and s 28G so far as relates to those sections) (SI 1981/1557) |
| | | 15 Mar 1982 (so far as inserts Education (Scotland) Act 1980, ss 28C, 28D, 28E (except s 28E(2)), 28F and s 28G so far as relates to those sections) (SI 1981/1557) |
| | | 1 Jan 1983 (so far as inserts Education (Scotland) Act 1980, ss 28B(1)(d), 28E(2)) (SI 1982/951) |
| | | 9 Mar 1983 (so far as inserts Education (Scotland) Act 1980, s 28G so far as relates to ss 28B(1)(d), 28E(2) and Sch A1) (SI 1983/371) |
| | | 5 Apr 1983 (so far as inserts Education (Scotland) Act 1980, s 28H) (SI 1982/1737) |
| | (2) | 15 Mar 1982 (SI 1981/1557) |
| | (3), (4) | 15 Feb 1982 (SI 1981/1557) |
| 2 | | 15 Feb 1982 (SI 1981/1557) |
| 3, 4 | | 1 Jan 1983 (SI 1982/951) |
| 5 | | 16 Aug 1982 (SI 1982/951) |
| 6–8 | | 1 Dec 1981 (SI 1981/1557) |
| 9–12 | | 30 Oct 1981 (SI 1981/1557) |
| 13 | (1)–(7) | 1 Jan 1982 (SI 1981/1557) |
| | (8) | 16 Aug 1982 (SI 1982/951) |
| 14 | | 1 Jan 1982 (SI 1981/1557) |
| 15 | | 10 Nov 1981 (SI 1981/1557) |
| 16 | | 1 Jan 1983 (SI 1982/1737) |
| 17–20 | | 30 Oct 1981 (SI 1981/1557) |
| 21 | (1) | See Sch 7 below |
| | (2) | See Sch 8 below |
| | (3) | See Sch 9 below |
| 22 | | 30 Oct 1981 (SI 1981/1557) |
| Sch 1 | | 15 Mar 1982 (SI 1981/1557) |

**Education (Scotland) Act 1981 (c 58)**—*contd*

| | | |
|---|---|---|
| Schs 2, 3 | | 1 Jan 1983 (SI 1982/951) |
| Sch 4 | | 16 Aug 1982 (SI 1982/951) |
| Sch 5 | | 1 Jan 1982 (SI 1981/1557) |
| Sch 6 | | 10 Nov 1981 (SI 1981/1557) |
| Sch 7 | paras 1–3 | 30 Oct 1981 (SI 1981/1557) |
| | para 4 | 1 Dec 1981 (SI 1981/1557) |
| | para 5 | 30 Oct 1981 (SI 1981/1557) |
| | para 6 | 15 Feb 1982 (so far as relates to Education (Scotland) Act 1980, ss 50, 51) (SI 1981/1557) |
| | | 1 Jan 1983 (so far as relates to Education (Scotland) Act 1980, ss 1(5)(c), (d), 28A(1) (as it has effect under the 1980 Act, Sch A2), 60–65F) (SI 1982/951) |
| | para 7 | 15 Feb 1982 (SI 1981/1557) |
| Sch 8 | para 1 | 1 Jan 1983 (SI 1982/951) |
| | para 2 | 15 Feb 1982 (SI 1981/1557) |
| | para 3 | 15 Mar 1982 (SI 1981/1557) |
| | para 4 | 1 Jan 1983 (SI 1982/951) |
| | para 5 | 30 Oct 1981 (SI 1981/1557) |
| | para 6 | 1 Jan 1982 (SI 1981/1557) |
| | para 7 | 30 Oct 1981 (SI 1981/1557) |
| Sch 9 | | 30 Oct 1981 (repeals of or in Education (Scotland) Act 1980, ss 98(1), 132(1), Sch 2, paras 1, 3, 4) (SI 1981/1557) |
| | | 10 Nov 1981 (repeals of or in Education (Scotland) Act 1980, ss 104(2), 105(5), 108(2), 110(3), 111(1)–(5), 112(6), 113, 114(1), 115, 116, 117 (proviso), 121(b)) (SI 1981/1557) |
| | | 1 Dec 1981 (repeals of or in Education (Scotland) Act 1980, ss 7(1)(c), (8), 17(1), 22(1), (4), proviso (ii), 29) (SI 1981/1557) |
| | | 1 Jan 1982 (repeals in Education (Scotland) Act 1980, s 129(3), (4)(e), (5)) (SI 1981/1557) |
| | | 15 Feb 1982 (repeals of or in Education (Scotland) Act 1980, ss 23(2) proviso, 28(2)) (SI 1981/1557) |
| | | 16 Aug 1982 (repeal of Education (Scotland) Act 1980, s 129(6)) (SI 1982/951) |
| | | 1 Jan 1983 (repeals of or in Education (Scotland) Act 1980, ss 4(b), (c), 5, 59, 135(1)) (SI 1982/951) |
| | | 1 Jan 1983 (repeal of Education (Scotland) Act 1980, s 66(2)) (SI 1982/1737) |

---

**Employment and Training Act 1981 (c 57)**

*RA*: 31 Jul 1981

*Commencement provisions:* s 11(3); Employment and Training Act 1981 (Commencement) Order 1982, SI 1982/126

| | | |
|---|---|---|
| 1 | | 31 Jul 1981 (RA) |
| 2 | | 1 Mar 1982 (for the purposes of specified industrial training boards) (SI 1982/126) |
| | | 1 Apr 1982 (for all other purposes) (SI 1982/126) |
| 3–11 | | 31 Jul 1981 (RA) |
| Sch 1 | para 1 | 1 Apr 1982 (except for the purposes of specified industrial training boards) (SI 1982/126) |
| | paras 2–6 | 31 Jul 1981 (RA) |
| | paras 7, 8 | 1 Apr 1982 (except for the purposes of specified industrial training boards) (SI 1982/126) |
| Sch 2 | | 31 Jul 1981 (RA) |
| Sch 3 | | 31 Jul 1981 (except entry relating to Industrial Training Act 1964, Sch) (RA) |

**Employment and Training Act 1981 (c 57)**—*contd*

> 1 Apr 1982 (entry relating to Industrial Training Act 1964,
> Schedule, except for the purposes of specified industrial
> training boards, but note whole of 1964 Act except s 16 was
> repealed as from 29 Jun 1982, except as applied to agricultural
> training boards) (SI 1982/126)

---

**Energy Conservation Act 1981 (c 17)**

*RA:* 21 May 1981

Whole Act in force 21 May 1981 (RA)

---

**English Industrial Estates Corporation Act 1981 (c 13)**

*RA:* 15 Apr 1981

*Commencement provisions:* s 10(2)

Whole Act in force 15 May 1981 (s 10(2))

---

**European Parliamentary Elections Act 1981 (c 8)**

*RA:* 19 Mar 1981

Whole Act in force 19 Mar 1981 (RA)

---

**Film Levy Finance Act 1981 (c 16)**

*RA:* 15 Apr 1981

*Commencement provisions:* s 11(2)

Whole Act in force 15 May 1981 (s 11(2))

---

**Finance Act 1981 (c 35)**

*Budget Day:* 10 Mar 1981

*RA:* 27 Jul 1981

The commencement details of Finance Acts are not set out, as the dates from which their provisions take
effect are usually stated clearly and unambiguously in the text of the Act, and charging provisions will
normally state for which year or years of assessment they are to have effect.

---

**Fisheries Act 1981 (c 29)**

*RA:* 2 Jul 1981

*Commencement provisions:* s 46(3), (4); Fisheries Act 1981 (Commencement No 1) Order 1981,
SI 1981/1357; Fisheries Act 1981 (Commencement No 2) Order 1981, SI 1981/1640

| | |
|---|---|
| 1–14 | 1 Oct 1981 (SI 1981/1357) |
| 15–30 | 2 Aug 1981 (s 46(3)) |
| 31 | 18 Nov 1981 (SI 1981/1640) |
| 32–45 | 2 Aug 1981 (s 46(3)) |
| 46 | 2 Aug 1981 (except as noted below) (s 46(3)) |
| | 1 Oct 1981 (for the purposes of Sch 5, Pt I) (SI 1981/1357) |
| Schs 1–3 | 1 Oct 1981 (SI 1981/1357) |
| Sch 4 | 2 Aug 1981 (s 46(3)) |

**Fisheries Act 1981 (c 29)**—*contd*

| Sch 5 | Pt I | 1 Oct 1981 (SI 1981/1357) |
| | Pt II | 2 Aug 1981 (s 46(3)) |

---

**Food and Drugs (Amendment) Act 1981 (c 26)**

*RA:* 2 Jul 1981

Whole Act in force 2 Jul 1981 (RA)

---

**Forestry Act 1981 (c 39)**

*RA:* 27 Jul 1981

Whole Act in force 27 Jul 1981 (RA)

---

**Forgery and Counterfeiting Act 1981 (c 45)**

*RA:* 27 Jul 1981

*Commencement provisions:* s 33

Whole Act in force 27 Oct 1981 (s 33)

---

**Friendly Societies Act 1981 (c 50)**

*RA:* 27 Jul 1981

Whole Act in force 27 Jul 1981 (RA)

---

**Gas Levy Act 1981 (c 3)**

*RA:* 19 Mar 1981

Whole Act in force 19 Mar 1981 (RA)

---

**Horserace Betting Levy Act 1981 (c 30)**

*RA:* 2 Jul 1981

Whole Act in force 2 Jul 1981 (RA)

---

**House of Commons Members' Fund and Parliamentary Pensions Act 1981 (c 7)**

*RA:* 19 Mar 1981

Whole Act in force 19 Mar 1981 (RA)

---

**Housing (Amendment) (Scotland) Act 1981 (c 72)**

*RA:* 22 Dec 1981

Whole Act in force 22 Dec 1981 (RA)

---

### Indecent Displays (Control) Act 1981 (c 42)

*RA:* 27 Jul 1981

*Commencement provisions:* s 5(5)

Whole Act in force 27 Oct 1981 (s 5(5))

---

### Industrial Diseases (Notification) Act 1981 (c 25)

*RA:* 2 Jul 1981

Whole Act in force 2 Jul 1981 (RA)

---

### Industry Act 1981 (c 6)

*RA:* 19 Mar 1981

*Commencement provisions:* s 7(2)

| | |
|---|---|
| 1 | 31 Mar 1981 (s 7(2)) |
| 2–7 | 19 Mar 1981 (RA) |
| Schedule | 19 Mar 1981 (RA) |

---

### Insurance Companies Act 1981 (c 31)

*RA:* 2 Jul 1981

*Commencement provisions:* s 37(1); Insurance Companies Act 1981 (Commencement) Order 1981, SI 1981/1657

Whole Act in force 1 Jan 1982 (SI 1981/1657)

---

### International Organisations Act 1981 (c 9)

*RA:* 15 Apr 1981

Whole Act in force 15 Apr 1981 (RA)

---

### Iron and Steel Act 1981 (c 46)

*RA:* 27 Jul 1981

Whole Act in force 27 Jul 1981 (RA)

---

### Iron and Steel (Borrowing Powers) Act 1981 (c 2)

*RA:* 26 Feb 1981

Whole Act in force 26 Feb 1981 (RA)

---

### Judicial Pensions Act 1981 (c 20)

*RA:* 21 May 1981

*Commencement provisions:* s 37(2)

Whole Act in force 21 Jun 1981 (s 37(2))

---

## Licensing (Alcohol Education and Research) Act 1981 (c 28)

*RA:* 2 Jul 1981

*Commencement provisions:* s 13(3); Licensing (Alcohol Education and Research) Act 1981 (Commencement) Order 1981, SI 1981/1324

Whole Act in force 1 Oct 1981 (SI 1981/1324)

## Licensing (Amendment) Act 1981 (c 40)

*RA:* 27 Jul 1981

*Commencement provisions:* s 3(2); Licensing (Amendment) Act 1981 (Commencement) Order 1982, SI 1982/1383

Whole Act in force 1 Oct 1982 (SI 1982/1383)

## Local Government and Planning (Amendment) Act 1981 (c 41)

*RA:* 27 Jul 1981

*Commencement provisions:* s 2(2), (3)

| | | |
|---|---|---|
| 1, 2 | | 27 Aug 1981 (s 2(3)) |
| Schedule | paras 1–5 | 27 Aug 1981 (s 2(3)) |
| | para 6 | 27 Nov 1981 (s 2(2)) |

## Local Government (Miscellaneous Provisions) (Scotland) Act 1981 (c 23)

*RA:* 11 Jun 1981

*Commencement provisions:* s 43(2)–(4); Local Government (Miscellaneous Provisions) (Scotland) Act 1981 (Commencement No 1) Order 1981, SI 1981/1402

| | |
|---|---|
| 1–3 | 11 Jun 1981 (RA) |
| 4–10 | 1 Apr 1982 (s 43(3)) |
| 11 | 1 Jan 1982 (s 43(2)) |
| 12–28 | 11 Jun 1981 (RA) |
| 29 | 1 Oct 1981 (SI 1981/1402) |
| 30–36 | 11 Jun 1981 (RA) |
| 37 | *Not yet in force* |
| 38–40 | 11 Jun 1981 (RA) |
| 41 | See Sch 4 below |
| 42, 43 | 11 Jun 1981 (RA) |
| Schs 1–3 | 11 Jun 1981 (RA) |
| Sch 4 | 11 Jun 1981 (RA) except repeals of— |
| |     Local Government (Financial Provisions etc) (Scotland) |
| |       Act 1962, s 4(2); |
| |     Social Work (Scotland) Act 1968, s 7 |
| | 1 Oct 1981 (repeal of Social Work (Scotland) Act 1968, s 7) |
| |     (SI 1981/1402) |
| | 1 Apr 1982 (repeal of Local Government (Financial Provisions etc) |
| |     (Scotland) Act 1962, s 4(2)) (s 43(3)) |

## Matrimonial Homes and Property Act 1981 (c 24)

*RA:* 2 Jul 1981

*Commencement provisions:* s 9; Matrimonial Homes and Property Act 1981 (Commencement No 1) Order 1981, SI 1981/1275; Matrimonial Homes and Property Act 1981 (Commencement No 2) Order 1983, SI 1983/50

## Matrimonial Homes and Property Act 1981 (c 24)—*contd*

| | | |
|---|---|---|
| 1–6 | | 14 Feb 1983 (SI 1983/50) |
| 7–9 | | 1 Oct 1981 (SI 1981/1275) |
| 10 | (1) | 1 Oct 1981 (SI 1981/1275) |
| | (2) | 14 Feb 1983 (SI 1983/50) |
| | (3) | 1 Oct 1981 (SI 1981/1275) |
| Schs 1–3 | | 14 Feb 1983 (SI 1983/50) |

## Matrimonial Homes (Family Protection) (Scotland) Act 1981 (c 59)

*RA:* 30 Oct 1981

*Commencement provisions:* s 23(3); Matrimonial Homes (Family Protection) (Scotland) Act 1981 (Commencement) Order 1982, SI 1982/972

| | |
|---|---|
| 1–22 | 1 Sep 1982 (SI 1982/972) |
| 23 | 30 Oct 1981 (RA) |

## Merchant Shipping Act 1981 (c 10)

*RA:* 15 Apr 1981

*Commencement provisions:* s 5(4); Merchant Shipping Act 1981 (Commencement No 1) Order 1981, SI 1981/1677; Merchant Shipping Act 1981 (Commencement No 2) Order 1983, SI 1983/1906; Merchant Shipping Act 1981 (Commencement No 3) Order 1984, SI 1984/1695

| | | |
|---|---|---|
| 1 | | 29 Nov 1984 (SI 1984/1695) |
| 2 | | 4 Feb 1984 (SI 1983/1906) |
| 3 | | 4 Feb 1984 (for purposes of Article IV of the Rules set out in the Sch to the Carriage of Goods by Sea Act 1971 as amended by s 2) (SI 1983/1906) |
| | | 29 Nov 1984 (for purposes of s 1) (SI 1984/1695) |
| 4 | (1) | 4 Feb 1984 (SI 1983/1906) |
| | (2) | 23 Dec 1981 (SI 1981/1677) |
| 5 | (1), (2) | 23 Dec 1981 (SI 1981/1677) |
| | (3) | See the Schedule below |
| | (4), (5) | 23 Dec 1981 (SI 1981/1677) |
| | (6) | 4 Feb 1984 (SI 1983/1906) |
| Schedule | | 4 Feb 1984 (repeal of the Carriage of Goods by Sea Act 1971, s 1(5)) (SI 1983/1906) |
| | | 29 Nov 1984 (repeals of or in Merchant Shipping (Liability of Shipowners and Others) Act 1958, s 1(1)–(4)) (SI 1984/1695) |

## National Film Finance Corporation Act 1981 (c 15)

*RA:* 15 Apr 1981

*Commencement provisions:* s 10(3)

Whole Act in force 15 May 1981 (s 10(3))

## New Towns Act 1981 (c 64)

*RA:* 30 Oct 1981

*Commencement provisions:* s 82(4)

Whole Act in force 30 Nov 1981 (s 82(4))

## Nuclear Industry (Finance) Act 1981 (c 71)

*RA:* 22 Dec 1981

Whole Act in force 22 Dec 1981 (RA)

---

## Parliamentary Commissioner (Consular Complaints) Act 1981 (c 11)

*RA:* 15 Apr 1981

Whole Act in force 15 Apr 1981 (RA)

---

## Ports (Financial Assistance) Act 1981 (c 21)

*RA:* 11 Jun 1981

Whole Act in force 11 Jun 1981 (RA)

---

## Public Passenger Vehicles Act 1981 (c 14)

*RA:* 15 Apr 1981

*Commencement provisions:* s 89(2); Public Passenger Vehicles Act 1981 (Commencement) Order 1981, SI 1981/1387

Whole Act in force 30 Oct 1981 (SI 1981/1387)

---

## Redundancy Fund Act 1981 (c 5)

*RA:* 19 Mar 1981

Whole Act in force 19 Mar 1981 (RA)

---

## Representation of the People Act 1981 (c 34)

*RA:* 2 Jul 1981

Whole Act in force 2 Jul 1981 (RA)

---

## Senior Courts Act 1981 (c 54)

*RA:* 28 Jul 1981

*Commencement provisions:* s 153(2), (3)

*Note:* This Act was originally cited as the Supreme Court Act 1981

| | | |
|---|---|---|
| 1–71 | | 1 Jan 1982 (s 153(2)) |
| 72 | | 28 Jul 1981 (s 153(3)) |
| 73–142 | | 1 Jan 1982 (s 153(2)) |
| 143 | | 28 Jul 1981 (s 153(3)) |
| 144–151 | | 1 Jan 1982 (s 153(2)) |
| 152 | (1) | 1 Jan 1982 (s 153(2)) |
| | (2) | 28 Jul 1981 (s 153(3)) |
| | (3)–(5) | 1 Jan 1982 (s 153(2)) |
| 153 | | 28 Jul 1981 (s 153(3)) |
| Schs 1–7 | | 1 Jan 1982 (s 153(2)) |

---

## Social Security Act 1981 (c 33)

*RA:* 2 Jul 1981

*Commencement provisions:* s 8(3); Social Security Act 1981 Commencement Order 1981, SI 1981/953

| | | |
|---|---|---|
| 1 | | 2 Jul 1981 (RA) |
| 2–7 | | 10 Aug 1981 (SI 1981/953) |
| 8 | (1)–(3) | 2 Jul 1981 (RA) |
| | (4), (5) | 10 Aug 1981 (SI 1981/953) |
| | (6) | 2 Jul 1981 (RA) |
| Schs 1, 2 | | 10 Aug 1981 (SI 1981/953) |

## Social Security (Contributions) Act 1981 (c 1)

*RA:* 29 Jan 1981

Whole Act in force 29 Jan 1981 (RA) but does not apply to any period prior to the tax year beginning with 6 Apr 1981

## Statute Law (Repeals) Act 1981 (c 19)

*RA:* 21 May 1981

Whole Act in force 21 May 1981 (RA)

## Supreme Court Act 1981 (c 54)

See Senior Courts Act 1981

## Town and Country Planning (Minerals) Act 1981 (c 36)

*RA:* 27 Jul 1981

*Commencement provisions:* s 35; Town and Country Planning (Minerals) Act 1981 (Commencement No 1) Order 1982, SI 1982/86; Town and Country Planning (Minerals) Act 1981 (Commencement No 2) Order 1982, SI 1982/1177; Town and Country Planning (Minerals) Act 1981 (Commencement No 3) Order 1986, SI 1986/760; Town and Country Planning (Minerals) Act 1981 (Commencement No 4) (Scotland) Order 1987, SI 1987/2002

| | | |
|---|---|---|
| 1 | | 19 May 1986 (SI 1986/760) |
| 2 | (1) | 19 May 1986 (SI 1986/760) |
| | (2)–(4) | 22 Feb 1982 (SI 1982/86) |
| 3 | | 19 May 1986 (SI 1986/760) |
| 4–7 | | 22 Feb 1982 (SI 1982/86) |
| 8–11 | | 19 May 1986 (SI 1986/760) |
| 12 | | 22 Feb 1982 (SI 1982/86) |
| 13 | | 17 Sep 1982 (SI 1982/1177) |
| 14 | | 19 May 1986 (SI 1986/760) |
| 15 | | 17 Sep 1982 (in so far as it inserts s 170B into the Town and Country Planning Act 1971) (SI 1982/1177) |
| 16 | | 17 Sep 1982 (SI 1982/1177) |
| 17, 18 | | 19 May 1986 (SI 1986/760) |
| 19, 20 | | 1 Jan 1988 (SI 1987/2002) |
| 21–24 | | 22 Feb 1982 (SI 1982/86) |
| 25–28 | | 1 Jan 1988 (SI 1987/2002) |
| 29 | | 30 Oct 1985 (SI 1985/1631) |
| 30 | | 30 Oct 1985 (in so far as inserts s 159B into the Town and Country Planning (Scotland) Act 1972) (SI 1985/1631) |

## Town and Country Planning (Minerals) Act 1981 (c 36)—*contd*

| | | |
|---|---|---|
| | | 1 Jan 1988 (in so far as inserts s 159A into the Town and Country Planning (Scotland) Act 1972) (SI 1987/2002) |
| 31 | | 30 Oct 1985 (SI 1985/1631) |
| 32 | | 1 Jan 1988 (SI 1987/2002) |
| 33 | | 27 Jul 1981 (RA) |
| 34 | | See the Schs below |
| 35, 36 | | 27 Jul 1981 (RA) |
| Sch 1 | paras 1–3 | 22 Feb 1982 (SI 1982/86) |
| | paras 4–6 | 17 Sep 1982 (SI 1982/1177) |
| | paras 7–10 | 19 May 1986 (SI 1986/760) |
| | para 11(a) | 22 Feb 1982 (SI 1982/86) |
| | para 11(b) | 19 May 1986 (SI 1986/760) |
| | para 11(c) | 22 Feb 1982 (in so far as relates to definition "mineral planning authority") (SI 1982/86) |
| | | 17 Sep 1982 (in so far as relates to definition "mineral corporation modifications") (SI 1982/1177) |
| | | 19 May 1986 (in so far as relates to definition "mineral-working deposit") (SI 1986/760) |
| | para 11(d) | 17 Sep 1982 (SI 1982/1177) |
| | para 11(e) | 22 Feb 1982 (in so far as relates to definition "restoration condition") (SI 1982/86) |
| | | 17 Sep 1982 (in so far as relates to definitions "restriction on the winning and working of minerals" and "special consultations") (SI 1982/1177) |
| | | 19 May 1986 (in so far as relates to definition "statutory maximum") (SI 1986/760) |
| | para 11(f), (g) | 19 May 1986 (SI 1986/760) |
| | para 12 | 22 Feb 1982 (SI 1982/86) |
| Sch 2 | paras 1–3 | 22 Feb 1982 (SI 1982/86) |
| | paras 4–6 | 30 Oct 1985 (SI 1985/1631) |
| | paras 7–10 | 1 Jan 1988 (SI 1987/2002) |
| | para 11(a) | 22 Feb 1982 (SI 1982/86) |
| | para 11(b) | 1 Jan 1988 (SI 1987/2002) |
| | para 11(c) | 30 Oct 1985 (in so far as relates to definition "mineral compensation modifications") (SI 1985/1631) |
| | | 1 Jan 1988 (in so far as relates to definition "mineral working deposit") (SI 1987/2002) |
| | para 11(d) | 30 Oct 1985 (SI 1985/1631) |
| | para 11(e) | 22 Feb 1982 (in so far as relates to definition "restoration condition") (SI 1982/86) |
| | | 30 Oct 1985 (in so far as relates to definitions "restriction on the winning and working of minerals" and "special consultations") (SI 1985/1631) |
| | | 1 Jan 1988 (in so far as relates to definition "the statutory maximum") (SI 1987/2002) |
| | para 11(f), (g) | 1 Jan 1988 (SI 1987/2002) |

## Transport Act 1962 (Amendment) Act 1981 (c 32)

*RA:* 2 Jul 1981

*Commencement provisions:* s 2(2)

Whole Act in force 2 Jul 1981 (s 2(2))

## Transport Act 1981 (c 56)

*RA:* 31 Jul 1981

*Commencement provisions:* ss 5, 15(1), (2), 18(3), 31 (repealed), 32(2), 35(5), 40(4); Transport Act 1981 (Commencement No 1) Order 1981, SI 1981/1331; Transport Act 1981 (Dissolution of National

**Transport Act 1981 (c 56)**—*contd*

Ports Council) (Appointed Day) Order 1981, SI 1981/1364; Transport Act 1981 (Commencement No 2) Order 1981, SI 1981/1617; Transport Act 1981 (Dissolution of National Ports Council) (Final) Order 1981, SI 1981/1665; Transport Act 1981 (Commencement No 3) Order 1982, SI 1982/300; Transport Act 1981 (Commencement No 4) Order 1982, SI 1982/310; Transport Act 1981 (Commencement No 5) Order 1982, SI 1982/866; Transport Act 1981 (Commencement No 6) Order 1982, SI 1982/1341; Transport Act 1981 (Commencement No 7) Order 1982, SI 1982/1451; Transport Act 1981 (Commencement No 8) Order 1982, SI 1982/1803; Transport Act 1981 (Commencement No 9) Order 1983, SI 1983/576; Transport Act 1981 (Commencement No 10) Order 1983, SI 1983/930; Transport Act 1981 (Commencement No 11) Order 1983, SI 1983/1089; Transport Act 1981 (Commencement No 12) Order 1988, SI 1988/1037; Transport Act 1981 (Commencement No 13) Order 1988, SI 1988/1170

| | | |
|---|---|---|
| 1–4 | | 31 Jul 1981 (RA) |
| 5 | | 31 Jul 1981 (RA) |
| | | 31 Dec 1982 (appointed day for reconstitution of the British Transport Docks Board) (s 5; SI 1982/1887) |
| 6–15 | | 31 Jul 1981 (RA) |
| | | 1 Oct 1981 (date on which the functions of the National Ports Council were determined) (s 15(1); SI 1981/1364) |
| | | 1 Dec 1981 (date on which the National Ports Council was dissolved) (s 15(2); SI 1981/1665) |
| 16, 17 | | 31 Jul 1981 (RA) |
| 18 | | See Sch 6 below |
| 19, 20 | | 1 Nov 1982 (s 31; SI 1982/1451) |
| 21, 22 | | 1 Dec 1981 (s 31; SI 1981/1617) |
| 23 | (1) | 1 Oct 1982 (s 31; SI 1982/866) |
| | (2), (3) | 1 Feb 1983 (s 31; SI 1982/866) |
| | (4), (5) | 1 Oct 1982 (s 31; SI 1982/866) |
| | (6), (7) | 29 Mar 1982 (s 31; SI 1982/300) |
| 24, 25 | | 6 May 1983 (s 31; SI 1983/576) |
| 26, 27 | | 1 Dec 1981 (s 31; SI 1981/1617) |
| 28 | | 31 Jan 1983 (s 31; SI 1982/1341) |
| 29 | | 31 Jul 1981 (RA) |
| 30 | | See ss 19–31 |
| 31 | | 31 Jul 1981 (RA) |
| 32 | | 25 Aug 1983 (s 32(2); SI 1983/1089) |
| 33, 34 | | 31 Jul 1981 (RA) |
| 35 | (1), (2) | 1 Apr 1982 (s 35(5); SI 1982/310) |
| | (3)–(5) | 12 Oct 1981 (s 35(5); SI 1981/1331) |
| 36–43 | | 31 Jul 1981 (RA) |
| Schs 1–5 | | 31 Jul 1981 (RA) |
| Sch 6 | paras 1–9 | 1 Oct 1981 (s 18(2); SI 1981/1364) |
| | para 10 | 2 Aug 1983 (s 18(3); SI 1983/930) |
| | paras 11–15 | 1 Oct 1981 (s 18(2); SI 1981/1364) |
| Sch 7 | | 1 Nov 1982 (s 31; SI 1982/1451) |
| Sch 8 | | 6 May 1983 (s 31; SI 1983/756) |
| Sch 9 | para 1 | 6 May 1983 (s 31; SI 1983/576) |
| | para 2 | 1 Nov 1982 (s 31; SI 1982/1451) |
| | para 3 | 6 May 1983 (s 31; SI 1983/576) |
| | paras 4–11 | 1 Nov 1982 (s 31; SI 1982/1451) |
| | para 12 | 20 Dec 1982 (save that: (a) the substitution provided for by that paragraph was not brought into force in so far as the Road Traffic Act 1972, s 101(7), relates to ss 5(1), 6(1) and 9(3) of that Act; and (b) the Road Traffic Act 1972, s 101(7A) as provided for by that paragraph was not brought into force so far as it relates to ss 5(1), 6(1)(a) and 8(7) of that Act) (s 31; SI 1982/1803) |
| | | 6 May 1983 (otherwise) (s 31; SI 1983/576) |
| | para 13 | 1 Nov 1982 (s 31; SI 1982/1451) |
| | para 14 | 1 Dec 1981 (s 31; SI 1981/1617) |

**Transport Act 1981 (c 56)**—*contd*

|  |  |  |
|---|---|---|
| | para 15 | 1 Nov 1982 (s 31; SI 1982/1451) |
| | para 16 | 13 Jul 1988 (SI 1988/1037) |
| | para 17 | 6 May 1983 (s 31; SI 1983/576) |
| | para 18(a) | 6 May 1983 (s 31; SI 1983/576) |
| | para 18(b), (c) | 1 Dec 1981 (in so far as they relate to the Road Traffic Act 1972, s 33A) (s 31; SI 1981/1617) |
| | | 6 May 1983 (otherwise) (s 31; SI 1983/576) |
| | paras 19–21 | 6 May 1983 (s 31; SI 1983/576) |
| | para 22 | 1 Dec 1981 (s 31; SI 1981/1617) |
| | paras 23–25 | 6 May 1983 (s 31; SI 1983/576) |
| Sch 10 | | 25 Aug 1983 (s 32(2); SI 1983/1089) |
| Sch 11 | | 31 Jul 1981 (RA) |
| Sch 12 | Pt I | 31 Dec 1982 (ss 5(4), 40(2)) |
| | Pt II | 1 Oct 1981 (except repeal of entry for National Ports Council in House of Commons Disqualification Act 1975, Sch 1, Pt II) (ss 5(3), 15(1)) |
| | | 1 Dec 1981 (exception noted above) (s 15(1)) |
| | Pt III | 31 Jul 1981 (s 40(4)), repeals of or in— |
| | | Railway Fires Act (1905) Amendment Act 1923; |
| | | Public Passenger Vehicles Act 1981 |
| | | 12 Oct 1981 (repeal of Town Police Clauses Act 1847, s 39) (s 40(4); SI 1981/1331) |
| | | 1 Apr 1982 (repeal in Metropolitan Public Carriage Act 1869) (s 40(4); SI 1982/310) |
| | | 1 Nov 1982 (repeals of or in Road Traffic Act 1972, ss 93(3), (5), 177(2)) (s 40(4); SI 1982/1451) |
| | | 6 May 1983 (repeals of or in Road Traffic Act 1972, ss 89, 90, 189, Sch 4, Pt V, para 1) (s 40(4); SI 1983/576) |
| | | 25 Aug 1983 (repeal of entry relating to Road Traffic Act 1974, s 17) (E) (W) (s 40(4); SI 1983/1089) |
| | | *Not yet in force*, repeals of or in— |
| | | Road Traffic Act 1974, Sch 3; |
| | | British Railways (No 2) Act 1975, s 21; |
| | | London Transport Act 1977, s 13(1); |
| | | British Railways Act 1977, s 14(1); |
| | | Criminal Justice (Scotland) Act 1980, Sch 7, para 22 |

**Trustee Savings Banks Act 1981 (c 65)**

*RA:* 30 Oct 1981

*Commencement provisions:* s 57(2)

Whole Act in force 30 Jan 1982 (s 57(2))

**Water Act 1981 (c 12)**

*RA:* 15 Apr 1981

*Commencement provisions:* ss 2(5), 6(8); Water Act 1981 (Commencement No 1) Order 1981, SI 1981/1755

|  |  |
|---|---|
| 1 | 15 Apr 1981 (RA) |
| 2 | *Never in force* (repealed) |
| 3–5 | 15 Apr 1981 (RA) |
| 6 | 1 Apr 1982 (SI 1981/1755) |
| 7 | 15 Apr 1981 (RA) |

## Wildlife and Countryside Act 1981 (c 69)

*RA:* 30 Oct 1981

*Commencement provisions:* s 74(2), (3); Wildlife and Countryside Act 1981 (Commencement No 1) Order 1982, SI 1982/44; Wildlife and Countryside Act 1981 (Commencement No 2) Order 1982, SI 1982/327; Wildlife and Countryside Act 1981 (Commencement No 3) Order 1982, SI 1982/990; Wildlife and Countryside Act 1981 (Commencement No 4) Order 1982, SI 1982/1136; Wildlife and Countryside Act 1981 (Commencement No 5) Order 1982, SI 1982/1217; Wildlife and Countryside Act 1981 (Commencement No 6) Order 1983, SI 1983/20; Wildlife and Countryside Act 1981 (Commencement No 7) Order 1983, SI 1983/87

| | | |
|---|---|---|
| 1–11 | | 28 Sep 1982 (SI 1982/1217) |
| 12 | | 16 Feb 1982 (SI 1982/44) |
| 13–27 | | 28 Sep 1982 (SI 1982/1217) |
| 28 | | 30 Nov 1981 (s 74(2)) |
| 29–31 | | 6 Sep 1982 (SI 1982/1136) |
| 32 | | 28 Feb 1983 (SI 1983/87) |
| 33–40 | | 30 Nov 1981 (s 74(2)) |
| 41 | | 28 Feb 1983 (SI 1983/87) |
| 42–45 | | 30 Nov 1981 (s 74(2)) |
| 46 | | 19 Aug 1982 (SI 1982/990) |
| 47 | | 1 Apr 1982 (SI 1982/327) |
| 48 | | 16 Feb 1982 (SI 1982/44) |
| 49–52 | | 30 Nov 1981 (s 74(2)) |
| 53–66 | | 28 Feb 1983 (SI 1983/20) |
| 67–71 | | 30 Nov 1981 (s 74(2)) |
| 72 | (1)–(3) | 30 Nov 1981 (s 74(2)) |
| | (4) | 28 Sep 1982 (SI 1982/1217) |
| | (5) | 30 Nov 1981 (s 74(2)) |
| | (6) | 28 Sep 1982 (SI 1982/1217) |
| | (7)–(13) | 30 Nov 1981 (s 74(2)) |
| 73 | (1) | See Sch 17 below |
| | (2)–(4) | 30 Nov 1981 (s 74(2)) |
| 74 | | 30 Nov 1981 (s 74(2)) |
| Schs 1–6 | | 28 Sep 1982 (SI 1982/1217) |
| Sch 7 | | 16 Feb 1982 (SI 1982/44) |
| Schs 8–10 | | 28 Sep 1982 (SI 1982/1217) |
| Sch 11 | | 30 Nov 1981 (so far as relates to orders under s 34) (s 74(2)) |
| | | 6 Sep 1982 (so far as relates to orders under s 29) (SI 1982/1136) |
| Sch 12 | | 30 Nov 1981 (s 74(2)) |
| Sch 13 | | 1 Apr 1982 (SI 1982/327) |
| Schs 14–16 | | 28 Feb 1983 (SI 1983/20) |
| Sch 17 | Pt I | 30 Nov 1981 (s 74(2)) |
| | Pt II | 16 Feb 1982 (SI 1982/44), repeals of or in— |
| | | Deer Act 1963, Sch 2; |
| | | Conservation of Seals Act 1970, s 10(1); |
| | | Badgers Act 1973, ss 6, 7, 8(2)(c), 11 |
| | | 1 Apr 1982 (SI 1982/327), repeals of or in— |
| | | National Parks and Access to the Countryside Act 1949, ss 2, 4, 95; |
| | | Countryside Act 1968, s 3 |
| | | 28 Sep 1982 (SI 1982/1217), repeals of or in— |
| | | Protection of Animals (Scotland) Act 1912, s 9; |
| | | Protection of Birds Act 1954 (Amendment) Act 1964; |
| | | Protection of Birds Act 1967; |
| | | Countryside Act 1968, s 1; |
| | | Local Government Act 1972, Sch 29, para 37; |
| | | Local Government (Scotland) Act 1973, Sch 27, Pt II, paras 115, 168; |
| | | Nature Conservancy Council Act 1973, s 5(3), Sch 1, paras 3, 5, 7, 12; |

**Wildlife and Countryside Act 1981 (c 69)**—*contd*
Water Act 1973, Sch 8, para 67;
Conservation of Wild Creatures and Wild Plants Act 1975;
Criminal Procedure (Scotland) Act 1975, Sch 7C;
Endangered Species (Import and Export) Act 1976, s 13(6);
Statute Law (Repeals) Act 1976, Sch 2, Pt II;
Criminal Law Act 1977, Sch 6;
Customs and Excise Management Act 1979, Sch 4, para 12;
Animal Health Act 1981, Sch 5, para 1;
Zoo Licensing Act 1981, s 4(5)
28 Feb 1983 (SI 1983/20), repeals of or in—
National Parks and Access to the Countryside Act 1949,
　ss 27–35, 38;
London Government Act 1963, s 60(1)–(4);
Countryside Act 1968, Sch 3;
Courts Act 1971, Sch 8, para 31, Sch 9, Pt II;
Town and Country Planning Act 1971, Sch 20;
Local Government Act 1972, Sch 17;
Highways Act 1980, ss 31(10), 340(2)(d)

**Zoo Licensing Act 1981 (c 37)**

*RA:* 27 Jul 1981

*Commencement provisions:* s 23(2); Zoo Licensing Act 1981 (Commencement) Order 1984, SI 1984/423

Whole Act in force 30 Apr 1984 (SI 1984/423)

# 1982 Acts

## Administration of Justice Act 1982 (c 53)

*RA:* 28 Oct 1982

*Commencement provisions:* s 76; Administration of Justice Act 1982 (Commencement No 1) Order 1983, SI 1983/236; Administration of Justice Act 1982 (Commencement No 2) Order 1984, SI 1984/1142; Administration of Justice Act 1982 (Commencement No 3) Order 1984, SI 1984/1287; Administration of Justice Act 1982 (Commencement No 4) Order 1985, SI 1985/858; Administration of Justice Act 1982 (Commencement No 5) Order 1986, SI 1986/2259; Administration of Justice Act 1982 (Commencement No 6) Order 1991, SI 1991/1245; Administration of Justice Act 1982 (Commencement No 7) Order 1991, SI 1991/1786

| | | |
|---|---|---|
| 1–5 | | 1 Jan 1983 (s 76(11)) |
| 6 | | 1 Jul 1985 (SI 1985/858) |
| 7–11 | | 1 Jan 1983 (s 76(11)) |
| 12 | | 1 Sep 1984 (SI 1984/1287) |
| 13 | | 1 Jan 1983 (s 76(11)) |
| 14 | (1) | 1 Jan 1983 (s 76(11)) |
| | (2) | 1 Sep 1984 (SI 1984/1287) |
| | (3), (4) | 1 Jan 1983 (s 76(11)) |
| 15, 16 | | 1 Apr 1983 (SI 1983/236) |
| 17–22 | | 1 Jan 1983 (s 76(11)) |
| 23–25 | | *Not yet in force* |
| 26 | | 1 Jan 1983 (s 76(11)) |
| 27, 28 | | *Not yet in force* |
| 29–31 | | 1 Jan 1983 (s 76(11)) |
| 32 | | 28 Oct 1982 (s 76(9), (10)) |
| 33 | | 1 Jan 1983 (s 76(11)) |
| 34, 35 | | 1 Sep 1984 (SI 1984/1142) |
| 36 | | 28 Oct 1982 (s 76(9), (10)) |
| 37 | | 1 Jan 1983 (s 76(11)) |
| 38–47 | | 2 Jan 1987 (SI 1986/2259) |
| 48 | | *Not yet in force* |
| 49–51 | | 1 Jan 1983 (s 76(11)) |
| 52 | | 28 Oct 1982 (s 76(9), (10)) |
| 53 | | 1 Jan 1983 (s 76(11)) |
| 54 | | 1 Apr 1983 (SI 1983/236) |
| 55, 56 | | 1 Jan 1983 (s 76(11)) |
| 57 | | 1 Apr 1983 (SI 1983/236) |
| 58, 59 | | 1 Jan 1983 (s 76(11)) |
| 60 | | 28 Oct 1982 (s 76(9), (10)) |
| 61–63 | | 1 Jan 1983 (s 76(11)) |
| 64, 65 | | 28 Oct 1982 (s 76(9), (10)) |
| 66, 67 | | 1 Jan 1983 (s 76(11)) |
| 68 | | See Sch 6 below |
| 69 | | 1 Jun 1983 (SI 1983/236) |
| 70 | | See Sch 8 below |
| 71, 72 | | 1 Jan 1983 (s 76(11)) |
| 73 | (1)–(7) | 1 Jan 1983 (s 76(11)) |

**Administration of Justice Act 1982 (c 53)**—*contd*

|          |           |                                                                            |
|----------|-----------|----------------------------------------------------------------------------|
|          | (8)       | *Never in force* (repealed)                                                |
|          | (9)       | 1 Jan 1983 (s 76(11))                                                       |
| 74       |           | 1 Jan 1983 (s 76(11))                                                       |
| 75       |           | See Sch 9 below                                                            |
| 76–78    |           | 28 Oct 1982 (s 76(9), (10))                                                 |
| Sch 1    |           | 1 Apr 1983 (SI 1983/236)                                                    |
| Sch 2    |           | *Not yet in force*                                                          |
| Schs 3–5 |           | 1 Jan 1983 (s 76(11))                                                       |
| Sch 6    | paras 1–9 | 1 Jan 1983 (s 76(11))                                                       |
|          | para 10   | 1 Sep 1991 (SI 1991/1786)                                                   |
| Sch 7    |           | 1 Jun 1983 (SI 1983/236)                                                    |
| Sch 8    | paras 1–5 | 1 Jan 1983 (s 76(11))                                                       |
|          | paras 6–8 | 13 Jun 1991 (SI 1991/1245)                                                  |
|          | paras 9–12| 1 Jan 1983 (s 76(11))                                                       |
| Sch 9    | Pt I      | 1 Jan 1983 (except repeals noted below) (s 76(11))                         |
|          |           | 1 Apr 1983 (repeal in Judicial Trustees Act 1896) (SI 1983/236)           |
|          |           | 1 Jun 1983 (repeal of Law Reform (Miscellaneous Provisions) Act (Northern Ireland) 1937, s 17) (SI 1983/236) |
|          |           | 1 Sep 1984 (repeal in County Courts Act 1959, s 148) (SI 1984/1142)       |
|          |           | 1 Sep 1984 (repeal in Damages (Scotland) Act 1976) (SI 1984/1287)         |
|          |           | 2 Jan 1987 (repeal of County Courts Act 1959, ss 99(3), 168–174A, 176) (SI 1986/2259) |
|          |           | 13 Jun 1991 (SI 1991/1245), repeals of—<br>Administration of Justice Act 1965, ss 1–16;<br>Judicature (Northern Ireland) Act 1978, s 83 |
|          |           | *Not yet in force*, repeals of or in—<br>Prevention of Fraud (Investments) Act 1958 (repealed);<br>Administration of Justice Act 1977;<br>Senior Courts Act 1981, s 126 |
|          | Pt II     | 1 Jan 1983 (s 76(11)) revocations of or in—<br>SI 1967/761;<br>SI 1977/1251 |
|          |           | *Not yet in force* (revocation in SI 1979/1575)                           |

**Agricultural Training Board Act 1982 (c 9)**

*RA:* 29 Mar 1982

*Commencement provisions:* s 12(3)

Whole Act in force 29 Jun 1982 (s 12(3))

**Appropriation Act 1982 (c 40)**

*RA:* 30 Jul 1982

Whole Act in force 30 Jul 1982 (RA)

**Aviation Security Act 1982 (c 36)**

*RA:* 23 Jul 1982

*Commencement provisions:* s 41(2)

Whole Act in force 23 Oct 1982 (s 41(2))

## Canada Act 1982 (c 11)

*RA:* 29 Mar 1982

Whole Act in force 29 Mar 1982 (RA)

## Children's Homes Act 1982 (c 20)

*RA:* 28 Jun 1982

*Never in force* (repealed)

## Cinematograph (Amendment) Act 1982 (c 33)

*RA:* 13 Jul 1982

*Commencement provisions:* s 11(3)

Whole Act in force 13 Oct 1982 (s 11(3))

## Civic Government (Scotland) Act 1982 (c 45)

*RA:* 28 Oct 1982

*Commencement provisions:* s 137(2)–(4); Civic Government (Scotland) Act 1982 (Commencement) Order 1983, SI 1983/201, as amended by SI 1984/573, SI 1984/774

| | | |
|---|---|---|
| 1–8 | | 1 Apr 1983 (for purpose only of enabling preliminary arrangements to be made for when provisions fully effective in operation) (SI 1983/201) |
| | | 1 Jul 1984 (otherwise) (SI 1983/201) |
| 9–23 | | 1 Apr 1983 (for purpose only of enabling preliminary arrangements to be made for when provisions fully effective in operation) (SI 1983/201) |
| | | 1 Jul 1984 (except in relation to areas of local authorities noted below) (SI 1983/201, as amended by SI 1984/744) |
| | | 2 Aug 1984 (as respects the area of Lochaber District Council) (SI 1984/744) |
| | | 20 Aug 1984 (as respects the area of the City of Glasgow District Council) (SI 1984/744) |
| | | 20 Sep 1984 (as respects the area of Wigtown District Council) (SI 1984/744) |
| | | 1 Nov 1984 (as respects the area of Cunninghame District Council) (SI 1984/744) |
| 24–27 | | As noted to ss 9–23 above, and in addition: |
| | | 1 Jan 1985 (as respects the area of Monklands District Council) (SI 1984/744) |
| 28–37 | | 1 Apr 1983 (for purpose only of enabling preliminary arrangements to be made for when provisions fully effective in operation) (SI 1983/201) |
| | | 1 Jul 1984 (otherwise) (SI 1983/201) |
| 38–44 | | As noted to ss 9–23, 24–27 above |
| 45–61 | | 1 Apr 1983 (SI 1983/201) |
| 62–66 | | 1 Apr 1983 (for purpose only of enabling preliminary arrangements to be made for when provisions fully effective in operation) (SI 1983/201) |
| | | 1 Jul 1984 (otherwise) (SI 1983/201) |
| 67–109 | | 1 Apr 1983 (SI 1983/201) |
| 110 | (1) | 1 Apr 1983 (so far as relates to s 110(2)) (SI 1983/201) |
| | | 1 Jul 1984 (otherwise) (SI 1983/201) |
| | (2) | 1 Apr 1983 (SI 1983/201) |

## Civic Government (Scotland) Act 1982 (c 45)—*contd*

|  |  |  |
|---|---|---|
| | (3) | 1 Jul 1984 (SI 1983/201) |
| 111–118 | | 1 Apr 1983 (SI 1983/201) |
| 119 | | 18 Apr 1984 (for purpose only of enabling preliminary arrangements to be made for when provisions fully effective in operation) (SI 1983/201, as amended by SI 1984/573) |
| | | 1 Jul 1984 (otherwise) (SI 1983/201) |
| 120–133 | | 1 Apr 1983 (SI 1983/201) |
| 134–136 | | 28 Oct 1982 (s 137(2)) |
| 137 | (1)–(6) | 28 Oct 1982 (s 137(2)) |
| | (7) | See Sch 3 below |
| | (8) | See Sch 4 below |
| | (9) | 28 Oct 1982 (s 137(2)) |
| Sch 1 | | 1 Apr 1983 (for purpose only of enabling preliminary arrangements to be made for when provisions fully effective in operation) (SI 1983/201) |
| | | 1 Jul 1984 (otherwise) (SI 1983/201) |
| Sch 2 | | 1 Apr 1983 (SI 1983/201) |
| Sch 3 | paras 1–4 | 1 Apr 1983 (SI 1983/201) |
| | para 5 | 1 Jul 1984 (SI 1983/201) |
| Sch 4 | | 1 Apr 1983 (SI 1983/201), repeals of or in— |
| | | Vagrancy Act 1824, s 4; |
| | | Prevention of Crime Act 1871, ss 7, 15; |
| | | Licensing (Scotland) Act 1903; |
| | | Dogs Act 1906, s 3(6), (7); |
| | | Countryside (Scotland) Act 1967, ss 56, 57(1), (2); |
| | | Theatres Act 1968, s 2(4)(c); |
| | | Sexual Offences (Scotland) Act 1976, s 13(3) |
| | | 1 Jul 1984 (otherwise) (SI 1983/201) |

## Civil Aviation Act 1982 (c 16)

*RA:* 27 May 1982

*Commencement provisions:* s 110(2)

Whole Act in force 27 Aug 1982 (s 110(2))

## Civil Aviation (Amendment) Act 1982 (c 1)

*RA: 2 Feb 1982*

Whole Act in force 2 Feb 1982 (RA)

## Civil Jurisdiction and Judgments Act 1982 (c 27)

*RA:* 13 Jul 1982

*Commencement provisions:* s 53(1), Sch 13, Pt I; Civil Jurisdiction and Judgments Act 1982 (Commencement No 1) Order 1984, SI 1984/1553; Civil Jurisdiction and Judgments Act 1982 (Commencement No 2) Order 1986, SI 1986/1781; Civil Jurisdiction and Judgments Act 1982 (Commencement No 3) Order 1986, SI 1986/2044

|  |  |  |
|---|---|---|
| 1–23 | | 1 Jan 1987 (SI 1986/2044) |
| 24 | (1)(a) | 24 Aug 1982 (s 53(1), Sch 13, Pt I) |
| | (1)(b) | 1 Jan 1987 (SI 1986/2044) |
| | (2)(a) | 24 Aug 1982 (s 53(1), Sch 13, Pt I) |
| | (2)(b) | 1 Jan 1987 (SI 1986/2044) |
| | (3) | 24 Aug 1982 (s 53(1), Sch 13, Pt I) |
| 25 | | 1 Jan 1987 (SI 1986/2044) |

**Civil Jurisdiction and Judgments Act 1982 (c 27)**—*contd*

| | | |
|---|---|---|
| 26 | | 1 Nov 1984 (SI 1984/1553) |
| 27, 28 | | 1 Jan 1987 (SI 1986/2044) |
| 29–34 | | 24 Aug 1982 (s 53(1), Sch 13, Pt I) |
| 35 | (1) | 14 Nov 1986 (SI 1986/1781) |
| | (2) | 1 Jan 1987 (SI 1986/2044) |
| | (3) | 24 Aug 1982 (s 53(1), Sch 13, Pt I) |
| 36, 37 | | 1 Jan 1987 (SI 1986/2044) |
| 38 | | 24 Aug 1982 (s 52(1), Sch 13, Pt I) |
| 39 | | 1 Jan 1987 (SI 1986/2044) |
| 40 | | 24 Aug 1982 (s 53(1), Sch 13, Pt I) |
| 41–48 | | 1 Jan 1987 (SI 1986/2044) |
| 49–52 | | 24 Aug 1982 (s 53(1), Sch 13, Pt I) |
| 53 | (1) | 13 Jul 1982 (s 53(1), Sch 13, Pt I) |
| | (2) | 24 Aug 1982 (so far as relates to Sch 13, Pt II, paras 7–10) (s 53(1), Sch 13, Pt I) |
| | | 1 Nov 1984 (so far as relates to Sch 13, Pt II, para 6) (SI 1984/1553) |
| | | 1 Jan 1987 (otherwise) (SI 1986/2044) |
| 54 | | 24 Aug 1982 (so far as relates to repeal in Foreign Judgments (Reciprocal Enforcement) Act 1933, s 4) (s 53(1), Sch 13, Pt I) |
| | | 1 Jan 1987 (otherwise) (SI 1986/2044) |
| 55 | | 13 Jul 1982 (s 53(1), Sch 13, Pt I) |
| Schs 1–9 | | 1 Jan 1987 (SI 1986/2044) |
| Sch 10 | | 14 Nov 1986 (SI 1986/1781) |
| Schs 11, 12 | | 1 Jan 1987 (SI 1986/2044) |
| Sch 13 | Pt I | 13 Jul 1982 (s 53(1), Sch 13, Pt I, para 2) |
| | Pt II, paras 1–5 | 1 Jan 1987 (SI 1986/2044) |
| | Pt II, para 6 | 1 Nov 1984 (SI 1984/1553) |
| | Pt II, paras 7–10 | 24 Aug 1982 (s 53(1), Sch 13, Pt I, para 2) |
| Sch 14 | | 24 Aug 1982 (repeals in Foreign Judgments (Reciprocal Enforcement) Act 1933, s 4) (s 53(1), Sch 13, Pt I) |
| | | 1 Jan 1987 (otherwise) (SI 1986/2044) |

---

**Clergy Pensions (Amendment) Measure 1982 (No 2)**

*RA:* 23 Jul 1982

Whole Measure in force 23 Jul 1982 (RA)

---

**Coal Industry Act 1982 (c 15)**

*RA:* 7 Apr 1982

Whole Act in force 7 Apr 1982 (RA)

---

**Commonwealth Development Corporation Act 1982 (c 54)**

*RA:* 22 Dec 1982

Whole Act in force 22 Dec 1982 (RA)

---

**Consolidated Fund Act 1982 (c 8)**

*RA:* 22 Mar 1982

Whole Act in force 22 Mar 1982 (RA)

---

## Copyright Act 1956 (Amendment) Act 1982 (c 35)

*RA:* 13 Jul 1982

Whole Act in force 13 Jul 1982 (RA)

---

## Criminal Justice Act 1982 (c 48)

*RA:* 28 Oct 1982

*Commencement provisions:* s 80; Criminal Justice Act 1982 (Commencement No 1) Order 1982, SI 1982/1857; Criminal Justice Act 1982 (Scotland) (Commencement No 1) Order 1983, SI 1983/24; Criminal Justice Act 1982 (Commencement No 2) Order 1983, SI 1983/182; Criminal Justice Act 1982 (Scotland) (Commencement No 2) Order 1983, SI 1983/758

| | | |
|---|---|---|
| 1–25 | | 24 May 1983 (SI 1983/182) |
| 26–28 | | 21 Jan 1983 (SI 1982/1857) |
| 29 | | 24 May 1983 (SI 1983/182) |
| 30, 31 | | 31 Jan 1983 (SI 1982/1857) |
| 32, 33 | | 28 Oct 1982 (s 80(1)) |
| 34 | | 31 Jan 1983 (SI 1982/1857) |
| 35–40 | | 11 Apr 1983 (SI 1982/1857) |
| 41, 42 | | 11 Apr 1983 (SI 1982/1857; SI 1983/24) |
| 43 | | 11 Apr 1983 (SI 1982/1857) |
| 44, 45 | | 11 Apr 1983 (SI 1982/1857; SI 1983/24) |
| 46 | | 11 Apr 1983 (SI 1982/1857) |
| 47 | (1) | 11 Apr 1983 (SI 1982/1857) |
| | (2) | 11 Apr 1983 (SI 1982/1857; SI 1983/24) |
| 48 | | 11 Apr 1983 (SI 1982/1857) |
| 49, 50 | | 11 Apr 1983 (SI 1982/1857; SI 1983/24) |
| 51 | | 24 May 1983 (SI 1983/182) |
| 52 | | 31 Jan 1983 (SI 1982/1857) |
| 53–56 | | 11 Apr 1983 (SI 1982/1857) |
| 57 | | 28 Oct 1982 (s 80(1)) |
| 58 | | 24 May 1983 (SI 1983/182; SI 1983/758) |
| 59–62 | | 24 May 1983 (SI 1983/182) |
| 63 | | 31 Jan 1983 (SI 1982/1857) |
| 64 | | 31 Jan 1983 (SI 1982/1857; SI 1983/24) |
| 65–67 | | 31 Jan 1983 (SI 1982/1857) |
| 68 | (1) | 24 May 1983 (SI 1983/182) |
| | (2) | 24 May 1983 (SI 1983/182; SI 1983/758) |
| 69 | | 24 May 1983 (SI 1983/182) |
| 70, 71 | | 31 Jan 1983 (SI 1982/1857) |
| 72 | | 24 May 1983 (SI 1983/182) |
| 73 | | 31 Jan 1983 (SI 1983/24) |
| 74–76 | | 28 Oct 1982 (s 80(1)) |
| 77 | | See Schs 14, 15 below |
| 78 | | See Sch 16 below |
| 79 | | See Sch 17 below |
| 80, 81 | | 28 Oct 1982 (s 80(1)) |
| Sch 1 | | 28 Oct 1982 (s 80(1)) |
| Schs 2–5 | | 11 Apr 1983 (SI 1982/1857) |
| Schs 6, 7 | | 11 Apr 1983 (SI 1982/24) |
| Sch 8 | | 24 May 1983 (SI 1983/182; SI 1983/758) |
| Sch 9 | | 24 May 1983 (SI 1983/182) |
| Sch 10 | | 31 Jan 1983 (SI 1982/1857; SI 1983/24) |
| Sch 11 | | 31 Jan 1983 (except provisions listed below) (SI 1982/1857) |
| | | 24 May 1983 (para 6(a)(iii), (v)) (SI 1983/182) |
| Sch 12 | | 24 May 1983 (SI 1983/182) |
| Sch 13 | | 24 May 1983 (SI 1983/182; SI 1983/758) |
| Sch 14 | para 1 | 31 Jan 1983 (SI 1982/1857) |

**Criminal Justice Act 1982 (c 48)**—*contd*

|  |  |  |
|---|---|---|
| | para 2 | 11 Apr 1983 (SI 1982/1857) |
| | para 3 | 31 Jan 1983 (SI 1983/24) |
| | para 4 | 24 May 1983 (SI 1983/182) |
| | para 5 | 31 Jan 1983 (SI 1982/1857) |
| | paras 6, 7 | 24 May 1983 (SI 1983/182) |
| | para 8(a) | 24 May 1983 (SI 1983/182; SI 1983/758) |
| | para 8(b), (c) | 24 May 1983 (SI 1983/182) |
| | para 9 | 24 May 1983 (SI 1983/182) |
| | para 10(a) | 31 Jan 1983 (SI 1982/1857) |
| | para 10(b) | 24 May 1983 (SI 1983/182) |
| | paras 11–13 | 24 May 1983 (SI 1983/182; SI 1983/758) |
| | para 14 | 24 May 1983 (SI 1983/182) |
| | paras 15–17 | 24 May 1983 (SI 1983/182; SI 1983/758) |
| | para 18(a) | 24 May 1983 (SI 1983/182; SI 1983/758) |
| | para 18(b) | 31 Jan 1983 (SI 1982/1857; SI 1983/24) |
| | para 18(c) | 24 May 1983 (SI 1983/182; SI 1983/758) |
| | para 19 | 24 May 1983 (SI 1983/182; SI 1983/758) |
| | para 20 | 28 Oct 1982 (s 80(1)) |
| | para 21 | 31 Jan 1983 (SI 1982/1857; SI 1983/24) |
| | para 22 | 31 Jan 1983 (SI 1982/1857) |
| | para 23 | 24 May 1983 (SI 1983/182) |
| | para 24 | 24 May 1983 (SI 1983/182; SI 1983/758) |
| | paras 25–28 | 24 May 1983 (SI 1983/182) |
| | para 29 | 24 May 1983 (SI 1983/182; SI 1983/758) |
| | para 30 | 24 May 1983 (SI 1983/182) |
| | para 31 | 31 Jan 1983 (SI 1982/1857; SI 1983/24) |
| | paras 32–35 | 24 May 1983 (SI 1983/182) |
| | paras 36, 37 | 24 May 1983 (SI 1983/182; SI 1983/758) |
| | para 38 | 24 May 1983 (SI 1983/182) |
| | para 39 | 24 May 1983 (SI 1983/182; SI 1983/758) |
| | paras 40, 41 | 31 Jan 1983 (SI 1982/1857) |
| | paras 42, 43 | 31 Jan 1983 (SI 1982/1857; SI 1983/24) |
| | paras 44–60 | 24 May 1983 (SI 1983/182) |
| Sch 15 | paras 1, 2 | 11 Apr 1983 (SI 1983/24) |
| | paras 3–5 | 31 Jan 1983 (SI 1983/24) |
| | paras 6–13 | 11 Apr 1983 (SI 1983/24) |
| | paras 14–16 | 31 Jan 1983 (SI 1983/24) |
| | para 17 | 11 Apr 1983 (SI 1983/24) |
| | paras 18, 19 | 31 Jan 1983 (SI 1983/24) |
| | paras 20–29 | 11 Apr 1983 (SI 1983/24) |
| | para 30 | 31 Jan 1983 (SI 1983/24) |
| Sch 16 | | 28 Oct 1982 (repeal of Imprisonment (Temporary Provisions) Act 1980) (s 80(1)) |

Sch 16 (contd)

31 Jan 1983 (SI 1982/1857; SI 1983/24), repeals of or in—
Merchant Shipping Act 1894, s 680(1);
Prison Act 1952, s 55(3);
Criminal Justice Act 1967, s 95(1);
Immigration Act 1971, s 6(5);
Powers of Criminal Courts Act 1973, ss 2, 4, 23(1), 47(d), 48–51, 57(1), Sch 1, para 7, Sch 3;
Criminal Procedure (Scotland) Act 1975, s 421(1);
Criminal Law Act 1977, Sch 9, para 10, Sch 12 (repeals in the entry relating to Powers of Criminal Courts Act 1973 only);
Customs and Excise Management Act 1979, ss 147(5), 156(3);
Criminal Justice (Scotland) Act 1980, s 55;
Magistrates' Courts Act 1980, s 108(3)(a);
Animal Health Act 1981, s 70

11 Apr 1983 (SI 1982/1857; SI 1983/24), repeals of or in—
Sea Fisheries (Scotland) Amendment Act 1885, s 4;

## Criminal Justice Act 1982 (c 48)—*contd*

|  |  |  |
|---|---|---|
|  |  | Electric Lighting (Clauses) Act 1899, Schedule; |
|  |  | Housing (Scotland) Act 1966, s 185(2); |
|  |  | Criminal Procedure (Scotland) Act 1975, ss 8(2), 289D(2), (3A), 291(1); |
|  |  | Criminal Law Act 1977, s 31; |
|  |  | National Health Service (Scotland) Act 1978, Sch 9, para 1(1), Sch 10, para 7(2)(b); |
|  |  | Electricity (Scotland) Act 1979, s 41(1)(b); |
|  |  | Merchant Shipping Act 1979, s 43; |
|  |  | Criminal Justice (Scotland) Act 1980, ss 7(3), 8, 46(1), Sch 7, para 50; |
|  |  | Water (Scotland) Act 1980, Sch 4, para 10(3) |
|  |  | 24 May 1983 (otherwise, except as noted below) (SI 1983/182; SI 1983/758) |
|  |  | *Not yet in force* (repeal of Criminal Justice Act 1961, s 38(5)(c), (d)) |
| Sch 17 | paras 1–14 | 24 May 1983 (SI 1983/182) |
|  | para 15 | 28 Oct 1982 (s 80(1)) |
|  | paras 16, 17 | 31 Jan 1983 (SI 1982/1857) |
|  | para 18 | 31 Jan 1983 (SI 1983/24) |

## Currency Act 1982 (c 3)

*RA:* 2 Feb 1982

Whole Act in force 2 Feb 1982 (RA)

## Deer (Amendment) (Scotland) Act 1982 (c 19)

*RA:* 28 Jun 1982

*Commencement provisions:* s 16(3), (4); commencement order made 27 Jun 1984 (not a statutory instrument)

| | |
|---|---|
| 1–10 | 28 Jul 1982 (s 16(3)) |
| 11 | 1 Jan 1985 (commencement order made 27 Jun 1984) |
| 12–16 | 28 Jul 1982 (s 16(3)) |
| Schs 1, 2 | 28 Jul 1982 (s 16(3)) |
| Sch 3 | 28 Jul 1982 (except repeal of Sale of Venison (Scotland) Act 1968) (s 16(3)) |
|  | 1 Jan 1985 (repeal of Sale of Venison (Scotland) Act 1968) (commencement order made 27 Jun 1984) |

## Derelict Land Act 1982 (c 42)

*RA:* 30 Jul 1982

*Commencement provisions:* s 5(3)

Whole Act in force 30 Aug 1982 (s 5(3))

## Duchy of Cornwall Management Act 1982 (c 47)

*RA:* 28 Oct 1982

Whole Act in force 28 Oct 1982 (RA)

## Electricity (Financial Provisions) (Scotland) Act 1982 (c 56)

*RA*: 22 Dec 1982

*Commencement provisions*: s 2(1)

Whole Act in force 22 Feb 1983 (s 2(1))

## Employment Act 1982 (c 46)

*RA*: 28 Oct 1982

*Commencement provisions*: s 22; Employment Act 1982 (Commencement) Order 1982, SI 1982/1656

| | | |
|---|---|---|
| 1 | | 1 Jan 1983 (not applicable to any director's report relating to a financial year before that date) (SI 1982/1656) |
| 2 | | 28 Oct 1982 (s 22(2)) |
| 3–7 | | 1 Dec 1982 (does not apply where the 'effective day' fell before that date) (SI 1982/1656) |
| 8 | | 1 Dec 1982 (does not apply where the complaint presented to tribunal before that date) (SI 1982/1656) |
| 9 | | 1 Dec 1982 (does not apply whereto dismissal during industrial action begun before that date) (SI 1982/1656) |
| 10 | | 1 Dec 1982 (does not apply where action short of dismissal taken before that date) (SI 1982/1656) |
| 11 | | 1 Dec 1982 (does not apply where the 'effective day' fell before that date) (SI 1982/1656) |
| 12–19 | | 1 Dec 1982 (SI 1982/1656) |
| 20 | | 2 Jan 1983 (SI 1982/1656) |
| 21 | (1) | 1 Dec 1982 (SI 1982/1656) |
| | (2) | See Sch 3 below |
| | (3) | See Sch 4 below |
| 22 | | 1 Dec 1982 (SI 1982/1656) |
| Sch 1 | | 28 Oct 1982 (s 22(2)) |
| Sch 2 | | 2 Jan 1983 (SI 1982/1656) |
| Sch 3 | | 1 Dec 1982 (SI 1982/1656)[1] |
| Sch 4 | | 1 Dec 1982 (all repeals except those listed below) (SI 1982/1656)[1] |
| | | 2 Jan 1983 (repeals of or in Employment Protection (Consolidation) Act 1978, ss 3, 4(4)(b), 5, 7, 73(3), 81(4), 143, 147, 149, Sch 4, paras 2, 7, Sch 13, para 13, Sch 16, para 23(9)) (SI 1982/1656) |

[1] For transitional provisions, see SI 1982/1656, art 3, Sch 2

## Finance Act 1982 (c 39)

*Budget Day*: 9 Mar 1982

*RA*: 30 Jul 1982

The commencement details of Finance Acts are not set out, as the dates from which their provisions take effect are usually stated clearly and unambiguously in the text of the Act, and charging provisions will normally state for which year or years of assessment they are to have effect.

## Fire Service College Board (Abolition) Act 1982 (c 13)

*RA*: 7 Apr 1982

*Commencement provisions*: s 2(2)

Whole Act in force 7 May 1982 (s 2(2))

## Firearms Act 1982 (c 31)

*RA:* 13 Jul 1982

*Commencement provisions:* s 4(3); Firearms Act 1982 (Commencement) Order 1983, SI 1983/1440

Whole Act in force 1 Nov 1983 (SI 1983/1440)

## Food and Drugs (Amendment) Act 1982 (c 26)

*RA:* 13 Jul 1982

*Commencement provisions:* s 12

| | |
|---|---|
| 1–3 | 1 Jan 1983 (s 12(2)) |
| 4 | 1 Nov 1982 (s 12(1)) |
| 5–8 | 1 Jan 1983 (s 12(2)) |
| 9 | 1 Nov 1982 (s 12(1)) |
| 10–13 | 1 Jan 1983 (s 12(2)) |

## Forfeiture Act 1982 (c 34)

*RA:* 13 Jul 1982

*Commencement provisions:* s 7(2); Forfeiture Act 1982 Commencement Order 1982, SI 1982/1731

| | |
|---|---|
| 1–3 | 13 Oct 1982 (s 7(2)) |
| 4 | 31 Dec 1982 (SI 1982/1731) |
| 5 | 13 Oct 1982 (s 7(2)) |
| 6, 7 | 13 Jul 1982 (RA) |

## Gaming (Amendment) Act 1982 (c 22)

*RA:* 28 Jan 1982

*Commencement provisions:* s 3(2)

Whole Act in force 28 Aug 1982 (s 3(2))

## Harbours (Scotland) Act 1982 (c 17)

*RA:* 27 May 1982

Whole Act in force 27 May 1982 (RA)

## Hops Marketing Act 1982 (c 5)

*RA:* 25 Feb 1982

Whole Act in force 25 Feb 1982 (RA); note that for practical purposes the majority of the Act came into effect on 1 Apr 1982, the day appointed for the revocation of the Hops Marketing Scheme under s 1(2)

## Industrial Development Act 1982 (c 52)

*RA:* 28 Oct 1982

*Commencement provisions:* s 20(2)

Whole Act in force 28 Jan 1983 (s 20(2))

## Industrial Training Act 1982 (c 10)

*RA:* 29 Mar 1982

*Commencement provisions:* s 21(3)

Whole Act in force 29 Jun 1982 (s 21(3))

---

## Industry Act 1982 (c 18)

*RA:* 27 May 1982

Whole Act in force 27 May 1982 (RA)

---

## Insurance Companies Act 1982 (c 50)

*RA:* 28 Oct 1982

*Commencement provisions:* ss 99(1), 100(2), Sch 4, para 6

| | |
|---|---|
| 1–35 | 28 Jan 1983 (s 100(2)) |
| 36 | *Never in force* (repealed) |
| 37–100 | 28 Jan 1983 (s 100(2)) |
| Schs 1–6 | 28 Jan 1983 (s 100(2)) |

---

## Iron and Steel Act 1982 (c 25)

*RA:* 13 Jul 1982

*Commencement provisions:* s 39(2)

Whole Act in force 13 Oct 1982 (s 39(2))

---

## Lands Valuation Amendment (Scotland) Act 1982 (c 57)

*RA:* 22 Dec 1982

Whole Act in force 22 Dec 1982 (RA)

---

## Legal Aid Act 1982 (c 44)

*RA:* 28 Oct 1982

*Commencement provisions:* s 16(5); Legal Aid Act 1982 (Commencement No 1) Order 1982, SI 1982/1893; Legal Aid Act 1982 (Commencement No 2) Order 1984, SI 1984/220; Legal Aid Act 1982 (Commencement No 3) Order 1984, SI 1984/730

| | | |
|---|---|---|
| 1 | | 1 Jan 1983 (SI 1982/1893) |
| 2 | | 1 Jul 1984 (SI 1984/730) |
| 3, 4 | | 1 Jan 1983 (SI 1982/1893) |
| 5–10 | | 1 Mar 1984 (SI 1984/220) |
| 11 | (1) | *Never in force* (repealed) |
| | (2) | 1 Mar 1984 (SI 1984/220) |
| 12 | (1) | 1 Mar 1984 (SI 1984/220) |
| | (2) | *Never in force* (repealed) |
| | (3)(a) | 1 Mar 1984 (SI 1984/220) |
| | (3)(b) | *Never in force* (repealed) |
| 13 | | *Never in force* (repealed) |
| 14 | | See Schedule below |
| 15, 16 | | 1 Mar 1984 (SI 1984/220) |

**Legal Aid Act 1982 (c 44)**—*contd*

| | |
|---|---|
| Schedule | 1 Mar 1984 (except repeal of Legal Aid Act 1974, s 36) (SI 1984/220) |
| | *Never in force* (exception noted above) (repealed) |

## Local Government and Planning (Scotland) Act 1982 (c 43)

*RA:* 30 Jul 1982

*Commencement provisions:* s 69(2); Local Government and Planning (Scotland) Act 1982 (Commencement No 1) Order 1982, SI 1982/1137; Local Government and Planning (Scotland) Act 1982 (Commencement No 2) Order 1982, SI 1982/1397; Local Government and Planning (Scotland) Act 1982 (Commencement No 3) Order 1984, SI 1984/239

| | | |
|---|---|---|
| 1–5 | | 1 Sep 1982 (SI 1982/1137) |
| 6 | | 1 Apr 1983 (SI 1982/1397) |
| 7 | | 1 Nov 1982 (in so far as it inserts Local Government (Scotland) Act 1973, s 154B) (SI 1982/1397) |
| 8 | | 1 Sep 1982 (SI 1982/1137) |
| 9–28 | | 1 Apr 1983 (SI 1982/1397) |
| 29 | | 1 Nov 1982 (SI 1982/1397) |
| 30, 31 | | 1 Apr 1983 (SI 1982/1397) |
| 32 | | 1 Nov 1982 (SI 1982/1397) |
| 33–35 | | 1 Sep 1982 (SI 1982/1137) |
| 36–40 | | 1 Nov 1982 (SI 1982/1397) |
| 41 | | 14 May 1984 (SI 1984/239) |
| 42, 43 | | 1 Nov 1982 (SI 1982/1397) |
| 44 | | 14 May 1984 (SI 1984/239) |
| 45, 46 | | 1 Nov 1982 (SI 1982/1397) |
| 47 | (a) | 14 May 1984 (SI 1984/239) |
| | (b), (c) | 1 Nov 1982 (SI 1982/1397) |
| 48 | | See Sch 2 below |
| 49–51 | | 1 Sep 1982 (SI 1982/1137) |
| 52 | | 1 Apr 1983 (SI 1982/1397) |
| 53–56 | | 1 Sep 1982 (SI 1982/1137) |
| 57 | | 1 Apr 1983 (SI 1982/1397) |
| 58–60 | | 1 Nov 1982 (SI 1982/1397) |
| 61–65 | | 1 Sep 1982 (SI 1982/1137) |
| 66 | (1) | See Sch 3 below |
| | (2) | See Sch 4 below |
| 67, 68 | | 1 Sep 1982 (SI 1982/1137) |
| 69 | | 30 Jul 1982 (RA) |
| Sch 1 | | 1 Apr 1983 (SI 1982/1397) |
| Sch 2 | paras 1–4 | 1 Nov 1982 (SI 1982/1397) |
| | para 5 | 14 May 1984 (SI 1984/239) |
| | paras 6, 7 | 1 Nov 1982 (SI 1982/1397) |
| | paras 8–12 | 14 May 1984 (SI 1984/239) |
| | paras 13–16 | 1 Nov 1982 (SI 1982/1397) |
| | paras 17–20 | 14 May 1984 (SI 1984/239) |
| | paras 21, 22 | 1 Nov 1982 (SI 1982/1397) |
| | para 23 | 14 May 1984 (SI 1984/239) |
| | para 24 | 1 Nov 1982 (SI 1982/1397) |
| | paras 25–27 | 14 May 1984 (SI 1984/239) |
| | paras 28–41 | 1 Nov 1982 (SI 1982/1397) |
| | para 42 | 14 May 1984 (SI 1984/239) |
| | para 43 | 1 Nov 1982 (SI 1982/1397) |
| Sch 3 | paras 1, 2 | 1 Apr 1983 (SI 1982/1397) |
| | para 3(a) | 1 Sep 1982 (SI 1982/1137) |
| | para 3(b) | 1 Apr 1983 (SI 1982/1397) |
| | para 4 | 1 Nov 1982 (SI 1982/1397) |

**Local Government and Planning (Scotland) Act 1982 (c 43)**—*contd*

|  |  |  |
|---|---|---|
| paras 5–7 | 1 Sep 1982 (SI 1982/1137) |
| paras 8–11 | 1 Nov 1982 (SI 1982/1397) |
| para 12 | 1 Apr 1983 (SI 1982/1397) |
| paras 13–15 | 1 Nov 1982 (SI 1982/1397) |
| para 16 | 1 Apr 1983 (SI 1982/1397) |
| paras 17–20 | 1 Sep 1982 (SI 1982/1137) |
| para 21 | 1 Apr 1983 (SI 1982/1397) |
| paras 22, 23 | 1 Nov 1982 (SI 1982/1397) |
| para 24 | 14 May 1984 (SI 1984/239) |
| paras 25–28 | 1 Nov 1982 (SI 1982/1397) |
| para 29 | 1 Apr 1983 (SI 1982/1397) |
| paras 30, 31 | 1 Sep 1982 (SI 1982/1137) |
| para 32 | 1 Apr 1983 (SI 1982/1397) |
| para 33(a) | 1 Apr 1983 (SI 1982/1397) |
| para 33(b) | 1 Sep 1982 (SI 1982/1137) |
| para 34 | 1 Nov 1982 (SI 1982/1397) |
| paras 35, 36 | 1 Sep 1982 (SI 1982/1137) |
| paras 37, 38 | 1 Apr 1983 (SI 1982/1397) |
| paras 39, 40 | 1 Sep 1982 (SI 1982/1137) |
| para 41 | 1 Apr 1983 (SI 1982/1397) |
| paras 42, 43 | 1 Sep 1982 (SI 1982/1137) |

Sch 4 1 Sep 1982 (SI 1982/1137), repeals of or in—

> Local Government (Scotland) Act 1966, s 5(1), Sch 1, Pt II, paras 2, 3;
> Local Government (Scotland) Act 1973, ss 216(2)–(5), 218, 221, 224(1)–(4), (6);
> Local Government (Scotland) Act 1975, Sch 1, paras 2, 2A, 3, 4, 4A;
> Electricity (Scotland) Act 1979, Sch 4, paras 1, 3, 5, 6;
> Tenants' Rights, Etc (Scotland) Act 1980, ss 1(1), 4(3)

1 Nov 1982 (SI 1982/1397), repeals of or in—

> Requisitioned Land and War Works Act 1945, s 52;
> Civic Restaurants Act 1947;
> Requisitioned Land and War Works Act 1948, Schedule, para 10;
> Highlands and Islands Development (Scotland) Act 1965, s 10(1), (3);
> Countryside (Scotland) Act 1967, ss 14(5), 34(5), 35A, Sch 3, paras 1(2), 2(1)–(3), 4;
> Social Work (Scotland) Act 1968, s 6(1)(d);
> Town and Country Planning (Scotland) Act 1972, ss 12(1), (2), 37(1), 54(2), 61(7), 84(6), 85(8), 92(1), 93(5)(b), 154(2), 164(6), 167C(2)(b), 215(1), 231(1)(b), (3)(f), 262(2), (3), 262A(3), (4), 262B(3), Sch 10, para 11(1);
> Local Government (Scotland) Act 1973, ss 49(2)(a), 164, Sch 22, Pt II, paras 5, 8, 9;
> Safety of Sports Grounds Act 1975, s 11;
> Scottish Development Agency Act 1975, s 10(1);
> Refuse Disposal (Amenity) Act 1978, s 8(1);
> Water (Scotland) Act 1980, Sch 3, para 7(5), Sch 4, para 23;
> Countryside (Scotland) Act 1981, s 5

1 Apr 1983 (SI 1982/1397), repeals of or in—

> Public Parks (Scotland) Act 1878;
> Burgh Police (Scotland) Act 1892, ss 107, 110, 112, 116, 277, 288, 307, 308;
> Public Health (Scotland) Act 1897, ss 29, 39;
> Burgh Police (Scotland) Act 1903, s 44;
> Physical Training and Recreation Act 1937, ss 4(1)–(4), 5, 7, 10(4)–(7), (11);
> Food and Drugs (Scotland) Act 1956, s 26(3);
> Physical Training and Recreation Act 1958;

**Local Government and Planning (Scotland) Act 1982 (c 43)**—*contd*

Caravan Sites and Control of Development Act 1960,
s 32(1)(h)(iii);
Social Work (Scotland) Act 1968, s 85;
Agriculture Act 1970, ss 95, 96;
Local Government (Scotland) Act 1973, ss 55, 91, 137(2), 139,
158, 162, 178, 219, 220, Sch 23, para 2(a);
Control of Pollution Act 1974, ss 22, 23, Sch 4;
Education (Scotland) Act 1980, s 1(3)(b), (5)(b)(iii);
Local Government, Planning and Land Act 1980, s 70(4)
14 May 1984 (otherwise) (SI 1984/239)

**Local Government Finance Act 1982 (c 32)**

*RA:* 13 Jul 1982

*Commencement provisions:* See notes to individual provisions below

| | |
|---|---|
| 1–6 | 13 Jul 1982 (ss 1–3, 6(1), (3) only effective for financial years 1 Apr 1982 onwards) (RA) |
| 7 | 13 Jul 1982 (RA) |
| 8–10 | 13 Jul 1982 (s 8 only effective in relation to block grant for years 1 Apr 1982 onwards, except s 8(2) so far as relates to consultation; s 8(4A) effective in relation to years 1 Apr 1987 onwards; s 8(8) which only applies to years 1 Apr 1983 onwards; s 10 (and Sch 2) only effective for years 1 Apr 1983 onwards) (RA) |
| 11 | 13 Jul 1982 (s 11 (and Sch 3) only effective from 21 Jan 1983) (RA; s 33(2); Accounts and Audit (First Appointed Day) Order 1982, SI 1982/1881) |
| 12–25 | 13 Jul 1982 (only effective for periods beginning on or after 1 Apr 1983) (RA; s 33(3); Accounts and Audit (Second Appointed Day) Order 1983, SI 1983/165) |
| 26–30 | 13 Jul 1982 (RA) |
| 31 | 13 Jul 1982 (so far as it relates to ss 12–25, only effective for periods beginning on or after 1 Apr 1983) (RA; s 33(3); Accounts and Audit (Second Appointed Day) Order 1983, SI 1983/165) |
| 32–39 | 13 Jul 1982 (RA) |
| Sch 1 | 13 Jul 1982 (RA; but only effective for financial years 1 Apr 1982 onwards) |
| Sch 2 | See ss 8–10 above |
| Sch 3 | See ss 11–18 above |
| Schs 4, 5 | 13 Jul 1982 (RA; only effective for periods 1 Apr 1983 onwards) |
| Sch 6 | Pt I | Effective for financial years 1 Apr 1982 onwards (s 38(2)) |
| | Pt II | Effective for financial years 1 Apr 1981 onwards (s 38(3)) |
| | Pt III | Effective for financial years 1 Apr 1983 onwards (s 38(4)) |
| | Pt IV | Effective for periods 1 Apr 1983 onwards (s 38(5)) |

**Local Government (Miscellaneous Provisions) Act 1982 (c 30)**

*RA:* 13 Jul 1982

*Commencement provisions:* ss 1(12), 7(3), 25(3), 40(10), 47(3), Sch 3, para 30(1); Local Government (Miscellaneous Provisions) Act 1982 (Commencement No 1) Order 1982, SI 1982/1119; Local Government (Miscellaneous Provisions) Act 1982 (Commencement No 2) Order 1982, SI 1982/1160

Note: certain provisions of this Act must be adopted by local authority resolution to have effect in particular areas

| | |
|---|---|
| 1 | 1 Jan 1983 (s 1(12)) |
| 2–6 | 13 Jul 1982 (RA) |

## Local Government (Miscellaneous Provisions) Act 1982 (c 30)—*contd*

| | | |
|---|---|---|
| 7 | (1), (2) | 13 Oct 1982 (s 7(3)) |
| | (3), (4) | 13 Jul 1982 (RA) |
| 8–24 | | 13 Jul 1982 (RA) |
| 25 | | 1 Sep 1982 (SI 1982/1160) |
| 26–39 | | 13 Jul 1982 (RA) |
| 40 | | 13 Sep 1982 (s 40(10)) |
| 41–46 | | 13 Jul 1982 (RA) |
| 47 | (1) | 13 Jul 1982 (RA) |
| | (2), (3) | See Sch 7 below |
| | (4) | 13 Jul 1982 (RA) |
| 48, 49 | | 13 Jul 1982 (RA) |
| Schs 1, 2 | | 1 Jan 1983 (s 1(12)) |
| Sch 3 | | 13 Jul 1982 (except in relation to sex cinemas) (RA) |
| | | 13 Oct 1982 (exception noted above) (SI 1982/1119) |
| Schs 4–6 | | 13 Jul 1982 (RA) |
| Sch 7 | Pts I, II | 1 Jan 1983 (s 47(3)) |
| | Pts III–XV | 13 Jul 1982 (RA) |
| | Pt XVI | 13 Jul 1982 (except as noted below) (RA) |
| | | 1 Sep 1982 (repeal of Health and Safety at Work etc Act 1974, s 63) (SI 1982/1160) |

## Mental Health (Amendment) Act 1982 (c 51)

*RA:* 28 Oct 1982

*Commencement provisions:* s 69; Mental Health (Amendment) Act 1982 (Commencement No 1) Order, SI 1983/890

| | | |
|---|---|---|
| 1–28 | | 30 Sep 1983 (s 69(1)) |
| 29–31 | | *Never in force* (repealed) |
| 32–55 | | 30 Sep 1983 (s 69(1)) |
| 56 | (1) | 1 Sep 1983 (SI 1983/890) |
| | (2)–(10) | 30 Sep 1983 (s 69(1)) |
| | (11) | 1 Sep 1983 (SI 1983/890) |
| 57–60 | | 30 Sep 1983 (s 69(1)) |
| 61 | | 28 Oct 1984 (ss 61(1), 69(4)) |
| 62 | | 1 Apr 1983 (s 69(5)) |
| 63, 64 | | 30 Sep 1983 (s 69(1)) |
| 65 | (1) | See Sch 3 below |
| | (2) | See Sch 4 below |
| 66–70 | | 30 Sep 1983 (s 69(1)) |
| Sch 1 | | 30 Sep 1983 (s 69(1)) |
| Sch 2 | | 1 Apr 1983 (s 69(5)) |
| Sch 3 | Pt I | 30 Sep 1983 (s 69(1)) |
| | Pt II | 28 Oct 1984 (s 69(4)) |
| Sch 4 | Pt I | 1 Apr 1983 (s 69(5)), repeals of or in— |
| | | Mental Health Act 1959, Sch 7; |
| | | Mental Health (Scotland) Act 1960; |
| | | Mental Health Act (Northern Ireland) 1961 |
| | | 30 Sep 1983 (otherwise) (s 69(1)) |
| | Pt II | 28 Oct 1984 (s 69(4)) |
| Sch 5 | | 30 Sep 1983 (s 69(1)) |

## Merchant Shipping (Liner Conferences) Act 1982 (c 37)

*RA:* 23 Jul 1982

*Commencement provisions:* s 15(2); Merchant Shipping (Liner Conferences) Act 1982 (Commencement) Order 1985, SI 1985/182

**Merchant Shipping (Liner Conferences) Act 1982 (c 37)**—*contd*
Whole Act in force 14 Mar 1985 (SI 1985/182)

---

**National Insurance Surcharge Act 1982 (c 55)**

*RA:* 22 Dec 1982

Whole Act in force 22 Dec 1982 (RA)

---

**New Towns Act 1982 (c 7)**

*RA:* 25 Feb 1982

Whole Act in force 25 Feb 1982 (RA)

---

**Northern Ireland Act 1982 (c 38)**

*RA:* 23 Jul 1982

Whole Act in force 23 Jul 1982 (RA)

---

**Oil and Gas (Enterprise) Act 1982 (c 23)**

*RA:* 28 Jun 1982

*Commencement provisions:* s 38(2); Oil and Gas (Enterprise) Act 1982 (Commencement No 1) Order 1982, SI 1982/895; Oil and Gas (Enterprise) Act 1982 (Commencement No 2) Order 1982, SI 1982/1059; Oil and Gas (Enterprise) Act 1982 (Commencement No 3) Order 1982, SI 1982/1431; Oil and Gas (Enterprise) Act 1982 (Commencement No 4) Order 1987, SI 1987/2272

| | | |
|---|---|---|
| 1–3 | | 2 Jul 1982 (SI 1982/895) |
| 4–6 | | 31 Dec 1982 (SI 1982/1431) |
| 7 | | 1 Nov 1982 (SI 1982/1431) |
| 8 | | 1 Apr 1983 (SI 1982/1431) |
| 9–11 | | 2 Jul 1982 (SI 1982/895) |
| 12–17 | | 18 Aug 1982 (SI 1982/1059) |
| 18 | | 23 Jul 1982 (SI 1982/895) |
| 19–21 | | 1 Oct 1982 (SI 1982/1059) |
| 22 | | 1 Feb 1988 (SI 1987/2272) |
| 23 | (1) | 1 Feb 1988 (SI 1987/2272) |
| | (2)–(4) | 31 Dec 1982 (amendments to Social Security Act 1975, Patents Act 1977 and Social Security and Housing Benefits Act 1982) (SI 1982/1431) |
| | | 1 Feb 1988 (otherwise) (SI 1987/2272) |
| | (5) | 1 Feb 1988 (SI 1987/2272) |
| | (6) | 31 Dec 1982 (amendments to Social Security Act 1975, Patents Act 1977 and Social Security and Housing Benefits Act 1982) (SI 1982/1431) |
| | | 1 Feb 1988 (otherwise) (SI 1987/2272) |
| 24 | | 1 Nov 1982 (SI 1982/1431) |
| 25 | | 1 Oct 1982 (SI 1982/1059) |
| 26 | | 1 Nov 1982 (SI 1982/1431) |
| 27 | (1)(a) | 1 Feb 1988 (SI 1987/2272) |
| | (1)(b)–(d) | 1 Oct 1982 (SI 1982/1059) |
| | (2)–(7) | 1 Oct 1982 (SI 1982/1059) |
| 28 | | 1 Oct 1982 (SI 1982/1059) |
| 29 | | 23 Jul 1982 (SI 1982/895) |
| 30, 31 | | 1 Oct 1982 (SI 1982/1059) |
| 32, 33 | | 2 Jul 1982 (SI 1982/895) |

**Oil and Gas (Enterprise) Act 1982 (c 23)**—*contd*

| | | |
|---|---|---|
| 34 | | 1 Nov 1982 (SI 1982/1431) |
| 35, 36 | | 2 Jul 1982 (SI 1982/895) |
| 37 | | See Schs 3, 4 below |
| 38 | | 2 Jul 1982 (SI 1982/895) |
| Sch 1 | | 2 Jul 1982 (SI 1982/895) |
| Sch 2 | | 1 Oct 1982 (SI 1982/1059) |
| Sch 3 | para 1 | 1 Oct 1982 (SI 1982/1059) |
| | paras 2, 3 | 1 Feb 1988 (SI 1987/2272) |
| | para 4 | 1 Oct 1982 (SI 1982/1059) |
| | paras 5, 6 | *Never in force* (repealed) |
| | paras 7–11 | 1 Nov 1982 (SI 1982/1431) |
| | para 12 | *Never in force* (repealed) |
| | paras 13–19 | 18 Aug 1982 (SI 1982/1059) |
| | para 20 | *Never in force* (repealed) |
| | para 21 | 31 Dec 1982 (SI 1982/1431) |
| | para 22 | 18 Aug 1982 (SI 1982/1059) |
| | para 23 | 1 Nov 1982 (SI 1982/1431) |
| | paras 24, 25 | *Never in force* (repealed) |
| | para 26 | 1 Nov 1982 (SI 1982/1431) |
| | para 27 | 31 Dec 1982 (SI 1982/1431) |
| | para 28 | 1 Nov 1982 (SI 1982/1431) |
| | para 29 | 1 Oct 1982 (SI 1982/1059) |
| | paras 30–33 | 1 Nov 1982 (SI 1982/1431) |
| | para 34 | 1 Feb 1988 (SI 1987/2272) |
| | paras 35, 36 | *Never in force* (repealed) |
| | para 37 | 18 Aug 1982 (SI 1982/1059) |
| | para 38 | *Never in force* (repealed) |
| | para 39 | 31 Dec 1982 (SI 1982/1431) |
| | paras 40, 41 | *Never in force* (repealed) |
| | paras 42, 43 | 1 Feb 1988 (SI 1987/2272) |
| | para 44 | 31 Dec 1982 (SI 1982/1431) |

Sch 4
    18 Aug 1982 (SI 1982/1059), repeals of or in—
      Petroleum (Production) Act 1934;
      Gas Act 1972 (except repeal in s 7(2));
      Oil Taxation Act 1975;
      Energy Act 1976;
      Gas Act 1980
    1 Oct 1982 (SI 1982/1059), repeals of or in—
      Continental Shelf Act 1964, s 2;
      Mineral Workings (Offshore Installations) Act 1971, s 10 (except
        in relation to offences within sub-s (1)(a));
      Petroleum and Submarine Pipe-lines Act 1975, ss 22, 26, 41;
      Customs and Excise Management Act 1979
    1 Nov 1982 (SI 1982/1431), repeals of or in—
      Mineral Workings (Offshore Installations) Act 1971, ss 6(2),
        12(1);
      Petroleum and Submarine Pipe-lines Act 1975, ss 1(3)(c), 3(3),
        44(1)–(4), 45(3)
    31 Dec 1982 (repeals of or in Petroleum and Submarine Pipe-lines
      Act 1975, ss 2(4)(d), 7(2), 14(4)(b), 40(2)(a), (c), (3)(a), (c))
      (SI 1982/1431)
    1 Apr 1983 (repeals of Petroleum and Submarine Pipe-lines
      Act 1975, s 40(1), (4), 40(3) (so far as not brought into force
      on 31 Dec 1982)) (SI 1982/1431)
    1 Feb 1988 (SI 1987/2272), repeals of or in—
      Continental Shelf Act 1964, ss 3, 11(3);
      Mineral Workings (Offshore Installations) Act 1971, ss 8, 9(5), 10
      (so far as not already repealed)
    *Never in force* (otherwise) (repealed)

## Planning Inquiries (Attendance of Public) Act 1982 (c 21)

*RA:* 28 Jun 1982

Whole Act in force 28 Jun 1982 (RA)

---

## Reserve Forces Act 1982 (c 14)

*RA:* 7 Apr 1982

Whole Act in force 7 Apr 1982 (RA)

---

## Shipbuilding Act 1982 (c 4)

*RA:* 25 Feb 1982

Whole Act in force 25 Feb 1982 (RA)

---

## Social Security and Housing Benefits Act 1982 (c 24)

*RA:* 28 Jun 1982

*Commencement provisions:* s 48(3); Social Security and Housing Benefits Act 1982 (Commencement No 1) Order 1982, SI 1982/893; Social Security and Housing Benefits Act 1982 (Commencement No 2) Order 1982, SI 1982/906

| | | |
|---|---|---|
| 1–6 | | 6 Apr 1983 (SI 1983/893) |
| 7 | | 28 Jun 1982 (scheme established under that section came into force on 6 Apr 1983) (s 48(3)) |
| 8–25 | | 6 Apr 1983 (SI 1982/893) |
| 26 | | 28 Jun 1982 (s 48(3)) |
| 27 | | 6 Apr 1983 (SI 1982/893) |
| 28 | (1)–(4) | 22 Nov 1982 (for specified purposes[1]) (SI 1982/906) |
| | | 1 Apr 1983 (to the extent that they are not then in operation in so far as they relate to rate rebate and in their application to a person, and his partner, where that person is not a tenant of a housing authority) (SI 1982/906) |
| | | 4 Apr 1983 (otherwise) (SI 1982/906) |
| | (5) | 4 Apr 1983 (SI 1982/906) |
| 29 | | 22 Nov 1982 (SI 1982/906) |
| 30, 31 | | 1 Apr 1983 (SI 1982/906) |
| 32 | (1)–(6) | 19 Jul 1982 (SI 1982/906) |
| | (7) | 4 Apr 1983 (SI 1982/906) |
| 33–35 | | 19 Jul 1982 (SI 1982/906) |
| 36 | (1)–(3) | 19 Jul 1982 (SI 1982/906) |
| | (4) | 4 Apr 1983 (SI 1982/906) |
| 37 | | 6 Apr 1983 (SI 1982/893) |
| 38 | | 18 Oct 1982 (SI 1982/893) |
| 39 | | 6 Apr 1983 (SI 1982/893) |
| 40 | | 28 Jun 1982 (s 48(3)) |
| 41 | | 1 Sep 1982 (SI 1982/893) |
| 42 | | 28 Jun 1982 (s 48(3)) |
| 43 | | 30 Aug 1982 (SI 1982/893) |
| 44–47 | | 28 Jun 1982 (s 48(3)) |
| 48 | (1)–(4) | 28 Jun 1982 (s 48(3)) |
| | (5), (6) | See Schs 4, 5 below |
| | (7) | 28 Jun 1982 (s 48(3)) |
| Schs 1–3 | | 6 Apr 1983 (SI 1982/893) |
| Sch 4 | paras 1–4 | 28 Jun 1982 (s 48(3)) |
| | paras 5, 6 | 4 Apr 1983 (SI 1982/906) |

**Social Security and Housing Benefits Act 1982 (c 24)**—*contd*

| | | |
|---|---|---|
| | para 7 | 28 Jun 1982 (s 48(3)) |
| | paras 8–10 | 6 Apr 1983 (SI 1982/893) |
| | para 11 | 28 Jun 1982 (s 48(3)) |
| | paras 12, 13 | 6 Apr 1983 (SI 1982/893) |
| | para 14(1) | 28 Jun 1982 (s 48(3)) |
| | para 14(2) | 6 Apr 1983 (SI 1982/893) |
| | para 14(3) | 28 Jun 1982 (s 48(3)) |
| | para 15 | 6 Apr 1983 (SI 1982/893) |
| | para 16 | 28 Jun 1982 (s 48(3)) |
| | para 17 | 6 Apr 1983 (SI 1982/893) |
| | para 18(1), (2) | 30 Jun 1982 (SI 1982/893) |
| | para 18(3), (4) | 6 Apr 1983 (SI 1982/893) |
| | para 19 | 1 Apr 1983 (SI 1982/906) |
| | para 20 | 30 Jun 1982 (SI 1982/893) |
| | para 21 | 28 Jun 1982 (s 48(3)) |
| | para 22 | 4 Apr 1983 (SI 1982/906) |
| | paras 23–25 | 28 Jun 1982 (s 48(3)) |
| | para 26 | 1 Sep 1982 (SI 1982/893) |
| | paras 27, 28 | 1 Apr 1983 (SI 1982/906) |
| | para 29 | 4 Apr 1983 (SI 1982/906) |
| | paras 30–34 | 28 Jun 1982 (s 48(3)) |
| | para 35(1) | 19 Jul 1982 (SI 1982/906) |
| | para 35(2), (3) | 4 Apr 1983 (SI 1982/906) |
| | para 36 | 4 Apr 1983 (SI 1982/906) |
| | paras 37, 38 | 28 Jun 1982 (RA) |
| | para 39 | 6 Apr 1983 (SI 1982/893) |
| Sch 5 | | 30 Jun 1982 (repeals of or in Social Security Act 1975, s 4, Sch 11) (SI 1982/893) |

6 Apr 1983 (SI 1982/893), repeals of or in—
Social Security Act 1975, except ss 4, 65, Sch 11;
Child Benefit Act 1975;
Social Security Act 1980;
Social Security (No 2) Act 1980

4 Apr 1983 (SI 1982/906), otherwise, except repeals in—
Social Security Act 1975, s 65(4) (repealed)[2];
Social Security Pensions Act 1975, Sch 4, para 22 (spent)[2]

---

[1] The specified purposes are: in so far as they relate to rate rebate or rent rebate; and in their application to a person and his partner where that person fulfils the following condition—

(i) he or his partner is a tenant of a housing authority and that if he is a joint tenant he is a joint tenant only with his partner,

(ii) he is entitled to qualifying supplementary benefit,

(iii) his dwelling is occupied as a home only by himself or persons who are members of his assessment unit,

(iv) the amount of qualifying supplementary benefit to which he is entitled exceeds his housing requirements, and

(v) he is not a person to whom section 8(1) or 9 of the Supplementary Benefits Act 1976 (persons affected by or returning to work after a trade dispute) applies

[2] It is unclear why the outstanding repeals were not brought into force; the whole of the Social Security Act 1975 was repealed (1 Jul 1992) by the Social Security (Consequential Provisions) Act 1992, s 3, Sch 1; the Social Security Pensions Act 1975, Sch 4, para 22 amended the Housing Finance Act 1972, Sch 3, which was repealed (4 Apr 1983) by Sch 5 to this Act

## Social Security (Contributions) Act 1982 (c 2)

*RA:* 2 Feb 1982

Whole Act in force 2 Feb 1982 (RA)

---

## Stock Transfer Act 1982 (c 41)

*RA:* 30 Jul 1982

*Commencement provisions:* s 6(2); Stock Transfer Act 1982 (Commencement) Order 1985, SI 1985/1137

| | |
|---|---|
| 1–3 | 23 Jul 1985 (SI 1985/1137) |
| 4–6 | 30 Oct 1982 (s 6(2)) |
| Schs 1, 2 | 23 Jul 1985 (SI 1985/1137) |

---

## Supply of Goods and Services Act 1982 (c 29)

*RA:* 13 Jul 1982

*Commencement provisions:* s 20(3); Supply of Goods and Services Act 1982 (Commencement) Order 1982, SI 1982/1770

| | |
|---|---|
| 1–11 | 4 Jan 1983 (s 20(3)) |
| 12–16 | 4 Jul 1983 (SI 1982/1770) |
| 17 | 4 Jan 1983 (s 20(3)) |
| 18, 19 | 4 Jan 1983 (so far as relate to ss 1–11) (s 20(3)) |
| | 4 Jul 1983 (so far as relate to ss 12–16) (SI 1982/1770) |
| 20 | 13 Jul 1982 (RA) |
| Schedule | 13 Jul 1982 (RA) |

---

## Taking of Hostages Act 1982 (c 28)

*RA:* 13 Jul 1982

*Commencement provisions:* s 6; Taking of Hostages Act 1982 (Commencement) Order 1982, SI 1982/1532

Whole Act in force 26 Nov 1982 (SI 1982/1532)

---

## Transport Act 1982 (c 49)

*RA:* 28 Oct 1982

*Commencement provisions:* s 76; Transport Act 1982 (Commencement No 1) Order 1982, SI 1982/1561; Transport Act 1982 (Commencement No 2) Order 1982, SI 1982/1804; Transport Act 1982 (Commencement No 3) Order 1983, SI 1983/276; Transport Act 1982 (Commencement No 4) Order 1983, SI 1983/577; Transport Act 1982 (Scotland) (Commencement No 1) Order 1983, SI 1983/650; Transport Act 1982 (Commencement No 5) Order 1984, SI 1984/175; Transport Act 1982 (Commencement No 6) Order 1986, SI 1986/1326; Transport Act 1982 (Scotland) (Commencement No 2) Order 1986, SI 1986/1874; Transport Act 1982 (Commencement No 7 and Transitional Provisions) Order 1996, SI 1996/1943

| | | |
|---|---|---|
| 1–7 | | 20 Dec 1982 (SI 1982/1804) |
| 8–15 | | *Not yet in force* |
| 16 | | 1 Nov 1982 (SI 1982/1561) |
| 17 | | *Not yet in force* (sub-s (3) repealed) |
| 18 | | 1 Aug 1996 (SI 1996/1943) |
| 19 | | *Never in force* (repealed) |
| 20 | | *Never in force* (substituted) |
| 21–26 | | *Not yet in force* |
| 27 | (1)–(4) | 1 Oct 1986 (SI 1986/1326) |
| | (5)–(9) | 30 Jun 1983 (S) (SI 1983/650) |

**Transport Act 1982 (c 49)**—*contd*

| | | |
|---|---|---|
| | | 1 Oct 1986 (E) (W) (SI 1986/1326) |
| 28 | | 1 Oct 1986 (SI 1986/1326) |
| 29 | (1) | 1 Oct 1986 (SI 1986/1326) |
| | (2)–(5) | 30 Jun 1983 (S) (SI 1983/650) |
| | | 1 Oct 1986 (E) (W) (SI 1986/1326) |
| | (6), (7) | 1 Oct 1986 (SI 1986/1326) |
| 30–32 | | 1 Oct 1986 (E) (W) (SI 1986/1326) |
| 33 | (1), (2) | 30 Jun 1983 (S) (SI 1983/650) |
| | | 1 Oct 1986 (E) (W) (SI 1986/1326) |
| | (3) | 1 Oct 1986 (SI 1986/1326) |
| | (4) | 30 Jun 1983 (S) (SI 1983/650) |
| | | 1 Oct 1986 (E) (W) (SI 1986/1326) |
| | (5)–(8) | 1 Oct 1986 (SI 1986/1326) |
| 34 | (1)–(5) | 1 Oct 1986 (SI 1986/1326) |
| | (6)–(10) | 30 Jun 1983 (S) (SI 1983/650) |
| | | 1 Oct 1986 (E) (W) (SI 1986/1326) |
| 35–38 | | 1 Oct 1986 (SI 1986/1326) |
| 39 | | *Never in force* (repealed) |
| 40, 41 | | 1 Oct 1986 (SI 1986/1326) |
| 42, 43 | | 1 Oct 1986 (E) (W) (SI 1986/1326) |
| | | 30 Jun 1983 (S) (SI 1983/650) |
| 44 | | 30 Jun 1983 (S) (in so far as relates to s 42) (SI 1983/650) |
| | | 1 Oct 1986 (E) (W) (SI 1986/1326) |
| 45–47 | | 1 Oct 1986 (SI 1986/1326) |
| 48 | | 30 Jun 1983 (S) (SI 1983/650) |
| | | 1 Oct 1986 (E) (W) (SI 1986/1326) |
| 49 | (1) | 30 Jun 1983 (S) (SI 1983/650) |
| | | 1 Oct 1986 (E) (W) (SI 1986/1326) |
| | (2)–(13) | 1 Oct 1986 (SI 1986/1326) |
| 50, 51 | | 1 Oct 1986 (SI 1986/1326) |
| 52 | | 1 Jun 1984 (SI 1984/175) |
| 53–56 | | 28 Oct 1982 (s 76(3)) |
| 57 | | 11 Apr 1983 (SI 1983/276) |
| 58 | | 1 Nov 1982 (SI 1982/1561) |
| 59 | | 6 May 1983 (SI 1983/577) |
| 60 | | 1 Nov 1982 (SI 1982/1561) |
| 61, 62 | | *Never in force* (repealed) |
| 63 | | 11 Apr 1983 (SI 1983/276) |
| 64 | | 20 Dec 1982 (SI 1982/1804) |
| 65 | | 11 Apr 1983 (SI 1983/276) |
| 66 | | *Not yet in force* |
| 67 | | 20 Dec 1982 (SI 1982/1804) |
| 68 | | 1 Nov 1982 (SI 1982/1561) |
| 69 | | *Never in force* (repealed) |
| 70 | | 1 Nov 1982 (SI 1982/1561) |
| 71 | | 20 Dec 1982 (SI 1982/1804) |
| 72 | (a) | *Not yet in force* |
| | (b) | 1 Nov 1982 (SI 1982/1561) |
| 73 | | 30 Jun 1983 (S) (SI 1983/650) |
| | | 1 Oct 1986 (E) (W) (SI 1986/1326) |
| 74 | | See Schs 5, 6 below |
| 75, 76 | | 30 Jun 1983 (S) (SI 1983/650) |
| | | 1 Oct 1986 (E) (W) (SI 1986/1326) |
| Sch 1 | | 30 Jun 1983 (S) (SI 1983/650) |
| | | 1 Oct 1986 (E) (W) (SI 1986/1326) |
| Sch 2 | | 30 Jun 1983 (SI 1983/650) |
| Sch 3 | | 1 Oct 1986 (SI 1986/1326) |
| Sch 4 | | 1 Jun 1984 (SI 1984/175) |
| Sch 5 | paras 1–5 | *Never in force* (repealed) |

**See Halsbury's Statutes Citator for amendments to these Acts**

**Transport Act 1982 (c 49)**—*contd*

|  |  |
|---|---|
| para 6 | 1 Jun 1984 (SI 1984/175) |
| paras 7–9 | *Never in force* (repealed) |
| para 10(a) | *Never in force* (repealed) |
| para 10(b) | 1 Apr 1983 (SI 1983/276) |
| paras 11, 12 | *Never in force* (repealed) |
| para 13 | 6 May 1983 (SI 1983/577) |
| paras 14–16 | *Never in force* (repealed) |
| para 17(1) | *Never in force* (repealed) |
| para 17(2) | *Not yet in force* |
| para 18(a) | *Never in force* (repealed) |
| para 18(b)–(f) | 28 Oct 1982 (s 76(3)) |
| para 19 | *Never in force* (repealed) |
| para 20 | *Not yet in force* |
| para 21 | *Never in force* (repealed) |
| paras 22–24 | *Not yet in force* |
| paras 25, 26 | 1 Nov 1982 (SI 1982/1561) |
| Sch 6 | 1 Nov 1982 (repeal of Road Traffic Regulation Act 1967, s 72(2), (4)) (SI 1982/1561) |
|  | 1 Jun 1984 (repeals in Transport Act 1968) (SI 1984/175) |
|  | *Not yet in force*, repeals or of in— |

Road Traffic Regulation Act 1967, ss 80, 81(4), 87, 107(2) (repealed);
Transport Act 1968, Sch 3, paras 3, 5 (repealed);
Road Traffic Act 1972, ss 45(4), (5), (6)(c) (i), (g), (8), (9), 50(1) (c), 188(4)(b), Sch 7 (repealed);
Heavy Commercial Vehicles (Controls and Regulations) Act 1973, s 1(7) (repealed);
Road Traffic Act 1974, ss 1, 3(1)(a), (2), (3)(a), (4), (5), 4(1), (4), (5), 5(1), (5), (8), Sch 2, Pt II, para 16, Sch 5, Pts II, III, Sch 6, para 8 (repealed);
Criminal Law Act 1977, Sch 12, para 3 (repealed);
Justices of the Peace Act 1979, Sch 2, para 15 (repealed);
Criminal Justice (Scotland) Act 1980, s 31 (repealed);
Transport Act 1980, s 66(2) (repealed);
Public Passenger Vehicles Act 1981, s 9(8), Sch 7, paras 13, 14 (repealed)

**Transport (Finance) Act 1982 (c 6)**

*RA:* 25 Feb 1982

Whole Act in force 25 Feb 1982 (RA)

**Travel Concessions (London) Act 1982 (c 12)**

*RA:* 29 Mar 1982

Whole Act in force 29 Mar 1982 (RA)

# 1983 Acts

### Agricultural Holdings (Amendment) (Scotland) Act 1983 (c 46)

*RA:* 13 May 1983

*Commencement provisions:* s 7(2)

Whole Act in force 13 Jul 1983 (s 7(2))

---

### Agricultural Marketing Act 1983 (c 3)

*RA:* 1 Mar 1983

*Commencement provisions:* s 9(3); Agricultural Marketing Act 1983 (Commencement) Order 1983, SI 1983/366

Whole Act in force 23 Mar 1983 (SI 1983/366)

---

### Appropriation Act 1983 (c 27)

*RA:* 13 May 1983

Whole Act in force 13 May 1983 (RA)

---

### Appropriation (No 2) Act 1983 (c 48)

*RA:* 26 Jul 1983

Whole Act in force 26 Jul 1983 (RA)

---

### British Fishing Boats Act 1983 (c 8)

*RA:* 28 Mar 1983

Whole Act in force 28 Mar 1983 (RA)

---

### British Nationality (Falkland Islands) Act 1983 (c 6)

*RA:* 28 Mar 1983

*Commencement provisions:* s 5(2)

Whole Act in force 1 Jan 1983 (retrospective: s 5(2))

---

### British Shipbuilders Act 1983 (c 15)

*RA:* 9 May 1983

*Commencement provisions:* s 3(4)

Whole Act in force 9 Jul 1983 (s 3(4))

---

### British Shipbuilders (Borrowing Powers) Act 1983 (c 58)

*RA:* 21 Dec 1983

Whole Act in force 21 Dec 1983 (RA)

---

### Car Tax Act 1983 (c 53)

*RA:* 26 Jul 1983

*Commencement provisions:* s 11(2)

Whole Act in force 26 Oct 1983 (s 11(2))

---

### Church of England (Miscellaneous Provisions) Measure 1983 (No 2)

*RA:* 9 May 1983

*Commencement provisions:* s 13(3)

Whole Act in force 9 Jun 1983 (s 13(3))

---

### Civil Aviation (Eurocontrol) Act 1983 (c 11)

*RA:* 11 Apr 1983

*Commencement provisions:* s 4(2); Civil Aviation (Eurocontrol) Act 1983 (Commencement No 1) Order 1983, SI 1983/1886; Civil Aviation (Eurocontrol) Act 1983 (Commencement No 2) Order 1985, SI 1985/1915

| | | |
|---|---|---|
| 1, 2 | | 1 Jan 1986 (SI 1985/1915) |
| 3 | (1) | 1 Jan 1986 (SI 1985/1915) |
| | (2) | 1 Jan 1984 (s 4(2); SI 1983/1886) |
| 4 | | 1 Jan 1984 (s 4(2); SI 1983/1886) |

---

### Coal Industry Act 1983 (c 60)

*RA:* 21 Dec 1983

Whole Act in force 21 Dec 1983 (RA)

---

### Companies (Beneficial Interests) Act 1983 (c 50)

*RA:* 26 Jul 1983

Whole Act in force 26 Jul 1983 (RA)

---

### Consolidated Fund Act 1983 (c 1)

*RA:* 8 Feb 1983

Whole Act in force 8 Feb 1983 (RA)

---

### Consolidated Fund (No 2) Act 1983 (c 5)

*RA:* 28 Mar 1983

Whole Act in force 28 Mar 1983 (RA)

---

### Consolidated Fund (No 3) Act 1983 (c 57)

*RA:* 21 Dec 1983

Whole Act in force 21 Dec 1983 (RA)

---

### Conwy Tunnel (Supplementary Powers) Act 1983 (c 7)

*RA:* 28 Mar 1983

Whole Act in force 28 Mar 1983 (RA)

---

### Copyright (Amendment) Act 1983 (c 42)

*RA:* 13 May 1983

*Commencement provisions:* s 3(2)

Whole Act in force 13 Jul 1983 (s 3(2))

---

### Coroners' Juries Act 1983 (c 31)

*RA:* 13 May 1983

*Commencement provisions:* s 3(2); Coroners' Juries Act 1983 (Commencement) Order 1983, SI 1983/1454

Whole Act in force 1 Jan 1984 (SI 1983/1454)

---

### County Courts (Penalties for Contempt) Act 1983 (c 45)

*RA:* 13 May 1983

Whole Act in force 13 May 1983 (RA)

---

### Currency Act 1983 (c 9)

*RA:* 28 Mar 1983

Whole Act in force 28 Mar 1983 (RA)

---

### Dentists Act 1983 (c 38)

*RA:* 13 May 1983

*Commencement provisions:* s 34(1)–(3)

| | | |
|---|---|---|
| 1 | (1) | 1 Jan 1984 (s 34(1)(a)) |

**Dentists Act 1983 (c 38)**—*contd*

|       |            |                               |
|-------|------------|-------------------------------|
|       | (2)–(6)    | 1 Oct 1984 (s 34(2)(a))       |
|       | (7)        | 1 Jan 1984 (s 34(1)(a))       |
| 2     |            | 1 Jan 1984 (s 34(1)(a))       |
| 3–10  |            | 1 Jan 1984 (s 34(1)(b))       |
| 11    |            | 1 Oct 1984 (s 34(2)(a))       |
| 12, 13|            | 1 Jan 1984 (s 34(1)(b))       |
| 14–16 |            | 1 Oct 1984 (s 34(2)(a))       |
| 17–21 |            | *Never in force* (repealed)   |
| 22    | (1)        | *Never in force* (repealed)   |
|       | (2)        | See Sch 1 below               |
| 23–25 |            | 1 Jan 1984 (s 34(1)(c))       |
| 26    | (1), (2)   | 1 Jan 1984 (s 34(1)(c))       |
|       | (3)        | 1 Oct 1984 (s 34(2)(a))       |
| 27    |            | 1 Jan 1984 (s 34(1)(c))       |
| 28    |            | 1 Oct 1984 (s 34(2)(a))       |
| 29–32 |            | 1 Jan 1984 (s 34(1)(d))       |
| 33    | (1)        | See Sch 2 below               |
|       | (2)        | See Sch 3 below               |
|       | (3)        | 1 Jan 1984 (s 34(1)(g))       |
| 34, 35|            | 1 Jan 1984 (s 34(1)(g))       |
| Sch 1 |            | *Never in force* (repealed)   |
| Sch 2 | para 1     | 1 Jan 1984 (s 34(1)(e))       |
|       | para 2     | 1 Oct 1984 (s 34(2)(b))       |
|       | paras 3–10 | 1 Jan 1984 (s 34(1)(e))       |
|       | para 11(a) | 1 Oct 1984 (s 34(2)(b))       |
|       | para 11(b) | 1 Jan 1984 (s 34(1)(e))       |
|       | para 12(a) | 1 Oct 1984 (s 34(2)(b))       |
|       | para 12(b) | 1 Jan 1984 (s 34(1)(e))       |
|       | paras 13, 14 | 1 Oct 1984 (s 34(2)(b))     |
|       | paras 15, 16 | 1 Jan 1984 (s 34(1)(e))     |
|       | para 17    | 1 Oct 1984 (s 34(2)(b))       |
|       | paras 18–22 | 1 Jan 1984 (s 34(1)(e))      |
|       | para 23    | *Never in force* (repealed)   |
|       | para 24    | 1 Jan 1984 (s 34(1)(e))       |
|       | para 25    | 1 Oct 1984 (s 34(2)(b))       |
| Sch 3 | Pt I       | 1 Jan 1984 (s 34(1)(f))       |
|       | Pt II      | 1 Oct 1984 (s 34(2)(c))       |
| Sch 4 |            | 1 Jan 1984 (s 34(1)(g))       |

**Diseases of Fish Act 1983 (c 30)**

*RA:* 13 May 1983

*Commencement provisions:* s 11(2); Diseases of Fish Act 1983 (Commencement) Order 1984, SI 1984/302

|          |                          |
|----------|--------------------------|
| 1–10     | 1 Apr 1984 (SI 1984/302) |
| 11       | 13 May 1983 (RA)         |
| Schedule | 1 Apr 1984 (SI 1984/302) |

**Divorce Jurisdiction, Court Fees and Legal Aid (Scotland) Act 1983 (c 12)**

*RA:* 11 Apr 1983

*Commencement provisions:* s 7(2), (3); Divorce Jurisdiction, Court Fees and Legal Aid (Scotland) Act 1983 (Commencement) Order 1984, SI 1984/253

|   |                          |
|---|--------------------------|
| 1 | 1 May 1984 (SI 1984/253) |
| 2 | 11 Jun 1983 (s 7(2))     |

**Divorce Jurisdiction, Court Fees and Legal Aid (Scotland) Act 1983 (c 12)**—*contd*

| | | |
|---|---|---|
| 3 | | 1 Apr 1984 (in so far as necessary to enable the Legal Aid (Scotland) Act 1967, s 14A to take effect only in relation to legal advice and assistance by virtue of the extension of the said s 14A by s 6(1) of the Legal Advice and Assistance Act 1972) (SI 1984/253) |
| | | 1 May 1984 (otherwise) (SI 1984/253) |
| 4, 5 | | 1 Apr 1984 (SI 1984/253) |
| 6 | (1) | See Sch 1 below |
| | (2) | See Sch 2 below |
| 7 | | 11 Jun 1983 (s 7(2)) |
| Sch 1 | para 1 | 1 May 1984 (SI 1984/253) |
| | para 2 | 11 Jun 1983 (s 7(2)) |
| | paras 3–5 | 1 May 1984 (SI 1984/253) |
| | paras 6–8 | 1 Apr 1984 (certain purposes) (SI 1984/253) |
| | | 1 May 1984 (otherwise) (SI 1984/253) |
| | paras 9, 10 | 1 Apr 1984 (SI 1984/253) |
| | paras 11–13 | 1 May 1984 (SI 1984/253) |
| | paras 14–17 | 1 Apr 1984 (SI 1984/253) |
| | paras 18–24 | 1 May 1984 (SI 1984/253) |
| Sch 2 | | 1 Apr 1984 (SI 1984/253), repeals of or in— |
| | | Court of Session Act 1821, s 31; |
| | | Sheriff Courts (Scotland) Act 1907, s 40; |
| | | Church of Scotland (Property and Endowments) Act 1925, s 1(3); |
| | | Juries Act 1949, s 26(1); |
| | | Legal Aid (Scotland) Act 1967, s 16(1)(b)(i), (2), (4); |
| | | Legal Advice and Assistance Act 1972, ss 3(3), 5(6) |
| | | 1 May 1984 (otherwise) (SI 1984/253) |

---

**Education (Fees and Awards) Act 1983 (c 40)**

*RA:* 13 May 1983

Whole Act in force 13 May 1983 (RA)

---

**Energy Act 1983 (c 25)**

*RA:* 9 May 1983

*Commencement provisions:* s 37(1); Energy Act 1983 (Commencement No 1) Order 1983, SI 1983/790; Energy Act 1983 (Commencement No 2) Order 1988, SI 1988/1587

| | | |
|---|---|---|
| 1–20 | | 1 Jun 1983 (SI 1983/790) |
| 21, 22 | | 1 Sep 1983 (SI 1983/790) |
| 23–26 | | 1 Jun 1983 (SI 1983/790) |
| 27–34 | | 1 Sep 1983 (SI 1983/790) |
| 35 | (a) | 1 Jun 1983 (SI 1983/790) |
| | (b) | 1 Sep 1983 (SI 1983/790) |
| 36 | | See Sch 4 below |
| 37 | (1), (2) | 1 Jun 1983 (SI 1983/790) |
| | (3) | 1 Sep 1983 (SI 1983/790) |
| 38 | | 1 Jun 1983 (SI 1983/790) |
| Sch 1 | | 1 Jun 1983 (SI 1983/790) |
| Sch 2 | | 1 Sep 1983 (SI 1983/790) |
| Sch 3 | | 1 Jun 1983 (SI 1983/790) |
| Sch 4 | Pt I | 1 Jun 1983 (SI 1983/790), repeals of or in— |
| | | Electric Lighting (Clauses) Act 1899, ss 2, 52, 54(2), Schedule; |
| | | Electric Lighting Act 1909, s 23; |
| | | Electricity (Supply) Act 1919, ss 11, 36; |

**Energy Act 1983 (c 25)**—*contd*

    Electricity (Supply) Act 1922, s 23;

    Electricity Supply (Meters) Act 1936, s 1(1), (3);

    Acquisition of Land (Authorisation Procedure) Act 1946, Sch 4;

    Electricity Act 1947 (except for s 60, in Sch 4, Pt I, the entry relating to Electricity (Supply) Act 1946, s 24, and in Sch 4, Pt III, the entry relating to Electric Lighting (Clauses) Act 1899, s 60, Schedule);

    South of Scotland Electricity Order Confirmation Act 1956, s 40;

    Electricity Act 1957 (except in Sch 4, Pt I, the entry relating to Electricity Act 1947, s 60);

    North of Scotland Electricity Order Confirmation Act 1958, s 27;

    Post Office Act 1969, Sch 4, para 11;

    Energy Act 1976, s 14(6)(b);

    Electricity (Scotland) Act 1979 (except reference to Electricity Act 1947, s 60 in Sch 10, para 13);

    Acquisition of Land Act 1981, Sch 4, para 1

    1 Oct 1988 (SI 1988/1587), repeals of or in—

    Electric Lighting (Clauses) Act 1899, ss 10, 38, 60, 69(1), (2), Schedule;

    Electricity Act 1947, s 60, Sch 4, Pt III, the entry relating to Electric Lighting (Clauses) Act 1899, s 60, Schedule;

    Electricity Act 1957, Sch 4, Pt I, the entry relating to Electricity Act 1947, s 60;

    Post Office Act 1969, Sch 4, para 8(c), (g);

    Electricity (Scotland) Act 1979, Sch 10, para 13, the reference to Electricity Act 1947, s 60

    *Never in force* (spent) repeals of or in—

    Electric Lighting Act 1888;

    Electricity (Supply) Act 1926, s 24;

    Electricity Act 1947, Sch 4, Pt I, the entry relating to Electricity (Supply) Act 1946, s 24;

    Electricity Reorganisation (Scotland) Act 1954, s 1(3), Sch 1, Pt III;

    Post Office Act 1969, Sch 4, para 8(b)

Pt II    1 Sep 1983 (SI 1983/790)

---

**Finance Act 1983 (c 28)**

*Budget Day*: 15 Mar 1983

*RA*: 13 May 1983

The commencement details of Finance Acts are not set out, as the dates from which their provisions take effect are usually stated clearly and unambiguously in the text of the Act, and charging provisions will normally state for which year or years of assessment they are to have effect.

---

**Finance (No 2) Act 1983 (c 49)**

*RA*: 26 Jul 1983

The commencement details of Finance Acts are not set out, as the dates from which their provisions take effect are usually stated clearly and unambiguously in the text of the Act, and charging provisions will normally state for which year or years of assessment they are to have effect.

---

## Health and Social Services and Social Security Adjudications Act 1983 (c 41)

*RA:* 13 May 1983

*Commencement provisions:* s 32(1), (2); Health and Social Services and Social Security Adjudications Act 1983 (Commencement No 1) Order 1983, SI 1983/974, as amended by SI 1983/1862; Health and Social Services and Social Security Adjudications Act 1983 (Commencement No 2) Order 1983, SI 1983/1862; Health and Social Services and Social Security Adjudications Act 1983 (Commencement No 3) Order 1984, SI 1984/216; Health and Social Services and Social Security Adjudications Act 1983 (Commencement No 4) Order 1984, SI 1984/957; Health and Social Services and Social Security Adjudications Act 1984 (Commencement No 5) Order 1984, SI 1984/1347; Health and Social Services and Social Security Adjudications Act 1983 (Scotland) (Commencement No 1) Order 1985, SI 1985/704; Health and Social Services and Social Security Adjudications Act 1983 (Commencement No 6) Order 1992, SI 1992/2974

| | | |
|---|---|---|
| 1 | | 15 Aug 1983 (so far as relates to (i) National Health Service Act 1977, s 28A(2)(a)–(d), but only for the purpose of giving effect to s 28B(1)(a) of that Act, and (ii) s 28B of the 1977 Act) (SI 1983/974) |
| | | 1 Apr 1984 (so far as relates to new s 28A of the 1977 Act) (SI 1984/216) |
| 2 | | 1 May 1985 (SI 1985/704) |
| 3 | | 15 Aug 1983 (SI 1983/974) |
| 4, 5 | | 1 Jan 1984 (SI 1983/974) |
| 6 | | See Sch 1 below |
| 7 | (1) | 15 Aug 1983 (SI 1983/974) |
| | (2), (3) | 30 Jan 1984 (SI 1983/1862) |
| 8 | | 30 Jan 1984 (SI 1983/1862) |
| 9 | | See Sch 2 below |
| 10 | | 1 Apr 1984 (SI 1983/974) |
| 11 | | 1 Oct 1984 (so far as relates to Sch 4, para 24 (repealed)) (SI 1984/957) |
| | | 1 Jan 1985 (otherwise) (SI 1984/1347) |
| 12 | | See Sch 5 below |
| 13, 14 | | 15 Aug 1983 (SI 1983/974) |
| 15, 16 | | 1 Oct 1984 (SI 1983/974) |
| 17–19 | | 1 Jan 1984 (SI 1983/974) |
| 20 | | 15 Aug 1983 (SI 1983/974) |
| 21–24 | | 12 Apr 1993 (SI 1992/2974) |
| 25 | | See Sch 8 below |
| 26–28 | | 15 Aug 1983 (SI 1983/974) |
| 29 | (1) | See Sch 9, Pt I below |
| | (2) | See Sch 9, Pt II below |
| 30 | (1) | See Sch 10, Pt I below |
| | (2) | See Sch 10, Pt II below |
| | (3) | 1 Jan 1985 (SI 1984/1347) |
| 31 | | 15 Aug 1983 (SI 1983/974) |
| 32–34 | | 13 May 1983 (s 32(1)) |
| Sch 1 | Pt I | 30 Jan 1984 (insertion of new ss 12A–12E, 12F(1), (2), 12G in the Child Care Act 1980) (SI 1983/1862) |
| | | 27 May 1984 (insertion of new s 12F(3), (4) in the 1980 Act) (SI 1983/1862) |
| | Pt II | 30 Jan 1984 (SI 1983/1862) |
| Sch 2 | paras 1, 2 | 15 Aug 1983 (SI 1983/974) |
| | para 3 | 1 Jan 1984 (SI 1983/974) |
| | paras 4–8 | 15 Aug 1983 (SI 1983/974) |
| | para 9 | 1 Jan 1984 (SI 1983/974) |
| | paras 10–16 | 15 Aug 1983 (SI 1983/974) |
| | paras 17, 18 | 1 Jan 1984 (SI 1983/974) |
| | para 19 | 15 Aug 1983 (SI 1983/974) |
| | para 20 | 1 Jan 1984 (SI 1983/974) |
| | paras 21–49 | 15 Aug 1983 (SI 1983/974) |

**Health and Social Services and Social Security Adjudications Act 1983 (c 41)**—*contd*

|  |  |  |
|---|---|---|
|  | para 50 | 1 Jan 1984 (SI 1983/974) |
|  | para 51 | 15 Aug 1983 (SI 1983/974) |
|  | paras 52–54 | 1 Jan 1984 (SI 1983/974) |
|  | paras 55, 56 | 15 Aug 1983 (SI 1983/974) |
|  | paras 57, 58 | 1 Jan 1984 (SI 1983/974) |
|  | paras 59–62 | 15 Aug 1983 (SI 1983/974) |
| Sch 3 |  | 1 Apr 1984 (SI 1983/974) |
| Sch 4 | paras 1–23 | 1 Jan 1985 (SI 1984/1347) |
|  | para 24 | 1 Oct 1984 (SI 1984/957) |
|  | paras 25–56 | 1 Jan 1985 (SI 1984/1347) |
| Sch 5 | para 1 | 15 Aug 1983 (SI 1983/974) |
|  | para 2 | 1 Apr 1984 (SI 1984/1347) |
|  | para 3 | 15 Aug 1983 (SI 1983/974) |
| Schs 6, 7 |  | 15 Aug 1983 (SI 1983/974) |
| Sch 8 | paras 1–19 | 23 Apr 1984 (SI 1984/216) |
|  | para 20 | 1 Jan 1984 (SI 1983/1862) |
|  | paras 21–29 | 23 Apr 1984 (SI 1984/216) |
|  | para 31(1)–(5) | 23 Apr 1984 (SI 1984/216) |
|  | para 31(6) | 5 Jul 1983 (SI 1983/974) |
| Sch 9 | Pt I, paras 1, 2 | 15 Aug 1983 (SI 1983/974) |
|  | Pt I, para 3 | 1 Apr 1984 (SI 1983/974) |
|  | Pt I, para 4 | 1 Jan 1985 (SI 1984/1347) |
|  | Pt I, para 5 | 15 Aug 1983 (SI 1983/974) |
|  | Pt I, para 6 | 1 Jan 1985 (SI 1984/1347) |
|  | Pt I, paras 7, 8 | 15 Aug 1983 (SI 1983/974) |
|  | Pt I, para 9 | 1 Jan 1985 (SI 1984/1347) |
|  | Pt I, para 10 | 23 Apr 1984 (SI 1984/216) |
|  | Pt I, paras 11–14 | 1 Jan 1985 (SI 1984/1347) |
|  | Pt I, para 15 | 23 Apr 1984 (SI 1984/216) |
|  | Pt I, paras 16, 17 | 1 Jan 1984 (SI 1983/974) |
|  | Pt I, para 18 | 23 Apr 1984 (SI 1984/216) |
|  | Pt I, para 19 | 1 Jan 1985 (SI 1984/1347) |
|  | Pt I, para 20 | 23 Apr 1984 (SI 1984/216) |
|  | Pt I, para 21 | 15 Aug 1983 (SI 1983/974) |
|  | Pt I, para 22 | 1 Jan 1984 (SI 1983/974) |
|  | Pt I, para 23 | 1 Apr 1984 (SI 1983/974) |
|  | Pt I, paras 24, 25 | 15 Aug 1983 (SI 1983/974) |
|  | Pt I, paras 26, 27 | 1 Jan 1985 (SI 1984/1347) |
|  | Pt I, para 28 | 15 Aug 1983 (SI 1983/974) |
|  | Pt II | 1 Jan 1984 (SI 1983/974) |
| Sch 10 | Pt I | 15 Aug 1983 (SI 1983/974, as partly revoked by SI 1983/1862), repeals of or in— |

Public Health Act 1936;

Food and Drugs Act 1955;

Health Services and Public Health Act 1968, ss 48(2), 64 (so far as relates to Scotland);

Social Work (Scotland) Act 1968, s 31(2);

Radiological Protection Act 1970;

Powers of Criminal Courts Act 1973;

Children Act 1975, s 109(3);

Adoption Act 1976;

Criminal Law Act 1977;

National Health Service Act 1977, ss 8(1A), 9, 100(2), 128(1), Sch 5;

Adoption (Scotland) Act 1978;

Employment Protection (Consolidation) Act 1978;

Child Care Act 1980, ss 71, 79(5)(h);

## Health and Social Services and Social Security Adjudications Act 1983 (c 41)—*contd*

Health Services Act 1980, ss 1, 4(1) (but only for the purpose of giving effect to new s 28B(1)(a) of National Health Service Act 1977), Sch 1;

Overseas Development and Co-operation Act 1980

1 Jan 1984 (SI 1983/974, as partly revoked by SI 1983/1862), repeals of or in—

National Assistance Act 1948;

Local Government Act 1966;

Health Services and Public Health Act 1968, s 45(2);

Social Work (Scotland) Act 1968, ss 14(2), 78(1)(b);

Children and Young Persons Act 1969;

Local Government Act 1972;

National Health Service Act 1977, Sch 8;

Domestic Proceedings and Magistrates' Courts Act 1978;

Child Care Act 1980, ss 10(2), 36(1), 39(2), 43(3), 44(5), 45(1)(ii), 87(1), Schs 1, 5;

Residential Homes Act 1980 (but only for the purposes of the repeal of s 8 of that Act);

Criminal Justice Act 1982

30 Jan 1984 (SI 1983/1862), repeals of or in—

Social Work (Scotland) Act 1968, s 59A(1), (3);

Children Act 1975, s 72

1 Apr 1984 (SI 1983/974, as partly revoked by SI 1983/1862), repeals of or in—

Health Visiting and Social Work (Training) Act 1962;

Local Authority Social Services Act 1970;

National Health Service Act 1977, Sch 15;

Nurses, Midwives and Health Visitors Act 1979

1 Apr 1984 (repeal of Health Services Act 1980, s 4(1) for remaining purposes) (SI 1984/216)

23 Apr 1984 (SI 1984/216), repeals of or in—

Family Income Supplements Act 1970;

Tribunals and Inquiries Act 1971;

House of Commons Disqualification Act 1975;

Social Security Act 1975;

Child Benefit Act 1975;

Supplementary Benefits Act 1976;

Social Security (Miscellaneous Provisions) Act 1977;

Social Security and Housing Benefits Act 1982

1 Jan 1985 (SI 1984/1347, as amended by SI 1984/1767), repeals of or in—

Nursing Homes Act 1975;

Child Care Act 1980, s 58, Sch 3;

Residential Homes Act 1980 (except s 8, repealed on 1 Jan 1984);

Children's Homes Act 1982

1 May 1985 (repeal of Health Services Act 1980, s 4(2)) (SI 1985/704)

Pt II      15 Aug 1983 (SI 1983/974)

## Importation of Milk Act 1983 (c 37)

*RA:* 13 May 1983

Whole Act in force 13 May 1983 (RA)

## International Monetary Arrangements Act 1983 (c 51)

*RA:* 26 Jul 1983

*Commencement provisions:* s 3(2); International Monetary Arrangements Act 1983 (Commencement) Order 1983, SI 1983/1643

| | |
|---|---|
| 1 | 14 Nov 1983 (SI 1983/1643) |
| 2, 3 | 26 Jul 1983 (RA) |

## International Transport Conventions Act 1983 (c 14)

*RA:* 11 Apr 1983

*Commencement provisions:* s 11(3); International Transport Convention Act 1983 (Certification of Commencement of Convention) Order 1985, SI 1985/612

| | |
|---|---|
| 1 | 1 May 1985 (SI 1985/612) |
| 2–10 | 11 Apr 1983 (RA) |
| 11 | 11 Apr 1983 (sub-s (2) effective from 1 May 1985, the day on which the Convention comes into force as regards the United Kingdom) (s 11(3); SI 1985/612) |
| Schs 1, 2 | 11 Apr 1983 (RA) |
| Sch 3 | 1 May 1985 (SI 1985/612) |

## Level Crossings Act 1983 (c 16)

*RA:* 9 May 1983

*Commencement provisions:* s 2(2)

Whole Act in force 9 Aug 1983 (s 2(2))

## Licensing (Occasional Permissions) Act 1983 (c 24)

*RA:* 9 May 1983

*Commencement provisions:* s 5(2)

Whole Act in force 9 Aug 1983 (s 5(2))

## Litter Act 1983 (c 35)

*RA:* 13 May 1983

*Commencement provisions:* s 13(2), (3)

| | | |
|---|---|---|
| 1–3 | | 13 Aug 1983 (s 13(3)) |
| 4 | | *Not yet in force* (sub-s (4) repealed) |
| 5–11 | | 13 Aug 1983 (s 13(3)) |
| 12 | (1), (2) | 13 Aug 1983 (s 13(3)) |
| | (3) | See Sch 2 below |
| 13 | | 13 Aug 1983 (s 13(3)) |
| Sch 1 | | 13 Aug 1983 (s 13(3)) |
| Sch 2 | | 13 Aug 1983 (except repeal of Control of Pollution Act 1974, s 24(1)–(3)) (s 13(2)) |
| | | *Not yet in force* (exception noted above) |

## Local Authorities (Expenditure Powers) Act 1983 (c 52)

*RA:* 26 Jul 1983

Whole Act in force 26 Jul 1983 (RA)

---

## Marriage Act 1983 (c 32)

*RA:* 13 May 1983

*Commencement provisions:* s 12(5); Marriage Act 1983 (Commencement) Order 1984, SI 1984/413

Whole Act in force 1 May 1984 (SI 1984/413)

---

## Matrimonial Homes Act 1983 (c 19)

*RA:* 9 May 1983

*Commencement provisions:* s 13(2)

Whole Act in force 9 Aug 1983 (s 13(2))

---

## Medical Act 1983 (c 54)

*RA:* 26 Jul 1983

*Commencement provisions:* s 57(2)

Whole Act in force 26 Oct 1983 (s 57(2))

---

## Mental Health Act 1983 (c 20)

*RA:* 9 May 1983

*Commencement provisions:* s 149(2), (3); Mental Health Act 1983 Commencement Order 1984, SI 1984/1357

| | | |
|---|---|---|
| 1–34 | | 30 Sep 1983 (s 149(2)) |
| 35, 36 | | 1 Oct 1984 (SI 1984/1357) |
| 37 | | 30 Sep 1983 (s 149(2)) |
| 38 | | 1 Oct 1984 (SI 1984/1357) |
| 39 | | 30 Sep 1983 (s 149(2)) |
| 40 | (1), (2) | 30 Sep 1983 (s 149(2)) |
| | (3) | 1 Oct 1984 (SI 1984/1357) |
| | (4), (5) | 30 Sep 1983 (s 149(2)) |
| 41–149 | | 30 Sep 1983 (s 149(2)) |
| Schs 1–6 | | 30 Sep 1983 (s 149(2)) |

---

## Mental Health (Amendment) (Scotland) Act 1983 (c 39)

*RA:* 13 May 1983

*Commencement provisions:* s 41(2); Mental Health (Amendment) (Scotland) Act 1983 (Commencement No 1) Order 1983, SI 1983/1199; Mental Health (Amendment) (Scotland) Act 1983 (Commencement No 2) Order 1983, SI 1983/1920

| | | |
|---|---|---|
| 1 | (1)–(3) | 31 Dec 1983 (SI 1983/1920) |
| | (4) | 30 Sep 1984 (SI 1983/1920) |
| 2–6 | | 30 Sep 1984 (SI 1983/1920) |
| 7 | (1), (2) | 16 Aug 1983 (SI 1983/1199) |
| | (3)–(5) | 30 Sep 1984 (SI 1983/1920) |

**Mental Health (Amendment) (Scotland) Act 1983 (c 39)**—*contd*

| | | |
|---|---|---|
| 8–25 | | 30 Sep 1984 (SI 1983/1920) |
| 26, 27 | | 31 Mar 1984 (SI 1983/1920) |
| 28–37 | | 30 Sep 1984 (SI 1983/1920) |
| 38 | | 16 Aug 1983 (SI 1983/1199) |
| 39 | (1) | See Sch 1 below |
| | (2) | See Sch 2 below |
| | (3) | See Sch 3 below |
| 40 | | 16 Aug 1983 (SI 1983/1199) |
| 41 | | 13 May 1983 (RA) |
| Sch 1 | para 1 | 16 Aug 1983 (SI 1983/1199) |
| | paras 2–12 | 30 Sep 1984 (SI 1983/1920) |
| Sch 2 | paras 1–5 | 30 Sep 1984 (SI 1983/1920) |
| | para 6(a) | 16 Aug 1983 (SI 1983/1199) |
| | para 6(b) | 30 Sep 1984 (SI 1983/1920) |
| | paras 7–37 | 30 Sep 1984 (SI 1983/1920) |
| | para 38 | 31 Mar 1984 (SI 1983/1920) |
| Sch 3 | | 16 Aug 1983 (repeals in Mental Health (Scotland) Act 1960, s 7) (SI 1983/1199) |
| | | 31 Dec 1983 (repeal in Mental Health (Scotland) Act 1960, s 2) (SI 1983/1920) |
| | | 31 Mar 1984 (repeal in National Health Service (Scotland) Act 1978) (SI 1983/1920) |
| | | 30 Sep 1984 (otherwise) (SI 1983/1920) |

---

**Merchant Shipping Act 1983 (c 13)**

*RA:* 11 Apr 1983

*Commencement provisions:* s 11(3); Merchant Shipping Act 1983 (Commencement No 1) Order 1983, SI 1983/1435; Merchant Shipping Act 1983 (Commencement Order No 2) 1983, SI 1983/1601

| | |
|---|---|
| 1–4 | *Never in force* (repealed) |
| 5–7 | 1 Nov 1983 (SI 1983/1435) |
| 8 | 17 Nov 1983 (SI 1983/1601) |
| 9 | 1 Nov 1983 (so far as it relates to any ship registered under s 5) (SI 1983/1435) |
| | *Never in force* (otherwise) (repealed) |
| 10, 11 | 1 Nov 1983 (SI 1983/1435) |
| Schedule | 1 Nov 1983 (SI 1983/1435) |

---

**Miscellaneous Financial Provisions Act 1983 (c 29)**

*RA:* 13 May 1983

*Commencement provisions:* s 9(1), (2); Miscellaneous Financial Provisions Act 1983 (Commencement of Provisions) Order 1983, SI 1983/1338

| | |
|---|---|
| 1 | 1 Apr 1984 (SI 1983/1338) |
| 2–7 | 13 Jul 1983 (s 9(2)) |
| 8 | 1 Apr 1984 (SI 1983/1338) |
| 9–11 | 13 Jul 1983 (s 9(2)) |
| Sch 1 | 1 Apr 1984 (SI 1983/1338) |
| Sch 2 | 13 Jul 1983 (s 9(2)) |
| Sch 3 | 1 Apr 1984 (SI 1983/1338) |

---

**Mobile Homes Act 1983 (c 34)**

*RA:* 13 May 1983

*Commencement provisions:* s 6(3)

**Mobile Homes Act 1983 (c 34)**—*contd*
Whole Act in force 20 May 1983 (s 6(3))

---

**National Audit Act 1983 (c 44)**

*RA:* 13 May 1983

*Commencement provisions:* s 15(2), (3)

| | |
|---|---|
| 1–15 | 1 Jan 1984 (s 15(2)) |
| Schs 1–4 | 1 Jan 1984 (s 15(2)) |
| Sch 5 | 1 Jan 1984 (s 15(2)), repeals of or in— |
| | Exchequer and Audit Departments Act 1866, s 24; |
| | Exchequer and Audit Departments Act 1921, in s 1(2), the proviso, ss 3(3), (4), 8(1) |
| | 1 Oct 1984 (repeal of Exchequer and Audit Departments Act 1921, s 8(2)) (s 15(3)) |

---

**National Heritage Act 1983 (c 47)**

*RA:* 13 May 1983

*Commencement provisions:* s 41(1)–(3); National Heritage Act 1983 (Commencement No 1) Order 1983, SI 1983/1062; National Heritage Act 1983 (Commencement No 2) Order 1983, SI 1983/1183; National Heritage Act 1983 (Commencement No 3) Order 1983, SI 1983/1437; National Heritage Act 1983 (Commencement No 4) Order 1984, SI 1984/208; National Heritage Act 1983 (Commencement No 5) Order 1984, SI 1984/217; National Heritage Act 1983 (Commencement No 6) Order 1984, SI 1984/225

| | | |
|---|---|---|
| 1 | (1) | 30 Sep 1983 (SI 1983/1062) |
| | (2) | See Sch 1, Pt I below |
| 2, 3 | | 1 Apr 1984 (SI 1984/225) |
| 4 | (1)–(4) | 1 Apr 1984 (SI 1984/225) |
| | (5) | 13 Jul 1983 (s 41(3)) |
| | (6) | 1 Apr 1984 (SI 1984/225) |
| | (7) | 13 Jul 1983 (s 41(3)) |
| | (8) | 1 Apr 1984 (SI 1984/225) |
| 5–8 | | 1 Apr 1984 (SI 1984/225) |
| 9 | (1) | 30 Sep 1983 (SI 1983/1062) |
| | (2) | See Sch 1, Pt II below |
| 10, 11 | | 1 Apr 1984 (SI 1984/225) |
| 12 | (1)–(4) | 1 Apr 1984 (SI 1984/225) |
| | (5), (6) | 13 Jul 1983 (s 41(3)) |
| | (7) | 1 Apr 1984 (SI 1984/225) |
| 13–16 | | 1 Apr 1984 (SI 1984/225) |
| 17 | | 1 Oct 1983 (SI 1983/1437) |
| 18 | | 1 Apr 1984 (SI 1984/208) |
| 19 | (1)–(3) | 1 Apr 1984 (SI 1984/208) |
| | (4), (5) | 13 Jul 1983 (s 41(3)) |
| | (6) | 1 Apr 1984 (SI 1984/208) |
| 20, 21 | | 1 Apr 1984 (SI 1984/208) |
| 22 | | 1 Oct 1983 (SI 1983/1437) |
| 23 | | 8 Aug 1983 (SI 1983/1183) |
| 24–28 | | 1 Apr 1984 (SI 1984/217) |
| 29 | | 8 Aug 1983 (SI 1983/1183) |
| 30, 31 | | 13 Jul 1983 (s 41(3)) |
| 32 | | 1 Oct 1983 (SI 1983/1437) |
| 33 | (1)–(4) | 1 Apr 1984 (SI 1984/208) |
| | (5) | 1 Oct 1983 (SI 1983/1437) |
| | (6)–(8) | 1 Apr 1984 (SI 1984/208) |
| 34 | | 1 Apr 1984 (SI 1984/208) |

**National Heritage Act 1983 (c 47)**—*contd*

| | | |
|---|---|---|
| 35 | | 1 Oct 1983 (SI 1983/1437) |
| 36, 37 | | 1 Apr 1984 (SI 1984/208) |
| 38 | | 1 Oct 1983 (SI 1983/1437) |
| 39 | | 1 Apr 1984 (SI 1984/208) |
| 40 | (1) | See Sch 5 below |
| | (2) | See Sch 6 below |
| 41–43 | | 13 Jul 1983 (s 41(3)) |
| Sch 1 | paras 1–8 | 30 Sep 1983 (SI 1983/1062) |
| | para 9 | 1 Apr 1984 (SI 1984/225) |
| | paras 10–18 | 30 Sep 1983 (SI 1983/1062) |
| | para 19 | 1 Apr 1984 (SI 1984/225) |
| | para 20 | 30 Sep 1983 (SI 1983/1062) |
| | paras 21–30 | 1 Oct 1983 (SI 1983/1437) |
| | paras 31–40 | 8 Aug 1983 (SI 1983/1183) |
| Sch 2 | | 13 Jul 1983 (s 41(3)) |
| Sch 3 | | 1 Oct 1983 (SI 1983/1437) |
| Sch 4 | paras 1–14 | 1 Apr 1984 (SI 1984/208) |
| | para 15 | 1 Oct 1984 (SI 1984/208) |
| | paras 16–71 | 1 Apr 1984 (SI 1984/208) |
| Sch 5 | para 1 | 3 Aug 1983 (SI 1983/1062) |
| | para 2 | 30 Sep 1983 (SI 1983/1062) |
| | para 3 | 8 Aug 1983 (so far as relates to Royal Botanic Gardens, Kew) (SI 1983/1183) |
| | | 30 Sep 1983 (so far as relates to Science Museum and Victoria and Albert Museum) (SI 1983/1062) |
| | | 1 Oct 1983 (so far as relates to Armouries, the Historic Buildings and Monuments Commission for England and Board of Trustees of the Armouries) (SI 1983/1437) |
| | para 4 | 8 Aug 1983 (so far as relates to Royal Botanic Gardens, Kew) (SI 1983/1183) |
| | | 30 Sep 1983 (so far as relates to Board of Trustees of the Science Museum and Victoria and Albert Museum) (SI 1983/1062) |
| | | 1 Oct 1983 (so far as relates to the Armouries, the Historic Buildings and Monuments Commission for England and Board of Trustees of the Armouries) (SI 1983/1437) |
| | para 5 | 3 Aug 1983 (SI 1983/1062) |
| | para 6 | 1 Apr 1984 (SI 1984/208) |
| | para 7 | 3 Aug 1983 (SI 1983/1062) |
| Sch 6 | | 3 Aug 1983 (repeal in National Gallery and Tate Gallery Act 1954, s 4(2)) (SI 1983/1062) |
| | | 1 Apr 1984 (SI 1984/208), repeals in— Historic Buildings and Ancient Monuments Act 1953; Town and Country Planning (Amendment) Act 1972; Ancient Monuments and Archaeological Areas Act 1979 |
| | | 1 Apr 1984 (SI 1984/225), repeals in— Patents and Designs Act 1907, s 47(1); Public Records Act 1958, Sch 1, para 3 (entries in Pt I of the Table relating to Victoria and Albert Museum and Science Museum) |

**Nuclear Material (Offences) Act 1983 (c 18)**

*RA:* 9 May 1983

*Commencement provisions:* s 8(2); Nuclear Material (Offences) Act 1983 (Commencement) Order 1991, SI 1991/1716

| | | |
|---|---|---|
| 1–6 | | 2 Oct 1991 (SI 1991/1716) |
| 7 | (1) | 2 Oct 1991 (SI 1991/1716) |
| | (2) | 24 Jul 1991 (in relation to any Order in Council) (SI 1991/1716) |

**Nuclear Material (Offences) Act 1983 (c 18)**—*contd*

|  | 2 Oct 1991 (otherwise) (SI 1991/1716) |
|---|---|
| 8 | 2 Oct 1991 (SI 1991/1716) |
| Schedule | 2 Oct 1991 (SI 1991/1716) |

**Oil Taxation Act 1983 (c 56)**

*RA:* 1 Dec 1983

Whole Act in force 1 Dec 1983 (RA) (though largely effective from 1 Jul 1982)

**Pastoral Measure 1983 (No 1)**

*RA:* 9 May 1983

*Commencement provisions:* s 94(4)

Whole Measure in force 1 Nov 1983 (s 94(4))

**Pet Animals Act 1951 (Amendment) Act 1983 (c 26)**

*RA:* 9 May 1983

*Commencement provisions:* s 2(2)

Whole Act in force 9 Nov 1983 (s 2(2))

**Petroleum Royalties (Relief) Act 1983 (c 59)**

*RA:* 21 Dec 1983

*Commencement provisions:* s 2(2)

Whole Act in force 21 Feb 1984 (s 2(2))

**Pig Industry Levy Act 1983 (c 4)**

*RA:* 1 Mar 1983

Whole Act in force 1 Mar 1983 (RA)

**Pilotage Act 1983 (c 21)**

*RA:* 9 May 1983

*Commencement provisions:* ss 30(7), (8), 70(4)

| 1–29 | 9 Aug 1983 (s 70(4)) |
|---|---|
| 30 | *Never in force* (repealed) |
| 31–70 | 9 Aug 1983 (s 70(4)) |
| Schs 1–4 | 9 Aug 1983 (s 70(4)) |

**Plant Varieties Act 1983 (c 17)**

*RA:* 9 May 1983

*Commencement provisions:* s 6(3)

Whole Act in force 9 Jul 1983 (s 6(3))

## Ports (Reduction of Debt) Act 1983 (c 22)

*RA:* 9 May 1983

Whole Act in force 9 May 1983 (RA)

---

## Representation of the People Act 1983 (c 2)

*RA:* 8 Feb 1983

*Commencement provisions:* s 207(2); Representation of the People Act 1983 (Commencement) Order 1983, SI 1983/153

Whole Act in force 15 Mar 1983 (SI 1983/153)

---

## Road Traffic (Driving Licences) Act 1983 (c 43)

*RA:* 13 May 1983

*Commencement provisions:* s 4(2)

Whole Act in force 13 Jul 1983 (s 4(2))

---

## Social Security and Housing Benefits Act 1983 (c 36)

*RA:* 13 May 1983

*Commencement provisions:* s 3(2)

Whole Act in force 16 Mar 1983 (s 3(2))

---

## Solvent Abuse (Scotland) Act 1983 (c 33)

*RA:* 13 May 1983

*Commencement provisions:* s 3(2)

Whole Act in force 13 Jul 1983 (s 3(2))

---

## Transport Act 1983 (c 10)

*RA:* 28 Mar 1983

*Commencement provisions:* s 10(1)(a)–(c)

This Act came into force on Royal Assent, subject to certain provisions of Pt I taking effect; see the relevant provisions as noted below:

| | | |
|---|---|---|
| 1 | | 28 Mar 1983 (s 10(1)) |
| 2 | | Effective in relation to any accounting period of an Executive ending after 31 Mar 1983 (s 10(1)(a)) |
| 3, 4 | | 1 Apr 1983 (s 10(1)(b)) |
| 5 | | Effective in relation to any year beginning on or after 1 Apr 1984 (s 10(1)(c)) |
| 6 | (1)–(6) | 1 Apr 1983 (s 10(1)(b)) |
| | (7) | Effective in relation to any accounting period of an Executive ending after 31 Mar 1983 (s 10(1)(a)) |
| 7, 8 | | 28 Mar 1983 (s 10(1)) |
| 9 | (1) | See Schedule below |
| | (2) | Effective in relation to any accounting period of an Executive ending after 31 Mar 1983 (so far as relates to the Transport Act 1968, ss 13(3), 15(3)) (s 10(1)(a)) |

**Transport Act 1983 (c 10)**—*contd*

|  |  |  |
|---|---|---|
|  | | Effective in relation to any year beginning on or after 1 Apr 1984 (otherwise) (s 10(1)(c)) |
| | (3)–(5) | Effective in relation to any accounting period of an Executive ending after 31 Mar 1983 (s 10(1)(a)) |
| 10 | | 28 Mar 1983 (s 10(1)) |
| 11, 12 | | 28 Mar 1983 (RA) |
| Schedule | | 31 Mar 1983 (repeals in Transport (London) Act 1969, ss 5, 7) (s 10(1)(a)) |
| | | 1 Apr 1983 (repeals in Transport (London) Act 1969, s 11) (s 10(1)(b)) |

---

**Value Added Tax Act 1983 (c 55)**

*RA:* 26 Jul 1983

*Commencement provisions:* s 51(2)

Whole Act in force 26 Oct 1983 (s 51(2))

---

**Water Act 1983 (c 23)**

*RA:* 9 May 1983

*Commencement provisions:* ss 3(1), 9(2), 11(4), (5); Water Act 1983 (Commencement No 1) Order 1983, SI 1983/1173; Water Act 1983 (Water Space Amenity Commission Appointed Day) Order 1983, SI 1983/1174; Water Act 1983 (Commencement No 2) Order 1983, SI 1983/1234; Water Act 1983 (National Water Council Appointed Day) Order 1983, SI 1983/1235; Water Act 1983 (Dissolution of the National Water Council) Order 1983, SI 1983/1927; Water Act 1983 (Representation of Consumers' Interests) (Appointed Date) Order 1984, SI 1984/71

| | | |
|---|---|---|
| 1 | | 1 Oct 1983 (SI 1983/1234) |
| 2–6 | | 9 May 1983 (s 11(4)) |
| 7, 8 | | 10 Aug 1983 (SI 1983/1173) |
| 9, 10 | | 9 May 1983 (s 11(4)) |
| 11 | (1) | 9 May 1983 (s 11(4)) |
| | (2), (3) | See Schs 4, 5 below |
| | (4)–(7) | 9 May 1983 (s 11(4)) |
| Sch 1 | | 1 Oct 1983 (SI 1983/1234) |
| Schs 2, 3 | | 9 May 1983 (s 11(4)) |
| Sch 4 | paras 1–3 | 1 Oct 1983 (SI 1983/1235) |
| | paras 4–7 | 1 Oct 1983 (SI 1983/1234) |
| | paras 8, 9 | 9 May 1983 (s 11(4)) |
| Sch 5 | Pt I | 10 Aug 1983 (SI 1983/1173), repeals of or in—<br>Development of Rural Wales Act 1976, Sch 7, para 11;<br>Water Charges Equalisation Act 1977;<br>Local Government Planning and Land Act 1980, s 158(1), (2);<br>New Towns Act 1981, Sch 12, para 12<br>1 Oct 1983 (repeals of or in Water Act 1973, ss 23, 24(12)(a), 25(5)(a), Sch 3, para 40, sub-para (1)(b) and word "and" immediately preceding it, and sub-para (5)) (SI 1983/1174)<br>1 Oct 1983 (SI 1983/1234), repeals of or in—<br>Public Bodies (Admission to Meetings) Act 1960;<br>Local Government Act 1972;<br>Water Act 1973, ss 6, 17(5);<br>House of Commons Disqualification Act 1975, Sch 1, Pt III;<br>Local Government, Planning and Land Act 1980, s 25(4)<br>1 Oct 1983 (SI 1983/1235), repeals of or in—<br>Public Health Act 1961, s 9(3);<br>Water Act 1973, ss 4, 5(3), 26(2)–(4), 29(2), 30(6), 38(1), Sch 3, Sch 8, para 90; |

**Water Act 1983 (c 23)**—*contd*

|  | House of Commons Disqualification Act 1975, Sch 1, Pt III; |
|  | Land Drainage Act 1976, Sch 5, para 8(1); |
|  | Water (Scotland) Act 1980, Sch 10 |
|  | *Not yet in force* (repeal of Local Government (Scotland) Act 1973, Sch 17, para 64) |
| Pt II | 9 May 1983 (revocation of SI 1982/944) (s 11(4)) |
|  | 1 Oct 1983 (otherwise) (SI 1983/1234) |

# 1984 Acts

## Agricultural Holdings Act 1984 (c 41)

*RA:* 12 Jul 1984

*Commencement provisions:* s 11(2)–(5); Agricultural Holdings Act 1984 (Commencement) Order 1985, SI 1985/1644

| | | |
|---|---|---|
| 1, 2 | | 12 Jul 1984 (s 11(3)) |
| 3–5 | | 12 Sep 1984 (s 11(2)) |
| 6 | (1)–(6) | 12 Sep 1984 (s 11(2)) |
| | (7) | 1 Mar 1984 (s 11(4)) |
| | (8), (9) | 12 Sep 1984 (s 11(2)) |
| 7 | | 12 Sep 1984 (s 11(2)) |
| 8 | | 1 Jan 1986 (SI 1985/1644) |
| 9 | | 12 Jul 1984 (s 11(3)) |
| 10 | | See Schs 3, 4 below |
| 11 | (1)–(5) | 12 Sep 1984 (s 11(2)) |
| | (6) | 12 Jul 1984 (s 11(3)) |
| | (7) | 12 Sep 1984 (s 11(2)) |
| Schs 1, 2 | | 12 Sep 1984 (s 11(2)) |
| Sch 3 | paras 1–4 | 12 Sep 1984 (s 11(2)) |
| | para 5(1), (2) | 12 Sep 1984 (s 11(2)) |
| | para 5(3) | 12 Jul 1984 (s 11(3)) |
| | para 5(4) | 12 Sep 1984 (s 11(2)) |
| | paras 6–22 | 12 Sep 1984 (s 11(2)) |
| | para 23 | 12 Jul 1984 (s 11(3)) |
| | paras 24–34 | 12 Sep 1984 (s 11(2)) |
| | para 35 | 12 Jul 1984 (s 11(3)) |
| | paras 36–43 | 12 Sep 1984 (s 11(2)) |
| Sch 4 | | 12 Jul 1984 (s 11(3)), repeals of or in— |
| | | Agricultural Holdings Act 1948, s 1(2); |
| | | Agriculture Act 1958, s 2; |
| | | Agricultural Holdings (Notices to Quit) Act 1977, s 2(3), Case H |
| | | 12 Sep 1984 (all other repeals except that mentioned below) (s 11(2)) |
| | | 1 Jan 1986 (repeal of Agricultural Holdings Act 1948, Sch 6, para 28) (SI 1985/1644) |
| Sch 5 | | 12 Jul 1984 (s 11(3)) |

## Agriculture (Amendment) Act 1984 (c 20)

*RA:* 24 May 1984

*Commencement provisions:* s 3(2)

Whole Act in force 24 Jul 1984 (s 3(2))

## Anatomy Act 1984 (c 14)

*RA:* 24 May 1984

*Commencement provisions:* s 13(3); Anatomy Act 1984 (Commencement) Order 1988, SI 1988/81

Whole Act in force 14 Feb 1988 (SI 1988/81)

## Animal Health and Welfare Act 1984 (c 40)

*RA:* 12 Jul 1984

*Commencement provisions:* s 17(2)–(4); Animal Health and Welfare Act 1984 (Commencement No 1) Order 1985, SI 1985/1267

| | | |
|---|---|---|
| 1–4 | | 12 Sep 1984 (s 17(2)) |
| 5 | | 12 Sep 1984 (except in relation to the slaughter of poultry chicks within the meaning of the Slaughter of Poultry Act 1967, s 1(2B)) (s 17(2)) |
| | | *Never in force* (repealed) (exception noted above) (s 17(4)) |
| 6–12 | | 12 Sep 1984 (s 17(2)) |
| 13 | | 16 Aug 1985 (SI 1985/1267) |
| 14–17 | | 12 Sep 1984 (s 17(2)) |
| Sch 1 | paras 1, 2 | 12 Sep 1984 (s 17(2)) |
| | para 3 | 16 Aug 1985 (SI 1985/1267) |
| | para 4 | 12 Sep 1984 (s 17(2)) |
| Sch 2 | | 12 Sep 1984 (except repeals in Medicines Act 1968) (s 17(2)) |
| | | 16 Aug 1985 (exception noted above) (SI 1985/1267) |

## Appropriation Act 1984 (c 44)

*RA:* 26 Jul 1984

Whole Act in force 26 Jul 1984 (RA)

## Betting, Gaming and Lotteries (Amendment) Act 1984 (c 25)

*RA:* 26 Jun 1984

*Commencement provisions:* s 4(2); Betting, Gaming and Lotteries (Amendment) Act 1984 (Commencement) Order 1986, SI 1986/102

| | |
|---|---|
| 1 | 26 Aug 1984 (s 4(2)) |
| 2 | 10 Mar 1986 (SI 1986/102) |
| 3 | 26 Aug 1984 (s 4(2)) |
| 4 | 26 Jun 1984 (RA) |

## Building Act 1984 (c 55)

*RA:* 31 Oct 1984

*Commencement provisions:* s 134; Building Act 1984 (Commencement No 1) Order 1985, SI 1985/1602; Building Act 1984 (Appointed Day and Repeal) Order 1985, SI 1985/1603; Building Act 1984 (Commencement No 2) Order 1998, SI 1998/1836

| | |
|---|---|
| 1–11 | 1 Dec 1984 (s 134(2)) |
| 12, 13 | 1 Dec 1984 (so far as enable regulations to be made) (s 134(1)(a)) |
| | *Not yet in force* (otherwise) (repealed in part) |
| 14, 15 | 1 Dec 1984 (s 134(2)) |
| 16 | 1 Dec 1984 (11 Nov 1985 being the appointed day under sub-s (13)) (SI 1985/1603) |
| 17–19 | 1 Dec 1984 (s 134(2)) |

**Building Act 1984 (c 55)**—*contd*

| | | |
|---|---|---|
| 20 | | *Not yet in force* |
| 21–30 | | 1 Dec 1984 (s 134(2)) |
| 31 | | 1 Dec 1984 (so far as enables regulations to be made) (s 134(1)(a)) |
| | | *Not yet in force* (otherwise) |
| 32 | | 1 Dec 1984 (s 134(2)) |
| 33 | | *Not yet in force* |
| 34–37 | | 1 Dec 1984 (s 134(2)) |
| 38 | | 1 Dec 1984 (so far as enables regulations to be made) (s 134(1)(a)) |
| | | *Not yet in force* (otherwise) |
| 39–41 | | 1 Dec 1984 (s 134(2)) |
| 42 | (1)–(3) | *Not yet in force* |
| | (4)–(6) | 1 Dec 1984 (so far as enable regulations to be made) (s 134(1)(a)) |
| | | *Not yet in force* (otherwise) |
| | (7) | 1 Dec 1984 (but no day appointed) |
| 43 | (1), (2) | *Not yet in force* |
| | (3) | 1 Dec 1984 (so far as enables regulations to be made) (s 134(1)(a)) |
| | | *Not yet in force* (otherwise) |
| 44, 45 | | *Not yet in force* |
| 46–49 | | 1 Dec 1984 (s 134(2)) |
| 50 | (1) | 1 Dec 1984 (s 134(2)) |
| | (2), (3) | 11 Nov 1985 (SI 1985/1602) |
| | (4)–(8) | 1 Dec 1984 (s 134(2)) |
| 51–132 | | 1 Dec 1984 (s 134(2)) |
| 133 | (1) | 1 Dec 1984 (s 134(2)) |
| | (2) | See Sch 7 below |
| 134, 135 | | 1 Dec 1984 (s 134(2)) |
| Sch 1 | paras 1–8 | 1 Dec 1984 (s 134(2)) |
| | para 9 | 7 Aug 1998 (SI 1998/1836) |
| | paras 10, 11 | 1 Dec 1984 (s 134(2)) |
| Schs 2–6 | | 1 Dec 1984 (s 134(2)) |
| Sch 7 | | 1 Dec 1984 (s 134(2)), except repeals of or in— |
| | | Town and Country Planning Act 1947 (repealed); |
| | | Atomic Energy Authority Act 1954 |
| | | *Not yet in force* (exceptions noted above) (s 134(1)(c)) |

---

## Cable and Broadcasting Act 1984 (c 46)

*RA:* 12 Jul 1984

*Commencement provisions:* s 59(4); Cable and Broadcasting Act 1984 (Commencement No 1) Order 1984, SI 1984/1796; Cable and Broadcasting Act 1984 (Commencement No 2) Order 1986, SI 1986/537; Cable and Broadcasting Act 1984 (Commencement No 3) Order 1987, SI 1987/672

| | | |
|---|---|---|
| 1 | | 1 Dec 1984 (SI 1984/1796) |
| 2–18 | | 1 Jan 1985 (SI 1984/1796) |
| 19–21 | | 1 Dec 1984 (SI 1984/1796) |
| 22–35 | | 1 Jan 1985 (SI 1984/1796) |
| 36 | | 1 Dec 1984 (SI 1984/1796) |
| 37–41 | | 1 Apr 1986 (SI 1986/537) |
| 42–44 | | *Never in force* (repealed) |
| 45, 46 | | 6 Apr 1987 (SI 1987/672) |
| 47–50 | | 1 Dec 1984 (SI 1984/1796) |
| 51 | | *Never in force* (repealed) |
| 52 | | 1 Dec 1984 (SI 1984/1796) |
| 53, 54 | | 1 Jan 1985 (SI 1984/1796) |
| 55, 56 | | 1 Dec 1984 (SI 1984/1796) |
| 57 | (1) | See Sch 5 below |
| | (2) | See Sch 6 below |
| 58 | | 1 Jan 1985 (SI 1984/1796) |

**Cable and Broadcasting Act 1984 (c 46)**—*contd*

| | | |
|---|---|---|
| 59 | | 1 Dec 1984 (SI 1984/1796) |
| Sch 1 | | 1 Dec 1984 (SI 1984/1796) |
| Sch 2 | | 1 Jan 1985 (SI 1984/1796) |
| Schs 3, 4 | | *Never in force* (repealed) |
| Sch 5 | paras 1–39 | 1 Jan 1985 (SI 1984/1796) |
| | para 40(1), (2) | 1 Jan 1985 (SI 1984/1796) |
| | para 40(3), (4) | 1 Apr 1986 (SI 1986/537) |
| | para 40(5), (6) | 1 Jan 1985 (SI 1984/1796) |
| | para 40(7) | 1 Dec 1984 (so far as relates to charges made for the reception of programmes broadcast in an additional teletext service) (SI 1984/1796) |
| | | 1 Apr 1986 (so far as it relates to charges made for the reception of programmes in a DBS service) (SI 1986/537) |
| | para 40(8), (9) | 1 Apr 1986 (SI 1986/537) |
| | para 40(10) | 1 Dec 1984 (SI 1984/1796) |
| Sch 6 | | 1 Dec 1984 (repeal of Broadcasting Act 1981, s 25(1)–(3), (5)) (SI 1984/1796) |
| | | 1 Jan 1985 (otherwise) (SI 1984/1796) |

**Capital Transfer Tax Act 1984 (c 51)**

See Inheritance Tax Act 1984

**Child Abduction Act 1984 (c 37)**

*RA:* 12 Jul 1984

*Commencement provisions:* s 13(2)

Whole Act in force 12 Oct 1984 (s 13(2))

**Consolidated Fund Act 1984 (c 1)**

*RA:* 13 Mar 1984

Whole Act in force 13 Mar 1984 (RA)

**Consolidated Fund (No 2) Act 1984 (c 61)**

*RA:* 20 Dec 1984

Whole Act in force 20 Dec 1984 (RA)

**Co-operative Development Agency and Industrial Development Act 1984 (c 57)**

*RA:* 31 Oct 1984

*Commencement provisions:* s 7(1); Co-operative Development Agency and Industrial Development Act 1984 (Commencement) Order 1984, SI 1984/1845

The days appointed for the winding up and dissolution of the Co-operative Development Agency were 30 Sep 1990 and 31 Dec 1990, by Co-operative Development Agency (Winding up and Dissolution) Order 1990 (SI 1990/279)

| | |
|---|---|
| 1–3 | 31 Oct 1984 (s 7(1)) |
| 4, 5 | 29 Nov 1984 (SI 1984/1845) |
| 6 | See Sch 2 below |
| 7, 8 | 31 Oct 1984 (s 7(1)) |

**Co-operative Development Agency and Industrial Development Act 1984 (c 57)**—*contd*

| | | |
|---|---|---|
| Sch 1 | | 29 Nov 1984 (SI 1984/1845) |
| Sch 2 | Pt I | 31 Oct 1984 (s 7(1)) |
| | Pt II | 31 Dec 1990 (see note below) |
| | Pt III | 29 Nov 1984 (SI 1984/1845) |

## County Courts Act 1984 (c 28)

*RA:* 26 Jun 1984

*Commencement provisions:* s 150

Whole Act in force 1 Aug 1984 (s 150)

## Cycle Tracks Act 1984 (c 38)

*RA:* 12 Jul 1984

*Commencement provisions:* s 9(2)

Whole Act in force 12 Sep 1984 (s 9(2))

## Data Protection Act 1984 (c 35)

*RA:* 12 Jul 1984

*Commencement provisions:* s 42; Data Protection Act 1984 (Appointed Day) Order 1985, SI 1985/1055

Whole Act in force 12 Jul 1984 (RA). Note that no application for registration under Pt II (ss 4–20) of the Act was to be made until 11 Nov 1985 (ie the day appointed by SI 1985/1055 for the purposes of s 42(1) of the Act) and certain provisions of the Act did not apply, or fully apply, until six months, or two years, after that date (s 42)

## Dentists Act 1984 (c 24)

*RA:* 26 Jun 1984

*Commencement provisions:* s 55(1)–(3); Dentists Act 1984 (Commencement) Order 1984, SI 1984/1815

| | | |
|---|---|---|
| 1 | | 1 Oct 1984 (s 55(1)) |
| 2 | (1)–(3) | 1 Oct 1984 (s 55(1)) |
| | (4), (5) | 1 Jan 1985 (SI 1984/1815) |
| 3–27 | | 1 Oct 1984 (s 55(1)) |
| 28 | | 1 Jan 1985 (SI 1984/1815) |
| 29 | | 1 Oct 1984 (except so far as relates to proceedings before Health Committee or any direction or order given or made by that Committee) (s 55(1)) |
| | | 1 Jan 1985 (otherwise) (SI 1984/1815) |
| 30 | | 1 Oct 1984 (except so far as relates to proceedings before Health Committee or any direction or order given or made by that Committee) (s 55(1)) |
| | | 1 Jan 1985 (otherwise) (SI 1984/1815) |
| 31 | | 1 Jan 1985 (SI 1984/1815) |
| 32 | | 1 Oct 1984 (s 55(1)) |
| 33 | | As noted to ss 29, 30 above |
| 34–48 | | 1 Oct 1984 (s 55(1)) |
| 49 | | 26 Jul 1984 (s 55(2)) |
| 50–53 | | 1 Oct 1984 (s 55(1)) |
| 54 | (1) | See Sch 5 below |
| | (2) | See Sch 6, Pt I below |

**Dentists Act 1984 (c 24)**—*contd*

|  |  |  |
|---|---|---|
|  | (3) | See Sch 6, Pt II below |
| 55, 56 |  | 1 Oct 1984 (s 55(1)) |
| Sch 1 | paras 1–7 | 1 Oct 1984 (s 55(1)) |
|  | para 8(1) | 1 Oct 1984 (s 55(1)) |
|  | para 8(2) | 1 Jan 1985 (SI 1984/1815) |
|  | para 8(3), (4) | 1 Oct 1984 (s 55(1)) |
|  | paras 9–12 | 1 Oct 1984 (s 55(1)) |
| Sch 2 |  | 1 Oct 1984 (s 55(1)) |
| Sch 3 | paras 1, 2 | As noted to ss 29, 30 above |
|  | para 3 | 1 Jan 1985 (SI 1984/1815) |
|  | paras 4, 5 | As noted to ss 29, 30 above |
|  | para 6 | 1 Jan 1985 (SI 1984/1815) |
|  | paras 7, 8 | As noted to ss 29, 30 above |
|  | para 9(1), (2) | As noted to ss 29, 30 above |
|  | para 9(3) | 1 Jan 1985 (SI 1984/1815) |
| Schs 4, 5 |  | 1 Oct 1984 (s 55(1)) |
| Sch 6 | Pt I | 26 Jul 1984 (repeal of Dentists Act 1983, s 29) (s 55(2)) |
|  |  | 1 Oct 1984 (otherwise) (s 55(1)) |
|  | Pt II | 1 Oct 1984 (s 55(1)) |
| Sch 7 |  | 1 Oct 1984 (s 55(1)) |

---

## Education (Amendment) (Scotland) Act 1984 (c 6)

*RA:* 13 Mar 1984

*Commencement provisions:* s 2

Whole Act in force 13 May 1984 (s 2)

---

## Education (Grants and Awards) Act 1984 (c 11)

*RA:* 12 Apr 1984

*Commencement provisions:* s 6(2)

Whole Act in force 12 Jun 1984 (s 6(2))

---

## Finance Act 1984 (c 43)

*Budget Day:* 13 Mar 1984

*RA:* 26 Jul 1984

The commencement details of Finance Acts are not set out, as the dates from which their provisions take effect are usually stated clearly and unambiguously in the text of the Act, and charging provisions will normally state for which year or years of assessment they are to have effect.

---

## Food Act 1984 (c 30)

*RA:* 26 Jun 1984

*Commencement provisions:* s 136(4)

Whole Act in force 26 Sep 1984 (s 136(4))

---

### Foreign Limitation Periods Act 1984 (c 16)

*RA:* 24 May 1984

*Commencement provisions:* s 7(2); Foreign Limitation Periods Act 1984 (Commencement) Order 1985, SI 1985/1276

Whole Act in force 1 Oct 1985 (SI 1985/1276)

---

### Fosdyke Bridge Act 1984 (c 17)

*RA:* 24 May 1984

Whole Act in force 24 May 1984 (RA)

---

### Foster Children (Scotland) Act 1984 (c 56)

*RA:* 31 Oct 1984

*Commencement provisions:* s 23(2)

Whole Act in force 31 Jan 1985 (s 23(2))

---

### Friendly Societies Act 1984 (c 62)

*RA:* 20 Dec 1984

Whole Act in force 20 Dec 1984 (RA)

---

### Health and Social Security Act 1984 (c 48)

*RA:* 26 Jul 1984

*Commencement provisions:* s 27; Health and Social Security Act 1984 (Commencement No 1) Order 1984, SI 1984/1302; Health and Social Security Act 1984 (Commencement No 1) Amendment Order 1984, SI 1984/1467; Health and Social Security Act 1984 (Commencement No 2) Order 1986, SI 1986/974

| | | |
|---|---|---|
| 1 | (1) | 1 Oct 1984 (SI 1984/1302) |
| | (2) | 16 Aug 1985 (SI 1984/1302) |
| | (3) | 1 Jul 1986 (SI 1986/974) |
| | (4) | 1 Apr 1985 (SI 1984/1302) |
| | (5)(a) | 1 Jul 1986 (SI 1986/974) |
| | (5)(b) | 1 Apr 1985 (SI 1984/1302) |
| | (6), (7) | 1 Jul 1986 (SI 1986/974) |
| 2 | | 1 Apr 1985 (SI 1984/1302) |
| 3, 4 | | 1 Nov 1984 (SI 1984/1302) |
| 5 | (1) | 26 Sep 1984 (SI 1984/1302) |
| | (2), (3) | 1 Apr 1985 (SI 1984/1302) |
| | (4) | See Sch 3 below |
| | (5)–(8) | 26 Sep 1984 (SI 1984/1302) |
| 6 | (1) | 26 Sep 1984 (SI 1984/1302) |
| | (2) | 1 Apr 1985 (SI 1984/1302) |
| | (3) | 26 Sep 1984 (SI 1984/1302) |
| | (4) | 26 Jul 1984 (s 27(2)) |
| 7 | (1) | *Never in force* (repealed) |
| | (2), (3) | *Not yet in force* |
| | (4) | 26 Jul 1984 (s 27(2)) |
| 8 | | 26 Sep 1984 (SI 1984/1302) |
| 9, 10 | | 26 Jul 1984 (s 27(2)) |
| 11 | | See Sch 4 below |

**Health and Social Security Act 1984 (c 48)**—*contd*

| | | |
|---|---|---|
| 12 | | 26 Nov 1984 (SI 1984/1302) |
| 13 | | See Sch 5 below |
| 14 | | 26 Nov 1984 (SI 1984/1302) |
| 15 | | 26 Jul 1984 (s 27(2)) |
| 16 | | 26 Sep 1984 (s 27(3)) |
| 17 | | 6 Apr 1985 (SI 1984/1302) |
| 18 | (1) | 6 Apr 1975 (ss 18(2), 27(2)) |
| | (2) | 26 Jul 1984 (s 27(2)) |
| | (3) | 6 Apr 1985 (SI 1984/1302) |
| 19 | | 26 Sep 1984 (s 27(3)) |
| 20 | | 1 Jan 1985 (SI 1984/1302) |
| 21 | | See Sch 7 below |
| 22, 23 | | 26 Jul 1984 (s 27(2)) |
| 24 | | See Sch 8 below |
| 25–29 | | 26 Jul 1984 (s 27(2)) |
| Sch 1 | | 1 Jul 1986 (SI 1986/974) |
| Sch 2 | | 1 Nov 1984 (SI 1984/1302) |
| Sch 3 | para 1 | 26 Sep 1984 (SI 1984/1302) |
| | paras 2–6 | 1 Apr 1985 (SI 1984/1302) |
| | para 7(a) | 1 Apr 1985 (SI 1984/1302) |
| | para 7(b)(i) | 1 Apr 1985 (SI 1984/1302) |
| | para 7(b)(ii) | 26 Sep 1984 (SI 1984/1302) |
| | para 7(c) | 26 Sep 1984 (SI 1984/1302) |
| | paras 8–11 | 1 Apr 1985 (SI 1984/1302) |
| | para 12 | 26 Sep 1984 (SI 1984/1302) |
| | paras 13–17 | 1 Apr 1985 (SI 1984/1302) |
| Sch 4 | | 10 Sep 1984 (claims for severe disablement allowance) (SI 1984/1302) |
| | | 29 Nov 1984 (for purposes of s 11(2) and Pt II of this Sch) (SI 1984/1302) |
| | | 29 Nov 1984 (in relation to (i) persons aged 50 or over on that day; (ii) persons born after 29 Nov 1949; (iii) any person who is incapable of work on or after 29 Nov 1984 on a day within the same period of interruption of employment as a day on which he was entitled to a non-contributory invalidity pension) (SI 1984/1302 as amended by SI 1984/1467) |
| | | The 50th birthday of any person for whom it falls between 30 Nov 1984 and 27 Nov 1985 (SI 1984/1302) |
| | | 28 Nov 1985 (otherwise) (SI 1984/1302) |
| Sch 5 | para 1 | 26 Nov 1984 (SI 1984/1302) |
| | para 2(a) | 29 Nov 1984 (SI 1984/1302) |
| | para 2(b) | 26 Nov 1984 (SI 1984/1302) |
| | para 3(a) | 29 Nov 1984 (SI 1984/1302) |
| | para 3(b), (c) | 26 Nov 1984 (SI 1984/1302) |
| | para 4 | 26 Nov 1984 (SI 1984/1302) |
| | paras 5, 6 | 28 Nov 1984 (SI 1984/1302) |
| | para 7 | 26 Nov 1984 (SI 1984/1302) |
| | para 8 | 29 Nov 1984 (SI 1984/1302) |
| Sch 6 | | 1 Jan 1985 (SI 1984/1302) |
| Sch 7 | paras 1, 2 | 26 Nov 1984 (SI 1984/1302) |
| | para 3 | 6 Apr 1985 (SI 1984/1302) |
| | paras 4, 5 | 26 Sep 1984 (s 27(3)) |
| | para 6 | 26 Jul 1984 (s 27(2)) |
| | para 7 | 26 Sep 1984 (s 27(3)) |
| | para 8 | 26 Jul 1984 (s 27(2)) |
| | para 9 | 26 Sep 1984 (s 27(3)) |
| Sch 8 | | 26 Sep 1984 (repeal in Social Security Pensions Act 1975, s 38(3)) (s 27(3)) |
| | | 26 Sep 1984 (SI 1984/1302), repeals of or in— |

**Health and Social Security Act 1984 (c 48)**—*contd*

> National Health Service Act 1977, ss 45(2), (3), 97(1)(a), (c), (2);
> National Health Service (Scotland) Act 1978, s 85(1);
> Health Services Act 1980, s 18, Sch 1, paras 30, 79, 88, 99;
> Social Security Act 1980, s 3(5)
> 1 Nov 1984 (repeal in Opticians Act 1958, s 13(3) (spent))
>   (SI 1984/1302)
> 26 Nov 1984 (repeals of or in Social Security Act 1975, ss 12(1)(d),
>   41(2)(d), (3), Sch 4, Pt IV, para 3) (SI 1984/1302)
> 28 Nov 1984 (repeal of Child Benefit Act 1975, Sch 4, para 25)
>   (SI 1984/1302)
> 29 Nov 1984 (SI 1984/1302), repeals of or in—
>   Social Security Act 1975, s 57(2), Sch 4, Pt IV, para 1(a), (c);
>   Social Security (Miscellaneous Provisions) Act 1977, s 22(2);
>   Social Security and Housing Benefits Act 1982, Sch 4,
>     para 18(4)
> 1 Apr 1985 (SI 1984/1302), repeals of or in—
>   Tribunals and Inquiries Act 1971, Sch 1 (repealed);
>   National Health Service Act 1977, ss 12(b), 15(1), (2), 39(c),
>     98(2), Sch 5, paras 9(1)–(3), 10;
>   National Health Service (Scotland) Act 1978, s 26(2)(c);
>   Health Services Act 1980, ss 1(6), 2, Sch 1, paras 35, 37, 56, 57,
>     69, 77(b), 82(2), (3), 87, 89–98
> 6 Apr 1985 (repeal in Social Security Pensions Act 1975, s 4(1))
>   (SI 1984/1302)
> 1 Jul 1986 (SI 1986/974), repeals of or in—
>   National Health Service Act 1977, ss 44, 46, 72, 81–83, Sch 5,
>     paras 1, 2, 6(3)(e), (5)(iv), Sch 12;
>   National Health Service (Scotland) Act 1978, ss 26 (except
>     sub-s (2)(c)), 29, 64, 73–75, Schs 8, 11;
>   Health Services Act 1980, Sch 5
> *Not yet in force*, repeals of or in—
>   Social Security Pensions Act 1975, s 38(4) (repealed);
>   National Health Service Act 1977, ss 19(1)(e), 128(1) (definition
>     of "dispensing optician"), Sch 5, para 6 (part) (repealed and
>     replaced), Sch 9, para 4(e) (now substituted);
>   National Health Service (Scotland) Act 1978, ss 9(1)(e), 108(1)
>     (definition of "dispensing optician")

**Housing and Building Control Act 1984 (c 29)**

*RA:* 26 Jun 1984

*Commencement provisions:* s 66(3)

Whole Act in force 26 Aug 1984 (s 66(3))

**Housing Defects Act 1984 (c 50)**

*RA:* 31 Jul 1984

*Commencement provisions:* s 29(2); Housing Defects Act 1984 (Commencement) Order 1984, SI 1984/1701

| | |
|---|---|
| 1–27 | 1 Dec 1984 (SI 1984/1701) |
| 28 | 31 Jul 1984 (s 29(2)) |
| 29 | 1 Dec 1984 (SI 1984/1701) |
| Schs 1–4 | 1 Dec 1984 (SI 1984/1701) |

## Inheritance Tax Act 1984 (c 51)

*RA:* 31 Jul 1984

*Commencement provisions:* s 274(1)

Whole Act in force 1 Jan 1985 (s 274(1)). Note that this Act does not apply to transfers of value made before 1985 or to other events before then on which tax is or would be chargeable. Note also s 275 of, and Sch 7 to, the Act in relation to continuity and construction of references to old and new law.

This Act was originally cited as the Capital Transfer Tax Act 1984. On and after 25 Jul 1986 the tax charged under this Act is known as inheritance tax and this Act may be cited as Inheritance Tax Act 1984 (Finance Act 1986, s 100).

## Inshore Fishing (Scotland) Act 1984 (c 26)

*RA:* 26 Jun 1984

*Commencement provisions:* s 11(2); Inshore Fishing (Scotland) Act 1984 (Commencement) Order 1985, SI 1985/961

Whole Act in force 26 Jul 1985 (SI 1985/961)

## Juries (Disqualification) Act 1984 (c 34)

*RA:* 12 Jul 1984

*Commencement provisions:* s 2(3); Juries (Disqualification) Act 1984 (Commencement) Order 1984, SI 1984/1599

Whole Act in force 1 Dec 1984 (SI 1984/1599)

## Law Reform (Husband and Wife) (Scotland) Act 1984 (c 15)

*RA:* 24 May 1984

*Commencement provisions:* s 10(2)

Whole Act in force 24 Jul 1984 (s 10(2))

## Local Government (Interim Provisions) Act 1984 (c 53)

*RA:* 31 Jul 1984

*Commencement provisions:* s 1(1); Local Government (Interim Provisions) Act 1984 (Appointed Day) Order 1985, SI 1985/2

| | |
|---|---|
| 1 | 31 Jul 1984 (RA) |
| 2, 3 | 1 Feb 1985 (SI 1985/2) |
| 4–13 | 31 Jul 1984 (RA) |

## London Regional Transport Act 1984 (c 32)

*RA:* 26 Jun 1984

*Commencement provisions:* s 72(2)–(6); London Regional Transport (Appointed Day) Order 1984, SI 1984/877

| | | |
|---|---|---|
| 1–39 | | 29 Jun 1984 (SI 1984/877) |
| 40 | (1)–(3) | 26 Jun 1984 (s 72(4)) |
| | (4)–(11) | 29 Jun 1984 (SI 1984/877) |
| | (12) | See Sch 3 below |

## London Regional Transport Act 1984 (c 32)—*contd*

| | | |
|---|---|---|
| 41–44 | | 29 Jun 1984 (SI 1984/877) |
| 45 | | 26 Aug 1984 (s 72(5)) |
| 46–59 | | 29 Jun 1984 (SI 1984/877) |
| 60 | | 26 Jun 1984 (s 72(3)) |
| 61–67 | | 29 Jun 1984 (SI 1984/877) |
| 68, 69 | | 26 Jun 1984 (s 72(3)) |
| 70 | | 29 Jun 1984 (SI 1984/877) |
| 71 | (1) | 29 Jun 1984 (SI 1984/877) |
| | (2) | See Sch 5 below |
| | (3) | See Schs 6, 7 below |
| | (4)–(7) | 29 Jun 1984 (SI 1984/877) |
| 72 | | 26 Jun 1984 (s 72(3)) |
| Schs 1, 2 | | 29 Jun 1984 (SI 1984/877) |
| Sch 3 | | 26 Jun 1984 (s 72(4)) |
| Sch 4 | | 29 Jun 1984 (SI 1984/877) |
| Sch 5 | paras 1–6 | 29 Jun 1984 (SI 1984/877) |
| | para 7 | 26 Jun 1984 (s 72(3)) |
| | para 8(1)–(5) | 26 Jun 1984 (s 72(3)) |
| | para 8(6)–(8) | 29 Jun 1984 (SI 1984/877) |
| | para 8(9) | 26 Jun 1984 (s 72(3)) |
| | para 8(10)(a) | 26 Jun 1984 (s 72(3)) |
| | para 8(10)(b) | 29 Jun 1984 (SI 1984/877) |
| | paras 9–19 | 29 Jun 1984 (SI 1984/877) |
| Sch 6 | | 29 Jun 1984 (SI 1984/877) |
| Sch 7 | | 1 Apr 1985 (s 72(6)), repeals of or in— |
| | | London Government Act 1963, Sch 2; |
| | | Local Government, Planning and Land Act 1980, Sch 13, para 9 |
| | | 29 Jun 1984 (otherwise) (SI 1984/877) |

## Lotteries (Amendment) Act 1984 (c 9)

*RA:* 12 Apr 1984

*Commencement provisions:* s 2(2)

Whole Act in force 12 Jun 1984 (s 2(2))

## Matrimonial and Family Proceedings Act 1984 (c 42)

*RA:* 12 Jul 1984

*Commencement provisions:* s 47; Matrimonial and Family Proceedings Act 1984 (Commencement No 1) Order 1984, SI 1984/1589; Matrimonial and Family Proceedings Act 1984 (Commencement No 2) Order 1985, SI 1985/1316; Matrimonial and Family Proceedings Act 1984 (Commencement No 3) Order 1986, SI 1986/635; Matrimonial and Family Proceedings Act 1984 (Commencement No 4) Order 1986, SI 1986/1049; Matrimonial and Family Proceedings Act 1984 (Commencement No 3) (Scotland) Order 1986, SI 1986/1226; Matrimonial and Family Proceedings Act 1984 (Commencement No 5) Order 1991, SI 1991/1211

| | |
|---|---|
| 1–9 | 12 Oct 1984 (s 47(1)) |
| 10 | 1 Oct 1986 (SI 1986/1049) |
| 11 | 12 Oct 1984 (s 47(1)) |
| 12–27 | 16 Sep 1985 (SI 1985/1316) |
| 28–31 | 1 Sep 1986 (SI 1986/1226) |
| 32–39 | 28 Apr 1986 (SI 1986/635) |
| 40, 41 | 14 Oct 1991 (SI 1991/1211) |
| 42, 43 | 28 Apr 1986 (SI 1986/635) |
| 44 | 12 Oct 1984 (SI 1984/1589) |
| 45 | *Never in force* (repealed) |
| 46 | See Schs 1–3 below |

**Matrimonial and Family Proceedings Act 1984 (c 42)**—*contd*

| | | |
|---|---|---|
| 47, 48 | | 12 Jul 1984 (s 47(1)) |
| Sch 1 | para 1(a) | 16 Sep 1985 (SI 1985/1316) |
| | para 1(b) | 1 Sep 1986 (SI 1986/1226) |
| | para 2 | 12 Oct 1984 (SI 1984/1589) |
| | para 3 | 28 Apr 1986 (SI 1986/635) |
| | para 4 | 12 Oct 1984 (SI 1984/1589) |
| | para 5 | 16 Sep 1985 (SI 1985/1316) |
| | paras 6, 7 | 1 Sep 1986 (SI 1986/1226) |
| | para 8 | 16 Sep 1985 (SI 1985/1316) |
| | paras 9–13 | 12 Oct 1984 (SI 1984/1589) |
| | para 14 | *Never in force (repealed)* |
| | para 15 | 16 Sep 1985 (SI 1985/1316) |
| | paras 16–18 | 28 Apr 1986 (SI 1986/635) |
| | para 19(a) | *Never in force (repealed)* |
| | para 19(b) | 28 Apr 1986 (SI 1986/635) |
| | para 20(a) | *Never in force (repealed)* |
| | para 20(b) | 28 Apr 1986 (SI 1986/635) |
| | para 21 | 1 Oct 1986 (SI 1986/1049) |
| | para 22 | 12 Oct 1984 (SI 1984/1589) |
| | para 23(a), (b) | 1 Oct 1986 (SI 1986/1049) |
| | para 23(c) | 12 Oct 1984 (except words from "after" to "to") (SI 1984/1589) |
| | | 1 Oct 1986 (words from "after" to "to") (SI 1986/1049) |
| | para 23(d), (e) | 1 Oct 1986 (SI 1986/1049) |
| | paras 24–26 | 1 Oct 1986 (SI 1986/1049) |
| | para 27 | 12 Oct 1984 (SI 1984/1589) |
| | para 28 | 1 Sep 1986 (SI 1986/1226) |
| | paras 29–31 | 28 Apr 1986 (SI 1986/635) |
| Sch 2 | paras 1, 2 | 12 Oct 1984 (s 47(1)) |
| | para 3 | *Not yet in force* |
| Sch 3 | | 12 Oct 1984 (repeal of Matrimonial Causes Act 1973, ss 43(9), 44(6)) (SI 1984/1589) |
| | | 28 Apr 1986 (SI 1986/635), repeals of or in— |
| | | Matrimonial Causes Act 1967; |
| | | Courts Act 1971; |
| | | Guardianship of Minors Act 1971; |
| | | Domicile and Matrimonial Proceedings Act 1973; |
| | | Matrimonial Causes Act 1973, s 45, Sch 2; |
| | | Children Act 1975; |
| | | Adoption Act 1976; |
| | | Domestic Proceedings and Magistrates' Courts Act 1978; |
| | | Matrimonial Homes and Property Act 1981; |
| | | Matrimonial Homes Act 1983; |
| | | County Courts Act 1984 |
| | | 14 Oct 1991 (otherwise) (SI 1991/1211) |

**Mental Health (Scotland) Act 1984 (c 36)**

*RA:* 12 Jul 1984

*Commencement provisions:* s 130

Whole Act in force 30 Sep 1984 (s 130)

**Merchant Shipping Act 1984 (c 5)**

*RA:* 13 Mar 1984

*Commencement provisions:* s 14(5)

## Merchant Shipping Act 1984 (c 5)—*contd*
Whole Act in force 13 May 1984 (s 14(5))

---

## Occupiers' Liability Act 1984 (c 3)

*RA:* 13 Mar 1984

*Commencement provisions:* s 4(2)

Whole Act in force 13 May 1984 (s 4(2))

---

## Ordnance Factories and Military Services Act 1984 (c 59)

*RA:* 31 Oct 1984

Whole Act in force 31 Oct 1984 (RA)

---

## Parliamentary Pensions etc Act 1984 (c 52)

*RA:* 31 Jul 1984

*Commencement provisions:* ss 1(5), 2(8), 4(5), 5(6)

| | | |
|---|---|---|
| 1 | (1) | 31 Jul 1984 (RA) |
| | (2)–(4) | 20 Jul 1983 (s 1(5)) |
| | (5) | 31 Jul 1984 (RA) |
| 2 | (1) | 31 Jul 1984 (RA) |
| | (2)–(7) | 20 Jul 1983 (s 2(8)) |
| | (8) | 31 Jul 1984 (RA) |
| 3 | | 31 Jul 1984 (RA) |
| 4 | (1) | 31 Jul 1984 (RA) |
| | (2)(a), (b) | 12 May 1983 (note modifications in relation to dissolution of Parliament on 13 May 1983) (s 4(5)) |
| | (2)(c) | 31 Jul 1984 (RA) |
| | (3)–(8) | 31 Jul 1984 (RA) |
| 5 | (1), (2) | 31 Jul 1984 (RA) |
| | (3) | 20 Jul 1983 (note sub-s (3) has no effect in relation to any pension first payable under the Parliamentary and other Pensions Act 1972 before that date) (s 5(6)) |
| | (4)–(7) | 31 Jul 1984 (RA) |
| 6–17 | | 31 Jul 1984 (RA) |
| Schedule | | 20 Jul 1983 (s 5(6)) repeals of or in (note repeals have no effect in relation to any pension payable under the 1972 Act before that date)— |
| | | Parliamentary and other Pensions Act 1972, s 6; |
| | | Parliamentary and other Pensions and Salaries Act 1975, s 1(2); |
| | | Parliamentary Pensions Act 1978, s 14 |
| | | 31 Jul 1984 (otherwise) (RA) |

---

## Pensions Commutation Act 1984 (c 7)

*RA:* 13 Mar 1984

*Commencement provisions:* s 3(2); Pensions Commutation Act 1984 (Commencement) Order 1984, SI 1984/1140

Whole Act in force 20 Aug 1984 (SI 1984/1140)

---

## Police and Criminal Evidence Act 1984 (c 60)

*RA:* 31 Oct 1984

*Commencement provisions:* s 121; Police and Criminal Evidence Act 1984 (Commencement No 1) Order 1984, SI 1984/2002; Police and Criminal Evidence Act 1984 (Commencement No 2) Order 1984, SI 1985/623; Police and Criminal Evidence Act 1984 (Commencement No 3) Order 1985/1934; Police and Criminal Evidence Act 1984 (Commencement No 4) Order 1991, SI 1991/2686; Police and Criminal Evidence Act 1984 (Commencement No 5) Order 1992, SI 1992/2802

| | | |
|---|---|---|
| 1 | | 1 Jan 1985 (so far as relates to search for stolen articles in localities in which, on 31 Dec 1984, an enactment (other than one contained in a public general Act or one relating to statutory undertakers) applies conferring power on a constable to search for stolen or unlawfully obtained goods) (SI 1984/2002) |
| | | 1 Jan 1986 (otherwise) (SI 1985/1934) |
| 2–6 | | 1 Jan 1986 (SI 1985/1934) |
| 7 | (1) | 1 Jan 1986 (SI 1985/1934) |
| | (2)(a) | 1 Jan 1986 (SI 1985/1934) |
| | (2)(b) | 1 Jan 1985 (SI 1984/2002) |
| | (3) | 1 Jan 1985 (SI 1984/2002) |
| 8–22 | | 1 Jan 1986 (SI 1985/1934) |
| 23 | | 1 Jan 1985 (SI 1984/2002) |
| 24–36 | | 1 Jan 1986 (SI 1985/1934) |
| 37 | (1)–(10) | 1 Jan 1986 (SI 1985/1934) |
| | (11)–(14) | *Never in force* (repealed) |
| | (15) | 1 Jan 1986 (SI 1985/1934) |
| 38–58 | | 1 Jan 1986 (SI 1985/1934) |
| 59 | | 1 Jan 1985 (SI 1984/2002) |
| 60 | (1)(a) | 1 Jan 1986 (SI 1985/1934) |
| | (1)(b) | 29 Nov 1991 (in the following police areas: Avon and Somerset, Bedfordshire, Cambridgeshire, Cheshire, City of London, Cleveland, Cumbria, Derbyshire, Devon and Cornwall, Dorset, Durham, Dyfed-Powys, Essex, Gloucestershire, Greater Manchester, Gwent, Hampshire, Hertfordshire, Humberside, Kent, Lancashire, Leicestershire, Lincolnshire, Merseyside, Metropolitan Police District, Norfolk, Northamptonshire, Northumbria, North Wales, North Yorkshire, Nottinghamshire, South Wales, South Yorkshire, Staffordshire, Suffolk, Surrey, Sussex, Warwickshire, West Mercia, West Midlands, West Yorkshire, Wiltshire) (SI 1991/2686) |
| | | 9 Nov 1992 (in the Thames Valley police area) (SI 1992/2802) |
| | (2) | 29 Nov 1991 (SI 1991/2686) |
| 61–65 | | 1 Jan 1986 (SI 1985/1934) |
| 66, 67 | | 1 Jan 1985 (SI 1984/2002) |
| 68–82 | | 1 Jan 1986 (SI 1985/1934) |
| 83–105 | | 29 Apr 1985 (SI 1985/623) |
| 106 | | 1 Jan 1985 (SI 1984/2002) |
| 107 | | 1 Jan 1986 (SI 1985/1934) |
| 108 | | 1 Mar 1985 (SI 1984/2002) |
| 109 | (a), (b) | 29 Apr 1985 (SI 1985/623) |
| | (c) | 1 Jan 1985 (SI 1984/2002) |
| 110, 111 | | 1 Mar 1985 (SI 1984/2002) |
| 112 | | 1 Jan 1985 (SI 1984/2002) |
| 113 | (1), (2) | 1 Jan 1986 (SI 1985/1934) |
| | (3)–(13) | 1 Jan 1985 (SI 1984/2002) |
| 114 | | 1 Jan 1986 (SI 1985/1934) |
| 115 | | 1 Jan 1985 (SI 1984/2002) |
| 116 | | 29 Apr 1985 (SI 1985/623) |
| 117 | | 1 Jan 1986 (SI 1985/1934) |
| 118 | | 1 Jan 1985 (SI 1984/2002) |

**Police and Criminal Evidence Act 1984 (c 60)**—*contd*

| | | |
|---|---|---|
| 119 | | See Schs 6, 7 below |
| 120–122 | | 31 Oct 1984 (RA) |
| Schs 1–3 | | 1 Jan 1986 (SI 1985/1934) |
| Schs 4, 5 | | 29 Apr 1985 (SI 1985/623) |
| Sch 6 | paras 1–13 | 1 Jan 1986 (SI 1985/1934) |
| | paras 14, 15 | 1 Mar 1985 (SI 1984/2002) |
| | para 16 | 29 Apr 1985 (SI 1985/623) |
| | paras 17–29 | 1 Jan 1986 (SI 1985/1934) |
| | paras 30–33 | 1 Mar 1985 (SI 1984/2002) |
| | para 34 | 1 Jan 1986 (SI 1985/1934) |
| | para 35 | 29 Apr 1985 (SI 1985/623) |
| | paras 36–41 | 1 Jan 1986 (SI 1985/1934) |
| Sch 7 | | 1 Mar 1985 (repeals in Police (Scotland) Act 1967) (SI 1984/2002, as amended by SI 1985/623) |
| | | 29 Apr 1985 (SI 1985/623), repeals of or in— |
| | | Police Act 1964; |
| | | Superannuation Act 1972; |
| | | House of Commons Disqualification Act 1975; |
| | | Northern Ireland Assembly Disqualification Act 1975; |
| | | Police Act 1976 |
| | | 1 Jan 1986 (otherwise) (SI 1985/1934) |

---

**Prescription and Limitation (Scotland) Act 1984 (c 45)**

*RA:* 26 Jul 1984

*Commencement provisions:* s 7(2)

Whole Act in force 26 Sep 1984 (s 7(2))

---

**Prevention of Terrorism (Temporary Provisions) Act 1984 (c 8)**

*RA:* 22 Mar 1984

Whole Act in force 22 Mar 1984 (RA)

---

**Public Health (Control of Disease) Act 1984 (c 22)**

*RA:* 26 Jun 1984

*Commencement provisions:* s 79(2)

Whole Act in force 26 Sep 1984 (s 79(2))

---

**Rates Act 1984 (c 33)**

*RA:* 26 Jun 1984

*Commencement provisions:* s 18

| | | |
|---|---|---|
| 1–8 | | 26 Jun 1984 (RA) (but maximum rate or precept may only be prescribed from financial year 1 Apr 1985 onwards (s 18(1))) |
| 9 | | 26 Jun 1984 (RA) |
| 10, 11 | | *Never in force* (repealed) |
| 12–15 | | 26 Jun 1984 (RA) |
| 16 | (1) | See Sch 1 below |
| | (2) | See Sch 2 below |
| | (3) | 26 Jun 1984 (RA) |
| 17–19 | | 26 Jun 1984 (RA) |

**Rates Act 1984 (c 33)**—*contd*

| | | |
|---|---|---|
| Sch 1 | para 1 | 26 Jun 1984 (RA) |
| | paras 2, 3 | Effective for rate periods beginning on or after the first date after 26 Jun 1984 on which new valuation lists come into force (paras 2(3), 3(1)) |
| | para 4 | Effective for rate periods beginning on or after 1 Apr 1984 (para 4(4)) |
| | paras 5, 6 | Effective for rate periods beginning on or after 1 Apr 1985 (para 9(2)) |
| | para 7 | 1 Jan 1973 (para 7(2)) |
| | para 8 | 26 Aug 1984 (para 8(3)) |
| | para 9 | Effective for rate periods beginning on or after 1 Apr 1985 (para 9(2)) |
| | para 10 | Deemed always to have had effect (para 10(2)) |
| | para 11 | Effective for rate periods beginning on or after 1 Apr 1985 (para 11(3)) |
| | paras 12–18 | Effective in relation to any proposal made or served on or after 1 Apr 1985 (para 19; but note sub-paras (a), (b)) |
| | para 19 | 26 Jun 1984 (RA) |
| | para 20 | 1 Jan 1985 (para 20(2)) |
| | para 21 | 26 Jun 1984 (para 21(2)) |
| | para 22 | Effective for any rate period beginning on or after 1 Apr 1985 (para 22(5)) |
| | para 23 | Effective for any financial year from 1 Apr 1983 (para 23(2)) |
| | para 24 | Effective for any financial year from 1 Apr 1984 (para 24(2)) |
| Sch 2 | Pt I | Effective for any rate period beginning on or after 1 Apr 1985 (para 1(3)) |
| | Pt II | No proposal for alteration of a valuation list may be made under Pt II before the first rate period beginning after 26 Jun 1984 (para 7) |

---

**Rating and Valuation (Amendment) (Scotland) Act 1984 (c 31)**

*RA:* 26 Jun 1984

*Commencement provisions:* s 23(1)

| | | |
|---|---|---|
| 1, 2 | | 26 Jun 1984 (s 23(1)(a)) |
| 3 | | 26 Aug 1984 (s 23(1)(c)) |
| 4 | | 26 Jun 1984 (s 23(1)(a)) |
| 5, 6 | | 26 Aug 1984 (s 23(1)(c)) |
| 7 | | 1 Apr 1985 (s 23(1)(b)) |
| 8 | | 26 Aug 1984 (s 23(1)(c)) |
| 9–13 | | 1 Apr 1985 (s 23(1)(b)) |
| 14–16 | | 26 Aug 1984 (s 23(1)(c)) |
| 17–19 | | 1 Apr 1985 (s 23(1)(b)) |
| 20 | | 26 Aug 1984 (s 23(1)(c)) |
| 21 | (1) | See Sch 2 below |
| | (2) | 26 Aug 1984 (s 23(1)(c)) |
| 22 | | 26 Aug 1984 (s 23(1)(c)) |
| 23 | | 26 Jun 1984 (s 23(1)(a)) |
| Sch 1 | | 26 Aug 1984 (s 23(1)(c)) |
| Sch 2 | paras 1–8 | 26 Aug 1984 (s 23(1)(c)) |
| | para 9 | 1 Apr 1985 (s 23(1)(b)) |
| | paras 10, 11 | 26 Aug 1984 (s 23(1)(c)) |
| | paras 12–15 | 1 Apr 1985 (s 23(1)(b)) |
| | para 16 | 26 Aug 1984 (s 23(1)(c)) |
| | para 17 | 1 Apr 1985 (s 23(1)(b)) |
| | para 18 | 26 Aug 1984 (s 23(1)(c)) |
| Sch 3 | | 26 Aug 1984 (s 23(1)(c)) |

## Registered Homes Act 1984 (c 23)

*RA:* 26 Jun 1984

*Commencement provisions:* s 59(2); Registered Homes Act 1984 (Commencement) Order 1984, SI 1984/1348

Whole Act in force 1 Jan 1985 (except s 1 so far as relates to an establishment which is a school referred to in s 1(5)(f), for which the date is 1 Jan 1986) (SI 1984/1348)

## Rent (Scotland) Act 1984 (c 58)

*RA:* 31 Oct 1984

*Commencement provisions:* s 118(2)

Whole Act in force 31 Jan 1985 (s 118(2))

## Repatriation of Prisoners Act 1984 (c 47)

*RA:* 26 Jul 1984

*Commencement provisions:* s 9(2); Repatriation of Prisoners (Commencement) Order 1985, SI 1985/550

Whole Act in force 15 Apr 1985 (SI 1985/550)

## Restrictive Trade Practices (Stock Exchange) Act 1984 (c 2)

*RA:* 13 Mar 1984

Whole Act in force 13 Mar 1984 (RA)

## Road Traffic (Driving Instruction) Act 1984 (c 13)

*RA:* 12 Apr 1984

*Commencement provisions:* s 5(3); Road Traffic (Driving Instruction) Act 1984 (Commencement No 1) Order 1985, SI 1985/578; Road Traffic (Driving Instruction) Act 1984 (Commencement No 2) Order 1986, SI 1986/1336

| | |
|---|---|
| 1 | 30 Sep 1986 (SI 1986/1336) |
| 2–5 | 20 May 1985 (SI 1985/578) |

## Road Traffic Regulation Act 1984 (c 27)

*RA:* 26 Jun 1984

*Commencement provisions:* s 145(1), (2); Road Traffic Regulation Act 1984 (Commencement No 1) Order 1986, SI 1986/1147

| | | |
|---|---|---|
| 1–89 | | 26 Sep 1984 (s 145(1)) |
| 90 | | 31 Jul 1986 (SI 1986/1147) |
| 91–147 | | 26 Sep 1984 (s 145(1)) |
| Schs 1–7 | | 26 Sep 1984 (s 145(1)) |
| Sch 8 | paras 1, 2 | 26 Sep 1984 (s 145(1)) |
| | para 3 | 22 Jul 2004 (by virtue of Statute Law (Repeals) Act 2004, s 1(1), Sch 1, Pt 14; note also s 1(2), Sch 2, para 16 thereof) |
| | paras 4–6 | 26 Sep 1984 (s 145(1)) |
| Schs 9–14 | | 26 Sep 1984 (s 145(1)) |

### Roads (Scotland) Act 1984 (c 54)

*RA:* 31 Oct 1984

*Commencement provisions:* s 157(2), (3); Roads (Scotland) Act 1984 (Commencement No 1) Order 1985, SI 1985/1953; Roads (Scotland) Act 1984 (Commencement No 2) Order 1989, SI 1989/1094; Roads (Scotland) Act 1984 (Commencement No 3) Order 1990, SI 1990/2622

| | | |
|---|---|---|
| 1–35 | | 1 Jan 1985 (s 157(2)) |
| 36–39 | | 1 Aug 1989 (so far as relates to areas of Tayside and Lothian Regional Councils) (SI 1989/1084) |
| | | 8 Jan 1991 (otherwise) (SI 1990/2622) |
| 40 | | 1 Aug 1989 (so far as relates to areas of Tayside and Lothian Regional Councils) (SI 1989/1084) |
| | | 8 Jan 1991 (otherwise) (SI 1990/2622) |
| 41–125 | | 1 Jan 1985 (s 157(2)) |
| 126 | | 1 Jan 1986 (SI 1985/1953) |
| 127–155 | | 1 Jan 1985 (s 157(2)) |
| 156 | (1), (2) | 1 Jan 1985 (s 157(2)) |
| | (3) | See Sch 11 below |
| 157 | | 31 Oct 1984 (RA) |
| Schs 1–6 | | 1 Jan 1985 (s 157(2)) |
| Sch 7 | | 1 Jan 1986 (SI 1985/1953) |
| Schs 8–10 | | 1 Jan 1985 (s 157(2)) |
| Sch 11 | | 1 Jan 1985 (except repeal of Road Traffic Regulation Act 1984, Sch 10, paras 14–16) (s 157(2)) |
| | | 1 Jan 1986 (exception noted above) (SI 1985/1953) |

### Somerset House Act 1984 (c 21)

*RA:* 26 Jun 1984

Whole Act in force 26 Jun 1984 (RA)

### Telecommunications Act 1984 (c 12)

*RA:* 12 Apr 1984

*Commencement provisions:* ss 60(1), 69(2), 110(2)–(5); Telecommunications Act 1984 (Appointed Day) (No 1) Order 1984, SI 1984/749; Telecommunications Act 1984 (Appointed Day) (No 2) Order 1984, SI 1984/876; British Telecommunications (Dissolution) Order 1994, SI 1994/2162

| | | |
|---|---|---|
| 1 | | 18 Jun 1984 (SI 1984/749) |
| 2–59 | | 5 Aug 1984 (SI 1984/876) |
| 60–73 | | 6 Aug 1984 (SI 1984/876) |
| 74–92 | | 16 Jul 1984 (SI 1984/876) |
| 93–95 | | 5 Aug 1984 (SI 1984/876) |
| 96 | | *Never in force* (repealed) |
| 97–107 | | 5 Aug 1984 (SI 1984/876) |
| 108 | | 18 Jun 1984 (SI 1984/749) |
| 109 | (1)–(3) | 5 Aug 1984 (SI 1984/876) |
| | (4) | See Sch 5 below |
| | (5) | 5 Aug 1984 (SI 1984/876) |
| | (6) | See Sch 7 below |
| | (7) | 5 Aug 1984 (SI 1984/876) |
| 110 | | 18 Jun 1984 (SI 1984/749) |
| Sch 1 | | 18 Jun 1984 (SI 1984/749) |
| Sch 2 | | 5 Aug 1984 (SI 1984/876) |
| Sch 3 | | 16 Jul 1984 (SI 1984/876) |
| Sch 4 | | 5 Aug 1984 (SI 1984/876) |
| Sch 5 | Pt I | 5 Aug 1984 (SI 1984/876) |

## Telecommunications Act 1984 (c 12)—*contd*

|        |        |                           |
|--------|--------|---------------------------|
|        | Pt II  | 6 Aug 1984 (SI 1984/876)  |
| Sch 6  |        | 6 Aug 1984 (SI 1984/876)  |
| Sch 7  | Pt I   | 5 Aug 1984 (SI 1984/876)  |
|        | Pt II  | 6 Aug 1984 (SI 1984/876)  |
|        | Pt III | 6 Sep 1994 (SI 1994/2162) |
|        | Pt IV  | 16 Jul 1984 (SI 1984/876) |

## Tenants' Rights, Etc (Scotland) Amendment Act 1984 (c 18)

*RA:* 24 May 1984

*Commencement provisions:* s 9(2)

Whole Act in force 24 Jul 1984 (s 9(2))

## Tourism (Overseas Promotion) (Scotland) Act 1984 (c 4)

*RA:* 13 Mar 1984

*Commencement provisions:* s 3

Whole Act in force 13 May 1984 (s 3)

## Town and Country Planning Act 1984 (c 10)

*RA:* 12 Apr 1984

*Commencement provisions:* s 7(2)

Whole Act in force 12 Aug 1984 (s 7(2))

## Trade Marks (Amendment) Act 1984 (c 19)

*RA:* 24 May 1984

*Commencement provisions:* s 2(2); Trade Marks (Amendment) Act 1984 (Commencement) Order 1986, SI 1986/1273

Whole Act in force 1 Oct 1986 (SI 1986/1273)

## Trade Union Act 1984 (c 49)

*RA:* 26 Jul 1984

*Commencement provisions:* s 22(2)–(5); Trade Union Act 1984 (Commencement) Order 1984, SI 1984/1490

|        |                           |
|--------|---------------------------|
| 1–3    | 1 Oct 1985 (SI 1984/1490) |
| 4      | 26 Jul 1984 (s 22(2))     |
| 5–9    | 1 Oct 1985 (SI 1984/1490) |
| 10, 11 | 26 Sep 1984 (s 22(4))     |
| 12–19  | 31 Mar 1985 (s 22(5))     |
| 20–22  | 26 Jul 1984 (RA)          |

## Video Recordings Act 1984 (c 39)

*RA:* 12 Jul 1984

*Commencement provisions:* s 23(2); Video Recordings Act 1984 (Commencement No 1) Order 1985, SI 1985/883; Video Recordings Act 1984 (Scotland) (Commencement No 1) Order 1985,

**Video Recordings Act 1984 (c 39)**—*contd*

SI 1985/904; Video Recordings Act 1984 (Commencement No 2) Order 1985, SI 1985/1264; Video Recordings Act 1984 (Scotland) (Commencement No 2) Order 1985, SI 1985/1265; Video Recordings Act 1984 (Commencement No 3) Order 1986, SI 1986/1125; Video Recordings Act 1984 (Scotland) (Commencement No 3) Order 1986, SI 1986/1182; Video Recordings Act 1984 (Commencement No 4) Order 1987, SI 1987/123; Video Recordings Act 1984 (Scotland) (Commencement No 4) Order 1987, SI 1987/160; Video Recordings Act 1984 (Commencement No 5) Order 1987, SI 1987/1142; Video Recordings Act 1984 (Scotland) (Commencement No 5) Order 1987, SI 1987/1249; Video Recordings Act 1984 (Commencement No 6) Order 1987, SI 1987/2155; Video Recordings Act 1984 (Scotland) (Commencement No 6) Order 1987, SI 1987/2273; Video Recordings Act 1984 (Commencement No 7) Order 1988, SI 1988/1018; Video Recordings Act 1984 (Scotland) (Commencement No 7) Order 1988, SI 1988/1079

| | |
|---|---|
| 1 | 10 Jun 1985 (SI 1985/883; SI 1985/904) |
| 2, 3 | 1 Sep 1985 (SI 1985/1264; SI 1985/1265) |
| 4, 5 | 10 Jun 1985 (SI 1985/883; SI 1985/904) |
| 6 | 1 Sep 1985 (SI 1985/1264; SI 1985/1265) |
| 7, 8 | 10 Jun 1985 (SI 1985/883; SI 1985/904) |
| 9, 10 | 1 Sep 1985 (for the purpose of prohibiting the supply, the offer to supply or the possession for the purpose of supply of a video recording containing a video work where— |

(a) a video recording containing such video work has not been sold, let on hire or offered for sale or hire in the United Kingdom to the public before 1 Sep 1985; and

(b) no classification certificate in respect of such video work has been issued) (SI 1985/1264; SI 1985/1265)

1 Sep 1986 (for the purpose of prohibiting the supply, the offer to supply or the possession for the purpose of supply of a video recording which has been sold, let on hire or offered for sale in the UK to the public in video form before 1 Sep 1985 where—

(a) its visual images, when shown as a moving picture, are not substantially the same as the moving picture produced on showing a film registered, or deemed to have been registered, under Films Act 1960, Pt II, on or after 1 Jan 1940;

(b) its visual images are accompanied by sound which comprises or includes words predominantly in the English language; and

(c) no classification certificate has been issued in respect of it.

Where such a video recording also contains another video work which does not satisfy the above requirements these sections are only brought into force for the above purpose in respect of the video work which does satisfy the requirements) (SI 1986/1125; SI 1986/1182)

1 Mar 1987 (for the purpose of prohibiting the supply, the offer to supply, or the possession for the purpose of supply of a video recording which has been sold, let on hire or offered for sale in the UK to the public in video form before 1 Sep 1985 where—

(a) its visual images, when shown as a moving picture, are substantially the same as the moving picture produced on showing a film registered, or deemed to have been registered, under Pt II of Films Act 1960 on or after 1 Jan 1980;

(b) its visual images are accompanied by sound which comprises or includes words predominantly in the English language; and

(c) no classification certificate has been issued in respect of it.

Where such a video recording also contains another video work which does not satisfy the above requirements these sections are only brought into force for the above purpose in respect of the video work which does satisfy the requirements) (SI 1987/123; SI 1987/160)

**Video Recordings Act 1984 (c 39)**—*contd*

1 Sep 1987 (for the purpose of prohibiting the supply, the offer to
supply or the possession for the purpose of supply of a video
recording which has been sold, let on hire or offered for sale in
the UK to the public in video form before 1 Sep 1985
where—

(a) its visual images, when shown as a moving picture, are
substantially the same as the moving picture produced on
showing a film registered, or deemed to have been registered,
under Pt II of Films Act 1960 on or after 1 Jan 1975;

(b) its visual images are accompanied by sound which comprises
or includes words predominantly in the English language; and

(c) no classification certificate has been issued in respect of it.

Where such a video recording also contains another video work
which does not satisfy the above requirements these sections are
only brought into force for the above purposes in respect of the
video work which does satisfy the requirements)
(SI 1987/1142; SI 1987/1249)

1 Mar 1988 (for the purpose of prohibiting the supply, the offer to
supply or the possession for the purpose of supply of a video
recording which has been sold, let on hire or offered for sale in
the UK to the public in video form before 1 Sep 1985
where—

(a) its visual images, when shown as a moving picture, are
substantially the same as the moving picture produced on
showing a film registered under Pt II of Films Act 1960 on or
after 1 Jan 1970;

(b) its visual images are accompanied by sound which comprises
or includes words predominantly in the English language; and

(c) no classification certificate has been issued in respect of it.

Where such a video recording also contains another video work
which does not satisfy the above requirements these sections are
only brought into force for the above purposes in respect of the
video work which does satisfy the requirements)
(SI 1987/2155; SI 1987/2273)

1 Sep 1988 (otherwise) (SI 1988/1018; SI 1988/1079)

| | |
|---|---|
| 11–17 | 1 Sep 1985 (SI 1985/1264; SI 1985/1265) |
| 18, 19 | 1 Sep 1985 (SI 1985/1264) |
| 20 | 1 Sep 1985 (SI 1985/1265) |
| 21 | 1 Sep 1985 (SI 1985/1264; SI 1985/1265) |
| 22, 23 | 10 Jun 1985 (SI 1985/883; SI 1985/904) |

## Video Recordings Act 1984 (c 39)—contd

...

# 1985 Acts

## Administration of Justice Act 1985 (c 61)

*RA:* 30 Oct 1985

*Commencement provisions:* s 69(2)–(4); Administration of Justice Act 1985 (Commencement No 1) Order 1986, SI 1986/364; Administration of Justice Act 1985 (Commencement No 2) Order 1986, SI 1986/1503; Administration of Justice Act 1985 (Commencement No 3) Order 1986, SI 1986/2260; Administration of Justice Act 1985 (Commencement No 4) Order 1987, SI 1987/787; Administration of Justice Act 1985 (Commencement No 5) Order 1988, SI 1988/1341; Administration of Justice Act 1985 (Commencement No 6) Order 1989, SI 1989/287; Administration of Justice Act 1985 (Commencement No 7) Order 1991, SI 1991/2683

| | | |
|---|---|---|
| 1 | | 1 Jan 1987 (SI 1986/2260) |
| 2 | | 12 Mar 1986 (except so far as relates to the investigation of any complaint made to the Law Society relating to the quality of any professional services provided by a solicitor) (SI 1986/364) |
| | | 1 Jan 1987 (exception noted above) (SI 1986/2260) |
| 3 | | 1 Jan 1987 (SI 1986/2260) |
| 4, 5 | | 12 Mar 1986 (SI 1986/364) |
| 6 | (1)–(3) | 11 May 1987 (SI 1987/787) |
| | (4) | 1 Dec 1987 (SI 1987/787) |
| | (5) | 11 May 1987 (SI 1987/787) |
| 7, 8 | | 12 Mar 1986 (SI 1986/364) |
| 9, 10 | | 1 Jan 1992 (SI 1991/2683) |
| 11 | | 11 May 1987 (SI 1987/787) |
| 12 | | 12 Mar 1986 (SI 1986/364) |
| 13 | | 1 Oct 1986 (SI 1986/1503) |
| 14–21 | | 11 May 1987 (SI 1987/787) |
| 22, 23 | | 1 Oct 1986 (SI 1986/1503) |
| 24–33 | | 11 May 1987 (SI 1987/787) |
| 34 | (1), (2) | 11 May 1987 (SI 1987/787) |
| | (3) | *Not yet in force* |
| 35–37 | | 11 May 1987 (SI 1987/787) |
| 38 | | 1 Oct 1986 (SI 1986/1503) |
| 39 | | 11 May 1987 (SI 1987/787) |
| 40–44 | | 1 Apr 1989 (SI 1989/287) |
| 45 | | 30 Dec 1985 (s 69(4)) |
| 46 | | 12 Mar 1986 (SI 1986/364) |
| 47 | | 1 Oct 1986 (SI 1986/1503) |
| 48 | | 1 Jan 1987 (SI 1986/2260) |
| 49 | | 30 Dec 1985 (s 69(4)) |
| 50 | | 28 Apr 1986 (SI 1986/364) |
| 51 | | 1 Oct 1986 (SI 1986/1503) |
| 52 | | 30 Dec 1985 (s 69(4)) |
| 53 | | 1 Oct 1988 (SI 1988/1341) |
| 54 | | 30 Dec 1985 (s 69(4)) |
| 55 | | 1 Oct 1986 (SI 1986/1503) |
| 56–62 | | 30 Dec 1985 (s 69(4)) |
| 63 | | 30 Oct 1985 (s 69(3)) |

**Administration of Justice Act 1985 (c 61)**—*contd*

| | | |
|---|---|---|
| 64, 65 | | 30 Dec 1985 (s 69(4)) |
| 66 | | *Never in force* (repealed) |
| 67 | (1) | See Sch 7 below |
| | (2) | See Sch 8 below |
| 68, 69 | | 30 Oct 1985 (s 69(3)) |
| Sch 1 | | 12 Mar 1986 (SI 1986/364) |
| Sch 2 | | 1 Jan 1992 (SI 1991/2683) |
| Sch 3 | | 12 Mar 1986 (SI 1986/364) |
| Schs 4–6 | | 11 May 1987 (SI 1987/787) |
| Sch 7 | paras 1–4 | *Never in force* (repealed) |
| | paras 5, 6 | *Not yet in force* |
| | para 7 | 1 Oct 1986 (SI 1986/1503) |
| | para 8 | 30 Dec 1985 (s 69(4)) |
| Sch 8 | Pt I | 30 Oct 1985 (s 69(3)) |
| | Pt II | 30 Dec 1985 (s 69(4)) |
| | Pt III | 12 Mar 1986 (repeals in Solicitors Act 1974) (SI 1986/364) |
| | | 1 Oct 1986 (SI 1986/1503), repeals in— |
| | | Supreme Court Act 1981; |
| | | County Courts Act 1984 |
| | | *Never in force* (repeals of Legal Aid Act 1974, ss 12(3)–(5), 38(2)–(6)) (repealed) |
| Sch 9 | | 30 Oct 1985 (s 69(3)) |

**Agricultural Training Board Act 1985 (c 36)**

*RA:* 16 Jul 1985

*Commencement provisions:* s 4(2)

Whole Act in force 16 Sep 1985 (s 4(2))

**Appropriation Act 1985 (c 55)**

*RA:* 25 Jul 1985

Whole Act in force 25 Jul 1985 (RA)

**Bankruptcy (Scotland) Act 1985 (c 66)**

*RA:* 30 Oct 1985

*Commencement provisions:* s 78(2); Bankruptcy (Scotland) Act 1985 (Commencement) Order 1985, SI 1985/1924; Bankruptcy (Scotland) Act 1985 (Commencement No 2) Order 1986, SI 1986/1913

| | | |
|---|---|---|
| 1 | (1)(a) | 1 Apr 1986 (SI 1985/1924) |
| | (1)(b) | 1 Feb 1986 (SI 1985/1924) |
| | (1)(c), (d) | 1 Apr 1986 (SI 1985/1924) |
| | (2) | 1 Feb 1986 (SI 1985/1924) |
| | (3)–(5) | 1 Apr 1986 (SI 1985/1924) |
| | (6) | 1 Feb 1986 (SI 1985/1924) |
| 2 | (1) | 1 Apr 1986 (SI 1985/1924) |
| | (2)–(4) | 1 Feb 1986 (SI 1985/1924) |
| 3–50 | | 1 Apr 1986 (SI 1985/1924) |
| 51 | (1) | 1 Apr 1986 (SI 1985/1924) |
| | (2) | 29 Dec 1986 (SI 1986/1913) |
| | (3)–(7) | 1 Apr 1986 (SI 1985/1924) |
| 52–71 | | 1 Apr 1986 (SI 1985/1924) |
| 72 | | 1 Feb 1986 (SI 1985/1924) |
| 73 | (1) | 1 Feb 1986 (except definition "preferred debt") (SI 1985/1924) |

**Bankruptcy (Scotland) Act 1985 (c 66)**—*contd*

|  |  |  |
|---|---|---|
|  |  | 29 Dec 1986 (exception noted above) (SI 1986/1913) |
|  | (2)–(5) | 1 Feb 1986 (SI 1985/1924) |
| 74, 75 |  | 1 Apr 1986 (SI 1985/1924) |
| 76 |  | 1 Feb 1986 (SI 1985/1924) |
| 77 |  | 1 Apr 1986 (SI 1985/1924) |
| 78 |  | 30 Oct 1985 (RA) |
| Schs 1, 2 |  | 1 Apr 1986 (SI 1985/1924) |
| Sch 3 |  | 29 Dec 1986 (SI 1986/1913) |
| Schs 4–6 |  | 1 Apr 1986 (SI 1985/1924) |
| Sch 7 | paras 1–12 | 1 Apr 1986 (SI 1985/1924) |
|  | para 13 | 29 Dec 1986 (SI 1986/1913) |
|  | para 14(1), (2) | 1 Apr 1986 (SI 1985/1924) |
|  | para 14(3) | 29 Dec 1986 (SI 1986/1913) |
|  | para 14(4) | 1 Apr 1986 (SI 1985/1924) |
|  | paras 15–25 | 1 Apr 1986 (SI 1985/1924) |
| Sch 8 |  | 1 Apr 1986 (SI 1985/1924), repeals of or in— |

> Bankruptcy Act 1621;
> Bankruptcy Act 1696;
> Titles to Land Consolidation (Scotland) Act 1868;
> Married Women's Property (Scotland) Act 1881;
> Judicial Factors (Scotland) Act 1889;
> Merchant Shipping Act 1894;
> Bankruptcy (Scotland) Act 1913 (except repeal of s 118);
> Married Women's Property (Scotland) Act 1920;
> Conveyancing (Scotland) Act 1924;
> Third Parties (Rights Against Insurers) Act 1930;
> Industrial Assurance and Friendly Societies Act 1948;
> Post Office Act 1969;
> Road Traffic Act 1972;
> Insolvency Act 1976;
> Banking Act 1979;
> Sale of Goods Act 1979;
> Law Reform (Miscellaneous Provisions) (Scotland) Act 1980;
> Matrimonial Homes (Family Protection) (Scotland) Act 1981;
> Companies Act 1985
> 29 Dec 1986 (otherwise) (SI 1986/1913)

---

**Betting, Gaming and Lotteries (Amendment) Act 1985 (c 18)**

*RA:* 9 May 1985

*Commencement provisions:* s 3(2), (3); Betting, Gaming and Lotteries (Amendment) Act 1985 (Commencement) Order 1985, SI 1985/1475

|  |  |  |
|---|---|---|
| 1 |  | 9 Jul 1985 (s 3(2)) |
| 2 | (1), (2) | 9 Jul 1985 (s 3(2)) |
|  | (3), (4) | 28 Oct 1985 (SI 1985/1475) |
|  | (5) | 9 Jul 1985 (s 3(2)) |
|  | (6) | 28 Oct 1985 (SI 1985/1475) |
| 3 |  | 9 Jul 1985 (s 3(2)) |
| Schedule |  | 9 Jul 1985 (s 3(2)) |

---

**Brunei and Maldives Act 1985 (c 3)**

*RA:* 11 Mar 1985

Whole Act in force 11 Mar 1985 (RA)

---

**Business Names Act 1985 (c 7)**

*RA:* 11 Mar 1985

*Commencement provisions:* s 10

Whole Act in force 1 Jul 1985 (s 10)

**Charities Act 1985 (c 20)**

*RA:* 23 May 1985

*Commencement provisions:* s 7(2); Charities Act 1985 (Commencement) Order 1985, SI 1985/1583

Whole Act in force 1 Jan 1986 (SI 1985/1583)

**Charter Trustees Act 1985 (c 45)**

*RA:* 16 Jul 1985

Whole Act in force 16 Jul 1985 (RA)

**Child Abduction and Custody Act 1985 (c 60)**

*RA:* 25 Jul 1985

*Commencement provisions:* s 29(2); Child Abduction and Custody Act 1985 (Commencement) Order 1986, SI 1986/1048

Whole Act in force 1 Aug 1986 (SI 1986/1048)

**Cinemas Act 1985 (c 13)**

*RA:* 27 Mar 1985

*Commencement provisions:* s 25(2)

Whole Act in force 27 Jun 1985 (s 25(2))

**Coal Industry Act 1985 (c 27)**

*RA:* 13 Jun 1985

Whole Act in force 13 Jun 1985 (RA)

**Companies Act 1985 (c 6)**

*RA:* 11 Mar 1985

*Commencement provisions:* ss 243(6), 746

Whole Act in force 1 Jul 1985 (s 746), except s 243(3), (4) (never in force and now repealed)

**Companies Consolidation (Consequential Provisions) Act 1985 (c 9)**

*RA:* 11 Mar 1985

*Commencement provisions:* s 34

**Companies Consolidation (Consequential Provisions) Act 1985 (c 9)**—*contd*
Whole Act in force 1 Jul 1985 (s 34)

---

**Company Securities (Insider Dealing) Act 1985 (c 8)**

*RA:* 11 Mar 1985

*Commencement provisions:* s 18

Whole Act in force 1 Jul 1985 (s 18)

---

**Consolidated Fund Act 1985 (c 1)**

*RA:* 24 Jan 1985

Whole Act in force 24 Jan 1985 (RA)

---

**Consolidated Fund (No 2) Act 1985 (c 11)**

*RA:* 27 Mar 1985

Whole Act in force 27 Mar 1985 (RA)

---

**Consolidated Fund (No 3) Act 1985 (c 74)**

*RA:* 19 Dec 1985

Whole Act in force 19 Dec 1985 (RA)

---

**Controlled Drugs (Penalties) Act 1985 (c 39)**

*RA:* 16 Jul 1985

*Commencement provisions:* s 2(1)

Whole Act in force 16 Sep 1985 (s 2(1))

---

**Copyright (Computer Software) Amendment Act 1985 (c 41)**

*RA:* 16 Jul 1985

*Commencement provisions:* s 4(3)

Whole Act in force 16 Sep 1985 (s 4(3))

---

**Dangerous Vessels Act 1985 (c 22)**

*RA:* 23 May 1985

*Commencement provisions:* s 8(2)

Whole Act in force 23 Jul 1985 (s 8(2))

---

### Elections (Northern Ireland) Act 1985 (c 2)

*RA:* 24 Jan 1985

*Commencement provisions:* s 7(2), (3); Elections (Northern Ireland) Act 1985 (Commencement) Order 1985, SI 1985/1221

| | | |
|---|---|---|
| 1–3 | | 24 Jan 1985 (so far as gives effect to s 5(1)) (s 7(3)) |
| | | 6 Aug 1985 (otherwise) (SI 1985/1221) |
| 4 | | 6 Aug 1985 (SI 1985/1221) |
| 5 | (1) | 24 Jan 1985 (s 7(3)) |
| | (2), (3) | 6 Aug 1985 (SI 1985/1221) |
| 6, 7 | | 24 Jan 1985 (s 7(3)) |

### Enduring Powers of Attorney Act 1985 (c 29)

*RA:* 26 Jun 1985

*Commencement provisions:* s 14(2); Enduring Powers of Attorney Act 1985 (Commencement) Order 1986, SI 1986/125

Whole Act in force 10 Mar 1986 (SI 1986/125)

### European Communities (Finance) Act 1985 (c 64)

*RA:* 30 Oct 1985

Whole Act in force 30 Oct 1985 (RA)

### European Communities (Spanish and Portuguese Accession) Act 1985 (c 75)

*RA:* 19 Dec 1985

19 Dec 1985 (RA); but note that the accession of Spain and Portugal to the European Communities did not take effect until 1 Jan 1986

### Family Law (Scotland) Act 1985 (c 37)

*RA:* 16 Jul 1985

*Commencement provisions:* s 29(2), (3); Family Law (Scotland) Act 1985 (Commencement No 1) Order 1986, SI 1986/1237; Family Law (Scotland) Act 1985 (Commencement No 2) Order 1988, SI 1988/1887

| | |
|---|---|
| 1–24 | 1 Sep 1986 (SI 1986/1237) |
| 25 | 30 Nov 1988 (SI 1988/1887) |
| 26–29 | 1 Sep 1986 (SI 1986/1237) |
| Schs 1, 2 | 1 Sep 1986 (SI 1986/1237) |

### Films Act 1985 (c 21)

*RA:* 23 May 1985

*Commencement provisions:* s 8(2)

| | | |
|---|---|---|
| 1–5 | | 23 May 1985 (RA) |
| 6 | | 23 Jul 1985 (s 8(2)) |
| 7 | (1) | See Sch 2 below |
| | (2)–(4) | 23 May 1985 (RA) |
| | (5), (6) | 23 Jul 1985 (s 8(2)) |
| | (7) | 23 May 1985 (RA) |

**Films Act 1985 (c 21)**—*contd*

| | |
|---|---|
| 8 | 23 May 1985 (RA) |
| Sch 1 | 23 Jul 1985 (s 8(2)) |
| Sch 2 | 23 May 1985 (except repeals noted below) (RA) |
| | 23 Jul 1985 (s 8(2)), repeals in— |
| | Finance Act 1982; |
| | Finance Act 1984 |

## Finance Act 1985 (c 54)

*Budget Day*: 19 Mar 1985

*RA*: 25 Jul 1985

The commencement details of Finance Acts are not set out, as the dates from which their provisions take
effect are usually stated clearly and unambiguously in the text of the Act, and charging provisions will
normally state for which year or years of assessment they are to have effect.

## Food and Environment Protection Act 1985 (c 48)

*RA*: 16 Jul 1985

*Commencement provisions*: s 27; Food and Environment Protection Act 1985 (Commencement No 1)
Order 1985, SI 1985/1390; Food and Environment Protection Act 1985 (Commencement No 2)
Order 1985, SI 1985/1698

| | |
|---|---|
| 1–4 | 16 Jul 1985 (s 27(2)) |
| 5–15 | 1 Jan 1986 (SI 1985/1698) |
| 16–19 | 5 Sep 1985 (SI 1985/1390) |
| 20–26 | 16 Jul 1985 (so far as relate to Pt I (ss 1–4)) (s 27(2)) |
| | 1 Jan 1986 (otherwise) (SI 1985/1698) |
| 27, 28 | 16 Jul 1985 (s 27(2)) |
| Sch 1 | 16 Jul 1985 (s 27(2)) |
| Sch 2 | 16 Jul 1985 (so far as relates to Pt I (ss 1–4)) (s 27(2)) |
| | 5 Sep 1985 (so far as relates to Pt III (ss 16–19)) (SI 1985/1390) |
| | 1 Jan 1986 (otherwise) (SI 1985/1698) |
| Schs 3, 4 | 1 Jan 1986 (SI 1985/1698) |
| Sch 5 | 5 Sep 1985 (SI 1985/1390) |

## Further Education Act 1985 (c 47)

*RA*: 16 Jul 1985

*Commencement provisions*: s 7; Further Education Act 1985 (Commencement) (No 1) Order 1985,
SI 1985/1429; Further Education Act 1985 (Commencement No 2) (Scotland) Order 1987,
SI 1987/1335

| | |
|---|---|
| 1–3 | 16 Sep 1985 (s 7(3)) |
| 4 | 16 Sep 1985 (E) (W) (SI 1985/1429) |
| | 17 Aug 1987 (S) (SI 1987/1335) |
| 5–8 | 16 Jul 1985 (s 7(2)) |

## Gaming (Bingo) Act 1985 (c 35)

*RA*: 16 Jul 1985

*Commencement provisions*: s 5(2); Gaming (Bingo) Act 1985 (Commencement) Order 1986, SI 1986/832

Whole Act in force 9 Jun 1986 (SI 1986/832)

## Hill Farming Act 1985 (c 32)

*RA:* 26 Jun 1985

*Commencement provisions:* s 2(3)

Whole Act in force 26 Aug 1985 (s 2(3))

## Hong Kong Act 1985 (c 15)

*RA:* 11 Mar 1985

Whole Act in force 11 Mar 1985 (RA)

## Hospital Complaints Procedure Act 1985 (c 42)

*RA:* 16 Jul 1985

*Commencement provisions:* s 2(2); Hospital Complaints Procedure Act 1985 (Commencement) Order 1989, SI 1989/1191

Whole Act in force 11 Jul 1989 (SI 1989/1191)

## Housing Act 1985 (c 68)

*RA:* 30 Oct 1985

*Commencement provisions:* s 625(2)

Whole Act in force 1 Apr 1986 (s 625(2))

## Housing Associations Act 1985 (c 69)

*RA:* 30 Oct 1985

*Commencement provisions:* s 107(2)

Whole Act in force 1 Apr 1986 (s 107(2))

## Housing (Consequential Provisions) Act 1985 (c 71)

*RA:* 30 Oct 1985

*Commencement provisions:* s 6(2)

Whole Act in force 1 Apr 1986 (s 6(2))

## Industrial Development Act 1985 (c 25)

*RA:* 13 Jun 1985

*Commencement provisions:* s 6(4)

| | |
|---|---|
| 1, 2 | 13 Aug 1985 (s 6(4)) |
| 3 | 1 Apr 1986 (s 6(4)) |
| 4–6 | 13 Aug 1985 (s 6(4)) |
| Schedule | 13 Aug 1985 (s 6(4)) |

## Insolvency Act 1985 (c 65)

*RA:* 30 Oct 1985

*Commencement provisions:* s 236(2); Insolvency Act 1985 (Commencement No 1) Order 1986, SI 1986/6; Insolvency Act 1985 (Commencement No 2) Order 1986, SI 1986/185; Insolvency Act 1985 (Commencement No 3) Order 1986, SI 1986/463; Insolvency Act 1985 (Commencement No 4) Order 1986, SI 1986/840; Insolvency Act 1985 (Commencement No 5) Order 1986, SI 1986/1924

| | | |
|---|---|---|
| 1, 2 | | 29 Dec 1986 (SI 1986/1924) |
| 3 | (1) | 1 Jul 1986 (SI 1986/840) |
| | (2) | 1 Jun 1986 (SI 1986/840) |
| | (3)–(5) | 1 Jul 1986 (SI 1986/840) |
| 4 | (1)(a), (b) | 1 Jul 1986 (SI 1986/840) |
| | (1)(c) | 1 Jun 1986 (SI 1986/840) |
| | (2)–(6) | 1 Jul 1986 (SI 1986/840) |
| 5 | (1) | 1 Jul 1986 (SI 1986/840) |
| | (2)(a) | 1 Jul 1986 (SI 1986/840) |
| | (2)(b) | 1 Jun 1986 (SI 1986/840) |
| | (3) | 1 Jun 1986 (SI 1986/840) |
| | (4), (5) | 1 Jul 1986 (SI 1986/840) |
| 6–9 | | 1 Jul 1986 (SI 1986/840) |
| 10, 11 | | 1 Feb 1986 (SI 1986/6) |
| 12–16 | | 28 Apr 1986 (SI 1986/463) |
| 17 | | 29 Dec 1986 (SI 1986/1924) |
| 18 | | 28 Apr 1986 (SI 1986/463) |
| 19–44 | | 29 Dec 1986 (SI 1986/1924) |
| 45 | | 1 Mar 1986 (SI 1986/6) |
| 46–105 | | 29 Dec 1986 (SI 1986/1924) |
| 106 | | 1 Feb 1986 (so far as it relates to the making of rules in relation to administrative receivers) (SI 1986/6) |
| | | 1 Mar 1986 (so far as it relates to the making of rules in relation to England and Wales and in relation to Scotland in respect of the matters specified in Sch 5, paras 26, 28–31) (SI 1986/185) |
| | | 29 Dec 1986 (otherwise) (SI 1986/1924) |
| 107 | | 29 Dec 1986 (SI 1986/1924) |
| 108 | (1) | 1 Feb 1986 (so far as they relate to the provisions of the Act brought into force on that date by SI 1986/6) (SI 1986/6) |
| | | 1 Mar 1986 (so far as they relate to the provisions of the Act brought into force on that date by SI 1986/6 and SI 1986/185) (SI 1986/6; SI 1986/185) |
| | | 28 Apr 1986 (otherwise) (SI 1986/463) |
| | (2) | 28 Apr 1986 (SI 1986/463) |
| | (3) | 1 Feb 1986 (so far as they relate to the provisions of the Act brought into force on that date by SI 1986/6) (SI 1986/6) |
| | | 1 Mar 1986 (so far as they relate to the provisions of the Act brought into force on that date by SI 1986/6 and SI 1986/185) (SI 1986/6; SI 1986/185) |
| | | 28 Apr 1986 (otherwise) (SI 1986/463) |
| | (4)–(7) | 28 Apr 1986 (SI 1986/463) |
| 109 | (1) | 1 Mar 1986 (SI 1986/185) |
| | (2) | 1 Mar 1986 (so far as it relates to general rules under Companies Act 1985, s 663(1)) (SI 1986/185) |
| | | 29 Dec 1986 (otherwise) (SI 1986/1924) |
| | (3) | 1 Mar 1986 (SI 1986/6) |
| 110–212 | | 29 Dec 1986 (SI 1986/1924) |
| 213 | (1) | 1 Apr 1986 (except so far as they relate to the assisting of the courts of any relevant country or territory) (SI 1986/185) |
| | | 29 Dec 1986 (otherwise) (SI 1986/1924) |
| | (2) | 1 Feb 1986 (SI 1986/6) |
| | (3)–(6) | 1 Apr 1986 (except so far as they relate to the assisting of the courts of any relevant country or territory) (SI 1986/185) |

**Insolvency Act 1985 (c 65)**—*contd*

| | | |
|---|---|---|
| | (7)–(9) | 1 Feb 1986 (SI 1986/6) |
| | (10) | 29 Dec 1986 (SI 1986/1924) |
| 214 | | 1 Apr 1986 (so far as it relates to the awarding by a court in Scotland of the sequestration of an individual's estate) (SI 1986/463) |
| | | 29 Dec 1986 (otherwise) (SI 1986/1924) |
| 215 | | 29 Dec 1986 (SI 1986/1924) |
| 216 | | 28 Apr 1986 (SI 1986/463) |
| 217–225 | | 29 Dec 1986 (SI 1986/1924) |
| 226 | | 1 Feb 1986 (so far as it relates to the making of rules in relation to administrative receivers under s 106) (SI 1986/6) |
| | | 1 Mar 1986 (so far as it relates to the making of rules under S106) (SI 1986/185) |
| | | 29 Dec 1986 (otherwise) (SI 1986/1924) |
| 227–231 | | 29 Dec 1986 (SI 1986/1924) |
| 232 | | 1 Feb 1986 (SI 1986/6) |
| 233 | | 29 Dec 1986 (SI 1986/1924) |
| 234 | | 1 Apr 1986 (SI 1986/185) |
| 235 | (1) | 1 Mar 1986 (SI 1986/185) |
| | (2) | 1 Mar 1986 (SI 1986/6) |
| | (3) | 1 Mar 1986 (SI 1986/185) |
| | (4), (5) | 29 Dec 1986 (SI 1986/1924) |
| 236 | (1)–(4) | 1 Feb 1986 (SI 1986/6) |
| | (5) | 29 Dec 1986 (SI 1986/1924) |
| Sch 1 | paras 1–3 | 1 Jul 1986 (SI 1986/840) |
| | para 4(1)–(3) | 1 Jul 1986 (SI 1986/840) |
| | para 4(4) | 1 Jun 1986 (SI 1986/840) |
| | para 4(5) | 1 Jul 1986 (SI 1986/840) |
| | paras 5, 6 | 1 Jul 1986 (SI 1986/840) |
| Sch 2 | | 28 Apr 1986 (SI 1986/463) |
| Schs 3, 4 | | 29 Dec 1986 (SI 1986/1924) |
| Sch 5 | | 1 Feb 1986 (so far as it relates to the making of rules in relation to administrative receivers) (SI 1986/6) |
| | | 1 Mar 1986 (so far as it relates to the making of rules in relation to England and Wales and in relation to Scotland in respect of the matters specified in paras 26, 28–31) (SI 1986/185) |
| | | 29 Dec 1986 (otherwise) (SI 1986/1924) |
| Sch 6 | paras 1–7 | 28 Apr 1986 (SI 1986/463) |
| | paras 8–14 | 29 Dec 1986 (SI 1986/1924) |
| | para 15(1), (2) | 28 Apr 1986 (SI 1986/463) |
| | para 15(3), (4) | 29 Dec 1986 (SI 1986/1924) |
| | paras 16–23 | 29 Dec 1986 (SI 1986/1924) |
| | para 24 | 1 Mar 1986 (so far as relates to the making of rules under s 106 in relation to England and Wales) (SI 1986/185) |
| | | 29 Dec 1986 (otherwise) (SI 1986/1924) |
| | paras 25–52 | 29 Dec 1986 (SI 1986/1924) |
| Sch 7 | | 29 Dec 1986 (SI 1986/1924) |
| Sch 8 | paras 1–26 | 29 Dec 1986 (SI 1986/1924) |
| | para 27 | 1 Apr 1986 (so far as relates to the awarding by a court in Scotland of the sequestration of an individual's estate) (SI 1986/463) |
| | | 29 Dec 1986 (otherwise) (SI 1986/1924) |
| | paras 28–31 | 29 Dec 1986 (SI 1986/1924) |
| | para 32(1)–(3) | 29 Dec 1986 (SI 1986/1924) |
| | para 32(4)(a) | 1 Mar 1986 (so far as it relates to the making of rules under s 106 in relation to England and Wales) (SI 1986/185) |
| | | 29 Dec 1986 (otherwise) (SI 1986/1924) |
| | para 32(4)(b) | 29 Dec 1986 (SI 1986/1924) |
| | paras 33–35 | 29 Dec 1986 (SI 1986/1924) |
| | para 36 | 1 Apr 1986 (SI 1986/185) |

**Insolvency Act 1985 (c 65)**—*contd*

|  |  |  |
|--|--|--|
| | para 37(1)–(3) | 29 Dec 1986 (SI 1986/1924) |
| | para 37(4) | 1 Mar 1986 (so far as relates to the making of rules under s 106 in relation to England and Wales) (SI 1986/185) |
| | | 29 Dec 1986 (otherwise) (SI 1986/1924) |
| | paras 38–40 | 29 Dec 1986 (SI 1986/1924) |
| Sch 9 | para 1 | 29 Dec 1986 (SI 1986/1924) |
| | paras 2–4 | 28 Apr 1986 (SI 1986/463) |
| | paras 5, 6 | 29 Dec 1986 (SI 1986/1924) |
| | paras 7, 8 | 1 Mar 1986 (SI 1986/6) |
| | paras 9–24 | 29 Dec 1986 (SI 1986/1924) |
| Sch 10 | | 1 Mar 1986 (SI 1986/185), repeals in— |

Sch 10 — 1 Mar 1986 (SI 1986/185), repeals in—

Insolvency Act 1976, s 10 (so far as it relates to the making of rules under Companies Act 1985, s 663);

Insolvency Act 1976, s 10(1) so far as the entry repeals reference to Companies Act 1985, s 663 in Insolvency Act 1976, s 10(1)(b);

Insurance Companies Act 1982, s 59 so far as the entries in respect thereof repeal the references therein to Companies Act 1985, s 663 so far as that section applies to the making of general rules in England and Wales;

Companies Act 1985, ss 663, 744 (so far as they relate to the making of general rules in relation to England and Wales);

Companies Consolidation (Consequential Provisions) Act 1985, Sch 2 (entries relating to Banking Act 1979, s 31 so far as the entry repeals reference to Companies Act 1985, s 663 in Banking Act 1979, s 31(7)(a))

1 Apr 1986 (SI 1986/185), repeals of or in—

Bankruptcy (Ireland) Amendment Act 1872, ss 65, 121(7);

Bankruptcy Act 1914, ss 121, 122 (so far as it relates to courts in the United Kingdom acting in aid of and being auxiliary to British courts elsewhere), 123;

Companies Act (Northern Ireland) 1960;

Irish Bankrupt and Insolvent Act 1976;

Criminal Law Act 1977;

Companies Act 1985, s 570

1 Apr 1986 (SI 1986/463), repeals of or in—

Bankruptcy Disqualification Act 1871;

Bankruptcy Act 1883;

Bankruptcy Act 1890;

Recess Elections Act 1975, s 1(2) all so far as they relate to the awarding by a court in Scotland of the sequestration of an individual's estate;

Civil Jurisdiction and Judgements Act 1982

28 Apr 1986 (SI 1986/463), repeals of or in—

Social Security Act 1975, s 152;

Companies Act 1985, s 300, Sch 12

29 Dec 1986 (otherwise) (SI 1986/1924)

---

**Insurance (Fees) Act 1985 (c 46)**

*RA:* 16 Jul 1985

Whole Act in force 16 Jul 1985 (RA)

---

**Interception of Communications Act 1985 (c 56)**

*RA:* 25 Jul 1985

*Commencement provisions:* s 12(2); Interception of Communications Act 1985 (Commencement) Order 1986, SI 1986/384

**Interception of Communications Act 1985 (c 56)**—*contd*
Whole Act in force 10 Apr 1986 (SI 1986/384)

---

**Intoxicating Substances (Supply) Act 1985 (c 26)**

*RA:* 13 Jun 1985

*Commencement provisions:* s 2(2)

Whole Act in force 13 Aug 1985 (s 2(2))

---

**Landlord and Tenant Act 1985 (c 70)**

*RA:* 30 Oct 1985

*Commencement provisions:* s 40(2)

Whole Act in force 1 Apr 1986 (s 40(2))

---

**Law Reform (Miscellaneous Provisions) (Scotland) Act 1985 (c 73)**

*RA:* 30 Oct 1985

*Commencement provisions:* s 60(3), (4); Law Reform (Miscellaneous Provisions) (Scotland) Act 1985 (Commencement No 1) Order 1985, SI 1985/1908; Law Reform (Miscellaneous Provisions) (Scotland) Act 1985 (Commencement No 2) Order 1985, SI 1985/2055; Law Reform (Miscellaneous Provisions) (Scotland) Act 1985 (Commencement No 3) Order 1986, SI 1986/1945; Law Reform (Miscellaneous Provisions) (Scotland) Act 1985 (Commencement No 4) Order 1988, SI 1988/1819

| | | |
|---|---|---|
| 1–13 | | 30 Dec 1985 (s 60(3)) |
| 14, 15 | | 8 Dec 1986 (SI 1986/1945) |
| 16, 17 | | 30 Dec 1985 (s 60(3)) |
| 18 | | 30 Nov 1988 (SI 1988/1819) |
| 19 | | 8 Dec 1986 (SI 1986/1945) |
| 20–25 | | 30 Dec 1985 (s 60(3)) |
| 26–29 | | 30 Oct 1985 (s 60(3)) |
| 30–34 | | 30 Dec 1985 (s 60(3)) |
| 35 | | 1 Jan 1986 (SI 1985/1908) |
| 36 | | 1 Jan 1986 (SI 1985/2055) |
| 37–49 | | 30 Dec 1985 (s 60(3)) |
| 50 | | 1 Feb 1986 (SI 1985/1908) |
| 51–53 | | 30 Dec 1985 (s 60(3)) |
| 54 | | 30 Oct 1985 (s 60(3)) |
| 55–58 | | 30 Dec 1985 (s 60(3)) |
| 59 | (1) | See Sch 2 below |
| | (2) | 30 Dec 1985 (s 60(3)) |
| 60 | | 30 Oct 1985 (s 60(3)) |
| Sch 1 | | 30 Dec 1985 (s 60(3)) |
| Sch 2 | paras 1–7 | 30 Dec 1985 (s 60(3)) |
| | para 8 | 8 Dec 1986 (SI 1986/1945) |
| | paras 9–11 | 30 Dec 1985 (s 60(3)) |
| | paras 12, 13 | 8 Dec 1986 (SI 1986/1945) |
| | paras 14–23 | 30 Dec 1985 (s 60(3)) |
| | para 24 | 8 Dec 1986 (SI 1986/1945) |
| | paras 25–27 | 30 Dec 1985 (s 60(3)) |
| | paras 28–30 | 30 Oct 1985 (s 60(3)) |
| | para 31 | 30 Dec 1985 (s 60(3)) |
| | para 32 | 30 Oct 1985 (s 60(3)) |
| Sch 3 | | 30 Oct 1985 (s 60(3)) |
| Sch 4 | | 30 Dec 1985 (s 60(3)) |

## Licensing (Amendment) Act 1985 (c 40)

*RA:* 16 Jul 1985

Whole Act in force 16 Jul 1985 (RA)

---

## Local Government (Access to Information) Act 1985 (c 43)

*RA:* 16 Jul 1985

*Commencement provisions:* s 5

Whole Act in force 1 Apr 1986 (s 5)

---

## Local Government Act 1985 (c 51)

*RA:* 16 Jul 1985

This Act largely came into force on the date of Royal Assent, but the effective date of operation for many of its provisions (except as otherwise provided) is 1 Apr 1986 (the date of abolition of the Greater London Council and the metropolitan county councils). In addition certain provisions come into force in different areas on dates appointed by order before and after 1 Apr 1986.

---

## London Regional Transport (Amendment) Act 1985 (c 10)

*RA:* 11 Mar 1985

Whole Act in force 11 Mar 1985 (RA)

---

## Milk (Cessation of Production) Act 1985 (c 4)

*RA:* 11 Mar 1985

*Commencement provisions:* s 7(2)

| | |
|---|---|
| 1–5 | 11 May 1985 (s 7(2)) |
| 6 | 11 Mar 1985 (RA) |
| 7 | 11 May 1985 (s 7(2)) |

---

## Mineral Workings Act 1985 (c 12)

*RA:* 27 Mar 1985

*Commencement provisions:* s 11(2)–(4)

| | |
|---|---|
| 1–6 | 1 Apr 1985 (s 11(2)) |
| 7, 8 | 27 May 1985 (s 11(3)) |
| 9, 10 | 1 Apr 1985 (s 11(2)) |
| 11 | 27 Mar 1985 (s 11(4)) |
| Schs 1, 2 | 1 Apr 1985 (s 11(2)) |

---

## Motor-Cycle Crash-Helmets (Restriction of Liability) Act 1985 (c 28)

*RA:* 13 Jun 1985

*Commencement provisions:* s 2(2)

Whole Act in force 13 Aug 1985 (s 2(2))

---

## National Heritage (Scotland) Act 1985 (c 16)

*RA:* 4 Apr 1985

*Commencement provisions:* s 25(1); National Heritage (Scotland) Act 1985 Commencement Order 1985, SI 1985/851

| | | |
|---|---|---|
| 1 | | 4 Jun 1985 (SI 1985/851) |
| 2–5 | | 1 Oct 1985 (SI 1985/851) |
| 6 | (1)–(4) | 1 Oct 1985 (SI 1985/851) |
| | (5)–(7) | 4 Jun 1985 (SI 1985/851) |
| 7–9 | | 1 Oct 1985 (SI 1985/851) |
| 10 | | 4 Jun 1985 (SI 1985/851) |
| 11–15 | | 1 Apr 1986 (SI 1985/851) |
| 16 | | 4 Jun 1985 (SI 1985/851) |
| 17 | | 4 Jun 1985 (so far as adds paras 1–7, 9 of Schedule to National Galleries of Scotland Act 1906) (SI 1985/851) |
| | | 1 Apr 1986 (so far as adds para 8 of that Schedule) (SI 1985/851) |
| 18 | (1)–(5) | 4 Jun 1985 (SI 1985/851) |
| | (6) | 1 Apr 1986 (SI 1985/851) |
| 19 | (1) | 1 Oct 1985 (SI 1985/851) |
| | (2), (3) | 4 Jun 1985 (SI 1985/851) |
| 20–23 | | 4 Jun 1985 (SI 1985/851) |
| 24 | | See Sch 2 below |
| 25 | | 4 Apr 1985 (RA) |
| Sch 1 | Pt I, paras 1–3 | 4 Jun 1985 (SI 1985/851) |
| | Pt I, para 4(1)–(5) | 4 Jun 1985 (SI 1985/851) |
| | Pt I, para 4(6) | 1 Oct 1985 (SI 1985/851) |
| | Pt I, paras 5–10 | 4 Jun 1985 (SI 1985/851) |
| | Pt II, paras 11–21 | 4 Jun 1985 (SI 1985/851) |
| Sch 2 | Pt I, para 1 | 1 Apr 1986 (SI 1985/851) |
| | Pt I, paras 2–4 | 1 Oct 1985 (SI 1985/851) |
| | Pt II | 4 Jun 1985 (repeal of words in National Library of Scotland Act 1925, s 2(f)) (SI 1985/851) |
| | | 1 Oct 1985 (SI 1985/851), repeals of or in— National Gallery and Tate Gallery Act 1954, Sch 1; National Museum of Antiquities of Scotland Act 1954 |
| | | 1 Apr 1986 (repeal of National Library of Scotland Act 1925, s 10) (SI 1985/851) |

## New Towns and Urban Development Corporations Act 1985 (c 5)

*RA:* 11 Mar 1985

*Commencement provisions:* s 15(2)

| | | |
|---|---|---|
| 1–4 | | 11 May 1985 (s 15(2)) |
| 5 | | 11 Mar 1985 (RA) |
| 6–15 | | 11 May 1985 (s 15(2)) |
| Schs 1, 2 | | 11 May 1985 (s 15(2)) |
| Sch 3 | paras 1–6 | 11 May 1985 (s 15(2)) |
| | para 7 | 11 Mar 1985 (RA) |
| | paras 8–16 | 11 May 1985 (s 15(2)) |

## Northern Ireland (Loans) Act 1985 (c 76)

*RA:* 19 Dec 1985

Whole Act in force 19 Dec 1985 (RA)

## Oil and Pipelines Act 1985 (c 62)

*RA:* 30 Oct 1985

*Commencement provisions:* s 8(2), (3); Oil and Pipelines Act 1985 (Commencement) Order 1985, SI 1985/1748; Oil and Pipelines Act 1985 (Appointed Day) Order 1985, SI 1985/1749; British National Oil Corporation (Dissolution) Order 1986, SI 1986/585

| | | |
|---|---|---|
| 1, 2 | | 1 Dec 1985 (SI 1985/1748) |
| 3 | | 1 Dec 1985 (SI 1985/1749) |
| 4–8 | | 1 Dec 1985 (SI 1985/1748) |
| Sch 1 | | 1 Dec 1985 (SI 1985/1748) |
| Sch 2 | | 1 Dec 1985 (SI 1985/1749) |
| Sch 3 | | 1 Dec 1985 (SI 1985/1748) |
| Sch 4 | Pt I | 1 Dec 1985 (SI 1985/1749) |
| | Pt II | 27 Mar 1986 (SI 1986/585) |

## Ports (Finance) Act 1985 (c 30)

*RA:* 26 Jun 1985

*Commencement provisions:* s 7(2); Ports (Finance) Act 1985 (Commencement) Order 1985, SI 1985/1153

| | |
|---|---|
| 1, 2 | 5 Aug 1985 (SI 1985/1153) |
| 3–5 | 1 Jan 1986 (SI 1985/1153) |
| 6, 7 | 5 Aug 1985 (SI 1985/1153) |
| Schedule | 5 Aug 1985 (SI 1985/1153) |

## Prohibition of Female Circumcision Act 1985 (c 38)

*RA:* 16 Jul 1985

*Commencement provisions:* s 4(2)

Whole Act in force 16 Sep 1985 (s 4(2))

## Prosecution of Offences Act 1985 (c 23)

*RA:* 23 May 1985

*Commencement provisions:* s 31(2); Prosecution of Offences Act 1985 (Commencement No 1) Order 1985, SI 1985/1849; Prosecution of Offences Act 1985 (Commencement No 2) Order 1986, SI 1986/1029; Prosecution of Offences Act 1985 (Commencement No 3) Order 1986, SI 1986/1334

| | |
|---|---|
| 1, 2 | 1 Apr 1986 (in the counties of Durham, Greater Manchester, Merseyside, Northumberland, South Yorkshire, Tyne and Wear, West Midlands and West Yorkshire only) (SI 1985/1849) |
| | 1 Oct 1986 (otherwise) (SI 1986/1029) |
| 3 | 1 Apr 1986 (in the counties noted to ss 1, 2 above only; but s 3(2) (a), (c), (d) does not apply in relation to proceedings transferred (whether on appeal or otherwise) to an area where those provisions are in force from an area where they are not) (SI 1985/1849) |
| | 1 Oct 1986 (otherwise) (SI 1986/1029) |
| 4–7 | 1 Apr 1986 (in the counties noted to ss 1, 2 above only) (SI 1985/1849) |
| | 1 Oct 1986 (otherwise) (SI 1986/1029) |
| 8 | 1 Apr 1986 (in the counties noted to ss 1, 2 above only) (SI 1985/1849) |
| | 1 Oct 1986 (otherwise) (SI 1986/1029) |
| 9 | 5 Apr 1987 (SI 1986/1029) |

**Prosecution of Offences Act 1985 (c 23)**—*contd*

| | | |
|---|---|---|
| 10 | | 1 Apr 1986 (in the counties noted to ss 1, 2 above only) (SI 1985/1849) |
| | | 1 Oct 1986 (otherwise) (SI 1986/1029) |
| 11–13 | | 23 May 1985 (s 31(2)) |
| 14 | | 1 Apr 1986 (in the counties noted to ss 1, 2 above only) (SI 1985/1849) |
| | | 1 Oct 1986 (otherwise) (SI 1986/1029) |
| 15 | | 23 May 1985 (so far as applies in relation to ss 11–13) (s 31(2)) |
| | | 1 Oct 1986 (otherwise) (SI 1986/1029) |
| 16–21 | | 1 Oct 1986 (SI 1986/1334) |
| 22 | | 1 Oct 1986 (SI 1986/1029) |
| 23 | | 1 Apr 1986 (in the counties noted to ss 1, 2 above only) (SI 1985/1849) |
| | | 1 Oct 1986 (otherwise) (SI 1986/1029) |
| 24 | | 1 Apr 1986 (SI 1985/1849) |
| 25–27 | | 1 Apr 1986 (in the counties noted to ss 1, 2 above only) (SI 1985/1849) |
| | | 1 Oct 1986 (otherwise) (SI 1986/1029) |
| 28 | | 1 Apr 1986 (SI 1985/1849) |
| 29, 30 | | 23 May 1985 (s 31(2)) |
| 31 | (1)–(4) | 23 May 1985 (s 31(2)) |
| | (5), (6) | 1 Apr 1986 (SI 1985/1849) |
| | (7) | 23 May 1985 (s 31(2)) |
| Sch 1 | paras 1–3 | 1 Apr 1986 (in the counties noted to ss 1, 2 above only) (SI 1985/1849) |
| | | 1 Oct 1986 (otherwise) (SI 1986/1029) |
| | paras 4, 5 | 1 Apr 1986 (SI 1985/1849) |
| | paras 6–10 | 1 Oct 1986 (otherwise) (SI 1986/1334) |
| | para 11 | *Not yet in force* |
| Sch 2 | | 1 Apr 1986 (SI 1985/1849), repeals of or in— |
| | | Perjury Act 1911; |
| | | Administration of Justice (Miscellaneous Provisions) Act 1933; |
| | | Industrial Development Act 1966; |
| | | Transport Act 1968; |
| | | European Communities Act 1972; |
| | | Bail Act 1976; |
| | | Representation of the People Act 1983 |
| | | 1 Apr 1986 (in the counties noted to ss 1, 2 above only) (SI 1985/1849) repeals of or in— |
| | | Prosecution of Offences Act 1979; |
| | | Magistrates' Courts Act 1980, s 25 |
| | | 1 Oct 1986 (in counties other than those noted above) (SI 1986/1029) repeals of or in— |
| | | Prosecution of Offences Act 1979; |
| | | Magistrates' Courts Act 1980, s 25 |
| | | 1 Oct 1986 (SI 1986/1334), repeals of or in— |
| | | Indictments Act 1915; |
| | | Criminal Justice Act 1967; |
| | | Criminal Appeal Act 1968; |
| | | Administration of Justice Act 1970; |
| | | Administration of Justice Act 1973; |
| | | Costs in Criminal Cases Act 1973; |
| | | Magistrates' Courts Act 1980, s 30(3); |
| | | Legal Aid Act 1982 |
| | | *Not yet in force* (repeal in Senior Courts Act 1981, s 77) |

## Rating (Revaluation Rebates) (Scotland) Act 1985 (c 33)

*RA:* 26 Jun 1985

*Commencement provisions:* s 3(1)

Whole Act in force 26 Aug 1985 (s 3(1))

---

## Rent (Amendment) Act 1985 (c 24)

*RA:* 23 May 1985

Whole Act in force 23 May 1985 (RA)

---

## Representation of the People Act 1985 (c 50)

*RA:* 16 Jul 1985

*Commencement provisions:* s 29(2), (3); Representation of the People Act 1985 (Commencement No 1) Order 1985, SI 1985/1185; Representation of the People Act 1985 (Commencement No 2) Order 1986, SI 1986/639; Representation of the People Act 1985 (Commencement No 3) Order 1986, SI 1986/1080; Representation of the People Act 1985 (Commencement No 4) Order 1987, SI 1987/207

| | | |
|---|---|---|
| 1–4 | | 11 Jul 1986 (SI 1986/1080) |
| 5–11 | | 16 Feb 1987 (SI 1986/1080) |
| 12 | (1), (2) | 11 Jul 1986 (SI 1986/1080) |
| | (3) | 16 Feb 1987 (SI 1986/1080) |
| | (4) | 11 Jul 1986 (SI 1986/1080) |
| 13, 14 | | 1 Oct 1985 (SI 1985/1185) |
| 15, 16 | | 16 Feb 1987 (SI 1986/1080) |
| 17 | | 1 Sep 1985 (SI 1985/1185) |
| 18 | | 1 Oct 1985 (SI 1985/1185) |
| 19 | (1)–(5) | 16 Feb 1987 (SI 1986/1080) |
| | (6)(a) | 1 Oct 1985 (SI 1985/1185) |
| | (6)(b), (c) | 16 Feb 1987 (SI 1986/1080) |
| 20 | | 1 Oct 1985 (SI 1985/1185) |
| 21 | | 16 Feb 1987 (SI 1986/1080) |
| 22–24 | | 1 Oct 1985 (SI 1985/1185) |
| 25 | (1) | 16 Jul 1985 (s 29(3)) |
| | (2) | 1 Oct 1985 (SI 1985/1185) |
| 26 | | 1 Oct 1985 (SI 1985/1185) |
| 27 | (1) | 16 Jul 1985 (s 29(3)) |
| | (2), (3) | 1 Oct 1985 (SI 1985/1185) |
| 28 | | 1 Oct 1985 (SI 1985/1185) |
| 29 | | 16 Jul 1985 (s 29(3)) |
| Sch 1 | | *Not yet in force* (para 7(2) repealed) |
| Sch 2 | | 16 Feb 1987 (SI 1986/1080) |
| Sch 3 | | 1 Oct 1985 (SI 1985/1185) |
| Sch 4 | paras 1–6 | 1 Oct 1985 (SI 1985/1185) |
| | para 7 | 16 Feb 1987 (SI 1986/1080) |
| | para 8 | 1 Oct 1985 (SI 1985/1185) |
| | para 9 | 16 Feb 1987 (SI 1986/1080) |
| | paras 10–17 | 1 Oct 1985 (SI 1985/1185) |
| | para 18 | 16 Jul 1985 (s 29(3)) |
| | paras 19–33 | 1 Oct 1985 (SI 1985/1185) |
| | para 34 | 30 Mar 1987 (except for the purposes of an election, notice of which is published before that date) (SI 1987/207) |
| | paras 35–68 | 1 Oct 1985 (SI 1985/1185) |
| | para 69 | 21 Apr 1986 (SI 1986/639) |
| | paras 70–72 | 1 Oct 1985 (SI 1985/1185) |

**Representation of the People Act 1985 (c 50)**—*contd*

| | | |
|---|---|---|
| | para 73 | 16 Feb 1987 (SI 1986/1080) |
| | paras 74–78 | 1 Oct 1985 (SI 1985/1185) |
| | paras 79, 80 | 16 Feb 1987 (SI 1986/1080) |
| | paras 81–83 | 1 Oct 1985 (SI 1985/1185) |
| | paras 84–86 | 16 Feb 1987 (SI 1986/1080) |
| | paras 87–90 | 1 Oct 1985 (SI 1985/1185) |

Sch 5  16 Jul 1985 (repeals in Police and Criminal Evidence Act 1984) (s 29(3))

1 Oct 1985 (SI 1985/1185), repeals of or in—
Meeting of Parliament Act 1797, ss 3–5;
Representation of the People Act 1918;
Local Government Act 1972, s 243(3);
Representation of the People Act 1983, ss 18(2)(b), (6)(b), 39(8), 49(1)(d), (2)(c), 51, 52(2), 53(2), 55, 56(1)(c), (6), 76(3), 103(2), 104(b), 106(4), 108(3), (4), 124(a), (b), 125(a), 126(3), 136(4), (5), (7), 140(5), (7), 141(3), (4), 142, 148(4)(a), 156(2)–(4), 161, 162, 163(1)(b), 168(5), (6), 169, 171, 172, 173(a), 176(1), (3), 181(3), (6), 187(1), 190, 191(1)(a), 192, 196, 199, 202(1), 203(4)(a), Sch 1, rr 5(1), 23(2)(c), (3), Appendix of Forms, Sch 2, para 9, Sch 7, paras 8, 9

16 Feb 1987 (SI 1986/1080), repeals of or in—
City of London (Various Powers) Act 1957;
Representation of the People Act 1983, ss 19–22, 32–34, 38, 40(1), 43(2)(b), 44, 49(3), 61, Sch 1, rr 2(3), 27, 40(1)(b), Sch 2, para 5(4), Sch 8

*Not yet in force* (repeals of or in Representation of the People Act 1983, s 160, Sch 1, r 5(3))

**Reserve Forces (Safeguard of Employment) Act 1985 (c 17)**

*RA:* 9 May 1985

*Commencement provisions:* s 23(3)

Whole Act in force 9 Aug 1985 (s 23(3))

**Road Traffic (Production of Documents) Act 1985 (c 34)**

*RA:* 16 Jul 1985

*Commencement provisions:* s 2(2)

Whole Act in force 16 Sep 1985 (s 2(2))

**Sexual Offences Act 1985 (c 44)**

*RA:* 16 Jul 1985

*Commencement provisions:* s 5(4)

Whole Act in force 16 Sep 1985 (s 5(4))

**Shipbuilding Act 1985 (c 14)**

*RA:* 27 Mar 1985

Whole Act in force 27 Mar 1985 (RA)

## Social Security Act 1985 (c 53)

*RA:* 22 Jul 1985

*Commencement provisions:* s 32; Social Security Act 1985 (Commencement No 1) Order 1985, SI 1985/1125; Social Security Act 1985 (Commencement No 2) Order 1985, SI 1985/1364

| | | |
|---|---|---|
| 1, 2 | | 1 Jan 1986 (SI 1985/1364) |
| 3 | | See Sch 2 below |
| 4 | | See Sch 3 below |
| 5 | | 1 Jan 1986 (SI 1985/1364) |
| 6 | (1)–(4) | 1 Jan 1986 (SI 1985/1364) |
| | (5), (6) | 22 Jul 1985 (s 32(2)) |
| 7 | | 6 Oct 1985 (SI 1985/1125) |
| 8 | | 22 Jul 1985 (s 32(2)) |
| 9 | | 16 Sep 1985 (SI 1985/1125) |
| 10, 11 | | 22 Jul 1985 (s 32(2)) |
| 12 | | 25 Nov 1985 (SI 1985/1125) |
| 13 | (1)–(5) | 16 Sep 1985 (SI 1985/1125) |
| | (6), (7) | 22 Jul 1985 (s 32(2)) |
| | (8) | 16 Sep 1985 (SI 1985/1125) |
| 14 | | 4 Nov 1985 (SI 1985/1364) |
| 15 | | 22 Jul 1985 (s 32(2)) |
| 16 | | 16 Sep 1985 (SI 1985/1125) |
| 17 | | *Never in force* (repealed) |
| 18 | | 6 Apr 1986 (s 32(5)) |
| 19 | | 22 Jul 1985 (s 32(2)) |
| 20 | | 6 Apr 1986 (s 32(5)) |
| 21 | | See Sch 4 below |
| 22 | (1)(a) | 6 Oct 1985 (SI 1985/1364) |
| | (1)(b), (c) | 22 Jul 1985 (s 32(2)) |
| | (2) | 22 Jul 1985 (s 32(2)) |
| 23–28 | | 22 Jul 1985 (s 32(2)) |
| 29 | (1) | See Sch 5 below |
| | (2) | See Sch 6 below |
| 30–33 | | 22 Jul 1985 (s 32(2)) |
| Sch 1 | | 1 Jan 1986 (SI 1985/1364) |
| Sch 2 | | 1 Jan 1986 (insertion in Social Security Pensions Act 1985 of ss 56A, 56E(1) (except para (c)), (2)–(8), 56L(1) (except the words "or (c)" in para (a), and para (b)), (2)–(4), (5)(a), (c) (except so far as it applies to the registrar), (d), (6)–(8)) (SI 1985/1364) |
| | | *Never in force* (otherwise) (repealed) |
| Sch 3 | Pt I | 22 Jul 1985 (s 32(2)) |
| | Pt II | 1 Jan 1986 (SI 1985/1364) |
| Sch 4 | paras 1, 2 | 16 Sep 1985 (SI 1985/1125) |
| | para 3 | 6 Apr 1985 (SI 1985/1125) |
| | paras 4, 5 | 16 Sep 1985 (SI 1985/1125) |
| | para 6 | 6 Apr 1985 (SI 1985/1125) |
| | para 7 | 16 Sep 1985 (SI 1985/1125) |
| Sch 5 | paras 1–4 | 1 Jan 1986 (SI 1985/1364) |
| | paras 5, 6 | 6 Oct 1985 (SI 1985/1125) |
| | paras 7, 8 | 5 Aug 1985 (s 32(3)) |
| | para 9 | 6 Oct 1985 (SI 1985/1125) |
| | para 10 | 16 Sep 1985 (SI 1985/1125) |
| | paras 11–13 | 6 Oct 1985 (SI 1985/1125) |
| | para 14 | 5 Aug 1985 (s 32(3)) |
| | paras 15–17 | 6 Oct 1985 (SI 1985/1125) |
| | paras 18–21 | 1 Jan 1986 (SI 1985/1364) |
| | para 22 | 22 Jul 1985 (s 32(2)) |
| | paras 23, 24 | 1 Jan 1986 (SI 1985/1364) |
| | para 25 | 6 Apr 1986 (SI 1985/1364) |

**Social Security Act 1985 (c 53)**—*contd*

| | | |
|---|---|---|
| | para 26 | 6 Oct 1985 (SI 1985/1364) |
| | para 27 | 1 Jan 1986 (SI 1985/1364) |
| | para 28 | 5 Aug 1985 (s 32(3)) |
| | para 29 | 6 Oct 1985 (SI 1985/1364) |
| | paras 30–32 | 1 Jan 1986 (SI 1985/1364) |
| | para 33 | 6 Oct 1985 (SI 1985/1364) |
| | para 34 | 22 Jul 1985 (s 32(2)) |
| | para 35 | *Never in force* (repealed) |
| | paras 36, 37 | 22 Jul 1985 (s 32(2)) |
| | para 38 | 6 Apr 1986 (SI 1985/1364) |
| | para 39 | 6 Oct 1985 (SI 1985/1125) |
| | para 40 | 6 Oct 1985 (SI 1985/1364) |

Sch 6   22 Jul 1985 (s 32(2)), repeals of or in—
Social Security Pensions Act 1975, s 41D;
Social Security (Miscellaneous Provisions) Act 1977, s 22(7);
Social Security Act 1981;
Health and Social Security Act 1984
23 Jul 1985 (SI 1985/1125), repeals of or in—
Social Security Act 1975, s 28(2);
Social Security Act 1979, Sch 1, para 11
5 Aug 1985 (repeals of or in Social Security Act 1975, ss 79, 82, 90) (s 32(3))
16 Sep 1985 (SI 1985/1125; SI 1985/1364), repeals of or in—
Social Security Act 1975, ss 5(3), (4), 125(1), 126A(1);
Social Security (Miscellaneous Provisions) Act 1977, s 5(1);
Social Security and Housing Benefits Act 1982, s 24, Sch 2, paras 7–11
6 Oct 1985 (SI 1985/1125; SI 1985/1364), repeals of or in—
Social Security Pensions Act 1975, ss 41B(4), 59(5)(b), Sch 4, para 36(b);
Social Security (Contributions) Act 1982, s 1(5), Sch 1, para 1(3)
25 Nov 1985 (repeals of or in Social Security Act 1975, s 39(2), Sch 4, Pt III, para 5) (SI 1985/1125)
1 Jan 1986 (SI 1985/1364), repeals of or in—
Social Security Act 1973, Sch 16, para 6(1)(a);
Social Security Pensions Act 1975, ss 26(2), 34(4), 41A(4)(i), 66;
Social Security (Miscellaneous Provisions) Act 1977, s 22(9)–(11);
Social Security Act 1980, s 3(6), (7)
6 Apr 1986 (remaining repeals in Social Security and Housing Benefits Act 1982) (SI 1985/1125)

**Sporting Events (Control of Alcohol etc) Act 1985 (c 57)**

*RA:* 25 Jul 1985

Whole Act in force 25 Jul 1985 (RA)

**Surrogacy Arrangements Act 1985 (c 49)**

*RA:* 16 Jul 1985

Whole Act in force 16 Jul 1985 (RA)

**Town and Country Planning (Amendment) Act 1985 (c 52)**

*RA:* 22 Jul 1985

*Commencement provisions:* s 3(3)

**Town and Country Planning (Amendment) Act 1985 (c 52)**—*contd*

Whole Act in force 22 Sep 1985 (s 3(3))

---

**Town and Country Planning (Compensation) Act 1985 (c 19)**

*RA:* 9 May 1985

Whole Act in force 9 May 1985 (RA)

---

**Transport Act 1985 (c 67)**

*RA:* 30 Oct 1985

*Commencement provisions:* s 140(2); Transport Act 1985 (Commencement No 1) Order 1985, SI 1985/1887; Transport Act 1985 (Commencement No 2) Order 1986, SI 1986/80; Transport Act 1985 (Commencement No 3) Order 1986, SI 1986/414; Transport Act 1985 (Commencement No 4) Order 1986, SI 1986/1088; Transport Act 1985 (Commencement No 5) Order 1986, SI 1986/1450; Transport Act 1985 (Commencement No 6) Order 1986, SI 1986/1794, as amended by SI 1988/2294; Transport Act 1985 (Commencement No 7) Order 1987, SI 1987/1228

| | | |
|---|---|---|
| 1 | (1), (2) | 26 Oct 1986 (SI 1986/1794) |
| | (3) | See Sch 1 below |
| 2, 3 | | 6 Jan 1986 (SI 1985/1887) |
| 4 | | 6 Jan 1986 (to the extent necessary to replace Public Passenger Vehicles Act 1981, s 54 with sub-ss (1), (2) only of the new s 54) (SI 1985/1887) |
| | | 26 Oct 1986 (otherwise) (SI 1986/1794) |
| 5 | | 6 Jan 1986 (SI 1985/1887) |
| 6 | | 26 Oct 1986 (SI 1986/1794) |
| 7–9 | | 14 Jul 1986 (SI 1986/1088) |
| 10, 11 | | 1 Aug 1986 (SI 1986/1088) |
| 12 | | 6 Jan 1986 (SI 1985/1887) |
| 13 | | 6 Jan 1986 (to the extent that it supplements s 12 of this Act) (SI 1985/1887) |
| | | 1 Aug 1986 (otherwise) (SI 1986/1088) |
| 14, 15 | | 1 Jan 1987 (SI 1986/1794) |
| 16 | | 6 Jan 1986 (SI 1985/1887) |
| 17 | | 1 Aug 1986 (SI 1986/1088) |
| 18 | | 1 Aug 1986 (so far as relates to the use of any vehicle under a permit granted under s 22 or the driving of any vehicle so used) (SI 1986/1088) |
| | | 13 Aug 1987 (otherwise) (SI 1987/1228) |
| 19–21 | | 13 Aug 1987 (SI 1987/1228) |
| 22, 23 | | 1 Aug 1986 (SI 1986/1088) |
| 24–28 | | 26 Oct 1986 (SI 1986/1794) |
| 29, 30 | | 6 Jan 1986 (SI 1985/1887) |
| 31 | | 15 Sep 1986 (SI 1986/1450) |
| 32 | | 6 Jan 1986 (to the extent that it applies to Public Passenger Vehicles Act 1981, s 28) (SI 1985/1887) |
| | | 26 Oct 1986 (otherwise) (SI 1986/1794) |
| 33 | | 1 Aug 1986 (SI 1986/1088) |
| 34 | | 6 Jan 1986 (SI 1985/1887) |
| 35–46 | | 26 Oct 1986 (SI 1986/1794) |
| 47–56 | | 6 Jan 1986 (SI 1985/1887) |
| 57 | (1)–(5) | 6 Jan 1986 (SI 1985/1887) |
| | (6) | See Sch 3 below |
| 58 | | 30 Oct 1985 (s 140(2)) |
| 59–84 | | 6 Jan 1986 (SI 1985/1887) |
| 85, 86 | | 13 Aug 1987 (SI 1987/1228) |
| 87–92 | | 6 Jan 1986 (SI 1985/1887) |

**Transport Act 1985 (c 67)**—*contd*

| | | |
|---|---|---|
| 93 | (1)–(7) | 14 Feb 1986 (SI 1986/80) |
| | (8)(a) | 14 Feb 1986 (SI 1986/80) |
| | (8)(b) | 1 Apr 1986 (SI 1986/414) |
| | (9), (10) | 14 Feb 1986 (SI 1986/80) |
| 94–101 | | 14 Feb 1986 (SI 1986/80) |
| 102 | | 1 Apr 1986 (SI 1986/414) |
| 103 | | 14 Feb 1986 (SI 1986/80) |
| 104 | | 15 Sep 1986 (SI 1986/1450) |
| 105 | | 14 Feb 1986 (SI 1986/80) |
| 106 | | 6 Jan 1986 (SI 1985/1887) |
| 107 | | 1 Apr 1986 (SI 1985/1887) |
| 108, 109 | | 1 Apr 1986 (SI 1986/414) |
| 110 | | 6 Jan 1986 (SI 1985/1887) |
| 111 | | 26 Oct 1986 (SI 1986/1794) |
| 112, 113 | | 6 Jan 1986 (SI 1985/1887) |
| 114, 115 | | 26 Jul 1986 (SI 1986/1088) |
| 116 | (1) | 1 Apr 1986 (SI 1986/414) |
| | (2), (3) | 26 Jul 1986 (SI 1986/1088) |
| 117 | | 15 Sep 1986 (SI 1986/1450) |
| 118–125 | | 6 Jan 1986 (SI 1985/1887) |
| 126 | (1), (2) | 1 Aug 1986 (so far as relate to fees chargeable in respect of applications for, and the grant of, permits under s 22) (SI 1986/1088) |
| | | 26 Oct 1986 (otherwise, except so far as sub-s (1) relates to applications for and the grant of permits under s 19) (SI 1986/1794) |
| | | 13 Aug 1987 (otherwise) (SI 1987/1228) |
| | (3)(a) | 26 Oct 1986 (SI 1986/1794) |
| | (3)(b) | 14 Jul 1986 (SI 1986/1088) |
| | (3)(c) | 26 Oct 1986 (SI 1986/1794) |
| 127 | (1), (2) | 1 Aug 1986 (SI 1986/1088) |
| | (3) | 6 Jan 1986 (SI 1985/1887) |
| | (4) | 6 Jan 1986 (so far as relates to s 30(2)) (SI 1985/1887) |
| | | 1 Aug 1986 (so far as relates to s 23(5)) (SI 1986/1088) |
| | | 26 Oct 1986 (otherwise) (SI 1986/1794) |
| | (5)–(7) | 6 Jan 1986 (SI 1985/1887) |
| 128–138 | | 6 Jan 1986 (SI 1985/1887) |
| 139 | (1)–(3) | See Schs 6–8 below |
| | (4), (5) | 6 Jan 1986 (SI 1985/1887) |
| 140 | | 30 Oct 1985 (s 140(2)) |
| Sch 1 | paras 1, 2 | 6 Jan 1986 (SI 1985/1887) |
| | para 3(1), (2) | 6 Jan 1986 (SI 1985/1887) |
| | para 3(3) | 26 Oct 1986 (SI 1986/1794) |
| | para 3(4) | 6 Jan 1986 (except omission of words "or Part III") (SI 1985/1887) |
| | | 26 Oct 1986 (exception noted above) (SI 1986/1794) |
| | para 3(5) | 6 Jan 1986 (SI 1985/1887) |
| | paras 4–6 | 6 Jan 1986 (SI 1985/1887) |
| | paras 7–11 | 26 Oct 1986 (SI 1986/1794) |
| | para 12 | 6 Jan 1986 (SI 1985/1887) |
| | para 13 | 6 Jan 1986 (except omission of definitions "excursion or tour", "road service licence" and "trial area") (SI 1985/1887) |
| | | 26 Oct 1986 (exceptions noted above) (SI 1986/1794) |
| | para 14 | 6 Jan 1986 (SI 1985/1887) |
| | para 15(1) | 6 Jan 1986 (SI 1985/1887) |
| | para 15(2), (3) | 26 Oct 1986 (SI 1986/1794) |
| | para 15(4), (5) | 6 Jan 1986 (SI 1985/1887) |
| | para 16 | 6 Jan 1986 (SI 1985/1887) |
| Sch 2 | | 6 Jan 1986 (SI 1985/1887) |
| Sch 3 | paras 1–7 | 6 Jan 1986 (SI 1985/1887) |

**Transport Act 1985 (c 67)**—*contd*

| | | |
|---|---|---|
| | para 8 | 1 Apr 1986 (SI 1986/414) |
| | paras 9–23 | 6 Jan 1986 (SI 1985/1887) |
| | para 24 | 6 Jan 1986 (to the extent that it relates to Local Government Act 1972, s 202(1), (4)–(7)) (SI 1985/1887) |
| | | 1 Apr 1986 (otherwise) (SI 1986/414) |
| | para 25 | 6 Jan 1986 (SI 1985/1887) |
| | para 26 | 1 Apr 1986 (SI 1986/414) |
| | paras 27–33 | 6 Jan 1986 (SI 1985/1887) |
| Sch 4 | | 15 Sep 1986 (SI 1986/1450) |
| Sch 5 | | 6 Jan 1986 (SI 1985/1887) |
| Sch 6 | paras 1–11 | 6 Jan 1986 (SI 1985/1887) |
| | para 12 | 30 Oct 1985 (s 140(2)) |
| | para 13 | 6 Jan 1986 (SI 1985/1887) |
| | para 14 | 26 Oct 1986 (SI 1986/1794) |
| | para 15 | 6 Jan 1986 (SI 1985/1887) |
| | paras 16–18 | 26 Oct 1986 (SI 1986/1794) |
| | paras 19–21 | 6 Jan 1986 (SI 1985/1887) |
| | paras 22, 23 | 14 Feb 1986 (SI 1986/80) (also purportedly brought into force, so far as not already in force, by SI 1986/414) |
| | paras 24, 25 | 15 Sep 1986 (SI 1986/1450) |
| | para 26 | 6 Jan 1986 (SI 1985/1887) |
| Sch 7 | para 1 | 6 Jan 1986 (SI 1985/1887) |
| | para 2 | 1 Aug 1986 (SI 1986/1088) |
| | para 3 | 1 Apr 1986 (SI 1986/414) |
| | para 4 | 6 Jan 1986 (SI 1985/1887) |
| | para 5 | 26 Oct 1986 (SI 1986/1794) |
| | para 6 | 6 Jan 1986 (SI 1985/1887) |
| | paras 7, 8 | 15 Sep 1986 (SI 1986/1450) |
| | para 9 | 1 Apr 1986 (SI 1986/414) |
| | paras 10–14 | 6 Jan 1986 (SI 1985/1887) |
| | para 15 | 15 Sep 1986 (SI 1986/1450) |
| | para 16 | 26 Oct 1986 (SI 1986/1794) |
| | para 17 | 1 Apr 1986 (SI 1986/414) |
| | para 18 | 6 Jan 1986 (SI 1985/1887) |
| | para 19 | 1 Apr 1986 (SI 1986/414) |
| | para 20 | 6 Jan 1986 (SI 1985/1887) |
| | para 21(1) | 6 Jan 1986 (SI 1985/1887) |
| | para 21(2) | 1 Aug 1986 (SI 1986/1088) |
| | para 21(3) | 15 Sep 1986 (SI 1986/1450) |
| | para 21(4) | 6 Jan 1986 (except words "sub-section (1A) below and") (SI 1985/1887) |
| | | 26 Oct 1986 (exception noted above) (SI 1986/1794) |
| | para 21(5) | 26 Oct 1986 (SI 1986/1794) |
| | para 21(6)–(8) | 6 Jan 1986 (SI 1985/1887) |
| | para 21(9), (10) | 26 Oct 1986 (SI 1986/1794) |
| | para 21(11) | 15 Sep 1986 (SI 1986/1450) |
| | para 21(12) | 6 Jan 1986 (SI 1985/1887) |
| | para 22 | 1 Apr 1986 (SI 1986/414) |
| | para 23 | 6 Jan 1986 (SI 1985/1887) |
| | para 24 | 1 Apr 1986 (SI 1986/414) |
| | paras 25, 26 | 26 Oct 1986 (SI 1986/1794) |
| Sch 8 | | 6 Jan 1986 (SI 1985/1887), repeals of or in— |
| | | Road Traffic Act 1930; |
| | | Transport Act 1962, ss 4, 92; |
| | | Finance Act 1965; |
| | | Transport Act 1968, ss 9, 10(2), 11(1), 12(3)(d), 14(3), 15, 15(A)(1), 16(2), 17–22, 24(3), 29(4), 34, 36, 54, 59(3), 90, 103(1), 159(1), Sch 5; |
| | | Post Office Act 1969; |

**Transport Act 1985 (c 67)**—*contd*

|  |  |
|---|---|
|  | Local Government Act 1972, ss 80(4), 202, Sch 24, Pt II; |
|  | Local Government Act 1974; |
|  | Energy Act 1976, Sch 1, para 1(2); |
|  | Transport Act 1978; |
|  | Transport Act 1980; |
|  | Public Passenger Vehicles Act 1981, ss 1, 2, 28, 46, 53(1) (word "the" before words "traffic commissioners"), 56, 60, 61(2), 62, 81(2), 82(1) (definitions "contract carriage", "express carriage", "express carriage service", "stage carriage" and "stage carriage service"), 83, Sch 1, paras 3, 4; |
|  | Transport Act 1982, s 73(4); |
|  | Transport Act 1983, s 9(2); |
|  | London Regional Transport Act 1984, s 28, Sch 6, paras 3, 6; |
|  | Road Traffic Regulation Act 1984, Sch 13, para 49 |

1 Apr 1986 (SI 1986/414), repeals of or in—
Finance Act 1970;
Local Government Act 1972, s 202(2), (3);
Local Government (Scotland) Act 1973, s 150;
Transport Act 1983, s 3;
Local Government Act 1985
26 Jul 1986 (repeal of London Regional Transport Act 1984, Sch 6, para 15(1)(a)) (SI 1986/1088)
15 Sep 1986 (SI 1986/1450), repeals of or in—
Transport Act 1962, s 57, Sch 10;
Transport Act 1968, s 88, Sch 10
26 Oct 1986 (SI 1986/1794) (otherwise), except those repeals of or in—
Town Police Clauses Act 1847 (repealed);
Public Passenger Vehicles Act 1981, ss 42–44, 52, 67, 76 (words "except sections 42 to 44" and word "thereof")
13 Aug 1987 (otherwise, except repeal of words "such number of" and "as they think fit" in Town Police Clauses Act 1847, s 37 (repealed)) (SI 1987/1228)

---

**Trustee Savings Banks Act 1985 (c 58)**

*RA:* 25 Jul 1985

*Commencement provisions:* ss 1(4), 2(4), 4(3)–(5), 7(2), Sch 1, Pt III, para 13; Trustee Savings Banks Act 1985 (Appointed Day) (No 1) Order 1985, SI 1986/1219; Trustee Savings Banks Act 1985 (Appointed Day) (No 2) Order 1986, SI 1986/1220; Trustee Savings Banks Act 1985 (Appointed Day) (No 3) Order 1986, SI 1986/1222; Trustee Savings Banks Act 1985 (Appointed Day) (No 4) Order 1986, SI 1986/1223; Trustee Savings Banks Act 1985 (Appointed Day) (No 6) Order 1988, SI 1988/1168; Trustee Savings Banks Act 1985 (Appointed Day) (No 7) Order 1990, SI 1990/1982 (*Note:* No (Appointed Day) (No 5) Order was made)

| | | |
|---|---|---|
| 1–7 | | 25 Sep 1985 (s 7(2)) (but note 21 Jul 1986 was the vesting day appointed under s 1(4) (SI 1986/1222); 31 Oct 1990 was the day appointed under s 2(4) on which the Trustee Savings Bank Central Board ceased to exist (SI 1990/1982)) |
| Sch 1 | paras 1–11 | 25 Sep 1985 (s 7(2)) |
| | para 12 | 25 Sep 1985 (s 7(2) but this paragraph never had any effect) |
| | para 13 | 20 Jul 1986 (SI 1986/1219) |
| Schs 2, 3 | | 25 Sep 1985 (s 7(2)) |
| Sch 4 | | 20 Jul 1986 (SI 1986/1220), repeals of or in— |
| | | Finance Act 1921; |
| | | Finance Act 1946; |
| | | Finance Act 1969; |
| | | National Savings Bank Act 1971; |

**Trustee Savings Banks Act 1985 (c 58)**—*contd*
Trustee Savings Banks Act 1981, Sch 7, para 10, para 12(a)
(words "4 to 7")
21 Jul 1986 (SI 1986/1223), repeals of or in—
Bankers' Books Evidence Act 1879;
Consolidated Fund (Permanent Charges Redemption) Act 1883;
Savings Banks Act 1887;
Bankruptcy Act 1914;
Agricultural Credits Act 1928;
Agricultural Credits (Scotland) Act 1929;
Government Annuities Act 1929;
Companies Act (Northern Ireland) 1960;
Payment of Wages Act 1960;
Clergy Pensions Measure 1961;
Trustee Investments Act 1961;
Building Societies Act 1962;
Administration of Estates (Small Payments) Act 1965;
Building Societies Act (Northern Ireland) 1967;
Friendly Societies Act (Northern Ireland) 1970;
Payment of Wages Act (Northern Ireland) 1970;
Northern Ireland Constitution Act 1973;
Friendly Societies Act 1974;
Pensions (Increase) Act 1974;
Solicitors Act 1974;
Financial Provisions (Northern Ireland) Order 1976;
Home Purchase Assistance and Housing Corporation Guarantee
Act 1978;
Banking Act 1979;
Credit Unions Act 1979, s 31(1)(b) in definition "authorised
bank";
Solicitors (Scotland) Act 1980;
British Telecommunications Act 1981;
Trustee Savings Banks Act 1981, ss 1, 2, 3(1), (2), 4, 5, 6(1),
7(3), (5), (6), 8–11, 13 (words "to the Central Board and" and
", and shall furnish such particulars of that person as the
Central Board may direct"), 14, 15(1)–(8), (11), 16(1), (3), (4),
17, 18, 19(1)–(4), 20–22, 25(1) (the words "to the Central
Board and"), (2), 26–50, 52, 55(1), (3), Schs 1, 2, paras 1(a),
(c), (3), (4), 4, 11, 13–16, Schs 4, 6, Sch 7, paras 5–8, 9(1), 11,
12, (so far as unrepealed), 13–15, Sch 8;
Housing (Northern Ireland) Order 1981;
Companies (Northern Ireland) Order 1982;
Companies Act 1985
5 Jul 1988 (SI 1988/1168), repeal of—
Trustee Savings Banks Act 1981, ss 12, 13 (so far as unrepealed),
23, 24, 25 (so far as unrepealed), 51, 53, Schs 3, 5, Sch 7,
para 9(2);
Insolvency Act 1986, s 220(3)
31 Oct 1990 (repeal of Trustee Savings Banks Act 1981, ss 3(3),
6(2), 7(1), (2), (4), 15(9), (10), 16(2), 19(5), 54, 55(2), (4), 56,
57, Sch 2 (so far as unrepealed), Sch 7, paras 1–4) (SI 1990/1982)

**Water (Fluoridation) Act 1985 (c 63)**

*RA:* 30 Oct 1985

Whole Act in force 30 Oct 1985 (RA)

**Weights and Measures Act 1985 (c 72)**

*RA:* 30 Oct 1985

*Commencement provisions:* ss 43(2), 99(2); Weights and Measures Act 1985 (Commencement) Order 1992, SI 1992/770 (revoked); Weights and Measures Act 1985 (Revocation) Order 1993, SI 1993/2698 (revoked Weights and Measures Act 1985 (Commencement) Order 1992, SI 1992/770, which appointed 1 Apr 1994 as the date on which s 43 was to come into force)

| | |
|---|---|
| 1–42 | 30 Jan 1986 (s 99(2)) |
| 43 | *Never in force* (repealed) |
| 44–99 | 30 Jan 1986 (s 99(2)) |
| Schs 1–13 | 30 Jan 1986 (s 99(2)) |

**Wildlife and Countryside (Amendment) Act 1985 (c 31)**

*RA:* 26 Jun 1985

*Commencement provisions:* s 5(3)

Whole Act in force 26 Aug 1985 (s 5(3))

**Wildlife and Countryside (Service of Notices) Act 1985 (c 59)**

*RA:* 25 Jul 1985

Whole Act in force 25 Jul 1985 (RA)

# 1986 Acts

## Advance Petroleum Revenue Tax Act 1986 (c 68)

*RA:* 18 Dec 1986

Whole Act in force 18 Dec 1986 (RA). Note that Petroleum Revenue Tax (levied in accordance with Oil Taxation Act 1975, Pt I (ss 1–12, Schs 1–8)) abolished for new oil and gas fields ("non-taxable fields") with effect from 16 Mar 1993, by Finance Act 1993, s 185

## Agricultural Holdings Act 1986 (c 5)

*RA:* 18 Mar 1986

*Commencement provisions:* s 102(2)

Whole Act in force 18 Jun 1986 (s 102(2)). Note that by virtue of Agricultural Tenancies Act 1995, s 4, this Act does not apply in relation to any tenancy beginning on or after 1 Sep 1995, with the exception of specified tenancies of an agricultural holding

## Agriculture Act 1986 (c 49)

*RA:* 25 Jul 1986

*Commencement provisions:* s 24(2), (3); Agriculture Act 1986 (Commencement) (No 1) Order 1986, SI 1986/1484; Agriculture Act 1986 (Commencement) (No 2) (Scotland) Order 1986, SI 1986/1485; Agriculture Act 1986 (Commencement No 3) Order 1986, SI 1986/1596; Agriculture Act 1986 (Commencement No 4) Order 1986, SI 1986/2301; Agriculture Act 1986 (Commencement No 5) Order 1991, SI 1991/2635; Agriculture Act 1986 (Commencement No 6) Order 1998, SI 1998/879

| | | |
|---|---|---|
| 1–7 | | 25 Sep 1986 (s 24(2)) |
| 8 | (1) | *Never in force* (repealed) |
| | (2) | 8 Sep 1986 (SI 1986/1596) |
| | (3) | *Never in force* (repealed) |
| | (4)–(6) | 1 Apr 1998 (SI 1998/879) |
| 9 | | 25 Sep 1986 (s 24(2)) |
| 10 | | 31 Dec 1986 (SI 1986/2301) |
| 11 | | 25 Sep 1986 (s 24(2)) |
| 12 | | 25 Jul 1986 (RA) |
| 13 | | 25 Sep 1986 (SI 1986/1484) |
| 14 | | 25 Sep 1986 (SI 1986/1485) |
| 15 | | 25 Sep 1986 (SI 1986/1484) |
| 16 | | 25 Sep 1986 (SI 1986/1485) |
| 17 | | 25 Sep 1986 (s 24(2)) |
| 18 | (1)–(12) | 25 Sep 1986 (s 24(2)) |
| | (13) | 25 Jul 1986 (RA) |
| 19–24 | | 25 Sep 1986 (s 24(2)) |
| Sch 1 | | 25 Sep 1986 (SI 1986/1484) |
| Sch 2 | | 25 Sep 1986 (SI 1986/1485) |
| Sch 3 | | 25 Sep 1986 (s 24(2)) |
| Sch 4 | | 25 Sep 1986 (except repeals consequential on ss 8–10) (s 24(2)) |

**Agriculture Act 1986 (c 49)**—*contd*

> 31 Dec 1986 (repeals consequential on ss 9, 10) (SI 1986/2301)
> 21 Nov 1991 (SI 1991/2635), repeals in—
>   House of Commons Disqualification Act 1975;
>   Northern Ireland Assembly Disqualification Act 1975
> 1 Apr 1998 (repeals consequential on s 8) (SI 1998/879)

---

**Airports Act 1986 (c 31)**

*RA:* 8 Jul 1986

*Commencement provisions:* s 85(2)–(6); Airports Act 1986 (Commencement No 1 and Appointed Day) Order 1986, SI 1986/1228; Airports Act 1986 (Commencement No 2) Order 1986, SI 1986/1487

| | | |
|---|---|---|
| 1 | | 8 Jul 1986 (s 85(2)) |
| 2 | | 1 Aug 1986 (SI 1986/1228) |
| 3 | | 8 Jul 1986 (s 85(2)) |
| 4–11 | | 1 Aug 1986 (SI 1986/1228) |
| 12–35 | | 8 Sep 1986 (s 85(4)) |
| 36–56 | | 1 Oct 1986 (SI 1986/1487) |
| 57–62 | | 31 Jul 1986 (SI 1986/1228) |
| 63–66 | | 1 Apr 1986 (SI 1986/1228) |
| 67 | | 1 Oct 1986 (SI 1986/1487) |
| 68 | | 8 Sep 1986 (s 85(4)) |
| 69 | | 1 Oct 1986 (SI 1986/1487) |
| 70–72 | | 8 Sep 1986 (s 85(4)) |
| 73, 74 | | 1 Oct 1986 (SI 1986/1487) |
| 75 | | 8 Jul 1986 (s 85(2)) |
| 76 | (1)–(4) | 8 Jul 1986 (s 85(2)) |
| | (5) | 1 Aug 1986 (SI 1986/1228) |
| 77 | (1)–(4) | 1 Aug 1986 (SI 1986/1228) |
| | (5), (6) | 8 Jul 1986 (s 85(2)) |
| 78 | | 8 Sep 1986 (s 85(4)) |
| 79–82 | | 8 Jul 1986 (s 85(2)) |
| 83 | (1) | See Sch 4 below |
| | (2) | 1 Aug 1986 (SI 1986/1228) |
| | (3) | 1 Oct 1986 (SI 1986/1487) |
| | (4) | 1 Aug 1986 (SI 1986/1228) |
| | (5) | See Sch 6 below |
| 84 | | 8 Sep 1986 (s 85(4)) |
| 85 | | 8 Jul 1986 (s 85(2)) |
| Sch 1 | | 1 Oct 1986 (SI 1986/1487) |
| Sch 2 | | 31 Jul 1986 (SI 1986/1228) |
| Sch 3 | | 1 Aug 1986 (SI 1986/1228) |
| Sch 4 | paras 1, 2 | 31 Jul 1986 (SI 1986/1228) |
| | paras 3–8 | 1 Oct 1986 (SI 1986/1487) |
| | para 9 | 1 Aug 1986 (SI 1986/1228) |
| | para 10 | 1 Aug 1986 (except the expression "60(3)(o)") (SI 1986/1228) |
| | | 1 Apr 1987 (exception noted above) (SI 1986/1487) |
| Sch 5 | | 1 Aug 1986 (SI 1986/1228) |
| Sch 6 | Pt I | 1 Aug 1986 (SI 1986/1228) |
| | Pt II | 1 Aug 1986 (SI 1986/1228), repeals of or in— |
| | | Civil Aviation Act 1982, ss 27, 29, 32, 33, 37, 40, 58, 99, Sch 5, Sch 13, Pt II (entries relating to ss 32(5), 33(1), 37, 40(2)), Sch 14; |
| | | Criminal Justice Act 1982 |
| | | 1 Oct 1986 (repeal in Fair Trading Act 1973) (SI 1986/1487) |
| | | 1 Apr 1987 (SI 1986/1487), repeals of or in— |
| | | Local Government, Planning and Land Act 1980; |

## Airports Act 1986 (c 31)—*contd*

Civil Aviation Act 1982, s 38, Sch 13, Pt II, entry relating to
s 61(6)

## Animals (Scientific Procedures) Act 1986 (c 14)

*RA:* 20 May 1986

*Commencement provisions:* s 30(3); Animals (Scientific Procedures) Act (Commencement) Order 1986, SI 1986/2088; Animals (Scientific Procedures) (1986 Act) (Commencement No 1) Order (Northern Ireland) 1986, SR 1986/364 (NI); Animals (Scientific Procedures) Act (Commencement No 2) Order 1989, SI 1989/2306; Animals (Scientific Procedures) (1986 Act) (Commencement No 2) Order (Northern Ireland) 1989, SR 1989/496 (NI)

| | | |
|---|---|---|
| 1–6 | | 1 Jan 1987 (SI 1986/2088) |
| 7 | | 1 Jan 1990 (SI 1989/2306; SR 1989/496) |
| 8, 9 | | 1 Jan 1987 (SI 1986/2088) |
| 10 | (1), (2) | 1 Jan 1987 (SI 1986/2088) |
| | (3) | 1 Jan 1990 (SI 1989/2306; SR 1989/496) |
| | (4)–(7) | 1 Jan 1987 (SI 1986/2088) |
| 11–28 | | 1 Jan 1987 (SI 1986/2088) |
| 29 | | 1 Jan 1987 (NI) (SR 1986/364) |
| 30 | | 1 Jan 1987 (SI 1986/2088) |
| Sch 1 | | 1 Jan 1987 (SI 1986/2088) |
| Sch 2 | | 1 Jan 1990 (SI 1989/2306; SR 1989/496) |
| Schs 3, 4 | | 1 Jan 1987 (SI 1986/2088) |

## Appropriation Act 1986 (c 42)

*RA:* 25 Jul 1986

Whole Act in force 25 Jul 1986 (RA)

## Armed Forces Act 1986 (c 21)

*RA:* 26 Jun 1986

*Commencement provisions:* s 17(2), (3); Armed Forces Act 1986 (Commencement No 1) Order 1986, SI 1986/2071; Armed Forces Act 1986 (Commencement No 2) Order 1986, SI 1986/2124; Armed Forces Act 1986 (Commencement No 3) Order 1987, SI 1987/1998

| | | |
|---|---|---|
| 1 | | 26 Jun 1986 (RA) |
| 2–8 | | 1 Jan 1987 (SI 1986/2124) |
| 9 | | 31 Dec 1987 (SI 1987/1998) |
| 10–13 | | 1 Jan 1987 (SI 1986/2124) |
| 14 | | 30 Dec 1986 (SI 1986/2071) |
| 15 | | 26 Jun 1986 (RA) |
| 16 | (1) | 1 Jan 1987 (SI 1986/2124) |
| | (2) | See Sch 2 below |
| | (3) | 1 Jan 1987 (SI 1986/2124) |
| 17 | | 26 Jun 1986 (RA) |
| Sch 1 | | 1 Jan 1987 (SI 1986/2124) |
| Sch 2 | | 1 Sep 1986 (repeal of Armed Forces Act 1981, s 1) (s 17(3)) |
| | | 30 Dec 1986 (repeal of Army Act 1955, s 213(a)) (SI 1986/2071) |
| | | 1 Jan 1987 (otherwise) (SI 1986/2124) |

## Atomic Energy Authority Act 1986 (c 3)

*RA:* 19 Feb 1986

*Commencement provisions:* s 10(2)

Whole Act in force 1 Apr 1986 (s 10(2))

## Australia Act 1986 (c 2)

*RA:* 17 Feb 1986

*Commencement provisions:* s 17(2); Australia Act 1986 (Commencement) Order 1986, SI 1986/319

Whole Act in force 3 Mar 1986 (at 5 am GMT) (SI 1986/319)

## Bishops (Retirement) Measure 1986 (No 1)

*RA:* 18 Mar 1986

*Commencement provisions:* s 13(3)

Whole Measure in force 1 Jun 1986 (the day appointed by the Archbishops of Canterbury and York under s 13(3))

## British Council and Commonwealth Institute Superannuation Act 1986 (c 51)

*RA:* 25 Jul 1986

*Commencement provisions:* s 3(2); British Council and Commonwealth Institute Superannuation Act 1986 (Commencement No 1) Order 1986, SI 1986/1860; British Council and Commonwealth Institute Superannuation Act 1986 (Commencement No 2) Order 1987, SI 1987/588

Whole Act in force as follows—

10 Nov 1986 (in relation to British Council) (SI 1986/1860)

1 Apr 1987 (in relation to Commonwealth Institute) (SI 1987/588)

## British Shipbuilders (Borrowing Powers) Act 1986 (c 19)

*RA:* 26 Jun 1986

Whole Act in force 26 Jun 1986 (RA)

## Building Societies Act 1986 (c 53)

*RA:* 25 Jul 1986

*Commencement provisions:* s 126(2)–(4); Building Societies Act 1986 (Commencement No 1) Order 1986, SI 1986/1560; Building Societies Act 1986 (Commencement No 2) Order 1989, SI 1989/1083

| | |
|---|---|
| 1–4 | 25 Sep 1986 (s 126(2)) |
| 5, 6 | 1 Jan 1987 (SI 1986/1560) |
| 7 | 25 Sep 1986 (so far as relates to orders under s 7(9)) (SI 1986/1560) |
| | 1 Jan 1987 (otherwise) (SI 1986/1560) |
| 8–17 | 1 Jan 1987 (SI 1986/1560) |
| 18 | 25 Sep 1986 (so far as relates to designation orders under s 18(2)(c)) (SI 1986/1560) |
| | 1 Jan 1987 (except so far as empowers building societies to invest in, or support, corresponding European bodies) (SI 1986/1560) |

**Building Societies Act 1986 (c 53)**—*contd*

|        |              |                                                                                                    |
|--------|--------------|----------------------------------------------------------------------------------------------------|
|        |              | 1 Jan 1988 (exception noted above) (SI 1986/1560)                                                  |
| 19–34  |              | 1 Jan 1987 (SI 1986/1560)                                                                          |
| 35     |              | *Never in force* (repealed)                                                                        |
| 36     | (1)–(4)      | 1 Jan 1987 (SI 1986/1560)                                                                          |
|        | (5), (6)     | 1 Jan 1988 (SI 1986/1560)                                                                          |
|        | (7)          | 1 Jan 1987 (SI 1986/1560)                                                                          |
|        | (8), (9)     | 1 Jan 1988 (SI 1986/1560)                                                                          |
|        | (10)         | 1 Jan 1987 (SI 1986/1560)                                                                          |
|        | (11)(a)      | 1 Jan 1987 (SI 1986/1560)                                                                          |
|        | (11)(b), (c) | 1 Jan 1988 (SI 1986/1560)                                                                          |
|        | (11)(d)      | 1 Jan 1987 (SI 1986/1560)                                                                          |
|        | (11)(e), (f) | 1 Jan 1988 (SI 1986/1560)                                                                          |
|        | (12)         | 1 Jan 1988 (SI 1986/1560)                                                                          |
| 37     |              | 1 Jan 1988 (SI 1986/1560)                                                                          |
| 38–40  |              | 25 Sep 1986 (so far as relate to procedure following directions under Sch 20, para 11(5)(c)) (SI 1986/1560) |
|        |              | 1 Jan 1987 (otherwise) (SI 1986/1560)                                                             |
| 41–82  |              | 1 Jan 1987 (SI 1986/1560)                                                                          |
| 83     | (1)–(5)      | 1 Jul 1987 (SI 1986/1560)                                                                          |
|        | (6)–(15)     | 1 Jan 1987 (SI 1986/1560)                                                                          |
| 84     | (1)–(7)      | 1 Jan 1987 (SI 1986/1560)                                                                          |
|        | (8)–(10)     | 1 Jul 1987 (SI 1986/1560)                                                                          |
|        | (11)         | 1 Jan 1987 (SI 1986/1560)                                                                          |
| 85     |              | 1 Jan 1987 (SI 1986/1560)                                                                          |
| 86–89  |              | 1 Jan 1988 (SI 1986/1560)                                                                          |
| 90     |              | 1 Jan 1987 (so far as relates to Sch 15, paras 58, 59) (SI 1986/1560)                             |
|        |              | 1 Jan 1988 (otherwise) (SI 1986/1560)                                                             |
| 91, 92 |              | 1 Jan 1988 (SI 1986/1560)                                                                          |
| 93–96  |              | 1 Jan 1987 (SI 1986/1560)                                                                          |
| 97–102 |              | 1 Jan 1988 (SI 1986/1560)                                                                          |
| 103    | (1)          | 1 Jan 1987 (so far as relates to societies dissolved by s 93(5) or 94(10)) (SI 1986/1560)         |
|        |              | 1 Jan 1988 (otherwise) (SI 1986/1560)                                                             |
|        | (2)–(9)      | 1 Jan 1987 (SI 1986/1560)                                                                          |
| 104–108|              | 1 Jan 1987 (SI 1986/1560)                                                                          |
| 109    |              | 25 Sep 1986 (so far as it relates to the exemption from stamp duties of any instrument referred to in s 109(1)(e) and required or authorised to be given, issued, signed, made or produced in pursuance of this Act) (SI 1986/1560) |
|        |              | 1 Jan 1987 (otherwise) (SI 1986/1560)                                                             |
| 110, 111|             | 1 Jan 1987 (SI 1986/1560)                                                                          |
| 112    | (1)          | 25 Sep 1986 (SI 1986/1560)                                                                         |
|        | (2)          | 1 Jan 1987 (SI 1986/1560)                                                                          |
|        | (3), (4)     | 25 Sep 1986 (SI 1986/1560)                                                                         |
| 113    |              | 25 Sep 1986 (so far as relates to a memorandum or rules agreed upon under Sch 20, para 2) (SI 1986/1560) |
|        |              | 1 Jan 1987 (otherwise) (SI 1986/1560)                                                             |
| 114    |              | 1 Jan 1987 (SI 1986/1560)                                                                          |
| 115, 116|             | 25 Sep 1986 (SI 1986/1560)                                                                         |
| 117    |              | 1 Jan 1987 (SI 1986/1560)                                                                          |
| 118, 119|             | 25 Sep 1986 (SI 1986/1560)                                                                         |
| 120    | (1)          | 1 Jan 1987 (SI 1986/1560)                                                                          |
|        | (2)          | See Sch 19 below                                                                                   |
|        | (3)          | 1 Jan 1987 (SI 1986/1560)                                                                          |
|        | (4)          | See Sch 20 below                                                                                   |
| 121    |              | 25 Jul 1986 (s 126(3))                                                                             |
| 122, 123|             | 25 Sep 1986 (SI 1986/1560)                                                                         |
| 124    |              | *Never in force* (repealed)                                                                        |

**Building Societies Act 1986 (c 53)**—*contd*

| | | |
|---|---|---|
| 125, 126 | | 25 Jul 1986 (s 126(3)) |
| Sch 1 | | 25 Sep 1986 (s 126(2)) |
| Sch 2 | paras 1–29 | 1 Jan 1987 (SI 1986/1560) |
| | para 30 | 1 Jan 1988 (SI 1986/1560) |
| | paras 31–36 | 1 Jan 1987 (SI 1986/1560) |
| Schs 3–14 | | 1 Jan 1987 (SI 1986/1560) |
| Sch 15 | paras 1–57 | 1 Jan 1988 (SI 1986/1560) |
| | paras 58, 59 | 1 Jan 1987 (SI 1986/1560) |
| Sch 16 | | 1 Jan 1987 (SI 1986/1560) |
| Sch 17 | | 1 Jan 1988 (SI 1986/1560) |
| Sch 18 | | 1 Jan 1987 (SI 1986/1560) |
| Sch 19 | Pt I | 1 Jan 1987 (SI 1986/1560), except repeals of or in— |
| | | Building Societies Act 1874; |
| | | Building Societies Act 1894; |
| | | Building Societies Act 1960, Sch 5; |
| | | Building Societies Act 1962, ss 28–31, Pt VII |
| | | 1 Jan 1988 (except repeal of 1962 Act, ss 28–31) (SI 1986/1560) |
| | | 17 Jul 1989 (repeal of 1962 Act, ss 28–31) (SI 1989/1083) |
| | Pt II | 1 Jan 1987 (SI 1986/1560) |
| | Pt III | 1 Jan 1987 (except repeal of Building Societies Act (Northern Ireland) 1967, ss 28–31, Pt VII) (SI 1986/1560) |
| | | 1 Jan 1988 (repeal of 1967 Act, Pt VII) (SI 1986/1560) |
| | | 17 Jul 1989 (repeal of 1967 Act, ss 28–31) (SI 1989/1083) |
| Sch 20 | paras 1, 2 | 25 Sep 1986 (SI 1986/1560) |
| | paras 3–6 | 1 Jan 1987 (SI 1986/1560) |
| | para 7 | 25 Jul 1986 (s 126(3)) |
| | paras 8–11 | 25 Sep 1986 (SI 1986/1560) |
| | paras 12–16 | 1 Jan 1987 (SI 1986/1560) |
| | para 17 | 25 Sep 1986 (SI 1986/1560) |
| | para 18 | 1 Jan 1987 (SI 1986/1560) |
| Sch 21 | | *Never in force* (repealed) |

---

**Children and Young Persons (Amendment) Act 1986 (c 28)**

*RA:* 8 Jul 1986

Whole Act in force 8 Jul 1986 (RA)

---

**Civil Protection in Peacetime Act 1986 (c 22)**

*RA:* 26 Jun 1986

*Commencement provisions:* s 3(2)

Whole Act in force 26 Aug 1986 (s 3(2))

---

**Commonwealth Development Corporation Act 1986 (c 25)**

*RA:* 26 Jun 1986

Whole Act in force 26 Jun 1986 (RA)

---

**Company Directors Disqualification Act 1986 (c 46)**

*RA:* 25 Jul 1986

*Commencement provisions:* s 25

**Company Directors Disqualification Act 1986 (c 46)**—*contd*
Whole Act in force 29 Dec 1986 (s 25)

---

**Consolidated Fund Act 1986 (c 4)**

*RA:* 18 Mar 1986

Whole Act in force 18 Mar 1986 (RA)

---

**Consolidated Fund (No 2) Act 1986 (c 67)**

*RA:* 18 Dec 1986

Whole Act in force 18 Dec 1986 (RA)

---

**Consumer Safety (Amendment) Act 1986 (c 29)**

*RA:* 8 Jul 1986

*Commencement provisions:* s 17(2)

Whole Act in force 8 Aug 1986 (s 17(2))

---

**Corneal Tissue Act 1986 (c 18)**

*RA:* 26 Jun 1986

*Commencement provisions:* s 2(2)

Whole Act in force 26 Aug 1986 (s 2(2))

---

**Crown Agents (Amendment) Act 1986 (c 43)**

*RA:* 25 Jul 1986

Whole Act in force 25 Jul 1986 (RA)

---

**Deacons (Ordination of Women) Measure 1986 (No 4)**

*RA:* 7 Nov 1986

*Commencement provisions:* s 5(2)

Whole Act in force 16 Feb 1987 (the day appointed by the Archbishops of Canterbury and York under s 5(2))

---

**Disabled Persons (Services, Consultation and Representation) Act 1986 (c 33)**

*RA:* 8 Jul 1986

*Commencement provisions:* s 18(2); Disabled Persons (Services, Consultation and Representation) Act 1986 (Commencement No 1) Order 1987, SI 1987/564; Disabled Persons (Services, Consultation and Representation) Act 1986 (Commencement No 2) Order 1987, SI 1987/729; Disabled Persons (Services, Consultation and Representation) Act 1986 (Commencement No 3) (Scotland) Order 1987, SI 1987/911; Disabled Persons (Services, Consultation and Representation) Act 1986 (Commencement No 4) Order 1988, SI 1988/51; Disabled Persons (Services, Consultation and Representation) Act 1986 (Commencement No 5) (Scotland) Order 1988, SI 1988/94; Disabled Persons (Services, Consultation and Representation) Act 1986 (Commencement No 5) Order 1989, SI 1989/2425

**Disabled Persons (Services, Consultation and Representation) Act 1986 (c 33)**—*contd*

| | | |
|---|---|---|
| 1–3 | | *Not yet in force* |
| 4 | (a) | 1 Apr 1987 (E) (W) (SI 1987/564) |
| | | 1 Oct 1987 (S) (SI 1987/911) |
| | (b) | *Not yet in force* |
| | (c) | 1 Apr 1987 (E) (W) (SI 1987/564) |
| | | 1 Oct 1987 (S) (SI 1987/911) |
| 5, 6 | | 1 Feb 1988 (SI 1988/51) |
| 7 | | *Not yet in force* |
| 8 | (1) | 1 Apr 1987 (E) (W) (SI 1987/564) |
| | | 1 Oct 1987 (S) (SI 1987/911) |
| | (2), (3) | *Not yet in force* |
| 9, 10 | | 1 Apr 1987 (E) (W) (SI 1987/564) |
| | | 1 Jun 1987 (S) (SI 1987/911) |
| 11 | | 1 Jun 1987 (S) (SI 1987/911) |
| | | 18 Dec 1989 (E) (W) (SI 1989/2425) |
| 12 | | 1 Jun 1987 (SI 1987/911) |
| 13 | | 1 Feb 1988 (SI 1988/94) |
| 14 | | 1 Jun 1987 (SI 1987/911) |
| 15 | | *Never in force* (repealed) |
| 16–18 | | 17 Apr 1987 (E) (W) (SI 1987/729) |
| | | 1 Jun 1987 (S) (SI 1987/911) |

**Dockyard Services Act 1986 (c 52)**

*RA:* 25 Jul 1986

*Commencement provisions:* s 5(2)

Whole Act in force 25 Sep 1986 (s 5(2))

**Drainage Rates (Disabled Persons) Act 1986 (c 17)**

*RA:* 26 Jun 1986

*Commencement provisions:* s 2(2)

Whole Act in force 1 Apr 1987 (s 2(2))

**Drug Trafficking Offences Act 1986 (c 32)**

*RA:* 8 Jul 1986

*Commencement provisions:* s 40(2) (repealed); Drug Trafficking Offences Act 1986 (Commencement No 1) Order 1986, SI 1986/1488; Drug Trafficking Offences Act 1986 (Commencement No 2) (Scotland) Order 1986, SI 1986/1546; Drug Trafficking Offences Act 1986 (Commencement No 3) Order 1986, SI 1986/2145; Drug Trafficking Offences Act 1986 (Commencement No 4) (Scotland) Order 1986, SI 1986/2266

| | | |
|---|---|---|
| 1 | (1), (2) | 12 Jan 1987 (SI 1986/2145) |
| | (3) | 30 Sep 1986 (SI 1986/1488) |
| | (4)–(8) | 12 Jan 1987 (SI 1986/2145) |
| 2 | (1) | 30 Sep 1986 (SI 1986/1488) |
| | (2)–(5) | 12 Jan 1987 (SI 1986/2145) |
| 3–6 | | 12 Jan 1987 (SI 1986/2145) |
| 7 | (1), (2) | 12 Jan 1987 (SI 1986/2145) |
| | (3), (4) | 12 Jan 1987 (SI 1986/2145; SI 1986/2266) |
| 8 | | 12 Jan 1987 (SI 1986/2145; SI 1986/2266) |
| 9, 10 | | 12 Jan 1987 (SI 1986/2145) |
| 11–13 | | 12 Jan 1987 (SI 1986/2145; SI 1986/2266) |

## Drug Trafficking Offences Act 1986 (c 32)—*contd*

| | | |
|---|---|---|
| 14 | | 12 Jan 1987 (SI 1986/2145) |
| 15–17 | | 12 Jan 1987 (SI 1986/2145; SI 1986/2266) |
| 18 | (1) | 12 Jan 1987 (SI 1986/2145; SI 1986/2266) |
| | (2) | 12 Jan 1987 (SI 1986/2145) |
| 19 | | 12 Jan 1987 (SI 1986/2145) |
| 20–23 | | 12 Jan 1987 (SI 1986/2266) |
| 24 | (1), (2) | 30 Sep 1986 (SI 1986/1488) |
| | (3)(a) | 30 Sep 1986 (SI 1986/1488; SI 1986/1546) |
| | (3)(b) | 30 Sep 1986 (SI 1986/1488) |
| | (4)–(6) | 30 Sep 1986 (SI 1986/1488) |
| 25, 26 | | 12 Jan 1987 (SI 1986/2145) |
| 27–29 | | 30 Dec 1986 (E) (W) (SI 1986/2145) |
| | | 1 Jan 1987 (S) (SI 1986/2266) |
| 30 | | 12 Jan 1987 (SI 1986/2145; SI 1986/2266) |
| 31 | | 30 Dec 1986 (SI 1986/2145) |
| 32 | | 12 Jan 1987 (SI 1986/2145) |
| 33 | | 30 Dec 1986 (SI 1986/2145) |
| 34 | | 30 Sep 1986 (SI 1986/1488; SI 1986/1546) |
| 35 | | 8 Jul 1986 (s 40(2)) |
| 36, 37 | | 12 Jan 1987 (SI 1986/2145) |
| 38 | | 30 Sep 1986 (SI 1986/1488; SI 1986/1546) |
| 39 | (1), (2) | 12 Jan 1987 (SI 1986/2145) |
| | (3), (4) | 12 Jan 1987 (SI 1986/2145; SI 1986/2266) |
| | (5) | 12 Jan 1987 (SI 1986/2145) |
| | (6) | 12 Jan 1987 (SI 1986/2145; SI 1986/2266) |
| 40 | | 30 Sep 1986 (SI 1986/1488; SI 1986/1546) |

## Ecclesiastical Fees Measure 1986 (No 2)

*RA:* 18 Mar 1986

*Commencement provisions:* s 12(3)

Whole Act in force 1 Sep 1986 (the day appointed by the Archbishops of Canterbury and York under s 12(3))

## Education Act 1986 (c 40)

*RA:* 18 Jul 1986

*Commencement provisions:* s 6(2)

| | |
|---|---|
| 1 | 18 Sep 1986 (s 6(2)) |
| 2–6 | 18 Jul 1986 (RA) |

## Education (Amendment) Act 1986 (c 1)

*RA:* 17 Feb 1986

Whole Act in force 17 Feb 1986 (RA)

## Education (No 2) Act 1986 (c 61)

*RA:* 7 Nov 1986

*Commencement provisions:* s 66(1)–(4); Education (No 2) Act 1986 (Commencement No 1) Order 1986, SI 1986/2203; Education (No 2) Act 1986 (Commencement No 2) Order 1987, SI 1987/344; Education (No 2) Act 1986 (Commencement No 3) Order 1987, SI 1987/1159

**Education (No 2) Act 1986 (c 61)**—*contd*

| | | |
|---|---|---|
| 1–16 | | 1 Sep 1987 (SI 1987/344) |
| 17 | | 7 Jan 1987 (SI 1986/2203) |
| 18–29 | | 1 Sep 1987 (SI 1987/344) |
| 30, 31 | | 7 Jan 1987 (SI 1986/2203) |
| 32 | | 1 Sep 1987 (SI 1987/344) |
| 33 | | 7 Jan 1987 (SI 1986/2203) |
| 34–43 | | 1 Sep 1987 (SI 1987/344) |
| 44–46 | | 7 Jan 1987 (SI 1986/2203) |
| 47 | (1)–(10) | 15 Aug 1987 (SI 1987/344) |
| | (11) | 7 Jan 1987 (SI 1986/2203) |
| 48 | | 15 Aug 1987 (SI 1987/344) |
| 49 | | 7 Jan 1987 (s 66(2)) |
| 50–53 | | 7 Jan 1987 (SI 1986/2203) |
| 54, 55 | | 1 Apr 1987 (SI 1986/2203) |
| 56 | | 7 Jan 1987 (SI 1986/2203) |
| 57, 58 | | 1 Sep 1987 (SI 1987/344) |
| 59 | | 7 Jan 1987 (s 66(2)) |
| 60 | | 7 Nov 1986 (s 66(1)) |
| 61, 62 | | 1 Sep 1987 (SI 1987/344) |
| 63–66 | | 7 Nov 1986 (s 66(1)) |
| 67 | (1)–(3) | 7 Nov 1986 (s 66(1)) |
| | (4) | See Sch 4 below |
| | (5) | See Sch 5 below |
| | (6) | See Sch 6 below |
| | (7) | 7 Nov 1986 (s 66(1)) |
| Schs 1–3 | | 1 Sep 1987 (SI 1987/344) |
| Sch 4 | para 1 | 1 Apr 1987 (SI 1986/2203) |
| | paras 2–4 | 1 Sep 1987 (SI 1987/344) |
| | para 5 | 1 Apr 1987 (SI 1986/2203) |
| | para 6 | 1 Sep 1987 (SI 1987/344) |
| | para 7 | 1 Apr 1987 (SI 1986/2203) |
| Sch 5 | | 1 Sep 1987 (SI 1987/344) |
| Sch 6 | Pt I | 7 Jan 1987 (SI 1986/2203), repeals of or in— |
| | | Education Act 1944, ss 4, 5, 67; |
| | | London Government Act 1963, s 31(7)(a); |
| | | Education Act 1980, ss 31, 32, Sch 6; |
| | | Education (Scotland) Act 1980; |
| | | Local Government, Planning and Land Act 1980 |
| | | 1 Sep 1987 (SI 1987/344), repeals of or in— |
| | | Education Act 1944, ss 17–21, 23, 24(1), 27(3); |
| | | Education Act 1962; |
| | | Education (No 2) Act 1968; |
| | | Education Act 1980, ss 2–4, 35(1) |
| | | 1 Sep 1987 (SI 1987/1159), repeals of or in— |
| | | London Government Act 1963, s 31(8); |
| | | Local Government Act 1966, Sch 5, para 6 |
| | Pt II | 7 Jan 1987 (SI 1986/2203) |

**European Communities (Amendment) Act 1986 (c 58)**

*RA:* 7 Nov 1986

Whole Act in force 7 Nov 1986 (RA); but note that the repeals and revocations in the Schedule took effect on 1 Jul 1987, the day on which the Single European Act came into force; see Art 33(2) thereof, Cmnd 9758

## Family Law Act 1986 (c 55)

*RA:* 7 Nov 1986

*Commencement provisions:* s 69(2), (3); Family Law Act 1986 (Commencement No 1) Order 1988, SI 1988/375

| | | |
|---|---|---|
| 1–63 | | 4 Apr 1988 (SI 1988/375) |
| 64–67 | | 7 Jan 1987 (s 69(2)) |
| 68, 69 | | 4 Apr 1988 (SI 1988/375) |
| Sch 1 | paras 1–9 | 4 Apr 1988 (SI 1988/375) |
| | para 10(1), (2) | 4 Apr 1988 (SI 1988/375) |
| | para 10(3) | *Never in force* (repealed) |
| | para 10(4) | 4 Apr 1988 (SI 1988/375) |
| | paras 11–34 | 4 Apr 1988 (SI 1988/375) |
| Sch 2 | | 4 Apr 1988 (SI 1988/375) |

## Finance Act 1986 (c 41)

*Budget Day:* 18 Mar 1986

*RA:* 25 Jul 1986

The commencement details of Finance Acts are not set out, as the dates from which their provisions take effect are usually stated clearly and unambiguously in the text of the Act, and charging provisions will normally state for which year or years of assessment they are to have effect.

## Financial Services Act 1986 (c 60)

*RA:* 7 Nov 1986

*Commencement provisions:* s 211(1), (2); Financial Services Act 1986 (Commencement No 1) Order 1986, SI 1986/1940; Financial Services Act 1986 (Commencement No 2) Order 1986, SI 1986/2031; Financial Services Act 1986 (Commencement No 3) Order 1986, SI 1986/2246; Financial Services Act 1986 (Commencement) (No 4) Order 1987, SI 1987/623; Financial Services Act 1986 (Commencement) (No 5) Order 1987, SI 1987/907; Financial Services Act 1986 (Commencement) (No 6) Order 1987, SI 1987/1997; Financial Services Act 1986 (Commencement) (No 7) Order 1987, SI 1987/2158; Financial Services Act 1986 (Commencement) (No 8) Order 1988, SI 1988/740; Financial Services Act 1986 (Commencement) (No 9) Order 1988, SI 1988/995; Financial Services Act 1986 (Commencement) (No 10) Order 1988, SI 1988/1960; Financial Services Act 1986 (Commencement) (No 11) Order 1988, SI 1988/2285; Financial Services Act 1986 (Commencement) (No 12) Order 1989, SI 1989/1583; Financial Services Act 1986 (Commencement) (No 13) Order 1995, SI 1995/1538; Financial Services Act 1986 (Commencement) (No 14) Order, 1999, SI 1999/727

| | |
|---|---|
| 1 | See Sch 1 below |
| 2 | 18 Dec 1986 (SI 1986/2246) |
| 3, 4 | 29 Apr 1988 (SI 1988/740) |
| 5 | 12 Jan 1987 (so far as necessary to identify agreements to which s 5(1) applies for the purposes of s 132, so far as that section is in force by virtue of SI 1986/2246) (SI 1986/2246) |
| | 29 Apr 1988 (otherwise) (SI 1988/740) |
| 6, 7 | 29 Apr 1988 (SI 1988/740) |
| 8–11 | 4 Jun 1987 (SI 1987/907) |
| 12 | 1 Dec 1987 (SI 1987/1997) |
| 13, 14 | 4 Jun 1987 (SI 1987/907) |
| 15 | 4 Jun 1987 (except so far as has effect of conferring authorisation) (SI 1987/907) |
| | 29 Apr 1988 (exception noted above) (SI 1988/740) |
| 16–19 | 4 Jun 1987 (SI 1987/907) |
| 20 | 1 Dec 1987 (SI 1987/1997) |
| 21 | 4 Jun 1987 (SI 1987/907) |

**Financial Services Act 1986 (c 60)**—*contd*

| | | |
|---|---|---|
| 22, 23 | | 29 Apr 1988 (SI 1988/740) |
| 24 | | 29 Apr 1988 (for purposes of Sch 15, para 10) (SI 1988/740) |
| | | 1 Oct 1989 (otherwise) (SI 1989/1583) |
| 25 | | 29 Apr 1988 (SI 1988/740) |
| 26–30 | | 1 Jan 1988 (SI 1987/2158) |
| 31 | (1)–(3) | 29 Apr 1988 (SI 1988/740) |
| | (4) | 1 Jan 1988 (so far as necessary to enable the Secretary of State to issue and revoke certificates) (SI 1987/2158) |
| | | 29 Apr 1988 (otherwise) (SI 1988/740) |
| | (5) | 29 Apr 1988 (SI 1988/740) |
| 32–34 | | 29 Apr 1988 (SI 1988/740) |
| 35 | | 18 Dec 1986 (so far as relevant for the purposes of s 105) (SI 1986/2246) |
| | | 29 Apr 1988 (otherwise) (SI 1988/740) |
| 36 | (1) | 29 Apr 1988 (SI 1988/740) |
| | (2), (3) | 4 Jun 1987 (SI 1987/907) |
| 37 | | 4 Jun 1987 (except so far as has effect in relation to a body or association of the kind described in s 40(1)) (SI 1987/907) |
| | | 23 Nov 1987 (exception noted above) (SI 1987/1997) |
| 38 | (1) | 29 Apr 1988 (SI 1988/740) |
| | (2), (3) | 4 Jun 1987 (SI 1987/907) |
| 39 | | 4 Jun 1987 (except so far as has effect in relation to a body or association of the kind described in s 40(1)) (SI 1987/907) |
| | | 23 Nov 1987 (exception noted above) (SI 1987/1997) |
| 40 | | 23 Nov 1987 (SI 1987/1997) |
| 41 | | 4 Jun 1987 (SI 1987/907) |
| 42 | | 18 Dec 1986 (for purposes of s 105) (SI 1986/2246) |
| | | 29 Apr 1988 (otherwise) (SI 1988/740) |
| 43 | | 1 Jan 1988 (SI 1987/2158) |
| 44 | | 29 Apr 1988 (SI 1988/740) |
| 45 | | 18 Dec 1986 (for purposes of s 105) (SI 1986/2246) |
| | | 29 Apr 1988 (otherwise) (SI 1988/740) |
| 46 | | 4 Jun 1987 (SI 1987/907) |
| 47 | | 29 Apr 1988 (SI 1988/740) |
| 48–52 | | 4 Jun 1987 (SI 1987/907) |
| 53 | | *Never in force* (repealed) |
| 54, 55 | | 4 Jun 1987 (SI 1987/907) |
| 56 | | 4 Jun 1987 (so far as necessary in order to enable regulations to be made under s 56(1)) (SI 1987/907) |
| | | 29 Apr 1988 (otherwise) (SI 1988/740) |
| 57 | | 6 May 1988 (so far as relates to an advertisement which is neither: (a) issued for valuable consideration in a newspaper, journal, magazine or other periodical published at intervals of less than seven days, nor; (b) issued for valuable consideration either (i) in any newspaper, journal, magazine or other publication published at intervals of seven or more days, or (ii) by way of sound broadcasting or television by the exhibition of cinematographic films or by the distribution of recordings, and which is issued or caused to be issued by a person who is not an authorised person except in relation to an advertisement issued on or after 6 May 1988 in an edition of a newspaper, magazine, journal or other publication first issued before 6 May 1988) (SI 1988/740) |
| | | 29 May 1988 (so far as it relates to an advertisement issued for valuable consideration in a newspaper, journal, magazine or other periodical publication which is published at intervals of less than seven days except in relation to an advertisement issued on or after 29 May 1988 in an edition of a newspaper, magazine, journal or other publication first issued before that date) (SI 1988/740) |

**Financial Services Act 1986 (c 60)**—*contd*

|  |  |  |
|---|---|---|
|  |  | 29 Jul 1988 (so far as relates to an advertisement issued for valuable consideration either (i) in any newspaper, journal, magazine or other publication which is published at intervals of seven or more days; or (ii) by way of sound broadcasting or television, by the exhibition of cinematographic films or by the distribution of recordings except in relation to an advertisement issued on or after 29 Jul 1988 in an edition of a newspaper, magazine, journal or other publication first issued before that date) (SI 1988/740) |
|  |  | 29 Apr 1988 (exception noted above) (SI 1988/740) |
| 58 | (1)(a)–(c) | 29 Apr 1988 (SI 1988/740) |
|  | (1)(d)(i) | 29 Apr 1988 (SI 1988/740) |
|  | (1)(d)(ii) | 29 Apr 1988 (except so far as relates to an advertisement required or permitted to be published by an approved exchange under Pt V of the Act) (SI 1988/740) |
|  |  | *Never in force* (exception noted above) (repealed) |
|  | (2) | *Never in force* (repealed) |
|  | (3)–(6) | 29 Apr 1988 (SI 1988/740) |
| 59–61 |  | 29 Apr 1988 (SI 1988/740) |
| 62 | (1) | 1 Dec 1987 (except so far as s 62(1) applies to a contravention such as is mentioned in s 62(2)) (SI 1987/1997) |
|  |  | 3 Oct 1988 (exception noted above) (SI 1987/1997) |
|  | (2)–(4) | 1 Dec 1987 (SI 1987/1997) |
| 63 |  | 23 Apr 1987 (SI 1987/623) |
| 64–75 |  | 29 Apr 1988 (SI 1988/740) |
| 76 |  | 29 Apr 1988 (except so far as has effect in relation to—<br>(a) a collective investment scheme which takes the form of an open-ended investment company, units in which are either included in the Official List of the International Stock Exchange of the United Kingdom and the Republic of Ireland Limited or are offered on terms such that any agreement for their acquisition is conditional upon their admission to that List, or;<br>(b) any prospectus issued by or on behalf of an open-ended investment company which complies with Chapter II of Pt III of Companies Act 1985 or the corresponding provisions of Companies (Northern Ireland) Order 1986 and the issue of which in the United Kingdom does not contravene s 74 or 75 of Companies Act 1985 or the corresponding provisions of Companies (Northern Ireland) Order 1986) (SI 1988/740)<br><br>31 Dec 1988 (except so far as has effect in relation to—<br>(a) an open-ended investment company units in which are either included in the Official List of the International Stock Exchange of the United Kingdom and the Republic of Ireland Limited or are offered on terms such that any agreement for their acquisition is conditional upon such listing being an open-ended investment company which either—<br>(i) is managed in and authorised under the law of a country or territory in respect of which an order under s 87 of Financial Services Act 1986 is in force on 31 Dec 1988 and which is of a class specified in that order; or,<br>(ii) is constituted in a member State in respect of which an order under para 10 of Sch 15 to Financial Services Act 1986 is in force on 31 Dec 1988 and which meets the requirements specified in that order, or; |

**Financial Services Act 1986 (c 60)**—*contd*

(b) any prospectus issued by or on behalf of an open-ended investment company which fulfils the conditions described in head (a)(i) or (a)(ii) immediately above being a prospectus which complies with Chapter II of Pt III of Companies Act 1985 or the corresponding provisions of Companies (Northern Ireland) Order 1986 and the issue of which in the United Kingdom does not contravene s 74 or 75 of Companies Act 1985 or the corresponding provisions of Companies (Northern Ireland) Order 1986 as the case may be) (SI 1988/1960, as amended by SI 1988/2285) (and also except so far as has effect in relation to (a) an open-ended investment company managed in and authorised under the law of Bermuda, units in which are, on 31 Dec 1988, included in the Official List of the International Stock Exchange of the United Kingdom and the Republic of Ireland Limited; or (b) any prospectus issued by or on behalf of an open-ended investment company which fulfils the conditions described in head (a) immediately above, being a prospectus which complies with Chapter II of Pt III of Companies Act 1985 or the corresponding provisions of Companies (Northern Ireland) Order 1986 and the issue of which in the United Kingdom does not contravene s 74 or 75 of Companies Act 1985 or the corresponding provisions of Companies (Northern Ireland) Order 1986 (as the case may be) (SI 1988/2285)

28 Feb 1989 (so far as has effect in relation to an open-ended investment company falling within head (a) immediately above but which is not a scheme of a class specified in the Schedule to Financial Services (Designated Countries and Territories) (Overseas Collective Investment Schemes) (Bermuda) Order 1988, SI 1988/2284, or to any prospectus which falls within head (b) immediately above issued by or on behalf of any such company) (SI 1988/2285)

1 Mar 1989 (otherwise, except so far as has effect in relation to (a) an open-ended investment company which fulfils the conditions described in head (a) immediately above and which is a scheme of a class specified in the Schedule to Financial Services (Designated Countries and Territories) (Overseas Collective Investment Schemes) (Bermuda) Order 1988, SI 1988/2284, or (b) any prospectus issued by or on behalf of such an open-ended investment company, being a prospectus which fulfils the conditions described in head (b) immediately above) (SI 1988/1960)

1 May 1989 (exception noted above) (SI 1988/2285)

| | | |
|---|---|---|
| 77–85 | | 29 Apr 1988 (SI 1988/740) |
| 86 | | 29 Apr 1988 (for purposes of Sch 15, para 10) (SI 1988/740) |
| | | 1 Oct 1989 (otherwise) (SI 1989/1583) |
| 87–95 | | 29 Apr 1988 (SI 1988/740) |
| 96 | | 1 Dec 1987 (SI 1987/1997) |
| 97–101 | | 29 Apr 1988 (SI 1988/740) |
| 102, 103 | | 4 Jun 1987 (SI 1987/907) |
| 104 | (1) | 29 Apr 1988 (SI 1988/740) |
| | (2), (3) | 4 Jun 1987 (SI 1987/907) |
| | (4) | 29 Apr 1988 (SI 1988/740) |
| 105, 106 | | 18 Dec 1986 (SI 1986/2246) |
| 107 | | 4 Jun 1987 (SI 1987/907) |
| 108, 109 | | 29 Apr 1988 (SI 1988/740) |
| 110 | | 4 Jun 1987 (SI 1987/907) |
| 111 | | 29 Apr 1988 (SI 1988/740) |
| 112 | (1)–(4) | 4 Jun 1987 (SI 1987/907) |
| | (5) | 1 Jan 1988 (so far as has effect in relation to applications under s 26) (SI 1987/2158) |

**Financial Services Act 1986 (c 60)**—*contd*

|  |  |  |
|---|---|---|
|  |  | 29 Apr 1988 (otherwise) (SI 1988/740) |
| 113 | (1) | 4 Jun 1987 (SI 1987/907) |
|  | (2)–(8) | 29 Apr 1988 (SI 1988/740) |
| 114–118 |  | 12 Jan 1987 (SI 1986/2246) |
| 119, 120 |  | 4 Jun 1987 (SI 1987/907) |
| 121 |  | 12 Jan 1987 (SI 1986/2246) |
| 122 |  | 12 Jan 1987 (for purposes of s 121) (SI 1986/2246) |
|  |  | 4 Jun 1987 (otherwise) (SI 1987/907) |
| 123 |  | 12 Jan 1987 (for purposes of any provision brought into force by SI 1986/2246) (SI 1986/2246) |
|  |  | 4 Jun 1987 (otherwise) (SI 1987/907) |
| 124 |  | 12 Jan 1987 (SI 1986/2246) |
| 125 | (1)–(7) | 4 Jun 1987 (SI 1987/907) |
|  | (8) | 1 Jul 1988 (SI 1988/995) |
| 126 |  | 12 Jan 1987 (SI 1986/2246) |
| 127 |  | 4 Jun 1987 (SI 1987/907) |
| 128 |  | 12 Jan 1987 (SI 1986/2246) |
| 129 |  | See Sch 10 below |
| 130, 131 |  | 29 Apr 1988 (SI 1988/740) |
| 132 | (1)–(5) | 12 Jan 1987 (SI 1986/2246) |
|  | (6) (first part) | 12 Jan 1987 (for purposes of any contract of insurance which is not an agreement to which s 5(1) applies) (SI 1986/2246) |
|  |  | 29 Apr 1988 (otherwise) (SI 1988/740) |
|  | (6) (second part) | 12 Jan 1987 (for purposes of any re-insurance contract entered into in respect of a contract of insurance which is not an agreement to which s 5(1) applies) (SI 1986/2246) |
|  |  | 29 Apr 1988 (otherwise) (SI 1988/740) |
| 133 |  | 29 Apr 1988 (SI 1988/740) |
| 134 |  | 12 Jan 1987 (for the purpose of a person who, on 12 Jan 1987 is not entitled (either alone or with any associate or associates) to exercise, or control the exercise of, 15 per cent or more of the voting power at any general meeting of an applicant under the Insurance Companies Act 1982, s 3, or of an insurance company in relation to which applicant or insurance company the question of who is its controller under that Act arises, or of a body corporate of which such an applicant or such an insurance company is a subsidiary) (SI 1986/2246) |
|  |  | *Never in force* (otherwise) (repealed) |
| 135, 136 |  | 29 Apr 1988 (SI 1988/740) |
| 137 |  | 12 Jan 1987 (SI 1986/2246) |
| 138 | (1), (2) | 4 Jun 1987 (SI 1987/907) |
|  | (3) | 12 Jan 1987 (SI 1986/2246) |
|  | (4) | 29 Apr 1988 (SI 1988/740) |
|  | (5) | 12 Jan 1987 (SI 1986/2246) |
|  | (6) | 4 Jun 1987 (SI 1987/907) |
| 139 | (1)(a) | 29 Apr 1988 (SI 1988/740) |
|  | (1)(b) | 12 Jan 1987 (SI 1986/2246) |
|  | (2)–(5) | 29 Apr 1988 (SI 1988/740) |
| 140 |  | See Sch 11 below |
| 141 |  | 12 Jan 1987 (SI 1986/2246) |
| 142–153 |  | 12 Jan 1987 (for all purposes relating to the admission of securities offered by or on behalf of a minister of the Crown or a body corporate controlled by a minister of the Crown or a subsidiary of such a body corporate to the Official List in respect of which an application is made after that date) (SI 1986/2246) |
|  |  | 16 Feb 1987 (for purposes relating to the admission of securities in respect of which an application is made after that date, other than those referred to in the preceding paragraph, and otherwise for all purposes) (SI 1986/2246) |

**Financial Services Act 1986 (c 60)**—*contd*

| | | |
|---|---|---|
| 154 | (1) | 12 Jan 1987 (for all purposes relating to the admission of securities offered by or on behalf of a minister of the Crown or a body corporate controlled by a minister of the Crown or a subsidiary of such a body corporate to the Official List in respect of which an application is made after that date) (SI 1986/2246) |
| | | 16 Feb 1987 (for purposes relating to the admission of securities in respect of which an application is made after that date, other than those referred to in the preceding paragraph, and otherwise for all purposes) (SI 1986/2246) |
| | (2)–(4) | 29 Apr 1988 (SI 1988/740) |
| | (5) | 12 Jan 1987 (for all purposes relating to the admission of securities offered by or on behalf of a minister of the Crown or a body corporate controlled by a minister of the Crown or a subsidiary of such a body corporate to the Official List in respect of which an application is made after that date) (SI 1986/2246) |
| | | 16 Feb 1987 (for purposes relating to the admission of securities in respect of which an application is made after that date, other than those referred to in the preceding paragraph, and otherwise for all purposes) (SI 1986/2246) |
| 155–157 | | 12 Jan 1987 (for all purposes relating to the admission of securities offered by or on behalf of a minister of the Crown or a body corporate controlled by a minister of the Crown or a subsidiary of such a body corporate to the Official List in respect of which an application is made after that date) (SI 1986/2246) |
| | | 16 Feb 1987 (for purposes relating to the admission of securities in respect of which an application is made after that date, other than those referred to in the preceding paragraph, and otherwise for all purposes) (SI 1986/2246) |
| 158, 159 | | *Never in force* (repealed) |
| 160 | | 29 Apr 1988 (in so far as is necessary to enable the Secretary of State to make an order under that section) (SI 1988/740) |
| | | *Never in force* (otherwise) (repealed) |
| 161 | | *Never in force* (repealed) |
| 162 | | 29 Apr 1988 (in so far as is necessary to enable the Secretary of State to make rules under that section and in so far as is necessary for the purposes of s 169) (SI 1988/740) |
| | | *Never in force* (otherwise) (repealed) |
| 163–168 | | *Never in force* (repealed) |
| 169 | | 29 Apr 1988 (SI 1988/740) |
| 170 | | 29 Apr 1988 (in so far as is necessary to enable the Secretary of State to make an order under that section) (SI 1988/740) |
| | | *Never in force* (otherwise) (repealed) |
| 171 | | *Never in force* (repealed) |
| 172 | | 30 Apr 1987 (SI 1986/2246) |
| 173 | | 12 Jan 1987 (SI 1986/2246) |
| 174 | (1), (2) | 18 Dec 1986 (SI 1986/2246) |
| | (3) | 29 Apr 1988 (SI 1988/740) |
| | (4)(a) | *Never in force* (repealed) |
| | (4)(b) | 29 Apr 1988 (SI 1988/740) |
| 175 | | 29 Apr 1988 (SI 1988/740) |
| 176 | | 12 Jan 1987 (SI 1986/2246) |
| 177 | | 15 Nov 1986 (SI 1986/1940) |
| 178 | (1) | 15 Nov 1986 (SI 1986/1940) |
| | (2)(a) | 15 Nov 1986 (SI 1986/1940) |
| | (2)(b) | 29 Apr 1988 (SI 1988/740) |
| | (3)–(9) | 29 Apr 1988 (SI 1988/740) |
| | (10) | 12 Jan 1987 (SI 1986/2246) |

**Financial Services Act 1986 (c 60)**—*contd*

| | | |
|---|---|---|
| 179 | | 15 Nov 1986 (for purposes of information obtained by a person mentioned in s 179(3)(h) so far as that provision applies to a person appointed or authorised to exercise any powers under s 177, or by a person mentioned in s 179(3)(i) who is an officer or servant of any such person) (SI 1986/1940) |
| | | 18 Dec 1986 (otherwise) (SI 1986/2246) |
| 180 | | 15 Nov 1986 (SI 1986/2246) |
| 181 | | 12 Jan 1987 (SI 1986/2246) |
| 182 | | See Sch 13 below |
| 183 | | 23 Apr 1987 (so far as relates to notices relating to the carrying on of insurance business or of a deposit-taking business as a recognised bank or licensed institution within the meaning of the Banking Act 1979) (SI 1987/623) |
| | | 29 Apr 1988 (otherwise) (SI 1988/740) |
| 184 | (1)–(3) | 23 Apr 1987 (so far as relate to notices relating to the carrying on of insurance business) (SI 1987/623) |
| | | 29 Apr 1988 (otherwise) (SI 1988/740) |
| | (4) | 29 Apr 1988 (SI 1988/740) |
| | (5) | 23 Apr 1987 (SI 1987/623) |
| | (6) | 29 Apr 1988 (SI 1988/740) |
| | (7) | 23 Apr 1987 (SI 1987/623) |
| | (8) | 29 Apr 1988 (SI 1988/740) |
| 185 | | 23 Apr 1987 (SI 1987/623) |
| 186 | (1)–(5) | 23 Apr 1987 (so far as relate to provisions brought into force by SI 1987/623) (SI 1987/623) |
| | | 29 Apr 1988 (otherwise) (SI 1988/740) |
| | (6) | 29 Apr 1988 (SI 1988/740) |
| | (7) | 23 Apr 1987 (so far as relates to provisions brought into force by SI 1987/623) (SI 1987/623) |
| | | 29 Apr 1988 (otherwise) (SI 1988/740) |
| 187 | (1), (2) | 4 Jun 1987 (SI 1987/907) |
| | (3), (4) | 12 Jan 1987 (SI 1986/2246) |
| | (5)–(7) | 4 Jun 1987 (SI 1987/907) |
| 188 | | 12 Jan 1987 (SI 1986/2246) |
| 189 | | See Sch 14 below |
| 190, 191 | | 4 Jun 1987 (SI 1987/907) |
| 192 | | 12 Jan 1987 (SI 1986/2246) |
| 193 | | *Never in force* (repealed) |
| 194 | | 29 Apr 1988 (SI 1988/740) |
| 195 | | 7 Nov 1986 (s 211(2)) |
| 196 | | 1 Dec 1987 (SI 1987/1997) |
| 197 | | 29 Apr 1988 (SI 1988/740) |
| 198 | (1)(a) | 29 Apr 1988 (SI 1988/740) |
| | (1)(b) | 18 Dec 1986 (SI 1986/2246) |
| | (2)(a) | 15 Nov 1986 (SI 1986/1940) |
| | (2)(b) | 18 Dec 1986 (SI 1986/2246) |
| | (3)(a) | 29 Apr 1988 (SI 1988/740) |
| | (3)(b) | 4 Jun 1987 (SI 1987/907) |
| 199 | (1)(a) | 15 Nov 1986 (for purposes relating to offences under Company Securities (Insider Dealing) Act 1985, ss 1, 2, 4, 5) (SI 1986/1940) |
| | | 29 Apr 1988 (otherwise) (SI 1988/740) |
| | (1)(b) | 29 Apr 1988 (SI 1988/740) |
| | (2) | 29 Apr 1988 (SI 1988/740) |
| | (3)–(6) | 15 Nov 1986 (for purposes relating to offences under Company Securities (Insider Dealing) Act 1985, ss 1, 2, 4, 5) (SI 1986/1940) |
| | | 29 Apr 1988 (otherwise) (SI 1988/740) |
| | (7) | 12 Jan 1987 (SI 1986/2246) |

**Financial Services Act 1986 (c 60)**—*contd*

|   |   |   |
|---|---|---|
| | (8), (9) | 15 Nov 1986 (for purposes relating to offences under Company Securities (Insider Dealing) Act 1985, ss 1, 2, 4, 5) (SI 1986/1940) |
| | | 29 Apr 1988 (otherwise) (SI 1988/740) |
| 200 | (1)(a) | 4 Jun 1987 (so far as has effect in relation to an application for a recognition order under Ch III or IV of Pt I) (SI 1987/907) |
| | | 1 Jan 1988 (so far as has effect in relation to an application for authorisation under s 26) (SI 1987/2158) |
| | | 29 Apr 1988 (otherwise) (SI 1988/740) |
| | (1)(b) | 15 Nov 1986 (so far as relates to a requirement imposed by or under s 177) (SI 1986/2246) |
| | | 12 Jan 1987 (so far as relates to a requirement imposed by or under any provision brought into force on 12 Jan 1987 by SI 1986/2246) (SI 1986/2246) |
| | | 4 Jun 1987 (so far as relates to a requirement imposed by or under any provision brought into force by SI 1987/907) (SI 1987/907) |
| | | 1 Jan 1988 (so far as relates to a requirement imposed by or under any provision brought into force by SI 1987/2158) (SI 1987/2158) |
| | | 29 Apr 1988 (otherwise) (SI 1988/740) |
| | (2) | 29 Apr 1988 (SI 1988/740) |
| | (3), (4) | 4 Jun 1987 (SI 1987/907) |
| | (5) | 15 Nov 1986 (so far as relates to a requirement imposed by or under s 177) (SI 1986/1940) |
| | | 18 Dec 1986 (so far as relates to a requirement imposed by or under s 105) (SI 1986/2246) |
| | | 12 Jan 1987 (so far as relates to a requirement imposed by or under any provision brought into force on 12 Jan 1987 by SI 1986/2246) (SI 1986/2246) |
| | | 4 Jun 1987 (so far as relates to a provision brought into force by SI 1987/907) (SI 1987/907) |
| | | 1 Jan 1988 (so far as relates to any provision brought into force by SI 1987/2158) (SI 1987/2158) |
| | | 29 Apr 1988 (otherwise) (SI 1988/740) |
| | (6)–(8) | 4 Jun 1987 (so far as relates to a provision brought into force by SI 1987/907) (SI 1987/907) |
| | | 29 Apr 1988 (otherwise) (SI 1988/740) |
| 201 | (1) | 15 Nov 1986 (so far as relates to a provision brought into force by SI 1986/1940) (SI 1986/1940) |
| | | 18 Dec 1986 (otherwise) (SI 1986/2246) |
| | (2) | 29 Apr 1988 (SI 1988/740) |
| | (3) | 23 Apr 1987 (SI 1987/623) |
| | (4) | 12 Jan 1987 (SI 1986/2246) |
| 202, 203 | | 15 Nov 1986 (for purposes of any provision brought into force by SI 1986/1940) (SI 1986/1940) |
| | | 18 Dec 1986 (otherwise) (SI 1986/2246) |
| 204 | | 12 Jan 1987 (SI 1986/2246) |
| 205 | | 15 Nov 1986 (for purposes of any provision brought into force by SI 1986/1940) (SI 1986/1940) |
| | | 18 Dec 1986 (otherwise) (SI 1986/2246) |
| 206 | (1)–(3) | 4 Jun 1987 (SI 1987/907) |
| | (4) | 15 May 1987 (SI 1987/907) |
| 207 | | 15 Nov 1986 (for purposes of any provision brought into force by SI 1986/1940) (SI 1986/1940) |
| | | 18 Dec 1986 (otherwise) (SI 1986/2246) |
| 208 | | 29 Apr 1988 (so far as has effect in relation to the application of s 130) (SI 1988/740) |
| | | *Never in force* (otherwise) (repealed) |

**Financial Services Act 1986 (c 60)**—*contd*

| | | |
|---|---|---|
| 209, 210 | | 15 Nov 1986 (for purposes of any provision brought into force by SI 1986/1940) (SI 1986/1940) |
| | | 18 Dec 1986 (otherwise) (SI 1986/2246) |
| 211 | (1), (2) | 7 Nov 1986 (RA) |
| | (3) | See Sch 15 below |
| 212 | (1) | 27 Nov 1986 (SI 1986/2031) |
| | (2) | See Sch 16 below |
| | (3) | See Sch 17 below |
| Sch 1 | paras 1–22 | 18 Dec 1986 (SI 1986/2246) |
| | para 23 | 1 Dec 1987 (SI 1987/1997) |
| | para 24 | 18 Dec 1986 (SI 1986/2246) |
| | para 25(1) | 18 Dec 1986 (SI 1986/2246) |
| | para 25(2), (3) | 18 Jan 1988 (SI 1987/2158) |
| | paras 26–33 | 18 Dec 1986 (SI 1986/2246) |
| Schs 2–4 | | 4 Jun 1987 (SI 1987/907) |
| Sch 5 | | 1 Jan 1988 (SI 1987/2158) |
| Sch 6 | | 1 Dec 1987 (SI 1987/1997) |
| Schs 7–9 | | 12 Jan 1987 (SI 1986/2246) |
| Sch 10 | para 1 | 12 Jan 1987 (SI 1986/2246) |
| | para 2 | 29 Apr 1988 (SI 1988/740) |
| | para 3(1), (2) | 4 Jun 1987 (SI 1987/907) |
| | para 3(3) | 12 Jan 1987 (SI 1986/2246) |
| | para 3(4) | 4 Jun 1987 (SI 1987/907) |
| | para 4(1)–(4) | 4 Jun 1987 (SI 1987/907) |
| | para 4(5) | 29 Apr 1988 (SI 1988/740) |
| | para 4(6) | 12 Jan 1987 (SI 1986/2246) |
| | para 5(1), (2) | 29 Apr 1988 (SI 1988/740) |
| | para 5(3), (4) | 1 Jul 1988 (SI 1988/995) |
| | paras 6, 7 | 29 Apr 1988 (SI 1988/740) |
| | para 8(1)–(5) | 29 Apr 1988 (SI 1988/740) |
| | para 8(6) | 12 Jan 1987 (SI 1986/2246) |
| | para 9 | 29 Apr 1988 (SI 1988/740) |
| | para 10 | 12 Jan 1987 (SI 1986/2246) |
| Sch 11 | para 1 | 12 Jan 1987 (SI 1986/2246) |
| | paras 2–5 | 4 Jun 1987 (SI 1987/907) |
| | para 6 | 1 Dec 1987 (SI 1987/1997) |
| | paras 7–16 | 4 Jun 1987 (SI 1987/907) |
| | para 17 | *Never in force* (repealed) |
| | paras 18–20 | 4 Jun 1987 (SI 1987/907) |
| | para 21 | 29 Apr 1988 (SI 1988/740) |
| | para 22(1)–(3) | 29 Apr 1988 (SI 1988/740) |
| | para 22(4) | 1 Dec 1987 (except for purposes of making a contravention of the kind described in para 22(4)(d) actionable at the suit of a person of the kind described in that paragraph) (SI 1987/1997) |
| | | 3 Oct 1988 (exception noted above) (SI 1987/1997) |
| | para 22(5) | 1 Dec 1987 (SI 1987/1997) |
| | para 23 | 29 Apr 1988 (SI 1988/740) |
| | para 24 | 4 Jun 1987 (SI 1987/907) |
| | paras 25–27 | 29 Apr 1988 (SI 1988/740) |
| | paras 28–37 | 12 Jan 1987 (SI 1986/2246) |
| | para 38 | 4 Jun 1987 (SI 1987/907) |
| | para 39 | 1 Jan 1988 (SI 1987/2158) |
| | paras 40, 41 | 12 Jan 1987 (SI 1986/2246) |
| | para 42 | 4 Jun 1987 (SI 1987/907) |
| | para 43 | 29 Apr 1988 (SI 1988/740) |
| | paras 44, 45 | 12 Jan 1987 (SI 1986/2246) |
| Sch 12 | | 30 Apr 1987 (SI 1986/2246) |
| Sch 13 | paras 1, 2 | 18 Dec 1986 (SI 1986/2246) |

**Financial Services Act 1986 (c 60)**—*contd*

| | |
|---|---|
| paras 3, 4 | 15 Nov 1986 (for purposes of anything done or which may be done under or by virtue of any provision brought into force by SI 1986/1940) (SI 1986/1940) |
| | 18 Dec 1986 (otherwise) (SI 1986/2246) |
| para 5 | 18 Dec 1986 (SI 1986/2246) |
| para 6 | 15 Nov 1986 (for purposes of anything done or which may be done under or by virtue of any provision brought into force by SI 1986/1940) (SI 1986/1940) |
| | 18 Dec 1986 (otherwise) (SI 1986/2246) |
| para 7 | 15 Nov 1986 (for purposes of anything done or which may be done under or by virtue of any provision brought into force by SI 1986/1940) (SI 1986/1940) |
| | 27 Nov 1986 (otherwise) (SI 1986/2031) |
| para 8 | 27 Nov 1986 (SI 1986/2031) |
| paras 9–11 | 15 Nov 1986 (for purposes of anything done or which may be done under or by virtue of any provision brought into force by SI 1986/1940) (SI 1986/1940) |
| | 27 Nov 1986 (otherwise) (SI 1986/2031) |
| para 12 | 27 Nov 1986 (SI 1986/2031) |
| paras 13, 14 | 15 Nov 1986 (for purposes of anything done or which may be done under or by virtue of any provision brought into force by SI 1986/1940) (SI 1986/1940) |
| | 27 Nov 1986 (otherwise) (SI 1986/2031) |
| Sch 14 | 12 Jan 1987 (so far as makes provision as to the application of— |

(i) Rehabilitation of Offenders Act 1974, s 4(1), in relation to the determination of proceedings of the kind specified in Sch 14, Pt I, para 4;

(ii) s 4(2) of the 1974 Act, in relation to a question put by or on behalf of a person specified in Sch 14, Pt II, para 5, first column;

(iii) s 4(3)(b) of the 1974 Act, in relation to action taken by the competent authority or by a person specified in Sch 14, Pt III, para 3, first column) (SI 1986/2246)

1 Dec 1987 (so far as makes provision as to the application of—

(i) Rehabilitation of Offenders Act 1974, s 4(1), in relation to the determination of proceedings of the kind described in Sch 14, Pt I, paras 2, 3 and 6; Rehabilitation of Offenders (Northern Ireland) Order 1978, art 5(1), in relation to the determination of proceedings of the kind described in those paras and in Sch 14, Pt I, para 4;

(ii) s 4(2) of the 1974 Act, in relation to a question put by or on behalf of a person specified in Sch 14, Pt II, para 6, first column; Rehabilitation of Offenders (Northern Ireland) Order 1978, art 5(2), in relation to a question put by or on behalf of a person specified in Sch 14, Pt II, para 5 or 6, first column;

(iii) s 4(2) of the 1974 Act and art 5(2) of the 1978 Order, in relation to a question put by or on behalf of a person specified in Sch 14, Pt II, para 2 or 3, first column; or to a question put by or on behalf of a person specified in Sch 14, Pt II, para 4, first column in so far as it relates to persons described in paras 2(a), (b) or (c) or 3(a), (b) or (c) or to a question put by or on behalf of a person specified in para 8 of that column;

(iv) s 4(3)(b) of the 1974 Act, in relation to action taken by a person of a kind described in sub-para (c) above and art 5(3)(b) of the 1978 Order in relation to action taken by a person described in sub-para (c) above or specified in Sch 14, Pt III, para 3, first column) (SI 1987/1977)

**Financial Services Act 1986 (c 60)**—*contd*

|  |  |  |
|---|---|---|
|  |  | 1 Jan 1988 (otherwise, except for the purposes of Rehabilitation of Offenders Act 1974 (Exceptions) (Amendment No 2) Order 1986, art 1(2)(b), and Rehabilitation of Offenders (Exceptions) (Amendment) Order (Northern Ireland) 1987, art 1(2)(b)) (SI 1987/2158) |
|  |  | *Never in force* (exception noted above) (repealed) |
| Sch 15 | para 1(1)–(3) | 27 Feb 1988 (SI 1987/2158) |
|  | para 1(4) | 29 Apr 1988 (SI 1988/740) |
|  | para 1(5) | 27 Feb 1988 (SI 1987/2158) |
|  | paras 2, 3 | 29 Apr 1988 (SI 1988/740) |
|  | paras 4–6 | 4 Jun 1987 (SI 1987/907) |
|  | paras 7–11 | 29 Apr 1988 (SI 1988/740) |
|  | para 12 | 12 Jan 1987 (SI 1986/2246) |
|  | para 13 | 27 Nov 1986 (SI 1986/2031) |
|  | paras 14, 15 | 29 Apr 1988 (SI 1988/740) |
|  | para 16 | 27 Feb 1988 (in relation to Sch 15, para 1(1)–(3), (5)) (SI 1987/2158) |
|  |  | 29 Apr 1988 (otherwise) (SI 1988/740) |
| Sch 16 | paras 1–12 | 29 Apr 1988 (SI 1988/740) |
|  | paras 13, 14 | 30 Apr 1987 (SI 1986/2246) |
|  | para 15 | 29 Apr 1988 (SI 1988/740) |
|  | para 16 | *Never in force* (repealed) |
|  | para 17(a), (b) | 29 Apr 1988 (SI 1988/740) |
|  | para 17(c) | 12 Jan 1987 (so far as relates to Companies Act 1985, s 173(2)(a)) (SI 1986/2246) |
|  |  | 29 Apr 1988 (otherwise) (SI 1988/740) |
|  | para 17(d) | 29 Apr 1988 (SI 1988/740) |
|  | paras 18–26 | 29 Apr 1988 (SI 1988/740) |
|  | para 27(a) | 29 Apr 1988 (SI 1988/740) |
|  | para 27(b) | 4 Jun 1987 (SI 1987/907) |
|  | para 28 | 12 Jan 1987 (SI 1986/2246) |
|  | paras 29, 30 | 29 Apr 1988 (SI 1988/740) |
|  | para 31 | *Never in force* (repealed) |
|  | para 32(a), (b) | 29 Apr 1988 (SI 1988/740) |
|  | para 32(c) | 12 Jan 1987 (so far as it relates to Companies (Northern Ireland) Order 1986, art 173(2)(a)) (SI 1986/2246) |
|  |  | 29 Apr 1988 (otherwise) (SI 1988/740) |
|  | para 32(d) | 29 Apr 1988 (SI 1988/740) |
|  | paras 33–43 | 29 Apr 1988 (SI 1988/740) |
| Sch 17 |  | 27 Nov 1986 (SI 1986/2031), repeals of or in— Banking Act 1979, s 20; Companies Act 1985, ss 433, 446(5); Companies Consolidation (Consequential Provisions) Act 1985, Sch 2 (entry relating to Banking Act 1979, s 20); Companies (Consequential Provisions) (Northern Ireland) Order 1986, Sch 2 (entry relating to Banking Act 1979, s 20) |
|  |  | 12 Jan 1987 (SI 1986/2246), repeals of or in— Banking Act 1979, Sch 1; Company Securities (Insider Dealing) Act 1985, s 3 |
|  |  | 12 Jan 1987 (for all purposes relating to the admission of securities offered by or on behalf of a minister of the Crown or a body corporate controlled by a minister of the Crown or a subsidiary of such a body corporate, to the Official List in respect of which an application is made after that date) (repeals of or in Companies Act 1985, Pt III, ss 81–87, 97, 693, 709, Schs 3, 22, 24 and corresponding provisions of Companies (Northern Ireland) Order 1986, to the extent to which they would apply in relation to any investment which is listed or the subject of an application for listing in accordance with Pt IV of the Act) (SI 1986/2246) |

**Financial Services Act 1986 (c 60)**—*contd*

16 Feb 1987 (in so far as not already in force, repeals of or in Companies Act 1985, Pt III, ss 81–87, 97, 693, 709, Schs 3, 22, 24 and corresponding provisions of Companies (Northern Ireland) Order 1986, to the extent to which they would apply in relation to any investment which is listed or the subject of an application for listing in accordance with Pt IV of the Act) (SI 1986/2246)

30 Apr 1987 (SI 1986/2246), repeals of or in—

Industry Act 1975;

Scottish Development Agency Act 1975;

Welsh Development Agency Act 1975;

Aircraft and Shipbuilding Industries Act 1977

29 Apr 1988 (SI 1988/740) otherwise, except repeals of or in—

such provisions of Prevention of Fraud (Investments) Act (Northern Ireland) 1940 as are necessary for the purposes of Sch 15, para 1(3) to this Act as it applies by virtue of para 16 of that Schedule;

such provisions of Prevention of Fraud (Investments) Act 1958 as are necessary for the purposes of Sch 15, para 1(3) to this Act;

Tribunals and Inquiries Act 1971;

House of Commons Disqualification Act 1975;

Restrictive Trade Practices (Stock Exchange) Act 1984;

Company Securities (Insider Dealing) Act 1985, s 13;

to the extent not yet repealed, and except in so far as is necessary to have the effect that those provisions cease to apply to a prospectus offering for subscription, or to any form of application for, units in a body corporate which is a recognised scheme, Companies Act 1985, Pt III, ss 81 to 87, 97, 449(1)(d), 693, 709, 744, so far as relates to the definition "prospectus issued generally", Schs 3, 22, 24, and corresponding provisions of Companies (Northern Ireland) Order 1986;

s 195 of this Act

1 Jul 1988 (repeal of Restrictive Trade Practices (Stock Exchange) Act 1984) (SI 1988/995)

31 Dec 1988 (so far as necessary to have the effect that, to the extent that they do apply, Companies Act 1985, Pt III, s 693, Sch 3, and corresponding provisions of Companies (Northern Ireland) Order 1986 cease to apply to a prospectus offering for subscription, or to any application form for, units in an open-ended investment company which does not fulfil the conditions described in head (a)(i) or (a)(ii) mentioned against s 76 above, except in relation to a prospectus offering for subscription, or to any application form for, units in an open-ended investment company which is managed in and authorised under the law of Bermuda, units in which are, on 31 Dec 1988, included in the Official List of the International Stock Exchange of the United Kingdom and the Republic of Ireland Limited) (SI 1988/1960 (amending SI 1988/740); SI 1988/2285)

**Financial Services Act 1986 (c 60)**—*contd*

28 Feb 1989 (so far as necessary to have the effect that, to the extent that they do apply, Companies Act 1985, Pt III, s 693, Sch 3, and corresponding provisions of Companies (Northern Ireland) Order 1986 cease to apply to a prospectus offering for subscription, or to any application form for, units in an open-ended investment company managed in and authorised under the law of Bermuda, units in which are, on 31 Dec 1988, included in the Official List of the International Stock Exchange of the United Kingdom and the Republic of Ireland Limited but which is not a scheme of a class specified in the Schedule to the Financial Services (Designated Countries and Territories) (Overseas Collective Investment Schemes) (Bermuda) Order 1988, SI 1988/2284) (SI 1988/2285)

1 Mar 1989 (so far as necessary to have the effect that to the extent that they do apply, Companies Act 1985, Pt III, s 693, Sch 3, and corresponding provisions of Companies (Northern Ireland) Order 1986 cease to apply to a prospectus offering for subscription, or to any application form for, units in an open-ended investment company which does fulfil the conditions described in head (a)(i) or (a)(ii) mentioned against s 76 above) (SI 1988/1960 (amending SI 1988/740), as amended by SI 1988/2285)

1 May 1989 (so far as necessary to have the effect that, to the extent that they do apply, Companies Act 1985, Pt III, s 693, Sch 3, and corresponding provisions of Companies (Northern Ireland) Order 1986 cease to apply to a prospectus offering for subscription, or to any application form for, units in an open-ended investment company managed in and authorised under the law of Bermuda, units in which are, on 31 Dec 1988, included in the Official List of the International Stock Exchange of the United Kingdom and the Republic of Ireland Limited and which is a scheme of a class specified in Financial Services (Designated Countries and Territories) (Overseas Collective Investment Schemes) (Bermuda) Order 1988, SI 1988/2284, Schedule) (SI 1988/2285)

1 Oct 1989 (SI 1989/1583), repeals of or in—

Prevention of Fraud (Investments) Act (Northern Ireland) 1940 (for all remaining purposes);

Prevention of Fraud (Investments) Act 1958 (for all remaining purposes);

Tribunals and Inquiries Act 1971;

House of Commons Disqualification Act 1975

19 Jun 1995 (SI 1995/1538), repeals of—

(i) Companies Act 1985, Pt III, Sch 3, Sch 22 (entry relating to Pt III), Sch 24 (entries relating to ss 56(4), 61, 64(5), 70(1), 78(1)), those repeals brought into force for all remaining purposes except for repeals of ss 58, 59, 60 (so far as necessary for purposes of ss 81, 83, 246, 248, 744), Sch 3, para 2 (so far as necessary for purposes of s 83(1)(a)) and s 62 (so far as necessary for purposes of s 744); and

(ii) corresponding provisions of Companies (Northern Ireland) Order 1986, SI 1986/1032 (NI 6)

10 May 1999 (SI 1999/727) repeals of or in—

(i) Companies Act 1985, ss 82, 83, and the corresponding provisions of Companies (Northern Ireland) Order 1986, SI 1986/1032, for all remaining purposes except for the purposes of prospectuses to which Public Offers of Securities Regulations 1995, SI 1995/1537, reg 8 applies; and

(ii) Companies Act 1985, ss 86, 87, and the corresponding provisions of Companies (Northern Ireland) Order 1986, SI 1986/1032, for all remaining purposes

**Financial Services Act 1986 (c 60)**—*contd*

*Never in force* (otherwise) (repealed)

**Forestry Act 1986 (c 30)**

*RA:* 8 Jul 1986

*Commencement provisions:* s 2(1)

Whole Act in force 8 Sep 1986 (s 2(1))

**Gaming (Amendment) Act 1986 (c 11)**

*RA:* 2 May 1986

*Commencement provisions:* s 3(3); Gaming (Amendment) Act 1986 (Commencement) Order 1988, SI 1988/1250

Whole Act in force 19 Sep 1988 (SI 1988/1250)

**Gas Act 1986 (c 44)**

*RA:* 25 Jul 1986

*Commencement provisions:* ss 3, 49(1), 57(2), 68(2)–(5); Gas Act 1986 (Commencement No 1) Order 1986, SI 1986/1315; Gas Act 1986 (Appointed Day) Order 1986, SI 1986/1316; Gas Act 1986 (Transfer Date) Order 1986, SI 1986/1318; Gas Act 1986 (Commencement No 2) Order 1986, SI 1986/1809; British Gas Corporation (Dissolution) Order 1990, SI 1990/147

| | | |
|---|---|---|
| 1 | | 18 Aug 1986 (SI 1986/1315) |
| 2 | | 23 Aug 1986 (SI 1986/1315) |
| 3–48 | | 23 Aug 1986 (s 68(2); SI 1986/1316) |
| 49–61 | | 24 Aug 1986 (s 68(3); SI 1986/1318) |
| 62 | | 14 Nov 1986 (SI 1986/1809) |
| 63, 64 | | 23 Aug 1986 (SI 1986/1315) |
| 65 | | 18 Aug 1986 (SI 1986/1315) |
| 66 | | 23 Aug 1986 (s 68(2); SI 1986/1316) |
| 67 | (1), (2) | 23 Aug 1986 (s 68(2); SI 1986/1316) |
| | (3) | See Sch 8 below |
| | (4) | See Sch 9 below |
| 68 | | 18 Aug 1986 (SI 1986/1315) |
| Sch 1 | | 18 Aug 1986 (SI 1986/1315) |
| Sch 2 | | 23 Aug 1986 (SI 1986/1315) |
| Schs 3–5 | | 23 Aug 1986 (s 68(2); SI 1986/1316) |
| Sch 6 | | 24 Aug 1986 (s 68(3); SI 1986/1318) |
| Sch 7 | | 23 Aug 1986 (s 68(2); SI 1986/1316) |
| Sch 8 | Pt I | 23 Aug 1986 (s 68(3); SI 1986/1316) |
| | Pt II | 24 Aug 1986 (s 68(3); SI 1986/1318) |
| Sch 9 | Pt I | 23 Aug 1986 (s 68(2); SI 1986/1316) |
| | Pt II | 24 Aug 1986 (s 68(3); SI 1986/1318) |
| | Pt III | 28 Feb 1990 (SI 1990/147) |

**Health Service Joint Consultative Committees (Access to Information) Act 1986 (c 24)**

*RA:* 26 Jun 1986

*Commencement provisions:* s 4(2)

Whole Act in force 26 Aug 1986 (s 4(2))

## Highways (Amendment) Act 1986 (c 13)

*RA:* 2 May 1986

*Commencement provisions:* s 2(2)

Whole Act in force 2 Jul 1986 (s 2(2))

---

## Horticultural Produce Act 1986 (c 20)

*RA:* 26 Jun 1986

*Commencement provisions:* s 7(3)

Whole Act in force 26 Aug 1986 (s 7(3))

---

## Housing and Planning Act 1986 (c 63)

*RA:* 7 Nov 1986

*Commencement provisions:* s 57(1), (2); Housing and Planning Act 1986 (Commencement No 1) Order 1986, SI 1986/2262; Housing and Planning Act 1986 (Commencement No 2) Order 1987, SI 1987/178 (revoked); Housing and Planning Act 1986 (Commencement No 3) Order 1987, SI 1987/304; Housing and Planning Act 1986 (Commencement No 4) Order 1987, SI 1987/348; Housing and Planning Act 1986 (Commencement No 5) Order 1987, SI 1987/754; Housing and Planning Act 1986 (Commencement No 6) Order 1987, SI 1987/1554 (revoked); Housing and Planning Act 1986 (Commencement No 7) (Scotland) Order 1987, SI 1987/1607; Housing and Planning Act 1986 (Commencement No 8) Order 1987, SI 1987/1759; Housing and Planning Act 1986 (Commencement No 9) Order 1987, SI 1987/1939; Housing and Planning Act 1986 (Commencement No 10) Order 1987, SI 1987/2277; Housing and Planning Act 1986 (Commencement No 11) Order 1988, SI 1988/283; Housing and Planning Act 1986 (Commencement No 12) Order 1988, SI 1988/1787; Housing and Planning Act 1986 (Commencement No 13) Order 1989, SI 1989/430; Housing and Planning Act 1986 (Commencement No 14) Order 1990, SI 1990/511; Housing and Planning Act 1986 (Commencement No 15) Order 1990, SI 1990/614; Housing and Planning Act 1986 (Commencement No 16) Order 1990, SI 1990/797 (bringing into force enabling provision in relation to Sch 11, paras 39, 40 only); Housing and Planning Act 1986 (Commencement No 17 and Transitional Provisions) Order 1992, SI 1992/1753; Housing and Planning Act 1986 (Commencement No 18 and Transitional Provisions) (Scotland) Order 1993, SI 1993/273; Housing and Planning Act 1986 (Commencement No 19) (Scotland) Order 1996, SI 1996/1276

| | | |
|---|---|---|
| 1–4 | | 7 Jan 1987 (SI 1986/2262) |
| 5 | | 13 Jul 1992 (SI 1992/1753) |
| 6 | | 11 Mar 1988 (SI 1988/283) |
| 7 | | *Never in force* (repealed) |
| 8 | | 5 Apr 1989 (SI 1989/430) |
| 9 | | 13 May 1987 (SI 1987/754) |
| 10–14 | | 7 Jan 1987 (SI 1986/2262) |
| 15 | | 17 Feb 1988 (SI 1987/2277) |
| 16, 17 | | 7 Jan 1987 (SI 1986/2262) |
| 18 | | See Sch 4 below |
| 19, 20 | | 7 Jan 1987 (SI 1986/2262) |
| 21 | | 7 Nov 1986 (s 57(1)) |
| 22, 23 | | 7 Jan 1987 (SI 1986/2262) |
| 24 | (1), (2) | See Sch 5 below (note sub-s (1)(j) came into force on 7 Nov 1986) (s 57(1)) |
| | (3) | See Sch 12, Pt I below |
| 25 | | 2 Nov 1987 (SI 1987/1759) |
| 26 | | 1 Oct 1987 (SI 1987/1607) |
| 27–29 | | 7 Jan 1987 (SI 1986/2262) |
| 30–34 | | *Never in force* (repealed) |

**Housing and Planning Act 1986 (c 63)**—*contd*

| | | |
|---|---|---|
| 35, 36 | | 18 Feb 1993 (so far as confers power or imposes duty on Secretary of State to make regulations, or makes provision with respect to exercise of any such power or duty) (SI 1993/273) |
| | | 1 May 1993 (otherwise) (subject to transitional provisions) (SI 1993/273) |
| 37 | | See Sch 7, Pt II below |
| 38 | | 18 Feb 1993 (so far as confers power or imposes duty on Secretary of State to make regulations, or makes provision with respect to exercise of any such power or duty) (SI 1993/273) |
| | | 1 May 1993 (otherwise) (SI 1993/273) |
| 39 | | 11 Dec 1987 (SI 1987/1939) |
| 40 | | 1 Apr 1987 (SI 1987/348) |
| 41 | | 2 Nov 1987 (SI 1987/1759) |
| 42 | | 17 Nov 1988 (SI 1988/1787) |
| 43 | | 31 Mar 1990 (SI 1990/614) |
| 44–48 | | 7 Jan 1987 (SI 1986/2262) |
| 49 | (1) | See Sch 11, Pt I below |
| | (2) | See Sch 12, Pt III below |
| 50, 51 | | 1 Oct 1987 (SI 1987/1607) |
| 52 | | 7 Nov 1986 (s 57(1)) |
| 53 | (1) | See Sch 11, Pt II below |
| | (2) | See Sch 12, Pt IV below |
| 54, 55 | | 7 Jan 1987 (SI 1986/2262) |
| 56–59 | | 7 Nov 1986 (s 57(1)) |
| Sch 1 | | 11 Mar 1988 (SI 1988/283) |
| Sch 2 | | 5 Apr 1989 (SI 1989/430) |
| Sch 3 | | 17 Feb 1988 (SI 1988/2277) |
| Sch 4 | paras 1–9 | 11 Dec 1987 (SI 1987/1939) |
| | para 10 | *Never in force* (repealed) |
| | para 11 | 11 Dec 1987 (SI 1987/1939) |
| Sch 5 | paras 1–7 | 7 Jan 1987 (SI 1986/2262) |
| | para 8 | 22 Sep 1987 (SI 1987/1554) |
| | para 9 | 17 Feb 1988 (SI 1987/2277) |
| | paras 10–13 | 7 Nov 1986 (s 57(1)) |
| | paras 14, 15 | 7 Jan 1987 (SI 1986/2262) |
| | para 16 | *Not yet in force* |
| | para 17 | 7 Jan 1987 (SI 1986/2262) |
| | paras 18–20 | 17 Aug 1992 (SI 1992/1753) |
| | paras 21–26 | 7 Jan 1987 (SI 1986/2262) |
| | para 27 | 17 Aug 1992 (so far as relates to definitions "consent" and "management agreement and manager") (SI 1992/1753) |
| | | *Not yet in force* (so far as relates to definition "landlord") |
| | para 28 | 7 Jan 1987 (SI 1986/2262) |
| | para 29 | 17 Aug 1992 (SI 1992/1753)[1] |
| | para 30 | 7 Jan 1987 (SI 1986/2262) |
| | para 31 | 17 Aug 1992 (SI 1992/1753) |
| | paras 32, 33 | 7 Jan 1987 (SI 1986/2262) |
| | paras 34–38 | 17 Aug 1992 (SI 1992/1753)[1] |
| | para 39 | 7 Jan 1987 (SI 1986/2262) |
| | para 40 | 17 Aug 1992 (SI 1992/1753)[1] |
| | paras 41, 42 | 7 Jan 1987 (SI 1986/2262) |
| Sch 6 | Pts I, II | 2 Nov 1987 (SI 1987/1759) |
| | Pts III, IV | 1 Oct 1987 (SI 1987/1607) |
| Sch 7 | Pt I | *Never in force* (repealed) |
| | Pt II, paras 1–3 | 1 May 1993 (SI 1993/273) |
| | Pt II, para 4 | 18 Feb 1993 (SI 1993/273) |
| | Pt II, paras 5–8 | 1 May 1993 (SI 1993/273) |
| Sch 8 | | 11 Dec 1987 (SI 1987/1939) |
| Sch 9 | Pt I | 1 Apr 1987 (SI 1987/348) |

**Housing and Planning Act 1986 (c 63)**—*contd*

| | | |
|---|---|---|
| | Pt II | 1 Oct 1987 (SI 1987/1607) |
| Sch 10 | | 2 Nov 1987 (SI 1987/1759) |
| Sch 11 | Pt I, paras 1–7 | 7 Jan 1987 (SI 1986/2262) |
| | Pt I, para 8 | 2 Mar 1987 (SI 1987/304) |
| | Pt I, para 9 | *Never in force* (repealed) |
| | Pt I, paras 10–14 | 7 Jan 1987 (SI 1986/2262) |
| | Pt I, para 15 | 2 Nov 1987 (SI 1987/1759) |
| | Pt I, paras 16–18 | 7 Jan 1987 (SI 1986/2262) |
| | Pt I, para 19 | *Never in force* (repealed) |
| | Pt I, paras 20–22 | 7 Jan 1987 (SI 1986/2262) |
| | Pt I, para 23 | 2 Nov 1987 (SI 1987/1759) |
| | Pt I, paras 24, 25 | 7 Jan 1987 (SI 1986/2262) |
| | Pt I, paras 26, 27 | 2 Nov 1987 (SI 1987/1759) |
| | Pt II, paras 28–38 | 7 Jan 1987 (SI 1986/2262) |
| | Pt II, paras 39, 40 | 31 Mar 1990 (SI 1990/511) |
| | Pt II, paras 41–56 | 7 Jan 1987 (SI 1986/2262) |
| | Pt II, paras 57, 58 | 1 Jun 1996 (SI 1996/1276) |
| | Pt II, paras 59–62 | 7 Jan 1987 (SI 1986/2262) |
| Sch 12 | Pt I | 7 Nov 1986 (repeals in Housing (Consequential Provisions) Act 1985 specified in first part of Sch 12, Pt I) (s 57(1)) |

Pt I *(contd)*

7 Jan 1987 (SI 1986/2262), repeals of or in—
Housing Rents and Subsidies (Scotland) Act 1975;
Rent Act 1977, s 70;
Housing Act 1980, s 56;
New Towns Act 1981;
Housing Act 1985, ss 30, 46, 127, Schs 4, 6;
Housing (Consequential Provisions) Act 1985, Sch 2, paras 27, 35(3), 45(2)

11 Dec 1987 (SI 1987/1939), repeals of or in—
Housing Act 1980, s 140;
Local Government Planning and Land Act 1980, s 156(3);
Local Government Act 1985, Sch 13, para 14(d), Sch 14, para 58(e)

*Not yet in force*, repeals of or in—
Rent Act 1977, s 69(1), Sch 12, para 3 (repealed);
Housing Act 1985, ss 452(2), 453(2)[2]

| | | |
|---|---|---|
| | Pt II | 11 Dec 1987 (SI 1987/1939) |
| | Pt III | 7 Jan 1987 (SI 1986/2262), repeals of or in— |

Electric Lighting (Clauses) Act 1899;
Electricity (Supply) Act 1926;
Requisitioned Land and War Works Act 1945;
Town and Country Planning Act 1947;
Electricity Act 1947;
Requisitioned Land and War Works Act 1948;
Electricity Act 1957;
Town and Country Planning Act 1971, ss 29A, 29B, 32(2), 66–86, 88B, 105, 147, 151, 165, 169, 180, 185, 191, 237, 250–252, 260, 287(4), (5), (7), 290, Schs 12, 13, 21, 24;
Town and Country Planning (Amendment) Act 1972;
Local Government Act 1972, s 182;
Local Government Act 1974;
Town and Country Amenities Act 1974, s 3;
Control of Office Development Act 1977;
Local Government, Planning and Land Act 1980 (except s 88);
Industrial Development Act 1982;
Local Government Act 1985, s 3

1 Apr 1987 (SI 1987/348), repeals of or in—
Town and Country Planning Act 1971, s 55(4);
Town and Country Amenities Act 1974, s 5;

**Housing and Planning Act 1986 (c 63)**—*contd*
> National Heritage Act 1983;
> Local Government Act 1985, Sch 2, para 1(8)
> 2 Nov 1987 (SI 1987/1759), repeals of or in—
> Local Government Act 1972, s 183(2), Sch 16, paras 1–3;
> Local Government, Planning and Land Act 1980, s 88;
> Local Government (Miscellaneous Provisions) Act 1982, Sch 6, para 7(b)
> 17 Nov 1988 (SI 1988/1787), repeals of or in—
> Public Expenditure and Receipts Act 1968;
> Local Government Act 1972, s 250(4);
> Land Drainage Act 1976;
> Road Traffic Regulation Act 1984
> 31 Mar 1990 (repeal in Acquisition of Land Act 1981, Sch 4, para 1) (SI 1990/614)
> *Never in force* (repeals of or in Town and Country Planning Act 1971, ss 110(1), 287(9) (repealed))

Pt IV
> 7 Jan 1987 (SI 1986/2262), repeals of or in—
> Town and Country Planning (Scotland) Act 1972, ss 29, 63, 64–83, 85, 136, 140, 154, 164, 174, 180, 226, 231, 233, 237–239, 247, 273(4), (5), (7), (8), 275, Schs 19, 22;
> Local Government Planning and Land 1980;
> Industrial Development Act 1982
> 1 Jun 1996 (SI 1996/1276), repeals of or in—
> Public Expenditure and Receipts Act 1968;
> Town and Country Planning (Scotland) Act 1972, ss 53(2), 53(4);
> Town and Country Amenities Act 1974;
> Road Traffic Regulation Act 1984
> *Never in force* (repeals of or in Town and Country Planning (Scotland) Act 1972, ss 158(5), (7), 169(4), 273(9) (repealed))

[1]   For transitional provisions, see SI 1992/1753, art 2, Schedule

[2]   Note that these repeals are also made by Sch 5, paras 35, 36 above, and have effectively been brought into force in accordance with those paragraphs

No further orders have been made under s 57(2) bringing the remainder of the repeals in this Part of this Sch into force, but these outstanding repeals can no longer take effect or have effectively been brought into force in accordance with certain provisions of Sch 5 to this Act.

---

**Housing (Scotland) Act 1986 (c 65)**

*RA:* 7 Nov 1986

*Commencement provisions:* s 26(2); Housing (Scotland) Act 1986 (Commencement) Order 1986, SI 1986/2137

| | |
|---|---|
| 1–25 | 7 Jan 1987 (SI 1986/2137) |
| 26 | 7 Nov 1986 (RA) |
| Schs 1, 2 | 7 Jan 1987 (SI 1986/2137) |

---

**Incest and Related Offences (Scotland) Act 1986 (c 36)**

*RA:* 18 Jul 1986

*Commencement provisions:* s 3(2); Incest and Related Offences (Scotland) Act 1986 (Commencement) Order 1986, SI 1986/1803

Whole Act in force 1 Nov 1986 (SI 1986/1803)

---

## Industrial Training Act 1986 (c 15)

*RA:* 20 May 1986

*Commencement provisions:* s 2(2)

Whole Act in force 20 Jul 1986 (s 2(2))

---

## Insolvency Act 1986 (c 45)

*RA:* 25 Jul 1986

*Commencement provisions:* s 443; Insolvency Act 1985 (Commencement No 5) Order 1986, SI 1986/1924

Whole Act in force 29 Dec 1986 (s 443; SI 1986/1924)

---

## Land Registration Act 1986 (c 26)

*RA:* 26 Jun 1986

*Commencement provisions:* s 6(4); Land Registration Act 1986 (Commencement) Order 1986, SI 1986/2117

Whole Act in force 1 Jan 1987 (SI 1986/2117)

---

## Latent Damage Act 1986 (c 37)

*RA:* 18 Jul 1986

*Commencement provisions:* s 5(3)

Whole Act in force 18 Sep 1986 (s 5(3))

---

## Law Reform (Parent and Child) (Scotland) Act 1986 (c 9)

*RA:* 26 Mar 1986

*Commencement provisions:* s 11(2); Law Reform (Parent and Child) (Scotland) Act 1986 (Commencement) Order 1986, SI 1986/1983

Whole Act in force 8 Dec 1986 (SI 1986/1983)

---

## Legal Aid (Scotland) Act 1986 (c 47)

*RA:* 25 Jul 1986

*Commencement provisions:* s 46(2); Legal Aid (Scotland) Act 1986 (Commencement No 1) Order 1986, SI 1986/1617; Legal Aid (Scotland) Act 1986 (Commencement No 2) Order 1987, SI 1987/289; Legal Aid (Scotland) Act 1986 (Commencement No 3) Order 1992, SI 1992/1226; Legal Aid (Scotland) Act 1986 (Commencement No 4) Order 2001, SSI 2001/393

| | | |
|---|---|---|
| 1 | (1) | 1 Oct 1986 (SI 1986/1617) |
| | (2) | 1 Apr 1987 (SI 1987/289) |
| | (3)–(6) | 1 Oct 1986 (SI 1986/1617) |
| 2 | (1) | 1 Apr 1987 (SI 1987/289) |
| | (2), (3) | 1 Oct 1986 (SI 1986/1617) |
| 3 | (1), (2) | 1 Oct 1986 (SI 1986/1617) |
| | (3) | 1 Apr 1987 (SI 1987/289) |
| | (4)–(6) | 1 Oct 1986 (SI 1986/1617) |
| 4–25 | | 1 Apr 1987 (SI 1987/289) |
| 26–28 | | 2 Nov 2001 (SSI 2001/393) |
| 29 | | 1 Apr 1987 (SI 1987/289) |

**Legal Aid (Scotland) Act 1986 (c 47)**—*contd*

| | | |
|---|---|---|
| 30 | | 1 Jul 1992 (SI 1992/1226) |
| 31–39 | | 1 Apr 1987 (SI 1987/289) |
| 40 | (1)(a) | 1 Apr 1987 (SI 1987/289) |
| | (1)(b) | 1 Oct 1986 (SI 1986/1617) |
| | (2)(a) | 1 Apr 1987 (SI 1987/289) |
| | (2)(b) | 1 Oct 1986 (SI 1986/1617) |
| | (3), (4) | 1 Apr 1987 (SI 1987/289) |
| 41 | | 1 Oct 1986 (SI 1986/1617) |
| 42–44 | | 1 Apr 1987 (SI 1987/289) |
| 45 | (1) | See Sch 3 below |
| | (2), (3) | 1 Apr 1987 (SI 1987/289) |
| 46 | | 25 Jul 1986 (RA) |
| Sch 1 | | 1 Oct 1986 (SI 1986/1617) |
| Sch 2 | | 1 Apr 1987 (SI 1987/289) |
| Sch 3 | paras 1, 2 | 1 Apr 1987 (SI 1987/289) |
| | paras 3, 4 | 1 Oct 1986 (SI 1986/1617) |
| | paras 5–9 | 1 Apr 1987 (SI 1987/289) |
| Schs 4, 5 | | 1 Apr 1987 (SI 1987/289) |

**Local Government Act 1986 (c 10)**

*RA:* 26 Mar 1986

*Commencement provisions:* s 12(2); Local Government Act 1986 (Commencement) Order 1987, SI 1987/2003

| | |
|---|---|
| 1 | 26 Mar 1986 (s 12(2)) |
| 2–4 | 1 Apr 1986 (s 12(2)) |
| 5 | 1 Apr 1988 (SI 1987/2003) |
| 6 | 1 Apr 1986 (s 12(2)) |
| 7 | 26 Mar 1986 (s 12(2)) |
| 8 | 1 Apr 1986 (s 12(2)) |
| 9–12 | 26 Mar 1986 (s 12(2)) |

**Marriage (Prohibited Degrees of Relationship) Act 1986 (c 16)**

*RA:* 20 May 1986

*Commencement provisions:* s 6(5); Marriage (Prohibited Degrees of Relationship) Act 1986 (Commencement) Order 1986, SI 1986/1343

Whole Act in force 1 Nov 1986 (SI 1986/1343)

**Marriage (Wales) Act 1986 (c 7)**

*RA:* 18 Mar 1986

Whole Act in force 18 Mar 1986 (RA)

**Museum of London Act 1986 (c 8)**

*RA:* 26 Mar 1986

*Commencement provisions:* s 7(2)

Whole Act in force 1 Apr 1986 (s 7(2))

## National Health Service (Amendment) Act 1986 (c 66)

*RA:* 7 Nov 1986

*Commencement provisions:* s 8(4), (5); National Health Service (Amendment) Act 1986 (Commencement No 1) Order 1987, SI 1987/399

| | |
|---|---|
| 1, 2 | 7 Feb 1987 (s 8(4)) |
| 3 | 1 Apr 1987 (SI 1987/399) |
| 4 | 7 Nov 1986 (RA) |
| 5 | 7 Nov 1986 (except so far as inserts National Health Service (Scotland) Act 1978, s 13B) (RA) |
| | *Not yet in force* (exception noted above) |
| 6–8 | 7 Nov 1986 (RA) |

## Outer Space Act 1986 (c 38)

*RA:* 18 Jul 1986

*Commencement provisions:* s 15(2); Outer Space Act 1986 (Commencement) Order 1989, SI 1989/1097

Whole Act in force 31 Jul 1989 (SI 1989/1097)

## Parliamentary Constituencies Act 1986 (c 56)

*RA:* 7 Nov 1986

*Commencement provisions:* s 9(2)

Whole Act in force 7 Feb 1986 (s 9(2))

## Patents, Designs and Marks Act 1986 (c 39)

*RA:* 18 Jul 1986

*Commencement provisions:* s 4(6), (7); Patents, Designs and Marks Act 1986 (Commencement No 1) Order 1986, SI 1986/1274; Patents, Designs and Marks Act 1986 (Commencement No 2) Order 1988, SI 1988/1824

| | | |
|---|---|---|
| 1 | | See Sch 1 below |
| 2 | | 1 Oct 1986 (s 4(7)) |
| 3 | | See Sch 3 below |
| 4 | | 18 Jul 1986 (RA) |
| Sch 1 | paras 1, 2 | 1 Oct 1986 (SI 1986/1274) |
| | paras 3, 4 | 1 Jan 1989 (SI 1988/1824) |
| Sch 2 | | 1 Oct 1986 (s 4(7)) |
| Sch 3 | Pt I | 1 Oct 1986 (repeals in Trade Marks Act 1938) (SI 1986/1274) |
| | | 1 Jan 1989 (SI 1988/1824), repeals of— |
| | | Registered Designs Act 1949, s 24; |
| | | Patents Act 1977, s 35 |
| | Pt II | 1 Oct 1986 (s 4(7)) |

## Patronage (Benefices) Measure 1986 (No 3)

*RA:* 18 Jul 1986

*Commencement provisions:* s 42(3)

The provisions of this Measure were brought into force on the following dates by an instrument made by the Archbishops of Canterbury and York and dated 31 Dec 1986 (made under s 42(3))

| | |
|---|---|
| 1, 2 | 1 Oct 1987 |

**Patronage (Benefices) Measure 1986 (No 3)**—*contd*

| | | |
|---|---|---|
| 3–5 | | 1 Jan 1989 |
| 6 | | 1 Oct 1987 |
| 7–25 | | 1 Jan 1989 |
| 26, 27 | | 1 Jan 1987 |
| 28–34 | | 1 Jan 1989 |
| 35 | (1)–(3) | 1 Oct 1987 |
| | (4)–(9) | 1 Jan 1989 |
| 36, 37 | | 1 Oct 1987 |
| 38, 39 | | 1 Jan 1987 |
| 40 | | 1 Oct 1987 |
| 41 | | 1 Jan 1989 |
| 42 | | 1 Jan 1987 |
| Sch 1 | | 1 Oct 1987 |
| Sch 2 | | 1 Jan 1989 |
| Sch 3 | | 1 Jan 1987 |
| Sch 4 | | 1 Jan 1989 |
| Sch 5 | | 1 Jan 1987 (repeal of Benefices (Diocesan Boards of Patronage) Measure 1932) |
| | | 1 Jan 1989 (otherwise) |

**Prevention of Oil Pollution Act 1986 (c 6)**

*RA:* 18 Mar 1986

*Commencement provisions:* s 2(2)

Whole Act in force 18 May 1986 (s 2(2))

**Protection of Children (Tobacco) Act 1986 (c 34)**

*RA:* 8 Jul 1986

*Commencement provisions:* s 3(3)

Whole Act in force 8 Oct 1986 (s 3(3))

**Protection of Military Remains Act 1986 (c 35)**

*RA:* 8 Jul 1986

*Commencement provisions:* s 10(2)

Whole Act in force 8 Sep 1986 (s 10(2))

**Public Order Act 1986 (c 64)**

*RA:* 7 Nov 1986

*Commencement provisions:* s 41(1); Public Order Act 1986 (Commencement No 1) Order 1986, SI 1986/2041; Public Order Act 1986 (Commencement No 2) Order 1987, SI 1987/198; Public Order Act 1986 (Commencement No 3) Order 1987, SI 1987/852

| | |
|---|---|
| 1–10 | 1 Apr 1987 (SI 1987/198) |
| 11 | 1 Jan 1987 (SI 1986/2041) |
| 12–15 | 1 Apr 1987 (SI 1987/198) |
| 16 | 1 Jan 1987 (SI 1986/2041) |
| 17–29 | 1 Apr 1987 (SI 1987/198) |
| 30–37 | 1 Aug 1987 (SI 1987/852) |
| 38 | 1 Jan 1987 (SI 1986/2041) |

**Public Order Act 1986 (c 64)**—*contd*

| | | |
|---|---|---|
| 39 | | 1 Apr 1987 (SI 1987/198) |
| 40 | (1) | See Sch 1 below |
| | (2) | See Sch 2 below |
| | (3) | See Sch 3 below |
| | (4), (5) | 1 Apr 1987 (SI 1987/198) |
| 41–43 | | 1 Jan 1987 (SI 1986/2041) |
| Sch 1 | | 1 Jan 1987 (SI 1986/2041) |
| Sch 2 | paras 1, 2 | 1 Apr 1987 (SI 1987/198) |
| | para 3(1), (2) | 1 Jan 1987 (SI 1986/2041) |
| | para 3(3)–(6) | 1 Apr 1987 (SI 1987/198) |
| | paras 4–7 | 1 Apr 1987 (SI 1987/198) |
| Sch 3 | | 1 Jan 1987 (SI 1986/2041), repeals in— |

      Erith Tramways and Improvement Act 1903;
      Middlesex County Council Act 1944;
      County of South Glamorgan Act 1976;
      Cheshire County Council Act 1980;
      County of Merseyside Act 1980;
      Isle of Wight Act 1980;
      West Midlands County Council Act 1980;
      East Sussex Act 1981;
      Greater Manchester Act 1981;
      Civic Government (Scotland) Act 1982, s 62;
      Sporting Events (Control of Alcohol etc) Act 1985
      1 Apr 1987 (otherwise) (SI 1987/198)

## Public Trustee and Administration of Funds Act 1986 (c 57)

*RA:* 7 Nov 1986

*Commencement provisions:* s 6(2); Public Trustee and Administration of Funds Act 1986 Commencement Order 1986, SI 1986/2261

Whole Act in force 2 Jan 1987 (SI 1986/2261)

## Rate Support Grants Act 1986 (c 54)

*RA:* 21 Oct 1986

Whole Act in force 21 Oct 1986 (RA)

## Road Traffic Regulation (Parking) Act 1986 (c 27)

*RA:* 8 Jul 1986

*Commencement provisions:* s 3(3)

Whole Act in force 8 Sep 1986 (s 3(3))

## Safety at Sea Act 1986 (c 23)

*RA:* 26 Jun 1986

*Commencement provisions:* s 15(3), (4); Safety at Sea Act 1986 (Commencement No 1) Order 1986, SI 1986/1759

| | | |
|---|---|---|
| 1–9 | | *Never in force* (repealed) |
| 10, 11 | | 30 Oct 1986 (SI 1986/1759) |
| 12, 13 | | *Never in force* (repealed) |
| 14 | (1) | *Never in force* (repealed) |

**Safety at Sea Act 1986 (c 23)**—*contd*

| | | |
|---|---|---|
| | (2), (3) | 30 Oct 1986 (SI 1986/1759) |
| | (4) | 30 Oct 1986 (so far as relates to sub-ss (2), (3)) (SI 1986/1759) |
| | | *Never in force* (otherwise) (repealed) |
| 15 | | 30 Oct 1986 (SI 1986/1759) |

---

**Salmon Act 1986 (c 62)**

*RA:* 7 Nov 1986

*Commencement provisions:* s 43(1), (2); Salmon Act 1986 (Commencement and Transitional Provisions) Order 1992, SI 1992/1973

| | |
|---|---|
| 1–20 | 7 Jan 1987 (s 43(1)) |
| 21 | 1 Jan 1993 (subject to transitional provisions) (SI 1992/1973) |
| 22–43 | 7 Jan 1987 (s 43(1)) |
| Schs 1–5 | 7 Jan 1987 (s 43(1)) |

---

**Sex Discrimination Act 1986 (c 59)**

*RA:* 7 Nov 1986

*Commencement provisions:* s 10(2)–(4); Sex Discrimination Act (Commencement) Order 1986, SI 1986/2313; Sex Discrimination Act 1986 (Commencement No 2) Order 1988, SI 1988/99

| | | |
|---|---|---|
| 1 | | 7 Feb 1987 (s 10(2)) |
| 2, 3 | | 7 Nov 1987 (s 10(4)) |
| 4, 5 | | 7 Nov 1986 (RA) |
| 6 | | 7 Feb 1987 (s 10(2)) |
| 7 | (1) | 26 Feb 1988 (SI 1988/99) |
| | (2), (3) | 27 Feb 1987 (SI 1986/2313) |
| | (4), (5) | 26 Feb 1988 (SI 1988/99) |
| 8 | | 27 Feb 1987 (SI 1986/2313) |
| 9 | (1) | 7 Feb 1987 (s 10(2)) |
| | (2) | 7 Nov 1986 (RA) |
| | (3) | 7 Feb 1987 (s 10(2)) |
| 10 | | 7 Nov 1986 (RA) |
| Sch | Pt I | 7 Nov 1986 (RA) |
| | Pt II | 7 Feb 1987 (s 10(2)) |
| | Pt III | 27 Feb 1987 (SI 1986/2313), repeals of or in— |
| | | Baking Industry (Hours of Work) Act 1954; |
| | | Mines and Quarries Act 1954, ss 125, 126, 128, 131; |
| | | Factories Act 1961; |
| | | Civil Evidence Act 1968; |
| | | Health and Safety at Work etc Act 1974; |
| | | Sex Discrimination Act 1975; |
| | | Companies Consolidation (Consequential Provisions) Act 1985 |
| | | 26 Feb 1988 (SI 1988/99), repeals in— |
| | | Hours of Employment (Conventions) Act 1936; |
| | | Mines and Quarries Act 1954, Sch 4 |

---

**Social Security Act 1986 (c 50)**

*RA:* 25 Jul 1986

*Commencement provisions:* s 88; Social Security Act 1986 (Commencement No 1) Order 1986, SI 1986/1609; Social Security Act 1986 (Commencement No 2) Order 1986, SI 1986/1719; Social Security Act (Commencement No 3) Order 1986, SI 1986/1958; Social Security Act 1986 (Commencement No 4) Order 1986, SI 1986/1959, as amended by SI 1987/354; Social Security Act 1986 (Commencement No 5) Order 1987, SI 1987/354; Social Security Act 1986 (Commencement No 6) Order 1987, SI 1987/543; Social Security Act 1986 (Commencement No 7)

**Social Security Act 1986 (c 50)**—*contd*

Order 1987, SI 1987/1096, as amended by SI 1987/1853; Social Security Act 1986 (Commencement No 8) Order 1987, SI 1987/1853; Social Security Act 1986 (Commencement No 9) Order 1988, SI 1988/567

| | | |
|---|---|---|
| 1 | | 1 Jan 1988 (SI 1987/543) |
| 2 | | 1 May 1987 (SI 1987/543) |
| 3–5 | | 1 Jan 1988 (SI 1987/543) |
| 6, 7 | | 6 Apr 1988 (SI 1987/543) |
| 8 | | 1 Nov 1986 (SI 1986/1719) |
| 9, 10 | | 6 Apr 1988 (SI 1987/543) |
| 11 | | 6 Apr 1987 (SI 1986/1719) |
| 12 | | 1 Jan 1988 (so far as relates to personal pension schemes) (SI 1987/543) |
| | | 6 Apr 1988 (so far as relates to occupational pension schemes) (SI 1987/543) |
| 13, 14 | | 1 May 1987 (SI 1987/543) |
| 15 | | 1 Jan 1988 (so far as relates to personal pension schemes) (SI 1987/543) |
| | | 6 Apr 1988 (so far as relates to occupational pension schemes) (SI 1987/543) |
| 16 | | 1 Nov 1986 (SI 1986/1719) |
| 17 | | 1 May 1987 (SI 1987/543) |
| 18 | (1) | 6 Apr 1987 (SI 1987/354) |
| | (2)–(6) | 6 Apr 1988 (SI 1987/543) |
| 19 | | 6 Apr 1988 (SI 1987/543) |
| 20 | (1) | 1 Apr 1988 (so far as relates to housing benefit in a case where rent is payable at intervals of one month or any other interval which is not a week or a multiple thereof or in a case where payments by way of rates are not made together with payments of rent at weekly intervals or multiples thereof) (SI 1987/1853, art 2(1)(a), (b)) |
| | | 4 Apr 1988 (so far as relates to housing benefit, in any other case) (SI 1987/1853, art 2(1)(c)) |
| | | 11 Apr 1988 (otherwise) (SI 1987/1853, art 2(2)) |
| | (2)–(6) | 11 Apr 1988 (SI 1987/1853) |
| | (7)–(9) | See s 20(1) above |
| | (10) | 11 Apr 1988 (SI 1987/1853) |
| | (11), (12) | See s 20(1) above |
| 21 | (1)–(3) | 11 Apr 1988 (SI 1987/1853) |
| | (4)–(7) | See s 20(1) above |
| 22 | | See s 20(1) above |
| 23–26 | | 11 Apr 1988 (SI 1987/1853) |
| 27 | | 6 Apr 1987 (so as to enable it to have effect under Sch 7, para 2 in relation to supplementary benefit) (SI 1986/1959) |
| | | 11 Apr 1988 (otherwise) (SI 1987/1853) |
| 28, 29 | | See the first two dates noted to s 20(1) above |
| 30 | (1)–(3) | See the first two dates noted to s 20(1) above |
| | (4) | 25 Jul 1986 (s 88(5)) |
| | (5)–(7) | See the first two dates noted to s 20(1) above |
| | (8)–(10) | 25 Jul 1986 (s 88(5)) |
| 31 | | See the first two dates noted to s 20(1) above |
| 32 | (1) | 6 Apr 1987 (SI 1986/1959) |
| | (2)(a) | 6 Apr 1987 (SI 1986/1959) |
| | (2)(b) | 11 Apr 1988 (SI 1987/1853) |
| | (3)–(7) | 6 Apr 1987 (SI 1986/1959) |
| | (8), (9) | 11 Apr 1988 (SI 1987/1853) |
| 33–35 | | 11 Apr 1988 (SI 1987/1853) |
| 36 | | 11 Apr 1988 (SI 1987/1096) |
| 37 | | 25 Jul 1986 (s 88(5)) |

**Social Security Act 1986 (c 50)**—*contd*

| | | |
|---|---|---|
| 38 | (1)–(3) | 6 Apr 1987 (to the extent that it is not already in force except to the extent that it repeals so much of the Social Security Act 1980, s 5(1) as amends the Social Security Act 1975, s 12(1)(d)) (SI 1986/1959) |
| | (4) | 25 Jul 1986 (s 88(5)) |
| 39 | | See Sch 3 below |
| 40, 41 | | 6 Apr 1987 (SI 1986/1959) |
| 42–44 | | 5 Oct 1986 (SI 1986/1609) except that— |
| | | (i) Social Security Act 1975, s 33(1)(a)–(c) shall continue in force where a person's days of unemployment, incapacity for work or maternity allowance period began before 5 Oct 1986 until the end of the period of interruption of employment or 4 Oct 1987, whichever is the earlier; |
| | | (ii) Social Security Act 1975, s 33(1)(a)–(c) shall continue in force in the case of a person who, on or after 5 Oct 1986, has a day of incapacity for work which is, or forms part of, a period of interruption of employment and falls within the period of 57 days immediately following the end of a period of entitlement to statutory sick pay which contains at least one day in the period between 10 Aug and 4 Oct 1986 (inclusive), until the end of the period of interruption or 4 Oct 1987, whichever is the earlier |
| 45 | | 25 Jul 1986 (s 88(5)) |
| 46 | (1)–(3) | 6 Apr 1987 (SI 1986/1959) |
| | (4), (5) | 15 Mar 1987 (SI 1986/1959) |
| | (6)–(8) | 6 Apr 1987 (SI 1986/1959) |
| 47, 48 | | 6 Apr 1987 (SI 1986/1959) |
| 49 | | See Sch 4 below |
| 50 | | 6 Apr 1987 (SI 1986/1959) |
| 51 | (1)(a) | 6 Apr 1987 (for the purpose of applying sub-s (1)(a)–(s) to benefits under Social Security Act 1975 and child benefit) (SI 1986/1959) |
| | | 11 Apr 1988 (otherwise) (SI 1987/1096) |
| | (1)(b)–(e) | 1 Oct 1986 (so far as relates to claims for mobility allowance) (SI 1986/1609) |
| | | 11 Apr 1988 (otherwise) (SI 1987/1096) |
| | (1)(f)–(u) | 6 Apr 1987 (for the purpose of applying sub-s (1)(a)–(s) to benefits under Social Security Act 1975 and child benefit) (SI 1986/1959) |
| | | 11 Apr 1988 (otherwise) (SI 1987/1096) |
| | (2)–(4) | 6 Apr 1987 (for the purpose of applying sub-s (1)(a)–(s) to benefits under Social Security Act 1975 and child benefit) (SI 1986/1959) |
| | | 11 Apr 1988 (otherwise) (SI 1987/1096) |
| 52 | | 6 Apr 1987 (SI 1986/1958) |
| 53–60 | | 6 Apr 1987 (SI 1986/1959) |
| 61 | | 25 Jul 1986 (s 88(5)) |
| 62 | | 1 Oct 1986 (SI 1986/1609) |
| 63, 64 | | 25 Jul 1986 (s 88(5)) |
| 65 | (1)–(3) | 11 Apr 1988 (SI 1987/1096) |
| | (4) | 11 Apr 1988 (SI 1987/1853) |
| 66 | | 11 Apr 1988 (SI 1987/1096) |
| 67 | (1) | 1 Oct 1986 (SI 1986/1609) |
| | (2) | 6 Apr 1987 (SI 1986/1959) |
| 68, 69 | | 6 Apr 1987 (SI 1986/1959) |
| 70 | | 25 Jul 1986 (s 88(5)) |
| 71 | (1)–(3) | 1 Oct 1986 (SI 1986/1609) |
| | (4), (5) | 25 Jul 1986 (s 88(5)) |
| 72 | | 25 Jul 1986 (s 88(5)) |
| 73 | | See Sch 7 below |

**Social Security Act 1986 (c 50)**—*contd*

| | | |
|---|---|---|
| 74 | | 25 Jul 1986 (s 88(5)) |
| 75 | | See Sch 8 below |
| 76 | | 25 Jul 1986 (s 88(5)) |
| 77 | | 11 Apr 1988 (SI 1987/1853) |
| 78 | | 11 Apr 1988 (SI 1987/1096) |
| 79 | (1), (2) | 1 May 1987 (SI 1987/543) |
| | (3) | 11 Apr 1988 (SI 1987/1853) |
| | (4)–(6) | 6 Apr 1987 (SI 1986/1959) |
| 80 | | 6 Apr 1987 (except in its application to Pt I (ss 1–19) of this Act) (SI 1986/1959) |
| | | 1 May 1987 (so far as relates to modification of Pt I (ss 1–19) of this Act) (SI 1987/543) |
| 81 | | 25 Jul 1986 (s 88(5)) |
| 82 | | 6 Apr 1987 (SI 1987/1853) |
| 83–85 | | 25 Jul 1986 (s 88(5)) |
| 86 | (1) | See Sch 10 below |
| | (2) | See Sch 11 below |
| 87–90 | | 25 Jul 1986 (s 88(5)) |
| Sch 1 | | 1 May 1987 (SI 1987/543) |
| Sch 2 | | 6 Apr 1988 (SI 1987/543) |
| Sch 3 | paras 1–3 | 1 Oct 1986 (SI 1986/1609) |
| | para 4 | 6 Apr 1987 (SI 1987/354) |
| | para 5(1) | 1 Oct 1986 (so far as inserts Social Security Act 1975, s 59A(1)–(9)) (SI 1986/1609) |
| | | 6 Apr 1987 (so far as inserts Social Security Act 1975, s 59A(10) (SI 1987/354) |
| | | *Never in force* (otherwise) (repealed) |
| | para 5(2) | 1 Oct 1986 (SI 1986/1609) |
| | para 5(3) | 6 Apr 1987 (SI 1987/354) |
| | para 5(4)–(8) | *Never in force* (repealed) |
| | paras 6, 7 | 6 Apr 1987 (SI 1987/354) |
| | para 8 | 11 Apr 1988 (so far as relates to Social Security Act 1975, s 67(2)(b)) (SI 1987/1853) |
| | | 11 Apr 1988 (otherwise) (SI 1987/567) |
| | para 9 | *Never in force* (repealed) |
| | para 10 | 11 Apr 1988 (SI 1987/567) |
| | paras 11, 12 | 11 Apr 1988 (SI 1987/1096) |
| | paras 13–15 | 1 Oct 1986 (SI 1986/1609) |
| | para 16 | 6 Apr 1987 (SI 1987/354) |
| | para 17 | 1 Oct 1986 (SI 1986/1609) |
| Sch 4 | paras 1–5 | 6 Apr 1987 (SI 1986/1959) |
| | para 6(a) | 15 Mar 1987 (SI 1986/1959) |
| | para 6(b) | 6 Apr 1987 (SI 1986/1959) |
| | paras 7–17 | 6 Apr 1987 (SI 1986/1959) |
| Sch 5 | Pt I, paras 1–6 | 6 Apr 1987 (SI 1986/1958) |
| | Pt I, para 7 | 6 Apr 1987 (but note that sub-paras (1) and (3), so far as they substitute a new sub-s (5A) for Social Security Act 1975, s 101(5), shall not have effect in relation to any decisions of social security appeal tribunals which are recorded in writing before 6 Apr 1987) (SI 1986/1958) |
| | Pt I, paras 8–20 | 6 Apr 1987 (SI 1986/1958) |
| | Pt II | 6 Apr 1987 (SI 1986/1958) |
| Sch 6 | | 11 Apr 1988 (SI 1987/1096) |
| Sch 7 | paras 1, 2 | 6 Apr 1987 (SI 1986/1959) |
| | para 3 | 6 Apr 1987 (except so far as applies to s 51(1)–(s) of this Act) (SI 1986/1959) |
| | | 11 Apr 1988 (otherwise) (SI 1987/1853) |
| | paras 4–7 | 6 Apr 1987 (SI 1986/1959) |
| | para 8 | *Never in force* (repealed) |

**Social Security Act 1986 (c 50)**—*contd*

| | | |
|---|---|---|
| Sch 8 | | 6 Apr 1987 (except para 7(1)(b)) (SI 1986/1959) |
| | | *Never in force* (para 7(1)(b)) (repealed) |
| Sch 9 | | 6 Apr 1987 (SI 1986/1958) |
| Sch 10 | para 1 | 6 Apr 1987 (SI 1987/354) |
| | para 2 | 25 Jul 1986 (s 88(5)) |
| | para 3 | 1 Nov 1986 (SI 1986/1719) |
| | paras 4–8 | 1 May 1987 (SI 1987/543) |
| | para 9 | 1 Nov 1986 (SI 1986/1719) |
| | paras 10, 11 | 6 Apr 1987 (SI 1987/354) |
| | para 12 | 1 Nov 1986 (SI 1986/1719) |
| | para 13 | 6 Apr 1987 (SI 1986/1719) |
| | para 14(a) | 6 Apr 1988 (SI 1987/543) |
| | para 14(b)(i) | 1 May 1987 (SI 1987/543) |
| | para 14(b)(ii) | 6 Apr 1988 (SI 1987/543) |
| | paras 15–19 | 1 Nov 1986 (SI 1986/1719) |
| | paras 20, 21 | 6 Apr 1988 (SI 1987/543) |
| | para 22 | 25 Jul 1986 (s 88(5)) |
| | para 23(1), (2) | 1 Nov 1986 (SI 1986/1719) |
| | para 23(3) | 25 Jul 1986 (s 88(5)) |
| | para 23(4), (5) | 1 Nov 1986 (SI 1986/1719) |
| | paras 24, 25 | 1 Nov 1986 (SI 1986/1719) |
| | para 26(1), (2) | 25 Jul 1986 (s 88(5)) |
| | para 26(3) | 1 Nov 1986 (SI 1986/1719) |
| | para 27 | 25 Jul 1986 (s 88(5)) |
| | paras 28, 29 | 1 May 1987 (SI 1987/543) |
| | para 30(a) | 6 Apr 1988 (SI 1987/543) |
| | para 30(b), (c) | 25 Jul 1986 (s 88(5)) |
| | para 30(d)(i) | 6 Apr 1988 (SI 1987/543) |
| | para 30(d)(ii) | 25 Jul 1986 (s 88(5)) |
| | para 30(d)(iii) | 6 Apr 1988 (SI 1987/543) |
| | para 31 | 4 Jan 1988 (SI 1987/543) |
| | paras 32–43 | 11 Apr 1988 (SI 1987/1853) |
| | para 44 | 1 Apr 1988 (so far as relates to housing benefit in a case where rent is payable at intervals of one month or any other interval which is not a week or a multiple thereof or in a case where payments by way of rates are not made together with payments of rent at weekly intervals or multiples thereof) (SI 1987/1853) |
| | | 4 Apr 1988 (otherwise) (SI 1987/1853) |
| | paras 45–47 | 11 Apr 1988 (SI 1987/1853) |
| | para 48 | See s 20(1) above |
| | para 49 | 1 Apr 1988 (so far as relates to housing benefit in a case where rent is payable at intervals of one month or any other interval which is not a week or a multiple thereof or in a case where payments by way of rates are not made together with payments of rent at weekly intervals or multiples thereof) (SI 1987/1853) |
| | | 4 Apr 1988 (otherwise) (SI 1987/1853) |
| | paras 50, 51 | 11 Apr 1988 (SI 1987/1853) |
| | paras 52, 53 | 1 Apr 1988 (so far as relates to housing benefit in a case where rent is payable at intervals of one month or any other interval which is not a week or a multiple thereof or in a case where payments by way of rates are not made together with payments of rent at weekly intervals or multiples thereof) (SI 1987/1853) |
| | | 4 Apr 1988 (otherwise) (SI 1987/1853) |
| | paras 54–57 | 11 Apr 1988 (SI 1987/1853) |
| | paras 58–60 | 1 Apr 1988 (so far as relates to housing benefit in a case where rent is payable at intervals of one month or any other interval which is not a week or a multiple thereof or in a case where payments by way of rates are not made together with payments of rent at weekly intervals or multiples thereof) (SI 1987/1853) |
| | | 4 Apr 1988 (otherwise) (SI 1987/1853) |

**Social Security Act 1986 (c 50)**—*contd*

| | | |
|---|---|---|
| para 61 | 11 Apr 1988 (SI 1987/1853) | |
| paras 62–66 | 11 Apr 1988 (SI 1987/1096) | |
| para 67 | 6 Apr 1987 (for certain purposes) (SI 1987/354) | |
| | 11 Apr 1988 (otherwise) (SI 1987/1096) | |
| para 68 | 1 Oct 1986 (SI 1986/1609) | |
| paras 69, 70 | 11 Apr 1988 (SI 1987/1096) | |
| paras 71, 72 | 6 Apr 1987 (SI 1986/1959) | |
| para 73 | 6 Apr 1987 (SI 1987/354) | |
| paras 74–81 | 6 Apr 1987 (SI 1986/1959) | |
| para 82 | 25 Jul 1986 (s 88(5)) | |
| paras 83, 84 | 1 Oct 1986 (SI 1986/1609) | |
| para 85 | 11 Apr 1988 (SI 1987/1096) | |
| para 86 | 25 Jul 1986 (s 88(5)) | |
| para 87 | 6 Apr 1987 (SI 1986/1959) | |
| paras 88–93 | 1 Oct 1986 (SI 1986/1609) | |
| para 94(a) | 25 Jul 1986 (s 88(5)) | |
| para 94(b) | 26 Jun 1987 (SI 1987/1096) | |
| para 95 | 1 Oct 1986 (SI 1986/1609) | |
| para 96 | 11 Apr 1988 (SI 1987/1096) | |
| para 97 | 1 Oct 1986 (SI 1986/1609) | |
| paras 98, 99 | 25 Jul 1986 (s 88(5)) | |
| para 100 | 1 Oct 1986 (SI 1986/1609) | |
| para 101(a) | 6 Apr 1987 (except in relation to widow's payments) (SI 1986/1959) | |
| | 11 Apr 1988 (in relation to widow's payments) (SI 1987/1096) | |
| para 101(b) | *Never in force* (repealed) | |
| para 102 | 26 Jun 1987 (SI 1987/1096) | |
| para 103 | 6 Apr 1987 (SI 1986/1959) | |
| paras 104, 105 | 1 Oct 1986 (SI 1986/1609) | |
| paras 106, 107 | 25 Jul 1986 (s 88(5)) | |
| para 108(a) | 6 Apr 1987 (SI 1986/1959) | |
| para 108(b) | 11 Apr 1988 (except so far as substitutes words for reference in Forfeiture Act 1982, s 4(5), to Family Income Supplements Act 1970 and Supplementary Benefits Act 1976) (SI 1987/1096) | |
| | 11 Apr 1988 (exception noted above) (SI 1987/1853) | |
| Sch 11 | 25 Jul 1986 (s 88(5)), repeals of or in— | |
| | Social Security Act 1975, ss 37, 141; | |
| | Social Security Pensions Act 1975, s 52D, Sch 1A; | |
| | Social Security (Miscellaneous Provisions) Act 1977, s 22(2) (reference to Social Security Act 1975, s 37(3)(b)); | |
| | Social Security Act 1980, s 10; | |
| | Social Security and Housing Benefits Act 1982, s 29 | |
| | 1 Oct 1986 (SI 1986/1609), repeals of or in— | |
| | Statute Law Revision (Consequential Repeals) Act 1965; | |
| | Child Benefit Act 1975, ss 5, 17(3), (4); | |
| | Social Security Act 1975, ss 12(3), 28, 34, 37A, 57, 60, 124–126A, Schs 14, 20 (definition "Up–rating Order"); | |
| | Social Security Pensions Act 1975, ss 22, 23; | |
| | Social Security Act 1979, s 13; | |
| | Social Security Act 1980, s 1; | |
| | Social Security (No 2) Act 1980, ss 1, 2; | |
| | Social Security Act 1981, s 1; | |
| | Social Security and Housing Benefits Act 1982, ss 7, 42; | |
| | Social Security and Housing Benefits Act 1983; | |
| | Social Security Act 1985, ss 15, 16, Sch 5, para 10 | |
| | 1 Nov 1986 (SI 1986/1719), repeals of or in— | |
| | Social Security Act 1973, s 99; | |

**Social Security Act 1986 (c 50)**—*contd*

> Social Security Pensions Act 1975, ss 30, 32–34, 36, 37, 39, 41, 44A, 46, 49, 66, Schs 2, 4, paras 31, 32(a);
>
> Social Security Act 1985, Sch 5, paras 19, 28
>
> 6 Apr 1987 (SI 1986/1959, as amended by SI 1987/354), repeals of or in—
>
> Supplementary Benefit Act 1966;
>
> Social Work (Scotland) Act 1968;
>
> Family Income Supplements Act 1970, ss 8(5), (6), 12;
>
> Income and Corporation Taxes Act 1970;
>
> Local Government Act 1972;
>
> Social Security Act 1973, s 92, Sch 23;
>
> National Insurance Act 1974, s 6(1) (the words "or the Social Security and Housing Benefits Act 1982");
>
> Child Benefit Act 1975, ss 9–11, 24, Sch 4, paras 11, 31;
>
> Industrial Injuries and Diseases (Old Cases) Act 1975, ss 9, 10;
>
> Social Security Act 1975, ss 13(1), 21, 32, 92, 95, 100, 104, 106, 107, 110, 114, 119(1)–(2A), (5), (6), 135(2)(g), 136, 144, 145, 146(3)(c), (5), 147, 164, Sch 3, Pt I, para 7, Pt II, paras 8(3), 12, Sch 4, Pt II, Sch 8, Sch 16, para 4;
>
> Social Security (Consequential Provisions) Act 1975, Sch 2, paras 5, 35;
>
> Social Security Pensions Act 1975, s 19, Sch 4, para 17;
>
> Adoption Act 1976;
>
> Supplementary Benefits Act 1976, s 20(1), (2), (5)–(7);
>
> Social Security (Miscellaneous Provisions) Act 1977, s 19;
>
> Social Security Act 1979, ss 6, 8;
>
> Child Care Act 1980;
>
> Social Security Act 1980, ss 5, 14, 15, 17, 20, Sch 1, paras 9, 10, Sch 2, paras 19(a), (b), (d), 21, Sch 3, Pt II, paras 16–18;
>
> Social Security Act 1981, Sch 1, paras 1–5;
>
> Social Security and Housing Benefits Act 1982, ss 8, 9, 11–16, 19–21, 25, 41, Schs 2, 3, Sch 4, paras 26, 38;
>
> Health and Social Services and Social Security Adjudications Act 1983, Sch 8, paras 18, 31, Sch 9;
>
> Health and Social Security Act 1984, Sch 4, para 12;
>
> Public Health (Control of Disease) Act 1984;
>
> Bankruptcy (Scotland) Act 1985;
>
> Insolvency Act 1985;
>
> Social Security Act 1985, s 17, Sch 4, Sch 5, paras 37, 38
>
> 6 Apr 1987 (SI 1987/354), repeals of or in—
>
> Social Security Act 1975, ss 1(1)(b), 122(4), 134(5)(b);
>
> Employment Protection Act 1975, s 40(2), (4);
>
> Supplementary Benefits Act 1976, s 26;
>
> Social Security (Miscellaneous Provisions) Act 1977, s 18(1)(c), (2)(a), (b);
>
> Employment Protection (Consolidation) Act 1978 (except ss 123(5), 127(3), 132(6));
>
> Social Security Act 1979, ss 3(2), 12, Sch 3, para 16;
>
> Social Security Act 1985, Sch 5, para 7
>
> 7 Apr 1987 (SI 1986/1959), repeals of or in—
>
> Child Benefit Act 1975, ss 7, 8 (except in relation to Social Security Act 1975, ss 82(3)), 17(5), (6), Sch 4, paras 5, 29, 33;
>
> Family Income Supplement Act 1970, s 8(3), (4);
>
> Social Security Act 1975, ss 86, 119(3), (4)(b)–(d);
>
> Social Security (Consequential Provisions) Act 1975, Sch 2, para 41;
>
> Social Security Pensions Act 1975, Sch 4, para 13;
>
> Supplementary Benefits Act 1979, s 7, Sch 3, para 9;
>
> Social Security Act 1980, s 4, Sch 1, para 12, Sch 2, paras 11, 19(c);

**Social Security Act 1986 (c 50)**—*contd*

Social Security and Housing Benefits Act 1982; Sch 4, para 22;
Health and Social Services and Social Security Adjudications Act 1983, Sch 8, para 17

26 Jun 1987 (SI 1987/1096), repeals of or in—

Attachment of Earnings Act 1971;
Social Security (Consequential Provisions) Act 1975, Sch 2, para 44;
Social Security and Housing Benefits Act 1982, s 45(2)(a)

4 Jan 1988 (SI 1987/543), repeals of or in—

Social Security Act 1975, ss 146(1), 151(1), 152(8);
Employment Protection (Consolidation) Act 1978, ss 123(5), 127(3)

1 Apr 1988 or 4 Apr 1988 (SI 1987/1853) repeals of or in—

Social Security Act 1980, Sch 3, Pt II, para 15B;
Social Security and Housing Benefits Act 1982, Pt II, ss 45(1), (2)(b), (c), (3), 47, Sch 4, paras 5, 19, 27, 28, 35(1), (2);
Social Security Act 1985, ss 22, 32(2)

6 Apr 1988 (repeal of or in Social Security Pensions Act 1975, s 6(2)) (SI 1987/543)

11 Apr 1988 (SI 1987/1096), repeals of or in—

Pensioners and Family Income Supplement Payments Act 1972 (except s 3 and s 4 so far as it refers to expenses attributable to s 3);
Pensioners' Payments and National Insurance Contributions Act 1972;
Pensioners' Payments and National Insurance Act 1973 (except s 7 and the Schedule);
Pensioners' Payments Act 1974;
Child Benefit Act 1975, ss 6, 8 (so far as not already in force), 15(1), Sch 4, paras 3, 4, 6, 27;
Industrial Injuries and Diseases (Old Cases) Act 1975, s 4(4);
Social Security Act 1975, ss 12(1)(h), (2), 13(1) (entry relating to widow's allowance), (5)(a), 25(3), 26(3), 41(2)(e), (2C), 50(2), 79–81, 82, 84(3), 88(a), 90, 101(3), Sch 3, Pt II, paras 8(2), 9, 10, Sch 4, Pt I, para 5, Pt IV, para 4, Pt V, paras 6, 11, Sch 20 (definitions "Relative" and "Short-term benefit");
Social Security Pensions Act 1975, s 56K(4), Sch 4, para 51;
Social Security (Miscellaneous Provisions) Act 1977, ss 9, 17(2), 22(2), (reference to Social Security Act 1975, s 24(2));
Pensioners' Payments Act 1977;
Pensioners' Payments Act 1978;
Pensioners' Payments and Social Security Act 1979;
Social Security (No 2) Act 1980, s 4(2);
Social Security and Housing Benefits Act 1982, s 44(1)(f), Sch 4, para 14;
Health and Social Security Act 1984, ss 22, 27(2), Sch 4, paras 3, 14, Sch 5, paras 5, 6;
Social Security Act 1985, ss 27, 32(2) (words "section 15"), Sch 5, para 6(a)

11 Apr 1988 (SI 1987/1853), repeals of or in—

National Assistance Act 1948;
Family Income Supplements Act 1970 (so far as it is not already repealed);
Pensioners and Family Income Supplement Payments Act 1972 (so far as it is not already repealed);
National Insurance Act 1974, s 6(1);
Social Security Act 1975, ss 67(2)(b), 143(1);

**Social Security Act 1986 (c 50)**—*contd*

> Supplementary Benefits Act 1976, ss 1–11, 13–19, 21, 24, 25, 27, 31–34, Sch 1, Sch 5, para 1(2), Sch 7, paras 1(b), (d), 3(a), 5, 19, 21, 23, 24, 31, 33, 37;
>
> Social Security (Miscellaneous Provisions) Act 1977, s 18(1);
>
> Employment Protection (Consolidation) Act 1978, s 132(6);
>
> Social Security Act 1979, Sch 3, paras 1, 2, 24–27;
>
> Social Security Act 1980, ss 7, 8(1), 9(7), 18(1), Sch 2, paras 1–10, 12–18, 22–30, Sch 3, Pt II, paras 11, 15;
>
> Social Security (No 2) Act 1980, s 6;
>
> Social Security Act 1981, s 4, Sch 1, paras 8, 9;
>
> Social Security and Housing Benefits Act 1982, ss 38, 44(1)(a), Sch 4, paras 2, 4, 23–25;
>
> Health and Social Services and Social Security Adjudications Act 1983, s 19(2), Sch 8, Pts III, IV (so far as not already repealed);
>
> Law Reform (Parent and Child) (Scotland) Act 1986
>
> 11 Apr 1988 (repeals of or in Social Security Act 1975, ss 67, 68, 70–75, 117(4), (5)) (SI 1988/567)
>
> *Not yet in force*, repeals of or in—
>
> Pensioners' Payments and National Insurance Act 1973, s 7, Schedule;
>
> Social Security Act 1975, ss 13(5A), 50(5), 91(2), 135(6), Sch 16, para 3 (all repealed);
>
> Social Security (Consequential Provisions) Act 1975, Sch 3, para 18 (repealed);
>
> Social Security Pensions Act 1975, s 6(5), Sch 4, paras 41, 42 (all repealed);
>
> Social Security Act 1985, Sch 5, paras 6(b), 16 (as to which, see note 1 to that Act)

---

**Statute Law (Repeals) Act 1986 (c 12)**

*RA:* 2 May 1986

Whole Act in force 2 May 1986 (RA)

---

**Wages Act 1986 (c 48)**

*RA:* 25 Jul 1986

*Commencement provisions:* s 33(2)–(5); Wages Act 1986 (Commencement) Order 1986, SI 1986/1998

| | | |
|---|---|---|
| 1–11 | | 1 Jan 1987 (SI 1986/1998) |
| 12–23 | | 25 Sep 1986 (s 33(4)) |
| 24 | | 25 Jul 1986 (s 33(2)) |
| 25 | (1)–(3) | 25 Jul 1986 (s 33(2)) |
| | (4)–(7) | 25 Sep 1986 (s 33(4)) |
| 26 | | 25 Sep 1986 (s 33(4)) |
| 27, 28 | | 1 Aug 1986 (s 33(5)) |
| 29 | | 25 Jul 1986 (s 33(2)) |
| 30 | | 1 Jan 1987 (so far as it relates to Pt I (ss 1–11)) (SI 1986/1998) |
| | | 25 Sep 1986 (so far as it relates to Pt II (ss 12–26)) (s 33(4)) |
| 31 | | 25 Jul 1986 (s 33(2)) |
| 32 | (1) | See Sch 4 below |
| | (2) | See Sch 5 below |
| | (3) | 25 Jul 1986 (s 33(2)) |
| 33 | | 25 Jul 1986 (s 33(2)) |
| Sch 1 | | 1 Jan 1987 (SI 1986/1998) |
| Schs 2, 3 | | 25 Sep 1986 (s 33(4)) |

**Wages Act 1986 (c 48)**—*contd*

| | | |
|---|---|---|
| Sch 4 | paras 1–3 | 1 Jan 1987 (SI 1986/1998) |
| | paras 4–7 | 25 Sep 1986 (s 33(4)) |
| | para 8 | 1 Aug 1986 (s 33(3)) |
| | paras 9, 10 | 1 Jan 1987 (SI 1986/1998) |
| | para 11 | 1 Aug 1986 (s 33(3)) |
| Sch 5 | Pt I | 1 Aug 1986 (s 33(3)) |
| | Pt II | 25 Sep 1986 (s 33(4)) |
| | Pt III | 1 Jan 1987 (SI 1986/1998) |
| Sch 6 | | 25 Jul 1986 (s 33(2)) |

# 1987 Acts

## Abolition of Domestic Rates Etc (Scotland) Act 1987 (c 47)

*RA:* 15 May 1987

*Commencement provisions:* s 35(2); Abolition of Domestic Rates Etc (Scotland) Act 1987 Commencement
Order 1987, SI 1987/1489

| | | |
|---|---|---|
| 1–5 | | 14 Sep 1987 (SI 1987/1489) |
| 6–8 | | 14 Sep 1987 (certain purposes) (SI 1987/1489) |
| | | 1 Apr 1989 (otherwise) (SI 1987/1489) |
| 9 | | 14 Sep 1987 (SI 1987/1489) |
| 10, 11 | | 14 Sep 1987 (certain purposes) (SI 1987/1489) |
| | | 1 Apr 1989 (otherwise) (SI 1987/1489) |
| 12–17 | | 14 Sep 1987 (SI 1987/1489) |
| 18–20 | | 1 Oct 1988 (SI 1987/1489) |
| 21–24 | | 14 Sep 1987 (SI 1987/1489) |
| 25 | (1) | 14 Sep 1987 (SI 1987/1489) |
| | (2), (3) | 14 Sep 1987 (certain purposes) (SI 1987/1489) |
| | | 1 Apr 1989 (otherwise) (SI 1987/1489) |
| 26 | (1) | 14 Sep 1987 (SI 1987/1489) |
| | (2) | 14 Sep 1987 (certain purposes) (SI 1987/1489) |
| | | 1 Apr 1989 (otherwise) (SI 1987/1489) |
| 27–33 | | 14 Sep 1987 (SI 1987/1489) |
| 34 | | 14 Sep 1987 (certain purposes) (SI 1987/1489) |
| | | 1 Apr 1989 (certain purposes) (SI 1987/1489) |
| | | 1 Apr 1994 (otherwise) (SI 1987/1489) |
| 35 | | 14 Sep 1987 (SI 1987/1489) |
| Sch 1 | paras 1–14 | 14 Sep 1987 (SI 1987/1489) |
| | para 15 | 14 Sep 1987 (certain purposes) (SI 1987/1489) |
| | | 1 Apr 1989 (otherwise) (SI 1987/1489) |
| | para 16 | 1 Apr 1989 (SI 1987/1489) |
| | para 17 | 14 Sep 1987 (certain purposes) (SI 1987/1489) |
| | | 1 Apr 1989 (otherwise) (SI 1987/1489) |
| | para 18 | 1 Apr 1989 (SI 1987/1489) |
| | para 19 | 14 Sep 1987 (certain purposes) (SI 1987/1489) |
| | | 1 Apr 1989 (otherwise) (SI 1987/1489) |
| | para 20 | 14 Sep 1987 (SI 1987/1489) |
| | para 21 | 14 Sep 1987 (certain purposes) (SI 1987/1489) |
| | | 1 Apr 1989 (otherwise) (SI 1987/1489) |
| | para 22 | 14 Sep 1987 (SI 1987/1489) |
| | para 23(a) | 14 Sep 1987 (certain purposes) (SI 1987/1489) |
| | | 1 Apr 1989 (otherwise) (SI 1987/1489) |
| | para 23(b) | 14 Sep 1987 (SI 1987/1489) |
| | para 24 | 1 Apr 1989 (SI 1987/1489) |
| | paras 25, 26 | 14 Sep 1987 (SI 1987/1489) |
| | para 27 | 1 Apr 1989 (SI 1987/1489) |
| | para 28 | 14 Sep 1987 (certain purposes) (SI 1987/1489) |
| | | 1 Apr 1989 (otherwise) (SI 1987/1489) |
| | paras 29–31 | 1 Apr 1989 (SI 1987/1489) |

**Abolition of Domestic Rates Etc (Scotland) Act 1987 (c 47)**—*contd*

|  |  |  |
|---|---|---|
|  | para 32 | 14 Sep 1987 (certain purposes) (SI 1987/1489) |
|  |  | 1 Apr 1989 (otherwise) (SI 1987/1489) |
|  | para 33 | 14 Sep 1987 (SI 1987/1489) |
|  | paras 34–36 | 1 Apr 1989 (SI 1987/1489) |
|  | paras 37, 38 | 14 Sep 1987 (certain purposes) (SI 1987/1489) |
|  |  | 1 Apr 1989 (otherwise) (SI 1987/1489) |
|  | para 39 | 1 Apr 1989 (SI 1987/1489) |
| Schs 2–4 |  | 14 Sep 1987 (SI 1987/1489) |
| Sch 5 | paras 1–22 | 14 Sep 1987 (certain purposes) (SI 1987/1489) |
|  |  | 1 Apr 1989 (otherwise) (SI 1987/1489) |
|  | paras 23, 24 | 1 Apr 1989 (SI 1987/1489) |
|  | paras 25, 26 | 14 Sep 1987 (certain purposes) (SI 1987/1489) |
|  |  | 1 Apr 1989 (otherwise) (SI 1987/1489) |
|  | para 27 | 1 Apr 1989 (SI 1987/1489) |
|  | paras 28, 29 | 14 Sep 1987 (certain purposes) (SI 1987/1489) |
|  |  | 1 Apr 1989 (otherwise) (SI 1987/1489) |
|  | para 30(a) | 14 Sep 1987 (certain purposes) (SI 1987/1489) |
|  |  | 1 Apr 1989 (otherwise) (SI 1987/1489) |
|  | para 30(b), (c) | 1 Apr 1989 (SI 1987/1489) |
|  | paras 31–37 | 14 Sep 1987 (certain purposes) (SI 1987/1489) |
|  |  | 1 Apr 1989 (otherwise) (SI 1987/1489) |
|  | para 38 | 1 Apr 1989 (SI 1987/1489) |
|  | paras 39–41 | 14 Sep 1987 (certain purposes) (SI 1987/1489) |
|  |  | 1 Apr 1989 (otherwise) (SI 1987/1489) |
|  | paras 42–46 | 1 Apr 1989 (SI 1987/1489) |
|  | paras 47–49 | 14 Sep 1987 (certain purposes) (SI 1987/1489) |
|  |  | 1 Apr 1989 (otherwise) (SI 1987/1489) |
| Sch 6 |  | 14 Sep 1987 (certain purposes) (SI 1987/1489) |
|  |  | 1 Apr 1989 (certain purposes) (SI 1987/1489) |
|  |  | 1 Apr 1994 (otherwise) (SI 1987/1489) |

---

**Access to Personal Files Act 1987 (c 37)**

*RA:* 15 May 1987

Whole Act in force 15 May 1987 (RA)

---

**Agricultural Training Board Act 1987 (c 29)**

*RA:* 15 May 1987

*Commencement provisions:* s 2(2)

Whole Act in force 15 May 1987 (s 2(2))

---

**AIDS (Control) Act 1987 (c 33)**

*RA:* 15 May 1987

Whole Act in force 15 May 1987 (RA)

---

**Animals (Scotland) Act 1987 (c 9)**

*RA:* 9 Apr 1987

*Commencement provisions:* s 9(2)

**Animals (Scotland) Act 1987 (c 9)**—*contd*

Whole Act in force 9 Jun 1987 (s 9(2))

---

**Appropriation Act 1987 (c 17)**

*RA:* 15 May 1987

Whole Act in force 15 May 1987 (RA)

---

**Appropriation (No 2) Act 1987 (c 50)**

*RA:* 23 Jul 1987

Whole Act in force 23 Jul 1987 (RA)

---

**Banking Act 1987 (c 22)**

*RA:* 15 May 1987

*Commencement provisions:* s 110(2); Banking Act 1987 (Commencement No 1) Order 1987, SI 1987/1189; Banking Act 1987 (Commencement No 2) Order 1987, SI 1987/1664; Banking Act 1987 (Commencement No 3) Order 1988, SI 1988/502; Banking Act 1987 (Commencement No 4) Order 1988, SI 1988/644

| | | |
|---|---|---|
| 1–37 | | 1 Oct 1987 (SI 1987/1664) |
| 38 | | 1 Apr 1988 (SI 1988/502) |
| 39–81 | | 1 Oct 1987 (SI 1987/1664) |
| 82–87 | | 15 Jul 1987 (SI 1987/1189) |
| 88–90 | | 1 Oct 1987 (SI 1987/1664) |
| 91 | | 15 May 1987 (s 110(2)) |
| 92–101 | | 1 Oct 1987 (SI 1987/1664) |
| 102 | | 15 Jul 1987 (SI 1987/1189) |
| 103–105 | | 1 Oct 1987 (SI 1987/1664) |
| 106 | | 15 Jul 1987 (SI 1987/1189) |
| 107 | | See Sch 5 below |
| 108 | (1) | See Sch 6 below |
| | (2) | See Sch 7 below |
| 109, 110 | | 15 Jul 1987 (SI 1987/1189) |
| Schs 1–4 | | 1 Oct 1987 (SI 1987/1664) |
| Sch 5 | paras 1–13 | 1 Oct 1987 (SI 1987/1664) |
| | para 14 | 15 Jul 1987 (SI 1987/1189) |
| Sch 6 | paras 1–25 | 1 Oct 1987 (SI 1987/1664) |
| | para 26(1)–(4) | 1 Oct 1987 (SI 1987/1189) |
| | para 26(5) | 15 Jul 1987 (SI 1987/1189) |
| | para 26(6)–(8) | 1 Oct 1987 (SI 1987/1664) |
| | paras 27–28 | 1 Oct 1987 (SI 1987/1664) |
| Sch 7 | | 15 Jul 1987 (SI 1987/1189), repeals of or in— |
| | | Banking Act 1979, s 20; |
| | | Building Societies Act 1986, s 54(4), (5); |
| | | Financial Services Act 1986, Sch 13, para 4 |
| | | 1 Oct 1987 (except repeal of Financial Services Act 1986, s 193) (SI 1987/1664) |
| | | 29 Apr 1988 (exception noted above) (SI 1988/644) |

---

**Billiards (Abolition of Restrictions) Act 1987 (c 19)**

*RA:* 15 May 1987

Whole Act in force 15 May 1987 (RA)

---

**British Shipbuilders (Borrowing Powers) Act 1987 (c 52)**

*RA:* 23 Jul 1987

Whole Act in force 23 Jul 1987 (RA)

---

**Broadcasting Act 1987 (c 10)**

*RA:* 9 Apr 1987

Whole Act in force 9 Apr 1987 (RA)

---

**Channel Tunnel Act 1987 (c 53)**

*RA:* 23 Jul 1987

Whole Act in force 23 Jul 1987 (RA)

---

**Chevening Estate Act 1987 (c 20)**

*RA:* 15 May 1987

*Commencement provisions:* s 5(2); Chevening Estate Act 1987 (Commencement) Order 1987, SI 1987/1254

Whole Act in force 1 Sep 1987 (SI 1987/1254)

---

**Coal Industry Act 1987 (c 3)**

*RA:* 5 Mar 1987

*Commencement provisions:* s 10(2)

| | |
|---|---|
| 1–5 | 5 Mar 1987 (RA) |
| 6–8 | 5 May 1987 (s 10(2)) |
| 9, 10 | 5 Mar 1987 (RA) |
| Schs 1–3 | 5 Mar 1987 (RA) |

---

**Consolidated Fund Act 1987 (c 8)**

*RA:* 25 Mar 1987

Whole Act in force 25 Mar 1987 (RA)

---

**Consolidated Fund (No 2) Act 1987 (c 54)**

*RA:* 17 Nov 1987

Whole Act in force 17 Nov 1987 (RA)

---

**Consolidated Fund (No 3) Act 1987 (c 55)**

*RA:* 10 Dec 1987

Whole Act in force 10 Dec 1987 (RA)

---

## Consumer Protection Act 1987 (c 43)

*RA:* 15 May 1987

*Commencement provisions:* s 50(2), (4), (5); Consumer Protection Act 1987 (Commencement No 1) Order 1987, SI 1987/1680; Consumer Protection Act 1987 (Commencement No 2) Order 1988, SI 1988/2041; Consumer Protection Act 1987 (Commencement No 3) Order 1988, SI 1988/2076

| | | |
|---|---|---|
| 1–9 | | 1 Mar 1988 (SI 1987/1680) |
| 10–19 | | 1 Oct 1987 (SI 1987/1680) |
| 20–26 | | 1 Mar 1989 (subject to transitional provisions in relation to s 20(1), (2)) (SI 1988/2076) |
| 27–35 | | 1 Oct 1987 (for purposes of or in relation to Pt II) (SI 1987/1680) |
| | | 1 Mar 1989 (otherwise) (SI 1988/2076) |
| 36 | | 1 Mar 1988 (SI 1987/1680) |
| 37–40 | | 1 Oct 1987 (for purposes of or in relation to Pt II) (SI 1987/1680) |
| | | 1 Mar 1989 (otherwise) (SI 1988/2076) |
| 41 | (1) | 1 Oct 1987 (for purposes of or in relation to Pt II) (SI 1987/1680) |
| | | 1 Mar 1989 (otherwise) (SI 1988/2076) |
| | (2) | 1 Oct 1987 (for purposes of or in relation to Pt II) (SI 1987/1680) |
| | | 1 Mar 1988 (for purposes of or in relation to Pt I) (SI 1987/1680) |
| | | 1 Mar 1989 (otherwise) (SI 1988/2076) |
| | (3)–(5) | 1 Oct 1987 (for purposes of or in relation to Pt II) (SI 1987/1680) |
| | | 1 Mar 1989 (otherwise) (SI 1988/2076) |
| | (6) | 1 Oct 1987 (for purposes of or in relation to Pt II) (SI 1987/1680) |
| | | 1 Mar 1988 (for purposes of or in relation to Pt I) (SI 1987/1680) |
| | | 1 Mar 1989 (otherwise) (SI 1988/2076) |
| 42–44 | | 1 Oct 1987 (so far as have effect for purposes of or in relation to Pt II) (SI 1987/1680) |
| | | 1 Mar 1989 (otherwise) (SI 1988/2076) |
| 45, 46 | | 1 Oct 1987 (so far as have effect for purposes of or in relation to Pt II) (SI 1987/1680) |
| | | 1 Mar 1988 (so far as have effect for purposes of or in relation to Pt I) (SI 1987/1680) |
| | | 1 Mar 1989 (otherwise) (SI 1988/2076) |
| 47 | | 1 Oct 1987 (for purposes of or in relation to Pt II) (SI 1987/1680) |
| | | 1 Mar 1989 (otherwise) (SI 1988/2076) |
| 48 | (1) | See Sch 4 below |
| | (2)(a) | 31 Dec 1988 (SI 1988/2041) |
| | (2)(b) | 1 Oct 1987 (SI 1987/1680) |
| | (3) | See Sch 5 below |
| 49, 50 | | 1 Oct 1987 (SI 1987/1680) |
| Sch 1 | | 1 Mar 1988 (SI 1987/1680) |
| Sch 2 | | 1 Oct 1987 (SI 1987/1680) |
| Sch 3 | | 1 Mar 1988 (SI 1987/1680) |
| Sch 4 | paras 1, 2 | 1 Oct 1987 (SI 1987/1680) |
| | para 3 | 1 Mar 1989 (SI 1988/2076) |
| | para 4 | 1 Oct 1987 (SI 1987/1680) |
| | para 5 | 1 Mar 1988 (SI 1987/1680) |
| | paras 6, 7 | 1 Oct 1987 (SI 1987/1680) |
| | para 8 | 1 Mar 1988 (SI 1987/1680) |
| | paras 9–11 | 1 Oct 1987 (SI 1987/1680) |
| | para 12 | 1 Mar 1988 (SI 1987/1680) |
| | para 13 | 1 Oct 1987 (SI 1987/1680) |
| Sch 5 | | 1 Oct 1987 (SI 1987/1680), repeals of or in— |
| | | Fabrics (Misdescription) Act 1913; |
| | | Criminal Justice Act 1967; |
| | | Fines Act (Northern Ireland) 1967; |
| | | Local Government Act 1972; |
| | | Local Government (Scotland) Act 1973; |
| | | Explosives (Age of Purchase etc) Act 1976; |
| | | Consumer Safety Act 1978; |

**Consumer Protection Act 1987 (c 43)**—*contd*

|  |  |
|---|---|
|  | Magistrates' Courts Act 1980; |
|  | Food Act 1984; |
|  | Telecommunications Act 1984; |
|  | Airports Act 1986; |
|  | Consumer Safety (Amendment) Act 1986; |
|  | Gas Act 1986 |
|  | 1 Mar 1988 (SI 1987/1680), repeals of or in— |
|  | Prescription and Limitation (Scotland) Act 1973; |
|  | Health and Safety at Work etc Act 1974 |
|  | 31 Dec 1988 (repeal of Trade Descriptions Act 1972) (SI 1988/2041) |
|  | 1 Mar 1989 (repeal of Trade Descriptions Act 1968, s 11) (SI 1988/2076) |

**Criminal Justice Act 1987 (c 38)**

*RA:* 15 May 1987

*Commencement provisions:* s 16; Criminal Justice Act 1987 (Commencement No 1) Order 1987, SI 1987/1061; Criminal Justice Act 1987 (Commencement No 2) Order 1988, SI 1988/397; Criminal Justice Act 1987 (Commencement No 3) Order 1988, SI 1988/1564

| | | |
|---|---|---|
| 1 | | 20 Jul 1987 (for purposes of appointment of a person to be Director of the Serious Fraud Office, staff for the Office and doing of such other things necessary or expedient for establishment of the Office) (SI 1987/1061) |
| | | 6 Apr 1988 (otherwise) (SI 1988/397) |
| 2, 3 | | 6 Apr 1988 (SI 1988/397) |
| 4–11 | | 31 Oct 1988 (SI 1988/1564) |
| 12 | | 20 Jul 1987 (except in relation to things done before that date) (SI 1987/1061) |
| 13 | | 15 May 1987 (s 16(3)) |
| 14 | | 20 Jul 1987 (SI 1987/1061) |
| 15 | | See Sch 2 below |
| 16–18 | | 15 May 1987 (s 16(3)) |
| Sch 1 | | See s 1 above |
| Sch 2 | paras 1–5 | 31 Oct 1988 (SI 1988/1564) |
| | para 6 | 6 Apr 1988 (SI 1988/397) |
| | paras 7–12 | 31 Oct 1988 (SI 1988/1564) |
| | para 13 | 6 Apr 1988 (SI 1988/397) |
| | paras 14–16 | 31 Oct 1988 (SI 1988/1564) |

**Criminal Justice (Scotland) Act 1987 (c 41)**

*RA:* 15 May 1987

*Commencement provisions:* s 72(2); Criminal Justice (Scotland) Act 1987 (Commencement No 1) Order 1987, SI 1987/1468; Criminal Justice (Scotland) Act 1987 (Commencement No 2) Order 1987, SI 1987/1594; Criminal Justice (Scotland) Act 1987 (Commencement No 3) Order 1987, SI 1987/2119; Criminal Justice (Scotland) Act 1987 (Commencement No 4) Order 1988, SI 1988/483; Criminal Justice (Scotland) Act 1987 (Commencement No 5) Order 1988, SI 1988/482; Criminal Justice (Scotland) Act 1987 (Commencement No 6) Order 1988, SI 1988/1710

| | | |
|---|---|---|
| 1–30 | | 1 Apr 1988 (SI 1988/482) |
| 31 | | 1 Apr 1988 (SI 1988/483) |
| 32–44 | | 1 Apr 1988 (SI 1988/482) |
| 45 | (1) | 1 Apr 1988 (SI 1988/483) |
| | (2), (3) | 1 Apr 1988 (SI 1988/482) |
| | (4) | 1 Apr 1988 (SI 1988/483) |

**Criminal Justice (Scotland) Act 1987 (c 41)**—*contd*

| | | |
|---|---|---|
| | (5), (6) | 1 Apr 1988 (SI 1988/482) |
| | (7)(a), (b) | 1 Apr 1988 (SI 1988/483) |
| | (7)(c) | 1 Apr 1988 (SI 1988/482) |
| | (7)(d), (e) | 1 Apr 1988 (SI 1988/483) |
| | (7)(f) | 1 Apr 1988 (SI 1988/482) |
| 46, 47 | | 1 Apr 1988 (SI 1988/482) |
| 48, 49 | | 1 Oct 1987 (SI 1987/1594) |
| 50 | | 1 Apr 1988 (SI 1988/482) |
| 51–56 | | 1 Jan 1988 (SI 1987/2119) |
| 57 | | 1 Sep 1987 (SI 1987/1468) |
| 58 | | 1 Jan 1988 (SI 1987/2119) |
| 59 | | 1 Apr 1988 (SI 1988/482) |
| 60 | | 1 Oct 1987 (SI 1987/1594) |
| 61–63 | | 1 Jan 1988 (SI 1987/2119) |
| 64 | | 1 Oct 1987 (SI 1987/1594) |
| 65 | | 1 Jan 1988 (SI 1987/2119) |
| 66 | | 12 Oct 1988 (SI 1988/1710) |
| 67 | | 1 Apr 1988 (SI 1988/482) |
| 68 | | 1 Jan 1988 (SI 1987/2119) |
| 69 | | 1 Oct 1987 (SI 1987/1594) |
| 70 | | See Schs 1, 2 below |
| 71 | | 1 Apr 1988 (SI 1988/482) |
| 72 | | 15 May 1987 (s 72(2)) |
| Sch 1 | paras 1, 2 | 1 Sep 1987 (SI 1987/1468) |
| | para 3 | 1 Oct 1987 (SI 1987/1594) |
| | paras 4–6 | 1 Sep 1987 (SI 1987/1468) |
| | paras 7–9 | 1 Jan 1988 (SI 1987/2119) |
| | para 10(a) | 1 Jan 1988 (SI 1987/2119) |
| | para 10(b) | 1 Oct 1987 (SI 1987/1594) |
| | paras 11–14 | 1 Oct 1987 (SI 1987/1594) |
| | para 15 | 12 Oct 1988 (SI 1988/1710) |
| | paras 16–19 | 1 Oct 1987 (SI 1987/1594) |

Sch 2 — 1 Sep 1987 (SI 1987/1468), repeals of or in—
Circuit Courts (Scotland) Act 1709;
Heritable Jurisdiction (Scotland) Act 1746;
Circuit Courts (Scotland) Act 1828;
Justiciary (Scotland) Act 1848;
Circuit Clerks (Scotland) Act 1898;
Criminal Procedure (Scotland) Act 1975, ss 5(1), 87, 88, 113, 115–119
1 Oct 1987 (SI 1987/1594), repeals of or in—
Road Traffic Act 1974, Sch 3, para 10(4);
Criminal Procedure (Scotland) Act 1975, s 263(2)
1 Jan 1988 (SI 1987/2119), repeals of or in—
Road Traffic Act 1972;
Criminal Procedure (Scotland) Act 1976, s 300(5);
Sexual Offences (Scotland) Act 1976;
Community Service by Offenders (Scotland) Act 1978
1 Apr 1988 (SI 1988/482), repeals of or in—
Children and Young Persons (Scotland) Act 1937;
Social Work (Scotland) Act 1968;
Criminal Procedure (Scotland) Act 1975, s 193B;
Law Reform (Miscellaneous Provisions) (Scotland) Act 1985;
Drug Trafficking Offences Act 1986
12 Oct 1988 (repeals of or in Criminal Procedure (Scotland)
Act 1975, ss 289B(3), (4), 289D(1A), (2)–(4)) (SI 1988/1710)

## Crossbows Act 1987 (c 32)

*RA:* 15 May 1987

*Commencement provisions:* s 8(2)

| | |
|---|---|
| 1–6 | 15 Jul 1987 (s 8(2)) |
| 7, 8 | 15 May 1987 (RA) |

## Crown Proceedings (Armed Forces) Act 1987 (c 25)

*RA:* 15 May 1987

Whole Act in force 15 May 1987 (RA)

## Debtors (Scotland) Act 1987 (c 18)

*RA:* 15 May 1987

*Commencement provisions:* s 109(2); Debtors (Scotland) Act 1987 (Commencement No 1) Order 1987, SI 1987/1838; Debtors (Scotland) Act 1987 (Commencement No 2) Order 1988, SI 1988/1818

| | |
|---|---|
| 1–74 | 30 Nov 1988 (SI 1988/1818) |
| 75, 76 | 2 Nov 1987 (SI 1987/1838) |
| 77–96 | 30 Nov 1988 (SI 1988/1818) |
| 97 | 2 Nov 1987 (SI 1987/1838) |
| 98–108 | 30 Nov 1988 (SI 1988/1818) |
| 109 | 15 May 1987 (RA) |
| Schs 1–8 | 30 Nov 1988 (SI 1988/1818) |

## Deer Act 1987 (c 28)

*RA:* 15 May 1987

*Commencement provisions:* s 2(2)

Whole Act in force 15 Jul 1987 (s 2(2))

## Diplomatic and Consular Premises Act 1987 (c 46)

*RA:* 15 May 1987

*Commencement provisions:* s 9(2); Diplomatic and Consular Premises Act 1987 (Commencement No 1) Order 1987, SI 1987/1022; Diplomatic and Consular Premises Act 1987 (Commencement No 2) Order 1987, SI 1987/2248; Diplomatic and Consular Premises Act 1987 (Commencement No 3) Order 1987, SI 1988/106

| | |
|---|---|
| 1–5 | 1 Jan 1988 (SI 1987/2248) |
| 6, 7 | 11 Jun 1987 (SI 1987/1022) |
| 8 | 1 Jan 1988 (SI 1987/2248) |
| 9 | 3 Feb 1988 (SI 1988/106) |
| Sch 1 | 1 Jan 1988 (SI 1987/2248) |
| Sch 2 | 11 Jun 1987 (SI 1987/1022) |

## Family Law Reform Act 1987 (c 42)

*RA:* 15 May 1987

*Commencement provisions:* s 34(2); Family Law Reform Act 1987 (Commencement No 1) Order 1988, SI 1988/425; Family Law Reform Act 1987 (Commencement No 2) Order 1989, SI 1989/382; Family Law Reform Act 1987 (Commencement No 3) Order 2001, SI 2001/777

**Family Law Reform Act 1987 (c 42)**—*contd*

| | | |
|---|---|---|
| 1 | | 4 Apr 1988 (SI 1988/425) |
| 2–8 | | 1 Apr 1989 (SI 1989/382) |
| 9 | | *Never in force* (repealed) |
| 10–17 | | 1 Apr 1989 (SI 1989/382) |
| 18–22 | | 4 Apr 1988 (SI 1988/425) |
| 23 | | 1 Apr 2001 (SI 2001/777) |
| 24, 25 | | 1 Apr 1989 (SI 1989/382) |
| 26–29 | | 4 Apr 1988 (SI 1988/425) |
| 30 | | 1 Apr 1989 (SI 1989/382) |
| 31 | | 4 Apr 1988 (SI 1988/425) |
| 32 | | *Never in force* (spent)[1] |
| 33 | | See Schs 2–4 below |
| 34 | | 4 Apr 1988 (SI 1988/425) |
| Sch 1 | | *Never in force* (spent)[1] |
| Sch 2 | para 1 | 1 Apr 1989 (SI 1989/382) |
| | paras 2–4 | 4 Apr 1988 (SI 1988/425) |
| | paras 5–8 | 1 Apr 1989 (SI 1989/382) |
| | paras 9–11 | 4 Apr 1988 (SI 1988/425) |
| | paras 12–15 | 1 Apr 1989 (SI 1989/382) |
| | para 16(a), (b) | 1 Apr 1989 (SI 1989/382) |
| | para 16(c) | 4 Apr 1988 (SI 1988/425) |
| | paras 17, 18 | 1 Apr 1989 (SI 1989/382) |
| | para 19 | 4 Apr 1988 (SI 1988/425) |
| | para 20 | 1 Apr 1989 (SI 1989/382) |
| | paras 21–25 | 1 Apr 2001 (SI 2001/777) |
| | paras 26–58 | 1 Apr 1989 (SI 1989/382) |
| | para 59 | 4 Apr 1988 (SI 1988/425) |
| | paras 60–72 | 1 Apr 1989 (SI 1989/382) |
| | paras 73, 74 | 4 Apr 1988 (SI 1988/425) |
| | paras 75–95 | 1 Apr 1989 (SI 1989/382) |
| | para 96 | 4 Apr 1988 (SI 1988/425) |
| Sch 3 | para 1 | 4 Apr 1988 (SI 1988/425) |
| | paras 2–7 | 1 Apr 1988 (SI 1989/382) |
| | paras 8–10 | 4 Apr 1988 (SI 1988/425) |
| | paras 11, 12 | 1 Apr 1989 (SI 1989/382) |
| Sch 4 | | 4 Apr 1988 (SI 1988/425), repeals of or in— |
| | | Domestic and Appellate Proceedings (Restriction of Publicity) Act 1968, s 2(1); |
| | | Family Law Reform Act 1969, ss 14, 15, 17; |
| | | Interpretation Act 1978, Sch 2, para 4 |
| | | 1 Apr 1989 (otherwise) (SI 1989/382) |

[1]  Provision not brought into force consequent on errors in Sch 1

---

**Finance Act 1987 (c 16)**

*Budget Day*: 17 Mar 1987

*RA*: 15 May 1987

The commencement details of Finance Acts are not set out, as the dates from which their provisions take effect are usually stated clearly and unambiguously in the text of the Act, and charging provisions will normally state for which year or years of assessment they are to have effect.

---

**Finance (No 2) Act 1987 (c 51)**

*RA*: 23 Jul 1987

The commencement details of Finance Acts are not set out, as the dates from which their provisions take effect are usually stated clearly and unambiguously in the text of the Act, and charging provisions will normally state for which year or years of assessment they are to have effect.

---

**See Halsbury's Statutes Citator for amendments to these Acts**  593

**Fire Safety and Safety of Places of Sport Act 1987 (c 27)**

*RA:* 15 May 1987

*Commencement provisions:* s 50(2); Fire Safety and Safety of Places of Sport Act 1987 (Commencement No 1) Order 1987, SI 1987/1762; Fire Safety and Safety of Places of Sport Act 1987 (Commencement No 2) Order 1988, SI 1988/485; Fire Safety and Safety of Places of Sport Act 1987 (Commencement No 3) (Scotland) Order 1988, SI 1988/626; Fire Safety and Safety of Places of Sport Act 1987 (Commencement No 4) Order 1988, SI 1988/1806; Fire Safety and Safety of Places of Sport Act 1987 (Commencement No 5) Order 1989, SI 1989/75; Fire Safety and Safety of Places of Sport Act 1987 (Commencement No 6) Order 1990, SI 1990/1984; Fire Safety and Safety of Places of Sport Act 1987 (Commencement No 7) Order 1993, SI 1993/1411

| | | |
|---|---|---|
| 1, 2 | | 1 Apr 1989 (SI 1989/75) |
| 3, 4 | | 1 Jan 1988 (SI 1987/1762) |
| 5–7 | | 1 Apr 1989 (SI 1989/75) |
| 8, 9 | | 1 Jan 1988 (SI 1987/1762) |
| 10 | | *Never in force* (repealed) |
| 11–14 | | 1 Jan 1988 (SI 1987/1762) |
| 15 | | 1 Aug 1993 (SI 1993/1411) |
| 16 | (1) | 1 Jan 1988 (SI 1987/1762) |
| | (2) | See Sch 1 below |
| | (3) | 1 Jan 1988 (SI 1987/1762) |
| 17 | | 1 Jan 1988 (SI 1987/1762) |
| 18 | (1) | See s 18(2)–(4) below |
| | (2) | 1 Jan 1988 (so far as it amends Fire Precautions Act 1971, s 40(1)(a), by insertion of a reference to "5(2A)") (SI 1987/1762) |
| | | 1 Apr 1989 (otherwise) (SI 1989/75) |
| | (3) | 1 Jan 1988 (so far as amends Fire Precautions Act 1971, s 40(1)(b), by insertion of references to "8B" and "10B") (SI 1987/1762) |
| | | 1 Apr 1989 (otherwise) (SI 1989/75) |
| | (4) | 1 Apr 1989 (SI 1989/75) |
| 19–25 | | 1 Jan 1988 (SI 1987/1762) |
| 26–41 | | 1 Jan 1989 (SI 1988/1806) |
| 42, 43 | | 1 Jun 1988 (SI 1988/485) |
| 44 | | 1 Jun 1988 (SI 1988/626) |
| 45 | | 1 Jun 1988 (SI 1988/485) |
| 46 | | 1 Jan 1988 (SI 1987/1762) |
| 47 | | 31 Dec 1990 (SI 1990/1984) |
| 48 | | 1 Jun 1988 (SI 1988/626) |
| 49 | | See Schs 4, 5 below |
| 50 | (1)–(3) | 1 Jan 1988 (SI 1987/1762) |
| | (4)–(7) | 1 Jan 1988 (so far as have effect in relation to Pt II of this Act) (SI 1987/1762) |
| | | 1 Jan 1989 (otherwise) (SI 1988/1806) |
| Sch 1 | | 1 Jan 1988 (so far as gives effect to Fire Precautions Act 1971, Sch 2, Pt I, Pt II, para 3(1)–(3) (so far as para 3(3) has effect in relation to references to the occupier in ss 5(2A), 7(3A), 7(4), 8B(1) of 1971 Act)) (SI 1987/1762) |
| | | 1 Apr 1989 (otherwise) (SI 1989/75) |
| Sch 2 | | 1 Jan 1988 (SI 1987/1762) |
| Sch 3 | | 1 Jun 1988 (SI 1988/485) |
| Sch 4 | | 1 Jan 1988 (SI 1987/1762) repeals of or in— Fire Precautions Act 1971, ss 2, 12(1), 43(1), (2); Safety of Sports Grounds Act 1975 |
| | | 1 Jun 1988 (repeals in London Government Act 1963, Sch 12) (SI 1988/485) |
| | | 1 Apr 1989 (repeal of Health and Safety at Work etc Act 1974, s 78(4)) (SI 1989/75) |
| | | 1 Aug 1993 (repeals in Fire Precautions Act 1971, ss 5(3)(c), 6(1)(d)) (SI 1993/1411) |

**Fire Safety and Safety of Places of Sport Act 1987 (c 27)**—*contd*

| Sch 5 | para 1 | 1 Jan 1988 (SI 1987/1762) |
| | para 2 | 1 Apr 1989 (SI 1989/75) |
| | paras 3–7 | 1 Jan 1988 (SI 1987/1762) |
| | para 8 | 1 Jun 1988 (SI 1988/485) |
| | para 9 | 1 Jan 1988 (SI 1987/1762) |
| | para 10 | 1 Jun 1988 (SI 1988/485) |

## Gaming (Amendment) Act 1987 (c 11)

*RA:* 9 Apr 1987

*Commencement provisions:* s 2(2); Gaming (Amendment) Act 1987 (Commencement) Order 1987, SI 1987/1200

Whole Act in force 1 Aug 1987 (SI 1987/1200)

## Housing (Scotland) Act 1987 (c 26)

*RA:* 15 May 1987

*Commencement provisions:* s 340(2)

Whole Act in force 15 Aug 1987 (s 340(2))

## Immigration (Carriers' Liability) Act 1987 (c 24)

*RA:* 15 May 1987

*Commencement provisions:* s 2(4)

The Act has effect in relation to persons arriving in UK after 4 Mar 1987 except persons arriving by voyage or flight for which they embarked before that date (s 2(4))

## Irish Sailors and Soldiers Land Trust Act 1987 (c 48)

*RA:* 15 May 1987

*Commencement provisions:* s 3(2); Irish Sailors and Soldiers Land Trust Act 1987 (Commencement) Order 1987, SI 1987/1909

Whole Act in force 4 Nov 1987 (SI 1987/1909)

## Landlord and Tenant Act 1987 (c 31)

*RA:* 15 May 1987

*Commencement provisions:* s 62(2); Landlord and Tenant Act 1987 (Commencement No 1) Order 1987, SI 1987/2177; Landlord and Tenant Act 1987 (Commencement No 2) Order 1988, SI 1988/480; Landlord and Tenant Act 1987 (Commencement No 3) Order 1988, SI 1988/1283

| 1–20 | 1 Feb 1988 (SI 1987/2177) |
| 21–40 | 18 Apr 1988 (SI 1988/480) |
| 41 | 1 Sep 1988 (SI 1988/1283) |
| 42 | 1 Apr 1989 (SI 1988/1283) |
| 43, 44 | 1 Sep 1988 (SI 1988/1283) |
| 45–51 | 1 Feb 1988 (SI 1987/2177) |
| 52 | 1 Feb 1988 (so far as relate to ss 1–20, 45–51) (SI 1987/2177) |
| | 18 Apr 1988 (so far as relate to ss 21–40) (SI 1988/480) |
| | 1 Sep 1988 (otherwise) (SI 1988/1283) |

**Landlord and Tenant Act 1987 (c 31)**—*contd*

| | | |
|---|---|---|
| 53–60 | | 1 Feb 1988 (so far as relate to ss 1–20, 45–51) (SI 1987/2177) |
| | | 18 Apr 1988 (so far as relate to ss 21–40) (SI 1988/480) |
| | | 1 Sep 1988 (otherwise) (SI 1988/1283) |
| 61 | (1) | See Sch 4 below |
| | (2) | See Sch 5 below |
| 62 | | 1 Feb 1988 (SI 1987/2177) |
| Sch 1 | Pt I | 1 Feb 1988 (SI 1987/2177) |
| | Pt II | 18 Apr 1988 (SI 1988/480) |
| Schs 2, 3 | | 1 Sep 1988 (SI 1988/1283) |
| Sch 4 | paras 1, 2 | 18 Apr 1988 (SI 1988/480) |
| | para 3(a) | 1 Sep 1988 (SI 1988/1283) |
| | para 3(b) | 1 Feb 1988 (SI 1987/2177) |
| | paras 4–6 | 1 Sep 1988 (SI 1988/1283) |
| | para 7 | 1 Feb 1988 (SI 1987/2177) |
| Sch 5 | | 1 Sep 1988 (SI 1988/1283) |

---

**Licensing (Restaurant Meals) Act 1987 (c 2)**

*RA:* 2 Mar 1987

*Commencement provisions:* s 3(2)

Whole Act in force 2 May 1987 (s 3(2))

---

**Local Government Act 1987 (c 44)**

*RA:* 15 May 1987

*Commencement provisions:* ss 1, 2(3), (4), 3(7)

| | | |
|---|---|---|
| 1 | | Year beginning with 1 Apr 1986 (s 1) |
| 2 | (1), (2) | 1988 and subsequent years (s 2(3)) |
| | (3) | 15 May 1987 (RA) |
| | (4) | Years beginning in 1986 and 1987 only (s 2(4)) |
| | (5) | 15 May 1987 (RA) |
| 3 | | 15 Jul 1987 (s 3(7)) |
| 4 | | 15 May 1987 (RA) |
| Schedule | | Year beginning with 1 Apr 1986 |

---

**Local Government Finance Act 1987 (c 6)**

*RA:* 12 Mar 1987

Whole Act in force 12 Mar 1987 (RA)

---

**Ministry of Defence Police Act 1987 (c 4)**

*RA:* 5 Mar 1987

*Commencement provisions:* s 8(2)

Whole Act in force 5 May 1987 (s 8(2))

---

**Minors' Contracts Act 1987 (c 13)**

*RA:* 9 Apr 1987

*Commencement provisions:* s 5(2)

**Minors' Contracts Act 1987 (c 13)**—*contd*
Whole Act in force 9 Jun 1987 (s 5(2))

---

**Motor Cycle Noise Act 1987 (c 34)**

*RA:* 15 May 1987

*Commencement provisions:* s 2(3); Motor Cycle Noise Act 1987 (Commencement) Order 1995, SI 1995/2367

Whole Act in force 1 Aug 1996 (SI 1995/2367)

---

**Northern Ireland (Emergency Provisions) Act 1987 (c 30)**

*RA:* 15 May 1987

*Commencement provisions:* s 26(1); Northern Ireland (Emergency Provisions) Act 1987 (Commencement No 1) Order 1987, SI 1987/1241; Northern Ireland (Emergency Provisions) Act 1987 (Commencement No 2) Order 1988, SI 1988/1105

| | |
|---|---|
| 1–11 | 15 Jun 1987 (s 26(1)) |
| 12 | 1 Jul 1988 (SI 1988/1105) |
| 13–16 | 15 Jun 1987 (s 26(1)) |
| 17 | 1 Jan 1988 (SI 1987/1241) |
| 18–20 | 1 Aug 1987 (SI 1987/1241) |
| 21 | 1 Jan 1988 (SI 1987/1241) |
| 22–24 | 1 Aug 1987 (SI 1987/1241) |
| 25–27 | 15 Jun 1987 (s 26(1)) |
| Schs 1, 2 | 15 Jun 1987 (s 26(1)) |

---

**Parliamentary and Health Service Commissioners Act 1987 (c 39)**

*RA:* 15 May 1987

*Commencement provisions:* s 10(3)

Whole Act in force 15 Jul 1987 (s 10(3))

---

**Parliamentary and other Pensions Act 1987 (c 45)**

*RA:* 15 May 1987

*Commencement provisions:* s 7(2); Parliamentary and other Pensions Act 1987 (Commencement No 1) Order 1987, SI 1987/1311; Parliamentary and other Pensions Act 1987 (Commencement No 2) Order 1989, SI 1989/892

| | | |
|---|---|---|
| 1–3 | | 24 May 1989 (SI 1989/892) |
| 4 | (1) | 23 Jul 1987 (SI 1987/1311) |
| | (2) | 24 May 1989 (SI 1989/892) |
| | (3) | 23 Jul 1987 (SI 1987/1311) |
| 5–7 | | 24 May 1989 (SI 1989/892) |
| Schs 1–4 | | 24 May 1989 (SI 1989/892) |

---

**Petroleum Act 1987 (c 12)**

*RA:* 9 Apr 1987

*Commencement provisions:* s 31(1), (2); Petroleum Act 1987 (Commencement No 1) Order 1987, SI 1987/820; Petroleum Act 1987 (Commencement No 2) Order 1987, SI 1987/1330

| | |
|---|---|
| 1–16 | 9 Apr 1987 (s 31(1)) |

**Petroleum Act 1987 (c 12)**—*contd*

| | |
|---|---|
| 17, 18 | 30 Jun 1987 (SI 1987/820) |
| 19, 20 | 9 Apr 1987 (s 31(1)) |
| 21–24 | 1 Sep 1987 (SI 1987/1330) |
| 25–32 | 9 Jun 1987 (s 31(1)) |
| Schs 1, 2 | 30 Jun 1987 (SI 1987/820) |
| Sch 3 | 9 Jun 1987 (except repeals of or in Oil and Gas (Enterprise) Act 1982, ss 21, 27) (s 31(1)) |
| | 1 Sep 1987 (exception noted above) (SI 1987/1330) |

---

**Pilotage Act 1987 (c 21)**

*RA:* 15 May 1987

*Commencement provisions:* s 33(2), (3); Pilotage Act 1987 (Commencement No 1) Order 1987, SI 1987/1306; Pilotage Act 1987 (Commencement No 2) Order 1987, SI 1987/2138; Pilotage Act 1987 (Commencement No 3) Order 1988, SI 1988/1137; Pilotage Act 1987 (Commencement No 4) Order 1991, SI 1991/1029

| | | |
|---|---|---|
| 1–23 | | 1 Oct 1988 (SI 1988/1137) |
| 24, 25 | | 1 Sep 1987 (SI 1987/1306) |
| 26 | | 1 Oct 1988 (SI 1988/1137) |
| 27 | | 15 May 1987 (RA) |
| 28 | | 1 Sep 1987 (SI 1987/1306) |
| 29 | | 1 Aug 1988 (SI 1988/1137) |
| 30, 31 | | 1 Sep 1987 (SI 1987/1306) |
| 32 | (1)–(3) | 1 Sep 1987 (SI 1987/1306) |
| | (4) | 1 Oct 1988 (SI 1988/1137) |
| | (5) | See Sch 3 below |
| 33 | | 1 Sep 1987 (SI 1987/1306) |
| Sch 1 | paras 1–4 | 1 Sep 1987 (SI 1987/1306) |
| | paras 5, 6 | 1 Oct 1988 (SI 1988/1137) |
| Sch 2 | | 1 Oct 1988 (SI 1988/1137) |
| Sch 3 | | 1 Feb 1988 (repeal of Pilotage Act 1983, s 15(1)(i)) (SI 1987/2138) |
| | | 1 Oct 1988 (except repeal of Pilotage Act 1983, ss 1(1), 2, 4, 5(4), 8, Sch 1) (SI 1988/1137) |
| | | 30 Apr 1991 (exception noted above) (SI 1991/1029) |

---

**Prescription (Scotland) Act 1987 (c 36)**

*RA:* 15 May 1987

Whole Act in force 15 May 1987 (RA)

---

**Protection of Animals (Penalties) Act 1987 (c 35)**

*RA:* 15 May 1987

*Commencement provisions:* s 2(3)

Whole Act in force 15 Jul 1987 (s 2(3))

---

**Rate Support Grants Act 1987 (c 5)**

*RA:* 12 Mar 1987

Whole Act in force 12 Mar 1987 (RA)

---

### Recognition of Trusts Act 1987 (c 14)

*RA:* 9 Apr 1987

*Commencement provisions:* s 3(2); Recognition of Trusts Act 1987 (Commencement) Order 1987, SI 1987/1177

Whole Act in force 1 Aug 1987 (SI 1987/1177)

### Register of Sasines (Scotland) Act 1987 (c 23)

*RA:* 15 May 1987

*Commencement provisions:* s 3(1)

Whole Act in force 15 Jul 1987 (s 3(1))

### Registered Establishments (Scotland) Act 1987 (c 40)

*RA:* 15 May 1987

*Commencement provisions:* s 8(2); commencement order dated 26 Sep 1988 (not a statutory instrument)

Whole Act in force 17 Oct 1988 (commencement order dated 26 Sep 1988)

### Reverter of Sites Act 1987 (c 15)

*RA:* 9 Apr 1987

*Commencement provisions:* s 9(2); Reverter of Sites (Commencement) Order 1987, SI 1987/1260

Whole Act in force 17 Aug 1987 (SI 1987/1260)

### Scottish Development Agency Act 1987 (c 56)

*RA:* 17 Dec 1987

Whole Act in force 17 Dec 1987 (RA)

### Social Fund (Maternity and Funeral Expenses) Act 1987 (c 7)

*RA:* 17 Mar 1987

Whole Act in force 17 Mar 1987 (RA)

### Teachers' Pay and Conditions Act 1987 (c 1)

*RA:* 2 Mar 1987

Whole Act in force 2 Mar 1987 (RA)

### Territorial Sea Act 1987 (c 49)

*RA:* 15 May 1987

*Commencement provisions:* s 4(2); Territorial Sea Act 1987 (Commencement) Order 1987, SI 1987/1270

Whole Act in force 1 Oct 1987 (SI 1987/1270)

## Urban Development Corporations (Financial Limits) Act 1987 (c 57)

*RA:* 17 Dec 1987

*Commencement provisions:* s 2(2)

Whole Act in force 17 Feb 1988 (s 2(2))

# 1988 Acts

## Access to Medical Reports Act 1988 (c 28)

*RA:* 29 Jul 1988

*Commencement provisions:* s 10(2)

Whole Act in force 1 Jan 1989 (s 10(2))

---

## Appropriation Act 1988 (c 38)

*RA:* 29 Jul 1988

Whole Act in force 29 Jul 1988 (RA)

---

## Arms Control and Disarmament (Privileges and Immunities) Act 1988 (c 2)

*RA:* 9 Feb 1988

Whole Act in force 9 Feb 1988 (RA)

---

## British Steel Act 1988 (c 35)

*RA:* 29 Jul 1988

*Commencement provisions:* ss 1(1), 10(2), 17(2)–(4); British Steel Act 1988 (Appointed Day) Order 1988, SI 1988/1375

| | | |
|---|---|---|
| 1 | | 5 Sep 1988 (SI 1988/1375) |
| 2 | | 29 Jul 1988 (s 17(2)) |
| 3–14 | | 5 Sep 1988 (SI 1988/1375) |
| 15 | (1) | 29 Jul 1988 (s 17(2)) |
| | (2) | 5 Sep 1988 (SI 1988/1375) |
| 16 | (1), (2) | 5 Sep 1988 (SI 1988/1375) |
| | (3) | See Sch 2 below |
| | (4) | 5 Sep 1988 (SI 1988/1375) |
| 17 | | 29 Jul 1988 (s 17(2)) |
| Sch 1 | | 5 Sep 1988 (SI 1988/1375) |
| Sch 2 | Pt I | 5 Sep 1988 (SI 1988/1375) |
| | Pt II | *Not yet in force* |
| Sch 3 | | 5 Sep 1988 (SI 1988/1375) |

---

## Church Commissioners (Assistance for Priority Areas) Measure 1988 (No 2)

*RA:* 3 May 1988

*Commencement provisions:* s 4(3)

**Church Commissioners (Assistance for Priority Areas) Measure 1988 (No 2)**—*contd*
Whole Measure in force 4 May 1988 (the day appointed by the Archbishops of Canterbury and York under
s 4(3))

**Church of England (Ecumenical Relations) Measure 1988 (No 3)**

*RA:* 29 Jul 1988

*Commencement provisions:* s 9(3)

Whole Measure in force 1 Nov 1988 (the day appointed by the Archbishops of Canterbury and York under
s 9(3))

**Church of England (Legal Aid and Miscellaneous Provisions) Measure 1988 (No 1)**

*RA:* 9 Feb 1988

*Commencement provisions:* s 15(2)

The provisions of this Measure were brought into force on the following dates by an instrument made by
the Archbishops of Canterbury and York and dated 19 Apr 1988 (made under s 15(2))

| | | |
|---|---|---|
| 1–4 | | 1 Aug 1988 |
| 5–15 | | 1 May 1988 |
| Sch 1 | | 1 Aug 1988 |
| Sch 2 | paras 1, 2 | 1 Aug 1988 |
| | para 3 | 1 May 1988 |
| | para 4 | 1 Aug 1988 |
| Sch 3 | | 1 May 1988, repeals of or in— |
| | | Pluralities Act 1838, ss 97, 98; |
| | | Parochial Church Councils (Powers) Measure 1956, s 7; |
| | | Clergy (Ordination and Miscellaneous Provisions) Measure 1964, ss 10, 12 |
| | | 1 Aug 1988 (otherwise) |

**Church of England (Pensions) Measure 1988 (No 4)**

*RA:* 27 Oct 1988

*Commencement provisions:* s 19(2)

The provisions of this Measure were brought into force on the following dates by an instrument made by
the Archbishops of Canterbury and York and dated 31 Oct 1988 (made under s 19(2))

| | |
|---|---|
| 1–15 | 1 Dec 1988 |
| 16 | 1 Nov 1988 |
| 17–19 | 1 Dec 1988 |
| Schs 1–3 | 1 Dec 1988 |

**Civil Evidence (Scotland) Act 1988 (c 32)**

*RA:* 29 Jul 1988

*Commencement provisions:* s 11(2); Civil Evidence (Scotland) Act 1988 (Commencement) Order 1989,
SI 1989/556

Whole Act in force 3 Apr 1989 (SI 1989/556)

## Community Health Councils (Access to Information) Act 1988 (c 24)

*RA:* 29 Jul 1988

*Commencement provisions:* s 3(2)

Whole Act in force 1 Apr 1989 (s 3(2))

## Consolidated Fund Act 1988 (c 6)

*RA:* 15 Mar 1988

Whole Act in force 15 Mar 1988 (RA)

## Consolidated Fund (No 2) Act 1988 (c 55)

*RA:* 20 Dec 1988

Whole Act in force 20 Dec 1988 (RA)

## Consumer Arbitration Agreements Act 1988 (c 21)

*RA:* 28 Jun 1988

*Commencement provisions:* s 9(2); Consumer Arbitration Act 1988 (Appointed Day No 1) Order 1988, SI 1988/1598; Consumer Arbitration Agreements Act 1988 (Appointed Day No 2) Order 1988, SI 1988/2291

| | |
|---|---|
| 1–5 | Have effect in relation to contracts made on or after 1 Oct 1988 (SI 1988/1598) |
| 6–8 | Have effect in relation to contracts made on or after 1 Feb 1989 (SI 1988/2291) |
| 9 | 28 Jun 1988 (RA) |

## Copyright, Designs and Patents Act 1988 (c 48)

*RA:* 15 Nov 1988

*Commencement provisions:* s 305; Copyright, Designs and Patents Act 1988 (Commencement No 1) Order 1989, SI 1989/816, as amended by SI 1989/1303; Copyright, Designs and Patents Act 1988 (Commencement No 2) Order 1989, SI 1989/955, as amended by SI 1989/1032; Copyright, Designs and Patents Act 1988 (Commencement No 3) Order 1989, SI 1989/1032; Copyright, Designs and Patents Act 1988 (Commencement No 4) Order 1989, SI 1989/1303; Copyright, Designs and Patents Act 1988 (Commencement No 5) Order 1990, SI 1990/1400; Copyright, Designs and Patents Act 1988 (Commencement No 6) Order 1990, SI 1990/2168

| | |
|---|---|
| 1–36 | 1 Aug 1989 (SI 1989/816) |
| 37–43 | 9 Jun 1989 (for purposes of making regulations) (SI 1989/955; SI 1989/1032) |
| | 1 Aug 1989 (otherwise) (SI 1989/816) |
| 44–46 | 1 Aug 1989 (SI 1989/816) |
| 47 | 9 Jun 1989 (for purposes of making orders) (SI 1989/955; SI 1989/1032) |
| | 1 Aug 1989 (otherwise) (SI 1989/816) |
| 48–51 | 1 Aug 1990 (SI 1989/816) |
| 52 | 9 Jun 1989 (for purposes of making orders) (SI 1989/955; SI 1989/1032) |
| | 1 Aug 1989 (otherwise) (SI 1989/816) |
| 53–60 | 1 Aug 1989 (SI 1989/816) |
| 61 | 9 Jun 1989 (for purposes of making orders) (SI 1989/955; SI 1989/1032) |

**Copyright, Designs and Patents Act 1988 (c 48)**—*contd*

| | |
|---|---|
| | 1 Aug 1989 (otherwise) (SI 1989/816) |
| 62–73 | 1 Aug 1989 (SI 1989/816) |
| 74, 75 | 9 Jun 1989 (for purposes of making orders) (SI 1989/955; SI 1989/1032) |
| | 1 Aug 1989 (otherwise) (SI 1989/816) |
| 76–99 | 1 Aug 1989 (SI 1989/816) |
| 100 | 9 Jun 1989 (for purposes of making orders) (SI 1989/955; SI 1989/1032) |
| | 1 Aug 1989 (otherwise) (SI 1989/816) |
| 101–111 | 1 Aug 1989 (SI 1989/816) |
| 112 | 9 Jun 1989 (for purposes of making regulations) (SI 1989/955; SI 1989/1032) |
| | 1 Aug 1989 (otherwise) (SI 1989/816) |
| 113–149 | 1 Aug 1989 (SI 1989/816) |
| 150 | 9 Jun 1989 (for purposes of making rules) (SI 1989/955; SI 1989/1032) |
| | 1 Aug 1989 (otherwise) (SI 1989/816) |
| 151 | 1 Aug 1989 (SI 1989/816) |
| 152 | 9 Jun 1989 (for purposes of making rules) (SI 1989/955; SI 1989/1032) |
| | 1 Aug 1989 (otherwise) (SI 1989/816) |
| 153–158 | 1 Aug 1989 (SI 1989/816) |
| 159 | 9 Jun 1989 (for purposes of making orders) (SI 1989/955; SI 1989/1032) |
| | 1 Aug 1989 (otherwise) (SI 1989/816) |
| 160–167 | 1 Aug 1989 (SI 1989/816) |
| 168 | 9 Jun 1989 (for purposes of making orders) (SI 1989/955; SI 1989/1032) |
| | 1 Aug 1989 (otherwise) (SI 1989/816) |
| 169 | 1 Aug 1989 (SI 1989/816) |
| 170 | See Sch 1 below |
| 171–173 | 1 Aug 1989 (SI 1989/816) |
| 174 | 9 Jun 1989 (for purposes of making orders) (SI 1989/955; SI 1989/1032) |
| | 1 Aug 1989 (otherwise) (SI 1989/816) |
| 175–188 | 1 Aug 1989 (SI 1989/816) |
| 189 | See Sch 2 below |
| 190–195 | 1 Aug 1989 (SI 1989/816) |
| 196 | 9 Jun 1989 (for purposes of making orders) (SI 1989/955; SI 1989/1032) |
| | 1 Aug 1989 (otherwise) (SI 1989/816) |
| 197–207 | 1 Aug 1989 (SI 1989/816) |
| 208 | 9 Jun 1989 (for purposes of making orders) (SI 1989/955; SI 1989/1032) |
| | 1 Aug 1989 (otherwise) (SI 1989/816) |
| 209–249 | 1 Aug 1989 (SI 1989/816) |
| 250 | 9 Jun 1989 (for purposes of making rules) (SI 1989/955; SI 1989/1032) |
| | 1 Aug 1989 (otherwise) (SI 1989/816) |
| 251–255 | 1 Aug 1989 (SI 1989/816) |
| 256 | 9 Jun 1989 (for purposes of making orders) (SI 1989/955; SI 1989/1032) |
| | 1 Aug 1989 (otherwise) (SI 1989/816) |
| 257–271 | 1 Aug 1989 (SI 1989/816) |
| 272 | See Sch 3 below |
| 273 | See Sch 4 below |
| 274–286 | 10 Jul 1990 (for purpose of making rules expressed to come into force on or after 13 Aug 1990) (SI 1990/1400) |
| | 13 Aug 1990 (otherwise) (SI 1990/1400) |
| 287–292 | 1 Aug 1989 (SI 1989/816) |

**Copyright, Designs and Patents Act 1988 (c 48)**—*contd*

| | | |
|---|---|---|
| 293, 294 | | 15 Jan 1989 (s 305(2)) |
| 295 | | See Sch 5 below |
| 296–300 | | 1 Aug 1989 (SI 1989/816) |
| 301 | | See Sch 6 below |
| 302 | | 1 Aug 1989 (SI 1989/816) |
| 303 | (1) | See Sch 7 below |
| | (2) | See Sch 8 below |
| 304 | (1)–(3) | 1 Aug 1989 (SI 1989/816) |
| | (4) | 28 Jul 1989 (SI 1989/816; SI 1989/1303) |
| | (5) | 1 Aug 1989 (SI 1989/816) |
| | (6) | 28 Jul 1989 (SI 1989/816; SI 1989/1303) |
| 305 | | 15 Nov 1988 (RA) |
| 306 | | 1 Aug 1989 (SI 1989/816) |
| Sch 1 | paras 1–33 | 1 Aug 1989 (SI 1989/816) |
| | para 34 | 9 Jun 1989 (for purposes of making rules) (SI 1989/955; SI 1989/1032) |
| | | 1 Aug 1989 (otherwise) (SI 1989/816) |
| | paras 35–46 | 1 Aug 1989 (SI 1989/816) |
| Sch 2 | | 1 Aug 1989 (SI 1989/816) |
| Sch 3 | paras 1–20 | 1 Aug 1989 (SI 1989/816) |
| | para 21 | 13 Aug 1990 (SI 1990/1400) |
| | paras 22–38 | 1 Aug 1989 (SI 1989/816) |
| Sch 4 | | 13 Aug 1990 (SI 1990/1400) |
| Sch 5 | paras 1–11 | 1 Nov 1990 (for purposes of making rules) (SI 1990/2168) |
| | | 7 Jan 1991 (otherwise) (SI 1990/2168) |
| | paras 12–16 | 1 Aug 1989 (SI 1989/816) |
| | paras 17–23 | 1 Nov 1990 (for purposes of making rules) (SI 1990/2168) |
| | | 7 Jan 1991 (otherwise) (SI 1990/2168) |
| | para 24 | 15 Nov 1988 (s 305(1)) |
| | paras 25, 26 | 1 Nov 1990 (for purposes of making rules) (SI 1990/2168) |
| | | 7 Jan 1991 (otherwise) (SI 1990/2168) |
| | para 27 | 13 Aug 1990 (SI 1990/1400) |
| | para 28 | 1 Nov 1990 (for purposes of making rules) (SI 1990/2168) |
| | | 7 Jan 1991 (otherwise) (SI 1990/2168) |
| | para 29 | 15 Nov 1988 (s 305(1)) |
| | para 30 | 1 Nov 1990 (for purposes of making rules) (SI 1990/2168) |
| | | 7 Jan 1991 (otherwise) (SI 1990/2168) |
| Sch 6 | | 15 Nov 1988 (s 305(1)) |
| Sch 7 | paras 1–14 | 1 Aug 1989 (SI 1989/816) |
| | para 15 | 13 Aug 1990 (SI 1990/1400) |
| | paras 16, 17 | 1 Aug 1989 (SI 1989/816) |
| | para 18(1) | 1 Aug 1989 (SI 1989/1400) |
| | para 18(2) | 13 Aug 1990 (SI 1990/1400) |
| | para 18(3) | 1 Aug 1989 (SI 1989/816) |
| | paras 19, 20 | 1 Aug 1989 (SI 1989/816) |
| | para 21 | 13 Aug 1990 (SI 1990/1400) |
| | paras 22–36 | 1 Aug 1989 (SI 1989/816) |
| Sch 8 | | 1 Aug 1989 (SI 1989/816), except repeals of or in— |
| | |   Registered Designs Act 1949, s 32; |
| | |   Patents Act 1977 (other than s 49(3), Sch 5, paras 1, 3) |
| | | 13 Aug 1990 (SI 1990/1400), repeals of or in— |
| | |   Registered Design Act 1949, s 32; |
| | |   Patents Act 1977, ss 84, 85, 104, 105, 114, 115, 123(2)(k), 130(1) |
| | | 7 Jan 1991 (repeals of or in Patents Act 1977 (so far as not already in force)) (SI 1990/2168) |

## Coroners Act 1988 (c 13)

*RA:* 10 May 1988

*Commencement provisions:* s 37(2)

Whole Act in force 10 Jul 1988 (s 37(2))

---

## Court of Session Act 1988 (c 36)

*RA:* 29 Jul 1988

*Commencement provisions:* s 53(2)

Whole Act in force 29 Sep 1988 (s 53(2))

---

## Criminal Justice Act 1988 (c 33)

*RA:* 29 Jul 1988

*Commencement provisions:* ss 166(4), 171; Extradition Act 1989, s 38(4)[1]; Criminal Justice Act 1988 (Commencement No 1) Order 1988, SI 1988/1408; Criminal Justice Act 1988 (Commencement No 2) Order 1988, SI 1988/1676; Criminal Justice Act 1988 (Commencement No 3) Order 1988, SI 1988/1817; Criminal Justice Act 1988 (Commencement No 4) Order 1988, SI 1988/2073; Criminal Justice Act 1988 (Commencement No 5) Order 1989, SI 1989/1; Criminal Justice Act 1988 (Commencement No 6) Order 1989, SI 1989/50; Criminal Justice Act 1988 (Commencement No 7) Order 1989, SI 1989/264; Criminal Justice Act 1988 (Commencement No 8) Order 1989, SI 1989/1085; Criminal Justice Act 1988 (Commencement No 9) Order 1989, SI 1989/1595; Criminal Justice Act 1988 (Commencement No 10) Order 1990, SI 1990/220; Criminal Justice Act 1988 (Commencement No 11) Order 1990, SI 1990/1145; Land Registration Act 1988 (Commencement) Order 1990, SI 1990/1359; Criminal Justice Act 1988 (Commencement No 12) Order 1990, SI 1990/2084; Criminal Justice Act 1988 (Commencement No 13) Order 1999, SI 1999/3425; Criminal Justice Act 1988 (Commencement No 14) Order 2004, SI 2004/2167

| | | |
|---|---|---|
| 1 | (1)–(8) | *Never in force* (repealed) |
| | (9) | See Sch 1 below |
| 2–21 | | *Never in force* (repealed) |
| 22 | | 5 Jun 1990 (SI 1990/1145) |
| 23–28 | | 3 Apr 1989 (except in relation to a trial, or proceedings before a magistrates' court acting as examining justices, which began before that date) (SI 1989/264) |
| 29 | (1)(a) | 12 Mar 1990 (SI 1990/220) |
| | (1)(b) | *Never in force* (repealed) |
| | (1)(c) | 12 Mar 1990 (SI 1990/220) |
| | (2), (3) | 12 Mar 1990 (SI 1990/220) |
| | (4), (5) | *Never in force* (repealed) |
| | (6) | 12 Mar 1990 (SI 1990/220) |
| 30, 31 | | 3 Apr 1989 (except in relation to a trial, or proceedings before a magistrates' court acting as examining justices, which began before that date) (SI 1989/264) |
| 32 | (1)(a) | 26 Nov 1990 (in relation only to proceedings for murder, manslaughter or any other offence of killing any person; proceedings being conducted by the Director of the Serious Fraud Office under Criminal Justice Act 1987, s 1(5); and proceedings for serious and complex fraud where there has been given a notice of transfer under s 4 of that Act) (subject to transitional provisions set out in SI 1990/2084, art 3) (SI 1990/2084) |
| | | 1 Sep 2004 (otherwise) (in relation only to proceedings to which sub-s (1A)(a) applies) (SI 2004/2167) |
| | | *Not yet in force* (otherwise) |
| | (1)(b) | 5 Jan 1989 (SI 1988/2073) |

**Criminal Justice Act 1988 (c 33)**—*contd*

|  |  |  |
|---|---|---|
|  | (2) | 5 Jan 1989 (SI 1988/2073) |
|  | (3) | 26 Nov 1990 (in relation only to proceedings for murder, manslaughter or any other offence of killing any person; proceedings being conducted by the Director of the Serious Fraud Office under Criminal Justice Act 1987, s 1(5); and proceedings for serious and complex fraud where there has been given a notice of transfer under s 4 of that Act) (subject to transitional provisions set out in SI 1990/2084, art 3) (SI 1990/2084) |
|  |  | 1 Sep 2004 (otherwise) (in relation only to proceedings to which sub-s (1A)(a) applies) (SI 2004/2167) |
|  |  | *Not yet in force* (otherwise) |
|  | (4), (5) | 5 Jan 1989 (SI 1988/2073) |
| 33, 34 |  | 12 Oct 1988 (SI 1988/1676) |
| 35, 36 |  | 1 Feb 1989 (SI 1989/1) |
| 37–42 |  | 12 Oct 1988 (SI 1988/1676) |
| 43 |  | 31 Jul 1989 (SI 1989/1085) |
| 44–48 |  | 29 Sep 1988 (s 171(6)) |
| 49 |  | 12 Oct 1988 (SI 1988/1676) |
| 50 |  | 5 Jan 1989 (SI 1988/2073) |
| 51–57 |  | 12 Oct 1988 (SI 1988/1676) |
| 58 |  | 29 Sep 1988 (s 171(6)) |
| 59 |  | 12 Oct 1988 (SI 1988/1676) |
| 60–62 |  | 5 Jan 1989 (SI 1988/2073) |
| 63 |  | 12 Oct 1988 (SI 1988/1676) |
| 64 |  | 29 Sep 1988 (s 171(6)) |
| 65 |  | 5 Jun 1990 (SI 1990/1145) |
| 66, 67 |  | 29 Jul 1988 (s 171(5)) |
| 68, 69 |  | 29 Sep 1988 (s 171(6)) |
| 70 |  | 12 Oct 1988 (SI 1988/1676) |
| 71–95 |  | 3 Apr 1989 (SI 1989/264) |
| 96, 97 |  | 12 Oct 1988 (SI 1988/1676) |
| 98–102 |  | 3 Apr 1989 (SI 1989/264) |
| 103 |  | See Sch 5 below |
| 104–107 |  | 12 Oct 1988 (SI 1988/1676) |
| 108–117 |  | *Never in force* (repealed) |
| 118 |  | 5 Jan 1989 (SI 1988/2073) |
| 119 |  | 15 Feb 1990 (SI 1989/1085) |
| 120 |  | 5 Jan 1989 (SI 1988/2073) |
| 121, 122 |  | 12 Oct 1988 (SI 1988/1676) |
| 123 |  | 1 Oct 1988 (SI 1988/1408) |
| 124 |  | 1 Nov 1988 (SI 1988/1817) |
| 125–128 |  | 1 Oct 1988 (SI 1988/1408) |
| 129 |  | 29 Jul 1988 (s 171(5)) |
| 130 |  | 5 Jan 1989 (SI 1988/2073) |
| 131 |  | 12 Oct 1988 (SI 1988/1676) |
| 132 |  | See Sch 11 below |
| 133 |  | 12 Oct 1988 (SI 1988/1676) |
| 134–140 |  | 29 Sep 1988 (s 171(6))[1] |
| 141–144 |  | 29 Jul 1988 (s 171(5)) |
| 145 |  | 12 Oct 1988 (SI 1988/1676) |
| 146 |  | See Sch 13 below |
| 147, 148 |  | 12 Oct 1988 (SI 1988/1676) |
| 149 |  | 29 Jul 1988 (s 171(5)) |
| 150 |  | *Not yet in force* |
| 151 | (1)–(4) | *Not yet in force* |
|  | (5) | 3 Apr 1989 (SI 1989/264) |
| 152–154 |  | 5 Jan 1989 (SI 1988/2073) |
| 155–157 |  | 12 Oct 1988 (SI 1988/1676) |

**Criminal Justice Act 1988 (c 33)**—*contd*

| | | |
|---|---|---|
| 158 | | 29 Sep 1988 (s 171(6)) |
| 159 | | 31 Jul 1989 (SI 1989/1085) |
| 160, 161 | | 29 Sep 1988 (s 171(6)) |
| 162 | | 1 Sep 1988 (s 171(7)) |
| 163–165 | | 12 Oct 1988 (SI 1988/1676) |
| 166 | (1) | 29 Jul 1988 (s 171(5)) |
| | (2), (3) | 1 Oct 1986 (retrospective) (s 166(4)) |
| | (4), (5) | 29 Jul 1988 (s 171(5)) |
| 167–169 | | 29 Jul 1988 (s 171(5)) |
| 170 | (1) | See Sch 15 below |
| | (2) | See Sch 16 below |
| 171–173 | | 29 Jul 1988 (s 171(5)) |
| Sch 1 | Pt I | *Never in force* (repealed)[1] |
| | Pt II | 26 Sep 1989 (SI 1989/1595) |
| | Pt III | *Never in force* (repealed) |
| Sch 2 | | 3 Apr 1989 (except in relation to a trial, or proceedings before a magistrates' court acting as examining justices, which began before that date) (SI 1989/264) |
| Sch 3 | | 1 Feb 1989 (SI 1989/1) |
| Sch 4 | | 3 Apr 1989 (SI 1989/264) |
| Sch 5 | Pt I, para 1 | 29 Jul 1988 (so far as relating to paras 3(2), 13, 15) (s 171(5)) |
| | | 23 Jan 1989 (so far as relating to paras 2, 3(1), 4–11, 16, 17) (SI 1989/50) |
| | | 3 Apr 1989 (otherwise) (SI 1989/264) |
| | Pt I, para 2 | 23 Jan 1989 (SI 1989/50) |
| | Pt I, para 3(1) | 23 Jan 1989 (SI 1989/50) |
| | Pt I, para 3(2) | 29 Jul 1988 (s 171(5)) |
| | Pt I, paras 4–11 | 23 Jan 1989 (SI 1989/50) |
| | Pt I, para 12 | 3 Apr 1989 (SI 1989/264) |
| | Pt I, para 13 | 29 Jul 1988 (s 171(5)) |
| | Pt I, para 14 | 3 Apr 1989 (SI 1989/264) |
| | Pt I, para 15 | 29 Jul 1988 (s 171(5)) |
| | Pt I, paras 16, 17 | 23 Jan 1989 (SI 1989/50) |
| | Pt II, paras 18–23 | 23 Jan 1989 (SI 1989/50) |
| Schs 6, 7 | | *Never in force* (repealed) |
| Sch 8 | | 1 Oct 1988 (SI 1988/1408) |
| Sch 9 | | 1 Nov 1988 (SI 1988/1817) |
| Sch 10 | | 1 Oct 1988 (SI 1988/1408) |
| Sch 11 | | 29 Jul 1988 (para 8) (s 171(5)) |
| | | 12 Oct 1988 (otherwise) (SI 1988/1676) |
| Sch 12 | | 12 Oct 1988 (SI 1988/1676) |
| Sch 13 | | 31 Jul 1989 (SI 1989/1085) |
| Sch 14 | | 29 Jul 1988 (s 171(5)) |
| Sch 15 | paras 1–4 | 12 Oct 1988 (SI 1988/1676) |
| | paras 5, 6 | 3 Apr 1989 (SI 1989/264) |
| | para 7 | 29 Jul 1988 (s 171(5)) |
| | para 8 | 12 Oct 1988 (SI 1988/1676) |
| | para 9 | 29 Jul 1988 (s 171(5)) |
| | para 10 | 12 Oct 1988 (SI 1988/1676) |
| | paras 11, 12 | 1 Oct 1988 (SI 1988/1408) |
| | paras 13–15 | 29 Jul 1988 (s 171(5)) |
| | para 16 | *Not yet in force* |
| | para 17 | 29 Jul 1988 (so far as relating to para 19) (s 171(5)) |
| | | 12 Oct 1988 (so far as relating to para 18) (SI 1988/1676) |
| | para 18 | 12 Oct 1988 (SI 1988/1676) |
| | para 19 | 29 Jul 1988 (s 171(5)) |
| | para 20 | 12 Oct 1988 (so far as relating to paras 21–24, 26–29, 31) (SI 1988/1676) |
| | | 31 Jul 1989 (so far as relating to paras 25, 30, 32) (SI 1989/1085) |

**Criminal Justice Act 1988 (c 33)**—*contd*

| | |
|---|---|
| paras 21–24 | 12 Oct 1988 (SI 1988/1676) |
| para 25 | 31 Jul 1989 (SI 1989/1085) |
| paras 26–29 | 12 Oct 1988 (SI 1988/1676) |
| para 30 | 31 Jul 1989 (SI 1989/1085) |
| para 31 | 12 Oct 1988 (SI 1988/1676) |
| para 32 | 31 Jul 1989 (SI 1989/1085) |
| para 33 | 12 Oct 1988 (SI 1988/1676) |
| para 34 | *Never in force* (repealed) |
| para 35 | 1 Oct 1988 (SI 1988/1408) |
| para 36 | 29 Jul 1988 (s 171(5)) |
| para 37 | *Never in force* (repealed) |
| para 38 | 1 Oct 1988 (so far as relating to para 38) (SI 1988/1408) |
| | 12 Oct 1988 (so far as relating to paras 39, 41) (SI 1988/1676) |
| | *Never in force* (otherwise) (repealed) |
| para 39 | 12 Oct 1988 (SI 1988/1676) |
| para 40 | *Never in force* (repealed) |
| para 41 | 12 Oct 1988 (SI 1988/1676) |
| para 42 | 1 Oct 1988 (SI 1988/1408) |
| para 43 | 12 Oct 1988 (SI 1988/1676) |
| para 44 | 31 Jul 1989 (except in relation to any register of electors or any part of any such register required to be used for elections in the twelve months ending on 15 Feb 1990) (SI 1990/1085) |
| para 45 | 29 Jul 1988 (s 171(5)) |
| para 46 | 5 Jan 1989 (SI 1988/2073) |
| para 47 | 3 Apr 1989 (SI 1989/264) |
| para 48 | 29 Jul 1988 (s 171(5)) |
| para 49 | 12 Oct 1988 (SI 1988/1676) |
| paras 50, 51 | 29 Jul 1988 (s 171(5)) |
| para 52 | 12 Oct 1988 (SI 1988/1676) |
| para 53 | 29 Sep 1988 (s 171(6)) |
| paras 54, 55 | *Never in force* (repealed) |
| para 56 | 1 Feb 1989 (SI 1989/1) |
| para 57 | *Never in force* (repealed) |
| paras 58, 59 | 12 Oct 1988 (SI 1988/1676) |
| paras 60–62 | 29 Sep 1988 (s 171(6)) |
| para 63 | 12 Oct 1988 (SI 1988/1676) |
| para 64 | 29 Jul 1988 (s 171(5)) |
| para 65 | 29 Jul 1988 (so far as relating to paras 67, 70) (s 171(5)) |
| | 29 Sep 1988 (so far as relating to para 66) (s 171(6)) |
| | 12 Oct 1988 (otherwise) (SI 1988/1676) |
| para 66 | 29 Sep 1988 (s 171(6)) |
| para 67 | 29 Jul 1988 (s 171(5)) |
| paras 68, 69 | 12 Oct 1988 (SI 1988/1676) |
| para 70 | 29 Jul 1988 (s 171(5)) |
| para 71 | 1 Feb 1989 (so far as relating to para 76) (SI 1989/1) |
| | 3 Apr 1989 (so far as relating to paras 72, 74, 75, 77) (SI 1989/264) |
| | 31 Jul 1989 (so far as relating to para 73) (SI 1989/1085) |
| para 72 | 3 Apr 1989 (SI 1989/264) |
| para 73 | 31 Jul 1989 (SI 1989/1085) |
| paras 74, 75 | 3 Apr 1989 (SI 1989/264) |
| para 76 | 1 Feb 1989 (SI 1989/1) |
| para 77 | 3 Apr 1989 (SI 1989/264) |
| para 78 | 31 Jul 1989 (SI 1989/1085) |
| para 79 | 31 Jul 1989 (SI 1989/1085); but note already in force 1 Feb 1989 (SI 1989/1) |
| para 80 | 1 Feb 1989 (SI 1989/1) |
| para 81 | *Never in force* (repealed) |
| para 82 | 12 Oct 1988 (SI 1988/1676) |

**Criminal Justice Act 1988 (c 33)**—*contd*

|  |  |
|---|---|
| paras 83–88 | *Never in force* (repealed) |
| paras 89–91 | 29 Jul 1988 (s 171(5)) |
| paras 92–94 | 12 Oct 1988 (SI 1988/1676) |
| paras 95, 96 | *Never in force* (repealed) |
| paras 97–104 | 29 Jul 1988 (s 171(5)) |
| para 105 | 12 Oct 1988 (SI 1988/1676) |
| paras 106–110 | 3 Apr 1989 (SI 1989/264) |
| paras 111–117 | 29 Jul 1988 (s 171(5)) |
| para 118 | 12 Oct 1988 (SI 1988/1676) |

Sch 16         29 Jul 1988 (s 171(5)), repeals of or in—
Criminal Justice Act 1967, s 49;
Children and Young Persons Act 1969, s 29;
Criminal Justice Act 1987
29 Sep 1988 (s 171(6)), repeals of or in—
Prevention of Corruption Act 1916;
Criminal Justice Act 1967, Sch 3;
Criminal Justice Act 1972, s 28(3);
Sexual Offences (Amendment) Act 1976;
Protection of Children Act 1978;
Cable and Broadcasting Act 1984;
Police and Criminal Evidence Act 1984, s 24(2)(e)
1 Oct 1988 (SI 1988/1408), repeals of or in—
Prison Act 1952;
Criminal Justice Act 1961;
Firearms Act 1968 (E) (W);
Children and Young Persons Act 1969, ss 16(10), 22(5), 34(1)(f);
Powers of Criminal Courts Act 1973, s 57(3);
Criminal Law Act 1977, Sch 12;
Reserve Forces Act 1980;
Criminal Justice Act 1982, ss 4–7, 12(1)–(5), (8), (9), 14, 20(1), Sch 8, paras 3(c), 7(d);
Repatriation of Prisoners Act 1984 (E) (W)
12 Oct 1988 (SI 1988/1676), repeals of or in—
Criminal Law Act 1826, s 30;
Offences Against the Person Act 1861, ss 42–44;
Criminal Justice Act 1925, s 39;
Children and Young Persons Act 1933, ss 1(5), (6), 38(1), Sch 1;
Children and Young Persons (Scotland) Act 1937, s 12(5), (6);
Criminal Appeal Act 1968, ss 10(3)(d), 42;
Criminal Justice Act 1972, Sch 5;
Road Traffic Act 1972, s 100;
Powers of Criminal Courts Act 1973, ss 22(5), 34A(1)(c), Sch 3, paras 2(4)(b), 7, Sch 5, para 29;
Juries Act 1974, s 16(2);
Criminal Law Act 1977, Sch 5, para 2, Sch 6;
Magistrates' Courts Act 1980;
Criminal Justice Act 1982, ss 43, 74, 75, 80(1);
Police and Criminal Evidence Act 1984, s 65;
Video Recordings Act 1984, s 15(2), (4), (5);
Cinemas Act 1985, Sch 2, para 11;
Local Government Act 1985, s 15(5);
Coroners Act 1988, Sch 3, para 14
1 Nov 1988 (SI 1988/1817), repeals of or in—
Prisons (Scotland) Act 1952;
Firearms Act 1968 (S);
Fire Precautions Act 1971, s 40(2)(b);
Repatriation of Prisoners Act 1984 (S)
5 Jan 1989 (SI 1988/2073), repeals of or in—
Offences Against the Person Act 1861, ss 46, 47;

**Criminal Justice Act 1988 (c 33)**—*contd*

Juries Act 1974, s 12(1)(a);

Criminal Law Act 1977, s 43;

Drug Trafficking Offences Act 1986, s 6(1)(b), (3), (5)

23 Jan 1989 (repeals of or in Drug Trafficking Offences Act 1986, ss 10(1), 15(5)(b), (c), 17(1), 38(11)) (SI 1989/50)

3 Apr 1989 (SI 1989/264), repeals of or in—

Administration of Justice Act 1970, s 41(8);

Police and Criminal Evidence Act 1984, s 68, Sch 3, paras 1–7, 13 (except in relation to a trial, or proceedings before a magistrates' court acting as examining justices, which began before that date);

Insolvency Act 1985, Sch 8, para 24;

Drug Trafficking Offences Act 1986, ss 19, 25

31 Jul 1989 (repeal in Criminal Appeal Act 1968, s 7(1)) (SI 1989/1085)

1 Jan 2000 (repeals of Power of Criminal Courts Act 1973, ss 39, 40) (SI 1999/3425)

*Not yet in force*, repeals of or in—

Fugitive Offenders Act 1967 (repealed);

Theft Act 1968, s 5(3) (repealed);

Children and Young Persons Act 1969, s 60(1)(b), (2) (repealed);

Genocide Act 1969, ss 2(1)(b), 3(1) (repealed);

Costs in Criminal Cases Act 1973, Sch 1, para 3 (repealed);

Suppression of Terrorism Act 1978, s 3(2) (repealed);

Aviation Security Act 1982, s 9(1)(b), (2), (3) (repealed);

Civil Aviation Act 1982, s 93(3) (repealed);

Taking of Hostages Act 1982, s 3(1)(b) (repealed), (3), (5);

Nuclear Material (Offences) Act 1983, s 5(1)(b), (2), (4) (repealed);

Prohibition of Female Circumcision Act 1985, s 3(1)(b) (repealed);

Insolvency Act 1986;

Criminal Justice (Scotland) Act 1987, s 45(7)(c)(ii) (repealed)

1    Extradition Act 1989, s 38(4) provided for s 136(1) of, and Sch 1, para 4 to, this Act to come into force immediately before 27 Sep 1989 and those provisions were then repealed on that date by s 37(1) of, and Sch 2 to, the 1989 Act

**Dartford–Thurrock Crossing Act 1988 (c 20)**

*RA:* 28 Jun 1988

*Commencement provisions:* s 47(2)

Whole Act in force on 28 Jun 1988 (date of royal assent), except ss 23, 24, 27, 28, 37–40 which came into force on 31 Jul 1988 by virtue of the Dartford–Thurrock Crossing Act 1988 (Appointed Day) Order 1988, SI 1988/1129 (made under s 4(1))

**Duchy of Lancaster Act 1988 (c 10)**

*RA:* 3 May 1988

Whole Act in force 3 May 1988 (RA)

## Education Reform Act 1988 (c 40)

*RA:* 29 Jul 1988

*Commencement provisions:* s 236; Education Reform Act 1988 (Commencement No 1) Order 1988, SI 1988/1459; Education Reform Act 1988 (Commencement No 2) Order 1988, SI 1988/1794; Education Reform Act 1988 (Commencement No 3) Order 1988, SI 1988/2002; Education Reform Act 1988 (Commencement No 4) Order 1988, SI 1988/2271, as amended by SI 1989/501, SI 1990/391; Education Reform Act 1988 (Commencement No 5) Order 1989, SI 1989/164; Education Reform Act 1988 (Commencement No 6) Order 1989, SI 1989/501; Education Reform Act 1988 (Commencement No 7) Order 1989, SI 1989/719; Education Reform Act 1988 (Commencement No 8 and Amendment) Order 1990, SI 1990/391; Education Reform Act 1988 (Commencement No 9) Order 1991, SI 1991/409

| | | |
|---|---|---|
| 1 | | 29 Jul 1988 (s 236(1)) |
| 2 | (1)(a) | 29 Sep 1988 (s 236(3)) |
| | (1)(b) | 29 Jul 1988 (s 236(1)) |
| | (2) | 29 Jul 1988 (s 236(1)) |
| | (3) | 29 Sep 1988 (s 236(3)) |
| 3, 4 | | 29 Jul 1988 (s 236(1)) |
| 5 | | 1 Aug 1989 (SI 1989/164) |
| 6 | | 29 Sep 1988 (s 236(3)) |
| 7 | | 1 Aug 1989 (except in relation to ILEA schools) (SI 1988/2271) |
| | | 1 Aug 1990 (above exception) (SI 1988/2271) |
| 8, 9 | | 29 Sep 1988 (s 236(3)) |
| 10 | (1) | 29 Sep 1988 (s 236(3)) |
| | (2) | 1 Aug 1989 (SI 1989/164) |
| | (3) | 1 Aug 1989 (only in relation to pupils at schools in England in the first, second and third key stage who do not have a statement of special educational needs) (SI 1989/164) |
| | | 1 Aug 1989 (so far as regards the core subjects, in relation to pupils at schools in Wales in the first, second and third key stage who do not have a statement of special educational needs) (SI 1989/501) |
| | | 1 Aug 1990 (in relation to pupils at schools in England in the first, second and third key stage who have a statement of special educational needs and, so far as regards the core subjects, in relation to pupils at such schools in the first year of the fourth key stage) (SI 1989/164) |
| | | 1 Aug 1990 (so far as regards the core subjects and other foundation subjects, in relation to pupils at schools in Wales in the first, second and third key stage (and who, in the former case, have a statement of special educational needs); and, so far as regards the core subjects in relation to pupils at schools in Wales in the first year of the fourth key stage) (SI 1989/501) |
| | | 1 Aug 1991 (so far as regards the core subjects, in relation to pupils at schools in England in the second year of the fourth key stage) (SI 1989/164) |
| | | 1 Aug 1991 (so far as regards the core subjects, in relation to pupils at schools in Wales in the second year of the fourth key stage) (SI 1989/501) |
| 11 | | 29 Sep 1988 (s 236(3)) |
| 12 | | 1 Mar 1989 (except in relation to ILEA county schools) (SI 1989/164) |
| | | 1 Apr 1990 (otherwise) (SI 1989/164) |
| 13 | | 29 Sep 1988 (s 236(3)) |
| 14, 15 | | 29 Jul 1988 (s 236(1)) |
| 16 | | 1 Aug 1989 (SI 1989/164) |
| 17–19 | | 1 Nov 1988 (SI 1988/1794) |
| 20–22 | | 29 Jul 1988 (s 236(1)) |
| 23 | (1) | 29 Jul 1988 (s 236(1)) |
| | (2) | 1 Sep 1989 (except in relation to ILEA schools) (SI 1989/164) |
| | | 1 Apr 1990 (otherwise) (SI 1989/164) |

**Education Reform Act 1988 (c 40)**—*contd*

| | | |
|---|---|---|
| 24 | | 31 Mar 1990 (SI 1990/391) |
| 25 | | 29 Jul 1988 (s 236(1)) |
| 26 | | 1 Sep 1989 (for the purpose of enabling proposals to be made under sub-ss (4)–(6) for fixing the number of pupils in any age group which it is intended to admit to a secondary school in the school year beginning next after 4 Aug 1990, and for purposes of sub-ss (7), (8), (10)) (SI 1988/1459) |
| | | 4 Aug 1990 (remaining purposes so far as relates to secondary schools) (SI 1988/1459) |
| | | 1 Sep 1991 (for the purpose of enabling proposals to be made under sub-ss (4)–(6) for fixing the number of pupils in any age group which it is intended to admit to a primary school in school year beginning next after 1 Aug 1992, and for purposes of sub-ss (7), (8), (10)) (SI 1991/409) |
| | | 1 Aug 1992 (remaining purposes so far as relates to primary schools) (SI 1991/409) |
| 27 | (1)–(3) | 1 Sep 1988 (so far as relates to secondary schools) (SI 1988/1459) |
| | | 12 Mar 1991 (so far as relates to primary schools) (SI 1991/409) |
| | (4)–(8) | 1 Sep 1988 (for purpose of enabling orders reducing any standard number applying to a secondary school to be made under sub-s (5) and applications for such orders to be made as mentioned in sub-s (6)) (SI 1988/1459) |
| | | 1 Sep 1989 (for purpose of enabling orders increasing any standard number applying to a secondary school to be made under sub-s (5) and applications for such orders to be made as mentioned in sub-s (7)) (SI 1988/1459) |
| | | 4 Aug 1990 (remaining purposes, so far as relates to secondary schools) (SI 1988/1459) |
| | | 1 May 1991 (for purpose of enabling orders reducing any standard number applying to a primary school to be made under sub-s (5) and applications for such orders to be made as mentioned in sub-s (6)) (SI 1991/409) |
| | | 1 Sep 1991 (for purpose of enabling orders increasing any standard number applying to a primary school to be made under sub-s (5) and applications for such orders to be made as mentioned in sub-s (7)) (SI 1991/409) |
| | (9) | 1 Sep 1988 (so far as relates to secondary schools) (SI 1988/1459) |
| | | 12 Mar 1991 (so far as relates to primary schools) (SI 1991/409) |
| 28 | | 1 Sep 1988 (so far as relates to secondary schools) (SI 1988/1459) |
| | | 12 Mar 1991 (so far as relates to primary schools) (SI 1991/409) |
| 29 | | 1 May 1991 (SI 1991/409) |
| 30 | | 1 Sep 1988 (SI 1988/1459) |
| 31 | (1) | 4 Aug 1990 (so far as relates to secondary schools) (SI 1988/1459) |
| | | 1 Aug 1992 (so far as relates to primary schools) (SI 1991/409) |
| | (2) | 1 Sep 1989 (so far as relates to the publication of admission arrangements for secondary schools for the school year beginning next after 4 Aug 1990 and subsequent school years) (SI 1988/1459) |
| | | 1 Sep 1991 (so far as relates to the publication of admission arrangements for primary schools for the school year beginning next after 1 Aug 1992 and subsequent school years) (SI 1991/409) |
| | (3) | 1 Aug 1991 (so far as relates to primary schools) (SI 1991/409) |
| | (4)–(6) | 1 May 1991 (so far as relates to primary schools) (SI 1991/409) |
| 32 | | 1 Sep 1988 (so far as relates to secondary schools) (SI 1988/1459) |
| | | 12 Mar 1991 (so far as relates to primary schools) (SI 1991/409) |
| 33–105 | | 29 Jul 1988 (s 236(1)) |
| 106–111 | | 1 Apr 1989 (SI 1988/1794) |
| 112, 113 | | 29 Jul 1988 (s 236(1)) |
| 114 | | 30 Nov 1988 (SI 1988/2002) |

**Education Reform Act 1988 (c 40)**—*contd*

| | | |
|---|---|---|
| 115 | | 1 May 1989 (SI 1989/164) |
| 116 | | 29 Jul 1988 (s 236(1)) |
| 117, 118 | | 1 Apr 1989 (SI 1988/1794) |
| 119 | | 29 Jul 1988 (s 236(1)) |
| 120 | | 1 Apr 1989 (SI 1988/2271) |
| 121 | | 21 Nov 1988 (except Southampton Institute of Higher Education) (SI 1988/1794) |
| | | 1 Feb 1989 (exception noted above) (SI 1988/2271) |
| 122–130 | | 21 Nov 1988 (SI 1988/1794) |
| 131–134 | | 1 Nov 1988 (SI 1988/1794) |
| 135 | | 21 Nov 1988 (SI 1988/1794) |
| 136 | | 1 Nov 1988 (SI 1988/1794) |
| 137–151 | | 29 Jul 1988 (s 236(1)) |
| 152 | (1)–(9) | 1 Apr 1990 (except in relation to an institution providing full-time education maintained by ILEA on 22 Dec 1988 in exercise of their further or higher education functions) (SI 1988/2271) |
| | | 1 Apr 1992 (in relation to an institution providing full-time education maintained by ILEA on 22 Dec 1988 in exercise of their further or higher education functions) (SI 1988/2271) |
| | (10) | 1 Jan 1989 (SI 1988/2271) |
| 153–208 | | 29 Jul 1988 (s 236(1)) |
| 209 | | 31 Mar 1990 (SI 1990/391) |
| 210, 211 | | 1 May 1989 (SI 1989/719) |
| 212, 213 | | 29 Jul 1988 (s 236(1)) |
| 214–216 | | 30 Nov 1988 (SI 1988/2002) |
| 217 | | 29 Jul 1988 (s 236(1)) |
| 218 | | 1 Apr 1989 (SI 1988/2002) |
| 219 | (1) | 1 Jan 1989 (SI 1988/2271) |
| | (2)(a) | 1 Jan 1989 (SI 1988/2271) |
| | (2)(b) | 29 Jul 1988 (s 236(1)) |
| | (2)(c), (d) | 1 Jan 1989 (SI 1988/2271) |
| | (2)(e) | 21 Nov 1988 (SI 1988/1794) |
| | (3)(a) | 1 Jan 1989 (SI 1988/2271) |
| | (3)(b) | 29 Jul 1988 (s 236(1)) |
| | (3)(c) | 1 Jan 1989 (SI 1988/2271) |
| 220 | | 1 Nov 1988 (SI 1988/1794) |
| 221–225 | | 29 Jul 1988 (s 236(1)) |
| 226 | | 21 Nov 1988 (SI 1988/1794) |
| 227 | (1) | 29 Jul 1988 (s 236(1)) |
| | (2)–(4) | 21 Nov 1988 (SI 1988/1794) |
| 228, 229 | | 21 Nov 1988 (SI 1988/1794) |
| 230–236 | | 29 Jul 1988 (s 236(1)) |
| 237 | (1) | See Sch 12 below |
| | (2) | See Sch 13 below |
| 238 | | 29 Jul 1988 (s 236(1)) |
| Sch 1 | | 29 Sep 1988 (s 236(3)) |
| Schs 2–6 | | 29 Jul 1988 (s 236(1)) |
| Sch 7 | | 21 Nov 1988 (SI 1988/1794) |
| Sch 8 | | 29 Jul 1988 (so far as relating to Education Assets Board) (s 236(1)) |
| | | 1 Nov 1988 (otherwise) (SI 1988/1754) |
| Schs 9–11 | | 29 Jul 1988 (s 236(1)) |
| Sch 12 | paras 1–39 | 29 Jul 1988 (s 236(1)) |
| | paras 40–53 | 1 Apr 1990 (s 236(4)) |
| | paras 54–57 | 1 Apr 1989 (SI 1988/2271) |
| | para 58 | 1 Mar 1989 (SI 1989/164) |
| | para 59 | 1 Apr 1989 (SI 1988/2271) |
| | para 60 | 29 Jul 1988 (s 236(1)) |
| | paras 61, 62 | 1 Apr 1989 (SI 1988/2271) |
| | para 63 | 1 Jan 1989 (SI 1988/2271) |

**Education Reform Act 1988 (c 40)**—*contd*

|  | para 64 | 21 Nov 1988 (SI 1988/1794) |
|---|---|---|
|  | paras 65, 66 | 1 Apr 1989 (SI 1988/2271) |
|  | para 67 | 29 Jul 1988 (s 236(1)) (NB also brought into force on 1 Jan 1989 by SI 1988/2271) |
|  | para 68 | 1 Apr 1989 (SI 1988/2002) |
|  | paras 69–76 | 1 Apr 1989 (SI 1988/2271) |
|  | para 77 | *Never in force* (repealed) |
|  | paras 78, 79 | 1 Apr 1989 (SI 1988/2271) |
|  | para 80 | 21 Nov 1988 (SI 1988/1794) |
|  | paras 81, 82 | 29 Jul 1988 (s 236(1)) |
|  | paras 83–85 | 1 Nov 1988 (SI 1988/1794) |
|  | paras 86–98 | 1 Apr 1989 (SI 1988/2271) |
|  | para 99 | 1 Aug 1989 (SI 1988/2271) |
|  | paras 100, 101 | 1 Apr 1989 (SI 1988/2271) |
|  | para 102 | 29 Jul 1988 (s 236(1)) |
|  | paras 103–105 | 1 Apr 1989 (SI 1988/2271) |
|  | para 106 | 31 Mar 1990 (SI 1990/391) |
|  | para 107 | 1 Apr 1989 (SI 1988/2271) |
| Sch 13 | Pt I | 1 Apr 1990 (s 236(5)) |
|  | Pt II | 30 Nov 1988 (SI 1988/2002), repeals of— |

Pt II (continued):

30 Nov 1988 (SI 1988/2002), repeals of—
> Education Act 1967, s 3;
> Education Act 1980, Sch 3, para 14

1 Jan 1989 (SI 1988/2271), repeals of—
> Education Act 1944, ss 25, 29(2)–(4);
> Education Act 1946, s 7;
> Education (No 2) Act 1968 (subject to transitional provisions)

1 Apr 1989 (repeal of Education Act 1944, s 61) (SI 1988/1794)

1 Apr 1989 (SI 1988/2002), repeals of or in—
> Education Act 1980, s 27;
> Education Act 1981, Sch 3, para 5

1 Apr 1989 (SI 1988/2271), repeals of or in—
> Education Act 1944, ss 8(1)(b), 42–46, 50, 52(1), 54, 60, 62(2), 69, 84, 114;
> Education Act 1946, s 8(3);
> London Government Act 1963, s 31(1), (4);
> Industrial Training Act 1964, s 16;
> Local Government Act 1972, ss 81(4)(a), 104(2);
> Sex Discrimination Act 1975, ss 24(2)(a), 25(6)(c)(ii);
> Race Relations Act 1976, ss 19(6)(c)(ii), 78(1);
> Education (No 2) Act 1986, s 56

1 Aug 1989 (repeals of or in Education (No 2) Act 1986, ss 17(1), (4), 18(3), (4), (6), (8), 19(3), 20) (SI 1988/2271)

1 May 1989 (SI 1989/719), repeals of or in—
> Education Act 1946, s 1(1);
> Employment Protection (Consolidation) Act 1978, s 29(1)(e);
> Education Act 1980, s 35(5), Sch 1, para 25;
> Local Government, Planning and Land Act 1980, Sch 10, Pt I;
> Local Government Act 1985, s 22;
> Education (No 2) Act 1986, ss 29, 47(5)(a)(ii), Sch 4, para 4;
> Local Government Act 1987, s 2

31 Mar 1990 (repeals in Local Government Act 1974) (SI 1990/391)

*Never in force* (repeal in Education Act 1980, s 35(3) (repealed))

---

**Electricity (Financial Provisions) (Scotland) Act 1988 (c 37)**

*RA:* 29 Jul 1988

Whole Act in force 29 Jul 1988 (RA)

---

## Employment Act 1988 (c 19)

*RA:* 26 May 1988

*Commencement provisions:* s 34(2); Employment Act 1988 (Commencement No 1) Order 1988, SI 1988/1118; Employment Act 1988 (Commencement No 2) Order 1988, SI 1988/2042

| | | |
|---|---|---|
| 1–7 | | 26 Jul 1988 (SI 1988/1118) |
| 8 | | 5 Dec 1988 (SI 1988/2042) |
| 9–11 | | 26 Jul 1988 (SI 1988/1118) |
| 12 | (1)–(5) | 26 Jul 1989 (SI 1988/1118) |
| | (6) | 26 Jul 1988 (so far as it defines the meaning of principal executive committee) (SI 1988/1118) |
| | | 26 Jul 1989 (otherwise) (SI 1988/1118) |
| 13, 14 | | 26 Jul 1988 (SI 1988/1118) |
| 15 | | 1 Feb 1989 (SI 1988/2042) |
| 16, 17 | | 26 Jul 1988 (SI 1988/1118) |
| 18 | | 26 May 1988 (RA) |
| 19–21 | | 5 Dec 1988 (SI 1988/2042) |
| 22, 23 | | 26 Jul 1988 (SI 1988/1118) |
| 24–32 | | 26 May 1988 (RA) |
| 33 | (1) | See Sch 3 below |
| | (2) | See Sch 4 below |
| 34 | | 26 May 1988 (RA) |
| Sch 1 | | 5 Dec 1988 (SI 1988/2042) |
| Sch 2 | | 26 May 1988 (RA) |
| Sch 3 | para 1 | 1 Feb 1989 (SI 1988/2042) |
| | paras 2–4 | 26 Jul 1988 (SI 1988/1118) |
| | para 5(1) | 26 Jul 1988 (SI 1988/1118) |
| | para 5(2)(a) | 1 Feb 1989 (SI 1988/2042) |
| | para 5(2)(b) | 26 Jul 1988 (SI 1988/1118) |
| | para 5(3) | 26 Jul 1988 (SI 1988/1118) |
| | para 5(4)(a) | 26 Jul 1988 (SI 1988/1118) |
| | para 5(4)(b) | 26 Jul 1988 (so far as relates to s 13) (SI 1988/1118) |
| | | 1 Feb 1989 (otherwise) (SI 1988/2042) |
| | para 5(4)(c) | 26 Jul 1988 (SI 1988/1118) |
| | para 5(5)(a) | 26 Jul 1989 (SI 1988/1118) |
| | para 5(5)(b) | 26 Jul 1988 (so far as relates to s 13) (SI 1988/1118) |
| | | 1 Feb 1989 (otherwise) (SI 1988/2042) |
| | para 5(5)(c), (d) | 26 Jul 1988 (SI 1988/1118) |
| | para 5(6) | *Never in force* (repealed) |
| | para 5(7)–(9) | 26 Jul 1988 (SI 1988/1118) |
| | para 6 | 26 Jul 1988 (SI 1988/1118) |
| | paras 7–15 | 26 May 1988 (RA) |
| Sch 4 | | 26 May 1988 (RA), repeals of or in— |

Parliamentary Commissioner Act 1967, Sch 2;
Employment and Training Act 1973, ss 4(2), 5(1), (4), 11(3), 12(4);
Employment Protection Act 1975, Sch 14, para 2(1);
House of Commons Disqualification Act 1975, Sch 1, Pt III;
Northern Ireland Assembly Disqualification Act 1975, Sch 1, Pt III;
Social Security Act 1975, s 20(1);
Social Security (Miscellaneous Provisions) Act 1977, s 22(6);
Social Security (No 2) Act 1980, s 7(7)
26 Jul 1988 (SI 1988/1118), repeals of or in—
Trade Union Act 1913, s 4(1F);
Trade Union (Amalgamations, etc) Act 1964, s 4(6), Sch 1;
Employment Protection (Consolidation) Act 1978, ss 23(1), (2A), (2B)[1], 58(1), (3)–(12)[1], 58A, 153(1);
Employment Act 1980, s 15(2);
Employment Act 1982, s 10(1), (2), Sch 3, para 16;

**Employment Act 1988 (c 19)**—*contd*

> Trade Union Act 1984, ss 3, 6(6), 9(1)
> 26 Jul 1989 (repeals of or in Trade Union Act 1984, ss 1(1)–(3), 8(1)) (SI 1988/1118)

[1] Note: repeal of Employment Protection (Consolidation) Act 1978, ss 23(2A), (2B), 58(3)–(12) effected on 26 Jul 1988 by virtue of the bringing into force on that date of s 11 (SI 1988/1118)

---

**Environment and Safety Information Act 1988 (c 30)**

*RA:* 29 Jul 1988

*Commencement provisions:* s 5(2)

Whole Act in force 1 Apr 1989 (s 5(2))

---

**European Communities (Finance) Act 1988 (c 46)**

*RA:* 15 Nov 1988

Whole Act in force 15 Nov 1989 (RA)

---

**Farm Land and Rural Development Act 1988 (c 16)**

*RA:* 10 May 1988

Whole Act in force 10 May 1988 (RA)

---

**Finance Act 1988 (c 39)**

*Budget Day:* 15 Mar 1988

*RA:* 29 Jul 1988

The commencement details of Finance Acts are not set out, as the dates from which their provisions take effect are usually stated clearly and unambiguously in the text of the Act, and charging provisions will normally state for which year or years of assessment they are to have effect.

---

**Firearms (Amendment) Act 1988 (c 45)**

*RA:* 15 Nov 1988

*Commencement provisions:* s 27(3); Firearms (Amendment) Act 1988 (Commencement No 1) Order 1988, SI 1988/2209; Firearms (Amendment) Act 1988 (Commencement No 2) Order 1989, SI 1989/853, amended by SI 1989/1673; Firearms (Amendment) Act 1988 (Commencement No 3) Order 1990, SI 1990/2620

| | | |
|---|---|---|
| 1 | | 1 Feb 1989 (subject to transitional provisions) (SI 1988/2209) |
| 2 | (1), (2) | 1 Jul 1989 (subject to transitional provisions) (SI 1989/853) |
| | (3) | 1 Jul 1989 (SI 1989/853) |
| 3 | (1) | 1 Jul 1989 (SI 1989/853) |
| | (2) | 1 Jul 1989 (subject to transitional provisions) (SI 1989/853) |
| 4 | (1) | 1 Jul 1989 (SI 1989/853) |
| | (2)(a) | 1 Jul 1989 (SI 1989/853) |
| | (2)(b) | 1 Jul 1989 (subject to transitional provisions) (SI 1989/853) |
| | (3) | 1 Jul 1989 (subject to transitional provisions) (SI 1989/853) |
| | (4), (5) | 1 Jul 1989 (SI 1989/853) |
| 5, 6 | | 1 Jul 1990 (SI 1989/853) |
| 7 | (1) | 1 Feb 1989 (subject to transitional provisions) (SI 1988/2209) |

**Firearms (Amendment) Act 1988 (c 45)**—*contd*

|  |  |  |
|---|---|---|
| | (2) | 1 Jul 1989 (subject to transitional provisions) (SI 1989/853) |
| | (3) | 1 Jul 1989 (SI 1989/853) |
| 8–10 | | 1 Feb 1988 (SI 1988/2209) |
| 11 | | 1 Jul 1989 (SI 1989/853) |
| 12 | | 1 Feb 1989 (SI 1989/2209) |
| 13 | (1) | 1 Jul 1989 (SI 1989/853) |
| | (2)–(5) | 1 Feb 1989 (SI 1988/2209) |
| 14 | | 1 Feb 1989 (SI 1988/2209) |
| 15 | | 1 Jul 1989 (SI 1989/853) |
| 16 | | 1 Feb 1989 (SI 1988/2209) |
| 17, 18 | | 1 Oct 1989 (SI 1989/853) |
| 19 | | See Schedule below |
| 20 | (1), (2) | 1 Jul 1989 (for purpose of enabling Secretary of State to make an order under Firearms Act 1968, s 6(1A), which is to come into force on the date on which this section comes into force for all other purposes) (SI 1989/853, as amended by Firearms (Amendment) Act 1988 (Commencement No 2) Order (Amendment) Order 1989, SI 1989/1673, art 3) |
| | | 2 Apr 1991 (otherwise) (SI 1990/2620) |
| | (3) | 2 Apr 1991 (SI 1990/2620) |
| 21, 22 | | 1 Feb 1989 (SI 1988/2209) |
| 23 | (1)–(3) | 1 Feb 1989 (SI 1988/2209) |
| | (4)–(6) | 1 Jul 1989 (SI 1989/853) |
| | (7) | 1 Feb 1989 (SI 1988/2209) |
| | (8) | 1 Oct 1989 (except in relation to a person who is in Great Britain on 1 Oct 1989) (SI 1989/853) |
| | | 31 Oct 1989 (exception noted above) (SI 1989/853) |
| 24 | (1) | 1 Feb 1989 (SI 1988/2209) |
| | (2) | 1 Jul 1989 (SI 1989/853) |
| 25 | | 1 Feb 1989 (SI 1988/2209) |
| 26, 27 | | 15 Nov 1988 (s 27(3)) |
| Schedule | | 1 Jul 1989 (SI 1989/853) |

---

**Foreign Marriage (Amendment) Act 1988 (c 44)**

*RA:* 2 Nov 1988

*Commencement provisions:* s 7(3); Foreign Marriage (Amendment) Act 1988 (Commencement) Order 1990, SI 1990/522

Whole Act in force 12 Apr 1990 (SI 1990/522)

---

**Health and Medicines Act 1988 (c 49)**

*RA:* 15 Nov 1988

*Commencement provisions:* ss 19(2), 26(1)–(5); Health and Medicines Act 1988 (Commencement No 1) Order 1988, SI 1988/2107; Health and Medicines Act 1988 (Commencement No 2) Order 1989, SI 1989/111; Health and Medicines Act 1988 (Commencement No 3) Order 1989, SI 1989/337; Health and Medicines Act 1988 (Commencement No 4) Order 1989, SI 1989/826; Health and Medicines Act 1988 (Commencement No 5) Order 1989, SI 1989/1174 (revoked); Health and Medicines Act 1988 (Commencement No 6) Order 1989, SI 1989/1229 (revoking SI 1989/1174); Health and Medicine Act 1988 (Commencement No 7) Order 1989, SI 1989/1896; Health and Medicines Act 1988 (Commencement No 8) Order 1989, SI 1989/1984

|  |  |  |
|---|---|---|
| 1–6 | | 15 Nov 1988 (s 26(3), (4)) |
| 7 | | 15 Jan 1989 (s 26(1)–(5)) |
| 8 | (1)(a) | 15 Oct 1989 (except words "or section 19 of the National Health Service (Scotland) Act 1978") (SI 1989/1896) |
| | | 31 Oct 1989 (exception noted above) (SI 1989/1984) |

**Health and Medicines Act 1988 (c 49)**—*contd*

|  |  |  |
|---|---|---|
|  | (1)(b) | 9 Jun 1989 (SI 1989/826) |
|  | (2) | 9 Jun 1989 (except words "(a) or") (SI 1989/826) |
|  |  | 15 Oct 1989 (words "(a) or" except so far as they have effect for the purposes of any list maintained under National Health Service (Scotland) Act 1978, s 19) (SI 1989/1896) |
|  |  | 31 Oct 1989 (exception noted above) (SI 1989/1984) |
|  | (3)–(7) | 9 Jun 1989 (SI 1989/826) |
| 9 |  | 1 Apr 1990 (SI 1989/826) |
| 10 |  | 15 Jan 1989 (s 26(1)–(5)) |
| 11 | (1) | 7 Mar 1989 (SI 1989/337) |
|  | (2) | 1 Apr 1989 (SI 1989/337) |
|  | (3) | 7 Mar 1989 (for purposes of regulations as to charges authorised by National Health Service Act 1977, s 78(1A)) (SI 1989/337) |
|  |  | 1 Apr 1989 (otherwise) (SI 1989/337) |
|  | (4) | 7 Mar 1989 (SI 1989/337) |
|  | (5) | 1 Apr 1989 (SI 1989/337) |
|  | (6) | 7 Mar 1989 (for purposes of regulations as to charges authorised by National Health Service (Scotland) Act 1978, s 70(1A)) (SI 1989/337) |
|  |  | 1 Apr 1989 (otherwise) (SI 1989/337) |
|  | (7) | 1 Jan 1989 (SI 1989/2107) |
|  | (8) | 1 Apr 1989 (SI 1989/337) |
| 12 |  | 1 Apr 1989 (SI 1989/337) |
| 13 | (1) | 7 Mar 1989 (for purposes of adding National Health Service Act 1977, s 38(2)–(6) and of adding s 38(7) thereof up to the words "are to be made" thereto) (SI 1989/337) |
|  |  | 1 Apr 1989 (otherwise) (SI 1989/337) |
|  | (2) | 7 Mar 1989 (for purposes of any regulations made to come into force on or after 1 Apr 1989) (SI 1989/337) |
|  |  | 1 Apr 1989 (otherwise) (SI 1989/337) |
|  | (3) | 7 Mar 1989 (SI 1989/337) |
|  | (4) | 7 Mar 1989 (for purposes of adding National Health Service (Scotland) Act 1978, s 26(1A)–(1E) and of adding s 26(1F) thereof up to the words "are to be made" thereto) (SI 1989/337) |
|  |  | 1 Apr 1989 (otherwise) (SI 1989/337) |
|  | (5) | 7 Mar 1989 (SI 1989/337) |
|  | (6), (7) | 1 Apr 1989 (SI 1989/337) |
| 14 |  | 20 Jul 1989 (so far as relates to Opticians Act 1988, s 20B(1), (3), (8), (9)) (SI 1989/1229) |
|  |  | 31 Jul 1989 (so far as relates to Opticians Act 1988, s 20B(2), (4)–(7)) (SI 1989/1229) |
| 15, 16 |  | 15 Jan 1989 (s 26(1)–(5)) |
| 17 | (1), (2) | 15 Jan 1989 (s 26(1)–(5)) |
|  | (3) | 15 Nov 1988 (s 26(3), (4)) |
| 18 |  | 15 Jan 1989 (s 26(1)–(5)) |
| 19 |  | 26 Nov 1987 (retrospective) (s 192)) |
| 20 |  | 15 Jan 1989 (s 26(1)–(5)) |
| 21, 22 |  | 15 Nov 1988 (s 26(3), (4)) |
| 23, 24 |  | 15 Jan 1989 (s 26(1)–(5)) |
| 25 | (1) | See Sch 2 below |
|  | (2) | See Sch 3 below |
| 26–28 |  | 15 Nov 1988 (s 26(3), (4)) |
| Sch 1 |  | 15 Nov 1988 (s 26(3), (4)) |
| Sch 2 | para 1 | 15 Jan 1989 (so far as relates to paras 2, 6, 7) (s 26(1)–(5)) |
|  |  | 7 Mar 1989 (so far as relates to para 8(1), (2)) (SI 1989/337) |
|  |  | 1 Apr 1989 (so far as relates to paras 5, 8(3)) (SI 1989/337) |
|  |  | 9 Jun 1989 (so far as relates to para 4) (SI 1989/826) |
|  |  | 15 Oct 1989 (so far as relates to para 3) (SI 1989/1896) |
|  | para 2 | 15 Jan 1989 (s 26(1)–(5)) |

**Health and Medicines Act 1988 (c 49)**—*contd*

|  |  |
|---|---|
| para 3 | 15 Oct 1989 (SI 1989/1896) |
| para 4 | 9 Jun 1989 (SI 1989/826) |
| para 5 | 1 Apr 1989 (SI 1989/337) |
| paras 6, 7 | 15 Jan 1989 (s 26(1)–(5)) |
| para 8(1) | 7 Mar 1989 (for purposes of any regulations made to come into force on or after 1 Apr 1989) (SI 1989/337) |
|  | 1 Apr 1989 (otherwise) (SI 1989/337) |
| para 8(2) | 7 Mar 1989 (SI 1989/337) |
| para 8(3) | 1 Apr 1989 (SI 1989/337) |
| para 9 | 15 Jan 1989 (so far as relates to paras 13, 14) (s 26(1)–(5)) |
|  | 7 Mar 1989 (so far as relates to para 15(1), (2)) (SI 1989/337) |
|  | 1 Apr 1989 (so far as relates to paras 12, 15(3)) (SI 1989/337) |
|  | 9 Jun 1989 (so far as relates to para 11) (SI 1989/826) |
|  | 31 Oct 1989 (so far as relates to para 10) (SI 1989/1984) |
| para 10 | 31 Oct 1989 (SI 1989/1984) |
| para 11 | 9 Jun 1989 (SI 1989/826) |
| para 12 | 1 Apr 1989 (SI 1989/337) |
| paras 13, 14 | 15 Jan 1989 (s 26(1)–(5)) |
| para 15(1) | 7 Mar 1989 (for purposes of any regulations made to come into force on or after 1 Apr 1989) (SI 1989/337) |
|  | 1 Apr 1989 (otherwise) (SI 1989/337) |
| para 15(2) | 7 Mar 1989 (SI 1989/337) |
| para 15(3) | 1 Apr 1989 (SI 1989/337) |
| Sch 3 | 15 Nov 1988 (repeal of National Health Service Act 1977, s 28(4)) (s 26(3), (4)) |
|  | 1 Jan 1989 (SI 1989/2107), repeals of or in— National Health Service Act 1977, s 79(1)(d) and word "or" preceding it; National Health Service (Scotland) Act 1978, s 71(1)(d) and word "or" preceding it |
|  | 15 Jan 1989 (s 26(1)–(5)), repeals of or in— Health Services and Public Health Act 1968, s 63(3); National Health Service Act 1977, ss 5(1)(a), 58, 61, 62, 63(2), 66A; National Health Service (Scotland) Act 1978, ss 39, 50, 53, 54, 55(2), 58A; Health Services Act 1980, ss 10, 11 |
|  | 27 Feb 1989 (SI 1989/111), repeals of or in— National Health Service Act 1966; Superannuation Act 1972; Health Services Act 1980, ss 17, 19; Health and Social Security Act 1984, s 8; Companies Consolidation (Consequential Provisions) Act 1985 |
|  | 1 Apr 1989 (otherwise) (SI 1989/337) |

---

**Housing Act 1988 (c 50)**

*RA:* 15 Nov 1988

*Commencement provisions:* ss 132(8), 141(2), (3); Housing Act 1988 (Commencement No 1) Order 1988, SI 1988/2056; Housing Act 1988 (Commencement No 2) Order 1988, SI 1988/2152; Housing Act 1988 (Commencement No 3) Order 1989, SI 1989/203; Housing Act 1988 (Commencement No 4) Order 1989, SI 1989/404; Housing Act 1988 (Commencement No 5 and Transitional Provisions) Order 1991, SI 1991/954; Housing Act 1988 (Commencement No 6) Order 1992, SI 1992/324

|  |  |  |
|---|---|---|
| 1–45 |  | 15 Jan 1989 (s 141(3)) |
| 46 | (1) | 1 Dec 1988 (SI 1988/2056) |
|  | (2) | See Sch 5 below |
|  | (3)–(5) | 1 Apr 1989 (SI 1989/404) |

**Housing Act 1988 (c 50)**—*contd*

| 47 | (1) | 1 Apr 1989 (SI 1989/404) |
|---|---|---|
| | (2) | 1 Dec 1988 (SI 1988/2056) |
| | (3)–(5) | 1 Apr 1989 (SI 1989/404) |
| | (6) | 1 Dec 1988 (so far as relates to s 47(2)) (SI 1988/2056) |
| | | 1 Apr 1989 (otherwise) (SI 1989/404) |
| 48 | | 1 Apr 1989 (SI 1989/404) |
| 49 | | 15 Jan 1989 (SI 1988/2152) |
| 50–56 | | 1 Apr 1989 (SI 1989/404) |
| 57 | | 15 Jan 1989 (SI 1988/2152) |
| 58 | | 1 Apr 1989 (SI 1989/404) |
| 59 | (1) | 15 Jan 1989 (SI 1988/2152) |
| | (2), (3) | See Sch 6 below |
| | (4) | 1 Apr 1989 (SI 1989/404) |
| 60–92 | | 15 Nov 1988 (RA) |
| 93 | | 5 Apr 1989 (SI 1989/404) |
| 94 | | 15 Jan 1989 (SI 1988/2152) |
| 95–105 | | 5 Apr 1989 (SI 1989/404) |
| 106 | | 15 Jan 1989 (SI 1988/2152) |
| 107 | | 5 Apr 1989 (SI 1989/404) |
| 108 | | See Sch 12 below |
| 109, 110 | | 5 Apr 1989 (SI 1989/404) |
| 111–114 | | 15 Jan 1989 (SI 1988/2152) |
| 115–118 | | 15 Jan 1989 (s 141(3)) |
| 119 | | See Sch 13 below |
| 120, 121 | | 15 Jan 1989 (s 141(3)) |
| 122 | | 10 Mar 1989 (SI 1989/203) |
| 123 | | 15 Jan 1989 (s 141(3)) |
| 124 | | 10 Mar 1989 (SI 1989/203) |
| 125, 126 | | 15 Jan 1989 (s 141(3)) |
| 127 | | 5 Apr 1989 (SI 1989/404) |
| 128 | | 21 Feb 1992 (SI 1992/324) |
| 129 | | 1 Apr 1989 (SI 1989/404) |
| 130, 131 | | 15 Jan 1989 (s 141(3)) |
| 132 | | 9 Jun 1988 (retrospective) (s 132(8)) |
| 133, 134 | | 15 Nov 1988 (RA; s 141(2), (3)) |
| 135 | (1) | 21 Feb 1992 (SI 1992/324) |
| | (2) | See Sch 16 below |
| | (3) | 21 Feb 1992 (SI 1992/324) |
| 136, 137 | | 15 Jan 1989 (s 141(3)) |
| 138, 139 | | 15 Nov 1988 (RA; s 141(2), (3)) |
| 140 | (1) | See Sch 17 below |
| | (2) | See Sch 18 below |
| 141 | | 15 Nov 1988 (RA; s 141(2), (3)) |
| Schs 1–4 | | 15 Jan 1989 (s 141(3)) |
| Sch 5 | | 1 Dec 1988 (SI 1988/2056) |
| Sch 6 | para 1 | 15 Jan 1989 (for the purposes only of s 59(1) of the Act and the Housing Associations Act 1985, s 36A) (SI 1988/2152) |
| | | 1 Apr 1989 (otherwise) (SI 1989/404) |
| | paras 2–7 | 1 Apr 1989 (SI 1989/404) |
| | para 8(1) | 1 Apr 1989 (SI 1989/404) |
| | para 8(2) | 15 Jan 1989 (SI 1988/2152) |
| | paras 9–24 | 1 Apr 1989 (SI 1989/404) |
| | para 25 | 15 Jan 1989 (SI 1988/2152) |
| | para 26(a) | 15 Jan 1989 (SI 1988/2152) |
| | para 26(b), (c) | 1 Apr 1989 (SI 1989/404) |
| | para 27 | *Never in force* (spent) |
| | para 28 | 1 Apr 1989 (SI 1989/404) |
| | para 29 | 1 Apr 1989 (except for purposes of hostel deficit grant payable under Housing Associations Act 1985, s 55) (SI 1989/404) |

**Housing Act 1988 (c 50)**—*contd*

| | | |
|---|---|---|
| | paras 30–37 | 1 Apr 1989 (SI 1989/404) |
| Schs 7–11 | | 15 Nov 1988 (RA) |
| Sch 12 | | 5 Apr 1989 (SI 1989/404) |
| Sch 13 | | 15 Jan 1989 (subject to transitional provisions) (SI 1988/2152) |
| Schs 14, 15 | | 15 Jan 1989 (s 141(3)) |
| Sch 16 | | 21 Feb 1992 (SI 1992/324) |
| Sch 17 | paras 1–16 | 15 Jan 1989 (SI 1988/2152) |
| | para 17(1) | 5 Apr 1989 (SI 1989/404) |
| | para 17(2) | 15 Jan 1989 (SI 1988/2152) |
| | paras 18–37 | 15 Jan 1989 (subject to transitional provision for para 21) (SI 1988/2152) |
| | paras 38, 39 | 5 Apr 1989 (SI 1989/404) |
| | para 40 | 15 Jan 1989 (SI 1988/2152) |
| | para 41 | 10 Mar 1989 (SI 1989/203) |
| | paras 42–65 | 15 Jan 1989 (SI 1988/2152) |
| | para 66 | 1 Apr 1989 (SI 1989/404) |
| | paras 67–76 | 15 Jan 1989 (SI 1988/2152) |
| | paras 77, 78 | 2 Jan 1989 (SI 1988/2152) |
| | para 79 | *Never in force* (repealed) |
| | paras 80–84 | 15 Jan 1989 (SI 1988/2152) |
| | paras 85–88 | 2 Jan 1989 (SI 1988/2152) |
| | para 89 | 1 Apr 1989 (SI 1989/404) |
| | para 90 | 2 Jan 1989 (SI 1988/2152) |
| | paras 91–96 | 1 Dec 1988 (SI 1988/2056) |
| | para 97 | 1 Apr 1989 (SI 1989/404) |
| | paras 98–102 | 1 Dec 1988 (SI 1988/2056) |
| | para 103 | 1 Apr 1989 (SI 1989/404) |
| | paras 104, 105 | 1 Dec 1988 (SI 1988/2056) |
| | paras 106–113 | 1 Apr 1989 (SI 1989/404) |
| | paras 114–116 | 1 Dec 1988 (SI 1988/2056) |
| Sch 18 | | 2 Jan 1989 (repeal in Housing (Scotland) Act 1988, s 38) (SI 1988/2152) |

15 Jan 1989 (SI 1988/2152) (subject to transitional provisions), repeals of or in—

Reserve and Auxiliary Forces (Protection of Civil Interests) Act 1951;

Rent (Agriculture) Act 1976;

Protection from Eviction Act 1977;

Rent Act 1977;

Housing Act 1980;

Housing Act 1985;

Local Government Act 1985;

Housing and Planning Act 1986, ss 7, 12, 13, Sch 4;

Landlord and Tenant Act 1987, ss 3, 4, 60;

Housing (Scotland) Act 1988, Sch 9, para 6

1 Apr 1989 (SI 1989/404), repeals of or in—

Housing Associations Act 1985, except s 55 and ss 56, 57 in relation to hostel deficit grants;

Housing and Planning Act 1986 (so far as not yet in force);

Housing (Scotland) Act 1986;

Landlord and Tenant Act 1987 (so far as not yet in force);

Local Government Act 1988;

Housing (Scotland) Act 1988 (so far as not yet in force)

1 Apr 1991 (repeals of or in Housing Associations Act 1985, ss 55–57, except in relation to hostel deficit grant payable to an association for a period which expires before 1 Apr 1991) (SI 1991/954)

*Not yet in force*, repeals of or in—

**Housing Act 1988 (c 50)**—*contd*

> Housing Associations Act 1985, ss 55–57, in relation to hostel
> deficit grant payable before 1 Apr 1991;
> Housing (Scotland) Act 1987, s 61(4)(b)

**Housing (Scotland) Act 1988 (c 43)**

*RA:* 2 Nov 1988

*Commencement provisions:* s 74(2); Housing (Scotland) Act 1988 Commencement Order 1988,
SI 1988/2038

| | | |
|---|---|---|
| 1 | (1) | 1 Dec 1988 (SI 1988/2038) |
| | (2) | See Sch 1 below |
| | (3) | 1 Dec 1988 (SI 1988/2038) |
| 2 | | 1 Dec 1988 (SI 1988/2038) |
| 3 | (1) | 1 Dec 1988 (SI 1988/2038) |
| | (2) | 1 Apr 1989 (SI 1988/2038) |
| | (3) | See Sch 2 below |
| | (4) | 1 Dec 1988 (SI 1988/2038) |
| 4 | (1)–(3) | 1 Dec 1988 (SI 1988/2038) |
| | (4) | See Sch 3 below |
| | (5)–(7) | 1 Dec 1988 (SI 1988/2038) |
| 5–11 | | 1 Dec 1988 (SI 1988/2038) |
| 12 | (1) | 2 Jan 1989 (SI 1988/2038) |
| | (2) | See Sch 4 below |
| 13–35 | | 2 Jan 1989 (SI 1988/2038) |
| 36–40 | | 2 Jan 1989 (s 74(2)(b)) |
| 41–45 | | 2 Jan 1989 (SI 1988/2038) |
| 46 | (1), (2) | 2 Jan 1989 (SI 1988/2038) |
| | (3), (4) | See Sch 6 below |
| 47–55 | | 2 Jan 1989 (SI 1988/2038) |
| 56–64 | | 1 Apr 1989 (SI 1988/2038) |
| 65 | | 2 Jan 1989 (s 74(2)(b)) |
| 66 | | 2 Jan 1989 (SI 1988/2038) |
| 67 | | 2 Jan 1989 (s 74(2)(b)) |
| 68 | | 2 Jan 1989 (SI 1988/2038) |
| 69 | | 2 Nov 1988 (s 74(2)(a)) |
| 70 | | 2 Jan 1989 (SI 1988/2038) |
| 71 | | 2 Jan 1989 (s 74(2)(b)) |
| 72 | (1) | See Schs 7, 8 below |
| | (2) | See Sch 9 below |
| | (3) | See Sch 10 below |
| 73 | | 1 Dec 1988 (SI 1988/2038) |
| 74 | | 2 Nov 1988 (s 74(2)(a)) |
| Sch 1 | | 1 Dec 1988 (SI 1988/2038) |
| Sch 2 | paras 1, 2 | 1 Apr 1989 (SI 1988/2038) |
| | para 3(a) | 1 Dec 1988 (SI 1988/2038) |
| | para 3(b) | 1 Apr 1989 (SI 1988/2038) |
| | paras 4–17 | 1 Apr 1989 (SI 1988/2038) |
| Sch 3 | | 1 Apr 1989 (SI 1988/2038) |
| Schs 4–6 | | 2 Jan 1989 (SI 1988/2038) |
| Sch 7 | | 2 Nov 1988 (s 74(2)(a)) |
| Sch 8 | | 2 Jan 1989 (s 74(2)(b)) |
| Sch 9 | paras 1–6 | 2 Jan 1989 (SI 1988/2038) |
| | para 7 | 1 Apr 1989 (SI 1988/2038) |
| | paras 8–16 | 2 Jan 1989 (SI 1988/2038) |
| | para 17 | 1 Apr 1989 (SI 1988/2038) |
| | paras 18–21 | 2 Apr 1989 (SI 1988/2038) |

## Housing (Scotland) Act 1988 (c 43)—*contd*

| | |
|---|---|
| Sch 10 | 2 Jan 1989 (repeals of or in Housing (Scotland) Act 1987, ss 62(11)–(13), 151) (s 74(2)(b)) |
| | 2 Jan 1989 (repeals of or in Rent (Scotland) Act 1984, ss 66(1), 68, 70(2), 71(1)) (SI 1988/2038) |
| | 1 Apr 1989 (repeal of Housing (Scotland) Act 1987, Sch 16, para 1(b)) (s 74(2)(c)) |
| | 1 Apr 1989 (otherwise) (SI 1988/2038) |

## Immigration Act 1988 (c 14)

*RA:* 10 May 1988

*Commencement provisions:* s 12(3), (4); Immigration Act 1988 (Commencement No 1) Order 1988, SI 1988/1133; Immigration Act 1988 (Commencement No 2) Order 1991, SI 1991/1001; Immigration Act 1988 (Commencement No 3) Order 1994, SI 1994/1923

| | | |
|---|---|---|
| 1–5 | | 1 Aug 1988 (subject to exceptions in relation to ss 1, 2, 4) (SI 1988/1133) |
| 6 | | 10 Jul 1988 (s 12(3)) |
| 7 | (1) | 20 Jul 1994 (SI 1994/1923) |
| | (2), (3) | 10 Jul 1988 (s 12(3)) |
| 8–12 | | 10 Jul 1988 (s 12(3)) |
| Schedule | para 1 | 16 May 1991 (SI 1991/1001) |
| | paras 2–10 | 10 Jul 1988 (s 12(3)) |

## Income and Corporation Taxes Act 1988 (c 1)

*RA:* 9 Feb 1988

*Commencement provisions:* s 843

In general, the Act came into force in relation to tax for the year 1988–89 and subsequent years of assessment, and for company accounting periods ending after 5 Apr 1988; but this is subject to a contrary intention, in particular as provided by ss 96, 380–384, 393, 394, 400, 470(3)[1], 703, 729(12)[2], 812

[1]  Appointed day for the purposes of s 470(3): 29 Apr 1988 (Income and Corporation Taxes Act 1988 (Appointed Day) Order 1988, SI 1988/745)

[2]  Appointed day for the purposes of s 729(12): 9 Jun 1988 (SI 1988/1002) (Income and Corporation Taxes Act 1988 (Appointed Day No 2) Order 1988, SI 1988/1002)

## Land Registration Act 1988 (c 3)

*RA:* 15 Mar 1988

*Commencement provisions:* s 3(2); Land Registration Act 1988 (Commencement) Order 1990, SI 1990/1359

Whole Act in force 3 Dec 1990 (SI 1990/1359)

## Landlord and Tenant Act 1988 (c 26)

*RA:* 29 Jul 1988

*Commencement provisions:* s 7(2)

Whole Act in force 29 Sep 1988 (s 7(2))

## Legal Aid Act 1988 (c 34)

*RA:* 29 Jul 1988

*Commencement provisions:* s 47; Legal Aid Act 1988 (Commencement No 1) Order 1988, SI 1988/1361; Legal Aid Act 1988 (Commencement No 2) (Scotland) Order 1988, SI 1988/1388; Legal Aid Act 1988 (Commencement No 3) Order 1989, SI 1989/288; Legal Aid Act 1988 (Commencement No 4) Order 1991, SI 1991/790

| | | |
|---|---|---|
| 1, 2 | | 1 Apr 1989 (SI 1989/288) |
| 3 | (1) | 20 Aug 1988 (SI 1988/1361) |
| | (2)–(4) | 1 Apr 1989 (SI 1989/288) |
| | (5)–(10) | 20 Aug 1988 (SI 1988/1361) |
| 4–28 | | 1 Apr 1989 (SI 1989/288) |
| 29 | | 1 May 1991 (SI 1991/790) |
| 30 | (1), (2) | 1 Apr 1989 (SI 1989/288) |
| | (3) | 1 May 1991 (SI 1991/790) |
| 31–34 | | 1 Apr 1989 (SI 1989/288) |
| 35 | | 29 Jul 1988 (s 47(4)) |
| 36–43 | | 1 Apr 1989 (SI 1989/288) |
| 44 | | See Sch 4 below |
| 45 | (1) | See Sch 5 below |
| | (2) | See Sch 6 below |
| | (3) | See Schs 5, 6 below |
| | (4) | See Sch 7 below |
| 46 | | 29 Jul 1988 (s 47(4)) |
| 47 | | 29 Jul 1988 (RA) |
| Sch 1 | | 20 Aug 1988 (SI 1988/1361) |
| Schs 2, 3 | | 1 Apr 1989 (SI 1989/288) |
| Sch 4 | paras 1, 2 | 29 Jul 1988 (SI 1988/1388) |
| | para 3 | *Never in force* (repealed) |
| | para 4 | 29 Jul 1988 (SI 1988/1388) |
| | para 5 | *Never in force* (repealed) |
| | paras 6–9 | 29 Jul 1988 (SI 1988/1388) |
| Sch 5 | | 1 Apr 1989 (SI 1989/288) |
| Sch 6 | | 29 Jul 1988 (repeal of Legal Aid Act 1974, s 21) (s 47(4)) |
| | | 1 Apr 1989 (otherwise) (SI 1989/288) |
| Sch 7 | paras 1–5 | 1 Apr 1989 (SI 1989/288) |
| | paras 6–8 | 20 Aug 1988 (SI 1988/1361) |
| | paras 9–11 | 1 Apr 1989 (SI 1989/288) |
| Sch 8 | | 29 Jul 1988 (s 47(4)) |

## Licensing Act 1988 (c 17)

*RA:* 19 May 1988

*Commencement provisions:* s 20(3); Licensing Act 1988 (Commencement No 1) Order 1988, SI 1988/1187; Licensing Act 1988 (Commencement No 2) Order 1988, SI 1988/1333

| | |
|---|---|
| 1 | 22 Aug 1988 (SI 1988/1333) |
| 2 | 1 Aug 1988 (SI 1988/1187) |
| 3 | 22 Aug 1988 (SI 1988/1333) |
| 4 | 1 Aug 1988 (SI 1988/1187) |
| 5 | 22 Aug 1988 (SI 1988/1333) |
| 6–8 | 1 Aug 1988 (SI 1988/1187) |
| 9 | 22 Aug 1988 (SI 1988/1333) |
| 10 | 1 Aug 1988 (SI 1988/1187) |
| 11 | 22 Aug 1988 (SI 1988/1333) |
| 12 | 1 Mar 1989 (SI 1988/1333) |
| 13, 14 | 22 Aug 1988 (SI 1988/1333) |
| 15 | 1 Mar 1989 (SI 1988/1333) |
| 16–18 | 1 Aug 1988 (SI 1988/1187) |

**Licensing Act 1988 (c 17)**—*contd*

| | | |
|---|---|---|
| 19 | (1) | See Sch 3 below |
| | (2) | See Sch 4 below |
| 20 | | 1 Aug 1988 (SI 1988/1187) |
| Schs 1, 2 | | 22 Aug 1988 (SI 1988/1333) |
| Sch 3 | para 1 | 22 Aug 1988 (SI 1988/1333) |
| | para 2 | 1 Aug 1988 (SI 1988/1187) |
| | paras 3–6 | 1 Mar 1989 (SI 1988/1333) |
| | para 7 | 22 Aug 1988 (SI 1988/1333) |
| | para 8(a) | 22 Aug 1988 (SI 1988/1333) |
| | para 8(b) | 1 Aug 1988 (SI 1988/1187) |
| | para 9 | 22 Aug 1988 (SI 1988/1333) |
| | para 10 | 1 Aug 1988 (SI 1988/1187) |
| | paras 11–14 | 22 Aug 1988 (SI 1988/1333) |
| | para 15(a) | 22 Aug 1988 (SI 1988/1333) |
| | para 15(b) | 1 Mar 1989 (SI 1988/1333) |
| | paras 16–18 | 1 Aug 1988 (SI 1988/1187) |
| | para 19 | 22 Aug 1988 (SI 1988/1333) |
| Sch 4 | | 1 Aug 1988 (repeals of or in Licensing Act 1964, ss 9(5), 71(3), 72(2), 73(1), 92(4), 169) (SI 1988/1187) |
| | | 22 Aug 1988 (SI 1988/1333), repeals of or in— |
| | | Licensing Act 1964, ss 2(3)(b), 6(4), 7, 60, 62(2), 80(2), 95, 151(5), Sch 2, para 9; |
| | | Finance Act 1967; |
| | | Criminal Law Act 1977; |
| | | Magistrates' Courts Act 1980; |
| | | Licensing (Restaurant Meals) Act 1987 |

---

**Licensing (Retail Sales) Act 1988 (c 25)**

*RA:* 29 Jul 1988

*Commencement provisions:* s 4(2); Licensing (Retail Sales) Act 1988 (Commencement) Order 1988, SI 1988/1670

Whole Act in force 1 Nov 1988 (SI 1988/1670)

---

**Local Government Act 1988 (c 9)**

*RA:* 24 Mar 1988

*Commencement provisions:* passim; Local Government Act 1988 (Commencement No 1) Order 1988, SI 1988/979; Local Government Act 1988 (Commencement No 2) (Scotland) Order 1988, SI 1988/1043

| | |
|---|---|
| 1–3 | 28 Mar 1988 (RA) |
| 4 | 24 Mar 1988 (but applies only where it is proposed to enter into the works contract on or after 1 Apr 1989) (RA; s 4(7)) |
| 5–8 | 24 Mar 1988 (RA) (in relation to s 6, see s 6(3)) |
| 9–11 | 24 Mar 1988 (apply in relation to work carried out in or after financial year beginning in 1989) (RA; ss 9(1), 10(1), 11(1)) |
| 12–16 | 24 Mar 1988 (RA) |
| 17–22 | 7 Apr 1988 (s 23) |
| 23–26 | 24 Mar 1988 (RA) |
| 27–30 | 24 May 1988 (ss 27(3), 28(2), 29(2), 30(3)) |
| 31 | See Sch 5 below |
| 32 | 24 Mar 1988 (RA); but see Sch 6 below |
| 33 | 11 Feb 1988 (s 33(4)) |
| 34 | The day any authority or body concerned was established (s 34(2)) |
| 35 | 24 May 1988 (s 35(5)) |
| 36, 37 | 24 Mar 1988 (RA) |

**Local Government Act 1988 (c 9)**—*contd*

| | | |
|---|---|---|
| 38 | | 24 May 1988 (s 35(4)) |
| 39 | | 24 May 1988 (s 39(6)) |
| 40 | | 24 Mar 1988 (RA) |
| 41 | | 24 Mar 1988 (RA); but see Sch 7 below |
| 42 | | 24 Mar 1988 (RA) |
| Sch 1 | | 24 Mar 1988 (RA) |
| Sch 2 | | 7 Apr 1988 (s 23) |
| Sch 3 | | 24 May 1988 (s 29(2)) |
| Sch 4 | | 24 May 1988 (s 30(3)) |
| Sch 5 | para 1 | 24 May 1988 (s 31(2)) |
| | para 2 | *Not yet in force* |
| | paras 3–6 | 24 May 1988 (s 31(2)) |
| Sch 6 | paras 1–3 | 24 Jun 1988 (SI 1988/979; SI 1988/1043) |
| | para 4 | 1 Oct 1988 (SI 1988/979; SI 1988/1043) |
| | paras 5–7 | 24 Jun 1988 (SI 1988/979; SI 1988/1043) |
| | para 8(1) | 24 Mar 1988 (s 32(3)) |
| | para 8(2) | 24 Jun 1988 (SI 1988/979; SI 1988/1043) |
| | para 8(3) | 24 Mar 1988 (s 32(3)) |
| | para 8(4) | 24 Jun 1988 (SI 1988/979; SI 1988/1043) |
| | para 9 | 24 Jun 1988 (SI 1988/979; SI 1988/1043) |
| | para 10(1) | 24 Jun 1988 (SI 1988/979; SI 1988/1043) |
| | para 10(2) | 1 Oct 1988 (SI 1988/979; SI 1988/1043) |
| | para 10(3)–(5) | 24 Jun 1988 (SI 1988/979; SI 1988/1043) |
| | para 10(6) | 24 Jun 1988 (so far as inserts Local Government, Planning and Land Act 1980, s 20(5)) (SI 1988/979; SI 1988/1043) |
| | | 1 Oct 1988 (so far as inserts Local Government, Planning and Land Act 1980, s 20(6)) (SI 1988/979; SI 1988/1043) |
| | para 10(7) | 24 Jun 1988 (SI 1988/979; SI 1988/1043) |
| | para 11 | 24 Mar 1988 (s 32(3)) |
| Sch 7 | Pt I | 7 Apr 1988 (s 23) |
| | Pt II | 24 May 1988 (s 29(2)) |
| | Pt III | 24 Jun 1988 or 1 Oct 1988 (dependent on relationship to s 32 and Sch 6) (SI 1988/979; SI 1988/1043) |
| | Pt IV | 29 May 1988 (Sch 7, Pt IV) |

---

**Local Government Finance Act 1988 (c 41)**

*RA:* 29 Jul 1988

*Commencement provisions:* ss 111(5), 131(8), 132(6), 143(1), (2), 150, Schs 12, 13; Local Government Finance Act 1988 (Commencement) (Scotland) Order 1988, SI 1988/1456 (partially revoked by SI 1990/573); Local Government Finance Act 1988 Commencement (Scotland) Amendment Order 1990, SI 1990/573 (partially revokes SI 1988/1456)

| | | |
|---|---|---|
| 1–110 | | 29 Jul 1988 (RA) |
| 111–116 | | 29 Sep 1988 (s 111(5)) |
| 117–126 | | 29 Jul 1988 (RA) |
| 127 | | 29 Jul 1988 (RA) (subject to prescribed savings made under s 127(2); section forbids levies under London Regional Transport Act 1984, s 13, after 31 Mar 1990) |
| 128 | | 22 Aug 1988 (SI 1988/1456) |
| 129 | | 22 Aug 1988 (only for the purposes of and in relation to the personal community charge and the personal community water charge in respect of the financial year 1989–90 and each subsequent financial year) (SI 1988/1456) |
| | | 1 Apr 1989 (otherwise) (SI 1988/1456) |
| 130 | | 29 Jul 1988 (RA) |
| 131 | | 10 Mar 1988 (retrospective) (s 131(8)) |
| 132 | (1), (2) | 10 Mar 1988 (retrospective) (s 131(8)) |
| | (3), (4) | 29 Jul 1988 (RA) |

**Local Government Finance Act 1988 (c 41)**—*contd*

| | | |
|---|---|---|
| | (5) | 10 Mar 1988 (retrospective) (s 131(8)) |
| | (6) | 29 Jul 1988 (RA) |
| 133–149 | | 29 Jul 1988 (RA) |
| 150 | | 22 Aug 1988 (SI 1988/1456) |
| 151, 152 | | 29 Jul 1988 (RA) |
| Schs 1–11 | | 29 Jul 1988 (RA) |
| Sch 12 | Pt I, para 1 | 31 Mar 1990 (as regards qualifying dates after that date) (Sch 12, Pt I, para 1(2)) |
| | Pt I, para 2 | 31 Mar 1990 (as regards any time after that date) (Sch 12, Pt I, para 2(2)) |
| | Pt I, para 3(1) | 29 Jul 1988 (RA) |
| | Pt I, para 3(2) | 1 Apr 1990 (Sch 12, Pt I, para 3(5)) |
| | Pt I, para 3(3) | 29 Jul 1988 (RA) |
| | Pt I, para 3(4) | 1 Apr 1990 (Sch 12, Pt I, para 3(5)) |
| | Pt I, para 3(5) | 29 Jul 1988 (RA) |
| | Pt II, paras 4–6 | 22 Aug 1988 (SI 1988/1456) |
| | Pt II, para 7 | 1 Apr 1990 (SI 1988/1456) |
| | Pt II, paras 8, 9 | 22 Aug 1988 (SI 1988/1456) |
| | Pt II, para 10 | 22 Aug 1988 (only for the purposes of and in relation to the financial year 1989–90 and in each subsequent financial year) (SI 1988/1456) |
| | | 1 Apr 1989 (otherwise) (SI 1988/1456) |
| | Pt II, paras 11–13 | 1 Apr 1990 (SI 1988/1456) |
| | Pt II, para 14 | 22 Aug 1988 (SI 1988/1456) |
| | Pt II, para 15 | 15 Sep 1988 (SI 1988/1456) |
| | Pt II, paras 16, 17 | 22 Aug 1988 (SI 1988/1456) |
| | Pt II, paras 18–21 | 22 Aug 1988 (only for purposes of and in relation to the community charge and the community water charge in respect of the financial year 1989–90 and each subsequent financial year) (SI 1988/1456) |
| | | 1 Apr 1989 (otherwise) (SI 1988/1456) |
| | Pt II, paras 22–26 | 22 Aug 1988 (SI 1988/1456) |
| | Pt II, para 27 | 1 Oct 1988 (SI 1988/1456) |
| | Pt II, para 28 | 22 Aug 1988 (SI 1988/1456) |
| | Pt II, paras 29, 30 | 1 Oct 1988 (SI 1988/1456) |
| | Pt II, paras 31–34 | 22 Aug 1988 (SI 1988/1456) |
| | Pt II, para 35 | 22 Aug 1988 (only for purposes of and in relation to the personal community charge and the personal community water charge in respect of the financial year 1989–90 and each subsequent financial year) (SI 1988/1456) |
| | | 1 Apr 1989 (otherwise) (SI 1988/1456) |
| | Pt II, paras 36–38 | 22 Aug 1988 (SI 1988/1456) |
| | Pt III, para 39 | 1 Apr 1989 (S) (Sch 12, Pt III, para 39(3)) |
| | | 1 Apr 1990 (E) (W) (Sch 12, Pt III, para 39(2)) |
| | Pt III, paras 40, 41 | 29 Jul 1988 (RA) |
| | Pt III, para 42 | 1 Apr 1989 (S) (Sch 12, Pt III, para 42(3)) |
| | | 1 Apr 1990 (E) (W) (Sch 12, Pt III, para 42(2)) |
| Sch 13 | Pt I | 1 Apr 1990 (subject to any saving under s 117(8)) (Sch 13, Pt I) |
| | Pt II | 1 Apr 1990 (Sch 13, Pt II) |
| | Pt III | See s 127 above |
| | Pt IV | 22 Aug 1988 (repeals of or in Abolition of Domestic Rates Etc (Scotland) Act 1987, ss 4(1), 11(11), 17(5), 30(2), Sch 2) (SI 1988/1456) |
| | | 15 Sep 1988 (repeals of or in Abolition of Domestic Rates Etc (Scotland) Act 1987, s 2) (SI 1988/1456) |
| | | 1 Oct 1988 (repeals of or in Abolition of Domestic Rates Etc (Scotland) Act 1987, s 20) (SI 1988/1456) |
| | | 1 Apr 1989 (repeal of or in Acquisition of Land (Authorisation Procedure) (Scotland) Act 1947, s 5) (SI 1988/1456) |

## Local Government Finance Act 1988 (c 41)—*contd*

> 1 Apr 1990 (otherwise, except repeal of or in Abolition of
> Domestic Rates Act (Scotland) Act 1987, s 24) (SI 1988/1456,
> as amended by SI 1990/573)
> *Not yet in force* (exception noted above)

## Malicious Communications Act 1988 (c 27)

*RA:* 29 Jul 1988

*Commencement provisions:* s 3(2)

| | |
|---|---|
| 1 | 29 Sep 1988 (s 3(2)) |
| 2, 3 | 29 Jul 1988 (RA) |

## Matrimonial Proceedings (Transfers) Act 1988 (c 18)

*RA:* 19 May 1988

Whole Act in force 19 May 1988 (RA)

## Merchant Shipping Act 1988 (c 12)

*RA:* 3 May 1988

*Commencement provisions:* s 58(2)–(4); Merchant Shipping Act 1988 (Commencement No 1) Order 1988,
SI 1988/1010; Merchant Shipping Act 1988 (Commencement No 2) Order 1988, SI 1988/1907;
Merchant Shipping (Transitional Provisions—Fishing Vessels) Order 1988, SI 1988/1911[1]; Merchant
Shipping Act 1988 (Commencement No 3) Order 1989, SI 1989/353; Merchant Shipping Act 1988
(Commencement No 4) Order 1994, SI 1994/1201

| | | |
|---|---|---|
| 1–3 | | 1 Apr 1989 (SI 1989/353) |
| 4 | (1)–(5) | 1 Apr 1989 (SI 1989/353) |
| | (6) | 1 Dec 1988 (SI 1988/1907) |
| | (7), (8) | 1 Apr 1989 (SI 1989/353) |
| 5–10 | | 1 Apr 1989 (SI 1989/353) |
| 11 | | 4 Jul 1988 (SI 1988/1010) |
| 12–25 | | 1 Dec 1988 (by virtue SI 1988/1926) |
| 26–33 | | 4 Jul 1988 (SI 1988/1010) |
| 34 | | *Never in force* (repealed) |
| 35–47 | | 4 Jul 1988 (SI 1988/1010) |
| 48 | | See Sch 5 below |
| 49–51 | | 4 Jul 1988 (SI 1988/1010) |
| 52 | | 1 Apr 1989 (1989/353) |
| 53 | | 4 Jul 1988 (SI 1988/1010) |
| 54 | | 1 Dec 1988 (so far as relates to notices under Pt II) (SI 1988/1907) |
| | | 1 Apr 1989 (otherwise) (1989/353) |
| 55, 56 | | 4 Jul 1988 (SI 1988/1010) |
| 57 | (1)–(3) | 4 Jul 1988 (SI 1988/1010) |
| | (4) | See Sch 6 below |
| | (5) | See Sch 7 below |
| 58 | (1)–(3) | 4 Jul 1988 (SI 1988/1010) |
| | (4) | See Sch 8 below |
| | (5) | 4 Jul 1988 (SI 1988/1010) |
| Sch 1 | | 1 Apr 1989 (SI 1989/353) |
| Sch 2 | | 1 Dec 1988 (by virtue SI 1988/1926) |
| Schs 3, 4 | | *Never in force* (repealed) |
| Sch 5 | | 4 Jul 1988 (all except: para 4 of entry for Merchant Shipping Act 1894; entry for Merchant Shipping 1906; para 7 of entry for Merchant Shipping Act 1970) (SI 1988/1010) |
| | | 1 Apr 1989 (entry for Merchant Shipping Act 1906) (SI 1989/353) |

**Merchant Shipping Act 1988 (c 12)**—*contd*

1 Jun 1994 (para 7 of entry for Merchant Shipping Act 1970) (SI 1994/1201)

*Never in force* (para 4 of entry for Merchant Shipping Act 1894) (repealed)

Sch 6    4 Jul 1988 (SI 1988/1010), entries relating to—

Merchant Shipping Act 1894;

Merchant Shipping (Amendment) Act 1920;

Merchant Shipping Act 1965;

Merchant Shipping Act 1970 (paras 1–4, 5(a) of the entry);

Merchant Shipping Act 1979;

Supreme Court Act 1981;

Merchant Shipping Act 1983 (para 2 of the entry);

Merchant Shipping Act 1984

1 Dec 1988 (SI 1988/1907), entries relating to—

Sea Fisheries Act 1868;

Contracts of Employment and Redundancy Payments Act (Northern Ireland) 1965;

Sea Fish (Conservation) Act 1967;

Sea Fisheries Act 1968;

Fishing Vessels (Safety Provisions) Act 1970;

Merchant Shipping Act 1970 (para 5(b) of the entry);

Fishery Limits Act 1976;

Employment Protection (Consolidation) Act 1978;

Customs and Excise Management Act 1979;

British Fishing Boats Act 1983;

Merchant Shipping Act 1983 (para 1(b) of the entry);

Inshore Fishing (Scotland) Act 1984;

Safety at Sea Act 1986

1 Apr 1989 (SI 1989/353), entries relating to—

Merchant Shipping Act 1906;

Merchant Shipping Act 1965 (already in force as from 4 Jul 1988 (SI 1988/1010));

Merchant Shipping Act 1983 (already mostly in force under previous orders)

Sch 7    4 Jul 1988 (SI 1988/1010) repeals of or in—

Merchant Shipping Act 1894, ss 463, 648(1), 652(4), 663, 676(1)(i), 677(i), 731, 744;

Merchant Shipping Act 1897;

Merchant Shipping (Mercantile Marine Fund) Act 1898;

Merchant Shipping Act 1906, ss 2(1), 83;

Merchant Shipping Act 1950;

National Loans Act 1968;

Merchant Shipping Act 1970 (except entries for ss 73, 75(1)(c), 89, 95(1));

Trade Union and Labour Relations Act 1974;

Merchant Shipping Act 1979 (except entries for ss 31, 38, Sch 6, Pt I, Pt II (entry relating to s 44(11) of 1894 Act), Pt VI);

Merchant Shipping Act 1983 (except entries relating to ss 5, 6)

1 Dec 1988 (SI 1988/1907), repeals of or in—

Sea Fishing Boats (Scotland) Act 1886;

Merchant Shipping Act 1894, ss 370, 372–374;

Sea Fisheries Act 1968, Sch 1, paras 23, 32, 33;

Fishery Limits Act 1976, s 2(8)(b), Sch 2, para 3;

British Fishing Boats Act 1983, s 11(2);

Inshore Fishing (Scotland) Act 1984, Sch 1 (entry relating to the 1894 Act)

1 Apr 1989 (SI 1989/353), repeals of or in—

**Merchant Shipping Act 1988 (c 12)**—*contd*

|  |  |  |
|---|---|---|
|  |  | Merchant Shipping Act 1894, ss 1–3, 4(2), 6, 7(1), (2), 9(iii), 11, 13, 19, 23, 26, 27(1)(b), (2), 32, 33, 38(1), (2), 39–46, 47(4), (5) 48(1), 54–57, 61(1), 62, 63(1), (2), 64(2)(a), (d), 65(1)–(4), 71, 73(1)–(3), 76(1), 85, 88–91, 695(2)(a), Sch 1, Pts I, II; |
|  |  | Merchant Shipping Act 1906, ss 51, 52; |
|  |  | Fees (Increase) Act 1923, s 2(1); |
|  |  | Merchant Shipping Act 1965, s 1(2)(c), Sch 1; |
|  |  | Merchant Shipping Act 1979, s 31, Sch 6, Pt I (entry relating to s 374(4) of 1894 Act), Pt II entry relating to s 44(11) of 1894 Act, Pt VI; |
|  |  | Merchant Shipping Act 1983, ss 5(5), 6 |
|  |  | 1 Jun 1994 (repeals of or in Merchant Shipping Act 1970, ss 73, 89, 95(1)) (SI 1994/1201) |
|  |  | *Never in force* (otherwise) (repealed) |
| Sch 8 | para 1 | 4 Jul 1988 (SI 1988/1010) |
|  | para 2 | 1 Apr 1989 (SI 1989/353) |
|  | para 3 | 4 Jul 1988 (SI 1988/1010) |
|  | para 4 | 1 Dec 1988 (SI 1988/1807) |
|  | para 5 | 1 Apr 1989 (SI 1989/353) |

[1] Specifies how certain references in documents under law in force before commencement of the 1988 Act are to be construed after commencement; provided that no fishing vessels to be registered under law in force before commencement during the period 17–30 Nov 1988 inclusive; and provided that no entries relating to fishing vessels to be made in registers of ships kept under Merchant Shipping Act 1894, Pt I except entries closing the registry

---

**Motor Vehicles (Wearing of Rear Seat Belts by Children) Act 1988 (c 23)**

*RA:* 28 Jun 1988

*Commencement provisions:* s 3(2)

Whole Act in force 1 Apr 1989 (s 3(2))

---

**Multilateral Investment Guarantee Agency Act 1988 (c 8)**

*RA:* 24 Mar 1988

*Commencement provisions:* s 9(2); Multilateral Investment Guarantee Agency Act 1988 (Commencement) Order 1988, SI 1988/715

Whole Act in force 12 Apr 1988 (SI 1988/715)

---

**Norfolk and Suffolk Broads Act 1988 (c 4)**

*RA:* 15 Mar 1988

*Commencement provisions:* s 26; Norfolk and Suffolk Broads Act 1988 (Commencement) Order 1988, SI 1988/955

|  |  |
|---|---|
| 1 | 15 Mar 1988 (s 26(1)) |
| 2–8 | 1 Apr 1989 (SI 1988/955) |
| 9 | 6 Jun 1988 (SI 1988/955) |
| 10–13 | 1 Apr 1989 (SI 1988/955) |
| 14–19 | 6 Jun 1988 (SI 1988/955) |
| 20 | 1 Apr 1989 (SI 1988/955) |
| 21 | See Sch 6 below |
| 22 | 1 Apr 1989 (SI 1988/955) |
| 23–27 | 15 Mar 1988 (s 26(1)) |

**Norfolk and Suffolk Broads Act 1988 (c 4)**—*contd*

| | | |
|---|---|---|
| Schs 1–5 | | 1 Apr 1989 (SI 1988/955)[1, 2] |
| Sch 6 | para 1 | 1 Apr 1989 (SI 1988/955) |
| | para 2 | 6 Jun 1988 (SI 1988/955) |
| | para 3 | 1 Apr 1989 (SI 1988/955) |
| | para 4 | 6 Jun 1988 (SI 1988/955) |
| | para 5 | 1 Apr 1989 (SI 1988/955) |
| | paras 6–10 | 6 Jun 1988 (SI 1988/955) |
| | para 11 | 1 Apr 1989 (SI 1988/955) |
| | paras 12–20 | 6 Jun 1988 (SI 1988/955) |
| | para 21 | 1 Apr 1989 (SI 1988/955) |
| | paras 22–28 | 6 Jun 1988 (SI 1988/955) |
| Sch 7 | | 15 Mar 1988 (s 26(1))[1] |

[1]   It is thought that Schs 1, 7 were brought into force on 15 Mar 1988 together with ss 1(7), 27(2) of this Act

[2]   It is thought that Sch 4 was brought into force on 6 Jun 1988 together with s 9(10) of this Act

**Protection against Cruel Tethering Act 1988 (c 31)**

*RA:* 29 Jul 1988

*Commencement provisions:* s 2(2)

Whole Act in force 29 Sep 1988 (s 2(2))

**Protection of Animals (Amendment) Act 1988 (c 29)**

*RA:* 29 Jul 1988

*Commencement provisions:* s 3(4)

Whole Act in force 29 Sep 1988 (s 3(4))

**Public Utility Transfers and Water Charges Act 1988 (c 15)**

*RA:* 10 May 1988

*Commencement provisions:* s 8(2) (repealed); Public Utility Transfers and Water Charges Act 1988 (Commencement No 1) Order 1988, SI 1988/879; Public Utility Transfers and Water Charges Act 1988 (Commencement No 2) Order 1988, SI 1988/1165

| | | |
|---|---|---|
| 1 | | 10 May 1988 (RA) |
| 2 | | 18 May 1988 (SI 1988/879) |
| 3 | (1)–(5) | 18 May 1988 (SI 1988/879) |
| | (6), (7) | 1 Oct 1988 (SI 1988/1165) |
| | (8) | 18 May 1988 (SI 1988/879) |
| 4 | | 18 May 1988 (SI 1988/879) |
| 5 | (1) | See Sch 1 below |
| | (2)–(5) | 18 May 1988 (SI 1988/879) |
| 6 | (1) | See Sch 2 below |
| | (2)–(4) | 11 Jul 1988 (SI 1988/879) |
| | (5) | See Sch 3 below |
| | (6) | 11 Jul 1988 (SI 1988/879) |
| 7, 8 | | 10 May 1988 (RA) |
| Sch 1 | para 1 | 1 Apr 1989 (SI 1988/1165) |
| | para 2(1)–(8) | 11 Jul 1988 (SI 1988/879) |
| | para 2(9) | 1 Apr 1989 (SI 1988/1165) |
| | paras 3–5 | 11 Jul 1988 (SI 1988/879) |

## Public Utility Transfers and Water Charges Act 1988 (c 15)—*contd*

| | | |
|---|---|---|
| | para 6 | 11 Jul 1988 (so far as it relates to paras 2(1)–(8) and 3) (SI 1988/879) |
| | | 1 Oct 1988 (so far as it relates to para 7) (SI 1988/1165) |
| | | 1 Apr 1989 (otherwise) (SI 1988/1165) |
| | paras 7, 8 | 1 Oct 1988 (SI 1988/1165) |
| | para 9(a) | 1 Apr 1989 (SI 1988/1165) |
| | para 9(b) | 11 Jul 1988 (SI 1988/879) |
| | para 9(c) | 11 Jul 1988 (so far as relevant to para 6) (SI 1988/879) |
| | | 1 Oct 1988 (so far as relevant to para 7) (SI 1988/1165) |
| | para 9(d) | 1 Oct 1988 (SI 1988/1165) |
| | para 9(e) | 11 Jul 1988 (so far as relevant to para 6) (SI 1988/879) |
| | | 1 Oct 1988 (so far as relevant to paras 7, 8) (SI 1988/1165) |
| | para 9(f) | 11 Jul 1988 (so far as relevant to para 6) (SI 1988/879) |
| | | 1 Oct 1988 (so far as relevant to para 7) (SI 1988/1165) |
| Sch 2 | paras 1, 2 | 18 May 1988 (SI 1988/879) |
| | para 3 | 11 Jul 1988 (SI 1988/879) |
| | para 4 | 18 May 1988 (SI 1988/879) |
| Sch 3 | | 18 May 1988 (SI 1988/879) |
| | | 11 Jul 1988 (SI 1988/879) |
| | | 1 Oct 1988 (SI 1988/1165) |

## Rate Support Grants Act 1988 (c 51)

*RA:* 15 Nov 1988

Whole Act in force 15 Nov 1988 (RA)

## Regional Development Grants (Termination) Act 1988 (c 11)

*RA:* 3 May 1988

Whole Act in force 3 May 1988 (RA)

## Road Traffic Act 1988 (c 52)

*RA:* 15 Nov 1988

*Commencement provisions:* s 197(2)

Whole Act in force 15 May 1989 (subject, in the case of ss 15, 195(3), (4), to transitory modifications specified in Road Traffic (Consequential Provisions) Act 1988, Sch 5 which applied until 21 Jul 1989 (Road Traffic Act 1988 (Appointed Day for Section 15) Order 1989, SI 1989/1086) or 1 Sep 1989 (Road Traffic Act 1988 (Appointed Day for Section 15) (No 2) Order 1989, SI 1989/1260)) (s 197(2))

## Road Traffic (Consequential Provisions) Act 1988 (c 54)

*RA:* 15 Nov 1988

*Commencement provisions:* s 8(2), (3)

| | | |
|---|---|---|
| 1–3 | | 15 May 1989 (s 8(2), (3)) |
| 4 | | See Schs 2, 3 below |
| 5–8 | | 15 May 1989 (s 8(2), (3)) |
| Sch 1 | | 15 May 1989 (s 8(2), (3)) |
| Sch 2 | para 1 | *Never in force* (repealed) |
| | paras 2–14 | 15 May 1989 (s 8(2), (3)) |
| | paras 15–20 | *Not yet in force* |
| | para 21 | *Never in force* (repealed) |

## Road Traffic (Consequential Provisions) Act 1988 (c 54)—*contd*

| | | |
|---|---|---|
| | para 22 | 15 May 1989 (so far as it relates to sub-ss (5)–(8) of the new section inserted by this paragraph) (s 8(2), (3)) |
| | | *Never in force* (otherwise) (repealed) |
| | paras 23–39 | *Never in force* (repealed) |
| Schs 3, 4 | | 15 May 1989 (s 8(2), (3)) |
| Sch 5 | | 15 May 1989 (s 8(2), (3)) |
| | | 21 Jun 1989 (appointed day for purposes of Road Traffic Act 1988, ss 15(3) (so far as relates to power to make regulations), (5), (6), 195(3), (4)) (SI 1989/1086) |
| | | 1 Sep 1989 (appointed day for purposes of Road Traffic Act 1988, s 15(3) (except in so far as relates to power to make regulations), (4), (7), (8)) (SI 1989/1260) |

## Road Traffic Offenders Act 1988 (c 53)

*RA:* 15 Nov 1988

*Commencement provisions:* s 99(2)–(5)

| | | |
|---|---|---|
| 1–26 | | 15 May 1989 (s 99(2)–(5)) |
| 27 | (1)–(3) | 15 May 1989 (s 99(2)–(5)) |
| | (4) | 15 May 1989 (E) (W) (s 99(2)–(5)) |
| | | *Never in force* (S) (repealed) |
| 28, 29 | | 15 May 1989 (s 99(2)–(5)) |
| 30 | | 15 May 1989 (E) (W) (s 99(2)–(5)) |
| | | 15 May 1989 (S) (so far as relates to ss 75–77) (s 99(2)–(5)) |
| | | *Never in force* (S) (otherwise) (repealed) |
| 31–51 | | 15 May 1989 (s 99(2)–(5)) |
| 52 | (1)–(3) | 15 May 1989 (s 99(2)–(5)) |
| | (4) | 15 May 1989 (E) (W) (s 99(2)–(5)) |
| | | *Never in force* (S) (repealed) |
| 53 | | 15 May 1989 (s 99(2)–(5)) |
| 54–58 | | 15 May 1989 (E) (W) (s 99(2)–(5)) |
| | | *Never in force* (S) (no longer applies in Scotland as a consequence of amendments made to s 54) |
| 59 | | *Never in force* (repealed) |
| 60 | | 15 May 1989 (E) (W) (s 99(2)–(5)) |
| | | *Never in force* (S) (repealed) |
| 61 | | 15 May 1989 (E) (W) (s 99(2)–(5)) |
| | | *Never in force* (S) (no longer applies in Scotland as a consequence of amendments made to s 54) |
| 62–78 | | 15 May 1989 (s 99(2)–(5)) |
| 79 | | 15 May 1989 (E) (W) (s 99(2)–(5)) |
| | | *Never in force* (S) (repealed) |
| 80, 81 | | 15 May 1989 (s 99(2)–(5)) |
| 82 | | 15 May 1989 (E) (W) (s 99(2)–(5)) |
| | | *Never in force* (S) (repealed) |
| 83–99 | | 15 May 1989 (s 99(2)–(5)) |
| Schs 1–5 | | 15 May 1989 (s 99(2)–(5)) |

## School Boards (Scotland) Act 1988 (c 47)

*RA:* 15 Nov 1988

*Commencement provisions:* s 24(2); School Boards (Scotland) Act 1988 (Commencement) Order 1989, SI 1989/272

| | |
|---|---|
| 1–23 | 1 Apr 1989 (SI 1989/272) |
| 24 | 15 Nov 1988 (RA) |
| Schs 1–3 | 1 Apr 1989 (SI 1989/272) |

## School Boards (Scotland) Act 1988 (c 47)—*contd*

| | | |
|---|---|---|
| Sch 4 | paras 1–5 | 1 Nov 1989 (SI 1989/272) |
| | para 6 | 1 Apr 1989 (SI 1989/272) |
| | para 7 | 1 Nov 1989 (SI 1989/272) |

## Scotch Whisky Act 1988 (c 22)

*RA:* 28 Jun 1988

*Commencement provisions:* s 5(2); Scotch Whisky Act 1988 (Commencement and Transitional Provisions) Order 1990, SI 1990/997

| | |
|---|---|
| 1–3 | 30 Apr 1990 (SI 1990/997) |
| 4, 5 | 28 Jun 1988 (RA; note that SI 1990/997 also purports to bring s 5 into force on 30 Apr 1990) |

## Social Security Act 1988 (c 7)

*RA:* 15 Mar 1988

*Commencement provisions:* s 18(1)–(4); Social Security Act 1988 (Commencement No 1) Order 1988, SI 1988/520; Social Security Act 1988 (Commencement No 2) Order 1988, SI 1988/1226; Social Security Act 1988 (Commencement No 3) Order 1988, SI 1988/1857

| | | |
|---|---|---|
| 1 | | 15 Mar 1988 (s 18(1), (2)) |
| 2 | (1), (2) | 10 Apr 1989 (SI 1988/1857) |
| | (3) | 15 Mar 1988 (s 18(1), (2)) |
| | (4)–(10) | 11 Apr 1988 (SI 1988/520) |
| 3 | | 11 Apr 1988 (SI 1988/520) |
| 4 | | 12 Sep 1988 (SI 1988/1226) |
| 5 | | *Never in force* (repealed) |
| 6 | | 2 Oct 1988 (SI 1988/520) |
| 7 | | 1 Jan 1989 (SI 1988/520) |
| 8 | | 15 Mar 1988 (s 18(1), (2)) |
| 9 | | 6 Apr 1988 (SI 1988/520) |
| 10 | | 15 Mar 1988 (s 18(1), (2)) |
| 11 | | 11 Apr 1988 (SI 1988/520) |
| 12 | | 15 Mar 1988 (s 18(1), (2)) |
| 13, 14 | | 17 Mar 1988 (SI 1988/520) |
| 15 | | 15 Mar 1988 (s 18(1), (2)) |
| 16 | (1) | See Sch 4 below |
| | (2) | See Sch 5 below |
| 17–20 | | 15 Mar 1988 (s 18(1), (2)) |
| Sch 1 | | 11 Apr 1988 (SI 1988/520) |
| Sch 2 | | 6 Apr 1988 (SI 1988/520) |
| Sch 3 | | 11 Apr 1988 (SI 1988/520) |
| Sch 4 | para 1 | 6 Apr 1988 (SI 1988/520) |
| | para 2 | 12 Sep 1988 (SI 1988/1226) |
| | para 3 | 11 Apr 1988 (SI 1988/520) |
| | para 4 | 15 Mar 1988 (s 18(1), (2)) |
| | para 5 | 11 Apr 1988 (SI 1988/520) |
| | paras 6–10 | 15 Mar 1988 (s 18(1), (2)) |
| | para 11 | 11 Apr 1988 (except for the insertion of sub-s (1A)(c)) (SI 1988/520) |
| | | 10 Apr 1989 (exception noted above) (SI 1988/1857) |
| | paras 12, 13 | 15 Mar 1988 (s 18(1), (2)) |
| | para 14 | 11 Apr 1988 (SI 1988/520) |
| | paras 15, 16 | 17 Mar 1988 (SI 1988/520) |
| | paras 17, 18 | 6 Apr 1988 (SI 1988/520) |
| | para 19 | 17 Mar 1988 (SI 1988/520) |
| | para 20 | 1 Apr 1988 (SI 1988/520) |

**Social Security Act 1988 (c 7)**—*contd*

| | | |
|---|---|---|
| | paras 21, 22 | 6 Apr 1988 (SI 1988/520) |
| | paras 23–25 | 11 Apr 1988 (SI 1988/520) |
| | paras 26–28 | 6 Apr 1987 (Sch 4, para 27; note also s 18(1), (2)) |
| | para 29 | 6 Apr 1988 (SI 1988/520) |
| | para 30 | 12 Sep 1988 (SI 1988/1226) |

Sch 5       15 Mar 1988 (s 18(1), (2)), repeals of or in—
        Social Security Act 1975, ss 45, 45A, 46, 47B, 66;
        Social Security Act 1980, Sch 1;
        Social Security Act 1985, s 13(4)(a)
      6 Apr 1988 (repeals in Social Security Act 1986, s 50(1))
        (SI 1988/520)
      11 Apr 1988 (SI 1988/520), repeals of or in—
        Emergency Laws (Re-enactments and Repeals) Act 1964;
        Health Services and Public Health Act 1968;
        Social Security Act 1975, ss 59A, 69;
        Adoption Act 1976;
        National Health Service Act 1977;
        Adoption (Scotland) Act 1978;
        National Health Service (Scotland) Act 1978;
        Social Security Act 1985, s 14;
        Social Security Act 1986, ss 20(6), 23(8), 32, 33(1), 34(1)(a),
          51(2), 52(6), 53(10), 63(7), 84(1), Sch 3
      12 Sep 1988 (repeal of Social Security Act 1986, Sch 10, para 45)
        (SI 1988/1226)
      2 Oct 1988 (repeals in Social Security Act 1975, Sch 3)
        (SI 1988/520)

---

**Solicitors (Scotland) Act 1988 (c 42)**

*RA:* 29 Jul 1988

*Commencement provisions:* s 7(2)

Whole Act in force 29 Jan 1989 (s 7(2))

---

**Welsh Development Agency Act 1988 (c 5)**

*RA:* 15 Mar 1988

Whole Act in force 15 Mar 1988 (RA)

---

# 1989 Acts

## Antarctic Minerals Act 1989 (c 21)

*RA:* 21 Jul 1989

*Commencement provisions:* s 20(2)

*Not yet in force* (repealed, except ss 14, 20)

---

## Appropriation Act 1989 (c 25)

*RA:* 27 Jul 1989

Whole Act in force 27 Jul 1989 (RA)

---

## Atomic Energy Act 1989 (c 7)

*RA:* 25 May 1989

*Commencement provisions:* s 7(2); Atomic Energy Act 1989 (Commencement) Order 1989, SI 1989/1317

Whole Act in force 1 Sep 1989 (SI 1989/1317)

---

## Brunei (Appeals) Act 1989 (c 36)

*RA:* 16 Nov 1989

*Commencement provisions:* s 2(2); Brunei (Appeals) Act 1989 (Commencement) Order 1989, SI 1989/2450

Whole Act in force 1 Feb 1990 (SI 1989/2450)

---

## Children Act 1989 (c 41)

*RA:* 16 Nov 1989

*Commencement provisions:* s 108(2), (3); Children Act 1989 (Commencement and Transitional Provisions) Order 1991, SI 1991/828; Children Act 1989 (Commencement No 2—Amendment and Transitional Provisions) Order 1991, SI 1991/1990

| | | |
|---|---|---|
| 1–4 | | 14 Oct 1991 (SI 1991/828) |
| 5 | (1)–(10) | 14 Oct 1991 (SI 1991/828) |
| | (11), (12) | 1 Feb 1992 (SI 1991/828; SI 1991/1990) |
| | (13) | 14 Oct 1991 (SI 1991/828) |
| 6–87 | | 14 Oct 1991 (SI 1991/828) |
| 88 | (1) | See Sch 10 below |
| | (2) | 14 Oct 1991 (SI 1991/828) |
| 89 | | 16 Nov 1989 (s 108(2)) |
| 90–95 | | 14 Oct 1991 (SI 1991/828) |
| 96 | (1), (2) | 14 Oct 1991 (SI 1991/828) |
| | (3)–(7) | 16 Nov 1989 (s 108(2)) |

**Children Act 1989 (c 41)**—*contd*

| | | |
|---|---|---|
| 97–107 | | 14 Oct 1991 (SI 1991/828) |
| 108 | | 16 Nov 1989 (RA) |
| Schs 1–9 | | 14 Oct 1991 (SI 1991/828) |
| Sch 10 | paras 1–20 | 14 Oct 1991 (SI 1991/828) |
| | para 21 | 1 May 1991 (SI 1991/828) |
| | paras 22–46 | 14 Oct 1991 (SI 1991/828) |
| Sch 11 | | 14 Oct 1991 (SI 1991/828) |
| Sch 12 | paras 1–34 | 14 Oct 1991 (SI 1991/828) |
| | para 35 | 16 Nov 1989 (s 108(2)) |
| | para 36 | 16 Jan 1989 (s 108(2)) |
| | paras 37–45 | 14 Oct 1991 (SI 1991/828) |
| Schs 13–15 | | 14 Oct 1991 (SI 1991/828) |

**Civil Aviation (Air Navigation Charges) Act 1989 (c 9)**

*RA:* 25 May 1989

Whole Act in force 25 May 1989 (RA)

**Common Land (Rectification of Registers) Act 1989 (c 18)**

*RA:* 21 Jul 1989

Whole Act in force 21 Jul 1989 (RA)

**Companies Act 1989 (c 40)**

*RA:* 16 Nov 1989

*Commencement provisions:* s 215(1)–(3); Companies Act 1989 (Commencement No 1) Order 1990, SI 1990/98; Companies Act 1989 (Commencement No 2) Order 1990, SI 1990/142; Companies Act 1989 (Commencement No 3, Transitional Provisions and Transfer of Functions under the Financial Services Act 1986) Order 1990, SI 1990/354 (which contains transitional provisions in relation to self-regulating organisations and professional bodies); Companies Act 1989 (Commencement No 4, Transitional and Saving Provisions) Order 1990, SI 1990/355, as amended by SI 1990/1707, SI 1990/2569, SI 1993/3246; Companies Act 1989 (Commencement No 5 and Transitional and Saving Provisions) Order 1990, SI 1990/713; Companies Act 1989 (Commencement No 6 and Transitional and Savings Provisions) Order 1990, SI 1990/1392, as amended by SI 1990/1707; Companies Act 1989 (Commencement No 7, Transitional and Saving Provisions) Order 1990, SI 1990/1707; Companies Act 1989 (Commencement No 8 and Transitional and Saving Provisions) Order 1990, SI 1990/2569; Companies Act 1989 (Commencement No 9 and Saving and Transitional Provisions) Order 1991, SI 1991/488; Companies Act 1989 (Commencement No 10 and Saving Provisions) Order 1991, SI 1991/878; Companies Act 1989 (Commencement No 11) Order 1991, SI 1991/1452; Companies Act 1989 (Commencement No 12 and Transitional Provision) Order 1991, SI 1991/1996; Companies Act 1989 (Commencement No 13) Order 1991, SI 1991/2173; Companies Act 1989 (Commencement No 14 and Transitional Provision) Order 1991, SI 1991/2945; Companies Act 1989 (Commencement No 15 and Transitional and Savings Provisions) Order 1995, SI 1995/1352; Companies Act 1989 (Commencement No 16) Order 1995, SI 1995/1591; Companies Act 1989 (Commencement No 17) Order 1998, SI 1998/1747; Companies (Audit, Investigations and Community Enterprise) Act 2004 (Commencement) and Companies Act 1989 (Commencement No 18) Order 2004, SI 2004/3322

| | |
|---|---|
| 1 | 1 Mar 1990 (so far as relates to s 15 below) (SI 1990/142) |
| | 1 Apr 1990 (so far as relates to any section or part thereof brought into force by SI 1990/355) (SI 1990/355)[1] |
| | 7 Jan 1991 (so far as relates to any section or part thereof brought into force by SI 1990/2569) (SI 1990/2569) |
| | 1 Jul 1992 (so far as relates to s 11) (subject to transitional provisions) (SI 1991/2945) |
| 2–6 | 1 Apr 1990 (SI 1990/355)[1] |

**Companies Act 1989 (c 40)**—*contd*

| | | |
|---|---|---|
| 7 | | 1 Apr 1990 (except so far as relates to Companies Act 1985, s 233(5)) (SI 1990/355)[1] |
| | | 7 Jan 1991 (exception noted above) (SI 1990/2569)[2] |
| 8–10 | | 1 Apr 1990 (SI 1990/355)[1] |
| 11 | | 1 Apr 1990 (except so far as relates to Companies Act 1985, s 242A) (SI 1990/355)[1] |
| | | 1 Jul 1992 (exception noted above) (subject to transitional provisions) (SI 1991/2945) |
| 12 | | 7 Jan 1991 (SI 1990/2569)[2] |
| 13, 14 | | 1 Apr 1990 (SI 1990/355)[1] |
| 15 | | 1 Mar 1990 (SI 1990/142) |
| 16–22 | | 1 Apr 1990 (SI 1990/355)[1] |
| 23 | | See Sch 10 below |
| 24 | | 1 Mar 1990 (for purposes of ss 30–33, 37–40, 41(1), (3)–(6), 42–45, 47(1), 48(1), (2), 49–54, Schs 11, 12, 14) (SI 1990/142) |
| | | 1 Oct 1991 (otherwise) (SI 1991/1996) |
| 25–27 | | 1 Oct 1991 (SI 1991/1996) |
| 28 | | 1 Oct 1991 (subject to transitional provisions in SI 1991/1996, art 4) (SI 1991/1996) |
| 29 | | 1 Oct 1991 (SI 1991/1996) |
| 30 | | 1 Mar 1990 (SI 1990/142) |
| 31 | | 1 Mar 1990 (so far as relates to recognition of supervisory bodies under Sch 11 and for purpose of enabling Secretary of State to approve a qualification under s 31(4), (5)) (SI 1990/142) |
| | | 1 Oct 1991 (otherwise) (SI 1991/1996) |
| 32, 33 | | 1 Mar 1990 (SI 1990/142) |
| 34 | | 1 Oct 1991 (SI 1991/1996) |
| 35, 36 | | 26 Jun 1991 (SI 1991/1452) |
| 37–40 | | 1 Mar 1990 (SI 1990/142) |
| 41 | (1) | 1 Mar 1990 (for purposes of an application under this section or under provisions specified under s 24 above or of any requirement imposed under such provisions) (SI 1990/142) |
| | | 1 Oct 1991 (otherwise) (SI 1991/1996) |
| | (2) | 1 Oct 1991 (SI 1991/1996) |
| | (3) | 1 Mar 1990 (SI 1990/142) |
| | (4) | 1 Mar 1990 (for purposes of an application under this section or under provisions specified under s 24 above or of any requirement imposed under such provisions) (SI 1990/142) |
| | | 1 Oct 1991 (otherwise) (SI 1991/1996) |
| | (5), (6) | 1 Mar 1990 (for purposes of s 41(3)) (SI 1990/142) |
| | | 1 Oct 1991 (otherwise) (SI 1991/1996) |
| 42–44 | | 1 Mar 1990 (for purposes of ss 30–33, 37–40, 41(1), (3)–(6), 42–45, 47(1), 48(1), (2), 49–54, Schs 11, 12, 14) (SI 1990/142) |
| | | 1 Oct 1991 (otherwise) (SI 1991/1996) |
| 45 | | 1 Mar 1990 (SI 1990/142) |
| 46 | | 1 Jan 2005 (SI 2004/3322) |
| 47 | (1) | 1 Mar 1990 (SI 1990/142) |
| | (2)–(6) | *Never in force* (repealed) |
| 48 | (1), (2) | 1 Mar 1990 (SI 1990/142) |
| | (3) | *Never in force* (repealed) |
| 49 | | 1 Mar 1990 (for purposes of ss 30–33, 37–40, 41(1), (3)–(6), 42–45, 47(1), 48(1), (2), 49–54, Schs 11, 12, 14) (SI 1990/142) |
| | | 1 Oct 1991 (otherwise) (SI 1991/1996) |
| 50, 51 | | 1 Mar 1990 (SI 1990/142) |
| 52–54 | | 1 Mar 1990 (for purposes of ss 30–33, 37–40, 41(1), (3)–(6), 42–45, 47(1), 48(1), (2), 49–54, Schs 11, 12, 14) (SI 1990/142) |
| | | 1 Oct 1991 (otherwise) (SI 1991/1996) |
| 55–64 | | 21 Feb 1990 (SI 1990/142) |
| 65 | (1) | 21 Feb 1990 (SI 1990/142) |

**Companies Act 1989 (c 40)**—*contd*

| | | |
|---|---|---|
| | (2) | 21 Feb 1990 (except so far as refers to Pt VII (ss 154–191) and so far as s 65(2)(g) refers to a body established under s 46) (SI 1990/142) |
| | | 25 Apr 1991 (so far as not already in force, except so far as s 65(2)(g) refers to a body established under s 46) (SI 1991/878) |
| | | *Never in force* (exception noted above) (repealed) |
| | (3)–(7) | 21 Feb 1990 (SI 1990/142) |
| 66–74 | | 21 Feb 1990 (SI 1990/142) |
| 75 | (1) | 21 Feb 1990 (SI 1990/142) |
| | (2) | 25 Jan 1990 (SI 1990/98) |
| | (3)(a)–(c) | 21 Feb 1990 (except so far as refers to Pt VII (ss 154–191) and so far as s 75(3)(c) refers to a body established under s 46) (SI 1990/142) |
| | | 25 Apr 1991 (so far as not already in force, except so far as s 75(3)(c) refers to a body established under s 46) (SI 1991/878) |
| | | *Never in force* (exception noted above) (repealed) |
| | (3)(d) | 25 Jan 1990 (SI 1990/98) |
| | (3)(e), (f) | 21 Feb 1990 (except so far as refers to Pt VII (ss 154–191)) (SI 1990/142) |
| | | 25 Apr 1991 (exception noted above) (SI 1991/878) |
| | (4) | 25 Jan 1990 (so far as relates to s 75(3)(d) above) (SI 1990/98) |
| | | 21 Feb 1990 (otherwise) (SI 1990/142) |
| | (5), (6) | 21 Feb 1990 (SI 1990/142) |
| | (7) | 25 Jan 1990 (SI 1990/98) |
| 76–79 | | 21 Feb 1990 (SI 1990/142) |
| 80 | | 21 Feb 1990 (except so far as refers to Pt VII (ss 154–191)) (SI 1990/142) |
| | | 25 Apr 1991 (exception noted above) (SI 1991/878) |
| 81 | (1) | 21 Feb 1990 (SI 1990/142) |
| | (2) | 21 Feb 1990 (except so far as refers to Pt VII (ss 154–191)) (SI 1990/142) |
| | | 25 Apr 1991 (exception noted above) (SI 1991/878) |
| | (3), (4) | 21 Feb 1990 (SI 1990/142) |
| | (5) | 21 Feb 1990 (except so far as refers to Pt VII (ss 154–191)) (SI 1990/142) |
| | | 25 Apr 1991 (exception noted above) (SI 1991/878) |
| 82–86 | | 21 Feb 1990 (SI 1990/142) |
| 87 | (1)–(3) | 21 Feb 1990 (SI 1990/142) |
| | (4) | 21 Feb 1990 (except so far as refers to Pt VII (ss 154–191)) (SI 1990/142) |
| | | 25 Apr 1991 (exception noted above) (SI 1991/878) |
| | (5), (6) | 21 Feb 1990 (SI 1990/142) |
| 88–91 | | 21 Feb 1990 (SI 1990/142) |
| 92–107 | | *Never in force* (repealed) |
| 108–112 | | 4 Feb 1991 (SI 1990/2569)[2] |
| 113, 114 | | 1 Apr 1990 (SI 1990/355) |
| 115 | | 1 Apr 1990 (SI 1990/355)[3] |
| 116, 117 | | 1 Apr 1990 (SI 1990/355) |
| 118–124 | | 1 Apr 1990 (SI 1990/355)[3] |
| 125 | | 7 Jan 1991 (SI 1990/2569) |
| 126 | | 1 Jul 1991 (SI 1991/488)[4] |
| 127 | (1), (2) | 7 Jan 1991 (SI 1990/2569) |
| | (3) | 1 Jul 1991 (SI 1991/488) |
| | (4) | 7 Jan 1991 (SI 1990/2569) |
| | (5), (6) | 1 Jul 1991 (SI 1991/488) |
| | (7) | 7 Jan 1991 (so far as inserts in Companies Act 1985, Sch 22, a reference to ss 706, 707, 715A of 1985 Act, as inserted by ss 125, 127(1) of this Act) (SI 1990/2569) |

**Companies Act 1989 (c 40)**—*contd*

|  |  |  |
|---|---|---|
|  |  | 1 Jul 1991 (otherwise) (SI 1991/488) |
| 128 |  | *Never in force* (repealed) |
| 129 |  | 1 Nov 1990 (SI 1990/1392) |
| 130 |  | 31 Jul 1990 (SI 1990/1392) |
| 131 |  | 1 Apr 1990 (not to be construed as affecting any right, privilege, obligation or liability acquired, accrued or incurred before 1 Apr 1990; see SI 1990/355, art 11) (SI 1990/355) |
| 132 |  | 1 Apr 1990 (SI 1990/355) |
| 133 |  | *Never in force* (repealed) |
| 134 | (1)–(3) | 31 May 1990 (SI 1990/713) |
|  | (4) | 1 Nov 1991 (SI 1991/1996) |
|  | (5), (6) | 31 May 1990 (SI 1990/713) |
| 135 |  | 7 Jan 1991 (SI 1990/2569) |
| 136 |  | 1 Apr 1990 (SI 1990/355; see, however, saving in art 12 thereof) |
| 137 | (1) | 1 Apr 1990 (SI 1990/355) |
|  | (2) | 1 Apr 1990 (for the purposes of a director's report of a company within the meaning of Companies Act 1985, s 735 (except in relation to a financial year commencing before 23 Dec 1989; see SI 1990/355, art 13)) (SI 1990/355) |
|  |  | *Never in force* (otherwise) (repealed) |
| 138 |  | 31 Jul 1990 (SI 1990/1392)[5] |
| 139 |  | 1 Oct 1990 (SI 1990/1707)[6] |
| 140 | (1)–(6) | 3 Jul 1995 (subject to transitional provisions and savings) (SI 1995/1352) |
|  | (7), (8) | *Not yet in force* |
| 141 |  | 16 Nov 1989 (s 215(1)) |
| 142 |  | *Never in force* (repealed) |
| 143 |  | 1 Nov 1991 (SI 1991/1996) |
| 144 |  | 1 Nov 1990 (SI 1990/1392)[7] |
| 145 |  | See Sch 19 below |
| 146 |  | 1 Apr 1990 (SI 1990/142) |
| 147–150 |  | 16 Nov 1989 (s 215(1)) |
| 151 |  | 1 Apr 1990 (SI 1990/142) |
| 152 |  | 1 Mar 1990 (SI 1990/142) |
| 153 |  | See Sch 20 below |
| 154–156 |  | 25 Mar 1991 (Pt VII (ss 154–191, Schs 21, 22) brought into force only in so far as is necessary to enable regulations to be made under ss 155(4), (5), 156(1) (so far as it relates to Sch 21), 158(4), (5), 160(5), 173(4), (5), 174(2)–(4), 185, 186, 187(3), Sch 21, para 2(3)) (SI 1991/488) |
|  |  | 25 Apr 1991 (otherwise) (SI 1991/878) |
| 157 |  | 25 Mar 1991 (see note to ss 154–156) (SI 1991/488) |
|  |  | 25 Apr 1991 (otherwise) (SI 1991/878)[8] |
| 158, 159 |  | 25 Mar 1991 (see note to ss 154–156) (SI 1991/488) |
|  |  | 25 Apr 1991 (otherwise) (SI 1991/878) |
| 160 |  | 25 Mar 1991 (see note to ss 154–156) (SI 1991/488) |
|  |  | 25 Apr 1991 (so far as not already in force, except in so far as imposing a duty (i) on any person where conflict with enactments in force in Northern Ireland relating to insolvency would arise, and (ii) on a relevant office-holder appointed under the general law of insolvency for the time being in force in Northern Ireland) (SI 1991/878)[8] |
|  |  | 1 Oct 1991 (exception noted above) (SI 1991/2173) |
| 161 |  | 25 Mar 1991 (see note to ss 154–156) (SI 1991/488) |
|  |  | 25 Apr 1991 (otherwise) (SI 1991/878) |
| 162 |  | 25 Mar 1991 (see note to ss 154–156) (SI 1991/488) |
|  |  | 25 Apr 1991 (except so far as would require an exchange or clearing house to supply a copy of a report to any relevant office-holder appointed under the general law of insolvency for the time being in force in Northern Ireland) (SI 1991/878) |

**Companies Act 1989 (c 40)**—*contd*

|  |  |  |
|---|---|---|
|  |  | 1 Oct 1991 (exception noted above) (SI 1991/2173) |
| 163–165 |  | 25 Mar 1991 (see note to ss 154–156) (SI 1991/488) |
|  |  | 25 Apr 1991 (otherwise) (SI 1991/878) |
| 166 |  | 25 Mar 1991 (see note to ss 154–156) (SI 1991/488) |
|  |  | 25 Apr 1991 (so far as not already in force, except where it would enable a direction to be given, where an order, appointment or resolution corresponding to those mentioned in s 166(6) has been made or passed in relation to the person in question under the general law of insolvency for the time being in force in Northern Ireland) (SI 1991/878)[8] |
|  |  | 1 Oct 1991 (exception noted above) (SI 1991/2173) |
| 167 |  | 25 Mar 1991 (see note to ss 154–156) (SI 1991/488) |
|  |  | 25 Apr 1991 (except where enabling an application to be made by a relevant office-holder appointed by, or in consequence of, or in connection with, an order or resolution corresponding to those mentioned in s 167(1) made or passed under the general law of insolvency for the time being in force in Northern Ireland) (1991/878) |
|  |  | 1 Oct 1991 (exception noted above) (SI 1991/2173) |
| 168 |  | 25 Mar 1991 (see note to ss 154–156) (SI 1991/488) |
|  |  | 25 Apr 1991 (otherwise) (SI 1991/878) |
| 169 | (1)–(3) | 25 Mar 1991 (see note to ss 154–156) (SI 1991/488) |
|  |  | 25 Apr 1991 (otherwise) (SI 1991/878) |
|  | (4) | 25 Mar 1991 (see note to ss 154–156) (SI 1991/488) |
|  |  | *Never in force* (otherwise) (repealed) |
|  | (5) | 25 Mar 1991 (see note to ss 154, 155) (SI 1991/488) |
|  |  | 25 Apr 1991 (otherwise) (SI 1991/878) |
| 170 |  | 25 Mar 1991 (see note to ss 154, 155) (SI 1991/488) |
|  |  | *Not yet in force* (otherwise) |
| 171 |  | 25 Mar 1991 (see note to ss 154–156) (SI 1991/488) |
|  |  | 4 Jul 1995 (otherwise) (SI 1995/1591) |
| 172 |  | 25 Mar 1991 (see note to ss 154, 155) (SI 1991/488) |
|  |  | *Not yet in force* (otherwise) |
| 173 |  | 25 Mar 1991 (see note to ss 154, 155) (SI 1991/488) |
|  |  | 25 Apr 1991 (otherwise) (SI 1991/878) |
| 174, 175 |  | 25 Mar 1991 (see note to ss 154, 155) (SI 1991/488) |
|  |  | 25 Apr 1991 (otherwise) (SI 1991/878)[8] |
| 176 |  | 25 Mar 1991 (see note to ss 154, 155) (SI 1991/488) |
|  |  | 4 Jul 1995 (otherwise) (SI 1995/1591) |
| 177 |  | 25 Mar 1991 (see note to ss 154, 155) (SI 1991/488) |
|  |  | 25 Apr 1991 (otherwise) (SI 1991/878)8 |
| 178 |  | 25 Mar 1991 (see note to ss 154, 155) (SI 1991/488) |
|  |  | *Not yet in force* (otherwise) |
| 179, 180 |  | 25 Mar 1991 (see note to ss 154, 155) (SI 1991/488) |
|  |  | 25 Apr 1991 (otherwise) (SI 1991/878)[8] |
| 181 |  | 25 Mar 1991 (see note to ss 154, 155) (SI 1991/488) |
|  |  | 4 Jul 1995 (otherwise) (SI 1995/1591) |
| 182, 183 |  | 25 Mar 1991 (see note to ss 154, 155) (SI 1991/488) |
|  |  | 25 Apr 1991 (otherwise) (SI 1991/878) |
| 184 | (1) | 25 Mar 1991 (see note to ss 154, 155) (SI 1991/488) |
|  |  | 25 Apr 1991 (so far as not already in force, except so far as has effect in relation to any relevant office-holder appointed under general law of insolvency for the time being in force in Northern Ireland) (SI 1991/878) |
|  |  | 1 Oct 1991 (exception noted above) (SI 1991/2173) |
|  | (2)–(5) | 25 Mar 1991 (see note to ss 154, 155) (SI 1991/488) |
|  |  | 25 Apr 1991 (otherwise) (SI 1991/878) |
| 185, 186 |  | 25 Mar 1991 (see note to ss 154, 155) (SI 1991/488) |
|  |  | 10 Aug 1998 (otherwise) (SI 1998/1747) |
| 187–191 |  | 25 Mar 1991 (see note to ss 154, 155) (SI 1991/488) |

**Companies Act 1989 (c 40)**—*contd*

|  |  |  |
|---|---|---|
|  |  | 25 Apr 1991 (otherwise) (SI 1991/878) |
| 192 |  | 15 Mar 1990 (so far as relates to Financial Services Act 1986, s 47A) (SI 1990/354) |
|  |  | *Never in force* (otherwise) (repealed) |
| 193 | (1) | 15 Mar 1990 (so far as relates to regulations under Financial Services Act 1986, s 62A) (SI 1990/354) |
|  |  | 1 Apr 1991 (otherwise) (SI 1991/488)[4] |
|  | (2) | 1 Apr 1991 (SI 1991/488)[4] |
|  | (3) | 15 Mar 1990 (so far as relates to regulations under Financial Services Act 1986, Sch 11, para 22A) (SI 1990/354) |
|  |  | 1 Apr 1991 (otherwise) (SI 1991/488)[4] |
|  | (4) | 1 Apr 1991 (SI 1991/488)[4] |
| 194–200 |  | 15 Mar 1990 (SI 1990/354) |
| 201 |  | 25 Apr 1991 (SI 1991/878)[8] |
| 202 |  | 16 Nov 1989 (s 215(1)) |
| 203–205 |  | 15 Mar 1990 (SI 1990/354) |
| 206 | (1) | See Sch 23 below |
|  | (2)–(4) | 15 Mar 1990 (SI 1990/354) |
| 207 |  | 1 Nov 1990 (SI 1990/1392, as amended by SI 1990/1707) |
| 208 |  | 1 Mar 1990 (SI 1990/142) |
| 209 |  | 21 Feb 1990 (SI 1990/142) |
| 210 |  | 1 Apr 1990 (SI 1990/142) |
| 211 | (1) | 1 Oct 1991 (SI 1991/1996) |
|  | (2) | 31 Jul 1990 (SI 1990/1392)[9] |
|  | (3) | 31 Jul 1990 (SI 1990/1392) |
| 212 |  | See Sch 24 below |
| 213, 214 |  | 2 Feb 1990 (SI 1990/142) |
| 215, 216 |  | 16 Nov 1989 (RA; see however SI 1990/98 which purports to bring s 216 into force on 25 Jan 1990) |
| Schs 1–9 |  | 1 Apr 1990 (SI 1990/355)[1] |
| Sch 10 | paras 1–18 | 1 Apr 1990 (SI 1990/355)[1, 10] |
|  | para 19 | 1 Aug 1990 (SI 1990/355)[1, 10] |
|  | paras 20–23 | 1 Apr 1990 (SI 1990/355)[1, 10] |
|  | para 24(1) | 1 Apr 1990 (SI 1990/355)[1, 10] |
|  | para 24(2) | 1 Apr 1990 (except so far as relates to Companies Act 1985, s 245(1), (2)) (SI 1990/355)[1, 10] |
|  |  | 7 Jan 1991 (exception noted above)[1] (SI 1990/2569)[2] |
|  | para 24(3) | 1 Apr 1990 (except so far as relates to Companies Act 1985, s 233(5)) (SI 1990/355)[1, 10] |
|  |  | 7 Jan 1991 (exception noted above)[1] (SI 1990/2569) |
|  | para 24(4) | 1 Apr 1990 (SI 1990/355)[1, 10] |
|  | paras 25–34 | 1 Apr 1990 (SI 1990/355)[1, 10] |
|  | para 35(1) | 1 Apr 1990 (SI 1990/355)[1, 10] |
|  | para 35(2)(a) | 1 Apr 1990 (SI 1990/355)[1, 10] |
|  | para 35(2)(b) | 7 Jan 1991 (SI 1990/2569) |
|  | para 35(3) | 1 Apr 1990 (SI 1990/355)[1, 10] |
|  | paras 36–39 | 1 Apr 1990 (SI 1990/355)[1, 10] |
| Schs 11, 12 |  | 1 Mar 1990 (SI 1990/142) |
| Sch 13 |  | 1 Jan 2005 (SI 2004/3322) |
| Sch 14 |  | 1 Mar 1990 (SI 1990/142) |
| Schs 15, 16 |  | *Never in force* (repealed) |
| Sch 17 |  | 31 Jul 1990 (SI 1990/1392) |
| Sch 18 |  | 1 Nov 1990 (SI 1990/1392)[7] |
| Sch 19 | para 1 | 1 Mar 1990 (SI 1990/142) |
|  | paras 2–6 | 1 Oct 1990 (SI 1990/1707)[6] |
|  | para 7 | 1 Oct 1990 (SI 1990/1707) |
|  | paras 8, 9 | 1 Mar 1990 (SI 1990/142) |
|  | para 10 | 7 Jan 1991 (SI 1990/2569) |
|  | para 11 | 4 Feb 1991 (SI 1990/2569) |

**Companies Act 1989 (c 40)**—*contd*

|  |  |  |
|---|---|---|
|  | para 12 | 1 Mar 1990 (SI 1990/142) |
|  | para 13 | *Never in force* (repealed) |
|  | para 14 | 1 Oct 1990 (SI 1990/1707) |
|  | paras 15–18 | 1 Apr 1990 (SI 1990/355) |
|  | para 19 | 1 Mar 1990 (SI 1990/142) |
|  | para 20 | 3 Jul 1995 (SI 1995/1352) |
|  | para 21 | 1 Mar 1990 (SI 1990/142) |
| Sch 20 | para 1 | 1 Apr 1990 (SI 1990/142) |
|  | paras 2–12 | 16 Nov 1989 (s 215(1)) |
|  | para 13 | 1 Apr 1990 (SI 1990/142) |
|  | paras 14–16 | 16 Nov 1989 (s 215(1)) |
|  | para 17 | 1 Apr 1990 (SI 1990/142) |
|  | paras 18–20 | 16 Nov 1989 (s 215(1)) |
|  | para 21 | 1 Apr 1990 (SI 1990/142) |
|  | paras 22–25 | 16 Nov 1989 (s 215(1)) |
|  | para 26 | 1 Apr 1990 (SI 1990/142) |
| Schs 21, 22 |  | 25 Mar 1991 (see note to ss 154–156) (SI 1991/488) |
|  |  | 25 Apr 1991 (otherwise) (SI 1991/878) |
| Sch 23 | paras 1–31 | 15 Mar 1990 (SI 1990/354) |
|  | para 32 | 15 Mar 1990 (so far as relates to Financial Services Act 1986, Sch 11, para 13A) (SI 1990/354) |
|  |  | *Never in force* (otherwise) (repealed) |
|  | paras 33–43 | 15 Mar 1990 (SI 1990/354) |
| Sch 24 |  | 16 Nov 1989 (repeals of or in Fair Trading Act 1973, ss 71, 74, 88, 89, Sch 9) (s 215(1)) |

Sch 24:

21 Feb 1990 (SI 1990/142), repeals of or in—
Companies Act 1985, ss 435, 440, 443, 446, 447, 449, 452, 735A;
Financial Services Act 1986, ss 94, 105, 179, 180, 198(1);
Banking Act 1987, s 84(1)

1 Mar 1990 (repeals of or in Company Directors Disqualification Act 1986, s 21(2)) (SI 1990/142)

1 Mar 1990 (repeal in Financial Services Act 1986, s 199(9)) (SI 1990/355)[11]

15 Mar 1990 (repeals of or in Financial Services Act 1986, ss 48, 55, 119, 159, 160, Sch 11, paras 4, 10, 14) (SI 1990/354)

1 Apr 1990 (repeals of or in Fair Trading Act 1973, ss 46(3), 85) (SI 1990/142)

1 Apr 1990 (SI 1990/355), repeals of or in—
Harbours Act 1964, s 42(6) (subject to transitional or saving provisions);
Companies Act 1985, ss 716, 717, 744 (definition of "authorised institution"), 746, Schs 2, 4, 9, 11, 22 (entry relating to ss 384–393), 24 (except entries relating to ss 245(1), (2), 365(3), 389(10)) (subject to transitional or saving provisions);
Insolvency Act 1985, Sch 6, paras 23, 45;
Financial Services Act 1986, Sch 16, para 22;
Insolvency Act 1986, Sch 13, Pt 1 (entries relating to ss 222(4), 225)

31 May 1990 (repeals of or in Companies Act 1985, ss 201, 202(1), 209(1)(j)) (SI 1990/713)

31 Jul 1990 (SI 1990/1392), repeals of or in—
Companies Act 1985, s 651(1), Sch 22 (entry relating to s 36(4));
Building Societies Act 1986, Schs 15, 18

1 Oct 1990 (SI 1990/1707)[6], repeals of or in—
Companies Act 1985, ss 466(2), 733(3), Sch 22 (entries relating to ss 363–365), Sch 24 (entries relating to s 365(3));
Insolvency Act 1986, Sch 13, Pt I (entry relating to s 733(3))

7 Jan 1991 (repeals of or in Companies Act 1985, s 708(1)(b), Schs 15, 24 (entries relating to s 245(1), (2))) (SI 1990/2569)[2, 6]

**Companies Act 1989 (c 40)**—*contd*

> 1 Jul 1991 (repeal of Companies Act 1985, ss 712, 715) (SI 1991/488)
>
> 1 Oct 1991 (SI 1991/1996), repeals of or in—
> Companies Act 1985, ss 389, 460(1);
> Financial Services Act 1986, s 196(3);
> Income and Corporation Taxes Act 1988, s 565(6)(b)
>
> 1 Nov 1991 (repeals of or in Companies Act 1985, ss 169(5), 175(6)(b), 191(1), (3)(a), (b), 219(1), 288(3), 318(7), 356(1), (2), (4), 383(1)–(3), Sch 13, para 25) (SI 1991/1996)
>
> 3 Jul 1995 (repeals of or in Companies Act 1985, ss 464(5)(c), 744 (definition "annual return")) (SI 1995/1352)
>
> *Not yet in force*, repeals of or in—
> Companies Act 1985, ss 160(3), 466(4)–(6), 744 (definitions of "authorised minimum", "expert", "floating charge", "joint stock company" and "undistributable reserves"), Sch 24 (the entry relating to s 389(10);
> Insolvency Act 1985, Sch 6, para 7(3);
> Financial Services Act 1986, s 13, Sch 11, para 14(3) (now repealed by SI 2001/3649) (but note that Sch 23, Pt I, para 1, Pt II, para 33(1), (4), which also repealed those provisions, was brought into force)[11];
> Insolvency Act 1986, ss 45(5), 53(2), 54(3), 62(5), Sch 10, column 5 (entries relating to ss 45(5), 53(2), 54(3), 62(5));
> Banking Act 1987, s 90, Sch 6 (now repealed by SI 2001/3649);
> Criminal Justice (Scotland) Act 1987;
> Copyright, Designs and Patents Act 1988;
> Criminal Justice Act 1988

[1] Subject to transitional and saving provisions set out in SI 1990/355, arts 6–9, Sch 2, as amended by SI 1990/2569, art 8, SI 1993/3246, reg 5(2), the principal effect being (with certain exceptions) that the existing rules relating to accounts and reports of companies continue to apply for financial years of a company commencing before 23 Dec 1989

[2] Subject to transitional and saving provisions set out in SI 1990/2569, arts 6, 7

[3] Subject to transitional and saving provisions set out in SI 1990/355, art 10, Sch 4, as amended by SI 1990/1707, art 8, with regard to annual returns and auditors

[4] Subject to transitional and saving provisions set out in SI 1991/488, arts 3, 4

[5] Subject to the saving provision set out in SI 1990/1392, art 5

[6] Subject to transitional and saving provisions set out in SI 1990/1707, arts 4–6

[7] Subject to the transitional provisions set out in SI 1990/1392, art 6

[8] Subject to saving provisions set out in SI 1991/878, art 3

[9] Subject to the saving provision set out in SI 1990/1392, art 7

[10] For transitional and savings provisions, see SI 1990/355, art 8, Sch 3

[11] The erroneous repeal of Financial Services Act 1986, s 199(1), by s 212, Sch 24, brought into force on 21 Feb 1990 by SI 1990/142, art 7(d), was revoked by SI 1990/355, art 16, as from 1 Mar 1990

---

**Consolidated Fund Act 1989 (c 2)**

*RA:* 5 Mar 1989

Whole Act in force 5 Mar 1989 (RA)

---

**Consolidated Fund (No 2) Act 1989 (c 46)**

*RA:* 21 Dec 1989

Whole Act in force 21 Dec 1989 (RA)

---

## Continental Shelf Act 1989 (c 35)

*RA:* 27 Jul 1989

Whole Act in force 27 Jul 1989 (RA)

---

## Control of Pollution (Amendment) Act 1989 (c 14)

*RA:* 6 Jul 1989

*Commencement provisions:* s 11(2); Control of Pollution (Amendment) Act 1989 (Commencement) Order 1991, SI 1991/1618

| 1 | (1), (2) | 1 Apr 1992 (SI 1991/1618) |
| | (3) | 16 Jul 1991 (SI 1991/1618) |
| | (4)–(6) | 1 Apr 1992 (SI 1991/1618) |
| 2 | | 16 Jul 1991 (SI 1991/1618) |
| 3 | | 16 Jul 1991 (so far as relates to making of regulations) (SI 1991/1618) |
| | | 14 Oct 1991 (otherwise) (SI 1991/1618) |
| 4 | (1)–(5) | 14 Oct 1991 (SI 1991/1618) |
| | (6) | 16 Jul 1991 (SI 1991/1618) |
| | (7), (8) | 14 Oct 1991 (SI 1991/1618) |
| 5 | (1), (2) | 1 Apr 1992 (SI 1991/1618) |
| | (3) | 16 Jul 1991 (so far as relates to making of regulations) (SI 1991/1618) |
| | | 1 Apr 1992 (otherwise) (SI 1991/1618) |
| | (4), (5) | 1 Apr 1992 (SI 1991/1618) |
| | (6) | 16 Jul 1991 (so far as relates to making of regulations) (SI 1991/1618) |
| | | 1 Apr 1992 (otherwise) (SI 1991/1618) |
| | (7) | 1 Apr 1992 (SI 1991/1618) |
| 6 | | 16 Jul 1991 (so far as relates to making of regulations) (SI 1991/1618) |
| | | 14 Oct 1991 (otherwise) (SI 1991/1618) |
| 7 | | 14 Oct 1991 (SI 1991/1618) |
| 8–11 | | 16 Jul 1991 (SI 1991/1618) |

---

## Control of Smoke Pollution Act 1989 (c 17)

*RA:* 21 Jul 1989

*Commencement provisions:* s 3(2)

Whole Act in force 21 Sep 1989 (s 3(2))

---

## Dangerous Dogs Act 1989 (c 30)

*RA:* 27 Jul 1989

*Commencement provisions:* s 2(4)

Whole Act in force 27 Aug 1989 (s 2(4))

---

## Disabled Persons (Northern Ireland) Act 1989 (c 10)

*RA:* 25 May 1989

*Commencement provisions:* s 12(2); Disabled Persons (1989 Act) (Commencement No 1) Order (Northern Ireland) 1989, SR 1989/474; Disabled Persons (1989 Act) (Commencement No 2) Order (Northern Ireland) 1990, SR 1990/456

## Disabled Persons (Northern Ireland) Act 1989 (c 10)—*contd*

| | | |
|---|---|---|
| 1–3 | | *Not yet in force* |
| 4 | | 1 Apr 1991 (except para (b)) (SR 1990/456) |
| | | *Not yet in force* (exception noted above) |
| 5, 6 | | 1 Apr 1991 (SR 1990/456) |
| 7 | | *Never in force* (substituted) |
| 8 | (1) | 1 Apr 1991 (SR 1990/456) |
| | (2), (3) | *Not yet in force* |
| 9, 10 | | 7 Dec 1989 (SR 1989/474) |
| 11 | (1)–(3) | 7 Dec 1989 (SR 1989/474) |
| | (4) | 1 Apr 1991 (SR 1990/456) |
| 12 | | 7 Dec 1989 (SR 1989/474) |

## Dock Work Act 1989 (c 13)

*RA:* 3 Jul 1989

*Commencement provisions:* s 8(3), (4); National Dock Labour Board (Date of Dissolution) Order 1990, SI 1990/1158

| | | |
|---|---|---|
| 1–6 | | 3 Jul 1989 (s 8(3)) |
| 7 | (1) | See Sch 1 below |
| | (2)–(5) | 3 Jul 1989 (s 8(3)) |
| 8 | | 3 Jul 1989 (s 8(3)) |
| Sch 1 | Pt I | 3 Jul 1989 (s 8(3)) |
| | Pt II | 30 Jun 1990 (SI 1990/1158) |
| Sch 2 | | 3 Jul 1989 (s 8(3)) |

## Elected Authorities (Northern Ireland) Act 1989 (c 3)

*RA:* 15 Mar 1989

*Commencement provisions:* s 13(2); Elected Authorities (Northern Ireland) Act 1989 (Commencement No 1) Order 1989, SI 1989/1093

| | | |
|---|---|---|
| 1 | (1) | 15 Mar 1989 (RA) |
| | (2) | 16 Feb 1990 (SI 1989/1093) |
| | (3), (4) | 15 Mar 1989 (RA) |
| 2–4 | | 15 Mar 1989 (RA) |
| 5 | | *Not yet in force* |
| 6, 7 | | 15 Mar 1989 (RA) |
| 8 | (1) | 15 Mar 1989 (RA) |
| | (2) | *Never in force* (spent) |
| 9–13 | | 15 Mar 1989 (RA) |
| Sch 1 | | 15 Mar 1989 (so far as relates to Representation of the People Act 1983, ss 3, 4) (RA) |
| | | 27 Jun 1989 (so far as relates to Representation of the People Act 1983, ss 53, 201, 202(1), Sch 2) (SI 1989/1093) |
| | | 1 Aug 1989 (otherwise except so far as relates to Representation of the People Act 1983, ss 49, 50) (SI 1989/1093) |
| | | 16 Feb 1990 (so far as relates to Representation of the People Act 1983, ss 49, 50) (SI 1989/1093) |
| Schs 2, 3 | | 15 Mar 1989 (RA) |

## Electricity Act 1989 (c 29)

*RA:* 27 Jul 1989

*Commencement provisions:* s 113(2); Electricity Act 1989 (Commencement No 1) Order 1989, SI 1989/1369; Electricity Act 1989 (Commencement No 2) Order 1990, SI 1990/117; Electricity Act 1989 (Commencement No 3) Order 2001, SI 2001/3419

**Electricity Act 1989 (c 29)**—*contd*

| | | |
|---|---|---|
| 1, 2 | | 1 Sep 1989 (SI 1989/1369) |
| 3–5 | | 31 Mar 1990 (SI 1990/117) |
| 6 | (1)–(8) | 31 Mar 1990 (SI 1990/117) |
| | (9) | 1 Sep 1989 (for the purpose of the interpretation of s 2(7)) (SI 1989/1369) |
| | | 31 Mar 1990 (otherwise) (SI 1990/117) |
| | (10), (11) | 31 Mar 1990 (SI 1990/117) |
| 7–63 | | 31 Mar 1990 (SI 1990/117) |
| 64 | | 1 Oct 1989 (definition "prescribed" for purposes of Schs 14, 15) (SI 1989/1369) |
| | | 31 Mar 1990 (otherwise) (SI 1990/117) |
| 65–69 | | 1 Oct 1989 (SI 1989/1369) |
| 70 | | See Sch 10 below |
| 71–84 | | 31 Mar 1990 (SI 1990/117) |
| 85 | | 1 Mar 1990 (SI 1990/117) |
| 86 | | 1 Sep 1989 (SI 1989/1369) |
| 87, 88 | | 31 Mar 1990 (SI 1990/117) |
| 89 | | 1 Oct 1989 (SI 1989/1369) |
| 90 | | See Sch 11 below |
| 91, 92 | | 1 Oct 1989 (SI 1989/1369) |
| 93 | | 31 Mar 1990 (SI 1990/117) |
| 94, 95 | | 1 Oct 1989 (SI 1989/1369) |
| 96 | | 31 Mar 1990 (SI 1990/117) |
| 97 | | See Sch 12 below |
| 98–103 | | 31 Mar 1990 (SI 1990/117) |
| 104 | | See Sch 14 below |
| 105 | | See Sch 15 below |
| 106, 107 | | 1 Sep 1989 (SI 1989/1369) |
| 108, 109 | | 31 Mar 1990 (SI 1990/117) |
| 110, 111 | | 1 Sep 1989 (SI 1989/1369) |
| 112 | (1)–(3) | 31 Mar 1990 (SI 1990/117) |
| | (4) | See Sch 18 below |
| 113 | | 1 Sep 1989 (SI 1989/1369) |
| Schs 1, 2 | | 1 Sep 1989 (SI 1989/1369) |
| Schs 3–9 | | 31 Mar 1990 (SI 1990/117) |
| Sch 10 | | 1 Oct 1989 (SI 1989/1369) |
| Sch 11 | | 31 Mar 1990 (SI 1990/117) |
| Sch 12 | | 1 Oct 1989 (SI 1989/1369) |
| Sch 13 | | 31 Mar 1990 (SI 1990/117) |
| Schs 14, 15 | | 1 Oct 1989 (SI 1989/1369) |
| Sch 16 | | 31 Mar 1990 (SI 1990/117) |
| Sch 17 | paras 1, 2 | 31 Mar 1990 (SI 1990/117) |
| | para 3(a) | 31 Mar 1990 (SI 1990/117) |
| | para 3(b) | 9 Nov 2001 (SI 2001/3419) |
| | paras 4–40 | 31 Mar 1990 (SI 1990/117) |
| Sch 18 | | 31 Mar 1990 (SI 1990/117), except repeals of or in— |

Electricity Act 1947, ss 1(2), (3), 3(1), (7), (8), 64(3), (4), 67(1), 69, Sch 1, column 1;

Electricity Act 1957, ss 2(1), 3(1), (6), (7), 40(1), 42, Sch 4, Pt I;

House of Commons Disqualification Act 1975, Sch 1, Pt II;

Electricity (Scotland) Act 1979, s 1, Sch 1, paras 2–6;

National Audit Act 1983, Sch 4;

Income and Corporation Taxes Act 1988, s 511(1)–(3), (6)

9 Nov 2001 (exceptions noted above) (SI 2001/3419)

## Employment Act 1989 (c 38)

*RA:* 16 Nov 1989

*Commencement provisions:* s 30(2)–(4); Employment Act 1989 (Commencement and Transitional Provisions) Order 1990, SI 1990/189; Employment Act 1989 (Commencement No 2) Order 1997, SI 1997/134

| | | |
|---|---|---|
| 1–7 | | 16 Jan 1990 (s 30(3)) |
| 8 | | 16 Nov 1989 (s 30(2)) |
| 9 | (1), (2) | 16 Jan 1990 (s 30(3)) |
| | (3) | 26 Feb 1990 (SI 1990/189) |
| | (4)–(6) | 16 Jan 1990 (s 30(3)) |
| 10 | (1), (2) | See Sch 3 below |
| | (3)–(6) | 16 Nov 1989 (s 30(2)) |
| 11, 12 | | 16 Nov 1989 (s 30(2)) |
| 13–15 | | 26 Feb 1990 (SI 1990/189)[1] |
| 16–19 | | 16 Jan 1990 (s 30(3)) |
| 20 | | 26 Feb 1990 (SI 1990/189) |
| 21 | | 16 Jan 1990 (s 30(3)) |
| 22–28 | | 16 Nov 1989 (s 30(2)) |
| 29 | (1), (2) | 16 Nov 1989 (s 30(2)) |
| | (3) | See Sch 6 below |
| | (4) | See Sch 7 below |
| | (5) | See Sch 8 below |
| | (6) | See Sch 9 below |
| 30 | | 16 Nov 1989 (s 30(2)) |
| Schs 1, 2 | | 16 Jan 1990 (s 30(3)) |
| Sch 3 | Pts I, II | 16 Jan 1990 (except repeals of or in Employment of Women, Young Persons and Children Act 1920, s 1(3), Schedule, Pt II; Factories Act 1961, s 119A) (s 30(3)) |
| | | 26 Feb 1990 (repeals of or in Employment of Women, Young Persons and Children Act 1920, s 1(3), Schedule, Pt II) (SI 1990/189) |
| | | 3 Mar 1997 (otherwise) (SI 1997/134) |
| | Pt III | 16 Jan 1990 (s 30(3)) |
| Schs 4, 5 | | 16 Nov 1989 (s 30(2)) |
| Sch 6 | paras 1, 2 | 26 Feb 1990 (SI 1990/189) |
| | paras 3–5 | 16 Jan 1990 (s 30(3)) |
| | para 6 | 3 Mar 1997 (SI 1997/134) |
| | paras 7, 8 | 16 Jan 1990 (s 30(3)) |
| | paras 9–15 | 16 Nov 1989 (s 30(2)) |
| | para 16 | 16 Jan 1990 (s 30(3)) |
| | para 17 | 16 Nov 1989 (s 30(2)) |
| | paras 18, 19 | 26 Feb 1990 (SI 1990/189) |
| | paras 20–25 | 16 Jan 1990 (s 30(3)) |
| | para 26 | 26 Feb 1990 (SI 1990/189) |
| | paras 27–29 | 16 Nov 1989 (s 30(2)) |
| | para 30 | 16 Jan 1990 (s 30(3)) |
| Sch 7 | Pt I | 16 Nov 1989 (s 30(2)) |
| | Pt II | 16 Jan 1990 (s 30(3)) |
| | Pt III | 26 Feb 1990 (SI 1990/189), except repeals of or in— Factories Act 1961, s 119A; Employment Medical Advisory Service Act 1972, ss 5(1), 8(1) (so far as relates to Factories Act 1961, s 119A); Employment and Training Act 1973, Sch 3, para 6 |
| | | 3 Mar 1997 (otherwise) (SI 1997/134) |
| Sch 8 | | 16 Jan 1990 (s 30(3)) |
| Sch 9 | | 16 Nov 1989 (s 30(2)) |

---

[1]   For transitional provisions (re ss 14, 15), see SI 1990/189, art 3

### Extradition Act 1989 (c 33)

*RA*: 27 Jul 1989

*Commencement provisions:* s 38(2), (3)

| | | |
|---|---|---|
| 1–6 | | 27 Sep 1989 (s 38(2)) |
| 7 | (1), (2) | 27 Sep 1989 (s 38(2)) |
| | (3) | 27 Jul 1989 (s 38(3)) |
| | (4)–(6) | 27 Sep 1989 (s 38(2)) |
| 8, 9 | | 27 Sep 1989 (s 38(2)) |
| 10 | (1), (2) | 27 Sep 1989 (s 38(2)) |
| | (3) | 27 Jul 1989 (s 38(3)) |
| | (4)–(13) | 27 Sep 1989 (s 38(2)) |
| 11–13 | | 27 Sep 1989 (s 38(2)) |
| 14 | (1) | 27 Sep 1989 (s 38(2)) |
| | (2), (3) | 27 Jul 1989 (s 38(3)) |
| | (4) | 27 Sep 1989 (s 38(2)) |
| 15–37 | | 27 Sep 1989 (s 38(2)) |
| 38 | | 27 Jul 1989 (s 38(3)) |
| Sch 1 | paras 1–8 | 27 Sep 1989 (s 38(3)) |
| | para 9(1) | 27 Sep 1989 (s 38(2)) |
| | para 9(2) | 27 Jul 1989 (s 38(3)) |
| | para 9(3), (4) | 27 Sep 1989 (s 38(2)) |
| | paras 10–20 | 27 Sep 1989 (s 38(2)) |
| Sch 2 | | 27 Sep 1989 (s 38(2)) |

### Fair Employment (Northern Ireland) Act 1989 (c 32)

*RA*: 27 Jul 1989

*Commencement provisions:* s 60(2); Fair Employment (Northern Ireland) Act 1989 (Commencement) Order 1989, SI 1989/1928

| | | |
|---|---|---|
| 1 | (1), (2) | 1 Jan 1990 (SI 1989/1928) |
| | (3) | 1 Nov 1989 (SI 1989/1928) |
| 2–28 | | 1 Jan 1990 (SI 1989/1928) |
| 29 | | 1 Nov 1989 (SI 1989/1928) |
| 30–46 | | 1 Jan 1990 (SI 1989/1928) |
| 47 | | 1 Nov 1989 (SI 1989/1928) |
| 48 | | 1 Jan 1990 (SI 1989/1928) |
| 49 | | 1 Jan 1990 (except for purposes of acts done before 1 Jan 1990) (SI 1990/1928) |
| 50–56 | | 1 Jan 1990 (SI 1989/1928) |
| 57 | | 1 Nov 1989 (SI 1989/1928) |
| 58–60 | | 1 Jan 1990 (SI 1989/1928) |
| Sch 1 | | 1 Jan 1990 (SI 1989/1928) |
| Sch 2 | paras 1–14 | 1 Jan 1990 (SI 1989/1928) |
| | para 15 | 1 Jan 1990 (except for purposes of any complaint or act to which s 50(2) applies) (SI 1989/1928) |
| | para 16(1), (2) | 1 Jan 1990 (SI 1989/1928) |
| | para 16(3)(a) | 1 Jan 1990 (SI 1989/1928) |
| | para 16(3)(b) | 1 Jan 1990 (except for purposes of any complaint or act to which s 50(2) applies) (SI 1989/1928) |
| | para 17 | 1 Jan 1990 (except for purposes of any complaint or act to which s 50(2) applies) (SI 1989/1928) |
| | paras 18–20 | 1 Jan 1990 (SI 1989/1928) |
| | para 21(a), (b) | 1 Jan 1990 (SI 1989/1928) |
| | para 21(c) | 1 Jan 1990 (except for purposes of any complaint or act to which s 50(2) applies) (SI 1989/1928) |
| | para 21(d)–(f) | 1 Jan 1990 (SI 1989/1928) |
| | paras 22, 23 | 1 Jan 1990 (SI 1989/1928) |

**Fair Employment (Northern Ireland) Act 1989 (c 32)**—*contd*

| | | |
|---|---|---|
| | paras 24–26 | 1 Jan 1990 (except for purposes of any complaint or act to which s 50(2) applies) (SI 1989/1928) |
| | paras 27–31 | 1 Jan 1990 (SI 1989/1928) |
| | paras 32, 33 | 1 Jan 1990 (except for purposes of any complaint or act to which s 50(2) applies) (SI 1989/1928) |
| Sch 3 | | 1 Jan 1990 (except repeals of or in Fair Employment (Northern Ireland) Act 1976, ss 44–48, 51, 53(4), 57(1) (definitions "complainant", "the county court", "finding" and "the injured person"), 59(2), Sch 1, para 11, for the purposes of any complaint or act to which s 50(2) of this Act applies) (SI 1989/1928) |

**Finance Act 1989 (c 26)**

*Budget Day:* 14 Mar 1989

*RA:* 27 Jul 1989

The commencement details of Finance Acts are not set out, as the dates from which their provisions take effect are usually stated clearly and unambiguously in the text of the Act, and charging provisions will normally state for which year or years of assessment they are to have effect.

**Football Spectators Act 1989 (c 37)**

*RA:* 16 Nov 1989

*Commencement provisions:* s 27(2), (3); Football Spectators Act 1989 (Commencement No 1) Order 1990, SI 1990/690; Football Spectators Act 1989 (Commencement No 2) Order 1990, SI 1990/926; Football Spectators Act 1989 (Commencement No 3) Order 1991, SI 1991/1071; Football Spectators Act 1989 (Commencement No 4) Order 1993, SI 1993/1690

| | | |
|---|---|---|
| 1 | (1), (2) | 22 Mar 1990 (SI 1990/690) |
| | (3) | *Never in force* (repealed) |
| | (4)(a) | 22 Mar 1990 (SI 1990/690) |
| | (4)(b), (5), (6) | *Never in force* (repealed) |
| | (7)–(11) | 22 Mar 1990 (SI 1990/690) |
| 2–7 | | *Never in force* (repealed) |
| 8 | | 1 Jun 1990 (SI 1990/690) |
| 9 | | 1 Aug 1993 (SI 1993/1690) |
| 10 | (1)–(5) | 1 Jun 1990 (SI 1990/690) |
| | (6), (7) | *Not yet in force* |
| | (8)(a), (b) | 1 Jun 1990 (SI 1990/690) |
| | (8)(c) | *Never in force* (repealed) |
| | (9)–(11) | 1 Jun 1990 (SI 1990/690) |
| | (12)(a) | *Not yet in force* |
| | (12)(b) | *Never in force* (repealed) |
| | (12)(c), (d) | 1 Jun 1990 (SI 1990/690) |
| | (13)–(17) | 1 Jun 1990 (SI 1990/690) |
| 11, 12 | | 1 Jun 1990 (SI 1990/690) |
| 13 | | 3 Jun 1991 (SI 1991/1071) |
| 14 | | 22 Mar 1990 (SI 1990/690) |
| 15–21 | | 24 Apr 1990 (SI 1990/690) |
| 22 | (1) | 22 Mar 1990 (SI 1990/690) |
| | (2)–(8) | 24 Apr 1990 (SI 1990/690) |
| | (9) | 22 Mar 1990 (SI 1990/690) |
| | (10), (11) | 24 Apr 1990 (SI 1990/690) |
| | (12) | 22 Mar 1990 (SI 1990/690) |
| 23–26 | | 24 Apr 1990 (SI 1990/690) |
| 27 | | 16 Nov 1989 (RA) |
| Sch 1 | | 24 Apr 1990 (SI 1990/690) |

**Football Spectators Act 1989 (c 37)**—*contd*

| | |
|---|---|
| Sch 2 | 1 Jun 1990 (SI 1990/690) |

**Hearing Aid Council (Amendment) Act 1989 (c 12)**

*RA:* 3 Jul 1989

*Commencement provisions:* s 6(2)

| | |
|---|---|
| 1–4 | 3 Sep 1989 (s 6(2)) |
| 5 | 1 Jan 1990 (s 6(2)) |
| 6 | 3 Sep 1989 (s 6(2)) |

**Human Organ Transplants Act 1989 (c 31)**

*RA:* 27 Jul 1989

*Commencement provisions:* s 7(3); Human Organ Transplants Act 1989 (Commencement) Order 1989, SI 1989/2106

| | | |
|---|---|---|
| 1 | | 28 Jul 1989 (s 7(3)) |
| 2 | (1) | 1 Apr 1990 (SI 1989/2106) |
| | (2)–(7) | 27 Jul 1989 (RA) |
| 3–7 | | 27 Jul 1989 (RA) |

**International Parliamentary Organisations (Registration) Act 1989 (c 19)**

*RA:* 21 Jul 1989

Whole Act in force 21 Jul 1989 (RA)

**Law of Property (Miscellaneous Provisions) Act 1989 (c 34)**

*RA:* 27 Jul 1989

*Commencement provisions:* s 5; Law of Property (Miscellaneous Provisions) Act 1989 (Commencement) Order 1990, SI 1990/1175

| | | |
|---|---|---|
| 1 | (1)–(7) | 31 Jul 1990 (SI 1990/1175) |
| | (8) | See Sch 1 below |
| | (9)–(11) | 31 Jul 1990 (SI 1990/1175) |
| 2, 3 | | 27 Sep 1989 (s 5) |
| 4 | | See Sch 2 below |
| 5, 6 | | 27 Jul 1989 (RA) |
| Sch 1 | | 31 Jul 1990 (SI 1990/1175) |
| Sch 2 | | 27 Sep 1989 (repeal of Law of Property Act 1925, s 40) (s 5) |
| | | 31 Jul 1990 (otherwise) (SI 1990/1175) |

**Licensing (Amendment) Act 1989 (c 20)**

*RA:* 21 Jul 1989

*Commencement provisions:* s 2(2)

Whole Act in force 21 Sep 1989 (s 2(2))

## Local Government and Housing Act 1989 (c 42)

*RA:* 16 Nov 1989

*Commencement provisions:* ss 154(3), 195(2), (3) (and individually as noted below: passim); Local Government and Housing Act 1989 (Commencement No 1) Order 1989, SI 1989/2180; Local Government and Housing Act 1989 (Commencement No 2) Order 1989, SI 1989/2186; Local Government and Housing Act 1989 (Commencement No 3) Order 1989, SI 1989/2445; Local Government and Housing Act 1989 (Commencement No 4) Order 1990, SI 1990/191; Local Government and Housing Act 1989 (Commencement No 5 and Transitional Provisions) Order 1990, SI 1990/431, as amended by SI 1990/672, SI 2004/533; Local Government and Housing Act 1989 (Commencement No 6 and Miscellaneous Provisions) Order 1990, SI 1990/762; Local Government and Housing Act 1989 (Commencement No 7) Order 1990, SI 1990/961; Local Government and Housing Act 1989 (Commencement No 8 and Transitional Provisions) Order 1990, SI 1990/1274, as amended by SI 1990/1335; Local Government and Housing Act 1989 (Commencement No 9 and Saving) Order 1990, SI 1990/1552; Local Government and Housing Act 1989 (Commencement No 10) Order 1990, SI 1990/2581; Local Government and Housing Act 1989 (Commencement No 11 and Savings) Order 1991, SI 1991/344; Local Government and Housing Act 1989 (Commencement No 12) Order 1991, SI 1991/953; Local Government and Housing Act 1989 (Commencement No 13) Order 1991, SI 1991/2940; Local Government and Housing Act 1989 (Commencement No 14) Order 1992, SI 1992/760; Local Government and Housing Act 1989 (Commencement No 15) Order 1993, SI 1993/105; Local Government and Housing Act 1989 (Commencement No 16) Order 1993, SI 1993/2410; Local Government and Housing Act 1989 (Commencement No 17) Order 1995, SI 1995/841; Local Government and Housing Act 1989 (Commencement No 18) Order 1996, SI 1996/1857

| | | |
|---|---|---|
| 1 | (1)–(4) | 1 Mar 1990 (SI 1989/2445) |
| | (5), (6) | 29 Nov 1989 (SI 1989/2186) |
| | (7), (8) | 1 Mar 1990 (SI 1989/2445) |
| 2 | | 29 Nov 1989 (SI 1989/2186) |
| 3 | | 16 Nov 1989 (RA) |
| 4, 5 | | 16 Jan 1990 (ss 4(7), 5(9)) |
| 6, 7 | | 16 Jan 1990 (ss 6(8), 7(3)) |
| 8 | | 16 Nov 1989 (RA) |
| 9 | | 16 Jan 1990 (orders etc)[2] (SI 1989/2445) |
| | | 1 Aug 1990 (E) (W) (otherwise) (SI 1990/1552) |
| | | *Not yet in force* (S) (otherwise) |
| 10 | | 1 Apr 1990 (SI 1990/431) |
| 11 | | 16 Nov 1989 (RA; note s 11(4)) |
| 12 | | 16 Jan 1990 (s 12(3)) |
| 13 | | 16 Jan 1990 (orders etc)[2] (SI 1989/2445) |
| | | 1 Aug 1990 (so far as not already in force, except in relation to a parish or community council until 1 Jan 1991) (SI 1990/1552) |
| 14 | | 16 Jan 1990 (orders etc)[2] (SI 1989/2445) |
| | | *Not yet in force* (otherwise) |
| 15 | | 16 Jan 1990 (orders etc)[2] (SI 1989/2445) |
| | | 1 Aug 1990 (E) (W) (otherwise) (SI 1990/1552) |
| | | *Not yet in force* (S) (otherwise) |
| 16 | | 1 Aug 1990 (E) (W) (SI 1990/1552) |
| | | *Not yet in force* (S) |
| 17 | | 16 Jan 1990 (orders etc)[2] (SI 1989/2445) |
| | | 1 Aug 1990 (E) (W) (otherwise) (SI 1990/1552) |
| | | *Not yet in force* (S) (otherwise) |
| 18 | | 16 Jan 1990 (SI 1989/2445) |
| 19 | | 16 Jan 1990 (orders etc)[2] (SI 1989/2445) |
| | | 8 May 1992 (otherwise) (SI 1992/760) |
| 20 | | 16 Jan 1990 (SI 1989/2445) |
| 21 | | 16 Nov 1989 (RA) |
| 22 | | 16 Jan 1990 (SI 1989/2445) |
| 23 | | 1 Apr 1990 (SI 1990/431) |
| 24 | | 16 Nov 1989 (RA) (note s 24(3)) |
| 25–29 | | 1 Apr 1990 (SI 1990/431) |

**See Halsbury's Statutes Citator for amendments to these Acts**

**Local Government and Housing Act 1989 (c 42)**—*contd*

| | | |
|---|---|---|
| 30 | (1) | 3 May 1990 (SI 1990/961) |
| | (2) | 3 May 1990 (so far as amends Local Government Act 1972, s 83(1)) (SI 1990/961) |
| | | 1 Jan 1991 (otherwise) (SI 1990/2581) |
| 31 | | 16 Jan 1990 (SI 1989/2445) |
| 32 | | 3 May 1990 (SI 1990/961) |
| 33–35 | | 16 Jan 1990 (orders etc)[2] (SI 1989/2445) |
| | | 1 Apr 1990 (otherwise) (SI 1990/762) |
| 36 | | 16 Jan 1990 (orders etc)[2] (SI 1989/2445) |
| | | 1 Apr 1990 (otherwise) (SI 1990/431) |
| 37, 38 | | 1 Apr 1990 (SI 1990/431) |
| 39–66 | | 16 Jan 1990 (SI 1989/2445) |
| 67–70 | | 16 Jan 1990 (orders etc)[2] (SI 1989/2445) |
| | | 7 Oct 1993 (otherwise) (SI 1993/2410) |
| 71 | (1) | 16 Jan 1990 (orders etc)[2] (SI 1989/2445) |
| | | 1 Apr 1995 (for purposes of sub-ss (4)–(6) only) (SI 1995/841) |
| | | *Not yet in force* (otherwise) |
| | (2), (3) | 16 Jan 1990 (orders etc)[2] (SI 1989/2445) |
| | | *Not yet in force* (otherwise) |
| | (4) | 16 Jan 1990 (orders etc)[2] (SI 1989/2445) |
| | | 1 Apr 1995 (subject to a transitional provision) (otherwise) (SI 1995/841) |
| | (5) | 16 Jan 1990 (orders etc)[2] (SI 1989/2445) |
| | | 1 Apr 1995 (for purposes of para (a) only) (subject to a transitional provision) (SI 1995/841) |
| | | *Not yet in force* (otherwise) |
| | (6) | 16 Jan 1990 (orders etc)[2] (SI 1989/2445) |
| | | 1 Apr 1995 (otherwise) (SI 1995/841) |
| | (7) | 16 Jan 1990 (orders etc)[2] (SI 1989/2445) |
| | | *Not yet in force* (otherwise) |
| | (8) | 16 Jan 1990 (orders etc)[2] (SI 1989/2445) |
| | | 1 Apr 1995 (SI 1995/841) (otherwise) |
| 72 | | 16 Jan 1990 (orders etc)[2] (SI 1989/2445) |
| | | 7 Oct 1993 (otherwise) (SI 1993/2410) |
| 73 | | 7 Oct 1993 (SI 1993/2410) |
| 74 | | 16 Nov 1989 (RA) |
| 75 | | See Sch 4 below |
| 76–88 | | 16 Nov 1989 (RA) |
| 89–92 | | 16 Jan 1990 (orders etc)[2] (SI 1989/2445) |
| | | 1 Apr 1990 (otherwise) (SI 1990/431) |
| 93, 94 | | 1 Apr 1990 (SI 1990/431) |
| 95, 96 | | 16 Jan 1990 (orders etc)[2] (SI 1989/2445) |
| | | 1 Apr 1990 (otherwise) (SI 1990/431) |
| 97 | | 1 Apr 1990 (SI 1990/431) |
| 98 | | 16 Jan 1990 (orders etc)[2] (SI 1989/2445) |
| | | 1 Apr 1990 (otherwise) (SI 1990/431) |
| 99 | | 16 Jan 1990 (SI 1989/2445) |
| 100 | | 1 Apr 1990 (SI 1990/431) |
| 101 | (1)–(4) | 1 Jul 1990 (SI 1990/1274) |
| | (5)(a) | 1 Jul 1990 (SI 1990/1274) |
| | (5)(b) | *Never in force* (repealed) |
| 102 | | 16 Jan 1990 (orders etc)[2] (SI 1989/2445) |
| | | 1 Jul 1990 (otherwise) (SI 1990/1274) |
| 103 | | 1 Jul 1990 (SI 1990/1274) |
| 104 | | 16 Jan 1990 (orders etc)[2] (SI 1989/2445) |
| | | 1 Jul 1990 (otherwise) (SI 1990/1274) |
| 105–108 | | 1 Jul 1990 (SI 1990/1274) |
| 109, 110 | | 16 Jan 1990 (orders etc)[2] (SI 1989/2445) |
| | | 1 Jul 1990 (otherwise) (SI 1990/1274) |

**Local Government and Housing Act 1989 (c 42)**—*contd*

| | | |
|---|---|---|
| 111, 112 | | 1 Jul 1990 (SI 1990/1274) |
| 113 | | 1 Jul 1990 (subject to transitional provisions) (SI 1990/1274) |
| 114 | | 1 Jul 1990 (SI 1990/1274) |
| 115 | | 16 Jan 1990 (orders etc)² (SI 1989/2445) |
| | | 1 Jul 1990 (otherwise) (SI 1990/1274) |
| 116–120 | | 1 Jul 1990 (SI 1990/1274) |
| 121 | | 16 Jan 1990 (orders etc)² (SI 1989/2445) |
| | | 1 Jul 1990 (otherwise) (SI 1990/1274) |
| 122–126 | | 1 Jul 1990 (SI 1990/1274) |
| 127 | | 16 Jan 1990 (orders etc)² (SI 1989/2445) |
| | | 1 Jul 1990 (otherwise) (SI 1990/1274) |
| 128, 129 | | 1 Jul 1990 (SI 1990/1274) |
| 130 | | 16 Jan 1990 (orders etc)² (SI 1989/2445) |
| | | 1 Jul 1990 (otherwise) (SI 1990/1274) |
| 131 | | 16 Jan 1990 (orders etc)² (SI 1989/2445) |
| | | 1 Apr 1990 (otherwise) (SI 1990/431) |
| 132 | (1)–(4) | 16 Jan 1990 (orders etc)² (SI 1989/2445) |
| | | 1 Apr 1990 (so far as relate to s 131 and not already in force) (SI 1990/431) |
| | (5) | 16 Jan 1990 (orders etc)² (SI 1989/2445) |
| | | 1 Jul 1990 (otherwise subject to transitional provisions) (SI 1990/1274) |
| 133–136 | | 1 Jul 1990 (SI 1990/1274) |
| 137, 138 | | 16 Jan 1990 (SI 1989/2445) |
| 139 | | See Sch 5 below |
| 140 | | 1 Dec 1989 (for purposes of, and in relation to, financial year 1990–91 and each subsequent financial year) (SI 1989/2180) |
| 141 | | *Never in force* (repealed) |
| 142 | | 1 Dec 1989 (for purposes of, and in relation to, financial year 1990–91 and each subsequent financial year) (SI 1989/2180) |
| 143, 144 | | 1 Dec 1989 (SI 1989/2180) |
| 145 | | See Sch 6 below |
| 146–149 | | 16 Nov 1989 (RA) |
| 150–152 | | 16 Jan 1990 (s 152(7)) |
| 153 | | 16 Nov 1989 (RA) |
| 154 | | 1 Jan 1992 (SI 1991/2940) |
| 155 | | 1 Apr 1990 (s 155(7)) |
| 156 | | 1 Apr 1990 (SI 1990/431) |
| 157, 158 | | 16 Nov 1989 (RA) |
| 159 | | 1 Dec 1989 (SI 1989/2180) |
| 160 | | See Sch 8 below |
| 161 | | 16 Nov 1989 (RA) |
| 162 | | 16 Jan 1990 (SI 1989/2445) |
| 163 | | 16 Nov 1989 (RA) |
| 164 | | 1 Mar 1990 (SI 1990/191) |
| 165 | (1) | See Sch 9 below |
| | (2) | 1 Apr 1990 (SI 1990/431) |
| | (3)–(9) | 1 Mar 1990 (SI 1990/191) |
| 166 | | 16 Nov 1989 (RA) |
| 167, 168 | | 16 Jan 1990 (SI 1989/2445) |
| 169 | (1) | 1 Apr 1990 (SI 1990/431) |
| | (2)(a) | 1 Apr 1990 (SI 1990/431) |
| | (2)(b), (c) | 1 Jul 1990 (SI 1990/1274) |
| | (2)(d) | 1 Apr 1990 (SI 1990/431) |
| | (3)–(9) | 1 Apr 1990 (SI 1990/431) |
| 170 | | 1 Apr 1990 (SI 1989/2180) |
| 171 | | 16 Jan 1990 (SI 1989/2445) |
| 172 | (1)–(5) | 1 Mar 1990 (SI 1989/2445) |
| | (6)–(8) | 16 Jan 1990 (SI 1989/2445) |

**Local Government and Housing Act 1989 (c 42)**—*contd*

| | | |
|---|---|---|
| | (9) | 1 Mar 1990 (SI 1989/2445) |
| 173 | | 1 Mar 1990 (SI 1989/2445) |
| 174 | | 16 Nov 1989 (RA) |
| 175 | | 16 Jan 1990 (SI 1989/2445) |
| 176–178 | | 16 Jan 1990 (SI 1989/2180) |
| 179 | | 1 Dec 1989 (SI 1989/2180) |
| 180 | | 16 Jan 1990 (SI 1989/2445) |
| 181 | | 16 Nov 1989 (RA) |
| 182 | | 16 Jan 1990 (SI 1989/2445) |
| 183 | | 1 Apr 1990 (SI 1990/431) |
| 184 | | 16 Nov 1989 (RA) |
| 185 | | 16 Jan 1990 (SI 1989/2180) |
| 186 | | 1 Apr 1990 (SI 1990/431) |
| 187–193 | | 16 Nov 1989 (RA) |
| 194 | (1) | See Sch 11 below |
| | (2)–(4) | See Sch 12 below |
| 195 | | 16 Nov 1989 (RA) |
| Sch 1 | | 16 Jan 1990 (orders etc)[2] (SI 1989/2445) |
| | | 1 Aug 1990 (E) (W) (otherwise) (SI 1990/1552) |
| | | *Not yet in force* (S) (otherwise) |
| Sch 2 | | 16 Jan 1990 (orders etc)[2] (SI 1989/2445) |
| | | 1 Apr 1990 (otherwise) (SI 1990/431) |
| Sch 3 | | 16 Jan 1990 (SI 1989/2445) |
| Sch 4 | | 16 Nov 1989 (RA) |
| Sch 5 | paras 1–6 | 16 Nov 1989 (RA)* |
| | paras 7, 8 | 16 Jan 1990 (para 79(1)) |
| | paras 9–48 | 16 Nov 1989 (RA)* |
| | para 49(1), (2) | 16 Nov 1989 (RA)* |
| | para 49(3) | 16 Jan 1990 (SI 1989/2445) |
| | paras 50, 51 | 16 Nov 1989 (RA)* |
| | para 52 | 16 Jan 1990 (para 79(1)) |
| | para 53 | 16 Nov 1989 (RA)* |
| | para 54 | 16 Jan 1990 (para 79(1)) |
| | para 55 | 16 Nov 1989 (RA)* |
| | para 56 | 16 Jan 1990 (para 79(1)) |
| | paras 57–59 | 16 Nov 1989 (RA)* |
| | para 60 | 16 Jan 1990 (SI 1989/2445) |
| | paras 61, 62 | 16 Nov 1989 (RA)* |
| | para 63 | 16 Jan 1990 (SI 1989/2445) |
| | paras 64, 65 | 16 Nov 1989 (RA) |
| | para 66 | 16 Jan 1990 (para 79(1)) |
| | paras 67–80 | 16 Nov 1989 (RA)* |
| Sch 6 | paras 1, 2 | 1 Apr 1990 (SI 1989/2180) |
| | paras 3, 4 | 1 Dec 1989 (for purposes of, and in relation to, financial year 1990–91 and each subsequent financial year) (SI 1989/2180) |
| | paras 5–8 | 1 Dec 1989 (SI 1989/2180) |
| | paras 9, 10 | 1 Apr 1990 (SI 1989/2180) |
| | paras 11, 12 | 1 Dec 1989 (SI 1989/2180) |
| | paras 13–15 | 1 Apr 1990 (SI 1989/2180) |
| | paras 16, 17 | 1 Dec 1989 (SI 1989/2180) |
| | paras 18, 19 | 1 Apr 1990 (SI 1989/2180) |
| | paras 20, 21 | 1 Dec 1989 (SI 1989/2180) |
| | para 22 | 1 Apr 1990 (SI 1989/2180) |
| | paras 23–27 | 1 Dec 1989 (SI 1989/2180) |
| | paras 28, 29 | 1 Dec 1989 (for purposes of, and in relation to, financial year 1990–91 and each subsequent financial year) (SI 1989/2180) |
| Sch 7 | | 16 Nov 1989 (RA) |
| Sch 8 | | *Never in force* (repealed) |
| Sch 9 | para 1(1)–(5) | 1 Apr 1990 (SI 1990/431) |

**Local Government and Housing Act 1989 (c 42)**—*contd*

| | | |
|---|---|---|
| | para 1(6) | 1 Jul 1990 (SI 1990/1274) |
| | para 2 | 1 Apr 1990 (SI 1990/431) |
| | para 3 | 1 Jul 1990 (SI 1990/1274) |
| | paras 4–43 | 1 Apr 1990 (SI 1990/431) |
| | para 44 | 16 Jan 1990 (for purposes of Housing Act 1985, s 369) (SI 1989/2445) |
| | | 1 Apr 1990 (otherwise) (SI 1990/431) |
| | paras 45–55 | 1 Apr 1990 (SI 1990/431) |
| | para 56(1), (2) | 16 Jan 1990 (SI 1989/2445) |
| | para 56(3), (4) | 1 Apr 1990 (SI 1990/431) |
| | paras 57, 58 | 1 Jul 1990 (SI 1990/1274) |
| | para 59 | 1 Apr 1990 (SI 1990/431) |
| | para 60 | 1 Jul 1990 (SI 1990/1274) |
| | paras 61–63 | 1 Apr 1990 (SI 1990/431) |
| | paras 64, 65 | 1 Jul 1990 (SI 1990/1274) |
| | paras 66–70 | 1 Apr 1990 (SI 1990/431) |
| | para 71(a), (b) | 1 Apr 1990 (SI 1990/431) |
| | para 71(c), (d) | 1 Jul 1990 (SI 1990/1274) |
| | paras 72–83 | 1 Apr 1990 (SI 1990/431) |
| | para 84 | 16 Jan 1990 (orders etc)[2] (SI 1989/2445) |
| | | 1 Apr 1990 (otherwise) (SI 1990/431) |
| | para 85 | 1 Apr 1990 (except so far as relating to Housing Act 1985, s 605(1)(e)) (SI 1990/431) |
| | | 1 Jul 1990 (exception noted above) (SI 1990/1274) |
| | paras 86–91 | 1 Apr 1990 (SI 1990/431) |
| Sch 10 | | 1 Apr 1990 (SI 1990/431) |
| Sch 11 | paras 1, 2 | 1 Apr 1990 (SI 1990/431) |
| | para 3 | *Never in force* (spent) |
| | para 4 | 26 Feb 1990 (SI 1990/191) |
| | paras 5–13 | 1 Apr 1990 (SI 1990/431)[1] |
| | para 14 | 25 Jan 1993 (SI 1993/105) |
| | para 15 | *Never in force* (repealed) |
| | para 16 | 1 Apr 1990 (SI 1990/431) |
| | paras 17, 18 | *Never in force* (spent) |
| | para 19 | 1 Apr 1990 (SI 1990/762) |
| | para 20 | 1 Apr 1990 (SI 1990/431) |
| | para 21 | *Not yet in force* |
| | paras 22, 23 | 1 Apr 1990 (SI 1990/431) |
| | paras 24, 25 | *Not yet in force* |
| | para 26 | 27 Feb 1991 (in relation only to power to make regulations relating to prescribed amount in Local Government Act 1972, s 173(1)) (SI 1991/344) |
| | | 1 Apr 1991 (otherwise) (SI 1991/344) |
| | para 27 | 1 Apr 1990 (orders etc)[2] (SI 1990/431) |
| | | 1 Apr 1991 (otherwise) (SI 1991/344) |
| | para 28(1), (2) | 1 Jul 1990 (orders etc)[2] (SI 1990/1274) |
| | | 1 Apr 1991 (otherwise) (SI 1991/344) |
| | para 28(3) | 16 Jan 1990 (orders etc)[2] (SI 1989/2445) |
| | | 1 Apr 1991 (otherwise) (SI 1991/344) |
| | para 28(4) | 16 Jan 1990 (SI 1989/2445) |
| | para 29 | 1 Apr 1991 (SI 1991/344) |
| | para 30 | 8 May 1992 (SI 1992/760) |
| | paras 31–33 | 1 Apr 1990 (SI 1990/431) |
| | para 34 | 1 Apr 1991 (SI 1991/344) |
| | para 35(1), (2) | *Not yet in force* |
| | para 35(3) | 16 Jan 1990 (orders etc)[2] (SI 1989/2445) |
| | | *Not yet in force* (otherwise) |
| | para 35(4) | 16 Jan 1990 (SI 1989/2445) |
| | para 36 | *Not yet in force* |

**Local Government and Housing Act 1989 (c 42)**—*contd*

| | | |
|---|---|---|
| | para 37 | 16 Jan 1990 (SI 1989/2445) |
| | paras 38–41 | 1 Apr 1990 (SI 1990/431) |
| | para 42 | 16 Jan 1990 (SI 1989/2445) |
| | para 43 | *Never in force* (repealed) |
| | paras 44–48 | 1 Apr 1990 (SI 1990/431) |
| | para 49 | 16 Jan 1990 (SI 1989/2445) |
| | paras 50, 51 | 1 Apr 1990 (SI 1990/431) |
| | para 52 | 1 Jul 1990 (SI 1990/1274) |
| | para 53(1) | 16 Jan 1990 (SI 1989/2445) |
| | para 53(2) | 1 Apr 1990 (SI 1990/431) |
| | para 54 | 1 Apr 1990 (SI 1990/431) |
| | paras 55–57 | *Not yet in force* |
| | para 58 | 16 Jan 1990 (SI 1989/2445) |
| | para 59 | 1 Apr 1990 (SI 1990/431) |
| | para 60 | *Not yet in force* |
| | para 61 | 1 Dec 1989 (SI 1989/2180) |
| | para 62 | 1 Apr 1990 (SI 1990/431) |
| | para 63 | 1 Jul 1990 (SI 1990/1274) |
| | paras 64, 65 | 1 Apr 1990 (SI 1990/431) |
| | paras 66–69 | 1 Jul 1990 (SI 1990/1274) |
| | paras 70–76 | 1 Apr 1990 (SI 1990/431) |
| | paras 77–84 | 16 Jan 1990 (SI 1989/2445) |
| | paras 85–87 | 1 Apr 1990 (SI 1990/431) |
| | para 88 | 16 Jan 1990 (orders etc)[2] (SI 1989/2445) |
| | | 1 Apr 1990 (otherwise) (SI 1990/431) |
| | para 89 | 16 Jan 1990 (SI 1989/2445) |
| | paras 90, 91 | 1 Jul 1990 (SI 1990/1274) |
| | para 92 | *Never in force* (repealed) |
| | paras 93, 94 | 16 Jan 1990 (SI 1989/2180) |
| | para 95 | 1 Dec 1989 (SI 1989/2180) |
| | para 96 | 1 Apr 1990 (SI 1990/431) |
| | paras 97, 98 | *Never in force* (repealed) |
| | paras 99, 100 | 16 Jan 1990 (SI 1989/2180) |
| | paras 101, 102 | 1 Apr 1990 (SI 1990/431) |
| | para 103 | 16 Jan 1990 (SI 1989/2445) |
| | paras 104–106 | 16 Nov 1989 (RA) |
| | para 107 | 16 Jan 1990 (SI 1989/2445) |
| | para 108 | 1 Apr 1990 (SI 1990/431) |
| | paras 109–112 | 16 Jan 1990 (SI 1989/2445) |
| | para 113 | 1 Apr 1991 (SI 1991/953) |
| Sch 12 | Pt I | 1 Apr 1990 (SI 1990/431)[1] |
| | Pt II | 1 Dec 1989 (SI 1988/2180), repeals of or in— |

                    Valuation and Rating (Scotland) Act 1956, s 22(4);
                    Local Government (Scotland) Act 1973, s 110A(2);
                    Housing (Scotland) Act 1988, s 2(6);
                    Local Government Finance Act 1988, s 128(2), Sch 12, para 16
            16 Jan 1990 (repeals of or in Housing (Scotland) Act 1987,
                    s 61(10)(a)(v)) (SI 1989/2180)
            16 Jan 1990 (SI 1989/2445), repeals of or in—
                    Race Relations Act 1976, s 47;
                    Housing Act 1985, ss 107, 417–420, 423(2), 434, 459, Sch 14;
                    Housing and Planning Act 1986, s 1;
                    Social Security Act 1986, s 30(10);
                    Housing (Scotland) Act 1987, s 80;
                    Housing Act 1988, s 129(5)(b)
            1 Mar 1990 (repeals of or in Housing Act 1985, ss 312–314,
                Sch 12 (in relation to any financial year beginning on or after
                1 Apr 1990)) (SI 1990/191)
            1 Apr 1990 (SI 1989/2180), repeals of or in—

**Local Government and Housing Act 1989 (c 42)**—*contd*

Local Government (Financial Provisions etc) (Scotland)
Act 1962, s 4(3), (4), Sch 1;

Water (Scotland) Act 1980, s 40(7);

Local Government Finance Act 1988, Sch 12, para 37

1 Apr 1990 (SI 1990/431)[1], repeals of or in—

Land Compensation Act 1961, s 10, Sch 2;

Local Government Act 1972, ss 101, 110;

Land Compensation Act 1973, ss 29, 37, 39, 73;

Housing Act 1974, Sch 13;

Local Government Act 1974, ss 23–25, 34;

Housing Act 1985 (so far as not already in force except those of
or in ss 370–372, 374, 379(1), 381(4) (figure '370'), 460–520,
524–526, 567, 569);

Housing (Consequential Provisions) Act 1985, Sch 2;

Housing and Planning Act 1986, s 42(1)(d), Sch 5;

Housing Act 1988, s 130(2);

Local Government Act 1988, s 25, Sch 3;

1 Jul 1990 (SI 1990/1274), repeals of or in—

Local Authorities (Expenditure Powers) Act 1983;

Housing Act 1985, ss 370–372, 374, 379(1), 381(4) (figure
'370'), 460–520, 567, 569 (subject to transitional provisions)

1 Aug 1990 (SI 1990/1552), repeals of or in—

Local Government Act 1972, s 102(3) (except in relation to a
parish or community council until 1 Jan 1991);

Local Government Act 1985, s 33

1 Apr 1991 (SI 1991/344), repeals of or in—

Local Government Act 1972, ss 177, 177A, 178;

Local Government (Scotland) Act 1973, ss 45, 45A, 49A;

Education Act 1980;

Local Government, Planning and Land Act 1980;

Local Government Act 1985, Sch 14;

Local Government Act 1986;

Norfolk and Suffolk Broads Act 1988

22 Jul 1996 (SI 1996/1857), repeals in—

Education (Grants and Awards) Act 1984;

Education (Amendment) Act 1986

*Not yet in force*, repeals of or in—

Town Development Act 1952;

Town and Country Planning Act 1962, Sch 12 (repealed);

Town and Country Planning Act 1968, s 99 (repealed);

Town and Country Planning Act 1971, Sch 23 (repealed);

Local Government Act 1972, ss 80(1)(a), 137(2A), (2B), (2C)(a),
(8), 185, 265A(1)(g), Sch 18;

Water Act 1973;

Local Government (Scotland) Act 1973, ss 31(1)(a)(ii), 49(1A),
57(3), 111(1)(a), (b), (d), 161(6) (repealed), Sch 10, para 11
(repealed), Sch 20, para 10 (repealed);

Local Government (Scotland) Act 1975;

Local Land Charges Act 1975;

Justices of the Peace Act 1979, s 59(1)(a) (repealed);

Acquisition of Land Act 1981;

New Towns Act 1981;

Housing Act 1985, ss 524–526;

Local Government Act 1985, Sch 8, paras 8, 9(2);

New Towns and Urban Development Corporations Act 1985;

Housing and Planning Act 1986, ss 15, 20, Sch 3;

Abolition of Domestic Rates Etc (Scotland) Act 1987, Sch 1,
para 28(a)(ii), (iii) (repealed);

Housing Act 1988, ss 103(4) (repealed), 131;

**Local Government and Housing Act 1989 (c 42)**—*contd*
Water Act 1989

\*   Note: certain amendments made by Sch 5 above (except those made by paras 7, 8, 12, 49(3), 52, 54, 57, 60, 63, 66 or 68) to Local Government Finance Act 1988 are, by virtue of para 79(3) thereof, retrospective in effect

[1]   For savings and transitional provisions see SI 1990/431, Sch 1

[2]   Abbreviation: "orders etc" means "so far as confers on Secretary of State powers to make orders, regulations or determinations, to give or make directions, to specify matters, to require information, to impose conditions or to give guidance or approvals, or make provision with respect to the exercise of any such power"

---

**National Maritime Museum Act 1989 (c 8)**

*RA:* 5 May 1989

*Commencement provisions:* s 3(3); National Maritime Museum Act 1989 (Commencement) Order 1989, SI 1989/1028

Whole Act in force 7 Jul 1989 (SI 1989/1028)

---

**Official Secrets Act 1989 (c 6)**

*RA:* 11 May 1989

*Commencement provisions:* s 16(6); Official Secrets Act 1989 (Commencement) Order 1990, SI 1990/199

Whole Act in force 1 Mar 1990 (SI 1990/199)

---

**Opticians Act 1989 (c 44)**

*RA:* 16 Nov 1989

*Commencement provisions:* s 38

Whole Act in force 16 Feb 1990 (s 38)

---

**Parking Act 1989 (c 16)**

*RA:* 21 Jul 1989

*Commencement provisions:* s 5(2); Parking Act 1989 (Commencement) Order 1990, SI 1990/933

Whole Act in force 16 May 1990 (SI 1990/933)

---

**Pesticides (Fees and Enforcement) Act 1989 (c 27)**

*RA:* 27 Jul 1989

*Commencement provisions:* s 3(2)

| | |
|---|---|
| 1 | 27 Jul 1989 (RA) |
| 2 | 27 Sep 1989 (s 3(2)) |
| 3 | 27 Jul 1989 (RA) |

---

## Petroleum Royalties (Relief) and Continental Shelf Act 1989 (c 1)

*RA:* 7 Feb 1989

Whole Act in force 7 Feb 1989 (RA)

## Police Officers (Central Service) Act 1989 (c 11)

*RA:* 3 Jul 1989

Whole Act in force 3 Jul 1989 (RA)

## Prevention of Terrorism (Temporary Provisions) Act 1989 (c 4)

*RA:* 15 Mar 1989

*Commencement provisions:* s 27(1)–(4) (see as to expiry of certain provisions on 22 Mar 1990, s 27(5), (10)–(12)); Prevention of Terrorism (Temporary Provisions) Act 1989 (Commencement No 1) Order 1989, SI 1989/1361; Prevention of Terrorism (Temporary Provisions) Act 1989 (Commencement No 2) Order 1990, SI 1990/215

| | | |
|---|---|---|
| 1–21 | | 22 Mar 1989 (s 27(1)) |
| 22–24 | | 16 Mar 1989 (s 27(2)) |
| 25–28 | | 22 Mar 1989 (s 27(1)) (ss 27(2), 28 in effect in force on 16 Mar 1989 for purposes of ss 22–24) |
| Schs 1, 2 | | 22 Mar 1989 (s 27(1)) |
| Sch 3 | | 1 Sep 1989 (in relation to a person detained under s 14, Sch 2, para 7 or Sch 5, para 6, after 31 Aug 1989, or a person given notice under Sch 5, para 2(4), after 31 Aug 1989 but not detained under Sch 5, para 6) (SI 1989/1361) |
| | | 5 Mar 1990 (otherwise) (SI 1990/215) |
| Sch 4 | paras 1–7 | 22 Mar 1989 (s 27(1)) |
| | paras 8, 9 | 1 Sep 1989 (SI 1989/1361) |
| | para 10 | 5 Mar 1990 (SI 1990/1361) |
| | paras 11–17 | 22 Mar 1989 (s 27(1)) |
| | paras 18–19 | 1 Sep 1989 (SI 1989/1361) |
| | para 20 | 5 Mar 1990 (SI 1990/215) |
| | paras 21–27 | 22 Mar 1989 (s 27(1)) |
| | paras 28, 29 | 1 Sep 1989 (SI 1989/1361) |
| | para 30 | 5 Mar 1990 (SI 1990/215) |
| | paras 31–33 | 22 Mar 1989 (s 27(1)) |
| | para 34 | 5 Mar 1990 (SI 1990/215) |
| | para 35 | 22 Mar 1989 (s 27(1)) |
| Schs 5–8 | | 22 Mar 1989 (s 27(1)) |
| Sch 9 | | 22 Mar 1989 (except repeal of Sch 7, para 9 of this Act) (s 27(1)) |
| | | 3 Dec 1990 (repeal of Sch 7, para 9 of this Act, which came into force on the coming into force of Land Registration Act 1988 (qv)) (s 27(4)) |

## Prisons (Scotland) Act 1989 (c 45)

*RA:* 16 Nov 1989

*Commencement provisions:* s 46(2)

Whole Act in force 16 Feb 1990 (s 46(2))

## Representation of the People Act 1989 (c 28)

*RA:* 27 Jul 1989

*Commencement provisions:* s 8(2); Representation of the People Act 1989 (Commencement No 1) Order 1989, SI 1989/1318; Representation of the People Act 1989 (Commencement No 2) Order 1990, SI 1990/519

| | |
|---|---|
| 1–4 | 1 Apr 1990 (SI 1990/519) |
| 5–8 | 1 Sep 1989 (SI 1989/1318) |

## Road Traffic (Driver Licensing and Information Systems) Act 1989 (c 22)

*RA:* 21 Jul 1989

*Commencement provisions:* s 17(2); Road Traffic (Driver Licensing and Information Systems) Act 1989 (Commencement No 1) Order 1989, SI 1989/1843; Road Traffic (Driver Licensing and Information Systems) Act 1989 (Commencement No 2) Order 1990, SI 1990/802; Road Traffic (Driver Licensing and Information Systems) Act 1989 (Commencement No 3) Order 1990, SI 1990/2228; Road Traffic (Driver Licensing and Information Systems) Act 1989 (Commencement No 4) Order 1990, SI 1990/2610

| | | |
|---|---|---|
| 1 | (1)–(5) | 1 Apr 1991 (SI 1990/2610) |
| | (6) | See Sch 1 below |
| | (7) | 1 Jun 1990 (so far as relates to definitions "the 1981 Act" and "the 1988 Act") (SI 1990/802) |
| | | 1 Apr 1991 (otherwise) (SI 1990/2610) |
| 2 | | 1 Apr 1991 (SI 1990/2610) |
| 3 | | 1 Jun 1990 (SI 1990/802) |
| 4 | | 1 Apr 1991 (SI 1990/2610) |
| 5 | (1) | 1 Jun 1990 (except so far as relates to s 5(5)) (SI 1990/802) |
| | | 1 Apr 1991 (exception noted above) (SI 1990/2610) |
| | (2)–(4) | 1 Jun 1990 (SI 1990/802) |
| | (5) | 1 Apr 1991 (SI 1990/2610) |
| | (6)–(10) | 1 Jun 1990 (SI 1990/802) |
| 6 | | 1 Dec 1990 (SI 1990/2228) |
| 7 | | See Sch 3 below |
| 8–15 | | 1 Jun 1990 (SI 1990/802) |
| 16 | | See Sch 6 below |
| 17 | | 8 Nov 1989 (SI 1989/1843) |
| Sch 1 | paras 1–9 | 1 Apr 1991 (SI 1990/2610) |
| | para 10 | 8 Nov 1989 (SI 1989/1843) |
| | para 11 | 1 Jun 1990 (SI 1990/802) |
| | para 12 | 1 Apr 1991 (SI 1990/2610) |
| Sch 2 | | 1 Apr 1991 (SI 1990/2610) |
| Sch 3 | paras 1–5 | 1 Apr 1991 (SI 1990/2610) |
| | para 6 | 1 Dec 1990 (SI 1990/2228) |
| | para 7 | 1 Jun 1990 (SI 1990/802) |
| | para 8(a) | 1 Apr 1991 (SI 1991/2610) |
| | para 8(b)(i) | 1 Apr 1991 (SI 1990/2610) |
| | para 8(b)(ii), (iii) | 1 Jun 1990 (SI 1990/802) |
| | para 8(c)–(e) | 1 Apr 1991 (SI 1990/2610) |
| | para 9(a) | 1 Apr 1991 (SI 1990/2610) |
| | para 9(b) | 1 Jun 1990 (SI 1990/802) |
| | para 9(c) | 1 Apr 1991 (SI 1990/2610) |
| | para 9(d) | 1 Jun 1990 (SI 1990/802) |
| | para 10 | 1 Dec 1990 (SI 1990/2228) |
| | para 11(a) | 1 Apr 1991 (SI 1990/2610) |
| | para 11(b) | 1 Jun 1990 (SI 1990/802) |
| | para 11(c) | 1 Dec 1990 (SI 1990/2228) |
| | para 11(d) | 1 Jun 1990 (SI 1990/802) |
| | para 12(a) | 1 Apr 1991 (SI 1990/2610) |

**Road Traffic (Driver Licensing and Information Systems) Act 1989 (c 22)**—*contd*

| | | |
|---|---|---|
| | para 12(b), (c) | 1 Jun 1990 (SI 1990/802) |
| | para 13 | 1 Apr 1991 (SI 1990/2610) |
| | para 14 | 1 Jun 1990 (SI 1990/802) |
| | para 15(a) | 1 Jun 1990 (SI 1990/802) |
| | para 15(b)–(d) | 1 Apr 1991 (SI 1990/2610) |
| | para 15(e) | 1 Jun 1990 (so far as relates to definitions "NI driving licence" and "NI licence") (SI 1990/802) |
| | | 1 Apr 1991 (so far as relates to definition "passenger carrying vehicle") (SI 1990/2610) |
| | para 15(f) | 1 Jun 1990 (SI 1990/802) |
| | para 15(g) | 1 Dec 1990 (SI 1990/2228) |
| | paras 16, 17 | 1 Jun 1990 (SI 1990/802) |
| | para 18(a) | 1 Apr 1991 (SI 1990/2610) |
| | para 18(b)–(d) | 1 Dec 1990 (SI 1990/2228) |
| | para 19 | 1 Jun 1990 (SI 1990/802) |
| | paras 20–23 | 1 Apr 1991 (SI 1990/2610) |
| | paras 24, 25 | 1 Jun 1990 (SI 1990/802) |
| | para 26 | 8 Nov 1989 (SI 1989/1843) |
| | para 27(a)–(c) | 1 Apr 1991 (SI 1990/2610) |
| | para 27(d) | 1 Jun 1990 (SI 1990/802) |
| | para 27(e) | 1 Apr 1991 (SI 1990/2610) |
| | para 28(a), (b) | 1 Jun 1990 (SI 1990/802) |
| | para 28(c), (d) | 1 Apr 1991 (SI 1990/2610) |
| | para 29 | 8 Nov 1989 (so far as relates to offences under Sch 1, para 10(4), (5)) (SI 1989/1843) |
| | | 1 Apr 1991 (otherwise) (SI 1990/2610) |
| | para 30(a) | 1 Jun 1990 (SI 1990/802) |
| | para 30(b), (c) | 1 Apr 1991 (SI 1990/2610) |
| | para 30(d) | 8 Nov 1989 (so far as relates to offences under Sch 1, para 10(4), (5)) (SI 1989/1843) |
| | | 1 Apr 1991 (otherwise) (SI 1990/2610) |
| Schs 4, 5 | | 1 Jun 1990 (SI 1990/802) |
| Sch 6 | | 1 Jun 1990 (SI 1990/802), repeals of or in— Road Traffic Act 1988, s 97(1); Road Traffic Offenders Act 1988, s 45(3), Sch 2, Pt I (entry relating to s 45 of that Act) |
| | | 1 Dec 1990 (repeals in Road Traffic Act 1988, s 97(3)) (SI 1990/2228) |
| | | 1 Apr 1991 (except repeal of Road Traffic (Driver Licensing and Information Systems) Act 1989, Sch 1, para 11) (SI 1990/2610) |
| | | *Never in force* (repeal of Road Traffic (Driver Licensing and Information Systems) Act 1989, Sch 1, para 11 (repealed)) |

---

## Security Service Act 1989 (c 5)

*RA:* 27 Apr 1989

*Commencement provisions:* s 7(2); Security Service Act 1989 (Commencement) Order 1989, SI 1989/2093

Whole Act in force 18 Dec 1989 (SI 1989/2093)

---

## Self-Governing Schools etc (Scotland) Act 1989 (c 39)

*RA:* 16 Nov 1989

*Commencement provisions:* s 81; Self-Governing Schools etc (Scotland) Act 1989 (Commencement) Order 1990, SI 1990/86; Self-Governing Schools etc (Scotland) Act 1989 (Commencement No 2) Order 1990, SI 1990/1108; Self-Governing Schools etc (Scotland) Act 1989 (Commencement No 3) Order 1997, SI 1997/391

**Self-Governing Schools etc (Scotland) Act 1989 (c 39)**—*contd*

| | | |
|---|---|---|
| 1–66 | | 16 Nov 1989 (s 81(1)) |
| 67 | | 1 Feb 1990 (SI 1990/86) |
| 68 | | 16 Nov 1989 (s 81(1)) |
| 69 | (1), (2) | 1 Feb 1990 (SI 1990/86) |
| | (3) | 16 Nov 1989 (s 81(1)) |
| 70 | | 19 Feb 1997 (SI 1997/391) |
| 71 | | 16 Nov 1989 (s 81(1)) |
| 72 | | 1 Jun 1990 (SI 1990/86) |
| 73–76 | | 1 Feb 1990 (SI 1990/86) |
| 77–81 | | 16 Nov 1989 (s 81(1)) |
| 82 | (1) | 16 Nov 1989 (s 81(1)) |
| | (2) | 1 Feb 1990 (SI 1990/86) |
| 83 | | 16 Nov 1989 (s 81(1)) |
| Schs 1–9 | | 16 Nov 1989 (s 81(1)) |
| Sch 10 | paras 1, 2 | 1 Feb 1990 (SI 1990/86) |
| | paras 3–7 | 16 Nov 1989 (s 81(1)) |
| | para 8(1)–(6) | 16 Nov 1989 (s 81(1)) |
| | para 8(7) | 1 Feb 1990 (SI 1990/86) |
| | para 8(8) | 16 Nov 1989 (s 81(1)) |
| | para 8(9)–(11) | 1 Feb 1990 (SI 1990/86) |
| | para 8(12) | 16 Nov 1989 (s 81(1)) |
| | para 8(13)–(21) | 1 Feb 1990 (SI 1990/86) |
| | para 8(22) | 16 Nov 1989 (s 81(1)) |
| | paras 9, 10 | 16 Nov 1989 (s 81(1)) |
| Sch 11 | | 1 Feb 1990 (SI 1990/86) |

**Social Security Act 1989 (c 24)**

*RA:* 21 Jul 1989

*Commencement provisions:* s 33(2), (3); Social Security Act 1989 (Commencement No 1) Order 1989, SI 1989/1238; Social Security Act 1989 (Commencement No 2) Order 1989, SI 1989/1262; Social Security Act 1989 (Commencement No 3) Order 1990, SI 1990/102; Social Security Act 1989 (Commencement No 4) Order 1990, SI 1990/312 (correcting defect in SI 1990/102); Social Security Act 1989 (Commencement No 5) Order 1994, SI 1994/1661; Social Security Act 1989 (Commencement No 6) Order 2007, SI 2007/2445

| | | |
|---|---|---|
| 1 | | 5 Oct 1989 (SI 1989/1238) |
| 2–4 | | 21 Jul 1989 (RA) |
| 5 | | 9 Oct 1989 (SI 1989/1238) |
| 6 | | 21 Jul 1989 (RA) |
| 7 | (1)–(5) | 1 Oct 1989 (SI 1989/1238) |
| | (6) | See Sch 1 below |
| 8 | | 9 Oct 1989 (SI 1989/1238) |
| 9–13 | | 25 Jul 1989 (for the purposes of regulations under Social Security Act 1975, Social Security (No 2) Act 1980 and Social Security Act 1986, expressed to come into force on or after 9 Oct 1989) (SI 1989/1262 (superseding SI 1989/1238)) |
| | | 9 Oct 1989 (for all remaining purposes) (SI 1989/1238) |
| 14 | | 21 Jul 1989 (s 14(1) deemed by s 14(2) to have come into force on 1 Apr 1988) (RA) |
| 15, 16 | | 21 Jul 1989 (RA) |
| 17 | | 21 Jul 1989 (s 17(3)–(6) deemed by s 17(7) to have come into force on 10 Apr 1989) (RA) |
| 18 | | 21 Jul 1989 (RA) |
| 19 | | 21 Jul 1989 (but see s 19(11) stating that s 19 comes into force on date of repeal of Official Secrets Act 1911, s 2, by Official Secrets Act 1989, s 16(4), Schedule) (RA) |
| 20 | | 21 Jul 1989 (RA) |
| 21 | | See Sch 3 below |

**Social Security Act 1989 (c 24)**—*contd*

| | | |
|---|---|---|
| 22 | (1), (2) | 3 Sep 1990 (SI 1990/102) |
| | (3) | 18 Jan 1990 (SI 1990/102) |
| | (4) | 18 Jan 1990 (for the purposes of regulations expressed to come into force on or after 2 Apr 1990) (SI 1990/102) |
| | | 1 Mar 1990 (otherwise) (SI 1990/102) |
| | (5) | 18 Jan 1990 (for purposes of regulations expressed to come into force on or after 2 Apr 1990) (SI 1990/102) |
| | | 3 Sep 1990 (otherwise) (SI 1990/102) |
| | (6) | 3 Sep 1990 (SI 1990/102) |
| | (7) | See Sch 4 below |
| | (8) | 3 Sep 1990 (SI 1990/102) |
| 23 | | See Sch 5 below |
| 24 | | See Sch 6 below |
| 25 | (1)–(3) | 1 Mar 1990 (for purposes of regulations expressed to come into force on 1 Jan 1991) (SI 1990/102) |
| | | 1 Jan 1991 (otherwise) (SI 1990/102) |
| | (4)–(6) | 1 Jan 1991 (SI 1990/102) |
| 26 | | See Sch 7 below |
| 27 | | *Never in force* (repealed) |
| 28–30 | | 21 Jul 1989 (RA) |
| 31 | (1) | See Sch 8 below |
| | (2) | See Sch 9 below |
| | (3) | 21 Jul 1989 (RA) |
| 32, 33 | | 21 Jul 1989 (RA) |
| Sch 1 | paras 1–7 | 1 Oct 1989 (SI 1989/1238) |
| | para 8(1)–(6) | 1 Oct 1989 (SI 1989/1238) |
| | para 8(7), (8) | *Never in force* (repealed) |
| | paras 9–11 | 1 Oct 1989 (SI 1989/1238) |
| Sch 2 | | 21 Jul 1989 (RA) |
| Sch 3 | para 1 | 21 Jul 1989 (RA) |
| | para 2 | 6 Apr 1990 (SI 1990/102) |
| | para 3(1) | 1 Feb 1990 (for purposes of regulations expressed to come into force on 6 Apr 1990) (SI 1990/102) |
| | | 6 Apr 1990 (otherwise) (SI 1990/102) |
| | para 3(2)–(4) | 6 Apr 1990 (SI 1990/102) |
| | paras 4–7 | 6 Apr 1990 (SI 1990/102) |
| | para 8 | 1 Feb 1990 (for purposes of regulations expressed to come into force on 6 Apr 1990) (SI 1990/102) |
| | | 6 Apr 1990 (otherwise) (SI 1990/102) |
| | para 9 | 6 Apr 1990 (SI 1990/102) |
| | para 10 | 1 Feb 1990 (for purposes of regulations expressed to come into force on 6 Apr 1990) (SI 1990/102) |
| | | 6 Apr 1990 (otherwise) (SI 1990/102) |
| | para 11(1) | 6 Apr 1990 (SI 1990/102) |
| | para 11(2) | 1 Feb 1990 (for purposes of regulations expressed to come into force on 6 Apr 1990) (SI 1990/102) |
| | | 6 Apr 1990 (otherwise) (SI 1990/102) |
| | para 11(3) | 6 Apr 1990 (SI 1990/102) |
| | para 11(4) | 1 Oct 1989 (SI 1989/1238) |
| | paras 12, 13 | 21 Jul 1989 (RA) |
| | paras 14, 15 | 6 Apr 1990 (SI 1990/102) |
| | para 16 | 1 Mar 1990 (SI 1990/102) |
| | paras 17–19 | 6 Apr 1990 (SI 1990/102) |
| Sch 4 | para 1 | 18 Jan 1990 (SI 1990/102) |
| | para 2 | 3 Sep 1990 (SI 1990/102) |
| | para 3 | 9 Jul 1990 (SI 1990/102) |
| | para 4 | 18 Jan 1990 (for purposes of regulations expressed to come into force on or after 2 Apr 1990) (SI 1990/102) |
| | | 3 Sep 1990 (otherwise) (SI 1990/102) |

**Social Security Act 1989 (c 24)**—*contd*

| | | |
|---|---|---|
| | paras 5–10 | 3 Sep 1990 (SI 1990/102) |
| | para 11 | 18 Jan 1990 (for purposes of regulations expressed to come into force on or after 2 Apr 1990) (SI 1990/102) |
| | | 3 Sep 1990 (otherwise) (SI 1990/102) |
| | para 12 | 3 Sep 1990 (SI 1990/102) |
| | para 13 | 18 Jan 1990 (for purposes of regulations expressed to come into force on or after 2 Apr 1990) (SI 1990/102) |
| | | 2 Apr 1990 (otherwise) (SI 1990/102) |
| | para 14 | 9 Jul 1990 (SI 1990/102) |
| | para 15(1)(a)(i) | 25 Jan 1990 (for purposes of making regulations expressed to come into force on 9 Jul 1990) (SI 1990/312) |
| | | *Never in force* (otherwise) (repealed) |
| | para 15(1)(a)(ii) | *Never in force* (repealed) |
| | para 15(1)(b) | 25 Jan 1990 (for purposes of making regulations expressed to come into force on 9 Jul 1990) (SI 1990/312) |
| | | *Never in force* (otherwise) (repealed) |
| | para 15(1)(c) | 3 Sep 1990 (SI 1990/102) |
| | para 15(2)–(5) | 3 Sep 1990 (SI 1990/102) |
| | para 16 | 9 Jul 1990 (SI 1990/102) |
| | para 17(1)–(3) | 3 Sep 1990 (SI 1990/102) |
| | para 17(4)(a) | 18 Jan 1990 (for purposes of regulations expressed to come into force on or after 2 Apr 1990) (SI 1990/102) |
| | | 3 Sep 1990 (otherwise) (SI 1990/102) |
| | para 17(4)(b) | 18 Jan 1990 (for purposes of regulations expressed to come into force on or after 2 Apr 1990) (SI 1990/102) |
| | | 9 Jul 1990 (otherwise) (SI 1990/102) |
| | para 17(5)–(9) | 3 Sep 1990 (SI 1990/102) |
| | para 17(10) | 18 Jan 1990 (for purposes of regulations expressed to come into force on or after 2 Apr 1990) (SI 1990/102) |
| | | 3 Sep 1990 (otherwise) (SI 1990/102) |
| | para 17(11) | 3 Sep 1990 (SI 1990/102) |
| | paras 18–20 | 3 Sep 1990 (SI 1990/102) |
| | para 21(1) | 3 Sep 1990 (SI 1990/102) |
| | para 21(2) | 18 Jan 1990 (for purposes of regulations expressed to come into force on or after 2 Apr 1990) (SI 1990/102) |
| | | 9 Jul 1990 (otherwise) (SI 1990/312) |
| | paras 22, 23 | 3 Sep 1990 (SI 1990/102) |
| Sch 5 | para 1 | 23 Jun 1994 (for purpose of giving effect to paras 5, 6 so far as brought into force by SI 1994/1661) (SI 1994/1661) |
| | | *Not yet in force* (for purpose of giving effect to paras 5(2)(b), (c), 6(3)(b), (c)) |
| | para 2(1), (2) | 23 Jun 1994 (for purpose of giving effect to paras 5, 6 so far as brought into force by SI 1994/1661) (SI 1994/1661) |
| | | *Not yet in force* (for purpose of giving effect to paras 5(2)(b), (c), 6(3)(b), (c)) |
| | para 2(3) | *Not yet in force* |
| | para 2(4)(a)(i) | *Never in force* (repealed) |
| | para 2(4)(a)(ii), (b) | *Not yet in force* |
| | para 2(4)(c) | 23 Jun 1994 (for purpose of giving effect to paras 5, 6 so far as brought into force by SI 1994/1661) (SI 1994/1661) |
| | | *Not yet in force* (for purpose of giving effect to paras 5(2)(b), (c), 6(3)(b), (c)) |
| | para 2(4)(d)–(g) | *Not yet in force* |
| | para 2(5) | 23 Jun 1994 (for purpose of giving effect to paras 5, 6 so far as brought into force by SI 1994/1661) (SI 1994/1661) |
| | | *Not yet in force* (for purpose of giving effect to paras 5(2)(b), (c), 6(3)(b), (c)) |
| | para 2(6)–(8) | *Not yet in force* |
| | para 2(9) | 23 Jun 1994 (for purpose of giving effect to paras 5, 6 so far as brought into force by SI 1994/1661) (SI 1994/1661) |

**Social Security Act 1989 (c 24)**—*contd*

| | | |
|---|---|---|
| | | *Not yet in force* (for purpose of giving effect to paras 5(2)(b), (c), 6(3)(b), (c)) |
| | para 3(1) | 23 Jun 1994 (for purpose of giving effect to paras 5, 6 so far as brought into force by SI 1994/1661) (SI 1994/1661) |
| | | 24 Aug 2007 (for the purpose of giving effect to paras 5A, 5B) (SI 2007/2445) |
| | | *Not yet in force* (for purpose of giving effect to paras 5(2)(b), (c), 6(3)(b), (c)) |
| | para 3(2) | *Not yet in force* |
| | para 3(3), (4) | 23 Jun 1994 (for purpose of giving effect to paras 5, 6 so far as brought into force by SI 1994/1661) (SI 1994/1661) |
| | | 24 Aug 2007 (for the purpose of giving effect to paras 5A, 5B) (SI 2007/2445) |
| | | *Not yet in force* (for purpose of giving effect to paras 5(2)(b), (c), 6(3)(b), (c)) |
| | para 4 | *Never in force* (repealed) |
| | para 5(1) | 23 Jun 1994 (SI 1994/1661) |
| | para 5(2)(a) | 23 Jun 1994 (SI 1994/1661) |
| | para 5(2)(b), (c) | *Never in force* (repealed) |
| | para 5(3) | 23 Jun 1994 (SI 1994/1661) |
| | para 6(1), (2) | 23 Jun 1994 (SI 1994/1661) |
| | para 6(3)(a) | 23 Jun 1994 (SI 1994/1661) |
| | para 6(3)(b), (c) | *Not yet in force* |
| | para 6(4) | 23 Jun 1994 (SI 1994/1661) |
| | para 7(a)–(c) | 23 Jun 1994 (for purpose of giving effect to paras 5, 6 so far as brought into force by SI 1994/1661) (SI 1994/1661) |
| | | *Not yet in force* (for purpose of giving effect to paras 5(2)(b), (c), 6(3)(b), (c)) |
| | para 7(d) | *Not yet in force* |
| | para 7(e) | 23 Jun 1994 (for purpose of giving effect to paras 5, 6 so far as brought into force by SI 1994/1661) (SI 1994/1661) |
| | | *Not yet in force* (for purpose of giving effect to paras 5(2)(b), (c), 6(3)(b), (c)) |
| | para 8 | *Not yet in force* |
| | paras 9, 10 | 23 Jun 1994 (for purpose of giving effect to paras 5, 6 so far as brought into force by SI 1994/1661) (SI 1994/1661) |
| | | *Not yet in force* (for purpose of giving effect to paras 5(2)(b), (c), 6(3)(b), (c)) |
| | para 11 | *Never in force* (repealed) |
| | para 12 | *Not yet in force* |
| | paras 13–15 | *Never in force* (repealed) |
| Sch 6 | paras 1–5 | 1 Oct 1989 (SI 1989/1238) |
| | paras 6–8 | 21 Jul 1989 (RA) |
| | paras 9–13 | 1 Oct 1989 (SI 1989/1238) |
| | para 14 | 21 Jul 1989 (RA) |
| | para 15 | 1 Oct 1989 (SI 1989/1238) |
| | paras 16–21 | 21 Jul 1989 (RA) |
| Sch 7 | para 1 | 1 Oct 1989 (SI 1989/1238) |
| | paras 2–7 | 21 Jul 1989 (RA) |
| | paras 8–10 | 1 Oct 1989 (SI 1989/1238) |
| | para 11 | *Never in force* (repealed) |
| | para 12 | 1 Oct 1989 (SI 1989/1238) |
| | para 13 | 21 Jul 1989 (RA) |
| | para 14 | 1 Oct 1989 (SI 1989/1238) |
| | para 15 | 21 Jul 1989 (RA) |
| | para 16 | 1 Oct 1989 (SI 1989/1238) |
| | para 17 | 6 Apr 1990 (SI 1990/102) |
| | paras 18–28 | 1 Oct 1989 (SI 1989/1238) |
| Sch 8 | para 1 | 21 Jul 1989 (RA) |
| | paras 2, 3 | 9 Oct 1989 (SI 1989/1238) |

**Social Security Act 1989 (c 24)**—*contd*

| | | |
|---|---|---|
| | paras 4–6 | 21 Jul 1989 (RA) |
| | para 7 | 9 Oct 1989 (SI 1989/1238) |
| | paras 8–13 | 21 Jul 1989 (RA) |
| | paras 14, 15 | 1 Oct 1989 (SI 1989/1238) |
| | para 16 | 9 Oct 1989 (SI 1989/1238) |
| | paras 17, 18 | 21 Jul 1989 (RA) |
| | para 19 | 25 Jul 1989 (SI 1989/1262 (superseding SI 1989/1238)) |
| Sch 9 | | 21 Jul 1989 (repeals consequential on bringing into force of provisions listed in s 33(3)(a)–(f) on 21 Jul 1989) (RA) |

1 Oct 1989 (SI 1989/1238), repeals of or in—
Social Security Act 1973, s 51(7);
Social Security Act 1975, ss 14(6), 15(6)(a), 27(3)–(5), 28(1)(a), 29(5)(a), 30(1), (3), (6)(a), 39(1)(b), 41(1), 48(2), (3), Sch 20 (in definition "week");
Social Security Pensions Act 1975, ss 8(1), 11, 45(3), Sch 4, para 39;
Social Security (Miscellaneous Provisions) Act 1977, s 21(1);
Social Security Act 1979, Sch 1, para 17;
Social Security and Housing Benefits Act 1982;
Social Security Act 1986, ss 50(1), 63(1)(a)(ii), Sch 6, para 3, Sch 10, para 96

5 Oct 1989 (SI 1989/1238), repeals of or in—
Social Security Act 1975, s 4(6F);
Social Security Contributions Act 1982, s 4(4), Sch 1, para 1(4)

9 Oct 1989 (SI 1989/1238), repeals of or in—
Merchant Shipping Act 1970, s 17(10);
Social Security Act 1975, ss 20(1A), 26(7);
Social Security Act 1986, s 26(3) and second paragraph of rubric at end of Sch 9

1 Feb 1990 (repeal of Social Security (Contributions) Act 1982, s 4(4)) (SI 1990/312)

6 Apr 1990 (repeals of or in Social Security Act 1975, ss 100(3), 101(6), (7), 112(4), (5), Sch 10, para 1(7), 2(2), Sch 11, para 4, Sch 13, paras 8, 9, Sch 20, definition "local office") (SI 1990/102)

*Never in force* (otherwise) (spent)

---

**Statute Law (Repeals) Act 1989 (c 43)**

*RA:* 16 Nov 1989

*Commencement provisions:* s 3(2); Statute Law (Repeals) Act 1989 (Commencement) Order 1992, SI 1992/1275

| | |
|---|---|
| 1–3 | 16 Nov 1989 (RA) |
| Sch 1 | 16 Nov 1989 (except repeal of Federation of Malaya Independence Act 1957, s 3; Malaysia Act 1963, s 5) (RA) |
| | 1 Jun 1992 (exceptions noted above) (SI 1992/1275) |
| Sch 2 | 16 Nov 1989 (RA) |

---

**Transport (Scotland) Act 1989 (c 23)**

*RA:* 21 Jul 1989

*Commencement provisions:* s 12(2)

| | |
|---|---|
| 1–17 | 21 Sep 1989 (s 12(2)) |
| 18 | 21 Jul 1989 (s 12(2)) |

---

## Water Act 1989 (c 15)

*RA:* 6 Jul 1989

*Commencement provisions:* s 194(2)–(5); Water Act 1989 (Commencement No 1) Order 1989, SI 1989/1146; Water Authorities (Transfer of Functions) (Appointed Day) Order 1989, SI 1989/1530; Water Act 1989 (Commencement No 2 and Transitional Provisions) Order 1989, SI 1989/1557; Water Act 1989 (Commencement No 3) (Scotland) Order 1989, SI 1989/1561; Water Act 1989 (Commencement No 4) Order 1989, SI 1989/2278

| | | |
|---|---|---|
| 1 | (1)–(5) | 7 Jul 1989 (SI 1989/1146) |
| | (6) | See Sch 1 below |
| 2, 3 | | 7 Jul 1989 (SI 1989/1146) |
| 4 | | 6 Jul 1989 (so far as relating to the making of subordinate legislation) (s 194(2)) |
| | | 7 Jul 1989 (E) (W) (otherwise) (SI 1989/1146) |
| | | 1 Sep 1989 (NI) (otherwise) (SI 1989/1557) |
| | | 1 Sep 1989 (S) (otherwise) (SI 1989/1561) |
| 5 | (1)–(4) | 7 Jul 1989 (SI 1989/1146) |
| | (5) | See Sch 3 below |
| 6 | | 1 Sep 1989 (SI 1989/1146; SI 1989/1530; SI 1989/1561) |
| 7 | | 7 Jul 1989 (SI 1989/1146) |
| 8, 9 | | 1 Sep 1989 (SI 1989/1146; SI 1989/1530) |
| 10 | | 6 Jul 1989 (so far as relating to the making of subordinate legislation) (s 194(2)) |
| | | 1 Sep 1989 (SI 1989/1146; SI 1989/1530) |
| 11 | (1)–(8) | 7 Jul 1989 (SI 1989/1146) |
| | (9) | 7 Jul 1989 (E) (W) (SI 1989/1146) |
| | | 1 Sep 1989 (NI) (SI 1989/1557) |
| 12 | | 6 Jul 1989 (so far as relating to the making of subordinate legislation) (s 194(2)) |
| | | *Never in force* (otherwise) (repealed) |
| 13 | | 6 Jul 1989 (so far as relating to the making of subordinate legislation) (s 194(2)) |
| | | 1 Sep 1989 (S) (so far as relates to schemes under Sch 5) (SI 1989/1561) |
| | | *Never in force* (otherwise) (repealed) |
| 14 | | 6 Jul 1989 (so far as relating to the making of subordinate legislation) (s 194(2)) |
| | | 7 Jul 1989 (E) (W) (otherwise) (SI 1989/1146) |
| | | *Never in force* (otherwise) (repealed) |
| 15–28 | | 6 Jul 1989 (so far as relating to the making of subordinate legislation) (s 194(2)) |
| | | 1 Sep 1989 (otherwise) (s 194(3)) |
| 29–31 | | *Never in force* (repealed) |
| 32 | | 6 Jul 1989 (so far as relating to the making of subordinate legislation) (s 194(2)) |
| | | 7 Jul 1989 (E) (W) (otherwise) (SI 1989/1146) |
| 33–36 | | *Never in force* (repealed) |
| 37–78 | | 6 Jul 1989 (so far as relating to the making of subordinate legislation) (s 194(2)) |
| | | 1 Sep 1989 (otherwise) (s 194(3)) |
| 79 | (1) | 1 Sep 1989 (SI 1989/1146; SI 1989/1530) |
| | (2) | 1 Apr 1990 (SI 1989/1146) |
| | (3)–(6) | 1 Sep 1989 (SI 1989/1146; SI 1989/1530) |
| 80, 81 | | 1 Sep 1989 (s 194(3)) |
| 82, 83 | | 6 Jul 1989 (so far as relating to the making of subordinate legislation) (s 194(2)) |
| | | 1 Sep 1989 (otherwise) (s 194(3)) |
| 84 | | 1 Sep 1989 (s 194(3)) |
| 85, 86 | | 6 Jul 1989 (so far as relating to the making of subordinate legislation) (s 194(2)) |

**Water Act 1989 (c 15)**—*contd*

| | | |
|---|---|---|
| | | 1 Sep 1989 (otherwise) (s 194(3)) |
| 87, 88 | | 1 Sep 1989 (s 194(3)) |
| 89 | | 6 Jul 1989 (so far as relating to the making of subordinate legislation) (s 194(2)) |
| | | 1 Sep 1989 (otherwise) (s 194(3)) |
| 90, 91 | | 1 Sep 1989 (s 194(3)) |
| 92 | | 6 Jul 1989 (so far as relating to the making of subordinate legislation) (s 194(2)) |
| | | 1 Sep 1989 (otherwise) (s 194(3)) |
| 93, 94 | | 1 Sep 1989 (s 194(3)) |
| 95 | | 6 Jul 1989 (so far as relating to the making of subordinate legislation) (s 194(2)) |
| | | 1 Sep 1989 (otherwise) (s 194(3)) |
| 96, 97 | | 1 Sep 1989 (s 194(3)) |
| 98 | (1) | 1 Sep 1989 (SI 1989/1557) |
| | (2)(a), (b) | 1 Sep 1989 (SI 1989/1557) |
| | (2)(c) | 1 Apr 1990 (SI 1989/2278) |
| | (3)–(7) | 1 Apr 1990 (SI 1989/2278) |
| | (8)–(10) | 1 Sep 1989 (SI 1989/1557) |
| 99, 100 | | 1 Sep 1989 (SI 1989/1557) |
| 101–132 | | 6 Jul 1989 (so far as relating to the making of subordinate legislation) (s 194(2)) |
| | | 1 Sep 1989 (otherwise) (s 194(3)) |
| 133–136 | | 1 Sep 1989 (s 194(3)) |
| 137, 138 | | 6 Jul 1989 (so far as relating to the making of subordinate legislation) (s 194(2)) |
| | | 1 Sep 1989 (otherwise) (s 194(3)) |
| 139, 140 | | 1 Sep 1989 (s 194(3)) |
| 141 | (1)–(4) | 1 Sep 1989 (s 194(3)) |
| | (5) | See Sch 17 below |
| | (6), (7) | 1 Sep 1989 (s 194(3)) |
| 142–154 | | 1 Sep 1989 (s 194(3)) |
| 155 | | 6 Jul 1989 (so far as relating to the making of subordinate legislation) (s 194(2)) |
| | | 1 Sep 1989 (otherwise) (s 194(3)) |
| 156 | | 1 Sep 1989 (s 194(3)) |
| 157, 158 | | 6 Jul 1989 (so far as relating to the making of subordinate legislation) (s 194(2)) |
| | | 1 Sep 1989 (otherwise) (s 194(3)) |
| 159–161 | | 1 Sep 1989 (s 194(3)) |
| 162 | | 6 Jul 1989 (so far as relating to the making of subordinate legislation) (s 194(2)) |
| | | 1 Sep 1989 (otherwise) (s 194(3)) |
| 163–167 | | 1 Sep 1989 (s 194(3)) |
| 168 | | See Sch 22 below |
| 169 | | See Sch 23 below |
| 170 | | 1 Sep 1989 (SI 1989/1146; SI 1989/1530) |
| 171 | | 6 Jul 1989 (s 194(2)) |
| 172 | | 7 Jul 1989 (E) (W) (SI 1989/1146) |
| | | 1 Sep 1989 (S) (SI 1989/1561) |
| 173 | | 6 Jul 1989 (so far as relating to the making of subordinate legislation) (s 194(2)) |
| | | 1 Sep 1989 (otherwise) (SI 1989/1146; SI 1989/1530) |
| 174 | | 6 Jul 1989 (so far as relating to the making of subordinate legislation) (s 194(2)) |
| | | 7 Jul 1989 (otherwise) (SI 1989/1146) |
| 175, 176 | | 1 Sep 1989 (SI 1989/1146; SI 1989/1530) |
| 177 | | 7 Jul 1989 (SI 1989/1146) |
| 178–184 | | 1 Sep 1989 (SI 1989/1146; SI 1989/1530) |

**Water Act 1989 (c 15)**—*contd*

| | | |
|---|---|---|
| 185 | | 6 Jul 1989 (s 194(2)) |
| 186 | | See Sch 24 below |
| 187 | | 7 Jul 1989 (SI 1989/1146) |
| 188 | | 1 Sep 1989 (SI 1989/1146; SI 1989/1530) |
| 189 | | 6 Jul 1989 (so far as relating to the making of subordinate legislation) (s 194(2)) |
| | | 7 Jul 1989 (otherwise) (SI 1989/1146) |
| 190 | | See Schs 25–27 below (6 Jul 1989 (so far as relating to the making of subordinate legislation)) (s 194(2)) |
| 191 | (1)–(5) | 6 Jul 1989 (s 194(2)) |
| | (6) | 7 Jul 1989 (SI 1989/1146) |
| 192 | | 7 Jul 1989 (SI 1989/1146) |
| 193 | | 6 Jul 1989 (so far as relating to the making of subordinate legislation) (s 194(2)) |
| | | 7 Jul 1989 (otherwise) (SI 1989/1146) |
| 194 | | 6 Jul 1989 (s 194(2)) |
| Sch 1 | paras 1–10 | 7 Jul 1989 (SI 1989/1146) |
| | para 11 | 7 Jul 1989 (E) (W) (SI 1989/1146) |
| | | 1 Sep 1989 (NI) (SI 1989/1557) |
| | | 1 Sep 1989 (S) (SI 1989/1561) |
| | para 12 | 7 Jul 1989 (SI 1989/1146) |
| | para 13 | 7 Jul 1989 (E) (W) (SI 1989/1146) |
| | | 1 Sep 1989 (NI) (SI 1989/1557) |
| | | 1 Sep 1989 (S) (SI 1989/1561) |
| | paras 14–23 | 6 Jul 1989 (so far as relating to the making of subordinate legislation) (see para 18) (s 194(2)) |
| | | 7 Jul 1989 (otherwise) (SI 1989/1146) |
| Sch 2 | | 6 Jul 1989 (so far as relating to the making of subordinate legislation) (s 194(2)) |
| | | 7 Jul 1989 (otherwise) (E) (W) (SI 1989/1146) |
| | | 1 Sep 1989 (otherwise) (NI) (SI 1989/1557) |
| | | 1 Sep 1989 (otherwise) (S) (SI 1989/1561) |
| Sch 3 | paras 1–5 | 7 Jul 1989 (SI 1989/1146) |
| | paras 6, 7 | 7 Jul 1989 (E) (W) (SI 1989/1146) |
| | | 1 Sep 1989 (NI) (SI 1989/1557) |
| | | 1 Sep 1989 (S) (SI 1989/1561) |
| Sch 4 | | 1 Sep 1989 (SI 1989/1146; SI 1989/1530; SI 1989/1557; SI 1989/1561) |
| Sch 5 | | 6 Jul 1989 (so far as relating to the making of subordinate legislation) (s 194(2)) |
| | | 1 Sep 1989 (otherwise) (s 194(3)) |
| Sch 6 | | 1 Sep 1989 (s 194(3)) |
| Sch 7 | | 6 Jul 1989 (s 194(2)) |
| Schs 8–10 | | 1 Sep 1989 (s 194(3)) |
| Sch 11 | | 6 Jul 1989 (s 194(2)) |
| Sch 12 | | 6 Jul 1989 (so far as relating to the making of subordinate legislation) (s 194(2)) |
| | | 1 Sep 1989 (otherwise) (s 194(3)) |
| Sch 13 | | 1 Sep 1989 (s 194(3)) |
| Sch 14 | | 6 Jul 1989 (s 194(2)) |
| Sch 15 | | 1 Sep 1989 (s 194(3)) |
| Sch 16 | | 6 Jul 1989 (s 194(2)) |
| Sch 17 | para 1 | 1 Sep 1989 (s 194(3)) |
| | para 2 | 6 Jul 1989 (s 194(2)) |
| | para 3 | 1 Sep 1989 (s 194(3)) |
| | para 4 | *Never in force* (repealed) |
| | paras 5–9 | 1 Sep 1989 (s 194(3)) |
| Sch 18 | | 1 Sep 1989 (s 194(3)) |

**Water Act 1989 (c 15)**—*contd*

| | | |
|---|---|---|
| Sch 19 | | 6 Jul 1989 (so far as relating to the making of subordinate legislation) (s 194(2)) |
| | | 1 Sep 1989 (otherwise) (s 194(3)) |
| Sch 20 | | 6 Jul 1989 (s 194(2)) |
| Schs 21, 22 | | 1 Sep 1989 (s 194(3)) |
| Sch 23 | | 1 Sep 1989 (except so far as relates to Control of Pollution Act 1974, s 33) (S) (s 194(3)) |
| | | 31 May 1991 (exception noted above) (S) (SI 1991/1172) |
| Sch 24 | | 6 Jul 1989 (so far as relating to the making of subordinate legislation) (s 194(2)) |
| | | 1 Sep 1989 (otherwise) (s 194(3)) |
| Sch 25 | | 1 Sep 1989 (for transitional provisions, see SI 1989/1557, art 6) (SI 1989/1146; SI 1989/1530; SI 1989/1557; SI 1989/1561) |
| Sch 26 | | 6 Jul 1989 (so far as relating to the making of subordinate legislation) (s 194(2)) |
| | | 1 Sep 1989 (otherwise) (s 194(3)) |
| Sch 27 | Pt I | 1 Sep 1989 (s 194(3)) |
| | Pt II | 1 Sep 1989 (SI 1989/1557; note savings therein), repeals of or in— |
| | | Water Act 1945, s 41(7), Sch 3, ss 75–77; |
| | | Rating and Valuation (Miscellaneous Provisions) Act 1955, s 11; |
| | | Trustee Investments Act 1961, Sch 4, para 3; |
| | | Water Act 1973, ss 34(1), (3), 35(1), (2), Sch 6, Pt I, Sch 8, para 50 |
| | | 1 Apr 1990 (repeals of or in Water Act 1945, s 59(3), Sch 3, ss 74, 81) (SI 1989/1557) |
| | | *Not yet in force,* repeals of or in— |
| | | Water Act 1973, ss 34(2), 35(3), 36(1), (2), Sch 6, Pt II; |
| | | Control of Pollution Act 1974; |
| | | House of Commons Disqualification Act 1975; |
| | | Water Act 1983; |
| | | Public Utility Transfers and Water Charges Act 1988 |

# 1990 Acts

## Access to Health Records Act 1990 (c 23)

*RA:* 13 Jul 1990

*Commencement provisions:* s 12(2)

Whole Act in force 1 Nov 1991 (s 12(2))

---

## Agricultural Holdings (Amendment) Act 1990 (c 15)

*RA:* 29 Jun 1990

*Commencement provisions:* s 3(2)

Whole Act in force 29 Jul 1990 (s 3(2))

---

## Appropriation Act 1990 (c 28)

*RA:* 26 Jul 1990

Whole Act in force 26 Jul 1990 (RA)

---

## Australian Constitution (Public Record Copy) Act 1990 (c 17)

*RA:* 29 Jul 1990

Whole Act in force 29 Jul 1990 (RA)

---

## Aviation and Maritime Security Act 1990 (c 31)

*RA:* 26 Jul 1990

*Commencement provisions:* s 54(2)

| | | |
|---|---|---|
| 1 | | 26 Sep 1990 (s 54(2)) |
| 2–4 | | 26 Jul 1990 (RA) |
| 5 | | 26 Sep 1990 (s 54(2)) |
| 6, 7 | | 26 Jul 1990 (RA) |
| 8 | | See Sch 1 below |
| 9–17 | | 26 Sep 1990 (s 54(2)) |
| 18–36 | | 26 Jul 1990 (RA) |
| 37–40 | | 26 Sep 1990 (s 54(2)) |
| 41–44 | | 26 Jul 1990 (RA) |
| 45 | | See Sch 2 below |
| 46–52 | | 26 Jul 1990 (RA) |
| 53 | (1) | See Sch 3 below |
| | (2) | See Sch 4 below |
| 54 | | 26 Jul 1990 (RA) |

**Aviation and Maritime Security Act 1990 (c 31)**—*contd*

| Sch 1 | para 1 | 26 Sep 1990 (s 54(2)) |
|---|---|---|
| | para 2(1)–(5) | 26 Jul 1990 (RA) |
| | para 2(6) | 26 Sep 1990 (s 54(2)) |
| | para 2(7) | 26 Jul 1990 (RA) |
| | para 3 | 26 Jul 1990 (RA) |
| | paras 4–6 | 26 Sep 1990 (s 54(2)) |
| | paras 7–10 | 26 Jul 1990 (RA) |
| | para 11(1)–(4) | 26 Jul 1990 (RA) |
| | para 11(5) | 26 Sep 1990 (s 54(2)) |
| Sch 2 | | 26 Jul 1990 (RA) |
| Sch 3 | | 26 Sep 1990 (s 54(2)) |
| Sch 4 | | 26 Jul 1990 (RA), except repeals of or in— |
| | | Criminal Jurisdiction Act 1975; |
| | | Aviation Security Act 1982, ss 11(5)(a), 14(7)(a), 20(5); |
| | | Extradition Act 1989 |
| | | 26 Sep 1990 (exception noted above) (s 54(2)) |

**British Nationality (Hong Kong) Act 1990 (c 34)**

*RA:* 26 Jul 1990

*Commencement provisions:* s 6(4); British Nationality (Hong Kong) Act 1990 (Commencement) Order 1990, SI 1990/2210

| 1 | (1) | See Sch 1 below |
|---|---|---|
| | (2), (3) | 7 Nov 1990 (SI 1990/2210) |
| | (4) | See Sch 2 below |
| | (5) | 7 Nov 1990 (SI 1990/2210) |
| 2 | (1) | 7 Nov 1990 (SI 1990/2210) |
| | (2) | *Not yet in force* |
| | (3) | 7 Nov 1990 (SI 1990/2210) |
| 3–6 | | 7 Nov 1990 (SI 1990/2210) |
| Schs 1, 2 | | 7 Nov 1990 (SI 1990/2210) |

**Broadcasting Act 1990 (c 42)**

*RA:* 1 Nov 1990

*Commencement provisions:* s 204(2); Broadcasting Act 1990 (Commencement No 1 and Transitional Provisions) Order 1990, SI 1990/2347

| 1 | (1), (2) | 1 Dec 1990 (SI 1990/2347) |
|---|---|---|
| | (3) | See Sch 1 below |
| 2 | (1) | 1 Jan 1991 (SI 1990/2347) |
| | (2)–(6) | 1 Dec 1990 (SI 1990/2347) |
| 3–9 | | 1 Dec 1990 (SI 1990/2347) |
| 10 | | 1 Jan 1991 (SI 1990/2347) |
| 11 | | 1 Dec 1990 (SI 1990/2347) |
| 12–22 | | 1 Jan 1991 (SI 1990/2347) |
| 23 | (1)–(5) | 1 Jan 1993 (SI 1990/2347) |
| | (6) | See Sch 3 below |
| 24, 25 | | 1 Jan 1993 (SI 1990/2347) |
| 26 | | 1 Jan 1991 (SI 1990/2347) |
| 27 | | 1 Jan 1993 (SI 1990/2347) |
| 28–33 | | 1 Jan 1991 (SI 1990/2347) |
| 34, 35 | | 1 Jan 1991 (for purposes of enabling conditions of type specified in ss 34(2), 35(1) to be included in a Channel 3 or Channel 5 licence or a licence to provide Channel 4) (SI 1990/2347) |
| | | 1 Jan 1993 (otherwise) (SI 1990/2347) |
| 36–42 | | 1 Jan 1991 (SI 1990/2347) |

**Broadcasting Act 1990 (c 42)**—*contd*

| | | |
|---|---|---|
| 43 | | 1 Dec 1990 (SI 1990/2347) |
| 44 | | 1 Jan 1991 (SI 1990/2347) |
| 45–47 | | 1 Dec 1990 (SI 1990/2347) |
| 48–55 | | 1 Jan 1991 (SI 1990/2347) |
| 56 | (1), (2) | 1 Jan 1991 (SI 1990/2347) |
| | (3) | See Sch 6 below |
| 57–70 | | 1 Jan 1991 (SI 1990/2347) |
| 71 | | 1 Dec 1990 (SI 1990/2347) |
| 72–82 | | 1 Jan 1991 (SI 1990/2347) |
| 83 | (1), (2) | 1 Dec 1990 (SI 1990/2347) |
| | (3) | See Sch 8 below |
| 84–125 | | 1 Jan 1991 (SI 1990/2347) |
| 126, 127 | | 1 Dec 1990 (SI 1990/2347) |
| 128, 129 | | 1 Jan 1991 (SI 1990/2347) |
| 130–133 | | 1 Dec 1990 (SI 1990/2347) |
| 134–140 | | 1 Jan 1991 (SI 1990/2347) |
| 141 | | 1 Dec 1990 (SI 1990/2347) |
| 142 | (1)–(3) | 1 Jan 1991 (SI 1990/2347) |
| | (4) | See Sch 13 below |
| 143–150 | | 1 Jan 1991 (SI 1990/2347) |
| 151 | (1), (2) | 1 Jan 1991 (SI 1990/2347) |
| | (3) | See Sch 14 below |
| 152–161 | | 1 Jan 1991 (SI 1990/2347) |
| 162 | (1) | 1 Jan 1991 (SI 1990/2347) |
| | (2) | See Sch 15 below |
| 163–170 | | 1 Jan 1991 (SI 1990/2347) |
| 171 | | See Sch 16 below |
| 172–174 | | 1 Jan 1991 (SI 1990/2347) |
| 175 | | 1 Feb 1991 (SI 1990/2347) |
| 176 | | See Sch 17 below |
| 177–179 | | 1 Jan 1991 (SI 1990/2347) |
| 180 | | See Sch 18 below |
| 181, 182 | | 1 Jan 1991 (SI 1990/2347) |
| 183 | | See Sch 19 below |
| 184 | | 1 Jan 1991 (SI 1990/2347) |
| 185 | | 1 Jan 1991 (for purposes of enabling conditions of type specified in s 185(3) to be included in a Channel 3 or Channel 5 licence or a licence to provide Channel 4) (SI 1990/2347) |
| | | 1 Jan 1993 (otherwise) (SI 1990/2347) |
| 186 | | 1 Jan 1991 (SI 1990/2347) |
| 187 | | 1 Jan 1993 (SI 1990/2347) |
| 188–197 | | 1 Jan 1991 (SI 1990/2347) |
| 198–202 | | 1 Dec 1990 (SI 1990/2347) |
| 203 | (1) | See Sch 20 below |
| | (2) | 1 Jan 1991 (SI 1990/2347) |
| | (3) | See Sch 21 below |
| | (4) | See Sch 22 below |
| 204 | | 1 Dec 1990 (SI 1990/2347) |
| Schs 1, 2 | | 1 Dec 1990 (SI 1990/2347) |
| Sch 3 | | 1 Jan 1993 (SI 1990/2347) |
| Schs 4–7 | | 1 Jan 1991 (SI 1990/2347) |
| Schs 8, 9 | | 1 Dec 1990 (SI 1990/2347) |
| Schs 10–16 | | 1 Jan 1991 (SI 1990/2347) |
| Sch 17 | | 1 Jan 1991 (for purposes of enabling publication of information about programmes to be included in a programme service on or after that date) (SI 1990/2347) |
| | | 1 Mar 1991 (otherwise) (SI 1990/2347) |
| Sch 18 | | 1 Apr 1991 (SI 1990/2347) |
| Sch 19 | | 1 Jan 1991 (SI 1990/2347) |

**Broadcasting Act 1990 (c 42)**—*contd*

| | | |
|---|---|---|
| Sch 20 | paras 1–35 | 1 Jan 1991 (SI 1990/2347) |
| | para 36 | 1 Jan 1991 (except so far as replaces reference to Independent Broadcasting Authority until that Authority is dissolved by order under s 127(3)) (SI 1990/2347) |
| | | 2 Oct 2003 (exception noted above) (the date on which that Authority was dissolved by SI 2003/2554) |
| | para 37 | 1 Jan 1993 (SI 1990/2347) |
| | paras 38–54 | 1 Jan 1991 (SI 1990/2347) |
| Sch 21 | | 1 Dec 1990 (repeal of or in Cable and Broadcasting Act 1984, s 8(1)(a), (b)) (SI 1990/2347) |
| | | 1 Jan 1991 (SI 1990/2347), all remaining repeals except repeals of or in— |
| | | Wireless Telegraphy (Blind Persons) Act 1955; |
| | | Wireless Telegraphy Act 1967; |
| | | House of Commons Disqualification Act 1975, Sch 1, Pt II (entries for Cable Authority and Independent Broadcasting Authority); |
| | | Northern Ireland Assembly Disqualification Act 1975, Sch 1, Pt II (subject to transitional provisions; see SI 1990/2347, art 3(3)) |
| | | 1 Apr 1991 (SI 1990/2347), repeals of or in— |
| | | Wireless Telegraphy (Blind Persons) Act 1955; |
| | | Wireless Telegraphy Act 1967 |
| | | *Not yet in force,* repeals of or in— |
| | | House of Commons Disqualification Act 1975, Sch 1, Pt II (entries for Cable Authority and Independent Broadcasting Authority); |
| | | Northern Ireland Assembly Disqualification Act 1975, Sch 1, Pt II |
| Sch 22 | paras 1–3 | 1 Dec 1990 (SI 1990/2347) |
| | paras 4–7 | 1 Jan 1991 (SI 1990/2347) |

---

**Caldey Island Act 1990 (c 44)**

*RA:* 1 Nov 1990

Whole Act in force 1 Nov 1990 (RA)

---

**Capital Allowances Act 1990 (c 1)**

*RA:* 19 Mar 1990

*Commencement provisions:* s 164

This Act (which was a consolidation) had effect, generally, as respects allowances and charges falling to be made for chargeable periods ending after 5 Apr 1990 and applied in relation to expenditure incurred in chargeable periods ending before 6 Apr 1990

---

**Care of Cathedrals Measure 1990 (No 2)**

*RA:* 26 Jul 1990

*Commencement provisions:* s 21(2)

The provisions of this Measure were brought into force on the following dates by an instrument made by the Archbishops of Canterbury and York and dated 28 Sep 1990 (made under s 21(2))

| | |
|---|---|
| 1–12 | 1 Mar 1991 |
| 13 | 1 Oct 1990 |
| 14, 15 | 1 Mar 1991 |

**Care of Cathedrals Measure 1990 (No 2)**—*contd*

| | |
|---|---|
| 16–21 | 1 Oct 1990 |
| Schs 1, 2 | 1 Mar 1991 |

---

**Civil Aviation Authority (Borrowing Powers) Act 1990 (c 2)**

*RA:* 19 Mar 1990

Whole Act in force 19 Mar 1990 (RA)

---

**Clergy (Ordination) Measure 1990 (No 1)**

*RA:* 22 Feb 1990

Whole Measure in force 22 Feb 1990 (RA)

---

**Coal Industry Act 1990 (c 3)**

*RA:* 19 Mar 1990

*Commencement provisions:* s 6(2)

| | |
|---|---|
| 1–3 | 19 Mar 1990 (RA) |
| 4 | 19 May 1990 (s 6(2)) |
| 5, 6 | 19 Mar 1990 (RA) |

---

**Computer Misuse Act 1990 (c 18)**

*RA:* 26 Jun 1990

*Commencement provisions:* s 18(2)

Whole Act in force 29 Aug 1990 (s 18(2))

---

**Consolidated Fund Act 1990 (c 4)**

*RA:* 28 Mar 1990

Whole Act in force 28 Mar 1990 (RA)

---

**Consolidated Fund (No 2) Act 1990 (c 46)**

*RA:* 20 Dec 1990

Whole Act in force 20 Dec 1990 (RA)

---

**Contracts (Applicable Law) Act 1990 (c 36)**

*RA:* 26 Jul 1990

*Commencement provisions:* s 7; Contracts (Applicable Law) Act 1990 (Commencement No 1) Order 1991, SI 1991/707; Contracts (Applicable Law) Act 1990 (Commencement No 2) Order 2004, SI 2004/3448

| | | |
|---|---|---|
| 1 | | 1 Apr 1991 (SI 1991/707) |
| 2 | (1) | 1 Apr 1991 (so far as relates to Rome Convention and Luxembourg Convention as defined in s 1) (SI 1991/707) |
| | | 1 Mar 2005 (so far as relates to the Brussels Protocol as defined in s 1) (SI 2004/3448) |

**Contracts (Applicable Law) Act 1990 (c 36)**—*contd*

| | | |
|---|---|---|
| | (2), (3) | 1 Apr 1991 (SI 1991/707) |
| | (4) | See Schs 1–3 below |
| 3 | (1), (2) | 1 Mar 2005 (SI 2004/3448) |
| | (3)(a) | 1 Apr 1991 (SI 1991/707) |
| | (3)(b) | 1 Mar 2005 (SI 2004/3448) |
| 4 | | 1 Apr 1991 (SI 1991/707) |
| 5 | | See Sch 4 below |
| 6–9 | | 1 Apr 1991 (SI 1991/707) |
| Schs 1–4 | | 1 Apr 1991 (SI 1991/707) |

**Courts and Legal Services Act 1990 (c 41)**

*RA:* 1 Nov 1990

*Commencement provisions:* s 124; Courts and Legal Services Act 1990 (Commencement No 1) Order 1990, SI 1990/2170; Courts and Legal Services Act 1990 (Commencement No 2) Order 1990, SI 1990/2484; Courts and Legal Services Act 1990 (Commencement No 3) Order 1991, SI 1991/608; Courts and Legal Services Act 1990 (Commencement No 4) Order 1991, SI 1991/985; Courts and Legal Services Act 1990 (Commencement No 5) Order 1991, SI 1991/1364; Courts and Legal Services Act 1990 (Commencement No 6) Order 1991, SI 1991/1883; Courts and Legal Services Act 1990 (Commencement No 7) Order 1991, SI 1991/2730; Courts and Legal Services Act 1990 (Commencement No 8) Order 1992, SI 1992/1221; Courts and Legal Services Act 1990 (Commencement No 9) Order 1993, SI 1993/2132; Courts and Legal Services Act 1990 (Commencement No 10) Order 1995, SI 1995/641; Courts and Legal Services Act 1990 (Commencement No 11) Order 2004, SI 2004/2950

| | | |
|---|---|---|
| 1 | | 1 Nov 1990 (RA) |
| 2, 3 | | 1 Jul 1991 (SI 1991/1364) |
| 4 | | 1 Oct 1991 (SI 1991/1883) |
| 5 | | 1 Nov 1990 (RA) |
| 6 | | 1 Jan 1991 (s 124(2)(a)) |
| 7 | (1) | 23 Jul 1993 (except so far as relates to s 7(2)) (SI 1993/2132) |
| | | 1 Oct 1993 (exception noted above) (SI 1993/2132) |
| | (2) | 1 Oct 1993 (SI 1993/2132) |
| | (3), (4) | 23 Jul 1993 (SI 1993/2132) |
| 8 | | 1 Jan 1991 (s 124(2)(a)) |
| 9 | | 1 Jan 1991 (SI 1990/2484) |
| 10 | | 1 Jul 1991 (SI 1991/1364) |
| 11 | | 1 Jan 1991 (s 124(2)(a)) |
| 12 | | *Never in force* (repealed) |
| 13 | | *Not yet in force* |
| 14 | | *Never in force* (repealed) |
| 15 | | 1 Jul 1991 (SI 1991/1364) |
| 16 | | 1 Jan 1991 (s 124(2)(a)) |
| 17, 18 | | 1 Apr 1991 (SI 1991/608) |
| 19 | (1)–(8) | 1 Apr 1991 (SI 1991/608) |
| | (9) | See Sch 1 below |
| 20 | (1) | 1 Apr 1991 (SI 1991/608) |
| | (2) | See Sch 2 below |
| | (3) | 1 Apr 1991 (SI 1991/608) |
| 21 | (1)–(5) | 1 Jan 1991 (SI 1990/2484) |
| | (6) | See Sch 3 below |
| 22, 23 | | 1 Jan 1991 (SI 1990/2484) |
| 24 | (1), (2) | 1 Jan 1991 (SI 1990/2484) |
| | (3) | 1 Apr 1991 (SI 1991/608) |
| 25–28 | | 1 Jan 1991 (SI 1990/2484) |
| 29 | | 1 Apr 1991 (SI 1991/608) |
| 30 | (1), (2) | 1 Apr 1991 (SI 1991/608) |
| | (3) | See Sch 4, Pt III below |
| | (4)–(6) | 1 Apr 1991 (SI 1991/608) |

**Courts and Legal Services Act 1990 (c 41)**—*contd*

| | | |
|---|---|---|
| 31 | (1), (2) | 1 Jan 1991 (SI 1990/2484) |
| | (3)–(9) | 1 Apr 1991 (SI 1991/608) |
| 32 | (1), (2) | 1 Jan 1991 (SI 1990/2484) |
| | (3)–(9) | 1 Apr 1991 (SI 1991/608) |
| 33 | (1), (2) | 1 Jan 1991 (SI 1990/2484) |
| | (3)–(9) | 1 Apr 1991 (SI 1991/608) |
| 34 | (1)–(7) | 1 Apr 1991 (SI 1991/608) |
| | (8) | See Sch 5 below |
| 35 | | 1 Apr 1991 (SI 1991/608) |
| 36–39 | | *Never in force* (repealed) |
| 40 | | 1 Apr 1991 (SI 1991/608) |
| 41 | (1)–(10) | *Never in force* (repealed) |
| | (11) | See Sch 6 below |
| 42 | | *Never in force* (repealed) |
| 43 | (1)–(3) | *Never in force* (repealed) |
| | (4) | See Sch 7 below |
| | (5)–(12) | *Never in force* (repealed) |
| 44, 45 | | *Never in force* (repealed) |
| 46 | (1)–(3) | *Never in force* (repealed) |
| 47–52 | | *Never in force* (repealed) |
| 53 | (1)–(6) | 1 Apr 1991 (except in relation to exemptions under s 55) (SI 1991/608) |
| | | 7 Dec 2004 (exception noted above) (SI 2004/2950) |
| | (7) | See Sch 8 below |
| | (8), (9) | 1 Apr 1991 (except in relation to exemptions under s 55) (SI 1991/608) |
| | | 7 Dec 2004 (exception noted above) (SI 2004/2950) |
| 54 | | *Never in force* (repealed) |
| 55 | (1)–(3) | 7 Dec 2004 (SI 2004/2950) |
| | (4) | See Sch 9 below |
| 56, 57 | | 1 Jul 1991 (SI 1991/1364) |
| 58 | | 23 Jul 1993 (SI 1993/2132) |
| 59 | | 1 Apr 1991 (SI 1991/608) |
| 60–62 | | 1 Jan 1991 (SI 1990/2484) |
| 63 | (1)(a) | 1 Apr 1991 (SI 1991/608) |
| | (1)(b), (c) | *Never in force* (repealed) |
| | (2) | 1 Apr 1991 (SI 1991/608) |
| | (3) | *Never in force* (repealed) |
| 64, 65 | | 1 Jan 1991 (s 124(2)(a)) |
| 66–68 | | 1 Jan 1991 (SI 1990/2484) |
| 69 | | 1 Apr 1991 (SI 1991/608) |
| 70 | | 1 Jan 1991 (except so far as relates to authorised practitioners) (SI 1990/2484) |
| | | *Never in force* (otherwise) (repealed) |
| 71 | (1) | 1 Jan 1991 (SI 1990/2484) |
| | (2) | See Sch 10 below |
| | (3)–(8) | 1 Jan 1991 (SI 1990/2484) |
| 72, 73 | | 1 Jan 1991 (s 124(2)(a)) |
| 74 | (1)–(3) | 1 Jan 1991 (SI 1990/2484) |
| | (4)–(7) | 1 Jul 1991 (SI 1991/1364) |
| 75 | | See Sch 11 below |
| 76–78 | | 1 Jan 1991 (SI 1990/2484) |
| 79 | (1) | 1 Jan 1992 (SI 1991/2730) |
| | (2) | See Sch 12 below |
| 80 | | 1 Jan 1992 (SI 1991/2730) |
| 81 | | See Sch 13 below |
| 82 | | 6 Mar 1995 (SI 1995/641) |
| 83, 84 | | 1 Jan 1991 (SI 1990/2484) |
| 85 | | 1 Jan 1991 (s 124(2)(a)) |

**Courts and Legal Services Act 1990 (c 41)**—*contd*

| | | |
|---|---|---|
| 86 | | 1 Jul 1991 (SI 1991/1364) |
| 87, 88 | | 1 Jan 1991 (s 124(2)(a)) |
| 89 | (1)–(7) | 14 Oct 1991 (SI 1991/1883) |
| | (8) | See Sch 14 below |
| | (9) | 14 Oct 1991 (SI 1991/1883) |
| 90–92 | | 1 Jan 1991 (s 124(2)(a)) |
| 93 | (1), (2) | 1 Apr 1991 (SI 1991/608) |
| | (3) | See Sch 15 below |
| | (4) | 1 Apr 1991 (SI 1991/608) |
| 94–98 | | 1 Jan 1991 (s 124(2)(a)) |
| 99–101 | | 1 Apr 1991 (SI 1991/608) |
| 102 | | 1 Jan 1992 (SI 1991/2730) |
| 103 | | 1 Apr 1991 (SI 1991/608) |
| 104–107 | | *Not yet in force* |
| 108–110 | | 1 Jan 1991 (s 124(2)(a)) |
| 111 | | 1 May 1991 (SI 1991/985) |
| 112 | | 1 Oct 1991 (SI 1991/1883) |
| 113–115 | | 1 Apr 1991 (SI 1991/608) |
| 116 | (1) | See Sch 16, Pt I below |
| | (2) | See Sch 16, Pt II below |
| | (3) | 1 Jan 1992 (SI 1991/2730) |
| 117 | | 1 Jul 1991 (SI 1991/1364) |
| 118 | | 1 Jan 1991 (SI 1990/2484) |
| 119–124 | | 1 Nov 1990 (RA) |
| 125 | (1) | 1 Nov 1990 (RA) |
| | (2) | See Sch 17 below |
| | (3) | See Sch 18 below |
| | (4), (5) | 14 Oct 1991 (SI 1991/1883) |
| | (6) | See Sch 19 below |
| | (7) | See Sch 20 below |
| Schs 1, 2 | | 1 Apr 1991 (SI 1991/608) |
| Sch 3 | | 1 Jan 1991 (SI 1990/2484) |
| Schs 4, 5 | | 1 Apr 1991 (SI 1991/608) |
| Schs 6, 7 | | *Never in force* (repealed) |
| Sch 8 | Pt I | 1 Apr 1991 (except in relation to exemptions under s 55) (SI 1991/608) |
| | | 7 Dec 2004 (in relation to exemptions under s 55) (SI 2004/2950) |
| | Pt II | 1 Apr 1991 (except in relation to exemptions under s 55) (SI 1991/608) |
| | | *Not yet in force* (exception noted above) (paras 13–20, 23 repealed) |
| Sch 9 | | 7 Dec 2004 (SI 2004/2950) |
| Schs 10, 11 | | 1 Jan 1991 (SI 1990/2484) |
| Sch 12 | | 1 Jan 1992 (SI 1991/2730) |
| Sch 13 | | *Not yet in force* |
| Sch 14 | | 14 Oct 1991 (SI 1991/1883) |
| Sch 15 | | 1 Apr 1991 (SI 1991/608) |
| Sch 16 | paras 1–7 | 14 Oct 1991 (SI 1991/1883) |
| | para 8 | 1 Jan 1991 (SI 1990/2484) |
| | paras 9–42 | 14 Oct 1991 (SI 1991/1883) |
| Sch 17 | para 1 | 1 Jan 1991 (s 124(2)(b)) |
| | paras 2, 3 | 1 Nov 1990 (RA) |
| | para 4 | 1 Apr 1991 (SI 1991/608) |
| | para 5 | *Not yet in force* |
| | para 6 | 1 Jul 1991 (SI 1991/1364) |
| | paras 7, 8 | 1 Apr 1991 (SI 1991/608) |
| | para 9 | 1 Jan 1991 (SI 1990/2484) |
| | para 10 | 1 Apr 1991 (SI 1991/608) |
| | paras 11, 12 | 1 Jan 1991 (s 124(2)(b)) |
| | para 13 | 1 Apr 1991 (SI 1991/608) |

**Courts and Legal Services Act 1990 (c 41)**—*contd*

| | | |
|---|---|---|
| | para 14 | 14 Oct 1991 (SI 1991/1883) |
| | para 15 | 1 Jan 1991 (SI 1990/2484) |
| | para 16 | 1 Jan 1991 (s 124(2)(b)) |
| | paras 17, 18 | 1 Jul 1991 (SI 1991/1364) |
| | para 19 | *Never in force* (repealed) |
| | para 20 | 1 Jan 1991 (s 124(2)(b)) |
| Sch 18 | para 1 | 1 Jan 1991 (so far as relates to Legal Services Ombudsman) (SI 1990/2484) |
| | | 1 Apr 1991 (so far as relates to Lord Chancellor's Advisory Committee on Legal Education and Conduct) (SI 1991/608) |
| | | *Never in force* (so far as relates to the Authorised Conveyancing Practitioners Board and the Conveyancing Ombudsman) (repealed) |
| | para 2 | *Never in force* (repealed) |
| | para 3 | 1 Jan 1991 (SI 1990/2484) |
| | para 4 | *Never in force* (repealed) |
| | para 5 | 1 Apr 1991 (SI 1991/608) |
| | para 6 | *Never in force* (repealed) |
| | paras 7, 8 | 1 Jan 1991 (s 124(2)(c)) |
| | paras 9, 10 | 1 Jul 1991 (SI 1991/1364) |
| | paras 11, 12 | *Never in force* (repealed) |
| | para 13 | 1 Jun 1992 (SI 1992/1221) |
| | paras 14–16 | 1 Jan 1991 (s 124(2)(c)) |
| | paras 17, 18 | 1 Jul 1991 (SI 1991/1364) |
| | para 19 | *Never in force* (spent) |
| | para 20 | 1 Jan 1991 (SI 1990/2484) |
| | para 21 | 14 Oct 1991 (SI 1991/1883) |
| | paras 22, 23 | *Never in force* (repealed) |
| | paras 24, 25 | 1 Jan 1991 (SI 1990/2484) |
| | paras 26–30 | 1 Jan 1992 (SI 1991/2730) |
| | para 31 | *Not yet in force* |
| | para 32 | 1 Jan 1991 (SI 1990/2484) |
| | paras 33–35 | 1 Jan 1992 (SI 1991/2730) |
| | paras 36–40 | 1 Jan 1991 (SI 1990/2484) |
| | para 41 | 1 Apr 1991 (SI 1991/608) |
| | para 42 | 1 Jan 1991 (SI 1990/2484) |
| | paras 43–46 | 1 Jul 1991 (SI 1991/1364) |
| | para 47 | 1 Jan 1991 (SI 1990/2484) |
| | paras 48, 49 | 1 Apr 1991 (SI 1991/608) |
| | paras 50, 51 | 1 Jan 1991 (SI 1990/2484) |
| | para 52 | 1 Apr 1991 (SI 1991/608) |
| | para 53 | 1 May 1991 (SI 1991/985) |
| | para 54 | 14 Oct 1991 (SI 1991/1883) |
| | para 55 | 1 Jan 1991 (s 124(2)(c)) |
| | para 56 | 1 Apr 1991 (SI 1991/608) |
| | para 57 | 1 Jan 1991 (s 124(2)(c)) |
| | paras 58–63 | 1 Apr 1991 (SI 1991/608) |
| Sch 19 | para 1 | 1 Jan 1991 (s 124(2)(d)) |
| | paras 2–8 | 1 Jan 1991 (SI 1990/2484) |
| | para 9 | 1 Jan 1992 (SI 1991/2730) |
| | paras 10, 11 | 1 Jan 1991 (SI 1990/2484) |
| | paras 12, 13 | 1 Jul 1991 (SI 1991/1364) |
| | paras 14, 15 | 1 Apr 1991 (SI 1991/608) |
| | para 16 | 1 Jan 1991 (SI 1990/2484) |
| | para 17 | 1 Apr 1991 (SI 1991/608) |
| Sch 20 | | 1 Nov 1990 (repeal of Administration of Justice Act 1956, s 53) (SI 1990/2170) |
| | | 1 Jan 1991 (SI 1990/2484), repeals of or in— Public Notaries Act 1801, ss 10, 14; |

**Courts and Legal Services Act 1990 (c 41)**—*contd*

Summary Jurisdiction Act 1857;
Naval Agency and Distribution Act 1864;
War Pensions (Administrative Provisions) Act 1919;
Pensions Appeal Tribunals Act 1943;
Lands Tribunal Act 1949;
Courts-Martial (Appeals) Act 1951;
Barristers (Qualification for Office) Act 1961;
Superannuation (Miscellaneous Provisions) Act 1967;
Superannuation (Miscellaneous Provisions) Act (Northern
   Ireland) 1969;
Courts Act 1971;
Administration of Justice Act 1973;
Solicitors Act 1974, ss 3–5, 7, 20(2)(c), 39, 45, 82, Sch 3,
   para 7;
Social Security Act 1975;
House of Commons Disqualification Act 1975;
Ministerial and other Salaries Act 1975;
Justices of the Peace Act 1979;
Social Security Act 1980;
Judicial Pensions Act 1981, s 33, Sch 1, Pt I;
Supreme Court Act 1981, ss 12(4), 94, 100(5), 101(2), 102(6),
   103(6);
County Courts Act 1984, ss 10, 60(1), (2);
Administration of Justice Act 1985, ss 3(1), 63, Sch 1, paras 4,
   11, Sch 2, paras 8, 15, Sch 7, para 4;
Prosecution of Offences Act 1985, s 4(5);
Coroners Act 1988
1 Apr 1991 (SI 1991/608), repeals of or in—
Commissioners for Oaths Act 1889, s 1;
Arbitration Act 1950, s 12(6)(b);
Solicitors Act 1974, ss 2(2), 44A, 47A, 81(5);
County Courts Act 1984, s 143(2);
Administration of Justice Act 1985, ss 1, 3(2), 26(3), 65(5),
   Sch 2, para 19, Sch 3, para 8, Sch 7, para 5;
Prosecution of Offences Act 1985, s 15(1)
1 Jul 1991 (SI 1991/1364), repeals of or in—
Public Notaries Act 1801, ss 1–5, 7–9;
Public Notaries Act 1833;
Public Notaries Act 1843;
Small Debts Act 1845;
Welsh Church Act 1914;
Administration of Justice Act 1956, s 37;
Administration of Justice Act 1969, s 29;
County Courts Act 1984, ss 19, 20, 22, 29, 34, 43, 44, 89(3),
   105, 106, Sch 1
14 Oct 1991 (SI 1991/1883), repeals of or in—
Maintenance Orders Act 1950;
Children and Young Persons Act 1969;
Family Law Reform Act 1969;
Administration of Justice Act 1970;
Maintenance Orders (Reciprocal Enforcement of Orders)
   Act 1972;
Domestic Proceedings and Magistrates' Courts Act 1978;
Magistrates' Courts Act 1980;
Matrimonial and Family Proceedings Act 1984;
Family Law Reform Act 1987;
Children Act 1989
1 Jan 1992 (repeals of or in Judicial Pensions Act 1981, ss 18(3),
   20(6), 22(5), 24, 25, Sch 1, para 15(3)) (SI 1991/2730)

**Courts and Legal Services Act 1990 (c 41)**—*contd*

    1 Jun 1992 (SI 1992/1221), repeals of or in—
        Solicitors Act 1974, ss 7, 33(4);
        County Courts Act 1984, s 45;
        Administration of Justice Act 1985, s 9(8), Sch 2, para 4(2)
    1 Oct 1993 (repeal of words in Supreme Court Act 1981, s 18)
      (SI 1993/2132)
    *Not yet in force*, repeals of or in—
        Rent (Agriculture) Act 1976;
        Rent Act 1977;
        Housing Act 1980;
        County Courts Act 1984, ss 63, 75(1), 112(5);
        Housing Act 1985;
        Landlord and Tenant Act 1985;
        Building Societies Act 1986;
        Landlord and Tenant Act 1987;
        Copyright, Designs and Patents Act 1988;
        Housing Act 1988

---

**Criminal Justice (International Co-operation) Act 1990 (c 5)**

*RA:* 5 Apr 1990

*Commencement provisions:* s 32(2); Criminal Justice (International Co-operation) Act 1990 (Commencement No 1) Order 1991, SI 1991/1072; Criminal Justice (International Co-operation) Act 1990 (Commencement No 2) Order 1991, SI 1991/2108

| | | |
|---|---|---|
| 1, 2 | | 10 Jun 1991 (SI 1991/1072) |
| 3 | (1), (2) | 10 Jun 1991 (SI 1991/1072) |
| | (3) | 23 Apr 1991 (for purpose of making any Order in Council, order, rules, or regulations) (SI 1991/1072) |
| | | 10 Jun 1991 (otherwise) (SI 1991/1072) |
| | (4)–(10) | 10 Jun 1991 (SI 1991/1072) |
| 4 | (1)–(5) | 10 Jun 1991 (SI 1991/1072) |
| | (6) | See Sch 1 below |
| 5, 6 | | 10 Jun 1991 (SI 1991/1072) |
| 7 | (1)–(6) | 10 Jun 1991 (SI 1991/1072) |
| | (7) | 23 Apr 1991 (for purpose of making any Order in Council, order, rules, or regulations) (SI 1991/1072) |
| | | 10 Jun 1991 (otherwise) (SI 1991/1072) |
| | (8), (9) | 10 Jun 1991 (SI 1991/1072) |
| 8 | (1)–(4) | 10 Jun 1991 (SI 1991/1072) |
| | (5) | 23 Apr 1991 (for purpose of making any Order in Council, order, rules, or regulations) (SI 1991/1072) |
| | | 10 Jun 1991 (otherwise) (SI 1991/1072) |
| | (6) | 10 Jun 1991 (SI 1991/1072) |
| 9, 10 | | 23 Apr 1991 (for purpose of making any Order in Council, order, rules, or regulations) (SI 1991/1072) |
| | | 10 Jun 1991 (otherwise) (SI 1991/1072) |
| 11 | | 10 Jun 1991 (SI 1991/1072) |
| 12 | (1)–(4) | 1 Jul 1991 (SI 1991/1072) |
| | (5) | 23 Apr 1991 (for purpose of making any Order in Council, order, rules, or regulations) (SI 1991/1072) |
| | | 1 Jul 1991 (otherwise) (SI 1991/1072) |
| 13 | | 23 Apr 1991 (for purpose of making any Order in Council, order, rules, or regulations) (SI 1991/1072) |
| | | 1 Jul 1991 (otherwise) (SI 1991/1072) |
| 14–24 | | 1 Jul 1991 (SI 1991/1072) |
| 25–27 | | 23 Sep 1991 (SI 1991/2108) |
| 28 | (1) | 23 Sep 1991 (SI 1991/2108) |

**Criminal Justice (International Co-operation) Act 1990 (c 5)**—*contd*

|        |              |                                                                                                      |
|--------|--------------|------------------------------------------------------------------------------------------------------|
|        | (2)          | 23 Apr 1991 (for purpose of making any Order in Council, order, rules, or regulations) (SI 1991/1072) |
|        |              | 23 Sep 1991 (otherwise) (SI 1991/2108)                                                                |
|        | (3)          | 23 Sep 1991 (SI 1991/2108)                                                                            |
| 29     | (1)          | 23 Sep 1991 (SI 1991/2108)                                                                            |
|        | (2)          | 23 Apr 1991 (for purpose of making any Order in Council, order, rules, or regulations) (SI 1991/1072) |
|        |              | 23 Sep 1991 (otherwise) (SI 1991/2108)                                                                |
|        | (3)          | 23 Sep 1991 (SI 1991/2108)                                                                            |
| 30     | (1)          | 10 Jun 1991 (SI 1991/1072)                                                                            |
|        | (2)          | 23 Sep 1991 (SI 1991/2108)                                                                            |
| 31     | (1)          | See Sch 4 below                                                                                       |
|        | (2)          | 1 Jul 1991 (SI 1991/1072)                                                                             |
|        | (3)          | See Sch 5 below                                                                                       |
|        | (4)          | 1 Jul 1991 (SI 1991/1072)                                                                             |
| 32     | (1)–(3)      | 10 Jun 1991 (SI 1991/1072)                                                                            |
|        | (4)          | 23 Apr 1991 (for purpose of making any Order in Council, order, rules, or regulations) (SI 1991/1072) |
|        |              | 10 Jun 1991 (otherwise) (SI 1991/1072)                                                                |
| Sch 1  |              | 10 Jun 1991 (SI 1991/1072)                                                                            |
| Sch 2  |              | 23 Apr 1991 (for purpose of making any Order in Council, order, rules, or regulations) (SI 1991/1072) |
|        |              | 1 Jul 1991 (otherwise) (SI 1991/1072)                                                                 |
| Sch 3  | para 1(1)(a), (b) | 1 Jul 1991 (SI 1991/1072)                                                                        |
|        | para 1(1)(c) | 23 Apr 1991 (for purpose of making any Order in Council, order, rules, or regulations) (SI 1991/1072) |
|        |              | 1 Jul 1991 (otherwise) (SI 1991/1072)                                                                 |
|        | para 1(2), (3) | 1 Jul 1991 (SI 1991/1072)                                                                           |
|        | paras 2–9    | 1 Jul 1991 (SI 1991/1072)                                                                             |
| Sch 4  | para 1       | 1 Jul 1991 (SI 1991/1072)                                                                             |
|        | para 2       | 10 Jun 1991 (SI 1991/1072)                                                                            |
|        | paras 3–5    | 1 Jul 1991 (SI 1991/1072)                                                                             |
|        | paras 6–8    | 10 Jun 1991 (SI 1991/1072)                                                                            |
| Sch 5  |              | 10 Jun 1991 (SI 1991/1072), repeals of or in—                                                        |
|        |              | Extradition Act 1873, s 5;                                                                            |
|        |              | Evidence (Proceedings in Other Jurisdictions) Act 1975, s 5;                                          |
|        |              | Suppression of Terrorism Act 1978, s 1(3)(d) (and word "and" immediately preceding it), (4), (5)(b) (and word "and" immediately preceding it); |
|        |              | Criminal Justice Act 1988, s 29                                                                       |
|        |              | 1 Jul 1991 (otherwise) (SI 1991/1072)                                                                 |

---

**Education (Student Loans) Act 1990 (c 6)**

*RA:* 26 Apr 1990

Whole Act in force 26 Apr 1990 (RA)

---

**Employment Act 1990 (c 38)**

*RA:* 1 Nov 1990

*Commencement provisions:* s 18(2)–(4); Employment Act 1990 (Commencement and Transitional Provisions) Order 1990, SI 1990/2378; Employment Act 1990 (Commencement and Transitional Provisions) Amendment Order 1991, SI 1991/89 (corrects defect in SI 1990/2378)

|      |          |                                                                          |
|------|----------|--------------------------------------------------------------------------|
| 1, 2 |          | 1 Jan 1991 (subject to transitional provisions) (SI 1990/2378; SI 1991/89) |
| 3    | (1)–(4)  | 1 Jan 1991 (SI 1990/2378)                                                 |

## Employment Act 1990 (c 38)—*contd*

| | | |
|---|---|---|
| | (5) | See Sch 1 below |
| 4–10 | | 1 Jan 1991 (subject to transitional provisions) (SI 1990/2378) |
| 11, 12 | | 1 Nov 1990 (s 18(2)) |
| 13 | | 1 Feb 1991 (SI 1990/2378) |
| 14, 15 | | 1 Nov 1990 (s 18(2)) |
| 16 | (1) | See Sch 2 below |
| | (2) | See Sch 3 below |
| 17 | | 1 Nov 1990 (s 18(2)) |
| 18 | | 1 Nov 1990 (RA) |
| Sch 1 | | 1 Jan 1991 (SI 1990/2378) |
| Sch 2 | para 1(1), (2) | 1 Feb 1991 (SI 1990/2378) |
| | para 1(3)–(6) | 1 Jan 1991 (SI 1990/2378) |
| | paras 2, 3 | 1 Jan 1991 (subject to transitional provisions) (SI 1990/2378) |
| Sch 3 | | 1 Jan 1991 (subject to transitional provisions) (SI 1990/2378) repeals of or in— |
| | | Employment Act 1980; |
| | | Employment Act 1982; |
| | | Trade Union Act 1984; |
| | | Employment Act 1988 |
| | | 1 Feb 1991 (otherwise) (SI 1990/2378) |

## Enterprise and New Towns (Scotland) Act 1990 (c 35)

*RA:* 26 Jul 1990

*Commencement provisions:* s 39(1), (3); Enterprise and New Towns (Scotland) Act 1990 Commencement Order 1990, SI 1990/1840

| | | |
|---|---|---|
| 1 | | 1 Oct 1990 (for purpose of establishing Scottish Enterprise and Highlands and Islands Enterprise, and bringing into force Sch 1) (SI 1990/1840) |
| | | 1 Apr 1991 (otherwise) (SI 1990/1840) |
| 2–18 | | 1 Apr 1991 (SI 1990/1840) |
| 19, 20 | | 26 Jul 1990 (for purposes of Sch 3, paras 4, 5) (s 39(1), (3)) |
| | | 1 Apr 1991 (otherwise) (SI 1990/1840) |
| 21 | (1)–(3) | 1 Apr 1991 (SI 1990/1840) |
| | (4) | 1 Oct 1990 (SI 1990/1840) |
| 22 | | 1 Oct 1990 (SI 1990/1840) |
| 23 | (1)–(3) | 1 Apr 1991 (SI 1990/1840) |
| | (4) | See Sch 3 below |
| 24 | | 1 Apr 1991 (SI 1990/1840) |
| 25 | (1) | See Sch 2 below |
| | (2)–(4) | 1 Apr 1991 (SI 1990/1840) |
| 26 | (1), (2) | 1 Oct 1990 (SI 1990/1840) |
| | (3), (4) | 1 Apr 1991 (SI 1990/1840) |
| 27 | | 1 Oct 1990 (SI 1990/1840) |
| 28 | | 1 Apr 1991 (SI 1990/1840) |
| 29, 30 | | 1 Oct 1990 (SI 1990/1840) |
| 31, 32 | | 1 Apr 1991 (SI 1990/1840) |
| 33–35 | | 1 Oct 1990 (SI 1990/1840) |
| 36, 37 | | 26 Jul 1990 (s 39(1), (3)) |
| 38 | (1) | See Sch 4 below |
| | (2) | See Sch 5 below |
| | (3), (4) | 1 Apr 1991 (SI 1990/1840) |
| 39, 40 | | 26 Jul 1990 (RA) |
| Sch 1 | | 1 Oct 1990 (SI 1990/1840) |
| Sch 2 | para 1 | 1 Oct 1990 (SI 1990/1840) |
| | paras 2–6 | 1 Apr 1991 (SI 1990/1840) |
| Sch 3 | paras 1–3 | 1 Apr 1991 (SI 1990/1840) |

**Enterprise and New Towns (Scotland) Act 1990 (c 35)**—*contd*

|         | paras 4, 5    | 26 Jul 1990 (s 39(1), (3))          |
|---------|---------------|-------------------------------------|
|         | paras 6–9     | 1 Apr 1991 (SI 1990/1840)           |
| Sch 4   | para 1        | 1 Oct 1990 (SI 1990/1840)           |
|         | paras 2–5     | 1 Apr 1991 (SI 1990/1840)           |
|         | para 6        | 1 Oct 1990 (SI 1990/1840)           |
|         | paras 7–18    | 1 Apr 1991 (SI 1990/1840)           |
| Sch 5   |               | 26 Jul 1990 (s 39(1), (3))          |

---

**Entertainments (Increased Penalties) Act 1990 (c 20)**

*RA:* 13 Jul 1990

Whole Act in force 13 Jul 1990 (RA)

---

**Environmental Protection Act 1990 (c 43)**

*RA:* 1 Nov 1990

*Commencement provisions:* ss 130(4), 131(3), 164(2), (3); Environmental Protection Act 1990 (Commencement No 1) Order 1990, SI 1990/2226; Environmental Protection Act 1990 (Commencement No 2) Order 1990, SI 1990/2243; Environmental Protection Act 1990 (Commencement No 3) Order 1990, SI 1990/2565, amended by SI 1990/2635; Environmental Protection Act 1990 (Commencement No 4) Order 1990, SI 1990/2635; Environmental Protection Act 1990 (Commencement No 5) Order 1991, SI 1991/96; Environmental Protection Act 1990 (Commencement No 6 and Appointed Day) Order 1991, SI 1991/685; Environmental Protection Act 1990 (Commencement No 7) Order 1991, SI 1991/1042; Environmental Protection Act 1990 (Commencement No 8) Order 1991, SI 1991/1319; Environmental Protection Act 1990 (Commencement No 9) Order 1991, SI 1991/1577; Environmental Protection Act 1990 (Commencement No 10) Order 1991, SI 1991/2829; Environmental Protection Act 1990 (Commencement No 11) Order 1992, SI 1992/266; Environmental Protection Act 1990 (Commencement No 12) Order 1992, SI 1992/3253; Environmental Protection Act 1990 (Commencement No 13) Order 1993, SI 1993/274; Environmental Protection Act 1990 (Commencement No 14) Order 1994, SI 1994/780; Environmental Protection Act 1990 (Commencement No 15) Order 1994, SI 1994/1096, amended by SI 1994/2487, SI 1994/3234; Environmental Protection Act 1990 (Commencement No 16) Order 1994, SI 1994/2854; Environmental Protection Act 1990 (Commencement No 17) Order 1995, SI 1995/2152; Environmental Protection Act 1990 (Commencement No 18) Order 1996, SI 1996/3056; Environmental Protection Act 1990 (Commencement No 19) Order 2012, SI 2012/898; Environmental Protection Act 1990 (Commencement No 20) (Scotland) Order 2015, SSI 2015/72

| 1, 2    |           | 1 Jan 1991 (SI 1990/2635)           |
|---------|-----------|-------------------------------------|
| 3       |           | 19 Dec 1991 (SI 1990/2635)          |
| 4–28    |           | 1 Jan 1991 (SI 1990/2635)           |
| 29–31   |           | 31 May 1991 (SI 1991/1319)          |
| 32      |           | See Sch 2 below                     |
| 33      | (1)(a), (b) | 1 May 1994 (except for the purposes of their application to specified activities[2]) (SI 1994/1096) |
|         |           | 1 Apr 1995 (subject to exceptions[3], in relation to an activity which involves treating, keeping or disposing of scrap metal or motor vehicles which are to be dismantled) (SI 1994/1096) |
|         | (1)(c)    | 1 Apr 1992 (SI 1991/2829)           |
|         | (2)       | 1 Apr 1992 (so far as relates to s 33(1)(c)) (SI 1991/2829) |
|         |           | 1 May 1994 (otherwise) (except for the purposes of its application to specified activities[2]) (SI 1994/1096) |
|         |           | 1 Apr 1995 (otherwise) (subject to exceptions[3], in relation to an activity which involves treating, keeping or disposing of scrap metal or motor vehicles which are to be dismantled) (SI 1994/1096) |
|         | (3), (4)  | 13 Dec 1991 (SI 1991/2829)          |

**Environmental Protection Act 1990 (c 43)**—*contd*

|  |  |  |
|---|---|---|
| | (5) | 1 May 1994 (otherwise) (except for the purposes of their application to specified activities²) (SI 1994/1096) |
| | | 1 Apr 1995 (otherwise) (subject to exceptions³, in relation to an activity which involves treating, keeping or disposing of scrap metal or motor vehicles which are to be dismantled) (SI 1994/1096) |
| | (6), (7) | 1 Apr 1992 (so far as relates to s 33(1)(c)) (SI 1991/2829) |
| | | 1 May 1994 (otherwise) (except for the purposes of their application to specified activities²) (SI 1994/1096) |
| | | 1 Apr 1995 (otherwise) (subject to exceptions³, in relation to an activity which involves treating, keeping or disposing of scrap metal or motor vehicles which are to be dismantled) (SI 1994/1096) |
| | (8), (9) | 1 Apr 1992 (so far as relates to s 33(1)(c)) (SI 1991/2829) |
| | | 1 May 1994 (otherwise) (except for the purposes of their application to specified activities²) (SI 1994/1096) |
| | | 1 Apr 1995 (otherwise) (subject to exceptions³, in relation to an activity which involves treating, keeping or disposing of scrap metal or motor vehicles which are to be dismantled) (SI 1994/1096) |
| 34 | (1)–(4) | 1 Apr 1992 (SI 1991/2829) |
| | (5) | 13 Dec 1991 (SI 1991/2829) |
| | (6) | 1 Apr 1992 (SI 1991/2829) |
| | (7)–(9) | 13 Dec 1991 (SI 1991/2829) |
| | (10) | 1 Apr 1992 (SI 1991/2829) |
| | (11) | 13 Dec 1991 (SI 1991/2829) |
| 35 | (1)–(5) | 1 May 1994 (except for the purposes of their application to specified activities²) (SI 1994/1096) |
| | | 1 Apr 1995 (subject to exceptions³, in relation to an activity which involves treating, keeping or disposing of scrap metal or motor vehicles which are to be dismantled) (SI 1994/1096) |
| | (6) | 18 Feb 1993 (SI 1993/274) |
| | (7)–(12) | 1 May 1994 (except for the purposes of their application to specified activities²) (SI 1994/1096) |
| | | 1 Apr 1995 (subject to exceptions³, in relation to an activity which involves treating, keeping or disposing of scrap metal or motor vehicles which are to be dismantled) (SI 1994/1096) |
| 36 | (1) | 18 Feb 1993 (SI 1993/274) |
| | (2)–(10) | 1 May 1994 (except for the purposes of their application to specified activities²) (SI 1994/1096) |
| | | 1 Apr 1995 (subject to exceptions³, in relation to an activity which involves treating, keeping or disposing of scrap metal or motor vehicles which are to be dismantled) (SI 1994/1096) |
| 37 | (1), (2) | 1 May 1994 (except for the purposes of their application to specified activities²) (SI 1994/1096) |
| | | 1 Apr 1995 (subject to exceptions³, in relation to an activity which involves treating, keeping or disposing of scrap metal or motor vehicles which are to be dismantled) (SI 1994/1096) |
| | (3) | 18 Feb 1993 (so far as enables Secretary of State to give directions) (SI 1993/274) |
| | | 1 May 1994 (otherwise) (except for the purposes of its application to specified activities²) (SI 1994/1096) |
| | | 1 Apr 1995 (otherwise) (subject to exceptions³, in relation to an activity which involves treating, keeping or disposing of scrap metal or motor vehicles which are to be dismantled) (SI 1994/1096) |
| | (4)–(6) | 1 May 1994 (except for the purposes of their application to specified activities²) (SI 1994/1096) |
| | | 1 Apr 1995 (subject to exceptions³, in relation to an activity which involves treating, keeping or disposing of scrap metal or motor vehicles which are to be dismantled) (SI 1994/1096) |

**Environmental Protection Act 1990 (c 43)**—*contd*

| | | |
|---|---|---|
| 38 | (1)–(6) | 1 May 1994 (except for the purposes of their application to specified activities[2]) (SI 1994/1096) |
| | | 1 Apr 1995 (subject to exceptions[3], in relation to an activity which involves treating, keeping or disposing of scrap metal or motor vehicles which are to be dismantled) (SI 1994/1096) |
| | (7) | 18 Feb 1993 (so far as enables Secretary of State to give directions) (SI 1993/274) |
| | | 1 May 1994 (otherwise) (except for the purposes of their application to specified activities[2]) (SI 1994/1096) |
| | | 1 Apr 1995 (otherwise) (subject to exceptions[3], in relation to an activity which involves treating, keeping or disposing of scrap metal or motor vehicles which are to be dismantled) (SI 1994/1096) |
| | (8)–(12) | 1 May 1994 (except for the purposes of their application to specified activities[2]) (SI 1994/1096) |
| | | 1 Apr 1995 (subject to exceptions[3], in relation to an activity which involves treating, keeping or disposing of scrap metal or motor vehicles which are to be dismantled) (SI 1994/1096) |
| 39 | (1), (2) | 1 May 1994 (except for the purposes of their application to specified activities[2]) (SI 1994/1096) |
| | | 1 Apr 1995 (subject to exceptions[3], in relation to an activity which involves treating, keeping or disposing of scrap metal or motor vehicles which are to be dismantled) (SI 1994/1096) |
| | (3) | 18 Feb 1993 (SI 1993/274) |
| | (4)–(11) | 1 May 1994 (except for the purposes of their application to specified activities[2]) (SI 1994/1096) |
| | | 1 Apr 1995 (subject to exceptions[3], in relation to an activity which involves treating, keeping or disposing of scrap metal or motor vehicles which are to be dismantled) (SI 1994/1096) |
| 40 | (1), (2) | 1 May 1994 (except for the purposes of their application to specified activities[2]) (SI 1994/1096) |
| | | 1 Apr 1995 (subject to exceptions[3], in relation to an activity which involves treating, keeping or disposing of scrap metal or motor vehicles which are to be dismantled) (SI 1994/1096) |
| | (3) | 18 Feb 1993 (SI 1993/274) |
| | (4)–(6) | 1 May 1994 (except for the purposes of their application to specified activities[2]) (SI 1994/1096) |
| | | 1 Apr 1995 (subject to exceptions[3], in relation to an activity which involves treating, keeping or disposing of scrap metal or motor vehicles which are to be dismantled) (SI 1994/1096) |
| 41 | (1) | 16 Mar 1994 (SI 1994/780) |
| | (2) | 18 Feb 1993 (SI 1993/274) |
| | (3) | 16 Mar 1994 (SI 1994/780) |
| | (4), (5) | 18 Feb 1993 (SI 1993/274) |
| | (6)–(8) | 16 Mar 1994 (SI 1994/780) |
| 42 | (1)–(7) | 1 May 1994 (except for the purposes of their application to specified activities[2]) (SI 1994/1096) |
| | | 1 Apr 1995 (subject to exceptions[3], in relation to an activity which involves treating, keeping or disposing of scrap metal or motor vehicles which are to be dismantled) (SI 1994/1096) |
| | (8) | 18 Feb 1993 (so far as enables Secretary of State to give directions) (SI 1993/274) |
| | | 1 May 1994 (otherwise) (except for the purposes of its application to specified activities[2]) (SI 1994/1096) |
| | | 1 Apr 1995 (otherwise) (subject to exceptions[3], in relation to an activity which involves treating, keeping or disposing of scrap metal or motor vehicles which are to be dismantled) (SI 1994/1096) |
| 43 | (1)–(7) | 1 May 1994 (except for the purposes of their application to specified activities[2]) (SI 1994/1096) |

**Environmental Protection Act 1990 (c 43)**—*contd*

|  |  |  |
|---|---|---|
|  |  | 1 Apr 1995 (subject to exceptions³, in relation to an activity which involves treating, keeping or disposing of scrap metal or motor vehicles which are to be dismantled) (SI 1994/1096) |
|  | (8) | 18 Feb 1993 (SI 1993/274) |
| 44 |  | 1 May 1994 (except for the purposes of its application to specified activities²) (SI 1994/1096) |
|  |  | 1 Apr 1995 (subject to exceptions³, in relation to an activity which involves treating, keeping or disposing of scrap metal or motor vehicles which are to be dismantled) (SI 1994/1096) |
| 45 | (1) | 14 Feb 1992 (so far as enables orders or regulations to be made) (SI 1992/266) |
|  |  | 1 Apr 1992 (otherwise) (SI 1992/266) |
|  | (2) | 14 Feb 1992 (so far as enables orders or regulations to be made) (SI 1992/266) |
|  |  | 1 Apr 1992 (otherwise) (S) (SI 1992/266) |
|  |  | *Not yet in force* (otherwise) (E) (W) |
|  | (3)–(10) | 14 Feb 1992 (so far as enable orders or regulations to be made) (SI 1992/266) |
|  |  | 1 Apr 1992 (otherwise) (SI 1992/266) |
|  | (11), (12) | 14 Feb 1992 (so far as enable orders or regulations to be made) (SI 1992/266) |
|  |  | 1 Apr 1992 (otherwise) (SI 1992/266) |
| 46, 47 |  | 1 Apr 1992 (SI 1992/266) |
| 48 | (1)–(6) | 1 Apr 1992 (SI 1992/266) |
|  | (7) | *Never in force* (repealed) |
|  | (8), (9) | 1 Apr 1992 (SI 1992/266) |
| 49 |  | 1 Aug 1991 (SI 1991/1577) |
| 50, 51 |  | 31 May 1991 (SI 1991/1319) |
| 52 | (1) | 1 Apr 1992 (SI 1992/266) |
|  | (2) | *Not yet in force* |
|  | (3)–(7) | 1 Apr 1992 (SI 1992/266) |
|  | (8) | 13 Dec 1991 (so far as relates to s 52(1), (3)) (SI 1991/2829) |
|  |  | *Not yet in force* (so far as relates to s 52(2), (4), (5)) |
|  | (9)–(11) | 1 Apr 1992 (SI 1992/266) |
| 53 |  | 1 Apr 1992 (SI 1992/266) |
| 54 | (1)–(13) | 1 May 1994 (SI 1994/1096) |
|  | (14) | 18 Feb 1993 (SI 1993/274) |
|  | (15)–(17) | 1 May 1994 (SI 1994/1096) |
| 55, 56 |  | 1 Apr 1992 (SI 1992/266) |
| 57 |  | 1 May 1994 (except for the purposes of its application to specified activities²) (SI 1994/1096) |
|  |  | 1 Apr 1995 (subject to exceptions³, in relation to an activity which involves treating, keeping or disposing of scrap metal or motor vehicles which are to be dismantled) (SI 1994/1096) |
| 58, 59 |  | 1 May 1994 (SI 1994/1096) |
| 60 |  | 31 May 1991 (so far as relates to anything deposited at a place for deposit of waste, or in a receptacle for waste, provided by a waste disposal contractor under arrangements made with a waste disposal authority) (SI 1991/1319) |
|  |  | 1 May 1994 (otherwise) (SI 1994/1096) |
| 61 |  | *Never in force* (repealed) |
| 62 |  | 11 Aug 1995 (SI 1995/2152) |
| 63 | (1) | 18 Feb 1993 (SI 1993/274) |
|  | (2)–(4) | *Never in force* (repealed) |
| 64 | (1) | 18 Feb 1993 (SI 1993/274) |
|  | (2), (3) | 1 May 1994 (SI 1994/1096) |
|  | (4) | 18 Feb 1993 (SI 1993/274) |
|  | (5)–(7) | 1 May 1994 (SI 1994/1096) |
|  | (8) | 18 Feb 1993 (SI 1993/274) |
| 65 | (1) | 1 May 1994 (SI 1994/1096) |

**Environmental Protection Act 1990 (c 43)**—*contd*

| | | |
|---|---|---|
| | (2) | 18 Feb 1993 (so far as enables Secretary of State to give directions) (SI 1993/274) |
| | | 1 May 1994 (otherwise) (SI 1994/1096) |
| | (3), (4) | 1 May 1994 (SI 1994/1096) |
| 66 | (1)–(6) | 1 May 1994 (SI 1994/1096) |
| | (7) | 18 Feb 1993 (so far as enables Secretary of State to give directions) (SI 1993/274) |
| | | 1 May 1994 (otherwise) (SI 1994/1096) |
| | (8)–(11) | 1 May 1994 (SI 1994/1096) |
| 67 | | 1 May 1994 (SI 1994/1096) |
| 68 | | 31 May 1991 (SI 1991/1319) |
| 69, 70 | | 1 Apr 1992 (SI 1991/2829) |
| 71, 72 | | 31 May 1991 (SI 1991/1319) |
| 73 | (1)–(5) | 1 Apr 1992 (SI 1992/266) |
| | (6)–(9) | 1 May 1994 (SI 1994/1096) |
| 74 | (1)–(5) | 1 May 1994 (SI 1994/1096) |
| | (6) | 18 Feb 1993 (SI 1993/274) |
| | (7) | 1 May 1994 (SI 1994/1096) |
| 75 | | 31 May 1991 (SI 1991/1319) |
| 76 | | *Never in force* (substituted) |
| 77 | | 31 May 1991 (SI 1991/1319) |
| 78 | | 13 Dec 1991 (SI 1991/2829) |
| 79–85 | | 1 Jan 1991 (s 164(2)) |
| 86 | (1) | 13 Feb 1991 (E) (W) (SI 1991/96) |
| | | 1 Apr 1991 (S) (SI 1991/1042) |
| | (2) | 14 Jan 1991 (SI 1991/96) |
| | (3) | 1 Apr 1991 (SI 1991/1042) |
| | (4), (5) | 13 Feb 1991 (E) (W) (SI 1991/96) |
| | | 1 Apr 1991 (S) (SI 1991/1042) |
| | (6)–(8) | 14 Jan 1991 (SI 1991/96) |
| | (9) | 13 Feb 1991 (SI 1991/96) |
| | (10) | 1 Apr 1991 (SI 1991/1042) |
| | (11) | 14 Jan 1991 (SI 1991/96) |
| | (12) | 1 Jun 1991 (SI 1991/1042) |
| | (13) | 13 Feb 1991 (E) (W) (SI 1991/96) |
| | | 1 Apr 1991 (S) (SI 1991/1042) |
| | (14), (15) | 14 Jan 1991 (SI 1991/96) |
| 87 | (1), (2) | 13 Feb 1991 (E) (W) (SI 1991/96) |
| | | 1 Apr 1991 (S) (SI 1991/1042) |
| | (3)(a)–(e) | 13 Feb 1991 (E) (W) (SI 1991/96) |
| | | 1 Apr 1991 (S) (SI 1991/1042) |
| | (3)(f) | 1 Jun 1991 (SI 1991/1042) |
| | (4)–(6) | 13 Feb 1991 (E) (W) (SI 1991/96) |
| | | 1 Apr 1991 (S) (SI 1991/1042) |
| | (7) | 1 Apr 1991 (SI 1991/1042) |
| 88 | (1)–(4) | 13 Feb 1991 (E) (W) (SI 1991/96) |
| | | 1 Apr 1991 (S) (SI 1991/1042) |
| | (5) | 14 Jan 1991 (SI 1991/96) |
| | (6) | 13 Feb 1991 (E) (W) (SI 1991/96) |
| | | 1 Apr 1991 (S) (SI 1991/1042) |
| | (7) | 14 Jan 1991 (SI 1991/96) |
| | (8) | 13 Feb 1991 (E) (W) (SI 1991/96) |
| | | 1 Apr 1991 (S) (SI 1991/1042) |
| | (9)(a) | 13 Feb 1991 (E) (W) (SI 1991/96) |
| | | 1 Apr 1991 (S) (SI 1991/1042) |
| | (9)(b) | 14 Jan 1991 (SI 1991/96) |
| | (9)(c), (d) | 13 Feb 1991 (E) (W) (SI 1991/96) |
| | | 1 Apr 1991 (S) (SI 1991/1042) |
| | (9)(e) | 13 Feb 1991 (E) (W) (SI 1991/96) |

**Environmental Protection Act 1990 (c 43)**—*contd*

|  |  |  |
|---|---|---|
|  |  | *Never in force* (S) (repealed) |
|  | (10) | 13 Feb 1991 (E) (W) (SI 1991/96) |
|  |  | 1 Apr 1991 (S) (SI 1991/1042) |
| 89 | (1)(a)–(f) | 1 Apr 1991 (SI 1991/1042) |
|  | (1)(g) | 1 Jun 1991 (SI 1991/1042) |
|  | (2), (3) | 1 Apr 1991 (SI 1991/1042) |
|  | (4) | 14 Jan 1991 (SI 1991/96) |
|  | (5), (6) | 1 Apr 1991 (SI 1991/1042) |
|  | (7)–(9) | 13 Nov 1990 (SI 1990/2243) |
|  | (10) | 1 Apr 1991 (SI 1991/1042) |
|  | (11)–(13) | 13 Nov 1990 (SI 1990/2243) |
|  | (14) | 1 Apr 1991 (SI 1991/1042) |
| 90 | (1), (2) | 14 Jan 1991 (SI 1991/96) |
|  | (3)–(6) | 1 Jun 1991 (SI 1991/1042) |
|  | (7) | 14 Jan 1991 (SI 1991/96) |
| 91 | (1)(a)–(f) | 1 Apr 1991 (SI 1991/1042) |
|  | (1)(g) | 1 Jun 1991 (SI 1991/1042) |
|  | (2)–(13) | 1 Apr 1991 (SI 1991/1042) |
| 92 | (1)(a)–(c) | 1 Apr 1991 (SI 1991/1042) |
|  | (1)(d) | 1 Jun 1991 (SI 1991/1042) |
|  | (2)–(10) | 1 Apr 1991 (SI 1991/1042) |
| 93 |  | 1 Apr 1991 (SI 1991/1042) |
| 94 | (1), (2) | 14 Jan 1991 (SI 1991/96) |
|  | (3)–(9) | 1 Apr 1991 (SI 1991/1042) |
| 95 |  | 1 Apr 1991 (SI 1991/1042) |
| 96 | (1) | 1 Apr 1991 (SI 1991/1042) |
|  | (2), (3) | 14 Jan 1991 (SI 1991/96) |
| 97 |  | 1 Jan 1991 (s 164(2)) |
| 98 | (1) | 13 Feb 1991 (E) (W) (SI 1991/96) |
|  |  | 1 Apr 1991 (S) (SI 1991/1042) |
|  | (2) | 13 Feb 1991 (SI 1991/96) |
|  | (3), (4) | 1 Apr 1991 (SI 1991/1042) |
|  | (5), (6) | 13 Feb 1991 (E) (W) (SI 1991/96) |
|  |  | 1 Apr 1991 (S) (SI 1991/1042) |
| 99 |  | See Sch 4 below |
| 100–104 |  | 1 Jan 1991 (SI 1990/2635) |
| 105 |  | See Sch 5 below |
| 106 | (1)–(3) | 1 Feb 1993 (SI 1992/3253) |
|  | (4), (5) | 1 Apr 1991 (SI 1991/1042) |
|  | (6), (7) | 1 Feb 1993 (SI 1992/3253) |
| 107 | (1)–(7) | 1 Feb 1993 (SI 1992/3253) |
|  | (8) | 1 Apr 1991 (SI 1991/1042) |
|  | (9)–(11) | 1 Feb 1993 (SI 1992/3253) |
| 108 | (1)(a) | 1 Feb 1993 (so far as relates to import or acquisition of genetically modified organisms) (SI 1992/3253) |
|  |  | *Not yet in force* (so far as relates to release or marketing of genetically modified organisms) |
|  | (1)(b) | 1 Apr 1991 (SI 1991/1042) |
|  | (2) | *Not yet in force* |
|  | (3)(a) | *Not yet in force* |
|  | (3)(b) | 1 Apr 1991 (SI 1991/1042) |
|  | (4) | *Not yet in force* |
|  | (5) | 1 Apr 1991 (SI 1991/1042) |
|  | (6) | *Not yet in force* (para (a) repealed) |
|  | (7) | 1 Apr 1991 (SI 1991/1042) |
|  | (8) | *Not yet in force* |
|  | (9) | 1 Apr 1991 (SI 1991/1042) |
|  | (10) | 1 Jan 1993 (SI 1992/3253) |
| 109 |  | *Not yet in force* |

**Environmental Protection Act 1990 (c 43)**—*contd*

| | | |
|---|---|---|
| 110 | | 1 Feb 1993 (so far as relates to import, acquisition, release or marketing of genetically modified organisms) (SI 1992/3253) |
| | | *Not yet in force* (so far as relates to the keeping of genetically modified organisms) |
| 111 | (1), (2) | 1 Apr 1991 (SI 1991/1042) |
| | (3) | *Not yet in force* |
| | (4), (5) | 1 Apr 1991 (SI 1991/1042) |
| | (6) | 1 Feb 1993 (SI 1992/3253) |
| | (7) | 1 Apr 1991 (SI 1991/1042) |
| | (8)–(10) | 1 Feb 1993 (SI 1992/3253) |
| | (11) | 1 Apr 1991 (SI 1991/1042) |
| 112 | (1), (2) | 1 Feb 1993 (SI 1992/3253) |
| | (3), (4) | *Not yet in force* |
| | (5)–(7) | 1 Feb 1993 (SI 1992/3253) |
| 113 | | 1 Apr 1991 (SI 1991/1042) |
| 114 | (1)–(3) | 1 Apr 1991 (SI 1991/1042) |
| | (4), (5) | 1 Feb 1993 (SI 1992/3253) |
| 115 | (1)–(3) | 1 Feb 1993 (SI 1992/3253) |
| | (4) | 1 Apr 1991 (SI 1991/1042) |
| | (5)–(10) | 1 Feb 1993 (SI 1992/3253) |
| 116 | | 1 Feb 1993 (so far as relates to import, acquisition, release or marketing of genetically modified organisms) (SI 1992/3253) |
| | | *Not yet in force* (so far as relates to the keeping of genetically modified organisms) |
| 117 | | 1 Feb 1993 (SI 1992/3253) |
| 118 | (1)(a) | 1 Feb 1993 (SI 1992/3253) |
| | (1)(b) | *Not yet in force* |
| | (1)(c) | 1 Feb 1993 (SI 1992/3253) |
| | (1)(d) | *Not yet in force* |
| | (1)(e)–(l) | 1 Feb 1993 (SI 1992/3253) |
| | (1)(m) | 1 Feb 1993 (so far as relates to s 111) (SI 1992/3253) |
| | | *Not yet in force* (so far as relates to s 108) |
| | (1)(n), (o) | 1 Feb 1993 (SI 1992/3253) |
| | (2)–(10) | 1 Feb 1993 (SI 1992/3253) |
| 119–121 | | 1 Feb 1993 (SI 1992/3253) |
| 122 | (1)(a), (b) | 1 Apr 1991 (so far as empower Secretary of State to make regulations) (SI 1991/1042) |
| | | *Not yet in force* (otherwise) |
| | (1)(c)–(h) | 1 Apr 1991 (so far as empower Secretary of State to make regulations) (SI 1991/1042) |
| | | 1 Feb 1993 (otherwise) (SI 1992/3253) |
| | (2), (3) | 1 Feb 1993 (SI 1992/3253) |
| | (4) | 1 Apr 1991 (SI 1991/1042) |
| 123 | (1)–(6) | 1 Feb 1993 (SI 1992/3253) |
| | (7) | 1 Apr 1991 (SI 1991/1042) |
| | (8) | 1 Feb 1993 (SI 1992/3253) |
| | (9) | 1 Apr 1991 (SI 1991/1042) |
| 124–126 | | 1 Apr 1991 (SI 1991/1042) |
| 127 | | 1 Feb 1993 (SI 1992/3253) |
| 128 | (1)–(4) | 5 Nov 1990 (save for amendments) (SI 1990/2226) |
| | | 1 Apr 1991 (otherwise) (SI 1991/685) |
| | (5) | See Schs 6, 7 below |
| 129 | | 5 Nov 1990 (SI 1990/2226) |
| 130 | | 1 Apr 1991 (SI 1991/685) |
| 131 | | 5 Nov 1990 (SI 1990/2226)[1] |
| 132 | (1)(a) | 1 Apr 1991 (SI 1991/685)[1] |
| | (1)(b)–(e) | 5 Nov 1990 (save for amendments) (SI 1990/2226)[1] |
| | | 1 Apr 1991 (otherwise) (SI 1991/685)[1] |
| | (2), (3) | 5 Nov 1990 (SI 1990/2226)[1] |

**Environmental Protection Act 1990 (c 43)**—*contd*

| | | |
|---|---|---|
| 133, 134 | | 5 Nov 1990 (SI 1990/2226)[1] |
| 135 | (1), (2) | 5 Nov 1990 (SI 1990/2226) |
| | (3) | See Sch 10, Pt I below |
| 136 | (1), (2) | 5 Nov 1990 (SI 1990/2226) |
| | (3) | See Sch 10, Pt II below |
| 137 | (1)–(3) | 5 Nov 1990 (SI 1990/2226) |
| | (4) | See Sch 10, Pt III below |
| 138 | | 5 Nov 1990 (SI 1990/2226) |
| 139 | | See Sch 11 below |
| 140 | (1)–(4) | 1 Jan 1991 (s 164(2)) |
| | (5) | See Sch 12 below |
| | (6)–(11) | 1 Jan 1991 (s 164(2)) |
| 141 | | 1 Jan 1991 (s 164(2)) |
| 142 | (1), (2) | 1 Jan 1991 (s 164(2)) |
| | (3) | See Sch 12 below |
| | (4)–(7) | 1 Jan 1991 (s 164(2)) |
| 143 | (1) | 14 Feb 1992 (E) (W) (SI 1992/266) |
| | | *Never in force* (S) (repealed) |
| | (2)–(4) | *Never in force* (repealed) |
| | (5), (6) | 14 Feb 1992 (E) (W) (SI 1992/266) |
| | | *Never in force* (S) (repealed) |
| 144 | | See Sch 13 below |
| 145, 146 | | 1 Jan 1991 (s 164(2)) |
| 147 | | 31 May 1991 (SI 1991/1319) |
| 148 | | See Sch 14 below |
| 149–151 | | 14 Feb 1992 (so far as enable orders or regulations to be made) (SI 1992/266) |
| | | 1 Apr 1992 (otherwise) (SI 1992/266) |
| 152 | | 10 Jul 1991 (SI 1991/1577) |
| 153–155 | | 1 Jan 1991 (s 164(2)) |
| 156 | | 1 Apr 1991 (SI 1991/1042) |
| 157 | | 1 Jan 1991 (s 164(2)) |
| 158 | | 1 Apr 1991 (SI 1991/1042) |
| 159 | | 1 Jan 1991 (SI 1990/2635) |
| 160, 161 | | 1 Jan 1991 (s 164(2)) |
| 162 | (1) | See Sch 15 below |
| | (2) | See Sch 16 below |
| | (3) | 1 Apr 1992 (SI 1992/266) |
| | (4) | *Not yet in force* |
| | (5) | 1 Jan 1991 (s 164(2)) |
| 163 | | 1 Jan 1991 (s 164(2)) |
| 164 | | 1 Nov 1990 (RA) |
| Sch 1 | | 1 Jan 1991 (SI 1990/2635) |
| Sch 2 | | 31 May 1991 (SI 1991/1319) |
| Schs 3, 4 | | 1 Jan 1991 (s 164(2)) |
| Sch 5 | paras 1–6 | 1 Jan 1991 (SI 1990/2635) |
| | para 7 | 1 Jan 1991 (s 164(2)) |
| | paras 8, 9 | *Never in force* (repealed) |
| | para 10 | 7 Dec 1990 (only to the extent that it confers power to make regulations under s 11D of the Radioactive Substances Act 1960) (SI 1990/2565) |
| | | *Never in force* (otherwise) (repealed) |
| | paras 11, 12 | *Never in force* (repealed) |
| | paras 13–15 | 1 Jan 1991 (s 164(2)) |
| | paras 16–20 | 1 Jan 1991 (SI 1990/2635) |
| Schs 6–9 | | 5 Nov 1990 (save for amendments) (SI 1990/2226) |
| | | 1 Apr 1991 (otherwise) (SI 1991/685) |
| Schs 10, 11 | | 5 Nov 1990 (SI 1990/2226) |
| Sch 12 | | 1 Jan 1991 (s 164(2)) |

**Environmental Protection Act 1990 (c 43)**—*contd*

| | | |
|---|---|---|
| Sch 13 | Pt I | 1 Jan 1992 (SI 1991/2829) |
| | Pt II, paras 11, 12 | 18 Feb 1993 (SI 1993/274) |
| | Pt II, para 13 | 1 May 1993 (SI 1993/274) |
| Sch 14 | | 1 Jan 1991 (s 164(2)) |
| Sch 15 | paras 1, 2 | 1 Apr 1991 (SI 1991/1042) |
| | para 3 | 1 Apr 1992 (SI 1992/266) |
| | paras 4, 5 | 1 Jan 1991 (s 164(2)) |
| | para 6 | 1 Apr 1991 (SI 1991/1042) |
| | paras 7–9 | 1 Jan 1991 (s 164(2)) |
| | para 10(1), (2) | 1 Apr 1992 (SI 1991/2829) |
| | para 10(3) | 14 Jan 1991 (SI 1991/96) |
| | paras 11–14 | 1 Apr 1991 (SI 1991/1042) |
| | para 15(1), (2) | *Not yet in force* (para 15(2) repealed) |
| | para 15(3)–(5) | 14 Jan 1991 (SI 1991/96) |
| | para 15(6)–(9) | 1 Apr 1991 (SI 1991/1042) |
| | para 16(1) | 1 Apr 1991 (SI 1991/1042) |
| | para 16(2) | 1 Apr 1991 (so far as inserts Control of Pollution Act 1974, s 31(2)(b)(v)) (SI 1991/1042) |
| | | *Never in force* (otherwise) (repealed) |
| | para 16(3) | 1 Apr 1991 (SI 1991/1042) |
| | para 17 | *Never in force* (repealed) |
| | para 18 | 1 Jan 1991 (s 164(2)) |
| | para 19 | 1 Apr 1992 (SI 1992/266) |
| | para 20 | 1 Apr 1991 (SI 1991/1042) |
| | para 21 | 18 Feb 1993 (SI 1993/274) |
| | para 22 | 1 Jan 1991 (so far as inserts Public Health (Control of Disease) Act 1984, s 7(4)(m)) (s 164(2)) |
| | | 1 Apr 1991 (otherwise) (SI 1991/1042) |
| | para 23 | 1 Apr 1991 (SI 1991/1042) |
| | para 24 | 1 Jan 1991 (s 164(2)) |
| | para 25 | *Never in force* (spent) |
| | para 26 | 1 May 1994 (except for the purposes of their application to specified activities[2]) (SI 1994/1096) |
| | | 1 Apr 1995 (subject to exceptions[3], in relation to an activity which involves treating, keeping or disposing of scrap metal or motor vehicles which are to be dismantled) (SI 1994/1096) |
| | para 27 | 1 May 1994 (SI 1994/1096) |
| | para 28 | 1 Apr 1991 (except in so far as it relates to the interpretation of section 74(2) of the Water Act 1989) (SI 1991/1042) |
| | | *Never in force* (otherwise) (repealed) |
| | paras 29, 30 | 1 Apr 1991 (SI 1991/1042) |
| | para 31(1)–(3) | 31 May 1991 (SI 1991/1319) |
| | para 31(4)(a) | 31 May 1991 (SI 1991/1319) |
| | para 31(4)(b) | 1 Jan 1991 (s 164(2)) |
| | para 31(4)(c) | 31 May 1991 (SI 1991/1319) |
| | para 31(5)(a) | 1 Apr 1992 (SI 1991/2829) |
| | para 31(5)(b), (c) | 31 May 1991 (SI 1991/1319) |
| | para 31(6) | 1 Apr 1992 (SI 1991/2829) |
| Sch 16 | Pt I | Repeal of Alkali, &c Works Regulation Act 1906 brought into force for purposes of application of 1906 Act to activities which fall within a description of a process which has been but has ceased to be a prescribed process (a) on 1 Dec 1994, or, if later, (b) on date on which that description of process ceases to be a prescribed process (SI 1994/2854) |
| | | 16 Dec 1996 (E) (W) (SI 1996/3056), repeals of or in— |
| | | Alkali, &c Works Regulation Act 1906 (so far as not already repealed); |
| | | Health and Safety at Work etc Act 1974; |
| | | Environmental Protection Act 1990 |
| | | 1 Apr 2015 (S) (SSI 2015/72), repeals of or in— |

**Environmental Protection Act 1990 (c 43)**—*contd*

                Alkali, &c Works Regulation Act 1906 (so far as not already
                   repealed);
                Control of Pollution Act 1974, s 105(1)
                *Not yet in force*, repeals or in—
                Clean Air Act 1956;
                Clean Air Act 1968;
                Local Government Act 1972;
                Local Government (Scotland) Act 1973;
                Control of Pollution Act 1974
                *Never in force* (repealed), repeals or in—
                Environmental Protection Act 1990 (S)

Pt II          31 May 1991 (SI 1991/1319), repeals of or in—
                Control of Pollution Act 1974, s 2;
                Control of Pollution (Amendment) Act 1989, ss 7(2), 9(1)
                1 Apr 1992 (repeal of Control of Pollution (Amendment)
                   Act 1989, s 9(2)) (SI 1991/2829)
                1 Apr 1992 (SI 1992/266), repeals of or in—
                Control of Pollution Act 1974, ss 12, 13, 14(1)–(5), (7)–(11)
                   (except so far as relate to industrial waste in England and
                   Wales), 15;
                Civic Government (Scotland) Act 1982
                1 May 1994 (repeal of Control of Pollution Act 1974, s 1)
                   (SI 1994/1096)
                1 May 1994 (S) (repeal of Control of Pollution Act 1974, s 11)
                   (SI 1994/1096)
                1 May 1994 (repeals of Control of Pollution Act 1974, ss 3–10, 18,
                   27, except for the purposes of its application to specified
                   activities[2]) (SI 1994/1096)
                1 Apr 1995 (repeals of Control of Pollution Act 1974, ss 3–10, 18,
                   27, subject to exceptions[3], in relation to an activity which
                   involves treating, keeping or disposing of scrap metal or motor
                   vehicles which are to be dismantled) (SI 1994/1096)
                1 Apr 2012 (repeal of Refuse Disposal (Amenity) Act 1978, s 1)
                   (SI 2012/898)
                1 Apr 2015 (S) (SSI 2015/72), repeals of or in—
                Control of Pollution Act 1974, ss 3–10, 14, 16–21, 27–30;
                Local Government Act 1988, Sch 1, para 1;
                Electricity Act 1989, Sch 16, para 18;
                Environment Act 1990, s 36(8)
                *Not yet in force*, repeals of or in—
                Control of Pollution Act 1974, ss 11(12), 12–14 (in relation to
                   industrial waste), 16, 17, 19–21, 28–30;
                Local Government Act 1988;
                Electricity Act 1989;
                Water Act 1989;
                Environmental Protection Act 1990

Pt III         1 Jan 1991 (s 164(2))
Pt IV          1 Apr 1991 (SI 1991/1042)
Pt V           1 Jan 1991 (SI 1990/2635)
Pt VI          1 Apr 1991 (SI 1991/685), repeals of or in—
                Countryside Act 1968;
                Wildlife and Countryside Act 1981
                1 Apr 1992 (repeals in Nature Conservancy Council Act 1973)
                 (SI 1991/2829)
Pt VII        1 Jan 1992 (repeals in Planning (Hazardous Substances) Act 1990)
                 (SI 1991/2829)
                18 Feb 1993 (repeals in Town and Country Planning (Scotland)
                 Act 1972) (SI 1993/274)
                1 May 1993 (repeal in Housing and Planning Act 1986)
                 (SI 1993/274)

**Environmental Protection Act 1990 (c 43)**—*contd*

|  |  |
|---|---|
|  | *Not yet in force*, repeals of in— |
|  | Electricity Act 1989; |
|  | Planning (Consequential Provisions) Act 1990 |
| Pt VIII | 1 Apr 2015 (S) (repeals in Food and Environment Protection Act 1985, ss 5, 6, Sch 4) |
|  | *Not yet in force* (otherwise) |
| Pt IX | 1 Jan 1991 (repeal of Control of Pollution Act 1974, s 100) (s 164(2)) |
|  | 1 Apr 1992 (SI 1992/266), repeals of or in— |
|  | Dogs Act 1906; |
|  | Civic Government (Scotland) Act 1982; |
|  | Local Government Act 1988 |
|  | 18 Feb 1993 (SI 1993/274), repeals of— |
|  | Criminal Justice Act 1982, s 43; |
|  | Criminal Justice Act 1988, s 58 |

[1]   1 Apr 1991 was the day appointed by SI 1991/685 as the day on and after which the Nature Conservancy Councils exercised functions under ss 132–134

[2]   The specified activities are—

(a)   an activity which on that date is the subject of a pending application for a disposal licence under Part I of the Control of Pollution Act 1974 (in which case the provision comes into force on the day immediately following the relevant date (see art 1(2)) in relation to the application in question);

(b)   an activity in respect of which on that date an appeal in pursuance of section 10(1)(d) of the Control of Pollution Act 1974 (appeals to Secretary of State where a disposal licence is revoked) is pending or where the period for making such an appeal has not expired (in which case the provision comes into force on the day immediately following the appropriate date (see art 1(2)) in relation to the appeal in question);

(c)   an activity which involves treating, keeping or disposing of scrap metal or motor vehicles which are to be dismantled;

(d)   an activity—

(i)   which on that date is the subject of a disposal licence under Part I of the Control of Pollution Act 1974;

(ii)   which is or forms part of an existing process for which no authorisation has been granted; and

(iii)   to which, if an authorisation were granted, section 33(1)(a) and (b) of the Environmental Protection Act 1990 would not apply by virtue of the Waste Management Licensing Regulations 1994

(in which case the provision comes into force on the day immediately following the prescribed date (see art 1(2)) in relation to the process in question)

[3]   The exceptions are that—

(a)   if on 1 Apr 1995 that activity is the subject of a pending application for a disposal licence under Part I of the Control of Pollution Act 1974, the provision shall come into force on the day immediately following the relevant date (see art 1(2)) in relation to the application in question;

(b)   if on 1 Apr 1995 an appeal in pursuance of section 10(1)(d) of the Control of Pollution Act 1974 (appeals to Secretary of State where a disposal licence is revoked) is pending in respect of that activity or the period for making such an appeal has not expired, the provision shall come into force on the day immediately following the appropriate date (see art 1(2)) in relation to that appeal

---

**Finance Act 1990 (c 29)**

*Budget Day*: 20 Mar 1990

*RA*: 26 Jul 1990

The commencement details of Finance Acts are not set out, as the dates from which their provisions take effect are usually stated clearly and unambiguously in the text of the Act, and charging provisions will normally state for which year or years of assessment they are to have effect.

---

## Food Safety Act 1990 (c 16)

*RA:* 29 Jun 1990

*Commencement provisions:* s 60(2)–(4); Food Safety Act 1990 (Commencement No 1) Order 1990, SI 1990/1383; Food Safety Act 1990 (Commencement No 2) Order 1990, SI 1990/2372; Food Safety Act 1990 (Commencement No 3) Order 1992, SI 1992/57

| | | |
|---|---|---|
| 1 | (1), (2) | 3 Jul 1990 (for purposes of ss 13, 51) (SI 1990/1383) |
| | | 1 Dec 1990 (otherwise) (SI 1990/2372) |
| | (3), (4) | 3 Jul 1990 (for purposes of s 13) (SI 1990/1383) |
| | | 1 Dec 1990 (otherwise) (SI 1990/2372) |
| 2, 3 | | 3 Jul 1990 (for purposes of s 13) (SI 1990/1383) |
| | | 1 Dec 1990 (otherwise) (SI 1990/2372) |
| 4 | (1) | 1 Dec 1990 (SI 1990/2372) |
| | (2) | 3 Jul 1990 (for purposes of s 13) (SI 1990/1383) |
| | | 1 Dec 1990 (otherwise) (SI 1990/2372) |
| 5, 6 | | 3 Jul 1990 (for purposes of s 13) (SI 1990/1383) |
| | | 1 Dec 1990 (otherwise) (SI 1990/2372) |
| 7 | (1), (2) | 1 Jan 1991 (SI 1990/2372) |
| | (3) | 3 Jul 1990 (for purposes of s 13) (SI 1990/1383) |
| | | 1 Jan 1991 (otherwise) (SI 1990/2372) |
| 8–12 | | 1 Jan 1991 (SI 1990/2372) |
| 13 | | 29 Jun 1990 (s 60(2)) |
| 14, 15 | | 1 Jan 1991 (SI 1990/2372) |
| 16 | (1), (2) | 1 Dec 1990 (SI 1990/2372) |
| | (3) | See Sch 1 below |
| | (4), (5) | 1 Dec 1990 (SI 1990/2372) |
| 17–19 | | 1 Dec 1990 (SI 1990/2372) |
| 20 | | 3 Jul 1990 (for purposes of s 13) (SI 1990/1383) |
| | | 1 Jan 1991 (otherwise) (SI 1990/2372) |
| 21 | (1) | 3 Jul 1990 (for purposes of s 13) (SI 1990/1383) |
| | | 1 Jan 1991 (otherwise) (SI 1990/2372) |
| | (2)–(4) | 1 Jan 1991 (SI 1990/2372) |
| | (5), (6) | 3 Jul 1990 (for purposes of s 13) (SI 1990/1383) |
| | | 1 Jan 1991 (otherwise) (SI 1990/2372) |
| 22 | | 3 Jul 1990 (for purposes of s 13) (SI 1990/1383) |
| | | 1 Jan 1991 (otherwise) (SI 1990/2372) |
| 23, 24 | | 1 Jan 1991 (SI 1990/2372) |
| 25, 26 | | 1 Dec 1990 (SI 1990/2372) |
| 27 | (1) | 1 Jan 1991 (SI 1990/2372) |
| | (2) | 1 Dec 1990 (SI 1990/2372) |
| | (3), (4) | 1 Jan 1991 (SI 1990/2372) |
| | (5) | 1 Dec 1990 (SI 1990/2372) |
| 28 | (1) | 1 Jan 1991 (SI 1990/2372) |
| | (2) | 1 Dec 1990 (SI 1990/2372) |
| 29 | | 3 Jul 1990 (for purposes of s 13) (SI 1990/1383) |
| | | 1 Jan 1991 (otherwise) (SI 1990/2372) |
| 30, 31 | | 1 Dec 1990 (SI 1990/2372) |
| 32–36 | | 3 Jul 1990 (for purposes of s 13) (SI 1990/1383) |
| | | 1 Jan 1991 (otherwise) (SI 1990/2372) |
| 37–39 | | 1 Jan 1991 (SI 1990/2372) |
| 40 | | 1 Dec 1990 (SI 1990/2372) |
| 41, 42 | | 3 Jul 1990 (for purposes of s 13) (SI 1990/1383) |
| | | 1 Jan 1991 (otherwise) (SI 1990/2372) |
| 43 | | 1 Jan 1991 (SI 1990/2372) |
| 44 | | 3 Jul 1990 (for purposes of s 13) (SI 1990/1383) |
| | | 1 Jan 1991 (otherwise) (SI 1990/2372) |
| 45 | | 1 Dec 1990 (SI 1990/2372) |
| 46 | | 3 Jul 1990 (for purposes of s 13) (SI 1990/1383) |
| | | 1 Jan 1991 (otherwise) (SI 1990/2372) |

**Food Safety Act 1990 (c 16)**—*contd*

| | | |
|---|---|---|
| 47 | | 1 Jan 1991 (SI 1990/2372) |
| 48 | (1)–(3) | 3 Jul 1990 (for purposes of s 13) (SI 1990/1383) |
| | | 1 Dec 1990 (otherwise) (SI 1990/2372) |
| | (4), (5) | 1 Dec 1990 (SI 1990/2372) |
| 49 | (1) | 3 Jul 1990 (for purposes of s 13) (SI 1990/1383) |
| | | 1 Jan 1991 (otherwise) (SI 1990/2372) |
| | (2) | 1 Dec 1990 (SI 1990/2372) |
| | (3)–(5) | 3 Jul 1990 (for purposes of s 13) (SI 1990/1383) |
| | | 1 Jan 1991 (otherwise) (SI 1990/2372) |
| 50 | | 3 Jul 1990 (for purposes of s 13) (SI 1990/1383) |
| | | 1 Jan 1991 (otherwise) (SI 1990/2372) |
| 51 | | 29 Jun 1990 (s 60(2)) |
| 52 | | See Sch 2 below |
| 53 | (1) | 3 Jul 1990 (for purposes of ss 13, 51) (SI 1990/1383) |
| | | 1 Dec 1990 (otherwise) (SI 1990/2372) |
| | (2)–(4) | 3 Jul 1990 (for purposes of s 13) (SI 1990/1383) |
| | | 1 Dec 1990 (otherwise) (SI 1990/2372) |
| | (5) | 1 Dec 1990 (SI 1990/2372) |
| 54 | | 1 Apr 1992 (SI 1990/2372) |
| 55, 56 | | 1 Jan 1991 (SI 1990/2372) |
| 57 | | 3 Jul 1990 (for purposes of s 13) (SI 1990/1383) |
| | | 1 Dec 1990 (otherwise) (SI 1990/2372) |
| 58 | (1) | 3 Jul 1990 (for purposes of s 13) (SI 1990/1383) |
| | | 1 Jan 1991 (otherwise) (SI 1990/2372) |
| | (2)–(4) | 1 Jan 1991 (SI 1990/2372) |
| 59 | (1) | See Sch 3 below |
| | (2) | 1 Dec 1990 (SI 1990/2372) |
| | (3) | See Sch 4 below |
| | (4) | See Sch 5 below |
| 60 | | 1 Jan 1991 (SI 1990/2372) |
| Sch 1 | | 1 Dec 1990 (SI 1990/2372) |
| Sch 2 | paras 1–11 | 1 Jan 1991 (SI 1990/2372) |
| | paras 12–15 | 29 Jun 1990 (s 60(2)) |
| | para 16 | 1 Jan 1991 (SI 1990/2372) |
| Sch 3 | paras 1–28 | 1 Jan 1991 (SI 1990/2372) |
| | paras 29, 30 | 13 Jul 1990 (for purposes of s 51) (SI 1990/1383) |
| | | 1 Jan 1991 (otherwise) (SI 1990/2372) |
| | paras 31–38 | 1 Jan 1991 (SI 1990/2372) |
| Sch 4 | | 1 Dec 1990 (SI 1990/2372) |
| Sch 5 | | 1 Dec 1990 (so far as relates to Public Analysts (Scotland) Regulations 1956, SI 1956/1162 or Public Analysts Regulations 1957, SI 1957/237, repeals of or in Food and Drugs (Scotland) Act 1956, ss 27, 29, 56 and Food Act 1984, ss 76(2), 79(5)) (SI 1990/2372) |
| | | 1 Jan 1991 (all repeals so far as not already in force except those of or in Food Act 1984, s 13 so far as relating to regulations (see following notes), ss 16–20, 62–67, ss 92, 93 (so far as relate to ss 16 and 18), s 132(1) so far as relates to regulations (see following notes)) (SI 1990/2372) |
| | | 1 Apr 1991 (repeals of Food Act 1984, ss 13, 132(1), so far as relate to Food Hygiene (Amendment) Regulations 1990, SI 1990/1431 (except reg 3(b), Sch 1 thereof)) (SI 1990/2372) |
| | | 1 Apr 1992 (repeals of Food Act 1984, ss 13, 132(1), so far as relate to Food Hygiene (Amendment) Regulations 1990, reg 3(b), Sch 1) (SI 1990/2372) |
| | | 3 Apr 1992 (repeals of or in Food Act 1984, ss 16–20, Pt IV (ss 62–67), ss 92 (so far as relates to s 16(2)), 93 (so far as relates to s 18(4))) (SI 1992/57) |

## Gaming (Amendment) Act 1990 (c 26)

*RA:* 13 Jul 1990

*Commencement provisions:* s 2(2), (3); Gaming (Amendment) Act 1990 (Commencement) Order 1991, SI 1991/59

| | | |
|---|---|---|
| 1 | | See Sch below |
| 2 | | 13 Sep 1990 (s 2(2)) |
| Schedule | paras 1, 2 | 13 Sep 1990 (s 2(2)) |
| | paras 3, 4 | 1 Apr 1991 (SI 1991/59) |
| | paras 5–10 | 13 Sep 1990 (s 2(2)) |

## Government Trading Act 1990 (c 30)

*RA:* 26 Jul 1990

*Commencement provisions:* s 4(3); Government Trading Act 1990 (Appointed Day) Order 1991, SI 1991/132

| | | |
|---|---|---|
| 1 | | 26 Jul 1990 (RA) |
| 2 | | See Sch 1 below |
| 3 | | 26 Jul 1990 (RA) |
| 4 | | See Sch 2, Pt I below |
| 5 | | See Sch 2, Pt II below |
| Sch 1 | | 26 Jul 1990 (RA) |
| Sch 2 | Pt I | 11 Feb 1991 (SI 1991/132) |
| | Pt II | 26 Jul 1990 (RA) |

## Greenwich Hospital Act 1990 (c 13)

*RA:* 29 Jun 1990

Whole Act in force 29 Jun 1990 (RA)

## Horses (Protective Headgear for Young Riders) Act 1990 (c 25)

*RA:* 13 Jul 1990

*Commencement provisions:* s 5(2); Horses (Protective Headgear for Young Riders) Act 1990 (Commencement) Order 1992, SI 1992/1200

| | |
|---|---|
| 1–3 | 30 Jun 1992 (SI 1992/1200) |
| 4, 5 | 13 Jul 1990 (s 5(2)) |

## Human Fertilisation and Embryology Act 1990 (c 37)

*RA:* 1 Nov 1990

*Commencement provisions:* s 49(2); Human Fertilisation and Embryology Act 1990 (Commencement No 1) Order 1990, SI 1990/2165; Human Fertilisation and Embryology Act 1990 (Commencement No 2 and Transitional Provision) Order 1991, SI 1991/480; Human Fertilisation and Embryology Act 1990 (Commencement No 3 and Transitional Provisions) Order 1991, SI 1991/1400, as amended by SI 1991/1781; Human Fertilisation and Embryology Act 1990 (Commencement No 5) Order 1994, SI 1994/1776

| | | |
|---|---|---|
| 1 | | 1 Aug 1991 (SI 1991/1400)[1] |
| 2 | (1) | 7 Nov 1990 (so far as relates to definition of "the Authority") (SI 1990/2165) |
| | | 1 Aug 1991 (otherwise) (SI 1991/1400)[1] |
| | (2), (3) | 1 Aug 1991 (SI 1991/1400)[1] |
| 3, 4 | | 1 Aug 1991 (SI 1991/1400)[1] |
| 5 | (1), (2) | 7 Nov 1990 (SI 1990/2165) |

**Human Fertilisation and Embryology Act 1990 (c 37)**—*contd*

| | | |
|---|---|---|
| | (3) | See Sch 1 below |
| 6, 7 | | 7 Nov 1990 (SI 1990/2165) |
| 8 | | 1 Aug 1991 (SI 1991/1400)[1] |
| 9 | (1)–(4) | 1 Aug 1991 (SI 1991/1400)[1] |
| | (5) | 8 Jul 1991 (for purpose of making regulations) (SI 1991/1400) |
| | | 1 Aug 1991 (otherwise) (SI 1991/1400)[1] |
| | (6)–(11) | 1 Aug 1991 (SI 1991/1400)[1] |
| 10 | | 8 Jul 1991 (for purpose of making regulations) (SI 1991/1400) |
| | | 1 Aug 1991 (otherwise) (SI 1991/1400)[1] |
| 11–13 | | 1 Aug 1991 (SI 1991/1400)[1] |
| 14 | (1)–(4) | 1 Aug 1991 (SI 1991/1400)[1] |
| | (5) | 8 Jul 1991 (for purpose of making regulations) (SI 1991/1400) |
| | | 1 Aug 1991 (otherwise) (SI 1991/1400)[1] |
| 15 | | 1 Aug 1991 (SI 1991/1400)[1] |
| 16 | (1) | 8 Jul 1991 (for purpose of requiring that an application for a licence be made in an approved form and be accompanied by initial fee) (SI 1991/1400) |
| | | 1 Aug 1991 (otherwise) (SI 1991/1400)[1] |
| | (2)–(5) | 1 Aug 1991 (SI 1991/1400)[1] |
| | (6) | 8 Jul 1991 (for purpose of fixing amount of initial fee) (SI 1991/1400) |
| | | 1 Aug 1991 (otherwise) (SI 1991/1400)[1] |
| | (7) | 1 Aug 1991 (SI 1991/1400)[1] |
| 17–25 | | 1 Aug 1991 (SI 1991/1400)[1] |
| 26 | | 7 Nov 1990 (SI 1990/2165) |
| 27–29 | | 1 Aug 1991 (SI 1991/1400)[1] |
| 30 | (1)–(8) | 1 Nov 1994 (SI 1994/1776) |
| | (9), (10) | 5 Jul 1994 (SI 1994/1776) |
| | (11) | 1 Nov 1994 (SI 1994/1776) |
| 31, 32 | | 1 Aug 1991 (SI 1991/1400)[1] |
| 33 | (1) | 7 Nov 1990 (SI 1990/2165) |
| | (2)(a) | 1 Aug 1991 (SI 1991/1400)[1] |
| | (2)(b) | 7 Nov 1990 (SI 1990/2165) |
| | (3) | 1 Aug 1991 (SI 1991/1400)[1] |
| | (4) | 7 Nov 1990 (SI 1990/2165) |
| | (5)–(8) | 1 Aug 1991 (SI 1991/1400)[1] |
| 34, 35 | | 1 Aug 1991 (SI 1991/1400)[1] |
| 36 | | 7 Nov 1990 (SI 1990/2165) |
| 37 | | 1 Apr 1991 (subject to transitional provisions) (SI 1991/480) |
| 38, 39 | | 1 Aug 1991 (SI 1991/1400)[1] |
| 40 | | 7 Nov 1990 (SI 1990/2165) |
| 41 | (1), (2) | 1 Aug 1991 (SI 1991/1400)[1] |
| | (3) | 8 Jul 1991 (SI 1991/1400) |
| | (4) | 8 Jul 1991 (so far as relates to s 41(3)) (SI 1991/1400) |
| | | 1 Aug 1991 (otherwise) (SI 1991/1400)[1] |
| | (5) | 7 Nov 1990 (so far as relates to s 33(1), (2)(b), (4)) (SI 1990/2165) |
| | | 1 Aug 1991 (otherwise) (SI 1991/1400)[1] |
| | (6) | 7 Nov 1990 (so far as relates to s 40) (SI 1990/2165) |
| | | 1 Aug 1991 (otherwise) (SI 1991/1400)[1] |
| | (7), (8) | 1 Aug 1991 (SI 1991/1400)[1] |
| | (9) | 7 Nov 1990 (so far as relates to s 40) (SI 1990/2165) |
| | | 1 Aug 1991 (otherwise) (SI 1991/1400)[1] |
| | (10), (11) | 1 Aug 1991 (SI 1991/1400)[1] |
| 42 | | 7 Nov 1990 (SI 1990/2165) |
| 43 | (1) | 8 Jul 1991 (for purpose of making regulations) (SI 1991/1400) |
| | | 1 Aug 1991 (otherwise) (SI 1991/1400)[1] |
| | (2), (3) | 1 Aug 1991 (SI 1991/1400)[1] |
| 44 | | 1 Aug 1991 (SI 1991/1400)[1] |
| 45 | | 8 Jul 1991 (SI 1991/1400) |

**Human Fertilisation and Embryology Act 1990 (c 37)**—*contd*

| | | |
|---|---|---|
| 46, 47 | | 1 Aug 1991 (SI 1991/1400)[1] |
| 48 | (1) | 7 Nov 1990 (so far as relates to provisions brought into force by SI 1990/2165) (SI 1990/2165) |
| | | 1 Apr 1991 (so far as relates to provisions brought into force by SI 1991/480) (SI 1991/480) |
| | | 8 Jul 1991 (so far as relates to provisions brought into force by SI 1991/1400) (SI 1991/1400) |
| | | 1 Aug 1991 (except so far as relates to s 30) (SI 1991/1400)[1] |
| | | 5 Jul 1994 (so far as relates to s 30(9), (10)) (SI 1994/1776) |
| | | 1 Nov 1994 (so far as relates to s 30(1)–(8), (11)) (SI 1994/1776) |
| | (2) | 1 Aug 1991 (SI 1991/1400)[1] |
| 49 | (1), (2) | 7 Nov 1990 (SI 1990/2165) |
| | (3), (4) | 1 Aug 1991 (SI 1991/1400)[1] |
| | (5) | See Sch 4 below |
| | (6), (7) | 7 Nov 1990 (SI 1990/2165) |
| Sch 1 | | 7 Nov 1990 (SI 1990/2165) |
| Schs 2–4 | | 1 Aug 1991 (SI 1991/1400)[1] |

[1] Subject to transitional provisions set out in SI 1991/1400, arts 3, 4, as amended by SI 1991/1781, art 2

---

**Import and Export Control Act 1990 (c 45)**

*RA:* 6 Dec 1990

Whole Act in force 6 Dec 1990 (RA)

---

**Landlord and Tenant (Licensed Premises) Act 1990 (c 39)**

*RA:* 1 Nov 1990

*Commencement provisions:* s 2(3)

| | | |
|---|---|---|
| 1 | (1) | 1 Jan 1991 (s 2(3)) |
| | (2), (3) | 1 Jan 1991 (subject to transitional provisions) (s 2(3)) |
| | (4) | 1 Jan 1991 (s 2(3)) |
| 2 | | 1 Jan 1991 (s 2(3)) |

---

**Law Reform (Miscellaneous Provisions) (Scotland) Act 1990 (c 40)**

*RA:* 1 Nov 1990

*Commencement provisions:* s 75(2)–(4); Law Reform (Miscellaneous Provisions) (Scotland) Act 1990 Commencement (No 1) Order 1990, SI 1990/2328; Law Reform (Miscellaneous Provisions) (Scotland) Act 1990 (Commencement No 2) Order 1990, SI 1990/2624; Law Reform (Miscellaneous Provisions) (Scotland) Act 1990 (Commencement No 3) Order 1991, SI 1991/330; Law Reform (Miscellaneous Provisions) (Scotland) Act 1990 (Commencement No 4) Order 1991, SI 1991/822; Law Reform (Miscellaneous Provisions) (Scotland) Act 1990 (Commencement No 5) Order 1991, SI 1991/850; Law Reform (Miscellaneous Provisions) (Scotland) Act 1990 (Commencement No 6) Order 1991, SI 1991/1252; Law Reform (Miscellaneous Provisions) (Scotland) Act 1990 (Commencement No 7) Order 1991, SI 1991/1903; Law Reform (Miscellaneous Provisions) (Scotland) Act 1990 (Commencement No 8) Order 1991, SI 1991/2151; Law Reform (Miscellaneous Provisions) (Scotland) Act 1990 (Commencement No 9) Order 1991, SI 1991/2862; Law Reform (Miscellaneous Provisions) (Scotland) Act 1990 (Commencement No 10) Order 1992, SI 1992/1599; Law Reform (Miscellaneous Provisions) (Scotland) Act 1990 (Commencement No 11) Order 1993, SI 1993/641; Law Reform (Miscellaneous Provisions) (Scotland) Act 1990 (Commencement No 12) Order 1993, SI 1993/2253; Law Reform (Miscellaneous Provisions) (Scotland) Act 1990 (Commencement No 13) Order 1995, SI 1995/364; Law Reform (Miscellaneous Provisions) (Scotland) Act 1990 (Commencement No 13) Order 1996, SI 1996/2894, as amended by

**Law Reform (Miscellaneous Provisions) (Scotland) Act 1990 (c 40)**—*contd*
SI 1996/2966[1]; Law Reform (Miscellaneous Provisions) (Scotland) Act 1990 (Commencement No 15) Order 2004, SSI 2004/382; Law Reform (Miscellaneous Provisions) (Scotland) Act 1990 (Commencement No 16) Order 2007, SSI 2007/141

| | | |
|---|---|---|
| 1, 2 | | 27 Jul 1992 (SI 1992/1599) |
| 3 | (1) | 4 Jul 1992 (for purpose of power to make orders) (SI 1992/1599) |
| | | 27 Jul 1992 (otherwise) (SI 1992/1599) |
| | (2)–(4) | 27 Jul 1992 (SI 1992/1599) |
| 4 | (1)–(3) | 30 Sep 1992 (SI 1992/1599) |
| | (4) | 4 Jul 1992 (SI 1992/1599) |
| 5 | (1), (2) | 30 Sep 1992 (SI 1992/1599) |
| | (3) | 4 Jul 1992 (SI 1992/1599) |
| | (4) | 30 Sep 1992 (SI 1992/1599) |
| | (5) | 4 Jul 1992 (SI 1992/1599) |
| | (6)–(14) | 30 Sep 1992 (SI 1992/1599) |
| 6 | | 27 Jul 1992 (SI 1992/1599) |
| 7 | (1)–(4) | 27 Jul 1992 (SI 1992/1599) |
| | (5) | 4 Jul 1992 (for purpose of power to make regulations) (SI 1992/1599) |
| | | 27 Jul 1992 (otherwise) (SI 1992/1599) |
| | (6)–(12) | 27 Jul 1992 (SI 1992/1599) |
| 8 | | 27 Jul 1992 (SI 1992/1599) |
| 9 | (1)–(4) | 27 Jul 1992 (SI 1992/1599) |
| | (5) | 4 Jul 1992 (for purpose of power to make orders) (SI 1992/1599) |
| | | 27 Jul 1992 (otherwise) (SI 1992/1599) |
| | (6), (7) | 27 Jul 1992 (SI 1992/1599) |
| 10–12 | | 15 Sep 1993 (SI 1993/2253) |
| 13, 14 | | 27 Jul 1992 (SI 1992/1599) |
| 15 | (1)–(4) | 27 Jul 1992 (SI 1992/1599) |
| | (5)(a) | 27 Jul 1992 (SI 1992/1599) |
| | (5)(b) | 4 Jul 1992 (for purpose of power to make orders) (SI 1992/1599) |
| | | 27 Jul 1992 (otherwise) (SI 1992/1599) |
| | (5)(c) | 27 Jul 1992 (SI 1992/1599) |
| | (5)(d) | 4 Jul 1992 (for purpose of power to make orders) (SI 1992/1599) |
| | | 27 Jul 1992 (otherwise) (SI 1992/1599) |
| | (6)–(10) | 27 Jul 1992 (SI 1992/1599) |
| | (11) | 4 Jul 1992 (SI 1992/1599) |
| 16 | (1)–(3) | 1 Apr 1991 (SI 1991/822) |
| | (4) | See Sch 1, Pt I below |
| 17 | (1), (2) | 1 Mar 1997 (SI 1996/2894) |
| | (3) | 30 Sep 1991 (SI 1991/2151) |
| | (4)–(10) | 1 Mar 1997 (SI 1996/2894) |
| | (11)–(15) | 30 Sep 1991 (SI 1991/2151) |
| | (16)–(24) | 1 Mar 1997 (SI 1996/2894) |
| 18 | (1)–(9) | 1 Mar 1997 (SI 1996/2894) |
| | (10), (11) | 30 Sep 1991 (SI 1991/2151) |
| | (12)–(15) | 1 Mar 1997 (SI 1996/2894) |
| 19 | | *Never in force* (repealed) |
| 20 | (1)–(11) | 1 Mar 1997 (SI 1996/2894) |
| | (12) | See Sch 1, Pt II below |
| | (13)–(17) | 1 Mar 1997 (SI 1996/2894) |
| 21 | | 1 Mar 1997 (SI 1996/2894) |
| 22 | (1)(a) | 1 Mar 1997 (SI 1996/2894) |
| | (1)(b) | *Never in force* (repealed) |
| | (2)(a), (b) | 1 Mar 1997 (SI 1996/2894) |
| | (2)(c) | *Never in force* (repealed) |
| 23 | | 1 Apr 1991 (SI 1991/822) |
| 24 | | 3 Jun 1991 (SI 1991/1252) |
| 25–29 | | 19 Mar 2007 (SSI 2007/141) |
| 30 | | 3 Jun 1991 (SI 1991/1252) |

**Law Reform (Miscellaneous Provisions) (Scotland) Act 1990 (c 40)**—*contd*

| | | |
|---|---|---|
| 31 | | 17 Mar 1993 (SI 1993/641) |
| 32 | | 17 Mar 1993 (for purpose of provisions relating to making of rules and orders in Solicitors (Scotland) Act 1980, s 60A(2), (3), (5)–(8)) (SI 1993/641) |
| | | 1 Oct 2004 (otherwise) (SSI 2004/382) |
| 33 | | 3 Jun 1991 (SI 1991/1252) |
| 34 | (1) | 1 Apr 1991 (SI 1991/822) |
| | (2)–(8) | 3 Jun 1991 (SI 1991/1252) |
| | (9)(a)–(c) | 1 Apr 1991 (SI 1991/822) |
| | (9)(d), (e) | 1 Mar 1997 (SI 1996/2894) |
| | (9)(f) | *Never in force* (repealed) |
| | (9)(g) | 1 Mar 1997 (SI 1996/2894) |
| | (9)(h) | *Never in force* (repealed) |
| | (10) | See Sch 3 below |
| 35 | | 1 Apr 1991 (SI 1991/822) |
| 36 | (1) | 20 Jul 1992 (SI 1992/1599) |
| | (2) | 4 Jul 1992 (for purpose of power to make act of sederunt) (SI 1992/1599) |
| | | 20 Jul 1992 (otherwise) (SI 1992/1599) |
| | (3) | 4 Jul 1992 (for purpose of power to make act of sederunt under Solicitors (Scotland) Act 1980, s 61A) (SI 1992/1599) |
| | | 20 Jul 1992 (otherwise) (SI 1992/1599) |
| | (4) | *Not yet in force* |
| 37 | | 20 Jul 1992 (SI 1992/1599) |
| 38–42 | | 30 Sep 1991 (SI 1991/2151) |
| 43 | | 3 Jun 1991 (SI 1991/1252) |
| 44 | | 1 Apr 1991 (SI 1991/822) |
| 45–48 | | 1 Jan 1991 (s 75(3)(a)) |
| 49 | (1)–(7) | 1 Jan 1991 (s 75(3)(a)) |
| | (8) | See Sch 5 below |
| | (9)–(11) | 1 Jan 1991 (s 75(3)(a)) |
| 50–55 | | 1 Jan 1991 (s 75(3)(a)) |
| 56 | | 30 Sep 1991 (for purposes of proceedings in the High Court of Justiciary sitting at Edinburgh or Glasgow and any sheriff court in sheriffdom of Glasgow and Strathkelvin or Lothian and Borders) (SI 1991/2151) |
| | | 3 Apr 1995 (otherwise) (SI 1995/364) |
| 57–59 | | 30 Sep 1991 (for purposes of proceedings in any sheriff court in sheriffdom of Glasgow and Strathkelvin or Lothian and Borders) (SI 1991/2151) |
| | | 3 Apr 1995 (otherwise) (SI 1995/364) |
| 60 | | 30 Sep 1991 (SI 1991/2151) |
| 61 | | 1 Apr 1991 (SI 1991/850) |
| 62 | (1)–(4) | 1 Apr 1991 (SI 1991/850) |
| | (5) | See Sch 6 below |
| | (6) | 1 Apr 1991 (SI 1991/850) |
| 63 | | 1 Dec 1990 (SI 1990/2328) |
| 64, 65 | | 1 Jan 1991 (SI 1990/2624) |
| 66 | | See Sch 7 below |
| 67 | | 1 Jan 1991 (s 73(3)(b)) |
| 68 | | 1 Apr 1991 (SI 1991/330) |
| 69 | | 1 Mar 1991 (SI 1991/330) |
| 70–72 | | 1 Jan 1991 (s 75(3)(b)) |
| 73 | (1)(a) | 17 Mar 1993 (SI 1993/641) |
| | (1)(b)–(e) | 1 Apr 1991 (SI 1991/822) |
| | (2) | 17 Mar 1993 (SI 1993/641) |
| 74 | (1) | See Sch 8 below |
| | (2) | See Sch 9 below |
| 75 | | 1 Nov 1990 (RA) |

**Law Reform (Miscellaneous Provisions) (Scotland) Act 1990 (c 40)**—*contd*

| | | |
|---|---|---|
| Sch 1 | Pt I | 1 Apr 1991 (SI 1991/822) |
| | Pt II | 1 Mar 1997 (SI 1996/2894) |
| Sch 2 | | 19 Mar 2007 (SSI 2007/141) |
| Schs 3, 4 | | 1 Apr 1991 (SI 1991/822) |
| Sch 5 | | 1 Jan 1991 (s 75(3)(a)) |
| Sch 6 | | See Sch 7 below |
| Sch 7 | | 1 Jan 1991 (s 75(3)(a)) |
| Sch 8 | paras 1–18 | 31 Dec 1991 (SI 1991/2892) |
| | paras 19, 20 | 1 Mar 1997 (SI 1996/2894) |
| | para 21 | 1 Jan 1991 (s 75(3)(b)) |
| | para 22(1) | 1 Mar 1997 (for all purposes except in relation to a recognised financial institution) (SI 1996/2894) |
| | | *Not yet in force* (exception noted above) |
| | para 22(2) | 1 Mar 1997 (SI 1996/2894) |
| | para 23 | 1 Apr 1991 (SI 1991/822) |
| | paras 24, 25 | 1 Mar 1997 (SI 1996/2894) |
| | para 26 | 1 Jan 1991 (SI 1990/2624) |
| | para 27(1), (2) | 3 Jun 1991 (SI 1991/1252) |
| | para 27(3) | 1 Nov 1990 (s 75(4)) |
| | para 28 | 1 Apr 1991 (SI 1991/850) |
| | para 29(1)–(4) | 3 Jun 1991 (SI 1991/1252) |
| | para 29(5)(a), (b) | 1 Mar 1997 (except in relation to a recognised financial institution) (SI 1996/2894) |
| | | *Not yet in force* (exception noted above) |
| | para 29(5)(c) | 17 Mar 1993 (SI 1993/641) |
| | para 29(5)(d) | 1 Mar 1997 (except in relation to a recognised financial institution) (SI 1996/2894) |
| | | *Not yet in force* (exception noted above) |
| | para 29(6)(a) | 1 Jan 1991 (SI 1990/2624) |
| | para 29(6)(b) | 1 Jan 1991 (in so far as it relates to insertion of Solicitors (Scotland) Act 1980, s 32(2B)) (SI 1990/2624) |
| | | 1 Mar 1997 (except in relation to a recognised financial institution) (SI 1996/2894) |
| | | *Not yet in force* (exception noted above) |
| | para 29(7) | 1 Jan 1991 (SI 1990/2624) |
| | para 29(8)–(14) | 3 Jun 1991 (SI 1991/1252) |
| | para 29(15)(a) | 3 Jun 1991 (SI 1991/1252) |
| | para 29(15)(b)–(d) | 17 Mar 1993 (SI 1993/641) |
| | para 29(15)(e) | 3 Jun 1991 (SI 1991/1252) |
| | para 29(15)(f) | 17 Mar 1993 (SI 1993/641) |
| | para 29(16), (17) | 3 Jun 1991 (SI 1991/1252) |
| | para 30 | 20 Jul 1992 (SI 1992/1599) |
| | paras 31, 32 | 1 Jan 1991 (SI 1990/2624) |
| | para 33 | 1 Dec 1990 (SI 1990/2328) |
| | para 34 | 1 Jan 1991 (s 75(3)(b)) |
| | para 35 | 1 Dec 1990 (SI 1990/2328) |
| | para 36(1) | *Not yet in force* |
| | para 36(2)–(5) | 30 Sep 1991 (SI 1991/2151) |
| | para 36(6) | 26 Aug 1991 (SI 1991/1903) |
| | para 36(7)–(9) | *Not yet in force* |
| | para 36(10)–(15) | 30 Sep 1991 (SI 1991/2151) |
| | para 36(16) | *Not yet in force* |
| | para 37 | 1 Jan 1991 (SI 1990/2624) |
| | para 38 | 3 Jun 1991 (SI 1991/1252) |
| | para 39 | 1 Jan 1991 (SI 1990/2624) |
| Sch 9 | | 1 Dec 1990 (SI 1990/2328), repeals of or in— |
| | | Companies Act 1985, ss 38(1), 39(3), 186, 188(2), 462(2); |
| | | Insolvency Act 1986, s 53(3); |
| | | Companies Act 1989, s 130(3), Sch 17, paras 1(2), 2(4), 8, 10 |

**Law Reform (Miscellaneous Provisions) (Scotland) Act 1990 (c 40)**—*contd*

    1 Jan 1991 (SI 1990/2624), repeals of or in—
        Matrimonial Homes (Family Protection) (Scotland) Act 1981,
        ss 6(3)(e), 8;
        Representation of the People Act 1983, s 42(3)(b)
    1 Apr 1991 (repeals of or in Unfair Contract Terms Act 1977,
        ss 15(1), 25(3)(d), (4)) (SI 1991/330)
    3 Jun 1991 (repeals of or in Solicitors (Scotland) Act 1980, ss 20(1),
        31(3), 63(1), Sch 4, paras 1, 17) (SI 1991/1252)
    15 Aug 1991 (SI 1991/1252), repeals of or in—
        House of Commons Disqualification Act 1975, Sch 1;
        Solicitors (Scotland) Act 1980, ss 49, 65(1), Sch 5
    26 Aug 1991 (repeal of Legal Aid Act 1988, Sch 4, para 3(c))
        (SI 1991/1903)
    30 Sep 1991 (SI 1991/2151), repeals of or in—
        Solicitors (Scotland) Act 1980, s 29;
        Legal Aid (Scotland) Act 1986, s 13(2)
    17 Mar 1993 (SI 1993/641), repeals of or in—
        Licensing (Scotland) Act 1976, ss 6, 18(1), 55, 61, 97(2), 131,
        132, 133(4), Sch 4, paras 1, 12–17, 19–22;
        Solicitors (Scotland) Act 1980, s 27;
        Family Law (Scotland) Act 1985, s 8(1)(a);
        Law Reform (Miscellaneous Provisions) (Scotland) Act 1985,
        Sch 1, Pt I, para 5
    1 Mar 1997 (SI 1996/2894), repeals of or in—
        Probate and Legacy Duties Act 1808;
        Confirmation of Executors (Scotland) Act 1858;
        Intestates Widows and Children (Scotland) Act 1875;
        Small Testate Estates (Scotland) Act 1876;
        Executors (Scotland) Act 1900
    *Not yet in force*, repeals of or in—
        Sheriff Courts (Scotland) Act 1907;
        Divorce Jurisdiction Court Fees and Legal Aid (Scotland)
        Act 1983;
        Law Reform (Miscellaneous Provisions) (Scotland) Act 1985,
        Sch 1, Pt I, para 4;
        Legal Aid (Scotland) Act 1986, ss 4(3)(a), (b), 17(3)–(5), 33(3)(c),
        (d);
        Legal Aid Act 1988, Sch 4, para 3(b);
        Court of Session Act 1988

[1]    The effect of this amendment is to change the commencement date from 5 Dec 1996 to 1 Mar 1997.
    (Note: it is thought that SI 1996/2894 should have been numbered as Commencement No 14)

**Licensing (Low Alcohol Drinks) Act 1990 (c 21)**

*RA:* 13 Jul 1990

*Commencement provisions:* s 3(2)

Whole Act in force 1 Jan 1994 (s 3(2)) (no day prior to that date was appointed by the Secretary of State)

**Marriage (Registration of Buildings) Act 1990 (c 33)**

*RA:* 26 Jul 1990

*Commencement provisions:* s 2(2)

Whole Act in force 26 Sep 1990 (s 2(2))

## National Health Service and Community Care Act 1990 (c 19)

*RA:* 29 Jun 1990

*Commencement provisions:* s 67(2); National Health Service and Community Care Act 1990 (Commencement No 1) Order 1990, SI 1990/1329, as amended by SI 1990/2511; National Health Service and Community Care Act 1990 (Commencement No 2) (Scotland) Order 1990, SI 1990/1520; National Health Service and Community Care Act 1990 (Commencement No 3 and Transitional Provisions) (Scotland) Order 1990, SI 1990/1793, as amended by SI 1990/2510, SI 1992/799; National Health Service and Community Care Act 1990 (Commencement No 4 and Transitional Provision) Order 1990, SI 1990/2218; National Health Service and Community Care Act 1990 (Commencement No 5 and Revocation) (Scotland) Order 1990, SI 1990/2510; National Health Service and Community Care Act 1990 (Commencement No 6–Amendment, and Transitional and Saving Provisions) Order 1990, SI 1990/2511; National Health Service and Community Care Act 1990 (Commencement No 7) Order 1991, SI 1991/388; National Health Service and Community Care Act 1990 (Commencement No 8 and Transitional Provisions) (Scotland) Order 1991, SI 1991/607; National Health Service and Community Care Act 1990 (Commencement No 9) Order 1992, SI 1992/567; National Health Service and Community Care Act 1990 (Commencement No 3 and Transitional Provisions) (Scotland) (Amendment) Order 1992, SI 1992/799; National Health Service and Community Care Act 1990 (Commencement No 10) Order 1992, SI 1992/2975; National Health Service and Community Care Act 1990 (Commencement No 11) (Scotland) Order 1994, SI 1994/2658

| | | |
|---|---|---|
| 1 | (1)(a) | 26 Jul 1990 (so far as relates to Regional Health Authorities) (SI 1990/1329) |
| | | 17 Sep 1990 (otherwise) (SI 1990/1329) |
| | (1)(b) | 17 Sep 1990 (SI 1990/1329) |
| | (1)(c) | 5 Jul 1990 (SI 1990/1329) |
| | (2) | See Sch 1, Pt I below |
| | (3) | See Sch 1, Pt III below |
| | (4)(a) | 25 Jul 1990 (so far as relates to Regional Health Authorities) (SI 1990/1329) |
| | | 16 Sep 1990 (otherwise) (SI 1990/1329) |
| | (4)(b) | 16 Sep 1990 (SI 1990/1329) |
| | (5) | 25 Jul 1990 (so far as relates to Regional Health Authorities) (SI 1990/1329) |
| | | 16 Sep 1990 (otherwise) (SI 1990/1329) |
| 2 | (1), (2) | 17 Sep 1990 (SI 1990/1329) |
| | (3)(a) | 17 Sep 1990 (SI 1990/1329) |
| | (3)(b) | 5 Jul 1990 (SI 1990/1329) |
| | (4) | See Sch 1, Pt II below |
| | (5) | 16 Sep 1990 (SI 1990/1329) |
| | (6), (7) | 17 Sep 1990 (SI 1990/1329) |
| 3 | (1), (2) | 1 Apr 1991 (SI 1990/1329) |
| | (3), (4) | 17 Sep 1990 (SI 1990/1329) |
| | (5)–(8) | 1 Apr 1991 (SI 1990/1329) |
| 4 | (1), (2) | 6 Mar 1991 (so far as relate to a reference under s 4(4)) (SI 1991/388) |
| | | 1 Apr 1991 (otherwise) (SI 1990/1329) |
| | (3) | 1 Apr 1991 (SI 1990/1329) |
| | (4) | 6 Mar 1991 (SI 1991/388) |
| | (5), (6) | 6 Mar 1991 (so far as relate to a reference under s 4(4)) (SI 1991/388) |
| | | 1 Apr 1991 (otherwise) (SI 1990/1329) |
| | (7), (8) | 1 Apr 1991 (SI 1990/1329) |
| | (9) | 6 Mar 1991 (so far as relates to a reference under s 4(4)) (SI 1991/388) |
| | | 1 Apr 1991 (otherwise) (SI 1990/1329) |
| 5 | | See Sch 2 below |
| 6–8 | | 5 Jul 1990 (SI 1990/1329) |
| 9 | | See Sch 3 below |
| 10, 11 | | 5 Jul 1990 (SI 1990/1329) |
| 12 | (1)–(3) | 17 Sep 1990 (subject to transitional provisions) (SI 1990/1329) |

**National Health Service and Community Care Act 1990 (c 19)**—*contd*

| | | |
|---|---|---|
| | (4) | 1 Oct 1991 (subject to savings) (SI 1990/2511) |
| | (5) | 17 Sep 1990 (SI 1990/1329) |
| 13 | | 1 Apr 1991 (SI 1990/1329) |
| 14 | | 17 Sep 1990 (SI 1990/1329) |
| 15–19 | | 1 Apr 1991 (SI 1990/1329) |
| 20 | (1) | See Sch 4 below |
| | (2), (3) | 1 Oct 1990 (SI 1990/1329) |
| | (4)–(7) | 5 Jul 1990 (SI 1990/1329) |
| | (8) | 1 Oct 1990 (SI 1990/1329) |
| 21 | | 17 Sep 1990 (SI 1990/1329) |
| 22 | | 1 Jan 1991 (SI 1990/1329) |
| 23 | (1)–(3) | 1 Jan 1991 (subject to transitional provisions) (SI 1990/1329, as amended by SI 1990/2511) |
| | (4) | 1 Jan 1991 (except so far as repeals second paragraph of National Health Service Act 1977, s 33(5)) (subject to transitional provisions) (SI 1990/1329, as amended by SI 1990/2511) |
| | | *Never in force* (exception noted above) (repealed) |
| | (5)–(8) | 1 Jan 1991 (subject to transitional provisions) (SI 1990/1329) |
| 24 | | 17 Sep 1990 (SI 1990/1329) |
| 25 | | 1 Apr 1991 (SI 1990/1329) |
| 26 | (1) | 5 Jul 1990 (SI 1990/1329) |
| | (2)(a) | 5 Jul 1990 (SI 1990/1329) |
| | (2)(b) | 17 Sep 1990 (SI 1990/1329) |
| | (2)(c) | 5 Jul 1990 (SI 1990/1329) |
| | (2)(d) | 5 Jul 1990 (so far as relates to definition "National Health Service trust") (SI 1990/1329) |
| | | 1 Apr 1991 (otherwise) (SI 1990/1329) |
| | (2)(e) | 5 Jul 1990 (SI 1990/1329) |
| | (2)(f) | 17 Sep 1990 (SI 1990/1329) |
| | (2)(g) | 5 Jul 1990 (SI 1990/1329) |
| | (2)(h) | 1 Apr 1991 (SI 1990/1329) |
| | (2)(i) | 5 Jul 1990 (SI 1990/1329) |
| 27 | (1), (2) | 31 Mar 1991 (so far as have effect in relation to members of a Health Board or management committee of Common Services Agency for Scottish Health Service) (SI 1990/1793) |
| | | 30 Jun 1992 (otherwise) (SI 1990/1793, as amended by SI 1992/799) |
| | (3) | See Sch 5 below |
| 28 | | 17 Sep 1990 (SI 1990/1793) |
| 29 | (1), (2) | 17 Sep 1990 (SI 1990/1793) |
| | (3)(a) | 24 Jul 1990 (subject to a transitional provision and saving) (SI 1990/1520) |
| | (3)(b), (c) | 24 Jul 1990 (SI 1990/1520) |
| | (4) | 24 Jul 1990 (SI 1990/1520) |
| 30 | | 1 Apr 1991 (SI 1990/1793) |
| 31 | | 24 Jul 1990 (SI 1990/1520) |
| 32 | | See Sch 6 below |
| 33 | | 24 Jul 1990 (SI 1990/1520) |
| 34 | | 17 Sep 1990 (so far as relates to provisions of ss 87A, 87B(1) (so far as s 87B(1) provides for meaning of "recognised fund-holding practice" and "allotted sum"), to be inserted into National Health Service (Scotland) Act 1978) (SI 1990/1793) |
| | | 1 Apr 1991 (otherwise) (SI 1990/1793) |
| 35 | | 1 Apr 1992 (SI 1990/1793) |
| 36 | (1) | See Sch 7 below |
| | (2)–(8) | 17 Sep 1990 (SI 1990/1793) |
| 37 | | 17 Sep 1990 (SI 1990/1793) |
| 38 | | 1 Apr 1991 (SI 1991/607) |
| 39 | (1)–(3) | 1 Apr 1991 (subject, in case of s 39(2), to transitional provisions) (SI 1991/607) |

**National Health Service and Community Care Act 1990 (c 19)**—*contd*

| | | |
|---|---|---|
| | (4) | 1 Apr 1991 (except repeal in second paragraph of National Health Service (Scotland) Act 1978, s 23(5)) (SI 1991/607) |
| | | *Not yet in force* (exception noted above) |
| | (5)–(8) | 1 Apr 1991 (SI 1991/607) |
| 40, 41 | | 17 Sep 1990 (SI 1990/1793) |
| 42 | (1)–(5) | 1 Apr 1993 (SI 1992/2975) |
| | (6), (7) | 1 Apr 1991 (SI 1990/2218) |
| 43, 44 | | 1 Apr 1993 (SI 1992/2975) |
| 45 | | 12 Apr 1993 (SI 1992/2975) |
| 46 | | 1 Apr 1991 (SI 1990/2218) |
| 47 | | 1 Apr 1993 (SI 1992/2975) |
| 48 | | 1 Apr 1991 (SI 1990/2218) |
| 49 | | 10 Dec 1992 (SI 1992/2975) |
| 50 | | 1 Apr 1991 (SI 1990/2218) |
| 51–54 | | 1 Apr 1991 (SI 1990/2510) |
| 55 | | 1 Apr 1993 (SI 1992/2975) |
| 56 | | 1 Apr 1991 (so far as relates to insertion of Social Work (Scotland) Act 1968, s 13B) (SI 1990/2510) |
| | | 1 Apr 1993 (otherwise) (SI 1992/2975) |
| 57 | | 1 Apr 1993 (SI 1992/2975) |
| 58 | | 1 Apr 1991 (SI 1990/2510) |
| 59 | (1) | 26 Jul 1990 (so far as has effect in relation to Regional Health Authorities) (SI 1990/1329) |
| | | 17 Sep 1990 (otherwise) (SI 1990/1329) |
| | (2) | 5 Jul 1990 (SI 1990/1329) |
| | (3) | 1 Apr 1991 (SI 1991/607) |
| 60 | | See Sch 8 below |
| 61, 62 | | 17 Sep 1990 (SI 1990/1329) |
| 63 | | 1 Apr 1991 (SI 1990/1329) |
| 64, 65 | | 5 Jul 1990 (SI 1990/1329) |
| 66 | (1) | See Sch 9 below |
| | (2) | See Sch 10 below |
| 67 | | 29 Jun 1990 (s 67(2)) |
| Sch 1 | Pt I, para 1 | 26 Jul 1990 (SI 1990/1329) |
| | Pt I, paras 2, 3 | 17 Sep 1990 (SI 1990/1329) |
| | Pt II, paras 4, 5 | 17 Sep 1990 (SI 1990/1329) |
| | Pt III, para 6 | 26 Jul 1990 (SI 1990/1329) |
| | Pt III, para 7 | 26 Jul 1990 (so far as has effect in relation to Regional Health Authorities) (SI 1990/1329) |
| | | 17 Sep 1990 (otherwise) (SI 1990/1329) |
| | Pt III, paras 8, 9 | 26 Jul 1990 (SI 1990/1329) |
| | Pt III, para 10 | 26 Jul 1990 (so far as has effect in relation to Regional Health Authorities) (SI 1990/1329) |
| | | 17 Sep 1990 (otherwise) (SI 1990/1329) |
| Schs 2, 3 | | 5 Jul 1990 (SI 1990/1329) |
| Sch 4 | paras 1–3 | 1 Oct 1990 (SI 1990/1329) |
| | para 4 | 5 Jul 1990 (SI 1990/1329) |
| | paras 5–24 | 1 Oct 1990 (SI 1990/1329) |
| Sch 5 | | 17 Sep 1990 (SI 1990/1793) |
| Sch 6 | | 24 Jul 1990 (SI 1990/1520) |
| Sch 7 | para 1 | See paras 2–13 below |
| | para 2 | 1 Dec 1994 (SI 1994/2658) |
| | para 3(1) | See sub-paras (2)–(7) below |
| | para 3(2)(a)–(c) | 1 Dec 1994 (SI 1994/2658) |
| | para 3(2)(d) | 24 Oct 1994 (SI 1994/2658) |
| | para 3(3), (4) | 1 Apr 1995 (SI 1994/2658) |
| | para 3(5) | 1 Dec 1994 (SI 1994/2658) |
| | para 3(6) | 24 Oct 1994 (SI 1994/2658) |
| | para 3(7) | 1 Apr 1995 (SI 1994/2658) |

**National Health Service and Community Care Act 1990 (c 19)**—*contd*

| | | |
|---|---|---|
| | paras 4–12 | 1 Apr 1995 (SI 1994/2658) |
| | para 13 | 1 Dec 1994 (SI 1994/2658) |
| | para 14 | 1 Apr 1995 (SI 1994/2658) |
| | para 15 | 1 Dec 1994 (SI 1994/2658) |
| Sch 8 | | 1 Apr 1991 (SI 1990/1329) |
| Sch 9 | para 1 | 24 Jul 1990 (SI 1990/1520) |
| | para 2 | 5 Jul 1990 (SI 1990/1329) |
| | paras 3, 4 | 24 Jul 1990 (SI 1990/1520) |
| | para 5(1)–(3) | 1 Apr 1993 (SI 1992/2975) |
| | para 5(4) | 5 Jul 1990 (SI 1990/1329) |
| | para 5(5) | 1 Apr 1993 (SI 1992/2975) |
| | para 5(6), (7) | 1 Apr 1991 (SI 1990/2218) |
| | para 5(8) | 1 Apr 1991 (SI 1990/2218; SI 1990/2510) |
| | para 5(9)(a) | 1 Apr 1993 (SI 1992/2975) |
| | para 5(9)(b) | 1 Apr 1991 (SI 1990/2510) |
| | paras 6–9 | 5 Jul 1990 (SI 1990/1329) |
| | para 10(1) | *Not yet in force* (repealed in part) |
| | para 10(2)–(6) | 1 Apr 1991 (SI 1990/2510) |
| | para 10(7), (8) | 1 Apr 1993 (SI 1992/2975) |
| | para 10(9)–(11) | 1 Apr 1991 (SI 1990/2510) |
| | para 10(12) | 24 Jul 1990 (SI 1990/1520) |
| | para 10(13) | 1 Apr 1991 (SI 1990/2510) |
| | para 10(14)(a) | 1 Apr 1991 (SI 1990/2510) |
| | para 10(14)(b) | 24 Jul 1990 (SI 1990/1520) |
| | para 11(a) | 1 Apr 1993 (SI 1992/2975) |
| | para 11(b) | 1 Apr 1991 (SI 1990/2218) |
| | para 11(c) | 1 Apr 1991 (so far as relates to s 46) (SI 1990/2218) |
| | | 1 Apr 1993 (otherwise) (SI 1992/2975) |
| | para 12 | 1 Apr 1991 (SI 1990/2218) |
| | para 13 | 5 Jul 1990 (SI 1990/1329) |
| | para 14 | 24 Jul 1990 (SI 1990/1520) |
| | para 15 | 1 Apr 1993 (SI 1992/2975) |
| | para 16 | 10 Dec 1992 (SI 1992/2975) |
| | para 17 | 5 Jul 1990 (SI 1990/1329) |
| | para 18(1)(a) | 17 Sep 1990 (SI 1990/1329) |
| | para 18(1)(b) | 5 Jul 1990 (SI 1990/1329) |
| | para 18(1)(c) | 17 Sep 1990 (SI 1990/1329) |
| | para 18(2) | 17 Sep 1990 (SI 1990/1329) |
| | para 18(3)–(13) | 5 Jul 1990 (SI 1990/1329) |
| | para 18(14) | 1 Apr 1993 (SI 1992/2975) |
| | para 19(1)–(3) | 17 Sep 1990 (SI 1990/1793) |
| | para 19(4), (5) | 24 Jul 1990 (SI 1990/1520) |
| | para 19(6) | 17 Sep 1990 (SI 1990/1793) |
| | para 19(7)(a)(i) | 17 Sep 1990 (SI 1990/1793) |
| | para 19(7)(a)(ii) | 24 Jul 1990 (SI 1990/1520) |
| | para 19(7)(a)(iii), (iv) | 17 Sep 1990 (SI 1990/1793) |
| | para 19(7)(b)–(d) | 17 Sep 1990 (SI 1990/1793) |
| | para 19(8) | 17 Sep 1990 (SI 1990/1793) |
| | para 19(9)–(14) | 24 Jul 1990 (SI 1990/1520) |
| | para 19(15) | 17 Sep 1990 (SI 1990/1793) |
| | para 19(16)–(19) | 24 Jul 1990 (SI 1990/1520) |
| | para 19(20) | 17 Sep 1990 (SI 1990/1793) |
| | para 19(21) | 24 Jul 1990 (SI 1990/1520) |
| | para 19(22)(a) | 17 Sep 1990 (SI 1990/1793) |
| | para 19(22)(b) | 24 Jul 1990 (SI 1990/1520) |
| | para 19(22)(c) | 24 Jul 1990 (so far as relates to definition "National Health Service trust") (SI 1990/1520) |
| | | 1 Apr 1991 (otherwise) (SI 1990/1793) |

See Halsbury's Statutes Citator for amendments to these Acts

**National Health Service and Community Care Act 1990 (c 19)**—*contd*

|  |  |
|---|---|
| para 19(22)(d) | 24 Jul 1990 (SI 1990/1520) |
| para 19(22)(e) | 17 Sep 1990 (SI 1990/1793) |
| para 19(23) | 1 Apr 1991 (SI 1990/1793) |
| para 19(24) | 24 Jul 1990 (SI 1990/1520) |
| para 20 | 5 Jul 1990 (SI 1990/1329) |
| para 21(a), (b) | 5 Jul 1990 (SI 1990/1329) |
| para 21(c) | 24 Jul 1990 (SI 1990/1520) |
| paras 22, 23 | 5 Jul 1990 (SI 1990/1329) |
| para 24(1), (2) | 5 Jul 1990 (SI 1990/1329) |
| para 24(3)(a), (b) | 5 Jul 1990 (SI 1990/1329) |
| para 24(3)(c) | 17 Sep 1990 (SI 1990/1329) |
| para 24(4), (5) | 5 Jul 1990 (SI 1990/1329) |
| para 24(6) | *Never in force* (repealed) |
| para 24(7)–(9) | 5 Jul 1990 (SI 1990/1329) |
| para 25(1) | 1 Apr 1993 (SI 1992/2975) |
| para 25(2) | 12 Apr 1993 (SI 1992/2975) |
| paras 26, 27 | 5 Jul 1990 (SI 1990/1329) |
| para 28 | 24 Jul 1990 (SI 1990/1520) |
| para 29 | 5 Jul 1990 (SI 1990/1329) |
| para 30(1)(a) | 5 Jul 1990 (SI 1990/1329) |
| para 30(1)(b), (c) | *Not yet in force* |
| para 30(2) | 5 Jul 1990 (SI 1990/1329) |
| paras 31–33 | 5 Jul 1990 (SI 1990/1329) |
| para 34 | 17 Sep 1990 (SI 1990/1329) |
| paras 35–37 | 5 Jul 1990 (SI 1990/1329) |

Sch 10
    5 Jul 1990 (repeals of or in National Health Service Act 1977, ss 8(5), 10(7)) (SI 1990/1329)

    17 Sep 1990 (SI 1990/1329), repeals of or in—
    National Health Service Act 1977, ss 8(1)–(3), 11(1), 12(a), 13(1), 14, 16, 18(3), 41(b), 55, 91(3)(b), 97(6), 99(1)(b), Sch 5, para 8;
    Health Services Act 1980, s 22, Sch 1;
    Public Health (Control of Disease) Act 1984

    17 Sep 1990 (SI 1990/1793), repeals of or in—
    National Health Service (Scotland) Act 1978, ss 5, 6, 10(4), 85(1)(a), 108(1), Sch 3;
    Health and Medicines Act 1988, Sch 2, para 11

    1 Oct 1990 (SI 1990/1329), repeals of or in—
    National Health Service Act 1977, s 98(1)(b), (3);
    Local Government and Housing Act 1989

    1 Jan 1991 (repeals of or in National Health Service Act 1977, s 33(7)) (SI 1990/1329)

    1 Jan 1991 (repeals of National Health Service (Scotland) Act 1978, s 23(7)) (SI 1990/1793)

    1 Apr 1991 (SI 1990/1329), repeals of or in—
    Nursing Homes Registration (Scotland) Act 1938;
    Fire Precautions Act 1971;
    Health Services Act 1976;
    National Health Service Act 1977, Sch 5, para 15(2);
    Employment Protection (Consolidation) Act 1978;
    National Health Service (Scotland) Act 1978;
    Health Services Act 1980, ss 12–15, Schs 2–4;
    Registered Homes Act 1984;
    National Health Service (Amendment) Act 1986

    1 Apr 1991 (repeals of or in National Health Service (Scotland) Act 1978, ss 7(2), 57(3)) (SI 1990/1793)

    1 Apr 1991 (SI 1990/2218), repeals of or in—

**National Health Service and Community Care Act 1990 (c 19)**—*contd*

National Assistance Act 1948, ss 35(2), (3), 36, 54 (so far as s 54 relates to England and Wales, and subject to a transitional provision (see SI 1990/2218, art 3));

Health Services and Public Health Act 1968, s 45(5);

Chronically Sick and Disabled Persons Act 1970, s 2(1) (E) (W)

1 Apr 1991 (S) (SI 1990/2510) so far as they apply to Scotland, repeals of or in—

National Assistance Act 1948, s 54;

Social Work (Scotland) Act 1968, s 1(4);

National Health Service (Scotland) Act 1978, ss 13A, 13B, Sch 15, para 15;

Mental Health (Scotland) Act 1984, s 13(1)(c)

6 Apr 1992 (repeal of National Assistance Act 1948, s 22(7)) (E) (W) (SI 1992/567)

10 Dec 1992 (repeal in Children Act 1975, s 99(1)(b)) (SI 1992/2975)

1 Apr 1993 (SI 1992/2975), repeals of or in—

National Assistance Act 1948, ss 21(8), 26;

National Health Service Act 1977, Sch 8, para 2;

Mental Health Act 1983, ss 124(3), 135(6);

Social Security Act 1986, Sch 10, para 32(2);

Local Government Act 1988, Sch 1, para 2(4)(b);

Local Government Finance Act 1988, Sch 1, para 9(2)(b)

1 Apr 1995 (SI 1994/2658), repeals of—

National Health Service (Scotland) Act 1978, s 86(2);

National Health Service and Community Care Act 1990, s 36(5)

*Not yet in force*, repeals of or in—

National Assistance Act 1948, s 41(1) (repealed);

Mental Health Act 1959;

Health Services and Public Health Act 1968, s 44(1);

Chronically Sick and Disabled Persons Act 1970, s 2(1) (except (E), (W));

Local Government Act 1972;

National Health Service Reorganisation Act 1973, Sch 4, para 45 (repealed);

Social Security Act 1975, s 35(6)(a) (repealed);

National Health Service Act 1977, s 85(1)(e), (3), (4), Sch 5, Pts I, II, Sch 14, para 13(1)(b), Sch 15, paras 5, 24(1), 63, 67;

Health and Social Services and Social Security Adjudications Act 1983;

Health and Social Security Act 1984;

Disabled Persons (Services, Consultation and Representation) Act 1986

---

**Pakistan Act 1990 (c 14)**

*RA:* 29 Jun 1990

*Commencement provisions:* s 2(3)

Whole Act in force 1 Oct 1989 (retrospective; s 2(3))

---

**Pensions (Miscellaneous Provisions) Act 1990 (c 7)**

*RA:* 24 May 1990

*Commencement provisions:* ss 1(8), 14(3)

| | | |
|---|---|---|
| 1 | (1) | 24 Jul 1990 (s 14(3)) |
| | (2)(a) | 24 Jul 1990 (s 14(3)) |

**Pensions (Miscellaneous Provisions) Act 1990 (c 7)**—*contd*

|  |  |  |
|---|---|---|
| | (2)(b) | 1 Jan 1993 (s 1(8)) |
| | (3) | 24 Jul 1990 (s 14(3)) |
| | (4) | 1 Jan 1993 (s 1(8)) |
| | (5)–(8) | 24 Jul 1990 (S 14(3)) |
| 2–11 | | 24 Jul 1990 (s 14(3)) |
| 12 | | 24 May 1990 (RA) |
| 13 | | 24 Jul 1990 (s 14(3)) |
| 14 | | 24 May 1990 (RA) |

---

## Planning (Consequential Provisions) Act 1990 (c 11)

*RA:* 24 May 1990

*Commencement provisions:* s 7(2), Sch 4, para 1(3), (4); Planning (Consequential Provisions) Act 1990 (Appointed Day No 1 and Transitional Provisions) Order 1991, SI 1991/2698

Whole Act in force 24 Aug 1990 (s 7(2)) (note that the Planning (Consequential Provisions) Act 1990 (Appointed Day No 1 and Transitional Provisions) Order 1991, SI 1991/2698 appointed 2 Jan 1992 as the appointed day under Sch 4, para 1(3)(a) for the purposes of paras 3–16 of that Schedule (transitory modifications), but only for the purposes of awards of costs in relation to proceedings which give rise to a hearing)

---

## Planning (Hazardous Substances) Act 1990 (c 10)

*RA:* 24 May 1990

*Commencement provisions:* s 41(2), (3); Planning (Hazardous Substances) Act 1990 (Commencement and Transitional Provisions) Order 1992, SI 1992/725

Whole Act in force as follows—

11 Mar 1992 (so far as provisions of this Act confer on the Secretary of State a power, or impose upon him a duty, to make regulations, or make provision with respect to the exercise of any such power or duty, for the purpose only of enabling or requiring the Secretary of State to make regulations) (SI 1992/725)

1 Jun 1992 (otherwise) (SI 1992/725)

See, for transitory provisions, Planning (Consequential Provisions) Act 1990, s 6, Sch 4; those transitory provisions partially ceased to have effect on 2 Jan 1992 (SI 1991/2698), so that on that day para 6(8) of the Schedule to this Act came partially into force

---

## Planning (Listed Buildings and Conservation Areas) Act 1990 (c 9)

*RA:* 24 May 1990

*Commencement provisions:* s 94(2)

Whole Act in force 24 Aug 1990 (s 94(2))

See, for transitory provisions, Planning (Consequential Provisions) Act 1990, s 6, Sch 4; those transitory provisions partially ceased to have effect on 2 Jan 1992 (SI 1991/2698), so that on that day, Sch 3, para 6(8) to this Act came partially into force

---

## Property Services Agency and Crown Suppliers Act 1990 (c 12)

*RA:* 29 Jun 1990

Whole Act in force 29 Jun 1990 (RA)

---

### Representation of the People Act 1990 (c 32)

*RA:* 26 Jul 1990

*Commencement provisions:* s 2(2); Representation of the People Act 1990 (Commencement No 1) Order 1991, SI 1991/1244; Representation of the People Act 1990 (Commencement No 2) Order 1991, SI 1991/1686

Whole Act in force as follows—

10 Jun 1991 (E) (W) (S) (SI 1991/1244)

7 Aug 1991 (NI) (SI 1991/1686)

### Rights of Way Act 1990 (c 24)

*RA:* 13 Jul 1990

*Commencement provisions:* s 6(2)

Whole Act in force 13 Aug 1990 (s 6(2))

### Social Security Act 1990 (c 27)

*RA:* 13 Jul 1990

*Commencement provisions:* s 23(2), (3); Social Security Act 1990 (Commencement No 1) Order 1990, SI 1990/1446; Social Security Act 1990 (Commencement No 2) Order 1990, SI 1990/1942; Social Security Act 1990 (Commencement No 3) Order 1991, SI 1991/558; Social Security Act 1990 (Commencement No 4) Order 1992, SI 1992/632; Social Security Act 1990 (Commencement No 5) Order 1992, SI 1992/1532; Social Security Act 1990 (Commencement No 6) Order 1997, SI 1997/1370

| | | |
|---|---|---|
| 1 | | 1 Oct 1990 (SI 1990/1446) |
| 2 | | 1 Oct 1990 (for the purpose of authorising the making of regulations) (SI 1990/1446) |
| | | 3 Dec 1990 (otherwise) (SI 1990/1942) |
| 3 | (1)–(5) | 1 Oct 1990 (SI 1990/1446) |
| | (6) | 13 Jul 1990 (s 23(2), (3)) |
| | (7), (8) | 1 Oct 1990 (SI 1990/1446) |
| 4 | | 6 Apr 1991 (SI 1991/558) |
| 5, 6 | | 13 Jul 1990 (s 23(2), (3)) |
| 7 | | See Sch 1 below |
| 8 | | 15 Oct 1990 (SI 1990/1446) |
| 9 | | *Never in force* (repealed) |
| 10 | | 13 Jul 1990 (s 23(2), (3)) |
| 11 | (1) | 17 Aug 1990 (for purpose only of giving effect to s 11(3)) (SI 1990/1446) |
| | (2) | See Sch 2 below |
| | (3)–(6) | 17 Aug 1990 (SI 1990/1446) |
| 12 | (1) | See Sch 3 below |
| | (2) | 1 Oct 1990 (SI 1990/1446) |
| 13 | | 18 Jul 1990 (SI 1990/1446) |
| 14 | | See Sch 4 below |
| 15 | (1)–(10) | 13 Jul 1990 (s 23(2), (3)) |
| | (11) | 9 Jun 1997 (SI 1997/1370) |
| 16 | (1) | 13 Jul 1990 (s 23(2), (3)) |
| | (2), (3) | 18 Jul 1990 (SI 1990/1446) |
| | (4)–(8) | 13 Jul 1990 (s 23(2), (3)) |
| | (9) | 18 Jul 1990 (SI 1990/1446) |
| | (10) | 13 Jul 1990 (s 23(2), (3)) |
| 17 | (1)–(6) | 6 Apr 1992 (SI 1992/632) |

**Social Security Act 1990 (c 27)**—*contd*

|  |  |  |
|---|---|---|
|  | (7) | See Sch 5 below |
|  | (8), (9) | *Never in force* (repealed) |
|  | (10) | 6 Apr 1992 (SI 1992/632) |
| 18–20 |  | 13 Jul 1990 (s 23(2), (3)) |
| 21 | (1) | See Sch 6 below |
|  | (2) | See Sch 7 below |
|  | (3) | 13 Jul 1990 (s 23(2), (3)) |
| 22, 23 |  | 13 Jul 1990 (s 23(2), (3)) |
| Sch 1 |  | 13 Jul 1990 (s 23(2), (3)) |
| Sch 2 |  | *Never in force* (repealed) |
| Sch 3 |  | 18 Jul 1990 (for the purpose of authorising the making of regulations under the Social Security Pensions Act 1975, s 59C(5) thereby inserted which are expressed to come into force on or after 1 Oct 1990) (SI 1990/1446) |
|  |  | 1 Oct 1990 (otherwise) (SI 1990/1446) |
| Sch 4 | para 1 | 22 Oct 1990 (for the purpose only of authorising the making of regulations) (SI 1990/1942) |
|  |  | 12 Nov 1990 (otherwise) (SI 1990/1942) |
|  | para 2 | 29 Jun 1992 (SI 1992/1532) |
|  | para 3 | 3 Dec 1990 (SI 1990/1942) |
|  | para 4 | 1 Jan 1991 (SI 1990/1942) |
|  | para 5 | 28 Feb 1991 (SI 1990/1942) |
|  | para 6 | 13 Jul 1990 (s 23(2), (3)) |
|  | para 7 | *Never in force* (repealed) |
|  | paras 8, 9 | 13 Jul 1990 (s 23(2), (3)) |
|  | para 10 | 13 May 1991 (for purposes of regulations expressed to come into force on or after 4 Nov 1991) (SI 1991/558) |
|  |  | 4 Nov 1991 (otherwise) (SI 1991/558) |
|  | para 11 | 1 Oct 1990 (SI 1990/1942) |
|  | paras 12–14 | 18 Jul 1990 (SI 1990/1446) |
|  | para 15 | 13 Jul 1990 (s 23(2), (3)) |
| Sch 5 |  | 18 Jul 1990 (SI 1990/1446) |
| Sch 6 | para 1 | 18 Jul 1990 (SI 1990/1446) |
|  | paras 2–9 | 13 Jul 1990 (s 23(2), (3)) |
|  | para 10 | 13 Jul 1990 (so far as consequential on any preceding provision brought into force on 13 Jul 1990) (s 23(2), (3)) |
|  |  | 18 Jul 1990 (for the purpose only of authorising the making of regulations which are expressed to come into force on or after 28 Oct 1990) (SI 1990/1446) |
|  |  | 28 Oct 1990 (otherwise) (SI 1990/1446) |
|  | para 11 | 13 Jul 1990 (so far as consequential on any preceding provision brought into force on 13 Jul 1990) (s 23(2), (3)) |
|  |  | 6 Apr 1991 (otherwise) (SI 1991/558) |
|  | paras 12–15 | 13 Jul 1990 (s 23(2), (3)) |
|  | para 16 | 13 Jul 1990 (so far as consequential on any preceding provision brought into force on 13 Jul 1990) (s 23(2), (3)) |
|  |  | 6 Apr 1991 (otherwise) (SI 1991/558) |
|  | paras 17–19 | 13 Jul 1990 (s 23(2), (3)) |
|  | para 20 | 13 Jul 1990 (so far as consequential on any preceding provision brought into force on 13 Jul 1990) (s 23(2), (3)) |
|  |  | 18 Jul 1990 (otherwise) (SI 1990/1446) |
|  | para 21 | 13 Jul 1990 (s 23(2), (3)) |
|  | para 22 | 13 Jul 1990 (so far as consequential on any preceding provision brought into force on 13 Jul 1990) (s 23(2), (3)) |
|  |  | 6 Apr 1991 (otherwise) (SI 1991/558) |
|  | para 23 | 13 Jul 1990 (so far as consequential on any preceding provision brought into force on 13 Jul 1990) (s 23(2), (3)) |
|  |  | 18 Jul 1990 (otherwise) (SI 1990/1446) |
|  | para 24 | 13 Jul 1990 (so far as consequential on any preceding provision brought into force on 13 Jul 1990) (s 23(2), (3)) |

**Social Security Act 1990 (c 27)**—*contd*

|  |  |  |
|---|---|---|
|  |  | 1 Oct 1990 (otherwise) (SI 1990/1942) |
|  | para 25 | 5 Aug 1990 (where the expected week of confinement is the week commencing 21 Oct 1990 or a later week) (SI 1990/1446) |
|  |  | *Never in force* (otherwise) (repealed) |
|  | paras 26, 27 | 13 Jul 1990 (s 23(2), (3)) |
|  | para 28 | 13 Jul 1990 (so far as consequential on any preceding provision brought into force on 13 Jul 1990) (s 23(2), (3)) |
|  |  | 18 Jul 1990 (otherwise) (SI 1990/1446) |
|  | para 29 | 13 Jul 1990 (so far as consequential on any preceding provision brought into force on 13 Jul 1990) (s 23(2), (3)) |
|  |  | *Not yet in force* (otherwise) |
|  | para 30 | 13 Jul 1990 (s 23(2), (3)) |
|  | para 31 | 1 Oct 1990 (SI 1990/1942) |
| Sch 7 |  | 13 Jul 1990 (so far as consequential on any preceding provision brought into force on 13 Jul 1990) (s 23(2), (3)) |

1 Oct 1990 (SI 1990/1942), repeals of or in—

Social Security Act 1975, ss 59B(1), (3), (4), (7)(b), (8), 152(6);
Social Security Pensions Act 1975, ss 33(2), 56B–56D, 56E(1)(c), 56F–56K, 56L(1)(a), (5)(b), (c), 56M, 56N;
Social Security and Housing Benefits Act 1982, s 46(3);
Social Security Act 1985, s 31(1), Sch 5, para 35;
Social Security Act 1986, s 85(4)(a);
Social Security Act 1988, s 2(8), (8A);
Social Security Act 1989, Sch 1, para 8(3), (4), (7), Sch 2, Pt II, paras 1(2), 4(b)

21 Oct 1990 (repeals of or in Social Security Act 1986, s 79) (SI 1990/1942)

28 Feb 1991 (repeals in Social Security Pensions Act 1975, Sch 1A, paras 1, 2, 11, 12) (SI 1990/1942)

9 Jun 1997 (repeals of Housing (Scotland) Act 1987, ss 252, 253) (SI 1997/1370)

*Not yet in force*, repeals of or in—

Social Security Act 1975, s 135(5) (repealed);
Social Security Pensions Act 1975, ss 32(2B)(d)(i), 56L(1)(b), (9), Sch 1A, para 7(4)(a), (b) (repealed);
Social Security (Miscellaneous Provisions) Act 1977, s 1(7)(b) (repealed);
National Health Service Act 1977, Sch 15, para 71;
National Health Service (Scotland) Act 1978, Sch 16, para 44;
Social Security Act 1979, s 4(2)(b) (repealed);
Social Security Act 1980, Sch 1, para 15 (repealed), Sch 2, Pt I, para 31(b), (c), (h);
Social Security Act 1985, Sch 5, paras 12, 22;
Social Security Act 1986, s 33(10A) (repealed), Sch 10, paras 68(1), 78, 79;
Social Security Act 1989, s 6(2), Sch 3, para 16 (repealed), Sch 6, paras 6, 7, para 8(1)(a) (repealed), Sch 8, para 2(6) (repealed), Sch 9 (entry relating to the Social Security Pensions Act 1975, s 41C(3)(a)(ii))

**Term and Quarter Days (Scotland) Act 1990 (c 22)**

*RA:* 13 Jul 1990

*Commencement provisions:* s 3(2)

| | | |
|---|---|---|
| 1 | (1)–(4) | 13 Jul 1991 (s 3(2)) |
|  | (5), (6) | 13 Jul 1990 (RA) |
|  | (7) | 13 Jul 1991 (s 3(2)) |
| 2 |  | 13 Jul 1991 (s 3(2)) |

**Term and Quarter Days (Scotland) Act 1990 (c 22)**—*contd*
3                                          13 Jul 1990 (RA)

**Town and Country Planning Act 1990 (c 8)**

*RA:* 24 May 1990

*Commencement provisions:* s 337(2)

Whole Act in force 24 Aug 1990 (s 337(2)) (however note also s 28 (repealed))

See, for transitory provisions, Planning (Consequential Provisions) Act 1990, s 6, Sch 4; those transitory
provisions partially ceased to have effect on 2 Jan 1992 (SI 1991/2698), so that on that day, s 322 of,
and Sch 6, para 6(5) to, this Act came partially into force

# 1991 Acts

## Age of Legal Capacity (Scotland) Act 1991 (c 50)

*RA:* 25 Jul 1991

*Commencement provisions:* s 11(2)

Whole Act in force 25 Sep 1991 (s 11(2))

---

## Agricultural Holdings (Scotland) Act 1991 (c 55)

*RA:* 25 Jul 1991

*Commencement provisions:* s 89(2)

Whole Act in force 25 Sep 1991 (s 89(2))

---

## Agriculture and Forestry (Financial Provisions) Act 1991 (c 33)

*RA:* 25 Jul 1991

*Commencement provisions:* ss 1(2)–(5), 5(2); Agricultural Mortgage Corporation (Specified Day for Repeals) Order 1991, SI 1991/1937; Scottish Agricultural Securities Corporation (Specified Day for Repeals) Order 1991, SI 1991/1978

| 1 | (1) | See Schedule below |
| | (2)–(7) | 25 Jul 1991 (RA) |
| 2 | | 25 Sep 1991 (s 5(2)) |
| 3–5 | | 25 Jul 1991 (RA) |
| Schedule | Pt I | 25 Sep 1991 (SI 1991/1937) |
| | Pt II | 25 Sep 1991 (by virtue of s 1(3), SI 1991/1937) |
| | Pt III | 25 Sep 1991 (SI 1991/1978) |
| | Pt IV | 25 Sep 1991 (by virtue of s 1(5), SI 1991/1978) |

---

## Appropriation Act 1991 (c 32)

*RA:* 25 Jul 1991

Whole Act in force 25 Jul 1991 (RA)

---

## Armed Forces Act 1991 (c 62)

*RA:* 25 Jul 1991

*Commencement provisions:* s 27(2)–(4); Armed Forces Act 1991 (Commencement No 1) Order 1991, SI 1991/2719; Armed Forces Act 1991 (Commencement No 2) Order 1996, SI 1996/1173

| 1 | 25 Jul 1991 (RA) |
| 2–5 | 1 Jan 1992 (SI 1991/2719) |

**Armed Forces Act 1991 (c 62)**—*contd*

| | | |
|---|---|---|
| 6 | | 1 Jan 1992 (with effect in relation to reception orders made after 31 Dec 1991) (SI 1991/2719) |
| 7–16 | | 1 Jan 1992 (SI 1991/2719) |
| 17–23 | | 1 Jun 1996 (SI 1996/1173) |
| 24 | (1), (2) | 1 Jan 1992 (SI 1991/2719) |
| | (3) | 1 Jun 1996 (SI 1996/1173) |
| | (4), (5) | 1 Jan 1992 (SI 1991/2719) |
| 25 | | 25 Jul 1991 (RA) |
| 26 | (1) | See Sch 2 below |
| | (2) | See Sch 3 below |
| 27 | | 25 Jul 1991 (RA) |
| Sch 1 | | 1 Jan 1992 (SI 1991/2719) |
| Sch 2 | paras 1–6 | 1 Jan 1992 (SI 1991/2719) |
| | para 7 | 1 Jan 1992 (with effect in relation to offences committed after 31 Dec 1991) (SI 1991/2719) |
| | para 8 | 1 Jan 1992 (with effect in relation to appeals lodged after 31 Dec 1991) (SI 1991/2719) |
| | paras 9–11 | 1 Jan 1992 (SI 1991/2719) |
| Sch 3 | | 1 Jan 1992 (repeal of Armed Forces Act 1986, s 1) (s 27(4)) |

1 Jan 1992 (SI 1991/2719), repeals of or in—

Naval and Marine Pay and Pensions Act 1865, ss 4, 5;

Naval Forces (Enforcement of Maintenance Liabilities) Act 1947, ss 1(3), (5), 2;

Army Act 1955, ss 71A(1B)(a), 71AA(1), (1A), (2), 93, 122(1), 127(2), 131(1), 145(1)(b), 150(1)(a), (5), 225(1), Sch 5A, paras 2, 6–9, 10(1A), 11(4), 15(3);

Air Force Act 1955, ss 71A(1B)(a), 71AA(1), (1A), (2), 93, 122(1), 127(2), 131(1), 145(1)(b), 150(1)(a), (5), 223(1), Sch 5A, paras 2, 6–9, 10(1A), 11(4), 15(3);

Naval Discipline Act 1957, ss 43A(1B)(a), 43AA, 60, 129(2), Sch 4A, paras 2, 6–9, 10(1A), 11(4), 15(3);

Courts-Martial (Appeals) Act 1968;

Rehabilitation of Offenders Act 1974;

Rehabilitation of Offenders (Northern Ireland) Order 1978;

Reserve Forces Act 1980;

Reserve Forces Act 1982;

Armed Forces Act 1986, Sch 1, para 12(3), (5);

Children Act 1989

1 Jun 1996 (SI 1996/1173), repeals of—

Army Act 1955, s 216(4);

Air Force Act 1955, s 214(4);

Naval Discipline Act 1957, s 125(3);

Armed Forces Act 1981, s 14 (except in relation to any order made under this section on or before 31 May 1996);

Armed Forces Act 1986, s 13

**Arms Control and Disarmament (Inspections) Act 1991 (c 41)**

*RA:* 25 Jul 1991

*Commencement provisions:* s 6(2); Arms Control and Disarmament (Inspections) Act 1991 (Commencement) Order 1992, SI 1992/1750

| | |
|---|---|
| 1–5 | 17 Jul 1992 (SI 1992/1750) |
| 6 | 25 Jul 1991 (RA) |
| Schedule | 17 Jul 1992 (SI 1992/1750) |

## Atomic Weapons Establishment Act 1991 (c 46)

*RA:* 25 Jul 1991

*Commencement provisions:* s 6(2)

Whole Act in force 25 Sep 1991 (s 6(2))

---

## Badgers Act 1991 (c 36)

*RA:* 25 Jul 1991

*Commencement provisions:* s 6(2)

Whole Act in force 25 Oct 1991 (s 6(2))

---

## Badgers (Further Protection) Act 1991 (c 35)

*RA:* 25 Jul 1991

*Commencement provisions:* s 2(3)

Whole Act in force 25 Sep 1991 (s 2(3))

---

## Breeding of Dogs Act 1991 (c 64)

*RA:* 25 Jul 1991

*Commencement provisions:* s 3(2)

Whole Act in force 25 Sep 1991 (s 3(2))

---

## British Railways Board (Finance) Act 1991 (c 63)

*RA:* 25 Jul 1991

Whole Act in force 25 Jul 1991 (RA)

---

## British Technology Group Act 1991 (c 66)

*RA:* 22 Oct 1991

*Commencement provisions:* ss 1(1), 11(2), 18(2)–(4); British Technology Group Act 1991 (Appointed Day) Order 1991, SI 1991/2721

| | | |
|---|---|---|
| 1 | (1)–(5) | 22 Oct 1991 (s 18(3)) |
| | (6) | See Sch 1 below |
| 2 | | 22 Oct 1991 (s 18(3)) |
| 3–13 | | 6 Jan 1992 (ss 1(1), 18(2); SI 1991/2721) |
| 14 | | 22 Oct 1991 (s 18(3)) |
| 15 | | 6 Jan 1992 (ss 1(1), 18(2); SI 1991/2721) |
| 16 | (1) | 22 Oct 1991 (s 18(3)) |
| | (2) | 6 Jan 1992 (ss 1(1), 18(2); SI 1991/2721) |
| 17 | (1) | 6 Jan 1992 (ss 1(1), 18(2); SI 1991/2721) |
| | (2) | See Sch 2 below |
| | (3) | See Sch 3 below |
| 18 | | 22 Oct 1991 (s 18(3)) |
| Sch 1 | para 1 | 22 Oct 1991 (s 18(3)) |
| | paras 2–5 | 6 Jan 1992 (ss 1(1), 18(2); SI 1991/2721) |
| Sch 2 | Pt I | 6 Jan 1992 (ss 1(1), 18(2); SI 1991/2721) |
| | Pt II | *Not yet in force* |

**British Technology Group Act 1991 (c 66)**—*contd*

| | | |
|---|---|---|
| | Pt III | 1 Jul 1996 (SI 1996/1448) |
| Sch 3 | | 6 Jan 1992 (ss 1(1), 18(2); SI 1991/2721) |

---

**Caravans (Standard Community Charge and Rating) Act 1991 (c 2)**

*RA:* 12 Feb 1991

Whole Act in force 12 Feb 1991 (RA)

---

**Care of Churches and Ecclesiastical Jurisdiction Measure 1991 (No 1)**

*RA:* 25 Jul 1991

*Commencement provisions:* s 33(2)

Whole Measure in force 1 Mar 1993 (the day appointed by the Archbishops of Canterbury and York under s 33(2))

---

**Census (Confidentiality) Act 1991 (c 6)**

*RA:* 7 Mar 1991

Whole Act in force 7 Mar 1991 (RA)

---

**Child Support Act 1991 (c 48)**

*RA:* 25 Jul 1991

*Commencement provisions:* s 58(2)–(7); Child Support Act 1991 (Commencement No 1) Order 1992, SI 1992/1431; Child Support Act 1991 (Commencement No 2) Order 1992, SI 1992/1938; Child Support Act 1991 (Commencement No 3 and Transitional Provisions) Order 1992, SI 1992/2644, as amended by SI 1993/966, SI 1999/1510

| | | |
|---|---|---|
| 1, 2 | | 5 Apr 1993 (SI 1992/2644) |
| 3 | (1), (2) | 5 Apr 1993 (SI 1992/2644) |
| | (3)(a), (b) | 5 Apr 1993 (SI 1992/2644) |
| | (3)(c) | 17 Jun 1992 (SI 1992/1431) |
| | (4)–(7) | 5 Apr 1993 (SI 1992/2644) |
| 4 | (1)–(3) | 5 Apr 1993 (subject to transitional provisions) (SI 1992/2644) |
| | (4) | 17 Jun 1992 (SI 1992/1431) |
| | (5), (6) | 5 Apr 1993 (subject to transitional provisions) (SI 1992/2644) |
| | (7), (8) | 17 Jun 1992 (SI 1992/1431) |
| | (9) | 5 Apr 1993 (subject to transitional provisions) (SI 1992/2644) |
| 5 | (1), (2) | 5 Apr 1993 (SI 1992/2644) |
| | (3) | 17 Jun 1992 (SI 1992/1431) |
| 6 | (1) | 17 Jun 1992 (so far as confers power to prescribe kinds of benefit for purposes of s 6(1)) (SI 1992/1431) |
| | | 5 Apr 1993 (otherwise) (SI 1992/2644) |
| | (2)–(8) | 5 Apr 1993 (SI 1992/2644) |
| | (9), (10) | 17 Jun 1992 (SI 1992/1431) |
| | (11), (12) | 5 Apr 1993 (SI 1992/2644) |
| | (13) | 17 Jun 1992 (SI 1992/1431) |
| | (14) | 5 Apr 1993 (SI 1992/2644) |
| 7 | (1)–(4) | 5 Apr 1993 (subject to transitional provisions) (SI 1992/2644) |
| | (5) | 17 Jun 1992 (SI 1992/1431) |
| | (6), (7) | 5 Apr 1993 (subject to transitional provisions) (SI 1992/2644) |
| | (8), (9) | 17 Jun 1992 (SI 1992/1431) |
| 8 | (1)–(4) | 5 Apr 1993 (subject to transitional provisions) (SI 1992/2644) |
| | (5) | 17 Jun 1992 (SI 1992/1431) |

**Child Support Act 1991 (c 48)**—*contd*

| | | |
|---|---|---|
| | (6)–(8) | 5 Apr 1993 (SI 1992/2644) |
| | (9) | 17 Jun 1992 (SI 1992/1431) |
| | (10) | 5 Apr 1993 (SI 1992/2644) |
| | (11)(a)–(e) | 5 Apr 1993 (SI 1992/2644) |
| | (11)(f) | 17 Jun 1992 (SI 1992/1431) |
| 9 | | 5 Apr 1993 (subject to transitional provisions) (SI 1992/2644) |
| 10 | | 17 Jun 1992 (SI 1992/1431) |
| 11 | (1) | 5 Apr 1993 (SI 1992/2644) |
| | (2), (3) | See Sch 1 below |
| 12 | (1) | 5 Apr 1993 (SI 1992/2644) |
| | (2), (3) | 17 Jun 1992 (SI 1992/1431) |
| | (4) | 5 Apr 1993 (SI 1992/2644) |
| | (5) | 17 Jun 1992 (SI 1992/1431) |
| 13 | | 1 Sep 1992 (SI 1992/1938) |
| 14 | (1) | 17 Jun 1992 (SI 1992/1431) |
| | (2) | 5 Apr 1993 (SI 1992/2644) |
| | (3) | 17 Jun 1992 (SI 1992/1431) |
| | (4) | See Sch 2 below |
| 15 | | 5 Apr 1993 (SI 1992/2644) |
| 16 | (1), (2) | 17 Jun 1992 (SI 1992/1431) |
| | (3), (4) | 5 Apr 1993 (subject to transitional provisions) (SI 1992/2644) |
| | (5), (6) | 17 Jun 1992 (SI 1992/1431) |
| 17 | (1)–(3) | 5 Apr 1993 (subject to transitional provisions) (SI 1992/2644) |
| | (4) | 17 Jun 1992 (SI 1992/1431) |
| | (5) | 5 Apr 1993 (subject to transitional provisions) (SI 1992/2644) |
| | (6)(a) | 5 Apr 1993 (subject to transitional provisions) (SI 1992/2644) |
| | (6)(b) | 17 Jun 1992 (SI 1992/1431) |
| 18 | (1)–(7) | 5 Apr 1993 (subject to transitional provisions) (SI 1992/2644) |
| | (8) | 17 Jun 1992 (SI 1992/1431) |
| | (9), (10) | 5 Apr 1993 (subject to transitional provisions) (SI 1992/2644) |
| | (11) | 17 Jun 1992 (SI 1992/1431) |
| | (12) | 5 Apr 1993 (subject to transitional provisions) (SI 1992/2644) |
| 19 | (1), (2) | 5 Apr 1993 (subject to transitional provisions) (SI 1992/2644) |
| | (3) | *Never in force* (substituted) |
| 20 | | 5 Apr 1993 (SI 1992/2644) |
| 21 | (1) | 1 Sep 1992 (SI 1992/1938) |
| | (2) | 17 Jun 1992 (SI 1992/1431) |
| | (3) | See Sch 3 below |
| 22 | (1), (2) | 1 Sep 1992 (SI 1992/1938) |
| | (3), (4) | 17 Jun 1992 (SI 1992/1431) |
| | (5) | See Sch 4 below |
| 23 | | 1 Sep 1992 (SI 1992/1938) |
| 24 | (1) | 5 Apr 1993 (SI 1992/2644) |
| | (2)–(5) | 5 Apr 1993 (SI 1992/2644) |
| | (6), (7) | 17 Jun 1992 (SI 1992/1431) |
| | (8) | 5 Apr 1993 (SI 1992/2644) |
| | (9) | 1 Sep 1992 (SI 1992/1938) |
| 25 | (1) | 5 Apr 1993 (SI 1992/2644) |
| | (2)(a) | 17 Jun 1992 (SI 1992/1431) |
| | (2)(b) | 5 Apr 1993 (SI 1992/2644) |
| | (3)(a), (b) | 5 Apr 1993 (SI 1992/2644) |
| | (3)(c) | 17 Jun 1992 (SI 1992/1431) |
| | (4) | 5 Apr 1993 (SI 1992/2644) |
| | (5), (6) | 17 Jun 1992 (SI 1992/1431) |
| 26–28 | | 5 Apr 1993 (SI 1992/2644) |
| 29 | (1) | 5 Apr 1993 (SI 1992/2644) |
| | (2), (3) | 17 Jun 1992 (SI 1992/1431) |
| 30 | (1) | 17 Jun 1992 (SI 1992/1431) |
| | (2) | *Never in force* (substituted) |

**Child Support Act 1991 (c 48)**—*contd*

|      |          |                                |
|------|----------|--------------------------------|
|      | (3)      | 5 Apr 1993 (SI 1992/2644)      |
|      | (4), (5) | 17 Jun 1992 (SI 1992/1431)     |
| 31   | (1)–(7)  | 5 Apr 1993 (SI 1992/2644)      |
|      | (8)      | 17 Jun 1992 (SI 1992/1431)     |
| 32   | (1)–(5)  | 17 Jun 1992 (SI 1992/1431)     |
|      | (6)      | 5 Apr 1993 (SI 1992/2644)      |
|      | (7)–(9)  | 17 Jun 1992 (SI 1992/1431)     |
|      | (10)–(11)| 5 Apr 1993 (SI 1992/2644)      |
| 33   |          | 5 Apr 1993 (SI 1992/2644)      |
| 34   | (1)      | 17 Jun 1992 (SI 1992/1431)     |
|      | (2)      | *Not yet in force*             |
| 35   | (1)      | 5 Apr 1993 (SI 1992/2644)      |
|      | (2)(a)   | 5 Apr 1993 (SI 1992/2644)      |
|      | (2)(b)   | 17 Jun 1992 (SI 1992/1431)     |
|      | (3)–(6)  | 5 Apr 1993 (SI 1992/2644)      |
|      | (7), (8) | 17 Jun 1992 (SI 1992/1431)     |
| 36   |          | 5 Apr 1993 (SI 1992/2644)      |
| 37   | (1)      | 5 Apr 1993 (SI 1992/2644)      |
|      | (2), (3) | *Not yet in force*             |
| 38   |          | 5 Apr 1993 (SI 1992/2644)      |
| 39   |          | 17 Jun 1992 (SI 1992/1431)     |
| 40   | (1)–(3)  | 5 Apr 1993 (SI 1992/2644)      |
|      | (4)(a)(i)| 5 Apr 1993 (SI 1992/2644)      |
|      | (4)(a)(ii)| 17 Jun 1992 (SI 1992/1431)    |
|      | (4)(b)   | 5 Apr 1993 (SI 1992/2644)      |
|      | (5)–(7)  | 5 Apr 1993 (SI 1992/2644)      |
|      | (8)      | 17 Jun 1992 (SI 1992/1431)     |
|      | (9), (10)| 5 Apr 1993 (SI 1992/2644)      |
|      | (11)     | 17 Jun 1992 (SI 1992/1431)     |
|      | (12)–(14)| 5 Apr 1993 (SI 1992/2644)      |
| 41   | (1)      | 5 Apr 1993 (SI 1992/2644)      |
|      | (2)–(4)  | 17 Jun 1992 (SI 1992/1431)     |
|      | (5), (6) | 5 Apr 1993 (SI 1992/2644)      |
| 42   |          | 17 Jun 1992 (SI 1992/1431)     |
| 43   | (1)(a)   | 5 Apr 1993 (SI 1992/2644)      |
|      | (1)(b)   | 17 Jun 1992 (SI 1992/1431)     |
|      | (2)(a)   | 17 Jun 1992 (SI 1992/1431)     |
|      | (2)(b)   | 5 Apr 1993 (SI 1992/2644)      |
| 44   | (1), (2) | 5 Apr 1993 (SI 1992/2644)      |
|      | (3)      | 17 Jun 1992 (SI 1992/1431)     |
| 45   |          | 17 Jun 1992 (SI 1992/1431)     |
| 46   | (1)–(10) | 5 Apr 1993 (SI 1992/2644)      |
|      | (11)     | 17 Jun 1992 (SI 1992/1431)     |
| 47   |          | 17 Jun 1992 (SI 1992/1431)     |
| 48   |          | 5 Apr 1993 (SI 1992/2644)      |
| 49   |          | 17 Jun 1992 (SI 1992/1431)     |
| 50   | (1)–(4)  | 5 Apr 1993 (SI 1992/2644)      |
|      | (5)      | 17 Jun 1992 (SI 1992/1431)     |
|      | (6)      | 5 Apr 1993 (SI 1992/2644)      |
|      | (7)(a)–(c)| 5 Apr 1993 (SI 1992/2644)     |
|      | (7)(d)   | 17 Jun 1992 (SI 1992/1431)     |
|      | (8)      | 5 Apr 1993 (SI 1992/2644)      |
| 51, 52 |        | 17 Jun 1992 (SI 1992/1431)     |
| 53   |          | 5 Apr 1993 (SI 1992/2644)      |
| 54, 55 |        | 17 Jun 1992 (SI 1992/1431)     |
| 56   | (1)      | 25 Jul 1991 (s 58(2))          |
|      | (2)–(4)  | 17 Jun 1992 (SI 1992/1431)     |
| 57   |          | 17 Jun 1992 (SI 1992/1431)     |
| 58   | (1)–(11) | 25 Jul 1991 (s 58(2))          |

**Child Support Act 1991 (c 48)**—*contd*

|         |                  |                              |
|---------|------------------|------------------------------|
|         | (12)             | *Never in force* (spent)     |
|         | (13)             | See Sch 5 below              |
|         | (14)             | 25 Jul 1991 (s 58(2))        |
| Sch 1   | para 1(1), (2)   | 5 Apr 1993 (SI 1992/2644)    |
|         | para 1(3)        | 17 Jun 1992 (SI 1992/1431)   |
|         | para 1(4)        | 5 Apr 1993 (SI 1992/2644)    |
|         | para 1(5)        | 17 Jun 1992 (SI 1992/1431)   |
|         | para 2(1)        | 17 Jun 1992 (SI 1992/1431)   |
|         | para 2(2), (3)   | 5 Apr 1993 (SI 1992/2644)    |
|         | para 3           | 5 Apr 1993 (SI 1992/2644)    |
|         | para 4(1)        | 17 Jun 1992 (SI 1992/1431)   |
|         | para 4(2)        | 5 Apr 1993 (SI 1992/2644)    |
|         | para 4(3)        | 17 Jun 1992 (SI 1992/1431)   |
|         | para 5(1), (2)   | 17 Jun 1992 (SI 1992/1431)   |
|         | para 5(3)        | 5 Apr 1993 (SI 1992/2644)    |
|         | para 5(4)        | 17 Jun 1992 (SI 1992/1431)   |
|         | para 6(1)        | 5 Apr 1993 (SI 1992/2644)    |
|         | para 6(2)–(6)    | 17 Jun 1992 (SI 1992/1431)   |
|         | paras 7–9        | 17 Jun 1992 (SI 1992/1431)   |
|         | para 10          | 5 Apr 1993 (SI 1992/2644)    |
|         | para 11          | 17 Jun 1992 (SI 1992/1431)   |
|         | paras 12, 13     | 5 Apr 1993 (SI 1992/2644)    |
|         | para 14          | 17 Jun 1992 (SI 1992/1431)   |
|         | para 15          | 5 Apr 1993 (SI 1992/2644)    |
|         | para 16(1)–(4)   | 5 Apr 1993 (SI 1992/2644)    |
|         | para 16(5)       | 17 Jun 1992 (SI 1992/1431)   |
|         | para 16(6)–(9)   | 5 Apr 1993 (SI 1992/2644)    |
|         | para 16(10), (11)| 17 Jun 1992 (SI 1992/1431)   |
| Sch 2   | para 1           | 5 Apr 1993 (SI 1992/2644)    |
|         | para 2(1), (2)   | 5 Apr 1993 (SI 1992/2644)    |
|         | para 2(3)        | 17 Jun 1992 (SI 1992/1431)   |
| Sch 3   | paras 1, 2       | 1 Sep 1992 (SI 1992/1938)    |
|         | para 3(1), (2)   | 1 Sep 1992 (SI 1992/1938)    |
|         | para 3(3)        | 17 Jun 1992 (SI 1992/1431)   |
|         | paras 4–8        | 1 Sep 1992 (SI 1992/1938)    |
| Sch 4   |                  | 1 Sep 1992 (SI 1992/1938)    |
| Sch 5   | paras 1–4        | 1 Sep 1992 (SI 1992/1938)    |
|         | paras 5–8        | 5 Apr 1993 (SI 1992/2644)    |

## Children and Young Persons (Protection from Tobacco) Act 1991 (c 23)

*RA*: 27 Jun 1991

*Commencement provisions:* s 8(2); Children and Young Persons (Protection from Tobacco) Act 1991 (Commencement No 1) Order 1991, SI 1991/2500; Children and Young Persons (Protection from Tobacco) Act 1991 (Commencement No 2) Order 1992, SI 1992/332; Children and Young Persons (Protection from Tobacco) Act 1991 (Commencement No 3) Order 1992, SI 1992/3227

|       |            |                                       |
|-------|------------|---------------------------------------|
| 1–3   |            | 1 Mar 1992 (SI 1992/332)              |
| 4     | (1), (2)   | 20 Feb 1993 (SI 1992/3227)            |
|       | (3)        | 17 Dec 1992 (SI 1992/3227)            |
|       | (4)–(8)    | 20 Feb 1993 (SI 1992/3227)            |
|       | (9)        | 17 Dec 1992 (SI 1992/3227)            |
| 5–7   |            | 1 Mar 1992 (SI 1992/332)              |
| 8     | (1)        | 1 Mar 1992 (SI 1992/332)              |
|       | (2)        | 27 Jun 1991 (RA)                      |
|       | (3)–(5)    | 1 Mar 1992 (SI 1992/332)              |
|       | (6), (7)   | 11 Nov 1991 (NI) (SI 1991/2500)       |
|       |            | 1 Mar 1992 (otherwise) (SI 1992/332)  |

## Civil Jurisdiction and Judgments Act 1991 (c 12)

*RA:* 9 May 1991

*Commencement provisions:* s 5(3); Civil Jurisdiction and Judgments Act 1991 (Commencement) Order 1992, SI 1992/745

Whole Act in force 1 May 1992 (SI 1992/745)

## Coal Mining Subsidence Act 1991 (c 45)

*RA:* 25 Jul 1991

*Commencement provisions:* s 54(2), (3); Coal Mining Subsidence Act 1991 (Commencement) Order 1991, SI 1991/2508

Whole Act in force 30 Nov 1991 (subject to transitional provision with respect to s 34(1)(a)) (SI 1991/2508)

## Community Charges (General Reduction) Act 1991 (c 9)

*RA:* 28 Mar 1991

Whole Act in force 28 Mar 1991 (RA)

## Community Charges (Substitute Setting) Act 1991 (c 8)

*RA:* 21 Mar 1991

Whole Act in force 21 Mar 1991 (RA)

## Consolidated Fund Act 1991 (c 7)

*RA:* 21 Mar 1991

Whole Act in force 21 Mar 1991 (RA)

## Consolidated Fund (No 2) Act 1991 (c 10)

*RA:* 9 May 1991

Whole Act in force 9 May 1991 (RA)

## Consolidated Fund (No 3) Act 1991 (c 68)

*RA:* 19 Dec 1991

Whole Act in force 19 Dec 1991 (RA)

## Criminal Justice Act 1991 (c 53)

*RA:* 25 Jul 1991

*Commencement provisions:* s 102(2), (3); Criminal Justice Act 1991 (Commencement No 1) Order 1991, SI 1991/2208; Criminal Justice Act 1991 (Commencement No 2 and Transitional Provisions) Order 1991, SI 1991/2706; Criminal Justice Act 1991 (Commencement No 3) Order 1992, SI 1992/333, as amended by SI 1992/2118, SI 1999/1280; Criminal Justice Act 1991 (Commencement No 4) Order 1994, SI 1994/3191; Criminal Justice Act 1991 (Commencement No 3) (Amendment) Order 1999, SI 1999/1280

**Criminal Justice Act 1991 (c 53)**—*contd*

| | | |
|---|---|---|
| 1–7 | | 1 Oct 1992 (SI 1992/333) |
| 8 | (1), (2) | 1 Oct 1992 (SI 1992/333) |
| | (3)(a) | See Sch 1, Pt I below |
| | (3)(b)–(d) | 1 Oct 1992 (SI 1992/333) |
| 9 | (1) | 1 Oct 1992 (SI 1992/333) |
| | (2) | See Sch 1, Pt II below |
| 10, 11 | | 1 Oct 1992 (SI 1992/333) |
| 12, 13 | | 9 Jan 1995 (SI 1994/3191) |
| 14 | (1) | See Sch 2 below |
| | (2) | 1 Oct 1992 (SI 1992/333) |
| 15, 16 | | 1 Oct 1992 (SI 1992/333) |
| 17 | | 1 Oct 1992 (but does not apply in relation to any offence committed before 1 Oct 1992) (SI 1992/333) |
| 18–25 | | 1 Oct 1992 (SI 1992/333) |
| 26 | (1), (2) | 1 Oct 1992 (SI 1992/333) |
| | (3) | 25 Oct 1991 (except so far as it would have effect with respect to the penalty provided by the Badgers Act 1973, s 10(2)(b), for an offence under s 9(3) of the 1973 Act (SI 1991/2208) |
| | | 25 Oct 1991 (S) (except so far as it would have effect with respect to the penalty provided by the Badgers Act 1973, s 10(2)(b), immediately before 9 Dec 1991, for an offence under s 9(3) of the 1973 Act (SI 1991/2706) |
| | | *Never in force* (otherwise) (repealed) |
| | (4), (5) | 31 Oct 1991 (SI 1991/2208) |
| 27–31 | | 1 Oct 1992 (SI 1992/333) |
| 32 | (1)–(6) | 1 Oct 1992 (SI 1992/333) |
| | (7) | See Sch 5 below |
| 33–52 | | 1 Oct 1992 (SI 1992/333) |
| 53 | (1)–(4) | 1 Oct 1992 (SI 1992/333) |
| | (5) | See Sch 6 below |
| | (6), (7) | 1 Oct 1992 (SI 1992/333) |
| 54–59 | | 1 Oct 1992 (SI 1992/333) |
| 60 | (1) | 1 Oct 1992 (SI 1992/333) |
| | (2)(a) | 1 Oct 1992 (SI 1992/333) |
| | (2)(b), (c) | 1 Jun 1999 (SI 1999/1280) |
| | (3) | 14 Oct 1991 (SI 1991/2208) |
| 61–65 | | 1 Oct 1992 (SI 1992/333) |
| 66 | | See Sch 7 below |
| 67 | | 1 Oct 1992 (SI 1992/333) |
| 68 | | See Sch 8 below |
| 69, 70 | | 1 Oct 1992 (SI 1992/333) |
| 71 | | See Sch 9 below |
| 72 | | 1 Oct 1992 (SI 1992/333) |
| 73, 74 | | 31 Oct 1991 (SI 1991/2208) |
| 75–79 | | 1 Apr 1992 (SI 1992/333) |
| 80–88 | | 31 Oct 1991 (SI 1991/2208) |
| 89 | (1) | 31 Oct 1991 (SI 1991/2208) |
| | (2) | See Sch 10 below |
| | (3) | 31 Oct 1991 (SI 1991/2208) |
| 90, 91 | | 31 Oct 1991 (SI 1991/2208) |
| 92 | (1) | 31 Oct 1991 (SI 1991/2208) |
| | (2) | 1 Apr 1992 (SI 1992/333) |
| | (3) | *Not yet in force* |
| 93–96 | | 31 Oct 1991 (SI 1991/2208) |
| 97 | | 1 Oct 1992 (SI 1992/333) |
| 98 | | 31 Oct 1991 (SI 1991/2208) |
| 99 | (1) | 14 Oct 1991 (except definitions "child" and "young person") (SI 1991/2208) |
| | | 1 Oct 1992 (exceptions noted above) (SI 1992/333) |

**Criminal Justice Act 1991 (c 53)**—*contd*

|       |                    |                                                                                                          |
|-------|--------------------|----------------------------------------------------------------------------------------------------------|
|       | (2)                | 1 Oct 1992 (SI 1992/333)                                                                                  |
| 100   |                    | See Sch 11 below                                                                                         |
| 101   | (1)                | See Sch 12 below                                                                                         |
|       | (2)                | See Sch 13 below                                                                                         |
| 102   |                    | 14 Oct 1991 (SI 1991/2208)                                                                               |
| Schs 1–7 |                 | 1 Oct 1992 (SI 1992/333)                                                                                  |
| Sch 8 | para 1(1)          | *Not yet in force*                                                                                       |
|       | para 1(2)          | 1 Oct 1992 (SI 1992/333)                                                                                  |
|       | para 1(3)          | 1 Oct 1992 (except to the extent that it would otherwise apply to Children and Young Persons Act 1933, s 34) (SI 1992/333) |
|       |                    | *Not yet in force* (exception noted above)                                                               |
|       | paras 2–6          | 1 Oct 1992 (SI 1992/333)                                                                                  |
| Sch 9 |                    | 1 Oct 1992 (SI 1992/333)                                                                                  |
| Sch 10|                    | 31 Oct 1991 (SI 1991/2208)                                                                               |
| Sch 11| para 1             | 1 Oct 1992 (SI 1992/333)                                                                                  |
|       | para 2(1)          | 1 Oct 1992 (SI 1992/333)                                                                                  |
|       | para 2(2)(a)       | 1 Oct 1992 (SI 1992/333)                                                                                  |
|       | para 2(2)(b)       | 1 Jun 1999 (SI 1999/1280)                                                                                 |
|       | para 2(3)          | 1 Oct 1992 (SI 1992/333)                                                                                  |
|       | para 2(4)(a), (b)  | 1 Oct 1992 (SI 1992/333)                                                                                  |
|       | para 2(4)(c)       | 1 Jun 1999 (SI 1999/1280)                                                                                 |
|       | paras 3–16         | 1 Oct 1992 (SI 1992/333)                                                                                  |
|       | para 17(1)         | 31 Oct 1991 (SI 1991/2208)                                                                               |
|       | para 17(2)         | 1 Oct 1992 (SI 1992/333)                                                                                  |
|       | paras 18–35        | 1 Oct 1992 (SI 1992/333)                                                                                  |
|       | para 36            | 14 Oct 1991 (SI 1991/2208)                                                                               |
|       | paras 37–41        | 1 Oct 1992 (SI 1992/333)                                                                                  |
| Sch 12| paras 1–6          | 1 Oct 1992 (SI 1992/333)                                                                                  |
|       | para 7             | 25 Oct 1991 (SI 1991/2208)                                                                               |
|       | paras 8–14         | 1 Oct 1992 (SI 1992/333)                                                                                  |
|       | para 15(1), (2)    | 1 Oct 1992 (SI 1992/333)                                                                                  |
|       | para 15(3)–(5)     | *Not yet in force*                                                                                       |
|       | para 16(1)         | 1 Oct 1992 (SI 1992/333)                                                                                  |
|       | para 16(2)–(4)     | 1 Jun 1999 (SI 1999/1280)                                                                                 |
|       | paras 17–22        | 1 Oct 1992 (SI 1992/333)                                                                                  |
|       | para 23            | 14 Oct 1991 (SI 1991/2208)                                                                               |
|       | para 24            | 1 Oct 1992 (SI 1992/333)                                                                                  |
| Sch 13|                    | 31 Oct 1991 (repeal of Metropolitan Police Act 1839, s 11) (SI 1991/2208)                                |
|       |                    | 1 Oct 1992 (otherwise, except repeal in Criminal Justice Act 1967, s 67(6)) (SI 1992/333)                |
|       |                    | 1 Jun 1999 (exception noted above) (SI 1999/1280)                                                        |

---

**Criminal Procedure (Insanity and Unfitness to Plead) Act 1991 (c 25)**

*RA:* 27 Jun 1991

*Commencement provisions:* s 9(2); Criminal Procedure (Insanity and Unfitness to Plead) Act 1991 (Commencement) Order 1991, SI 1991/2488

Whole Act in force 1 Jan 1992 (SI 1991/2488)

---

**Crofter Forestry (Scotland) Act 1991 (c 18)**

*RA:* 27 Jun 1991

*Commencement provisions:* s 4(2); Crofter Forestry (Scotland) Act 1991 (Commencement) Order 1992, SI 1992/504

**Crofter Forestry (Scotland) Act 1991 (c 18)**—*contd*
Whole Act in force 1 Apr 1992 (SI 1992/504)

---

**Dangerous Dogs Act 1991 (c 65)**

*RA:* 25 Jul 1991

*Commencement provisions:* s 10(4); Dangerous Dogs Act 1991 (Commencement and Appointed Day) Order 1991, SI 1991/1742

| | |
|---|---|
| 1–7 | 12 Aug 1991 (SI 1991/1742) |
| 8 | 25 Jul 1991 (s 10(4)) |
| 9, 10 | 12 Aug 1991 (SI 1991/1742) |

---

**Deer Act 1991 (c 54)**

*RA:* 25 Jul 1991

*Commencement provisions:* s 18(3)

Whole Act in force 25 Oct 1991 (s 18(3))

---

**Development Board for Rural Wales Act 1991 (c 1)**

*RA:* 12 Feb 1991

Whole Act in force 12 Feb 1991 (RA)

---

**Diocesan Boards of Education Measure 1991 (No 2)**

*RA:* 12 Jul 1991

*Commencement provisions:* s 13(3)

Whole Measure in force 1 Aug 1991 (the day appointed by the Archbishops of Canterbury and York under s 13(3))

---

**Disability Living Allowance and Disability Working Allowance Act 1991 (c 21)**
*RA:* 27 Jun 1991

*Commencement provisions:* s 15(2), (3); Disability Living Allowance and Disability Working Allowance Act 1991 (Commencement No 1) Order 1991, SI 1991/1519; Disability Living Allowance and Disability Working Allowance Act 1991 (Commencement No 2) Order 1991, SI 1991/2617

| | |
|---|---|
| 1 | 19 Nov 1991 (for the purpose of authorising the making, under the Social Security Act 1975, Social Security (Miscellaneous Provisions) Act 1977 or Social Security Act 1986, as amended by this section, of regulations expressed to come into force on or after 3 Feb 1992) (SI 1991/2617) |
| | 3 Feb 1992 (for the purposes of— |
| | (i) the making of claims for and the determination of claims and questions relating to, disability living allowance, and |
| | (ii) the making by persons who will have attained the age of 65 on 6 Apr 1992 of claims for, and the determination of claims and questions relating to, attendance allowance) (SI 1991/2617) |
| | 6 Apr 1992 (otherwise) (SI 1991/2617) |

**Disability Living Allowance and Disability Working Allowance Act 1991 (c 21)**—*contd*

| | | |
|---|---|---|
| 2 | (1) | 19 Nov 1991 (for the purpose of authorising the making, under the Social Security Act 1975, Social Security (Miscellaneous Provisions) Act 1977 or Social Security Act 1986 as amended by this section, of regulations expressed to come into force on or after 3 Feb 1992) (SI 1991/2617) |
| | | 3 Feb 1992 (for the purposes of—<br>(i) the making of claims for and the determination of claims and questions relating to, disability living allowance, and<br>(ii) the making by persons who will have attained the age of 65 on 6 Apr 1992 of claims for, and the determination of claims and questions relating to, attendance allowance) (SI 1991/2617) |
| | | 6 Apr 1992 (otherwise) (SI 1991/2617) |
| | (2), (3) | 6 Apr 1992 (SI 1991/2617) |
| 3 | | 3 Jul 1991 (for the purpose of authorising the making of regulations expressed to come into force on 12 Aug 1991) (SI 1991/1519) |
| | | 12 Aug 1991 (otherwise) (1991/1519) |
| 4 | (1) | See Sch 1 below |
| | (2) | See Sch 2 below |
| 5 | | 19 Nov 1991 (SI 1991/2617) |
| 6 | | 19 Nov 1991 (for the purpose of authorising the making, under the Social Security Act 1975, Social Security (Miscellaneous Provisions) Act 1977 or Social Security Act 1986, as amended by this section, of regulations expressed to come into force on or after 3 Feb 1992) (SI 1991/2617) |
| | | 10 Mar 1992 (for purposes of making claims for, and the determination of claims and questions relating to, disability living allowance) (SI 1991/2617) |
| | | 6 Apr 1992 (otherwise) (SI 1991/2617) |
| 7 | (1) | 19 Nov 1991 (for the purpose of authorising the making, under the Social Security Act 1975, Social Security (Miscellaneous Provisions) Act 1977 or Social Security Act 1986, as amended by this section, of regulations expressed to come into force on or after 3 Feb 1992) (SI 1991/2617) |
| | | 10 Mar 1992 (for purposes of making claims for, and the determination of claims and questions relating to, disability living allowance) (SI 1991/2617) |
| | | 6 Apr 1992 (otherwise) (SI 1991/2617) |
| | (2) | See Sch 3 below |
| 8 | | 19 Nov 1991 (for the purpose of authorising the making, under the Social Security Act 1975, Social Security (Miscellaneous Provisions) Act 1977 or Social Security Act 1986, as amended by this section, of regulations expressed to come into force on or after 3 Feb 1992) (SI 1991/2617) |
| | | 6 Apr 1992 (otherwise) (SI 1991/2617) |
| 9 | | 10 Mar 1992 (for purposes of making claims for, and the determination of claims and questions relating to, disability living allowance) (SI 1991/2617) |
| | | 6 Apr 1992 (otherwise) (SI 1991/2617) |
| 10 | | See Sch 4 below |
| 11 | | 19 Nov 1991 (SI 1991/2617) |
| 12–15 | | 27 Jun 1991 (s 15(2), (3)) |
| Sch 1 | | 19 Nov 1991 (for the purpose of authorising the making, under the Social Security Act 1975, Social Security (Miscellaneous Provisions) Act 1977 or Social Security Act 1986, as amended by this Schedule, of regulations expressed to come into force on or after 3 Feb 1992) (SI 1991/2617) |

**Disability Living Allowance and Disability Working Allowance Act 1991
(c 21)**—*contd*

|  |  |  |
|---|---|---|
|  |  | 3 Feb 1992 (for the purposes of— |
|  |  | (i) the making of claims for and the determination of claims and questions relating to, disability living allowance, and |
|  |  | (ii) the making by persons who will have attained the age of 65 on 6 Apr 1992 of claims for, and the determination of claims and questions relating to, attendance allowance) (SI 1991/2617) |
|  |  | 6 Apr 1992 (otherwise) (SI 1991/2617) |
| Sch 2 | paras 1–7 | 3 Feb 1992 (for the purposes of— |
|  |  | (i) the making of claims for and the determination of claims and questions relating to, disability living allowance, and |
|  |  | (ii) the making by persons who will have attained the age of 65 on 6 Apr 1992 of claims for, and the determination of claims and questions relating to, attendance allowance) (SI 1991/2617) |
|  |  | 6 Apr 1992 (otherwise) (SI 1991/2617) |
|  | para 8 | 19 Nov 1991 (for the purpose of authorising the making, under the Social Security Act 1975, Social Security (Miscellaneous Provisions) Act 1977 or Social Security Act 1986, as amended by this Schedule, of regulations expressed to come into force on or after 3 Feb 1992) (SI 1991/2617) |
|  |  | 3 Feb 1992 (for the purposes of— |
|  |  | (i) the making of claims for and the determination of claims and questions relating to, disability living allowance, and |
|  |  | (ii) the making by persons who will have attained the age of 65 on 6 Apr 1992 of claims for, and the determination of claims and questions relating to, attendance allowance) (SI 1991/2617) |
|  |  | 6 Apr 1992 (otherwise) (SI 1991/2617) |
|  | paras 9–15 | 3 Feb 1992 (for the purposes of— |
|  |  | (i) the making of claims for and the determination of claims and questions relating to, disability living allowance, and |
|  |  | (ii) the making by persons who will have attained the age of 65 on 6 Apr 1992 of claims for, and the determination of claims and questions relating to, attendance allowance) (SI 1991/2617) |
|  |  | 6 Apr 1992 (otherwise) (SI 1991/2617) |
|  | para 16 | 3 Feb 1992 (for the purposes of— |
|  |  | (i) the making of claims for and the determination of claims and questions relating to, disability living allowance, and |
|  |  | (ii) the making by persons who will have attained the age of 65 on 6 Apr 1992 of claims for, and the determination of claims and questions relating to, attendance allowance) (SI 1991/2617) |
|  |  | 1 May 1992 (otherwise) (SI 1991/2617) |
|  | paras 17–22 | 3 Feb 1992 (for the purposes of— |
|  |  | (i) the making of claims for and the determination of claims and questions relating to, disability living allowance, and |
|  |  | (ii) the making by persons who will have attained the age of 65 on 6 Apr 1992 of claims for, and the determination of claims and questions relating to, attendance allowance) (SI 1991/2617) |
|  |  | 6 Apr 1992 (otherwise) (SI 1991/2617) |
| Sch 3 |  | 19 Nov 1991 (for the purpose of authorising the making, under the Social Security Act 1975, Social Security (Miscellaneous Provisions) Act 1977 or Social Security Act 1986, as amended by this Schedule, of regulations expressed to come into force on or after 3 Feb 1992) (SI 1991/2617) |

**Disability Living Allowance and Disability Working Allowance Act 1991 (c 21)**—*contd*

|   | 10 Mar 1992 (for purposes of making claims for, and the determination of claims and questions relating to, disability living allowance) (SI 1991/2617) |
|---|---|
|   | 6 Apr 1992 (otherwise) (SI 1991/2617) |
| Sch 4 | 6 Apr 1992 (SI 1991/2617) |

**Export and Investment Guarantees Act 1991 (c 67)**

*RA:* 22 Oct 1991

*Commencement provisions:* s 15(6); Export and Investment Guarantees Act 1991 (Commencement) Order 1991, SI 1991/2430

Whole Act in force 23 Oct 1991 (SI 1991/2430)

**Finance Act 1991 (c 31)**

*Budget Day:* 19 Mar 1991

*RA:* 25 Jul 1991

The commencement details of Finance Acts are not set out, as the dates from which their provisions take effect are usually stated clearly and unambiguously in the text of the Act, and charging provisions will normally state for which year or years of assessment they are to have effect.

**Football (Offences) Act 1991 (c 19)**

*RA:* 27 Jun 1991

*Commencement provisions:* s 6(2); Football (Offences) Act 1991 (Commencement) Order 1991, SI 1991/1564

Whole Act in force 10 Aug 1991 (SI 1991/1564)

**Foreign Corporations Act 1991 (c 44)**

*RA:* 25 Jul 1991

*Commencement provisions:* s 2(3)

Whole Act in force 25 Sep 1991 (s 2(3))

**Forestry Act 1991 (c 43)**

*RA:* 25 Jul 1991

*Commencement provisions:* s 2(2)

Whole Act in force 25 Sep 1991 (s 2(2))

**Land Drainage Act 1991 (c 59)**

*RA:* 25 Jul 1991

*Commencement provisions:* s 76(2)

Whole Act in force 1 Dec 1991 (s 76(2))

## Local Government Finance and Valuation Act 1991 (c 51)

*RA:* 25 Jul 1991

*Commencement provisions:* s 7(5)

| | | |
|---|---|---|
| 1, 2 | | 25 Sep 1991 (s 7(5)) |
| 3 | | 25 Jul 1991 (RA) |
| 4 | | 25 Sep 1991 (s 7(5)) |
| 5 | | 25 Jul 1991 (RA) |
| 6, 7 | | 25 Sep 1991 (s 7(5)) |
| Schedule | | 25 Jul 1991 (RA) |

## Local Government Finance (Publicity for Auditors' Reports) Act 1991 (c 15)

*RA:* 27 Jun 1991

*Commencement provisions:* s 2(2)

Whole Act in force 27 Aug 1991 (s 2(2))

## Maintenance Enforcement Act 1991 (c 17)

*RA:* 27 Jun 1991

*Commencement provisions:* s 12(2); Maintenance Enforcement Act 1991 (Commencement No 1) Order 1991, SI 1991/2042; Maintenance Enforcement Act 1991 (Commencement No 2) Order 1992, SI 1992/455

| | | |
|---|---|---|
| 1–9 | | 1 Apr 1992 (SI 1992/455) |
| 10 | | See Sch 1 below |
| 11 | (1) | See Sch 2 below |
| | (2) | See Sch 3 below |
| 12 | | 27 Jun 1991 (RA) |
| Sch 1 | paras 1–14 | 1 Apr 1992 (SI 1992/455) |
| | paras 15–17 | *Never in force* (repealed) |
| | paras 18–21 | 1 Apr 1992 (SI 1992/455) |
| Sch 2 | paras 1–10 | 1 Apr 1992 (SI 1992/455) |
| | para 11 | 14 Oct 1991 (SI 1991/2042) |
| Sch 3 | | 1 Apr 1992 (SI 1992/455) |

## Medical Qualifications (Amendment) Act 1991 (c 38)

*RA:* 25 Jul 1991

*Commencement provisions:* s 2(2); Medical Qualifications (Amendment) Act 1991 (Commencement) Order 1992, SI 1992/804

| | |
|---|---|
| 1 | 30 Mar 1992 (SI 1992/804) |
| 2 | 25 Jul 1991 (RA) |

## Mental Health (Detention) (Scotland) Act 1991 (c 47)

*RA:* 25 Jul 1991

*Commencement provisions:* s 4(2); Mental Health (Detention) (Scotland) Act 1991 (Commencement) Order 1992, SI 1992/357

Whole Act in force 9 Mar 1992 (SI 1992/357)

## Ministerial and other Pensions and Salaries Act 1991 (c 5)

*RA:* 28 Feb 1991

Whole Act in force 28 Feb 1991 (RA)

---

## Motor Vehicles (Safety Equipment for Children) Act 1991 (c 14)

*RA:* 27 Jun 1991

Whole Act in force 27 Jun 1991 (RA)

---

## Namibia Act 1991 (c 4)

*RA:* 28 Feb 1991

*Commencement provisions:* s 2(2)

Whole Act in force 21 Mar 1990 (s 2(2))

---

## Natural Heritage (Scotland) Act 1991 (c 28)

*RA:* 27 Jun 1991

*Commencement provisions:* s 28(2); Natural Heritage (Scotland) Act 1991 (Commencement No 1) Order 1991, SI 1991/2187; Natural Heritage (Scotland) Act 1991 (Commencement No 2) Order 1991, SI 1991/2633

| | | |
|---|---|---|
| 1 | | 27 Nov 1991 (SI 1991/2633) |
| 2 | (1) | 27 Nov 1991 (SI 1991/2633) |
| | (2) | 1 Apr 1992 (SI 1991/2633) |
| 3 | | 27 Nov 1991 (SI 1991/2633) |
| 4–7 | | 1 Apr 1992 (SI 1991/2633) |
| 8 | | 27 Nov 1991 (SI 1991/2633) |
| 9 | | 1 Apr 1992 (SI 1991/2633) |
| 10, 11 | | 27 Nov 1991 (SI 1991/2633) |
| 12, 13 | | 1 Apr 1992 (SI 1991/2633) |
| 14 | (1), (2) | 27 Nov 1991 (SI 1991/2633) |
| | (3), (4) | 1 Apr 1992 (SI 1991/2633) |
| | (5) | 27 Nov 1991 (SI 1991/2633) |
| 15–26 | | 1 Oct 1991 (SI 1991/2187) |
| 27 | (1) | See Sch 10 below |
| | (2) | See Sch 11 below |
| 28 | | 27 Nov 1991 (SI 1991/2633) |
| Sch 1 | | 27 Nov 1991 (SI 1991/2633) |
| Schs 2, 3 | | 1 Apr 1992 (SI 1991/2633) |
| Sch 4 | | 27 Nov 1991 (SI 1991/2633) |
| Schs 5–9 | | 1 Oct 1991 (SI 1991/2187) |
| Sch 10 | para 1 | 1 Oct 1991 (SI 1991/2187) |
| | para 2 | 27 Nov 1991 (so far as inserts reference to Scottish Natural Heritage in Superannuation Act 1965, s 39(1), para 7) (SI 1991/2633) |
| | | 1 Apr 1992 (otherwise) (SI 1991/2633) |
| | para 3 | 27 Nov 1991 (SI 1991/2633) |
| | para 4 | 1 Apr 1992 (SI 1991/2633) |
| | paras 5–7 | 1 Oct 1991 (SI 1991/2187) |
| | para 8 | 1 Apr 1992 (SI 1991/2633) |
| | para 9 | 1 Oct 1991 (SI 1991/2187) |
| | para 10 | 27 Nov 1991 (SI 1991/2633) |
| | paras 11–13 | 1 Apr 1992 (SI 1991/2633) |
| Sch 11 | | 1 Oct 1991 (SI 1991/2187), repeals of or in— |

**Natural Heritage (Scotland) Act 1991 (c 28)**—*contd*
> Spray Irrigation (Scotland) Act 1964;
> Water (Scotland) Act 1980, ss 77–79, Schs 5, 6
> 1 Apr 1992 (otherwise) (SI 1991/2633)

---

**New Roads and Street Works Act 1991 (c 22)**

*RA:* 27 Jun 1991

*Commencement provisions:* s 170(1); New Roads and Street Works Act 1991 (Commencement No 1) (Scotland) Order 1991, SI 1991/2286; New Roads and Street Works Act 1991 (Commencement No 1) Order 1991, SI 1991/2288; New Roads and Street Works Act 1991 (Commencement No 3) Order 1992, SI 1992/1686; New Roads and Street Works Act 1991 (Commencement No 4) (Scotland) Order 1992, SI 1992/1671; New Roads and Street Works Act 1991 (Commencement No 5 and Transitional Provisions and Savings) Order 1992, SI 1992/2984; New Roads and Street Works Act 1991 (Commencement No 6 and Transitional Provisions and Savings) (Scotland) Order 1992, SI 1992/2990; New Roads and Street Works Act 1991 (Commencement No 7) (England) Order 2002, SI 2002/3267; New Roads and Street Works Act 1991 (Commencement No 1) (Wales) Order 2004, SI 2004/1780

| | | |
|---|---|---|
| 1–5 | | 1 Nov 1991 (SI 1991/2288) |
| 6 | (1), (2) | 1 Nov 1991 (SI 1991/2288) |
| | (3) | See Sch 2 below |
| | (4)–(6) | 1 Nov 1991 (SI 1991/2288) |
| 7–26 | | 1 Nov 1991 (SI 1991/2288) |
| 27–42 | | 21 Oct 1991 (SI 1991/2286) |
| 43, 44 | | 1 Nov 1991 (SI 1991/2286) |
| 45–47 | | 21 Oct 1991 (SI 1991/2286) |
| 48, 49 | | 14 Jul 1992 (SI 1992/1686) |
| 50 | (1)–(3) | 1 Jan 1993 (SI 1992/2984) |
| | (4) | See Sch 3 below |
| | (5)–(7) | 1 Jan 1993 (SI 1992/2984) |
| 51 | | 1 Jan 1993 (SI 1992/2984) |
| 52 | | 14 Jul 1992 (SI 1992/1686) |
| 53 | (1)–(3) | 28 Nov 1992 (SI 1992/2984) |
| | (4)–(6) | 14 Jul 1992 (SI 1992/1686) |
| 54 | | 14 Jul 1992 (SI 1992/1686) |
| 55 | | 28 Nov 1992 (for purpose of making regulations) (SI 1992/2984) |
| | | 1 Jan 1993 (otherwise) (SI 1992/2984) |
| 56 | | 14 Jul 1992 (SI 1992/1686) |
| 57, 58 | | 28 Nov 1992 (SI 1992/2984) |
| 59 | (1), (2) | 1 Jan 1993 (SI 1992/2984) |
| | (3) | 14 Jul 1992 (SI 1992/1686) |
| | (4)–(6) | 1 Jan 1993 (SI 1992/2984) |
| 60 | (1) | 1 Jan 1993 (SI 1992/2984) |
| | (2) | 14 Jul 1992 (SI 1992/1686) |
| | (3) | 1 Jan 1993 (SI 1992/2984) |
| 61 | | 1 Jan 1993 (SI 1992/2984) |
| 62 | | 14 Jul 1992 (SI 1992/1686) |
| 63 | (1) | See Sch 4 below |
| | (2)–(4) | 14 Jul 1992 (SI 1992/1686) |
| 64 | | 14 Jul 1992 (SI 1992/1686) |
| 65 | (1), (2) | 1 Apr 1993 (SI 1992/2984) |
| | (3) | 14 Jul 1992 (SI 1992/1686) |
| | (4)–(6) | 1 Apr 1993 (SI 1992/2984) |
| 66 | | 1 Jan 1993 (SI 1992/2984) |
| 67 | | 14 Jul 1992 (SI 1992/1686) |
| 68, 69 | | 1 Jan 1993 (SI 1992/2984) |
| 70 | (1)–(3) | 1 Jan 1993 (SI 1992/2984) |
| | (4) | 14 Jul 1992 (SI 1992/1686) |
| | (5)–(7) | 1 Jan 1993 (SI 1992/2984) |

**New Roads and Street Works Act 1991 (c 22)**—*contd*

| | | |
|---|---|---|
| 71 | | 14 Jul 1992 (SI 1992/1686) |
| 72–74 | | 1 Jan 1993 (SI 1992/2984) |
| 75 | | 14 Jul 1992 (SI 1992/1686) |
| 76–78 | | 1 Jan 1993 (SI 1992/2984) |
| 79 | (1)(a), (b) | 1 May 2003 (E) (SI 2002/3267) |
| | | 23 Jul 2004 (W) (SI 2004/1780) |
| | (1)(c) | *Not yet in force* |
| | (2)–(6) | 1 May 2003 (E) (SI 2002/3267) |
| | | 23 Jul 2004 (W) (SI 2004/1780) |
| 80 | | *Not yet in force* |
| 81 | (1), (2) | 1 Jan 1993 (SI 1992/2984) |
| | (3), (4) | 14 Jul 1992 (SI 1992/1686) |
| | (5)–(7) | 1 Jan 1993 (SI 1992/2984) |
| 82, 83 | | 1 Jan 1993 (SI 1992/2984) |
| 84 | (1) | 1 Jan 1993 (SI 1992/2984) |
| | (2) | 14 Jul 1992 (SI 1992/1686) |
| | (3), (4) | 1 Jan 1993 (SI 1992/2984) |
| 85–87 | | 14 Jul 1992 (SI 1992/1686) |
| 88–96 | | 1 Jan 1993 (SI 1992/2984) |
| 97–99 | | 14 Jul 1992 (SI 1992/1686) |
| 100–103 | | 1 Jan 1993 (SI 1992/2984) |
| 104–106 | | 14 Jul 1992 (SI 1992/1686) |
| 107, 108 | | 14 Jul 1992 (SI 1992/1671) |
| 109, 110 | | 1 Jan 1993 (SI 1992/2990) |
| 111 | | 14 Jul 1992 (SI 1992/1671) |
| 112 | (1)–(3) | 30 Nov 1992 (SI 1992/2990) |
| | (4)–(6) | 14 Jul 1992 (SI 1992/1671) |
| 113 | | 14 Jul 1992 (SI 1992/1671) |
| 114 | | 30 Nov 1992 (for purpose of making regulations) (SI 1992/2990) |
| | | 1 Jan 1993 (otherwise) (SI 1992/2990) |
| 115 | | 14 Jul 1992 (SI 1992/1671) |
| 116, 117 | | 30 Nov 1992 (SI 1992/2990) |
| 118 | (1), (2) | 1 Jan 1993 (SI 1992/2990) |
| | (3) | 14 Jul 1992 (SI 1992/1671) |
| | (4)–(6) | 1 Jan 1993 (SI 1992/2990) |
| 119 | (1) | 1 Jan 1993 (SI 1992/2990) |
| | (2) | 14 Jul 1992 (SI 1992/1671) |
| | (3) | 1 Jan 1993 (SI 1992/2990) |
| 120 | | 1 Jan 1993 (SI 1992/2990) |
| 121 | | 14 Jul 1992 (SI 1992/1671) |
| 122 | (1) | See Sch 6 below |
| | (2)–(5) | 14 Jul 1992 (SI 1992/1671) |
| 123 | | 14 Jul 1992 (SI 1992/1671) |
| 124 | (1), (2) | 1 Apr 1993 (SI 1992/2990) |
| | (3) | 14 Jul 1992 (SI 1992/1671) |
| | (4)–(6) | 1 Apr 1993 (SI 1992/2990) |
| 125 | | 1 Jan 1993 (SI 1992/2990) |
| 126 | | 14 Jul 1992 (SI 1992/1671) |
| 127, 128 | | 1 Jan 1993 (SI 1992/2990) |
| 129 | (1)–(3) | 1 Jan 1993 (SI 1992/2990) |
| | (4) | 14 Jul 1992 (SI 1992/1671) |
| | (5)–(7) | 1 Jan 1993 (SI 1992/2990) |
| 130 | | 14 Jul 1992 (SI 1992/1671) |
| 131–133 | | 1 Jan 1993 (SI 1992/2990) |
| 134 | | 14 Jul 1992 (SI 1992/1671) |
| 135–137 | | 1 Jan 1993 (SI 1992/2990) |
| 138, 139 | | *Not yet in force* |
| 140 | (1), (2) | 1 Jan 1993 (SI 1992/2990) |
| | (3), (4) | 14 Jul 1992 (SI 1992/1671) |

**New Roads and Street Works Act 1991 (c 22)**—*contd*

| | | |
|---|---|---|
| | (5)–(7) | 1 Jan 1993 (SI 1992/2990) |
| 141, 142 | | 1 Jan 1993 (SI 1992/2990) |
| 143 | (1) | 1 Jan 1993 (SI 1992/2990) |
| | (2) | 14 Jul 1992 (SI 1992/1671) |
| | (3), (4) | 1 Jan 1993 (SI 1992/2990) |
| 144–146 | | 14 Jul 1992 (SI 1992/1671) |
| 147–155 | | 1 Jan 1993 (SI 1992/2990) |
| 156–158 | | 14 Jul 1992 (SI 1992/1671) |
| 159–162 | | 1 Jan 1993 (SI 1992/2990) |
| 163–165 | | 14 Jul 1992 (SI 1992/1671) |
| 166 | (1) | 21 Oct 1991 (S) (so far as relates to an offence committed under Pt II (ss 27–47)) (SI 1991/2286) |
| | | 1 Nov 1991 (E) (W) (SI 1991/2288) |
| | | 1 Jan 1993 (S) (otherwise) (SI 1992/2990) |
| | (2) | 21 Oct 1991 (so far as relates to an offence committed under Pt II (ss 27–47)) (SI 1991/2286) |
| | | 1 Jan 1993 (otherwise) (SI 1992/2990) |
| 167 | (1)–(3) | 21 Oct 1991 (S) (so far as relate to Pt II (ss 27–47)) (SI 1991/2286) |
| | | 1 Nov 1991 (E) (W) (SI 1991/2288) |
| | | *Not yet in force* (S) (so far as relate to Pt I (ss 1–26, Schs 1, 2)) |
| | (4), (5) | 14 Jul 1992 (S) (SI 1992/1671) |
| | | 14 Jul 1992 (E) (W) (SI 1992/1686) |
| | (6) | 21 Oct 1991 (S) (so far as relates to Pt II (ss 27–47)) (SI 1991/2286) |
| | | 1 Nov 1991 (E) (W) (SI 1991/2288) |
| | | *Not yet in force* (S) (so far as relates to Pt I (ss 1–26, Schs 1, 2)) |
| 168 | (1) | See Sch 8 below |
| | (2) | See Sch 9 below |
| 169 | (1) | 1 Nov 1991 (SI 1991/2288) |
| | (2) | 14 Jul 1992 (SI 1992/1671) |
| | (3) | *Not yet in force* |
| 170, 171 | | 1 Nov 1991 (SI 1991/2288) |
| Schs 1, 2 | | 1 Nov 1991 (SI 1991/2288) |
| Sch 3 | | 1 Jan 1993 (SI 1992/2984) |
| Sch 4 | | 14 Jul 1992 (SI 1992/1686) |
| Sch 5 | | 1 Jan 1993 (SI 1992/2984) |
| Sch 6 | | 14 Jul 1992 (SI 1992/1671) |
| Sch 7 | | 1 Jan 1993 (SI 1992/2990) |
| Sch 8 | Pt I | 1 Jan 1993 (SI 1992/2984) |
| | Pt II | 1 Nov 1991 (SI 1991/2286; SI 1991/2288) |
| | Pt III, paras 81–92 | 1 Jan 1993 (SI 1992/2990) |
| | Pt III, para 93(a) | 21 Oct 1991 (SI 1991/2286) |
| | Pt III, para 93(b) | 1 Jan 1993 (SI 1992/2990) |
| | Pt III, para 93(c) | 21 Oct 1991 (SI 1991/2286) |
| | Pt III, para 94(a) | 1 Jan 1993 (SI 1992/2990) |
| | Pt III, para 94(b) | 21 Oct 1991 (SI 1991/2286) |
| | Pt III, para 95 | 1 Jan 1993 (SI 1992/2990) |
| | Pt III, paras 96, 97 | 21 Oct 1991 (SI 1991/2286) |
| | Pt IV, para 98 | 21 Oct 1991 (so far as it relates to Pt II of the Act) (SI 1991/2286) |
| | | 1 Nov 1991 (so far as it relates to Pt II of the Act) (SI 1991/2288) |
| | | 1 Jan 1993 (otherwise) (SI 1992/2984; SI 1992/2990) |
| | Pt IV, para 99(1), (2) | 1 Nov 1991 (SI 1991/2286; SI 1991/2288) |
| | Pt IV, para 99(3)(a) | 1 Nov 1991 (SI 1991/2288) |
| | Pt IV, para 99(3)(b) | 1 Jan 1993 (SI 1992/2990) |
| | Pt IV, paras 100, 101 | 1 Jan 1993 (SI 1992/2984; SI 1992/2990) |
| | Pt IV, para 102 | 1 Nov 1991 (SI 1991/2286) |

**New Roads and Street Works Act 1991 (c 22)**—*contd*

| | |
|---|---|
| Pt IV, para 103 | 1 Jan 1993 (SI 1992/2990) |
| Pt IV, para 104(a) | 1 Nov 1991 (SI 1991/2286) |
| Pt IV, para 104(b) | 1 Jan 1993 (SI 1992/2990) |
| Pt IV, para 105 | 1 Jan 1993 (SI 1992/2990) |
| Pt IV, para 106 | 1 Jan 1993 (SI 1992/2984) |
| Pt IV, para 107 | 1 Nov 1991 (SI 1991/2288) |
| Pt IV, para 108 | 1 Jan 1993 (SI 1992/2990) |
| Pt IV, paras 109–111 | 1 Jan 1993 (SI 1992/2984; SI 1992/2990) |
| Pt IV, para 112 | 1 Nov 1991 (SI 1991/2288) |
| Pt IV, paras 113–115 | 1 Jan 1993 (SI 1992/2984; SI 1992/2990) |
| Pt IV, para 116 | 1 Nov 1991 (SI 1991/2288) |
| Pt IV, para 117 | 1 Nov 1991 (SI 1991/2286; SI 1991/2288) |
| Pt IV, para 118(1), (2) | 1 Nov 1991 (SI 1991/2286; SI 1991/2288) |
| Pt IV, para 118(3) | 1 Jan 1993 (SI 1992/2984; SI 1992/2990) |
| Pt IV, para 119(1)–(6) | 1 Jan 1993 (SI 1992/2984; SI 1992/2990) |
| Pt IV, para 119(7) | 1 Jan 1993 (SI 1992/2990) |
| Pt IV, para 120 | 1 Jan 1993 (SI 1992/2984; SI 1992/2990) |
| Pt IV, para 121(1) | 1 Nov 1991 (SI 1991/2286; SI 1991/2288) |
| Pt IV, para 121(2) | 1 Jan 1993 (SI 1992/2984; SI 1992/2990) |
| Pt IV, para 121(3) | 1 Nov 1991 (SI 1991/2286; SI 1991/2288) |
| Pt IV, para 121(4) | 1 Nov 1991 (SI 1991/2288) |
| Pt IV, paras 122, 123 | 1 Jan 1993 (SI 1992/2984; SI 1992/2990) |
| Pt IV, para 124 | 1 Jan 1993 (SI 1992/2990) |
| Pt IV, para 125 | 1 Jan 1993 (SI 1992/2984; SI 1992/2990) |
| Pt IV, para 126(1), (2) | 1 Nov 1991 (SI 1991/2288) |
| Pt IV, para 126(3) | 1 Jan 1993 (SI 1992/2984) |
| Pt IV, para 127 | 1 Jan 1993 (SI 1992/2990) |
| Sch 9 | 21 Oct 1991 (repeal in Roads (Scotland) Act 1984, s 143(2)(b)(ii)) (SI 1991/2286) |
| | 1 Nov 1991 (S) (SI 1991/2286), repeals of or in— |
| | Road Traffic Regulation Act 1984, ss 1(2), (4), (5), 3(1), 5(2), 16(3), (4), 17(6), 19(3), 23(5), 34(1), 55(5), 68(1)(a), 86(4), 91, 106(8), 124(2), 132(6), 132A, Sch 9, paras 20(1), 21, 27(1); |
| | Roads (Scotland) Act 1984, s 127, Sch 7, paras 2, 3(a), (b), 4, Sch 9, para 93(2)–(22), (23)(a), (24)–(38), (40), (42), (44)(a), (b), (d), (e), (45)(b); |
| | Transport Act 1985, s 137(1); |
| | Road Traffic Offenders Act 1988, Sch 3 (the entry relating to Road Traffic Regulation Act 1984, s 29(3)); |
| | Environmental Protection Act 1990, Sch 8, para 7 |
| | 1 Nov 1991 (E) (W) (SI 1991/2288), repeals of or in— |
| | Road Traffic Regulation Act 1984; |
| | Transport Act 1985; |
| | Road Traffic Offenders Act 1988; |
| | Environmental Protection Act 1990 |
| | 1 Nov 1991 (repeals in Local Government Act 1985, Sch 5) (SI 1991/2288) |
| | 1 Jan 1993 (otherwise) (SI 1992/2984; 1992/2990) |

---

**Northern Ireland (Emergency Provisions) Act 1991 (c 24)**

*RA:* 27 Jun 1991

*Commencement provisions:* s 69(1); Northern Ireland (Emergency Provisions) Act 1991 (Commencement)
Order 1992, SI 1992/1181; Northern Ireland (Emergency Provisions) Act 1991 (Continuance)

**Northern Ireland (Emergency Provisions) Act 1991 (c 24)**—*contd*
Order 1992, SI 1992/1390; Northern Ireland (Emergency and Prevention of Terrorism Provisions) (Continuance) Order 1992, SI 1992/1413; Northern Ireland (Emergency and Prevention of Terrorism Provisions) (Continuance) Order 1993, SI 1993/1522; Northern Ireland (Emergency and Prevention of Terrorism Provisions) (Continuance) Order 1994, SI 1994/1569; Northern Ireland (Emergency and Prevention of Terrorism Provisions) (Continuance) Order 1995, SI 1995/1566[1]

| | | |
|---|---|---|
| 1–33 | | 27 Aug 1991 (s 69(1)) |
| 34 | | See Sch 3 below |
| 35–46 | | 27 Aug 1991 (s 69(1)) |
| 47–54 | | 1 Jun 1992 (SI 1992/1181) |
| 55 | | See Sch 4 below |
| 56 | | 1 Jun 1992 (SI 1992/1181) |
| 57–59 | | 27 Aug 1991 (s 69(1)) |
| 60 | (1), (2) | 27 Aug 1991 (s 69(1)) |
| | (3) | See Sch 6 below |
| | (4)–(6) | 27 Aug 1991 (s 69(1)) |
| 61–69 | | 27 Aug 1991 (s 69(1)) |
| 70 | (1), (2) | 27 Aug 1991 (s 69(1)) |
| | (3) | See Sch 7 below |
| | (4) | See Sch 8 below |
| 71 | | 27 Aug 1991 (s 69(1)) |
| Schs 1, 2 | | 27 Aug 1991 (s 69(1)) |
| Sch 3 | | 27 Aug 1991 (s 69(1)); but note s 69(3), (4) which provide that s 34 and Sch 3 are deemed to have ceased to have effect immediately after coming into force[2] |
| Sch 4 | | 1 Jun 1992 (SI 1992/1181) |
| Schs 5–8 | | 27 Aug 1991 (s 69(1)) |

[1]   Note that the temporary provisions of this Act (Pts I–VIII except ss 7, 63, 64, Sch 1, Pt III, Sch 4, para 20, and, so far as they relate to offences which are scheduled offences by virtue of Sch 1, Pt III, ss 3, 9, 10), except s 34 and Sch 3, were continued in force for twelve months from 16 Jun 1995 (SI 1995/2695)

[2]   S 34 and Sch 3 are brought into force again immediately before the end of 15 Jun 1992, continued in force from the beginning of 16 Jun 1992, and then cease to be in force immediately after the coming into effect of their continuance (SI 1992/1390)

---

**Oversea Superannuation Act 1991 (c 16)**

*RA:* 27 Jun 1991

*Commencement provisions:* s 3(2)

Whole Act in force 27 Aug 1991 (s 3(2))

---

**Planning and Compensation Act 1991 (c 34)**

*RA:* 25 Jul 1991

*Commencement provisions:* s 84(2)–(4); Planning and Compensation Act 1991 (Commencement No 1 and Transitional Provisions) Order 1991, SI 1991/2067; Planning and Compensation Act 1991 (Commencement No 2 and Transitional Provisions) (Scotland) Order 1991, SI 1991/2092; Planning and Compensation Act 1991 (Commencement No 3) Order 1991, SI 1991/2272; Planning and Compensation Act 1991 (Commencement No 4 and Transitional Provisions) Order 1991, SI 1991/2728; Planning and Compensation Act 1991 (Commencement No 5 and Transitional Provisions) Order 1991, SI 1991/2905; Planning and Compensation Act 1991 (Commencement No 6) (Scotland) Order 1992, SI 1992/71; Planning and Compensation Act 1991 (Commencement No 7 and Transitional Provisions) Order 1992, SI 1992/334; Planning and Compensation Act 1991 (Commencement No 8) Order 1992, SI 1992/665; Planning and Compensation Act 1991 (Commencement No 9 and Transitional Provision) Order 1992, SI 1992/1279; Planning and Compensation Act 1991 (Commencement No 10 and Transitional Provision) Order 1992,

**Planning and Compensation Act 1991 (c 34)**—*contd*

SI 1992/1491; Planning and Compensation Act 1991 (Commencement No 11 and Transitional Provisions) Order 1992, SI 1992/1630; Planning and Compensation Act 1991 (Commencement No 12 and Transitional Provisions) (Scotland) Order 1992, SI 1992/1937; Planning and Compensation Act 1991 (Commencement No 13 and Transitional Provision) Order 1992, SI 1992/2413; Planning and Compensation Act 1991 (Commencement No 14 and Transitional Provision) Order 1992, SI 1992/2831; Planning and Compensation Act 1991 (Commencement No 15) (Scotland) Order 1993, SI 1993/275; Planning and Compensation Act 1991 (Commencement No 16) (Scotland) Order 1994, SI 1994/398; Planning and Compensation Act 1991 (Commencement No 17 and Transitional Provision) (Scotland) Order 1994, SI 1994/3292; Planning and Compensation Act 1991 (Commencement No 18 and Transitional Provision) (Scotland) Order 1995, SI 1995/2045

| | | |
|---|---|---|
| 1 | | 2 Jan 1992 (SI 1991/2905) |
| 2 | | 27 Jul 1992 (SI 1992/1630) |
| 3 | | 25 Nov 1991 (rules, etc[1]) (SI 1991/2728) |
| | | 2 Jan 1992 (otherwise) (SI 1991/2905) |
| 4 | | 2 Jan 1992 (except so far as relates to breach of condition notices) (SI 1991/2905) |
| | | 27 Jul 1992 (exception noted above) (SI 1992/1630) |
| 5 | | 25 Nov 1991 (rules, etc[1]) (SI 1991/2728) |
| | | 2 Jan 1992 (otherwise) (SI 1991/2905) |
| 6 | (1)–(4) | 2 Jan 1992 (SI 1991/2905) |
| | (5) | 25 Nov 1991 (rules, etc[1]) (SI 1991/2728) |
| | | 2 Jan 1992 (otherwise) (SI 1991/2905) |
| | (6) | 13 Oct 1991 (SI 1991/2272) |
| 7–9 | | 2 Jan 1992 (SI 1991/2905) |
| 10 | | 25 Nov 1991 (rules, etc[1]) (SI 1991/2728) |
| | | 27 Jul 1992 (otherwise) (SI 1992/1630) |
| 11 | | 2 Jan 1992 (SI 1991/2905) |
| 12 | (1) | 25 Oct 1991 (so far as substitutes Town and Country Planning Act 1990, s 106) (SI 1991/2272) |
| | | 25 Nov 1991 (so far as substitutes Town and Country Planning Act 1990, ss 106A, 106B) (rules, etc[1]) (SI 1991/2728) |
| | | 9 Nov 1992 (otherwise) (SI 1992/2831) |
| | (2), (3) | 25 Oct 1991 (SI 1991/2272) |
| 13 | (1) | 27 Jul 1992 (SI 1992/1279) |
| | (2) | 25 Nov 1991 (rules, etc[1]) (SI 1991/2728) |
| | | 27 Jul 1992 (otherwise) (SI 1992/1279) |
| | (3) | 27 Jul 1992 (SI 1992/1279) |
| 14 | | 2 Jan 1992 (SI 1991/2905) |
| 15 | | 25 Sep 1991 (SI 1991/2067) |
| 16 | | 25 Nov 1991 (rules, etc[1]) (SI 1991/2728) |
| | | 17 Jul 1992 (otherwise) (SI 1992/1491) |
| 17, 18 | | 25 Sep 1991 (SI 1991/2067) |
| 19 | | 25 Nov 1991 (rules, etc[1]) (SI 1991/2728) |
| | | 2 Jan 1992 (otherwise, except so far as relates to Town and Country Planning Act 1990, Sch 1, para 4(1), as it concerns applications for consent to the display of advertisements) (SI 1991/2905) |
| | | 6 Apr 1992 (exception noted above) (SI 1992/665) |
| 20 | | 25 Nov 1991 (rules, etc[1]) (SI 1991/2728) |
| | | 17 Jul 1992 (otherwise) (SI 1992/1491) |
| 21 | | See Sch 1 below |
| 22 | | 25 Sep 1991 (SI 1991/2067) |
| 23 | (1)–(6) | 2 Jan 1992 (SI 1991/2905) |
| | (7) | 25 Nov 1991 (so far as relates to Town and Country Planning Act 1990, s 214A(2)) (rules, etc[1]) (SI 1991/2728) |
| | | 2 Jan 1992 (otherwise) (SI 1991/2905) |
| | (8) | 2 Jan 1992 (SI 1991/2905) |
| 24 | | 6 Apr 1992 (SI 1992/665) |
| 25 | | See Sch 3 below |

**Planning and Compensation Act 1991 (c 34)**—*contd*

| | | |
|---|---|---|
| 26 | | 25 Sep 1991 (SI 1991/2067) |
| 27 | | See Sch 4 below |
| 28 | | See Sch 5 below |
| 29 | | 25 Sep 1991 (SI 1991/2067) |
| 30 | | 2 Jan 1992 (subject to certain exceptions and savings; see SI 1991/2728, arts 3, 4) (SI 1991/2728) |
| | | *Not yet in force* (exceptions noted above) |
| 31 | (1) | 25 Sep 1991 (SI 1991/2067) |
| | (2), (3) | 25 Jul 1991 (s 84(4)) |
| | (4) | See Sch 6 below |
| | (5), (6) | 25 Sep 1991 (SI 1991/2067) |
| | (7), (8) | 25 Jul 1991 (s 84(4)) |
| 32 | | See Sch 7 below |
| 33 | | 26 Mar 1992 (SI 1992/334) |
| 34 | | 10 Aug 1992 (so far as inserts definition of breach of condition notice into Town and Country Planning (Scotland) Act 1972) (SI 1992/1937) |
| | | 25 Sep 1992 (otherwise) (SI 1992/1937) |
| 35 | | 26 Mar 1992 (SI 1992/334) |
| 36 | | 26 Mar 1992 (except so far as relates to breach of condition notices) (SI 1992/334) |
| | | 25 Sep 1992 (exception noted above) (SI 1992/1937) |
| 37 | | 24 Feb 1992 (for purpose of enabling Secretary of State to make regulations under Town and Country Planning (Scotland) Act 1972, s 84AA(10)) (SI 1992/334) |
| | | 26 Mar 1992 (otherwise) (SI 1992/334) |
| 38–41 | | 26 Mar 1992 (SI 1992/334) |
| 42 | | 10 Aug 1992 (for purpose of enabling Secretary of State to make regulations or development order under Town and Country Planning (Scotland) Act 1972, s 90B) (SI 1992/1937) |
| | | 25 Sep 1992 (otherwise) (SI 1992/1937) |
| 43 | | 26 Mar 1992 (SI 1992/334) |
| 44 | | 3 Feb 1995 (subject to a transitional provision) (SI 1994/3292) |
| 45 | | 10 Aug 1992 (SI 1992/1937) |
| 46 | | 3 Feb 1995 (SI 1994/3292) |
| 47, 48 | | 25 Sep 1991 (SI 1991/2092) |
| 49 | | 24 Jan 1992 (SI 1992/71) |
| 50 | | 25 Sep 1991 (SI 1991/2092) |
| 51 | | See Sch 8 below |
| 52, 53 | | 24 Jan 1992 (SI 1992/71) |
| 54 | | 26 Mar 1992 (SI 1992/334) |
| 55 | | 10 Aug 1992 (SI 1992/1937) |
| 56 | | 26 Mar 1992 (SI 1992/334) |
| 57 | | See Sch 10 below |
| 58 | | 7 Mar 1994 (SI 1994/398) |
| 59 | | See Sch 11 below |
| 60 | (1) | 25 Sep 1991 (SI 1991/2092) |
| | (2), (3) | 25 Jul 1991 (s 84(4)) |
| | (4) | 25 Sep 1991 (SI 1991/2092) |
| | (5) | 25 Jul 1991 (s 84(4)) |
| | (6) | See Sch 12 below |
| | (7), (8) | 25 Sep 1991 (SI 1991/2092) |
| 61 | | See Sch 13 below |
| 62–69 | | 25 Sep 1991 (SI 1991/2067) |
| 70 | | See Sch 15 below |
| 71–78 | | 25 Sep 1991 (SI 1991/2092) |
| 79 | | See Sch 17 below |
| 80 | | 25 Sep 1991 (E) (W) (except in relation to entries noted to Sch 18 below) (SI 1991/2067) |

**Planning and Compensation Act 1991 (c 34)**—*contd*

|  |  |  |
|---|---|---|
|  |  | 25 Sep 1991 (S) (except in relation to entries noted to Sch 18 below) (SI 1991/2092) |
|  |  | 2 Jan 1992 (E) (W) (otherwise) (SI 1991/2728) |
|  |  | 30 Aug 1995 (S) (otherwise) (SI 1995/2045) |
| 81 |  | 25 Sep 1991 (SI 1991/2067) |
| 82 |  | 26 Mar 1992 (SI 1992/334) |
| 83 |  | 25 Oct 1991 (SI 1991/2272) |
| 84 | (1)–(5) | 25 Jul 1991 (RA) |
|  | (6) | See Sch 19 below |
|  | (7)–(9) | 25 Jul 1991 (RA) |
| Schs 1, 2 |  | 25 Sep 1991 (SI 1991/2067) |
| Sch 3 | para 1 | 25 Sep 1991 (SI 1991/2067) |
|  | paras 2–6 | 2 Jan 1992 (SI 1991/2905) |
|  | para 7 | 25 Nov 1991 (rules, etc[1]) (SI 1991/2728) |
|  |  | 2 Jan 1992 (otherwise) (SI 1991/2905) |
|  | paras 8–14 | 2 Jan 1992 (SI 1991/2905) |
|  | para 15 | 25 Nov 1991 (rules, etc[1]) (SI 1991/2728) |
|  |  | 2 Jan 1992 (otherwise) (SI 1991/2905) |
|  | paras 16–32 | 2 Jan 1992 (SI 1991/2905) |
| Sch 4 | paras 1, 2 | 25 Nov 1991 (rules, etc[1]) (SI 1991/2728) |
|  |  | 10 Feb 1992 (otherwise) (SI 1991/2905) |
|  | para 3 | 10 Feb 1992 (SI 1991/2905) |
|  | paras 4–25 | 25 Nov 1991 (rules, etc[1]) (SI 1991/2728) |
|  |  | 10 Feb 1992 (otherwise) (SI 1991/2905) |
|  | para 26 | 10 Feb 1992 (SI 1991/2905) |
|  | paras 27–51 | 25 Nov 1991 (rules, etc[1]) (SI 1991/2728) |
|  |  | 10 Feb 1992 (otherwise) (SI 1991/2905) |
| Sch 5 |  | 25 Nov 1991 (rules, etc[1]) (SI 1991/2728) |
|  |  | 9 Nov 1992 (otherwise; but note that amendments do not apply with respect to proposals which are or have been made available for inspection in accordance with Town and Country Planning Act 1990, Sch 7, para 5 or 6 before 12 Oct 1992 but simplified planning zone scheme had not yet come into operation on that date) (SI 1992/2413) |
| Sch 6 | para 1 | 25 Jul 1991 (s 84(4)) |
|  | paras 2–4 | 25 Sep 1991 (SI 1991/2067) |
|  | para 5 | 25 Jul 1991 (s 84(4)) |
|  | paras 6–12 | 25 Sep 1991 (SI 1991/2067) |
|  | para 13 | 25 Jul 1991 (s 84(4)) |
|  | paras 14–49 | 25 Sep 1991 (SI 1991/2067) |
| Sch 7 | para 1 | 27 Jul 1992 (SI 1992/1630) |
|  | para 2 | 2 Jan 1992 (SI 1991/2905) |
|  | para 3 | 27 Jul 1992 (SI 1992/1630) |
|  | para 4 | 2 Jan 1992 (SI 1991/2905) |
|  | para 5 | 2 Jan 1992 (except so far as relates to reference to s 187A) (SI 1991/2905) |
|  |  | 27 Jul 1992 (exception noted above) (SI 1992/1630) |
|  | para 6 | 25 Oct 1991 (SI 1991/2272) |
|  | para 7 | 2 Jan 1992 (SI 1991/2905) |
|  | para 8 | 25 Sep 1991 (SI 1991/2067) |
|  | para 9(1) | 2 Jan 1992 (SI 1991/2905) |
|  | para 9(2)(a) | 10 Feb 1992 (SI 1991/2905) |
|  | para 9(2)(b) | 27 Jul 1992 (SI 1992/1630) |
|  | para 9(2)(c) | 25 Sep 1991 (SI 1991/2067) |
|  | para 9(2)(d) | 2 Jan 1992 (so far as relates to reference to s 171C) (SI 1991/2905) |
|  |  | 9 Nov 1992 (otherwise) (SI 1992/2831) |
|  | para 9(2)(e) | 2 Jan 1992 (SI 1991/2905) |
|  | para 9(2)(f) | 2 Jan 1992 (so far as relates to reference to s 187B) (SI 1991/2905) |
|  |  | 27 Jul 1992 (otherwise) (SI 1992/1630) |

**Planning and Compensation Act 1991 (c 34)**—*contd*

| | |
|---|---|
| para 9(2)(g) | 2 Jan 1992 (SI 1991/2905) |
| para 9(2)(h) | 25 Oct 1991 (SI 1991/2272) |
| para 9(2)(i) | 2 Jan 1992 (except so far as relates to substitution of reference to "section 316(1) to (3)" by reference to "section 316") (SI 1991/2905) |
| | 17 Jul 1992 (exception noted above) (SI 1992/1491) |
| para 10(1) | 25 Sep 1991 (SI 1991/2067) |
| para 10(2) | 27 Jul 1992 (SI 1992/1279) |
| para 11 | 2 Jan 1992 (SI 1991/2905) |
| para 12 | 27 Jul 1992 (SI 1992/1630) |
| para 13 | 2 Jan 1992 (SI 1991/2905) |
| paras 14, 15 | 17 Jul 1992 (SI 1992/1491) |
| para 16 | 2 Jan 1992 (SI 1991/2905) |
| para 17 | 17 Jul 1992 (SI 1992/1491) |
| paras 18, 19 | 2 Jan 1992 (so far as relate to inclusion in Town and Country Planning Act 1990, ss 77(4), 79(4), of reference to s 73A) (SI 1991/2905) |
| | 17 Jul 1992 (otherwise) (SI 1992/1491) |
| paras 20–23 | 2 Jan 1992 (SI 1991/2905) |
| para 24(1)(a) | 2 Jan 1992 (SI 1991/2905) |
| para 24(1)(b) | 27 Jul 1992 (SI 1992/1630) |
| para 24(2), (3) | 2 Jan 1992 (SI 1991/2905) |
| para 25 | 2 Jan 1992 (SI 1991/2905) |
| para 26 | 2 Jan 1992 (except so far as relates to breach of condition notices) (SI 1991/2905) |
| | 27 Jul 1992 (exception noted above) (SI 1992/1630) |
| paras 27–29 | 2 Jan 1992 (SI 1991/2905) |
| para 30 | 27 Jul 1992 (SI 1992/1630) |
| para 31 | 2 Jan 1992 (SI 1991/2905) |
| paras 32, 33 | 27 Jul 1992 (SI 1992/1630) |
| para 34 | 17 Jul 1992 (SI 1992/1491) |
| para 35 | 2 Jan 1992 (SI 1991/2905) |
| para 36 | 25 Sep 1991 (SI 1991/2067) |
| para 37 | 17 Jul 1992 (SI 1992/1491) |
| para 38 | 6 Apr 1992 (SI 1992/665) |
| paras 39–41 | 27 Jul 1992 (SI 1992/1630) |
| para 42 | 2 Jan 1992 (SI 1991/2905) |
| paras 43, 44 | 27 Jul 1992 (SI 1992/1630) |
| para 45(1) | 2 Jan 1992 (SI 1991/2905) |
| para 45(2) | 2 Jan 1992 (except so far as relates to reference to s 187A) (SI 1991/2905) |
| | 27 Jul 1992 (exception noted above) (SI 1992/1630) |
| para 46 | 27 Jul 1992 (SI 1992/1630) |
| para 47 | 2 Jan 1992 (SI 1991/2905) |
| para 48 | 25 Nov 1991 (rules, etc[1]) (SI 1991/2728) |
| | 17 Jul 1992 (otherwise) (SI 1992/1491) |
| para 49 | 25 Nov 1991 (rules, etc[1]) (SI 1991/2728) |
| | 27 Jul 1992 (otherwise) (SI 1992/1630) |
| para 50 | 2 Jan 1992 (SI 1991/2905) |
| para 51 | 25 Sep 1991 (SI 1991/2067) |
| para 52(1) | 2 Jan 1992 (SI 1991/2905) |
| para 52(2)(a) | 2 Jan 1992 (except so far as relates to definition "breach of condition notice") (SI 1991/2905) |
| | 27 Jul 1992 (exception noted above) (SI 1992/1630) |
| para 52(2)(b) | 2 Jan 1992 (SI 1991/2905) |
| para 52(2)(c) | 27 Jul 1992 (but not relating to demolition of building on land where, before 27 Jul 1992, planning permission has been granted under Town and Country Planning Act 1990, Pt III, or has been deemed to have been granted under that Part of that Act, for the redevelopment of the land) (SI 1992/1279) |

**Planning and Compensation Act 1991 (c 34)**—*contd*

| | |
|---|---|
| para 52(2)(d) | 27 Jul 1992 (SI 1992/1630) |
| para 52(2)(e) | 17 Jul 1992 (SI 1992/1491) |
| para 52(2)(f), (g) | 2 Jan 1992 (SI 1991/2905) |
| para 52(3) | 17 Jul 1992 (SI 1992/1491) |
| para 52(4) | 2 Jan 1992 (SI 1991/2905) |
| para 53(1) | See sub-paras (2)–(9) below |
| para 53(2) | 27 Jul 1992 (SI 1992/1630) |
| para 53(3) | 2 Jan 1992 (except so far as relates to applications for consent to the display of advertisements) (SI 1991/2905) |
| | 6 Apr 1992 (exception noted above) (SI 1992/665) |
| para 53(4) | 17 Jul 1992 (SI 1992/1491) |
| para 53(5) | 2 Jan 1992 (so far as confers on the Secretary of State a power to make provision by development order) (SI 1991/2905) |
| | 9 Nov 1992 (otherwise; but note that it does not apply to application for planning permission or application for approval of matter reserved under outline planning permission (within meaning of Town and Country Planning Act 1990, s 92, made before 6 Nov 1992 nor to any alteration to that application accepted by the authority)) (SI 1992/2831) |
| para 53(6) | 2 Jan 1992 (so far as relates to insertion of the words "planning contravention notices under s 171C or") (SI 1991/2905) |
| | 27 Jul 1992 (otherwise) (SI 1992/1630) |
| para 53(7), (8) | 2 Jan 1992 (SI 1991/2905) |
| para 53(9) | 25 Oct 1991 (SI 1991/2272) |
| para 54(1) | 25 Sep 1991 (SI 1991/2067) |
| para 54(2) | 9 Nov 1992 (SI 1992/2831) |
| para 54(3)(a) | 25 Sep 1991 (SI 1991/2067) |
| para 54(3)(b) | 9 Nov 1992 (SI 1992/2831) |
| para 54(3)(c) | 2 Jan 1992 (SI 1991/2905) |
| para 54(3)(d) | 27 Jul 1992 (SI 1992/1630) |
| para 54(3)(e) | 2 Jan 1992 (SI 1991/2905) |
| para 54(3)(f) | 9 Nov 1992 (SI 1992/2831) |
| para 54(3)(g) | 27 Jul 1992 (SI 1992/1630) |
| para 54(4) | 17 Jul 1992 (SI 1992/1491) |
| para 55 | 17 Jul 1992 (SI 1992/1491) |
| para 56 | 25 Sep 1991 (SI 1991/2067) |
| para 57(1) | 25 Sep 1991 (SI 1991/2067) |
| para 57(2)(a) | 2 Jan 1992 (so far as relates to omission of reference to s 63) (SI 1991/2905) |
| | 27 Jul 1992 (otherwise) (SI 1992/1630) |
| para 57(2)(b) | 25 Sep 1991 (SI 1991/2067) |
| para 57(2)(c) | 2 Jan 1992 (SI 1991/2905) |
| para 57(2)(d), (e) | 17 Jul 1992 (SI 1992/1491) |
| para 57(2)(f) | 9 Nov 1992 (SI 1992/2831) |
| para 57(2)(g) | 2 Jan 1992 (so far as relates to references to ss 196A–196C) (SI 1991/2905) |
| | 27 Jul 1992 (otherwise) (SI 1992/1630) |
| para 57(2)(h), (i) | 2 Jan 1992 (SI 1991/2905) |
| para 57(2)(j), (k) | 17 Jul 1992 (SI 1992/1491) |
| para 57(3)(a) | 17 Jul 1992 (SI 1992/1491) |
| para 57(3)(b) | 25 Sep 1991 (SI 1991/2067) |
| para 57(3)(c) | 2 Jan 1992 (SI 1991/2905) |
| para 57(3)(d) | 2 Jan 1992 (except so far as relates to s 187A) (SI 1991/2905) |
| | 27 Jul 1992 (exception noted above) (SI 1992/1630) |
| para 57(4) | 25 Sep 1991 (SI 1991/2067) |
| para 57(5) | 17 Jul 1992 (except so far as relates to omission of reference to Pt IV) (SI 1992/1491) |
| | 27 Jul 1992 (exception noted above) (SI 1992/1630) |
| para 57(6)(a), (b) | 17 Jul 1992 (SI 1992/1491) |
| para 57(6)(c) | 27 Jul 1992 (SI 1992/1630) |

**Planning and Compensation Act 1991 (c 34)**—*contd*

| | | |
|---|---|---|
| | para 57(6)(d) | 17 Jul 1992 (SI 1992/1491) |
| | paras 58–61 | 2 Jan 1992 (SI 1991/2905) |
| Schs 8, 9 | | 24 Jan 1992 (SI 1992/71) |
| Sch 10 | paras 1, 2 | 25 Sep 1991 (SI 1991/2092) |
| | para 3 | 18 Feb 1993 (SI 1993/275) |
| | paras 4–8 | 26 Mar 1992 (SI 1992/334) |
| | para 9 | 18 Feb 1993 (SI 1993/275) |
| | para 10 | 26 Mar 1992 (SI 1992/334) |
| | para 11 | 1 May 1993 (SI 1993/275) |
| | paras 12, 13 | 26 Mar 1992 (SI 1992/334) |
| Sch 11 | | 30 Aug 1995 (subject to a transitional provision) (SI 1995/2045) |
| Sch 12 | | 25 Sep 1991 (SI 1991/2092) |
| Sch 13 | para 1 | 25 Sep 1992 (SI 1992/1937) |
| | para 2 | 25 Sep 1991 (SI 1991/2092) |
| | paras 3, 4 | 7 Mar 1994 (SI 1994/398) |
| | paras 5, 6 | 25 Sep 1991 (SI 1991/2092) |
| | para 7(a)(i) | 3 Feb 1995 (SI 1994/3292) |
| | para 7(a)(ii), (iii) | 25 Sep 1991 (SI 1991/2092) |
| | para 7(b) | 25 Sep 1991 (SI 1991/2092) |
| | para 8 | 26 Mar 1992 (SI 1992/334) |
| | para 9 | 25 Sep 1991 (SI 1991/2092) |
| | para 10(a) | 26 Mar 1992 (so far as relates to substitution of reference to "27(1), 27A, 28A and 29") (SI 1992/334) |
| | | 3 Feb 1995 (otherwise) (SI 1994/3292) |
| | para 10(b) | 3 Feb 1995 (SI 1994/3292) |
| | para 11(a) | 25 Sep 1991 (SI 1991/2092) |
| | para 11(b)(i), (ii) | 3 Feb 1995 (SI 1994/3292) |
| | para 11(b)(iii) | 26 Mar 1992 (SI 1992/334) |
| | para 11(b)(iv) | 3 Feb 1995 (SI 1994/3292) |
| | para 11(c) | 25 Sep 1991 (SI 1991/2092) |
| | para 12 | 25 Sep 1991 (SI 1991/2092) |
| | para 13 | 26 Mar 1992 (SI 1992/334) |
| | para 14 | 25 Sep 1991 (SI 1991/2092) |
| | para 15 | 3 Feb 1995 (SI 1994/3292) |
| | para 16 | 26 Mar 1992 (SI 1992/334) |
| | paras 17, 18 | 25 Sep 1992 (SI 1992/1937) |
| | para 19 | 26 Mar 1992 (SI 1992/334) |
| | para 20(a), (b) | 26 Mar 1992 (SI 1992/334) |
| | para 20(c) | 26 Mar 1992 (except so far as para 20(c)(ii) relates to substitution of Town and Country Planning (Scotland) Act 1972, s 85(5)(d)) (SI 1992/334) |
| | | 25 Sep 1992 (exception noted above) (SI 1992/1937) |
| | para 20(d) | 25 Sep 1992 (SI 1992/1937) |
| | para 20(e)–(g) | 26 Mar 1992 (SI 1992/334) |
| | para 21 | 26 Mar 1992 (SI 1992/334) |
| | para 22 | 10 Aug 1992 (SI 1992/1937) |
| | paras 23, 24 | 26 Mar 1992 (SI 1992/334) |
| | para 25 | 26 Mar 1992 (except so far as substituted s 89A relates to breach of condition notice) (SI 1992/334) |
| | | 25 Sep 1992 (exception noted above) (SI 1992/1937) |
| | para 26 | 25 Sep 1992 (SI 1992/1937) |
| | para 27 | 26 Mar 1992 (SI 1992/334) |
| | para 28 | 25 Sep 1991 (SI 1991/2092) |
| | paras 29, 30 | 26 Mar 1992 (SI 1992/334) |
| | paras 31–34 | 25 Sep 1992 (SI 1992/1937) |
| | para 35 | 26 Mar 1992 (SI 1992/334) |
| | para 36 | 25 Sep 1991 (SI 1991/2092) |
| | para 37 | 26 Mar 1992 (except insertion of reference to s 87AA) (SI 1992/334) |

**Planning and Compensation Act 1991 (c 34)**—*contd*

|  |  |  |
|---|---|---|
|  |  | 25 Sep 1992 (exception noted above) (SI 1992/1937) |
|  | para 38(a)–(d) | 26 Mar 1992 (SI 1992/334) |
|  | para 38(e) | 25 Sep 1991 (SI 1991/2092) |
|  | para 38(f) | 26 Mar 1992 (SI 1992/334) |
|  | para 39 | 26 Mar 1992 (SI 1992/334) |
|  | para 40(1)(a) | 26 Mar 1992 (so far as inserts definition "breach of planning control") (SI 1992/334) |
|  |  | 10 Aug 1992 (otherwise) (SI 1992/1937) |
|  | para 40(1)(b), (c) | 3 Feb 1995 (SI 1994/3292) |
|  | para 40(1)(d) | 25 Sep 1992 (SI 1992/1937) |
|  | para 40(1)(e), (f) | 26 Mar 1992 (SI 1992/334) |
|  | para 40(2) | 30 Aug 1995 (SI 1995/2045) |
|  | para 41(1) | 25 Sep 1991 (SI 1991/2092) |
|  | para 41(2) | 26 Mar 1992 (SI 1992/334) |
|  | para 41(3), (4) | 3 Feb 1995 (SI 1994/3292) |
|  | para 42 | 3 Feb 1995 (SI 1994/3292) |
|  | para 43(a)(i) | 25 Sep 1991 (SI 1991/2092) |
|  | para 43(a)(ii) | 25 Sep 1992 (SI 1992/1937) |
|  | para 43(a)(iii) | 26 Mar 1992 (except insertion of reference to "section 90A") (SI 1992/334) |
|  |  | 25 Sep 1992 (exception noted above) (SI 1992/1937) |
|  | para 43(a)(iv) | 26 Mar 1992 (SI 1992/334) |
|  | para 43(b)(i) | 25 Sep 1991 (SI 1991/2092) |
|  | para 43(b)(ii) | 26 Mar 1992 (SI 1992/334) |
|  | para 43(b)(iii) | 25 Sep 1992 (SI 1992/1937) |
|  | para 43(c) | 26 Mar 1992 (SI 1992/334) |
|  | para 44 | *Never in force* (repealed) |
|  | para 45 | 13 Oct 1991 (SI 1991/2272; but note that SI 1992/334 also purports to bring this provision into force on 26 Mar 1992) |
|  | para 46 | 26 Mar 1992 (except insertion of reference to "section 87AA") (SI 1992/334) |
|  |  | 25 Sep 1992 (exception noted above) (SI 1992/1937) |
|  | para 47 | 25 Sep 1992 (SI 1992/1937) |
| Sch 14 |  | 25 Sep 1991 (SI 1991/2067) |
| Sch 15 | paras 1–31 | 25 Sep 1991 (SI 1991/2067) |
|  | para 32 | 2 Jan 1992 (SI 1991/2728) |
| Schs 16, 17 |  | 25 Sep 1991 (SI 1991/2092) |
| Sch 18 | Pt I | 25 Sep 1991 (E) (W) (except entries relating to Planning (Hazardous Substances) Act 1990) (SI 1991/2067) |
|  |  | 25 Sep 1991 (S) (except entries relating to Town and Country Planning (Scotland) Act 1972, ss 56J(8), 56K(12)) (SI 1991/2092) |
|  |  | 2 Jan 1992 (E) (W) (exception noted above) (SI 1991/2728) |
|  |  | 30 Aug 1995 (S) (exception noted above) (SI 1995/2045) |
|  | Pt II | 25 Sep 1991 (SI 1991/2067; SI 1991/2092) |
| Sch 19 | Pt I | 25 Sep 1991 (SI 1991/2067), repeals of or in— |
|  |  | Town and Country Planning Act 1990, ss 55(6), 97(5), 219(6), 336(1) (definitions of "development consisting of the winning and working of minerals", "mineral compensation modifications", "relevant order", "restriction on the winning and working of minerals" and "special consultations"), Sch 1, para 1(2), Sch 5, para 1(6), Sch 11, Sch 16, Pt III (entries relating to ss 312(2), 324(4)); |
|  |  | Planning (Listed Buildings and Conservation Areas) Act 1990, s 9(5) |
|  |  | 2 Jan 1992 (SI 1991/2905), repeals of or in— |

**Planning and Compensation Act 1991 (c 34)**—*contd*

Town and Country Planning Act 1990, ss 63, 69(1), (3), 178(2), 186(1)(c), 190(4), 210(3), (5), 285, 324, 336(1) (definition of "planning permission"), Sch 1, para 4(1) (except so far as concerns applications for consent to the display of advertisements), Sch 16 (entry relating to s 285);

Planning (Listed Buildings and Conservation Areas) Act 1990, ss 38(2), 39(7), 42(7), 55(6), 88(6), 90(6)(b), 92(2)(b);

Planning (Hazardous Substances) Act 1990, ss 25(1)(c), 36(5);

Planning (Consequential Provisions) Act 1990, Sch 2, para 38

10 Feb 1992 (SI 1991/2905), repeals of or in—

Town and Country Planning Act 1990, ss 12(4)(a), 14(3), 21(2), 22, 23(2)–(4), (9), (10), 49, 50, 51(1), 52(2), (3), 53(1), (2)(b), (g), (5), 284(1)(a), 287(1)–(3), (5), 306(2), Sch 2, Pt I, paras 3, 5, 6, Pt II, paras 3–16, 18, Sch 13;

Planning (Consequential Provisions) Act 1990, Sch 4

6 Apr 1992 (repeal of Town and Country Planning Act 1990, Sch 1, para 4(1) (so far as not already in force)) (SI 1992/665)

17 Jul 1992 (repeals of or in Town and Country Planning Act 1990, ss 74(2), 198(4)(a), 220(3)(a), 336(1) (definition of "owner"), (9), Sch 16, Pt I, entries relating to ss 77–79, Pt V) (SI 1992/1491)

27 Jul 1992 (SI 1992/1630), repeals of or in—

Local Government (Miscellaneous Provisions) Act 1976, s 7(5)(a)(iii);

Town and Country Planning Act 1990, ss 64, 188(1), 196, 250(2), 266(3), 284(3)(g), 286(1)(b), 290, 336(1) (so far as not already in force), Sch 6, para 2(1)(c), (8), Sch 16, Pt IV;

Planning (Consequential Provisions) Act 1990, Sch 2, paras 3(2), 35(1)(b)

9 Nov 1992 (repeals of or in Town and Country Planning Act 1990, Sch 1, para 9(2), (3), Sch 7, para 13(2)(e)) (SI 1992/2831)

*Not yet in force* (repeal of Town and Country Planning Act 1990, s 221(7)–(9))

Pt II      25 Jul 1991 (s 84(4)), repeals of or in—

Land Compensation Act 1961, s 15(4)(a), (b);

Land Compensation Act 1973, s 5(3)(a), (b);

Town and Country Planning Act 1990, s 114;

Planning (Listed Buildings and Conservation Areas) Act 1990, s 27

25 Sep 1991 (otherwise) (SI 1991/2067)

Pt III      25 Sep 1991 (SI 1991/2067)

Pt IV      25 Jul 1991 (repeals of Town and Country Planning (Scotland) Act 1972, ss 158, 160) (s 84(4))

25 Sep 1991 (repeal in Land Compensation (Scotland) Act 1973, Sch 2, Pt II) (SI 1991/2067)

25 Sep 1991 (SI 1991/2092), repeals of or in—

Land Compensation (Scotland) Act 1963;

Gas Act 1965;

Public Expenditure and Receipts Act 1968;

Town and Country Planning (Scotland) Act 1972, ss 19(5), 35, 36, 58(2)(a), 106, Pt VII (except s 145), 155(5), (6), 156, 157(1), (3), (4), 158, 160, 169(3), 231(3)(c), 244(2), 245, 246, 248, 249, 263, 264, 265(5) (the words "Part VII of"), 275(1) (definitions of "new development" and "previous apportionment"), Sch 6, paras 3–9, 12, Sch 19, Pt I;

Land Compensation (Scotland) Act 1973, ss 5(3)(a), (b), 27(1), (5), 31(6), 48(9)(b);

Local Government, Planning and Land Act 1980;

Civil Aviation Act 1982;

**Planning and Compensation Act 1991 (c 34)**—*contd*

|  | Airports Act 1986 |
|---|---|
|  | 26 Mar 1992 (repeals of or in Town and Country Planning (Scotland) Act 1972, ss 85(5), (11), 88(1), (2), 93(1)(k), (5), 98(1), (3), 166(2)(c), 265 (so far as not already in force), 275(1) (in definition "planning permission", words from "and in construing" to the end)) (SI 1992/334) |
|  | 25 Sep 1992 (repeals of or in Town and Country Planning (Scotland) Act 1972, ss 51, 91(3), (5), 201(5) (definition of "lawful access"), 214(3), 234, 275(1) (definition of "established use certificate")) (subject to transitional provisions) (SI 1992/1937) |
|  | 3 Feb 1995 (repeal in Town and Country Planning (Scotland) Act 1972, s 28(1)) (SI 1994/3292) |
|  | 30 Aug 1995 (repeals of or in Town and Country Planning (Scotland) Act 1972, s 61(6), Sch 6A, para 12(2)(e), Sch 7, para 2(1)(c), Schs 12–15) (SI 1995/2045) |
|  | *Never in force* (repeals of or in Town and Country Planning (Scotland) Act 1972, ss 41A(6), (7), 101(1), (2), 153A, 159A, 159B, 167B, 167C, 251(1A), 275(1) (definition of "development consisting of the winning and working of minerals") (repealed)) |
| Pt V | 25 Sep 1991 (SI 1991/2067) |

[1] "rules, etc" means "so much of the provision as enables provision to be made by rules of court, confers on the Secretary of State a power or imposes on him a duty to make or to make provision by development order or other order or regulations or to give or revoke directions, or makes provision with respect to the exercise of any such power or performance of any such duty, is brought into force on the specified date"

---

**Ports Act 1991 (c 52)**

*RA:* 25 Jul 1991

*Commencement provisions:* ss 32(8), 42(2); Ports Act 1991 (Transfer of Local Lighthouses: Appointed Day) Order 1992, SI 1992/2381

| 1–30 | 25 Jul 1991 (RA) |
|---|---|
| 31–34 | 1 Apr 1993 (SI 1992/2381) |
| 35–42 | 25 Jul 1991 (RA) |
| Schs 1, 2 | 25 Jul 1991 (RA) |

---

**Property Misdescriptions Act 1991 (c 29)**

*RA:* 27 Jun 1991

Whole Act in force 27 Jun 1991 (RA)

---

**Radioactive Material (Road Transport) Act 1991 (c 27)**

*RA:* 27 Jun 1991

*Commencement provisions:* s 9(3)

| 1–7 |  | 27 Aug 1991 (s 9(3)) |
|---|---|---|
| 8 |  | 27 Jun 1991 (RA) |
| 9 | (1) | 27 Aug 1991 (s 9(3)) |
|  | (2) | See Schedule below |
|  | (3), (4) | 27 Aug 1991 (s 9(3)) |
| Schedule |  | 27 Aug 1991 (s 9(3)) |

### Registered Homes (Amendment) Act 1991 (c 20)

*RA:* 27 Jun 1991

*Commencement provisions:* s 2(2); Registered Homes (Amendment) Act 1991 (Commencement) Order 1992, SI 1992/2240

Whole Act in force 1 Apr 1993 (SI 1992/2240)

---

### Representation of the People Act 1991 (c 11)

*RA:* 9 May 1991

*Commencement provisions:* s 3(2); Representation of the People Act 1991 (Commencement) Order 1991, SI 1991/1634

Whole Act in force 22 Jul 1991 (SI 1991/1634)

---

### Road Traffic Act 1991 (c 40)

*RA:* 25 Jul 1991

*Commencement provisions:* s 84(1); Road Traffic Act 1991 (Commencement No 1) Order 1991, SI 1991/2054; Road Traffic Act 1991 (Commencement No 2) Order 1992, SI 1992/199; Road Traffic Act 1991 (Commencement No 3) Order 1992, SI 1992/421; Road Traffic Act 1991 (Commencement No 4 and Transitional Provisions) Order 1992, SI 1992/1286, as amended by SI 1992/1410; Road Traffic Act 1991 (Commencement No 5 and Transitional Provisions) Order 1992, SI 1992/2010; Road Traffic Act 1991 (Commencement No 6) Order 1993, SI 1993/975; Road Traffic Act 1991 (Commencement No 6 and Transitional Provisions) Order 1993, SI 1993/1461, as amended by SI 1993/1686, SI 1993/2229, SI 1998/967; Road Traffic Act 1991 (Commencement No 6 and Transitional Provisions) (Amendment) Order 1993, SI 1993/1686; Road Traffic Act 1991 (Commencement No 7 and Transitional Provisions) Order 1993, SI 1993/2229, as amended by SI 1998/967; Road Traffic Act 1991 (Commencement No 8 and Transitional Provisions) Order 1993, SI 1993/2803, as amended by SI 1998/967; Road Traffic Act 1991 (Commencement No 9 and Transitional Provisions) Order 1993, SI 1993/3238, as amended by SI 1994/81, SI 1998/967; Road Traffic Act 1991 (Commencement No 10 and Transitional Provisions) Order 1994, SI 1994/81, as amended by SI 1998/967; Road Traffic Act 1991 (Commencement No 11 and Transitional Provisions) Order 1994, SI 1994/1482, as amended by SI 1998/967; Road Traffic Act 1991 (Commencement No 12 and Transitional Provisions) Order 1994, SI 1994/1484, as amended by SI 1998/967; Road Traffic Act 1991 (Commencement No 13) (Scotland) Order 1997, SI 1997/1580; Road Traffic Act 1991 (Commencement No 14) (Scotland) Order 1997, SI 1997/2260; Road Traffic Act 1991 (Commencement No 15 and Transitional Provisions) Order 1998, SI 1998/967

| | | |
|---|---|---|
| 1–21 | | 1 Jul 1992 (SI 1992/1286) |
| 22 | | See Sch 1 below |
| 23–25 | | 1 Jul 1992 (SI 1992/1286) |
| 26 | | See Sch 2 below |
| 27–34 | | 1 Jul 1992 (SI 1992/1286) |
| 35 | (1) | 1 Oct 1991 (so far as relates to s 35(2), (5)) (SI 1991/2054) |
| | | 2 Mar 1992 (otherwise) (SI 1992/199) |
| | (2) | 1 Oct 1991 (SI 1991/2054) |
| | (3), (4) | 2 Mar 1992 (SI 1992/199) |
| | (5) | 1 Oct 1991 (SI 1991/2054) |
| | (6) | 2 Mar 1992 (SI 1992/199) |
| 36–40 | | 1 Jul 1992 (SI 1992/1286) |
| 41, 42 | | 5 Jul 1993 (E) (W) (SI 1993/1461) |
| | | 10 Oct 1997 (S) (SI 1997/2260) |
| 43 | | 1 Oct 1991 (E) (W) (SI 1991/2054) |
| | | 16 Jun 1997 (S) (SI 1997/1580) |
| 44 | | 1 Oct 1991 (SI 1991/2054) |
| 45, 46 | | 1 Jul 1992 (SI 1992/1286) |
| 47 | | 1 Apr 1992 (SI 1992/421) |

**Road Traffic Act 1991 (c 40)**—*contd*

| | | |
|---|---|---|
| 48 | | See Sch 4 below |
| 49 | | 1 Jul 1992 (SI 1992/1286) |
| 50, 51 | | 1 Oct 1991 (SI 1991/2054) |
| 52 | (1) | 1 Oct 1991 (SI 1991/2054) |
| | (2) | See Sch 5 below |
| | (3)–(9) | 1 Oct 1991 (SI 1991/2054) |
| 53–63 | | 1 Oct 1991 (SI 1991/2054) |
| 64 | (1) | Ss 64(1), 65, 66(1)–(6), 67(4), (6), 68(2)(b), 69, 81 (so far as relate to Sch 7 as noted below), Sch 7, para 5(2), (3), brought into force, subject to transitional provisions relating to ss 66(2), 67(4), (6), 68(2)(b), on various dates and in respect of various London boroughs as follows— |
| | | 5 Jul 1993 (only in London borough of Wandsworth) (subject to transitional provisions) (SI 1993/1461) |
| | | 4 Oct 1993 (only in London boroughs of Bromley, Hammersmith and Fulham and Lewisham) (SI 1993/2229) |
| | | 6 Dec 1993 (only in London boroughs of Camden, Hackney and Hounslow) (SI 1993/2803) |
| | | 31 Jan 1994 (only in London borough of Richmond upon Thames) (SI 1993/3238, as amended by SI 1994/81) |
| | | 5 Apr 1994 (only in London borough of Southwark) (SI 1994/81) |
| | | 4 Jul 1994 (only in City of London and London boroughs of Barking and Dagenham, Barnet, Brent, Croydon, Ealing, Enfield, Greenwich, Haringey, Harrow, Havering, Hillingdon, Islington, Royal borough of Kensington and Chelsea, Royal borough of Kingston upon Thames, Lambeth, Merton, Newham, Redbridge, Sutton, Tower Hamlets, Waltham Forest, City of Westminster) (SI 1994/1482) |
| | | 4 Jul 1994 (only in London borough of Bexley, and not in relation to ss 67(4), (6), 68(2)(b), 69) (SI 1994/1484) |
| | | 10 Apr 1998 (in relation to ss 67(4), 68(2)(b), 69 (so far as those provisions are not already in force)) (SI 1998/967) |
| | (2) | 1 Oct 1991 (SI 1991/2054) |
| 65 | | See s 64 above |
| 66 | (1)–(6) | See s 64 above |
| | (7) | See Sch 6 below |
| 67 | (1)–(3) | 5 Jul 1993 (subject to transitional provisions) (SI 1993/1461) |
| | (4) | See s 64 above |
| | (5) | 5 Jul 1993 (subject to transitional provisions) (SI 1993/1461) |
| | (6) | See s 64 above |
| | (7) | 5 Jul 1993 (subject to transitional provisions) (SI 1993/1461) |
| 68 | (1) | 5 Jul 1993 (subject to transitional provisions) (SI 1993/1461) |
| | (2)(a) | 5 Jul 1993 (subject to transitional provisions) (SI 1993/1461) |
| | (2)(b) | See s 64 above |
| | (3), (4) | 5 Jul 1993 (subject to transitional provisions) (SI 1993/1461) |
| 69 | | See s 64 above |
| 70–72 | | 5 Jul 1993 (SI 1993/1461) |
| 73–78 | | 1 Oct 1991 (SI 1991/2054) |
| 79 | | 5 Jul 1993 (SI 1993/1461) |
| 80 | | 1 Oct 1991 (SI 1991/2054) |
| 81 | | See Sch 7 below |
| 82 | | 1 Oct 1991 (SI 1991/2054) |
| 83 | | See Sch 8 below |
| 84–87 | | 25 Jul 1991 (RA) |
| Schs 1, 2 | | 1 Jul 1992 (SI 1992/1286) |
| Sch 3 | | 1 Oct 1991 (E) (W) (SI 1991/2054) |
| | | 16 Jun 1997 (S) (SI 1997/1580) |
| Sch 4 | paras 1–26 | 1 Jul 1992 (SI 1992/1286) |
| | paras 27, 28 | 1 Oct 1991 (SI 1991/2054) |
| | paras 29, 30 | 1 Jul 1992 (SI 1992/1286) |

**Road Traffic Act 1991 (c 40)**—*contd*

| | | |
|---|---|---|
| | paras 31–35 | 1 Oct 1991 (SI 1991/2054) |
| | para 36 | 1 Apr 1992 (SI 1992/421) |
| | paras 37–49 | 1 Jul 1992 (SI 1992/1286) |
| | para 50 | 1 Apr 1992 (SI 1992/421) |
| | paras 51–72 | 1 Jul 1992 (SI 1992/1286) |
| | para 73(1) | 1 Apr 1992 (so far as relates to para 73(2), (3)) (SI 1992/421) |
| | | 1 Jul 1992 (otherwise) (SI 1992/1286) |
| | para 73(2), (3) | 1 Apr 1992 (SI 1992/421) |
| | para 73(4)–(6) | 1 Jul 1992 (SI 1992/1286) |
| | para 74 | 1 Jul 1992 (SI 1992/1286) |
| | para 75 | 1 Apr 1992 (SI 1992/421) |
| | paras 76–78 | 1 Jul 1992 (SI 1992/1286) |
| | para 79 | *Never in force* (repealed) |
| | paras 80–84 | 1 Jul 1992 (SI 1992/1286) |
| | para 85 | 1 Apr 1993 (for purposes of summary criminal proceedings in Scotland commenced on or after that date) (SI 1993/975) |
| | paras 86–101 | 1 Jul 1992 (SI 1992/1286) |
| | para 102 | 1 Apr 1992 (but does not apply to offence alleged to have been committed before 1 Apr 1992) (SI 1992/199) |
| | paras 103–105 | 1 Jul 1992 (SI 1992/1286) |
| | para 106 | 1 Oct 1991 (SI 1991/2054) |
| | paras 107–114 | 1 Jul 1992 (SI 1992/1286) |
| Sch 5 | | 1 Oct 1991 (SI 1991/2054) |
| Sch 6 | | 5 Jul 1993 (SI 1993/1461) |
| Sch 7 | para 1 | 1 Oct 1991 (SI 1991/2054) |
| | para 2 | 1 Jul 1992 (SI 1992/1286) |
| | paras 3, 4 | 1 Oct 1991 (SI 1991/2054) |
| | para 5(1) | 1 Oct 1991 (SI 1991/2054) |
| | para 5(2), (3) | See s 64 above |
| | para 5(4) | 1 Oct 1991 (SI 1991/2054) |
| | para 6 | 10 Apr 1998 (SI 1998/967) |
| | para 7 | 1 Oct 1991 (SI 1991/2054) |
| | para 8 | 1 Sep 1992 (subject to transitional provisions with respect to a notice of a proposal to exercise a power to which Local Government Act 1985, Sch 5, para 5(2), applies, given before 1 Sep 1992) (SI 1992/2010) |
| | paras 9–11 | 1 Oct 1991 (SI 1991/2054) |
| | para 12 | 10 Apr 1998 (SI 1998/967) |
| Sch 8 | | 1 Oct 1991 (SI 1991/2054), repeals of or in— |
| | | Chronically Sick and Disabled Persons Act 1970, s 21(5); |
| | | Road Traffic Regulation Act 1984, ss 35(9), 51(5), 55(4)(c), 99(2), 104(10), 105(3)(b), 106(2)–(6), (9), (10), 117(3) |
| | | 1 Apr 1992 (repeal of Road Traffic Act 1988, s 41(3)(b), (c)) (SI 1992/421) |
| | | 1 Jul 1992 (SI 1992/1286) otherwise, except repeals in— |
| | | Public Passenger Vehicles Act 1981, s 66A; |
| | | Road Traffic Regulation Act 1984, s 102 |
| | | 5 Jul 1993 (repeals in Road Traffic Regulation Act 1984, s 102) (SI 1993/1461) |
| | | *Not yet in force* (repeal in Public Passenger Vehicles Act 1981, s 66A) |

**Road Traffic (Temporary Restrictions) Act 1991 (c 26)**

*RA:* 27 Jun 1991

*Commencement provisions:* s 2(7); Road Traffic (Temporary Restrictions) Act 1991 (Commencement) Order 1992, SI 1992/1218

Whole Act in force 1 Jul 1992 (SI 1992/1218)

## School Teachers' Pay and Conditions Act 1991 (c 49)

*RA:* 25 Jul 1991

*Commencement provisions:* s 6(5); School Teachers' Pay and Conditions Act 1991 (Commencement No 1) Order 1991, SI 1991/1874; School Teachers' Pay and Conditions Act 1991 (Commencement No 2 and Transitional Provision) Order 1992, SI 1992/532; School Teachers' Pay and Conditions Act 1991 (Commencement No 3) Order 1992, SI 1992/988; School Teachers' Pay and Conditions Act 1991 (Commencement No 4) Order 1992, SI 1992/3070

| | | |
|---|---|---|
| 1 | | 22 Aug 1991 (SI 1991/1874) |
| 2 | (1)–(6) | 6 Mar 1992 SI 1992/532) |
| | (7) | 4 Dec 1992 (SI 1992/3070) |
| | (8) | 6 Mar 1992 (SI 1992/532) |
| | (9) | 30 Mar 1992 (SI 1992/988) |
| 3 | | 6 Mar 1992 (SI 1992/532) |
| 4, 5 | | 22 Aug 1991 (SI 1991/1874) |
| 6 | (1), (2) | 22 Aug 1991 (SI 1991/1874) |
| | (3) | See Sch 2 below |
| | (4), (5) | 22 Aug 1991 (SI 1991/1874) |
| Sch 1 | | 22 Aug 1991 (SI 1991/1874) |
| Sch 2 | | 6 Mar 1992 (SI 1992/532) |

## Smoke Detectors Act 1991 (c 37)

*RA:* 25 Jul 1991

*Commencement provisions:* s 7(3)

*Never in force* (repealed)

## Social Security (Contributions) Act 1991 (c 42)

*RA:* 25 Jul 1991

*Commencement provisions:* s 6(4)

Whole Act in force 25 Jul 1991 (RA). Note that in so far as this Act amends an enactment not in force at the time this Act was passed, it comes into force on the day on which that enactment comes into force (s 6(4))

## Statute Law Revision (Isle of Man) Act 1991 (c 61)

*RA:* 25 Jul 1991

Whole Act in force 25 Jul 1991 (RA)

## Statutory Sick Pay Act 1991 (c 3)

*RA:* 12 Feb 1991

*Commencement provisions:* s 4(2); Statutory Sick Pay Act 1991 (Commencement) Order 1991, SI 1991/260

| | | |
|---|---|---|
| 1 | | 6 Apr 1991 (SI 1991/260) |
| 2 | | 14 Feb 1991 (for the purpose of authorising the making of regulations expressed to come into force on 6 Apr 1991) (SI 1991/260) |
| | | 6 Apr 1991 (otherwise) (SI 1991/260) |
| 3 | para (1) | 12 Feb 1991 (s 4(2)) |
| | para (2) | See Schedule below |
| | paras (3)–(6) | 12 Feb 1991 (s 4(2)) |

**Statutory Sick Pay Act 1991 (c 3)**—*contd*

| | |
|---|---|
| 4 | 12 Feb 1991 (s 4(2)) |
| Schedule | 6 Apr 1991 (SI 1991/260) |

**Statutory Water Companies Act 1991 (c 58)**

*RA:* 25 Jul 1991

*Commencement provisions:* s 17(2)

Whole Act in force 1 Dec 1991 (s 17(2))

**War Crimes Act 1991 (c 13)**

*RA:* 9 May 1991

*Commencement provisions:* s 3(4)

| | | |
|---|---|---|
| 1 | (1)–(3) | 9 May 1991 (s 3(4)) |
| | (4) | *Never in force* (repealed or spent) |
| 2, 3 | | 9 May 1991 (s 3(4)) |
| Schedule | | *Never in force* (repealed) |

**Water Consolidation (Consequential Provisions) Act 1991 (c 60)**

*RA:* 25 Jul 1991

*Commencement provisions:* s 4(2)

Whole Act in force 1 Dec 1991 (s 4(2))

**Water Industry Act 1991 (c 56)**

*RA:* 25 Jul 1991

*Commencement provisions:* s 223(2)

Whole Act in force 1 Dec 1991 (s 223(2))

**Water Resources Act 1991 (c 57)**

*RA:* 25 Jul 1991

*Commencement provisions:* s 225(2)

Whole Act in force 1 Dec 1991 (s 225(2))

**Welfare of Animals at Slaughter Act 1991 (c 30)**

*RA:* 27 Jun 1991

*Commencement provisions:* s 7(2)

Whole Act in force 27 Aug 1991 (s 7(2))

**Welsh Development Agency Act 1991 (c 69)**

*RA:* 19 Dec 1991

Whole Act in force 19 Dec 1991 (RA)

---

**Wildlife and Countryside (Amendment) Act 1991 (c 39)**

*RA:* 25 Jul 1991

*Commencement provisions:* s 3(3)

Whole Act in force 25 Sep 1991 (s 3(3))

---

# 1992 Acts

## Access to Neighbouring Land Act 1992 (c 23)

*RA:* 16 Mar 1992

*Commencement provisions:* s 9(2); Access to Neighbouring Land Act 1992 (Commencement) Order 1992, SI 1992/3349

Whole Act in force 31 Jan 1993 (SI 1992/3349)

---

## Aggravated Vehicle-Taking Act 1992 (c 11)

*RA:* 6 Mar 1992

*Commencement provisions:* s 4(2); Aggravated Vehicle-Taking Act 1992 (Commencement) Order 1992, SI 1992/764

Whole Act in force 1 Apr 1992 (SI 1992/764)

---

## Appropriation Act 1992 (c 22)

*RA:* 16 Mar 1992

Whole Act in force 16 Mar 1992 (RA)

---

## Appropriation (No 2) Act 1992 (c 47)

*RA:* 16 Jul 1992

Whole Act in force 16 Jul 1992 (RA)

---

## Army Act 1992 (c 39)

*RA:* 16 Mar 1992

*Commencement provisions:* s 5

Whole Act in force 1 Jul 1992 (s 5)

---

## Bingo Act 1992 (c 10)

*RA:* 6 Mar 1992

*Commencement provisions:* s 2(2)

Whole Act in force 6 May 1992 (s 2(2))

---

## Boundary Commissions Act 1992 (c 55)

*RA:* 12 Nov 1992

Whole Act in force 12 Nov 1992 (RA)

---

## Car Tax (Abolition) Act 1992 (c 58)

*RA:* 3 Dec 1992

*Commencement provisions:* s 5

Whole Act in force 13 Nov 1992 (s 5)

---

## Carriage of Goods by Sea Act 1992 (c 50)

*RA:* 16 Jul 1992

*Commencement provisions:* s 6(3)

Whole Act in force 16 Sep 1992 (s 6(3))

---

## Charities Act 1992 (c 41)

*RA:* 16 Mar 1992

*Commencement provisions:* s 79(2); Charities Act 1992 (Commencement No 1 and Transitional Provisions) Order 1992, SI 1992/1900; Charities Act 1992 (Commencement No 2) Order 1994, SI 1994/3023

| | |
|---|---|
| 1 | 1 Sep 1992 (except definitions "financial year", "independent examiner" and "special trust" in sub-s (1), and except sub-s (3) (now repealed)) (SI 1992/1900) |
| | *Never in force* (exceptions noted above) (repealed) |
| 2 | 1 Sep 1992 (SI 1992/1900) |
| 3 | 1 Jan 1993 (SI 1992/1900) |
| 4–7 | 1 Sep 1992 (SI 1992/1900) |
| 8–10 | 1 Nov 1992 (SI 1992/1900) |
| 11 | 1 Sep 1992 (SI 1992/1900) |
| 12 | 1 Nov 1992 (SI 1992/1900) |
| 13, 14 | 1 Sep 1992 (SI 1992/1900) |
| 15 | 1 Jan 1993 (SI 1992/1900) |
| 16, 17 | 1 Sep 1992 (SI 1992/1900) |
| 18 | 1 Jan 1993 (SI 1992/1900) |
| 19–27 | *Never in force* (repealed) |
| 28 | 1 Jan 1992 (SI 1992/1900) |
| 29–31 | 1 Sep 1992 (SI 1992/1900) |
| 32–37 | 1 Jan 1993 (SI 1992/1900) |
| 38, 39 | 1 Sep 1992 (SI 1992/1900) |
| 40–42 | 1 Jan 1993 (SI 1992/1900) |
| 43, 44 | 1 Sep 1992 (SI 1992/1900) |
| 45, 46 | 1 Jan 1993 (SI 1992/1900) |
| 47 | 1 Sep 1992 (SI 1992/1900) |
| 48 | 1 Jan 1993 (SI 1992/1900) |
| 49–57 | 1 Sep 1992 (SI 1992/1900) |
| 58 | 1 Mar 1995 (SI 1994/3023) |
| 59 | 28 Nov 1994 (regulations, etc) (SI 1994/3023) |
| | 1 Mar 1995 (otherwise) (SI 1994/3023) |
| 60–63 | 1 Mar 1995 (SI 1994/3023) |
| 64 | 28 Nov 1994 (regulations, etc) (SI 1994/3023) |
| | 1 Mar 1995 (otherwise) (SI 1994/3023) |
| 65–74 | *Never in force* (repealed) |

**Charities Act 1992 (c 41)**—*contd*

| | | |
|---|---|---|
| 75–78 | | 1 Sep 1992 (SI 1992/1900) |
| 79 | | 16 Mar 1992 (RA) |
| Sch 1 | | 1 Sep 1992 (so far as relates to the Charities Act 1960, s 4) (SI 1992/1900) |
| | | 1 Jan 1993 (so far as relates to the Charities Act 1960, s 20) (SI 1992/1900) |
| Sch 2 | | 1 Jan 1993 (SI 1992/1900) |
| Sch 3 | para 1 | 1 Sep 1992 (SI 1992/1900) |
| | para 2 | *Never in force* (repealed) |
| | paras 3–7 | 1 Sep 1992 (SI 1992/1900) |
| | para 8(a) | 1 Nov 1992 (SI 1992/1900) |
| | para 8(b) | 1 Sep 1992 (SI 1992/1900) |
| | para 9 | 1 Sep 1992 (SI 1992/1900) |
| | para 10 | 1 Jan 1993 (SI 1992/1900) |
| | paras 11, 12 | 1 Sep 1992 (SI 1992/1900) |
| | para 13 | *Never in force* (repealed) |
| | paras 14–21 | 1 Sep 1992 (SI 1992/1900) |
| | para 22 | *Never in force* (repealed) |
| Sch 4 | | 1 Jan 1993 (SI 1992/1900) |
| Sch 5 | | 1 Sep 1992 (SI 1992/1900) |
| Sch 6 | para 1 | 1 Jan 1993 (SI 1992/1900) |
| | para 2 | 1 Sep 1992 (SI 1992/1900) |
| | paras 3–8 | 1 Jan 1993 (SI 1992/1900) |
| | para 9 | *Never in force* (repealed) |
| | para 10(a) | 1 Sep 1992 (SI 1992/1900) |
| | para 10(b) | *Not yet in force* |
| | paras 11, 12 | 1 Sep 1992 (SI 1992/1900) |
| | para 13(1) | 1 Jan 1993 (SI 1992/1900) |
| | para 13(2) | *Never in force* (repealed) |
| | para 13(3) | 1 Jan 1993 (SI 1992/1900) |
| | paras 14–17 | 1 Sep 1992 (SI 1992/1900) |

Sch 7     1 Sep 1992 (SI 1992/1900), repeals of or in—

> War Charities Act 1940;
> National Assistance Act 1948, s 41;
> Trading Representations (Disabled Persons) Act 1958, s 1(2)(b);
> Mental Health Act 1959, s 8(3);
> Charities Act 1960, ss 4(6), 6(6), (9) (subject to transitional provisions), 7(4), 16(2), 19(6), 22(6), (9), 30C(1)(c), 31, 45(3), 46, Sch 1, para 1(3), Sch 6;
> Local Government Act 1966, Sch 3, Pt II, column 1, para 20;
> Local Authority Social Services Act 1970, Sch 1;
> Local Government Act 1972, s 210(8);
> Health and Social Services and Social Security Adjudications Act 1983, s 30(3);
> National Heritage Act 1983, Sch 4, paras 13, 14;
> Charities Act 1985 (except s 1) (subject to transitional provisions);
> Companies Consolidation (Consequential Provisions) Act 1985, Sch 2;
> Finance Act 1986, s 33

1 Jan 1993 (SI 1992/1900), repeals of or in—

> Charitable Trustees Incorporation Act 1872, ss 2, 4, 5, 7, Schedule;
> Charities Act 1960, ss 27 (subject to transitional provisions), 29, 44

*Not yet in force*, repeals of or in—

> Police, Factories &c (Miscellaneous Provisions) Act 1916;
> House to House Collections Act 1939;
> Charities Act 1960, s 8(1), (2), (6)(a), (7) (repealed);

**Charities Act 1992 (c 41)**—*contd*

> Theft Act 1968, Sch 2, Pt III;
> Local Government Act 1972, Sch 29, paras 22, 23;
> Charities Act 1985, s 1 (repealed)

**Cheques Act 1992 (c 32)**

*RA:* 16 Mar 1992

*Commencement provisions:* s 4(2)

Whole Act in force 16 Jun 1992 (s 4(2))

**Church of England (Miscellaneous Provisions) Measure 1992 (No 1)**

*RA:* 6 Mar 1992

*Commencement provisions:* s 19(2)

The provisions of this Measure were brought into force on the following dates by instruments made by the
Archbishops of Canterbury and York, and dated 27 May 1992, 11 Jul 1992 and 11 Sep 1992 (made
under s 19(2))

| | | |
|---|---|---|
| 1 | | 1 Jun 1992 |
| 2, 3 | | 11 Jul 1992 |
| 4 | | 1 Jan 1993 |
| 5–14 | | 1 Jun 1992 |
| 15 | | 11 Jul 1992 |
| 16–19 | | 1 Jun 1992 |
| Sch 1 | | 1 Jan 1993 |
| Sch 2 | | 1 Jun 1992 |
| Sch 3 | para 1 | 11 Jul 1992 |
| | paras 2–4 | 1 Jun 1992 |
| | para 5 | 11 Jul 1992 |
| | paras 6–11 | 1 Jun 1992 |
| | para 12 | 11 Jul 1992 |
| | paras 13–27 | 1 Jun 1992 |
| Sch 4 | Pt I | 1 Jun 1992 |
| | Pt II | 1 Jun 1992 (except entry relating to Cremation Act 1902, s 11) |
| | | 11 Jul 1992 (exception noted above) |

**Civil Service (Management Functions) Act 1992 (c 61)**

*RA:* 17 Dec 1992

Whole Act in force 17 Dec 1992 (RA)

**Coal Industry Act 1992 (c 17)**

*RA:* 6 Mar 1992

*Commencement provisions:* s 3(4); Coal Industry Act 1992 (Commencement) Order 1993, SI 1993/2514

| | | |
|---|---|---|
| 1 | | 6 Mar 1992 (RA) |
| 2 | | 20 Nov 1993 (SI 1993/2514) |
| 3 | (1), (2) | 6 Mar 1992 (RA) |
| | (3) | See Schedule below |
| | (4), (5) | 6 Mar 1992 (RA) |
| Schedule | Pt I | 6 Mar 1992 (RA) |
| | Pt II | 20 Nov 1993 (SI 1993/2514) |

## Community Care (Residential Accommodation) Act 1992 (c 49)

*RA:* 16 Jul 1992

*Commencement provisions:* s 2(2); Community Care (Residential Accommodation) Act 1992 (Commencement) Order 1992, SI 1992/2976

| | |
|---|---|
| 1 | 1 Apr 1993 (SI 1992/2976) |
| 2 | 16 Jul 1992 (RA) |

## Competition and Service (Utilities) Act 1992 (c 43)

*RA:* 16 Mar 1992

*Commencement provisions:* s 56(2); Competition and Service (Utilities) Act 1992 (Commencement No 1) Order 1992, dated 29 May 1992 (note that, due to a drafting error, commencement orders under this Act are not made by statutory instrument)

In the following table, the abbreviation "No 1" means the Competition and Service (Utilities) Act 1992 (Commencement No 1) Order 1992

| | | |
|---|---|---|
| 1–4 | | 1 Jul 1992 (No 1) |
| 5 | | 1 Sep 1992 (No 1) |
| 6 | (1) | 1 Jul 1992 (except so far as inserts Telecommunications Act 1984, s 27G(8)) (No 1) |
| | | *Never in force* (exception noted above) (repealed) |
| | (2) | 1 Jul 1992 (No 1) |
| 7 | | 1 Jul 1992 (except so far as inserts Telecommunications Act 1984, s 27H(4)) (No 1) |
| | | *Never in force* (exception noted above) (repealed) |
| 8–15 | | 1 Jul 1992 (No 1) |
| 16 | | 1 Sep 1992 (No 1) |
| 17 | | *Not yet in force* |
| 18–22 | | 1 Jul 1992 (No 1) |
| 23 | | *Not yet in force* |
| 24–33 | | 1 Jul 1992 (No 1) |
| 34, 35 | | 1 Sep 1992 (No 1) |
| 36 | | *Not yet in force* |
| 37 | | 30 May 1992 (No 1) |
| 38–50 | | 1 Jul 1992 (No 1) |
| 51 | | 1 Sep 1992 (No 1) |
| 52, 53 | | 1 Jul 1992 (No 1) |
| 54 | | 16 Mar 1992 (s 56(2)) |
| 55 | | 30 May 1992 (No 1) |
| 56 | (1)–(5) | 16 Mar 1992 (s 56(2)) |
| | (6) | See Sch 1 below |
| | (7) | See Sch 2 below |
| Sch 1 | paras 1–30 | 1 Jul 1992 (No 1) |
| | para 31 | 1 Sep 1992 (No 1) |
| Sch 2 | | 1 Jul 1992 (No 1) |

## Consolidated Fund Act 1992 (c 1)

*RA:* 13 Feb 1992

Whole Act in force 13 Feb 1992 (RA)

## Consolidated Fund (No 2) Act 1992 (c 21)

*RA:* 16 Mar 1992

Whole Act in force 16 Mar 1992 (RA)

## Consolidated Fund (No 3) Act 1992 (c 59)

*RA:* 17 Dec 1992

Whole Act in force 17 Dec 1992 (RA)

---

## Education (Schools) Act 1992 (c 38)

*RA:* 16 Mar 1992

*Commencement provisions:* s 21(3); Education (Schools) Act 1992 (Commencement No 1) Order 1992, SI 1992/1157; Education (Schools) Act 1992 (Commencement No 2 and Transitional Provision) Order 1993, SI 1993/1190; Education (Schools) Act 1992 (Commencement No 3) Order 1993, SI 1993/1491; Education (Schools) Act 1992 (Commencement No 4) Order 1996, SI 1996/1325

| | | |
|---|---|---|
| 1 | (1)–(4) | 16 May 1992 (SI 1992/1154) |
| | (5), (6) | 31 Aug 1992 (SI 1992/1154) |
| 2 | (1), (2) | 31 Aug 1992 (SI 1992/1154) |
| | (3)(a), (b) | 31 Aug 1992 (SI 1992/1154) |
| | (3)(c), (d) | 15 May 1996 (SI 1996/1325) |
| | (3)(e) | 31 Aug 1992 (SI 1992/1154) |
| | (4)–(6) | 31 Aug 1992 (SI 1992/1154) |
| 3 | (1) | 31 Aug 1992 (SI 1992/1154) |
| | (2) | 15 May 1996 (SI 1996/1325) |
| | (3)–(5) | 31 Aug 1992 (SI 1992/1154) |
| 4 | | 31 Aug 1992 (SI 1992/1154) |
| 5 | (1)–(4) | 16 May 1992 (SI 1992/1154) |
| | (5), (6) | 31 Aug 1992 (SI 1992/1154) |
| 6 | (1), (2) | 31 Aug 1992 (SI 1992/1154) |
| | (3)(a), (b) | 31 Aug 1992 (SI 1992/1154) |
| | (3)(c), (d) | 15 May 1996 (SI 1996/1325) |
| | (3)(e) | 31 Aug 1992 (SI 1992/1154) |
| | (4)–(6) | 31 Aug 1992 (SI 1992/1154) |
| 7 | (1) | 31 Aug 1992 (SI 1992/1154) |
| | (2) | 15 May 1996 (SI 1996/1325) |
| | (3)–(5) | 31 Aug 1992 (SI 1992/1154) |
| 8 | | 31 Aug 1992 (SI 1992/1154) |
| 9 | (1)–(6) | 12 Jun 1993 (SI 1993/1491) |
| | (7) | See Sch 2 below |
| 10 | (1)–(3), (4)(a) | 31 Aug 1992 (SI 1992/1154) |
| | (4)(b) | 16 May 1992 (SI 1992/1154) |
| | (5)–(9) | 31 Aug 1992 (SI 1992/1154) |
| 11, 12 | | 31 Aug 1992 (SI 1992/1154) |
| 13 | | 12 Jun 1993 (SI 1993/1491) |
| 14 | | 1 May 1993 (note that SI 1993/1491 purports to bring this section into force on 12 Jun 1993) |
| 15 | | 1 Sep 1992 (in relation to secondary schools) (SI 1993/1491) |
| | | 1 Sep 1994 (in relation to other schools) (SI 1993/1491) |
| 16 | | 16 May 1992 (SI 1992/1154) |
| 17 | | 1 May 1993 (SI 1993/1190) |
| 18 | (1) | 16 May 1992 (SI 1992/1154) |
| | (2), (3) | 31 Aug 1992 (SI 1992/1154) |
| | (4) | 16 May 1992 (SI 1992/1154) |
| 19, 20 | | 16 May 1992 (SI 1992/1154) |
| 21 | (1)–(6) | 16 Mar 1992 (s 21(3)) |
| | (7) | See Sch 4 below |
| | (8) | See Sch 5 below |
| Sch 1 | paras 1–6 | 31 Aug 1992 (SI 1992/1154) |
| | paras 7–9 | 31 Aug 1992 (E) (W) (SI 1992/1154) |
| | | 1 May 1993 (S) (SI 1993/1190) |
| Sch 2 | paras 1–3 | 1 May 1993 (SI 1993/1190) |

**Education (Schools) Act 1992 (c 38)**—*contd*

| | | |
|---|---|---|
| | paras 4, 5 | 31 Aug 1992 (SI 1992/1154) |
| | paras 6–12 | 12 Jun 1993 (SI 1993/1491) |
| Sch 3 | | 31 Aug 1992 (SI 1992/1154) |
| Sch 4 | para 1 | *Never in force* (repealed) |
| | paras 2, 3 | 31 Aug 1992 (SI 1992/1154) |
| | para 4 | 1 May 1993 (SI 1993/1190) |
| | paras 5, 6 | 16 May 1992 (SI 1992/1154) |
| | para 7 | 31 Aug 1992 (SI 1992/1154) |
| Sch 5 | | 16 May 1992 (SI 1992/1154), repeals in Education Reform Act 1988, s 22 |
| | | 12 Jun 1993 (SI 1993/1491), repeal of Education Act 1944, s 77(6) |
| | | 1 Sep 1993 (in relation to secondary schools) (SI 1993/1491), repeals of or in Education Act 1944, s 77(1), (5) |
| | | 1 Sep 1993 (in relation to other schools) (SI 1993/1491), repeals of or in Education Act 1944, s 77(1), (5) |
| | | *Never in force* (repeal of Education Reform Act 1988, Sch 1, para 5) (repealed) |

**Finance Act 1992 (c 20)**

*Budget Day*: 10 Mar 1992

*RA*: 16 Mar 1992

The commencement details of Finance Acts are not set out, as the dates from which their provisions take effect are usually stated clearly and unambiguously in the text of the Act, and charging provisions will normally state for which year or years of assessment they are to have effect.

**Finance (No 2) Act 1992 (c 48)**

*Budget Day*: 10 Mar 1992

*RA*: 16 Jul 1992

The commencement details of Finance Acts are not set out, as the dates from which their provisions take effect are usually stated clearly and unambiguously in the text of the Act, and charging provisions will normally state for which year or years of assessment they are to have effect.

**Firearms (Amendment) Act 1992 (c 31)**

*RA*: 16 Mar 1992

Whole Act in force 16 Mar 1992 (RA)

**Friendly Societies Act 1992 (c 40)**

*RA*: 16 Mar 1992

*Commencement provisions*: s 126(2); Friendly Societies Act 1992 (Commencement No 1) Order 1992, SI 1992/1325; Friendly Societies Act 1992 (Commencement No 2) Order 1992, SI 1992/3117; Friendly Societies Act 1992 (Commencement No 3 and Transitional Provisions) Order 1993, SI 1993/16; Friendly Societies Act 1992 (Commencement No 4) Order 1993, SI 1993/197; Friendly Societies Act 1992 (Commencement No 5 and Savings) Order 1993, SI 1993/1186; Friendly Societies Act 1992 (Commencement No 6 and Transitional Provisions) Order 1993, SI 1993/2213; Friendly Societies Act 1992 (Commencement No 7 and Transitional Provisions and Savings) Order 1993, SI 1993/3226; Friendly Societies Act 1992 (Commencement No 8) Order 1994, SI 1994/2543

| | | |
|---|---|---|
| 1–4 | | 8 Jun 1992 (SI 1992/1325) |
| 5 | (1)–(5) | 1 Feb 1993 (SI 1993/16) |
| | (6) | See Sch 3 below |

**Friendly Societies Act 1992 (c 40)**—*contd*

| | | |
|---|---|---|
| | (7) | 1 Feb 1993 (SI 1993/16) |
| 6–26 | | 1 Feb 1993 (SI 1993/16) |
| 27 | (1)–(4) | 13 Jan 1993 (for purpose of management and administration of incorporated friendly societies) (SI 1993/16) |
| | | 1 Jan 1994 (otherwise) (SI 1993/2213) |
| | (5) | See Sch 11 below |
| 28, 29 | | 13 Jan 1993 (for purpose of management and administration of incorporated friendly societies) (SI 1993/16) |
| | | 1 Jan 1994 (otherwise) (subject to transitional provisions) (SI 1993/2213) |
| 30 | | See Sch 12 below |
| 31 | | 13 Jan 1993 (for purpose of carrying on business by incorporated friendly societies) (SI 1993/16) |
| | | 1 Jan 1994 (in relation to registered friendly societies the value of whose specified income for the relevant year exceeded £3,000 and which do not apply for authorisation before 1 Jan 1994) (SI 1993/2213) |
| | | 1 Jan 1994 (for purpose of carrying on by a registered friendly society of insurance business in respect of which the society is deemed to be granted authorisation under s 32(7)) (SI 1993/2213) |
| | | 1 Jul 1994 (in relation to registered friendly societies the value of whose specified income for the relevant year exceeded £3,000 and which apply for authorisation before 1 Jan 1994) (SI 1993/2213) |
| | | 1 Nov 1994 (in relation to carrying on of any insurance business or non-insurance business by a registered friendly society (other than one to which SI 1993/2213, art 2(2), (3) or (4) applies) which does not duly apply to the Commission before 1 Nov 1994 under s 32 or 33 for authorisation to carry on or continue to carry on any class or part of a class of insurance business or any description of non-insurance business) (SI 1994/2543) |
| | | 1 Jan 1995 (in relation to carrying on of any insurance or non-insurance business by a friendly society to which s 96(2) of this Act applies) (SI 1993/3226) |
| | | 1 Apr 1995 (all remaining purposes) (SI 1994/2543) |
| 32 | (1)–(5) | 13 Jan 1993 (for purpose of authorisation of incorporated friendly societies following application from such societies and from registered friendly societies seeking to be incorporated under this Act) (SI 1993/16) |
| | | 13 Sep 1993 (otherwise) (SI 1993/2213) |
| | (6) | See Sch 13 below |
| | (7) | 13 Jan 1993 (for purpose of authorisation of incorporated friendly societies following application from such societies and from registered friendly societies seeking to be incorporated under this Act) (SI 1993/16) |
| | | 1 Jan 1994 (otherwise) (SI 1993/2213) |
| | (8), (9) | 13 Jan 1993 (for purpose of authorisation of incorporated friendly societies following application from such societies and from registered friendly societies seeking to be incorporated under this Act) (SI 1993/16) |
| | | 13 Sep 1993 (otherwise) (SI 1993/2213) |
| 33 | | 13 Jan 1993 (for purpose of applications from registered friendly societies seeking to be incorporated under this Act and from incorporated friendly societies for authorisation to carry on existing business as incorporated friendly societies) (SI 1993/16) |
| | | 13 Sep 1993 (otherwise) (SI 1993/2213) |

**Friendly Societies Act 1992 (c 40)**—*contd*

| | | |
|---|---|---|
| 34, 35 | | 13 Jan 1993 (for purpose of grant and extension of authorisation of incorporated friendly societies following applications from incorporated friendly societies and from registered friendly societies seeking to be incorporated under Friendly Societies Act 1992) (SI 1993/16) |
| | | 13 Sep 1993 (otherwise) (SI 1993/2213) |
| 36 | | 13 Jan 1993 (for purpose of control of conduct of business by incorporated friendly societies) (SI 1993/16) |
| | | 13 Sep 1993 (otherwise) (SI 1993/2213) |
| 37–43 | | 13 Jan 1993 (for purpose of control of conduct of business by incorporated friendly societies) (SI 1993/16) |
| | | 13 Sep 1993 (otherwise) (SI 1993/2213) |
| 44 | (1)–(7) | 13 Jan 1993 (for purpose of regulation of business of incorporated friendly societies) (SI 1993/16) |
| | | 1 Jan 1994 (otherwise) (SI 1993/2213) |
| | (8) | 13 Jan 1993 (for purpose of regulation of business of incorporated friendly societies) (SI 1993/16) |
| | | 13 Sep 1993 (otherwise) (SI 1993/2213) |
| 45 | | 13 Jan 1993 (for purpose of regulation of business of incorporated friendly societies) (SI 1993/16) |
| | | 13 Sep 1993 (otherwise) (SI 1993/2213) |
| 46 | (1) | 13 Jan 1993 (for purpose of regulation of business of incorporated friendly societies) (SI 1993/16) |
| | | 13 Sep 1993 (otherwise) (SI 1993/2213) |
| | (2) | 13 Jan 1993 (for purpose of regulation of business of incorporated friendly societies) (SI 1993/16)[1] |
| | | 1 Jan 1994 (otherwise) (SI 1993/2213) |
| | (3) | 13 Jan 1993 (for purpose of regulation of business of incorporated friendly societies) (SI 1993/16) |
| | | 13 Sep 1993 (otherwise) (SI 1993/2213) |
| | (4), (5) | 13 Jan 1993 (for purpose of regulation of business of incorporated friendly societies) (SI 1993/16) |
| | | 1 Jan 1994 (otherwise) (SI 1993/2213) |
| | (6) | 13 Jan 1993 (for purpose of regulation of business of incorporated friendly societies) (SI 1993/16) |
| | | 13 Sep 1993 (otherwise) (SI 1993/2213) |
| | (7) | 13 Jan 1993 (for purpose of regulation of business of incorporated friendly societies) (SI 1993/16) |
| | | 1 Jan 1994 (otherwise) (SI 1993/2213) |
| | (8) | 13 Jan 1993 (for purpose of regulation of business of incorporated friendly societies) (SI 1993/16) |
| | | 13 Sep 1993 (otherwise) (SI 1993/2213) |
| 47 | | 13 Jan 1993 (for purpose of regulation of business of incorporated friendly societies) (SI 1993/16)[1] |
| | | 1 Jan 1994 (otherwise) (SI 1993/2213) |
| 48 | (1), (2) | 13 Jan 1993 (for purpose of regulation of business of incorporated friendly societies) (SI 1993/16) |
| | | 13 Sep 1993 (so far as confers powers to make regulations for purposes of section) (SI 1993/2213) |
| | | 1 Jan 1994 (otherwise) (SI 1993/2213) |
| | (3)–(5) | 13 Jan 1993 (for purpose of regulation of business of incorporated friendly societies) (SI 1993/16) |
| | | 1 Jan 1994 (otherwise) (SI 1993/2213) |
| | (6), (7) | 13 Jan 1993 (for purpose of regulation of business of incorporated friendly societies) (SI 1993/16) |
| | | 13 Sep 1993 (so far as confers powers to make regulations for purposes of section) (SI 1993/2213) |
| | | 1 Jan 1994 (otherwise) (SI 1993/2213) |
| 49 | (1) | 13 Jan 1993 (for purpose of regulation of business of incorporated friendly societies) (SI 1993/16) |

**Friendly Societies Act 1992 (c 40)**—*contd*

|  |  |  |
|---|---|---|
|  |  | 13 Sep 1993 (otherwise) (SI 1993/2213) |
|  | (2), (3) | 13 Jan 1993 (for purpose of regulation of business of incorporated friendly societies) (SI 1993/16) |
|  |  | 1 Jan 1994 (otherwise) (SI 1993/2213) |
| 50 |  | 13 Jan 1993 (for purpose of regulation of business of incorporated friendly societies) (SI 1993/16) |
|  |  | 13 Sep 1993 (otherwise) (SI 1993/2213) |
| 51, 52 |  | 13 Jan 1993 (for purpose of regulation of business of incorporated friendly societies) (SI 1993/16) |
|  |  | 28 Apr 1993 (otherwise) (SI 1993/1186) |
| 53, 54 |  | 13 Jan 1993 (for purpose of regulation of business of incorporated friendly societies) (SI 1993/16) |
|  |  | 28 Apr 1993 (otherwise) (SI 1993/1186) |
| 55 |  | 13 Jan 1993 (for purpose of regulation of business of incorporated friendly societies) (SI 1993/16) |
|  |  | 1 Jan 1994 (otherwise) (SI 1993/2213) |
| 56 |  | 13 Jan 1993 (for purpose of regulation of business of incorporated friendly societies) (SI 1993/16) |
|  |  | 28 Apr 1993 (otherwise) (SI 1993/1186) |
| 57 |  | 13 Jan 1993 (for purpose of regulation of business of incorporated friendly societies) (SI 1993/16) |
|  |  | 28 Apr 1993 (otherwise) (SI 1993/1186) |
| 58–61 |  | 13 Jan 1993 (SI 1993/16) |
| 62–67 |  | 13 Jan 1993 (for purpose of regulation of business of incorporated friendly societies) (SI 1993/16) |
|  |  | 28 Apr 1993 (otherwise) (SI 1993/1186) |
| 68, 69 |  | 13 Jan 1993 (for purpose of accounts and audit of incorporated friendly societies) (SI 1993/16) |
|  |  | 1 Jan 1994 (otherwise) (SI 1993/2213) |
| 70 | (1)–(4) | 13 Jan 1993 (for purpose of accounts and audit of incorporated friendly societies) (SI 1993/16) |
|  |  | 1 Jan 1994 (otherwise) (SI 1993/2213) |
|  | (5)–(7) | 13 Jan 1993 (for purpose of accounts and audit of incorporated friendly societies) (SI 1993/16) |
|  |  | 13 Sep 1993 (otherwise) (SI 1993/2213) |
|  | (8)–(11) | 13 Jan 1993 (for purpose of accounts and audit of incorporated friendly societies) (SI 1993/16) |
|  |  | 1 Jan 1994 (otherwise) (SI 1993/2213) |
| 71 | (1), (2) | 13 Jan 1993 (for purpose of accounts and audit of incorporated friendly societies) (SI 1993/16) |
|  |  | 13 Sep 1993 (so far as confers powers to make regulations for purposes of section) (SI 1993/2213) |
|  |  | 1 Jan 1994 (otherwise) (SI 1993/2213) |
|  | (3) | 13 Jan 1993 (for purpose of accounts and audit of incorporated friendly societies) (SI 1993/16) |
|  |  | 1 Jan 1994 (otherwise) (SI 1993/2213) |
| 72 | (1) | 13 Jan 1993 (for purpose of accounts and audit of incorporated friendly societies) (SI 1993/16) |
|  |  | 1 Jan 1994 (otherwise) (SI 1993/2213) |
|  | (2) | See Sch 14 below |
| 73–79 |  | 13 Jan 1993 (for purpose of accounts and audit of incorporated friendly societies) (SI 1993/16) |
|  |  | 1 Jan 1994 (otherwise) (SI 1993/2213) |
| 80 |  | 13 Jan 1993 (subject to transitional provisions) (SI 1993/16) |
| 81 |  | 13 Jan 1993 (SI 1993/16) |
| 82 | (1)–(4) | 13 Jan 1993 (SI 1993/16) |
|  | (5) | 1 Jan 1994 (SI 1993/3226) |
| 83 |  | 13 Jan 1993 (SI 1993/16) |
| 84 |  | 1 Jan 1993 (subject to transitional provisions) (SI 1992/3117) |
| 85–92 |  | 13 Sep 1993 (subject to transitional provisions) (SI 1993/2213) |

**Friendly Societies Act 1992 (c 40)**—*contd*

| | | |
|---|---|---|
| 93 | (1)–(4) | 1 Feb 1993 (SI 1993/16) |
| | (5)–(15) | 1 Jan 1994 (SI 1993/2213) |
| 94 | | 1 Feb 1993 (SI 1993/16) |
| 95 | | See Sch 16 below |
| 96 | | 1 Jan 1994 (SI 1993/3226) |
| 97 | | *Never in force* (repealed) |
| 98 | | See Sch 18 below |
| 99 | | 1 Feb 1993 (SI 1993/16) |
| 100 | | See Sch 19 below |
| 101 | | See Sch 20 below |
| 102–113 | | 1 Feb 1993 (SI 1993/16) |
| 114 | | 13 Jan 1993 (SI 1993/16) |
| 115 | | 1 Feb 1993 (SI 1993/16) |
| 116–119 | | 8 Jun 1992 (SI 1992/1325) |
| 120 | (1) | See Sch 21 below |
| | (2) | See Sch 22 below |
| 121–123 | | 8 Jun 1992 (SI 1992/1325) |
| 124 | | 1 Jan 1994 (SI 1993/3226) |
| 125 | | 1 Feb 1993 (SI 1993/16) |
| 126 | | 8 Jun 1992 (SI 1992/1325) |
| Sch 1 | | 8 Jun 1992 (SI 1992/1325) |
| Sch 2 | | 1 Feb 1993 (SI 1993/16) |
| Sch 3 | paras 1–8 | 1 Feb 1993 (SI 1993/16) |
| | para 9(1) | 1 Feb 1993 (SI 1993/16) |
| | para 9(2) | *Never in force* (repealed) |
| | para 9(3)–(7) | 1 Feb 1993 (SI 1993/16) |
| | paras 10–15 | 1 Feb 1993 (SI 1993/16) |
| Schs 4–10 | | 1 Feb 1993 (SI 1993/16) |
| Sch 11 | paras 1–15 | 13 Jan 1993 (for purpose of committee of management of incorporated friendly societies) (SI 1993/16) |
| | | 1 Jan 1994 (otherwise) (SI 1993/2213) |
| | para 16 | 13 Jan 1993 (for purpose of committee of management of incorporated friendly societies) (SI 1993/16) |
| | | 13 Sep 1993 (otherwise) (SI 1993/2213) |
| Sch 12 | paras 1–6 | 13 Jan 1993 (for purpose of meetings and resolutions of incorporated friendly societies) (SI 1993/16) |
| | | 1 Jan 1994 (otherwise) (SI 1993/2213) |
| | para 7 | 13 Jan 1993 (for purpose of meetings and resolutions of incorporated friendly societies) (SI 1993/16) |
| | | 13 Sep 1993 (otherwise) (SI 1993/2213) |
| | paras 8, 9 | 13 Jan 1993 (for purpose of meetings and resolutions of incorporated friendly societies) (SI 1993/16) |
| | | 1 Jan 1994 (otherwise) (SI 1993/2213) |
| Sch 13 | | 13 Jan 1993 (for purpose of authorisation of incorporated friendly societies and applications for authorisation from registered friendly societies to carry on business as incorporated friendly societies) (SI 1993/16) |
| | | 13 Sep 1993 (otherwise) (SI 1993/2213) |
| Sch 14 | paras 1–6 | 13 Jan 1993 (for purpose of auditors of incorporated friendly societies) (SI 1993/16) |
| | | 1 Jan 1994 (otherwise) (SI 1993/2213) |
| | para 7(1)–(3) | 1 Jan 1994 (SI 1993/2213) |
| | para 7(4) | 13 Sep 1993 (SI 1993/2213) |
| | para 7(5)–(7) | 1 Jan 1994 (SI 1993/2213) |
| | paras 8–16 | 13 Jan 1993 (for purpose of auditors of incorporated friendly societies) (SI 1993/16) |
| | | 1 Jan 1994 (otherwise) (SI 1993/2213) |
| | para 17 | 13 Jan 1993 (for purpose of auditors of incorporated friendly societies) (SI 1993/16) |
| | | 13 Sep 1993 (otherwise) (SI 1993/2213) |

**Friendly Societies Act 1992 (c 40)**—*contd*

| | | |
|---|---|---|
| Sch 15 | | 13 Sep 1993 (SI 1993/2213) |
| Sch 16 | para 1 | See paras 2–52 below |
| | para 2(1)(a) | 13 Jan 1993 (SI 1993/16) |
| | para 2(1)(b) | 1 Jan 1994 (SI 1993/3226) |
| | para 2(2) | 1 Jan 1994 (SI 1993/3226) |
| | para 2(3) | 13 Jan 1993 (SI 1993/16) |
| | para 3 | 28 Apr 1993 (SI 1993/1186) |
| | para 4(a) | 1 Feb 1993 (SI 1993/16) |
| | para 4(b) | 1 Jan 1994 (subject to transitional provisions) (SI 1993/2213) |
| | para 4(c) | 1 Feb 1993 (SI 1993/16) |
| | paras 5–7 | 1 Feb 1993 (SI 1993/16) |
| | paras 8, 9 | 1 Jan 1994 (SI 1993/2213) |
| | para 10 | 1 Feb 1993 (SI 1993/16) |
| | paras 11, 12 | 1 Jan 1994 (subject to transitional provisions) (SI 1993/2213) |
| | paras 13, 14 | 1 Jan 1994 (SI 1993/3226) |
| | para 15 | 1 Jan 1994 (SI 1993/2213) |
| | para 16 | 1 Feb 1993 (SI 1993/16) |
| | para 17 | 1 Jan 1994 (SI 1993/2213) |
| | para 18(a) | 1 Jan 1994 (SI 1993/2213) |
| | para 18(b) | 1 Jan 1994 (SI 1993/3226) |
| | para 19 | 1 Feb 1993 (SI 1993/16) |
| | paras 20, 21 | 1 Jan 1994 (SI 1993/3226) |
| | paras 22, 23 | 1 Jan 1994 (subject to transitional provisions) (SI 1993/2213) |
| | para 24 | 1 Feb 1993 (so far as repeals Friendly Societies Act 1974, ss 70–73, 75) (subject to transitional provisions) (SI 1993/16) |
| | | *Never in force* (repeal of Friendly Societies Act 1974, s 74 (repealed)) |
| | paras 25, 26 | 13 Jan 1993 (subject to transitional provisions) (SI 1993/16) |
| | para 27 | 1 Jan 1994 (SI 1993/3226) |
| | para 28 | 13 Jan 1993 (SI 1993/16) |
| | para 29 | 13 Sep 1993 (subject to transitional provisions) (SI 1993/2213) |
| | para 30 | 1 Jan 1994 (SI 1993/3226) |
| | para 31 | 13 Sep 1993 (SI 1993/2213) |
| | para 32 | 1 Feb 1993 (insertion of Friendly Societies Act 1974, s 84A(1)–(7)) (SI 1993/16)[1] |
| | | 1 Jan 1994 (insertion of Friendly Societies Act 1974, s 84A(8)) (SI 1993/3226) |
| | para 33 | 13 Sep 1993 (subject to transitional provisions) (SI 1993/2213) |
| | paras 34–36 | 28 Apr 1993 (SI 1993/1186) |
| | para 37 | 1 Feb 1993 (SI 1993/16) |
| | para 38(a) | 1 Feb 1993 (subject to transitional provisions) (SI 1993/16) |
| | para 38(b) | 28 Apr 1993 (SI 1993/1186) |
| | para 38(c) | 28 Apr 1993 (so far as relates to Friendly Societies Act 1974, s 93(3)(a), (b)) (SI 1993/1186) |
| | | 1 Jan 1994 (so far as relates to Friendly Societies Act 1974, s 93(3)(c)) (SI 1993/3226) |
| | paras 39–41 | 28 Apr 1993 (SI 1993/1186) |
| | para 42(a) | 1 Feb 1993 (SI 1993/16) |
| | para 42(b), (c) | 1 Jan 1994 (SI 1993/3226) |
| | para 43 | 1 Jan 1994 (SI 1993/2213) |
| | para 44 | 1 Jan 1994 (SI 1993/3226) |
| | para 45 | 1 Feb 1993 (SI 1993/16) |
| | para 46 | 1 Jan 1994 (SI 1993/3226) |
| | para 47 | 1 Feb 1993 (SI 1993/16) |
| | para 48(a) | 1 Jan 1994 (SI 1993/3226) |
| | para 48(b) | 1 Feb 1993 (SI 1993/16) |
| | para 48(c), (d) | 1 Jan 1994 (SI 1993/3226) |
| | para 48(e) | 1 Feb 1993 (SI 1993/16) |
| | paras 49, 50 | 1 Jan 1994 (SI 1993/3226) |
| | para 51 | 1 Jan 1994 (SI 1993/2213) |

**Friendly Societies Act 1992 (c 40)**—*contd*

| | | |
|---|---|---|
| | para 52 | 1 Feb 1993 (SI 1993/16) |
| Sch 17 | | *Never in force* (repealed) |
| Sch 18 | Pt I, paras 1, 2 | 1 Feb 1993 (for purpose of application of Financial Services Act 1986 to incorporated friendly societies) (SI 1993/16) |
| | | 1 Jan 1994 (otherwise) (SI 1993/2213) |
| | Pt I, para 3 | 1 Feb 1993 (for purpose of application of Financial Services Act 1986 to incorporated friendly societies) (SI 1993/16) |
| | | 28 Apr 1993 (otherwise) (SI 1993/1186) |
| | Pt I, paras 4–9 | 1 Feb 1993 (for purpose of application of Financial Services Act 1986 to incorporated friendly societies) (SI 1993/16) |
| | | 1 Jan 1994 (otherwise) (SI 1993/2213) |
| | Pt II, paras 10–12 | 1 Feb 1993 (for purpose of application of Financial Services Act 1986 to incorporated friendly societies) (SI 1993/16) |
| | | 1 Jan 1994 (otherwise) (SI 1993/2213) |
| | Pt II, para 13 | 1 Feb 1993 (for purpose of application of Financial Services Act 1986 to incorporated friendly societies) (SI 1993/16) |
| | | 1 Jan 1994 (otherwise) (SI 1993/3226) |
| | Pt II, paras 14–22 | 1 Feb 1993 (for purpose of application of Financial Services Act 1986 to incorporated friendly societies) (SI 1993/16) |
| | | 1 Jan 1994 (otherwise) (SI 1993/2213) |
| Sch 19 | Pt I, para 1 | See paras 2–16 below |
| | Pt I, para 2(1) | 1 Feb 1993 (SI 1993/16) |
| | Pt I, para 2(2) | 1 Feb 1993 (in relation to incorporated friendly societies and industrial assurance companies) (SI 1993/16) |
| | | 28 Apr 1993 (otherwise) (SI 1993/1186) |
| | Pt I, para 3 | 1 Feb 1993 (in relation to incorporated friendly societies and industrial assurance companies) (SI 1993/16) |
| | | 28 Apr 1993 (otherwise) (SI 1993/1186) |
| | Pt I, para 4 | 1 Feb 1993 (in relation to incorporated friendly societies and industrial assurance companies) (SI 1993/16) |
| | | 28 Apr 1993 (otherwise) (SI 1993/1186) |
| | Pt I, para 5(1)(a), (b) | 1 Feb 1993 (in relation to incorporated friendly societies and industrial assurance companies) (SI 1993/16) |
| | | 28 Apr 1993 (otherwise) (SI 1993/1186) |
| | Pt I, para 5(1)(c) | 1 Jan 1994 (SI 1993/2213) |
| | Pt I, para 5(1)(d), (e) | 1 Feb 1993 (in relation to incorporated friendly societies and industrial assurance companies) (SI 1993/16) |
| | | 28 Apr 1993 (otherwise) (SI 1993/1186) |
| | Pt I, para 5(2)(a) | 1 Feb 1993 (in relation to incorporated friendly societies and industrial assurance companies) (SI 1993/16) |
| | | 28 Apr 1993 (otherwise) (SI 1993/1186) |
| | Pt I, para 5(2)(b) | 1 Jan 1994 (SI 1993/2213) |
| | Pt I, para 6 | 1 Feb 1993 (SI 1993/16) |
| | Pt I, para 7 | 1 Jan 1994 (SI 1993/2213) |
| | Pt I, para 8 | *Never in force* (repealed) |
| | Pt I, para 9 | 13 Jan 1993 (SI 1993/16) |
| | Pt I, para 10 | *Never in force* (repealed) |
| | Pt I, para 11 | 1 Feb 1993 (in relation to incorporated friendly societies and industrial assurance companies) (SI 1993/16) |
| | | 28 Apr 1993 (otherwise, subject to a saving) (SI 1993/1186) |
| | Pt I, para 12 | 1 Feb 1993 (SI 1993/16) |
| | Pt I, para 13 | 1 Feb 1993 (in relation to incorporated friendly societies and industrial assurance companies) (SI 1993/16) |
| | | 28 Apr 1993 (otherwise) (SI 1993/1186) |
| | Pt I, para 14 | 1 Feb 1993 (in relation to incorporated friendly societies and industrial assurance companies) (subject to transitional provisions) (SI 1993/16) |
| | | 13 Sep 1993 (otherwise) (subject to transitional provisions) (SI 1993/2213) |

**Friendly Societies Act 1992 (c 40)**—*contd*

|  |  |  |
|---|---|---|
| | Pt I, paras 15, 16 | 1 Feb 1993 (in relation to incorporated friendly societies and industrial assurance companies) (SI 1993/16) |
| | | 28 Apr 1993 (otherwise) (SI 1993/1186) |
| | Pt II, para 17 | See paras 18–32 below |
| | Pt II, paras 18–25 | 1 Jan 1994 (subject to savings) (SI 1993/3226) |
| | Pt II, para 26 | *Never in force* (repealed) |
| | Pt II, para 27 | 1 Jan 1994 (SI 1993/3226) |
| | Pt II, para 28 | *Never in force* (repealed) |
| | Pt II, paras 29–32 | 1 Jan 1994 (SI 1993/3226) |
| Sch 20 | | 1 Feb 1993 (SI 1993/16) |
| Sch 21 | Pt I, para 1 | 1 Feb 1993 (SI 1993/16) |
| | Pt I, paras 2–4 | 1 Jan 1993 (SI 1992/3117) |
| | Pt I, paras 5–11 | 1 Feb 1993 (SI 1993/16) |
| | Pt I, paras 12–17 | *Never in force* (repealed) |
| | Pt I, paras 18, 19 | 1 Jan 1994 (SI 1993/3226) |
| | Pt II | 1 Jan 1994 (SI 1993/3226) |
| Sch 22 | Pt I | 13 Jan 1993 (repeals of or in Friendly Societies Act 1974, ss 76(1)(c)–(e), (5), 77, 78(1)_(3), 79(1), 80(1)) (subject to transitional provisions) (SI 1993/16) |

1 Feb 1993 (subject to transitional provisions) (SI 1993/16), repeals of or in—

Industrial Assurance Act 1923, ss 2(1) (words "and anything which under" to the end), 4, 7, 8(3), Sch 1;

Industrial Assurance and Friendly Societies Act 1948, ss 6, 7, 10(1)(b), (c) (and words from "and shall, on demand" to the end of sub-s (1)), (2), (3), 11, Sch 1;

Friendly Societies Act 1974, ss 8, 11(1), 13(2), 15 (words "society or", in each place they appear[2]), 17, 70–73, 75

1 Feb 1993 (SI 1993/16), in relation to incorporated friendly societies which are collecting societies, repeals of or in—

Industrial Assurance Act 1923, ss 8(2), (4), 15, 16, 18, 19(1)–(3), 35;

Industrial Assurance and Friendly Societies Act 1948, s 13(3)

5 Feb 1993 (SI 1993/197), repeals of—

Industrial Assurance Act 1923, s 8(1)(b), in relation to collecting societies (as defined by s 1(1A) thereof) to which the criteria of prudent management described in Friendly Societies Act 1992, s 50(3) apply;

Friendly Societies Act 1974, Sch 5

28 Apr 1993 (in relation to incorporated friendly societies, repeals of or in Financial Services Act 1986, ss 139(3)–(5), 207(1), Sch 11, paras 1, 26(1), (3), 27, 38(1)(a), 43, Sch 15, para 14(1), (3)) (SI 1993/1186)

28 Apr 1993 (SI 1993/1186), repeals of or in—

Friendly Societies Act 1974, ss 6(2), 16, 88, 89, 106;

Industrial Assurance Act 1948, s 17A(2)

13 Sep 1993 (subject to transitional provisions) (SI 1993/2213), repeals of or in—

Industrial Assurance Act 1923, ss 36, 38;

Friendly Societies Act 1974, s 82, Sch 9, para 5

1 Jan 1994 (SI 1993/2213) (so far as not brought into force on 1 Feb and 28 Apr 1993 by SI 1993/16, SI 1993/1186), repeals of or in—

Industrial Assurance Act 1923, ss 8(2), (4), 15, 16, 18, 19(1)–(3), 35;

Industrial Assurance and Friendly Societies Act 1948, s 13(3);

Financial Services Act 1986, ss 139(3)–(5), 207(1), Sch 11, paras 1, 26(1), (3), 27, 38(1)(a), 43, Sch 15, para 14(1), (3)

1 Jan 1994 (subject to transitional provisions) (SI 1993/2213), repeals of or in—

**Friendly Societies Act 1992 (c 40)**—*contd*

Loan Societies Act 1840;
Friendly Societies Act 1896;
Industrial Assurance Act 1923, ss 20(1)(b), 31, 44, 45(2);
Industrial Assurance and Friendly Societies Act 1929;
Industrial Assurance and Friendly Societies Act 1948, ss 1, 4, 23(1), Schs 2, 3;
Friendly Societies Act 1955, s 3(2);
Industrial Assurance Act 1948 (Amendment) Act 1958;
Friendly Societies Act 1974, ss 9(2), (3), 27, 28, 30(5), 46, 53(3), 107(1), Schs 1–3, Sch 9, paras 2, 6, 8, 10(1);
Banking Act 1987, s 84(1);
Income and Corporation Taxes Act 1988;
Companies Act 1989

1 Jan 1994 (SI 1993/3226), repeals of or in—
Industrial Assurance and Friendly Societies Act 1948, ss 2, 10(1)(a) (words "signed by two of the committee of management and by the secretary" only);
Consumer Credit Act 1974, s 189(1);
Friendly Societies Act 1974, ss 98, 111(6), 115, 117(3), Sch 3;
Finance Act 1984;
Friendly Societies Act 1984, s 3;
Companies Act 1985, s 449;
Building Societies Act 1986, s 7;
Banking Act 1987, s 96, Sch 2

1 Nov 1994 (repeal of Industrial Assurance Act 1923, s 2(1) (so far as not already in force), (2)) (SI 1994/2543)

*Never in force* (repeal of Trade Union and Labour Relations (Consolidation) Act 1992, s 19(2)) (repealed)

*Not yet in force*, repeals of or in—
Industrial Assurance Act 1923, ss 3, 6, 8(1) (part), 19(4) (repealed);
Industrial Assurance and Friendly Societies Act 1948, s 10(1)(a) (part) (repealed);
Friendly Societies Act 1955, s 6 (repealed);
Industrial and Provident Societies Act 1965, s 60(3);
Companies Act 1967, Sch 6, Pt II (repealed);
Friendly Societies Act 1974, s 74, Sch 6 (repealed);
Financial Services Act 1986, s 189(5)(c) (repealed)

Pt II     1 Jan 1994 (except so far as repeals Industrial Assurance (Northern Ireland) Order 1979, SI 1979/1574, arts 4(1) (other than words "and in the exercise and performance of his powers and duties as Registrar under the Friendly Societies Act in relation to collecting societies" which are repealed), (3), 5, 9(1)(a) (other than words "signed by two of the committee of management and by the secretary" which are repealed)) (subject to transitional provisions) (SI 1993/3226)

1 Nov 1994 (revocation of Industrial Assurance (Northern Ireland) Order 1979, SI 1979/1574, art 4(1) (so far as not already in force), (3)) (SI 1994/2543)

*Never in force* (repeal of Industrial Assurance (Northern Ireland) Order 1979, SI 1979/1574, arts 5, 9(1)(a) (part) (revoked))

---

¹   Note that SI 1993/16 purports to bring into force Sch 16, para 32 (except sub-para (8)). As para 32 contains no sub-paragraphs, it is thought that it was intended to bring into force s 84A(1)–(7) of the 1974 Act, but not sub-s (8) thereof. Note also that SI 1993/2213 purports to bring Sch 16, para 32 (except s 84A(8)) into force for all remaining purposes on 13 Sep 1993

²   Note that the repeal of those words by the Friendly Societies Act 1992, s 120(2), Sch 22, Pt I, is made to the Friendly Societies Act 1974, s 16, and not to s 15 thereof

**Further and Higher Education Act 1992 (c 13)**

*RA:* 6 Mar 1992

*Commencement provisions:* s 94(3); Further and Higher Education Act 1992 (Commencement No 1 and Transitional Provisions) Order 1992, SI 1992/831, as amended by SI 1992/2041; Further and Higher Education Act 1992 (Commencement No 2) Order 1992, SI 1992/2377; Further and Higher Education Act 1992 (Commencement No 2) Order 1992, SI 1992/3057; Further and Higher Education Act 1992 (Commencement No 3) Order 1996, SI 1996/1897

| | | |
|---|---|---|
| 1 | | 6 May 1992 (SI 1992/831) |
| 2–4 | | 1 Apr 1993 (SI 1992/831) |
| 5 | (1), (2) | 1 Apr 1993 (SI 1992/831) |
| | (3) | 30 Sep 1992 (SI 1992/831) |
| | (4) | 1 Apr 1993 (SI 1992/831) |
| | (5)–(8) | 6 May 1992 (SI 1992/831) |
| 6 | (1) | 1 Apr 1993 (SI 1992/831) |
| | (2)–(4) | 6 May 1992 (SI 1992/831) |
| | (5), (6) | 30 Sep 1992 (SI 1992/831) |
| 7, 8 | | 6 May 1992 (SI 1992/831) |
| 9 | (1)–(3) | 1 Apr 1993 (SI 1992/831) |
| | (4) | 1 Apr 1993 (SI 1992/2377) |
| | (5) | 1 Apr 1993 (SI 1992/831) |
| 10, 11 | | 1 Apr 1993 (SI 1992/831) |
| 12, 13 | | 1 Aug 1993 (SI 1992/831) |
| 14 | (1)–(4) | 6 May 1992 (for the purposes of the provisions of this Act also brought into force on that date) (SI 1992/831) |
| | | 30 Sep 1992 (for the purposes of the provisions of this Act also brought into force on that date) (SI 1992/831) |
| | | 1 Apr 1993 (otherwise) (SI 1992/831) |
| | (5) | 1 Apr 1993 (SI 1992/831) |
| | (6) | 1 Aug 1993 (SI 1992/831) |
| 15 | (1)–(3) | 6 May 1992 (SI 1992/831) |
| | (4) | 30 Sep 1992 (SI 1992/831) |
| | (5)–(7) | 6 May 1992 (SI 1992/831) |
| 16 | | 30 Sep 1992 (SI 1992/831) |
| 17 | | 6 May 1992 (SI 1992/831) |
| 18–25 | | 30 Sep 1992 (SI 1992/831) |
| 26 | | 30 Sep 1992 (except in respect of persons employed by a local authority to work solely at the institution the corporation is established to conduct and who are so employed in connection with an arrangement for the supply by that local authority of goods or services for the purposes of that institution in pursuance of a bid prepared under Local Government Act 1988, s 7) (SI 1992/831) |
| | | *Never in force* (exception noted above) (repealed) |
| 27 | | 30 Sep 1992 (SI 1992/831) |
| 28–33 | | 6 May 1992 (SI 1992/831) |
| 34, 35 | | 1 Apr 1993 (SI 1992/831) |
| 36 | | 30 Sep 1992 (SI 1992/831) |
| 37, 38 | | 1 Apr 1993 (SI 1992/831) |
| 39–43 | | 6 May 1992 (SI 1992/831) |
| 44, 45 | | 1 Apr 1993 (in respect of institutions which, before they became institutions within the further education sector, were schools maintained by a local education authority or grant-maintained schools) (SI 1992/831) |
| | | *Not yet in force* (in respect of any other institutions within the further education sector which are principally concerned with the provision of full-time education suitable to the requirements of persons over compulsory school age who have not attained the age of nineteen years) |
| 46–50 | | 1 Apr 1993 (SI 1992/831) |

**Further and Higher Education Act 1992 (c 13)**—*contd*

| | | |
|---|---|---|
| 51 | | 30 Sep 1992 (SI 1992/831) |
| 52 | | 1 Apr 1993 (SI 1992/831) |
| 53 | | 30 Sep 1992 (SI 1992/831) |
| 54 | (1) | 6 May 1992 (SI 1992/831) |
| | (2) | 1 Apr 1993 (SI 1992/831) |
| 55 | (1)–(3) | 1 Apr 1993 (E) (SI 1992/831) |
| | | 1 Aug 1996 (W) (SI 1996/1897) |
| | (4)–(7) | 1 Apr 1993 (SI 1992/831) |
| 56 | | 6 May 1992 (SI 1992/831) |
| 57 | (1), (2) | 1 Apr 1993 (SI 1992/831) |
| | (3)–(6) | 6 May 1992 (so far as apply to the Further Education Funding Councils) (SI 1992/831) |
| | | 1 Apr 1993 (otherwise) (SI 1992/831) |
| 58 | | 30 Sep 1992 (SI 1992/831) |
| 59 | (1), (2) | 30 Sep 1992 (SI 1992/831) |
| | (3)–(5) | 6 May 1992 (SI 1992/831) |
| 60 | | 1 Apr 1993 (SI 1992/831) |
| 61, 62 | | 6 May 1992 (SI 1992/831) |
| 63 | | 1 Apr 1993 (SI 1992/831) |
| 64 | | 6 May 1992 (SI 1992/831) |
| 65, 66 | | 1 Apr 1993 (SI 1992/831) |
| 67 | (1) | 1 Apr 1993 (SI 1992/831) |
| | (2)–(5) | 6 May 1992 (SI 1992/831) |
| 68–73 | | 6 May 1992 (SI 1992/831) |
| 74 | | 1 Apr 1993 (SI 1992/831) |
| 75–84 | | 6 May 1992 (SI 1992/831) |
| 85 | | 1 Apr 1993 (SI 1992/831) |
| 86 | | 6 May 1992 (SI 1992/831) |
| 87 | | 30 Sep 1992 (SI 1992/831) |
| 88–92 | | 6 May 1992 (SI 1992/831) |
| 93 | (1) | See Sch 8 below |
| | (2) | See Sch 9 below |
| 94 | | 6 May 1992 (SI 1992/831) |
| Sch 1 | | 6 May 1992 (SI 1992/831) |
| Sch 2 | | 30 Sep 1992 (SI 1992/831) |
| Sch 3 | | 6 May 1992 (SI 1992/831) |
| Schs 4, 5 | | 30 Sep 1992 (SI 1992/831) |
| Sch 6 | | 6 May 1992 (SI 1992/831) |
| Sch 7 | | 30 Sep 1992 (SI 1992/831) |
| Sch 8 | Pt I, para 1 | 6 May 1992 (SI 1992/831) |
| | Pt I, paras 2–8 | 1 Apr 1993 (SI 1992/831) |
| | Pt I, para 9 | 6 May 1992 (SI 1992/831) |
| | Pt I, para 10 | 1 Sep 1992 (in so far as relates to institutions within the PCFC funding sector) (except in relation to Wales) (SI 1992/831) |
| | | 1 Sep 1992 (in so far as relates to institutions within the PCFC funding sector) (W) (SI 1992/2377) |
| | | 1 Apr 1993 (otherwise) (except in relation to Wales) (SI 1992/831) |
| | | 1 Apr 1993 (otherwise) (W) (SI 1992/2377) |
| | Pt I, paras 11, 12 | 1 Apr 1993 (SI 1992/831) |
| | Pt I, para 13(1) | 6 May 1992 (SI 1992/831) |
| | Pt I, para 13(2)(a) | 6 May 1992 (in relation to references to "further education" in provisions of the Act as they are brought into force) (SI 1992/831) |
| | | 1 Apr 1993 (otherwise except for para 13(2)(d)) (SI 1992/831) |
| | Pt I, para 13(2)(b), (c) | 1 Apr 1993 (SI 1992/831) |
| | Pt I, para 13(2)(d) | 1 Aug 1993 (SI 1992/831) |
| | Pt I, para 13(2)(e)–(g) | 1 Apr 1993 (SI 1992/831) |

**Further and Higher Education Act 1992 (c 13)**—*contd*

| | |
|---|---|
| Pt I, paras 14–16 | 1 Apr 1993 (SI 1992/831) |
| Pt I, para 17 | 1 Aug 1993 (SI 1992/831) |
| Pt I, para 18 | 6 May 1992 (SI 1992/831) |
| Pt I, paras 19, 20 | 1 Apr 1993 (SI 1992/831) |
| Pt I, para 21 | 30 Sep 1992 (SI 1992/831) |
| Pt I, paras 22, 23 | 1 Apr 1993 (SI 1992/831) |
| Pt I, para 24 | 1 Apr 1993 (the amendments by para 24(a) not having effect in relation to provision for further education made by a local education authority before 1 Apr 1993) (SI 1992/831) |
| Pt I, paras 25, 26 | 1 Apr 1993 (SI 1992/831) |
| Pt I, para 27 | 6 May 1992 (SI 1992/831) |
| Pt I, para 28 | 1 Apr 1993 (SI 1992/831) |
| Pt I, para 29 | 1 Aug 1993 (SI 1992/831) |
| Pt I, para 30 | 1 Apr 1993 (SI 1992/831) |
| Pt I, para 31 | 6 May 1992 (SI 1992/831) |
| Pt I, para 32(a) | 1 Apr 1993 (SI 1992/831) |
| Pt I, para 32(b) | 6 May 1992 (SI 1992/831) |
| Pt I, para 33 | 1 Apr 1993 (SI 1992/831) |
| Pt I, para 34 | 6 May 1992 (SI 1992/831) |
| Pt I, para 35 | 1 Apr 1993 (SI 1992/831) |
| Pt I, para 36(a) | 6 May 1992 (SI 1992/831) |
| Pt I, para 36(b) | 1 Apr 1993 (SI 1992/831) |
| Pt I, para 37(a) | 1 Apr 1993 (SI 1992/831) |
| Pt I, para 37(b) | 6 May 1992 (SI 1992/831) |
| Pt I, para 38 | 6 May 1992 (SI 1992/831) |
| Pt I, paras 39–42 | 1 Apr 1993 (SI 1992/831) |
| Pt I, para 43 | 6 May 1992 (SI 1992/831) |
| Pt I, paras 44–47 | 1 Apr 1993 (SI 1992/831) |
| Pt I, para 48 | 6 May 1992 (SI 1992/831) |
| Pt I, para 49 | 1 Apr 1993 (SI 1992/831) |
| Pt I, para 50 | 6 May 1992 (so far as it relates to the Education Reform Act 1988, s 219(2)(e)) (SI 1992/831) |
| Pt I, para 51 | 6 May 1992 (SI 1992/831) |
| Pt I, paras 52, 53 | 1 Apr 1993 (SI 1992/831) |
| Pt I, para 54 | 6 May 1992 (SI 1992/831) |
| Pt I, para 55 | 1 Apr 1993 (SI 1992/831) |
| Pt I, para 56(a) | 1 Apr 1993 (SI 1992/831) |
| Pt I, para 56(b), (c) | 6 May 1992 (SI 1992/831) |
| Pt I, paras 57, 58 | 1 Apr 1993 (SI 1992/831) |
| Pt I, para 59 | 6 May 1992 (SI 1992/831) |
| Pt I, para 60 | 1 Apr 1993 (SI 1992/831) |
| Pt I, paras 61–65 | 6 May 1992 (subject to saving in relation to any matter notified to the Secretary of State by the Education Assets Board pursuant to Education Reform Act 1988, Sch 10, para 3, before 6 May 1992) (SI 1992/831) |
| Pt I, paras 66, 67 | 1 Apr 1993 (SI 1992/831) |
| Pt II, para 68 | 6 May 1992 (SI 1992/831) |
| Pt II, para 69 | 30 Sep 1992 (SI 1992/831) |
| Pt II, paras 70–74 | 1 Apr 1993 (SI 1992/831) |
| Pt II, paras 75, 76 | 6 May 1992 (SI 1992/831) |
| Pt II, para 77 | 1 Aug 1993 (SI 1992/831) |
| Pt II, paras 78, 79 | 6 May 1992 (SI 1992/831) |
| Pt II, para 80 | 1 Aug 1993 (SI 1992/831) |
| Pt II, paras 81–83 | 1 Apr 1993 (SI 1992/831) |
| Pt II, paras 84, 85 | 6 May 1992 (SI 1992/831) |
| Pt II, para 86 | 1 Aug 1993 (SI 1992/831) |
| Pt II, paras 87, 88 | 6 May 1992 (SI 1992/831) |
| Pt II, para 89 | 30 Sep 1992 (SI 1992/831) |
| Pt II, paras 90–92 | 1 Apr 1993 (SI 1992/831) |

**Further and Higher Education Act 1992 (c 13)**—*contd*

|  |  |  |
|---|---|---|
|  | Pt II, para 93(a) | 1 Apr 1993 (SI 1992/831) |
|  | Pt II, para 93(b) | 6 May 1992 (SI 1992/831) |
|  | Pt II, paras 94, 95 | 1 Apr 1993 (SI 1992/831) |
| Sch 9 |  | 6 May 1992 (repeals of or in Education Reform Act 1988, ss 122(2)–(5), 129(3), (4), 136(3)–(7), 137(2) (expression "or 129(3)"), 156 (so far as relates to institutions designated under Education Reform Act 1988, s 129), 219(2)(e), 227(2)–(4), 232(3) (expression "or 227"), 232(4)(b) (expression "227"), Sch 7, para 19) (SI 1992/831) |
|  |  | 1 Apr 1993 (SI 1992/831), repeals of or in— |
|  |  | Education Act 1944, ss 8(3), 67(4A), 85(2), (3), 114(1), (1A)–(1C); |
|  |  | Education (Miscellaneous Provisions) Act 1948, s 3(3); |
|  |  | Superannuation Act 1972, Sch 1; |
|  |  | House of Commons Disqualification Act 1975, Sch 1, Pt III; |
|  |  | Education (No 2) Act 1986, ss 43(5)(c), (7), 49(3)(d), (da), 51(2)(b), (5), (6), 58(3), (4), (5)(a), (ab); |
|  |  | Education Reform Act 1988, ss 120, 124(4), 131, 132, 134, Pt II, Chapter III (ss 139–155), s 156 (so far as still in force), ss 157, 158(2), 159(2)(b), 161(1)(c), 205(6), 211(c), 218(10)(b), 219, 221(1)(c), (3), 222(2)(b), (3)(c), 230(1), (3)(c)(ii), 232(2), 234(2)(b), 235(2)(a), (h), Sch 12, paras 68, 69(2), 70, 100(2), 101(4); |
|  |  | Environmental Protection Act 1990, s 98(2)(a) |
|  |  | 1 Aug 1993 (repeal in Education Reform Act 1988, s 105(2)(b)) (SI 1992/831) |

**Further and Higher Education (Scotland) Act 1992 (c 37)**

*RA:* 16 Mar 1992

*Commencement provisions:* s 63(2); Further and Higher Education (Scotland) Act 1992 (Commencement No 1 and Saving Provisions) Order 1992, SI 1992/817; Further and Higher Education (Scotland) Act 1992 (Commencement No 2) Order 1998, SI 1998/2886

|  |  |  |
|---|---|---|
| 1 | (1), (2) | 1 Apr 1993 (SI 1992/817) |
|  | (3)–(5) | 16 May 1992 (SI 1992/817) |
|  | (6) | 1 Apr 1993 (SI 1992/817) |
| 2 |  | 1 Apr 1993 (SI 1992/817) |
| 3 | (1)–(4) | 1 Apr 1993 (SI 1992/817) |
|  | (5) | 16 May 1992 (SI 1992/817) |
|  | (6) | 1 Apr 1993 (SI 1992/817) |
| 4, 5 |  | 1 Apr 1993 (SI 1992/817) |
| 6 |  | 16 May 1992 (SI 1992/817) |
| 7–10 |  | 21 Nov 1998 (SI 1998/2886) |
| 11, 12 |  | 16 May 1992 (SI 1992/817) |
| 13, 14 |  | 1 Apr 1993 (SI 1992/817) |
| 15 |  | 16 May 1992 (SI 1992/817) |
| 16 |  | 1 Sep 1992 (SI 1992/817) |
| 17 |  | 1 Apr 1993 (SI 1992/817) |
| 18 |  | 16 May 1992 (SI 1992/817) |
| 19–25 |  | 1 Apr 1993 (SI 1992/817) |
| 26–36 |  | 16 May 1992 (SI 1992/817) |
| 37 |  | 1 Jun 1992 (SI 1992/817) |
| 38 |  | 16 May 1992 (SI 1992/817) |
| 39 |  | 1 Jun 1992 (so far as relates to institutions for whose activities the Council are considering providing financial support) (SI 1992/817) |
|  |  | 1 Apr 1993 (otherwise) (SI 1992/817) |
| 40, 41 |  | 1 Apr 1993 (SI 1992/817) |

**Further and Higher Education (Scotland) Act 1992 (c 37)**—*contd*

| | | |
|---|---|---|
| 42 | (1) | 1 Jun 1992 (SI 1992/817) |
| | (2), (3) | 1 Apr 1993 (SI 1992/817) |
| | (4) | 1 Jun 1992 (SI 1992/817) |
| 43 | (1) | 1 Jun 1992 (SI 1992/817) |
| | (2) | 1 Apr 1993 (SI 1992/817) |
| | (3)–(8) | 1 Jun 1992 (SI 1992/817) |
| 44 | | 25 Apr 1992 (for purpose of authorising the making under s 44 of an Order which is expressed to come into force on or after 16 May 1992) (SI 1992/817) |
| | | 16 May 1992 (otherwise) (SI 1992/817) |
| 45–49 | | 16 May 1992 (SI 1992/817) |
| 50, 51 | | 1 Jun 1992 (SI 1992/817) |
| 52 | | 16 May 1992 (SI 1992/817) |
| 53 | | 1 Apr 1993 (SI 1992/817) |
| 54 | (1), (2) | 1 Jun 1992 (SI 1992/817) |
| | (3) | 1 Apr 1993 (SI 1992/817) |
| 55–61 | | 16 May 1992 (SI 1992/817) |
| 62 | (1) | See Sch 8 below |
| | (2) | See Sch 9 below |
| | (3) | See Sch 10 below |
| 63 | | 25 Apr 1992 (SI 1992/817) |
| Sch 1 | | 21 Nov 1998 (SI 1998/2886) |
| Sch 2 | | 16 May 1992 (SI 1992/817) |
| Schs 3, 4 | | 1 Sep 1992 (SI 1992/817) |
| Schs 5, 6 | | 16 May 1992 (SI 1992/817) |
| Sch 7 | | 1 Jun 1992 (SI 1992/817) |
| Sch 8 | | 16 May 1992 (SI 1992/817) |
| Sch 9 | para 1 | 16 May 1992 (SI 1992/817) |
| | para 2(a) | 1 Apr 1993 (SI 1992/817) |
| | para 2(b), (c) | 16 May 1992 (SI 1992/817) |
| | para 3 | 16 May 1992 (SI 1992/817) |
| | para 4(1), (2) | 16 May 1992 (SI 1992/817) |
| | para 4(3) | 1 Jun 1992 (so far as relates to the Scottish Higher Education Funding Council) (SI 1992/817) |
| | | 21 Nov 1998 (otherwise) (SI 1998/2886) |
| | para 4(4)–(6) | 16 May 1992 (SI 1992/817) |
| | para 5(1), (2) | 16 May 1992 (SI 1992/817) |
| | para 5(3) | 1 Jun 1992 (so far as relates to the Scottish Higher Education Funding Council) (SI 1992/817) |
| | | 21 Nov 1998 (otherwise) (SI 1998/2886) |
| | para 5(4), (5) | 16 May 1992 (SI 1992/817) |
| | para 6 | 16 May 1992 (SI 1992/817) |
| | para 7(1) | 16 May 1992 (SI 1992/817) |
| | para 7(2)–(6) | 1 Apr 1993 (SI 1992/817) |
| | para 7(7) | 16 May 1992 (SI 1992/817) |
| | para 8(1), (2) | 16 May 1992 (SI 1992/817) |
| | para 8(3) | 1 Apr 1993 (SI 1992/817) |
| | para 9 | 1 Apr 1993 (SI 1992/817) |
| | para 10 | 1 Jun 1992 (SI 1992/817) |
| | para 11 | 1 Apr 1993 (SI 1992/817) |
| | para 12(1), (2) | 16 May 1992 (SI 1992/817) |
| | para 12(3) | 1 Apr 1993 (SI 1992/817) |
| | para 13(a) | 1 Apr 1993 (SI 1992/817) |
| | para 13(b), (c) | 16 May 1992 (SI 1992/817) |
| Sch 10 | | 16 May 1992 (SI 1992/817), repeals of or in— |
| | | Employment Protection (Consolidation) Act 1978, s 29; |
| | | Education (Scotland) Act 1980, ss 3, 7, 77, 135(1) |
| | | 1 Apr 1993 (SI 1992/817), repeals of or in— |
| | | School Boards (Scotland) Act 1988, ss 8, 22; |

**Further and Higher Education (Scotland) Act 1992 (c 37)**—*contd*

Self-Governing Schools etc (Scotland) Act 1989, ss 54–66, 80

**Human Fertilisation and Embryology (Disclosure of Information) Act 1992 (c 54)**

*RA:* 16 Jul 1992

Whole Act in force 16 Jul 1992 (RA)

**Licensing (Amendment) (Scotland) Act 1992 (c 18)**

*RA:* 6 Mar 1992

*Commencement provisions:* s 2(2); Licensing (Amendment) (Scotland) Act 1992 (Commencement and Savings) Order 1992, SI 1992/819

| | |
|---|---|
| 1 | 15 Apr 1992 (subject to savings with respect to any licence temporarily transferred under Licensing (Scotland) Act 1976, s 25(1), before 15 Apr 1992) (SI 1992/819) |
| 2 | 6 Mar 1992 (RA) |

**Local Government Act 1992 (c 19)**

*RA:* 6 Mar 1992

*Commencement provisions:* s 30(2), (3); Local Government Act 1992 (Commencement No 1) Order 1992, SI 1992/2371; Local Government Act 1992 (Commencement No 2) Order 1992, SI 1992/3241; Local Government Act 1992 (Commencement No 3) Order 1993, SI 1993/3169; Local Government Act 1992 (Commencement No 4) Order 1994, SI 1994/1445; Local Government Act 1992 (Commencement No 5) Order 1996, SI 1996/1888

| | | |
|---|---|---|
| 1–7 | | 6 May 1992 (s 30(2)) |
| 8 | | *Never in force* (repealed) |
| 9 | | 4 Jan 1993 (SI 1992/3241) |
| 10 | | 14 Feb 1993 (SI 1992/3241) |
| 11 | | See Sch 1 below |
| 12–23 | | 6 Mar 1992 (RA) |
| 24 | | 31 Oct 1992 (SI 1992/2371) |
| 25–30 | | 6 Mar 1992 (RA) |
| Sch 1 | para 1 | 14 Feb 1993 (SI 1992/3241) |
| | para 2(1) | 13 Jun 1994 (SI 1994/1445) |
| | para 2(2), (3) | 14 Mar 1994 (SI 1992/3241) |
| | paras 3–5 | 13 Jun 1994 (SI 1994/1445) |
| | paras 6, 7 | 4 Jan 1993 (SI 1992/3241) |
| | para 8 | 14 Mar 1994 (SI 1992/3241) |
| | paras 9, 10 | 13 Jun 1994 (SI 1994/1445) |
| | para 11 | 14 Feb 1993 (SI 1992/3241) |
| | para 12 | 6 Jan 1994 (SI 1993/3169) |
| | paras 13, 14 | 4 Jan 1993 (SI 1992/3241) |
| Sch 2 | | 6 Mar 1992 (RA) |
| Sch 3 | | 31 Oct 1992 (SI 1992/2371) |
| Sch 4 | Pt I | 6 May 1992 (repeal in Local Government Finance Act 1982, s 15(1)) (s 30(2)) |
| | | 8 Aug 1996 (repeals in Local Government, Planning and Land Act 1980) (SI 1996/1888) |
| | | *Never in force* (repeal in Local Government Act 1988, s 7(3)(a) (repealed)) |
| | Pt II | 31 Oct 1992 (SI 1992/2371) |

## Local Government Finance Act 1992 (c 14)

*RA:* 6 Mar 1992

*Commencement provisions:* s 119(2); Local Government Finance Act 1992 (Commencement No 1) Order 1992, SI 1992/473; Local Government Finance Act 1992 (Commencement No 2) Order 1992, SI 1992/818; Local Government Finance Act 1992 (Commencement No 3) Order 1992, SI 1992/1460; Local Government Finance Act 1992 (Commencement No 4) Order 1992, SI 1992/1755; Local Government Finance Act 1992 (Commencement No 5 and Transitional Provisions) Order 1992, SI 1992/2183; Local Government Finance Act 1992 (Commencement No 6 and Transitional Provisions) Order 1992, SI 1992/2454, as amended by SI 1993/194; Local Government Finance Act 1992 (Commencement No 7 and Amendment) Order 1993, SI 1993/194; Local Government Finance Act 1992 (Commencement No 8 and Transitional Provisions) Order 1993, SI 1993/575; Local Government Finance Act 1992 (Commencement No 9 and Transitional Provision) Order 1994, SI 1994/3152; Local Government Finance Act 1992 (Commencement No 10) Order 1996, SI 1996/918

| | | |
|---|---|---|
| 1–98 | | 6 Mar 1992 (RA) |
| 99 | (1) | 6 Mar 1992 (RA) |
| | (2) | 1 Apr 1993 (SI 1993/575) |
| | (3) | 6 Mar 1992 (RA) |
| 100–103 | | 6 Mar 1992 (RA) |
| 104 | | See Sch 10 below |
| 105, 106 | | 6 Mar 1992 (RA) |
| 107 | | See Sch 11 below |
| 108, 109 | | 6 Mar 1992 (RA) |
| 110 | (1) | 1 Oct 1992 (subject to transitional provisions in relation to any financial year beginning before 1 Apr 1993) (SI 1992/2183) |
| | (2), (3) | 31 Mar 1995 (subject to a saving) (SI 1994/3152) |
| | (4) | 1 Oct 1992 (subject to transitional provisions in relation to any financial year beginning before 1 Apr 1993) (SI 1992/2183) |
| 111 | | 1 Apr 1993 (SI 1993/575) |
| 112–116 | | 6 Mar 1992 (RA) |
| 117 | (1) | See Sch 13 below |
| | (2) | See Sch 14 below |
| 118, 119 | | 6 Mar 1992 (RA) |
| Schs 1–9 | | 6 Mar 1992 (RA) |
| Sch 10 | para 1 | 18 Jun 1992 (SI 1992/1460) |
| | para 2 | 7 Mar 1992 (SI 1992/473) |
| | para 3 | 1 Apr 1992 (SI 1992/473) |
| | para 4 | 7 Mar 1992 (so far as enables provision to be made by regulations) (SI 1992/473) |
| | | 1 Apr 1992 (otherwise) (SI 1992/473) |
| | paras 5–24 | 6 Mar 1992 (RA) |
| Sch 11 | paras 1–28 | 6 Mar 1992 (RA) |
| | para 29(a) | 1 Apr 1993 (SI 1993/575) |
| | para 29(b) | 6 Mar 1992 (RA) |
| | para 30 | 1 Apr 1993 (SI 1993/575) |
| | para 31(a) | 6 Mar 1992 (RA) |
| | para 31(b) | 1 Oct 1992 (subject to transitional provisions in relation to any financial year beginning before 1 Apr 1993) (SI 1992/2183) |
| | paras 32–36 | 1 Apr 1993 (SI 1993/575) |
| | para 37 | 1 Oct 1992 (subject to transitional provisions in relation to any financial year beginning before 1 Apr 1993) (SI 1992/2183) |
| | para 38(a) | 1 Oct 1992 (subject to transitional provisions in relation to any financial year beginning before 1 Apr 1993) (SI 1992/2183) |
| | para 38(b) | 1 Apr 1993 (SI 1993/575) |
| | para 38(c) | 1 Oct 1992 (subject to transitional provisions in relation to any financial year beginning before 1 Apr 1993) (SI 1992/2183) |
| | para 38(d) | 6 Mar 1992 (RA) |
| | para 38(e) | 1 Apr 1993 (SI 1993/575) |
| | para 38(f) | 6 Mar 1992 (RA) |

**Local Government Finance Act 1992 (c 14)**—*contd*

| | | |
|---|---|---|
| Sch 12 | | 6 Mar 1992 (RA) |
| Sch 13 | para 1 | 1 Apr 1993 (SI 1993/194) |
| | para 2 | 1 Apr 1993 (SI 1993/575) |
| | paras 3–5 | 1 Apr 1993 (SI 1992/2454) |
| | paras 6–8 | 2 Nov 1992 (SI 1992/2454) |
| | para 9 | 1 Apr 1993 (SI 1993/575) |
| | paras 10, 11 | 1 Apr 1992 (SI 1992/818) |
| | paras 12–14 | 2 Nov 1992 (SI 1992/2454) |
| | paras 15–25 | 6 Mar 1992 (RA) |
| | para 26 | 2 Nov 1992 (SI 1992/2454) |
| | paras 27, 28 | 1 Apr 1993 (SI 1993/194) |
| | paras 29, 30 | 2 Nov 1992 (SI 1992/2454) |
| | para 31 | *Never in force* (repealed) |
| | para 32 | 1 Feb 1993 (SI 1992/2454) |
| | para 33 | *Never in force* (spent) |
| | para 34 | 1 Apr 1993 (SI 1992/2454) |
| | para 35 | 1 Apr 1993 (SI 1993/575) |
| | para 36 | 1 Oct 1992 (subject to transitional provisions in relation to any financial year beginning before 1 Apr 1993) (SI 1992/2183) |
| | para 37 | 6 Mar 1992 (RA) |
| | para 38 | 1 Oct 1992 (so far as relates to Local Government (Scotland) Act 1973, s 110A) (subject to transitional provisions in relation to any financial year beginning before 1 Apr 1993) (SI 1992/2183) |
| | | 1 Apr 1993 (otherwise) (SI 1993/575) |
| | para 39 | 1 Apr 1996 (SI 1996/918) |
| | para 40 | 1 Apr 1993 (SI 1993/575) |
| | para 41 | 1 Apr 1992 (SI 1992/818) |
| | para 42 | 6 Mar 1992 (RA) |
| | para 43 | 1 Oct 1992 (subject to transitional provisions in relation to any financial year beginning before 1 Apr 1993) (SI 1992/2183) |
| | para 44(a), (b) | 1 Apr 1993 (SI 1993/575) |
| | para 44(c) | 6 Mar 1992 (RA) |
| | para 44(d) | 1 Apr 1993 (SI 1993/575) |
| | paras 45–47 | 6 Mar 1992 (RA) |
| | para 48 | 2 Nov 1992 (SI 1992/2454) |
| | para 49 | 1 Oct 1992 (subject to transitional provisions in relation to any financial year beginning before 1 Apr 1993) (SI 1992/2183) |
| | paras 50–52 | 2 Nov 1992 (SI 1992/2454) |
| | paras 53–56 | 1 Apr 1993 (SI 1993/575) |
| | paras 57, 58 | 1 Apr 1993 (SI 1992/2454) |
| | paras 59–74 | 6 Mar 1992 (RA) |
| | para 75 | 1 Oct 1992 (subject to transitional provisions in relation to any financial year beginning before 1 Apr 1993) (SI 1992/2183) |
| | paras 76–88 | 6 Mar 1992 (RA) |
| | para 89 | 1 Apr 1992 (SI 1992/818) |
| | paras 90, 91 | 2 Nov 1992 (SI 1992/2454) |
| | para 92 | 6 Mar 1992 (RA) |
| | para 93 | 1 Apr 1993 (SI 1993/575) |
| | para 94 | 1 Apr 1993 (SI 1993/194) |
| | para 95 | 1 Aug 1992 (subject to transitional provisions in relation to any financial year beginning before 1 Apr 1993) (SI 1992/1755) |
| | paras 96–98 | 1 Aug 1992 (subject to transitional provisions in relation to any financial year beginning before 1 Apr 1993) (SI 1992/1755) |
| | paras 99, 100 | 6 Mar 1992 (RA) |
| Sch 14[1] | | 6 Mar 1992 (RA), repeals of or in— |
| | | Local Government Finance Act 1988 (except Sch 12); |
| | | Social Security Contributions and Benefits Act 1992; |
| | | Social Security Administration Act 1992 |

**Local Government Finance Act 1992 (c 14)**—*contd*

1 Apr 1992 (SI 1992/818), repeals of or in—
  Local Government (Financial Provisions) (Scotland) Act 1963,
    s 10;
  Local Government (Scotland) Act 1975, s 37(1);
  Local Government, Planning and Land Act 1980, s 46;
  Abolition of Domestic Rates etc (Scotland) Act 1987, Sch 1,
    para 19;
  Local Government Finance Act 1988, Sch 12, para 5;
  Local Government and Housing Act 1989, Sch 6, para 8
1 Aug 1992 (subject to transitional provisions) (SI 1992/1755),
    repeals of or in—
  Local Government and Housing Act 1989, Sch 5, para 30(4);
  Water Resources Act 1991, ss 11, 135, 136
1 Oct 1992 (SI 1992/2183), repeals of or in—
  Local Government (Scotland) Act 1973, s 110A;
  Abolition of Domestic Rates Etc (Scotland) Act 1987, ss 3A, 9,
    10(7A), 11B, 28, Sch 2, paras 1(2), 2(1), Sch 5, paras 2–5, 9,
    10, 14, 15, 17–19, 21, 25;
  Local Government Finance Act 1988, Sch 12, paras 10, 13
    (subject to transitional provisions in relation to any financial
    year beginning before 1 Apr 1993)
1 Apr 1993 (SI 1992/2454), repeals of or in—
  Education Reform Act 1988, s 81(8A);
  Local Government and Housing Act 1989, s 146 (subject to
    transitional provisions), Sch 5, paras 2–18, 43, 49–54, 55(3), 56,
    58, 59, 61, 63–65, 70, 71, 73, 74, 76(3), 77, 78, Sch 11,
    para 98;
  Community Charges (Substitute Setting) Act 1991
1 Apr 1993 (repeal of Local Government Finance and Valuation
    Act 1991) (SI 1993/194)
1 Apr 1993 (subject to transitional provisions) (SI 1993/575),
    repeals of or in—
  Registration of Births, Deaths and Marriages (Scotland)
    Act 1965, s 28B;
  Local Government (Scotland) Act 1966, Sch 1, Pt I, para 2A;
  Local Government (Scotland) Act 1973, ss 110, 118(1)(b);
  Local Government (Scotland) Act 1975, Sch 3, para 31;
  Water (Scotland) Act 1980, ss 41(2), (2A), 54(3)(b), 109(1);
  Abolition of Domestic Rates Etc (Scotland) Act 1987, ss 1–7,
    14, 18(2A), 20(10), 25(1), (3), 26(1), (2), 27, 33, Sch 1, Sch 3,
    paras 1–4, 5(1), 7, Sch 5, paras 1, 6, 12, 13, 16, 19A, 20,
    22–24, 26–49;
  Debtors (Scotland) Act 1987, s 106;
  Local Government Finance Act 1988, Sch 12, paras 8, 15, 17,
    23, 27;
  Local Government and Housing Act 1989, ss 140, 141, Sch 6,
    paras 20, 21;
  Environmental Protection Act 1990, Sch 15, para 1;
  Caravans (Standard Community Charge and Rating) Act 1991,
    s 2
1 Apr 1996 (SI 1996/918), repeals of—
  Local Government (Scotland) Act 1973, s 111(1)(a), (b), (d);
  Water (Scotland) Act 1980, s 9(6)
*Not yet in force*, repeals of or in—
  Civil Jurisdiction and Judgments Act 1982;
  Abolition of Domestic Rates Etc (Scotland) Act 1987, ss 8, 10
    (except sub-s (7A)), 11, 11A, 12, 13, 15–17, 18 (except
    sub-s (2A)), 19, 20(1)–(9), (11), 21–24, 25(2), 26 (except
    sub-ss (1), (2)), 29–32, 34, 35, Sch 2, paras 1(1), 2(2)–(4), 3–9,
    Sch 3, paras 5(2), (3), 6, Sch 4, Sch 5, paras 7, 8, 11, Sch 6;

**Local Government Finance Act 1992 (c 14)**—*contd*
> Local Government Finance Act 1988, Sch 12, paras 18–22,
> 24–26, 28–36, 38;
> Local Government and Housing Act 1989, ss 142–144, Sch 6,
> paras 10–15, 22, 24–29

[1]   For savings in relation to the repeals of the Abolition of Domestic Rates (Scotland) Act 1987, Sch 2, para 7A, and the Local Government Finance Act 1988, Sch 4, para 6, see the Local Government Finance Act 1992 (Recovery of Community Charge) Saving Order 1993, SI 1993/1780

---

**Maintenance Orders (Reciprocal Enforcement) Act 1992 (c 56)**

*RA:* 12 Nov 1992

*Commencement provisions:* s 3; Maintenance Orders (Reciprocal Enforcement) Act 1992 (Commencement) Order 1993, SI 1993/618

Whole Act in force 5 Apr 1993 (SI 1993/618)

---

**Mauritius Republic Act 1992 (c 45)**

*RA:* 18 Jun 1992

Whole Act in force 18 Jun 1992 (RA); but note that s 1 is deemed to have come into force on 12 Mar 1992 (s 1(4))

---

**Medicinal Products: Prescription by Nurses etc Act 1992 (c 28)**

*RA:* 16 Mar 1992

*Commencement provisions:* s 6(2); Medicinal Products: Prescription by Nurses etc Act 1992 (Commencement No 1) Order 1994, SI 1994/2408; Medicinal Products: Prescription by Nurses etc Act 1992 (Commencement No 2) Order 1996, SI 1996/1505

| | |
|---|---|
| 1, 2 | 3 Oct 1994 (SI 1994/2408) |
| 3 | 1 Jul 1996 (SI 1996/1505) |
| 4–6 | 16 Mar 1992 (RA) |

---

**Museums and Galleries Act 1992 (c 44)**

*RA:* 16 Mar 1992

*Commencement provisions:* s 11(4); Museums and Galleries Act 1992 (Commencement) Order 1992, SI 1992/1874

| | | |
|---|---|---|
| 1–8 | | 1 Sep 1992 (SI 1992/1874) |
| 9 | | 1 Apr 1993 (SI 1992/1874) |
| 10, 11 | | 1 Sep 1992 (SI 1992/1874) |
| Schs 1–7 | | 1 Sep 1992 (SI 1992/1874) |
| Sch 8 | para 1(1)–(6) | 1 Sep 1992 (SI 1992/1874) |
| | para 1(7) | *Never in force* (repealed) |
| | para 1(8), (9) | 1 Sep 1992 (SI 1992/1874) |
| | para 2 | *Never in force* (repealed) |
| | paras 3–9 | 1 Sep 1992 (SI 1992/1874) |
| | para 10(1) | 1 Sep 1992 (SI 1992/1874) |
| | para 10(2) | *Never in force* (repealed) |
| | paras 11–14 | 1 Sep 1992 (SI 1992/1874) |
| Sch 9 | | 1 Sep 1992 (except repeal of Charities Act 1960, Sch 2, paras (da)–(dd)) (SI 1992/1874) |

**Museums and Galleries Act 1992 (c 44)**—*contd*

*Never in force* (repeal of Charities Act 1960, Sch 2, paras (da)–(dd))
(repealed)

---

**Non-Domestic Rating Act 1992 (c 46)**

*RA:* 18 Jun 1992

*Commencement provisions:* s 10(2); Non-Domestic Rating Act 1992 (Commencement No 1) Order 1992, SI 1992/1486; Non-Domestic Rating Act 1992 (Commencement No 2) Order 1992, SI 1992/1642

| | | |
|---|---|---|
| 1–4 | | 16 Jul 1992 (SI 1992/1642) |
| 5 | (1) | 16 Jul 1992 (SI 1992/1642) |
| | (2) | 23 Jun 1992 (SI 1992/1486) |
| 6 | | 16 Jul 1992 (SI 1992/1642) |
| 7 | | 23 Jun 1992 (SI 1992/1486) |
| 8 | | 16 Jul 1992 (SI 1992/1642) |
| 9 | | 23 Jun 1992 (SI 1992/1486) |
| 10 | | 18 Jun 1992 (RA) |

---

**Nurses, Midwives and Health Visitors Act 1992 (c 16)**

*RA:* 6 Mar 1992

*Commencement provisions:* s 17(3); Nurses, Midwives and Health Visitors Act 1992 (Commencement No 1) Order 1993, SI 1993/588

| | | |
|---|---|---|
| 1 | (1) | 1 Apr 1993 (SI 1993/588) |
| | (2) | See Sch 1 below |
| 2 | | 6 Mar 1992 (RA) |
| 3 | | 1 Apr 1993 (SI 1993/588) |
| 4 | | 1 Apr 1993 (except so far as substitutes Nurses, Midwives and Health Visitors Act 1979, s 5(8)(e) and s 5(9) (so far as that substitution consists of removal of that provision in its application to Sch 2, para 7 to the 1979 Act)) (SI 1993/588) |
| | | *Never in force* (exceptions noted above) (repealed) |
| 5 | (1) | 1 Apr 1993 (SI 1993/588) |
| | (2) | 1 Apr 1993 (except in Northern Ireland) (SI 1993/588) |
| | | *Never in force* (exception noted above) (repealed) |
| | (3)–(5) | 1 Apr 1993 (SI 1993/588) |
| 6–14 | | 1 Apr 1993 (SI 1993/588) |
| 15 | | 6 Mar 1992 (RA) |
| 16 | (1) | See Sch 2 below |
| | (2) | See Sch 3 below |
| 17 | (1), (2) | 1 Apr 1993 (SI 1993/588) |
| | (3) | 6 Mar 1992 (RA) |
| | (4) | 1 Apr 1993 (except so far as applies to s 5(2)) (SI 1993/588) |
| | | *Never in force* (exception noted above) (repealed) |
| Schs 1, 2 | | 1 Apr 1993 (SI 1993/588) |
| Sch 3 | | 1 Apr 1993 (except repeal of Nurses, Midwives and Health Visitors Act 1979, Sch 2, para 7) (SI 1993/588) |
| | | *Never in force* (exception noted above) (repealed) |

---

**Offshore Safety Act 1992 (c 15)**

*RA:* 6 Mar 1992

*Commencement provisions:* s 7(3); Offshore Safety Act 1992 (Commencement No 1) Order 1993, SI 1993/2406; Offshore Safety Act 1992 (Commencement No 2) Order 1996, SI 1996/487

| | | |
|---|---|---|
| 1 | | 6 Mar 1992 (RA) |

**Offshore Safety Act 1992 (c 15)**—*contd*

| | | |
|---|---|---|
| 2 | (1), (2) | 6 Mar 1992 (RA) |
| | (3)(a) | 6 Mar 1992 (RA) |
| | (3)(b), (c) | 1 Mar 1996 (SI 1996/487) |
| | (4) | 6 Mar 1992 (RA) |
| 3 | (1)(a) | 30 Nov 1993 (SI 1993/2406) |
| | (1)(b)–(d) | 6 Mar 1992 (RA) |
| | (1)(e) | 30 Nov 1993 (SI 1993/2406) |
| | (2) | 30 Nov 1993 (SI 1993/2406) |
| | (3)(a) | 6 Mar 1992 (RA) |
| | (3)(b) | 1 Mar 1996 (SI 1996/487) |
| | (3)(c), (d) | 6 Mar 1992 (RA) |
| | (4) | 6 Mar 1992 (RA) |
| 4–6 | | 6 Mar 1992 (RA) |
| 7 | (1) | 6 Mar 1992 (RA) |
| | (2) | See Sch 2 below |
| | (3), (4) | 6 Mar 1992 (RA) |
| Sch 1 | | 30 Nov 1993 (SI 1993/2406) |
| Sch 2 | | 6 Mar 1992 (RA), except repeals in— |
| | | Continental Shelf Act 1964; |
| | | Gas Act 1986, s 47(5) |
| | | 30 Nov 1993 (repeal in Continental Shelf Act 1964) |
| | | (SI 1993/2406) |
| | | 1 Mar 1996 (repeal of Gas Act 1986, s 47(5)) (SI 1996/487) |

---

**Offshore Safety (Protection Against Victimisation) Act 1992 (c 24)**

*RA:* 16 Mar 1992

Whole Act in force 16 Mar 1992 (RA)

---

**Parliamentary Corporate Bodies Act 1992 (c 27)**

*RA:* 16 Mar 1992

Whole Act in force 16 Mar 1992 (RA)

---

**Prison Security Act 1992 (c 25)**

*RA:* 16 Mar 1992

*Commencement provisions:* s 3(2)

Whole Act in force 16 May 1992 (s 3(2))

---

**Protection of Badgers Act 1992 (c 51)**

*RA:* 16 Jul 1992

*Commencement provisions:* s 15(3)

Whole Act in force 16 Oct 1992 (s 15(3))

---

## Sea Fish (Conservation) Act 1992 (c 60)

*RA:* 17 Dec 1992

*Commencement provisions:* s 11(1), (2)

| | | |
|---|---|---|
| 1 | (1) | 17 Dec 1992 (RA) |
| | (2) | 17 Jan 1993 (except in relation to vessels of an overall length of 10 metres or less) (s 11(1), (2)) |
| | | *Not yet in force* (exception noted above) |
| | (3) | 17 Dec 1992 (RA) |
| | (4), (5) | 17 Jan 1993 (s 11(1)) |
| 2 | | 17 Dec 1992 (RA) |
| 3 | | 17 Jan 1993 (s 11(1)) |
| 4 | | 17 Dec 1992 (RA) |
| 5 | | 17 Jan 1993 (s 11(1)) |
| 6–13 | | 17 Dec 1992 (RA) |

## Sea Fisheries (Wildlife Conservation) Act 1992 (c 36)

*RA:* 16 Mar 1992

*Commencement provisions:* s 2(2)

Whole Act in force 16 May 1992 (s 2(2))

## Severn Bridges Act 1992 (c 3)

Local application only; amendments to this enactment are not noted.

## Sexual Offences (Amendment) Act 1992 (c 34)

*RA:* 16 Mar 1992

*Commencement provisions:* s 8(3)–(5); Sexual Offences (Amendment) Act 1992 (Commencement) Order 1992, SI 1992/1336

| | |
|---|---|
| 1–7 | 1 Aug 1992 (SI 1992/1336) |
| 8 | 16 Mar 1992 (s 8(3)) |

## Social Security Administration Act 1992 (c 5)

*RA:* 13 Feb 1992

*Commencement provisions:* s 192(4)

Whole Act in force 1 Jul 1992 (s 192(4)); but note transitory modifications in Social Security (Consequential Provisions) Act 1992, Sch 4

## Social Security Administration (Northern Ireland) Act 1992 (c 8)

*RA:* 13 Feb 1992

*Commencement provisions:* s 168(4)

Whole Act in force 1 Jul 1992 (s 168(4)); but note transitory modifications in Social Security (Consequential Provisions) (Northern Ireland) Act 1992, Sch 4

## Social Security (Consequential Provisions) Act 1992 (c 6)

*RA:* 13 Feb 1992

*Commencement provisions:* s 7(2), Sch 4, para 1(3); Social Security (Consequential Provisions) Act 1992 Appointed Day Order 1993, SI 1993/1025[1]

Whole Act in force 1 Jul 1992 (s 7(2))[1]

[1]   This order appointed 19 Apr 1993 as the appointed day in respect of Sch 4, paras 8, 9

## Social Security (Consequential Provisions) (Northern Ireland) Act 1992 (c 9)

*RA:* 13 Feb 1992

*Commencement provisions:* s 7(2)

Whole Act in force 1 Jul 1992 (s 7(2))

## Social Security Contributions and Benefits Act 1992 (c 4)

*RA:* 13 Feb 1992

*Commencement provisions:* s 177(4)

Whole Act in force 1 Jul 1992 (s 177(4)); but note transitory modifications in Social Security (Consequential Provisions) Act 1992, Sch 4; those transitory modifications partially ceased to have effect on 19 Apr 1993 (SI 1993/1025) so that, on that day, Sch 2, para 6(2) to this Act came into force

## Social Security Contributions and Benefits (Northern Ireland) Act 1992 (c 7)

*RA:* 13 Feb 1992

*Commencement provisions:* s 173(4)

Whole Act in force 1 Jul 1992 (s 173(4)); but note transitory modifications in Social Security (Consequential Provisions) (Northern Ireland) Act 1992, Sch 4

## Social Security (Mortgage Interest Payments) Act 1992 (c 33)

*RA:* 16 Mar 1992

Whole Act in force 16 Mar 1992 (RA); but note that s 1(1) ceased to have effect on 1 Jul 1992, by virtue of s 1(2)

## Sporting Events (Control of Alcohol etc) (Amendment) Act 1992 (c 57)

*RA:* 3 Dec 1992

Whole Act in force 3 Dec 1992 (RA)

## Stamp Duty (Temporary Provisions) Act 1992 (c 2)

*RA:* 13 Feb 1992

*Commencement provisions:* s 1(4)

| | |
|---|---|
| 1 | 16 Jan 1992 (s 1(4)) |
| 2, 3 | 13 Feb 1992 (RA) |

## Still–Birth (Definition) Act 1992 (c 29)

*RA:* 16 Mar 1992

*Commencement provisions:* s 4(2)

| | |
|---|---|
| 1, 2 | 1 Oct 1992 (s 4(2)) |
| 3 | 16 Mar 1992 (RA) |
| 4 | 1 Oct 1992 (s 4(2)) |

## Taxation of Chargeable Gains Act 1992 (c 12)

*RA:* 6 Mar 1992

*Commencement provisions:* s 289

Except where the context otherwise requires, this Act has effect in relation to tax for the year 1992–93 and subsequent years of assessment, and tax for the accounting periods of companies beginning on or after 6 Apr 1992 (s 289)

## Timeshare Act 1992 (c 35)

*RA:* 16 Mar 1992

*Commencement provisions:* s 13(2); Timeshare Act 1992 (Commencement) Order 1992, SI 1992/1941

Whole Act in force 12 Oct 1992 (SI 1992/1941)

## Tourism (Overseas Promotion) (Wales) Act 1992 (c 26)

*RA:* 16 Mar 1992

*Commencement provisions:* s 3

Whole Act in force 16 May 1992 (s 3)

## Trade Union and Labour Relations (Consolidation) Act 1992 (c 52)

*RA:* 16 Jul 1992

*Commencement provisions:* s 302

Whole Act in force 16 Oct 1992 (s 302)

## Traffic Calming Act 1992 (c 30)

*RA:* 16 Mar 1992

*Commencement provisions:* s 3

Whole Act in force 16 May 1992 (s 3)

## Transport and Works Act 1992 (c 42)

*RA:* 16 Mar 1992

*Commencement provisions:* s 70; Transport and Works Act 1992 (Commencement No 1) Order 1992, SI 1992/1347; Transport and Works Act 1992 (Commencement No 2) Order 1992, SI 1992/2043; Transport and Works Act 1992 (Commencement No 3 and Transitional Provisions) Order 1992, SI 1992/2784; Transport and Works Act 1992 (Commencement No 4) Order 1992, SI 1992/3144; Transport and Works Act 1992 (Commencement No 5 and Transitional Provisions) Order 1994,

**Transport and Works Act 1992 (c 42)**—*contd*

SI 1994/718; Transport and Works Act 1992 (Commencement No 6) Order 1996, SI 1996/1609; Transport and Works Act 1992 (Commencement No 7) Order 1998, SI 1998/274

| | | |
|---|---|---|
| 1–25 | | 1 Jan 1993 (SI 1992/2784) |
| 26–40 | | 7 Dec 1992 (SI 1992/2043) |
| 41, 42 | | 31 Jan 1993 (SI 1992/3144) |
| 43, 44 | | *Never in force* (repealed) |
| 45, 46 | | 15 Jul 1992 (SI 1992/1347) |
| 47 | (1) | See Sch 2 below |
| | (2) | 31 Jan 1993 (SI 1992/3144) |
| 48 | | 31 Jan 1993 (SI 1992/3144) |
| 49 | | 15 Jul 1992 (SI 1992/1347) |
| 50 | | 8 Jul 1996 (SI 1996/1609) |
| 51 | | 31 Jan 1993 (SI 1992/3144) |
| 52–56 | | 8 Jul 1996 (SI 1996/1609) |
| 57–60 | | 15 Jul 1992 (SI 1992/1347) |
| 61 | | 31 Jan 1993 (SI 1992/3144) |
| 62 | | 8 Jul 1996 (SI 1996/1609) |
| 63 | | 15 Jul 1992 (subject to transitional provisions with respect to certain Harbour Revision Orders and Harbour Empowerment Orders) (SI 1992/1347) |
| 64 | | 31 Jan 1993 (SI 1992/3144) |
| 65 | (1)(a) | 15 Jul 1992 (SI 1992/1347) |
| | (1)(b) | 1 Jan 1993 (except words "in section 25, the words 'and shall not be opened' onwards," and "section 48,") (SI 1992/2784) |
| | | 5 Apr 1994 (words "in section 25, the words 'and shall not be opened' onwards,") (subject to transitional provisions) (SI 1994/718) |
| | | 8 Jul 1996 (words "section 48,") (SI 1996/1609) |
| | (1)(c), (d) | 1 Jan 1993 (SI 1992/2784) |
| | (1)(e) | 15 Jul 1992 (SI 1992/1347) |
| | (1)(f) | 1 Jan 1993 (SI 1992/2784) |
| | (2) | 15 Jul 1992 (SI 1992/1347) |
| 66, 67 | | 15 Jul 1992 (SI 1992/1347) |
| 68 | (1) | See Sch 4 below |
| | (2) | 26 Feb 1998 (SI 1998/274) |
| 69 | | 15 Jul 1992 (SI 1992/1347) |
| 70–72 | | 16 Mar 1992 (s 70) |
| Sch 1 | | 1 Jan 1993 (SI 1992/2784) |
| Sch 2 | | 22 Dec 1992 (for purpose of conferring on Secretary of State power to make regulations in relation to rail crossing extinguishment orders or rail crossing diversion orders) (SI 1992/3144) |
| | | 31 Jan 1993 (otherwise) (SI 1992/3144) |
| Sch 3 | | 15 Jul 1992 (subject to transitional provisions with respect to certain Harbour Revision Orders and Harbour Empowerment Orders) (SI 1992/1347) |
| Sch 4 | Pt I | 15 Jul 1992 (subject to transitional provisions with respect to certain Harbour Revision Orders and Harbour Empowerment Orders) (SI 1992/1347), repeals of or in— |
| | | British Railways Act 1965; |
| | | London Transport Act 1965; |
| | | Criminal Justice Act 1967; |
| | | British Railways Act 1977; |
| | | London Transport Act 1977 |
| | | 7 Dec 1992 (repeal in Railway Regulation Act 1842) (SI 1992/2043) |
| | | 1 Jan 1993 (subject to transitional provisions) (SI 1992/2784), repeals of or in— |

**Transport and Works Act 1992 (c 42)**—*contd*

    Tramways Act 1870 (except words "and shall not be opened"
      onwards in s 25, and s 48);
    Municipal Corporations Act 1882;
    Military Tramways Act 1887;
    Light Railways Act 1896;
    Railways (Electrical Power) Act 1903;
    Light Railways Act 1912;
    Railways Act 1921;
    Transport Act 1962;
    Administration of Justice Act 1965;
    Transport Act 1968 (except ss 124, 125(4));
    Local Government Act 1972;
    Supply Powers Act 1975;
    Administration of Justice Act 1982;
    Roads (Scotland) Act 1984;
    Telecommunications Act 1984;
    Insolvency Act 1986
    31 Jan 1993 (SI 1992/3144), repeals of or in—
    Regulation of Railways Act 1871, s 3;
    Highways Act 1980
    5 Apr 1994 (subject to transitional provisions) (SI 1994/718),
      repeals of—
    Tramways Act 1870, s 25 (words "and shall not be opened"
      onwards);
    Road and Rail Traffic Act 1933, s 41;
    Transport Act 1968, s 125(4)
    8 Jul 1996 (SI 1996/1609), repeals of—
    Tramways Act 1870, s 48;
    Transport Act 1968, s 124, subject to a saving
    26 Feb 1998 (SI 1998/274), repeals of or in—
    Town Police Clauses Act 1889;
    Notice of Accidents Act 1894;
    Notice of Accidents Act 1906;
    Road and Rail Traffic Act 1933, s 43;
    Transport Charges &c (Miscellaneous Provisions) Act 1954;
    Public Service Vehicles (Arrest of Offenders) Act 1975;
    Channel Tunnel Act 1987
    *Never in force* (repeals of or in Railway Employment (Prevention of
      Accidents) Act 1900, s 13(2) (repealed); Road Traffic Act 1960,
      Sch 17 (repealed))

  Pt II    15 Jul 1992 (subject to transitional provisions with respect to
    certain Harbour Revision Orders and Harbour Empowerment
    Orders) (SI 1992/1347)

**Tribunals and Inquiries Act 1992 (c 53)**

*RA:* 16 Jul 1992

*Commencement provisions:* s 19(2)

Whole Act in force 1 Oct 1992 (s 19(2))

# 1993 Acts

## Agriculture Act 1993 (c 37)

*RA:* 27 Jul 1993

*Commencement provisions:* ss 1(2)–(4), 21(2), (3), 26(2)–(4), 54(2), 55(3), 65(2), (3); Agriculture Act 1993 (Commencement No 1) Order 1993, SI 1993/2038; Potato Marketing Scheme (Commencement of Revocation Period) Order 1996, SI 1996/336

| | | |
|---|---|---|
| 1 | (1) | 1 Nov 1994 (SI 1994/2921) |
| | (2)–(5) | 27 Jul 1993 (RA) |
| 2–11 | | 27 Jul 1993 (RA) |
| 12 | | See Sch 2 below |
| 13–20 | | 27 Jul 1993 (RA) |
| 21 | (1) | 1 Nov 1994 (s 21(2), (3); SI 1994/2922) |
| | (2), (3) | 27 Jul 1993 (RA) |
| 22–25 | | 27 Jul 1993 (RA) |
| 26 | (1) | 1 Jul 1996 (SI 1996/336) |
| | (2)–(5) | 27 Jul 1993 (RA) |
| 27–35 | | 27 Jul 1993 (RA) |
| 36 | | See Sch 4 below |
| 37–49 | | 27 Jul 1993 (RA) |
| 50–53 | | 27 Sep 1993 (s 65(2)) |
| 54 | | 27 Jul 1993 (RA) |
| 55 | | 4 Aug 1993 (SI 1993/2038) |
| 56–58 | | 27 Jul 1993 (RA) |
| 59 | | 4 Aug 1993 (SI 1993/2038) |
| 60–65 | | 27 Jul 1993 (RA) |
| Schs 1–4 | | 27 Jul 1993 (RA) |
| Sch 5 | | 27 Jul 1993 (except so far as repeals relate to potatoes and revocation of Potato Marketing Scheme, para 67) (RA) |
| | | 4 Aug 1993 (exceptions noted above) (SI 1993/2038) |

## Appropriation Act 1993 (c 33)

*RA:* 27 Jul 1993

Whole Act in force 27 Jul 1993 (RA)

## Asylum and Immigration Appeals Act 1993 (c 23)

*RA:* 1 Jul 1993

*Commencement provisions:* s 14; Asylum and Immigration Appeals Act 1993 (Commencement and Transitional Provisions) Order 1993, SI 1993/1655

| | |
|---|---|
| 1 | 1 Jul 1993 (except so far as relates to ss 4–11) (RA) |
| | 26 Jul 1993 (exception noted above) (SI 1993/1655) |
| 2, 3 | 1 Jul 1993 (RA) |
| 4–7 | 26 Jul 1993 (SI 1993/1655) |

**Asylum and Immigration Appeals Act 1993 (c 23)**—*contd*

| | |
|---|---|
| 8, 9 | 26 Jul 1993 (subject to savings) (SI 1993/1655) |
| 10, 11 | 26 Jul 1993 (SI 1993/655) |
| 12–16 | 1 Jul 1993 (RA) |
| Schs 1, 2 | 26 Jul 1993 (SI 1993/1655) |

---

**Bail (Amendment) Act 1993 (c 26)**

*RA:* 20 Jul 1993

*Commencement provisions:* s 2(2); Bail (Amendment) Act 1993 (Commencement) Order 1994, SI 1994/1437

| | |
|---|---|
| 1 | 27 Jun 1994 (SI 1994/1437) |
| 2 | 20 Jul 1993 (s 2(2)) |

---

**Bankruptcy (Scotland) Act 1993 (c 6)**

*RA:* 18 Feb 1993

*Commencement provisions:* s 12(3)–(6); Bankruptcy (Scotland) Act 1993 Commencement and Savings Order 1993, SI 1993/438

| | | |
|---|---|---|
| 1–7 | | 1 Apr 1993 (SI 1993/438) |
| 8, 9 | | 18 Feb 1993 (s 12(3)) |
| 10 | | 1 Apr 1993 (SI 1993/438) |
| 11 | (1), (2) | 1 Apr 1993 (SI 1993/438) |
| | (3) | See Sch 1 below |
| | (4) | See Sch 2 below |
| 12 | | 18 Feb 1993 (s 12(3)) |
| Sch 1 | paras 1–21 | 1 Apr 1993 (SI 1993/438) |
| | para 22(1)–(4) | 1 Apr 1993 (SI 1993/438) |
| | para 22(5) | 18 Feb 1993 (s 12(3)) |
| | para 23 | 18 Feb 1993 (s 12(3)) |
| | paras 24–30 | 1 Apr 1993 (SI 1993/438) |
| | para 31(1)–(3) | 1 Apr 1993 (SI 1993/438) |
| | para 31(4), (5) | 18 Feb 1993 (s 12(3)) |
| | para 32 | 1 Apr 1993 (SI 1993/438) |
| Sch 2 | | 1 Apr 1993 (SI 1993/438) |

---

**British Coal and British Rail (Transfer Proposals) Act 1993 (c 2)**

*RA:* 19 Jan 1993

Whole Act in force 19 Jan 1993 (RA)

---

**Cardiff Bay Barrage Act 1993 (c 42)**

*RA:* 5 Nov 1993

Whole Act in force 5 Nov 1993 (RA)

---

**Carrying of Knives etc (Scotland) Act 1993 (c 13)**

*RA:* 27 May 1993

Whole Act in force 27 May 1993 (RA)

---

## Charities Act 1993 (c 10)

*RA:* 27 May 1993

*Commencement provisions:* s 99; Charities Act 1993 (Commencement and Transitional Provisions) Order 1995, SI 1995/2695

| | | |
|---|---|---|
| 1–4 | | 1 Aug 1993 (s 99(1)) |
| 5 | (1) | 1 Aug 1993 (subject to transitional provisions) (s 99(1), (4)) |
| | (2)–(6) | 1 Aug 1993 (s 99(1)) |
| 6–40 | | 1 Aug 1993 (s 99(1)) |
| 41–49 | | 15 Oct 1995 (for purposes of making orders or regulations) (SI 1995/2695) |
| | | 1 Mar 1996 (otherwise, subject to a transitional provision) (SI 1995/2695) |
| 50–68 | | 1 Aug 1993 (s 99(1)) |
| 69 | | 1 Mar 1996 (SI 1995/2695) |
| 70–73 | | 1 Aug 1993 (s 99(1)) |
| 74 | (1)(a) | 1 Aug 1993 (subject to transitional provisions) (s 99(1), (4)) |
| | (1)(b) | 1 Aug 1993 (s 99(1)) |
| | (2)–(12) | 1 Aug 1993 (s 99(1)) |
| 75 | (1)(a) | 1 Aug 1993 (s 99(1)) |
| | (1)(b) | 1 Aug 1993 (subject to transitional provisions) (s 99(1), (4)) |
| | (2)–(10) | 1 Aug 1993 (s 99(1)) |
| 76–97 | | 1 Aug 1993 (s 99(1)) |
| 98 | (1) | See Sch 6 below |
| | (2) | See Sch 7 below |
| 99, 100 | | 1 Aug 1993 (s 99(1)) |
| Schs 1–5 | | 1 Aug 1993 (s 99(1)) |
| Sch 6 | paras 1–20 | 1 Aug 1993 (s 99(1)) |
| | para 21(1), (2) | 1 Aug 1993 (s 99(1)) |
| | para 21(3) | 1 Mar 1996 (SI 1995/2695) |
| | para 21(4), (5) | 1 Aug 1993 (s 99(1)) |
| | paras 22–30 | 1 Aug 1993 (s 99(1)) |
| Sch 7 | | 1 Aug 1993 (subject to transitional provisions) (s 99(1)–(3)) |
| Sch 8 | | 1 Aug 1993 (s 99(1)) |

## Clean Air Act 1993 (c 11)

*RA:* 27 May 1993

*Commencement provisions:* s 68(2)

Whole Act in force 27 Aug 1993 (s 68(2))

## Consolidated Fund Act 1993 (c 4)

*RA:* 18 Feb 1993

Whole Act in force 18 Feb 1993 (RA)

## Consolidated Fund (No 2) Act 1993 (c 7)

*RA:* 29 Mar 1993

Whole Act in force 29 Mar 1993 (RA)

## Consolidated Fund (No 3) Act 1993 (c 52)

*RA:* 17 Dec 1993

Whole Act in force 17 Dec 1993 (RA)

---

## Criminal Justice Act 1993 (c 36)

*RA:* 27 Jul 1993

*Commencement provisions:* s 78; Criminal Justice Act 1993 (Commencement No 1) Order 1993, SI 1993/1968; Criminal Justice Act 1993 (Commencement No 2 Transitional Provisions and Savings) (Scotland) Order 1993, SI 1993/2035; Criminal Justice Act 1993 (Commencement No 3) Order 1993, SI 1993/2734; Criminal Justice Act 1993 (Commencement No 4) Order 1994, SI 1994/71; Criminal Justice Act 1993 (Commencement No 5) Order 1994, SI 1994/242; Criminal Justice Act 1993 (Commencement No 6) Order 1994, SI 1994/700; Criminal Justice Act 1993 (Commencement No 7) Order 1994, SI 1994/1951; Criminal Justice Act 1993 (Commencement No 8) Order 1995, SI 1995/43; Criminal Justice Act 1993 (Commencement No 9) Order 1995, SI 1995/1958; Criminal Justice Act 1993 (Commencement No 10) Order 1999, SI 1999/1189; Criminal Justice Act 1993 (Commencement No 11) Order 1999, SI 1999/1499

| | | |
|---|---|---|
| 1–4 | | 1 Jun 1999 (SI 1999/1189) |
| 5 | (1) | *Never in force* (repealed) |
| | (2) | 1 Jun 1999 (SI 1999/1189) |
| | (3)–(5) | 1 Jun 1999 (SI 1999/1499) |
| 6 | | 1 Jun 1999 (SI 1999/1189) |
| 7–15 | | *Never in force* (repealed) |
| 16, 17 | | 15 Feb 1994 (SI 1994/71) |
| 18, 19 | | 1 Apr 1994 (SI 1994/700) |
| 20–23 | | 1 Dec 1993 (SI 1993/2734) |
| 24 | (1)–(11) | *Never in force* (repealed) |
| | (12)–(15) | 3 Feb 1995 (SI 1995/43) |
| 25 | | *Never in force* (repealed) |
| 26 | | 1 Apr 1994 (SI 1994/700) |
| 27, 28 | | 3 Feb 1995 (SI 1995/43) |
| 29–31 | | 15 Feb 1994 (SI 1994/71) |
| 32 | | 1 Apr 1994 (SI 1994/700) |
| 33 | | 15 Feb 1994 (SI 1994/71) |
| 34, 35 | | 1 Dec 1993 (SI 1993/2734) |
| 36–43 | | 3 Feb 1995 (SI 1995/43) |
| 44–46 | | 1 Dec 1993 (SI 1993/2734) |
| 47 | | 15 Feb 1994 (SI 1994/71) |
| 48 | | 1 Apr 1994 (SI 1994/700) |
| 49 | | 15 Feb 1994 (SI 1994/71) |
| 50, 51 | | 1 Apr 1994 (SI 1994/700) |
| 52–64 | | 1 Mar 1994 (SI 1994/242) |
| 65 | | 20 Sep 1993 (SI 1993/1968) |
| 66 | | 16 Aug 1993 (SI 1993/1968) |
| 67 | (1) | 16 Aug 1993 (E) (W) (SI 1993/1968) |
| | | 16 Aug 1993 (S) (subject to savings) (SI 1993/2035) |
| | (2) | 16 Aug 1993 (SI 1993/1968) |
| 68, 69 | | 27 Jul 1993 (s 78(2)) |
| 70, 71 | | 27 Sep 1993 (s 78(1)) |
| 72 | | 22 Aug 1994 (SI 1994/1951) |
| 73 | | 1 Dec 1993 (SI 1993/2734) |
| 74 | | 15 Feb 1994 (SI 1994/71) |
| 75, 76 | | 27 Jul 1993 (s 78(2)) |
| 77 | | 1 Apr 1994 (SI 1994/700) |
| 78 | | 27 Jul 1993 (partly) (RA) |
| | | 15 Feb 1994 (otherwise) (SI 1994/71) |
| 79 | (1)–(12) | 27 Jul 1993 (s 78(2)) |

**Criminal Justice Act 1993 (c 36)**—*contd*

|  |  |  |
|---|---|---|
|  | (13) | See Sch 5 below |
|  | (14) | See Sch 6 below |
| Schs 1, 2 |  | 1 Mar 1994 (SI 1994/242) |
| Sch 3 |  | 20 Sep 1993 (SI 1993/1968) |
| Sch 4 |  | 1 Apr 1994 (SI 1994/700) |
| Sch 5 | para 1 | 14 Aug 1995 (SI 1995/1958) |
|  | para 2 | 27 Jul 1993 (s 78(2)) |
|  | para 3 | 3 Feb 1995 (SI 1995/43) |
|  | para 4 | 1 Mar 1994 (SI 1994/242) |
|  | paras 5, 6 | *Never in force* (repealed) |
|  | paras 7–13 | 1 Mar 1994 (SI 1994/242) |
|  | para 14 | 15 Feb 1994 (SI 1994/71) |
|  | para 15 | 1 Apr 1994 (SI 1994/700) |
|  | para 16 | 1 Mar 1994 (SI 1994/242) |
|  | para 17(1) | 1 Apr 1994 (SI 1994/700) |
|  | para 17(2), (3) | 3 Feb 1995 (SI 1995/43) |
|  | para 17(4), (5) | 1 Apr 1994 (SI 1994/700) |
|  | para 17(6), (7) | 3 Feb 1995 (SI 1995/43) |
|  | paras 18–22 | 1 Mar 1994 (SI 1994/242) |
| Sch 6 | Pt I | 27 Jul 1993 (s 78(2)), repeals in— |
|  |  | Criminal Procedure (Scotland) Act 1975; |
|  |  | Prisoners and Criminal Proceedings (Scotland) Act 1993 |
|  |  | 20 Sep 1993 (SI 1993/1968), repeals in— |
|  |  | Magistrates' Courts Act 1980; |
|  |  | Criminal Justice Act 1991 |
|  |  | 15 Feb 1994 (SI 1994/71), repeals of or in— |
|  |  | Drug Trafficking Offences Act 1986, ss 1(5)(b)(iii), 27(5); |
|  |  | Criminal Justice Act 1988, ss 48 (E) (W), 98; |
|  |  | Prevention of Terrorism (Temporary Provisions) Act 1989; |
|  |  | Criminal Justice (International Co-operation) Act 1990; |
|  |  | Northern Ireland (Emergency Provisions) Act 1991, ss 50(2), 67(6) |
|  |  | 1 Mar 1994 (SI 1994/242), repeals of or in— |
|  |  | Company Securities (Insider Dealing) Act 1985; |
|  |  | Financial Services Act 1986; |
|  |  | Banking Act 1987; |
|  |  | Criminal Justice Act 1987; |
|  |  | Companies Act 1989 |
|  |  | 3 Feb 1995 (repeals of or in Northern Ireland (Emergency Provisions) Act 1991, ss 48(3), 51(3)) (SI 1995/43) |
|  |  | *Never in force* (repeals of or in Drug Trafficking Offences Act 1986, ss 1(8), 5(3), 26A(3), 38(2) (repealed)) |
|  | Pt II | 1 Mar 1994 (SI 1994/242) |

**Crofters (Scotland) Act 1993 (c 44)**

*RA:* 5 Nov 1993

*Commencement provisions:* ss 28(17), 64(2)

|  |  |
|---|---|
| 1–27 | 5 Jan 1994 (s 64(2)) |
| 28 | *Never in force* (repealed) |
| 29–64 | 5 Jan 1994 (s 64(2)) |
| Schs 1–7 | 5 Jan 1994 (s 64(2)) |

**Damages (Scotland) Act 1993 (c 5)**

*RA:* 18 Feb 1993

*Commencement provisions:* s 8(3)

**Damages (Scotland) Act 1993 (c 5)**—*contd*

Whole Act in force 18 Apr 1993 (s 8(3))

---

**Disability (Grants) Act 1993 (c 14)**

*RA:* 27 May 1993

Whole Act in force 27 May 1993 (RA)

---

**Education Act 1993 (c 35)**

*RA:* 27 Jul 1993

*Commencement provisions:* s 308(3); Education Act 1993 (Commencement No 1 and Transitional Provisions) Order 1993, SI 1993/1975; Education Act 1993 (Commencement No 2 and Transitional Provisions) Order 1993, SI 1993/3106, as amended by SI 1994/436; Education Act 1993 (Commencement No 3 and Transitional Provisions) Order 1994, SI 1994/507; Education Act 1993 (Commencement No 4) Order 1994, SI 1994/1558; Education Act 1993 (Commencement No 5 and Transitional Provisions) Order 1994, SI 1994/2038, as amended by SI 1994/2248

| | | |
|---|---|---|
| 1, 2 | | 1 Oct 1993 (SI 1993/1975) |
| 3, 4 | | 1 Apr 1994 (SI 1994/507) |
| 5 | | 1 Sep 1993 (SI 1993/1975) |
| 6–21 | | 1 Apr 1994 (SI 1994/507) |
| 22 | (1) | 1 Jan 1994 (SI 1994/3106) |
| | (2)(a) | 1 Jan 1994 (SI 1994/3106) |
| | (2)(b) | 1 Jan 1994 (for purpose of defining expression "proposals for the establishment of a new grant-maintained school") (SI 1994/3106) |
| | | 1 Apr 1994 (otherwise) (SI 1994/507) |
| | (2)(c) | 1 Apr 1994 (SI 1994/507) |
| | (3) | 1 Jan 1994 (SI 1994/3106) |
| | (4) | 1 Apr 1994 (SI 1994/507) |
| 23 | | 1 Jan 1994 (subject to transitional provisions) (SI 1994/3106) |
| 24 | | 9 Dec 1993 (SI 1994/3106) |
| 25–35 | | 1 Jan 1994 (subject to transitional provisions) (SI 1994/3106) |
| 36 | (1), (2) | 1 Jan 1994 (subject to transitional provisions) (SI 1994/3106) |
| | (3)–(5) | 1 Apr 1994 (SI 1994/507) |
| 37–46 | | 1 Jan 1994 (subject to transitional provisions) (SI 1994/3106) |
| 47 | (1)–(4) | 1 Apr 1994 (SI 1994/507) |
| | (5)–(9) | 1 Jan 1994 (subject to transitional provisions) (SI 1994/3106) |
| 48–54 | | 1 Apr 1994 (SI 1994/507) |
| 55–58 | | 1 Jan 1994 (SI 1994/3106) |
| 59–67 | | 1 Jan 1994 (subject to transitional provisions) (SI 1994/3106) |
| 68–70 | | 1 Apr 1994 (SI 1994/507) |
| 71–77 | | 1 Jan 1994 (subject to transitional provisions) (SI 1994/3106) |
| 78 | | 1 Apr 1994 (SI 1994/507) |
| 79, 80 | | 1 Jan 1994 (SI 1994/3106) |
| 81–91 | | 1 Apr 1994 (SI 1994/507) |
| 92 | | 1 Jan 1994 (SI 1994/3106) |
| 93–135 | | 1 Apr 1994 (subject to transitional provisions relating to ss 96(3), 96(6)(a), 99(1), 104(2)) (SI 1994/507) |
| 136 | (1) | 1 Jan 1994 (SI 1994/3106) |
| | (2) | 1 Apr 1994 (SI 1994/507) |
| | (3) | 1 Jan 1994 (SI 1994/3106) |
| 137 | | 1 Jan 1994 (SI 1994/3106) |
| 138–151 | | 1 Apr 1994 (subject to transitional provisions relating to s 147(1)) (SI 1994/507) |
| 152 | | 1 Jan 1994 (SI 1994/3106) |
| 153 | (1), (2) | 1 Jan 1994 (SI 1994/3106) |

**Education Act 1993 (c 35)**—*contd*

| | | |
|---|---|---|
| | (3) | 1 Apr 1994 (SI 1994/507) |
| | (4) | 1 Jan 1994 (SI 1994/3106) |
| | (5) | 1 Apr 1994 (SI 1994/507) |
| 154 | | 1 Apr 1994 (SI 1994/507) |
| 155–158 | | 1 Jan 1994 (SI 1994/3106) |
| 159 | | 1 Apr 1994 (SI 1994/507) |
| 160 | | 1 Sep 1994 (SI 1994/2038) |
| 161 | (1)–(4) | 1 Apr 1994 (SI 1994/507) |
| | (5) | 1 Jan 1994 (SI 1994/3106) |
| 162, 163 | | 1 Apr 1994 (SI 1994/507) |
| 164, 165 | | 1 Sep 1994 (SI 1994/2038) |
| 166 | (1)–(3) | 1 Sep 1994 (SI 1994/2038) |
| | (4) | 1 Apr 1994 (SI 1994/507) |
| | (5) | 1 Sep 1994 (SI 1994/2038) |
| 167 | (1)–(4) | 1 Sep 1994 (SI 1994/2038) |
| | (5) | See Sch 9 below |
| | (6) | 1 Sep 1994 (subject to transitional provisions) (SI 1994/2038) |
| 168 | (1)–(6) | 1 Sep 1994 (subject to transitional provisions) (SI 1994/2038) |
| | (7) | See Sch 10 below |
| 169–171 | | 1 Sep 1994 (subject to transitional provisions) (SI 1994/2038) |
| 172 | (1) | 3 Mar 1994 (SI 1994/507) |
| | (2)–(5) | 1 Sep 1994 (SI 1994/2038) |
| | (6) | 3 Mar 1994 (SI 1994/507) |
| 173–176 | | 1 Sep 1994 (SI 1994/2038) |
| 177 | (1) | 1 Sep 1994 (SI 1994/2038) |
| | (2)–(6) | 1 Jan 1994 (SI 1994/3106) |
| 178, 179 | | 1 Jan 1994 (SI 1994/3106) |
| 180 | (1), (2) | 1 Jan 1994 (SI 1994/3106) |
| | (3) | 1 Sep 1994 (SI 1994/2038) |
| | (4) | 1 Apr 1994 (SI 1994/507) |
| | (5), (6) | 1 Sep 1994 (SI 1994/2038) |
| 181 | | 1 Jan 1994 (SI 1994/3106) |
| 182 | (1)–(3) | 3 Mar 1994 (for purpose of defining "special school", "maintained special school" and "grant-maintained special school" in relation to regulations made under Pt III and s 228) (SI 1994/507) |
| | | 1 Apr 1994 (otherwise) (SI 1994/507) |
| | (4) | See Sch 11 below |
| 183–185 | | 1 Apr 1994 (subject to transitional provisions) (SI 1994/507) |
| 186 | (1), (2) | 3 Mar 1994 (SI 1994/507) |
| | (3) | 1 Apr 1994 (SI 1994/507) |
| | (4) | 3 Mar 1994 (SI 1994/507) |
| 187 | | 3 Mar 1994 (SI 1994/507) |
| 188, 189 | | 1 Apr 1994 (SI 1994/507) |
| 190 | | *Never in force* (repealed) |
| 191 | | 1 Apr 1994 (SI 1994/507) |
| 192 | (1)–(5) | 1 Oct 1993 (SI 1993/1975) |
| | (6), (7) | 1 Oct 1993 (for purposes of school attendance orders with respect to children other than those for whom a statement is maintained under the Education Act 1981, s 7) (SI 1993/1975) |
| | | 1 Sep 1994 (otherwise) (SI 1994/2038) |
| | (8) | 1 Oct 1993 (SI 1993/1975) |
| 193 | (1) | 1 Oct 1993 (subject to transitional provisions) (SI 1993/1975) |
| | (2)–(6) | 1 Oct 1993 (SI 1993/1975) |
| 194 | (1) | 1 Oct 1993 (SI 1993/1975) |
| | (2) | 1 Oct 1993 (subject to transitional provisions) (SI 1993/1975) |
| | (3)–(8) | 1 Oct 1993 (SI 1993/1975) |
| 195 | (1) | 1 Oct 1993 (subject to transitional provisions) (SI 1993/1975) |
| | (2)–(4) | 1 Oct 1993 (SI 1993/1975) |

**Education Act 1993 (c 35)**—*contd*

| | | |
|---|---|---|
| 196 | | 1 Sep 1994 (subject to transitional provisions) (SI 1994/2038) |
| 197 | (1)–(4) | 1 Oct 1993 (SI 1993/1975) |
| | (5) | 1 Sep 1994 (SI 1994/2038) |
| | (6) | 1 Oct 1993 (SI 1993/1975) |
| 198–203 | | 1 Oct 1993 (SI 1993/1975) |
| 204–212 | | 1 Sep 1993 (subject to transitional provisions) (SI 1993/1975) |
| 213–216 | | 1 Jan 1994 (SI 1994/3106) |
| 217 | (1) | 1 Jan 1994 (SI 1994/3106) |
| | (2) | 1 Apr 1994 (SI 1994/507) |
| 218–223 | | 1 Jan 1994 (subject to transitional provisions) (SI 1994/3106) |
| 224–226 | | 1 Dec 1994 (SI 1994/2038) |
| 227 | | 1 Jan 1994 (SI 1994/3106) |
| 228 | (1)–(3) | 1 Jan 1994 (SI 1994/3106) |
| | (4) | 1 Dec 1994 (SI 1994/2038) |
| 229 | (1) | 1 Oct 1993 (so far as amends Education Act 1980, s 12(1)(d) (insertion of words "or to transfer a county school to a new site in the area")) (SI 1993/1975) |
| | | 1 Apr 1994 (otherwise) (subject to transitional provisions) (SI 1994/507) |
| | (2) | 1 Apr 1994 (subject to transitional provisions) (SI 1994/507) |
| | (3) | 1 Apr 1994 (SI 1994/507) |
| 230 | (1) | 1 Oct 1993 (so far as amends Education Act 1980, s 13(1)(b) (insertion of words "or to transfer the school to a new site")) (SI 1993/1975) |
| | | 1 Apr 1994 (otherwise) (subject to transitional provisions) (SI 1994/507) |
| | (2) | 1 Apr 1994 (subject to transitional provisions) (SI 1994/507) |
| | (3)–(5) | 1 Oct 1993 (SI 1993/1975) |
| | (6) | 1 Apr 1994 (SI 1994/507) |
| 231–237 | | 1 Apr 1994 (SI 1994/507) |
| 238, 239 | | 1 Jan 1994 (SI 1994/3106) |
| 240 | | 27 Jul 1993 (RA) |
| 241 | | 1 Sep 1994 (SI 1994/2038) |
| 242–245 | | 1 Oct 1993 (SI 1993/1975) |
| 246 | | 1 Jan 1994 (SI 1994/3106) |
| 247–251 | | 1 Oct 1993 (SI 1993/1975) |
| 252 | | 3 Mar 1994 (SI 1994/507) |
| 253–258 | | 1 Apr 1994 (SI 1994/507) |
| 259 | (1) | 1 Oct 1993 (SI 1993/1975) |
| | (2) | 1 Oct 1993 (subject to transitional provisions) (SI 1993/1975) |
| | (3) | 1 Oct 1993 (SI 1993/1975) |
| 260 | | 1 Oct 1993 (SI 1993/1975) |
| 261, 262 | | 1 Sep 1994 (SI 1994/2038) |
| 263–265 | | 1 Oct 1993 (SI 1993/1975) |
| 266–268 | | 1 Jan 1994 (subject to transitional provisions) (SI 1994/3106) |
| 269 | | 1 Oct 1993 (subject to transitional provisions) (SI 1993/1975) |
| 270 | | 1 Oct 1993 (SI 1993/1975) |
| 271 | | 1 Jan 1994 (SI 1994/3106) |
| 272, 273 | | 1 Apr 1994 (SI 1994/507) |
| 274–276 | | 1 Jan 1994 (subject to transitional provisions) (SI 1994/3106) |
| 277 | | *Never in force (repealed)* |
| 278 | (1)–(5) | 3 Mar 1994 (SI 1994/507) |
| | (6) | 1 Apr 1994 (subject to transitional provisions) (SI 1994/507) |
| 279 | | 15 Jun 1994 (for purposes of enabling regulations to be made under Education (No 2) Act 1986, s 51(1)–(4)) (SI 1994/1558) |
| | | 1 Apr 1995 (otherwise) (SI 1994/1558) |
| 280 | | 1 Oct 1993 (SI 1993/1975) |
| 281 | | 1 Jan 1994 (SI 1994/3106) |
| 282–286 | | 1 Oct 1993 (SI 1993/1975) |

**Education Act 1993 (c 35)**—*contd*

| | | |
|---|---|---|
| 287, 288 | | 1 Jan 1994 (SI 1994/3106) |
| 289 | | 1 Apr 1994 (SI 1994/507) |
| 290–292 | | 1 Jan 1994 (SI 1994/3106) |
| 293, 294 | | 1 Oct 1993 (SI 1993/1975) |
| 295–297 | | 1 Apr 1994 (SI 1994/507) |
| 298 | (1) | 1 Sep 1994 (SI 1994/2038) |
| | (2) | 1 Aug 1994 (for purpose of defining "pupil referral unit" in relation to regulations made under Sch 18, para 3) (SI 1994/2038) |
| | | 1 Sep 1994 (otherwise) (SI 1994/2038) |
| | (3)–(7) | 1 Sep 1994 (SI 1994/2038) |
| | (8) | See Sch 18 below |
| 299, 300 | | 1 Jan 1994 (SI 1994/3106) |
| 301–303 | | 27 Jul 1993 (RA) |
| 304 | | 1 Apr 1994 (SI 1994/507) |
| 305, 306 | | 27 Jul 1993 (RA) |
| 307 | (1) | See Sch 19 below |
| | (2) | See Sch 20 below |
| | (3) | See Sch 21 below |
| 308 | | 27 Jul 1993 (RA) |
| Schs 1, 2 | | 1 Apr 1994 (SI 1994/507) |
| Sch 3 | Pt I | 1 Jan 1994 (subject to transitional provisions) (SI 1994/3106) |
| | Pt II | 1 Apr 1994 (SI 1994/507) |
| Schs 4–7 | | 1 Jan 1994 (subject to transitional provisions) (SI 1994/3106) |
| Sch 8 | | 1 Apr 1994 (SI 1994/507) |
| Sch 9 | paras 1, 2 | 1 Sep 1994 (subject to transitional provisions) (SI 1994/2038) |
| | para 3 | 1 Apr 1994 (SI 1994/507) |
| | paras 4, 5 | 1 Sep 1994 (subject to transitional provisions) (SI 1994/2038) |
| Sch 10 | paras 1–4 | 1 Sep 1994 (subject to transitional provisions) (SI 1994/2038) |
| | para 5(1), (2) | 1 Sep 1994 (subject to transitional provisions) (SI 1994/2038) |
| | para 5(3) | 1 Apr 1994 (SI 1994/507) |
| | para 5(4) | 1 Sep 1994 (subject to transitional provisions) (SI 1994/2038) |
| | para 6 | 1 Sep 1994 (SI 1994/2038) |
| | para 7 | 1 Apr 1994 (SI 1994/507) |
| | para 8(1)–(4) | 1 Sep 1994 (SI 1994/2038) |
| | para 8(5) | 1 Apr 1994 (SI 1994/507) |
| | para 8(6) | 1 Sep 1994 (SI 1994/2038) |
| | paras 9–11 | 1 Sep 1994 (subject to transitional provisions) (SI 1994/2038) |
| Sch 11 | paras 1–13 | 1 Apr 1994 (SI 1994/507) |
| | para 14 | 1 Jan 1994 (SI 1994/3106) |
| Sch 12 | | 1 Jan 1994 (SI 1994/3106) |
| Sch 13 | | 1 Jan 1994 (subject to transitional provisions) (SI 1994/3106) |
| Sch 14 | | 1 Oct 1993 (SI 1993/1975) |
| Sch 15 | | 1 Apr 1994 (SI 1994/507) |
| Schs 16, 17 | | 1 Jan 1994 (SI 1994/3106) |
| Sch 18 | paras 1, 2 | 1 Sep 1994 (SI 1994/2038) |
| | para 3 | 1 Aug 1994 (SI 1994/2038) |
| | paras 4–14 | 1 Sep 1994 (SI 1994/2038) |
| Sch 19 | para 1 | 1 Oct 1993 (SI 1993/1975) |
| | para 2 | *Never in force* (repealed) |
| | paras 3–5 | 1 Oct 1993 (SI 1993/1975) |
| | para 6 | 1 Apr 1994 (subject to transitional provisions) (SI 1994/507) |
| | para 7 | 1 Jan 1994 (SI 1994/3106) |
| | para 8 | 1 Oct 1993 (SI 1993/1975) |
| | para 9 | 1 Apr 1994 (SI 1994/507) |
| | para 10 | *Never in force* (repealed) |
| | para 11 | 1 Oct 1993 (SI 1993/1975) |
| | paras 12, 13 | 1 Apr 1994 (SI 1994/507) |
| | paras 14, 15 | 1 Oct 1993 (SI 1993/1975) |

**See Halsbury's Statutes Citator for amendments to these Acts**

**Education Act 1993 (c 35)**—*contd*

| | |
|---|---|
| para 16 | 1 Sep 1994 (SI 1994/2038) |
| para 17 | *Never in force* (repealed) |
| paras 18, 19 | 1 Apr 1994 (SI 1994/507) |
| para 20(a) | 1 Oct 1993 (SI 1993/1975) |
| para 20(b) | 1 Apr 1994 (SI 1994/507) |
| para 21 | 1 Apr 1994 (SI 1994/507) |
| para 22 | 1 Jan 1994 (SI 1994/3106) |
| para 23(a)(i) | 1 Oct 1993 (so far as amends Education Act 1944, s 105(2)(c)(i) (insertion of words "or on a transfer of the school to a new site")) (SI 1993/1975) |
| | 1 Jan 1994 (otherwise) (SI 1994/3106) |
| para 23(a)(ii)–(iv) | 1 Jan 1994 (SI 1994/3106) |
| para 23(b) | 1 Apr 1994 (SI 1994/507) |
| para 24(a)(i) | *Never in force* (repealed) |
| para 24(a)(ii), (iii) | 1 Oct 1993 (SI 1993/1975) |
| para 24(a)(iv) | 1 Jan 1994 (SI 1994/3106) |
| para 24(b) | 1 Jan 1994 (subject to transitional provisions) (SI 1994/3106) |
| para 25 | 1 Oct 1993 (SI 1993/1975) |
| paras 26, 27 | 1 Apr 1994 (SI 1994/507) |
| para 28 | 1 Oct 1993 (SI 1993/1975) |
| para 29 | 1 Jan 1994 (SI 1994/3106) |
| para 30 | 1 Oct 1993 (SI 1993/1975) |
| para 31(a) | 1 Sep 1994 (SI 1994/2038) |
| para 31(b)–(f) | *Never in force* (repealed) |
| para 32 | 1 Oct 1993 (SI 1993/1975) |
| para 33 | *Never in force* (repealed) |
| para 34 | 1 Oct 1993 (so far as relates to the Curriculum Council for Wales and the School Curriculum and Assessment Authority) (SI 1993/1975) |
| | 1 Apr 1994 (otherwise) (SI 1994/507) |
| para 35 | 1 Oct 1993 (SI 1993/1975) |
| paras 36, 37 | *Never in force* (repealed) |
| para 38 | 1 Apr 1994 (SI 1994/507) |
| para 39 | 1 Jan 1994 (SI 1994/3106) |
| paras 40–43 | 1 Oct 1993 (SI 1993/1975) |
| para 44 | 1 Sep 1994 (SI 1994/2038) |
| para 45 | *Never in force* (repealed) |
| paras 46–52 | 1 Apr 1994 (subject to transitional provisions relating to paras 49, 50) (SI 1994/507) |
| para 53 | *Never in force* (repealed) |
| para 54(a) | 1 Sep 1994 (SI 1994/2038) |
| para 54(b) | *Never in force* (repealed) |
| para 55(a) | 1 Apr 1994 (SI 1994/507) |
| para 55(b) | 1 Jan 1994 (SI 1994/3106) |
| para 56 | 1 Oct 1993 (SI 1993/1975) |
| para 57 | 1 Apr 1994 (SI 1994/507) |
| para 58 | *Never in force* (repealed) |
| para 59 | 1 Apr 1994 (SI 1994/507) |
| para 60 | *Never in force* (repealed) |
| paras 61, 62 | 1 Apr 1994 (SI 1994/507) |
| para 63 | *Never in force* (repealed) |
| para 64 | 1 Oct 1993 (SI 1993/1975) (also purported to be brought into force on 1 Apr 1994 by SI 1994/507) |
| paras 65, 66 | 1 Apr 1994 (SI 1994/507) |
| para 67 | *Never in force* (repealed) |
| paras 68, 69 | 1 Oct 1993 (SI 1993/1975) |
| para 70 | 1 Apr 1994 (SI 1994/507) |
| para 71 | *Never in force* (repealed) |
| para 72 | 1 Oct 1993 (SI 1993/1975) |

**Education Act 1993 (c 35)**—*contd*

| | |
|---|---|
| para 73 | 1 Apr 1994 (SI 1994/507) |
| para 74 | 1 Sep 1994 (SI 1994/2038) |
| para 75 | 1 Oct 1993 (SI 1993/1975) |
| para 76 | 1 Apr 1994 (SI 1994/507) |
| para 77(a) | 1 Oct 1993 (SI 1993/1975) |
| para 77(b) | 1 Apr 1994 (SI 1994/507) |
| para 78 | 1 Oct 1993 (SI 1993/1975) |
| para 79 | 1 Apr 1994 (SI 1994/507) |
| para 80 | 1 Oct 1993 (SI 1993/1975) |
| para 81 | 1 Apr 1994 (SI 1994/507) |
| para 82 | 1 Jan 1994 (so far as repeals Education Act 1981, s 1) (SI 1994/3106) |
| | 3 Mar 1994 (so far as repeals Education Act 1981, s 7(10)) (subject to a saving) (SI 1994/507) |
| | 1 Apr 1994 (so far as repeals Education Act 1981, ss 2(4)–(7), 3, 11(2), (3), 12–14, Sch 1, paras 1(3), 4, Sch 3, paras 1, 2, 10, 13) (subject to transitional provisions and savings) (SI 1994/507) |
| | 1 Sep 1994 (otherwise) (subject to transitional provisions and savings) (SI 1994/2038) |
| para 83 | 1 Jan 1994 (SI 1994/3106) |
| para 84 | 1 Oct 1993 (SI 1993/1975) |
| paras 85, 86 | 1 Apr 1994 (SI 1994/507) |
| para 87(a) | 1 Sep 1994 (SI 1994/2038) |
| para 87(b) | 1 Apr 1994 (SI 1994/507) |
| para 87(c) | 1 Sep 1994 (SI 1994/2038) |
| para 88 | 1 Sep 1994 (SI 1994/2038) |
| para 89 | 1 Apr 1994 (SI 1994/507) |
| para 90 | 1 Jan 1994 (so far as provides for Education (No 2) Act 1986, s 9(5), to have effect as if the transfer of a school to a new site in pursuance of Education Act 1980, s 16(1A)(c) were an alteration of the kind mentioned in sub-s (5) of that section) (SI 1994/3106) |
| | 1 Apr 1994 (otherwise) (SI 1994/507) |
| paras 91–94 | 1 Apr 1994 (SI 1994/507) |
| paras 95, 96 | 1 Sep 1994 (SI 1994/2038) |
| para 97(a) | 1 Aug 1994 (for purpose of prescribing the period within which, under the articles of government for county, voluntary controlled and maintained special schools, the governing body are to be required to express their views to the local education authority as to the reinstatement of a permanently excluded pupil) (SI 1994/2038) |
| | 1 Sep 1994 (otherwise) (SI 1994/2038) |
| para 97(b)–(d) | 1 Sep 1994 (SI 1994/2038) |
| para 98(a) | 1 Aug 1994 (for purpose of prescribing the period within which, under the articles of government for voluntary aided and special agreement schools, the governing body are to be required to express their views to the local education authority as to the reinstatement of a permanently excluded pupil) (SI 1994/2038) |
| | 1 Sep 1994 (otherwise) (SI 1994/2038) |
| para 98(b) | 1 Sep 1994 (SI 1994/2038) |
| paras 99, 100 | 1 Apr 1994 (SI 1994/507) |
| para 101(a) | 1 Sep 1994 (SI 1994/2038) |
| para 101(b) | 1 Apr 1994 (SI 1994/507) |
| para 102 | 1 Apr 1994 (subject to transitional provisions) (SI 1994/507) |
| paras 103, 104 | 1 Apr 1995 (SI 1994/1558) |
| paras 105, 106 | 1 Apr 1994 (SI 1994/507) |
| para 107 | 1 Apr 1995 (SI 1994/1558) |
| para 108 | 1 Apr 1994 (SI 1994/507) |

**Education Act 1993 (c 35)**—*contd*

| | |
|---|---|
| para 109(a) | 1 Jan 1994 (SI 1994/3106) |
| para 109(b)(i) | 1 Jan 1994 (SI 1994/3106) |
| para 109(b)(ii) | 1 Apr 1994 (SI 1994/507) |
| para 109(c), (d) | 1 Apr 1994 (SI 1994/507) |
| para 109(e) | 1 Jan 1994 (SI 1994/3106) |
| paras 110, 111 | 1 Apr 1994 (subject to transitional provisions) (SI 1994/507) |
| para 112 | 1 Oct 1993 (SI 1993/1975) |
| para 113(a) | 1 Apr 1994 (SI 1994/507) |
| para 113(b) | *Never in force* (repealed) |
| paras 114–117 | 1 Apr 1994 (SI 1994/507) |
| para 118(a) | 1 Jan 1994 (SI 1994/3106) |
| para 118(b)–(d) | 1 Oct 1993 (subject to transitional provisions) (SI 1993/1975) |
| para 118(e) | 1 Jan 1994 (SI 1994/3106) |
| para 119 | 1 Oct 1993 (SI 1993/1975) |
| paras 120, 121 | 1 Sep 1994 (SI 1994/2038) |
| para 122 | 1 Oct 1993 (SI 1993/1975) |
| para 123 | 1 Jan 1994 (SI 1994/3106) |
| para 124 | 1 Oct 1993 (SI 1993/1975) |
| para 125(a) | 3 Mar 1994 (SI 1994/507) |
| para 125(b) | 1 Apr 1994 (SI 1994/507) |
| para 126 | 1 Jan 1994 (so far as repeals Education Reform Act 1988, ss 52(3)–(9), 53–56, 58–72, 74–78, 104(1)(a), (b), (f)–(h), (2), (3) (definition "incorporation date" only)) (subject to transitional provisions) (SI 1994/3106) |
| | 1 Apr 1994 (otherwise) (subject to transitional provisions) (SI 1994/507) |
| paras 127–129 | 1 Apr 1994 (SI 1994/507) |
| para 130 | 1 Jan 1994 (so far as repeals reference to "52(4)" in Education Reform Act 1988, s 119(2)) (subject to transitional provisions) (SI 1994/3106) |
| | 1 Apr 1994 (otherwise) (SI 1994/507) |
| paras 131, 132 | 1 Oct 1993 (SI 1993/1975) |
| paras 133–135 | 1 Jan 1994 (subject to transitional provisions) (SI 1994/3106) |
| para 136 | 1 Apr 1994 (SI 1994/507) |
| para 137 | 1 Jan 1994 (so far as repeals words "section 74 (taken with Schedule 10)" in Education Reform Act 1988, s 230(1)) (subject to transitional provisions) (SI 1994/3106) |
| | 1 Apr 1994 (otherwise) (SI 1994/507) |
| para 138(a) | 1 Jan 1994 (SI 1994/3106) |
| para 138(b)(i) | 1 Jan 1994 (so far as repeals references to "58(2), 59(1)" and "102" in Education Reform Act 1988, s 232(2)) (SI 1994/3106) |
| | 1 Apr 1994 (otherwise) (SI 1994/507) |
| para 138(b)(ii) | 1 Jan 1994 (SI 1994/3106) |
| para 139(a)(i) | 1 Sep 1994 (SI 1994/2038) |
| para 139(a)(ii) | 1 Jan 1994 (subject to transitional provisions) (SI 1994/3106) |
| para 139(b), (c) | 1 Jan 1994 (subject to transitional provisions) (SI 1994/3106) |
| para 140 | 1 Apr 1994 (SI 1994/507) |
| para 141 | 1 Oct 1993 (SI 1993/1975) |
| para 142 | 1 Apr 1994 (SI 1994/507) |
| paras 143, 144 | 1 Jan 1994 (subject to transitional provisions) (SI 1994/3106) |
| para 145 | 1 Apr 1994 (so far as repeals Education Reform Act 1988, Sch 12, paras 26, 33) (SI 1994/507) |
| | 1 Sep 1994 (otherwise) (SI 1994/2038) |
| para 146 | *Never in force* (repealed) |
| paras 147, 148 | 1 Sep 1994 (SI 1994/2038) |
| para 149 | 1 Oct 1993 (SI 1993/1975) |
| para 150 | 1 Jan 1994 (SI 1994/3106) |
| para 151 | 1 Sep 1994 (SI 1994/2038) |
| para 152 | 1 Oct 1993 (SI 1993/1975) |

**Education Act 1993 (c 35)**—*contd*

| | | |
|---|---|---|
| | para 153 | 1 Jan 1994 (SI 1994/3106) |
| | para 154 | 1 Oct 1993 (so far as relates to Children Act 1989, Sch 12, para 4) (SI 1993/1975) |
| | | 1 Sep 1994 (otherwise) (SI 1994/2038) |
| | para 155 | 1 Oct 1993 (SI 1993/1975) |
| | paras 156–159 | 1 Apr 1994 (subject to transitional provisions relating to para 156(a), (b), (d)) (SI 1994/507) |
| | para 160 | 1 Sep 1994 (SI 1994/2038) |
| | para 161 | 1 Apr 1994 (SI 1994/507) |
| | para 162 | 1 Jan 1994 (SI 1994/3106) |
| | para 163(a) | 1 Jan 1994 (subject to transitional provisions) (SI 1994/3106) |
| | para 163(b) | 1 Apr 1994 (SI 1994/507) |
| | para 163(c) | 1 Jan 1994 (subject to transitional provisions) (SI 1994/3106) |
| | para 164 | 1 Jan 1994 (subject to transitional provisions) (SI 1994/3106) |
| | paras 165, 166 | 1 Jan 1994 (SI 1994/3106) |
| | para 167(a) | 1 Apr 1994 (SI 1994/507) |
| | para 167(b) | 1 Jan 1994 (SI 1994/3106) |
| | paras 168, 169 | 1 Apr 1994 (SI 1994/507) |
| | para 170 | 1 Oct 1993 (SI 1993/1975) |
| | paras 171, 172 | 1 Apr 1994 (SI 1994/507) |
| | para 173(1)(a) | 1 Apr 1994 (SI 1994/507) |
| | para 173(1)(b) | 1 Oct 1993 (SI 1993/1975) |
| | para 173(1)(c) | 1 Sep 1993 (SI 1993/1975) |
| | para 173(2), (3) | 1 Aug 1993 (for purpose of prescribing matters which fall to be prescribed under Education (Schools) Act 1992, Sch 2) (SI 1993/1975) |
| | | 1 Sep 1993 (otherwise) (SI 1993/1975) |
| | para 173(4) | 1 Sep 1993 (SI 1993/1975) |
| | para 173(5), (6) | 1 Aug 1993 (for purpose of prescribing matters which fall to be prescribed under Education (Schools) Act 1992, Sch 2) (subject to transitional provisions) (SI 1993/1975) |
| | | 1 Sep 1993 (otherwise) (subject to transitional provisions) (SI 1993/1975) |
| | para 173(7) | 1 Sep 1993 (SI 1993/1975) |
| | para 173(8)(a) | 1 Aug 1993 (for purpose of prescribing matters which fall to be prescribed under Education (Schools) Act 1992, Sch 2) (SI 1993/1975) |
| | | 1 Oct 1993 (otherwise) (SI 1993/1975) |
| | para 173(8)(b) | 1 Oct 1993 (SI 1993/1975) |
| | para 173(9)(a) | 1 Aug 1993 (for purpose of prescribing matters which fall to be prescribed under Education (Schools) Act 1992, Sch 2) (SI 1993/1975) |
| | | 1 Oct 1993 (otherwise) (SI 1993/1975) |
| | para 173(9)(b) | 1 Oct 1993 (SI 1993/1975) |
| | para 174 | 1 Jan 1994 (SI 1994/3106) |
| | para 175 | 1 Oct 1993 (SI 1993/1975) |
| Sch 20 | para 1 | 1 Jan 1994 (SI 1994/3106) |
| | para 2 | 1 Apr 1994 (SI 1994/507) |
| | para 3 | 1 Jan 1994 (SI 1994/3106) |
| | para 4 | 1 Apr 1994 (SI 1994/507) |
| | paras 5–7 | 1 Jan 1994 (SI 1994/3106) |
| Sch 21 | | 1 Oct 1993 (SI 1993/1975), repeals of or in— |
| | | Children and Young Persons Act 1933, s 10; |
| | | Education Act 1944, ss 1, 6, 16, 37, 39, 40, 114, Sch 8; |
| | | Education (Miscellaneous Provisions) Act 1948, s 9; |
| | | Education (Miscellaneous Provisions) Act 1953, s 10; |
| | | Criminal Justice Act 1967; |
| | | Education Act 1968, s 3, Sch 1, para 1; |
| | | Children and Young Persons Act 1969; |
| | | Criminal Law Act 1977; |

**See Halsbury's Statutes Citator for amendments to these Acts**

**Education Act 1993 (c 35)**—*contd*

Education Act 1980, ss 10, 11, Sch 1, para 10;
Education Reform Act 1988, ss 14(4), (5), 25, Sch 2, para 18;
Children Act 1989, s 36, Sch 13

1 Jan 1994 (subject to transitional provisions) (SI 1994/3106),
repeals of or in—
Education Act 1944, ss 102, 103, 105(2);
Education Act 1967, s 1;
Superannuation Act 1972, Sch 1;
House of Commons Disqualification Act 1975, Sch 1;
Education Act 1981, s 1;
Education Reform Act 1988, ss 14(1), 42, 52(3)–(9), 53–56,
58–72, 74–78, 102, 103, 104(1)(a), (b), (f)–(h), (2), (3)
(definition "incorporation date" only), 119(2) (reference to
"52(4)" only), 198(1), 200, 230(1) (words "section 74 (taken
with Schedule 10)" only), 232(2) (references to "58(2), 59(1)"
and "102" only), (4)(b), 235 (except definition "the 1981 Act"
in sub-s (1)), Sch 2, paras 1, 9 (entries relating to membership
of the National Curriculum Council and the School
Examinations and Assessment Council only), 10(5) (entries
relating to National Curriculum Council and the School
Examinations and Assessment Council only), Sch 4, para 2,
Sch 5;
Children Act 1989, Sch 12, para 4;
Diocesan Boards of Education Measure 1991, s 3(6)

3 Mar 1994 (subject to a saving) (SI 1994/507), repeals of or in—
Education Act 1981, s 7(10);
Education (Grants and Awards) Act 1984

1 Apr 1994 (subject to savings and transitional provisions), repeals
of or in—
Education Act 1944, ss 9(5), 50(1), 52(1), Sch 1, Pts I, II, Sch 5,
para 13;
Local Government Act 1972;
Education Act 1973, s 1;
Education Act 1980, ss 12(3), 13(1), (3), 14(4), Sch 2, para 1,
Sch 3, paras 4, 13;
Education Act 1981, ss 2(4)–(7), 3, 11(2), (3), 12–14, Sch 1,
paras 1(3), 4, Sch 3, paras 1, 2, 10, 13;
Education (No 2) Act 1986, ss 5(4), 9(5), 11, 12(3), 13(2), 38,
50, 54(12), 65(1), Sch 2;
Education Reform Act 1988, ss 52(1), (2), 57, 73, 79–101,
104(1)(c)–(e), (i), (j), (3) (except definition "incorporation
date"), (4), 111, 119(2) (so far as repeals in that section not
already in force), 230 (so far as repeals in that section not
already in force), 232 (so far as repeals in that section not
already in force), Sch 1, para 9, Sch 2, paras 9, 10, Sch 12,
paras 26, 33;
Local Government Act 1988;
Local Government and Housing Act 1989;
Planning (Consequential Provisions) Act 1990;
Further and Higher Education Act 1992, ss 13, 59(5), Sch 8,
paras 18, 29;
Local Government Finance Act 1992

1 Sep 1994 (SI 1994/2038) (subject to transitional provisions and
savings), repeals of or in—
Education Act 1944, s 56;
Education Act 1981, ss 2(2), (3), 3A, 4–6, 7(1)–(9), (11), 8–10,
15, 16, 18, 19, 20(1) (except definition "principal Act"), Sch 1,
paras 1(1), (2), 2, 3, 5–7, Sch 2, paras 2–8, Sch 3, paras 8(2)(a),
(c), 9, 15, 16;
Education (No 2) Act 1986, ss 23–25;

**Education Act 1993 (c 35)**—*contd*

> Education Reform Act 1988, s 235(1) (definition "the 1981
> Act"), Sch 12, paras 27, 28, 83–85;
> Children Act 1989, s 27(4), Sch 12, para 36;
> National Health Service and Community Care Act 1990
> 1 Apr 1995 (repeals of Education (No 2) Act 1986, ss 51(9), (13),
> 63(4)) (SI 1994/1558)
> *Never in force* (otherwise) (repealed)

---

**European Communities (Amendment) Act 1993 (c 32)**

*RA:* 20 Jul 1993

*Commencement provisions:* s 7

Whole Act in force 23 Jul 1993 (s 7)

---

**European Economic Area Act 1993 (c 51)**

*RA:* 5 Nov 1993

Whole Act in force 5 Nov 1993 (RA)

---

**European Parliamentary Elections Act 1993 (c 41)**

*RA:* 5 Nov 1993

*Commencement provisions:* s 3(3); European Parliamentary Elections Act 1993 (Commencement)
Order 1994, SI 1994/1089

| | |
|---|---|
| 1 | 1 May 1994 (SI 1994/1089) |
| 2, 3 | 5 Nov 1993 (RA) |
| Schedule | 5 Nov 1993 (RA) |

---

**Finance Act 1993 (c 34)**

*Budget Day:* 16 Mar 1993

*RA:* 27 Jul 1993

The commencement details of Finance Acts are not set out, as the dates from which their provisions take
effect are usually stated clearly and unambiguously in the text of the Act, and charging provisions will
normally state for which year or years of assessment they are to have effect.

---

**Foreign Compensation (Amendment) Act 1993 (c 16)**

*RA:* 27 May 1993

*Commencement provisions:* s 3(1)

Whole Act in force 27 Jul 1993 (s 3(1))

---

**Gas (Exempt Supplies) Act 1993 (c 1)**

*RA:* 19 Jan 1993

*Commencement provisions:* s 4(2); Gas (Exempt Supplies) Act 1993 (Commencement) Order 1994,
SI 1994/2568

**Gas (Exempt Supplies) Act 1993 (c 1)**—*contd*

Whole Act in force 31 Oct 1994 (SI 1994/2568)

**Health Service Commissioners Act 1993 (c 46)**

*RA:* 5 Nov 1993

*Commencement provisions:* s 22(4)

Whole Act in force 5 Feb 1994 (s 22(4))

**Incumbents (Vacation of Benefices) (Amendment) Measure 1993 (No 1)**

*RA:* 27 Jul 1993

*Commencement provisions:* s 16(2)

The provisions of this Measure are brought into force on 1 Sep 1994 by an appointed day notice signed by the Archbishops of Canterbury and York and dated 25 Jul 1994 (made under s 16(2))

**Judicial Pensions and Retirement Act 1993 (c 8)**

*RA:* 29 Mar 1993

*Commencement provisions:* s 31(2); Judicial Pensions and Retirement Act 1993 (Commencement) Order 1995, SI 1995/631

Whole Act in force 31 Mar 1995 (SI 1995/631)

**Leasehold Reform, Housing and Urban Development Act 1993 (c 28)**

*RA:* 20 Jul 1993

*Commencement provisions:* ss 138(2), 188(2), (3); Leasehold Reform, Housing and Urban Development Act 1993 (Commencement and Transitional Provisions No 1) Order 1993, SI 1993/2134; Leasehold Reform, Housing and Urban Development Act 1993 (Commencement No 2) (Scotland) Order 1993, SI 1993/2163; Leasehold Reform, Housing and Urban Development Act 1993 (Commencement and Transitional Provisions No 3) Order 1993, SI 1993/2762; Leasehold Reform, Housing and Urban Development Act 1993 (Commencement No 4) Order 1994, SI 1994/935

| | | |
|---|---|---|
| 1–25 | | 1 Nov 1993 (SI 1993/2134) |
| 26 | (1)–(8) | 1 Nov 1993 (SI 1993/2134) |
| | (9) | 2 Sep 1993 (SI 1993/2134) |
| 27–66 | | 1 Nov 1993 (SI 1993/2134) |
| 67, 68 | | 1 Nov 1993 (subject to savings) (SI 1993/2134) |
| 69–74 | | 1 Nov 1993 (SI 1993/2134) |
| 75 | | 2 Sep 1993 (so far as confers on Secretary of State a power to make orders, regulations or declarations) (SI 1993/2134) |
| | | 1 Nov 1993 (otherwise) (SI 1993/2134) |
| 76–84 | | 1 Nov 1993 (SI 1993/2134) |
| 85, 86 | | 1 Nov 1993 (subject to savings) (SI 1993/2134) |
| 87 | | 1 Nov 1993 (SI 1993/2134) |
| 88 | | 2 Sep 1993 (so far as confers on Secretary of State a power to make orders, regulations or declarations) (SI 1993/2134) |
| | | 1 Nov 1993 (otherwise) (SI 1993/2134) |
| 89, 90 | | 1 Nov 1993 (SI 1993/2134) |
| 91 | | 2 Sep 1993 (so far as confers on Secretary of State a power to make orders, regulations or declarations) (SI 1993/2134) |
| | | 1 Nov 1993 (otherwise) (SI 1993/2134) |
| 92–97 | | 1 Nov 1993 (SI 1993/2134) |

**Leasehold Reform, Housing and Urban Development Act 1993 (c 28)**—*contd*

| | | |
|---|---|---|
| 98 | | 2 Sep 1993 (SI 1993/2134) |
| 99 | | 2 Sep 1993 (so far as confers on Secretary of State a power to make orders, regulations or declarations) (SI 1993/2134) |
| | | 1 Nov 1993 (otherwise) (SI 1993/2134) |
| 100 | | 2 Sep 1993 (SI 1993/2134) |
| 101–103 | | 1 Nov 1993 (SI 1993/2134) |
| 104–107 | | 11 Oct 1993 (subject to savings) (SI 1993/2134) |
| 108 | | 2 Sep 1993 (so far as confers on Secretary of State a power to make orders, regulations or declarations) (SI 1993/2134) |
| | | 11 Oct 1993 (otherwise) (subject to savings) (SI 1993/2134) |
| 109–120 | | 11 Oct 1993 (subject to savings) (SI 1993/2134) |
| 121 | | 1 Dec 1993 (subject to transitional provisions) (SI 1993/2762) |
| 122 | | 1 Feb 1994 (subject to transitional provisions) (SI 1993/2762) |
| 123 | | 11 Oct 1993 (SI 1993/2134) |
| 124, 125 | | 11 Oct 1993 (subject to savings) (SI 1993/2134) |
| 126, 127 | | 20 Jul 1993 (RA) |
| 128, 129 | | 11 Oct 1993 (SI 1993/2134) |
| 130 | | 11 Oct 1993 (subject to savings) (SI 1993/2134) |
| 131 | | 11 Oct 1993 (SI 1993/2134) |
| 132 | | 10 Nov 1993 (so far as confers on the Secretary of State a power to make regulations) (SI 1993/2762) |
| | | 1 Apr 1994 (otherwise) (SI 1994/935) |
| 133, 134 | | 11 Oct 1993 (subject to savings) (SI 1993/2134) |
| 135–137 | | 20 Jul 1993 (RA) |
| 138 | | 1 Jan 1993 (s 138(2)) |
| 139 | | 1 Jan 1993 (s 139(7)) |
| 140 | | 20 Jul 1993 (RA) |
| 141–145 | | 27 Sep 1993 (SI 1993/2163) |
| 146, 147 | | 1 Apr 1994 (SI 1993/2163) |
| 148 | | 27 Sep 1993 (SI 1993/2163) |
| 149–151 | | 20 Jul 1993 (RA) |
| 152, 153 | | 1 Apr 1994 (SI 1993/2163) |
| 154–157 | | 27 Sep 1993 (SI 1993/2163) |
| 158–173 | | 10 Nov 1993 (SI 1993/2762) |
| 174 | | 11 Oct 1993 (SI 1993/2134) |
| 175 | | 10 Nov 1993 (SI 1993/2762) |
| 176 | | 11 Oct 1993 (SI 1993/2134) |
| 177 | | 10 Nov 1993 (SI 1993/2762) |
| 178 | | 11 Oct 1993 (subject to savings) (SI 1993/2134) |
| 179 | | 11 Oct 1993 (SI 1993/2134) |
| 180 | | 11 Oct 1993 (except so far as relates to insertion of s 165A(2) of the 1980 Act) (SI 1993/2134) |
| | | 10 Nov 1993 (otherwise) (SI 1993/2762) |
| 181 | (1), (2) | 20 Jul 1993 (RA) |
| | (3) | 10 Nov 1993 (SI 1993/2762) |
| | (4) | 20 Jul 1993 (RA) |
| 182 | | 11 Oct 1993 (SI 1993/2134) |
| 183 | | 10 Nov 1993 (SI 1993/2762) |
| 184 | | 1 Apr 1994 (subject to transitional provisions) (SI 1994/935) |
| 185 | | 10 Nov 1993 (SI 1993/2762) |
| 186 | | 20 Jul 1993 (RA) |
| 187 | (1) | See Sch 21 below |
| | (2) | See Sch 22 below |
| 188 | | 20 Jul 1993 (RA) |
| Schs 1–15 | | 1 Nov 1993 (SI 1993/2134) |
| Sch 16 | | 11 Oct 1993 (subject to savings) (SI 1993/2134) |
| Schs 17–20 | | 10 Nov 1993 (SI 1993/2762) |
| Sch 21 | para 1 | 1 Nov 1993 (SI 1993/2134) |
| | para 2 | *Never in force* (repealed) |

**Leasehold Reform, Housing and Urban Development Act 1993 (c 28)**—*contd*

|  |  |  |
|--|--|--|
| | para 3 | 10 Nov 1993 (SI 1993/2762) |
| | para 4 | 2 Sep 1993 (SI 1993/2134) |
| | para 5 | 1 Nov 1993 (subject to savings) (SI 1993/2134) |
| | para 6 | 10 Nov 1993 (SI 1993/2762) |
| | para 7 | 2 Sep 1993 (SI 1993/2134) |
| | para 8 | 10 Nov 1993 (SI 1993/2762) |
| | para 9 | 1 Nov 1993 (SI 1993/2134) |
| | para 10 | 11 Oct 1993 (SI 1993/2134) |
| | paras 11–25 | 11 Oct 1993 (subject to savings) (SI 1993/2134) |
| | para 26 | 1 Nov 1993 (SI 1993/2134) |
| | para 27 | 2 Sep 1993 (SI 1993/2134) |
| | paras 28, 29 | 10 Nov 1993 (SI 1993/2762) |
| | para 30 | 1 Nov 1993 (SI 1993/2134) |
| | paras 31, 32 | 10 Nov 1993 (SI 1993/2762) |

Sch 22　　　　　　　20 Jul 1993 (repeal in Local Government and Housing Act 1989,
　　　　　　　　　　　　s 80(1)) (RA)

　　　　　　　　　　2 Sep 1993 (SI 1993/2134), repeals of—
　　　　　　　　　　Housing Act 1988, s 41(1);
　　　　　　　　　　Local Government and Housing Act 1989, Sch 11, para 51

　　　　　　　　　　27 Sep 1993 (repeals in Housing Scotland Act 1987)
　　　　　　　　　　　　(SI 1993/2163)

　　　　　　　　　　11 Oct 1993 (SI 1993/2134), repeals in—
　　　　　　　　　　Local Government, Planning and Land Act 1980;
　　　　　　　　　　Housing Act 1988, s 69(2)

　　　　　　　　　　11 Oct 1993 (subject to savings) (SI 1993/2134), repeals of or in—
　　　　　　　　　　Housing Act 1985, ss 124(3), 128(6), 132–135, 137, 138(1),
　　　　　　　　　　　　139(3), 140(5), 142, 153A(1), 153B(1), 164(6), 166(6), 169(3),
　　　　　　　　　　　　171C(2), 171H, 177, 180, 181(1), 182(1), 187, 188, Schs 6–9;
　　　　　　　　　　Housing and Planning Act 1986, Sch 5, para 5;
　　　　　　　　　　Housing Act 1988, s 79;
　　　　　　　　　　Local Government and Housing Act 1989, s 164

　　　　　　　　　　1 Nov 1993 (SI 1993/2134), repeals in—
　　　　　　　　　　Housing Act 1980;
　　　　　　　　　　Housing (Consequential Provisions) Act 1985

　　　　　　　　　　1 Nov 1993 (repeals in Landlord and Tenant Act 1987) (subject to
　　　　　　　　　　　　savings) (SI 1993/2134)

　　　　　　　　　　10 Nov 1993 (repeal in Land Compensation Act 1961)
　　　　　　　　　　　　(SI 1993/2762)

　　　　　　　　　　1 Apr 1994 (repeal of English Industrial Estates Corporation
　　　　　　　　　　　　Act 1981) (subject to transitional provisions) (SI 1994/935)

　　　　　　　　　　*Not yet in force*, repeals of or in—
　　　　　　　　　　House of Commons Disqualification Act 1975;
　　　　　　　　　　Northern Ireland Assembly Disqualification Act 1975;
　　　　　　　　　　Industrial Development Act 1982;
　　　　　　　　　　Miscellaneous Financial Provisions Act 1983;
　　　　　　　　　　Housing Act 1985, s 27C;
　　　　　　　　　　Industrial Development Act 1985;
　　　　　　　　　　Housing Act 1988, Sch 9, para 12(2);
　　　　　　　　　　Planning (Consequential Provisions) Act 1990

---

**Licensing (Amendment) (Scotland) Act 1993 (c 20)**

*RA:* 1 Jul 1993

Whole Act in force 1 Jul 1993 (RA)

---

## Local Government (Amendment) Act 1993 (c 27)

*RA:* 20 Jul 1993

*Commencement provisions:* s 3(2)

Whole Act in force 20 Sep 1993 (s 3(2))

## Local Government (Overseas Assistance) Act 1993 (c 25)

*RA:* 20 Jul 1993

*Commencement provisions:* s 2(2)

Whole Act in force 20 Sep 1993 (s 2(2))

## Merchant Shipping (Registration, etc) Act 1993 (c 22)

*RA:* 1 Jul 1993

*Commencement provisions:* s 10(2), (3); Merchant Shipping (Registration, etc) Act 1993 (Commencement No 1 and Transitional Provisions) Order 1993, SI 1993/3137

| | | |
|---|---|---|
| 1–7 | | 21 Mar 1994 (SI 1993/3137) |
| 8 | (1) | See Sch 2 below |
| | (2) | See Sch 3 below |
| | (3) | See Sch 4 below |
| | (4) | See Sch 5 below |
| 9, 10 | | 21 Mar 1994 (SI 1993/3137) |
| Schs 1–3 | | 21 Mar 1994 (SI 1993/3137) |
| Sch 4 | paras 1–17 | 1 May 1994 (SI 1993/3137) |
| | para 18 | *Never in force* (repealed) |
| | paras 19–35 | 1 May 1994 (SI 1993/3137) |
| | para 36 | *Never in force* (repealed) |
| | paras 37–51 | 1 May 1994 (SI 1993/3137) |
| | para 52 | *Never in force* (repealed) |
| | para 53 | 1 May 1994 (SI 1993/3137) |
| | para 54 | 1 May 1994 (except so far as repeals Merchant Shipping (Mercantile Marine Fund) Act 1898, s 2(3), so far as that provision applies to the lighthouse at Sombrero in the Leeward Islands) (SI 1993/3137) |
| | | *Never in force* (exception noted above) (repealed) |
| | paras 55–79 | 1 May 1994 (SI 1993/3137) |
| Sch 5 | Pt I | 21 Mar 1994 (SI 1993/3137)[1] |
| | Pt II | 1 May 1994 (SI 1993/3137), except repeals of or in— |
| | | Merchant Shipping Act 1894, ss 634, 669; |
| | | Merchant Shipping (Mercantile Marine Fund) Act 1898, s 2(3), so far as that provision applies to the lighthouse at Sombrero in the Leeward Islands; |
| | | Merchant Shipping (Safety Convention) Act 1949, ss 28(1), 33(2) |
| | | *Never in force* (exceptions noted above) (repealed) |

[1]  For savings relating to registration under, and instruments made under, certain provisions repealed by this Act, see SI 1993/3137, arts 4, 5, 7, Sch 3. Note also that by SI 1993/3137, art 3(2), Sch 2, Appendix, the Merchant Shipping (Safety Convention) Act 1949, s 28(1), remains in force for the sole purpose of enabling exemptions to be made from the requirements of rules made under the Merchant Shipping Act 1894, s 427, and rules made under s 3 of the 1949 Act, and that s 33(2) of the 1949 Act remains in force for the sole purpose of enabling regulations to be made prescribing maximum fees for measurement of a ship's tonnage

## National Lottery etc Act 1993 (c 39)

*RA:* 21 Oct 1993

*Commencement provisions:* s 65; National Lottery etc Act 1993 (Commencement No 1 and Transitional Provisions) Order 1993, SI 1993/2632; National Lottery etc Act 1993 (Commencement No 2 and Transitional Provisions) Order 1994, SI 1994/1055; National Lottery etc Act 1993 (Commencement No 3) Order 1994, SI 1994/2659

| | | |
|---|---|---|
| 1–15 | | 25 Oct 1993 (SI 1993/2632) |
| 16 | | 21 Dec 1993 (SI 1993/2632) |
| 17 | | 25 Oct 1993 (SI 1993/2632) |
| 18 | | 21 Dec 1993 (subject to transitional provisions) (SI 1993/2632) |
| 19, 20 | | 25 Oct 1993 (SI 1993/2632) |
| 21–25 | | 21 Dec 1993 (SI 1993/2632) |
| 26 | (1) | 25 Oct 1993 (SI 1993/2632) |
| | (2) | 21 Dec 1993 (SI 1993/2632) |
| | (3)–(5) | 25 Oct 1993 (SI 1993/2632) |
| 27–39 | | 21 Dec 1993 (SI 1993/2632) |
| 40–44 | | 25 Oct 1993 (SI 1993/2632) |
| 45–47 | | 21 Dec 1993 (SI 1993/2632) |
| 48, 49 | | 3 May 1994 (subject to transitional provisions relating to s 48(3)) (SI 1994/1055) |
| 50 | | 3 Oct 1994 (SI 1994/1055) |
| 51–55 | | 3 May 1994 (subject to transitional provisions relating to s 52(4), (7), (8)) (SI 1994/1055) |
| 56–59 | | 14 Nov 1994 (SI 1994/2659) |
| 60–63 | | 25 Oct 1993 (SI 1993/2632) |
| 64 | | See Sch 10 below |
| 65, 66 | | 25 Oct 1993 (SI 1993/2632) |
| Schs 1–3 | | 25 Oct 1993 (SI 1993/2632) |
| Schs 4, 5 | | 21 Dec 1993 (SI 1993/2632) |
| Sch 6 | | 25 Oct 1993 (SI 1993/2632) |
| Schs 7, 8 | | 3 May 1994 (subject to transitional provisions relating to Sch 7, Pt I, para 7) (SI 1994/1055) |
| Sch 9 | | 3 Oct 1994 (SI 1994/1055) |
| Sch 10 | | 21 Dec 1993 (SI 1993/2632), repeals in— |
| | | Revenue Act 1898; |
| | | National Heritage Act 1980 |
| | | 3 May 1994 (otherwise) (SI 1994/1055) |

## Noise and Statutory Nuisance Act 1993 (c 40)

*RA:* 5 Nov 1993

*Commencement provisions:* s 12

| | |
|---|---|
| 1–8 | 5 Jan 1994 (s 12(1)) |
| 9 | *Never in force* (repealed) |
| 10–14 | 5 Jan 1994 (s 12(1)) |
| Schs 1, 2 | 5 Jan 1994 (s 12(1)) |
| Sch 3 | *Never in force* (repealed) |

## Non-Domestic Rating Act 1993 (c 17)

*RA:* 27 May 1993

*Commencement provisions:* s 6(2); Non-Domestic Rating Act 1993 (Commencement No 1) Order 1993, SI 1993/1418; Non-Domestic Rating Act 1993 (Commencement No 2) Order 1993, SI 1993/1512

| | | |
|---|---|---|
| 1 | (1) | 6 Jul 1993 (SI 1993/1512) |
| | (2) | 4 Jun 1993 (SI 1993/1418) |

**Non-Domestic Rating Act 1993 (c 17)**—*contd*

|  |  |  |
|---|---|---|
| (3)–(5) | 6 Jul 1993 (SI 1993/1512) |
| 2, 3 | 6 Jul 1993 (SI 1993/1512) |
| 4 | 4 Jun 1993 (SI 1993/1418) |
| 5, 6 | 6 Jul 1993 (SI 1993/1512) |

---

**Ordination of Women (Financial Provisions) Measure 1993 (No 3)**

*RA:* 5 Nov 1993

Whole Measure in force 5 Nov 1993 (RA)

---

**Osteopaths Act 1993 (c 21)**

*RA:* 1 Jul 1993

*Commencement provisions:* s 42(2)–(5); Osteopaths Act 1993 (Commencement No 1 and Transitional Provision) Order 1997, SI 1997/34; Osteopaths Act 1993 (Commencement No 2) Order 1998, SI 1998/872; Osteopaths Act 1993 (Commencement No 3) Order 1998, SI 1998/1138; Osteopaths Act 1993 (Commencement No 4) Order 1999, SI 1999/1767; Osteopaths Act 1993 (Commencement No 5) Order 2000, SI 2000/217; Osteopaths Act 1993 (Commencement No 6 and Transitional Provision) Order 2000, SI 2000/1065; Osteopaths Act 1993 (Commencement No 7) Order 2002, SI 2002/500

| | | |
|---|---|---|
| 1 | (1) | 14 Jan 1997 (SI 1997/34) |
| | (2) | 14 Jan 1997 (for limited purposes referred to in SI 1997/34, art 2, Sch) (SI 1997/34) |
| | | 9 May 1998 (otherwise) (SI 1998/1138) |
| | (3) | 14 Jan 1997 (so far as it relates to the other provisions of the Act brought into force by SI 1997/34) (SI 1997/34) |
| | | 1 Apr 1998 (so far as it relates to the other provisions of the Act brought into force by SI 1998/872) (SI 1998/872) |
| | | 9 May 1998 (so far as it relates to the other provisions of the Act brought into force by SI 1998/1138) (SI 1998/1138) |
| | | 8 Mar 2000 (otherwise) (SI 2000/217) |
| | (4) | See Sch below |
| | (5)(a) | 1 Apr 1998 (SI 1998/872) |
| | (5)(b) | 1 Apr 1998 (SI 1998/872)[1] |
| | | 5 Jul 1999 (otherwise) (SI 1999/1767) |
| | (5)(c), (d) | 1 Apr 1998 (SI 1998/872)[1] |
| | | 8 Mar 2000 (otherwise) (SI 2000/217) |
| | (6) | 1 Apr 1998 (SI 1998/872) |
| | (7) | 1 Apr 1998 (SI 1998/872)[1] |
| | | 5 Jul 1999 (so far as relates to the other provisions of this Act brought into force by SI 1999/1767) (SI 1999/1767) |
| | | 8 Mar 2000 (otherwise) (SI 2000/217) |
| | (8) | 14 Jan 1997 (SI 1997/34) |
| | (9) | 1 Apr 1998 (SI 1998/872)[1] |
| | | 5 Jul 1999 (so far as relates to the other provisions of this Act brought into force by SI 1999/1767) (SI 1999/1767) |
| | | 8 Mar 2000 (otherwise) (SI 2000/217) |
| | (10)–(12) | 14 Jan 1997 (SI 1997/34) |
| 2 | (1), (2) | 14 Jan 1997 (SI 1997/34) |
| | (3) | 9 May 1998 (SI 1998/1138) |
| | (4)–(6) | 14 Jan 1997 (SI 1997/34) |
| 3, 4 | | 1 Apr 1998 (for limited purposes referred to in SI 1998/872, art 2(1)(b)) (SI 1998/872) |
| | | 9 May 1998 (otherwise) (SI 1998/1138) |
| 5 | | 8 Mar 2000 (SI 2000/217) |
| 6 | (1) | 9 May 1998 (SI 1998/1138) |

**Osteopaths Act 1993 (c 21)**—*contd*

| | | |
|---|---|---|
| | (2) | 1 Apr 1998 (SI 1998/872) |
| | (3)(a) | 9 May 1998 (SI 1998/1138) |
| | (3)(b)–(l) | 1 Apr 1998 (SI 1998/872) |
| | (3)(m) | 9 May 1998 (SI 1998/1138) |
| | (4)(a) | 1 Apr 1998 (SI 1998/872) |
| | (4)(b)–(e) | 9 May 1998 (SI 1998/1138) |
| | (5) | 9 May 1998 (SI 1998/1138) |
| 7 | (1), (2) | 5 Jul 1999 (so far as they relate to the other provisions of this Act brought into force by SI 1999/1767) (SI 1999/1767) |
| | | 8 Mar 2000 (otherwise) (SI 2000/217) |
| | (3) | 9 May 2000 (SI 2000/1065) |
| 8 | | 8 Mar 2000 (SI 2000/217) |
| 9 | | 9 May 1998 (SI 1998/1138) |
| 10 | (1) | 9 May 1998 (SI 1998/1138) |
| | (2) | 5 Jul 1999 (except the words "or section 8, or under rules made by virtue of section 8(8),") (SI 1999/1767) |
| | | 8 Mar 2000 (otherwise) (SI 2000/217) |
| | (3)–(12) | 5 Jul 1999 (SI 1999/1767) |
| 11 | | 1 Apr 1998 (SI 1998/872) |
| 12 | | 9 May 1998 (SI 1998/1138) |
| 13 | | 1 Apr 1998 (SI 1998/872) |
| 14–16 | | 9 May 1998 (SI 1998/1138) |
| 17 | | 8 Mar 2000 (SI 2000/217) |
| 18 | | 9 May 1998 (SI 1998/1138) |
| 19 | | 1 Apr 1998 (SI 1998/872) |
| 20, 21 | | 5 Jul 1999 (SI 1999/1767) |
| 22–26 | | 8 Mar 2000 (SI 2000/217) |
| 27, 28 | | 5 Jul 1999 (SI 1999/1767) |
| 29 | | 9 May 1998 (SI 1998/1138) |
| 30, 31 | | 8 Mar 2000 (SI 2000/217) |
| 32 | (1) | 9 May 2000 (subject to a transitional provision) (SI 2000/1065) |
| | (2) | 8 Mar 2000 (SI 2000/217) |
| | (3) | 8 Mar 2000 (except so far as relates to s 32(1)) (SI 2000/217) |
| | | 9 May 2000 (exception noted above) (SI 2000/1065) |
| 33 | | 9 May 1998 (SI 1998/1138) |
| 34 | | 14 Jan 1997 (SI 1997/34) |
| 35 | (1), (2) | 14 Jan 1997 (SI 1997/34) |
| | (3) | 8 Mar 2000 (SI 2000/217) |
| | (4) | 14 Jan 1997 (SI 1997/34) |
| 36 | (1), (2) | 14 Jan 1997 (SI 1997/34) |
| | (3) | 8 Mar 2000 (SI 2000/217) |
| | (4)–(6) | 14 Jan 1997 (SI 1997/34) |
| 37 | | 1 Apr 1998 (SI 1998/872) |
| 38 | | 9 May 1998 (SI 1998/1138) |
| 39 | | 1 Apr 1998 (SI 1998/872) |
| 40 | | 14 Jan 1997 (SI 1997/34) |
| 41 | | 14 Jan 1997 (so far as relates to definitions "the General Council", "prescribed" and "the Registrar") (SI 1997/34) |
| | | 1 Apr 1998 (otherwise, except definitions "interim suspension order", "provisionally registered osteopath", "registered address", "unacceptable professional conduct" and "visitor") (SI 1998/872) |
| | | 5 Jul 1999 (exceptions noted above) (SI 1999/1767) |
| 42 | (1)–(6) | 14 Jan 1997 (SI 1997/34) |
| | (7) | 14 Jan 1997 (words "This Act extends to the United Kingdom") (SI 1997/34) |
| | | 9 May 1998 (otherwise) (SI 1998/1138) |
| Schedule | paras 1, 2 | 14 Jan 1997 (SI 1997/34) |
| | para 3 | 3 Mar 2002 (SI 2002/500) |

**Osteopaths Act 1993 (c 21)**—*contd*

| | | |
|---|---|---|
| | para 4 | 14 Jan 1997 (SI 1997/34) |
| | para 5 | 14 Jan 1997 (subject to a transitional provision) (SI 1997/34) |
| | para 6 | 14 Jan 1997 (SI 1997/34) |
| | para 7 | 8 Mar 2000 (SI 2000/217) |
| | para 8 | 14 Jan 1997 (SI 1997/34) |
| | paras 9, 10 | 3 Mar 2002 (SI 2002/500) |
| | para 11 | 14 Jan 1997 (SI 1997/34) |
| | para 12 | 3 Mar 2002 (SI 2002/500) |
| | para 13 | 14 Jan 1997 (SI 1997/34) |
| | para 14(1) | 3 Mar 2002 (SI 2002/500) |
| | para 14(2) | 14 Jan 1997 (subject to a transitional provision) (SI 1997/34) |
| | para 14(3)(a)–(c) | 14 Jan 1997 (SI 1997/34) |
| | para 14(3)(d) | 3 Mar 2002 (SI 2002/500) |
| | para 14(4) | 3 Mar 2002 (SI 2002/500) |
| | para 14(5)(a) | 3 Mar 2002 (SI 2002/500) |
| | para 14(5)(b) | 1 Apr 1998 (SI 1998/872) |
| | para 15 | 14 Jan 1997 (SI 1997/34) |
| | paras 16–21 | 1 Apr 1998 (SI 1998/872)[1] |
| | | 5 Jul 1999 (so far as not already in force, in relation to the Investigating Committee only) (SI 1999/1767) |
| | | 8 Mar 2000 (otherwise) (SI 2000/217) |
| | para 22 | 5 Jul 1999 (in relation to the Investigating Committee only) (SI 1999/1767) |
| | | 8 Mar 2000 (otherwise) (SI 2000/217) |
| | para 23 | 1 Apr 1998 (SI 1998/872)[1] |
| | | 5 Jul 1999 (so far as not already in force, in relation to the Investigating Committee only) (SI 1999/1767) |
| | | 8 Mar 2000 (otherwise) (SI 2000/217) |
| | para 24(1) | 1 Apr 1998 (SI 1998/872)[1] |
| | | 5 Jul 1999 (so far as not already in force, in relation to the Investigating Committee only) (SI 1999/1767) |
| | | 8 Mar 2000 (otherwise) (SI 2000/217) |
| | para 24(2) | 8 Mar 2000 (SI 2000/217) |
| | paras 25–29 | 1 Apr 1998 (SI 1998/872) |
| | paras 30–33 | 1 Apr 1998 (SI 1998/872)[1] |
| | | 5 Jul 1999 (otherwise) (SI 1999/1767) |
| | paras 34–41 | 1 Apr 1998 (SI 1998/872)[1] |
| | | 8 Mar 2000 (otherwise) (SI 2000/217) |
| | paras 42–48 | 14 Jan 1997 (SI 1997/34) |

[1] For the purpose only of enabling the Investigating Committee, the Professional Conduct Committee and the Health Committee and any sub-committees of those committees to be established and to carry out work preparatory to the exercise of any function which may be, or if the relevant provision were in force could become, exercisable under any provision of the Act

---

**Pension Schemes Act 1993 (c 48)**

*RA:* 5 Nov 1993

*Commencement provisions:* s 193(2), (3); Pension Schemes Act 1993 (Commencement No 1) Order 1994, SI 1994/86

| | | |
|---|---|---|
| 1–187 | | 7 Feb 1994 (SI 1994/86) |
| 188 | (1), (2) | See Sch 5 below |
| | (3) | 7 Feb 1994 (SI 1994/86) |
| 189 | | 7 Feb 1994 (SI 1994/86) |
| 190 | | See Schs 7, 8 below |
| 191–193 | | 7 Feb 1994 (SI 1994/86) |
| Schs 1–4 | | 7 Feb 1994 (SI 1994/86) |

**Pension Schemes Act 1993 (c 48)**—*contd*

| | | |
|---|---|---|
| Sch 5 | Pt I | 7 Feb 1994 (SI 1994/86) |
| | Pt II | *Not yet in force* |
| | Pts III, IV | 7 Feb 1994 (SI 1994/86) |
| Sch 6 | | 7 Feb 1994 (SI 1994/86) |
| Sch 7 | | *Not yet in force* (paras 1, 3 repealed) |
| Schs 8, 9 | | 7 Feb 1994 (SI 1994/86) |

---

**Pension Schemes (Northern Ireland) Act 1993 (c 49)**

*RA:* 5 Nov 1993

*Commencement provisions:* s 186(2), (3); Pension Schemes (1993 Act) (Commencement No 1) Order (Northern Ireland) 1994, SR 1994/17

| | | |
|---|---|---|
| 1–181 | | 7 Feb 1994 (SR 1994/17) |
| 182 | (1), (2) | See Sch 4 below |
| | (3) | 7 Feb 1994 (SR 1994/17) |
| 183 | | 7 Feb 1994 (SR 1994/17) |
| 184 | | See Schs 6, 7 below |
| 185, 186 | | 7 Feb 1994 (SR 1994/17) |
| Schs 1–3 | | 7 Feb 1994 (SR 1994/17) |
| Sch 4 | Pt I | 7 Feb 1994 (SR 1994/17) |
| | Pt II | *Not yet in force* |
| | Pt III | 7 Feb 1994 (SR 1994/17) |
| Sch 5 | | 7 Feb 1994 (SR 1994/17) |
| Sch 6 | | *Not yet in force* |
| Schs 7, 8 | | 7 Feb 1994 (SR 1994/17) |

---

**Priests (Ordination of Women) Measure 1993 (No 2)**

*RA:* 5 Nov 1993

*Commencement provisions:* s 12(2)

The provisions of this Measure are brought into force on 1 Feb 1994 by an appointed day notice signed by the Archbishops of Canterbury and York and dated 31 Jan 1994 (made under s 12)

---

**Prisoners and Criminal Proceedings (Scotland) Act 1993 (c 9)**

*RA:* 29 Mar 1993

*Commencement provisions:* s 48(2)–(4); Prisoners and Criminal Proceedings (Scotland) Act 1993 Commencement, Transitional Provisions and Savings Order 1993, SI 1993/2050

| | | |
|---|---|---|
| 1–5 | | 1 Oct 1993 (SI 1993/2050) |
| 6 | (1), (2) | 1 Oct 1993 (SI 1993/2050) |
| | (3) | 18 Aug 1993 (for purpose of enabling orders to be made so as to come into force on or after 1 Oct 1993) (SI 1993/2050) |
| | | 1 Oct 1993 (otherwise) (SI 1993/2050) |
| 7 | (1)–(5) | 1 Oct 1993 (SI 1993/2050) |
| | (6) | 18 Aug 1993 (for purpose of enabling orders to be made so as to come into force on or after 1 Oct 1993) (SI 1993/2050) |
| | | 1 Oct 1993 (otherwise) (SI 1993/2050) |
| | (7) | 1 Oct 1993 (SI 1993/2050) |
| 8–19 | | 1 Oct 1993 (SI 1993/2050) |
| 20 | (1), (2) | 1 Oct 1993 (SI 1993/2050) |
| | (3) | 18 Aug 1993 (for purpose of enabling orders to be made so as to come into force on or after 1 Oct 1993) (SI 1993/2050) |
| | | 1 Oct 1993 (otherwise) (SI 1993/2050) |

**Prisoners and Criminal Proceedings (Scotland) Act 1993 (c 9)**—*contd*

| | | |
|---|---|---|
| | (4), (5) | 18 Aug 1993 (for purpose of enabling rules to be made, and directions to be given, so as to come into force on or after 1 Oct 1993) (SI 1993/2050) |
| | | 1 Oct 1993 (otherwise) (SI 1993/2050) |
| | (6) | 1 Oct 1993 (SI 1993/2050) |
| 21–23 | | 1 Oct 1993 (SI 1993/2050) |
| 24, 25 | | 18 Aug 1993 (SI 1993/2050) |
| 26 | | 1 Oct 1993 (SI 1993/2050) |
| 27 | (1) | 18 Aug 1993 (for purpose of enabling an order to be made so as to come into force on or after 1 Oct 1993) (SI 1993/2050) |
| | | 1 Oct 1993 (otherwise) (SI 1993/2050) |
| | (2), (3) | 18 Aug 1993 (for purpose of enabling an order to be made so as to come into force on or after 1 Oct 1993) (SI 1993/2050) |
| | | 1 Oct 1993 (otherwise) (SI 1993/2050) |
| | (4)–(7) | 1 Oct 1993 (SI 1993/2050) |
| 28, 29 | | 1 Oct 1993 (subject to a saving) (SI 1993/2050) |
| 30 | | 1 Jan 1994 (subject to a saving) (SI 1993/2050) |
| 31 | | 18 Sep 1993 (subject to a saving) (SI 1993/2050) |
| 32 | | 1 Oct 1993 (subject to a saving) (SI 1993/2050) |
| 33–35 | | 1 Jan 1994 (subject to a saving) (SI 1993/2050) |
| 36 | | 18 Sep 1993 (subject to a saving) (SI 1993/2050) |
| 37 | | 1 Oct 1993 (subject to a saving) (SI 1993/2050) |
| 38–41 | | 18 Sep 1993 (subject to a saving) (SI 1993/2050) |
| 42 | | 1 Oct 1993 (subject to a saving) (SI 1993/2050) |
| 43 | | 18 Sep 1993 (subject to a saving) (SI 1993/2050) |
| 44 | | 1 Oct 1993 (SI 1993/2050) |
| 45, 46 | | 18 Aug 1993 (SI 1993/2050) |
| 47 | (1) | See Sch 5 below |
| | (2) | See Sch 6 below |
| | (3) | See Sch 7 below |
| 48 | | 29 Mar 1993 (s 48(4)) |
| Schs 1–4 | | 1 Oct 1993 (subject to a saving) (SI 1993/2050) |
| Sch 5 | para 1(1), (2) | 1 Oct 1993 (subject to a saving) (SI 1993/2050) |
| | para 1(3)–(6) | 18 Sep 1993 (subject to a saving) (SI 1993/2050) |
| | para 1(7)–(26) | 1 Oct 1993 (subject to a saving) (SI 1993/2050) |
| | para 1(27) | 18 Aug 1993 (for purpose of enabling an order to be made under s 275(3) of the 1975 Act so as to come into force on or after 1 Oct 1993) (subject to a saving) (SI 1993/2050) |
| | | 1 Oct 1993 (subject to a saving) (SI 1993/2050) |
| | para 1(28) | 18 Sep 1993 (SI 1993/2050) |
| | para 1(29) | 1 Oct 1993 (subject to a saving) (SI 1993/2050) |
| | para 1(30), (31) | 18 Sep 1993 (subject to a saving) (SI 1993/2050) |
| | para 1(32)–(38) | 1 Oct 1993 (subject to a saving) (SI 1993/2050) |
| | paras 2–4 | 1 Oct 1993 (SI 1993/2050) |
| | para 5 | 29 Mar 1993 (s 48(4)) |
| | para 6(1)–(4) | 18 Aug 1993 (SI 1993/2050) |
| | para 6(5) | 1 Oct 1993 (SI 1993/2050) |
| | para 6(6) | 18 Aug 1993 (SI 1993/2050) |
| | para 6(7) | 1 Oct 1993 (SI 1993/2050) |
| | para 6(8) | 18 Aug 1993 (SI 1993/2050) |
| | para 6(9) | 1 Oct 1993 (SI 1993/2050) |
| Sch 6 | | 1 Oct 1993 (SI 1993/2050) |
| Sch 7 | | 18 Sep 1993 (subject to savings) (SI 1993/2050), repeals of or in— Criminal Procedure (Scotland) Act 1975, ss 108, 289D, 328; Criminal Justice (Scotland) Act 1980, Sch 3; Criminal Justice (Scotland) Act 1987, s 62 |
| | | 1 Oct 1993 (otherwise) (subject to savings) (SI 1993/2050) |

**1993**                                    *Is it in Force? Winter 2022–23*

## Probation Service Act 1993 (c 47)

*RA:* 5 Nov 1993

*Commencement provisions:* s 33(2)

Whole Act in force 5 Feb 1994 (s 33(2))

## Protection of Animals (Scotland) Act 1993 (c 15)

*RA:* 27 May 1993

*Commencement provisions:* s 2(2)

Whole Act in force 27 Jul 1993 (s 2(2))

## Radioactive Substances Act 1993 (c 12)

*RA:* 27 May 1993

*Commencement provisions:* s 51(2)

Whole Act in force 27 Aug 1993 (s 51(2))

## Railways Act 1993 (c 43)

*RA:* 5 Nov 1993

*Commencement provisions:* s 154(2); Railways Act 1993 (Commencement No 1) Order 1993, SI 1993/3237; Railways Act 1993 (Commencement No 2) Order 1994, SI 1994/202; Railways Act 1993 (Commencement No 3) Order 1994, SI 1994/447; Railways Act 1993 (Commencement No 4 and Transitional Provision) Order 1994, SI 1994/571; Railways Act 1993 (Commencement No 5 and Transitional Provisions) Order 1994, SI 1994/1648; Railways Act 1993 (Commencement No 6) Order 1994, SI 1994/2142

| | | |
|---|---|---|
| 1 | | 5 Nov 1993 (s 154(2)) |
| 2, 3 | | 1 Apr 1994 (SI 1994/571) |
| 4 | (1) | 24 Dec 1993 (for purposes of functions of Secretary of State under s 33) (SI 1993/3237) |
| | | 22 Feb 1994 (for purpose of functions of Regulator under s 70) (SI 1994/447) |
| | | 21 Mar 1994 (otherwise) (SI 1994/571) |
| | (2) | 22 Feb 1994 (for purpose of functions of Regulator under s 70) (SI 1994/447) |
| | | 21 Mar 1994 (otherwise) (SI 1994/571) |
| | (3) | 24 Dec 1993 (for purposes of functions of Secretary of State under s 33) (SI 1993/3237) |
| | | 22 Feb 1994 (for purpose of functions of Regulator under s 70) (SI 1994/447) |
| | | 21 Mar 1994 (otherwise) (SI 1994/571) |
| | (4) | 21 Mar 1994 (SI 1994/571) |
| | (5) | 22 Feb 1994 (for purpose of functions of Regulator under s 70) (SI 1994/447) |
| | | 21 Mar 1994 (otherwise) (SI 1994/571) |
| | (6) | 22 Feb 1994 (for purpose of functions of Regulator under s 70) (SI 1994/447) |
| | | 21 Mar 1994 (otherwise) (SI 1994/571) |
| | (7) | 24 Dec 1993 (for purposes of functions of Secretary of State under s 33) (SI 1993/3237) |
| | | 21 Mar 1994 (otherwise) (SI 1994/571) |
| | (8) | 21 Mar 1994 (SI 1994/571) |

**Railways Act 1993 (c 43)**—*contd*

| | | |
|---|---|---|
| | (9) | 24 Dec 1993 (for purposes of definitions "environment" and "through ticket") (SI 1993/3237) |
| | | 21 Mar 1994 (otherwise) (SI 1994/571) |
| 5 | | 21 Mar 1994 (SI 1994/571) |
| 6 | (1) | 1 Apr 1994 (SI 1994/571) |
| | (2) | 6 Jan 1994 (SI 1993/3237) |
| | (3), (4) | 1 Apr 1994 (SI 1994/571) |
| 7–16 | | 1 Apr 1994 (SI 1994/571) |
| 17–22 | | 2 Apr 1994 (SI 1994/571) |
| 23 | (1), (2) | 1 Apr 1994 (SI 1994/571) |
| | (3), (4) | 6 Jan 1994 (SI 1993/3237) |
| 24 | | 1 Apr 1994 (SI 1994/571) |
| 25 | (1), (2) | 6 Jan 1994 (for purpose of providing definition "public sector operator") (SI 1993/3237) |
| | | 1 Apr 1994 (otherwise) (SI 1994/571) |
| | (3)–(9) | 1 Apr 1994 (SI 1994/571) |
| 26–28 | | 1 Apr 1994 (SI 1994/571) |
| 29 | (1)–(7) | 1 Apr 1994 (SI 1994/571) |
| | (8) | 6 Jan 1994 (SI 1993/3237) |
| 30, 31 | | 1 Apr 1994 (SI 1994/571) |
| 32, 33 | | 24 Dec 1993 (SI 1993/3237) |
| 34–51 | | 1 Apr 1994 (SI 1994/571) |
| 52 | | 21 Mar 1994 (SI 1994/571) |
| 53 | | 1 Apr 1994 (SI 1994/571) |
| 54 | (1) | 1 Apr 1994 (SI 1994/571) |
| | (2) | 21 Mar 1994 (SI 1994/571) |
| | (3) | 21 Mar 1994 (for purpose of definitions "franchising functions", in relation to the Franchising Director, and "railway investment") (SI 1994/571) |
| | | 1 Apr 1994 (otherwise) (SI 1994/571) |
| 55–69 | | 1 Apr 1994 (SI 1994/571) |
| 70 | | 22 Feb 1994 (SI 1994/447) |
| 71–80 | | 1 Apr 1994 (SI 1994/571) |
| 81, 82 | | 24 Dec 1993 (SI 1993/3237) |
| 83 | (1) | 24 Dec 1993 (for purposes of definitions "goods", "light maintenance services", "locomotive", "network", "network services", "premises", "passenger service operator", "railway", "railway services", "railway vehicle", "rolling stock", "station", "station services", "track", "train" and "vehicle") (SI 1993/3237) |
| | | 6 Jan 1994 (for purposes of definitions "additional railway asset", "the Director", "franchise agreement", "franchise operator", "franchise term", "franchised services", "franchisee", "information", ""licence" and "licence holder"", "light maintenance depot", "operator", "passenger licence", "private sector operator", "public sector operator", "railway asset", "railway passenger service", "records" and "station licence") (SI 1993/3237) |
| | | 22 Feb 1994 (for purposes of definitions "network licence" and "railway facility") (SI 1994/447) |
| | | 1 Apr 1994 (otherwise) (SI 1994/571) |
| | (2) | 24 Dec 1993 (SI 1993/3237) |
| 84, 85 | | 6 Jan 1994 (SI 1993/3237) |
| 86 | | 1 Apr 1994 (SI 1994/571) |
| 87 | (1) | 6 Jan 1994 (for purpose of enabling Secretary of State to transfer functions to himself) (SI 1993/3237) |
| | | 1 Apr 1994 (otherwise) (SI 1994/571) |
| | (2) | 6 Jan 1994 (SI 1993/3237) |
| | (3), (4) | 1 Apr 1994 (SI 1994/571) |
| | (5) | 6 Jan 1994 (SI 1993/3237) |

**Railways Act 1993 (c 43)**—*contd*

| | | |
|---|---|---|
| 88–92 | | 6 Jan 1994 (SI 1993/3237) |
| 93 | (1), (2) | 6 Jan 1994 (SI 1993/3237) |
| | (3)(a) | 6 Jan 1994 (SI 1993/3237) |
| | (3)(b) | 1 Apr 1994 (SI 1994/571) |
| | (4)–(13) | 6 Jan 1994 (SI 1993/3237) |
| 94–116 | | 6 Jan 1994 (SI 1993/3237) |
| 117 | | 2 Feb 1994 (SI 1994/202) |
| 118–121 | | 8 Mar 1994 (SI 1994/571) |
| 122–127 | | 1 Apr 1994 (SI 1994/571) |
| 128 | | 6 Jan 1994 (SI 1993/3237) |
| 129 | | 1 Apr 1994 (SI 1994/571) |
| 130, 131 | | 6 Jan 1994 (SI 1993/3237) |
| 132 | (1)–(7) | 8 Mar 1994 (SI 1994/571) |
| | (8) | See Sch 10 below |
| | (9), (10) | 8 Mar 1994 (SI 1994/571) |
| 133 | | 8 Mar 1994 (SI 1994/571) |
| 134 | (1) | See Sch 11 below |
| | (2), (3) | 6 Jan 1994 (SI 1993/3237) |
| 135–137 | | 1 Apr 1994 (SI 1994/571) |
| 138 | | 21 Mar 1994 (SI 1994/571) |
| 139, 140 | | 15 Jul 1994 (subject to transitional provisions) (SI 1994/1648) |
| 141 | (1) | 6 Jan 1994 (except para (a)) (SI 1993/3237) |
| | | 1 Apr 1994 (para (a)) (SI 1994/571) |
| | (2)–(5) | 6 Jan 1994 (SI 1993/3237) |
| 142–144 | | 24 Dec 1993 (SI 1993/3237) |
| 145 | (1)–(6) | 24 Dec 1993 (except for purposes of sub-s (5)(a), (b)(i)) (SI 1993/3237) |
| | | 1 Apr 1994 (exceptions noted above) (SI 1994/571) |
| | (7) | 1 Apr 1994 (SI 1994/571) |
| 146–149 | | 24 Dec 1993 (SI 1993/3237) |
| 150 | (1)–(3) | 24 Dec 1993 (SI 1993/3237) |
| | (4) | 1 Apr 1994 (SI 1994/571) |
| 151 | (1) | 24 Dec 1993 (for purposes of definitions "the Board", "body corporate", "company", "contravention", "the Franchising Director", "functions", "local authority", "the Monopolies Commission", "notice", "the Regulator", "subsidiary" and "wholly owned subsidiary") (SI 1993/3237) |
| | | 6 Jan 1994 (otherwise) (SI 1993/3237) |
| | (2)–(4) | 6 Jan 1994 (SI 1993/3237) |
| | (5) | 24 Dec 1993 (SI 1993/3237) |
| | (6)–(9) | 6 Jan 1994 (SI 1993/3237) |
| 152 | (1) | See Sch 12 below |
| | (2) | See Sch 13 below |
| | (3) | See Sch 14 below |
| 153 | | 6 Jan 1994 (SI 1993/3237) |
| 154 | | 24 Dec 1993 (SI 1993/3237) |
| Sch 1 | | 5 Nov 1993 (s 154(2)) |
| Schs 2, 3 | | 1 Apr 1994 (SI 1994/571) |
| Sch 4 | | 2 Apr 1994 (SI 1994/571) |
| Schs 5–7 | | 1 Apr 1994 (SI 1994/571) |
| Schs 8, 9 | | 6 Jan 1994 (SI 1993/3237) |
| Sch 10 | paras 1, 2 | 8 Mar 1994 (subject to transitional provisions) (SI 1994/571) |
| | para 3(1) | 8 Mar 1994 (so far as repeals Transport Act 1962, ss 69, 71) (SI 1994/571) |
| | | *Never in force* (otherwise) (repealed) |
| | para 3(2), (3) | 8 Mar 1994 (SI 1994/571) |
| Sch 11 | paras 1–8 | 6 Jan 1994 (SI 1993/3237) |
| | para 9(1), (2) | 6 Jan 1994 (SI 1993/3237) |

**Railways Act 1993 (c 43)**—*contd*

|   |   |   |
|---|---|---|
|   | para 9(3) | 6 Jan 1994 (for purpose of inserting Transport Act 1980, s 52D(6)–(8)) (SI 1993/3237) |
|   |   | 16 Aug 1994 (otherwise) (SI 1994/2142) |
|   | para 9(4) | 6 Jan 1994 (SI 1993/3237) |
|   | para 10 | 6 Jan 1994 (SI 1993/3237) |
|   | para 11 | 16 Aug 1994 (SI 1994/2142) |
|   | paras 12–14 | 6 Jan 1994 (SI 1993/3237) |
| Sch 12 | paras 1–3 | 1 Apr 1994 (SI 1994/571) |
|   | paras 4, 5 | 6 Jan 1994 (SI 1993/3237) |
|   | para 6(1)–(5) | 6 Jan 1994 (SI 1993/3237) |
|   | para 6(6) | 1 Apr 1994 (SI 1994/571) |
|   | para 6(7) | 6 Jan 1994 (SI 1993/3237) |
|   | paras 7, 8 | 6 Jan 1994 (SI 1993/3237) |
|   | para 9 | 1 Apr 1994 (SI 1994/571) |
|   | paras 10–13 | 6 Jan 1994 (SI 1993/3237) |
|   | para 14(1)–(3) | 6 Jan 1994 (SI 1993/3237) |
|   | para 14(4)–(6) | 1 Apr 1994 (SI 1994/571) |
|   | paras 15–22 | 1 Apr 1994 (SI 1994/571) |
|   | paras 23, 24 | 6 Jan 1994 (SI 1993/3237) |
|   | para 25 | 1 Apr 1994 (SI 1994/571) |
|   | para 26 | 6 Jan 1994 (SI 1993/3237) |
|   | para 27 | 1 Apr 1994 (SI 1994/571) |
|   | para 28 | 6 Jan 1994 (SI 1993/3237) |
|   | para 29 | 1 Apr 1994 (SI 1994/571) |
|   | paras 30, 31 | 6 Jan 1994 (SI 1993/3237) |
|   | para 32 | *Not yet in force* |
| Sch 13 |   | 1 Apr 1994 (SI 1994/571) |
| Sch 14 |   | 6 Jan 1994 (SI 1993/3237), repeals of or in— |

British Transport Commission Act 1950, s 43;
Transport Act 1962, ss 4, 5, 13, 53;
Transport Act 1968, ss 42, 45, 50, 137

8 Mar 1994 (repeals of Transport Act 1962, ss 54(1)(b), (2), 69, 71) (SI 1994/571)

31 Mar 1994 (repeal of Transport Act 1981, Pt I, Sch 1) (SI 1994/571)

1 Apr 1994 (SI 1994/571), all repeals so far as not already in force except repeals of—
Transport Act 1962, s 70;
Railways Act 1974, s 8;
Transport Act 1981, s 36

15 Jul 1994 (subject to transitional provisions) (SI 1994/1648), repeals of—
Railways Act 1974, s 8;
Transport Act 1981, s 36

*Not yet in force* (repeal of Transport Act 1962, s 70)

---

**Reinsurance (Acts of Terrorism) Act 1993 (c 18)**

*RA*: 27 May 1993

Whole Act in force 27 May 1993 (RA)

---

**Representation of the People Act 1993 (c 29)**

*RA*: 20 Jul 1993

Whole Act in force 20 Jul 1993 (RA)

---

## Road Traffic (Driving Instruction by Disabled Persons) Act 1993 (c 31)

*RA:* 20 Jul 1993

*Commencement provisions:* s 7(2); Road Traffic (Driving Instruction by Disabled Persons) Act 1993 (Commencement) Order 1996, SI 1996/1980

Whole Act in force 9 Sep 1996 (SI 1996/1980)

## Scottish Land Court Act 1993 (c 45)

*RA:* 5 Nov 1993

*Commencement provisions:* s 2(3)

Whole Act in force 5 Jan 1994 (s 2(3))

## Sexual Offences Act 1993 (c 30)

*RA:* 20 Jul 1993

*Commencement provisions:* s 2(2)

Whole Act in force 20 Sep 1993 (s 2(2))

## Social Security Act 1993 (c 3)

*RA:* 29 Jan 1993

Whole Act in force 29 Jan 1993 (RA; but note s 5(2))

## Statute Law (Repeals) Act 1993 (c 50)

*RA:* 5 Nov 1993

*Commencement provisions:* s 4(2), (3); Statute Law (Repeals) Act 1993 (Commencement) Order 1996, SI 1996/509

| | | |
|---|---|---|
| 1 | (1) | See Sch 1 below |
| | (2) | See Sch 2 below |
| 2–4 | | 5 Nov 1993 (RA) |
| Sch 1 | | 5 Nov 1993[1] (RA), except repeals of or in— |
| | | Shipbuilding (Redundancy Payments) Act 1978; |
| | | Shipbuilding Act 1985, s 1 |
| | | 1 Apr 1996 (exceptions noted above) (SI 1996/509) |
| Sch 2 | | 5 Nov 1993 (RA) |

[1] By s 4(2), repeals of National Loans Act 1939, Sch 2, para 5, Bank of England Act 1946, Sch 1, para 10, Coal Industry Nationalisation Act 1946, s 33(8) have effect, so far as relating to stock registered in the National Savings Stock Register, on the coming into force of the first regulations made by virtue of the National Debt Act 1972, s 3(1)(bb)

## Trade Union Reform and Employment Rights Act 1993 (c 19)

*RA:* 1 Jul 1993

*Commencement provisions:* ss 7(4), 52; Trade Union Reform and Employment Rights Act 1993 (Commencement No 1 and Transitional Provisions) Order 1993, SI 1993/1908; Trade Union Reform and Employment Rights Act 1993 (Commencement No 2 and Transitional Provisions) Order 1993, SI 1993/2503; Trade Union Reform and Employment Rights Act 1993 (Commencement No 3 and Transitional Provisions) Order 1994, SI 1994/1365

**Trade Union Reform and Employment Rights Act 1993 (c 19)**—*contd*

| | | |
|---|---|---|
| 1, 2 | | 30 Aug 1993 (subject to transitional provisions) (SI 1993/1908) |
| 3 | | See Sch 1 below |
| 4–6 | | 30 Aug 1993 (subject to transitional provisions) (SI 1993/1908) |
| 7 | (1) | 1 Apr 1996 (s 7(4)) |
| | (2)–(4) | 1 Apr 1996 (SI 1993/1908) |
| 8, 9 | | 1 Jan 1994 (SI 1993/1908) |
| 10–12 | | 30 Aug 1993 (SI 1993/1908) |
| 13 | | 30 Aug 1993 (subject to transitional provisions) (SI 1993/1908) |
| 14 | | 30 Nov 1993 (SI 1993/1908) |
| 15, 16 | | 30 Aug 1993 (SI 1993/1908) |
| 17 | | 30 Aug 1993 (subject to transitional provisions) (SI 1993/1908) |
| 18 | (1) | 30 Aug 1993 (SI 1993/1908) |
| | (2) | 30 Aug 1993 (subject to transitional provisions) (SI 1993/1908) |
| 19–21 | | 30 Aug 1993 (subject to transitional provisions) (SI 1993/1908) |
| 22 | | 30 Aug 1993 (SI 1993/1908) |
| 23 | | 10 Jun 1994 (SI 1994/1365)[1] |
| 24 | (1) | 10 Jun 1994 (SI 1994/1365)[1, 2] |
| | (2), (3) | 30 Aug 1993 (except for purpose of giving effect to s 60(a)–(f) of the 1978 Act) (subject to transitional provisions) (SI 1993/1908) |
| | | 10 Jun 1994 (exception noted above) (SI 1994/1365)[1, 2] |
| | (4) | 10 Jun 1994 (SI 1994/1365)[1, 2] |
| 25 | | 10 Jun 1994 (SI 1994/1365)[1] |
| 26, 27 | | 30 Nov 1993 (SI 1993/2503) |
| 28 | | See Sch 5 below |
| 29, 30 | | 30 Aug 1993 (subject to transitional provisions) (SI 1993/1908) |
| 31 | | *Never in force* (repealed) |
| 32 | | 30 Nov 1993 (SI 1993/2503) |
| 33 | | 30 Aug 1993 (SI 1993/1908) |
| 34 | | 30 Aug 1993 (subject to transitional provisions) (SI 1993/1908) |
| 35 | | 30 Aug 1993 (SI 1993/1908) |
| 36 | (1), (2) | 30 Nov 1993 (subject to transitional provisions) (SI 1993/2503) |
| | (3) | 30 Aug 1993 (for purpose of inserting s 128(5) of the 1978 Act) (SI 1993/1908) |
| | | 30 Nov 1993 (otherwise) (subject to transitional provisions) (SI 1993/2503) |
| 37 | | 30 Nov 1993 (SI 1993/2503) |
| 38 | | 30 Aug 1993 (SI 1993/1908) |
| 39 | (1) | 30 Aug 1993 (SI 1993/1908) |
| | (2) | See Sch 6 below |
| 40, 41 | | 30 Aug 1993 (SI 1993/1908) |
| 42 | | 30 Nov 1993 (SI 1993/2503) |
| 43, 44 | | 30 Aug 1993 (SI 1993/1908) |
| 45 | | 30 Nov 1993 (so far as substitutes 1973 Act, s 10(7)) (SI 1993/2503) |
| | | 1 Apr 1994 (otherwise) (E) (S) (SI 1993/2503) |
| | | 1 Apr 1995 (otherwise) (SI 1993/2503) |
| 46 | | 1 Apr 1994 (E) (S) (SI 1993/2503) |
| | | 1 Apr 1995 (otherwise) (SI 1993/2503) |
| 47, 48 | | 30 Aug 1993 (SI 1993/1908) |
| 49 | (1) | See Sch 7 below |
| | (2) | See Sch 8 below |
| 50 | | See Sch 9 below |
| 51 | | See Sch 10 below |
| 52–55 | | 1 Jul 1993 (RA) |
| Sch 1 | | 30 Aug 1993 (subject to transitional provisions) (SI 1993/1908) |
| Schs 2, 3 | | 10 Jun 1994 (SI 1994/1365)[1] |
| Sch 4 | | 30 Nov 1993 (SI 1993/2503) |
| Sch 5 | | 30 Aug 1993 (subject to transitional provisions) (SI 1993/1908) |
| Sch 6 | | 30 Aug 1993 (SI 1993/1908) |

**Trade Union Reform and Employment Rights Act 1993 (c 19)**—*contd*

| | | |
|---|---|---|
| Sch 7 | paras 1, 2 | 30 Aug 1993 (SI 1993/1908) |
| | para 3(a) | 30 Nov 1993 (SI 1993/2503) |
| | para 3(b) | 30 Nov 1993 (except so far as relates to s 60 of the 1978 Act) (SI 1993/2503) |
| | | 10 Jun 1994 (exception noted above) (SI 1994/1365)[1] |
| | para 4 | 30 Nov 1993 (SI 1993/2503) |
| | para 5 | 30 Nov 1993 (except so far as relates to s 60 of the 1978 Act) (SI 1993/2503) |
| | | 10 Jun 1994 (exception noted above) (SI 1994/1365)[1] |
| | para 6(a) | 30 Nov 1993 (SI 1993/2503) |
| | para 6(b) | 30 Nov 1993 (except so far as relates to s 60 of the 1978 Act) (SI 1993/2503) |
| | | 10 Jun 1994 (exception noted above) (SI 1994/1365)[1] |
| | para 7 | 15 Oct 1993 (SI 1993/2503) |
| | paras 8–12 | 30 Nov 1993 (SI 1993/2503) |
| | paras 13–27 | 30 Aug 1993 (SI 1993/1908) |
| Sch 8 | para 1 | 1 Apr 1994 (E) (S) (SI 1993/2503) |
| | | 1 Apr 1995 (otherwise) (SI 1993/2503) |
| | para 2 | 30 Aug 1993 (SI 1993/1908) |
| | paras 3–5 | 1 Apr 1994 (E) (S) (SI 1993/2503) |
| | | 1 Apr 1995 (otherwise) (SI 1993/2503) |
| | paras 6, 7 | 30 Aug 1993 (SI 1993/1908) |
| | paras 8, 9 | 1 Apr 1994 (E) (S) (SI 1993/2503) |
| | | 1 Apr 1995 (otherwise) (SI 1993/2503) |
| | para 10 | 30 Nov 1993 (SI 1993/2503) |
| | para 11 | 30 Aug 1993 (SI 1993/1908) |
| | paras 12, 13 | 10 Jun 1994 (SI 1994/1365)[1] |
| | para 14 | 30 Aug 1993 (SI 1993/1908) |
| | para 15 | 10 Jun 1994 (SI 1994/1365)[1] |
| | para 16 | 30 Aug 1993 (so far as relates to s 60A(1) of the 1978 Act) (SI 1993/1908) |
| | | 10 Jun 1994 (otherwise) (SI 1994/1365)[1] |
| | paras 17–19 | 10 Jun 1994 (SI 1994/1365)[1] |
| | para 20(a) | 30 Aug 1993 (SI 1993/1908) |
| | para 20(b) | 10 Jun 1994 (SI 1994/1365)[1] |
| | para 21 | 30 Aug 1993 (SI 1993/1908) |
| | paras 22, 23 | 30 Nov 1993 (SI 1993/2503) |
| | para 24 | 30 Aug 1993 (SI 1993/1908) |
| | para 25(a) | 10 Jun 1994 (SI 1994/1365)[1] |
| | para 25(b) | 30 Nov 1993 (SI 1993/2503) |
| | para 26(a)(i) | 30 Aug 1993 (SI 1993/1908) |
| | para 26(a)(ii), (iii) | 10 Jun 1994 (SI 1994/1365)[1] |
| | para 26(b)–(e) | 10 Jun 1994 (SI 1994/1365)[1] |
| | para 27 | 10 Jun 1994 (SI 1994/1365)[1] |
| | para 28(a) | 10 Jun 1994 (SI 1994/1365)[1] |
| | para 28(b), (c) | 15 Oct 1993 (SI 1993/2503) |
| | para 29 | 30 Aug 1993 (SI 1993/1908) |
| | para 30 | 15 Oct 1993 (SI 1993/2503) |
| | para 31 | 10 Jun 1994 (SI 1994/1365)[1] |
| | para 32(a) | 10 Jun 1994 (SI 1994/1365)[1] |
| | para 32(b) | 30 Aug 1993 (SI 1993/1908) |
| | paras 33, 34 | 1 Apr 1994 (E) (S) (SI 1993/2503) |
| | | 1 Apr 1995 (otherwise) (SI 1993/2503) |
| | para 35 | 10 Jun 1994 (SI 1994/1365)[1] |
| | paras 36–41 | 30 Aug 1993 (SI 1993/1908) |
| | para 42 | 1 Jan 1994 (SI 1993/1908) |
| | para 43(a) | 1 Jan 1994 (SI 1993/1908) |
| | para 43(b) | 30 Aug 1993 (SI 1993/1908) |
| | paras 44, 45 | 1 Jan 1994 (SI 1993/1908) |

**Trade Union Reform and Employment Rights Act 1993 (c 19)**—*contd*

|  |  |  |
|---|---|---|
|  | paras 46, 47 | 30 Aug 1993 (SI 1993/1908) |
|  | para 48 | 30 Nov 1993 (SI 1993/1908) |
|  | para 49 | 30 Aug 1993 (SI 1993/1908) |
|  | paras 50, 51 | 30 Nov 1993 (SI 1993/1908) |
|  | paras 52–61 | 30 Aug 1993 (SI 1993/1908) |
|  | para 62(a) | 1 Jan 1994 (SI 1993/1908) |
|  | para 62(b) | 30 Aug 1993 (SI 1993/1908) |
|  | para 63 | 30 Aug 1993 (SI 1993/1908) |
|  | para 64(a) | 1 Jan 1994 (SI 1993/1908) |
|  | para 64(b), (c) | 30 Aug 1993 (SI 1993/1908) |
|  | para 65 | 30 Aug 1993 (SI 1993/1908) |
|  | para 66(a) | 1 Jan 1994 (SI 1993/1908) |
|  | para 66(b) | 30 Aug 1993 (SI 1993/1908) |
|  | paras 67–75 | 30 Aug 1993 (SI 1993/1908) |
|  | paras 76, 77 | 30 Aug 1993 (so far as relate to s 57A of the 1978 Act) (SI 1993/1908) |
|  |  | 10 Jun 1994 (otherwise) (SI 1994/1365)[1] |
|  | paras 78–84 | 30 Aug 1993 (SI 1993/1908) |
|  | para 85 | 30 Nov 1993 (SI 1993/2503) |
|  | paras 86–89 | 30 Aug 1993 (SI 1993/1908) |
| Sch 9 | para 1 | 30 Aug 1993 (SI 1993/1908) |
|  | para 2 | 30 Aug 1993 (subject to savings) (SI 1993/1908) |
|  | para 3 | 30 Nov 1993 (SI 1993/2503) |
|  | paras 4, 5 | 30 Aug 1993 (SI 1993/1908) |
| Sch 10 |  | 30 Aug 1993 (SI 1993/1908), repeals of or in— |

    Factories Act 1961;

    Contracts of Employment and Redundancy Payments Act (Northern Ireland) 1965;

    Transport Act 1968;

    House of Commons Disqualification Act 1975;

    Northern Ireland Assembly Disqualification Act 1975;

    Industrial Relations (Northern Ireland) Order 1976;

    Employment Protection (Consolidation) Act 1978, ss 18, 53, 55, 64A, 93–95, 100, 123, 149, Schs 12, 13;

    Employment Act 1980, s 8, Sch 1;

    Transfer of Undertakings (Protection of Employment) Regulations 1981;

    Wages Act 1986;

    Income and Corporation Taxes Act 1988;

    Enterprise and New Towns (Scotland) Act 1990;

    Offshore Safety (Protection Against Victimisation) Act 1992;

    Trade Union and Labour Relations (Consolidation) Act 1992, ss 24, 34, 43, 52, 65, 74, 78, 118, 135, 154, 188, 190, 209, 246, 249, 256, 273, 283, 299, Sch 2, paras 15, 34

    15 Oct 1993 (repeal in Employment Protection (Consolidation) Act 1978, Sch 9, para 1A) (SI 1993/2503)

    30 Nov 1993 (repeals in Trade Union and Labour Relations (Consolidation) Act 1992, ss 67, 288, 290, 291) (SI 1993/1908)

    30 Nov 1993 (SI 1993/2503), repeals of or in—

    Employment Protection (Consolidation) Act 1978, ss 11(3), (7), 128(4), 133(1), 138(1), (2) (so far as words repealed relate to sub-ss (4), (5)), 139(1), 146(4), Sch 9, para 8;

    Employment Act 1982;

    Dock Work Act 1989;

    Employment Act 1989;

    Trade Union and Labour Relations (Consolidation) Act 1992, s 277(2), Sch 2, para 24(3)

    1 Jan 1994 (repeal in Trade Union and Labour Relations (Consolidation) Act 1992, s 32) (SI 1993/1908)

**Trade Union Reform and Employment Rights Act 1993 (c 19)**—*contd*

> 1 Apr 1994 (E) (S) and 1 Apr 1995 (otherwise) (SI 1993/2503), repeals in—
> Finance Act 1969;
> Chronically Sick and Disabled Persons Act 1970;
> Employment and Training Act 1973;
> Education (Scotland) Act 1980;
> Agricultural Training Board Act 1982;
> Industrial Training Act 1982
>
> 10 Jun 1994 (so far as not already in force, except repeal of words "subject to subsections (3)–(5)" in Employment Protection (Consolidation) Act 1978, s 138, so far as they relate to sub-s (3)) (SI 1994/1365)[1]
>
> 1 Apr 1996 (repeals of Trade Union and Labour Relations (Consolidation) Act 1992, ss 115, 116) (SI 1993/1908)
>
> *Never in force* (repeal of words "subject to subsections (3)–(5)" in Employment Protection (Consolidation) Act 1978, s 138(2), so far as relating to sub-s (3) (repealed))

[1] By SI 1994/1365, art 3(1), the amendments and repeals made by provisions of this Act brought into force by that Order have effect only in relation to women whose expected week of childbirth begins on or after 16 Oct 1994

[2] By SI 1994/1365, art 3(2), the amendments made by s 24 of this Act (so far as brought into force by that Order) apply to any dismissal where the effective date of termination in relation to that dismissal falls on or after 10 Jun 1994

---

**Video Recordings Act 1993 (c 24)**

*RA:* 20 Jul 1993

*Commencement provisions:* s 6(2)

Whole Act in force 20 Sep 1993 (s 6(2))

---

**Welsh Language Act 1993 (c 38)**

*RA:* 21 Oct 1993

*Commencement provisions:* s 36; Welsh Language Act 1993 (Commencement) Order 1994, SI 1994/115

| | | |
|---|---|---|
| 1–29 | | 21 Dec 1993 (s 36(1)) |
| 30 | (1) | 25 Jan 1994 (so far as enables prescription of description of documents for purpose of Companies Act 1985, s 710B(3)(a) and so far as enables prescription of manner in which a translation is to be certified for purpose of s 710B(8) of the 1985 Act) (SI 1994/115) |
| | | 1 Feb 1994 (otherwise) (SI 1994/115) |
| | (2)–(5) | 1 Feb 1994 (SI 1994/115) |
| | (6) | 25 Jan 1994 (so far as enables prescription of description of documents for purpose of Companies Act 1985, s 710B(3)(a) and so far as enables prescription of manner in which a translation is to be certified for purpose of s 710B(8) of the 1985 Act) (SI 1994/115) |
| | | 1 Feb 1994 (otherwise) (SI 1994/115) |
| 31 | | 1 Feb 1994 (SI 1994/115) |
| 32–34 | | 21 Dec 1993 (s 36(1)) |
| 35 | (1) | See Sch 2 below |
| | (2) | 1 Feb 1994 (SI 1994/115) |
| | (3)–(5) | 21 Dec 1993 (s 36(1)) |
| 36, 37 | | 21 Dec 1993 (s 36(1)) |
| Sch 1 | | 21 Dec 1993 (s 36(1)) |

**Welsh Language Act 1993 (c 38)**—*contd*
Sch 2                            21 Dec 1993 (except repeals in Companies Act 1985) (s 36(1), (2))
                                         1 Feb 1994 (exceptions noted above) (SI 1994/115)

# 1994 Acts

## Antarctic Act 1994 (c 15)

*RA:* 5 Jul 1994

*Commencement provisions:* s 35; Antarctic Act 1994 (Commencement) Order 1995, SI 1995/2748; Antarctic Act 1994 (Commencement) Order 1996, SI 1996/2666; Antarctic Act 1994 (Commencement) Order 1997, SI 1997/1411; Antarctic Act 1994 (Commencement No 2) Order 1997, SI 1997/2298; Antarctic Act 1994 (Commencement No 3) Order 1997, SI 1997/3068

| | |
|---|---|
| 1, 2 | 1 Nov 1995 (SI 1995/2748) |
| 3, 4 | 14 Jan 1998 (SI 1997/3068) |
| 5 | 1 Jun 1997 (SI 1997/1411) |
| 6 | 1 Oct 1997 (SI 1997/2298) |
| 7 | 1 Nov 1996 (SI 1996/2666) |
| 8–32 | 1 Nov 1995 (SI 1995/2748) |
| 33 | See Schedule below |
| 34–36 | 1 Nov 1995 (SI 1995/2748) |
| Schedule | 1 Nov 1995 (except repeals of Antarctic Treaty Act 1967, ss 6, 7(2)(b), (7), 8–11) (SI 1995/2748) |
| | *Not yet in force* (exceptions noted above) |

## Appropriation Act 1994 (c 24)

*RA:* 21 Jul 1994

Whole Act in force 21 Jul 1994 (RA)

## Care of Cathedrals (Supplementary Provisions) Measure 1994 (No 2)

*RA:* 21 Jul 1994

*Commencement provisions:* s 11(2)

The provisions of this Measure are brought into force on 1 Oct 1994 by an appointed day notice signed by the Archbishops of Canterbury and York and dated 25 Jul 1994 (made under s 11(2))

## Chiropractors Act 1994 (c 17)

*RA:* 5 Jul 1994

*Commencement provisions:* s 44(2)–(6); Chiropractors Act 1994 (Commencement No 1 and Transitional Provision) Order 1998, SI 1998/2031; Chiropractors Act 1994 (Commencement No 2) Order 1999, SI 1999/1309; Chiropractors Act 1994 (Commencement No 3) Order 1999, SI 1999/1496; Chiropractors Act 1994 (Commencement No 4) Order 2000, SI 2000/2388; Chiropractors Act 1994 (Commencement Order No 5 and Transitional Provision) Order 2001, SI 2001/2028; Chiropractors Act 1994 (Commencement No 6) Order 2002, SI 2002/312; Chiropractors Act 1994 (Commencement No 7) Order 2004, SI 2004/1521

| | | |
|---|---|---|
| 1 | (1) | 14 Aug 1998 (SI 1998/2031) |

**Chiropractors Act 1994 (c 17)**—*contd*

| | | |
|---|---|---|
| | (2) | 14 Aug 1998 (for the purpose of enabling the Chiropractic Council to prepare for the exercise of any functions which may be, or if the relevant provisions were in force could become, exercisable under any provision of the Act including this subsection) (SI 1998/2031) |
| | | 13 May 1999 (so far as relates to the other provisions of this Act brought into force by SI 1999/1309) (SI 1999/1309) |
| | | 15 Jun 1999 (so far as relates to the other provisions of this Act brought into force by SI 1999/1496) (SI 1999/1496) |
| | | 7 Sep 2000 (so far as relates to the other provisions of this Act brought into force by SI 2000/2388) (SI 2000/2388) |
| | | *Not yet in force* (so far as relates to provisions of this Act not yet in force) |
| | (3) | 14 Aug 1998 (so far as relates to the other provisions of this Act brought into force by SI 1998/2031) (SI 1998/2031) |
| | | 13 May 1999 (so far as relates to the other provisions of this Act brought into force by SI 1999/1309) (SI 1999/1309) |
| | | 15 Jun 1999 (so far as relates to the other provisions of this Act brought into force by SI 1999/1496) (SI 1999/1496) |
| | | 7 Sep 2000 (so far as relates to the other provisions of this Act brought into force by SI 2000/2388) (SI 2000/2388) |
| | | *Not yet in force* (so far as relates to provisions of this Act not yet in force) |
| | (4) | 14 Aug 1998 (so far as relates to Sch 1, Pt I, paras 1, 2, 4–6, 8, 11, 13, 14(2), (3)(a)–(c), 15) (SI 1998/2031) |
| | | 13 May 1999 (so far as relates to Sch 1, Pt 1, paras 7, 14(5)(b)) (SI 1999/1309) |
| | | 1 Feb 2002 (so far as relates to Sch 1, Pt 1, paras 9, 10, 14(5)(a)) (SI 2002/312) |
| | | 16 Jun 2002 (so far as it relates to Sch 1, Pt 1, paras 3 (in so far as it relates to elected members), 14(1), (3)(d), (4)) (SI 2002/312) |
| | | 15 Feb 2003 (so far as it relates to Sch 1, Pt 1, para 12 (for the purpose of enabling consultation on appointments by the Education Committee)) (SI 2002/312) |
| | | 16 Jun 2003 (so far as relates to Sch 1, Pt 1, para 12 (otherwise)) (SI 2001/312) |
| | | 16 Jun 2003 (so far as relates to Sch 1, Pt 1, para 3 (in so far as it relates to education members and members appointed by the Secretary of State)) (SI 2001/312) |
| | | 16 Jun 2004 (so far as relates to Sch 1, Pt 1, para 3 (otherwise)) (SI 2002/312) |
| | (5)–(7) | 13 May 1999 (so far as they relate to the Education Committee) (SI 1999/1309) |
| | | 7 Sep 2000 (otherwise) (SI 2000/2388) |
| | (8) | 14 Aug 1998 (SI 1998/2031) |
| | (9) | 13 May 1999 (so far as relates to the provisions of Sch 1, Pt II brought into force by SI 1999/1309) (SI 1999/1309) |
| | | 7 Sep 2000 (so far as not already in force) (SI 2000/2388) |
| | | *Not yet in force* (otherwise) |
| | (10)–(12) | 14 Aug 1998 (SI 1998/2031) |
| 2 | (1), (2) | 14 Aug 1998 (SI 1998/2031) |
| | (3) | 15 Jun 1999 (SI 1999/1496) |
| | (4)–(6) | 14 Aug 1998 (SI 1998/2031) |
| 3, 4 | | 15 Jun 1999 (SI 1999/1496) |
| 5 | | *Not yet in force* |
| 6 | | 15 Jun 1999 (SI 1999/1496) |
| 7 | (1)–(2) | 7 Sep 2000 (SI 2000/2388) |
| | (3) | 15 Jun 2001 (SI 2001/2028) |
| 8 | (1)–(7) | 7 Sep 2000 (SI 2000/2388) |

**Chiropractors Act 1994 (c 17)**—*contd*

| | | |
|---|---|---|
| | (8) | 7 Sep 2000 (so far as relates to restoration to register of conditionally registered chiropractors) (SI 2000/2388) |
| | | *Not yet in force* (otherwise) |
| 9 | | 15 Jun 1999 (SI 1999/1496) |
| 10 | (1) | 15 Jun 1999 (SI 1999/1496) |
| | (2)–(12) | 7 Sep 2000 (SI 2000/2388) |
| 11–16 | | 13 May 1999 (SI 1999/1309) |
| 17 | | 1 Jul 2004 (SI 2004/1521) |
| 18 | | 13 May 1999 (SI 1999/1309) |
| 19 | | 15 Jun 1999 (SI 1999/1496) |
| 20–28 | | 7 Sep 2000 (SI 2000/2388) |
| 29 | | 15 Jun 1999 (SI 1999/1496) |
| 30, 31 | | 7 Sep 2000 (SI 2000/2388) |
| 32 | (1) | 15 Jun 2001 (subject to a transitional provision) (SI 2001/2028) |
| | (2) | 7 Sep 2000 (SI 2000/2388) |
| | (3) | 7 Sep 2000 (so far as relates to sub-s (2)) (SI 2000/2388) |
| | | 15 Jun 2001 (otherwise) (SI 2001/2028) |
| 33 | | 13 May 1999 (SI 1999/1309) |
| 34 | | 14 Aug 1998 (SI 1998/2031) |
| 35 | (1), (2) | 14 Aug 1998 (SI 1998/2031) |
| | (3) | 7 Sep 2000 (SI 2000/2388) |
| | (4) | 14 Aug 1998 (SI 1998/2031) |
| 36 | (1), (2) | 14 Aug 1998 (SI 1998/2031) |
| | (3) | 15 Jun 1999 (SI 1999/1496) |
| | (4)–(6) | 14 Aug 1998 (SI 1998/2031) |
| 37, 38 | | 15 Jun 1999 (SI 1999/1496) |
| 39 | | 13 May 1999 (SI 1999/1309) |
| 40 | | 15 Jun 1999 (SI 1999/1496) |
| 41 | | 14 Aug 1998 (SI 1998/2031) |
| 42 | | See Sch 2 below |
| 43 | | 14 Aug 1998 (so far as it provides the definitions "the General Council", "prescribed" and "the Registrar") (SI 1998/2031) |
| | | 13 May 1999 (so far as it provides the definitions "recognised qualification", "the required standard of proficiency", "the statutory committees" and "visitor") (SI 1999/1309) |
| | | 15 Jun 1999 (so far as it provides the definitions "conditionally registered chiropractor", "fully registered chiropractor", "opening of the register", "the register", "registered", "registered address", "registered chiropractor" and "unacceptable professional conduct") (SI 1999/1496) |
| | | 7 Sep 2000 (so far as provides the definition "interim suspension order") (SI 2000/2388) |
| | | *Not yet in force* (so far as it provides the definition "provisionally registered chiropractor") |
| 44 | (1) | 14 Aug 1998 (SI 1998/2031) |
| | (2) | 5 Jul 1994 (s 44(2)) |
| | (3)–(6) | 14 Aug 1998 (SI 1998/2031) |
| | (7) | See Sch 1, Pt III below |
| | (8) | 14 Aug 1998 (so far as it relates to provisions of this Act already in force or brought into force by SI 1998/2031) (SI 1998/2031) |
| | | 13 May 1999 (so far as it relates to the provisions of this Act brought into force by SI 1999/1309) (SI 1999/1309) |
| | | 15 Jun 1999 (otherwise) (SI 1999/1496) |
| Sch 1 | Pt I, paras 1, 2 | 14 Aug 1998 (SI 1998/2031) |
| | Pt I, para 3 | 16 Jun 2002 (in so far as it relates to elected members) (SI 2002/312) |
| | | 16 Jun 2003 (in so far as relates to education members and the member appointed by Secretary of State) (SI 2002/312) |
| | | 16 Jun 2004 (otherwise) (SI 2002/312) |
| | Pt I, para 4 | 14 Aug 1998 (SI 1998/2031) |

**Chiropractors Act 1994 (c 17)**—*contd*

| | | |
|---|---|---|
| | Pt I, para 5 | 14 Aug 1998 (subject to a transitional provision) (SI 1998/2031) |
| | Pt I, para 6 | 14 Aug 1998 (SI 1998/2031) |
| | Pt I, para 7 | 13 May 1999 (SI 1999/1309) |
| | Pt I, para 8 | 14 Aug 1998 (SI 1998/2031) |
| | Pt I, paras 9, 10 | 1 Feb 2002 (SI 2002/312) |
| | Pt I, para 11 | 14 Aug 1998 (SI 1998/2031) |
| | Pt I, para 12 | 15 Feb 2003 (for purposes of enabling consultation on appointments by the Education Committee) (SI 2002/312) |
| | | 16 Jun 2003 (otherwise) (SI 2002/312) |
| | Pt I, para 13 | 14 Aug 1998 (SI 1998/2031) |
| | Pt I, para 14(1) | 16 Jun 2002 (SI 2002/312) |
| | Pt I, para 14(2) | 14 Aug 1998 (subject to a transitional provision) (SI 1998/2031) |
| | Pt I, para 14(3)(a)–(c) | 14 Aug 1998 (SI 1998/2031) |
| | Pt I, para 14(3)(d) | 16 Jun 2002 (SI 2002/312) |
| | Pt I, para 14(4) | 16 Jun 2002 (SI 2002/312) |
| | Pt I, para 14(5)(a) | 1 Feb 2002 (SI 2002/312) |
| | Pt I, para 14(5)(b) | 13 May 1999 (SI 1999/1309) |
| | Pt I, para 15 | 14 Aug 1998 (SI 1998/2031) |
| | Pt II, paras 16, 17 | 13 May 1999 (SI 1999/1309) |
| | Pt II, paras 18–20 | 13 May 1999 (so far as they relate to the Education Committee) (SI 1999/1309) |
| | | 7 Sep 2000 (otherwise) (SI 2000/2388) |
| | Pt II, para 21(1) | 7 Sep 2000 (SI 2000/2388) |
| | Pt II, para 21(2) | 13 May 1999 (so far as relates to the Education Committee) (SI 1999/1309) |
| | | 7 Sep 2000 (otherwise) (SI 2000/2388) |
| | Pt II, paras 22, 23 | 13 May 1999 (so far as they relate to the Education Committee) (SI 1999/1309) |
| | | 7 Sep 2000 (otherwise) (SI 2000/2388) |
| | Pt II, para 24 | 7 Sep 2000 (SI 2000/2388) |
| | Pt II, paras 25–29 | 13 May 1999 (SI 1999/1309) |
| | Pt II, paras 30–41 | 7 Sep 2000 (SI 2000/2388) |
| | Pt III | 14 Aug 1998 (SI 1998/2031) |
| Sch 2 | | 5 Jul 1994 (s 44(2)) |

---

**Church of England (Legal Aid) Measure 1994 (No 3)**

*RA:* 21 Jul 1994

*Commencement provisions:* s 8(2)

The provisions of this Measure are brought into force on 1 Sep 1994 by an appointed day notice signed by the Archbishops of Canterbury and York and dated 25 Jul 1994 (made under s 8(2))

---

**Coal Industry Act 1994 (c 21)**

*RA:* 5 Jul 1994

*Commencement provisions:* s 68(2)–(6); Coal Industry Act 1994 (Commencement No 1) Order 1994, SI 1994/2189; Coal Industry Act 1994 (Commencement No 2 and Transitional Provision) Order 1994, SI 1994/2552; Coal Industry (Restructuring Date) Order 1994, SI 1994/2553; Coal Industry Act 1994 (Commencement No 3) Order 1994, SI 1994/3063; Coal Industry Act 1994 (Commencement No 4) Order 1995, SI 1995/159; Coal Industry Act 1994 (Commencement No 5) Order 1995, SI 1995/273; Coal Industry Act 1994 (Commencement No 6) and Membership of the British Coal Corporation (Appointed Day) Order 1995, SI 1995/1507; Coal Industry Act 1994 (Commencement No 7) and Dissolution of the British Coal Corporation Order 2004, SI 2004/144; Coal Industry Act 1994 (Commencement No 8 and Transitional Provision) Order 2014, SI 2014/888

| | |
|---|---|
| 1 | 19 Sep 1994 (SI 1994/2189) |

**Coal Industry Act 1994 (c 21)**—*contd*

| | | |
|---|---|---|
| 2, 3 | | 31 Oct 1994 (SI 1994/2552) |
| 4–6 | | 19 Sep 1994 (SI 1994/2189) |
| 7–9 | | 5 Jul 1994 (s 68(4), (6)) |
| 10, 11 | | 31 Oct 1994 (SI 1994/2553) |
| 12–14 | | 5 Jul 1994 (s 68(4), (6)) |
| 15, 16 | | 31 Oct 1994 (SI 1994/2552) |
| 17 | | 5 Jul 1994 (s 68(4), (6)) |
| 18 | | 31 Oct 1994 (SI 1994/2553) |
| 19, 20 | | 31 Oct 1994 (SI 1994/2552) |
| 21 | | 19 Sep 1994 (SI 1994/2189) |
| 22 | (1) | 31 Oct 1994 (SI 1994/2552) |
| | (2) | *Not yet in force* |
| | (3) | 31 Oct 1994 (SI 1994/2552) |
| 23 | | 31 Oct 1994 (SI 1994/2553) |
| 24 | | 31 Jan 1995 (SI 1995/159) |
| 25–30 | | 31 Oct 1994 (SI 1994/2552) |
| 31–34 | | 31 Oct 1994 (SI 1994/2553) |
| 35 | | 31 Oct 1994 (SI 1994/2552) |
| 36 | | 31 Oct 1994 (SI 1994/2553) |
| 37 | | 31 Oct 1994 (SI 1994/2552) |
| 38–44 | | 31 Oct 1994 (SI 1994/2553) |
| 45–47 | | 31 Oct 1994 (SI 1994/2552) |
| 48–53 | | 31 Oct 1994 (SI 1994/2553) |
| 54 | | 5 Jul 1994 (s 68(4), (6)) |
| 55 | | 31 Oct 1994 (SI 1994/2553) |
| 56–61 | | 31 Oct 1994 (SI 1994/2552) |
| 62–66 | | 5 Jul 1994 (s 68(4), (6)) |
| 67 | (1) | See Sch 9 below |
| | (2)–(6) | 5 Jul 1994 (s 68(4), (6)) |
| | (7) | See Sch 10 below |
| | (8) | See Sch 11 below |
| 68 | | 5 Jul 1994 (s 68(4), (6)) |
| Sch 1 | | 19 Sep 1994 (SI 1994/2189) |
| Sch 2 | | 5 Jul 1994 (s 68(4), (6)) |
| Sch 3 | | 31 Oct 1994 (SI 1994/2552) |
| Sch 4 | | 19 Sep 1994 (SI 1994/2189) |
| Sch 5 | | 31 Oct 1994 (SI 1994/2552) |
| Schs 6–8 | | 31 Oct 1994 (SI 1994/2553) |
| Sch 9 | paras 1–6 | 31 Oct 1994 (SI 1994/2553) |
| | para 7 | 27 Mar 2004 (s 68(3); SI 2004/144) |
| | para 8 | 31 Oct 1994 (SI 1994/2552) |
| | paras 9, 10 | 31 Oct 1994 (SI 1994/2553) |
| | para 11(1)(a) | 31 Oct 1994 (SI 1994/2553) |
| | para 11(1)(b) | 31 Oct 1994 (SI 1994/2552) |
| | para 11(2)(a) | 31 Oct 1994 (SI 1994/2553) |
| | para 11(2)(b) | 31 Oct 1994 (SI 1994/2552) |
| | para 11(3)–(5) | 31 Oct 1994 (SI 1994/2553) |
| | para 12 | 31 Oct 1994 (SI 1994/2552) |
| | para 13(1), (2) | 31 Oct 1994 (SI 1994/2553) |
| | para 13(3) | 1 Nov 1994 (SI 1994/2552) |
| | paras 14–23 | 31 Oct 1994 (SI 1994/2553) |
| | para 24 | 27 Mar 2004 (s 68(3); SI 2004/144) |
| | paras 25–28 | 31 Oct 1994 (SI 1994/2553) |
| | paras 29, 30 | 27 Mar 2004 (s 68(3); SI 2004/144) |
| | paras 31–38 | 31 Oct 1994 (SI 1994/2553) |
| | para 39(1) | 31 Oct 1994 (SI 1994/2553) |
| | para 39(2), (3) | 1 Nov 1994 (SI 1994/2552) |
| | para 39(4) | 31 Oct 1994 (SI 1994/2553) |
| | paras 40–44 | 31 Oct 1994 (SI 1994/2553) |

**Coal Industry Act 1994 (c 21)**—*contd*

|          |        |                                      |
|----------|--------|--------------------------------------|
|          | para 45 | 27 Mar 2004 (s 68(3); SI 2004/144)  |
| Sch 10   |        | 31 Oct 1994 (SI 1994/2552)           |
| Sch 11   | Pt I   | 5 Jul 1994 (s 68(4), (6))            |
|          | Pt II  | 31 Oct 1994 (SI 1994/2553)           |
|          | Pt III | 31 Oct 1994 (SI 1994/2552), repeals of or in— |

             Coal Act 1938;
             Coal Act 1943;
             Coal Industry Nationalisation Act 1946, ss 52, 57, 58, 63(2);
             Opencast Coal Act 1958;
             Land Commission Act 1967;
             Electricity Act 1989
        1 Nov 1994 (SI 1994/2552), repeals in—
             Town and Country Planning (Scotland) Act 1972;
             Town and Country Planning Act 1990
        24 Dec 1994 (SI 1994/3063), repeals of or in—
             Coal Industry Nationalisation Act 1946, s 45 (for purposes specified in sub-s (1) thereof);
             Housing and Planning Act 1986, Sch 8, para 8;
             Coal Industry Act 1987, Sch 1, paras 9, 17, 20
        1 Mar 1995 (SI 1995/273), repeals of or in—
             Coal Industry Nationalisation Act 1946, s 4 (subject to a saving in relation to sub-s (6));
             Coal Consumers' Councils (Northern Irish Interests) Act 1962 (subject to a saving in relation to s 2);
             Chronically Sick and Disabled Persons Act 1970, s 14(1)
        30 Jun 1995 (SI 1995/1507), repeals of or in—
             Coal Industry Nationalisation Act 1946, s 2(2), (3), (5);
             Coal Industry Act 1949, s 1(2), (4)
        27 Mar 2004 (SI 2004/144), repeals of or in—
             Coal Industry Nationalisation Act 1946, ss 4(6) (so far as not already in force), 27, 28, 34(1), 35, 55, 64(2), (4), (6)–(9);
             Coal Consumers' Councils (Northern Irish Interests) Act 1962, s 2 (so far as not already in force);
             Coal Industry Act 1962;
             Coal Industry Act 1965;
             Coal Industry Act 1967;
             National Loans Act 1968;
             Coal Industry Act 1971;
             Coal Industry Act 1973;
             Statutory Corporations (Financial Provisions) Act 1975;
             National Coal Board (Finance) Act 1976;
             Coal Industry Act 1977, ss 1, 15, Schs 1, 4, 5;
             Coal Industry Act 1980, ss 1, 2, 9;
             Coal Industry Act 1982;
             Coal Industry Act 1983, ss 1, 2;
             Miscellaneous Financial Provisions Act 1983;
             Companies Consolidation (Consequential Provisions) Act 1985, Sch 2, entries relating to the Coal Industry Act 1965 and the Coal Industry Act 1971;
             Coal Industry Act 1987, ss 3, 4, 6, 10(3), (4), Schs 2, 3;
             Companies Act 1989, Sch 18, para 18;
             Coal Industry Act 1990;
             Coal Mining Subsidence Act 1991;
             Coal Industry Act 1992;
             British Coal and British Rail (Transfer Proposals) Act 1993
        28 Apr 2014 (SI 2014/888), repeals of or in—
             Coal Industry Act 1977, s 7(1), (2)[1];
             Coal Industry Act 1980, ss 7, 10–11;
             Coal Industry Act 1983, ss 4–6, Schedule;

**Coal Industry Act 1994 (c 21)**—*contd*

          Coal Industry Act 1985, ss 3–5

          *Not yet in force*, repeals of or in—

          Coal Industry Nationalisation Act 1946, ss 37, 41, 56, 59–62, 63(1), (3), (4), 64(1), (3), (10), 65, Sch 2A;

          Coal Industry Act 1949, ss 4, 7, 8, 13;

          Miners' Welfare Act 1952;

          Coal Industry Act 1977, ss 7(3)–(10), 11(1), 12(1), (2), 13, 14, 16, Sch 3;

          Companies Consolidation (Consequential Provisions) Act 1985, Sch 2, entry relating to the Coal Industry Act 1977;

          Coal Industry Act 1987, ss 7–9, 10(2), Sch 1, paras 1(3), (4), 3, 8, 11(1), (2), 16, 18(1), (2), 21, 27, 30, 34(1)–(3), 36, 41;

          Companies Act 1989, Sch 18, para 1

       Pt IV          27 Mar 2004 (s 68(3); SI 2004/144)

[1]   For transitional provision, see SI 2014/889, art 3

---

**Consolidated Fund Act 1994 (c 4)**

*RA:* 24 Mar 1994

Whole Act in force 24 Mar 1994 (RA)

---

**Consolidated Fund (No 2) Act 1994 (c 41)**

*RA:* 16 Dec 1994

Whole Act in force 16 Dec 1994 (RA)

---

**Criminal Justice and Public Order Act 1994 (c 33)**

*RA:* 3 Nov 1994

*Commencement provisions:* ss 82(3), 172(2)–(4), (6); Criminal Justice and Public Order Act 1994 (Commencement No 1) Order 1994, SI 1994/2935; Criminal Justice and Public Order Act 1994 (Commencement No 2) Order 1994, SI 1994/3192; Criminal Justice and Public Order Act 1994 (Commencement No 3) Order 1994, SI 1994/3258; Criminal Justice and Public Order Act 1994 (Commencement No 4) Order 1995, SI 1995/24; Criminal Justice and Public Order Act 1994 (Commencement No 5 and Transitional Provisions) Order 1995, SI 1995/127; Criminal Justice and Public Order Act 1994 (Commencement No 6) Order 1995, SI 1995/721; Criminal Justice and Public Order Act 1994 (Commencement No 7) Order 1995, SI 1995/1378; Criminal Justice and Public Order Act 1994 (Commencement No 8 and Transitional Provision) Order 1995, SI 1995/1957; Criminal Justice and Public Order Act 1994 (Commencement No 9) Order 1996, SI 1996/625; Criminal Justice and Public Order Act 1994 (Commencement No 10) Order 1996, SI 1996/1608; Criminal Justice and Public Order Act 1994 (Commencement No 11 and Transitional Provision) Order 1997, SI 1997/882; Criminal Justice and Public Order Act 1994 (Commencement No 12 and Transitional Provision) Order 1998, SI 1998/277; Criminal Justice and Public Order Act 1994 (Commencement No 13) Order 2002, SI 2002/447; Criminal Justice and Public Order Act 1994 (Commencement No 14) Order 2007, SI 2007/621

| | |
|---|---|
| 1 | 1 Mar 1998 (subject to a transitional provision) (SI 1998/277) |
| 2–4 | 1 Mar 1998 (SI 1998/277) |
| 5–15 | 3 Nov 1994 (s 172(4)) |
| 16 | 9 Jan 1995 (SI 1994/3192) |
| 17, 18 | 3 Feb 1995 (subject to a saving relating to s 17) (SI 1995/127) |
| 19 | 30 May 1995 (SI 1995/1378) |
| 20, 21 | *Never in force* (repealed) |
| 22 | 8 Mar 1996 (SI 1996/625) |
| 23, 24 | 3 Feb 1995 (subject to a saving relating to s 23) (SI 1995/127) |

**Criminal Justice and Public Order Act 1994 (c 33)**—*contd*

| | | |
|---|---|---|
| 25–30 | | 10 Apr 1995 (SI 1995/721) |
| 31–33 | | 3 Feb 1995 (subject to a saving relating to s 31) (SI 1995/127) |
| 34–39 | | 10 Apr 1995 (SI 1995/721) |
| 40–43 | | 3 Feb 1995 (SI 1995/127) |
| 44 | | Repealed (deemed to have been enacted with this repeal) |
| 45 | | See Sch 5 below |
| 46–51 | | 3 Feb 1995 (subject to a saving relating to s 50) (SI 1995/127) |
| 52 | | 11 Jan 1995 (SI 1994/3258) |
| 53 | | 2 Feb 1995 (SI 1995/24) |
| 54–60 | | 10 Apr 1995 (SI 1995/721) |
| 61 | | 3 Nov 1994 (s 172(4)) |
| 62 | | 10 Apr 1995 (SI 1995/721) |
| 63 | | 3 Nov 1994 (s 172(4)) |
| 64 | (1)–(3) | 3 Feb 1995 (so far as relating to powers conferred on a constable by s 63) (SI 1995/127) |
| | | *Not yet in force* (otherwise) |
| | (4)–(6) | 10 Apr 1995 (SI 1995/721) |
| 65 | | 3 Nov 1994 (s 172(4)) |
| 66 | (1)–(5) | 10 Apr 1995 (SI 1995/721) |
| | (6) | 3 Feb 1995 (SI 1995/127) |
| | (7)–(9) | 10 Apr 1995 (SI 1995/721) |
| | (10)–(13) | 3 Feb 1995 (SI 1995/127) |
| 67 | (1), (2) | 10 Apr 1995 (SI 1995/721) |
| | (3)–(5) | 3 Feb 1995 (SI 1995/127) |
| | (6), (7) | 10 Apr 1995 (SI 1995/721) |
| | (8), (9) | 3 Feb 1995 (SI 1995/127) |
| 68–71 | | 3 Nov 1994 (s 172(4)) |
| 72–74 | | 3 Feb 1995 (SI 1995/127) |
| 75, 76 | | 24 Aug 1995 (SI 1995/1957) |
| 77–81 | | 3 Nov 1994 (s 172(4)) |
| 82 | | 3 Jan 1995 (s 82(3)) |
| 83 | | 3 Nov 1994 (s 172(4)) |
| 84–88 | | 3 Feb 1995 (subject to a saving relating to s 88) (SI 1995/127) |
| 89 | | 1 Nov 1995 (subject to a transitional provision) (SI 1995/1957) |
| 90 | | 3 Nov 1994 (s 172(4)) |
| 91, 92 | | 3 Feb 1995 (SI 1995/127) |
| 93–101 | | 3 Nov 1994 (s 172(4)) |
| 102–117 | | 3 Feb 1995 (SI 1995/127) |
| 118–125 | | 10 Apr 1995 (SI 1995/721) |
| 126–128 | | 3 Nov 1994 (s 172(4)) |
| 129–133 | | 3 Feb 1995 (subject to a saving relating to s 129) (SI 1995/127) |
| 134 | (1), (2) | 3 Feb 1995 (SI 1995/127) |
| | (3) | 3 Feb 1995 (for purpose of making rules under Prisons (Scotland) Act 1989, s 18(3A)) (SI 1995/127) |
| | | 1 Jun 1995 (otherwise) (subject to a saving) (SI 1995/127) |
| | (4)–(6) | 3 Feb 1995 (SI 1995/127) |
| 135–141 | | 3 Feb 1995 (SI 1995/127) |
| 142–148 | | 3 Nov 1994 (s 172(4)) |
| 149 | | 1 Jul 1996 (SI 1996/1608) |
| 150 | | 3 Nov 1994 (s 172(4)) |
| 151 | | 9 Jan 1995 (SI 1994/3192) |
| 152–155 | | 3 Feb 1995 (SI 1995/127) |
| 156 | | 10 Apr 1995 (SI 1995/721) |
| 157 | | 3 Feb 1995 (subject to a saving) (SI 1995/127) |
| 158 | (1) | 3 Nov 1994 (s 172(4)) |
| | (2) | 1 Apr 1997 (SI 1997/882) |
| | (3), (4) | 3 Nov 1994 (s 172(4)) |
| | (5)–(8) | 1 Apr 1997 (subject to transitional provisions relating to sub-ss (5), (8)) (SI 1997/882) |

**Criminal Justice and Public Order Act 1994 (c 33)**—*contd*

| | | |
|---|---|---|
| 159 | (1), (2) | 19 Dec 1994 (SI 1994/2935) |
| | (3) | 20 Mar 2002 (SI 2002/447) |
| | (4) | 19 Dec 1994 (SI 1994/2935) |
| | (5) | 1 Apr 1997 (SI 1997/882) |
| 160–164 | | 3 Feb 1995 (SI 1995/127) |
| 165 | | 6 Apr 2007 (SI 2007/621) |
| 166, 167 | | 3 Nov 1994 (s 172(4)) |
| 168 | (1) | See Sch 9 below |
| | (2) | See Sch 10 below |
| | (3) | See Sch 11 below |
| 169, 170 | | 3 Feb 1995 (SI 1995/127) |
| 171, 172 | | 3 Nov 1994 (s 172(4)) |
| Schs 1, 2 | | 3 Nov 1994 (s 172(4)) |
| Sch 3 | | 10 Apr 1995 (SI 1995/721) |
| Sch 4 | | Repealed (deemed to have been enacted with this repeal) |
| Sch 5 | | 4 Sep 1995 (SI 1995/1957) |
| Sch 6 | | 3 Feb 1995 (SI 1995/127) |
| Sch 7 | | 10 Apr 1995 (SI 1995/721) |
| Sch 8 | | 3 Feb 1995 (subject to a saving) (SI 1995/127) |
| Sch 9 | paras 1–14 | 3 Feb 1995 (SI 1995/127) |
| | para 15 | 3 Feb 1995 (subject to a saving) (SI 1995/127) |
| | paras 16–32 | 3 Feb 1995 (SI 1995/127) |
| | para 33 | 3 Feb 1995 (subject to a saving) (SI 1995/127) |
| | para 34 | 9 Jan 1995 (SI 1994/3192) |
| | paras 35, 36 | 3 Feb 1995 (SI 1995/127) |
| | para 37 | 3 Feb 1995 (save for para 37(3)) (SI 1995/127) |
| | | 10 Apr 1995 (para 37(3)) (SI 1995/721) |
| | para 38 | *Never in force* (repealed) |
| | para 39 | 3 Feb 1995 (SI 1995/127) |
| | para 40 | 3 Feb 1995 (subject to a saving) (SI 1995/127) |
| | para 41 | 9 Jan 1995 (SI 1994/3192) |
| | paras 42–45 | 3 Feb 1995 (SI 1995/127) |
| | para 46 | 3 Nov 1994 (s 172(4)) |
| | paras 47–53 | 3 Feb 1995 (SI 1995/127) |
| Sch 10 | paras 1–3 | 10 Apr 1995 (SI 1995/721) |
| | para 4 | 1 Mar 1998 (SI 1998/277) |
| | paras 5, 6 | 10 Apr 1995 (SI 1995/721) |
| | paras 7, 8 | 3 Feb 1995 (SI 1995/127) |
| | para 9 | 1 Mar 1998 (SI 1998/277) |
| | para 10 | 10 Apr 1995 (SI 1995/721) |
| | para 11 | 3 Feb 1995 (SI 1995/127) |
| | para 12 | 1 Mar 1998 (SI 1998/277) |
| | paras 13, 14 | 3 Feb 1995 (SI 1995/127) |
| | para 15 | 10 Apr 1995 (SI 1995/721) |
| | para 16 | 1 Mar 1998 (SI 1998/277) |
| | paras 17, 18 | 3 Feb 1995 (SI 1995/127) |
| | paras 19–23 | 10 Apr 1995 (SI 1995/721) |
| | para 24 | 1 Mar 1998 (SI 1998/277) |
| | para 25 | 3 Feb 1995 (SI 1995/127) |
| | para 26 | 3 Nov 1994 (s 172(4), (6)) |
| | paras 27–29 | 3 Feb 1995 (SI 1995/127) |
| | para 30 | 1 Mar 1998 (SI 1998/277) |
| | para 31 | 3 Feb 1995 (SI 1995/127) |
| | paras 32–34 | 10 Apr 1995 (SI 1995/721) |
| | paras 35, 36 | 3 Nov 1994 (s 172(4), (6)) |
| | paras 37, 38 | 3 Feb 1995 (SI 1995/127) |
| | para 39 | 1 Mar 1998 (SI 1998/277) |
| | para 40 | 9 Jan 1995 (SI 1994/3192) |
| | paras 41–44 | 10 Apr 1995 (SI 1995/721) |

**Criminal Justice and Public Order Act 1994 (c 33)**—*contd*

|  |  |
|---|---|
| para 45 | 3 Feb 1995 (SI 1995/127) |
| para 46 | 1 Mar 1998 (SI 1998/277) |
| para 47 | 3 Feb 1995 (SI 1995/127) |
| para 48 | 10 Apr 1995 (SI 1995/721) |
| paras 49, 50 | 1 Mar 1998 (SI 1998/277) |
| para 51 | 10 Apr 1995 (SI 1995/721) |
| para 52 | 3 Feb 1995 (SI 1995/127) |
| para 53 | 24 Aug 1995 (SI 1995/1957) |
| paras 54–58 | 10 Apr 1995 (SI 1995/721) |
| paras 59, 60 | 3 Nov 1994 (s 172(4), (6)) |
| paras 61, 62 | 10 Apr 1995 (SI 1995/721) |
| para 63(1) | 3 Nov 1994 (s 172(4), (6)) |
| para 63(2) | 3 Feb 1995 (SI 1995/127) |
| para 63(3)–(5) | 3 Nov 1994 (s 172(4), (6)) |
| para 64 | 9 Jan 1995 (so far as substitutes for reference to s 41 references to ss 41 and 41B in Prisons (Scotland) Act 1989, s 19(4)) (SI 1994/3192) |
|  | 3 Feb 1995 (so far as not already in force) (SI 1995/127) |
| para 65 | 4 Sep 1995 (SI 1995/1957) |
| para 66 | 1 Mar 1998 (SI 1998/277) |
| para 67 | 10 Apr 1995 (SI 1995/721) |
| para 68 | 3 Feb 1995 (SI 1995/127) |
| para 69 | 9 Jan 1995 (SI 1994/3192) |
| para 70 | 1 Jul 1996 (SI 1996/1608) |
| para 71 | 10 Apr 1995 (SI 1995/721) |
| paras 72, 73 | 1 Mar 1998 (SI 1998/277) |
| Sch 11[1] | 3 Nov 1994 (s 172(4))[2], repeals in— |
|  | Sexual Offences Act 1967; |
|  | Caravan Sites Act 1968; |
|  | Sexual Offences (Amendment) Act 1976; |
|  | Criminal Justice (Scotland) Act 1980; |
|  | Homosexual Offences (Northern Ireland) Order 1982, SI 1982/1536; |
|  | Public Order Act 1986 |
|  | 9 Jan 1995 (SI 1994/3192), repeals of or in— |
|  | Magistrates' Courts Act 1980, s 24; |
|  | Criminal Justice Act 1988, s 126; |
|  | Criminal Justice Act 1991, s 64; |
|  | Criminal Justice Act 1993, s 67(2) |
|  | 3 Feb 1995 (SI 1995/127), repeals of or in— |
|  | Indictable Offences Act 1848; |
|  | Sexual Offences Act 1956; |
|  | Children and Young Persons Act 1963; |
|  | Police (Scotland) Act 1967; |
|  | Children and Young Persons Act 1969[3]; |
|  | Police Act 1969; |
|  | Police Act (Northern Ireland) 1970; |
|  | Juries Act 1974; |
|  | Rehabilitation of Offenders Act 1974; |
|  | Criminal Law Act 1977, s 38; |
|  | Protection of Children Act 1978; |
|  | Magistrates' Courts Act 1980, ss 22(1), 38(2)(b); |
|  | Criminal Justice Act 1982, s 12(6), (7), (11); |
|  | Video Recordings Act 1984; |
|  | Prisons (Scotland) Act 1989; |
|  | Broadcasting Act 1990; |
|  | Northern Ireland (Emergency Provisions) Act 1991; |
|  | Criminal Justice Act 1991 (so far as not already in force); |
|  | Parole Board (Transfer of Functions) Order 1992, SI 1992/1829; |

## Criminal Justice and Public Order Act 1994 (c 33)—*contd*

Video Recordings Act 1993;
Criminal Justice Act 1993 (so far as not already in force)
10 Apr 1995 (SI 1995/721), repeals in—
Criminal Evidence Act 1898;
Criminal Evidence Act (Northern Ireland) 1923;
Bail Act 1976;
Police and Criminal Evidence Act 1984;
Criminal Evidence (Northern Ireland) Order 1988,
SI 1988/1987
4 Sep 1995 (SI 1995/1957), repeals in—
Prosecution of Offences Act 1985;
Criminal Justice Act 1988, ss 25, 34, 160
1 Mar 1998 (SI 1998/277), repeals of or in—
Prison Act 1952, s 43(1), the word "and" at end of para (b);
Criminal Justice Act 1967, s 67(5)(a);
Criminal Justice Act 1982, Sch 14, para 8
20 Mar 2002 (repeals in Backing of Warrants (Republic of Ireland)
Act 1965) (SI 2002/447)
*Not yet in force*, repeals of or in—
Prison Act 1952, s 43(1)(a), (2)(b), (c);
Criminal Law Act 1977, s 6(3);
Criminal Justice Act 1982, s 67(5) (repealed);
Criminal Justice Act 1988, s 32A(10) (repealed)

[1]   Certain repeals made by Sch 11 have been repealed by Criminal Procedure and Investigations Act 1996, s 44, and Sch 11 is deemed to have been enacted as such

[2]   In relation to repeal of Criminal Justice Act 1991, s 50(4), note that s 150 of this Act (which also effects that repeal) is brought into force on 3 Nov 1994 as noted above

[3]   The entry relating to Children and Young Persons Act 1969, s 57(4) is to be treated as always having been an entry relating to Children and Young Persons Act 1969, s 57(4), by virtue of Youth Justice and Criminal Evidence Act 1999, s 67, Sch 4, para 24, as from a day to be appointed under s 68(3) of the 1999 Act

## Deregulation and Contracting Out Act 1994 (c 40)

*RA:* 3 Nov 1994

*Commencement provisions:* s 82(2)–(7); Deregulation and Contracting Out Act 1994 (Commencement No 1) Order 1994, SI 1994/3037; Deregulation and Contracting Out Act 1994 (Commencement No 2) Order 1994, SI 1994/3188; Industrial Relations (Deregulation and Contracting Out Act 1994) (Commencement) Order (Northern Ireland) 1994, SR 1994/488; Deregulation and Contracting Out Act 1994 (Commencement No 3) Order 1995, SI 1995/1433; Deregulation and Contracting Out Act 1994 (Commencement No 4 and Transitional Provisions) Order 1995, SI 1995/2835

| | | |
|---|---|---|
| 1–6 | | 3 Nov 1994 (s 82(3)) |
| 7 | | 3 Jan 1995 (s 82(2)) |
| 8 | | 3 Jan 1995 (SI 1994/3188) |
| 9, 10 | | 3 Jan 1995 (s 82(2)) |
| 11 | | 3 Jan 1995 (SI 1994/3188) |
| 12 | | 3 Jan 1995 (s 82(2)) |
| 13 | (1) | See Sch 5 below |
| | (2) | See Sch 6 below |
| 14 | | 3 Nov 1994 (s 82(3)) |
| 15–17 | | 3 Jan 1995 (s 82(2)) |
| 18 | | 3 Nov 1994 (s 82(3)) |
| 19 | | 3 Jan 1995 (SI 1994/3188) |
| 20, 21 | | 3 Jan 1995 (s 82(2)) |
| 22–24 | | 1 Dec 1994 (SI 1994/3037) |
| 25–30 | | 3 Nov 1994 (s 82(3)) |

**Deregulation and Contracting Out Act 1994 (c 40)**—*contd*

| | | |
|---|---|---|
| 31 | | 3 Jan 1995 (s 82(2)) |
| 32 | | 3 Nov 1994 (s 82(3)) |
| 33 | | 3 Nov 1994 (s 82(3)) (but deemed always to have had effect, subject to a transitional provision (s 33(2), (3)) |
| 34 | | 3 Nov 1994 (s 82(3)) |
| 35 | | See Sch 10 below |
| 36 | (1) | 3 Jan 1995 (subject to transitional provisions) (SI 1994/3188) |
| | (2) | 3 Jan 1995 (subject to transitional provisions) (SR 1994/488) |
| 37 | | 3 Nov 1994 (s 82(3)) |
| 38 | | 1 Jan 1996 (SI 1995/2835) |
| 39 | | See Sch 11 below |
| 40, 41 | | 3 Nov 1994 (s 82(3)) |
| 42–50 | | *Never in force* (repealed) |
| 51 | | 3 Jan 1995 (SI 1994/3188) |
| 52, 53 | | *Never in force* (repealed) |
| 54, 55 | | 3 Nov 1994 (s 82(3)) |
| 56 | | *Never in force* (repealed) |
| 57 | | See Sch 13 below |
| 58 | | 3 Jan 1995 (SI 1994/3188) |
| 59 | | 1 Jan 1996 (subject to transitional provisions) (SI 1995/2835) |
| 60 | | 1 Apr 1995 (subject to transitional provisions) (SI 1994/3188) |
| 61 | | 1 Jan 1996 (subject to transitional provisions) (SI 1995/2835) |
| 62 | | 3 Jan 1995 (SI 1994/3188) |
| 63 | | 1 Jan 1996 (subject to transitional provisions) (SI 1995/2835) |
| 64 | | 3 Jan 1995 (SI 1994/3188) |
| 65, 66 | | 1 Jan 1996 (subject to transitional provisions) (SI 1995/2835) |
| 67 | | 3 Jan 1995 (SI 1994/3188) |
| 68 | | See Sch 14 below |
| 69–79 | | 3 Jan 1995 (s 82(2)) |
| 80 | | 1 Jan 1996 (subject to transitional provisions) (SI 1995/2835) |
| 81 | | See Sch 17 below |
| 82 | | 3 Nov 1994 (s 82(3)) |
| Sch 1 | | 3 Nov 1994 (s 82(3)) |
| Schs 2–4 | | 3 Jan 1995 (s 82(2)) |
| Sch 5 | | 1 Jul 1995 (SI 1995/1433) |
| Sch 6 | paras 1, 2 | 1 Jul 1995 (so far as enables regulations to be made under Companies (Northern Ireland) Order 1986, SI 1986/1032, arts 603B(6)(f), 603C(2)(f)) (SI 1995/1433) |
| | | 1 Nov 1995 (otherwise) (SI 1995/1433) |
| | paras 3, 4 | 1 Nov 1995 (SI 1995/1433) |
| Sch 7 | | 3 Jan 1995 (SI 1994/3188) |
| Schs 8, 9 | | 3 Jan 1995 (s 82(2)) |
| Sch 10 | | 3 Jan 1995 (SI 1994/3188) |
| Sch 11 | | 3 Nov 1994 (s 82(3)), amendments relating to— Road Traffic Regulation Act 1984; Charities Act 1993 |
| | | 3 Jan 1995 (s 82(2)), amendments relating to— Fair Trading Act 1973, ss 93A, 133; Energy Act 1976; Competition Act 1980; Building Societies Act 1986; Financial Services Act 1986; Companies Act 1989; Companies (Northern Ireland) Order 1990 |
| | | 3 Jan 1995 (SI 1994/3188), amendments relating to— Licensing Act 1964; Fair Trading Act 1973, s 77 |
| | | 1 Jul 1995 (amendment relating to Company Directors Disqualification Act 1986) (SI 1995/1433) |

**Deregulation and Contracting Out Act 1994 (c 40)**—*contd*

|  |  |  |
|---|---|---|
|  |  | 1 Nov 1995 (amendment relating to Companies (Northern Ireland) Order 1989, SI 1989/2404) (SI 1995/1433) |
| Sch 12 |  | *Never in force* (repealed) |
| Sch 13 | paras 1–13 | *Never in force* (repealed) |
|  | para 14(1)(a), (b) | *Never in force* (repealed) |
|  | para 14(1)(c), (d) | 3 Nov 1994 (s 82(3)) |
|  | para 14(1)(e) | *Never in force* (repealed) |
|  | para 14(2)–(6) | *Never in force* (repealed) |
|  | paras 15–18 | *Never in force* (repealed) |
| Sch 14 | para 1 | See paras 2–8 below |
|  | para 2 | 1 Jan 1996 (subject to transitional provisions) (SI 1995/2835) |
|  | para 3 | 3 Jan 1995 (SI 1994/3188) |
|  | para 4 | 1 Jan 1996 (subject to transitional provisions) (SI 1995/2835) |
|  | para 5(1) | 1 Jan 1996 (subject to transitional provisions) (SI 1995/2835) |
|  | para 5(2)(a) | 1 Jan 1996 (subject to transitional provisions) (SI 1995/2835) |
|  | para 5(2)(b) | 3 Jan 1995 (SI 1994/3188) |
|  | paras 6–8 | 1 Jan 1996 (subject to transitional provisions) (SI 1995/2835) |
| Schs 15, 16 |  | 3 Jan 1995 (s 82(2)) |
| Sch 17 |  | 3 Nov 1994 (s 82(3)), repeals in— |
|  |  | Road Traffic Regulation Act 1984; |
|  |  | Weights and Measures Act 1985; |
|  |  | Charities Act 1992; |
|  |  | Charities Act 1993 |
|  |  | 1 Dec 1994 (SI 1994/3037), repeals of or in— |
|  |  | Shops Act 1950; |
|  |  | Shops (Airports) Act 1962; |
|  |  | Shops (Early Closing Days) Act 1965; |
|  |  | Local Government Act 1972; |
|  |  | Local Government (Scotland) Act 1973; |
|  |  | Cinemas Act 1985; |
|  |  | Employment Act 1989; |
|  |  | Sunday Trading Act 1994 |
|  |  | 3 Jan 1995 (s 82(2)), repeals in— |
|  |  | Fair Trading Act 1973; |
|  |  | Competition Act 1980; |
|  |  | Telecommunications Act 1984; |
|  |  | Building Societies Act 1986; |
|  |  | Financial Services Act 1986; |
|  |  | Gas Act 1986; |
|  |  | Companies Act 1989; |
|  |  | Electricity Act 1989; |
|  |  | Companies (Northern Ireland) Order 1990; |
|  |  | Electricity (Northern Ireland) Order 1992; |
|  |  | Railways Act 1993 |
|  |  | 3 Jan 1995 (SI 1994/3188), repeals of or in— |
|  |  | Merchant Shipping Act 1894; |
|  |  | Licensing Act 1964; |
|  |  | Employment Agencies Act 1973; |
|  |  | Employment Protection Act 1975; |
|  |  | House of Commons Disqualification Act 1975; |
|  |  | Employment Protection (Consolidation) Act 1978; |
|  |  | Merchant Shipping Act 1979; |
|  |  | Public Passenger Vehicles Act 1981, ss 14A(3), 17(2)(b), 27; |
|  |  | Employment (Miscellaneous Provisions) (Northern Ireland) Order 1981, SI 1981/839; |
|  |  | Income and Corporation Taxes Act 1988 |
|  |  | 1 Jan 1996 (so far as not already in force) (SI 1995/2835) |

### Drug Trafficking Act 1994 (c 37)

*RA:* 3 Nov 1994

*Commencement provisions:* s 69(2)

Whole Act in force 3 Feb 1995 (s 69(2))

---

### Education Act 1994 (c 30)

*RA:* 21 Jul 1994

*Commencement provisions:* s 26; Education Act 1994 (Commencement) Order 1994, SI 1994/2204

| | | |
|---|---|---|
| 1–21 | | 21 Sep 1994 (SI 1994/2204) |
| 22 | (1), (2) | 21 Sep 1994 (SI 1994/2204) |
| | (3)–(5) | 1 Apr 1995 (SI 1994/2204) |
| | (6)–(9) | 21 Sep 1994 (SI 1994/2204) |
| 23–27 | | 21 Sep 1994 (SI 1994/2204) |
| Schs 1, 2 | | 21 Sep 1994 (SI 1994/2204) |

---

### European Union (Accessions) Act 1994 (c 38)

*RA:* 3 Nov 1994

Whole Act in force 3 Nov 1994 (RA)

---

### Finance Act 1994 (c 9)

*Budget Day:* 30 Nov 1993

*RA:* 3 May 1994

The commencement details of Finance Acts are not set out, as the dates from which their provisions take effect are usually stated clearly and unambiguously in the text of the Act, and charging provisions will normally state for which year or years of assessment they are to have effect.

---

### Firearms (Amendment) Act 1994 (c 31)

*RA:* 21 Jul 1994

*Commencement provisions:* s 4(2)

Whole Act in force 21 Sep 1994 (s 4(2))

---

### Inshore Fishing (Scotland) Act 1994 (c 27)

*RA:* 21 Jul 1994

*Commencement provisions:* s 5(1); Inshore Fishing (Scotland) Act 1994 (Commencement) Order 1994, SI 1994/2124

Whole Act in force 8 Aug 1994 (SI 1994/2124)

---

### Insolvency Act 1994 (c 7)

*RA:* 24 Mar 1994

Whole Act in force 24 Mar 1994 (RA; but note ss 1(7), 2(4), 3(5), Sch 1, para 3)

---

## Insolvency (No 2) Act 1994 (c 12)

*RA:* 26 May 1994

*Commencement provisions:* s 6(2)

Whole Act in force 26 Jul 1994 (s 6(2))

---

## Intelligence Services Act 1994 (c 13)

*RA:* 26 May 1994

*Commencement provisions:* s 12(2); Intelligence Services Act 1994 (Commencement) Order 1994, SI 1994/2734

Whole Act in force 15 Dec 1994 (SI 1994/2734; though note that for purposes of making any Order in Council under s 12(4) it is brought into force on 2 Nov 1994)

---

## Land Drainage Act 1994 (c 25)

*RA:* 21 Jul 1994

*Commencement provisions:* s 3(2)

Whole Act in force 21 Sep 1994 (s 3(2))

---

## Law of Property (Miscellaneous Provisions) Act 1994 (c 36)

*RA:* 3 Nov 1994

*Commencement provisions:* s 23; Law of Property (Miscellaneous Provisions) Act 1994 (Commencement No 1) Order 1995, SI 1995/145; Law of Property (Miscellaneous Provisions) Act 1994 (Commencement No 2) Order 1995, SI 1995/1317

| | | |
|---|---|---|
| 1–20 | | 1 Jul 1995 (SI 1995/1317) |
| 21 | (1) | See Sch 1 below |
| | (2)–(4) | 1 Jul 1995 (SI 1995/1317) |
| 22–24 | | 1 Jul 1995 (SI 1995/1317) |
| Sch 1 | para 1 | 1 Jul 1995 (SI 1995/1317) |
| | para 2 | 15 Feb 1995 (SI 1995/145) |
| | paras 3–12 | 1 Jul 1995 (SI 1995/1317) |
| Sch 2 | | 1 Jul 1995 (SI 1995/1317) |

---

## Local Government etc (Scotland) Act 1994 (c 39)

*RA:* 3 Nov 1994

*Commencement provisions:* s 184(2), (3); Local Government etc (Scotland) Act 1994 (Commencement No 1) Order 1994, SI 1994/2850, as amended by SI 1994/3150; Local Government etc (Scotland) Act 1994 (Commencement No 2) Order 1994, SI 1994/3150; Local Government etc (Scotland) Act 1994 (Commencement No 3) Order 1995, SI 1995/702; Local Government etc (Scotland) Act 1994 (Commencement No 4) Order 1995, SI 1995/1898; Local Government etc (Scotland) Act 1994 (Commencement No 5) Order 1995, SI 1995/2866; Local Government etc (Scotland) Act 1994 (Commencement No 6 and Saving) Order 1995, SI 1995/3326; Local Government etc (Scotland) Act 1994 (Commencement No 7 and Savings) Order 1996, SI 1996/323; Local Government etc (Scotland) Act 1994 (Commencement No 8) Order 1998, SI 1998/2532; Local Government etc (Scotland) Act 1994 (Commencement No 9) Order 2016, SSI 2016/31

| | |
|---|---|
| 1 | 8 Nov 1994 (SI 1994/2850) |
| 2–4 | 6 Apr 1995 (SI 1995/702) |
| 5 | 8 Nov 1994 (SI 1994/2850) |
| 6 | 1 Apr 1996 (SI 1996/323) |

**Local Government etc (Scotland) Act 1994 (c 39)**—*contd*

| | | |
|---|---|---|
| 7 | | 8 Nov 1994 (SI 1994/2850) |
| 8–11 | | 4 Jan 1995 (SI 1994/2850) |
| 12 | | 8 Nov 1994 (SI 1994/2850) |
| 13–17 | | 4 Jan 1995 (SI 1994/2850) |
| 18, 19 | | 6 Apr 1995 (SI 1995/702) |
| 20 | | 1 Apr 1996 (SI 1995/702) |
| 21, 22 | | 1 Apr 1996 (SI 1996/323) |
| 23 | | 6 Apr 1995 (SI 1995/702) |
| 24 | | 4 Jan 1995 (SI 1994/2850) |
| 25–29 | | 6 Apr 1995 (SI 1995/702) (but note s 29(1) effective from 1 Apr 1996) |
| 30–32 | | 1 Apr 1996 (SI 1996/323) |
| 33 | | 1 Apr 1996 (SI 1995/702) |
| 34 | | 4 Jan 1995 (SI 1994/2850) |
| 35 | | 1 Apr 1996 (SI 1996/323) |
| 36 | | 6 Apr 1995 (subject to a transitional provision) (SI 1995/702) |
| 37 | | *Never in force* (repealed) |
| 38 | | 4 Jan 1995 (SI 1994/2850) |
| 39 | | 6 Apr 1995 (SI 1995/702) |
| 40 | | 4 Jan 1995 (SI 1994/2850) |
| 41 | | 1 Apr 1996 (SI 1996/323) |
| 42, 43 | | 6 Apr 1995 (SI 1995/702) |
| 44 | | 4 Jan 1995 (SI 1994/2850) |
| 45 | | 1 Apr 1996 (SI 1996/323) |
| 46 | | 19 Feb 1996 (SI 1996/323) |
| 47 | | 4 Jan 1995 (SI 1994/2850) |
| 48 | | 1 Apr 1996 (SI 1996/323) |
| 49, 50 | | 4 Jan 1995 (SI 1994/2850) |
| 51 | (1), (2) | 1 Apr 1996 (SI 1996/323) |
| | (3) | 4 Jan 1995 (SI 1994/2850) |
| | (4), (5) | 1 Apr 1996 (SI 1996/323) |
| 52 | | 1 Apr 1996 (SI 1995/702) |
| 53 | | 1 Apr 1996 (SI 1996/323) |
| 54 | (1)–(4) | 1 Apr 1996 (SI 1996/323) |
| | (5) | *Never in force* (repealed) |
| 55, 56 | | 6 Apr 1995 (SI 1995/702) |
| 57 | | 8 Nov 1994 (SI 1994/2850) |
| 58 | | 1 Aug 1995 (so far as enables a new local authority to enter into an agreement with any other new local authority for carrying out an activity or service on and after 1 Apr 1996) (SI 1995/702) |
| | | 1 Apr 1996 (otherwise) (SI 1996/323) |
| 59 | | 6 Apr 1995 (SI 1995/702) |
| 60 | | 4 Jan 1995 (SI 1994/2850) |
| 61 | | 8 Nov 1994 (SI 1994/2850) |
| 62–64 | | 17 Jul 1995 (SI 1995/1898) |
| 65 | (1) | 1 Apr 1996 (SI 1996/323) |
| | (2) | 17 Jul 1995 (SI 1995/1898) |
| 66 | | 17 Jul 1995 (SI 1995/1898) |
| 67 | | 30 Oct 1995 (SI 1995/2866) |
| 68 | (1) | 30 Oct 1995 (SI 1995/2866) |
| | (2), (3) | 1 Apr 1996 (SI 1996/323) |
| | (4), (5) | 30 Oct 1995 (SI 1995/2866) |
| 69–71 | | 30 Oct 1995 (SI 1995/2866) |
| 72 | | 1 Apr 1996 (SI 1996/323) |
| 73, 74 | | 17 Jul 1995 (SI 1995/1898) |
| 75 | | 1 Apr 1996 (SI 1996/323) |
| 76, 77 | | 17 Jul 1995 (SI 1995/1898) |
| 78 | | 1 Apr 1996 (SI 1996/323) |
| 79 | (1)–(3) | 17 Jul 1995 (SI 1995/1898) |

**Local Government etc (Scotland) Act 1994 (c 39)**—*contd*

| | | |
|---|---|---|
| | (4) | 1 Apr 1996 (SI 1996/323) |
| | (5) | 17 Jul 1995 (SI 1995/1898) |
| 80 | | 1 Apr 1996 (SI 1996/323) |
| 81 | | 17 Jul 1995 (SI 1995/1898) |
| 82 | | 1 Apr 1996 (SI 1996/323) |
| 83–90 | | 17 Jul 1995 (SI 1995/1898) |
| 91–96 | | 10 Mar 1995 (SI 1995/702) |
| 97 | (1)–(5) | 4 Jan 1995 (SI 1994/2850) |
| | (6) | 8 Nov 1994 (SI 1994/2850) |
| | (7), (8) | 4 Jan 1995 (SI 1994/2850) |
| 98 | | 17 Jul 1995 (SI 1995/1898) |
| 99, 100 | | 1 Apr 1996 (SI 1996/323) |
| 101 | | 4 Jan 1995 (subject to a transitional provision) (SI 1994/2850) |
| 102 | | 1 Apr 1996 (SI 1996/323) |
| 103 | | 30 Jun 1999 (SI 1998/2532) |
| 104 | | 4 Jan 1995 (SI 1994/2850) |
| 105–112 | | 1 Apr 1996 (SI 1996/323) |
| 113–115 | | 4 Jan 1995 (SI 1994/2850) |
| 116 | | 17 Jul 1995 (SI 1995/1898) |
| 117 | | 1 Apr 1996 (SI 1996/323) |
| 118 | (1) | 17 Jul 1995 (SI 1995/1898) |
| | (2), (3) | 1 Apr 1996 (SI 1996/323) |
| 119 | | 1 Apr 1996 (SI 1996/323) |
| 120 | (1) | 17 Jul 1995 (SI 1995/1898) |
| | (2) | 1 Apr 1996 (SI 1996/323) |
| 121 | | 1 Apr 1996 (SI 1996/323) |
| 122, 123 | | 17 Jul 1995 (SI 1995/1898) |
| 124 | | 4 Jan 1995 (SI 1994/2850) |
| 125 | | 8 Nov 1994 (SI 1994/2850) |
| 126 | | 4 Jan 1995 (SI 1994/2850) |
| 127–131 | | 6 Apr 1995 (except so far as s 127(1) provides for the transfer of functions referred to therein or repeals Social Work (Scotland) Act 1968, s 36(1)) (SI 1995/702) |
| | | 1 Apr 1996 (exceptions relating to s 127(1) noted above) (SI 1996/323) |
| 132 | | 1 Apr 1996 (SI 1996/323) |
| 133–136 | | 6 Apr 1995 (SI 1995/702) |
| 137 | (1) | 8 Nov 1994 (so far as applies to s 12) (SI 1994/2850) |
| | | 4 Jan 1995 (otherwise) (SI 1994/2850) |
| | (2)–(5) | 4 Jan 1995 (SI 1994/2850) |
| 138 | | 6 Apr 1995 (SI 1995/702) |
| 139, 140 | | 1 Apr 1996 (SI 1996/323) |
| 141 | | 4 Jan 1995 (SI 1994/2850) |
| 142 | | 1 Apr 1996 (SI 1996/323) |
| 143 | | 4 Jan 1995 (SI 1994/2850) |
| 144, 145 | | 1 Apr 1996 (SI 1996/323) |
| 146–151 | | 4 Jan 1995 (SI 1994/2850) |
| 152 | | 1 Apr 1995 (SI 1994/3150) |
| 153 | | 4 Jan 1995 (SI 1994/3150) |
| 154–156 | | 1 Apr 1995 (SI 1994/3150) |
| 157 | | 8 Nov 1994 (SI 1994/2850) |
| 158, 159 | | 1 Apr 1995 (SI 1994/3150) |
| 160, 161 | | 4 Jan 1995 (SI 1994/3150) |
| 162 | (1) | 1 Apr 1995 (SI 1994/3150) |
| | (2) | 1 Apr 1996 (SI 1996/323) |
| 163 | | 3 Nov 1994 (RA) |
| 164 | (1), (2) | 1 Apr 1995 (SI 1995/702) |
| | (3)–(5) | 1 Apr 1996 (SI 1996/323) |
| 165–167 | | 4 Jan 1995 (SI 1994/2850) |

**Local Government etc (Scotland) Act 1994 (c 39)**—*contd*

| | | |
|---|---|---|
| 168 | | 1 Apr 1995 (subject to a transitional provision) (SI 1995/702) |
| 169 | | 6 Apr 1995 (SI 1995/702) |
| 170 | | 4 Jan 1995 (SI 1994/2850) |
| 171 | | 30 Oct 1995 (so far as enables a local authority to comply with their duties under Local Government (Scotland) Act 1973, s 171A(5) before the beginning of the financial year commencing 1 Apr 1996, and so far as enables the Secretary of State to approve under s 171A(6) of the 1973 Act the proposals submitted by the local authority under sub-s (5) of that section) (SI 1995/2866) |
| | | 1 Apr 1996 (otherwise) (SI 1995/2866) |
| 172, 173 | | 4 Jan 1995 (SI 1994/2850) |
| 174 | | 1 Apr 1996 (SI 1996/323) |
| 175 | | 4 Jan 1995 (SI 1994/2850) |
| 176 | | 1 Apr 1996 (SI 1995/2866) |
| 177 | (1) | See sub-ss (2), (3) below |
| | (2) | 6 Apr 1995 (so far as relates to entry in House of Commons Disqualification Act 1975, Sch 1, Pt II, concerning Scottish Children's Reporter Administration) (SI 1995/702) |
| | | 17 Jul 1995 (so far as relates to entry in House of Commons Disqualification Act 1975, Sch 1, Pt II, concerning East of Scotland Water Authority, North of Scotland Water Authority and West of Scotland Water Authority) (SI 1995/1898) |
| | | 30 Oct 1995 (otherwise) (SI 1995/2866) |
| | (3) | 8 Nov 1994 (so far as relates to entry in House of Commons Disqualification Act 1975, Pt III, concerning any member of the staff commission) (SI 1994/2850) |
| | | 6 Apr 1995 (so far as not already in force) (SI 1995/702) |
| 178 | | 8 Nov 1994 (SI 1994/2850) |
| 179 | | 4 Jan 1995 (SI 1994/2850) |
| 180 | (1) | See Sch 13 below |
| | (2) | See Sch 14 below |
| 181 | (1), (2) | 8 Nov 1994 (SI 1994/2850) |
| | (3)–(7) | 6 Apr 1995 (SI 1995/702) |
| | (8), (9) | 8 Nov 1994 (SI 1994/2850) |
| 182 | | 4 Jan 1995 (SI 1994/2850) |
| 183 | (1) | 8 Nov 1994 (SI 1994/2850) |
| | (2) | 1 Apr 1996 (SI 1996/323) |
| | (3) | 6 Apr 1995 (SI 1995/702) |
| | (4), (5) | 1 Apr 1996 (SI 1996/323) |
| | (6) | 6 Apr 1995 (SI 1995/702) |
| 184 | | 8 Nov 1994 (SI 1994/2850) |
| Schs 1, 2 | | 8 Nov 1994 (SI 1994/2850) |
| Sch 3 | | 6 Apr 1995 (SI 1995/702) |
| Sch 4 | | 1 Apr 1996 (SI 1995/702) |
| Sch 5 | | 4 Jan 1995 (SI 1994/2850) |
| Sch 6 | | 1 Apr 1996 (SI 1995/702) |
| Schs 7, 8 | | 17 Jul 1995 (SI 1995/1898) |
| Sch 9 | | 30 Oct 1995 (SI 1995/2866) |
| Sch 10 | | 1 Apr 1996 (SI 1996/323) |
| Sch 11 | | 10 Mar 1995 (SI 1995/702) |
| Sch 12 | | 6 Apr 1995 (SI 1995/702) |
| Sch 13 | paras 1, 2 | 1 Apr 1996 (SI 1996/323) |
| | para 3 | 4 Jan 1995 (SI 1994/2850) |
| | para 4(1) | 4 Jan 1995 (SI 1994/2850) |
| | para 4(2) | 1 Apr 1996 (SI 1996/323) |
| | para 4(3) | 4 Jan 1995 (SI 1994/2850) |
| | paras 5, 6 | 1 Apr 1996 (SI 1996/323) |
| | para 7 | *Never in force* (repealed) |
| | paras 8–26 | 1 Apr 1996 (SI 1996/323) |

**Local Government etc (Scotland) Act 1994 (c 39)**—*contd*

| | |
|---|---|
| para 27(1), (2) | 4 Jan 1995 (SI 1994/2850) |
| para 27(3)(a)(i) | 4 Jan 1995 (SI 1994/2850) |
| para 27(3)(a)(ii) | 1 Apr 1996 (SI 1996/323) |
| para 27(3)(b)–(o) | 1 Apr 1996 (SI 1996/323) |
| para 27(3)(p) | 6 Apr 1995 (SI 1995/702) |
| para 27(3)(q) | 1 Apr 1996 (SI 1996/323) |
| para 27(4) | 1 Apr 1996 (SI 1996/323) |
| paras 28–33 | 1 Apr 1996 (SI 1996/323) |
| para 34 | *Not yet in force* |
| paras 35–37 | 1 Apr 1996 (SI 1996/323) |
| para 38(1) | See sub-paras (2)–(8) below |
| para 38(2)–(7) | *Never in force* (repealed) |
| para 38(8) | 1 Apr 1996 (SI 1996/323) |
| paras 39–56 | 1 Apr 1996 (SI 1996/323) |
| para 57 | 1 Apr 1995 (SI 1994/3150) |
| paras 58, 59 | 1 Apr 1996 (SI 1996/323) |
| para 60(1) | 4 Jan 1995 (SI 1994/2850) |
| para 60(2) | 1 Apr 1996 (SI 1996/323) |
| para 60(3)(a)–(c) | 4 Jan 1995 (SI 1994/2850) |
| para 60(3)(d) | 1 Apr 1996 (SI 1996/323) |
| para 60(4) | 1 Apr 1995 (SI 1994/3150) |
| para 60(5) | 1 Apr 1996 (SI 1996/323) |
| para 61 | 1 Apr 1996 (SI 1996/323) |
| para 62 | *Not yet in force* |
| paras 63–66 | 1 Apr 1996 (SI 1996/323) |
| para 67(1), (2) | 1 Apr 1995 (SI 1994/3150) |
| para 67(3), (4) | 1 Apr 1996 (SI 1996/323) |
| para 67(5) | 1 Apr 1995 (SI 1994/3150) |
| paras 68–70 | 1 Apr 1996 (SI 1996/323) |
| para 71(1) | 4 Jan 1995 (SI 1994/2850) |
| para 71(2)–(5) | 1 Apr 1996 (SI 1996/323) |
| para 71(6) | 4 Jan 1995 (SI 1994/2850) |
| para 71(7)–(17) | 1 Apr 1996 (SI 1996/323) |
| para 72(1), (2) | 1 Apr 1995 (SI 1995/702) |
| para 72(3)–(9) | 1 Apr 1996 (SI 1996/323) |
| paras 73, 74 | 1 Apr 1996 (SI 1996/323) |
| para 75(1) | 4 Jan 1995 (SI 1994/2850) |
| para 75(2)(a) | 1 Apr 1996 (SI 1996/323) |
| para 75(2)(b) | 4 Jan 1995 (subject to a transitional provision) (SI 1994/2850) |
| para 75(2)(c) | 1 Apr 1996 (SI 1996/323) |
| para 75(2)(d) | 4 Jan 1995 (subject to a transitional provision) (SI 1994/2850) |
| para 75(2)(e) | 4 Jan 1995 (SI 1994/2850) |
| para 75(3)–(12) | 1 Apr 1996 (SI 1996/323) |
| para 75(13)(a)(i) | 1 Apr 1996 (SI 1996/323) |
| para 75(13)(a)(ii) | 4 Jan 1995 (SI 1994/2850) |
| para 75(13)(b), (c) | 1 Apr 1996 (SI 1996/323) |
| para 75(14) | 4 Jan 1995 (subject to a transitional provision) (SI 1994/2850) |
| para 75(15), (16) | 1 Apr 1996 (SI 1996/323) |
| para 75(17)(a)–(c) | 1 Apr 1996 (SI 1996/323) |
| para 75(17)(d) | 4 Jan 1995 (subject to a transitional provision) (SI 1994/2850) |
| para 75(18)(a), (b) | 1 Apr 1996 (SI 1996/323) |
| para 75(18)(c) | 4 Jan 1995 (SI 1994/2850) |
| para 75(19)(a) | 1 Apr 1996 (SI 1996/323) |
| para 75(19)(b) | 4 Jan 1995 (subject to a transitional provision) (SI 1994/2850) |
| para 75(20) | 4 Jan 1995 (subject to a transitional provision) (SI 1994/2850) |
| para 75(21)–(23) | 1 Apr 1996 (SI 1996/323) |
| para 75(24) | 4 Jan 1995 (subject to a transitional provision) (SI 1994/2850) |
| para 75(25)(a) | 1 Apr 1996 (SI 1996/323) |
| para 75(25)(b) | 17 Jul 1995 (SI 1995/1898) |

**Local Government etc (Scotland) Act 1994 (c 39)**—*contd*

| | |
|---|---|
| para 75(26)–(28) | 1 Apr 1996 (SI 1996/323) |
| paras 76–84 | 1 Apr 1996 (SI 1996/323) |
| para 85(1), (2) | 1 Apr 1996 (SI 1996/323) |
| para 85(3)(a) | *Never in force* (repealed) |
| para 85(3)(b)(i) | *Never in force* (repealed) |
| para 85(3)(b)(ii) | 1 Apr 1996 (SI 1996/323) |
| para 85(3)(c) | 1 Apr 1996 (SI 1996/323) |
| para 85(4) | *Never in force* (repealed) |
| paras 86–91 | 1 Apr 1996 (SI 1996/323) |
| para 92(1) | 4 Jan 1995 (SI 1994/2850) |
| para 92(2)–(19) | 1 Apr 1996 (SI 1996/323) |
| para 92(20) | 4 Jan 1995 (SI 1994/2850) |
| para 92(21) | 1 Apr 1996 (SI 1996/323) |
| para 92(22) | 4 Jan 1995 (SI 1994/2850) |
| para 92(23), (24) | 1 Apr 1996 (SI 1996/323) |
| para 92(25) | 1 Apr 1995 (SI 1995/702) |
| para 92(26), (27) | 4 Jan 1995 (SI 1994/2850) |
| para 92(28)–(33) | 1 Apr 1996 (SI 1996/323) |
| para 92(34), (35) | *Never in force* (repealed) |
| para 92(36)–(47) | 1 Apr 1996 (SI 1996/323) |
| para 92(48) | *Not yet in force* |
| para 92(49)–(59) | 1 Apr 1996 (SI 1996/323) |
| para 92(60) | 4 Jan 1995 (SI 1994/2850) |
| para 92(61)–(69) | 1 Apr 1996 (SI 1996/323) |
| para 92(70) | 4 Jan 1995 (SI 1994/2850) |
| para 92(71)–(74) | 1 Apr 1996 (SI 1996/323) |
| para 93(1) | See sub-paras (2), (3) below |
| para 93(2) | *Never in force* (repealed) |
| para 93(3) | 1 Apr 1996 (SI 1996/323) |
| para 94 | 1 Apr 1996 (SI 1996/323) |
| para 95(1), (2) | 4 Jan 1995 (SI 1994/2850) |
| para 95(3) | 1 Apr 1996 (SI 1996/323) |
| para 95(4) | *Never in force* (repealed) |
| para 95(5)–(7) | 1 Apr 1996 (SI 1996/323) |
| para 95(8), (9) | *Never in force* (repealed) |
| para 95(10) | 1 Apr 1996 (SI 1996/323) |
| paras 96–99 | 1 Apr 1996 (SI 1996/323) |
| para 100(1) | 4 Jan 1995 (SI 1994/2850) |
| para 100(2) | 1 Apr 1995 (SI 1994/3150) |
| para 100(3) | *Not yet in force* |
| para 100(4), (5) | 1 Apr 1995 (SI 1994/3150) |
| para 100(6)(a)(i) | 6 Apr 1995 (SI 1995/702) |
| para 100(6)(a)(ii) | 1 Apr 1996 (SI 1996/323) |
| para 100(6)(b) | 1 Apr 1996 (SI 1996/323) |
| para 100(7), (8) | 1 Apr 1996 (SI 1996/323) |
| para 100(9)(a)–(e) | 1 Apr 1996 (SI 1996/323) |
| para 100(9)(f), (g) | 4 Jan 1995 (SI 1994/2850) |
| para 100(9)(h) | 31 Mar 1996 (SI 1996/323) |
| para 100(9)(i) | 1 Apr 1996 (SI 1996/323) |
| para 100(9)(j) | *Not yet in force* |
| paras 101–115 | 1 Apr 1996 (SI 1996/323) |
| para 116(1)–(5) | 1 Apr 1996 (SI 1996/323) |
| para 116(6) | *Never in force* (repealed) |
| paras 117, 118 | 1 Apr 1996 (SI 1996/323) |
| para 119(1) | 4 Jan 1995 (SI 1994/2850) |
| para 119(2)–(4) | 1 Apr 1996 (SI 1996/323) |
| para 119(5)(a)–(c) | 1 Apr 1996 (SI 1996/323) |
| para 119(5)(d) | 4 Jan 1995 (SI 1994/2850) |
| para 119(5)(e) | 1 Apr 1996 (SI 1996/323) |

**Local Government etc (Scotland) Act 1994 (c 39)**—*contd*

| | |
|---|---|
| para 119(6) | 1 Apr 1996 (SI 1996/323) |
| para 119(7)(a), (b) | 1 Apr 1996 (SI 1996/323) |
| para 119(7)(c)(i) | 1 Apr 1996 (SI 1996/323) |
| para 119(7)(c)(ii) | 4 Jan 1995 (SI 1994/2850) |
| para 119(7)(d) | 1 Apr 1996 (SI 1996/323) |
| para 119(8)–(33) | 1 Apr 1996 (SI 1996/323) |
| para 119(34) | 4 Jan 1995 (SI 1994/2850) |
| para 119(35) | 1 Apr 1996 (SI 1996/323) |
| para 119(36) | 4 Jan 1995 (SI 1994/2850) |
| para 119(37)–(41) | 1 Apr 1996 (SI 1996/323) |
| para 119(42)–(45) | 4 Jan 1995 (SI 1994/2850) |
| para 119(46) | 4 Jan 1995 (so far as relates to definition "wholesome" in Water (Scotland) Act 1980, s 76L(1)) (SI 1994/2850) |
| | 1 Apr 1996 (otherwise) (SI 1996/323) |
| para 119(47)–(50) | 1 Apr 1996 (SI 1996/323) |
| para 119(51) | 4 Jan 1995 (SI 1994/2850) |
| para 119(52) | 1 Apr 1996 (SI 1996/323) |
| para 119(53)(a) (i)–(iii) | 1 Apr 1996 (SI 1996/323) |
| para 119(53)(a)(iv) | 4 Jan 1995 (SI 1994/2850) |
| para 119(53)(a)(v) | 1 Apr 1996 (SI 1996/323) |
| para 119(53)(a)(vi) | 4 Jan 1995 (SI 1994/2850) |
| para 119(53)(b) | 1 Apr 1996 (SI 1996/323) |
| para 119(54) | 1 Apr 1996 (except paras (a)(ii), (h)(ii)) (SI 1996/323) |
| | *Never in force* (exception noted above) (repealed) |
| para 119(55)–(58) | 1 Apr 1996 (SI 1996/323) |
| paras 120–128 | 1 Apr 1996 (SI 1996/323) |
| para 129(1) | 4 Jan 1995 (SI 1994/2850) |
| para 129(2)–(19) | 1 Apr 1996 (SI 1996/323) |
| para 129(20)(a) | 1 Apr 1996 (SI 1996/323) |
| para 129(20)(b) | 4 Jan 1995 (SI 1994/2850) |
| para 129(21), (22) | 1 Apr 1996 (SI 1996/323) |
| paras 130–148 | 1 Apr 1996 (SI 1996/323) |
| para 149 | *Never in force* (repealed) |
| paras 150–155 | 1 Apr 1996 (SI 1996/323) |
| para 156(1) | 4 Jan 1995 (SI 1994/2850) |
| para 156(2) | 1 Apr 1996 (SI 1996/323) |
| para 156(3), (4) | 4 Jan 1995 (SI 1994/2850) |
| para 156(5), (6) | 1 Apr 1996 (SI 1996/323) |
| paras 157–161 | 1 Apr 1996 (SI 1996/323) |
| para 162(1), (2) | 22 Dec 1995 (subject to a saving) (SI 1995/3326) |
| para 162(3), (4) | 1 Apr 1996 (SI 1995/3326) |
| paras 163–166 | 1 Apr 1996 (SI 1996/323) |
| para 167 | 1 Apr 1996 (except para 167(2), (4), (5), (7), (9)) (SI 1996/323) |
| | *Never in force* (exception noted above) (repealed) |
| paras 168–175 | 1 Apr 1996 (SI 1996/323) |
| para 176(1) | 31 Dec 1994 (SI 1994/3150) |
| para 176(2) | 19 Feb 1996 (subject to a saving) (SI 1996/323) |
| para 176(3)–(9) | 1 Apr 1996 (SI 1996/323) |
| para 176(10) | 19 Feb 1996 (subject to a saving) (SI 1996/323) |
| para 176(11) | 1 Apr 1996 (SI 1996/323) |
| para 176(12)(a) | 1 Apr 1996 (SI 1996/323) |
| para 176(12)(b) | 19 Feb 1996 (subject to a saving) (SI 1996/323) |
| para 176(12)(c), (d) | 1 Apr 1996 (SI 1996/323) |
| para 176(13)–(15) | 1 Apr 1996 (SI 1996/323) |
| para 176(16)(a)–(c) | 19 Feb 1996 (subject to a saving) (SI 1996/323) |
| para 176(16)(d) | 1 Apr 1996 (SI 1996/323) |
| para 176(17), (18) | 1 Apr 1996 (SI 1996/323) |
| para 176(19)(a) | 1 Apr 1996 (SI 1996/323) |

**Local Government etc (Scotland) Act 1994 (c 39)**—*contd*

|  |  |
|---|---|
| para 176(19)(b) | 31 Dec 1994 (subject to a transitional provision) (SI 1994/3150) |
| para 176(19)(c), (d) | 4 Jan 1995 (SI 1994/2850) |
| para 177 | 4 Jan 1995 (SI 1994/2850) |
| paras 178–184 | 1 Apr 1996 (SI 1996/323) |

Sch 14        4 Jan 1995 (SI 1994/2850), repeals of or in—

    Burial Grounds (Scotland) Act 1855;

    Fire Services Act 1947, ss 15(2), 36(2);

    Local Government (Scotland) Act 1973, s 84(2), (4);

    Water (Scotland) Act 1980, ss 64–67, 76H(8), 76L(1) (definition "wholesome" only), 109(1) (definition "owner" only);

    Civic Government (Scotland) Act 1982, s 121

    4 Jan 1995 (SI 1994/3150), repeals of—

    Local Government (Scotland) Act 1973, s 116(6);

    Local Government (Miscellaneous Provisions) (Scotland) Act 1981, Sch 2, paras 41, 42;

    Water Act 1989, Sch 25, para 60(2)

    1 Apr 1995 (SI 1994/3150), repeals of or in—

    Sporting Lands Rating (Scotland) Act 1886;

    Local Government (Scotland) Act 1947, ss 243, 243A, 243B, 244;

    Valuation and Rating (Scotland) Act 1956, s 22A;

    Local Government and Miscellaneous Financial Provisions (Scotland) Act 1958, s 7;

    Local Government (Scotland) Act 1966;

    Town and Country Planning (Scotland) Act 1972, Sch 21;

    Local Government (Scotland) Act 1973, Sch 9, para 11;

    Local Government (Scotland) Act 1975, Sch 6, Pt II, paras 6, 13, 34;

    Local Government Planning and Land Act 1980, Sch 32, para 33 (except repeal of definition "rates" in sub-para (4));

    Local Government (Miscellaneous Provisions) (Scotland) Act 1981, s 6, Sch 3, para 26;

    Local Government and Planning (Scotland) Act 1982, s 4;

    Rating and Valuation (Amendment) (Scotland) Act 1984, ss 6, 7, Sch 2, para 7;

    Local Government Finance Act 1988, s 128, Sch 12, Pt II, para 6;

    Local Government and Housing Act 1989, Sch 6, para 7;

    Water Act 1989, Sch 25, para 22;

    Local Government Finance Act 1992, Sch 13, para 75

    1 Apr 1995 (SI 1995/702), repeals of or in—

    Local Government (Scotland) Act 1973, ss 83(4B)(d), 96(5), 100(3);

    Criminal Procedure (Scotland) Act 1975, Sch 7D, para 59;

    Local Government (Scotland) Act 1975, Sch 3, para 22(1), head (c) and para 24A;

    Local Government Act 1988, Sch 6, para 11;

    Local Government Finance Act 1992, Sch 7, para 1(6)

    19 Feb 1996 (repeals of or in Local Government Finance Act 1992, ss 93(1)(a), 97(2), 112(2)(d), Sch 2, Sch 11, Pts I, II, and paras 26, 27) (subject to a saving) (SI 1996/323)

    1 Apr 1996 (repeals in Prisons (Scotland) Act 1989, ss 14(2), 16(2)) (SI 1995/3326)

    1 Apr 1996 (SI 1996/323), repeals of or in—

    Rural Water Supplies and Sewerage Act 1944;

    Fire Services Act 1947 (remainder);

    Local Government (Scotland) Act 1947 (remainder);

    National Assistance Act 1948;

    Coast Protection Act 1949;

    National Parks and Access to the Countryside Act 1949;

**Local Government etc (Scotland) Act 1994 (c 39)**—*contd*

 Rural Water Supplies and Sewerage Act 1955;

 Valuation and Rating (Scotland) Act 1956 (remainder);

 Deer (Scotland) Act 1959;

 Caravan Sites and Control of Development Act 1960;

 Flood Prevention (Scotland) Act 1961;

 Registration of Births, Deaths and Marriages (Scotland) Act 1965;

 Police (Scotland) Act 1967;

 Water (Scotland) Act 1967;

 Countryside (Scotland) Act 1967;

 New Towns (Scotland) Act 1968;

 Health Services and Public Health Act 1968;

 Sewerage (Scotland) Act 1968;

 Social Work (Scotland) Act 1968;

 Transport Act 1968;

 Rural Water Supplies and Sewerage (Scotland) Act 1970;

 Rural Water Supplies and Sewerage Act 1971;

 Town and Country Planning (Scotland) Act 1972 (remainder);

 Local Government (Scotland) Act 1973, ss 1–3, 3A, 4, 5, 11, 24(5), 31(4), 47(4), (5), 51(1), (3), 56(6), (9), 63(2), (5), 64(5), 69(4), 74(3), 83(2), (2A), (2B), (3A), 87(1)–(3), 90A, 106(1), 109, 111(1), 116(1)–(5), (7), (8), 118(1), (5), 127, 131, 132, 133(1), 134(1), 137(1), 138(1), 140, 142, 143, 146(7), 148(1), 153(1)–(3), 154(1)–(3B), 154A, 154B, 155(1), 156(1), 159, 161, 163(1)–(3), 166(1), (2), 168, 170A(5), 170B(2), 171(1), (2), 173, 174, 176, 177, 179, 181–183, 202(1), (1A), (13), 215(3)–(7), 222–224, 226, 230, 235(1), 236(2), Schs 1, 2, Sch 6, para 2, Sch 9, para 53, Schs 10, 13, 14, Sch 17, paras 1, 2, Schs 20, 22, Sch 27, Pt II, paras 159, 180, 182 (subject to a saving relating to s 223);

 Control of Pollution Act 1974, s 106(3);

 Children Act 1975;

 District Courts (Scotland) Act 1975;

 House of Commons Disqualification Act 1975;

 Local Government (Scotland) Act 1975, ss 1(3), (7), 4, 6(1A), 7(1A), 13, 16, 23(1), (2), 29A(3), Sch 3, paras 1(4), 22(2), 28(1), Sch 6, Pt II, paras 23, 53;

 Licensing (Scotland) Act 1976;

 Supplementary Benefits Act 1976;

 Inner Urban Areas Act 1978;

 National Health Service (Scotland) Act 1978;

 Education (Scotland) Act 1980;

 Local Government, Planning and Land Act 1980 (remainder);

 Reserve Forces Act 1980;

 Water (Scotland) Act 1980 (remainder);

 Local Government (Miscellaneous Provisions) (Scotland) Act 1981, s 11, Sch 3, paras 24, 28, 38;

 Civic Government (Scotland) Act 1982 (remainder);

 Civil Aviation Act 1982;

 Local Government and Planning (Scotland) Act 1982 (remainder);

 Representation of the People Act 1983;

 Roads (Scotland) Act 1984;

 Road Traffic Regulation Act 1984;

 Housing Associations Act 1985;

 Water (Fluoridation) Act 1985;

 Disabled Persons (Services, Consultation and Representation) Act 1986;

 Housing (Scotland) Act 1987;

 Housing (Scotland) Act 1988;

**Local Government etc (Scotland) Act 1994 (c 39)**—*contd*

Local Government Act 1988 (remainder);
School Boards (Scotland) Act 1988;
Electricity Act 1989;
Local Government and Housing Act 1989 (remainder);
Environmental Protection Act 1990, ss 53(4), 88(9), 90(3), 92(1), 93(1), 95(1);
Natural Heritage (Scotland) Act 1991;
New Roads and Street Works Act 1991;
Planning and Compensation Act 1991;
Social Security Administration Act 1992;
Social Security Contributions and Benefits Act 1992;
Local Government Finance Act 1992, ss 74(1), 84(1), (2), 85(2)–(5), 86(4), (10), (11), 87(9), 90(3), 94(9), 95, 99(1), (2), 107(1), Sch 9, paras 9, 25, Sch 11, paras 24, 25, 31–34, 36–38, Sch 13, paras 37, 93;
Railways Act 1993
1 Apr 2016 (SSI 2016/31), repeals of or in—
Local Government (Scotland) Act 1975, Sch 3, paras 1–4, 6–21, 26, 29, 30;
Local Government (Miscellaneous Provisions) (Scotland) Act 1981, s 27;
Local Government Finance Act 1992, Sch 13, para 44(a), (b), (d)
*Not yet in force*, repeals of or in—
Local Government (Scotland) Act 1973, ss 135(5)(a), (6)(d), (8), 193(2), 200(1)–(6), (8), (9), (11)(b), 225;
Control of Pollution Act 1974, s 32(6) (repealed);
Local Government (Scotland) Act 1975, Sch 3, para 5
Stock Transfer Act 1982;
Environmental Protection Act 1990, ss 36(6), (10), 39(8), 50(5)(a)(iv), 54(4)(c);
Local Government Finance Act 1992, Sch 8, paras 3(2), 4(2)

---

**Local Government (Wales) Act 1994 (c 19)**

*RA:* 5 Jul 1994

*Commencement provisions:* s 66(2)–(4); Local Government (Wales) Act 1994 (Commencement No 1) Order 1994, SI 1994/2109; Local Government (Wales) Act 1994 (Commencement No 2) Order 1994, SI 1994/2790; Local Government (Wales) Act 1994 (Commencement No 3) Order 1995, SI 1995/546, as amended by SI 1995/851; Local Government (Wales) Act 1994 (Commencement No 4) Order 1995, SI 1995/852; Local Government (Wales) Act 1994 (Commencement No 5) Order 1995, SI 1995/2490; Local Government (Wales) Act 1994 (Commencement No 6) Order 1995, SI 1995/3198; Local Government (Wales) Act 1994 (Commencement No 7) Order 1996, SI 1996/396

| | | |
|---|---|---|
| 1 | (1), (2) | 5 Jul 1994 (s 66(2)(a)) |
| | (3) | See Sch 2 below |
| | (4) | See sub-ss (5)–(8) below |
| | (5), (6) | 24 Oct 1994 (in relation to sub-ss (5), (6), for interpretation of Pt IV of Local Government Act 1972) (subject to a saving) (SI 1994/2790) |
| | | 20 Mar 1995 (in relation to sub-s (5), for interpretation of Local Government Act 1972, ss 21, 25, 26, 79, 80, 270(1), (3) and s 17 of this Act) (subject to a saving) (SI 1995/546) |
| | | 3 Apr 1995 (in relation to sub-ss (5), (6), for interpretation of provisions of Local Government Act 1972 falling to be applied in consequence of SI 1995/852) (subject to a saving) (SI 1995/852) |
| | | 1 Oct 1995 (in relation to sub-s (5), for interpretation of Local Government Finance Act 1982, Pt III) (subject to a transitional provision) (SI 1995/2490) |

**Local Government (Wales) Act 1994 (c 19)**—*contd*

|  |  |  |
|---|---|---|
|  |  | 1 Apr 1996 (otherwise) (SI 1995/3198) |
|  | (7) | 5 Jul 1994 (s 66(2)(a)) |
|  | (8) | 24 Oct 1994 (for interpretation of Pt IV of Local Government Act 1972) (subject to a saving) (SI 1994/2790) |
|  |  | 20 Mar 1995 (for interpretation of Local Government Act 1972, ss 21, 25, 26, 79, 80, 270(1), (3) and s 17 of this Act) (subject to a saving) (SI 1995/546) |
|  |  | 3 Apr 1995 (for interpretation of provisions of Local Government Act 1972 falling to be applied in consequence of SI 1995/852) (subject to a saving) (SI 1995/852) |
|  |  | 1 Oct 1995 (for interpretation of Environment Act 1995, s 65(4), Sch 7, para 2) (SI 1995/2490) |
|  |  | 1 Apr 1996 (otherwise) (SI 1995/3198) |
| 2 |  | 20 Mar 1995 (subject to a saving) (SI 1995/546) |
| 3 |  | 5 Jul 1994 (s 66(2)(a)) |
| 4 |  | 20 Mar 1995 (subject to a saving) (SI 1995/546) |
| 5 |  | 3 Apr 1995 (subject to a saving) (SI 1995/852) |
| 6, 7 |  | 5 Jul 1994 (s 66(2)(a)) |
| 8–13 |  | 1 Apr 1996 (SI 1995/3198) |
| 14, 15 |  | 3 Apr 1995 (SI 1995/852) |
| 16 |  | 1 Apr 1996 (SI 1995/3198) |
| 17 |  | 20 Mar 1995 (only for purposes of legislative provisions specified in SI 1995/546, art 5, and subject to a transitional provision) (SI 1995/546, as amended by SI 1995/851) |
|  |  | 1 Apr 1996 (otherwise) (SI 1996/396) |
| 18 | (1)–(6) | 3 Apr 1995 (for purposes specified in SI 1995/852, art 4(2), and subject to savings) (SI 1995/852) |
|  |  | 1 Apr 1996 (otherwise) (SI 1995/852) |
|  | (7) | 1 Apr 1996 (SI 1995/3198) |
| 19 |  | 3 Apr 1995 (SI 1995/852) |
| 20 | (1)–(3) | 1 Apr 1996 (SI 1995/3198) |
|  | (4) | See Sch 6 below |
| 21 |  | 1 Apr 1996 (SI 1996/396) |
| 22 | (1)–(5) | See Schs 7–11 below |
|  | (6) | 1 Apr 1996 (SI 1996/396) |
| 23 | (1) | 1 Apr 1996 (SI 1995/3198) |
|  | (2)–(6) | 3 Apr 1995 (SI 1995/852) |
| 24 |  | *Never in force* (repealed) |
| 25–34 |  | 3 Apr 1995 (SI 1995/852) |
| 35 |  | 3 Apr 1995 (subject to a saving) (SI 1995/852) |
| 36–38 |  | 3 Apr 1995 (SI 1995/852) |
| 39, 40 |  | 5 Jul 1994 (s 66(2)(a)) |
| 41 |  | 15 Aug 1994 (SI 1994/2109) |
| 42 |  | 3 Apr 1995 (SI 1995/852) |
| 43 |  | 5 Jul 1994 (s 66(2)(a)) |
| 44, 45 |  | 3 Apr 1995 (SI 1995/852) |
| 46–48 |  | 5 Jul 1994 (s 66(2)(a)) |
| 49, 50 |  | 1 Apr 1996 (SI 1995/3198) |
| 51 |  | 3 Apr 1995 (SI 1995/852) |
| 52 |  | 15 Aug 1994 (SI 1994/2109) |
| 53 |  | 3 Apr 1995 (SI 1995/852) |
| 54, 55 |  | 5 Jul 1994 (s 66(2)(a)) |
| 56–60 |  | 3 Apr 1995 (SI 1995/852) |
| 61 |  | 1 Apr 1996 (SI 1996/396) |
| 62 |  | 1 Apr 1996 (SI 1995/3198) |
| 63, 64 |  | 5 Jul 1994 (s 66(2)(a)) |
| 65 |  | 15 Aug 1994 (SI 1994/2109) |
| 66 | (1)–(4) | 5 Jul 1994 (s 66(2)(c)) |
|  | (5) | See Sch 15 below |

**Local Government (Wales) Act 1994 (c 19)**—*contd*

|  |  |  |
|---|---|---|
|  | (6) | See Sch 16 below |
|  | (7) | See Sch 17 below |
|  | (8) | See Sch 18 below |
|  | (9) | 5 Jul 1994 (s 66(2)(c)) |
| Sch 1 |  | 5 Jul 1994 (s 66(2)(b)) |
| Sch 2 | paras 1–3 | 1 Apr 1996 (SI 1995/3198) |
|  | paras 4, 5 | 24 Oct 1994 (subject to a saving) (SI 1994/2790) |
|  | paras 6, 7 | 1 Apr 1996 (SI 1995/3198) |
|  | paras 8, 9 | 3 Apr 1995 (SI 1995/852) |
|  | paras 10–12 | 1 Apr 1996 (SI 1995/3198) |
|  | para 13 | 1 Oct 1995 (SI 1995/2490) |
| Sch 3 |  | 5 Jul 1994 (s 66(2)(b)) |
| Schs 4, 5 |  | 1 Apr 1996 (SI 1995/3198) |
| Sch 6 | para 1 | 1 Apr 1996 (SI 1996/396) |
|  | paras 2–4 | 3 Apr 1995 (SI 1995/852) |
|  | paras 5–10 | *Never in force* (repealed) |
|  | paras 11, 12 | 3 Apr 1995 (subject to a saving) (SI 1995/852) |
|  | paras 13–17 | 1 Apr 1996 (SI 1996/396) |
|  | para 18 | *Never in force* (repealed) |
|  | paras 19, 20 | 1 Apr 1996 (SI 1996/396) |
|  | para 21 | 3 Apr 1995 (SI 1995/852) |
|  | para 22 | 1 Apr 1996 (SI 1996/396) |
|  | para 23 | 3 Apr 1995 (SI 1995/852) |
|  | para 24(1)(a) | *Never in force* (repealed) |
|  | para 24(1)(b) | 3 Apr 1995 (SI 1995/852) |
|  | para 24(2)–(9) | 1 Apr 1996 (SI 1996/396) |
|  | para 24(10)(a) | 1 Apr 1996 (SI 1996/396) |
|  | para 24(10)(b) | 1 Oct 1995 (SI 1995/2490) |
|  | para 24(11)–(16) | 1 Apr 1996 (SI 1996/396) |
|  | para 24(17)(a) | 1 Oct 1995 (SI 1995/2490) |
|  | para 24(17)(b) | 1 Apr 1996 (SI 1996/396) |
|  | para 24(18), (19) | 1 Apr 1996 (SI 1996/396) |
|  | paras 25–27 | 1 Apr 1996 (SI 1996/396) |
|  | paras 28, 29 | *Never in force* (repealed) |
| Sch 7 | para 1 | 3 Apr 1995 (for purposes specified in SI 1995/852, art 4(5), and subject to a transitional provision) (SI 1995/852) |
|  |  | 1 Apr 1996 (otherwise) (SI 1996/396) |
|  | paras 2–26 | 1 Apr 1996 (SI 1996/396) |
|  | para 27(1)–(3) | 1 Apr 1996 (SI 1996/396) |
|  | para 27(4) | 1 Oct 1995 (SI 1995/2490) |
|  | paras 28–43 | 1 Apr 1996 (SI 1996/396) |
| Sch 8 | paras 1, 2 | 1 Apr 1996 (SI 1996/396) |
|  | para 3(1) | 1 Apr 1996 (SI 1996/396) |
|  | para 3(2) | 1 Oct 1995 (for purposes specified in SI 1995/2490, art 4(2), and subject to a transitional provision) (SI 1995/2490) |
|  | para 3(3)–(5) | 1 Apr 1996 (SI 1996/396) |
|  | paras 4–11 | 1 Apr 1996 (SI 1996/396) |
| Sch 9 | paras 1–16 | 1 Apr 1996 (SI 1996/396) |
|  | para 17(1)–(3) | 1 Apr 1996 (SI 1996/396) |
|  | para 17(4) | *Never in force* (repealed) |
|  | para 17(5)–(13) | 1 Apr 1996 (SI 1996/396) |
|  | para 18 | 1 Apr 1996 (SI 1996/396) |
| Sch 10 | paras 1–10 | 1 Apr 1996 (SI 1996/396) |
|  | para 11(1) | *Never in force* (repealed) |
|  | para 11(2)–(4) | 1 Apr 1996 (SI 1996/396) |
|  | paras 12, 13 | 1 Apr 1996 (SI 1996/396) |
|  | para 14 | 3 Apr 1995 (SI 1995/852) |
| Sch 11 | paras 1, 2 | 1 Apr 1996 (SI 1996/396) |
|  | para 3(1), (2) | *Never in force* (repealed) |

**Local Government (Wales) Act 1994 (c 19)**—*contd*

| | | |
|---|---|---|
| | para 3(3)–(11) | 1 Apr 1996 (SI 1996/396) |
| | paras 4, 5 | 1 Apr 1996 (SI 1996/396) |
| Sch 12 | | 3 Apr 1995 (subject to savings) (SI 1995/852) |
| Schs 13, 14 | | 5 Jul 1994 (s 66(2)(b)) |
| Sch 15 | para 1 | 24 Oct 1994 (SI 1994/2790) |
| | para 2 | 1 Apr 1996 (SI 1996/396) |
| | para 3 | 3 Apr 1995 (SI 1995/852) |
| | paras 4, 5 | 1 Apr 1996 (SI 1996/396) |
| | para 6 | 20 Mar 1995 (SI 1995/546) |
| | para 7 | 24 Oct 1994 (subject to a saving) (SI 1994/2790) |
| | para 8(1)–(4) | 1 Apr 1996 (SI 1996/396) |
| | para 8(5) | 24 Oct 1994 (subject to a saving) (SI 1994/2790) |
| | para 9(1)–(3) | 1 Apr 1996 (SI 1996/396) |
| | para 9(4)(a) | 1 Apr 1996 (SI 1996/396) |
| | para 9(4)(b) | 24 Oct 1994 (subject to a saving) (SI 1994/2790) |
| | para 10(1) | 1 Oct 1995 (SI 1995/2490) |
| | para 10(2), (3) | 1 Apr 1996 (SI 1996/396) |
| | para 11(1) | 1 Apr 1996 (SI 1996/396) |
| | para 11(2) | 24 Oct 1994 (subject to a saving) (SI 1994/2790) |
| | para 12(a) | 1 Apr 1996 (SI 1996/396) |
| | para 12(b) | 24 Oct 1994 (subject to a saving) (SI 1994/2790) |
| | paras 13–17 | 1 Apr 1996 (SI 1996/396) |
| | paras 18, 19 | 24 Oct 1994 (subject to a saving) (SI 1994/2790) |
| | para 20 | 3 Apr 1995 (subject to a saving) (SI 1995/852) |
| | paras 21, 22 | 1 Apr 1996 (SI 1996/396) |
| | para 23 | 3 Apr 1995 (SI 1995/852) |
| | paras 24, 25 | 1 Apr 1996 (SI 1996/396) |
| | para 26 | 3 Apr 1995 (subject to a saving) (SI 1995/852) |
| | paras 27–51 | 1 Apr 1996 (SI 1996/396) |
| | para 52 | 1 Oct 1995 (SI 1995/2490) |
| | paras 53, 54 | 1 Apr 1996 (SI 1996/396) |
| | para 55 | 3 Apr 1995 (subject to a saving) (SI 1995/852) |
| | para 56 | 1 Apr 1996 (SI 1996/396) |
| | para 57 | 24 Oct 1994 (subject to a saving) (SI 1994/2790) |
| | paras 58–61 | 1 Oct 1995 (SI 1995/2490) |
| | paras 62–66 | 1 Apr 1996 (SI 1996/396) |
| Sch 16 | paras 1–10 | 1 Apr 1996 (SI 1996/396) |
| | para 11 | *Never in force* (repealed) |
| | para 12 | 1 Oct 1995 (for purposes specified in SI 1995/2490, art 5(2), and subject to a transitional provision) (SI 1995/2490) |
| | | 1 Apr 1996 (otherwise) (SI 1995/2490) |
| | paras 13–25 | 1 Apr 1996 (SI 1996/396) |
| | para 26 | 1 Oct 1995 (for purposes specified in SI 1995/2490, art 5(4), and subject to a transitional provision) (SI 1995/2490) |
| | | 1 Apr 1996 (otherwise) (SI 1995/2490) |
| | paras 27–39 | 1 Apr 1996 (SI 1996/396) |
| | para 40(1) | 1 Apr 1996 (SI 1996/396) |
| | para 40(2)(a) | 1 Apr 1996 (SI 1996/396) |
| | para 40(2)(b) | *Never in force* (repealed) |
| | para 40(3) | 1 Apr 1996 (SI 1996/396) |
| | paras 41–53 | 1 Apr 1996 (SI 1996/396) |
| | para 54(1) | 1 Apr 1996 (SI 1996/396) |
| | para 54(2) | 1 Jan 1996 (subject to a saving) (SI 1995/3198) |
| | paras 55, 56 | 1 Apr 1996 (SI 1996/396) |
| | para 57(1)–(5) | 3 Apr 1995 (subject to a saving) (SI 1995/852) |
| | para 57(6) | *Never in force* (repealed) |
| | paras 58–66 | 1 Apr 1996 (SI 1996/396) |
| | para 67 | *Never in force* (repealed) |
| | para 68(1)–(5) | 1 Apr 1996 (SI 1996/396) |

**Local Government (Wales) Act 1994 (c 19)**—*contd*

| | | |
|---|---|---|
| | para 68(6) | 20 Mar 1995 (subject to savings and transitional provisions) (SI 1995/546) |
| | para 68(7) | 20 Mar 1995 (but not in respect of Representation of the People Act 1983, s 35(1A)(b)) (subject to a saving) (SI 1995/546) |
| | | 1 Apr 1996 (otherwise) (SI 1996/396) |
| | para 68(8), (9) | 20 Mar 1995 (subject to savings and transitional provisions in respect of sub-para (8)) (SI 1995/546) |
| | para 68(10)–(12) | 1 Apr 1996 (SI 1996/396) |
| | para 68(13)–(16) | 20 Mar 1995 (subject to transitional provisions in respect of sub-para (16)) (SI 1995/546) |
| | para 68(17), (18) | 1 Apr 1996 (SI 1996/396) |
| | para 68(19) | 20 Mar 1995 (SI 1995/546) |
| | para 68(20) | 1 Apr 1996 (SI 1996/396) |
| | para 69 | 1 Apr 1996 (SI 1996/396) |
| | para 70 | *Never in force* (repealed) |
| | paras 71–81 | 1 Apr 1996 (SI 1996/396) |
| | para 82(1)–(3) | 3 Apr 1995 (for purposes of orders made under Coroners Act 1988, s 4A, and subject to transitional provisions) (SI 1995/852) |
| | | 1 Apr 1996 (otherwise) (SI 1995/852) |
| | para 82(4) | 3 Apr 1995 (subject to transitional provisions) (SI 1995/852) |
| | para 82(5) | 3 Apr 1995 (only in respect of Coroners Act 1988, s 4A(1), (2), (7), (9), (10)) (SI 1995/852) |
| | | 1 Apr 1996 (otherwise) (SI 1996/396) |
| | para 82(6)–(10) | 1 Apr 1996 (SI 1996/396) |
| | para 83 | 1 Apr 1996 (SI 1996/396) |
| | paras 84–86 | 3 Apr 1995 (SI 1995/852) |
| | para 87 | 1 Apr 1996 (SI 1996/396) |
| | para 88 | 3 Apr 1995 (SI 1995/852) |
| | paras 89–92 | 1 Apr 1996 (SI 1996/396) |
| | para 93 | *Never in force* (repealed) |
| | paras 94, 95 | 1 Apr 1996 (SI 1996/396) |
| | paras 96, 97 | 3 Apr 1995 (SI 1995/852) |
| | para 98 | 1 Oct 1995 (to have effect only in relation to any financial year beginning on or after 1 Apr 1996) (SI 1995/2490) |
| | paras 99–105 | 1 Apr 1996 (SI 1996/396) |
| | para 106 | 3 Apr 1995 (SI 1995/852) |
| | paras 107–109 | 1 Apr 1996 (SI 1996/396) |
| Sch 17 | para 1 | 5 Jul 1994 (s 66(2)(b)) |
| | paras 2, 3 | 3 Apr 1995 (SI 1995/852) |
| | para 4 | 5 Jul 1994 (s 66(2)(b)) |
| | para 5 | 3 Apr 1995 (SI 1995/852) |
| | para 6 | 5 Jul 1994 (s 66(2)(b)) |
| | paras 7, 8 | 20 Mar 1995 (SI 1995/546) |
| | para 9 | 5 Jul 1994 (s 66(2)(b)) |
| | paras 10–14 | 3 Apr 1995 (SI 1995/852) |
| | para 15 | 1 Apr 1996 (SI 1995/3198) |
| | para 16 | 1 Apr 1996 (SI 1996/396) |
| | para 17 | 1 Apr 1996 (SI 1995/3198) |
| | paras 18–23 | 3 Apr 1995 (SI 1995/852) |
| Sch 18 | | 24 Oct 1994 (repeals in Local Government Act 1972, ss 55(5)(a), 59(2), 72(2)) (subject to a saving) (SI 1994/2790) |
| | | 20 Mar 1995 (repeals in Representation of the People Act 1983, ss 35(1), 36(3)(b)) (SI 1995/546) |
| | | 3 Apr 1995 (SI 1995/852), repeals in— Local Government Act 1972, s 74(3), (4); Local Government, Planning and Land Act 1980, ss 4(7), 20(1); Town and Country Planning Act 1990, ss 1(3), 2(1) |

**Local Government (Wales) Act 1994 (c 19)**—*contd*

        1 Oct 1995 (repeals of or in Local Government Act 1972, Sch 4,
            Pt IV, Sch 8, para 8, Sch 10, Sch 11, para 3(2)(b), (c))
            (SI 1995/2490)

        1 Jan 1996 (subject to a saving) (repeal in European Parliamentary
            Elections Act 1978, Sch 2, para 5A(4)(a)) (SI 1995/3198)

        1 Apr 1996 (SI 1996/396), repeals of or in—
            Game Licences Act 1860;
            Finance Act 1908;
            Public Health Act 1936;
            Education Act 1944;
            Coast Protection Act 1949;
            Disabled Persons (Employment) Act 1958;
            Opencast Coal Act 1958;
            Caravan Sites and Control of Development Act 1960;
            Pipe-lines Act 1962;
            Harbours Act 1964;
            Licensing Act 1964;
            Public Libraries and Museums Act 1964;
            Gas Act 1965;
            Agriculture Act 1967;
            Slaughter of Poultry Act 1967;
            Theatres Act 1968;
            Mines and Quarries (Tips) Act 1969;
            Post Office Act 1969;
            Agriculture Act 1970;
            Chronically Sick and Disabled Persons Act 1970;
            Fire Precautions Act 1971;
            Local Government Act 1972, ss 30, 60(5), 67(5)(f), 69(4),
              76(2), (3), 97(1)–(3), 195(3), 200, 207, 213(1), 226(5),
              227(1), (2), 245(6)–(9), Sch 11, para 1(2)(c), (d), Sch 26,
              paras 4(a), 11(1);
            Poisons Act 1972;
            Employment Agencies Act 1973;
            Breeding of Dogs Act 1973;
            Consumer Credit Act 1974;
            Control of Pollution Act 1974;
            Health and Safety at Work etc Act 1974;
            Slaughterhouses Act 1974;
            Guard Dogs Act 1975;
            Reservoirs Act 1975;
            Safety of Sports Grounds Act 1975;
            Dangerous Wild Animals Act 1976;
            Development of Rural Wales Act 1976;
            European Parliamentary Elections Act 1978, Sch 1, para 4(5)(a);
            Ancient Monuments and Archaeological Areas Act 1979;
            Local Government, Planning and Land Act 1980, ss 116(4)(a),
              165(9)(a), Sch 32, para 2(2)(a)(ii);
            Wildlife and Countryside Act 1981;
            Zoo Licensing Act 1981;
            Civil Aviation Act 1982;
            Level Crossings Act 1983;
            Representation of the People Act 1983, ss 8(2), 18(2), 36(5),
              39(6)(b), 52(4)(a);
            Road Traffic Regulation Act 1984;
            Telecommunications Act 1984;
            Cinemas Act 1985;
            Representation of the People Act 1985;
            Transport Act 1985;
            Airports Act 1986;

**Local Government (Wales) Act 1994 (c 19)**—*contd*

Building Societies Act 1986;
Gas Act 1986;
Fire Safety and Safety of Places of Sport Act 1987;
Road Traffic Act 1988;
Road Traffic Offenders Act 1988;
Children Act 1989;
Electricity Act 1989;
Broadcasting Act 1990;
Caldey Island Act 1990;
Environmental Protection Act 1990, ss 30(3)(a), 143(6)(b), 149(11);
Food Safety Act 1990;
Planning (Listed Buildings and Conservation Areas) Act 1990;
Town and Country Planning Act 1990, Sch 1, para 8(1), (2)(a);
Coal Mining Subsidence Act 1991;
Road Traffic Act 1991;
Severn Bridges Act 1992;
Social Security Administration Act 1992;
Clean Air Act 1993;
Health Service Commissioners Act 1993;
Radioactive Substances Act 1993

---

**Marriage Act 1994 (c 34)**

*RA:* 3 Nov 1994

*Commencement provisions:* s 3(2); Marriage Act 1994 (Commencement No 1) Order 1994, SI 1994/3116; Marriage Act 1994 (Commencement No 2) Order 1995, SI 1995/424

| | | |
|---|---|---|
| 1 | (1) | 1 Apr 1995 (SI 1995/424) |
| | (2) | 24 Feb 1995 (so far as inserts Marriage Act 1949, ss 46A, 46B(2)) (SI 1995/424) |
| | | 1 Apr 1995 (otherwise) (SI 1995/424) |
| | (3) | See Schedule below |
| 2 | (1) | 1 Jan 1995 (so far as inserts Marriage Act 1949, s 35(2A)) (SI 1994/3116) |
| | | 1 Apr 1995 (so far as not already in force) (SI 1995/424) |
| | (2) | 1 Jan 1995 (SI 1994/3116) |
| 3 | | 1 Jan 1995 (SI 1994/3116) |
| Schedule | para 1 | See paras 2–8 below |
| | paras 2–4 | 1 Apr 1995 (SI 1995/424) |
| | para 5 | 24 Feb 1995 (SI 1995/424) |
| | paras 6–9 | 1 Apr 1995 (SI 1995/424) |

---

**Mental Health (Amendment) Act 1994 (c 6)**

*RA:* 24 Mar 1994

*Commencement provisions:* s 2(3)

Whole Act in force 14 Apr 1994 (s 2(3))

---

**Merchant Shipping (Salvage and Pollution) Act 1994 (c 28)**

*RA:* 21 Jul 1994

*Commencement provisions:* s 10(4); Merchant Shipping (Salvage and Pollution) Act 1994 (Commencement No 1) Order 1994, SI 1994/1988; Merchant Shipping (Salvage and Pollution) Act 1994 (Commencement No 2) Order 1994, SI 1994/2971

**Merchant Shipping (Salvage and Pollution) Act 1994 (c 28)**—*contd*

| | | |
|---|---|---|
| 1, 2 | | 1 Jan 1995 (SI 1994/2971) |
| 3 | | 28 Jul 1994 (SI 1994/1988) |
| 4 | | 1 Jan 1995 (SI 1994/2971) |
| 5 | | *Never in force* (repealed) |
| 6 | (1) | See Sch 3 below |
| | (2) | 1 Oct 1994 (SI 1994/1988) |
| | (3), (4) | *Never in force* (repealed) |
| 7, 8 | | 1 Oct 1994 (SI 1994/1988) |
| 9 | | 28 Jul 1994 (SI 1994/1988) |
| 10 | (1), (2) | 28 Jul 1994 (SI 1994/1988) |
| | (3) | See Sch 4 below |
| | (4), (5) | 28 Jul 1994 (SI 1994/1988) |
| Schs 1, 2 | | 1 Jan 1995 (SI 1994/2971) |
| Sch 3 | Pt I | 1 Oct 1994 (SI 1994/1988) |
| | Pts II, III | *Never in force* (repealed) |
| Sch 4 | | 1 Oct 1994 (SI 1994/1988), repeals in— |

Merchant Shipping (Oil Pollution) Act 1971;
Prevention of Oil Pollution Act 1971;
Merchant Shipping Act 1974

1 Jan 1995 (SI 1994/2971), repeals in—
Merchant Shipping Act 1894;
Maritime Conventions Act 1911;
Crown Proceedings Act 1947;
Merchant Shipping (Safety Convention) Act 1949;
Administration of Justice Act 1956;
Merchant Shipping Act 1988 (except repeal of Sch 4, para 12);
Merchant Shipping (Registration, etc) Act 1993 (except repeal of Sch 4, para 18)

*Never in force* (repealed), repeals of or in—
Merchant Shipping Act 1988, Sch 4, para 12;
Merchant Shipping (Registration, etc) Act 1993, Sch 4, para 18 (repealed)

---

**New Towns (Amendment) Act 1994 (c 5)**

*RA:* 24 Mar 1994

Whole Act in force 24 Mar 1994 (RA)

---

**Non-Domestic Rating Act 1994 (c 3)**

*RA:* 24 Feb 1994

Whole Act in force 24 Feb 1994 (RA)

---

**Parliamentary Commissioner Act 1994 (c 14)**

*RA:* 5 Jul 1994

*Commencement provisions:* s 3(2)

Whole Act in force 5 Sep 1994 (s 3(2))

---

**Pastoral (Amendment) Measure 1994 (No 1)**

*RA:* 24 Mar 1994

*Commencement provisions:* s 15(2)

**Pastoral (Amendment) Measure 1994 (No 1)**—*contd*
The provisions of this Measure are brought into force on 1 Apr 1994 by an appointed day notice signed by
the Archbishops of Canterbury and York and dated 25 Mar 1994 (made under s 15(2))

---

**Police and Magistrates' Courts Act 1994 (c 29)**

*RA:* 21 Jul 1994

*Commencement provisions:* s 94; Police and Magistrates' Courts Act 1994 (Commencement No 1 and
Transitional Provisions) Order 1994, SI 1994/2025; Police and Magistrates' Courts Act 1994
(Commencement No 2) Order 1994, SI 1994/2151; Police and Magistrates' Courts Act 1994
(Commencement No 3 and Transitional Provisions) Order 1994, SI 1994/2594; Police and
Magistrates' Courts Act 1994 (Commencement No 4 and Transitional Provisions) (Scotland)
Order 1994, SI 1994/3075; Police and Magistrates' Courts Act 1994 (Commencement No 5 and
Transitional Provisions) Order 1994, SI 1994/3262, as amended by SI 1995/246, SI 1995/899; Police
and Magistrates' Courts Act 1994 (Commencement No 6 and Transitional Provisions) Order 1995,
SI 1995/42; Police and Magistrates' Courts Act 1994 (Commencement No 7 and Transitional
Provisions) (Scotland) Order 1995, SI 1995/492, as amended by SI 1995/3003; Police and
Magistrates' Courts Act 1994 (Commencement No 8 and Transitional Provisions) Order 1995,
SI 1995/685; Police and Magistrates' Courts Act 1994 (Commencement No 9 and Amendment)
Order 1995, SI 1995/3003; Police and Magistrates' Courts Act 1994 (Commencement No 10 and
Savings) (Scotland) Order 1996, SI 1996/1646

| | |
|---|---|
| 1 | 8 Aug 1994 (for purposes specified in SI 1994/2025, art 4(1) and subject to modifications specified in art 4(3)–(6) thereof) (SI 1994/2025) |
| | 1 Apr 1995 (otherwise) (SI 1994/3262) |
| 2 | 8 Aug 1994 (so far as substitutes new s 3 of Police Act 1964) (for purposes specified in SI 1994/2025, art 4(1) and subject to modifications specified in art 4(3)–(6) thereof) (SI 1994/2025) |
| | 1 Apr 1995 (otherwise) (SI 1994/3262) |
| 3 | 8 Aug 1994 (for purposes specified in SI 1994/2025, art 4(1) and subject to modifications specified in art 4(3)–(6) thereof) (SI 1994/2025) |
| | 1 Apr 1995 (otherwise) (SI 1994/3262) |
| 4 | 1 Oct 1994 (for purposes specified in SI 1994/2025, art 6(1) and subject to modifications specified in art 6(3)–(6) thereof) (SI 1994/2025) |
| | 1 Apr 1995 (otherwise) (SI 1994/3262) |
| 5–7 | 1 Apr 1995 (SI 1994/3262) |
| 8 | 1 Oct 1994 (for purposes specified in SI 1994/2025, art 6(1) and subject to modifications specified in art 6(3)–(6) thereof) (SI 1994/2025) |
| | 1 Apr 1995 (otherwise) (SI 1994/3262) |
| 9 | 1 Apr 1995 (SI 1994/3262) |
| 10, 11 | 1 Oct 1994 (for purposes specified in SI 1994/2025, art 6(1) and subject to modifications specified in art 6(3)–(6) thereof) (SI 1994/2025) |
| | 1 Apr 1995 (otherwise) (SI 1994/3262) |
| 12 | 1 Apr 1995 (SI 1994/3262) |
| 13 | 21 Jul 1994 (s 9(3)(b)) |
| 14 | 1 Oct 1994 (so far as substitutes new ss 21A, 21C of the Police Act 1994) (SI 1994/2025) |
| | 1 Apr 1995 (otherwise) (SI 1994/3262) |
| 15 | 1 Oct 1994 (except so far as substitutes new s 28D of the 1964 Act) (for purposes specified in SI 1994/2025, art 6(1) and subject to modifications specified in art 6(3)–(6) thereof) (SI 1994/2025) |
| | 1 Apr 1995 (otherwise) (SI 1994/3262) |
| 16 | 1 Oct 1994 (for purposes specified in SI 1994/2025, art 6(1) and subject to modifications specified in art 6(3)–(6) thereof) (SI 1994/2025) |

**Police and Magistrates' Courts Act 1994 (c 29)**—*contd*

|  |  |  |
|---|---|---|
|  |  | 1 Apr 1995 (otherwise) (SI 1994/3262) |
| 17 |  | 1 Nov 1994 (for purposes of any financial year beginning on or after 1 Apr 1995, and subject to SI 1994/2025, art 7(3), (4)) (SI 1994/2025) |
| 18 |  | 8 Aug 1994 (except so far as sub-s (3) inserts Police Act 1964, s 33(3)) (SI 1994/2025) |
|  |  | *Never in force* (exception noted above) (repealed) |
| 19 |  | *Never in force* (repealed) |
| 20, 21 |  | 1 Apr 1995 (subject to a transitional provision) (SI 1994/3262) |
| 22 |  | 1 Oct 1994 (SI 1994/2025) |
| 23, 24 |  | 1 Apr 1995 (SI 1994/3262) |
| 25 |  | 1 Oct 1994 (SI 1994/2025) |
| 26 |  | 21 Jul 1994 (so far as relates to service in accordance with arrangements made under Police Act 1964, s 15A(2)) (s 94(3)(c)) |
|  |  | 1 Apr 1995 (otherwise) (SI 1994/3262) |
| 27, 28 |  | 1 Nov 1994 (for purposes of any financial year beginning on or after 1 Apr 1995, and subject to SI 1994/2025, art 7(3), (4)) (SI 1994/2025) |
| 29 |  | 1 Apr 1995 (SI 1994/3262) |
| 30 |  | 15 Mar 1995 (for purposes of issuing a basic credit approval under the Local Government and Housing Act 1989, s 53, to a new police authority in respect of the financial year beginning on 1 Apr 1995) (SI 1994/3262) |
|  |  | 1 Apr 1995 (otherwise) (SI 1994/3262) |
| 31 |  | 1 Oct 1994 (for purposes specified in SI 1994/2025, art 6(1) and subject to modifications specified in art 6(3)–(6) thereof) (SI 1994/2025) |
|  |  | 1 Apr 1995 (otherwise) (SI 1994/3262) |
| 32 |  | 1 Oct 1994 (only in respect of new police authorities which have come into existence) (SI 1994/2025) |
|  |  | *Never in force* (otherwise) (repealed) |
| 33 |  | 1 Oct 1994 (SI 1994/2025) |
| 34–38 |  | *Never in force* (repealed) |
| 39 | (1) | 1 Oct 1994 (SI 1994/2025) |
|  | (2), (3) | 1 Apr 1995 (SI 1994/3262) |
|  | (4)–(7) | 1 Oct 1994 (SI 1994/2025) |
| 40 |  | 1 Apr 1995 (SI 1994/3262) |
| 41 |  | 8 Aug 1994 (SI 1994/2025) |
| 42 |  | 1 Oct 1994 (SI 1994/2025) |
| 43 |  | See Sch 4 below |
| 44 |  | See Sch 5 below |
| 45 |  | 1 Oct 1994 (for purposes specified in SI 1994/2025, art 6(1) and subject to modifications specified in art 6(3)–(6) thereof) (SI 1994/2025) |
|  |  | 1 Apr 1995 (otherwise) (SI 1994/3262) |
| 46 |  | 8 Aug 1994 (SI 1994/2025) |
| 47 | (1) | 13 Dec 1995 (SI 1995/3003)[1] |
|  | (2)(a) | 1 Apr 1995 (subject to transitional provisions) (SI 1995/492) |
|  | (2)(b) | 13 Dec 1995 (SI 1995/3003)[1] |
|  | (3) | 1 Apr 1996 (SI 1995/492) |
|  | (4), (5) | 13 Dec 1995 (SI 1995/3003)[1] |
| 48 |  | 1 Jan 1995 (for purpose of regulations under Police (Scotland) Act 1967, Pt II, relating to appointments and promotions to rank of assistant chief constable) (SI 1994/3075) |
|  |  | 1 Apr 1995 (otherwise) (SI 1995/492) |
| 49 |  | 1 Apr 1996 (SI 1995/492) |
| 50 |  | 21 Jul 1994 (s 94(3)(b)) |
| 51 | (a) | 1 Jan 1996 (subject to a transitional provision) (SI 1994/3075) |
|  | (b) | 1 Jan 1995 (SI 1994/3075) |

**Police and Magistrates' Courts Act 1994 (c 29)**—*contd*

| | | |
|---|---|---|
| | (c) | 1 Jan 1996 (subject to a transitional provision) (SI 1994/3075) |
| 52 | (1) | See sub-ss (2)–(4) below |
| | (2) | 1 Aug 1996 (subject to a saving) (SI 1996/1646) |
| | (3) | 8 Aug 1994 (so far as inserts Police (Scotland) Act 1967, s 26(2B)) (SI 1994/2025) |
| | | 1 Jan 1995 (for purpose of regulations under Police (Scotland) Act 1967, s 26, for purposes mentioned in sub-ss (2A), (2C) thereof) (SI 1994/3075) |
| | | 1 Aug 1996 (otherwise) (SI 1996/1646) |
| | (4) | 1 Aug 1996 (subject to a saving) (SI 1996/1646) |
| 53 | (1) | 1 Jan 1995 (SI 1994/3075) |
| | (2) | 1 Apr 1995 (SI 1995/492) |
| 54 | | 1 Apr 1996 (SI 1995/492) |
| 55 | (1) | 1 Jan 1995 (for purpose of rules under Police (Scotland) Act 1967, s 30(3), (4), (6)) (SI 1994/3075) |
| | | 1 Aug 1996 (otherwise) (SI 1996/1646) |
| | (2) | 1 Aug 1996 (subject to a saving) (SI 1996/1646) |
| 56–58 | | 1 Jan 1995 (SI 1994/3075) |
| 59 | | 1 Jan 1995 (for purpose of substitution of Police (Scotland) Act 1967, s 36(1), in relation to consultation by Secretary of State with the Joint Central Committee etc, and for purpose of power to make regulations or orders under s 36) (SI 1994/3075) |
| | | 1 Apr 1995 (otherwise) (SI 1994/3075, but see further SI 1995/492 below) |
| | | 1 Apr 1995 (so far as not already in force (though already brought fully into force by SI 1994/3075)) (SI 1995/492) |
| 60 | | 21 Jul 1994 (so far as relates to service in accordance with arrangements made under Police (Scotland) Act 1967, s 12A(2)) (s 94(3)(c)) |
| | | 1 Apr 1995 (otherwise) (SI 1995/492) |
| 61 | | 1 Aug 1996 (SI 1996/1646) |
| 62 | | 1 Jan 1995 (SI 1994/3075) |
| 63 | (1) | 1 Jan 1995 (SI 1994/3075) |
| | (2) | 1 Apr 1995 (SI 1995/492) |
| | (3) | 1 Aug 1996 (subject to a saving) (SI 1996/1646) |
| | (4) | 21 Jul 1994 (so far as relates to service in accordance with arrangements made under Police (Scotland) Act 1967, s 12A(2)) (s 94(3)(c)) |
| | | 1 Apr 1995 (otherwise) (SI 1995/492) |
| | (5) | 1 Apr 1995 (SI 1995/492) |
| | (6) | 1 Jan 1995 (SI 1994/3075) |
| | (7)(a) | 21 Jul 1994 (so far as relates to service in accordance with arrangements made under Police (Scotland) Act 1967, s 12A(2)) (s 94(3)(c)) |
| | | 1 Apr 1995 (otherwise) (SI 1995/492) |
| | (7)(b) | 1 Jan 1995 (SI 1994/3075) |
| | (8) | 1 Aug 1996 (subject to a saving) (SI 1996/1646) |
| | (9)(a) | 13 Dec 1995 (SI 1995/3003)[1] |
| | (9)(b) | 1 Jan 1995 (SI 1994/3075) |
| | (10) | 1 Aug 1996 (subject to a saving) (SI 1996/1646) |
| 64 | | 1 Apr 1996 (SI 1995/492) |
| 65 | | 8 Aug 1994 (SI 1994/2025) |
| 66–68 | | 23 Aug 1994 (SI 1994/2151) |
| 69–71 | | 1 Nov 1994 (subject to transitional provisions and savings relating to ss 70, 71) (SI 1994/2594) |
| 72 | (1)–(5) | 1 Apr 1995 (subject to transitional provisions) (SI 1995/685) |
| | (6) | 1 Apr 1995 (in relation to magistrates' courts committee for inner London area) (SI 1995/685) |

**Police and Magistrates' Courts Act 1994 (c 29)**—*contd*

|  |  |  |
|---|---|---|
|  |  | 1 Oct 1995 (so far as inserts Justices of the Peace Act 1979, s 22(9)–(11), except in relation to magistrates' courts committee for inner London area) (SI 1995/685) |
|  |  | 1 Jan 1996 (so far as inserts Justices of the Peace Act 1979, s 22(8), except in relation to magistrates' courts committee for inner London area) (SI 1995/685) |
| 73 |  | 1 Apr 1995 (SI 1995/685) |
| 74 |  | 1 Nov 1994 (SI 1994/2594) |
| 75 |  | 1 Apr 1995 (except so far as inserts Justices of the Peace Act 1979, s 24D(5), in relation to appointments of justices' chief executives by magistrates' courts committees for Hampshire, Kent and Lincolnshire) (SI 1995/685) |
|  |  | *Never in force* (exception noted above) (repealed) |
| 76, 77 |  | 1 Apr 1995 (SI 1995/685) |
| 78 |  | 1 Nov 1994 (SI 1994/2594) |
| 79 |  | 1 Nov 1994 (for purpose only of enabling a magistrates' courts committee for inner London area to be constituted in accordance with regulations made under s 21 of the 1979 Act as amended by s 71 of this Act) (SI 1994/2594) |
|  |  | 1 Apr 1995 (so far as not already in force) (SI 1995/685) |
| 80, 81 |  | 1 Apr 1995 (SI 1995/685) |
| 82 |  | *Never in force* (repealed) |
| 83 | (1) | 1 Apr 1995 (except in relation to inner London area) (SI 1995/685) |
|  |  | *Never in force* (exception noted above) (repealed) |
|  | (2) | 1 Apr 1995 (so far as applies to Justices of the Peace Act 1979, s 57) (SI 1995/685) |
|  |  | *Never in force* (otherwise) (repealed) |
| 84 |  | 1 Apr 1995 (SI 1995/685) |
| 85–87 |  | 1 Nov 1994 (SI 1994/2594) |
| 88 | (1)–(5) | 1 Nov 1994 (SI 1994/2594) |
|  | (6) | 1 Apr 1995 (SI 1995/685) |
| 89, 90 |  | 1 Nov 1994 (SI 1994/2594) |
| 91 | (1) | See Sch 8 below |
|  | (2), (3) | 1 Apr 1995 (SI 1995/685) |
| 92 |  | 1 Nov 1994 (SI 1994/2594) |
| 93 |  | See Sch 9 below |
| 94–97 |  | 21 Jul 1994 (RA) |
| Sch 1 |  | 8 Aug 1994 (for purposes specified in SI 1994/2025, art 4(1) and subject to modifications specified in art 4(3)–(6) thereof) (SI 1994/2025) |
|  |  | 1 Apr 1995 (otherwise) (SI 1994/3262) |
| Sch 2 |  | 21 Jul 1994 (for purpose of power to make regulations under Police Act 1964, Sch 1C, para 11) (s 94(3)(a)(ii)) |
|  |  | 8 Aug 1994 (for purposes specified in SI 1994/2025, art 4(1) and subject to modifications specified in art 4(3)–(6) thereof) (SI 1994/2025) |
|  |  | 1 Apr 1995 (otherwise) (SI 1994/3262) |
| Sch 3 |  | *Never in force* (repealed) |
| Sch 4 | paras 1–4 | 1 Apr 1995 (SI 1994/3262) |
|  | paras 5–14 | 1 Oct 1994 (for purposes specified in SI 1994/2025, art 6(1) and subject to modifications specified in art 6(3)–(6) thereof) (SI 1994/2025) |
|  |  | 1 Apr 1995 (otherwise) (SI 1994/3262) |
|  | para 15(1) | 1 Oct 1994 (for purposes specified in SI 1994/2025, art 6(1) and subject to modifications specified in art 6(3)–(6) thereof) (SI 1994/2025) |
|  |  | 1 Apr 1995 (otherwise) (SI 1994/3262) |
|  | para 15(2) | 1 Apr 1995 (SI 1994/3262) |

**Police and Magistrates' Courts Act 1994 (c 29)**—*contd*

| | | |
|---|---|---|
| | para 15(3), (4) | 1 Oct 1994 (for purposes specified in SI 1994/2025, art 6(1) and subject to modifications specified in art 6(3)–(6) thereof) (SI 1994/2025) |
| | | 1 Apr 1995 (otherwise) (SI 1994/3262) |
| | paras 16–41 | 1 Oct 1994 (for purposes specified in SI 1994/2025, art 6(1) and subject to modifications specified in art 6(3)–(6) thereof) (SI 1994/2025) |
| | | 1 Apr 1995 (otherwise) (SI 1994/3262) |
| | para 42 | 1 Apr 1995 (SI 1994/3262) |
| | paras 43–63 | 1 Oct 1994 (for purposes specified in SI 1994/2025, art 6(1) and subject to modifications specified in art 6(3)–(6) thereof) (SI 1994/2025) |
| | | 1 Apr 1995 (otherwise) (SI 1994/3262) |
| Sch 5 | para 1 | 31 Dec 1994 (subject to a transitional provision in respect of para 1(2)(a)) (SI 1994/3262) |
| | paras 2–4 | 1 Apr 1995 (SI 1994/3262) |
| | para 5 | 8 Aug 1994 (for purposes specified in SI 1994/2025, art 4(1) and subject to modifications specified in art 4(3)–(6) thereof) (SI 1994/2025) |
| | | 1 Apr 1995 (otherwise) (SI 1994/3262) |
| | paras 6, 7 | 1 Apr 1995 (SI 1994/3262) |
| | para 8 | 31 Dec 1994 (subject to a transitional provision in respect of para 8(3)) (SI 1994/3262) |
| | para 9 | 1 Apr 1995 (SI 1994/3262) |
| | para 10(1) | 1 Oct 1994 (SI 1994/2025) |
| | para 10(2) | 1 Apr 1995 (SI 1994/3262) |
| | para 10(3) | 1 Oct 1994 (SI 1994/2025) |
| | para 11 | 1 Aug 1996 (S) (SI 1996/1646) |
| | | *Never in force* (otherwise) (repealed) |
| | para 12 | *Never in force* (repealed) |
| | paras 13, 14 | 1 Apr 1995 (SI 1994/3262) |
| | para 15 | 8 Aug 1994 (for purposes specified in SI 1994/2025, art 4(1) and subject to modifications specified in art 4(3)–(6) thereof) (SI 1994/2025) |
| | | 1 Apr 1995 (otherwise) (SI 1994/3262) |
| | para 16 | 1 Oct 1994 (SI 1994/2025) |
| | paras 17–20 | 21 Jul 1994 (so far as relate to service in accordance with arrangements made under Police Act 1964, s 15A(2), Police (Scotland) Act 1967, s 12A(2)) (s 94(3)(c)) |
| | | 1 Apr 1995 (otherwise) (SI 1994/3262) |
| | para 21 | 1 Oct 1994 (SI 1994/2025) |
| | paras 22, 23 | 1 Apr 1995 (SI 1994/3262) |
| | para 24(a) | 1 Apr 1995 (SI 1994/3262) |
| | para 24(b) | *Never in force* (repealed) |
| | paras 25–28 | *Never in force* (repealed) |
| | paras 29, 30 | 1 Apr 1995 (SI 1994/3262) |
| | paras 31–34 | *Never in force* (repealed) |
| | paras 35–38 | 1 Apr 1995 (SI 1994/3262) |
| | para 39(a) | *Never in force* (repealed) |
| | para 39(b) | 1 Aug 1996 (SI 1996/1646) |
| | para 40(1) | 1 Aug 1996 (SI 1996/1646) |
| | para 40(2) | *Never in force* (repealed) |
| | para 40(3) | 1 Aug 1996 (SI 1996/1646) |
| Sch 6 | | 1 Aug 1996 (subject to a saving) (SI 1996/1646) |
| Sch 7 | | *Never in force* (repealed) |
| Sch 8 | Pt I, para 1 | *Never in force* (repealed) |
| | Pt I, paras 2–4 | 1 Nov 1994 (SI 1994/2594) |
| | Pt I, para 5 | 1 Apr 1995 (SI 1995/685) |
| | Pt I, paras 6–9 | 1 Nov 1994 (SI 1994/2594) |
| | Pt I, paras 10–16 | 1 Apr 1995 (SI 1995/685) |

**Police and Magistrates' Courts Act 1994 (c 29)**—*contd*

| | | |
|---|---|---|
| | Pt I, para 17 | 1 Nov 1994 (SI 1994/2594) |
| | Pt I, para 18 | 1 Apr 1995 (SI 1995/685) |
| | Pt I, para 19(1) | See sub-paras (2), (3) below |
| | Pt I, para 19(2) | 3 Feb 1995 (subject to a saving) (SI 1995/42) |
| | Pt I, para 19(3) | 1 Apr 1995 (except so far as definition "responsible authority" relates to inner London area) (SI 1995/685) |
| | | *Never in force* (exception noted above) (repealed) |
| | Pt I, paras 20, 21 | 1 Apr 1995 (SI 1995/685) |
| | Pt I, para 22 | 1 Nov 1994 (subject to a saving) (SI 1994/2594) |
| | Pt I, para 23 | *Never in force* (repealed) |
| | Pt II, para 24 | *Never in force* (repealed) |
| | Pt II, paras 25–32 | 1 Apr 1995 (SI 1995/685) |
| | Pt II, para 33(1)–(4) | 1 Apr 1995 (SI 1995/685) |
| | Pt II, para 33(5) | *Never in force* (repealed) |
| | Pt II, para 33(6) | 1 Apr 1995 (SI 1995/685) |
| | Pt II, para 34 | 1 Apr 1995 (SI 1995/685) |
| | Pt II, para 35 | *Never in force* (repealed) |
| Sch 9 | Pt I | 8 Aug 1994 (SI 1994/2025), repeals of or in— |

Metropolitan Police Act 1856;
Police Act 1964, ss 25(5) (for certain purposes), 33(5);
Drug Trafficking Offences Act 1986
23 Aug 1994 (repeals in Police Act (Northern Ireland) 1970) (SI 1994/2151)
1 Oct 1994 (SI 1994/2025), repeals in—
Licensing Act 1902;
Police Negotiating Board Act 1980;
Local Government Act 1985, s 30(2)
31 Dec 1994 (repeals in Police Act 1964, s 12) (SI 1994/3262)
1 Jan 1995 (repeals of or in Police (Scotland) Act 1967, ss 24(3), 38(1)–(3), (5), Sch 4) (SI 1994/3075)
1 Apr 1995 (SI 1994/3262), all entries so far as relate to enactments as they apply in England and Wales, except those in respect of—
Metropolitan Police Act 1856;
Licensing Act 1902;
Police Act 1964, ss 12, 33(5), 53(1), 60;
Police Act (Northern Ireland) 1970;
Police Negotiating Board Act 1980;
Police and Criminal Evidence Act 1984, ss 67(8), 85(8), 90(3), (4), (6), (8), 91, 92, 94, 97(4), 99(2), 101, 103, 104(1), (2), 105, Sch 4;
Local Government Act 1985, s 30(2);
Drug Trafficking Offences Act 1986;
Courts and Legal Services Act 1990
1 Apr 1995 (repeal of Police Act 1964, s 25(5) (for remaining purposes)) (SI 1994/3262)
1 Apr 1995 (S) (SI 1995/492), repeals in—
Police (Overseas Service) Act 1945;
Police Act 1969;
Police Pensions Act 1976;
Overseas Development and Cooperation Act 1980
1 Apr 1995 (repeals in Police (Scotland) Act 1967, ss 6(2), 7(1), 31(2), (4)) (subject to transitional provisions) (SI 1995/492)
13 Dec 1995 (SI 1995/3003)[1], repeals of or in—
Police (Scotland) Act 1967, ss 7(2), 14(1), 26(2)(d), 51(1);
Police and Criminal Evidence Act 1984, Sch 4, para 11
1 Apr 1996 (repeal in Police (Scotland) Act 1967, s 8(1)) (SI 1995/492)
1 Aug 1996 (repeals in Police (Scotland) Act 1967 so far as not already in force, subject to savings) (SI 1996/1646)

**Police and Magistrates' Courts Act 1994 (c 29)**—*contd*

*Never in force* (entries relating to Police Act 1964, ss 53(1), 60(1), 60(2); Police and Criminal Evidence Act 1984 (except s 108, Schs 4, 6); Courts and Legal Services Act 1990) (repealed)

Pt II
1 Nov 1994 (repeals of or in Justices of the Peace Act 1979, ss 12(7), 18(2), 19(3), (4), 21(1), 23(1), 24(1)(a), (2), (5), 24A(1), 70 (definition "joint committee area" only) and (for purpose specified in entry to s 79 of this Act above), repeal of s 35 of the 1979 Act) (SI 1994/2594)

1 Apr 1995 (subject to transitional provisions) (SI 1995/685), repeals of or in—

Reserve and Auxiliary Forces (Protection of Civil Interests) Act 1951, s 48;

Administration of Justice Act 1964, Sch 3, Pt II, para 29;

Gaming Act 1968, Sch 2, para 2(2);

Juries Act 1974, Sch 1, Pt I, Group B;

Justices of the Peace Act 1979, ss 22(2), 26(1), (2), (4), (5), 27(1)–(5), (7), (9), 28(1A), 30(1), 35 (so far as not already in force), 36–38, 53(6), 57, 63(2), (4);

Magistrates' Courts Act 1980, ss 68(7), 141(3), 145(1)(d);

Local Government Act 1985, s 12;

Criminal Justice Act 1988, ss 164(3), 165;

Courts and Legal Services Act 1990, s 10(3)–(5), Sch 18, para 25;

Criminal Justice Act 1991, s 76(3), 79 (so far as applies to Justices of the Peace Act 1979, s 55(2)), 93(1), Sch 11, paras 40(2)(k), 41(2)(c))

*Not yet in force*, repeals of or in—

Metropolitan Police Courts Act 1897, ss 3, 4, 7, 11 (repealed);

London Building Acts (Amendment) Act 1939, s 151(1)(bb) (repealed);

Metropolitan Magistrates' Courts Act 1959, ss 3(1), 4(2) (repealed);

Justices of the Peace Act 1979, ss 58, 59(1)(b), 70 (definition of "the Receiver") (repealed);

Criminal Justice Act 1991, ss 79 (part) (spent), 93(2);

Social Security (Consequential Provisions) Act 1992, Sch 2, para 58;

Pension Schemes Act 1993, Sch 8, para 12 (spent)

[1]  Note that these provisions were to come into force on 1 Apr 1996 by virtue of SI 1995/492, which was subsequently amended by SI 1995/3003

---

**Race Relations (Remedies) Act 1994 (c 10)**

*RA*: 3 May 1994

*Commencement provisions*: s 3(3)

Whole Act in force 3 Jul 1994 (s 3(3))

---

**Road Traffic Regulation (Special Events) Act 1994 (c 11)**

*RA*: 3 May 1994

Whole Act in force 3 May 1994 (RA)

---

## Sale and Supply of Goods Act 1994 (c 35)

*RA:* 3 Nov 1994

*Commencement provisions:* s 8(2)

Whole Act in force 3 Jan 1995 (s 8(2))

---

## Sale of Goods (Amendment) Act 1994 (c 32)

*RA:* 3 Nov 1994

*Commencement provisions:* s 3(3)

Whole Act in force 3 Jan 1995 (s 3(3))

---

## Social Security (Contributions) Act 1994 (c 1)

*RA:* 10 Feb 1994

Whole Act in force 10 Feb 1994 (RA; but note ss 1(2), 2(3), 3(2))

---

## Social Security (Incapacity for Work) Act 1994 (c 18)

*RA:* 5 Jul 1994

*Commencement provisions:* s 16(2), (3); Social Security (Incapacity for Work) Act 1994 (Commencement) Order 1994, SI 1994/2926

| | | |
|---|---|---|
| 1 | | 13 Apr 1995 (SI 1994/2926) |
| 2 | (1) | 18 Nov 1994 (for purpose of authorising the making of regulations expressed to come into force on 13 Apr 1995) (SI 1994/2926) |
| | | 13 Apr 1995 (otherwise) (SI 1994/2926) |
| | (2) | 13 Apr 1995 (SI 1994/2926) |
| | (3) | 18 Nov 1994 (SI 1994/2926) |
| | (4) | 13 Apr 1995 (SI 1994/2926) |
| | (5) | 18 Nov 1994 (for purpose of authorising the making of regulations expressed to come into force on 13 Apr 1995) (SI 1994/2926) |
| | | 13 Apr 1995 (otherwise) (SI 1994/2926) |
| | (6) | 13 Apr 1995 (SI 1994/2926) |
| | (7) | 18 Nov 1994 (SI 1994/2926) |
| 3 | (1) | 18 Nov 1994 (for purpose of authorising the making of regulations expressed to come into force on 13 Apr 1995) (SI 1994/2926) |
| | | 13 Apr 1995 (otherwise) (SI 1994/2926) |
| | (2) | 13 Apr 1995 (SI 1994/2926) |
| 4 | | 18 Nov 1994 (SI 1994/2926) |
| 5, 6 | | 18 Nov 1994 (for purpose of authorising the making of regulations expressed to come into force on 13 Apr 1995) (SI 1994/2926) |
| | | 13 Apr 1995 (otherwise) (SI 1994/2926) |
| 7 | | 18 Nov 1994 (SI 1994/2926) |
| 8 | (1) | 6 Apr 1995 (SI 1994/2926) |
| | (2) | 18 Nov 1994 (SI 1994/2926) |
| | (3), (4) | 6 Apr 1995 (SI 1994/2926) |
| 9 | (1)–(3) | 18 Nov 1994 (for purpose of authorising the making of regulations expressed to come into force on 13 Apr 1995) (SI 1994/2926) |
| | | 13 Apr 1995 (otherwise) (SI 1994/2926) |
| | (4) | 18 Nov 1994 (SI 1994/2926) |
| 10 | (1) | 18 Nov 1994 (for purpose of authorising the making of regulations expressed to come into force on 13 Apr 1995) (SI 1994/2926) |
| | | 13 Apr 1995 (otherwise) (SI 1994/2926) |
| | (2) | 13 Apr 1995 (SI 1994/2926) |

**Social Security (Incapacity for Work) Act 1994 (c 18)**—*contd*

| | |
|---|---|
| (3) | 18 Nov 1994 (for purpose of authorising the making of regulations expressed to come into force on 13 Apr 1995) (SI 1994/2926) |
| | 13 Apr 1995 (otherwise) (SI 1994/2926) |
| 11 | 13 Apr 1995 (SI 1994/2926) |
| 12 | 18 Nov 1994 (SI 1994/2926) |
| 13 | 13 Apr 1995 (SI 1994/2926) |
| 14–16 | 5 Jul 1994 (s 16(2)) |
| Schs 1, 2 | 13 Apr 1995 (SI 1994/2926) |

**State Hospitals (Scotland) Act 1994 (c 16)**

*RA:* 5 Jul 1994

*Commencement provisions:* s 3(2), (3); State Hospitals (Scotland) Act 1994 Commencement Order 1995, SI 1995/576

Whole Act in force 1 Apr 1995 (SI 1995/576)

**Statutory Sick Pay Act 1994 (c 2)**

*RA:* 10 Feb 1994

*Commencement provisions:* s 5(2)

| | |
|---|---|
| 1 | 6 Apr 1994 (s 5(2)) |
| 2–5 | 10 Feb 1994 (s 5(2)) |

**Sunday Trading Act 1994 (c 20)**

*RA:* 5 Jul 1994

*Commencement provisions:* ss 1, 9(3); Sunday Trading Act 1994 Appointed Day Order 1994, SI 1994/1841

| | | |
|---|---|---|
| 1 | | 5 Jul 1994 (RA) |
| 2–5 | | 26 Aug 1994 (SI 1994/1841) |
| 6–8 | | 5 Jul 1994 (RA) |
| 9 | (1) | 5 Jul 1994 (RA) |
| | (2) | 26 Aug 1994 (SI 1994/1841) |
| | (3), (4) | 5 Jul 1994 (RA) |
| Schs 1–5 | | 26 Aug 1994 (SI 1994/1841) |

**Trade Marks Act 1994 (c 26)**

*RA:* 21 Jul 1994

*Commencement provisions:* s 109; Trade Marks Act 1994 (Commencement) Order 1994, SI 1994/2550

Whole Act in force 31 Oct 1994 (SI 1994/2550; though note that, for certain purposes relating to the making of subordinate legislation, ss 4(4), 13(2), 25(1), (5), (6), 34(1), 35(5), 38(1), (2), 39(3), 40(4), 41(1), (3), 43(2), (3), (5), (6), 44(3), 45(2), 63(2), (3), 64(4), 65(1), (3)–(5), 66(2), 67(1), (2), 68(1), (3), 69, 76(1), 78, 79, 80(3), 81, 82, 88, 90, Sch 1, para 6(2), Sch 2, para 7(2), Sch 3, paras 10(2), 11(2), 12, 14(5) are brought into force on 29 Sep 1994, and note that ss 66(1), 80(1), (3) are brought into force on that date for certain purposes relating to the exercise of the registrar's powers)

**Transport Police (Jurisdiction) Act 1994 (c 8)**

*RA:* 24 Mar 1994

*Commencement provisions:* s 2(2)

**Transport Police (Jurisdiction) Act 1994 (c 8)**—*contd*
Whole Act in force 1 Apr 1994 (s 2(2))

---

**Value Added Tax Act 1994 (c 23)**

*RA:* 5 Jul 1994

*Commencement provisions:* s 101(1)

Whole Act in force 1 Sep 1994 (s 101(1))

---

**Vehicle Excise and Registration Act 1994 (c 22)**

*RA:* 5 Jul 1994

*Commencement provisions:* s 66, Sch 4, para 9

Whole Act in force 1 Sep 1994 (s 66); though note that by Sch 4, para 9 to the Act, s 20 and the references thereto in ss 45(1)(b), 57(5) do not come into force until a day to be appointed by the Secretary of State

---

# 1995 Acts

## Activity Centres (Young Persons' Safety) Act 1995 (c 15)

*RA:* 28 Jun 1995

*Commencement provisions:* s 5

Whole Act in force 28 Aug 1995 (s 5)

---

## Agricultural Tenancies Act 1995 (c 8)

*RA:* 9 May 1995

*Commencement provisions:* s 41(2)

Whole Act in force 1 Sep 1995 (s 41(2))

---

## Appropriation Act 1995 (c 19)

*RA:* 19 Jul 1995

Whole Act in force 19 Jul 1995 (RA)

---

## Atomic Energy Authority Act 1995 (c 37)

*RA:* 8 Nov 1995

Whole Act in force 8 Nov 1995 (RA)

---

## Building Societies (Joint Account Holders) Act 1995 (c 5)

*RA:* 1 May 1995

Whole Act in force 1 May 1995 (RA) (and see s 2(2))

---

## Carers (Recognition and Services) Act 1995 (c 12)

*RA:* 28 Jun 1995

*Commencement provisions:* s 5(2)

Whole Act in force 1 Apr 1996 (s 5(2))

---

## Charities (Amendment) Act 1995 (c 48)

*RA:* 8 Nov 1995

Whole Act in force 8 Nov 1995 (RA)

---

## Child Support Act 1995 (c 34)

*RA:* 19 Jul 1995

*Commencement provisions:* s 30(3), (4); Child Support Act 1995 (Commencement No 1) Order 1995, SI 1995/2302; Child Support Act 1995 (Commencement No 2) Order 1995, SI 1995/3262; Child Support Act 1995 (Commencement No 3) Order 1996, SI 1996/2630

| | | |
|---|---|---|
| 1 | (1) | 14 Oct 1996 (for the purpose of regulations under Child Support Act 1991, s 28A) (SI 1996/2630) |
| | | 2 Dec 1996 (otherwise) (SI 1996/2630) |
| | (2) | See Sch 1 below |
| 2 | | 14 Oct 1996 (in respect of insertion of Child Support Act 1991, s 28B(2), (3), for the purpose of regulations under s 28B(2) thereof) (SI 1996/2630) |
| | | 2 Dec 1996 (in respect of insertion of Child Support Act 1991, s 28B(1), (2) (so far as not already in force), (3) (so far as not already in force), (4), (5)) (SI 1996/2630) |
| | | *Not yet in force* (in respect of insertion of Child Support Act 1991, s 28B(6) (substituted by Social Security Act 1998, s 86, Sch 7, para 35, Sch 8)) (repealed in part) |
| 3 | | 14 Oct 1996 (for the purpose of regulations under Child Support Act 1991, s 28C) (SI 1996/2630) |
| | | 2 Dec 1996 (otherwise) (SI 1996/2630) |
| 4 | | 2 Dec 1996 (SI 1996/2630) |
| 5 | | 14 Oct 1996 (for the purpose of regulations under Child Support Act 1991, s 28E) (SI 1996/2630) |
| | | 2 Dec 1996 (otherwise) (SI 1996/2630) |
| 6 | (1) | 14 Oct 1996 (for the purpose of regulations under Child Support Act 1991, s 28F) (SI 1996/2630) |
| | | 2 Dec 1996 (otherwise) (SI 1996/2630) |
| | (2) | See Sch 2 below |
| 7 | | 14 Oct 1996 (for the purpose of regulations under Child Support Act 1991, s 28G) (SI 1996/2630) |
| | | 2 Dec 1996 (otherwise) (SI 1996/2630) |
| 8 | | 2 Dec 1996 (SI 1996/2630) |
| 9 | | 22 Jan 1996 (in respect of insertion of Child Support Act 1991, s 28I(4)) (SI 1995/3262) |
| | | 14 Oct 1996 (in respect of the insertion of Child Support Act 1991, s 28I(5)) (SI 1996/2630) |
| | | *Not yet in force* (in respect of insertion of Child Support Act 1991, s 28I(1)–(3)) (repealed in part) |
| 10 | | 14 Oct 1996 (SI 1996/2630) |
| 11 | | 22 Jan 1996 (SI 1995/3262) |
| 12 | (1) | See sub-ss (2)–(7) below |
| | (2)–(4) | 22 Jan 1996 (SI 1995/3262) |
| | (5) | 1 Oct 1995 (for the purpose of regulations under Child Support Act 1991, s 17(5)) (SI 1995/2302) |
| | | 22 Jan 1996 (otherwise) (SI 1995/3262) |
| | (6) | 22 Jan 1996 (SI 1995/3262) |
| | (7) | 1 Oct 1995 (for the purpose of regulations under Child Support Act 1991, s 17(7)) (SI 1995/2302) |
| | | 22 Jan 1996 (otherwise) (SI 1995/3262) |
| 13–15 | | 22 Jan 1996 (SI 1995/3262) |
| 16, 17 | | 18 Dec 1995 (SI 1995/3262) |
| 18–21 | | 4 Sep 1995 (SI 1995/2302) |

**Child Support Act 1995 (c 34)**—*contd*

| | | |
|---|---|---|
| 22 | | *Not yet in force* (repealed in part) |
| 23 | | 4 Sep 1995 (so far as inserts Child Support Act 1991, s 41B(1), (2), (7)) (SI 1995/2302) |
| | | 1 Oct 1995 (otherwise) (SI 1995/2302) |
| 24, 25 | | 1 Oct 1995 (SI 1995/2302) |
| 26 | (1)–(3) | 4 Sep 1995 (SI 1995/2302) |
| | (4)(a) | 14 Oct 1996 (SI 1996/2630) |
| | (4)(b) | 4 Sep 1995 (SI 1995/2302) |
| | (4)(c) | 1 Oct 1995 (SI 1995/2302) |
| | (5), (6) | 4 Sep 1995 (SI 1995/2302) |
| 27, 28 | | 4 Sep 1995 (SI 1995/2302) |
| 29 | | 19 Jul 1995 (s 30(3)) |
| 30 | (1)–(4) | 19 Jul 1995 (s 30(3)) |
| | (5) | See Sch 3 below |
| | (6) | 19 Jul 1995 (s 30(3)) |
| Sch 1 | | 14 Oct 1996 (for the purpose of regulations under Child Support Act 1991, Sch 4A) (SI 1996/2630) |
| | | 2 Dec 1996 (otherwise) (SI 1996/2630) |
| Sch 2 | | 14 Oct 1996 (for the purpose of regulations under Child Support Act 1991, Sch 4B) (SI 1996/2630) |
| | | 2 Dec 1996 (otherwise) (SI 1996/2630) |
| Sch 3 | para 1 | 1 Oct 1995 (so far as inserts Income and Corporation Taxes Act 1988, s 617(2)(ae)) (SI 1995/2302) |
| | | 14 Oct 1996 (otherwise) (SI 1996/2630) |
| | para 2 | 4 Sep 1995 (SI 1995/2302) |
| | para 3(1) | 1 Oct 1995 (SI 1995/2302) |
| | para 3(2) | 4 Sep 1995 (SI 1995/2302) |
| | para 4 | 4 Sep 1995 (SI 1995/2302) |
| | para 5 | *Never in force* (repealed) |
| | paras 6, 7 | 2 Dec 1996 (SI 1996/2630) |
| | para 8 | 4 Sep 1995 (SI 1995/2302) |
| | para 9 | *Never in force* (repealed) |
| | para 10 | 4 Sep 1995 (SI 1995/2302) |
| | paras 11, 12 | 1 Oct 1995 (SI 1995/2302) |
| | para 13 | *Not yet in force* |
| | paras 14–16 | 4 Sep 1995 (SI 1995/2302) |
| | para 17 | 2 Dec 1996 (SI 1996/2630) |
| | para 18 | 18 Dec 1995 (SI 1995/3262) |
| | para 19 | 4 Sep 1995 (SI 1995/2302) |
| | para 20 | 14 Oct 1996 (SI 1996/2630) |

**Children (Scotland) Act 1995 (c 36)**

*RA:* 19 Jul 1995

*Commencement provisions:* s 105(1), (2); Children (Scotland) Act 1995 (Commencement No 1) Order 1995, SI 1995/2787; Children (Scotland) Act 1995 (Commencement No 2 and Transitional Provisions) Order 1996, SI 1996/2203, as amended by SI 1996/2708, SI 1997/137; Children (Scotland) Act 1995 (Commencement No 3) Order 1996, SI 1996/3201[2], as amended by SI 1997/744; Children (Scotland) Act 1995 (Commencement No 4) Order 2001, SSI 2001/475; Children (Scotland) Act 1995 (Commencement No 5) Order 2002, SSI 2002/12

| | | |
|---|---|---|
| 1 | (1)–(3) | 1 Nov 1995 (for purpose of bringing into force ss 15, 103, Sch 4, para 12) (SI 1995/2787) |
| | | 1 Nov 1996 (otherwise) (SI 1996/2203) |
| | (4) | 1 Nov 1996 (SI 1996/2203) |
| 2 | | 1 Nov 1996 (SI 1996/2203) |
| 3 | | 1 Nov 1996 (SI 1996/2203)[1] |
| 4 | | 1 Sep 1996 (for purpose of making regulations so as to come into force on or after 1 Nov 1996) (SI 1996/2203) |

**See Halsbury's Statutes Citator for amendments to these Acts**

**Children (Scotland) Act 1995 (c 36)**—*contd*

|  |  |
|---|---|
|  | 1 Nov 1996 (otherwise) (SI 1996/2203) |
| 5, 6 | 1 Nov 1996 (SI 1996/2203) |
| 7 | 1 Nov 1996 (SI 1996/2203)[1] |
| 8–10 | 1 Nov 1996 (SI 1996/2203) |
| 11 | 1 Nov 1996 (SI 1996/2203)[1] |
| 12–14 | 1 Nov 1996 (SI 1996/2203) |
| 15 | 1 Nov 1995 (SI 1995/2787) |
| 16 | 1 Apr 1997 (SI 1996/3201) |
| 17 | 12 Dec 1996 (for the purpose of enabling directions, rules or regulations to be made so as to come into force on or after 1 Apr 1997) (SI 1996/3201) |
|  | 1 Apr 1997 (otherwise) (SI 1996/3201) |
| 18 | 1 Apr 1997 (SI 1996/3201) |
| 19, 20 | 12 Dec 1996 (for the purpose of enabling directions, rules or regulations to be made so as to come into force on or after 1 Apr 1997) (SI 1996/3201) |
|  | 1 Apr 1997 (otherwise) (SI 1996/3201) |
| 21–30 | 1 Apr 1997 (SI 1996/3201) |
| 31 | 12 Dec 1996 (for the purpose of enabling directions, rules or regulations to be made so as to come into force on or after 1 Apr 1997) (SI 1996/3201) |
|  | 1 Apr 1997 (otherwise) (SI 1996/3201) |
| 32 | 1 Apr 1997 (SI 1996/3201) |
| 33 | 12 Dec 1996 (for the purpose of enabling directions, rules or regulations to be made so as to come into force on or after 1 Apr 1997) (SI 1996/3201) |
|  | 1 Apr 1997 (otherwise) (SI 1996/3201) |
| 34 | 1 Apr 1997 (SI 1996/3201) |
| 35 | 1 Nov 1995 (SI 1995/2787) |
| 36 | 1 Apr 1997 (SI 1996/3201) |
| 37 | 1 Nov 1995 (SI 1995/2787) |
| 38 | 12 Dec 1996 (for the purpose of enabling directions, rules or regulations to be made so as to come into force on or after 1 Apr 1997) (SI 1996/3201) |
|  | 1 Apr 1997 (otherwise) (SI 1996/3201) |
| 39 | 1 Apr 1997 (SI 1996/3201) |
| 40 | 12 Dec 1996 (for the purpose of enabling directions, rules or regulations to be made so as to come into force on or after 1 Apr 1997) (SI 1996/3201) |
|  | 1 Apr 1997 (otherwise) (SI 1996/3201) |
| 41 | 1 Apr 1997 (SI 1996/3201) |
| 42 | 12 Dec 1996 (for the purpose of enabling directions, rules or regulations to be made so as to come into force on or after 1 Apr 1997) (SI 1996/3201) |
|  | 1 Apr 1997 (otherwise) (SI 1996/3201) |
| 43–53 | 1 Apr 1997 (SI 1996/3201) |
| 54 | 1 Nov 1996 (subject to transitional provisions) (SI 1996/2203) |
| 55–61 | 1 Apr 1997 (SI 1996/3201) |
| 62 | 12 Dec 1996 (for the purpose of enabling directions, rules or regulations to be made so as to come into force on or after 1 Apr 1997) (SI 1996/3201) |
|  | 1 Apr 1997 (otherwise) (SI 1996/3201) |
| 63–69 | 1 Apr 1997 (SI 1996/3201) |
| 70 | 12 Dec 1996 (for the purpose of enabling directions, rules or regulations to be made so as to come into force on or after 1 Apr 1997) (SI 1996/3201) |
|  | 1 Apr 1997 (otherwise) (SI 1996/3201) |
| 71–73 | 1 Apr 1997 (SI 1996/3201) |

**Children (Scotland) Act 1995 (c 36)**—*contd*

| | | |
|---|---|---|
| 74, 75 | | 12 Dec 1996 (for the purpose of enabling directions, rules or regulations to be made so as to come into force on or after 1 Apr 1997) (SI 1996/3201) |
| | | 1 Apr 1997 (otherwise) (SI 1996/3201) |
| 76–86 | | 1 Apr 1997 (SI 1996/3201) |
| 87 | | 12 Dec 1996 (for the purpose of enabling directions, rules or regulations to be made so as to come into force on or after 1 Apr 1997) (SI 1996/3201) |
| | | 1 Apr 1997 (otherwise) (SI 1996/3201) |
| 88–90 | | 1 Apr 1997 (SI 1996/3201) |
| 91 | | 1 Oct 1996 (SI 1996/2203) |
| 92 | | 1 Apr 1997 (SI 1996/3201) |
| 93 | | 1 Nov 1996 (SI 1996/2203) |
| 94 | | 12 Dec 1996 (for the purpose of enabling directions, rules or regulations to be made so as to come into force on or after 1 Apr 1997) (SI 1996/3201) |
| | | 1 Apr 1997 (otherwise) (SI 1996/3201) |
| 95–97 | | 1 Apr 1997 (SI 1996/3201) |
| 98 | (1) | See Sch 2 below |
| | (2) | 1 Nov 1996 (SI 1996/2203) |
| 99 | | 1 Nov 1995 (SI 1995/2787) |
| 100 | | 1 Apr 1997 (SI 1996/3201) |
| 101 | | 12 Dec 1996 (for the purpose of enabling directions, rules or regulations to be made so as to come into force on or after 1 Apr 1997) (SI 1996/3201) |
| | | 22 Jan 2002 (otherwise) (SSI 2001/475) |
| 102 | | 1 Apr 1997 (SI 1996/3201) |
| 103, 104 | | 1 Nov 1995 (SI 1995/2787) |
| 105 | (1), (2) | 19 Jul 1995 (RA) |
| | (3) | See Sch 3 below |
| | (4) | See Sch 4 below |
| | (5) | See Sch 5 below |
| | (6)–(10) | 19 Jul 1995 (RA) |
| Sch 1 | | 1 Apr 1997 (SI 1996/3201) |
| Sch 2 | para 1 | 1 Nov 1996 (SI 1996/2203) |
| | para 2 | 1 Apr 1997 (SI 1996/3201) |
| | para 3 | 12 Dec 1996 (for the purposes of inserting Adoption (Scotland) Act 1978, s 3(3)(aa), for the purpose of enabling regulations to be made, so as to come into force on or after 1 Apr 1997) (SI 1996/3201) |
| | | 1 Apr 1997 (otherwise) (SI 1996/3201) |
| | para 4 | 1 Apr 1997 (SI 1996/3201) |
| | para 5 | 12 Dec 1996 (for the purpose of amending Adoption Act 1978, s 9, and inserting s 9(3A) for the purpose of enabling regulations to be made so as to come into force on or after 1 Apr 1997) (SI 1996/3201) |
| | | 1 Apr 1997 (otherwise) (SI 1996/3201) |
| | para 6 | 1 Apr 1997 (SI 1996/3201) |
| | para 7(a)(i) | 1 Nov 1996 (SI 1996/2203) |
| | para 7(a)(ii) | 1 Apr 1997 (SI 1996/3201) |
| | para 7(b), (c) | 1 Nov 1996 (SI 1996/2203) |
| | para 7(d) | 1 Apr 1997 (SI 1996/3201) |
| | para 8(a) | 1 Nov 1996 (SI 1996/2203) |
| | para 8(b) | 1 Apr 1997 (SI 1996/3201) |
| | para 9(a) | 1 Nov 1996 (SI 1996/2203) |
| | para 9(b) | 1 Apr 1997 (SI 1996/3201) |
| | para 10 | 1 Apr 1997 (SI 1996/3201) |
| | para 11(a) | 1 Apr 1997 (SI 1996/3201) |
| | para 11(b), (c) | 1 Nov 1996 (SI 1996/2203) |
| | para 11(d) | 1 Apr 1997 (SI 1996/3201) |

**Children (Scotland) Act 1995 (c 36)**—*contd*

| | | |
|---|---|---|
| | para 12(a) | 1 Apr 1997 (SI 1996/3201) |
| | para 12(b)(i) | 1 Nov 1996 (SI 1996/2203) |
| | para 12(b)(ii) | 1 Apr 1997 (SI 1996/3201) |
| | para 12(c), (d) | 1 Apr 1997 (SI 1996/3201) |
| | para 13(a)(i) | 1 Apr 1997 (SI 1996/3201) |
| | para 13(a)(ii) | 1 Nov 1996 (SI 1996/2203) |
| | para 13(b) | 1 Apr 1997 (SI 1996/3201) |
| | para 13(c)(i) | 1 Apr 1997 (SI 1996/3201) |
| | para 13(c)(ii) | 1 Nov 1996 (SI 1996/2203) |
| | para 13(d) | 1 Nov 1996 (SI 1996/2203) |
| | para 13(e), (f) | 1 Apr 1997 (SI 1996/3201) |
| | para 14 | 1 Nov 1996 (SI 1996/2203) |
| | paras 15, 16 | 1 Apr 1997 (SI 1996/3201) |
| | para 17(a) | 1 Apr 1997 (SI 1996/3201) |
| | para 17(b) | 1 Nov 1996 (SI 1996/2203) |
| | para 18 | 1 Apr 1997 (SI 1996/3201) |
| | para 19 | 12 Dec 1996 (for the purpose of substituting new Adoption (Scotland) Act 1978, s 27(1), (2), for the purpose of enabling regulations to be made, so as to come into force on or after 1 Apr 1997) (SI 1996/3201) |
| | | 1 Apr 1997 (otherwise) (SI 1996/3201) |
| | paras 20–22 | 1 Apr 1997 (SI 1996/3201) |
| | para 23 | 1 Nov 1996 (SI 1996/2203) |
| | para 24 | 1 Apr 1997 (SI 1996/3201) |
| | para 25 | 12 Dec 1996 (for the purpose of inserting Adoption (Scotland) Act 1978, s 51A, for the purpose of enabling regulations to be made, so as to come into force on or after 1 Apr 1998, or enabling the Secretary of State to make a direction) (SI 1996/3201) |
| | | 1 Apr 1997 (so far as it relates to insertion of Adoption (Scotland) Act 1978, s 51B) (SI 1996/3201) |
| | | 1 Apr 1998 (otherwise) (SI 1996/3201) |
| | para 26 | 1 Nov 1996 (SI 1996/2203) |
| | paras 27, 28 | 1 Apr 1997 (SI 1996/3201) |
| | para 29(a)(i), (ii) | 1 Apr 1997 (SI 1996/3201) |
| | para 29(a)(iii) | 1 Nov 1996 (SI 1996/2203) |
| | para 29(a)(iv) | 1 Apr 1997 (SI 1996/3201) |
| | para 29(a)(v), (vi) | 1 Nov 1996 (SI 1996/2203) |
| | para 29(a)(vii) | 1 Apr 1997 (SI 1996/3201) |
| | para 29(b), (c) | 1 Apr 1997 (SI 1996/3201) |
| Sch 3 | paras 1–6 | 1 Apr 1997 (SI 1996/3201) |
| | para 7 | 1 Nov 1996 (SI 1996/2203) |
| | paras 8–11 | 1 Apr 1997 (SI 1996/3201) |
| Sch 4 | paras 1–6 | 1 Nov 1996 (SI 1996/2203) |
| | para 7(1)–(5) | 1 Nov 1996 (SI 1996/2203) |
| | para 7(6)(a) | 1 Nov 1996 (SI 1996/2203) |
| | para 7(6)(b), (c) | 1 Apr 1997 (SI 1996/3201) |
| | paras 8, 9 | 1 Nov 1996 (SI 1996/2203) |
| | para 10(a) | 1 Apr 1997 (SI 1996/3201) |
| | para 10(b) | 1 Nov 1996 (SI 1996/2203) |
| | para 11 | 1 Nov 1996 (SI 1996/2203) |
| | paras 12, 13 | 1 Nov 1995 (SI 1995/2787) |
| | para 14 | 1 Nov 1996 (SI 1996/2203) |
| | para 15(1) | 1 Nov 1996 (SI 1996/2203) |
| | para 15(2)–(4) | 12 Dec 1996 (for the purpose of amending Social Work (Scotland) Act 1968 for the purpose of enabling regulations to be made, so as to come into force on or after 1 Apr 1997) (SI 1996/3201) |
| | | 1 Apr 1997 (otherwise) (SI 1996/3201) |
| | para 15(5) | 1 Nov 1996 (SI 1996/2203) |

**Children (Scotland) Act 1995 (c 36)**—*contd*

| | |
|---|---|
| para 15(6)–(16) | 12 Dec 1996 (for the purpose of amending Social Work (Scotland) Act 1968 for the purpose of enabling regulations to be made, so as to come into force on or after 1 Apr 1997) (SI 1996/3201) |
| | 1 Apr 1997 (otherwise) (SI 1996/3201) |
| para 15(17)(a)(i) | 12 Dec 1996 (for the purpose of amending Social Work (Scotland) Act 1968 for the purpose of enabling regulations to be made, so as to come into force on or after 1 Apr 1997) (SI 1996/3201) |
| | 1 Apr 1997 (otherwise) (SI 1996/3201) |
| para 15(17)(a)(ii) | 1 Nov 1996 (SI 1996/2203) |
| para 15(17)(b) | 12 Dec 1996 (for the purpose of amending Social Work (Scotland) Act 1968 for the purpose of enabling regulations to be made, so as to come into force on or after 1 Apr 1997) (SI 1996/3201) |
| | 1 Apr 1997 (otherwise) (SI 1996/3201) |
| para 15(18), (19) | 12 Dec 1996 (for the purpose of amending Social Work (Scotland) Act 1968 for the purpose of enabling regulations to be made, so as to come into force on or after 1 Apr 1997) (SI 1996/3201) |
| | 1 Apr 1997 (otherwise) (SI 1996/3201) |
| para 15(20)(a), (b) | 12 Dec 1996 (for the purpose of amending Social Work (Scotland) Act 1968 for the purpose of enabling regulations to be made, so as to come into force on or after 1 Apr 1997) (SI 1996/3201) |
| | 1 Apr 1997 (otherwise) (SI 1996/3201) |
| para 15(20)(c) | 1 Nov 1996 (SI 1996/2203) |
| para 15(20)(d) | 12 Dec 1996 (for the purpose of amending Social Work (Scotland) Act 1968 for the purpose of enabling regulations to be made, so as to come into force on or after 1 Apr 1997) (SI 1996/3201) |
| | 1 Apr 1997 (otherwise) (SI 1996/3201) |
| para 15(21)–(27) | 12 Dec 1996 (for the purpose of amending Social Work (Scotland) Act 1968 for the purpose of enabling regulations to be made, so as to come into force on or after 1 Apr 1997) (SI 1996/3201) |
| | 1 Apr 1997 (otherwise) (SI 1996/3201) |
| para 15(28)(a)–(c) | 12 Dec 1996 (for the purpose of amending Social Work (Scotland) Act 1968 for the purpose of enabling regulations to be made, so as to come into force on or after 1 Apr 1997) (SI 1996/3201) |
| | 1 Apr 1997 (otherwise) (SI 1996/3201) |
| para 15(28)(d), (e) | 1 Nov 1996 (SI 1996/2203) |
| para 15(28)(f)–(k) | 12 Dec 1996 (for the purpose of amending Social Work (Scotland) Act 1968 for the purpose of enabling regulations to be made, so as to come into force on or after 1 Apr 1997) (SI 1996/3201) |
| | 1 Apr 1997 (otherwise) (SI 1996/3201) |
| para 15(29), (30) | 12 Dec 1996 (for the purpose of amending Social Work (Scotland) Act 1968 for the purpose of enabling regulations to be made, so as to come into force on or after 1 Apr 1997) (SI 1996/3201) |
| | 1 Apr 1997 (otherwise) (SI 1996/3201) |
| paras 16, 17 | 1 Apr 1997 (SI 1996/3201) |
| para 18(1) | See sub-paras (2), (3) below |
| para 18(2) | 1 Nov 1995 (SI 1995/2787) |
| para 18(3) | 1 Nov 1996 (SI 1996/2203) |
| paras 19, 20 | 1 Nov 1996 (SI 1996/2203) |
| paras 21, 22 | 1 Apr 1997 (SI 1996/3201) |
| para 23(1) | 1 Nov 1996 (SI 1996/2203) |
| para 23(2), (3) | 1 Apr 1997 (SI 1996/3201) |

**Children (Scotland) Act 1995 (c 36)**—*contd*

| | | |
|---|---|---|
| para 23(4)(a) | 1 Nov 1996 (for purpose of the substitution of Rehabilitation of Offenders Act 1974, s 7(2)(c)) (SI 1996/2203) | |
| | 1 Apr 1997 (otherwise) (SI 1996/3201) | |
| para 23(4)(b) | 1 Apr 1997 (SI 1996/3201) | |
| para 23(4)(c) | 1 Nov 1996 (SI 1996/2203) | |
| para 24(1) | 1 Nov 1996 (SI 1996/2203) | |
| para 24(2), (3) | 1 Apr 1997 (SI 1996/3201) | |
| para 24(4), (5) | 1 Nov 1996 (SI 1996/2203) | |
| para 24(6)–(9) | 1 Apr 1997 (SI 1996/3201) | |
| para 24(10), (11) | 1 Nov 1996 (SI 1996/2203) | |
| para 24(12)–(18) | 1 Apr 1997 (SI 1996/3201) | |
| para 25 | 1 Apr 1997 (SI 1996/3201) | |
| para 26(1)–(3) | 1 Nov 1996 (SI 1996/2203) | |
| para 26(4)(a) | 1 Nov 1996 (SI 1996/2203) | |
| para 26(4)(b) | 1 Apr 1997 (SI 1996/3201) | |
| para 26(4)(c) | 1 Nov 1996 (SI 1996/2203) | |
| para 26(5)–(7) | 1 Nov 1996 (SI 1996/2203) | |
| para 26(8) | 1 Apr 1997 (except in so far as relates to Children Act 1975, s 103) (SI 1996/3201) | |
| | 22 Jan 2002 (exception noted above) (SSI 2002/12) | |
| para 26(9), (10) | 1 Apr 1997 (SI 1996/3201) | |
| para 27 | 1 Nov 1996 (SI 1996/2203) | |
| para 28(1) | 1 Nov 1996 (SI 1996/2203) | |
| para 28(2)–(4) | 1 Apr 1997 (SI 1996/3201) | |
| para 28(5)(a) | 1 Nov 1996 (SI 1996/2203) | |
| para 28(5)(b)–(d) | 1 Apr 1997 (SI 1996/3201) | |
| para 29 | 1 Apr 1997 (SI 1996/3201) | |
| paras 30, 31 | 1 Nov 1996 (SI 1996/2203) | |
| para 32 | 1 Apr 1997 (SI 1996/3201) | |
| para 33(1) | 1 Nov 1996 (SI 1996/2203) | |
| para 33(2), (3) | 1 Apr 1997 (SI 1996/3201) | |
| para 33(4) | 1 Nov 1996 (SI 1996/2203) | |
| para 34 | 1 Nov 1996 (SI 1996/2203) | |
| para 35 | 1 Apr 1997 (SI 1996/3201) | |
| para 36 | 1 Nov 1996 (SI 1996/2203) | |
| para 37(1) | 1 Nov 1996 (SI 1996/2203) | |
| para 37(2)–(4) | 1 Apr 1997 (SI 1996/3201) | |
| para 37(5) | 1 Nov 1996 (SI 1996/2203) | |
| para 37(6)(a)(i), (ii) | 1 Nov 1996 (SI 1996/2203) | |
| para 37(6)(a)(iii), (iv) | 1 Apr 1997 (SI 1996/3201) | |
| para 37(6)(b), (c) | 1 Apr 1997 (SI 1996/3201) | |
| para 38 | 1 Nov 1996 (SI 1996/2203) | |
| para 39(1) | 1 Nov 1996 (SI 1996/2203) | |
| para 39(2)(a) | 1 Nov 1996 (SI 1996/2203) | |
| para 39(2)(b) | 1 Apr 1997 (SI 1996/3201) | |
| para 39(3)(a) | 1 Nov 1996 (SI 1996/2203) | |
| para 39(3)(b) | 1 Apr 1997 (SI 1996/3201) | |
| para 39(4) | 1 Nov 1996 (SI 1996/2203) | |
| para 39(5)(a) | 1 Apr 1997 (SI 1996/3201) | |
| para 39(5)(b) | 1 Nov 1996 (SI 1996/2203) | |
| para 39(5)(c), (d) | 1 Apr 1997 (SI 1996/3201) | |
| para 40(a) | 1 Apr 1997 (SI 1996/3201) | |
| para 40(b) | 1 Nov 1995 (SI 1995/2787) | |
| para 41 | 1 Nov 1996 (SI 1996/2203) | |
| para 42 | 1 Apr 1997 (SI 1996/3201) | |
| para 43 | 1 Nov 1996 (SI 1996/2203) | |
| para 44 | 1 Apr 1997 (SI 1996/3201) | |
| para 45 | 1 Nov 1995 (SI 1995/2787) | |

**Children (Scotland) Act 1995 (c 36)**—*contd*

| | | |
|---|---|---|
| paras 46, 47 | 1 Nov 1996 (SI 1996/2203) |
| para 48(1) | 1 Nov 1996 (SI 1996/2203) |
| para 48(2), (3) | 1 Apr 1997 (SI 1996/3201) |
| para 48(4) | 1 Nov 1996 (SI 1996/2203) |
| para 48(5) | 1 Apr 1997 (SI 1996/3201) |
| para 49 | 1 Apr 1997 (SI 1996/3201) |
| paras 50–52 | 1 Nov 1996 (SI 1996/2203) |
| para 53(1) | See sub-paras (2)–(5) below |
| para 53(2) | 1 Nov 1996 (SI 1996/2203) |
| para 53(3) | 1 Nov 1995 (SI 1995/2787) |
| para 53(4), (5) | 1 Nov 1996 (SI 1996/2203) |
| para 54(1) | 1 Nov 1996 (SI 1996/2203) |
| para 54(2)–(4) | 1 Apr 1997 (SI 1996/3201) |
| para 54(5) | 1 Nov 1996 (SI 1996/2203) |
| paras 55–60 | 1 Apr 1997 (SI 1996/3201) |
| Sch 5 | 1 Nov 1995 (repeals in Registration of Births, Deaths and Marriages (Scotland) Act 1965, s 43) (SI 1995/2787) |

1 Nov 1996 (SI 1996/2203), repeals of or in—
  Lands Clauses Consolidation (Scotland) Act 1845;
  Judicial Factors Act 1849;
  Improvement of Land Act 1864;
  Judicial Factors (Scotland) Act 1880;
  Sheriff Courts (Scotland) Act 1907;
  Children and Young Persons (Scotland) Act 1937;
  Nursing Homes Registration (Scotland) Act 1938;
  Reserve and Auxiliary Forces (Protection of Civil Interests) Act 1951;
  Matrimonial Proceedings (Children) Act 1958;
  Social Work (Scotland) Act 1968, ss 5B(5), 94(1) relating to the definition "guardian";
  Maintenance Orders (Reciprocal Enforcement) Act 1972;
  Guardianship Act 1973;
  Rehabilitation of Offenders Act 1974, s 7(2) (the words from "In the application" to the end);
  Children Act 1975, ss 47–49, 53;
  Adoption (Scotland) Act 1978, ss 12(3)(b), (4), 14(1), 15(1), (3), 65(1) relating to the definition "guardian";
  Law Reform (Husband and Wife) (Scotland) Act 1984;
  Mental Health (Scotland) Act 1984, s 55(4);
  Family Law (Scotland) Act 1985;
  Law Reform (Parent and Child) (Scotland) Act 1986;
  Disabled Persons (Services, Consultation and Representation) Act 1986;
  Family Law Act 1986;
  Court of Session Act 1988;
  Children Act 1989;
  Age of Legal Capacity (Scotland) Act 1991;
  Child Support Act 1991;
  Education Act 1993

1 Apr 1997 (SI 1996/3201), repeals of or in—
  Social Work (Scotland) Act 1968 (so far as not already in force);
  Children and Young Persons Act 1969;
  Social Work (Scotland) Act 1972;
  Local Government (Scotland) Act 1973;
  Rehabilitation of Offenders Act 1974 (so far as not already in force);
  Children Act 1975, ss 73–84, 99, 100, 102, 105, 107, Sch 3, paras 52–57;
  Criminal Procedure (Scotland) Act 1975;

**Children (Scotland) Act 1995 (c 36)**—*contd*

> Adoption (Scotland) Act 1978 (so far as not already in force);
> Criminal Justice (Scotland) Act 1980;
> Education (Scotland) Act 1980;
> Health and Social Services and Social Security Adjudications Act 1983;
> Solvent Abuse (Scotland) Act 1983;
> Foster Children (Scotland) Act 1984;
> Mental Health (Scotland) Act 1984 (so far as not already in force);
> Child Abduction and Custody Act 1985;
> Civil Evidence (Scotland) Act 1988;
> Local Government and Housing Act 1989;
> Prisoners and Criminal Proceedings (Scotland) Act 1993;
> Local Government etc (Scotland) Act 1994
> 22 Jan 2002 (repeal of Children Act 1975, s 103) (SSI 2002/12)
> *Not yet in force* (repeal of or in Trusts (Scotland) Act 1921)

1    For transitional provisions, see SI 1996/2203, arts 4–7

2    For transitional provisions, see SI 1996/3201, arts 4–6

---

**Church of England (Miscellaneous Provisions) Measure 1995 (No 2)**

*RA:* 19 Jul 1995

*Commencement provisions:* s 15(2)

The provisions of this Measure (except s 6) were brought into force on 1 Sep 1995 by an instrument made by the Archbishops of Canterbury and York and dated 26 Jul 1995 (made under s 15(2))

---

**Civil Evidence Act 1995 (c 38)**

*RA:* 8 Nov 1995

*Commencement provisions:* s 16(2); Civil Evidence Act 1995 (Commencement No 1) Order 1996, SI 1996/3217

| | | |
|---|---|---|
| 1–9 | | 31 Jan 1997 (SI 1996/3217) |
| 10 | | *Not yet in force* |
| 11–15 | | 31 Jan 1997 (SI 1996/3217) |
| 16 | (1)–(4) | 31 Jan 1997 (SI 1996/3217) |
| | (5) | *Not yet in force* |
| | (6) | 31 Jan 1997 (SI 1996/3217) |
| Schs 1, 2 | | 31 Jan 1997 (SI 1996/3217) |

---

**Civil Evidence (Family Mediation) (Scotland) Act 1995 (c 6)**

*RA:* 1 May 1995

*Commencement provisions:* s 3(3); Civil Evidence (Family Mediation) (Scotland) Act 1995 (Commencement and Transitional Provision) Order 1996, SI 1996/125

Whole Act in force 19 Feb 1996 (but Act not to apply to any civil proceedings in which any evidence has been given or heard (in whole or in part) at any time prior to that date) (SI 1996/125)

---

## Commonwealth Development Corporation Act 1995 (c 9)

*RA:* 28 Jun 1995

Whole Act in force 28 Jun 1995 (RA)

---

## Consolidated Fund Act 1995 (c 2)

*RA:* 23 Mar 1995

Whole Act in force 23 Mar 1995 (RA)

---

## Consolidated Fund (No 2) Act 1995 (c 54)

*RA:* 19 Dec 1995

Whole Act in force 19 Dec 1995 (RA)

---

## Criminal Appeal Act 1995 (c 35)

*RA:* 19 Jul 1995

*Commencement provisions:* s 32; Criminal Appeal Act 1995 (Commencement No 1 and Transitional Provisions) Order 1995, SI 1995/3061; Criminal Appeal Act 1995 (Commencement No 2) Order 1996, SI 1996/3041; Criminal Appeal Act 1995 (Commencement No 3) Order 1996, SI 1996/3149; Criminal Appeal Act 1995 (Commencement No 4 and Transitional Provisions) Order 1997, SI 1997/402

| | | |
|---|---|---|
| 1, 2 | | 1 Jan 1996 (subject to transitional provisions) (SI 1995/3061) |
| 3 | | 31 Mar 1997 (subject to transitional provisions) (SI 1997/402) |
| 4 | | 1 Jan 1996 (subject to transitional provisions) (SI 1995/3061) |
| 5 | | 31 Mar 1997 (subject to transitional provisions) (SI 1997/402) |
| 6 | | 1 Jan 1996 (subject to transitional provisions) (SI 1995/3061) |
| 7 | | 1 Jan 1996 (subject to transitional provisions, and except in so far as relating to references by the Criminal Cases Review Commission) (SI 1995/3061) |
| | | 31 Mar 1997 (exception noted above) (SI 1997/402) |
| 8 | (1)–(6) | 12 Dec 1996 (for the purposes of making recommendations and appointments) (SI 1996/3041) |
| | | 1 Jan 1997 (otherwise) (SI 1996/3149) |
| | (7) | See Sch 1 below |
| 9–25 | | 31 Mar 1997 (subject to transitional provisions) (SI 1997/402) |
| 26–28 | | 1 Jan 1996 (subject to transitional provisions) (SI 1995/3061) |
| 29 | | See Schs 2, 3 below |
| 30 | | 1 Jan 1996 (subject to transitional provisions) (SI 1995/3061) |
| 31 | (1)(a) | 1 Jan 1997 (SI 1996/3149) |
| | (1)(b) | 1 Jan 1996 (subject to transitional provisions) (SI 1995/3061) |
| | (2) | 1 Jan 1996 (subject to transitional provisions) (SI 1995/3061) |
| 32–34 | | 1 Jan 1996 (subject to transitional provisions) (SI 1995/3061) |
| Sch 1 | paras 1, 2 | 12 Dec 1996 (for the purposes of making recommendations and appointments) (SI 1996/3041) |
| | | 1 Jan 1997 (otherwise) (SI 1996/3149) |
| | paras 3–11 | 1 Jan 1997 (SI 1996/3149) |
| Sch 2 | paras 1, 2 | 1 Jan 1996 (subject to transitional provisions) (SI 1995/3061) |
| | para 3 | 31 Mar 1997 (subject to transitional provisions) (SI 1997/402) |
| | para 4(1)–(3) | 1 Jan 1996 (subject to transitional provisions) (SI 1995/3061) |
| | para 4(4) | 31 Mar 1997 (subject to transitional provisions) (SI 1997/402) |
| | para 4(5) | 1 Jan 1996 (subject to transitional provisions) (SI 1995/3061) |
| | paras 5, 6 | 1 Jan 1996 (subject to transitional provisions) (SI 1995/3061) |
| | paras 7–11 | 1 Jan 1997 (SI 1996/3149) |

**Criminal Appeal Act 1995 (c 35)**—*contd*

| | | |
|---|---|---|
| | para 12(1)–(4) | 1 Jan 1996 (subject to transitional provisions) (SI 1995/3061) |
| | para 12(5) | 31 Mar 1997 (subject to transitional provisions) (SI 1997/402) |
| | para 12(6) | 1 Jan 1996 (subject to transitional provisions) (SI 1995/3061) |
| | paras 13, 14 | 31 Mar 1997 (subject to transitional provisions) (SI 1997/402) |
| | para 15 | 1 Jan 1996 (subject to transitional provisions) (SI 1995/3061) |
| | para 16 | 31 Mar 1997 (subject to transitional provisions) (SI 1997/402) |
| | para 17 | 1 Jan 1996 (subject to transitional provisions) (SI 1995/3061) |
| | para 18 | 31 Mar 1997 (subject to transitional provisions) (SI 1997/402) |
| | para 19 | 31 Mar 1997 (subject to transitional provisions) (SI 1997/402) |
| Sch 3 | | 1 Jan 1996 (subject to transitional provisions) (SI 1995/3061), repeals of or in— |

      Criminal Appeal Act 1968, s 23(3);
      Courts-Martial (Appeals) Act 1968;
      Criminal Law Act 1977;
      Criminal Appeal (Northern Ireland) Act 1980, ss 16(1), 25(3);
      Magistrates' Courts Act 1980;
      Supreme Court Act 1981;
      Criminal Justice Act 1988;
      Criminal Procedure (Insanity and Unfitness to Plead) Act 1991, Sch 3, para 3(1)
   31 Mar 1997 (otherwise) (subject to transitional provisions) (SI 1997/402)

**Criminal Injuries Compensation Act 1995 (c 53)**

*RA:* 8 Nov 1995

Whole Act in force 8 Nov 1995 (RA)

**Criminal Justice (Scotland) Act 1995 (c 20)**

*RA:* 19 Jul 1995

*Commencement provisions:* s 118(2), (3); Criminal Justice (Scotland) Act 1995 (Commencement No 1, Transitional Provisions and Savings) Order 1995, SI 1995/2295; Criminal Justice (Scotland) Act 1995 (Commencement No 2, Transitional Provisions and Savings) Order 1996, SI 1996/517

Whole Act in force (in so far as not already in force), subject to transitional provisions and savings, and with the exception of s 66 (repealed), on 5 Mar 1996 and 31 Mar 1996

**Criminal Law (Consolidation) (Scotland) Act 1995 (c 39)**

*RA:* 8 Nov 1995

*Commencement provisions:* s 53(2)

Whole Act in force 1 Apr 1996 (s 53(2)), subject to transitional provisions and savings in Criminal Procedure (Consequential Provisions) (Scotland) Act 1995, in particular for consolidated provisions which are not yet in force at that date; see s 4, Sch 3 thereto

**Criminal Procedure (Consequential Provisions) (Scotland) Act 1995 (c 40)**

*RA:* 8 Nov 1995

*Commencement provisions:* s 7(2)

Whole Act in force 1 Apr 1996 (s 7(2)), subject to transitional provisions and savings, in particular for amendments by consolidated enactments which are not yet in force at that date; see s 4, Sch 3 thereto

## Criminal Procedure (Scotland) Act 1995 (c 46)

*RA:* 8 Nov 1995

*Commencement provisions:* s 309(2)

Whole Act in force 1 Apr 1996 (s 309(2)), subject to transitional provisions and savings in Criminal Procedure (Consequential Provisions) (Scotland) Act 1995, in particular for consolidated provisions which are not yet in force at that date; see s 4, Sch 3 thereto

## Crown Agents Act 1995 (c 24)

*RA:* 19 Jul 1995

Whole Act in force 19 Jul 1995 (RA) (note that certain provisions of this Act have effect as from "the appointed day": 21 Mar 1997 is the appointed day under s 1(1) (Crown Agents Act 1995 (Appointed Day) Order 1997, SI 1997/1139))

## Disability Discrimination Act 1995 (c 50)

*RA:* 8 Nov 1995

*Commencement provisions:* s 70(2), (3); Disability Discrimination Act 1995 (Commencement No 1) Order 1995, SI 1995/3330; Disability Discrimination Act 1995 (Commencement No 1) Order (Northern Ireland) 1996, SR 1996/1; Disability Discrimination Act 1995 (Commencement No 2) Order 1996, SI 1996/1336; Disability Discrimination Act 1995 (Commencement No 2) Order (Northern Ireland) 1996, SR 1996/219; Disability Discrimination Act 1995 (Commencement No 3 and Saving and Transitional Provisions) Order 1996, SI 1996/1474; Disability Discrimination Act 1995 (Commencement No 3 and Saving and Transitional Provisions) Order (Northern Ireland) 1996, SR 1996/280; Disability Discrimination Act 1995 (Commencement No 4) Order 1996, SI 1996/3003; Disability Discrimination Act 1995 (Commencement No 4) Order (Northern Ireland) 1996, SR 1996/560; Disability Discrimination Act 1995 (Commencement No 5) Order 1998, SI 1998/1282; Disability Discrimination Act (Commencement No 5) Order (Northern Ireland) 1998, SR 1998/183; Disability Discrimination Act 1995 (Commencement No 6) Order 1999, SI 1999/1190; Disability Discrimination Act (Commencement No 6) Order (Northern Ireland) 1999, SR 1999/196; Disability Discrimination Act 1995 (Commencement No 7) Order 2000, SI 2000/1969; Disability Discrimination Act 1995 (Commencement No 7) Order (Northern Ireland) 2001, SR 2001/163; Disability Discrimination Act 1995 (Commencement No 8) Order 2000, SI 2000/2989; Disability Discrimination Act 1995 (Commencement No 9) Order 2001, SI 2001/2030; Disability Discrimination Act 1995 (Commencement No 8) Order (Northern Ireland) 2001, SR 2001/439; Disability Discrimination Act 1995 (Commencement No 9) Order (Northern Ireland) 2003, SR 2003/24; Disability Discrimination Act 1995 (Commencement No 10) (Scotland) Order 2003, SI 2003/215; Disability Discrimination Act 1995 (Commencement No 11) Order 2005, SI 2005/1122; Disability Discrimination Act 1995 (Commencement No 10) Order (Northern Ireland) 2008, SR 2008/236; Disability Discrimination Act 1995 (Commencement No 11) Order (Northern Ireland) 2015, SR 2015/333

| | | |
|---|---|---|
| 1–3 | | 17 May 1996 (E) (W) (S) (SI 1996/1336) |
| | | 30 May 1996 (NI) (SR 1996/219) |
| 4 | | 2 Dec 1996 (SI 1996/1474; SR 1996/280) |
| 5 | (1)–(5) | 2 Dec 1996 (SI 1996/1474; SR 1996/280) |
| | (6), (7) | 6 Jun 1996 (E) (W) (S) (SI 1996/1474) |
| | | 11 Jul 1996 (NI) (SR 1996/280) |
| 6 | (1)–(7) | 2 Dec 1996 (SI 1996/1474; SR 1996/280) |
| | (8)–(10) | 6 Jun 1996 (E) (W) (S) (SI 1996/1474) |
| | | 11 Jul 1996 (NI) (SR 1996/280) |
| | (11), (12) | 2 Dec 1996 (SI 1996/1474; SR 1996/280) |
| 7 | | 2 Dec 1996 (SI 1996/1474; SR 1996/280) |
| 8 | (1)–(5) | 2 Dec 1996 (SI 1996/1474; SR 1996/280) |
| | (6), (7) | 6 Jun 1996 (E) (W) (S) (SI 1996/1474) |
| | | 11 Jul 1996 (NI) (SR 1996/280) |
| | (8) | 2 Dec 1996 (SI 1996/1474; SR 1996/280) |

**Disability Discrimination Act 1995 (c 50)**—*contd*

| | | |
|---|---|---|
| 9 | | 2 Dec 1996 (SI 1996/1474; SR 1996/280) |
| 10 | | 2 Dec 1996 (SI 1996/1474; SR 1996/280) |
| 11 | | 2 Dec 1996 (SI 1996/1474; SR 1996/280) |
| 12 | (1), (2) | 2 Dec 1996 (SI 1996/1474; SR 1996/280) |
| | (3) | 6 Jun 1996 (E) (W) (S) (SI 1996/1474) |
| | | 11 Jul 1996 (NI) (SR 1996/280) |
| | (4), (5) | 2 Dec 1996 (SI 1996/1474; SR 1996/280) |
| | (6) | 6 Jun 1996 (E) (W) (S) (SI 1996/1474) |
| | | 11 Jul 1996 (NI) (SR 1996/280) |
| 13 | | 2 Dec 1996 (SI 1996/1474; SR 1996/280) |
| 14 | (1) | 2 Dec 1996 (SI 1996/1474; SR 1996/280) |
| | (2) | 1 Oct 1999 (SI 1999/1190; SR 1999/196) |
| | (3) | 2 Dec 1996 (SI 1996/1474; SR 1996/280) |
| | (4), (5) | 1 Oct 1999 (SI 1999/1190; SR 1999/196) |
| | (6) | 6 Jun 1996 (E) (W) (S) (SI 1996/1474) |
| | | 11 Jul 1996 (NI) (SR 1996/280) |
| 15 | (1)(a) | 1 Oct 1999 (SI 1999/1190; SR 1999/196) |
| | (1)(b) | *Never in force* (repealed) |
| | (2)–(10) | 1 Oct 1999 (SI 1999/1190; SR 1999/196) |
| 16 | (1), (2) | 2 Dec 1996 (SI 1996/1474; SR 1996/280) |
| | (3) | 17 May 1996 (E) (W) (S) (so far as it relates to definitions "sub-lease" and "sub-tenancy") (SI 1996/1336) |
| | | 30 May 1996 (NI) (so far as it relates to definitions "sub-lease" and "sub-tenancy") (SR 1996/219) |
| | | 2 Dec 1996 (otherwise) (SI 1996/3003; SR 1996/560) |
| | (4) | 2 Dec 1996 (SI 1996/1474; SR 1996/280) |
| | (5) | See Sch 4, paras 1–4 below |
| 17 | (1), (2) | 2 Dec 1996 (SI 1996/1474; SR 1996/280) |
| | (3) | 6 Jun 1996 (E) (W) (S) (SI 1996/1474) |
| | | 11 Jul 1996 (NI) (SR 1996/280) |
| | (4) | 2 Dec 1996 (SI 1996/1474; SR 1996/280) |
| 18 | (1), (2) | 2 Dec 1996 (SI 1996/1474; SR 1996/280) |
| | (3), (4) | 6 Jun 1996 (E) (W) (S) (SI 1996/1474) |
| | | 11 Jul 1996 (NI) (SR 1996/280) |
| 19 | (1)(a) | 2 Dec 1996 (SI 1996/1474; SR 1996/280) |
| | (1)(b) | 1 Oct 1999 (SI 1999/1190; SR 1999/196) |
| | (1)(c), (d) | 2 Dec 1996 (SI 1996/1474; SR 1996/280) |
| | (2)–(4) | 2 Dec 1996 (SI 1996/1474; SR 1996/280) |
| | (5)(a), (b) | 2 Dec 1996 (SI 1996/1474; SR 1996/280) |
| | (5)(c) | 6 Jun 1996 (E) (W) (S) (SI 1996/1474) |
| | | 11 Jul 1996 (NI) (SR 1996/280) |
| | (6) | 2 Dec 1996 (SI 1996/1474; SR 1996/280); |
| 20 | (1) | 2 Dec 1996 (SI 1996/1474; SR 1996/280) |
| | (2) | 1 Oct 1999 (SI 1999/1190; SR 1999/196) |
| | (3), (4) | 2 Dec 1996 (SI 1996/1474; SR 1996/280) |
| | (5) | 1 Oct 1999 (SI 1999/1190; SR 1999/196) |
| | (6)–(8) | 6 Jun 1996 (E) (W) (S) (SI 1996/1474) |
| | | 11 Jul 1996 (NI) (SR 1996/280) |
| | (9) | 1 Oct 1999 (SI 1999/1190; SR 1999/196) |
| 21 | (1) | 1 Oct 1999 (SI 1999/1190; SR 1999/196) |
| | (2)(a)–(c) | 1 Oct 2004 (SI 2001/2030; SR 2001/439) |
| | (2)(d) | 1 Oct 1999 (SI 1999/1190; SR 1999/196) |
| | (3) | 26 Apr 1999 (SI 1999/1190; SR 1999/196) |
| | (4) | 1 Oct 1999 (SI 1999/1190; SR 1999/196) |
| | (5) | 26 Apr 1999 (SI 1999/1190; SR 1999/196) |
| | (6) | 1 Oct 1999 (SI 1999/1190; SR 1999/196) |
| | (7)–(9) | *Never in force* (repealed) |
| | (10) | 1 Oct 1999 (SI 1999/1190; SR 1999/196) |
| 22, 23 | | 2 Dec 1996 (SI 1996/1474; SR 1996/280) |

**Disability Discrimination Act 1995 (c 50)**—*contd*

| | | |
|---|---|---|
| 24 | (1)–(4) | 2 Dec 1996 (SI 1996/1474; SR 1996/280) |
| | (5) | 6 Jun 1996 (E) (W) (S) (SI 1996/1474) |
| | | 11 Jul 1996 (NI) (SR 1996/280) |
| 25, 26 | | 2 Dec 1996 (SI 1996/1474; SR 1996/280) |
| 27 | (1), (2) | 1 Oct 2004 (SI 2001/2030; SR 2001/439) |
| | (3) | 9 May 2001 (E) (W) (S) (SI 2001/2030) |
| | | 31 Dec 2001 (NI) (SR 2001/439) |
| | (4) | 1 Oct 2004 (SI 2001/2030; SR 2001/439) |
| | (5) | See Sch 4, paras 5–9 below |
| 28 | | 17 May 1996 (SI 1996/1336) |
| 29 | (1), (2) | *Never in force* (repealed) |
| | (3) | 31 Jul 1996 (SI 1996/1474) |
| 30 | (1)–(6) | 31 Jul 1996 (SI 1996/1474) |
| | (7)–(9) | *Never in force* (repealed) |
| 31 | | 31 Jul 1996 (SI 1996/1474) |
| 32 | | 18 Sep 2015 (NI) (SR 2015/333) |
| 33–35 | | *Never in force* (repealed) |
| 36 | | 26 Jan 2009 (so far as applies to designated vehicles) (s 70(2A)(a)) |
| | | *Never in force* (repealed) (otherwise) |
| 37 | | 1 Dec 2000 (E) (W) (for the purposes of the issue of certificates of exemption by licensing authorities pursuant to s 37(5)–(7), the prescription of the notices of exemption pursuant to s 37(8)(b)) (SI 2000/2989) |
| | | 31 Mar 2001 (E) (W) (otherwise) (SI 2000/2989) |
| | | 1 Jun 2001 (NI) (for the purposes of the issue of certificates of exemption by the Department of the Environment pursuant to s 37(5)–(7), the prescription of the notices of exemption pursuant to s 37(8)(b)) (SR 2001/163) |
| | | 1 Aug 2001 (NI) (otherwise) (SR 2001/163) |
| | | *Never in force* (repealed) (S) |
| 38 | | 1 Dec 2000 (E) (W) (SI 2000/2989) |
| | | 1 Jun 2001 (NI) (SR 2001/163) |
| | | 26 Jan 2009 (S) (s 70(2A)(c)) |
| 39 | | 5 Feb 2003 (S) (SI 2003/215) |
| 40–45 | | 30 Aug 2000 (E) (W) (S) (SI 2000/1969) |
| | | 21 Jan 2003 (NI) (SR 2003/24) |
| 46, 47 | | 13 May 1998 (SI 1998/1282; SR 1998/183) |
| 48 | | 13 May 1998 (so far as relates to s 46) (SI 1998/1282; SR 1998/183) |
| | | 30 Aug 2000 (E) (W) (S) (otherwise) (SI 2000/1969) |
| | | 21 Jan 2003 (NI) (otherwise) (SR 2003/24) |
| 49 | | 6 Apr 2005 (E) (W) (S) (so far as relates to a certificate of exemption issued under s 37 or 37A, a notice of a kind mentioned in s 37(8)(b) or 37A(8)(b), an accessibility certificate and an approval certificate) (SI 2005/1122) |
| | | 3 Jun 2008 (NI) (so far as relates to a certificate of exemption issued under s 37 or 37A, a notice of a kind mentioned in s 37(8)(b) or 37A(8)(b), an accessibility certificate and an approval certificate) (SR 2008/236) |
| | | *Never in force* (repealed) (in relation to a certificate of exemption issued under s 36, and a notice of a kind mentioned in s 36(9)(b)) |
| 50–52 | | 1 Jan 1996 (E) (W) (S) (SI 1995/3330) |
| | | 2 Jan 1996 (NI) (SR 1996/1) |
| 53, 54 | | 6 Jun 1996 (E) (W) (S) (SI 1996/1474) |
| | | 11 Jul 1996 (NI) (SR 1996/280) |
| 55 | | 2 Dec 1996 (SI 1996/1474; SR 1996/280) |
| 56 | | 6 Jun 1996 (E) (W) (S) (SI 1996/1474) |
| | | 11 Jul 1996 (NI) (SR 1996/280) |
| 57, 58 | | 2 Dec 1996 (SI 1996/1474; SR 1996/280) |

**Disability Discrimination Act 1995 (c 50)**—*contd*

| | | |
|---|---|---|
| 59 | | 17 May 1996 (E) (W) (S) (SI 1996/1336) |
| | | 30 May 1996 (NI) (SR 1996/219) |
| 60 | | 2 Dec 1996 (SI 1996/1474; SR 1996/280) |
| 61 | | 2 Dec 1996 (subject to a saving and transitional provisions) (SI 1996/1474; SR 1996/280) |
| 62 | (1), (2) | 17 May 1996 (E) (W) (S) (SI 1996/1336) |
| | | 30 May 1996 (NI) (SR 1996/219) |
| | (3)–(6) | *Never in force* (repealed) |
| | (7) | 17 May 1996 (E) (W) (S) (SI 1996/1336) |
| | | 30 May 1996 (NI) (SR 1996/219) |
| 63 | (1), (2) | 17 May 1996 (E) (W) (S) (SI 1996/1336) |
| | | *Never in force* (NI) (repealed) |
| | (3) | *Never in force* (repealed) |
| | (4)–(6) | 17 May 1996 (E) (W) (S) (SI 1996/1336) |
| | | *Never in force* (NI) (repealed) |
| 64 | | 2 Dec 1996 (SI 1996/1474; SR 1996/280) |
| 65 | | 2 Dec 1996 (SI 1996/1474) |
| 66 | | 2 Dec 1996 (E) (W) (S) (SI 1996/1474) |
| | | *Never in force* (NI) (repealed) |
| 67 | | 17 May 1996 (SI 1996/1336) |
| 68 | (1) | 17 May 1996 (E) (W) (S) (SI 1996/1336) |
| | | 30 May 1996 (NI) (SR 1996/219) |
| | (2)–(5) | 2 Dec 1996 (SI 1996/1474; SR 1996/280) |
| 69 | | 17 May 1996 (E) (W) (S) (SI 1996/1336) |
| | | 30 May 1996 (NI) (SR 1996/219) |
| 70 | (1)–(3) | 8 Nov 1995 (s 70(2)) |
| | (4) | 2 Dec 1996 (SI 1996/1474; SR 1996/280) |
| | (5) | See Sch 7 below |
| | (6) | 8 Nov 1995 (s 70(2)) |
| | (7) | 17 May 1996 (E) (W) (S) (SI 1996/1336) |
| | | 30 May 1996 (NI) (SR 1996/219) |
| | (8) | 8 Nov 1995 (s 70(2)) |
| Sch 1 | paras 1–6 | 17 May 1996 (E) (W) (S) (SI 1996/1336) |
| | | 30 May 1996 (NI) (SR 1996/219) |
| | para 7 | 2 Dec 1996 (SI 1996/1474; SR 1996/280) |
| | para 8 | 17 May 1996 (E) (W) (S) (SI 1996/1336) |
| | | 30 May 1996 (NI) (SR 1996/219) |
| Sch 2 | | 17 May 1996 (E) (W) (S) (SI 1996/1336) |
| | | 30 May 1996 (NI) (SR 1996/219) |
| Sch 3 | | 2 Dec 1996 (SI 1996/1474; SR 1996/280) |
| Sch 4 | paras 1, 2 | 2 Dec 1996 (SI 1996/1474; SR 1996/280) |
| | para 3 | 6 Jun 1996 (E) (W) (S) (SI 1996/1474) |
| | | 11 Jul 1996 (NI) (SR 1996/280) |
| | para 4 | 17 May 1996 (E) (W) (S) (SI 1996/1336) |
| | | 30 May 1996 (NI) (SR 1996/219) |
| | paras 5–7 | 1 Oct 2004 (SI 2001/2030; SR 2001/439) |
| | paras 8, 9 | 9 May 2001 (E) (W) (S) (SI 2001/2030) |
| | | 31 Dec 2001 (NI) (SR 2001/439) |
| Sch 5 | | 1 Jan 1996 (SI 1995/3330) |
| | | 2 Jan 1996 (NI) (SR 1996/1) |
| Sch 6 | | 2 Dec 1996 (SI 1996/1474; SR 1996/280) |
| Sch 7 | | 2 Dec 1996 (E) (W) (S) (SI 1996/1474), repeals of or in— |
| | | Disabled Persons (Employment) Act 1944, ss 1, 6–14, 19, 21 (subject to a saving and transitional provisions); |
| | | Disabled Persons (Employment) Act 1958 |
| | | 2 Dec 1996 (NI) (SR 1996/280), repeals of— |
| | | Disabled Persons (Employment) Act (Northern Ireland) 1945, ss 1, 6–14, 19, 21 (subject to saving and transitional provisions); |
| | | Disabled Persons (Employment) Act (Northern Ireland) 1960 |

**Disability Discrimination Act 1995 (c 50)**—*contd*

|  |  |
|---|---|
|  | *Never in force* (repealed) repeals of or in— |
|  | Disabled Persons (Employment) Act 1944, s 22(4); |
|  | Disabled Persons (Employment) Act (Northern Ireland) 1945, s 22; |
|  | Chronically Sick and Disabled Persons Act 1970; |
|  | Industrial Relations (Northern Ireland) Order 1976, SI 1976/1043 (NI 16), art 68(6) (revoked); |
|  | Employment Protection (Consolidation) Act 1978, Sch 13, para 20(3) (repealed); |
|  | Local Government and Housing Act 1989; |
|  | Education Act 1993 |
| Sch 8 | 8 Nov 1995 (s 70(2)) |

**Environment Act 1995 (c 25)**

*RA:* 19 Jul 1995

*Commencement provisions:* s 125(2)–(5); Environment Act 1995 (Commencement No 1) Order 1995, SI 1995/1983; Environment Act 1995 (Commencement No 2) Order 1995, SI 1995/2649; Environment Act 1995 (Commencement No 3) Order 1995, SI 1995/2765; Environment Act 1995 (Commencement No 4 and Saving Provisions) Order 1995, SI 1995/2950; Environment Act 1995 (Commencement No 5) Order 1996, SI 1996/186; Environment Act (Commencement No 6 and Repeal Provisions) Order 1996, SI 1996/2560; Environment Act 1995 (Commencement No 7) (Scotland) Order 1996, SI 1996/2857; Environment Act 1995 (Commencement No 8 and Saving Provisions) Order 1996, SI 1996/2909; Environment Act 1995 (Commencement No 9 and Transitional Provisions) Order 1997, SI 1997/1626; Environment Act 1995 (Commencement No 10) Order 1997, SI 1997/3044; Environment Act 1995 (Commencement No 11) Order 1998, SI 1998/604; Environment Act 1995 (Commencement No 12 and Transitional Provisions) (Scotland) Order 1998, SI 1998/781; Environment Act 1995 (Commencement No 13) (Scotland) Order 1998, SI 1998/3272; Environment Act 1995 (Commencement No 14) Order 1999, SI 1999/803; Environment Act 1995 (Commencement No 15) Order 1999, SI 1999/1301; Environment Act 1995 (Commencement No 16 and Saving Provision) (England) Order 2000, SI 2000/340; Environment Act 1995 (Commencement No 17 and Savings Provision) (Scotland) Order 2000, SSI 2000/180; Environment Act 1995 (Commencement No 18) (Scotland) Order 2000, SI 2000/1986; Environment Act 1995 (Commencement No 18) (England and Wales) Order 2000, SI 2000/3033; Environment Act 1995 (Commencement No 19) (Scotland) Order 2000, SSI 2000/433; Environment Act 1995 (Commencement and Saving Provision) (Wales) Order 2001, SI 2001/2351[1]; Environment Act 1995 (Commencement No 20 and Saving Provision) (Wales) Order 2001, SI 2001/3211[2]; Environment Act 1995 (Commencement No 21) (Scotland) Order 2003, SSI 2003/206; Environment Act 1995 (Commencement No 22) (Scotland) Order 2004, SSI 2004/541; Environment Act 1995 (Commencement No 23) (England and Wales) Order 2006, SI 2006/934; Environment Act 1995 (Commencement No 24) (Scotland) Order 2015, SS1 2015/73; Environment Act 1995 (Commencement No 25) Order 2017, SI 2017/1045; Environment Act 1995 (Commencement No 26) Order 2020, SI 2020/216

| | | |
|---|---|---|
| 1 | | 28 Jul 1995 (SI 1995/1983) |
| 2 | | 1 Apr 1996 (SI 1996/186) |
| 3 | (1) | 1 Apr 1996 (SI 1996/186) |
| | (2)–(8) | 28 Jul 1995 (SI 1995/1983) |
| 4 | | 28 Jul 1995 (SI 1995/1983) |
| 5 | (1) | 1 Apr 1996 (SI 1996/186) |
| | (2) | 1 Feb 1996 (SI 1996/186) |
| | (3), (4) | 1 Apr 1996 (SI 1996/186) |
| | (5) | 1 Feb 1996 (SI 1996/186) |
| 6 | | 1 Apr 1996 (SI 1996/186) |
| 7 | | 28 Jul 1995 (SI 1995/1983) |
| 8 | | 1 Apr 1996 (SI 1996/186) |
| 9 | | 28 Jul 1995 (SI 1995/1983) |
| 10, 11 | | 1 Apr 1996 (SI 1996/186) |
| 12 | | 28 Jul 1995 (SI 1995/1983) |
| 13 | | 1 Apr 1996 (SI 1996/186) |

**See Halsbury's Statutes Citator for amendments to these Acts**

**Environment Act 1995 (c 25)**—*contd*

| | | |
|---|---|---|
| 14 | | See Sch 4 below |
| 15–18 | | 1 Apr 1996 (SI 1996/186) |
| 19 | | See Sch 5 below |
| 20–23 | | 12 Oct 1995 (SI 1995/2649) |
| 24 | | *Never in force* (repealed) |
| 25–29 | | 1 Apr 1996 (SI 1996/186) |
| 30–32 | | 12 Oct 1995 (SI 1995/2649) |
| 33–35 | | 1 Apr 1996 (SI 1996/186) |
| 36 | | 12 Oct 1995 (SI 1995/2649) |
| 37 | (1), (2) | 28 Jul 1995 (SI 1995/1983) |
| | (3)–(8) | 1 Apr 1996 (SI 1996/186) |
| | (9) | 28 Jul 1995 (SI 1995/1983) |
| 38–40 | | 28 Jul 1995 (SI 1995/1983) |
| 41 | | 21 Sep 1995 (so far as confers power to make schemes imposing charges) (SI 1995/1983) |
| | | 1 Feb 1996 (so far as confers power on Secretary of State to make regulations and makes provision in relation to the exercise of that power) (SI 1996/186) |
| | | 1 Apr 1996 (otherwise) (SI 1996/186) |
| 42 | | 21 Sep 1995 (SI 1995/1983) |
| 43–52 | | 28 Jul 1995 (SI 1995/1983) |
| 53, 54 | | 1 Apr 1996 (SI 1996/186) |
| 55 | (1)–(6) | 1 Apr 1996 (SI 1996/186) |
| | (7)–(10) | 1 Feb 1996 (SI 1996/186) |
| 56 | | 28 Jul 1995 (SI 1995/1983) |
| 57 | | 21 Sep 1995 (so far as it confers power on Secretary of State to make regulations or orders, give directions or issue guidance, or so far as makes provision with respect to the exercise of any such power) (SI 1995/1983) |
| | | 1 Apr 2000 (E) (otherwise) (SI 2000/340) |
| | | 14 Jul 2000 (S) (except so far as inserts Environmental Protection Act 1990, s 78S) (SSI 2000/180) |
| | | 14 Jul 2000 (S) (otherwise) (SI 2000/1986) |
| | | 15 Sep 2001 (W) (otherwise) (SI 2001/3211) |
| 58 | | 21 Sep 1995 (so far as it confers power on Secretary of State to make regulations or orders, give directions or issue guidance, or so far as makes provision with respect to the exercise of any such power) (SI 1995/1983) |
| | | 1 Jul 1998 (otherwise) (SI 1998/604) |
| 59 | | 12 Oct 1995 (so far as confers power on Secretary of State to make regulations) (SI 1995/2649) |
| | | 1 Jan 1999 (otherwise) (SI 1998/3272) |
| 60 | (1), (2) | 1 Jul 1998 (SI 1998/604) |
| | (3), (4) | 1 Jul 1997 (subject to transitional provisions) (SI 1997/1626) |
| | (5)(a) | 1 Jul 1997 (subject to transitional provisions) (SI 1997/1626) |
| | (5)(b) | 1 Jul 1998 (SI 1998/604) |
| | (6) | 1 Jul 1998 (SI 1998/604) |
| | (7) | 1 Jul 1997 (subject to transitional provisions) (SI 1997/1626) |
| 61–73 | | 19 Sep 1995 (s 125(2)) |
| 74 | | 19 Jul 1995 (s 125(3)) |
| 75–77 | | 19 Sep 1995 (s 125(2)) |
| 78 | | See Sch 10 below |
| 79 | | 19 Sep 1995 (s 125(2)) |
| 80 | | 1 Feb 1996 (SI 1996/186) |
| 81 | | 1 Apr 1996 (SI 1996/186) |
| 82–86 | | 23 Dec 1997 (SI 1997/3044) |
| 87–89 | | 1 Feb 1996 (SI 1996/186) |
| 90 | | See Sch 11 below |
| 91 | | 1 Feb 1996 (SI 1996/186) |
| 92 | | 1 Apr 1996 (SI 1996/186) |

**Environment Act 1995 (c 25)**—*contd*

| | | |
|---|---|---|
| 93–95 | | 21 Sep 1995 (SI 1995/1983) |
| 96 | (1) | See Schs 13, 14 below |
| | (2) | 1 Nov 1995 (SI 1995/2765) |
| | (3) | 1 Jan 1997 (SI 1996/2857) |
| | (4) | 1 Nov 1995 (repeal of Town and Country Planning Act 1990, s 105) (SI 1995/2765) |
| | | 1 Jan 1997 (repeal of Town and Country Planning (Scotland) Act 1972, s 251A) (SI 1996/2857) |
| | (5), (6) | 1 Nov 1995 (E) (W) (SI 1995/2765) |
| | | 1 Jan 1997 (S) (SI 1996/2857) |
| 97–103 | | 21 Sep 1995 (SI 1995/1983) |
| 104 | | 1 Apr 1996 (SI 1996/186) |
| 105 | | See Sch 15 below |
| 106 | | See Sch 16 below |
| 107 | | See Sch 17 below |
| 108 | (1)–(13) | 1 Apr 1996 (SI 1996/186) |
| | (14) | See Sch 18 below |
| | (15), (16) | 1 Apr 1996 (SI 1996/186) |
| 109–111 | | 1 Apr 1996 (SI 1996/186) |
| 112 | | See Sch 19 below |
| 113 | | 1 Apr 1996 (SI 1996/186) |
| 114 | (1)–(3) | 1 Apr 1996 (SI 1996/186) |
| | (4) | See Sch 20 below |
| 115 | | 1 Apr 1996 (SI 1995/2950; SI 1996/186) |
| 116 | | See Sch 21 below |
| 117 | | 1 Feb 1996 (SI 1996/186) |
| 118 | (1)–(3) | 1 Feb 1996 (SI 1996/186) |
| | (4), (5) | 1 Feb 1996 (so far as confers power to make orders or make provision in relation to the exercise of that power) (SI 1996/186) |
| | | 1 Apr 2020 (otherwise) (SI 2020/216) |
| | (6) | 1 Feb 1996 (SI 1996/186) |
| 119 | | 1 Feb 1996 (SI 1996/186) |
| 120 | (1) | 28 Jul 1995 (so far as confers powers to make regulations) (SI 1995/1983) |
| | | See Sch 22 below (otherwise) |
| | (2) | See Sch 23 below |
| | (3) | See Sch 24 below |
| | (4)–(6) | 28 Jul 1995 (SI 1995/1983) |
| 121–124 | | 28 Jul 1995 (SI 1995/1983) |
| 125 | | 19 Jul 1995 (s 125(3)) |
| Sch 1 | | 28 Jul 1995 (SI 1995/1983) |
| Sch 2 | | 28 Jul 1995 (so far as relates to s 3) (SI 1995/1983) |
| | | 12 Oct 1995 (so far as relates to s 22) (SI 1995/2649) |
| Sch 3 | | 28 Jul 1995 (SI 1995/1983) |
| Schs 4, 5 | | 1 Apr 1996 (SI 1996/186) |
| Sch 6 | | 12 Oct 1995 (SI 1995/2649) |
| Sch 7 | paras 1–6 | 19 Sep 1995 (s 125(2)) |
| | para 7(1) | 19 Sep 1995 (s 125(2)) |
| | para 7(2) | 1 Apr 1997 (SI 1996/2560) |
| | para 7(3)–(5) | 19 Sep 1995 (s 125(2)) |
| | paras 8–20 | 19 Sep 1995 (s 125(2)) |
| Schs 8, 9 | | 19 Sep 1995 (s 125(2)) |
| Sch 10 | para 1 | 23 Nov 1995 (SI 1995/2950) |
| | para 2(1) | 23 Nov 1995 (SI 1995/2950) |
| | para 2(2) | 1 Apr 1996 (SI 1995/2950) |
| | para 2(3)–(8) | 23 Nov 1995 (SI 1995/2950) |
| | para 2(9)(a) | 23 Nov 1995 (SI 1995/2950) |
| | para 2(9)(b) | 1 Apr 1996 (SI 1995/2950) |

**Environment Act 1995 (c 25)**—*contd*

| | | |
|---|---|---|
| | para 2(9)(c), (d) | 23 Nov 1995 (SI 1995/2950) |
| | paras 3–7 | 23 Nov 1995 (SI 1995/2950) |
| | para 8(1) | 1 Apr 1996 (SI 1995/2950) |
| | para 8(2) | 23 Nov 1995 (SI 1995/2950) |
| | para 8(3) | 1 Apr 1996 (SI 1995/2950) |
| | para 9 | 23 Nov 1995 (SI 1995/2950) |
| | para 10(1) | 23 Nov 1995 (SI 1995/2950) |
| | para 10(2)(a) | *Never in force* (spent) |
| | para 10(2)(b) | 1 Apr 1997 (SI 1996/2560) |
| | para 10(3) | 23 Nov 1995 (SI 1995/2950) |
| | paras 11, 12 | 23 Nov 1995 (SI 1995/2950) |
| | para 13 | 1 Apr 1996 (SI 1995/2950) |
| | paras 14, 15 | 23 Nov 1995 (SI 1995/2950) |
| | para 16 | 1 Apr 1996 (SI 1995/2950) |
| | paras 17–19 | 23 Nov 1995 (SI 1995/2950) |
| | para 20 | 1 Apr 1996 (SI 1995/2950) |
| | para 21 | 23 Nov 1995 (SI 1995/2950) |
| | para 22(1), (2) | 1 Apr 1997 (SI 1996/2560) |
| | para 22(3) | 1 Apr 1996 (SI 1995/2950) |
| | para 22(4)(a), (b) | 1 Apr 1996 (SI 1995/2950) |
| | para 22(4)(c) | 1 Apr 1997 (SI 1996/2560) |
| | para 22(5) | 1 Apr 1996 (SI 1995/2950) |
| | para 22(6), (7) | 1 Apr 1997 (SI 1996/2560) |
| | paras 23–26 | 23 Nov 1995 (SI 1995/2950) |
| | para 27 | 1 Apr 1997 (SI 1996/2560) |
| | paras 28–31 | 23 Nov 1995 (SI 1995/2950) |
| | para 32(1)–(13) | 23 Nov 1995 (subject to a saving in relation to sub-para (2)) (SI 1995/2950) |
| | para 32(14) | 1 Apr 1997 (SI 1996/2560) |
| | para 32(15)–(18) | 23 Nov 1995 (SI 1995/2950) |
| | para 33(1)–(5) | 23 Nov 1995 (SI 1995/2950) |
| | para 33(6)–(8) | 1 Apr 1997 (SI 1996/2560) |
| | para 34 | 23 Nov 1995 (SI 1995/2950) |
| | para 35 | 23 Nov 1995 (so far as inserts Local Government Finance Act 1992, s 35(5)(c) and the word "or" immediately preceding it) (SI 1995/2950) |
| | | 1 Apr 1997 (otherwise) (SI 1996/2560) |
| | paras 36, 37 | 23 Nov 1995 (SI 1995/2950) |
| | para 38(1) | 23 Nov 1995 (SI 1995/2950) |
| | para 38(2) | 1 Apr 1997 (SI 1996/2560) |
| Sch 11 | para 1 | 23 Dec 1997 (SI 1997/3044) |
| | paras 2, 3 | 1 Feb 1996 (SI 1996/186) |
| | para 4 | 23 Dec 1997 (SI 1997/3044) |
| | para 5 | 1 Feb 1996 (SI 1996/186) |
| Sch 12 | | 1 Apr 1996 (SI 1996/186) |
| Schs 13, 14 | | 1 Nov 1995 (E) (W) (SI 1995/2765) |
| | | 1 Jan 1997 (S) (1996/2875) |
| Sch 15 | paras 1, 2 | 1 Apr 1996 (SI 1996/186) |
| | para 3 | 1 Feb 1996 (SI 1996/186) |
| | para 4 | 1 Apr 1996 (SI 1996/186) |
| | para 5(1) | 1 Feb 1996 (SI 1996/186) |
| | para 5(2), (3) | 1 Apr 1996 (SI 1996/186) |
| | paras 6–12 | 1 Apr 1996 (SI 1996/186) |
| | para 13 | 1 Jan 1999 (SI 1995/1983) |
| | para 14(1) | 1 Jan 1999 (SI 1995/1983) |
| | para 14(2), (3) | 1 Apr 1996 (SI 1996/186) |
| | para 14(4) | 1 Jan 1999 (SI 1995/1983) |
| | paras 15, 16 | 1 Apr 1996 (SI 1996/186) |
| | para 17 | 1 Jan 1999 (SI 1995/1983) |

**Environment Act 1995 (c 25)**—*contd*

| | | |
|---|---|---|
| | paras 18, 19 | 1 Apr 1996 (SI 1996/186) |
| | para 20 | 1 Jan 1999 (SI 1995/1983) |
| | paras 21–24 | 1 Apr 1996 (SI 1996/186) |
| | para 25 | 21 Sep 1995 (SI 1995/1983) |
| | para 26(1) | 21 Sep 1995 (SI 1995/1983) |
| | para 26(2) | 1 Jan 1999 (SI 1995/1983) |
| Schs 16–20 | | 1 Apr 1996 (SI 1996/186) |
| Sch 21 | para 1 | 1 Dec 2000 (SI 2000/3033) |
| | para 2(1)–(3) | 21 Sep 1995 (SI 1995/1983) |
| | para 2(4) | 1 Jul 1997 (except for purposes of the application of substituted Water Resources Act 1991, s 222 to Pt II of the Act) (subject to transitional provisions) (SI 1997/1626) |
| | | 1 Jan 2018 (exception noted above) (SI 2017/1045) |
| | para 3 | *Never in force* (repealed) |
| | para 4 | 8 Apr 1998 (subject to transitional provisions) (SI 1998/781) |
| | para 5 | *Not yet in force* |
| | para 6 | *Never in force* (repealed) |
| Sch 22 | para 1 | 1 Apr 1996 (SI 1996/186) |
| | para 2 | 1 Feb 1996 (SI 1996/186) |
| | para 3 | 1 Apr 1996 (SI 1996/186) |
| | para 4 | 28 Jul 1995 (SI 1995/1983) |
| | paras 5–12 | 1 Apr 1996 (SI 1996/186) |
| | para 13 | 1 Feb 1996 (SI 1996/186) |
| | para 14 | 1 Apr 1996 (SI 1996/186) |
| | para 15 | 12 Oct 1995 (SI 1995/2649) |
| | para 16 | *Never in force* (repealed) |
| | paras 17–26 | 1 Apr 1996 (SI 1996/186) |
| | para 27(a) | 1 Apr 1996 (SI 1996/186) |
| | para 27(b), (c) | 1 Jan 2005 (S) (SSI 2004/541) |
| | | 15 May 2006 (E) (W) (SI 2006/934) |
| | para 28 | 1 Apr 1996 (SI 1996/186) |
| | para 29(1) | See sub-paras (2)–(35) below |
| | para 29(2)–(20) | 1 Apr 1996 (SI 1996/186) |
| | para 29(21)(a)(i) | 1 Apr 2003 (SSI 2003/206) |
| | para 29(21)(a)(ii) | 1 Apr 1996 (SI 1996/186) |
| | para 29(21)(b)–(e) | 1 Apr 2003 (SSI 2003/206) |
| | para 29(22) | 12 Oct 1995 (so far as confers power on Secretary of State to make regulations) (SI 1995/2649) |
| | | 1 Apr 2003 (otherwise) (SSI 2003/206) |
| | para 29(23)–(25) | 1 Apr 1996 (SI 1996/186) |
| | para 29(26) | 1 Jan 2001 (SSI 2000/433) |
| | para 29(27)–(35) | 1 Apr 1996 (SI 1996/186) |
| | para 30 | 1 Apr 1996 (SI 1996/186) |
| | para 31 | 28 Jul 1995 (SI 1995/1983) |
| | paras 32–35 | 1 Apr 1996 (SI 1996/186) |
| | para 36 | 1 Feb 1996 (SI 1996/186) |
| | para 37(1) | 21 Sep 1995 (SI 1995/1983) |
| | para 37(2)(a) | 1 Apr 1998 (SI 1998/604) |
| | para 37(2)(b) | 1 Feb 1996 (SI 1996/186) |
| | para 37(3) | 1 Apr 1996 (SI 1996/186) |
| | para 37(4) | 21 Sep 1995 (SI 1995/1983) |
| | para 37(5)–(8) | 1 Apr 1996 (SI 1996/186) |
| | paras 38, 39 | 21 Sep 1995 (SI 1995/1983) |
| | paras 40, 41 | 1 Apr 1996 (SI 1996/186) |
| | para 42 | 28 Jul 1995 (SI 1995/1983) |
| | paras 43, 44 | 1 Feb 1996 (SI 1996/186) |
| | para 45 | 1 Apr 1996 (SI 1996/186) |
| | para 46(1)–(4) | 1 Apr 1996 (SI 1996/186) |
| | para 46(5) | 23 Dec 1997 (SI 1997/3044) |

**Environment Act 1995 (c 25)**—*contd*

| | |
|---|---|
| para 46(6)–(11) | 1 Apr 1996 (SI 1996/186) |
| paras 47–50 | 1 Apr 1996 (SI 1996/186) |
| para 51(1)–(3) | 12 Oct 1995 (SI 1995/2649) |
| para 51(4) | 1 Apr 1996 (SI 1996/186) |
| para 51(5) | 12 Oct 1995 (SI 1995/2649) |
| para 52 | 1 Apr 1996 (SI 1996/186) |
| para 53 | 12 Oct 1995 (SI 1995/2649) |
| paras 54–66 | 1 Apr 1996 (SI 1996/186) |
| para 67 | 1 Feb 1996 (so far as confers power to make regulations or makes provision in relation to the exercise of that power) (SI 1996/186) |
| | 1 Apr 1998 (so far as it imposes a duty, or confers power, to make regulations) (SI 1998/604) |
| | 1 Apr 1999 (otherwise) (SI 1999/803) |
| para 68(1) | 1 Apr 1996 (SI 1996/186) |
| para 68(2) | 1 Apr 1996 (so far as requires an application to be accompanied by the prescribed charge) (subject to a saving) (SI 1996/186) |
| | 1 Apr 1998 (otherwise) (SI 1998/604) |
| para 68(3), (4) | 1 Apr 1996 (subject to a saving relating to sub-para (3)) (SI 1996/186) |
| para 68(5) | 1 Apr 1998 (SI 1998/604) |
| para 68(6) | 1 Apr 1996 (subject to a saving) (SI 1996/186) |
| para 69 | 1 Apr 1998 (so far as confers power to make regulations) (SI 1998/604) |
| | 1 Apr 1999 (otherwise) (SI 1999/803) |
| para 70(1), (2) | 1 Apr 1996 (SI 1996/186) |
| para 70(3) | 1 Apr 1999 (SI 1999/803) |
| para 71 | 1 Apr 1998 (so far as confers power to make regulations) (SI 1998/604) |
| | 1 Apr 1999 (otherwise) (SI 1999/803) |
| para 72(1) | 1 Apr 1998 (so far as confers power to make regulations) (SI 1998/604) |
| | 1 Apr 1999 (otherwise) (SI 1999/803) |
| para 72(2) | 1 Apr 1996 (SI 1996/186) |
| para 73(1) | 1 Apr 1996 (SI 1996/186) |
| para 73(2) | 1 Apr 1996 (so far as requires an application to be accompanied by the prescribed charge) (SI 1996/186) |
| | 1 Apr 1998 (otherwise) (SI 1998/604) |
| para 73(3)–(6) | 1 Apr 1996 (SI 1996/186) |
| para 74 | 1 Apr 1996 (so far as requires an application to be accompanied by the prescribed charge) (SI 1996/186) |
| | 1 Apr 1998 (otherwise) (SI 1998/604) |
| para 75 | 1 Apr 1996 (SI 1996/186) |
| para 76(1) | 21 Sep 1995 (SI 1995/1983) |
| para 76(2) | 1 Apr 1996 (SI 1996/186) |
| para 76(3) | 21 Sep 1995 (SI 1995/1983) |
| para 76(4)–(7) | 1 Apr 1996 (SI 1996/186) |
| para 76(8)(a) | 19 Jul 1995 (s 125(3)) |
| para 76(8)(b) | 1 Apr 1996 (SI 1996/186) |
| paras 77, 78 | 1 Apr 1996 (SI 1996/186) |
| para 79 | 1 Apr 2000 (E) (SI 2000/340) |
| | 14 Jul 2000 (S) (SSI 2000/180) |
| | 15 Sep 2001 (W) (SI 2001/3211) |
| para 80(1), (2) | 21 Sep 1995 (SI 1995/1983) |
| para 80(3) | 1 Apr 1996 (SI 1996/186) |
| para 81 | 1 Apr 2015 (S) (SSI 2015/73) |
| | *Not yet in force* (E) (W) |
| para 82(1) | See sub-paras (2)–(5) below |
| para 82(2)–(4) | 1 Apr 1996 (SI 1996/186) |

**Environment Act 1995 (c 25)**—*contd*

| | |
|---|---|
| para 82(5) | 21 Sep 1995 (so far as confers power on Secretary of State to make regulations or makes provision with respect to the exercise of any such power) (SI 1995/1983) |
| | 1 Apr 1996 (otherwise) (SI 1996/186) |
| paras 83–87 | 1 Apr 1996 (SI 1996/186) |
| para 88 | 1 Apr 2003 (S) (for the purposes of the Landfill (Scotland) Regulations 2003, SSI 2003/208[3]) (SSI 2003/206) |
| | 1 Jan 2005 (S) (otherwise) (SSI 2004/541) |
| | 15 May 2006 (E) (W) (SI 2006/934) |
| para 89 | 1 Apr 2000 (E) (subject to a saving) (SI 2000/340) |
| | 14 Jul 2000 (S) (subject to a saving) (SSI 2000/180) |
| | 15 Sep 2001 (W) (subject to a saving) (SI 2001/3211) |
| para 90 | Apr 1996 (SI 1996/186) |
| paras 91, 92 | 1 Apr 2000 (E) (SI 2000/340) |
| | 14 Jul 2000 (S) (SSI 2000/180) |
| | 15 Sep 2001 (W) (SI 2001/3211) |
| paras 93, 94 | 1 Apr 1996 (SI 1996/186) |
| para 95 | 1 Jan 2005 (S) (SSI 2004/541) |
| | 15 May 2006 (E) (W) (SI 2006/934) |
| paras 96–101 | 1 Apr 1996 (SI 1996/186) |
| para 102 | 1 Feb 1996 (SI 1996/186) |
| para 103 | 1 Feb 1996 (so far as confers power to issue guidance or makes provision in relation to the exercise of that power) (SI 1996/186) |
| | 1 Apr 1996 (otherwise) (SI 1996/186) |
| paras 104–132 | 1 Apr 1996 (SI 1996/186) |
| para 133(1) | 21 Sep 1995 (SI 1995/1983) |
| para 133(2) | 1 Apr 1996 (SI 1996/186) |
| para 134 | 1 Apr 1996 (SI 1996/186) |
| para 135 | 19 Jul 1995 (s 125(3)) |
| para 136 | 1 Apr 1996 (SI 1996/186) |
| paras 137–139 | 21 Sep 1995 (SI 1995/1983) |
| paras 140, 141 | 1 Apr 1996 (SI 1996/186) |
| para 142 | 21 Nov 1996 (so far as confers power to make regulations) (SI 1996/2909) |
| | 31 Dec 1996 (otherwise) (SI 1996/2909) |
| para 143 | 21 Nov 1996 (so far as confers power to make regulations) (SI 1996/2909) |
| | 31 Dec 1996 (otherwise) (SI 1996/2909) |
| paras 144–146 | 1 Apr 1996 (SI 1996/186) |
| para 147 | 21 Sep 1995 (SI 1995/1983) |
| paras 148–152 | 1 Apr 1996 (SI 1996/186) |
| para 153 | 21 Sep 1995 (SI 1995/1983) |
| paras 154–160 | 1 Apr 1996 (SI 1996/186) |
| para 161 | 29 Apr 1999 (SI 1999/1301) |
| para 162 | 21 Sep 1995 (so far as confers power on Secretary of State to make regulations or makes provision with respect to the exercise of any such power) (SI 1995/1983) |
| | 16 Mar 1999 (so far as confers power to make regulations in relation to Water Resources Act 1991, ss 161A–161D) (SI 1999/803) |
| | 29 Apr 1999 (otherwise) (SI 1999/1301) |
| para 163 | 29 Apr 1999 (SI 1999/1301) |
| paras 164–168 | 1 Apr 1996 (SI 1996/186) |
| paras 169, 170 | 21 Nov 1996 (so far as confers power to make regulations) (SI 1996/2909) |
| | 31 Dec 1996 (otherwise) (SI 1996/2909) |
| paras 171–181 | 1 Apr 1996 (SI 1996/186) |
| para 182 | 21 Sep 1995 (SI 1995/1983) |

**Environment Act 1995 (c 25)**—*contd*

| | | |
|---|---|---|
| | para 183 | 21 Nov 1996 (so far as confers power to make regulations) (SI 1996/2909) |
| | | 31 Dec 1996 (otherwise, but subject to savings) (SI 1996/2909) |
| | paras 184, 185 | 1 Apr 1996 (SI 1996/186) |
| | para 186 | *Never in force* (repealed) |
| | para 187(1) | 21 Sep 1995 (SI 1995/1983) |
| | para 187(2) | 1 Apr 1996 (SI 1996/186) |
| | paras 188–191 | 1 Apr 1996 (SI 1996/186) |
| | para 192 | 21 Sep 1995 (SI 1995/1983) |
| | paras 193–212 | 1 Apr 1996 (SI 1996/186) |
| | para 213(1) | 28 Jul 1995 (SI 1995/1983) |
| | para 213(2)(a) | 1 Apr 1996 (SI 1996/186) |
| | para 213(2)(b) | 28 Jul 1995 (SI 1995/1983) |
| | para 213(3) | 28 Jul 1995 (SI 1995/1983) |
| | para 213(4), (5) | 1 Apr 1996 (SI 1996/186) |
| | paras 214–222 | 1 Apr 1996 (SI 1996/186) |
| | para 223(1)(a), (b) | 1 Apr 1996 (SI 1996/186) |
| | para 223(1)(c) | 28 Jul 1995 (SI 1995/1983) |
| | para 223(2) | 1 Apr 1996 (SI 1996/186) |
| | paras 224–231 | 1 Apr 1996 (SI 1996/186) |
| | para 232(1) | 1 Feb 1996 (SI 1996/186) |
| | para 232(2) | *Not yet in force* |
| | para 233 | 1 Apr 1996 (SI 1996/186) |
| Sch 23 | paras 1–6 | 1 Apr 1996 (SI 1996/186) |
| | para 7 | *Not yet in force* |
| | paras 8–10 | 1 Apr 1996 (SI 1996/186) |
| | para 11 | *Not yet in force* |
| | paras 12, 13 | 1 Apr 1996 (SI 1996/186) |
| | para 14(1)–(4) | 1 Apr 1996 (SI 1996/186) |
| | para 14(5), (6) | 1 Jan 1999 (SI 1995/1983) |
| | para 14(7) | 1 Apr 1996 (SI 1996/186) |
| | para 14(8) | 1 Jan 1999 (definitions "grating" and "the substitution date") (SI 1995/1983) |
| | | 1 Apr 1996 (otherwise) (SI 1996/186) |
| | para 15 | *Not yet in force* |
| | paras 16–24 | 1 Apr 1996 (SI 1996/186) |
| Sch 24 | | 21 Sep 1995 (repeal of Water Resources Act 1991, ss 68, 69(5), 126(6), 129(4)) (SI 1995/1983) |
| | | 1 Nov 1995 (repeal of Town and Country Planning Act 1990, s 105) (SI 1995/2765) |
| | | 1 Feb 1996 (repeals in Local Government etc (Scotland) Act 1994, except the repeal in relation to s 165(6)) (SI 1996/186) |
| | | 1 Apr 1996 (SI 1996/186), repeals of or in— |
| | | Public Health (Scotland) Act 1897; |
| | | Alkali, &c, Works Regulation Act 1906; |
| | | Rivers (Prevention of Pollution) (Scotland) Act 1951; |
| | | Mines and Quarries Act 1954; |
| | | Nuclear Installations Act 1965; |
| | | Rivers (Prevention of Pollution) (Scotland) Act 1965; |
| | | Parliamentary Commissioner Act 1967; |
| | | Hovercraft Act 1968; |
| | | Sewerage (Scotland) Act 1968; |
| | | Agriculture Act 1970; |
| | | Clyde River Purification Act 1972; |
| | | Local Government Act 1972, s 223(2); |
| | | Local Government (Scotland) Act 1973; |
| | | Clean Air Enactments (Repeals and Modifications) Regulations 1974; |
| | | Control of Pollution Act 1974 (except repeal relating to s 30(1)); |

**Environment Act 1995 (c 25)**—*contd*

        Health and Safety at Work etc Act 1974;

        House of Commons Disqualification Act 1975;

        Local Government (Scotland) Act 1975;

        Northern Ireland Assembly Disqualification Act 1975;

        Salmon and Freshwater Fisheries Act 1975, ss 5(2), 10, 15;

        Water (Scotland) Act 1980;

        Roads (Scotland) Act 1984;

        Control of Industrial Air Pollution (Transfer of Powers of
         Enforcement) Regulations 1987;

        Control of Pollution (Amendment) Act 1989, ss 7(2), (8), 11(3);

        Water Act 1989;

        Environmental Protection Act 1990 (except repeals relating to
         ss 33(1), 36(11), (12), 39(12), (13), 54, 61, 75(3), 88, 143,
         Sch 8);

        Natural Heritage (Scotland) Act 1991;

        Water Industry Act 1991 (except repeals in s 4(6));

        Water Resources Act 1991, ss 1–14, 16–19, 58, 105(1), 113(1),
         114, 117, 121–124, 131, 132, 144, 146, 150–153, 187, 196,
         202(5), 206(2), 209(1), (2), (4), 213–215, 218, 219, 221(1),
         Schs 1, 3, 4;

        Land Drainage Act 1991, s 72(1);

        Water Consolidation (Consequential Provisions) Act 1991;

        Clean Air Act 1993;

        Noise and Statutory Nuisance Act 1993;

        Radioactive Substances Act 1993;

        Local Government etc (Scotland) Act 1994, s 165(6);

        Local Government (Wales) Act 1994, Sch 9, para 17(4), Sch 11,
         para 3(1), (2)

     31 Dec 1996 (repeals in Water Resources Act 1991, ss 91, 190(1))
        (subject to savings relating to s 91)[1] (SI 1996/2909)

     1 Jan 1997 (repeal of Town and Country Planning (Scotland)
        Act 1972, s 251A) (SI 1996/2857)

     1 Apr 1997 (SI 1996/2560), repeals of or in—

        National Parks and Access to the Countryside Act 1949;

        Caravan Sites and Control of Development Act 1960;

        Agriculture Act 1967;

        Countryside Act 1968;

        Local Government Act 1972;

        Local Government Act 1974;

        Welsh Development Agency Act 1975;

        Race Relations Act 1976;

        Highways Act 1980;

        Local Government, Planning and Land Act 1980 (except repeals
         relating to s 103(2)(c) and Sch 2, para 9(2), (3));

        Acquisition of Land Act 1981;

        Wildlife and Countryside Act 1981;

        Derelict Land Act 1982;

        Local Government (Miscellaneous Provisions) Act 1982;

        Litter Act 1983;

        Housing Act 1985;

        Local Government Act 1985;

        Local Government Act 1988;

        Local Government Finance Act 1988;

        Norfolk and Suffolk Broads Act 1988;

        Electricity Act 1989;

        Local Government and Housing Act 1989 (except repeal relating
         to the word "and" in s 21(1));

        Environmental Protection Act 1990 (remainder, except repeals
         relating to ss 33(1), 54, 61, 75(3), 143);

        Planning (Consequential Provisions) Act 1990;

**Environment Act 1995 (c 25)**—*contd*

> Planning (Hazardous Substances) Act 1990;
> Planning (Listed Buildings and Conservation Areas) Act 1990;
> Town and Country Planning Act 1990 (remainder);
> Land Drainage Act 1991;
> Planning and Compensation Act 1991;
> Water Industry Act 1991 (remainder);
> Water Resources Act 1991 (remainder, except repeal relating to s 190(1));
> Local Government Finance Act 1992 (except repeal relating to Sch 13, para 95);
> Local Government (Overseas Assistance) Act 1993;
> Local Government (Wales) Act 1994 (remainder, except repeals relating to Sch 9, para 17(12), Sch 16, para 65(5));
> Environment Act 1995 (except repeals relating to Sch 22)
> 1 Jan 1999 (repeals in Salmon and Freshwater Fisheries Act 1975, ss 30, 41(1)) (SI 1995/1983)
> 1 Apr 2000 (E) (repeals of or in Environmental Protection Act 1990, ss 61, 143) (SI 2000/340)
> 14 Jul 2000 (S) (repeals of or in Environmental Protection Act 1990, ss 61, 143) (SSI 2000/180)
> 15 Sep 2001 (W) (repeals of or in Environmental Protection Act 1990, ss 61, 143) (SI 2001/3211)
> 1 Jan 2005 (S) (SSI 2004/541), repeals of or in—
> Control of Pollution Act 1974, s 30(1);
> Environmental Protection Act 1990, s 75(3)
> 15 May 2006 (E) (W) (SI 2006/934), repeals of or in—
> Control of Pollution Act 1974, s 30(1);
> Environmental Protection Act 1990, s 75(3)
> 1 Apr 2015 (S) (SSI 2015/73), repeals of or in—
> Environmental Protection Act 1990, ss 33(1), 54;
> Environment Act 1995, Sch 22, paras 19, 20–24, 26, 27
> *Not yet in force*, repeals of or in—
> Local Government, Planning and Land Act 1980, s 103(2)(c), Sch 2, para 9(2), (3);
> Criminal Justice Act 1982;
> Control of Pollution (Amendment) Act 1989, s 2(3)(e);
> Local Government and Housing Act 1989, s 21(1) (part);
> Environmental Protection Act 1990, s 33(1) (E) (W);
> Water Resources Act 1991, s 190(1);
> Local Government Finance Act 1992, Sch 13, para 95;
> Local Government (Wales) Act 1994, Sch 9, para 17(12), Sch 16, para 65(5);
> Environment Act 1995, Sch 22, paras 19–27, 46(11)(a) 182, 231 (E) (W)

[1]    SI 2001/2351 was made by the National Assembly for Wales and purported to bring into force certain provisions of this Act; the National Assembly for Wales subsequently found it did not have the power to make that commencement order and those provisions are now brought into force on a later date by SI 2001/3211

[2]    For saving see SI 2001/3211, art 3

[3]    Note that SSI 2003/208 is void due to having been made without proper authority

---

**European Communities (Finance) Act 1995 (c 1)**

*RA:* 16 Jan 1995

Whole Act in force 16 Jan 1995 (RA)

---

## Finance Act 1995 (c 4)

*Budget Day:* 29 Nov 1994

*RA:* 1 May 1995

The commencement details of Finance Acts are not set out, as the dates from which their provisions take effect are usually stated clearly and unambiguously in the text of the Act, and charging provisions will normally state for which year or years of assessment they are to have effect.

## Gas Act 1995 (c 45)

*RA:* 8 Nov 1995

*Commencement provisions:* s 18(2)–(4); Gas Act 1995 (Appointed Day and Commencement) Order 1996, SI 1996/218

| | | |
|---|---|---|
| 1–7 | | 1 Mar 1996 (SI 1996/218) |
| 8 | (1) | 1 Mar 1996 (SI 1996/218) |
| | (2) | 8 Nov 1995 (RA) |
| 9, 10 | | 1 Mar 1996 (SI 1996/218) |
| 11 | (1)–(5) | 8 Nov 1995 (RA) |
| | (6), (7) | 1 Mar 1996 (SI 1996/218) |
| 12 | | 1 Mar 1996 (SI 1996/218) |
| 13 | | 8 Nov 1995 (RA) |
| 14–16 | | 1 Mar 1996 (SI 1996/218) |
| 17 | (1), (2) | 8 Nov 1995 (RA) |
| | (3), (4) | 1 Mar 1996 (SI 1996/218) |
| | (5) | See Sch 6 below |
| 18 | | 8 Nov 1995 (RA) |
| Schs 1–4 | | 1 Mar 1996 (SI 1996/218) |
| Sch 5 | | 8 Nov 1995 (RA) |
| Sch 6 | | 8 Nov 1995 (repeal of Gas Act 1986, s 62(7)) (RA) |
| | | 1 Mar 1996 (otherwise) (SI 1996/218) |

## Geneva Conventions (Amendment) Act 1995 (c 27)

*RA:* 19 Jul 1995

*Commencement provisions:* s 7(2); Geneva Conventions (Amendment) Act 1995 (Commencement) Order 1998, SI 1998/1505

Whole Act in force 20 Jul 1998 (SI 1998/1505)

## Goods Vehicles (Licensing of Operators) Act 1995 (c 23)

*RA:* 19 Jul 1995

*Commencement provisions:* ss 50(2), 61; Goods Vehicles (Licensing of Operators) Act 1995 (Commencement and Transitional Provisions) Order 1995, SI 1995/2181

| | |
|---|---|
| 1–49 | 1 Jan 1996 (subject to transitional provisions) (SI 1995/2181) |
| 50 | *Not yet in force* |
| 51–62 | 1 Jan 1996 (SI 1995/2181) |
| Schs 1–4 | 1 Jan 1996 (SI 1995/2181) |
| Sch 5 | *Not yet in force* |
| Schs 6–8 | 1 Jan 1996 (SI 1995/2181) |

## Health Authorities Act 1995 (c 17)

*RA:* 28 Jun 1995

*Commencement provisions:* ss 1(2), 2(3), 4(2), 5(2), 8(1)

| | | |
|---|---|---|
| 1 | (1) | 28 Jun 1995 (regulations etc)[1] (s 8(1)) |
| | | 1 Apr 1996 (otherwise) (s 1(2)) |
| | (2) | 28 Jun 1995 (RA) |
| 2 | (1) | See Sch 1 below |
| | (2), (3) | 28 Jun 1995 (RA) |
| 3 | | 28 Jun 1995 (RA) |
| 4 | (1) | See Sch 2 below |
| | (2) | 28 Jun 1995 (RA) |
| 5 | (1) | See Sch 3 below |
| | (2) | 28 Jun 1995 (RA) |
| 6–10 | | 28 Jun 1995 (RA) |
| Sch 1 | | 28 Jun 1995 (regulations etc)[1] (s 8(1)) |
| | | 1 Apr 1996 (otherwise) (s 2(3)) |
| Sch 2 | | 28 Jun 1995 (regulations etc)[1] (s 8(1)) |
| | | 1 Apr 1996 (otherwise) (s 4(2)) |
| Sch 3 | | 28 Jun 1995 (repeal in National Health Service Act 1977, s 18(3)) (RA) |
| | | 1 Apr 1996 (otherwise) (s 5(2)) |

[1] "regulations etc" means "so far as is necessary for enabling the making of any regulations, orders, directions, schemes or appointments" (s 8(1))

## Home Energy Conservation Act 1995 (c 10)

*RA:* 28 Jun 1995

*Commencement provisions:* s 9(2), (3); Home Energy Conservation Act 1995 (Commencement) Order (Northern Ireland) 1995, SR 1995/455; Home Energy Conservation Act 1995 (Commencement No 2) (England) Order 1995, SI 1995/3340; Home Energy Conservation Act 1995 (Commencement No 3) (Scotland) Order 1996, SI 1996/2797; Home Energy Conservation Act 1995 (Commencement No 4) (Wales) Order 1996, SI 1996/3181

| | | |
|---|---|---|
| 1, 2 | | 1 Apr 1996 (E) (NI) (SI 1995/3340; SR 1995/455) |
| | | 1 Dec 1996 (S) (SI 1996/2797) |
| | | 1 Apr 1997 (W) (SI 1996/3181) |
| 3 | (1) | 1 Jan 1996 (NI) (SR 1995/455) |
| | | 15 Jan 1996 (E) (SI 1995/3340) |
| | | 1 Dec 1996 (S) (SI 1996/2797) |
| | | 10 Jan 1997 (W) (SI 1996/3181) |
| | (2)–(4) | 1 Apr 1996 (E) (NI) (SI 1995/3340; SR 1995/455) |
| | | 1 Dec 1996 (S) (SI 1996/2797) |
| | | 1 Apr 1997 (W) (SI 1996/3181) |
| 4 | (1), (2) | 1 Jan 1996 (NI) (SR 1995/455) |
| | | 15 Jan 1996 (E) (SI 1995/3340) |
| | | 1 Dec 1996 (S) (SI 1996/2797) |
| | | 10 Jan 1997 (W) (SI 1996/3181) |
| | (3) | 1 Apr 1996 (E) (NI) (SI 1995/3340; SR 1995/455) |
| | | 1 Dec 1996 (S) (SI 1996/2797) |
| | | 1 Apr 1997 (W) (SI 1996/3181) |
| 5–9 | | 1 Apr 1996 (E) (NI) (SI 1995/3340; SR 1995/455) |
| | | 1 Dec 1996 (S) (SI 1996/2797) |
| | | 1 Apr 1997 (W) (SI 1996/3181) |

## Insurance Companies (Reserves) Act 1995 (c 29)

*RA:* 19 Jul 1995

*Commencement provisions:* s 4(2); Insurance Companies (Reserves) Act 1995 (Commencement) Order 1996, SI 1996/945

| | | |
|---|---|---|
| 1 | | 30 Apr 1996 (SI 1996/945) |
| 2 | | 19 Jul 1995 (RA) |
| 3 | | 30 Apr 1996 (SI 1996/945) |
| 4 | | 19 Jul 1995 (RA) |

## Jobseekers Act 1995 (c 18)

*RA:* 28 Jun 1995

*Commencement provisions:* s 41(2), (3); Jobseekers Act 1995 (Commencement No 1) Order 1995, SI 1995/3228; Jobseekers Act 1995 (Commencement No 2) Order 1996, SI 1996/1126; Jobseekers Act 1995 (Commencement No 3) Order 1996, SI 1996/1509; Jobseekers Act 1995 (Commencement No 4) Order 1996, SI 1996/2208

| | | |
|---|---|---|
| 1 | | 7 Oct 1996 (SI 1996/2208) |
| 2 | (1)(a), (b) | 7 Oct 1996 (SI 1996/2208) |
| | (1)(c) | 12 Dec 1995 (for purpose of authorising regulations to be made) (SI 1995/3228) |
| | | 7 Oct 1996 (otherwise) (SI 1996/2208) |
| | (1)(d) | 7 Oct 1996 (SI 1996/2208) |
| | (2), (3) | 7 Oct 1996 (SI 1996/2208) |
| | (4)(a) | 7 Oct 1996 (SI 1996/2208) |
| | (4)(b) | 12 Dec 1995 (for purpose of authorising regulations to be made) (SI 1995/3228) |
| | | 7 Oct 1996 (otherwise) (SI 1996/2208) |
| | (4)(c) | 7 Oct 1996 (SI 1996/2208) |
| 3 | (1)(a)–(e) | 7 Oct 1996 (SI 1996/2208) |
| | (1)(f)(i), (ii) | 7 Oct 1996 (SI 1996/2208) |
| | (1)(f)(iii) | 12 Dec 1995 (for purpose of authorising regulations to be made) (SI 1995/3228) |
| | | 7 Oct 1996 (otherwise) (SI 1996/2208) |
| | (2)–(4) | 12 Dec 1995 (for purpose of authorising regulations to be made) (SI 1995/3228) |
| | | 7 Oct 1996 (otherwise) (SI 1996/2208) |
| 4 | (1)(a) | 7 Oct 1996 (SI 1996/2208) |
| | (1)(b) | 12 Dec 1995 (for purpose of authorising regulations to be made) (SI 1995/3228) |
| | | 7 Oct 1996 (otherwise) (SI 1996/2208) |
| | (2) | 12 Dec 1995 (for purpose of authorising regulations to be made) (SI 1995/3228) |
| | | 7 Oct 1996 (otherwise) (SI 1996/2208) |
| | (3) | 7 Oct 1996 (SI 1996/2208) |
| | (4), (5) | 12 Dec 1995 (for purpose of authorising regulations to be made) (SI 1995/3228) |
| | | 7 Oct 1996 (otherwise) (SI 1996/2208) |
| | (6)–(11) | 7 Oct 1996 (SI 1996/2208) |
| | (12) | 12 Dec 1995 (for purpose of authorising regulations to be made) (SI 1995/3228) |
| | | 7 Oct 1996 (otherwise) (SI 1996/2208) |
| 5 | (1), (2) | 7 Oct 1996 (SI 1996/2208) |
| | (3) | 12 Dec 1995 (for purpose of authorising regulations to be made) (SI 1995/3228) |
| | | 7 Oct 1996 (otherwise) (SI 1996/2208) |
| 6 | (1) | 7 Oct 1996 (SI 1996/2208) |

**Jobseekers Act 1995 (c 18)**—*contd*

| | | |
|---|---|---|
| | (2)–(5) | 12 Dec 1995 (for purpose of authorising regulations to be made) (SI 1995/3228) |
| | | 7 Oct 1996 (otherwise) (SI 1996/2208) |
| | (6) | 7 Oct 1996 (SI 1996/2208) |
| | (7), (8) | 12 Dec 1995 (for purpose of authorising regulations to be made) (SI 1995/3228) |
| | | 7 Oct 1996 (otherwise) (SI 1996/2208) |
| | (9) | 7 Oct 1996 (SI 1996/2208) |
| 7 | (1) | 7 Oct 1996 (SI 1996/2208) |
| | (2)–(6) | 12 Dec 1995 (for purpose of authorising regulations to be made) (SI 1995/3228) |
| | | 7 Oct 1996 (otherwise) (SI 1996/2208) |
| | (7) | 7 Oct 1996 (SI 1996/2208) |
| | (8) | 12 Dec 1995 (for purpose of authorising regulations to be made) (SI 1995/3228) |
| | | 7 Oct 1996 (otherwise) (SI 1996/2208) |
| 8 | | 12 Dec 1995 (for purpose of authorising regulations to be made) (SI 1995/3228) |
| | | 7 Oct 1996 (otherwise) (SI 1996/2208) |
| 9 | (1) | 12 Dec 1995 (for purpose of authorising regulations to be made) (SI 1995/3228) |
| | | 7 Oct 1996 (otherwise) (SI 1996/2208) |
| | (2)–(7) | 7 Oct 1996 (SI 1996/2208) |
| | (8) | 12 Dec 1995 (for purpose of authorising regulations to be made) (SI 1995/3228) |
| | | 7 Oct 1996 (otherwise) (SI 1996/2208) |
| | (9) | 7 Oct 1996 (SI 1996/2208) |
| | (10)–(12) | 12 Dec 1995 (for purpose of authorising regulations to be made) (SI 1995/3228) |
| | | 7 Oct 1996 (otherwise) (SI 1996/2208) |
| | (13) | 12 Dec 1995 (SI 1995/3228) |
| 10 | (1) | 12 Dec 1995 (for purpose of authorising regulations to be made) (SI 1995/3228) |
| | | 7 Oct 1996 (otherwise) (SI 1996/2208) |
| | (2)–(5) | 7 Oct 1996 (SI 1996/2208) |
| | (6)(a), (b) | 7 Oct 1996 (SI 1996/2208) |
| | (6)(c) | 12 Dec 1995 (for purpose of authorising regulations to be made) (SI 1995/3228) |
| | | 7 Oct 1996 (otherwise) (SI 1996/2208) |
| | (6)(d) | 7 Oct 1996 (SI 1996/2208) |
| | (7) | 12 Dec 1995 (for purpose of authorising regulations to be made) (SI 1995/3228) |
| | | 7 Oct 1996 (otherwise) (SI 1996/2208) |
| | (8) | 7 Oct 1996 (SI 1996/2208) |
| 11 | (1) | 7 Oct 1996 (SI 1996/2208) |
| | (2) | 12 Dec 1995 (for purpose of authorising regulations to be made) (SI 1995/3228) |
| | | 7 Oct 1996 (otherwise) (SI 1996/2208) |
| | (3), (4) | 7 Oct 1996 (SI 1996/2208) |
| | (5) | 12 Dec 1995 (for purpose of authorising regulations to be made) (SI 1995/3228) |
| | | 7 Oct 1996 (otherwise) (SI 1996/2208) |
| | (6) | 7 Oct 1996 (SI 1996/2208) |
| | (7), (8) | 12 Dec 1995 (for purpose of authorising regulations to be made) (SI 1995/3228) |
| | | 7 Oct 1996 (otherwise) (SI 1996/2208) |
| | (9) | 7 Oct 1996 (SI 1996/2208) |
| 12, 13 | | 12 Dec 1995 (for purpose of authorising regulations to be made) (SI 1995/3228) |
| | | 7 Oct 1996 (otherwise) (SI 1996/2208) |

**Jobseekers Act 1995 (c 18)**—*contd*

| | | |
|---|---|---|
| 14 | | 7 Oct 1996 (SI 1996/2208) |
| 15 | (1) | 12 Dec 1995 (for purpose of authorising regulations to be made) (SI 1995/3228) |
| | | 7 Oct 1996 (otherwise) (SI 1996/2208) |
| | (2)(a)–(c) | 7 Oct 1996 (SI 1996/2208) |
| | (2)(d) | 12 Dec 1995 (for purpose of authorising regulations to be made) (SI 1995/3228) |
| | | 7 Oct 1996 (otherwise) (SI 1996/2208) |
| | (3), (4) | 7 Oct 1996 (SI 1996/2208) |
| | (5), (6) | 12 Dec 1995 (for purpose of authorising regulations to be made) (SI 1995/3228) |
| | | 7 Oct 1996 (otherwise) (SI 1996/2208) |
| | (7)–(10) | 7 Oct 1996 (SI 1996/2208) |
| 16 | | 7 Oct 1996 (SI 1996/2208) |
| 17 | (1) | 12 Dec 1995 (for purpose of authorising regulations to be made) (SI 1995/3228) |
| | | 7 Oct 1996 (otherwise) (SI 1996/2208) |
| | (2)–(5) | 7 Oct 1996 (SI 1996/2208) |
| 18 | | 7 Oct 1996 (SI 1996/2208) |
| 19 | (1) | 7 Oct 1996 (SI 1996/2208) |
| | (2) | 12 Dec 1995 (for purpose of authorising regulations to be made) (SI 1995/3228) |
| | | 7 Oct 1996 (otherwise) (SI 1996/2208) |
| | (3) | 7 Oct 1996 (SI 1996/2208) |
| | (4) | 12 Dec 1995 (for purpose of authorising regulations to be made) (SI 1995/3228) |
| | | 7 Oct 1996 (otherwise) (SI 1996/2208) |
| | (5), (6) | 7 Oct 1996 (SI 1996/2208) |
| | (7), (8) | 12 Dec 1995 (for purpose of authorising regulations to be made) (SI 1995/3228) |
| | | 7 Oct 1996 (otherwise) (SI 1996/2208) |
| | (9) | 7 Oct 1996 (SI 1996/2208) |
| | (10)(a) | 12 Dec 1995 (SI 1995/3228) |
| | (10)(b) | 7 Oct 1996 (SI 1996/2208) |
| | (10)(c) | 12 Dec 1995 (for purpose of authorising regulations to be made) (SI 1995/3228) |
| | | 7 Oct 1996 (otherwise) (SI 1996/2208) |
| 20 | (1), (2) | 7 Oct 1996 (SI 1996/2208) |
| | (3)–(8) | 12 Dec 1995 (for purpose of authorising regulations to be made) (SI 1995/3228) |
| | | 7 Oct 1996 (otherwise) (SI 1996/2208) |
| 21, 22 | | 12 Dec 1995 (for purpose of authorising regulations to be made) (SI 1995/3228) |
| | | 7 Oct 1996 (SI 1996/2208) |
| 23 | (1) | 12 Dec 1995 (for purpose of authorising regulations to be made) (SI 1995/3228) |
| | | 7 Oct 1996 (otherwise) (SI 1996/2208) |
| | (2) | 7 Oct 1996 (SI 1996/2208) |
| | (3), (4) | 12 Dec 1995 (for purpose of authorising regulations to be made) (SI 1995/3228) |
| | | 7 Oct 1996 (otherwise) (SI 1996/2208) |
| | (5) | 7 Oct 1996 (SI 1996/2208) |
| 24, 25 | | 7 Oct 1996 (SI 1996/2208) |
| 26 | | 12 Dec 1995 (for purpose of authorising regulations to be made) (SI 1995/3228) |
| | | 7 Oct 1996 (otherwise) (SI 1996/2208) |
| 27 | | 12 Dec 1995 (for purpose of authorising regulations to be made) (SI 1995/3228) |
| | | 6 Apr 1996 (otherwise) (SI 1995/3228) |

**Jobseekers Act 1995 (c 18)**—*contd*

| | | |
|---|---|---|
| 28 | | 12 Dec 1995 (for purpose of authorising regulations to be made) (SI 1995/3228) |
| | | 1 Apr 1996 (otherwise) (SI 1995/3228) |
| 29 | | 1 Jan 1996 (SI 1995/3228) |
| 30 | | 1 Apr 1996 (SI 1995/3228) |
| 31 | | 12 Dec 1995 (for purpose of authorising regulations to be made) (SI 1995/3228) |
| | | 7 Oct 1996 (otherwise) (SI 1996/2208) |
| 32 | | 7 Oct 1996 (SI 1996/2208) |
| 33 | | 6 Apr 1996 (SI 1995/3228) |
| 34 | (1), (2) | 6 Apr 1996 (SI 1995/3228) |
| | (3) | 12 Dec 1995 (for purpose of authorising regulations to be made) (SI 1995/3228) |
| | | 6 Apr 1996 (otherwise) (SI 1995/3228) |
| | (4)–(6) | 6 Apr 1996 (SI 1995/3228) |
| | (7) | 12 Dec 1995 (for purpose of authorising regulations to be made) (SI 1995/3228) |
| | | 6 Apr 1996 (otherwise) (SI 1995/3228) |
| 35–37 | | 12 Dec 1995 (SI 1995/3228) |
| 38 | (1)(a) | 7 Oct 1996 (SI 1996/2208) |
| | (1)(b) | 6 Apr 1996 (SI 1995/3228) |
| | (2)–(4) | 7 Oct 1996 (SI 1996/2208) |
| | (5) | 6 Apr 1996 (SI 1995/3228) |
| | (6)–(8) | 7 Oct 1996 (SI 1996/2208) |
| 39 | | 28 Jun 1995 (s 41(2)) |
| 40 | | 12 Dec 1995 (for purpose of authorising regulations to be made) (SI 1995/3228) |
| | | 7 Oct 1996 (otherwise) (SI 1996/2208) |
| 41 | (1)–(3) | 28 Jun 1995 (s 41(2)) |
| | (4) | See Sch 2 below |
| | (5) | See Sch 3 below |
| | (6) | 28 Jun 1995 (s 41(2)) |
| Sch 1 | | 12 Dec 1995 (for purpose of authorising regulations to be made) (SI 1995/3228) |
| | | 7 Oct 1996 (otherwise) (SI 1996/2208) |
| Sch 2 | para 1 | 7 Oct 1996 (SI 1996/2208) |
| | para 2 | 2 Sep 1996 (SI 1996/2208) |
| | paras 3–9 | 7 Oct 1996 (SI 1996/2208) |
| | para 10 | 11 Jun 1996 (SI 1996/1509) |
| | para 11 | 7 Oct 1996 (SI 1996/2208) |
| | para 12 | 2 Sep 1996 (SI 1996/2208) |
| | para 13 | 7 Oct 1996 (SI 1996/2208) |
| | para 14 | 2 Sep 1996 (SI 1996/2208) |
| | paras 15–17 | 7 Oct 1996 (SI 1996/2208) |
| | para 18 | 11 Jun 1996 (SI 1996/1509) |
| | paras 19, 20 | 7 Oct 1996 (SI 1996/2208) |
| | para 21 | 11 Jun 1996 (SI 1996/1509) |
| | paras 22–29 | 7 Oct 1996 (SI 1996/2208) |
| | para 30(1)–(4) | 7 Oct 1996 (SI 1996/2208) |
| | para 30(5) | 12 Dec 1995 (for purpose of authorising regulations to be made) (SI 1995/3228) |
| | | 7 Oct 1996 (otherwise) (SI 1996/2208) |
| | paras 31–37 | 7 Oct 1996 (SI 1996/2208) |
| | paras 38–40 | 22 Apr 1996 (SI 1996/1126) |
| | para 41 | 6 Apr 1996 (SI 1995/3228) |
| | para 42 | 11 Jun 1996 (SI 1996/1509) |
| | para 43 | 7 Oct 1996 (SI 1996/2208) |
| | paras 44, 45 | 22 Apr 1996 (SI 1996/1126) |
| | para 46 | 11 Jun 1996 (SI 1996/1509) |

**Jobseekers Act 1995 (c 18)**—*contd*

| | | |
|---|---|---|
| | para 47 | 22 Apr 1996 (SI 1996/1126) |
| | para 48 | 7 Oct 1996 (SI 1996/2208) |
| | paras 49–51 | 11 Jun 1996 (SI 1996/1509) |
| | para 52 | 22 Apr 1996 (SI 1996/1126) |
| | paras 53–64 | 11 Jun 1996 (SI 1996/1509) |
| | para 65 | 7 Oct 1996 (SI 1996/2208) |
| | para 66 | 11 Jun 1996 (SI 1996/1509) |
| | paras 67–70 | 22 Apr 1996 (SI 1996/1126) |
| | paras 71, 72 | 11 Jun 1996 (SI 1996/1509) |
| | para 73 | 22 Apr 1996 (SI 1996/1126) |
| | para 74 | 11 Jun 1996 (SI 1996/1509) |
| | paras 75, 76 | 22 Apr 1996 (SI 1996/1126) |
| Sch 3 | | 1 Apr 1996 (repeals of Supplementary Benefits Act 1976, s 30, Sch 5) |
| | | 7 Oct 1996 (otherwise) (SI 1996/2208) |

**Land Registers (Scotland) Act 1995 (c 14)**

*RA:* 28 Jun 1995

*Commencement provisions:* s 2(2); Land Registers (Scotland) Act 1995 (Commencement) Order 1996, SI 1996/94

Whole Act in force 1 Apr 1996 (SI 1996/94)

**Landlord and Tenant (Covenants) Act 1995 (c 30)**

*RA:* 19 Jul 1995

*Commencement provisions:* s 31; Landlord and Tenant (Covenants) Act 1995 (Commencement) Order 1995, SI 1995/2963

Whole Act in force 1 Jan 1996 (SI 1995/2963)

**Law Reform (Succession) Act 1995 (c 41)**

*RA:* 8 Nov 1995

Whole Act in force 8 Nov 1995 (RA)

**Licensing (Sunday Hours) Act 1995 (c 33)**

*RA:* 19 Jul 1995

*Commencement provisions:* s 5; Licensing (Sunday Hours) Act 1995 (Commencement) Order 1995, SI 1995/1930

Whole Act in force 6 Aug 1995 (SI 1995/1930)

**Medical (Professional Performance) Act 1995 (c 51)**

*RA:* 8 Nov 1995

*Commencement provisions:* s 6; Medical (Professional Performance) Act 1995 (Commencement No 1) Order 1996, SI 1996/271; Medical (Professional Performance) Act 1995 (Commencement No 2) Order 1996, SI 1996/1631; Medical (Professional Performance) Act 1995 (Commencement No 3) Order 1997, SI 1997/1315; Medical (Professional Performance) Act 1995 (Commencement No 4) Order 2000, SI 2000/1344

**Medical (Professional Performance) Act 1995 (c 51)**—*contd*

| | | |
|---|---|---|
| 1 | | 1 Jul 1997 (SI 1997/1315) |
| 2 | | 18 May 2000 (SI 2000/1344) |
| 3 | | 1 May 1996 (SI 1996/271) |
| 4 | | See Schedule below |
| 5, 6 | | 1 May 1996 (SI 1996/271) |
| 7 | (1) | 1 May 1996 (SI 1996/271) |
| | (2) | 1 May 1996 (so far as relates to provisions brought into force by SI 1996/271) (SI 1996/271) |
| | | 1 Sep 1996 (so far as relates to provisions brought into force by SI 1996/1631) (SI 1996/1631) |
| | | 1 Jan 1997 (so far as relates to provisions brought into force by SI 1996/1631) (SI 1996/1631) |
| | | 1 Jul 1997 (so far as relates to provisions brought into force by SI 1997/1315) (SI 1997/1315) |
| | | 18 May 2000 (otherwise) (SI 2000/1344) |
| Schedule | para 1 | See paras 2–27 below |
| | para 2 | 1 Jan 1997 (SI 1996/1631) |
| | para 3 | 18 May 2000 (SI 2000/1344) |
| | paras 4–6 | 1 May 1996 (SI 1996/271) |
| | paras 7–9 | 1 Jul 1997 (SI 1997/1315) |
| | para 10(a), (b) | 1 Jul 1997 (SI 1997/1315) |
| | para 10(c) | 1 May 1996 (SI 1996/271) |
| | para 11 | 1 Jul 1997 (SI 1997/1315) |
| | para 12 | 1 Sep 1996 (for the purpose of enabling the General Medical Council in accordance with rules to determine the membership of its statutory committees as from 1 Jan 1997) (SI 1996/1631) |
| | | 1 Jan 1997 (otherwise) (SI 1996/1631) |
| | para 13 | 1 Jan 1997 (SI 1996/1631) |
| | para 14 | 1 Sep 1996 (SI 1996/1631) |
| | paras 15–21 | 1 Jul 1997 (SI 1997/1315) |
| | para 22(a) | 1 Jul 1997 (SI 1997/1315) |
| | para 22(b) | 1 May 1996 (SI 1996/271) |
| | paras 23–27 | 1 Jul 1997 (SI 1997/1315) |
| | para 28(a) | 1 May 1996 (SI 1996/271) |
| | para 28(b) | 1 Jul 1997 (SI 1997/1315) |
| | para 29(a) | 1 May 1996 (SI 1996/271) |
| | para 29(b) | 1 Jul 1997 (SI 1997/1315) |
| | para 30(a) | 1 May 1996 (SI 1996/271) |
| | para 30(b) | 1 Jul 1997 (SI 1997/1315) |

---

**Mental Health (Patients in the Community) Act 1995 (c 52)**

*RA*: 8 Nov 1995

*Commencement provisions:* s 7(2)

Whole Act in force 1 Apr 1996 (s 7(2))

---

**Merchant Shipping Act 1995 (c 21)**

*RA*: 19 Jul 1995

*Commencement provisions:* s 316(2), Sch 14, para 5; Merchant Shipping Act 1995 (Appointed Day No 2) Order 1997, SI 1997/3107[1]

| | | |
|---|---|---|
| 1–59 | | 1 Jan 1996 (s 316(2)) |
| 60 | | *Not yet in force* |
| 61–79 | | 1 Jan 1996 (s 316(2)) |
| 80 | (1) | 1 Jan 1996 (s 316(2)) |
| | (2) | *Not yet in force* |

**Merchant Shipping Act 1995 (c 21)**—*contd*

|  |  |  |
|---|---|---|
|  | (3) | 1 Jan 1996 (s 316(2)) |
|  | (4) | *Not yet in force* |
| 81–110 |  | 1 Jan 1996 (s 316(2)) |
| 111 |  | *Not yet in force* |
| 112–114 |  | 1 Jan 1996 (s 316(2)) |
| 115 |  | *Not yet in force* |
| 116 |  | 1 Feb 1998 (SI 1997/3107) |
| 117 |  | 1 Jan 1996 (s 316(2)) |
| 118 |  | *Not yet in force* |
| 119 | (1) | 1 Jan 1996 (s 316(2)) |
|  | (2), (3) | *Not yet in force* |
| 120–126 |  | 1 Jan 1996 (s 316(2)) |
| 127 |  | *Not yet in force* |
| 128–313 |  | 1 Jan 1996 (s 316(2)) |
| 314 | (1) | See Sch 12 below |
|  | (2)–(4) | 1 Jan 1996 (s 316(2)) |
| 315, 316 |  | 1 Jan 1996 (s 316(2)) |
| Schs 1–11 |  | 1 Jan 1996 (s 316(2)) |
| Sch 12 |  | 1 Jan 1996 (s 316(2)), except repeals in— |
|  |  | Aliens Restriction (Amendment) Act 1919; |
|  |  | Local Government etc (Scotland) Act 1994 |
|  |  | *Not yet in force* (exceptions noted above) |
| Sch 13 |  | 1 Jan 1996 (s 316(2)) |
| Sch 14 |  | 1 Jan 1996 (s 316(2)) (note paras 5, 6 and 9) |

---

[1]    Only appointed day orders that are relevant to the commencement of this Act will be noted in this work

---

## National Health Service (Amendment) Act 1995 (c 31)

*RA:* 19 Jul 1995

*Commencement provisions:* s 14(3), (4); National Health Service (Amendment) Act 1995 (Commencement No 1 and Saving) Order 1995, SI 1995/3090; National Health Service (Amendment) Act 1995 (Commencement No 2 and Saving) (Scotland) Order 1995, SI 1995/3214; National Health Service (Amendment) Act 1995 (Commencement No 3) Order 1996, SI 1996/552

|  |  |  |
|---|---|---|
| 1, 2 |  | 21 Dec 1995 (subject to transitional provisions) (for the purposes of amending National Health Service Act 1977 in relation to general medical services and general dental services only) (SI 1995/3090) |
|  |  | 1 Apr 1996 (otherwise) (SI 1996/552) |
| 3–6 |  | 21 Dec 1995 (subject to transitional provisions) (SI 1995/3090) |
| 7, 8 |  | 1 Jan 1996 (subject to transitional provisions) (for the purposes of amending National Health Service (Scotland) Act 1978 in relation to general medical services and general dental services only) (SI 1995/3214) |
|  |  | 1 Apr 1996 (otherwise) (SI 1996/552) |
| 9–12 |  | 1 Jan 1996 (subject to transitional provisions) (SI 1995/3214) |
| 13 |  | 19 Jul 1995 (RA) |
| 14 | (1) | 19 Jul 1995 (RA) |
|  | (2) | See Schedule below |
|  | (3)–(6) | 19 Jul 1995 (RA) |
| Schedule |  | 21 Dec 1995 (subject to transitional provisions) (SI 1995/3090), repeals in— |
|  |  | National Health Service Act 1977; |
|  |  | Health Authorities Act 1995 |
|  |  | 1 Jan 1996 (subject to transitional provisions) (repeals in National Health Service (Scotland) Act 1978) (SI 1995/3214) |

## Northern Ireland (Remission of Sentences) Act 1995 (c 47)

*RA:* 8 Nov 1995

*Commencement provisions:* s 2; Northern Ireland (Remission of Sentences) Act 1995 (Commencement) Order 1995, SI 1995/2945

Whole Act in force 17 Nov 1995 (SI 1995/2945)

---

## Olympic Symbol etc (Protection) Act 1995 (c 32)

*RA:* 19 Jul 1995

*Commencement provisions:* s 19(2); Olympic Symbol etc (Protection) Act 1995 (Commencement) Order 1995, SI 1995/2472

Whole Act in force 20 Sep 1995 (SI 1995/2472)

---

## Pensions Act 1995 (c 26)

*RA:* 19 Jul 1995

*Commencement provisions:* ss 135, 150(2), 180, Sch 4; Pensions Act 1995 (Commencement No 1) Order 1995, SI 1995/2548; Pensions Act 1995 (Commencement No 2) Order 1995, SI 1995/3104; Pensions Act 1995 (Commencement No 3) Order 1996, SI 1996/778; Pensions Act 1995 (Commencement No 4) Order 1996, SI 1996/1412; Pensions Act 1995 (Commencement No 5) Order 1996, SI 1996/1675; Pensions Act 1995 (Commencement No 6) Order 1996, SI 1996/1843; Pensions Act 1995 (Commencement No 7) Order 1996, SI 1996/1853[1]; Pensions Act 1995 (Commencement No 8) Order 1996, SI 1996/2637; Pensions Act 1995 (Commencement No 9) Order 1997, SI 1997/216; Pensions Act 1995 (Commencement No 10) Order 1997, SI 1997/664

| | | |
|---|---|---|
| 1 | (1)–(4) | 1 Apr 1996 (SI 1996/778) |
| | (5) | See Sch 1 below |
| | (6) | 1 Apr 1996 (SI 1996/778) |
| 2 | | 1 Apr 1996 (SI 1996/778) |
| 3 | (1) | 6 Apr 1997 (SI 1997/664) |
| | (2) | 16 Oct 1996 (for purpose of making regulations) (SI 1996/2637) |
| | | 6 Apr 1997 (otherwise) (SI 1997/664) |
| | (3), (4) | 6 Apr 1997 (SI 1997/664) |
| 4–9 | | 6 Apr 1997 (SI 1997/664) |
| 10 | (1) | 1 Jun 1996 (for purpose of authorising the making of regulations) (SI 1996/1412) |
| | | 6 Apr 1997 (otherwise) (SI 1997/664) |
| | (2), (3) | 6 Apr 1996 (for purpose of authorising the making of regulations) (SI 1996/778) |
| | | 6 Apr 1997 (otherwise) (SI 1997/664) |
| | (4)–(9) | 6 Apr 1997 (SI 1997/664) |
| 11–15 | | 6 Apr 1997 (SI 1997/664) |
| 16–20 | | 6 Apr 1996 (for purpose of authorising the making of regulations) (SI 1996/778) |
| | | 6 Apr 1997 (otherwise) (SI 1997/664) |
| 21 | (1), (2) | 6 Apr 1996 (for purpose of authorising the making of regulations) (SI 1996/778) |
| | | 6 Apr 1997 (otherwise) (SI 1997/664) |
| | (3) | 6 Apr 1996 (for purpose of authorising the making of regulations) (SI 1996/778) |
| | | 6 Oct 1996 (for purpose of any transitional provision in regulations made under ss 16–21) (SI 1996/778) |
| | | 6 Apr 1997 (otherwise) (SI 1997/664) |
| | (4)–(8) | 6 Apr 1996 (for purpose of authorising the making of regulations) (SI 1996/778) |
| | | 6 Apr 1997 (otherwise) (SI 1997/664) |

**Pensions Act 1995 (c 26)**—*contd*

| | | |
|---|---|---|
| 22 | | 6 Apr 1997 (SI 1997/664) |
| 23 | | 1 Jun 1996 (for purpose of authorising the making of regulations) (SI 1996/1412) |
| | | 6 Apr 1997 (otherwise) (SI 1997/664) |
| 24–26 | | 6 Apr 1997 (SI 1997/664) |
| 27 | | 6 Apr 1996 (for purpose of authorising the making of regulations) (SI 1996/778) |
| | | 6 Apr 1997 (otherwise) (SI 1997/664) |
| 28–31 | | 6 Apr 1997 (SI 1997/664) |
| 32, 33 | | 6 Apr 1996 (for purpose of authorising the making of regulations) (SI 1996/778) |
| | | 6 Apr 1997 (otherwise) (SI 1997/664) |
| 34 | | 6 Apr 1997 (SI 1997/664) |
| 35 | | 6 Apr 1996 (for purpose of authorising the making of regulations) (SI 1996/778) |
| | | 6 Apr 1997 (otherwise) (SI 1997/664) |
| 36 | | 6 Apr 1997 (SI 1997/664) |
| 37 | | 6 Apr 1996 (for purpose of authorising the making of regulations) (SI 1996/778) |
| | | 6 Apr 1997 (otherwise) (SI 1997/664) |
| 38 | | 6 Apr 1996 (for purpose of authorising the making of regulations) (SI 1996/778) |
| | | 6 Apr 1997 (otherwise) (SI 1997/664) |
| 39 | | 1 Jan 1996 (SI 1995/3104) |
| 40, 41 | | 6 Apr 1996 (for purpose of authorising the making of regulations) (SI 1996/778) |
| | | 6 Apr 1997 (otherwise) (SI 1997/664) |
| 42–46 | | *Never in force (repealed)* |
| 47 | | 6 Apr 1996 (for purpose of authorising the making of regulations) (SI 1996/778) |
| | | 6 Apr 1997 (otherwise) (SI 1997/664) |
| 48 | (1) | 6 Apr 1997 (SI 1997/664) |
| | (2) | *Never in force (repealed)* |
| | (3)–(6) | 6 Apr 1997 (SI 1997/664 |
| | (7)–(13) | *Never in force (repealed)* |
| 49–51 | | 6 Apr 1996 (for purpose of authorising the making of regulations) (SI 1996/778) |
| | | 6 Apr 1997 (otherwise) (SI 1997/664) |
| 52–54 | | 6 Apr 1997 (SI 1997/664) |
| 55 | | 4 Feb 1997 (SI 1997/216) |
| 56–61 | | 6 Apr 1996 (for purpose of authorising the making of regulations) (SI 1996/778) |
| | | 6 Apr 1997 (otherwise) (SI 1997/664) |
| 62–66 | | 4 Dec 1995 (for purpose of authorising the making of regulations under ss 63(5), 64(2), (3), 66(4)) (SI 1995/3104) |
| | | 1 Jan 1996 (otherwise) (SI 1995/3104) |
| 67 | | 6 Apr 1996 (for purpose of authorising the making of regulations) (SI 1996/778) |
| | | 6 Apr 1997 (otherwise) (SI 1997/664) |
| 68 | | 6 Apr 1996 (for purpose of authorising the making of regulations) (SI 1996/778) |
| | | 6 Oct 1996 (for purpose of any transitional provision in regulations made under ss 16–21) (SI 1996/778) |
| | | 6 Apr 1997 (otherwise) (SI 1997/664) |
| 69 | | 6 Apr 1996 (for purpose of authorising the making of regulations) (SI 1996/778) |
| | | 6 Apr 1997 (otherwise) (SI 1997/664) |
| 70–72 | | 6 Apr 1997 (SI 1997/664) |
| 73 | | 6 Apr 1996 (for purpose of authorising the making of regulations) (SI 1996/778) |

**Pensions Act 1995 (c 26)**—*contd*

|  |  |  |
|---|---|---|
|  |  | 6 Apr 1997 (otherwise) (SI 1997/664) |
| 74 | (1) | 16 Oct 1996 (for purpose of making regulations) (SI 1996/2637) |
|  |  | 6 Apr 1997 (otherwise) (SI 1997/664) |
|  | (2), (3) | 6 Apr 1996 (for purpose of authorising the making of regulations) (SI 1996/778) |
|  |  | 6 Apr 1997 (otherwise) (SI 1997/664) |
|  | (4) | 6 Apr 1997 (SI 1997/664) |
|  | (5)(a) | 16 Oct 1996 (for purpose of making regulations) (SI 1996/2637) |
|  |  | 6 Apr 1997 (otherwise) (SI 1997/664) |
|  | (5)(b) | 6 Apr 1996 (for purpose of authorising the making of regulations) (SI 1996/778) |
|  |  | 6 Apr 1997 (otherwise) (SI 1997/664) |
| 75 |  | 6 Apr 1996 (for purpose of authorising the making of regulations) (SI 1996/778) |
|  |  | 6 Apr 1997 (otherwise) (SI 1997/664) |
| 76, 77 |  | 6 Apr 1996 (for purpose of authorising the making of regulations) (SI 1996/778) |
|  |  | 6 Apr 1997 (otherwise) (SI 1997/664) |
| 78 | (1)–(3) | 1 Aug 1996 (SI 1996/1412) |
|  | (4) | 6 Apr 1997 (SI 1997/664) |
|  | (5) | 1 Aug 1996 (SI 1996/1412) |
|  | (6) | 1 Jun 1996 (for purpose of authorising the making of regulations) (SI 1996/1412) |
|  |  | 1 Aug 1996 (otherwise) (SI 1996/1412) |
|  | (7) | 1 Aug 1996 (SI 1996/1412) |
|  | (8) | See Sch 2 below |
| 79 |  | 6 Apr 1997 (SI 1997/664) |
| 80 | (1)–(3) | 6 Apr 1997 (SI 1997/664) |
|  | (4) | 4 Feb 1997 (for purpose of authorising the making of regulations) (SI 1997/216) |
|  |  | 6 Apr 1997 (otherwise) (SI 1997/216) |
|  | (5) | 6 Apr 1997 (SI 1997/664) |
| 81 | (1)(a), (b) | 6 Apr 1997 (SI 1997/664) |
|  | (1)(c) | 1 Jun 1996 (for purpose of authorising the making of regulations) (SI 1996/1412) |
|  |  | 6 Apr 1997 (otherwise) (SI 1997/664) |
|  | (1)(d), (e) | 6 Apr 1997 (SI 1997/664) |
|  | (2) | 1 Jun 1996 (for purpose of authorising the making of regulations) (SI 1996/1412) |
|  |  | 6 Apr 1997 (otherwise) (SI 1997/664) |
|  | (3)(a)–(e) | 6 Apr 1997 (SI 1997/664) |
|  | (3)(f)(i) | 1 Jun 1996 (for purpose of authorising the making of regulations) (SI 1996/1412) |
|  |  | 6 Apr 1997 (otherwise) (SI 1997/664) |
|  | (3)(f)(ii) | 6 Apr 1997 (SI 1997/664) |
|  | (4)–(6) | 6 Apr 1997 (SI 1997/664) |
|  | (7) | 6 Mar 1997 (for purpose of making regulations relating to the compensation regulations) (SI 1997/664) |
|  |  | 6 Apr 1997 (otherwise) (SI 1997/664) |
|  | (8) | 6 Apr 1997 (SI 1997/664) |
| 82 | (1) | 1 Jun 1996 (for purpose of authorising the making of regulations) (SI 1996/1412) |
|  |  | 6 Apr 1997 (otherwise) (SI 1997/664) |
|  | (2)–(5) | 6 Apr 1997 (SI 1997/664) |
| 83 | (1) | 6 Apr 1997 (SI 1997/664) |
|  | (2) | 1 Jun 1996 (for purpose of authorising the making of regulations) (SI 1996/1412) |
|  |  | 6 Apr 1997 (otherwise) (SI 1997/664) |
|  | (3)(a) | 1 Jun 1996 (for purpose of authorising the making of regulations) (SI 1996/1412) |

**Pensions Act 1995 (c 26)**—*contd*

| | | |
|---|---|---|
| | | 6 Apr 1997 (otherwise) (SI 1997/664) |
| | (3)(b) | 6 Apr 1997 (SI 1997/664) |
| 84 | (1)(a) | 6 Apr 1997 (SI 1997/664) |
| | (1)(b) | 1 Jun 1996 (for purpose of authorising the making of regulations) (SI 1996/1412) |
| | | 6 Apr 1997 (otherwise) (SI 1997/664) |
| | (2), (3) | 1 Jun 1996 (for purpose of authorising the making of regulations) (SI 1996/1412) |
| | | 6 Apr 1997 (otherwise) (SI 1997/664) |
| 85 | (1), (2) | 6 Apr 1997 (SI 1997/664) |
| | (3)(a) | 1 Aug 1996 (SI 1996/1412) |
| | (3)(b) | 6 Apr 1997 (SI 1997/664) |
| 86 | | 1 Jun 1996 (for purpose of authorising the making of regulations) (SI 1996/1412) |
| | | 6 Apr 1997 (otherwise) (SI 1997/664) |
| 87–89 | | 6 Apr 1996 (for purpose of authorising the making of regulations) (SI 1996/778) |
| | | 6 Apr 1997 (otherwise) (SI 1997/664) |
| 90 | | 2 Oct 1995 (SI 1995/2548) |
| 91 | (1), (2) | 6 Apr 1996 (for purpose of authorising the making of regulations) (SI 1996/778) |
| | | 6 Apr 1997 (otherwise) (SI 1997/664) |
| | (3) | 6 Apr 1996 (for purpose of authorising the making of regulations) (SI 1996/778) |
| | | *Never in force* (otherwise) (repealed) |
| | (4)–(7) | 6 Apr 1996 (for purpose of authorising the making of regulations) (SI 1996/778) |
| | | 6 Apr 1997 (otherwise) (SI 1997/664) |
| 92–94 | | 6 Apr 1996 (for purpose of authorising the making of regulations) (SI 1996/778) |
| | | 6 Apr 1997 (otherwise) (SI 1997/664) |
| 95 | | 6 Apr 1996 (for purpose of authorising the making of regulations) (SI 1996/778) |
| | | *Never in force* (otherwise) (repealed) |
| 96 | (1) | 6 Apr 1997 (SI 1997/664) |
| | (2) | 1 Jun 1996 (for purpose of authorising the making of regulations) (SI 1996/1412) |
| | | 6 Apr 1997 (otherwise) (SI 1997/664) |
| | (3), (4) | 6 Apr 1997 (SI 1997/664) |
| | (5) | 1 Jun 1996 (for purpose of authorising the making of regulations) (SI 1996/1412) |
| | | 6 Apr 1997 (otherwise) (SI 1997/664) |
| | (6) | 6 Apr 1997 (SI 1997/664) |
| 97–115 | | 6 Apr 1997 (SI 1997/664) |
| 116 | (1) | 16 Jul 1996 (SI 1996/1853) |
| | (2), (3) | 6 Apr 1997 (SI 1997/664) |
| 117 | | 1 Jan 1996 (so far as relates to s 39) (SI 1995/3104) |
| | | 4 Dec 1995 and 1 Jan 1996 (so far as relates to ss 62–66) (SI 1995/3104) |
| | | 6 Oct 1996 (for purpose of any transitional provision in regulations made under ss 16–21) (SI 1996/778) |
| | | 6 Apr 1997 (otherwise) (SI 1997/664) |
| 118 | | 6 Apr 1996 (so far as relates to authorising the making of regulations relating to certain provisions of Pt I of this Act) (SI 1996/778) |
| | | 16 Oct 1996 (otherwise) (SI 1996/2637) |
| 119 | | 6 Apr 1996 (SI 1996/778) |
| 120 | | 4 Dec 1995 and 1 Jan 1996 (so far as relates to ss 62–66) (SI 1995/3104) |
| | | 6 Apr 1996 (otherwise) (SI 1996/778) |

**Pensions Act 1995 (c 26)**—*contd*

| | | |
|---|---|---|
| 121 | | 1 Jan 1996 (so far as relates to s 39) (SI 1995/3104) |
| | | 4 Dec 1995 and 1 Jan 1996 (so far as relates to ss 62–66) (SI 1995/3104) |
| | | 6 Apr 1996 (otherwise) (SI 1996/778) |
| 122 | | See Sch 3 below |
| 123 | (1), (2) | 6 Apr 1997 (SI 1997/664) |
| | (3) | 6 Apr 1996 (SI 1996/778) |
| 124 | | 1 Jan 1996 (so far as relates to s 39) (SI 1995/3104) |
| | | 4 Dec 1995 and 1 Jan 1996 (so far as relates to ss 62–66) (SI 1995/3104) |
| | | 6 Apr 1996 (otherwise) (SI 1996/778) |
| 125 | (1) | 6 Apr 1996 (so far as relates to authorising the making of regulations relating to certain provisions of Pt I of this Act) (SI 1996/778) |
| | | 6 Apr 1997 (otherwise) (SI 1997/664) |
| | (2)–(4) | 6 Apr 1996 (so far as relates to authorising the making of regulations relating to certain provisions of Pt I of this Act) (SI 1996/778) |
| | | 16 Oct 1996 (otherwise) (SI 1996/2637) |
| 126 | | See Sch 4 below |
| 127–134 | | 19 Jul 1995 (s 180(2)) |
| 135 | | *Not yet in force* |
| 136 | | 6 Apr 1996 (for purpose of authorising the making of regulations) (SI 1996/778) |
| | | 6 Apr 1997 (otherwise) (SI 1996/778) |
| 137 | (1)–(5) | 13 Mar 1996 (for purpose of authorising the making of orders) (SI 1996/778) |
| | | 6 Apr 1996 (for purpose of authorising the making of regulations) (SI 1996/778) |
| | | 6 Apr 1997 (otherwise) (SI 1997/664) |
| | (6), (7) | 6 Apr 1996 (for purpose of authorising the making of regulations) (SI 1996/778) |
| | | 6 Apr 1997 (otherwise) (SI 1997/664) |
| 138 | (1)–(4) | 6 Apr 1997 (SI 1997/664) |
| | (5) | 13 Mar 1996 (for purpose of authorising the making of orders) (SI 1996/778) |
| | | 6 Apr 1997 (otherwise) (SI 1997/664) |
| 139 | | 6 Apr 1996 (for purpose of authorising the making of regulations) (SI 1996/778) |
| | | 6 Apr 1997 (otherwise) (SI 1997/664) |
| 140 | (1) | 6 Apr 1996 (for purpose of authorising the making of regulations) (SI 1996/778) |
| | | 6 Apr 1997 (otherwise) (SI 1997/664) |
| | (2) | 13 Mar 1996 (for purpose of authorising the making of regulations) (SI 1996/778) |
| | | 6 Apr 1996 (otherwise) (SI 1996/778) |
| | (3) | 6 Apr 1997 (subject to savings) (SI 1997/664) |
| 141 | | 6 Apr 1996 (for purpose of authorising the making of regulations) (SI 1996/778) |
| | | 6 Apr 1997 (otherwise) (SI 1997/664) |
| 142–144 | | 13 Mar 1996 (for purpose of authorising the making of regulations) (SI 1996/778) |
| | | 6 Apr 1996 (otherwise) (SI 1996/778) |
| 145 | | *Never in force* (repealed) |
| 146 | | 13 Mar 1996 (for purpose of authorising the making of regulations) (SI 1996/778) |
| | | 6 Apr 1996 (otherwise) (SI 1996/778) |
| 147 | | 6 Apr 1997 (SI 1997/664) |
| 148 | | 6 Apr 1996 (SI 1996/778) |

**Pensions Act 1995 (c 26)**—*contd*

| | | |
|---|---|---|
| 149 | | 1 Jun 1996 (for purpose of authorising the making of regulations) (SI 1996/778) |
| | | 6 Apr 1997 (otherwise) (SI 1997/664) |
| 150 | | 6 Apr 1997 (SI 1997/664) |
| 151 | | See Sch 5 below |
| 152–154 | | 6 Apr 1996 (for purpose of authorising the making of regulations) (SI 1996/778) |
| | | 6 Apr 1997 (otherwise) (SI 1997/664) |
| 155 | | 6 Apr 1996 (for purpose of authorising the making of regulations relating to Pension Schemes Act 1993, s 113) (SI 1996/778) |
| | | 1 Jun 1996 (for purpose of authorising the making of other regulations) (SI 1996/1412) |
| | | 6 Apr 1997 (otherwise) (SI 1997/664) |
| 156 | | 2 Oct 1995 (SI 1995/2548) |
| 157 | (1) | 6 Apr 1997 (SI 1997/664) |
| | (2) | 1 Jun 1996 (for purpose of authorising the making of regulations) (SI 1996/1412) |
| | | 6 Apr 1997 (otherwise) (SI 1997/664) |
| | (3)–(12) | 6 Apr 1997 (SI 1997/664) |
| 158 | | 1 Jun 1996 (for purpose of authorising the making of regulations) (SI 1996/1412) |
| | | 16 Oct 1996 (for purpose of making rules) (SI 1996/2637) |
| | | 6 Apr 1997 (otherwise) (SI 1997/664) |
| 159 | | 6 Apr 1997 (SI 1997/664) |
| 160 | | 1 Jun 1996 (for purpose of authorising the making of regulations) (SI 1996/1412) |
| | | 6 Apr 1997 (otherwise) (SI 1997/664) |
| 161 | | 6 Apr 1997 (subject to savings) (SI 1997/664) |
| 162–164 | | 6 Apr 1997 (SI 1997/664) |
| 165 | | 16 Oct 1996 (for purpose of making regulations) (SI 1996/2637) |
| | | 6 Apr 1997 (otherwise) (SI 1997/664) |
| 166 | | 27 Jun 1996 (in relation to the insertion of Matrimonial Causes Act 1973, s 25D(2)–(4)) (SI 1996/1675) |
| | | 1 Aug 1996 (otherwise, but subject to savings) (SI 1996/1675)[2] |
| 167 | | 15 Jul 1996 (for the purpose of bringing into force the provisions relating to the making of regulations in Family Law (Scotland) Act 1985, ss 10(8)–(10), 12A(8)–(10)) (SI 1996/1843) |
| | | 19 Aug 1996 (otherwise, but subject to savings) (SI 1996/1843) |
| 168 | | 19 Jul 1995 (s 180(2)) |
| 169 | | 2 Oct 1995 (SI 1995/2548) |
| 170, 171 | | 19 Jul 1995 (s 180(2)) |
| 172 | | 2 Oct 1995 (SI 1995/2548) |
| 173 | | See Sch 6 below |
| 174, 175 | | 2 Oct 1995 (so far as they relate to s 172) (SI 1995/2548) |
| | | 4 Dec 1995 and 1 Jan 1996 (so far as relates to ss 62–66) (SI 1995/3104) |
| | | 6 Apr 1996 (otherwise) (SI 1996/778) |
| 176 | | 6 Apr 1996 (SI 1996/778) |
| 177 | | See Sch 7 below |
| 178 | | 6 Apr 1997 (SI 1997/664) |
| 179 | | 19 Jul 1995 (s 180(2)) |
| 180, 181 | | See ss 1–179 above |
| Sch 1 | paras 1–12 | 1 Apr 1996 (SI 1996/778) |
| | para 13 | 1 Jun 1996 (SI 1996/1412) |
| | paras 14–17 | 1 Apr 1996 (SI 1996/778) |
| | para 18 | 6 Apr 1997 (SI 1997/664) |
| | paras 19, 20 | 1 Apr 1996 (SI 1996/778) |
| Sch 2 | paras 1–11 | 1 Aug 1996 (SI 1996/1412) |
| | para 12 | 4 Feb 1997 (for purpose of authorising the making of regulations) (SI 1997/216) |

**Pensions Act 1995 (c 26)**—*contd*

|  |  |  |
|---|---|---|
|  |  | 6 Apr 1997 (otherwise) (SI 1997/216) |
|  | para 13 | 1 Aug 1996 (SI 1996/1412) |
|  | para 14(1)–(4) | 1 Aug 1996 (SI 1996/1412) |
|  | para 14(5) | 6 Apr 1997 (SI 1997/664) |
|  | para 15 | 6 Apr 1997 (SI 1997/664) |
|  | paras 16, 17 | 1 Aug 1996 (SI 1996/1412) |
|  | para 18(1) | 1 Aug 1996 (SI 1996/1412) |
|  | para 18(2) | 6 Apr 1997 (SI 1997/664) |
|  | paras 19, 20 | 1 Aug 1996 (SI 1996/1412) |
| Sch 3 | paras 1–10 | *Never in force* (repealed) |
|  | paras 11–22 | 6 Apr 1997 (SI 1997/664) |
|  | para 23 | 16 Oct 1996 (for purpose of making regulations) (SI 1996/2637) |
|  |  | 1 Apr 1997 (otherwise) (SI 1997/664) |
|  | para 24 | 6 Apr 1997 (SI 1997/664) |
|  | para 25 | 6 Apr 1997 (subject to savings) (SI 1997/664) |
|  | para 26 | 6 Apr 1997 (SI 1997/664) |
|  | para 27 | 6 Apr 1997 (subject to savings) (SI 1997/664) |
|  | para 28 | 6 Apr 1997 (SI 1997/664) |
|  | para 29 | 1 Jan 1996 (SI 1995/3104) |
|  | paras 30, 31 | 6 Apr 1997 (SI 1997/664) |
|  | paras 32–37 | 1 Jan 1996 (SI 1995/3104) |
|  | para 38 | 6 Apr 1997 (SI 1997/664) |
|  | para 39(a) | 6 Apr 1997 (SI 1997/664) |
|  | para 39(b) | 1 Jan 1996 (SI 1995/3104) |
|  | para 39(c), (d) | 6 Apr 1997 (SI 1997/664) |
|  | paras 40, 41 | 6 Apr 1997 (SI 1997/664) |
|  | para 42 | 1 Jan 1996 (SI 1995/3104) |
|  | para 43 | 6 Apr 1997 (SI 1997/664) |
|  | para 44(a)(i) | 1 Jan 1996 (SI 1995/3104) |
|  | para 44(a)(ii) | 16 Oct 1996 (for purpose of making regulations) (SI 1996/2637) |
|  |  | 6 Apr 1997 (otherwise) (SI 1997/664) |
|  | para 44(b) | 6 Apr 1997 (SI 1997/664) |
|  | paras 45, 46 | 6 Apr 1997 (SI 1997/664) |
|  | para 47 | 1 Jan 1996 (SI 1995/3104) |
| Sch 4 |  | 19 Jul 1995 (s 180(2))[3] |
| Sch 5 | paras 1–19 | 6 Apr 1997 (SI 1997/664) |
|  | para 20 | 1 Apr 1997 (SI 1997/664) |
|  | para 21 | 6 Apr 1996 (for purpose of authorising the making of regulations so far as relates to Pension Schemes Act 1993, ss 11(5)(d), 34(2)(a), 50(4), 163(6)) (SI 1996/778) |
|  |  | 6 Apr 1997 (otherwise) (SI 1997/664) |
|  | para 22(a) | 6 Apr 1996 (for purpose of authorising the making of regulations so far as relates to Pension Schemes Act 1993, s 7(1)) (SI 1996/778) |
|  |  | 6 Apr 1997 (otherwise and subject to transitional provisions) (SI 1997/664) |
|  | para 22(b) | 6 Apr 1997 (SI 1997/664) |
|  | paras 23–27 | 6 Apr 1997 (SI 1997/664) |
|  | para 28(a) | 6 Apr 1996 (for purpose of authorising the making of regulations) (SI 1996/778) |
|  |  | 6 Apr 1997 (otherwise) (SI 1997/664) |
|  | para 28(b) | 6 Apr 1997 (SI 1997/664) |
|  | paras 29–32 | 6 Apr 1997 (SI 1997/664) |
|  | para 33(a) | 6 Apr 1997 (SI 1997/664) |
|  | para 33(b) | 6 Apr 1996 (for purpose of authorising the making of regulations) (SI 1996/778) |
|  |  | 6 Apr 1997 (otherwise) (SI 1997/664) |
|  | para 34(a) | 6 Apr 1996 (for purpose of authorising the making of regulations) (SI 1996/778) |

**Pensions Act 1995 (c 26)**—*contd*

|  |  |  |
|---|---|---|
|  |  | 6 Apr 1997 (otherwise) (SI 1997/664) |
|  | para 34(b) | 6 Apr 1997 (SI 1997/664) |
|  | para 35 | 6 Apr 1996 (for purpose of authorising the making of regulations) (SI 1996/778) |
|  |  | 6 Apr 1997 (otherwise) (SI 1997/664) |
|  | para 36 | 1 Jun 1996 (for purpose of authorising the making of regulations) (SI 1996/1412) |
|  |  | 6 Apr 1997 (otherwise) (SI 1997/664) |
|  | para 37 | 6 Apr 1996 (for purpose of authorising the making of regulations) (SI 1996/778) |
|  |  | 6 Apr 1997 (otherwise) (SI 1997/664) |
|  | para 38 | *Not yet in force* |
|  | para 39 | 6 Apr 1996 (for purpose of authorising the making of regulations) (SI 1996/778) |
|  |  | 6 Apr 1997 (otherwise) (SI 1997/664) |
|  | paras 40–44 | 6 Apr 1997 (SI 1997/664) |
|  | para 45(a) | 6 Apr 1997 (SI 1997/664) |
|  | para 45(b) | 6 Apr 1996 (for purpose of authorising the making of regulations) (SI 1996/778) |
|  |  | 6 Apr 1997 (otherwise) (SI 1997/664) |
|  | para 45(c) | 6 Apr 1997 (SI 1997/664) |
|  | para 46 | 6 Apr 1996 (for purpose of authorising the making of regulations) (SI 1996/778) |
|  |  | 6 Apr 1997 (otherwise) (SI 1997/664) |
|  | para 47 | 6 Apr 1997 (SI 1997/664) |
|  | para 48(a), (b) | 6 Apr 1997 (SI 1997/664) |
|  | para 48(c) | 6 Apr 1996 (for purpose of authorising the making of regulations) (SI 1996/778) |
|  |  | 6 Apr 1997 (otherwise) (SI 1997/664) |
|  | para 48(d) | 6 Apr 1997 (SI 1997/664) |
|  | para 49(a) | 6 Apr 1996 (for purpose of authorising the making of regulations) (SI 1996/778) |
|  |  | 6 Apr 1997 (otherwise) (SI 1997/664) |
|  | para 49(b) | 6 Apr 1997 (SI 1997/664) |
|  | paras 50–64 | 6 Apr 1997 (subject to savings) (SI 1997/664) |
|  | para 65 | 6 Apr 1996 (for purpose of authorising the making of regulations) (SI 1996/778) |
|  |  | 6 Apr 1997 (otherwise) (SI 1997/664) |
|  | paras 66–69 | 6 Apr 1997 (SI 1997/664) |
|  | para 70(a), (b) | 6 Apr 1997 (subject to savings) (SI 1997/664) |
|  | para 70(c) | 6 Apr 1996 (for purpose of authorising the making of regulations) (SI 1996/778) |
|  |  | 6 Apr 1997 (otherwise) (SI 1997/664) |
|  | para 71 | 6 Apr 1997 (subject to savings) (SI 1997/664) |
|  | para 72 | 6 Apr 1997 (SI 1997/664) |
|  | para 73 | 1 Apr 1997 (SI 1997/664) |
|  | paras 74–79 | 6 Apr 1997 (SI 1997/664) |
|  | para 80(a)–(e) | 6 Apr 1997 (SI 1997/664) |
|  | para 80(f) | 16 Oct 1996 (for purpose of making regulations) (SI 1996/2637) |
|  |  | 6 Apr 1997 (otherwise) (SI 1997/664) |
|  | paras 81–83 | 6 Apr 1997 (SI 1997/664) |
|  | para 84 | 6 Apr 1996 (for purpose of authorising the making of regulations) (SI 1996/778) |
|  |  | 6 Apr 1997 (otherwise) (SI 1997/664) |
| Sch 6 | para 1 | 2 Oct 1995 (SI 1995/2548) |
|  | paras 2, 3 | 6 Apr 1997 (SI 1997/664) |
|  | paras 4, 5 | 6 Apr 1996 (for purpose of authorising the making of regulations) (SI 1996/778) |
|  |  | 6 Apr 1997 (otherwise) (SI 1997/664) |
|  | para 6(a), (b) | 6 Apr 1997 (SI 1997/664) |

**Pensions Act 1995 (c 26)**—*contd*

| | | |
|---|---|---|
| | para 6(c) | 6 Apr 1996 (for purpose of authorising the making of regulations) (SI 1996/778) |
| | | 6 Apr 1997 (otherwise) (SI 1997/664) |
| | para 6(d) | 6 Apr 1997 (SI 1997/664) |
| | para 6(e) | 6 Apr 1996 (for purpose of authorising the making of regulations) (SI 1996/778) |
| | | 6 Apr 1997 (otherwise) (SI 1997/664) |
| | paras 7, 8 | 6 Apr 1997 (SI 1997/664) |
| | para 9 | 6 Apr 1996 (SI 1996/778) |
| | paras 10–16 | 6 Apr 1997 (SI 1997/664) |
| Sch 7 | Pt I | 6 Apr 1997 (subject to savings relating to Pension Schemes Act 1993, ss 108, 114) (SI 1997/664) |
| | Pt II | Has effect in accordance with Sch 4 (s 180(2)) |
| | Pt III | 6 Apr 1996 (so far as relates to Pension Schemes Act 1993, s 48(2)(b), (c)) (SI 1996/778) |
| | | 6 Apr 1997 (otherwise, except repeals relating to Pension Schemes Act 1993, ss 35, 36, and subject to savings relating to 1993 Act, ss 55–68, 170(1), 171(1)) (SI 1997/664) |
| | | *Not yet in force* (exceptions noted above) |
| | Pt IV | 19 Jul 1995 (repeal in Pensions (Increase) Act 1971) (s 180(2)) |
| | | 6 Apr 1997 (otherwise, subject to savings relating to Pension Schemes Act 1993, ss 136–140) (SI 1997/664) |

[1]  SI 1996/1853 (originally issued as Commencement No 6) was renumbered as Commencement No 7 by the Pensions Act 1995 (Commencement No 6: SI 1996/1853: C 38) (Amendment) Order 1996, SI 1996/2150

[2]  Orders under Matrimonial Causes Act 1973, s 23 requiring periodical payments made by a pension fund to a spouse without pension rights may not be ordered so as to commence before 6 Apr 1997

[3]  Certain provisions of Sch 4 have effect as follows: para 2 has effect on or after 6 Apr 2010 (para 2(2)); para 4 has effect in relation to any person attaining pensionable age on or after 6 Apr 2010 (para 4(2)); para 6(1) comes into force on 6 Apr 2010; and para 6(2)–(4) have effect in relation to incremental periods beginning on or after that date (para 6(5)); paras 18, 19 have effect on or after 6 Apr 2010 (para 20)

**Prisoners (Return to Custody) Act 1995 (c 16)**

*RA:* 28 Jun 1995

*Commencement provisions:* s 3(2); Prisoners (Return to Custody) Act 1995 (Commencement) Order 1995, SI 1995/2021

Whole Act in force 5 Sep 1995 (SI 1995/2021)

**Private International Law (Miscellaneous Provisions) Act 1995 (c 42)**

*RA:* 8 Nov 1995

*Commencement provisions:* s 16; Private International Law (Miscellaneous Provisions) Act 1995 (Commencement) Order 1996, SI 1996/995; Private International Law (Miscellaneous Provisions) Act 1995 (Commencement No 2) Order 1996, SI 1996/2515

| | |
|---|---|
| 1, 2 | 1 Nov 1996 (SI 1996/2515) |
| 3 | *Never in force* (repealed) |
| 4 | 1 Nov 1996 (SI 1996/2515) |
| 5–8 | 8 Jan 1996 (s 16(2)) |
| 9–15 | 1 May 1996 (SI 1996/995) |
| 16–19 | 8 Nov 1995 (RA) |
| Schedule | 8 Jan 1996 (s 16(2)) |

## Proceeds of Crime Act 1995 (c 11)

*RA:* 28 Jun 1995

*Commencement provisions:* s 16(3)–(6); Proceeds of Crime Act 1995 (Commencement) Order 1995, SI 1995/2650

| | |
|---|---|
| 1–13 | 1 Nov 1995 (SI 1995/2650) |
| 14 | 28 Jun 1995 (s 16(4)) |
| 15 | 1 Nov 1995 (SI 1995/2650) |
| 16 | 28 Jun 1995 (s 16(4)) |
| Schs 1, 2 | 1 Nov 1995 (SI 1995/2650) |

## Proceeds of Crime (Scotland) Act 1995 (c 43)

*RA:* 8 Nov 1995

*Commencement provisions:* s 50(2)

Whole Act in force 1 Apr 1996 (s 50(2)), subject to transitional provisions and savings in Criminal Procedure (Consequential Provisions) (Scotland) Act 1995, in particular for consolidated provisions which are not yet in force at that date; see s 4, Sch 3 thereto

## Requirements of Writing (Scotland) Act 1995 (c 7)

*RA:* 1 May 1995

*Commencement provisions:* s 15(2)

Whole Act in force 1 Aug 1995 (s 15(2))

## Road Traffic (New Drivers) Act 1995 (c 13)

*RA:* 28 Jun 1995

*Commencement provisions:* s 10(2), (3); Road Traffic (New Drivers) Act 1995 (Commencement) Order 1997, SI 1997/267

| | | |
|---|---|---|
| 1–4 | | 1 Jun 1997 (SI 1997/267) |
| 5 | (1), (2) | 1 Mar 1997 (SI 1997/267) |
| | (3)–(7) | 1 Jun 1997 (SI 1997/267) |
| | (8)–(10) | 1 Mar 1997 (SI 1997/267) |
| 6 | | See Sch 1 below |
| 7–9 | | 1 Jun 1997 (SI 1997/267) |
| 10 | (1) | 1 Mar 1997 (SI 1997/267) |
| | (2)–(4) | 1 Jun 1997 (SI 1997/267) |
| | (5) | 1 Mar 1997 (SI 1997/267) |
| Sch 1 | paras 1–10 | 1 Jun 1997 (SI 1997/267) |
| | para 11 | 1 Mar 1997 (SI 1997/267) |
| Sch 2 | | 1 Jun 1997 (SI 1997/267) |

## Sale of Goods (Amendment) Act 1995 (c 28)

*RA:* 19 Jul 1995

*Commencement provisions:* s 3(2)

Whole Act in force 19 Sep 1995 (s 3(2))

**Shipping and Trading Interests (Protection) Act 1995 (c 22)**

*RA:* 19 Jul 1995

*Commencement provisions:* s 9(4)

Whole Act in force 1 Jan 1996 (s 9(4))

---

**South Africa Act 1995 (c 3)**

*RA:* 23 Mar 1995

Whole Act in force 23 Mar 1995 (RA)

---

**Statute Law (Repeals) Act 1995 (c 44)**

*RA:* 8 Nov 1995

Whole Act in force 8 Nov 1995 (RA)

**Team and Group Ministries Measure 1995 (No 1)**

*RA:* 28 Jun 1995

*Commencement provisions:* s 20(2); Order dated 12 Feb 1996

| | |
|---|---|
| 1 | 1 May 1996 (order dated 12 Feb 1996) |
| 2 | 28 Jun 1995 (s 20(2)) |
| 3–12 | 1 May 1996 (order dated 12 Feb 1996) |
| 13 | 12 Feb 1996 (order dated 12 Feb 1996) |
| 14–19 | 1 May 1996 (order dated 12 Feb 1996) |
| 20 | See ss 1–19 above |
| Schs 1, 2 | 1 May 1996 (order dated 12 Feb 1996) |

---

**Town and Country Planning (Costs of Inquiries etc) Act 1995 (c 49)**

*RA:* 8 Nov 1995

Whole Act in force 8 Nov 1995 (RA)

---

# 1996 Acts

## Appropriation Act 1996 (c 45)

*RA:* 24 Jul 1996

Whole Act in force 24 Jul 1996 (RA)

---

## Arbitration Act 1996 (c 23)

*RA:* 17 Jun 1996

*Commencement provisions:* s 109; Arbitration Act 1996 (Commencement No 1) Order 1996, SI 1996/3146

| | | |
|---|---|---|
| 1–84 | | 31 Jan 1997 (subject to transitional provisions) (SI 1996/3146) |
| 85–87 | | *Not yet in force* |
| 88–90 | | 31 Jan 1997 (subject to transitional provisions) (SI 1996/3146) |
| 91 | | 17 Dec 1996 (so far as it relates to the power to make orders) (SI 1996/3146) |
| | | 31 Jan 1997 (otherwise, and subject to transitional provisions) (SI 1996/3146) |
| 92–104 | | 31 Jan 1997 (subject to transitional provisions) (SI 1996/3146) |
| 105 | | 17 Dec 1996 (SI 1996/3146) |
| 106 | | 31 Jan 1997 (subject to transitional provisions) (SI 1996/3146) |
| 107 | (1) | See Sch 3 below |
| | (2) | See Sch 4 below |
| 108–110 | | 17 Dec 1996 (SI 1996/3146) |
| Schs 1, 2 | | 31 Jan 1997 (subject to transitional provisions) (SI 1996/3146) |
| Sch 3 | | 17 Dec 1996 (so far as it relates to the provision that may be made by county court rules) (SI 1996/3146) |
| | | 31 Jan 1997 (otherwise, and subject to transitional provisions) (SI 1996/3146) |
| Sch 4 | | 17 Dec 1996 (repeal relating to the County Courts (Northern Ireland) Order 1980 (NI 3), so far as it relates to the provision that may be made by county court rules) (SI 1996/3146) |
| | | 31 Jan 1997 (otherwise, and subject to transitional provisions) (SI 1996/3146) |

---

## Armed Forces Act 1996 (c 46)

*RA:* 24 Jul 1996

*Commencement provisions:* s 36; Armed Forces Act 1996 (Commencement No 1) Order 1996, SI 1996/2474; Armed Forces Act 1996 (Commencement No 2) Order 1997, SI 1997/304; Armed Forces Act 1996 (Commencement No 3 and Transitional Provisions) Order 1997, SI 1997/2164; Armed Forces Act 1996 (Commencement No 4) Order 2001, SI 2001/1519; Armed Forces Act 1996 (Commencement No 5) Order 2005, SI 2005/1119

| | |
|---|---|
| 1 | 24 Jul 1996 (s 36) |
| 2 | 1 Oct 1996 (SI 1996/2474) |
| 3, 4 | 1 May 2001 (SI 2001/1519) |

**Armed Forces Act 1996 (c 46)**—*contd*

| | | |
|---|---|---|
| 5 | | See Sch 1 below |
| 6 | | 1 Oct 1996 (with a saving for any service disciplinary proceedings which began on or before 30 Sep 1996) (SI 1996/2474) |
| 7 | | 1 Oct 1996 (SI 1996/2474) |
| 8 | | *Never in force* (repealed) |
| 9 | | 1 Apr 1997 (with savings) (SI 1997/304) |
| 10 | | See Sch 3 below |
| 11, 12 | | 1 Oct 1996 (with a saving for convictions on or before 30 Sep 1996) (SI 1996/2474) |
| 13, 14 | | 1 Oct 1996 (SI 1996/2474) |
| 15 | | 1 Apr 1997 (with savings) (SI 1997/304) |
| 16 | | See Sch 5 below |
| 17 | | 1 Apr 1997 (with savings) (SI 1997/304) |
| 18, 19 | | 1 Oct 1996 (SI 1996/2474) |
| 20 | | 1 Oct 1997 (SI 1997/2164) |
| 21 | (1)–(3) | 1 Oct 1997 (SI 1997/2164) |
| | (4) | 1 Oct 1997 (subject to transitional provisions) (SI 1997/2164) |
| | (5), (6) | 1 Oct 1997 (SI 1997/2164) |
| 22 | (1)–(3) | 1 Oct 1997 (SI 1997/2164) |
| | (4) | 1 Oct 1997 (subject to transitional provisions) (SI 1997/2164) |
| | (5)–(7) | 1 Oct 1997 (SI 1997/2164) |
| 23 | | 1 Oct 1997 (subject to transitional provisions) (SI 1997/2164) |
| 24 | (1) | 1 Oct 1997 (SI 1997/2164) |
| | (2) | 1 Oct 1997 (subject to transitional provisions) (SI 1997/2164) |
| 25 | (1) | 1 Oct 1997 (SI 1997/2164) |
| | (2) | 1 Oct 1997 (subject to transitional provisions) (SI 1997/2164) |
| 26, 27 | | 1 Oct 1997 (SI 1997/2164) |
| 28, 29 | | 1 Apr 1997 (with savings) (SI 1997/304) |
| 30–33 | | 1 Oct 1996 (SI 1996/2474) |
| 34 | | 24 Jul 1996 (s 36) |
| 35 | (1) | See Sch 6 below |
| | (2) | See Sch 7 below |
| 36 | | 24 Jul 1996 (RA) (repealed in part) |
| Sch 1 | | 1 Apr 1997 (with savings) (SI 1997/304) |
| Sch 2 | | *Never in force* (repealed) |
| Sch 3 | | 1 Apr 1997 (with savings) (SI 1997/304) |
| Sch 4 | | 1 Oct 1996 (SI 1996/2474) |
| Sch 5 | | 1 Apr 1997 (with savings) (SI 1997/304) |
| Sch 6 | paras 1–3 | 1 Oct 1996 (SI 1996/2474) |
| | para 4 | 1 Apr 1997 (with savings) (SI 1997/304) |
| | paras 5, 6 | 1 Oct 1996 (SI 1996/2474) |
| | paras 7–9 | 1 Apr 1997 (with savings) (SI 1997/304) |
| | paras 10–13 | 1 Oct 1996 (SI 1996/2474) |
| | paras 14, 15 | 1 Apr 1997 (with savings) (SI 1997/304) |
| Sch 7 | Pts I, II | 1 Apr 1997 (with savings) (SI 1997/304) |
| | Pt III | 1 Sep 1996 (repeal of or in Armed Forces Act 1991) (s 36) |
| | | 1 Oct 1996 (SI 1996/2474), repeals of or in— |
| | | Greenwich Hospital Act 1869; |
| | | Army Act 1955, s 122(1)(e), Sch 7, para 8; |
| | | Air Force Act 1955, s 122(1)(e); |
| | | Naval Discipline Act 1957, ss 82(1)(d), 111(2), 132(5); |
| | | Rehabilitation of Offenders Act 1974; |
| | | Armed Forces Act 1976, s 17, Sch 9, para 20(2); |
| | | Rehabilitation of Offenders (Northern Ireland) Order 1978, SI 1978/1908 (NI 27); |
| | | Armed Forces Act 1981 |
| | | 1 Apr 1997 (SI 1997/304), repeals of or in— |
| | | Army Act 1955, s 108; |
| | | Air Force Act 1955, s 108; |

## Armed Forces Act 1996 (c 46)—*contd*

Naval Discipline Act 1957, s 72;
Courts-Martial (Appeals) Act 1968;
Firearms Act 1968;
Armed Forces Act 1976, Sch 3, para 19;
Criminal Appeal Act 1995

1 May 2001 (SI 2001/1519) otherwise, except repeals of or in—
Mental Health Act 1983, s 46;
Mental Health (Scotland) Act 1984, s 69;
Mental Health (Northern Ireland) Order 1986, SI 1986/595 (NI 4), art 52

29 Apr 2005 (exceptions noted above) (SI 2005/1119)

## Asylum and Immigration Act 1996 (c 49)

*RA:* 24 Jul 1996

*Commencement provisions:* s 13(3); Asylum and Immigration Act 1996 (Commencement No 1) Order 1996, SI 1996/2053; Asylum and Immigration Act 1996 (Commencement No 2) Order 1996, SI 1996/2127; Asylum and Immigration Act 1996 (Commencement No 3 and Transitional Provisions) Order 1996, SI 1996/2970

| | | |
|---|---|---|
| 1 | | 7 Oct 1996 (for the purpose only of designating countries or territories) (SI 1996/2127) |
| | | 21 Oct 1996 (otherwise) (SI 1996/2127) |
| 2 | | 1 Sep 1996 (SI 1996/2053) |
| 3 | (1), (2) | 1 Sep 1996 (SI 1996/2053) |
| | (3) | 26 Jul 1996 (SI 1996/2053) |
| | (4) | 1 Sep 1996 (SI 1996/2053) |
| | (5) | 26 Jul 1996 (SI 1996/2053) |
| | (6) | 1 Sep 1996 (SI 1996/2053) |
| 4–7 | | 1 Oct 1996 (SI 1996/2053) |
| 8 | (1), (2) | 1 Dec 1996 (for the purpose only of making orders) (SI 1996/2970) |
| | | 27 Jan 1997 (otherwise, but subject to a saving for employment beginning before 27 Jan 1997) (SI 1996/2970) |
| | (3)–(8) | 27 Jan 1997 (subject to a saving for employment beginning before 27 Jan 1997) (SI 1996/2970) |
| 9 | (1), (2) | 26 Jul 1996 (for purpose only of making orders) (SI 1996/2053) |
| | | 19 Aug 1996 (otherwise) (SI 1996/2127) |
| | (3) | 26 Jul 1996 (SI 1996/2053) |
| | (4) | 19 Aug 1996 (SI 1996/2127) |
| 10 | | 19 Aug 1996 (for the purpose only of prescribing conditions) (SI 1996/2127) |
| | | 7 Oct 1996 (otherwise) (SI 1996/2127) |
| 11 | | 24 Jul 1996 (RA) |
| 12 | (1) | See Sch 2 below |
| | (2) | See Sch 3 below |
| | (3) | See Sch 4 below |
| 13 | | 26 Jul 1996 (SI 1996/2053) |
| Sch 1 | | 24 Jul 1996 (RA) |
| Sch 2 | para 1(1) | 1 Nov 1996 (SI 1996/2127) |
| | para 1(2), (3) | 1 Oct 1996 (SI 1996/2053) |
| | para 2 | 1 Oct 1996 (SI 1996/2053) |
| | para 3(1) | 1 Nov 1996 (SI 1996/2127) |
| | para 3(2) | 1 Sep 1996 (SI 1996/2053) |
| | paras 4–7 | 1 Oct 1996 (SI 1996/2053) |
| | paras 8–12 | 1 Sep 1996 (SI 1996/2053) |
| | para 13 | 1 Oct 1996 (SI 1996/2053) |
| Sch 3 | paras 1–3 | 1 Sep 1996 (SI 1996/2053) |
| | para 4 | *Never in force* (spent) |

**Asylum and Immigration Act 1996 (c 49)**—*contd*

| | |
|---|---|
| para 5 | 1 Sep 1996 (SI 1996/2053) |
| Sch 4 | 1 Sep 1996 (repeals of or in Asylum and Immigration Appeals Act 1993) (SI 1996/2053) |
| | 1 Oct 1996 (repeals of or in Immigration Act 1971) (SI 1996/2053) |

---

**Audit (Miscellaneous Provisions) Act 1996 (c 10)**

*RA:* 29 Apr 1996

*Commencement provisions:* s 1(2)

| | |
|---|---|
| 1 | 29 Jun 1996 (s 1(2)) |
| 2–7 | 29 Apr 1996 (RA) |

---

**Broadcasting Act 1996 (c 55)**

*RA:* 24 Jul 1996

*Commencement provisions:* s 149(1), (2); Broadcasting Act 1996 (Commencement No 1 and Transitional Provisions) Order 1996, SI 1996/2120; Broadcasting Act 1996 (Commencement No 2) Order 1997, SI 1997/1005; Broadcasting Act 1996 (Commencement No 3) Order 1998, SI 1998/188

| | |
|---|---|
| 1 | 1 Oct 1996 (SI 1996/2120) |
| 2 | 15 Sep 1996 (for the purposes of the notification by the independent analogue broadcasters of their intention to provide their respective services for broadcasting in digital form) (SI 1996/2120) |
| | 1 Oct 1996 (otherwise) (SI 1996/2120) |
| 3–40 | 1 Oct 1996 (SI 1996/2120) |
| 41 | 1 Oct 1996 (except for the purposes of the notification by the independent national broadcasters of their intention to provide a service for broadcasting in digital form pursuant to s 41(2) of this Act) (SI 1996/2120) |
| | 29 Jan 1998 (exception noted above) (SI 1998/188) |
| 42–72 | 1 Oct 1996 (SI 1996/2120) |
| 73 | See Sch 2 below |
| 74–78 | 24 Jul 1996 (s 149(1)) |
| 79 | 1 Oct 1996 (SI 1996/2120) |
| 80 | 24 Jul 1996 (s 149(1)) |
| 81 | 1 Oct 1996 (SI 1996/2120) |
| 82 | *Never in force* (repealed) |
| 83 | 24 Jul 1996 (s 149(1)) |
| 84 | 1 Oct 1996 (SI 1996/2120) |
| 85 | 1 Apr 1997 (SI 1997/1005) |
| 86 | 1 Oct 1996 (SI 1996/2120) |
| 87 | 1 Nov 1996 (SI 1996/2120) |
| 88 | 24 Jul 1996 (s 149(1)) |
| 89 | 1 Nov 1996 (SI 1996/2120) |
| 90 | 24 Jul 1996 (s 149(1)) |
| 91 | 1 Oct 1996 (SI 1996/2120) |
| 92 | 24 Jul 1996 (s 149(1)) |
| 93, 94 | 1 Nov 1996 (SI 1996/2120) |
| 95 | 1 Apr 1997 (SI 1997/1005) |
| 96 | 1 Nov 1996 (SI 1996/2120) |
| 97–103 | 1 Oct 1996 (SI 1996/2120) |
| 104 | 10 Aug 1996 (subject to a transitional provision) (SI 1996/2120) |
| 105 | 1 Oct 1996 (SI 1996/2120) |
| 106–130 | 1 Apr 1997 (SI 1997/1005) |
| 131–136 | 24 Jul 1996 (s 149(1)) |
| 137, 138 | 1 Oct 1996 (SI 1996/2120) |

**Broadcasting Act 1996 (c 55)**—*contd*

| | | |
|---|---|---|
| 139 | | 1 Nov 1996 (SI 1996/2120) |
| 140–142 | | 1 Oct 1996 (SI 1996/2120) |
| 143–146 | | 1 Nov 1996 (SI 1996/2120) |
| 147 | (1) | 24 Jul 1996 (s 149(1)) |
| | (2)(a), (b) | 1 Oct 1996 (SI 1996/2120) |
| | (2)(c) | 1 Apr 1997 (SI 1997/1005) |
| | (2)(d) | 1 Oct 1996 (SI 1996/2120) |
| 148 | (1) | See Sch 10 below |
| | (2) | See Sch 11 below |
| 149, 150 | | 24 Jul 1996 (s 149(1)) |
| Sch 1 | | 1 Oct 1996 (SI 1996/2120) |
| Sch 2 | paras 1–5 | 10 Aug 1996 (in relation to the interpretation of Broadcasting Act 1990, Sch 2, Pt IV, paras 12, 13) (SI 1996/2120) |
| | | 1 Nov 1996 (otherwise) (SI 1996/2120) |
| | para 6 | 1 Nov 1996 (SI 1996/2120) |
| | paras 7, 8 | 24 Jul 1996 (so far as relating to BBC companies) (s 149(1)) |
| | | 1 Nov 1996 (otherwise) (SI 1996/2120) |
| | para 9 | 24 Jul 1996 (so far as relating to BBC companies) (s 149(1)) |
| | | 1 Oct 1996 (otherwise) (SI 1996/2120) |
| | para 10 | 1 Nov 1996 (except so far as relating to Broadcasting Act 1990, Sch 2, Pt III, paras 1(2)(b), 2(7)) (SI 1996/2120) |
| | | 1 Apr 1997 (exception noted above) (SI 1997/1005) |
| | para 11 | 10 Aug 1996 (so far as relates to Broadcasting Act 1990, Sch 2, Pt IV, paras 12, 13 and in relation to paras 1–3, 9, 10, 14 of that substituted Part in so far as those paras apply to the interpretation of the said paras 12, 13 to the 1990 Act) (subject to a transitional provision) (SI 1996/2120) |
| | | 1 Nov 1996 (except so far as relating to Broadcasting Act 1990, Sch 2, Pt IV, para 15(2)) (SI 1996/2120) |
| | | 1 Apr 1997 (exception noted above) (SI 1997/1005) |
| | paras 12, 13 | 1 Nov 1996 (SI 1996/2120) |
| Schs 3, 4 | | 1 Apr 1997 (SI 1997/1005) |
| Schs 5–8 | | 24 Jul 1996 (s 149(1)) |
| Sch 9 | | 1 Oct 1996 (SI 1996/2120) |
| Sch 10 | paras 1–11 | 1 Oct 1996 (SI 1996/2120) |
| | para 12 | 1 Apr 1997 (SI 1997/1005) |
| | para 13 | 1 Nov 1996 (SI 1996/2120) |
| | para 14 | 1 Oct 1996 (SI 1996/2120) |
| | para 15 | 24 Jul 1996 (so far as relating to BBC companies) (s 149(1)) |
| | | 1 Oct 1996 (otherwise) (SI 1996/2120) |
| | para 16 | 1 Oct 1996 (so far as relating to a multiplex service) (SI 1996/2120) |
| | | 1 Apr 1997 (otherwise) (SI 1997/1005) |
| | paras 17, 18 | 1 Apr 1997 (SI 1997/1005) |
| | para 19 | 24 Jul 1996 (so far as relating to BBC companies) (s 149(1)) |
| | | 1 Oct 1996 (otherwise) (SI 1996/2120) |
| | para 20 | 1 Apr 1997 (SI 1997/1005) |
| | para 21(a) | 1 Oct 1996 (SI 1996/2120) |
| | para 21(b) | 1 Nov 1996 (SI 1996/2120) |
| | para 21(c) | 1 Oct 1996 (SI 1996/2120) |
| | paras 22–26 | 1 Apr 1997 (SI 1997/1005) |
| | paras 27–30 | 1 Oct 1996 (SI 1996/2120) |
| | para 31 | 1 Oct 1996 (so far as relating to anything done under ss 1–72 of this Act) (SI 1996/2120) |
| | | 1 Apr 1997 (otherwise) (SI 1997/1005) |
| | para 32 | 1 Oct 1996 (except so far as relating to anything done in pursuance of ss 115(4), (6), 116(5), 117 of this Act) (SI 1996/2120) |
| | | 1 Apr 1997 (otherwise) (SI 1997/1005) |

**Broadcasting Act 1996 (c 55)**—*contd*

| | | |
|---|---|---|
| Sch 11 | Pt I | 24 Jul 1996 (repeals of or in Broadcasting Act 1990, ss 32(9), 45(8), (9), 47(11), (12)) (s 149(1)) |
| | | 1 Oct 1996 (repeals of or in Broadcasting Act 1990, ss 2(1)(a), (4), 32(10), (13)(a), 72(2)(d), 84(1)(b), 182, Sch 20, para 50) (SI 1996/2120) |
| | | 1 Nov 1996 (repeals of or in Broadcasting Act 1990, s 104(5), (6)(a), Sch 2) (SI 1996/2120) |
| | | 1 Apr 1997 (otherwise) (SI 1997/1005) |
| | Pt II | 1 Oct 1996 (revocation of Cable (Excepted Programmes) Order 1991, SI 1991/1246) (SI 1996/2120) |
| | | 1 Nov 1996 (SI 1996/2120), revocations of or in— |
| | | Broadcasting (Restrictions on the Holding of Licences) Order 1991, SI 1991/1176; |
| | | Broadcasting (Restrictions on the Holding of Licences) (Amendment) Order 1993, SI 1993/3199; |
| | | Broadcasting (Restrictions on the Holding of Licences) (Amendment) Order 1995, SI 1995/1924 |

---

**Channel Tunnel Rail Link Act 1996 (c 61)**

*RA:* 18 Dec 1996

Whole Act in force 18 Dec 1996 (RA)

---

**Chemical Weapons Act 1996 (c 6)**

*RA:* 3 Apr 1996

*Commencement provisions:* s 39(1); Chemical Weapons Act 1996 (Commencement) Order 1996, SI 1996/2054

| | |
|---|---|
| 1–38 | 16 Sep 1996 (SI 1996/2054) |
| 39 | 3 Apr 1996 (RA) |
| Schedule | 16 Sep 1996 (SI 1996/2054) |

---

**Civil Aviation (Amendment) Act 1996 (c 39)**

*RA:* 18 Jul 1996

Whole Act in force 18 Jul 1996 (RA)

---

**Commonwealth Development Corporation Act 1996 (c 28)**

*RA:* 4 Jul 1996

*Commencement provisions:* s 2(3)

Whole Act in force 4 Sep 1996 (s 2(3))

---

**Community Care (Direct Payments) Act 1996 (c 30)**

*RA:* 4 Jul 1996

*Commencement provisions:* s 7(2); Community Care (Direct Payments) Act 1996 (Commencement) Order 1997, SI 1997/756

| | |
|---|---|
| 1–5 | 1 Apr 1997 (SI 1997/756) |
| 6 | 4 Jul 1996 (s 7(2)) |
| 7 | 1 Apr 1997 (SI 1997/756) |

---

## Consolidated Fund Act 1996 (c 4)

*RA:* 21 Mar 1996

Whole Act in force 21 Mar 1996 (RA)

---

## Consolidated Fund (No 2) Act 1996 (c 60)

*RA:* 18 Dec 1996

Whole Act in force 18 Dec 1996 (RA)

---

## Criminal Procedure and Investigations Act 1996 (c 25)

*RA:* 4 Jul 1996

*Commencement provisions:* Criminal Procedure and Investigations Act 1996 (Appointed Day No 1) Order 1996, SI 1996/2343; Criminal Procedure and Investigations Act 1996 (Appointed Day No 2) Order 1997, SI 1997/36; Criminal Procedure and Investigations Act 1996 (Appointed Day No 3) Order 1997, SI 1997/682; Criminal Procedure and Investigations Act 1996 (Commencement) (Section 65 and Schedules 1 and 2) Order 1997, SI 1997/683; Criminal Procedure and Investigations Act 1996 (Appointed Day No 4) Order 1997, SI 1997/1019; Criminal Procedure and Investigations Act 1996 (Appointed Day No 5) Order 1997, SI 1997/1504; Criminal Procedure and Investigations Act 1996 (Appointed Day No 6) Order 1997, SI 1997/2199; Criminal Procedure and Investigations Act 1996 (Appointed Day No 7) Order 1997, SI 1997/3108; Criminal Procedure and Investigations Act 1996 (Appointed Day No 8) Order 1998, SI 1998/851; Criminal Procedure and Investigations Act 1996 (Commencement) (Section 67) Order 1999, SI 1999/716; Criminal Procedure and Investigations Act 1996 (Appointed Day No 9) Order 1999, SI 1999/718; Criminal Procedure and Investigations Act 1996 (Appointed Day No 10) Order 2000, SI 2000/1968

The text of this Act generally states clearly the dates from which the provisions of the Act are to have effect. Only those provisions for which a date is specified by an order made under a provision of the Act are set out below:

| | |
|---|---|
| 1–21 | 1 Apr 1997 (E) (W) (SI 1997/682) |
| | 1 Jan 1998 (NI) (SI 1997/3108) |
| 28–38 | 15 Apr 1997 (SI 1997/1019) |
| 39–43 | 1 Oct 1996 (E) (W) (S) (SI 1996/2343) |
| | 1 Jan 1998 (NI) (SI 1997/3108) |
| 45 | 1 Apr 1998 (E) (W) (insofar as relates to notices of transfer served under the Criminal Justice Act 1991, s 53) (SI 1998/851) |
| | *Never in force* (otherwise) (repealed) |
| 47 | In force in relation to any alleged offence into which no criminal investigation has begun before 1 Apr 1997 (SI 1997/682; SI 1997/683) |
| 48 | 1 Oct 1996 (SI 1996/2343) |
| 49 | 1 Oct 1997 (SI 1997/2199) |
| 50 | 1 Oct 1996 (SI 1996/2343) |
| 51 | 1 Apr 1997 (E) (W) (SI 1997/682) |
| 52 | 1 Feb 1997 (SI 1997/36) |
| 53 | 1 Oct 1996 (SI 1996/2343) |
| 54 | 15 Apr 1997 (E) (W) (SI 1997/1019) |
| | 30 Jun 1997 (NI) (SI 1997/1504) |
| 61 | 1 Apr 1997 (E) (W) (S) (SI 1997/682) |
| | 15 Apr 1997 (E) (W) (SI 1997/1019) |
| 63 | 1 Apr 1997 (E) (W) (S) (SI 1997/682) |
| 65 | In force in relation to any alleged offence into which no criminal investigation has begun before 1 Apr 1997 (SI 1997/682; SI 1997/683) |
| 66 | 1 Apr 1999 (E) (W) (SI 1999/718) |
| | 21 Aug 2000 (NI) (SI 2000/1968) |

**Criminal Procedure and Investigations Act 1996 (c 25)**—*contd*

| | |
|---|---|
| 67 | In force in relation to any proceedings for the purpose of which no witness summons has been issued under the Criminal Procedure (Attendance of Witnesses) Act 1965, s 2 before 1 Apr 1999 (SI 1999/716) |
| 68 | In force in relation to any alleged offence into which no criminal investigation has begun before 1 Apr 1997 (SI 1997/682; SI 1997/683) |
| 69 | 1 Apr 1997 (E) (W) (SI 1997/682)<br>1 Jan 1998 (NI) (SI 1997/3108) |
| 70, 71 | 1 Oct 1996 (SI 1996/2343) |
| Schs 1, 2 | In force in relation to any alleged offence into which no criminal investigation has begun before 1 Apr 1997 (SI 1997/682; SI 1997/683) |
| Sch 3 | 15 Apr 1997 (SI 1997/1019) |

---

**Damages Act 1996 (c 48)**

*RA:* 24 Jul 1996

*Commencement provisions:* s 8(3)

Whole Act in force 24 Sep 1996 (s 8(3))

---

**Deer (Amendment) (Scotland) Act 1996 (c 44)**

*RA:* 18 Jul 1996

*Commencement provisions:* s 14(2)

Whole Act in force 18 Oct 1996 (s 14(2))

---

**Deer (Scotland) Act 1996 (c 58)**

*RA:* 24 Jul 1996

*Commencement provisions:* s 48(6)

Whole Act in force 18 Nov 1996 (s 48(6))

---

**Defamation Act 1996 (c 31)**

*RA:* 4 Jul 1996

*Commencement provisions:* s 19; Defamation Act 1996 (Commencement No 1) Order 1999, SI 1999/817; Defamation Act 1996 (Commencement No 2) Order 2000, SI 2000/222; Defamation Act 1996 (Commencement No 3 and Transitional Provision) (Scotland) Order 2001, SSI 2001/98[1]; Defamation Act 1996 (Commencement No 4) Order 2009, SI 2009/2858

| | | |
|---|---|---|
| 1 | | 4 Sep 1996 (s 19) |
| 2 | | 28 Feb 2000 (E) (W) (SI 2000/222)<br>31 Mar 2001 (S) (SSI 2001/98)<br>6 Jan 2010 (NI) (SI 2009/2858) |
| 3 | (1)–(7) | 28 Feb 2000 (E) (W) (SI 2000/222)<br>31 Mar 2001 (S) (SSI 2001/98)<br>6 Jan 2010 (NI) (SI 2009/2858) |
| | (8) | 28 Feb 2000 (E) (W) (SI 2000/222)<br>6 Jan 2010 (NI) (SI 2009/2858) |
| | (9) | 31 Mar 2001 (S) (SSI 2001/98) |
| | (10) | 28 Feb 2000 (E) (W) (SI 2000/222)<br>31 Mar 2001 (S) (SSI 2001/98) |

**Defamation Act 1996 (c 31)**—*contd*

| | | |
|---|---|---|
| | | 6 Jan 2010 (NI) (SI 2009/2858) |
| 4 | | 28 Feb 2000 (E) (W) (SI 2000/222) |
| | | 31 Mar 2001 (S) (SSI 2001/98) |
| | | 6 Jan 2010 (NI) (SI 2009/2858) |
| 5, 6 | | 4 Sep 1996 (s 19) |
| 7–10 | | 28 Feb 2000 (E) (W) (SI 2000/222) |
| | | 6 Jan 2010 (NI) (SI 2009/2858) |
| 11 | | 6 Jan 2010 (NI) (SI 2009/2858) |
| 12, 13 | | 4 Sep 1996 (s 19) |
| 14, 15 | | 1 Apr 1999 (SI 1999/817) |
| 16 | | See Sch 2 below |
| 17 | (1) | 4 Sep 1996 (so far as relates to ss 1, 5, 6, 12, 13, 16, Sch 2 (so far as consequential to ss 1, 5, 6, 12, 13, 16)) (s 19) |
| | | 1 Apr 1999 (so far as applies to ss 14, 15, Sch 1) (SI 1999/817) |
| | | 28 Feb 2000 (E) (W) (otherwise) (SI 2000/222) |
| | | 31 Mar 2001 (S) (otherwise) (SSI 2001/98) |
| | | 6 Jan 2010 (NI) (otherwise) (SI 2009/2858) |
| | (2) | 4 Sep 1996 (so far as relates to ss 1, 5, 6, 12, 13, 16, Sch 2 (so far as consequential to ss 1, 5, 6, 12, 13, 16)) (s 19) |
| | | 1 Apr 1999 (so far as applies to ss 14, 15, Sch 1) (SI 1999/817) |
| | | 31 Mar 2001 (S) (otherwise) (SSI 2001/98) |
| 18–20 | | 4 Jul 1996 (RA) |
| Sch 1 | | 1 Apr 1999 (SI 1999/817) |
| Sch 2 | | 4 Sep 1996 (so far as consequential on ss 1, 5, 6, 12, 13, 16) (s 19) |

1 Apr 1999 (SI 1999/817), so far as consequential on ss 14, 15, 17, Sch 1, except repeals of—
Defamation Act 1952, ss 4, 16(3);
Defamation Act (Northern Ireland) 1955, ss 4, 14(2);
Broadcasting Act 1990, Sch 20, para 3
28 Feb 2000 (E) (W) (SI 2000/222) (otherwise) (subject to a saving in relation to Defamation Act 1952, s 4), except repeals of or in—
Defamation Act (Northern Ireland) 1955;
Local Government Act (Northern Ireland) 1972;
British Nationality Act 1981, Sch 7 (entry relating to Defamation Act (Northern Ireland) 1955);
Local Government (Access to Information) Act 1985, Sch 2, para 3;
Education and Libraries (Northern Ireland) Order 1986, SI 1986/594 (NI 3);
Broadcasting Act 1990, Sch 20, para 3
31 Mar 2001 (S) (so far as extends to and is not already in force in relation to Scotland) (SSI 2001/98)[1]
6 Jan 2010 (NI) (otherwise) (SI 2009/2858)[2]
*Not yet in force* (exceptions noted above)

[1] For a transitional provision, see SSI 2001/98, art 4

[2] For a transitional provision, see SI 2009/2858, art 4

---

**Dogs (Fouling of Land) Act 1996 (c 20)**

*RA:* 17 Jun 1996

*Commencement provisions:* s 8(2)

Whole Act in force 17 Aug 1996 (s 8(2))

---

## Education Act 1996 (c 56)

*RA:* 24 Jul 1996

*Commencement provisions:* s 583(2), (3); the Education Act 1996 (Commencement No 1) Order 1996, SI 1996/2904; Education Act 1996 (Commencement No 2 and Appointed Day) Order 1997, SI 1997/1623; Education Act 1996 (Commencement No 3) Order 1997, SI 1997/2352

| | | |
|---|---|---|
| 1–7 | | 1 Nov 1996 (s 583(2)) |
| 8 | | 1 Sep 1997 (SI 1997/1623) |
| 9–316 | | 1 Nov 1996 (s 583(2)) |
| 317 | (1)–(5) | 1 Nov 1996 (s 583(2)) |
| | (6) | 1 Jan 1997 (SI 1996/2904) |
| | (7) | 1 Nov 1996 (s 583(2)) |
| 318–347 | | 1 Nov 1996 (s 583(2)) |
| 348 | | 1 Sep 1997 (SI 1997/1623) |
| 349–527 | | 1 Nov 1996 (s 583(2)) |
| 528 | | 1 Aug 1997 (E) (SI 1997/1623) |
| | | 30 Oct 1997 (W) (SI 1997/2352) |
| 529–581 | | 1 Nov 1996 (s 583(2)) |
| 582 | (1) | See Sch 37 below |
| | (2) | See Sch 38 below |
| | (3), (4) | 1 Nov 1996 (s 583(2)) |
| 583 | | 1 Nov 1996 (s 583(2)) |
| Schs 1–36 | | 1 Nov 1996 (s 583(2)) |
| Sch 37 | Pt I | 1 Nov 1996 (s 583(2)) |
| | Pt II | 1 Sep 1997 (SI 1997/1623) |
| Sch 38 | Pt I | 1 Nov 1996 (s 583(2)) |
| | Pt II | 1 Sep 1997 (SI 1997/1623) |
| | Pt III | 1 Nov 1996 (s 583(2)) |
| Sch 39 | | 1 Nov 1996 (s 583(2)) |

## Education (Scotland) Act 1996 (c 43)

*RA:* 18 Jul 1996

*Commencement provisions:* s 37(2); Education (Scotland) Act 1996 (Commencement) Order 1996, SI 1996/2250; Education (Scotland) Act 1996 (Commencement No 2) Order 1997, SI 1997/365

| | | |
|---|---|---|
| 1 | | 18 Sep 1996 (SI 1996/2250) |
| 2–8 | | 1 Apr 1997 (SI 1997/365) |
| 9–35 | | 18 Sep 1996 (SI 1996/2250) |
| 36 | (1) | See Sch 5 below |
| | (2) | See Sch 6 below |
| | (3) | 18 Sep 1996 (SI 1996/2250) |
| 37 | | 18 Sep 1996 (SI 1996/2250) |
| Schs 1–4 | | 18 Sep 1996 (SI 1996/2250) |
| Sch 5 | paras 1–5 | 18 Sep 1996 (SI 1996/2250) |
| | paras 6–9 | 1 Apr 1997 (SI 1997/365) |
| Sch 6 | | 18 Sep 1996 (SI 1996/2250), repeals of or in— |
| | | Education (Scotland) Act 1980, ss 2, 19(1), 20, 65F; |
| | | School Boards (Scotland) Act 1988; |
| | | Self-Governing Schools etc (Scotland) Act 1989 |
| | | 1 Apr 1997 (otherwise) (SI 1997/365) |

## Education (Student Loans) Act 1996 (c 9)

*RA:* 29 Apr 1996

Whole Act in force 29 Apr 1996 (RA)

## Employment Rights Act 1996 (c 18)

*RA:* 22 May 1996

*Commencement provisions:* s 243

Whole Act in force 22 Aug 1996 (s 243)

## Employment Tribunals Act 1996 (c 17)

*RA:* 22 May 1996

*Commencement provisions:* s 46

Whole Act in force 22 Aug 1996 (s 46)

*Note:* This Act was originally cited as the Industrial Tribunals Act 1996

## Energy Conservation Act 1996 (c 38)

*RA:* 18 Jul 1996

*Commencement provisions:* s 2(2); Energy Conservation Act 1996 (Commencement No 1) (Scotland) Order 1996, SI 1996/2796; Energy Conservation Act (Commencement) Order (Northern Ireland) 1996, SR 1996/559; Energy Conservation Act 1996 (Commencement No 3 and Adaptations) Order 1997, SI 1997/47

Whole Act in force as follows—

1 Dec 1996 (S)

5 Dec 1996 (NI)

14 Jan 1997 (E) (W) (for the purposes of Home Energy Conservation Act 1995, ss 3(1), 4(1), (2))

1 Apr 1997 (E) (W) (otherwise)

## Family Law Act 1996 (c 27)

*RA:* 4 Jul 1996

*Commencement provisions:* s 67(2), (3); Family Law Act 1996 (Commencement No 1) Order 1997, SI 1997/1077; Family Law Act 1996 (Commencement No 2) Order 1997, SI 1997/1892; Family Law Act 1996 (Commencement) (No 3) Order 1998, SI 1998/2572

| | | |
|---|---|---|
| 1 | | 21 Mar 1997 (SI 1997/1077) |
| 2–21 | | *Never in force* (repealed) |
| 22 | | 21 Mar 1997 (SI 1997/1077) |
| 23–25 | | *Never in force* (repealed) |
| 26–29 | | 21 Mar 1997 (SI 1997/1077) |
| 30–56 | | 1 Oct 1997 (SI 1997/1892) |
| 57 | | 28 Jul 1997 (SI 1997/1892) |
| 58, 59 | | 1 Oct 1997 (SI 1997/1892) |
| 60 | | *Not yet in force* |
| 61–63 | | 1 Oct 1997 (SI 1997/1892) |
| 64 | | *Not yet in force* (repealed in part) |
| 65 | | 4 Jul 1996 (s 67(2)) |
| 66 | (1) | See Sch 8 below |
| | (2) | See Sch 9 below |
| | (3) | See Sch 10 below |
| 67 | | 4 Jul 1996 (s 67(2)) |
| Schs 1–3 | | *Never in force* (repealed) |
| Schs 4–6 | | 1 Oct 1997 (SI 1997/1892) |
| Sch 7 | para 1 | 1 Oct 1997 (SI 1997/1892) |

**Family Law Act 1996 (c 27)**—*contd*

| | | |
|---|---|---|
| | para 2(1) | 1 Oct 1997 (SI 1997/1892) |
| | para 2(2) | 1 Oct 1997 (subject to a transitional provision) (SI 1997/1892) |
| | paras 3–6 | 1 Oct 1997 (SI 1997/1892) |
| | para 7(1), (2) | 1 Oct 1997 (SI 1997/1892) |
| | para 7(3), (4) | 1 Oct 1997 (subject to a transitional provision) (SI 1997/1892) |
| | para 7(5) | 1 Oct 1997 (SI 1997/1892) |
| | para 7(6) | 1 Oct 1997 (subject to a transitional provision) (SI 1997/1892) |
| | paras 8–11 | 1 Oct 1997 (SI 1997/1892) |
| | para 12 | 1 Oct 1997 (subject to a transitional provision) (SI 1997/1892) |
| | para 13(1) | 1 Oct 1997 (subject to a transitional provision) (SI 1997/1892) |
| | para 13(2) | 1 Oct 1997 (SI 1997/1892) |
| | paras 14, 15 | 1 Oct 1997 (SI 1997/1892) |
| Sch 8 | paras 1–3 | *Never in force* (repealed) |
| | para 4 | *Not yet in force* |
| | paras 5–15 | *Never in force* (repealed) |
| | para 16(1) | *Not yet in force* |
| | para 16(2)–(4) | *Never in force* (repealed) |
| | para 16(5)(a) | 1 Nov 1998 (SI 1998/2572) |
| | para 16(5)(b) | *Never in force* (repealed) |
| | para 16(6)(a) | *Never in force* (repealed) |
| | para 16(6)(b) | 1 Nov 1998 (SI 1998/2572) |
| | para 16(7) | 1 Nov 1998 (subject to transitional provisions) (SI 1998/2572) |
| | paras 17–38 | *Never in force* (repealed) |
| | para 39 | *Never in force* (repealed) |
| | paras 40–43 | *Never in force* (repealed) |
| | para 44 | 21 Mar 1997 (SI 1997/1077) |
| | paras 45–51 | 1 Oct 1997 (SI 1997/1892) |
| | para 52 | 1 Oct 1997 (subject to a transitional provision) (SI 1997/1892) |
| | paras 53–60 | 1 Oct 1997 (SI 1997/1892) |
| | para 61 | 1 Oct 1997 (SI 1997/1892) |
| Sch 9 | paras 1, 2 | *Never in force* (repealed) |
| | paras 3, 4 | 28 Jul 1997 (SI 1997/1892) |
| | paras 5, 6 | *Not yet in force* |
| | paras 7–15 | 1 Oct 1997 (SI 1997/1892) |
| Sch 10 | | 21 Mar 1997 (repeal in Legal Aid Act 1988) (SI 1997/1077) |

1 Oct 1997 (SI 1997/1892), repeals of or in—
Domestic Violence and Matrimonial Proceedings Act 1976;
Domestic Proceedings and Magistrates' Courts Act 1978, ss 16–18, 28(2), Sch 2, para 53;
Matrimonial Homes Act 1983;
Administration of Justice Act 1985;
Housing (Consequential Provisions) Act 1985;
Housing Act 1988;
Children Act 1989, s 8(4);
Courts and Legal Services Act 1990;
Private International Law (Miscellaneous Provisions) Act 1995
*Not yet in force*, repeals of or in—
Domestic and Appellate Proceedings (Restriction of Publicity) Act 1968;
Magistrates' Courts Act 1980;
Building Societies Act 1986;
Children Act 1989, Sch 11, para 6(b)
*Never in force* (repealed), repeals of or in—
Matrimonial Causes Act 1973;
Domicile and Matrimonial Proceedings Act 1973;
Domestic Proceedings and Magistrates' Courts Act 1978, ss 1, 7(1), 63(3), Sch 2, para 38;
Senior Courts Act 1981;
Administration of Justice Act 1982;

**Family Law Act 1996 (c 27)**—*contd*

> Matrimonial and Family Proceedings Act 1984;
> Family Law Act 1986;
> Children Act 1989, Sch 13, paras 33(1), 65(1)

**Finance Act 1996 (c 8)**

*Budget Day*: 28 Nov 1995

*RA*: 29 Apr 1996

The commencement details of Finance Acts are not set out, as the dates from which their provisions take effect are usually stated clearly and unambiguously in the text of the Act, and charging provisions will normally state for which year or years of assessment they are to have effect.

**Health Service Commissioners (Amendment) Act 1996 (c 5)**

*RA*: 21 Mar 1996

*Commencement provisions:* s 14; Health Service Commissioners (Amendment) Act 1996 (Commencement) Order 1996, SI 1996/970

Whole Act in force 1 Apr 1996 (SI 1996/970)

**Hong Kong Economic and Trade Office Act 1996 (c 63)**

*RA*: 18 Dec 1996

Whole Act in force 18 Dec 1996 (RA)

**Hong Kong (Overseas Public Servants) Act 1996 (c 2)**

*RA*: 29 Feb 1996

Whole Act in force 29 Feb 1996 (RA)

**Hong Kong (War Wives and Widows) Act 1996 (c 41)**

*RA*: 18 Jul 1996

Whole Act in force 18 Jul 1996 (RA)

**Housing Act 1996 (c 52)**

*RA*: 24 Jul 1996

*Commencement provisions:* s 232; Housing Act 1996 (Commencement No 1) Order 1996, SI 1996/2048; Housing Act 1996 (Commencement No 2 and Savings) Order 1996, SI 1996/2212; Housing Act 1996 (Commencement No 3 and Transitional Provisions) Order 1996, SI 1996/2402; Housing Act 1996 (Commencement No 4) Order 1996, SI 1996/2658; Housing Act 1996 (Commencement No 5 and Transitional Provisions) Order 1996, SI 1996/2959; Housing Act 1996 (Commencement No 6 and Savings) Order 1997, SI 1997/66; Housing Act 1996 (Commencement No 7 and Savings) Order 1997, SI 1997/225; Housing Act 1996 (Commencement No 8) Order 1997, SI 1997/350; Housing Act 1996 (Commencement No 9) Order 1997, SI 1997/596; Housing Act 1996 (Commencement No 10 and Transitional Provisions) Order 1997, SI 1997/618; Housing Act 1996 (Commencement No 11 and Savings) Order 1997, SI 1997/1851; Housing Act 1996 (Commencement No 12 and Transitional Provision) Order 1998, SI 1998/1768; Housing Act 1996 (Commencement No 13) Order 2001, SI 2001/3164

**Housing Act 1996 (c 52)**—*contd*

Abbreviation: "orders etc" means "so much of the provision as to confer on the Corporation or the Secretary of State a power to consult, to make determinations, directions, orders or regulations or prepare schemes"

| | | |
|---|---|---|
| 1 | | 1 Oct 1996 (subject to transitional provisions) (SI 1996/2402) |
| 2 | (1)–(6) | 1 Oct 1996 (subject to transitional provisions) (SI 1996/2402) |
| | (7), (8) | 1 Aug 1996 (SI 1996/2048) |
| 3 | (1) | 1 Oct 1996 (subject to transitional provisions) (SI 1996/2402) |
| | (2) | 1 Aug 1996 (for the purpose of conferring upon the Secretary of State, the Housing Corporation or Housing for Wales a power to consult, to make determinations, to give consents and to delegate functions) (SI 1996/2048) |
| | | 1 Oct 1996 (otherwise) (subject to transitional provisions) (SI 1996/2402) |
| | (3), (4) | 1 Oct 1996 (subject to transitional provisions) (SI 1996/2402) |
| 4 | | 1 Oct 1996 (subject to transitional provisions) (SI 1996/2402) |
| 5 | | 1 Aug 1996 (SI 1996/2048) |
| 6 | | 1 Oct 1996 (subject to savings and transitional provisions) (SI 1996/2402) |
| 7 | | See Sch 1 below |
| 8 | | 1 Oct 1996 (subject to transitional provisions) (SI 1996/2402) |
| 9 | (1), (2) | 1 Oct 1996 (subject to transitional provisions) (SI 1996/2402) |
| | (3) | 1 Aug 1996 (SI 1996/2048) |
| | (4)–(8) | 1 Oct 1996 (subject to savings and transitional provisions) (SI 1996/2402) |
| 10–15 | | 1 Oct 1996 (subject to transitional provisions) (SI 1996/2402) |
| 16 | | 1 Apr 1997 (subject to a saving relating to sub-s (2)(c)) (SI 1997/618) |
| 17 | | 1 Aug 1996 (SI 1996/2048) |
| 18 | (1) | 1 Apr 1997 (SI 1997/618) |
| | (2) | 1 Oct 1996 (orders etc) (SI 1996/2402) |
| | | 1 Apr 1997 (otherwise) (SI 1997/618) |
| | (3)–(6) | 1 Apr 1997 (SI 1997/618) |
| | (7) | 1 Oct 1996 (orders etc) (SI 1996/2402) |
| | | 1 Apr 1997 (otherwise) (SI 1997/618) |
| | (8) | 1 Apr 1997 (SI 1997/618) |
| 19 | | 1 Apr 1997 (SI 1997/618) |
| 20 | (1), (2) | 1 Apr 1997 (SI 1997/618) |
| | (3) | 1 Oct 1996 (orders etc) (SI 1996/2402) |
| | | 1 Apr 1997 (otherwise) (SI 1997/618) |
| | (4) | 1 Apr 1997 (SI 1997/618) |
| 21 | (1), (2) | 1 Apr 1997 (SI 1997/618) |
| | (3) | 1 Oct 1996 (orders etc) (SI 1996/2402) |
| | | 1 Apr 1997 (otherwise) (SI 1997/618) |
| | (4) | 1 Apr 1997 (SI 1997/618) |
| 22, 23 | | 1 Oct 1996 (subject to transitional provisions) (SI 1996/2402) |
| 24 | | 1 Aug 1996 (for the purposes of conferring upon the Secretary of State, the Housing Corporation or Housing for Wales a power to consult, to make determinations, to give consents and to delegate functions) (SI 1996/2048) |
| | | 1 Apr 1997 (otherwise) (SI 1997/618) |
| 25 | | 1 Oct 1996 (orders etc) (SI 1996/2402) |
| | | 1 Apr 1997 (otherwise) (SI 1997/618) |
| 26 | | 1 Apr 1997 (SI 1997/618) |
| 27 | | 1 Oct 1996 (orders etc) (SI 1996/2402) |
| | | 1 Apr 1997 (otherwise) (SI 1997/618) |
| 28 | (1), (2) | 1 Apr 1997 (SI 1997/618) |
| | (3) | 1 Oct 1996 (for the purpose of enabling a determination to be made under Housing Act 1988, s 52(2), as amended by this Act) (SI 1996/2402) |

**Housing Act 1996 (c 52)**—*contd*

|  |  |  |
|---|---|---|
|  |  | 1 Apr 1997 (otherwise) (SI 1997/618) |
|  | (4) | 1 Aug 1996 (SI 1996/2048) |
|  | (5), (6) | 1 Apr 1997 (SI 1997/618) |
| 29 |  | 1 Aug 1996 (for the purposes of conferring upon the Secretary of State, the Housing Corporation or Housing for Wales a power to consult, to make determinations, to give consents and to delegate functions) (SI 1996/2048) |
|  |  | 1 Apr 1997 (otherwise) (SI 1997/618) |
| 30–34 |  | 1 Oct 1996 (subject to transitional provisions) (SI 1996/2402) |
| 35 | (1)–(3) | 1 Apr 1997 (SI 1997/618) |
|  | (4) | 1 Apr 1998 (SI 1997/618) |
|  | (5) | 1 Apr 1997 (SI 1997/618) |
| 36 | (1)–(6) | 1 Aug 1996 (SI 1996/2048) |
|  | (7) | 1 Oct 1996 (subject to transitional provisions) (SI 1996/2402) |
| 37, 38 |  | 1 Oct 1996 (subject to transitional provisions) (SI 1996/2402) |
| 39–50 |  | 1 Oct 1996 (SI 1996/2402) |
| 51 | (1) | See Sch 2 below |
|  | (2)–(6) | 1 Apr 1997 (SI 1997/618) |
| 52–54 |  | 1 Aug 1996 (SI 1996/2048) |
| 55 | (1) | See Sch 3 below |
|  | (2), (3) | 1 Aug 1996 (SI 1996/2048) |
| 56–64 |  | 1 Aug 1996 (SI 1996/2048) |
| 65, 66 |  | 1 Oct 1996 (orders etc) (SI 1996/2402) |
|  |  | 3 Mar 1997 (otherwise) (SI 1997/350) |
| 67–71 |  | 3 Mar 1997 (SI 1997/350) |
| 72 |  | 1 Oct 1996 (orders etc) (SI 1996/2402) |
|  |  | 3 Mar 1997 (otherwise) (SI 1997/350) |
| 73 |  | *Never in force* (repealed) |
| 74 |  | 3 Mar 1997 (SI 1997/350) |
| 75 |  | 1 Oct 1996 (orders etc) (SI 1996/2402) |
|  |  | 3 Mar 1997 (otherwise) (SI 1997/350) |
| 76, 77 |  | 1 Oct 1996 (SI 1996/2402) |
| 78, 79 |  | 3 Mar 1997 (SI 1997/350) |
| 80 | (1), (2) | 3 Mar 1997 (SI 1997/350) |
|  | (3) | 1 Oct 1996 (SI 1996/2402) |
| 81, 82 |  | 24 Sep 1996 (s 232(2)) |
| 83 | (1) | 1 Sep 1997 (subject to savings) (SI 1997/1851) |
|  | (2) | 1 Sep 1997 (subject to savings) (SI 1997/1851) |
|  |  | 11 Aug 1998 (otherwise, subject to a transitional provision) (SI 1998/1768) |
|  | (3) | 23 Aug 1996 (for the purpose of conferring power to make orders, regulations or rules) (SI 1996/2212) |
|  |  | 1 Sep 1997 (otherwise, but subject to savings) (SI 1997/1851) |
|  | (4)–(6) | 1 Sep 1997 (subject to savings) (SI 1997/1851) |
|  |  | 11 Aug 1998 (otherwise, subject to a transitional provision) (SI 1998/1768) |
| 84 |  | 1 Oct 1996 (SI 1996/2212) |
| 85 |  | 24 Sep 1996 (s 232(2)) |
| 86 | (1)–(3) | 1 Sep 1997 (subject to savings) (SI 1997/1851) |
|  | (4), (5) | 23 Aug 1996 (for the purpose of conferring power to make orders, regulations or rules) (SI 1996/2212) |
|  |  | 1 Sep 1997 (otherwise, but subject to savings) (SI 1997/1851) |
|  | (6) | 1 Sep 1997 (subject to savings) (SI 1997/1851) |
| 87 |  | *Not yet in force* |
| 88–91 |  | 1 Oct 1996 (subject to savings) (SI 1996/2212) |
| 92 | (1) | See Sch 6 below |
|  | (2), (3) | 1 Oct 1996 (subject to savings) (SI 1996/2212) |
| 93 |  | 1 Oct 1996 (subject to savings) (SI 1996/2212) |
| 94, 95 |  | 24 Sep 1996 (s 232(2)) |

**Housing Act 1996 (c 52)**—*contd*

| | | |
|---|---|---|
| 96 | (1) | 28 Feb 1997 (SI 1997/225) |
| | (2) | See Sch 7 below |
| 97 | | 28 Feb 1997 (SI 1997/225) |
| 98 | | 28 Feb 1997 (subject to savings) (SI 1997/225) |
| 99, 100 | | 28 Feb 1997 (SI 1997/225) |
| 101, 102 | | 28 Feb 1997 (subject to savings) (SI 1997/225) |
| 103 | | 28 Feb 1997 (SI 1997/225) |
| 104 | | See Sch 8 below |
| 105 | | 1 Oct 1996 (subject to savings) (SI 1996/2212) |
| 106 | | See Sch 9 below |
| 107–109 | | 1 Oct 1996 (subject to savings) (SI 1996/2212) |
| 110 | | 24 Jul 1996 (s 232(1)) |
| 111–115 | | 1 Oct 1996 (subject to savings) (SI 1996/2212) |
| 116, 117 | | 1 Oct 1996 (SI 1996/2212) |
| 118 | | 1 Apr 1997 (subject to transitional provisions) (SI 1997/618) |
| 119 | | 23 Aug 1996 (for the purpose of conferring power to make orders, regulations or rules) (SI 1996/2212) |
| | | *Never in force* (otherwise) (repealed) |
| 120 | | 24 Jul 1996 (s 232(1)) |
| 121 | | See Sch 12 below |
| 122 | | 1 Apr 1997 (SI 1997/618) |
| 123 | | See Sch 13 below |
| 124–128 | | 12 Feb 1997 (SI 1997/66) |
| 129 | (1), (2) | 12 Feb 1997 (SI 1997/66) |
| | (3), (4) | 1 Oct 1996 (SI 1996/2402) |
| | (5), (6) | 12 Feb 1997 (SI 1997/66) |
| 130–134 | | 12 Feb 1997 (SI 1997/66) |
| 135 | | 1 Oct 1996 (SI 1996/2402) |
| 136, 137 | | 12 Feb 1997 (SI 1997/66) |
| 138 | (1)–(3) | 12 Feb 1997 (SI 1997/66) |
| | (4)–(6) | 1 Oct 1996 (SI 1996/2402) |
| 139, 140 | | 1 Oct 1996 (SI 1996/2402) |
| 141 | (1) | See Sch 14 below |
| | (2), (3) | 1 Oct 1996 (SI 1996/2402) |
| 142, 143 | | 1 Oct 1996 (SI 1996/2402) |
| 144–146 | | 12 Feb 1997 (subject to savings) (SI 1997/66) |
| 147 | | 1 Oct 1996 (orders etc) (SI 1996/2402) |
| | | 12 Feb 1997 (otherwise, but subject to savings) (SI 1997/66) |
| 148–151 | | 28 Feb 1997 (subject to savings) (SI 1997/225) |
| 152–154 | | 1 Sep 1997 (SI 1997/1851) |
| 155 | (1) | 1 Sep 1997 (SI 1997/1851) |
| | (2)(a) | 1 Sep 1997 (SI 1997/1851) |
| | (2)(b) | 15 Oct 2001 (SI 2001/3164) |
| | (3)–(7) | 15 Oct 2001 (SI 2001/3164) |
| 156 | | 15 Oct 2001 (SI 2001/3164) |
| 157, 158 | | 1 Sep 1997 (SI 1997/1851) |
| 159 | | 1 Apr 1997 (SI 1996/2959) |
| 160 | (1)–(3) | 1 Apr 1997 (SI 1996/2959) |
| | (4), (5) | 1 Oct 1996 (SI 1996/2402) |
| 161 | (1) | 1 Apr 1997 (SI 1996/2959) |
| | (2), (3) | 1 Oct 1996 (orders etc) (SI 1996/2402) |
| | | 1 Apr 1997 (otherwise) (SI 1996/2959) |
| | (4)–(6) | 1 Apr 1997 (SI 1996/2959) |
| 162 | (1)–(3) | 1 Apr 1997 (SI 1996/2959) |
| | (4) | 1 Oct 1996 (orders etc) (SI 1996/2402) |
| | | 1 Apr 1997 (otherwise) (SI 1996/2959) |
| | (5) | 1 Apr 1997 (SI 1996/2959) |
| 163 | (1)–(6) | 1 Apr 1997 (SI 1996/2959) |
| | (7) | 1 Oct 1996 (orders etc) (SI 1996/2402) |

**Housing Act 1996 (c 52)**—*contd*

| | | |
|---|---|---|
| | | 1 Apr 1997 (otherwise) (SI 1996/2959) |
| 164 | | 1 Apr 1997 (SI 1996/2959) |
| 165 | (1), (2) | 1 Oct 1996 (SI 1996/2402) |
| | (3), (4) | 1 Apr 1997 (SI 1996/2959) |
| | (5) | 1 Oct 1996 (SI 1996/2402) |
| | (6) | 1 Apr 1997 (SI 1996/2959) |
| 166 | | 1 Apr 1997 (SI 1996/2959) |
| 167 | (1), (2) | 23 Oct 1996 (for the purposes of requiring a local housing authority to consult on an allocation scheme prior to its adoption and enabling them to adopt a scheme) (SI 1996/2658) |
| | | 1 Apr 1997 (otherwise) (SI 1996/2959) |
| | (3), (4) | 1 Oct 1996 (SI 1996/2402) |
| | (5) | 1 Oct 1996 (SI 1996/2402) |
| | (6)–(8) | 23 Oct 1996 (for the purposes of requiring a local housing authority to consult on an allocation scheme prior to its adoption and enabling them to adopt a scheme) (SI 1996/2658) |
| | | 1 Apr 1997 (otherwise) (SI 1996/2959) |
| 168 | | 1 Apr 1997 (SI 1996/2959) |
| 169 | | 1 Oct 1996 (SI 1996/2402) |
| 170, 171 | | 1 Apr 1997 (SI 1996/2959) |
| 172 | | 1 Oct 1996 (SI 1996/2402) |
| 173 | | See Sch 16 below |
| 174 | | 1 Oct 1996 (SI 1996/2402) |
| 175, 176 | | 20 Jan 1997 (SI 1996/2959) |
| 177 | (1), (2) | 20 Jan 1997 (SI 1996/2959) |
| | (3) | 1 Oct 1996 (SI 1996/2402) |
| 178–181 | | 20 Jan 1997 (SI 1996/2959) |
| 182 | | 1 Oct 1996 (SI 1996/2402) |
| 183 | (1) | 20 Jan 1997 (SI 1996/2959) |
| | (2) | 1 Oct 1996 (SI 1996/2402) |
| | (3) | 20 Jan 1997 (SI 1996/2959) |
| 184 | | 20 Jan 1997 (SI 1996/2959) |
| 185 | (1) | 20 Jan 1997 (SI 1996/2959) |
| | (2), (3) | 1 Oct 1996 (orders etc) (SI 1996/2402) |
| | | 20 Jan 1997 (otherwise) (SI 1996/2959) |
| | (4) | 20 Jan 1997 (SI 1996/2959) |
| 186–188 | | 20 Jan 1997 (SI 1996/2959) |
| 189 | (1) | 20 Jan 1997 (SI 1996/2959) |
| | (2)–(4) | 1 Oct 1996 (SI 1996/2402) |
| 190–193 | | 20 Jan 1997 (SI 1996/2959) |
| 194 | (1)–(5) | 20 Jan 1997 (SI 1996/2959) |
| | (6) | 1 Oct 1996 (orders etc) (SI 1996/2402) |
| | | 20 Jan 1997 (otherwise) (SI 1996/2959) |
| 195–197 | | 20 Jan 1997 (SI 1996/2959) |
| 198 | (1)–(3) | 20 Jan 1997 (SI 1996/2959) |
| | (4)–(7) | 1 Oct 1996 (orders etc) (SI 1996/2402) |
| | | 20 Jan 1997 (otherwise) (SI 1996/2959) |
| 199 | (1)–(4) | 20 Jan 1997 (SI 1996/2959) |
| | (5) | 1 Oct 1996 (SI 1996/2402) |
| 200–202 | | 20 Jan 1997 (SI 1996/2959) |
| 203 | (1), (2) | 1 Oct 1996 (SI 1996/2402) |
| | (3)–(6) | 20 Jan 1997 (SI 1996/2959) |
| | (7) | 1 Oct 1996 (SI 1996/2402) |
| | (8) | 20 Jan 1997 (SI 1996/2959) |
| 204–206 | | 20 Jan 1997 (SI 1996/2959) |
| 207 | (1)–(3) | 20 Jan 1997 (SI 1996/2959) |
| | (4)–(6) | 1 Oct 1996 (orders etc) (SI 1996/2402) |
| | | 20 Jan 1997 (otherwise) (SI 1996/2959) |
| 208, 209 | | 20 Jan 1997 (SI 1996/2959) |

**Housing Act 1996 (c 52)**—*contd*

| | | |
|---|---|---|
| 210 | (1) | 20 Jan 1997 (SI 1996/2959) |
| | (2) | 1 Oct 1996 (SI 1996/2402) |
| 211–214 | | 20 Jan 1997 (SI 1996/2959) |
| 215 | | 1 Oct 1996 (SI 1996/2402) |
| 216 | (1), (2) | 20 Jan 1997 (SI 1996/2959) |
| | (3) | See Sch 17 below |
| 217, 218 | | 1 Oct 1996 (SI 1996/2402) |
| 219, 220 | | 24 Sep 1996 (SI 1996/2402) |
| 221 | | 24 Sep 1996 (s 232(2)) |
| 222 | | See Sch 18 below |
| 223–226 | | 24 Jul 1996 (s 232(1)) |
| 227 | | See Sch 19 below |
| 228–233 | | 24 Jul 1996 (s 232(1)) |
| Sch 1 | para 1 | 1 Oct 1996 (subject to transitional provisions) (SI 1996/2402) |
| | para 2(1) | 1 Oct 1996 (subject to transitional provisions) (SI 1996/2402) |
| | para 2(2)(a)–(e) | 1 Oct 1996 (subject to transitional provisions) (SI 1996/2402) |
| | para 2(2)(f) | 1 Aug 1996 (for the purpose of conferring upon the Secretary of State, the Housing Corporation or Housing for Wales a power to consult, to make determinations, to give consents and to delegate functions) (SI 1996/2048) |
| | | 1 Oct 1996 (otherwise) (subject to transitional provisions) (SI 1996/2402) |
| | para 2(3), (4) | 1 Oct 1996 (subject to transitional provisions) (SI 1996/2402) |
| | para 3(1), (2) | 1 Aug 1996 (SI 1996/2048) |
| | para 3(3) | 1 Oct 1996 (subject to transitional provisions) (SI 1996/2402) |
| | paras 4–15 | 1 Oct 1996 (subject to transitional provisions) (SI 1996/2402) |
| | para 16(1), (2) | 1 Aug 1996 (SI 1996/2048) |
| | para 16(3)–(5) | 1 Oct 1996 (subject to transitional provisions) (SI 1996/2402) |
| | paras 17–26 | 1 Oct 1996 (subject to transitional provisions) (SI 1996/2402) |
| | para 27(1)–(3) | 1 Oct 1996 (subject to transitional provisions) (SI 1996/2402) |
| | para 27(4) | 1 Aug 1996 (for the purpose of conferring upon the Secretary of State, the Housing Corporation or Housing for Wales a power to consult, to make determinations, to give consents and to delegate functions) (SI 1996/2048) |
| | | 1 Oct 1996 (otherwise) (subject to transitional provisions) (SI 1996/2402) |
| | para 27(5), (6) | 1 Oct 1996 (subject to transitional provisions) (SI 1996/2402) |
| | paras 28, 29 | 1 Oct 1996 (subject to transitional provisions) (SI 1996/2402) |
| Sch 2 | para 1 | 1 Apr 1997 (subject to a saving for complaints against any social landlord which is or at any time was registered with Housing for Wales) (SI 1997/618) |
| | paras 2–6 | 1 Aug 1996 (subject to a saving for complaints against any social landlord which is or at any time was registered with Housing for Wales) (SI 1996/2048) |
| | paras 7–9 | 1 Apr 1997 (subject to a saving for complaints against any social landlord which is or at any time was registered with Housing for Wales) (SI 1997/618) |
| | para 10 | 1 Aug 1996 (subject to a saving for complaints against any social landlord which is or at any time was registered with Housing for Wales) (SI 1996/2048) |
| | para 11(1) | 1 Aug 1996 (subject to a saving for complaints against any social landlord which is or at any time was registered with Housing for Wales) (1996/2048) |
| | para 11(2) | 1 Apr 1997 (subject to a saving for complaints against any social landlord which is or at any time was registered with Housing for Wales) (SI 1997/618) |
| | para 11(3), (4) | 1 Aug 1996 (subject to a saving for complaints against any social landlord which is or at any time was registered with Housing for Wales) (SI 1996/2048) |

**Housing Act 1996 (c 52)**—*contd*

| | | |
|---|---|---|
| Sch 3 | para 1(1)–(4) | 1 Oct 1996 (subject to transitional provisions and savings) (SI 1996/2402) |
| | para 1(5) | 1 Apr 1997 (SI 1997/618) |
| | paras 2–5 | 1 Oct 1996 (subject to transitional provisions and savings) (SI 1996/2402) |
| | para 6 | 1 Aug 1996 (SI 1996/2048) |
| | para 7 | 1 Aug 1996 (for the purposes of enabling a determination to be made under Housing Associations Act 1985, s 87(3) with respect to financial assistance under that section) (SI 1996/2048) |
| | | 1 Oct 1996 (otherwise) (subject to transitional provisions and savings) (SI 1996/2402) |
| | para 8 | 1 Oct 1996 (subject to transitional provisions and savings) (SI 1996/2402) |
| | para 9 | 1 Aug 1996 (SI 1996/2048) |
| | paras 10, 11 | 1 Oct 1996 (subject to transitional provisions and savings) (SI 1996/2402) |
| Sch 4 | | 1 Oct 1996 (SI 1996/2212) |
| Sch 5 | | *Not yet in force* |
| Sch 6 | Pts I–III | 1 Oct 1996 (SI 1996/2212) |
| | Pt IV, paras 1–6 | 1 Oct 1996 (subject to savings) (SI 1996/2212) |
| | Pt IV, para 7 | 23 Aug 1996 (for the power of conferring power to make orders, regulations or rules) (SI 1996/2212) |
| | | 1 Oct 1996 (otherwise, but subject to savings) (SI 1996/2212) |
| | Pt IV, paras 8–11 | 1 Oct 1996 (subject to savings) (SI 1996/2212) |
| Sch 7 | | 23 Aug 1996 (so far as relates to the insertion of Housing Act 1988, Sch 2A, paras 7(2)(a), 9(2)(a) for the purpose of conferring power to make orders, regulations or rules) (SI 1996/2212) |
| | | 28 Feb 1997 (otherwise) (SI 1997/225) |
| Sch 8 | | 28 Feb 1997 (SI 1997/225) |
| Sch 9 | para 1 | 23 Aug 1996 (for the purpose of conferring power to make orders, regulations or rules) (SI 1996/2212) |
| | | 1 Apr 1997 (otherwise and subject to savings) (SI 1997/618) |
| | paras 2–5 | 1 Apr 1997 (subject to savings) (SI 1997/618) |
| Schs 10, 11 | | 1 Oct 1996 (SI 1996/2212) |
| Schs 12, 13 | | 1 Apr 1997 (SI 1997/618) |
| Sch 14 | | 12 Feb 1997 (SI 1997/66) |
| Sch 15 | | 15 Oct 2001 (SI 2001/3164) |
| Sch 16 | para 1 | 1 Apr 1997 (SI 1996/2959) |
| | para 2 | 1 Apr 1997 (subject to transitional provisions) (SI 1996/2959) |
| | para 3 | 1 Apr 1997 (SI 1996/2959) |
| Sch 17 | | 20 Jan 1997 (SI 1996/2959) |
| Sch 18 | paras 1–23 | 1 Oct 1996 (SI 1996/2402) |
| | para 24 | 24 Sep 1996 (s 232(2)) |
| | para 25 | 1 Oct 1996 (SI 1996/2402) |
| | paras 26–29 | 24 Sep 1996 (s 232(2)) |
| | para 30 | 24 Sep 1996 (SI 1996/2402) |
| Sch 19 | Pt I | 1 Oct 1996 (subject to savings) (SI 1996/2402) |
| | Pt II | 3 Mar 1997 (SI 1997/596) |
| | Pt III | 1 Oct 1996 (repeals in Landlord and Tenant Act 1987, subject to savings) (SI 1996/2212) |
| | | 1 Sep 1997 (SI 1997/1851), repeals in— Landlord and Tenant Act 1985; Arbitration Act 1996 |
| | Pt IV | 28 Feb 1997 (SI 1997/225) |
| | Pt V | 1 Oct 1996 (except repeal in Leasehold Reform, Housing and Urban Development Act 1993, s 39(3) and subject to savings) (SI 1996/2212) |
| | | 1 Apr 1997 (exception noted above) (SI 1997/618) |

**Housing Act 1996 (c 52)**—*contd*

|  |  |
|---|---|
| Pt VI | 1 Apr 1997 (subject to transitional provisions and savings) (SI 1997/618) |
| Pt VII | 1 Apr 1997 (SI 1996/2959) |
| Pt VIII | 20 Jan 1997 (subject to transitional provisions) (SI 1996/2959) |
| Pt IX | 1 Oct 1996 (except repeal in Housing Act 1988, s 79(2)(a) and subject to savings) (SI 1996/2402) |
|  | *Not yet in force* (exception noted above, which is now superseded) |
| Pts X–XIII | 1 Oct 1996 (subject to savings) (SI 1996/2402) |
| Pt XIV | 24 Sep 1996 (repeals in Housing Act 1985) (s 232(2)) |
|  | 24 Sep 1996 (repeal in Local Government (Wales) Act 1994) (SI 1996/2402) |
|  | *Not yet in force*, repeals of or in— Consumer Credit Act 1974; Building Societies Act 1986 |

## Housing Grants, Construction and Regeneration Act 1996 (c 53)

*RA:* 24 Jul 1996

*Commencement provisions:* s 150(1)–(3); Housing Grants, Construction and Regeneration Act 1996 (Commencement No 1) Order 1996, SI 1996/2352; Housing Grants, Construction and Regeneration Act 1996 (Commencement No 2 and Revocation, Savings, Supplementary and Transitional Provisions) Order 1996, SI 1996/2842; Housing Grants, Construction and Regeneration Act 1996 (Commencement No 3) Order 1997, SI 1997/2846; Housing Grants, Construction and Regeneration Act (England and Wales) (Commencement No 4) Order 1998, SI 1998/650; Housing Grants, Construction and Regeneration Act 1996 (Scotland) (Commencement No 5) Order 1998, SI 1998/894

In the following table, the abbreviation "orders etc" means "so far as confers on the Secretary of State or the Lord Advocate a power to consult, to make orders, regulations or determinations, to give directions, guidance, approvals or consents, to specify matters, or to impose conditions"

| | |
|---|---|
| 1 | 17 Dec 1996 (SI 1996/2842) |
| 2, 3 | 11 Sep 1996 (orders etc) (SI 1996/2352) |
| | 17 Dec 1996 (otherwise) (SI 1996/2842) |
| 4–6 | 17 Dec 1996 (SI 1996/2842) |
| 7 | 11 Sep 1996 (orders etc) (SI 1996/2352) |
| | 17 Dec 1996 (otherwise) (SI 1996/2842) |
| 8–11 | 17 Dec 1996 (SI 1996/2842) |
| 12 | 11 Sep 1996 (orders etc) (SI 1996/2352) |
| | 17 Dec 1996 (otherwise) (SI 1996/2842) |
| 13–16 | 17 Dec 1996 (SI 1996/2842) |
| 17 | 11 Sep 1996 (orders etc) (SI 1996/2352) |
| | 17 Dec 1996 (otherwise) (SI 1996/2842) |
| 18 | 17 Dec 1996 (SI 1996/2842) |
| 19 | 11 Sep 1996 (orders etc) (SI 1996/2352) |
| | 17 Dec 1996 (otherwise) (SI 1996/2842) |
| 20–24 | 17 Dec 1996 (SI 1996/2842) |
| 25 | 11 Sep 1996 (orders etc) (SI 1996/2352) |
| | 17 Dec 1996 (otherwise) (SI 1996/2842) |
| 26 | 17 Dec 1996 (SI 1996/2842) |
| 27 | 11 Sep 1996 (orders etc) (SI 1996/2352) |
| | 17 Dec 1996 (otherwise) (SI 1996/2842) |
| 28, 29 | 17 Dec 1996 (SI 1996/2842) |
| 30 | 11 Sep 1996 (orders etc) (SI 1996/2352) |
| | 17 Dec 1996 (otherwise) (SI 1996/2842) |
| 31 | 13 Nov 1996 (so far as confers on the Secretary of State a power to make regulations) (SI 1996/2842) |
| | 17 Dec 1996 (otherwise) (SI 1996/2842) |
| 32 | 17 Dec 1996 (SI 1996/2842) |

**Housing Grants, Construction and Regeneration Act 1996 (c 53)**—*contd*

| | |
|---|---|
| 33 | 11 Sep 1996 (orders etc) (SI 1996/2352) |
| | 17 Dec 1996 (otherwise) (SI 1996/2842) |
| 34–43 | 17 Dec 1996 (SI 1996/2842) |
| 44–47 | 11 Sep 1996 (orders etc) (SI 1996/2352) |
| | 17 Dec 1996 (otherwise) (SI 1996/2842) |
| 48–50 | 17 Dec 1996 (SI 1996/2842) |
| 51, 52 | 11 Sep 1996 (orders etc) (SI 1996/2352) |
| | 17 Dec 1996 (otherwise) (SI 1996/2842) |
| 53–60 | 17 Dec 1996 (SI 1996/2842) |
| 61 | 11 Sep 1996 (orders etc) (SI 1996/2352) |
| | 17 Dec 1996 (otherwise) (SI 1996/2842) |
| 62 | 17 Dec 1996 (SI 1996/2842) |
| 63, 64 | 11 Sep 1996 (orders etc) (SI 1996/2352) |
| | 17 Dec 1996 (otherwise) (SI 1996/2842) |
| 65, 66 | 17 Dec 1996 (SI 1996/2842) |
| 67, 68 | 11 Sep 1996 (orders etc) (SI 1996/2352) |
| | 17 Dec 1996 (otherwise) (SI 1996/2842) |
| 69–73 | 17 Dec 1996 (SI 1996/2842) |
| 74 | 11 Sep 1996 (SI 1996/2352) |
| 75 | 17 Dec 1996 (SI 1996/2842) |
| 76 | 11 Sep 1996 (orders etc) (SI 1996/2352) |
| | 17 Dec 1996 (otherwise) (SI 1996/2842) |
| 77, 78 | 17 Dec 1996 (SI 1996/2842) |
| 79 | 11 Sep 1996 (SI 1996/2352) |
| 80–84 | 17 Dec 1996 (SI 1996/2842) |
| 85 | 11 Sep 1996 (orders etc) (SI 1996/2352) |
| | 17 Dec 1996 (otherwise) (SI 1996/2842) |
| 86 | 11 Sep 1996 (SI 1996/2352) |
| 87 | 11 Sep 1996 (orders etc) (SI 1996/2352) |
| | 17 Dec 1996 (otherwise) (SI 1996/2842) |
| 88 | 17 Dec 1996 (SI 1996/2842) |
| 89 | 11 Sep 1996 (SI 1996/2352) |
| 90, 91 | 17 Dec 1996 (SI 1996/2842) |
| 92 | 11 Sep 1996 (orders etc) (SI 1996/2352) |
| | 17 Dec 1996 (otherwise) (SI 1996/2842) |
| 93 | 17 Dec 1996 (SI 1996/2842) |
| 94 | 11 Sep 1996 (SI 1996/2352) |
| 95–100 | 17 Dec 1996 (SI 1996/2842) |
| 101 | 11 Sep 1996 (orders etc) (SI 1996/2352) |
| | 17 Dec 1996 (otherwise) (SI 1996/2352) |
| 102 | 11 Sep 1996 (orders etc) (SI 1996/2352) |
| | 17 Dec 1996 (otherwise, and subject to transitional provisions) (SI 1996/2842) |
| 103 | 17 Dec 1996 (SI 1996/2842) |
| 104–106 | 11 Sep 1996 (orders etc) (SI 1996/2352) |
| | 1 May 1998 (E) (W) (otherwise) (SI 1998/650) |
| | 1 May 1998 (S) (otherwise) (SI 1998/894) |
| 107 | 1 May 1998 (E) (W) (SI 1998/650) |
| | 1 May 1998 (S) (SI 1998/894) |
| 108 | 11 Sep 1996 (orders etc) (SI 1996/2352) |
| | 1 May 1998 (E) (W) (otherwise) (SI 1998/650) |
| | 1 May 1998 (S) (otherwise) (SI 1998/894) |
| 109–113 | 1 May 1998 (E) (W) (SI 1998/650) |
| | 1 May 1998 (S) (SI 1998/894) |
| 114 | 11 Sep 1996 (orders etc) (SI 1996/2352) |
| | 1 May 1998 (E) (W) (otherwise) (SI 1998/650) |
| | 1 May 1998 (S) (otherwise) (SI 1998/894) |
| 115–117 | 1 May 1998 (E) (W) (SI 1998/650) |
| | 1 May 1998 (S) (SI 1998/894) |

**Housing Grants, Construction and Regeneration Act 1996 (c 53)**—*contd*

| | | |
|---|---|---|
| 118–124 | | 1 Apr 1997 (SI 1996/2842) |
| 125 | (1) | See Sch 2 below |
| | (2)–(4) | 1 Apr 1997 (SI 1996/2842) |
| 126–130 | | 24 Sep 1996 (s 150(2)) |
| 131–135 | | 11 Sep 1996 (orders etc) (SI 1996/2352) |
| | | 16 Dec 1997 (otherwise) (SI 1997/2846) |
| 136–138 | | 16 Dec 1997 (SI 1997/2846) |
| 139, 140 | | 11 Sep 1996 (orders etc) (SI 1996/2352) |
| | | 16 Dec 1997 (otherwise) (SI 1997/2846) |
| 141–145 | | 24 Sep 1996 (s 150(2)) |
| 146 | | 24 Jul 1996 (s 150(1)) |
| 147 | | See Sch 3 below |
| 148–151 | | 24 Jul 1996 (s 150(1)) |
| Sch 1 | | 17 Dec 1996 (SI 1996/2842) |
| Sch 2 | paras 1–20 | 1 Apr 1997 (SI 1996/2842) |
| | para 21(1)–(3) | 1 Oct 1996 (SI 1996/2352) |
| | para 21(4) | 1 Apr 1997 (SI 1996/2842) |
| | paras 22–35 | 1 Apr 1997 (SI 1996/2842) |
| Sch 3 | Pt I | 17 Dec 1996 (subject to savings and transitional provisions relating to Local Government and Housing Act 1989) (SI 1996/2842) |
| | Pt II | 1 Apr 1997 (SI 1996/2842) |
| | Pt III | 24 Sep 1996 (s 150(2)) |

---

**Humber Bridge (Debts) Act 1996 (c 1)**

*RA:* 29 Feb 1996

Whole Act in force 29 Feb 1996 (RA)

---

**Industrial Tribunals Act 1996 (c 17)**

See Employment Tribunals Act 1996

---

**Law Reform (Year and a Day Rule) Act 1996 (c 19)**

*RA:* 17 Jun 1996

*Commencement provisions:* s 3(3)

| | |
|---|---|
| 1 | 17 Jun 1996 (subject to a saving) (RA) |
| 2 | 17 Aug 1996 (but applies to the institution of proceedings after 17 Aug 1996 in any case where the death occurred between 17 Jun 1996 and 17 Aug 1996) (s 3(3)) |
| 3 | 17 Jun 1996 (RA) |

---

**Licensing (Amendment) (Scotland) Act 1996 (c 36)**

*RA:* 18 Jul 1996

*Commencement provisions:* s 3(2); Licensing (Amendment) (Scotland) Act 1996 Commencement Order 1996, SI 1996/2670

Whole Act in force 21 Oct 1996 (SI 1996/2670)

---

## London Regional Transport Act 1996 (c 21)

*RA:* 17 Jun 1996

*Commencement provisions:* s 6(2)

Whole Act in force 17 Aug 1996 (s 6(2))

## Marriage Ceremony (Prescribed Words) Act 1996 (c 34)

*RA:* 18 Jul 1996

*Commencement provisions:* s 2(2); Marriage Ceremony (Prescribed Words) Act 1996 (Commencement) Order 1996, SI 1996/2506

Whole Act in force 1 Feb 1997 (SI 1996/2506)

## National Health Service (Residual Liabilities) Act 1996 (c 15)

*RA:* 22 May 1996

Whole Act in force 22 May 1996 (RA)

## Noise Act 1996 (c 37)

*RA:* 18 Jul 1996

*Commencement provisions:* s 14(2); Noise Act 1996 (Commencement No 1) Order 1996, SI 1996/2219; Noise Act 1996 (Commencement No 2) Order 1997, SI 1997/1695; Noise Act 1996 (Commencement) Order (Northern Ireland) 1997, SR 1997/366

| | | |
|---|---|---|
| 1–9 | | 23 Jul 1997 (E) (W) (SI 1997/1695) |
| | | 1 Sep 1997 (NI) (SR 1997/366) |
| 10 | (1)–(6) | 23 Jul 1997 (E) (W) (SI 1997/1695) |
| | | 1 Sep 1997 (NI) (SR 1997/366) |
| | (7) | 19 Sep 1996 (SI 1996/2219) |
| | (8) | 19 Sep 1996 (E) (W) (so far as relates to the power of a local authority under Environmental Protection Act 1990, s 81(3), to abate a statutory nuisance by virtue of s 79(1)(g) of that Act) (SI 1996/2219) |
| | | 23 Jul 1997 (E) (W) (otherwise) (SI 1997/1695) |
| | | 1 Sep 1997 (NI) (SR 1997/366) |
| | (9) | See Schedule below |
| 11, 12 | | 19 Sep 1996 (E) (W) (so far as relates to the power of a local authority under Environmental Protection Act 1990, s 81(3), to abate a statutory nuisance by virtue of s 79(1)(g) of that Act) (SI 1996/2219) |
| | | 23 Jul 1997 (E) (W) (otherwise) (SI 1997/1695) |
| | | 1 Sep 1997 (NI) (SR 1997/366) |
| 13 | | 19 Sep 1996 (E) (W) (SI 1996/2219) |
| | | 1 Sep 1997 (NI) (SR 1997/366) |
| 14 | (1)–(3) | 19 Sep 1996 (E) (W) (SI 1996/2219) |
| | | 1 Sep 1997 (NI) (SR 1997/366) |
| | (4) | 23 Jul 1997 (E) (W) (SI 1997/1695) |
| | | 1 Sep 1997 (NI) (SR 1997/366) |
| Schedule | | 19 Sep 1996 (E) (W) (so far as relates to the power of a local authority under Environmental Protection Act 1990, s 81(3), to abate a statutory nuisance by virtue of s 79(1)(g) of that Act) (SI 1996/2219) |
| | | 23 Jul 1997 (E) (W) (otherwise) (SI 1997/1695) |
| | | 1 Sep 1997 (NI) (SR 1997/366) |

## Non-Domestic Rating (Information) Act 1996 (c 13)

*RA:* 22 May 1996

Whole Act in force 22 May 1996 (RA)

---

## Northern Ireland (Emergency Provisions) Act 1996 (c 22)

*RA:* 17 Jun 1996

*Commencement provisions:* s 62(1)

Whole Act in force 25 Aug 1996 (s 62(1))

---

## Northern Ireland (Entry to Negotiations, etc) Act 1996 (c 11)

*RA:* 29 Apr 1996

Whole Act in force 29 Apr 1996 (RA)

---

## Nursery Education and Grant-Maintained Schools Act 1996 (c 50)

*RA:* 24 Jul 1996

*Commencement provisions:* s 11(3); Nursery Education and Grant-Maintained Schools Act 1996 (Commencement No 1) Order 1996, SI 1996/2022; Nursery Education and Grant-Maintained Schools Act 1996 (Commencement No 2) Order 1996, SI 1996/3192

| | | |
|---|---|---|
| 1–4 | | 1 Sep 1996 (SI 1996/2022) |
| 5 | | See Sch 1 below |
| 6–11 | | 1 Sep 1996 (SI 1996/2022) |
| Sch 1 | paras 1–5 | 1 Sep 1996 (SI 1996/2022) |
| | para 6(1)(a) | 1 Sep 1996 (except in so far as it relates to inspections under this sub-para) (SI 1996/2022) |
| | | 10 Dec 1996 (for the purpose of empowering the making of regulations under this sub-para) (SI 1996/3192) |
| | | 1 Jan 1997 (otherwise) (SI 1996/3192) |
| | para 6(1)(b), (c) | 1 Sep 1996 (SI 1996/2022) |
| | para 6(2) | 1 Jan 1997 (SI 1996/3192) |
| | para 6(3) | 1 Sep 1996 (except in so far as it relates to inspections under para 6(1)(a)) (SI 1996/2022) |
| | | 1 Jan 1997 (otherwise) (SI 1996/3192) |
| | para 6(4) | 1 Sep 1996 (SI 1996/2022) |
| | para 6(5) | 10 Dec 1996 (SI 1996/3192) |
| | para 6(6) | 1 Sep 1996 (SI 1996/2022) |
| | para 7 | 1 Sep 1996 (SI 1996/2022) |
| | para 8(1) | 1 Sep 1996 (SI 1996/2022) |
| | para 8(2) | 1 Sep 1996 (except in so far as it relates to inspections under para 6(1)(a)) (SI 1996/2022) |
| | | 1 Jan 1997 (otherwise) (SI 1996/3192) |
| | para 8(3)–(9) | 1 Sep 1996 (SI 1996/2022) |
| | paras 9–13 | 1 Sep 1996 (SI 1996/2022) |
| | para 14 | 1 Sep 1996 (except in so far as it relates to inspections under para 6(1)(a)) (SI 1996/2022) |
| | | 1 Apr 1997 (otherwise) (SI 1996/3192) |
| | para 15 | 1 Sep 1996 (SI 1996/2022) |
| | para 16 | 1 Jan 1997 (SI 1996/3192) |
| | para 17 | 1 Sep 1996 (SI 1996/2022) |
| Schs 2–4 | | 1 Sep 1996 (SI 1996/2022) |

## Offensive Weapons Act 1996 (c 26)

*RA:* 4 Jul 1996

*Commencement provisions:* ss 4(4), 6(3); Offensive Weapons Act 1996 (Commencement No 1) Order 1996, SI 1996/2071; Offensive Weapons Act 1996 (Commencement No 2) Order 1996, SI 1996/3063

| | | |
|---|---|---|
| 1–3 | | 4 Jul 1996 (RA) |
| 4 | (1)–(3) | 1 Sep 1996 (SI 1996/2071) |
| | (4) | 4 Jul 1996 (RA) |
| 5 | | 4 Jul 1996 (RA) |
| 6 | (1), (2) | 1 Jan 1997 (SI 1996/3063) |
| | (3) | 4 Jul 1996 (RA) |
| 7 | | 4 Jul 1996 (RA) |

## Party Wall etc Act 1996 (c 40)

*RA:* 18 Jul 1996

*Commencement provisions:* s 22(2); Party Wall etc Act 1996 (Commencement) Order 1997, SI 1997/670

Whole Act in force 1 Jul 1997 (SI 1997/670) (subject to transitional provisions relating to ss 1, 2 and 6)

## Police Act 1996 (c 16)

*RA:* 22 May 1996

*Commencement provisions:* s 104; Police Act 1996 (Commencement and Transitional Provisions) Order 1999, SI 1999/533

| | | |
|---|---|---|
| 1–49 | | 22 Aug 1996 (s 104(1)) |
| 50 | (1), (2) | 22 Aug 1996 (s 104(1)) |
| | (3) | 1 Apr 1999 (SI 1999/533) |
| | (4)–(8) | 22 Aug 1996 (s 104(1)) |
| 51–64 | | 22 Aug 1996 (s 104(1)) |
| 65–74 | | 1 Apr 1999 (SI 1999/533) |
| 75 | | 1 Apr 1999 (subject to transitional provisions) (SI 1999/533) |
| 76–84 | | 1 Apr 1999 (SI 1999/533) |
| 85 | | 1 Apr 1999 (subject to transitional provisions) (SI 1999/533) |
| 86, 87 | | 1 Apr 1999 (SI 1999/533) |
| 88–102 | | 22 Aug 1996 (s 104(1)) |
| 103 | (1) | See Sch 7 below |
| | (2) | See Sch 8 below |
| | (3) | See Sch 9 below |
| 104–106 | | 22 Aug 1996 (s 104(1)) |
| Schs 1–4 | | 22 Aug 1996 (s 104(1)) |
| Schs 5, 6 | | 1 Apr 1999 (SI 1999/533) |
| Sch 7 | paras 1–42 | 22 Aug 1996 (s 104(1)) |
| | para 43 | 1 Apr 1999 (SI 1999/533) |
| | para 44 | 22 Aug 1996 (s 104(1)) |
| | paras 45, 46 | 1 Apr 1999 (SI 1999/533) |
| | para 47 | 22 Aug 1996 (s 104(1)) |
| Sch 8 | paras 1–11 | 22 Aug 1996 (s 104(1)) |
| | para 12 | 1 Apr 1999 (SI 1999/533) |
| | para 13 | 22 Aug 1996 (s 104(1)) |
| Sch 9 | Pt I | 22 Aug 1996 (s 104(1)) |
| | Pt II | 1 Apr 1999 (SI 1999/533) |
| | Pt III | 22 Aug 1996 (s 104(1)) |

**Prevention of Terrorism (Additional Powers) Act 1996 (c 7)**

*RA:* 3 Apr 1996

Whole Act in force 3 Apr 1996 (RA)

---

**Prisoners' Earnings Act 1996 (c 33)**

*RA:* 18 Jul 1996

*Commencement provisions:* s 5(2); Prisoners' Earnings Act 1996 (Commencement) (England and Wales) Order 2011, SI 2011/1658

| | | |
|---|---|---|
| 1–3 | | 26 Sep 2011 (SI 2011/1658) |
| 4 | (1), (2) | 26 Sep 2011 (SI 2011/1658) |
| | (3) | *Not yet in force* |
| 5 | | 26 Sep 2011 (SI 2011/1658) |

---

**Public Order (Amendment) Act 1996 (c 59)**

*RA:* 17 Oct 1996

Whole Act in force 17 Oct 1996 (RA)

---

**Railway Heritage Act 1996 (c 42)**

*RA:* 18 Jul 1996

*Commencement provisions:* s 8(3)

Whole Act in force 18 Sep 1996 (s 8(3))

---

**Rating (Caravans and Boats) Act 1996 (c 12)**

*RA:* 29 Apr 1996

Whole Act in force 29 Apr 1996 (RA)

---

**Reserve Forces Act 1996 (c 14)**

*RA:* 22 May 1996

*Commencement provisions:* ss 121(2), 132(4); Reserve Forces Act 1996 (Commencement No 1) Order 1997, SI 1997/305

| | | |
|---|---|---|
| 1–120 | | 1 Apr 1997 (SI 1997/305) |
| 121 | (1) | 1 Apr 1997 (SI 1997/305) |
| | (2) | 22 May 1996 (s 121(2)) |
| 122–130 | | 1 Apr 1997 (SI 1997/305) |
| 131 | (1) | 1 Apr 1997 (SI 1997/305) |
| | (2) | See Sch 11 below |
| Schs 1–10 | | 1 Apr 1997 (SI 1997/305) |
| Sch 11 | | 1 Apr 1997 (except repeals of or in Reserve Forces Act 1980, ss 10, 11, 13(2)–(4), 16, 17, 18(1), (2), 19, 20(1), 21, 22, 24–26, 28, 29, 30(1), (2), 31, 32, 34(1)–(3), 35, 36, 38, 39(1)(a), (b), 40–42, 44, 47, 50, 57, 58, 63, 67, 69, 70, 83(1), (2), 87, 93, 100, 101, 120, 139(1), 141–144, 145(1)(b), (2), 146(1)(b), (2), 154(1), 155, Sch 2, Sch 8, paras 1, 4, 5(1), (3), 6–8, 10–15, 16(2), (3), (5)–(10), 17, 19, 20) (SI 1997/305) |
| | | *Not yet in force* (exceptions noted above) |

---

## School Inspections Act 1996 (c 57)

*RA:* 24 Jul 1996

*Commencement provisions:* s 48(2)

Whole Act in force 1 Nov 1996 (s 48(2))

---

## Security Service Act 1996 (c 35)

*RA:* 18 Jul 1996

*Commencement provisions:* s 4(2); Security Service Act 1996 (Commencement) Order 1996, SI 1996/2454

Whole Act in force 14 Oct 1996 (SI 1996/2454)

---

## Sexual Offences (Conspiracy and Incitement) Act 1996 (c 29)

*RA:* 4 Jul 1996

*Commencement provisions:* s 7(2); Sexual Offences (Conspiracy and Incitement) Act 1996 (Commencement) Order 1996, SI 1996/2262

Whole Act in force 1 Oct 1996 (SI 1996/2262)

---

## Social Security (Overpayments) Act 1996 (c 51)

*RA:* 24 Jul 1996

Whole Act in force 24 Jul 1996 (RA)

---

## Statutory Instruments (Production and Sale) Act 1996 (c 54)

*RA:* 24 Jul 1996

Whole Act in force 24 Jul 1996 (RA)

---

## Theft (Amendment) Act 1996 (c 62)

*RA:* 18 Dec 1996

Whole Act in force 18 Dec 1996 (RA)

---

## Trading Schemes Act 1996 (c 32)

*RA:* 4 Jul 1996

*Commencement provisions:* s 5(2); Trading Schemes Act 1996 (Commencement) Order 1997, SI 1997/29

Whole Act in force 6 Feb 1997 (SI 1997/29)

---

## Treasure Act 1996 (c 24)

*RA:* 4 Jul 1996

*Commencement provisions:* s 15(2); Treasure Act 1996 (Commencement No 1) Order 1997, SI 1997/760; Treasure Act 1996 (Commencement No 2) Order 1997, SI 1997/1977

| | |
|---|---|
| 1–10 | 24 Sep 1997 (SI 1997/1977) |
| 11 | 13 Mar 1997 (SI 1997/760) |

**Treasure Act 1996 (c 24)**—*contd*

12–15  24 Sep 1997 (SI 1997/1977)

**Trusts of Land and Appointment of Trustees Act 1996 (c 47)**

*RA:* 24 Jul 1996

*Commencement provisions:* s 27(2); Trusts of Land and Appointment of Trustees Act 1996 (Commencement)
Order 1996, SI 1996/2974

Whole Act in force 1 Jan 1997 (SI 1996/2974)

**Wild Mammals (Protection) Act 1996 (c 3)**

*RA:* 29 Feb 1996

*Commencement provisions:* s 7(2)

Whole Act in force 29 Apr 1996 (s 7(2))

# 1997 Acts

## Appropriation Act 1997 (c 31)

*RA:* 21 Mar 1997

Whole Act in force 21 Mar 1997 (RA)

---

## Appropriation (No 2) Act 1997 (c 57)

*RA:* 31 Jul 1997

Whole Act in force 31 Jul 1997 (RA)

---

## Architects Act 1997 (c 22)

*RA:* 19 Mar 1997

*Commencement provisions:* s 28(2); Architects Act 1997 (Commencement) Order 1997, SI 1997/1672

| | |
|---|---|
| 1–27 | 21 Jul 1997 (SI 1997/1672) |
| 28 | 19 Mar 1997 (RA) |
| Schs 1–3 | 21 Jul 1997 (SI 1997/1672) |

---

## Birds (Registration Charges) Act 1997 (c 55)

*RA:* 21 Mar 1997

Whole Act in force 21 Mar 1997 (RA)

---

## British Nationality (Hong Kong) Act 1997 (c 20)

*RA:* 19 Mar 1997

Whole Act in force 19 Mar 1997 (RA)

---

## Building Societies Act 1997 (c 32)

*RA:* 21 Mar 1997

*Commencement provisions:* s 47(3); Building Societies Act 1997 (Commencement No 1) Order 1997, SI 1997/1307; Building Societies Act 1997 (Commencement No 2) Order 1997, SI 1997/1427; Building Societies Act 1997 (Commencement No 3) Order 1997, SI 1997/2668

| | | |
|---|---|---|
| 1–6 | | 1 Dec 1997 (SI 1997/2668)[1] |
| 7 | | 1 Dec 1997 (SI 1997/2668) |
| 8–10 | | 1 Dec 1997 (SI 1997/2668)[1] |
| 11 | | 9 Jun 1997 (SI 1997/1427) |
| 12 | (1)(a) | 1 Dec 1997 (so far as relates to Building Societies Act 1986, s 13(7), Sch 4) (SI 1997/2668) |

**Building Societies Act 1997 (c 32)**—*contd*

| | | |
|---|---|---|
| | | 1 Dec 1997 (otherwise) (SI 1997/2668)[1] |
| | (1)(b)–(d) | 1 Dec 1997 (SI 1997/2668)[1] |
| | (2) | 1 Dec 1997 (SI 1997/2668) |
| | (3) | 1 Dec 1997 (SI 1997/2668)[1] |
| | (4) | 1 Dec 1997 (SI 1997/2668) |
| 13–15 | | 1 Dec 1997 (SI 1997/2668)[1] |
| 16–20 | | 9 Jun 1997 (SI 1997/1427) |
| 21 | | 1 Dec 1997 (SI 1997/2668)[1] |
| 22 | | 1 Dec 1997 (SI 1997/2668) |
| 23, 24 | | 9 Jun 1997 (so far as relates to conditions imposed or varied under Building Societies Act 1986, s 42A or directions under ss 42B(1), 43A of that Act) (SI 1997/1427) |
| | | 1 Dec 1997 (otherwise) (SI 1997/2668)[1] |
| 25–29 | | 1 Dec 1997 (SI 1997/2668)[1] |
| 30 | | 1 Dec 1997 (SI 1997/2668) |
| 31–33 | | 9 Jun 1997 (SI 1997/1427) |
| 34–36 | | 1 Dec 1997 (SI 1997/2668) |
| 37 | | 9 Jun 1997 (SI 1997/1427) |
| 38 | | 1 Dec 1997 (SI 1997/2668)[1] |
| 39 | | 1 Dec 1997 (SI 1997/2668) |
| 40, 41 | | 21 Mar 1997 (RA) |
| 42 | | 9 Jun 1997 (SI 1997/1427) |
| 43 | | See Sch 7 below |
| 44 | | 9 Jun 1997 (SI 1997/1427) |
| 45 | (1) | 9 Jun 1997 (SI 1997/1427) |
| | (2) | 1 Dec 1997 (SI 1997/2668)[1] |
| 46 | (1) | See Sch 8 below |
| | (2) | See Sch 9 below |
| 47 | | 21 Mar 1997 (RA) |
| Sch 1 | | 1 Dec 1997 (SI 1997/2668)[1] |
| Sch 2 | | 1 May 1999 (SI 1997/2668)[2] |
| Sch 3 | | 1 Dec 1997 (SI 1997/2668)[1] |
| Sch 4 | | 9 Jun 1997 (SI 1997/1427) |
| Schs 5, 6 | | 1 Dec 1997 (SI 1997/2668) |
| Sch 7 | para 1 | 1 Dec 1997 (SI 1997/2668)[1] |
| | para 2 | 2 Dec 1997 (SI 1997/2668) |
| | para 3(1)–(3) | 1 Dec 1997 (SI 1997/2668)[1] |
| | para 3(4) | 1 Dec 1997 (SI 1997/2668) |
| | para 4 | 1 Dec 1997 (SI 1997/2668) |
| | paras 5, 6 | 9 Jun 1997 (SI 1997/1427) |
| | para 7(1) | 9 Jun 1997 (SI 1997/1427) |
| | para 7(2)–(4) | 1 Dec 1997 (SI 1997/2668) |
| | paras 8, 9 | 9 Jun 1997 (SI 1997/1427) |
| | para 10 | 1 Dec 1997 (SI 1997/2668) |
| | para 11 | 1 Dec 1997 (SI 1997/2668)[1] |
| | para 12(1) | 9 Jun 1997 (SI 1997/1427) |
| | para 12(2) | 1 Dec 1997 (SI 1997/2668)[1] |
| | para 12(3) | 9 Jun 1997 (SI 1997/1427) |
| | para 12(4), (5) | 1 Dec 1997 (SI 1997/2668)[1] |
| | para 13(1) | 1 Dec 1997 (SI 1997/2668)[1] |
| | para 13(2) | 9 Jun 1997 (SI 1997/1427) |
| | para 14(1) | 9 Jun 1997 (so far as relates to a direction under Building Societies Act 1986, s 42B(1)) (SI 1997/1427) |
| | | 1 Dec 1997 (otherwise) (SI 1997/2668) |
| | para 14(2) | 1 Dec 1997 (SI 1997/2668) |
| | para 15(1) | 1 Dec 1997 (SI 1997/2668)[1] |
| | para 15(2) | 1 Dec 1997 (SI 1997/2668) |
| | para 15(3), (4) | 1 Dec 1997 (SI 1997/2668)[1] |
| | para 16 | 1 Dec 1997 (SI 1997/2668)[1] |

**Building Societies Act 1997 (c 32)**—*contd*

| | |
|---|---|
| para 17(1) | 9 Jun 1997 (SI 1997/1427) |
| para 17(2)–(4) | 1 Dec 1997 (SI 1997/2668)[1] |
| para 17(5)(a), (b) | 1 Dec 1997 (SI 1997/2668)[1] |
| para 17(5)(c) | 9 Jun 1997 (SI 1997/1427) |
| para 17(6)–(8) | 9 Jun 1997 (SI 1997/1427) |
| para 18 | 9 Jun 1997 (SI 1997/1427) |
| para 19(1), (2) | 9 Jun 1997 (SI 1997/1427) |
| para 19(3) | 1 Dec 1997 (SI 1997/2668)[1] |
| para 19(4) | 9 Jun 1997 (SI 1997/1427) |
| para 20 | 9 Jun 1997 (SI 1997/1427) |
| paras 21–25 | 1 Dec 1997 (SI 1997/2668)[1] |
| para 26 | 9 Jun 1997 (SI 1997/1427) |
| para 27(1) | 1 Dec 1997 (SI 1997/2668)[1] |
| para 27(2), (3) | 9 Jun 1997 (SI 1997/1427) |
| para 28 | 9 Jun 1997 (SI 1997/1427) |
| para 29(1) | 1 Dec 1997 (SI 1997/2668)[1] |
| para 29(2) | 9 Jun 1997 (SI 1997/1427) |
| para 29(3), (4) | 1 Dec 1997 (SI 1997/2668)[1] |
| paras 30–32 | 1 Dec 1997 (SI 1997/2668)[1] |
| para 33(1) | 1 Dec 1997 (SI 1997/2668)[1] |
| para 33(2) | 9 Jun 1997 (SI 1997/1427) |
| paras 34, 35 | 1 Dec 1997 (SI 1997/2668)[1] |
| para 36 | 1 Dec 1997 (SI 1997/2668) |
| paras 37, 38 | 9 Jun 1997 (SI 1997/1427) |
| paras 39, 40 | 1 Dec 1997 (SI 1997/2668)[1] |
| para 41(a) | 1 Dec 1997 (SI 1997/2668) |
| para 41(b) | 1 Dec 1997 (SI 1997/2668)[1] |
| para 42 | 1 Dec 1997 (SI 1997/2668)[1] |
| paras 43, 44 | 1 Dec 1997 (SI 1997/2668) |
| para 45(1) | 9 Jun 1997 (SI 1997/1427) |
| para 45(2), (3) | 1 Dec 1997 (SI 1997/2668)[1] |
| para 45(4) | 9 Jun 1997 (SI 1997/1427) |
| para 46 | 1 Dec 1997 (SI 1997/2668) |
| para 47 | 1 Dec 1997 (SI 1997/2668)[1] |
| para 48 | 1 Dec 1997 (SI 1997/2668) |
| para 49 | 1 Dec 1997 (SI 1997/2668)[1] |
| para 50 | 1 Dec 1997 (SI 1997/2668) |
| para 51 | 9 Jun 1997 (SI 1997/1427) |
| para 52 | 1 Dec 1997 (SI 1997/2668)[1] |
| para 53(1)(a) | 1 Dec 1997 (for purpose of defining expressions used in provisions falling within SI 1997/2668, Schedule, Pt I) (SI 1997/2668) |
| | 1 Dec 1997 (otherwise) (SI 1997/2668)[1] |
| para 53(1)(b) | 9 Jun 1997 (SI 1997/1427) |
| para 53(1)(c) | 1 Dec 1997 (for purpose of defining expressions used in provisions falling within SI 1997/2668, Schedule, Pt I) (SI 1997/2668) |
| | 1 Dec 1997 (otherwise) (SI 1997/2668)[1] |
| para 53(1)(d) | 9 Jun 1997 (for purpose of construing the words "connected undertaking" in Building Societies Act 1986, ss 43A(3)(c), 52(5A), (6), (9)) (SI 1997/1427) |
| | 1 Dec 1997 (for purpose of defining expressions used in provisions falling within SI 1997/2668, Schedule, Pt I) (SI 1997/2668) |
| | 1 Dec 1997 (otherwise) (SI 1997/2668)[1] |
| para 53(1)(e)–(o) | 1 Dec 1997 (for purpose of defining expressions used in provisions falling within SI 1997/2668, Schedule, Pt I) (SI 1997/2668) |
| | 1 Dec 1997 (otherwise) (SI 1997/2668)[1] |
| para 53(2) | 1 Dec 1997 (for the purpose of defining expressions used in provisions falling within SI 1997/2668, Schedule, Pt I) (SI 1997/2668) |
| | 1 Dec 1997 (otherwise) (SI 1997/2668)[1] |

**Building Societies Act 1997 (c 32)**—*contd*

| | | |
|---|---|---|
| | para 53(3)(a) | 9 Jun 1997 (SI 1997/1427) |
| | para 53(3)(b) | 1 Dec 1997 (for the purpose of defining expressions used in provisions falling within SI 1997/2668, Schedule, Pt I) (SI 1997/2668) |
| | | 1 Dec 1997 (otherwise) (SI 1997/2668)[1] |
| | para 53(4), (5) | 1 Dec 1997 (for the purpose of defining expressions used in provisions falling within SI 1997/2668, Schedule, Pt I) (SI 1997/2668) |
| | | 1 Dec 1997 (otherwise) (SI 1997/2668)[1] |
| | para 54 | 1 Dec 1997 (SI 1997/2668)[1] |
| | para 55 | 9 Jun 1997 (SI 1997/1427) |
| | para 56(1)–(8) | 1 Dec 1997 (SI 1997/2668)[1] |
| | para 56(9) | 9 Jun 1997 (SI 1997/1427) |
| | para 56(10) | 1 Dec 1997 (SI 1997/2668)[1] |
| | para 57 | 1 Dec 1997 (SI 1997/2668)[1] |
| | para 58 | 9 Jun 1997 (SI 1997/1427) |
| | para 59 | 1 Dec 1997 (SI 1997/2668)[1] |
| | para 60(1) | 9 Jun 1997 (SI 1997/1427) |
| | para 60(2), (3) | 1 Dec 1997 (SI 1997/2668)[1] |
| | paras 61–63 | 1 Dec 1997 (SI 1997/2668) |
| | para 64(1)–(4) | 1 Dec 1997 (SI 1997/2668)[1] |
| | para 64(5) | 1 Dec 1997 (SI 1997/2668) |
| | para 65 | 1 Dec 1997 (SI 1997/2668) |
| | para 66(1)(a) | 1 Dec 1997 (SI 1997/2668)[1] |
| | para 66(1)(b) | 1 Dec 1997 (SI 1997/2668) |
| | para 66(2)–(4) | 1 Dec 1997 (SI 1997/2668) |
| | para 67(a) | 1 Dec 1997 (SI 1997/2668)[1] |
| | para 67(b) | 1 Dec 1997 (so far as relates to Building Societies Act 1986, Sch 20, paras 2–4, 18) (SI 1997/2668) |
| | | 1 Dec 1997 (so far as relates to Building Societies Act 1986, Sch 20, paras 7–13, 15, 17) (SI 1997/2668)[1] |
| | | 1 May 1999 (so far as it relates to the Building Societies Act 1986, Sch 20, para 14) (SI 1997/2668)[2] |
| Sch 8 | para 1 | 21 May 1997 (SI 1997/1307) |
| | paras 2, 3 | 1 Dec 1997 (SI 1997/2668) |
| | paras 4–8 | 1 Dec 1997 (SI 1997/2668)[1] |
| | paras 9, 10 | 21 Mar 1997 (s 47(3)(b)) |
| Sch 9 | | 21 Mar 1997 (s 47(3)(c)), repeals and revocations in— |

Building Societies Act 1986, s 100;

Building Societies (Transfer of Business) Regulations 1988, SI 1988/1153

1 Dec 1997 (SI 1997/2668), repeals and revocations of or in—

Solicitors Act 1974, s 86;

Building Societies Act 1986, ss 13(7), 28(2), 41, 84(1), 95, 108, 119(3)(a), Sch 4, Sch 12, Pt II, Sch 16, para 1(5), Sch 20, paras 2–4, 18;

Credit Institutions (Protection of Depositors) Regulations 1995, SI 1995/1442

1 Dec 1997 (SI 1997/2668)[1], repeals and revocations of or in—

Home Purchase Assistance and Housing Corporation Guarantee Act 1978;

Housing (Northern Ireland) Order 1981, SI 1981/156 (NI 3);

Housing Act 1985;

Building Societies Act 1986, s 9(3), Pt III (so far as not already repealed), s 33, Pt V, ss 38–40, 51, 52(3), 60(17), 65(10), 71(10A), 79(5), 82, 97(3), 105, 118, 119(1), 122(1), Schs 2, 10, 18, Sch 20, paras 1, 7–13, 15, 17;

Banking Act 1987;

Deregulation and Contracting Out Act 1994

1 May 1999 (SI 1997/2668)[2], repeals of—

**Building Societies Act 1997 (c 32)**—*contd*

Building Societies Act 1986, s 4(2), Sch 20, para 14

¹ The Building Societies Act 1997 (Commencement No 3) Order 1997, SI 1997/2668, art 2(2)–(5), provides that:

(1) in the case of any existing building society which sends the central office a record of alterations to its purpose or principal purpose, its powers and its rules, in accordance with the Building Societies Act 1986, Sch 8, para 1(1), where—

(a) the alterations are specified as taking effect on or before 1 Dec 1997; and

(b) the record of the alterations is registered by the central office under Sch 8, para 1(3) to the 1986 Act on or before 1 Dec 1997,

the provisions of the Act specified in Pt II of the Schedule to that Order (ie those marked as "¹") are to come into force for all purposes, subject to any specified purposes, on 1 Dec 1997

(2) In the case of any other existing building society, the provisions of the Act specified in Pt II of the Schedule to that Order are to come into force for all purposes, except for the purpose and to the extent stated in para (3) below and subject to any specified purposes, on the date on which the record of alterations to its purpose or principal purpose, its powers and its rules takes effect under Sch 8, para 1(5) or 2(6) to the 1986 Act, or as the case may be, is registered under para 3(3)(a) of that Schedule

(3) For the purpose of ending the period mentioned in Sch 8, para 1(1) to the 1986 Act and of construing the definitions of "existing building society" and "the transitional period" in para 2(7) or 3(6) of that Schedule, ss 1, 2 of this Act are to come into force in the case of a building society falling within para (2) above on 1 Dec 1997

(4) In the case of any building society registered after 30 Nov 1997 the provisions of the Act specified in Pt II of the Schedule to that Order are to come into force for all purposes, subject to any specified purposes, on 1 Dec 1997

² The Building Societies Act 1997 (Commencement No 3) Order 1997, SI 1997/2668, art 2(6), provides that the provisions of the Act specified in Pt III of the Schedule to that Order (ie those marked as "²") are to come into force on the day after the transitional period defined in Sch 8, para 2(7) to the 1986 Act ends. That period ended on 30 Apr 1999 by virtue of the Building Societies Act 1997 (Expiry of Transitional Period) Order 1998, SI 1998/2835

---

**Building Societies (Distributions) Act 1997 (c 41)**

*RA:* 21 Mar 1997

*Commencement provisions:* s 2(2)

Whole Act in force 22 Jan 1997 (s 2(2)). This Act applies to any transfer of business of a building society where the decision of the board of directors of the building society to enter the transfer is made public after 22 Jan 1997

---

**Civil Procedure Act 1997 (c 12)**

*RA:* 27 Feb 1997

*Commencement provisions:* s 11(2); Civil Procedure Act 1997 (Commencement No 1) Order 1997, SI 1997/841; Civil Procedure Act 1997 (Commencement No 2) Order 1999, SI 1999/1009

| | | |
|---|---|---|
| 1 | (1) | 27 Apr 1997 (SI 1997/841) |
| | (2) | See Sch 1 below |
| | (3) | 27 Apr 1997 (SI 1997/841) |
| 2–9 | | 27 Apr 1997 (SI 1997/841) |
| 10 | | See Sch 2 below |
| 11 | | 27 Feb 1997 (RA) |
| Sch 1 | | 27 Apr 1997 (SI 1997/841) |
| Sch 2 | para 1(1), (2) | 27 Apr 1997 (SI 1997/841) |
| | para 1(3) | 26 Apr 1999 (SI 1999/1009) |

## Civil Procedure Act 1997 (c 12)—*contd*

| | |
|---|---|
| para 1(4)(a), (b) | 26 Apr 1999 (SI 1999/1009) |
| para 1(4)(c) | 27 Apr 1997 (SI 1997/841) |
| para 1(4)(d) | 26 Apr 1999 (SI 1999/1009) |
| para 1(5)–(7) | 26 Apr 1999 (SI 1999/1009) |
| para 2(1), (2) | 27 Apr 1997 (SI 1997/841) |
| para 2(3) | 26 Apr 1999 (SI 1999/1009) |
| para 2(4), (5) | 27 Apr 1997 (SI 1997/841) |
| para 2(6)–(9) | 26 Apr 1999 (SI 1999/1009) |
| para 3(a) | 14 Mar 1997 (SI 1997/841) |
| para 3(b) | 26 Apr 1999 (SI 1999/1009) |
| para 4 | 27 Apr 1997 (SI 1997/841) |

## Confiscation of Alcohol (Young Persons) Act 1997 (c 33)

*RA:* 21 Mar 1997

*Commencement provisions:* s 2(2); Confiscation of Alcohol (Young Persons) Act 1997 (Commencement) Order 1997, SI 1997/1725

| | |
|---|---|
| 1 | 1 Aug 1997 (SI 1997/1725) |
| 2 | 21 Mar 1997 (RA) |

## Consolidated Fund Act 1997 (c 15)

*RA:* 19 Mar 1997

Whole Act in force 19 Mar 1997 (RA)

## Consolidated Fund (No 2) Act 1997 (c 67)

*RA:* 17 Dec 1997

Whole Act in force 17 Dec 1997 (RA)

## Contract (Scotland) Act 1997 (c 34)

*RA:* 21 Mar 1997

*Commencement provisions:* s 4(2)

Whole Act in force 21 Jun 1997 (s 4(2))

## Crime and Punishment (Scotland) Act 1997 (c 48)

*RA:* 21 Mar 1997

*Commencement provisions:* s 65(2)–(4); Crime and Punishment (Scotland) Act 1997 (Commencement and Transitional Provisions) Order 1997, SI 1997/1712; Crime and Punishment (Scotland) Act 1997 (Commencement No 2 and Transitional and Consequential Provisions) Order 1997, SI 1997/2323; Crime and Punishment (Scotland) Act 1997 (Commencement No 3) Order 1997, SI 1997/2694; Crime and Punishment (Scotland) Act 1997 (Commencement No 4) Order 1997, SI 1997/3004; Crime and Punishment (Scotland) Act 1997 (Commencement No 5 and Transitional Provisions and Savings) Order 1999, SI 1999/652; Crime and Punishment (Scotland) Act 1997 (Commencement No 6 and Savings) Order 2004, SSI 2004/176

| | |
|---|---|
| 1 | *Never in force* (repealed) |
| 2 | 20 Oct 1997 (SI 1997/2323) |

**Crime and Punishment (Scotland) Act 1997 (c 48)**—*contd*

| | | |
|---|---|---|
| 3 | | 20 Oct 1997 (for purpose of inserting Criminal Procedure (Scotland) Act 1995, s 205C(1) for the purpose of the interpretation of s 205B of that Act) (SI 1997/2323) |
| | | *Not yet in force* (insertion of Criminal Procedure (Scotland) Act 1995, s 205C(1), for the purpose of the interpretation of s 205A of that Act, and s 205C(2), (3)) |
| 4 | | *Never in force* (repealed) |
| 5 | | 20 Oct 1997 (for purpose of enabling the Secretary of State to make regulations, notify courts and make arrangements, including contractual arrangements, under Criminal Procedure (Scotland) Act 1995, ss 245A–245C) (SI 1997/2323) |
| | | 1 Jul 1998 (otherwise) (SI 1997/2323) |
| 6–11 | | 1 Jan 1998 (SI 1997/2323) |
| 12 | | 1 Aug 1997 (SI 1997/1712)[1] |
| 13 | (1) | 1 May 2004 (SSI 2004/176)[1] |
| | (2) | *Never in force* (repealed) |
| | (3), (4) | 1 May 2004 (SSI 2004/176)[1] |
| 14 | | 1 Aug 1997 (subject to a transitional provision) (SI 1997/1712) |
| 15 | | 20 Oct 1997 (for purpose of enabling the Secretary of State to make an order under Criminal Procedure (Scotland) Act 1995, s 248C) (SI 1997/2323) |
| | | 1 Jan 1998 (otherwise, but subject to transitional provisions) (SI 1997/2323) |
| 16 | | 20 Oct 1997 (except for the purpose of substituting into Prisoners and Criminal Proceedings (Scotland) Act 1993, s 2(1) a reference to sentences imposed under Criminal Procedure (Scotland) Act 1995, s 205A(2)) (SI 1997/2323) |
| | | *Not yet in force* (exception noted above) |
| 17 | | 1 Aug 1997 (SI 1997/1712) |
| 18 | | 20 Oct 1997 (except for purpose of inserting references to ss 205A, 209(1A) into Criminal Procedure (Scotland) Act 1995) (SI 1997/2323) |
| | | *Not yet in force* (exception noted above) |
| 19 | | 20 Oct 1997 (except for purposes of inserting Criminal Procedure (Scotland) Act 1995, ss 106A(1), 106A(3) (so far as refers to s 205A(2) of the 1995 Act)) (SI 1997/2323) |
| | | *Not yet in force* (exceptions noted above) |
| 20 | | 1 Aug 1997 (so far as relates to Criminal Procedure (Scotland) Act 1995, s 303A(1), (2), (4)–(6)) (SI 1997/1712) |
| | | 1 Apr 1999 (otherwise, subject to transitional provisions and savings) (SI 1999/652) |
| 21 | | 1 Aug 1997 (SI 1997/1712) |
| 22 | | 1 Jan 1998 (SI 1997/2323) |
| 23 | | 1 Aug 1997 (SI 1997/1712) |
| 24 | | 1 Aug 1997 (so far as relates to Criminal Procedure (Scotland) Act 1995, ss 121A(1)–(3), (4)(a)–(c), 193A(1)–(3), (4)(a)–(c)) (SI 1997/1712) |
| | | 1 Jul 1998 (otherwise) (SI 1997/2323) |
| 25 | | 1 Jan 1998 (for purpose of inserting Criminal Procedure (Scotland) Act 1995, ss 194A, 194E, 194G, Sch 9A) (SI 1997/3004) |
| | | 1 Apr 1999 (otherwise, subject to transitional provisions and savings) (SI 1999/652) |
| 26–32 | | 1 Aug 1997 (SI 1997/1712) |
| 33–41 | | *Never in force* (repealed) |
| 42–44 | | 1 Jan 1998 (SI 1997/2323) |
| 45, 46 | | 21 Mar 1997 (RA) |
| 47 | (1)(a), (b) | 1 Aug 1997 (SI 1997/1712) |
| | (1)(c) | 17 Nov 1997 (SI 1997/2694) |
| | (1)(d) | 1 Aug 1997 (SI 1997/1712) |
| | (2)–(5) | 1 Aug 1997 (SI 1997/1712) |

**See Halsbury's Statutes Citator for amendments to these Acts**          943

**Crime and Punishment (Scotland) Act 1997 (c 48)**—*contd*

| | | |
|---|---|---|
| 48 | | 17 Nov 1997 (SI 1997/2694) |
| 49 | | 1 Oct 1997 (for purpose of bringing into force Legal Aid (Scotland) Act 1986, ss 25A(5), (6) (for purposes of enabling the Scottish Legal Aid Board to determine the form of the application for entry on the Register and to specify the documents which are to accompany the application), 25B) (SI 1997/2323) |
| | | 1 Apr 1998 (for purpose of bringing into force Legal Aid (Scotland) Act 1986, ss 25A(1), (5)–(15), 25F(1)) (SI 1997/2323) |
| | | 1 Oct 1998 (for purpose of bringing into force Legal Aid (Scotland) Act 1986, ss 25A(2)–(4), 25C–25E, 25F(2), (3)) (SI 1997/2323) |
| 50–54 | | 1 Oct 1997 (SI 1997/2323) |
| 55, 56 | | 1 Aug 1997 (SI 1997/1712) |
| 57 | (1) | 1 Aug 1997 (subject to a transitional provision) (SI 1997/1712) |
| | (2) | 1 Aug 1997 (SI 1997/1712) |
| 58–61 | | 1 Aug 1997 (SI 1997/1712) |
| 62 | (1) | See Sch 1 below |
| | (2) | See Sch 3 below |
| 63 | (1)(a)(i) | 20 Oct 1997 (SI 1997/2323) |
| | (1)(a)(ii) | 1 Jan 1998 (SI 1997/3004) |
| | (1)(a)(iii) | 1 Aug 1997 (SI 1997/1712) |
| | (1)(b) | 1 Oct 1997 (SI 1997/2323) |
| | (1)(c) | 1 Aug 1997 (SI 1997/1712) |
| | (2) | 1 Aug 1997 (SI 1997/1712) |
| 64 | | 1 Aug 1997 (SI 1997/1712) |
| 65 | (1) | 1 Aug 1997 (SI 1997/1712) |
| | (2)–(4) | *Not yet in force* |
| | (5) | 1 Aug 1997 (SI 1997/1712) |
| | (6) | *Not yet in force* |
| | (7) | 1 Aug 1997 (SI 1997/1712) |
| Sch 1 | para 1 | *Never in force (repealed)* |
| | para 2 | 1 Aug 1997 (SI 1997/1712) |
| | para 3 | *Not yet in force* |
| | paras 4, 5 | 1 Jan 1998 (SI 1997/3004) |
| | para 6 | 1 Aug 1997 (SI 1997/1712) |
| | para 7 | 1 Jan 1998 (SI 1997/3004) |
| | para 8 | 1 Aug 1997 (SI 1997/1712) |
| | para 9(1) | 1 Aug 1997 (SI 1997/1712) |
| | para 9(2) | 1 Jan 1998 (SI 1997/2323) |
| | para 9(3)(a) | 1 Jan 1998 (SI 1997/2323) |
| | para 9(3)(b) | 1 Aug 1997 (SI 1997/1712) |
| | para 9(4)–(6) | 1 Aug 1997 (SI 1997/1712) |
| | para 9(7) | *Never in force (repealed)* |
| | para 9(8), (9) | 1 Jan 1998 (SI 1997/2323) |
| | para 9(10)–(14) | 1 Aug 1997 (SI 1997/1712) |
| | para 9(15), (16) | 1 Jan 1998 (SI 1997/2323) |
| | para 10(1) | 1 Aug 1997 (SI 1997/1712) |
| | para 10(2)(a) | *Never in force (repealed)* |
| | para 10(2)(b) | 1 Aug 1997 (SI 1997/1712) |
| | para 10(3) | 20 Oct 1997 (SI 1997/2323) |
| | para 11 | 1 Aug 1997 (SI 1997/1712) |
| | para 12(1) | 1 Aug 1997 (SI 1997/1712) |
| | para 12(2)–(4) | 1 Oct 1997 (SI 1997/2323) |
| | para 12(5), (6) | 20 Oct 1997 (SI 1997/2323) |
| | para 12(7) | 1 Aug 1997 (SI 1997/1712) |
| | para 12(8)–(10) | 1 Oct 1997 (SI 1997/2323) |
| | para 13(1), (2) | 1 Jan 1998 (SI 1997/2323) |

**Crime and Punishment (Scotland) Act 1997 (c 48)**—*contd*

| | |
|---|---|
| para 13(3) | *Never in force* (repealed) |
| para 13(4) | 1 Jan 1998 (SI 1997/2323) |
| para 14(1) | 20 Oct 1997 (SI 1997/2323) |
| para 14(2)(a) | *Never in force* (repealed) |
| para 14(2)(b) | 20 Oct 1997 (SI 1997/2323) |
| para 14(3)(a)–(d) | 20 Oct 1997 (SI 1997/2323) |
| para 14(3)(e) | *Never in force* (repealed) |
| para 14(4)–(7) | *Never in force* (repealed) |
| para 14(8) | 20 Oct 1997 (SI 1997/2323) |
| para 14(9) | *Never in force* (repealed) |
| para 14(10)(a) | *Never in force* (repealed) |
| para 14(10)(b) | 20 Oct 1997 (SI 1997/2323) |
| para 14(11)(a) | 20 Oct 1997 (SI 1997/2323) |
| para 14(11)(b) | *Never in force* (repealed) |
| para 14(12)–(15) | *Never in force* (repealed) |
| para 14(16) | 1 Aug 1997 (SI 1997/1712) |
| para 14(17) | *Never in force* (repealed) |
| para 14(18) | 20 Oct 1997 (SI 1997/2323) |
| para 15 | 1 Jan 1998 (SI 1997/2323) |
| paras 16, 17 | 1 Aug 1997 (SI 1997/1712) |
| para 18(1) | 1 Aug 1997 (SI 1997/1712) |
| para 18(2)(a) | *Not yet in force* |
| para 18(2)(b) | 1 Aug 1997 (SI 1997/1712) |
| para 18(3)–(8) | 1 Aug 1997 (SI 1997/1712) |
| paras 19, 20 | 1 Aug 1997 (SI 1997/1712) |
| para 21(1), (2) | 1 Aug 1997 (SI 1997/1712) |
| para 21(3) | *Never in force* (repealed) |
| para 21(4) | 1 Aug 1997 (SI 1997/1712) |
| para 21(5)–(8) | 1 Jan 1998 (SI 1997/2323) |
| para 21(9)–(15) | 1 Aug 1997 (SI 1997/1712) |
| para 21(16) | 1 Apr 1999 (subject to transitional provisions and savings) (SI 1999/652) |
| para 21(17) | 1 Aug 1997 (SI 1997/1712) |
| para 21(18) | 1 Apr 1999 (subject to transitional provisions and savings) (SI 1999/652) |
| para 21(19)–(22) | 1 Aug 1997 (SI 1997/1712) |
| para 21(23) | 20 Oct 1997 (except for purpose of inserting references to s 205A into Criminal Procedure (Scotland) Act 1995) (SI 1997/2323) |
| | *Not yet in force* (exception noted above) |
| para 21(24) | *Not yet in force* |
| para 21(25) | 20 Oct 1997 (except for purpose of inserting references to s 205A into Criminal Procedure (Scotland) Act 1995) (SI 1997/2323) |
| | *Not yet in force* (exception noted above) |
| para 21(26) | 1 Apr 1999 (subject to transitional provisions and savings) (SI 1999/652) |
| para 21(27), (28) | 1 Jul 1998 (SI 1997/2323) |
| para 21(29) | *Never in force* (repealed) |
| para 21(30) | 1 Aug 1997 (SI 1997/1712) |
| para 21(31) | 20 Oct 1997 (except for purpose of inserting references to s 205A into Criminal Procedure (Scotland) Act 1995) (SI 1997/2323) |
| | *Not yet in force* (exception noted above) |
| para 21(32) | 1 Aug 1997 (SI 1997/1712) |
| para 21(33)(a) | 20 Oct 1997 (SI 1997/2323) |
| para 21(33)(b) | 1 Apr 1999 (subject to transitional provisions and savings) (SI 1999/652) |
| para 21(34)(a) | 1 Apr 1999 (subject to transitional provisions and savings) (SI 1999/652) |
| para 21(34)(b) | 1 Aug 1997 (SI 1997/1712) |
| para 21(35) | 1 Jan 1998 (SI 1997/2323) |

**See Halsbury's Statutes Citator for amendments to these Acts**

**Crime and Punishment (Scotland) Act 1997 (c 48)**—*contd*

| | |
|---|---|
| Sch 2 | *Never in force* (repealed) |
| Sch 3 | 1 Aug 1997 (SI 1997/1712), repeals of or in— |

      Police (Scotland) Act 1967;
      Social Work (Scotland) Act 1968;
      Sexual Offences (Scotland) Act 1976;
      Video Recordings Act 1993;
      Criminal Justice (Scotland) Act 1995;
      Environment Act 1995;
      Children (Scotland) Act 1995;
      Criminal Procedure (Consequential Provisions) (Scotland) Act 1995;
      Criminal Procedure (Scotland) Act 1995 (except ss 18, 44, 53, 63, 124, 252)
     20 Oct 1997 (SI 1997/2323), repeals of or in—
      Repatriation of Prisoners Act 1984;
      Prisoners and Criminal Proceedings (Scotland) Act 1993, s 2(2)
     17 Nov 1997 (repeal of Criminal Procedure (Scotland) Act 1995, s 18(7)) (SI 1997/2694)
     1 Jan 1998 (SI 1997/2323), repeals of or in—
      Mental Health (Scotland) Act 1984;
      Prisons (Scotland) Act 1989, s 3(1);
      Criminal Procedure (Scotland) Act 1995, ss 53, 63, 252(2)
     1 Apr 1999 (repeal of Criminal Procedure (Scotland) Act 1995, s 124(3)–(5), subject to transitional provisions and savings) (SI 1999/652)
     *Not yet in force* (repeals of or in Prisoners and Criminal Proceedings (Scotland) 1993, s 14(2), s 27(1), (definition "supervised release order", words "(as inserted by section 14 of this Act)"))
     *Never in force* (repealed), repeals of or in—
      Prisons (Scotland) Act 1989, s 39(7);
      Prisoners and Criminal Proceedings (Scotland) Act 1993, ss 1, 3, 5–7, 9, 12, 14(4), 16, 17, 20, 24, 27(2), (3), (5), (6), Sch 1, in s 27(1), definitions "short term prisoner", "long term prisoner", and in definition "supervised release order", words from "but" to the end;
      Criminal Procedure (Scotland) Act 1995, s 44

[1]   For savings, see SSI 2004/176, art 3

---

**Crime (Sentences) Act 1997 (c 43)**

*RA:* 21 Mar 1997

*Commencement provisions:* s 57(2); Crime (Sentences) Act 1997 (Commencement) (No 1) Order 1997, SI 1997/1581; Crime (Sentences) Act 1997 (Commencement No 2 and Transitional Provisions) Order 1997, SI 1997/2200; Crime (Sentences) Act 1997 (Commencement No 3) Order 1999, SI 1999/3096; Crime (Sentences) Act 1997 (Commencement No 4) Order 2005, SI 2005/932; Crime (Sentences) Act 1997 (Commencement No 5) Order 2012, SI 2012/2901

| | | |
|---|---|---|
| 1 | (1), (2) | 1 Oct 1997 (SI 1997/2200) |
| | (3) | 1 Oct 1997 (so far as relates to s 3) (SI 1997/2200) |
| | | *Never in force* (repealed) (otherwise) |
| 2 | | 1 Oct 1997 (SI 1997/2200) |
| 3 | (1)–(5) | 1 Oct 1997 (SI 1997/2200) |
| | (6) | 1 Oct 1997 (so far as relates to s 3) (SI 1997/2200) |
| | | 1 Dec 1999 (otherwise) (SI 1999/3096) |
| 4 | | 1 Dec 1999 (SI 1999/3096) |
| 5 | | 1 Oct 1997 (so far as relates to sentences imposed under ss 2(2), 3(2)) (SI 1997/2200) |
| | | 1 Dec 1999 (otherwise) (SI 1999/3096) |

**Crime (Sentences) Act 1997 (c 43)**—*contd*

| | | |
|---|---|---|
| 6 | | 1 Oct 1997 (so far as relates to serious offences within the meaning of s 2 or class A drug trafficking offences within the meaning of s 3) (SI 1997/2200) |
| | | 1 Dec 1999 (otherwise) (SI 1999/3096) |
| 7 | | 1 Oct 1997 (SI 1997/2200) |
| 8–27 | | *Never in force* (repealed) |
| 28–34 | | 1 Oct 1997 (SI 1997/2200)[1] |
| 35 | | 1 Jan 1998 (SI 1997/2200) |
| 36 | | 1 Oct 1997 (SI 1997/2200) |
| 37 | | 1 Jan 1998 (SI 1997/2200) |
| 38 | | 1 Oct 1997 (SI 1997/2200)[1] |
| 39 | (1) | 1 Jan 1998 (subject to a saving) (SI 1997/2200)[1] |
| | (2) | 1 Jan 1998 (so far as relates to offences the sentences for which are fixed by law or fall to be imposed under ss 2(2), 3(2)) (SI 1997/2200)[1] |
| | | 1 Dec 1999 (otherwise) (SI 1999/3096) |
| | (3)–(6) | 1 Jan 1998 (SI 1997/2200) |
| 40 | | 1 Jan 1998 (SI 1997/2200) |
| 41 | | See Sch 1 below |
| 42 | | See Sch 2 below |
| 43 | | 1 Jan 1998 (SI 1997/2200)[1] |
| 44–47 | | 1 Oct 1997 (SI 1997/2200)[1] |
| 48 | | See Sch 3 below |
| 49 | | 1 Oct 1997 (SI 1997/2200) |
| 50 | | 1 Mar 1998 (SI 1997/2200) |
| 51–54 | | 1 Oct 1997 (SI 1997/2200)[1] |
| 55 | (1) | See Sch 4 below |
| | (2)(a) | 1 Oct 1997 (so far as relates to sentences falling to be imposed under ss 2(2), 3(2)) (SI 1997/2200) |
| | | 1 Dec 1999 (otherwise) (SI 1999/3096) |
| | (2)(b) | 1 Oct 1997 (SI 1997/2200) |
| 56 | (1) | See Sch 5 below |
| | (2) | See Sch 6 below |
| 57 | | 1 Oct 1997 (SI 1997/2200) |
| Sch 1 | paras 1–13 | 1 Oct 1997 (SI 1997/2200)[1] |
| | para 14 | 25 Jun 1997 (SI 1997/1581) |
| | paras 15–18 | 1 Oct 1997 (SI 1997/2200)[1] |
| | para 19 | 25 Jun 1997 (SI 1997/1581) |
| | para 20 | 1 Oct 1997 (SI 1997/2200)[1] |
| Sch 2 | paras 1–3 | 1 Oct 1997 (SI 1997/2200)[1] |
| | para 4 | *Never in force* (repealed) |
| | paras 5–7 | 1 Oct 1997 (SI 1997/2200)[1] |
| | para 8 | *Never in force* (repealed) |
| | paras 9–11 | 1 Oct 1997 (SI 1997/2200)[1] |
| Sch 3 | | 1 Oct 1997 (SI 1997/2200) |
| Sch 4 | para 1(1) | 1 Oct 1997 (so far as relates to offences whose corresponding civil offences are offences to which s 2 would apply) (SI 1997/2200) |
| | | *Not yet in force* (so far as relates to offences whose corresponding civil offences are offences to which s 3 or 4 would apply) |
| | para 1(2) | 1 Oct 1997 (SI 1997/2200) |
| | para 1(3) | *Not yet in force* |
| | para 1(4) | 1 Oct 1997 (SI 1997/2200) |
| | para 1(5) | *Not yet in force* |
| | para 2(1) | 1 Oct 1997 (so far as relates to offences whose corresponding civil offences are offences to which s 2 would apply) (SI 1997/2200) |
| | | *Not yet in force* (so far as relates to offences whose corresponding civil offences are offences to which s 3 or 4 would apply) |
| | para 2(2) | 1 Oct 1997 (SI 1997/2200) |
| | para 2(3) | *Not yet in force* |

**Crime (Sentences) Act 1997 (c 43)**—*contd*

| | | |
|---|---|---|
| | para 2(4) | 1 Oct 1997 (SI 1997/2200) |
| | para 2(5) | *Not yet in force* |
| | para 3(1) | 1 Oct 1997 (so far as relates to offences whose corresponding civil offences are offences to which s 2 would apply) (SI 1997/2200) |
| | | *Not yet in force* |
| | para 3(2) | 1 Oct 1997 (SI 1997/2200) |
| | para 3(3) | *Not yet in force* |
| | para 3(4) | 1 Oct 1997 (SI 1997/2200) |
| | para 3(5) | *Not yet in force* |
| | paras 4, 5 | 1 Oct 1997 (SI 1997/2200)[1] |
| | para 6(1)(a) | 1 Oct 1997 (SI 1997/2200) |
| | para 6(1)(b), (2) | *Never in force (repealed)* |
| | para 7 | *Never in force (repealed)* |
| | para 8(1)–(3) | 1 Oct 1997 (so far as relates to offences the sentences for which fall to be imposed under ss 2(2), 3(2)) (SI 1997/2200) |
| | | 1 Dec 1999 (otherwise) (SI 1999/3096) |
| | para 8(4) | 1 Oct 1997 (SI 1997/2200) |
| | para 9 | *Never in force (repealed)* |
| | para 10(1) | 1 Oct 1997 (SI 1997/2200) |
| | para 10(2) | 1 Jan 1998 (SI 1997/2200) |
| | para 11 | *Never in force (repealed)* |
| | para 12(1) | 1 Oct 1997 (SI 1997/2200) |
| | para 12(2) | 1 Oct 1997 (so far as relates to offences the sentences for which would otherwise fall to be imposed under s 3(2)) (SI 1997/2200) |
| | | 1 Dec 1999 (otherwise) (SI 1999/3096) |
| | para 12(3) | 1 Oct 1997 (SI 1997/2200) |
| | para 12(4) | *Never in force (repealed)* |
| | para 12(5)–(19) | 1 Oct 1997 (SI 1997/2200) |
| | para 13 | 1 Oct 1997 (so far as relates to sentences required by ss 2(2), 3(2)) (SI 1997/2200) |
| | | 1 Dec 1999 (otherwise) (SI 1999/3096) |
| | para 14 | *Not yet in force* |
| | para 15(1) | 1 Oct 1997 (so far as relates to offences the sentences for which fall to be imposed under ss 2(2), 3(2)) (SI 1997/2200) |
| | | 1 Dec 1999 (otherwise) (SI 1999/3096) |
| | para 15(2), (3) | 1 Oct 1997 (SI 1997/2200)[1] |
| | para 15(4) | 1 Oct 1997 (so far as relates to s 3(2)) (SI 1997/2200) |
| | | 1 Dec 1999 (otherwise) (SI 1999/3096) |
| | para 15(5) | 1 Oct 1997 (so far as relates to sentences falling to be imposed under s 3(2)) (SI 1997/2200) |
| | | 1 Dec 1999 (otherwise) (SI 1999/3096) |
| | para 15(6), (7) | 1 Oct 1997 (SI 1997/2200) |
| | para 15(8), (9) | 1 Oct 1997 (so far as relates to offences the sentences for which fall to be imposed under ss 2(2), 3(2)) (SI 1997/2200) |
| | | 1 Dec 1999 (otherwise) (SI 1999/3096) |
| | para 15(10)–(13) | 1 Oct 1997 (SI 1997/2200)[1] |
| | para 16 | 1 Oct 1997 (SI 1997/2200) |
| | para 17 | 1 Oct 1997 (so far as relates to offences the sentences for which fall to be imposed under s 3(2)) (SI 1997/2200) |
| | | 1 Dec 1999 (otherwise) (SI 1999/3096) |
| Sch 5 | paras 1–4 | *Never in force (repealed)* |
| | para 5 | 1 Oct 1997 (SI 1997/2200) |
| | para 6 | *Never in force (repealed)* |
| | paras 7–13 | 1 Oct 1997 (SI 1997/2200) |
| Sch 6 | | 1 Oct 1997 (subject to savings) (SI 1997/2200), repeals of or in— |
| | | Criminal Justice Act 1961[1]; |
| | | Powers of Criminal Courts Act 1973[1]; |
| | | Mental Health Act 1983; |

**Crime (Sentences) Act 1997 (c 43)**—*contd*

> Criminal Justice Act 1991, ss 4(1)[1], 12[1], 34, 35(2), (3), 36(1) (so far as relating to life prisoners), 36(2) (the words "or life"), 37(3), 37(4) and (5) (so far as relating to life prisoners), 39(1) (the words "or life"), 39(5) (the words "direction or"), (5)(a), 39(5)(b) (the word "other"), 43(2), (3) (the words "(whether short-term, long-term or life prisoners)" and "or (2)"), 48, 51(1) (the definitions "discretionary life prisoner", "life prisoner"), 51(3), Sch 2[1]
>
> 4 Apr 2005 (repeal of Criminal Justice Act 1967, s 67) (SI 2005/932)[2]
>
> 3 Dec 2012 (repeal of Criminal Justice Act 1967, s 67, in so far as it remains in force by virtue of transitional provisions in SI 2005/932, art 2(3)) (SI 2012/2901)
>
> *Never in force* (repeals of Criminal Justice Act 1991, ss 33–51, 65 (so far as not already in force))

[1]   For transitional provisions, see SI 1997/2200, art 5

[2]   For transitional provisions, see SI 2005/932, art 2(3)

---

**Criminal Evidence (Amendment) Act 1997 (c 17)**

*RA:* 19 Mar 1997

Whole Act in force 19 Mar 1997 (RA)

---

**Dangerous Dogs (Amendment) Act 1997 (c 53)**

*RA:* 21 Mar 1997

*Commencement provisions:* s 6(3); Dangerous Dogs (Amendment) Act 1997 (Commencement) Order 1997, SI 1997/1151

Whole Act in force 8 Jun 1997 (SI 1997/1151)

---

**Education Act 1997 (c 44)**

*RA:* 21 Mar 1997

*Commencement provisions:* s 58(3), (4); Education Act 1997 (Commencement No 1) Order 1997, SI 1997/1153; Education Act 1997 (Commencement No 2 and Transitional Provisions) Order 1997, SI 1997/1468, as amended by SI 2005/3239; Education Act 1997 (Commencement No 3 and Transitional Provisions) Order 1998, SI 1998/386; Education Act 1997 (Commencement No 4) Order 2001, SI 2001/1215

| | | |
|---|---|---|
| 1 | | 4 Apr 1997 (SI 1997/1153) |
| 2, 3 | | 1 Apr 1998 (subject to transitional provisions) (SI 1998/386) |
| 4 | | 1 Sep 1998 (SI 1998/386) |
| 5–8 | | 1 Sep 1998 (subject to transitional provisions) (SI 1998/386) |
| 9 | | 1 Apr 1998 (SI 1998/386) |
| 10, 11 | | 1 Sep 1997 (SI 1997/1468) |
| 12 | (1) | 1 Sep 1997 (SI 1997/1468) |
| | (2) | See Sch 2 below |
| 13 | | *Never in force* (repealed) |
| 14 | (1) | 1 Sep 1997 (so far as relates to Education Act 1996, Sch 33B, paras 3, 4) (SI 1997/1468) |
| | (2) | See Sch 3 below |
| 15 | | 1 Nov 1997 (SI 1997/1468) |
| 16 | (1) | 1 Apr 1998 (E) (SI 1998/386) |
| | | 1 Apr 1999 (W) (SI 1998/386) |

**Education Act 1997 (c 44)**—*contd*

| | | |
|---|---|---|
| | (2), (3) | 1 Nov 1997 (SI 1997/1468) |
| | (4) | 1 Nov 1997 (E) (SI 1997/1468) |
| | | 1 Nov 1998 (W) (SI 1998/386) |
| | (5) | 1 Apr 1998 (E) (SI 1998/386) |
| | | 1 Apr 1999 (W) (SI 1998/386) |
| | (6) | 1 Nov 1997 (SI 1997/1468) |
| 17 | (1)–(3) | 1 Aug 1998 (E) (SI 1998/386) |
| | | 1 Sep 1999 (W) (SI 1998/386) |
| | (4) | 1 Nov 1997 (SI 1997/1468) |
| | (5)–(7) | 1 Aug 1998 (E) (SI 1998/386) |
| | | 1 Sep 1999 (W) (SI 1998/386) |
| | (8) | 1 Nov 1997 (SI 1997/1468) |
| 18 | | 1 Nov 1997 (SI 1997/1468) |
| 19 | | 1 Apr 1998 (SI 1998/386) |
| 20 | | 14 Jun 1997 (SI 1997/1468) |
| 21 | (1)–(4) | 1 Oct 1997 (SI 1997/1468) |
| | (5) | See Sch 4 below |
| 22–26 | | 1 Oct 1997 (SI 1997/1468) |
| 27 | (1)–(4) | 1 Oct 1997 (SI 1997/1468) |
| | (5) | See Sch 5 below |
| 28–32 | | 1 Oct 1997 (SI 1997/1468) |
| 33 | | 1 Mar 1998 (SI 1998/386) |
| 34, 35 | | 1 Sep 1997 (SI 1997/1468) |
| 36 | | 1 Dec 1997 (SI 1997/1468) |
| 37 | (1)–(4) | 1 Sep 1997 (SI 1997/1468) |
| | (5) | 1 Sep 2001 (SI 2001/1215) |
| 38–41 | | 1 Sep 1997 (SI 1997/1468) |
| 42 | | See Sch 6 below |
| 43 | | 1 Sep 1998 (SI 1998/386) |
| 44–46 | | 1 Sep 1997 (SI 1997/1468) |
| 47 | | 1 Sep 1998 (SI 1998/386) |
| 48 | | 1 Dec 1997 (SI 1997/1468) |
| 49 | (1) | 1 Oct 1997 (so far as relates to s 49(2), (3)) (SI 1997/1468) |
| | | 1 Mar 1998 (otherwise) (SI 1998/386) |
| | (2), (3) | 1 Oct 1997 (SI 1997/1468) |
| | (4) | 1 Mar 1998 (SI 1998/386) |
| 50 | | 21 Mar 1997 (s 58(4)) |
| 51 | | 1 Sep 1997 (SI 1997/1468) |
| 52 | (1)–(3) | 1 Aug 1998 (SI 1998/386) |
| | (4) | 1 Sep 1997 (SI 1997/1468) |
| | (5) | *Never in force* (repealed) |
| 53 | | 1 Oct 1997 (SI 1997/1468) |
| 54 | | 21 Mar 1997 (s 58(4)) |
| 55, 56 | | 14 Jun 1997 (SI 1997/1468) |
| 57 | (1) | See Sch 7 below |
| | (2), (3) | 1 Sep 1997 (SI 1997/1468) |
| | (4) | See Sch 8 below |
| 58 | | 21 Mar 1997 (s 58(4)) |
| Sch 1 | | 1 Sep 1998 (subject to transitional provisions) (SI 1998/386) |
| Sch 2 | | 1 Sep 1997 (SI 1997/1468) |
| Sch 3 | | 1 Sep 1997 (so far as relates to Education Act 1996, Sch 33B, paras 3, 4) (SI 1997/1468) |
| | | *Never in force* (otherwise) (repealed) |
| Schs 4, 5 | | 1 Oct 1997 (SI 1997/1468) |
| Sch 6 | | 1 Sep 1997 (subject to transitional provisions) (SI 1997/1468) |
| Sch 7 | para 1 | 1 Oct 1997 (SI 1997/1468) |
| | para 2(1) | 1 Oct 1997 (except so far as it provides that the definition of "public body" ceases to include SCAA) (SI 1997/1468) |
| | | 1 Mar 1998 (exception noted above) (SI 1998/386) |

**Education Act 1997 (c 44)**—*contd*

| | |
|---|---|
| para 2(2) | 1 Oct 1997 (SI 1997/1468) |
| para 3(1) | 1 Oct 1997 (except so far as it omits entry relating to SCAA) (SI 1997/1468) |
| | 1 Mar 1998 (exception noted above) (SI 1998/386) |
| para 3(2) | 1 Mar 1998 (SI 1998/386) |
| para 4(1) | 1 Oct 1997 (SI 1997/1468) |
| para 4(2) | 1 Oct 1997 (except so far as it omits entry relating to SCAA) (SI 1997/1468) |
| | 1 Mar 1998 (exception noted above) (SI 1998/386) |
| para 4(3), (4) | 1 Oct 1997 (SI 1997/1468) |
| para 5 | 1 Sep 1997 (SI 1997/1468) |
| paras 6, 7 | 1 Oct 1997 (subject to transitional provisions) (SI 1997/1468) |
| para 8 | 1 Aug 1998 (SI 1998/386) |
| para 9 | 1 Sep 1997 (SI 1997/1468) |
| para 10 | 1 Sep 1998 (SI 1998/386) |
| paras 11–14 | 1 Aug 1998 (SI 1998/386) |
| para 15 | 14 Jun 1997 (SI 1997/1468) |
| para 16 | 1 Sep 1998 (SI 1998/386) |
| para 17 | 1 Aug 1998 (SI 1998/386) |
| para 18 | 14 Jun 1997 (SI 1997/1468) |
| para 19 | 1 Aug 1998 (SI 1998/386) |
| para 20(a) | 14 Jun 1997 (SI 1997/1468) |
| para 20(b) | 1 Apr 1998 (except so far as it substitutes "307A" for "307") (SI 1998/386) |
| | 1 Sep 1998 (exception noted above) (SI 1998/386) |
| para 21 | 1 Aug 1998 (SI 1998/386) |
| para 22 | 1 Sep 1998 (SI 1998/386) |
| paras 23–25 | 1 Aug 1998 (SI 1998/386) |
| para 26 | 1 Oct 1997 (repeals of or in Education Act 1996, ss 360, 361) (SI 1997/1468) |
| | 1 Mar 1998 (otherwise) (SI 1998/386) |
| paras 27–29 | 1 Oct 1997 (subject to transitional provisions) (SI 1997/1468) |
| para 30(a) | 1 Oct 1997 (SI 1997/1468) |
| para 30(b) | 1 Sep 2001 (SI 2001/1215) |
| para 31(1) | 1 Sep 1997 (SI 1997/1468) |
| para 31(2) | 1 Sep 1997 (except so far as it inserts words "section 413B(3) (home-school partnership documents)") (SI 1997/1468) |
| | *Never in force* (exception noted above) (repealed) |
| para 31(3), (4) | 1 Sep 1997 (SI 1997/1468) |
| paras 32, 33 | 1 Sep 1997 (SI 1997/1468) |
| para 34(a) | 1 Sep 1997 (except so far as substitutes words "413A and 413B" for the word "413") (SI 1997/1468) |
| | *Never in force* (exception noted above) (repealed) |
| para 34(b), (c) | 1 Aug 1998 (SI 1998/386) |
| para 34(d) | 1 Sep 1997 (SI 1997/1468) |
| paras 35, 36 | 1 Aug 1998 (SI 1998/386) |
| para 37 | 14 Jun 1997 (SI 1997/1468) |
| para 38 | 1 Sep 1998 (SI 1998/386) |
| para 39 | 14 Jun 1997 (SI 1997/1468) |
| para 40 | *Never in force* (repealed) |
| paras 41–43 | 14 Jun 1997 (SI 1997/1468) |
| para 44 | 14 Jun 1997 (so far as it inserts reference to "school year" into Education Act 1996, s 580) (SI 1997/1468) |
| | 1 Sep 1997 (otherwise) (SI 1997/1468) |
| para 45 | 14 Jun 1997 (SI 1997/1468) |
| para 46 | 1 Aug 1998 (SI 1998/386) |
| para 47 | 1 Sep 1998 (SI 1998/386) |
| para 48(1) | 1 Apr 1998 (SI 1998/386) |
| para 48(2) | 21 Mar 1997 (s 58(4)) |

**Education Act 1997 (c 44)**—*contd*

| | | |
|---|---|---|
| | para 48(3) | 1 Apr 1998 (SI 1998/386) |
| | para 49(1) | 1 Sep 1997 (SI 1997/1468) |
| | para 49(2) | *Never in force* (repealed) |
| | para 49(3) | 1 Sep 1997 (except so far as it inserts Sch 23, para 6(2A)(a) in Education Act 1996) (SI 1997/1468) |
| | | 1 Sep 1998 (exception noted above) (SI 1998/386) |
| | para 50 | 1 Apr 1998 (SI 1998/386) |
| | para 51 | 1 Aug 1998 (SI 1998/386) |
| Sch 8 | | 4 Apr 1997 (repeal in Education Act 1996, s 479(2)) (SI 1997/1153) |
| | | 14 Jun 1997 (repeals of or in Education Act 1996, ss 355(5), 571(2)) (SI 1997/1468) |
| | | 1 Sep 1997 (repeal of Education Act 1996, s 423(6)) (SI 1997/1468) |
| | | 1 Oct 1997 (SI 1997/1468), repeals of or in— |
| | |   Superannuation Act 1972 (to the extent that the provisions relate to the Curriculum and Assessment Authority for Wales); |
| | |   House of Commons Disqualification Act 1975 (to the extent that the provisions relate to the Curriculum and Assessment Authority for Wales); |
| | |   Education Act 1996, ss 360, 361, Schs 30, 37 (except in so far as Sch 37 relates to SCAA) |
| | | 1 Mar 1998 (SI 1998/386), repeals of or in— |
| | |   Superannuation Act 1972 (to the extent that the provisions relate to SCAA); |
| | |   House of Commons Disqualification Act 1975 (to the extent that the provisions relate to NCVQ and SCAA); |
| | |   Education Act 1996, ss 358, 359, Schs 29, 37 (in so far as Sch 37 relates to SCAA) |
| | | 1 Aug 1998 (repeal in Education Act 1996, s 312(2)(c)) (SI 1998/386) |
| | | 1 Sep 1998 (repeals in Education Act 1996, ss 4(2), 19(1), (4), Sch 16, para 15(1)) (SI 1998/386) |
| | | 1 Sep 2001 (repeals of or in Education Act 1996, ss 400, 401, 408(4)(f)) (SI 2001/1215) |
| | | *Never in force* (repeal in Education Act 1996, Sch 23, para 4(1) (repealed)) |

---

**Education (Schools) Act 1997 (c 59)**

*RA:* 31 Jul 1997

*Commencement provisions:* s 7(3); Education (Schools) Act 1997 (Commencement) Order 1997, SI 1997/2774

| | | |
|---|---|---|
| 1, 2 | | 1 Sep 1997 (s 7(3)(a)) |
| 3, 4 | | 31 Jul 1997 (RA) |
| 5 | (1) | 31 Jul 1997 (RA) |
| | (2) | 1 Dec 1997 (SI 1997/2774) |
| 6 | (1) | 1 Sep 1997 (s 7(3)(a)) |
| | (2) | 31 Jul 1997 (RA) |
| | (3) | See Schedule below |
| 7 | | 31 Jul 1997 (RA) |
| Schedule | Pt I | 1 Sep 1997 (s 7(3)(a)) |
| | Pt II | 1 Dec 1997 (SI 1997/2774) |

---

### Finance Act 1997 (c 16)

*Budget Day:* 26 Nov 1996

*RA:* 19 Mar 1997

The commencement details of Finance Acts are not set out, as the dates from which their provisions take effect are usually stated clearly and unambiguously in the text of the Act, and charging provisions will normally state for which year or years of assessment they are to have effect.

---

### Finance (No 2) Act 1997 (c 58)

*Budget Day:* 2 Jul 1997

*RA:* 31 Jul 1997

The commencement details of Finance Acts are not set out, as the dates from which their provisions take effect are usually stated clearly and unambiguously in the text of the Act, and charging provisions will normally state for which year or years of assessment they are to have effect.

---

### Firearms (Amendment) Act 1997 (c 5)

*RA:* 27 Feb 1997

*Commencement provisions:* s 53(3); Firearms (Amendment) Act 1997 (Commencement) (No 1) Order 1997, SI 1997/1076; Firearms (Amendment) Act 1997 (Commencement) (No 2) Order 1997, SI 1997/1535, as amended by SI 1997/1536

| | | |
|---|---|---|
| 1 | (1) | 1 Jul 1997 (SI 1997/1535) |
| | (2), (3) | 1 Jul 1997 (subject to a saving) (SI 1997/1535) |
| | (4)–(9) | 1 Jul 1997 (SI 1997/1535) |
| 2–8 | | 1 Jul 1997 (SI 1997/1535) |
| 9 | | 1 Jul 1997 (subject to a saving) (SI 1997/1535) |
| 10 | | 1 Jul 1997 (SI 1997/1535) |
| 11–14 | | *Never in force* (repealed) |
| 15 | | 10 Jun 1997 (SI 1997/1535) |
| 16–18 | | 17 Mar 1997 (for purposes of making a compensation scheme) (SI 1997/1076) |
| | | 1 Jul 1997 (otherwise) (SI 1997/1535) |
| 19–31 | | *Never in force* (repealed) |
| 32–36 | | 1 Oct 1997 (SI 1997/1535) |
| 37, 38 | | 1 Jul 1997 (SI 1997/1535) |
| 39 | | 1 Oct 1997 (SI 1997/1535) |
| 40 | | 1 Jul 1997 (SI 1997/1535) |
| 41 | | 1 Jul 1997 (subject to a saving) (SI 1997/1535) |
| 42, 43 | | 1 Jul 1997 (SI 1997/1535) |
| 44, 45 | | 1 Oct 1997 (SI 1997/1535) |
| 46 | | *Never in force* (repealed) |
| 47–50 | | 1 Jul 1997 (SI 1997/1535) |
| 51 | | 10 Jun 1997 (SI 1997/1535) |
| 52 | | See Sch 2, 3 below |
| 53 | | 27 Feb 1997 (RA) |
| Sch 1 | | *Never in force* (repealed) |
| Sch 2 | paras 1, 2 | 1 Jul 1997 (SI 1997/1535) |
| | para 3 | 1 Oct 1997 (SI 1997/1535) |
| | para 4 | 1 Jul 1997 (SI 1997/1535) |
| | paras 5, 6 | 1 Oct 1997 (SI 1997/1535) |
| | paras 7, 8 | 1 Jul 1997 (SI 1997/1535) |
| | para 9 | *Never in force* (repealed) |
| | paras 10–12 | 1 Jul 1997 (SI 1997/1535) |
| | para 13 | *Never in force* (repealed) |
| | paras 14–20 | 1 Jul 1997 (SI 1997/1535) |

**Firearms (Amendment) Act 1997 (c 5)**—*contd*

Sch 3                                    1 Jul 1997 (SI 1997/1535), repeals of or in—
                                         Firearms Act 1968, ss 5, 5A, 23, 28;
                                         Firearms (Amendment) Act 1988, ss 9, 10, 12;
                                         Firearms (Amendment) Act 1992
                                         1 Oct 1997 (SI 1997/1535), repeals of or in—
                                         Firearms Act 1968, ss 42, 54, Sch 6;
                                         Firearms (Amendment) Act 1988, s 4

---

**Firearms (Amendment) (No 2) Act 1997 (c 64)**

*RA:* 27 Nov 1997

*Commencement provisions:* s 3(3), (4); Firearms (Amendment) (No 2) Act 1997 (Commencement)
    Order 1997, SI 1997/3114

| | | |
|---|---|---|
| 1 | | 1 Feb 1998 (subject to savings) (SI 1997/3114) |
| 2 | (1), (2) | 17 Dec 1997 (SI 1997/3114) |
| | (3), (4) | 17 Dec 1997 (for purposes of making a compensation scheme) (SI 1997/3114) |
| | | 1 Feb 1998 (otherwise, but subject to savings) (SI 1997/3114) |
| | (5), (6) | 17 Dec 1997 (SI 1997/3114) |
| | (7) | See Schedule below |
| 3 | | 27 Nov 1997 (RA) |
| Schedule | | 17 Dec 1997 (SI 1997/3114), repeals of or in— |

Firearms Act 1968, s 32(2B);
Firearms (Amendment) Act 1988;
Firearms (Amendment) Act 1997, ss 11–14, 19–31, 45(2), 46,
    49(2), 50(1), Sch 1, Sch 2, para 13
1 Feb 1998 (so far as not already in force) (subject to savings)
    (SI 1997/3114)

---

**Flood Prevention and Land Drainage (Scotland) Act 1997 (c 36)**

*RA:* 21 Mar 1997

*Commencement provisions:* s 9(2)–(4); Flood Prevention and Land Drainage (Scotland) Act 1997
    (Commencement) Order 1997, SI 1997/1322

| | | |
|---|---|---|
| 1 | | 26 May 1997 (SI 1997/1322) |
| 2 | | 28 Jul 1997 (SI 1997/1322) |
| 3, 4, 5 | | 26 May 1997 (SI 1997/1322) |
| 6 | (1) | 21 Mar 1997 (s 9(2)) |
| | (2) | 1 Apr 1999 (s 9(3)) |
| 7 | | 21 Mar 1997 (s 9(2)) |
| 8 | | See Schedule below |
| 9 | | 21 Mar 1997 (s 9(2)) |
| Schedule | | 1 Apr 1999 (SI 1997/1322), repeals of or in— |

Land Drainage (Scotland) Act 1930;
Land Drainage (Scotland) Act 1941
26 May 1997 (otherwise) (SI 1997/1322)

---

**Horserace Totalisator Board Act 1997 (c 1)**

*RA:* 27 Feb 1997

Whole Act in force 27 Feb 1997 (RA)

---

## Justices of the Peace Act 1997 (c 25)

*RA:* 19 Mar 1997

*Commencement provisions:* s 74(1)–(4)

Whole Act in force 19 Jun 1997 (s 74(1); but note sub-ss (2), (4))

## Knives Act 1997 (c 21)

*RA:* 19 Mar 1997

*Commencement provisions:* s 11(2), (3); Knives Act 1997 (Commencement) (No 1) Order 1997, SI 1997/1906; Knives Act 1997 (Commencement) (No 2) Order 1999, SI 1999/5

| | |
|---|---|
| 1–7 | 1 Sep 1997 (SI 1997/1906) |
| 8 | 1 Mar 1999 (SI 1999/5) |
| 9, 10 | 1 Sep 1997 (SI 1997/1906) |
| 11 | 19 Mar 1997 (s 11(2)) |

## Land Registration Act 1997 (c 2)

*RA:* 27 Feb 1997

*Commencement provisions:* s 5; Land Registration Act 1997 (Commencement) Order 1997, SI 1997/3036

| | | |
|---|---|---|
| 1 | | 1 Apr 1998 (SI 1997/3036) |
| 2, 3 | | 27 Apr 1997 (s 5(3)) |
| 4 | (1) | See Sch 1 below |
| | (2) | See Sch 2 below |
| 5 | | 27 Apr 1997 (s 5(3)) |
| Sch 1 | Pt I | 1 Apr 1998 (in relation to dispositions made on or after 1 Apr 1998) (SI 1997/3036) |
| | Pt II | 27 Apr 1997 (s 5(3)) |
| Sch 2 | Pt I | 1 Apr 1998 (SI 1997/3036) |
| | Pt II | 27 Apr 1997 (s 5(3)) |

## Law Officers Act 1997 (c 60)

*RA:* 31 Jul 1997

*Commencement provisions:* s 3(3)

Whole Act in force 30 Sep 1997 (s 3(3))

## Lieutenancies Act 1997 (c 23)

*RA:* 19 Mar 1997

*Commencement provisions:* s 9(2)

Whole Act in force 1 Jul 1997 (s 9(2))

## Local Government and Rating Act 1997 (c 29)

*RA:* 19 Mar 1997

*Commencement provisions:* s 34(1)–(3); Local Government and Rating Act 1997 (Commencement No 1) Order 1997, SI 1997/1097; Local Government and Rating Act 1997 (Commencement No 2) Order 1997, SI 1997/2752; Local Government and Rating Act 1997 (Commencement No 3)

**Local Government and Rating Act 1997 (c 29)**—*contd*
Order 1997, SI 1997/2826; Local Government and Rating Act 1997 (Commencement No 4) Order 1998, SI 1998/694; Local Government and Rating Act 1997 (Commencement No 5 and Transitional Provision) Order 1998, SI 1998/2329

| | | |
|---|---|---|
| 1 | | 19 Nov 1997 (subject to a saving) (SI 1997/2752) |
| 2 | | 1 Apr 1997 (SI 1997/1097) |
| 3 | | 1 Apr 2000 (subject to a transitional provision) (SI 1998/2329) |
| 4 | | 1 Oct 1998 (SI 1998/2329) |
| 5 | | See Sch 2 below |
| 6 | | 1 Apr 2000 (subject to a transitional provision) (SI 1998/2329) |
| 7 | | 1 Oct 1998 (SI 1998/2329) |
| 8 | | 1 Dec 1997 (subject to a transitional provision) (SI 1997/2826) |
| 9–25 | | 19 May 1997 (s 34(2)) |
| 26–31 | | 19 May 1997 (SI 1997/1097) |
| 32 | | 19 Mar 1997 (s 34(3)) |
| 33 | (1) | See Sch 3 below |
| | (2) | See Sch 4 below |
| 34, 35 | | 19 Mar 1997 (s 34(3)) |
| Sch 1 | | 19 Nov 1997 (subject to a saving) (SI 1997/2752) |
| Sch 2 | | 1 Dec 1997 (subject to a transitional provision) (SI 1997/2826) |
| Sch 3 | para 1 | 19 May 1997 (SI 1997/1097) |
| | para 2 | 1 Apr 1997 (SI 1997/1097) |
| | para 3 | 1 Apr 2000 (subject to a transitional provision) (SI 1998/2329) |
| | paras 4–10 | 19 May 1997 (s 34(2)) |
| | paras 11–16 | 19 May 1997 (SI 1997/1097) |
| | para 17 | 18 Mar 1998 (SI 1998/694) |
| | paras 18–20 | 1 Apr 2000 (subject to a transitional provision) (SI 1998/2329) |
| | para 21 | 19 May 1997 (s 34(2)) |
| | para 22 | 1 Apr 1997 (so far as relates to Local Government Finance Act 1988, s 47(7) only) (SI 1997/1097) |
| | | 1 Apr 2000 (otherwise) (subject to a transitional provision) (SI 1998/2329) |
| | para 23 | 1 Apr 1997 (SI 1997/1097) |
| | paras 24–28 | 1 Apr 2000 (subject to a transitional provision) (SI 1998/2329) |
| | para 29(a) | 1 Apr 2000 (subject to a transitional provision) (SI 1998/2329) |
| | para 29(b) | 1 Dec 1997 (subject to a transitional provision) (SI 1997/2826) |
| Sch 4 | | 19 May 1997 (SI 1997/1097), except repeals of or in— |

Valuation and Rating (Scotland) Act 1956, s 20;
Local Government Act 1972, ss 9(2), (3), (5), 11(5), 12(1);
National Heritage Act 1983, Sch 1, paras 2(5), 12(5), 22(3), 32(5), Sch 3, para 2(5);
National Heritage (Scotland) Act 1985, s 20;
Dockyard Services Act 1986, s 3(1);
Local Government Finance Act 1988, ss 64(4)(d), (5)–(7D), 65(9), Sch 5, paras 10, 14(3);
Local Government and Housing Act 1989, Sch 5, paras 33, 35(2);
National Maritime Museum Act 1989, s 1(6)
18 Mar 1998 (repeals in Local Government Act 1972) (SI 1998/694)
1 Apr 2000 (otherwise) (subject to a transitional provision) (SI 1998/2329)

**Local Government (Contracts) Act 1997 (c 65)**

*RA:* 27 Nov 1997

*Commencement provisions:* s 12(2); Local Government (Contracts) Act 1997 (Commencement No 1) Order 1997, SI 1997/2843; Local Government (Contracts) Act 1997 (Commencement No 2) Order 1997, SI 1997/2878

**Local Government (Contracts) Act 1997 (c 65)**—*contd*

| | | |
|---|---|---|
| 1 | | 27 Nov 1997 (RA) |
| 2 | | 30 Dec 1997 (E) (W) (SI 1997/2843) |
| | | 1 Jan 1998 (S) (SI 1997/2878) |
| 3 | (1) | 30 Dec 1997 (E) (W) (SI 1997/2843) |
| | | 1 Jan 1998 (S) (SI 1997/2878) |
| | (2)(a)–(d) | 30 Dec 1997 (E) (W) (SI 1997/2843) |
| | | 1 Jan 1998 (S) (SI 1997/2878) |
| | (2)(e), (f) | 1 Dec 1997 (so far as they confer power on the Secretary of State to make regulations) (E) (W) (SI 1997/2843) |
| | | 2 Dec 1997 (so far as they confer power on the Secretary of State to make regulations) (S) (SI 1997/2878) |
| | | 30 Dec 1997 (otherwise) (E) (W) (SI 1997/2843) |
| | | 1 Jan 1998 (otherwise) (S) (SI 1997/2878) |
| | (2)(g) | 30 Dec 1997 (E) (W) (SI 1997/2843) |
| | | 1 Jan 1998 (S) (SI 1997/2878) |
| | (3) | 1 Dec 1997 (so far as it confers power on the Secretary of State to make regulations) (E) (W) (SI 1997/2843) |
| | | 2 Dec 1997 (so far as it confers power on the Secretary of State to make regulations) (S) (SI 1997/2878) |
| | | 30 Dec 1997 (otherwise) (E) (W) (SI 1997/2843) |
| | | 1 Jan 1998 (otherwise) (S) (SI 1997/2878) |
| | (4) | 30 Dec 1997 (E) (W) (SI 1997/2843) |
| | | 1 Jan 1998 (S) (SI 1997/2878) |
| 4–9 | | 30 Dec 1997 (E) (W) (SI 1997/2843) |
| | | 1 Jan 1998 (S) (SI 1997/2878) |
| 10–12 | | 27 Nov 1997 (RA) |

---

**Local Government Finance (Supplementary Credit Approvals) Act 1997 (c 63)**

*RA:* 6 Nov 1997

Whole Act in force 6 Nov 1997 (RA)

---

**Local Government (Gaelic Names) (Scotland) Act 1997 (c 6)**

*RA:* 27 Feb 1997

*Commencement provisions:* s 2(2)

Whole Act in force 27 Apr 1997 (s 2(2))

---

**Merchant Shipping and Maritime Security Act 1997 (c 28)**

*RA:* 19 Mar 1997

*Commencement provisions:* s 31(3), (4); Merchant Shipping and Maritime Security Act 1997 (Commencement No 1) Order 1997, SI 1997/1082; Merchant Shipping and Maritime Security Act 1997 (Commencement No 2) Order 1997, SI 1997/1539

| | | |
|---|---|---|
| 1 | | 23 Mar 1997 (SI 1997/1082) |
| 2–4 | | 17 Jul 1997 (SI 1997/1539) |
| 5 | | 19 Mar 1997 (s 31(4)) |
| 6, 7 | | 17 Jul 1997 (SI 1997/1539) |
| 8 | | 19 Mar 1997 (s 31(4)) |
| 9 | | See Sch 1 below |
| 10 | | 23 Mar 1997 (SI 1997/1082) |
| 11, 12 | | 19 Mar 1997 (s 31(4)) |
| 13 | | See Sch 2 below |
| 14 | (1) | 17 Jul 1997 (SI 1997/1539) |

**Merchant Shipping and Maritime Security Act 1997 (c 28)**—*contd*

| | | |
|---|---|---|
| | (2) | See Sch 3 below |
| 15 | | 17 Jul 1997 (SI 1997/1539) |
| 16 | | 19 Mar 1997 (s 31(4)) |
| 17–23 | | 17 Jul 1997 (SI 1997/1539) |
| 24 | | 19 Mar 1997 (s 31(4)) |
| 25 | | See Sch 4 below |
| 26 | (1) | See Sch 5 below |
| | (2)–(6) | 17 Jul 1997 (SI 1997/1539) |
| 27 | | 17 Jul 1997 (SI 1997/1539) |
| 28 | | 19 Mar 1997 (s 31(4)) |
| 29 | (1) | See Sch 6 below |
| | (2) | See Sch 7 below |
| 30, 31 | | 19 Mar 1997 (s 31(4)) |
| Sch 1 | paras 1–5 | 23 Mar 1997 (SI 1997/1082) |
| | para 6 | *Never in force* (repealed) |
| Sch 2 | | 19 Mar 1997 (s 31(4)) |
| Schs 3–5 | | 17 Jul 1997 (SI 1997/1539) |
| Sch 6 | paras 1–15 | 17 Jul 1997 (SI 1997/1539) |
| | para 16 | 19 Mar 1997 (s 31(4)) |
| | para 17 | 17 Jul 1997 (SI 1997/1539) |
| | para 18(1) | 23 Mar 1997 (SI 1997/1082) |
| | para 18(2) | 17 Jul 1997 (SI 1997/1539) |
| | para 18(3) | 23 Mar 1997 (SI 1997/1082) |
| | para 18(4) | 17 Jul 1997 (SI 1997/1539) |
| | para 18(5) | 23 Mar 1997 (SI 1997/1082) |
| | para 19(1) | 23 Mar 1997 (SI 1997/1082) |
| | para 19(2)(a) | 17 Jul 1997 (SI 1997/1539) |
| | para 19(2)(b), (c) | 23 Mar 1997 (SI 1997/1082) |
| | para 19(2)(d) | 17 Jul 1997 (SI 1997/1539) |
| | para 19(3) | 23 Mar 1997 (SI 1997/1082) |
| | para 20 | 23 Mar 1997 (SI 1997/1082) |
| Sch 7 | Pt I | 23 Mar 1997 (repeals of Merchant Shipping Act 1995, ss 85(3), 86(5), (6)) (SI 1997/1082) |
| | | 17 Jul 1997 (otherwise) (SI 1997/1539) |
| | Pt II | 17 Jul 1997 (SI 1997/1539) |

**Ministerial and other Salaries Act 1997 (c 62)**

*RA:* 6 Nov 1997

Whole Act in force 6 Nov 1997 (RA)

**National Health Service (Primary Care) Act 1997 (c 46)**

*RA:* 21 Mar 1997

*Commencement provisions:* s 41(2), (3); National Health Service (Primary Care) Act 1997 (Commencement No 1) Order 1997, SI 1997/1780; National Health Service (Primary Care) Act 1997 (Commencement No 2) Order 1997, SI 1997/2457; National Health Service (Primary Care) Act 1997 (Commencement No 3) Order 1997, SI 1997/2620; National Health Service (Primary Care) Act 1997 (Commencement No 4) Order 1998, SI 1998/631, as amended by SSI 2001/58, SI 2004/287, SI 2005/2926; National Health Service (Primary Care) Act 1997 (Commencement No 5) Order 1998, SI 1998/1998, as amended by SSI 2001/58, SI 2004/287, SI 2005/2926; National Health Service (Primary Care) Act 1997 (Commencement No 6) Order 1998, SI 1998/2840, as amended by SI 2005/2926; National Health Service (Primary Care) Act 1997 (Commencement No 7) (Scotland) Order 2001, SSI 2001/58; National Health Service (Primary Care) Act 1997 (Commencement No 8) Order 2002, SI 2002/1616; National Health Service (Primary Care) Act 1997 (Commencement No 9) Order 2004, SI 2004/287; National Health Service (Primary Care)

**National Health Service (Primary Care) Act 1997 (c 46)**—*contd*
Act 1997 (Commencement No 10) Order 2005, SI 2005/2926; National Health Service
(Pre-consolidation Amendments) Order 2006, SI 2006/1407

| | | |
|---|---|---|
| 1, 2 | | 28 Nov 1997 (SI 1997/2620) |
| 3 | | 14 Aug 1998 (SI 1998/1998) |
| 4 | | 22 Aug 1997 (so far as relates to pilot schemes under which personal medical services are provided) (SI 1997/1780) |
| | | 30 Oct 1997 (otherwise) (SI 1997/2620) |
| 5, 6 | | 28 Nov 1997 (so far as they relate to pilot schemes under which personal medical services are provided) (SI 1997/2620) |
| | | 1 Apr 1998 (otherwise) (SI 1998/631) |
| 7, 8 | | 1 Apr 1998 (so far as they relate to pilot schemes under which personal medical services are provided) (SI 1998/631) |
| | | 1 Oct 1998 (otherwise) (SI 1998/1998) |
| 9 | (1), (2) | 15 Aug 1997 (SI 1997/1780) |
| | (3) | 1 Apr 1998 (so far as it relates to pilot schemes under which personal medical services are provided) (SI 1998/631) |
| | | 1 Oct 1998 (otherwise) (SI 1998/1998) |
| 10 | | 15 Aug 1997 (SI 1997/1780) |
| 11, 12 | | 1 Apr 1998 (SI 1998/631) |
| 13 | (1) | 15 Aug 1997 (SI 1997/1780) |
| | (2) | 1 Apr 1998 (SI 1998/631) |
| | (3)–(8) | 15 Aug 1997 (SI 1997/1780) |
| | (9) | 1 Apr 1998 (SI 1998/631) |
| 14 | | *Never in force* (repealed) |
| 15 | | 1 Apr 1998 (SI 1998/631) |
| 16 | | 30 Oct 1997 (so far as relates to pilot schemes under which personal medical services are provided) (SI 1997/2620) |
| | | 11 May 1998 (otherwise) (SI 1998/631) |
| 17 | | 1 Oct 1998 (SI 1998/1998) |
| 18 | (1) | 15 Aug 1997 (SI 1997/1780) |
| | (2)(a) | 15 Aug 1997 (SI 1997/1780) |
| | (2)(b) | 28 Nov 1997 (so far as relates to pilot schemes under which personal medical services are provided) (SI 1997/2620) |
| | | 1 Apr 1998 (otherwise) (SI 1998/631) |
| | (3) | 15 Aug 1997 (SI 1997/1780) |
| 19 | | 1 Apr 1998 (SI 1998/631) |
| 20 | | 1 Oct 1998 (SI 1998/1998) |
| 21 | (1) | 1 Mar 2004 (E) (for the purposes of making an order or regulations) (SI 2004/287) |
| | | 1 Apr 2004 (E) (otherwise) (so far as relates to personal medical services) (SI 2004/287) |
| | | 1 Dec 2005 (E) (otherwise) (SI 2005/2926) |
| | | 1 Dec 2005 (W) (so far as relates to personal dental services) (SI 2005/2926) |
| | | 1 Mar 2007 (immediately before the National Health Service Act 2006 comes into force) (otherwise) (SI 2006/1407)[1] |
| | (2) | 5 Mar 2001 (S) (so far as relates to personal medical services) (SSI 2001/58) |
| | | *Not yet in force* (S) (so far as relates to personal dental services) |
| | (3) | 5 Mar 2001 (S) (so far as relates to personal medical services) (SSI 2001/58) |
| | | 1 Mar 2004 (E) (for the purposes of making an order or regulations) (SI 2004/287) |
| | | 1 Apr 2004 (E) (otherwise) (so far as relates to personal medical services) (SI 2004/287) |
| | | 1 Dec 2005 (E) (otherwise) (SI 2005/2926) |
| | | 1 Dec 2005 (W) (so far as relates to personal dental services) (SI 2005/2926) |

**National Health Service (Primary Care) Act 1997 (c 46)**—*contd*

|  |  |  |
|---|---|---|
|  |  | 1 Mar 2007 (immediately before the National Health Service Act 2006 comes into force) (otherwise) (SI 2006/1407)[1] |
| 22 | (1) | 1 Mar 2004 (E) (SI 2004/287) |
|  |  | 1 Dec 2005 (W) (so far as relates to personal dental services) (SI 2005/2926) |
|  |  | 1 Mar 2007 (immediately before the National Health Service Act 2006 comes into force) (otherwise) (SI 2006/1407)[1] |
|  | (2) | 5 Mar 2001 (S) (so far as relates to personal medical services) (SSI 2001/58) |
|  |  | *Not yet in force* (S) (so far as relates to personal dental services) |
| 23 |  | 1 Apr 1998 (SI 1998/631)[1] |
| 24 |  | 1 Oct 1998 (SI 1998/1998) |
| 25 | (1) | *Never in force* (repealed) |
|  | (2) | 5 Mar 2001 (S) (so far as relates to personal medical services) (SSI 2001/58) |
|  |  | *Not yet in force* (S) (so far as relates to general medical services) |
| 26 | (1) | *Never in force* (repealed) |
|  | (2) | *Not yet in force* |
| 27, 28 |  | 15 Aug 1997 (SI 1997/1780) |
| 29 |  | 1 Apr 1998 (SI 1998/631) |
| 30 |  | 15 Aug 1997 (SI 1997/1780) |
| 31 |  | 1 Sep 1997 (SI 1997/1780) |
| 32 |  | 10 Dec 1998 (SI 1998/2840) |
| 33 |  | *Never in force* (repealed) |
| 34, 35 |  | 1 Apr 1998 (SI 1998/631) |
| 36 |  | 14 Oct 1997 (subject to a saving) (SI 1997/2457) |
| 37 |  | 1 Apr 1998 (SI 1998/631) |
| 38–40 |  | 21 Mar 1997 (s 41(2)) |
| 41 | (1)–(9) | 21 Mar 1997 (s 41(2)) |
|  | (10), (11) | See Sch 2 below |
|  | (12) | See Sch 3 below |
|  | (13), (14) | 21 Mar 1997 (s 41(2)) |
| Sch 1 |  | 1 Apr 1998 (subject to transitional provisions relating to paras 1(2)(c), 2(2), (4)) (SI 1998/631) |
| Sch 2 | Pt I, paras 1, 2 | 1 Apr 1998 (SI 1998/631) |
|  | Pt I, para 3 | See paras 4–31 below |
|  | Pt I, paras 4–8 | 1 Apr 1998 (SI 1998/631) |
|  | Pt I, paras 9–11 | 10 Dec 1998 (subject to a saving) (SI 1998/2840) |
|  | Pt I, para 12 | 1 Oct 1998 (SI 1998/1998) |
|  | Pt I, paras 13, 14 | 15 Aug 1997 (SI 1997/1780) |
|  | Pt I, paras 15–18 | 1 Oct 1998 (SI 1998/1998) |
|  | Pt I, para 19 | *Never in force* (repealed) |
|  | Pt I, para 20 | 15 Aug 1997 (SI 1997/1780) |
|  | Pt I, para 21 | 1 Apr 1998 (so far as it relates to pilot schemes under which personal medical services are provided) (SI 1998/631) |
|  |  | 1 Oct 1998 (otherwise) (SI 1998/1998) |
|  | Pt I, paras 22, 23 | 1 Apr 1998 (subject to a saving) (SI 1998/631) |
|  | Pt I, paras 24–26 | 1 Apr 1998 (SI 1998/631) |
|  | Pt I, para 27 | 15 Aug 1997 (SI 1997/1780) |
|  | Pt I, para 28 | 1 Apr 1998 (for the purpose of inserting the definition "section 28C arrangements") (SI 1998/631) |
|  |  | 10 Dec 1998 (for the purpose of inserting the definition "medical list") (SI 1998/2840) |
|  |  | 24 Jun 2002 (E) (for the purpose of inserting the definition "health service body") (SI 2002/1616) |
|  |  | 1 Apr 2004 (W) (for the purpose of inserting the definition "health service body") (SI 2004/287) |
|  |  | 1 Mar 2007 (immediately before the National Health Service Act 2006 comes into force) (otherwise) (SI 2006/1407)[1] |
|  | Pt I, paras 29–31 | 1 Apr 1998 (SI 1998/631) |

**National Health Service (Primary Care) Act 1997 (c 46)**—*contd*

| | | |
|---|---|---|
| Pt I, para 32 | See paras 33–60 below |
| Pt I, para 33 | *Never in force* (repealed) |
| Pt I, para 34 | 5 Mar 2001 (S) (SSI 2001/58) |
| Pt I, paras 35–39 | 1 Apr 1998 (SI 1998/631) |
| Pt I, paras 40–42 | *Never in force* (repealed) |
| Pt I, para 43 | 1 Oct 1998 (SI 1998/1998) |
| Pt I, paras 44, 45 | 15 Aug 1997 (SI 1997/1780) |
| Pt I, para 46 | *Not yet in force* |
| Pt I, paras 47–50 | 1 Oct 1998 (SI 1998/1998) |
| Pt I, para 51 | 15 Aug 1997 (SI 1997/1780) |
| Pt I, para 52 | 1 Oct 1998 (SI 1998/1998) |
| Pt I, paras 53, 54 | 1 Apr 1998 (SI 1998/631) |
| Pt I, para 55 | *Not yet in force* |
| Pt I, para 56 | 5 Mar 2001 (S) (SSI 2001/58) |
| Pt I, para 57 | 1 Apr 1998 (for the purpose of inserting the definition "section 17C arrangements") (SI 1998/631) |
| | 5 Mar 2001 (for purpose of inserting the definition "personal medical services" (repealed)) (SSI 2001/58) |
| | *Not yet in force* (for the purpose of inserting the definitions "health service body" and "personal dental services") |
| | *Never in force* (repealed) (for purpose of inserting the definition "medical list") |
| Pt I, paras 58–61 | 1 Apr 1998 (SI 1998/631) |
| Pt I, para 62 | 18 Nov 1998 (SI 1998/2840) |
| Pt I, para 63 | 1 Apr 1998 (SI 1998/631) |
| Pt I, para 64(1) | See sub-paras (2)–(4) below |
| Pt I, para 64(2) | 1 Apr 1998 (SI 1998/631) |
| Pt I, para 64(3) | *Not yet in force* |
| Pt I, para 64(4) | 1 Apr 1998 (SI 1998/631) |
| Pt I, para 65(1) | See paras (2)–(11) below |
| Pt I, para 65(2) | 1 Apr 2004 (E) (so far as relates to personal medical services) (SI 2004/287) |
| | 1 Dec 2005 (E) (otherwise) (SI 2005/2926) |
| | 1 Dec 2005 (W) (so far as relates to personal dental services) (SI 2005/2926) |
| | 1 Mar 2007 (immediately before the National Health Service Act 2006 comes into force) (otherwise) (SI 2006/1407)[1] |
| Pt I, para 65(3)–(7) | *Never in force* (repealed) |
| Pt I, para 65(8)–(11) | 1 Apr 1998 (SI 1998/631) |
| Pt I, paras 66–68 | 1 Apr 1998 (SI 1998/631) |
| Pt II | *Never in force* (repealed) |
| Sch 3    Pt I | 1 Apr 1998 (SI 1998/631), repeals of or in— |
| |   National Health Service Act 1977, ss 29(2), 97A(9)(c)(i) (subject to a saving), Sch 10; |
| |   National Health Service (Scotland) Act 1978, s 19(2), Sch 9; |
| |   National Health Service and Community Care Act 1990, s 12(1)(c); |
| |   Health Authorities Act 1995, Sch 1, paras 6(c), 36 |
| | 1 Oct 1998 (SI 1998/1998), repeals of or in— |
| |   National Health Service Act 1977, s 36(1)(c); |
| |   National Health Service (Scotland) Act 1978, s 25(2)(c) |
| | 10 Dec 1998 (subject to a saving) (SI 1998/2840), repeals in— |
| |   National Health Service Act 1977 (so far as not already in force); |
| |   Health Services Act 1980; |
| |   Health and Social Security Act 1984; |
| |   Health and Medicines Act 1988; |
| |   National Health Service and Community Care Act 1990 (so far as not already in force); |
| |   Health Authorities Act 1995 (so far as not already in force) |

**National Health Service (Primary Care) Act 1997 (c 46)**—*contd*

> *Not yet in force* (repeal in National Health Service (Scotland)
>   Act 1978, s 23)
> *Never in force* (repealed) repeals in or of National Health Service
>   (Scotland) Act 1978, ss 3, 20, 24

| | |
|---|---|
| Pt II | *Not yet in force* |
| Pt III | 10 Dec 1998 (SI 1998/2840) |

[1]  For a saving, see SI 2006/1407, art 4

---

**National Health Service (Private Finance) Act 1997 (c 56)**

*RA:* 15 Jul 1997

Whole Act in force 15 Jul 1997 (RA)

---

**National Heritage Act 1997 (c 14)**

*RA:* 27 Feb 1997

*Commencement provisions:* s 4(2); National Heritage Act 1997 (Commencement) Order 1998, SI 1998/292

| | |
|---|---|
| 1–3 | 4 Mar 1998 (SI 1998/292) |
| 4 | 27 Feb 1997 (RA) |
| Schedule | 4 Mar 1998 (SI 1998/292) |

---

**Northern Ireland Arms Decommissioning Act 1997 (c 7)**

*RA:* 27 Feb 1997

*Commencement provisions:* s 7(6); Northern Ireland Arms Decommissioning Act 1997 (Commencement of Section 7) Order 1997, SI 1997/2111

| | |
|---|---|
| 1–6 | 27 Feb 1997 (RA) |
| 7 | 1 Sep 1997 (SI 1997/2111) |
| 8–11 | 27 Feb 1997 (RA) |
| Schedule | 27 Feb 1997 (RA) |

---

**Nurses, Midwives and Health Visitors Act 1997 (c 24)**

*RA:* 19 Mar 1997

*Commencement provisions:* s 24(2)

Whole Act in force 19 Jun 1997 (s 24(2))

---

**Pensions Measure 1997 (No 1)**

*RA:* 21 Mar 1997

*Commencement provisions:* s 11(2)

The provisions of this Measure were brought into force on 1 Jan 1998 by an instrument made by the Archbishops of Canterbury and York dated 28 Nov 1997 (made under s 11(2))

---

## Pharmacists (Fitness to Practise) Act 1997 (c 19)

*RA:* 19 Mar 1997

*Commencement provisions:* s 2(1), (2)

| | |
|---|---|
| 1 | *Never in force* (repealed) |
| 2, 3 | 19 Mar 1997 (RA) |
| Schedule | *Never in force* (repealed) |

## Planning (Consequential Provisions) (Scotland) Act 1997 (c 11)

*RA:* 27 Feb 1997

*Commencement provisions:* s 6

| | | |
|---|---|---|
| 1, 2 | | 27 May 1997 (s 6(2)) |
| 3 | (1) | See Sch 1 below |
| | (2), (3) | 27 May 1997 (s 6(2)) |
| 4 | | See Sch 2 below |
| 5 | (1) | See Sch 3 below |
| | (2) | 27 May 1997 (s 6(2)) |
| 6 | | 27 May 1997 (s 6(2)) |
| Sch 1 | Pt I | 27 May 1997 (except repeal relating to Town and Country Planning (Scotland) Act 1997, s 186) (s 6(2)) |
| | | *Not yet in force* (exception noted above) |
| | Pts II, III | 27 May 1997 (s 6(2)) |
| Schs 2, 3 | | 27 May 1997 (s 6(2)) |

## Planning (Hazardous Substances) (Scotland) Act 1997 (c 10)

*RA:* 27 Feb 1997

*Commencement provisions:* s 40(2)

Whole Act in force 27 May 1997 (s 40(2))

## Planning (Listed Buildings and Conservation Areas) (Scotland) Act 1997 (c 9)

*RA:* 27 Feb 1997

*Commencement provisions:* s 83(2)

Whole Act in force 27 May 1997 (s 83(2))

## Plant Varieties Act 1997 (c 66)

*RA:* 27 Nov 1997

*Commencement provisions:* s 54(2)–(4); Plant Varieties Act 1997 (Commencement) Order 1998, SI 1998/1028

| | |
|---|---|
| 1–48 | 8 May 1998 (SI 1998/1028) |
| 49 | 27 Nov 1997 (s 54(2)) |
| 50–52 | 8 May 1998 (SI 1998/1028) |
| 53, 54 | 27 Nov 1997 (s 54(2)) |
| Schs 1–4 | 8 May 1998 (SI 1998/1028) |

## Police Act 1997 (c 50)

*RA:* 21 Mar 1997

*Commencement provisions:* s 135; Police Act 1997 (Commencement No 1 and Transitional Provisions) Order 1997, SI 1997/1377; Police Act 1997 (Commencement No 2) Order 1997, SI 1997/1696; Police Act 1997 (Commencement No 3 and Transitional Provisions) Order 1997, SI 1997/1930; Police Act 1997 (Commencement No 4 and Transitional Provisions) Order 1997, SI 1997/2390, as amended by SI 1998/354; Police Act 1997 (Commencement No 5 and Transitional Provisions) Order 1998, SI 1998/354; Police Act 1997 (Commencement No 6) Order 1999, SI 1999/151; Police Act 1997 (Commencement No 7) Order 2001, SI 2001/1097; Police Act 1997 (Commencement No 8) (Scotland) Order 2001, SSI 2001/482; Police Act 1997 (Commencement No 9) Order 2002, SI 2002/413; Police Act 1997 (Commencement No 10) (Scotland) Order 2002, SSI 2002/124; Police Act 1997 (Commencement No 10) Order 2007, SI 2007/3342[1]; Police Act 1997 (Commencement No 11) Order 2008, SI 2008/692[2]; Police Act 1997 (Commencement No 12) (England and Wales) Order 2014, SI 2014/237

| | | |
|---|---|---|
| 1 | (1)–(6) | 25 Jun 1997 (for purposes of the appointment of members of the Service Authority for the National Criminal Intelligence Service) (SI 1997/1377) |
| | | 23 Jul 1997 (otherwise) (SI 1997/1377) |
| | (7) | See Schs 1, 2 below |
| 2 | (1)–(5) | 1 Apr 1998 (SI 1998/354) |
| | (6) | 1 Sep 1997 (so far as relates to any directions given under s 27) (SI 1997/1930) |
| | | 8 Oct 1997 (so far as relates to any directions given under Sch 3 below) (SI 1997/1930) |
| | | 1 Apr 1998 (otherwise) (SI 1998/354) |
| 3 | (1) | 1 Apr 1998 (SI 1998/354) |
| | (2), (3) | 1 Sep 1997 (SI 1997/1930) |
| | (4)(a) | 1 Sep 1997 (subject to a transitional provision) (SI 1997/1930) |
| | (4)(b)–(d) | 1 Sep 1997 (SI 1997/1930) |
| 4 | | 31 Oct 1997 (subject to a transitional provision) (SI 1997/2390) |
| 5 | | 1 Apr 1998 (SI 1998/354) |
| 6 | | 23 Jul 1997 (SI 1997/1377) |
| 7 | | 1 Apr 1998 (SI 1998/354) |
| 8, 9 | | 31 Oct 1997 (subject to transitional provisions) (SI 1997/2390) |
| 10–12 | | 1 Apr 1998 (SI 1998/354) |
| 13–16 | | 23 Jul 1997 (SI 1997/1377) |
| 17 | (1) | 8 Oct 1997 (SI 1997/1930) |
| | (2)–(5) | 25 Jun 1997 (SI 1997/1377) |
| | (6) | 8 Oct 1997 (SI 1997/1930) |
| 18 | | 23 Jul 1997 (SI 1997/1377) |
| 19 | | 31 Oct 1997 (SI 1997/2390) |
| 20 | | 1 Apr 1998 (SI 1998/354) |
| 21 | | 31 Oct 1997 (SI 1997/2390) |
| 22 | (1)–(3) | 1 Apr 1998 (SI 1998/354) |
| | (4)–(8) | 31 Oct 1997 (subject to a transitional provision) (SI 1997/2390) |
| 23, 24 | | 1 Apr 1998 (SI 1998/354) |
| 25 | | 1 Sep 1997 (SI 1997/1930) |
| 26 | (1) | 1 Sep 1997 (SI 1997/1930) |
| | (2)(a) | 1 Sep 1997 (SI 1997/1930) |
| | (2)(b) | 1 Sep 1997 (subject to a transitional provision) (SI 1997/1930) |
| | (2)(c)–(e) | 1 Sep 1997 (SI 1997/1930) |
| | (2)(f) | 1 Sep 1997 (subject to a transitional provision) (SI 1997/1930) |
| | (2)(g) | 1 Sep 1997 (SI 1997/1930) |
| 27 | | 1 Sep 1997 (SI 1997/1930) |
| 28 | | 31 Oct 1997 (SI 1997/2390) |
| 29–36 | | 1 Apr 1998 (SI 1998/354) |
| 37 | | 31 Oct 1997 (SI 1997/2390) |
| 38 | | 31 Oct 1997 (for purpose of making orders) (SI 1997/2390) |
| | | 1 Apr 1998 (otherwise) (SI 1998/354) |

**Police Act 1997 (c 50)**—*contd*

| | | |
|---|---|---|
| 39 | | 31 Oct 1997 (SI 1997/2390) |
| 40–43 | | 1 Apr 1998 (SI 1998/354) |
| 44–46 | | 25 Jun 1997 (SI 1997/1377) |
| 47 | (1)–(6) | 25 Jun 1997 (for purposes of the appointment of members of the Service Authority for the National Crime Squad) (SI 1997/1377) |
| | | 23 Jul 1997 (otherwise) (SI 1997/1377) |
| | (7) | See Schs 1, 2 below |
| 48 | (1)–(6) | 1 Apr 1998 (SI 1998/354) |
| | (7) | 1 Sep 1997 (so far as relates to any directions given under s 72) (SI 1997/1930) |
| | | 8 Oct 1997 (so far as relates to any directions given under Sch 5) (SI 1997/1930) |
| | | 1 Apr 1998 (otherwise) (SI 1998/354) |
| 49 | (1) | 1 Apr 1998 (SI 1998/354) |
| | (2), (3) | 1 Sep 1997 (SI 1997/1930) |
| | (4)(a) | 1 Sep 1997 (subject to a transitional provision) (SI 1997/1930) |
| | (4)(b), (c) | 1 Sep 1997 (SI 1997/1930) |
| 50 | | 31 Oct 1997 (subject to a transitional provision) (SI 1997/2390) |
| 51 | | 1 Apr 1998 (SI 1998/354) |
| 52 | | 23 Jul 1997 (SI 1997/1377) |
| 53 | | 1 Apr 1998 (SI 1998/354) |
| 54, 55 | | 31 Oct 1997 (subject to transitional provisions) (SI 1997/2390) |
| 56, 57 | | 1 Apr 1998 (SI 1998/354) |
| 58–61 | | 23 Jul 1997 (SI 1997/1377) |
| 62 | (1) | 8 Oct 1997 (SI 1997/1930) |
| | (2)–(5) | 25 Jun 1997 (SI 1997/1377) |
| | (6) | See Sch 5 below |
| 63 | | 23 Jul 1997 (SI 1997/1377) |
| 64 | | 31 Oct 1997 (SI 1997/2390) |
| 65 | | 1 Apr 1998 (SI 1998/354) |
| 66 | | 31 Oct 1997 (SI 1997/2390) |
| 67 | | 1 Apr 1998 (subject to a transitional provision) (SI 1998/354) |
| 68, 69 | | 1 Apr 1998 (SI 1998/354) |
| 70 | | 1 Sep 1997 (SI 1997/1930) |
| 71 | (1) | 1 Sep 1997 (SI 1997/1930) |
| | (2)(a) | 1 Sep 1997 (SI 1997/1930) |
| | (2)(b) | 1 Sep 1997 (subject to a transitional provision) (SI 1997/1930) |
| | (2)(c)–(e) | 1 Sep 1997 (SI 1997/1930) |
| | (2)(f) | 1 Sep 1997 (subject to a transitional provision) (SI 1997/1930) |
| | (3) | 1 Sep 1997 (SI 1997/1930) |
| 72 | | 1 Sep 1997 (SI 1997/1930) |
| 73 | | 31 Oct 1997 (SI 1997/2390) |
| 74–80 | | 1 Apr 1998 (SI 1998/354) |
| 81 | | 31 Oct 1997 (SI 1997/2390) |
| 82 | | 31 Oct 1997 (for purpose of making orders) (SI 1997/2390) |
| | | 1 Apr 1998 (otherwise) (SI 1998/354) |
| 83 | | 31 Oct 1997 (SI 1997/2390) |
| 84–87 | | 1 Apr 1998 (SI 1998/354) |
| 88 | | See Sch 6 below |
| 89, 90 | | 25 Jun 1997 (SI 1997/1377) |
| 91 | (1)–(9) | 1 Sep 1997 (SI 1997/1930) |
| | (10) | 22 Feb 1999 (SI 1999/151) |
| 92–95 | | 22 Feb 1999 (SI 1999/151) |
| 96 | | 1 Sep 1997 (for purpose of making orders) (SI 1997/1930) |
| | | 22 Feb 1999 (otherwise) (SI 1999/151) |
| 97–100 | | 22 Feb 1999 (SI 1999/151) |
| 101 | | 5 Aug 1997 (SI 1997/1696) |
| 102–108 | | 22 Feb 1999 (SI 1999/151) |

**Police Act 1997 (c 50)**—*contd*

| | | |
|---|---|---|
| 109 | (1) | 1 Sep 1997 (SI 1997/1930) |
| | (2) | See Sch 8 below |
| | (3) | 1 Sep 1997 (for purpose of making orders) (SI 1997/1930) |
| | | 1 Apr 1998 (otherwise) (SI 1998/354) |
| | (4) | 1 Apr 1998 (SI 1998/354) |
| | (5) | 1 Sep 1997 (for purpose of making orders) (SI 1997/1930) |
| | | 1 Apr 1998 (otherwise) (SI 1998/354) |
| | (6) | 1 Apr 1998 (SI 1998/354) |
| 110 | | 1 Apr 1998 (SI 1998/354) |
| 111 | (1)(a), (b) | 1 Sep 1997 (SI 1997/1930) |
| | (1)(c), (d) | 1 Apr 1998 (SI 1998/354) |
| | (2)(a)–(c) | 1 Sep 1997 (SI 1997/1930) |
| | (2)(d), (e) | 1 Apr 1998 (SI 1998/354) |
| | (3)(a), (b) | 1 Sep 1997 (SI 1997/1930) |
| | (3)(c), (d) | 1 Apr 1998 (SI 1998/354) |
| 112 | | 31 Jul 2002 (S) (SSI 2002/124) |
| | | 1 Apr 2008 (NI) (SI 2008/692) |
| | | 10 Mar 2014 (E) (W) (SI 2014/237) |
| 113 | | 1 Mar 2002 (E) (W) (SI 2002/413) |
| | | 25 Apr 2002 (S) (SSI 2002/124) |
| 114 | | 1 Mar 2002 (E) (W) (SI 2002/413) |
| | | 25 Apr 2002 (S) (SSI 2002/124) |
| | | 1 Apr 2008 (NI) (SI 2008/692) |
| 115 | (1), (2) | 1 Mar 2002 (E) (W) (SI 2002/413) |
| | | 25 Apr 2002 (S) (SSI 2002/124) |
| | (3) | 1 Mar 2002 (E) (W) (SI 2002/413) |
| | | 25 Apr 2002 (S) (SSI 2002/124) |
| | (4) | 1 Mar 2002 (E) (W) (SI 2002/413) |
| | | 11 Mar 2002 (S) (for the purpose of making regulations under para (a)) (SSI 2002/124) |
| | | 25 Apr 2002 (S) (otherwise) (SSI 2002/124) |
| | (5)–(10) | 1 Mar 2002 (E) (W) (SI 2002/413) |
| | | 25 Apr 2002 (S) (SSI 2002/124) |
| 116–119 | | 1 Mar 2002 (E) (W) (SI 2002/413) |
| | | 25 Apr 2002 (S) (SSI 2002/124) |
| | | 1 Apr 2008 (NI) (SI 2008/692) |
| 120 | (1), (2) | 1 May 2001 (E) (W) (SI 2001/1097) |
| | | 1 Feb 2002 (S) (SSI 2001/482) |
| | | 3 Dec 2007 (NI) (SI 2007/3342) |
| | (3) | 19 Mar 2001 (E) (W) (SI 2001/1097) |
| | | 1 Jan 2002 (S) (SSI 2001/482) |
| | | 3 Dec 2007 (NI) (SI 2007/3342) |
| | (4)–(7) | 1 May 2001 (E) (W) (SI 2001/1097) |
| | | 1 Feb 2002 (S) (SSI 2001/482) |
| | | 3 Dec 2007 (NI) (SI 2007/3342) |
| 121 | | 25 Apr 2002 (S) (SSI 2002/124) |
| 122 | (1), (2) | 19 Mar 2001 (E) (W) (SI 2001/1097) |
| | | 1 Jan 2002 (S) (SSI 2001/482) |
| | | 3 Dec 2007 (NI) (SI 2007/3342) |
| | (3) | 1 Mar 2002 (E) (W) (SI 2002/413) |
| | | 25 Apr 2002 (S) (SSI 2002/124) |
| | | 3 Dec 2007 (NI) (SI 2007/3342) |
| 123, 124 | | 1 Mar 2002 (E) (W) (SI 2002/413) |
| | | 25 Apr 2002 (S) (SSI 2002/124) |
| | | 3 Dec 2007 (NI) (SI 2007/3342) |
| 125 | | 19 Mar 2001 (E) (W) (SI 2001/1097) |
| | | 1 Jan 2002 (S) (SSI 2001/482) |
| | | 3 Dec 2007 (NI) (SI 2007/3342) |
| 126, 127 | | 1 Mar 2002 (E) (W) (SI 2002/413) |

**Police Act 1997 (c 50)**—*contd*

|  |  |  |
|---|---|---|
|  |  | 25 Apr 2002 (S) (SSI 2002/124) |
|  |  | 3 Dec 2007 (NI) (SI 2007/3342) |
| 128 |  | 25 Jun 1997 (SI 1997/1377) |
| 129 | (a) | *Not yet in force* |
|  | (b)–(d) | 25 Jun 1997 (SI 1997/1377) |
| 130–132 |  | 25 Jun 1997 (SI 1997/1377) |
| 133 |  | *Not yet in force* |
| 134 | (1) | See Sch 9 below |
|  | (2) | See Sch 10 below |
| 135–138 |  | 21 Mar 1997 (RA) |
| Schs 1, 2 |  | 25 Jun 1997 (for purposes of the appointment of members of the Service Authority for the National Criminal Intelligence Service and members of the Service Authority for the National Crime Squad) (SI 1997/1377) |
|  |  | 23 Jul 1997 (otherwise) (SI 1997/1377) |
| Sch 3 | para 1(1)–(3) | 8 Oct 1997 (SI 1997/1930) |
|  | para 1(4)(a) | 8 Oct 1997 (subject to a transitional provision) (SI 1997/1930) |
|  | para 1(4)(b)–(f) | 8 Oct 1997 (SI 1997/1930) |
|  | para 1(5), (6) | 8 Oct 1997 (SI 1997/1930) |
|  | paras 2–5 | 8 Oct 1997 (SI 1997/1930) |
| Sch 4 |  | 1 Sep 1997 (SI 1997/1930) |
| Sch 5 | para 1(1)–(3) | 8 Oct 1997 (SI 1997/1930) |
|  | para 1(4)(a) | 8 Oct 1997 (subject to a transitional provision) (SI 1997/1930) |
|  | para 1(4)(b)–(f) | 8 Oct 1997 (SI 1997/1930) |
|  | para 1(5), (6) | 8 Oct 1997 (SI 1997/1930) |
|  | paras 2–5 | 8 Oct 1997 (SI 1997/1930) |
| Sch 6 | paras 1, 2 | 31 Oct 1997 (SI 1997/2390) |
|  | para 3 | 1 Sep 1997 (SI 1997/1930) |
|  | para 4 | 1 Apr 1998 (SI 1998/354) |
|  | para 5 | 1 Sep 1997 (SI 1997/1930) |
|  | para 6 | 31 Oct 1997 (subject to a transitional provision) (SI 1997/2390) |
|  | paras 7, 8 | 1 Apr 1998 (SI 1998/354) |
|  | para 9(a)–(d) | 1 Apr 1998 (SI 1998/354) |
|  | para 9(e) | 31 Oct 1997 (SI 1997/2390) |
|  | para 10 | 1 Sep 1997 (SI 1997/1930) |
|  | paras 11–13 | 1 Apr 1998 (SI 1998/354) |
|  | para 14 | *Never in force* (repealed) |
|  | paras 15–24 | 1 Apr 1998 (SI 1998/354) |
|  | paras 25, 26 | *Never in force* (repealed) |
|  | paras 27, 28 | 1 Apr 1998 (SI 1998/354) |
|  | para 29 | 31 Oct 1997 (subject to a transitional provision) (SI 1997/2390) |
|  | paras 30, 31 | 1 Apr 1998 (SI 1998/354) |
|  | para 32 | 31 Oct 1997 (SI 1997/2390) |
| Sch 7 |  | 22 Feb 1999 (SI 1999/151) |
| Sch 8 | para 1(1) | 1 Sep 1997 (SI 1997/1930) |
|  | para 1(2) | 1 Sep 1997 (subject to a modification) (SI 1997/1930) |
|  | para 1(3)(a)–(d) | 1 Sep 1997 (SI 1997/1930) |
|  | para 1(3)(e), (f) | *Never in force* (repealed) |
|  | para 1(3)(g) | 1 Sep 1997 (SI 1997/1930) |
|  | para 2(1)–(5) | 1 Sep 1997 (SI 1997/1930) |
|  | para 2(6) | *Never in force* (repealed) |
|  | para 3 | 1 Apr 1998 (SI 1998/354) |
|  | para 4 | 1 Sep 1997 (SI 1997/1930) |
|  | paras 5–7 | 1 Apr 1998 (SI 1998/354) |
|  | para 8(1) | 1 Sep 1997 (SI 1997/1930) |
|  | para 8(2) | 1 Apr 1998 (SI 1998/354) |
|  | para 9 | 1 Sep 1997 (SI 1997/1930) |

**Police Act 1997 (c 50)**—*contd*

| | | |
|---|---|---|
| | para 10 | 1 Sep 1997 (except the reference to para 1(3)(e) in sub-para (1)(a) and the reference to para 1(3)(f) in sub-para (1)(b)) (SI 1997/1930) |
| | | *Never in force* (exceptions noted above) (repealed) |
| | para 11 | 1 Sep 1997 (SI 1997/1930) |
| | paras 12–17 | 1 Apr 1998 (SI 1998/354) |
| | para 18 | 1 Sep 1997 (SI 1997/1930) |
| Sch 9 | paras 1, 2 | 1 Apr 1998 (SI 1998/354) |
| | para 3 | 1 Sep 1997 (SI 1997/1930) |
| | paras 4–7 | 1 Apr 1998 (SI 1998/354) |
| | paras 8, 9 | 1 Sep 1997 (SI 1997/1930) |
| | paras 10–12 | 1 Apr 1998 (SI 1998/354) |
| | paras 13, 14 | 31 Oct 1997 (SI 1997/2390) |
| | paras 15–20 | 1 Apr 1998 (SI 1998/354) |
| | paras 21, 22 | 1 Apr 1998 (SI 1998/354) |
| | para 23 | 31 Oct 1997 (SI 1997/2390) |
| | paras 24–26 | 1 Apr 1998 (SI 1998/354) |
| | para 27 | 23 Jul 1997 (so far as relates to members of the service authorities for the National Crime Intelligence Service and the National Crime Squad) (SI 1997/1377) |
| | | 1 Apr 1998 (otherwise) (SI 1998/354) |
| | para 28 | 23 Jul 1997 (SI 1997/1377) |
| | para 29(1), (2) | 1 Apr 1998 (SI 1998/354) |
| | para 29(3) | 1 Sep 1997 (SI 1997/1930) |
| | paras 30–37 | 1 Apr 1998 (SI 1998/354) |
| | paras 38, 39 | 31 Oct 1997 (SI 1997/2390) |
| | para 40 | 23 Jul 1997 (SI 1997/1377) |
| | para 41 | 23 Jul 1997 (so far as relates to members of the service authorities for the National Crime Intelligence Service and the National Crime Squad) (SI 1997/1377) |
| | | 1 Apr 1998 (otherwise) (SI 1998/354) |
| | para 42 | 1 Apr 1998 (SI 1998/354) |
| | para 43 | 31 Oct 1997 (SI 1997/2390) |
| | paras 44–48 | 1 Apr 1998 (SI 1998/354) |
| | paras 49–52 | 31 Oct 1997 (SI 1997/2390) |
| | paras 53, 54 | 1 Apr 1998 (SI 1998/354) |
| | para 55 | 31 Oct 1997 (SI 1997/2390) |
| | para 56 | 1 Apr 1998 (SI 1998/354) |
| | para 57 | 31 Oct 1997 (SI 1997/2390) |
| | paras 58–64 | 1 Apr 1998 (SI 1998/354) |
| | para 65 | 1 Mar 2002 (SI 2002/413) |
| | paras 66–68 | 31 Oct 1997 (SI 1997/2390) |
| | paras 69–71 | 1 Apr 1998 (SI 1998/354) |
| | paras 72, 73 | 31 Oct 1997 (SI 1997/2390) |
| | paras 74–80 | 1 Apr 1998 (SI 1998/354) |
| | para 81 | 31 Oct 1997 (SI 1997/2390) |
| | paras 82, 83 | 1 Sep 1997 (SI 1997/1930) |
| | paras 84, 85 | 1 Apr 1998 (SI 1998/354) |
| | para 86 | 31 Oct 1997 (SI 1997/2390) |
| | para 87 | 1 Apr 1998 (SI 1998/354) |
| | para 88 | 23 Jul 1997 (SI 1997/1377) |
| | paras 89, 90 | 1 Apr 1998 (SI 1998/354) |
| | para 91 | 31 Oct 1997 (SI 1997/2390) |
| | para 92 | 1 Apr 1998 (SI 1998/354) |
| Sch 10 | | 1 Apr 1998 (SI 1998/354), repeals in— |
| | | Leasehold Reform Act 1967; |
| | | Police (Scotland) Act 1967; |
| | | Local Government Act 1972; |
| | | Local Government (Miscellaneous Provisions) Act 1976; |

**Police Act 1997 (c 50)**—*contd*

> Police Pensions Act 1976;
> Security Service Act 1989;
> Aviation and Maritime Security Act 1990;
> Environment Act 1995;
> Police Act 1996;
> Security Service Act 1996
> 1 Mar 2002 (repeal in Road Traffic Act 1991) (SI 2002/413)
> *Not yet in force*, repeals of or in—
> Financial Services Act 1986, s 189, Sch 14 (repealed);
> Banking Act 1987, s 95 (repealed);
> National Lottery etc Act 1993;
> Osteopaths Act 1993;
> Chiropractors Act 1994

[1] Note that SI 2007/3342 also purports to bring ss 120ZA, 120A, 120AA, 120AB, 122A and 124A into force on 3 Dec 2007 in relation to Northern Ireland. For further information on these inserted sections, please consult Halsbury's Statutes Citator

[2] Note that SI 2008/692 also purports to bring ss 113A, 113B, 113C, 113D and 113F into force on 1 Apr 2008 in relation to Northern Ireland. For further information on these inserted sections, please consult Halsbury's Statutes Citator

**Police and Firemen's Pensions Act 1997 (c 52)**

*RA:* 21 Mar 1997

*Commencement provisions:* s 4

| | |
|---|---|
| 1 | 21 Mar 1997 (RA) |
| 2, 3 | 21 May 1997 (s 4(2)) |
| 4 | 21 Mar 1997 (RA) |

**Police (Health and Safety) Act 1997 (c 42)**

*RA:* 21 Mar 1997

*Commencement provisions:* s 9(2); Police (Health and Safety) Act 1997 (Commencement) Order 1998, SI 1998/1542

| | |
|---|---|
| 1–6 | 1 Jul 1998 (SI 1998/1542) |
| 7–9 | 21 Mar 1997 (s 9(2)) |

**Police (Insurance of Voluntary Assistants) Act 1997 (c 45)**

*RA:* 21 Mar 1997

Whole Act in force 21 Mar 1997 (RA)

**Police (Property) Act 1997 (c 30)**

*RA:* 19 Mar 1997

*Commencement provisions:* s 7(2)

Whole Act in force 19 May 1997 (s 7(2))

## Policyholders Protection Act 1997 (c 18)

*RA:* 19 Mar 1997

*Commencement provisions:* s 23(2), (3); Policyholders Protection Act 1997 (Commencement No 1) Order 2000, SI 2000/971; Policyholders Protection Act 1997 (Commencement No 2) Order 2000, SI 2000/3111

| | | |
|---|---|---|
| 1, 2 | | *Never in force* (repealed) |
| 3 | | 5 Apr 2000 (subject to savings, in relation to petitions for the winding-up of a company leading to the appointment of a provisional liquidator or where the petition for the winding-up of a company was presented before the specified date, or applications for the sanctioning of a compromise or arrangement made before that date) (SI 2000/971) |
| | | *Never in force* (exceptions noted above) (repealed) |
| 4, 5 | | 23 Nov 2000 (SI 2000/3111) |
| 6–15 | | *Never in force* (repealed) |
| 16 | | 5 Apr 2000 (subject to savings, for the purposes of Policyholders Protection Act 1975, ss 5–11, in relation to resolutions passed or petitions presented before that date, and for the purposes of ss 15–17 of the 1975 Act in relation to petitions for the winding-up of a company leading to the appointment of a provisional liquidator or where the petition for the winding-up of a company was presented before that date, or applications for the sanctioning of a compromise or arrangement made before that date) (SI 2000/971) |
| | | *Never in force* (exceptions noted above) (repealed) |
| 17–19 | | *Never in force* (repealed) |
| 20 | (1), (2) | See Sch 4 below |
| | (3) | 19 Mar 1997 (s 23(2)) |
| 21 | | 5 Apr 2000 (SI 2000/971) |
| 22 | | See Sch 5 below |
| 23 | | 19 Mar 1997 (s 23(2)) |
| Schs 1–3 | | *Never in force* (repealed) |
| Sch 4 | Pt I | 19 Mar 1997 (s 23(2)) |
| | Pt II | *Never in force* (repealed) |
| Sch 5 | | 19 Mar 1997 (so far as relates to Friendly Societies Act 1992) (s 23(2)) |
| | | *Never in force* (otherwise) (repealed) |

## Prisons (Alcohol Testing) Act 1997 (c 38)

*RA:* 21 Mar 1997

*Commencement provisions:* s 3(2)

Whole Act in force 21 May 1997 (s 3(2))

## Protection from Harassment Act 1997 (c 40)

*RA:* 21 Mar 1997

*Commencement provisions:* s 15(1)–(3); Protection from Harassment Act 1997 (Commencement) (No 1) Order 1997, SI 1997/1418; Protection from Harassment Act 1997 (Commencement) (No 2) Order 1997, SI 1997/1498; Protection from Harassment Act 1997 (Commencement No 3) Order 1998, SI 1998/1902

| | | |
|---|---|---|
| 1, 2 | | 16 Jun 1997 (SI 1997/1418) |
| 3 | (1), (2) | 16 Jun 1997 (SI 1997/1498) |
| | (3)–(9) | 1 Sep 1998 (SI 1998/1902) |
| 4, 5 | | 16 Jun 1997 (SI 1997/1418) |

## Protection from Harassment Act 1997 (c 40)—*contd*

| | |
|---|---|
| 6 | 16 Jun 1997 (SI 1997/1498) |
| 7–12 | 16 Jun 1997 (SI 1997/1418) |
| 13–16 | 21 Mar 1997 (RA) |

## Public Entertainments Licences (Drug Misuse) Act 1997 (c 49)

*RA:* 21 Mar 1997

*Commencement provisions:* s 4(2); Public Entertainments Licences (Drug Misuse) Act 1997 (Commencement and Transitional Provisions) Order 1998, SI 1998/1009

| | |
|---|---|
| 1–3 | 1 May 1998 (subject to a transitional provision relating to ss 1(5), 2(5)) (SI 1998/1009) |
| 4 | 21 Mar 1997 (RA) |

## Referendums (Scotland and Wales) Act 1997 (c 61)

*RA:* 31 Jul 1997

Whole Act in force 31 Jul 1997 (RA)

## Road Traffic Reduction Act 1997 (c 54)

*RA:* 21 Mar 1997

*Commencement provisions:* s 4(3); Road Traffic Reduction Act 1997 (Commencement) (Scotland) Order 2000, SI 2000/101; Road Traffic Reduction Act 1997 (Commencement) (England and Wales) Order 2000, SI 2000/735

Whole Act in force as follows—

10 Mar 2000 (E) (W) (SI 2000/735)

21 Apr 2000 (S) (SI 2000/101)

## Scottish Legal Services Ombudsman and Commissioner for Local Administration in Scotland Act 1997 (c 35)

*RA:* 21 Mar 1997

*Commencement provisions:* s 11; Scottish Legal Services Ombudsman and Commissioner for Local Administration in Scotland Act 1997 (Commencement) Order 1998, SI 1998/252

| | | |
|---|---|---|
| 1–7 | | 21 May 1997 (s 11(2)) |
| 8 | (1) | 21 May 1997 (s 11(2)) |
| | (2) | 21 May 1997 (repeal of Local Government (Scotland) Act 1975, s 23(1)(ee)) (s 11(2)) |
| | | 1 Apr 1998 (otherwise) (SI 1998/252) |
| | (3) | 1 Apr 1998 (SI 1998/252) |
| | (4)–(6) | 21 May 1997 (s 11(2)) |
| 9 | | 21 May 1997 (s 11(2)) |
| 10 | | See Schedule below |
| 11 | | 21 Mar 1997 (RA) |
| Schedule | | 21 May 1997 (s 11(2)), repeals of or in— |
| | | Local Government (Scotland) Act 1975, ss 23(1)(ee), 29A(3), 32(2A); |
| | | Local Government and Housing Act 1989, s 27(2); |
| | | Law Reform (Miscellaneous Provisions) (Scotland) Act 1990, ss 33(3), (4), 34(2), (3), Sch 1, paras 1, 7, 8; |

**Scottish Legal Services Ombudsman and Commissioner for Local Administration in Scotland Act 1997 (c )**—*contd*

Local Government etc (Scotland) Act 1994, Sch 13,
para 100(6)(a)
1 Apr 1998 (otherwise) (SI 1998/252)

---

**Sea Fisheries (Shellfish) (Amendment) Act 1997 (c 3)**

*RA:* 27 Feb 1997

Whole Act in force 27 Feb 1997 (RA)

---

**Senior Courts (Offices) Act 1997 (c 69)**

*RA:* 17 Dec 1997

Whole Act in force 17 Dec 1997 (RA)

*Note:* This Act was originally cited as the Supreme Court (Offices) Act 1997

---

**Sex Offenders Act 1997 (c 51)**

*RA:* 21 Mar 1997

*Commencement provisions:* s 10(2); Sex Offenders Act 1997 (Commencement) Order 1997, SI 1997/1920

Whole Act in force 1 Sep 1997 (SI 1997/1920)

---

**Sexual Offences (Protected Material) Act 1997 (c 39)**

*RA:* 21 Mar 1997

*Commencement provisions:* s 11(2)

*Not yet in force*

---

**Social Security Administration (Fraud) Act 1997 (c 47)**

*RA:* 21 Mar 1997

*Commencement provisions:* s 25(1), (2); Social Security Administration (Fraud) Act 1997 (Commencement No 1) Order 1997, SI 1997/1577; Social Security Administration (Fraud) Act 1997 (Commencement No 2) Order 1997, SI 1997/2056; Social Security Administration (Fraud) Act 1997 (Commencement No 3) Order 1997, SI 1997/2417; Social Security Administration (Fraud) Act 1997 (Commencement No 4) Order 1997, SI 1997/2669; Social Security Administration (Fraud) Act 1997 (Commencement No 5) Order 1997, SI 1997/2766; Social Security Administration (Fraud) Act 1997 (Commencement No 6) Order 1998, SI 1998/2779; Social Security Administration (Fraud) Act 1997 (Commencement No 7) Order 1999, SI 1999/1046; Social Security Administration (Fraud) Act 1997 (Commencement No 8) Order 2004, SI 2004/564

| | |
|---|---|
| 1, 2 | 1 Jul 1997 (SI 1997/1577) |
| 3 | 1 Jul 1997 (except so far as it inserts s 122E(3), (4) into Social Security Administration Act 1992) (SI 1997/1577) |
| | 2 Mar 2004 (exception noted above) (SI 2004/564) |
| 4–10 | 1 Jul 1997 (SI 1997/1577) |
| 11 | 8 Oct 1997 (SI 1997/2417) |
| 12–14 | 1 Jul 1997 (SI 1997/1577) |
| 15 | 21 Nov 1997 (for purposes of authorising the making of regulations) (SI 1997/2766) |
| | 18 Dec 1997 (otherwise) (SI 1997/2766) |

**Social Security Administration (Fraud) Act 1997 (c 47)**—*contd*

| | | |
|---|---|---|
| 16 | | 8 Oct 1997 (for purpose of authorising the making of regulations) (SI 1997/2417) |
| | | 3 Nov 1997 (otherwise) (SI 1997/2417) |
| 17, 18 | | 1 Jul 1997 (SI 1997/1577) |
| 19 | | 7 Nov 1997 (for purpose of authorising the making of regulations) (SI 1997/2669) |
| | | 1 Dec 1997 (otherwise) (SI 1997/2669) |
| 20 | (1) | 25 Aug 1997 (so far as relates to the area falling within the London Borough of Richmond and the area falling within the London Borough of Hounslow) (SI 1997/2056) |
| | | 16 Nov 1998 (otherwise) (SI 1998/2779) |
| | (2) | 5 Apr 1999 (SI 1999/1046) |
| 21 | (1) | 16 Nov 1998 (SI 1998/2779) |
| | (2) | 5 Apr 1999 (SI 1999/1046) |
| 22 | | See Schs 1, 2 below |
| 23–26 | | 21 Mar 1997 (RA) |
| Sch 1 | paras 1–7 | 1 Jul 1997 (SI 1997/1577) |
| | para 8 | 18 Dec 1997 (SI 1997/2766) |
| | paras 9–14 | 1 Jul 1997 (SI 1997/1577) |
| Sch 2 | | 1 Jul 1997 (except repeal of Social Security Administration Act 1992, s 128A and the heading preceding that section) (SI 1997/1577) |
| | | *Not yet in force* (exception noted above) (partly superseded) |

**Social Security (Recovery of Benefits) Act 1997 (c 27)**

*RA:* 19 Mar 1997

*Commencement provisions:* s 34(2); Social Security (Recovery of Benefits) Act 1997 (Commencement) Order 1997, SI 1997/2085

| | | |
|---|---|---|
| 1 | (1) | 6 Oct 1997 (SI 1997/2085) |
| | (2) | 3 Sep 1997 (for purpose of conferring on the Secretary of State the powers to make regulations, so far as it relates to Sch 1, Pt I, paras 4, 8) (SI 1997/2085) |
| | | 6 Oct 1997 (otherwise) (SI 1997/2085) |
| | (3), (4) | 6 Oct 1997 (SI 1997/2085) |
| 2, 3 | | 6 Oct 1997 (SI 1997/2085) |
| 4 | (1)–(8) | 6 Oct 1997 (SI 1997/2085) |
| | (9) | 3 Sep 1997 (for purpose of conferring on the Secretary of State the powers to make regulations) (SI 1997/2085) |
| | | 6 Oct 1997 (otherwise) (SI 1997/2085) |
| 5–10 | | 6 Oct 1997 (SI 1997/2085) |
| 11 | (1)–(4) | 6 Oct 1997 (SI 1997/2085) |
| | (5) | 3 Sep 1997 (for purpose of conferring on the Secretary of State the powers to make regulations) (SI 1997/2085) |
| | | 6 Oct 1997 (otherwise) (SI 1997/2085) |
| | (6) | 3 Sep 1997 (for purpose of conferring on the Secretary of State the powers to make regulations) (SI 1997/2085) |
| | | 6 Oct 1997 (otherwise) (SI 1997/2085) |
| 12 | (1)–(5) | 6 Oct 1997 (SI 1997/2085) |
| | (6) | 3 Sep 1997 (for purpose of conferring on the Secretary of State the powers to make regulations) (SI 1997/2085) |
| | | 6 Oct 1997 (otherwise) (SI 1997/2085) |
| | (7) | 3 Sep 1997 (for purpose of conferring on the Secretary of State the powers to make regulations) (SI 1997/2085) |
| | | 6 Oct 1997 (otherwise) (SI 1997/2085) |
| | (8) | 6 Oct 1997 (SI 1997/2085) |
| 13 | (1), (2) | 6 Oct 1997 (SI 1997/2085) |

**Social Security (Recovery of Benefits) Act 1997 (c 27)**—*contd*

|        |          |                                                                                                          |
|--------|----------|----------------------------------------------------------------------------------------------------------|
|        | (3)      | 3 Sep 1997 (for purpose of conferring on the Secretary of State the powers to make regulations) (SI 1997/2085) |
|        |          | 6 Oct 1997 (otherwise) (SI 1997/2085)                                                                    |
|        | (4)      | 6 Oct 1997 (SI 1997/2085)                                                                                |
| 14     | (1)      | 6 Oct 1997 (SI 1997/2085)                                                                                |
|        | (2)–(4)  | 3 Sep 1997 (for purpose of conferring on the Secretary of State the powers to make regulations) (SI 1997/2085) |
|        |          | 6 Oct 1997 (otherwise) (SI 1997/2085)                                                                    |
| 15     |          | 6 Oct 1997 (SI 1997/2085)                                                                                |
| 16     | (1), (2) | 3 Sep 1997 (for purpose of conferring on the Secretary of State the powers to make regulations) (SI 1997/2085) |
|        |          | 6 Oct 1997 (otherwise) (SI 1997/2085)                                                                    |
|        | (3), (4) | 6 Oct 1997 (SI 1997/2085)                                                                                |
| 17     |          | 6 Oct 1997 (SI 1997/2085)                                                                                |
| 18, 19 |          | 3 Sep 1997 (for purpose of conferring on the Secretary of State the powers to make regulations) (SI 1997/2085) |
|        |          | 6 Oct 1997 (otherwise) (SI 1997/2085)                                                                    |
| 20     |          | 6 Oct 1997 (SI 1997/2085)                                                                                |
| 21     | (1), (2) | 6 Oct 1997 (SI 1997/2085)                                                                                |
|        | (3)      | 3 Sep 1997 (for purpose of conferring on the Secretary of State the powers to make regulations) (SI 1997/2085) |
|        |          | 6 Oct 1997 (otherwise) (SI 1997/2085)                                                                    |
|        | (4)–(6)  | 6 Oct 1997 (SI 1997/2085)                                                                                |
| 22     |          | 6 Oct 1997 (SI 1997/2085)                                                                                |
| 23     | (1), (2) | 3 Sep 1997 (for purpose of conferring on the Secretary of State the powers to make regulations) (SI 1997/2085) |
|        |          | 6 Oct 1997 (otherwise) (SI 1997/2085)                                                                    |
|        | (3), (4) | 6 Oct 1997 (SI 1997/2085)                                                                                |
|        | (5)      | 3 Sep 1997 (for purpose of conferring on the Secretary of State the powers to make regulations) (SI 1997/2085) |
|        |          | 6 Oct 1997 (otherwise) (SI 1997/2085)                                                                    |
|        | (6)      | 6 Oct 1997 (SI 1997/2085)                                                                                |
|        | (7)      | 3 Sep 1997 (for purpose of conferring on the Secretary of State the powers to make regulations) (SI 1997/2085) |
|        |          | 6 Oct 1997 (otherwise) (SI 1997/2085)                                                                    |
|        | (8)      | 6 Oct 1997 (SI 1997/2085)                                                                                |
| 24     |          | 6 Oct 1997 (SI 1997/2085)                                                                                |
| 25     |          | 19 Mar 1997 (RA)                                                                                         |
| 26–28  |          | 6 Oct 1997 (SI 1997/2085)                                                                                |
| 29–32  |          | 19 Mar 1997 (RA)                                                                                         |
| 33     |          | 6 Oct 1997 (SI 1997/2085)                                                                                |
| 34     |          | 19 Mar 1997 (RA)                                                                                         |
| Schs 1–4 |        | 6 Oct 1997 (SI 1997/2085)                                                                                |

**Special Immigration Appeals Commission Act 1997 (c 68)**

*RA:* 17 Dec 1997

*Commencement provisions:* s 9(2); Special Immigration Appeals Commission Act 1997 (Commencement No 1) Order 1998, SI 1998/1336; Special Immigration Appeals Commission Act 1997 (Commencement No 2) Order 1998, SI 1998/1892

|          |                            |
|----------|----------------------------|
| 1–4      | 3 Aug 1998 (SI 1998/1892)  |
| 5        | 11 Jun 1998 (SI 1998/1336) |
| 6, 7     | 3 Aug 1998 (SI 1998/1892)  |
| 8        | 11 Jun 1998 (SI 1998/1336) |
| 9        | 17 Dec 1997 (RA)           |
| Schs 1–3 | 3 Aug 1998 (SI 1998/1892)  |

**Supreme Court (Offices) Act 1997 (c 69)**

See Senior Courts (Offices) Act 1997

---

**Telecommunications (Fraud) Act 1997 (c 4)**

*RA:* 27 Feb 1997

*Commencement provisions:* s 3(3)

Whole Act in force 27 Apr 1997 (s 3(3))

---

**Town and Country Planning (Scotland) Act 1997 (c 8)**

*RA:* 27 Feb 1997

*Commencement provisions:* s 278(2)

Whole Act in force 27 May 1997 (s 278(2)) (except as provided in the Planning (Consequential Provisions) (Scotland) Act 1997, Sch 3)

---

**Transfer of Crofting Estates (Scotland) Act 1997 (c 26)**

*RA:* 19 Mar 1997

*Commencement provisions:* s 8(2); Transfer of Crofting Estates (Scotland) Act 1997 Commencement Order 1997, SI 1997/1430

Whole Act in force 6 Jun 1997 (SI 1997/1430)

---

**United Nations Personnel Act 1997 (c 13)**

*RA:* 27 Feb 1997

*Commencement provisions:* s 10(2)

Whole Act in force 27 Apr 1997 (s 10(2))

---

**Welsh Development Agency Act 1997 (c 37)**

*RA:* 21 Mar 1997

*Commencement provisions:* s 2(3)

Whole Act in force 21 May 1997 (s 2(3))

---

# 1998 Acts

## Animal Health (Amendment) Act 1998 (c 13)

*RA:* 21 May 1998

*Commencement provisions:* s 2(2)

Whole Act in force 21 Jul 1998 (s 2(2))

---

## Appropriation Act 1998 (c 28)

*RA:* 16 Jul 1998

Whole Act in force 16 Jul 1998 (RA)

---

## Audit Commission Act 1998 (c 18)

*RA:* 11 Jun 1998

*Commencement provisions:* s 55(2)

Whole Act in force 11 Sep 1998 (s 55(2))

---

## Bank of England Act 1998 (c 11)

*RA:* 23 Apr 1998

*Commencement provisions:* s 46; Bank of England Act 1998 (Commencement) Order 1998, SI 1998/1120

Whole Act in force 1 Jun 1998 (SI 1998/1120)

---

## Community Care (Residential Accommodation) Act 1998 (c 19)

*RA:* 11 Jun 1998

*Commencement provisions:* s 3(2)

Whole Act in force 11 Aug 1998 (s 3(2))

---

## Competition Act 1998 (c 41)

*RA:* 9 Nov 1998

*Commencement provisions:* s 76(2), (3); Competition Act 1998 (Commencement No 1) Order 1998, SI 1998/2750; Competition Act 1998 (Commencement No 2) Order 1998, SI 1998/3166; Competition Act 1998 (Commencement No 3) Order 1999, SI 1999/505; Competition Act 1998 (Commencement No 4) Order 1999, SI 1999/2859; Competition Act 1998 (Commencement No 5) Order 2000, SI 2000/344; Competition Act 1998 (Commencement No 6) Order 2013, SI 2013/284

1      (a)      10 Mar 2013 (SI 2013/284)

**Competition Act 1998 (c 41)**—*contd*

| | | |
|---|---|---|
| | (b)–(d) | 1 Mar 2000 (SI 2000/344) |
| 2 | | 1 Mar 2000 (SI 2000/344) |
| 3 | (1)(a) | 11 Jan 1999 (SI 1998/3166) |
| | (1)(b) | See Sch 2 below |
| | (1)(c)–(d) | 11 Jan 1999 (SI 1998/3166) |
| | (2)–(6) | 11 Jan 1999 (SI 1998/3166) |
| 4–11 | | 1 Mar 2000 (SI 2000/344) |
| 12 | (1), (2) | 1 Mar 2000 (SI 2000/344) |
| | (3) | 11 Jan 1999 (SI 1998/3166) |
| 13–18 | | 1 Mar 2000 (SI 2000/344) |
| 19 | | 11 Jan 1999 (SI 1998/3166) |
| 20–37 | | 1 Mar 2000 (SI 2000/344) |
| 38 | (1)–(7) | 11 Jan 1999 (SI 1998/3166) |
| | (8)–(10) | 1 Mar 2000 (SI 2000/344) |
| 39–44 | | 1 Mar 2000 (SI 2000/344) |
| 45 | | 1 Apr 1999 (SI 1999/505) |
| 46, 47 | | 1 Mar 2000 (SI 2000/344) |
| 48 | | 1 Apr 1999 (SI 1999/505) |
| 49 | (1), (2) | 1 Mar 2000 (SI 2000/344) |
| | (3) | 1 Apr 1999 (SI 1999/505) |
| | (4) | 1 Mar 2000 (SI 2000/344) |
| 50 | | 11 Jan 1999 (SI 1998/3166) |
| 51, 52 | | 26 Nov 1998 (SI 1998/2750) |
| 53 | | 11 Jan 1999 (SI 1998/3166) |
| 54 | (1) | 1 Mar 2000 (SI 2000/344) |
| | (2), (3) | See Sch 10 below |
| | (4)–(7) | 11 Jan 1999 (SI 1998/3166) |
| 55 | (1)–(5) | 1 Mar 2000 (SI 2000/344) |
| | (6) | 11 Jan 1999 (SI 1998/3166) |
| | (7), (8) | 1 Mar 2000 (SI 2000/344) |
| 56 | | 1 Mar 2000 (SI 2000/344) |
| 57 | | 11 Jan 1999 (SI 1998/3166) |
| 58 | | 1 Mar 2000 (SI 2000/344) |
| 59 | | 26 Nov 1998 (for the purposes of ss 51, 52, Sch 9) (SI 1998/2750) |
| | | 11 Jan 1999 (so far as not already in force) (SI 1998/3166) |
| 60 | | 11 Jan 1999 (SI 1998/3166) |
| 61–65 | | 1 Mar 2000 (SI 2000/344) |
| 66–68 | | 1 Apr 1999 (SI 1999/505) |
| 69 | | 11 Jan 1999 (SI 1998/3166) |
| 70 | | 1 Mar 2000 (SI 2000/344) |
| 71 | | 9 Nov 1998 (s 76(2)) |
| 72, 73 | | 1 Mar 2000 (SI 2000/344) |
| 74 | (1) | See Sch 12 below |
| | (2) | See Sch 13 below |
| | (3) | See Sch 14 below |
| 75, 76 | | 9 Nov 1998 (s 76(2)) |
| Sch 1 | | 11 Jan 1999 (SI 1998/3166) |
| Sch 2 | paras 1–5 | 1 Mar 2000 (SI 2000/344) |
| | para 6 | 11 Jan 1999 (SI 1998/3166) |
| Schs 3, 4 | | 11 Jan 1999 (SI 1998/3166) |
| Sch 5 | paras 1–6 | 1 Mar 2000 (SI 2000/344) |
| | para 7 | *Never in force* (repealed) |
| Sch 6 | paras 1–6 | 1 Mar 2000 (SI 2000/344) |
| | para 7 | *Never in force* (repealed) |
| Sch 7 | | 1 Apr 1999 (SI 1999/505) |
| Sch 8 | Pt I, para 1 | 1 Apr 1999 (SI 1999/505) |
| | Pt I, paras 2–4 | 1 Mar 2000 (SI 2000/344) |
| | Pt II | 1 Apr 1999 (SI 1999/505) |
| Sch 9 | | 26 Nov 1998 (SI 1998/2750) |

**Competition Act 1998 (c 41)**—*contd*

| | | |
|---|---|---|
| Sch 10 | para 1 | 1 Apr 1999 (SI 1999/505) |
| | paras 2–8 | 26 Nov 1998 (for the purposes of ss 51, 52, Sch 9) (subject to a saving) (SI 1998/2750) |
| | | 1 Mar 2000 (otherwise) (SI 2000/344) |
| | para 9(1), (2) | 1 Apr 1999 (SI 1999/505) |
| | para 9(3), (4) | 1 Mar 2000 (SI 2000/344) |
| | para 9(5) | 1 Apr 1999 (SI 1999/505) |
| | para 9(6) | 1 Mar 2000 (SI 2000/344) |
| | para 9(7)(a) | 1 Mar 2000 (SI 2000/344) |
| | para 9(7)(b) | 11 Jan 1999 (SI 1998/3166) |
| | para 9(8) | 1 Mar 2000 (SI 2000/344) |
| | para 10(1), (2) | 1 Apr 1999 (SI 1999/505) |
| | para 10(3)–(5) | 1 Mar 2000 (SI 2000/344) |
| | para 10(6)(a) | 1 Mar 2000 (SI 2000/344) |
| | para 10(6)(b) | 11 Jan 1999 (SI 1998/3166) |
| | para 10(7) | 1 Mar 2000 (SI 2000/344) |
| | para 11(a) | 1 Mar 2000 (SI 2000/344) |
| | para 11(b) | 11 Jan 1999 (SI 1998/3166) |
| | para 12(1), (2) | 1 Apr 1999 (SI 1999/505) |
| | para 12(3)–(5) | 1 Mar 2000 (SI 2000/344) |
| | para 12(6) | 1 Apr 1999 (SI 1999/505) |
| | para 12(7)(a) | 1 Mar 2000 (SI 2000/344) |
| | para 12(7)(b) | 11 Jan 1999 (SI 1998/3166) |
| | para 12(8) | 1 Mar 2000 (SI 2000/344) |
| | para 13(1) | 1 Apr 1999 (SI 1999/505) |
| | para 13(2) | 1 Mar 2000 (SI 2000/344) |
| | para 13(3) | 1 Apr 1999 (SI 1999/505) |
| | para 13(4)–(7) | 1 Mar 2000 (SI 2000/344) |
| | para 13(8) | 1 Apr 1999 (SI 1999/505) |
| | para 13(9) | 1 Mar 2000 (SI 2000/344) |
| | para 13(10)(a) | 1 Mar 2000 (SI 2000/344) |
| | para 13(10)(b) | 11 Jan 1999 (SI 1998/3166) |
| | para 14(a) | 1 Mar 2000 (SI 2000/344) |
| | para 14(b) | 11 Jan 1999 (SI 1998/3166) |
| | para 15(1), (2) | 1 Apr 1999 (SI 1999/505) |
| | para 15(3)–(8) | 1 Mar 2000 (SI 2000/344) |
| | para 15(9)(a) | 1 Mar 2000 (SI 2000/344) |
| | para 15(9)(b) | 11 Jan 1999 (SI 1998/3166) |
| | para 15(10) | 1 Mar 2000 (SI 2000/344) |
| | para 16 | 1 Mar 2000 (SI 2000/344) |
| | para 17(1), (2) | 1 Apr 1999 (SI 1999/505) |
| | para 17(3)–(5) | 1 Mar 2000 (SI 2000/344) |
| | para 17(6) | 1 Apr 1999 (SI 1999/505) |
| | para 17(7)(a) | 1 Mar 2000 (SI 2000/344) |
| | para 17(7)(b) | 11 Jan 1999 (SI 1998/3166) |
| | para 17(8), (9) | 1 Mar 2000 (SI 2000/344) |
| | para 18(1), (2) | 1 Apr 1999 (SI 1999/505) |
| | para 18(3)–(5) | 1 Mar 2000 (SI 2000/344) |
| | para 18(6)(a) | 1 Mar 2000 (SI 2000/344) |
| | para 18(6)(b) | 11 Jan 1999 (SI 1998/3166) |
| | para 18(7) | 1 Mar 2000 (SI 2000/344) |
| Sch 11 | | 1 Mar 2000 (SI 2000/344) |
| Sch 12 | para 1(1), (2) | 1 Apr 1999 (SI 1999/505) |
| | para 1(3)(a), (b) | 10 Nov 1999 (SI 1999/2859) |
| | para 1(3)(c) | 1 Mar 2000 (SI 2000/344) |
| | para 1(3)(d) | 10 Nov 1999 (SI 1999/2859) |
| | para 1(4)–(8) | 1 Mar 2000 (SI 2000/344) |
| | para 1(9)–(13) | 1 Apr 1999 (SI 1999/505) |
| | para 1(14) | 11 Jan 1999 (SI 1998/3166) |

**Competition Act 1998 (c 41)**—*contd*

|         |                |                                          |
|---------|----------------|------------------------------------------|
|         | para 1(15)     | 1 Apr 1999 (SI 1999/505)                 |
|         | para 2         | 1 Mar 2000 (SI 2000/344)                 |
|         | para 3(a)      | 1 Mar 2000 (SI 2000/344)                 |
|         | para 3(b)      | 11 Jan 1999 (SI 1998/3166)               |
|         | para 4(1)      | 1 Apr 1999 (SI 1999/505)                 |
|         | para 4(2)      | 1 Mar 2000 (SI 2000/344)                 |
|         | para 4(3)      | 1 Apr 1999 (SI 1999/505)                 |
|         | para 4(4)–(8)  | 1 Mar 2000 (SI 2000/344)                 |
|         | para 4(9)      | 11 Jan 1999 (SI 1998/3166)               |
|         | para 4(10)     | 1 Mar 2000 (SI 2000/344)                 |
|         | para 4(11)     | 11 Jan 1999 (SI 1998/3166)               |
|         | para 4(12)     | 1 Apr 1999 (SI 1999/505)                 |
|         | para 4(13)–(15)| 1 Mar 2000 (SI 2000/344)                 |
|         | para 5         | 1 Mar 2000 (SI 2000/344)                 |
|         | para 6(a)      | 1 Apr 1999 (SI 1999/505)                 |
|         | para 6(b)      | 1 Mar 2000 (SI 2000/344)                 |
|         | para 7(1), (2) | 1 Apr 1999 (SI 1999/505)                 |
|         | para 7(3)–(5)  | 1 Mar 2000 (SI 2000/344)                 |
|         | paras 8, 9     | 1 Mar 2000 (SI 2000/344)                 |
|         | para 10(a)     | 1 Mar 2000 (SI 2000/344)                 |
|         | para 10(b)     | 11 Jan 1999 (SI 1998/3166)               |
|         | paras 11–13    | 1 Mar 2000 (SI 2000/344)                 |
|         | para 14(1)     | 1 Apr 1999 (SI 1999/505)                 |
|         | para 14(2)     | 1 Mar 2000 (SI 2000/344)                 |
|         | para 14(3)     | 1 Apr 1999 (SI 1999/505)                 |
|         | para 15        | 1 Apr 1999 (SI 1999/505)                 |
|         | paras 16, 17   | 1 Mar 2000 (SI 2000/344)                 |
|         | para 18(a)     | 1 Mar 2000 (SI 2000/344)                 |
|         | para 18(b)     | 11 Jan 1999 (SI 1998/3166)               |
|         | para 19        | 1 Mar 2000 (SI 2000/344)                 |
|         | para 20(1), (2)| 1 Apr 1999 (SI 1999/505)                 |
|         | para 20(3)–(6) | 1 Mar 2000 (SI 2000/344)                 |
|         | para 21        | 1 Mar 2000 (SI 2000/344)                 |
| Sch 13  | paras 1–7      | 9 Nov 1998 (s 76(2))                     |
|         | paras 8, 9     | 1 Mar 2000 (SI 2000/344)                 |
|         | para 10(1)–(4) | 1 Mar 2000 (SI 2000/344)                 |
|         | para 10(5)     | 11 Jan 1999 (SI 1998/3166)               |
|         | para 10(6)     | 1 Mar 2000 (SI 2000/344)                 |
|         | para 11        | 11 Jan 1999 (for the purpose of prescribing modifications to Restrictive Trade Practices Act 1976) (SI 1998/3166) |
|         |                | *Not yet in force* (otherwise)           |
|         | para 12(1)     | 11 Jan 1999 (for the purpose of prescribing modifications to Restrictive Trade Practices Act 1976) (SI 1998/3166) |
|         |                | 1 Mar 2000 (otherwise) (SI 2000/344)     |
|         | para 12(2)     | 1 Mar 2000 (SI 2000/344)                 |
|         | paras 13–18    | 1 Mar 2000 (SI 2000/344)                 |
|         | para 19(1), (2)| 1 Mar 2000 (SI 2000/344)                 |
|         | para 19(3)     | 11 Jan 1999 (SI 1998/3166)               |
|         | paras 20–34    | 1 Mar 2000 (SI 2000/344)                 |
|         | para 35        | 9 Nov 1998 (s 76(2))                     |
|         | paras 36–39    | 1 Mar 2000 (SI 2000/344)                 |
|         | paras 40, 41   | 10 Nov 1999 (SI 1999/2859)               |
|         | paras 42–46    | 1 Mar 2000 (SI 2000/344)                 |
| Sch 14  | Pt I           | 11 Jan 1999 (SI 1998/3166), repeals of or in— |
|         |                | Fair Trading Act 1973, s 83;             |
|         |                | Competition Act 1980, s 22               |
|         |                | 1 Apr 1999 (repeals of or in Fair Trading Act 1973, ss 4, 45, 81, 135, Sch 3) (SI 1999/505) |

**Competition Act 1998 (c 41)**—*contd*

|  |  |  |
|---|---|---|
|  |  | 10 Nov 1999 (repeals of or in Fair Trading Act 1973, ss 10(2), 54(5), Sch 8, para 3(1), (2)) (SI 1999/2859) |
|  |  | 1 Mar 2000 (except repeal of Restrictive Practices Court Act 1976) (SI 2000/344) |
|  |  | 10 Mar 2013 (exception noted above) (SI 2013/284) |
|  | Pt II | 1 Apr 1999 (repeal of entry relating to Fair Trading Act 1973 in Agricultural Marketing (Northern Ireland) Order 1982, SI 1982/1080) (SI 1999/505) |
|  |  | 1 Mar 2000 (otherwise) (SI 2000/344) |

---

**Consolidated Fund Act 1998 (c 4)**

*RA:* 18 Mar 1998

Whole Act in force 18 Mar 1998 (RA)

---

**Consolidated Fund (No 2) Act 1998 (c 49)**

*RA:* 17 Dec 1998

Whole Act in force 17 Dec 1998 (RA)

---

**Crime and Disorder Act 1998 (c 37)**

*RA:* 31 Jul 1998

*Commencement provisions:* s 121(2); Crime and Disorder Act 1998 (Commencement No 1) Order 1998, SI 1998/1883; Crime and Disorder Act 1998 (Commencement No 2 and Transitional Provisions) Order 1998, SI 1998/2327, as amended by SI 1998/2412, SI 1998/2906, SI 2000/924; Crime and Disorder Act 1998 (Commencement No 3 and Appointed Day) Order 1998, SI 1998/3263; Crime and Disorder Act 1998 (Commencement No 4) Order 1999, SI 1999/1279; Crime and Disorder Act 1998 (Commencement No 5) Order 1999, SI 1999/2976; Crime and Disorder Act 1998 (Commencement No 6) Order 1999, SI 1999/3426; Crime and Disorder Act 1998 (Commencement No 7) Order 2000, SI 2000/924; Crime and Disorder Act 1998 (Commencement No 8) Order 2000, SI 2000/3283

| | | |
|---|---|---|
| 1 | | 1 Apr 1999 (SI 1998/3263) |
| 2, 3 | | 1 Dec 1998 (SI 1998/2327) |
| 4 | | 1 Dec 1998 (so far as relating to a sex offender order) (SI 1998/2327) |
| | | 1 Apr 1999 (otherwise) (SI 1998/3263) |
| 5–9 | | 30 Sep 1998 (SI 1998/2327) |
| 10 | (1)–(5) | 30 Sep 1998 (SI 1998/2327) |
| | (6), (7) | 1 Jun 2000 (SI 2000/924) |
| 11, 12 | | 30 Sep 1998 (SI 1998/2327) |
| 13 | (1), (2) | 30 Sep 1998 (SI 1998/2327) |
| | (3) | 1 Jun 2000 (SI 2000/924) |
| 14, 15 | | 30 Sep 1998 (SI 1998/2327) |
| 16 | | 1 Dec 1998 (SI 1998/2327) |
| 17, 18 | | 30 Sep 1998 (SI 1998/2327) |
| 19 | | 1 Apr 1999 (SI 1998/3263) |
| 20 | | 1 Dec 1998 (SI 1998/2327) |
| 21 | | 1 Dec 1998 (for the purposes of sex offender orders made under s 20, and orders made under s 20(4)(a)) (SI 1998/2327) |
| | | 1 Apr 1999 (otherwise) (SI 1998/3263) |
| 22 | (1)–(5) | 1 Dec 1998 (for the purposes of their application to an order under s 20(4)(a), and to a sex offender order made under s 20) (SI 1998/2327) |
| | | 1 Apr 1999 (otherwise) (SI 1998/3263) |

**Crime and Disorder Act 1998 (c 37)**—*contd*

| | | |
|---|---|---|
| | (6), (7) | 1 Dec 1998 (SI 1998/2327) |
| 23, 24 | | 1 Dec 1998 (SI 1998/2327) |
| 25 | | 1 Mar 1999 (SI 1998/3263) |
| 26 | | 1 Dec 1998 (for the purpose of making regulations under Criminal Justice and Public Order Act 1994, s 60A) (SI 1998/2327) |
| | | 1 Mar 1999 (otherwise) (SI 1998/3263) |
| 27 | | 1 Mar 1999 (SI 1998/3263) |
| 28–37 | | 30 Sep 1998 (SI 1998/2327) |
| 38 | (1)–(3) | 30 Sep 1998 (in the areas of the counties of Bedfordshire, Devon and Hampshire, the Isle of Wight, the cities of Portsmouth, Sheffield, Southampton and Westminster, the Royal borough of Kensington and Chelsea, the London boroughs of Hammersmith and Fulham, and Lewisham, the Metropolitan boroughs of St Helens and Wolverhampton, and the boroughs of Blackburn with Darwen, and Luton) (subject to transitional provisions) (SI 1998/2327) |
| | | 1 Apr 2000 (otherwise) (SI 2000/924) |
| | (4) | 30 Sep 1998 (subject to transitional provisions) (SI 1998/2327)[1] |
| | (5) | 30 Sep 1998 (in the areas of the counties of Bedfordshire, Devon and Hampshire, the Isle of Wight, the cities of Portsmouth, Sheffield, Southampton and Westminster, the Royal borough of Kensington and Chelsea, the London boroughs of Hammersmith and Fulham, and Lewisham, the Metropolitan boroughs of St Helens and Wolverhampton, and the boroughs of Blackburn with Darwen, and Luton) (subject to transitional provisions) (SI 1998/2327) |
| | | 1 Apr 2000 (otherwise) (SI 2000/924) |
| 39 | | 30 Sep 1998 (in the areas of the counties of Bedfordshire, Devon and Hampshire, the Isle of Wight, the cities of Portsmouth, Sheffield, Southampton and Westminster, the Royal borough of Kensington and Chelsea, the London boroughs of Hammersmith and Fulham, and Lewisham, the Metropolitan boroughs of St Helens and Wolverhampton, and the boroughs of Blackburn with Darwen, and Luton) (subject to transitional provisions) (SI 1998/2327) |
| | | 1 Apr 2000 (otherwise) (SI 2000/924) |
| 40 | | 30 Sep 1998 (in the areas of the counties of Bedfordshire, Devon and Hampshire, the Isle of Wight, the cities of Portsmouth, Sheffield, Southampton and Westminster, the Royal borough of Kensington and Chelsea, the London boroughs of Hammersmith and Fulham, and Lewisham, the Metropolitan boroughs of St Helens and Wolverhampton, and the boroughs of Blackburn with Darwen, and Luton) (subject to transitional provisions) (SI 1998/2327) |
| | | 1 Jan 2000 (otherwise) (SI 1999/3426) |
| 41 | (1)–(10) | 1 Aug 1998 (for the purpose of making appointments) (SI 1998/1883) |
| | | 30 Sep 1998 (otherwise) (SI 1998/2327) |
| | (11) | See Sch 2 below |
| 42 | | 30 Sep 1998 (SI 1998/2327) |
| 43 | (1) | 30 Sep 1998 (SI 1998/2327) |
| | (2)–(8) | 1 Jun 1999 (SI 1999/1279) |
| 44, 45 | | 1 Jun 1999 (SI 1999/1279) |

**Crime and Disorder Act 1998 (c 37)**—*contd*

| | | |
|---|---|---|
| 46 | | 30 Sep 1998 (in the petty sessions areas of Bromley, Croydon, and Sutton, the petty sessional divisions of Aberconwy, Arfon, Blackburn, Darwen and Ribble Valley, Burnley and Pendle, Colwyn, Corby, Daventry, Dyffryn Clwyd, Eifionydd and Pwllheli, Gateshead, Kettering, Meirionnydd, Newcastle-under-Lyme and Pirehill North, Newcastle-upon-Tyne, Northampton, Rhuddlan, Staffordshire Moorlands, Stoke-on-Trent, Towcester, Wellingborough, and Ynys Mon/Anglesey) (SI 1999/2327) |
| | | 1 Nov 1999 (otherwise) (SI 1999/2976) |
| 47, 48 | | 30 Sep 1998 (SI 1998/2327) |
| 49 | (1) | 1 Aug 1998 (for the purpose of making rules which make such provision as is mentioned in sub-s (2) of that section) (SI 1998/1883) |
| | | 30 Sep 1998 (in the petty sessions areas of Bromley, Croydon, and Sutton, the petty sessional divisions of Aberconwy, Arfon, Blackburn, Darwen and Ribble Valley, Burnley and Pendle, Colwyn, Corby, Daventry, Dyffryn Clwyd, Eifionydd and Pwllheli, Gateshead, Kettering, Meirionnydd, Newcastle-under-Lyme and Pirehill North, Newcastle-upon-Tyne, Northampton, Rhuddlan, Staffordshire Moorlands, Stoke-on-Trent, Towcester, Wellingborough, and Ynys Mon/Anglesey) (SI 1999/2327) |
| | | 1 Nov 1999 (otherwise) (SI 1999/2976) |
| | (2) | 1 Aug 1998 (SI 1998/1883) |
| | (3)–(5) | 30 Sep 1998 (in the petty sessions areas of Bromley, Croydon, and Sutton, the petty sessional divisions of Aberconwy, Arfon, Blackburn, Darwen and Ribble Valley, Burnley and Pendle, Colwyn, Corby, Daventry, Dyffryn Clwyd, Eifionydd and Pwllheli, Gateshead, Kettering, Meirionnydd, Newcastle-under-Lyme and Pirehill North, Newcastle-upon-Tyne, Northampton, Rhuddlan, Staffordshire Moorlands, Stoke-on-Trent, Towcester, Wellingborough, and Ynys Mon/Anglesey) (SI 1999/2327) |
| | | 1 Nov 1999 (otherwise) (SI 1999/2976) |
| 50 | | 30 Sep 1998 (SI 1998/2327) |
| 51 | | 4 Jan 1999 (for the purpose of sending any person for trial under s 51 from the petty sessions areas of Bromley, Croydon, and Sutton, the petty sessional divisions of Aberconwy, Arfon, Blackburn, Darwen and Ribble Valley, Burnley and Pendle, Colwyn, Corby, Daventry, Dyffryn Clwyd, Eifionydd and Pwllheli, Gateshead, Kettering, Meirionnydd, Newcastle-under-Lyme and Pirehill North, Newcastle-upon-Tyne, Northampton, Rhuddlan, Staffordshire Moorlands, Stoke-on-Trent, Towcester, Wellingborough, and Ynys Mon/Anglesey) (SI 1998/2327) |
| | | 15 Jan 2001 (otherwise) (SI 2000/3283)[2] |
| 52 | (1)–(5) | 4 Jan 1999 (for the purpose of sending any person for trial under s 51 from the petty sessions areas of Bromley, Croydon, and Sutton, the petty sessional divisions of Aberconwy, Arfon, Blackburn, Darwen and Ribble Valley, Burnley and Pendle, Colwyn, Corby, Daventry, Dyffryn Clwyd, Eifionydd and Pwllheli, Gateshead, Kettering, Meirionnydd, Newcastle-under-Lyme and Pirehill North, Newcastle-upon-Tyne, Northampton, Rhuddlan, Staffordshire Moorlands, Stoke-on-Trent, Towcester, Wellingborough, and Ynys Mon/Anglesey) (SI 1998/2327) |
| | | 15 Jan 2001 (otherwise) (SI 2000/3283)[2] |
| | (6) | See Sch 3 below |
| 53–58 | | 30 Sep 1998 (SI 1998/2327) |
| 59 | | 30 Sep 1998 (subject to transitional provisions) (SI 1998/2327) |

**Crime and Disorder Act 1998 (c 37)**—*contd*

| | | |
|---|---|---|
| 60–64 | | 30 Sep 1998 (SI 1998/2327) |
| 65, 66 | | 30 Sep 1998 (in the areas, for the purpose of reprimanding or warning a person under s 65, of the county of Hampshire, the Isle of Wight, the cities of Portsmouth, Sheffield, Southampton and Westminster, the Royal borough of Kensington and Chelsea, the London borough of Hammersmith and Fulham, the Metropolitan borough of Wolverhampton, and the borough of Blackburn with Darwen) (SI 1998/2327) |
| | | 1 Apr 2000 (in the areas, for the purpose of reprimanding or warning a person under s 65, of the counties of Oxfordshire, Norfolk, the cities of Cardiff, Sunderland, the London boroughs of Lewisham, Greenwich, Southwark, the Metropolitan borough of Gateshead) (SI 2000/924) |
| | | 1 Jun 2000 (otherwise) (SI 2000/924) |
| 67–70 | | 30 Sep 1998 (SI 1998/2327) |
| 71 | (1)–(3) | 1 Jun 2000 (SI 2000/924) |
| | (4) | 1 Apr 1999 (SI 1998/3263) |
| | (5) | 30 Sep 1998 (SI 1998/2327) |
| 72 | | 30 Sep 1998 (SI 1998/2327) |
| 73–79[1] | | 1 Apr 2000 (subject to transitional provisions and savings) (SI 1999/3426) |
| 80, 81 | | 1 Jul 1999 (SI 1998/3263) |
| 82, 83 | | 30 Sep 1998 (SI 1998/2327) |
| 84 | | 7 Aug 1998 (SI 1998/1883) |
| 85 | | 30 Sep 1998 (SI 1998/2327) |
| 86 | | 30 Sep 1998 (subject to transitional provisions) (SI 1998/2327) |
| 87–96 | | 30 Sep 1998 (SI 1998/2327) |
| 97 | | 30 Sep 1998 (for the purpose of making an order under Children and Young Persons Act 1969, s 23) (SI 1998/2327) |
| | | 1 Jun 1999 (otherwise) (SI 1999/1279) |
| 98 | | 1 Jun 1999 (SI 1999/1279) |
| 99 | | 28 Jan 1999 (SI 1998/3263) |
| 100 | (1) | 30 Sep 1998 (for the purpose of making orders under Criminal Justice Act 1991, s 37A) (subject to a transitional provision) (SI 1998/2327) |
| | | 28 Jan 1999 (otherwise) (SI 1998/3263) |
| | (2) | 28 Jan 1999 (SI 1998/3263) |
| 101, 102 | | 30 Sep 1998 (SI 1998/2327) |
| 103 | | 1 Jan 1999 (SI 1998/3263) |
| 104–108 | | 30 Sep 1998 (SI 1998/2327) |
| 109 | | 31 Jul 1998 (s 121(2)) |
| 110 | | 30 Sep 1998 (SI 1998/2327) |
| 111 | (1)–(7) | 30 Sep 1998 (SI 1998/2327) |
| | (8) | 31 Jul 1998 (s 121(2)) |
| 112, 113 | | 30 Sep 1998 (SI 1998/2327) |
| 114 | | 1 Aug 1998 (SI 1998/1883) |
| 115 | | 30 Sep 1998 (SI 1998/2327) |
| 116, 117 | | 1 Aug 1998 (SI 1998/1883) |
| 118 | | 30 Sep 1998 (SI 1998/2327) |
| 119 | | See Sch 8 below |
| 120 | (1) | 30 Sep 1998 (SI 1998/2327) |
| | (2) | See Sch 10 below |
| 121 | | 31 Jul 1998 (s 121(2)) |
| Sch 1 | | 1 Dec 1998 (SI 1998/2327) |
| Sch 2 | paras 1, 2 | 1 Aug 1998 (for the purpose of making appointments under s 41 and para 1) (SI 1998/1883) |
| | | 30 Sep 1998 (otherwise) (SI 1998/2327) |
| | paras 3–11 | 30 Sep 1998 (SI 1998/2327) |
| Sch 3 | para 1 | 30 Sep 1998 (for the purpose of making regulations) (SI 1998/2327) |

**Crime and Disorder Act 1998 (c 37)**—*contd*

|  |  |  |
|---|---|---|
|  |  | 4 Jan 1999 (for the purpose of sending any person for trial under s 51 from the petty sessions areas of Bromley, Croydon, and Sutton, the petty sessional divisions of Aberconwy, Arfon, Blackburn, Darwen and Ribble Valley, Burnley and Pendle, Colwyn, Corby, Daventry, Dyffryn Clwyd, Eifionydd and Pwllheli, Gateshead, Kettering, Meirionnydd, Newcastle-under-Lyme and Pirehill North, Newcastle-upon-Tyne, Northampton, Rhuddlan, Staffordshire Moorlands, Stoke-on-Trent, Towcester, Wellingborough, and Ynys Mon/Anglesey) (SI 1998/2327) |
|  |  | 15 Jan 2001 (otherwise) (SI 2000/3283)[2] |
|  | para 2(1)–(6) | 4 Jan 1999 (for the purpose of sending any person for trial under s 51 from the petty sessions areas of Bromley, Croydon, and Sutton, the petty sessional divisions of Aberconwy, Arfon, Blackburn, Darwen and Ribble Valley, Burnley and Pendle, Colwyn, Corby, Daventry, Dyffryn Clwyd, Eifionydd and Pwllheli, Gateshead, Kettering, Meirionnydd, Newcastle-under-Lyme and Pirehill North, Newcastle-upon-Tyne, Northampton, Rhuddlan, Staffordshire Moorlands, Stoke-on-Trent, Towcester, Wellingborough, and Ynys Mon/Anglesey) (SI 1998/2327) |
|  |  | 15 Jan 2001 (otherwise) (SI 2000/3283)[2] |
|  | para 2(7) | 30 Sep 1998 (for the purpose of making rules) (SI 1998/2327) |
|  |  | 4 Jan 1999 (for the purpose of sending any person for trial under s 51 from the petty sessions areas of Bromley, Croydon, and Sutton, the petty sessional divisions of Aberconwy, Arfon, Blackburn, Darwen and Ribble Valley, Burnley and Pendle, Colwyn, Corby, Daventry, Dyffryn Clwyd, Eifionydd and Pwllheli, Gateshead, Kettering, Meirionnydd, Newcastle-under-Lyme and Pirehill North, Newcastle-upon-Tyne, Northampton, Rhuddlan, Staffordshire Moorlands, Stoke-on-Trent, Towcester, Wellingborough, and Ynys Mon/Anglesey) (SI 1998/2327) |
|  |  | 15 Jan 2001 (otherwise) (SI 2000/3283)[2] |
|  | paras 3–15 | 4 Jan 1999 (for the purpose of sending any person for trial under s 51 from the petty sessions areas of Bromley, Croydon, and Sutton, the petty sessional divisions of Aberconwy, Arfon, Blackburn, Darwen and Ribble Valley, Burnley and Pendle, Colwyn, Corby, Daventry, Dyffryn Clwyd, Eifionydd and Pwllheli, Gateshead, Kettering, Meirionnydd, Newcastle-under-Lyme and Pirehill North, Newcastle-upon-Tyne, Northampton, Rhuddlan, Staffordshire Moorlands, Stoke-on-Trent, Towcester, Wellingborough, and Ynys Mon/Anglesey) (SI 1998/2327) |
|  |  | 15 Jan 2001 (otherwise) (SI 2000/3283)[2] |
| Schs 4–6 |  | 30 Sep 1998 (SI 1998/2327) |
| Sch 7 |  | 30 Sep 1998 (subject to transitional provisions) (SI 1998/2327) |
| Sch 8 | para 1 | 1 Apr 2000 (subject to transitional provisions and savings) (SI 1999/3426) |
|  | para 2 | 30 Sep 1998 (SI 1998/2327) |
|  | para 3 | 4 Jan 1999 (for the purpose of sending any person for trial under s 51 from the petty sessions areas and petty sessional divisions noted to s 51 above only) (SI 1998/2327) |
|  |  | 15 Jan 2001 (otherwise) (SI 2000/3283) |
|  | para 4 | 30 Sep 1998 (SI 1998/2327) |

**See Halsbury's Statutes Citator for amendments to these Acts**

**Crime and Disorder Act 1998 (c 37)**—*contd*

| | |
|---|---|
| para 5(1)(a) | 4 Jan 1999 (for the purpose of sending any person for trial under s 51 from the petty sessions areas of Bromley, Croydon, and Sutton, the petty sessional divisions of Aberconwy, Arfon, Blackburn, Darwen and Ribble Valley, Burnley and Pendle, Colwyn, Corby, Daventry, Dyffryn Clwyd, Eifionydd and Pwllheli, Gateshead, Kettering, Meirionnydd, Newcastle-under-Lyme and Pirehill North, Newcastle-upon-Tyne, Northampton, Rhuddlan, Staffordshire Moorlands, Stoke-on-Trent, Towcester, Wellingborough, and Ynys Mon/Anglesey) (SI 1998/2327) |
| | 15 Jan 2001 (otherwise) (SI 2000/3283)[2] |
| para 5(1)(b) | 1 Jun 1999 (SI 1999/1279) |
| para 5(2) | 4 Jan 1999 (for the purpose of sending any person for trial under s 51 from the petty sessions areas of Bromley, Croydon, and Sutton, the petty sessional divisions of Aberconwy, Arfon, Blackburn, Darwen and Ribble Valley, Burnley and Pendle, Colwyn, Corby, Daventry, Dyffryn Clwyd, Eifionydd and Pwllheli, Gateshead, Kettering, Meirionnydd, Newcastle-under-Lyme and Pirehill North, Newcastle-upon-Tyne, Northampton, Rhuddlan, Staffordshire Moorlands, Stoke-on-Trent, Towcester, Wellingborough, and Ynys Mon/Anglesey) (SI 1998/2327) |
| | 15 Jan 2001 (otherwise) (SI 2000/3283)[2] |
| para 6 | 1 Apr 2000 (SI 1999/3426) |
| para 7 | 1 Apr 2000 (subject to transitional provisions and savings) (SI 1999/3426) |
| para 8 | 4 Jan 1999 (for the purpose of sending any person for trial under s 51 from the petty sessions areas of Bromley, Croydon, and Sutton, the petty sessional divisions of Aberconwy, Arfon, Blackburn, Darwen and Ribble Valley, Burnley and Pendle, Colwyn, Corby, Daventry, Dyffryn Clwyd, Eifionydd and Pwllheli, Gateshead, Kettering, Meirionnydd, Newcastle-under-Lyme and Pirehill North, Newcastle-upon-Tyne, Northampton, Rhuddlan, Staffordshire Moorlands, Stoke-on-Trent, Towcester, Wellingborough, and Ynys Mon/Anglesey) (SI 1998/2327) |
| | 15 Jan 2001 (otherwise) (SI 2000/3283)[2] |
| para 9(1)(a) | 1 Apr 2000 (SI 1999/3426) |
| para 9(1)(b) | 30 Sep 1998 (SI 1998/2327) |
| para 9(2) | 1 Apr 2000 (SI 1999/3426) |
| para 10(a) | 30 Sep 1998 (SI 1998/2327) |
| para 10(b) | 1 Apr 2000 (SI 1999/3426) |
| para 11 | 30 Sep 1998 (SI 1998/2327) |
| para 12 | 4 Jan 1999 (for the purpose of sending any person for trial under s 51 from the petty sessions areas of Bromley, Croydon, and Sutton, the petty sessional divisions of Aberconwy, Arfon, Blackburn, Darwen and Ribble Valley, Burnley and Pendle, Colwyn, Corby, Daventry, Dyffryn Clwyd, Eifionydd and Pwllheli, Gateshead, Kettering, Meirionnydd, Newcastle-under-Lyme and Pirehill North, Newcastle-upon-Tyne, Northampton, Rhuddlan, Staffordshire Moorlands, Stoke-on-Trent, Towcester, Wellingborough, and Ynys Mon/Anglesey) (SI 1998/2327) |
| | 15 Jan 2001 (otherwise) (SI 2000/3283)[2] |
| para 13 | 30 Sep 1998 (SI 1998/2327) |
| para 14 | 1 Apr 2000 (SI 1999/3426) |
| para 15 | 1 Apr 2000 (subject to transitional provisions and savings) (SI 1999/3426) |
| para 16 | 30 Sep 1998 (SI 1998/2327) |
| para 17 | 30 Sep 1998 (in the areas noted to s 38(1)–(3) above only) (SI 1998/2327) |

**Crime and Disorder Act 1998 (c 37)**—*contd*

|  |  |
|---|---|
|  | 1 Apr 2000 (otherwise) (SI 2000/924) |
| para 18 | 30 Sep 1998 (SI 1998/2327) |
| para 19 | 30 Sep 1998 (in the areas noted to s 38(1)–(3) above only) (SI 1998/2327) |
|  | 1 Apr 2000 (otherwise) (SI 2000/924) |
| paras 20, 21 | 30 Sep 1998 (SI 1998/2327) |
| para 22 | 1 Apr 2000 (SI 1999/3426) |
| para 23 | 30 Sep 1998 (in the areas noted to s 38(1)–(3) above only) (SI 1998/2327) |
|  | 1 Apr 2000 (otherwise) (SI 2000/924) |
| para 24 | 30 Sep 1998 (SI 1998/2327) |
| para 25 | 30 Sep 1998 (in the areas, for the purpose of reprimanding or warning a person under s 65, noted to ss 65, 66 above only) (SI 1998/2327) |
|  | 1 Apr 2000 (so far as relates to the counties of Oxfordshire and Norfolk, the cities of Cardiff and Sunderland, the London boroughs of Lewisham, Greenwich and Southwark, and the Metropolitan borough of Gateshead) (SI 2000/924) |
|  | 1 Jun 2000 (otherwise) (SI 2000/924) |
| paras 26, 27 | 30 Sep 1998 (in the areas noted to s 38(1)–(3) above only) (SI 1998/2327) |
|  | 1 Apr 2000 (otherwise) (SI 2000/924) |
| paras 28, 29 | 4 Jan 1999 (for the purpose of sending any person for trial under s 51 from the petty sessions areas and petty sessional divisions noted to s 51 above only) (SI 1998/2327) |
|  | 15 Jan 2001 (otherwise) (SI 2000/3283) |
| para 30 | 30 Sep 1998 (SI 1998/2327) |
| para 31 | 1 Apr 2000 (SI 1999/3426) |
| paras 32, 33 | 30 Sep 1998 (in the areas noted to s 38(1)–(3) above only) (SI 1998/2327) |
|  | 1 Apr 2000 (otherwise) (SI 2000/924) |
| para 34(1), (2) | 30 Sep 1998 (SI 1998/2327) |
| para 34(3) | 30 Sep 1998 (in the areas noted to s 38(1)–(3) above only) (SI 1998/2327) |
|  | 1 Apr 2000 (otherwise) (SI 2000/924) |
| para 35 | 1 Apr 2000 (SI 1999/3426) |
| para 36 | 1 Dec 1998 (SI 1998/2327) |
| para 37 | 4 Jan 1999 (for the purpose of sending any person for trial under s 51 from the petty sessions areas of Bromley, Croydon, and Sutton, the petty sessional divisions of Aberconwy, Arfon, Blackburn, Darwen and Ribble Valley, Burnley and Pendle, Colwyn, Corby, Daventry, Dyffryn Clwyd, Eifionydd and Pwllheli, Gateshead, Kettering, Meirionnydd, Newcastle-under-Lyme and Pirehill North, Newcastle-upon-Tyne, Northampton, Rhuddlan, Staffordshire Moorlands, Stoke-on-Trent, Towcester, Wellingborough, and Ynys Mon/Anglesey) (SI 1998/2327) |
|  | 15 Jan 2001 (otherwise) (SI 2000/3283)[2] |
| para 38 | 30 Sep 1998 (SI 1998/2327) |
| para 39 | 1 Apr 2000 (SI 1999/3426) |
| para 40(1) | 30 Sep 1998 (SI 1998/2327) |
| para 40(2) | 4 Jan 1999 (for the purpose of sending any person for trial under s 51 from the petty sessions areas of Bromley, Croydon, and Sutton, the petty sessional divisions of Aberconwy, Arfon, Blackburn, Darwen and Ribble Valley, Burnley and Pendle, Colwyn, Corby, Daventry, Dyffryn Clwyd, Eifionydd and Pwllheli, Gateshead, Kettering, Meirionnydd, Newcastle-under-Lyme and Pirehill North, Newcastle-upon-Tyne, Northampton, Rhuddlan, Staffordshire Moorlands, Stoke-on-Trent, Towcester, Wellingborough, and Ynys Mon/Anglesey) (SI 1998/2327) |

**Crime and Disorder Act 1998 (c 37)**—*contd*

|  |  |
|---|---|
| | 15 Jan 2001 (otherwise) (SI 2000/3283)[2] |
| para 41 | 1 Apr 2000 (SI 1999/3426) |
| paras 42, 43 | 30 Sep 1998 (SI 1998/2327) |
| para 44 | 4 Jan 1999 (for the purpose of sending any person for trial under s 51 from the petty sessions areas and petty sessional divisions noted to s 51 above only) (SI 1998/2327) |
| | 15 Jan 2001 (otherwise) (SI 2000/3283)[2] |
| para 45 | 4 Jan 1999 (for the purpose of sending any person for trial under s 51 from the petty sessions areas of Bromley, Croydon, and Sutton, the petty sessional divisions of Aberconwy, Arfon, Blackburn, Darwen and Ribble Valley, Burnley and Pendle, Colwyn, Corby, Daventry, Dyffryn Clwyd, Eifionydd and Pwllheli, Gateshead, Kettering, Meirionnydd, Newcastle-under-Lyme and Pirehill North, Newcastle-upon-Tyne, Northampton, Rhuddlan, Staffordshire Moorlands, Stoke-on-Trent, Towcester, Wellingborough, and Ynys Mon/Anglesey) (SI 1998/2327) |
| | 15 Jan 2001 (otherwise) (SI 2000/3283)[2] |
| paras 46, 47 | 30 Sep 1998 (SI 1998/2327) |
| paras 48, 49 | 4 Jan 1999 (for the purpose of sending any person for trial under s 51 from the petty sessions areas of Bromley, Croydon, and Sutton, the petty sessional divisions of Aberconwy, Arfon, Blackburn, Darwen and Ribble Valley, Burnley and Pendle, Colwyn, Corby, Daventry, Dyffryn Clwyd, Eifionydd and Pwllheli, Gateshead, Kettering, Meirionnydd, Newcastle-under-Lyme and Pirehill North, Newcastle-upon-Tyne, Northampton, Rhuddlan, Staffordshire Moorlands, Stoke-on-Trent, Towcester, Wellingborough, and Ynys Mon/Anglesey) (SI 1998/2327) |
| | 15 Jan 2001 (otherwise) (SI 2000/3283)[2] |
| para 50(1) | 1 Apr 2000 (subject to transitional provisions and savings) (SI 1999/3426) |
| para 50(2)–(4) | 1 Apr 2000 (SI 1999/3426) |
| para 50(5) | 30 Sep 1998 (SI 1998/2327) |
| para 51 | 1 Apr 2000 (SI 1999/3426) |
| para 52(1) | 1 Apr 2000 (SI 1999/3426) |
| para 52(2) | 4 Jan 1999 (for the purpose of sending any person for trial under s 51 from the petty sessions areas and petty sessional divisions noted to s 51 above only) (SI 1998/2327) |
| | 15 Jan 2001 (otherwise) (SI 2000/3283)[2] |
| paras 53, 54 | 30 Sep 1998 (SI 1998/2327) |
| para 55 | 31 Jul 1998 (s 121(2)) |
| paras 56–60 | 30 Sep 1998 (SI 1998/2327) |
| para 61 | 30 Sep 1998 (in the areas, for the purpose of reprimanding or warning a person under s 65, noted to ss 65, 66 above only) (SI 1998/2327) |
| | 1 Apr 2000 (so far as not already in force, only for the purpose and in the areas noted to ss 65, 66 above) (SI 2000/924) |
| | 1 Jun 2000 (otherwise) (SI 2000/924) |
| para 62 | 30 Sep 1998 (SI 1998/2327) |
| paras 63–67 | 4 Jan 1999 (for the purpose of sending any person for trial under s 51 from the petty sessions areas of Bromley, Croydon, and Sutton, the petty sessional divisions of Aberconwy, Arfon, Blackburn, Darwen and Ribble Valley, Burnley and Pendle, Colwyn, Corby, Daventry, Dyffryn Clwyd, Eifionydd and Pwllheli, Gateshead, Kettering, Meirionnydd, Newcastle-under-Lyme and Pirehill North, Newcastle-upon-Tyne, Northampton, Rhuddlan, Staffordshire Moorlands, Stoke-on-Trent, Towcester, Wellingborough, and Ynys Mon/Anglesey) (SI 1998/2327) |
| | 15 Jan 2001 (otherwise) (SI 2000/3283)[2] |

**Crime and Disorder Act 1998 (c 37)**—*contd*

| | |
|---|---|
| paras 68–72 | 30 Sep 1998 (SI 1998/2327) |
| para 73 | 30 Sep 1998 (in the areas noted to s 38(1)–(3) above only) (SI 1998/2327) |
| | 1 Apr 2000 (otherwise) (SI 2000/924) |
| paras 74, 75 | 30 Sep 1998 (SI 1998/2327) |
| para 76 | 30 Sep 1998 (in the areas noted to s 38(1)–(3) above only) (SI 1998/2327) |
| | 1 Apr 2000 (otherwise) (SI 2000/924) |
| para 77(a) | 30 Sep 1998 (in the areas noted to s 38(1)–(3) above only) (SI 1998/2327) |
| | 1 Apr 2000 (otherwise) (SI 2000/924) |
| para 77(b) | 30 Sep 1998 (SI 1998/2327) |
| para 78(a) | 30 Sep 1998 (SI 1998/2327) |
| para 78(b) | 1 Apr 2000 (SI 1999/3426) |
| para 78(c) | 30 Sep 1998 (SI 1998/2327) |
| paras 79–82 | 30 Sep 1998 (SI 1998/2327) |
| para 83(1)(a) | 30 Sep 1998 (SI 1998/2327) |
| para 83(1)(b) | 1 Jan 1999 (SI 1998/3263) |
| para 83(2), (3) | 1 Jan 1999 (SI 1998/3263) |
| para 83(4)–(6) | 30 Sep 1998 (SI 1998/2327) |
| para 84, 85 | 30 Sep 1998 (SI 1998/2327) |
| para 86 | *Never in force* (repealed) |
| para 87 | 30 Sep 1998 (SI 1998/2327) |
| para 88(1), (2) | 30 Sep 1998 (SI 1998/2327) |
| para 88(3)(a) | 1 Jan 1999 (SI 1998/3263) |
| para 88(3)(b) | 30 Sep 1998 (SI 1998/2327) |
| para 89 | 30 Sep 1998 (SI 1998/2327) |
| para 90 | *Never in force* (repealed) |
| paras 91, 92 | 30 Sep 1998 (SI 1998/2327) |
| para 93 | 4 Jan 1999 (for the purpose of sending any person for trial under s 51 from the petty sessions areas of Bromley, Croydon, and Sutton, the petty sessional divisions of Aberconwy, Arfon, Blackburn, Darwen and Ribble Valley, Burnley and Pendle, Colwyn, Corby, Daventry, Dyffryn Clwyd, Eifionydd and Pwllheli, Gateshead, Kettering, Meirionnydd, Newcastle-under-Lyme and Pirehill North, Newcastle-upon-Tyne, Northampton, Rhuddlan, Staffordshire Moorlands, Stoke-on-Trent, Towcester, Wellingborough, and Ynys Mon/Anglesey) (SI 1998/2327) |
| | 15 Jan 2001 (otherwise) (SI 2000/3283)[2] |
| paras 94, 95 | 30 Sep 1998 (in the areas noted to s 38(1)–(3) above only) (SI 1998/2327) |
| | 1 Apr 2000 (otherwise) (SI 2000/924) |
| para 96(1)–(5) | 30 Sep 1998 (SI 1998/2327) |
| para 96(6) | 30 Sep 1998 (in the areas noted to s 38(1)–(3) above only) (SI 1998/2327) |
| | 1 Apr 2000 (otherwise) (SI 2000/924) |
| para 96(7) | 30 Sep 1998 (SI 1998/2327) |
| para 97 | 30 Sep 1998 (SI 1998/2327) |
| para 98 | 30 Sep 1998 (subject to transitional provisions) (SI 1998/2327) |
| para 99 | 31 Jul 1998 (s 121(2)) |
| paras 100–104 | 30 Sep 1998 (subject to transitional provisions) (SI 1998/2327) |
| paras 105–108 | 30 Sep 1998 (SI 1998/2327) |
| para 109 | 1 Apr 2000 (subject to transitional provisions and savings) (SI 1999/3426) |
| paras 110–112 | 1 Apr 2000 (SI 1999/3426) |
| para 113 | 30 Sep 1998 (SI 1998/2327) |
| para 114 | 1 Apr 2000 (SI 1999/3426) |
| paras 115, 116 | 30 Sep 1998 (SI 1998/2327) |
| para 117 | 31 Jul 1998 (s 121(2)) |

**Crime and Disorder Act 1998 (c 37)**—*contd*

| | | |
|---|---|---|
| | paras 118–124 | 30 Sep 1998 (SI 1998/2327) |
| | para 125(a) | 4 Jan 1999 (for the purpose of sending any person for trial under s 51 from the petty sessions areas of Bromley, Croydon, and Sutton, the petty sessional divisions of Aberconwy, Arfon, Blackburn, Darwen and Ribble Valley, Burnley and Pendle, Colwyn, Corby, Daventry, Dyffryn Clwyd, Eifionydd and Pwllheli, Gateshead, Kettering, Meirionnydd, Newcastle-under-Lyme and Pirehill North, Newcastle-upon-Tyne, Northampton, Rhuddlan, Staffordshire Moorlands, Stoke-on-Trent, Towcester, Wellingborough, and Ynys Mon/Anglesey) (SI 1998/2327) |
| | | 15 Jan 2001 (otherwise) (SI 2000/3283)[2] |
| | para 125(b) | 1 Jun 1999 (SI 1999/1279) |
| | para 126 | 4 Jan 1999 (for the purpose of sending any person for trial under s 51 from the petty sessions areas of Bromley, Croydon, and Sutton, the petty sessional divisions of Aberconwy, Arfon, Blackburn, Darwen and Ribble Valley, Burnley and Pendle, Colwyn, Corby, Daventry, Dyffryn Clwyd, Eifionydd and Pwllheli, Gateshead, Kettering, Meirionnydd, Newcastle-under-Lyme and Pirehill North, Newcastle-upon-Tyne, Northampton, Rhuddlan, Staffordshire Moorlands, Stoke-on-Trent, Towcester, Wellingborough, and Ynys Mon/Anglesey) (SI 1998/2327) |
| | | 15 Jan 2001 (otherwise) (SI 2000/3283)[2] |
| | para 127(a) | 4 Jan 1999 (for the purpose of sending any person for trial under s 51 from the petty sessions areas and petty sessional divisions noted to s 51 above only) (SI 1998/2327) |
| | | *Never in force* (otherwise) (repealed) |
| | para 127(b) | 1 Jun 1999 (SI 1999/1279) |
| | paras 128, 129 | 4 Jan 1999 (for the purpose of sending any person for trial under s 51 from the petty sessions areas of Bromley, Croydon, and Sutton, the petty sessional divisions of Aberconwy, Arfon, Blackburn, Darwen and Ribble Valley, Burnley and Pendle, Colwyn, Corby, Daventry, Dyffryn Clwyd, Eifionydd and Pwllheli, Gateshead, Kettering, Meirionnydd, Newcastle-under-Lyme and Pirehill North, Newcastle-upon-Tyne, Northampton, Rhuddlan, Staffordshire Moorlands, Stoke-on-Trent, Towcester, Wellingborough, and Ynys Mon/Anglesey) (SI 1998/2327) |
| | | 15 Jan 2001 (otherwise) (SI 2000/3283)[2] |
| | para 130 | 30 Sep 1998 (SI 1998/2327) |
| | para 131(1), (2) | 30 Sep 1998 (in the areas noted to s 38(1)–(3) above only) (SI 1998/2327) |
| | | 1 Apr 2000 (otherwise) (SI 2000/924) |
| | para 131(3) | 30 Sep 1998 (SI 1998/2327) |
| | paras 132–134 | 30 Sep 1998 (SI 1998/2327) |
| | para 135(1) | 30 Sep 1998 (SI 1998/2327) |
| | para 135(2)(a) | 1 Apr 2000 (SI 1999/3426) |
| | para 135(2)(b) | 30 Sep 1998 (SI 1998/2327) |
| | para 135(3)–(8) | 30 Sep 1998 (SI 1998/2327) |
| | para 135(9), (10) | 1 Apr 2000 (SI 1999/3426) |
| | paras 136–143 | 30 Sep 1998 (SI 1998/2327) |
| | para 144 | 1 Apr 2000 (SI 1999/3426) |
| Sch 9 | paras 1–4 | 30 Sep 1998 (SI 1998/2327) |
| | para 5 | 30 Sep 1998 (in the areas, for the purpose of reprimanding or warning a person under s 65, of the county of Hampshire, the Isle of Wight, the cities of Portsmouth, Sheffield, Southampton and Westminster, the Royal borough of Kensington and Chelsea, the London borough of Hammersmith and Fulham, the Metropolitan borough of Wolverhampton, and the borough of Blackburn with Darwen) (SI 1998/2327) |

**Crime and Disorder Act 1998 (c 37)**—*contd*

|  |  |
|---|---|
|  | 1 Apr 2000 (in the areas, for the purpose of reprimanding or warning a person under s 65, of the counties of Oxfordshire, Norfolk, the cities of Cardiff, Sunderland, the London boroughs of Lewisham, Greenwich, Southwark, the Metropolitan borough of Gateshead) (SI 2000/924) |
|  | 1 Jun 2000 (otherwise) (SI 2000/924) |
| para 6 | 30 Sep 1998 (SI 1998/2327) |
| para 7 | 1 Jul 1999 (SI 1998/3263) |
| para 8 | 30 Sep 1998 (SI 1998/2327) |
| para 9 | 7 Aug 1998 (SI 1998/1883) |
| para 10 | 28 Jan 1999 (SI 1998/3263) |
| para 11 | 30 Sep 1998 (SI 1998/2327) |
| para 12(1) | 30 Sep 1998 (SI 1998/2327) |
| para 12(2) | 1 Jan 1999 (SI 1998/3263) |
| para 12(3)–(9) | 30 Sep 1998 (SI 1998/2327) |
| paras 13–15 | 30 Sep 1998 (SI 1998/2327) |
| Sch 10 | 30 Sep 1998 (SI 1998/2327), repeals of or in— |

Treason Act 1790;

Treason Act 1795;

Treason by Women Act (Ireland) 1796;

Treason Act 1817;

Treason Felony Act 1848;

Sentence of Death (Expectant Mothers) Act 1931;

Children and Young Persons Act 1933;

Criminal Justice Act (Northern Ireland) 1945;

Criminal Justice Act 1967, s 56(3), (13);

Criminal Appeal Act 1968;

Children and Young Persons Act 1969;

Criminal Justice Act 1972;

Powers of Criminal Courts Act 1973, ss 1B, 1C, in s 2(1), the words "For the purposes" to "available evidence", ss 11 (subject to transitional provisions), 14, 31, 32, Schs 1A, 5;

Bail Act 1976;

Magistrates' Courts Act 1980, ss 38, 38A, 108, Sch 7;

Criminal Justice Act 1982, ss 3, 18, 19, 66, Sch 14;

Family Law Reform Act 1987;

Criminal Justice Act 1988;

Prisons (Scotland) Act 1989;

Criminal Justice Act 1991, ss 6, 33, 37(4), Schs 2, 11;

Prisoners and Criminal Proceedings (Scotland) Act 1993 (subject to transitional provisions);

Criminal Justice and Public Order Act 1994, ss 35, 130(4);

Criminal Procedure (Scotland) Act 1995;

Crime and Punishment (Scotland) Act 1997;

Crime (Sentences) Act 1997, ss 1, 8, 10–27, 35, 43, 54, Schs 1, 2, 4–6;

Police Act 1997

30 Sep 1998 (in the areas noted to s 38(1)–(3) above only) (SI 1998/2327), repeals of—

Powers of Criminal Courts Act 1973, in s 2(1) (the words "by a probation officer");

Crime (Sentences) Act 1997, s 31(2) (in the areas of the counties of Bedfordshire, Devon and Hampshire, the Isle of Wight, the cities of Portsmouth, Sheffield, Southampton and Westminster, the Royal borough of Kensington and Chelsea, the London boroughs of Hammersmith and Fulham, and Lewisham, the Metropolitan boroughs of St Helens and Wolverhampton, and the boroughs of Blackburn with Darwen, and Luton)

1 Jan 1999 (repeals of or in Criminal Justice Act 1991, ss 37(1), 38, 45) (SI 1998/3263)

**Crime and Disorder Act 1998 (c 37)**—*contd*

4 Jan 1999 (repeals in Magistrates' Courts Act 1980, ss 125, 126)
(for the purpose of sending any person for trial under s 51
from the petty sessions areas of Bromley, Croydon, and Sutton,
the petty sessional divisions of Aberconwy, Arfon, Blackburn,
Darwen and Ribble Valley, Burnley and Pendle, Colwyn,
Corby, Daventry, Dyffryn Clwyd, Eifionydd and Pwllheli,
Gateshead, Kettering, Meirionnydd, Newcastle-under-Lyme
and Pirehill North, Newcastle-upon-Tyne, Northampton,
Rhuddlan, Staffordshire Moorlands, Stoke-on-Trent, Towcester,
Wellingborough, and Ynys Mon/Anglesey) (SI 1998/2327)

1 Jun 1999 (SI 1999/1279), repeals of—
Criminal Justice Act 1991, s 62;
Criminal Justice and Public Order Act 1994, s 20

1 Apr 2000 (subject to transitional provisions and savings)
(SI 1999/3426), repeals of or in—
Criminal Justice Act 1967, ss 56(6), 67;
Powers of Criminal Courts Act 1973, ss 1, 42;
Magistrates' Courts Act 1980, s 37;
Criminal Justice Act 1982, ss 1A–1C;
Criminal Justice Act 1991, ss 31, 61, Sch 12;
Probation Service Act 1993, s 17;
Criminal Justice and Public Order Act 1994, ss 1–4, Sch 10;
Drug Trafficking Act 1994, s 2

1 Apr 2000 (SI 2000/924), repeals of—
Powers of Criminal Courts Act 1973, s 2(1) (the words "by a
probation officer") (otherwise);
Crime (Sentences) Act 1997, s 31(2) (otherwise)

15 Jan 2001 (repeals of or in Magistrates' Courts Act 1980, ss 125,
126) (otherwise) (SI 2000/3283)[2]

[1]   SI 1998/2327 contains transitional provisions relating to the commencement of ss 75–77

[2]   For transitional provisions, see SI 2000/3283, art 3

---

**Criminal Justice (International Co-operation) (Amendment) Act 1998 (c 27)**

*RA:* 9 Jul 1998

*Commencement provisions:* s 2(2)

Whole Act in force 9 Sep 1998 (s 2(2))

---

**Criminal Justice (Terrorism and Conspiracy) Act 1998 (c 40)**

*RA:* 8 Apr 1998

Whole Act in force 8 Apr 1998 (RA)

---

**Data Protection Act 1998 (c 29)**

*RA:* 16 Jul 1998

*Commencement provisions:* s 75(2), (3); Data Protection Act 1998 (Commencement) Order 2000,
SI 2000/183; Data Protection Act 1998 (Commencement No 2) Order 2008, SI 2008/1592; Data
Protection Act 1998 (Commencement No 3) Order 2011, SI 2011/601; Data Protection Act 1998
(Commencement No 4) Order 2015, SI 2015/312

| | | |
|---|---|---|
| 1–3 | | 16 Jul 1998 (s 75(2)) |
| 4 | (1) | See Sch 1, Pt I below |
| | (2) | See Sch 1, Pt II below |

**Data Protection Act 1998 (c 29)**—*contd*

| | | |
|---|---|---|
| | (3) | See Schs 2–4 below |
| | (4) | 1 Mar 2000 (SI 2000/183) |
| 5, 6 | | 1 Mar 2000 (SI 2000/183) |
| 7 | (1)–(6) | 1 Mar 2000 (SI 2000/183) |
| | (7) | 16 Jul 1998 (so far as conferring power to make subordinate legislation) (s 75(2)) |
| | | 1 Mar 2000 (otherwise) (SI 2000/183) |
| | (8)–(11) | 1 Mar 2000 (SI 2000/183) |
| 8 | (1) | 16 Jul 1998 (so far as conferring power to make subordinate legislation) (s 75(2)) |
| | | 1 Mar 2000 (otherwise) (SI 2000/183) |
| | (2)–(7) | 1 Mar 2000 (SI 2000/183) |
| 9 | (1), (2) | 1 Mar 2000 (SI 2000/183) |
| | (3) | 16 Jul 1998 (so far as conferring power to make subordinate legislation) (s 75(2)) |
| | | 1 Mar 2000 (otherwise) (SI 2000/183) |
| 10 | (1) | 1 Mar 2000 (SI 2000/183) |
| | (2) | 16 Jul 1998 (so far as conferring power to make subordinate legislation) (s 75(2)) |
| | | 1 Mar 2000 (otherwise) (SI 2000/183) |
| | (3)–(5) | 1 Mar 2000 (SI 2000/183) |
| 11 | | 1 Mar 2000 (SI 2000/183) |
| 12 | (1)–(4) | 1 Mar 2000 (SI 2000/183) |
| | (5) | 16 Jul 1998 (so far as conferring power to make subordinate legislation) (s 75(2)) |
| | | 1 Mar 2000 (otherwise) (SI 2000/183) |
| | (6)–(9) | 1 Mar 2000 (SI 2000/183) |
| 13–16 | | 1 Mar 2000 (SI 2000/183) |
| 17 | (1), (2) | 1 Mar 2000 (SI 2000/183) |
| | (3) | 16 Jul 1998 (so far as conferring power to make subordinate legislation) (s 75(2)) |
| | | 1 Mar 2000 (otherwise) (SI 2000/183) |
| | (4) | 1 Mar 2000 (SI 2000/183) |
| 18 | (1) | 1 Mar 2000 (SI 2000/183) |
| | (2) | 16 Jul 1998 (so far as conferring power to make subordinate legislation) (s 75(2)) |
| | | 1 Mar 2000 (otherwise) (SI 2000/183) |
| | (3) | 1 Mar 2000 (SI 2000/183) |
| | (4)–(6) | 16 Jul 1998 (so far as conferring power to make subordinate legislation) (s 75(2)) |
| | | 1 Mar 2000 (otherwise) (SI 2000/183) |
| 19 | (1), (2) | 1 Mar 2000 (SI 2000/183) |
| | (3), (4) | 16 Jul 1998 (so far as conferring power to make subordinate legislation) (s 75(2)) |
| | | 1 Mar 2000 (otherwise) (SI 2000/183) |
| | (5), (6) | 1 Mar 2000 (SI 2000/183) |
| | (7) | 16 Jul 1998 (so far as conferring power to make subordinate legislation) (s 75(2)) |
| | | 1 Mar 2000 (otherwise) (SI 2000/183) |
| 20 | (1) | 16 Jul 1998 (so far as conferring power to make subordinate legislation) (s 75(2)) |
| | | 1 Mar 2000 (otherwise) (SI 2000/183) |
| | (2)–(4) | 1 Mar 2000 (SI 2000/183) |
| 21 | | 1 Mar 2000 (SI 2000/183) |
| 22 | (1) | 16 Jul 1998 (so far as conferring power to make subordinate legislation) (s 75(2)) |
| | | 1 Mar 2000 (SI 2000/183) |
| | (2)–(6) | 1 Mar 2000 (SI 2000/183) |
| | (7) | 16 Jul 1998 (so far as conferring power to make subordinate legislation) (s 75(2)) |

**Data Protection Act 1998 (c 29)**—*contd*

| | | |
|---|---|---|
| | | 1 Mar 2000 (otherwise) (SI 2000/183) |
| 23 | (1) | 16 Jul 1998 (so far as conferring power to make subordinate legislation) (s 75(2)) |
| | | 1 Mar 2000 (otherwise) (SI 2000/183) |
| | (2) | 1 Mar 2000 (SI 2000/183) |
| 24 | (1), (2) | 1 Mar 2000 (SI 2000/183) |
| | (3) | 16 Jul 1998 (so far as conferring power to make subordinate legislation) (s 75(2)) |
| | | 1 Mar 2000 (otherwise) (SI 2000/183) |
| | (4), (5) | 1 Mar 2000 (SI 2000/183) |
| 25 | (1) | 16 Jul 1998 (s 75(2)) |
| | (2), (3) | 1 Mar 2000 (SI 2000/183) |
| | (4) | 16 Jul 1998 (s 75(2)) |
| 26 | | 16 Jul 1998 (s 75(2)) |
| 27–29 | | 1 Mar 2000 (SI 2000/183) |
| 30 | (1)–(3) | 16 Jul 1998 (so far as conferring power to make subordinate legislation) (s 75(2)) |
| | | 1 Mar 2000 (otherwise) (SI 2000/183) |
| | (4), (5) | 1 Mar 2000 (SI 2000/183) |
| 31 | | 1 Mar 2000 (SI 2000/183) |
| 32 | (1), (2) | 1 Mar 2000 (SI 2000/183) |
| | (3) | 16 Jul 1998 (so far as conferring power to make subordinate legislation) (s 75(2)) |
| | | 1 Mar 2000 (otherwise) (SI 2000/183) |
| | (4)–(6) | 1 Mar 2000 (SI 2000/183) |
| 33–37 | | 1 Mar 2000 (SI 2000/183) |
| 38 | | 16 Jul 1998 (so far as conferring power to make subordinate legislation) (s 75(2)) |
| | | 1 Mar 2000 (otherwise) (SI 2000/183) |
| 39–50 | | 1 Mar 2000 (SI 2000/183) |
| 51 | (1), (2) | 1 Mar 2000 (SI 2000/183) |
| | (3) | 16 Jul 1998 (so far as conferring power to make subordinate legislation) (s 75(2)) |
| | | 1 Mar 2000 (otherwise) (SI 2000/183) |
| | (4)–(9) | 1 Mar 2000 (SI 2000/183) |
| 52, 53 | | 1 Mar 2000 (SI 2000/183) |
| 54 | (1) | 1 Mar 2000 (SI 2000/183) |
| | (2)–(4) | 16 Jul 1998 (so far as conferring power to make subordinate legislation) (s 75(2)) |
| | | 1 Mar 2000 (otherwise) (SI 2000/183) |
| | (5)–(8) | 1 Mar 2000 (SI 2000/183) |
| 55 | | 1 Mar 2000 (SI 2000/183) |
| 56 | (1)–(6) | 7 Jul 2008 (in so far as it relates to the entries in sub-s (6) which relate to the functions of the Secretary of State or the Independent Barring Board under the Safeguarding Vulnerable Groups Act 2006 or SI 2007/1351 (NI 11)) (SI 2008/1592) |
| | | 3 Mar 2011 (in so far as it relates to a record containing information relating to the Scottish Ministers' functions under the Protection of Vulnerable Groups (Scotland) Act 2007, Pts 1, 2) (SI 2011/601) |
| | | 10 Mar 2015 (otherwise) (SI 2015/312) |
| | (7) | 7 Jul 2008 (in so far as it relates to the entries in sub-s (6) which relate to the functions of the Secretary of State or the Independent Barring Board under the Safeguarding Vulnerable Groups Act 2006 or SI 2007/1351 (NI 11)) (SI 2008/1592) |
| | | 3 Mar 2011 (in so far as it relates to a record containing information relating to the Scottish Ministers' functions under the Protection of Vulnerable Groups (Scotland) Act 2007, Pts 1, 2) (SI 2011/601) |
| | | 10 Mar 2015 (otherwise) (SI 2015/312) |

**Data Protection Act 1998 (c 29)**—*contd*

| | | |
|---|---|---|
| | (8) | 16 Jul 1998 (so far as conferring power to make subordinate legislation) (s 75(2)) |
| | | 7 Jul 2008 (in so far as it relates to the entries in sub-s (6) which relate to the functions of the Secretary of State or the Independent Barring Board under the Safeguarding Vulnerable Groups Act 2006 or SI 2007/1351 (NI 11)) (SI 2008/1592) |
| | | 3 Mar 2011 (in so far as it relates to a record containing information relating to the Scottish Ministers' functions under the Protection of Vulnerable Groups (Scotland) Act 2007, Pts 1, 2) (SI 2011/601) |
| | | 10 Mar 2015 (otherwise) (SI 2015/312) |
| | (9), (10) | 7 Jul 2008 (in so far as it relates to the entries in sub-s (6) which relate to the functions of the Secretary of State or the Independent Barring Board under the Safeguarding Vulnerable Groups Act 2006 or SI 2007/1351 (NI 11)) (SI 2008/1592) |
| | | 3 Mar 2011 (in so far as it relates to a record containing information relating to the Scottish Ministers' functions under the Protection of Vulnerable Groups (Scotland) Act 2007, Pts 1, 2) (SI 2011/601) |
| | | 10 Mar 2015 (otherwise) (SI 2015/312) |
| 57–61 | | 1 Mar 2000 (SI 2000/183) |
| 62 | | 1 Mar 2000 (subject to transitional provisions) (SI 2000/183) |
| 63 | | 1 Mar 2000 (SI 2000/183) |
| 64 | (1), (2) | 1 Mar 2000 (SI 2000/183) |
| | (3) | 16 Jul 1998 (so far as conferring power to make subordinate legislation) (s 75(2)) |
| | | 1 Mar 2000 (otherwise) (SI 2000/183) |
| 67–71 | | 16 Jul 1998 (s 75(2)) |
| 72 | | 1 Mar 2000 (SI 2000/183) |
| 73 | | See Sch 14 below |
| 74 | | 1 Mar 2000 (SI 2000/183) |
| 75 | | 16 Jul 1998 (s 75(2)) |
| Sch 1 | Pt I | 1 Mar 2000 (SI 2000/183) |
| | Pt II | 16 Jul 1998 (so far as conferring power to make subordinate legislation) (s 75(2)) |
| | | 1 Mar 2000 (otherwise) (SI 2000/183) |
| Sch 2 | paras 1–5 | 1 Mar 2000 (SI 2000/183) |
| | para 6(1) | 1 Mar 2000 (SI 2000/183) |
| | para 6(2) | 16 Jul 1998 (so far as conferring power to make subordinate legislation) (s 75(2)) |
| | | 1 Mar 2000 (otherwise) (SI 2000/183) |
| Sch 3 | para 1 | 1 Mar 2000 (SI 2000/183) |
| | para 2(1) | 1 Mar 2000 (SI 2000/183) |
| | para 2(2) | 16 Jul 1998 (so far as conferring power to make subordinate legislation) (s 75(2)) |
| | | 1 Mar 2000 (otherwise) (SI 2000/183) |
| | paras 3–6 | 1 Mar 2000 (SI 2000/183) |
| | para 7(1) | 1 Mar 2000 (SI 2000/183) |
| | para 7(2) | 16 Jul 1998 (so far as conferring power to make subordinate legislation) (s 75(2)) |
| | | 1 Mar 2000 (otherwise) (SI 2000/183) |
| | para 8 | 1 Mar 2000 (SI 2000/183) |
| | para 9(1) | 1 Mar 2000 (SI 2000/183) |
| | para 9(2) | 16 Jul 1998 (so far as conferring power to make subordinate legislation) (s 75(2)) |
| | | 1 Mar 2000 (otherwise) (SI 2000/183) |
| | para 10 | 16 Jul 1998 (so far as conferring power to make subordinate legislation) (s 75(2)) |
| | | 1 Mar 2000 (otherwise) (SI 2000/183) |
| Sch 4 | paras 1–3 | 1 Mar 2000 (SI 2000/183) |

**See Halsbury's Statutes Citator for amendments to these Acts**          995

**Data Protection Act 1998 (c 29)**—*contd*

| | | |
|---|---|---|
| | para 4(1) | 1 Mar 2000 (SI 2000/183) |
| | para 4(2) | 16 Jul 1998 (so far as conferring power to make subordinate legislation) (s 75(2)) |
| | | 1 Mar 2000 (otherwise) (SI 2000/183) |
| | paras 5–9 | 1 Mar 2000 (SI 2000/183) |
| Sch 5 | paras 1–16 | 1 Mar 2000 (SI 2000/183) |
| | para 17 | 16 Jul 1998 (s 75(2)) |
| Sch 6 | paras 1–6 | 1 Mar 2000 (SI 2000/183) |
| | para 7 | 16 Jul 1998 (so far as conferring power to make subordinate legislation) (s 75(2)) |
| | | 1 Mar 2000 (otherwise) (SI 2000/183) |
| | para 8 | 1 Mar 2000 (SI 2000/183) |
| Sch 7 | paras 1–3 | 1 Mar 2000 (SI 2000/183) |
| | para 4 | 16 Jul 1998 (so far as conferring power to make subordinate legislation) (s 75(2)) |
| | | 1 Mar 2000 (otherwise) (SI 2000/183) |
| | para 5 | 1 Mar 2000 (SI 2000/183) |
| | para 6(1) | 1 Mar 2000 (SI 2000/183) |
| | para 6(2) | 16 Jul 1998 (so far as conferring power to make subordinate legislation) (s 75(2)) |
| | | 1 Mar 2000 (otherwise) (SI 2000/183) |
| | para 6(3) | 1 Mar 2000 (SI 2000/183) |
| | paras 7–11 | 1 Mar 2000 (SI 2000/183) |
| Schs 8–10 | | 1 Mar 2000 (SI 2000/183) |
| Schs 11, 12 | | 16 Jul 1998 (s 75(2)) |
| Sch 13 | | 1 Mar 2000 (SI 2000/183) |
| Sch 14 | | 16 Jul 1998 (so far as conferring power to make subordinate legislation) (s 75(2)) |
| | | 1 Mar 2000 (otherwise) (SI 2000/183) |
| Schs 15, 16 | | 1 Mar 2000 (SI 2000/183) |

**Education (Student Loans) Act 1998 (c 1)**

*RA:* 27 Jan 1998

*Commencement provisions:* s 7(4); Education (Student Loans) Act 1998 (Commencement) Order 1998, SI 1998/210

| | | |
|---|---|---|
| 1 | | 27 Jan 1998 (RA) |
| 2, 3 | | 1 Mar 1998 (SI 1998/210) |
| 4, 5 | | 27 Jan 1998 (RA) |
| 6 | (1) | 27 Jan 1998 (RA) |
| | (2) | 1 Mar 1998 (SI 1998/210) |
| 7 | | 27 Jan 1998 (RA) |
| Schedule | | 1 Mar 1998 (SI 1998/210) |

**Employment Rights (Dispute Resolution) Act 1998 (c 8)**

*RA:* 8 Apr 1998

*Commencement provisions:* s 17(1), (2); Employment Rights (Dispute Resolution) Act 1998 (Commencement No 1 and Transitional and Saving Provisions) Order 1998, SI 1998/1658

| | | |
|---|---|---|
| 1, 2 | | 1 Aug 1998 (SI 1998/1658) |
| 3 | (1)–(3) | 1 Aug 1998 (subject to a transitional provision) (SI 1998/1658) |
| | (4)–(6) | 1 Aug 1998 (SI 1998/1658) |
| 4 | | *Not yet in force* |
| 5 | | 1 Aug 1998 (SI 1998/1658) |
| 6 | | 1 Aug 1998 (subject to a transitional provision) (SI 1998/1658) |
| 7 | | 1 Aug 1998 (SI 1998/1658) |

## Employment Rights (Dispute Resolution) Act 1998 (c 8)—*contd*

| | | |
|---|---|---|
| 8 | (1), (2) | 1 Aug 1998 (subject to a transitional provision) (SI 1998/1658) |
| | (3) | 1 Aug 1998 (SI 1998/1658) |
| | (4) | 1 Aug 1998 (subject to a transitional provision) (SI 1998/1658) |
| | (5) | 1 Aug 1998 (SI 1998/1658) |
| 9, 10 | | 1 Aug 1998 (SI 1998/1658) |
| 11 | | 1 Oct 1998 (subject to a saving) (SI 1998/1658) |
| 12 | | 1 Aug 1998 (SI 1998/1658) |
| 13 | | 1 Jan 1999 (subject to a transitional provision) (SI 1998/1658) |
| 14 | | 1 Aug 1998 (subject to a saving) (SI 1998/1658) |
| 15 | | See Schs 1, 2 below |
| 16–18 | | 8 Apr 1998 (s 17(1)) |
| Sch 1 | paras 1–11 | 1 Aug 1998 (SI 1998/1658) |
| | para 12(1), (2) | 1 Aug 1998 (SI 1998/1658) |
| | para 12(3) | 1 Aug 1998 (subject to a transitional provision) (SI 1998/1658) |
| | para 12(4) | 1 Aug 1998 (SI 1998/1658) |
| | paras 13–16 | 1 Aug 1998 (SI 1998/1658) |
| | para 17(1) | 1 Aug 1998 (SI 1998/1658) |
| | para 17(2) | 8 Apr 1998 (amendment made by this sub-paragraph is deemed always to have had effect) (s 17(1), (3)) |
| | para 17(3) | 1 Aug 1998 (SI 1998/1658) |
| | para 18 | 1 Aug 1998 (subject to a saving) (SI 1998/1658) |
| | paras 19–21 | 1 Jan 1999 (subject to a transitional provision) (SI 1998/1658) |
| | para 22 | 1 Aug 1998 (SI 1998/1658) |
| | para 23 | 1 Jan 1999 (subject to a transitional provision) (SI 1998/1658) |
| | paras 24, 25 | 1 Aug 1998 (SI 1998/1658) |
| | para 26 | 1 Jan 1999 (subject to a transitional provision) (SI 1998/1658) |
| Sch 2 | | 1 Aug 1998 (except repeals in Employment Rights Act 1996, ss 166(2)(a), 168(1)(a)) (subject to a transitional provision and savings) (SI 1998/1658) |
| | | 1 Oct 1998 (exceptions noted above) (subject to a saving) (SI 1998/1658) |

## European Communities (Amendment) Act 1998 (c 21)

*RA:* 11 Jun 1998

Whole Act in force 11 Jun 1998 (RA)

## Finance Act 1998 (c 36)

*Budget Day:* 17 Mar 1998

*RA:* 31 Jul 1998

The commencement details of Finance Acts are not set out, as the dates from which their provisions take effect are usually stated clearly and unambiguously in the text of the Act, and charging provisions will normally state for which year or years of assessment they are to have effect.

## Fossil Fuel Levy Act 1998 (c 5)

*RA:* 18 Mar 1998

*Commencement provisions:* s 2(2); Fossil Fuel Levy Act 1998 (Commencement) Order 1998, SI 1998/930

Whole Act in force 1 Apr 1998 (SI 1998/930)

## Government of Wales Act 1998 (c 38)

*RA:* 31 Jul 1998

*Commencement provisions:* s 158; Government of Wales Act 1998 (Commencement No 1) Order 1998, SI 1998/2244; Government of Wales Act 1998 (Commencement No 2) Order 1998, SI 1998/2789; Government of Wales Act 1998 (Commencement No 3) Order 1999, SI 1999/118; Government of Wales Act 1998 (Commencement No 4) Order 1999, SI 1999/782; Government of Wales Act 1998 (Commencement No 5) Order 1999, SI 1999/1290; Government of Wales Act 1998 (Commencement No 6) Order 2001, SI 2001/1756

| | | |
|---|---|---|
| 1–49 | | 1 Dec 1998 (SI 1998/2789) |
| 50, 51 | | 31 Jul 1998 (s 158(1)) |
| 52–103 | | 1 Dec 1998 (SI 1998/2789) |
| 104 | (1)–(4) | 1 Jul 1999 (SI 1999/1290) |
| | (5) | 1 Jul 1999 (SI 1999/1290) |
| | (6) | See Sch 6 below |
| 105 | (1)–(3) | 14 May 2001 (SI 2001/1756)[1] |
| | (4) | 14 May 2001 (SI 2001/1756)[2] |
| | (5) | See Sch 7 below |
| 106 | | 1 Dec 1998 (SI 1998/2789) |
| 107 | | 1 Apr 1999 (SI 1999/782) |
| 108–110 | | 1 Dec 1998 (SI 1998/2789) |
| 111 | (1) | 1 Feb 1999 (SI 1999/118) |
| | (2) | See Sch 9 below |
| 112 | | See Sch 10 below |
| 113–115 | | 1 Dec 1998 (SI 1998/2789) |
| 116–118 | | 1 Apr 1999 (SI 1999/782) |
| 119–124 | | 1 Dec 1998 (SI 1998/2789) |
| 125 | | See Sch 12 below |
| 126 | | 1 Oct 1998 (SI 1998/2244) |
| 127 | | See Sch 13 below |
| 128 | | See Sch 14 below |
| 129 | (1) | 1 Oct 1998 (SI 1998/2244) |
| | (2) | See Sch 15 below |
| 130 | (1)–(3) | 1 Oct 1998 (SI 1998/2244) |
| | (4), (5) | 2 Sep 1998 (SI 1998/2244) |
| 131 | | 1 Oct 1998 (SI 1998/2244) |
| 132 | (1) | 2 Sep 1998 (SI 1998/2244) |
| | (2)–(5) | 1 Oct 1998 (SI 1998/2244) |
| | (6) | 2 Sep 1998 (SI 1998/2244) |
| | (7) | 1 Oct 1998 (SI 1998/2244) |
| 133 | (1), (2) | 1 Oct 1998 (SI 1998/2244) |
| | (3), (4) | 2 Sep 1998 (SI 1998/2244) |
| 134, 135 | | 1 Oct 1998 (SI 1998/2244) |
| 136 | (1)–(3) | 1 Oct 1998 (SI 1998/2244) |
| | (4), (5) | 2 Sep 1998 (SI 1998/2244) |
| 137 | | 1 Oct 1998 (SI 1998/2244) |
| 138 | (1) | 2 Sep 1998 (SI 1998/2244) |
| | (2)–(5) | 1 Oct 1998 (SI 1998/2244) |
| | (6) | 2 Sep 1998 (SI 1998/2244) |
| | (7) | 1 Oct 1998 (SI 1998/2244) |
| 139 | (1), (2) | 1 Oct 1998 (SI 1998/2244) |
| | (3), (4) | 2 Sep 1998 (SI 1998/2244) |
| 140 | (1)–(4) | 1 Nov 1998 (SI 1998/2244) |
| | (5), (6) | 2 Sep 1998 (SI 1998/2244) |
| 141 | | 1 Nov 1998 (SI 1998/2244) |
| 142 | (1) | 2 Sep 1998 (SI 1998/2244) |
| | (2)–(6) | 1 Nov 1998 (SI 1998/2244) |
| | (7), (8) | 2 Sep 1998 (SI 1998/2244) |
| 143 | (1), (2) | 1 Nov 1998 (SI 1998/2244) |
| | (3), (4) | 2 Sep 1998 (SI 1998/2244) |

**Government of Wales Act 1998 (c 38)**—*contd*

| | | |
|---|---|---|
| 144–149 | | 1 Dec 1998 (SI 1998/2789) |
| 150 | | 2 Sep 1998 (SI 1998/2244) |
| 151 | | 31 Jul 1998 (s 158(1)) |
| 152 | | See Sch 18 below |
| 153–159 | | 31 Jul 1998 (s 158(1)) |
| Schs 1–5 | | 1 Dec 1998 (SI 1998/2789) |
| Sch 6 | paras 1, 2 | 1 May 1999 (SI 1999/1290) |
| | paras 3–9 | 1 Jul 1999 (SI 1999/1290) |
| Sch 7 | para 1(1), (2) | 1 Apr 1999 (SI 1999/782) |
| | para 1(3) | 14 May 2001 (SI 2001/1756)[1] |
| | paras 2–7 | 14 May 2001 (SI 2001/1756)[1] |
| | para 8 | 1 Apr 1999 (SI 1999/782) |
| | para 9(1) | 14 May 2001 (SI 2001/1756)[1] |
| | para 9(2) | 1 Apr 1999 (so far as relates to an examination under National Audit Act 1983, s 6) (SI 1999/782) |
| | | 14 May 2001 (otherwise) (SI 2001/1756)[1] |
| | paras 10, 11 | 14 May 2001 (SI 2001/1756)[1] |
| Sch 8 | | 1 Dec 1998 (SI 1998/2789) |
| Sch 9 | Pt I | 1 Feb 1999 (SI 1999/118) |
| | Pt II, paras 14–16 | 1 Jul 1999 (SI 1999/1290) |
| | Pt II, para 17(1)–(8) | 1 Jul 1999 (SI 1999/1290) |
| | Pt II, para 17(9) | 1 May 1999 (SI 1999/1290) |
| | Pt II, para 17(10) | 1 Jul 1999 (SI 1999/1290) |
| | Pt II, paras 18–27 | 1 Jul 1999 (SI 1999/1290) |
| Sch 10 | para 1 | 1 Apr 1999 (SI 1999/782) |
| | para 2 | 1 Jul 1999 (SI 1999/1290) |
| | para 3(1), (2) | 1 Apr 1999 (SI 1999/782) |
| | para 3(3), (4) | 1 Jul 1999 (SI 1999/1290) |
| | para 4 | 1 Apr 1999 (SI 1999/782) |
| | para 5 | 1 Jul 1999 (SI 1999/1290) |
| | paras 6, 7 | 1 Apr 1999 (s 1999/782) |
| | paras 8–12 | 1 Jul 1999 (SI 1999/1290) |
| | paras 13, 14 | 1 Apr 1999 (SI 1999/782) |
| | para 15(1), (2) | 1 Apr 1999 (SI 1999/782) |
| | para 15(3) | 1 Jul 1999 (SI 1999/1290) |
| | para 15(4) | 1 Apr 1999 (SI 1999/782) |
| | paras 16, 17 | 1 Jul 1999 (SI 1999/1290) |
| Sch 11 | | 1 Dec 1998 (SI 1998/2789) |
| Sch 12 | para 1 | 1 Feb 1999 (SI 1999/118) |
| | paras 2–4 | 1 Apr 1999 (SI 1999/782) |
| | paras 5, 6 | 1 Jul 1999 (SI 1999/1290) |
| | para 7 | 1 Apr 1999 (SI 1999/782) |
| | paras 8, 9 | 1 Jul 1999 (SI 1999/1290) |
| | paras 10–14 | 1 Apr 1999 (SI 1999/782) |
| | para 15(1), (2) | 1 Apr 1999 (SI 1999/782) |
| | para 15(3) | 1 Jul 1999 (SI 1999/1290) |
| | para 16 | 1 Apr 1999 (SI 1999/782) |
| | para 17 | 1 Jul 1999 (SI 1999/1290) |
| | paras 18, 19 | 1 Feb 1999 (SI 1999/118) |
| | paras 20–30 | 1 Apr 1999 (SI 1999/782) |
| | paras 31, 32 | 1 Feb 1999 (SI 1999/118) |
| | paras 33–36 | 1 Apr 1999 (SI 1999/782) |
| Schs 13–15 | | 1 Oct 1998 (SI 1998/2244) |
| Sch 16 | | 1 Nov 1998 (SI 1998/2244) |
| Sch 17 | | 1 Dec 1998 (SI 1998/2789) |
| Sch 18 | Pt I | 1 Feb 1999 (repeal in Finance Act 1989, s 182) (SI 1999/118) |
| | | 1 Apr 1999 (SI 1999/782), repeals of or in— |
| | | Health Service Commissioners Act 1993, ss 2(2)(b), 18(3); |
| | | Health Authorities Act 1995 |

**Government of Wales Act 1998 (c 38)**—*contd*

|  | 1 Jul 1999 (otherwise) (SI 1999/1290) |
| Pt II | 1 Apr 1999 (except the reference to the General Teaching Council for Wales) (SI 1999/782) |
|  | *Not yet in force* (exception noted above) |
| Pts III–V | 1 Oct 1998 (SI 1998/2244) |
| Pt VI | 1 Nov 1998 (SI 1998/2244) |
| Pt VII | 2 Sep 1998 (SI 1998/2244) |

1   This provision does not apply in relation to the financial year beginning on 1 Apr 2000, or any earlier financial year; see SI 2001/1756, art 2(2)

2   This provision does not apply in relation to the financial year beginning on 1 Apr 2001, or any earlier financial year; see SI 2001/1756, art 2(3)

---

**Greater London Authority (Referendum) Act 1998 (c 3)**

*RA:* 23 Feb 1998

Whole Act in force 23 Feb 1998 (RA)

---

**Human Rights Act 1998 (c 42)**

*RA:* 9 Nov 1998

*Commencement provisions:* s 22(2), (3); Human Rights Act 1998 (Commencement) Order 1998, SI 1998/2882; Human Rights Act 1998 (Commencement No 2) Order 2000, SI 2000/1851

| 1–17 |  | 2 Oct 2000 (SI 2000/1851) |
| 18 |  | 9 Nov 1998 (s 22(2)) |
| 19 |  | 24 Nov 1998 (SI 1998/2882) |
| 20 |  | 9 Nov 1998 (s 22(2)) |
| 21 | (1)–(4) | 2 Oct 2000 (SI 2000/1851) |
|  | (5) | 9 Nov 1998 (s 22(2)) |
| 22 |  | 9 Nov 1998 (s 22(2)) |
| Schs 1–3 |  | 2 Oct 2000 (SI 2000/1851) |
| Sch 4 |  | 9 Nov 1998 (s 22(2)) |

---

**Landmines Act 1998 (c 33)**

*RA:* 28 Jul 1998

*Commencement provisions:* s 29(2); Landmines Act 1998 (Commencement) Order 1999, SI 1999/448

| 1–28 | 1 Mar 1999 (SI 1999/448) |
| 29 | 28 Jul 1998 (s 29(2)) |

---

**Late Payment of Commercial Debts (Interest) Act 1998 (c 20)**

*RA:* 11 Jun 1998

*Commencement provisions:* s 17(2); Late Payment of Commercial Debts (Interest) Act 1998 (Commencement No 1) Order 1998, SI 1998/2479; Late Payment of Commercial Debts (Interest) Act 1998 (Commencement No 2) Order 1999, SI 1999/1816; Late Payment of Commercial Debts (Interest) Act 1998 (Commencement No 3) Order 2000, SI 2000/2225; Late Payment of Commercial Debts (Interest) Act 1998 (Commencement No 4) Order 2000, SI 2000/2740; Late Payment of Commercial Debts (Interest) Act 1998 (Commencement No 5) Order 2002, SI 2002/1673; Late Payment of Commercial Debts (Interest) Act 1998 (Commencement No 6) (Scotland) Order 2002, SSI 2002/337

## Late Payment of Commercial Debts (Interest) Act 1998 (c 20)—*contd*

| | |
|---|---|
| 1–16 | 1 Nov 1998 (in relation to contracts for the supply of goods or services made on or after 1 Nov 1998 made between a small business supplier and a purchaser who is a United Kingdom public authority, or made between a small business supplier and a large business supplier) (SI 1998/2479) |
| | 1 Jul 1999 (in relation to contracts for the supply of goods or services made on or after 1 Jul 1999 between a small business supplier and any purchaser who is a United Kingdom public authority) (SI 1999/1816) |
| | 1 Sep 2000 (in relation to contracts for the supply of goods or services made on or after 1 Sep 2000 between a small business supplier and the Comptroller and Auditor General for Northern Ireland, the Metropolitan Police Authority or the London Fire and Emergency Planning Authority) (SI 2000/2225) |
| | 1 Nov 2000 (in relation to contracts for the supply of goods or services made on or after 1 Nov 2000 between a small business supplier and a small business purchaser) (SI 2000/2740) |
| | 7 Aug 2002 (otherwise) (SI 2002/1673; SSI 2002/337) |
| 17 | 11 Jun 1998 (s 17(2)) |

## Magistrates' Courts (Procedure) Act 1998 (c 15)

*RA:* 21 May 1998

*Commencement provisions:* s 5(2), (3); Magistrates' Courts (Procedure) Act 1998 (Commencement No 1) Order 1998, SI 1998/1837; Magistrates' Courts (Procedure) Act 1998 (Commencement No 2) Order 1999, SI 1999/1197

| | |
|---|---|
| 1 | 4 May 1999 (in cases where a summons is issued on or after that date) (SI 1999/1197) |
| 2 | 1 Sep 1998 (subject to a transitional provision) (SI 1998/1837) |
| 3 | 1 Sep 1998 (in relation to where the information is substantiated on oath, or the accused is convicted, on or after 1 Sep 1998) (SI 1998/1837) |
| 4 | 1 Sep 1998 (SI 1998/1837) |
| 5 | 21 May 1998 (s 5(2)) |

## National Institutions Measure 1998 (No 1)

*RA:* 2 Jul 1998

*Commencement provisions:* s 15; Instrument of the Archbishops of 14 Oct 1998

Whole Measure in force 1 Jan 1999 (Instrument of the Archbishops of 14 Oct 1998)

## National Lottery Act 1998 (c 22)

*RA:* 2 Jul 1998

*Commencement provisions:* s 27(3)–(5); National Lottery Act 1998 (Commencement) Order 1999, SI 1999/650

| | |
|---|---|
| 1 | 1 Apr 1999 (SI 1999/650) |
| 2–5 | 2 Sep 1998 (s 27(5)) |
| 6–12 | 2 Jul 1998 (s 27(4)) |
| 13, 14 | 2 Sep 1998 (s 27(5)) |
| 15–25 | 2 Jul 1998 (s 27(4)) |
| 26 | See Sch 5 below |
| 27 | 2 Jul 1998 (s 27(4)) |
| Sch 1 | 1 Apr 1999 (SI 1999/650) |

**National Lottery Act 1998 (c 22)**—*contd*

| | | |
|---|---|---|
| Schs 2–4 | | 2 Jul 1998 (s 27(4)) |
| Sch 5 | Pt I | 1 Apr 1999 (SI 1999/650) |
| | Pt II | 2 Jul 1998 (repeals in National Lottery etc Act 1993, s 22, Sch 5, paras 2, 3, 6) (s 27(4)) |
| | | 2 Sep 1998 (otherwise) (s 27(5)) |

---

**National Minimum Wage Act 1998 (c 39)**

*RA:* 31 Jul 1998

*Commencement provisions:* s 56(2); National Minimum Wage Act 1998 (Commencement No 1 and Transitional Provisions) Order 1998, SI 1998/2574; National Minimum Wage Act 1998 (Commencement No 2 and Transitional Provisions) Order 1999, SI 1999/685

| | | |
|---|---|---|
| 1 | (1), (2) | 1 Apr 1999 (SI 1998/2574) |
| | (3), (4) | 31 Jul 1998 (so far as confers power to make subordinate legislation) (s 56(2)) |
| | | 1 Apr 1999 (otherwise) (SI 1998/2574) |
| | (5) | 1 Apr 1999 (SI 1998/2574) |
| 2–4 | | 31 Jul 1998 (s 56(2)) |
| 5–8 | | 1 Nov 1998 (SI 1998/2574) |
| 9 | | 31 Jul 1998 (s 56(2)) |
| 10, 11 | | 1 Apr 1999 (SI 1998/2574) |
| 12 | (1), (2) | 31 Jul 1998 (so far as confers power to make subordinate legislation) (s 56(2)) |
| | | 1 Apr 1999 (otherwise) (SI 1998/2574) |
| | (3), (4) | 1 Apr 1999 (SI 1998/2574) |
| 13 | | 1 Nov 1998 (SI 1998/2574) |
| 14–20 | | 1 Apr 1999 (SI 1998/2574) |
| 21 | (1)–(3) | 1 Apr 1999 (SI 1998/2574) |
| | (4) | 31 Jul 1998 (so far as confers power to make subordinate legislation) (s 56(2)) |
| | | 1 Apr 1999 (otherwise) (SI 1998/2574) |
| | (5)–(8) | 1 Apr 1999 (SI 1998/2574) |
| 22 | | 1 Apr 1999 (SI 1998/2574) |
| 23, 24 | | 1 Nov 1998 (SI 1998/2574) |
| 25 | | 1 Nov 1998 (subject to transitional provisions) (SI 1998/2574) |
| 26 | (1)–(4) | 1 Nov 1998 (subject to transitional provisions) (SI 1998/2574) |
| | (5) | *Never in force* (repealed) |
| | (6) | 31 Jul 1998 (so far as confers power to make subordinate legislation) (s 56(2)) |
| 27, 28 | | 1 Apr 1999 (SI 1998/2574) |
| 29 | | 1 Nov 1998 (SI 1998/2574) |
| 30 | | 1 Nov 1998 (so far as it relates to s 24) (SI 1998/2574) |
| | | 1 Apr 1999 (otherwise) (SI 1998/2574) |
| 31–33 | | 1 Apr 1999 (SI 1998/2574) |
| 34–40 | | 1 Nov 1998 (SI 1998/2574) |
| 41, 42 | | 31 Jul 1998 (s 56(2)) |
| 43, 44, 45 | | 1 Nov 1998 (SI 1998/2574) |
| 46 | | 1 Apr 1999 (SI 1999/685) |
| 47 | (1) | 1 Apr 1999 (SI 1999/685) |
| | (2) | 31 Jul 1998 (so far as confers power to make subordinate legislation) (s 56(2)) |
| | | 1 Apr 1999 (otherwise) (SI 1999/685) |
| | (3) | 1 Apr 1999 (SI 1999/685) |
| | (4) | 31 Jul 1998 (so far as confers power to make subordinate legislation) (s 56(2)) |
| | | 1 Apr 1999 (otherwise) (SI 1999/685) |
| | (5), (6) | 1 Apr 1999 (SI 1999/685) |
| 48 | | 1 Nov 1998 (SI 1998/2574) |

**National Minimum Wage Act 1998 (c 39)**—*contd*

| | | |
|---|---|---|
| 49 | (1)–(8) | 1 Nov 1998 (SI 1998/2574) |
| | (9), (10) | *Not yet in force* |
| | (11) | 31 Jul 1998 (so far as confers power to make subordinate legislation) (s 56(2)) |
| | | 1 Nov 1998 (otherwise) (SI 1998/2574) |
| 50 | | 1 Nov 1998 (SI 1998/2574) |
| 51 | | *Not yet in force* |
| 52 | | 1 Nov 1998 (SI 1998/2574) |
| 53 | | See Sch 3 below |
| 54, 55 | | 1 Nov 1998 (SI 1998/2574) |
| 56 | | 31 Jul 1998 (s 56(2)) |
| Sch 1 | | 1 Nov 1998 (SI 1998/2574) |
| Sch 2 | paras 1, 2 | 1 Apr 1999 (subject to transitional provisions) (SI 1999/685) |
| | para 3 | 1 Apr 1999 (except the words "(f) any reference to a pay reference period shall be disregarded") (subject to transitional provisions) (SI 1999/685) |
| | | *Not yet in force* (exception noted above) (repealed in part) |
| | paras 4–12 | 1 Apr 1999 (subject to transitional provisions) (SI 1999/685) |
| | para 13 | 1 Apr 1999 (except the words "(f) any reference to a pay reference period shall be disregarded") (subject to transitional provisions) (SI 1999/685) |
| | | *Not yet in force* (exception noted above) (repealed in part) |
| | paras 14–25 | 1 Apr 1999 (subject to transitional provisions) (SI 1999/685) |
| | para 26 | 1 Apr 1999 (except the words "(f) any reference to a pay reference period shall be disregarded") (subject to transitional provisions) (SI 1999/685) |
| | | *Not yet in force* (exception noted above) |
| | para 27 | 1 Apr 1999 (subject to transitional provisions) (SI 1999/685) |
| Sch 3 | | 1 Nov 1998 (SI 1998/2574), repeals in— |
| | | Employment Rights Act 1996; |
| | | Employment Tribunals Act 1996 |
| | | 1 Apr 1999 (subject to transitional provisions) (SI 1999/685), repeals in— |
| | | Agricultural Wages Act 1948; |
| | | Agricultural Wages (Scotland) Act 1949 |
| | | *Not yet in force* (repeal in Employment Rights (Northern Ireland) Order 1996, SI 1996/1919) |

## Northern Ireland Act 1998 (c 47)

*RA:* 19 Nov 1998

*Commencement provisions:* s 101(2), (3); Northern Ireland Act 1998 (Commencement No 1) Order 1999, SI 1999/340; Northern Ireland Act 1998 (Commencement No 2) Order 1999, SI 1999/1753; Northern Ireland Act 1998 (Commencement No 3) Order 1999, SI 1999/2204; Northern Ireland Act 1998 (Commencement No 4) Order 1999, SI 1999/2936; Northern Ireland Act 1998 (Appointed Day) Order 1999, SI 1999/3208; Northern Ireland Act 1998 (Commencement No 5) Order 1999, SI 1999/3209

| | | |
|---|---|---|
| 1, 2 | | 2 Dec 1999 (SI 1999/3209) |
| 3 | | 19 Nov 1998 (s 101(2)) |
| 4–39 | | 2 Dec 1999 (SI 1999/3209) |
| 40 | (1)–(9) | 2 Dec 1999 (SI 1999/3209) |
| | (10) | See Sch 5 below |
| 41–48 | | 2 Dec 1999 (SI 1999/3209) |
| 49 | (1) | 1 Mar 1999 (SI 1999/340) |
| | (2)–(4) | 2 Dec 1999 (SI 1999/3209) |
| 50–54 | | 2 Dec 1999 (SI 1999/3209) |
| 55 | | 19 Nov 1998 (s 101(2)) |
| 56–67 | | 2 Dec 1999 (SI 1999/3209) |

**Northern Ireland Act 1998 (c 47)**—*contd*

| | | |
|---|---|---|
| 68 | (1)–(3) | 15 Feb 1999 (for the purpose of making appointments to the Northern Ireland Human Rights Commission) (SI 1999/340)<br>1 Mar 1999 (otherwise) (SI 1999/340) |
| | (4) | See Sch 7 below |
| 69 | (1), (2) | 1 Mar 1999 (SI 1999/340) |
| | (3) | 1 Mar 1999 (so far as provides for the Commission to advise the Secretary of State) (SI 1999/340)<br>2 Dec 1999 (otherwise) (SI 1999/3209) |
| | (4) | 2 Dec 1999 (SI 1999/3209) |
| | (5) | 1 Jun 1999 (SI 1999/340) |
| | (6)–(11) | 1 Mar 1999 (SI 1999/340) |
| 70 | | 1 Jun 1999 (SI 1999/340) |
| 71 | (1) | 1 Jun 1999 (to the extent that it makes provision about s 69(5) of this Act) (SI 1999/340)<br>2 Dec 1999 (otherwise) (SI 1999/3209) |
| | (2) | 1 Jun 1999 (SI 1999/340) |
| | (3), (4) | 2 Dec 1999 (SI 1999/3209) |
| | (5) | 1 Jun 1999 (SI 1999/340) |
| 72 | | 1 Mar 1999 (SI 1999/340) |
| 73 | (1) | 15 Feb 1999 (for the purpose of making appointments to the Equality Commission for Northern Ireland and appointing the Chief Commissioner and the Deputy Chief Commissioner) (SI 1999/340)<br>2 Aug 1999 (except for the purposes of Employment and Treatment (Northern Ireland) Order 1998, SI 1998/3162, Sch 4, para 6) (SI 1999/2204)<br>1 Oct 1999 (exception noted above) (SI 1999/2204) |
| | (2)–(4) | 2 Aug 1999 (SI 1999/2204) |
| | (5) | See Sch 8 below |
| 74 | (1)–(4) | 1 Oct 1999 (SI 1999/2204) |
| | (5), (6) | 21 Jun 1999 (for the purpose of making orders) (SI 1999/1753)<br>1 Oct 1999 (otherwise) (SI 1999/2204) |
| 75 | (1), (2) | 1 Jan 2000 (SI 1999/2204) |
| | (3)(a) | 1 Mar 1999 (for the purpose of making designations under s 75(3)(a), (d)) (SI 1999/340)<br>1 Jan 2000 (otherwise) (SI 1999/2204) |
| | (3)(b), (c) | 1 Jan 2000 (SI 1999/2204) |
| | (3)(d) | 1 Mar 1999 (for the purpose of making designations under s 75(3)(a), (d)) (SI 1999/340)<br>1 Jan 2000 (otherwise) (SI 1999/2204) |
| | (4) | See Sch 9 below |
| | (5) | 1 Jan 2000 (SI 1999/2204) |
| 76–78 | | 2 Dec 1999 (SI 1999/3209) |
| 79 | | See Sch 10 below |
| 80, 81 | | 2 Dec 1999 (SI 1999/3209) |
| 82 | (1), (2) | 2 Dec 1999 (SI 1999/3209) |
| | (3)–(5) | 1 Mar 1999 (SI 1999/340) |
| 83–85 | | 2 Dec 1999 (SI 1999/3209) |
| 86 | | 19 Nov 1998 (s 101(2)) |
| 87–89 | | 2 Dec 1999 (SI 1999/3209) |
| 90 | | 2 Aug 1999 (SI 1999/2204) |
| 91 | (1) | See Sch 11 below |
| | (2)–(6) | 1 Mar 1999 (SI 1999/340) |
| | (7)–(9) | 2 Aug 1999 (SI 1999/2204) |
| 92 | (1), (2) | 2 Aug 1999 (SI 1999/2204) |
| | (3), (4) | 1 Mar 1999 (SI 1999/340) |
| 93 | | 19 Nov 1998 (s 101(2)) |
| 94 | | 2 Dec 1999 (SI 1999/3209) |
| 95 | (1)–(4) | 2 Dec 1999 (SI 1999/3209) |

**Northern Ireland Act 1998 (c 47)**—*contd*

| | | |
|---|---|---|
| | (5) | See Sch 12 below |
| 96 | | 19 Nov 1998 (s 101(2)) |
| 97 | | 1 Mar 1999 (SI 1999/340) |
| 98 | | 19 Nov 1998 (s 101(2)) |
| 99 | | See Sch 13 below |
| 100 | (1) | See Sch 14 below |
| | (2) | See Sch 15 below |
| 101 | | 19 Nov 1998 (s 101(2)) |
| Schs 1–4 | | 2 Dec 1999 (SI 1999/3209) |
| Sch 5 | paras 1–5 | 2 Dec 1999 (SI 1999/3209) |
| | para 6 | 28 Oct 1999 (SI 1999/2936) |
| Sch 6 | | 2 Dec 1999 (SI 1999/3209) |
| Sch 7 | paras 1, 2 | 15 Feb 1999 (for the purpose of making appointments to the Northern Ireland Human Rights Commission) (SI 1999/340) |
| | | 1 Mar 1999 (otherwise) (SI 1999/340) |
| | paras 3–11 | 1 Mar 1999 (SI 1999/340) |
| Sch 8 | paras 1, 2 | 15 Feb 1999 (for the purpose of making appointments to the Equality Commission for Northern Ireland and appointing the Chief Commissioner and Deputy Chief Commissioner) (SI 1999/340) |
| | | 2 Aug 1999 (otherwise) (SI 1999/2204) |
| | paras 3–12 | 2 Aug 1999 (SI 1999/2204) |
| Sch 9 | para 1(a) | 1 Jan 2000 (SI 1999/2204) |
| | para 1(b) | 1 Oct 1999 (except for the purposes of para 2 of this Schedule) (SI 1999/2204) |
| | | 1 Jan 2000 (exception noted above) (SI 1999/2204) |
| | para 1(c) | 1 Jan 2000 (SI 1999/2204) |
| | paras 2–12 | 1 Jan 2000 (SI 1999/2204) |
| Sch 10 | paras 1–37 | 2 Dec 1999 (SI 1999/3209) |
| | para 38 | 1 Mar 1999 (SI 1999/340) |
| | paras 39–41 | 2 Dec 1999 (SI 1999/3209) |
| Sch 11 | paras 1–3 | 15 Feb 1999 (for the purpose of making appointments and nominations in connection with the Tribunal established under s 91 of this Act) (SI 1999/340) |
| | | 2 Aug 1999 (otherwise) (SI 1999/2204) |
| | paras 4–7 | 2 Aug 1999 (SI 1999/2204) |
| | para 8 | 15 Feb 1999 (for the purpose of making appointments and nominations in connection with the Tribunal established under s 91 of this Act) (SI 1999/340) |
| | | 2 Aug 1999 (otherwise) (SI 1999/2204) |
| | paras 9–11 | 2 Aug 1999 (SI 1999/2204) |
| Sch 12 | para 1 | 1 Oct 1999 (SI 1999/2204) |
| | paras 2–12 | 2 Dec 1999 (SI 1999/3209) |
| | para 13 | 1 Oct 1999 (SI 1999/2204) |
| Sch 13 | para 1 | *Never in force* (repealed) |
| | para 2 | 1 Oct 1999 (SI 1999/2204) |
| | paras 3–9 | 2 Dec 1999 (SI 1999/3209) |
| | para 10 | *Never in force* (repealed) |
| | paras 11–15 | 2 Dec 1999 (SI 1999/3209) |
| | para 16 | 1 Oct 1999 (SI 1999/2204) |
| | paras 17, 18 | 2 Dec 1999 (SI 1999/3209) |
| | para 19 | 1 Oct 1999 (SI 1999/2204) |
| | para 20 | 19 Nov 1998 (s 101(2)) |
| | para 21 | 2 Dec 1999 (SI 1999/3209) |
| Sch 14 | para 1 | 1 Jun 1999 (so far as refers to s 71 of this Act) (SI 1999/340) |
| | | 2 Dec 1999 (otherwise) (SI 1999/3209) |
| | paras 2–17 | 2 Dec 1999 (SI 1999/3209) |
| | para 18 | 2 Aug 1999 (SI 1999/2204) |
| | paras 19–23 | 2 Dec 1999 (SI 1999/3209) |

**Northern Ireland Act 1998 (c 47)**—*contd*

| | |
|---|---|
| Sch 15 | 19 Nov 1998 (repeal of Northern Ireland Constitution Act 1973, s 31(4)–(6)) (s 101(2)) |
| | 1 Mar 1999 (repeal of Northern Ireland Constitution Act 1973, s 20) (SI 1999/340) |
| | 1 Oct 1999 (SI 1999/2204), repeals of or in— |
| | House of Commons Disqualification Act 1975; |
| | Northern Ireland Assembly Disqualification Act 1975, Sch 1; |
| | Sex Discrimination (Northern Ireland) Order 1976; |
| | Commissioner for Complaints (Northern Ireland) Order 1996, Sch 2; |
| | Race Relations (Northern Ireland) Order 1997 |
| | 2 Dec 1999 (SI 1999/3209), so far as not already in force, except repeals of or in— |
| | Fair Employment (Northern Ireland) Act 1976; |
| | Fair Employment (Northern Ireland) Act 1989; |
| | Northern Ireland (Emergency Provisions) Act 1996; |
| | Northern Ireland Act 1998 |
| | *Not yet in force* (exceptions noted above) |

**Northern Ireland (Elections) Act 1998 (c 12)**

*RA:* 7 May 1998

*Commencement provisions:* s 8; Northern Ireland (Elections) Act 1998 (Commencement) Order 1998, SI 1998/1313

| | | |
|---|---|---|
| 1 | | 28 May 1998 (SI 1998/1313) |
| 2 | (1)–(4) | 28 May 1998 (SI 1998/1313) |
| | (5), (6) | 7 May 1998 (s 8(1)) |
| 3 | | 7 May 1998 (s 8(1)) |
| 4, 5 | | 28 May 1998 (SI 1998/1313) |
| 6 | | 7 May 1998 (s 8(1)) |
| 7 | | 28 May 1998 (SI 1998/1313) |
| 8 | | 7 May 1998 (s 8(1)) |
| 9 | | 28 May 1998 (SI 1998/1313) |
| Schedule | | 28 May 1998 (SI 1998/1313) |

**Northern Ireland (Emergency Provisions) Act 1998 (c 9)**

*RA:* 8 Apr 1998

Whole Act in force 8 Apr 1998 (RA)

**Northern Ireland (Sentences) Act 1998 (c 35)**

*RA:* 28 Jul 1998

*Commencement provisions:* s 22; Northern Ireland (Sentences) Act 1998 (Commencement) Order 1998, SI 1998/1858

Whole Act in force 28 Jul 1998 (SI 1998/1858)

**Nuclear Explosions (Prohibition and Inspections) Act 1998 (c 7)**

*RA:* 18 Mar 1998

*Commencement provisions:* s 15(1)

**Nuclear Explosions (Prohibition and Inspections) Act 1998 (c 7)**—*contd*
*Not yet in force*

**Pesticides Act 1998 (c 26)**

*RA:* 9 Jul 1998

*Commencement provisions:* s 3(b)

Whole Act in force 9 Sep 1998 (s 3(b))

**Petroleum Act 1998 (c 17)**

*RA:* 11 Jun 1998

*Commencement provisions:* s 52; Petroleum Act 1998 (Commencement No 1) Order 1999, SI 1999/161

| | | |
|---|---|---|
| 1–4 | | 15 Feb 1999 (SI 1999/161) |
| 5 | (1)–(4) | 11 Jun 1998 (s 52(1)) |
| | (5)–(10) | 15 Feb 1999 (SI 1999/161) |
| | (11) | 11 Jun 1998 (s 52(1)) |
| 6–49 | | 15 Feb 1999 (SI 1999/161) |
| 50 | | See Sch 4 below |
| 51 | | See Sch 5 below |
| 52 | | 11 Jun 1998 (s 52(1)) |
| 53 | | 15 Feb 1999 (SI 1999/161) |
| Sch 1 | | 11 Jun 1998 (so far as relates to s 5(1)–(4), (11)) (s 52(1)) |
| | | 15 Feb 1999 (otherwise) (SI 1999/161) |
| Schs 2, 3 | | 15 Feb 1999 (SI 1999/161) |
| Sch 4 | paras 1–7 | 15 Feb 1999 (SI 1999/161) |
| | para 8 | *Not yet in force* |
| | para 9 | 15 Feb 1999 (SI 1999/161) |
| | para 10 | *Never in force* (repealed) |
| | para 11 | *Not yet in force* |
| | para 12 | 15 Feb 1999 (SI 1999/161) |
| | para 13 | *Not yet in force* |
| | paras 14–33 | 15 Feb 1999 (SI 1999/161) |
| | para 34 | *Not yet in force* |
| | paras 35–39 | 15 Feb 1999 (SI 1999/161) |
| | para 40 | *Not yet in force* |
| | para 41 | 15 Feb 1999 (SI 1999/161) |
| Sch 5 | | 15 Feb 1999 (SI 1999/161), except repeals of— |
| | | Employment (Continental Shelf) Act 1978; |
| | | Trade Union and Labour Relations (Consolidation) Act 1992, |
| | | s 287(5); |
| | | Employment Rights Act 1996, s 201(5) |
| | | *Not yet in force* (exceptions noted above) |

**Police (Northern Ireland) Act 1998 (c 32)**

*RA:* 24 Jul 1998

*Commencement provisions:* s 75; Police (1998 Act) (Commencement No 1) Order (Northern Ireland) 1998, SR 1998/346; Police (1998 Act) (Commencement No 2) Order (Northern Ireland) 1999, SR 1999/48; Police (1998 Act) (Commencement No 3) Order (Northern Ireland) 1999, SR 1999/176; Police (Northern Ireland) Act 1998 (Commencement) Order (Northern Ireland) 2000, SR 2000/399[2]; Police (Northern Ireland) Act 1998 (Commencement No 5) Order (Northern Ireland) 2003, SR 2003/142

| | | |
|---|---|---|
| 1 | (1) | 1 Apr 1999 (subject to transitional provisions and savings) (SR 1999/176) |

**Police (Northern Ireland) Act 1998 (c 32)**—*contd*

| | | |
|---|---|---|
| | (2) | 9 Feb 1999 (subject to transitional provisions and savings) (SR 1999/48) |
| | (3) | 1 Apr 1999 (subject to transitional provisions and savings) (SR 1999/176) |
| 2 | (1)–(3) | 1 Apr 1999 (subject to transitional provisions and savings) (SR 1999/176) |
| | (4)(a) | *Never in force* (repealed) |
| | (4)(b) | 1 Apr 1999 (subject to transitional provisions and savings) (SR 1999/176) |
| | (5)(a)–(c) | 8 Oct 1998 (SR 1998/346) |
| | (5)(d), (e) | 9 Feb 1999 (subject to transitional provisions and savings) (SR 1999/48) |
| 3–6 | | 1 Apr 1999 (subject to transitional provisions and savings) (SR 1999/176) |
| 7 | | 8 Oct 1998 (SR 1998/346) |
| 8 | | 9 Feb 1999 (subject to transitional provisions and savings) (SR 1999/48) |
| 9–13 | | 1 Apr 1999 (subject to transitional provisions and savings) (SR 1999/176) |
| 14 | | 8 Oct 1998 (SR 1998/346) |
| 15 | | 8 Oct 1998 (subject to transitional provisions) (SR 1998/346) |
| 16 | | 8 Oct 1998 (SR 1998/346) |
| 17 | | 8 Oct 1998 (subject to transitional provisions) (SR 1998/346) |
| 18 | | 9 Feb 1999 (subject to transitional provisions and savings) (SR 1999/48) |
| 19 | (1) | 1 Apr 1999 (subject to transitional provisions and savings) (SR 1999/176) |
| | (2)(a) | 8 Oct 1998 (SR 1998/346) |
| | (2)(b) | 9 Feb 1999 (subject to transitional provisions and savings) (SR 1999/48) |
| 20–23 | | 1 Apr 1999 (subject to transitional provisions and savings) (SR 1999/176) |
| 24 | | 8 Oct 1998 (SR 1998/346) |
| 25 | (1)–(3) | 9 Feb 1999 (subject to transitional provisions and savings) (SR 1999/48) |
| | (4) | *Not yet in force* |
| | (5)–(8) | 9 Feb 1999 (subject to transitional provisions and savings) (SR 1999/48) |
| 26 | (1)–(3) | 9 Feb 1999 (subject to transitional provisions and savings) (SR 1999/48) |
| | (4) | 1 Apr 1999 (subject to transitional provisions and savings) (SR 1999/176) |
| | (5), (6) | 9 Feb 1999 (subject to transitional provisions and savings) (SR 1999/48) |
| 27, 28 | | 9 Feb 1999 (subject to transitional provisions and savings) (SR 1999/48) |
| 29 | | 1 Apr 1999 (subject to transitional provisions and savings) (SR 1999/176) |
| 30 | | 9 Feb 1999 (subject to transitional provisions and savings) (SR 1999/48) |
| 31 | | 1 Apr 1999 (subject to transitional provisions and savings) (SR 1999/176) |
| 32–35 | | 9 Feb 1999 (subject to transitional provisions and savings) (SR 1999/48) |
| 36 | | 1 Apr 1999 (subject to transitional provisions and savings) (SR 1999/176) |
| 37–39 | | 9 Feb 1999 (subject to transitional provisions and savings) (SR 1999/48) |
| 40 | (1), (2) | 1 Apr 1999 (subject to transitional provisions and savings) (SR 1999/176) |

**Police (Northern Ireland) Act 1998 (c 32)**—*contd*

| | | |
|---|---|---|
| | (3), (4) | *Never in force* (repealed) |
| 41–46 | | 1 Apr 1999 (subject to transitional provisions and savings) (SR 1999/176) |
| 47 | (1) | 8 Oct 1998 (subject to transitional provisions) (SR 1998/346) |
| | (2)–(6) | 8 Oct 1998 (SR 1998/346) |
| 48, 49 | | 8 Oct 1998 (SR 1998/346) |
| 50 | | 6 Nov 2000 (SR 2000/399)[2] |
| 51 | (1), (2) | 6 Nov 2000 (SR 2000/399)[2] |
| | (3) | See Sch 3 below |
| | (4), (5) | 6 Nov 2000 (SR 2000/399)[2] |
| 52–65 | | 6 Nov 2000 (SR 2000/399)[2] |
| 66–69 | | 9 Feb 1999 (subject to transitional provisions and savings) (SR 1999/48) |
| 70–73 | | 1 Apr 1999 (subject to transitional provisions and savings) (SR 1999/176) |
| 74 | (1) | See Sch 4 below |
| | (2) | See Sch 5 below |
| | (3) | See Sch 6 below |
| | (4) | 1 Apr 1999 (subject to transitional provisions and savings) (SR 1999/176) |
| 75 | | 8 Oct 1998 (SR 1998/346) |
| 76 | (1) | 8 Oct 1998 (SR 1998/346) |
| | (2) | 21 Feb 2003 (SR 2003/142) |
| | (3) | 1 Apr 1999 (subject to transitional provisions and savings) (SR 1999/176) |
| 77 | | 8 Oct 1998 (SR 1998/346) |
| Sch 1 | | 1 Apr 1999 (subject to transitional provisions and savings) (SR 1999/176) |
| Sch 2 | | 8 Oct 1998 (SR 1998/346) |
| Sch 3 | | 6 Nov 2000 (SR 2000/399)[2] |
| Sch 4 | para 1 | 1 Apr 1999 (subject to transitional provisions and savings) (SR 1999/176) |
| | para 2 | 9 Feb 1999 (subject to transitional provisions and savings) (SR 1999/48) |
| | para 3 | 1 Apr 1999 (subject to transitional provisions and savings) (SR 1999/176) |
| | para 4 | 21 Feb 2003 (SR 2003/142) |
| | paras 5–7 | 9 Feb 1999 (subject to transitional provisions and savings) (SR 1999/48) |
| | paras 8, 9 | 21 Feb 2003 (SR 2003/142) |
| | paras 10, 11 | 1 Apr 1999 (subject to transitional provisions and savings) (SR 1999/176) |
| | para 12(1) | 1 Apr 1999 (subject to transitional provisions and savings) (SR 1999/176) |
| | para 12(2) | 9 Feb 1999 (subject to transitional provisions and savings) (SR 1999/48) |
| | para 12(3), (4) | 1 Apr 1999 (subject to transitional provisions and savings) (SR 1999/176) |
| | paras 13, 14 | 1 Apr 1999 (subject to transitional provisions and savings) (SR 1999/176) |
| | paras 15, 16 | 9 Feb 1999 (subject to transitional provisions and savings) (SR 1999/48) |
| | para 17 | 1 Apr 1999 (subject to transitional provisions and savings) (SR 1999/176) |
| | para 18(1) | 1 Apr 1999 (subject to transitional provisions and savings) (SR 1999/176) |
| | para 18(2)–(4) | 8 Oct 1998 (SR 1998/346) |
| | para 18(5) | 9 Feb 1999 (subject to transitional provisions and savings) (SR 1999/48) |

**Police (Northern Ireland) Act 1998 (c 32)**—*contd*

| | | |
|---|---|---|
| | para 18(6) | 1 Apr 1999 (subject to transitional provisions and savings) (SR 1999/176) |
| | para 19 | 1 Apr 1999 (subject to transitional provisions and savings) (SR 1999/176) |
| | para 20(1), (2) | 1 Apr 1999 (subject to transitional provisions and savings) (SR 1999/176) |
| | para 20(3)–(5) | 21 Feb 2003 (SR 2003/142) |
| | para 20(6) | 1 Apr 1999 (subject to transitional provisions and savings) (SR 1999/176) |
| | para 21 | 21 Feb 2003 (SR 2003/142) |
| | para 22(1) | 1 Apr 1999 (subject to transitional provisions and savings) (SR 1999/176)[1] |
| | para 22(2)–(5) | 9 Feb 1999 (subject to transitional provisions and savings) (SR 1999/48)[1] |
| | para 22(6), (7) | 1 Apr 1999 (subject to transitional provisions and savings) (SR 1999/176) |
| | para 22(8) | 21 Feb 2003 (SR 2003/142) |
| | para 22(9) | 9 Feb 1999 (subject to transitional provisions and savings) (SR 1999/48)[1] |
| | paras 23–25 | 1 Apr 1999 (subject to transitional provisions and savings) (SR 1999/176) |
| Sch 5 | para 1 | 9 Feb 1999 (subject to transitional provisions and savings) (SR 1999/48) |
| | para 2 | 1 Apr 1999 (subject to transitional provisions and savings) (SR 1999/176) |
| | para 3 | 9 Feb 1999 (subject to transitional provisions and savings) (SR 1999/48) |
| | paras 4–11 | 21 Feb 2003 (SR 2003/142) |
| Sch 6 | | 8 Oct 1998 (SR 1998/346), repeals of— Constabulary (Ireland) Act 1836, ss 5, 17; Constabulary Act (Northern Ireland) 1922, s 7(1)(c), Sch 2; Police Act (Northern Ireland) 1970, s 15 (subject to transitional provisions); Police and Criminal Evidence (Northern Ireland) Order 1989, art 82 |
| | | 9 Feb 1999 (subject to transitional provisions and savings) (SR 1999/48), repeals of— Constabulary (Ireland) Act 1836; Constabulary and Police (Ireland) Act 1919; Game Preservation Act (Northern Ireland) 1928, in s 1, the words "notwithstanding anything in Section 15 of the Constabulary (Ireland) Act 1836, as it applies to the said Constabulary"; Police (Overseas Service) Act 1945, s 3(4); Criminal Justice Act (Northern Ireland) 1953, s 20(2); Fisheries Act (Northern Ireland) 1966, in s 167(1), the words "notwithstanding" to the end, and in s 167(2), the words "as provided" to "any case"; Criminal Justice (Miscellaneous Provisions) Act (Northern Ireland) 1968, s 7(1)(a); Police Act (Northern Ireland) 1970, ss 17, 21, 25, 26, 28, 34; Police (Amendment) (Northern Ireland) Order 1995, in Pt III, Sch 1, the amendments to Police Act (Northern Ireland) 1970 |
| | | 1 Apr 1999 (subject to transitional provisions and savings) (SR 1999/176), except repeals in— Superannuation Act (Northern Ireland) 1972; Superannuation (Northern Ireland) Order 1972; House of Commons Disqualification Act 1975; Northern Ireland Assembly Disqualification Act 1975; Police (Northern Ireland) Order 1987; |

### Police (Northern Ireland) Act 1998 (c 32)—*contd*

Police (Amendment) (Northern Ireland) Order 1995, in
Art 2(2), the definition "the 1987 Order" and Pt IV
*Not yet in force* (exceptions noted above)

1. It is assumed that the reference in SR 1999/48, art 3, with regards to Sch 4, para 20 to the Police (Northern Ireland) Act 1998 is a reference to Sch 4, para 22

2. For transitional provisions, see SR 2000/399, arts 4, 5

### Private Hire Vehicles (London) Act 1998 (c 34)

*RA:* 28 Jul 1998

*Commencement provisions:* s 40(2), Private Hire Vehicles (London) Act 1998 (Commencement No 1) Order 2000, SI 2000/3144; Private Hire Vehicles (London) Act 1998 (Commencement No 2) Order 2003, SI 2003/580; Private Hire Vehicles (London) Act 1998 (Commencement No 3) Order 2004, SI 2004/241

| | | |
|---|---|---|
| 1 | | 22 Jan 2001 (SI 2000/3144) |
| 2 | | 22 Oct 2001 (SI 2000/3144) |
| 3 | | 22 Jan 2001 (SI 2000/3144) |
| 4 | (1) | 22 Jan 2001 (SI 2000/3144) |
| | (2) | 8 Jun 2004 (SI 2004/241) |
| | (3), (4) | 22 Jan 2001 (SI 2000/3144) |
| | (5), (6) | 22 Oct 2001 (SI 2000/3144) |
| 5 | (1)–(4) | 22 Oct 2001 (SI 2000/3144) |
| | (5) | 22 Jan 2001 (SI 2000/3144) |
| 6 | | 8 Jun 2004 (SI 2004/241) |
| 7–11 | | 8 Mar 2004 (for the purposes of existing private hire vehicles as defined by Private Hire Vehicles (London) (Transitional Provisions) Regulations 2004, SI 2004/242, reg 2) (SI 2004/241) |
| | | 8 Apr 2004 (otherwise) (SI 2004/241) |
| 12 | (1)–(6) | 1 Jun 2003 (SI 2003/580) |
| | (7) | 8 Jun 2004 (SI 2004/241) |
| 13 | (1) | 1 Apr 2003 (SI 2003/580) |
| | (2)(a) | 1 Apr 2003 (SI 2003/580) |
| | (2)(b) | 1 Apr 2003 (except so far as relates to the requirement mentioned in s 13(3)) (SI 2003/580) |
| | | 1 Apr 2006 (exception noted above) (in relation to applications for London PHV drivers' licences received by Transport for London on or after that day) (SI 2003/580) |
| | (3) | 1 Apr 2006 (in relation to applications for London PHV drivers' licences received by Transport for London on or after that day) (SI 2003/580) |
| | (4)–(7) | 1 Apr 2003 (SI 2003/580) |
| 14 | (1), (2) | 1 Apr 2003 (SI 2003/580) |
| | (3) | 1 Jun 2003 (SI 2003/580) |
| | (4) | 1 Apr 2003 (SI 2003/580) |
| | (5) | 1 Jun 2003 (SI 2003/580) |
| 15 | (1)–(3) | 22 Jan 2001 (SI 2000/3144) |
| | (4) | 1 Apr 2003 (SI 2003/580) |
| | (5) | 22 Jan 2001 (SI 2000/3144) |
| 16 | (1), (2) | 22 Jan 2001 (SI 2000/3144) |
| | (3) | 8 Jun 2004 (SI 2004/241) |
| | (4) | 1 Apr 2003 (SI 2003/580) |
| 17–20 | | 22 Jan 2001 (SI 2000/3144) |
| 21 | (1) | 22 Jan 2001 (SI 2000/3144) |
| | (2) | 8 Jun 2004 (SI 2004/241) |
| | (3) | 22 Jan 2001 (SI 2000/3144) |

**Private Hire Vehicles (London) Act 1998 (c 34)**—*contd*

| | | |
|---|---|---|
| | (4) | 22 Oct 2001 (SI 2000/3144) |
| 22 | (1) | 22 Jan 2001 (SI 2000/3144) |
| | (2) | 8 Mar 2004 (for the purposes of existing private hire vehicles as defined by the Private Hire Vehicles (London) (Transitional Provisions) Regulations 2004, SI 2004/242, reg 2) (SI 2004/241) |
| | | 8 Apr 2004 (otherwise) (SI 2004/241) |
| | (3) | 1 Apr 2003 (SI 2003/580) |
| | (4) | 22 Jan 2001 (SI 2000/3144) |
| | (5), (6) | 22 Oct 2001 (SI 2000/3144) |
| | (7) | 8 Jun 2004 (SI 2004/241) |
| 23–29 | | 22 Jan 2001 (SI 2000/3144) |
| 30 | | 8 Jun 2004 (SI 2004/241) |
| 31 | | 1 Jun 2003 (SI 2003/580) |
| 32, 33 | | 22 Jan 2001 (SI 2000/3144) |
| 34 | (1), (2) | 22 Jan 2001 (SI 2000/3144) |
| | (3) | 8 Mar 2004 (for the purposes of existing private hire vehicles as defined by the Private Hire Vehicles (London) (Transitional Provisions) Regulations 2004, SI 2004/242, reg 2) (SI 2004/241) |
| | | 8 Apr 2004 (otherwise) (SI 2004/241) |
| 35 | | 8 Mar 2004 (for the purposes of existing private hire vehicles as defined by the Private Hire Vehicles (London) (Transitional Provisions) Regulations 2004, SI 2004/242, reg 2) (SI 2004/241) |
| | | 8 Apr 2004 (otherwise) (SI 2004/241) |
| 36–38 | | 22 Jan 2001 (SI 2000/3144) |
| 39 | | See Schs 1, 2 below |
| 40 | | 28 Jul 1998 (s 40(2)) |
| Sch 1 | | 8 Jun 2004 (SI 2004/241) |
| Sch 2 | | 1 Jun 2003 (SI 2003/580), repeals of or in— London Cab Act 1968, s 4; Broadcasting Act 1990; Transport and Works Act 1992 |
| | | 8 Jun 2004 (otherwise) (SI 2004/241) |

**Public Interest Disclosure Act 1998 (c 23)**

*RA:* 2 Jul 1998

*Commencement provisions:* s 18(3), (4); Public Interest Disclosure Act 1998 (Commencement) Order 1999, SI 1999/1547

| | |
|---|---|
| 1 | 2 Jul 1998 (so far as relates to the power to make an order under Employment Rights Act 1996, s 43F) (s 18(4)) |
| | 2 Jul 1999 (otherwise) (SI 1999/1547) |
| 2–7 | 2 Jul 1999 (SI 1999/1547) |
| 8 | 2 Jul 1998 (so far as relates to the power to make regulations under the Employment Rights Act 1996, s 127B) (s 18(4)) |
| | 2 Jul 1999 (otherwise) (SI 1999/1547) |
| 9–16 | 2 Jul 1999 (SI 1999/1547) |
| 17, 18 | 2 Jul 1998 (s 18(4)) |

**Public Processions (Northern Ireland) Act 1998 (c 2)**

*RA:* 16 Feb 1998

*Commencement provisions:* s 19(2)–(4); Public Processions (Northern Ireland) Act 1998 (Commencement) Order 1998, SI 1998/717

**Public Processions (Northern Ireland) Act 1998 (c 2)**—*contd*

| | | |
|---|---|---|
| 1 | (1) | 16 Feb 1998 (RA) |
| | (2) | See Sch 1 below |
| 2 | | 2 Mar 1998 (SI 1998/717) |
| 3 | (1), (2) | 16 Feb 1998 (RA) |
| | (3) | See Sch 2 below |
| 4 | (1)–(4) | 16 Feb 1998 (RA) |
| | (5) | See Sch 2 below |
| 5 | | 16 Feb 1998 (RA) |
| 6, 7 | | 2 Mar 1998 (SI 1998/717) |
| 8 | (1)–(5) | 2 Mar 1998 (SI 1998/717) |
| | (6) | 16 Feb 1998 (RA) |
| | (7)–(9) | 2 Mar 1998 (SI 1998/717) |
| 9–15 | | 2 Mar 1998 (SI 1998/717) |
| 16, 17 | | 16 Feb 1998 (RA) |
| 18 | (1) | See Sch 3 below |
| | (2) | See Sch 4 below |
| 19 | | 16 Feb 1998 (RA) |
| Schs 1, 2 | | 16 Feb 1998 (RA) |
| Sch 3 | paras 1, 2 | 16 Feb 1998 (RA) |
| | para 3 | 2 Mar 1998 (SI 1998/717) |
| Sch 4 | | 2 Mar 1998 (SI 1998/717) |

**Regional Development Agencies Act 1998 (c 45)**

*RA:* 19 Nov 1998

*Commencement provisions:* s 43; Regional Development Agencies Act 1998 (Commencement No 1) Order 1998, SI 1998/2952; Regional Development Agencies Act 1998 (Commencement No 2) Order 2000, SI 2000/1173

| | | |
|---|---|---|
| 1 | | 25 Nov 1998 (except in so far as it relates to the establishment of a regional development agency for London) (SI 1998/2952) |
| | | 3 Jul 2000 (exception noted above) (SI 2000/1173) |
| 2 | | 25 Nov 1998 (for the purposes of regional development agencies established on 25 Nov 1998) (SI 1998/2952) |
| | | 8 May 2000 (for the purpose only of enabling the Mayor to consult on the appointment of persons to be members of the London Development Agency) (SI 2000/1173) |
| | | 3 Jul 2000 (otherwise) (SI 2000/1173) |
| 3–5 | | 25 Nov 1998 (for the purposes of regional development agencies established on 25 Nov 1998) (SI 1998/2952) |
| | | 3 Jul 2000 (otherwise) (SI 2000/1173) |
| 6 | (1), (2) | 25 Nov 1998 (for the purposes of regional development agencies established on 25 Nov 1998) (SI 1998/2952) |
| | | 8 May 2000 (otherwise) (SI 2000/1173) |
| | (3)–(5) | 25 Nov 1998 (for the purposes of regional development agencies established on 25 Nov 1998) (SI 1998/2952) |
| | | 3 Jul 2000 (otherwise) (SI 2000/1173) |
| | (6) | See Sch 3 below |
| 7–42 | | 25 Nov 1998 (for the purposes of regional development agencies established on 25 Nov 1998) (SI 1998/2952) |
| | | 3 Jul 2000 (otherwise) (SI 2000/1173) |
| 43–45 | | 19 Nov 1998 (s 43) |
| Schs 1, 2 | | 25 Nov 1998 (for the purposes of regional development agencies established on 25 Nov 1998) (SI 1998/2952) |
| | | 3 Jul 2000 (otherwise) (SI 2000/1173) |
| Sch 3 | para 1(1) | 25 Nov 1998 (for the purposes of regional development agencies established on 25 Nov 1998) (SI 1998/2952) |
| | | 8 May 2000 (otherwise) (SI 2000/1173) |

**Regional Development Agencies Act 1998 (c 45)**—*contd*

| | | |
|---|---|---|
| | para 1(2) | 25 Nov 1998 (for the purposes of regional development agencies established on 25 Nov 1998) (SI 1998/2952) |
| | | 3 Jul 2000 (otherwise) (SI 2000/1173) |
| | paras 2–10 | 25 Nov 1998 (for the purposes of regional development agencies established on 25 Nov 1998) (SI 1998/2952) |
| | | 8 May 2000 (otherwise) (SI 2000/1173) |
| | paras 11, 12 | 25 Nov 1998 (for the purposes of regional development agencies established on 25 Nov 1998) (SI 1998/2952) |
| | | 3 Jul 2000 (otherwise) (SI 2000/1173) |
| | para 13 | 25 Nov 1998 (for the purposes of regional development agencies established on 25 Nov 1998) (SI 1998/2952) |
| | | 8 May 2000 (otherwise) (SI 2000/1173) |
| Schs 4–9 | | 25 Nov 1998 (for the purposes of regional development agencies established on 25 Nov 1998) (SI 1998/2952) |
| | | 3 Jul 2000 (otherwise) (SI 2000/1173) |

---

**Registered Establishments (Scotland) Act 1998 (c 25)**

*RA:* 9 Jul 1998

Whole Act in force 9 Jul 1998 (RA)

---

**Registration of Political Parties Act 1998 (c 48)**

*RA:* 19 Nov 1998

*Commencement provisions:* s 25; Registration of Political Parties Act 1998 (Commencement) Order 1999, SI 1999/393

| | | |
|---|---|---|
| 1, 2 | | 3 Dec 1998 (s 25) |
| 3 | (1)(a)–(e) | 3 Dec 1998 (s 25) |
| | (1)(f) | 19 Nov 1998 (so far as conferring power to make subordinate legislation) (s 25) |
| | | 3 Dec 1998 (otherwise) (s 25) |
| | (2) | 3 Dec 1998 (s 25) |
| 4, 5 | | 3 Dec 1998 (s 25) |
| 6 | (1)–(6) | 3 Dec 1998 (s 25) |
| | (7) | 19 Nov 1998 (so far as conferring power to make subordinate legislation) (s 25) |
| | | 3 Dec 1998 (otherwise) (s 25) |
| 7 | (1), (2) | 3 Dec 1998 (s 25) |
| | (3)(a), (b) | 3 Dec 1998 (s 25) |
| | (3)(c) | 19 Nov 1998 (so far as conferring power to make subordinate legislation) (s 25) |
| | | 3 Dec 1998 (otherwise) (s 25) |
| 8–10 | | 3 Dec 1998 (s 25) |
| 11 | | 19 Nov 1998 (so far as conferring power to make subordinate legislation) (s 25) |
| | | 3 Dec 1998 (otherwise) (s 25) |
| 12 | | 3 Dec 1998 (s 25) |
| 13 | | See Sch 2 below |
| 14, 15 | | 24 Mar 1999 (SI 1999/393) |
| 16–19 | | 3 Dec 1998 (s 25) |
| 20–22 | | 19 Nov 1998 (s 25) |
| 23 | | See Sch 3 below |
| 24–26 | | 19 Nov 1998 (s 25) |
| Sch 1 | para 1 | 19 Nov 1998 (so far as conferring power to make subordinate legislation) (s 25) |
| | | 3 Dec 1998 (otherwise) (s 25) |

**Registration of Political Parties Act 1998 (c 48)**—*contd*

| | | |
|---|---|---|
| | paras 2–6 | 3 Dec 1998 (s 25) |
| | para 7 | 19 Nov 1998 (so far as conferring power to make subordinate legislation) (s 25) |
| | | 3 Dec 1998 (otherwise) (s 25) |
| | para 8 | 3 Dec 1998 (s 25) |
| Sch 2 | | 24 Mar 1999 (SI 1999/393) |
| Sch 3 | paras 1, 2 | 3 Dec 1998 (s 25) |
| | para 3 | 24 Mar 1999 (SI 1999/393) |
| | paras 4, 5 | 3 Dec 1998 (s 25) |

**Road Traffic Reduction (National Targets) Act 1998 (c 24)**

*RA:* 2 Jul 1998

Whole Act in force 2 Jul 1998 (RA)

**School Standards and Framework Act 1998 (c 31)**

*RA:* 24 Jul 1998

*Commencement provisions:* s 145(3)–(5); School Standards and Framework Act 1998 (Commencement No 1) Order 1998, SI 1998/2048; School Standards and Framework Act 1998 (Commencement No 2 and Supplemental, Saving and Transitional Provisions) Order 1998, SI 1998/2212, as amended by SI 1998/2459, SI 1999/1016; School Standards and Framework Act 1998 (Commencement No 3 and Saving and Transitional Provisions) Order 1998, SI 1998/2791; School Standards and Framework Act 1998 (Commencement No 4 and Transitional Provisions) Order 1998, SI 1998/3198; School Standards and Framework Act 1998 (Commencement No 5 and Saving and Transitional Provisions) Order 1999, SI 1999/120; School Standards and Framework Act 1998 (Commencement No 6 and Saving and Transitional Provisions) Order 1999, SI 1999/1016[1], as amended by SI 1999/2484; School Standards and Framework Act 1998 (Commencement No 7 and Saving and Transitional Provisions) Order 1999, SI 1999/2323[2], as amended by SI 1999/2484; School Standards and Framework Act 1998 (Commencement No 8 and Supplemental Provisions) Order 2001, SI 2001/1195; School Standards and Framework Act 1998 (Commencement No 9 and Supplemental Provisions) Order 2001, SI 2001/2663

| | | |
|---|---|---|
| 1–4 | | 24 Jul 1998 (s 145(4)) |
| 5–9 | | 1 Oct 1998 (SI 1998/2212) |
| 10–12 | | 8 Aug 1998 (SI 1998/2048) |
| 13 | | 1 Sep 1998 (SI 1998/2048) |
| 14, 15 | | 1 Oct 1998 (SI 1998/2212) |
| 16 | (1)–(5) | 1 Oct 1998 (SI 1998/2212) |
| | (6)–(12) | 1 Sep 1999 (SI 1999/2323) |
| | (13) | 1 Oct 1998 (SI 1998/2212) |
| 17–19 | | 1 Oct 1998 (SI 1998/2212) |
| 20, 21 | | 24 Jul 1998 (s 145(4)) |
| 22, 23 | | 1 Sep 1999 (SI 1999/2323) |
| 24 | (1) | 1 Apr 1999 (SI 1999/1016) |
| | (2)–(5) | 1 Oct 1998 (SI 1998/2212) |
| 25 | | 1 Oct 1998 (SI 1998/2212) |
| 26 | (1) | 1 Apr 1999 (SI 1999/1016) |
| | (2)–(8) | 1 Oct 1998 (SI 1998/2212) |
| 27 | | 1 Sep 1999 (SI 1999/2323) |
| 28 | (1)–(4) | 1 Sep 1999 (SI 1999/2323) |
| | (5) | 1 Apr 1999 (SI 1999/1016) |
| | (6)–(8) | 1 Sep 1999 (SI 1999/2323) |
| | (9) | 1 Feb 1999 (SI 1998/3198) |
| | (10) | 1 Apr 1999 (SI 1999/1016) |
| | (11), (12) | 1 Sep 1999 (SI 1999/2323) |
| 29 | (1)–(3) | 1 Sep 1999 (SI 1999/2323) |
| | (4) | 1 Apr 1999 (SI 1999/1016) |

**School Standards and Framework Act 1998 (c 31)**—*contd*

| | | |
|---|---|---|
| | (5)–(7) | 1 Sep 1999 (SI 1999/2323) |
| | (8) | 1 Feb 1999 (SI 1998/3198) |
| | (9) | 1 Apr 1999 (SI 1999/1016) |
| | (10) | 1 Sep 1999 (SI 1999/2323) |
| 30 | | 1 Sep 1999 (SI 1999/2323) |
| 31 | (1)–(3) | 1 Sep 1999 (SI 1999/2323) |
| | (4) | 1 Apr 1999 (SI 1999/1016) |
| | (5)–(8) | 1 Sep 1999 (SI 1999/2323) |
| | (9) | 1 Apr 1999 (SI 1999/1016) |
| 32 | | 1 Sep 1999 (SI 1999/2323) |
| 33 | (1)–(3) | 1 Sep 1999 (SI 1999/2323) |
| | (4) | 1 Feb 1999 (SI 1998/3198) |
| 34 | | 1 Sep 1999 (SI 1999/2323) |
| 35 | | 1 Apr 1999 (SI 1999/1016) |
| 36 | (1), (2) | 24 Jul 1998 (for purposes of the preparation of instruments of government and the constitution of governing bodies and the exercise (in relation to those or any other matters) of any power to make regulations) (s 145(5)) |
| | | 1 Sep 1999 (otherwise) (SI 1999/2323) |
| | (3) | 24 Jul 1998 (s 145(4)) |
| 37 | (1), (2) | 24 Jul 1998 (for purposes of the preparation of instruments of government and the constitution of governing bodies and the exercise (in relation to those or any other matters) of any power to make regulations) (s 145(5)) |
| | | 1 Sep 1999 (otherwise) (SI 1999/2323) |
| | (3) | 1 Sep 1999 (SI 1999/2323) |
| 38 | (1), (2) | 1 Sep 1999 (SI 1999/2323) |
| | (3) | 1 Oct 1998 (SI 1998/2212) |
| | (4) | 1 Sep 1999 (SI 1999/2323) |
| 39 | (1) | 1 Oct 1998 (as far as relates to the power to make regulations) (SI 1998/2212) |
| | | *Never in force* (otherwise) (repealed) |
| | (2), (3) | 1 Sep 1999 (SI 1999/2323) |
| 40, 41 | | 1 Sep 1999 (SI 1999/2323) |
| 42 | (1), (2) | 1 Apr 1999 (so far as relates to the power to make regulations) (SI 1999/1016) |
| | | 1 Sep 1999 (otherwise) (SI 1999/2323) |
| | (3)–(5) | 1 Sep 1999 (SI 1999/2323) |
| 43 | (1)–(3) | 1 Sep 1999 (SI 1999/2323) |
| | (4) | 1 Apr 1999 (SI 1999/1016) |
| 44 | (1)–(4) | 1 Sep 1999 (SI 1999/2323) |
| | (5), (6) | 1 Oct 1998 (SI 1998/2212) |
| | (7)–(9) | 1 Sep 1999 (SI 1999/2323) |
| 45–48 | | 1 Oct 1998 (subject to supplemental, saving and transitional provisions) (SI 1998/2212) |
| 49 | | 1 Apr 1999 (SI 1998/2212) |
| 50 | (1), (2) | 1 Apr 1999 (SI 1998/2212) |
| | (3), (4) | 1 Oct 1998 (subject to supplemental, saving and transitional provisions) (SI 1998/2212) |
| | (5)–(7) | 1 Apr 1999 (SI 1998/2212) |
| 51 | | 1 Apr 1999 (SI 1998/2212) |
| 52 | | 1 Oct 1998 (subject to supplemental, saving and transitional provisions) (SI 1998/2212) |
| 53 | | 1 Apr 1999 (SI 1998/2212) |
| 54 | | See Sch 16 below |
| 55 | | See Sch 17 below |
| 56 | | 1 Sep 1999 (SI 1999/2323) |
| 57 | | 1 Apr 1999 (SI 1999/1016) |
| 58–61 | | 1 Sep 1999 (SI 1999/2323) |
| 62, 63 | | 1 Oct 1998 (SI 1998/2212) |

**School Standards and Framework Act 1998 (c 31)**—*contd*

| | | |
|---|---|---|
| 64, 65 | | 1 Sep 1999 (SI 1999/2323) |
| 66 | (1)–(7) | 1 Sep 1999 (SI 1999/2323) |
| | (8) | 1 Dec 1998 (SI 1998/2212) |
| 67 | (1) | 1 Sep 1999 (SI 1999/2323) |
| | (2) | See Sch 18 below |
| | (3), (4) | 1 Sep 1999 (SI 1999/2323) |
| 68 | | 1 Sep 1999 (SI 1999/2323) |
| 69 | (1) | 1 Sep 1999 (SI 1999/2323) |
| | (2)–(5) | 1 Oct 1998 (SI 1998/2212) |
| 70 | | 1 Sep 1999 (SI 1999/2323) |
| 71 | (1)–(6) | 1 Sep 1999 (SI 1999/2323) |
| | (7) | 1 Oct 1998 (SI 1998/2212) |
| 72 | | 1 Oct 1998 (SI 1998/2212) |
| 73, 74 | | 1 Apr 1999 (SI 1999/1016) |
| 75, 76 | | 1 Sep 1999 (SI 1999/2323) |
| 77 | (1) | 1 Oct 1998 (SI 1998/2212) |
| | (2)(a) | 1 Oct 1998 (SI 1998/2212) |
| | (2)(b) | 1 Feb 1999 (SI 1998/3198) |
| | (3)–(9) | 1 Oct 1998 (SI 1998/2212) |
| 78–80 | | 1 Sep 1999 (SI 1999/2323) |
| 81 | | 1 Oct 1998 (SI 1998/2212) |
| 82 | | 24 Jul 1998 (s 145(4)) |
| 83 | | 1 Sep 1999 (SI 1999/2323) |
| 84, 85 | | 24 Jul 1998 (s 145(4)) |
| 86, 87 | | 1 Apr 1999 (SI 1999/1016) |
| 88 | | 1 Oct 1998 (SI 1998/2212) |
| 89 | (1) | 6 Jan 1999 (subject to transitional provisions) (SI 1998/3198) |
| | (2)–(8) | 1 Oct 1998 (as far as relate to the power to make regulations) (SI 1998/2212) |
| | | 6 Jan 1999 (subject to transitional provisions) (otherwise) (SI 1998/3198) |
| | (9) | 6 Jan 1999 (subject to transitional provisions) (SI 1998/3198) |
| 90 | (1)–(3) | 1 Oct 1998 (as far as relate to the power to make regulations) (SI 1998/2212) |
| | | 1 Apr 1999 (otherwise) (SI 1999/1016) |
| | (4) | 1 Apr 1999 (SI 1999/1016) |
| | (5) | 1 Oct 1998 (as far as relates to the power to make regulations) (SI 1998/2212) |
| | | 1 Apr 1999 (otherwise) (SI 1999/1016) |
| | (6)–(8) | 1 Apr 1999 (SI 1999/1016) |
| | (9), (10) | 1 Oct 1998 (as far as relate to the power to make regulations) (SI 1998/2212) |
| | | 1 Apr 1999 (otherwise) (SI 1999/1016) |
| 91 | (1) | 1 Apr 1999 (subject to saving and transitional provisions) (SI 1999/1016) |
| | (2)–(4) | 1 Oct 1998 (as far as relate to the power to make regulations) (SI 1998/2212) |
| | | 1 Apr 1999 (subject to saving and transitional provisions) (otherwise) (SI 1999/1016) |
| | (5) | 1 Apr 1999 (subject to saving and transitional provisions) (SI 1999/1016) |
| | (6) | 1 Oct 1998 (as far as relates to the power to make regulations) (SI 1998/2212) |
| | | 1 Apr 1999 (subject to saving and transitional provisions) (otherwise) (SI 1999/1016) |
| | (7), (8) | 1 Apr 1999 (subject to saving and transitional provisions) (SI 1999/1016) |
| | (9) | 1 Oct 1998 (as far as relates to the power to make regulations) (SI 1998/2212) |

**School Standards and Framework Act 1998 (c 31)**—*contd*

| | | |
|---|---|---|
| | | 1 Apr 1999 (subject to saving and transitional provisions) (otherwise) (SI 1999/1016) |
| | (10) | 1 Apr 1999 (subject to saving and transitional provisions) (SI 1999/1016) |
| 92 | | 1 Oct 1998 (as far as relates to the power to make regulations) (SI 1998/2212) |
| | | 1 Apr 1999 (subject to saving and transitional provisions) (otherwise) (SI 1999/1016) |
| 93 | (1), (2) | 1 Apr 1999 (subject to saving and transitional provisions) (SI 1999/1016) |
| | (3) | 1 Oct 1998 (SI 1998/2212) |
| | (4)–(7) | 1 Sep 1999 (subject to saving and transitional provisions) (SI 1999/1016) |
| | (8), (9) | 1 Oct 1998 (SI 1998/2212) |
| | (10) | 1 Apr 1999 (subject to saving and transitional provisions) (SI 1999/1016) |
| 94–97 | | 1 Apr 1999 (subject to savings and transitional provisions) (SI 1999/1016) |
| 98 | (1)–(4) | 1 Apr 1999 (SI 1999/1016) |
| | (5) | 1 Oct 1998 (as far as relates to the power to make regulations) (SI 1998/2212) |
| | | 1 Apr 1999 (otherwise) (SI 1999/1016) |
| | (6), (7) | 1 Apr 1999 (SI 1999/1016) |
| | (8) | 1 Oct 1998 (as far as relates to the power to make regulations) (SI 1998/2212) |
| | | 1 Apr 1999 (otherwise) (SI 1999/1016) |
| | (9) | 1 Oct 1998 (as far as relates to the power to make regulations) (SI 1998/2212) |
| | | 1 Apr 1999 (otherwise) (SI 1999/1016) |
| | (10) | 1 Oct 1998 (as far as relates to the power to make regulations) (SI 1998/2212) |
| | | 1 Apr 1999 (otherwise) (SI 1999/1016) |
| 99 | (1) | 1 Oct 1998 (subject to supplemental, saving and transitional provisions) (SI 1998/2212) |
| | (2) | 1 Oct 1998 (SI 1998/2212) |
| | (3), (4) | 1 Apr 1999 (SI 1999/1016) |
| | (5) | 1 Oct 1998 (SI 1998/2212) |
| 100 | | 1 Oct 1998 (so far as relates to s 99(2)(a)) (SI 1998/2212) |
| | | 1 Apr 1999 (otherwise) (SI 1999/1016) |
| 101 | (1)–(3) | 1 Oct 1998 (SI 1998/2212) |
| | (4) | 1 Oct 1998 (subject to supplemental, saving and transitional provisions) (SI 1998/2212) |
| | (5) | 1 Apr 1999 (SI 1999/1016) |
| 102 | (1) | 1 Oct 1998 (as far as relates to the power to make regulations) (SI 1998/2212) |
| | | 1 Apr 1999 (otherwise) (SI 1999/1016) |
| | (2), (3) | 1 Apr 1999 (SI 1999/1016) |
| | (4) | 1 Oct 1998 (as far as relates to the power to make regulations) (SI 1998/2212) |
| | | 1 Apr 1999 (otherwise) (SI 1999/1016) |
| | (5) | 1 Apr 1999 (SI 1999/1016) |
| 103 | (1), (2) | 1 Apr 1999 (SI 1999/1016) |
| | (3) | 1 Oct 1998 (SI 1998/2212) |
| 104 | (1)–(3) | 1 Sep 1998 (SI 1998/2048) |
| | (4)(a) | 1 Oct 1998 (SI 1998/2212) |
| | (4)(b) | 1 Sep 1999 (SI 1999/2323) |
| | (5)–(7) | 1 Sep 1998 (SI 1998/2048) |
| 105, 106 | | 1 Oct 1998 (SI 1998/2212) |
| 107 | | 1 Dec 1998 (SI 1998/2212) |
| 108 | | 1 Oct 1998 (SI 1998/2212) |

**School Standards and Framework Act 1998 (c 31)**—*contd*

| | | |
|---|---|---|
| 109 | (1), (2) | 1 Sep 1999 (SI 1999/2323) |
| | (3), (4) | 1 Feb 1999 (SI 1998/3198) |
| | (5) | 1 Sep 1999 (SI 1999/2323) |
| 110, 111 | | 1 Feb 1999 (SI 1998/2212) |
| 112 | (1), (2) | 1 Oct 1998 (SI 1998/2212) |
| | (3) | *Not yet in force* |
| 113 | | 1 Oct 1998 (SI 1998/2212) |
| 114 | | 1 Apr 1999 (SI 1999/1016) |
| 115 | (1) | 1 Apr 1999 (SI 1999/1016) |
| | (2), (3) | 1 Apr 2001 (E) (SI 2001/1195) |
| | | 20 Jul 2001 (W) (SI 2001/2663) |
| | (4), (5) | 1 Apr 1999 (SI 1999/1016) |
| 116 | | 1 Feb 1999 (SI 1998/3198) |
| 117 | | 1 Oct 1998 (SI 1998/2212) |
| 118 | | 1 Apr 1999 (SI 1998/2212) |
| 119 | | 1 Oct 1998 (SI 1998/2212) |
| 120, 121 | | 1 Apr 1999 (SI 1999/1016) |
| 122, 123 | | 1 Oct 1998 (SI 1998/2212) |
| 124 | | 1 Apr 1999 (SI 1998/2212) |
| 125 | (1)–(4) | 1 Sep 1999 (SI 1999/2323) |
| | (5) | 1 Apr 1999 (SI 1998/2212) |
| 126 | | 1 Sep 1999 (SI 1999/2323) |
| 127 | | 1 Oct 1998 (SI 1998/2212) |
| 128 | | *Never in force* (repealed) |
| 129 | | 1 Feb 1999 (subject to transitional provisions) (SI 1999/120) |
| 130 | | 24 Jul 1998 (s 145(4)) |
| 131 | | 1 Sep 1999 (SI 1999/2323) |
| 132, 133 | | 1 Apr 1999 (SI 1999/1016) |
| 134 | (1) | 1 Oct 1998 (SI 1998/2212) |
| | (2) | *Never in force* (repealed) |
| | (3) | 1 Oct 1998 (SI 1998/2212) |
| 135 | | See Sch 28 below |
| 136 | | 1 Oct 1998 (SI 1998/2212) |
| 137 | | 1 Feb 1999 (subject to transitional provisions) (SI 1999/120) |
| 138, 139 | | 24 Jul 1998 (s 145(4)) |
| 140 | (1) | See Sch 30 below |
| | (2) | 1 Sep 1999 (SI 1999/2323) |
| | (3) | See Sch 31 below |
| | (4) | 1 Sep 1999 (SI 1999/2323) |
| 141–145 | | 24 Jul 1998 (s 145(4)) |
| Sch 1 | | 8 Aug 1998 (SI 1998/2048) |
| Sch 2 | | 24 Jul 1998 (s 145(4)) |
| Sch 3 | | 1 Sep 1999 (SI 1999/2323) |
| Sch 4 | paras 1, 2 | 1 Oct 1998 (SI 1998/2212) |
| | paras 3, 4 | 1 Sep 1999 (SI 1999/2323) |
| | para 5 | 1 Oct 1998 (SI 1998/2212) |
| | paras 6–10 | 1 Sep 1999 (SI 1999/2323) |
| Sch 5 | | 1 Oct 1998 (SI 1998/2212) |
| Sch 6 | Pt I, paras 1–4 | 1 Sep 1999 (SI 1999/2323) |
| | Pt I, para 5(1)–(3) | 1 Sep 1999 (SI 1999/2323) |
| | Pt I, para 5(4) | 1 Feb 1999 (so far as confers power to provide for ss 28, 29, 31 and Sch 6, Pt I to have effect with modifications) (SI 1998/3198) |
| | | 1 Sep 1999 (otherwise) (SI 1999/2323) |
| | Pt I, para 5(5)–(9) | 1 Sep 1999 (SI 1999/2323) |
| | Pt II, paras 6–9 | 1 Sep 1999 (SI 1999/2323) |
| | Pt II, para 10(1)–(3) | 1 Sep 1999 (SI 1999/2323) |

**School Standards and Framework Act 1998 (c 31)**—*contd*

| | | |
|---|---|---|
| | Pt II, para 10(4) | 1 Feb 1999 (so far as confers power to provide for ss 28, 29, 31 and Sch 6, Pt I to have effect with modifications) (SI 1998/3198) |
| | | 1 Sep 1999 (otherwise) (SI 1999/2323) |
| | Pt II, para 10(5), (6) | 1 Sep 1999 (SI 1999/2323) |
| | Pts III–V | 1 Sep 1999 (SI 1999/2323) |
| Sch 7 | | 1 Sep 1999 (SI 1999/2323) |
| Sch 8 | | 1 Apr 1999 (SI 1999/1016) |
| Schs 9, 10 | | 24 Jul 1998 (for purposes of the preparation of instruments of government and the constitution of governing bodies and the exercise (in relation to those or any other matters) of any power to make regulations) (s 145(5)) |
| | | 1 Sep 1999 (otherwise) (SI 1999/2323) |
| Sch 11 | Pt I | 24 Jul 1998 (s 145(4)) |
| | Pt II, para 6 | 1 Oct 1998 (SI 1998/2212) |
| | Pt II, para 7 | 1 Sep 1999 (SI 1999/2323) |
| | Pt III | 24 Jul 1998 (s 145(4)) |
| Sch 12 | | 24 Jul 1998 (for purposes of the preparation of instruments of government and the constitution of governing bodies and the exercise (in relation to those or any other matters) of any power to make regulations) (s 145(5)) |
| | | 1 Sep 1999 (otherwise) (SI 1999/2323) |
| Sch 13 | | 1 Sep 1999 (SI 1999/2323) |
| Sch 14 | | 1 Oct 1998 (subject to supplemental, saving and transitional provisions) (SI 1998/2212) |
| Sch 15 | | 1 Apr 1999 (subject to supplemental, saving and transitional provisions) (SI 1998/2212) |
| Sch 16 | paras 1–29 | 1 Sep 1999 (SI 1999/2323) |
| | para 30 | 1 Feb 1999 (SI 1999/120) |
| | para 31 | 1 Sep 1999 (SI 1999/2323) |
| Sch 17 | para 1(1) | 1 Feb 1999 (SI 1999/120) |
| | para 1(2), (3) | 1 Sep 1999 (SI 1999/2323) |
| | paras 2–26 | 1 Sep 1999 (SI 1999/2323) |
| | para 27(1), (2) | 1 Sep 1999 (SI 1999/2323) |
| | para 27(3) | 1 Feb 1999 (SI 1999/120) |
| | paras 28–30 | 1 Sep 1999 (SI 1999/2323) |
| Sch 18 | paras 1–3 | 1 Sep 1999 (SI 1999/2323) |
| | para 4 | 1 Apr 1999 (SI 1999/1016) |
| | paras 5–18 | 1 Sep 1999 (SI 1999/2323) |
| Sch 19 | para 1 | 1 Oct 1998 (SI 1998/2212) |
| | para 2(1)–(3) | 1 Sep 1999 (SI 1999/2323) |
| | para 2(4) | 1 Oct 1998 (for the purpose of making orders) (SI 1998/2212) |
| | | 1 Sep 1999 (otherwise) (SI 1999/2323) |
| | para 2(5) | 1 Sep 1999 (SI 1999/2323) |
| | para 3(1)–(3) | 1 Sep 1999 (SI 1999/2323) |
| | para 3(4) | 1 Oct 1998 (for the purpose of making orders) (SI 1998/2212) |
| | | 1 Sep 1999 (otherwise) (SI 1999/2323) |
| | para 4 | 1 Sep 1999 (SI 1999/2323) |
| Schs 20–22 | | 1 Sep 1999 (SI 1999/2323) |
| Sch 23 | paras 1–4 | 1 Sep 1999 (SI 1999/1016) |
| | para 5(1) | 1 Oct 1998 (as far as relates to the power to make regulations) (SI 1998/2212) |
| | | 1 Sep 1999 (otherwise) (SI 1999/1016) |
| | para 5(2)–(4) | 1 Sep 1999 (SI 1999/1016) |
| | para 5(5), (6) | 1 Oct 1998 (as far as relate to the power to make regulations) (SI 1998/2212) |
| | | 1 Sep 1999 (otherwise) (SI 1999/1016) |
| | para 6(1)–(6) | 1 Sep 1999 (SI 1999/1016) |

**School Standards and Framework Act 1998 (c 31)**—*contd*

| | | |
|---|---|---|
| | para 6(7) | 1 Oct 1998 (as far as relates to the power to make regulations) (SI 1998/2212) |
| | | 1 Sep 1999 (otherwise) (SI 1999/1016) |
| | para 6(8), (9) | 1 Sep 1999 (SI 1999/1016) |
| | para 6(10) | 1 Oct 1998 (as far as relates to the power to make regulations) (SI 1998/2212) |
| | | 1 Sep 1999 (otherwise) (SI 1999/1016) |
| | para 6(11) | 1 Sep 1999 (SI 1999/1016) |
| | paras 7, 8 | 1 Sep 1999 (SI 1999/1016) |
| | para 9(1) | 1 Oct 1998 (as far as relates to the power to make regulations) (SI 1998/2212) |
| | | 1 Sep 1999 (otherwise) (SI 1999/1016) |
| | para 9(2)–(5) | 1 Sep 1999 (SI 1999/1016) |
| | para 9(6), (7) | 1 Oct 1998 (as far as relate to the power to make regulations) (SI 1998/2212) |
| | | 1 Sep 1999 (otherwise) (SI 1999/1016) |
| | para 10(1)–(6) | 1 Sep 1999 (SI 1999/1016) |
| | para 10(7) | 1 Oct 1998 (as far as relates to the power to make regulations) (SI 1998/2212) |
| | | 1 Sep 1999 (otherwise) (SI 1999/1016) |
| | para 11 | 1 Sep 1999 (SI 1999/1016) |
| Schs 24, 25 | | 1 Apr 1999 (SI 1999/1016) |
| Sch 26 | | 1 Oct 1998 (SI 1998/2212) |
| Sch 27 | | 1 Apr 1999 (so far as relates to the power to make regulations) (SI 1998/2212) |
| | | 1 Sep 1999 (otherwise) (SI 1999/2323) |
| Sch 28 | Pt I, paras 1–3 | 1 Oct 1998 (SI 1998/2212) |
| | Pt I, para 4(1) | 1 Jan 2000 (so far as it applies in relation to the inspection of schools in England) (SI 1999/2323) |
| | | 1 Aug 2000 (so far as it applies in relation to the inspection of schools in Wales) (SI 1999/2323) |
| | Pt I, para 4(2) | 1 Oct 1998 (subject to a transitional provision) (SI 1998/2212) |
| | Pt I, para 5 | *Never in force* (repealed) |
| | Pt II | 1 Sep 1999 (SI 1999/2323) |
| Sch 29 | | 1 Feb 1999 (SI 1999/120) |
| Sch 30 | para 1 | 1 Sep 1999 (SI 1999/2323) |
| | para 2 | 1 Oct 1998 (SI 1998/2212) |
| | para 3 | 1 Apr 1999 (SI 1999/1016) |
| | para 4 | 1 Apr 1999 (except so far as substitutes Local Government Act 1974, s 25(5)(b)) (SI 1999/1016) |
| | | 1 Sep 1999 (exception noted above) (SI 1999/2323) |
| | paras 5–13 | 1 Sep 1999 (SI 1999/2323) |
| | para 14 | 1 Apr 1999 (subject to transitional provisions and savings) (SI 1999/1016) |
| | para 15 | 1 Sep 1999 (SI 1999/2323) |
| | para 16 | 1 Oct 1998 (SI 1998/2212) |
| | paras 17–19 | 1 Sep 1999 (SI 1999/2323) |
| | para 20 | 1 Oct 1998 (SI 1998/2212) |
| | paras 21–23 | 1 Sep 1999 (SI 1999/2323) |
| | para 24 | 1 Oct 1998 (SI 1998/2212) |
| | para 25 | 1 Sep 1999 (SI 1999/2323) |
| | para 26(a), (b) | 1 Sep 1999 (SI 1999/2323) |
| | para 26(c), (d) | 1 Oct 1998 (SI 1998/2212) |
| | para 26(e), (f) | 1 Sep 1999 (SI 1999/2323) |
| | para 27 | 1 Sep 1999 (SI 1999/2323) |
| | para 28(1) | 1 Jun 1999 (for the purpose of making orders under School Teachers' Pay and Conditions Act 1991, to come into force on or after 1 Sep 1999) (SI 1999/1016) |
| | | 1 Sep 1999 (otherwise) (SI 1999/2323) |

**School Standards and Framework Act 1998 (c 31)**—*contd*

| | |
|---|---|
| para 28(2)(a) | 1 Jun 1999 (for the purpose of making orders under School Teachers' Pay and Conditions Act 1991, to come into force on or after 1 Sep 1999) (SI 1999/1016) |
| | 1 Sep 1999 (otherwise) (SI 1999/2323) |
| para 28(2)(b) | *Never in force* (repealed) |
| para 28(2)(c) | 1 Jun 1999 (for the purpose of making orders under School Teachers' Pay and Conditions Act 1991, to come into force on or after 1 Sep 1999) (SI 1999/1016) |
| | 1 Sep 1999 (otherwise) (SI 1999/2323) |
| para 28(3) | 1 Sep 1999 (SI 1999/2323) |
| paras 29–32 | 1 Sep 1999 (SI 1999/2323) |
| para 33 | 1 Apr 1999 (SI 1998/2212) |
| paras 34–39 | 1 Sep 1999 (SI 1999/2323) |
| para 40 | 1 Apr 1999 (SI 1998/2212) |
| paras 41–46 | 1 Sep 1999 (SI 1999/2323) |
| para 47 | 1 Apr 1999 (except so far as substitutes Tribunal and Inquiries Act 1992, Sch 1, para 15(b)) (subject to savings and transitional provisions) (SI 1999/1016) |
| | 1 Sep 1999 (exception noted above) (SI 1999/2323) |
| para 48 | 1 Feb 1999 (SI 1999/120) |
| paras 49–51 | 1 Sep 1999 (SI 1999/2323) |
| para 52 | 1 Apr 1999 (SI 1998/2212) |
| para 53 | 1 Sep 1999 (SI 1999/2323) |
| para 54(a), (b) | 1 Sep 1999 (SI 1999/2323) |
| para 54(c) | 1 Apr 1999 (SI 1998/2212) |
| para 55 | 1 Sep 1999 (SI 1999/2323) |
| para 56 | 1 Apr 1999 (SI 1999/1016) |
| para 57 | 1 Oct 1998 (SI 1998/2212) |
| paras 58–60 | 1 Sep 1999 (SI 1999/2323) |
| para 61 | 1 Apr 1999 (SI 1999/1016) |
| paras 62, 63 | 1 Sep 1999 (SI 1999/2323) |
| para 64 | *Never in force* (repealed) |
| para 65 | *Not yet in force* |
| para 66 | 1 Apr 1999 (so far as relates to the repeal of Education Act 1996, ss 21, 22(1)(b), (c), (2), 27) (SI 1999/1016) |
| | 1 Nov 1999 (otherwise) (SI 1999/2323) |
| paras 67, 68 | 1 Nov 1999 (SI 1999/2323) |
| para 69 | 1 Oct 1998 (so far as it relates to the repeal of Education Act 1996, s 155(1), (4)) (SI 1998/2212) |
| | 10 Mar 1999 (so far as it relates to the repeal of Education Act 1996, ss 54(6)(c), 89(1), (2), 90, 91, 92(1), (2), (4), 94, 95) (subject to savings) (SI 1999/120) |
| | 1 Apr 1999 (so far as it relates to the repeal of Education Act 1996, Pt II, Chapter V) (SI 1998/2212) |
| | 1 Apr 1999 (so far as relates to the repeals of or in Education Act 1996, ss 35(8), 36(3), 37(4), (7)–(9), 42(4), 43(2) (the words "(subject to subsections (3) to (6))"), (3)–(6), 139, 155 (so far as not already repealed), 167(1) (the words "(subject to subsection (6)"), (6), 168(3), 169(4), (5) (the words "(subject to subsection (6)"), (6) (SI 1999/1016) |
| | 1 Sep 1999 (otherwise) (SI 1999/2323) |
| para 70 | 1 Oct 1998 (repeals of or in Education Act 1996, ss 184–199, 200(4), 202, 203, 209, 212 (subject to a saving), 213(2), (3), 232–240, 290) (SI 1998/2212) |

**School Standards and Framework Act 1998 (c 31)**—*contd*

1 Apr 1999 (repeals of or in Education Act 1996, ss 183(4), 211, 213 (so far as not already repealed), 214, 215, 216(2) (subject to a transitional provision), (3)–(9), 217, 244 (except in relation to the payment of maintenance grants in respect of any financial year beginning before 1 Apr 1999), 245 (except in so far as it applies to the payment of special purpose grant in England by the Secretary of State on or after 1 Apr 1999), 246–248 (except in so far as they apply to the payment of special purpose and capital grants by the Secretary of State on or after 1 Apr 1999), 249 (except in so far as it applies to the application of ss 250–254 in their application to the payment of capital grant by the Secretary of State on or after 1 Apr 1999), 250, 251, 253 and 254 (except in so far as they apply to the payment of capital grant by the Secretary of State on or after 1 Apr 1999), 255–258, 260, 261(2), (3) (the words "under subsection (1) or (2) any" and "(and, in the case of proposals published under section 268, the funding authority)"), (4), (5), 263(4)(b), 264, 265, 268, 269(2), (3) (the words "under subsection (1) or (2) any" and "(and, in the case of proposals published under section 268, the funding authority)"), (5), (6), 270(2)(b)(ii), 271–273, 310, (subject to a saving)) (SI 1999/1016)

1 Sep 1999 (repeal of Education Act 1996, Pt III, Chapters I–V, s 252, Chapters VII–X) (SI 1999/2323)

| | |
|---|---|
| paras 71–74 | 1 Sep 1999 (SI 1999/2323) |
| para 75(1)–(3) | 1 Sep 1999 (SI 1999/2323) |
| para 75(4) | 1 Oct 1998 (SI 1998/2212) |
| para 76 | 1 Sep 1999 (SI 1999/2323) |
| para 77(a) | 1 Sep 1999 (SI 1999/2323) |
| para 77(b) | 1 Oct 1998 (SI 1998/2212) |
| paras 78–80 | 1 Sep 1999 (SI 1999/2323) |
| para 81 | 1 Apr 1999 (so far as relates to the repeal of Education Act 1996, ss 338, 339(2), and in 339(4)(a), the words "or the funding authority") (SI 1999/1016) |
| | 1 Sep 1999 (otherwise) (SI 1999/2323) |
| para 82 | 1 Sep 1999 (SI 1999/2323) |
| para 83 | 1 Oct 1998 (repeal of Education Act 1996, s 346) (SI 1998/2212) |
| | 1 Apr 1999 (repeal of Education Act 1996, s 345) (SI 1999/1016) |
| | 1 Sep 1999 (otherwise) (SI 1999/2323) |
| paras 84–86 | 1 Sep 1999 (SI 1999/2323) |
| para 87(a) | 1 Oct 1998 (SI 1998/2212) |
| para 87(b) | 1 Apr 1999 (SI 1999/1016) |
| para 88 | 1 Oct 1998 (SI 1998/2212) |
| paras 89, 90 | 1 Sep 1999 (SI 1999/2323) |
| para 91 | 1 Oct 1998 (repeal of Education Act 1996, ss 370–373) (SI 1998/2212) |
| | 1 Sep 1999 (otherwise) (SI 1999/2323) |
| paras 92–95 | 1 Sep 1999 (SI 1999/2323) |
| para 96 | 1 Apr 1999 (SI 1999/1016) |
| paras 97–102 | 1 Sep 1999 (SI 1999/2323) |
| para 103(a) | 1 Sep 1999 (SI 1999/2323) |
| para 103(b) | 1 Oct 1998 (SI 1998/2212) |
| paras 104, 105 | 1 Sep 1999 (SI 1999/2323) |
| para 106(a) | 1 Sep 1999 (SI 1999/2323) |
| para 106(b) | 1 Oct 1998 (SI 1998/2212) |
| para 106(c), (d) | 1 Sep 1999 (SI 1999/2323) |
| para 107 | 1 Sep 1999 (SI 1999/2323) |
| para 108 | 1 Sep 1999 (SI 1999/1016) |
| para 109 | 1 Apr 1999 (repeal of Education Act 1996, ss 426(6), 428, 431, 432) (SI 1999/1016) |

**School Standards and Framework Act 1998 (c 31)**—*contd*

|  |  |
|---|---|
|  | 1 Sep 1999 (repeal of Education Act 1996, ss 411, 411A, 412–421, 421A, 422, 423, 423A, 424, 425, 425A, 425B, 426(1)–(5), 426A, 427, 429, 430, 436) (SI 1999/1016) |
| para 110 | 1 Oct 1998 (SI 1998/2212) |
| paras 111–113 | 1 Sep 1999 (SI 1999/2323) |
| para 114 | 1 Sep 1999 (except in so far as substitutes Education Act 1996, s 438(5)(b)) (SI 1999/2323) |
|  | *Not yet in force* (exception noted above) |
| para 115 | 1 Sep 1999 (SI 1999/2323) |
| para 116 | 1 Sep 1999 (except in so far as substitutes Education Act 1996, s 440(3)(b)) (SI 1999/2323) |
|  | *Not yet in force* (exception noted above) |
| paras 117–124 | 1 Sep 1999 (SI 1999/2323) |
| paras 125, 126 | 1 Feb 1999 (SI 1999/120) |
| para 127 | 1 Sep 1999 (SI 1999/2323) |
| para 128 | 1 Apr 1999 (SI 1998/2212) |
| paras 129–131 | 1 Sep 1999 (SI 1999/2323) |
| para 132 | 1 Apr 1999 (repeals of or in Education Act 1996, ss 500(2), and in (3), (4) (the words "or (2)" in each place they appear), 501(1)(a), 502(6)) (SI 1999/1016) |
|  | 1 Sep 1999 (otherwise) (SI 1999/2323) |
| para 133(a) | 1 Sep 1999 (SI 1999/2323) |
| para 133(b) | 1 Apr 1999 (SI 1998/2212) |
| paras 134–136 | 1 Sep 1999 (SI 1999/2323) |
| para 137 | 1 Apr 1999 (SI 1998/2212) |
| para 138 | *Not yet in force* |
| para 139 | 20 Nov 1998 (for the purpose of making schemes and regulations under Education Act 1996, s 519) (subject to saving and transitional provisions) (SI 1998/2791) |
|  | 1 Apr 1999 (otherwise) (SI 1998/2791) |
| paras 140–147 | 1 Sep 1999 (SI 1999/2323) |
| para 148 | 1 Apr 1999 (SI 1999/1016) |
| paras 149–152 | 1 Sep 1999 (SI 1999/2323) |
| para 153 | 20 Nov 1998 (subject to saving and transitional provisions) (SI 1998/2791) |
| para 154 | 1 Sep 1999 (SI 1999/2323) |
| para 155 | 1 Nov 1999 (SI 1999/2323) |
| paras 156–158 | 1 Sep 1999 (SI 1999/2323) |
| para 159 | 1 Feb 1999 (SI 1998/2212) |
| para 160(a) | 1 Apr 1999 (SI 1999/1016) |
| para 160(b) | 1 Sep 1999 (SI 1999/2323) |
| paras 161–166 | 1 Sep 1999 (SI 1999/2323) |
| para 167 | 1 Apr 1999 (repeal of Education Act 1996, s 552(1)–(3)) (SI 1999/1016) |
|  | 1 Sep 1999 (otherwise) (SI 1999/2323) |
| paras 168–176 | 1 Sep 1999 (SI 1999/2323) |
| para 177 | 1 Apr 1999 (SI 1999/1016) |
| paras 178–181 | 1 Sep 1999 (SI 1999/2323) |
| para 182 | 1 Feb 1999 (SI 1999/120) |
| para 183 | 1 Sep 1999 (SI 1999/2323) |
| para 184(a) | 1 Oct 1998 (SI 1998/2212) |
| para 184(b), (c) | 1 Sep 1999 (SI 1999/2323) |
| para 185 | 1 Oct 1998 (repeals of Education Act 1996, Sch 4, paras 7, 8, Sch 20, Pt 1, Sch 21) (SI 1998/2212) |
|  | 1 Apr 1999 (repeals of Education Act 1996, Sch 22, para 15) (SI 1998/2212) |
|  | 1 Apr 1999 (repeals of Education Act 1996, Schs 3, 4, 20 (so far as not already repealed)) (SI 1999/1016) |
|  | 1 Sep 1999 (repeals of Education Act 1996, Schs 5–10, 14–16) (SI 1999/2323) |

**School Standards and Framework Act 1998 (c 31)**—*contd*

|  |  |
|---|---|
|  | 1 Nov 1999 (repeals of Education Act 1996, Sch 2) (SI 1999/2323) |
|  | *Not yet in force* (repeals of or in Education Act 1996, Schs 11–13, 17–19, Sch 22, paras 1–14, 16, Schs 23–25A) |
| paras 186–188 | 1 Sep 1999 (SI 1999/2323) |
| para 189(a)–(d) | 1 Sep 1999 (subject to savings and transitional provisions) (SI 1999/1016) |
| para 189(e), (f) | 1 Sep 1999 (SI 1999/2323) |
| para 189(g) | 1 Oct 1998 (SI 1998/2212) |
| para 190 | 1 Oct 1998 (subject to a saving) (SI 1998/2212) |
| para 191 | 1 Sep 1999 (SI 1999/2323) |
| para 192(1)–(3) | 1 Sep 1999 (SI 1999/2323) |
| para 192(4)(a) | 1 Sep 1999 (SI 1999/2323) |
| para 192(4)(b) | 1 Apr 1999 (SI 1999/1016) |
| paras 193–196 | 1 Sep 1999 (SI 1999/2323) |
| para 197(a) | 1 Sep 1999 (SI 1999/2323) |
| para 197(b) | 1 Apr 1999 (SI 1999/1016) |
| para 198(a) | 1 Sep 1999 (SI 1999/2323) |
| para 198(b) | 1 Apr 1999 (SI 1999/1016) |
| para 199 | 1 Sep 1999 (SI 1999/2323) |
| paras 200, 201 | 1 Oct 1998 (SI 1998/2212) |
| para 202(1), (2) | 1 Sep 1999 (SI 1999/2323) |
| para 202(3), (4) | 1 Apr 1999 (SI 1999/1016) |
| paras 203–206 | 1 Sep 1999 (SI 1999/2323) |
| para 207 | 1 Oct 1998 (SI 1998/2212) |
| para 208(a), (b) | 1 Sep 1999 (SI 1999/2323) |
| para 208(c) | 1 Feb 1999 (repeal of Education Act 1997, s 13) (SI 1998/2212) |
|  | 1 Sep 1999 (otherwise) (SI 1999/1016) |
| paras 209–215 | 1 Sep 1999 (SI 1999/2323) |
| para 216 | 1 Oct 1998 (SI 1998/2212) |
| para 217 | 1 Sep 1999 (SI 1999/2323) |
| para 218 | 1 Apr 1999 (SI 1999/1016) |
| para 219 | 1 Oct 1998 (SI 1998/2212) |
| para 220 | 1 Sep 1999 (SI 1999/1016) |
| para 221 | 1 Sep 1999 (SI 1999/2323) |
| para 222(a) | 1 Feb 1999 (repeals of or in Education Act 1996, Sch 33B, paras, 1, 2 set out in Education Act 1997, Sch 3) (SI 1998/2212) |
|  | 1 Sep 1999 (repeal of Education Act 1997, Sch 3, so far as that repeal is not already in force) (SI 1999/1016) |
|  | 1 Sep 1999 (otherwise) (SI 1999/2323) |
| para 222(b) | 1 Oct 1998 (SI 1998/2212) |
| para 223 | 1 Sep 1999 (repeals of or in Education Act 1997, Sch 7, paras 31–34, 49(3), so far as those repeals are not already in force) (SI 1999/1016) |
|  | 1 Sep 1999 (otherwise) (SI 1999/2323) |
| para 224 | 24 Jul 1998 (s 145(4)) |
| para 225 | 1 Apr 1999 (SI 1999/1016) |
| Sch 31 | 1 Oct 1998 (SI 1998/2212), repeals of or in— |
|  | Local Government Act 1974; |
|  | Education Reform Act 1988, Sch 8; |
|  | School Teachers Pay and Conditions Act 1991, s 2(4); |
|  | Education Act 1996, ss 155(1), (4), 184–199, 200(4), 202, 203, 209, 212 (subject to a saving), 213(2), (3), 232–240, 290, 346, 357(2), 370–373, 404(3), 433(4), Sch 4, paras 7, 8, Sch 20, Pt I, Schs 21, 40; |
|  | Nursery Education and Grant-Maintained Schools Act 1996; |
|  | School Inspections Act 1996, Pt II (subject to a saving), ss 44, 45; |
|  | Education Act 1997, ss 42, 52(4), (5), Sch 6, para 5 |
|  | 1 Feb 1999 (SI 1998/2212), repeals of or in— |

**School Standards and Framework Act 1998 (c 31)**—*contd*

Education Act 1996, Sch 33B, paras, 1, 2 set out in Education Act 1997, Sch 3;

Education Act 1997, s 13

10 Mar 1999 (repeals of or in Education Act 1996, ss 54(6)(c), 89(1), (2), 90, 91, 92(1), (2), (4), 94, 95) (subject to savings) (SI 1999/120)

1 Apr 1999 (repeals of Education Act 1996, Pt II, Chapter V (subject to a saving), s 516, Sch 22, para 15) (SI 1998/2212)

1 Apr 1999 (SI 1999/1016), repeals of or in—

Public Records Act 1958;

Building Act 1984, s 4(1)(a)(iv);

Education Act 1996, ss 356(5)(a)(ii), 393, 544(1), and the provisions repealed by Sch 30, paras 66, 69, 70, 81, 83, 109, 132, 167, 177, 185 to this Act, to the extent that they are brought into force by SI 1999/1016 as noted above;

Education (No 2) Act 1986, s 49(3)(ba);

Schools Inspections Act 1996, ss 11(5)(b), 20(3), 21(4), 46(1);

Education Act 1997, s 50;

Audit Commission Act 1998

1 Sep 1999 (so far it relates to the repeals of or in Education Acts of 1996 and 1997 by Sch 30, paras 109, 189, 208, 220, 222, 223 to this Act, to the extent that they are brought into force by SI 1999/1016 as noted above) (SI 1999/1016)

1 Sep 1999 (SI 1999/2323), repeals of or in—

London Government Act 1963, s 31;

Superannuation Act 1972, Sch 1 (entry relating to the Schools Funding Council for Wales);

Local Government Act 1972;

House of Commons Disqualification Act 1975, Sch 1, Pt III (the entries "Any member of an education association in receipt of remuneration" and "Any member of the Funding Council for Wales in receipt of remuneration";

Sex Discrimination Act 1975, ss 22, 23C, 25;

Race Relations Act 1976;

National Health Service Act 1977;

Education (Scotland) Act 1980;

Acquisition of Land Act 1981, s 17(4)(ab);

Representation of the People Act 1983;

Building Act 1984, s 4(1)(a)(ii), (iii);

Education Reform Act 1988, ss 166, 167, 197(7), 236(1), Sch 12;

Children Act 1989;

Diocesan Boards of Education Measure 1991;

School Teachers' Pay and Conditions Act 1991, ss 1(5), (6), 2(2), (5), (6);

Further and Higher Education Act 1992;

Charities Act 1993;

Education Act 1994;

Value Added Tax Act 1994;

Disability Discrimination Act 1995;

Education Act 1996, ss 391(8), (9), 392(4), 560(6), and the provisions repealed by Sch 30, paras 58, 62, 69–71, 74, 79, 81, 83, 90–92, 94, 95, 106, 107, 111–118, 120–124, 127, 132, 133(a), 134, 140–143, 149, 151, 152, 158, 160(b), 161–167, 172, 174, 175, 178–181, 183–185, 187–189, to this Act, to the extent that they are brought into force by SI 1999/2323 as noted above;

Employment Rights Act 1996;

**School Standards and Framework Act 1998 (c 31)**—*contd*

School Inspections Act 1996 (the provisions repealed by Sch 30, paras 191, 192, 194, 195, 199, 202, 205, 206 to this Act, to the extent that they are brought into force by SI 1999/2323 as noted above);

Education Act 1997 (the provisions repealed by Sch 30, paras 208, 212, 217, 221–223 to this Act, to the extent that they are brought into force by SI 1999/2323 as noted above);

Education (Schools) Act 1997

1 Nov 1999 (SI 1999/2323), repeals of or in—

Superannuation Act 1972, Sch 1 (the entry relating to the Funding Agency for Schools);

House of Commons Disqualification Act 1975, Sch 1, Pt III (the entry "Any member of the Funding Agency for Schools in receipt of remuneration");

Education Act 1996 (the provisions repealed by Sch 30, paras 66–68, 155, 185 to this Act, to the extent that they are brought into force by SI 1999/2323 as noted above)

*Not yet in force*, repeals of or in—

Sex Discrimination Act 1975, Sch 2, para 1;

Acquisition of Land Act 1981, s 17(4)(ac);

Education Act 1996, ss 517, Schs 11–13, 17–19, Sch 22, paras 1–14, 16, Schs 23–25A

*Never in force* (repeals of or in Education Act 1996, s 16(1)(c); School Inspections Act 1996, s 9(3)(a); Education Act 1997, s 17(7)(a)) (repealed)

Sch 32     24 Jul 1998 (s 145(4))

---

[1] For transitional and saving provisions relating to the admission of children to maintained schools, see SI 1999/1016, art 6, Sch 4, as amended by SI 1999/2484

[2] For transitional and saving provisions, see SI 1999/2323, arts 3–23, Schs 5–7, as amended by SI 1999/2484

---

## Scotland Act 1998 (c 46)

*RA:* 19 Nov 1998

*Commencement provisions:* s 130; Scotland Act (Commencement) Order 1998, SI 1998/3178

| | | |
|---|---|---|
| 1–18 | | 19 Nov 1998 (RA) |
| 19, 20 | | 6 May 1999 (SI 1998/3178) |
| 21 | (1)–(7) | 6 May 1999 (SI 1998/3178) |
| | (8) | See Sch 2 below |
| 22 | | 6 May 1999 (SI 1998/3178) |
| 23 | | 6 May 1999 (for the purpose of enabling the Parliament to require any member of the Scottish Executive or his staff to attend its proceedings for the purpose of giving evidence or to produce documents in his custody or under his control) (SI 1998/3178) |
| | | 1 Jul 1999 (otherwise) (SI 1998/3178) |
| 24–26 | | 6 May 1999 (SI 1998/3178) |
| 27 | | 20 May 1999 (SI 1998/3178) |
| 28, 29 | | 1 Jul 1999 (SI 1998/3178) |
| 30 | | 6 May 1999 (SI 1998/3178) |
| 31–36 | | 1 Jul 1999 (SI 1998/3178) |
| 37 | | 25 Jan 1999 (SI 1998/3178) |
| 38 | (1), (2) | 6 May 1999 (SI 1998/3178) |
| | (3) | 25 Jan 1999 (SI 1998/3178) |
| | (4)–(6) | 6 May 1999 (SI 1998/3178) |
| 39 | | 1 Jul 1999 (SI 1998/3178) |
| 40–43 | | 6 May 1999 (SI 1998/3178) |

**Scotland Act 1998 (c 46)**—*contd*

| | | |
|---|---|---|
| 44 | (1)(a), (b) | 6 May 1999 (SI 1998/3178) |
| | (1)(c) | 20 May 1999 (SI 1998/3178) |
| | (2)–(4) | 6 May 1999 (SI 1998/3178) |
| 45–47 | | 6 May 1999 (SI 1998/3178) |
| 48 | (1) | 6 May 1999 (for the purpose of enabling the First Minister to recommend the appointment of the Lord Advocate and Solicitor General for Scotland to take effect from a date not earlier than 20 May 1999) (SI 1998/3178) |
| | | 20 May 1999 (otherwise) (SI 1998/3178) |
| | (2)–(6) | 20 May 1999 (SI 1998/3178) |
| 49, 50 | | 6 May 1999 (SI 1998/3178) |
| 51 | (1)–(3) | 6 May 1999 (SI 1998/3178) |
| | (4) | 25 Jan 1999 (for the purpose of enabling any delegation of civil service management functions or any determination of payments to be made to come into force not earlier than 6 May 1999) (SI 1998/3178) |
| | | 6 May 1999 (otherwise) (SI 1998/3178) |
| | (5), (6) | 6 May 1999 (SI 1998/3178) |
| | (7) | 25 Jan 1999 (for the purpose of enabling any delegation of civil service management functions or any determination of payments to be made to come into force not earlier than 6 May 1999) (SI 1998/3178) |
| | | 6 May 1999 (otherwise) (SI 1998/3178) |
| | (8), (9) | 6 May 1999 (SI 1998/3178) |
| 52 | | 6 May 1999 (except so far as relating to the Lord Advocate) (SI 1998/3178) |
| | | 20 May 1999 (exception noted above) (SI 1998/3178) |
| 53–55 | | 1 Jul 1999 (SI 1998/3178) |
| 56 | (1) | 1 Jul 1999 (SI 1998/3178) |
| | (2) | 25 Jan 1999 (for the purpose of enabling subordinate legislation to be made to come into force not earlier than 1 Jul 1999) (SI 1998/3178) |
| | | 1 Jul 1999 (otherwise) (SI 1998/3178) |
| | (3)–(5) | 1 Jul 1999 (SI 1998/3178) |
| 57 | (1) | 1 Jul 1999 (SI 1998/3178) |
| | (2) | 6 May 1999 (SI 1998/3178) |
| | (3) | 20 May 1999 (SI 1998/3178) |
| 58, 59 | | 6 May 1999 (SI 1998/3178) |
| 60 | | 25 Jan 1999 (for the purpose of enabling subordinate legislation to be made to come into force not earlier than 1 Jul 1999) (SI 1998/3178) |
| | | 6 May 1999 (otherwise) (SI 1998/3178) |
| 61 | (1)–(3) | 20 May 1999 (SI 1998/3178) |
| | (4) | 6 May 1999 (SI 1998/3178) |
| 62 | | 25 Jan 1999 (for the purpose of enabling subordinate legislation to be made to come into force not earlier than 20 May 1999) (SI 1998/3178) |
| | | 20 May 1999 (otherwise) (SI 1998/3178) |
| 63 | | 6 May 1999 (for the purpose of enabling subordinate legislation to be made to come into force not earlier than 1 Jul 1999) (SI 1998/3178) |
| | | 1 Jul 1999 (otherwise) (SI 1998/3178) |
| 64 | (1), (2) | 1 Apr 1999 (SI 1998/3178) |
| | (3)–(7) | 1 Jul 1999 (SI 1998/3178) |
| | (8) | 1 Apr 1999 (SI 1998/3178) |
| 65–68 | | 1 Jul 1999 (SI 1998/3178) |
| 69 | | 6 May 1999 (SI 1998/3178) |
| 70 | | 1 Jul 1999 (SI 1998/3178) |
| 71 | (1)–(5) | 1 Jul 1999 (SI 1998/3178) |

**Scotland Act 1998 (c 46)**—*contd*

| | | |
|---|---|---|
| | (6) | 25 Jan 1999 (for the purpose of enabling subordinate legislation to be made to come into force not earlier than 1 Jul 1999) (SI 1998/3178) |
| | | 1 Jul 1999 (otherwise) (SI 1998/3178) |
| | (7), (8) | 1 Jul 1999 (SI 1998/3178) |
| 72 | | 1 Jul 1999 (SI 1998/3178) |
| 73–85 | | 6 May 1999 (SI 1998/3178) |
| 86 | | 1 Jul 1999 (SI 1998/3178) |
| 87 | | 20 May 1999 (SI 1998/3178) |
| 88 | | 25 Jan 1999 (for the purpose of enabling subordinate legislation to be made to come into force not earlier than 1 Jul 1999) (SI 1998/3178) |
| | | 1 Jul 1999 (otherwise) (SI 1998/3178) |
| 89 | | 6 May 1999 (for the purpose of enabling subordinate legislation to be made to come into force not earlier than 1 Jul 1999) (SI 1998/3178) |
| | | 1 Jul 1999 (otherwise) (SI 1998/3178) |
| 90, 91 | | 1 Jul 1999 (SI 1998/3178) |
| 92 | | 6 May 1999 (SI 1998/3178) |
| 93 | | 6 May 1999 (for the purpose of enabling subordinate legislation to be made to come into force not earlier than 1 Jul 1999) (SI 1998/3178) |
| | | 1 Jul 1999 (otherwise) (SI 1998/3178) |
| 94, 95 | | 1 Jul 1999 (SI 1998/3178) |
| 96 | | 6 May 1999 (SI 1998/3178) |
| 97 | | 25 Jan 1999 (for the purpose of enabling subordinate legislation to be made to come into force not earlier than 6 May 1999) (SI 1998/3178) |
| | | 6 May 1999 (otherwise) (SI 1998/3178) |
| 98–100 | | 6 May 1999 (SI 1998/3178) |
| 101, 102 | | 1 Jul 1999 (SI 1998/3178) |
| 103 | (1), (2) | 6 May 1999 (SI 1998/3178) |
| | (3) | 25 Jan 1999 (for the purpose of enabling subordinate legislation to be made to come into force not earlier than 6 May 1999) (SI 1998/3178) |
| | | 6 May 1999 (otherwise) (SI 1998/3178) |
| | (4) | 6 May 1999 (SI 1998/3178) |
| 104 | | 1 Jul 1999 (SI 1998/3178) |
| 105, 106 | | 25 Jan 1999 (SI 1998/3178) |
| 107 | | 1 Jul 1999 (SI 1998/3178) |
| 108–111 | | 6 May 1999 (SI 1998/3178) |
| 112–116 | | 19 Nov 1998 (RA) |
| 117–119 | | 1 Jul 1999 (SI 1998/3178) |
| 120 | | 1 Apr 2000 (SI 1998/3178) |
| 121, 122 | | 1 Jul 1999 (SI 1998/3178) |
| 123 | | 6 May 1999 (except so far as relating to the Lord Advocate) (SI 1998/3178) |
| | | 20 May 1999 (exception noted above) (SI 1998/3178) |
| 124 | | 1 Jul 1999 (SI 1998/3178) |
| 125 | (1) | See Sch 8 below |
| | (2) | See Sch 9 below |
| 126–132 | | 19 Nov 1998 (RA) |
| Sch 1 | | 19 Nov 1998 (RA) |
| Sch 2 | para 1 | 6 May 1999 (SI 1998/3178) |
| | para 2(1) | 6 May 1999 (SI 1998/3178) |
| | para 2(2)–(4) | 25 Jan 1999 (for the purpose of enabling subordinate legislation to be made to come into force not earlier than 6 May 1999) (SI 1998/3178) |
| | | 6 May 1999 (otherwise) (SI 1998/3178) |
| | paras 3–6 | 6 May 1999 (SI 1998/3178) |

**Scotland Act 1998 (c 46)**—*contd*

|  |  |  |
|---|---|---|
|  | para 7 | 25 Jan 1999 (for the purpose of enabling subordinate legislation to be made to come into force not earlier than 6 May 1999) (SI 1998/3178) |
|  |  | 6 May 1999 (otherwise) (SI 1998/3178) |
| Sch 3 |  | 6 May 1999 (SI 1998/3178) |
| Sch 4 |  | 1 Jul 1999 (SI 1998/3178) |
| Schs 5, 6 |  | 6 May 1999 (SI 1998/3178) |
| Sch 7 |  | 19 Nov 1998 (RA) |
| Sch 8 | para 1 | 1 Jul 1999 (SI 1998/3178) |
|  | para 2 | 20 May 1999 (SI 1998/3178) |
|  | paras 3–6 | 1 Jul 1999 (SI 1998/3178) |
|  | para 7 | 20 May 1999 (SI 1998/3178) |
|  | paras 8, 9 | 1 Jul 1999 (SI 1998/3178) |
|  | paras 10, 11 | 19 Nov 1998 (RA) |
|  | para 12 | 1 Jul 1999 (SI 1998/3178) |
|  | paras 13, 14 | 6 May 1999 (SI 1998/3178) |
|  | paras 15–17 | 1 Jul 1999 (SI 1998/3178) |
|  | para 18 | 6 May 1999 (SI 1998/3178) |
|  | para 19 | 19 Nov 1998 (RA) |
|  | para 20 | 1 Apr 2000 (SI 1998/3178) |
|  | paras 21, 22 | 1 Jul 1999 (SI 1998/3178) |
|  | para 23(1) | 19 Nov 1998 (RA) |
|  | para 23(2)–(5) | 1 Jul 1999 (SI 1998/3178) |
|  | para 23(6) | 19 Nov 1998 (RA) |
|  | paras 24–26 | 6 May 1999 (SI 1998/3178) |
|  | para 27 | 1 Jul 1999 (SI 1998/3178) |
|  | para 28 | 6 May 1999 (SI 1998/3178) |
|  | para 29 | 1 Jul 1999 (SI 1998/3178) |
|  | paras 30, 31 | 6 May 1999 (SI 1998/3178) |
|  | para 32 | 20 May 1999 (SI 1998/3178) |
|  | para 33 | 6 May 1999 (SI 1998/3178) |
|  | para 34 | 1 Jul 1999 (SI 1998/3178) |
| Sch 9 |  | 20 May 1999 (SI 1998/3178), repeals in— House of Commons Disqualification Act 1975; Ministerial and other Salaries Act 1975 |
|  |  | 1 Jul 1999 (otherwise) (SI 1998/3178) |

---

**Social Security Act 1998 (c 14)**

*RA:* 21 May 1998

*Commencement provisions:* s 87(2), (3); Social Security Act 1998 (Commencement No 1) Order 1998, SI 1998/2209; Social Security Act 1998 (Commencement No 2) Order 1998, SI 1998/2780; Social Security Act 1998 (Commencement No 3) Order 1999, SI 1999/418; Social Security Act 1998 (Commencement No 4) Order 1999, SI 1999/526; Social Security Act 1998 (Commencement No 5) Order 1999, SI 1999/528; Social Security Act 1998 (Commencement No 6) Order 1999, SI 1999/1055; Social Security Act 1998 (Commencement No 7 and Consequential and Transitional Provisions) Order 1999, SI 1999/1510[1]; Social Security Act 1998 (Commencement No 8, and Savings and Consequential and Transitional Provisions) Order 1999, SI 1999/1958; Social Security Act 1998 (Commencement No 9, and Savings and Consequential and Transitional Provisions) Order 1999, SI 1999/2422, as amended by SI 2006/2540; Social Security Act 1998 (Commencement No 10 and Transitional Provisions) Order 1999, SI 1999/2739[4]; Social Security Act 1998 (Commencement No 11, and Savings and Consequential and Transitional Provisions) Order 1999, SI 1999/2860[5], as amended by SI 2006/2540; Social Security Act 1998 (Commencement No 12 and Consequential and Transitional Provisions) Order 1999, SI 1999/3178[6]; Social Security Act 1998 (Commencement No 13) Order 2001, SI 2001/2316; Social Security Act 1998 (Commencement No 14) Order 2006, SI 2006/2376

| 1 | (a) | 5 Jul 1999 (for certain purposes)[2] (SI 1999/1958) |
|---|---|---|

**Social Security Act 1998 (c 14)**—*contd*

|   |   |   |
|---|---|---|
| | | 6 Sep 1999 (so far as not already in force for certain purposes)[3] (SI 1999/2422) |
| | | 5 Oct 1999 (so far as not already in force for certain purposes)[4] (SI 1999/2739) |
| | | 18 Oct 1999 (so far as not already in force for certain purposes)[5] (SI 1999/2860) |
| | | 29 Nov 1999 (so far as not already in force for certain purposes)[6] (SI 1999/3178) |
| | | 29 Nov 1999 (so far as not already in force except for certain purposes)[6] (SI 1999/3178) |
| | | *Not yet in force* (exceptions noted above) |
| | (b) | 29 Nov 1999 (for certain purposes)[6] (SI 1999/3178) |
| | | 29 Nov 1999 (so far as not already in force except for certain purposes)[6] (SI 1999/3178) |
| | | *Not yet in force* (exceptions noted above) |
| | (c) | 1 Jun 1999 (SI 1999/1510) |
| 2 | (1) | 8 Sep 1998 (SI 1998/2209) |
| | (2)(a) | 5 Jul 1999 (for certain purposes)[2] (SI 1999/1958) |
| | | 6 Sep 1999 (so far as not already in force for certain purposes)[3] (SI 1999/2422) |
| | | 5 Oct 1999 (so far as not already in force for certain purposes)[4] (SI 1999/2739) |
| | | 18 Oct 1999 (so far as not already in force for certain purposes)[5] (SI 1999/2860) |
| | | 29 Nov 1999 (so far as not already in force except for certain purposes)[6] (SI 1999/3178) |
| | | *Not yet in force* (exceptions noted above) |
| | (2)(b)–(h) | 8 Sep 1998 (SI 1998/2209) |
| | (3) | 8 Sep 1998 (SI 1998/2209) |
| 3 | | 8 Sep 1998 (SI 1998/2209) |
| 4 | (1)(a) | 5 Jul 1999 (for certain purposes[2] and so far as it relates to social security appeal tribunals and medical appeal tribunals) (SI 1999/1958) |
| | | 6 Sep 1999 (so far as not already in force for certain purposes[3] and so far as it relates to social security appeal tribunals and medical appeal tribunals) (SI 1999/2422) |
| | | 5 Oct 1999 (so far as not already in force for certain purposes[4] and so far as it relates to social security appeal tribunals and disability appeal tribunals) (SI 1999/2739) |
| | | 18 Oct 1999 (so far as not already in force for certain purposes)[5] (SI 1999/2860) |
| | | 29 Nov 1999 (so far as not already in force for certain purposes)[6] (SI 1999/3178) |
| | | 29 Nov 1999 (so far as not already in force except for certain purposes)[6] (SI 1999/3178) |
| | | *Never in force* (exceptions noted above) (repealed) |
| | (1)(b) | 1 Jun 1999 (SI 1999/1510) |
| | (1)(c) | 18 Oct 1999 (for certain purposes)[5] (SI 1999/2860) |
| | | 29 Nov 1999 (so far as not already in force for certain purposes)[6] (SI 1999/3178) |
| | | 29 Nov 1999 (so far as not already in force except for certain purposes)[6] (SI 1999/3178) |
| | | *Never in force* (exceptions noted above) (repealed) |
| | (2)(a) | 5 Jul 1999 (for certain purposes)[2] (SI 1999/1958) |
| | | 6 Sep 1999 (so far as not already in force for certain purposes)[3] (SI 1999/2422) |
| | | 5 Oct 1999 (so far as not already in force for certain purposes)[4] (SI 1999/2739) |
| | | 18 Oct 1999 (so far as not already in force for certain purposes)[5] (SI 1999/2860) |

## Social Security Act 1998 (c 14)—*contd*

|   |   |   |
|---|---|---|
|   |   | 29 Nov 1999 (so far as not already in force for certain purposes)[6] (SI 1999/3178) |
|   |   | 29 Nov 1999 (so far as not already in force except for certain purposes)[6] (SI 1999/3178) |
|   |   | *Never in force* (exceptions noted above) (repealed) |
|   | (2)(b) | 1 Jun 1999 (SI 1999/1510) |
|   | (2)(c) | 18 Oct 1999 (for certain purposes)[5] (SI 1999/2860) |
|   |   | 29 Nov 1999 (so far as not already in force for certain purposes)[6] (SI 1999/3178) |
|   |   | 29 Nov 1999 (so far as not already in force except for certain purposes)[6] (SI 1999/3178) |
|   |   | *Never in force* (exceptions noted above) (repealed) |
|   | (2)(d) | 29 Nov 1999 (so far as not already in force for certain purposes)[6] (SI 1999/3178) |
|   |   | 29 Nov 1999 (so far as not already in force except for certain purposes)[6] (SI 1999/3178) |
|   |   | *Never in force* (exceptions noted above) (repealed) |
| 5 |   | 1 Jun 1999 (SI 1999/1510) |
| 6 | (1), (2) | 1 Jun 1999 (SI 1999/1510) |
|   | (3) | 4 Mar 1999 (so far as authorising the making of regulations) (SI 1999/528) |
|   |   | 1 Jun 1999 (otherwise) (SI 1999/1510) |
|   | (4)–(6) | 1 Jun 1999 (SI 1999/1510) |
| 7 | (1)–(5) | 1 Jun 1999 (SI 1999/1510) |
|   | (6) | 4 Mar 1999 (so far as authorising the making of regulations) (SI 1999/528) |
|   |   | 1 Jun 1999 (otherwise) (SI 1999/1510) |
|   | (7) | See Sch 1 below |
| 8 | (1)(a) | 5 Jul 1999 (for certain purposes)[2] (SI 1999/1958) |
|   |   | 6 Sep 1999 (so far as not already in force for certain purposes)[3] (SI 1999/2422) |
|   |   | 5 Oct 1999 (so far as not already in force for certain purposes)[4] (SI 1999/2739) |
|   |   | 18 Oct 1999 (so far as not already in force for certain purposes)[5] (SI 1999/2860) |
|   |   | 29 Nov 1999 (so far as not already in force except for certain purposes)[6] (SI 1999/3178) |
|   |   | *Not yet in force* (exceptions noted above) |
|   | (1)(b) | 29 Nov 1999 (except for certain purposes)[6] (SI 1999/3178) |
|   |   | *Never in force* (exceptions noted above) (repealed) |
|   | (1)(c) | 5 Jul 1999 (for certain purposes)[2] (SI 1999/1958) |
|   |   | 6 Sep 1999 (so far as not already in force for certain purposes)[3] (SI 1999/2422) |
|   |   | 5 Oct 1999 (so far as not already in force for certain purposes)[4] (SI 1999/2739) |
|   |   | 18 Oct 1999 (so far as not already in force for certain purposes)[5] (SI 1999/2860) |
|   |   | 29 Nov 1999 (so far as not already in force except for certain purposes)[6] (SI 1999/3178) |
|   |   | *Not yet in force* (exceptions noted above) |
|   | (1)(d) | 29 Nov 1999 (except for certain purposes)[6] (SI 1999/3178) |
|   |   | *Never in force* (exceptions referred to above) (repealed) |
|   | (2) | 5 Jul 1999 (for certain purposes)[2] (SI 1999/1958) |
|   |   | 6 Sep 1999 (so far as not already in force for certain purposes)[3] (SI 1999/2422) |
|   |   | 5 Oct 1999 (so far as not already in force for certain purposes)[4] (SI 1999/2739) |
|   |   | 18 Oct 1999 (so far as not already in force for certain purposes)[5] (SI 1999/2860) |

**Social Security Act 1998 (c 14)**—*contd*

|  |  |  |
|---|---|---|
|  | 29 Nov 1999 (so far as not already in force except for certain purposes)[6] (SI 1999/3178) |
|  | *Not yet in force* (exceptions noted above) |
| (3)(a) | 5 Jul 1999 (for certain purposes)[2] (SI 1999/1958) |
|  | 6 Sep 1999 (so far as not already in force for certain purposes)[3] (SI 1999/2422) |
|  | 18 Oct 1999 (so far as not already in force for certain purposes)[5] (SI 1999/2860) |
|  | 29 Nov 1999 (so far as not already in force except for certain purposes)[6] (SI 1999/3178) |
|  | *Not yet in force* (exceptions noted above) |
| (3)(b) | 18 Oct 1999 (for certain purposes)[5] (SI 1999/2860) |
|  | 29 Nov 1999 (so far as not already in force except for certain purposes)[6] (SI 1999/3178) |
|  | *Not yet in force* (exceptions noted above) |
| (3)(c) | 29 Nov 1999 (except for certain purposes)[6] (SI 1999/3178) |
|  | *Not yet in force* (exceptions noted above) |
| (3)(d), (e) | 5 Oct 1999 (for certain purposes)[4] (SI 1999/2739) |
|  | 29 Nov 1999 (so far as not already in force except for certain purposes)[6] (SI 1999/3178) |
|  | *Never in force* (exceptions noted above) (repealed) |
| (3)(f) | 29 Nov 1999 (except for certain purposes)[6] (SI 1999/3178) |
|  | *Not yet in force* (exceptions noted above) |
| (3)(g) | 5 Jul 1999 (for certain purposes)[2] (SI 1999/1958) |
|  | 29 Nov 1999 (so far as not already in force except for certain purposes)[6] (SI 1999/3178) |
|  | *Not yet in force* (exceptions noted above) |
| (3)(h) | 29 Nov 1999 (except for certain purposes)[6] (SI 1999/3178) |
|  | *Not yet in force* (exceptions noted above) |
| (4), (5) | 5 Jul 1999 (for certain purposes)[2] (SI 1999/1958) |
|  | 6 Sep 1999 (so far as not already in force for certain purposes)[3] (SI 1999/2422) |
|  | 5 Oct 1999 (so far as not already in force for certain purposes)[4] (SI 1999/2739) |
|  | 18 Oct 1999 (so far as not already in force for certain purposes)[5] (SI 1999/2860) |
|  | 29 Nov 1999 (so far as not already in force except for certain purposes)[6] (SI 1999/3178) |
|  | *Not yet in force* (exceptions noted above) |
| 9 | (1) | 4 Mar 1999 (so far as authorising the making of regulations) (SI 1999/528) |
|  | 5 Jul 1999 (for certain purposes)[2] (SI 1999/1958) |
|  | 6 Sep 1999 (so far as not already in force for certain purposes)[3] (SI 1999/2422) |
|  | 5 Oct 1999 (so far as not already in force for certain purposes)[4] (SI 1999/2739) |
|  | 18 Oct 1999 (so far as not already in force for certain purposes)[5] (SI 1999/2860) |
|  | 29 Nov 1999 (so far as not already in force except for certain purposes)[6] (SI 1999/3178) |
|  | *Not yet in force* (exceptions noted above) |
| (2), (3) | 5 Jul 1999 (for certain purposes)[2] (SI 1999/1958) |
|  | 6 Sep 1999 (so far as not already in force for certain purposes)[3] (SI 1999/2422) |
|  | 5 Oct 1999 (so far as not already in force for certain purposes)[4] (SI 1999/2739) |
|  | 18 Oct 1999 (so far as not already in force for certain purposes)[5] (SI 1999/2860) |
|  | 29 Nov 1999 (so far as not already in force except for certain purposes)[6] (SI 1999/3178) |

**Social Security Act 1998 (c 14)**—*contd*

|  |  |  |
|---|---|---|
| | | *Not yet in force* (exceptions noted above) |
| (4) | | 4 Mar 1999 (so far as authorising the making of regulations) (SI 1999/528) |
| | | 5 Jul 1999 (for certain purposes)[2] (SI 1999/1958) |
| | | 6 Sep 1999 (so far as not already in force for certain purposes)[3] (SI 1999/2422) |
| | | 5 Oct 1999 (so far as not already in force for certain purposes)[4] (SI 1999/2739) |
| | | 18 Oct 1999 (so far as not already in force for certain purposes)[5] (SI 1999/2860) |
| | | 29 Nov 1999 (so far as not already in force except for certain purposes)[6] (SI 1999/3178) |
| | | *Not yet in force* (exceptions noted above) |
| (5) | | 5 Jul 1999 (for certain purposes)[2] (SI 1999/1958) |
| | | 6 Sep 1999 (so far as not already in force for certain purposes)[3] (SI 1999/2422) |
| | | 5 Oct 1999 (so far as not already in force for certain purposes)[4] (SI 1999/2739) |
| | | 18 Oct 1999 (so far as not already in force for certain purposes)[5] (SI 1999/2860) |
| | | 29 Nov 1999 (so far as not already in force except for certain purposes)[6] (SI 1999/3178) |
| | | *Not yet in force* (exceptions noted above) |
| (6) | | 4 Mar 1999 (so far as authorising the making of regulations) (SI 1999/528) |
| | | 5 Jul 1999 (for certain purposes)[2] (SI 1999/1958) |
| | | 6 Sep 1999 (so far as not already in force for certain purposes)[3] (SI 1999/2422) |
| | | 5 Oct 1999 (so far as not already in force for certain purposes)[4] (SI 1999/2739) |
| | | 18 Oct 1999 (so far as not already in force for certain purposes)[5] (SI 1999/2860) |
| | | 29 Nov 1999 (so far as not already in force except for certain purposes)[6] (SI 1999/3178) |
| | | *Not yet in force* (exceptions noted above) |
| 10 | (1), (2) | 5 Jul 1999 (for certain purposes)[2] (SI 1999/1958) |
| | | 6 Sep 1999 (so far as not already in force for certain purposes)[3] (SI 1999/2422) |
| | | 5 Oct 1999 (so far as not already in force for certain purposes)[4] (SI 1999/2739) |
| | | 18 Oct 1999 (so far as not already in force for certain purposes)[5] (SI 1999/2860) |
| | | 29 Nov 1999 (so far as not already in force except for certain purposes)[6] (SI 1999/3178) |
| | | *Not yet in force* (exceptions noted above) |
| (3) | | 4 Mar 1999 (so far as authorising the making of regulations) (SI 1999/528) |
| | | 5 Jul 1999 (for certain purposes)[2] (SI 1999/1958) |
| | | 6 Sep 1999 (so far as not already in force for certain purposes)[3] (SI 1999/2422) |
| | | 5 Oct 1999 (so far as not already in force for certain purposes)[4] (SI 1999/2739) |
| | | 18 Oct 1999 (so far as not already in force for certain purposes)[5] (SI 1999/2860) |
| | | 29 Nov 1999 (so far as not already in force except for certain purposes)[6] (SI 1999/3178) |
| | | *Not yet in force* (exceptions noted above) |
| (4) | | 5 Jul 1999 (for certain purposes)[2] (SI 1999/1958) |
| | | 6 Sep 1999 (so far as not already in force for certain purposes)[3] (SI 1999/2422) |

**Social Security Act 1998 (c 14)**—*contd*

|  |  |  |
|---|---|---|
|  |  | 5 Oct 1999 (so far as not already in force for certain purposes)[4] (SI 1999/2739) |
|  |  | 18 Oct 1999 (so far as not already in force for certain purposes)[5] (SI 1999/2860) |
|  |  | 29 Nov 1999 (so far as not already in force except for certain purposes)[6] (SI 1999/3178) |
|  |  | *Never in force* (exceptions noted above) (repealed) |
|  | (5) | 5 Jul 1999 (for certain purposes)[2] (SI 1999/1958) |
|  |  | 6 Sep 1999 (so far as not already in force for certain purposes)[3] (SI 1999/2422) |
|  |  | 5 Oct 1999 (so far as not already in force for certain purposes)[4] (SI 1999/2739) |
|  |  | 18 Oct 1999 (so far as not already in force for certain purposes)[5] (SI 1999/2860) |
|  |  | 29 Nov 1999 (so far as not already in force except for certain purposes)[6] (SI 1999/3178) |
|  |  | *Not yet in force* (exceptions noted above) |
|  | (6) | 4 Mar 1999 (so far as authorising the making of regulations) (SI 1999/528) |
|  |  | 5 Jul 1999 (for certain purposes)[2] (SI 1999/1958) |
|  |  | 6 Sep 1999 (so far as not already in force for certain purposes)[3] (SI 1999/2422) |
|  |  | 5 Oct 1999 (so far as not already in force for certain purposes)[4] (SI 1999/2739) |
|  |  | 18 Oct 1999 (so far as not already in force for certain purposes)[5] (SI 1999/2860) |
|  |  | 29 Nov 1999 (so far as not already in force except for certain purposes)[6] (SI 1999/3178) |
|  |  | *Not yet in force* (exceptions noted above) |
| 11 | (1) | 4 Mar 1999 (so far as authorising the making of regulations) (SI 1999/528) |
|  |  | 5 Jul 1999 (for certain purposes)[2] (SI 1999/1958) |
|  |  | 6 Sep 1999 (so far as not already in force for certain purposes)[3] (SI 1999/2422) |
|  |  | 5 Oct 1999 (so far as not already in force for certain purposes)[4] (SI 1999/2739) |
|  |  | 18 Oct 1999 (so far as not already in force for certain purposes)[5] (SI 1999/2860) |
|  |  | 29 Nov 1999 (so far as not already in force except for certain purposes)[6] (SI 1999/3178) |
|  |  | *Not yet in force* (exceptions noted above) |
|  | (2) | 5 Jul 1999 (for certain purposes)[2] (SI 1999/1958) |
|  |  | 6 Sep 1999 (so far as not already in force for certain purposes)[3] (SI 1999/2422) |
|  |  | 5 Oct 1999 (so far as not already in force for certain purposes)[4] (SI 1999/2739) |
|  |  | 18 Oct 1999 (so far as not already in force for certain purposes)[5] (SI 1999/2860) |
|  |  | 29 Nov 1999 (so far as not already in force except for certain purposes)[6] (SI 1999/3178) |
|  |  | *Not yet in force* (exceptions noted above) |
|  | (3) | 5 Jul 1999 (for certain purposes[2], except the definitions "the current legislation" (so far as it relates to Jobseekers Act 1995 and Social Security (Recovery of Benefits) Act 1997) and "the former legislation" (so far as it relates to Social Security Act 1986, Pt II)) (SI 1999/1958) |

**Social Security Act 1998 (c 14)**—*contd*

6 Sep 1999 (so far as not already in force for certain purposes[3], except the definitions "the current legislation" (so far as it relates to Jobseekers Act 1995 and Social Security (Recovery of Benefits) Act 1997) and "the former legislation" (so far as it relates to Social Security Act 1986, Pt II)) (SI 1999/2422)

5 Oct 1999 (so far as not already in force for certain purposes[4], except the definitions "the current legislation" (so far as it relates to Jobseekers Act 1995 and Social Security (Recovery of Benefits) Act 1997) and "the former legislation" (so far as it relates to National Insurance Acts 1965–1974, National Insurance (Industrial Injuries) Acts 1965–1974, Social Security Act 1975)) (SI 1999/2739)

18 Oct 1999 (so far as not already in force for certain purposes[5], except the definitions "the current legislation" (so far as it relates to Social Security (Recovery of Benefits) Act 1997) and "the former legislation" (so far as it relates to National Insurance Acts 1965–1974, National Insurance (Industrial Injuries) Acts 1965–1974, Social Security Act 1986, Pt II)) (SI 1999/2860)

29 Nov 1999 (so far as not already in force except for certain purposes)[6] (SI 1999/3178)

*Not yet in force* (exceptions noted above)

| | | |
|---|---|---|
| 12 | (1) | See Schs 2, 3 below |
| | (2), (3) | 4 Mar 1999 (so far as authorising the making of regulations) (SI 1999/528) |

5 Jul 1999 (for certain purposes)[2] (SI 1999/1958)

6 Sep 1999 (so far as not already in force for certain purposes)[3] (SI 1999/2422)

5 Oct 1999 (so far as not already in force for certain purposes)[4] (SI 1999/2739)

18 Oct 1999 (so far as not already in force for certain purposes)[5] (SI 1999/2860)

29 Nov 1999 (so far as not already in force except for certain purposes)[6] (SI 1999/3178)

*Not yet in force* (exceptions noted above)

(4)   5 Jul 1999 (for certain purposes[2] except so far as relates to Social Security Administration Act 1992, s 74) (SI 1999/1958)

6 Sep 1999 (so far as not already in force for certain purposes[3], except so far as relates to Social Security Administration Act 1992, s 74) (SI 1999/2422)

5 Oct 1999 (so far as not already in force for certain purposes[4], except so far as relates to Social Security Administration Act 1992, s 74) (SI 1999/2739)

18 Oct 1999 (so far as not already in force for certain purposes)[5] (SI 1999/2860)

29 Nov 1999 (so far as not already in force except for certain purposes)[6] (SI 1999/3178)

*Not yet in force* (exceptions noted above)

(5)   5 Jul 1999 (for certain purposes)[2] (SI 1999/1958)

29 Nov 1999 (so far as not already in force except for certain purposes)[6] (SI 1999/3178)

*Not yet in force* (exceptions noted above)

(6), (7)   4 Mar 1999 (so far as authorising the making of regulations) (SI 1999/528)

5 Jul 1999 (for certain purposes)[2] (SI 1999/1958)

6 Sep 1999 (so far as not already in force for certain purposes)[3] (SI 1999/2422)

5 Oct 1999 (so far as not already in force for certain purposes)[4] (SI 1999/2739)

18 Oct 1999 (so far as not already in force for certain purposes)[5] (SI 1999/2860)

**Social Security Act 1998 (c 14)**—*contd*

|  |  |
|---|---|
|  | 29 Nov 1999 (so far as not already in force except for certain purposes)[6] (SI 1999/3178) |
|  | *Not yet in force* (exceptions noted above) |
| (8), (9) | 5 Jul 1999 (for certain purposes)[2] (SI 1999/1958) |
|  | 6 Sep 1999 (so far as not already in force for certain purposes)[3] (SI 1999/2422) |
|  | 5 Oct 1999 (so far as not already in force for certain purposes)[4] (SI 1999/2739) |
|  | 18 Oct 1999 (so far as not already in force for certain purposes)[5] (SI 1999/2860) |
|  | 29 Nov 1999 (so far as not already in force except for certain purposes)[6] (SI 1999/3178) |
|  | *Not yet in force* (exceptions noted above) |
| 13 | 5 Jul 1999 (for certain purposes)[2] (SI 1999/1958) |
|  | 6 Sep 1999 (so far as not already in force for certain purposes)[3] (SI 1999/2422) |
|  | 5 Oct 1999 (so far as not already in force for certain purposes)[4] (SI 1999/2739) |
|  | 18 Oct 1999 (so far as not already in force for certain purposes)[5] (SI 1999/2860) |
|  | 29 Nov 1999 (so far as not already in force except for certain purposes)[6] (SI 1999/3178) |
|  | *Not yet in force* (exceptions noted above) |
| 14 | (1), (2) |
|  | 5 Jul 1999 (for certain purposes)[2] (SI 1999/1958) |
|  | 6 Sep 1999 (so far as not already in force for certain purposes)[3] (SI 1999/2422) |
|  | 5 Oct 1999 (so far as not already in force for certain purposes)[4] (SI 1999/2739) |
|  | 18 Oct 1999 (so far as not already in force for certain purposes)[5] (SI 1999/2860) |
|  | 29 Nov 1999 (so far as not already in force except for certain purposes)[6] (SI 1999/3178) |
|  | *Never in force* (exceptions noted above) (repealed) |
| (3) | 4 Mar 1999 (so far as authorising the making of regulations) (SI 1999/528) |
|  | 5 Jul 1999 (for certain purposes)[2] (SI 1999/1958) |
|  | 6 Sep 1999 (so far as not already in force for certain purposes)[3] (SI 1999/2422) |
|  | 5 Oct 1999 (so far as not already in force for certain purposes)[4] (SI 1999/2739) |
|  | 18 Oct 1999 (so far as not already in force for certain purposes)[5] (SI 1999/2860) |
|  | 29 Nov 1999 (so far as not already in force except for certain purposes)[6] (SI 1999/3178) |
|  | *Not yet in force* (exceptions noted above) |
| (4)–(6) | 5 Jul 1999 (for certain purposes)[2] (SI 1999/1958) |
|  | 6 Sep 1999 (so far as not already in force for certain purposes)[3] (SI 1999/2422) |
|  | 5 Oct 1999 (so far as not already in force for certain purposes)[4] (SI 1999/2739) |
|  | 18 Oct 1999 (so far as not already in force for certain purposes)[5] (SI 1999/2860) |
|  | 29 Nov 1999 (so far as not already in force except for certain purposes)[6] (SI 1999/3178) |
|  | *Not yet in force* (exceptions noted above) |
| (7)–(9) | 5 Jul 1999 (for certain purposes)[2] (SI 1999/1958) |
|  | 6 Sep 1999 (so far as not already in force for certain purposes)[3] (SI 1999/2422) |
|  | 5 Oct 1999 (so far as not already in force for certain purposes)[4] (SI 1999/2739) |

**Social Security Act 1998 (c 14)**—*contd*

|  |  |  |
|---|---|---|
| | | 18 Oct 1999 (so far as not already in force for certain purposes)[5] (SI 1999/2860) |
| | | 29 Nov 1999 (so far as not already in force except for certain purposes)[6] (SI 1999/3178) |
| | | *Never in force* (exceptions noted above) (repealed) |
| | (10), (11) | 4 Mar 1999 (so far as authorising the making of regulations) (SI 1999/528) |
| | | 5 Jul 1999 (for certain purposes)[2] (SI 1999/1958) |
| | | 6 Sep 1999 (so far as not already in force for certain purposes)[3] (SI 1999/2422) |
| | | 5 Oct 1999 (so far as not already in force for certain purposes)[4] (SI 1999/2739) |
| | | 18 Oct 1999 (so far as not already in force for certain purposes)[5] (SI 1999/2860) |
| | | 29 Nov 1999 (so far as not already in force except for certain purposes)[6] (SI 1999/3178) |
| | | *Never in force* (exceptions noted above) (repealed) |
| | (12) | See Sch 4 below |
| 15 | (1) | 5 Jul 1999 (for certain purposes)[2] (SI 1999/1958) |
| | | 6 Sep 1999 (so far as not already in force for certain purposes)[3] (SI 1999/2422) |
| | | 5 Oct 1999 (so far as not already in force for certain purposes)[4] (SI 1999/2739) |
| | | 18 Oct 1999 (so far as not already in force for certain purposes)[5] (SI 1999/2860) |
| | | 29 Nov 1999 (so far as not already in force except for certain purposes)[6] (SI 1999/3178) |
| | | *Never in force* (exceptions noted above) (repealed) |
| | (2), (3) | 4 Mar 1999 (so far as authorising the making of regulations) (SI 1999/528) |
| | | 5 Jul 1999 (for certain purposes)[2] (SI 1999/1958) |
| | | 6 Sep 1999 (so far as not already in force for certain purposes)[3] (SI 1999/2422) |
| | | 5 Oct 1999 (so far as not already in force for certain purposes)[4] (SI 1999/2739) |
| | | 18 Oct 1999 (so far as not already in force for certain purposes)[5] (SI 1999/2860) |
| | | 29 Nov 1999 (so far as not already in force except for certain purposes)[6] (SI 1999/3178) |
| | | *Not yet in force* (exceptions noted above) (sub-s (2) repealed) |
| | (4), (5) | 5 Jul 1999 (for certain purposes)[2] (SI 1999/1958) |
| | | 6 Sep 1999 (so far as not already in force for certain purposes)[3] (SI 1999/2422) |
| | | 5 Oct 1999 (so far as not already in force for certain purposes)[4] (SI 1999/2739) |
| | | 18 Oct 1999 (so far as not already in force for certain purposes)[5] (SI 1999/2860) |
| | | 29 Nov 1999 (so far as not already in force except for certain purposes)[6] (SI 1999/3178) |
| | | *Not yet in force* (exceptions noted above) |
| 16 | (1)–(3) | 4 Mar 1999 (so far as authorising the making of regulations) (SI 1999/528) |
| | | 5 Jul 1999 (for certain purposes)[2] (SI 1999/1958) |
| | | 6 Sep 1999 (so far as not already in force for certain purposes)[3] (SI 1999/2422) |
| | | 5 Oct 1999 (so far as not already in force for certain purposes)[4] (SI 1999/2739) |
| | | 18 Oct 1999 (so far as not already in force for certain purposes)[5] (SI 1999/2860) |

**Social Security Act 1998 (c 14)**—*contd*

|  |  |  |
|---|---|---|
|  |  | 29 Nov 1999 (so far as not already in force except for certain purposes)[6] (SI 1999/3178) |
|  |  | *Not yet in force* (exceptions noted above) (sub-s (2) repealed) |
|  | (4)(a) | 8 Sep 1998 (SI 1998/2209) |
|  | (4)(b) | 6 Apr 1999 (SI 1998/2209) |
|  | (5) | 8 Sep 1998 (SI 1998/2209) |
|  | (6)–(9) | 5 Jul 1999 (for certain purposes)[2] (SI 1999/1958) |
|  |  | 6 Sep 1999 (so far as not already in force for certain purposes)[3] (SI 1999/2422) |
|  |  | 5 Oct 1999 (so far as not already in force for certain purposes)[4] (SI 1999/2739) |
|  |  | 18 Oct 1999 (so far as not already in force for certain purposes)[5] (SI 1999/2860) |
|  |  | 29 Nov 1999 (so far as not already in force except for certain purposes)[6] (SI 1999/3178) |
|  |  | *Never in force* (exceptions noted above) (repealed) |
| 17 |  | 4 Mar 1999 (so far as authorising the making of regulations) (SI 1999/528) |
|  |  | 5 Jul 1999 (for certain purposes)[2] (SI 1999/1958) |
|  |  | 6 Sep 1999 (so far as not already in force for certain purposes)[3] (SI 1999/2422) |
|  |  | 5 Oct 1999 (so far as not already in force for certain purposes)[4] (SI 1999/2739) |
|  |  | 18 Oct 1999 (so far as not already in force for certain purposes)[5] (SI 1999/2860) |
|  |  | 29 Nov 1999 (so far as not already in force except for certain purposes)[6] (SI 1999/3178) |
|  |  | *Not yet in force* (exceptions noted above) |
| 18 | (1) | 4 Mar 1999 (so far as authorising the making of regulations) (SI 1999/528) |
|  |  | 5 Jul 1999 (for certain purposes)[2] (SI 1999/1958) |
|  |  | 6 Sep 1999 (so far as not already in force for certain purposes)[3] (SI 1999/2422) |
|  |  | 5 Oct 1999 (so far as not already in force for certain purposes)[4] (SI 1999/2739) |
|  |  | 18 Oct 1999 (so far as not already in force for certain purposes)[5] (SI 1999/2860) |
|  |  | 29 Nov 1999 (so far as not already in force except for certain purposes)[6] (SI 1999/3178) |
|  |  | *Not yet in force* (exceptions noted above) |
|  | (2) | 18 Oct 1999 (SI 1999/2860) |
| 19 |  | 5 Jul 1999 (for certain purposes)[2] (SI 1999/1958) |
|  |  | 6 Sep 1999 (so far as not already in force for certain purposes)[3] (SI 1999/2422) |
|  |  | 5 Oct 1999 (so far as not already in force for certain purposes)[4] (SI 1999/2739) |
|  |  | 18 Oct 1999 (so far as not already in force for certain purposes)[5] (SI 1999/2860) |
|  |  | 29 Nov 1999 (so far as not already in force except for certain purposes)[6] (SI 1999/3178) |
|  |  | *Not yet in force* (exceptions noted above) |
| 20 | (1), (2) | 4 Mar 1999 (so far as authorising the making of regulations) (SI 1999/528) |
|  |  | 5 Jul 1999 (for certain purposes)[2] (SI 1999/1958) |
|  |  | 6 Sep 1999 (so far as not already in force for certain purposes)[3] (SI 1999/2422) |
|  |  | 5 Oct 1999 (so far as not already in force for certain purposes)[4] (SI 1999/2739) |
|  |  | 18 Oct 1999 (so far as not already in force for certain purposes)[5] (SI 1999/2860) |

**Social Security Act 1998 (c 14)**—*contd*

|  |  |  |
|---|---|---|
|  |  | 29 Nov 1999 (so far as not already in force except for certain purposes)[6] (SI 1999/3178) |
|  |  | *Not yet in force* (exceptions noted above) |
|  | (3)(a) | 4 Mar 1999 (so far as authorising the making of regulations) (SI 1999/528) |
|  |  | 5 Jul 1999 (for certain purposes)[2] (SI 1999/1958) |
|  |  | 6 Sep 1999 (so far as not already in force for certain purposes)[3] (SI 1999/2422) |
|  |  | 5 Oct 1999 (so far as not already in force for certain purposes)[4] (SI 1999/2739) |
|  |  | 18 Oct 1999 (so far as not already in force for certain purposes)[5] (SI 1999/2860) |
|  |  | 29 Nov 1999 (so far as not already in force except for certain purposes)[6] (SI 1999/3178) |
|  |  | *Not yet in force* (exceptions noted above) |
|  | (3)(b) | 4 Mar 1999 (so far as authorising the making of regulations) (SI 1999/528) |
|  |  | 18 Oct 1999 (so far as not already in force for certain purposes)[5] (SI 1999/2860) |
|  |  | 29 Nov 1999 (so far as not already in force except for certain purposes)[6] (SI 1999/3178) |
|  |  | *Not yet in force* (exceptions noted above) |
| 21–24 |  | 4 Mar 1999 (so far as authorising the making of regulations) (SI 1999/528) |
|  |  | 5 Jul 1999 (for certain purposes)[2] (SI 1999/1958) |
|  |  | 6 Sep 1999 (so far as not already in force for certain purposes)[3] (SI 1999/2422) |
|  |  | 5 Oct 1999 (so far as not already in force for certain purposes)[4] (SI 1999/2739) |
|  |  | 18 Oct 1999 (so far as not already in force for certain purposes)[5] (SI 1999/2860) |
|  |  | 29 Nov 1999 (so far as not already in force except for certain purposes)[6] (SI 1999/3178) |
|  |  | *Not yet in force* (exceptions noted above) |
| 25 | (1), (2) | 5 Jul 1999 (for certain purposes)[2] (SI 1999/1958) |
|  |  | 6 Sep 1999 (so far as not already in force for certain purposes)[3] (SI 1999/2422) |
|  |  | 5 Oct 1999 (so far as not already in force for certain purposes)[4] (SI 1999/2739) |
|  |  | 18 Oct 1999 (so far as not already in force for certain purposes)[5] (SI 1999/2860) |
|  |  | 29 Nov 1999 (so far as not already in force except for certain purposes)[6] (SI 1999/3178) |
|  |  | *Not yet in force* (exceptions noted above) |
|  | (3)(a) | 5 Jul 1999 (for certain purposes)[2] (SI 1999/1958) |
|  |  | 6 Sep 1999 (so far as not already in force for certain purposes)[3] (SI 1999/2422) |
|  |  | 5 Oct 1999 (so far as not already in force for certain purposes)[4] (SI 1999/2739) |
|  |  | 18 Oct 1999 (so far as not already in force for certain purposes)[5] (SI 1999/2860) |
|  |  | 29 Nov 1999 (so far as not already in force except for certain purposes)[6] (SI 1999/3178) |
|  |  | *Not yet in force* (exceptions noted above) |
|  | (3)(b) | 4 Mar 1999 (so far as authorising the making of regulations) (SI 1999/528) |
|  |  | 5 Jul 1999 (for certain purposes)[2] (SI 1999/1958) |
|  |  | 6 Sep 1999 (so far as not already in force for certain purposes)[3] (SI 1999/2422) |

**Social Security Act 1998 (c 14)**—*contd*

|  |  |
|---|---|
|  | 5 Oct 1999 (so far as not already in force for certain purposes)[4] (SI 1999/2739) |
|  | 18 Oct 1999 (so far as not already in force for certain purposes)[5] (SI 1999/2860) |
|  | 29 Nov 1999 (so far as not already in force except for certain purposes)[6] (SI 1999/3178) |
|  | *Not yet in force* (exceptions noted above) |
| (4) | 5 Jul 1999 (for certain purposes)[2] (SI 1999/1958) |
|  | 6 Sep 1999 (so far as not already in force for certain purposes)[3] (SI 1999/2422) |
|  | 5 Oct 1999 (so far as not already in force for certain purposes)[4] (SI 1999/2739) |
|  | 18 Oct 1999 (so far as not already in force for certain purposes)[5] (SI 1999/2860) |
|  | 29 Nov 1999 (so far as not already in force except for certain purposes)[6] (SI 1999/3178) |
|  | *Not yet in force* (exceptions noted above) |
| (5)(a), (b) | 5 Jul 1999 (for certain purposes)[2] (SI 1999/1958) |
|  | 6 Sep 1999 (so far as not already in force for certain purposes)[3] (SI 1999/2422) |
|  | 5 Oct 1999 (so far as not already in force for certain purposes)[4] (SI 1999/2739) |
|  | 18 Oct 1999 (so far as not already in force for certain purposes)[5] (SI 1999/2860) |
|  | 29 Nov 1999 (so far as not already in force except for certain purposes)[6] (SI 1999/3178) |
|  | *Not yet in force* (exceptions noted above) |
| (5)(c) | 4 Mar 1999 (so far as authorising the making of regulations) (SI 1999/528) |
|  | 5 Jul 1999 (for certain purposes)[2] (SI 1999/1958) |
|  | 6 Sep 1999 (so far as not already in force for certain purposes)[3] (SI 1999/2422) |
|  | 5 Oct 1999 (so far as not already in force for certain purposes)[4] (SI 1999/2739) |
|  | 18 Oct 1999 (so far as not already in force for certain purposes)[5] (SI 1999/2860) |
|  | 29 Nov 1999 (so far as not already in force except for certain purposes)[6] (SI 1999/3178) |
|  | *Not yet in force* (exceptions noted above) |
| (6) | 5 Jul 1999 (for certain purposes)[2] (SI 1999/1958) |
|  | 6 Sep 1999 (so far as not already in force for certain purposes)[3] (SI 1999/2422) |
|  | 5 Oct 1999 (so far as not already in force for certain purposes)[4] (SI 1999/2739) |
|  | 18 Oct 1999 (so far as not already in force for certain purposes)[5] (SI 1999/2860) |
|  | 29 Nov 1999 (so far as not already in force except for certain purposes)[6] (SI 1999/3178) |
|  | *Not yet in force* (exceptions noted above) |
| 26 (1)–(5) | 5 Jul 1999 (for certain purposes)[2] (SI 1999/1958) |
|  | 6 Sep 1999 (so far as not already in force for certain purposes)[3] (SI 1999/2422) |
|  | 5 Oct 1999 (so far as not already in force for certain purposes)[4] (SI 1999/2739) |
|  | 18 Oct 1999 (so far as not already in force for certain purposes)[5] (SI 1999/2860) |
|  | 29 Nov 1999 (so far as not already in force except for certain purposes)[6] (SI 1999/3178) |
|  | *Not yet in force* (exceptions noted above) |
| (6)(a), (b) | 5 Jul 1999 (for certain purposes)[2] (SI 1999/1958) |

**Social Security Act 1998 (c 14)**—*contd*

6 Sep 1999 (so far as not already in force for certain purposes)[3] (SI 1999/2422)

5 Oct 1999 (so far as not already in force for certain purposes)[4] (SI 1999/2739)

18 Oct 1999 (so far as not already in force for certain purposes)[5] (SI 1999/2860)

29 Nov 1999 (so far as not already in force except for certain purposes)[6] (SI 1999/3178)

*Not yet in force* (exceptions noted above)

(6)(c)  4 Mar 1999 (so far as authorising the making of regulations) (SI 1999/528)

5 Jul 1999 (for certain purposes)[2] (SI 1999/1958)

6 Sep 1999 (so far as not already in force for certain purposes)[3] (SI 1999/2422)

5 Oct 1999 (so far as not already in force for certain purposes)[4] (SI 1999/2739)

18 Oct 1999 (so far as not already in force for certain purposes)[5] (SI 1999/2860)

29 Nov 1999 (so far as not already in force except for certain purposes)[6] (SI 1999/3178)

*Not yet in force* (exceptions noted above)

(7)  5 Jul 1999 (for certain purposes)[2] (SI 1999/1958)

6 Sep 1999 (so far as not already in force for certain purposes)[3] (SI 1999/2422)

5 Oct 1999 (so far as not already in force for certain purposes)[4] (SI 1999/2739)

18 Oct 1999 (so far as not already in force for certain purposes)[5] (SI 1999/2860)

29 Nov 1999 (so far as not already in force except for certain purposes)[6] (SI 1999/3178)

*Not yet in force* (exceptions noted above)

(8)  1 Jun 1999 (SI 1999/1510)

27   5 Jul 1999 (for certain purposes)[2] (SI 1999/1958)

6 Sep 1999 (so far as not already in force for certain purposes)[3] (SI 1999/2422)

5 Oct 1999 (so far as not already in force for certain purposes)[4] (SI 1999/2739)

18 Oct 1999 (so far as not already in force for certain purposes)[5] (SI 1999/2860)

29 Nov 1999 (so far as not already in force except for certain purposes)[6] (SI 1999/3178)

*Not yet in force* (exceptions noted above)

28   (1)  4 Mar 1999 (so far as authorising the making of regulations) (SI 1999/528)

5 Jul 1999 (for certain purposes)[2] (SI 1999/1958)

6 Sep 1999 (so far as not already in force for certain purposes)[3] (SI 1999/2422)

5 Oct 1999 (so far as not already in force for certain purposes)[4] (SI 1999/2739)

18 Oct 1999 (so far as not already in force for certain purposes)[5] (SI 1999/2860)

29 Nov 1999 (so far as not already in force except for certain purposes)[6] (SI 1999/3178)

*Not yet in force* (exceptions noted above)

(2)  4 Mar 1999 (so far as authorising the making of regulations) (SI 1999/528)

5 Jul 1999 (for certain purposes)[2] (SI 1999/1958)

6 Sep 1999 (so far as not already in force for certain purposes)[3] (SI 1999/2422)

**Social Security Act 1998 (c 14)**—*contd*

|  |  |  |
|---|---|---|
|  |  | 5 Oct 1999 (so far as not already in force for certain purposes)[4] (SI 1999/2739) |
|  |  | 18 Oct 1999 (so far as not already in force for certain purposes)[5] (SI 1999/2860) |
|  |  | 29 Nov 1999 (so far as not already in force except for certain purposes)[6] (SI 1999/3178) |
|  |  | *Not yet in force* (exceptions noted above) |
|  | (3)(a), (b) | 4 Mar 1999 (so far as authorising the making of regulations) (SI 1999/528) |
|  |  | 5 Jul 1999 (for certain purposes)[2] (SI 1999/1958) |
|  |  | 6 Sep 1999 (so far as not already in force for certain purposes)[3] (SI 1999/2422) |
|  |  | 5 Oct 1999 (so far as not already in force for certain purposes)[4] (SI 1999/2739) |
|  |  | 18 Oct 1999 (so far as not already in force for certain purposes)[5] (SI 1999/2860) |
|  |  | 29 Nov 1999 (so far as not already in force except for certain purposes)[6] (SI 1999/3178) |
|  |  | *Not yet in force* (exceptions noted above) |
|  | (3)(c) | 4 Mar 1999 (so far as authorising the making of regulations) (SI 1999/528) |
|  |  | 5 Jul 1999 (for certain purposes)[2] (SI 1999/1958) |
|  |  | 29 Nov 1999 (so far as not already in force except for certain purposes)[6] (SI 1999/3178) |
|  |  | *Not yet in force* (exceptions noted above) |
|  | (3)(d) | 4 Mar 1999 (so far as authorising the making of regulations) (SI 1999/528) |
|  |  | 18 Oct 1999 (so far as not already in force for certain purposes)[5] (SI 1999/2860) |
|  |  | 29 Nov 1999 (so far as not already in force except for certain purposes)[6] (SI 1999/3178) |
|  |  | *Not yet in force* (exceptions noted above) |
|  | (3)(e) | 4 Mar 1999 (so far as authorising the making of regulations) (SI 1999/528) |
|  |  | 29 Nov 1999 (so far as not already in force except for certain purposes)[6] (SI 1999/3178) |
|  |  | *Not yet in force* (exceptions noted above) |
| 29, 30 |  | 5 Jul 1999 (for certain purposes)[2] (SI 1999/1958) |
|  |  | *Not yet in force* (otherwise) (s 29(2) repealed) |
| 31 | (1) | 6 Sep 1999 (SI 1999/2422) |
|  | (2), (3) | 4 Mar 1999 (so far as authorising the making of regulations) (SI 1999/528) |
|  |  | 6 Sep 1999 (otherwise) (SI 1999/2422) |
| 32 |  | 18 Oct 1999 (SI 1999/2860) |
| 33 |  | 29 Nov 1999 (except for certain purposes)[6] (SI 1999/3178) |
|  |  | *Not yet in force* (exceptions noted above) |
| 34 |  | 18 Oct 1999 (SI 1999/2860) |
| 35 |  | *Never in force* (repealed) |
| 36, 37 |  | 29 Nov 1999 (except for certain purposes)[6] (SI 1999/3178) |
|  |  | *Never in force* (exceptions noted above) (repealed) |
| 38 | (1)(a) | 4 Mar 1999 (so far as authorising the making of regulations) (SI 1999/528) |
|  |  | 29 Nov 1999 (so far as not already in force except for certain purposes)[6] (SI 1999/3178) |
|  |  | *Never in force* (exceptions noted above) (repealed) |
|  | (1)(b), (c) | 29 Nov 1999 (except for certain purposes)[6] (SI 1999/3178) |
|  |  | *Never in force* (exceptions noted above) (repealed) |
|  | (2) | 29 Nov 1999 (except for certain purposes)[6] (SI 1999/3178) |
|  |  | *Never in force* (exceptions noted above) (repealed) |

**Social Security Act 1998 (c 14)**—*contd*

| | | |
|---|---|---|
| | (3) | 4 Mar 1999 (so far as authorising the making of regulations) (SI 1999/528) |
| | | 29 Nov 1999 (so far as not already in force except for certain purposes)[6] (SI 1999/3178) |
| | | *Never in force* (exceptions noted above) (repealed) |
| | (4)–(13) | 29 Nov 1999 (except for certain purposes)[6] (SI 1999/3178) |
| | | *Never in force* (exceptions noted above) (repealed) |
| 39 | (1), (2) | 5 Jul 1999 (for certain purposes)[2] (SI 1999/1958) |
| | | 6 Sep 1999 (so far as not already in force for certain purposes)[3] (SI 1999/2422) |
| | | 5 Oct 1999 (so far as not already in force for certain purposes)[4] (SI 1999/2739) |
| | | 18 Oct 1999 (so far as not already in force for certain purposes)[5] (SI 1999/2860) |
| | | 29 Nov 1999 (so far as not already in force except for certain purposes)[6] (SI 1999/3178) |
| | | *Not yet in force* (exceptions noted above) |
| | (3) | 5 Jul 1999 (for certain purposes)[2] (SI 1999/1958) |
| | | 6 Sep 1999 (so far as not already in force for certain purposes[3] and so far as relates to the repeal of Social Security Administration Act 1992, s 61A) (subject to a saving) (SI 1999/2422) |
| | | 5 Oct 1999 (so far as not already in force for certain purposes)[4] (SI 1999/2739) |
| | | 18 Oct 1999 (so far as not already in force for certain purposes[5] and so far as relates to the repeal of Social Security Administration Act 1992, s 63) (subject to a saving) (SI 1999/2860) |
| | | 29 Nov 1999 (so far as not already in force for certain purposes)[6] (SI 1999/3178) |
| | | *Not yet in force* (exceptions noted above) |
| 40 | | 16 Nov 1998 (so far as it introduces the making of regulations) (subject to transitional provisions and savings) (SI 1998/2780) |
| | | 7 Dec 1998 (otherwise) (subject to transitional provisions and savings) (SI 1998/2780) |
| 41 | | 4 Mar 1999 (so far as authorising the making of regulations, and in so far as substitutes Child Support Act 1991, s 17(3), (5)) (SI 1999/528) |
| | | 1 Jun 1999 (otherwise) (SI 1999/1510) |
| 42 | | 4 Mar 1999 (so far as authorising the making of regulations, and in so far as substitutes Child Support Act 1991, s 20(4)–(6)) (SI 1999/528) |
| | | 1 Jun 1999 (otherwise) (SI 1999/1510) |
| 43 | | 4 Mar 1999 (so far as authorising the making of regulations and in so far as inserts Child Support Act 1991, ss 28ZA(2)(b), (4)(c), 28ZB(6)(c)) (SI 1999/528) |
| | | 1 Jun 1999 (otherwise) (SI 1999/1510) |
| 44 | | 4 Mar 1999 (so far as authorising the making of regulations and in so far as inserts Child Support Act 1991, s 28ZD) (SI 1999/528) |
| | | 1 Jun 1999 (otherwise) (SI 1999/1510) |
| 45 | | 4 Mar 1999 (so far as authorising the making of regulations and in so far as inserts Vaccine Damage Payments Act 1979, s 3A(1), (3), (4)) (SI 1999/528) |
| | | 18 Oct 1999 (so far as not already in force for certain purposes)[5] (SI 1999/2860) |
| | | *Not yet in force* (so far as inserts Vaccine Damage Payments Act 1979, s 3A(2), (5), (6), except for certain purposes)[5] |
| 46 | | 4 Mar 1999 (so far as authorising the making of regulations, and in so far as substitutes Vaccine Damage Payments Act 1979, s 4(2), (3)) (SI 1999/528) |

**Social Security Act 1998 (c 14)**—*contd*

|  |  |  |
|---|---|---|
|  |  | 18 Oct 1999 (so far as not already in force for certain purposes)[5] (SI 1999/2860) |
|  |  | *Not yet in force* (so far as substitutes Vaccine Damage Payments Act 1979, s 4(1), (4), except for certain purposes)[5] |
| 47 |  | 4 Mar 1999 (so far as authorising the making of regulations) (SI 1999/528) |
|  |  | 18 Oct 1999 (so far as not already in force for certain purposes)[5] (SI 1999/2860) |
|  |  | *Not yet in force* (otherwise) |
| 48, 49 |  | 8 Sep 1998 (SI 1998/2209) |
| 50 | (1) | 21 May 1998 (so far as relating to a sum which is chargeable to tax by virtue of Income and Corporation Taxes Act 1998, s 313) (s 87(2)) |
|  |  | 8 Sep 1998 (otherwise) (SI 1998/2209) |
|  | (2)–(4) | 21 May 1998 (s 87(2)) |
| 51 |  | 23 Feb 1999 (for the purpose of authorising the making of regulations) (SI 1999/418) |
|  |  | 6 Apr 1999 (otherwise) (SI 1999/418) |
| 52 |  | 8 Sep 1998 (SI 1998/2209) |
| 53 |  | 8 Sep 1998 (for the purpose of authorising the making of regulations or orders) (SI 1998/2209) |
|  |  | 6 Apr 1999 (otherwise) (SI 1998/2209) |
| 54 |  | 4 Mar 1999 (for the purpose of authorising the making of regulations or schemes) (SI 1999/526) |
|  |  | 6 Apr 1999 (otherwise) (SI 1999/526) |
| 55 |  | 8 Sep 1998 (SI 1998/2209) |
| 56 | (1) | 6 Apr 1999 (SI 1999/526) |
|  | (2) | 4 Mar 1999 (for the purpose of authorising the making of regulations or schemes) (SI 1999/526) |
|  |  | 6 Apr 1999 (otherwise) (SI 1999/526) |
| 57 |  | 4 Mar 1999 (for the purpose of authorising the making of regulations or schemes) (SI 1999/526) |
|  |  | 6 Apr 1999 (otherwise) (SI 1999/526) |
| 58 |  | *Never in force* (repealed) |
| 59 |  | 8 Sep 1998 (subject to a saving) (SI 1998/2209) |
| 60 |  | 4 Mar 1999 (for the purpose of authorising the making of regulations or schemes) (SI 1999/526) |
|  |  | 6 Apr 1999 (otherwise) (SI 1999/526) |
| 61 |  | 4 Mar 1999 (for the purpose of authorising the making of regulations or schemes, except so far as relates to Social Security Administration Act 1992, s 114A) (SI 1999/526) |
|  |  | 6 Apr 1999 (except so far as relates to Social Security Administration Act 1992, s 114A) (SI 1999/526) |
|  |  | *Never in force* (substitution of Social Security Administration Act 1992, s 114A) (repealed) |
| 62 |  | 6 Apr 1999 (SI 1999/526) |
| 63 |  | 4 Mar 1999 (for the purpose of authorising the making of regulations or schemes) (SI 1999/526) |
|  |  | 6 Apr 1999 (otherwise) (SI 1999/526) |
| 64 |  | 6 Apr 1999 (SI 1999/526) |
| 65 |  | 8 Sep 1998 (for purpose of authorising the making of regulations or orders) (SI 1998/2209) |
|  |  | 6 Apr 1999 (otherwise) (SI 1998/2209) |
| 66 |  | 21 May 1998 (s 87(2)) |
| 67 |  | 1 Oct 2006 (in respect of women whose expected week of confinement falls on or after 1 Apr 2007) (SI 2006/2376) |
|  |  | *Not yet in force* (otherwise) |
| 68 |  | 8 Sep 1998 (SI 1998/2209) |
| 69 |  | 21 May 1998 (s 87(2)) |
| 70, 71 |  | 5 Apr 1999 (subject to a transitional provision) (SI 1999/1055) |

**Social Security Act 1998 (c 14)**—*contd*

| | | |
|---|---|---|
| 72 | | 21 May 1998 (s 87(2)) |
| 73 | | 6 Apr 1999 (SI 1998/2209) |
| 74 | | 4 Mar 1999 (so far as authorising the making of regulations) (SI 1999/528) |
| | | 29 Nov 1999 (so far as not already in force except for certain purposes)[7] (SI 1999/3178) |
| | | *Not yet in force* (exceptions noted above) |
| 75 | | 5 Oct 1998 (SI 1998/2209) |
| 76 | | 16 Nov 1998 (subject to transitional provisions and savings) (SI 1998/2780) |
| 77–82 | | 21 May 1998 (s 87(2)) |
| 83 | | See Sch 6 below |
| 84, 85 | | 21 May 1998 (s 87(2)) |
| 86 | (1) | See Sch 7 below |
| | (2) | See Sch 8 below |
| 87 | | 21 May 1998 (s 87(2)) |
| Sch 1 | paras 1–6 | 1 Jun 1999 (SI 1999/1510) |
| | para 7 | 4 Mar 1999 (so far as authorising the making of regulations) (SI 1999/528) |
| | | 1 Jun 1999 (otherwise) (SI 1999/1510) |
| | paras 8, 9 | 1 Jun 1999 (SI 1999/1510) |
| | para 10 | 31 Mar 2000 (SI 1999/3178) |
| | paras 11, 12 | 4 Mar 1999 (so far as authorising the making of regulations) (SI 1999/528) |
| | | 1 Jun 1999 (otherwise) (SI 1999/1510) |
| | para 13 | 1 Jun 1999 (SI 1999/1510) |
| Sch 2 | para 1 | 18 Oct 1999 (for certain purposes)[5] (SI 1999/2860) |
| | | 29 Nov 1999 (so far as not already in force except for certain purposes)[6] (SI 1999/3178) |
| | | *Not yet in force* (exceptions noted above) |
| | para 2 | 29 Nov 1999 (except for certain purposes)[6] (SI 1999/3178) |
| | | *Not yet in force* (exceptions noted above) |
| | para 3 | 18 Oct 1999 (for certain purposes)[5] (SI 1999/2860) |
| | | 29 Nov 1999 (so far as not already in force except for certain purposes)[6] (SI 1999/3178) |
| | | *Not yet in force* (exceptions noted above) |
| | para 4 | 5 Jul 1999 (for certain purposes)[2] (SI 1999/1958) |
| | | 29 Nov 1999 (so far as not already in force except for certain purposes)[6] (SI 1999/3178) |
| | | *Not yet in force* (exceptions noted above) |
| | para 5 | 5 Jul 1999 (for certain purposes)[2] (SI 1999/1958) |
| | | 6 Sep 1999 (so far as not already in force for certain purposes)[3] (SI 1999/2422) |
| | | 18 Oct 1999 (so far as not already in force for certain purposes)[5] (SI 1999/2860) |
| | | 29 Nov 1999 (so far as not already in force except for certain purposes)[6] (SI 1999/3178) |
| | | *Not yet in force* (exceptions noted above) |
| | para 6(a) | 5 Jul 1999 (for certain purposes)[2] (SI 1999/1958) |
| | | 6 Sep 1999 (so far as not already in force for certain purposes)[3] (SI 1999/2422) |
| | | 5 Oct 1999 (so far as not already in force for certain purposes)[4] (SI 1999/2739) |
| | | 18 Oct 1999 (so far as not already in force for certain purposes)[5] (SI 1999/2860) |
| | | 29 Nov 1999 (so far as not already in force except for certain purposes)[6] (SI 1999/3178) |
| | | *Not yet in force* (exceptions noted above) |
| | para 6(b)(i) | 29 Nov 1999 (except for certain purposes)[6] (SI 1999/3178) |
| | | *Not yet in force* (exceptions noted above) |

**Social Security Act 1998 (c 14)**—*contd*

para 6(b)(ii)  18 Oct 1999 (for certain purposes)[5] (SI 1999/2860)

29 Nov 1999 (so far as not already in force except for certain purposes)[6] (SI 1999/3178)

*Not yet in force* (exceptions noted above)

para 7  5 Jul 1999 (for certain purposes)[2] (SI 1999/1958)

18 Oct 1999 (so far as not already in force for certain purposes)[5] (SI 1999/2860)

29 Nov 1999 (so far as not already in force except for certain purposes)[6] (SI 1999/3178)

*Not yet in force* (exceptions noted above)

para 8  5 Jul 1999 (for certain purposes)[2] (SI 1999/1958)

5 Oct 1999 (so far as not already in force for certain purposes)[4] (SI 1999/2739)

18 Oct 1999 (so far as not already in force for certain purposes)[5] (SI 1999/2860)

29 Nov 1999 (so far as not already in force except for certain purposes)[6] (SI 1999/3178)

*Not yet in force* (exceptions noted above)

para 9  4 Mar 1999 (so far as authorising the making of regulations) (SI 1999/528)

5 Jul 1999 (for certain purposes)[2] (SI 1999/1958)

6 Sep 1999 (so far as not already in force for certain purposes)[3] (SI 1999/2422)

5 Oct 1999 (so far as not already in force for certain purposes)[4] (SI 1999/2739)

18 Oct 1999 (so far as not already in force for certain purposes)[5] (SI 1999/2860)

29 Nov 1999 (so far as not already in force except for certain purposes)[6] (SI 1999/3178)

*Not yet in force* (exceptions noted above)

Sch 3  para 1  4 Mar 1999 (so far as authorising the making of regulations) (SI 1999/528)

5 Jul 1999 (for certain purposes)[2] (SI 1999/1958)

6 Sep 1999 (so far as not already in force for certain purposes)[3] (SI 1999/2422)

5 Oct 1999 (so far as not already in force for certain purposes)[4] (SI 1999/2739)

18 Oct 1999 (so far as not already in force for certain purposes)[5] (SI 1999/2860)

29 Nov 1999 (so far as not already in force except for certain purposes)[6] (SI 1999/3178)

*Not yet in force* (exceptions noted above)

para 2  5 Jul 1999 (for certain purposes)[2] (SI 1999/1958)

6 Sep 1999 (so far as not already in force for certain purposes)[3] (SI 1999/2422)

5 Oct 1999 (so far as not already in force for certain purposes)[4] (SI 1999/2739)

18 Oct 1999 (so far as not already in force for certain purposes)[5] (SI 1999/2860)

29 Nov 1999 (so far as not already in force except for certain purposes)[6] (SI 1999/3178)

*Not yet in force* (exceptions noted above)

para 3(a)  5 Jul 1999 (for certain purposes)[2] (SI 1999/1958)

6 Sep 1999 (so far as not already in force for certain purposes)[3] (SI 1999/2422)

5 Oct 1999 (so far as not already in force for certain purposes)[4] (SI 1999/2739)

18 Oct 1999 (so far as not already in force for certain purposes)[5] (SI 1999/2860)

**Social Security Act 1998 (c 14)**—*contd*

|  |  |
|---|---|
|  | 29 Nov 1999 (so far as not already in force except for certain purposes)[6] (SI 1999/3178) |
|  | *Not yet in force* (exceptions noted above) |
| para 3(b) | 18 Oct 1999 (for certain purposes)[5] (SI 1999/2860) |
|  | 29 Nov 1999 (so far as not already in force except for certain purposes)[6] (SI 1999/3178) |
|  | *Not yet in force* (exceptions noted above) |
| para 3(c) | 5 Jul 1999 (for certain purposes)[2] (SI 1999/1958) |
|  | 6 Sep 1999 (so far as not already in force for certain purposes)[3] (SI 1999/2422) |
|  | 5 Oct 1999 (so far as not already in force for certain purposes)[4] (SI 1999/2739) |
|  | 18 Oct 1999 (so far as not already in force for certain purposes)[5] (SI 1999/2860) |
|  | 29 Nov 1999 (so far as not already in force except for certain purposes)[6] (SI 1999/3178) |
|  | *Not yet in force* (exceptions noted above) |
| para 3(d) | 18 Oct 1999 (for certain purposes)[5] (SI 1999/2860) |
|  | 29 Nov 1999 (so far as not already in force except for certain purposes)[6] (SI 1999/3178) |
|  | *Never in force* (exceptions noted above) (repealed) |
| para 4 | 4 Mar 1999 (so far as authorising the making of regulations) (SI 1999/528) |
|  | 5 Jul 1999 (for certain purposes)[2] (SI 1999/1958) |
|  | 6 Sep 1999 (so far as not already in force for certain purposes)[3] (SI 1999/2422) |
|  | 5 Oct 1999 (so far as not already in force for certain purposes)[4] (SI 1999/2739) |
|  | 18 Oct 1999 (so far as not already in force for certain purposes)[5] (SI 1999/2860) |
|  | 29 Nov 1999 (so far as not already in force except for certain purposes)[6] (SI 1999/3178) |
|  | *Not yet in force* (exceptions noted above) |
| para 5 | 5 Jul 1999 (for certain purposes[2], except so far as relates to Social Security Administration Act 1992, s 71A) (SI 1999/1958) |
|  | 6 Sep 1999 (so far as not already in force for certain purposes[3], except so far as relates to Social Security Administration Act 1992, s 71A) (SI 1999/2422) |
|  | 5 Oct 1999 (so far as not already in force for certain purposes[4], except so far as relates to Social Security Administration Act 1992, s 71A) (SI 1999/2739) |
|  | 18 Oct 1999 (so far as not already in force for certain purposes)[5] (SI 1999/2860) |
|  | 29 Nov 1999 (so far as not already in force except for certain purposes)[6] (SI 1999/3178) |
|  | *Not yet in force* (exceptions noted above) |
| para 6 | 5 Jul 1999 (for certain purposes)[2] (SI 1999/1958) |
|  | 6 Sep 1999 (so far as not already in force for certain purposes)[3] (SI 1999/2422) |
|  | 5 Oct 1999 (so far as not already in force for certain purposes)[4] (SI 1999/2739) |
|  | 18 Oct 1999 (so far as not already in force for certain purposes)[5] (SI 1999/2860) |
|  | 29 Nov 1999 (so far as not already in force except for certain purposes)[6] (SI 1999/3178) |
|  | *Not yet in force* (exceptions noted above) |
| para 7 | 5 Jul 1999 (for certain purposes)[2] (SI 1999/1958) |
|  | 29 Nov 1999 (so far as not already in force except for certain purposes)[6] (SI 1999/3178) |
|  | *Not yet in force* (exceptions noted above) |

## Social Security Act 1998 (c 14)—*contd*

| | | |
|---|---|---|
| | para 8 | 18 Oct 1999 (for certain purposes)[5] (SI 1999/2860) |
| | | 29 Nov 1999 (so far as not already in force except for certain purposes)[6] (SI 1999/3178) |
| | | *Not yet in force* (exceptions noted above) (repealed in part) |
| | para 9 | 4 Mar 1999 (so far as authorising the making of regulations) (SI 1999/528) |
| | | 5 Jul 1999 (for certain purposes)[2] (SI 1999/1958) |
| | | 6 Sep 1999 (so far as not already in force for certain purposes)[3] (SI 1999/2422) |
| | | 5 Oct 1999 (so far as not already in force for certain purposes)[4] (SI 1999/2739) |
| | | 18 Oct 1999 (so far as not already in force for certain purposes)[5] (SI 1999/2860) |
| | | 29 Nov 1999 (so far as not already in force except for certain purposes)[6] (SI 1999/3178) |
| | | *Not yet in force* (exceptions noted above) |
| | paras 10–15 | 29 Nov 1999 (so far as not already in force except for certain purposes)[6] (SI 1999/3178) |
| | | *Never in force* (exceptions referred to above) (repealed) |
| | paras 16, 17 | 18 Oct 1999 (for certain purposes)[5] (SI 1999/2860) |
| | | 29 Nov 1999 (so far as not already in force except for certain purposes)[6] (SI 1999/3178) |
| | | *Not yet in force* (exceptions noted above) |
| | paras 18–29 | 29 Nov 1999 (except for certain purposes)[6] (SI 1999/3178) |
| | | *Never in force* (exceptions referred to above) (repealed) |
| Sch 4 | paras 1–5 | 5 Jul 1999 (for certain purposes)[2] (SI 1999/1958) |
| | | 6 Sep 1999 (so far as not already in force for certain purposes)[3] (SI 1999/2422) |
| | | 5 Oct 1999 (so far as not already in force for certain purposes)[4] (SI 1999/2739) |
| | | 18 Oct 1999 (so far as not already in force for certain purposes)[5] (SI 1999/2860) |
| | | 29 Nov 1999 (so far as not already in force except for certain purposes)[6] (SI 1999/3178) |
| | | *Never in force* (exceptions noted above) (repealed) |
| | para 6 | 4 Mar 1999 (so far as authorising the making of regulations) (SI 1999/528) |
| | | 5 Jul 1999 (for certain purposes)[2] (SI 1999/1958) |
| | | 6 Sep 1999 (so far as not already in force for certain purposes)[3] (SI 1999/2422) |
| | | 5 Oct 1999 (so far as not already in force for certain purposes)[4] (SI 1999/2739) |
| | | 18 Oct 1999 (so far as not already in force for certain purposes)[5] (SI 1999/2860) |
| | | 29 Nov 1999 (so far as not already in force except for certain purposes)[6] (SI 1999/3178) |
| | | *Never in force* (exceptions noted above) (repealed) |
| | para 7 | 5 Jul 1999 (for certain purposes)[2] (SI 1999/1958) |
| | | 6 Sep 1999 (so far as not already in force for certain purposes)[3] (SI 1999/2422) |
| | | 5 Oct 1999 (so far as not already in force for certain purposes)[4] (SI 1999/2739) |
| | | 18 Oct 1999 (so far as not already in force for certain purposes)[5] (SI 1999/2860) |
| | | 29 Nov 1999 (so far as not already in force except for certain purposes)[6] (SI 1999/3178) |
| | | *Never in force* (exceptions noted above) (repealed) |
| | para 8 | 4 Mar 1999 (so far as authorising the making of regulations) (SI 1999/528) |
| | | 5 Jul 1999 (for certain purposes)[2] (SI 1999/1958) |

**Social Security Act 1998 (c 14)**—*contd*

|  |  |  |
|---|---|---|
| | | 6 Sep 1999 (so far as not already in force for certain purposes)[3] (SI 1999/2422) |
| | | 5 Oct 1999 (so far as not already in force for certain purposes)[4] (SI 1999/2739) |
| | | 18 Oct 1999 (so far as not already in force for certain purposes)[5] (SI 1999/2860) |
| | | 29 Nov 1999 (so far as not already in force except for certain purposes)[6] (SI 1999/3178) |
| | | *Never in force* (exceptions noted above) (repealed) |
| Sch 5 | | 4 Mar 1999 (so far as authorising the making of regulations) (SI 1999/528) |
| | | 5 Jul 1999 (for certain purposes)[2] (SI 1999/1958) |
| | | 6 Sep 1999 (so far as not already in force for certain purposes)[3] (SI 1999/2422) |
| | | 5 Oct 1999 (so far as not already in force for certain purposes)[4] (SI 1999/2739) |
| | | 18 Oct 1999 (so far as not already in force for certain purposes)[5] (SI 1999/2860) |
| | | 29 Nov 1999 (so far as not already in force except for certain purposes)[6] (SI 1999/3178) |
| | | *Not yet in force* (exceptions noted above) |
| Sch 6 | | 21 May 1998 (s 87(2)) |
| Sch 7 | paras 1, 2 | 1 Jun 1999 (SI 1999/1510) |
| | para 3 | *Not yet in force* (sub-para (1) repealed; sub-para (2) superseded) |
| | para 4(1) | 29 Nov 1999 (except for certain purposes)[6] (SI 1999/3178) |
| | | *Not yet in force* (exceptions noted above) |
| | para 4(2) | 1 Jun 1999 (so far as applies to the entries relating to regional or other full-time chairmen of child support appeal tribunals, the Chief Child Support Officer and members of a panel appointed under Tribunals and Inquiries Act 1992, s 6, of persons to act as chairmen of child support appeal tribunals) (SI 1999/1510) |
| | | 18 Oct 1999 (so far as not already in force for certain purposes[5] as applies to the entries relating to regional or other full-time chairmen of disability appeal tribunals, members of a panel appointed under Tribunals and Inquiries Act 1992, s 6, of persons to act as chairmen of disability appeal tribunals and members of a panel of persons appointed to serve on a vaccine damage tribunal) (SI 1999/2860) |
| | | 29 Nov 1999 (so far as not already in force except for certain purposes)[6] (SI 1999/3178) |
| | | *Not yet in force* (exceptions noted above) |
| | para 4(3) | 1 Jun 1999 (SI 1999/1510) |
| | paras 5–7 | 18 Oct 1999 (for certain purposes)[5] (SI 1999/2860) |
| | | *Not yet in force* (otherwise) |
| | paras 8, 9 | 4 Mar 1999 (so far as authorising the making of regulations) (SI 1999/528) |
| | | 18 Oct 1999 (so far as not already in force for certain purposes)[5] (SI 1999/2860) |
| | | *Not yet in force* (otherwise) |
| | para 10 | 18 Oct 1999 (for certain purposes)[5] (SI 1999/2860) |
| | | *Not yet in force* (otherwise) |
| | para 11 | 5 Jul 1999 (for certain purposes)[2] (SI 1999/1958) |
| | | 6 Sep 1999 (so far as not already in force for certain purposes)[3] (SI 1999/2422) |
| | | 29 Nov 1999 (so far as not already in force except for certain purposes)[6] (SI 1999/3178) |
| | | *Never in force* (exceptions noted above) (repealed) |
| | paras 12–14 | 6 Apr 1999 (SI 1999/526) |
| | para 15 | 18 Oct 1999 (for certain purposes)[5] (SI 1999/2860) |

**Social Security Act 1998 (c 14)**—*contd*

| | |
|---|---|
| | 29 Nov 1999 (so far as not already in force except for certain purposes)[6] (SI 1999/3178) |
| | *Not yet in force* (exceptions noted above) |
| para 16 | 6 Apr 1999 (SI 1999/418) |
| para 17 | 18 Oct 1999 (for certain purposes)[5] (SI 1999/2860) |
| | 29 Nov 1999 (so far as not already in force except for certain purposes)[6] (SI 1999/3178) |
| | *Not yet in force* (exceptions noted above) |
| paras 18–26 | 1 Jun 1999 (SI 1999/1510) |
| para 27(a) | 8 Sep 1998 (SI 1998/2209) |
| para 27(b) | 1 Jun 1999 (SI 1999/1510) |
| paras 28–34 | 1 Jun 1999 (SI 1999/1510) |
| para 35(1) | 1 Jun 1999 (SI 1999/1510) |
| para 35(2) | 4 Mar 1999 (so far as authorising the making of regulations) (SI 1999/528) |
| | 1 Jun 1999 (otherwise) (SI 1999/1510) |
| paras 36–38 | 1 Jun 1999 (SI 1999/1510) |
| paras 39, 40 | 4 Mar 1999 (so far as authorising the making of regulations) (SI 1999/528) |
| | 1 Jun 1999 (otherwise) (SI 1999/1510) |
| paras 41, 42 | 1 Jun 1999 (SI 1999/1510) |
| para 43(1), (2) | 1 Jun 1999 (SI 1999/1510) |
| para 43(3) | 4 Mar 1999 (so far as authorising the making of regulations) (SI 1999/528) |
| | 1 Jun 1999 (otherwise) (SI 1999/1510) |
| para 43(4) | 1 Jun 1999 (SI 1999/1510) |
| para 44 | 4 Mar 1999 (so far as authorising the making of regulations and in so far as relates to the insertions of Child Support Act 1991, ss 46A(2), 46B) (SI 1999/528) |
| | 1 Jun 1999 (otherwise) (SI 1999/1510) |
| para 45 | 1 Jun 1999 (SI 1999/1510) |
| para 46(a) | 16 Nov 1998 (subject to transitional provisions and savings) (SI 1998/2780) |
| para 46(b) | 4 Mar 1999 (so far as authorising the making of regulations) (SI 1999/528) |
| | 1 Jun 1999 (otherwise) (SI 1999/1510) |
| para 47(a) | 1 Jun 1999 (SI 1999/1510) |
| para 46(b) | 1 Jun 1999 (so far as relates to the definitions "Chief Child Support Officer", "child support appeal tribunal" and "child support officer") (SI 1999/1510) |
| | 29 Nov 1999 (so far as not already in force except for certain purposes)[6] (SI 1999/3178) |
| | *Never in force* (exceptions noted above) (repealed) |
| para 48 | 1 Jun 1999 (SI 1999/1510) |
| para 49 | 8 Sep 1998 (SI 1998/2209) |
| paras 50, 51 | 1 Jun 1999 (SI 1999/1510) |
| para 52(1)–(3) | 1 Jun 1999 (SI 1999/1510) |
| para 52(4) | 4 Mar 1999 (so far as authorising the making of regulations) (SI 1999/528) |
| | 1 Jun 1999 (otherwise) (SI 1999/1510) |
| para 53(1)–(4) | 1 Jun 1999 (SI 1999/1510) |
| para 53(5) | 4 Mar 1999 (so far as authorising the making of regulations) (SI 1999/528) |
| | 1 Jun 1999 (otherwise) (SI 1999/1510) |
| para 53(6) | 1 Jun 1999 (SI 1999/1510) |
| para 54 | 4 Mar 1999 (so far as authorising the making of regulations) (SI 1999/528) |
| | 1 Jun 1999 (otherwise) (SI 1999/1510) |
| para 55 | 18 Oct 1999 (for certain purposes)[5] (SI 1999/2860) |

**Social Security Act 1998 (c 14)**—*contd*

|  |  |
|---|---|
|  | 29 Nov 1999 (so far as not already in force except for certain purposes)[6] (SI 1999/3178) |
|  | *Not yet in force* (exceptions noted above) |
| para 56 | 8 Sep 1998 (for purpose of authorising the making of regulations or orders) (SI 1998/2209) |
|  | 6 Apr 1999 (otherwise) (SI 1998/2209) |
| para 57 | 6 Apr 1999 (SI 1998/2209) |
| para 58(1) | 6 Apr 1999 (SI 1999/418) |
| para 58(2) | 6 Apr 1999 (SI 1998/2209) |
| paras 59–61 | 6 Apr 1999 (SI 1999/418) |
| para 62 | 6 Sep 1999 (for certain purposes)[3] (SI 1999/2422) |
|  | *Not yet in force* (otherwise) |
| para 63 | 5 Jul 1999 (for certain purposes, coming into force immediately before Social Security Contributions (Transfer of Functions) Act 1999, Sch 7, para 4 comes into force)[2] (SI 1999/1958) |
| paras 64, 65 | 5 Jul 1999 (for certain purposes)[2] (SI 1999/1958) |
|  | *Not yet in force* (otherwise) |
| paras 66–70 | 5 Jul 1999 (for certain purposes)[2] (SI 1999/1958) |
|  | 6 Sep 1999 (so far as not already in force for certain purposes)[3] (SI 1999/2422) |
|  | 18 Oct 1999 (so far as not already in force for certain purposes)[5] (SI 1999/2860) |
|  | 29 Nov 1999 (so far as not already in force except for certain purposes)[6] (SI 1999/3178) |
|  | *Not yet in force* (exceptions noted above) |
| para 71(a) | 5 Jul 1999 (for certain purposes)[2] (SI 1999/1958) |
|  | 6 Sep 1999 (so far as not already in force for certain purposes)[3] (SI 1999/2422) |
|  | 18 Oct 1999 (so far as not already in force for certain purposes)[5] (SI 1999/2860) |
|  | 29 Nov 1999 (so far as not already in force except for certain purposes)[6] (SI 1999/3178) |
|  | *Not yet in force* (exceptions noted above) |
| para 71(b), (c) | 6 Apr 1999 (SI 1999/418) |
| para 71(d) | 8 Sep 1998 (for purpose of authorising the making of regulations or orders) (SI 1998/2209) |
|  | 6 Apr 1999 (otherwise) (SI 1998/2209) |
| para 71(e) | 6 Apr 1999 (SI 1999/418) |
| para 72(1), (2) | 29 Nov 1999 (except for certain purposes)[6] (SI 1999/3178) |
|  | *Not yet in force* (exceptions noted above) |
| para 72(3), (4) | 5 Apr 1999 (subject to a transitional provision) (SI 1999/1055) |
| para 72(5) | 29 Nov 1999 (except for certain purposes)[6] (SI 1999/3178) |
|  | *Not yet in force* (exceptions noted above) |
| para 73 | 29 Nov 1999 (except for certain purposes)[6] (SI 1999/3178) |
|  | *Not yet in force* (exceptions noted above) |
| paras 74, 75 | 6 Apr 1999 (SI 1999/418) |
| para 76 | 6 Sep 1999 (for certain purposes)[3] (SI 1999/2422) |
|  | *Not yet in force* (otherwise) |
| para 77(1) | 6 Apr 1999 (SI 1998/2209) |
| para 77(2)–(5) | 6 Apr 1999 (SI 1999/418) |
| para 77(6) | 8 Sep 1998 (SI 1998/2209) |
| para 77(7)–(9) | 8 Sep 1998 (for purpose of authorising the making of regulations or orders) (SI 1998/2209) |
|  | 6 Apr 1999 (otherwise) (SI 1998/2209) |
| para 77(10) | *Never in force* (repealed) |
| para 77(11) | 8 Sep 1998 (for purpose of authorising the making of regulations or orders) (SI 1998/2209) |
|  | 6 Apr 1999 (otherwise) (SI 1998/2209) |
| para 77(12) | 6 Apr 1999 (SI 1998/2209) |
| para 77(13) | *Never in force* (repealed) |

**Social Security Act 1998 (c 14)**—*contd*

| | |
|---|---|
| para 77(14)–(16) | 8 Sep 1998 (for purpose of authorising the making of regulations or orders) (SI 1998/2209) |
| | 6 Apr 1999 (otherwise) (SI 1998/2209) |
| para 78 | 6 Sep 1999 (for certain purposes)[3] (SI 1999/2422) |
| | *Never in force* (otherwise) (repealed) |
| para 79(1)(a) | 5 Jul 1999 (for certain purposes)[2] (SI 1999/1958) |
| | 6 Sep 1999 (so far as not already in force for certain purposes)[3] (SI 1999/2422) |
| | 5 Oct 1999 (so far as not already in force for certain purposes)[4] (SI 1999/2739) |
| | 18 Oct 1999 (so far as not already in force for certain purposes)[5] (SI 1999/2860) |
| | 29 Nov 1999 (so far as not already in force except for certain purposes)[6] (SI 1999/3178) |
| | *Not yet in force* (exceptions noted above) |
| para 79(1)(b) | 5 Jul 1999 (for certain purposes)[2] (SI 1999/1958) |
| | 6 Sep 1999 (so far as not already in force for certain purposes)[3] (SI 1999/2422) |
| | 5 Oct 1999 (so far as not already in force for certain purposes)[4] (SI 1999/2739) |
| | 18 Oct 1999 (so far as not already in force for certain purposes)[5] (SI 1999/2860) |
| | 29 Nov 1999 (so far as not already in force except for certain purposes)[6] (SI 1999/3178) |
| | 2 Jul 2001 (in so far as relates to housing benefit) (SI 2001/2316) |
| | *Not yet in force* (exceptions noted above) |
| para 79(2) | 2 Jul 2001 (SI 2001/2316) |
| para 80 | 2 Jul 2001 (SI 2001/2316) |
| para 81 | 5 Jul 1999 (for certain purposes)[2] (SI 1999/1958) |
| | 6 Sep 1999 (so far as not already in force for certain purposes)[3] (SI 1999/2422) |
| | 5 Oct 1999 (so far as not already in force for certain purposes)[4] (SI 1999/2739) |
| | 18 Oct 1999 (so far as not already in force for certain purposes)[5] (SI 1999/2860) |
| | 29 Nov 1999 (so far as not already in force except for certain purposes)[6] (SI 1999/3178) |
| | *Not yet in force* (exceptions noted above) (sub-para (2) repealed) |
| para 82 | 18 Oct 1999 (for certain purposes)[5] (SI 1999/2860) |
| | *Not yet in force* (otherwise) |
| para 83 | 29 Nov 1999 (except for certain purposes)[6] (SI 1999/3178) |
| | *Not yet in force* (exceptions noted above) |
| para 84 | 5 Jul 1999 (for certain purposes)[2] (SI 1999/1958) |
| | 29 Nov 1999 (so far as not already in force except for certain purposes)[6] (SI 1999/3178) |
| | *Not yet in force* (exceptions noted above) |
| para 85 | 6 Apr 1999 (SI 1999/526) |
| para 86(1) | 6 Apr 1999 (SI 1999/526) |
| para 86(2)(a) | 6 Apr 1999 (SI 1998/2209) |
| para 86(2)(b) | 6 Apr 1999 (SI 1999/526) |
| para 86(3)(a) | 6 Apr 1999 (SI 1998/2209) |
| para 86(3)(b) | 6 Apr 1999 (SI 1999/526) |
| para 86(4) | 6 Apr 1999 (SI 1998/2209) |
| para 86(5) | 6 Apr 1999 (SI 1999/526) |
| para 86(6) | 6 Apr 1999 (SI 1998/2209) |
| para 87 | 6 Apr 1999 (SI 1999/526) |
| paras 88, 89 | 5 Jul 1999 (for certain purposes)[2] (SI 1999/1958) |
| | 6 Sep 1999 (so far as not already in force for certain purposes)[3] (SI 1999/2422) |

**Social Security Act 1998 (c 14)**—*contd*

|  |  |
|---|---|
|  | 5 Oct 1999 (so far as not already in force for certain purposes)[4] (SI 1999/2739) |
|  | 18 Oct 1999 (so far as not already in force for certain purposes)[5] (SI 1999/2860) |
|  | 29 Nov 1999 (so far as not already in force except for certain purposes)[6] (SI 1999/3178) |
|  | *Not yet in force* (exceptions noted above) |
| para 90 | 6 Apr 1999 (SI 1999/418) |
| para 91 | 8 Sep 1998 (for purpose of authorising the making of regulations or orders) (SI 1998/2209) |
|  | 6 Apr 1999 (otherwise) (SI 1998/2209) |
| paras 92–94 | 6 Apr 1999 (SI 1999/418) |
| para 95 | 29 Nov 1999 (except for certain purposes)[6] (SI 1999/3178) |
|  | *Not yet in force* (exceptions noted above) |
| para 96 | 18 Oct 1999 (for certain purposes)[5] (SI 1999/2860) |
|  | *Not yet in force* (otherwise) |
| para 97 | 29 Nov 1999 (except for certain purposes)[6] (SI 1999/3178) |
|  | *Not yet in force* (exceptions noted above) |
| para 98 | 18 Oct 1999 (for certain purposes)[5] (SI 1999/2860) |
|  | *Not yet in force* (otherwise) |
| para 99(1) | 8 Sep 1998 (SI 1998/2209) |
| para 99(2) | 6 Apr 1999 (SI 1999/526) |
| para 99(3) | 6 Apr 1999 (SI 1999/418) |
| para 99(4) | 8 Sep 1998 (for purpose of authorising the making of regulations or orders) (SI 1998/2209) |
|  | 6 Apr 1999 (otherwise) (SI 1998/2209) |
| para 100(1) | 6 Apr 1999 (SI 1998/2209) |
| para 100(2) | 6 Apr 1999 (SI 1999/526) |
| para 101 | 5 Jul 1999 (for certain purposes)[2] (SI 1999/1958) |
|  | 29 Nov 1999 (so far as not already in force except for certain purposes)[6] (SI 1999/3178) |
|  | *Not yet in force* (exceptions noted above) |
| para 102 | 5 Jul 1999 (for certain purposes, coming into force immediately before Social Security Contributions (Transfer of Functions) Act 1999, Sch 7, para 14 comes into force)[2] (SI 1999/1958) |
|  | 6 Sep 1999 (so far as not already in force for certain purposes)[3] (SI 1999/2422) |
|  | 18 Oct 1999 (so far as not already in force for certain purposes)[5] (SI 1999/2860) |
|  | 29 Nov 1999 (so far as not already in force except for certain purposes)[6] (SI 1999/3178) |
|  | *Not yet in force* (exceptions noted above) |
| para 103 | 29 Nov 1999 (except for certain purposes)[6] (SI 1999/3178) |
|  | *Not yet in force* (exceptions noted above) |
| para 104 | 4 Mar 1999 (SI 1999/528) |
| para 105 | 5 Jul 1999 (subject to transitional provisions and savings) (SI 1999/1958) |
| para 106 | 5 Jul 1999 (for certain purposes)[2] (SI 1999/1958) |
|  | 5 Oct 1999 (so far as not already in force for certain purposes)[4] (SI 1999/2739) |
|  | 18 Oct 1999 (so far as not already in force for certain purposes)[5] (SI 1999/2860) |
|  | 29 Nov 1999 (so far as not already in force except for certain purposes)[6] (SI 1999/3178) |
|  | *Never in force* (exceptions noted above) (spent) |
| paras 107, 108 | 5 Jul 1999 (for certain purposes)[2] (SI 1999/1958) |
|  | 6 Sep 1999 (so far as not already in force for certain purposes)[3] (SI 1999/2422) |
|  | 5 Oct 1999 (so far as not already in force for certain purposes)[4] (SI 1999/2739) |

**Social Security Act 1998 (c 14)**—*contd*

| | |
|---|---|
| | 18 Oct 1999 (so far as not already in force for certain purposes)[5] (SI 1999/2860) |
| | 29 Nov 1999 (so far as not already in force except for certain purposes)[6] (SI 1999/3178) |
| | *Not yet in force* (exceptions noted above) |
| para 109 | 6 Sep 1999 (for certain purposes)[3] (SI 1999/2422) |
| | 5 Oct 1999 (so far as not already in force for certain purposes)[4] (SI 1999/2739) |
| | 18 Oct 1999 (so far as not already in force for certain purposes)[5] (SI 1999/2860) |
| | 29 Nov 1999 (so far as not already in force except for certain purposes)[6] (SI 1999/3178) |
| | *Not yet in force* (exceptions noted above) |
| para 110(1)(a) | 8 Sep 1998 (for purpose of authorising the making of regulations or orders) (SI 1998/2209) |
| | 6 Apr 1999 (otherwise) (SI 1998/2209) |
| para 110(1)(b) | 6 Apr 1999 (SI 1999/418) |
| para 110(2) | 29 Nov 1999 (except for certain purposes)[6] (SI 1999/3178) |
| | *Not yet in force* (exceptions noted above) |
| para 111(a) | 29 Nov 1999 (except for certain purposes)[6] (SI 1999/3178) |
| | *Not yet in force* (exceptions noted above) |
| para 111(b) | 5 Jul 1999 (for certain purposes)[2] (SI 1999/1958) |
| | 29 Nov 1999 (so far as not already in force except for certain purposes)[6] (SI 1999/3178) |
| | *Not yet in force* (exceptions noted above) |
| para 112 | 6 Sep 1999 (so far as not already in force for certain purposes)[3] (SI 1999/2422) |
| | 5 Oct 1999 (so far as not already in force for certain purposes)[4] (SI 1999/2739) |
| | 29 Nov 1999 (so far as not already in force except for certain purposes)[6] (SI 1999/3178) |
| | *Not yet in force* (exceptions noted above) |
| para 113 | 29 Nov 1999 (except for certain purposes)[6] (SI 1999/3178) |
| | *Not yet in force* (exceptions noted above) (sub-para (b) repealed) |
| para 114 | 8 Sep 1998 (for purpose of authorising the making of regulations or orders) (SI 1998/2209) |
| | 6 Apr 1999 (otherwise) (SI 1998/2209) |
| para 115 | 5 Jul 1999 (for certain purposes)[2] (SI 1999/1958) |
| | *Not yet in force* (otherwise) |
| para 116 | 29 Nov 1999 (except for certain purposes)[6] (SI 1999/3178) |
| | *Not yet in force* (exceptions noted above) |
| para 117 | 18 Oct 1999 (for certain purposes)[5] (SI 1999/2860) |
| | 29 Nov 1999 (so far as not already in force except for certain purposes)[6] (SI 1999/3178) |
| | *Not yet in force* (exceptions noted above) |
| para 118(1) | 1 Jun 1999 (so far as substitutes words "paragraph 7(b)" for the words "paragraph 7") (SI 1999/1510) |
| | 18 Oct 1999 (for certain purposes[5] so far as substitutes for the words "paragraph 38(a), 41(b), 41(e) or 43" the words "paragraph 38(a)") (SI 1999/2860) |
| | 29 Nov 1999 (so far as not already in force except for certain purposes)[6] (SI 1999/3178) |
| | *Not yet in force* (exceptions noted above) |
| para 118(2) | 18 Oct 1999 (for certain purposes[5] so far as relates to the tribunals specified in Tribunals and Inquiries Act 1992, Sch 1, para 41(b)) (SI 1999/2860) |
| | 29 Nov 1999 (so far as not already in force except for certain purposes)[6] (SI 1999/3178) |
| | *Not yet in force* (exceptions noted above) |
| para 119 | 18 Oct 1999 (for certain purposes)[5] (SI 1999/2860) |

**Social Security Act 1998 (c 14)**—*contd*

|  |  |
|---|---|
| | *Not yet in force* (otherwise) |
| para 120(a) | *Not yet in force* |
| para 120(b) | 29 Nov 1999 (except for certain purposes)[6] (SI 1999/3178) |
| | *Not yet in force* (exceptions noted above) |
| para 121(1) | 4 Mar 1999 (so far as authorising the making of regulations) (SI 1999/528) |
| | 1 Jun 1999 (otherwise) (SI 1999/1510) |
| para 121(2)(a) | 4 Mar 1999 (so far as authorising the making of regulations) (SI 1999/528) |
| | 6 Sep 1999 (so far as not already in force for certain purposes)[3] (SI 1999/2422) |
| | 5 Oct 1999 (so far as not already in force for certain purposes)[4] (SI 1999/2739) |
| | 18 Oct 1999 (so far as not already in force for certain purposes[5] and so far as relates to Tribunals and Inquiries Act 1992, Sch 1, para 41(b), (e)) (SI 1999/2860) |
| | 29 Nov 1999 (so far as not already in force except for certain purposes)[6] (SI 1999/3178) |
| | *Not yet in force* (exceptions noted above) |
| para 121(2)(b) | 4 Mar 1999 (so far as authorising the making of regulations) (SI 1999/528) |
| | 18 Oct 1999 (so far as not already in force for certain purposes[5] and so far as relates to Tribunals and Inquiries Act 1992, Sch 1, para 41(b), (e)) (SI 1999/2860) |
| | 29 Nov 1999 (so far as not already in force except for certain purposes)[6] (SI 1999/3178) |
| | *Not yet in force* (exceptions noted above) |
| para 121(2)(c) | 4 Mar 1999 (so far as authorising the making of regulations) (SI 1999/528) |
| | 6 Sep 1999 (so far as not already in force for certain purposes)[3] (SI 1999/2422) |
| | 5 Oct 1999 (so far as not already in force for certain purposes)[4] (SI 1999/2739) |
| | 29 Nov 1999 (so far as not already in force except for certain purposes)[6] (SI 1999/3178) |
| | *Not yet in force* (exceptions noted above) |
| para 122 | 1 Jun 1999 (SI 1999/1510) |
| para 123(1)(a) | 6 Sep 1999 (for certain purposes)[3] (SI 1999/2422) |
| | 5 Oct 1999 (so far as not already in force for certain purposes)[4] (SI 1999/2739) |
| | 29 Nov 1999 (so far as not already in force except for certain purposes)[6] (SI 1999/3178) |
| | *Not yet in force* (exceptions noted above) |
| para 123(1)(b) | 1 Jun 1999 (SI 1999/1510) |
| para 123(2) | 1 Jun 1999 (so far as it applies to the entry "Chairman of child support appeal tribunals") (SI 1999/1510) |
| | 18 Oct 1999 (for certain purposes[5] and so far as it applies to the entries relating to chairmen of disability appeal tribunals in Judicial Pensions and Retirement Act 1993, Sch 1, Pt II) (SI 1999/2860) |
| | 29 Nov 1999 (so far as not already in force except for certain purposes)[6] (SI 1999/3178) |
| | *Not yet in force* (exceptions noted above) |
| para 124(1)(a) | 6 Sep 1999 (for certain purposes)[3] (SI 1999/2422) |
| | 5 Oct 1999 (so far as not already in force for certain purposes)[4] (SI 1999/2739) |
| | 29 Nov 1999 (so far as not already in force except for certain purposes)[6] (SI 1999/3178) |
| | *Not yet in force* (exceptions noted above) |
| para 124(1)(b) | 1 Jun 1999 (SI 1999/1510) |

**Social Security Act 1998 (c 14)**—*contd*

| | |
|---|---|
| para 124(2) | 1 Jun 1999 (so far as it applies to the entry "Chairman of child support appeal tribunals") (SI 1999/1510) |
| | 18 Oct 1999 (for certain purposes[5] and so far as it applies to the entries relating to chairmen of disability appeal tribunals and vaccine damage tribunals in Judicial Pensions and Retirement Act 1993, Sch 5) (SI 1999/2860) |
| | 29 Nov 1999 (so far as not already in force except for certain purposes)[6] (SI 1999/3178) |
| | *Not yet in force* (exceptions noted above) |
| para 125 | 29 Nov 1999 (except for certain purposes)[6] (SI 1999/3178) |
| | *Not yet in force* (exceptions noted above) |
| paras 126–128 | 6 Apr 1999 (SI 1999/418) |
| para 129 | 5 Jul 1999 (for certain purposes)[2] (SI 1999/1958) |
| | 29 Nov 1999 (so far as not already in force except for certain purposes)[6] (SI 1999/3178) |
| | *Not yet in force* (exceptions noted above) |
| para 130(1) | *Never in force* (repealed) |
| para 130(2) | 5 Jul 1999 (for certain purposes)[2] (SI 1999/1958) |
| | *Never in force* (otherwise) (repealed) |
| para 131 | 4 Mar 1999 (so far as authorising the making of regulations) (SI 1999/528) |
| | 5 Jul 1999 (for certain purposes)[3] (SI 1999/1958) |
| | *Not yet in force* (otherwise) |
| para 132 | *Never in force* (repealed) |
| para 133 | 6 Apr 1999 (SI 1999/418) |
| paras 134–146 | 18 Oct 1999 (for certain purposes)[5] (SI 1999/2860) |
| | *Not yet in force* (otherwise) (para 141 repealed) |
| para 147 | 18 Oct 1999 (for certain purposes)[5] (SI 1999/2860) |
| | 29 Nov 1999 (so far as not already in force except for certain purposes)[6] (SI 1999/3178) |
| | *Not yet in force* (exceptions noted above) |
| para 148 | *Never in force* (repealed) |
| para 149(1) | 4 Mar 1999 (so far as authorising the making of regulations) (SI 1999/528) |
| | 29 Nov 1999 (so far as not already in force except for certain purposes)[6] (SI 1999/3178) |
| | *Not yet in force* (exceptions noted above) |
| para 149(2) | 29 Nov 1999 (except for certain purposes)[6] (SI 1999/3178) |
| | *Not yet in force* (exceptions noted above) |
| paras 150–153 | 29 Nov 1999 (except for certain purposes)[6] (SI 1999/3178) |
| | *Not yet in force* (exceptions noted above) (paras 152(1), (3), 153 repealed) |
| Sch 8 | 8 Sep 1998 (SI 1998/2209), repeals of or in— |
| | Child Support Act 1991, s 14(2), (2A), Sch 2, para 2; |
| | Social Security Contributions and Benefits Act 1992, Sch 2, paras 3(1)(b), 6(2); |
| | Social Security Contributions and Benefits (Northern Ireland) Act 1992, Sch 2, paras 3(1)(b), 6(2); |
| | Child Support Act 1995, Sch 3, para 3(2); |
| | Jobseekers Act 1995, Sch 2, para 20(3) |
| | 5 Apr 1999 (repeal of Social Security Contributions and Benefits Act 1992, ss 139(3), 140(4)(e)) (subject to a transitional provision) (SI 1999/1055) |
| | 6 Apr 1999 (repeals in Social Security Contributions and Benefits Act 1992, Sch 1, para 6(2)(b), Sch 11, para 2(d)) (SI 1998/2209) |
| | 6 Apr 1999 (SI 1999/418), repeals of or in— |
| | Social Security Administration Act 1992, ss 146, 147(1)–(3), 190(1)(a); |
| | Social Security Contributions and Benefits Act 1992, s 122(1); |

**Social Security Act 1998 (c 14)**—*contd*

Pensions Act 1995, s 137(2)

6 Apr 1999 (repeals of or in Social Security Administration
  Act 1992, ss 118(4), 119(2), 120(1), (5), 121(1), (2))
  (SI 1999/526)

1 Jun 1999 (SI 1999/1510), repeals of or in—

House of Commons Disqualification Act 1975, Sch 1, Pt III (so
  far as applies to the entries relating to regional or other
  full-time chairmen of child support appeal tribunals, the Chief
  Child Support Officer and members of a panel appointed
  under Tribunals and Inquiries Act 1992, s 6, of persons to act as
  chairmen of child support appeal tribunals);

Debtors (Scotland) Act 1987;

Child Support Act 1991;

Social Security Administration Act 1992, Sch 2, para 3;

Tribunals and Inquiries Act 1992, Sch 2, para 3;

Judicial Pensions and Retirement Act 1993, Sch 1, Pt II (entry
  relating to chairmen of child support appeal tribunals), Sch 5
  (entry relating to chairmen of child support appeal tribunals),
  Sch 6, para 23(1), Sch 8, para 21(1);

Child Support Act 1995

5 Jul 1999 (SI 1999/1958), for certain purposes[2], repeals of—

Social Security Administration Act 1992, s 164(5)(a);

Pension Schemes Act 1993, s 167(4)

6 Sep 1999 (repeal of Social Security Administration Act 1992,
  s 61A) (SI 1999/2422)

18 Oct 1999 (repeal of Social Security Administration Act 1992,
  s 63) (SI 1999/2860)

18 Oct 1999 (SI 1999/2860), for certain purposes[5], repeals of or
  in—

House of Commons Disqualification Act 1975, Pt III (so far as
  applies to the entries relating to regional or other full-time
  chairmen of disability appeal tribunals, members of a panel
  appointed under Tribunals and Inquiries Act 1992, s 6, of
  persons to act as chairmen of disability appeal tribunals,
  members of a panel of persons who may be appointed to serve
  on a vaccine damage tribunal, and the President of disability
  appeals tribunals);

Vaccine Damage Payments Act 1979;

Judicial Pensions and Retirement Act 1993, Sch 1, Pt II, Sch 5
  (entries relating to chairmen of disability appeal tribunals and
  to chairmen of vaccine damage tribunals);

Jobseekers Act 1995

29 Nov 1999 (SI 1999/3178), except for certain purposes[6], repeals
  of or in—

House of Commons Disqualification Act 1975;

Health and Social Services and Social Security Adjudications
  Act 1983;

Local Government Finance Act 1992;

Social Security Administration Act 1992, ss 17–70, 116(6), 189,
  190(4), 191, 192(5), Sch 4, Pt I;

Social Security (Consequential Provisions) Act 1992;

Tribunals and Inquiries Act 1992;

Judicial Pensions and Retirement Act 1993;

Pension Schemes Act 1993;

Deregulation and Contracting Out Act 1994;

Social Security (Incapacity for Work) Act 1994;

Pensions Act 1995;

Arbitration Act 1996;

Industrial Tribunals Act 1996;

Social Security (Recovery of Benefits) Act 1997;

**Social Security Act 1998 (c 14)**—*contd*

    Social Security Administration (Fraud) Act 1997;
    Social Security Act 1998
    2 Jul 2001 (repeals of Social Security Administration Act 1992,
      ss 5(1)(n), (o), (4), 6(1)(n), (o)) (SI 2001/2316)
    *Not yet in force*, repeals of or in—
    Parliamentary Commissioner Act 1967, Sch 4 (repealed or
      superseded);
    Jobseekers Act 1995 (except Sch 2, para 20(3))
    *Not yet in force* (except for certain purposes[5]), repeals of or in—
    Vaccine Damage Payments Act 1979
    *Not yet in force* (for the purposes of housing benefit, council tax
      benefit and decisions given before 1 Apr 1999 relating to
      contributions, statutory sick pay, statutory maternity pay and
      certain pension matters) repeals of or in—
    House of Commons Disqualification Act 1975, Sch 1, Pt III
      (except entries relating to regional or other full-time chairmen
      of child support appeal tribunals, the Chief Child Support
      Officer and members of a panel appointed under Tribunals and
      Inquiries Act 1992, s 6, of persons to act as chairmen of child
      support appeal tribunals);
    Health and Social Services and Social Security Adjudications
      Act 1983;
    Local Government Finance Act 1992;
    Social Security Administration Act 1992, ss 17–61, 62, 64–70,
      116, 164, 189, 190(4), 191, 192, Sch 2, paras 1, 2, 4–8, Sch 3,
      Sch 4, Pt I;
    Social Security (Consequential Provisions) Act 1992;
    Tribunals and Inquiries Act 1992, ss 6, 13, Sch 1, Sch 3;
    Judicial Pensions and Retirement Act 1993, Sch 1, Pt II and
      Sch 5 (other than entries relating to chairmen of child support
      appeal tribunals), Sch 6, para 21, Sch 7, Sch 8, para 23;
    Pension Schemes Act 1993;
    Deregulation and Contracting Out Act 1994;
    Social Security (Incapacity for Work) Act 1994;
    Pensions Act 1995, Sch 5;
    Arbitration Act 1996;
    Industrial Tribunals Act 1996;
    Social Security Act 1998;
    Social Security Administration (Fraud) Act 1997;
    Social Security (Recovery of Benefits) Act 1997

[1]   For transitional provisions, see SI 1999/1510, arts 48–50

[2]   Subject to transitional provisions and savings, "for certain purposes" means for the purposes of guardian's allowance under the Social Security Contributions and Benefits Act 1992 ("the Act"), Pt III, benefits under Pt V of the Act, child benefit, and any matter to which, by virtue of Pension Schemes Act 1993, s 170, provisions of Chapter II of Pt I of the Act are to apply

[3]   Subject to transitional provisions in SI 1999/2422, art 4, Sch 14, "for certain purposes" means for the purposes of benefits under the Social Security Contributions and Benefits Act 1992 ("the Act"), Pt II (except child's special allowance), severe disablement allowance under ss 68, 69 of the Act, benefits for the aged under ss 78, 79 of the Act, increases for dependants under Pt IV of the Act, and graduated retirement benefit under the National Insurance Act 1965, ss 36, 37

[4]   Subject to transitional provisions in SI 1999/2739, art 3, Sch 2, "for certain purposes" means for the purposes of family credit and disability working allowance under Pt VII of the Social Security Contributions and Benefits Act 1992

[5]   Subject to transitional provisions in SI 1999/2860, art 4, Schs 16–18, "for certain purposes" means for the purposes of (i) attendance allowance, disability living allowance and invalid care allowance under Social Security Contributions and Benefits Act 1992, Pt III, (ii) jobseeker's allowance under Jobseekers Act 1995, Pt I and any sums payable under s 26 of that Act, (iii) vaccine damage payments under Vaccine Damage Payments Act 1979, (iv) decisions whether a person is entitled to be credited with

**Social Security Act 1998 (c 14)**—*contd*

earnings or contributions in accordance with regulations made under Social Security Contributions and Benefits Act 1992, s 22(5), and (v) decisions whether a person was, within the meaning of regulations, precluded from regular employment by responsibilities at home

[6]    Subject to transitional provisions in SI 1999/3178, art 4, Schs 21–23, "for certain purposes" means for the purposes of statutory sick pay and statutory maternity pay under Social Security Contributions and Benefits Act 1992, Pts XI, XII, and "except for certain purposes" means for the purposes of housing benefit, council Tax benefit and decisions to which the Social Security Contributions (Transfer of Functions, etc) Act 1999 (Commencement No 1 and Transitional Provisions) Order 1999, SI 1999/527, art 4(6), applies

**Statute Law (Repeals) Act 1998 (c 43)**

*RA:* 19 Nov 1998

*Commencement provisions:* s 2

| | | |
|---|---|---|
| 1 | (1) | See Sch 1 below |
| | (2) | See Sch 2 below |
| 2, 3 | | 19 Nov 1998 (RA) |
| Sch 1 | | 19 Nov 1998 (RA), except repeals of or in— |
| | | Public Notaries Act 1843 as it applies to the Isle of Man; |
| | | Statute Law (Repeals) Act 1993, s 3(3) |
| | | *Not yet in force* (exceptions noted above) |
| Sch 2 | | 19 Nov 1998 (RA) |

**Tax Credits (Initial Expenditure) Act 1998 (c 16)**

*RA:* 21 May 1998

Whole Act in force 21 May 1998 (RA)

**Teaching and Higher Education Act 1998 (c 30)**

*RA:* 16 Jul 1998

*Commencement provisions:* s 46(3), (4); Teaching and Higher Education Act 1998 (Commencement No 1) Order 1998, SI 1998/1729; Teaching and Higher Education Act 1998 (Commencement No 2 and Transitional Provisions) Order 1998, SI 1998/2004; Teaching and Higher Education Act 1998 (Commencement No 3) Order 1998, SI 1998/2215; Teaching and Higher Education Act 1998 (Commencement No 4 and Transitional Provisions) Order 1998, SI 1998/3237; Teaching and Higher Education Act 1998 (Commencement No 5) Order 1999, SI 1999/987; Teaching and Higher Education Act 1998 (Commencement No 6) Order 2000, SI 2000/970; Teaching and Higher Education Act 1998 (Commencement No 7) Order 2000, SI 2000/2199; Teaching and Higher Education Act 1998 (Commencement No 8) Order 2001, SI 2001/1211

| | | |
|---|---|---|
| 1 | (1) | 1 Oct 1998 (so far as defines "the Council") (SI 1998/2215) |
| | | 1 Sep 2000 (otherwise) (SI 2000/970) |
| | (2)–(10) | 1 Oct 1998 (SI 1998/2215) |
| 2 | (1)–(3) | 1 Sep 2000 (SI 2000/970) |
| | (4) | 30 Apr 2001 (W) (SI 2001/1211) |
| | | 1 Jun 2001 (E) (SI 2001/1211) |
| | (5)–(7) | 1 Sep 2000 (SI 2000/970) |
| 3 | (1), (2) | 1 Sep 2000 (SI 2000/970) |
| | (3)(a)–(c) | 1 Sep 2000 (SI 2000/970) |
| | (3)(d) | 5 Apr 2000 (for the purpose of making regulations) (SI 2000/970) |
| | | 1 Sep 2000 (otherwise) (SI 2000/970) |
| | (4) | 5 Apr 2000 (for the purpose of making regulations) (SI 2000/970) |
| | | 1 Sep 2000 (otherwise) (SI 2000/970) |
| 4, 5 | | 5 Apr 2000 (SI 2000/970) |

**Teaching and Higher Education Act 1998 (c 30)**—*contd*

| | | |
|---|---|---|
| 6 | | See Sch 2 below |
| 7 | (1)–(4) | 5 Apr 2000 (SI 2000/970) |
| | (5) | 1 Sep 2000 (SI 2000/970) |
| 8 | | 1 Oct 1998 (SI 1998/2215) |
| 9, 10 | | 1 Sep 2000 (SI 2000/970) |
| 11, 12 | | 5 Apr 2000 (SI 2000/970) |
| 13 | | 1 Sep 2000 (SI 2000/970) |
| 14 | (1), (2) | 1 Sep 2000 (SI 2000/970) |
| | (3) | 5 Apr 2000 (SI 2000/970) |
| | (4), (5) | 1 Sep 2000 (SI 2000/970) |
| 15 | | 15 Aug 2000 (SI 2000/2199) |
| 16, 17 | | 1 Oct 1998 (SI 1998/2215) |
| 18 | | *Never in force* (repealed) |
| 19 | (1)–(8) | 1 Oct 1998 (SI 1998/2215) |
| | (9) | 1 Apr 1999 (SI 1998/2215) |
| | (10)(a) | 1 Apr 1999 (SI 1998/2215) |
| | (10)(b), (c) | 1 Oct 1998 (SI 1998/2215) |
| 20, 21 | | 1 Oct 1998 (SI 1998/2215) |
| 22–31 | | 16 Jul 1998 (s 46(3)) |
| 32, 33 | | 1 Sep 1999 (SI 1999/987) |
| 34, 35 | | 1 Oct 1998 (SI 1998/2215) |
| 36 | | 1 Apr 1999 (SI 1998/3237) |
| 37, 38 | | 1 Jan 1999 (SI 1998/3237) |
| 39 | | 1 Feb 1999 (SI 1998/3237) |
| 40, 41 | | 1 Oct 1998 (SI 1998/2215) |
| 42, 43 | | 16 Jul 1998 (s 46(3)) |
| 44 | (1) | See Sch 3 below |
| | (2) | See Sch 4 below |
| 45, 46 | | 16 Jul 1998 (s 46(3)) |
| Sch 1 | | 1 Oct 1998 (SI 1998/2215) |
| Sch 2 | paras 1, 2 | 28 Feb 2001 (SI 2001/1211) |
| | para 3(1)–(3) | 30 Apr 2001 (W) (SI 2001/1211) |
| | | 1 Jun 2001 (E) (SI 2001/1211) |
| | para 3(4) | 28 Feb 2001 (for the purpose of making regulations) (SI 2001/1211) |
| | | 30 Apr 2001 (W) (otherwise) (SI 2001/1211) |
| | | 1 Jun 2001 (E) (otherwise) (SI 2001/1211) |
| | para 3(5) | 28 Feb 2001 (SI 2001/1211) |
| | para 4 | 30 Apr 2001 (W) (SI 2001/1211) |
| | | 1 Jun 2001 (E) (SI 2001/1211) |
| | para 5(1) | 28 Feb 2001 (for the purpose of making regulations) (SI 2001/1211) |
| | | 30 Apr 2001 (W) (otherwise) (SI 2001/1211) |
| | | 1 Jun 2001 (E) (otherwise) (SI 2001/1211) |
| | para 5(2) | 30 Apr 2001 (W) (SI 2001/1211) |
| | | 1 Jun 2001 (E) (SI 2001/1211) |
| | para 6(1) | 28 Feb 2001 (SI 2001/1211) |
| | para 6(2), (3) | 30 Apr 2001 (W) (SI 2001/1211) |
| | | 1 Jun 2001 (E) (SI 2001/1211) |
| | paras 7, 8 | 28 Feb 2001 (SI 2001/1211) |
| Sch 3 | paras 1–3 | 1 Sep 2000 (SI 2000/970) |
| | para 4 | 18 Jul 1998 (SI 1998/1729) |
| | paras 5–9 | 1 Oct 1998 (SI 1998/2215) |
| | paras 10–14 | 1 Sep 1999 (SI 1999/987) |
| | para 15 | 1 Oct 1998 (SI 1998/2215) |
| Sch 4 | | 13 Aug 1998 (subject to transitional and saving provisions) (SI 1998/2004), repeals of— |
| | | Education (Student Loans) Act 1990; |
| | | Education (Student Loans) Act 1996; |

**Teaching and Higher Education Act 1998 (c 30)**—*contd*
Education (Student Loans) Act 1998
1 Oct 1998 (repeals in Education Reform Act 1988, ss 218(1)(c), 232(6)) (SI 1998/2215)
1 Jan 1999 (subject to transitional and saving provisions) (SI 1998/3237), repeals of or in—
Education Act 1962;
Education Act 1973, s 3;
Education Act 1980, s 19, Sch 5;
Education (Fees and Awards) Act 1983, s 2(3);
Education Reform Act 1988, s 209;
Education Act 1996, s 578
1 Jan 1999 (repeal of Charities Act 1993, Sch 2, paras (h), (j)) (SI 1998/3237)
*Not yet in force* (repeal of Education Act 1996, Sch 37, paras 4–7, 98)

**Waste Minimisation Act 1998 (c 44)**

*RA:* 19 Nov 1998

Whole Act in force 19 Nov 1998 (RA)

**Wireless Telegraphy Act 1998 (c 6)**

*RA:* 18 Mar 1998

*Commencement provisions:* s 10(2)

Whole Act in force 18 Jun 1998 (s 10(2))

# 1999 Acts

## Access to Justice Act 1999 (c 22)

*RA:* 27 Jul 1999

*Commencement provisions:* s 108; Access to Justice Act 1999 (Commencement No 1) Order 1999,
SI 1999/2657; Access to Justice Act 1999 (Commencement No 2 and Transitional Provisions)
Order 1999, SI 1999/3344; Access to Justice Act 1999 (Commencement No 3, Transitional Provisions
and Savings) Order 2000, SI 2000/7741; Access to Justice Act 1999 (Commencement No 4 and
Transitional Provisions) Order 2000, SI 2000/19202; Access to Justice Act 1999 (Commencement
No 5 and Transitional Provisions) Order 2000, SI 2000/32803; Access to Justice Act 1999
(Commencement No 6 and Transitional Provisions) Order 2001, SI 2001/1684; Access to Justice
Act 1999 (Commencement No 7, Transitional Provisions and Savings) Order 2001, SI 2001/9165;
Access to Justice Act 1999 (Commencement No 8) Order 2001, SI 2001/1655; Access to Justice
Act 1999 (Commencement No 9 and Transitional Provisions) (Scotland) Order 2003, SSI 2003/207;
Access to Justice Act 1999 (Commencement No 10) Order 2003, SI 2003/1241; Access to Justice
Act 1999 (Commencement No 11) Order 2003, SI 2003/2571

| | | |
|---|---|---|
| 1–11 | | 1 Apr 2000 (SI 2000/774) |
| 12–18 | | 2 Apr 2001 (SI 2001/916) |
| 19–23 | | 1 Apr 2000 (SI 2000/774) |
| 24 | | See Sch 4 below |
| 25–27 | | 1 Apr 2000 (SI 2000/774) |
| 28 | | *Not yet in force* |
| 29, 30 | | 1 Apr 2000 (SI 2000/774) |
| 31 | | 2 Jun 2003 (SI 2003/1241) |
| 32–34 | | 27 Sep 1999 (s 108(3)) |
| 35 | | 1 Jan 2000 (SI 1999/3344) |
| 36 | | 27 Sep 1999 (SI 1999/2657) |
| 37–39 | | 31 Jul 2000 (SI 2000/1920) |
| 40 | | 27 Sep 1999 (SI 1999/2657) |
| 41 | | See Sch 5 below |
| 42 | | 27 Sep 1999 (SI 1999/2657) |
| 43 | | See Sch 6 below |
| 44 | | 31 Jul 2000 (SI 2000/1920) |
| 45 | | 27 Jul 1999 (s 108(2)) |
| 46 | | 27 Sep 1999 (SI 1999/2657) |
| 47 | | 25 May 2001 (SI 2001/1655) |
| 48 | | See Sch 7 below |
| 49 | | 27 Sep 1999 (SI 1999/2657) |
| 50 | | 1 Nov 2003 (SI 2003/2571) |
| 51 | (1)–(4) | 1 Nov 2003 (SI 2003/2571) |
| | (5) | See Sch 8 below |
| 52 | | 1 Nov 2003 (SI 2003/2571) |
| 53 | | 1 Nov 1999 (SI 1999/2657) |
| 54–65 | | 27 Sep 1999 (s 108(3)) |
| 66 | | See Sch 9 below |
| 67 | (1) | 27 Sep 1999 (s 108(3)) |

**Access to Justice Act 1999 (c 22)**—*contd*

| | | |
|---|---|---|
| | (2) | 27 Sep 1999 (in the petty sessions areas of Aberconwy, Arfon, Blackburn, Darwen and Ribble Valley, Bromley, Burnley and Pendle, Colwyn, Corby, Croydon, Daventry, Denbighshire, Dwyfor, Flintshire, Gateshead, Kettering, Meirionnydd, Newcastle-under-Lyme and Pirehill North, Newcastle-upon-Tyne, Northampton, Rhuddlan, Staffordshire Moorlands, Stoke-on-Trent, Sutton, Towcester, Wellingborough, Wrexham Maelor, Ynys Môn/Anglesey) (SI 1999/2657) |
| | | 8 Jan 2001 (otherwise) (SI 2000/3280) |
| | (3) | 27 Sep 1999 (s 108(3)) |
| 68–70 | | 27 Sep 1999 (s 108(3)) |
| 71 | | 1 Jan 2000 (SI 1999/3344) |
| 72–76 | | 27 Sep 1999 (s 108(3)) |
| 77 | | *Never in force* (repealed) |
| 78 | (1) | 31 Aug 2000 (SI 2000/1920) |
| | (2) | See Sch 11 below |
| 79 | | 12 Nov 1999 (SI 1999/2657) |
| 80 | | *Never in force* (repealed) |
| 81, 82 | | 27 Sep 1999 (s 108(3)) |
| 83 | (1) | 27 Sep 1999 (so far as it inserts Justices of the Peace Act 1997, s 30B) (SI 1999/2657) |
| | | 1 Mar 2000 (so far as it inserts Justices of the Peace Act 1997, ss 30A(1), 30C) (SI 1999/3344) |
| | | 1 Apr 2001 (otherwise) (SI 2001/916) |
| | (2) | 1 Apr 2001 (SI 2001/916) |
| | (3) | See Sch 12 below |
| 84 | | 27 Sep 1999 (s 108(3)) |
| 85 | | 1 Jan 2000 (SI 1999/3344) |
| 86, 87 | | 27 Sep 1999 (s 108(3)) |
| 88, 89 | | 27 Sep 1999 (SI 1999/2657) |
| 90, 91 | | 1 Apr 2001 (SI 2001/916) |
| 92–95 | | 8 Jan 2001 (SI 2000/3280) |
| 96, 97 | | 19 Feb 2001 (SI 2001/168) |
| 98–100 | | 1 Apr 2001 (SI 2001/916) |
| 101–103 | | 1 Apr 2001 (E) (W) (NI) (SI 2001/916) |
| | | 31 Mar 2003 (S) (SSI 2003/207)[6] |
| 104 | | 27 Sep 1999 (s 108(3)) |
| 105 | | See Sch 14 below |
| 106 | | See Sch 15 below |
| 107 | | 27 Sep 1999 (s 108(3)) |
| 108–110 | | 27 Jul 1999 (RA) |
| Schs 1, 2 | | 1 Apr 2000 (SI 2000/774) |
| Sch 3 | | 2 Apr 2001 (SI 2001/916) |
| Sch 4 | paras 1, 2 | 1 Apr 2000 (SI 2000/774) |
| | paras 3, 4 | 2 Apr 2001 (SI 2001/916) |
| | para 5 | *Never in force* (repealed) |
| | paras 6–8 | 2 Apr 2001 (SI 2001/916) |
| | para 9 | *Never in force* (repealed) |
| | para 10(1) | 1 Apr 2000 (SI 2000/774) |
| | para 10(2) | 2 Apr 2001 (SI 2001/916) |
| | para 10(3)(a) | 2 Apr 2001 (SI 2001/916) |
| | para 10(3)(b) | 1 Apr 2000 (SI 2000/774) |
| | para 10(4), (5) | 2 Apr 2001 (SI 2001/916) |
| | paras 11–15 | 1 Apr 2000 (SI 2000/774) |
| | paras 16–18 | 2 Apr 2001 (SI 2001/916) |
| | paras 19, 20 | 1 Apr 2000 (SI 2000/774) |
| | paras 21–23 | 2 Apr 2001 (SI 2001/916) |
| | paras 24, 25 | *Never in force* (repealed) |

**Access to Justice Act 1999 (c 22)**—*contd*

| | | |
|---|---|---|
| | para 26 | 1 Apr 2000 (SI 2000/774) |
| | paras 27–30 | 2 Apr 2001 (SI 2001/916) |
| | paras 31–34 | 1 Apr 2000 (SI 2000/774) |
| | para 35 | 2 Apr 2001 (SI 2001/916) |
| | paras 36, 37 | 1 Apr 2000 (SI 2000/774) |
| | paras 38–40 | 2 Apr 2001 (SI 2001/916) |
| | paras 41–46 | 1 Apr 2000 (SI 2000/774) |
| | para 47 | 2 Apr 2001 (SI 2001/916) |
| | para 48 | 1 Apr 2000 (SI 2000/774) |
| | para 49 | 2 Apr 2001 (SI 2001/916) |
| | paras 50–52 | 1 Apr 2000 (SI 2000/774) |
| | paras 53–55 | 2 Apr 2001 (SI 2001/916) |
| | para 56 | 1 Apr 2000 (SI 2000/774) |
| Sch 5 | | 1 Jan 2000 (subject to transitional provisions) (SI 1999/3344) |
| Sch 6 | paras 1–5 | 1 Jan 2000 (SI 1999/3344) |
| | paras 6, 7 | 27 Sep 1999 (SI 1999/2657) |
| | para 8 | 1 Jan 2000 (SI 1999/3344) |
| | paras 9, 10 | 27 Sep 1999 (SI 1999/2657) |
| | para 11 | 1 Jan 2000 (SI 1999/3344) |
| Sch 7 | | 27 Sep 1999 (SI 1999/2657) |
| Sch 8 | | 1 Nov 2003 (SI 2003/2571) |
| Sch 9 | | 27 Sep 1999 (SI 1999/2657) |
| Sch 10 | | 27 Sep 1999 (s 108(3)) |
| Sch 11 | | 31 Aug 2000 (SI 2000/1920) |
| Sch 12 | paras 1–8 | 1 Apr 2001 (SI 2001/916) |
| | para 9 | 1 Mar 2000 (SI 1999/3344) |
| | para 10 | 1 Apr 2001 (SI 2001/916) |
| | para 11 | 27 Sep 1999 (SI 1999/2657) |
| | para 12 | 1 Mar 2000 (SI 1999/3344) |
| | paras 13–19 | 1 Apr 2001 (SI 2001/916) |
| Sch 13 | | 1 Apr 2001 (SI 2001/916) |
| Sch 14 | | 27 Sep 1999 (s 108(3)) |
| Sch 15 | Pt I | 1 Apr 2000 (SI 2000/774), repeals of or in— |

Parliamentary Commissioner Act 1967;

House of Commons Disqualification Act 1975;

Northern Ireland Assembly Disqualification Act 1975;

Legal Aid Act 1988, ss 3(5)–(10), 4(5), (8), 5–18, 31, 32, 34–40, 42, 45, 46, Schs 1, 2, Sch 5, paras 2, 4, 5, 6(a), 7(a), 8, 16–18, 20, 21, Schs 6–8;

Children Act 1989 (except s 99(3));

Civil Legal Aid (Matrimonial Proceedings) Regulations 1989, SI 1989/549;

Courts and Legal Services Act 1990 (except s 59);

Legal Aid Act 1988 (Children Act 1989) Order 1991, SI 1991/1924;

Companies Act 1989 (Eligibility for Appointment as Company Auditor) (Consequential Amendments) Regulations 1991, SI 1991/1997;

Civil Legal Aid (General) (Amendment) (No 2) Regulations 1991, SI 1991/2036;

Social Security (Consequential Provisions) Act 1992;

Tribunals and Inquiries Act 1992;

Trade Union Reform and Employment Rights Act 1993;

Civil Legal Aid (Scope) Regulations 1993, SI 1993/1354;

Legal Aid (Scope) Regulations 1994, SI 1994/2768;

Employment Rights Act 1996;

Family Law Act 1996

2 Apr 2001 (otherwise) (SI 2001/916)

| | | |
|---|---|---|
| | Pt II | 27 Sep 1999 (SI 1999/2657), repeals of or in— |

**Access to Justice Act 1999 (c 22)**—*contd*

|  |  |
|---|---|
|  | Solicitors Act 1974, ss 32(4), 87(1);<br>Courts and Legal Services Act 1990, ss 27(2), (3), (6), 28(2), (3), (5), 71(7), (8), Schs 3, 19<br>1 Nov 1999 (SI 1999/2657), repeals of or in—<br>Public Notaries Act 1801, s 13;<br>Public Notaries Act 1843, s 6;<br>Courts and Legal Services Act 1990, ss 57(11), 113(1), (10)<br>1 Jan 2000 (SI 1999/3344), repeals of or in—<br>House of Commons Disqualification Act 1975;<br>Northern Ireland Assembly Disqualification Act 1975;<br>Administration of Justice Act 1985, ss 9(2)(g), 65, Sch 2;<br>Courts and Legal Services Act 1990, ss 19 (and the heading preceding it), 20, 24(3), 123(1), (f), (2)(e), Schs 1, 2<br>31 Jul 2000 (otherwise) (SI 2000/1920) |
| Pt III | 27 Sep 1999 (s 108(3)) |
| Pt IV | 27 Sep 1999 (SI 1999/2657) |
| Pt V(1) | 27 Sep 1999 (s 108(3)), except repeals of or in—<br>Magistrates' Courts Act 1980, s 67(8) (substituted);<br>Children Act 1989, Sch 11<br>*Not yet in force* (exceptions noted above) |
| Pt V(2) | *Not yet in force* |
| Pt V(3) | 31 Aug 2000 (SI 2000/1920) |
| Pt V(4) | 12 Nov 1999 (SI 1999/2657) |
| Pt V(5) | 27 Sep 1999 (s 108(3)) |
| Pt V(6) | 1 Mar 2000 (repeals of or in Justices of the Peace Act 1997, s 56(4)) (SI 1999/3344)<br>1 Apr 2001 (so far as not already in force) (SI 2001/916) |
| Pt V(7) | 27 Sep 1999 (repeals of or in Justices of the Peace Act 1997, ss 31(2), 40(5), Sch 4, para 15) (SI 1999/2657)<br>1 Apr 2001 (otherwise) (SI 2001/916) |
| Pt V(8) | 8 Jan 2001 (SI 2000/3280), repeals of or in—<br>Magistrates' Courts Act 1980, s 125(2);<br>Criminal Justice Act 1988, s 65;<br>Courts and Legal Services Act 1990, Sch 17, para 11<br>19 Feb 2001 (otherwise) (SI 2001/168) |
| Pt VI | 1 Apr 2001 (SI 2001/916) |

[1]   For transitional and saving provisions, see SI 2000/774, arts 3–11

[2]   For transitional provisions, see SI 2000/1920, art 4

[3]   For transitional provisions, see SI 2000/3280, art 3

[4]   For transitional provisions, see SI 2001/168, art 3

[5]   For transitional provisions and savings, see SI 2001/916, art 4, Schs 1, 2

[6]   For transitional provisions in relation to s 102, see SSI 2003/207, art 3

---

**Adoption (Intercountry Aspects) Act 1999 (c 18)**

*RA:* 27 Jul 1999

*Commencement provisions:* s 18(3); Adoption (Intercountry Aspects) Act 1999 (Commencement No 1) Order 2000, SI 2000/52; Adoption (Intercountry Aspects) Act 1999 (Commencement No 2) (Scotland) Order 2000, SSI 2000/223; Adoption (Intercountry Aspects) Act 1999 (Commencement No 3) Order 2000, SI 2000/2821; Adoption (Intercountry Aspects) Act 1999 (Commencement No 4) (Scotland) Order 2000, SSI 2000/390[1]; Adoption (Intercountry Aspects) Act 1999 (Commencement No 5) Order 2001, SI 2001/1279; Adoption (Intercountry Aspects) Act 1999 (Commencement No 6) Order 2001, SSI 2001/235; Adoption (Intercountry Aspects) Act 1999 (Commencement No 7) (Scotland) Order 2002, SSI 2002/562; Adoption (Intercountry Aspects) Act 1999 (Commencement

**Adoption (Intercountry Aspects) Act 1999 (c 18)**—*contd*
No 8) Order 2003, SI 2003/189; Adoption (Intercountry Aspects) Act 1999 (Commencement No 9) Order 2003, SI 2003/362; Adoption (Intercountry Aspects) Act 1999 (Commencement No 10) (Scotland) Order 2003, SSI 2003/121

| | | |
|---|---|---|
| 1 | | 14 Jan 2003 (S) (SSI 2002/562) |
| | | 23 Jan 2003 (E) (W) (SI 2003/189) |
| 2 | (1), (2) | 1 Jun 2003 (SI 2003/189; SSI 2003/121) |
| | (3) | 1 Jun 2003 (S) (SSI 2003/121) |
| | | *Not yet in force* (E) (W) |
| | (4) | 1 Jun 2003 (SI 2003/189; SSI 2003/121) |
| | (5) | *Never in force* (substituted) |
| | (6) | 1 Jun 2003 (SI 2003/121) |
| 3 | | 23 Jan 2003 (for the purpose of making regulations) (E) (W) (SI 2003/189) |
| | | 1 Jun 2003 (E) (W) (otherwise) (SI 2003/189) |
| | | 1 Jun 2003 (S) (SSI 2003/121) |
| 4 | | 1 Jun 2003 (E) (W) (SI 2003/189) |
| 5 | | 1 Jun 2003 (S) (SSI 2003/121) |
| 6 | | 1 Jun 2003 (SI 2003/189; SSI 2003/121) |
| 7 | | 1 Jun 2003 (SI 2003/362) |
| 8 | | 23 Jan 2003 (E) (W) (for the purpose of making regulations in so far as it relates to the meaning of "Convention adoption" and "Convention adoption order") (SI 2003/189) |
| | | 1 Jun 2003 (E) (W) (otherwise) (SI 2003/189) |
| | | 1 Jun 2003 (S) (SSI 2003/121) |
| 9 | | 30 Apr 2001 (so far as amends Adoption Act 1976) (SI 2001/1279) |
| | | 2 Jul 2001 (so far as amends Adoption (Scotland) Act 1978) (SSI 2001/235) |
| 10 | | *Never in force* (repealed) |
| 11 | | 1 Jun 2003 (S) (SSI 2003/121) |
| | | *Never in force* (repealed) (E) (W) |
| 12 | | 14 Jan 2003 (so far as it amends Adoption (Scotland) Act 1978) (SSI 2002/562) |
| | | 23 Jan 2003 (E) (W) (for the purpose of making regulations) (SI 2003/189) |
| | | 1 Jun 2003 (E) (W) (otherwise) (SI 2003/189) |
| 13 | | 31 Jan 2000 (so far as it inserts Adoption Act 1976, s 72(3A)) (SI 2000/52) |
| | | 10 Nov 2000 (so far as it inserts Adoption (Scotland) Act 1978, s 65(3A)) (S) (SSI 2000/390) |
| | | *Never in force* (so far as inserts Adoption Act 1976, s 72(3B), Adoption (Scotland) Act 1978, s 65(3B)) (repealed) |
| 14 | | 30 Apr 2001 (so far as amends Adoption Act 1976) (SI 2001/1279) |
| | | 2 Jul 2001 (so far as amends Adoption (Scotland) Act 1978) (SSI 2001/235) |
| 15 | | See Schs 2, 3 below |
| 16 | (1) | 23 Jan 2003 (E) (W) (SI 2003/189) |
| | | *Not yet in force* (S) |
| | (2) | 16 Oct 2000 (SI 2000/2821) |
| 17 | | 1 Jun 2003 (SI 2003/189; SSI 2003/121) |
| 18 | | 27 Jul 1999 (RA) |
| Sch 1 | | 23 Jan 2003 (E) (W) (SI 2003/189) |
| | | 1 Jun 2003 (S) (SSI 2003/121) |
| Sch 2 | para 1 | 1 Jun 2003 (E) (W) (SI 2003/189) |
| | para 2 | 1 Jun 2003 (SI 2003/362) |
| | para 3 | 1 Jun 2003 (E) (W) (SI 2003/189) |
| | para 4 | 1 Jun 2003 (S) (SSI 2003/121) |
| | para 5 | 1 Jun 2003 (E) (W) (SI 2003/189) |
| Sch 3 | | 1 Jun 2003 (SI 2003/189; SSI 2003/121) |

**Adoption (Intercountry Aspects) Act 1999 (c 18)**—*contd*

1   SSI 2000/390 replaces SSI 2000/223 which incorrectly purported to bring s 13 into force on 2 Jun 2000

---

**Appropriation Act 1999 (c 13)**

*RA:* 15 Jul 1999

Whole Act in force 15 Jul 1999 (RA)

---

**Breeding and Sale of Dogs (Welfare) Act 1999 (c 11)**

*RA:* 30 Jun 1999

*Commencement provisions:* s 11(2)

Whole Act in force 31 Dec 1999 (s 11(2))

---

**Care of Places of Worship Measure 1999 (No 2)**

*RA:* 30 Jun 1999

*Commencement provisions:* s 7(2)

The provisions of this Measure were brought into force on 1 Jul 2001 by an instrument made by the Archbishops of Canterbury and York and dated 21 Jun 2001 (made under s 7(2))

---

**Cathedrals Measure 1999 (No 1)**

*RA:* 30 Jun 1999

Whole Act in force 30 Jun 1999 (RA)

---

**Commonwealth Development Corporation Act 1999 (c 20)**

*RA:* 27 Jul 1999

Whole Act in force 27 Jul 1999 (RA)

---

**Company and Business Names (Chamber of Commerce, Etc) Act 1999 (c 19)**

*RA:* 27 Jul 1999

*Commencement provisions:* s 5(2) Company and Business Names (Chamber of Commerce Etc) Act 1999 (Commencement) Order 2001, SI 2001/258

Whole Act in force 10 May 2001 (SI 2001/258)

---

**Consolidated Fund Act 1999 (c 4)**

*RA:* 25 Mar 1999

Whole Act in force 25 Mar 1999 (RA)

---

## Consolidated Fund (No 2) Act 1999 (c 35)

*RA:* 20 Dec 1999

Whole Act in force 20 Dec 1999 (RA)

---

## Contracts (Rights of Third Parties) Act 1999 (c 31)

*RA:* 11 Nov 1999

Whole Act in force 11 Nov 1999 (RA), but the Act does not apply in relation to contracts entered into before the end of the period of six months beginning on 11 Nov 1999, except in certain limited circumstances

---

## Criminal Cases Review (Insanity) Act 1999 (c 25)

*RA:* 27 Jul 1999

Whole Act in force 27 Jul 1999 (RA)

---

## Disability Rights Commission Act 1999 (c 17)

*RA:* 27 Jul 1999

*Commencement provisions:* s 16(2); Disability Rights Commission Act 1999 (Commencement No 1 and Transitional Provision) Order 1999, SI 1999/2210; Disability Rights Commission Act 1999 (Commencement No 2 and Transitional Provision) Order 2000, SI 2000/880; Disability Rights Commission Act 1999 (Commencement No 3) Order 2006, SI 2006/3189

| | | |
|---|---|---|
| 1 | (1)–(3) | 6 Aug 1999 (SI 1999/2210) |
| | (4) | 25 Apr 2000 (SI 2000/880) |
| 2 | | 25 Apr 2000 (SI 2000/880) |
| 3 | (1)–(4) | 25 Apr 2000 (SI 2000/880) |
| | (5) | 23 Mar 2000 (in so far as relates to the Secretary of State's regulation making powers contained in Sch 3, para 26(a)) (SI 2000/880) |
| | | 25 Apr 2000 (otherwise) (SI 2000/880) |
| 4 | (1)–(5) | 25 Apr 2000 (SI 2000/880) |
| | (6) | 23 Mar 2000 (in so far as bringing into effect the Secretary of State's powers to prescribe any matter in regulations made by him contained in Sch 3, paras 15(3), 16(3), 16(4), 17(4), 18(2), 18(3)(a), (b) of this Act and the Secretary of State's regulation making powers contained in Sch 3 para 26(a) of this Act) (SI 2000/880) |
| | | 25 Apr 2000 (otherwise) (SI 2000/880) |
| 5–11 | | 25 Apr 2000 (SI 2000/880) |
| 12, 13 | | 6 Aug 1999 (SI 1999/2210) |
| 14 | (1) | See Sch 4 below |
| | (2) | See Sch 5 below |
| 15 | | 6 Aug 1999 (SI 1999/2210) |
| 16 | | 27 Jul 1999 (RA) |
| Sch 1 | | 6 Aug 1999 (SI 1999/2210) |
| Sch 2 | | 25 Apr 2000 (SI 2000/880) |
| Sch 3 | paras 1–14 | 25 Apr 2000 (SI 2000/880) |
| | para 15(1), (2) | 25 Apr 2000 (SI 2000/880) |
| | para 15(3) | 23 Mar 2000 (in so far as relates to the Secretary of State's powers to prescribe any matter in regulations made by him) (SI 2000/880) |
| | | 25 Apr 2000 (otherwise) (SI 2000/880) |
| | para 16(1), (2) | 25 Apr 2000 (SI 2000/880) |

**Disability Rights Commission Act 1999 (c 17)**—*contd*

| | | |
|---|---|---|
| | para 16(3), (4) | 23 Mar 2000 (in so far as relates to the Secretary of State's powers to prescribe any matter in regulations made by him) (SI 2000/880) |
| | | 25 Apr 2000 (otherwise) (SI 2000/880) |
| | para 17(1)–(3) | 25 Apr 2000 (SI 2000/880) |
| | para 17(4) | 23 Mar 2000 (in so far as relates to the Secretary of State's powers to prescribe any matter in regulations made by him) (SI 2000/880) |
| | | 25 Apr 2000 (otherwise) (SI 2000/880) |
| | para 18(1) | 25 Apr 2000 (SI 2000/880) |
| | para 18(2), (3) | 23 Mar 2000 (in so far as relates to the Secretary of State's powers to prescribe any matter in regulations made by him) (SI 2000/880) |
| | | 25 Apr 2000 (otherwise) (SI 2000/880) |
| | paras 19–25 | 25 Apr 2000 (SI 2000/880) |
| | para 26(a) | 23 Mar 2000 (SI 2000/880) |
| | para 26(b) | 25 Apr 2000 (SI 2000/880) |
| Sch 4 | paras 1, 2 | 6 Aug 1999 (SI 1999/2210) |
| | para 3(1), (2) | 25 Apr 2000 (SI 2000/880) |
| | para 3(3) | 25 Apr 2000 (SI 2000/880)[1] |
| | para 4 | 6 Aug 1999 (SI 1999/2210)[2] |
| Sch 5 | | 25 Apr 2000 (SI 2000/880), repeals of or in— House of Commons Disqualification Act 1975; Northern Ireland Assembly Disqualification Act 1975; Disability Discrimination Act 1995, ss 50, 51(1), (2), 52(1)–(10), (12), 53(1)–(3), (8), (9), 54(1)–(7), (9), 70(7), Sch 5 |
| | | 4 Dec 2006 (repeals of or in Disability Discrimination Act 1995, ss 51(3)–(6), 52(11), 53(4)–(7), 54(8)) (SI 2006/3189) |

[1]　For transitional provisions, see SI 2000/880, art 3

[2]　For a transitional provision, see SI 1999/2210, art 3

---

**Employment Relations Act 1999 (c 26)**

*RA:* 27 Jul 1999

*Commencement provisions:* s 45(1); Employment Relations Act 1999 (Commencement No 1 and Transitional Provisions) Order 1999, SI 1999/2509; Employment Relations Act 1999 (Commencement No 2 and Transitional and Saving Provisions) Order 1999, SI 1999/2830[1]; Employment Relations Act 1999 (Commencement No 3 and Transitional Provision) Order 1999, SI 1999/3374; Employment Relations Act 1999 (Commencement No 4 and Transitional Provision) Order 2000, SI 2000/420; Employment Relations Act 1999 (Commencement No 5 and Transitional Provision) Order 2000, SI 2000/875; Employment Relations Act 1999 (Commencement No 6 and Transitional Provisions) Order 2000, SI 2000/1338; Employment Relations Act 1999 (Commencement No 7 and Transitional Provisions) Order 2000, SI 2000/2242; Employment Relations Act 1999 (Commencement No 8) Order 2001, SI 2001/1187, as amended by SI 2001/1461; Employment Relations Act 1999 (Commencement No 9) Order 2003, SI 2003/3357

| | | |
|---|---|---|
| 1 | (1), (2) | 6 Jun 2000 (SI 2000/1338) |
| | (3) | See Sch 1 below |
| 2 | | See Sch 2 below |
| 3 | | 25 Oct 1999 (SI 1999/2830) |
| 4 | | 18 Sep 2000 (SI 2000/2242) |
| 5 | | 6 Jun 2000 (SI 2000/1338) |
| 6 | | 6 Jun 2000 (subject to a transitional provision) (SI 2000/1338) |
| 7–9 | | See Sch 4 below |
| 10–12 | | 4 Sep 2000 (subject to a transitional provision in relation to s 10) (SI 2000/2242) |
| 13 | (1)–(3) | 25 Oct 1999 (SI 1999/2830) |
| | (4)–(6) | 4 Sep 2000 (SI 2000/2242) |

**Employment Relations Act 1999 (c 26)**—*contd*

| | | |
|---|---|---|
| 14, 15 | | 4 Sep 2000 (SI 2000/2242) |
| 16 | | See Sch 5 below |
| 17 | | *Never in force* (repealed) |
| 18 | (1)–(5) | 25 Oct 1999 (SI 1999/2830) |
| | (6) | 30 Sep 1999 (in respect of fixed term contracts which expire on or after that date) (SI 1999/2509) |
| 19–23 | | 25 Oct 1999 (SI 1999/2830) |
| 24 | | 22 Feb 2000 (subject to a transitional provision) (SI 2000/420) |
| 25 | | 6 Jun 2000 (SI 2000/1338) |
| 26–28 | | 25 Oct 1999 (SI 1999/2830) |
| 29 | | See Sch 6 below |
| 30 | | 25 Oct 1999 (SI 1999/2830) |
| 31 | | See Sch 7 below |
| 32, 33 | | 25 Oct 1999 (SI 1999/2830) |
| 34 | (1)–(3) | 17 Dec 1999 (subject to a transitional provision) (SI 1999/3374) |
| | (4) | 25 Oct 1999 (SI 1999/2830) |
| | (5), (6) | 17 Dec 1999 (SI 1999/3374) |
| 35 | | 25 Oct 1999 (SI 1999/2830) |
| 36 | (1)(a) | 17 Dec 1999 (SI 1999/3374) |
| | (1)(b) | 25 Oct 1999 (so far as repeals Trade Union and Labour Relations (Consolidation) Act 1992, s 159(1)(b)) (SI 1999/2830) |
| | | 17 Dec 1999 (otherwise) (SI 1999/3374) |
| | (2), (3) | 17 Dec 1999 (SI 1999/3374) |
| 37 | | 25 Oct 1999 (SI 1999/2830) |
| 38 | | 9 Sep 1999 (SI 1999/2509) |
| 39, 40 | | 25 Oct 1999 (SI 1999/2830) |
| 41 | | See Sch 8 below |
| 42 | | 9 Sep 1999 (SI 1999/2509) |
| 43 | | 25 Oct 1999 (SI 1999/2830) |
| 44 | | See Sch 9 below |
| 45–47 | | 27 Jul 1999 (RA) |
| Sch 1 | | 6 Jun 2000 (subject to a transitional provision) (SI 2000/1338) |
| Sch 2 | | 25 Oct 1999 (SI 1999/2830) |
| Sch 3 | | 18 Sep 2000 (SI 2000/2242) |
| Sch 4 | | 15 Dec 1999 (SI 1999/2830) |
| Sch 5 | | 24 Apr 2000 (subject to a transitional provision) (SI 2000/875) |
| Sch 6 | | 25 Oct 1999 (SI 1999/2830) |
| Sch 7 | paras 1, 2 | 25 Oct 1999 (SI 1999/2830) |
| | para 3 | 6 Apr 2004 (SI 2003/3357) |
| | para 4(1)–(5) | 6 Apr 2004 (SI 2003/3357) |
| | para 4(6) | *Not yet in force* |
| | para 5 | 25 Oct 1999 (so far as inserts Employment Agencies Act 1973, s 11A) (SI 1999/2830) |
| | | 6 Apr 2004 (otherwise) (SI 2003/3357) |
| | para 6 | 25 Oct 1999 (SI 1999/2830) |
| | para 7 | 6 Jul 2004 (SI 2003/3357) |
| | para 8 | 25 Oct 1999 (SI 1999/2830) |
| Sch 8 | | 16 Jul 2001 (SI 2001/1187)[2] |
| Sch 9 | (1) | *Not yet in force* |
| | (2) | 15 Dec 1999 (SI 1999/2830) |
| | (3) | 25 Oct 1999 (except repeal of Trade Union and Labour Relations (Consolidation) Act 1992, Sch A1, para 163) (SI 1999/2830) |
| | | *Not yet in force* (exception noted above) |
| | (4)–(7) | 25 Oct 1999 (SI 1999/2830) |
| | (8) | *Not yet in force* |
| | (9) | 25 Oct 1999 (SI 1999/2830) |
| | (10) | 25 Oct 1999 (SI 1999/2830), repeals of or in— |
| | | Trade Union and Labour Relations (Consolidation) Act 1992, ss 157, 158, 159(1)(b); |

**Employment Relations Act 1999 (c 26)**—*contd*
Employment Rights Act 1996, s 117(4)(b) (and the word "or"
before it), (5), (6), 118(2), (3), 125;
Employment Rights (Dispute Resolution) Act 1998, s 14(1)
17 Dec 1999 (SI 1999/3374), repeals of or in—
Trade Union and Labour Relations (Consolidation) Act 1992,
ss 159(1)(a), (2), (3), 176(7), (8);
Employment Rights Act 1996, ss 120(2), 124(2), 186(2), 208,
227(2)–(4),
*Not yet in force* (repeals of or in Employment Rights Act 1996,
s 236, Sch 1)

|       |                                      |
|-------|--------------------------------------|
| (11)  | 25 Oct 1999 (SI 1999/2830)           |
| (12)  | 16 Jul 2001 (SI 2001/1187)[2]        |

1   For transitional and saving provisions relating to the provisions brought into force by SI 1999/2830,
see Sch 3 of that Order

2   SI 2001/1187 purported to bring s 41 and Sch 8 into force on 18 Apr 2001, but was amended by
SI 2001/1461, which alters the date for the coming into force of these provisions to 16 Jul 2001

---

**European Parliamentary Elections Act 1999 (c 1)**

*RA:* 14 Jan 1999

*Commencement provisions:* s 5(1); European Parliamentary Elections Act 1999 (Commencement)
Order 1999, SI 1999/717

| 1       | 16 Mar 1999 (so far as confers power to make subordinate legislation) (subject to a saving) (SI 1999/717) |
|---------|------|
|         | 1 May 1999 (otherwise) (subject to a saving) (SI 1999/717) |
| 2–4     | 1 May 1999 (otherwise) (SI 1999/717) |
| 5, 6    | 14 Jan 1999 (RA) |
| Sch 1   | 1 May 1999 (otherwise) (SI 1999/717) |
| Sch 2   | 16 Mar 1999 (so far as confers power to make subordinate legislation) (subject to a saving) (SI 1999/717) |
|         | 1 May 1999 (otherwise) (subject to a saving) (SI 1999/717) |
| Schs 3, 4 | 1 May 1999 (otherwise) (SI 1999/717) |

---

**Finance Act 1999 (c 16)**

*Budget Day:* 9 Mar 1999

*RA:* 27 Jul 1999

The commencement details of Finance Acts are not set out, as the dates from which their provisions take
effect are usually stated clearly and unambiguously in the text of the Act, and charging provisions will
normally state for which year or years of assessment they are to have effect.

---

**Food Standards Act 1999 (c 28)**

*RA:* 11 Nov 1999

*Commencement provisions:* s 43(2); Food Standards Act 1999 (Commencement No 1) Order 2000,
SI 2000/92; Food Standards Act 1999 (Commencement No 2) Order 2000, SI 2000/1066

| 1 | (1)      | 11 Jan 2000 (SI 2000/92) |
|---|----------|--------------------------|
|   | (2), (3) | 1 Apr 2000 (SI 2000/1066) |
| 2 |          | 11 Jan 2000 (SI 2000/92) |
| 3 | (1)–(3)  | 11 Jan 2000 (SI 2000/92) |
|   | (4), (5) | 11 Jan 2000 (W) (S) (SI 2000/92) |
|   |          | 1 Apr 2000 (otherwise) (SI 2000/1066) |

**Food Standards Act 1999 (c 28)**—*contd*

| | | |
|---|---|---|
| | (6) | 11 Jan 2000 (so far as (i) it is concerned with the chief executive, and (ii) it is concerned with directors and relates to Wales and Scotland) (SI 2000/92) |
| | | 1 Apr 2000 (otherwise) (SI 2000/1066) |
| 4 | | 1 Apr 2000 (SI 2000/1066) |
| 5 | (1) | 11 Jan 2000 (W) (S) (SI 2000/92) |
| | | 1 Apr 2000 (otherwise) (SI 2000/1066) |
| | (2), (3) | 1 Apr 2000 (SI 2000/1066) |
| | (4) | See Sch 2 below |
| 6–35 | | 1 Apr 2000 (SI 2000/1066) |
| 36 | (1) | 11 Jan 2000 (so far as it relates to the definitions "Agency" and "appropriate authority") (SI 2000/92) |
| | | 1 Apr 2000 (otherwise) (SI 2000/1066) |
| | (2) | 11 Jan 2000 (SI 2000/92) |
| | (3)–(5) | 1 Apr 2000 (SI 2000/1066) |
| 37–40 | | 1 Apr 2000 (SI 2000/1066) |
| 41, 42 | | 11 Jan 2000 (SI 2000/92) |
| 43 | | 11 Nov 1999 (RA) |
| Sch 1 | | 11 Jan 2000 (SI 2000/92) |
| Sch 2 | para 1 | 11 Jan 2000 (SI 2000/92) |
| | paras 2–4 | 1 Apr 2000 (SI 2000/1066) |
| | paras 5, 6 | 11 Jan 2000 (SI 2000/92) |
| | paras 7, 8 | 1 Apr 2000 (SI 2000/1066) |
| Schs 3, 4 | | 1 Apr 2000 (SI 2000/1066) |
| Sch 5 | paras 1–5 | 1 Apr 2000 (SI 2000/1066) |
| | para 6(1) | 1 Apr 2000 (SI 2000/1066) |
| | para 6(2) | 11 Nov 1999 (RA) |
| | para 6(3), (4) | 1 Apr 2000 (SI 2000/1066) |
| | para 6(5) | 11 Nov 1999 (RA) |
| | para 6(6) | 1 Apr 2000 (SI 2000/1066) |
| | paras 7–45 | 1 Apr 2000 (SI 2000/1066) |
| Sch 6 | | 1 Apr 2000 (SI 2000/1066) |

---

## Football (Offences and Disorder) Act 1999 (c 21)

*RA:* 27 Jul 1999

*Commencement provisions:* s 12(2)

Whole Act in force 27 Sep 1999 (s 12(2))

---

## Greater London Authority Act 1999 (c 29)

*RA:* 11 Nov 1999

*Commencement provisions:* s 425(2); Greater London Authority Act 1999 (Commencement No 1) Order 1999, SI 1999/3271; Greater London Authority Act 1999 (Commencement No 2) Order 1999, SI 1999/3376; Greater London Authority Act 1999 (Commencement No 3 and Transitional Finance Provisions) Order 1999, SI 1999/3434; Greater London Authority Act 1999 (Commencement No 4 and Adaptation) Order 2000, SI 2000/801; Greater London Authority Act 1999 (Commencement No 5 and Appointment of Reconstitution Day) Order 2000, SI 2000/1094; Greater London Authority Act 1999 (Commencement No 6 and Preliminary Arrangements for the Metropolitan Police Authority) Order 2000, SI 2000/1095; Greater London Authority Act 1999 (Commencement No 7, Transitional Provisions and Amendment) Order 2000, SI 2000/1648; Greater London Authority Act 1999 (Commencement No 8 and Consequential Provisions) Order 2000, SI 2000/3145; Greater London Authority Act 1999 (Commencement No 9) Order 2000, SI 2000/3379; Greater London Authority Act 1999 (Commencement No 10) Order 2001, SI 2001/3603; Greater London Authority Act 1999 (Commencement No 11) Order 2003, SI 2003/1920

| | |
|---|---|
| 1–29 | 14 Dec 1999 (SI 1999/3376) |

**Greater London Authority Act 1999 (c 29)**—*contd*

| | | |
|---|---|---|
| 30 | (1)–(6) | 3 Jul 2000 (SI 2000/801) |
| | (7) | 8 May 2000 (SI 2000/801) |
| | (8) | 3 Jul 2000 (SI 2000/801) |
| | (9) | 8 May 2000 (SI 2000/801) |
| | (10) | 3 Jul 2000 (SI 2000/801) |
| 31 | | 11 Nov 1999 (for the purpose of making orders) (s 425(2)) |
| | | 3 Jul 2000 (otherwise) (SI 2000/801) |
| 32, 33 | | 3 Jul 2000 (SI 2000/801) |
| 34–36 | | 8 May 2000 (SI 2000/801) |
| 37 | | See Sch 4 below |
| 38–40 | | 8 May 2000 (SI 2000/801) |
| 41–44 | | 3 Jul 2000 (SI 2000/801) |
| 45 | | 8 May 2000 (SI 2000/801) |
| 46–48 | | 3 Jul 2000 (SI 2000/801) |
| 49–59 | | 8 May 2000 (SI 2000/801) |
| 60–62 | | 3 Jul 2000 (SI 2000/801) |
| 63 | | *Not yet in force*[1] |
| 64, 65 | | 3 Jul 2000 (SI 2000/801) |
| 66–75 | | 8 May 2000 (SI 2000/801) |
| 76 | | 3 Jul 2000 (SI 2000/801) |
| 77 | (1)–(3) | 3 Jul 2000 (SI 2000/801) |
| | (4) | See Sch 5 below |
| | (5)–(7) | 3 Jul 2000 (SI 2000/801) |
| 78, 79 | | 3 Jul 2000 (SI 2000/801) |
| 80 | | 8 May 2000 (SI 2000/801) |
| 81 | | 12 Jan 2000 (SI 1999/3434)[2] |
| 82 | (1), (2) | 12 Jan 2000 (SI 1999/3434)[2] |
| | (3) | 12 Jan 2000 (so far as relates to the exercise of functions by the London Fire and Civil Defence Authority in respect of the financial year beginning on 1 Apr 2000 and subsequent years) (SI 1999/3434) |
| | | 1 Jan 2001 (otherwise)[6] (SI 2000/3379) |
| 83 | | 12 Jan 2000 (SI 1999/3434)[2] |
| 84 | | 3 Jul 2000 (SI 1999/3434) |
| 85 | | 12 Jan 2000 (SI 1999/3434)[2] |
| 86 | | 11 Nov 1999 (for the purpose of making regulations) (s 425(2)) |
| | | 12 Jan 2000 (so far as not already in force) (SI 1999/3434)[2] |
| 87 | | See Sch 6 below |
| 88, 89 | | 11 Nov 1999 (for the purpose of making regulations) (s 425(2)) |
| | | 12 Jan 2000 (so far as not already in force) (SI 1999/3434)[2] |
| 90, 91 | | 12 Jan 2000 (SI 1999/3434) |
| 92, 93 | | 12 Jan 2000 (SI 1999/3434)[2] |
| 94 | | 3 Jul 2000 (SI 1999/3434)[2] |
| 95, 96 | | 3 Jul 2000 (SI 1999/3434) |
| 97 | (1), (2) | 12 Jan 2000 (SI 1999/3434)[2] |
| | (3) | 3 Jul 2000 (SI 1999/3434) |
| 98 | | See Sch 7 below |
| 99 | | 12 Jan 2000 (SI 1999/3434) |
| 100 | (1)–(4) | 12 Jan 2000 (SI 1999/3434) |
| | (5) | 3 Jul 2000 (SI 1999/3434) |
| | (6) | 12 Jan 2000 (SI 1999/3434) |
| 101 | | 12 Jan 2000 (SI 1999/3434)[2] |
| 102 | (1)–(4) | 12 Jan 2000 (SI 1999/3434)[2] |
| | (5) | 3 Jul 2000 (SI 1999/3434) |
| | (6)–(8) | 12 Jan 2000 (SI 1999/3434)[2] |
| 103, 104 | | 3 Jul 2000 (SI 1999/3434) |
| 105 | | 12 Jan 2000 (SI 1999/3434)[2] |
| 106, 107 | | 12 Jan 2000 (SI 1999/3434) |
| 108–110 | | 3 Jul 2000 (SI 1999/3434) |

**Greater London Authority Act 1999 (c 29)**—*contd*

| | | |
|---|---|---|
| 111 | | 8 May 2000 (except in so far as relates to a functional body) (SI 2000/801) |
| | | 3 Jul 2000 (exception noted above) (SI 2000/801) |
| 112 | | 8 May 2000 (except in so far as relates to a functional body) (SI 2000/801) |
| | | 3 Jul 2000 (exception noted above) (SI 2000/801) |
| 113 | (1) | 8 May 2000 (SI 2000/801) |
| | (2) | 3 Jul 2000 (SI 2000/801) |
| | (3)–(6) | 8 May 2000 (SI 2000/801) |
| 114 | | 8 May 2000 (SI 2000/801) |
| 115 | (1) | 3 Jul 2000 (SI 2000/801) |
| | (2) | 3 Jul 2000 (so far as relates to financial years beginning in or after 2001) (SI 2000/801) |
| | | *Never in force* (otherwise)[1] (repealed) |
| | (3) | 3 Jul 2000 (SI 2000/801) |
| 116 | | 11 Nov 1999 (for the purpose of making regulations) (s 425(2)) |
| | | 3 Jul 2000 (otherwise) (SI 2000/801) |
| 117 | | 8 May 2000 (SI 2000/801) |
| 118 | | 3 Jul 2000 (SI 2000/801) |
| 119 | | 11 Nov 1999 (for the purpose of making regulations) (s 425(2)) |
| | | 3 Jul 2000 (otherwise) (SI 2000/801) |
| 120, 121 | | 3 Jul 2000 (SI 2000/801) |
| 122–124 | | 3 Jul 2000 (so far as relates to capital spending plans for financial years beginning in or after 2001) (SI 2000/801) |
| 125 | | 3 Jul 2000 (SI 2000/801) |
| 126 | | 8 May 2000 (SI 2000/801) |
| 127 | | 8 May 2000 (so far as applies to the Greater London Authority) (SI 1999/3434) |
| | | Operative date[4] (so far as applies to the Metropolitan Police Authority, and for the purposes only of SI 2000/1095, arts 5, 6, which provide for the first meeting of the Authority) (SI 2000/1095) |
| | | 3 Jul 2000 (otherwise) (SI 1999/3434) |
| 128–133 | | 8 May 2000 (so far as applies to the Greater London Authority) (SI 1999/3434) |
| | | 3 Jul 2000 (otherwise) (SI 1999/3434) |
| 134 | | 8 May 2000 (SI 1999/3434) |
| 135 | | 3 Jul 2000 (SI 1999/3434) |
| 136 | (1) | 12 Jan 2000 (SI 1999/3434) |
| | (2) | See Sch 9 below |
| 137 | | 8 May 2000 (SI 1999/3434) |
| 138–140 | | 3 Jul 2000 (SI 1999/3434) |
| 141–153 | | 3 Jul 2000 (SI 2000/801) |
| 154 | (1) | 8 May 2000 (SI 2000/801) |
| | (2), (3) | 3 Jul 2000 (SI 2000/801) |
| | (4) | See Sch 10 below |
| 155 | | 3 Jul 2000 (SI 2000/801) |
| 156 | (1)–(7) | 3 Jul 2000 (SI 2000/801) |
| | (8) | See Sch 11 below |
| 157, 158 | | 11 Nov 1999 (for the purpose of making orders) (s 425(2)) |
| | | 3 Jul 2000 (otherwise) (SI 2000/801) |
| 159–162 | | 3 Jul 2000 (SI 2000/801) |
| 163 | | 11 Nov 1999 (for the purpose of making orders) (s 425(2)) |
| | | 3 Jul 2000 (otherwise) (SI 2000/801) |
| 164 | | 3 Jul 2000 (SI 2000/801) |
| 165 | (1)–(3) | 3 Jul 2000 (SI 2000/801) |
| | (4) | See Sch 12 below |
| 166 | | 3 Jul 2000 (SI 2000/801) |
| 167 | (1)–(4) | 3 Jul 2000 (SI 2000/801) |

**Greater London Authority Act 1999 (c 29)**—*contd*

| | | |
|---|---|---|
| | (5) | See Sch 13 below |
| | (6)–(9) | 3 Jul 2000 (SI 2000/801) |
| 168, 169 | | 3 Jul 2000 (SI 2000/801) |
| 170–172 | | 12 Jan 2000 (SI 1999/3434) |
| 173–198 | | 3 Jul 2000 (SI 2000/801) |
| 199 | | 11 Nov 1999 (s 425(2)) |
| 200–209 | | 3 Jul 2000 (SI 2000/801) |
| 210–216 | | 12 Jan 2000 (SI 1999/3434) |
| 217 | | 15 Jul 2003 (SI 2003/1920) |
| 218, 219 | | 12 Jan 2000 (SI 1999/3434) |
| 220–224 | | 15 Jul 2003 (SI 2003/1920) |
| 225–239 | | 12 Jan 2000 (SI 1999/3434) |
| 240–244 | | 3 Jul 2000 (SI 2000/801) |
| 245 | | See Sch 17 below |
| 246 | | 3 Jul 2000 (SI 2000/801) |
| 247 | (1)–(6) | 3 Jul 2000 (SI 2000/801) |
| | (7) | See Sch 18 below |
| 248–251 | | 3 Jul 2000 (SI 2000/801) |
| 252 | (1) | 3 Jul 2000 (SI 2000/801) |
| | (2) | See Sch 19 below |
| 253 | | See Sch 20 below |
| 254 | | 22 Jan 2001 (so far as relates to Sch 21, paras 1–18) (SI 2000/3145) |
| | | 7 Nov 2001 (otherwise) (SI 2001/3603) |
| 255 | | 11 Nov 1999 (for the purposes of making orders) (s 425(2)) |
| | | 1 Apr 2000 (otherwise) (SI 2000/801) |
| 256, 257 | | 3 Jul 2000 (SI 2000/801) |
| 258 | | 12 Jan 2000 (SI 1999/3434) |
| 259 | | 3 Jul 2000 (SI 2000/801) |
| 260 | | 12 Jan 2000 (SI 1999/3434) |
| 261–265 | | 3 Jul 2000 (SI 2000/801) |
| 266 | | 8 May 2000 (for the purposes of enabling directions to be given under Highways Act 1980, s 301A(9)) (SI 2000/801) |
| | | 3 Jul 2000 (otherwise) (SI 2000/801) |
| 267–269 | | 3 Jul 2000 (SI 2000/801) |
| 270 | | See Sch 22 below |
| 271 | | 3 Jul 2000 (SI 2000/801) |
| 272 | | 12 Jan 2000 (SI 1999/3434) |
| 273–286 | | 3 Jul 2000 (SI 2000/801) |
| 287 | (1) | 3 Jul 2000 (SI 2000/801) |
| | (2) | *Not yet in force*[5] |
| | (3)–(5) | 3 Jul 2000 (SI 2000/801) |
| 288 | | 1 Apr 2000 (SI 2000/801) |
| 289, 290 | | 3 Jul 2000 (SI 2000/801) |
| 291 | | 8 May 2000 (for the purposes of enabling directions to be given under Road Traffic Regulation Act 1984, s 121B(9)) (SI 2000/801) |
| | | 3 Jul 2000 (otherwise) (SI 2000/801) |
| 292–294 | | 3 Jul 2000 (SI 2000/801) |
| 295 | (1) | 8 May 2000 (except in relation to Transport for London) (SI 2000/801) |
| | | 3 Jul 2000 (exception noted above) (SI 2000/801) |
| | (2) | See Sch 23 below |
| | (3) | 8 May 2000 (except in relation to Transport for London) (SI 2000/801) |
| | | 3 Jul 2000 (exception noted above) (SI 2000/801) |
| 296 | (1) | 8 May 2000 (except in relation to Transport for London) (SI 2000/801) |
| | | 3 Jul 2000 (exception noted above) (SI 2000/801) |
| | (2) | See Sch 24 below |

**Greater London Authority Act 1999 (c 29)**—*contd*

| | | |
|---|---|---|
| 297 | | 1 Apr 2000 (SI 2000/801) |
| 298 | (1), (2) | 12 Jan 2000 (SI 1999/3434) |
| | (3)–(9) | 3 Jul 2000 (SI 2000/801) |
| 299, 300 | | 3 Jul 2000 (SI 2000/801) |
| 301 | | 15 Jul 2003 (SI 2003/1920) |
| 302 | | 11 Nov 1999 (s 425(2)) |
| 303 | | 1 Apr 2000 (for the purposes of s 297) (SI 2000/801) |
| | | 15 Jul 2003 (otherwise) (SI 2003/1920) |
| 304 | | 8 May 2000 (for the purpose only of enabling the Mayor to consult on the appointment of persons to be members of the London Development Agency) (SI 2000/801) |
| | | 3 Jul 2000 (otherwise) (SI 2000/801) |
| 305 | | 8 May 2000 (SI 2000/801) |
| 306–308 | | 3 Jul 2000 (SI 2000/801) |
| 309 | | See Sch 25 below |
| 310 | (1) | 1 Jan 2000 (for the purposes of giving effect to those parts of Police Act 1996, Schs 2A, 3 relating to the appointment of members of the Metropolitan Police Authority) (SI 1999/3271) |
| | | Operative date[4] (for the purposes only of SI 2000/1095, arts 5, 6, which provide for the first meeting of the Metropolitan Police Authority) (SI 2000/1095) |
| | | 3 Jul 2000 (otherwise) (SI 2000/1095) |
| | (2) | See Sch 26 below |
| 311–322 | | 3 Jul 2000 (SI 2000/1648) |
| 323 | | 1 Apr 2000 (SI 1999/3271) |
| 324 | | 1 Jan 2000 (SI 1999/3271) |
| 325 | | See Sch 27 below |
| 326 | | *Never in force* (repealed) |
| 327 | | 11 Nov 1999 (s 425(2)) |
| 328 | | 1 May 2000 (for the purpose only of nominating or appointing the first members of the Fire etc Authority) (SI 2000/1094) |
| | | 3 Jul 2000 (otherwise) (SI 2000/1094) |
| 329–333 | | 3 Jul 2000 (SI 2000/1094) |
| 334–342 | | 3 Jul 2000 (SI 2000/801) |
| 343 | | 11 Nov 1999 (for the purpose of making regulations) (s 425(2)) |
| | | 3 Jul 2000 (otherwise) (SI 2000/801) |
| 344 | | 12 Jan 2000 (SI 1999/3434) |
| 345–348 | | 3 Jul 2000 (SI 2000/801) |
| 349 | | 1 Apr 2000 (SI 2000/801) |
| 350–373 | | 3 Jul 2000 (SI 2000/801) |
| 374 | | 1 Apr 2000 (SI 2000/801) |
| 375 | (1) | 8 May 2000 (SI 2000/801) |
| | (2) | 3 Jul 2000 (SI 2000/801) |
| | (3) | See Sch 30 below |
| 376–379 | | 3 Jul 2000 (SI 2000/801) |
| 380 | | 8 May 2000 (SI 2000/801) |
| 381 | | 3 Jul 2000 (SI 2000/801) |
| 382 | (1) | 3 Jul 2000 (SI 2000/801) |
| | (2), (3) | 8 May 2000 (SI 2000/801) |
| 383, 384 | | 1 Oct 2000 (SI 2000/801) |
| 385, 386 | | 8 May 2000 (SI 2000/801) |
| 387 | | 8 May 2000 (for the purposes of its application to the Greater London Authority) (SI 1999/3434) |
| | | 3 Jul 2000 (other than for the purposes of sub-s (3)(b), so far as not already in force) (SI 1999/3434) |
| | | 3 Jul 2000 (otherwise) (SI 2000/801) |
| 388 | | 8 May 2000 (for the purposes of para (a)) (SI 1999/3434) |
| | | 3 Jul 2000 (otherwise) (SI 1999/3434) |
| 389, 390 | | 12 Jan 2000 (SI 1999/3434) |

**Greater London Authority Act 1999 (c 29)**—*contd*

| | | |
|---|---|---|
| 391 | | 8 May 2000 (SI 2000/801) |
| 392 | | 8 May 2000 (for the purposes of sub-s (3)(a)) (SI 1999/3434) |
| | | 3 Jul 2000 (for the purposes of sub-s (3)(b)) (SI 1999/3434) |
| | | 3 Jul 2000 (otherwise) (SI 2000/801) |
| 393 | | 8 May 2000 (for the purposes of its application to the Greater London Authority) (SI 1999/3434) |
| | | 3 Jul 2000 (otherwise) (SI 1999/3434) |
| 394 | | 8 May 2000 (SI 2000/801) |
| 395 | | 3 Jul 2000 (SI 2000/801) |
| 396 | (1)–(9) | 11 Nov 1999 (for the purpose of making regulations) (s 425(2)) |
| | | 8 May 2000 (otherwise) (SI 2000/801) |
| | (10)–(12) | 1 Apr 2000 (SI 2000/801) |
| 397–400 | | 8 May 2000 (SI 2000/801) |
| 401 | | 12 Jan 2000 (SI 1999/3434) |
| 402, 403 | | 3 Jul 2000 (SI 2000/801) |
| 404 | | 8 May 2000 (SI 2000/801) |
| 405, 406 | | 11 Nov 1999 (s 425(2)) |
| 407 | | 12 Jan 2000 (SI 1999/3434) |
| 408 | | 11 Nov 1999 (s 425(2)) |
| 409, 410 | | 12 Jan 2000 (SI 1999/3434) |
| 411 | | 11 Nov 1999 (s 425(2)) |
| 412 | | 12 Jan 2000 (SI 1999/3434) |
| 413 | | *Not yet in force*[1] |
| 414–419 | | 12 Jan 2000 (SI 1999/3434) |
| 420 | | 11 Nov 1999 (s 425(2)) |
| 421, 422 | | 12 Jan 2000 (SI 1999/3434) |
| 423 | | See Sch 34 below |
| 424 | | 14 Dec 1999 (so far as relates to Pt I, Schs 1–3 of this Act) (SI 1999/3376) |
| | | 12 Jan 2000 (so far as not already in force and subject to transitional provisions) (SI 1999/3434)[2] |
| 425 | | 11 Nov 1999 (s 425(2)) |
| Schs 1–3 | | 14 Dec 1999 (SI 1999/3376) |
| Sch 4 | | 8 May 2000 (SI 2000/801) |
| Sch 5 | | 3 Jul 2000 (SI 2000/801) |
| Schs 6, 7 | | 3 Jul 2000 (SI 1999/3434) |
| Sch 8 | | *Not yet in force*[1] |
| Sch 9 | | 3 Jul 2000 (SI 1999/3434) |
| Sch 10 | | 8 May 2000 (SI 2000/801) |
| Schs 11–13 | | 3 Jul 2000 (SI 2000/801)[7] |
| Schs 14, 15 | | 15 Jul 2003 (SI 2003/1920) |
| Sch 16 | | 3 Jul 2000 (SI 2000/801) |
| Sch 17 | paras 1–9 | 3 Jul 2000 (SI 2000/801) |
| | para 10 | 11 Nov 1999 (for the purpose of making orders) (s 425(2)) |
| | | 3 Jul 2000 (otherwise) (SI 2000/801) |
| | para 11 | 15 Jul 2003 (SI 2003/1920) |
| Schs 18–20 | | 3 Jul 2000 (SI 2000/801) |
| Sch 21 | paras 1–18 | 22 Jan 2001 (SI 2000/3145) |
| | para 19 | 7 Nov 2001 (SI 2001/3603) |
| Sch 22 | | 3 Jul 2000 (SI 2000/801) |
| Schs 23, 24 | | 8 May 2000 (except in relation to Transport for London) (SI 2000/801) |
| | | 3 Jul 2000 (exception noted above) (SI 2000/801)[1] |
| Sch 25 | | 3 Jul 2000 (SI 2000/801) |
| Sch 26 | | 1 Jan 2000 (for the purposes of giving effect to those parts of Police Act 1996, Schs 2A, 3 relating to the appointment of members of the Metropolitan Police Authority) (SI 1999/3271) |

**Greater London Authority Act 1999 (c 29)**—*contd*

|  |  |  |
|---|---|---|
|  |  | Operative date[4] (for the purposes only of SI 2000/1095, arts 5, 6, which provide for the first meeting of the Metropolitan Police Authority) (SI 2000/1095) |
|  |  | 3 Jul 2000 (otherwise) (SI 2000/1095) |
| Sch 27 | para 1 | 3 Jul 2000 (subject to a transitional provision) (save in so far as Metropolitan Police Act 1829, ss 10–12, relate to the Receiver's functions in relation to purposes other than police purposes) (SI 2000/1648) |
|  |  | *Not yet in force*[1] |
|  | para 2 | 3 Jul 2000 (SI 2000/1648) |
|  | para 3 | 3 Jul 2000 (so far as Metropolitan Police (Receiver) Act 1861, ss 1, 5, relate to the Receiver's functions in relation to police purposes) (SI 2000/1648) |
|  |  | *Not yet in force*[1] (repeals of Metropolitan Police (Receiver) Act 1861, ss 1, 5 (except so far as they relate to the Receiver's functions in relation to police purposes), 9) |
|  | para 4 | 30 Mar 2000 (subject to adaptation)[3] (SI 2000/801) |
|  | para 5 | 3 Jul 2000 (so far as Metropolitan Police Act 1886, ss 2, 4, 6, relate to the Receiver's functions in relation to police purposes) (SI 2000/1648) |
|  |  | *Not yet in force*[1] (repeals of Metropolitan Police Act 1866, ss 2, 4, 6 (except so far as they relate to the Receiver's functions in relation to police purposes), 7) |
|  | para 6 | 3 Jul 2000 (SI 2000/1648) |
|  | para 7 | 3 Jul 2000 (so far as Metropolitan Police Act 1887 relates to the Receiver's functions in relation to police purposes) (SI 2000/1648) |
|  |  | *Not yet in force*[1] (repeal of Metropolitan Police Act 1887 (except so far as it relates to the Receiver's functions in relation to police purposes)) |
|  | paras 8, 9 | *Not yet in force*[1] |
|  | para 10 | 3 Jul 2000 (SI 2000/1648) |
|  | para 11 | 3 Jul 2000 (save in so far as Metropolitan Police Act 1899, s 1, relates to the Receiver) (SI 2000/1648) |
|  |  | *Not yet in force*[1] (saving noted above) |
|  | para 12 | 3 Jul 2000 (SI 2000/1648) |
|  | para 13 | 3 Jul 2000 (save in so far as Crown Lands Act 1936, s 3(2), relates to the Receiver's functions in relation to purposes other than police purposes) (SI 2000/1648) |
|  |  | *Not yet in force*[1] (saving noted above) |
|  | para 14 | *Not yet in force*[1] |
|  | paras 15–17 | 3 Jul 2000 (SI 2000/1648) |
|  | para 18 | *Not yet in force*[1] |
|  | para 19 | 3 Jul 2000 (SI 2000/1648) |
|  | para 20 | 3 Jul 2000 (subject to a transitional provision) (SI 2000/1648) |
|  | paras 21–38 | 3 Jul 2000 (SI 2000/1648) |
|  | para 39(1) | 3 Jul 2000 (SI 2000/1648) |
|  | para 39(2)(a), (b) | 3 Jul 2000 (SI 2000/1648) |
|  | para 39(2)(c) | *Not yet in force*[1] |
|  | para 40(1) | 3 Jul 2000 (SI 2000/1648) |
|  | para 40(2)(a), (b) | 3 Jul 2000 (SI 2000/1648) |
|  | para 40(2)(c) | *Not yet in force*[1] |
|  | paras 41–61 | 3 Jul 2000 (SI 2000/1648) |
|  | para 62 | Operative date[4] (for the purposes only of SI 2000/1095, arts 5, 6, which provide for the first meeting of the Metropolitan Police Authority) (SI 2000/1095) |
|  |  | 3 Jul 2000 (otherwise) (SI 2000/1095) |
|  | para 63 | 3 Jul 2000 (SI 2000/1648) |

**Greater London Authority Act 1999 (c 29)**—*contd*

| | | |
|---|---|---|
| | para 64 | 3 Jul 2000 (except that the substitution of Local Government and Housing Act 1989, s 157(6)(f), shall not have effect in so far as it relates to the Receiver's functions in relation to purposes other than police purposes) (SI 2000/1648) |
| | | *Not yet in force*[1] (exception noted above) |
| | para 65 | 3 Jul 2000 (SI 2000/1648) |
| | para 66(a) | *Not yet in force*[1] |
| | para 66(b) | 3 Jul 2000 (subject to a transitional provision) (SI 2000/1648) |
| | para 67 | 3 Jul 2000 (SI 2000/1648) |
| | para 68 | *Not yet in force*[1] |
| | para 69 | 1 Apr 2000 (SI 1999/3271) |
| | paras 70–74 | 3 Jul 2000 (SI 2000/1648) |
| | paras 75, 76 | Operative date[4] (for the purposes only of SI 2000/1095, arts 5, 6, which provide for the first meeting of the Metropolitan Police Authority) (SI 2000/1095) |
| | | 3 Jul 2000 (otherwise) (SI 2000/1095) |
| | paras 77–83 | 3 Jul 2000 (SI 2000/1648) |
| | para 84(1) | 1 Apr 2000 (SI 1999/3271) |
| | para 84(2) | 3 Jul 2000 (SI 2000/1648) |
| | para 84(3) | 1 Apr 2000 (SI 1999/3271) |
| | paras 85–104 | 3 Jul 2000 (SI 2000/1648) |
| | para 105 | 1 Apr 2000 (SI 1999/3271) |
| | para 106 | 1 Jan 2000 (for the purposes of giving effect to those parts of Police Act 1996, Schs 2A, 3 relating to the appointment of members of the Metropolitan Police Authority) (SI 1999/3271) |
| | | 3 Jul 2000 (otherwise) (SI 2000/1648) |
| | paras 107–115 | 3 Jul 2000 (SI 2000/1648) |
| | para 116 | *Not yet in force*[1] |
| Sch 28 | | 1 May 2000 (for the purpose only of nominating or appointing the first members of the Fire etc Authority) (SI 2000/1094) |
| | | 3 Jul 2000 (otherwise) (SI 2000/1094) |
| Sch 29 | | 3 Jul 2000 (SI 2000/1094) |
| Sch 30 | | 8 May 2000 (SI 2000/801) |
| Sch 31 | | 12 Jan 2000 (SI 1999/3434) |
| Sch 32 | | 11 Nov 1999 (s 425(2)) |
| Sch 33 | | 12 Jan 2000 (SI 1999/3434) |
| Sch 34 | Pt I | 12 Jan 2000 (repeals of or in Local Government Finance Act 1992, ss 39(1)(e) (in respect of the exercise of functions in relation to the financial year beginning on 1 Apr 2000 and subsequent years), 43(5A)(b) and the word "and" immediately preceding it, 46(2)(d), (3)(d), (4)) (SI 1999/3434) |
| | | 3 Jul 2000 (SI 1999/3434), repeals of or in— |
| | | Public Works Loans Act 1965; |
| | | National Loans Act 1968 |
| | | 1 Jan 2001 (repeals of or in Local Government Finance Act 1992, ss 39(1)(f), 65(3)) (SI 2000/3379)[6] |
| | | *Not yet in force*, repeals of or in— |
| | | Trustee Investments Act 1961; |
| | | Local Government Act 1972; |
| | | Stock Transfer Act 1982; |
| | | Local Government Finance Act 1988; |
| | | Local Government and Housing Act 1989; |
| | | Local Government Finance Act 1992, ss 19(3)(e), 53(1), Sch 4, para 5(8)(a); |
| | | Access to Justice Act 1999 |
| | Pt II | 3 Jul 2000 (repeals of or in Railways Act 1993, s 2(1)) (SI 2000/801) |
| | | 15 Jul 2003 (otherwise) (except repeal of Transport Act 1985, Pt II) (SI 2003/1920) |
| | | *Not yet in force* (exception noted above) |

**Greater London Authority Act 1999 (c 29)**—*contd*

| | |
|---|---|
| Pts III, IV | 3 Jul 2000 (SI 2000/801) |
| Pt V | 3 Jul 2000 (except repeal of or in Private Hire Vehicles (London) Act 1998, s 38) (SI 2000/801) |
| | *Not yet in force* (exception noted above) |
| Pt VI | 3 Jul 2000 (SI 2000/801) |
| Pt VII | 1 Apr 2000 (repeals of or in Police Act 1996, ss 1(3), 32(5), Sch 2) (SI 1999/3271) |

3 Jul 2000 (SI 2000/1648), repeals of or in—
Metropolitan Police Act 1856;
Riot (Damages) Act 1886;
Police (Property) Act 1897;
Police Act 1909;
Crown Lands Act 1936, ss 1, 3(1);
Local Government Act 1948;
Metropolitan Magistrates' Courts Act 1959;
Leasehold Reform Act 1967;
Firearms Act 1968;
Local Government Act 1972;
Local Government Act 1974;
House of Commons Disqualification Act 1975 (except entry relating to the Receiver);
Northern Ireland Assembly Disqualification Act 1975 (except entry relating to the Receiver);
Local Government, Planning and Land Act 1980;
Aviation Security Act 1982;
Insurance Companies Act 1982;
Rates Act 1984;
Road Traffic Regulation Act 1984;
Local Government Finance Act 1988;
Road Traffic Act 1988;
Police Act 1996, ss 22, 25, 26, 28, 29, 32(3), 33, 44, 55, 65, 93, 95, 96, 101, Sch 6;
Police Act 1997;
Police (Insurance of Voluntary Assistants) Act 1997

*Not yet in force*, repeals of or in—
Metropolitan Police Act 1829;
Metropolitan Police (Receiver) Act 1861;
Metropolitan Police (Receiver) Act 1867;
Metropolitan Police Act 1886;
Metropolitan Police Act 1887;
Metropolitan Police (Receiver) Act 1895;
Metropolitan Police Courts Act 1897;
Metropolitan Police Act 1899;
Crown Lands Act 1936, s 3(2);
London Building Acts (Amendment) Act 1939;
Administration of Justice Act 1964;
House of Commons Disqualification Act 1975, Sch 1, Pt III (entry relating to the Receiver);
Northern Ireland Assembly Disqualification Act 1975, Sch 1, Pt III (entry relating to the Receiver);
Town and Country Planning Act 1990;
Value Added Tax Act 1994;
Local Government (Contracts) Act 1997

| | |
|---|---|
| Pt VIII | 3 Jul 2000 (SI 2000/1094) |
| Pt IX | 3 Jul 2000 (repeal in Local Government Act 1974, s 25(1)) (SI 2000/801) |

*Not yet in force*, repeals of or in—
Trafalgar Square Act 1844;
Local Government Act 1985;

**Greater London Authority Act 1999 (c 29)**—*contd*
> Town and Country Planning Act 1990;
> Deregulation and Contracting Out Act 1994

1    But, note that any power of a Minister of the Crown to make regulations or an order under this Act came into force on 11 Nov 1999 (s 425(2))

2    The transitional provisions are set out in the Greater London Authority Act 1999 (Commencement No 3 and Transitional Finance Provisions) Order 1999, SI 1999/3434, Sch 1, Tables 1, 2. The transitional provisions in Tables 1, 2 modify certain provisions of this Act with effect for the financial year beginning on 1 Apr 2000 and the exercise before 3 Jul 2000 or 3 Apr 2001 respectively of functions under those provisions, or under any provisions modified by any of those provisions

3    For the adaptation to this provision, see SI 2000/801, art 3

4    The "operative date" means the date on which appointments to the Metropolitan Police Authority are first made under Police Act 1996, Sch 2A, para 3(3) (appointment of independent members), as inserted by the Greater London Authority Act 1999, s 310(2), Sch 26

5    SI 2000/801 purported to bring s 287(2) into force on 3 Jul 2000. However SI 2000/1648, art 3, amends SI 2000/801 so as to provide that s 287(2) has not yet come into force

6    For saving provisions, see SI 2000/3379, art 3

7    S 217(7) which is one of the enabling provisions for Sch 12 was brought into force on 15 Jul 2003 by SI 2003/1920. It is therefore thought that the intention was to commence Sch 12 (so far as not already in force) on 3 Jul 2000 (in so far as it relates to s 165), and on 15 Jul 2003 (in so far as it relates to s 217)

---

**Health Act 1999 (c 8)**

*RA:* 30 Jun 1999

*Commencement provisions:* s 67; Health Act 1999 (Commencement No 1) Order 1999, SI 1999/2177; Health Act 1999 (Commencement No 2) Order 1999, SI 1999/2342; Health Act 1999 (Commencement No 3) Order 1999, SI 1999/2540; Health Act 1999 (Commencement No 4) Order 1999, SSI 1999/90; Health Act 1999 (Commencement No 5) Order 1999, SI 1999/2793; Health Act 1999 (Commencement No 6) (Scotland) Order 1999, SSI 1999/115; Health Act 1999 (Commencement No 1) (Wales) Order 1999, SI 1999/3184; Health Act 1999 (Commencement No 7) (Scotland) Order 2000, SSI 2000/38; Health Act 1999 (Commencement No 8) Order 2000, SI 2000/779; Health Act 1999 (Commencement No 9) Order 2000, SI 2000/1041; Health Act 1999 (Commencement No 2) (Wales) Order 2000, SI 2000/1026; Health Act 1999 (Commencement No 3) (Wales) Order 2000, SI 2000/2991; Health Act 1999 (Commencement No 10) Order 2001, SI 2001/270; Health Act 1999 (Commencement No 11) Order 2001, SI 2001/1985; Health Act 1999 (Commencement No 12) Order 2002, SI 2002/1167; Health Act 1999 (Commencement No 13) Order 2003, SI 2003/1689; Health Act 1999 (Commencement No 14) Order 2004, SI 2004/289; Health Act 1999 (Commencement No 14) (Scotland) Order 2004, SSI 2004/32; Health Act 1999 (Commencement No 15) Order 2004, SI 2004/1859; National Health Service (Pre-consolidation Amendments) Order 2006, SI 2006/1407; Health Act 1999 (Commencement No 16) Order 2007, SI 2007/1179; Health Act 1999 (Commencement No 17) Order 2017, SI 2017/810

| | | |
|---|---|---|
| 1 | | 1 Oct 1999 (E) (SI 1999/2540) |
| | | 1 Apr 2000 (W) (SI 2000/1026) |
| 2 | (1) | 8 Sep 1999 (E) (so far as relates to National Health Service Act 1977, s 16A(4)–(6), Sch 5A, paras 20(2), (3), 23(3)) (SI 1999/2342) |
| | | 4 Jan 2000 (E) (otherwise) (SI 1999/2342) |
| | | *Never in force* (W) (repealed) |
| | (2) | See Sch 1 below |
| 3 | | 1 Apr 2000 (E) (for the purposes of the financial year 2000–2001 and subsequent financial years) (SI 1999/2342) |
| | | *Never in force* (W) (repealed) |
| 4 | (1) | 1 Sep 1999 (E) (so far as it inserts National Health Service Act 1977, Sch 12A, paras 1–3, 7, except in so far as para 7(3) relates to a Primary Care Trust) (SI 1999/2342) |

**Health Act 1999 (c 8)**—*contd*

|  |  |  |
|---|---|---|
|  |  | 1 Apr 2000 (E) (except that the provisions of National Health Service Act 1977, Sch 12A, relating to Primary Care Trusts are brought into force only for the purposes of the financial year 2000–2001 and subsequent financial years) (SI 1999/2342) |
|  |  | In force (otherwise) immediately before the National Health Service Act 2006 comes into force (SI 2006/1407)[2] |
|  | (2)(a), (b) | 1 Sep 1999 (E) (SI 1999/2342) |
|  |  | In force (W) immediately before the National Health Service Act 2006 comes into force (SI 2006/1407)[2] |
|  | (2)(c) | 1 Sep 1999 (E) (so far as it relates to the provisions in s 4(1) brought into force on 1 Sep 1999 by SI 1999/2342) (SI 1999/2342) |
|  |  | 1 Apr 2000 (E) (except that the provisions of National Health Service Act 1977, Sch 12A, relating to Primary Care Trusts are brought into force only for the purposes of the financial year 2000–2001 and subsequent financial years) (SI 1999/2342) |
|  |  | In force (W) immediately before the National Health Service Act 2006 comes into force (SI 2006/1407)[2] |
|  | (3) | 1 Sep 1999 (E) (SI 1999/2342) |
|  |  | In force (W) immediately before the National Health Service Act 2006 comes into force (SI 2006/1407)[2] |
|  | (4) | 1 Sep 1999 (E) (so far as it relates to the provisions of s 4 brought into force on 1 Sep 1999 by SI 1999/2342) (SI 1999/2342) |
|  |  | 1 Apr 2000 (E) (except that the provisions of National Health Service Act 1977, Sch 12A, relating to Primary Care Trusts are brought into force only for the purposes of the financial year 2000–2001 and subsequent financial years) (SI 1999/2342) |
|  |  | In force (W) immediately before the National Health Service Act 2006 comes into force (SI 2006/1407)[2] |
| 5 |  | 4 Jan 2000 (E) (except that the references in National Health Service Act 1977, s 18A to arrangements made under s 28C of the 1977 Act are brought into force for the purposes only of pilot schemes under National Health Service (Primary Care) Act 1997, Pt I) (SI 1999/2342) |
|  |  | *Never in force* (E) (exception noted above) (repealed) |
|  |  | *Never in force* (W) (repealed) |
| 6 | (1) | 4 Jan 2000 (E) (SI 1999/2342) |
|  |  | *Never in force* (W) (repealed) |
|  | (2) | 1 Apr 2004 (E) (SI 2004/289) |
|  |  | *Never in force* (W) (repealed) |
| 7 |  | 4 Jan 2000 (E) (SI 1999/2342) |
|  |  | *Never in force* (W) (repealed) |
| 8 |  | 1 Sep 1999 (E) (SI 1999/2342) |
|  |  | *Never in force* (W) (repealed) |
| 9 |  | 1 Apr 2000 (E) (SI 1999/2793) |
|  |  | 1 Apr 2000 (W) (SI 2000/1041) |
| 10 |  | *Never in force* (repealed) |
| 11 |  | 1 Sep 1999 (E) (except that the references in National Health Service Act 1977, s 44(3) to arrangements made under s 28C of the 1977 Act are brought into force for the purposes only of pilot schemes under National Health Service (Primary Care) Act 1997, Pt I) (SI 1999/2342) |
|  |  | 1 Apr 2000 (W) (except that the references in National Health Service Act 1977, s 44(3) to arrangements made under s 28C of the 1977 Act are brought into force for the purposes only of pilot schemes under National Health Service (Primary Care) Act 1997, Pt I) (SI 2000/1026) |
|  |  | *Never in force* (E) (W) (exceptions noted above) (repealed) |
| 12 | (1) | 1 Sep 1999 (E) (so far as it substitutes National Health Service Act 1977, ss 16D, 17, except in so far as they relate to Primary Care Trusts and s 28 of the 1999 Act) (SI 1999/2342) |

**Health Act 1999 (c 8)**—*contd*

|  |  |  |
|---|---|---|
|  |  | 1 Dec 1999 (W) (so far as it substitutes National Health Service Act 1977, ss 16D, 17, except in so far as they relate to Primary Care Trusts, and s 28 of the 1999 Act) (SI 1999/3184) |
|  |  | 4 Jan 2000 (E) (otherwise) (SI 1999/2342) |
|  |  | *Never in force* (W) (otherwise) (repealed) |
|  | (2) | 1 Sep 1999 (E) (SI 1999/2342) |
|  |  | 1 Dec 1999 (W) (SI 1999/3184) |
|  | (3), (4) | 1 Sep 1999 (E) (so far as relates to s 12(1)) (SI 1999/2342) |
|  |  | 1 Dec 1999 (W) (so far as relates to s 12(1)) (SI 1999/3184) |
|  |  | 4 Jan 2000 (E) (otherwise) (SI 1999/2342) |
|  |  | *Never in force* (W) (otherwise) (repealed) |
|  | (5) | 1 Sep 1999 (E) (SI 1999/2342) |
|  |  | 1 Dec 1999 (W) (SI 1999/3184) |
| 13, 14 |  | 1 Oct 1999 (E) (SI 1999/2540) |
|  |  | 1 Nov 1999 (W) (SI 1999/3184) |
| 15–17 |  | 1 Sep 1999 (E) (SI 1999/2342) |
|  |  | 1 Nov 1999 (W) (SI 1999/3184) |
| 18 |  | 1 Nov 1999 (except so far as relates to Primary Care Trusts) (SI 1999/2793; SI 1999/3184) |
|  |  | 4 Jan 2000 (E) (exception noted above) (SI 1999/2793) |
|  |  | *Never in force* (W) (exception noted above) (repealed) |
| 19 |  | 1 Nov 1999 (SI 1999/2793) |
| 20 |  | 1 Nov 1999 (E) (W) (except so far as relates to Primary Care Trusts) (SI 1999/2793) |
|  |  | 4 Jan 2000 (E) (otherwise) (SI 1999/2793) |
|  |  | *Never in force* (W) (exception noted above) (repealed) |
| 21 |  | 4 Jan 2000 (E) (SI 1999/2793) |
|  |  | 1 Apr 2000 (W) (SI 2000/1041) |
| 22 |  | *Never in force* (repealed) |
| 23–25 |  | 1 Nov 1999 (SI 1999/2793) |
| 26 |  | 1 Apr 2000 (E) (SI 1999/2793) |
|  |  | 1 Dec 2000 (W) (except so far as relates to Primary Care Trusts) (SI 2000/2991) |
|  |  | *Never in force* (W) (exception noted above) (repealed) |
| 27 |  | 1 Apr 2000 (E) (SI 1999/2793) |
|  |  | 1 Dec 2000 (W) (except so far as National Health Service Act 1977, s 22(1A) relates to Primary Care Trusts) (SI 2000/2991) |
|  |  | *Never in force* (W) (exception noted above) (repealed) |
| 28 |  | 1 Nov 1999 (W) (except so far as relates to Primary Care Trusts) (SI 1999/3184) |
|  |  | 1 Apr 2000 (E) (SI 1999/2793) |
|  |  | *Never in force* (W) (exception noted above) (repealed) |
| 29 | (1) | 1 Nov 1999 (E) (so far as relates to s 29(2)(a), (3) below) (SI 1999/2793) |
|  |  | 1 Apr 2000 (E) (otherwise) (SI 1999/2793) |
|  |  | 1 Dec 2000 (W) (so far as relates to s 29(2)(a), (3)) (SI 2000/2991) |
|  |  | In force (otherwise) immediately before the National Health Service Act 2006 comes into force (SI 2006/1407)[2] |
|  | (2)(a) | 1 Nov 1999 (E) (SI 1999/2793) |
|  |  | 1 Dec 2000 (W) (except so far as National Health Service Act 1977, s 28A(2B) relates to Primary Care Trusts) (SI 2000/2991) |
|  |  | In force (otherwise) immediately before the National Health Service Act 2006 comes into force (SI 2006/1407)[2] |
|  | (2)(b) | 1 Apr 2000 (E) (SI 1999/2793) |
|  |  | In force (otherwise) immediately before the National Health Service Act 2006 comes into force (SI 2006/1407)[2] |
|  | (3) | 1 Nov 1999 (E) (SI 1999/2793) |
|  |  | 1 Dec 2000 (W) (so far as relates to s 29(2)(a)) (SI 2000/2991) |

**Health Act 1999 (c 8)**—*contd*

|   |   |   |
|---|---|---|
| | | In force (otherwise) immediately before the National Health Service Act 2006 comes into force (SI 2006/1407)[2] |
| 30 | | 1 Apr 2000 (E) (SI 1999/2793) |
| | | 1 Dec 2000 (W) (except so far as National Health Service Act 1977, s 28BB(2) relates to Primary Care Trusts) (SI 2000/2991) |
| | | In force (otherwise) immediately before the National Health Service Act 2006 comes into force (SI 2006/1407)[2] |
| 31 | | 1 Apr 2000 (E) (SI 1999/2793) |
| | | 1 Dec 2000 (W) (except so far as relates to Primary Care Trusts) (SI 2000/2991) |
| | | In force (otherwise) immediately before the National Health Service Act 2006 comes into force (SI 2006/1407)[2] |
| 32 | | 1 Apr 2000 (E) (SI 1999/2793) |
| | | 1 Jan 2001 (W) (SI 2000/2991) |
| 33 | (1)–(6) | 1 Sep 1999 (except in so far as relates to s 35) (SI 1999/2177) |
| | | *Not yet in force* (exception noted above) |
| | (7) | 3 Apr 2007 (except in so far as relates to ss 33(8), 35) (SI 2007/1179) |
| | | *Not yet in force* (exceptions noted above) |
| | (8) | 7 Aug 2017 (SI 2017/810) |
| 34 | | 3 Aug 1999 (for the purpose only of consulting the industry body) (SI 1999/2177) |
| | | 1 Nov 1999 (otherwise) (SI 1999/2177) |
| 35 | | 7 Aug 2017 (SI 2017/810) |
| 36 | | 3 Aug 1999 (for the purpose only of consulting the industry body and so far as relates to the introduction of a limit under s 34) (SI 1999/2177) |
| | | 3 Apr 2007 (otherwise) (SI 2007/1179) |
| 37 | (1)–(9) | 3 Aug 1999 (for the purpose only of consulting the industry body) (SI 1999/2177) |
| | | 1 Nov 1999 (otherwise) (SI 1999/2177) |
| | (10) | 3 Aug 1999 (for the purpose only of consulting the industry body) (SI 1999/2177) |
| | | 7 Aug 2017 (otherwise) (SI 2017/810) |
| 38 | (1)–(4) | 1 Sep 1999 (so far as relates to the exercise of any power conferred by s 33(6)) (SI 1999/2177) |
| | | 1 Nov 1999 (so far as relates to the exercise of any power conferred by ss 34, 37) (SI 1999/2177) |
| | | 3 Apr 2007 (so far as relates to the exercise of any power conferred by ss 33(7), 36) (SI 2007/1179) |
| | | 7 Aug 2017 (so far as relates to the exercise of any power conferred by ss 33(8), 35) (SI 2017/810) |
| | (5) | 1 Sep 1999 (so far as relates to the exercise of any power conferred by s 33(6)) (SI 1999/2177) |
| | | 1 Nov 1999 (otherwise) (SI 1999/2177) |
| | (6) | 3 Aug 1999 (for the purpose only of consulting the industry body, except in so far as relates to ss 33, 35) (SI 1999/2177) |
| | | 1 Sep 1999 (so far as relates to the exercise of any power conferred by s 33(6)) (SI 1999/2177) |
| | | 1 Nov 1999 (so far as relates to the exercise of any power conferred by ss 34, 37) (SI 1999/2177) |
| | | 3 Apr 2007 (so far as relates to the exercise of any power conferred by ss 33(7), 36) (SI 2007/1179) |
| | | *Not yet in force* (so far as relates to the exercise of any power conferred by ss 33(8), 35) |
| | (7), (8) | 1 Sep 1999 (so far as relates to the exercise of any power conferred by s 33(6)) (SI 1999/2177) |
| | | 1 Nov 1999 (so far as relates to the exercise of any power conferred by ss 34, 37) (SI 1999/2177) |

**Health Act 1999 (c 8)**—*contd*

| | | |
|---|---|---|
| | | 3 Apr 2007 (so far as relates to the exercise of any power conferred by ss 33(7), 36) (SI 2007/1179) |
| | | *Not yet in force* (so far as relates to the exercise of any power conferred by ss 33(8), 35) |
| 39 | | 1 Nov 1999 (E) (SI 1999/2793) |
| | | 9 Feb 2001 (W) (SI 2001/270) |
| 40 | | *Never in force* (repealed) |
| 41 | | 1 Apr 2000 (SI 1999/2793) |
| 42 | | 1 Oct 1999 (SI 1999/2540) |
| 43 | | 1 Oct 1999 (E) (W) (SI 1999/2540) |
| | | 1 Mar 2000 (S) (SSI 2000/38) |
| 44 | | 1 Oct 1999 (SI 1999/2540) |
| 45–55 | | 1 Oct 1999 (SSI 1999/90) |
| 56 | | 1 Mar 2000 (S) (SSI 2000/38) |
| 57 | | 1 Oct 1999 (SSI 1999/90) |
| 58 | | 31 Jan 2004 (for the purpose of making regulations to come into force not earlier than 4 Mar 2004 under National Health Service (Scotland) Act 1978, ss 29–30) (SSI 2004/32) |
| | | 4 Mar 2004 (otherwise) (SSI 2004/32) |
| 59 | | 14 Oct 1999 (SSI 1999/115) |
| 60 | (1), (2) | 15 Mar 2000 (SI 2000/779) |
| | (3) | 1 Jul 1999 (repeal of Professions Supplementary to Medicine Act 1960, s 10) (s 67(3)) |
| | | 11 May 2001 (SI 2001/1985), so far as relates to— |
| | | Professions Supplementary to Medicine Act 1960, Sch 1, para 16(2) (so far as it provides that not more than one third of members of a committee appointed by the Council or a board under para 16(1) may be persons who are not members of the body appointing the committee) and Sch 2, para 1(1) (so far as it provides that, subject to sub-para (2)(b), a person shall not be eligible for membership of the investigating committee or disciplinary committee set up by a board unless he is a member of that board); |
| | | Nurses, Midwives and Health Visitors Act 1997, s 10(5), Sch 1, para 7(4) |
| | | 1 Apr 2002 (SI 2002/1167), so far as relates to— |
| | | Professions Supplementary to Medicine Act 1960, ss 1, 2(1)–(4), 3–5, 8, 9(1), (2), (5), (6), 11, 12, Schs 1, 2; |
| | | Nurses, Midwives and Health Visitors Act 1997, ss 1–8, 10, 11, 14, 15, 17–20, 22(1) (so far as relates to the definitions "by order", "the Central Council", "the Council", "elected members", "electoral scheme", "the National Boards", "the Boards", "prescribed" and "rules"), 22(2), (3), 24(2)–(5), Schs 1–3, Sch 4, paras 1, 2 |
| | | 9 Jul 2003 (so far as relates to Professions Supplementary to Medicine Act 1960, ss 6, 7, 9(3), (4), 13) (SI 2003/1689) |
| | | 1 Aug 2004 (otherwise) (SI 2004/1859) |
| | (4) | See Sch 3 below |
| 61 | | *Not yet in force* |
| 62–64 | | 3 Aug 1999 (SI 1999/2177) |
| | | 1 Oct 1999 (S) (SSI 1999/90) |
| 65 | (1) | See Sch 4 below |
| | (2) | See Sch 5 below |
| 66 | (1) | 30 Jun 1999 (s 67(4)) |
| | (2) | 1 Jul 1999 (s 67(4)) |
| | (3)–(6) | 30 Jun 1999 (s 67(4)) |
| 67–69 | | 30 Jun 1999 (RA) |
| Sch 1 | | 8 Sep 1999 (E) (so far as inserts National Health Service Act 1977, Sch 5A, paras 20(2), (3), 23(3)) (SI 1999/2342) |

**Health Act 1999 (c 8)**—*contd*

|  |  |  |
|--|--|--|
|  |  | 4 Jan 2000 (E) (except so far as it inserts National Health Service Act 1977, Sch 5A, paras 16, 17) (SI 1999/2342) |
|  |  | 1 Apr 2000 (E) (except that the provisions of National Health Service Act 1977, Sch 5A, paras 16, 17 are brought into force only for the purposes of the financial year 2000–2001 and subsequent financial years) (SI 1999/2342) |
|  |  | *Never in force* (E) (exception noted above) (repealed) |
|  |  | *Never in force* (W) (repealed) |
| Sch 2 | paras 1–14 | 1 Nov 1999 (E) (W) (SI 1999/2793) |
|  | paras 15–19 | 1 Nov 1999 (E) (W) (SI 1999/2793) |
|  |  | 11 May 2001 (S) (SI 2001/1985) |
| Sch 3 |  | 15 Mar 2000 (SI 2000/779) |
| Sch 4 | para 1 | 1 Oct 1999 (S) (SSI 1999/90) |
|  |  | 4 Jan 2000 (E) (SI 1999/2342) |
|  |  | *Never in force* (otherwise) (repealed) |
|  | para 2 | 1 Oct 1999 (S) (SSI 1999/90) |
|  |  | *Never in force* (otherwise) (repealed) |
|  | para 3 | 4 Jan 2000 (E) (SI 1999/2342) |
|  |  | *Not yet in force* (otherwise) |
|  | para 4 | See paras 5–41 below |
|  | para 5 | 1 Dec 1999 (W) (SI 1999/3184) |
|  |  | 4 Jan 2000 (E) (SI 1999/2342) |
|  | para 6 | 1 Sep 1999 (E) (SI 1999/2342) |
|  |  | 1 Dec 1999 (W) (SI 1999/3184) |
|  | para 7 | 4 Jan 2000 (E) (SI 1999/2342) |
|  |  | In force (otherwise) immediately before the National Health Service Act 2006 comes into force (SI 2006/1407)[2] |
|  | para 8 | 1 Oct 1999 (E) (so far as relates to fund-holding practices) (SI 1999/2540) |
|  |  | 1 Apr 2000 (W) (so far as relates to fund-holding practices) (SI 2000/1026) |
|  |  | 1 Aug 2004 (E) (otherwise) (SI 2004/1859) |
|  |  | In force (otherwise) immediately before the National Health Service Act 2006 comes into force (SI 2006/1407)[2] |
|  | para 9 | 1 Sep 1999 (E) (so far as substitutes National Health Service Act 1977, s 16, except in so far as relates to Primary Care Trusts) (SI 1999/2342) |
|  |  | 1 Dec 1999 (W) (so far as substitutes National Health Service Act 1977, s 16, except in so far as relates to Primary Care Trusts) (SI 1999/3184) |
|  |  | 4 Jan 2000 (E) (otherwise) (SI 1999/2342) |
|  |  | In force (otherwise) immediately before the National Health Service Act 2006 comes into force (SI 2006/1407)[2] |
|  | paras 10, 11 | 4 Jan 2000 (E) (SI 1999/2342) |
|  |  | In force (otherwise) immediately before the National Health Service Act 2006 comes into force (SI 2006/1407)[2] |
|  | para 12(1) | See sub-paras (2), (3) below |
|  | para 12(2) | 4 Jan 2000 (E) (SI 1999/2342) |
|  |  | In force (otherwise) immediately before the National Health Service Act 2006 comes into force (SI 2006/1407)[2] |
|  | para 12(3)(a) | 4 Jan 2000 (E) (SI 1999/2342) |
|  |  | In force (otherwise) immediately before the National Health Service Act 2006 comes into force (SI 2006/1407)[2] |
|  | para 12(3)(b) | 1 Sep 1999 (E) (SI 1999/2342) |
|  |  | 1 Dec 1999 (W) (SI 1999/3184) |
|  | para 13 | 4 Jan 2000 (E) (SI 1999/2342) |
|  |  | In force (otherwise) immediately before the National Health Service Act 2006 comes into force (SI 2006/1407)[2] |
|  | para 14(1) | See sub-paras (2)–(4) below |
|  | para 14(2) | 1 Nov 1999 (E) (SI 1999/2793) |

**Health Act 1999 (c 8)**—*contd*

| | |
|---|---|
| | 1 Dec 2000 (W) (SI 2000/2991) |
| para 14(3) | 1 Nov 1999 (E) (SI 1999/2793) |
| | 1 Dec 2000 (W) (so far as relates to payments made under National Health Service Act 1977 s 28A(2A)) (SI 2000/2991) |
| | 1 Jan 2001 (W) (otherwise) (SI 2000/2991) |
| para 14(4)(a) | 1 Nov 1999 (E) (SI 1999/2793) |
| | 1 Dec 2000 (W) (so far as relates to payments made under National Health Service Act 1977 s 28A(2A)) (SI 2000/2991) |
| | 1 Jan 2001 (W) (otherwise) (SI 2000/2991) |
| para 14(4)(b) | 1 Nov 1999 (E) (SI 1999/2793) |
| | 1 Dec 2000 (W) (SI 2000/2991) |
| para 14(4)(c), (d) | 1 Apr 2000 (E) (SI 1999/2793) |
| | 1 Jan 2001 (W) (SI 2000/2991) |
| para 14(4)(e) | 1 Nov 1999 (E) (so far as relates to payments made under section National Health Service Act 1977, s 28A(2A)) (SI 1999/2793) |
| | 1 Apr 2000 (E) (otherwise) (SI 1999/2793) |
| | 1 Dec 2000 (W) (so far as relates to payments made under National Health Service Act 1977 s 28A(2A)) (SI 2000/2991) |
| | 1 Jan 2001 (W) (otherwise) (SI 2000/2991) |
| para 15 | 1 Oct 1999 (E) (SI 1999/2540) |
| | 1 Dec 1999 (W) (SI 1999/3184) |
| para 16 | 4 Jan 2000 (E) (SI 1999/2540) |
| | In force (otherwise) immediately before the National Health Service Act 2006 comes into force (SI 2006/1407)[2] |
| paras 17–22 | *Never in force* (repealed) |
| para 23 | 4 Jan 2000 (E) (SI 1999/2342) |
| | In force (otherwise) immediately before the National Health Service Act 2006 comes into force (SI 2006/1407)[2] |
| para 24 | 1 Sep 1999 (E) (SI 1999/2342) |
| | 1 Apr 2000 (W) (SI 2000/1026) |
| para 25 | 4 Jan 2000 (E) (SI 1999/2342) |
| | In force (otherwise) immediately before the National Health Service Act 2006 comes into force (SI 2006/1407)[2] |
| para 26 | 1 Sep 1999 (E) (SI 1999/2342) |
| | 1 Dec 1999 (W) (SI 1999/3184) |
| para 27(a) | 1 Oct 1999 (E) (except so far as substitutes National Health Service Act 1977, s 91(3)(b)–(d), in so far as those paras relate to NHS trusts) (SI 1999/2540) |
| | 4 Jan 2000 (E) (exception noted above) (SI 1999/2342) |
| | 1 Apr 2000 (W) (except so far as substitutes National Health Service Act 1977, s 91(3)(b)–(d), in so far as those paras relate to Primary Care Trusts) (SI 2000/1026) |
| | In force (otherwise) immediately before the National Health Service Act 2006 comes into force (SI 2006/1407)[2] |
| para 27(b) | 1 Apr 2000 (SI 1999/2793) |
| paras 28, 29 | 4 Jan 2000 (E) (SI 1999/2342) |
| | In force (otherwise) immediately before the National Health Service Act 2006 comes into force (SI 2006/1407)[2] |
| para 30(1) | See sub-paras (2)–(4) below |
| para 30(2) | 1 Sep 1999 (E) (SI 1999/2342) |
| | 1 Dec 1999 (W) (SI 1999/3184) |
| para 30(3), (4) | 4 Jan 2000 (E) (SI 1999/2342) |
| | In force (otherwise) immediately before the National Health Service Act 2006 comes into force (SI 2006/1407)[2] |
| para 31(1) | See sub-paras (2)–(4) below |
| para 31(2) | *Never in force* (W) (repealed) |
| para 31(3) | 1 Sep 1999 (E) (SI 1999/2342) |
| | 1 Dec 1999 (W) (SI 1999/3184) |
| para 31(4) | 1 Apr 2000 (E) (SI 1999/2342) |

**Health Act 1999 (c 8)**—*contd*

|  |  |
|---|---|
|  | In force (otherwise) immediately before the National Health Service Act 2006 comes into force (SI 2006/1407)[2] |
| para 32 | 1 Sep 1999 (E) (SI 1999/2342) |
|  | 1 Dec 1999 (W) (SI 1999/3184) |
| para 33 | 1 Apr 2000 (E) (for the purposes of the financial year 2000–2001 and subsequent financial years) (SI 1999/2342) |
|  | *Not yet in force* (otherwise) (repealed in part) |
| para 34(a) | 4 Jan 2000 (E) (SI 1999/2342) |
|  | *Never in force* (otherwise) (repealed) |
| para 34(b) | 1 Sep 1999 (E) (SI 1999/2342) |
|  | 1 Dec 1999 (W) (SI 1999/3184) |
| para 35 | *Never in force* (W) (repealed) |
| para 36 | 1 Nov 1999 (E) (SI 1999/2793) |
|  | Never specifically brought into force as respects (W) but effective from 9 Feb 2001 by entry into force on that date of equivalent provision in Sch 5 as respects (W) |
| para 37(1) | See sub-paras (2)–(6) below |
| para 37(2), (3) | 4 Jan 2000 (E) (SI 1999/2342) |
|  | In force (otherwise) immediately before the National Health Service Act 2006 comes into force (SI 2006/1407)[2] |
| para 37(4) | 1 Sep 1999 (E) (so far as relates to the substitution of National Health Service Act 1977, ss 16D, 17) (SI 1999/2342) |
|  | 1 Dec 1999 (W) (so far as relates to the substitution of National Health Service Act 1977, ss 16D, 17) (SI 1999/3184) |
|  | 4 Jan 2000 (E) (otherwise) (SI 1999/2342) |
|  | In force (otherwise) immediately before the National Health Service Act 2006 comes into force (SI 2006/1407)[2] |
| para 37(5), (6) | 1 Sep 1999 (E) (SI 1999/2342) |
|  | 1 Nov 1999 (W) (SI 1999/3184) |
| para 38(1) | See sub-paras (2), (3) below |
| para 38(2)(a) | 4 Jan 2000 (E) (SI 1999/2342) |
|  | In force (otherwise) immediately before the National Health Service Act 2006 comes into force (SI 2006/1407)[2] |
| para 38(2)(b) | 1 Apr 2000 (E) (W) (SI 1999/2793) |
| para 38(2)(c) | 4 Jan 2000 (E) (SI 1999/2342) |
|  | In force (otherwise) immediately before the National Health Service Act 2006 comes into force (SI 2006/1407)[2] |
| para 38(2)(d) | 1 Apr 2000 (E) (W) (SI 1999/2793) |
| para 38(3) | 1 Sep 1999 (E) (so far as inserts National Health Service Act 1977, s 128(1A), except in so far as that subsection relates to s 17A of the 1977 Act and Primary Care Trusts) (SI 1999/2342) |
|  | 1 Dec 1999 (W) (so far as inserts National Health Service Act 1977, s 128(1A), except in so far as that subsection relates to s 17A of the 1977 Act and Primary Care Trusts) (SI 1999/3184) |
|  | 4 Jan 2000 (E) (otherwise) (SI 1999/2342) |
|  | In force (otherwise) immediately before the National Health Service Act 2006 comes into force (SI 2006/1407)[2] |
| para 39 | 1 Sep 1999 (E) (SI 1999/2342) |
|  | 1 Dec 1999 (W) (SI 1999/3184) |
| para 40 | 4 Jan 2000 (E) (SI 1999/2342) |
|  | *Never in force* (otherwise) (repealed) |
| para 41 | *Never in force* (repealed) |
| paras 42–47 | 1 Oct 1999 (SSI 1999/90) |
| para 48 | *Never in force* (repealed) |
| para 49 | 4 Mar 2004 (SSI 2004/32) |
| para 50 | 31 Jan 2004 (for the purpose of making regulations to come into force not earlier than 4 Mar 2004 under National Health Service (Scotland) Act 1978, s 32) (SSI 2004/32) |
|  | 4 Mar 2004 (otherwise) (SSI 2004/32) |

**Health Act 1999 (c 8)**—*contd*

| | |
|---|---|
| para 51 | 4 Mar 2004 (SSI 2004/32) |
| para 52(a) | 4 Mar 2004 (SSI 2004/32) |
| para 52(b) | *Never in force* (repealed) |
| para 52(c), (d) | 4 Mar 2004 (SSI 2004/32) |
| para 53 | 4 Mar 2004 (SSI 2004/32) |
| paras 54–63 | 1 Oct 1999 (SSI 1999/90) |
| para 64 | 4 Mar 2004 (SSI 2004/32) |
| paras 65–69 | 1 Apr 2000 (E) (W) (SI 1999/2793) |
| para 70 | 1 Oct 1999 (SSI 1999/90) |
| para 71(a), (b) | 1 Oct 1999 (E) (except so far as inserts Hospital Complaints Procedure Act 1985, s 1(1B), and s 1(1C) in so far as it relates to s 1(1B)) (SI 1999/2540) |
| | 1 Oct 1999 (S) (SSI 1999/90) |
| | 4 Jan 2000 (E) (exception noted above) (SI 1999/2342) |
| | 1 Apr 2000 (W) (SI 2000/1026) |
| para 71(c) | 1 Oct 1999 (E) (except so far as inserts Hospital Complaints Procedure Act 1985, s 1(1B), and s 1(1C) in so far as it relates to s 1(1B)) (SI 1999/2540) |
| | 1 Oct 1999 (S) (SSI 1999/90) |
| | 4 Jan 2000 (E) (exception noted above) (SI 1999/2342) |
| | *Never in force* (otherwise) (repealed) |
| para 72 | 1 Apr 2000 (E) (SI 1999/2793) |
| | 1 Jan 2001 (W) (SI 2000/2991) |
| para 73 | 1 Apr 2000 (E) (W) (SI 1999/2342) |
| | 11 May 2001 (otherwise) (SI 2001/1985) |
| para 74 | See paras 75–84 below |
| para 75 | 1 Sep 1999 (E) (SI 1999/2342) |
| | 1 Dec 1999 (W) (SI 1999/3184) |
| para 76(a)(i) | 4 Jan 2000 (E) (W) (SI 1999/2342) |
| para 76(a)(ii) | 1 Nov 1999 (E) (W) (SI 1999/2793) |
| para 76(b) | 1 Sep 1999 (E) (SI 1999/2342) |
| | 1 Dec 1999 (W) (SI 1999/3184) |
| paras 77, 78 | 4 Jan 2000 (E) (SI 1999/2342) |
| | In force (otherwise) immediately before the National Health Service Act 2006 comes into force (SI 2006/1407)[2] |
| para 79(1) | See sub-paras (2)–(4) below |
| para 79(2)(a) | 1 Nov 1999 (W) (SI 1999/3184) |
| | 1 Apr 2000 (E) (SI 1999/2342) |
| para 79(2)(b) | 1 Apr 2000 (E) (SI 1999/2342) |
| | In force (otherwise) immediately before the National Health Service Act 2006 comes into force (SI 2006/1407)[2] |
| para 79(2)(c) | 1 Nov 1999 (W) (SI 1999/3184) |
| | 1 Apr 2000 (E) (SI 1999/2342) |
| para 79(3), (4) | 1 Apr 2000 (E) (SI 1999/2342) |
| | In force (otherwise) immediately before the National Health Service Act 2006 comes into force (SI 2006/1407)[2] |
| para 80 | *Not yet in force* |
| para 81(1) | See sub-paras (2), (3) below |
| para 81(2)(a) | 4 Jan 2000 (E) (SI 1999/2342) |
| | In force (otherwise) immediately before the National Health Service Act 2006 comes into force (SI 2006/1407)[2] |
| para 81(2)(b) | 1 Nov 1999 (E) (W) (SI 1999/2793) |
| para 81(3) | 4 Jan 2000 (E) (SI 1999/2342) |
| | In force (otherwise) immediately before the National Health Service Act 2006 comes into force (SI 2006/1407)[2] |
| para 82 | 1 Apr 2000 (E) (W) (SI 1999/2342) |
| para 83(1) | See sub-paras (2)–(7) below |
| para 83(2) | 4 Jan 2000 (E) (SI 1999/2342) |
| | *Never in force* (otherwise) (repealed) |

**Health Act 1999 (c 8)**—*contd*

| | |
|---|---|
| para 83(3) | 1 Oct 1999 (S) (SSI 1999/90) |
| | 4 Jan 2000 (E) (SI 1999/2342) |
| | *Never in force* (otherwise) (repealed) |
| para 83(4) | 1 Sep 1999 (E) (SI 1999/2342) |
| | 1 Oct 1999 (S) (SSI 1999/90) |
| | 1 Dec 1999 (W) (subject to a saving)[1] (SI 1999/3184) |
| para 83(5) | 4 Jan 2000 (E) (SI 1999/2342) |
| | *Never in force* (otherwise) (repealed) |
| para 83(6) | 1 Oct 1999 (E) (SI 1999/2540) |
| | 1 Apr 2000 (W) (SI 2000/1026) |
| para 83(7) | 4 Jan 2000 (E) (SI 1999/2342) |
| | *Never in force* (otherwise) (repealed) |
| para 84 | 1 Sep 1999 (E) (SI 1999/2342) |
| | 1 Apr 2000 (W) (SI 2000/1026) |
| para 85(1) | See sub-paras (2)–(4) below |
| para 85(2)(a) | 4 Jan 2000 (E) (W) (SI 1999/2342) |
| | *Never in force* (otherwise) (repealed) |
| para 85(2)(b) | *Never in force* (repealed) |
| para 85(3) | 1 Oct 1999 (E) (S) (SI 1999/2540; SSI 1999/90) |
| | *Not yet in force* (otherwise) |
| para 85(4) | 1 Oct 1999 (E) (S) (SI 1999/2540; SSI 1999/90) |
| | 1 Apr 2000 (W) (SI 2000/1026) |
| para 86 | 1 Apr 2000 (E) (W) (SI 1999/2342) |
| | 11 May 2001 (otherwise) (SI 2001/1985) |
| para 87 | 4 Jan 2000 (E) (SI 1999/2342) |
| | *Never in force* (otherwise) (repealed) |
| para 88(1) | See sub-paras (2)–(6) below |
| para 88(2)–(4) | 1 Oct 1999 (S) (SSI 1999/90) |
| | 4 Jan 2000 (E) (SI 1999/2342) |
| | *Not yet in force* (otherwise) (repealed in part) |
| para 88(5) | 1 Sep 1999 (E) (SI 1999/2342) |
| | 1 Oct 1999 (S) (SSI 1999/90) |
| | 1 Dec 1999 (W) (SI 1999/3184) |
| para 88(6) | 1 Oct 1999 (E) (SI 1999/2540) |
| | 1 Oct 1999 (S) (SSI 1999/90) |
| | *Not yet in force* (otherwise) (repealed in part) |
| para 89 | 4 Jan 2000 (E) (SI 1999/2342) |
| | *Never in force* (otherwise) (repealed) |
| para 90 | 1 Oct 1999 (E) (SI 1999/2540) |
| | 1 Apr 2000 (W) (SI 2000/1026) |
| | *Not yet in force* (otherwise) |
| Sch 5 | 1 Jul 1999 (repeal of Professions Supplementary to Medicine Act 1960, s 10) (s 67(3)) |
| | 1 Oct 1999 (E) (SI 1999/2540), repeals of or in— |
| | National Health Service Act 1977, ss 15(1B)–(1D) (so far as relates to fund-holding practices), 28E(4), 98(2B), 128(1) (so far as relates to the definition "fund-holding practice"); |
| | National Health Service and Community Care Act 1990, ss 4(2)(f), 14–17, 18(2), 20(2)(b); |
| | Health Service Commissioners Act 1993, ss 3(1B), 19; |
| | Health Authorities Act 1995, Sch 1, paras 6(c), (d), 50(c), 58(b), 73–76, Sch 2, para 13(5); |
| | Health Service Commissioners (Amendment) Act 1996, Sch 1, para 6(2), (7); |
| | National Health Service (Primary Care) Act 1997, ss 14, 19, Sch 2, paras 4(3), (4) (so far as relates to fund-holding practices), 65(3)–(7); |
| | Audit Commission Act 1998 |
| | 1 Oct 1999 (S) (SSI 1999/90), repeals of or in— |

**Health Act 1999 (c 8)**—*contd*

National Health Service Act 1966, s 10;

Local Government (Scotland) Act 1973, s 97(2)(a)(iii), (2A), (2B) (the definitions "recognised fund-holding practice" and "allotted sum");

National Health Service (Scotland) Act 1978, ss 12E(5), (6), 17A(2)(d), (j), (3)(a) and the word "and" following it, 17E(4), 86(1A), (1C), (5), 87A–87D, Sch 7A, paras 6(2), 16(c) (the words from "which purposes shall include" to the end), para 22(1) (the words "or Health Authority" and in sub-para (c), the words following "Health Board"), 23, Sch 7B, paras 1(3)–(5), 3(2), 5(2), Sch 16, para 22;

Hospital Complaints Procedure Act 1985, s 1(1) (the words from "under" to "functions)" and the words "for the management of"), (1A) (the words "for the management of");

Health Service Commissioners Act 1993, ss 3(1B), 19 (the definitions "allotted sum" and "recognised fund-holding practice");

National Health Service (Primary Care) Act 1997, ss 14, 19

1 Nov 1999 (repeal of National Health Service and Community Care Act 1990, s 62) (SI 1999/2793)

1 Nov 1999 (E) (W) (repeal of Health Service Commissioners Act 1993, s 15) (SI 1999/2793)

1 Apr 2000 (E) (W) (SI 1999/2793), repeal of or in—

National Health Service Act 1977, ss 91(4), 128(1) (so far as it relates to the definition "special hospital");

Mental Health Act 1983

1 Apr 2000 (E) (W) (so far as not already in force) (SI 2000/1041), repeals of or in—

National Health Service Act 1977, ss 8(4), 13, 27(3), 44(1)(a), (b), 45(2), 65(3), 86(b), 96A(5)(b), 97(7), 97A(5), 99(3), s 15(1B)–(1D) (in relation to "fund-holding practices" only, so far as not already in force), ss 28E(4), 98(2B), 128(1) (so far as not already in force), Sch 5, para 10(3);

Hospital Complaints Procedure Act 1985, s 1(1), (1A);

National Health Service and Community Care Act 1990, ss 4, 14–17, 18(2), 20(2)(b) (so far as not already in force), ss 5(1), 8(1), 9(5), (6), Sch 2, paras 6, 19, 20, Sch 3, paras 1(3)–(5), 3(3), 5(2);

Health Service Commissioners Act 1993, ss 3(1B), 19 (so far as not already in force), s 15;

Health Authorities Act 1995, Sch 1, paras 4, 6(c), (d), 50(c), 58(b), 73–76, 85(d), Sch 2, para 13(5) (so far as not already in force);

Health Service Commissioners (Amendment) Act 1996, Sch 1, para 6(2), (7) (so far as not already in force);

National Health Service (Primary Care) Act 1997, ss 14, 19 (so far as not already in force), Sch 2, paras 4 (in relation to "fund-holding practices" only, so far as not already in force), 65(3)–(7);

Audit Commission Act 1998, ss 6(3), 53(1), (3), Sch 2, para 3

5 Feb 2001 (E) (W) (SI 2001/270), repeals of or in—

National Health Service Act 1977, ss 22(2)–(6), 28A(4), (8)(a), 122(2);

Health Service Joint Consultative Committee (Access to Information) Act 1986

11 May 2001 (SI 2001/1985), repeals of or in—

**Health Act 1999 (c 8)**—*contd*

Professions Supplementary to Medicine Act 1960, Sch 1,
para 16(2) (so far as it provides that not more than one third of
members of a committee appointed by the Council or a board
under para 16(1) may be persons who are not members of the
body appointing the committee) and Sch 2, para 1(1) (so far as
it provides that, subject to sub-para (2)(b), a person shall not be
eligible for membership of the investigating committee or
disciplinary committee set up by a board unless he is a member
of that board);
Nurses, Midwives and Health Visitors Act 1997, s 10(5), Sch 1,
para 7(4)

1 Apr 2002 (SI 2002/1167), repeals of or in—
Professions Supplementary to Medicine Act 1960, ss 1, 2(1)–(4),
3–5, 8, 9(1), (2), (5), (6), 11, 12, Schs 1, 2;
Nurses, Midwives and Health Visitors Act 1997, ss 1–8, 10, 11,
14, 15, 17–20, 22(1) (so far as relates to the definitions "by
order", "the Central Council", "the Council", "elected
members", "electoral scheme", "the National Boards", "the
Boards", "prescribed" and "rules"), 22(2), (3), 24(2)–(5),
Schs 1–3, Sch 4, paras 1, 2

9 Jul 2003 (repeals of or in Professions Supplementary to Medicine
Act 1960, ss 6, 7, 9(3), (4), 13) (SI 2003/1689)

4 Mar 2004 (repeals of or in National Health Service (Scotland)
Act 1978, ss 32A, 32B) (SSI 2004/32)

1 Aug 2004 (SI 2004/1859), repeals of or in—
Professions Supplementary to Medicine Act 1960 (so far as not
already in force);
Nurses, Midwives and Health Visitors Act 1997 (so far as not
already in force)

1 Aug 2004 (E) (repeals of or in National Health Service Act 1977,
s 15(1B)–(1D)) (SI 2004/1859)

In force immediately before the National Health Service Act 2006
comes into force (repeals in Health Authorities Act 1995
(except repeal relating to Sch 1, para 77) in so far as not
already in force) (SI 2006/1407)[2]

*Not yet in force*, repeals of or in—
National Health Service Act 1966, s 10 (E) (W);
National Health Service Act 1977, ss 12(1), 49A(5), (6)(a),
49B(4), 97(2), (6), Sch 15, para 37;
Mental Health Act 1983, s 122 (S);
National Health Service and Community Care Act 1990,
ss 15(4) (S), 18(1), (3)–(8), 34, 35, Sch 7, para 14(3);
Health Service Commissioners Act 1993, s 15(1A), (1B) (NI);
Health Authorities Act 1995, Sch 1, para 77;
National Health Service (Amendment) Act 1995;
National Health Service (Primary Care) Act 1997, Sch 2,
paras 4(3), (4) (except in relation to fund-holding practices),
53–55, 65(5) (S), (8)–(10), 69, 71(4) (repeal now superseded),
77, 78

[1]   For a saving, see SI 1999/3184, art 3

[2]   For a saving, see SI 2006/1407, art 4

---

**House of Lords Act 1999 (c 34)**

*RA:* 11 Nov 1999

*Commencement provision:* s 5

1–4                              11 Nov 1999 (s 5(1))

**House of Lords Act 1999 (c 34)**—*contd*

| | |
|---|---|
| 5, 6 | 11 Nov 1999 (RA) |
| Schs 1, 2 | 11 Nov 1999 (s 5(1)) |

---

## Immigration and Asylum Act 1999 (c 33)

*RA:* 11 Nov 1999

*Commencement provisions:* s 170(2)–(5); Immigration and Asylum Act 1999 (Commencement No 1) Order 1999, SI 1999/3190; Immigration and Asylum Act 1999 (Commencement No 2 and Transitional Provisions) Order 2000, SI 2000/168; Immigration and Asylum Act 1999 (Commencement No 3) Order 2000, SI 2000/464; Immigration and Asylum Act 1999 (Commencement No 4) Order 2000, SI 2000/1282; Immigration and Asylum Act 1999 (Commencement No 5 and Transitional Provisions) Order 2000, SI 2000/1985[4]; Immigration and Asylum Act 1999 (Commencement No 6, Transitional and Consequential Provisions) Order 2000, SI 2000/2444[5]; Immigration and Asylum Act 1999 (Commencement No 7) Order 2000, SI 2000/2698[6]; Immigration and Asylum Act 1999 (Commencement No 8 and Transitional Provisions) Order 2000, SI 2000/3099[7]; Immigration and Asylum Act 1999 (Commencement No 9) Order 2001, SI 2001/239; Immigration and Asylum Act 1999 (Commencement No 10) Order 2001, SI 2001/1394; Immigration and Asylum Act 1999 (Commencement No 11) Order 2002, SI 2002/2815; Immigration and Asylum Act 1999 (Commencement No 12) Order 2003, SI 2003/2; Immigration and Asylum Act 1999 (Commencement No 13) Order 2003, SI 2003/758; Immigration and Asylum Act 1999 (Commencement No 14) Order 2003, SI 2003/1469; Immigration and Asylum Act 1999 (Commencement No 15) Order 2003, SI 2003/1862; Immigration and Asylum Act 1999 (Commencement No 16) Order 2004, SI 2004/2997

| | | |
|---|---|---|
| 1, 2 | | 14 Feb 2000 (SI 2000/168) |
| 3 | | 2 Oct 2000 (SI 2000/2444)[5] |
| 4 | | 11 Nov 1999 (s 170(3)) |
| 5 | | 1 Apr 2003 (SI 2003/758) |
| 6–8 | | 1 Mar 2000 (SI 2000/168) |
| 9 | | 11 Nov 1999 (s 170(3)) |
| 10 | (1)–(5) | 2 Oct 2000 (SI 2000/2444)[1, 5] |
| | (6) | 22 May 2000 (SI 2000/1282) |
| | (7)–(9) | 2 Oct 2000 (SI 2000/2444)[1, 5] |
| 11 | | 2 Oct 2000 (SI 2000/2444)[5] |
| 12 | (1) | 22 May 2000 (for the purposes of enabling subordinate legislation to be made under it) (SI 2000/1282) |
| | | 2 Oct 2000 (otherwise) (SI 2000/2444)[5] |
| | (2)–(8) | 2 Oct 2000 (SI 2000/2444)[5] |
| 13 | | 11 Dec 2000 (SI 2000/3099) |
| 14 | | 1 Mar 2000 (SI 2000/168) |
| 15 | | 11 Nov 1999 (s 170(3)) |
| 16, 17 | | *Not yet in force* |
| 18 | | 1 Mar 2000 (so far as conferring power to make subordinate legislation) (SI 2000/464) |
| | | 3 Apr 2000 (otherwise) (SI 2000/464) |
| 19 | | 3 Apr 2000 (SI 2000/464) |
| 20, 21 | | 1 Jan 2000 (SI 1999/3190) |
| 22 | | 19 Feb 2001 (for purposes of laying a draft code before Parliament and enabling subordinate legislation to be made under Asylum and Immigration Act 1996, s 8A) (SI 2001/239) |
| | | 2 May 2001 (otherwise) (SI 2001/1394) |
| 23 | | 2 Oct 2000 (SI 2000/2444)[5] |
| 24 | | 1 Jan 2001 (SI 2000/2698) |
| 25 | | 17 Feb 2003 (for purpose of enabling Secretary of State to exercise power to make subordinate legislation) (SI 2003/2) |
| | | 1 Apr 2003 (otherwise) (SI 2003/2) |
| 26 | | 5 Jun 2003 (for the purpose of enabling the Secretary of State to make subordinate legislation) (SI 2003/1469) |
| | | 30 Jun 2003 (otherwise) (SI 2003/1469) |

**Immigration and Asylum Act 1999 (c 33)**—*contd*

| | | |
|---|---|---|
| 27 | | 11 Nov 1999 (s 170(3)) |
| 28 | | 14 Feb 2000 (SI 2000/168) |
| 29 | (1) | See sub-ss (2)–(4) below |
| | (2) | 14 Feb 2000 (SI 2000/168) |
| | (3) | 2 Oct 2000 (SI 2000/2444)[5] |
| | (4) | 14 Feb 2000 (SI 2000/168) |
| 30 | | 14 Feb 2000 (SI 2000/168) |
| 31 | | 11 Nov 1999 (s 170(3)) |
| 32 | (1) | 3 Apr 2000 (for the purposes of clandestine entrants, within the meaning of s 32(1) of this Act, other than those who (a) within the meaning of Pt II of this Act, arrive in the United Kingdom concealed otherwise than in a vehicle, and (b) are clandestine entrants by virtue of s 32(1)(a) of this Act) (SI 2000/464) |
| | | 18 Sep 2000 (for the purposes of s 39 of this Act and any regulations made under it (in addition to the purposes specified in relation to these provisions in SI 2000/464)) (SI 2000/2444)[5] |
| | | 8 Dec 2002 (for the purposes of clandestine entrants, within the meaning of s 32(1) of this Act, who arrive in the United Kingdom concealed in a rail freight wagon as defined in s 43) (SI 2002/2815) |
| | | *Not yet in force* (for the purpose of clandestine entrants who arrive in the United Kingdom concealed in a ship or aircraft) |
| | (2)(a) | 6 Dec 1999 (so far as conferring power to make subordinate legislation) (SI 1999/3190) |
| | | 3 Apr 2000 (for the purposes of clandestine entrants, within the meaning of s 32(1) of this Act, other than those who (a) within the meaning of Pt II of this Act, arrive in the United Kingdom concealed otherwise than in a vehicle, and (b) are clandestine entrants by virtue of s 32(1)(a) of this Act) (SI 2000/464) |
| | | 18 Sep 2000 (for the purposes of s 39 of this Act and any regulations made under it (in addition to the purposes specified in relation to these provisions in SI 2000/464)) (SI 2000/2444)[5] |
| | | 8 Dec 2002 (for the purposes of clandestine entrants, within the meaning of s 32(1) of this Act, who arrive in the United Kingdom concealed in a rail freight wagon as defined in s 43) (SI 2002/2815) |
| | | *Not yet in force* (for the purpose of clandestine entrants who arrive in the United Kingdom concealed in a ship or aircraft) |
| | (2)(b) | 3 Apr 2000 (for the purposes of clandestine entrants, within the meaning of s 32(1) of this Act, other than those who (a) within the meaning of Pt II of this Act, arrive in the United Kingdom concealed otherwise than in a vehicle, and (b) are clandestine entrants by virtue of s 32(1)(a) of this Act) (SI 2000/464) |
| | | 18 Sep 2000 (for the purposes of s 39 of this Act and any regulations made under it (in addition to the purposes specified in relation to these provisions in SI 2000/464)) (SI 2000/2444)[5] |
| | | 8 Dec 2002 (for the purposes of clandestine entrants, within the meaning of s 32(1) of this Act, who arrive in the United Kingdom concealed in a rail freight wagon as defined in s 43) (SI 2002/2815) |
| | | *Not yet in force* (for the purpose of clandestine entrants who arrive in the United Kingdom concealed in a ship or aircraft) |
| | (3) | 6 Dec 1999 (so far as conferring power to make subordinate legislation) (SI 1999/3190) |
| | | 3 Apr 2000 (for the purposes of clandestine entrants, within the meaning of s 32(1) of this Act, other than those who (a) within the meaning of Pt II of this Act, arrive in the United Kingdom concealed otherwise than in a vehicle, and (b) are clandestine entrants by virtue of s 32(1)(a) of this Act) (SI 2000/464) |

**Immigration and Asylum Act 1999 (c 33)**—*contd*

|  |  |  |
|---|---|---|
|  |  | 18 Sep 2000 (for the purposes of s 39 of this Act and any regulations made under it (in addition to the purposes specified in relation to these provisions in SI 2000/464)) (SI 2000/2444)[5] |
|  |  | 8 Dec 2002 (for the purposes of clandestine entrants, within the meaning of s 32(1) of this Act, who arrive in the United Kingdom concealed in a rail freight wagon as defined in s 43) (SI 2002/2815) |
|  |  | *Not yet in force* (for the purpose of clandestine entrants who arrive in the United Kingdom concealed in a ship or aircraft) |
|  | (4)–(9) | 3 Apr 2000 (for the purposes of clandestine entrants, within the meaning of s 32(1) of this Act, other than those who (a) within the meaning of Pt II of this Act, arrive in the United Kingdom concealed otherwise than in a vehicle, and (b) are clandestine entrants by virtue of s 32(1)(a) of this Act) (SI 2000/464) |
|  |  | 18 Sep 2000 (for the purposes of s 39 of this Act and any regulations made under it (in addition to the purposes specified in relation to these provisions in SI 2000/464)) (SI 2000/2444)[5] |
|  |  | 8 Dec 2002 (for the purposes of clandestine entrants, within the meaning of s 32(1) of this Act, who arrive in the United Kingdom concealed in a rail freight wagon as defined in s 43) (SI 2002/2815) |
|  |  | *Not yet in force* (for the purpose of clandestine entrants who arrive in the United Kingdom concealed in a ship or aircraft) |
|  | (10) | 6 Dec 1999 (so far as conferring power to make subordinate legislation) (SI 1999/3190) |
|  |  | 3 Apr 2000 (for the purposes of clandestine entrants, within the meaning of s 32(1) of this Act, other than those who (a) within the meaning of Pt II of this Act, arrive in the United Kingdom concealed otherwise than in a vehicle, and (b) are clandestine entrants by virtue of s 32(1)(a) of this Act) (SI 2000/464) |
|  |  | 18 Sep 2000 (for the purposes of s 39 of this Act and any regulations made under it (in addition to the purposes specified in relation to these provisions in SI 2000/464)) (SI 2000/2444)[5] |
|  |  | 8 Dec 2002 (for the purposes of clandestine entrants, within the meaning of s 32(1) of this Act, who arrive in the United Kingdom concealed in a rail freight wagon as defined in s 43) (SI 2002/2815) |
|  |  | *Not yet in force* (for the purpose of clandestine entrants who arrive in the United Kingdom concealed in a ship or aircraft) |
| 33 |  | 6 Dec 1999 (SI 1999/3190) |
| 34 |  | 3 Apr 2000 (for the purposes of clandestine entrants, within the meaning of s 32(1) of this Act, other than those who (a) within the meaning of Pt II of this Act, arrive in the United Kingdom concealed otherwise than in a vehicle, and (b) are clandestine entrants by virtue of s 32(1)(a) of this Act) (SI 2000/464) |
|  |  | 18 Sep 2000 (for the purposes of s 39 of this Act and any regulations made under it (in addition to the purposes specified in relation to these provisions in SI 2000/464)) (SI 2000/2444)[5] |
|  |  | 8 Dec 2002 (for the purposes of clandestine entrants, within the meaning of s 32(1) of this Act, who arrive in the United Kingdom concealed in a rail freight wagon as defined in s 43) (SI 2002/2815) |
|  |  | *Not yet in force* (for the purpose of clandestine entrants who arrive in the United Kingdom concealed in a ship or aircraft) (sub-s (5) repealed) |
| 35 | (1)–(6) | 3 Apr 2000 (for the purposes of clandestine entrants, within the meaning of s 32(1) of this Act, other than those who (a) within the meaning of Pt II of this Act, arrive in the United Kingdom concealed otherwise than in a vehicle, and (b) are clandestine entrants by virtue of s 32(1)(a) of this Act) (SI 2000/464) |

**Immigration and Asylum Act 1999 (c 33)**—*contd*

|  |  |
|---|---|
|  | 18 Sep 2000 (for the purposes of s 39 of this Act and any regulations made under it (in addition to the purposes specified in relation to these provisions in SI 2000/464)) (SI 2000/2444)[5] |
|  | 8 Dec 2002 (for the purposes of clandestine entrants, within the meaning of s 32(1) of this Act, who arrive in the United Kingdom concealed in a rail freight wagon as defined in s 43) (SI 2002/2815) |
|  | *Not yet in force* (for the purpose of clandestine entrants who arrive in the United Kingdom concealed in a ship or aircraft) |
| (7)–(9) | 6 Dec 1999 (so far as conferring power to make subordinate legislation) (SI 1999/3190) |
|  | 3 Apr 2000 (for the purposes of clandestine entrants, within the meaning of s 32(1) of this Act, other than those who (a) within the meaning of Pt II of this Act, arrive in the United Kingdom concealed otherwise than in a vehicle, and (b) are clandestine entrants by virtue of s 32(1)(a) of this Act) (SI 2000/464) |
|  | 18 Sep 2000 (for the purposes of s 39 of this Act and any regulations made under it (in addition to the purposes specified in relation to these provisions in SI 2000/464)) (SI 2000/2444)[5] |
|  | 8 Dec 2002 (for the purposes of clandestine entrants, within the meaning of s 32(1) of this Act, who arrive in the United Kingdom concealed in a rail freight wagon as defined in s 43) (SI 2002/2815) |
|  | *Not yet in force* (for the purpose of clandestine entrants who arrive in the United Kingdom concealed in a ship or aircraft) |
| (10) | 3 Apr 2000 (for the purposes of clandestine entrants, within the meaning of s 32(1) of this Act, other than those who (a) within the meaning of Pt II of this Act, arrive in the United Kingdom concealed otherwise than in a vehicle, and (b) are clandestine entrants by virtue of s 32(1)(a) of this Act) (SI 2000/464) |
|  | 18 Sep 2000 (for the purposes of s 39 of this Act and any regulations made under it (in addition to the purposes specified in relation to these provisions in SI 2000/464)) (SI 2000/2444)[5] |
|  | 8 Dec 2002 (for the purposes of clandestine entrants, within the meaning of s 32(1) of this Act, who arrive in the United Kingdom concealed in a rail freight wagon as defined in s 43) (SI 2002/2815) |
|  | *Not yet in force* (for the purpose of clandestine entrants who arrive in the United Kingdom concealed in a ship or aircraft) |
| 36   (1) | 3 Apr 2000 (for the purposes of clandestine entrants, within the meaning of s 32(1) of this Act, other than those who (a) within the meaning of Pt II of this Act, arrive in the United Kingdom concealed otherwise than in a vehicle, and (b) are clandestine entrants by virtue of s 32(1)(a) of this Act) (SI 2000/464) |
|  | 18 Sep 2000 (for the purposes of s 39 of this Act and any regulations made under it (in addition to the purposes specified in relation to these provisions in SI 2000/464)) (SI 2000/2444)[5] |
|  | 8 Dec 2002 (for the purposes of clandestine entrants, within the meaning of s 32(1) of this Act, who arrive in the United Kingdom concealed in a rail freight wagon as defined in s 43) (SI 2002/2815) |
|  | *Not yet in force* (for the purpose of clandestine entrants who arrive in the United Kingdom concealed in a ship or aircraft) |
| (2)(a) | 6 Dec 1999 (so far as conferring power to make subordinate legislation) (SI 1999/3190) |
|  | 3 Apr 2000 (for the purposes of clandestine entrants, within the meaning of s 32(1) of this Act, other than those who (a) within the meaning of Pt II of this Act, arrive in the United Kingdom concealed otherwise than in a vehicle, and (b) are clandestine entrants by virtue of s 32(1)(a) of this Act) (SI 2000/464) |

**Immigration and Asylum Act 1999 (c 33)**—*contd*

|  |  |  |
|---|---|---|
|  |  | 18 Sep 2000 (for the purposes of s 39 of this Act and any regulations made under it (in addition to the purposes specified in relation to these provisions in SI 2000/464)) (SI 2000/2444)[5] |
|  |  | 8 Dec 2002 (for the purposes of clandestine entrants, within the meaning of s 32(1) of this Act, who arrive in the United Kingdom concealed in a rail freight wagon as defined in s 43) (SI 2002/2815) |
|  |  | *Not yet in force* (for the purpose of clandestine entrants who arrive in the United Kingdom concealed in a ship or aircraft) |
|  | (2)(b) | 3 Apr 2000 (for the purposes of clandestine entrants, within the meaning of s 32(1) of this Act, other than those who (a) within the meaning of Pt II of this Act, arrive in the United Kingdom concealed otherwise than in a vehicle, and (b) are clandestine entrants by virtue of s 32(1)(a) of this Act) (SI 2000/464) |
|  |  | 18 Sep 2000 (for the purposes of s 39 of this Act and any regulations made under it (in addition to the purposes specified in relation to these provisions in SI 2000/464)) (SI 2000/2444)[5] |
|  |  | 8 Dec 2002 (for the purposes of clandestine entrants, within the meaning of s 32(1) of this Act, who arrive in the United Kingdom concealed in a rail freight wagon as defined in s 43) (SI 2002/2815) |
|  |  | *Not yet in force* (for the purpose of clandestine entrants who arrive in the United Kingdom concealed in a ship or aircraft) |
|  | (3)–(5) | 3 Apr 2000 (for the purposes of clandestine entrants, within the meaning of s 32(1) of this Act, other than those who (a) within the meaning of Pt II of this Act, arrive in the United Kingdom concealed otherwise than in a vehicle, and (b) are clandestine entrants by virtue of s 32(1)(a) of this Act) (SI 2000/464) |
|  |  | 18 Sep 2000 (for the purposes of s 39 of this Act and any regulations made under it (in addition to the purposes specified in relation to these provisions in SI 2000/464)) (SI 2000/2444)[5] |
|  |  | 8 Dec 2002 (for the purposes of clandestine entrants, within the meaning of s 32(1) of this Act, who arrive in the United Kingdom concealed in a rail freight wagon as defined in s 43) (SI 2002/2815) |
|  |  | *Not yet in force* (for the purpose of clandestine entrants who arrive in the United Kingdom concealed in a ship or aircraft) |
| 37 | (1)–(5) | 3 Apr 2000 (for the purposes of clandestine entrants, within the meaning of s 32(1) of this Act, other than those who (a) within the meaning of Pt II of this Act, arrive in the United Kingdom concealed otherwise than in a vehicle, and (b) are clandestine entrants by virtue of s 32(1)(a) of this Act) (SI 2000/464) |
|  |  | 18 Sep 2000 (for the purposes of s 39 of this Act and any regulations made under it (in addition to the purposes specified in relation to these provisions in SI 2000/464)) (SI 2000/2444)[5] |
|  |  | 8 Dec 2002 (for the purposes of clandestine entrants, within the meaning of s 32(1) of this Act, who arrive in the United Kingdom concealed in a rail freight wagon as defined in s 43) (SI 2002/2815) |
|  |  | *Not yet in force* (for the purpose of clandestine entrants who arrive in the United Kingdom concealed in a ship or aircraft) |
|  | (6) | See Sch 1 below |
| 38 |  | 3 Apr 2000 (SI 2000/464) |
| 39 |  | 6 Dec 1999 (SI 1999/3190) |
| 40 | (1)–(8) | *Never in force* (repealed) |
|  | (9), (10) | 6 Dec 1999 (SI 1999/3190) |
|  | (11)–(13) | *Never in force* (repealed) |
| 41 |  | 8 Dec 2002 (SI 2002/2815) |
| 42 | (1)–(7) | *Never in force* (repealed) |
|  | (8) | See Sch 1 below |
| 43 |  | 6 Dec 1999 (SI 1999/3190) |

**Immigration and Asylum Act 1999 (c 33)**—*contd*

| | | |
|---|---|---|
| 44–52 | | *Never in force* (repealed) |
| 53 | (1)–(4) | 10 Feb 2003 (SI 2003/2) |
| | (5) | *Never in force* (repealed) |
| | (6), (7) | 10 Feb 2003 (SI 2003/2) |
| 54 | | 10 Feb 2003 (SI 2003/2) |
| 55 | | *Never in force* (repealed) |
| 56, 57 | | 14 Feb 2000 (subject to transitional provisions) (SI 2000/168) |
| 58 | (1) | 2 Oct 2000 (SI 2000/2444) |
| | (2) | See Sch 4 below |
| | (3)–(10) | 2 Oct 2000 (SI 2000/2444)[5] |
| 59 | | 2 Oct 2000 (SI 2000/2444)[5] |
| 60 | (1)–(5) | 2 Oct 2000 (SI 2000/2444)[5] |
| | (6) | 22 May 2000 (SI 2000/1282) |
| | (7)–(9) | 2 Oct 2000 (SI 2000/2444)[5] |
| | (10) | 22 May 2000 (SI 2000/1282) |
| 61–71 | | 2 Oct 2000 (SI 2000/2444)[5] |
| 72 | (1), (2) | 2 Oct 2000 (SI 2000/2444)[5] |
| | (3) | 22 May 2000 (for the purposes of enabling subordinate legislation to be made under it) (SI 2000/1282) |
| | | 2 Oct 2000 (otherwise) (SI 2000/2444)[5] |
| 73 | | 2 Oct 2000 (SI 2000/2444)[5] |
| 74, 75 | | 22 May 2000 (for the purposes of enabling subordinate legislation to be made under them) (SI 2000/1282) |
| | | 2 Oct 2000 (otherwise) (SI 2000/2444)[5] |
| 76 | (1)–(5) | 2 Oct 2000 (SI 2000/2444)[5] |
| | (6) | 22 May 2000 (SI 2000/1282) |
| 77, 78 | | 2 Oct 2000 (SI 2000/2444)[5] |
| 79 | | *Never in force* (repealed) |
| 80 | | 22 May 2000 (SI 2000/1282) |
| 81 | | 2 Oct 2000 (SI 2000/2444)[5] |
| 82 | | 22 May 2000 (SI 2000/1282) |
| 83 | (1)–(3) | 22 May 2000 (SI 2000/1282) |
| | (4) | See Sch 5 below |
| | (5) | 22 May 2000 (so far as relates to the regulatory functions set out in Sch 5, paras 1(1), (2), (4), 2(1)–(4), (6)–(8), 3(1)–(3), (5)–(7), 4, 5(1)–(3), 6(1), 11–25) (SI 2000/1282) |
| | | 30 Oct 2000 (otherwise) (SI 2000/1985) |
| | (6), (7) | 22 May 2000 (SI 2000/1282) |
| 84 | (1) | 30 Apr 2001 (SI 2001/1394) |
| | (2)(a), (b) | 30 Oct 2000 (so far as relates to the provisions of s 85 below as commenced by this order) (SI 2000/1985) |
| | | 30 Apr 2001 (otherwise) (SI 2001/1394) |
| | (2)(c)–(f) | 30 Apr 2001 (SI 2001/1394) |
| | (3) | 30 Apr 2001 (SI 2001/1394) |
| | (4)(a) | 30 Oct 2000 (so far as to enable the Commissioner to certify a person as exempt under it) (SI 2000/1985) |
| | | 30 Apr 2001 (otherwise) (SI 2001/1394) |
| | (4)(b), (c) | 30 Apr 2001 (SI 2001/1394) |
| | (4)(d) | 30 Oct 2000 (so far as conferring power to make subordinate legislation) (SI 2000/1985) |
| | | 30 Apr 2001 (otherwise) (SI 2001/1394) |
| | (5) | 30 Oct 2000 (SI 2000/1985) |
| | (6) | 30 Apr 2001 (SI 2001/1394) |
| | (7) | 30 Oct 2000 (SI 2000/1985) |
| 85 | (1), (2) | 30 Oct 2000 (SI 2000/1985) |
| | (3) | See Sch 6 below |
| 86 | (1)–(9) | 22 May 2000 (SI 2000/1282) |
| | (10)–(12) | 30 Oct 2000 (so far as conferring power to make subordinate legislation) (SI 2000/1985) |

**Immigration and Asylum Act 1999 (c 33)**—*contd*

| | | |
|---|---|---|
| | | 30 Apr 2001 (otherwise) (SI 2001/1394) |
| 87 | (1)–(4) | 30 Oct 2000 (SI 2000/1985) |
| | (5) | See Sch 7 below |
| 88, 89 | | 30 Oct 2000 (SI 2000/1985) |
| 90 | | 1 Aug 2000 (so far as conferring power to make subordinate legislation) (SI 2000/1985) |
| | | 30 Apr 2001 (otherwise) (SI 2001/1394) |
| 91, 92 | | 30 Apr 2001 (SI 2001/1394) |
| 93 | | 22 May 2000 (SI 2000/1282) |
| 94 | | 11 Nov 1999 (s 170(3)) |
| 95 | (1), (2) | 1 Jan 2000 (so far as conferring power to make subordinate legislation) (SI 1999/3190) |
| | | 3 Apr 2000 (otherwise) (SI 2000/464) |
| | (3)–(8) | 6 Dec 1999 (for the purposes of ss 116, 117(1), (2) of (and the amendments to other legislation effected by those sections), and Sch 9, para 3 to, this Act) (SI 1999/3190) |
| | | 1 Jan 2000 (so far as conferring power to make subordinate legislation) (SI 1999/3190) |
| | | 3 Apr 2000 (otherwise) (SI 2000/464) |
| | (9)–(11) | 1 Jan 2000 (so far as conferring power to make subordinate legislation) (SI 1999/3190) |
| | | 3 Apr 2000 (otherwise) (SI 2000/464) |
| | (12) | 1 Jan 2000 (SI 1999/3190) |
| | (13) | 11 Nov 1999 (s 170(3)) |
| 96 | | 3 Apr 2000 (SI 2000/464) |
| 97 | | 1 Jan 2000 (so far as conferring power to make subordinate legislation) (SI 1999/3190) |
| | | 3 Apr 2000 (otherwise) (SI 2000/464) |
| 98 | (1), (2) | 3 Apr 2000 (SI 2000/464) |
| | (3) | 1 Mar 2000 (for the purposes of enabling subordinate legislation to be made under s 95 of this Act as applied by s 98(3)) (SI 2000/464) |
| | | 3 Apr 2000 (otherwise) (SI 2000/464) |
| 99 | (1)–(3) | 3 Apr 2000 (SI 2000/464) |
| | (4), (5) | 11 Nov 1999 (s 170(3)) |
| 100–103 | | 3 Apr 2000 (SI 2000/464) |
| 104 | | 1 Jan 2000 (SI 1999/3190) |
| 105–109 | | 11 Nov 1999 (s 170(3)) |
| 110 | (1), (2) | 11 Nov 1999 (s 170(3)) |
| | (3)–(7) | 3 Apr 2000 (SI 2000/464) |
| | (8) | 11 Nov 1999 (so far as relates to sub-ss (1), (2) above) (s 170(3)) |
| | | 3 Apr 2000 (otherwise) (SI 2000/464) |
| | (9) | 6 Dec 1999 (SI 1999/3190) |
| 111 | | 11 Nov 1999 (s 170(3)) |
| 112, 113 | | 3 Apr 2000 (SI 2000/464) |
| 114 | | 1 Jan 2000 (so far as conferring power to make subordinate legislation) (SI 1999/3190) |
| | | 3 Apr 2000 (otherwise) (SI 2000/464) |
| 115 | | 1 Jan 2000 (so far as conferring power to make subordinate legislation) (SI 1999/3190)[2] |
| | | 3 Apr 2000 (otherwise) (SI 2000/464) |
| 116 | | 6 Dec 1999 (SI 1999/3190) |
| 117 | (1), (2) | 6 Dec 1999 (SI 1999/3190) |
| | (3), (4) | 3 Apr 2000 (SI 2000/464) |
| | (5) | *Not yet in force* |
| | (6) | 3 Apr 2000 (SI 2000/464) |
| 118, 119 | | 1 Jan 2000 (so far as conferring power to make subordinate legislation) (SI 1999/3190) |
| | | 1 Mar 2000 (otherwise) (SI 2000/464) |

**Immigration and Asylum Act 1999 (c 33)**—*contd*

| | | |
|---|---|---|
| 120, 121 | | 1 Mar 2000 (for the purpose of enabling subordinate legislation to be made under s 95 of this Act as applied by any provision inserted by ss 120, 121) (SI 2000/464) |
| | | 3 Apr 2000 (otherwise) (SI 2000/464) |
| 122 | | 1 Mar 2000 (so far as conferring power to make subordinate legislation) (SI 2000/464) |
| | | 3 Apr 2000 (otherwise) (SI 2000/464) |
| 123 | | 1 Jan 2000 (so far as conferring power to make subordinate legislation) (SI 1999/3190) |
| | | 3 Apr 2000 (otherwise) (SI 2000/464) |
| 124 | | 11 Nov 1999 (s 170(3)) |
| 125–127 | | 3 Apr 2000 (SI 2000/464) |
| 128–139 | | 14 Feb 2000 (SI 2000/168) |
| 140 | | 11 Nov 1999 (s 170(3)) |
| 141–144 | | 11 Dec 2000 (SI 2000/3099) |
| 145 | | 11 Nov 1999 (s 170(3)) |
| 146 | (1) | 11 Nov 1999 (s 170(3)) |
| | (2) | *Never in force* (substituted) |
| 147 | | 1 Aug 2000 (SI 2000/1985) |
| 148 | (1), (2) | 2 Apr 2001 (SI 2001/239) |
| | (3) | 1 Aug 2000 (so far as conferring power to make subordinate legislation) (SI 2000/1985) |
| | | 2 Apr 2001 (otherwise) (SI 2001/239) |
| | (4), (5) | 2 Apr 2001 (SI 2001/239) |
| 149 | (1) | 1 Aug 2000 (SI 2000/1985) |
| | (2) | 2 Apr 2001 (SI 2001/239) |
| | (3) | 1 Aug 2000 (SI 2000/1985) |
| | (4), (5) | 2 Apr 2001 (SI 2001/239) |
| | (6)(a) | 1 Aug 2000 (SI 2000/1985) |
| | (6)(b) | 2 Apr 2001 (SI 2001/239) |
| | (7), (8) | 2 Apr 2001 (SI 2001/239) |
| | (9) | 1 Aug 2000 (SI 2000/1985) |
| 150, 151 | | 2 Apr 2001 (SI 2001/239) |
| 152 | (1) | 2 Apr 2001 (SI 2001/239) |
| | (2), (3) | 1 Aug 2000 (so far as conferring power to make subordinate legislation) (SI 2000/1985) |
| | | 2 Apr 2001 (otherwise) (SI 2001/239) |
| | (4), (5) | 2 Apr 2001 (SI 2001/239) |
| 153 | | 1 Aug 2000 (so far as conferring power to make subordinate legislation) (SI 2000/1985) |
| | | 2 Apr 2001 (otherwise) (SI 2001/239) |
| 154 | (1)–(6) | 2 Apr 2001 (SI 2001/239) |
| | (7) | See Sch 11 below |
| 155 | (1) | 2 Apr 2001 (SI 2001/239) |
| | (2) | See Sch 12 below |
| 156 | (1)–(4) | 2 Apr 2001 (SI 2001/239) |
| | (5) | See Sch 13 below |
| | (6), (7) | 2 Apr 2001 (SI 2001/239) |
| 157 | | 1 Aug 2000 (so far as conferring power to make subordinate legislation) (SI 2000/1985) |
| | | 2 Apr 2001 (otherwise) (SI 2001/239) |
| 158, 159 | | 2 Apr 2001 (SI 2001/239) |
| 160–163 | | 1 Jan 2001 (SI 2000/2698) |
| 164 | | 1 Dec 2004 (SI 2004/2997) |
| 165 | | 22 May 2000 (for the purposes of enabling subordinate legislation to be made under Immigration Act 1971, s 31A, as inserted by this section) (SI 2000/1282) |
| | | 1 Aug 2003 (otherwise) (SI 2003/1862) |
| 166–168 | | 11 Nov 1999 (s 170(3)) |

**Immigration and Asylum Act 1999 (c 33)**—*contd*

| | | |
|---|---|---|
| 169 | (1) | See Sch 14 below |
| | (2) | See Sch 15 below |
| | (3) | See Sch 16 below |
| 170 | | 11 Nov 1999 (s 170(3)) |
| Sch 1 | para 1 | 3 Apr 2000 (for the purposes of s 37 of this Act) (SI 2000/464) |
| | | *Not yet in force* (for the purposes of s 42 of this Act) |
| | para 2 | 6 Dec 1999 (SI 1999/3190) |
| | paras 3, 4 | 3 Apr 2000 (for the purposes of s 37 of this Act) (SI 2000/464) |
| | | *Not yet in force* (for the purposes of s 42 of this Act) |
| | para 5 | 6 Dec 1999 (SI 1999/3190) |
| Schs 2, 3 | | 14 Feb 2000 (subject to transitional provisions) (SI 2000/168) |
| Sch 4 | para 1 | 22 May 2000 (SI 2000/1282) |
| | para 2 | 2 Oct 2000 (SI 2000/2444)[5] |
| | paras 3–5 | 14 Feb 2000 (subject to a transitional provision relating to para 5) (SI 2000/168) |
| | paras 6–24 | 2 Oct 2000 (SI 2000/2444)[5] |
| Sch 5 | para 1(1), (2) | 22 May 2000 (SI 2000/1282) |
| | para 1(3) | 30 Oct 2000 (SI 2000/1985) |
| | para 1(4) | 22 May 2000 (SI 2000/1282) |
| | para 2(1)–(4) | 22 May 2000 (SI 2000/1282) |
| | para 2(5) | 30 Oct 2000 (SI 2000/1985) |
| | para 2(6)–(8) | 22 May 2000 (SI 2000/1282) |
| | para 3(1)–(3) | 22 May 2000 (SI 2000/1282) |
| | para 3(4) | 30 Oct 2000 (SI 2000/1985) |
| | para 3(5)–(7) | 22 May 2000 (SI 2000/1282) |
| | para 4 | 22 May 2000 (SI 2000/1282) |
| | para 5(1)–(3) | 22 May 2000 (SI 2000/1282) |
| | para 5(4), (5) | 30 Oct 2000 (SI 2000/1985) |
| | para 6(1) | 22 May 2000 (SI 2000/1282) |
| | para 6(2), (3) | 30 Oct 2000 (SI 2000/1985) |
| | paras 7–10 | 30 Oct 2000 (SI 2000/1985) |
| | paras 11–25 | 22 May 2000 (SI 2000/1282) |
| Sch 6 | paras 1–4 | 30 Oct 2000 (SI 2000/1985) |
| | para 5(1) | 1 Aug 2000 (so far as conferring power to make subordinate legislation) (SI 2000/1985) |
| | | 30 Oct 2000 (otherwise) (SI 2000/1985) |
| | para 5(2) | 30 Oct 2000 (SI 2000/1985) |
| | para 6 | 30 Oct 2000 (SI 2000/1985) |
| Sch 7 | paras 1–6 | 30 Oct 2000 (SI 2000/1985) |
| | para 7 | 1 Aug 2000 (SI 2000/1985) |
| | para 8(1), (2) | 30 Oct 2000 (SI 2000/1985) |
| | para 8(3) | 1 Aug 2000 (SI 2000/1985) |
| | paras 9–13 | 30 Oct 2000 (SI 2000/1985) |
| Sch 8 | | 1 Jan 2000 (SI 1999/3190) |
| Sch 9 | | 11 Nov 1999 (s 170(3)) |
| Sch 10 | | *Never in force* (repealed) |
| Sch 11 | para 1 | 3 Apr 2000 (SI 2000/464) |
| | para 2(1)(a) | 1 Aug 2000 (so far as conferring power to make subordinate legislation) (SI 2000/1985) |
| | | 2 Apr 2001 (otherwise) (SI 2001/239) |
| | para 2(1)(b) | 2 Apr 2001 (SI 2001/239) |
| | para 2(2)–(4) | 2 Apr 2001 (SI 2001/239) |
| | paras 3–6 | 2 Apr 2001 (SI 2001/239) |
| | para 7(1) | 3 Apr 2000 (SI 2000/464) |
| | para 7(2), (3) | 1 Aug 2000 (so far as conferring power to make subordinate legislation) (SI 2000/1985) |
| | | 2 Apr 2001 (otherwise) (SI 2001/239) |
| Sch 12 | paras 1, 2 | 1 Aug 2000 (so far as conferring power to make subordinate legislation) (SI 2000/1985) |

**Immigration and Asylum Act 1999 (c 33)**—*contd*

|  |  |  |
|---|---|---|
|  |  | 2 Apr 2001 (otherwise) (SI 2001/239) |
|  | para 3(1)–(6) | 2 Apr 2001 (SI 2001/239) |
|  | para 3(7) | 1 Aug 2000 (so far as conferring power to make subordinate legislation) (SI 2000/1985) |
|  |  | 2 Apr 2001 (otherwise) (SI 2001/239) |
|  | paras 4–8 | 2 Apr 2001 (SI 2001/239) |
| Sch 13 | para 1 | 2 Apr 2001 (SI 2001/239) |
|  | para 2(1)(a) | 1 Aug 2000 (so far as conferring power to make subordinate legislation) (SI 2000/1985) |
|  |  | 2 Apr 2001 (otherwise) (SI 2001/239) |
|  | para 2(1)(b) | 2 Apr 2001 (SI 2001/239) |
|  | para 2(2), (3) | 2 Apr 2001 (SI 2001/239) |
|  | para 2(4) | 1 Aug 2000 (so far as conferring power to make subordinate legislation) (SI 2000/1985) |
|  |  | 2 Apr 2001 (otherwise) (SI 2001/239) |
|  | para 2(5) | 2 Apr 2001 (SI 2001/239) |
|  | para 3 | 2 Apr 2001 (SI 2001/239) |
| Sch 14 | paras 1–32 | 1 Jan 2001 (SI 2000/2698) |
|  | paras 33–36 | *Not yet in force* |
|  | paras 37–42 | 1 Jan 2001 (SI 2000/2698) |
|  | para 43 | See paras 44–70 below |
|  | para 44(1) | 14 Feb 2000 (SI 2000/168) |
|  | para 44(2) | 2 Oct 2000 (SI 2000/2444)[5] |
|  | para 45 | 14 Feb 2000 (SI 2000/168) |
|  | para 46 | 2 Oct 2000 (SI 2000/2444)[5] |
|  | paras 47, 48 | *Not yet in force* |
|  | para 49 | 14 Feb 2000 (so far as relates to repeal of Immigration Act 1971, s 12) (SI 2000/168) |
|  |  | 2 Oct 2000 (except in relation to Immigration Act 1971, s 22, so far as that section has effect for the purposes of Sch 2, para 25 to that Act) (SI 2000/2444)[5] |
|  |  | *Not yet in force* (exception noted above) |
|  | paras 50, 51 | 14 Feb 2000 (SI 2000/168) |
|  | para 52(1) | See sub-paras (2), (3) below |
|  | para 52(2) | 2 Oct 2000 (SI 2000/2444)[5] |
|  | para 52(3)(a) | 1 Mar 2000 (SI 2000/464) |
|  | para 52(3)(b) | 3 Apr 2000 (SI 2000/464) |
|  | para 53 | 14 Feb 2000 (SI 2000/168) |
|  | para 54 | 6 Dec 1999 (SI 1999/3190) |
|  | para 55 | 2 Oct 2000 (SI 2000/2444)[5] |
|  | paras 56–60 | 14 Feb 2000 (SI 2000/168) |
|  | para 61 | 11 Dec 2000 (SI 2000/3099) |
|  | para 62(1) | 14 Feb 2000 (SI 2000/168) |
|  | para 62(2) | 11 Nov 1999 (s 170(3)) |
|  | para 62(3), (4) | 14 Feb 2000 (SI 2000/168) |
|  | paras 63, 64 | 14 Feb 2000 (SI 2000/168) |
|  | paras 65, 66 | 2 Oct 2000 (SI 2000/2444)[5] |
|  | paras 67, 68 | 14 Feb 2000 (SI 2000/168) |
|  | paras 69, 70 | 2 Oct 2000 (SI 2000/2444)[5] |
|  | paras 71, 72 | 14 Feb 2000 (subject to transitional provisions) (SI 2000/168) |
|  | para 73 | 11 Nov 1999 (s 170(3)) |
|  | para 74 | 3 Apr 2000 (SI 2000/464) |
|  | para 75 | *Not yet in force* |
|  | para 76 | 3 Apr 2000 (SI 2000/464) |
|  | para 77 | 1 Jan 2001 (SI 2000/2698) |
|  | paras 78, 79 | 11 Nov 1999 (s 170(3)) |
|  | para 80(1) | See sub-paras (2)–(4) below |
|  | para 80(2), (3) | 14 Feb 2000 (SI 2000/168) |
|  | para 80(4) | *Not yet in force* |

**Immigration and Asylum Act 1999 (c 33)**—*contd*

| | | |
|---|---|---|
| | paras 81, 82 | 11 Nov 1999 (s 170(3)) |
| | para 83 | See paras 84–86 below |
| | para 84 | 2 Oct 2000 (SI 2000/2444)[5] |
| | para 85 | *Not yet in force* |
| | para 86 | 30 Jun 2003 (SI 2003/1469) |
| | paras 87, 88 | 11 Nov 1999 (s 170(3)) |
| | para 89 | *Never in force (repealed)* |
| | para 90(1) | See sub-paras (2)–(4) below |
| | para 90(2), (3) | 14 Feb 2000 (SI 2000/168) |
| | para 90(4) | *Not yet in force* |
| | para 91 | 14 Feb 2000 (subject to transitional provisions) (SI 2000/168) |
| | paras 92, 93 | 3 Apr 2000 (SI 2000/464) |
| | para 94 | See paras 95–97 below |
| | paras 95, 96 | 14 Feb 2000 (SI 2000/168) |
| | para 97 | *Never in force (repealed)* |
| | para 98 | 14 Feb 2000 (subject to transitional provisions) (SI 2000/168) |
| | para 99 | See paras 100–107 below |
| | para 100 | *Not yet in force* |
| | para 101 | 3 Apr 2000 (SI 2000/464) |
| | para 102 | 11 Nov 1999 (s 170(3)) |
| | paras 103–106 | 2 Oct 2000 (SI 2000/2444)[5] |
| | para 107 | *Not yet in force* |
| | para 108 | See paras 109–115 below |
| | para 109 | 14 Feb 2000 (SI 2000/168) |
| | para 110 | 1 Mar 2000 (SI 2000/464) |
| | paras 111–113 | 3 Apr 2000 (SI 2000/464) |
| | paras 114, 115 | 2 Oct 2000 (SI 2000/2444)[5] |
| | para 116 | *Not yet in force* |
| | para 117 | 6 Dec 1999 (SI 1999/3190) |
| | para 118 | See paras 119–129 below |
| | para 119 | *Never in force (repealed)* |
| | para 120 | 2 Oct 2000 (SI 2000/2444)[5] |
| | para 121 | 2 Oct 2000 (so far as relates to Special Immigration Appeals Commission Act 1997, s 2A(1)–(6)) (SI 2000/2444)[5] |
| | | *Never in force (otherwise) (repealed)* |
| | paras 122–124 | 2 Oct 2000 (SI 2000/2444)[5] |
| | para 125 | 14 Feb 2000 (SI 2000/168) |
| | paras 126–128 | 2 Oct 2000 (SI 2000/2444)[5] |
| | para 129 | 1 Aug 2000 (so far as conferring power to make subordinate legislation) (SI 2000/1985) |
| | | 2 Oct 2000 (otherwise) (SI 2000/2444)[5] |
| Sch 15 | para 1 | 14 Feb 2000 (SI 2000/168) |
| | para 2 | 11 Nov 1999 (s 170(3)) |
| | para 3 | 14 Feb 2000 (SI 2000/168) |
| | para 4(a) | *Not yet in force* |
| | para 4(b) | 14 Feb 2000 (SI 2000/168) |
| | paras 5, 6 | 6 Dec 1999 (SI 1999/3190) |
| | paras 7, 8 | *Not yet in force* |
| | para 9 | 6 Dec 1999 (SI 1999/3190) |
| | para 10 | *Never in force (repealed)* |
| | paras 11, 12 | 2 Oct 2000 (SI 2000/2444)[1, 5] |
| | para 13 | 11 Nov 1999 (s 170(3)) |
| | para 14 | 14 Feb 2000 (SI 2000/168) |
| Sch 16 | | 26 Jul 1993 (with retrospective effect) (ss 169(1), 170(3)(s), Sch 14, para 102(2)), repeals of or in— |
| | | Asylum and Immigration Appeals Act 1993, s 6 |
| | | 14 Feb 2000 (SI 2000/168), repeals of or in— |
| | | Immigration Act 1971, ss 12, 24, 25, Sch 2, paras 21, 26, Sch 5; House of Commons Disqualification Act 1975; |

**Immigration and Asylum Act 1999 (c 33)**—*contd*

Northern Ireland Assembly Disqualification Act 1975;

Courts and Legal Services Act 1990;

Judicial Pensions and Retirement Act 1993;

Asylum and Immigration Act 1996, s 7

1 Mar 2000 (SI 2000/464), repeals of or in—

Asylum and Immigration Act 1996, s 9;

Housing Act 1996, Sch 16, para 3

3 Apr 2000 (SI 2000/464)[3], repeals of or in—

Social Security Contributions and Benefits Act 1992;

Social Security Contributions and Benefits (Northern Ireland) Act 1992;

Asylum and Immigration Appeals Act 1993, ss 4, 5, Sch 1;

Asylum and Immigration Act 1996, ss 10, 11

2 Oct 2000 (SI 2000/2444)[5], repeals of or in—

Immigration Act 1971, Pt II (ss 13–23), Schs 2, 3 (except s 22 of the 1971 Act, so far as that section has effect for the purposes of Sch 2, para 25 to the 1971 Act) so far as not already in force;

Immigration Act 1988, s 5;

Asylum and Immigration Appeals Act 1993, ss 7–11, Sch 2;

Asylum and Immigration Act 1996, ss 1–3, Schs 2, 3;

Special Immigration Appeals Commission Act 1997

11 Dec 2000 (repeal of Asylum and Immigration Act 1993, s 3) (SI 2000/3099)

1 Jan 2001 (SI 2000/2698), repeals of or in—

Marriage Act 1949;

Family Law Reform Act 1969;

Marriage (Registrar General's Licence) Act 1970

8 Dec 2002 (SI 2002/2815), repeal of—

Immigration (Carriers' Liability) Act 1987;

Asylum and Immigration Appeals Act 1993, s 12

30 Jun 2003 (repeal of Immigration Act 1988, s 9) (SI 2003/1469)

*Not yet in force*, repeals of or in—

Immigration Act 1971, ss 10(1), 22 (so far as that section has effect for the purposes of Sch 2, para 25 to the 1971 Act);

Immigration Act 1988, s 8;

Asylum and Immigration Act 1996, s 4;

Housing Act 1996, ss 183(2), 186

[1] But, note that s 10 of, and Sch 15, para 12 to, this Act come into force on the day after that on which the "regularisation period" ends. As to the meaning of "regularisation period", see s 9 of the 1999 Act

[2] Sub-ss (1), (2) of s 115 are to come into force on the day on which the first regulations made under Sch 8 of this Act come into force

[3] The Queen's Printer's copy of SI 2000/464 erroneously purports to bring into force the repeal by Sch 16 to this Act of Asylum and Immigration Act 1996, Sch 1. Sch 16 to this Act does not repeal Sch 1 to the 1996 Act; Sch 1 is repealed by Sch 14, para 113 to this Act

[4] For transitional provisions relating to the provisions brought into force by SI 2000/1985, see art 3 of that Order

[5] For transitional provisions relating to the provisions brought into force by SI 2000/2444, see arts 3, 4, Sch 2 of that Order

[6] For transitional provisions relating to the provisions brought into force by SI 2000/2698, see SI 2000/3099, art 4, which inserts SI 2000/2698, art 3

[7] For transitional provisions made by SI 2000/3099, relating to Pt IV of this Act, see art 5 of that Order

## Local Government Act 1999 (c 27)

*RA:* 27 Jul 1999

*Commencement provisions:* s 27; Local Government Act 1999 (Commencement No 1) Order 1999, SI 1999/2169; Local Government Act 1999 (Commencement) (Wales) Order 1999, SI 1999/2815; Local Government Act 1999 (Commencement No 3) (England) Order 2000, SI 2000/1724

| | | |
|---|---|---|
| 1 | (1)(a), (b) | 10 Aug 1999 (SI 1999/2169)[2] |
| | | 1 Oct 1999 (otherwise) (SI 1999/2815)[1] |
| | (1)(c) | 10 Aug 1999 (SI 1999/2169)[2] |
| | (1)(d), (e) | 10 Aug 1999 (SI 1999/2169) |
| | (1)(f) | 3 Jul 2000 (SI 2000/1724)[1] |
| | (1)(g) | 10 Aug 1999 (SI 1999/2169)[2] |
| | | 1 Oct 1999 (otherwise) (SI 1999/2815)[1] |
| | (1)(h) | 10 Aug 1999 (SI 1999/2169)[2] |
| | (1)(i), (j) | 3 Jul 2000 (SI 2000/1724)[1] |
| | (2)(a)–(c) | 10 Aug 1999 (SI 1999/2169)[2] |
| | (2)(d) | 3 Jul 2000 (SI 2000/1724)[1] |
| | (3) | 1 Oct 1999 (SI 1999/2815)[1] |
| | (4)(a), (b) | 10 Aug 1999 (SI 1999/2169) |
| | (4)(c) | 3 Jul 2000 (SI 2000/1724)[1] |
| | (5)(a) | 10 Aug 1999 (SI 1999/2169)[2] |
| | | 1 Oct 1999 (otherwise) (SI 1999/2815)[1] |
| | (5)(b) | 10 Aug 1999 (SI 1999/2169)[2] |
| 2 | (1)–(3) | 27 Sep 1999 (SI 1999/2169)[2] |
| | | 1 Oct 1999 (otherwise) (SI 1999/2815)[1] |
| | (4) | 3 Jul 2000 (SI 2000/1724)[1] |
| | (5) | 27 Sep 1999 (SI 1999/2169)[2] |
| | | 1 Oct 1999 (otherwise) (SI 1999/2815)[1] |
| | (6) | 27 Sep 1999 (SI 1999/2169)[2] |
| | | 27 Jul 2000 (otherwise) (s 27(1))[1] |
| 3 | (1) | 1 Apr 2000 (SI 1999/2169)[2] |
| | | 1 Apr 2000 (otherwise) (SI 1999/2815)[1] |
| | (2)–(4) | 10 Aug 1999 (SI 1999/2169)[2] |
| | | 1 Oct 1999 (otherwise) (SI 1999/2815)[1] |
| 4 | (1), (2) | 27 Sep 1999 (SI 1999/2169)[2] |
| | | 1 Oct 1999 (otherwise) (SI 1999/2815)[1] |
| | (3), (4) | 10 Aug 1999 (SI 1999/2169)[2] |
| | | 1 Oct 1999 (otherwise) (SI 1999/2815)[1] |
| | (5) | 1 Apr 2000 (SI 1999/2169)[2] |
| | | 1 Apr 2000 (otherwise) (SI 1999/2815)[1] |
| 5 | (1) | 1 Apr 2000 (SI 1999/2169)[2] |
| | | 1 Apr 2000 (otherwise) (SI 1999/2815)[1] |
| | (2) | 27 Sep 1999 (SI 1999/2169)[2] |
| | | 1 Oct 1999 (otherwise) (SI 1999/2815)[1] |
| | (3) | 1 Apr 2000 (SI 1999/2169)[2] |
| | | 1 Apr 2000 (otherwise) (SI 1999/2815)[1] |
| | (4) | 27 Sep 1999 (SI 1999/2169)[2] |
| | | 1 Oct 1999 (otherwise) (SI 1999/2815)[1] |
| | (5)–(7) | 27 Sep 1999 (SI 1999/2169)[2] |
| | | 1 Oct 1999 (otherwise) (SI 1999/2815)[1] |
| 6 | | 27 Sep 1999 (SI 1999/2169)[2] |
| | | 1 Oct 1999 (otherwise) (SI 1999/2815)[1] |
| 7 | | 1 Apr 2000 (SI 1999/2169)[2] |
| | | 1 Apr 2000 (otherwise) (SI 1999/2815)[1] |
| 8 | (1) | 1 Apr 2000 (SI 1999/2169)[2] |
| | | 1 Apr 2000 (otherwise) (SI 1999/2815)[1] |
| | (2)–(7) | 27 Sep 1999 (SI 1999/2169)[2] |
| | | 1 Oct 1999 (otherwise) (SI 1999/2815)[1] |
| 9 | | 1 Apr 2000 (SI 1999/2169)[2] |

**Local Government Act 1999 (c 27)**—*contd*

|    |              |                                                                                           |
|----|--------------|-------------------------------------------------------------------------------------------|
|    |              | 1 Apr 2000 (otherwise) (SI 1999/2815)[1]                                                   |
| 10 | (1)–(3)      | 1 Apr 2000 (SI 1999/2169)[2]                                                               |
|    |              | 1 Apr 2000 (otherwise) (SI 1999/2815)[1]                                                   |
|    | (4)          | 27 Sep 1999 (for the purposes of the issue of guidance by the Secretary of State) (SI 1999/2169)[2] |
|    |              | 1 Oct 1999 (W) (otherwise) (SI 1999/2815)[1]                                               |
|    |              | 1 Apr 2000 (E) (otherwise) (SI 1999/2815)[1]                                               |
| 11 |              | 1 Apr 2000 (SI 1999/2169)[2]                                                               |
|    |              | 1 Apr 2000 (otherwise) (SI 1999/2815)[1]                                                   |
| 12 | (1)          | 27 Sep 1999 (SI 1999/2169)[2]                                                              |
|    |              | 1 Oct 1999 (otherwise) (SI 1999/2815)[1]                                                   |
|    | (2), (3)     | 1 Apr 2000 (SI 1999/2169)[2]                                                               |
|    |              | 1 Apr 2000 (otherwise) (SI 1999/2815)[1]                                                   |
|    | (4)          | 10 Aug 1999 (SI 1999/2169)[2]                                                              |
|    |              | 1 Oct 1999 (otherwise) (SI 1999/2815)[1]                                                   |
| 13 |              | 1 Apr 2000 (SI 1999/2169)[2]                                                               |
|    |              | 1 Apr 2000 (otherwise) (SI 1999/2815)[1]                                                   |
| 14 |              | 1 Apr 2000 (SI 1999/2169)                                                                  |
| 15 | (1)–(6)      | 1 Apr 2000 (SI 1999/2169)[2]                                                               |
|    |              | 1 Apr 2000 (otherwise) (SI 1999/2815)[1]                                                   |
|    | (7), (8)     | 27 Sep 1999 (SI 1999/2169)[2]                                                              |
|    |              | 1 Apr 2000 (otherwise) (SI 1999/2815)[1]                                                   |
|    | (9)–(13)     | 1 Apr 2000 (SI 1999/2169)[2]                                                               |
|    |              | 1 Apr 2000 (otherwise) (SI 1999/2815)[1]                                                   |
| 16 |              | 27 Sep 1999 (SI 1999/2169)                                                                 |
| 17 |              | 10 Aug 1999 (SI 1999/2169)                                                                 |
| 18 |              | 27 Sep 1999 (SI 1999/2169)                                                                 |
| 19 | (1), (2)     | 27 Sep 1999 (SI 1999/2169)[2]                                                              |
|    |              | 1 Oct 1999 (otherwise) (SI 1999/2815)[1]                                                   |
|    | (3)          | 27 Sep 1999 (SI 1999/2169)[2]                                                              |
|    |              | 27 Jul 2000 (otherwise) (s 27(1))[1]                                                       |
|    | (4)          | 27 Sep 1999 (SI 1999/2169)[2]                                                              |
|    |              | 1 Oct 1999 (otherwise) (SI 1999/2815)[1]                                                   |
| 20 |              | 27 Sep 1999 (SI 1999/2169)[2]                                                              |
|    |              | 1 Oct 1999 (otherwise) (SI 1999/2815)[1]                                                   |
| 21 |              | 27 Jul 1999 (RA)                                                                           |
| 22 |              | 27 Sep 1999 (SI 1999/2169)[2]                                                              |
|    |              | 1 Oct 1999 (otherwise) (SI 1999/2815)[1]                                                   |
| 23 | (1)–(3)      | 27 Sep 1999 (SI 1999/2169)[2]                                                              |
|    |              | 1 Oct 1999 (otherwise) (SI 1999/2815)[1]                                                   |
|    | (4)          | 10 Aug 1999 (SI 1999/2169)[2]                                                              |
|    |              | 1 Oct 1999 (otherwise) (SI 1999/2815)[1]                                                   |
|    | (5), (6)     | 27 Sep 1999 (SI 1999/2169)[2]                                                              |
|    |              | 1 Oct 1999 (otherwise) (SI 1999/2815)[1]                                                   |
| 24 | (1)          | 27 Sep 1999 (SI 1999/2169)                                                                 |
|    | (2), (3)     | 1 Apr 2000 (SI 1999/2169)                                                                  |
| 25 | (1)          | 27 Sep 1999 (SI 1999/2169)[2]                                                              |
|    |              | 1 Oct 1999 (otherwise) (SI 1999/2815)[1]                                                   |
|    | (2)(a)       | 27 Sep 1999 (SI 1999/2169)[2]                                                              |
|    |              | 1 Oct 1999 (otherwise) (SI 1999/2815)[1]                                                   |
|    | (2)(b), (c)  | 27 Sep 1999 (SI 1999/2169)[2]                                                              |
|    |              | 27 Jul 2000 (otherwise) (s 27(1))[1]                                                       |
|    | (2)(d), (e)–(h) | 27 Sep 1999 (SI 1999/2169)[2]                                                           |
|    |              | 1 Oct 1999 (otherwise) (SI 1999/2815)[1]                                                   |
|    | (2)(i)       | 27 Sep 1999 (SI 1999/2169)[2]                                                              |
|    |              | 27 Jul 2000 (otherwise) (s 27(1))[1]                                                       |
|    | (3)          | 27 Sep 1999 (SI 1999/2169)[2]                                                              |
|    |              | 1 Oct 1999 (otherwise) (SI 1999/2815)[1]                                                   |
| 26 | (1)          | 27 Sep 1999 (SI 1999/2169)[2]                                                              |

**Local Government Act 1999 (c 27)**—*contd*

|  |  |  |
|---|---|---|
|  |  | 1 Oct 1999 (otherwise) (SI 1999/2815)[1] |
|  | (2)(a), (b) | 27 Sep 1999 (SI 1999/2169)[2] |
|  |  | 1 Oct 1999 (otherwise) (SI 1999/2815)[1] |
|  | (2)(c) | 10 Aug 1999 (SI 1999/2169)[2] |
|  |  | 1 Oct 1999 (otherwise) (SI 1999/2815)[1] |
|  | (2)(d) | 27 Sep 1999 (SI 1999/2169)[2] |
|  |  | 1 Oct 1999 (otherwise) (SI 1999/2815)[1] |
|  | (3), (4) | 10 Aug 1999 (SI 1999/2169)[2] |
|  |  | 1 Oct 1999 (otherwise) (SI 1999/2815)[1] |
| 27–29 |  | 27 Jul 1999 (RA) |
| 30 |  | See Sch 1 below |
| 31 |  | 27 Jul 1999 (RA) (this section applies as regards the financial year beginning with 1 Apr 1999, subject to modifications, and subsequent financial years) |
| 32, 33 |  | 27 Jul 1999 (RA) |
| 34 |  | See Sch 2 below |
| 35, 36 |  | 27 Jul 1999 (RA) |
| Sch 1 |  | 27 Jul 1999 (RA) (applies in relation to the limitation of council tax and precepts as regards the financial year beginning with 1 Apr 2000 and subsequent financial years) |
| Sch 2 |  | 27 Jul 1999 (RA) |

[1]   The Secretary of State may by order provide for:

(i)   any of ss 1–13, 15, 19, 20, 22, 23, 25, 26 to be brought into force in relation to England before the time appointed by s 27(1) of this Act (i e 27 Jul 2000);

(ii)   any of those sections, in so far as it relates to an authority falling within s 1(1)(d), (e) to be brought into force in relation to Wales before that time; and

(iii)   any of ss 14, 16–18, 24 to be brought into force before that time, and the National Assembly for Wales may by order provide for any of ss 1–13, 15, 19, 20, 22, 23, 25, 26, except in so far as it relates to an authority falling within s 1(1)(d), (e), to be brought into force in relation to Wales before that time

[2]   In relation to England, and in relation to Wales so far as they relate to an authority falling within s 1(1)(d), (e) of the Act

---

**Mental Health (Amendment) (Scotland) Act 1999 (c 32)**

*RA:* 11 Nov 1999

*Commencement provisions:* s 2(2)

Whole Act in force 11 Jan 2000 (s 2(2))

---

**Mental Health (Public Safety and Appeals) (Scotland) Act 1999 (asp 1)**

*RA:* 13 Sep 1999

Whole Act in force 13 Sep 1999 (RA)

---

**Northern Ireland (Location of Victims' Remains) Act 1999 (c 7)**

*RA:* 26 May 1999

*Commencement provisions:* s 2(5); Northern Ireland (Location of Victims' Remains) Act 1999 (Commencement of Section 2) Order 1999, SI 1999/1511

| | |
|---|---|
| 1 | 26 May 1999 (RA) |
| 2 | 26 May 1999 (SI 1999/1511) |
| 3–7 | 26 May 1999 (RA) |

## Pollution Prevention and Control Act 1999 (c 24)

*RA:* 27 Jul 1999

*Commencement provisions:* s 7(3); Pollution Prevention and Control Act 1999 (Commencement No 1) (England and Wales) Order 2000, SI 2000/800; Pollution Prevention and Control Act 1999 (Commencement No 2) (Scotland) Order 2000, SSI 2000/322; Pollution Prevention and Control Act 1999 (Commencement No 3) (Scotland) Order 2015, SSI 2015/74, as amended by SI 2015/139; Pollution Prevention and Control Act 1999 (Commencement No 4 and Amendment) (Scotland) Order 2015, SSI 2015/139

| | | |
|---|---|---|
| 1 | (1) | See Sch 1 below |
| | (2), (3) | 27 Jul 1999 (RA) |
| 2–5 | | 27 Jul 1999 (RA) |
| 6 | (1) | See Sch 2 below |
| | (2) | See Sch 3 below |
| 7 | | 27 Jul 1999 (RA) |
| Sch 1 | | 27 Jul 1999 (RA) |
| Sch 2 | para 1 | 21 Mar 2000 (E) (W) (SI 2000/800) |
| | | 29 Sep 2000 (S) (SSI 2000/322) |
| | para 2 | 21 Mar 2000 (E) (W) (SI 2000/800) |
| | para 3 | 21 Mar 2000 (E) (W) (SI 2000/800) |
| | | 29 Sep 2000 (S) (SSI 2000/322) |
| | para 4 | 21 Mar 2000 (E) (W) (SI 2000/800) |
| | paras 5, 6 | 21 Mar 2000 (E) (W) (SI 2000/800) |
| | | 29 Sep 2000 (S) (SSI 2000/322) |
| | paras 7, 8 | 21 Mar 2000 (E) (W) (SI 2000/800) |
| | paras 9–12 | 21 Mar 2000 (E) (W) (SI 2000/800) |
| | | 29 Sep 2000 (S) (SSI 2000/322) |
| | para 13 | 21 Mar 2000 (E) (W) (SI 2000/800) |
| | | 1 Apr 2015 (S) (SSI 2015/74) |
| | | *Not yet in force* (NI) |
| | para 14 | 21 Mar 2000 (E) (W) (SI 2000/800) |
| | | 29 Sep 2000 (S) (SSI 2000/322) |
| | para 15 | 21 Mar 2000 (E) (W) (SI 2000/800) |
| | | 1 Apr 2015 (S) (SSI 2015/74) |
| | para 16 | 29 Sep 2000 (S) (SSI 2000/322) |
| | paras 17, 18 | 21 Mar 2000 (E) (W) (SI 2000/800) |
| | | 29 Sep 2000 (S) (SSI 2000/322) |
| | paras 19, 20 | 21 Mar 2000 (E) (W) (SI 2000/800) |
| Sch 3 | | 1 Apr 2015 (S) (SSI 2015/74), repeals of or in— |
| | | Prevention of Oil Pollution Act 1971, s 11A(1); |
| | | Environmental Protection Act 1990, ss 1–19, 22–28, Sch 1; |
| | | Water Consolidation (Consequential Provisions) Act 1990, Sch 1, para 56; |
| | | Clean Air Act 1993, ss 33(1), 35(3), 36(3), 41; |
| | | Radioactive Substances Act 1993, Sch 4, para 6; |
| | | Merchant Shipping Act 1995, s 136A; |
| | | Environment Act 1995, ss 5(5)(e), 56(1), 108(15) |
| | | 1 Apr 2015 (S) (SSI 2015/139), repeals of or in— |
| | | Environment Act 1995, ss 111(6), 113(5), 114(2), Sch 20, para 4(3)(b), Sch 22, paras 45–61 |
| | | *Not yet in force* (E) (W) |

## Protection of Children Act 1999 (c 14)

*RA:* 15 Jul 1999

*Commencement provisions:* s 14(2); Protection of Children Act 1999 (Commencement No 1) Order 2000, SI 2000/1459; Protection of Children Act 1999 (Commencement No 2) Order 2000, SI 2000/2337; Protection of Children Act 1999 (Commencement No 3) Order 2002, SI 2002/1436

**Protection of Children Act 1999 (c 14)**—*contd*

| | | |
|---|---|---|
| 1 | | 2 Oct 2000 (SI 2000/2337) |
| 2 | (1) | 2 Oct 2000 (SI 2000/2337) |
| | (2)(a)–(c) | 1 Sep 2000 (so far as relate to s 3 below) (SI 2000/2337) |
| | | 2 Oct 2000 (otherwise) (SI 2000/2337) |
| | (2)(d) | 2 Oct 2000 (SI 2000/2337) |
| | (3)–(10) | 2 Oct 2000 (SI 2000/2337) |
| 3 | (1), (2) | 5 Jun 2000 (SI 2000/1459) |
| | (3) | 1 Sep 2000 (except so far as provides for inclusion of any individual in list kept by Secretary of State under s 1 above) (SI 2000/2337) |
| | | 2 Oct 2000 (otherwise) (SI 2000/2337) |
| 4 | | 2 Oct 2000 (SI 2000/2337) |
| 5, 6 | | 1 Sep 2000 (SI 2000/2337) |
| 7 | | 2 Oct 2000 (SI 2000/2337) |
| 8 | | 12 Mar 2002 (E) (W) (SI 2002/1436) |
| | | *Never in force* (NI) (repealed) |
| 9 | (1)–(3) | 1 Sep 2000 (for purpose of making regulations) (SI 2000/2337) |
| | | 2 Oct 2000 (otherwise) (SI 2000/2337) |
| | (4)–(6) | 1 Sep 2000 (for purpose of making regulations) (SI 2000/2337) |
| | | 2 Oct 2000 (otherwise) (SI 2000/2337) |
| | (7) | See Schedule below |
| 10 | | *Never in force* (repealed) |
| 11 | | 2 Oct 2000 (SI 2000/2337) |
| 12 | | 1 Sep 2000 (SI 2000/2337) |
| 13, 14 | | 2 Oct 2000 (SI 2000/2337) |
| Schedule | | 2 Oct 2000 (SI 2000/2337) |

---

**Rating (Valuation) Act 1999 (c 6)**

*RA:* 26 May 1999

*Commencement provisions:* s 2(1)–(3)

| | |
|---|---|
| 1 | 1 Apr 1990 (in relation to rating lists compiled before 26 May 1999) (subject to a saving) (s 2(2), (3)) |
| | 26 May 1999 (in relation to rating lists to be compiled on or after 26 May 1999) (s 2(1)) |
| 2, 3 | 26 May 1999 (RA) |

---

**Road Traffic (NHS Charges) Act 1999 (c 3)**

*RA:* 10 Mar 1999

*Commencement provisions:* s 21(2), (3); Road Traffic (NHS Charges) Act 1999 (Commencement No 1) Order 1999, SI 1999/1075

| | |
|---|---|
| 1–20 | 5 Apr 1999 (except in relation to military hospitals) (SI 1999/1075) |
| | *Never in force* (repealed) (exception noted above) |
| 21 | 10 Mar 1999 (RA) |

---

**Road Traffic (Vehicle Testing) Act 1999 (c 12)**

*RA:* 30 Jun 1999

*Commencement provisions:* s 9(2); Road Traffic (Vehicle Testing) Act 1999 (Commencement No 1) Order 2001, SI 2001/1896; Road Traffic (Vehicle Testing) Act 1999 (Commencement No 2) Order 2003, SI 2003/1095

| | | |
|---|---|---|
| 1 | (1), (2) | 11 Apr 2003 (SI 2003/1095) |

## Road Traffic (Vehicle Testing) Act 1999 (c 12)—*contd*

| | | |
|---|---|---|
| | (3) | 1 Jun 2001 (so far as relates to the insertion of Road Traffic Act 1988, s 45(6B)) (SI 2001/1896) |
| | | 11 Apr 2003 (otherwise) (SI 2003/1095) |
| 2 | | 11 Apr 2003 (SI 2003/1095) |
| 3 | | 1 Jun 2001 (SI 2001/1896) |
| 4, 5 | | 11 Apr 2003 (SI 2003/1095) |
| 6 | | 30 Jun 1999 (RA) |
| 7 | (1) | See Schedule below |
| | (2) | *Not yet in force* |
| 8, 9 | | 30 Jun 1999 (RA) |
| Schedule | paras 1, 2 | *Not yet in force* |
| | para 3 | 11 Apr 2003 (SI 2003/1095) |

## Scottish Enterprise Act 1999 (c 5)

*RA:* 26 May 1999

*Commencement provisions:* s 2(3)

Whole Act in force 26 Jul 1999 (s 2(3))

## Social Security Contributions (Transfer of Functions, etc) Act 1999 (c 2)

*RA:* 25 Feb 1999

*Commencement provisions:* s 28(2), (3); Social Security Contributions (Transfer of Functions, etc) Act 1999 (Commencement No 1 and Transitional Provisions) Order 1999, SI 1999/527[1]; Social Security Contributions (Transfer of Functions, etc) Act 1999 (Commencement No 2 and Consequential and Transitional Provisions) Order 1999, SI 1999/1662

| | | |
|---|---|---|
| 1 | (1) | See Sch 1 below |
| | (2) | See Sch 2 below |
| 2 | | See Sch 3 below |
| 3 | (1), (2) | 1 Apr 1999 (SI 1999/527) |
| | (3)(a), (b) | 1 Apr 1999 (SI 1999/527) |
| | (3)(c) | *Never in force* (repealed) |
| | (3)(d)–(f) | 1 Apr 1999 (SI 1999/527) |
| | (4)–(7) | 1 Apr 1999 (SI 1999/527) |
| 4 | (a) | 1 Apr 1999 (except so far as relates to Class 1B contributions) (SI 1999/527) |
| | | 6 Apr 1999 (exception noted above) (SI 1999/527) |
| | (b) | 1 Apr 1999 (SI 1999/527) |
| | (c) | 6 Apr 1999 (SI 1999/527) |
| 5 | | See Sch 5 below |
| 6 | | See Sch 6 below |
| 7 | | 1 Apr 1999 (SI 1999/527) |
| 8 | (1)(a)–(g) | 25 Feb 1999 (so far as conferring power to make subordinate legislation) (s 28(2)) |
| | | 1 Apr 1999 (otherwise) (SI 1999/527) |
| | (1)(h) | 25 Feb 1999 (so far as conferring power to make subordinate legislation) (s 28(2)) |
| | | 6 Apr 1999 (otherwise) (SI 1999/527) |
| | (1)(i) | 25 Feb 1999 (so far as conferring power to make subordinate legislation) (s 28(2)) |
| | | 1 Apr 1999 (otherwise) (SI 1999/527) |
| | (1)(j) | 1 Apr 1999 (SI 1999/527) |
| | (1)(k), (l) | 25 Feb 1999 (so far as conferring power to make subordinate legislation) (s 28(2)) |
| | | 6 Apr 1999 (otherwise) (SI 1999/527) |

**Social Security Contributions (Transfer of Functions, etc) Act 1999 (c 2)**—*contd*

| | | |
|---|---|---|
| | (1)(m) | 25 Feb 1999 (so far as conferring power to make subordinate legislation) (s 28(2)) |
| | | 1 Apr 1999 (otherwise) (SI 1999/527) |
| | (2)–(4) | 25 Feb 1999 (so far as conferring power to make subordinate legislation) (s 28(2)) |
| | | 1 Apr 1999 (otherwise) (SI 1999/527) |
| 9, 10 | | 25 Feb 1999 (so far as conferring power to make subordinate legislation) (s 28(2)) |
| | | 1 Apr 1999 (otherwise) (SI 1999/527) |
| 11 | (1)–(3) | 25 Feb 1999 (so far as conferring power to make subordinate legislation) (s 28(2)) |
| | | 1 Apr 1999 (otherwise) (SI 1999/527) |
| | (4) | 25 Feb 1999 (so far as conferring power to make subordinate legislation) (s 28(2)) |
| | | 6 Apr 1999 (otherwise) (SI 1999/527) |
| 12 | | 25 Feb 1999 (so far as conferring power to make subordinate legislation) (s 28(2)) |
| | | 1 Apr 1999 (except for the words from "section 121D" to "and to" in sub-s (4)) (SI 1999/527) |
| | | 6 Apr 1999 (exception noted above) (SI 1999/527) |
| 13–15 | | 25 Feb 1999 (so far as conferring power to make subordinate legislation) (s 28(2)) |
| | | 1 Apr 1999 (otherwise) (SI 1999/527) |
| 16 | (1) | 5 Jul 1999 (SI 1999/1662) |
| | (2) | 14 Jun 1999 (for the purpose of authorising the making of regulations) (SI 1999/1662) |
| | | 5 Jul 1999 (otherwise) (subject to a transitional provision) (SI 1999/1662) |
| 17 | | 25 Feb 1999 (s 28(2)) |
| 18 | | See Sch 7 below |
| 19 | | 4 Mar 1999 (for purposes connected with the making of regulations) (SI 1999/527) |
| | | 1 Apr 1999 (otherwise) (SI 1999/527) |
| 20 | | 25 Feb 1999 (s 28(2)) |
| 21 | | 1 Apr 1999 (SI 1999/527) |
| 22 | (1)–(3) | 1 Apr 1999 (SI 1999/527) |
| | (4) | 25 Feb 1999 (so far as conferring power to make an order) (s 28(2)) |
| | | 1 Apr 1999 (otherwise) (SI 1999/527) |
| | (5) | 1 Apr 1999 (SI 1999/527) |
| 23 | | 1 Apr 1999 (SI 1999/527) |
| 24, 25 | | 25 Feb 1999 (s 28(2)) |
| 26 | (1) | See Sch 8 below |
| | (2) | See Sch 9 below |
| | (3) | See Sch 10 below |
| 27, 28 | | 25 Feb 1999 (s 28(2)) |
| Sch 1 | paras 1–16 | 25 Feb 1999 (so far as enabling the Secretary of State to make subordinate legislation conferring functions on the Board) (s 28(2)) |
| | | 1 Apr 1999 (otherwise) (SI 1999/527) |
| | para 17(a), (b) | 25 Feb 1999 (so far as enabling the Secretary of State to make subordinate legislation conferring functions on the Board) (s 28(2)) |
| | | 1 Apr 1999 (otherwise) (SI 1999/527) |
| | para 17(c) | 25 Feb 1999 (so far as enabling the Secretary of State to make subordinate legislation conferring functions on the Board) (s 28(2)) |
| | | 1 Apr 1999 (except in so far as amends Social Security Contributions and Benefits Act 1992, Sch 1, para 6(8)) (SI 1999/527) |

**Social Security Contributions (Transfer of Functions, etc) Act 1999 (c 2)**—*contd*

| | | |
|---|---|---|
| | | *Not yet in force* (exception noted above) |
| | paras 18–65 | 25 Feb 1999 (so far as enabling the Secretary of State to make subordinate legislation conferring functions on the Board) (s 28(2)) |
| | | 1 Apr 1999 (otherwise) (SI 1999/527) |
| | para 66(1), (2) | 25 Feb 1999 (so far as enabling the Secretary of State to make subordinate legislation conferring functions on the Board) (s 28(2)) |
| | | 1 Apr 1999 (otherwise) (SI 1999/527) |
| | para 66(3) | *Never in force* (repealed) |
| | para 66(4)–(6) | 25 Feb 1999 (so far as enabling the Secretary of State to make subordinate legislation conferring functions on the Board) (s 28(2)) |
| | | 1 Apr 1999 (otherwise) (SI 1999/527) |
| | paras 67, 68 | 25 Feb 1999 (so far as enabling the Secretary of State to make subordinate legislation conferring functions on the Board) (s 28(2)) |
| | | 1 Apr 1999 (otherwise) (SI 1999/527) |
| Sch 2 | | 1 Apr 1999 (except in relation to functions which are, by virtue of SI 1997/664, art 4, exercisable under SI 1984/380, reg 20(2)(b)) (SI 1999/527) |
| | | *Not yet in force* (exception noted above) |
| Sch 3 | | 1 Apr 1999 (SI 1999/527) |
| Sch 4 | | 1 Apr 1999 (except so far as relates to Class 1B contributions) (SI 1999/527) |
| | | 6 Apr 1999 (exception noted above) (SI 1999/527) |
| Sch 5 | paras 1–4 | 1 Apr 1999 (SI 1999/527) |
| | para 5 | 6 Apr 1999 (SI 1999/527) |
| | para 6 | 1 Apr 1999 (SI 1999/527) |
| | para 7 | 6 Apr 1999 (SI 1999/527) |
| | paras 8–12 | 1 Apr 1999 (SI 1999/527) |
| Sch 6 | | 1 Apr 1999 (SI 1999/527) |
| Sch 7 | paras 1–3 | 4 Mar 1999 (for purposes connected with the making of regulations) (SI 1999/527) |
| | | 1 Apr 1999 (otherwise) (SI 1999/527) |
| | para 4 | 5 Jul 1999 (SI 1999/1662) |
| | paras 5–8 | 4 Mar 1999 (for purposes connected with the making of regulations) (SI 1999/527) |
| | | 1 Apr 1999 (otherwise) (SI 1999/527) |
| | paras 9, 10 | 4 Mar 1999 (for purposes connected with the making of regulations) (SI 1999/527) |
| | | 6 Apr 1999 (otherwise) (SI 1999/527) |
| | para 11 | 4 Mar 1999 (for purposes connected with the making of regulations) (SI 1999/527) |
| | | 1 Apr 1999 (otherwise) (SI 1999/527) |
| | para 12 | 5 Jul 1999 (SI 1999/1662) |
| | para 13 | 1 Apr 1999 (SI 1999/527) |
| | para 14 | 5 Jul 1999 (SI 1999/1662) |
| | paras 15, 16 | 1 Apr 1999 (SI 1999/527) |
| | para 17 | 4 Mar 1999 (for purposes connected with the making of regulations) (SI 1999/527) |
| | | 1 Apr 1999 (otherwise) (SI 1999/527) |
| | para 18(1), (2) | 1 Apr 1999 (SI 1999/527) |
| | para 18(3) | 5 Jul 1999 (SI 1999/1662) |
| | paras 19, 20 | 5 Jul 1999 (SI 1999/1662) |
| | paras 21–23 | 1 Apr 1999 (SI 1999/527) |
| | para 24 | 14 Jun 1999 (for the purpose of authorising the making of regulations) (SI 1999/1662) |
| | | 5 Jul 1999 (otherwise) (SI 1999/1662) |
| | paras 25–27 | 1 Apr 1999 (SI 1999/527) |

**Social Security Contributions (Transfer of Functions, etc) Act 1999 (c 2)**—*contd*

| | | |
|---|---|---|
| | para 28 | *Not yet in force* |
| | paras 29–32 | 1 Apr 1999 (SI 1999/527) |
| | para 33 | 14 Jun 1999 (for the purpose of authorising the making of regulations) (SI 1999/1662) |
| | | 5 Jul 1999 (otherwise) (SI 1999/1662) |
| | para 34 | 5 Jul 1999 (SI 1999/1662) |
| | para 35 | 1 Apr 1999 (SI 1999/527) |
| | para 36 | 1 Apr 1999 (except so far as relates to Social Security Act 1998, Sch 3, para 23) (SI 1999/527) (note that there is thought to be an error in SI 1999/527) |
| | | 5 Jul 1999 (so far as relates to Social Security Act 1998, Sch 3, para 23) (SI 1999/1662) |
| Sch 8 | | 25 Feb 1999 (s 28(2)) |
| Sch 9 | paras 1, 2 | 6 Apr 1999 (SI 1999/527) |
| | para 3 | 1 Apr 1999 (SI 1999/527) |
| | paras 4–7 | 4 Mar 1999 (for purposes connected with the making of regulations) (SI 1999/527) |
| | | 1 Apr 1999 (otherwise) (SI 1999/527) |
| | para 8 | 1 Apr 1999 (SI 1999/527) |
| Sch 10 | | 1 Apr 1999 (SI 1999/527), except repeals of or in— |
| | | Social Security Administration Act 1992, s 118; |
| | | Pension Schemes Act 1993, s 167(3); |
| | | Social Security Act 1998, ss 16, 62, Sch 3, para 23, Sch 7, paras 130, 132 |
| | | 6 Apr 1999 (SI 1999/527), repeals of or in— |
| | | Social Security Administration Act 1992, s 118; |
| | | Social Security Act 1998, s 62 |
| | | 5 Jul 1999 (SI 1999/1662), repeals of— |
| | | Pension Schemes Act 1993, s 167(3); |
| | | Social Security Act 1998, Sch 3, para 23, Sch 7, paras 130(1), 132 |
| | | *Not yet in force* (repeal of or in Social Security Act 1998, s 16, Sch 7, para 130(2)) |

[1]  For transitional provisions relating to the provisions brought into force by SI 1999/527, see arts 3–6 of that Order

---

**Tax Credits Act 1999 (c 10)**

*RA:* 30 Jun 1999

*Commencement provisions:* ss 6(4), 14(9), 20(2)

| | | |
|---|---|---|
| 1–5 | | 5 Oct 1999 (s 20(2)) |
| 6 | | 6 Apr 2000 (s 6(4)) |
| 7–13 | | 5 Oct 1999 (s 20(2)) |
| 14 | (1) | 5 Oct 1999 (so far as relates to s 14(3) of this Act) (s 20(2)) |
| | | 1 Oct 2000 (otherwise) (s 14(9)) |
| | (2) | 1 Oct 2000 (s 14(9)) |
| | (3) | 5 Oct 1999 (s 20(2)) |
| | (4)–(9) | 1 Oct 2000 (s 14(9)) |
| 15–18 | | 5 Oct 1999 (s 20(2)) |
| 19 | (1) | 30 Jun 1999 (RA) |
| | (2)–(4) | 5 Oct 1999 (s 20(2)) |
| 20 | | 30 Jun 1999 (RA) |
| Schs 1–6 | | 5 Oct 1999 (s 20(2)) |

---

## Trustee Delegation Act 1999 (c 15)

*RA:* 15 Jul 1999

*Commencement provisions:* s 13(1); Trustee Delegation Act 1999 (Commencement) Order 2000, SI 2000/216

| | |
|---|---|
| 1–12 | 1 Mar 2000 (SI 2000/216) |
| 13 | 15 Jul 1999 (RA) |
| Schedule | 1 Mar 2000 (SI 2000/216) |

## Water Industry Act 1999 (c 9)

*RA:* 30 Jun 1999

*Commencement provisions:* s 17(2), (3); Water Industry Act 1999 (Commencement No 1) (Scotland) Order 1999, SSI 1999/133; Water Industry Act 1999 (Commencement No 2) Order 1999, SI 1999/3440

| | | |
|---|---|---|
| 1, 2 | | 30 Jun 1999 (s 17(2)) |
| 3 | | 1 Apr 2000 (SI 1999/3440) |
| 4, 5 | | 30 Jun 1999 (so far as confers power to make subordinate legislation) (s 17(2)) |
| | | 23 Dec 1999 (otherwise) (SI 1999/3440) |
| 6, 7 | | 30 Jun 1999 (so far as confers power to make subordinate legislation) (s 17(2)) |
| | | 1 Apr 2000 (otherwise) (SI 1999/3440) |
| 8 | | 30 Jun 1999 (s 17(2)) |
| 9–11 | | 1 Apr 2000 (SI 1999/3440) |
| 12 | | 30 Jun 1999 (so far as confers power to make subordinate legislation) (s 17(2)) |
| | | 1 Nov 1999 (otherwise) (SSI 1999/133) |
| 13 | | 1 Nov 1999 (SSI 1999/133) |
| 14 | | 30 Jun 1999 (s 17(2)) |
| 15 | (1) | See Sch 3 below |
| | (2) | See Sch 4 below |
| 16 | | 23 Dec 1999 (SI 1999/3440) |
| 17 | | 30 Jun 1999 (RA) |
| Sch 1 | | 30 Jun 1999 (s 17(2)) |
| Sch 2 | | 1 Nov 1999 (SSI 1999/133) |
| Sch 3 | Pt I, paras 1–3 | 1 Apr 2000 (SI 1999/3440) |
| | Pt I, para 4 | 23 Dec 1999 (SI 1999/3440) |
| | Pt II | 1 Nov 1999 (SSI 1999/133) |
| Sch 4 | Pt I | 30 Jun 1999 (repeal of Water Industry Act 1991, s 145 and the heading preceding it) (s 17(2)) |
| | | 1 Apr 2000 (otherwise) (SI 1999/3440) |
| | Pt II | 1 Nov 1999 (SSI 1999/133) |

## Welfare Reform and Pensions Act 1999 (c 30)

*RA:* 11 Nov 1999

*Commencement provisions:* s 89; Welfare Reform and Pensions Act 1999 (Commencement No 1) Order 1999, SI 1999/3309; Welfare Reform and Pensions Act 1999 (Commencement No 2) Order 1999, SI 1999/3420; Welfare Reform and Pensions Act 1999 (Commencement No 3) Order 2000, SI 2000/629; Welfare Reform and Pensions Act 1999 (Commencement No 4) Order 2000, SI 2000/1047; Welfare Reform and Pensions Act 1999 (Commencement No 5) Order 2000, SI 2000/1116; Welfare Reform and Pensions Act 1999 (Scotland) (Commencement No 6) Order 2000, SSI 2000/111; Welfare Reform and Pensions Act 1999 (Commencement No 7) Order 2000, SI 2000/1382; Welfare Reform and Pensions Act 1999 (Scotland) (Commencement No 8) Order 2000, SSI 2000/238; Welfare Reform and Pensions Act 1999 (Commencement No 9, and Transitional and Savings Provisions) Order 2000, SI 2000/2958; Welfare Reform and Pensions Act 1999 (Commencement No 10, and Transitional Provisions) Order 2001, SI 2001/933; Welfare

**Welfare Reform and Pensions Act 1999 (c 30)**—*contd*

Reform and Pensions Act 1999 (Commencement No 11) Order 2001, SI 2001/1219; Welfare Reform and Pensions Act 1999 (Commencement No 12) Order 2001, SI 2001/4049, as amended by SI 2002/153; Welfare Reform and Pensions Act 1999 (Commencement No 13) Order 2002, SI 2002/153, amended by SI 2002/818; Welfare Reform and Pensions Act 1999 (Commencement No 14) Order 2002, SI 2002/381; Welfare Reform and Pensions Act 1999 (Commencement No 15) Order 2002, SI 2002/818; Welfare Reform and Pensions Act 1999 (Commencement No 16) Order 2003, SI 2003/936

| | | |
|---|---|---|
| 1, 2 | | 11 Nov 1999 (for the purpose of the exercise of any power to make regulations) (s 89(5)(a)) |
| | | 1 Oct 2000 (otherwise) (SI 2000/1047) |
| 3 | (1) | 11 Nov 1999 (for the purpose of the exercise of any power to make regulations) (s 89(5)(a)) |
| | | 6 Apr 2001 (so far as relates to the provisions of s 3 brought into force on that date) (SI 2001/933) |
| | | 8 Oct 2001 (otherwise) (SI 2001/933) |
| | (2) | 11 Nov 1999 (for the purpose of the exercise of any power to make regulations) (s 89(5)(a)) |
| | | 6 Apr 2001 (second paragraph only) (SI 2001/933) |
| | | 8 Oct 2001 (otherwise) (SI 2001/933) |
| | (3)–(5) | 11 Nov 1999 (for the purpose of the exercise of any power to make regulations) (s 89(5)(a)) |
| | | 8 Oct 2001 (otherwise) (SI 2001/933) |
| | (6) | 11 Nov 1999 (for the purpose of the exercise of any power to make regulations) (s 89(5)(a)) |
| | | 6 Apr 2001 (otherwise) (SI 2001/933) |
| | (7) | 11 Nov 1999 (for the purpose of the exercise of any power to make regulations) (s 89(5)(a)) |
| | | 6 Apr 2001 (so far as relates to s 3(6) and the second paragraph of s 3(2)) (SI 2001/933) |
| | | 8 Oct 2001 (otherwise) (SI 2001/933) |
| | (8) | 11 Nov 1999 (for the purpose of the exercise of any power to make regulations) (s 89(5)(a)) |
| | | 6 Apr 2001 (otherwise) (SI 2001/933) |
| | (9) | 11 Nov 1999 (for the purpose of the exercise of any power to make regulations) (s 89(5)(a)) |
| | | 6 Apr 2001 (so far as relates to definitions "employer" and "relevant employees") (SI 2001/933) |
| | | 8 Oct 2001 (otherwise) (SI 2001/933) |
| 4, 5 | | 11 Nov 1999 (for the purpose of the exercise of any power to make regulations) (s 89(5)(a)) |
| | | 8 Oct 2001 (otherwise) (SI 2000/1047) |
| 6 | (1), (2) | 11 Nov 1999 (for the purpose of the exercise of any power to make regulations) (s 89(5)(a)) |
| | | 8 Oct 2001 (otherwise) (SI 2000/1047) |
| | (3) | See Sch 1 below |
| | (4) | 11 Nov 1999 (for the purpose of the exercise of any power to make regulations) (s 89(5)(a)) |
| | | 8 Oct 2001 (otherwise) (SI 2000/1047) |
| 7 | | 11 Nov 1999 (for the purpose of the exercise of any power to make regulations) (s 89(5)(a)) |
| | | 1 Oct 2000 (otherwise) (SI 2000/1047) |
| 8 | | 11 Nov 1999 (for the purpose of the exercise of any power to make regulations) (s 89(5)(a)) |
| | | 1 Oct 2000 (otherwise, except the definition "designated scheme") (SI 2000/1047) |
| | | 8 Oct 2001 (exception noted above) (SI 2000/1047) |
| 9 | | 11 Nov 1999 (for the purpose of the exercise of any power to make regulations) (s 89(5)(a)) |
| | | 6 Apr 2001 (otherwise) (SI 2000/2958) |

**Welfare Reform and Pensions Act 1999 (c 30)**—*contd*

| | | |
|---|---|---|
| 10 | | 11 Nov 1999 (for the purpose of the exercise of any power to make regulations) (s 89(5)(a)) |
| | | 3 Apr 2000 (otherwise) (SI 2000/629) |
| 11 | (1)–(3) | 11 Nov 1999 (for the purpose of the exercise of any power to make regulations) (s 89(5)(a)) |
| | | 29 May 2000 (otherwise) (SI 2000/1382) |
| | (4)–(10) | 11 Nov 1999 (for the purpose of the exercise of any power to make regulations) (s 89(5)(a)) |
| | | 6 Apr 2002 (otherwise) (SI 2002/153) |
| | (11) | 11 Nov 1999 (for the purpose of the exercise of any power to make regulations) (s 89(5)(a)) |
| | | 29 May 2000 (otherwise) (SI 2000/1382) |
| | (12) | 11 Nov 1999 (for the purpose of the exercise of any power to make regulations) (s 89(5)(a)) |
| | | 1 Dec 2000 (otherwise) (SI 2000/1382) |
| 12 | | 11 Nov 1999 (for the purpose of the exercise of any power to make regulations) (s 89(5)(a)) |
| | | 6 Apr 2002 (otherwise) (SI 2002/153) |
| 13 | (1), (2) | 11 Nov 1999 (for the purpose of the exercise of any power to make regulations) (s 89(5)(a)) |
| | | 29 May 2000 (so far as relates to s 11(1)–(3), (11) of this Act) (SI 2000/1382) |
| | | 6 Apr 2002 (otherwise) (SI 2002/153) |
| | (3) | 11 Nov 1999 (for the purpose of the exercise of any power to make regulations) (s 89(5)(a)) |
| | | 6 Apr 2002 (otherwise) (SI 2002/153) |
| 14–16 | | 11 Nov 1999 (for the purpose of the exercise of any power to make regulations) (s 89(5)(a)) |
| | | 6 Apr 2002 (otherwise) (SI 2002/153) |
| 17 | | 11 Nov 1999 (for the purpose of the exercise of any power to make regulations) (s 89(5)(a)) |
| | | 23 Apr 2001 (otherwise) (SI 2001/1219) |
| 18 | | See Sch 2 below |
| 19 | | 11 Nov 1999 (for the purpose of the exercise of any power to make regulations) (s 89(5)(a)) |
| | | 1 Dec 2000 (otherwise) (SI 2000/1116) |
| 20 | | 11 Nov 1999 (for the purpose of the exercise of any power to make regulations) (s 89(5)(a)) |
| | | 1 Dec 2000 (otherwise) (SI 2000/1047) |
| 21, 22 | | 11 Nov 1999 (for the purpose of the exercise of any power to make regulations) (s 89(5)(a)) |
| | | 1 Dec 2000 (otherwise) (SI 2000/1116) |
| 23, 24 | | 11 Nov 1999 (for the purpose of the exercise of any power to make regulations) (s 89(5)(a)) |
| | | 1 Dec 2000 (otherwise) (SI 2000/1047) |
| 25 | | *Not yet in force* |
| 26–51 | | 11 Nov 1999 (for the purpose of the exercise of any power to make regulations) (s 89(5)(a)) |
| | | 1 Dec 2000 (otherwise) (SI 2000/1047) |
| 52 | | 11 Nov 1999 (s 89(4)(a)) |
| 53 | | 12 Jan 2000 (for the purpose of the exercise of any power to make regulations) (SI 1999/3309) |
| | | 2 Apr 2000 (otherwise) (SI 1999/3309) |
| 54–56 | | 24 Apr 2000 (for the purpose of making regulations) (SI 2000/1047) |
| | | 9 Apr 2001 (otherwise) (SI 2000/1047) |
| 57, 58 | | 11 Nov 1999 (s 89(4)(a)) |
| 59 | | 11 Nov 1999 (for the purpose of the exercise of any power to make regulations) (s 89(5)(b)) |
| | | 19 Mar 2001 (otherwise) (SI 2000/2958) |

**Welfare Reform and Pensions Act 1999 (c 30)**—*contd*

| | | |
|---|---|---|
| 60 | | 11 Nov 1999 (s 89(4)(a)) |
| 61 | | 11 Nov 1999 (for the purpose of the exercise of any power to make regulations) (s 89(5)(b)) |
| | | 3 Apr 2000 (otherwise) (SI 1999/3309) |
| 62, 63 | | 3 Nov 2000 (for the purpose of authorising the making of regulations) (SI 2000/2958) |
| | | 6 Apr 2001 (otherwise) (subject to transitional provisions) (SI 2000/2958) |
| 64 | | 3 Nov 2000 (for the purpose of authorising the making of regulations) (SI 2000/2958) |
| | | 6 Apr 2001 (otherwise) (SI 2000/2958) |
| 65 | | 3 Nov 2000 (for the purpose of authorising the making of regulations) (SI 2000/2958) |
| | | 6 Apr 2001 (otherwise) (subject to a saving) (SI 2000/2958) |
| 66 | | 12 Jan 2000 (SI 1999/3309) |
| 67 | (1), (2) | 12 Jan 2000 (SI 1999/3309) |
| | (3), (4) | 9 Apr 2001 (SI 2000/1382) |
| 68 | | 11 Nov 1999 (s 89(4)(a)) |
| 69 | | 17 Apr 2000 (for the purpose of the exercise of powers to make regulations) (SI 2000/1047) |
| | | 15 May 2000 (otherwise) (SI 2000/1047) |
| 70 | | See Sch 8 below |
| 71, 72 | | 11 Nov 1999 (s 89(4)(a), (c)) |
| 73, 74 | | 22 Dec 1999 (for the purpose of the exercise of any power to make regulations) (SI 1999/3420) |
| | | 6 Apr 2000 (otherwise) (SI 1999/3420) |
| 75, 76 | | 22 Dec 1999 (SI 1999/3420) |
| 77, 78 | | 6 Apr 2000 (SI 1999/3420) |
| 79–83 | | 11 Nov 1999 (s 89(4)(d)) |
| 84 | (1) | See Sch 12 below |
| | (2)–(4) | 11 Nov 1999 (s 89(4)(f)) |
| 85 | (1), (2) | 11 Nov 1999 (s 89(4)(g)) |
| | (3), (4) | 1 Dec 2000 (SI 2000/1116) |
| | (5) | 1 Dec 2000 (SI 2000/1047) |
| | (6), (7) | 11 Nov 1999 (s 89(4)(g)) |
| 86, 87 | | 11 Nov 1999 (s 89(4)(h)) |
| 88 | | See Sch 13 below |
| 89–91 | | 11 Nov 1999 (s 89(4)(h)) |
| Sch 1 | para 1(1), (2) | 1 Oct 2000 (SI 2000/1047) |
| | para 1(3) | 8 Oct 2001 (SI 2000/1047) |
| | para 1(4), (5) | 1 Oct 2000 (SI 2000/1047) |
| | paras 2, 3 | 1 Oct 2000 (SI 2000/1047) |
| Sch 2 | paras 1, 2 | 29 May 2000 (SI 2000/1382) |
| | paras 3, 4 | 25 Apr 2000 (SI 2000/1047) |
| | para 5 | 11 Nov 1999 (for the purpose of the exercise of any power to make regulations) (s 89(5)(a)) |
| | | 1 Jan 2002 (otherwise) (SI 2001/4049) |
| | para 6 | 6 Apr 2002 (SI 2002/153) |
| | para 7 | 11 Nov 1999 (for the purpose of the exercise of any power to make regulations) (s 89(5)(a)) |
| | | 6 Apr 2002 (otherwise) (SI 2001/4049) |
| | paras 8–13 | 25 Apr 2000 (SI 2000/1047) |
| | para 14 | 19 Mar 2002 (SI 2002/381) |
| | paras 15–19 | 25 Apr 2000 (SI 2000/1047) |
| Schs 3, 4 | | 1 Dec 2000 (SI 2000/1116) |
| Schs 5, 6 | | 1 Dec 2000 (SI 2000/1047) |
| Sch 7 | | 19 Mar 2001 (SI 2000/2958) |
| Sch 8 | paras 1–19 | 24 Apr 2000 (for the purpose of making regulations) (SI 2000/1047) |

**Welfare Reform and Pensions Act 1999 (c 30)**—*contd*

|  |  |  |
|---|---|---|
|  |  | 9 Apr 2001 (otherwise) (SI 2000/1047) |
| para 20 |  | 3 Nov 2000 (SI 2000/2958) |
| para 21 |  | 3 Nov 2000 (for the purpose of authorising the making of regulations) (SI 2000/2958) |
|  |  | 6 Apr 2001 (otherwise) (SI 2000/2958) |
| para 22 |  | 3 Nov 2000 (for the purpose of authorising the making of regulations) (SI 2000/2958) |
|  |  | 6 Apr 2001 (otherwise) (subject to transitional provisions) (SI 2000/2958) |
| para 23(1), (2) |  | 11 Nov 1999 (for the purpose of the exercise of any power to make regulations) (s 89(5)(c)) |
|  |  | 13 Dec 1999 (otherwise) (SI 1999/3309) |
| para 23(3) |  | 11 Nov 1999 (for the purpose of the exercise of any power to make regulations) (s 89(5)(c)) |
|  |  | 3 Apr 2000 (otherwise) (SI 1999/3309) |
| para 23(4) |  | 11 Nov 1999 (for the purpose of the exercise of any power to make regulations) (s 89(5)(c)) |
|  |  | 13 Dec 1999 (otherwise) (SI 1999/3309) |
| para 24 |  | 3 Apr 2000 (SI 1999/3309) |
| para 25 |  | 3 Nov 2000 (SI 2000/2958) |
| para 26 |  | 3 Nov 2000 (for the purpose of authorising the making of regulations) (SI 2000/2958) |
|  |  | 6 Apr 2001 (otherwise) (subject to a saving) (SI 2000/2958) |
| para 27 |  | 6 Apr 2001 (SI 2000/2958) |
| para 28 |  | 19 Mar 2001 (SI 2001/933) |
| para 29 |  | 11 Nov 1999 (s 89(4)(b)) |
| paras 30–32 |  | 12 Jan 2000 (for the purpose of the exercise of any power to make regulations) (SI 1999/3309) |
|  |  | 2 Apr 2000 (otherwise) (SI 1999/3309) |
| para 33 |  | 1 Dec 2000 (SI 2000/1047) |
| para 34 |  | 6 Apr 2003 (SI 2003/936) |
| Schs 9, 10 |  | 22 Dec 1999 (for the purpose of the exercise of any power to make regulations) (SI 1999/3420) |
|  |  | 6 Apr 2000 (otherwise) (SI 1999/3420) |
| Sch 11 |  | 11 Nov 1999 (s 89(4)(d)) |
| Sch 12 | paras 1–4 | 1 Dec 2000 (SI 2000/1116) |
|  | paras 5–7 | 1 Dec 2000 (SI 2000/1047) |
|  | para 8(1), (2) | 1 Dec 2000 (SI 2000/1047) |
|  | para 8(3), (4) | 15 Apr 2000 (SSI 2000/111) |
|  | para 8(5), (6) | 1 Dec 2000 (SI 2000/1047) |
|  | para 9 | 1 Dec 2000 (SI 2000/1047) |
|  | para 10 | 1 Dec 2000 (SSI 2000/238) |
|  | paras 11, 12 | 1 Dec 2000 (SI 2000/1047) |
|  | para 13 | 11 Nov 1999 (s 89(4)(e)) |
|  | paras 14–63 | 1 Dec 2000 (SI 2000/1047) |
|  | paras 64–66 | 1 Dec 2000 (SI 2000/1116) |
|  | paras 67–72 | 26 Mar 2002 (for the purpose of the exercise of any power to make regulations) (SI 2002/818) |
|  |  | 6 Apr 2002 (otherwise) (SI 2002/818) |
|  | para 73 | 25 Apr 2000 (SI 2000/1047) |
|  | para 74 | 6 Apr 2000 (SI 1999/3420) |
|  | para 75 | 25 Apr 2000 (SI 2000/1047) |
|  | paras 76–78 | 6 Apr 2000 (SI 1999/3420) |
|  | paras 79–83 | 11 Nov 1999 (s 89(4)(e)) |
|  | paras 84–86 | 6 Apr 2000 (SI 1999/3420) |
|  | para 87 | 11 Nov 1999 (s 89(4)(e)) |
| Sch 13 | Pt I | 25 Apr 2000 (SI 2000/1047), repeals of or in— |
|  |  | Pension Schemes Act 1993, ss 73(2)(a)(ii), 96(2)(a), 181(1); |
|  |  | Pensions Act 1995, s 8(4); |

**Welfare Reform and Pensions Act 1999 (c 30)**—*contd*

|  |  |
|---|---|
| | Scotland Act 1998, s 126(1) |
| | 19 Mar 2001 (repeal of Pensions Act 1995, Sch 5, para 80(f)) (SI 2001/933) |
| | 23 Apr 2001 (repeal of or in Pensions Act 1995, s 83(3)(a)) (SI 2001/1219) |
| | 1 Jan 2002 (repeal of or in Pension Schemes Act 1993, s 28(1)) (SI 2001/4049) |
| | 19 Mar 2002 (repeals of or in Pensions Act 1995, s 58(6)(a)) (SI 2002/381) |
| | 6 Apr 2002 (SI 2001/4049), repeals of or in— |
| | Pension Schemes Act 1993, s 55(2A); |
| | Pension Schemes (Northern Ireland) Act 1993, s 51(2A) |
| | 6 Apr 2002 (SI 2002/153), repeals of or in— |
| | Pension Schemes Act 1993, s 159(5); |
| | Pensions Act 1995, ss 91(3), 92(2), 94(3), 95 |
| | *Never in force* (repeals of or in Pensions Act 1995, s 142 (repealed)) |
| Pt II | 1 Dec 2000 (repeals of or in Family Law (Scotland) Act 1985) (SI 2000/1047) |
| | 1 Dec 2000 (SI 2000/1116), repeals of or in— |
| | Matrimonial Causes Act 1973; |
| | Matrimonial and Family Proceedings Act 1984; |
| | Family Law Act 1996, ss 9(8), 16 |
| | 6 Apr 2002 (repeal of or in Family Law Act 1996, s 17) (SI 2001/4049) |
| Pt III | 1 Dec 2000 (SI 2000/1047) |
| Pt IV | 3 Nov 2000 (for the purpose of authorising the making of regulations) (SI 2000/2958) |
| | 6 Apr 2001 (otherwise) (subject to a saving) (SI 2000/2958) |
| Pt V | 2 Apr 2000 (SI 1999/3309), repeals of or in— |
| | Social Security Contributions and Benefits Act 1992, s 21, Sch 3, Pt I, Sch 4, Pt I; |
| | Maternity Allowance and Statutory Maternity Pay Regulations 1994, SI 1994/1230 |
| | 9 Apr 2001 (SI 2000/1047), repeals of or in— |
| | Income and Corporation Taxes Act 1988; |
| | Social Security Act 1998, Sch 7, para 78; |
| | Social Security Contributions and Benefits Act 1992, s 20(1)(e)(i) |
| | 6 Apr 2002 (SI 2001/4049), repeals of or in— |
| | Pension Schemes Act 1993, Sch 8, para 24; |
| | Jobseekers Act 1995, s 1(4) |
| Pts VI, VII | 6 Apr 2000 (SI 1999/3420) |

**Youth Justice and Criminal Evidence Act 1999 (c 23)**

*RA:* 27 Jul 1999

*Commencement provisions:* s 68(3), (4); Youth Justice and Criminal Evidence Act 1999 (Commencement No 1) Order 1999, SI 1999/3427; Youth Justice and Criminal Evidence Act 1999 (Commencement No 2) Order 2000, SI 2000/1034; Youth Justice and Criminal Evidence Act 1999 (Commencement No 3) Order 2000, SI 2000/1587; Youth Justice and Criminal Evidence Act 1999 (Commencement No 4) Order 2000, SI 2000/2091; Youth Justice and Criminal Evidence Act 1999 (Commencement No 5) Order 2000, SI 2000/3075; Youth Justice and Criminal Evidence Act 1999 (Commencement No 6) (Scotland) Order 2000, SSI 2000/445; Youth Justice and Criminal Evidence Act 1999 (Commencement No 7) Order 2002, SI 2002/1739; Youth Justice and Criminal Evidence Act 1999 (Commencement No 8) Order 2003, SI 2003/707; Youth Justice and Criminal Evidence Act 1999 (Commencement No 9) Order 2004, SI 2004/299; Youth Justice and Criminal Evidence Act 1999 (Commencement No 10) (England and Wales) Order 2004, SI 2004/2428; Youth Justice and Criminal Evidence Act 1999 (Commencement No 11) (Scotland) Order 2004, SSI 2004/408; Youth Justice and Criminal Evidence Act 1999 (Commencement Order No 1) (Northern Ireland) Order 2004, SR 2004/467; Youth Justice and Criminal Evidence Act 1999 (Commencement No 12) Order 2006,

**Youth Justice and Criminal Evidence Act 1999 (c 23)**—*contd*

SI 2006/2885; Youth Justice and Criminal Evidence Act 1999 (Commencement No 13) Order 2013, SI 2013/3236; Youth Justice and Criminal Evidence Act 1999 (Commencement No 14) (England and Wales) Order 2015, SI 2015/818; Youth Justice and Criminal Evidence Act 1999 (Commencement No 15) Order 2016, SI 2016/1201; Youth Justice and Criminal Evidence Act 1999 (Commencement No 16) Order 2019, SI 2019/947; Youth Justice and Criminal Evidence Act 1999 (Commencement No 17) Order 2020, SI 2020/155; Youth Justice and Criminal Evidence Act 1999 (Commencement No 18) Order 2020, SI 2020/888; Youth Justice and Criminal Evidence Act 1999 (Commencement No 19) Order 2020, SI 2020/1159; Youth Justice and Criminal Evidence Act 1999 (Commencement No 20) Order 2020, SI 2020/1331; Youth Justice and Criminal Evidence Act 1999 (Commencement No 21) Order 2021, SI 2021/244; Youth Justice and Criminal Evidence Act 1999 (Commencement No 22) Order 2021, SI 2021/1036; Youth Justice and Criminal Evidence Act 1999 (Commencement No 23) Order 2022, SI 2022/456; Youth Justice and Criminal Evidence Act 1999 (Commencement No 24) Order 2022, SI 2022/536; Youth Justice and Criminal Evidence Act 1999 (Commencement No 25) Order 2022, SI 2022/623; Youth Justice and Criminal Evidence Act 1999 (Commencement No 26) Order 2022, SI 2022/713; Youth Justice and Criminal Evidence Act 1999 (Commencement No 27) Order 2022, SI 2022/773; Youth Justice and Criminal Evidence Act 1999 (Commencement No 28) Order 2022, SI 2022/951; Youth Justice and Criminal Evidence Act 1999 (Commencement No 29) Order 2022, SI 2022/992

| | | |
|---|---|---|
| 1–5 | | 26 Jun 2000 (SI 2000/1587) |
| 6 | (1)–(3) | 26 Jun 2000 (SI 2000/1587) |
| | (4) | 27 Jul 1999 (s 68(4)(a)) |
| | (5)–(7) | 26 Jun 2000 (SI 2000/1587) |
| 7–15 | | 26 Jun 2000 (SI 2000/1587) |
| 16–19 | | 24 Jul 2002 (SI 2002/1739) |
| 20 | (1)–(5) | 24 Jul 2002 (SI 2002/1739) |
| | (6) | 27 Jul 1999 (s 68(4)(b)) |
| 21–26 | | 24 Jul 2002 (SI 2002/1739) |
| 27 | (1)–(3), (4)(a) | 24 Jul 2002 (SI 2002/1739) |
| | (4)(b) | 27 Jul 1999 (s 68(4)(b)) |
| | (5)–(11) | 24 Jul 2002 (SI 2002/1739) |
| 28 | (1) | 30 Dec 2013 (in relation to proceedings taking place before the Crown Court sitting at Kingston-upon-Thames, Leeds, or Liverpool and the witness is eligible for assistance by virtue of either s 16(1)(a) where the witness is under the age of 16 at the time of the hearing, or s 16(1)(b) of this Act) (SI 2013/3236) |
| | | 2 Jan 2017 (in relation to proceedings taking place before the Crown Court sitting at Kingston-upon-Thames, Leeds, or Liverpool and the witness is eligible for assistance by virtue of s 16(1)(a) where the witness is aged 16 or 17 at the time of the hearing) (SI 2016/1201) |
| | | 3 Jun 2019 (in relation to proceedings taking place before the Crown Court sitting at Kingston-upon-Thames, Leeds or Liverpool and the witness is eligible for assistance by virtue of s 17(4), and in relations to proceedings taking place before the Crown Court sitting at Bradford, Carlisle, Chester, Durham, Mold or Sheffield and the witness is eligible for assistance by virtue of s 16) (SI 2019/947) |
| | | 24 Feb 2020 (in relation to proceedings taking place before the Crown Court sitting at Aylesbury, Bristol, Leicester, Northampton, Oxford, Portsmouth, Reading, Swansea or Wolverhampton and the witness is eligible for assistance by virtue of s 16) (SI 2020/155) |
| | | 24 Aug 2020 (in relation to proceedings taking place before the Crown Court sitting at Basildon, Canterbury, the Central Criminal Court, Chelmsford, Croydon, Guildford, Harrow, the Inner London Sessions House, Isleworth, Lewes, Maidstone, Snaresbrook, Southwark, Stafford, Wood Green, or Woolwich and the witness is eligible for assistance by virtue of s 16) (SI 2020/888) |

**Youth Justice and Criminal Evidence Act 1999 (c 23)**—*contd*

26 Oct 2020 (in relation to proceedings taking place before the Crown Court sitting at Amersham Law Courts, Bolton, Burnley Combined Court Centre, Caernarfon Justice Centre, Cardiff, Doncaster Justice Centre South, Exeter Law Courts, Gloucester, Ipswich, King's Lynn, Lancaster, Manchester (Crown Square), Manchester (Minshull Street), Merthyr Tydfil Combined Court Centre, Newcastle Moot Hall, Newport (South Wales), Norwich Combined Court Centre, Plymouth Combined Court, Preston Crown Court and Family Court (Sessions House), Salisbury Law Courts, Southampton Combined Court Centre, St Albans, Swindon Combined Court, Teesside Combined Court Centre, Warrington, Winchester Combined Court Centre, Worcester Combined Court, or York, where the witness is eligible for assistance by virtue of s 16) (SI 2020/1159)

23 Nov 2020 (in relation to proceedings taking place before the Crown Court sitting at Birmingham; Bournemouth Combined Court; Cambridge; Coventry Combined Court Centre; Derby Combined Court Centre; Great Grimsby Combined Court Centre; Hereford; Hove Trial Centre; Isle of Wight Combined Court; Kingston-Upon-Hull Combined Court Centre; Lincoln; Luton; Newcastle-upon-Tyne Combined Court Centre; Nottingham; Peterborough Combined Court Centre; Shrewsbury; Southend; Stoke-on-Trent Combined Court; Taunton Crown, County and Family Court; Truro Combined Court, or Warwick Combined Court, where the witness is eligible for assistance by virtue of s 16) (SI 2020/1331)

4 Mar 2021 (in relation to proceedings taking place before the Crown Court sitting at Preston Combined Court Centre, where the witness is eligible for assistance by virtue of s 16) (SI 2020/244)

30 Sep 2021 (in relation to proceedings taking place before the Crown Court sitting at Durham; Harrow; Isleworth; or Wood Green, where the witness is eligible for assistance by virtue of s 17(4) (SI 2021/1036)

31 Mar 2022 (in relation to proceedings taking place before the Crown Court sitting at Great Grimsby Combined Court, Kingston-upon-Hull Combined Court Centre, York, where the witness is eligible for assistance by virtue of s 17(4) (SI 2022/456)

4 Apr 2022 (in relation to proceedings taking place before the Crown Court sitting at Bradford Combined Court Centre, where the witness is eligible for assistance by virtue of s 17(4)) (SI 2022/456)

11 Apr 2022 (in relation to proceedings taking place before the Crown Court sitting at Teesside Combined Court Centre, where the witness is eligible for assistance by virtue of s 17(4)) (SI 2022/456)

12 May 2022 (in relation to proceedings taking place before the Crown Court sitting at Sheffield Combined Court Centre, Newcastle-upon-Tyne, Doncaster Justice Centre South, Portsmouth Combined Court Centre, Southampton Combined Court Centre, Winchester Combined Court Centre, Truro Combined Court Centre, Bristol, Plymouth Combined Court, Isle of Wight Combined Court, Gloucester, Bournemouth Combined Court, Exeter, Salisbury, where the witness is eligible for assistance by virtue of s 17(4)) (SI 2022/536)

**Youth Justice and Criminal Evidence Act 1999 (c 23)**—*contd*

8 Jun 2022 (in relation to proceedings taking place before the Crown Court sitting at Stafford Combined Court Centre; Stoke-on-Trent Combined Court; Shrewsbury; Hereford; Worcester Combined Court; Nottingham; Lincoln; Leicester; Northampton Crown, County and Family Court; or Taunton Crown, County and Family Court, where the witness is eligible for assistance by virtue of s 17(4)) (SI 2022/623)

28 Jun 2022 (in relation to proceedings taking place before the Crown Court sitting at Bolton Crown Court; Burnley Combined Court Centre; Preston Combined Court Centre; Carlisle Combined Court; Lancaster Crown Court; Chester Crown Court; Swindon Combined Court; Warrington Crown Court; Manchester Crown Court (Crown Square); or Manchester Crown Court (Minshull Street); and where the witness is eligible for assistance by virtue of s 17(4)) (SI 2022/713)

11 Jul 2022 (in relation to proceedings taking place before the Crown Court sitting at Caernarfon Justice Centre; Cardiff Crown Court; Merthyr Tydfil Combined Court Centre; Mold Justice Centre; Newport (South Wales) Crown Court; Preston Crown Court and Family Court (Sessions House) or Swansea Crown Court and where the witness is eligible for assistance by virtue of s 17(4)) (SI 2022/773)

18 Jul 2022 (in relation to proceedings taking place before the Crown Court sitting at Birmingham Crown Court; Coventry Combined Court Centre; Derby Combined Court Centre; or Wolverhampton Combined Court Centre and where the witness is eligible for assistance by virtue of s 17(4)) (SI 2022/773)

9 Sep 2022 (in relation to proceedings taking place before the Crown Court sitting at Ipswich; Luton; Maidstone Combined Court Centre; Oxford Combined Court Centre; or St Albans and where where the witness is eligible for assistance by virtue of s 17(4)) (SI 2022/951)

26 Sep 2022 (in relation to proceedings taking place before the Crown Court sitting at the Amersham Law Courts; Aylesbury; the Basildon Combined Court; Cambridge; the Canterbury Combined Court Centre; the Central Criminal Court; Chelmsford; Croydon; Guildford; the Hove Trial Centre; the Inner London Sessions House; King's Lynn; the Lewes Combined Court Centre; the Norwich Combined Court Centre; the Peterborough Combined Court Centre; Reading; Snaresbrook; Southend; Southwark; or Woolwich and where the witness is eligible for assistance by virtue of s 17(4) and in relation to proceedings before the youth court sitting at Leeds Magistrates' Court and the witness is eligible for assistance by virtue of s 16) (SI 2022/992)

*Not yet in force* (otherwise)

(2)    27 Jul 1999 (so far as confers power to make rules of court) (s 68(4)(b))

30 Dec 2013 (in relation to proceedings taking place before the Crown Court sitting at Kingston-upon-Thames, Leeds, or Liverpool and the witness is eligible for assistance by virtue of either s 16(1)(a) where the witness is under the age of 16 at the time of the hearing, or s 16(1)(b) of this Act) (SI 2013/3236)

**Youth Justice and Criminal Evidence Act 1999 (c 23)**—*contd*

    26 Oct 2020 (in relation to proceedings taking place before the Crown Court sitting at Amersham Law Courts, Bolton, Burnley Combined Court Centre, Caernarfon Justice Centre, Cardiff, Doncaster Justice Centre, Exeter Law Courts, Gloucester, Ipswich, King's Lynn, Lancaster, Manchester (Crown Square), Manchester (Minshull Street), Merthyr Tydfil Combined Court Centre, Newcastle Moot Hall, Newport (South Wales), Norwich Combined Court Centre, Plymouth Combined Court, Preston Crown Court and Family Court (Sessions House), Salisbury Law Courts, Southampton Combined Court Centre, St Albans, Swindon Combined Court, Teesside Combined Court Centre, Warrington, Winchester Combined Court Centre, Worcester Combined Court, or York, where the witness is eligible for assistance by virtue of s 16) (SI 2020/1159)

    23 November 2020 (in relation to proceedings taking place before the Crown Court sitting at Birmingham; Bournemouth Combined Court; Cambridge; Coventry Combined Court Centre; Derby Combined Court Centre; Great Grimsby Combined Court Centre; Hereford; Hove Trial Centre; Isle of Wight Combined Court; Kingston-Upon-Hull Combined Court Centre; Lincoln; Luton; Newcastle-upon-Tyne Combined Court Centre; Nottingham; Peterborough Combined Court Centre; Shrewsbury; Southend; Stoke-on-Trent Combined Court; Taunton Crown, County and Family Court; Truro Combined Court, or Warwick Combined Court,where the witness is eligible for assistance by virtue of s 16) (SI 2020/1331)

    4 Mar 2021 (in relation to proceedings taking place before the Crown Court sitting at Preston Combined Court Centre, where the witness is eligible for assistance by virtue of s 16) (SI 2020/244)

    30 Sep 2021 (in relation to proceedings taking place before the Crown Court sitting at Durham; Harrow; Isleworth; or Wood Green, where the witness is eligible for assistance by virtue of s 17(4) (SI 2021/1036)

    31 Mar 2022 (in relation to proceedings taking place before the Crown Court sitting at Great Grimsby Combined Court, Kingston-upon-Hull Combined Court Centre, York, where the witness is eligible for assistance by virtue of s 17(4) (SI 2022/456)

    4 Apr 2022 (in relation to proceedings taking place before the Crown Court sitting at Bradford Combined Court Centre, where the witness is eligible for assistance by virtue of s 17(4) (SI 2022/456)

    11 Apr 2022 (in relation to proceedings taking place before the Crown Court sitting at Teesside Combined Court Centre, where the witness is eligible for assistance by virtue of s 17(4) (SI 2022/456)

    12 May 2022 (in relation to proceedings taking place before the Crown Court sitting at Sheffield Combined Court Centre, Newcastle-upon-Tyne, Doncaster Justice Centre South, Portsmouth Combined Court Centre, Southampton Combined Court Centre, Winchester Combined Court Centre, Truro Combined Court Centre, Bristol, Plymouth Combined Court, Isle of Wight Combined Court, Gloucester, Bournemouth Combined Court, Exeter, Salisbury, where the witness is eligible for assistance by virtue of s 17(4)) (SI 2022/536)

**Youth Justice and Criminal Evidence Act 1999 (c 23)**—*contd*

8 Jun 2022 (in relation to proceedings taking place before the Crown Court sitting at Stafford Combined Court Centre; Stoke-on-Trent Combined Court; Shrewsbury; Hereford; Worcester Combined Court; Nottingham; Lincoln; Leicester; Northampton Crown, County and Family Court; or Taunton Crown, County and Family Court, where the witness is eligible for assistance by virtue of s 17(4)) (SI 2022/623)

28 Jun 2022 (in relation to proceedings taking place before the Crown Court sitting at Bolton Crown Court; Burnley Combined Court Centre; Preston Combined Court Centre; Carlisle Combined Court; Lancaster Crown Court; Chester Crown Court; Swindon Combined Court; Warrington Crown Court; Manchester Crown Court (Crown Square); or Manchester Crown Court (Minshull Street); and where the witness is eligible for assistance by virtue of s 17(4)) (SI 2022/713)

11 Jul 2022 (in relation to proceedings taking place before the Crown Court sitting at Caernarfon Justice Centre; Cardiff Crown Court; Merthyr Tydfil Combined Court Centre; Mold Justice Centre; Newport (South Wales) Crown Court; Preston Crown Court and Family Court (Sessions House) or Swansea Crown Court and where the witness is eligible for assistance by virtue of s 17(4)) (SI 2022/773)

18 Jul 2022 (in relation to proceedings taking place before the Crown Court sitting at Birmingham Crown Court; Coventry Combined Court Centre; Derby Combined Court Centre; or Wolverhampton Combined Court Centre and where the witness is eligible for assistance by virtue of s 17(4)) (SI 2022/773)

9 Sep 2022 (in relation to proceedings taking place before the Crown Court sitting at Ipswich; Luton; Maidstone Combined Court Centre; Oxford Combined Court Centre; or St Albans and where where the witness is eligible for assistance by virtue of s 17(4)) (SI 2022/951)

26 Sep 2022 (in relation to proceedings taking place before the Crown Court sitting at the Amersham Law Courts; Aylesbury; the Basildon Combined Court; Cambridge; the Canterbury Combined Court Centre; the Central Criminal Court; Chelmsford; Croydon; Guildford; the Hove Trial Centre; the Inner London Sessions House; King's Lynn; the Lewes Combined Court Centre; the Norwich Combined Court Centre; the Peterborough Combined Court Centre; Reading; Snaresbrook; Southend; Southwark; or Woolwich and where the witness is eligible for assistance by virtue of s 17(4) and in relation to proceedings before the youth court sitting at Leeds Magistrates' Court and the witness is eligible for assistance by virtue of s 16) (SI 2022/992)

*Not yet in force* (otherwise)

(3)–(7)      30 Dec 2013 (in relation to proceedings taking place before the Crown Court sitting at Kingston-upon-Thames, Leeds, or Liverpool and the witness is eligible for assistance by virtue of either s 16(1)(a) where the witness is under the age of 16 at the time of the hearing, or s 16(1)(b) of this Act) (SI 2013/3236)

2 Jan 2017 (in relation to proceedings taking place before the Crown Court sitting at Kingston-upon-Thames, Leeds, or Liverpool and the witness is eligible for assistance by virtue of s 16(1)(a) where the witness is aged 16 or 17 at the time of the hearing) (SI 2016/1201)

**Youth Justice and Criminal Evidence Act 1999 (c 23)**—*contd*

26 Oct 2020 (in relation to proceedings taking place before the Crown Court sitting at Amersham Law Courts, Bolton, Burnley Combined Court Centre, Caernarfon Justice Centre, Cardiff, Doncaster Justice Centre South, Exeter Law Courts, Gloucester, Ipswich, King's Lynn, Lancaster, Manchester (Crown Square), Manchester (Minshull Street), Merthyr Tydfil Combined Court Centre, Newcastle Moot Hall, Newport (South Wales), Norwich Combined Court Centre, Plymouth Combined Court, Preston Crown Court and Family Court (Sessions House), Salisbury Law Courts, Southampton Combined Court Centre, St Albans, Swindon Combined Court, Teesside Combined Court Centre, Warrington, Winchester Combined Court Centre, Worcester Combined Court, or York, where the witness is eligible for assistance by virtue of s 16) (SI 2020/1159)

23 November 2020 (in relation to proceedings taking place before the Crown Court sitting at Birmingham; Bournemouth Combined Court; Cambridge; Coventry Combined Court Centre; Derby Combined Court Centre; Great Grimsby Combined Court Centre; Hereford; Hove Trial Centre; Isle of Wight Combined Court; Kingston-Upon-Hull Combined Court Centre; Lincoln; Luton; Newcastle-upon-Tyne Combined Court Centre; Nottingham; Peterborough Combined Court Centre; Shrewsbury; Southend; Stoke-on-Trent Combined Court; Taunton Crown, County and Family Court; Truro Combined Court, or Warwick Combined Court,where the witness is eligible for assistance by virtue of s 16) (SI 2020/1331)

4 Mar 2021 (in relation to proceedings taking place before the Crown Court sitting at Preston Combined Court Centre, where the witness is eligible for assistance by virtue of s 16) (SI 2020/244)

30 Sep 2021 (in relation to proceedings taking place before the Crown Court sitting at Durham; Harrow; Isleworth; or Wood Green, where the witness is eligible for assistance by virtue of s 17(4) (SI 2021/1036)

31 Mar 2022 (in relation to proceedings taking place before the Crown Court sitting at Great Grimsby Combined Court, Kingston-upon-Hull Combined Court Centre, York, where the witness is eligible for assistance by virtue of s 17(4) (SI 2022/456)

4 Apr 2022 (in relation to proceedings taking place before the Crown Court sitting at Bradford Combined Court Centre, where the witness is eligible for assistance by virtue of s 17(4) (SI 2022/456)

11 Apr 2022 (in relation to proceedings taking place before the Crown Court sitting at Teesside Combined Court Centre, where the witness is eligible for assistance by virtue of s 17(4) (SI 2022/456)

12 May 2022 (in relation to proceedings taking place before the Crown Court sitting at Sheffield Combined Court Centre, Newcastle-upon-Tyne, Doncaster Justice Centre South, Portsmouth Combined Court Centre, Southampton Combined Court Centre, Winchester Combined Court Centre, Truro Combined Court Centre, Bristol, Plymouth Combined Court, Isle of Wight Combined Court, Gloucester, Bournemouth Combined Court, Exeter, Salisbury, where the witness is eligible for assistance by virtue of s 17(4)) (SI 2022/536)

**Youth Justice and Criminal Evidence Act 1999 (c 23)**—*contd*

　　　　　　　8 Jun 2022 (in relation to proceedings taking place before the Crown Court sitting at Stafford Combined Court Centre; Stoke-on-Trent Combined Court; Shrewsbury; Hereford; Worcester Combined Court; Nottingham; Lincoln; Leicester; Northampton Crown, County and Family Court; or Taunton Crown, County and Family Court, where the witness is eligible for assistance by virtue of s 17(4)) (SI 2022/623)

　　　　　　　28 Jun 2022 (in relation to proceedings taking place before the Crown Court sitting at Bolton Crown Court; Burnley Combined Court Centre; Preston Combined Court Centre; Carlisle Combined Court; Lancaster Crown Court; Chester Crown Court; Swindon Combined Court; Warrington Crown Court; Manchester Crown Court (Crown Square); or Manchester Crown Court (Minshull Street); and where the witness is eligible for assistance by virtue of s 17(4)) (SI 2022/713)

　　　　　　　11 Jul 2022 (in relation to proceedings taking place before the Crown Court sitting at Caernarfon Justice Centre; Cardiff Crown Court; Merthyr Tydfil Combined Court Centre; Mold Justice Centre; Newport (South Wales) Crown Court; Preston Crown Court and Family Court (Sessions House) or Swansea Crown Court and where the witness is eligible for assistance by virtue of s 17(4)) (SI 2022/773)

　　　　　　　18 Jul 2022 (in relation to proceedings taking place before the Crown Court sitting at Birmingham Crown Court; Coventry Combined Court Centre; Derby Combined Court Centre; or Wolverhampton Combined Court Centre and where the witness is eligible for assistance by virtue of s 17(4)) (SI 2022/773)

　　　　　　　9 Sep 2022 (in relation to proceedings taking place before the Crown Court sitting at Ipswich; Luton; Maidstone Combined Court Centre; Oxford Combined Court Centre; or St Albans and where the witness is eligible for assistance by virtue of s 17(4)) (SI 2022/951)

　　　　　　　26 Sep 2022 (in relation to proceedings taking place before the Crown Court sitting at the Amersham Law Courts; Aylesbury; the Basildon Combined Court; Cambridge; the Canterbury Combined Court Centre; the Central Criminal Court; Chelmsford; Croydon; Guildford; the Hove Trial Centre; the Inner London Sessions House; King's Lynn; the Lewes Combined Court Centre; the Norwich Combined Court Centre; the Peterborough Combined Court Centre; Reading; Snaresbrook; Southend; Southwark; or Woolwich and where the witness is eligible for assistance by virtue of s 17(4) and in relation to proceedings before the youth court sitting at Leeds Magistrates' Court and the witness is eligible for assistance by virtue of s 16) (SI 2022/992)

　　　　　　　*Not yet in force* (otherwise)

| | | |
|---|---|---|
| 29 | (1), (2) | 23 Feb 2004 (SI 2004/299) |
| | (3) | 27 Jul 1999 (so far as confers power to make rules of court) (s 68(4)(b)) |
| | | 23 Feb 2004 (otherwise) (SI 2004/299) |
| | (4) | 23 Feb 2004 (SI 2004/299) |
| | (5) | 27 Jul 1999 (so far as confers power to make rules of court) (s 68(4)(b)) |
| | | 23 Feb 2004 (otherwise) (SI 2004/299) |
| | (6), (7) | 23 Feb 2004 (SI 2004/299) |
| 30–33 | | 27 Jul 1999 (so far as confers power to make rules of court) (s 68(4)(b)) |
| | | 24 Jul 2002 (otherwise) (SI 2002/1739) |

**See Halsbury's Statutes Citator for amendments to these Acts**　　1127

**Youth Justice and Criminal Evidence Act 1999 (c 23)**—*contd*

| | | |
|---|---|---|
| 34, 35 | | 27 Jul 1999 (so far as confers power to make rules of court) (s 68(4)(b)) |
| | | 4 Sep 2000 (otherwise) (SI 2000/2091) |
| 36 | | 24 Jul 2002 (SI 2002/1739) |
| 37 | (1)–(4) | 24 Jul 2002 (otherwise) (SI 2002/1739) |
| | (5) | 27 Jul 1999 (s 68(4)(b)) |
| 38 | (1)–(5) | 4 Sep 2000 (SI 2000/2091) |
| | (6), (7) | 27 Jul 1999 (s 68(4)(b)) |
| | (8) | 4 Sep 2000 (SI 2000/2091) |
| 39 | | 4 Sep 2000 (SI 2000/2091) |
| 40 | (1) | 27 Jul 1999 (s 68(4)(c)) |
| | (2) | *Never in force* (repealed) |
| 41, 42 | | 4 Dec 2000 (SI 2000/3075) |
| 43 | (1), (2) | 4 Dec 2000 (SI 2000/3075) |
| | (3) | 27 Jul 1999 (s 68(4)(b)) |
| 44 | (1)–(10) | *Not yet in force* |
| | (11) | 27 Jul 1999 (so far as confers power to make rules of court) (s 68(4)(b)) |
| | | *Not yet in force* (otherwise) |
| | (12), (13) | *Not yet in force* |
| 45 | | 13 Apr 2015 (E) (W) (SI 2015/818) |
| | | *Not yet in force* (S) (NI) |
| 46 | | 7 Oct 2004 (E) (W) (SI 2004/2428) |
| | | 7 Oct 2004 (S) (for the purpose of the prosecution in Scotland of an offence under s 49) (SSI 2004/408) |
| | | 8 Nov 2004 (NI) (SR 2004/467) |
| | | *Not yet in force* (S) (otherwise) |
| 47 | | 27 Jul 1999 (so far as confers power to make rules of court) (s 68(4)(b)) |
| | | 24 Jul 2002 (E) (W) (otherwise) (SI 2002/1739) |
| | | 7 Oct 2004 (S) (for the purpose of the prosecution in Scotland of an offence under s 49) (SSI 2004/408) |
| | | 8 Nov 2004 (NI) (SR 2004/467) |
| | | *Not yet in force* (S) (otherwise) |
| 48 | | See Sch 2 below |
| 49–52 | | 7 Oct 2004 (E) (W) (S) (for the purposes of ss 46, 47) (SI 2004/2428; SSI 2004/408) |
| | | 8 Nov 2004 (NI) (for the purposes of ss 46, 47) (SR 2004/467) |
| | | 13 Apr 2015 (for the purposes of ss 45, 45A) (SI 2015/818) |
| | | *Not yet in force* (for the purposes of s 44) |
| 53–57 | | 24 Jul 2002 (SI 2002/1739) |
| 58 | (1)–(4) | 1 Apr 2003 (SI 2003/707) |
| | (5) | 27 Jul 1999 (so far as confers power to make orders) (s 68(4)(d)) |
| | | 1 Apr 2003 (otherwise) (SI 2003/707) |
| 59 | | See Sch 3 below |
| 60 | | 14 Apr 2000 (SI 2000/1034) |
| 61 | (1) | 27 Jul 1999 (s 68(4)(e)) |
| | (2) | 27 Jul 1999 (so far as confers power to make orders) (s 68(4)(d)) |
| | | 6 Dec 2006 (otherwise) (SI 2006/2885) |
| | (3) | 27 Jul 1999 (s 68(4)(e)) |
| 62–66 | | 27 Jul 1999 (s 68(4)(e)) |
| 67 | (1) | See Sch 4 below |
| | (2) | 1 Jan 2000 (SI 1999/3427) |
| | (3) | See Sch 6 below |
| | (4) | See Sch 7 below |
| 68 | | 27 Jul 1999 (s 68(4)) |
| Sch 1 | | 26 Jun 2000 (SI 2000/1587) |
| Sch 2 | para 1 | 13 Apr 2015 (SI 2015/818) |
| | para 2 | *Never in force* (repealed) |

**Youth Justice and Criminal Evidence Act 1999 (c 23)**—*contd*

|  |  |  |
|---|---|---|
| | para 3(1)–(8) | 13 Apr 2015 (SI 2015/818) |
| | para 3(9) | *Not yet in force* |
| | para 3(10) | 13 Apr 2015 (SI 2015/818) |
| | para 4 | 7 Oct 2004 (E) (W) (SI 2004/2428) |
| | | 8 Nov 2004 (NI) (SR 2004/467) |
| | para 5 | 8 Nov 2004 (NI) (SR 2004/467) |
| | paras 6–13 | 7 Oct 2004 (E) (W) (SI 2004/2428) |
| | | 7 Oct 2004 (S) (for the purposes of the prosecution in Scotland of an offence under Sexual Offences (Amendment) Act 1992, s 5) (SSI 2004/408) |
| | | 8 Nov 2004 (NI) (SR 2004/467) |
| | | *Not yet in force* (S) (otherwise) (paras 9, 13 repealed) |
| | para 14 | 7 Oct 2004 (E) (W) (S) (SI 2004/2428; SSI 2004/408) |
| | | 8 Nov 2004 (NI) (SR 2004/467) |
| | para 15 | 8 Nov 2004 (NI) (SR 2004/467) |
| Sch 3 | | 14 Apr 2000 (E) (W) (NI) (SI 2000/1034) |
| | | 1 Jan 2001 (S) (SSI 2000/445) |
| Sch 4 | para 1 | 24 Jul 2002 (E) (W) (SI 2002/1739) |
| | | *Not yet in force* (S) (sub-para (5) repealed) |
| | paras 2, 3 | *Not yet in force* |
| | para 4(1) | *Not yet in force* |
| | para 4(2) | *Never in force* (repealed) |
| | para 4(3) | *Not yet in force* |
| | paras 5–9 | 26 Jun 2000 (SI 2000/1587) |
| | para 10 | 24 Jul 2002 (SI 2002/1739) |
| | para 11 | 26 Jun 2000 (SI 2000/1587) |
| | paras 12–14 | 24 Jul 2002 (E) (W) (SI 2002/1739) |
| | paras 15–17 | 14 Apr 2000 (SI 2000/1034) |
| | para 18 | *Never in force* (repealed) |
| | para 19 | *Not yet in force* |
| | para 20 | 26 Jun 2000 (SI 2000/1587) |
| | para 21 | *Not yet in force* |
| | para 22 | 14 Apr 2000 (SI 2000/1034) |
| | para 23 | 26 Jun 2000 (SI 2000/1587) |
| | para 24 | *Not yet in force* |
| | paras 25–30 | 26 Jun 2000 (SI 2000/1587) |
| Sch 5 | | *Never in force* (repealed) |
| Sch 6 | | 1 Apr 2000 (repeals of or in Youth Justice and Criminal Evidence Act 1999) (SI 1999/3427) |
| | | 14 Apr 2000 (E) (W) (SI 2000/1034), repeals of or in— |
| | | Registered Designs Act 1949; |
| | | Children and Young Persons Act 1969; |
| | | Patents Act 1977; |
| | | Customs and Excise Management Act 1979; |
| | | Police and Criminal Evidence Act 1984, ss 69, 70, Sch 3; |
| | | Companies Act 1985; |
| | | Criminal Justice Act 1988, ss 23, 24; |
| | | Finance Act 1994; |
| | | Value Added Tax Act 1994; |
| | | Civil Evidence Act 1995[1]; |
| | | Criminal Procedure and Investigations Act 1996, Sch 1, para 27; |
| | | Finance Act 1996; |
| | | Crime and Disorder Act 1998 |
| | | 4 Sep 2000 (repeal of or in Criminal Justice Act 1988, s 34A) (subject to a saving) (SI 2000/2091) |
| | | 4 Dec 2000 (SI 2000/3075), repeals of or in— |
| | | Sexual Offences (Amendment) Act 1976, ss 2, 3 (although commencement of repeal of ss 2, 3(3) does not apply in relation to any trial before a court-martial); |

**Youth Justice and Criminal Evidence Act 1999 (c 23)**—*contd*

Magistrates' Courts Act 1980, Sch 7, para 148;
Criminal Justice and Public Order Act 1994, Sch 10, para 35(3)
(although the commencement does not apply in relation to any
trial before a court-martial);
Criminal Procedure and Investigations Act 1996, Sch 1, para 23

24 Jul 2002 (E) (W) (SI 2002/1739), repeals of or in—
Criminal Evidence Act 1898;
Police and Criminal Evidence Act 1984, s 80(1), (5), (8);
Criminal Justice Act 1988, ss 32 (except so far as applied to
proceedings before Service courts by SI 1996/2592), 32A
(except so far as applied to proceedings before Service courts
by SI 1996/2592), 33A;
Criminal Justice Act 1991, ss 52, 54 (except so far as required
for proceedings before Service courts), 55(2)(b), (4), (6) (except
so far as required for proceedings before Service courts);
Criminal Justice and Public Order Act 1994, s 50, Sch 9,
para 33;
Criminal Appeal Act 1995;
Criminal Procedure and Investigations Act 1996, s 62, Sch 1,
para 33

7 Oct 2004 (E) (W) (SI 2004/2428), repeals of or in—
Sexual Offences (Amendment) Act 1976;
Sexual Offences (Amendment) Act 1992

7 Oct 2004 (S) (repeals of or in Sexual Offences (Amendment)
Act 1992, in so far as is necessary for the purpose of
prosecution in Scotland of an offence under s 5 of that Act)
(SSI 2004/408)

8 Nov 2004 (NI) (SR 2004/467), repeals of or in—
Sexual Offences (Northern Ireland) Order 1978, SI 1978/460
(NI 5);
Criminal Justice (Northern Ireland) Order 1994, SI 1994/2795
(NI 15);
Sexual Offences (Amendment) Act 1976;
Sexual Offences (Amendment) Act 1992

6 Dec 2006 (SI 2006/2885), repeals of or in—
Army Act 1955;
Air Force Act 1955;
Naval Discipline Act 1957;
Courts-Martial (Appeals) Act 1968;
Armed Forces Act 1976;
Armed Forces Act 1981;
Criminal Justice Act 1988, ss 32(1), (2), (3A)–(3E), (6) and 32A
(in so far as not already in force), Sch 13, para 8;
Criminal Justice and Public Order Act 1994, Sch 10, para 35(3)
(in so far as not already in force)

*Not yet in force*, repeals of or in—
Criminal Evidence Act 1898, s 1 (S);
Children and Young Persons Act 1933;
Children and Young Persons Act 1963;
Criminal Appeal Act 1968, s 10(2)(b) (however, note that the
words in s 10(2)(b) which would be repealed, were never
inserted);
Theft Act 1968;
Sexual Offences (Amendment) Act 1976, ss 2, 3(3) (in relation
to any trial before a court-martial (S)), ss 4, 5, 7(4), (5) (S);
Judicature (Northern Ireland) Act 1978;
Magistrates' Courts Act 1980, ss 125(4)(c)(iii), 126(d);
Police and Criminal Evidence Act 1984, s 82(1);
Criminal Justice Act 1988, s 158(2)–(4), Sch 15, para 53;
Broadcasting Act 1990;

**Youth Justice and Criminal Evidence Act 1999 (c 23)**—*contd*

|  |  |  |
|---|---|---|
|  |  | Criminal Justice Act 1991, s 54 (so far as required for proceedings before Service courts), s 55(2)(b), (4) and (6) (so far as required for proceedings before Service courts), (7), Sch 9, paras 3, 7, Sch 11, paras 1, 37; |
|  |  | Sexual Offences (Amendment) Act 1992, ss 5(2), 6(1), 7(3) (S) (except so far as is necessary for the purpose of prosecution in Scotland of an offence under s 5 of that Act); |
|  |  | Criminal Justice and Public Order Act 1994, Sch 9, paras 11(1)(a), 13, Sch 10, para 32, para 36; |
|  |  | Armed Forces Act 1996; |
|  |  | Criminal Justice (Children) (Northern Ireland) Order 1998, SI 1998/1504 (NI 9) |
| Sch 7 | para 1 | 26 Jun 2000 (E) (W) (NI) (SI 2000/1587) |
|  |  | 7 Oct 2004 (S) (so far as relates to para 6) (SSI 2004/408) |
|  | para 2 | 26 Jun 2000 (SI 2000/1587) |
|  | para 3 | 24 Jul 2002 (SI 2002/1739) |
|  | para 4 | 4 Sep 2000 (SI 2000/2091) |
|  | para 5 | 4 Dec 2000 (SI 2000/3075) |
|  | para 6 | 7 Oct 2004 (E) (W) (S) (so far as relates to s 46) (SI 2004/2428; SSI 2004/408) |
|  |  | 8 Nov 2004 (NI) (so far as relates to s 46) (SR 2004/467) |
|  |  | 13 Apr 2015 (in so far as relates to s 45) (SI 2015/818) |
|  |  | *Not yet in force* (so far as relates to s 44) |
|  | para 7 | 24 Jul 2002 (SI 2002/1739) |
|  | para 8 | 1 Apr 2003 (SI 2003/707) |

---

[1] The Queen's Printer's copy of SI 2000/1034 erroneously purports to bring into force the repeal by Sch 6 to this Act in Criminal Evidence Act 1995; it is assumed that the reference is to Civil Evidence Act 1995

# 2000 Acts

## Abolition of Feudal Tenure etc (Scotland) Act 2000 (asp 5)

*RA:* 9 Jun 2000

*Commencement provisions:* s 77; Abolition of Feudal Tenure etc (Scotland) Act 2000 (Commencement No 1) Order 2003, SSI 2003/455; Abolition of Feudal Tenure etc (Scotland) Act 2000 (Commencement No 2) (Appointed Day) Order 2003, SSI 2003/456; Abolition of Feudal Tenure etc (Scotland) Act 2000 (Commencement No 3) Order 2003, SSI 2003/620

| | | |
|---|---|---|
| 1, 2 | | 28 Nov 2004 (SSI 2003/456) |
| 3 | | 9 Jun 2000 (RA) |
| 4–13 | | 28 Nov 2004 (SSI 2003/456) |
| 14–16 | | 9 Jun 2000 (RA) |
| 17–22 | | 1 Nov 2003 (SSI 2003/455) |
| 23 | | *Never in force* (repealed) |
| 24, 25 | | 1 Nov 2003 (SSI 2003/455) |
| 26 | | *Never in force* (repealed) |
| 27, 28 | | 1 Nov 2003 (SSI 2003/455) |
| 29–32 | | *Never in force* (repealed) |
| 33, 34 | | 1 Nov 2003 (SSI 2003/455) |
| 35–37 | | 28 Nov 2004 (SSI 2003/456) |
| 38–45 | | 1 Nov 2003 (SSI 2003/455) |
| 46 | | 28 Nov 2004 (SSI 2003/456) |
| 47–49 | | 1 Nov 2003 (SSI 2003/455) |
| 50, 51 | | 28 Nov 2004 (SSI 2003/456) |
| 52, 53 | | 9 Jun 2000 (RA) |
| 54–57 | | 28 Nov 2004 (SSI 2003/456) |
| 58 | | 9 Jun 2000 (RA) |
| 59–61 | | 28 Nov 2004 (SSI 2003/456) |
| 62 | | 9 Jun 2000 (RA) |
| 63 | | 28 Nov 2004 (SSI 2003/620) |
| 64–66 | | 28 Nov 2004 (SSI 2003/456) |
| 67 | | 9 Jun 2000 (RA) |
| 68–70 | | 28 Nov 2004 (SSI 2003/456) |
| 71, 72 | | 9 Jun 2000 (RA) |
| 73 | | 28 Nov 2004 (SSI 2003/456) |
| 74 | | 9 Jun 2000 (RA) |
| 75 | | 28 Nov 2004 (SSI 2003/456) |
| 76 | (1) | See Sch 12 below |
| | (2) | See Sch 13 below |
| | (3), (4) | 9 Jun 2000 (RA) |
| 77 | | 9 Jun 2000 (RA) |
| Schs 1–3 | | 28 Nov 2004 (SSI 2003/456) |
| Sch 4 | | 9 Jun 2000 (RA) |
| Schs 5–11 | | 1 Nov 2003 (SSI 2003/455) |
| Sch 12 | para 1 | 28 Nov 2004 (SSI 2003/456) |
| | para 2 | *Never in force* (repealed) |
| | paras 3–29 | 28 Nov 2004 (SSI 2003/456) |
| | para 30(1) | 28 Nov 2004 (SSI 2003/456) |

**Abolition of Feudal Tenure etc (Scotland) Act 2000 (asp 5)**—*contd*

|  |  |  |
|---|---|---|
|  | para 30(2), (3) | *Never in force* (repealed) |
|  | para 30(4) | 28 Nov 2004 (SSI 2003/456) |
|  | para 30(5) | *Never in force* (repealed) |
|  | para 30(6)–(21) | 28 Nov 2004 (SSI 2003/456) |
|  | para 30(22) | *Never in force* (repealed) |
|  | para 30(23)(a) | 9 Jun 2000 (RA) |
|  | para 30(23)(b), (c) | 28 Nov 2004 (SSI 2003/456) |
|  | para 30(24)–(26) | 28 Nov 2004 (SSI 2003/456) |
|  | paras 31–38 | 28 Nov 2004 (SSI 2003/456) |
|  | para 39(1)–(5) | 28 Nov 2004 (SSI 2003/456) |
|  | para 39(6) | *Never in force* (repealed) |
|  | para 39(7)–(11) | 28 Nov 2004 (SSI 2003/456) |
|  | paras 40–63 | 28 Nov 2004 (SSI 2003/456) |
| Sch 13 |  | 28 Nov 2004 (in so far as not already repealed) (SSI 2003/456) |
|  |  | *Never in force* (repealed), repeals of or in— |
|  |  | Conveyancing (Scotland) Act 1874, s 32, Sch H; |
|  |  | Conveyancing (Scotland) Act 1924, s 9; |
|  |  | Church of Scotland (Property and Endowments) Act 1925, s 22(2)(h); |
|  |  | Conveyancing and Feudal Reform (Scotland) Act 1970, s 2, Sch 1; |
|  |  | Land Registration (Scotland) Act 1979, ss 3(6), 15(2)(a) |

**Adults with Incapacity (Scotland) Act 2000 (asp 4)**

*RA:* 9 May 2000

*Commencement provisions:* s 89(2); Adults with Incapacity (Scotland) Act 2000 (Commencement No 1) Order 2001, SSI 2001/81, as amended by SSI 2002/172; Adults with Incapacity (Scotland) Act 2000 (Commencement No 2) Order 2002, SSI 2002/189; Adults with Incapacity (Scotland) Act 2000 (Commencement No 3) Order 2003, SSI 2003/136, as amended by SSI 2003/227; Adults with Incapacity (Scotland) Act 2000 (Commencement No 4) Order 2003, SSI 2003/267; Adults with Incapacity (Scotland) Act 2000 (Commencement No 5) Order 2003, SSI 2003/516

|  |  |  |
|---|---|---|
| 1–5 |  | 2 Apr 2001 (SSI 2001/81) |
| 6 | (1) | 2 Apr 2001 (SSI 2001/81) |
|  | (2)(a) | 1 Apr 2002 (SSI 2001/81) |
|  | (2)(b)(i)–(iii) | 2 Apr 2001 (SSI 2001/81) |
|  | (2)(b)(iv), (v) | 1 Apr 2002 (SSI 2001/81) |
|  | (2)(c)(i), (ii) | 2 Apr 2001 (SSI 2001/81) |
|  | (2)(c)(iii) | 1 Apr 2002 (SSI 2001/81) |
|  | (2)(d) | 2 Apr 2001 (SSI 2001/81) |
|  | (2)(e) | 2 Apr 2001 (in so far as relates to continuing attorneys or withdrawers) (SSI 2001/81) |
|  |  | 1 Apr 2002 (otherwise) (SSI 2001/81) |
|  | (2)(f) | 2 Apr 2001 (SSI 2001/81) |
|  | (3)(a) | 1 Apr 2002 (SSI 2001/81) |
|  | (3)(b) | 2 Apr 2001 (SSI 2001/81) |
| 7, 8 |  | 2 Apr 2001 (SSI 2001/81) |
| 9 | (1)(a)–(c) | 2 Apr 2001 (SSI 2001/81) |
|  | (1)(d)(i) | 2 Apr 2001 (SSI 2001/81) |
|  | (1)(d)(ii) | 1 Apr 2002 (SSI 2001/81) |
|  | (1)(e), (f) | 2 Apr 2001 (SSI 2001/81) |
|  | (1)(g) | 2 Apr 2001 (in so far as relates to welfare attorneys) (SSI 2001/81) |
|  |  | 1 Apr 2002 (otherwise) (SSI 2001/81) |
|  | (2) | 2 Apr 2001 (in so far as relates to welfare attorneys) (SSI 2001/81) |
|  |  | 1 Apr 2002 (otherwise) (SSI 2001/81) |
|  | (3)(a) | 1 Apr 2002 (SSI 2001/81) |
|  | (3)(b) | 2 Apr 2001 (SSI 2001/81) |
| 10 | (1)(a) | 1 Apr 2002 (SSI 2001/81) |

**Adults with Incapacity (Scotland) Act 2000 (asp 4)**—*contd*

| | | |
|---|---|---|
| | (1)(b) | 2 Apr 2001 (SSI 2001/81) |
| | (1)(c)(i) | 2 Apr 2001 (SSI 2001/81) |
| | (1)(c)(ii) | 1 Apr 2002 (SSI 2001/81) |
| | (1)(d) | 2 Apr 2001 (SSI 2001/81) |
| | (1)(e) | 2 Apr 2001 (in so far as relates to welfare attorneys) (SSI 2001/81) |
| | | 1 Apr 2002 (otherwise) (SSI 2001/81) |
| | (2) | 2 Apr 2001 (SSI 2001/81) |
| | (3)(a) | 1 Apr 2002 (SSI 2001/81) |
| | (3)(b)(i) | 1 Apr 2002 (SSI 2001/81) |
| | (3)(b)(ii) | 2 Apr 2001 (SSI 2001/81) |
| | (4)(a) | 1 Apr 2002 (SSI 2001/81) |
| | (4)(b) | 2 Apr 2001 (SSI 2001/81) |
| 11 | | 2 Apr 2001 (SSI 2001/81) |
| 12 | | 2 Apr 2001 (in so far as relates to investigations in relation to continuing attorneys, welfare attorneys and intromission with funds under Pt 3 of this Act) (SSI 2001/81) |
| | | 1 Apr 2002 (otherwise) (SSI 2001/81) |
| 13–23 | | 2 Apr 2001 (SSI 2001/81) |
| 24 | (1) | 2 Apr 2001 (SSI 2001/81) |
| | (2), (3) | 1 Apr 2002 (SSI 2001/81) |
| | (4) | 2 Apr 2001 (SSI 2001/81) |
| 25–34 | | 2 Apr 2001 (SSI 2001/81) |
| 35, 36 | | 1 Oct 2003 (SSI 2003/267) |
| 37 | (1) | 1 Oct 2003 (SSI 2003/267) |
| | (2) | 6 Mar 2003 (for the purpose of making regulations to come into force on 1 Apr 2003) (SSI 2003/136) |
| | | 29 May 2003 (for the purpose of making regulations (otherwise)) (SSI 2003/267) |
| | | 1 Oct 2003 (otherwise) (SSI 2003/267) |
| | (3)–(8) | 1 Oct 2003 (SSI 2003/267) |
| | (9) | 6 Mar 2003 (for the purpose of making regulations to come into force on 1 Apr 2003) (SSI 2003/136) |
| | | 29 May 2003 (for the purpose of making regulations (otherwise)) (SSI 2003/267) |
| | | 1 Oct 2003 (otherwise) (SSI 2003/267) |
| 38 | | 1 Oct 2003 (SSI 2003/267) |
| 39 | (1), (2) | 1 Oct 2003 (SSI 2003/267) |
| | (3) | 6 Mar 2003 (for the purpose of making regulations to come into force on 1 Apr 2003) (SSI 2003/136) |
| | | 29 May 2003 (for the purpose of making regulations (otherwise)) (SSI 2003/267) |
| | | 1 Oct 2003 (otherwise) (SSI 2003/267) |
| | (4), (5) | 1 Oct 2003 (SSI 2003/267) |
| 40 | | 1 Oct 2003 (SSI 2003/267) |
| 41 | (a)–(c) | 1 Oct 2003 (SSI 2003/267) |
| | (d) | 6 Mar 2003 (for the purpose of making regulations to come into force on 1 Apr 2003) (SSI 2003/136) |
| | | 29 May 2003 (for the purpose of making regulations (otherwise)) (SSI 2003/267) |
| | | 1 Oct 2003 (otherwise) (SSI 2003/267) |
| | (e)–(i) | 1 Oct 2003 (SSI 2003/267) |
| 42–46 | | 1 Oct 2003 (SSI 2003/267) |
| 47–52 | | 1 Jul 2002 (SSI 2002/189) |
| 53–80 | | 1 Apr 2002 (SSI 2001/81) |
| 81 | (1)(a)–(c) | 2 Apr 2001 (SSI 2001/81) |
| | (1)(d), (e) | 1 Apr 2002 (SSI 2001/81) |
| | (1)(f) | *Not yet in force* |
| | (2) | 2 Apr 2001 (in so far as relates to s 82 below) (SSI 2001/81) |
| | | 1 Apr 2002 (otherwise) (except so far as relates to managers of an authorised establishment) (SSI 2001/81) |

**Adults with Incapacity (Scotland) Act 2000 (asp 4)**—*contd*

| | | |
|---|---|---|
| | | *Not yet in force* (exception noted above) |
| 82 | (1) | 2 Apr 2001 (in so far as relates to continuing attorneys, welfare attorneys and withdrawers) (SSI 2001/81) |
| | | 1 Apr 2002 (otherwise) (except so far as relates to managers of an authorised establishment) (SSI 2001/81) |
| | | *Not yet in force* (exception noted above) |
| | (2)(a) | 1 Apr 2002 (SSI 2001/81) |
| | (2)(b), (c) | 2 Apr 2001 (SSI 2001/81) |
| 83 | | 2 Apr 2001 (SSI 2001/81) |
| 84 | | 1 Apr 2002 (SSI 2001/81) |
| 85 | | See Sch 3 below |
| 86, 87 | | 2 Apr 2001 (SSI 2001/81) |
| 88 | (1) | See Sch 4 below |
| | (2) | See Sch 5 below |
| | (3) | See Sch 6 below |
| 89 | | *Not yet in force* |
| Sch 1 | | 1 Oct 2003 (SSI 2003/267) |
| Sch 2 | | 1 Apr 2002 (SSI 2001/81) |
| Sch 3 | para 1(1) | 2 Apr 2001 (SSI 2001/81) |
| | para 1(2)–(4) | 4 Nov 2003 (SSI 2003/516) |
| | para 1(5) | 2 Apr 2001 (SSI 2001/81) |
| | para 2(1) | 2 Apr 2001 (SSI 2001/81) |
| | para 2(2) | 4 Nov 2003 (SSI 2003/516) |
| | para 2(3), (4) | 2 Apr 2001 (SSI 2001/81) |
| | paras 3–6 | 2 Apr 2001 (SSI 2001/81) |
| | para 7(1) | 2 Apr 2001 (SSI 2001/81) |
| | para 7(2)(a) | 2 Apr 2001 (SSI 2001/81) |
| | para 7(2)(b) | 4 Nov 2003 (SSI 2003/516) |
| | para 7(3)(a)–(d) | 2 Apr 2001 (SSI 2001/81) |
| | para 7(3)(e) | 4 Nov 2003 (SSI 2003/516) |
| | paras 8–10 | 2 Apr 2001 (SSI 2001/81) |
| | paras 11, 12 | 4 Nov 2003 (SSI 2003/516) |
| | paras 13, 14 | 2 Apr 2001 (SSI 2001/81) |
| Sch 4 | paras 1–3 | 1 Apr 2002 (SSI 2001/81) |
| | para 4 | 2 Apr 2001 (SSI 2001/81) |
| | para 5 | 1 Oct 2003 (SSI 2003/267) |
| | para 6 | 1 Apr 2002 (SSI 2001/81) |
| | para 7(a)–(c) | 2 Apr 2001 (SSI 2001/81) |
| | para 7(d) | *Not yet in force* |
| | para 8 | 2 Apr 2001 (SSI 2001/81) |
| Sch 5 | para 1 | 1 Apr 2002 (SSI 2001/81) |
| | paras 2, 3 | 2 Apr 2001 (SSI 2001/81) |
| | para 4 | *Never in force* (repealed) |
| | paras 5, 6 | 2 Apr 2001 (SSI 2001/81) |
| | para 7 | 2 Apr 2001 (in so far as relates to continuing and welfare attorneys and withdrawers) (SSI 2001/81) |
| | | 1 Apr 2002 (otherwise) (SSI 2001/81) |
| | para 8 | 1 Apr 2002 (SSI 2001/81) |
| | para 9 | 2 Apr 2001 (in so far as relates to continuing and welfare attorneys and withdrawers) (SSI 2001/81) |
| | | 1 Apr 2002 (otherwise) (SSI 2001/81) |
| | paras 10, 11 | *Never in force* (repealed) |
| | para 12 | 1 Apr 2002 (SSI 2001/81) |
| | paras 13, 14 | 2 Apr 2001 (SSI 2001/81) |
| | paras 15, 16 | 1 Apr 2002 (SSI 2001/81) |
| | para 17(1), (2) | 1 Apr 2002 (SSI 2001/81) |
| | para 17(3)–(21) | 2 Apr 2001 (in so far as relate to welfare attorneys) (SSI 2001/81) |
| | | 1 Apr 2002 (otherwise) (SSI 2001/81) |
| | para 17(22) | *Never in force* (repealed) |

## Adults with Incapacity (Scotland) Act 2000 (asp 4)—*contd*

|  |  |  |
|---|---|---|
| | para 17(23) | 1 Oct 2003 (SSI 2003/267) |
| | para 17(24)(a) | 1 Apr 2002 (SSI 2001/81) |
| | para 17(24)(b) | 2 Apr 2001 (in so far as relates to welfare attorneys) (SSI 2001/81) |
| | | 1 Apr 2002 (otherwise) (SSI 2001/81) |
| | para 18 | 1 Apr 2002 (SSI 2001/81) |
| | para 19 | 2 Apr 2001 (SSI 2001/81) |
| | paras 20, 21 | 1 Apr 2002 (SSI 2001/81) |
| | paras 22, 23 | 2 Apr 2001 (in so far as relate to welfare attorneys) (SSI 2001/81) |
| | | 1 Apr 2002 (otherwise) (SSI 2001/81) |
| | para 24 | 1 Apr 2002 (SSI 2001/81) |
| | para 25 | 2 Apr 2001 (SSI 2001/81) |
| | para 26 | 1 Apr 2002 (SSI 2001/81) |
| Sch 6 | | 2 Apr 2001 (repeal of Law Reform (Miscellaneous Provisions) (Scotland) Act 1990) (SSI 2001/81) |
| | | 1 Apr 2002 (SSI 2001/81) (otherwise), except repeals of or in— Improvement of Land Act 1864; Mental Health (Scotland) Act 1984, ss 5(2), 94 |
| | | 1 Oct 2003 (repeals of Mental Health (Scotland) Act 1984, ss 5(2), 94) (SSI 2003/267) |
| | | *Not yet in force* (repeal in Improvement of Land Act 1864) |

## Appropriation Act 2000 (c 9)

*RA:* 20 Jul 2000

Whole Act in force 20 Jul 2000 (RA)

## Armed Forces Discipline Act 2000 (c 4)

*RA:* 25 May 2000

*Commencement provisions:* s 28(2), (3); Armed Forces Discipline Act 2000 (Commencement and Transitional Provisions) Order 2000, SI 2000/2366

|  |  |
|---|---|
| 1–25 | 2 Oct 2000 (subject to transitional provisions and savings) (SI 2000/2366) |
| 26 | 25 May 2000 (RA) |
| 27 | 2 Oct 2000 (subject to transitional provisions and savings) (SI 2000/2366) |
| 28 | 25 May 2000 (RA) |
| Schs 1–4 | 2 Oct 2000 (subject to transitional provisions and savings) (SI 2000/2366) |

## Bail, Judicial Appointments etc (Scotland) Act 2000 (asp 9)

*RA:* 9 Aug 2000

Whole Act in force 9 Aug 2000 (RA)

## Budget (Scotland) Act 2000 (asp 2)

*RA:* 20 Mar 2000

Whole Act in force 20 Mar 2000 (RA)

## Care Standards Act 2000 (c 14)

*RA:* 20 Jul 2000

*Commencement provisions:* s 122; Care Standards Act 2000 (Commencement No 1) Order 2000, SI 2000/2544; Care Standards Act 2000 (Commencement No 1 (England) and Transitional Provisions) Order 2000, SI 2000/2795; Care Standards Act 2000 (Commencement No 1) (Wales) Order 2000, SI 2000/2992; Care Standards Act 2000 (Commencement No 2 and Transitional Provisions) (Wales) Order 2001, SI 2001/139[1]; Care Standards Act 2000 (Commencement No 2 (England) and Transitional Provisions) Order 2001, SI 2001/290[2]; Care Standards Act 2000 (Commencement No 3) (England) Order 2001, SI 2001/731; Care Standards Act 2000 (Commencement No 4) (England) Order 2001, SI 2001/1193; Care Standards Act 2000 (Commencement No 5) (England) Order 2001, SI 2001/1210; Care Standards Act 2000 (Commencement No 6) (England) Order 2001, SI 2001/1536; Care Standards Act 2000 (Commencement No 7 and Transitional, Transitory and Savings (England)) Order 2001, SI 2001/2041[4]; Care Standards Act 2000 (Commencement No 3) (Wales) Order 2001, SI 2001/2190; Care Standards Act 2000 (Commencement No 4) (Wales) Order 2001, SI 2001/2354; Care Standards Act 2000 (Commencement No 5 and Transitional Provisions) (Wales) Order 2001, SI 2001/2504[5]; Care Standards Act 2000 (Commencement No 6) (Wales) Order 2001, SI 2001/2538; Care Standards Act 2000 (Commencement No 7) (Wales) Order 2001, SI 2001/2782; Care Standards Act 2000 (Commencement No 8) (England) Order 2001, SI 2001/3331; Care Standards Act 2000 (Commencement No 9) (England) and Transitional and Savings Provisions) Order 2001, SI 2001/3852[6], as amended by SI 2001/4150, SI 2002/1493, SI 2002/1790, SI 2002/2001, SI 2002/3210[13], SI 2005/3397; Care Standards Act 2000 (Commencement No 10 (England) and Transitional, Savings and Amendment Provisions) Order 2001, SI 2001/4150[10], as amended by SI 2002/1493, SI 2002/1790, SI 2002/2001, SI 2002/3210[13]; Care Standards Act 2000 (Commencement No 11) Order 2002, SI 2002/629; Care Standards Act 2000 (Commencement No 8 (Wales) and Transitional, Savings and Consequential Provisions) Order 2002, SI 2002/920; Care Standards Act 2000 (Commencement No 9) (Wales) Order 2002, SI 2002/1175; Care Standards Act 2000 (Commencement No 12) (England) Order 2002, SI 2002/1245; Care Standards Act 2000 (Commencement No 13) (England) Order 2002, SI 2002/839; Care Standards Act 2000 (Commencement No 14 (England) and Transitional, Savings and Amendment Provisions) Order 2002, SI 2002/1493[11]; Care Standards Act 2000 (Commencement No 16) (England) Order 2002, SI 2002/2215; Care Standards Act 2000 (Commencement No 10) and Transitional Provisions (Wales) Order 2003, SI 2003/152[14]; Care Standards Act 2000 (Commencement No 17 (England) and Transitional and Savings Provisions) Order 2003, SI 2003/365[15]; Care Standards Act 2000 (Commencement No 11) (Wales) Order 2003, SI 2003/501; Care Standards Act 2000 (Commencement No 18) (England) Order 2003, SI 2003/933; Care Standards Act 2000 (Commencement No 12) (Wales) Order 2003, SI 2003/2528; Care Standards Act 2000 (Commencement No 19) (England) Order 2004, SI 2004/484; Care Standards Act 2000 (Commencement No 13) (Wales) Order 2004, SI 2004/1015; Care Standards Act 2000 (Commencement No 14) (Wales) Order 2004, SI 2004/1730; Care Standards Act 2000 (Commencement No 20) Order 2004, SI 2004/1757; Care Standards Act 2000 (Commencement No 21) Order 2005, SI 2005/375

| | | |
|---|---|---|
| 1–3 | | 1 Jul 2001 (W) (SI 2001/2190) |
| | | 20 Nov 2001 (E) (for the purpose only of the exercise of any power to make regulations) (SI 2001/3852) |
| | | 1 Jan 2002 (E) (for specified purposes)[7] (SI 2001/3852) |
| | | 1 Apr 2002 (E) (otherwise) (SI 2001/3852) |
| 4 | (1) | See sub-ss (2)–(9) below |
| | (2), (3) | 1 Jul 2001 (W) (SI 2001/2190) |
| | | 20 Nov 2001 (E) (for the purpose only of the exercise of any power to make regulations) (SI 2001/3852) |
| | | 1 Jan 2002 (E) (for specified purposes)[7] (SI 2001/3852) |
| | | 1 Apr 2003 (E) (otherwise) (SI 2001/3852) |
| | (4) | 1 Jul 2001 (W) (SI 2001/2190) |
| | | 20 Nov 2001 (E) (for the purpose only of the exercise of any power to make regulations) (SI 2001/3852) |
| | | 1 Jan 2002 (E) (for specified purposes)[7] (SI 2001/3852) |
| | | 1 Apr 2002 (E) (otherwise) (SI 2001/3852) |
| | (5) | 1 Jul 2001 (W) (SI 2001/2190) |
| | | 20 Nov 2001 (E) (for the purpose only of the exercise of any power to make regulations) (SI 2001/3852) |
| | | 1 Jan 2002 (E) (for specified purposes)[7] (SI 2001/3852) |

**Care Standards Act 2000 (c 14)**—*contd*

|  |  |  |
|---|---|---|
| | | 1 Apr 2003 (E) (otherwise) (SI 2001/3852) |
| (6) | | 1 Jul 2001 (W) (SI 2001/2190) |
| | | 20 Nov 2001 (E) (for the purpose only of the exercise of any power to make regulations) (SI 2001/3852) |
| | | 1 Jan 2002 (E) (for specified purposes)[7] (SI 2001/3852) |
| | | 1 Apr 2002 (E) (so far as it relates to s 4(4)) (SI 2001/3852) |
| | | 1 Apr 2003 (E) (otherwise) (SI 2001/3852) |
| (7) | | 1 Jul 2001 (W) (SI 2001/2190) |
| | | 20 Nov 2001 (E) (for the purpose only of the exercise of any power to make regulations) (SI 2001/3852) |
| | | 25 Feb 2003 (E) (for specified purposes)[16] (SI 2003/365) |
| | | 30 Apr 2003 (E) (otherwise) (SI 2003/365) |
| (8) | | 1 Jul 2001 (W) (SI 2001/2190) |
| | | 20 Nov 2001 (E) (for the purpose only of the exercise of any power to make regulations) (SI 2001/3852) |
| | | 1 Jan 2002 (E) (for specified purposes)[7] (SI 2001/3852) |
| | | 1 Apr 2002 (E) (except in so far as it relates to residential family centres) (SI 2001/3852) |
| | | 1 Apr 2003 (E) (otherwise) (SI 2001/3852) |
| (9) | | 1 Jul 2001 (W) (SI 2001/2190) |
| | | 20 Nov 2001 (E) (for the purpose only of the exercise of any power to make regulations) (SI 2001/3852) |
| | | 1 Jan 2002 (E) (for specified purposes)[7] (except in so far as it relates to voluntary adoption agencies) (SI 2001/3852) |
| | | 1 Apr 2002 (E) (otherwise) (except in so far as it relates to domiciliary care agencies, nurses agencies and voluntary adoption agencies) (SI 2001/3852) |
| | | 25 Feb 2003 (E) (for specified purposes)[16] (in so far as it relates to a voluntary adoption agency) (SI 2003/365) |
| | | 1 Apr 2003 (E) (otherwise) (in so far as it relates to domiciliary care agencies and nurses agencies) (SI 2001/3852) |
| | | 30 Apr 2003 (E) (otherwise) (in so far as it relates to a voluntary adoption agency) (SI 2003/365) |
| 5 | | 1 Jul 2001 (W) (SI 2001/2190) |
| | | 1 Apr 2002 (E) (in so far as it relates to the Commission) (SI 2001/3852) |
| | | *Not yet in force* (otherwise) |
| 6 | (1), (2) | 9 Apr 2001 (SI 2001/1193) |
| | (3) | See Sch 1 below |
| | (4) | 9 Apr 2001 (SI 2001/1193) |
| 7 | (1)–(6) | 1 Apr 2002 (E) (SI 2001/3852) |
| | | *Never in force* (W) (repealed) |
| | (7) | 1 Jul 2001 (W) (SI 2001/2190) |
| | | 1 Apr 2002 (E) (SI 2001/3852) |
| 8 | | 1 Jul 2001 (W) (for purpose of enabling subordinate legislation to be made) (SI 2001/2190) |
| | | 1 Apr 2002 (W) (in relation to children's homes, independent hospitals, independent clinics and care homes) (SI 2002/920)[12] |
| | | 30 Jan 2003 (W) (in relation to residential family centres, fostering agencies and voluntary adoption agencies) (SI 2003/152)[14] |
| | | 2 Oct 2003 (W) (in relation to nurses agencies) (SI 2003/2528) |
| | | 1 Apr 2004 (W) (in relation to domiciliary care agencies) (SI 2004/1015) |
| | | 7 Jul 2004 (W) (so far as relates to regulations made under s 42, so far as not already in force) (SI 2004/1730) |
| | | *Not yet in force* (W) (in relation to an independent medical agency, except for the purpose of enabling subordinate legislation to be made) |
| 9 | | 1 Jul 2001 (W) (SI 2001/2190) |
| | | *Never in force* (otherwise) (repealed) |

**Care Standards Act 2000 (c 14)**—*contd*

10 (1)   1 Apr 2002 (E) (SI 2001/3852)

*Never in force* (otherwise) (repealed)

(2)–(5)   1 Apr 2002 (E) (SI 2001/3852)

1 Apr 2002 (W) (in relation to children's homes, independent hospitals, independent clinics and care homes) (SI 2002/920)[12]

30 Jan 2003 (W) (in relation to residential family centres, fostering agencies and voluntary adoption agencies) (SI 2003/152)[14]

1 Apr 2004 (W) (in relation to domiciliary care agencies) (SI 2004/1015)

7 Jul 2004 (W) (so far as they relate to regulations made under s 42, so far as not already in force) (SI 2004/1730)

*Not yet in force* (W) (in relation to an independent medical agency)

(6)   1 Apr 2002 (W) (in relation to children's homes, independent hospitals, independent clinics and care homes) (SI 2002/920)[12]

30 Jan 2003 (W) (in relation to residential family centres, fostering agencies and voluntary adoption agencies) (SI 2003/152)[14]

1 Apr 2004 (W) (in relation to domiciliary care agencies) (SI 2004/1015)

7 Jul 2004 (W) (so far as relates to regulations made under s 42, so far as not already in force) (SI 2004/1730)

*Never in force* (W) (in relation to an independent medical agency) (repealed)

(7)   1 Apr 2002 (E) (SI 2001/3852)

1 Apr 2002 (W) (in relation to children's homes, independent hospitals, independent clinics and care homes) (SI 2002/920)[12]

30 Jan 2003 (W) (in relation to residential family centres, fostering agencies and voluntary adoption agencies) (SI 2003/152)[14]

1 Apr 2004 (W) (in relation to domiciliary care agencies) (SI 2004/1015)

7 Jul 2004 (W) (so far as relates to regulations made under s 42, so far as not already in force) (SI 2004/1730)

*Not yet in force* (W) (in relation to an independent medical agency)

11   1 Jul 2001 (W) (for purpose of enabling subordinate legislation to be made) (SI 2001/2190)

20 Nov 2001 (E) (for the purpose only of the exercise of any power to make regulations) (SI 2001/3852)

1 Apr 2002 (E) (otherwise) (SI 2001/3852)

1 Apr 2002 (W) (in relation to children's homes, independent hospitals, independent clinics and care homes) (SI 2002/920)[12]

30 Jan 2003 (W) (in relation to residential family centres, fostering agencies and voluntary adoption agencies) (SI 2003/152)[14]

2 Oct 2003 (W) (in relation to nurses agencies) (SI 2003/2528)

1 Apr 2004 (W) (in relation to domiciliary care agencies) (SI 2004/1015)

7 Jul 2004 (W) (so far as relates to regulations made under s 42, so far as not already in force) (SI 2004/1730)

*Not yet in force* (W) (in relation to an independent medical agency, except for the purpose of enabling subordinate legislation to be made)

12   1 Jul 2001 (W) (for purpose of enabling subordinate legislation to be made) (SI 2001/2190)

20 Nov 2001 (E) (for the purpose only of the exercise of any power to make regulations) (SI 2001/3852)

1 Jan 2002 (E) (for specified purposes)[7] (SI 2001/3852)

1 Apr 2002 (E) (otherwise) (SI 2001/3852)

1 Apr 2002 (W) (in relation to children's homes, independent hospitals, independent clinics and care homes) (SI 2002/920)[12]

30 Jan 2003 (W) (in relation to residential family centres, fostering agencies and voluntary adoption agencies) (SI 2003/152)[14]

2 Oct 2003 (W) (in relation to nurses agencies) (SI 2003/2528)

**Care Standards Act 2000 (c 14)**—*contd*

|  |  |
|---|---|
|  | 1 Apr 2004 (W) (in relation to domiciliary care agencies) (SI 2004/1015) |
|  | 7 Jul 2004 (W) (so far as relates to regulations made under s 42, so far as not already in force) (SI 2004/1730) |
|  | *Not yet in force* (W) (in relation to an independent medical agency, except for the purpose of enabling subordinate legislation to be made) |
| 13 | 1 Jan 2002 (E) (for specified purposes)[7] (SI 2001/3852) |
|  | 1 Apr 2002 (E) (otherwise) (SI 2001/3852) |
|  | 1 Apr 2002 (W) (in relation to children's homes, independent hospitals, independent clinics and care homes) (SI 2002/920)[12] |
|  | 30 Jan 2003 (W) (in relation to residential family centres, fostering agencies and voluntary adoption agencies) (SI 2003/152)[14] |
|  | 2 Oct 2003 (W) (in relation to nurses agencies) (SI 2003/2528) |
|  | 1 Apr 2004 (W) (in relation to domiciliary care agencies) (SI 2004/1015) |
|  | 7 Jul 2004 (W) (so far as relates to regulations made under s 42, so far as not already in force) (SI 2004/1730) |
|  | *Not yet in force* (W) (in relation to an independent medical agency) |
| 14, 15 | 1 Jul 2001 (W) (for purpose of enabling subordinate legislation to be made) (SI 2001/2190) |
|  | 20 Nov 2001 (E) (for the purpose only of the exercise of any power to make regulations) (SI 2001/3852) |
|  | 1 Apr 2002 (E) (otherwise) (SI 2001/3852) |
|  | 1 Apr 2002 (W) (in relation to children's homes, independent hospitals, independent clinics and care homes) (SI 2002/920)[12] |
|  | 30 Jan 2003 (W) (in relation to residential family centres, fostering agencies and voluntary adoption agencies) (SI 2003/152)[14] |
|  | 2 Oct 2003 (W) (in relation to nurses agencies) (SI 2003/2528) |
|  | 1 Apr 2004 (W) (in relation to domiciliary care agencies) (SI 2004/1015) |
|  | 7 Jul 2004 (W) (so far as they relate to regulations made under s 42, so far as not already in force) (SI 2004/1730) |
|  | *Not yet in force* (W) (in relation to an independent medical agency, except for purpose of enabling subordinate legislation to be made) |
| 16 | 1 Jul 2001 (W) (SI 2001/2190) |
|  | 20 Nov 2001 (E) (for the purpose only of the exercise of any power to make regulations) (SI 2001/3852) |
|  | 1 Apr 2002 (otherwise) (E) (SI 2001/3852) |
| 17–20 | 1 Apr 2002 (E) (SI 2001/3852) |
|  | 1 Apr 2002 (W) (in relation to children's homes, independent hospitals, independent clinics and care homes) (SI 2002/920)[12] |
|  | 30 Jan 2003 (W) (in relation to residential family centres, fostering agencies and voluntary adoption agencies) (SI 2003/152)[14] |
|  | 2 Oct 2003 (W) (in relation to nurses agencies) (SI 2003/2528) |
|  | 1 Apr 2004 (W) (in relation to domiciliary care agencies) (SI 2004/1015) |
|  | 7 Jul 2004 (W) (so far as they relate to regulations made under s 42, so far as not already in force) (SI 2004/1730) |
|  | *Not yet in force* (W) (in relation to an independent medical agency) |
| 21 | 20 Nov 2001 (E) (for the purpose only of enabling a person to bring an appeal against a determination which is treated under Sch 1, para 5(6) to SI 2001/3852, as a decision of the Commission for the purposes of that section) (SI 2001/3852) |
|  | 1 Apr 2002 (E) (otherwise) (SI 2001/3852) |
|  | 1 Apr 2002 (W) (in relation to children's homes, independent hospitals, independent clinics and care homes) (SI 2002/920)[12] |
|  | 30 Jan 2003 (W) (in relation to residential family centres, fostering agencies and voluntary adoption agencies) (SI 2003/152)[14] |

**Care Standards Act 2000 (c 14)**—*contd*

|  |  |  |
|---|---|---|
|  |  | 2 Oct 2003 (W) (in relation to nurses agencies) (SI 2003/2528) |
|  |  | 1 Apr 2004 (W) (in relation to domiciliary care agencies) (SI 2004/1015) |
|  |  | 7 Jul 2004 (W) (so far as relates to regulations made under s 42, so far as not already in force) (SI 2004/1730) |
|  |  | *Not yet in force* (W) (in relation to an independent medical agency) |
| 22 |  | 1 Jul 2001 (W) (SI 2001/2190) |
|  |  | 20 Nov 2001 (E) (SI 2001/3852) |
| 23 | (1)–(3) | 2 Mar 2001 (E) (SI 2001/731) |
|  |  | 1 Jul 2001 (W) (SI 2001/2190) |
|  | (4) | 1 Jul 2001 (W) (SI 2001/2190) |
|  |  | 1 Jan 2002 (E) (in relation to certain applications)[8] (SI 2001/3852) |
|  |  | 1 Apr 2002 (E) (otherwise) (SI 2001/3852) |
| 24 |  | 1 Apr 2002 (E) (SI 2001/3852) |
|  |  | 1 Apr 2002 (W) (in relation to children's homes, independent hospitals, independent clinics and care homes) (SI 2002/920)[12] |
|  |  | 30 Jan 2003 (W) (in relation to residential family centres, fostering agencies and voluntary adoption agencies) (SI 2003/152)[14] |
|  |  | 2 Oct 2003 (W) (in relation to nurses agencies) (SI 2003/2528) |
|  |  | 1 Apr 2004 (W) (in relation to domiciliary care agencies) (SI 2004/1015) |
|  |  | 7 Jul 2004 (W) (so far as relates to regulations made under s 42, so far as not already in force) (SI 2004/1730) |
|  |  | *Not yet in force* (W) (in relation to an independent medical agency) |
| 25 |  | 1 Jul 2001 (W) (SI 2001/2190) |
|  |  | 20 Nov 2001 (E) (for the purpose only of the exercise of any power to make regulations) (SI 2001/3852) |
|  |  | 1 Apr 2002 (E) (otherwise) (SI 2001/3852) |
| 26 |  | 1 Apr 2002 (E) (SI 2001/3852) |
|  |  | 1 Apr 2002 (W) (in relation to children's homes, independent hospitals, independent clinics and care homes) (SI 2002/920)[12] |
|  |  | 30 Jan 2003 (W) (in relation to residential family centres, fostering agencies and voluntary adoption agencies) (SI 2003/152)[14] |
|  |  | 2 Oct 2003 (W) (in relation to nurses agencies) (SI 2003/2528) |
|  |  | 1 Apr 2004 (W) (in relation to domiciliary care agencies) (SI 2004/1015) |
|  |  | 7 Jul 2004 (W) (so far as relates to regulations made under s 42, so far as not already in force) (SI 2004/1730) |
|  |  | *Not yet in force* (W) (in relation to an independent medical agency) |
| 27 |  | 1 Jan 2002 (E) (in relation to certain applications)[8] (SI 2001/3852) |
|  |  | 1 Apr 2002 (E) (otherwise) (SI 2001/3852) |
|  |  | 1 Apr 2002 (W) (in relation to children's homes, independent hospitals, independent clinics and care homes) (SI 2002/920)[12] |
|  |  | 30 Jan 2003 (W) (in relation to residential family centres, fostering agencies and voluntary adoption agencies) (SI 2003/152)[14] |
|  |  | 2 Oct 2003 (W) (in relation to nurses agencies) (SI 2003/2528) |
|  |  | 1 Apr 2004 (W) (in relation to domiciliary care agencies) (SI 2004/1015) |
|  |  | 7 Jul 2004 (W) (so far as relates to regulations made under s 42, so far as not already in force) (SI 2004/1730) |
|  |  | *Not yet in force* (W) (in relation to an independent medical agency) |
| 28–30 |  | 1 Apr 2002 (E) (SI 2001/3852) |
|  |  | 1 Apr 2002 (W) (in relation to children's homes, independent hospitals, independent clinics and care homes) (SI 2002/920)[12] |
|  |  | 30 Jan 2003 (W) (in relation to residential family centres, fostering agencies and voluntary adoption agencies) (SI 2003/152)[14] |
|  |  | 2 Oct 2003 (W) (in relation to nurses agencies) (SI 2003/2528) |
|  |  | 1 Apr 2004 (W) (in relation to domiciliary care agencies) (SI 2004/1015) |

**Care Standards Act 2000 (c 14)**—*contd*

|   | |
|---|---|
|   | 7 Jul 2004 (W) (so far as they relate to regulations made under s 42, so far as not already in force) (SI 2004/1730) |
|   | *Not yet in force* (W) (in relation to an independent medical agency) |
| 31 | 20 Nov 2001 (E) (for the purpose only of the exercise of any power to make regulations) (SI 2001/3852) |
|   | 1 Jan 2002 (E) (for certain purposes)[9] (SI 2001/3852) |
|   | 1 Apr 2002 (E) (otherwise) (SI 2001/3852) |
|   | 1 Apr 2002 (W) (in relation to children's homes, independent hospitals, independent clinics and care homes) (SI 2002/920)[12] |
|   | 30 Jan 2003 (W) (in relation to residential family centres, fostering agencies and voluntary adoption agencies) (SI 2003/152)[14] |
|   | 2 Oct 2003 (W) (in relation to nurses agencies) (SI 2003/2528) |
|   | 1 Apr 2004 (W) (in relation to domiciliary care agencies) (SI 2004/1015) |
|   | 7 Jul 2004 (W) (so far as relates to regulations made under s 42, so far as not already in force) (SI 2004/1730) |
|   | *Not yet in force* (W) (in relation to an independent medical agency) |
| 32 | 1 Jan 2002 (E) (for certain purposes)[9] (SI 2001/3852) |
|   | 1 Apr 2002 (E) (otherwise) (SI 2001/3852) |
|   | 1 Apr 2002 (W) (in relation to children's homes, independent hospitals, independent clinics and care homes) (SI 2002/920)[12] |
|   | 30 Jan 2003 (W) (in relation to residential family centres, fostering agencies and voluntary adoption agencies) (SI 2003/152)[14] |
|   | 2 Oct 2003 (W) (in relation to nurses agencies) (SI 2003/2528) |
|   | 1 Apr 2004 (W) (in relation to domiciliary care agencies) (SI 2004/1015) |
|   | 7 Jul 2004 (W) (so far as relates to regulations made under s 42, so far as not already in force) (SI 2004/1730) |
|   | *Not yet in force* (W) (in relation to an independent medical agency) (sub-s (8) repealed) |
| 33–35 | 1 Jul 2001 (W) (SI 2001/2190) |
|   | 20 Nov 2001 (E) (for the purpose only of the exercise of any power to make regulations) (SI 2001/3852) |
|   | 1 Apr 2002 (E) (otherwise) (SI 2001/3852) |
| 36 | 1 Jul 2001 (W) (for purpose of enabling subordinate legislation to be made) (SI 2001/2190) |
|   | 20 Nov 2001 (E) (for the purpose only of the exercise of any power to make regulations) (SI 2001/3852) |
|   | 1 Apr 2002 (E) (otherwise) (SI 2001/3852) |
|   | 1 Apr 2002 (W) (in relation to children's homes, independent hospitals, independent clinics and care homes) (SI 2002/920)[12] |
|   | 30 Jan 2003 (W) (in relation to residential family centres, fostering agencies and voluntary adoption agencies) (SI 2003/152)[14] |
|   | 2 Oct 2003 (W) (in relation to nurses agencies) (SI 2003/2528) |
|   | 1 Apr 2004 (W) (in relation to domiciliary care agencies) (SI 2004/1015) |
|   | 7 Jul 2004 (W) (so far as relates to regulations made under s 42, so far as not already in force) (SI 2004/1730) |
|   | *Not yet in force* (W) (in relation to an independent medical agency) |
| 37 | 1 Apr 2002 (E) (SI 2001/3852) |
|   | 1 Apr 2002 (W) (in relation to children's homes, independent hospitals, independent clinics and care homes) (SI 2002/920)[12] |
|   | 30 Jan 2003 (W) (in relation to residential family centres, fostering agencies and voluntary adoption agencies) (SI 2003/152)[14] |
|   | 2 Oct 2003 (W) (in relation to nurses agencies) (SI 2003/2528) |
|   | 1 Apr 2004 (W) (in relation to domiciliary care agencies) (SI 2004/1015) |
|   | 7 Jul 2004 (W) (so far as relates to regulations made under s 42, so far as not already in force) (SI 2004/1730) |
|   | *Not yet in force* (W) (in relation to an independent medical agency) |

**Care Standards Act 2000 (c 14)**—*contd*

| | | |
|---|---|---|
| 38 | | 1 Jul 2001 (W) (SI 2001/2190) |
| | | 20 Nov 2001 (E) (SI 2001/3852) |
| 39 | | 19 Feb 2001 (E) (for purposes of enabling an application for registration to be made under Registered Homes Act 1984, s 23(3)) (SI 2001/290) |
| | | 19 Mar 2001 (E) (otherwise) (SI 2001/290) |
| | | 31 Jul 2001 (W) (for purposes of enabling an application for registration to be made under Registered Homes Act 1984, s 23(3)) (SI 2001/2504) |
| | | 31 Aug 2001 (W) (otherwise) (SI 2001/2504) |
| 40 | | 15 Oct 2000 (E) (for purposes of enabling application for registration to be made under Children Act 1989, Sch 6, para 1(1), (2)) (SI 2000/2795) |
| | | 1 Jan 2001 (E) (otherwise) (SI 2000/2795) |
| | | 1 Feb 2001 (W) (for purposes only of enabling application for registration to be made under Children Act 1989, Sch 6, para 1(1), (2)) (SI 2001/139) |
| | | 28 Feb 2001 (W) (otherwise) (SI 2001/139) |
| 41 | | 1 Jan 2001 (E) (SI 2000/2795) |
| | | 28 Feb 2001 (W) (SI 2001/139) |
| 42 | | 1 Jul 2001 (W) (SI 2001/2190) |
| | | 1 Sep 2003 (E) (SI 2003/933) |
| 43 | (1) | 1 Jul 2001 (W) (SI 2001/2190) |
| | | 20 Nov 2001 (E) (for the purpose only of the exercise of any power to make regulations, in so far as they relate to relevant fostering functions) (SI 2001/3852) |
| | | 1 Apr 2002 (E) (otherwise) (in so far as relates to relevant fostering functions) (SI 2001/3852) |
| | | 24 Feb 2003 (E) (for the purpose only of the exercise of any power to make regulations, in so far as they relate to relevant adoption functions) (SI 2003/365) |
| | | 30 Apr 2003 (E) (otherwise) (in so far as it relates to relevant adoption functions) (SI 2003/365) |
| | (2) | 1 Jul 2001 (W) (SI 2001/2190) |
| | | 20 Nov 2001 (E) (for the purpose only of the exercise of any power to make regulations, in so far as they relate to relevant fostering functions) (SI 2001/3852) |
| | | 1 Apr 2002 (E) (otherwise) (in so far as relates to relevant fostering functions) (SI 2001/3852) |
| | | 24 Feb 2003 (E) (for the purpose only of the exercise of any power to make regulations, in so far as they relate to relevant adoption functions) (SI 2003/365) |
| | | 30 Apr 2003 (E) (otherwise) (in so far as it relates to relevant adoption functions) (SI 2003/365) |
| | (3)(a) | 1 Jul 2001 (W) (SI 2001/2190) |
| | | 24 Feb 2003 (E) (for the purpose only of the exercise of any power to make regulations, in so far as they relate to relevant adoption functions) (SI 2003/365) |
| | | 30 Apr 2003 (E) (otherwise) (in so far as it relates to relevant adoption functions) (SI 2003/365) |
| | (3)(b) | 1 Jul 2001 (W) (SI 2001/2190) |
| | | 20 Nov 2001 (E) (for the purpose only of the exercise of any power to make regulations, in so far as they relate to relevant fostering functions) (SI 2001/3852) |
| | | 1 Apr 2002 (E) (otherwise) (in so far as relates to relevant fostering functions) (SI 2001/3852) |
| 44 | (1) | 1 Apr 2002 (E) (SI 2001/3852) |
| | | *Never in force* (otherwise) (repealed) |
| 45 | (1)–(3) | 1 Apr 2002 (E) (SI 2001/3852) |
| | | 30 Jan 2003 (W) (SI 2003/152) |

**Care Standards Act 2000 (c 14)**—*contd*

|   |   |   |
|---|---|---|
| | (4) | 20 Nov 2001 (E) (for the purpose only of the exercise of any power to make regulations, in so far as they relate to relevant fostering functions) (SI 2001/3852) |
| | | 1 Apr 2002 (E) (in so far as relates to relevant fostering functions) (SI 2001/3852) |
| | | 30 Jan 2003 (W) (SI 2003/152)[14] |
| | | 24 Feb 2003 (E) (for the purpose only of the exercise of any power to make regulations, in so far as they relate to relevant adoption functions) (SI 2003/365) |
| | | 30 Apr 2003 (E) (otherwise) (in so far as it relates to relevant adoption functions) (SI 2003/365) |
| | (5) | 1 Apr 2002 (E) (SI 2001/3852) |
| | | 30 Jan 2003 (W) (SI 2003/152) |
| 46 | (1)–(6) | 1 Apr 2002 (E) (SI 2001/3852) |
| | | 30 Jan 2003 (W) (SI 2003/152) |
| | (7)(a), (b) | 1 Apr 2002 (E) (SI 2001/3852) |
| | | 30 Jan 2003 (W) (SI 2003/152) |
| | (7)(c) | 30 Jan 2003 (W) (SI 2003/152) |
| | | *Never in force* (E) (repealed) |
| | (8) | 1 Apr 2002 (E) (SI 2001/3852) |
| | | 30 Jan 2003 (W) (SI 2003/152) |
| 47 | | 1 Apr 2002 (E) (SI 2001/3852) |
| | | *Never in force* (W) (repealed) |
| 48 | | 1 Jul 2001 (W) (SI 2001/2190) |
| | | 20 Nov 2001 (E) (for the purpose only of the exercise of any power to make regulations) (SI 2001/3852) |
| | | 1 Apr 2002 (E) (in so far as relates to relevant fostering functions) (SI 2001/3852) |
| 49 | | 1 Jul 2001 (W) (SI 2001/2190) |
| | | 20 Nov 2001 (E) (for the purpose only of issuing statements of national minimum standards so far as they relate to the exercise of relevant fostering functions by local authorities) (SI 2001/3852) |
| | | 1 Apr 2002 (E) (otherwise) (in so far as relates to relevant fostering functions) (SI 2001/3852) |
| | | 24 Feb 2003 (E) (for the purpose only of issuing statements of national minimum standards so far as they relate to the exercise of relevant adoption functions by local authorities) (SI 2003/365) |
| | | 30 Apr 2003 (E) (otherwise) (in so far as relates to relevant adoption functions) (SI 2003/365) |
| 50–52 | | 1 Jul 2001 (W) (SI 2001/2190) |
| | | 20 Nov 2001 (E) (for the purpose only of the exercise of any power to make regulations, in so far as they relate to relevant fostering functions) (SI 2001/3852) |
| | | 1 Apr 2002 (E) (in so far as they relate to relevant fostering functions) (otherwise) (SI 2001/3852) |
| | | *Not yet in force* (E) (so far as they relate to relevant adoption functions) (s 51 repealed) |
| 53 | | 1 Apr 2002 (E) (in so far as it relates to relevant fostering functions) (SI 2001/3852) |
| | | 30 Jan 2003 (W) (in so far as it relates to relevant fostering functions) (SI 2003/152)[14] |
| | | 30 Apr 2003 (E) (in so far as relates to relevant adoption functions) (SI 2003/365) |
| | | *Not yet in force* (W) (in so far as relates to relevant adoption functions) |
| 54 | (1)(a) | 7 May 2001 (SI 2001/1536) |
| | (1)(b) | 1 Apr 2001 (SI 2000/2992) |
| | (2) | 25 Mar 2002 (SI 2002/1245) |

**Care Standards Act 2000 (c 14)**—*contd*

|  |  |  |
|---|---|---|
|  | (3) | 1 Apr 2001 (SI 2000/2992) |
|  | (4), (5) | 1 Apr 2001 (W) (so far as relates to Care Council for Wales) (SI 2000/2992) |
|  |  | 7 May 2001 (E) (so far as relates to the General Social Care Council) (SI 2001/1536) |
|  | (6) | See Sch 1 below |
|  | (7)(a) | 7 May 2001 (SI 2001/1536) |
|  | (7)(b) | 1 Apr 2001 (SI 2000/2992) |
| 55 | (1) | 1 Apr 2001 (W) (SI 2000/2992) |
|  |  | 7 May 2001 (E) (so far as relates to ss 54(1)(a), (4)–(6), (7)(a), 59, 60, 62, 63, 65, 66, 71, Sch 1, paras 1–5, 7, 8, 12–14, 16, 18–26) (SI 2001/1536) |
|  |  | 25 Mar 2002 (E) (so far as relates to ss 54(2), 62, 63, 66, 67(1)–(5), (7), 71) (SI 2002/1245) |
|  |  | 7 Mar 2003 (E) (otherwise) (in so far as relates to the General Social Care Council) (SI 2003/933) |
|  | (2)(a) | 1 Apr 2001 (W) (SI 2000/2992) |
|  |  | 7 May 2001 (E) (so far as relates to ss 54(1)(a), (4)–(6), (7)(a), 59, 60, 62, 63, 65, 66, 71, Sch 1, paras 1–5, 7, 8, 12–14, 16, 18–26) (SI 2001/1536) |
|  |  | 25 Mar 2002 (E) (so far as relates to ss 54(2), 62, 63, 66, 67(1)–(5), (7), 71) (SI 2002/1245) |
|  |  | 7 Mar 2003 (E) (otherwise) (in so far as relates to the General Social Care Council) (SI 2003/933) |
|  | (2)(b)–(d) | 1 Apr 2001 (W) (SI 2000/2992) |
|  |  | 7 May 2001 (E) (so far as they relate to ss 54(1)(a), (4)–(6), (7)(a), 59, 60, 62, 63, 65, 66, 71, Sch 1, paras 1–5, 7, 8, 12–14, 16, 18–26) (SI 2001/1536) |
|  |  | 25 Mar 2002 (E) (so far as they relate to ss 54(2), 62, 63, 66, 67(1)–(5), (7), 71) (SI 2002/1245) |
|  |  | *Not yet in force* (E) (so far as they relate to provisions of Pt IV applying to England which are not listed above and remain in force) |
|  | (3)(a)–(f) | 1 Apr 2001 (W) (SI 2000/2992) |
|  |  | 7 May 2001 (E) (so far as they relate to ss 54(1)(a), (4)–(6), (7)(a), 59, 60, 62, 63, 65, 66, 71, Sch 1, paras 1–5, 7, 8, 12–14, 16, 18–26) (SI 2001/1536) |
|  |  | 25 Mar 2002 (E) (so far as they relate to ss 54(2), 62, 63, 66, 67(1)–(5), (7), 71) (SI 2002/1245) |
|  |  | *Not yet in force* (E) (so far as they relate to provisions of Pt IV applying to England which are not listed above and remain in force) |
|  | (3)(g) | 1 Apr 2001 (W) (SI 2000/2992) |
|  |  | 7 May 2001 (E) (so far as relates to ss 54(1)(a), (4)–(6), (7)(a), 59, 60, 62, 63, 65, 66, 71, Sch 1, paras 1–5, 7, 8, 12–14, 16, 18–26) (SI 2001/1536) |
|  |  | 25 Mar 2002 (E) (so far as relates to ss 54(2), 62, 63, 66, 67(1)–(5), (7), 71) (SI 2002/1245) |
|  |  | 1 Mar 2004 (E) (in so far as relates to s 56) (SI 2004/484) |
|  |  | *Not yet in force* (E) (so far as relates to provisions of Pt IV applying to England which are not listed above and remain in force) |
|  | (4) | 1 Apr 2001 (W) (SI 2000/2992) |
|  |  | 7 May 2001 (E) (so far as relates to ss 54(1)(a), (4)–(6), (7)(a), 59, 60, 62, 63, 65, 66, 71, Sch 1, paras 1–5, 7, 8, 12–14, 16, 18–26) (SI 2001/1536) |
|  |  | 25 Mar 2002 (E) (so far as relates to ss 54(2), 62, 63, 66, 67(1)–(5), (7), 71) (SI 2002/1245) |
|  |  | 7 Mar 2003 (E) (otherwise) (in so far as relates to the General Social Care Council) (SI 2003/933) |
|  | (5) | 1 Apr 2001 (W) (SI 2000/2992) |

**Care Standards Act 2000 (c 14)**—*contd*

|  |  |  |
|---|---|---|
|  |  | 7 May 2001 (E) (so far as relates to ss 54(1)(a), (4)–(6), (7)(a), 59, 60, 62, 63, 65, 66, 71, Sch 1, paras 1–5, 7, 8, 12–14, 16, 18–26) (SI 2001/1536) |
|  |  | 25 Mar 2002 (E) (so far as relates to ss 54(2), 62, 63, 66, 67(1)–(5), (7), 71) (SI 2002/1245) |
|  |  | *Not yet in force* (E) (so far as relates to provisions of Pt IV applying to England which are not listed above and remain in force) |
| 56 | (1)(a) | 30 Apr 2002 (W) (for the purpose only of the exercise of any power to make orders, regulations or rules or prepare and publish codes of practice) (SI 2002/1175) |
|  |  | 1 Apr 2003 (E) (in so far as relates to the General Social Care Council) (SI 2003/933) |
|  |  | 1 Jun 2003 (W) (otherwise) (SI 2003/501) |
|  | (1)(b) | 30 Apr 2002 (W) (for the purpose only of the exercise of any power to make orders, regulations or rules or prepare and publish codes of practice) (SI 2002/1175) |
|  |  | 1 Jun 2003 (W) (otherwise) (SI 2003/501) |
|  |  | 1 Mar 2004 (E) (in so far as relates to the General Social Care Council) (SI 2004/484) |
|  | (2)–(4) | 30 Apr 2002 (W) (for the purpose only of the exercise of any power to make orders, regulations or rules or prepare and publish codes of practice) (SI 2002/1175) |
|  |  | 1 Jun 2003 (W) (otherwise) (SI 2003/501) |
|  |  | 1 Mar 2004 (E) (in so far as they relate to the General Social Care Council) (SI 2004/484) |
| 57 |  | 30 Apr 2002 (W) (for the purpose only of the exercise of any power to make orders, regulations or rules or prepare and publish codes of practice) (SI 2002/1175) |
|  |  | 7 Mar 2003 (E) (in so far as relates to the General Social Council) (SI 2003/933) |
|  |  | 1 Apr 2003 (W) (otherwise) (SI 2003/501) |
| 58 |  | 30 Apr 2002 (W) (for the purpose only of the exercise of any power to make orders, regulations or rules or prepare and publish codes of practice) (SI 2002/1175) |
|  |  | 1 Apr 2003 (E) (in so far as relates to the General Social Care Council) (SI 2003/933) |
|  |  | 1 Jun 2003 (W) (otherwise) (SI 2003/501) |
| 59 |  | 7 May 2001 (E) (so far as relates to the General Social Care Council, for purpose only of the exercise of any power to make rules and prepare codes of practice) (SI 2001/1536) |
|  |  | 30 Apr 2002 (W) (for the purpose only of the exercise of any power to make orders, regulations or rules or prepare and publish codes of practice) (SI 2002/1175) |
|  |  | 1 Apr 2003 (E) (otherwise) (in so far as relates to the General Social Care Council) (SI 2003/933) |
|  |  | 1 Jun 2003 (W) (otherwise) (SI 2003/501) |
| 60 | (a) | 7 May 2001 (E) (so far as relates to the General Social Care Council, for purpose only of the exercise of any power to make rules and prepare codes of practice) (SI 2001/1536) |
|  |  | 30 Apr 2002 (W) (for the purpose only of the exercise of any power to make orders, regulations or rules or prepare and publish codes of practice) (SI 2002/1175) |
|  |  | 1 Apr 2003 (E) (otherwise) (in so far as relates to the General Social Care Council) (SI 2003/933) |
|  |  | 1 Jun 2003 (W) (otherwise) (SI 2003/501) |
|  | (b) | 7 May 2001 (E) (so far as relates to the General Social Care Council, for purpose only of the exercise of any power to make rules and prepare codes of practice) (SI 2001/1536) |
|  |  | 30 Apr 2002 (W) (for the purpose only of the exercise of any power to make orders, regulations or rules or prepare and publish codes of practice) (SI 2002/1175) |

**Care Standards Act 2000 (c 14)**—*contd*

|   |   |   |
|---|---|---|
|   |   | 1 Apr 2003 (W) (so far as relates to the documentary and other evidence to be produced by those applying for registration) (SI 2003/501) |
|   |   | 1 Apr 2003 (E) (otherwise) (in so far as relates to the General Social Care Council) (SI 2003/933) |
|   |   | 1 Jun 2003 (W) (otherwise) (SI 2003/501) |
|   | (c) | 7 May 2001 (E) (so far as relates to the General Social Care Council, for purpose only of the exercise of any power to make rules and prepare codes of practice) (SI 2001/1536) |
|   |   | 30 Apr 2002 (W) (for the purpose only of the exercise of any power to make orders, regulations or rules or prepare and publish codes of practice) (SI 2002/1175) |
|   |   | 1 Apr 2003 (E) (otherwise) (in so far as relates to the General Social Care Council) (SI 2003/933) |
|   |   | 1 Jun 2003 (W) (otherwise) (SI 2003/501) |
| 61 | (1) | 30 Apr 2002 (W) (for the purpose only of the exercise of any power to make orders, regulations or rules or prepare and publish codes of practice) (SI 2002/1175) |
|   |   | 1 Apr 2005 (otherwise) (SI 2005/375) |
|   | (2)(a) | 30 Apr 2002 (W) (for the purpose only of the exercise of any power to make orders, regulations or rules or prepare and publish codes of practice) (SI 2002/1175) |
|   |   | 1 Apr 2005 (otherwise) (SI 2005/375) |
|   | (2)(b) | 30 Apr 2002 (W) (for the purpose only of the exercise of any power to make orders, regulations or rules or prepare and publish codes of practice) (SI 2002/1175) |
|   |   | 1 Mar 2005 (E) (for the purpose only of the exercise of the power to make regulations) (SI 2005/375) |
|   |   | 1 Apr 2005 (otherwise) (SI 2005/375) |
|   | (3) | 30 Apr 2002 (W) (for the purpose only of the exercise of any power to make orders, regulations or rules or prepare and publish codes of practice) (SI 2002/1175) |
|   |   | 1 Apr 2005 (otherwise) (SI 2005/375) |
| 62 |   | 7 May 2001 (E) (so far as relates to the General Social Care Council, for purpose only of the exercise of any power to make rules and prepare codes of practice) (SI 2001/1536) |
|   |   | 25 Mar 2002 (E) (otherwise, so far as relates to the General Social Care Council) (SI 2002/1245) |
|   |   | 30 Apr 2002 (W) (for the purpose only of the exercise of any power to make orders, regulations or rules or prepare and publish codes of practice) (SI 2002/1175) |
|   |   | 1 Jun 2003 (W) (otherwise) (SI 2003/501) |
| 63 |   | 7 May 2001 (E) (so far as relates to the General Social Care Council, for purpose only of the exercise of any power to make rules and prepare codes of practice) (SI 2001/1536) |
|   |   | 31 Jul 2001 (W) (SI 2001/2538) |
|   |   | 25 Mar 2002 (E) (otherwise) (so far as relates to the General Social Care Council) (SI 2002/1245) |
| 64 | (1)(a) | *Never in force* (repealed) |
|   | (1)(b) | 1 Apr 2003 (E) (in so far as relates to the General Social Care Council) (SI 2003/933) |
|   | (2) | 30 Apr 2002 (W) (for the purpose only of the exercise of any power to make orders, regulations or rules or prepare and publish codes of practice) (SI 2002/1175) |
|   |   | 1 Jun 2003 (W) (otherwise) (SI 2003/501) |
|   | (3), (4) | 30 Apr 2002 (W) (for the purpose only of the exercise of any power to make orders, regulations or rules or prepare and publish codes of practice) (SI 2002/1175) |
|   |   | 1 Jun 2003 (W) (otherwise) (SI 2003/501) |
|   |   | *Never in force* (E) (repealed) |
|   | (5) | 1 Jun 2003 (W) (SI 2003/501) |

**Care Standards Act 2000 (c 14)**—*contd*

*Never in force* (E) (repealed)

| | | |
|---|---|---|
| 65 | | 7 May 2001 (E) (so far as relates to the General Social Care Council, for purpose only of the exercise of any power to make rules and prepare codes of practice) (SI 2001/1536) |
| | | 30 Apr 2002 (W) (for the purpose only of the exercise of any power to make orders, regulations or rules or prepare and publish codes of practice) (SI 2002/1175) |
| | | 1 Apr 2003 (E) (otherwise) (in so far as relates to the General Social Care Council) (SI 2003/933) |
| | | 1 Jun 2003 (W) (otherwise) (SI 2003/501) |
| 66 | | 7 May 2001 (E) (so far as relates to the General Social Care Council, for purpose only of the exercise of any power to make rules and prepare codes of practice) (SI 2001/1536) |
| | | 31 Jul 2001 (W) (SI 2001/2538) |
| | | 25 Mar 2002 (E) (otherwise) (so far as relates to the General Social Care Council) (SI 2002/1245) |
| 67 | (1)–(4) | 1 Oct 2001 (W) (SI 2001/2538) |
| | | 25 Mar 2002 (E) (so far as they confer functions on the Secretary of State) (SI 2002/1245) |
| | (5) | 1 Oct 2001 (W) (SI 2001/2538) |
| | | 25 Mar 2002 (E) (SI 2002/1245) |
| | (6) | 1 Oct 2001 (W) (SI 2001/2538) |
| | (7) | 1 Oct 2001 (W) (SI 2001/2538) |
| | | 25 Mar 2002 (E) (so far as relates to s 67(5) and the Secretary of State) (SI 2002/1245) |
| 68, 69 | | 1 Apr 2003 (E) (in so far as they relate to the General Social Care Council) (SI 2003/933) |
| | | 1 Jun 2003 (W) (SI 2003/501) |
| 70 | (1) | 1 Oct 2001 (W) (SI 2001/2538) |
| | | 1 Apr 2002 (E) (SI 2002/1245) |
| | (2)–(5) | 20 Jul 2000 (RA) |
| 71 | | 7 May 2001 (E) (so far as relates to the General Social Care Council, for purpose only of the exercise of any power to make rules and prepare codes of practice) (SI 2001/1536) |
| | | 31 Jul 2001 (W) (so far as it applies to ss 63, 66 of this Act) (SI 2001/2538) |
| | | 25 Mar 2002 (E) (otherwise, so far as relates to the General Social Care Council) (SI 2002/1245) |
| | | 30 Apr 2002 (W) (otherwise) (SI 2002/1175) |
| 72 | | 13 Nov 2000 (SI 2000/2992) |
| 73–78 | | 26 Aug 2001 (SI 2001/2782) |
| 79 | (1) | 16 Mar 2001 (E) (for the purpose of enabling the Secretary of State to make regulations under Children Act 1989, ss 79C(1), 79E(2)(a), 79F(1)(b), (2)(b), 79H(1), 79N(5), 79Q(2), (3), 79R(1), (3)(b), 79V, 79W(4)) (SI 2001/1210) |
| | | 1 Jul 2001 (W) (for purpose of enabling subordinate legislation to be made under a provision inserted by it into Children Act 1989 and for purposes of inserting Children Act 1989, s 79B(2), (9) (to the extent necessary for the purposes of enabling subordinate legislation to be made under Sch 9A to the 1989 Act)) (SI 2001/2190) |
| | | 2 Jul 2001 (E) (except for the purposes of Pt XA, ss 79B(8), 79K(5), 79L(6), (7), 79M, 79P(1)–(4), 79Q(2), (3)) (SI 2001/2041) |
| | | 1 Apr 2002 (E) (for purpose of giving effect to Pt XA, ss 79B(8), 79K(5), 79L(6), (7), 79M) (SI 2002/839) |
| | | 1 Apr 2002 (W) (otherwise) (SI 2002/920)[12] |
| | | 2 Sep 2002 (E) (for purpose of giving effect to Pt XA, ss 79P(1), (2), 79Q(2), (3)) (SI 2001/2041) |

**Care Standards Act 2000 (c 14)**—*contd*

|  |  |  |
|---|---|---|
|  |  | 2 Sep 2002 (E) (for purpose of giving effect to Pt XA, s 79P(3), (4)(a)–(c)) (SI 2002/2215) |
|  |  | *Never in force* (E) (in so far as relates to Pt XA, s 79P(4)(d)) (spent) |
|  | (2) | See Sch 3 below |
|  | (3), (4) | 16 Mar 2001 (E) (SI 2001/1210) |
|  |  | 1 Jul 2001 (W) (SI 2001/2190) |
|  | (5) | 2 Jul 2001 (E) (SI 2001/2041) |
|  |  | 1 Apr 2002 (W) (SI 2002/920)[12] |
| 80 | (1) | 26 Jul 2004 (SI 2004/1757) |
|  | (2)(a) | 26 Jul 2004 (SI 2004/1757) |
|  | (2)(b) | *Never in force* (repealed) |
|  | (2)(c) | 26 Jul 2004 (SI 2004/1757) |
|  | (3) | 26 Jul 2004 (in so far as relates to positions mentioned in sub-s (2)(a), (c)) (SI 2004/1757) |
|  |  | *Never in force* (in so far as relates to positions mentioned in sub-s (2)(b), (d)) (repealed) |
|  | (4), (5) | 26 Jul 2004 (SI 2004/1757) |
|  | (6)(a), (b) | 26 Jul 2004 (SI 2004/1757) |
|  | (6)(c) | *Never in force* (repealed) |
|  | (7)(a), (b) | 26 Jul 2004 (SI 2004/1757) |
|  | (7)(c), (d) | *Never in force* (repealed) |
|  | (8) | 2 Oct 2000 (for purposes only of regulations under s 103 of this Act) (SI 2000/2544) |
|  |  | 26 Jul 2004 (otherwise) (SI 2004/1757) |
| 81–90 |  | 26 Jul 2004 (SI 2004/1757) |
| 91 |  | *Never in force* (repealed) |
| 92, 93 |  | 26 Jul 2004 (SI 2004/1757) |
| 94 |  | 2 Oct 2000 (SI 2000/2544) |
| 95 |  | 1 Apr 2002 (E) (SI 2002/1493) |
|  |  | 1 Apr 2002 (W) (SI 2002/920)[12] |
| 96 |  | 15 Sep 2000 (so far as inserts Protection of Children Act 1999, s 2B, for purposes only of definition "relevant enquiry" in s 3(7) of 1999 Act) (SI 2000/2544) |
|  |  | 2 Oct 2000 (otherwise) (SI 2000/2544) |
| 97 |  | 26 Jul 2004 (SI 2004/1757) |
| 98 |  | 1 Apr 2001 (E) (SI 2001/1193) |
|  |  | 1 Jul 2001 (W) (SI 2001/2354) |
| 99 |  | 15 Sep 2000 (SI 2000/2544) |
| 100, 101 |  | 2 Oct 2000 (SI 2000/2544) |
| 102 |  | 18 Mar 2002 (E) (W) (SI 2002/629) |
|  |  | *Never in force* (S) (NI) (repealed) |
| 103 |  | 2 Oct 2000 (SI 2000/2544) |
| 104 | (1) | See sub-ss (2)–(3) below |
|  | (2)(a) | 18 Mar 2002 (E) (W) (SI 2002/629) |
|  |  | *Never in force* (S) (NI) (repealed) |
|  | (2)(b) | 18 Mar 2002 (E) (W) (except so far as inserts Police Act 1997, s 113(3E)(a), (b)) (SI 2002/629) |
|  |  | 1 Apr 2002 (E) (W) (in so far as inserts Police Act 1997, s 113(3E)(a)) (SI 2002/629) |
|  |  | 1 Apr 2003 (W) (in so far as inserts Police Act 1997, s 113(3E)(b)) (SI 2003/501) |
|  |  | 1 Apr 2003 (E) (otherwise) (in so far as relates to the General Social Care Council) (SI 2003/933) |
|  | (3)(a)(i) | 1 Apr 2002 (E) (W) (in so far as inserts Police Act 1997, s 115(5)(ea)) (SI 2002/629) |
|  |  | 1 Apr 2003 (W) (in so far as inserts Police Act 1997, s 115(5)(eb)) (SI 2003/501) |
|  |  | 1 Apr 2003 (E) (otherwise) (in so far as relates to the General Social Care Council) (SI 2003/933) |
|  | (3)(a)(ii) | 18 Mar 2002 (E) (W) (SI 2002/629) |

**Care Standards Act 2000 (c 14)**—*contd*

|  |  |  |
|---|---|---|
|  |  | *Never in force* (S) (NI) (repealed) |
|  | (3)(b) | 18 Mar 2002 (E) (W) (SI 2002/629) |
|  |  | *Never in force* (S) (NI) (repealed) |
| 105 | (1)–(4) | 20 Nov 2001 (E) (for the purpose only of the exercise of any power to make regulations) (SI 2001/3852) |
|  |  | 1 Apr 2002 (E) (otherwise) (SI 2001/3852) |
|  |  | 1 Feb 2003 (W) (SI 2003/152)[14] |
|  | (5) | 1 Apr 2002 (E) (SI 2001/3852) |
|  |  | 1 Feb 2003 (W) (SI 2003/152)[14] |
| 106 |  | 1 Apr 2002 (E) (SI 2001/3852) |
|  |  | 1 Feb 2003 (W) (SI 2003/152)[14] |
| 107 |  | 1 Jul 2001 (W) (SI 2001/2190) |
|  |  | 20 Nov 2001 (E) (for the purpose only of issuing statements of national minimum standards for safeguarding and promoting the welfare of children for whom accommodation is provided in schools and colleges) (SI 2001/3852) |
|  |  | 1 Apr 2002 (E) (otherwise) (SI 2001/3852) |
| 108 |  | 1 Jul 2001 (W) (SI 2001/2190) |
|  |  | 20 Nov 2001 (E) (for the purpose only of the exercise of any power to make regulations) (SI 2001/3852) |
|  |  | 1 Apr 2002 (E) (otherwise) (SI 2001/3852) |
| 109 |  | 1 Apr 2002 (E) (SI 2001/3852) |
|  |  | *Not yet in force* (W) |
| 110 |  | 1 Apr 2002 (E) (SI 2001/3852) |
|  |  | 1 Apr 2002 (W) (SI 2002/920)[12] |
| 111 | (1) | 1 Apr 2003 (E) (SI 2001/3852) |
|  |  | 2 Oct 2003 (W) (SI 2003/2528) |
|  | (2) | 1 Apr 2003 (E) (in so far as it omits Employment Agencies Act 1973, s 13(7)(b), (c), and the proviso thereto) (SI 2001/3852) |
|  |  | 2 Oct 2003 (W) (in so far as it omits Employment Agencies Act 1973, s 13(7)(b), (c), and the proviso thereto) (SI 2003/2528) |
|  |  | *Not yet in force* (E) (W) (in so far as it substitutes Employment Agencies Act 1973, s 13(8)) |
| 112 |  | 1 Jul 2001 (W) (SI 2001/2190) |
|  |  | 4 Oct 2001 (E) (SI 2001/3331) |
| 113 | (1) | 25 Mar 2002 (E) (so far as confers power on the Secretary of State in relation to the functions of the General Social Care Council) (SI 2002/1245) |
|  | (2) | 1 Apr 2001 (SI 2000/2992) |
|  | (3), (4) | 1 Apr 2001 (W) (so far as they relate to Care Council for Wales) (SI 2000/2992) |
|  |  | 25 Mar 2002 (E) (so far as they confer power on the Secretary of State in relation to the functions of the General Social Care Council) (SI 2002/1245) |
|  |  | *Not yet in force* (so far as they relate to the National Care Standards Commission) |
| 114 |  | 16 Mar 2001 (E) (SI 2001/1210) |
|  |  | 1 Apr 2001 (W) (so far as relates to an Order in Council, or a recommendation to Her Majesty to make an Order in Council, under s 70 containing a scheme for the transfer of staff from the Central Council for Education and Training in Social Work to the Care Council for Wales) (SI 2000/2992) |
|  |  | 1 Jul 2001 (W) (otherwise) (SI 2001/2190) |
|  |  | *Not yet in force* (S) (NI) |
| 115 |  | 16 Mar 2001 (E) (SI 2001/1210) |
|  |  | 1 Jul 2001 (W) (SI 2001/2190) |
|  |  | *Not yet in force* (S) (NI) |
| 116 |  | See Sch 4 below |

**Care Standards Act 2000 (c 14)**—*contd*

| | | |
|---|---|---|
| 117 | (1) | See Sch 5 below |
| | (2) | See Sch 6 below |
| 118–123 | | 20 Jul 2000 (RA) |
| Sch 1 | para 1 | 16 Mar 2001 (E) (so far as relates to the National Care Standards Commission) (SI 2001/1193) |
| | | 1 Apr 2001 (W) (so far as relates to Care Council for Wales) (SI 2000/2992) |
| | | 7 May 2001 (E) (so far as relates to the General Social Care Council) (SI 2001/1536) |
| | paras 2–5 | 1 Apr 2001 (W) (so far as they relate to the Care Council for Wales) (SI 2000/2992) |
| | | 9 Apr 2001 (E) (so far as they relate to the National Care Standards Commission) (SI 2001/1193) |
| | | 7 May 2001 (E) (so far as they relate to the General Social Care Council) (SI 2001/1536) |
| | para 6 | 16 Mar 2001 (E) (so far as relates to the National Care Standards Commission) (SI 2001/1193) |
| | | 1 Apr 2001 (W) (so far as relates to Care Council for Wales) (SI 2000/2992) |
| | | 10 Apr 2001 (E) (so far as relates to the General Social Care Council) (SI 2001/1536) |
| | paras 7, 8 | 1 Apr 2001 (W) (so far as they relate to Care Council for Wales) (SI 2000/2992) |
| | | 9 Apr 2001 (E) (so far as they relate to the National Care Standards Commission) (SI 2001/1193) |
| | | 7 May 2001 (E) (so far as they relate to the General Social Care Council) (SI 2001/1536) |
| | paras 9–11 | 1 Apr 2001 (SI 2001/1193) |
| | paras 12–14 | 1 Apr 2001 (W) (so far as they relate to Care Council for Wales) (SI 2000/2992) |
| | | 9 Apr 2001 (E) (so far as they relate to the National Care Standards Commission) (SI 2001/1193) |
| | | 7 May 2001 (E) (so far as they relate to the General Social Care Council) (SI 2001/1536) |
| | para 15 | 1 Apr 2001 (SI 2001/1193) |
| | para 16 | 1 Apr 2001 (W) (so far as relates to Care Council for Wales) (SI 2000/2992) |
| | | 9 Apr 2001 (E) (so far as relates to the National Care Standards Commission) (SI 2001/1193) |
| | | 7 May 2001 (E) (so far as relates to the General Social Care Council) (SI 2001/1536) |
| | para 17 | 1 Apr 2001 (SI 2001/1193) |
| | paras 18–26 | 1 Apr 2001 (W) (so far as they relate to Care Council for Wales) (SI 2000/2992) |
| | | 9 Apr 2001 (E) (so far as they relate to the National Care Standards Commission) (SI 2001/1193) |
| | | 7 May 2001 (E) (so far as they relate to the General Social Care Council) (SI 2001/1536) |
| | para 27 | 1 Apr 2001 (SI 2000/2992) |
| Sch 2 | | 13 Nov 2000 (SI 2000/2992) |
| Sch 3 | | 16 Mar 2001 (E) (for the purpose of enabling the Secretary of State to make regulations under Children Act 1989, Sch 9A, paras 1(1), 4(1), (3), 6(2), (4), 7) (SI 2001/1210) |
| | | 1 Jul 2001 (W) (for the purpose of enabling subordinate legislation to be made under Children Act 1989, Sch 9A) (SI 2001/2190) |
| | | 2 Jul 2001 (E) (otherwise) (SI 2001/2041)[4] |
| | | 1 Apr 2002 (W) (otherwise) (SI 2002/920)[12] |
| Sch 4 | paras 1–4 | 1 Apr 2002 (E) (SI 2001/4150) |
| | | 1 Apr 2002 (W) (SI 2002/920)[12] |
| | | *Not yet in force* (S) (paras 2, 3 repealed) |

**Care Standards Act 2000 (c 14)**—*contd*

| | |
|---|---|
| para 5(1) | 1 Apr 2002 (E) (SI 2001/4150) |
| | 1 Apr 2002 (W) (SI 2002/920)[12] |
| para 5(2)(a) | 30 Jan 2003 (W) (SI 2003/152)[15] |
| | 30 Apr 2003 (E) (SI 2003/365) |
| para 5(2)(b) | 30 Jan 2003 (W) (SI 2003/152)[15] |
| | 24 Feb 2003 (E) (for the purpose only of the exercise of any power to make regulations) (SI 2003/365) |
| | 30 Apr 2003 (E) (otherwise) (SI 2003/365) |
| para 5(3) | 1 Apr 2002 (E) (SI 2001/4150) |
| | 1 Apr 2002 (W) (SI 2002/920)[12] |
| para 5(4), (5) | 30 Jan 2003 (W) (SI 2003/152)[15] |
| | 30 Apr 2003 (E) (SI 2003/365) |
| para 5(6)(a)–(c) | 1 Jul 2001 (W) (SI 2001/2190) |
| | 24 Feb 2003 (E) (for the purpose only of the exercise of any power to make regulations) (SI 2003/365) |
| | 30 Apr 2003 (E) (otherwise) (SI 2003/365) |
| para 5(6)(d) | 1 Jul 2001 (W) (SI 2001/2190) |
| | *Never in force* (otherwise) (repealed) |
| para 5(7)(a) | 30 Jan 2003 (W) (SI 2003/152)[15] |
| | 30 Apr 2003 (E) (SI 2003/365) |
| para 5(7)(b) | *Never in force* (repealed) |
| para 5(8) | 1 Apr 2002 (E) (SI 2001/4150) |
| | 1 Apr 2002 (W) (SI 2002/920)[12] |
| para 5(9)–(11) | 30 Jan 2003 (W) (SI 2003/152)[15] |
| | 30 Apr 2003 (E) (SI 2003/365) |
| para 6 | *Never in force* (repealed) |
| para 7 | 2 Jul 2001 (E) (SI 2001/2041) |
| | 1 Apr 2002 (W) (SI 2002/920)[12] |
| | *Never in force* (S) (repealed) |
| para 8 | 1 Apr 2002 (E) (SI 2001/4150) |
| | 1 Apr 2002 (W) (SI 2002/920)[12] |
| | *Never in force* (S) (repealed) |
| para 9 | 1 Apr 2002 (E) (SI 2001/4150) |
| | 1 Apr 2002 (W) (SI 2002/920)[12] |
| | *Not yet in force* (S) |
| para 10 | 1 Apr 2002 (E) (SI 2001/4150) |
| para 11 | 1 Apr 2002 (E) (SI 2001/4150) |
| | 1 Apr 2002 (W) (SI 2002/920)[12] |
| | *Not yet in force* (S) |
| para 12 | *Not yet in force* |
| para 13 | 2 Jul 2001 (E) (SI 2001/2041) |
| | 1 Apr 2002 (W) (SI 2002/920)[12] |
| | *Never in force* (S) (NI) (repealed) |
| para 14(1), (2) | 2 Jul 2001 (E) (SI 2001/2041) |
| | 1 Apr 2002 (W) (SI 2002/920)[12] |
| para 14(3) | 1 Apr 2002 (E) (SI 2001/4150) |
| | 1 Apr 2002 (W) (SI 2002/920)[12] |
| para 14(4)–(6) | *Never in force* (repealed) |
| para 14(7)–(9) | 1 Apr 2002 (E) (SI 2001/4150) |
| | 1 Apr 2002 (W) (SI 2002/920)[12] |
| para 14(10)(a) | 1 Apr 2002 (E) (SI 2001/4150) |
| | 1 Apr 2002 (W) (SI 2002/920)[12] |
| para 14(10)(b) | *Not yet in force* |
| para 14(11), (12) | 1 Apr 2002 (E) (SI 2001/4150) |
| | 1 Apr 2002 (W) (SI 2002/920)[12] |
| para 14(13), (14) | 1 Apr 2002 (E) (SI 2002/1493)[11] |
| | 1 Apr 2002 (W) (SI 2002/920)[12] |
| para 14(15) | 1 Jan 2001 (E) (SI 2000/2795) |
| | 28 Feb 2001 (W) (SI 2001/139) |

**Care Standards Act 2000 (c 14)**—*contd*

| | |
|---|---|
| para 14(16)(a) | 1 Apr 2002 (E) (SI 2001/4150) |
| | 1 Apr 2002 (W) (SI 2002/920)[12] |
| para 14(16)(b) | 2 Jul 2001 (E) (SI 2001/2041) |
| | 1 Apr 2002 (W) (SI 2002/920)[12] |
| para 14(16)(c) | 1 Apr 2002 (E) (SI 2001/4150) |
| | 1 Apr 2002 (W) (SI 2002/920)[12] |
| para 14(16)(d) | 2 Jul 2001 (E) (SI 2001/2041) |
| | 1 Apr 2002 (W) (SI 2002/920)[12] |
| para 14(17)–(20) | 1 Apr 2002 (E) (SI 2001/4150) |
| | 1 Apr 2002 (W) (SI 2002/920)[12] |
| para 14(21) | 1 Apr 2002 (E) (SI 2001/4150) |
| | 1 Feb 2003 (W) (SI 2003/152)[17] |
| para 14(22) | 1 Apr 2002 (W) (SI 2002/920)[12] |
| | *Not yet in force* (E) |
| para 14(23)(a) (i)–(iii) | 1 Apr 2002 (E) (SI 2001/4150) |
| | 1 Apr 2002 (W) (SI 2002/920)[12] |
| para 14(23)(a)(iv), (v) | 2 Jul 2001 (E) (SI 2001/2041) |
| | 1 Apr 2002 (W) (SI 2002/920)[12] |
| para 14(23)(a)(vi), (vii) | 1 Apr 2002 (E) (SI 2001/4150) |
| | 1 Apr 2002 (W) (SI 2002/920)[12] |
| para 14(23)(b) | 2 Jul 2001 (E) (SI 2001/2041) |
| | 1 Apr 2002 (W) (SI 2002/920)[12] |
| para 14(24)–(28) | 1 Apr 2002 (E) (SI 2001/4150) |
| | 1 Apr 2002 (W) (SI 2002/920)[12] |
| para 14(29) | 1 Apr 2002 (W) (SI 2002/920)[12] |
| | *Never in force* (E) (spent) |
| paras 15–18 | 1 Apr 2002 (E) (SI 2001/4150) |
| | 1 Apr 2002 (W) (SI 2002/920)[12] |
| para 19 | 2 Jul 2001 (E) (SI 2001/2041) |
| | 1 Apr 2002 (W) (SI 2002/920)[12] |
| para 20 | 1 Apr 2002 (E) (SI 2001/4150) |
| | 1 Apr 2002 (W) (SI 2002/920)[12] |
| para 21 | 1 Apr 2002 (E) (except words "and vulnerable adults") (SI 2001/4150) |
| | 1 Apr 2002 (W) (except words "and vulnerable adults") (SI 2002/920)[12] |
| | *Never in force* (E) (W) (words "and vulnerable adults") (repealed) |
| para 22 | *Never in force* (spent) |
| para 23 | 1 Apr 2002 (E) (SI 2001/4150) |
| | *Not yet in force* (W) (S) |
| para 24(1), (2) | 1 Apr 2002 (E) (SI 2001/4150) |
| | 1 Apr 2002 (W) (SI 2002/920)[12] |
| | *Never in force* (S) (repealed) |
| para 24(3), (4) | *Never in force* (repealed) |
| para 25 | 2 Jul 2001 (E) (SI 2001/2041) |
| | 1 Apr 2002 (W) (SI 2002/920)[12] |
| | *Never in force* (S) (NI) (repealed) |
| para 26(1), (2)[3] | 2 Oct 2000 (SI 2000/2544) |
| para 26(3) | 1 Apr 2002 (E) (except in so far as it inserts Protection of Children Act 1999, s 9(2)(b) and 9(2)(d) (in so far as s 9(2)(d) relates to ss 68, 87, 88 of the 2000 Act) and s 9(3A)) (SI 2001/3852) |
| | 1 Apr 2002 (W) (except in so far as it inserts Protection of Children Act 1999, s 9(2)(b) and 9(2)(d) (in so far as s 9(2)(d) relates to ss 68, 87, 88 of the 2000 Act) and s 9(3A)) (SI 2002/920)[12] |

**Care Standards Act 2000 (c 14)**—*contd*

|  |  |  |
|---|---|---|
|  |  | 5 Mar 2003 (W) (in so far as it inserts Protection of Children Act 1999, s 9(2)(d) in so far as it relates to s 68 of the 2000 Act) (SI 2003/501) |
|  |  | 7 Mar 2003 (E) (in so far as it inserts Protection of Children Act 1999, s 9(2)(d) in so far as it relates to s 68 of the 2000 Act) (SI 2003/933) |
|  |  | 26 Jul 2004 (otherwise) (SI 2004/1757) |
|  | para 26(4) | 2 Oct 2000 (SI 2000/2544) |
|  | para 27 | 1 Jun 2003 (E) (SI 2003/365) |
|  |  | 30 Apr 2003 (W) (SI 2003/501) |
|  | para 28 | 1 Apr 2002 (E) (SI 2001/4150) |
|  |  | 1 Apr 2002 (W) (SI 2002/920)[12] |
|  | paras 29, 30 | 1 Apr 2002 (E) (SI 2001/4150) |
| Sch 5 | para 1 | 1 Jul 2001 (W) (SI 2001/2190) |
|  |  | *Not yet in force* (E) |
|  | para 2 | 1 Jul 2001 (W) (for purpose of enabling subordinate legislation to be made) (SI 2001/2190) |
|  |  | 30 Jan 2003 (W) (otherwise) (SI 2003/152)[15] |
|  |  | *Not yet in force* (E) |
|  | para 3 | 26 Aug 2001 (SI 2001/2782) |
| Sch 6 |  | 2 Oct 2000 (repeals of or in Protection of Children Act 1999, ss 10, 13(3), (4)) (SI 2000/2544) |
|  |  | 4 Oct 2001 (E) (repeals of or in Chronically Sick and Disabled Persons Act 1970, s 18(1), (3)) (SI 2001/3331) |

1 Apr 2002 (E) (SI 2001/3852), repeals of or in—
Registered Homes Act 1984;
Children Act 1989, ss 60, 63, Schs 5, 6

1 Apr 2002 (E) (SI 2001/4150), repeals of or in—
National Assistance Act 1948;
London Government Act 1963;
Local Authority Social Services Act 1970;
Greater London Council (General Powers) Act 1981;
Mental Health Act 1983;
Greater London Council (General Powers) Act 1984;
Public Health (Control of Disease) Act 1984;
Children Act 1989 (in so far as not already in force, except definition "child minder" in s 105(1));
National Health Service and Community Care Act 1990;
Registered Homes (Amendment) Act 1991;
Arbitration Act 1996;
Education Act 1996;
Nurses, Midwives and Health Visitors Act 1997

1 Apr 2002 (W) (SI 2002/920)[12], repeals of or in—
National Assistance Act 1948;
Local Authority Social Services Act 1970;
Chronically Sick and Disabled Persons Act 1970, s 18(1), (3);
Mental Health Act 1983;
Registered Homes Act 1984;
Children Act 1989;
National Health Service and Community Care Act 1990;
Registered Homes (Amendment) Act 1991;
Arbitration Act 1996;
Education Act 1996;
Nurses, Midwives and Health Visitors Act 1997

30 Jan 2003 (W) (repeals of or in Adoption Act 1976) (SI 2003/152)[14]

1 Apr 2003 (E) (SI 2001/3852), repeals of or in—
Nurses Agencies Act 1957;
Employment Agencies Act 1973

**Care Standards Act 2000 (c 14)**—*contd*

> 1 Apr 2003 (E) (SI 2001/4150), repeals of or in—
> Local Government Act 1972;
> Nurses, Midwives and Health Visitors Act 1979
> 30 Apr 2003 (E) (repeals of or in Adoption Act 1976)
> (SI 2003/365)
> 30 Apr 2003 (W) (repeals of or in Adoption (Intercountry Aspects)
> Act 1999) (SI 2003/501)
> 1 Jun 2003 (E) (repeals of or in Adoption (Intercountry Aspects)
> Act 1999) (SI 2003/365)
> 2 Oct 2003 (W) (SI 2003/2528), repeals of or in—
> Nurses Agencies Act 1957;
> Employment Agencies Act 1973
> *Not yet in force* (E), repeals of or in—
> Public Records Act 1958, Sch 1;
> Chronically Sick and Disabled Persons Act 1970, s 18(2);
> Health and Social Services and Social Security Adjudication
> Act 1983, Sch 2, para 29;
> Children Act 1989, s 105(1) (definition "child minder");
> Tribunals and Inquiries Act 1992, Sch 1;
> Judicial Pensions and Retirement Act 1993, Sch 5, Sch 6,
> para 55, Sch 7, para 5(5)(xxxi);
> Protection of Children Act 1999, ss 2(9), 7(2), 12(1)
> *Not yet in force* (W), repeals of or in—
> Public Records Act 1958, Sch 1;
> London Government Act 1963, s 40;
> Chronically Sick and Disabled Persons Act 1970, s 18(2);
> Local Government Act 1972, Sch 29, para 30;
> Nurses, Midwives and Health Visitors Act 1979, Sch 7,
> paras 8–10;
> Health and Social Services and Social Security Adjudication
> Act 1983, Sch 2, para 29;
> Public Health (Control of Disease) Act 1984, s 7(4);
> Tribunals and Inquiries Act 1992, Sch 1;
> Judicial Pensions and Retirement Act 1993, Sch 5, Sch 6,
> para 55, Sch 7, para 5(5)(xxxi);
> Local Government (Wales) Act 1994, Sch 9, para 5;
> Protection of Children Act 1999, ss 2(9), 7(2), 12(1)
> *Not yet in force* (S)

[1]   For transitional provisions, see SI 2001/139, art 3

[2]   For transitional provisions, see SI 2001/290, art 3

[3]   The Queen's Printer's copy of the Care Standards Act 2000, Sch 4, para 26, contains 2 sub-paras (2)

[4]   For transitional, transitory and savings provisions, see SI 2001/2041, art 3, Schedule

[5]   For transitional provisions, see SI 2001/2504, art 3

[6]   For transitional provisions, see SI 2001/3852, Schs 1, 2

[7]   The specified purposes are—

(a)   to enable the Commission to consider or obtain information in relation to an application within note 8 below;

(b)   to enable the Commission to determine such an application, except for the purpose of enabling any effect to be given to the determination of any such application before—

(i)   in the case of an application to which paragraph 13(2) of Sch 1 to SI 2001/3852 applies, 1 Apr 2003;

(ii)   in the case of an application to which paragraph 14(2) of Sch 1 applies, 1 Sep 2002;

(iii)   in the case of an application for registration under the Care Standards Act 2000, Pt II in respect of a residential family centre, a nurses agency or a domiciliary care agency, 1 Apr 2003;

**Care Standards Act 2000 (c 14)**—*contd*

    (iv)   in the case of any other application 1 Apr 2001

8    The relevant applications are—

(a)   an application which is to be determined by the Commission by virtue of Sch 1, para 1 or 14 to SI 2001/3852;

(b)   an application for registration under Part II of the 2000 Act in respect of an establishment or an agency referred to in para 15(1) or (2) of Sch 1 to SI 2001/3852 and which is made by a person to whom that paragraph applies

9    The relevant purposes are—

(a)   an application to which note 8 above applies;

(b)   an establishment or agency to which Sch 1, para 5(2) and (3) apply

10    For transitional provisions, see SI 2001/4150, art 4

11    For transitional provisions, see SI 2002/1493, art 4

12    For transitional provisions, see SI 2002/920, arts 2, 3(2), (4)–(10), Schs 1–3

13    For transitional provisions, see SI 2002/3210, art 4

14    For transitional provisions, see SI 2003/152, art 3

15    For transitional provisions, see SI 2003/365, art 2, Schedule

16    The specified purposes are—

(a)   to enable the Commission to consider or obtain information—

(i)   about an existing provider for the purposes of SI 2003/365, Schedule, para 2;

(ii)   in relation to an application that is to be determined by the Commission by virtue of SI 2003/365, Schedule, para 6

(b)   to enable the Commission to determine an application for registration for the purposes of the Care Standards Act 2000, Pt II, in respect of a voluntary organisation that is not an existing agency, except for the purpose of enabling any effect to be given to the determination of such an application before 30 Apr 2003

17    SI 2003/152, art 2(2) purports to bring Sch 4, para 21 into force in relation to Wales on 1 Feb 2003. It is thought that the intention was in fact to bring Sch 4, para 14(21) into force on that date

---

**Carers and Disabled Children Act 2000 (c 16)**

*RA:* 20 Jul 2000

*Commencement provisions:* s 12(2)–(4); Carers and Disabled Children Act 2000 (Commencement No 1) (England) Order 2001, SI 2001/510; Carers and Disabled Children Act 2000 (Commencement No 1) (Wales) Order 2001, SI 2001/2196; Carers and Disabled Children Act 2000 (Commencement No 2) (England) Order 2003, SI 2003/1183

| | | |
|---|---|---|
| 1, 2 | | 1 Apr 2001 (E) (SI 2001/510) |
| | | 1 Jul 2001 (W) (SI 2001/2196) |
| 3 | | 30 Apr 2003 (E) (SI 2003/1183) |
| | | *Never in force* (repealed) (W) |
| 4–6 | | 1 Apr 2001 (E) (SI 2001/510) |
| | | 1 Jul 2001 (W) (SI 2001/2196) |
| 7 | (1) | 30 Apr 2003 (E) (so far as inserts Children Act 1989, s 17B) (SI 2003/1183) |
| | | *Never in force* (repealed) (W) (so far as inserts Children Act 1989, s 17B) |
| | (2), (3) | 1 Apr 2001 (E) (SI 2001/510) |
| | | 1 Jul 2001 (W) (SI 2001/2196) |
| 8 | | 1 Apr 2001 (E) (SI 2001/510) |
| | | 1 Jul 2001 (W) (SI 2001/2196) |
| 9 | | 1 Apr 2001 (E) (except so far as relates to provision of vouchers) (SI 2001/510) |

**Carers and Disabled Children Act 2000 (c 16)**—*contd*

|   |   | 1 Jul 2001 (W) (except so far as relates to provision of vouchers) (SI 2001/2196) |
|---|---|---|
|   |   | 30 Apr 2003 (E) (exception noted above) (SI 2003/1183) |
|   |   | *Never in force* (repealed) (W) (exception noted above) |
| 10 |   | 1 Apr 2001 (E) (SI 2001/510) |
|   |   | 1 Jul 2001 (W) (SI 2001/2196) |
| 11 | (1)–(3) | 1 Apr 2001 (E) (SI 2001/510) |
|   |   | 1 Jul 2001 (W) (SI 2001/2196) |
|   | (4) | 1 Apr 2001 (E) (SI 2001/510) |
| 12 |   | 20 Jul 2000 (RA) |

**Census (Amendment) Act 2000 (c 24)**

*RA:* 28 Jul 2000

Whole Act in force 28 Jul 2000 (RA)

**Census (Amendment) (Scotland) Act 2000 (asp 3)**

*RA:* 10 Apr 2000

Whole Act in force 10 Apr 2000 (RA)

**Children (Leaving Care) Act 2000 (c 35)**

*RA:* 30 Nov 2000

*Commencement provisions:* s 8(2)–(5); Children (Leaving Care) Act 2000 (Commencement No 1) (England) Order 2001, SI 2001/2878; Children (Leaving Care) Act 2000 (Commencement No 2 and Consequential Provisions) Order 2001, SI 2001/3070, as amended by SI 2006/217; Children (Leaving Care) Act 2000 (Commencement) (Wales) Order 2001, SI 2001/2191

| 1–3 |   | 1 Oct 2001 (E) (SI 2001/2878) |
|---|---|---|
|   |   | 1 Oct 2001 (W) (SI 2001/2191) |
| 4 |   | 1 Oct 2001 (E) (SI 2001/2878) |
|   |   | 1 Oct 2001 (W) (except so far as Children Act 1989, s 24C(2) relates to Primary Care Trusts) (SI 2001/2191) |
| 5 |   | 1 Oct 2001 (E) (SI 2001/2878) |
|   |   | 1 Oct 2001 (W) (SI 2001/2191) |
| 6 |   | 10 Sep 2001 (for the purpose of making Regulations) (SI 2001/3070) |
|   |   | 1 Oct 2001 (otherwise) (SI 2001/3070) |
| 7 | (1)–(4) | 1 Oct 2001 (E) (SI 2001/2878) |
|   |   | 1 Oct 2001 (W) (SI 2001/2191) |
|   | (5) | 30 Nov 2000 (RA) |
| 8 |   | 30 Nov 2000 (RA) |

**Child Support, Pensions and Social Security Act 2000 (c 19)**

*RA:* 28 Jul 2000

*Commencement provisions:* s 86; Child Support, Pensions and Social Security Act 2000 (Commencement No 1) Order 2000, SI 2000/2666; Child Support, Pensions and Social Security Act 2000 (Commencement No 2) Order 2000, SI 2000/2950, as amended by SI 2000/3166; Child Support, Pensions and Social Security Act 2000 (Commencement No 3) Order 2000, SI 2000/2994, Child Support, Pensions and Social Security Act 2000 (Commencement No 4) Order 2000, SI 2000/3166, as amended by SI 2001/1252; Child Support, Pensions and Social Security Act 2000 (Commencement No 5) Order 2000, SI 2000/3354; Child Support, Pensions and Social Security Act 2000 (Commencement No 6) Order 2001, SI 2001/153; Child Support, Pensions and Social Security

**Child Support, Pensions and Social Security Act 2000 (c 19)**—*contd*

Act 2000 (Commencement No 7) Order 2001, SI 2001/774; Child Support, Pensions and Social Security Act 2000 (Commencement No 8) Order 2001, SI 2001/1252; Child Support, Pensions and Social Security Act 2000 (Commencement No 9) Order 2001, SI 2001/2295, as amended by SI 2002/437; Child Support, Pensions and Social Security Act 2000 (Commencement No 10) Order 2001, SI 2001/2619; Child Support, Pensions and Social Security Act 2000 (Commencement No 11) Order 2002, SI 2002/437; Child Support, Pensions and Social Security Act 2000 (Commencement No 12) Order 2003, SI 2003/192, as amended by SI 2003/346; Child Support, Pensions and Social Security Act 2000 (Commencement No 13) Order 2003, SI 2003/346; Child Support, Pensions and Social Security Act 2000 (Commencement No 14) Order 2008, SI 2008/2545; Child Support, Pensions and Social Security Act 2000 (Commencement No 15) Order 2014, SI 2014/1263

| | | |
|---|---|---|
| 1 | (1), (2) | 3 Mar 2003 (for certain purposes[2]) (SI 2003/192) |
| | | *Not yet in force* (otherwise) |
| | (3) | See Sch 1 below |
| 2 | (1), (2) | 4 Feb 2003 (for the purpose of making regulations) (SI 2003/192) |
| | | 3 Mar 2003 (otherwise) (for certain purposes[2]) (SI 2003/192) |
| | | *Not yet in force* (otherwise) |
| | (3) | 3 Mar 2003 (for certain purposes[2]) (SI 2003/192) |
| | | *Not yet in force* (otherwise) |
| 3 | | 10 Nov 2000 (for purpose of making regulations and Acts of Sederunt) (SI 2000/2994) |
| | | 3 Mar 2003 (otherwise) (for certain purposes[3]) (SI 2003/192) |
| | | *Never in force* (otherwise). (repealed) |
| 4, 5 | | 10 Nov 2000 (for purpose of making regulations and Acts of Sederunt) (SI 2000/2994) |
| | | 3 Mar 2003 (otherwise) (for certain purposes[2]) (SI 2003/192) |
| | | *Not yet in force* (otherwise) |
| 6 | | See Sch 2 below |
| 7 | | 10 Nov 2000 (except in so far as it relates to s 28G(2)) (for the purpose of making regulations and Acts of Sederunt) (SI 2000/2994) |
| | | 10 Nov 2000 (in so far as it relates to s 28G(2)) (for purpose of making regulations) (SI 2000/2994) |
| | | 1 Jan 2001 (in so far as it relates to s 28G(2)) (for all other purposes) (SI 2000/2994) |
| | | 3 Mar 2003 (otherwise) (for certain purposes[2]) (SI 2003/192) |
| | | *Not yet in force* (in so far as it relates to s 28G(1), (3), except for the purpose of making regulations and Acts of Sederunt and for certain purposes[2]) |
| 8 | | 3 Mar 2003 (for certain purposes[2]) (SI 2003/192) |
| | | *Not yet in force* (otherwise) |
| 9, 10 | | 10 Nov 2000 (for purpose of making regulations and Acts of Sederunt) (SI 2000/2994) |
| | | 3 Mar 2003 (for certain purposes[2]) (SI 2003/192) |
| | | *Not yet in force* (otherwise) |
| 11 | | 15 Feb 2001 (SI 2000/3354) |
| 12 | | 3 Mar 2003 (for certain purposes[2]) (SI 2003/192) |
| | | 26 Sep 2008 (otherwise) (SI 2008/2545) |
| 13–15 | | 31 Jan 2001 (SI 2000/3354) |
| 16, 17 | | 10 Nov 2000 (for purpose of making regulations and Acts of Sederunt) (SI 2000/2994) |
| | | 2 Apr 2001 (otherwise) (SI 2000/3354) |
| 18–21 | | 10 Nov 2000 (for purpose of making regulations and Acts of Sederunt) (SI 2000/2994) |
| | | 3 Mar 2003 (otherwise) (for certain purposes[2]) (SI 2003/192) |
| | | *Not yet in force* (otherwise) (s 19 repealed) |
| 22 | (1), (2) | 31 Jan 2001 (SI 2000/3354) |
| | (3) | 10 Nov 2000 (for purpose of making regulations and Acts of Sederunt) (SI 2000/2994) |
| | | 31 Jan 2001 (otherwise) (SI 2000/3354) |

**Child Support, Pensions and Social Security Act 2000 (c 19)**—*contd*

|       |          |                                                                                                                                                      |
|-------|----------|------------------------------------------------------------------------------------------------------------------------------------------------------|
|       | (4)      | 3 Mar 2003 (for certain purposes[2]) (SI 2003/192)                                                                                                    |
|       |          | *Not yet in force* (otherwise)                                                                                                                        |
| 23    |          | 3 Mar 2003 (for certain purposes[5]) (SI 2003/192)                                                                                                    |
|       |          | 27 Oct 2008 (otherwise) (SI 2008/2545)                                                                                                                |
| 24    |          | 28 Jul 2000 (RA)                                                                                                                                      |
| 25    |          | 10 Nov 2000 (for purpose of making regulations and Acts of Sederunt) (SI 2000/2994)                                                                   |
|       |          | 3 Mar 2003 (otherwise) (for certain purposes[2]) (SI 2003/192)                                                                                        |
|       |          | 15 May 2014 (otherwise) (SI 2014/1263)                                                                                                                |
| 26    |          | See Sch 3 below                                                                                                                                       |
| 27    |          | 10 Nov 2000 (for purpose of making regulations) (SI 2000/2994)                                                                                        |
|       |          | 1 Jan 2001 (otherwise) (SI 2000/2994)                                                                                                                 |
| 28    |          | *Never in force* (repealed)                                                                                                                           |
| 29    |          | 10 Nov 2000 (for purpose of making regulations and Acts of Sederunt) (SI 2000/2994)                                                                   |
|       |          | 3 Mar 2003 (otherwise) (SI 2003/192)                                                                                                                  |
| 30, 31 |         | 8 Jan 2001 (for purposes of making regulations and of making an order appointing the first or second appointed year) (SI 2000/2950)                   |
|       |          | 25 Jan 2001 (for purposes of making reports and orders under Pension Schemes Act 1993, ss 42, 42B and 45A) (SI 2001/153)                              |
|       |          | 6 Apr 2002 (otherwise) (SI 2001/153)                                                                                                                  |
| 32    |          | 8 Jan 2001 (for purposes of making regulations and of making an order appointing the first or second appointed year) (SI 2000/2950)                   |
|       |          | 9 Apr 2001 (otherwise) (SI 2001/153)                                                                                                                  |
| 33    | (1), (2) | 8 Jan 2001 (for purposes of making regulations and of making an order appointing the first or second appointed year) (SI 2000/2950)                   |
|       |          | 25 Jan 2001 (for purposes of an order under Social Security Administration Act 1992, s 148A, as inserted by Child Support, Pensions and Social Security Act 2000, s 33(1)) (SI 2001/153) |
|       |          | 6 Apr 2002 (otherwise) (SI 2001/153)                                                                                                                  |
|       | (3), (4) | 8 Jan 2001 (for purposes of making regulations and of making an order appointing the first or second appointed year) (SI 2000/2950)                   |
|       |          | 25 Jan 2001 (otherwise) (SI 2001/153)                                                                                                                 |
| 34, 35 |         | 8 Jan 2001 (for purposes of making regulations and of making an order appointing the first or second appointed year) (SI 2000/2950)                   |
|       |          | 25 Jan 2001 (for purposes of making reports and orders under Pension Schemes Act 1993, ss 42, 42B and 45A) (SI 2001/153)                              |
|       |          | 6 Apr 2002 (otherwise) (SI 2001/153)                                                                                                                  |
| 36    |          | 1 Nov 2000 (SI 2000/2950)                                                                                                                             |
| 37    |          | 1 Dec 2000 (SI 2000/3166)                                                                                                                             |
| 38, 39 |         | 28 Jul 2000 (RA)                                                                                                                                      |
| 40    |          | 8 Jan 2001 (SI 2000/3166)                                                                                                                             |
| 41    |          | 29 Sep 2000 (SI 2000/2666)                                                                                                                            |
| 42    |          | 1 Dec 2000 (for purposes of authorising the making of regulations) (SI 2000/3166)                                                                    |
|       |          | 1 Jan 2001 (otherwise) (SI 2000/3166)                                                                                                                 |
| 43–46 |          | *Never in force* (repealed)                                                                                                                           |
| 47, 48 |         | 1 Mar 2002 (for the purpose of making regulations and rules) (SI 2002/437)                                                                            |
|       |          | 1 Apr 2002 (otherwise) (SI 2002/437)                                                                                                                  |
| 49    | (1)      | 1 Mar 2002 (so far as it inserts Pensions Act 1995, s 72A(1), (2), (3) (except for words "Subject to subsection (4)," and "(apart from any postponement under subsection (4))"), (7), (8)(a), (9) (for the purpose of making regulations and rules)) (SI 2002/437) |

## Child Support, Pensions and Social Security Act 2000 (c 19)—*contd*

|  |  |  |
|---|---|---|
|  |  | 1 Apr 2002 (so far as it inserts Pensions Act 1995, s 72A(1), (2), (3) (except for words "Subject to subsection (4)," and "(apart from any postponement under subsection (4))"), (7), (8)(a), (9) (otherwise)) (SI 2002/437) |
|  |  | *Not yet in force* (so far as it inserts Pensions Act 1995, s 72A(3) (words "Subject to subsection (4)," and "(apart from any postponement under subsection (4))"), (4)–(6), (8)(b), (c)) |
|  | (2), (3) | 1 Mar 2002 (for the purpose of making regulations and rules) (SI 2002/437) |
|  |  | 1 Apr 2002 (otherwise) (SI 2002/437) |
| 50 |  | 1 Mar 2002 (for the purpose of making regulations and rules) (SI 2002/437) |
|  |  | 1 Apr 2002 (otherwise) (SI 2002/437) |
| 51 |  | 1 Dec 2000 (SI 2000/3166) |
| 52 |  | 1 Jan 2001 (except so far as inserts Pension Schemes Act 1993, s 113(3B)) (SI 2000/3166) |
|  |  | *Not yet in force* (exception noted above) |
| 53 |  | 1 Dec 2000 (SI 2000/3166) |
| 54 |  | 1 Mar 2002 (for the purpose of making regulations and rules) (SI 2002/437) |
|  |  | *Never in force* (otherwise) (repealed) |
| 55 |  | 23 Jul 2001 (SI 2001/2295) |
| 56 |  | See Sch 5 below |
| 57, 58 |  | 15 Nov 2000 (for purpose of the exercise of the power to make regulations) (SI 2000/2994) |
|  |  | 9 Apr 2001 (for all other purposes) (SI 2000/2994) |
| 59 |  | 1 Jan 2001 (SI 2000/2994) |
| 60 |  | 9 Apr 2001 (SI 2000/2994) |
| 61 |  | 1 Jan 2001 (SI 2000/2994) |
| 62 | (1)–(10) | 1 Dec 2000 (for the purposes of making regulations) (SI 2000/2950) |
|  |  | 15 Oct 2001 (in so far as not already in force, for the purposes of its application to any person who, as a result of a relevant community order (as defined in s 62(8) of this Act) being made in accordance with s 64(1) of this Act in relation to him, falls to be supervised by an officer of the local probation board for any of the probation areas of Derbyshire, Hertfordshire, Teesside and West Midlands) (SI 2001/2619) |
|  |  | *Never in force* (otherwise) (repealed) |
|  | (11) | 1 Dec 2000 (for the purposes of making regulations) (SI 2000/2950) |
|  |  | *Never in force* (otherwise) (repealed) |
| 63 |  | 1 Dec 2000 (for the purposes of making regulations) (SI 2000/2950) |
|  |  | 15 Oct 2001 (in so far as not already in force, for the purposes of its application to any person who, as a result of a relevant community order (as defined in s 62(8) of this Act) being made in accordance with s 64(1) of this Act in relation to him, falls to be supervised by an officer of the local probation board for any of the probation areas of Derbyshire, Hertfordshire, Teesside and West Midlands) (SI 2001/2619) |
|  |  | *Never in force* (otherwise) (repealed) |
| 64 | (1), (2) | 1 Dec 2000 (for the purposes of making regulations) (SI 2000/2950) |
|  |  | 15 Oct 2001 (for the purposes of its application to any person who, as a result of a relevant community order (as defined in s 62(8) of this Act) being made in accordance with s 64(1) of this Act in relation to him, falls to be supervised by an officer of the local probation board for any of the probation areas of Derbyshire, Hertfordshire, Teesside and West Midlands) (SI 2001/2619) |

**Child Support, Pensions and Social Security Act 2000 (c 19)**—*contd*

| | |
|---|---|
| | *Never in force* (otherwise) (repealed) |
| (3) | 1 Dec 2000 (for the purposes of making regulations) (SI 2000/2950) |
| | *Never in force* (otherwise) (repealed) |
| (4)(a) | 1 Dec 2000 (for the purposes of making regulations) (SI 2000/2950) |
| | 15 Oct 2001 (in so far as not already in force, for the purposes of its application to any person who, as a result of a relevant community order (as defined in s 62(8) of this Act) being made in accordance with s 64(1) of this Act in relation to him, falls to be supervised by an officer of the local probation board for any of the probation areas of Derbyshire, Hertfordshire, Teesside and West Midlands) (SI 2001/2619) |
| | *Never in force* (otherwise) (repealed) |
| (4)(b) | 1 Dec 2000 (for the purposes of making regulations) (SI 2000/2950) |
| | *Never in force* (otherwise) (repealed) |
| (5), (6) | 1 Dec 2000 (for the purposes of making regulations) (SI 2000/2950) |
| | 15 Oct 2001 (in so far as not already in force, for the purposes of its application to any person who, as a result of a relevant community order (as defined in s 62(8) of this Act) being made in accordance with s 64(1) of this Act in relation to him, falls to be supervised by an officer of the local probation board for any of the probation areas of Derbyshire, Hertfordshire, Teesside and West Midlands) (SI 2001/2619) |
| | *Never in force* (otherwise) (repealed) |
| (7)(a)–(c) | 1 Dec 2000 (for the purposes of making regulations) (SI 2000/2950) |
| | 15 Oct 2001 (in so far as not already in force, for the purposes of its application to any person who, as a result of a relevant community order (as defined in s 62(8) of this Act) being made in accordance with s 64(1) of this Act in relation to him, falls to be supervised by an officer of the local probation board for any of the probation areas of Derbyshire, Hertfordshire, Teesside and West Midlands) (SI 2001/2619) |
| | *Never in force* (otherwise) (repealed) |
| (7)(d) | 1 Dec 2000 (for the purposes of making regulations) (SI 2000/2950) |
| | *Never in force* (otherwise) (repealed) |
| (8) | 1 Dec 2000 (for the purposes of making regulations) (SI 2000/2950) |
| | 15 Oct 2001 (in so far as not already in force, for the purposes of its application to any person who, as a result of a relevant community order (as defined in s 62(8) of this Act) being made in accordance with s 64(1) of this Act in relation to him, falls to be supervised by an officer of the local probation board for any of the probation areas of Derbyshire, Hertfordshire, Teesside and West Midlands) (SI 2001/2619) |
| | *Never in force* (otherwise) (repealed) |
| (9) | 1 Dec 2000 (for the purposes of making regulations) (SI 2000/2950) |
| | *Never in force* (otherwise) (repealed) |
| (10) | 1 Dec 2000 (for the purposes of making regulations) (SI 2000/2950) |

**Child Support, Pensions and Social Security Act 2000 (c 19)**—*contd*

15 Oct 2001 (in so far as not already in force, for the purposes of its application to any person who, as a result of a relevant community order (as defined in s 62(8) of this Act) being made in accordance with s 64(1) of this Act in relation to him, falls to be supervised by an officer of the local probation board for any of the probation areas of Derbyshire, Hertfordshire, Teesside and West Midlands) (SI 2001/2619)

*Never in force* (otherwise) (repealed)

(11)      1 Dec 2000 (for the purposes of making regulations) (SI 2000/2950)

*Never in force* (otherwise) (repealed)

65    (1)–(6)    1 Dec 2000 (for the purposes of making regulations) (SI 2000/2950)

15 Oct 2001 (in so far as not already in force, for the purposes of its application to any person who, as a result of a relevant community order (as defined in s 62(8) of this Act) being made in accordance with s 64(1) of this Act in relation to him, falls to be supervised by an officer of the local probation board for any of the probation areas of Derbyshire, Hertfordshire, Teesside and West Midlands) (SI 2001/2619)

*Never in force* (otherwise) (repealed)

(7)      1 Dec 2000 (for the purposes of making regulations) (SI 2000/2950)

*Never in force* (otherwise) (repealed)

(8)      1 Dec 2000 (for the purposes of making regulations) (SI 2000/2950)

15 Oct 2001 (in so far as not already in force, for the purposes of its application to any person who, as a result of a relevant community order (as defined in s 62(8) of this Act) being made in accordance with s 64(1) of this Act in relation to him, falls to be supervised by an officer of the local probation board for any of the probation areas of Derbyshire, Hertfordshire, Teesside and West Midlands) (SI 2001/2619)

*Never in force* (otherwise) (repealed)

66      15 Oct 2001 (for the purposes of its application to any person who, as a result of a relevant community order (as defined in s 62(8) of this Act) being made in accordance with s 64(1) of this Act in relation to him, falls to be supervised by an officer of the local probation board for any of the probation areas of Derbyshire, Hertfordshire, Teesside and West Midlands) (SI 2001/2619)

*Never in force* (otherwise) (repealed)

67      See Sch 6 below

68      See Sch 7 below

69      1 Nov 2000 (SI 2000/2950) (for purposes of making regulations)
       2 Jul 2001 (otherwise) (SI 2001/1252)

70      26 Jun 2001 (for the purpose of making an order) (SI 2001/2295)
       2 Jul 2001 (otherwise) (SI 2001/2295)

71      1 Nov 2000 (for purposes of making regulations) (SI 2000/2950)
       1 Oct 2001 (otherwise) (SI 2001/2295)

72      9 Oct 2000 (SI 2000/2666)

73      1 Nov 2000 (SI 2000/2950) (so far as inserts into Social Security Administration Act 1992, s 170(5), new para (af) into definitions "relevant enactments" and "relevant Northern Ireland enactments", so far as each new para (af) refers to—

         (i)   s 69;

         (ii)   Sch 7, paras 3, 4, 6, 8–10, 12–16, 19–21, 23 and so far as relating to those paras, para 1 and s 68)

**Child Support, Pensions and Social Security Act 2000 (c 19)**—*contd*

|  |  |  |
|---|---|---|
|  |  | 1 Dec 2000 (for purpose of insertion of Social Security Administration Act 1992, s 170(5), para (af) into definitions "relevant enactments" and "relevant Northern Ireland enactments" so far as each new para (af) refers to ss 62–65) (SI 2000/2950) |
|  |  | 1 Dec 2000 (for purpose of insertion of Social Security Administration Act 1992, s 170(5), para (af) into each definition of "relevant enactments" and "relevant Northern Ireland enactments", so far as each new para (af) refers to s 42) (SI 2000/3166) |
|  |  | *Not yet in force* (so far as inserts into Social Security Administration Act 1992, s 170(5), new para (af) into definitions "relevant enactments" and "relevant Northern Ireland enactments", so far as each new para (af) refers to— |
|  |  | (i)  s 70; |
|  |  | (ii)  Sch 7, paras 2, 5, 7, 11, 17, 18, 22 and so far as relating to those paras, para 1 and s 68) |
| 74–81 |  | 28 Jul 2000 (RA) |
| 82, 83 |  | 1 Apr 2001 (SI 2001/774) |
| 84 |  | 28 Jul 2000 (RA) |
| 85 |  | See Sch 9 below |
| 86, 87 |  | 28 Jul 2000 (RA) |
| Schs 1, 2 |  | 10 Nov 2000 (for purpose of making regulations and Acts of Sederunt) (SI 2000/2994) |
|  |  | 3 Mar 2003 (for certain purposes[2]) (SI 2003/192) |
|  |  | *Not yet in force* (otherwise) |
| Sch 3 | paras 1–10 | 3 Mar 2003 (for certain purposes[2]) (SI 2003/192) |
|  |  | *Not yet in force* (otherwise) (para 8(2) repealed) |
|  | para 11(1) | 3 Mar 2003 (for certain purposes[2]) (SI 2003/192) |
|  |  | *Not yet in force* (otherwise) |
|  | para 11(2) | 31 Jan 2001 (in so far as affects Child Support Act 1991, s 3(2), for the purposes of ss 15(4A), 44(2A) of the 1991 Act, as inserted respectively by ss 14 and 22(3), and s 44(1) of that Act amended by s 22(2)) (SI 2000/3354) |
|  |  | 3 Mar 2003 (otherwise) (for certain purposes[2]) (SI 2003/192) |
|  |  | *Not yet in force* (so far as it changes "absent parent" to "non-resident parent" in the Child Support Act 1991, other than in ss 15(4A) and 44(1), (2A) of that Act and for certain purposes[2]) |
|  | para 11(3) | 3 Mar 2003 (for certain purposes[2]) (SI 2003/192) |
|  |  | *Not yet in force* (otherwise) (sub-para (b) repealed) |
|  | para 11(4)(a) | 3 Mar 2003 (for certain purposes[2]) (SI 2003/192) |
|  |  | *Never in force* (otherwise) (repealed) |
|  | para 11(4)(b)(i), (ii) | 4 Feb 2003 (for the purpose of making regulations) (SI 2003/192) |
|  |  | 3 Mar 2003 (otherwise) (for certain purposes[2]) (SI 2003/192) |
|  |  | *Not yet in force* (otherwise) |
|  | para 11(4)(b)(iii) | 3 Mar 2003 (for certain purposes[2]) (SI 2003/192) |
|  |  | *Not yet in force* (otherwise) |
|  | para 11(5)–(14) | 3 Mar 2003 (for certain purposes[2]) (SI 2003/192) |
|  |  | *Not yet in force* (otherwise) (repealed in part) |
|  | para 11(15) | 3 Mar 2003 (SI 2003/192) |
|  | para 11(16) | 3 Mar 2003 (for certain purposes[2]) (SI 2003/192) |
|  |  | 26 Sep 2008 (for the purpose of making regulations) (SI 2008/2545) |
|  |  | 27 Oct 2008 (otherwise) (SI 2008/2545) |
|  | para 11(17) | 1 Jan 2001 (SI 2000/2994) |
|  | para 11(18) | 10 Nov 2000 (for purpose of making regulations and Acts of Sederunt) (SI 2000/2994) |
|  |  | 3 Mar 2003 (otherwise) (for certain purposes[2]) (SI 2003/192) |
|  |  | *Not yet in force* (otherwise) |
|  | para 11(19)–(22) | 3 Mar 2003 (for certain purposes[2]) (SI 2003/192) |

**Child Support, Pensions and Social Security Act 2000 (c 19)**—*contd*

|  |  |  |
|---|---|---|
|  |  | *Not yet in force* (otherwise) (sub-para (22)(b) repealed) |
|  | para 12 | 3 Mar 2003 (for certain purposes²) (SI 2003/192) |
|  |  | *Not yet in force* (otherwise) |
|  | para 13(1) | 2 Apr 2001 (SI 2001/1252) |
|  | para 13(2) | 3 Mar 2003 (for certain purposes²) (SI 2003/192) |
|  |  | *Not yet in force* (otherwise) |
|  | para 13(3) | 2 Apr 2001 (SI 2001/1252) |
|  | paras 14, 15 | 3 Mar 2003 (for certain purposes²) (SI 2003/192) |
|  |  | *Not yet in force* (otherwise) |
| Sch 4 |  | 8 Jan 2001 (for purposes of making regulations and of making an order appointing the first or second appointed year) (SI 2000/2950) |
|  |  | 25 Jan 2001 (for purposes of making reports and orders under Pension Schemes Act 1993, ss 42, 42B and 45A) (SI 2001/153) |
|  |  | 6 Apr 2002 (otherwise) (SI 2001/153) |
| Sch 5 | paras 1–3 | 1 Jan 2001 (SI 2000/3166) |
|  | paras 4–6 | 28 Jul 2000 (RA) |
|  | para 7 | 1 Jan 2001 (SI 2000/3166) |
|  | para 8(1) | 28 Jul 2000 (RA) |
|  | para 8(2) | 1 Jan 2001 (SI 2000/3166) |
|  | para 8(3), (4) | 28 Jul 2000 (RA) |
|  | para 9 | 1 Jan 2001 (SI 2000/3166) |
|  | para 10 | 1 Nov 2000 (SI 2000/2950) |
|  | para 11 | 2 Apr 2001 (SI 2001/1252) |
|  | para 12(1) | 1 Jan 2001 (SI 2000/3166) |
|  | para 12(2)–(4) | *Never in force* (repealed) |
|  | para 13 | 28 Jul 2000 (RA) |
|  | paras 14–17 | 12 Feb 2001 (for purposes of authorising making of regulations and orders) (SI 2000/3166) |
|  |  | *Never in force* (repealed) |
| Sch 6 | para 1 | See paras 2–8 below |
|  | paras 2–6 | 2 Apr 2001 (SI 2001/1252) |
|  | para 7 | 1 Nov 2000 (SI 2000/2950) |
|  | para 8 | 1 Nov 2000 (SI 2000/2950) (so far as inserts Social Security Administration Act 1992, s 121DA(1), (7) for purpose of construing s 113 of that Act, as amended by para 7) |
|  |  | 2 Apr 2001 (otherwise) (SI 2001/1252) |
|  | para 9 | 2 Apr 2001 (SI 2001/1252) |
| Sch 7 | para 1 | 1 Nov 2000 (SI 2000/2950) (so far as relates to paras 3, 4, 6, 8–10, 12–16, 19–21, 23 of this Schedule, for purposes of making regulations) |
|  |  | 2 Jul 2001 (otherwise) (SI 2001/1252) |
|  | para 2 | 2 Jul 2001 (SI 2001/1252) |
|  | paras 3, 4 | 1 Nov 2000 (SI 2000/2950) (for purposes of making regulations) |
|  |  | 2 Jul 2001 (otherwise) (SI 2001/1252) |
|  | para 5 | 2 Jul 2001 (SI 2001/1252) |
|  | para 6 | 1 Nov 2000 (SI 2000/2950) (for purposes of making regulations) |
|  |  | 2 Jul 2001 (otherwise) (SI 2001/1252) |
|  | para 7 | 2 Jul 2001 (SI 2001/1252) |
|  | paras 8–10 | 1 Nov 2000 (SI 2000/2950) (for purposes of making regulations) |
|  |  | 2 Jul 2001 (otherwise) (SI 2001/1252) |
|  | para 11 | 2 Jul 2001 (SI 2001/1252) |
|  | paras 12–16 | 1 Nov 2000 (SI 2000/2950) (for purposes of making regulations) |
|  |  | 2 Jul 2001 (otherwise) (SI 2001/1252) |
|  | para 17 | *Not yet in force* (repealed in part) |
|  | para 18(1) | 2 Jul 2001 (SI 2001/1252) |
|  | para 18(2)(a) | 2 Jul 2001 (SI 2001/1252) |
|  | para 18(2)(b) | *Not yet in force* (repealed in part) |
|  | para 18(3)–(9) | 2 Jul 2001 (SI 2001/1252) |

**Child Support, Pensions and Social Security Act 2000 (c 19)**—*contd*

| | | |
|---|---|---|
| | paras 19–21 | 1 Nov 2000 (SI 2000/2950) (for purposes of making regulations) |
| | | 2 Jul 2001 (otherwise) (SI 2001/1252) |
| | para 22(1) | 2 Jul 2001 (except for certain purposes[1]) (SI 2001/1252) |
| | | *Not yet in force* (otherwise) (repealed in part) |
| | para 22(2), (3) | 2 Jul 2001 (SI 2001/1252) |
| | para 23 | 1 Nov 2000 (SI 2000/2950) (for purposes of making regulations) |
| | | 2 Jul 2001 (otherwise) (SI 2001/1252) |
| Sch 8 | | 1 Apr 2001 (SI 2001/774) |
| Sch 9 | Pt I | 2 Apr 2001 (SI 2001/1252), repeals of or in— |

Child Support Act 1991, ss 15(10), 40(1), (2);
Child Support Act 1995, s 24;
Social Security Act 1998, Sch 7, para 28;
Social Security Act 1998 (Commencement No 2) Order 1998,
   SI 1998/2780

3 Mar 2003 (otherwise) (for certain purposes[2]) (except repeal of
   Child Support Act 1995, s 10) (SI 2003/192)

3 Mar 2003 (for certain purposes[5]) (repeal of Child Support
   Act 1995, s 10) (SI 2003/192)

*Not yet in force*, except for certain purposes[2], repeals of or in—
Naval Forces (Enforcement of Maintenance Liabilities) Act 1947,
   s 1(1)(aaa);
Army Act 1955, s 150A(2), (3);
Air Force Act 1955, s 150A(2), (3);
Matrimonial Causes Act 1973, s 29(7), (8);
Domestic Proceedings and Magistrates' Courts Act 1978,
   s 5(7), (8);
Children Act 1989, Sch 1, para 3(7), (8);
Child Support Act 1991, ss 17(1), 28D(2)(a), 28H, 28I,
   41(3)–(5), 44(3), 46B(3), 54, Sch 1, paras 13, 16, Sch 4C;
Social Security Administration Act 1992, s 170(5);
Social Security (Consequential Provisions) Act 1992, Sch 2,
   para 113;
Child Support Act 1995, ss 1–3, 6–9, 11, 14(2), (3), 18(3), (5),
   19, 22, 26(4)(c), Schs 1, 2, Sch 3, paras 12, 15, 20(a);
Jobseekers Act 1995, Sch 2, para 20(2), (4), (7);
Social Security Act 1998, s 42, Sch 7, paras 20, 24, 25, 34–40,
   43, 46, 48(1)–(3), (5)(a)–(c), 53, 54;
Tax Credits Act 1999, Sch 1, para 6(i), Sch 2, para 17(a)

*Not yet in force*, (except for certain purposes[5]) (repeal of Child
   Support Act 1995, s 10)

| | | |
|---|---|---|
| | Pt II | 8 Apr 2001 (SI 2001/153) |
| | Pt III(1) | *Not yet in force* |
| | Pt III(2) | 1 Mar 2002 (for the purpose of making regulations and rules) (SI 2002/437) |
| | | 1 Apr 2002 (otherwise) (SI 2002/437) |
| | Pt III(3) | 1 Dec 2000 (except so far as relates to Pensions Act 1995) (SI 2000/3166) |
| | | *Not yet in force* (exception noted above) |
| | Pt III(4)–(9) | 1 Dec 2000 (SI 2000/3166) |
| | Pt III(10) | *Never in force* (repealed) |
| | Pt III(11) | 6 Apr 2002 (SI 2002/437) |
| | Pt IV | 9 Apr 2001 (SI 2000/2994) |
| | Pt V | *Not yet in force* |
| | Pt VI | 2 Apr 2001 (SI 2001/1252) |
| | Pt VII | 2 Jul 2001 (except for certain purposes[1]) (SI 2001/1252) |
| | Pt VIII | 28 Jul 2000 (RA) |
| | Pt IX | 1 Apr 2001 (SI 2001/774) |

[1]   The "certain purposes" are where, pursuant to a request for a further review of a determination under
   Social Security Act 1998, s 34 relating to housing benefit or council tax benefit:

**Child Support, Pensions and Social Security Act 2000 (c 19)**—*contd*

(a)   an oral hearing by a Review Board constituted under the Housing Benefit (General) Regulations 1987, SI 1987/1971, or the Council Tax Benefit (General) Regulations 1992, SI 1992/1814, has been held and completed before 2 Jul 2001, the purpose of enabling the Review Board on or after that date to record its decision, or to give or send its decision to persons likely to be affected by it; or

(b)   a decision on the further review has been given by such a Review Board, whether before, on or after that date—

(i)   the purpose of enabling the Review Board to correct any accidental error in the record of its decision,

(ii)   where proceedings are brought by way of judicial review in connection with that decision, the purpose of enabling the Review Board to participate in those proceedings or in any appeal arising out of those proceedings, or

(iii)   the purpose of giving effect to the Review Board's decision

2    The "certain purposes" are cases:

(a)   where an application for child support maintenance is made to the Secretary of State (whether or not in writing) and the effective date (as defined in SI 2003/192, art 8) would be on or after 3 Mar 2003;

(b)   where there is an existing assessment and a related decision (as defined in SI 2003/192, art 3(2)) falls to be made; and

(c)   where there is an existing assessment and where—

(i)   an application is made or treated as made which would but for that assessment result in a maintenance calculation being made,

(ii)   the non-resident parent in relation to the application referred to above is the absent parent in relation to the existing assessment, and

(iii)   the person with care in relation to the application referred to above is a different person to the person with care in relation to the existing assessment

3    The "certain purposes" are cases:

(a)   where, on or after 3 Mar 2003, income support, an income-based jobseeker's allowance or any other benefit prescribed for the purposes of the Child Support Act 1991, s 6, as substituted by s 3 of this Act is claimed by or in respect of, or paid to or in respect of, the parent of a qualifying child who is also the person with care of the child, and when the claim is made—

(i)   there is no maintenance assessment or maintenance calculation in force in respect of that parent, and

(ii)   there has been no maintenance assessment in force during the previous 8 weeks in respect of that child;

(b)   where—

(i)   before 3 Mar 2003, the Child Support Act 1991, s 6(1), before its substitution by this Act, applied to the parent with care,

(ii)   a maintenance assessment has been made with an effective date (as defined in SI 2003/192, art 8) which is before 3 Mar 2003, and

(iii)   on or after 3 Mar 2003 the parent with care withdraws her authorisation under s 6(1) at a date when she continues to fall within s 6(1);

(c)   where, immediately before 3 Mar 2003, the Child Support Act 1991, s 6(1), before its substitution by this Act, applied to the parent with care, and a maintenance assessment has not been made because:

(i)   the Secretary of State was in the process of considering whether the parent with care should be required to give the authorisation referred to in that subsection,

(ii)   subsection (2) of that section applied,

(iii)   subsection (2) of that section did not apply and a reduced benefit direction was given under the Child Support Act 1991, s 46(5), before its substitution by this Act, or

(iv)   the parent with care failed to comply with a requirement imposed on her under s 6(1), and

**Child Support, Pensions and Social Security Act 2000 (c 19)**—*contd*

the Secretary of State was in the process of serving a notice or considering reasons given by the parent with care under the Child Support Act 1991, s 46(2) or (3) before its substitution by this Act

[4] The "certain purposes" are cases where an application for child support maintenance is made to the Secretary of State (whether or not in writing) and the effective date (as defined in SI 2003/192, art 8) would be on or after 3 Mar 2003

[5] The provisions come into force on varying dates for the purposes of the cases listed in footnotes 2 and 3 above and for the purposes of cases not referred to in either of the footnotes, where, on or after 3 Mar 2003, relevant maintenance is first paid, as follows:

(a) as respects any case specified in head (a) of footnote 2 where, before 3 Mar 2003, relevant maintenance is paid or payable:

(i) where 3 Mar 2003 is the day on which the maintenance calculation in relation to that case takes effect, 3 Mar 2003,

(ii) where the maintenance calculation in relation to that case takes effect on a day later than 3 Mar 2003, that later day;

(b) as respects any other case specified in head (a) of footnote 2, 3 Mar 2003;

(c) as respects any case which is specified in head (b) or (c) of footnote 2:

(i) where 3 Mar 2003 is the case conversion date in relation to that case, 3 Mar 2003,

(ii) where a day later than 3 Mar 2003 is the case conversion date in relation to that case, that later day;

(d) as respects any case specified in footnote 3 which is referred to:

(i) in head (a) of that footnote, the day on which the claim for the benefit mentioned in that head is made,

(ii) in head (b) of that footnote, the day on which the Secretary of State is notified that the authorisation mentioned in head (b)(iii) of that footnote is withdrawn,

(iii) in head (c) of that footnote, 3 Mar 2003;

(e) as respects any case which is not referred to in footnotes 2 and 3 where relevant maintenance is first paid after 3 Mar 2003, the day on which the relevant maintenance is first paid

**Church of England (Miscellaneous Provisions) Measure 2000 (No 1)**

*RA:* 28 Jul 2000

*Commencement provisions:* s 22(2)

The provisions of this Measure were brought into force on the following dates by instruments made by the Archbishops of Canterbury and York, and dated 30 Aug 2000 and 14 Dec 2000 (made under s 22(2))

| | |
|---|---|
| 1–11 | 1 Jan 2001 |
| 12–18 | 1 Sep 2000 |
| 19, 20 | 1 Jan 2001 |
| 21, 22 | 1 Sep 2000 |
| Sch 1 | 1 Jan 2001 |
| Sch 2 | 1 Jan 2001 (except in so far as relates to para 5(a)) |
| Schs 3–8 | 1 Jan 2001 |

**Consolidated Fund Act 2000 (c 3)**

*RA:* 21 Mar 2000

Whole Act in force 21 Mar 2000 (RA)

## Consolidated Fund (No 2) Act 2000 (c 45)

*RA:* 21 Dec 2000

Whole Act in force 21 Dec 2000 (RA)

---

## Countryside and Rights of Way Act 2000 (c 37)

*RA:* 30 Nov 2000

*Commencement provisions:* s 103; Countryside and Rights of Way Act 2000 (Commencement No 1) Order 2001, SI 2001/114; Countryside and Rights of Way Act 2000 (Commencement No 1) (Wales) Order 2001, SI 2001/203; Countryside and Rights of Way Act 2000 (Commencement No 2) (Wales) Order 2001, SI 2001/1410; Countryside and Rights of Way Act 2000 (Commencement No 3) (Wales) Order 2002, SI 2002/2615; Countryside and Rights of Way Act 2000 (Commencement No 2) Order 2002, SI 2002/2833; Countryside and Rights of Way Act 2000 (Commencement No 3) Order 2003, SI 2003/272; Countryside and Rights of Way Act 2000 (Commencement No 4) Order 2004, SI 2004/292; Countryside and Rights of Way Act 2000 (Commencement No 4) (Wales) Order 2004, SI 2004/315; Countryside and Rights of Way Act 2000 (Commencement No 5) (Wales) Order 2004, SI 2004/1489; Countryside and Rights of Way Act 2000 (Commencement No 5) Order 2004, SI 2004/2173; Countryside and Rights of Way Act 2000 (Commencement No 6) Order 2004, SI 2004/3088; Countryside and Rights of Way Act 2000 (Commencement No 6) (Wales) Order 2005, SI 2005/423; Countryside and Rights of Way Act 2000 (Commencement No 7) Order 2005, SI 2005/827; Countryside and Rights of Way Act 2000 (Commencement No 7) (Wales) Order 2005, SI 2005/1314; Countryside and Rights of Way Act 2000 (Commencement No 8) Order 2005, SI 2005/1901; Countryside and Rights of Way Act 2000 (Commencement No 9) Order 2005, SI 2005/2459; Countryside and Rights of Way Act 2000 (Commencement No 10) Order 2005, SI 2005/2752; Countryside and Rights of Way Act 2000 (Commencement No 11 and Savings) Order 2006, SI 2006/1172; Countryside and Rights of Way Act 2000 (Commencement No 8 and Transitional Provisions) (Wales) Order 2006, SI 2006/1279; Countryside and Rights of Way Act 2000 (Commencement No 9 and Saving) (Wales) Order 2006, SI 2006/3257; Countryside and Rights of Way Act 2000 (Commencement No 12) Order 2007, SI 2007/1493; Countryside and Rights of Way Act 2000 (Commencement No 13) Order 2007, SI 2007/2335; Countryside and Rights of Way Act 2000 (Commencement No 14) Order 2007, SI 2007/2595; Countryside and Rights of Way Act 2000 (Commencement No 15) Order 2008, SI 2008/308

| | |
|---|---|
| 1 | 30 Jan 2001 (s 103(2)) |
| 2 | 19 Sep 2004 (E) (in so far as it relates to any access land which is access land by virtue of s 1(1)(a) or (b) and which lies within an area covered by one of the maps in conclusive form issued by the Countryside Agency for the purposes of Pt I on 4 May 2004 (South East) and 2 Jun 2004 (Lower North West)) (SI 2004/2173) |
| | 19 Sep 2004 (E) (or the end of a period of six months beginning with the day on which the land is dedicated for the purposes of Pt I under s 16, whichever is the later) (in so far as it relates to any access land which is access land by virtue of s 1(1)(e) and which lies within an area covered by one of the maps in conclusive form issued by the Countryside Agency for the purposes of Pt I on 4 May 2004 (South East) and 2 Jun 2004 (Lower North West)) (SI 2004/2173) |
| | 14 Dec 2004 (E) (in so far as it relates to any access land which is access land by virtue of s 1(1)(a) or (b) and which lies within an area covered by the map in conclusive form issued by the Countryside Agency for the purposes of Pt I on 28 Sep 2004 (Central Southern England)) (SI 2004/3088) |
| | 14 Dec 2004 (E) (or the end of a period of six months beginning with the day on which the land is dedicated for the purposes of Pt I under s 16, whichever is the later) (in so far as it relates to any access land which is access land by virtue of s 1(1)(e) and which lies within an area covered by the map in conclusive form issued by the Countryside Agency for the purposes of Pt I on 28 Sep 2004 (Central Southern England)) (SI 2004/3088) |

**Countryside and Rights of Way Act 2000 (c 37)**—*contd*

28 May 2005 (W) (SI 2005/423)

28 May 2005 (E) (in so far as it relates to any access land which is access land by virtue of s 1(1)(a) or (b) and which lies within an area covered by one of the maps in conclusive form issued by the Countryside Agency for the purposes of Pt I on 25 Jan 2005 (Upper North West) and 7 Mar 2005 (North East)) (SI 2005/827)

28 May 2005 (E) (or the end of a period of six months beginning with the day on which the land is dedicated for the purposes of Pt I under s 16, whichever is the later) (in so far as it relates to any access land which is access land solely by virtue of s 1(1)(e) and which lies within an area covered by one of the maps in conclusive form issued by the Countryside Agency for the purposes of Pt I on 25 Jan 2005 (Upper North West) and 7 Mar 2005 (North East)) (SI 2005/827)

28 Aug 2005 (E) (in so far as it relates to any access land which is access land by virtue of s 1(1)(a) or (b) and which lies within an area covered by the map in conclusive form issued by the Countryside Agency for the purposes of Pt I on 9 May 2005 (South West)) (SI 2005/1901)

28 Aug 2005 (E) (or the end of a period of six months beginning with the day on which the land is dedicated for the purposes of Pt I under s 16, whichever is the later) (in so far as it relates to any access land which is access land solely by virtue of s 1(1)(e) and which lies within an area covered by the map in conclusive form issued by the Countryside Agency for the purposes of Pt I on 9 May 2005 (South West)) (SI 2005/1901)

31 Oct 2005 (E) (in so far as it relates to any access land which is access land by virtue of s 1(1)(a) or (b) and which lies within an area covered by one of the maps in conclusive form issued by the Countryside Agency for the purposes of Pt I on 1 Jul 2005 (West) and 16 Aug 2005 (East)) (SI 2005/2752)

31 Oct 2005 (E) (or the end of a period of six months beginning with the day on which the land is dedicated for the purposes of Pt I under s 16, whichever is the later) (in so far as it relates to any access land which is access land solely by virtue of s 1(1)(e) and which lies within an area covered by one of the maps in conclusive form issued by the Countryside Agency for the purposes of Pt I on 1 Jul 2005 (West) and 16 Aug 2005 (East)) (SI 2005/2752)

*Not yet in force* (E) (in so far as relates to access land which is access land by virtue of s 1(1)(c), (d))[6]

| | | |
|---|---|---|
| 3–7 | | 30 Jan 2001 (s 103(2)) |
| 8 | (1) | 30 Jan 2001 (s 103(2)) |
| | (2) | See Sch 3 below |
| 9–11 | | 30 Jan 2001 (s 103(2)) |
| 12–14 | | 19 Sep 2004 (E) (SI 2004/2173) |
| | | 28 May 2005 (W) (SI 2005/423) |
| 15–17 | | 30 Jan 2001 (s 103(2)) |
| 18 | | 21 Jun 2004 (W) (SI 2004/1489) |
| | | 19 Sep 2004 (E) (SI 2004/2173) |
| 19 | | 30 Jan 2001 (s 103(2)) |
| 20 | | 21 Jun 2004 (W) (SI 2004/1489) |
| | | 19 Sep 2004 (E) (SI 2004/2173) |
| 21–45 | | 30 Jan 2001 (s 103(2)) |
| 46 | (1)(a) | 21 Jun 2004 (W) (SI 2004/1489)[2] |
| | | *Never in force* (E) (repealed) |
| | (1)(b) | 1 Apr 2001 (E) (SI 2001/114) |
| | | 1 May 2001 (W) (SI 2001/1410) |
| | (2) | *Not yet in force* |
| | (3) | See Sch 4 below |

**Countryside and Rights of Way Act 2000 (c 37)**—*contd*

| | | |
|---|---|---|
| 47, 48 | | 2 May 2006 (E) (SI 2006/1172)[7] |
| | | 11 May 2006 (W) (SI 2006/1279)[8] |
| 49, 50 | | 2 May 2006 (E) (SI 2006/1172) |
| | | 11 May 2006 (W) (SI 2006/1279) |
| 51 | | See Sch 5 below |
| 52 | | 30 Jan 2001 (s 103(2)) |
| 53–56 | | *Not yet in force* |
| 57 | | See Sch 6 below |
| 58, 59 | | 30 Jan 2001 (s 103(2)) |
| 60, 61 | | 1 Nov 2002 (W) (SI 2002/2615) |
| | | 21 Nov 2002 (E) (SI 2002/2833) |
| 62 | | 21 Nov 2002 (E) (SI 2002/2833) |
| 63 | | 13 Feb 2004 (E) (SI 2004/292) |
| | | 1 Apr 2004 (W) (SI 2004/315) |
| 64–66 | | 30 Jan 2001 (s 103(2)) |
| 67 | | See Sch 7 below |
| 68 | | 1 Apr 2001 (E) (SI 2001/114) |
| | | 1 May 2001 (W) (SI 2001/1410) |
| 69 | (1) | 6 Dec 2006 (W) (in so far as it provides the power to issue guidance) (SI 2006/3257) |
| | | 1 Apr 2007 (W) (otherwise) (SI 2006/3257) |
| | | 1 Oct 2007 (E) (SI 2007/2595) |
| | (2) | 27 Sep 2005 (E) (SI 2005/2459) |
| | | 11 May 2006 (W) (SI 2006/1279) |
| | (3) | 6 Dec 2006 (W) (in so far as it provides the power to issue guidance) (SI 2006/3257) |
| | | 1 Apr 2007 (W) (otherwise) (SI 2006/3257) |
| | | 1 Oct 2007 (E) (SI 2007/2595) |
| | (4), (5) | 1 Apr 2007 (W) (SI 2006/3257) |
| | | 1 Oct 2007 (E) (SI 2007/2595) |
| 70 | (1) | 13 Feb 2004 (E) (SI 2004/292) |
| | | 1 Apr 2004 (W) (SI 2004/315) |
| | (2) | 1 Apr 2001 (E) (repeal of Highways Act 1980, s 134(5), shall not have effect in relation to any offence under s 134 of the 1980 Act committed before 1 Apr 2001) (SI 2001/114) |
| | | 1 May 2001 (W) (repeal of Highways Act 1980, s 134(5), shall not have effect in relation to any offence under s 134 of the 1980 Act committed before 1 May 2001) (SI 2001/1410) |
| | (3) | 13 Feb 2004 (E) (SI 2004/292) |
| | | 1 Apr 2004 (W) (SI 2004/315) |
| | (4) | 1 Apr 2001 (E) (SI 2001/114) |
| | | 1 May 2001 (W) (SI 2001/1410) |
| 71 | | *Not yet in force* |
| 72 | | 30 Jan 2001 (E) (SI 2001/114) |
| | | 1 May 2001 (W) (SI 2001/1410) |
| 73 | (1)–(3) | 30 Jan 2001 (s 103(2)) |
| | (4) | See Sch 8 below |
| 74 | | 30 Jan 2001 (s 103(2)) |
| 75 | (1) | See Sch 9 below |
| | (2)–(4) | 30 Jan 2001 (s 103(2)) |
| 76 | (1) | See Sch 10 below |
| | (2) | See Sch 11 below |
| 77–80 | | 30 Jan 2001 (s 103(2)) |
| 81 | (1) | 30 Jan 2001 (s 103(2)) |
| | (2), (3) | 30 Nov 2000 (RA) |
| 82–85 | | 1 Apr 2001 (E) (SI 2001/114) |
| | | 1 May 2001 (W) (SI 2001/1410) |
| 86 | (1) | 1 Apr 2001 (E) (SI 2001/114) |
| | | 1 May 2001 (W) (SI 2001/1410) |

**Countryside and Rights of Way Act 2000 (c 37)**—*contd*

|       |            |                                                                                         |
|-------|------------|-----------------------------------------------------------------------------------------|
|       | (2)        | See Sch 13 below                                                                        |
|       | (3)–(10)   | 1 Apr 2001 (E) (SI 2001/114)                                                            |
|       |            | 1 May 2001 (W) (SI 2001/1410)                                                           |
| 87    | (1)–(5)    | 1 Apr 2001 (E) (SI 2001/114)                                                            |
|       |            | 1 May 2001 (W) (SI 2001/1410)                                                           |
|       | (6)        | See Sch 14 below                                                                        |
|       | (7)        | 1 Apr 2001 (E) (SI 2001/114)                                                            |
|       |            | 1 May 2001 (W) (SI 2001/1410)                                                           |
| 88–92 |            | 1 Apr 2001 (E) (SI 2001/114)                                                            |
|       |            | 1 May 2001 (W) (SI 2001/1410)                                                           |
| 93    |            | See Sch 15 below                                                                        |
| 94, 95|            | 30 Jan 2001 (s 103(2))                                                                  |
| 96    |            | 1 Apr 2001 (E) (SI 2001/114)                                                            |
|       |            | 1 May 2001 (W) (SI 2001/1410)                                                           |
| 97    |            | 1 Apr 2001 (SI 2001/114)                                                                |
| 98    |            | 30 Jan 2001 (s 103(2))                                                                  |
| 99    |            | 30 Jan 2001 (W) (SI 2001/203)                                                           |
| 100   | (1), (2)   | 30 Jan 2001 (E) (SI 2001/114)                                                           |
|       | (3)        | 1 Apr 2001 (E) (SI 2001/114)                                                            |
|       | (4)        | 30 Jan 2001 (E) (SI 2001/114)                                                           |
|       | (5)(a)     | *Not yet in force*                                                                      |
|       | (5)(b)     | 30 Jan 2001 (E) (SI 2001/114)                                                           |
| 101   |            | *Not yet in force* (para (a) repealed)                                                  |
| 102   |            | See Sch 16 below                                                                        |
| 103, 104|          | 30 Nov 2000 (RA)                                                                        |
| Sch 1 |            | 30 Jan 2001 (s 103(2))                                                                  |
| Sch 2 |            | 19 Sep 2004 (E) (SI 2004/2173)                                                          |
|       |            | 28 May 2005 (W) (SI 2005/423)                                                           |
| Sch 3 |            | 30 Jan 2001 (s 103(2))                                                                  |
| Sch 4 | para 1     | 1 Apr 2001 (E) (SI 2001/114)                                                            |
|       |            | 1 May 2001 (W) (SI 2001/1410)                                                           |
|       | paras 2, 3 | 19 Sep 2004 (E) (SI 2004/2173)                                                          |
|       |            | 28 May 2005 (W) (SI 2005/423)                                                           |
|       | paras 4–6  | 1 Apr 2001 (E) (SI 2001/114)                                                            |
|       |            | 1 May 2001 (W) (SI 2001/1410)                                                           |
| Sch 5 | para 1     | 2 May 2006 (E) (SI 2006/1172)                                                           |
|       |            | 11 May 2006 (W) (SI 2006/1279)                                                          |
|       | para 2     | 27 Sep 2005 (E) (in so far as inserts the Wildlife and Countryside Act 1981, s 53B) (SI 2005/2459) |
|       |            | 21 Nov 2005 (W) (SI 2005/1314)                                                          |
|       |            | 18 Feb 2008 (E) (in so far as inserts s 53A of the 1981 Act) (SI 2008/308)             |
|       | paras 3, 4 | *Not yet in force*                                                                      |
|       | para 5     | 27 Sep 2005 (E) (SI 2005/2459)                                                          |
|       |            | 11 May 2006 (W) (SI 2006/1279)                                                          |
|       | para 6     | 2 May 2006 (E) (SI 2006/1172)                                                           |
|       |            | 11 May 2006 (W) (SI 2006/1279)                                                          |
|       | para 7     | 2 May 2006 (E) (SI 2006/1172)                                                           |
|       |            | *Not yet in force* (W)                                                                  |
|       | para 8     | 13 Feb 2004 (E) (SI 2004/292)[5]                                                        |
|       |            | 31 May 2005 (W) (SI 2005/1314)                                                          |
|       | para 9     | 2 May 2006 (E) (SI 2006/1172)                                                           |
|       |            | 11 May 2006 (W) (SI 2006/1279)                                                          |
|       | para 10    | 13 Feb 2004 (E) (SI 2004/292)[5]                                                        |
|       |            | 31 May 2005 (W) (SI 2005/1314)                                                          |
|       | para 11    | 13 Feb 2004 (E) (SI 2004/292)[1, 5]                                                     |
|       |            | 31 May 2005 (W) (SI 2005/1314)                                                          |
|       | paras 12–17| 2 May 2006 (E) (SI 2006/1172)                                                           |
|       |            | 11 May 2006 (W) (SI 2006/1279)                                                          |

**Countryside and Rights of Way Act 2000 (c 37)**—*contd*

| Sch 6 | para 1 | 12 Feb 2003 (E) (SI 2003/272) |
| | | 1 Apr 2004 (W) (SI 2004/315)[9] |
| | para 2 | 12 Feb 2003 (E) (SI 2003/272) |
| | | 31 May 2005 (W) (SI 2005/1314) |
| | para 3 | 13 Feb 2004 (E) (SI 2004/292)[1, 5] |
| | | 31 May 2005 (W) (SI 2005/1314)[3] |
| | para 4 | 21 Nov 2005 (W) (SI 2005/1314) |
| | | 1 Oct 2007 (E) (SI 2007/2335) |
| | para 5 | 12 Feb 2003 (E) (except so far as relates to a highway created in consequence of an SSSI diversion order) (SI 2003/272) |
| | | 15 Jul 2005 (W) (so far as relates to a highway created in consequence of a special diversion order to which s 119B(1)(b) applies) (SI 2005/1314, art 3) |
| | | 21 May 2007 (E) (exception noted above) (SI 2007/1493) |
| | | *Not yet in force* (W) (so far as relates to a highway created in consequence of an SSSI diversion order or a special diversion order to which s 119B(1)(a) applies) |
| | para 6 | 12 Feb 2003 (E) (SI 2003/272) |
| | | 1 Apr 2004 (W) (SI 2004/315)[9] |
| | para 7 | *Not yet in force* |
| | para 8 | 12 Feb 2003 (E) (so far as inserts Highways Act 1980, s 118B) (SI 2003/272) |
| | | 15 Jul 2005 (W) (so far as inserts Highways Act 1980, s 118B for the purposes of sub-s (1)(b)) (SI 2005/1314, art 3) |
| | | *Not yet in force* (E) (so far as inserts Highways Act 1980, s 118C) |
| | | *Not yet in force* (W) (so far as inserts Highways Act 1980, ss 118B (for the purposes of sub-s (1)(a)), 118C) |
| | para 9(1)–(3) | 12 Feb 2003 (E) (SI 2003/272) |
| | | 31 May 2005 (W) (SI 2005/1314) |
| | para 9(4) | *Not yet in force* |
| | para 9(5) | 12 Feb 2003 (E) (SI 2003/272) |
| | | 1 Apr 2004 (W) (SI 2004/315)[9] |
| | para 10 | *Not yet in force* |
| | para 11 | 12 Feb 2003 (E) (SI 2003/272) |
| | | 31 May 2005 (W) (SI 2005/1314) |
| | para 12 | 12 Feb 2003 (E) (so far as inserts Highways Act 1980, s 119B) (SI 2003/272) |
| | | 15 Jul 2005 (W) (so far as inserts Highways Act 1980, s 119B for the purposes of sub-s (1)(b)) (SI 2005/1314, art 3) |
| | | 21 May 2007 (E) (so far as inserts Highways Act 1980, ss 119D, 119E) (SI 2007/1493) |
| | | *Not yet in force* (E) (so far as inserts Highways Act 1980, s 119C) |
| | | *Not yet in force* (W) (so far as inserts Highways Act 1980, ss 119B (for the purposes of sub-s (1)(a)), 119C–119E) |
| | para 13(1)–(4) | 12 Feb 2003 (E) (except so far as they relate to (1) an SSSI diversion order or (2) any order or confirmation of an order on appeal under Highways Act 1980, s 121D(1)) (SI 2003/272) |
| | | 15 Jul 2005 (W) (for certain purposes[4]) (SI 2005/1314, art 3) |
| | | 21 May 2007 (E) (in so far as they relate to an SSSI diversion order) (SI 2007/1493) |
| | | *Not yet in force* (E) (exception (2) noted above) |
| | | *Not yet in force* (W) (except in so far as they relate to a provision brought into force by SI 2005/1314, art 3) |
| | para 13(5)(a)–(d) | 12 Feb 2003 (E) (except so far as they relate to (1) an SSSI diversion order or (2) any order or confirmation of an order on appeal under Highways Act 1980, s 121D(1)) (SI 2003/272) |
| | | 15 Jul 2005 (W) (for certain purposes[4]) (SI 2005/1314, art 3) |
| | | 21 May 2007 (E) (in so far as they relate to an SSSI diversion order) (SI 2007/1493) |
| | | *Not yet in force* (E) (exception (2) noted above) |

**Countryside and Rights of Way Act 2000 (c 37)**—*contd*

|  |  |
|---|---|
|  | *Not yet in force* (W) (except in so far as they relate to a provision brought into force by SI 2005/1314, art 3) |
| para 13(5)(e) | 12 Feb 2003 (E) (except so far as relates to (1) an SSSI diversion order or (2) any order or confirmation of an order on appeal under Highways Act 1980, s 121D(1)) (SI 2003/272) |
|  | 21 May 2007 (E) (in so far as relates to an SSSI diversion order) (SI 2007/1493) |
|  | *Not yet in force* (E) (exception (2) noted above) |
|  | *Not yet in force* (W) |
| para 13(6) | *Not yet in force* |
| para 13(7)–(9) | 12 Feb 2003 (E) (except so far as they relate to (1) an SSSI diversion order or (2) any order or confirmation of an order on appeal under Highways Act 1980, s 121D(1)) (SI 2003/272) |
|  | 15 Jul 2005 (W) (for certain purposes[4]) (SI 2005/1314, art 3) |
|  | 21 May 2007 (E) (in so far as they relate to an SSSI diversion order) (SI 2007/1493) |
|  | *Not yet in force* (E) (exception (2) noted above) |
|  | *Not yet in force* (W) (except in so far as they relate to a provision brought into force by SI 2005/1314, art 3) |
| para 13(10) | 21 May 2007 (E) (in so far as relates to an SSSI diversion order) (SI 2007/1493) |
|  | *Not yet in force* (W) |
| para 14(1) | 12 Feb 2003 (E) (except so far as relates to (1) an SSSI diversion order or (2) any order made on an application or on an appeal under Highways Act 1980, s 121D(1)(a)) (SI 2003/272) |
|  | 31 May 2005 (W) (SI 2005/1314) |
|  | 21 May 2007 (E) (in so far as relates to an SSSI diversion order) (SI 2007/1493) |
|  | *Not yet in force* (E) (exception (2) noted above) |
| para 14(2), (3) | 12 Feb 2003 (E) (except so far as they relate to (1) an SSSI diversion order or (2) any order made on an application or on an appeal under Highways Act 1980, s 121D(1)(a)) (SI 2003/272) |
|  | 15 Jul 2005 (W) (for certain purposes[4]) (SI 2005/1314, art 3) |
|  | 21 May 2007 (E) (in so far as they relate to an SSSI diversion order) (SI 2007/1493) |
|  | *Not yet in force* (E) (exception (2) noted above) |
|  | *Not yet in force* (W) (except in so far as they relate to a provision brought into force by SI 2005/1314, art 3) |
| para 14(4)(a) | 12 Feb 2003 (E) (except so far as relates to (1) an SSSI diversion order or (2) any order made on an application or on an appeal under Highways Act 1980, s 121D(1)(a)) (SI 2003/272) |
|  | 31 May 2005 (W) (SI 2005/1314) |
|  | 21 May 2007 (E) (so far as relates to an SSSI diversion order) (SI 2007/1493) |
|  | *Not yet in force* (E) (exception (2) noted above) |
| para 14(4)(b), (c) | 12 Feb 2003 (E) (except so far as they relate to (1) an SSSI diversion order or (2) any order made on an application or on an appeal under Highways Act 1980, s 121D(1)(a)) (SI 2003/272) |
|  | 15 Jul 2005 (W) (for certain purposes[4]) (SI 2005/1314, art 3) |
|  | 21 May 2007 (E) (in so far as they relate to an SSSI diversion order) (SI 2007/1493) |
|  | *Not yet in force* (E) (exception (2) noted above) |
|  | *Not yet in force* (W) (except in so far as they relate to a provision brought into force by SI 2005/1314, art 3) |
| para 14(5)–(7) | 12 Feb 2003 (E) (except so far as they relate to (1) an SSSI diversion order or (2) any order made on an application or on an appeal under Highways Act 1980, s 121D(1)(a)) (SI 2003/272) |

**Countryside and Rights of Way Act 2000 (c 37)**—*contd*

|            | 15 Jul 2005 (W) (for certain purposes[4]) (SI 2005/1314, art 3) |
|------------|------------------------------------------------------------------|
|            | 21 May 2007 (E) (in so far as relates to an SSSI diversion order) (SI 2007/1493) |
|            | *Not yet in force* (E) (exception (2) noted above) |
|            | *Not yet in force* (W) (except in so far as they relate to a provision brought into force by SI 2005/1314, art 3) |
| para 15    | 21 Nov 2005 (W) (in so far as inserts Highways Act 1980, s 121B) (SI 2005/1314) |
|            | *Not yet in force* (W) (in so far as inserts Highways Act 1980, ss 121A, 121C–121E) |
|            | *Not yet in force* (E) |
| para 16    | *Not yet in force* |
| para 17(a) | 12 Feb 2003 (E) (SI 2003/272) |
|            | 15 Jul 2005 (W) (for certain purposes[4]) (SI 2005/1314, art 3) |
|            | *Not yet in force* (W) (except in so far as relates to a provision brought into force by SI 2005/1314, art 3) |
| para 17(b) | 12 Feb 2003 (E) (except so far as relates to an SSSI diversion order) (SI 2003/272) |
|            | 15 Jul 2005 (W) (for certain purposes[4]) (SI 2005/1314, art 3) |
|            | 21 May 2007 (E) (exception noted above) (SI 2007/1493) |
|            | *Not yet in force* (W) (except in so far as relates to a provision brought into force by SI 2005/1314, art 3) |
| para 18(a) | 30 Jan 2001 (E) (in so far as substitutes in Highways Act 1980, s 325(1)(d) references to ss 118, 118A, 119, 119A) (SI 2001/114) |
|            | 1 May 2001 (W) (in so far as substitutes in Highways Act 1980, s 325(1)(d) references to ss 118, 118A, 119, 119A) (SI 2001/1410) |
|            | 12 Feb 2003 (E) (in so far as substitutes in Highways Act 1980, s 325(1)(d) references to ss 118B(4), 119B(4)) (SI 2003/272) |
|            | 15 Jul 2005 (W) (in so far as substitutes in Highways Act 1980, s 325(1)(d) references to ss 118B(4), 119B(4); for certain purposes[4]) (SI 2005/1314, art 3) |
|            | 21 May 2007 (E) (otherwise) (SI 2007/1493) |
|            | *Not yet in force* (W) (in so far as substitutes in Highways Act 1980, s 325(1)(d) references to ss 118, 118A, 119, 119A, 119D, and to ss 118B(4), 119B(4) (except for certain purposes[4])) |
| para 18(b) | 12 Feb 2003 (E) (SI 2003/272) |
|            | 15 Jul 2005 (W) (for certain purposes[4]) (SI 2005/1314, art 3) |
|            | *Not yet in force* (W) (except in so far as relates to a provision brought into force by SI 2005/1314, art 3) |
| para 19    | 30 Jan 2001 (E) (in so far as substitutes in Highways Act 1980, s 326(5) references to a rail crossing extinguishment order, a public path diversion order and a rail crossing diversion order) (SI 2001/114) |
|            | 1 May 2001 (W) (in so far as substitutes in Highways Act 1980, s 326(5) references to a rail crossing extinguishment order, a public path diversion order and a rail crossing diversion order) (SI 2001/1410) |
|            | 12 Feb 2003 (E) (in so far as substitutes in Highways Act 1980, s 326(5) references to a special extinguishment order and a special diversion order) (SI 2003/272) |
|            | 15 Jul 2005 (W) (in so far as substitutes in Highways Act 1980, s 326(5) references to a special extinguishment order and a special diversion order; for certain purposes[4]) (SI 2005/1314, art 3) |
|            | 21 May 2007 (E) (otherwise) (SI 2007/1493) |
|            | *Not yet in force* (W) (in so far as substitutes in the Highways Act 1980, s 326(5) references to a special extinguishment order and a special diversion order (except for certain purposes[4]), and to an SSSI diversion order) |

**Countryside and Rights of Way Act 2000 (c 37)**—*contd*

| | |
|---|---|
| para 20(a)–(c) | 12 Feb 2003 (E) (SI 2003/272) |
| | 31 May 2005 (W) (SI 2005/1314) |
| para 20(d), (e) | 12 Feb 2003 (E) (SI 2003/272) |
| | 15 Jul 2005 (W) (for certain purposes[4]) (SI 2005/1314, art 3) |
| | *Not yet in force* (W) (except in so far as relates to a provision brought into force by SI 2005/1314, art 3) |
| para 20(f) | 12 Feb 2003 (E) (SI 2003/272) |
| | *Not yet in force* (W) |
| para 21 | 12 Feb 2003 (E) (except so far as relates to an SSSI diversion order) (SI 2003/272) |
| | 15 Jul 2005 (W) (in so far as substitutes in Highways Act 1980, s 334(2) references to a special extinguishment order and a special diversion order; for certain purposes[4]) (SI 2005/1314, art 3) |
| | 21 May 2007 (E) (exception noted above) (SI 2007/1493) |
| | *Not yet in force* (W) (in so far as substitutes in the Highways Act 1980, s 334(2) references to a special extinguishment order and a special diversion order (except for certain purposes[4]), and to a public path diversion order and an SSSI diversion order) |
| para 22 | *Not yet in force* |
| para 23(1) | 12 Feb 2003 (E) (except so far as relates to an SSSI diversion order or a draft SSSI diversion order) (SI 2003/272) |
| | 15 Jul 2005 (W) (for certain purposes[4]) (SI 2005/1314, art 3) |
| | 21 May 2007 (E) (exception noted above) (SI 2007/1493) |
| | *Not yet in force* (W) (except in so far as relates to a provision brought into force by SI 2005/1314, art 3) |
| para 23(2)(a) | 12 Feb 2003 (E) (except so far as relates to an SSSI diversion order or a draft SSSI diversion order) (SI 2003/272) |
| | 15 Jul 2005 (W) (for certain purposes[4]) (SI 2005/1314, art 3) |
| | 21 May 2007 (E) (exception noted above) (SI 2007/1493) |
| | *Not yet in force* (W) (except in so far as relates to a provision brought into force by SI 2005/1314, art 3) |
| para 23(2)(b) | 12 Feb 2003 (E) (except so far as relates to an SSSI diversion order or a draft SSSI diversion order) (SI 2003/272) |
| | 15 Jul 2005 (W) (in so far as substitutes in Highways Act 1980, Sch 6, para 1(1), (2) a reference to a special diversion order; for certain purposes[4]) (SI 2005/1314, art 3) |
| | 21 May 2007 (E) (exceptions noted above) (SI 2007/1493) |
| | *Not yet in force* (W) (in so far as substitutes in Highways Act 1980, Sch 6, para 1(1), (2) a reference to a special diversion order (except for certain purposes[4]), a rail crossing diversion order or an SSSI diversion order) |
| para 23(3)(a) | 12 Feb 2003 (E) (except so far as relates to an SSSI diversion order or a draft SSSI diversion order) (SI 2003/272) |
| | 15 Jul 2005 (W) (for certain purposes[4]) (SI 2005/1314, art 3) |
| | 21 May 2007 (E) (exceptions noted above) (SI 2007/1493) |
| | *Not yet in force* (W) (except in so far as relates to a provision brought into force by SI 2005/1314, art 3) |
| para 23(3)(b) | 12 Feb 2003 (E) (except so far as relates to an SSSI diversion order or a draft SSSI diversion order) (SI 2003/272) |
| | 15 Jul 2005 (W) (in so far as substitutes in Highways Act 1980, Sch 6, para 1(3A) a reference to a special diversion order; for certain purposes[4]) (SI 2005/1314, art 3) |
| | 21 May 2007 (E) (exceptions noted above) (SI 2007/1493) |
| | *Not yet in force* (W) (in so far as substitutes in Highways Act 1980, Sch 6, para 1(3A) a reference to a special diversion order (except for certain purposes[4]), a rail crossing diversion order or an SSSI diversion order) |
| para 23(4)(a) | 12 Feb 2003 (E) (except so far as relates to an SSSI diversion order or a draft SSSI diversion order) (SI 2003/272) |

**Countryside and Rights of Way Act 2000 (c 37)**—*contd*

|  |  |
|---|---|
|  | 15 Jul 2005 (W) (for certain purposes[4]) (SI 2005/1314, art 3) |
|  | 21 May 2007 (E) (exceptions noted above) (SI 2007/1493) |
|  | *Not yet in force* (W) (except in so far as relates to a provision brought into force by SI 2005/1314, art 3) |
| para 23(4)(b) | 12 Feb 2003 (E) (except so far as relates to an SSSI diversion order or a draft SSSI diversion order) (SI 2003/272) |
|  | 15 Jul 2005 (W) (in so far as substitutes in Highways Act 1980, Sch 6, para 1(3B) a reference to a special diversion order; for certain purposes[4]) (SI 2005/1314, art 3) |
|  | 21 May 2007 (E) (exceptions noted above) (SI 2007/1493) |
|  | *Not yet in force* (W) (in so far as substitutes in Highways Act 1980, Sch 6, para 1(3B) a reference to a special diversion order (except for certain purposes[4]), a public path diversion order or an SSSI diversion order) |
| para 23(5)(a) | *Not yet in force* |
| para 23(5)(b) | 12 Feb 2003 (E) (except so far as relates to an SSSI diversion order) (SI 2003/272) |
|  | 15 Jul 2005 (W) (in so far as substitutes in Highways Act 1980, Sch 6, para 2(2), (3) a reference to a special diversion order; for certain purposes[4]) (SI 2005/1314, art 3) |
|  | 21 May 2007 (E) (exception noted above) (SI 2007/1493) |
|  | *Not yet in force* (W) (in so far as substitutes in Highways Act 1980, Sch 6, para 2(2), (3) a reference to a special diversion order (except for certain purposes[4]), a public path diversion order or an SSSI diversion order) |
| para 23(5)(c) | *Not yet in force* |
| para 23(6) | *Not yet in force* |
| para 23(7) | 12 Feb 2003 (E) (except so far as relates to an SSSI diversion order or a draft SSSI diversion order, and except so far as substitutes Highways Act 1980, Sch 6, para 2A(1)(b)) (SI 2003/272) |
|  | 15 Jul 2005 (W) (except in so far as substitutes in Highways Act 1980, Sch 6, para 2A(1)(b); for certain purposes[4]) (SI 2005/1314, art 3) |
|  | 21 May 2007 (E) (except in so far as substitutes Highways Act 1980, Sch 6, para 2A(1)(b)) (SI 2007/1493) |
|  | *Not yet in force* (exceptions noted above) |
| para 23(8) | 12 Feb 2003 (E) (except so far as relates to an SSSI diversion order or a draft SSSI diversion order) (SI 2003/272) |
|  | 15 Jul 2005 (W) (for certain purposes[4]) (SI 2005/1314, art 3) |
|  | 11 May 2006 (W) (otherwise) (SI 2006/1279) |
|  | 21 May 2007 (E) (exceptions noted above) (SI 2007/1493) |
| para 23(9)(a) | 12 Feb 2003 (E) (except so far as relates to an SSSI diversion order or a draft SSSI diversion order) (SI 2003/272) |
|  | 15 Jul 2005 (W) (for certain purposes[4]) (SI 2005/1314, art 3) |
|  | 21 May 2007 (E) (exceptions noted above) (SI 2007/1493) |
|  | *Not yet in force* (W) (except in so far as relates to a provision brought into force by SI 2005/1314, art 3) |
| para 23(9)(b) | 12 Feb 2003 (E) (except so far as relates to an SSSI diversion order or a draft SSSI diversion order) (SI 2003/272) |
|  | 15 Jul 2005 (W) (in so far as substitutes in Highways Act 1980, Sch 6, para 3(2) a reference to a special diversion order; for certain purposes[4]) (SI 2005/1314, art 3) |
|  | 21 May 2007 (E) (exceptions noted above) (SI 2007/1493) |
|  | *Not yet in force* (W) (in so far as substitutes in Highways Act 1980, Sch 6, para 3(2) a reference to a special diversion order (except for certain purposes[4]), a rail crossing diversion order or an SSSI diversion order) |
| para 23(10) | *Not yet in force* |

**Countryside and Rights of Way Act 2000 (c 37)**—*contd*

|  |  |  |
|---|---|---|
|  | para 24 | 12 Feb 2003 (E) (except so far as relates to (1) an SSSI diversion order or (2) any order made on an application or on an appeal under Highways Act 1980, s 121D(1)(a)) (SI 2003/272) |
|  |  | 31 May 2005 (W) (SI 2005/1314) |
|  |  | 21 May 2007 (E) (in so far as relates to an SSSI diversion order) (SI 2007/1493) |
|  |  | *Not yet in force* (E) (exception (2) noted above) |
|  | para 25 | 12 Feb 2003 (E) (SI 2003/272) |
|  | para 26 | 12 Feb 2003 (E) (SI 2003/272) |
|  |  | 6 Dec 2006 (W) (SI 2006/3257) |
| Sch 7 | paras 1–5 | 30 Jan 2001 (s 103(2)) |
|  | paras 6, 7 | *Never in force* (repealed) |
|  | paras 8, 9 | 30 Jan 2001 (s 103(2)) |
| Schs 8–12 |  | 30 Jan 2001 (s 103(2)) |
| Schs 13–15 |  | 1 Apr 2001 (E) (SI 2001/114) |
|  |  | 1 May 2001 (W) (SI 2001/1410) |
| Sch 16 | Pt I | 1 Apr 2001 (E) (SI 2001/114), except repeals of or in— |
|  |  | Law of Property Act 1925, s 193(2); |
|  |  | Local Government Act 1972, Sch 17, para 35A; |
|  |  | Local Government (Wales) Act 1994 |
|  |  | 1 May 2001 (W) (SI 2001/1410), except repeals of or in— |
|  |  | Law of Property Act 1925, s 193(2)[9, 10]; |
|  |  | Local Government Act 1972, Sch 17, para 35A; |
|  |  | Local Government (Wales) Act 1994 |
|  |  | 21 Jun 2004 (W) (repeal of Law of Property Act 1925, s 193(2)) (SI 2004/1489)[2] |
|  |  | 28 May 2005 (W) (otherwise) (SI 2005/423) |
|  |  | 31 Oct 2005 (E) (SI 2005/2752), repeals of or in— |
|  |  | Local Government Act 1972, Sch 17, para 35A; |
|  |  | Local Government (Wales) Act 1994 |
|  |  | *Not yet in force* (E) (repeal of Law of Property Act 1925, s 193(2)) |
|  | Pt II | 30 Jan 2001 (E) (repeals of or in Road Traffic Regulation Act 1984, s 22(1)(a)) (SI 2001/114) |
|  |  | 1 Apr 2001 (E) (repeals of or in Highways Act 1980, s 134(5); note that the repeal of Highways Act 1980, s 134(5), shall not have effect in relation to any offence under s 134 of the 1980 Act committed before 1 Apr 2001) (SI 2001/114) |
|  |  | 1 May 2001 (W) (SI 2001/1410), repeals of or in— |
|  |  | Road Traffic Regulation Act 1984, s 22(1)(a); |
|  |  | Highways Act 1980, s 134(5); note that the repeal of Highways Act 1980, s 134(5), shall not have effect in relation to any offence under s 134 of the 1980 Act committed before 1 May 2001 |
|  |  | 2 May 2006 (E) (repeal of Wildlife and Countryside Act 1981, s 54) (SI 2006/1172) |
|  |  | 11 May 2006 (W) (repeals of or in Wildlife and Countryside Act 1981, ss 54, 56(5), 57(1)) (SI 2006/1279) |
|  |  | 6 Dec 2006 (W) (repeals of or in Wildlife and Countryside Act 1981, Sch 15, para 9) (SI 2006/3257) |
|  |  | *Not yet in force* (E), repeals of or in— |
|  |  | Wildlife and Countryside Act 1981, ss 56(5), 57(1), Sch 15, para 9; |
|  |  | Transport and Works Act 1992, Sch 2, paras 5(2), (4)(a), (d), (e), (6), (7), 6(2)(b), 10(4)(a) |
|  |  | *Not yet in force* (W) (repeals of or in Transport and Works Act 1992, Sch 2, paras 5(2), (4)(a), (d), (e), (6), (7), 6(2)(b), 10(4)(a)) |
|  | Pts III, IV | 30 Jan 2001 (E) (s 103(2)) (SI 2001/114) |
|  |  | 1 May 2001 (W) (SI 2001/1410) |
|  | Pts V, VI | 1 Apr 2001 (E) (SI 2001/114) |

### Countryside and Rights of Way Act 2000 (c 37)—*contd*
1 May 2001 (W) (SI 2001/1410)

[1]  For transitional provisions, see SI 2004/292, art 3

[2]  For a saving, see SI 2004/1489, art 3

[3]  For transitional provisions, see SI 2005/1314, art 5

[4]  This provision is brought into force in so far as it relates to a provision brought into force by SI 2005/1314, art 3

[5]  Note that SI 2004/292 did not expressly bring ss 51, 57 into force in so far as they introduce the provisions of Schs 5, 6 brought into force by that order; accordingly, SI 2005/2549 brings Sch 5, paras 8, 10, 11 and Sch 6, para 3 and ss 51, 57, in so far as they relate thereto, into force in relation to England, in so far as they are not already in force by virtue of SI 2004/292, on 27 Sep 2005

[6]  Maps in conclusive form showing open country and registered common land have now been issued for all areas of England and Wales, therefore it is thought that no land would fall within the scope of s 1(1)(c), (d). However, no registered common land was included in the conclusive map for the South East area, due to the destruction of the relevant records by fire at the time when the provisional map was prepared. It is unclear whether registered common land in East Sussex would fall within s 1(1)(c)

[7]  For savings, see SI 2006/1172, art 3

[8]  For transitional provisions, see SI 2006/1279, art 3

[9]  Note that SI 2004/315 did not expressly bring ss 57, 102 into force in so far as they introduce the provisions of Schs 6, 16, Pt 1, brought into force by that order; accordingly, SI 2006/3257 brings Sch 6, paras 1, 6, 9(5), Sch 16, Pt 1 (repeal of Law of Property Act 1925, s 193(2)), and ss 57, 102, in so far as they relate thereto, into force in relation to Wales, on 6 Dec 2006

[10]  For savings, see SI 2006/3257, art 4

---

### Criminal Justice and Court Services Act 2000 (c 43)

*RA:* 30 Nov 2000

*Commencement provisions:* s 80; Criminal Justice and Court Services Act 2000 (Commencement No 1) Order 2000, SI 2000/3302; Criminal Justice and Court Services Act 2000 (Commencement No 2) Order 2001, SI 2001/340; Criminal Justice and Court Services Act 2000 (Commencement No 3) Order 2001, SI 2001/562; Criminal Justice and Court Services Act 2000 (Commencement No 4) Order 2001, SI 2001/919; Criminal Justice and Court Services Act 2000 (Commencement No 5) (Scotland) Order 2001, SSI 2001/166; Criminal Justice and Court Services Act 2000 (Commencement No 6) Order 2001, SI 2001/1651; Criminal Justice and Court Services Act 2000 (Commencement No 7) Order 2001, SI 2001/2232; Criminal Justice and Court Services Act 2000 (Commencement No 8) Order 2001, SI 2001/3385; Criminal Justice and Court Services Act 2000 (Commencement No 9) Order 2002, SI 2002/1149; Criminal Justice and Court Services Act 2000 (Commencement No 10) Order 2002, SI 2002/1862; Criminal Justice and Court Services Act 2000 (Commencement No 11) Order 2003, SI 2003/709; Criminal Justice and Court Services Act 2000 (Commencement No 12) Order 2004, SI 2004/780; Criminal Justice and Court Services Act 2000 (Commencement No 13) Order 2004, SI 2004/2171; Criminal Justice and Court Services Act 2000 (Commencement No 14) Order 2005, SI 2005/596; Criminal Justice and Court Services Act 2000 (Commencement No 15) Order 2005, SI 2005/3054

| | | |
|---|---|---|
| 1–3 | | 1 Apr 2001 (SI 2001/919) |
| 4 | (1), (2) | 1 Apr 2001 (SI 2001/919) |
| | (3) | See Sch 1 below |
| | (4), (6) | 1 Apr 2001 (SI 2001/919) |
| 5–10 | | 1 Apr 2001 (SI 2001/919) |
| 11 | (1) | 1 Apr 2001 (SI 2001/919) |
| | (2) | See Sch 2 below |
| | (3) | 1 Apr 2001 (SI 2001/919) |
| 12–18 | | 1 Apr 2001 (SI 2001/919) |
| 19–22 | | 30 Nov 2000 (s 80(3)) |
| 23–25 | | 1 Apr 2001 (SI 2001/919) |
| 26 | | See Sch 4 below |

**Criminal Justice and Court Services Act 2000 (c 43)**—*contd*

| | |
|---|---|
| 27–42 | 11 Jan 2001 (SI 2000/3302) |
| 43–45 | 1 Apr 2001 (SI 2001/919) |
| 46 | 2 Sep 2004 (SI 2004/2171) |
| 47–50 | 20 Jun 2001 (for purpose of exercising any power conferred on the Secretary of State to make orders) (SI 2001/2232) |
| | 2 Jul 2001 (otherwise) (SI 2001/2232) |
| 51 | *Never in force* (repealed) |
| 52 | 20 Jun 2001 (for purpose of exercising any power conferred on the Secretary of State to make orders, except so far as it relates to exclusion orders and exclusion requirements) (SI 2001/2232) |
| | 2 Jul 2001 (otherwise) (except so far as it relates to exclusion orders and exclusion requirements) (SI 2001/2232) |
| | 2 Sep 2004 (otherwise) (except so far as it relates to exclusion requirements) (SI 2004/2171) |
| | *Not yet in force* (so far as it relates to exclusion requirements) |
| 53 | *Never in force* (repealed) |
| 54, 55 | 1 Apr 2001 (SI 2001/919) |
| 56 | 1 Feb 2001 (SI 2000/3302) |
| 57 | 20 Jun 2001 (for purpose of exercising any power conferred on the Secretary of State to make orders, within the following police areas only: Nottinghamshire; Staffordshire; the metropolitan police district) (SI 2001/2232) |
| | 2 Jul 2001 (otherwise, within the following police areas only: Nottinghamshire; Staffordshire; the metropolitan police district) (SI 2001/2232) |
| | 20 May 2002 (within the following police areas only: Bedfordshire; Devon and Cornwall; Lancashire; Merseyside; South Yorkshire; North Wales) (SI 2002/1149) |
| | 2 Sep 2002 (within the following police areas only: Avon and Somerset; Greater Manchester; Thames Valley; West Yorkshire) (SI 2002/1862) |
| | 1 Apr 2003 (within the following police areas only: Cleveland; Humber) (SI 2003/709) |
| | 1 Apr 2004 (within the following police areas only: Cambridgeshire; Leicestershire; Northumbria; West Midlands) (SI 2004/780) |
| | 1 Apr 2005 (within the following police areas only: Gwent; Northamptonshire; South Wales) (SI 2005/596) |
| | 1 Dec 2005 (otherwise, ie within the following police areas: Cheshire; City of London; Cumbria; Derbyshire; Dorset; Durham; Essex; Gloucestershire; Hampshire; Hertfordshire; Kent; Lincolnshire; Norfolk; North Yorkshire; Suffolk; Surrey; Sussex; Warwickshire; West Mercia; Wiltshire; Dyfed Powys) (SI 2005/3054) |
| 58 | 20 Jun 2001 (for purpose of exercising any power conferred on the Secretary of State to make orders) (SI 2001/2232) |
| | 2 Jul 2001 (otherwise) (SI 2001/2232) |
| 59 | *Not yet in force* |
| 60 | 30 Nov 2000 (s 80(3)) |
| 61 | *Not yet in force* |
| 62 | 1 Feb 2001 (SI 2000/3302) |
| 63 | 1 Feb 2001 (so far as inserts Criminal Justice Act 1991, s 65(5A)(a), (b), s 65(5C) (so far as it applies to sub-s (5A)(a), (b))) (SI 2000/3302) |
| | 20 Jun 2001 (so far as inserts Criminal Justice Act 1991, s 65(5A)(c), (5B), (5C) (so far as it applies to sub-s (5A)(c)), s 65(5D), (9), (10)) (for purpose of exercising any power conferred on the Secretary of State to make orders) (SI 2001/2232) |

**Criminal Justice and Court Services Act 2000 (c 43)**—*contd*

|  |  |  |
|---|---|---|
| | | 2 Jul 2001 (so far as inserts Criminal Justice Act 1991, s 65(5A)(c), (5B), (5C) (so far as it applies to sub-s (5A)(c)), s 65(5D), (9), (10)) (otherwise) (SI 2001/2232) |
| 64 | | 20 Jun 2001 (for purpose of exercising any power conferred on the Secretary of State to make orders) (SI 2001/2232) |
| | | 2 Jul 2001 (otherwise) (SI 2001/2232) |
| 65 | | 1 Mar 2001 (SI 2001/340) |
| 66 | | See Sch 5 below |
| 67–69 | | 1 Apr 2001 (SI 2001/919) |
| 70 | | 20 Jun 2001 (for purpose of exercising any power conferred on the Secretary of State to make orders) (SI 2001/2232) |
| | | 2 Jul 2001 (otherwise) (SI 2001/2232) |
| 71 | (1)–(4) | 29 Oct 2001 (SI 2001/3385) |
| | (5) | *Never in force* (repealed) |
| 72 | | 1 Mar 2001 (SI 2001/562) |
| 73 | | 1 Apr 2001 (SI 2001/919) |
| 74 | | See Sch 7 below |
| 75 | | See Sch 8 below |
| 76–82 | | 30 Nov 2000 (s 80(3)) |
| Schs 1–3 | | 1 Apr 2001 (SI 2001/919) |
| Sch 4 | | 11 Jan 2001 (SI 2000/3302) |
| Sch 5 | | 2 May 2001 (E) (W) (NI) (for purpose of exercising any power conferred on the Secretary of State to make regulations or an order) (SI 2001/1651) |
| | | 31 May 2001 (S) (SSI 2001/166) |
| | | 1 Jun 2001 (E) (W) (NI) (otherwise) (SI 2001/1651) |
| Sch 6 | | 20 Jun 2001 (for purpose of exercising any power conferred on the Secretary of State to make orders) (SI 2001/2232) |
| | | 2 Jul 2001 (otherwise) (SI 2001/2232) |
| Sch 7 | paras 1–4 | 1 Apr 2001 (SI 2001/919) |
| | para 5 | *Not yet in force* |
| | para 6 | 1 Apr 2001 (SI 2001/919) |
| | paras 7–11 | *Not yet in force* |
| | para 12 | 11 Jan 2001 (SI 2000/3302) |
| | para 13 | *Not yet in force* |
| | para 14 | 11 Jan 2001 (SI 2000/3302) |
| | para 15(1)(a)–(d) | *Not yet in force* |
| | para 15(1)(e) | 30 Nov 2000 (s 80(3)) |
| | para 15(1)(f), (g) | *Not yet in force* |
| | para 15(2) | 30 Nov 2000 (s 80(3)) |
| | paras 16, 17 | *Not yet in force* |
| | para 18(1), (2) | *Not yet in force* |
| | para 18(3)(a), (b) | *Not yet in force* |
| | para 18(3)(c)(i) | 30 Nov 2000 (s 80(3)) |
| | para 18(3)(c)(ii) | *Not yet in force* |
| | para 18(4) | 30 Nov 2000 (s 80(3)) |
| | para 19 | 11 Jan 2001 (SI 2000/3302) |
| | para 20 | *Not yet in force* |
| | para 21 | 11 Jan 2001 (SI 2000/3302) |
| | para 22(1)(a)–(d) | *Not yet in force* |
| | para 22(1)(e) | 30 Nov 2000 (s 80(3)) |
| | para 22(1)(f), (g) | *Not yet in force* |
| | para 22(2) | 30 Nov 2000 (s 80(3)) |
| | paras 23, 24 | *Not yet in force* |
| | para 25(1), (2) | *Not yet in force* |
| | para 25(3)(a), (b) | *Not yet in force* |
| | para 25(3)(c)(i) | 30 Nov 2000 (s 80(3)) |
| | para 25(3)(c)(ii) | *Not yet in force* |
| | para 25(4) | 30 Nov 2000 (s 80(3)) |

**Criminal Justice and Court Services Act 2000 (c 43)**—*contd*

| | |
|---|---|
| para 26 | 11 Jan 2001 (SI 2000/3302) |
| para 27 | *Not yet in force* |
| para 28 | 11 Jan 2001 (SI 2000/3302) |
| para 29(1)(a)–(d) | *Not yet in force* |
| para 29(1)(e) | 30 Nov 2000 (s 80(3)) |
| para 29(1)(f), (g) | *Not yet in force* |
| para 29(2) | 30 Nov 2000 (s 80(3)) |
| paras 30, 31 | *Not yet in force* |
| para 32(1), (2) | *Not yet in force* |
| para 32(3)(a), (b) | *Not yet in force* |
| para 32(3)(c)(i) | 30 Nov 2000 (s 80(3)) |
| para 32(3)(c)(ii) | *Not yet in force* |
| para 32(4) | 30 Nov 2000 (s 80(3)) |
| paras 33–36 | *Not yet in force* |
| paras 37, 38 | 1 Apr 2001 (SI 2001/919) |
| para 39 | *Never in force* (repealed) |
| paras 40–53 | 1 Apr 2001 (SI 2001/919) |
| paras 54–56 | *Not yet in force* |
| paras 57, 58 | 1 Apr 2001 (SI 2001/919) |
| paras 59, 60 | *Not yet in force* |
| para 61 | 1 Apr 2001 (SI 2001/919) |
| paras 62–70 | *Not yet in force* (para 69 repealed) |
| paras 71, 72 | 1 Apr 2001 (SI 2001/919) |
| para 73 | *Not yet in force* |
| paras 74, 75 | 1 Apr 2001 (SI 2001/919) |
| para 76 | *Not yet in force* |
| para 77 | *Never in force* (repealed) |
| para 78 | 2 Jul 2001 (SI 2001/2232) |
| paras 79–82 | 1 Apr 2001 (SI 2001/919) |
| para 83 | 11 Jan 2001 (SI 2000/3302) |
| paras 84–97 | 1 Apr 2001 (SI 2001/919) |
| para 98 | *Not yet in force* |
| paras 99, 100 | 1 Apr 2001 (SI 2001/919) |
| para 101 | *Never in force* (repealed) |
| paras 102, 103 | 1 Apr 2001 (SI 2001/919) |
| para 104 | *Never in force* (repealed) |
| para 105 | 2 Jul 2001 (SI 2001/2232) |
| paras 106, 107 | *Never in force* (repealed) |
| paras 108, 109 | *Not yet in force* |
| para 110 | 1 Apr 2001 (SI 2001/919) |
| para 111(a) | 1 Apr 2001 (SI 2001/919) |
| para 111(b) | *Never in force* (repealed) |
| paras 112–115 | *Not yet in force* |
| paras 116–118 | 1 Apr 2001 (SI 2001/919) |
| para 119 | *Not yet in force* |
| paras 120–126 | 1 Apr 2001 (SI 2001/919) |
| paras 127–130 | 11 Jan 2001 (SI 2000/3302) |
| paras 131–133 | 1 Apr 2001 (SI 2001/919) |
| para 134 | *Not yet in force* |
| paras 135–138 | 30 Nov 2000 (s 80(3)) |
| paras 139, 140 | *Never in force* (repealed) |
| para 141 | 1 Apr 2001 (SI 2001/919) |
| para 142 | 30 Nov 2000 (s 80(3)) |
| para 143 | 1 Apr 2001 (SI 2001/919) |
| paras 144–148 | 30 Nov 2000 (s 80(3)) |
| para 149 | *Not yet in force* |
| paras 150–153 | 1 Apr 2001 (SI 2001/919) |
| paras 154–159 | 11 Jan 2001 (SI 2000/3302) |
| para 160 | See paras 161–204 below |

**Criminal Justice and Court Services Act 2000 (c 43)**—*contd*

| | |
|---|---|
| para 161(a) | 2 Sep 2004 (SI 2004/2171) |
| para 161(b) | 2 Jul 2001 (SI 2001/2232) |
| paras 162, 163 | 2 Jul 2001 (SI 2001/2232) |
| para 164 | 20 Jun 2001 (for purpose of exercising any power conferred on the Secretary of State to make orders, except for the reference in sub-para (b) to Powers of Criminal Courts (Sentencing) Act 2000, Sch 3, paras 2A(4), (5)) (SI 2001/2232) |
| | 2 Jul 2001 (otherwise) (except for the reference in sub-para (b) to Powers of Criminal Courts (Sentencing) Act 2000, Sch 3, paras 2A(4), (5)) (SI 2001/2232) |
| | *Never in force* (exception noted above) (repealed) |
| para 165 | *Never in force* (repealed) |
| para 166 | 1 Apr 2001 (SI 2001/919) |
| para 167 | *Never in force* (repealed) |
| paras 168, 169 | 1 Apr 2001 (SI 2001/919) |
| para 170 | *Never in force* (repealed) |
| para 171 | 1 Apr 2001 (SI 2001/919) |
| para 172 | *Never in force* (repealed) |
| para 173 | *Not yet in force* |
| paras 174, 175 | 1 Apr 2001 (SI 2001/919) |
| para 176 | *Not yet in force* |
| para 177 | *Never in force* (repealed) |
| para 178 | *Not yet in force* |
| para 179 | *Never in force* (repealed) |
| paras 180–188 | *Not yet in force* |
| para 189 | *Never in force* (repealed) |
| paras 190–194 | *Not yet in force* (para 192 repealed) |
| para 195 | 1 Apr 2001 (SI 2001/919) |
| para 196 | 20 Jun 2001 (for purpose of exercising any power conferred on the Secretary of State to make orders, except for references to Powers of Criminal Courts (Sentencing) Act 2000, ss 40A(6), 40C(1), (2), Sch 2, para 8, Sch 3, para 1(1A)) (SI 2001/2232) |
| | 2 Jul 2001 (otherwise) (except for references to Powers of Criminal Courts (Sentencing) Act 2000, ss 40A(6), 40C(1), (2), Sch 2, para 8, Sch 3, para 1(1A)) (SI 2001/2232) |
| | 2 Sep 2004 (otherwise) (except sub-para (c)(iii) and references to Powers of Criminal Courts (Sentencing) Act 2000, Sch 2, para 8) (SI 2004/2171) |
| | *Not yet in force* (exceptions noted above) |
| para 197(a) | *Not yet in force* |
| para 197(b) | 1 Apr 2001 (SI 2001/919) |
| para 197(c), (d) | *Never in force* (repealed) |
| para 197(e) | *Not yet in force* |
| para 197(f) | 1 Apr 2001 (so far as relates to definitions "community rehabilitation period" and "local probation board") (SI 2001/919) |
| | 2 Jul 2001 (otherwise, so far as relates to drug abstinence orders) (SI 2001/2232) |
| | 2 Sep 2004 (so far as relates to an exclusion order) (SI 2004/2171) |
| | *Not yet in force* (so far as relates to definition "affected person") |
| para 197(g)(i) | 2 Sep 2004 (SI 2004/2171) |
| para 197(g)(ii) | 2 Jul 2001 (SI 2001/2232) |
| para 198 | 1 Apr 2001 (SI 2001/919) |
| para 199(1) | 1 Apr 2001 (SI 2001/919) |
| para 199(2)(a) | 2 Jul 2001 (so far as relates to drug abstinence orders) (SI 2001/2232) |
| | 2 Sep 2004 (otherwise) (SI 2004/2171) |
| para 199(2)(b) | 1 Apr 2001 (save in so far as relates to exclusion and drug abstinence orders) (SI 2001/919) |

**See Halsbury's Statutes Citator for amendments to these Acts** 1183

**Criminal Justice and Court Services Act 2000 (c 43)**—*contd*

|  |  |
|---|---|
|  | 2 Jul 2001 (otherwise, so far as relates to drug abstinence orders) (SI 2001/2232) |
|  | 2 Sep 2004 (otherwise) (SI 2004/2171) |
| para 199(2)(c) | 2 Jul 2001 (SI 2001/2232) |
| para 199(3), (4) | 1 Apr 2001 (SI 2001/919) |
| para 199(5) | 1 Apr 2001 (save in so far as relates to exclusion and drug abstinence orders) (SI 2001/919) |
|  | 2 Jul 2001 (otherwise, so far as relates to drug abstinence orders) (SI 2001/2232) |
|  | 2 Sep 2004 (otherwise) (SI 2004/2171) |
| para 199(6) | 2 Jul 2001 (SI 2001/2232) |
| para 199(7)–(9) | *Never in force* (repealed) |
| para 199(10) | 1 Apr 2001 (so far as it substitutes cross-heading preceding Powers of Criminal Courts (Sentencing) Act 2000, Sch 3, para 7) (SI 2001/919) |
|  | *Never in force* (otherwise) (repealed) |
| para 199(11)(a) | *Never in force* (repealed) |
| para 199(11)(b)(i) | 2 Jul 2001 (SI 2001/2232) |
| para 199(11)(b)(ii) | *Never in force* (repealed) |
| para 199(11)(c) | *Never in force* (repealed) |
| para 199(12) | *Never in force* (repealed) |
| para 199(13) | 2 Jul 2001 (SI 2001/2232) |
| para 199(14)–(18) | 1 Apr 2001 (SI 2001/919) |
| para 199(19) | *Never in force* (repealed) |
| para 199(20) | 1 Apr 2001 (SI 2001/919) |
| para 199(21)(a)(i), (ii) | 2 Sep 2004 (SI 2004/2171) |
| para 199(21)(a)(iii) | 1 Apr 2001 (save in so far as relates to exclusion orders) (SI 2001/919) |
|  | *Never in force* (otherwise) (repealed) |
| para 199(21)(b) | 2 Jul 2001 (so far as inserts Powers of Criminal Courts (Sentencing) Act 2000, Sch 3, para 19(2)(aa)) (SI 2001/2232) |
|  | 2 Sep 2004 (otherwise) (SI 2004/2171) |
| para 199(21)(c) | 2 Jul 2001 (SI 2001/2232) |
| para 199(21)(d) | 2 Jul 2001 (so far as inserts Powers of Criminal Courts (Sentencing) Act 2000, Sch 3, para 19(6)) (SI 2001/2232) |
|  | 2 Sep 2004 (otherwise) (SI 2004/2171) |
| para 199(21)(e) | 1 Apr 2001 (save in so far as relates to exclusion orders) (SI 2001/919) |
|  | 2 Sep 2004 (otherwise) (SI 2004/2171) |
| para 199(22), (23) | 1 Apr 2001 (SI 2001/919) |
| para 199(24), (25)(a) | 2 Jul 2001 (SI 2001/2232) |
| para 199(25)(b), (c), (26) | *Never in force* (repealed) |
| para 199(27) | 1 Apr 2001 (SI 2001/919) |
| para 200 | 1 Apr 2001 (SI 2001/919) |
| para 201(1), (2)(a) | 2 Jul 2001 (SI 2001/2232) |
| para 201(2)(b), (3) | *Never in force* (repealed) |
| para 202(1), (2)(a) | 2 Jul 2001 (SI 2001/2232) |
| para 202(2)(b) | *Never in force* (repealed) |
| para 202(3) | *Not yet in force* |
| para 203(1) | 1 Apr 2001 (SI 2001/919) |
| para 203(2) | 1 Apr 2001 (so far as relates to Powers of Criminal Courts (Sentencing) Act 2000, Sch 9, paras 34(a), 153–156) (SI 2001/919) |
|  | *Not yet in force* (so far as relates to Powers of Criminal Courts (Sentencing) Act 2000, Sch 9, paras 5(3), 9, 10, 12, 14, 15, 17, 19, 20, 22, 56, 57, 66, 68, 70, 77, 78, 111(4), 143(b), 152, 166(3)) |

**Criminal Justice and Court Services Act 2000 (c 43)**—*contd*

| | | |
|---|---|---|
| | para 203(3), (4) | 30 Nov 2000 (s 80(3)) |
| | para 203(5) | *Not yet in force* |
| | para 204 | *Never in force* (repealed) |
| | paras 205–210 | 1 Apr 2001 (SI 2001/919) |
| | para 211 | *Not yet in force* |
| Sch 8 | | 30 Nov 2000 (s 80(3)), repeals of or in— |

            Crime (Sentences) Act 1997, ss 28, 34, Sch 5, para 5;
            Powers of Criminal Courts (Sentencing) Act 2000, Sch 9,
              paras 182, 188
        11 Jan 2001 (repeal of Protection of Children Act 1999, s 6)
          (SI 2000/3302)
        1 Apr 2001 (SI 2001/919), repeals of or in—
          Metropolitan Magistrates' Courts Act 1959;
          Children and Young Persons Act 1969, s 46(1), Sch 3,
            para 9(2)(a);
          Local Government Act 1972;
          Juries Act 1974;
          Adoption Act 1976;
          Magistrates' Courts Act 1980, s 72;
          Health and Social Services and Social Security Adjudications
            Act 1983;
          Children Act 1989;
          Courts and Legal Services Act 1990;
          Probation Service Act 1993;
          Criminal Justice and Public Order Act 1994, Sch 10, paras 72,
            73;
          Local Government (Wales) Act 1994;
          Crime and Disorder Act 1998;
          Access to Justice Act 1999;
          Greater London Authority Act 1999;
          Learning and Skills Act 2000;
          Powers of Criminal Courts (Sentencing) Act 2000, ss 46(13),
            47(5), 64(2), 163, Sch 9, paras 34(a), 153–156
        2 Jul 2001 (repeals of Powers of Criminal Courts (Sentencing)
          Act 2000, ss 38, 40(1)(a)) (SI 2001/2232)
        *Not yet in force*, repeals of or in—
          Criminal Justice Act 1948;
          Prison Act 1952;
          Air Force Act 1955;
          Army Act 1955;
          Naval Discipline Act 1957;
          Criminal Justice Act 1967;
          Finance Act 1968;
          Firearms Act 1968;
          Children and Young Persons Act 1969, s 23;
          Fire Precautions Act 1971;
          Imprisonment (Temporary Provisions) Act 1980;
          Magistrates' Courts Act 1980, ss 11, 31, 77, 96A, 133, 135, 136,
            Sch 6A;
          Mental Health Act 1983;
          Criminal Justice Act 1988;
          Road Traffic Act 1988;
          Criminal Justice Act 1991;
          Criminal Procedure (Insanity and Unfitness to Plead) Act 1991;
          Local Government Finance Act 1992;
          Criminal Justice and Public Order Act 1994, ss 117, 125;
          Drug Trafficking Act 1994;
          Prisoners' Earnings Act 1996;
          Criminal Justice and Court Services Act 2000;

**Criminal Justice and Court Services Act 2000 (c 43)**—*contd*

> Powers of Criminal Courts (Sentencing) Act 2000, ss 76, 78, 87,
> 93–99, 106, 108, 110, 111, 137, 139, 140, Schs 3, 7, 8, Sch 9,
> paras 5, 9, 10, 12, 14, 15, 17, 19, 20, 22, 56, 57, 66, 68, 70,
> 77, 78, 111, 143, 152, 163, 183, 188

**Crown Prosecution Service Inspectorate Act 2000 (c 10)**

*RA:* 20 Jul 2000

*Commencement provisions:* s 3(2); Crown Prosecution Service Inspectorate Act 2000 (Commencement) Order 2000, SI 2000/2423

| | |
|---|---|
| 1, 2 | 1 Oct 2000 (SI 2000/2423) |
| 3 | 20 Jul 2000 (RA) |

**Disqualifications Act 2000 (c 42)**

*RA:* 30 Nov 2000

Whole Act in force 30 Nov 2000 (RA)

**Education and Training (Scotland) Act 2000 (asp 8)**

*RA:* 9 Aug 2000

Whole Act in force 9 Aug 2000 (RA)

**Electronic Communications Act 2000 (c 7)**

*RA:* 25 May 2000

*Commencement provisions:* s 16(2)–(4); Electronic Communications Act 2000 (Commencement No 1) Order 2000, SI 2000/1798

| | |
|---|---|
| 1–6 | *Never in force* (repealed) |
| 7 | 25 Jul 2000 (SI 2000/1798) |
| 8–10 | 25 May 2000 (RA) |
| 11, 12 | 25 Jul 2000 (SI 2000/1798) |
| 13–16 | 25 May 2000 (RA) |

**Ethical Standards in Public Life etc (Scotland) Act 2000 (asp 7)**

*RA:* 24 Jul 2000

*Commencement provisions:* s 37(2), (3); Ethical Standards in Public Life etc (Scotland) Act 2000 (Commencement No 1) Order 2001, SSI 2001/113; Ethical Standards in Public Life etc (Scotland) Act 2000 (Commencement No 2 and Transitional Provisions) Order 2001, SSI 2001/474; Ethical Standards in Public Life etc (Scotland) Act 2000 (Commencement No 3) Order 2003, SSI 2003/74

| | | |
|---|---|---|
| 1–3 | | 29 Mar 2001 (SSI 2001/113) |
| 4, 5 | | 1 May 2003 (SSI 2003/74) |
| 6 | | 21 Feb 2003 (SSI 2003/74) |
| 7 | (1) | 1 May 2003 (SSI 2003/74) |
| | (2) | 21 Feb 2003 (for the purpose of making regulations) (SSI 2003/74) |
| | | 1 May 2003 (otherwise) (SSI 2003/74) |
| | (3)–(5) | 1 May 2003 (SSI 2003/74) |
| 8, 9 | | 29 Mar 2001 (SSI 2001/113) |
| 10–24 | | 1 May 2003 (SSI 2003/74) |
| 25 | (1)–(8) | 21 Feb 2003 (SSI 2003/74) |

**Ethical Standards in Public Life etc (Scotland) Act 2000 (asp 7)**—*contd*

| | | |
|---|---|---|
| | (9)–(13) | 1 May 2003 (SSI 2003/74) |
| 26 | | 1 May 2003 (SSI 2003/74) |
| 27 | | 21 Feb 2003 (SSI 2003/74) |
| 28 | | 29 Mar 2001 (SSI 2001/113) |
| 29 | | 1 May 2003 (SSI 2003/74) |
| 30, 31 | | 29 Mar 2001 (SSI 2001/113) |
| 32 | | 1 May 2003 (SSI 2003/74) |
| 33 | | 1 Jan 2002 (SSI 2001/474) |
| 34, 35 | | 29 Mar 2001 (SSI 2001/113) |
| 36 | (1) | See Sch 4 below |
| | (2) | 1 May 2003 (SSI 2003/74) |
| 37 | | 24 Jul 2000 (RA) |
| Schs 1–3 | | 29 Mar 2001 (SSI 2001/113) |
| Sch 4 | | 29 Mar 2001 (repeal of Local Government Act 1988, s 28) (SSI 2001/113) |
| | | 1 May 2003 (otherwise) (SSI 2003/74) |

**Finance Act 2000 (c 17)**

*Budget Day:* 21 Mar 2000

*RA:* 28 Jul 2000

The commencement details of Finance Acts are not set out, as the dates from which their provisions take effect are usually stated clearly and unambiguously in the text of the Act, and charging provisions will normally state for which year or years of assessment they are to have effect.

**Financial Services and Markets Act 2000 (c 8)**

*RA:* 14 Jun 2000

*Commencement provisions:* s 431; Financial Services and Markets Act 2000 (Commencement No 1) Order 2001, SI 2001/516; Financial Services and Markets Act 2000 (Commencement No 2) Order 2001, SI 2001/1282; Financial Services and Markets Act 2000 (Commencement No 3) Order 2001, SI 2001/1820; Financial Services and Markets Act 2000 (Commencement No 4 and Transitional Provisions) Order 2001, SI 2001/2364[1]; Financial Services and Markets Act 2000 (Commencement No 5) Order 2001, SI 2001/2632; Financial Services and Markets Act 2000 (Commencement No 6) Order 2001, SI 2001/3436; Financial Services and Markets Act 2000 (Commencement No 7) Order 2001, SI 2001/3538

| | | |
|---|---|---|
| 1–11 | | 18 Jun 2001 (SI 2001/1820) |
| 12–19 | | 1 Dec 2001 (SI 2001/3538) |
| 20 | (1), (2) | 1 Dec 2001 (SI 2001/3538) |
| | (3) | 25 Feb 2001 (for the purpose of making orders or regulations) (SI 2001/516) |
| | | 1 Dec 2001 (otherwise) (SI 2001/3538) |
| 21 | | 25 Feb 2001 (for the purpose of making orders or regulations) (SI 2001/516) |
| | | 1 Dec 2001 (otherwise) (SI 2001/3538) |
| 22 | | 25 Feb 2001 (SI 2001/516) |
| 23–30 | | 1 Dec 2001 (SI 2001/3538) |
| 31 | (1)(a) | 1 Dec 2001 (SI 2001/3538) |
| | (1)(b) | See Sch 3 below |
| | (1)(c) | See Sch 4 below |
| | (1)(d) | 1 Dec 2001 (SI 2001/3538) |
| | (2) | 1 Dec 2001 (SI 2001/3538) |
| 32–36 | | 1 Dec 2001 (SI 2001/3538) |
| 37 | | See Sch 3 below |
| 38 | | 25 Feb 2001 (SI 2001/516) |

**Financial Services and Markets Act 2000 (c 8)**—*contd*

| | | |
|---|---|---|
| 39 | (1) | 25 Feb 2001 (for the purpose of making orders or regulations) (SI 2001/516) |
| | | 1 Dec 2001 (otherwise) (SI 2001/3538) |
| | (2)–(6) | 1 Dec 2001 (SI 2001/3538) |
| 40 | | 3 Sep 2001 (SI 2001/2632) |
| 41 | (1) | 25 Feb 2001 (SI 2001/516) |
| | (2), (3) | 3 Sep 2001 (SI 2001/2632) |
| 42, 43 | | 3 Sep 2001 (for the purposes of permissions coming into force not sooner than the day on which s 19 of this Act comes into force, and applications for such permissions) (SI 2001/2632) |
| | | 1 Dec 2001 (otherwise) (SI 2001/3538) |
| 44–46 | | 3 Sep 2001 (for the purposes of variations or cancellations taking effect not sooner than the day on which s 19 of this Act comes into force, and applications for such variations or cancellations) (SI 2001/2632) |
| | | 1 Dec 2001 (otherwise) (SI 2001/3538) |
| 47 | (1) | 25 Feb 2001 (for the purpose of making orders or regulations) (SI 2001/516) |
| | | 3 Sep 2001 (for the purposes of variations or cancellations taking effect not sooner than the day on which s 19 of this Act comes into force, and applications for such variations or cancellations) (SI 2001/2632) |
| | | 1 Dec 2001 (otherwise) (SI 2001/3538) |
| | (2) | 3 Sep 2001 (for the purposes of variations or cancellations taking effect not sooner than the day on which s 19 of this Act comes into force, and applications for such variations or cancellations) (SI 2001/2632) |
| | | 1 Dec 2001 (otherwise) (SI 2001/3538) |
| | (3) | 25 Feb 2001 (for the purpose of making orders or regulations) (SI 2001/516) |
| | | 3 Sep 2001 (for the purposes of variations or cancellations taking effect not sooner than the day on which s 19 of this Act comes into force, and applications for such variations or cancellations) (SI 2001/2632) |
| | | 1 Dec 2001 (otherwise) (SI 2001/3538) |
| | (4)–(7) | 3 Sep 2001 (for the purposes of variations or cancellations taking effect not sooner than the day on which s 19 of this Act comes into force, and applications for such variations or cancellations) (SI 2001/2632) |
| | | 1 Dec 2001 (otherwise) (SI 2001/3538) |
| 48–50 | | 3 Sep 2001 (SI 2001/2632) |
| 51 | | 18 Jun 2001 (for the purpose of giving directions or imposing requirements as mentioned in sub-s (3)) (SI 2001/1820) |
| | | 3 Sep 2001 (otherwise) (SI 2001/2632) |
| 52 | | 3 Sep 2001 (SI 2001/2632) |
| 53, 54 | | 3 Sep 2001 (for the purposes of variations and cancellations taking effect not sooner than the day on which s 19 of this Act comes into force) (SI 2001/2632) |
| | | 1 Dec 2001 (otherwise) (SI 2001/3538) |
| 55 | | 3 Sep 2001 (SI 2001/2632) |
| 56–58 | | 3 Sep 2001 (for the purposes of prohibition orders coming into force not sooner than the day on which s 19 of this Act comes into force) (SI 2001/2632) |
| | | 1 Dec 2001 (otherwise) (SI 2001/3538) |
| 59 | | 18 Jun 2001 (for the purpose of making rules) (SI 2001/1820) |
| | | 3 Sep 2001 (for the purposes of approvals coming into force not sooner than the day on which s 19 of this Act comes into force, and applications for such approvals) (SI 2001/2632) |
| | | 1 Dec 2001 (otherwise) (SI 2001/3538) |

**Financial Services and Markets Act 2000 (c 8)**—*contd*

| | | |
|---|---|---|
| 60 | | 18 Jun 2001 (for the purpose of giving directions or imposing requirements as mentioned in sub-s (2) or (4)) (SI 2001/1820) |
| | | 3 Sep 2001 (for the purposes of approvals coming into force not sooner than the day on which s 19 of this Act comes into force, and applications for such approvals) (SI 2001/2632) |
| | | 1 Dec 2001 (otherwise) (SI 2001/3538) |
| 61–63 | | 3 Sep 2001 (for the purposes of approvals coming into force not sooner than the day on which s 19 of this Act comes into force, and applications for such approvals) (SI 2001/2632) |
| | | 1 Dec 2001 (otherwise) (SI 2001/3538) |
| 64, 65 | | 18 Jun 2001 (SI 2001/1820) |
| 66–68 | | 1 Dec 2001 (SI 2001/3538) |
| 69, 70 | | 18 Jun 2001 (SI 2001/1820) |
| 71 | (1) | 1 Dec 2001 (SI 2001/3538) |
| | (2), (3) | 25 Feb 2001 (for the purpose of making orders or regulations) (SI 2001/516) |
| | | 1 Dec 2001 (otherwise) (SI 2001/3538) |
| 72, 73 | | 18 Jun 2001 (SI 2001/1820) |
| 74 | (1)–(3) | 1 Dec 2001 (SI 2001/3538) |
| | (4), (5) | 18 Jun 2001 (SI 2001/1820) |
| 75 | (1) | 18 Jun 2001 (for the purpose of making listing rules) (SI 2001/1820) |
| | | 1 Dec 2001 (otherwise) (SI 2001/3538) |
| | (2) | 1 Dec 2001 (SI 2001/3538) |
| | (3) | 25 Feb 2001 (for the purpose of making orders or regulations) (SI 2001/516) |
| | | 1 Dec 2001 (otherwise) (SI 2001/3538) |
| | (4)–(6) | 1 Dec 2001 (SI 2001/3538) |
| 76 | | 1 Dec 2001 (SI 2001/3538) |
| 77 | (1), (2) | 18 Jun 2001 (for the purpose of making listing rules) (SI 2001/1820) |
| | | 1 Dec 2001 (otherwise) (SI 2001/3538) |
| | (3) | 1 Dec 2001 (SI 2001/3538) |
| | (4) | 18 Jun 2001 (for the purpose of making listing rules) (SI 2001/1820) |
| | | 1 Dec 2001 (otherwise) (SI 2001/3538) |
| | (5) | 1 Dec 2001 (SI 2001/3538) |
| 78 | | 1 Dec 2001 (SI 2001/3538) |
| 79 | (1), (2) | 18 Jun 2001 (SI 2001/1820) |
| | (3) | 25 Feb 2001 (SI 2001/516) |
| | (4) | 18 Jun 2001 (SI 2001/1820) |
| 80 | | 1 Dec 2001 (SI 2001/3538) |
| 81 | (1) | 18 Jun 2001 (for the purpose of making listing rules) (SI 2001/1820) |
| | | 1 Dec 2001 (otherwise) (SI 2001/3538) |
| | (2)–(4) | 1 Dec 2001 (SI 2001/3538) |
| | (5) | 18 Jun 2001 (for the purpose of making listing rules) (SI 2001/1820) |
| | | 1 Dec 2001 (otherwise) (SI 2001/3538) |
| 82 | (1) | 18 Jun 2001 (for the purpose of making listing rules) (SI 2001/1820) |
| | | 1 Dec 2001 (otherwise) (SI 2001/3538) |
| | (2)–(4) | 1 Dec 2001 (SI 2001/3538) |
| | (5) | 18 Jun 2001 (for the purpose of making listing rules) (SI 2001/1820) |
| | | 1 Dec 2001 (otherwise) (SI 2001/3538) |
| | (6) | 1 Dec 2001 (SI 2001/3538) |
| | (7) | 18 Jun 2001 (for the purpose of making listing rules) (SI 2001/1820) |
| | | 1 Dec 2001 (otherwise) (SI 2001/3538) |

**Financial Services and Markets Act 2000 (c 8)**—*contd*

| | | |
|---|---|---|
| 83 | | 1 Dec 2001 (SI 2001/3538) |
| 84 | | 18 Jun 2001 (SI 2001/1820) |
| 85 | | 1 Dec 2001 (SI 2001/3538) |
| 86 | | 25 Feb 2001 (SI 2001/516) |
| 87 | (1)–(3) | 18 Jun 2001 (SI 2001/1820) |
| | (4), (5) | 25 Feb 2001 (SI 2001/516) |
| 88 | (1)–(3) | 18 Jun 2001 (SI 2001/1820) |
| | (4)–(7) | 1 Dec 2001 (SI 2001/3538) |
| 89 | (1) | 18 Jun 2001 (SI 2001/1820) |
| | (2)–(4) | 1 Dec 2001 (SI 2001/3538) |
| 90–92 | | 1 Dec 2001 (SI 2001/3538) |
| 93, 94 | | 18 Jun 2001 (SI 2001/1820) |
| 95 | | 1 Dec 2001 (SI 2001/3538) |
| 96 | | 18 Jun 2001 (SI 2001/1820) |
| 97 | | 1 Dec 2001 (SI 2001/3538) |
| 98 | (1) | 18 Jun 2001 (for the purpose of making listing rules) (SI 2001/1820) |
| | | 1 Dec 2001 (otherwise) (SI 2001/3538) |
| | (2)–(5) | 1 Dec 2001 (SI 2001/3538) |
| 99–102 | | 18 Jun 2001 (SI 2001/1820) |
| 103 | | 25 Feb 2001 (SI 2001/516) |
| 104 | | 1 Dec 2001 (for the purpose of insurance business transfer schemes only) (SI 2001/3538) |
| | | *Never in force* (repealed) (for the purpose of banking business transfer schemes) |
| 105–107 | | 1 Dec 2001 (SI 2001/3538) |
| 108 | | 25 Feb 2001 (for the purpose of making orders or regulations) (SI 2001/516) |
| | | 1 Dec 2001 (otherwise) (SI 2001/3538) |
| 109, 110 | | 1 Dec 2001 (SI 2001/3538) |
| 111 | (1) | 1 Dec 2001 (SI 2001/3538) |
| | (2) | 25 Feb 2001 (for the purpose of introducing Sch 12, Pt I to the extent brought into force by SI 2001/516) (SI 2001/516) |
| | | 1 Dec 2001 (otherwise) (SI 2001/3538) |
| | (3) | 1 Dec 2001 (SI 2001/3538) |
| 112–117 | | 1 Dec 2001 (SI 2001/3538) |
| 118 | (1), (2) | 1 Dec 2001 (SI 2001/3538) |
| | (3), (4) | 25 Feb 2001 (SI 2001/516) |
| | (5)–(9) | 1 Dec 2001 (SI 2001/3538) |
| | (10) | 25 Feb 2001 (SI 2001/516) |
| 119–121 | | 18 Jun 2001 (SI 2001/1820) |
| 122, 123 | | 1 Dec 2001 (SI 2001/3538) |
| 124, 125 | | 18 Jun 2001 (SI 2001/1820) |
| 126–131 | | 1 Dec 2001 (SI 2001/3538) |
| 132 | (1) | 25 Feb 2001 (for the purpose of the definition "the Tribunal") (SI 2001/516) |
| | | 3 Sep 2001 (otherwise) (SI 2001/2632) |
| | (2) | 3 Sep 2001 (SI 2001/2632) |
| | (3) | 25 Feb 2001 (SI 2001/516) |
| | (4) | See Sch 13 below |
| 133 | | 3 Sep 2001 (SI 2001/2632) |
| 134, 135 | | 25 Feb 2001 (SI 2001/516) |
| 136 | | 18 Jun 2001 (for the purpose of making rules) (SI 2001/1820) |
| | | 3 Sep 2001 (otherwise) (SI 2001/2632) |
| 137 | (1)–(5) | 3 Sep 2001 (SI 2001/2632) |
| | (6) | 25 Feb 2001 (SI 2001/516) |
| 138–141 | | 18 Jun 2001 (SI 2001/1820) |
| 142 | (1)–(4) | 25 Feb 2001 (SI 2001/516) |
| | (5) | 1 Dec 2001 (SI 2001/3538) |

**Financial Services and Markets Act 2000 (c 8)**—*contd*

| | | |
|---|---|---|
| | (6) | 25 Feb 2001 (SI 2001/516) |
| 143 | | 18 Jun 2001 (for the purpose of making rules) (SI 2001/1820) |
| | | 1 Dec 2001 (otherwise) (SI 2001/3538) |
| 144 | (1)–(3) | 18 Jun 2001 (SI 2001/1820) |
| | (4), (5) | 25 Feb 2001 (SI 2001/516) |
| | (6), (7) | 18 Jun 2001 (SI 2001/1820) |
| 145 | (1)–(4) | 18 Jun 2001 (SI 2001/1820) |
| | (5) | 25 Feb 2001 (SI 2001/516) |
| 146, 147 | | 18 Jun 2001 (SI 2001/1820) |
| 148 | | 18 Jun 2001 (for the purpose of giving directions as mentioned in sub-s (3)) (SI 2001/1820) |
| | | 3 Sep 2001 (otherwise) (SI 2001/2632) |
| 149 | | 18 Jun 2001 (SI 2001/1820) |
| 150 | (1), (2) | 18 Jun 2001 (for the purpose of making rules) (SI 2001/1820) |
| | | 1 Dec 2001 (otherwise) (SI 2001/3538) |
| | (3)–(5) | 25 Feb 2001 (for the purpose of making orders or regulations) (SI 2001/516) |
| | | 18 Jun 2001 (for the purpose of making rules) (SI 2001/1820) |
| | | 1 Dec 2001 (otherwise) (SI 2001/3538) |
| 151 | | 1 Dec 2001 (SI 2001/3538) |
| 152–164 | | 18 Jun 2001 (SI 2001/1820) |
| 165–167 | | 3 Sep 2001 (SI 2001/2632) |
| 168 | (1)–(3) | 3 Sep 2001 (SI 2001/2632) |
| | (4)(a) | 3 Sep 2001 (SI 2001/2632) |
| | (4)(b) | 25 Feb 2001 (for the purpose of making orders or regulations) (SI 2001/516) |
| | | 3 Sep 2001 (otherwise) (SI 2001/2632) |
| | (4)(c)–(i) | 3 Sep 2001 (SI 2001/2632) |
| | (5), (6) | 3 Sep 2001 (SI 2001/2632) |
| 169 | | 18 Jun 2001 (for the purpose of preparing a statement of policy as mentioned in sub-s (9)) (SI 2001/1820) |
| | | 3 Sep 2001 (otherwise) (SI 2001/2632) |
| 170–177 | | 3 Sep 2001 (SI 2001/2632) |
| 178–181 | | 1 Dec 2001 (SI 2001/3538) |
| 182 | | 18 Jun 2001 (for the purpose of imposing requirements as mentioned in sub-s (1)(b)) (SI 2001/1820) |
| | | 1 Dec 2001 (otherwise) (SI 2001/3538) |
| 183 | (1) | 1 Dec 2001 (SI 2001/3538) |
| | (2) | 25 Feb 2001 (for the purpose of making orders or regulations) (SI 2001/516) |
| | | 1 Dec 2001 (otherwise) (SI 2001/3538) |
| | (3) | 1 Dec 2001 (SI 2001/3538) |
| 184–187 | | 1 Dec 2001 (SI 2001/3538) |
| 188 | (1) | 1 Dec 2001 (SI 2001/3538) |
| | (2) | 25 Feb 2001 (for the purpose of making orders or regulations) (SI 2001/516) |
| | | 1 Dec 2001 (otherwise) (SI 2001/3538) |
| | (3)–(6) | 1 Dec 2001 (SI 2001/3538) |
| 189–191 | | 1 Dec 2001 (SI 2001/3538) |
| 192 | (a) | 25 Feb 2001 (SI 2001/516) |
| | (b)–(e) | 1 Dec 2001 (SI 2001/3538) |
| 193 | | 3 Sep 2001 (SI 2001/2632) |
| 194–197 | | 3 Sep 2001 (for the purposes of requirements (as mentioned in s 196) taking effect not sooner than the day on which s 19 of this Act comes into force) (SI 2001/2632) |
| | | 1 Dec 2001 (otherwise) (SI 2001/3538) |
| 198 | | 1 Dec 2001 (SI 2001/3538) |
| 199 | | 3 Sep 2001 (for the purposes of requirements (as mentioned in s 196) taking effect not sooner than the day on which s 19 of this Act comes into force) (SI 2001/2632) |

**Financial Services and Markets Act 2000 (c 8)**—*contd*

|  |  |  |
|---|---|---|
|  |  | 1 Dec 2001 (otherwise) (SI 2001/3538) |
| 200, 201 |  | 3 Sep 2001 (SI 2001/2632) |
| 202 | (1) | 3 Sep 2001 (SI 2001/2632) |
|  | (2) | 25 Feb 2001 (for the purpose of making orders or regulations) (SI 2001/516) |
|  |  | 3 Sep 2001 (otherwise) (SI 2001/2632) |
| 203–209 |  | 1 Dec 2001 (SI 2001/3538) |
| 210–212 |  | 18 Jun 2001 (SI 2001/1820) |
| 213 | (1)–(9) | 18 Jun 2001 (SI 2001/1820) |
|  | (10) | 25 Feb 2001 (for the purpose of making orders or regulations) (SI 2001/516) |
|  |  | 18 Jun 2001 (otherwise) (SI 2001/1820) |
| 214 | (1)–(4) | 18 Jun 2001 (SI 2001/1820) |
|  | (5) | 25 Feb 2001 (for the purpose of making orders or regulations) (SI 2001/516) |
|  |  | 18 Jun 2001 (otherwise) (SI 2001/1820) |
|  | (6) | 18 Jun 2001 (SI 2001/1820) |
| 215 | (1)–(5) | 18 Jun 2001 (SI 2001/1820) |
|  | (6) | 25 Feb 2001 (SI 2001/516) |
|  | (7) | 18 Jun 2001 (SI 2001/1820) |
|  | (8), (9) | 25 Feb 2001 (SI 2001/516) |
| 216–218 |  | 18 Jun 2001 (SI 2001/1820) |
| 219–221 |  | 1 Dec 2001 (SI 2001/3538) |
| 222 |  | 18 Jun 2001 (SI 2001/1820) |
| 223 |  | 18 Jun 2001 (for the purpose of fixing an amount by the scheme as mentioned in sub-s (1)) (SI 2001/1820) |
|  |  | 1 Dec 2001 (otherwise) (SI 2001/3538) |
| 224 | (1)–(3) | 1 Dec 2001 (SI 2001/3538) |
|  | (4) | 25 Feb 2001 (for the purpose of making orders or regulations) (SI 2001/516) |
|  |  | 1 Dec 2001 (otherwise) (SI 2001/3538) |
|  | (5) | 1 Dec 2001 (SI 2001/3538) |
| 225 |  | 18 Jun 2001 (SI 2001/1820) |
| 226, 227 |  | 18 Jun 2001 (for the purpose of the making of rules by the Authority and the scheme operator) (SI 2001/1820) |
|  |  | 1 Dec 2001 (otherwise) (SI 2001/3538) |
| 228 |  | 1 Dec 2001 (SI 2001/3538) |
| 229 |  | 18 Jun 2001 (for the purpose of the making of rules by the Authority and the scheme operator) (SI 2001/1820) |
|  |  | 1 Dec 2001 (otherwise) (SI 2001/3538) |
| 230 |  | 18 Jun 2001 (SI 2001/1820) |
| 231–233 |  | 1 Dec 2001 (SI 2001/3538) |
| 234 |  | 18 Jun 2001 (SI 2001/1820) |
| 235–237 |  | 25 Feb 2001 (SI 2001/516) |
| 238 |  | 25 Feb 2001 (for the purpose of making orders or regulations) (SI 2001/516) |
|  |  | 18 Jun 2001 (for the purpose of making rules) (SI 2001/1820) |
|  |  | 1 Dec 2001 (otherwise) (SI 2001/3538) |
| 239 | (1)–(3) | 25 Feb 2001 (SI 2001/516) |
|  | (4), (5) | 18 Jun 2001 (SI 2001/1820) |
| 240, 241 |  | 1 Dec 2001 (SI 2001/3538) |
| 242 |  | 18 Jun 2001 (for the purpose of giving directions or imposing requirements as mentioned in sub-s (3)) (SI 2001/1820) |
|  |  | 3 Sep 2001 (for the purposes of authorisation orders coming into force not sooner than the day on which s 19 of this Act comes into force) (SI 2001/2632) |
|  |  | 1 Dec 2001 (otherwise) (SI 2001/3538) |
| 243–245 |  | 3 Sep 2001 (for the purposes of authorisation orders coming into force not sooner than the day on which s 19 of this Act comes into force) (SI 2001/2632) |

**Financial Services and Markets Act 2000 (c 8)**—*contd*

|  |  |  |
|---|---|---|
|  |  | 1 Dec 2001 (otherwise) (SI 2001/3538) |
| 246 |  | 3 Sep 2001 (for the purposes of certificates coming into force not sooner than the day on which s 19 of this Act comes into force) (SI 2001/2632) |
|  |  | 1 Dec 2001 (otherwise) (SI 2001/3538) |
| 247, 248 |  | 18 Jun 2001 (SI 2001/1820) |
| 249 |  | 1 Dec 2001 (SI 2001/3538) |
| 250 |  | 3 Sep 2001 (SI 2001/2632) |
| 251 | (1)–(3) | 3 Sep 2001 (for the purposes of the giving of notice of any proposal to alter a scheme, or to replace its trustee or manager, not sooner than the day on which s 19 of this Act comes into force, and the giving of approval to any such proposal) (SI 2001/2632) |
|  |  | 1 Dec 2001 (otherwise) (SI 2001/3538) |
|  | (4)(a) | 3 Sep 2001 (for the purposes of the giving of notice of any proposal to alter a scheme, or to replace its trustee or manager, not sooner than the day on which s 19 of this Act comes into force, and the giving of approval to any such proposal) (SI 2001/2632) |
|  |  | 1 Dec 2001 (otherwise) (SI 2001/3538) |
|  | (4)(b) | 1 Dec 2001 (SI 2001/3538) |
|  | (5) | 3 Sep 2001 (for the purposes of the giving of notice of any proposal to alter a scheme, or to replace its trustee or manager, not sooner than the day on which s 19 of this Act comes into force, and the giving of approval to any such proposal) (SI 2001/2632) |
|  |  | 1 Dec 2001 (otherwise) (SI 2001/3538) |
| 252 |  | 3 Sep 2001 (for the purposes of the giving of notice of any proposal to alter a scheme, or to replace its trustee or manager, not sooner than the day on which s 19 of this Act comes into force, and the giving of approval to any such proposal) (SI 2001/2632) |
|  |  | 1 Dec 2001 (otherwise) (SI 2001/3538) |
| 253 |  | 1 Dec 2001 (SI 2001/3538) |
| 254–256 |  | 3 Sep 2001 (SI 2001/2632) |
| 257 |  | 3 Sep 2001 (for the purposes of directions coming into force not sooner than the day on which s 19 of this Act comes into force) (SI 2001/2632) |
|  |  | 1 Dec 2001 (otherwise) (SI 2001/3538) |
| 258 |  | 1 Dec 2001 (SI 2001/3538) |
| 259–261 |  | 3 Sep 2001 (for the purposes of directions coming into force not sooner than the day on which s 19 of this Act comes into force) (SI 2001/2632) |
|  |  | 1 Dec 2001 (otherwise) (SI 2001/3538) |
| 262 |  | 25 Feb 2001 (SI 2001/516) |
| 263 |  | 1 Dec 2001 (SI 2001/3538) |
| 264 | (1) | 25 Feb 2001 (for the purpose of making orders or regulations) (SI 2001/516) |
|  |  | 3 Sep 2001 (for the purposes of— |
|  |  | (a) the giving of notice under sub-s (1) of intention to make invitations not sooner than the day on which s 19 of this Act comes into force; and |
|  |  | (b) the giving of notice under sub-ss (2) or (6)) (SI 2001/2632) |
|  |  | 1 Dec 2001 (otherwise) (SI 2001/3538) |
|  | (2) | 3 Sep 2001 (for the purposes of— |
|  |  | (a) the giving of notice under sub-s (1) of intention to make invitations not sooner than the day on which s 19 of this Act comes into force; and |
|  |  | (b) the giving of notice under sub-ss (2) or (6)) (SI 2001/2632) |
|  |  | 1 Dec 2001 (otherwise) (SI 2001/3538) |

**Financial Services and Markets Act 2000 (c 8)**—*contd*

| | | |
|---|---|---|
| | (3)(a), (b) | 3 Sep 2001 (for the purposes of— |

(a) the giving of notice under sub-s (1) of intention to make invitations not sooner than the day on which s 19 of this Act comes into force; and

(b) the giving of notice under sub-ss (2) or (6)) (SI 2001/2632)

1 Dec 2001 (otherwise) (SI 2001/3538)

| | (3)(c) | 25 Feb 2001 (for the purpose of making orders or regulations) (SI 2001/516) |
|---|---|---|

3 Sep 2001 (for the purposes of—

(a) the giving of notice under sub-s (1) of intention to make invitations not sooner than the day on which s 19 of this Act comes into force; and

(b) the giving of notice under sub-ss (2) or (6)) (SI 2001/2632)

1 Dec 2001 (otherwise) (SI 2001/3538)

| | (4)–(7) | 3 Sep 2001 (for the purposes of— |
|---|---|---|

(a) the giving of notice under sub-s (1) of intention to make invitations not sooner than the day on which s 19 of this Act comes into force; and

(b) the giving of notice under sub-ss (2) or (6)) (SI 2001/2632)

1 Dec 2001 (otherwise) (SI 2001/3538)

| 265 | (1), (2) | 3 Sep 2001 (SI 2001/2632) |
|---|---|---|
| | (3) | 1 Dec 2001 (SI 2001/3538) |
| | (4), (5) | 3 Sep 2001 (SI 2001/2632) |
| 266 | | 18 Jun 2001 (SI 2001/1820) |
| 267–269 | | 1 Dec 2001 (SI 2001/3538) |
| 270 | | 25 Feb 2001 (for the purpose of making orders or regulations) (SI 2001/516) |

3 Sep 2001 (for the purposes of—

(a) the giving of notices under sub-s (1)(c); and

(b) the giving of notice of approval under sub-s (1)(d)(i) coming into force not sooner than the day on which s 19 of this Act comes into force) (SI 2001/2632)

1 Dec 2001 (otherwise) (SI 2001/3538)

| 271 | (1) | 3 Sep 2001 (SI 2001/2632) |
|---|---|---|
| | (2) | 1 Dec 2001 (SI 2001/3538) |
| | (3) | 3 Sep 2001 (SI 2001/2632) |
| 272, 273 | | 3 Sep 2001 (for the purposes of orders (and applications for orders) coming into force not sooner than the day on which s 19 of this Act comes into force) (SI 2001/2632) |

1 Dec 2001 (otherwise) (SI 2001/3538)

| 274 | | 18 Jun 2001 (for the purpose of giving directions or imposing requirements as mentioned in sub-s (2)) (SI 2001/1820) |
|---|---|---|

3 Sep 2001 (for the purposes of orders (and applications for orders) coming into force not sooner than the day on which s 19 of this Act comes into force) (SI 2001/2632)

1 Dec 2001 (otherwise) (SI 2001/3538)

| 275, 276 | | 3 Sep 2001 (for the purposes of orders (and applications for orders) coming into force not sooner than the day on which s 19 of this Act comes into force) (SI 2001/2632) |
|---|---|---|

1 Dec 2001 (otherwise) (SI 2001/3538)

| 277 | (1) | 3 Sep 2001 (for the purposes of— |
|---|---|---|

(a) the giving of notice under sub-s (1) of any proposal to alter a scheme not sooner than the day on which s 19 of this Act comes into force, and the giving of approval to any such proposal; and

(b) the giving of notice under sub-s (3) of any proposal to replace an operator, trustee or depositary not sooner than the day on which s 19 of this Act comes into force) (SI 2001/2632)

1 Dec 2001 (otherwise) (SI 2001/3538)

| | (2)(a) | 3 Sep 2001 (for the purposes of— |
|---|---|---|

**Financial Services and Markets Act 2000 (c 8)**—*contd*

|  |  |  |
|---|---|---|
|  |  | (a) the giving of notice under sub-s (1) of any proposal to alter a scheme not sooner than the day on which s 19 of this Act comes into force, and the giving of approval to any such proposal; and |
|  |  | (b) the giving of notice under sub-s (3) of any proposal to replace an operator, trustee or depositary not sooner than the day on which s 19 of this Act comes into force) (SI 2001/2632) |
|  |  | 1 Dec 2001 (otherwise) (SI 2001/3538) |
|  | (2)(b) | 1 Dec 2001 (SI 2001/3538) |
|  | (3) | 3 Sep 2001 (for the purposes of— |
|  |  | (a) the giving of notice under sub-s (1) of any proposal to alter a scheme not sooner than the day on which s 19 of this Act comes into force, and the giving of approval to any such proposal; and |
|  |  | (b) the giving of notice under sub-s (3) of any proposal to replace an operator, trustee or depositary not sooner than the day on which s 19 of this Act comes into force) (SI 2001/2632) |
|  |  | 1 Dec 2001 (otherwise) (SI 2001/3538) |
| 278 |  | 18 Jun 2001 (SI 2001/1820) |
| 279–282 |  | 3 Sep 2001 (SI 2001/2632) |
| 283 | (1) | 18 Jun 2001 (SI 2001/1820) |
|  | (2), (3) | 1 Dec 2001 (SI 2001/3538) |
| 284 | (1) | 1 Dec 2001 (SI 2001/3538) |
|  | (2) | 25 Feb 2001 (for the purpose of making orders or regulations) (SI 2001/516) |
|  |  | 1 Dec 2001 (otherwise) (SI 2001/3538) |
|  | (3)–(11) | 1 Dec 2001 (SI 2001/3538) |
| 285 |  | 1 Dec 2001 (SI 2001/3538) |
| 286 |  | 25 Feb 2001 (SI 2001/516) |
| 287, 288 |  | 18 Jun 2001 (for the purpose of giving directions or imposing requirements as mentioned in sub-s (2)) (SI 2001/1820) |
|  |  | 3 Sep 2001 (otherwise) (SI 2001/2632) |
| 289 |  | 3 Sep 2001 (SI 2001/2632) |
| 290 |  | 3 Sep 2001 (for the purposes of recognition orders coming into force not sooner than the day on which s 19 of this Act comes into force) (SI 2001/2632) |
|  |  | 1 Dec 2001 (otherwise) (SI 2001/3538) |
| 291 |  | 1 Dec 2001 (SI 2001/3538) |
| 292 | (1) | 3 Sep 2001 (SI 2001/2632) |
|  | (2)–(5) | 3 Sep 2001 (for the purposes of recognition orders coming into force not sooner than the day on which s 19 of this Act comes into force) (SI 2001/2632) |
|  |  | 1 Dec 2001 (otherwise) (SI 2001/3538) |
| 293 |  | 18 Jun 2001 (for the purpose of making rules) (SI 2001/1820) |
|  |  | 1 Dec 2001 (otherwise) (SI 2001/3538) |
| 294 |  | 18 Jun 2001 (for the purpose of giving directions as mentioned in sub-s (2)) (SI 2001/1820) |
|  |  | 3 Sep 2001 (otherwise) (SI 2001/2632) |
| 295 |  | 18 Jun 2001 (for the purpose of making rules) (SI 2001/1820) |
|  |  | 1 Dec 2001 (otherwise) (SI 2001/3538) |
| 296 |  | 1 Dec 2001 (SI 2001/3538) |
| 297 |  | 3 Sep 2001 (SI 2001/2632) |
| 298 |  | 3 Sep 2001 (for the purposes of revocation orders under s 297) (SI 2001/2632) |
|  |  | 1 Dec 2001 (otherwise) (SI 2001/3538) |
| 299 |  | 18 Jun 2001 (SI 2001/1820) |
| 300, 301 |  | 1 Dec 2001 (SI 2001/3538) |
| 302, 303 |  | 3 Sep 2001 (SI 2001/2632) |
| 304 |  | 1 Dec 2001 (SI 2001/3538) |
| 305 |  | 3 Sep 2001 (for the purposes of s 303) (SI 2001/2632) |

**Financial Services and Markets Act 2000 (c 8)**—*contd*

|  |  |  |
|---|---|---|
|  |  | 1 Dec 2001 (otherwise) (SI 2001/3538) |
| 306 |  | 3 Sep 2001 (for the purposes of reports issued by the Director under s 303) (SI 2001/2632) |
|  |  | 1 Dec 2001 (otherwise) (SI 2001/3538) |
| 307 |  | 3 Sep 2001 (SI 2001/2632) |
| 308, 309 |  | 1 Dec 2001 (SI 2001/3538) |
| 310 |  | 3 Sep 2001 (for the purposes of s 307) (SI 2001/2632) |
|  |  | 1 Dec 2001 (otherwise) (SI 2001/3538) |
| 311, 312 |  | 3 Sep 2001 (SI 2001/2632) |
| 313 |  | 25 Feb 2001 (SI 2001/516) |
| 314 |  | 3 Sep 2001 (SI 2001/2632) |
| 315 | (1), (2) | 1 Dec 2001 (SI 2001/3538) |
|  | (3)–(5) | 3 Sep 2001 (SI 2001/2632) |
| 316 |  | 18 Jun 2001 (for the purpose of giving directions as mentioned in sub-s (1) coming into force not sooner than the day on which s 19 of the Act comes into force) (SI 2001/1820) |
|  |  | 1 Dec 2001 (otherwise) (SI 2001/3538) |
| 317 |  | 18 Jun 2001 (SI 2001/1820) |
| 318 |  | 18 Jun 2001 (for the purpose of giving directions as mentioned in sub-s (1) coming into force not sooner than the day on which s 19 of the Act comes into force) (SI 2001/1820) |
|  |  | 1 Dec 2001 (otherwise) (SI 2001/3538) |
| 319 |  | 18 Jun 2001 (SI 2001/1820) |
| 320 | (1), (2) | 1 Dec 2001 (SI 2001/3538) |
|  | (3), (4) | 3 Sep 2001 (for the purposes of requirements taking effect not sooner than the day on which s 19 of this Act comes into force) (SI 2001/2632) |
|  |  | 1 Dec 2001 (otherwise) (SI 2001/3538) |
| 321 |  | 3 Sep 2001 (for the purposes of requirements taking effect not sooner than the day on which s 19 of this Act comes into force) (SI 2001/2632) |
|  |  | 1 Dec 2001 (otherwise) (SI 2001/3538) |
| 322 |  | 18 Jun 2001 (for the purpose of making rules coming into force not sooner than the day on which s 19 of the Act comes into force) (SI 2001/1820) |
|  |  | 1 Dec 2001 (otherwise) (SI 2001/3538) |
| 323, 324 |  | 18 Jun 2001 (SI 2001/1820) |
| 325 | (1)–(3) | 1 Dec 2001 (SI 2001/3538) |
|  | (4) | 3 Sep 2001 (SI 2001/2632) |
| 326 |  | 25 Feb 2001 (SI 2001/516) |
| 327 | (1)–(5) | 1 Dec 2001 (SI 2001/3538) |
|  | (6) | 25 Feb 2001 (for the purpose of making orders or regulations) (SI 2001/516) |
|  |  | 1 Dec 2001 (otherwise) (SI 2001/3538) |
|  | (7), (8) | 1 Dec 2001 (SI 2001/3538) |
| 328–331 |  | 3 Sep 2001 (SI 2001/2632) |
| 332 |  | 18 Jun 2001 (SI 2001/1820) |
| 333 |  | 1 Dec 2001 (SI 2001/3538) |
| 334 | (1), (2) | 25 Feb 2001 (SI 2001/516) |
|  | (3), (4) | 1 Dec 2001 (SI 2001/3538) |
| 335 |  | 25 Feb 2001 (SI 2001/516) |
| 336 | (1), (2) | 25 Feb 2001 (SI 2001/516) |
|  | (3) | 1 Dec 2001 (SI 2001/3538) |
| 337 |  | 25 Feb 2001 (SI 2001/516) |
| 338 | (1), (2) | 25 Feb 2001 (SI 2001/516) |
|  | (3), (4) | 1 Dec 2001 (SI 2001/3538) |
| 339 |  | 25 Feb 2001 (SI 2001/516) |
| 340 |  | 18 Jun 2001 (SI 2001/1820) |
| 341 |  | 1 Dec 2001 (SI 2001/3538) |
| 342 | (1)–(4) | 1 Dec 2001 (SI 2001/3538) |

**Financial Services and Markets Act 2000 (c 8)**—*contd*

| | | |
|---|---|---|
| | (5) | 25 Feb 2001 (SI 2001/516) |
| | (6), (7) | 1 Dec 2001 (SI 2001/3538) |
| 343 | (1)–(4) | 1 Dec 2001 (SI 2001/3538) |
| | (5) | 25 Feb 2001 (SI 2001/516) |
| | (6)–(9) | 1 Dec 2001 (SI 2001/3538) |
| 344–346 | | 1 Dec 2001 (SI 2001/3538) |
| 347 | (1)(a) | 1 Dec 2001 (for the purpose of enabling the Authority to maintain a record of the approved persons listed below) (SI 2001/3538) |
| | | 1 May 2002 (for the purpose of requiring the Authority to maintain a record of persons who appear to the Authority to be authorised persons who are EEA firms or Treaty firms) (SI 2001/3538) |
| | | 1 Aug 2002 (for the purpose of requiring the Authority to maintain a record of persons who appear to the Authority to be authorised persons who were, immediately before the appointed day, authorised under Financial Services Act 1986 by virtue of holding a certificate issued for the purposes of Part I of that Act by a recognised professional body, within the meaning of that Act) (SI 2001/3538) |
| | (1)(b)–(g) | 1 Dec 2001 (SI 2001/3538) |
| | (1)(h) | 1 Dec 2001 (for the purpose of enabling the Authority to maintain a record of approved persons) (SI 2001/3538) |
| | | 1 Dec 2002 (for the purpose of requiring the Authority to maintain a record of approved persons) (SI 2001/3538) |
| | (1)(i) | 1 Dec 2001 (SI 2001/3538) |
| | (2)(a) | 1 Dec 2001 (for the purpose of enabling the Authority to maintain a record of the approved persons listed below) (SI 2001/3538) |
| | | 1 May 2002 (for the purpose of requiring the Authority to maintain a record of persons who appear to the Authority to be authorised persons who are EEA firms or Treaty firms) (SI 2001/3538) |
| | | 1 Aug 2002 (for the purpose of requiring the Authority to maintain a record of persons who appear to the Authority to be authorised persons who were, immediately before the appointed day, authorised under Financial Services Act 1986 by virtue of holding a certificate issued for the purposes of Part I of that Act by a recognised professional body (within the meaning of that Act)) (SI 2001/3538) |
| | (2)(b)–(f) | 1 Dec 2001 (SI 2001/3538) |
| | (2)(g) | 1 Dec 2001 (for the purpose of enabling the Authority to maintain a record of approved persons) (SI 2001/3538) |
| | | 1 Dec 2002 (for the purpose of requiring the Authority to maintain a record of approved persons) (SI 2001/3538) |
| | (3)–(9) | 1 Dec 2001 (SI 2001/3538) |
| 348 | | 18 Jun 2001 (SI 2001/1820) |
| 349 | | 25 Feb 2001 (for the purpose of making orders or regulations) (SI 2001/516) |
| | | 18 Jun 2001 (otherwise) (SI 2001/1820) |
| 350 | (1), (2) | 3 Sep 2001 (SI 2001/2632) |
| | (3) | 18 Jun 2001 (SI 2001/1820) |
| | (4)–(6) | 3 Sep 2001 (SI 2001/2632) |
| | (7) | 18 Jun 2001 (SI 2001/1820) |
| 351 | (1)–(6) | 18 Jun 2001 (SI 2001/1820) |
| | (7) | 25 Feb 2001 (SI 2001/516) |
| 352 | | 18 Jun 2001 (for the purpose of any contravention of s 348) (SI 2001/1820) |
| | | 3 Sep 2001 (otherwise) (SI 2001/2632) |
| 353 | | 25 Feb 2001 (SI 2001/516) |
| 354 | | 3 Sep 2001 (SI 2001/2632) |
| 355 | | 20 Jul 2001 (SI 2001/2632) |

**Financial Services and Markets Act 2000 (c 8)**—*contd*

| | | |
|---|---|---|
| 356–359 | | 1 Dec 2001 (SI 2001/3538) |
| 360 | | 20 Jul 2001 (SI 2001/2632) |
| 361–371 | | 1 Dec 2001 (SI 2001/3538) |
| 372 | | 20 Jul 2001 (for the purpose of making rules) (SI 2001/2632) |
| | | 1 Dec 2001 (otherwise) (SI 2001/3538) |
| 373–377 | | 1 Dec 2001 (SI 2001/3538) |
| 378, 379 | | 20 Jul 2001 (SI 2001/2632) |
| 380 | | 18 Jun 2001 (SI 2001/1820) |
| 381 | | 1 Dec 2001 (SI 2001/3538) |
| 382 | | 18 Jun 2001 (SI 2001/1820) |
| 383–386 | | 1 Dec 2001 (SI 2001/3538) |
| 387–394 | | 3 Sep 2001 (SI 2001/2632) |
| 395, 396 | | 18 Jun 2001 (SI 2001/1820) |
| 397 | (1)–(8) | 1 Dec 2001 (SI 2001/3538) |
| | (9)–(14) | 25 Feb 2001 (SI 2001/516) |
| 398–401 | | 18 Jun 2001 (SI 2001/1820) |
| 402 | (1)(a) | 1 Dec 2001 (SI 2001/3538) |
| | (1)(b) | 25 Feb 2001 (for the purpose of making orders or regulations) (SI 2001/516) |
| | | 19 Oct 2001 (for the purposes of proceedings for offences under prescribed regulations relating to money laundering) (SI 2001/3436) |
| | (2), (3) | 19 Oct 2001 (for the purposes of proceedings for offences under prescribed regulations relating to money laundering) (SI 2001/3436) |
| | | 1 Dec 2001 (otherwise) (SI 2001/3538) |
| 403 | | 18 Jun 2001 (SI 2001/1820) |
| 404 | | 1 Dec 2001 (SI 2001/3538) |
| 405 | (1)(a), (b) | 3 Sep 2001 (SI 2001/2632) |
| | (1)(c), (d) | 1 Dec 2001 (SI 2001/3538) |
| | (2)–(5) | 3 Sep 2001 (SI 2001/2632) |
| 406 | | 1 Dec 2001 (SI 2001/3538) |
| 407 | (1), (2) | 3 Sep 2001 (SI 2001/2632) |
| | (3) | 1 Dec 2001 (SI 2001/3538) |
| 408 | | 3 Sep 2001 (for the purposes of determinations coming into force not sooner than the day on which s 19 of this Act comes into force) (SI 2001/2632) |
| | | 1 Dec 2001 (otherwise) (SI 2001/3538) |
| 409 | | 25 Feb 2001 (SI 2001/516) |
| 410 | | 18 Jun 2001 (SI 2001/1820) |
| 411 | | 1 Dec 2001 (SI 2001/3538) |
| 412 | | 25 Feb 2001 (for the purpose of making orders or regulations) (SI 2001/516) |
| | | 1 Dec 2001 (otherwise) (SI 2001/3538) |
| 413 | | 3 Sep 2001 (SI 2001/2632) |
| 414 | (1)–(3) | 25 Feb 2001 (SI 2001/516) |
| | (4) | 18 Jun 2001 (SI 2001/1820) |
| 415 | | 18 Jun 2001 (SI 2001/1820) |
| 416 | (1)(a), (b) | 1 Dec 2001 (SI 2001/3538) |
| | (1)(c) | 30 Apr 2001 (SI 2001/1282) |
| | (2) | 1 Dec 2001 (SI 2001/3538) |
| | (3)(a) | 30 Apr 2001 (SI 2001/1282) |
| | (3)(b), (c) | 2 Mar 2002 (SI 2001/3538) |
| | (3)(d) | 1 Dec 2001 (SI 2001/3538) |
| | (4), (5) | 25 Feb 2001 (SI 2001/516) |
| 417 | | 25 Feb 2001 (SI 2001/516) |
| 418 | | 3 Sep 2001 (SI 2001/2632) |
| 419–423 | | 25 Feb 2001 (SI 2001/516) |
| 424 | (1), (2) | 25 Feb 2001 (SI 2001/516) |

**Financial Services and Markets Act 2000 (c 8)**—*contd*

|  |  |  |
|---|---|---|
|  | (3) | 25 Feb 2001 (for the purpose of making orders or regulations) (SI 2001/516) |
|  |  | 1 Dec 2001 (otherwise) (SI 2001/3538) |
| 425–427 |  | 25 Feb 2001 (SI 2001/516) |
| 428 |  | 14 Jun 2000 (s 431(1)) |
| 429 |  | 25 Feb 2001 (SI 2001/516) |
| 430, 431 |  | 14 Jun 2000 (s 431(1)) |
| 432 | (1) | See Sch 20 below |
|  | (2) | See Sch 21 below |
|  | (3) | See Sch 22 below |
| 433 |  | 14 Jun 2000 (s 431(1)) |
| Sch 1 | paras 1–6 | 18 Jun 2001 (SI 2001/1820) |
|  | paras 7, 8 | 19 Jul 2001 (for the purpose of enabling the Authority to make the complaints scheme and appoint the investigator) (SI 2001/2364) |
|  |  | 3 Sep 2001 (otherwise) (SI 2001/2632) |
|  | paras 9–21 | 18 Jun 2001 (SI 2001/1820) |
| Sch 2 |  | 25 Feb 2001 (SI 2001/516) |
| Sch 3 | paras 1–18 | 25 Feb 2001 (for the purpose of making orders or regulations) (SI 2001/516) |
|  |  | 18 Jun 2001 (for the purpose of making rules) (SI 2001/1820) |
|  |  | 1 Dec 2001 (otherwise) (SI 2001/3538) |
|  | para 19 | 25 Feb 2001 (for the purpose of making orders or regulations) (SI 2001/516) |
|  |  | 18 Jun 2001 (for the purpose of making rules) (SI 2001/1820) |
|  |  | 3 Sep 2001 (for the purposes of the giving of notice under sub-para (2) of intention to establish a branch not sooner than the day on which s 19 of this Act comes into force) (SI 2001/2632) |
|  |  | 1 Dec 2001 (otherwise) (SI 2001/3538) |
|  | para 20 | 25 Feb 2001 (for the purpose of making orders or regulations) (SI 2001/516) |
|  |  | 18 Jun 2001 (for the purpose of making rules) (SI 2001/1820) |
|  |  | 3 Sep 2001 (for the purposes of the giving of notice under sub-para (1) of intention to provide services not sooner than the day on which s 19 of this Act comes into force) (SI 2001/2632) |
|  |  | 1 Dec 2001 (otherwise) (SI 2001/3538) |
|  | paras 21–24 | 25 Feb 2001 (for the purpose of making orders or regulations) (SI 2001/516) |
|  |  | 18 Jun 2001 (for the purpose of making rules) (SI 2001/1820) |
|  |  | 1 Dec 2001 (otherwise) (SI 2001/3538) |
| Sch 4 | para 1 | 3 Sep 2001 (SI 2001/2632) |
|  | para 2 | 1 Dec 2001 (SI 2001/3538) |
|  | para 3 | 3 Sep 2001 (for the purposes of issuing certificates under sub-para (4)) (SI 2001/2632) |
|  |  | 1 Dec 2001 (otherwise) (SI 2001/3538) |
|  | para 4 | 1 Dec 2001 (SI 2001/3538) |
|  | para 5 | 3 Sep 2001 (for the purposes of giving notice under sub-para (2) of intention to carry on regulated activities not sooner than the day on which s 19 of this Act comes into force) (SI 2001/2632) |
|  |  | 1 Dec 2001 (otherwise) (SI 2001/3538) |
|  | para 6 | 1 Dec 2001 (SI 2001/3538) |
| Sch 5 |  | 1 Dec 2001 (SI 2001/3538) |
| Sch 6 | paras 1–7 | 3 Sep 2001 (SI 2001/2632) |
|  | paras 8, 9 | 25 Feb 2001 (for the purpose of making orders or regulations) (SI 2001/516) |
|  |  | 3 Sep 2001 (otherwise) (SI 2001/2632) |
| Schs 7, 8 |  | 18 Jun 2001 (SI 2001/1820) |
| Sch 9 | paras 1–6 | 25 Feb 2001 (SI 2001/516) |
|  | para 7 | 18 Jun 2001 (SI 2001/1820) |

**Financial Services and Markets Act 2000 (c 8)**—*contd*

| | | |
|---|---|---|
| Sch 10 | | 1 Dec 2001 (SI 2001/3538) |
| Sch 11 | | 25 Feb 2001 (SI 2001/516) |
| Sch 12 | paras 1–5 | 1 Dec 2001 (SI 2001/3538) |
| | para 6(1) | 1 Dec 2001 (SI 2001/3538) |
| | para 6(2) | 25 Feb 2001 (SI 2001/516) |
| | para 6(3) | 1 Dec 2001 (SI 2001/3538) |
| | paras 7–10 | 1 Dec 2001 (SI 2001/3538) |
| Sch 13 | paras 1–8 | 3 Sep 2001 (SI 2001/2632) |
| | para 9 | 25 Feb 2001 (SI 2001/516) |
| | paras 10–13 | 3 Sep 2001 (SI 2001/2632) |
| Sch 14 | | 18 Jun 2001 (SI 2001/1820) |
| Sch 15 | | 3 Sep 2001 (SI 2001/2632) |
| Sch 16 | | 1 Dec 2001 (SI 2001/3538) |
| Sch 17 | | 18 Jun 2001 (SI 2001/1820) |
| Sch 18 | Pts I–IV | 1 Dec 2001 (SI 2001/3538) |
| | Pt V | 2 Jul 2002 (SI 2001/3538) |
| Sch 19 | Pt I | 18 Jun 2001 (SI 2001/1820) |
| | Pt II, paras 1–18 | 18 Jun 2001 (SI 2001/1820) |
| | Pt II, para 19 | 25 Feb 2001 (for the purpose of making orders or regulations) (SI 2001/516) |
| | | 18 Jun 2001 (otherwise) (SI 2001/1820) |
| Sch 20 | para 1(a) | 1 Dec 2001 (SI 2001/3538) |
| | para 1(b) | 3 Sep 2001 (SI 2001/2632) |
| | para 2(a) | 1 Dec 2001 (SI 2001/3538) |
| | para 2(b) | 3 Sep 2001 (SI 2001/2632) |
| | para 3 | 3 Sep 2001 (SI 2001/2632) |
| | paras 4, 5 | 1 Dec 2001 (SI 2001/3538) |
| | para 6 | 3 Jul 2001[1] (SI 2001/2364) |
| | para 7(1), (2) | 3 Sep 2001 (SI 2001/2632) |
| | para 7(3)(a) | 1 Dec 2001 (SI 2001/3538) |
| | para 7(3)(b) | 3 Sep 2001 (SI 2001/2632) |
| Sch 21 | | 14 Jun 2000 (s 431(1)) |
| Sch 22 | | 30 Apr 2001 (repeal of Insurance Brokers (Registration) Act 1977) (SI 2001/1282) |
| | | 1 Dec 2001 (otherwise, except repeals in Credit Unions Act 1979) (SI 2001/3538) |
| | | 2 Jul 2002 (repeals in Credit Unions Act 1979) (SI 2001/3538) |

[1] For transitional provision, see SI 2001/2364, art 3

---

**Football (Disorder) Act 2000 (c 25)**

*RA:* 28 Jul 2000

*Commencement provisions:* s 5(1); Football (Disorder) Act 2000 (Commencement) Order 2000, SI 2000/2125

| | |
|---|---|
| 1 | 28 Aug 2000 (SI 2000/2125) |
| 2–7 | 28 Jul 2000 (s 5(1)) |
| Schs 1–3 | 28 Aug 2000 (SI 2000/2125) |

---

**Freedom of Information Act 2000 (c 36)**

*RA:* 30 Nov 2000

*Commencement provisions:* s 87; Freedom of Information Act 2000 (Commencement No 1) Order 2001, SI 2001/1637; Freedom of Information Act 2000 (Commencement No 2) Order 2002, SI 2002/2812, as amended by SI 2005/3239, SI 2006/63, SI 2006/64; Freedom of Information Act 2000 (Commencement No 3) Order 2003, SI 2003/2603, as amended by virtue of the Natural

**Freedom of Information Act 2000 (c 36)**—*contd*

Environment and Rural Communities Act 2006, s 105(1), Sch 11, Pt 2, para 175(1); Freedom of Information Act 2000 (Commencement No 4) Order 2004, SI 2004/1909; Freedom of Information Act 2000 (Commencement No 5) Order 2004, SI 2004/3122

| | | |
|---|---|---|
| 1, 2 | | 1 Jan 2005 (SI 2004/3122) |
| 3–8 | | 30 Nov 2000 (RA) |
| 9, 10 | | 30 Nov 2000 (so far as confers power to make any order, regulations or code of practice) (RA) |
| | | 1 Jan 2005 (otherwise) (SI 2004/3122) |
| 11 | | 1 Jan 2005 (SI 2004/3122) |
| 12, 13 | | 30 Nov 2000 (so far as confers power to make any order, regulations or code of practice) (RA) |
| | | 1 Jan 2005 (otherwise) (SI 2004/3122) |
| 14 | | 1 Jan 2005 (SI 2004/3122) |
| 15 | (1)–(3) | 1 Jan 2005 (SI 2004/3122) |
| | (4), (5) | 1 Jan 2005 (SI 2004/1909; SI 2004/3122) |
| 16, 17 | | 1 Jan 2005 (SI 2004/3122) |
| 18 | (1) | 30 Jan 2001 (s 87(2)) |
| | (2), (3) | 14 May 2001 (SI 2001/1637) |
| | (4) | See Sch 2 below |
| | (5)–(7) | 14 May 2001 (SI 2001/1637) |
| 19 | (1)–(4) | 30 Nov 2000 (RA) (so far as relates to approval of publication schemes) |
| | | 30 Nov 2002 (so far as relates to public authorities listed in Sch 1, paras 1 (except the Crown Prosecution Service and the Serious Fraud Office), 2, 3, 5 to the Act and SI 2002/2812, Sch 1) (SI 2002/2812) |
| | | 28 Feb 2003 (so far as relates to the Common Council of the City of London, in respect of information held in its capacity as a local authority or port health authority and public authorities listed in Sch 1, paras 7, 8, 10–16, 18–36 to the Act and SI 2002/2812, Sch 2) (SI 2002/2812) |
| | | 30 Jun 2003 (so far as relates to the Crown Prosecution Service and the Serious Fraud Office, the Common Council of the City of London, in respect of information held in its capacity as a police authority, and public authorities listed in Sch 1, paras 6, 57–64 to the Act and SI 2002/2812, Sch 3) (SI 2002/2812) |
| | | 31 Oct 2003 (so far as relates to the public authorities listed in Sch 1, Pt III to the Act, the Distinction and Meritorious Service Awards Committee, Invest Northern Ireland and The Northern Ireland Council for Postgraduate Medical and Dental Education) (SI 2003/2603) |
| | | 29 Feb 2004 (so far as relates to the public authorities listed in Sch 1, Pt IV to the Act (except for those specified in para 52(b)), the public authorities listed in SI 2003/2603, Sch 1 and any publicly-owned company as defined in s 6 of the Act) (SI 2003/2603) |
| | | 30 Jun 2004 (so far as relates to all public authorities in respect of which these provisions have not been commenced elsewhere, except for that public authority listed in Sch 1, para 17 to the Act and the consultative Civic Forum referred to in the Northern Ireland Act 1998, s 56(4)) (SI 2003/2603) |
| | | 1 Jan 2005 (otherwise) (SI 2004/3122) |
| | (5)–(7) | 30 Nov 2000 (RA) (so far as relates to approval of publication schemes) |
| | | 30 Nov 2002 (otherwise) (SI 2002/2812) |
| 20 | | 30 Nov 2000 (RA) (so far as relates to approval and preparation by the Commissioner of model publication schemes) |
| | | 30 Nov 2002 (otherwise) (SI 2002/2812) |
| 21–44 | | 1 Jan 2005 (SI 2004/3122) |

**Freedom of Information Act 2000 (c 36)**—*contd*

| | | |
|---|---|---|
| 45, 46 | | 30 Nov 2000 (so far as confers power to make any order, regulations or code of practice) (RA) |
| | | 30 Nov 2002 (otherwise) (SI 2002/2812) |
| 47 | (1) | 30 Nov 2002 (SI 2002/2812) |
| | (2)–(6) | 30 Nov 2000 (RA) |
| 48 | (1), (2) | 30 Nov 2002 (SI 2002/2812), so far as relates to: |
| | | (i) the issue of practice recommendations, and |
| | | (ii) the issue and enforcement of information notices, relating to the conformity with the code of practice under s 45 of the practice of public authorities in relation to the exercise of their functions under the publication scheme provisions |
| | | 1 Jan 2005 (otherwise) (SI 2004/1909; SI 2004/3122) |
| | (3), (4) | 1 Jan 2005 (SI 2004/1909; SI 2004/3122) |
| 49 | | 30 Nov 2000 (RA) |
| 50 | | 1 Jan 2005 (SI 2004/1909; SI 2004/3122) |
| 51 | | 30 Nov 2002 (SI 2002/2812), so far as relates to the enforcement of the requirements on public authorities under the publication scheme provisions and so far as relates to: |
| | | (i) the issue of practice recommendations, and |
| | | (ii) the issue and enforcement of information notices, relating to the conformity with the code of practice under s 45 of the practice of public authorities in relation to the exercise of their functions under the publication scheme provisions |
| | | 1 Jan 2005 (otherwise) (SI 2004/1909; SI 2004/3122) |
| 52 | | 30 Nov 2002 (so far as relates to the enforcement of the requirements on public authorities under the publication scheme provisions) (SI 2002/2812) |
| | | 1 Jan 2005 (otherwise) (SI 2004/1909; SI 2004/3122) |
| 53 | | 30 Nov 2000 (so far as confers power to make any order, regulations or code of practice) (RA) |
| | | 1 Jan 2005 (otherwise) (SI 2004/1909; SI 2004/3122) |
| 54 | | 30 Nov 2002 (SI 2002/2812) so far as relates to the enforcement of the requirements on public authorities under the publication scheme provisions and so far as relates to: |
| | | (i) the issue of practice recommendations, and |
| | | (ii) the issue and enforcement of information notices, relating to the conformity with the code of practice under s 45 of the practice of public authorities in relation to the exercise of their functions under the publication scheme provisions |
| | | 1 Jan 2005 (otherwise) (SI 2004/1909; SI 2004/3122) |
| 55 | | See Sch 3 below |
| 56 | | 30 Nov 2002 (SI 2002/2812) |
| 57 | (1) | 1 Jan 2005 (SI 2004/1909; SI 2004/3122) |
| | (2) | 30 Nov 2002 (SI 2002/2812) |
| | (3) | 1 Jan 2005 (SI 2004/1909; SI 2004/3122) |
| 58, 59 | | 30 Nov 2002 (SI 2002/2812) |
| 60 | | 1 Jan 2005 (SI 2004/1909; SI 2004/3122) |
| 61 | (1) | See Sch 4 below |
| | (2) | 14 May 2001 (so far as relating to Sch 4, paras 1, 4) (SI 2001/1637) |
| | | 30 Nov 2002 (otherwise) (SI 2002/2812) |
| 62 | | 1 Jan 2005 (SI 2004/1909; SI 2004/3122) |
| 63–66 | | 1 Jan 2005 (SI 2004/3122) |
| 67 | | See Sch 5 below |
| 68 | | 1 Jan 2005 (SI 2004/1909; SI 2004/3122) |
| 69 | | 30 Nov 2000 (so far as confers power to make any order, regulations or code of practice) (RA) |
| | | 1 Jan 2005 (otherwise) (SI 2004/1909; SI 2004/3122) |
| 70, 71 | | 1 Jan 2005 (SI 2004/1909; SI 2004/3122) |
| 72 | | 30 Nov 2002 (SI 2002/2812) |

**Freedom of Information Act 2000 (c 36)**—*contd*

| | | |
|---|---|---|
| 73 | | See Sch 6 below |
| 74, 75 | | 30 Nov 2000 (RA) |
| 76 | | 30 Jan 2001 (s 87(2)) |
| 77 | | 1 Jan 2005 (SI 2004/1909; SI 2004/3122) |
| 78–85 | | 30 Nov 2000 (RA) |
| 86 | | See Sch 8 below |
| 87 | | 30 Nov 2000 (RA) |
| 88 | | 30 Nov 2002 (SI 2002/2812) |
| Sch 1 | | 30 Nov 2000 (RA) |
| Sch 2 | para 1(1) | 30 Jan 2001 (s 87(2)) |
| | para 1(2) | 14 May 2001 (SI 2001/1637) |
| | para 2 | 30 Nov 2000 (RA) |
| | para 3(1) | 30 Jan 2001 (s 87(2)) |
| | para 3(2) | 14 May 2001 (SI 2001/1637) |
| | para 4 | 30 Jan 2001 (s 87(2)) |
| | para 5 | 14 May 2001 (SI 2001/1637) |
| | paras 6, 7 | 30 Jan 2001 (s 87(2)) |
| | para 8(1) | 14 May 2001 (SI 2001/1637) |
| | para 8(2) | 30 Jan 2001 (s 87(2)) |
| | para 9(1) | 14 May 2001 (SI 2001/1637) |
| | para 9(2) | 30 Jan 2001 (s 87(2)) |
| | para 10(a) | 30 Jan 2001 (s 87(2)) |
| | para 10(b) | 30 Nov 2002 (SI 2002/2812) |
| | paras 11, 12 | 14 May 2001 (SI 2001/1637) |
| | para 13(1), (2) | 30 Jan 2001 (s 87(2)) |
| | para 13(3) | 14 May 2001 (SI 2001/1637) |
| | para 14(a) | 30 Jan 2001 (s 87(2)) |
| | para 14(b) | 14 May 2001 (SI 2001/1637) |
| | para 15(1), (2) | 30 Jan 2001 (s 87(2)) |
| | para 15(3) | 14 May 2001 (SI 2001/1637) |
| | para 16 | 14 May 2001 (SI 2001/1637) |
| | paras 17–22 | 30 Nov 2000 (RA) |
| Sch 3 | | 30 Nov 2002 (so far as relates to the enforcement of the requirements on public authorities under the publication scheme provisions and so far as relates to: (i) the issue of practice recommendations, and (ii) the issue and enforcement of information notices, relating to the conformity with the code of practice under s 45 of the practice of public authorities in relation to the exercise of their functions under the publication scheme provisions) (SI 2002/2812) |
| | | 1 Jan 2005 (otherwise) (SI 2004/1909; SI 2004/3122) |
| Sch 4 | para 1 | 14 May 2001 (SI 2001/1637) |
| | para 2 | 1 Jan 2005 (SI 2004/1909; SI 2004/3122) |
| | para 3 | 30 Nov 2002 (SI 2002/2812) |
| | para 4 | 14 May 2001 (SI 2001/1637) |
| Sch 5 | para 1 | 30 Nov 2002 (SI 2002/2812) |
| | paras 2, 3 | 1 Jan 2005 (SI 2004/3122) |
| | para 4 | 30 Nov 2000 (RA) |
| | para 5 | 1 Jan 2005 (SI 2004/3122) |
| Sch 6 | para 1 | 14 May 2001 (SI 2001/1637) |
| | paras 2–5 | 1 Jan 2005 (SI 2004/1909; SI 2004/3122) |
| | paras 6, 7 | 14 May 2001 (SI 2001/1637) |
| | para 8 | 30 Nov 2000 (RA) |
| Sch 7 | | 30 Jan 2001 (s 87(2)) |
| Sch 8 | Pt I | 30 Nov 2000 (RA) |
| | Pt II | 30 Jan 2001 (s 87(2)) |
| | Pt III | 1 Jan 2005 (SI 2004/3122) |

## Fur Farming (Prohibition) Act 2000 (c 33)

*RA:* 23 Nov 2000

*Commencement provisions:* s 7(2), (3); Fur Farming (Prohibition) Act 2000 (Commencement) Order 2001,
SI 2001/3854

| | |
|---|---|
| 1–4 | 1 Jan 2003 (SI 2001/3854) |
| 5 | 23 Jan 2001 (s 7(3)) |
| 6, 7 | 23 Nov 2000 (RA) |

## Government Resources and Accounts Act 2000 (c 20)

*RA:* 28 Jul 2000

*Commencement provisions:* s 30(1), (2); Government Resources and Accounts Act 2000 (Commencement
No 1 and Transitional Provision) Order 2000, SI 2000/3349[1]; Government Resources and Accounts
Act 2000 (Commencement No 2 and Transitional Provision) Order 2010, SI 2010/516

| | | |
|---|---|---|
| 1 | | 1 Apr 2001 (SI 2000/3349) |
| 2 | (1), (2) | 22 Dec 2000 (SI 2000/3349) |
| | (3)–(6) | 1 Apr 2001 (SI 2000/3349) |
| 3 | | 1 Apr 2001 (SI 2000/3349) |
| 4 | | 22 Dec 2000 (SI 2000/3349) |
| 5–9 | | 1 Apr 2001 (SI 2000/3349) |
| 10 | | 22 Dec 2000 (SI 2000/3349) |
| 11 | | 2 Mar 2010 (SI 2010/516)[2] |
| 12, 13 | | 22 Dec 2000 (so far as relate to the specifying of amounts and the giving of directions) (E) (S) (NI) (SI 2000/3349) |
| | | 1 Apr 2001 (otherwise) (E) (S) (NI) (SI 2000/3349) |
| | | *Never in force* (W) (repealed) |
| 14 | | 1 Apr 2001 (SI 2000/3349) |
| 15 | | 22 Dec 2000 (SI 2000/3349) |
| 16–20 | | 28 Jul 2000 (s 30(1)) |
| 21, 22 | | 1 Apr 2001 (SI 2000/3349) |
| 23, 24 | | 22 Dec 2000 (SI 2000/3349) |
| 25, 26 | | 1 Apr 2001 (SI 2000/3349) |
| 27, 28 | | 22 Dec 2000 (SI 2000/3349) |
| 29 | (1) | See Sch 1 below |
| | (2) | See Sch 2 below |
| 30–31 | | 28 Jul 2000 (s 30(1)) |
| Sch 1 | paras 1–16 | 1 Apr 2001 (SI 2000/3349) |
| | para 17 | 22 Dec 2000 (so far as relates to the preparation and laying of estimates, the giving of directions, and the making of any provision described in House of Commons (Administration) Act 1978, s 3(4)(b), as substituted by Sch 1, para 17 to this Act) (SI 2000/3349) |
| | | 1 Apr 2001 (otherwise) (SI 2000/3349) |
| | paras 18–23 | 1 Apr 2001 (SI 2000/3349) |
| | para 24 | 22 Dec 2000 (so far as relates to the giving of directions under Government of Wales Act 1998, s 101A(4), as inserted by Sch 1, para 24 to this Act) (SI 2000/3349) |
| | | 1 Apr 2001 (otherwise) (except so far as relates to Government of Wales Act 1998, s 101A(7)–(12)) (SI 2000/3349) |
| | | *Never in force* (exception noted above) (repealed) |
| | paras 25–27 | 1 Apr 2001 (SI 2000/3349) |
| Sch 2 | | 1 Apr 2001 (SI 2000/3349) |

[1]  None of the provisions brought into force by this Order shall have effect in relation to the business of
any financial year ending with or before 31 Mar 2001, with the exception of s 4, Sch 1, paras 19, 23

[2]  For a transitional provision, see SI 2010/516, art 3

## Health Service Commissioners (Amendment) Act 2000 (c 28)

*RA:* 23 Nov 2000

*Commencement provisions:* s 4(2)

Whole Act in force 23 Feb 2001 (s 4(2))

## Insolvency Act 2000 (c 39)

*RA:* 30 Nov 2000

*Commencement provisions:* s 16; Insolvency Act 2000 (Commencement No 1 and Transitional Provisions) Order 2001, SI 2001/766; Insolvency Act 2000 (Commencement No 2) Order 2001, SI 2001/1751; Insolvency Act 2000 (Commencement No 3 and Transitional Provisions) Order 2002, SI 2002/2711

| | | |
|---|---|---|
| 1 | | See Sch 1 below |
| 2–4 | | 1 Jan 2003 (SI 2002/2711)[2] |
| 5–13 | | 2 Apr 2001 (SI 2001/766)[1] |
| 14 | | 30 Nov 2000 (s 16(2)) |
| 15 | (1) | See Sch 5 below |
| | (2), (3) | 1 Jan 2003 (SI 2002/2711)[2] |
| 16–18 | | 30 Nov 2000 (RA) |
| Sch 1 | paras 1–3 | 1 Jan 2003 (SI 2002/2711)[2] |
| | para 4 | 11 May 2001 (only in so far as gives effect to Insolvency Act 1986, Sch A1, paras 5, 45(1)–(3), (5)) (SI 2001/1751) |
| | | 1 Jan 2003 (otherwise) (SI 2002/2711)[2] |
| | paras 5–12 | 1 Jan 2003 (SI 2002/2711)[2] |
| Schs 2, 3 | | 1 Jan 2003 (SI 2002/2711)[2] |
| Sch 4 | | 2 Apr 2001 (SI 2001/766)[1] |
| Sch 5 | | 2 Apr 2001 (SI 2001/766), repeals of or in— |
| | | Company Directors Disqualification Act 1986, ss 9(1), 22(4); |
| | | Insolvency Act 1986, s 218(2), (6)(b); |
| | | Companies Act 1989, s 78 |
| | | 1 Jan 2003 (otherwise) (SI 2002/2711)[2] |

[1]   For transitional provisions, see SI 2001/766, art 3

[2]   For transitional provisions, see SI 2002/2711, arts 3–5

## Learning and Skills Act 2000 (c 21)

*RA:* 28 Jul 2000

*Commencement provisions:* s 154; Learning and Skills Act 2000 (Commencement No 1) Order 2000, SI 2000/2114; Learning and Skills Act (Commencement No 1) (Wales) Order 2000, SI 2000/2540; Learning and Skills Act (Commencement No 2 and Savings) Order 2000, SI 2000/2559[1]; Learning and Skills Act 2000 (Commencement No 2) (Wales) Order 2000, SI 2000/3230; Learning and Skills Act 2000 (Commencement No 3 and Savings and Transitional Provisions) Order 2001, SI 2001/654[2]; Learning and Skills Act 2000 (Commencement No 3 and Transitional Provisions) (Wales) Order 2001, SI 2001/1274[3]; Learning and Skills Act 2000 (Commencement No 4) (Wales) Order 2001, SI 2001/2705; Learning and Skills Act 2000 (Commencement No 4) and Transitional Provisions Order 2002, SI 2002/279[4]

| | | |
|---|---|---|
| 1 | (1)–(3) | 1 Sep 2000 (SI 2000/2114) |
| | (4) | See Sch 1 below |
| | (5) | 1 Sep 2000 (SI 2000/2114) |
| 2–4 | | 1 Apr 2001 (SI 2001/654) |
| 5 | (1)(a)–(e) | 1 Mar 2001 (SI 2001/654) |
| | (1)(f) | 1 Sep 2000 (SI 2000/2114) |
| | (1)(g)–(i) | 1 Mar 2001 (SI 2001/654) |
| | (2) | 1 Sep 2000 (SI 2000/2114) |

**Learning and Skills Act 2000 (c 21)**—*contd*

| | | |
|---|---|---|
| | (3) | 1 Mar 2001 (SI 2001/654) |
| 6 | (1), (2) | 1 Sep 2000 (SI 2000/2114) |
| | (3), (4) | 1 Mar 2001 (SI 2001/654) |
| | (5) | 1 Sep 2000 (SI 2000/2114) |
| | (6) | 1 Mar 2001 (SI 2001/654) |
| 7 | | 1 Mar 2002 (SI 2002/279) |
| 8, 9 | | 1 Mar 2001 (SI 2001/654) |
| 10, 11 | | 1 Apr 2001 (SI 2001/654) |
| 12 | (1) | 1 Sep 2000 (SI 2000/2114) |
| | (2) | 1 Mar 2001 (SI 2001/654) |
| | (3)–(5) | 1 Sep 2000 (SI 2000/2114) |
| | (6) | 1 Mar 2001 (SI 2001/654) |
| 13 | | 1 Apr 2001 (SI 2001/654) |
| 14–18 | | 1 Sep 2000 (SI 2000/2114) |
| 19 | (1)–(4) | 1 Sep 2000 (SI 2000/2114) |
| | (5) | See Sch 2 below |
| 20–22 | | 1 Sep 2000 (SI 2000/2114) |
| 23 | | 1 Apr 2001 (SI 2001/654) |
| 24, 25 | | 1 Sep 2000 (SI 2000/2114) |
| 26 | | See Sch 3 below |
| 27 | | 1 Sep 2000 (SI 2000/2114) |
| 28 | | 1 Apr 2001 (SI 2001/654) |
| 29 | | 1 Sep 2000 (SI 2000/2114) |
| 30 | | 19 Sep 2000 (SI 2000/2540) |
| 31–35 | | 1 Apr 2001 (SI 2001/1274) |
| 36 | | 1 Apr 2002 (SI 2001/2705) |
| 37–41 | | 1 Apr 2001 (SI 2001/1274) |
| 42–44 | | 1 Jan 2001 (SI 2000/3230) |
| 45 | | 1 Apr 2001 (SI 2001/1274) |
| 46 | | 1 Jan 2001 (SI 2000/3230) |
| 47 | | 19 Sep 2000 (SI 2000/2540) |
| 48 | | 1 Jan 2001 (SI 2000/3230) |
| 49 | | 19 Sep 2000 (SI 2000/2540) |
| 50 | | 1 Apr 2001 (SI 2001/1274) |
| 51 | | 19 Sep 2000 (SI 2000/2540) |
| 52 | (1)–(7) | 3 Aug 2000 (SI 2000/2114) |
| | (8) | See Sch 6 below |
| 53 | | 3 Aug 2000 (SI 2000/2114) |
| 54–59 | | 1 Apr 2001 (SI 2001/654) |
| 60 | | 3 Aug 2000 (SI 2000/2114) |
| 61–68 | | 1 Apr 2001 (SI 2001/654) |
| 69, 70 | | 3 Aug 2000 (SI 2000/2114) |
| 71 | (1), (2) | 1 Oct 2000 (SI 2000/2559) |
| | (3) | 1 Apr 2001 (SI 2001/654) |
| 72 | | 1 Apr 2001 (SI 2001/654) |
| 73 | | 1 Jan 2001 (SI 2000/3230) |
| 74–86 | | 1 Apr 2001 (SI 2001/1274) |
| 87 | | 1 Jan 2001 (SI 2000/3230) |
| 88 | | 1 Apr 2001 (SI 2001/1274) |
| 89 | | 1 Apr 2001 (SI 2001/654) |
| 90 | | 1 Oct 2000 (SI 2000/2559) |
| 91 | | 1 Apr 2001 (SI 2001/1274) |
| 92 | | 1 Sep 2000 (SI 2000/2114) |
| 93 | | 1 Jan 2001 (SI 2000/3230) |
| 94 | | 1 Sep 2000 (SI 2000/2114) |
| 95 | | 1 Sep 2000 (E) (SI 2000/2114) |
| | | 1 Jan 2001 (W) (SI 2000/3230) |
| 96 | | 1 Sep 2001 (SI 2001/654; SI 2001/1274) |
| 97 | | 1 Aug 2002 (E) (SI 2002/279) |

**Learning and Skills Act 2000 (c 21)**—*contd*

| | | |
|---|---|---|
| | | 1 Sep 2002 (W) (SI 2001/2705) |
| 98 | | 1 Apr 2001 (SI 2001/654) |
| 99 | | 1 Apr 2001 (SI 2001/1274) |
| 100 | (1) | 1 Sep 2001 (SI 2001/654) |
| | (2) | 1 Sep 2001 (SI 2001/1274) |
| 101 | | 1 Sep 2001 (SI 2001/654) |
| 102 | | 1 Sep 2001 (SI 2001/1274) |
| 103 | (1) | 1 Apr 2001 (W) (SI 2001/1274) |
| | | 1 Sep 2001 (E) (SI 2001/654) |
| | (2), (3) | 1 Apr 2001 (W) (so far as necessary for the purposes of s 103(4)(b)) (SI 2001/1274) |
| | | 1 Apr 2002 (E) (SI 2002/279) |
| | | *Never in force* (otherwise) (repealed) |
| | (4) | 1 Apr 2001 (SI 2001/1274) |
| | (5) | 1 Sep 2001 (SI 2001/654; SI 2001/1274) |
| 104–109 | | 3 Aug 2000 (SI 2000/2114) |
| 110 | (1) | 1 Sep 2000 (E) (so far as inserts Education Act 1996, s 2(2A)) (SI 2000/2114) |
| | | 1 Apr 2001 (W) (SI 2001/1274) |
| | | 1 Apr 2001 (E) (otherwise) (SI 2001/654) |
| | (2) | 1 Sep 2000 (E) (so far as relates to s 110(3)) (SI 2000/2114) |
| | | 1 Apr 2001 (W) (SI 2001/1274) |
| | | 1 Aug 2002 (E) (otherwise) (SI 2002/279) |
| | (3) | 1 Sep 2000 (E) (SI 2000/2114) |
| | | 1 Apr 2001 (W) (SI 2001/1274) |
| | (4), (5) | 1 Apr 2001 (W) (SI 2001/1274) |
| | | 1 Aug 2002 (E) (SI 2002/279) |
| 111, 112 | | 1 Oct 2000 (E) (SI 2000/2559) |
| | | 1 Apr 2001 (W) (SI 2001/1274) |
| 113 | (1), (2) | See Sch 7 below |
| | (3) | 1 Apr 2001 (E) (SI 2001/654) |
| | | 1 Apr 2002 (W) (SI 2001/2705) |
| 114–122 | | 1 Apr 2001 (SI 2001/654) |
| 123–129 | | 1 Apr 2001 (SI 2001/1274) |
| 130, 131 | | 28 Jul 2000 (RA) |
| 132–136 | | 1 Oct 2000 (SI 2000/2559) |
| 137 | | 1 Apr 2001 (SI 2001/654; SI 2001/1274) |
| 138 | | 1 Apr 2001 (SI 2001/1274) |
| 139 | | 3 Aug 2000 (E) (except so far as inserts Teaching and Higher Education Act 1998, s 19(12)) (SI 2000/2114) |
| | | 1 Oct 2000 (E) (exception as noted above) (SI 2000/2559) |
| | | 1 Jan 2001 (W) (SI 2000/3230) |
| 140 | (1), (2) | 1 Apr 2002 (W) (SI 2001/2705) |
| | | 1 Apr 2002 (E) (SI 2002/279)[4] |
| | (3) | 1 Apr 2001 (SI 2001/654; SI 2001/1274) |
| | (4) | 1 Apr 2001 (W) (so far as necessary for the purposes of sub-s (3) above) (SI 2001/1274) |
| | | 1 Apr 2001 (E) (SI 2001/654) |
| | | 1 Apr 2002 (W) (otherwise) (SI 2001/2705) |
| | (5) | 1 Mar 2001 (E) (SI 2001/654) |
| | | 1 Apr 2001 (W) (so far as necessary for the purposes of sub-s (3) above) (SI 2001/1274) |
| | | 1 Apr 2002 (W) (otherwise) (SI 2001/2705) |
| | (6) | 1 Apr 2001 (W) (so far as necessary for the purposes of sub-s (3) above) (SI 2001/1274) |
| | | 1 Apr 2002 (W) (otherwise) (SI 2001/2705) |
| 141 | | 10 Aug 2000 (E) (SI 2000/2114) |
| | | 1 Jan 2001 (W) (SI 2000/3230) |
| 142 | | 1 Apr 2001 (SI 2001/654; SI 2001/1274) |

**Learning and Skills Act 2000 (c 21)**—*contd*

| | | |
|---|---|---|
| 143 | (1)(a) | 1 Apr 2001 (SI 2001/654; SI 2001/1274) |
| | (1)(b), (c) | 1 Oct 2000 (E) (SI 2000/2559) |
| | | 1 Apr 2001 (W) (SI 2001/1274) |
| | (2) | 1 Oct 2000 (E) (SI 2000/2559) |
| | | 1 Apr 2001 (W) (SI 2001/1274) |
| | (3) | 1 Apr 2001 (SI 2001/654; SI 2001/1274) |
| | (4) | 1 Oct 2000 (E) (SI 2000/2559) |
| | | 1 Apr 2001 (W) (SI 2001/1274) |
| | (5) | 1 Apr 2001 (W) (SI 2001/1274) |
| | (6), (7) | 1 Oct 2000 (E) (SI 2000/2559) |
| | | 1 Apr 2001 (W) (SI 2001/1274) |
| 144 | | 1 Oct 2000 (E) (SI 2000/2559) |
| | | 1 Apr 2001 (W) (SI 2001/1274) |
| 145 | | 1 Oct 2000 (E) (SI 2000/2559) |
| | | 1 Jan 2001 (W) (SI 2000/3230) |
| 146, 147 | | 1 Oct 2000 (SI 2000/2559) |
| 148 | | 1 Nov 2000 (E) (SI 2000/2559) |
| | | 1 Sep 2001 (W) (SI 2001/1274) |
| 149 | | See Sch 9 below |
| 150–152 | | 28 Jul 2000 (RA) |
| 153 | | See Sch 11 below |
| 154–156 | | 28 Jul 2000 (RA) |
| Schs 1–3 | | 1 Sep 2000 (SI 2000/2114) |
| Sch 4 | | 19 Sep 2000 (SI 2000/2540) |
| Sch 5 | | 1 Jan 2001 (SI 2000/3230) |
| Sch 6 | | 3 Aug 2000 (SI 2000/2114) |
| Sch 7 | | 1 Oct 2000 (E) (for purpose of authorising the making of Regulations) (SI 2000/2559) |
| | | 1 Apr 2001 (E) (otherwise) (SI 2001/654) |
| | | 1 Apr 2002 (W) (SI 2001/2705) |
| Sch 8 | | 28 Jul 2000 (RA) |
| Sch 9 | para 1 | See paras 2–94 below |
| | para 2 | 28 Jul 2000 (RA) (so far as consequential upon ss 130, 131, Sch 8) |
| | | 3 Aug 2000 (so far as relates to Adult Learning Inspectorate) (SI 2000/2114) |
| | | 1 Sep 2000 (so far as relates to Learning and Skills Council for England) (SI 2000/2114) |
| | para 3 | 28 Jul 2000 (RA) (so far as consequential upon ss 130, 131, Sch 8) |
| | | 3 Aug 2000 (so far as relates to Adult Learning Inspectorate) (SI 2000/2114) |
| | | 1 Sep 2000 (so far as relates to Learning and Skills Council for England) (SI 2000/2114) |
| | | 19 Sep 2000 (so far as relates to National Council for Education and Training for Wales) (SI 2000/2540) |
| | para 4 | 28 Jul 2000 (RA) (so far as consequential upon ss 130, 131, Sch 8) |
| | | 1 Sep 2000 (so far as relates to Learning and Skills Council for England) (SI 2000/2114) |
| | | 19 Sep 2000 (so far as relates to National Council for Education and Training for Wales) (SI 2000/2540) |
| | paras 5–10 | 28 Jul 2000 (RA) (so far as consequential upon ss 130, 131, Sch 8) |
| | | 1 Apr 2001 (W) (otherwise) (SI 2001/1274) |
| | | 1 Apr 2001 (E) (otherwise) (SI 2001/654) |
| | para 11 | 28 Jul 2000 (RA) (so far as consequential upon ss 130, 131, Sch 8) |
| | | 1 Apr 2001 (otherwise) (SI 2001/654) |
| | paras 12, 13 | 28 Jul 2000 (RA) (so far as consequential upon ss 130, 131, Sch 8) |
| | | 1 Apr 2001 (W) (otherwise) (SI 2001/1274) |
| | | 1 Apr 2001 (E) (otherwise) (SI 2001/654) |
| | para 14 | 28 Jul 2000 (RA) (so far as consequential upon ss 130, 131, Sch 8) |
| | | 1 Oct 2000 (otherwise) (SI 2000/2559) |

**Learning and Skills Act 2000 (c 21)**—*contd*

| | |
|---|---|
| paras 15–17 | 28 Jul 2000 (RA) (so far as consequential upon ss 130, 131, Sch 8) |
| | 1 Apr 2001 (W) (otherwise) (SI 2001/1274) |
| | 1 Apr 2001 (E) (otherwise) (SI 2001/654) |
| paras 18, 19 | 28 Jul 2000 (RA) |
| para 20 | 28 Jul 2000 (RA) (so far as consequential upon ss 130, 131, Sch 8) |
| | 1 Apr 2001 (W) (otherwise) (SI 2001/1274) |
| | 1 Apr 2001 (E) (otherwise) (SI 2001/654) |
| para 21(a) | 28 Jul 2000 (RA) (so far as consequential upon ss 130, 131, Sch 8) |
| | 1 Apr 2001 (W) (otherwise) (SI 2001/1274) |
| | 1 Apr 2001 (E) (otherwise) (SI 2001/654) |
| para 21(b) | 28 Jul 2000 (RA) (so far as consequential upon ss 130, 131, Sch 8) |
| | 1 Jan 2001 (W) (otherwise) (SI 2000/3230) |
| | 1 Apr 2001 (E) (otherwise) (SI 2001/654) |
| para 22 | 28 Jul 2000 (RA) (so far as consequential upon ss 130, 131, Sch 8) |
| | 1 Apr 2001 (W) (otherwise) (SI 2001/1274) |
| | 1 Apr 2001 (E) (otherwise) (SI 2001/654) |
| para 23 | 28 Jul 2000 (RA) (so far as consequential upon ss 130, 131, Sch 8) |
| | 1 Oct 2000 (E) (otherwise) (SI 2000/2559) |
| | 1 Apr 2001 (W) (otherwise) (SI 2001/1274) |
| para 24(1) | 28 Jul 2000 (RA) (so far as consequential upon ss 130, 131, Sch 8) |
| | 1 Oct 2000 (E) (otherwise) (SI 2000/2559) |
| | 1 Apr 2001 (W) (otherwise) (SI 2001/1274) |
| para 24(2), (3) | 28 Jul 2000 (RA) (so far as consequential upon ss 130, 131, Sch 8) |
| | 1 Apr 2001 (W) (otherwise) (SI 2001/1274) |
| | 1 Apr 2001 (E) (otherwise) (SI 2001/654) |
| para 24(4) | 28 Jul 2000 (RA) (so far as consequential upon ss 130, 131, Sch 8) |
| | 1 Oct 2000 (E) (otherwise) (SI 2000/2559) |
| | 1 Apr 2001 (W) (otherwise) (SI 2001/1274) |
| para 25 | 28 Jul 2000 (RA) (so far as consequential upon ss 130, 131, Sch 8) |
| | 1 Apr 2001 (W) (otherwise) (SI 2001/1274) |
| | 1 Apr 2001 (E) (otherwise) (SI 2001/654) |
| para 26 | 1 Apr 2001 (W) (SI 2001/1274) |
| | 1 Oct 2000 (E) (SI 2000/2559) |
| paras 27, 28 | 28 Jul 2000 (RA) (so far as consequential upon ss 130, 131, Sch 8) |
| | 1 Oct 2000 (E) (SI 2000/2559) (for the purposes of application of Further and Higher Education Act 1992, ss 44, 45, to any institution which— |
| | (a) becomes an institution within the further education sector (within the meaning of s 91(3) of that Act) on or after 1 Oct 2000, or |
| | (b) was an institution within that sector before 1 Oct 2000 and before that, was a school maintained by a local education authority) |
| | 1 Apr 2001 (W) (otherwise) (SI 2001/1274) |
| | *Not yet in force* (E) (otherwise) |
| paras 29, 30 | 28 Jul 2000 (RA) (so far as consequential upon ss 130, 131, Sch 8) |
| | 1 Apr 2001 (W) (otherwise) (SI 2001/1274) |
| | 1 Apr 2001 (E) (otherwise) (SI 2001/654) |
| para 31 | 28 Jul 2000 (RA) |
| paras 32, 33 | 28 Jul 2000 (RA) (so far as consequential upon ss 130, 131, Sch 8) |
| | 1 Apr 2001 (W) (otherwise) (SI 2001/1274) |
| | 1 Apr 2001 (E) (otherwise) (SI 2001/654) |
| para 34 | 28 Jul 2000 (RA) (so far as consequential upon ss 130, 131, Sch 8) |
| | 1 Jan 2001 (W) (otherwise) (SI 2000/3230) |
| | 1 Apr 2001 (E) (otherwise) (SI 2001/654) |
| para 35 | 28 Jul 2000 (RA) (so far as consequential upon ss 130, 131, Sch 8) |
| | 1 Apr 2001 (otherwise) (SI 2001/654) |
| para 36 | 28 Jul 2000 (RA) (so far as consequential upon ss 130, 131, Sch 8) |
| | 1 Jan 2001 (W) (otherwise) (SI 2000/3230) |

**Learning and Skills Act 2000 (c 21)**—*contd*

| | |
|---|---|
| paras 37–39 | 28 Jul 2000 (RA) (so far as consequential upon ss 130, 131, Sch 8) |
| | 1 Apr 2001 (otherwise) (SI 2001/654) |
| para 40 | 28 Jul 2000 (RA) (so far as consequential upon ss 130, 131, Sch 8) |
| | 1 Apr 2001 (W) (otherwise) (SI 2001/1274) |
| | 1 Apr 2001 (E) (otherwise) (SI 2001/654) |
| paras 41–43 | 28 Jul 2000 (RA) (so far as consequential upon ss 130, 131, Sch 8) |
| | 1 Apr 2001 (otherwise) (SI 2001/654) |
| para 44(1), (2) | 28 Jul 2000 (RA) (so far as consequential upon ss 130, 131, Sch 8) |
| | 1 Apr 2001 (W) (otherwise) (SI 2001/1274) |
| | 1 Apr 2001 (E) (otherwise) (SI 2001/654) |
| para 44(3), (4) | 28 Jul 2000 (RA) (so far as consequential upon ss 130, 131, Sch 8) |
| | 1 Oct 2000 (E) (otherwise) (SI 2000/2559) |
| | 1 Jan 2001 (W) (otherwise) (SI 2000/3230) |
| para 45 | 28 Jul 2000 (RA) (so far as consequential upon ss 130, 131, Sch 8) |
| | 1 Jan 2001 (otherwise) (SI 2000/3230) |
| para 46 | 28 Jul 2000 (RA) (so far as consequential upon ss 130, 131, Sch 8) |
| | 1 Apr 2001 (W) (otherwise) (SI 2001/1274) |
| paras 47–50 | 28 Jul 2000 (RA) (so far as consequential upon ss 130, 131, Sch 8) |
| | 1 Apr 2001 (otherwise) (SI 2001/654) |
| para 51 | 28 Jul 2000 (RA) (so far as consequential upon ss 130, 131, Sch 8) |
| | 1 Apr 2001 (W) (otherwise) (SI 2001/1274) |
| | 1 Apr 2001 (E) (otherwise) (SI 2001/654) |
| para 52(1), (2) | 28 Jul 2000 (RA) (so far as consequential upon ss 130, 131, Sch 8) |
| | 1 Apr 2001 (W) (otherwise) (SI 2001/1274) |
| | 1 Apr 2001 (E) (otherwise) (SI 2001/654) |
| para 52(3) | 28 Jul 2000 (RA) (so far as consequential upon ss 130, 131, Sch 8) |
| | 1 Apr 2001 (otherwise) (SI 2001/654) |
| paras 53–56 | 28 Jul 2000 (RA) (so far as consequential upon ss 130, 131, Sch 8) |
| | 1 Apr 2001 (W) (otherwise) (SI 2001/1274) |
| | 1 Apr 2001 (E) (otherwise) (SI 2001/654) |
| para 57 | 28 Jul 2000 (RA) (so far as consequential upon ss 130, 131, Sch 8) |
| | 1 Sep 2001 (W) (otherwise) (SI 2001/1274) |
| | 1 Sep 2001 (E) (otherwise) (SI 2001/654) |
| para 58 | 28 Jul 2000 (RA) |
| para 59 | 28 Jul 2000 (RA) (so far as consequential upon ss 130, 131, Sch 8) |
| | 1 Apr 2001 (W) (otherwise) (SI 2001/1274) |
| | 1 Apr 2001 (E) (otherwise) (SI 2001/654) |
| paras 60–63 | 28 Jul 2000 (RA) |
| para 64 | 28 Jul 2000 (RA) (so far as consequential upon ss 130, 131, Sch 8) |
| | 1 Oct 2000 (E) (otherwise) (SI 2000/2559) |
| | 1 Jan 2001 (W) (otherwise) (SI 2000/3230) |
| paras 65, 66 | 28 Jul 2000 (RA) (so far as consequential upon ss 130, 131, Sch 8) |
| | 1 Apr 2001 (otherwise) (SI 2001/1274) |
| para 67(1) | See paras (2)–(5) below |
| para 67(2) | 28 Jul 2000 (RA) |
| para 67(3) | 28 Jul 2000 (RA) (so far as consequential upon ss 130, 131, Sch 8) |
| | 1 Apr 2001 (E) (otherwise) (SI 2001/654) |
| | 1 Apr 2002 (W) (otherwise) (SI 2001/2705) |
| para 67(4) | 28 Jul 2000 (RA) |
| para 67(5) | 28 Jul 2000 (RA) (so far as consequential upon ss 130, 131, Sch 8) |
| | 1 Apr 2001 (otherwise) (SI 2001/1274) |
| para 68 | 28 Jul 2000 (RA) (so far as consequential upon ss 130, 131, Sch 8) |
| | 1 Apr 2001 (W) (otherwise) (SI 2001/1274) |
| | 1 Apr 2001 (E) (otherwise) (SI 2001/654) |
| para 69 | 28 Jul 2000 (RA) (so far as consequential upon ss 130, 131, Sch 8) |
| | 10 Sep 2000 (E) (otherwise) (SI 2000/2114) |
| | *Never in force* (W) (repealed) |
| para 70 | 28 Jul 2000 (RA) (so far as consequential upon ss 130, 131, Sch 8) |
| | 1 Jan 2001 (W) (otherwise) (SI 2000/3230) |

**Learning and Skills Act 2000 (c 21)**—*contd*

| | | |
|---|---|---|
| | para 71 | 28 Jul 2000 (RA) |
| | paras 72–74 | 28 Jul 2000 (RA) (so far as consequential upon ss 130, 131, Sch 8) |
| | | 1 Apr 2001 (W) (otherwise) (SI 2001/1274) |
| | | 1 Apr 2001 (E) (otherwise) (SI 2001/654) |
| | para 75(a), (b) | 28 Jul 2000 (RA) (so far as consequential upon ss 130, 131, Sch 8) |
| | | 1 Apr 2001 (W) (otherwise) (SI 2001/1274) |
| | | 1 Apr 2001 (E) (otherwise) (SI 2001/654) |
| | para 75(c) | 28 Jul 2000 (RA) (so far as consequential upon ss 130, 131, Sch 8) |
| | | 1 Apr 2001 (W) (so far as relates to s 34 of this Act) (SI 2001/1274) |
| | | 1 Apr 2001 (so far as relates to s 5 of this Act) (SI 2001/654) |
| | paras 76, 77 | 28 Jul 2000 (RA) (so far as consequential upon ss 130, 131, Sch 8) |
| | | 1 Apr 2001 (otherwise) (SI 2001/1274) |
| | paras 78, 79 | 28 Jul 2000 (RA) (so far as consequential upon ss 130, 131, Sch 8) |
| | | 1 Apr 2001 (W) (otherwise) (SI 2001/1274) |
| | | 1 Apr 2001 (E) (otherwise) (SI 2001/654) |
| | para 80 | 28 Jul 2000 (RA) (so far as consequential upon ss 130, 131, Sch 8) |
| | | 1 Jan 2001 (E) (otherwise) (SI 2000/2559) |
| | | 1 Apr 2001 (W) (otherwise) (SI 2001/1274) |
| | para 81 | 28 Jul 2000 (RA) (so far as consequential upon ss 130, 131, Sch 8) |
| | | 1 Jan 2001 (E) (otherwise) (SI 2000/2559) |
| | | 1 Jan 2001 (W) (otherwise) (SI 2000/3230) |
| | para 82 | 28 Jul 2000 (RA) (so far as consequential upon ss 130, 131, Sch 8) |
| | | 1 Apr 2002 (otherwise) (SI 2001/2705) |
| | para 83 | 28 Jul 2000 (RA) (so far as consequential upon ss 130, 131, Sch 8) |
| | | 1 Apr 2001 (otherwise) (SI 2001/654) |
| | para 84 | 28 Jul 2000 (RA) (so far as consequential upon ss 130, 131, Sch 8) |
| | | 1 Apr 2001 (E) (otherwise) (SI 2001/654) |
| | | 1 Apr 2002 (W) (otherwise) (SI 2001/2705) |
| | para 85 | 28 Jul 2000 (RA) |
| | para 86 | 28 Jul 2000 (RA) (so far as consequential upon ss 130, 131, Sch 8) |
| | | 1 Jan 2001 (otherwise) (SI 2000/3230) |
| | para 87 | 28 Jul 2000 (RA) (so far as consequential upon ss 130, 131, Sch 8) |
| | | 1 Sep 2000 (otherwise) (SI 2000/2114) |
| | para 88 | 28 Jul 2000 (RA) (so far as consequential upon ss 130, 131, Sch 8) |
| | | 1 Apr 2001 (otherwise) (SI 2001/654) |
| | para 89 | 28 Jul 2000 (RA) (so far as consequential upon ss 130, 131, Sch 8) |
| | | 1 Apr 2001 (E) (otherwise) (SI 2001/654) |
| | para 90(1)–(4) | 28 Jul 2000 (RA) (so far as consequential upon ss 130, 131, Sch 8) |
| | | 1 Apr 2001 (E) (otherwise) (SI 2001/654) |
| | para 90(5), (6) | 28 Jul 2000 (RA) (so far as consequential upon ss 130, 131, Sch 8) |
| | | 1 Apr 2001 (E) (otherwise) (SI 2001/654) |
| | | 1 Apr 2002 (W) (otherwise) (SI 2001/2705) |
| | para 91 | 28 Jul 2000 (RA) (so far as consequential upon ss 130, 131, Sch 8) |
| | | 1 Apr 2001 (E) (otherwise) (SI 2001/654) |
| | | 1 Apr 2002 (W) (otherwise) (SI 2001/2705) |
| | para 92 | 28 Jul 2000 (RA) (so far as consequential upon ss 130, 131, Sch 8) |
| | | 1 Jan 2001 (otherwise) (SI 2000/3230) |
| | para 93 | 28 Jul 2000 (RA) (so far as consequential upon ss 130, 131, Sch 8) |
| | | 19 Sep 2000 (otherwise) (SI 2000/2540) |
| | para 94 | 28 Jul 2000 (RA) (so far as consequential upon ss 130, 131, Sch 8) |
| | | 1 Apr 2001 (otherwise) (SI 2001/1274) |
| Sch 10 | Pts I–III | 28 Jul 2000 (RA) |
| | Pt IV | 1 Apr 2001 (SI 2001/654) |
| Sch 11 | | 28 Jul 2000 (RA) (so far as consequential upon ss 130, 131, Sch 8) |
| | | 3 Aug 2000 (E) (repeals of or in Teaching and Higher Education Act 1998, s 19) (SI 2000/2114) |
| | | 1 Oct 2000 (E) (SI 2000/2559), repeals of or in— |

**Learning and Skills Act 2000 (c 21)**—*contd*

Further and Higher Education Act 1992, ss 28(2)(b), 44(6), 45(6);

School Standards and Framework Act 1998, Sch 30, paras 41, 42;

Teaching and Higher Education Act 1998, s 22(2)(h), (7)

1 Nov 2000 (E) (the repeal in Education Act 1996, s 403(1)) (SI 2000/2559)

1 Jan 2001 (W) (SI 2000/3230), repeals of or in—

Further and Higher Education Act 1992, ss 18(4)–(6), 60A, Sch 5A;

Education Act 1996, Sch 37, para 113;

Government of Wales Act 1998, s 104(4);

School Standards and Framework Act 1998, ss 125, 126, Sch 27;

Teaching and Higher Education Act 1998, ss 19, 22

1 Apr 2001 (W) (SI 2001/1274), repeals of or in—

Superannuation Act 1972, Sch 1, in the list of "Other Bodies" the words "Further Education Funding Council for Wales in receipt of remuneration.";

House of Commons Disqualification Act 1975, Sch 1, Pt III the words "Any member of the Further Education Funding Council for Wales in receipt of remuneration.";

Sex Discrimination Act 1975;

Race Relations Act 1976;

Education Reform Act 1988;

Further and Higher Education Act 1992, ss 1–9, 28(2)(b), 32(2A), 44(6), 45(6), 52(1), 55(1)–(3), (7)(a), (b), 56, Sch 2;

Disability Discrimination Act 1995, ss 19(6)(f), 30(2)–(4);

Education Act 1996, ss 15, 509(1)(d) and word "or" immediately preceding it, Sch 37, paras 70, 112;

Education Act 1997, s 30(1), (3);

Audit Commission Act 1998, s 36(1), (2);

School Standards and Framework Act 1998, Sch 30, paras 41, 42;

Teaching and Higher Education Act 1998, ss 26(1), (2), 28(1)(a), 34

1 Apr 2001 (SI 2001/654), repeals of or in—

Superannuation Act 1972, Sch 1, in the list of "Other Bodies" the words "Further Education Funding Council for England in receipt of remuneration";

House of Commons Disqualification Act 1975, Sch 1, Pt III, the words "Any member of the Further Education Funding Council for England in receipt of remuneration";

Sex Discrimination Act 1975 (so far as relates to England);

Race Relations Act 1976 (so far as relates to England);

Education Reform Act 1988 (so far as relates to England);

Further and Higher Education Act 1992, ss 1–9, 32(2A), s 52(1) word "full-time", ss 55, 56, Sch 1, para 9, Sch 2 (all so far as they relate to England), s 91(2);

Disability Discrimination Act 1995, s 19(6)(e), s 30(2)–(4) (so far as relates to England);

Education Act 1996, ss 15, 482, 509(1), Sch 37, paras 70, 112, 113 (so far as they relate to England);

Audit Commission Act 1998 (so far as relates to England);

School Standards and Framework Act 1998, Schs 6, 7, 22 (so far as relate to England), s 142(1);

Teaching and Higher Education Act 1998, ss 26(1), (2), 28(1) (so far as relate to England)

1 Sep 2001 (W) (SI 2001/1274), repeals of or in—

Education Act 1996, s 403(1);

Education Act 1997, s 37(1)–(4), (5)

**Learning and Skills Act 2000 (c 21)**—*contd*

1 Sep 2001 (E) (repeal of or in Education Act 1997, s 37)
(SI 2001/654)
1 Apr 2002 (W) (repeals of School Standards and Framework
Act 1998, Sch 7, para 13(4), (7), Sch 22, para 5(1))
(SI 2001/2705)

[1] For savings provisions, see SI 2000/2559, art 3

[2] For savings and transitional provisions, see SI 2001/654, art 3

[3] For savings and transitional provisions, see SI 2001/1274, arts 3, 4

[4] For transitional provisions, see SI 2002/279, art 3

---

**Licensing (Young Persons) Act 2000 (c 30)**

*RA:* 23 Nov 2000

*Commencement provisions:* s 3(2)

Whole Act in force 23 Jan 2000 (s 3(2))

---

**Limited Liability Partnerships Act 2000 (c 12)**

*RA:* 20 Jul 2000

*Commencement provisions:* s 19(1), (2); Limited Liability Partnerships Act 2000 (Commencement) Order 2000, SI 2000/3316

| | |
|---|---|
| 1–18 | 6 Apr 2001 (SI 2000/3316) |
| 19 | 20 Jul 2000 (s 19(1)) |
| Schedule | 6 Apr 2001 (SI 2000/3316) |

---

**Local Government Act 2000 (c 22)**

*RA:* 28 Jul 2000

*Commencement provisions:* s 108; Local Government Act 2000 (Commencement No 1) Order 2000, SI 2000/2187; Local Government Act 2000 (Commencement No 2) Order 2000, SI 2000/2420; Local Government Act 2000 (Commencement No 3) Order 2000, SI 2000/2836; Local Government Act 2000 (Commencement No 4) Order 2000, SI 2000/2849; Local Government Act 2000 (Commencement) (Wales) Order 2000, SI 2000/2948; Local Government Act 2000 (Commencement No 5) Order 2000, SI 2000/3335; Local Government Act 2000 (Commencement No 6) Order 2001, SI 2001/415; Local Government Act 2000 (Commencement) (No 2) (Wales) Order 2001, SI 2001/1411[3]; Local Government Act 2000 (Commencement No 7) Order 2001, SI 2001/2684; Local Government Act 2000 (Commencement No 3) (Wales) Order 2002, SI 2002/1359; Local Government Act 2000 (Commencement No 8) Order 2002, SI 2002/1718; Local Government Act 2000 (Commencement No 9) Order 2012, SI 2012/1358

| | | |
|---|---|---|
| 1, 2 | | 18 Oct 2000 (E) (SI 2000/2836) |
| | | 9 Apr 2001 (W) (SI 2001/1411)[3] |
| 3 | (1), (2) | 18 Oct 2000 (E) (SI 2000/2836) |
| | | 9 Apr 2001 (W) (SI 2001/1411)[3] |
| | (3)–(7) | 18 Oct 2000 (E) (SI 2000/2836) |
| | | 1 Nov 2000 (W) (SI 2000/2948) |
| | (8) | 18 Oct 2000 (E) (SI 2000/2836) |
| | | 9 Apr 2001 (W) (SI 2001/1411)[3] |
| 4 | (1), (2) | 18 Oct 2000 (E) (SI 2000/2836) |
| | | 9 Apr 2001 (W) (SI 2001/1411)[3] |
| | (3)(a) | 18 Oct 2000 (E) (SI 2000/2836) |
| | | 9 Apr 2001 (W) (SI 2001/1411)[3] |
| | (3)(b) | 18 Oct 2000 (E) (SI 2000/2836) |

**Local Government Act 2000 (c 22)**—*contd*

| | | |
|---|---|---|
| | | 1 Nov 2000 (W) (SI 2000/2948) |
| | (4), (5) | 18 Oct 2000 (E) (SI 2000/2836) |
| | | 1 Nov 2000 (W) (SI 2000/2948) |
| 5 | (1)–(4) | 18 Oct 2000 (E) (SI 2000/2836) |
| | | 9 Apr 2001 (W) (SI 2001/1411)[3] |
| | (5) | 18 Oct 2000 (E) (SI 2000/2836) |
| | | 1 Nov 2000 (W) (SI 2000/2948) |
| | (6) | 18 Oct 2000 (E) (SI 2000/2836) |
| | | 9 Apr 2001 (W) (SI 2001/1411)[3] |
| 6 | (1)–(5) | 18 Oct 2000 (E) (SI 2000/2836) |
| | | 9 Apr 2001 (W) (SI 2001/1411)[3] |
| | (6) | 18 Oct 2000 (E) (SI 2000/2836) |
| | | 1 Nov 2000 (W) (SI 2000/2948) |
| | (7), (8) | 18 Oct 2000 (E) (SI 2000/2836) |
| | | 9 Apr 2001 (W) (SI 2001/1411)[3] |
| 7 | | 18 Oct 2000 (E) (SI 2000/2836) |
| | | 1 Nov 2000 (W) (SI 2000/2948) |
| 8, 9 | | 18 Oct 2000 (E) (SI 2000/2836) |
| | | 9 Apr 2001 (W) (SI 2001/1411)[3] |
| 10 | | 7 Aug 2000 (E) (SI 2000/2187) |
| | | 28 Jul 2001 (s 108(4)–(6)) (otherwise) |
| 11 | (1)–(4) | 7 Aug 2000 (E) (so far as they confer power to make orders or regulations) (SI 2000/2187) |
| | | 26 Oct 2000 (E) (otherwise) (SI 2000/2849) |
| | | 28 Jul 2001 (s 108(4)–(6)) (otherwise) |
| | (5), (6) | 7 Aug 2000 (E) (so far as they confer power to make orders or regulations) (SI 2000/2187) |
| | | 26 Oct 2000 (E) (otherwise) (SI 2000/2849) |
| | | 1 Nov 2000 (W) (SI 2000/2948) |
| | (7), (8) | 7 Aug 2000 (E) (so far as they confer power to make orders or regulations) (SI 2000/2187) |
| | | 26 Oct 2000 (E) (otherwise) (SI 2000/2849) |
| | | 28 Jul 2001 (W) (s 108(4)–(6)) |
| | (9) | 7 Aug 2000 (E) (so far as confers power to make orders or regulations) (SI 2000/2187) |
| | | 26 Oct 2000 (E) (otherwise) (SI 2000/2849) |
| | | 1 Nov 2000 (W) (SI 2000/2948) |
| | (10) | 7 Aug 2000 (E) (so far as confers power to make orders or regulations) (SI 2000/2187) |
| | | 26 Oct 2000 (E) (otherwise) (SI 2000/2849) |
| | | 28 Jul 2001 (W) (s 108(4)–(6)) |
| 12 | (1) | 7 Aug 2000 (E) (SI 2000/2187) |
| | | 1 Nov 2000 (W) (SI 2000/2948) |
| | (2)–(4) | 7 Aug 2000 (E) (SI 2000/2187) |
| | | 28 Jul 2001 (W) (s 108(4)–(6)) |
| 13 | (1), (2) | 7 Aug 2000 (E) (so far as they confer power to make orders or regulations) (SI 2000/2187) |
| | | 26 Oct 2000 (E) (otherwise) (SI 2000/2849) |
| | | 28 Jul 2001 (W) (s 108(4)–(6)) |
| | (3) | 7 Aug 2000 (E) (so far as confers power to make orders or regulations) (SI 2000/2187) |
| | | 26 Oct 2000 (E) (otherwise) (SI 2000/2849) |
| | | 1 Nov 2000 (W) (SI 2000/2948) |
| | (4) | 7 Aug 2000 (E) (so far as confers power to make orders or regulations) (SI 2000/2187) |
| | | 26 Oct 2000 (E) (otherwise) (SI 2000/2849) |
| | | 28 Jul 2001 (W) (s 108(4)–(6)) |
| | (5), (6) | 7 Aug 2000 (E) (so far as they confer power to make orders or regulations) (SI 2000/2187) |

**Local Government Act 2000 (c 22)**—*contd*

|  |  |  |
|---|---|---|
|  |  | 26 Oct 2000 (E) (otherwise) (SI 2000/2849) |
|  |  | 1 Nov 2000 (W) (SI 2000/2948) |
|  | (7)–(11) | 7 Aug 2000 (E) (so far as they confer power to make orders or regulations) (SI 2000/2187) |
|  |  | 26 Oct 2000 (E) (otherwise) (SI 2000/2849) |
|  |  | 28 Jul 2001 (W) (s 108(4)–(6)) |
|  | (12)–(14) | 7 Aug 2000 (E) (so far as they confer power to make orders or regulations) (SI 2000/2187) |
|  |  | 26 Oct 2000 (E) (otherwise) (SI 2000/2849) |
|  |  | 1 Nov 2000 (W) (SI 2000/2948) |
| 14–16 |  | 26 Oct 2000 (E) (SI 2000/2849) |
|  |  | 28 Jul 2001 (W) (s 108(4)–(6)) |
| 17–20 |  | 7 Aug 2000 (E) (SI 2000/2187) |
|  |  | 1 Nov 2000 (W) (SI 2000/2948) |
| 21 |  | 26 Oct 2000 (E) (SI 2000/2849) |
|  |  | 28 Jul 2001 (W) (s 108(4)–(6)) |
| 22 | (1)–(5) | 7 Aug 2000 (E) (so far as they confer power to make orders or regulations) (SI 2000/2187) |
|  |  | 26 Oct 2000 (E) (otherwise) (SI 2000/2849) |
|  |  | 28 Jul 2001 (W) (s 108(4)–(6)) |
|  | (6)–(13) | 7 Aug 2000 (E) (so far as they confer power to make orders or regulations) (SI 2000/2187) |
|  |  | 26 Oct 2000 (E) (otherwise) (SI 2000/2849) |
|  |  | 1 Nov 2000 (W) (SI 2000/2948) |
| 23 |  | See Sch 1 below |
| 24 |  | 26 Oct 2000 (E) (SI 2000/2849) |
|  |  | 28 Jul 2001 (W) (s 108(4)–(6)) |
| 25 | (1)–(4) | 7 Aug 2000 (E) (so far as they confer power to make orders or regulations) (SI 2000/2187) |
|  |  | 26 Oct 2000 (E) (otherwise) (SI 2000/2849) |
|  |  | 28 Jul 2001 (W) (s 108(4)–(6)) |
|  | (5), (6) | 7 Aug 2000 (E) (so far as they confer power to make orders or regulations) (SI 2000/2187) |
|  |  | 26 Oct 2000 (E) (otherwise) (SI 2000/2849) |
|  |  | 1 Nov 2000 (W) (SI 2000/2948) |
|  | (7) | 7 Aug 2000 (E) (so far as confers power to make orders or regulations) (SI 2000/2187) |
|  |  | 26 Oct 2000 (E) (otherwise) (SI 2000/2849) |
|  |  | 28 Jul 2001 (W) (s 108(4)–(6)) |
|  | (8) | 7 Aug 2000 (E) (so far as confers power to make orders or regulations) (SI 2000/2187) |
|  |  | 26 Oct 2000 (E) (otherwise) (SI 2000/2849) |
|  |  | 1 Nov 2000 (W) (SI 2000/2948) |
| 26 |  | 26 Oct 2000 (E) (SI 2000/2849) |
|  |  | 28 Jul 2001 (W) (s 108(4)–(6)) |
| 27 | (1)–(8) | 7 Aug 2000 (E) (so far as they confer power to make orders or regulations) (SI 2000/2187) |
|  |  | 26 Oct 2000 (E) (otherwise) (SI 2000/2849) |
|  |  | 28 Jul 2001 (W) (s 108(4)–(6)) |
|  | (9)–(10) | 7 Aug 2000 (E) (so far as they confer power to make orders or regulations) (SI 2000/2187) |
|  |  | 26 Oct 2000 (E) (otherwise) (SI 2000/2849) |
|  |  | 1 Nov 2000 (W) (SI 2000/2948) |
|  | (11)–(13) | 7 Aug 2000 (E) (so far as they confer power to make orders or regulations) (SI 2000/2187) |
|  |  | 26 Oct 2000 (E) (otherwise) (SI 2000/2849) |
|  |  | 28 Jul 2001 (W) (s 108(4)–(6)) |
| 28 | (1), (2) | 7 Aug 2000 (E) (so far as they confer power to make orders or regulations) (SI 2000/2187) |
|  |  | 26 Oct 2000 (E) (otherwise) (SI 2000/2849) |

**Local Government Act 2000 (c 22)**—*contd*

|  |  |  |
|---|---|---|
|  |  | 1 Nov 2000 (W) (SI 2000/2948) |
|  | (3) | 7 Aug 2000 (E) (so far as confers power to make orders or regulations) (SI 2000/2187) |
|  |  | 26 Oct 2000 (E) (otherwise) (SI 2000/2849) |
|  |  | *Not yet in force* (W) |
| 29 |  | 26 Oct 2000 (E) (SI 2000/2849) |
|  |  | 28 Jul 2001 (W) (s 108(4)–(6)) |
| 30 |  | 7 Aug 2000 (E) (SI 2000/2187) |
|  |  | 1 Nov 2000 (W) (SI 2000/2948) |
| 31 | (1)(a) | 7 Aug 2000 (E) (so far as confers power to make orders or regulations) (SI 2000/2187) |
|  |  | 26 Oct 2000 (E) (otherwise) (SI 2000/2849) |
|  |  | 28 Jul 2001 (W) (s 108(4)–(6)) |
|  | (1)(b) | 7 Aug 2000 (E) (so far as confers power to make orders or regulations) (SI 2000/2187) |
|  |  | 26 Oct 2000 (E) (otherwise) (SI 2000/2849) |
|  |  | 1 Nov 2000 (W) (SI 2000/2948) |
|  | (2)–(9) | 7 Aug 2000 (E) (so far as they confer power to make orders or regulations) (SI 2000/2187) |
|  |  | 26 Oct 2000 (E) (otherwise) (SI 2000/2849) |
|  |  | 28 Jul 2001 (W) (s 108(4)–(6)) |
| 32 |  | 7 Aug 2000 (E) (SI 2000/2187) |
|  |  | 1 Nov 2000 (W) (SI 2000/2948) |
| 33 | (1)–(4) | 7 Aug 2000 (E) (so far as they confer power to make orders or regulations) (SI 2000/2187) |
|  |  | 26 Oct 2000 (E) (otherwise) (SI 2000/2849) |
|  |  | 28 Jul 2001 (W) (s 108(4)–(6)) |
|  | (5)–(11) | 7 Aug 2000 (E) (so far as they confer power to make orders or regulations) (SI 2000/2187) |
|  |  | 26 Oct 2000 (E) (otherwise) (SI 2000/2849) |
|  |  | 1 Nov 2000 (W) (SI 2000/2948) |
| 34–36 |  | 7 Aug 2000 (E) (SI 2000/2187) |
|  |  | 1 Nov 2000 (W) (SI 2000/2948) |
| 37 | (1)(a) | 7 Aug 2000 (E) (so far as confers power to make orders or regulations) (SI 2000/2187) |
|  |  | 26 Oct 2000 (E) (otherwise) (SI 2000/2849) |
|  |  | 1 Nov 2000 (W) (SI 2000/2948) |
|  | (1)(b)–(d) | 7 Aug 2000 (E) (so far as they confer power to make orders or regulations) (SI 2000/2187) |
|  |  | 26 Oct 2000 (E) (otherwise) (SI 2000/2849) |
|  |  | 28 Jul 2001 (W) (s 108(4)–(6)) |
|  | (2)–(3) | 7 Aug 2000 (E) (so far as they confer power to make orders or regulations) (SI 2000/2187) |
|  |  | 26 Oct 2000 (E) (otherwise) (SI 2000/2849) |
|  |  | 28 Jul 2001 (W) (s 108(4)–(6)) |
| 38 |  | 7 Aug 2000 (E) (SI 2000/2187) |
|  |  | 1 Nov 2000 (W) (SI 2000/2948) |
| 39 | (1) | 7 Aug 2000 (E) (so far as confers power to make orders or regulations) (SI 2000/2187) |
|  |  | 26 Oct 2000 (E) (otherwise) (SI 2000/2849) |
|  |  | 1 Nov 2000 (W) (SI 2000/2948) |
|  | (2) | 7 Aug 2000 (E) (so far as confers power to make orders or regulations) (SI 2000/2187) |
|  |  | 26 Oct 2000 (E) (otherwise) (SI 2000/2849) |
|  |  | 28 Jul 2001 (W) (s 108(4)–(6)) |
|  | (3) | 7 Aug 2000 (E) (so far as confers power to make orders or regulations) (SI 2000/2187) |
|  |  | 1 Nov 2000 (W) (SI 2000/2948) |
|  |  | *Not yet in force* (E) (otherwise) |

**Local Government Act 2000 (c 22)**—*contd*

| | | |
|---|---|---|
| | (4), (5) | 7 Aug 2000 (E) (so far as they confer power to make orders or regulations) (SI 2000/2187) |
| | | 26 Oct 2000 (E) (otherwise) (SI 2000/2849) |
| | | 1 Nov 2000 (W) (SI 2000/2948) |
| | (6) | 7 Aug 2000 (E) (so far as confers power to make orders or regulations) (SI 2000/2187) |
| | | 26 Oct 2000 (E) (otherwise) (SI 2000/2849) |
| | | 28 Jul 2001 (W) (s 108(4)–(6)) |
| 40 | | 28 Jul 2001 (s 108(4)–(6)) |
| 41 | | 7 Aug 2000 (E) (SI 2000/2187) |
| | | 1 Nov 2000 (W) (SI 2000/2948) |
| 42, 43 | | 28 Jul 2001 (s 108(4)–(6)) |
| 44 | | 7 Aug 2000 (E) (so far as confers power to make orders or regulations) (SI 2000/2187) |
| | | 1 Nov 2000 (W) (SI 2000/2948) |
| | | *Not yet in force* (E) (otherwise) |
| 45 | (1)–(4) | 7 Aug 2000 (E) (so far as they confer power to make orders or regulations) (SI 2000/2187) |
| | | 19 Feb 2001 (E) (otherwise) (SI 2001/415) |
| | | 28 Jul 2001 (W) (s 108(4)–(6)) |
| | (5)–(9) | 7 Aug 2000 (E) (so far as they confer power to make orders or regulations) (SI 2000/2187) |
| | | 1 Nov 2000 (W) (SI 2000/2948) |
| | | 19 Feb 2001 (E) (otherwise) (SI 2001/415) |
| 46 | | See Sch 3 below |
| 47, 48 | | 7 Aug 2000 (E) (SI 2000/2187) |
| | | 1 Nov 2000 (W) (SI 2000/2948) |
| 49 | (1) | 19 Dec 2000 (E) (SI 2000/3335) |
| | | 19 Dec 2000 (W) (in relation to police authorities) (SI 2000/3335) |
| | | 28 Jul 2001 (W) (otherwise) (s 108(4)–(6)) |
| | (2) | 1 Nov 2000 (W) (SI 2000/2948)[1] |
| | | 19 Dec 2000 (E) (SI 2000/3335) |
| | | 19 Dec 2000 (W) (in relation to police authorities) (SI 2000/3335) |
| | (3), (4) | 19 Dec 2000 (E) (SI 2000/3335) |
| | | 19 Dec 2000 (W) (in relation to police authorities) (SI 2000/3335) |
| | | 28 Jul 2001 (W) (otherwise) (s 108(4)–(6)) |
| | (5) | 1 Nov 2000 (W) (SI 2000/2948)[1] |
| | | 19 Dec 2000 (E) (SI 2000/3335) |
| | | 19 Dec 2000 (W) (in relation to police authorities) (SI 2000/3335) |
| | (6)(a), (b) | 1 Nov 2000 (W) (SI 2000/2948)[1] |
| | | 19 Dec 2000 (E) (SI 2000/3335) |
| | | 19 Dec 2000 (W) (in relation to police authorities) (SI 2000/3335) |
| | (6)(c)–(e) | 19 Dec 2000 (E) (SI 2000/3335) |
| | | 19 Dec 2000 (W) (in relation to police authorities) (SI 2000/3335) |
| | | 28 Jul 2001 (W) (otherwise) (s 108(4)–(6)) |
| | (6)(f) | 1 Nov 2000 (W) (SI 2000/2948)[1] |
| | | 19 Dec 2000 (E) (SI 2000/3335) |
| | | 19 Dec 2000 (W) (in relation to police authorities) (SI 2000/3335) |
| | (6)(g)–(k) | 19 Dec 2000 (E) (SI 2000/3335) |
| | | 19 Dec 2000 (W) (in relation to police authorities) (SI 2000/3335) |
| | | 28 Jul 2001 (W) (otherwise) (s 108(4)–(6)) |
| | (6)(l) | 1 Nov 2000 (W) (SI 2000/2948)[1] |
| | | 19 Dec 2000 (E) (SI 2000/3335) |
| | (6)(m) | 1 Nov 2000 (W) (SI 2000/2948)[1] |
| | | 19 Dec 2000 (E) (SI 2000/3335) |
| | | 19 Dec 2000 (W) (in relation to police authorities) (SI 2000/3335) |
| | (6)(n), (o) | 19 Dec 2000 (E) (SI 2000/3335) |
| | | 19 Dec 2000 (W) (in relation to police authorities) (SI 2000/3335) |
| | | 28 Jul 2001 (W) (otherwise) (s 108(4)–(6)) |

**Local Government Act 2000 (c 22)**—*contd*

| | | |
|---|---|---|
| | (6)(p) | 1 Nov 2000 (W) (SI 2000/2948)[1] |
| | | 19 Dec 2000 (E) (SI 2000/3335) |
| | | 19 Dec 2000 (W) (in relation to police authorities) (SI 2000/3335) |
| | (7) | 1 Nov 2000 (W) (SI 2000/2948)[1] |
| | | 19 Dec 2000 (E) (SI 2000/3335) |
| | | 19 Dec 2000 (W) (in relation to police authorities) (SI 2000/3335) |
| 50 | (1) | 19 Dec 2000 (E) (SI 2000/3335) |
| | | 19 Dec 2000 (W) (in relation to police authorities) (SI 2000/3335) |
| | | 28 Jul 2001 (W) (otherwise) (s 108(4)–(6)) |
| | (2)–(7) | 1 Nov 2000 (W) (SI 2000/2948)[1] |
| | | 19 Dec 2000 (E) (SI 2000/3335) |
| | | 19 Dec 2000 (W) (in relation to police authorities) (SI 2000/3335) |
| 51, 52 | | 19 Dec 2000 (E) (SI 2000/3335) |
| | | 19 Dec 2000 (W) (in relation to police authorities) (SI 2000/3335) |
| | | 28 Jul 2001 (W) (otherwise) (s 108(4)–(6)) |
| 53 | (1)–(10) | 19 Dec 2000 (E) (SI 2000/3335) |
| | | 19 Dec 2000 (W) (in relation to police authorities) (SI 2000/3335) |
| | | 28 Jul 2001 (W) (otherwise) (s 108(4)–(6)) |
| | (11), (12) | 1 Nov 2000 (W) (SI 2000/2948)[1] |
| | | 19 Dec 2000 (E) (SI 2000/3335) |
| | | 19 Dec 2000 (W) (in relation to police authorities) (SI 2000/3335) |
| 54 | (1)–(4) | 19 Dec 2000 (E) (SI 2000/3335) |
| | | 19 Dec 2000 (W) (in relation to police authorities) (SI 2000/3335) |
| | | 28 Jul 2001 (W) (otherwise) (s 108(4)–(6)) |
| | (5) | 1 Nov 2000 (W) (SI 2000/2948)[1] |
| | | 19 Dec 2000 (E) (SI 2000/3335) |
| | | 19 Dec 2000 (W) (in relation to police authorities) (SI 2000/3335) |
| | (6) | 19 Dec 2000 (E) (SI 2000/3335) |
| | | 19 Dec 2000 (W) (in relation to police authorities) (SI 2000/3335) |
| | | 28 Jul 2001 (W) (otherwise) (s 108(4)–(6)) |
| | (7) | 1 Nov 2000 (W) (SI 2000/2948)[1] |
| | | 19 Dec 2000 (E) (SI 2000/3335) |
| | | 19 Dec 2000 (W) (in relation to police authorities) (SI 2000/3335) |
| 55 | | 19 Dec 2000 (E) (SI 2000/3335) |
| | | 19 Dec 2000 (W) (in relation to police authorities) (SI 2000/3335) |
| | | 28 Jul 2001 (W) (otherwise) (s 108(4)–(6)) |
| 56 | | 28 Jul 2001 (s 108(4)–(6)) |
| 57–67 | | 19 Dec 2000 (E) (SI 2000/3335) |
| | | 19 Dec 2000 (W) (in relation to police authorities) (SI 2000/3335) |
| | | 28 Jul 2001 (W) (otherwise) (s 108(4)–(6)) |
| 68 | (1), (2) | 28 Jul 2001 (s 108(4)–(6)) |
| | (3)–(5) | 1 Nov 2000 (W) (SI 2000/2948) |
| 69 | | 28 Jul 2001 (s 108(4)–(6)) |
| 70 | (1), (2) | 1 Nov 2000 (W) (SI 2000/2948) |
| | (3)–(5) | 28 Jul 2001 (s 108(4)–(6)) |
| 71, 72 | | 28 Jul 2001 (s 108(4)–(6)) |
| 73 | (1)–(6) | 1 Nov 2000 (W) (SI 2000/2948) |
| | (7) | 28 Jul 2001 (s 108(4)–(6)) |
| 74 | | 28 Jul 2001 (s 108(4)–(6)) |
| 75 | (1) | 19 Dec 2000 (E) (SI 2000/3335) |
| | | 19 Dec 2000 (W) (in relation to police authorities) (SI 2000/3335) |
| | | 28 Jul 2001 (W) (otherwise) (s 108(4)–(6)) |
| | (2) | 1 Nov 2000 (W) (SI 2000/2948)[1] |
| | | 19 Dec 2000 (E) (SI 2000/3335) |
| | | 19 Dec 2000 (W) (in relation to police authorities) (SI 2000/3335) |
| | (3), (4) | 19 Dec 2000 (E) (SI 2000/3335) |
| | | 19 Dec 2000 (W) (in relation to police authorities) (SI 2000/3335) |
| | | 28 Jul 2001 (W) (otherwise) (s 108(4)–(6)) |
| | (5), (6) | 1 Nov 2000 (W) (SI 2000/2948)[1] |

**Local Government Act 2000 (c 22)**—*contd*

| | | |
|---|---|---|
| | | 19 Dec 2000 (E) (SI 2000/3335) |
| | | 19 Dec 2000 (W) (in relation to police authorities) (SI 2000/3335) |
| | (7) | 19 Dec 2000 (E) (SI 2000/3335) |
| | | 19 Dec 2000 (W) (in relation to police authorities) (SI 2000/3335) |
| | | 28 Jul 2001 (W) (otherwise) (s 108(4)–(6)) |
| | (8) | 1 Nov 2000 (W) (SI 2000/2948)[1] |
| | | 19 Dec 2000 (E) (SI 2000/3335) |
| | | 19 Dec 2000 (W) (in relation to police authorities) (SI 2000/3335) |
| | (9)–(11) | 19 Dec 2000 (E) (SI 2000/3335) |
| | | 19 Dec 2000 (W) (in relation to police authorities) (SI 2000/3335) |
| | | 28 Jul 2001 (W) (otherwise) (s 108(4)–(6)) |
| 76 | (1)–(12) | 19 Dec 2000 (E) (SI 2000/3335) |
| | | 19 Dec 2000 (W) (in relation to police authorities) (SI 2000/3335) |
| | | 28 Jul 2001 (W) (otherwise) (s 108(4)–(6)) |
| | (13) | 1 Nov 2000 (W) (SI 2000/2948)[1] |
| | | 19 Dec 2000 (E) (SI 2000/3335) |
| | | 19 Dec 2000 (W) (in relation to police authorities) (SI 2000/3335) |
| | (14) | 19 Dec 2000 (E) (SI 2000/3335) |
| | | 19 Dec 2000 (W) (in relation to police authorities) (SI 2000/3335) |
| | | 28 Jul 2001 (W) (otherwise) (s 108(4)–(6)) |
| 77 | (1)–(3) | 19 Dec 2000 (E) (SI 2000/3335) |
| | | 19 Dec 2000 (W) (in relation to police authorities) (SI 2000/3335) |
| | | 28 Jul 2001 (W) (otherwise) (s 108(4)–(6)) |
| | (4) | 1 Nov 2000 (W) (SI 2000/2948)[1] |
| | | 19 Dec 2000 (E) (SI 2000/3335) |
| | | 19 Dec 2000 (W) (in relation to police authorities) (SI 2000/3335) |
| | (5) | 19 Dec 2000 (E) (SI 2000/3335) |
| | | 19 Dec 2000 (W) (in relation to police authorities) (SI 2000/3335) |
| | | 28 Jul 2001 (W) (otherwise) (s 108(4)–(6)) |
| | (6) | 1 Nov 2000 (W) (SI 2000/2948)[1] |
| | | 19 Dec 2000 (E) (SI 2000/3335) |
| | | 19 Dec 2000 (W) (in relation to police authorities) (SI 2000/3335) |
| | (7), (8) | 19 Dec 2000 (E) (SI 2000/3335) |
| | | 19 Dec 2000 (W) (in relation to police authorities) (SI 2000/3335) |
| | | 28 Jul 2001 (W) (otherwise) (s 108(4)–(6)) |
| 78–80 | | 19 Dec 2000 (E) (SI 2000/3335) |
| | | 19 Dec 2000 (W) (in relation to police authorities) (SI 2000/3335) |
| | | 28 Jul 2001 (W) (otherwise) (s 108(4)–(6)) |
| 81 | (1)–(4) | 19 Dec 2000 (E) (SI 2000/3335) |
| | | 19 Dec 2000 (W) (in relation to police authorities) (SI 2000/3335) |
| | | 28 Jul 2001 (W) (otherwise) (s 108(4)–(6)) |
| | (5) | 1 Nov 2000 (W) (SI 2000/2948)[1] |
| | | 19 Dec 2000 (E) (SI 2000/3335) |
| | | 19 Dec 2000 (W) (in relation to police authorities) (SI 2000/3335) |
| | (6), (7) | 19 Dec 2000 (E) (SI 2000/3335) |
| | | 19 Dec 2000 (W) (in relation to police authorities) (SI 2000/3335) |
| | | 28 Jul 2001 (W) (otherwise) (s 108(4)–(6)) |
| | (8) | 1 Nov 2000 (W) (SI 2000/2948)[1] |
| | | 19 Dec 2000 (E) (SI 2000/3335) |
| | | 19 Dec 2000 (W) (in relation to police authorities) (SI 2000/3335) |
| 82 | (1) | 19 Dec 2000 (E) (SI 2000/3335) |
| | | 19 Dec 2000 (W) (in relation to police authorities) (SI 2000/3335) |
| | | 28 Jul 2001 (W) (otherwise) (s 108(4)–(6)) |
| | (2), (3) | 1 Nov 2000 (W) (SI 2000/2948)[1] |
| | | 19 Dec 2000 (E) (SI 2000/3335) |
| | | 19 Dec 2000 (W) (in relation to police authorities) (SI 2000/3335) |
| | (4), (5) | 19 Dec 2000 (E) (SI 2000/3335) |
| | | 19 Dec 2000 (W) (in relation to police authorities) (SI 2000/3335) |
| | | 28 Jul 2001 (W) (otherwise) (s 108(4)–(6)) |

**Local Government Act 2000 (c 22)**—*contd*

|       |            |                                                                                            |
|-------|------------|--------------------------------------------------------------------------------------------|
|       | (6)        | 1 Nov 2000 (W) (SI 2000/2948)[1]                                                           |
|       |            | 19 Dec 2000 (E) (SI 2000/3335)                                                              |
|       |            | 19 Dec 2000 (W) (in relation to police authorities) (SI 2000/3335)                         |
|       | (7)        | 19 Dec 2000 (E) (SI 2000/3335)                                                              |
|       |            | 19 Dec 2000 (W) (in relation to police authorities) (SI 2000/3335)                         |
|       |            | 28 Jul 2001 (W) (otherwise) (s 108(4)–(6))                                                  |
|       | (8), (9)   | 1 Nov 2000 (W) (SI 2000/2948)[1]                                                           |
|       |            | 19 Dec 2000 (E) (SI 2000/3335)                                                              |
|       |            | 19 Dec 2000 (W) (in relation to police authorities) (SI 2000/3335)                         |
| 83    | (1)–(3)    | 1 Nov 2000 (W) (SI 2000/2948)[1]                                                           |
|       |            | 19 Dec 2000 (E) (SI 2000/3335)                                                              |
|       |            | 19 Dec 2000 (W) (in relation to police authorities) (SI 2000/3335)                         |
|       | (4)        | 19 Dec 2000 (E) (SI 2000/3335)                                                              |
|       |            | 19 Dec 2000 (W) (in relation to police authorities) (SI 2000/3335)                         |
|       |            | 28 Jul 2001 (W) (otherwise) (s 108(4)–(6))                                                  |
|       | (5)–(11)   | 1 Nov 2000 (W) (SI 2000/2948)[1]                                                           |
|       |            | 19 Dec 2000 (E) (SI 2000/3335)                                                              |
|       |            | 19 Dec 2000 (W) (in relation to police authorities) (SI 2000/3335)                         |
|       | (12)       | 19 Dec 2000 (E) (SI 2000/3335)                                                              |
|       |            | 19 Dec 2000 (W) (in relation to police authorities) (SI 2000/3335)                         |
|       |            | 28 Jul 2001 (W) (otherwise) (s 108(4)–(6))                                                  |
|       | (13), (14) | 1 Nov 2000 (W) (SI 2000/2948)[1]                                                           |
|       |            | 19 Dec 2000 (E) (SI 2000/3335)                                                              |
|       |            | 19 Dec 2000 (W) (in relation to police authorities) (SI 2000/3335)                         |
|       | (15), (16) | 19 Dec 2000 (E) (SI 2000/3335)                                                              |
|       |            | 19 Dec 2000 (W) (in relation to police authorities) (SI 2000/3335)                         |
|       |            | 28 Jul 2001 (W) (otherwise) (s 108(4)–(6))                                                  |
| 84–89 |            | 28 Sep 2000 (s 108(2))                                                                      |
| 90    |            | 27 Jul 2002 (E) (SI 2002/1718)                                                              |
|       |            | 27 Jul 2002 (W) (in relation to police authorities) (SI 2002/1718)                         |
| 91    |            | 19 Dec 2000 (E) (SI 2000/3335)[2]                                                          |
|       |            | 19 Dec 2000 (W) (in relation to police authorities) (SI 2000/3335)[2]                      |
| 92    |            | 19 Dec 2000 (E) (SI 2000/3335)                                                              |
|       |            | 19 Dec 2000 (W) (in relation to police authorities) (SI 2000/3335)                         |
|       |            | 28 Jul 2001 (W) (otherwise) (s 108(4)–(6))                                                  |
| 93    | (1)        | 19 Dec 2000 (E) (SI 2000/3335)[2]                                                          |
|       | (2)        | 19 Dec 2000 (E) (SI 2000/3335)[2]                                                          |
|       |            | 19 Dec 2000 (W) (in relation to police authorities) (SI 2000/3335)[2]                      |
|       |            | 30 Jun 2002 (W) (SI 2002/1359)                                                              |
|       | (3)–(12)   | 19 Dec 2000 (E) (SI 2000/3335)[2]                                                          |
|       |            | 19 Dec 2000 (W) (in relation to police authorities) (SI 2000/3335)[2]                      |
|       |            | 30 Jun 2002 (W) (SI 2002/1359)                                                              |
| 94, 95 |           | 1 Aug 2001 (E) (SI 2001/2684)                                                               |
|       |            | *Never in force* (W) (S) (repealed)                                                         |
| 96    |            | *Not yet in force*                                                                         |
| 97, 98 |           | 1 Oct 2000 (E) (SI 2000/2187)                                                               |
|       |            | 28 Jul 2001 (W) (s 108(4)–(6))                                                              |
| 99    | (1), (2)   | 19 Feb 2001 (E) (SI 2001/415)                                                               |
|       |            | 28 Jul 2001 (W) (s 108(4))                                                                  |
|       | (3)        | 19 Feb 2001 (E) (except in so far as relates to s 99(4) as noted below) (SI 2001/415)       |
|       |            | *Not yet in force* (E) (exception noted above)                                             |
|       |            | 28 Jul 2001 (W) (s 108(4))                                                                  |
|       | (4)        | 28 Jul 2001 (s 108(4))                                                                      |
|       | (5)–(9)    | 19 Feb 2001 (E) (SI 2001/415)                                                               |
|       |            | 28 Jul 2001 (W) (s 108(4))                                                                  |

**Local Government Act 2000 (c 22)**—*contd*

| | | |
|---|---|---|
| 100 | | 1 Nov 2000 (W) (SI 2000/2948) |
| | | 19 Feb 2001 (E) (SI 2001/415) |
| 101 | (1) | 28 Jul 2001 (s 108(4)) |
| | (2)–(5) | 1 Nov 2000 (W) (SI 2000/2948) |
| | | 28 Jul 2001 (E) (s 108(4)) |
| 102 | | 26 Oct 2000 (E) (SI 2000/2849) |
| | | 28 Jul 2001 (W) (s 108(4)) |
| 103 | | 25 Aug 2000 (E) (SI 2000/2420) |
| | | 28 Jul 2001 (W) (s 108(4)–(6)) |
| 104 | | 28 Sep 2000 (s 108(2)) |
| 105, 106 | | 28 Jul 2000 (RA) |
| 107 | (1) | 28 Jul 2001 (s 108(4)–(6)) |
| | (2) | See Sch 6 below |
| 108, 109 | | 28 Jul 2000 (RA) |
| Sch 1 | paras 1–5 | 26 Oct 2000 (E) (SI 2000/2849) |
| | | 28 Jul 2001 (otherwise) (s 108(4)–(6)) |
| | paras 6, 7 | 7 Aug 2000 (E) (SI 2000/2187) |
| | | 28 Jul 2001 (otherwise) (s 108(4)–(6)) |
| | para 8(1)–(3) | 28 Jul 2001 (s 108(4)–(6)) |
| | para 8(4), (5) | 1 Nov 2000 (W) (SI 2000/2948) |
| | | 28 Jul 2001 (E) (s 108(4)–(6)) |
| | para 8(6), (7) | 28 Jul 2001 (s 108(4)–(6)) |
| | para 8(8) | 1 Nov 2000 (W) (SI 2000/2948) |
| | | 28 Jul 2001 (E) (s 108(4)–(6)) |
| | para 9(1)–(3) | 7 Aug 2000 (E) (SI 2000/2187) |
| | | 28 Jul 2001 (otherwise) (s 108(4)–(6)) |
| | para 9(4)–(6) | 7 Aug 2000 (E) (SI 2000/2187) |
| | | 1 Nov 2000 (W) (SI 2000/2948) |
| | paras 10, 11 | 7 Aug 2000 (E) (SI 2000/2187) |
| | | 1 Nov 2000 (W) (SI 2000/2948) |
| Sch 2 | | 28 Jul 2001 (s 108(4)–(6)) |
| Sch 3 | | 26 Oct 2000 (E) (SI 2000/2849) |
| | | 28 Jul 2001 (otherwise) (s 108(4)–(6)) |
| Sch 4 | | 19 Dec 2000 (E) (SI 2000/3335) |
| | | 19 Dec 2000 (W) (in relation to police authorities) (SI 2000/3335) |
| | | 28 Jul 2001 (W) (otherwise) (s 108(4)–(6)) |
| Sch 5 | paras 1–7 | 26 Oct 2000 (E) (SI 2000/2849) |
| | | 28 Jul 2001 (s 108(4)) (otherwise) |
| | para 8 | 27 Jul 2002 (in relation to England and police authorities in Wales) (SI 2002/1718)[4] |
| | | 22 May 2012 (otherwise) (SI 2012/1358) |
| | paras 9–11 | 19 Dec 2000 (E) (SI 2000/3335) |
| | | 19 Dec 2000 (W) (in relation to police authorities) (SI 2000/3335) |
| | | 28 Jul 2001 (W) (otherwise) (s 108(4)–(6)) |
| | paras 12, 13 | 22 May 2012 (SI 2012/1358) |
| | para 14 | 19 Dec 2000 (E) (SI 2000/3335) |
| | | 19 Dec 2000 (W) (in relation to police authorities) (SI 2000/3335) |
| | | 28 Jul 2001 (W) (otherwise) (s 108(4)–(6)) |
| | para 15 | 22 May 2012 (SI 2012/1358) |
| | para 16 | 26 Oct 2000 (E) (SI 2000/2849) |
| | | 28 Jul 2001 (otherwise) (s 108(4)–(6)) |
| | paras 17–20 | 26 Oct 2000 (E) (SI 2000/2849) |
| | | 28 Jul 2001 (otherwise) (s 108(4)) |
| | para 21 | 26 Oct 2000 (E) (SI 2000/2849) |
| | | 28 Jul 2001 (otherwise) (s 108(4)–(6)) |
| | paras 22, 23 | 26 Oct 2000 (E) (SI 2000/2849) |
| | | 28 Jul 2001 (otherwise) (s 108(4)) |
| | para 24 | 28 Jul 2001 (s 108(4)) |
| | paras 25, 26 | 22 May 2012 (SI 2012/1358) |

**Local Government Act 2000 (c 22)**—*contd*

| | |
|---|---|
| para 27 | 28 Jul 2001 (s 108(4)–(6)) |
| para 28 | 19 Dec 2000 (E) (SI 2000/3335) |
| | 19 Dec 2000 (W) (in relation to police authorities) (SI 2000/3335) |
| | 28 Jul 2001 (W) (otherwise) (s 108(4)–(6)) |
| para 29 | 26 Oct 2000 (E) (SI 2000/2849) |
| | 28 Jul 2001 (otherwise) (s 108(4)–(6)) |
| paras 30–32 | 19 Dec 2000 (E) (SI 2000/3335) |
| | 19 Dec 2000 (W) (in relation to police authorities) (SI 2000/3335) |
| | 28 Jul 2001 (W) (otherwise) (s 108(4)–(6)) |
| para 33 | 26 Oct 2000 (E) (SI 2000/2849) |
| | 28 Jul 2001 (otherwise) (s 108(4)–(6)) |
| para 34 | 22 May 2012 (SI 2012/1358) |
| Sch 6 | 28 Sep 2000 (repeal of Education Act 1996, Sch 37, para 63) (s 108(2)) |
| | 1 Oct 2000 (E) (repeal of or in Local Government Act 1972, s 100D(2)) (SI 2000/2187) |
| | 18 Oct 2000 (E) (SI 2000/2836), repeals of or in— |
| | Local Government (Miscellaneous Provisions) Act 1976, s 25(8); |
| | Inner Urban Areas Act 1978, s 13; |
| | Housing Act 1985, s 11A(4); |
| | Local Government and Housing Act 1989, ss 34, 35 |
| | 26 Oct 2000 (E) (repeals of or in Local Authority Social Services Act 1970, ss 2(2), 3(1), 6(5), 107 (to the extent that it relates to those repeals and to Local Government Act 2000, Sch 5, paras 1–7, 16–23, 29, 33)) (SI 2000/2849) |
| | 9 Apr 2001 (W) (SI 2001/1411[3]), repeals of or in— |
| | Local Government (Miscellaneous Provisions) Act 1976; |
| | Inner Urban Areas Act 1978; |
| | Housing Act 1985; |
| | Local Government and Housing Act 1989, ss 34, 35 |
| | 28 Jul 2001 (otherwise) (s 108(4)–(6)), except repeals of or in— |
| | Local Government Act 1972, ss 80(1)(e), 94–98, 105, 265A(1)(b); |
| | Local Government Act 1974; |
| | Local Government Act 1985; |
| | Transport Act 1985; |
| | Financial Services Act 1986; |
| | Local Government and Housing Act 1989, ss 19, 31, 32(1), Sch 11; |
| | Local Government Finance Act 1992; |
| | Local Government (Wales) Act 1994; |
| | Police and Magistrates' Courts Act 1994; |
| | Environment Act 1995; |
| | Police Act 1996; |
| | Police Act 1997; |
| | Audit Commission Act 1998; |
| | Greater London Authority Act 1999 |
| | 27 Jul 2002 (E) (SI 2002/1718), repeals of or in— |
| | Local Government Act 1972, s 80(1)(e); |
| | Audit Commission Act 1998, ss 16(1)(a), 17(1)(b), (2), (3), (5)(b), (7), (8), 18 |
| | 27 Jul 2002 (W) (in relation to police authorities) (SI 2002/1718), repeals of or in— |
| | Local Government Act 1972, s 80(1)(e); |
| | Audit Commission Act 1998, ss 16(1)(a), 17(1)(b), (2), (3), (5)(b), (7), (8), 18 |
| | 22 May 2012 (SI 2012/1358), repeals of or in— |
| | Local Government Act 1972, 94–98, 105, 265A(1)(b); |
| | Local Government Act 1974; |

**Local Government Act 2000 (c 22)**—*contd*

Local Government and Housing Act 1989, ss 19, 31, 32(1);
Environment Act 1995;
Greater London Authority Act 1999, s 66
*Not yet in force* (exceptions noted above)

[1]   As to the powers of the Secretary of State and the National Assembly for Wales to bring into force provisions of this Act in relation to Wales, see s 108(5)(c), (6) of this Act

[2]   SI 2000/3335, made under s 108(5), (7), purports to bring this section into force in relation to England and in relation to police authorities in Wales. However, provision for the commencement of this section is made in s 108(3)

[3]   Previously incorrectly numbered as SI 2001/1471

[4]   SI 2002/1718, art 2(b)(i) does not commence Sch 5, para 8, but it does bring into force the identical repeal in Sch 6 to this Act and it is thought that the intention was to bring this paragraph into force at the same time

---

**National Parks (Scotland) Act 2000 (asp 10)**

*RA:* 9 Aug 2000

*Commencement provisions:* s 37(1); National Parks (Scotland) Act 2000 (Commencement) Order 2000, SSI 2000/312

| | | |
|---|---|---|
| 1–36 | | 8 Sep 2000 (SSI 2000/312) |
| 37 | | 9 Aug 2000 (RA) |
| Schs 1–5 | | 8 Sep 2000 (SSI 2000/312) |

---

**Northern Ireland Act 2000 (c 1)**

*RA:* 10 Feb 2000

*Commencement provisions:* s 9(2); Northern Ireland Act 2000 (Commencement) Order 2000, SI 2000/396

| | | |
|---|---|---|
| 1–8 | | 12 Feb 2000 (SI 2000/396) |
| 9 | (1), (2) | 10 Feb 2000 (s 9(2)) |
| | (3) | 12 Feb 2000 (SI 2000/396) |
| Schedule | | 12 Feb 2000 (SI 2000/396) |

---

**Nuclear Safeguards Act 2000 (c 5)**

*RA:* 25 May 2000

*Commencement provisions:* s 12(2); Nuclear Safeguards Act Commencement (No 1) Order 2004, SI 2004/1242

| | | |
|---|---|---|
| 1–4 | | 1 May 2004 (SI 2004/1242) |
| 5 | (1)(a) | 1 May 2004 (SI 2004/1242) |
| | (1)(b) | *Not yet in force* |
| | (1)(c) | 1 May 2004 (SI 2004/1242) |
| | (2) | 1 May 2004 (except the words "or Article 9 (if it falls within subsection (1)(b))" and "procedural arrangements for wide-area environmental sampling approved under Article 9") (SI 2004/1242) |
| | | *Not yet in force* (exception noted above) |
| | (3)–(8) | 1 May 2004 (SI 2004/1242) |
| 6–11 | | 1 May 2004 (SI 2004/1242) |
| 12 | | 25 May 2000 (RA) |

## Police (Northern Ireland) Act 2000 (c 32)

*RA:* 23 Nov 2000

*Commencement provisions:* s 79; Police (Northern Ireland) Act 2000 (Commencement) Order 2000, SR 2000/412; Police (Northern Ireland) Act 2000 (Commencement No 2) Order 2001, SR 2001/132; Police (Northern Ireland) Act 2000 (Commencement No 3 and Transitional Provisions) Order 2001, SR 2001/396; Police (Northern Ireland) Act 2000 (Commencement No 4) Order 2002, SR 2002/146

| | | |
|---|---|---|
| 1 | | 4 Nov 2001 (SR 2001/396) |
| 2 | (1) | 4 Nov 2001 (SR 2001/396) |
| | (2) | See Sch 1 below |
| | (3) | 4 Nov 2001 (SR 2001/396) |
| | (4) | See Sch 2 below |
| 3 | (1), (2) | 4 Nov 2001 (SR 2001/396) |
| | (3)(a)–(c) | 4 Nov 2001 (SR 2001/396) |
| | (3)(d)(i), (ii) | 4 Nov 2001 (SR 2001/396) |
| | (3)(d)(iii) | 15 Apr 2002 (SR 2002/146) |
| | (3)(d)(iv) | 4 Nov 2001 (SR 2001/396) |
| | (3)(e) | 4 Nov 2001 (SR 2001/396) |
| | (4) | 4 Nov 2001 (SR 2001/396) |
| 4–13 | | 4 Nov 2001 (SR 2001/396) |
| 14–19 | | 15 Apr 2002 (SR 2002/146) |
| 20 | | 30 Mar 2001 (SR 2001/132) |
| 21–23 | | 15 Apr 2002 (SR 2002/146) |
| 24–27 | | 4 Nov 2001 (SR 2001/396) |
| 28–31 | | *Not yet in force* |
| 32–38 | | 4 Nov 2001 (SR 2001/396) |
| 39–41 | | 30 Mar 2001 (SR 2001/132) |
| 42 | | 4 Nov 2001 (SR 2001/396) |
| 43, 44 | | 22 Dec 2000 (SR 2000/412) |
| 45 | | 4 Nov 2001 (SR 2001/396) |
| 46, 47 | | 30 Mar 2001 (SR 2001/132) |
| 48 | | 4 Nov 2001 (SR 2001/396) |
| 49 | | 23 Nov 2000 (s 79(2)) |
| 50 | | 30 Mar 2001 (SR 2001/132) |
| 51–56 | | 4 Nov 2001 (SR 2001/396)[1] |
| 57 | (1) | 4 Nov 2001 (SR 2001/396) |
| | (2)(a)–(h) | 4 Nov 2001 (SR 2001/396) |
| | (2)(i), (j) | 15 Apr 2002 (SR 2002/146) |
| | (3)–(6) | 4 Nov 2001 (SR 2001/396) |
| 58–61 | | 4 Nov 2001 (SR 2001/396) |
| 62 | | 22 Dec 2000 (SR 2000/412) |
| 63, 64 | | 4 Nov 2001 (SR 2001/396) |
| 65 | | 22 Dec 2000 (SR 2000/412) |
| 66 | | 4 Nov 2001 (SR 2001/396) |
| 67, 68 | | 23 Nov 2000 (s 79(2)) |
| 69 | | 4 Nov 2001 (SR 2001/396) |
| 70 | | 30 Mar 2001 (SR 2001/132) |
| 71 | | 4 Nov 2001 (SR 2001/396) |
| 72 | | 15 Apr 2002 (SR 2002/146) |
| 73, 74 | | 4 Nov 2001 (SR 2001/396) |
| 75–77 | | 23 Nov 2000 (s 79(2)) |
| 78 | (1) | See Sch 6 below |
| | (2) | 4 Nov 2001 (SR 2001/396) |
| | (3) | See Sch 7 below |
| | (4) | See Sch 8 below |
| 79–81 | | 23 Nov 2000 (RA) |
| Sch 1 | Pts I, II | 4 Nov 2001 (SR 2001/396) |
| | Pt III | 23 Nov 2000 (s 79(2)) |
| | Pts IV–VI | 4 Nov 2001 (SR 2001/396) |

**Police (Northern Ireland) Act 2000 (c 32)**—*contd*

| | | |
|---|---|---|
| Sch 2 | | 4 Nov 2001 (SR 2001/396) |
| Sch 3 | | 15 Apr 2002 (SR 2002/146) |
| Sch 4 | | 23 Nov 2000 (s 79(2)) |
| Sch 5 | | 4 Nov 2001 (SR 2001/396) |
| Sch 6 | paras 1, 2 | 4 Nov 2001 (SR 2001/396) |
| | para 3(1)–(3) | 4 Nov 2001 (SR 2001/396) |
| | para 3(4) | 23 Nov 2000 (s 79(2)) |
| | para 4(1), (2) | 4 Nov 2001 (SR 2001/396) |
| | para 4(3) | 23 Nov 2000 (s 79(2)) |
| | paras 5–13 | 4 Nov 2001 (SR 2001/396) |
| | para 14 | 15 Apr 2002 (SR 2002/146) |
| | paras 15–19 | 4 Nov 2001 (SR 2001/396) |
| | para 20(1)–(5) | 4 Nov 2001 (SR 2001/396) |
| | para 20(6) | 22 Dec 2000 (SR 2000/412) |
| | para 20(7) | 4 Nov 2001 (SR 2001/396) |
| | paras 21–22 | 4 Nov 2001 (SR 2001/396) |
| | para 23(1)–(5) | 4 Nov 2001 (SR 2001/396) |
| | para 23(6)(a) | 22 Dec 2000 (SR 2000/412) |
| | para 23(6)(b) | 4 Nov 2001 (SR 2001/396) |
| | para 23(7), (8) | 4 Nov 2001 (SR 2001/396) |
| | para 24(1), (2) | 4 Nov 2001 (SR 2001/396) |
| | para 24(3) | 30 Mar 2001 (SR 2001/132) |
| | para 24(4) | 4 Nov 2001 (SR 2001/396) |
| | para 25 | 4 Nov 2001 (SR 2001/396) |
| Sch 7 | para 1 | 23 Nov 2000 (s 79(2)) |
| | para 2 | 22 Dec 2000 (SR 2000/412) |
| | para 3 | 15 Apr 2002 (SR 2002/146) |
| | para 4 | 22 Dec 2000 (SR 2000/412) |
| Sch 8 | | 4 Nov 2001 (SR 2001/396) |

[1]    Note that the Queen's Printer's copy of SR 2001/396 purports to bring s 54 into force twice. However it is thought that this should be a reference to ss 53 and 54

---

## Political Parties, Elections and Referendums Act 2000 (c 41)

*RA:* 30 Nov 2000

*Commencement provisions:* s 163(2)–(6); Political Parties, Elections and Referendums Act 2000 (Commencement No 1 and Transitional Provisions) Order 2001, SI 2001/222; Political Parties, Elections and Referendums Act 2000 (Commencement No 2) Order 2001, SI 2001/3526; Political Parties, Elections and Referendums Act 2000 (Commencement No 3 and Transitional Provisions) Order 2006, SI 2006/3416; Political Parties, Elections and Referendums Act 2000 (Commencement No 4 and Transitional Provisions) Order 2021, SI 2021/890

| | | |
|---|---|---|
| 1–3 | | 30 Nov 2000 (RA) |
| 4, 5 | | 16 Feb 2001 (SI 2001/222) |
| 6 | (1)(a), (b) | 16 Feb 2001 (SI 2001/222) |
| | (1)(c) | *Not yet in force* |
| | (1)(d) | 30 Oct 2001 (SI 2001/3526) |
| | (1)(e)–(g) | 16 Feb 2001 (SI 2001/222) |
| | (2)–(6) | 16 Feb 2001 (SI 2001/222) |
| 7, 8 | | 16 Feb 2001 (SI 2001/222) |
| 9 | | 1 Jul 2001 (SI 2001/222)[2] |
| 10, 11 | | 16 Feb 2001 (SI 2001/222) |
| 12 | | 30 Nov 2000 (so far as confers power to make an order or regulations) (RA) |
| | | 16 Feb 2001 (otherwise) (SI 2001/222) |
| 13 | | 30 Nov 2000 (so far as confers power to make an order or regulations) (RA) |

**Political Parties, Elections and Referendums Act 2000 (c 41)**—*contd*

|  | 1 Jul 2001 (otherwise) (SI 2001/222)[2] |
|---|---|
| 14 | 30 Oct 2001 (so far as relates to Boundary Committee for England) (SI 2001/3526) |
|  | *Never in force* (so far as relates to Boundary Committees for Scotland, Wales and Northern Ireland) (repealed) |
| 15 | 30 Oct 2001 (SI 2001/3526) |
| 16 | 30 Nov 2000 (so far as confers power to make an order or regulations) (RA) |
|  | *Never in force* (otherwise) (repealed) |
| 17 | *Never in force* |
| 18 | 30 Nov 2000 (so far as confers power to make an order or regulations) (RA) |
|  | 30 Oct 2001 (otherwise) (SI 2001/3526) |
| 19, 20 | 30 Nov 2000 (so far as they confer power to make an order or regulations) (RA) |
|  | *Never in force* (otherwise) (repealed) |
| 21 | 16 Feb 2001 (SI 2001/222) |
| 22 | 14 Dec 2000 (for the purposes of the operation of Sch 23, paras 1–7) (s 163(4)) |
|  | 16 Feb 2001 (otherwise) (SI 2001/222) |
| 23 | 30 Nov 2000 (so far as confers power to make an order or regulations) (RA) |
|  | 14 Dec 2000 (for the purposes of the operation of Sch 23, paras 1–7) (s 163(4)) |
|  | 16 Feb 2001 (otherwise) (SI 2001/222) |
| 24, 25 | 14 Dec 2000 (for the purposes of the operation of Sch 23, paras 1–7) (s 163(4)) |
|  | 16 Feb 2001 (otherwise) (SI 2001/222) |
| 26 | 30 Nov 2000 (so far as confers power to make an order or regulations) (RA) |
|  | 14 Dec 2000 (for the purposes of the operation of Sch 23, paras 1–7) (s 163(4)) |
|  | 16 Feb 2001 (otherwise) (SI 2001/222) |
| 27 | 14 Dec 2000 (for the purposes of the operation of Sch 23, paras 1–7) (s 163(4)) |
|  | 16 Feb 2001 (otherwise) (SI 2001/222) |
| 28 | 30 Nov 2000 (so far as confers power to make an order or regulations) (RA) |
|  | 14 Dec 2000 (for the purposes of the operation of Sch 23, paras 1–7) (s 163(4)) |
|  | 16 Feb 2001 (otherwise) (SI 2001/222) |
| 29–31 | 14 Dec 2000 (for the purposes of the operation of Sch 23, paras 1–7) (s 163(4)) |
|  | 16 Feb 2001 (otherwise) (SI 2001/222) |
| 32 | 30 Nov 2000 (so far as confers power to make an order or regulations) (RA) |
|  | 14 Dec 2000 (for the purposes of the operation of Sch 23, paras 1–7) (s 163(4)) |
|  | 16 Feb 2001 (otherwise) (SI 2001/222) |
| 33 | 14 Dec 2000 (for the purposes of the operation of Sch 23, paras 1–7) (s 163(4)) |
|  | 16 Feb 2001 (otherwise) (SI 2001/222) |
| 34 | 30 Nov 2000 (so far as confers power to make an order or regulations) (RA) |
|  | 14 Dec 2000 (for the purposes of the operation of Sch 23, paras 1–7) (s 163(4)) |
|  | 16 Feb 2001 (otherwise) (SI 2001/222) |
| 35 | 14 Dec 2000 (for the purposes of the operation of Sch 23, paras 1–7) (s 163(4)) |
|  | 16 Feb 2001 (otherwise) (SI 2001/222) |

**Political Parties, Elections and Referendums Act 2000 (c 41)**—*contd*

| | | |
|---|---|---|
| 36 | | 14 Dec 2000 (s 163(4)) |
| 37–40 | | 14 Dec 2000 (for the purposes of the operation of Sch 23, paras 1–7) (s 163(4)) |
| | | 16 Feb 2001 (otherwise) (SI 2001/222) |
| 41 | | 1 Jan 2002 (SI 2001/3526) |
| 42, 43 | | 30 Nov 2000 (so far as they confer power to make an order or regulations) (RA) |
| | | 1 Jan 2002 (otherwise) (SI 2001/3526) |
| 44–47 | | 1 Jan 2002 (SI 2001/3526) |
| 48 | | 30 Nov 2000 (so far as confers power to make an order or regulations) (RA) |
| | | 1 Jan 2002 (otherwise) (SI 2001/3526) |
| 49 | | 1 Jan 2002 (SI 2001/3526) |
| 50 | | 16 Feb 2001 (SI 2001/222)[1] |
| 51 | | 30 Nov 2000 (so far as confers power to make an order or regulations) (RA) |
| | | 16 Feb 2001 (otherwise) (SI 2001/222)[1] |
| 52–66 | | 16 Feb 2001 (SI 2001/222)[1] |
| 67 | | 30 Nov 2000 (so far as confers power to make an order or regulations) (RA) |
| | | 16 Feb 2001 (otherwise) (SI 2001/222)[1] |
| 68, 69 | | 16 Feb 2001 (SI 2001/222)[1] |
| 70 | | 30 Nov 2000 (so far as confers power to make an order or regulations) (RA) |
| | | 16 Feb 2001 (otherwise) (SI 2001/222)[1] |
| 71 | | 16 Feb 2001 (SI 2001/222)[1] |
| 72–79 | | 16 Feb 2001 (SI 2001/222) |
| 80 | | 30 Nov 2000 (so far as confers power to make an order or regulations) (RA) |
| | | 16 Feb 2001 (otherwise) (SI 2001/222) |
| 81–95 | | 16 Feb 2001 (SI 2001/222) |
| 96 | | 30 Nov 2000 (so far as confers power to make an order or regulations) (RA) |
| | | 16 Feb 2001 (otherwise) (SI 2001/222) |
| 97–100 | | 16 Feb 2001 (SI 2001/222) |
| 101 | | 30 Nov 2000 (so far as confers power to make an order or regulations) (RA) |
| | | 16 Feb 2001 (otherwise) (SI 2001/222) |
| 102–107 | | 16 Feb 2001 (SI 2001/222) |
| 108, 109 | | 30 Nov 2000 (so far as they confer power to make an order or regulations) (RA) |
| | | 16 Feb 2001 (otherwise) (SI 2001/222) |
| 110–119 | | 16 Feb 2001 (SI 2001/222) |
| 120 | | 30 Nov 2000 (so far as confers power to make an order or regulations) (RA) |
| | | 16 Feb 2001 (otherwise) (SI 2001/222) |
| 121–125 | | 16 Feb 2001 (SI 2001/222) |
| 126 | | 30 Nov 2000 (so far as confers power to make an order or regulations) (RA) |
| | | 16 Feb 2001 (otherwise) (SI 2001/222) |
| 127, 128 | | 16 Feb 2001 (SI 2001/222) |
| 129 | | 30 Nov 2000 (so far as confers power to make an order or regulations) (RA) |
| | | 16 Feb 2001 (otherwise) (SI 2001/222) |
| 130 | | 1 Jul 2001 (SI 2001/222)[2] |
| 131 | | 16 Feb 2001 (SI 2001/222) |
| 132 | (1) | 16 Feb 2001 (SI 2001/222) |
| | (2)–(4) | 1 Jul 2001 (SI 2001/222)[2] |
| | (5) | 16 Feb 2001 (SI 2001/222) |
| | (6) | 1 Jul 2001 (SI 2001/222)[2] |

**Political Parties, Elections and Referendums Act 2000 (c 41)**—*contd*

| | | |
|---|---|---|
| 133 | | 30 Nov 2000 (so far as confers power to make an order or regulations) (RA) |
| | | 16 Feb 2001 (otherwise) (SI 2001/222) |
| 134, 135 | | 1 Jul 2001 (SI 2001/222)[2] |
| 136 | | 16 Feb 2001 (SI 2001/222)[1] |
| 137–140 | | 16 Feb 2001 (SI 2001/222) |
| 141 | | 1 Apr 2002 (SI 2001/3526) |
| 142 | | 16 Feb 2001 (SI 2001/222) |
| 143 | | 30 Nov 2000 (so far as confers power to make an order or regulations) (RA) |
| | | 1 Jan 2007 (E) (W) (S) (Gibraltar) (otherwise) (SI 2006/3416)[4] |
| | | 11 Aug 2021 (NI)[3] (SI 2021/890)[5] |
| 144 | | 16 Feb 2001 (for purposes of drawing up codes referred to in Representation of the People Act 1983, s 93) (SI 2001/222) |
| | | 16 Mar 2001 (otherwise) (SI 2001/222) |
| 145 | | 30 Nov 2000 (so far as confers power to make an order or regulations) (RA) |
| | | 16 Feb 2001 (otherwise) (SI 2001/222) |
| 146–154 | | 16 Feb 2001 (SI 2001/222) |
| 155 | | 30 Nov 2000 (so far as confers power to make an order or regulations) (RA) |
| | | 16 Feb 2001 (otherwise) (SI 2001/222) |
| 156 | | 30 Nov 2000 (RA) |
| 157, 158 | | 16 Feb 2001 (SI 2001/222) |
| 159, 160 | | 30 Nov 2000 (RA) |
| 161, 162 | | 16 Feb 2001 (SI 2001/222) |
| 163 | | 30 Nov 2000 (RA) |
| Schs 1, 2 | | 30 Nov 2000 (RA) |
| Sch 3 | | *Never in force* (repealed) |
| Sch 4 | | 30 Nov 2000 (so far as confers power to make an order or regulations) (RA) |
| | | 16 Feb 2001 (otherwise) (SI 2001/222)[1] |
| Sch 5 | | 1 Jan 2002 (SI 2001/3526) |
| Schs 6, 7 | | 30 Nov 2000 (so far as they confer power to make an order or regulations) (RA) |
| | | 16 Feb 2001 (otherwise) (SI 2001/222)[1] |
| Sch 8 | | 30 Nov 2000 (so far as confers power to make an order or regulations) (RA) |
| | | 16 Feb 2001 (otherwise) (SI 2001/222)[1] |
| Sch 9 | paras 1, 2 | 16 Feb 2001 (SI 2001/222) |
| | para 3(1) | 16 Feb 2001 (SI 2001/222) |
| | para 3(2)(a) | 16 Feb 2001 (SI 2001/222)[1] |
| | para 3(2)(b) | 16 Feb 2001 (SI 2001/222) |
| | para 3(3) | 16 Feb 2001 (SI 2001/222) |
| | para 3(4) | 16 Feb 2001 (SI 2001/222)[1] |
| | para 3(5), (6) | 16 Feb 2001 (SI 2001/222) |
| | para 3(7)(a) | 16 Feb 2001 (SI 2001/222)[1] |
| | para 3(7)(b) | 16 Feb 2001 (SI 2001/222) |
| | paras 4–11 | 16 Feb 2001 (SI 2001/222)[2] |
| Sch 10 | paras 1, 2 | 16 Feb 2001 (SI 2001/222) |
| | para 3(1) | 16 Feb 2001 (SI 2001/222) |
| | para 3(2) | 16 Feb 2001 (SI 2001/222)[1] |
| | para 3(3)(a) | 16 Feb 2001 (SI 2001/222)[1] |
| | para 3(3)(b) | 16 Feb 2001 (SI 2001/222) |
| | paras 4–11 | 16 Feb 2001 (SI 2001/222) |
| Sch 11 | | 30 Nov 2000 (so far as confers power to make an order or regulations) (RA) |
| | | 16 Feb 2001 (otherwise) (SI 2001/222) |
| Sch 12 | | 16 Feb 2001 (SI 2001/222) |

**Political Parties, Elections and Referendums Act 2000 (c 41)**—*contd*

| | | |
|---|---|---|
| Schs 13–15 | | 30 Nov 2000 (so far as confers power to make an order or regulations) (RA) |
| | | 16 Feb 2001 (otherwise) (SI 2001/222) |
| Sch 16 | | 30 Nov 2000 (so far as confers power to make an order or regulations) (RA) |
| | | 1 Jul 2001 (otherwise) (SI 2001/222)[2] |
| Sch 17 | paras 1–6 | 16 Feb 2001 (SI 2001/222) |
| | paras 7, 8 | 16 Feb 2001 (SI 2001/222)[1] |
| | paras 9, 10 | 16 Feb 2001 (SI 2001/222) |
| Sch 18 | paras 1, 2 | 16 Feb 2001 (SI 2001/222) |
| | paras 3–5 | 1 Jul 2001 (SI 2001/222)[2] |
| | para 6 | 16 Feb 2001 (SI 2001/222) |
| | para 7 | 30 Nov 2000 (so far as confers power to make an order or regulations) (RA) |
| | | 1 Jul 2001 (otherwise) (SI 2001/222)[2] |
| | paras 8, 9 | 16 Feb 2001 (SI 2001/222) |
| | para 10 | 1 Jul 2001 (SI 2001/222)[2] |
| | para 11(a), (b) | 1 Jul 2001 (SI 2001/222)[2] |
| | para 11(c) | 16 Feb 2001 (SI 2001/222) |
| | para 11(d) | 1 Jul 2001 (SI 2001/222)[2] |
| | para 12 | 16 Feb 2001 (SI 2001/222) |
| | para 13 | 16 Feb 2001 (otherwise) (SI 2001/222) |
| | para 14 | 30 Nov 2000 (so far as confers power to make an order or regulations) (RA) |
| | | 1 Jan 2007 (E) (W) (S) (Gibraltar) (otherwise) (SI 2006/3416)[4] |
| | | 11 Aug 2021 (NI)[3] (SI 2021/890)[5] |
| | paras 15, 16 | 1 Jul 2001 (SI 2001/222)[2] |
| | paras 17–19 | 16 Feb 2001 (SI 2001/222) |
| Sch 19 | | 30 Nov 2000 (so far as confers power to make an order or regulations) (RA) |
| | | 16 Feb 2001 (otherwise) (SI 2001/222) |
| Sch 20 | | 16 Feb 2001 (SI 2001/222) |
| Sch 21 | paras 1–5 | 16 Feb 2001 (SI 2001/222) |
| | para 6(1) | 16 Feb 2001 (SI 2001/222) |
| | para 6(2) | 1 Jul 2001 (SI 2001/222)[2] |
| | para 6(3) | 30 Nov 2000 (so far as confers power to make an order or regulations) (RA) |
| | | *Not yet in force* (otherwise) |
| | para 6(4) | *Not yet in force* |
| | para 6(5), (6) | 16 Feb 2001 (SI 2001/222) |
| | para 6(7)(a) | 30 Nov 2000 (so far as confers power to make an order or regulations) (RA) |
| | para 6(7)(b) | 16 Feb 2001 (SI 2001/222)[1] |
| | para 6(7)(c) | 16 Feb 2001 (SI 2001/222) |
| | para 6(7)(d) | 1 Jul 2001 (SI 2001/222)[2] |
| | para 6(8), (9) | 16 Feb 2001 (SI 2001/222) |
| | para 7 | *Not yet in force* |
| | paras 8–11 | 16 Feb 2001 (SI 2001/222) |
| | para 12(1) | 30 Nov 2000 (RA) |
| | para 12(2), (3) | 16 Feb 2001 (SI 2001/222) |
| | para 12(4) | 30 Nov 2000 (RA) |
| | paras 13–15 | 16 Feb 2001 (SI 2001/222) |
| | paras 16–18 | 1 Jul 2001 (SI 2001/222)[2] |
| Sch 22 | | 16 Feb 2001 (SI 2001/222), repeals of or in— |
| | | Representation of the People Act 1983, ss 72, 75(1B), (1C), 78(6), 79(3), 82(4), 86(9), 101–105, 106(8), 108, 122(8), 138(1), 148–153, 157(5), 159(2), 167(4), 174(6), Sch 1, r 30(5); |
| | | Representation of the People Act 1985, s 14(3)–(5), Sch 3, paras 6, 7; |

**Political Parties, Elections and Referendums Act 2000 (c 41)**—*contd*

Representation of the People Act 1989, s 6;
Local Government Act 1992, s 13;
Government of Wales Act 1998, s 11(2);
Scotland Act 1998, s 12(2);
Greater London Authority Act 1999, Sch 3 (except so far as relates to para 28);
Registration of Political Parties Act 1998
16 Mar 2001 (SI 2001/222), repeals of or in—
Representation of the People Act 1985, Sch 4, para 35;
Broadcasting Act 1996, Sch 10;
Greater London Authority Act 1999, Sch 3, para 28
1 Jul 2001 (repeals of or in Representation of the People Act 1983, ss 73, 81, Sch 3) (SI 2001/222)[2]
*Not yet in force*, repeals in or of—
House of Commons Disqualification Act 1975;
Northern Ireland Assembly Disqualification Act 1975;
Representation of the People Act 1983, s 201(1);
Representation of the People Act 1991;
Representation of the People Act 2000
*Never in force* (repeals in or of Parliamentary Constituencies Act 1986; Boundary Commissions Act 1992) (repealed)

| | | |
|---|---|---|
| Sch 23 | paras 1–7 | 14 Dec 2000 (s 163(4)) |
| | paras 8–13 | 30 Nov 2000 (RA) |

[1]  For transitional provisions, see SI 2001/222, Sch 1, Pt II

[2]  For transitional provisions, see SI 2001/222, Sch 2, Pt II

[3]  This provision was originally brought into force, for all purposes other than the power to make an order or regulations, on 16 Feb 2001 by SI 2001/222; however, by virtue of the Election Publications Act 2001, s 1, this provision is deemed not to have come into force on the commencement date

[4]  For a transitional provision, see SI 2006/3416, art 5

[5]  For transitional provisions, see SI 2021/890, art 2(3)

---

**Postal Services Act 2000 (c 26)**

*RA:* 28 Jul 2000

*Commencement provisions:* s 130; Postal Services Act 2000 (Commencement No 1 and Transitional Provisions) Order 2000, SI 2000/2957[1], as amended by SI 2001/1148, art 43; Postal Services Act 2000 (Commencement No 2) Order 2001, SI 2001/534; Postal Services Act 2000 (Commencement No 3 and Transitional and Saving Provisions) Order 2001, SI 2001/878[2]; Postal Services Act 2000 (Commencement No 4 and Transitional and Saving Provisions) Order 2001, SI 2001/1148[3]; Postal Services Act 2000 (Commencement No 5) Order 2007, SI 2007/1181

| | | |
|---|---|---|
| 1 | | 6 Nov 2000 (SI 2000/2957) |
| 2 | | 1 Jan 2001 (SI 2000/2957) |
| 3–5 | | 6 Nov 2000 (SI 2000/2957) |
| 6–10 | | 26 Mar 2001 (SI 2000/2957) |
| 11 | | 6 Nov 2000 (SI 2000/2957) |
| 12 | (1), (2) | 6 Nov 2000 (SI 2000/2957) |
| | (3)(a) | 6 Nov 2000 (SI 2000/2957) |
| | (3)(b) | 1 Jan 2001 (SI 2000/2957) |
| | (3)(c) | 6 Nov 2000 (SI 2000/2957) |
| | (4) | 6 Nov 2000 (SI 2000/2957) |
| | (5) | 1 Jan 2001 (SI 2000/2957) |
| 13 | | 6 Nov 2000 (SI 2000/2957) |
| 14–29 | | 26 Mar 2001 (SI 2000/2957) |
| 30 | (1) | 26 Mar 2001 (SI 2000/2957) |
| | (2) | 6 Nov 2000 (SI 2000/2957) |

**Postal Services Act 2000 (c 26)**—*contd*

| | | |
|---|---|---|
| | (3) | 26 Mar 2001 (SI 2000/2957) |
| 31 | | 1 Jan 2001 (SI 2000/2957) |
| 32–37 | | 26 Mar 2001 (SI 2000/2957) |
| 38, 39 | | 6 Nov 2000 (SI 2000/2957) |
| 40 | | 26 Mar 2001 (SI 2000/2957) |
| 41 | | 1 Jan 2001 (SI 2000/2957) |
| 42 | (1), (2) | 1 Jan 2001 (SI 2000/2957) |
| | (3) | 6 Nov 2000 (SI 2000/2957) |
| 43 | (1), (2) | 6 Nov 2000 (SI 2000/2957) |
| | (3)(a) | 6 Nov 2000 (SI 2000/2957) |
| | (3)(b) | 1 Jan 2001 (SI 2000/2957) |
| | (3)(c)–(e) | 6 Nov 2000 (SI 2000/2957) |
| | (4)–(8) | 6 Nov 2000 (SI 2000/2957) |
| 44 | (1)–(4) | 6 Nov 2000 (SI 2000/2957) |
| | (5) | 1 Jan 2001 (SI 2000/2957) |
| | (6) | 6 Nov 2000 (SI 2000/2957) |
| 45, 46 | | 6 Nov 2000 (SI 2000/2957) |
| 47 | | 6 Nov 2000 (in so far as it relates to information required in connection with exercise of Commission's functions under s 44(4)) (SI 2000/2957) |
| | | 1 Jan 2001 (in so far as it relates to information required in connection with exercise of Commission's functions under ss 42, 44(5)) (SI 2000/2957) |
| | | 26 Mar 2001 (otherwise) (SI 2000/2957) |
| 48 | | 6 Nov 2000 (SI 2000/2957) |
| 49 | | 26 Mar 2001 (SI 2000/2957) |
| 50–58 | | 1 Jan 2001 (SI 2000/2957) |
| 59 | (1) | 1 Jan 2001 (SI 2000/2957) |
| | (2) | 6 Nov 2000 (SI 2000/2957) |
| | (3) | 1 Jan 2001 (SI 2000/2957) |
| 60, 61 | | 1 Jan 2001 (SI 2000/2957) |
| 62–82 | | 6 Nov 2000 (SI 2000/2957) |
| 83–88 | | 26 Mar 2001 (SI 2001/878) |
| 89 | (1)–(6) | 26 Feb 2001 (SI 2001/534) |
| | (7) | 26 Mar 2001 (SI 2001/1148)[3] |
| | (8) | 26 Feb 2001 (SI 2001/534) |
| 90 | | 26 Mar 2001 (SI 2001/1148)[3] |
| 91, 92 | | 26 Feb 2001 (so far as relate to s 89(1)–(6)) (SI 2001/534) |
| | | 26 Mar 2001 (otherwise) (SI 2001/1148)[3] |
| 93, 94 | | 1 Jan 2001 (SI 2000/2957) |
| 95 | | 26 Mar 2001 (SI 2000/2957) |
| 96 | | 26 Mar 2001 (SI 2001/1148)[3] |
| 97–100 | | 26 Mar 2001 (SI 2000/2957) |
| 101–103 | | 6 Nov 2000 (SI 2000/2957) |
| 104 | | 26 Mar 2001 (SI 2001/1148)[3] |
| 105 | (1) | 26 Mar 2001 (SI 2001/1148)[3] |
| | (2) | 26 Feb 2001 (SI 2001/534) |
| | (3)–(5) | 26 Mar 2001 (SI 2001/1148)[3] |
| 106–108 | | 26 Mar 2001 (SI 2001/1148)[3] |
| 109 | | 26 Mar 2001 (SI 2001/878) |
| 110, 111 | | 26 Mar 2001 (SI 2001/1148)[3] |
| 112 | (1) | 26 Mar 2001 (SI 2001/1148)[3] |
| | (2)–(7) | 26 Feb 2001 (SI 2001/534) |
| | (8) | 26 Mar 2001 (SI 2001/1148)[3] |
| | (9), (10) | 26 Feb 2001 (SI 2001/534) |
| 113 | | 26 Mar 2001 (SI 2001/1148)[3] |
| 114 | (1), (2) | 26 Feb 2001 (so far as relate to s 112(2)–(7)) (SI 2001/534) |
| | | 26 Mar 2001 (otherwise) (SI 2001/1148)[3] |
| | (3) | 26 Feb 2001 (SI 2001/534) |

**Postal Services Act 2000 (c 26)**—*contd*

| | | |
|---|---|---|
| 115 | | 28 Sep 2000 (s 130(2)) |
| 116 | | 25 Mar 2001 (SI 2001/1148) |
| 117, 118 | | 6 Nov 2000 (SI 2000/2957) |
| 119 | | See Sch 7 below |
| 120–126 | | 28 Jul 2000 (RA) |
| 127 | (1)–(3) | 28 Jul 2000 (RA) |
| | (4) | See Sch 8 below |
| | (5) | 28 Jul 2000 (RA) |
| | (6) | See Sch 9 below |
| 128–131 | | 28 Jul 2000 (RA) |
| Sch 1 | | 6 Nov 2000 (SI 2000/2957) |
| Sch 2 | | 1 Jan 2001 (SI 2000/2957) |
| Schs 3, 4 | | 6 Nov 2000 (SI 2000/2957) |
| Sch 5 | | 26 Mar 2001 (SI 2000/2957) |
| Sch 6 | para 1 | 6 Nov 2000 (SI 2000/2957) |
| | paras 2–10 | 26 Mar 2001 (SI 2000/2957) |
| Sch 7 | paras 1, 2 | 6 Nov 2000 (SI 2000/2957) |
| | para 3(1)(a) | 6 Nov 2000 (except in relation to Competition Commission and Council) (SI 2000/2957) |
| | | 1 Jan 2001 (in relation to Council) (SI 2000/2957) |
| | | 26 Mar 2001 (otherwise) (SI 2000/2957) |
| | para 3(1)(b)–(n) | 6 Nov 2000 (SI 2000/2957) |
| | para 3(2), (3) | 6 Nov 2000 (SI 2000/2957) |
| | paras 4–6 | 6 Nov 2000 (SI 2000/2957) |
| Sch 8 | paras 1–5 | 26 Mar 2001 (SI 2001/1148)[3] |
| | paras 6, 7 | 6 Nov 2000 (SI 2000/2957) |
| | para 8 | 6 Nov 2000 (in so far as it relates to Post Office company) (SI 2000/2957) |
| | | 1 Jan 2001 (otherwise) (SI 2000/2957) |
| | para 9 | 1 Jan 2001 (SI 2000/2957) |
| | para 10 | 6 Nov 2000 (SI 2000/2957) |
| | paras 11, 12 | 26 Mar 2001 (SI 2001/1148)[3] |
| | para 13 | 1 Jan 2001 (SI 2000/2957) |
| | para 14(1) | 6 Nov 2000 (SI 2000/2957) |
| | para 14(2) | 1 Jan 2001 (SI 2000/2957) |
| | para 14(3) | 6 Nov 2000 (SI 2000/2957) |
| | para 15 | 6 Nov 2000 (SI 2000/2957) |
| | paras 16–26 | 26 Mar 2001 (SI 2001/1148)[3] |
| | para 27 | 6 Nov 2000 (SI 2000/2957) |
| Sch 9 | | 6 Nov 2000 (SI 2000/2957), repeals of or in— |
| | | Post Office (Banking Services) Act 1976; |
| | | Postal Services Regulations 1999, SI 1999/2107, regs 2, 3 |
| | | 1 Jan 2001 (SI 2000/2957), repeals of or in— |
| | | Post Office Act 1953, ss 29, 44, 45; |
| | | Parliamentary Commissioner Act 1967, Sch 2; |
| | | Post Office Act 1969, ss 14, 15; |
| | | Chronically Sick and Disabled Persons Act 1970, s 14(1), (2); |
| | | House of Commons Disqualification Act 1975, Sch 1, Pt III; |
| | | British Telecommunications Act 1981, s 65; |
| | | Merchant Shipping Act 1995, Sch 13, para 28 |
| | | 26 Mar 2001 (SI 2000/2957), repeals of or in— |
| | | Official Secrets Act 1920; |
| | | Post Office Act 1969, ss 33, 40, 41, 43, 44, 46–48, 55–63, 66, 67, 72, 73, 84, 119, 129, 135, Schs 2, 3, Sch 4, para 21; |
| | | Northern Ireland (Modification of Enactments—No 1) Order 1973, SI 1973/2163; |
| | | British Telecommunications Act 1981, ss 58(1)–(3), 59–61, 63, 64, 66–69, 71–74, 76; |
| | | Banking Act 1987, Sch 6, para 10; |

**Postal Services Act 2000 (c 26)**—*contd*

    Scotland Act 1998 (Consequential Modifications) (No 1)
      Order 1999, SI 1999/1042;

    Postal Services Regulations 1999, SI 1999/2107, regs 1(3), 4–6

    26 Mar 2001 (SI 2001/878), repeals of or in—

    Post Office Act 1953, ss 11, 25–28, 32, 52–65, 68–70, 72, 79;

    Criminal Justice Act 1967;

    Forgery and Counterfeiting Act 1981;

    Interception of Communications Act 1985;

    Post Office (Abolition of Import Restrictions) Regulations 1993,
      SI 1993/1324

    26 Mar 2001 (SI 2001/1148)[3], repeals of or in—

    Post Office Act 1953 (the whole Act, other than the sections
      noted above);

    Post Office Act 1969, ss 7, 8, 10–12, 28–30, 37–39, 64, 69–71,
      75(2), s 80 (except in so far as it extends to the Bailiwick of
      Guernsey), s 81, Sch 9, para 3(2);

    Local Government Act 1972, Sch 29, para 36;

    British Telecommunications Act 1981, s 75, Sch 3,
      para 51(1), (3);

    Mental Health Act 1983, s 134(9);

    Miscellaneous Financial Provisions Act 1983, Sch 2;

    Telecommunications Act 1984, s 99(1), Sch 4, paras 50, 78;

    Transport Act 1985, Sch 3, para 22, Sch 7, para 13;

    Gas Act 1986, Sch 7, para 10;

    Companies Act 1989, Sch 10, para 30;

    Electricity Act 1989, Sch 16, para 15;

    Water Act 1989, Sch 25, para 39;

    Electricity (Northern Ireland) Order 1992, SI 1992/231 (NI 1),
      Sch 12, para 7;

    Police and Magistrates' Courts Act 1994, Sch 4, para 49;

    Gas Act 1995, Sch 4, para 9;

    Police Act 1996;

    Gas (Northern Ireland) Order 1996, SI 1996/275 (NI 2), Sch 6

    1 May 2007 (SI 2007/1181), repeals of or in—

    Post Office Act 1969, ss 6, 74(2), 75(1), 87, Sch 1;

    House of Commons Disqualification Act 1975, Sch 1, Pt II

    *Not yet in force*, repeals of or in—

    Post Office Act 1969, ss 74(1), 80 (so far as it extends to the
      Bailiwick of Guernsey)

[1]    For transitional provisions, see SI 2000/2957, arts 3–8

[2]    For transitional and saving provisions, see SI 2001/878, arts 3–17

[3]    For transitional and saving provisions, see SI 2001/1148, arts 3–42

---

**Powers of Criminal Courts (Sentencing) Act 2000 (c 6)**

*RA:* 25 May 2000

*Commencement provisions:* s 168(1)

Whole Act in force 25 Aug 2000 (s 168(1))

---

**Protection of Animals (Amendment) Act 2000 (c 40)**

*RA:* 30 Nov 2000

*Commencement provisions:* s 5(3)

**Protection of Animals (Amendment) Act 2000 (c 40)**—*contd*
Whole Act in force 30 Jan 2001 (s 5(3))

---

**Public Finance and Accountability (Scotland) Act 2000 (asp 1)**

*RA:* 17 Jan 2000

*Commencement provisions:* s 30(1), (2); Public Finance and Accountability (Scotland) Act 2000 (Commencement) Order 2000, SSI 2000/10)

| | | |
|---|---|---|
| 1–3 | | 1 Apr 2001 (SSI 2000/10) |
| 4 | (1) | 1 Apr 2000 (SSI 2000/10) |
| | (2)–(5) | 1 Apr 2001 (SSI 2000/10) |
| 5 | | 1 Feb 2000 (for the purpose of enabling credits to be granted to take effect no earlier than 1 Apr 2000) (SSI 2000/10) |
| | | 1 Apr 2000 (otherwise) (SSI 2000/10) |
| 6–9 | | 1 Apr 2000 (SSI 2000/10) |
| 10 | (1), (2) | 1 Feb 2000 (SSI 2000/10) |
| | (3) | 1 Apr 2000 (SSI 2000/10) |
| | (4) | 1 Feb 2000 (for the purpose of enabling directions to be given to take effect no earlier than 1 Apr 2000) (SSI 2000/10) |
| | | 1 Apr 2000 (otherwise) (SSI 2000/10) |
| | (5) | 1 Apr 2000 (SSI 2000/10) |
| | (6) | See Sch 2 below |
| 11 | (1)–(6) | 1 Apr 2000 (SSI 2000/10) |
| | (7) | 1 Feb 2000 (SSI 2000/10) |
| | (8) | 1 Apr 2000 (SSI 2000/10) |
| | (9) | 1 Feb 2000 (for the purpose of requiring the preparation and examination of proposals under this subsection relating to the financial year beginning with 1 Apr 2000) (SSI 2000/10) |
| | | 1 Apr 2000 (otherwise) (SSI 2000/10) |
| 12, 13 | | 1 Feb 2000 (SSI 2000/10) |
| 14 | (1) | 1 Feb 2000 (SSI 2000/10) |
| | (2)–(5) | 1 Apr 2000 (SSI 2000/10) |
| 15 | (1), (2) | 1 Feb 2000 (for the purpose of enabling designations of accountable officers and determinations of their functions to be made to take effect no earlier than 1 Apr 2000) (SSI 2000/10) |
| | | 1 Apr 2000 (otherwise) (SSI 2000/10) |
| | (3)–(5) | 1 Apr 2000 (SSI 2000/10) |
| | (6), (7) | 1 Feb 2000 (for the purpose of enabling designations of accountable officers and determinations of their functions to be made to take effect no earlier than 1 Apr 2000) (SSI 2000/10) |
| | | 1 Apr 2000 (otherwise) (SSI 2000/10) |
| | (8) | 1 Apr 2000 (SSI 2000/10) |
| 16–23 | | 1 Apr 2000 (SSI 2000/10) |
| 24 | (1)–(4) | 1 Apr 2000 (SSI 2000/10) |
| | (5), (6) | 1 Feb 2000 (for the purpose of enabling an order to be made under sub-s (5) to come into force no earlier than 1 Apr 2000) (SSI 2000/10) |
| | | 1 Apr 2000 (otherwise) (SSI 2000/10) |
| | (7) | 1 Apr 2000 (SSI 2000/10) |
| 25, 26 | | 1 Apr 2000 (SSI 2000/10) |
| 27–29 | | 19 Jan 2000 (SSI 2000/10) |
| 30 | | 17 Jan 2000 (RA) |
| Sch 1 | | 1 Apr 2000 (SSI 2000/10) |
| Sch 2 | paras 1–4 | 1 Apr 2000 (SSI 2000/10) |
| | paras 5, 6 | 1 Feb 2000 (for the purpose of enabling Audit Scotland to exercise powers under these paragraphs so as to make provision to take effect no earlier than 1 Apr 2000) (SSI 2000/10) |
| | | 1 Apr 2000 (otherwise) (SSI 2000/10) |
| | paras 7–9 | 1 Apr 2000 (SSI 2000/10) |

**Public Finance and Accountability (Scotland) Act 2000 (asp 1)**—*contd*

| | |
|---|---|
| Sch 3 | 1 Feb 2000 (SSI 2000/10) |
| Sch 4 | 1 Apr 2000 (SSI 2000/10) |

## Race Relations (Amendment) Act 2000 (c 34)

*RA:* 30 Nov 2000

*Commencement provisions:* s 10(2)–(4); Race Relations (Amendment) Act 2000 (Commencement) Order 2001, SI 2001/566

| | |
|---|---|
| 1 | 26 Mar 2001 (for the purpose of the imposition of a requirement or the giving of an express authorisation by a Minister of the Crown acting personally in accordance with Race Relations Act 1976, s 19D(3)) (SI 2001/566) |
| | 2 Apr 2001 (otherwise) (SI 2001/566) |
| 2–9 | 2 Apr 2001 (SI 2001/566) |
| 10 | 30 Nov 2000 (RA) |
| Schs 1–3 | 2 Apr 2001 (SI 2001/566) |

## Regulation of Investigatory Powers Act 2000 (c 23)

*RA:* 28 Jul 2000

*Commencement provisions:* s 83(2); Regulation of Investigatory Powers Act 2000 (Commencement No 1 and Transitional Provisions) Order 2000, SI 2000/2543; Regulation of Investigatory Powers Act 2000 (Commencement No 2) Order 2001, SI 2001/2727; Regulation of Investigatory Powers Act 2000 (Commencement No 3) Order 2003, SI 2003/3140; Regulation of Investigatory Powers Act 2000 (Commencement No 4) Order 2007, SI 2007/2196

| | | |
|---|---|---|
| 1 | (1), (2) | 2 Oct 2000 (SI 2000/2543) |
| | (3) | 24 Oct 2000 (SI 2000/2543) |
| | (4)–(8) | 2 Oct 2000 (SI 2000/2543) |
| 2–20 | | 2 Oct 2000 (SI 2000/2543) |
| 21 | (1)–(3) | 5 Jan 2004 (SI 2003/3140) |
| | (4) | 2 Oct 2000 (for purpose of giving effect to definition "related communications data" in s 20 of this Act) (SI 2000/2543) |
| | | 5 Jan 2004 (otherwise) (SI 2003/3140) |
| | (5)–(7) | 5 Jan 2004 (SI 2003/3140) |
| 22–25 | | 5 Jan 2004 (SI 2003/3140) |
| 26–48 | | 25 Sep 2000 (SI 2000/2543) |
| 49–56 | | 1 Oct 2007 (SI 2007/2196) |
| 57 | (1) | 2 Oct 2000 (SI 2000/2543) |
| | (2)(a) | 2 Oct 2000 (SI 2000/2543) |
| | (2)(b) | 5 Jan 2004 (SI 2003/3140) |
| | (2)(c) | 1 Oct 2007 (SI 2007/2196) |
| | (2)(d)(i) | 2 Oct 2000 (SI 2000/2543) |
| | (2)(d)(ii) | 1 Oct 2007 (SSI 2007/2196) |
| | (3)–(8) | 2 Oct 2000 (SI 2000/2543) |
| 58 | (1)(a)–(f) | 2 Oct 2000 (SI 2000/2543) |
| | (1)(g), (h) | 5 Jan 2004 (SI 2003/3140) |
| | (1)(i) | 1 Oct 2007 (SI 2007/2196) |
| | (1)(j) | 2 Oct 2000 (except so far as relates to s 58(1)(h), (i) of this Act) (SI 2000/2543) |
| | | 5 Jan 2004 (otherwise) (SI 2003/3140) |
| | (2)–(7) | 2 Oct 2000 (SI 2000/2543) |
| 59 | (1) | 2 Oct 2000 (SI 2000/2543) |
| | (2)(a) | 2 Oct 2000 (SI 2000/2543) |
| | (2)(b) | 2 Oct 2000 (so far as relate to Pt II (ss 26–48) of this Act) (SI 2000/2543) |
| | | 1 Oct 2007 (otherwise) (SI 2007/2196) |

**Regulation of Investigatory Powers Act 2000 (c 23)**—*contd*

|  |  |  |
|---|---|---|
| | (2)(c)–(e) | 2 Oct 2000 (so far as relate to Pt II (ss 26–48) of this Act) (SI 2000/2543) |
| | | *Not yet in force* (so far as relate to Pt III (ss 49–56) of this Act) |
| | (3)–(10) | 2 Oct 2000 (SI 2000/2543) |
| 60 | | 2 Oct 2000 (SI 2000/2543) |
| 61 | | 25 Sep 2000 (SI 2000/2543) |
| 62 | (1)(a) | 25 Sep 2000 (SI 2000/2543) |
| | (1)(b), (c) | 1 Oct 2007 (SI 2007/2196) |
| | (2), (3) | 25 Sep 2000 (SI 2000/2543) |
| 63, 64 | | 25 Sep 2000 (SI 2000/2543) |
| 65 | (1) | 2 Oct 2000 (subject to transitional provisions in SI 2000/2543, art 6) (SI 2000/2543) |
| | (2)(a)–(b) | 2 Oct 2000 (subject to transitional provisions in SI 2000/2543, art 6) (SI 2000/2543) |
| | (2)(c), (d) | *Not yet in force* |
| | (3)(a), (b) | 2 Oct 2000 (SI 2000/2543) |
| | (3)(c) | 1 Oct 2007 (SI 2007/2196) |
| | (3)(d) | 2 Oct 2000 (SI 2000/2543) |
| | (4) | 2 Oct 2000 (SI 2000/2543) |
| | (5)(a), (b) | 2 Oct 2000 (SI 2000/2543) |
| | (5)(c) | 5 Jan 2004 (SI 2003/3140) |
| | (5)(d) | 2 Oct 2000 (SI 2000/2543) |
| | (5)(e) | 1 Oct 2007 (SI 2007/2196) |
| | (5)(f) | 2 Oct 2000 (SI 2000/2543) |
| | (6), (7) | 2 Oct 2000 (SI 2000/2543) |
| | (8)(a) | 2 Oct 2000 (SI 2000/2543) |
| | (8)(b) | 5 Jan 2004 (SI 2003/3140) |
| | (8)(c) | 2 Oct 2000 (SI 2000/2543) |
| | (8)(d), (e) | 1 Oct 2007 (SI 2007/2196) |
| | (8)(f) | 2 Oct 2000 (SI 2000/2543) |
| | (9) | 2 Oct 2000 (SI 2000/2543) |
| | (10) | 1 Oct 2007 (SI 2007/2196) |
| | (11) | 2 Oct 2000 (SI 2000/2543) |
| 66 | | *Not yet in force* |
| 67 | (1) | 2 Oct 2000 (so far as relates to s 65(2)(a), (b) of this Act) (SI 2000/2543) |
| | | *Not yet in force* (so far as relates to s 65(2)(c), (d) of this Act) |
| | (2)–(8) | 2 Oct 2000 (SI 2000/2543) |
| | (9) | *Not yet in force* |
| | (10)–(12) | 2 Oct 2000 (SI 2000/2543) |
| 68 | (1)–(6) | 2 Oct 2000 (SI 2000/2543) |
| | (7)(a)–(f) | 2 Oct 2000 (SI 2000/2543) |
| | (7)(g), (h) | 5 Jan 2004 (SI 2003/3140) |
| | (7)(i)–(l) | 2 Oct 2000 (SI 2000/2543) |
| | (7)(m) | 1 Oct 2007 (SI 2007/2196) |
| | (7)(n) | 2 Oct 2000 (except so far as relates to para (m)) (SI 2000/2543) |
| | | 1 Oct 2007 (otherwise) (SI 2007/2196) |
| | (8) | 2 Oct 2000 (SI 2000/2543) |
| 69, 70 | | 2 Oct 2000 (SI 2000/2543) |
| 71, 72 | | 25 Sep 2000 (so far as relate to Pt II (ss 26–48) of this Act, Intelligence Services Act 1994, s 5, or Police Act 1997, Pt III (ss 91–108)) (SI 2000/2543) |
| | | 2 Oct 2000 (so far as relate to Pt I, Chapter I (ss 1–20) of this Act) (SI 2000/2543) |
| | | 13 Aug 2001 (so far as relate to Pt I, Chapter II (ss 21–25) of this Act) (SI 2007/2727) |
| | | 1 Oct 2007 (otherwise) (SI 2007/2196) |
| 73 | | 2 Oct 2000 (SI 2000/2543) |
| 74–78 | | 25 Sep 2000 (SI 2000/2543) |

### Regulation of Investigatory Powers Act 2000 (c 23)—*contd*

| | | |
|---|---|---|
| 79 | | 2 Oct 2000 (SI 2000/2543) |
| 80, 81 | | 25 Sep 2000 (SI 2000/2543) |
| 82 | (1) | See Sch 4 below |
| | (2) | See Sch 5 below |
| | (3)–(6) | 2 Oct 2000 (subject to transitional provisions in arts 5,6 in SI 2000/2543) (SI 2000/2543) |
| 83 | | 28 Jul 2000 (RA) |
| Sch 1 | | 25 Sep 2000 (SI 2000/2543) |
| Sch 2 | | 1 Oct 2007 (SI 2007/2196) |
| Sch 3 | | 2 Oct 2000 (SI 2000/2543) |
| Sch 4 | paras 1–3 | 2 Oct 2000 (SI 2000/2543) |
| | para 4 | 25 Sep 2000 (SI 2000/2543) |
| | para 5 | 2 Oct 2000 (subject to transitional provisions in SI 2000/2543, art 5) (SI 2000/2543) |
| | para 6 | 25 Sep 2000 (SI 2000/2543) |
| | para 7 | 2 Oct 2000 (subject to transitional provisions in SI 2000/2543, art 5) (SI 2000/2543) |
| | para 8 | 25 Sep 2000 (SI 2000/2543) |
| | paras 9–12 | 2 Oct 2000 (subject to transitional provisions in SI 2000/2543, art 5) (SI 2000/2543) |
| Sch 5 | | 25 Sep 2000 (SI 2000/2543); so far as relates to— Intelligence Services Act 1994, ss 6, 7; Police Act 1997[1]; Crime and Disorder Act 1998 |
| | | 2 Oct 2000 (otherwise and subject to transitional provisions in SI 2000/2543, art 6) (SI 2000/2543) |

[1]  In the Queen's Printer's copy of SI 2000/2543, art 2 purports to bring the entry in Sch 5 of this Act relating to Police Act 1997 into force on 25 Sep 2000, however art 6 of the 2000 SI purports to bring the entry in Sch 5 of this Act relating to s 102 of, Sch 7 to, the 1997 Act into force on 2 Oct 2000

### Regulation of Investigatory Powers (Scotland) Act 2000 (asp 11)

*RA:* 28 Sep 2000

*Commencement provisions:* s 32(2); Regulation of Investigatory Powers (Scotland) Act 2000 (Commencement) Order 2000, SSI 2000/341

Whole Act in force 29 Sep 2000 (SSI 2000/341)

### Representation of the People Act 2000 (c 2)

*RA:* 9 Mar 2000

*Commencement provisions:* s 17(3); Representation of the People Act 2000 (Commencement) Order 2001, SI 2001/116[1]

| | | |
|---|---|---|
| 1–7 | | 29 Jan 2001 (so far as they confer power to make regulations) (SI 2001/116) |
| | | 16 Feb 2001 (otherwise) (SI 2001/116) |
| 8 | | See Schs 1–3 below |
| 9 | | 16 Feb 2001 (SI 2001/116) |
| 10, 11 | | 9 Mar 2000 (s 17(3)) |
| 12 | (1) | See Sch 4 below |
| | (2), (3) | 29 Jan 2001 (so far as they confer power to make regulations) (SI 2001/116) |
| | | 16 Feb 2001 (otherwise) (SI 2001/116) |
| 13 | | 29 Jan 2001 (so far as they confer power to make regulations) (SI 2001/116) |
| | | 16 Feb 2001 (otherwise) (SI 2001/116) |

**Representation of the People Act 2000 (c 2)**—*contd*

| | | |
|---|---|---|
| 14 | (1)–(3) | 9 Mar 2000 (s 17(3)) |
| | (4) | See Sch 5 below |
| 15 | (1) | See Sch 6 below |
| | (2) | See Sch 7 below |
| 16, 17 | | 9 Mar 2000 (s 17(3)) |
| Schs 1–4 | | 29 Jan 2001 (so far as they confer power to make regulations) (SI 2001/116) |
| | | 16 Feb 2001 (otherwise) (SI 2001/116) |
| Sch 5 | | 9 Mar 2000 (s 17(3)) |
| Sch 6 | paras 1–5 | 29 Jan 2001 (so far as they confer power to make regulations) (SI 2001/116) |
| | | 16 Feb 2001 (otherwise) (SI 2001/116) |
| | para 6 | 9 Mar 2000 (s 17(3)) |
| | paras 7–19 | 29 Jan 2001 (so far as they confer power to make regulations) (SI 2001/116) |
| | | 16 Feb 2001 (otherwise) (SI 2001/116) |
| Sch 7 | | 29 Jan 2001 (so far as confers power to make regulations) (SI 2001/116) |
| | | 16 Feb 2001 (otherwise) (SI 2001/116) |

[1]   For savings, see SI 2001/116, art 2(3)–(5)

---

**Royal Parks (Trading) Act 2000 (c 13)**

*RA:* 20 Jul 2000

Whole Act in force 20 Jul 2000 (RA)

---

**Sea Fishing Grants (Charges) Act 2000 (c 18)**

*RA:* 28 Jul 2000

Whole Act in force 28 Jul 2000 (RA)

---

**Sexual Offences (Amendment) Act 2000 (c 44)**

*RA:* 30 Nov 2000

*Commencement provisions:* s 7(3); Sexual Offences (Amendment) Act 2000 (Commencement No 1) Order 2000, SI 2000/3303; Sexual Offences (Amendment) Act 2000 (Commencement No 2) (Scotland) Order 2000, SSI 2000/452; Sexual Offences (Amendment) Act 2000 (Commencement No 3) Order 2003, SI 2003/1935; Sexual Offences (Amendment) Act 2000 (Commencement No 4) (Scotland) Order 2003, SSI 2003/378

| | | |
|---|---|---|
| 1 | (1), (2) | 8 Jan 2001 (E) (W) (NI) (SI 2000/3303) |
| | (3) | 8 Jan 2001 (SSI 2000/452)[2] |
| | (4) | 8 Jan 2001 (SI 2000/3303) |
| | (5) | 8 Jan 2001 (E) (W) (NI) (SI 2000/3303) |
| | | 8 Jan 2001 (S) (SSI 2000/452)[2] |
| 2 | (1)–(3) | 8 Jan 2001 (SI 2000/3303) |
| | (4) | 8 Jan 2001 (SSI 2000/452)[2] |
| | (5) | 8 Jan 2001 (SI 2000/3303) |
| 3 | | 8 Jan 2001 (E) (W) (NI) (SI 2000/3303) |
| | | 8 Jan 2001 (S) (SSI 2000/452)[2] |
| 4 | (1), (2) | 8 Jan 2001 (E) (W) (NI) (SI 2000/3303) |
| | | 8 Jan 2001 (S) (SSI 2000/452)[2] |
| | (3)(a), (b) | 8 Jan 2001 (SI 2000/3303) |
| | (3)(c) | 8 Jan 2001 (SSI 2000/452)[2] |

**Sexual Offences (Amendment) Act 2000 (c 44)**—*contd*

|   |   |   |
|---|---|---|
|   | (4)(a)–(c) | 8 Jan 2001 (E) (W) (NI) (SI 2000/3303) |
|   |   | 8 Jan 2001 (S) (SSI 2000/452)[2] |
|   | (4)(d) | 8 Jan 2001 (SI 2000/3303) |
|   | (5)–(9) | 8 Jan 2001 (E) (W) (NI) (SI 2000/3303) |
|   |   | 8 Jan 2001 (S) (SSI 2000/452)[2] |
| 5 | (1) | 8 Jan 2001 (E) (W) (NI) (SI 2000/3303) |
|   |   | 8 Jan 2001 (S) (SSI 2000/452)[2] |
|   | (2) | 8 Jan 2001 (SI 2000/3303) |
|   | (3) | 8 Jan 2001 (SSI 2000/452)[2] |
|   | (4) | 8 Jan 2001 (SI 2000/3303) |
| 6 | (1) | 8 Jan 2001 (SI 2000/3303) |
|   | (2) | 8 Jan 2001 (S) (SSI 2000/452)[2] |
| 7 | (1) | 30 Nov 2000 (RA) |
|   | (2) | 30 Nov 2000 (RA) |
|   |   | 1 Aug 2003 (SI 2003/1935)[1] |
|   | (3), (4) | 30 Nov 2000 (RA) |

[1]  SI 2003/1935 brings s 7(2) into force to the extent, if any, that it is not already in force. It is intended to address the doubts expressed by the Subordinate Legislation Committee of the Scottish Parliament as to whether s 7(2) had been brought into force

[2]  SSI 2003/378 brings these provisions into force on 11 Aug 2003, to the extent, if any, that they are not already in force. It is intended, together with SI 2003/1935, to address the doubts expressed by the Subordinate Legislation Committee of the Scottish Parliament as to whether the power to make SSI 2000/452 had devolved to the Scottish Ministers

**Standards in Scotland's Schools etc Act 2000 (asp 6)**

*RA:* 14 Jul 2000

*Commencement provisions:* s 61(2)–(4); Standards in Scotland's Schools etc Act 2000 (Commencement No 1) Order 2000, SSI 2000/258; Standards in Scotland's Schools etc Act 2000 (Commencement No 2 and Transitional Provisions), SSI 2000/298[1]; Standards in Scotland's Schools etc Act 2000 (Commencement No 3 and Transitional Provisions), SSI 2000/361[2], as amended by SSI 2001/400; Standards in Scotland's Schools etc Act 2000 (Commencement No 4) Order 2001, SSI 2001/102; Standards in Scotland's Schools etc Act 2000 (Commencement No 5) Order 2002, SSI 2002/72; Standards in Scotland's Schools etc Act 2000 (Commencement No 6) Order 2003, SSI 2003/84; Standards in Scotland's Schools etc Act 2000 (Commencement No 7) Order 2004, SSI 2004/528; Standards in Scotland's Schools etc Act 2000 (Commencement No 8 and Savings) Order 2006, SSI 2006/232

|   |   |   |
|---|---|---|
| 1–8 |   | 13 Oct 2000 (SSI 2000/361) |
| 9, 10 |   | 23 Aug 2000 (SSI 2000/298) |
| 11–14 |   | 13 Oct 2000 (SSI 2000/361) |
| 15 |   | 1 Aug 2003 (SSI 2003/84) |
| 16–21 |   | 13 Oct 2000 (SSI 2000/361) |
| 22 |   | 28 Jul 2000 (SSI 2000/258) |
| 23 |   | 14 Jul 2000 (RA) |
| 24–27 |   | 13 Oct 2000 (SSI 2000/361) |
| 28 |   | 23 Aug 2000 (SSI 2000/298) |
| 29–31 |   | 13 Oct 2000 (SSI 2000/361) |
| 32–37 |   | 4 Mar 2002 (SSI 2002/72) |
| 38 |   | 13 Oct 2000 (SSI 2000/361) |
| 39 |   | 1 Apr 2002 (SSI 2002/72) |
| 40–43 |   | 13 Oct 2000 (SSI 2000/361) |
| 44 | (1)–(3) | 13 Oct 2000 (SSI 2000/361) |
|   | (4) | 13 Oct 2000 (except words "or (vii)" to "numbers") (SSI 2000/361) |
|   |   | 31 Dec 2004 (otherwise) (SSI 2004/528) |
|   | (5)–(7) | 13 Oct 2000 (SSI 2000/361) |

**Standards in Scotland's Schools etc Act 2000 (asp 6)**—*contd*

| | | |
|---|---|---|
| 45 | | 13 Oct 2000 (SSI 2000/361) |
| 46 | (1), (2) | 13 Oct 2000 (for the purpose of enabling elections to be held and appointments and nominations to be made amending Teaching Council (Scotland) Act 1965 and bringing those amendments into force to enable elections to be held prior to 1 Nov 2001 for the Council to be constituted in accordance with the 1965 Act as amended by s 46(1), (2) on that date) (SSI 2000/361) |
| | | 1 Nov 2001 (otherwise) (SSI 2000/361) |
| | (3) | 13 Oct 2000 (SSI 2000/361) |
| | (4) | 1 Nov 2001 (SSI 2000/361) |
| | (5) | 13 Oct 2000 (SSI 2000/361) |
| | (6), (7) | 1 Nov 2001 (SSI 2000/361) |
| 47, 48 | | 13 Oct 2000 (SSI 2000/361) |
| 49 | | 13 Oct 2000 (so far as inserts Teaching Council (Scotland) Act 1965, ss 9B(a)(i), (b), 9C) (SSI 2000/361) |
| | | 1 Jul 2006 (otherwise) (SSI 2006/232)[3] |
| 50 | | 1 Nov 2001 (so far as substitutes Teaching Council (Scotland) Act 1965, ss 10, 10A(1), 10B, 10C, 11(1) (except head (ii) and (iii)), 11(8), 11(9) (except the words "or (2) above"), 11(10), 11(11), 11B) (SSI 2000/361) |
| | | 1 Jul 2006 (so far as substitutes Teaching Council (Scotland) Act 1965, ss 11(1)(ii), (iii), (2)–(7), (9) (so far as not already in force), 11A(1), (2)) (SSI 2006/232)[3] |
| | | *Never in force* (so far as substitutes Teaching Council (Scotland) Act 1965, ss 10A(2)–(5), 11A(3)) (repealed) |
| 51 | | 13 Oct 2000 (so far as substitutes Teaching Council (Scotland) Act 1965, s 12(1), except words from "(a) such person" to "or" in the third place it occurs) (SSI 2000/361) |
| | | *Never in force* (so far as substitutes Teaching Council (Scotland) Act 1965, s 12(1)(a), (b), (1A), (4)–(9), and amends sub-ss (2), (3) thereof) (repealed) |
| 52 | | 13 Oct 2000 (so far as inserts Teaching Council (Scotland) Act 1965, s 17(1), definition "the register") (SSI 2000/361) |
| | | 1 Nov 2001 (otherwise) (SSI 2000/361) |
| 53, 54 | | 13 Oct 2000 (SSI 2000/361) |
| 55 | | 23 Mar 2001 (SSI 2001/102) |
| 56–59 | | 13 Oct 2000 (SSI 2000/361) |
| 60 | (1) | See Sch 2 below |
| | (2) | See Sch 3 below |
| 61 | | 14 Jul 2000 (RA) |
| Sch 1 | | *Never in force* (repealed) |
| Sch 2 | para 1(1) | 13 Oct 2000 (as far as relates to sub-paras (2), (4), (5)(d)(i) below) (SSI 2000/361) |
| | | 1 Nov 2001 (otherwise) (SSI 2000/361) |
| | para 1(2) | 13 Oct 2000 (SSI 2000/361) |
| | para 1(3) | 1 Nov 2001 (SSI 2000/361) |
| | para 1(4) | 13 Oct 2000 (SSI 2000/361) |
| | para 1(5)(a)–(c) | 1 Nov 2001 (SSI 2000/361) |
| | para 1(5)(d)(i) | 13 Oct 2000 (SSI 2000/361) |
| | para 1(5)(d)(ii) | 1 Nov 2001 (SSI 2000/361) |
| | para 1(6) | 1 Nov 2001 (SSI 2000/361) |
| | para 2 | 31 Dec 2004 (SSI 2004/528) |
| | para 3(1), (2) | 13 Oct 2000 (SSI 2000/361) |
| | para 3(3), (4) | 31 Dec 2004 (SSI 2004/528) |
| | para 3(5)–(8) | 13 Oct 2000 (SSI 2000/361) |
| | para 3(9) | 31 Dec 2004 (SSI 2004/528) |
| Sch 3 | | 14 Jul 2000 (so far as relates to Self-Governing Schools etc (Scotland) Act 1989, ss 13–22, 24, Schs 3, 5) (RA) |
| | | 13 Oct 2000 (SSI 2000/361), repeals of or in— |
| | | Teaching Council (Scotland) Act 1965; |

## Standards in Scotland's Schools etc Act 2000 (asp 6)—*contd*

Education (Scotland) Act 1980, s 1(5)(a);

School Boards (Scotland) Act 1988

31 Dec 2004 (otherwise, except repeal in Race Relations Act 1976, s 19(6)(c)(i)) (SSI 2004/528)

*Never in force* (repeal in Race Relations Act 1976, s 19(6)(c)(i) (repealed))

1   For transitional provisions, see SSI 2000/298, art 4

2   For transitional provisions, see SSI 2000/361, art 4

3   For savings, see SSI 2006/232, art 3

---

## Television Licences (Disclosure of Information) Act 2000 (c 15)

*RA:* 20 Jul 2000

Whole Act in force 20 Jul 2000 (RA)

---

## Terrorism Act 2000 (c 11)

*RA:* 20 Jul 2000

*Commencement provisions:* s 128; Terrorism Act 2000 (Commencement No 1) Order 2000, SI 2000/2800; Terrorism Act 2000 (Commencement No 2) Order 2000, SI 2000/2944; Terrorism Act 2000 (Commencement No 3) Order 2000, SI 2001/421; Terrorism Act 2000 (Continuance of Part VII) Order 2002, SI 2002/365; Terrorism Act 2000 (Continuance of Part VII) Order 2003, SI 2003/427; Terrorism Act 2000 (Continuance of Part VII) Order 2004, SI 2004/431; Terrorism Act 2000 (Continuance of Part VII) Order 2005, SI 2005/350; Terrorism (Northern Ireland) Act 2006, s 1(1), (2)

| | | |
|---|---|---|
| 1 | | 19 Feb 2001 (SI 2001/421) |
| 2 | (1)(a) | 19 Feb 2001 (SI 2001/421) |
| | (1)(b) | 20 Jul 2000 (RA) |
| | (2) | 20 Jul 2000 (RA) |
| 3 | | 19 Feb 2001 (SI 2001/421) |
| 4 | (1), (2) | 19 Feb 2001 (SI 2001/421) |
| | (3), (4) | 31 Oct 2000 (SI 2000/2944) |
| 5 | (1) | 31 Oct 2000 (SI 2000/2944) |
| | (2)–(5) | 19 Feb 2001 (SI 2001/421) |
| | (6) | See Sch 3 below |
| 6–23 | | 19 Feb 2001 (SI 2001/421) |
| 24 | (1) | 19 Feb 2001 (SI 2001/421) |
| | (2)(a)–(d) | 19 Feb 2001 (SI 2001/421) |
| | (2)(e) | 31 Oct 2000 (SI 2000/2944) |
| 25–30 | | 19 Feb 2001 (SI 2001/421) |
| 31 | | 31 Oct 2000 (SI 2000/2944) |
| 32–40 | | 19 Feb 2001 (SI 2001/421) |
| 41 | (1) | 19 Feb 2001 (SI 2001/421) |
| | (2) | See Sch 8 below |
| | (3)–(9) | 19 Feb 2001 (SI 2001/421) |
| 42–52 | | 19 Feb 2001 (SI 2001/421) |
| 53 | (1) | See Sch 7 below |
| | (2), (3) | 19 Feb 2001 (SI 2001/421) |
| 54–98 | | 19 Feb 2001 (SI 2001/421) |
| 99 | | 12 Oct 2000 (SI 2000/2800) |
| 100 | | *Never in force* (repealed) |
| 101 | (1)–(5) | 12 Oct 2000 (SI 2000/2800) |
| | (6)–(9) | 19 Feb 2001 (SI 2001/421) |
| 102–114 | | 19 Feb 2001 (SI 2001/421) |

**Terrorism Act 2000 (c 11)**—*contd*

| | | |
|---|---|---|
| 115 | | See Sch 14 below |
| 116, 117 | | 19 Feb 2001 (SI 2001/421) |
| 118 | | 20 Jul 2000 (RA) |
| 119 | | 31 Oct 2000 (SI 2000/2944) |
| 120–122 | | 19 Feb 2001 (SI 2001/421) |
| 123 | | 31 Oct 2000 (SI 2000/2944) |
| 124–127 | | 19 Feb 2001 (SI 2001/421) |
| 128–131 | | 20 Jul 2000 (RA) |
| Sch 1 | | 20 Jul 2000 (RA) |
| Sch 2 | | 19 Feb 2001 (SI 2001/421) |
| Sch 3 | paras 1–5 | 31 Oct 2000 (SI 2000/2944) |
| | paras 6–8 | 19 Feb 2001 (SI 2001/421) |
| Sch 4 | paras 1–12 | 19 Feb 2001 (SI 2001/421) |
| | para 13(1) | 19 Feb 2001 (SI 2001/421) |
| | para 13(2)(a) | 19 Feb 2001 (SI 2001/421) |
| | para 13(2)(b) | 31 Oct 2000 (SI 2000/2944) |
| | para 13(3), (4) | 31 Oct 2000 (SI 2000/2944) |
| | para 13(5)–(9) | 19 Feb 2001 (SI 2001/421) |
| | paras 14–26 | 19 Feb 2001 (SI 2001/421) |
| | para 27(1) | 19 Feb 2001 (SI 2001/421) |
| | para 27(2)(a) | 19 Feb 2001 (SI 2001/421) |
| | para 27(2)(b) | 31 Oct 2000 (SI 2000/2944) |
| | para 27(3), (4) | 31 Oct 2000 (SI 2000/2944) |
| | para 27(5)–(10) | 19 Feb 2001 (SI 2001/421) |
| | paras 28–42 | 19 Feb 2001 (SI 2001/421) |
| | para 43(1) | 19 Feb 2001 (SI 2001/421) |
| | para 43(2)(a) | 19 Feb 2001 (SI 2001/421) |
| | para 43(2)(b) | 31 Oct 2000 (SI 2000/2944) |
| | para 43(3), (4) | 31 Oct 2000 (SI 2000/2944) |
| | para 43(5)–(9) | 19 Feb 2001 (SI 2001/421) |
| | paras 44–51 | 19 Feb 2001 (SI 2001/421) |
| | para 52 | 31 Oct 2000 (SI 2000/2944) |
| | para 53 | 19 Feb 2001 (SI 2001/421) |
| Sch 5 | paras 1–9 | 19 Feb 2001 (SI 2001/421) |
| | para 10(1) | 19 Feb 2001 (SI 2001/421) |
| | para 10(2), (3) | 31 Oct 2000 (SI 2000/2944) |
| | paras 11–33 | 19 Feb 2001 (SI 2001/421) |
| Sch 6 | paras 1–3 | 19 Feb 2001 (SI 2001/421) |
| | para 4 | 31 Oct 2000 (SI 2000/2944) |
| | para 5 | 19 Feb 2001 (SI 2001/421) |
| | para 6(1) | 19 Feb 2001 (SI 2001/421) |
| | para 6(2) | 31 Oct 2000 (SI 2000/2944) |
| | para 6(3) | 19 Feb 2001 (SI 2001/421) |
| | para 7(1), (2) | 19 Feb 2001 (SI 2001/421) |
| | para 7(3) | 31 Oct 2000 (SI 2000/2944) |
| | paras 8, 9 | 19 Feb 2001 (SI 2001/421) |
| Sch 7 | paras 1–5 | 19 Feb 2001 (SI 2001/421) |
| | para 6(1), (2) | 19 Feb 2001 (SI 2001/421) |
| | para 6(3) | See Sch 8 below |
| | para 6(4) | 19 Feb 2001 (SI 2001/421) |
| | paras 7–15 | 19 Feb 2001 (SI 2001/421) |
| | para 16(1), (2) | 31 Oct 2000 (SI 2000/2944) |
| | para 16(3) | 19 Feb 2001 (SI 2001/421) |
| | para 17(1)–(3) | 19 Feb 2001 (SI 2001/421) |
| | para 17(4) | 31 Oct 2000 (SI 2000/2944) |
| | para 17(5), (6) | 19 Feb 2001 (SI 2001/421) |
| | para 18 | 19 Feb 2001 (SI 2001/421) |
| Sch 8 | para 1(1) | 31 Oct 2000 (SI 2000/2944) |
| | para 1(2)–(6) | 19 Feb 2001 (SI 2001/421) |

## Terrorism Act 2000 (c 11)—*contd*

|  |  |  |
|---|---|---|
|  | para 2 | 19 Feb 2001 (SI 2001/421) |
|  | para 3 | 12 Oct 2000 (SI 2000/2800) |
|  | para 4(1)–(5) | 12 Oct 2000 (SI 2000/2800) |
|  | para 4(6), (7) | 19 Feb 2001 (SI 2001/421) |
|  | paras 5–18 | 19 Feb 2001 (SI 2001/421) |
|  | para 19 | 31 Oct 2000 (SI 2000/2944) |
|  | paras 20–37 | 19 Feb 2001 (SI 2001/421) |
| Schs 9–13 |  | 19 Feb 2001 (SI 2001/421) |
| Sch 14 | para 1 | 12 Oct 2000 (SI 2000/2800) |
|  | paras 2–5 | 19 Feb 2001 (SI 2001/421) |
|  | para 6(1) | 12 Oct 2000 (SI 2000/2800) |
|  | para 6(2), (3) | 19 Feb 2001 (SI 2001/421) |
|  | para 6(4) | 12 Oct 2000 (SI 2000/2800) |
|  | para 7 | 12 Oct 2000 (SI 2000/2800) |
| Schs 15, 16 |  | 19 Feb 2001 (SI 2001/421) |

## Transport Act 2000 (c 38)

*RA:* 30 Nov 2000

*Commencement provisions:* s 275; Transport Act 2000 (Commencement No 1 and Transitional Provisions) Order 2000, SI 2000/3229[1]; Transport Act 2000 (Commencement No 2) Order 2000, SI 2000/3376; Transport Act 2000 (Commencement No 3) Order 2001, SI 2001/57, as amended by SI 2001/115[2]; Transport Act 2000 (Commencement No 4) Order 2001, SI 2001/242; Transport Act 2000 (Commencement No 5) Order 2001, SI 2001/869; Transport Act 2000 (Commencement No 6) Order 2001, SI 2001/1498; Transport Act 2000 (Commencement No 1) (Wales) Order 2001, SI 2001/2788; Transport Act 2000 (Commencement No 7) Order 2001, SI 2001/3342; Transport Act 2000 (Commencement No 8 and Transitional Provisions) Order 2002, SI 2002/658[6], as amended by SI 2002/846; Transport Act 2000 (Commencement No 9 and Transitional Provisions) Order 2002, SI 2002/1014[7]; Transport Act 2000 (Commencement No 10) Order 2003, SI 2003/1694; Transport Act 2000 (Commencement No 2) (Wales) Order 2002, SI 2002/2024; Transport Act 2000 (Commencement No 11) Order 2005, SI 2005/2862; Transport Act 2000 (Commencement No 12) Order 2006, SI 2006/1933

|  |  |  |
|---|---|---|
| 1, 2 |  | 1 Feb 2001 (SI 2001/57) |
| 3 |  | 1 May 2001 (SI 2001/1498) |
| 4–29 |  | 1 Feb 2001 (SI 2001/57) |
| 30 | (1)–(3) | 1 Feb 2001 (SI 2001/57) |
|  | (4) | See Schs 1, 2 below |
|  | (5)–(7) | 1 Feb 2001 (SI 2001/57) |
| 31, 32 |  | 1 Feb 2001 (SI 2001/57) |
| 33 |  | See Sch 3 below |
| 34, 35 |  | 1 Feb 2001 (SI 2001/57) |
| 36, 37 |  | 1 Apr 2001 (SI 2001/869) |
| 38–62 |  | 1 Feb 2001 (SI 2001/57) |
| 63 |  | See Sch 6 below |
| 64 |  | See Sch 7 below |
| 65–96 |  | 1 Feb 2001 (SI 2001/57) |
| 97 |  | See Sch 8 below |
| 98–101 |  | 1 Feb 2001 (SI 2001/57) |
| 102 |  | See Sch 9 below |
| 103–107 |  | 1 Feb 2001 (SI 2001/57) |
| 108–113 |  | 1 Feb 2001 (E) (SI 2001/57) |
|  |  | 1 Aug 2001 (W) (SI 2001/2788) |
| 114–118 |  | 1 Aug 2001 (W) (SI 2001/2788) |
|  |  | 26 Oct 2001 (E) (SI 2001/3342) |
| 119 |  | 1 Feb 2001 (E) (SI 2001/57) |
|  |  | 1 Aug 2001 (W) (SI 2001/2788) |
| 120–123 |  | 1 Aug 2001 (W) (SI 2001/2788) |
|  |  | 26 Oct 2001 (E) (SI 2001/3342) |

**Transport Act 2000 (c 38)**—*contd*

| | | |
|---|---|---|
| 124–127 | | 1 Aug 2001 (W) (in relation to powers to make regulations under specified provisions[3]) (SI 2001/2788) |
| | | 26 Oct 2001 (E) (SI 2001/3342) |
| | | *Not yet in force* (otherwise) |
| 128 | (1)–(3) | 1 Aug 2001 (W) (in relation to powers to make regulations under specified provisions[3]) (SI 2001/2788) |
| | | 26 Oct 2001 (E) (SI 2001/3342) |
| | | *Not yet in force* (otherwise) |
| | (4) | 1 Aug 2001 (W) (SI 2001/2788) |
| | | 26 Oct 2001 (E) (SI 2001/3342) |
| | (5) | 1 Aug 2001 (W) (in relation to powers to make regulations under specified provisions[3]) (SI 2001/2788) |
| | | 26 Oct 2001 (E) (SI 2001/3342) |
| | | *Not yet in force* (otherwise) |
| 129 | | 1 Aug 2001 (W) (in relation to powers to make regulations under specified provisions[3]) (SI 2001/2788) |
| | | 26 Oct 2001 (E) (SI 2001/3342) |
| | | *Not yet in force* (otherwise) |
| 130 | (1)–(7) | 1 Aug 2001 (W) (in relation to powers to make regulations under specified provisions[3]) (SI 2001/2788) |
| | | 26 Oct 2001 (E) (SI 2001/3342) |
| | | *Not yet in force* (otherwise) |
| | (8) | 1 Aug 2001 (W) (SI 2001/2788) |
| | | 26 Oct 2001 (E) (SI 2001/3342) |
| 131 | (1) | 1 Aug 2001 (W) (in relation to powers to make regulations under specified provisions[3]) (SI 2001/2788) |
| | | 26 Oct 2001 (E) (SI 2001/3342) |
| | | *Not yet in force* (otherwise) |
| | (2)–(4) | 1 Aug 2001 (W) (SI 2001/2788) |
| | | 26 Oct 2001 (E) (SI 2001/3342) |
| | (5) | 1 Aug 2001 (W) (in relation to powers to make regulations under specified provisions[3]) (SI 2001/2788) |
| | | 26 Oct 2001 (E) (SI 2001/3342) |
| | | *Not yet in force* (otherwise) |
| 132 | (1)–(4), (5) | 1 Aug 2001 (W) (in relation to powers to make regulations under specified provisions[3]) (SI 2001/2788) |
| | | 26 Oct 2001 (E) (SI 2001/3342) |
| | | *Not yet in force* (otherwise) |
| | (6) | 1 Aug 2001 (W) (SI 2001/2788) |
| | | 26 Oct 2001 (E) (SI 2001/3342) |
| 133, 134 | | 1 Aug 2001 (W) (SI 2001/2788) |
| | | 26 Oct 2001 (E) (SI 2001/3342) |
| 135–143 | | 1 Feb 2001 (E) (SI 2001/57) |
| | | 1 Aug 2001 (W) (SI 2001/2788) |
| 144 | | 1 Feb 2001 (E) (except for purpose of enabling regulations to be made as respects civil penalties for bus lane contraventions in relation to roads in Greater London) (SI 2001/57) |
| | | 1 Aug 2001 (W) (SI 2001/2788) |
| | | 1 Apr 2002 (E) (exception noted above) (SI 2002/658) |
| 145 | (1)–(3) | 1 Jan 2001 (E) (for purposes of s 150) (SI 2000/3229) |
| | | 1 Feb 2001 (E) (for purposes of s 145(4), (5), (7), (8)) (SI 2000/3229) |
| | | 1 Jun 2001 (E) (otherwise) (SI 2000/3229) |
| | | 1 Apr 2002 (W) (SI 2001/2788) |
| | (4), (5) | 1 Feb 2001 (E) (SI 2000/3229) |
| | | 1 Aug 2001 (W) (SI 2001/2788) |
| | (6) | 1 Feb 2001 (E) (for purposes of s 145(4), (5), (7), (8)) (SI 2000/3229) |
| | | 1 Jun 2001 (E) (otherwise) (SI 2000/3229) |
| | | 1 Aug 2001 (W) (SI 2001/2788) |

**Transport Act 2000 (c 38)**—*contd*

| | | |
|---|---|---|
| | (7), (8) | 1 Feb 2001 (E) (SI 2000/3229) |
| | | 1 Aug 2001 (W) (SI 2001/2788) |
| 146 | | 1 Jan 2001 (E) (definition "travel concession authority", and the remainder thereof for the purposes of s 150) (SI 2000/3229) |
| | | 1 Feb 2001 (E) (definition of "disabled person") (SI 2000/3229) |
| | | 1 Jun 2001 (E) (otherwise) (SI 2000/3229) |
| | | 1 Aug 2001 (W) (SI 2001/2788) |
| 147, 148 | | 1 Jun 2001 (E) (SI 2000/3229) |
| | | 1 Aug 2001 (W) (SI 2001/2788) |
| 149 | (1), (2) | 1 Jan 2001 (E) (for purposes of s 150) (SI 2000/3229) |
| | | 1 Jun 2001 (E) (otherwise) (SI 2000/3229) |
| | | 1 Aug 2001 (W) (SI 2001/2788) |
| | (3) | 1 Jan 2001 (E) (SI 2000/3229) |
| | | 1 Aug 2001 (W) (SI 2001/2788) |
| 150 | | 1 Jan 2001 (E) (SI 2000/3229) |
| | | 1 Aug 2001 (W) (SI 2001/2788) |
| 151 | | 1 Apr 2001 (SI 2000/3229) |
| 152 | | 1 Feb 2001 (E) (SI 2001/57) |
| | | 1 Aug 2001 (W) (SI 2001/2788) |
| 153 | | See Sch 10 below |
| 154 | (1)–(5) | 1 Feb 2001 (E) (SI 2000/57) |
| | | 1 Aug 2001 (W) (SI 2001/2788) |
| | (6) | 1 May 2002 (E) (SI 2002/1014)[7] |
| | | 14 Aug 2002 (W) (SI 2002/2024) |
| 155 | | 1 Aug 2001 (W) (SI 2001/2788) |
| | | 1 May 2002 (E) (SI 2002/1014)[7] |
| 156–160 | | 1 Feb 2001 (E) (SI 2001/57) |
| | | 1 Aug 2001 (W) (SI 2001/2788) |
| 161 | | See Sch 11 below |
| 162 | (1) | 1 Jan 2001 (E) (definition "travel concession authority") (SI 2000/3229) |
| | | 1 Feb 2001 (E) (definition "disabled person") (SI 2000/3229) |
| | | 1 Jun 2001 (E) (definitions "elderly person", "eligible service", "half-price travel concession" and "relevant time") (SI 2000/3229) |
| | | 1 Feb 2001 (E) (otherwise) (SI 2001/57) |
| | | 1 Aug 2001 (W) (SI 2001/2788) |
| | (2) | 1 Jun 2001 (E) (so far as relates to meaning of "fares") (SI 2000/3229) |
| | | 1 Feb 2001 (E) (otherwise) (SI 2001/57) |
| | | 1 Aug 2001 (W) (SI 2001/2788) |
| | (3) | 1 Jan 2001 (E) (so far as relates to meaning of "local service") (SI 2000/3229) |
| | | 1 Jun 2001 (E) (so far as relates to meaning of "public passenger transport services") (SI 2000/3229) |
| | | 1 Feb 2001 (E) (otherwise) (SI 2001/57) |
| | | 1 Aug 2001 (W) (SI 2001/2788) |
| | (4) | 1 Feb 2001 (E) (SI 2001/57) |
| | | 1 Aug 2001 (W) (SI 2001/2788) |
| | (5) | 1 Jan 2001 (E) (SI 2000/3229) |
| | | 1 Aug 2001 (W) (SI 2001/2788) |
| | (6), (7) | 1 Feb 2001 (E) (SI 2001/57) |
| | | 1 Aug 2001 (W) (SI 2001/2788) |
| 163 | (1) | 1 Feb 2001 (E) (SI 2001/57) |
| | | 1 Aug 2001 (W) (in relation to powers to make regulations under specified provisions[4]) (SI 2001/2788) |
| | | *Not yet in force* (otherwise) |
| | (2)(a) | 1 Feb 2001 (E) (SI 2001/57) |

**Transport Act 2000 (c 38)**—*contd*

|  |  |  |
|---|---|---|
|  |  | 1 Aug 2001 (W) (in relation to powers to make regulations under specified provisions[4]) (SI 2001/2788) |
|  |  | *Not yet in force* (otherwise) |
|  | (2)(b) | 1 Feb 2001 (E) (SI 2001/57) |
|  |  | 1 Aug 2001 (W) (SI 2001/2788) |
|  | (3)–(6) | 1 Feb 2001 (E) (SI 2001/57) |
|  |  | 1 Aug 2001 (W) (in relation to powers to make regulations under specified provisions[4]) (SI 2001/2788) |
|  |  | *Not yet in force* (otherwise) |
| 164, 165 |  | 1 Feb 2001 (E) (SI 2001/57) |
|  |  | 1 Aug 2001 (W) (in relation to powers to make regulations under specified provisions[4]) (SI 2001/2788) |
|  |  | *Not yet in force* (otherwise) |
| 166 |  | 1 Feb 2001 (E) (SI 2001/57) |
| 167 |  | 1 Feb 2001 (E) (SI 2001/57) |
|  |  | 1 Aug 2001 (W) (in relation to powers to make regulations under specified provisions[4]) (SI 2001/2788) |
|  |  | *Not yet in force* (otherwise) |
| 168 | (1), (2) | 1 Feb 2001 (E) (SI 2001/57) |
|  |  | 1 Aug 2001 (W) (in relation to powers to make regulations under specified provisions[4]) (SI 2001/2788) |
|  |  | *Not yet in force* (otherwise) |
|  | (3) | 1 Feb 2001 (E) (SI 2001/57) |
|  |  | 1 Aug 2001 (W) (SI 2001/2788) |
|  | (4) | 1 Feb 2001 (E) (SI 2001/57) |
|  |  | 1 Aug 2001 (W) (in relation to powers to make regulations under specified provisions[4]) (SI 2001/2788) |
|  |  | *Not yet in force* (otherwise) |
| 169–171 |  | 1 Feb 2001 (E) (SI 2001/57) |
|  |  | 1 Aug 2001 (W) (in relation to powers to make regulations under specified provisions[4]) (SI 2001/2788) |
|  |  | *Not yet in force* (otherwise) |
| 172 | (1) | 1 Feb 2001 (E) (SI 2001/57) |
|  |  | 1 Aug 2001 (W) (SI 2001/2788) |
|  | (2)–(4) | 1 Feb 2001 (E) (SI 2001/57) |
|  |  | 1 Aug 2001 (W) (in relation to powers to make regulations under specified provisions[4]) (SI 2001/2788) |
|  |  | *Not yet in force* (otherwise) (sub-s (3) substituted) |
| 173 | (1)–(4) | 1 Feb 2001 (E) (SI 2001/57) |
|  |  | 1 Aug 2001 (W) (SI 2001/2788) |
|  | (5)–(9) | 1 Feb 2001 (E) (SI 2001/57) |
|  |  | 1 Aug 2001 (W) (in relation to powers to make regulations under specified provisions[4]) (SI 2001/2788) |
|  |  | *Not yet in force* (otherwise) |
| 174 | (1), (2) | 1 Feb 2001 (E) (SI 2001/57) |
|  |  | 1 Aug 2001 (W) (SI 2001/2788) |
|  | (3), (4) | 1 Feb 2001 (E) (SI 2001/57) |
|  |  | 1 Aug 2001 (W) (in relation to powers to make regulations under specified provisions[4]) (SI 2001/2788) |
|  |  | *Not yet in force* (otherwise) |
|  | (5) | 1 Feb 2001 (E) (SI 2001/57) |
|  |  | 1 Aug 2001 (W) (SI 2001/2788) |
|  | (6) | 1 Feb 2001 (E) (SI 2001/57) |
|  |  | 1 Aug 2001 (W) (in relation to powers to make regulations under specified provisions[4]) (SI 2001/2788) |
|  |  | *Not yet in force* (otherwise) |
| 175 | (1) | 1 Feb 2001 (E) (SI 2001/57) |
|  |  | 1 Aug 2001 (W) (SI 2001/2788) |
|  | (2)–(8) | 1 Feb 2001 (E) (SI 2001/57) |

**Transport Act 2000 (c 38)**—*contd*

|  |  |  |
|---|---|---|
|  |  | 1 Aug 2001 (W) (in relation to powers to make regulations under specified provisions[4]) (SI 2001/2788) |
|  |  | *Not yet in force* (otherwise) |
| 176 | (1) | 1 Feb 2001 (E) (SI 2001/57) |
|  |  | 1 Aug 2001 (W) (in relation to powers to make regulations under specified provisions[4]) (SI 2001/2788) |
|  |  | *Not yet in force* (otherwise) |
|  | (2) | 1 Feb 2001 (E) (SI 2001/57) |
|  |  | 1 Aug 2001 (W) (SI 2001/2788) |
|  | (3) | 1 Feb 2001 (E) (SI 2001/57) |
|  |  | 1 Aug 2001 (W) (in relation to powers to make regulations under specified provisions[4]) (SI 2001/2788) |
|  |  | *Not yet in force* (otherwise) |
| 177 |  | 1 Feb 2001 (E) (SI 2001/57) |
|  |  | 1 Aug 2001 (W) (in relation to powers to make regulations under specified provisions[4]) (SI 2001/2788) |
|  |  | *Not yet in force* (otherwise) |
| 178 | (1) | 1 Feb 2001 (E) (SI 2001/57) |
|  |  | 1 Aug 2001 (W) (in relation to powers to make regulations under specified provisions[5]) (SI 2001/2788) |
|  |  | *Not yet in force* (otherwise) |
|  | (2)(a) | 1 Feb 2001 (E) (SI 2001/57) |
|  |  | 1 Aug 2001 (W) (in relation to powers to make regulations under specified provisions[5]) (SI 2001/2788) |
|  |  | *Not yet in force* (otherwise) |
|  | (2)(b) | 1 Feb 2001 (E) (SI 2001/57) |
|  |  | 1 Aug 2001 (W) (SI 2001/2788) |
|  | (3)–(7) | 1 Feb 2001 (E) (SI 2001/57) |
|  |  | 1 Aug 2001 (W) (in relation to powers to make regulations under specified provisions[5]) (SI 2001/2788) |
|  |  | *Not yet in force* (otherwise) |
| 179, 180 |  | 1 Feb 2001 (E) (SI 2001/57) |
|  |  | 1 Aug 2001 (W) (in relation to powers to make regulations under specified provisions[5]) (SI 2001/2788) |
|  |  | *Not yet in force* (otherwise) |
| 181 |  | 1 Feb 2001 (E) (SI 2001/57) |
|  |  | *Not yet in force* (otherwise) |
| 182 | (1)–(4) | 1 Feb 2001 (E) (SI 2001/57) |
|  |  | 1 Aug 2001 (W) (in relation to powers to make regulations under specified provisions[5]) (SI 2001/2788) |
|  |  | *Not yet in force* (otherwise) |
|  | (5) | 1 Feb 2001 (E) (SI 2001/57) |
|  |  | 1 Aug 2001 (W) (SI 2001/2788) |
| 183 | (1), (2) | 1 Feb 2001 (E) (SI 2001/57) |
|  |  | 1 Aug 2001 (W) (in relation to powers to make regulations under specified provisions[5]) (SI 2001/2788) |
|  |  | *Not yet in force* (otherwise) |
|  | (3) | 1 Feb 2001 (E) (SI 2001/57) |
|  |  | 1 Aug 2001 (W) (SI 2001/2788) |
|  | (4) | 1 Feb 2001 (E) (SI 2001/57) |
|  |  | 1 Aug 2001 (W) (in relation to powers to make regulations under specified provisions[5]) (SI 2001/2788) |
|  |  | *Not yet in force* (otherwise) |
| 184–186 |  | 1 Feb 2001 (E) (SI 2001/57) |
|  |  | 1 Aug 2001 (W) (in relation to powers to make regulations under specified provisions[5]) (SI 2001/2788) |
|  |  | *Not yet in force* (otherwise) |
| 187 | (1) | 1 Feb 2001 (E) (SI 2001/57) |
|  |  | 1 Aug 2001 (W) (SI 2001/2788) |
|  | (2)–(4) | 1 Feb 2001 (E) (SI 2001/57) |

**Transport Act 2000 (c 38)**—*contd*

|  |  |  |
|---|---|---|
|  |  | 1 Aug 2001 (W) (in relation to powers to make regulations under specified provisions[5]) (SI 2001/2788) |
|  |  | *Not yet in force* (otherwise) |
| 188 |  | 1 Feb 2001 (E) (SI 2001/57) |
|  |  | 1 Aug 2001 (W) (in relation to powers to make regulations under specified provisions[5]) (SI 2001/2788) |
|  |  | *Not yet in force* (otherwise) |
| 189 | (1), (2) | 1 Feb 2001 (E) (SI 2001/57) |
|  |  | 1 Aug 2001 (W) (SI 2001/2788) |
|  | (3)(a) | 1 Feb 2001 (E) (SI 2001/57) |
|  |  | 1 Aug 2001 (W) (in relation to powers to make regulations under specified provisions[5]) (SI 2001/2788) |
|  |  | *Not yet in force* (otherwise) |
|  | (3)(b) | 1 Feb 2001 (E) (SI 2001/57) |
|  |  | 1 Aug 2001 (W) (SI 2001/2788) |
|  | (4) | 1 Feb 2001 (E) (SI 2001/57) |
|  |  | 1 Aug 2001 (W) (SI 2001/2788) |
| 190 |  | 1 Feb 2001 (E) (SI 2001/57) |
|  |  | 1 Aug 2001 (W) (in relation to powers to make regulations under specified provisions[5]) (SI 2001/2788) |
|  |  | *Not yet in force* (otherwise) |
| 191 |  | See Sch 12 below |
| 192–198 |  | 1 Feb 2001 (E) (SI 2001/57) |
|  |  | 1 Aug 2001 (W) (SI 2001/2788) |
| 199 |  | See Sch 13 below |
| 200 |  | 1 Feb 2001 (E) (SI 2001/57) |
|  |  | 1 Aug 2001 (W) (SI 2001/2788) |
| 201–203 |  | 15 Jan 2001 (SI 2000/3376) |
| 204 |  | See Sch 14 below |
| 205–210 |  | 15 Jan 2001 (SI 2000/3376) |
| 211 |  | See Sch 15 below |
| 212–214 |  | 1 Feb 2001 (SI 2001/57) |
| 215 | (1) | See Sch 16 below |
|  | (2)–(9) | 1 Feb 2001 (SI 2001/57) |
| 216 |  | See Sch 17 below |
| 217 |  | See Sch 18 below |
| 218 |  | See Sch 19 below |
| 219 | (1), (2) | 1 Feb 2001 (SI 2001/57) |
|  | (3) | See Sch 20 below |
|  | (4) | 1 Feb 2001 (SI 2001/57) |
| 220 |  | See Sch 21 below |
| 221 |  | 1 Feb 2001 (SI 2000/57) |
| 222 |  | 15 Jan 2001 (SI 2000/3376) |
| 223 |  | 15 Oct 2005 (SI 2005/2862) |
| 224–226 |  | 1 Feb 2001 (SI 2001/57) |
| 227 | (1) | 1 Feb 2001 (SI 2001/57) |
|  | (2) | See Sch 22 below |
|  | (3) | 1 Feb 2001 (SI 2001/57) |
| 228 |  | 29 Jul 2003 (SI 2003/1694) |
| 229 |  | See Sch 23 below |
| 230 |  | 1 Feb 2001 (SI 2001/57) |
| 231 |  | 30 Nov 2000 (s 275(4)) |
| 232–240 |  | 1 Feb 2001 (SI 2001/57) |
| 241 |  | 15 Jan 2001 (SI 2000/3376) |
| 242–244 |  | 1 Feb 2001 (SI 2001/57) |
| 245 | (1) | 10 May 2000 (s 275(5)) |
|  | (2) | 10 May 2000 (so far as relates to sub-ss (3)–(5)) (s 275(5)) |
|  |  | 1 Feb 2001 (otherwise) (SI 2001/57) |
|  | (3)–(5) | 10 May 2000 (s 275(5)) |

**Transport Act 2000 (c 38)**—*contd*

|  |  |  |
|---|---|---|
|  | (6), (7) | 1 Feb 2001 (SI 2001/57) |
|  | (8) | 10 May 2000 (so far as relates to sub-ss (3)–(5)) (s 275(5)) |
|  |  | 1 Feb 2001 (otherwise) (SI 2001/57) |
| 246, 247 |  | 1 Feb 2001 (SI 2001/57) |
| 248 |  | 1 Oct 2006 (SI 2006/1933) |
| 249 |  | 1 Feb 2001 (SI 2001/57) |
| 250 |  | See Sch 26 below |
| 251 |  | 1 Feb 2001 (SI 2001/57) |
| 252 |  | See Sch 27 below |
| 253 |  | See Sch 28 below |
| 254 |  | 30 Jan 2001 (SI 2001/57) |
| 255, 256 |  | 1 Feb 2001 (SI 2001/57) |
| 257 |  | 1 May 2002 (SI 2002/1014) |
| 258, 259 |  | 1 Apr 2002 (SI 2002/658) |
| 260 |  | See Sch 29 below |
| 261 |  | 1 Feb 2001 (SI 2001/57) |
| 262 | (1) | 1 Feb 2001 (SI 2001/57) |
|  | (2) | See Sch 30 below |
| 263 |  | *Not yet in force* |
| 264 |  | 1 Feb 2001 (SI 2001/57) |
| 265 |  | 1 Jul 2001 (SI 2001/1498) |
| 266 |  | 1 Feb 2001 (SI 2001/57) |
| 267 | (1) | See sub-ss (2)–(8) below |
|  | (2) | 1 Apr 2002 (SI 2002/658) |
|  | (3) | 1 Feb 2001 (E) (for the purposes of making regulations with regard to appeals under Greater London Authority Act 1999, s 189 made after the date on which s 267 is fully in force) (SI 2001/57) |
|  |  | 1 Apr 2002 (otherwise) (SI 2002/658) |
|  | (4) | 1 Apr 2002 (SI 2002/658) |
|  | (5) | 1 Feb 2001 (E) (for the purposes of making regulations with regard to appeals under Greater London Authority Act 1999, s 189 made after the date on which s 267 is fully in force) (SI 2001/57) |
|  |  | 1 Apr 2002 (otherwise) (SI 2002/658) |
|  | (6), (7) | 1 Apr 2002 (SI 2002/658) |
|  | (8) | 1 Feb 2001 (E) (for the purposes of making regulations with regard to appeals under Greater London Authority Act 1999, s 189 made after the date on which s 267 is fully in force) (SI 2001/57) |
|  |  | 1 Apr 2002 (otherwise) (SI 2002/658) |
| 268 |  | 1 Feb 2001 (SI 2001/57) |
| 269 |  | 30 Nov 2000 (s 275(4)) |
| 270 |  | 30 Jan 2001 (SI 2001/57) |
| 271–273 |  | 1 Feb 2001 (SI 2001/57) |
| 274 |  | See Sch 31 below |
| 275–280 |  | 30 Nov 2000 (RA) |
| Schs 1–3 |  | 1 Feb 2001 (SI 2001/57) |
| Schs 4, 5 |  | 1 Apr 2001 (SI 2001/869) |
| Schs 6, 7 |  | 1 Feb 2001 (SI 2000/57) |
| Sch 8 | paras 1, 2 | 1 Feb 2001 (SI 2001/57) |
|  | paras 3–10 | 1 Apr 2001 (SI 2001/869) |
|  | paras 11–17 | 1 Feb 2001 (SI 2001/57) |
|  | para 18 | 1 Apr 2001 (SI 2001/869) |
|  | para 19 | 1 Feb 2001 (SI 2001/57) |
| Sch 9 |  | 1 Feb 2001 (SI 2001/57) |
| Sch 10 | para 1(1)(a) | 26 Oct 2001 (E) (SI 2001/3342) |
|  |  | *Not yet in force* (otherwise) |
|  | para 1(1)(b), (c) | 1 Feb 2001 (E) (SI 2001/57) |

**Transport Act 2000 (c 38)**—*contd*

|  |  |  |
|---|---|---|
|  |  | 1 Aug 2001 (W) (SI 2001/2788) |
|  | para 1(2)(a) | 26 Oct 2001 (E) (SI 2001/3342) |
|  |  | *Not yet in force* (otherwise) |
|  | para 1(2)(b), (c) | 1 Feb 2001 (E) (SI 2001/57) |
|  |  | 1 Aug 2001 (W) (SI 2001/2788) |
|  | paras 2–11 | 1 Feb 2001 (E) (SI 2001/57) |
|  |  | 1 Aug 2001 (W) (SI 2001/2788) |
|  | para 12(1) | 1 Feb 2001 (E) (SI 2001/57) |
|  |  | 1 Aug 2001 (W) (SI 2001/2788) |
|  | para 12(2) | 1 Feb 2001 (E) (except words "a quality partnership scheme or") (SI 2001/57) |
|  |  | 1 Aug 2001 (W) (except words "a quality partnership scheme or") (SI 2001/2788) |
|  |  | 26 Oct 2001 (E) (exception noted above) (SI 2001/3342) |
|  |  | *Not yet in force* (W) (exception noted above) |
|  | para 12(3)–(5) | 1 Feb 2001 (E) (SI 2001/57) |
|  |  | 1 Aug 2001 (W) (SI 2001/2788) |
|  | paras 13–16 | 1 Feb 2001 (E) (SI 2001/57) |
|  |  | 1 Aug 2001 (W) (SI 2001/2788) |
| Sch 11 | para 1 | 1 Aug 2001 (W) (SI 2001/2788) |
|  |  | 26 Oct 2001 (E) (SI 2001/3342) |
|  | paras 2–5 | 1 Feb 2001 (E) (SI 2001/57) |
|  |  | 1 Aug 2001 (W) (SI 2001/2788) |
|  | paras 6–8 | 1 Aug 2001 (W) (SI 2001/2788) |
|  |  | 26 Oct 2001 (E) (SI 2001/3342) |
|  | para 9 | 1 Feb 2001 (E) (SI 2001/57) |
|  |  | 1 Aug 2001 (W) (SI 2001/2788) |
|  | para 10(1) | 1 Feb 2001 (E) (SI 2001/57) |
|  |  | 1 Aug 2001 (W) (SI 2001/2788) |
|  | para 10(2) | 1 Aug 2001 (W) (SI 2001/2788) |
|  |  | 26 Oct 2001 (E) (SI 2001/3342) |
|  | para 10(3) | 1 Feb 2001 (E) (SI 2001/57) |
|  |  | 1 Aug 2001 (W) (SI 2001/2788) |
|  | paras 11–13 | 1 Feb 2001 (E) (SI 2001/57) |
|  |  | 1 Aug 2001 (W) (SI 2001/2788) |
|  | para 14 | 1 Aug 2001 (W) (SI 2001/2788) |
|  |  | 26 Oct 2001 (E) (SI 2001/3342) |
|  | paras 15–19 | 1 Jun 2001 (E) (SI 2000/3229) |
|  |  | 1 Apr 2002 (W) (SI 2001/2788) |
|  | para 20 | 1 Apr 2002 (SI 2001/2788) |
|  | para 21 | 1 Aug 2001 (W) (SI 2001/2788) |
|  |  | 26 Oct 2001 (E) (SI 2001/3342) |
|  | para 22(1) | 1 Feb 2001 (E) (except entry relating to Transport Act 1985, s 111(1)(b)) (SI 2001/57) |
|  |  | 1 Aug 2001 (W) (SI 2001/2788) |
|  |  | 26 Oct 2001 (E) (exception noted above) (SI 2001/3342) |
|  | para 22(2) | 1 Feb 2001 (E) (except entry relating to Transport Act 1985, s 111(1)(b)) (SI 2001/57) |
|  |  | 20 Feb 2001 (E) (so far as relates to words "operated a local service in contravention of that section" in Transport Act 1985, s 111(1)(b)) (SI 2001/242) |
|  |  | 26 Oct 2001 (E) (so far as relates to words "or section 118(4) or 129(1)(b) of the Transport Act 2000; or" in Transport Act 1985, s 111(1)(b)) (SI 2001/3342) |
|  |  | 1 Aug 2001 (W) (SI 2001/2788) |
|  | para 23 | 1 Apr 2001 (SI 2000/3229) |
| Sch 12 |  | 1 Feb 2001 (E) (SI 2001/57) |
|  |  | *Not yet in force* (W) |
| Sch 13 |  | 1 Feb 2001 (E) (SI 2001/57) |

**Transport Act 2000 (c 38)**—*contd*

| | | |
|---|---|---|
| Sch 14 | | 15 Jan 2001 (SI 2000/3376) |
| Sch 15 | | 30 Jan 2001 (SI 2001/57) |
| Sch 16 | | 1 Feb 2001 (SI 2001/57) |
| Sch 17 | Pts I, II | 1 Feb 2001 (SI 2001/57) |
| | Pt III | 30 Jan 2001 (SI 2001/57) |
| Sch 18 | | 1 Feb 2001 (SI 2001/57) |
| Sch 19 | | 30 Jan 2001 (SI 2001/57) |
| Schs 20–23 | | 1 Feb 2001 (SI 2001/57) |
| Sch 24 | | 30 Nov 2000 (s 275(4)) |
| Sch 25 | | 1 Feb 2001 (SI 2001/57) |
| Sch 26 | | 15 Jan 2001 (SI 2000/3376) |
| Sch 27 | paras 1–15 | 1 Feb 2001 (SI 2001/57) |
| | para 16 | *Not yet in force* |
| | paras 17–49 | 1 Feb 2001 (SI 2001/57) |
| | para 50 | 15 Jan 2001 (SI 2000/3376) |
| | paras 51–63 | 1 Feb 2001 (SI 2001/57) |
| Sch 28 | | 30 Nov 2000 (s 275(4)) |
| Sch 29 | para 1 | See paras 2–12 below |
| | paras 2–6 | *Not yet in force* |
| | paras 7–12 | 1 Apr 2002[6] (SI 2002/658) |
| Sch 30 | | 1 Feb 2001 (SI 2001/57) |
| Sch 31 | Pt I | 1 Apr 2001 (SI 2001/869) |
| | Pt II | 1 Feb 2001 (E) (SI 2001/57), repeals of or in— |

Transport Act 1968;
Transport Act 1983;
Local Government Act 1985;
Transport Act 1985 (except ss 94(4), 104(2), 108(1), 110, 111, 112(2))
1 Apr 2001 (repeals in Greater London Authority Act 1999) (SI 2000/3229)
1 Jun 2001 (E) (SI 2000/3229), revocations in—
SI 1986/1385;
SI 1989/2293
26 Oct 2001 (E) (repeal in Transport Act 1985, s 104(2)) (SI 2001/3342)
1 May 2002 (E) (SI 2002/1014), repeals of or in—
Finance Act 1965;
Finance Act 1974;
Excise Duties (Surcharges or Rebates) Act 1979;
Magistrates' Courts Act 1980;
Finance Act 1981;
Transport Act 1985, ss 94(4), 110, 111[7], 112(2);
Transport Act 2000
14 Aug 2002 (W) (SI 2002/2024)
*Not yet in force* (E), repeals of or in—
Transport Act 1985, 108(1);
London Local Authorities Act 1996;
London Local Authorities Act 2000

| | | |
|---|---|---|
| | Pt III | 1 Feb 2001 (E) (SI 2001/57) |
| | Pt IV | 15 Jan 2001 (repeals of or in Railways Act 1993, ss 7(10), 113) (SI 2000/3376) |

1 Feb 2001 (SI 2001/57), repeals of or in—
British Transport Commission Act 1949;
British Transport Commission Act 1962;
Transport Act 1962, s 1(3);
Harbours Act 1964;
Docks and Harbours Act 1966;
Parliamentary Commissioner Act 1967;
Transport (Grants) Act 1972;

**Transport Act 2000 (c 38)**—*contd*

House of Commons Disqualification Act 1975 (except entry in Sch 1, Pt II, relating to British Railways Board);

Channel Tunnel Act 1987, ss 40, 42;

Transport and Works Act 1992;

Railways Act 1993 (except entries relating to ss 7(10), 84–116, 129, Schs 7–9, Sch 12, paras 5, 6(2)–(5), 32;

Railway Pensions (Protection and Designation of Schemes) Order 1994, SI 1994/1432;

Competition Act 1998;

Greater London Authority Act 1999;

Parliamentary Commissioner Order 1999, SI 1999/277;

Scotland Act 1998 (Transfer of Functions to the Scottish Ministers etc) Order 1999, SI 1999/1750

15 Oct 2005 (repeal of Railways Act 1993, s 129) (SI 2005/2862)

*Not yet in force*, repeals of or in—

Transport Act 1962, ss 1(1), 3–4A, 12(1), 13(1A), (9)–(12), 14(4), 18(6), 19(6), 21A, 22, 27(2), (7), (8), 31(2), (6), 32(6), 52(2), 54(1), 65(1), (4), 67, First Schedule, para 3, Sixth Schedule, para 1(5), Seventh Schedule, paras 23, 24;

Transport Act 1968;

Post Office Act 1969;

Railways Act 1974;

House of Commons Disqualification Act 1975, Sch 1, Pt II;

Northern Ireland Assembly Disqualification Act 1975;

Transport Act 1978;

Transport Act 1980;

Transport Act 1981;

Transport (Finance) Act 1982;

National Audit Act 1983, Sch 4, Pt I;

Transport Act 1985;

Channel Tunnel Act 1987, ss 22, 39, 41(1), (2), (4), Sch 6, para 6;

British Railways Board (Finance) Act 1991;

Heathrow Express Railway Act 1991;

Railways Act 1993, ss 84–112, 114–116, Sch 7, paras 2(7), 7(3), (4), Schs 8, 9, Sch 12, paras 5, 6(2)–(5), 32;

Railways Act 1993 (Consequential Modifications) (No 2) Order 1994, SI 1994/1649;

Employment Rights Act 1996;

Freedom of Information Act 2000

*Never in force* (repeals in Railway Heritage Act 1996) (repealed)

Pt V(1)    1 Apr 2002 (repeals of or in Road Traffic Act 1988, ss 130, 131(5), Sch 3)[6] (SI 2002/658)

*Not yet in force*, repeals of or in—

Road Traffic Act 1988, ss 89(2A), (5A), 97(3), (3A), (3B), 98(3), 108(1);

Road Traffic (Driving Licensing and Information Systems) Act 1989

Pt V(2)    *Not yet in force*

---

[1]   For transitional provisions, see SI 2000/3229, arts 3, 4

[2]   For transitional provisions and savings, see SI 2001/57, Sch 2, Pt II, Sch 3, Pt II

[3]   The specified provisions are ss 128(4), 130(8), 131(2)–(4), 132(6), 133 and 134 of this Act

[4]   The specified provisions are ss 163(2)(b), 168(3), 172(1), 173(1)–(4), 174(1), (2), (5), 175(1), and 176(2) of this Act

[5]   The specified provisions are ss 178(2)(b), 182(5), 183(3), 187(1), 189(1), (2), (3)(b), and (4) of this Act

[6]   For transitional provisions, see SI 2002/658, art 3

**Transport Act 2000 (c 38)**—*contd*
[7]    For transitional provisions, see SI 2002/1014, art 3

---

**Trustee Act 2000 (c 29)**

*RA:* 23 Nov 2000

*Commencement provisions:* s 42(1)–(3); Trustee Act 2000 (Commencement) Order 2001, SI 2001/49

| | |
|---|---|
| 1–40 | 1 Feb 2001 (SI 2001/49) |
| 41–43 | 23 Nov 2000 (RA) |
| Schs 1–4 | 1 Feb 2001 (SI 2001/49) |

---

**Utilities Act 2000 (c 27)**

*RA:* 28 Jul 2000

*Commencement provisions:* s 110(2); Utilities Act 2000 (Commencement No 1 and Saving) Order 2000, SI 2000/2412; Utilities Act 2000 (Commencement No 2) Order 2000, SI 2000/2917; Utilities Act 2000 (Commencement No 3 and Transitional Provisions) Order 2000, SI 2000/2974[1]; Utilities Act 2000 (Commencement No 4 and Transitional Provisions) Order 2000, SI 2000/3343[2], as amended by SI 2001/1780; Utilities Act 2000 (Commencement No 5 and Transitional Provisions) Order 2001, SI 2001/1781[3]; Utilities Act 2000 (Commencement No 6 and Transitional Provisions) Order 2001, SI 2001/3266[4]

| | | |
|---|---|---|
| 1 | (1), (2) | 1 Nov 2000 (SI 2000/2917) |
| | (3) | 1 Oct 2001 (SI 2001/3266) |
| | (4) | 1 Nov 2000 (SI 2000/2917) |
| 2 | (1), (2) | 1 Nov 2000 (SI 2000/2917) |
| | (3) | 7 Nov 2000 (SI 2000/2974) |
| | (4) | 1 Nov 2000 (SI 2000/2917) |
| 3 | (1), (2) | 20 Dec 2000 (SI 2000/3343) |
| | (3)–(5) | 1 Nov 2000 (SI 2000/2917) |
| | (6), (7) | 7 Nov 2000 (SI 2000/2974) |
| | (8) | 1 Nov 2000 (SI 2000/2917) |
| 4 | | 7 Nov 2000 (for purpose of requiring the Gas Consumers' Council to prepare and publish its forward work programme) (SI 2000/2974) |
| | | 20 Dec 2000 (otherwise) (SI 2000/3343) |
| 5 | (1)–(9) | 20 Dec 2000 (SI 2000/3343) |
| | (10) | 20 Dec 2000 (subject to saving in respect of Sch 7, para 29) (SI 2000/3343) |
| | | 1 Oct 2001 (otherwise) (SI 2001/3266) |
| 6–16 | | 20 Dec 2000 (SI 2000/3343) |
| 17 | | 7 Nov 2000 (SI 2000/2974) |
| 18 | (1)–(4) | 7 Nov 2000 (SI 2000/2974) |
| | (5), (6) | 20 Dec 2000 (SI 2000/3343) |
| | (7) | 7 Nov 2000 (SI 2000/2974) |
| 19 | (1)–(3) | 7 Nov 2000 (SI 2000/2974) |
| | (4)(a) | 7 Nov 2000 (SI 2000/2974)[1] |
| | (4)(b) | 20 Dec 2000 (SI 2000/3343) |
| | (5), (6) | 7 Nov 2000 (SI 2000/2974)[1] |
| 20 | (1)–(4) | 7 Nov 2000 (SI 2000/2974) |
| | (5), (6) | 7 Nov 2000 (for purpose of requiring the Gas Consumers' Council to publish statistical information in relation to complaints made by consumers) (SI 2000/2974)[1] |
| | | 1 Oct 2001 (otherwise) (SI 2001/3266) |
| | (7) | *Not yet in force* |
| 21 | (1)–(3) | 7 Nov 2000 (SI 2000/2974) |
| | (4)(a) | 7 Nov 2000 (SI 2000/2974)[1] |
| | (4)(b) | 20 Dec 2000 (SI 2000/3343) |

**Utilities Act 2000 (c 27)**—*contd*

|  |  |  |
|--|--|--|
| | (5) | 7 Nov 2000 (SI 2000/2974)[1] |
| 22, 23 | | 7 Nov 2000 (SI 2000/2974)[1] |
| 24 | (1)–(3) | 7 Nov 2000 (for purpose of enabling the Council to direct gas or electricity licence holder to supply information to it) (SI 2000/2974) |
| | | 20 Dec 2000 (otherwise) (SI 2000/3343) |
| | (4) | 20 Dec 2000 (SI 2000/3343) |
| 25, 26 | | 20 Dec 2000 (SI 2000/3343) |
| 27 | (1) | 29 Sep 2000 (so far as relates to the power to make regulations) (SI 2000/2412) |
| | | 7 Nov 2000 (so far as not already in force) (SI 2000/2974) |
| | (2) | 29 Sep 2000 (so far as relates to the power to make regulations) (SI 2000/2412) |
| | | 20 Dec 2000 (otherwise) (SI 2000/3343) |
| | (3)–(7) | 29 Sep 2000 (so far as they relate to the power to make regulations) (SI 2000/2412) |
| | | 7 Nov 2000 (so far as not already in force) (SI 2000/2974) |
| 28 | (1), (2) | 1 Oct 2001 (SI 2001/3266) |
| | (3)(a) | 7 Nov 2000 (for purpose of defining a "distribution system" wherever it occurs in Pt III (ss 7–27) of this Act) (SI 2000/2974) |
| | | 20 Dec 2000 (for purpose of defining a "distribution system" where that term is used in Pts I, II) (SI 2000/3343) |
| | | 1 Oct 2001 (otherwise) (SI 2001/3266) |
| | (3)(b) | 1 Oct 2001 (SI 2001/3266) |
| 29 | | 1 Oct 2001 (SI 2001/3266) |
| 30 | | 16 May 2001 (SI 2001/1781)[3], for purpose of enabling the Gas and Electricity Markets Authority to make regulations prescribing— |
| | | (i) the form and manner in which an application for a generation licence, transmission licence, distribution licence or supply licence, as defined in Electricity Act 1989, s 6(1) or an application for the extension or restriction of a distribution or supply licence is to be made; |
| | | (ii) the information, documents and any fee which should accompany any application; and |
| | | (iii) the period within which, after the making of the application, the applicant shall publish a notice of the application and the manner of that publication |
| | | 1 Oct 2001 (otherwise) (SI 2001/3266)[4] |
| 31 | | 1 Oct 2001 (SI 2001/3266) |
| 32 | (1) | 20 Dec 2000 (as far as relates to sub-s (2) of this section) (SI 2000/3343) |
| | | 16 May 2001 (for the purpose of the determination by the Secretary of State of standard licence conditions pursuant to s 33(1) of this Act) (SI 2001/1781) |
| | | 1 Oct 2001 (otherwise) (SI 2001/3266)[4] |
| | (2) | 20 Dec 2000 (SI 2000/3343) |
| | (3)–(8) | 16 May 2001 (for the purpose of the determination by the Secretary of State of standard licence conditions pursuant to s 33(1) of this Act) (SI 2001/1781) |
| | | 1 Oct 2001 (otherwise) (SI 2001/3266)[4] |
| 33 | (1), (2) | 16 May 2001 (SI 2001/1781) |
| | (3) | 1 Oct 2001 (SI 2001/3266) |
| 34 | | 1 Oct 2001 (SI 2001/3266) |
| 35 | | 16 May 2001 (for the purpose of enabling the Secretary of State to make an order prescribing the percentages and weighting referred to in Electricity Act 1989, s 11A(6), (7) respectively) (SI 2001/1781) |
| | | 1 Oct 2001 (otherwise) (SI 2001/3266) |

## Utilities Act 2000 (c 27)—*contd*

| | | |
|---|---|---|
| 36–45 | | 1 Oct 2001 (SI 2001/3266)[4] |
| 46 | (1) | 16 May 2001 (for purposes of enabling the Secretary of State to consult with the Gas and Electricity Markets Authority and to make regulations relating to the recovery and application of reasonably incurred expenditure by an electricity distributor as provided for in Electricity Act 1989, s 19(2), (3)) (SI 2001/1781) |
| | | 1 Oct 2001 (otherwise) (SI 2001/3266)[4] |
| | (2) | 1 Oct 2001 (SI 2001/3266)[4] |
| | (3)–(5) | 16 May 2001 (for purposes of enabling the Secretary of State to consult with the Gas and Electricity Markets Authority and to make regulations relating to the recovery and application of reasonably incurred expenditure by an electricity distributor as provided for in Electricity Act 1989, s 19(2), (3)) (SI 2001/1781)[3] |
| | | 1 Oct 2001 (otherwise) (SI 2001/3266)[4] |
| 47–50 | | 1 Oct 2001 (SI 2001/3266)[4] |
| 51 | (1) | 1 Oct 2001 (SI 2001/3266)[4] |
| | (2) | See Sch 4 below |
| 52 | | See Sch 5 below |
| 53 | | 1 Oct 2001 (SI 2001/3266) |
| 54 | (1) | 1 Oct 2001 (SI 2001/3266)[4] |
| | (2) | 16 May 2001 (for the purpose of enabling the Gas and Electricity Markets Authority to make and the Secretary of State to consent to the making of regulations prescribing standards of performance in connection with the activities of electricity distributors as provided for in Electricity Act 1989, s 39A and the person (where this is not the Authority) by whom a reference shall be determined and the practice and procedure to be followed in connection with any determination of any dispute arising under Electricity Act 1989, ss 39 or 39A or regulations made under either of those sections, as provided for in Electricity Act 1989, s 39B) (SI 2001/1781) |
| | | 1 Oct 2001 (otherwise) (SI 2001/3266) |
| 55 | | 16 May 2001 (for purpose of enabling the Gas and Electricity Markets Authority to determine and arrange for the publication of overall standards of performance in connection with the activities of electricity distributors as provided for in Electricity Act 1989, s 40A(1), (2)) (SI 2001/1781) |
| | | 1 Oct 2001 (otherwise) (SI 2001/3266) |
| 56 | | 16 May 2001 (for purpose of enabling the Gas and Electricity Markets Authority to comply with the procedures for prescribing or determining standards of performance required by Electricity Act 1989, s 40B) (SI 2001/1781) |
| | | 1 Oct 2001 (otherwise) (SI 2001/3266) |
| 57 | | 1 Oct 2001 (SI 2001/3266) |
| 58 | | 16 May 2001 (for purpose of enabling the Gas and Electricity Markets Authority to make regulations as provided for in Electricity Act 1989, s 42A) (SI 2001/1781)[3] |
| | | 1 Oct 2001 (otherwise) (SI 2001/3266)[4] |
| 59 | (1) | 20 Dec 2000 (for purposes of enabling the Secretary of State to make an order determining turnover and enabling the Authority to consult upon, prepare and publish a statement of policy with respect to the imposition of penalties and the determination of their amount) (SI 2000/3343) |
| | | 1 Oct 2001 (otherwise) (SI 2001/3266) |
| | (2), (3) | 1 Oct 2001 (SI 2001/3266) |
| 60, 61 | | 1 Oct 2001 (SI 2001/3266)[4] |

**Utilities Act 2000 (c 27)**—*contd*

| | | |
|---|---|---|
| 62 | | 16 May 2001 (for the purpose of enabling the Secretary of State to undertake the consultation required by Electricity Act 1989, s 32(7) before an order may be made by him under s 32(1) of that Act) (SI 2001/1781)[3] |
| | | 1 Oct 2001 (otherwise) (SI 2001/3266) |
| 63–65 | | 1 Oct 2001 (SI 2001/3266) |
| 66 | | 21 Nov 2000 (subject to a saving) (SI 2000/2412) |
| 67 | | 29 Sep 2000 (SI 2000/2412) |
| 68 | | 28 Jul 2000 (RA) |
| 69–73 | | 1 Oct 2001 (SI 2001/3266) |
| 74 | (1) | See sub-ss (2)–(7) below |
| | (2) | 1 Oct 2001 (SI 2001/3266)[4] |
| | (3) | 20 Dec 2000 (SI 2000/3343) |
| | (4)–(6) | 16 May 2001 (for purpose of the determination by the Secretary of State of standard licence conditions pursuant to s 81(2) of the 2000 Act) (SI 2001/1781) |
| | | 1 Oct 2001 (otherwise) (SI 2001/3266)[4] |
| | (7) | 16 May 2001 (SI 2001/1781), for purpose of enabling the Gas and Electricity Markets Authority to make regulations prescribing— |
| | | (i) the form and manner in which an application for the grant, extension or restriction of a licence under Gas Act 1986, s 7 or s 7A is to be made; |
| | | (ii) the information, documents and fee which accompany any application; and |
| | | (iii) the period within which, after the making of the application, the applicant should publish a notice of the application and the manner of that publication |
| | | 1 Oct 2001 (otherwise) (SI 2001/3266)[4] |
| 75 | | *Not yet in force* |
| 76–80 | | 1 Oct 2001 (SI 2001/3266) |
| 81 | (1), (2) | 16 May 2001 (SI 2001/1781) |
| | (3) | 1 Oct 2001 (SI 2001/3266) |
| 82 | (1)–(3) | 1 Oct 2001 (SI 2001/3266) |
| | (4) | 16 May 2001 (for the purpose of enabling the Secretary of State to make an order prescribing the percentages and weighting referred to in Gas Act 1986, s 23(7), (8) respectively) (SI 2001/1781)[3] |
| | | 1 Oct 2001 (otherwise) (SI 2001/3266) |
| 83–89 | | 1 Oct 2001 (SI 2001/3266) |
| 90 | (1) | 1 Oct 2001 (SI 2001/3266) |
| | (2) | 16 May 2001 (for the purpose of enabling the Gas and Electricity Markets Authority to make and the Secretary of State to consent to the making of regulations prescribing standards of performance in connection with the activities of gas transporters as provided for in Gas Act 1986, s 33AA and the person (where this is not an Authority) by whom a reference shall be determined and the practice and procedure to be followed in connection with any determination of any dispute arising under Gas Act 1986, ss 33A or 33AA or regulations made under either of those sections, as provided for in Gas Act 1986, s 33AB) (SI 2001/1781) |
| | | 1 Oct 2001 (otherwise) (SI 2001/3266) |
| 91 | | 16 May 2001 (for the purpose of enabling the Gas and Electricity Markets Authority to determine and arrange for the publication of overall standards of performance in connection with the activities of gas transporters as provided for in Gas Act 1986, s 33BA) (SI 2001/1781) |
| | | 1 Oct 2001 (otherwise) (SI 2001/3266) |

**Utilities Act 2000 (c 27)**—*contd*

| | | |
|---|---|---|
| 92 | | 16 May 2001 (for purpose of enabling the Gas and Electricity Markets Authority to comply with the procedures for prescribing or determining standards of performance required by Gas Act 1986, s 33BAA) (SI 2001/1781) |
| | | 1 Oct 2001 (otherwise) (SI 2001/3266) |
| 93 | | 1 Oct 2001 (SI 2001/3266) |
| 94 | | 16 May 2001 (for purpose of enabling the Gas and Electricity Markets Authority to make regulations as provided for in Gas Act 1986, s 33D) (SI 2001/1781)[3] |
| | | 1 Oct 2001 (otherwise) (SI 2001/3266) |
| 95 | (1) | 20 Dec 2000 (for purposes of enabling the Secretary of State to make an order determining turnover and enabling the Authority to consult upon, prepare and publish a statement of policy with respect to the imposition of penalties and the determination of their amount) (SI 2000/3343) |
| | | 1 Oct 2001 (otherwise) (SI 2001/3266) |
| | (2)–(5) | 1 Oct 2001 (SI 2001/3266) |
| 96–99 | | 1 Oct 2001 (SI 2001/3266)[4] |
| 100 | | 20 Dec 2000 (SI 2000/3343) |
| 101–103 | | 1 Oct 2001 (SI 2001/3266) |
| 104 | | 16 May 2001 (SI 2001/1781) |
| 105 | (1)–(7) | 7 Nov 2000 (SI 2000/2974) |
| | (8)(a) | 7 Nov 2000 (SI 2000/2974) |
| | (8)(b) | 20 Dec 2000 (SI 2000/3343) |
| | (8)(c) | 7 Nov 2000 (SI 2000/2974) |
| | (9)–(12) | 7 Nov 2000 (SI 2000/2974) |
| 106, 107 | | 29 Sep 2000 (SI 2000/2412) |
| 108 | | See Schs 6–8 below |
| 109 | | 29 Sep 2000 (SI 2000/2412) |
| 110 | | 28 Jul 2000 (RA) |
| Sch 1 | | 1 Nov 2000 (SI 2000/2917) |
| Sch 2 | paras 1–9 | 1 Nov 2000 (SI 2000/2917) |
| | paras 10–14 | 7 Nov 2000 (SI 2000/2974) |
| | paras 15–17 | 1 Nov 2000 (SI 2000/2917) |
| Sch 3 | | 1 Nov 2000 (SI 2000/2917) |
| Sch 4 | | 20 Dec 2000 (for purpose of inserting Electricity Act 1989, Sch 6, para 3(1), (6)–(10)) (SI 2000/3343) |
| | | 1 Oct 2001 (otherwise) (SI 2001/3266)[4] |
| Sch 5 | para 1 | 16 May 2001 (for purpose of enabling the Gas and Electricity Markets Authority to make and the Secretary of State to consent to the making of regulations under Electricity Act 1989, Sch 7, para 1(1A)) (SI 2001/1781) |
| | | 1 Oct 2001 (otherwise) (SI 2001/3266) |
| | para 2 | 1 Oct 2001 (SI 2001/3266) |
| | para 3(1), (2) | 16 May 2001 (for purpose of enabling the Gas and Electricity Markets Authority to make and the Secretary of State to consent to the making of regulations under Electricity Act 1989, Sch 7, para 1(1A)) (SI 2001/1781) |
| | | 1 Oct 2001 (otherwise) (SI 2001/3266) |
| | para 3(3)–(5) | 1 Oct 2001 (SI 2001/3266) |
| | para 4 | 16 May 2001 (for purpose of enabling the Gas and Electricity Markets Authority to make and the Secretary of State to consent to the making of regulations under Electricity Act 1989, Sch 7, para 1(1A)) (SI 2001/1781) |
| | | 1 Oct 2001 (otherwise) (SI 2001/3266) |
| | paras 5–8 | 1 Oct 2001 (SI 2001/3266)[4] |
| Sch 6 | para 1 | See paras 2–23 below |
| | para 2(1) | 16 May 2001 (so far as relates to Gas Act 1986, s 7B and for the purpose of the determination by the Secretary of State of standard licence conditions) (SI 2001/1781) |

**Utilities Act 2000 (c 27)**—*contd*

|  | 1 Oct 2001 (otherwise) (SI 2001/3266)[4] |
|---|---|
| para 2(2) | 1 Oct 2001 (SI 2001/3266)[4] |
| paras 3, 4 | 1 Oct 2001 (SI 2001/3266)[1] |
| para 5 | 7 Nov 2000 (SI 2000/2974)[4] |
| paras 6, 7 | 1 Oct 2001 (SI 2001/3266)[4] |
| para 8(1) | 20 Dec 2000 (for purpose of entry in sub para (3) below) (SI 2000/3343) |
|  | 1 Oct 2001 (otherwise) (SI 2001/3266) |
| para 8(2) | 1 Oct 2001 (SI 2001/3266) |
| para 8(3) | 20 Dec 2000 (SI 2000/3343) |
| para 8(4) | 1 Oct 2001 (SI 2001/3266) |
| paras 9, 10 | 1 Oct 2001 (SI 2001/3266) |
| para 11 | 20 Dec 2000 (SI 2000/3343) |
| para 12(a)–(e) | 1 Oct 2001 (SI 2001/3266) |
| para 12(f) | 7 Nov 2000 (SI 2000/2974) |
| para 13 | 16 May 2001 (for purpose of enabling the Gas and Electricity Markets Authority to make and the Secretary of State to consent to the making of regulations prescribing standards of performance in connection with the activities of gas suppliers as provided for in Gas Act 1986, s 33A) (SI 2001/1781)[3] |
|  | 1 Oct 2001 (otherwise) (SI 2001/3266) |
| para 14 | 1 Oct 2001 (SI 2001/3266) |
| para 15 | 7 Nov 2000 (SI 2000/2974) |
| para 16 | 1 Oct 2001 (SI 2001/3266) |
| para 17 | 20 Dec 2000 (SI 2000/3343) |
| para 18 | 1 Oct 2001 (SI 2001/3266) |
| para 19(a) | 7 Nov 2000 (so far as relates to definition "authorised supplier", for purposes of Pt III of this Act) (SI 2000/2974) |
|  | 1 Oct 2001 (otherwise) (SI 2001/3266) |
| para 19(b)–(d) | 1 Oct 2001 (SI 2001/3266) |
| paras 20, 21 | 1 Oct 2001 (SI 2001/3266) |
| para 22(a) | 20 Dec 2000 (SI 2000/3343) |
| para 22(b) | 7 Nov 2000 (SI 2000/2974) |
| para 23 | 1 Oct 2001 (SI 2001/3266) |
| para 24 | See paras 25–40 below |
| para 25 | 20 Dec 2000 (SI 2000/3343) |
| para 26 | 1 Oct 2001 (SI 2001/3266)[4] |
| para 27 | 20 Dec 2000 (SI 2000/3343) |
| para 28 | 7 Nov 2000 (for the purpose of insertion of "or section 27(4)(b) of the Utilities Act 2000 (order to comply with a direction under section 24 of that Act)" in Electricity Act 1989, s 25(8)) (SI 2000/2974) |
|  | 1 Oct 2001 (otherwise) (SI 2001/3266)[4] |
| para 29 | 20 Dec 2000 (SI 2000/3343)[4] |
| paras 30, 31 | 1 Oct 2001 (SI 2001/3266)[1] |
| para 32 | 16 May 2001 (for purpose of enabling the Gas and Electricity Markets Authority to make and the Secretary of State to consent to the making of regulations prescribing standards of performance in connection with the activities of electricity suppliers as provided for in Electricity Act 1989, s 39) (SI 2001/1781)[3] |
|  | 1 Oct 2001 (otherwise) (SI 2001/3266)[4] |
| para 33 | 16 May 2001 (for purpose of enabling the Gas and Electricity Markets Authority to determine and arrange for the publication of overall standards of performance in connection with the activities of electricity suppliers as provided for in Electricity Act 1989, s 40) (SI 2001/1781) |
|  | 1 Oct 2001 (otherwise) (SI 2001/3266)[4] |
| para 34 | 1 Oct 2001 (SI 2001/3266)[1] |
| para 35 | 7 Nov 2000 (SI 2000/2974) |

**Utilities Act 2000 (c 27)**—*contd*

| | | |
|---|---|---|
| | paras 36, 37 | 1 Oct 2001 (SI 2001/3266) |
| | para 38(1) | 1 Oct 2001 (SI 2001/3266) |
| | para 38(2) | 7 Nov 2000 (so far as relates to definition "authorised supplier", for purposes of Part III of this Act) (SI 2000/2974) |
| | | 1 Oct 2001 (otherwise) (SI 2001/3266) |
| | para 38(3)–(8) | 1 Oct 2001 (SI 2001/3266) |
| | para 39 | 1 Oct 2001 (SI 2001/3266) |
| | para 40(a) | 20 Dec 2000 (SI 2000/3343) |
| | para 40(b) | 7 Nov 2000 (SI 2000/2974) |
| | para 41 | 1 Oct 2001 (SI 2001/3266) |
| | paras 42–44 | 1 Nov 2000 (SI 2000/2917) |
| | para 45 | 1 Nov 2000 (so far as inserts in House of Commons Disqualification Act 1975, references to "Gas and Electricity Markets Authority" and "Gas and Electricity Consumer Council") (SI 2000/2917) |
| | | 7 Nov 2000 (otherwise) (SI 2000/2974) |
| | paras 46, 47 | 1 Oct 2001 (SI 2001/3266) |
| Sch 7 | paras 1–23 | 16 May 2001 (SI 2001/1781) |
| | paras 24, 25 | 7 Nov 2000 (SI 2000/2974) |
| | para 26 | 1 Nov 2000 (SI 2000/2917) |
| | para 27 | 20 Dec 2000 (SI 2000/3343) |
| | para 28 | 7 Nov 2000 (SI 2000/2974) |
| | para 29 | 1 Oct 2001 (SI 2001/3266) |
| | paras 30–32 | 7 Nov 2000 (SI 2000/2974) |
| Sch 8 | | 7 Nov 2000 (SI 2000/2974), repeals of or in— |

Parliamentary Commissioner Act 1967;

Chronically Sick and Disabled Persons Act 1970;

House of Commons Disqualification Act 1975 (for purposes of references to Gas Consumers' Council and Chairman of a consumers' committee appointed under Electricity Act 1989, s 2);

Northern Ireland Assembly Disqualification Act 1975 (for purposes of references to Gas Consumers' Council and Chairman of a consumers' committee appointed under Electricity Act 1989, s 2);

Gas Act 1986, ss 2, 3, 7B(4)(d) and word "and" preceding it, 31, 32A, in s 33A(6)(a) the words "or, with the agreement of either party, by the Council", ss 33E(2)(a), 40, 42, and in s 48(1) the definition of "the Council" (for all purposes save for its use in Gas Act 1986, s 41 (so long as it remains in force)), Sch 2;

Electricity Act 1989, s 2, in s 39(5)(b) the word "either" and words "or, if he thinks fit, by the consumers' committee to which the supplier is allocated or any sub-committee of that committee", ss 42B(2)(a), 45, 47(4), 51–55, 57, Sch 2

20 Dec 2000 (SI 2000/3343), repeals of or in—

Gas Act 1986, s 39 (save in respect of Sch 7, para 29);

Electricity Act 1989, s 50 (save in respect of Sch 7, para 29)

16 May 2001 (repeals of or in House of Commons Disqualification Act 1975 (for the purpose of reference to the Chairman of the Gas Consumers' Council only)) (SI 2001/1781)

1 Oct 2001 (SI 2001/3266)[4], repeals of or in—

House of Commons Disqualification Act 1975 (for purposes of references to Director General of Gas Supply and Director General of Electricity Supply);

Northern Ireland Assembly Disqualification Act 1975 (for purposes of references to Director General of Gas Supply and Director General of Electricity Supply);

Gas Act 1986 (in so far as not already in force, except entries relating to ss 5, 7A(12), 8A(1), 36 and Schs 2A, 2B);

Insolvency Act 1986;

**Utilities Act 2000 (c 27)**—*contd*

> Electricity Act 1989 (in so far as not already in force);
> Competition and Service (Utilities) Act 1992;
> Offshore Safety Act 1992;
> Environment Act 1995;
> Gas Act 1995 (except s 3(2), Schs 1, 3);
> Competition Act 1998;
> Fossil Fuel Levy Act 1998
> *Not yet in force,* repeals of or in—
> Gas Act 1986, ss 5(1), (2), 7A(12), 8A(1), 36(1), (2)(a), (c), (d),
> Schs 2A, Sch 2B, paras 7(2), 8(2)(b), 8(4)–(6), (8), 9(5);
> Consumer Protection Act 1987;
> Gas Act 1995, s 3(2), Schs 1, 3

¹   For transitional provisions, see SI 2000/2974, arts 3–12

²   For transitional provisions, see SI 2000/3343, arts 3–15, as amended by SI 2001/1780

³   For transitional provisions, see SI 2001/1781, arts 3–10

⁴   For transitional provisions, see SI 2001/3266, arts 3–20

---

**Warm Homes and Energy Conservation Act 2000 (c 31)**

*RA:* 23 Nov 2000

*Commencement provisions:* s 4(3); Warm Homes and Energy Conservation Act 2000 (Commencement) (Wales) Order 2002, SI 2002/758

| | |
|---|---|
| 1 | 23 Nov 2000 (RA) |
| 2 | 23 Nov 2000 (E) (RA) |
| | 1 Apr 2002 (W) (SI 2002/758) |
| 3, 4 | 23 Nov 2000 (RA) |

---

# 2001 Acts

## Abolition of Poindings and Warrant Sales Act 2001 (asp 1)

*RA:* 17 Jan 2001

*Commencement provisions:* s 4(1)

| | |
|---|---|
| 1–3 | 31 Dec 2002 (s 4(1)) |
| 4 | 17 Jan 2001 (RA) |
| Schedule | 31 Dec 2002 (s 4(1)) |

## Anti-terrorism, Crime and Security Act 2001 (c 24)

*RA:* 14 Dec 2001

*Commencement provisions:* s 127; Anti-terrorism, Crime and Security Act 2001 (Commencement No 1 and Consequential Provisions) Order 2001, SI 2001/4019[1]; Anti-terrorism, Crime and Security Act 2001 (Commencement No 2) (Scotland) Order 2001, SI 2001/4104; Anti-terrorism, Crime and Security Act 2001 (Commencement No 3) Order 2002, SI 2002/228; Anti-terrorism, Crime and Security Act 2001 (Commencement No 4) Order 2002, SI 2002/1279; Anti-terrorism, Crime and Security Act 2001 (Commencement No 5) Order 2002, SI 2002/1558

| | | |
|---|---|---|
| 1–3 | | 20 Dec 2001 (SI 2001/4019) |
| 4–57 | | 14 Dec 2001 (RA) |
| 58–75 | | 31 May 2002 (SI 2002/1279) |
| 76, 77 | | 14 Dec 2001 (RA) |
| 78 | | *Not yet in force* (sub-s (2) repealed) |
| 79–83 | | 14 Dec 2001 (RA) |
| 84 | | 14 Feb 2002 (s 127(3)) |
| 85, 86 | | 14 Dec 2001 (RA) |
| 87 | | 14 Feb 2002 (s 127(3)) |
| 88–97 | | 14 Dec 2001 (RA) |
| 98, 99 | | 14 Dec 2001 (E) (W) (NI) (RA) |
| | | 7 Jan 2002 (S) (SI 2001/4104) |
| 100 | | 14 Dec 2001 (E) (W) (RA) |
| | | 7 Jan 2002 (S) (SI 2001/4104) |
| 101 | | See Sch 7 below |
| 102–107 | | 14 Dec 2001 (RA) |
| 108–110 | | 14 Feb 2002 (SI 2002/228) |
| 111–120 | | 14 Dec 2001 (RA) |
| 121 | | 7 Jul 2002 (SI 2002/1558) |
| 122–124 | | 14 Dec 2001 (RA) |
| 125 | | See Sch 8 below |
| 126–129 | | 14 Dec 2001 (RA) |
| Schs 1, 2 | | 20 Dec 2001 (SI 2001/4019) |
| Schs 3, 4 | | 14 Dec 2001 (RA) |
| Schs 5, 6 | | 31 May 2002 (SI 2002/1279) |
| Sch 7 | paras 1–7 | 7 Jan 2002 (SI 2001/4104) |
| | paras 8–33 | 14 Dec 2001 (RA) |
| Sch 8 | Pt 1 | 20 Dec 2001 (SI 2001/4019)[1] |

**Anti-terrorism, Crime and Security Act 2001 (c 24)**—*contd*

| | |
|---|---|
| Pts 2–4 | 14 Dec 2001 (RA) |
| Pt 5 | 14 Dec 2001 (except repeals of or in Nuclear Installations Act 1965) (RA) |
| | *Not yet in force* (exception noted above) |
| Pt 6 | 14 Dec 2001 (RA), except insofar as following repeals extend to Scotland— |
| | British Transport Commission Act 1962; |
| | Ministry of Defence Police Act 1987 |
| | 7 Jan 2002 (S) (SI 2001/4104), repeals of or in— |
| | British Transport Commission Act 1962; |
| | Ministry of Defence Police Act 1987 |
| Pt 7 | 14 Dec 2001 (except repeals of or in Terrorism Act 2000, Sch 5) (RA) |
| | *Not yet in force* (exception noted above) |

[1]    For transitional provisions, see SI 2001/4019, art 2(2)

---

**Appropriation Act 2001 (c 8)**

*RA:* 11 May 2001

Whole Act in force 11 May 2001 (RA)

---

**Appropriation (No 2) Act 2001 (c 21)**

*RA:* 19 Jul 2001

Whole Act in force 19 Jul 2001 (RA)

---

**Armed Forces Act 2001 (c 19)**

*RA:* 11 May 2001

*Commencement provisions:* s 39(2)–(6); Armed Forces Act 2001 (Commencement No 1) Order 2001, SI 2001/3234[1]; Armed Forces Act 2001 (Commencement No 2) Order 2002, SI 2002/345; Armed Forces Act 2001 (Commencement No 3) Order 2003, SI 2003/2268; Armed Forces Act 2001 (Commencement No 4) Order 2004, SI 2004/1938; Armed Forces Act 2001 (Commencement No 5) Order 2005, SI 2005/2861; Armed Forces Act 2001 (Commencement No 6) Order 2006, SI 2006/235; Armed Forces Act 2001 (Commencement No 7) Order 2006, SI 2006/2309; Armed Forces Act 2001 (Commencement No 8) Order 2007, SI 2007/662; Armed Forces Act 2001 (Commencement No 9) Order 2007, SI 2007/3434

| | |
|---|---|
| 1 | 11 May 2001 (RA) |
| 2–11 | 30 Sep 2003 (SI 2003/2268) |
| 12 | *Never in force* (repealed) |
| 13–16 | 30 Sep 2003 (SI 2003/2268) |
| 17 | See Sch 1 below |
| 18 | 28 Feb 2002 (SI 2002/345) |
| 19 | See Sch 2 below |
| 20 | 22 Jul 2004 (SI 2004/1938) |
| 21 | 28 Feb 2007 (SI 2007/662) |
| 22 | *Never in force* (repealed) |
| 23 | 28 Feb 2002 (SI 2002/345)[2] |
| 24 | 28 Feb 2002 (SI 2002/345) |
| 25 | 1 Jan 2008 (SI 2007/3434) |
| 26–28 | 14 Oct 2005 (SI 2005/2861) |
| 29, 30 | 25 Aug 2006 (SI 2006/2309) |
| 31 | 30 Sep 2003 (SI 2003/2268) |

## Armed Forces Act 2001 (c 19)—*contd*

| | | |
|---|---|---|
| 32 | (1)–(8) | 3 Feb 2006 (in relation to incidents which occur on or after 3 Feb 2006) (SI 2006/235) |
| | (9) | See Sch 5 below |
| 33 | | 3 Feb 2006 (in relation to incidents which occur on or after 3 Feb 2006) (SI 2006/235) |
| 34 | | See Sch 6 below |
| 35–37 | | 11 May 2001 (RA) |
| 38 | | See Sch 7 below |
| 39 | | 11 May 2001 (RA) |
| Schs 1, 2 | | 28 Feb 2002 (SI 2002/345) |
| Schs 3, 4 | | *Never in force* (repealed) |
| Sch 5 | para 1 | 3 Feb 2006 (SI 2006/235) |
| | paras 2–4 | 3 Feb 2006 (in relation to incidents which occur on or after 3 Feb 2006) (SI 2006/235) |
| | para 5(1) | 3 Feb 2006 (SI 2006/235) |
| | para 5(2)(a) | 3 Feb 2006 (SI 2006/235) |
| | para 5(2)(b) | 28 Feb 2002 (SI 2002/345) |
| | para 5(3) | 3 Feb 2006 (SI 2006/235) |
| | para 5(4) | 28 Feb 2002 (SI 2002/345) |
| | paras 6, 7 | 3 Feb 2006 (in relation to incidents which occur on or after 3 Feb 2006) (SI 2006/235) |
| Sch 6 | Pts 1–3 | 1 Oct 2001 (SI 2001/3234)[1] |
| | Pts 4, 5 | 11 May 2001 (RA) |
| | Pt 6, paras 31–40 | 1 Oct 2001 (SI 2001/3234)[1] |
| | Pt 6, paras 41, 42 | 30 Sep 2003 (SI 2003/2268)[3] |
| | Pt 6, paras 43–49 | 1 Oct 2001 (SI 2001/3234) |
| | Pt 6, para 50(1) | See sub-paras (2)–(4) below |
| | Pt 6, para 50(2) | *Never in force* (repealed) |
| | Pt 6, para 50(3), (4) | 1 Oct 2001 (SI 2001/3234) |
| | Pt 6, paras 51–54 | 1 Oct 2001 (SI 2001/3234) |
| | Pt 6, paras 55, 56 | *Never in force* (repealed) |
| | Pt 6, paras 57, 58 | 1 Oct 2001 (SI 2001/3234) |
| | Pt 6, para 59 | 28 Feb 2002 (SI 2002/345) |
| Sch 7 | Pt 1 | 28 Feb 2002 (SI 2002/345) |
| | Pt 2 | *Not yet in force* |
| | Pt 3 | 1 Oct 2001 (SI 2001/3234) |
| | Pts 4–6 | 11 May 2001 (RA) |
| | Pt 7 | 1 Sep 2001 (repeal of Armed Forces Act 1996, s 1) (s 39(4)) |
| | | 1 Oct 2001 (otherwise) (SI 2001/3234)[1], except repeals of or in— |
| | | Naval Discipline Act 1957, s 12A(1); |
| | | Courts-Martial (Appeals) Act 1968, s 42 |
| | | *Not yet in force* (exceptions noted above) |

[1]   For transitional provisions, see SI 2001/3234, art 3(1), (2)

[2]   For transitional provisions, see SI 2002/345, art 3

[3]   For transitional provisions, see SI 2003/2268, arts 3, 4

---

## Budget (Scotland) Act 2001 (asp 4)

*RA:* 15 Mar 2001

Whole Act in force 15 Mar 2001 (RA)

---

## Capital Allowances Act 2001 (c 2)

*RA:* 22 Mar 2001

*Commencement provisions:* s 579(1)

**Capital Allowances Act 2001 (c 2)**—*contd*

The Act has effect (a) for income tax purposes, as respects allowances and charges falling to be made for chargeable periods ending on or after 6 Apr 2001; and (b) for corporation tax purposes, as respects allowances and charges falling to be made for chargeable periods ending on or after 1 Apr 2001.

---

**Children's Commissioner for Wales Act 2001 (c 18)**

*RA:* 11 May 2001

*Commencement provisions:* s 9(1); Children's Commissioner for Wales Act 2001 (Commencement) Order 2001, SI 2001/2783[1]

| | |
|---|---|
| 1–8 | 26 Aug 2001 (SI 2001/2783)[1] |
| 9 | 11 May 2001 (RA) |
| Schedule | 26 Aug 2001 (SI 2001/2783) |

[1]  Note that in the Queen's Printer's copy of SI 2001/2783, the list of sections brought into force refers to s 5 twice and does not include s 8, however it is thought that the intention was to bring the whole Act into force

---

**Churchwardens Measure 2001 (No 1)**

*RA:* 10 Apr 2001

*Commencement provisions:* s 16(2)

The provisions of this Measure were brought into force on 1 Jan 2002 by an instrument made by the Archbishops of Canterbury and York and dated 13 Nov 2001 (made under s 16(2))

---

**Consolidated Fund Act 2001 (c 1)**

*RA:* 22 Mar 2001

Whole Act in force 22 Mar 2001 (RA)

---

**Consolidated Fund (No 2) Act 2001 (c 25)**

*RA:* 18 Dec 2001

Whole Act in force 18 Dec 2001 (RA)

---

**Convention Rights (Compliance) (Scotland) Act 2001 (asp 7)**

*RA:* 5 Jul 2001

*Commencement provisions:* s 15(2), (3); Convention Rights (Compliance) (Scotland) Act 2001 (Commencement) Order 2001, SSI 2001/274

| | | |
|---|---|---|
| 1, 2 | | 8 Oct 2001 (SSI 2001/274) |
| 3 | (1)(a) | 8 Oct 2001 (SSI 2001/274) |
| | (1)(b) | 27 Jul 2001 (in so far as it inserts s 10(2U) of Prisoners and Criminal Proceedings (Scotland) Act 1993) (SSI 2001/274) |
| | | 8 Oct 2001 (otherwise) (SSI 2001/274) |
| | (1)(c)–(e) | 8 Oct 2001 (SSI 2001/274) |
| | (2)–(3) | 8 Oct 2001 (SSI 2001/274) |
| 4 | | See Schedule below |
| 5 | (1), (2) | 27 Jul 2001 (SSI 2001/274) |
| | (3) | 8 Oct 2001 (SSI 2001/274) |

**Convention Rights (Compliance) (Scotland) Act 2001 (asp 7)**—*contd*

|  |  |  |
|---|---|---|
|  | (4) | 27 Jul 2001 (for the purpose of enabling the Scottish Ministers to make regulations under Sch 2, para 3D to Prisoners and Criminal Proceedings (Scotland) Act 1993) (SSI 2001/274) |
|  |  | 8 Oct 2001 (otherwise) (SSI 2001/274) |
|  | (5) | 27 Jul 2001 (SSI 2001/274) |
|  | (6) | 8 Oct 2001 (SSI 2001/274) |
| 6–10 |  | 6 Jul 2001 (s 15(3)) |
| 11 |  | 5 Sep 2001 (SSI 2001/274) |
| 12–14 |  | 6 Jul 2001 (s 15(3)) |
| 15 |  | 5 Jul 2001 (RA) |
| Schedule | paras 1–20 | 8 Oct 2001 (SSI 2001/274) |
|  | para 21 | 27 Jul 2001 (SSI 2001/274) |
|  | paras 22–67 | 8 Oct 2001 (SSI 2001/274) |
|  | para 68 | 27 Jul 2001 (SSI 2001/274) |
|  | paras 69–76 | 8 Oct 2001 (SSI 2001/274) |
|  | para 77 | 27 Jul 2001 (for the purpose of applying para 68 of this Schedule) (SSI 2001/274) |
|  |  | 8 Oct 2001 (otherwise) (SSI 2001/274) |
|  | paras 78–83 | 8 Oct 2001 (SSI 2001/274) |

---

**Criminal Defence Service (Advice and Assistance) Act 2001 (c 4)**

*RA:* 10 Apr 2001

Whole Act in force 10 Apr 2001 (RA)

---

**Criminal Justice and Police Act 2001 (c 16)**

*RA:* 11 May 2001

*Commencement provisions:* s 138(2)–(4); Criminal Justice and Police Act 2001 (Commencement No 1) Order 2001, SI 2001/2223; Criminal Justice and Police Act 2001 (Commencement No 2) Order 2001, SI 2001/3150; Criminal Justice and Police Act 2001 (Commencement No 3) Order 2001, SI 2001/3736; Criminal Justice and Police Act 2001 (Commencement No 4 and Transitional Provisions) Order 2002, SI 2002/344[1]; Criminal Justice and Police Act 2001 (Commencement No 5) Order 2002, SI 2002/533; Criminal Justice and Police Act 2001 (Commencement No 6) Order 2002, SI 2002/1097; Criminal Justice and Police Act 2001 (Commencement No 7) Order 2002, SI 2002/2050; Criminal Justice and Police Act 2001 (Commencement No 8) Order 2002, SI 2002/3032; Criminal Justice and Police Act 2001 (Commencement No 9) Order 2003, SI 2003/708; Criminal Justice and Police Act 2001 (Commencement No 10) Order 2004, SI 2004/1376

|  |  |  |
|---|---|---|
| 1 |  | 1 Mar 2002 (for the purpose of making orders) (SI 2002/344) |
|  |  | 12 Aug 2002 (otherwise) (SI 2002/2050) |
| 2 | (1)–(5) | 12 Aug 2002 (SI 2002/2050) |
| 3 |  | 1 Mar 2002 (SI 2002/344) |
| 4–11 |  | 12 Aug 2002 (SI 2002/2050) |
| 12 |  | 1 Sep 2001 (SI 2001/2223) |
| 13 |  | 19 Jun 2001 (for the purpose of making orders or regulations) (SI 2001/2223) |
|  |  | 1 Sep 2001 (otherwise) (SI 2001/2223) |
| 14–16 |  | 1 Sep 2001 (SI 2001/2223) |
| 17–28 |  | 1 Dec 2001 (SI 2001/3736) |
| 29 |  | 1 Sep 2001 (SI 2001/2223) |
| 30–32 |  | 1 Dec 2001 (SI 2001/3736) |
| 33–36 |  | 1 Apr 2002 (SI 2002/344) |
| 37 |  | 19 Jun 2001 (for the purpose of making orders or regulations) (SI 2001/2223) |
|  |  | 1 Apr 2002 (otherwise) (SI 2002/344) |
| 38 |  | *Never in force* (repealed) |

**Criminal Justice and Police Act 2001 (c 16)**—*contd*

| | | |
|---|---|---|
| 39–41 | | 1 Aug 2001 (SI 2001/2223) |
| 42, 43 | | 11 May 2001 (RA) |
| 44 | | 1 Aug 2001 (SI 2001/2223) |
| 45 | | 19 Jun 2001 (for the purpose of making orders or regulations) (SI 2001/2223) |
| | | 2 Apr 2002 (otherwise) (SI 2002/533) |
| 46, 47 | | 1 Sep 2001 (SI 2001/2223) |
| 48, 49 | | 1 Aug 2001 (SI 2001/2223) |
| 50–63 | | 1 Apr 2003 (SI 2003/708) |
| 64 | (1) | 1 Apr 2003 (except words "subject to subsection (2),") (SI 2003/708) |
| | | 1 Jun 2004 (exception noted above) (SI 2004/1376) |
| | (2), (3) | 1 Jun 2004 (SI 2004/1376) |
| 65–70 | | 1 Apr 2003 (SI 2003/708) |
| 71, 72 | | 1 Oct 2001 (SI 2001/3150) |
| 73, 74 | | 1 Apr 2003 (SI 2003/708) |
| 75 | | 1 Aug 2001 (SI 2001/2223) |
| 76, 77 | | 19 Jun 2001 (SI 2001/2223) |
| 78 | (1) | 1 Jan 2003 (SI 2002/3032) |
| | (2) | 1 Apr 2003 (SI 2003/708) |
| | (3)–(6) | 1 Jan 2003 (SI 2002/3032) |
| | (7) | *Never in force* (repealed) |
| | (8), (9) | 1 Jan 2003 (SI 2002/3032) |
| 79 | | 1 Apr 2003 (SI 2003/708) |
| 80 | (1) | 1 Apr 2003 (SI 2003/708) |
| | (2) | *Never in force* (repealed) |
| | (3) | 1 Jan 2003 (SI 2002/3032) |
| | (4) | *Never in force* (repealed) |
| | (5), (6) | 1 Jan 2003 (SI 2002/3032) |
| 81–84 | | 11 May 2001 (RA) |
| 85 | | 11 Jul 2001 (s 138(4)) |
| 86 | | 1 Aug 2001 (SI 2001/2223) |
| 87–96 | | 1 Apr 2002 (SI 2002/533) |
| 97 | (1)–(3) | 1 Oct 2001 (SI 2001/3150) |
| | (4)(a) | 1 Apr 2002 (SI 2002/533) |
| | (4)(b)–(d) | 1 Oct 2001 (SI 2001/3150) |
| | (5), (6) | 1 Oct 2001 (SI 2001/3150) |
| 98, 99 | | 1 Apr 2002 (SI 2002/533) |
| 100 | | 1 Oct 2001 (SI 2001/3150) |
| 101–103 | | 1 Apr 2002 (SI 2002/533) |
| 104 | (1), (2) | 19 Jun 2001 (SI 2001/2223) |
| | (3) | 1 Apr 2002 (SI 2002/344) |
| | (4)(a), (b) | 19 Jun 2001 (SI 2001/2223) |
| | (4)(c) | 1 Apr 2002 (SI 2002/344) |
| | (5) | 19 Jun 2001 (except so far as relates to Police Act 1997) (SI 2001/2223) |
| | | 1 Apr 2002 (exception noted above) (SI 2002/344) |
| | (6), (7) | 19 Jun 2001 (SI 2001/2223) |
| | (8) | 1 Apr 2002 (SI 2002/344) |
| | (9) | 19 Jun 2001 (SI 2001/2223) |
| 105 | | 19 Jun 2001 (SI 2001/2223) |
| 106 | (1)(a) | 19 Jun 2001 (SI 2001/2223) |
| | (1)(b) | 1 Apr 2002 (SI 2002/344) |
| | (2) | 19 Jun 2001 (SI 2001/2223) |
| 107 | (1)(a), (b) | 1 Dec 2001 (SI 2001/3736) |
| | (1)(c) | 1 Apr 2002 (SI 2002/344) |
| | (2), (3) | 1 Dec 2001 (SI 2001/3736) |
| | (4) | 1 Apr 2002 (SI 2002/344) |
| 108 | | 1 Apr 2002 (SI 2002/344) |

**Criminal Justice and Police Act 2001 (c 16)**—*contd*

| | | |
|---|---|---|
| 109 | | 11 May 2001 (RA) |
| 110, 111 | | 1 Aug 2001 (SI 2001/2223) |
| 112 | | 1 Apr 2002 (SI 2002/344) |
| 113, 114 | | 1 Aug 2001 (SI 2001/2223) |
| 115 | | 1 Apr 2002 (SI 2002/344) |
| 116 | (1)–(6) | 1 Apr 2002 (SI 2002/344) |
| | (7) | 11 May 2001 (RA) |
| 117, 118 | | 1 Apr 2002 (SI 2002/344) |
| 119 | (1)–(6) | 1 Apr 2002 (SI 2002/344) |
| | (7) | 11 May 2001 (RA) |
| 120, 121 | | 1 Apr 2002 (SI 2002/344) |
| 122–125 | | 1 Jan 2002 (SI 2001/3736) |
| 126 | | 1 Apr 2002 (SI 2002/344) |
| 127 | | 1 Sep 2002 (SI 2002/2050) |
| 128 | | See Sch 6 below |
| 129 | | 1 Aug 2001 (SI 2001/2223) |
| 130 | | 22 Apr 2002 (so far as relates to remands and committals by a court in the following police areas: Avon and Somerset, City of London, Greater Manchester, Lancashire, Merseyside, Metropolitan police district, Nottinghamshire, South Yorkshire, Thames Valley, West Midlands and West Yorkshire) (SI 2002/1097) |
| | | 16 Sep 2002 (otherwise) (SI 2002/1097) |
| 131, 132 | | 1 Mar 2002 (SI 2002/344) |
| 133 | | 1 Dec 2001 (SI 2001/3736) |
| 134–136 | | 19 Jun 2001 (SI 2001/2223) |
| 137 | | See Sch 7 below |
| 138 | | 11 May 2001 (RA) |
| Sch 1 | Pt 1, paras 1–34 | 1 Apr 2003 (SI 2003/708) |
| | Pt 1, para 35 | 8 Oct 2004 (SI 2004/1376) |
| | Pt 1, paras 36–41 | 1 Apr 2003 (SI 2003/708) |
| | Pt 1, para 42 | 1 Jun 2004 (SI 2004/1376) |
| | Pt 1, paras 43–66 | 1 Apr 2003 (SI 2003/708) |
| | Pt 1, para 67 | 1 Jun 2004 (SI 2004/1376) |
| | Pt 1, paras 68–73 | 1 Apr 2003 (SI 2003/708) |
| | Pts 2, 3 | 1 Apr 2003 (SI 2003/708) |
| Sch 2 | paras 1–25 | 1 Apr 2003 (SI 2003/708) |
| | para 26 | 1 Oct 2001 (SI 2001/3150) |
| | para 27 | 1 Apr 2003 (SI 2003/708) |
| Schs 3, 4 | | 1 Apr 2002 (SI 2002/533) |
| Sch 5 | | 1 Apr 2003 (SI 2003/708) |
| Sch 6 | paras 1, 2 | 1 Apr 2002 (SI 2002/344) |
| | para 3 | 1 Aug 2001 (SI 2001/2223) |
| | paras 4–11 | 1 Apr 2002 (SI 2002/344) |
| | para 12 | 1 Aug 2001 (SI 2001/2223) |
| | paras 13–20 | 1 Apr 2002 (SI 2002/344) |
| | para 21 | 1 Apr 2002 (except for insertion of para 4 of Sch 2A to the 1997 Act) (SI 2002/344) |
| | | *Never in force* (exception noted above) (repealed) |
| | paras 22–80 | 1 Apr 2002 (SI 2002/344) |
| Sch 7 | Pt 1 | 1 Dec 2001 (SI 2001/3736) |
| | Pt 2(1) | 19 Jun 2001 (repeal of Police and Criminal Evidence Act 1984, s 64(4)) (SI 2001/2223) |
| | | 1 Jan 2003 (repeal of Criminal Justice Act 1948, s 39) (SI 2002/3032) |
| | | 1 Apr 2003 (otherwise) (SI 2003/708) |
| | Pt 2(2) | 19 Jun 2001 (SI 2001/2223) |
| | Pt 3 | 1 Apr 2002 (SI 2002/533) |
| | Pt 4 | 19 Jun 2001 (SI 2001/2223), repeals of or in— |

**Criminal Justice and Police Act 2001 (c 16)**—*contd*

|  |  |
|---|---|
|  | Police Act 1996, Sch 2, paras 10, 16, Sch 3; Greater London Authority Act 1999 |
|  | 1 Dec 2001 (repeals of or in Police Act 1996, Sch 2, para 25(1), Sch 2A, para 20(1), (2)) (SI 2001/3736) |
|  | 1 Jan 2002 (repeals of or in Police Act 1996, ss 12(4)–(6), 13(2)) (SI 2001/3736) |
|  | 1 Apr 2002 (repeals of or in Police Act 1997) (SI 2002/344) |
| Pt 5(1) | 1 Aug 2001 (SI 2001/2223), repeals of or in— |
|  | Local Government Finance Act 1992, ss 32(6A), 43(5A); |
|  | Police Act 1997, ss 2(6), 18, 48(7), 63, 137(2)(d), Schs 3, 5; |
|  | Greater London Authority Act 1999, s 86(3), Sch 27, paras 110, 111, 114, 115 |
|  | 1 Apr 2002 (otherwise) (SI 2002/344) |
| Pt 5(2) | 1 Apr 2002 (SI 2002/344) |
| Pt 6 | 1 Aug 2001 (repeal of or in Bail Act 1976) (SI 2001/2223) |
|  | *Not yet in force* (repeal in Criminal Justice Act 1988) |

[1]    For transitional provisions, see SI 2002/344, art 4

---

**Education (Graduate Endowment and Student Support) (Scotland) Act 2001 (asp 6)**

*RA:* 3 May 2001

*Commencement provisions:* s 5; Education (Graduate Endowment and Student Support) (Scotland) Act 2001 (Commencement) Order 2001, SSI 2001/191

| | |
|---|---|
| 1–3 | 3 May 2001 (RA) |
| 4 | 1 Jun 2001 (SSI 2001/191) |
| 5 | 3 May 2001 (RA) |

---

**Election Publications Act 2001 (c 5)**

*RA:* 10 Apr 2001

Whole Act in force 10 Apr 2001 (RA)

---

**Elections Act 2001 (c 7)**

*RA:* 10 Apr 2001

Whole Act in force 10 Apr 2001 (RA)

---

**European Communities (Finance) Act 2001 (c 22)**

*RA:* 4 Dec 2001

Whole Act in force 4 Dec 2001 (RA)

---

**Finance Act 2001 (c 9)**

*Budget Day:* 7 Mar 2001

*RA:* 11 May 2001

The commencement details of Finance Acts are not set out, as the dates from which their provisions take effect are usually stated clearly and unambiguously in the text of the Act, and charging provisions will normally state for which year or years of assessment they are to have effect.

---

**Health and Social Care Act 2001 (c 15)**

*RA:* 11 May 2001

*Commencement provisions:* s 70(2); Health and Social Care Act 2001 (Commencement No 1) (England) Order 2001, SI 2001/2804; Health and Social Care Act 2001 (Commencement No 2) (England) Order 2001, SI 2001/3167; Health and Social Care Act 2001 (Commencement No 3) (England) Order 2001, SI 2001/3294; Health and Social Care Act 2001 (Commencement No 4) (England) Order 2001, SI 2001/3619; Health and Social Care Act 2001 (Commencement No 5) Order 2001, SI 2001/3752; Health and Social Care Act 2001 (Commencement No 6) (England) Order 2001, SI 2001/3738; Health and Social Care Act 2001 (Commencement No 1) (Wales) Order 2001, SI 2001/3807; Health and Social Care Act 2001 (Commencement No 7) (England) Order 2001, SI 2001/4149; Health and Social Care Act 2001 (Commencement No 8) Order 2002, SI 2002/1095, as amended by SI 2002/1170; Health and Social Care Act 2001 (Commencement No 9) Order 2002, SI 2002/1312; Health and Social Care Act 2001 (Commencement No 9) (Scotland) Order 2002, SSI 2002/75; Health and Social Care Act 2001 (Commencement No 2) (Wales) Order 2002, SI 2002/1475; Health and Social Care Act 2001 (Commencement No 3) (Wales) Order 2002, SI 2002/1919; Health and Social Care Act 2001 (Commencement No 10) (England) Order 2002, SI 2002/2363; Health and Social Care Act 2001 (Commencement No 11) (England) Order 2002, SI 2003/53; Health and Social Care Act 2001 (Commencement No 4) (Wales) Order 2003, SI 2003/713; Health and Social Care Act 2001 (Commencement No 12) (England) Order 2003, SI 2003/850; Health and Social Care Act 2001 (Commencement No 5) (Wales) Order 2003, SI 2003/939; Health and Social Care Act 2001 (Commencement No 13) (England) Order 2003, SI 2003/2245; Health and Social Care Act 2001 (Commencement No 6) (Wales) Order 2004, SI 2004/103; Health and Social Care Act 2001 (Commencement No 7) (Wales) Order 2004, SI 2004/1754; Health and Social Care Act 2001 (Commencement No 14) (England) Order 2006, SI 2006/481; National Health Service (Pre-consolidation Amendments) Order 2006, SI 2006/1407

| | | |
|---|---|---|
| 1 | | 11 May 2001 (in so far as conferring any power to make an order or regulations which is exercisable by the Secretary of State) (RA) |
| | | 22 Oct 2001 (E) (otherwise) (SI 2001/3619)[2] |
| | | *Never in force* (W) (otherwise) (repealed) |
| 2 | | 11 May 2001 (in so far as conferring any power to make an order or regulations which is exercisable by the Secretary of State) (RA) |
| | | 30 Sep 2002 (E) (for the purposes of the year ending 31 Mar 2003 and subsequent years) (SI 2002/2363) |
| | | *Never in force* (W) (otherwise) (repealed) |
| 3 | (1), (2) | 1 Aug 2001 (E) (SI 2001/2804) |
| | | 1 Jul 2002 (W) (SI 2002/1475) |
| | (3), (4) | *Never in force* (W) (repealed) |
| 4 | | 11 May 2001 (in so far as conferring any power to make an order or regulations which is exercisable by the Secretary of State) (RA) |
| | | 1 Aug 2001 (E) (otherwise) (SI 2001/2804) |
| | | In force (otherwise) immediately before the National Health Service Act 2006 comes into force (SI 2006/1407)[10] |
| 5 | | 1 Jul 2002 (W) (SI 2002/1475) |
| | | 12 Sep 2002 (E) (SI 2002/2363) |
| | | *Not yet in force* (S) |
| 6 | (1) | 11 May 2001 (in so far as conferring any power to make an order or regulations which is exercisable by the Secretary of State) (RA) |
| | | 1 Oct 2001 (E) (otherwise) (SI 2001/3294) |
| | | In force (otherwise) immediately before the National Health Service Act 2006 comes into force (SI 2006/1407)[10] |
| | (2) | 11 May 2001 (in so far as conferring any power to make an order or regulations which is exercisable by the Secretary of State) (RA) |
| | | 1 Oct 2001 (E) (otherwise) (SI 2001/3294) |
| | | *Never in force* (W) (otherwise) (repealed) |

**Health and Social Care Act 2001 (c 15)**—*contd*

| | | |
|---|---|---|
| | (3) | 11 May 2001 (in so far as conferring any power to make an order or regulations which is exercisable by the Secretary of State) (RA) |
| | | 1 Oct 2001 (E) (otherwise) (SI 2001/3294) |
| | | 24 Jan 2004 (W) (otherwise) (SI 2004/103) |
| 7–10 | | 11 May 2001 (in so far as conferring any power to make an order or regulations which is exercisable by the Secretary of State) (RA) |
| | | 1 Jan 2003 (E) (SI 2003/53) |
| | | In force (otherwise) immediately before the National Health Service Act 2006 comes into force (SI 2006/1407)[10] |
| 11 | | 1 Dec 2002 (W) (SI 2002/1475) |
| | | 1 Jan 2003 (E) (SI 2003/53) |
| 12 | | 1 Sep 2003 (E) (SI 2003/2245) |
| | | 31 Jan 2004 (W) (SI 2004/103) |
| 13 | | 11 May 2001 (in so far as conferring any power to make an order or regulations which is exercisable by the Secretary of State) (RA) |
| | | 1 Aug 2001 (E) (otherwise) (SI 2001/2804) |
| | | 17 Mar 2003 (W) (otherwise) (SI 2003/713) |
| 14 | | 1 Apr 2002 (SI 2002/1095)[5] |
| 15 | (1), (2) | 8 Mar 2002 (for the purpose of making regulations) (SI 2002/1095) |
| | | 1 Apr 2002 (otherwise) (SI 2002/1095) |
| | (3) | 8 Mar 2002 (for the purpose of making regulations) (SI 2002/1095) |
| | | 1 Apr 2002 (E) (otherwise) (SI 2002/1095)[5] |
| | | *Never in force* (W) (otherwise) (repealed) |
| 16 | | 14 Dec 2001 (E) (SI 2001/3738)[4] |
| | | 26 Aug 2002 (W) (SI 2002/1919)[8] |
| 17 | | 11 May 2001 (in so far as conferring any power to make an order or regulations which is exercisable by the Secretary of State) (RA) |
| | | 14 Dec 2001 (E) (for all purposes except those relating to the provision of pharmaceutical services) (SI 2001/3738) |
| | | *Never in force* (otherwise) (repealed) |
| 18 | | 11 May 2001 (in so far as conferring any power to make an order or regulations which is exercisable by the Secretary of State) (RA) |
| | | 12 Sep 2002 (E) (otherwise) (SI 2002/2363) |
| | | *Never in force* (otherwise) (repealed) |
| 19 | | 1 Apr 2002 (E) (SI 2002/1095) |
| | | 1 Jul 2002 (W) (SI 2002/1475) |
| | | *Never in force* (S) (NI) (repealed) |
| 20 | (1) | See sub-ss (2)–(7) below |
| | (2)–(5) | 22 Nov 2001 (E) (for the purpose of making regulations) (SI 2001/3738) |
| | (6) | 1 Jul 2002 (W) (SI 2002/1475) |
| | | 1 Feb 2003 (E) (SI 2003/53) |
| | (7) | 1 Jul 2002 (W) (SI 2002/1475) |
| | | In force (otherwise) immediately before the National Health Service Act 2006 comes into force (SI 2006/1407)[10] |
| 21, 22 | | 22 Nov 2001 (E) (SI 2001/3738) |
| | | 1 Jul 2002 (W) (SI 2002/1475) |
| 23 | (1) | See sub-ss (2)–(5) below |
| | (2)–(5) | 1 Jul 2002 (W) (SI 2002/1475) |
| | | In force (otherwise) immediately before the National Health Service Act 2006 comes into force (SI 2006/1407)[10] |
| 24 | | 22 Nov 2001 (E) (SI 2001/3738) |
| | | 1 Jul 2002 (W) (SI 2002/1475) |

**Health and Social Care Act 2001 (c 15)**—*contd*

| | | |
|---|---|---|
| 25 | | 22 Nov 2001 (E) (in so far as inserts ss 49O–49R) (SI 2001/3738) |
| | | 22 Nov 2001 (E) (in so far as inserts ss 49F, 49I, 49L–49N for the purpose of making regulations) (SI 2001/3738) |
| | | 14 Dec 2001 (E) (in so far as inserts ss 49F, 49I, 49L–49N for all other purposes except those relating to the provision of pharmaceutical services) (SI 2001/3738) |
| | | 14 Dec 2001 (E) (in so far as inserts ss 49G, 49H, 49J and 49K for all purposes except those relating to the provision of pharmaceutical services) (SI 2001/3738) |
| | | 1 Jul 2002 (W) (SI 2002/1475) |
| | | 1 Feb 2003 (E) (otherwise) (SI 2003/53) |
| 26 | (1) | 1 Jul 2002 (W) (SI 2002/1475) |
| | | *Never in force* (E) (repealed) |
| | (2) | 31 May 2002 (E) (SI 2002/1095) |
| | | 1 Jul 2002 (W) (SI 2002/1475) |
| | (3) | 1 Jul 2002 (W) (SI 2002/1475) |
| | | *Never in force* (E) (repealed) |
| 27 | | 1 Oct 2001 (E) (for the purpose of constituting the Family Health Services Appeal Authority and for making rules or regulations in respect of it) (SI 2001/3294) |
| | | 1 Dec 2001 (E) (otherwise) (SI 2001/3294) |
| | | 26 Aug 2002 (W) (SI 2002/1919) |
| 28–39 | | 8 Mar 2002 (E) (SI 2002/1095) |
| | | 1 Jul 2002 (W) (SI 2002/1475) |
| 40 | | 28 Feb 2006 (E) (for the purpose of making regulations) (SI 2006/481) |
| | | 1 Apr 2006 (E) (otherwise) (SI 2006/481) |
| | | *Never in force* (W) (repealed) |
| 41 | | 11 May 2001 (in so far as conferring any power to make an order or regulations which is exercisable by the Secretary of State) (RA) |
| | | 8 Mar 2002 (E) (otherwise) (SI 2002/1095) |
| | | 1 Jul 2002 (W) (otherwise) (SI 2002/1475) |
| 42 | | 8 Mar 2002 (E) (for the purpose of making regulations) (SI 2002/1095) |
| | | 1 Apr 2002 (E) (otherwise) (SI 2002/1095) |
| | | 1 Jul 2002 (W) (SI 2002/1475) |
| 43 | | 1 Apr 2002 (E) (SI 2002/1095) |
| | | 1 Jul 2002 (W) (SI 2002/1475) |
| 44 | | 11 May 2001 (in so far as conferring any power to make an order or regulations which is exercisable by the Secretary of State) (RA) |
| | | 1 Apr 2002 (S) (otherwise) (SSI 2002/75) |
| 45 | | 11 May 2001 (in so far as conferring any power to make an order or regulations which is exercisable by the Secretary of State) (RA) |
| | | 19 Dec 2001 (E) (otherwise) (SI 2001/4149) |
| | | In force (otherwise) immediately before the National Health Service Act 2006 comes into force (SI 2006/1407)[10] |
| 46 | | 11 May 2001 (in so far as conferring any power to make an order or regulations which is exercisable by the Secretary of State) (RA) |
| | | 1 Aug 2001 (E) (otherwise) (SI 2001/2804) |
| | | In force (otherwise) immediately before the National Health Service Act 2006 comes into force (SI 2006/1407)[10] |
| 47 | (1)–(4) | 11 May 2001 (in so far as conferring any power to make an order or regulations which is exercisable by the Secretary of State) (RA) |
| | | 1 Aug 2001 (E) (otherwise) (SI 2001/2804) |

**See Halsbury's Statutes Citator for amendments to these Acts** 1271

**Health and Social Care Act 2001 (c 15)**—*contd*

|  |  |  |
|---|---|---|
|  |  | In force (otherwise) immediately before the National Health Service Act 2006 comes into force (SI 2006/1407)[10] |
|  | (5), (6) | 11 May 2001 (in so far as conferring any power to make an order or regulations which is exercisable by the Secretary of State) (RA) |
|  |  | 1 Aug 2001 (E) (except in so far as relates to directions given under s 45) (SI 2001/2804) |
|  |  | 19 Dec 2001 (E) (otherwise) (SI 2001/4149) |
|  |  | In force (otherwise) immediately before the National Health Service Act 2006 comes into force (SI 2006/1407)[10] |
|  | (7), (8) | 11 May 2001 (in so far as conferring any power to make an order or regulations which is exercisable by the Secretary of State) (RA) |
|  |  | 1 Aug 2001 (E) (otherwise) (SI 2001/2804) |
|  |  | In force (otherwise) immediately before the National Health Service Act 2006 comes into force (SI 2006/1407)[10] |
| 48 |  | 1 Aug 2001 (E) (SI 2001/2804) |
|  |  | 1 Nov 2004 (W) (SI 2004/1754) |
| 49 |  | 11 May 2001 (in so far as conferring any power to make an order or regulations which is exercisable by the Secretary of State) (RA) |
|  |  | 1 Oct 2001 (E) (in so far as it relates to certain persons only[1]) (SI 2001/3294) |
|  |  | 3 Dec 2001 (W) (in so far as it relates to certain persons only[3]) (SI 2001/3807) |
|  |  | 1 Apr 2003 (E) (otherwise) (SI 2003/850) |
|  |  | 1 Apr 2004 (W) (otherwise) (SI 2004/103) |
| 50 | (1) | 8 Apr 2002 (SI 2001/3752) |
|  | (2)–(7) | 19 Dec 2001 (W) (SI 2001/3807) |
|  |  | 20 Dec 2001 (E) (SI 2001/3752) |
|  |  | 1 Apr 2002 (S) (SSI 2002/75) |
|  | (8) | 11 May 2001 (in so far as conferring any power to make an order or regulations which is exercisable by the Secretary of State) (RA) |
|  |  | 19 Dec 2001 (W) (otherwise) (SI 2001/3807) |
|  |  | 20 Dec 2001 (E) (otherwise) (SI 2001/3752) |
|  |  | 1 Apr 2002 (S) (otherwise) (SSI 2002/75) |
|  | (9) | 11 May 2001 (in so far as conferring any power to make an order or regulations which is exercisable by the Secretary of State) (RA) |
|  |  | 19 Dec 2001 (W) (otherwise) (SI 2001/3807) |
|  |  | 1 Apr 2002 (S) (SSI 2002/75) |
|  |  | *Not yet in force* (E) (otherwise) |
|  | (10) | 19 Dec 2001 (W) (SI 2001/3807) |
|  |  | 20 Dec 2001 (E) (SI 2001/3752) |
|  |  | 1 Apr 2002 (S) (SSI 2002/75) |
| 51, 52 |  | 11 May 2001 (in so far as conferring any power to make an order or regulations which is exercisable by the Secretary of State) (RA) |
|  |  | 8 Nov 2001 (otherwise) (SI 2001/3752) |
| 53 |  | 1 Oct 2001 (E) (SI 2001/3167) |
|  |  | 1 Apr 2003 (W) (SI 2003/939) |
|  |  | *Not yet in force* (S) |
| 54 |  | 11 May 2001 (in so far as conferring any power to make an order or regulations which is exercisable by the Secretary of State) (RA) |
|  |  | 1 Oct 2001 (E) (otherwise) (SI 2001/3167) |
|  |  | 1 Apr 2003 (W) (otherwise) (SI 2003/939) |

**Health and Social Care Act 2001 (c 15)**—*contd*

| | | |
|---|---|---|
| 55 | (1)–(6) | 1 Oct 2001 (E) (for the purpose of enabling a local authority to enter into a deferred payment agreement with a resident who has a beneficial interest in property which he occupies or formerly occupied as his only or main residence) (SI 2001/3167) |
| | | 1 Apr 2003 (W) (SI 2003/939) |
| | | *Not yet in force* (E) (otherwise) |
| | (7) | 1 Apr 2003 (W) (SI 2003/939) |
| | | *Never in force* (substituted) (E) |
| | (8) | 1 Oct 2001 (E) (for the purpose of enabling a local authority to enter into a deferred payment agreement with a resident who has a beneficial interest in property which he occupies or formerly occupied as his only or main residence) (SI 2001/3167) |
| | | 1 Apr 2003 (W) (SI 2003/939) |
| | | *Not yet in force* (E) (otherwise) |
| 56 | | 11 May 2001 (in so far as conferring any power to make an order or regulations which is exercisable by the Secretary of State) (RA) |
| | | *Not yet in force* (otherwise) |
| 57 | | 11 May 2001 (in so far as conferring any power to make an order or regulations which is exercisable by the Secretary of State) (RA) |
| | | 16 Mar 2003 (E) (otherwise) (SI 2003/850) |
| | | 1 Nov 2004 (W) (otherwise) (SI 2004/1754) |
| 58 | | 16 Mar 2003 (E) (for the purpose of making regulations under the Children Act 1989, s 17A) (SI 2003/850) |
| | | 8 Apr 2003 (E) (otherwise) (SI 2003/850) |
| | | 8 Jul 2004 (W) (in so far as confers powers to make regulations) (SI 2004/1754) |
| | | 1 Nov 2004 (W) (otherwise) (SI 2004/1754) |
| 59–61 | | 11 May 2001 (RA) |
| 62 | | 11 May 2001 (in so far as conferring any power to make an order or regulations which is exercisable by the Secretary of State) (RA) |
| | | 15 Apr 2002 (E) (S) (SI 2002/1312) |
| | | *Not yet in force* (W) (otherwise) |
| 63 | | 6 Mar 2002 (for the purpose of making orders) (SI 2002/1095) |
| | | 1 Apr 2002 (otherwise) (SI 2002/1095) |
| 64–66 | | 11 May 2001 (RA) |
| 67 | (1) | See Sch 5 below |
| | (2) | See Sch 6 below |
| 68–70 | | 11 May 2001 (RA) |
| Sch 1 | | 11 May 2001 (in so far as conferring any power to make an order or regulations which is exercisable by the Secretary of State) (RA) |
| | | 1 Jan 2003 (E) (otherwise) (SI 2003/53) |
| | | *Never in force* (W) (otherwise) (repealed) |
| Sch 2 | | 11 May 2001 (in so far as conferring any power to make an order or regulations which is exercisable by the Secretary of State) (RA) |
| | | 8 Mar 2002 (E) (otherwise) (SI 2002/1095) |
| | | 1 Jul 2002 (W) (otherwise) (SI 2002/1475) |
| Sch 3 | | 1 Jul 2002 (W) (SI 2002/1475) |
| | | 28 Feb 2006 (E) (for the purpose of making regulations) (SI 2006/481) |
| | | 1 Apr 2006 (E) (otherwise) (SI 2006/481) |
| Sch 4 | | 1 Aug 2001 (E) (SI 2001/2804) |
| | | 1 Nov 2004 (W) (SI 2004/1754) |
| Sch 5 | para 1 | 1 Jul 2002 (W) (SI 2002/1475) |

**Health and Social Care Act 2001 (c 15)**—*contd*

|  |  |
|---|---|
| | 1 Jan 2003 (E) (SI 2003/53) |
| | *Not yet in force* (S) (NI) |
| para 2 | 1 Apr 2002 (E) (SI 2002/1095) |
| | 1 Jul 2002 (W) (SI 2002/1475) |
| | *Never in force* (spent) (S)[6] |
| para 3 | 1 Oct 2001 (E) (for the purpose of constituting the Family Health Services Appeal Authority and for making rules or regulations in respect of it) (SI 2001/3294) |
| | 1 Dec 2001 (E) (otherwise) (SI 2001/3294) |
| | 1 Jul 2002 (W) (SI 2002/1475) |
| | 26 Aug 2002 (W) (SI 2002/1919)[9] |
| para 4 | 1 Jul 2002 (W) (SI 2002/1475) |
| | 1 Jan 2003 (E) (SI 2003/53) |
| | *Not yet in force* (S) (NI) |
| para 5(1) | See sub-paras (2)–(17) below |
| para 5(2) | 1 Apr 2002 (SI 2002/1095)[7] |
| | 1 Jul 2002 (W) (SI 2002/1475) |
| para 5(3) | 22 Oct 2001 (E) (SI 2001/3619) |
| | In force (otherwise) immediately before the National Health Service Act 2006 comes into force (SI 2006/1407)[10] |
| para 5(4) | 11 May 2001 (in so far as conferring any power to make an order or regulations which is exercisable by the Secretary of State) (RA) |
| | 22 Nov 2001 (E) (for the purpose of making regulations) (SI 2001/3738) |
| | 14 Dec 2001 (E) (for all other purposes except those relating to the provision of pharmaceutical services) (SI 2001/3738) |
| | *Never in force* (otherwise) (repealed) |
| para 5(5), (6) | 11 May 2001 (in so far as conferring any power to make an order or regulations which is exercisable by the Secretary of State) (RA) |
| | 1 Apr 2002 (otherwise) (SI 2002/1095) |
| para 5(7) | 1 Apr 2002 (E) (SI 2002/1095) |
| | 1 Jul 2002 (W) (SI 2002/1475) |
| | 14 Dec 2001 (E) (SI 2001/3738)[4] |
| | 1 Jul 2002 (W) (SI 2002/1475) |
| | 26 Aug 2002 (W) (SI 2002/1919)[8, 9] |
| para 5(8) | 14 Dec 2001 (E) (SI 2001/3738)[4] |
| | 1 Jul 2002 (W) (SI 2002/1475) |
| | 26 Aug 2002 (W) (SI 2002/1919)[8, 9] |
| para 5(9) | 1 Apr 2002 (SI 2002/1095) |
| para 5(10)(a) | 1 Apr 2002 (SI 2002/1095) |
| para 5(10)(b) | 1 Oct 2001 (E) (for the purpose of constituting the Family Health Services Appeal Authority and for making rules or regulations in respect of it) (SI 2001/3294) |
| | 1 Dec 2001 (E) (otherwise) (SI 2001/3294) |
| | 26 Aug 2002 (W) (SI 2002/1919) |
| para 5(11) | In force immediately before the National Health Service Act 2006 comes into force (SI 2006/1407)[10] |
| para 5(12)(a) | 1 Apr 2006 (E) (SI 2006/481) |
| | In force (otherwise) immediately before the National Health Service Act 2006 comes into force (SI 2006/1407)[10] |
| para 5(12)(b), (c) | *Never in force* (repealed) |
| para 5(13)(a), (b) | 1 Oct 2001 (E) (for the purpose of constituting the Family Health Services Appeal Authority and for making rules or regulations in respect of it) (SI 2001/3294) |
| | 1 Dec 2001 (E) (otherwise) (SI 2001/3294) |
| | 26 Aug 2002 (W) (SI 2002/1919) |
| para 5(13)(c) | *Never in force* (repealed) |

**Health and Social Care Act 2001 (c 15)**—*contd*

| | |
|---|---|
| para 5(13)(d) | 1 Oct 2001 (E) (for the purpose of constituting the Family Health Services Appeal Authority and for making rules or regulations in respect of it) (SI 2001/3294) |
| | 1 Dec 2001 (E) (otherwise) (SI 2001/3294) |
| | 26 Aug 2002 (W) (SI 2002/1919) |
| para 5(14) | 22 Nov 2001 (E) (for the purpose of making regulations) (SI 2001/3738) |
| | 14 Dec 2001 (E) (for all other purposes except those relating to the provision of pharmaceutical services) (SI 2001/3738) |
| | 1 Feb 2003 (E) (otherwise) (SI 2003/53) |
| | In force (otherwise) immediately before the National Health Service Act 2006 comes into force (SI 2006/1407)[10] |
| para 5(15) | *Never in force* (repealed) |
| para 5(16) | 14 Dec 2001 (E) (SI 2001/3738)[4] |
| | 26 Aug 2002 (W) (SI 2002/1919)[8] |
| para 5(17) | 1 Jan 2003 (E) (SI 2003/53) |
| | In force (otherwise) immediately before the National Health Service Act 2006 comes into force (SI 2006/1407)[10] |
| para 6 | 1 Jul 2002 (W) (SI 2002/1475) |
| | 1 Sep 2003 (E) (SI 2003/2245) |
| para 7 | 1 Jul 2002 (W) (SI 2002/1475) |
| | 1 Jan 2003 (E) (SI 2003/53) |
| | *Not yet in force* (S) (NI) |
| para 8 | 1 Jul 2002 (W) (SI 2002/1475) |
| | *Never in force* (E) (repealed) |
| para 9 | 1 Jul 2002 (W) (SI 2002/1475) |
| | 1 Jan 2003 (E) (SI 2003/53) |
| | *Not yet in force* (S) |
| para 10 | 1 Oct 2001 (E) (for the purpose of constituting the Family Health Services Appeal Authority and for making rules or regulations in respect of it) (SI 2001/3294) |
| | 1 Dec 2001 (E) (otherwise) (SI 2001/3294) |
| | 1 Jul 2002 (W) (SI 2002/1475) |
| | 26 Aug 2002 (W) (SI 2002/1919)[9] |
| para 11(1) | See sub-paras (2)–(4) below |
| para 11(2)(a) | 1 Jul 2002 (W) (SI 2002/1475) |
| | 1 Jan 2003 (E) (SI 2003/53) |
| | *Never in force* (S) (repealed) |
| para 11(2)(b) | 1 Jul 2002 (W) (SI 2002/1475) |
| | *Never in force* (otherwise) (repealed) |
| para 11(3) | 1 Apr 2002 (E) (SI 2002/1095) |
| | 1 Jul 2002 (W) (SI 2002/1475) |
| | *Never in force* (S) (repealed) |
| para 11(4) | 1 Jul 2002 (W) (SI 2002/1475) |
| | 1 Apr 2006 (E) (SI 2006/481) |
| para 12(1) | 14 Dec 2001 (E) (for all purposes except those relating to the provision of pharmaceutical services) (SI 2001/3738) |
| | *Never in force* (otherwise) (repealed) |
| para 12(2) | 14 Dec 2001 (E) (for all purposes except those relating to the provision of pharmaceutical services) (SI 2001/3738) |
| | *Never in force* (otherwise) (repealed) |
| para 12(3) | *Never in force* (repealed) |
| para 13 | 1 Jan 2003 (E) (SI 2003/53) |
| | *Not yet in force* (W) |
| para 14 | 1 Jul 2002 (W) (SI 2002/1475) |
| | 1 Jan 2003 (E) (SI 2003/53) |
| | *Not yet in force* (S) (NI) |
| para 15(1) | See sub-paras (2), (3) below |
| para 15(2) | 8 Apr 2003 (E) (SI 2003/850) |

**Health and Social Care Act 2001 (c 15)**—*contd*

|  |  |  |
|---|---|---|
|  |  | 1 Nov 2004 (W) (SI 2004/1754) |
|  | para 15(3) | 22 Oct 2001 (E) (in so far as relating to functions in relation to the provision of residential accommodation only) (SI 2001/3619) |
|  |  | 8 Apr 2003 (E) (in so far as relating to the making of direct payments to a person in respect of his securing provision of community care services or services to carers) (SI 2003/850) |
|  |  | 1 Nov 2004 (W) (in so far as inserts words "making of direct payments to a person in respect of his securing provision of community care services or services to carers", and the related references to Part 4 of the Act, into the Local Authority Social Services Act 1970, Sch 1) (SI 2004/1754) |
|  |  | *Not yet in force* (W) (in so far as inserts words "Functions in relation to the provision of residential accommodation.", and the related references to Part 4 of the Act, into the Local Authority Social Services Act 1970, Sch 1) |
|  | para 16 | *Not yet in force* |
|  | paras 17, 18 | 11 May 2001 (RA) |
| Sch 6 | Pt 1 | 14 Dec 2001 (E) (repeals of or in National Health Service Act 1977, s 29(4), for all purposes except those relating to the provision of pharmaceutical services) (SI 2001/3738) |

para 15(3)

Sch 6    Pt 1

14 Dec 2001 (E) (SI 2001/3738)[4], repeals of or in—
National Health Service Act 1977, ss 46–49E, Sch 9;
National Health Service (Amendment) Act 1995

1 Apr 2002 (SI 2002/1095), repeals of or in—
National Health Service Act 1977, ss 7, 33(1B), 34, 85(1)(d), 100(1)(c), 102;
Parliamentary Commissioners Act 1967, Sch 2;
Police Act 1997, s 115

1 Jul 2002 (W) (SI 2002/1475), repeals of or in—
National Health Service Act 1977, s 102;
National Health Service (Amendment) Act 1995;
Police Act 1997

26 Aug 2002 (W) (SI 2002/1919)[8], repeals of or in—
National Health Service Act 1977, ss 46–49E, Sch 9;
National Health Service (Amendment) Act 1995

1 Feb 2003 (E) (repeals of or in National Health Service Act 1977, s 42(3)(d)) (SI 2003/53)

In force (otherwise) immediately before the National Health Service Act 2006 comes into force (SI 2006/1407)[10], repeals of or in—
National Health Service Act 1977;
National Health Service and Community Care Act 1990;
Health Authorities Act 1995;
National Health Service (Primary Care) Act 1997;
Health Act 1999

*Not yet in force* (repeals in Government Resources and Accounts Act 2000)

Pt 2    1 Jul 2002 (W) (SI 2002/1475), repeals of or in—
Health Services Act 1980;
National Health Service and Community Care Act 1990;
Health Authorities Act 1995;
National Health Service (Primary Care) Act 1997

1 Apr 2006 (E) (SI 2006/481)

*Not yet in force* (W) (superseded) (repeal in Medicinal Products: Prescription by Nurses etc Act 1992)

Pt 3    15 Apr 2002 (SI 2002/1312), repeals of or in—
National Assistance Act 1948, s 26A;
Social Work (Scotland) Act 1968, s 86A;
National Health Service and Community Care Act 1990, ss 43, 57;

**Health and Social Care Act 2001 (c 15)**—*contd*

Social Security Contributions and Benefits Act 1992,
s 135(3), (4)

8 Apr 2003 (E) (SI 2003/850), repeals of or in—
Community Care (Direct Payments) Act 1996;
Carers and Disabled Children Act 2000

1 Nov 2004 (W) (SI 2004/1754), repeals in—
Community Care (Direct Payments) Act 1996;
Carers and Disabled Children Act 2000

*Not yet in force*, repeals of or in—
Local Authorities Social Services Act 1970;
Community Care (Residential Accommodation) Act 1998, ss 1,
3(2)

1    "Certain persons" means any person:

(a) who is provided with accommodation by a local authority under National Assistance Act 1948,
s 21(1); and

(b) who, if the local authority were also to provide the nursing care in connection with that
accommodation, would be liable to make a payment under s 22(3) or 26(3) of that Act either at the
standard rate or at a lower rate which is not less than the standard rate minus £110

Notwithstanding that a person ceases to satisfy head (b) above, the Health and Social Care Act 2001,
s 49 shall continue to apply to him

2    S 1 has effect in England in relation to the determination of allotments and resource limits for the
financial year beginning with 1 Apr 2002 and subsequent financial years; see SI 2001/3619, art 2(2)

3    "Certain persons" means any person:

(a) who is provided with accommodation by a local authority under National Assistance Act 1948,
s 21(1); and

(b) who, if the local authority were also to provide the nursing care in connection with that
accommodation, would be liable to make a payment under s 22 or 26 of that Act either at the standard
rate or at a lower rate which is not less than the standard rate minus £100

Notwithstanding that a person ceases to satisfy head (b) above, the Health and Social Care Act 2001,
s 49 shall continue to apply to him

4    For transitional provisions, see SI 2001/3738, art 2(5), (6)

5    For transitional provisions, see SI 2002/1095, arts 3, 4

6    Although the provision amended by para 2 extends to Scotland, the amendment made by para 2 does
not, for practical purposes, affect its application to Scotland, and accordingly para 2 may never be
brought into force in relation to Scotland

7    It is unclear from the drafting of SI 2002/1095, whether this provision was intended to be brought
into force on 1 Apr 2002 for both England and Wales or England only

8    For transitional provisions, see SI 2002/1919, art 2(2), (3)

9    Note that SI 2002/1919 purports to bring this provision into force in relation to Wales. As this
provision has already been brought into force in relation to Wales by SI 2002/1475, it is thought that
there is an error in either SI 2002/1475 or SI 2002/1919

10    For saving, see SI 2006/1407, art 4

---

**House of Commons (Removal of Clergy Disqualification) Act 2001 (c 13)**

*RA:* 11 May 2001

Whole Act in force 11 May 2001 (RA)

---

**Housing (Scotland) Act 2001 (asp 10)**

*RA:* 18 Jul 2001

*Commencement provisions:* s 113(1), (2); Housing (Scotland) Act 2001 (Commencement No 1, Transitional
Provisions and Savings) Order 2001, SSI 2001/336, as amended by SSI 2001/397; Housing (Scotland)

**Housing (Scotland) Act 2001 (asp 10)**—*contd*
Act 2001 (Commencement No 2, Transitional Provisions, Savings and Variation) Order 2001,
SSI 2001/397; Housing (Scotland) Act 2001 (Commencement No 3, Transitional Provisions and
Savings) Order 2001, SSI 2001/467; Housing (Scotland) Act 2001 (Commencement No 4,
Transitional Provisions and Savings) Order 2002, SSI 2002/168; Housing (Scotland) Act 2001
(Commencement No 5, Transitional Provisions and Savings) Order 2002, SSI 2002/321, as amended
by SSI 2002/433; Housing (Scotland) Act 2001 (Commencement No 6 and Amendment)
Order 2002, SSI 2002/433; Housing (Scotland) Act 2001 (Commencement No 7, Transitional
Provisions and Savings) Order 2003, SSI 2003/434

| | | |
|---|---|---|
| 1, 2 | | 1 Oct 2001 (SSI 2001/336) |
| 3 | (1)(a) | 1 Apr 2002 (SSI 2002/168)[4] |
| | (1)(b) | 30 Sep 2002 (SSI 2002/321)[5] |
| | (1)(c) | 1 Apr 2002 (SSI 2002/168)[4] |
| | (1)(d) | 30 Sep 2002 (SSI 2002/321)[5] |
| | (2), (3) | 30 Sep 2002 (SSI 2002/321)[5] |
| | (4)(a) | 30 Sep 2002 (SSI 2002/321)[5] |
| | (4)(b) | 1 Apr 2002 (SSI 2002/168)[4] |
| | (4)(c) | 30 Sep 2002 (SSI 2002/321)[5] |
| | (5), (6) | 30 Sep 2002 (SSI 2002/321)[5] |
| 4 | | 1 Apr 2002 (SSI 2002/168)[4] |
| 5–7 | | 30 Sep 2002 (SSI 2002/321)[5] |
| 8–10 | | 1 Apr 2002 (SSI 2002/168)[4] |
| 11–56 | | 30 Sep 2002 (SSI 2002/321)[5] |
| 57–83 | | 1 Nov 2001 (SSI 2001/336)[1] |
| 84 | | 1 Nov 2001 (for the purpose of transferring all of the functions of Scottish Homes to the Scottish Ministers except the functions conferred by Housing (Scotland) Act 1988, s 1(3)(b)) (SSI 2001/397)[2] |
| | | *Not yet in force* (exception noted above) |
| 85 | | 1 Nov 2001 (SSI 2001/397) |
| 86 | | *Not yet in force* |
| 87 | | 1 Nov 2001 (SSI 2001/397) |
| 88 | | 1 Oct 2001 (SSI 2001/336) |
| 89 | | 1 Nov 2001 (SSI 2001/397) |
| 90–94 | | 1 Nov 2001 (SSI 2001/336) |
| 95 | | 1 Oct 2001 (SSI 2001/336) |
| 96–105 | | 1 Oct 2003 (SSI 2003/434)[6] |
| 106, 107 | | 1 Nov 2001 (SSI 2001/336) |
| 108 | | 1 Oct 2001 (SSI 2001/336) |
| 109, 110 | | 18 Jul 2001 (RA) |
| 111 | | 1 Oct 2001 (SSI 2001/336) |
| 112 | | See Sch 10 below |
| 113 | | 18 Jul 2001 (RA) |
| Schs 1–6 | | 30 Sep 2002 (SSI 2002/321)[5] |
| Schs 7–9 | | 1 Nov 2001 (SSI 2001/336)[1] |
| Sch 10 | para 1 | 1 Nov 2001 (SSI 2001/397)[2] |
| | para 2 | 1 Nov 2001 (SSI 2001/336) |
| | paras 3, 4 | 30 Sep 2002 (SSI 2002/321)[5] |
| | paras 5, 6 | *Not yet in force* |
| | para 7 | 30 Sep 2002 (SSI 2002/321)[5] |
| | para 8 | *Not yet in force* |
| | para 9(1) | See sub-paras (2)–(4) below |
| | para 9(2) | 1 Nov 2001 (SSI 2001/336) |
| | para 9(3) | 30 Sep 2002 (SSI 2002/321)[5] |
| | para 9(4) | 1 Nov 2001 (SSI 2001/336) |
| | para 10 | 30 Sep 2002 (SSI 2002/321)[5] |
| | paras 11, 12 | 1 Nov 2001 (SSI 2001/336) |
| | para 13(1) | See sub-paras (2)–(42) below |
| | para 13(2) | 19 Dec 2001 (repeal of Housing (Scotland) Act 1987, s 12A) (SSI 2001/467)[3] |

**Housing (Scotland) Act 2001 (asp 10)**—*contd*

| | |
|---|---|
| | *Not yet in force* (repeals of Housing (Scotland) Act 1987, ss 1, 17C) |
| para 13(3) | 1 Apr 2002 (SSI 2002/168)[4] |
| para 13(4) | 30 Sep 2002 (SSI 2002/433) |
| para 13(5)–(16) | 30 Sep 2002 (SSI 2002/321)[5] |
| para 13(17) | 19 Dec 2001 (repeal of Housing (Scotland) Act 1987, s 81B) (SSI 2001/467)[3] |
| | 30 Sep 2002 (otherwise) (SSI 2002/321)[5] |
| para 13(18)–(22) | 30 Sep 2002 (SSI 2002/321)[5] |
| para 13(23) | 1 Oct 2003 (SSI 2003/434)[6] |
| para 13(24) | 1 Nov 2001 (SSI 2001/336) |
| para 13(25)–(34) | 1 Oct 2003 (SSI 2003/434)[6] |
| para 13(35) | 1 Nov 2001 (SSI 2001/336) |
| para 13(36)–(40) | 30 Sep 2002 (SSI 2002/321)[5] |
| para 13(41)(a), (b) | 30 Sep 2002 (SSI 2002/321)[5] |
| para 13(41)(c) | 1 Oct 2003 (SSI 2003/434)[6] |
| para 13(42) | 19 Dec 2001 (repeal of Housing (Scotland) Act 1987, Sch 6A) (SSI 2001/467)[3] |
| | 30 Sep 2002 (repeal of Housing (Scotland) Act 1987, Schs 2–5) (SSI 2002/321)[5] |
| | 1 Oct 2003 (otherwise) (SSI 2003/434)[6] |
| para 14(1) | See sub-paras (2)–(15) below |
| para 14(2)–(4) | 1 Nov 2001 (SSI 2001/397)[2] |
| para 14(5)(a) | 1 Nov 2001 (SSI 2001/336) |
| para 14(5)(b) | *Not yet in force* |
| para 14(5)(c) | 30 Sep 2002 (SSI 2002/321)[5] |
| para 14(6)–(8) | 1 Nov 2001 (SSI 2001/336) |
| para 14(9) | 30 Sep 2002 (SSI 2002/321)[5] |
| para 14(10) | 1 Nov 2001 (SSI 2001/397)[2] |
| para 14(11) | 1 Nov 2001 (so far as relates to para 6) (SSI 2001/336) |
| | *Not yet in force* (so far as relates to paras 2, 3(a), 4 and 14) |
| para 14(12)(a), (b) | 30 Sep 2002 (SSI 2002/321)[5] |
| para 14(12)(c) | 1 Nov 2001 (SSI 2001/336) |
| para 14(13) | *Not yet in force* |
| para 14(14) | 30 Sep 2002 (SSI 2002/321)[5] |
| para 14(15) | 1 Nov 2001 (so far as relates to paras 6, 8, 9) (SSI 2001/336) |
| | 30 Sep 2002 (otherwise) (SSI 2002/321)[5] |
| para 15(1) | See sub-paras (1)–(9) below |
| para 15(2) | 1 Nov 2001 (SSI 2001/336) |
| para 15(3), (4) | 1 Nov 2001 (SSI 2001/397)[2] |
| para 15(5) | 30 Sep 2002 (repeal of Housing Act 1988, s 55) (SSI 2002/321)[5] |
| | *Not yet in force* (repeal of Housing Act 1988, s 54) |
| para 15(6) | 1 Nov 2001 (SSI 2001/397)[2] |
| para 15(7) | 30 Sep 2002 (SSI 2002/321)[5] |
| para 15(8) | 1 Nov 2001 (SSI 2001/336) |
| para 15(9) | 30 Sep 2002 (SSI 2002/321)[5] |
| para 16 | 30 Sep 2002 (SSI 2002/321)[5] |
| para 17 | 1 Apr 2002 (SSI 2002/168) |
| para 18 | *Not yet in force* |
| para 19(1) | 30 Sep 2002 (SSI 2002/321)[5] |
| para 19(2) | *Not yet in force* |
| para 20 | 1 Apr 2002 (repeal of Leasehold Reform, Housing and Urban Development Act 1993, s 155(2)) (SSI 2002/168) |
| | 30 Sep 2002 (otherwise) (SSI 2002/321)[5] |
| paras 21–23 | 30 Sep 2002 (SSI 2002/321)[5] |
| para 24 | 1 Nov 2001 (SSI 2001/397)[2] |
| para 25 | 30 Sep 2002 (SSI 2002/321)[5] |
| para 26 | *Not yet in force* |
| para 27 | 30 Sep 2002 (SSI 2002/321)[5] |
| para 28 | 1 Nov 2001 (SSI 2001/397)[2] |

**Housing (Scotland) Act 2001 (asp 10)**—*contd*

        para 29        *Not yet in force*

[1]    For transitional provisions and savings, see SSI 2001/336, art 3

[2]    For transitional provisions and savings, see SSI 2001/397, arts 3–6

[3]    For transitional provisions and savings, see SSI 2001/467, art 3

[4]    For transitional provisions and savings, see SSI 2002/168, art 3

[5]    For transitional provisions and savings, see SSI 2002/321, arts 3–5

[6]    For transitional provisions and savings, see SSI 2003/434, arts 3, 4

---

## Human Reproductive Cloning Act 2001 (c 23)

*RA:* 4 Dec 2001

Whole Act in force 4 Dec 2001 (RA)

---

## International Criminal Court Act 2001 (c 17)

*RA:* 11 May 2001

*Commencement provisions:* s 82; International Criminal Court Act 2001 (Commencement) Order 2001, SI 2001/2161, as amended by SI 2001/2304

| | | |
|---|---|---|
| 1–6 | | 1 Sep 2001 (SI 2001/2161) |
| 7 | (1), (2) | 1 Sep 2001 (SI 2001/2161) |
| | (3) | 13 Jun 2001 (for purposes of making any Order in Council, order, rules or regulations) (SI 2001/2161) |
| | | 1 Sep 2001 (otherwise) (SI 2001/2161) |
| | (4)–(6) | 1 Sep 2001 (SI 2001/2161) |
| 8–12 | | 1 Sep 2001 (SI 2001/2161) |
| 13 | (1), (2) | 1 Sep 2001 (SI 2001/2161) |
| | (3) | 13 Jun 2001 (for purposes of making any Order in Council, order, rules or regulations) (SI 2001/2161) |
| | | 1 Sep 2001 (otherwise) (SI 2001/2161) |
| | (4)–(6) | 1 Sep 2001 (SI 2001/2161) |
| 14–48 | | 1 Sep 2001 (SI 2001/2161) |
| 49 | | 13 Jun 2001 (for purposes of making any Order in Council, order, rules or regulations) (SI 2001/2161) |
| | | 1 Sep 2001 (otherwise) (SI 2001/2161) |
| 50 | (1), (2) | 1 Sep 2001 (SI 2001/2161) |
| | (3), (4) | 13 Jun 2001 (for purposes of making any Order in Council, order, rules or regulations) (SI 2001/2161) |
| | | 1 Sep 2001 (otherwise) (SI 2001/2161) |
| | (5), (6) | 1 Sep 2001 (SI 2001/2161) |
| 51–78 | | 1 Sep 2001 (SI 2001/2161) |
| 79 | (1), (2) | 1 Sep 2001 (SI 2001/2161) |
| | (3) | 13 Jun 2001 (for purposes of making any Order in Council, order, rules or regulations) (SI 2001/2161) |
| | | 1 Sep 2001 (otherwise) (SI 2001/2161) |
| | (4), (5) | 1 Sep 2001 (SI 2001/2161) |
| 80 | (1), (2) | 1 Sep 2001 (SI 2001/2161) |
| | (3) | 13 Jun 2001 (for purposes of making any Order in Council, order, rules or regulations) (SI 2001/2161) |
| | | 1 Sep 2001 (otherwise) (SI 2001/2161) |
| 81–84 | | 1 Sep 2001 (SI 2001/2161) |
| Sch 1 | para 1 | 13 Jun 2001 (for purposes of making any Order in Council, order, rules or regulations) (SI 2001/2161) |
| | | 1 Sep 2001 (otherwise) (SI 2001/2161) |

### International Criminal Court Act 2001 (c 17)—*contd*

| | | |
|---|---|---|
| | paras 2–7 | 1 Sep 2001 (SI 2001/2161) |
| Schs 2–10 | | 1 Sep 2001 (SI 2001/2161) |

### International Criminal Court (Scotland) Act 2001 (asp 13)

*RA:* 24 Sep 2001

*Commencement provisions:* s 30(2); International Criminal Court (Scotland) Act 2001 (Commencement) Order 2001, SSI 2001/456

| | |
|---|---|
| 1–29 | 17 Dec 2001 (SSI 2001/456) |
| 30 | 24 Sep 2001 (RA) |
| Schs 1–6 | 17 Dec 2001 (SSI 2001/456) |

### Leasehold Casualties (Scotland) Act 2001 (asp 5)

*RA:* 12 Apr 2001

*Commencement provisions:* ss 1(3), 5(3), 6(2), 7(4)

| | |
|---|---|
| 1 | 10 May 2000 (s 1(3)) |
| 2–4 | 12 Apr 2001 (RA) |
| 5 | 10 May 2000 (s 5(3)) |
| 6 | 12 Feb 2001 (s 6(2)) |
| 7 | 10 May 2000 (s 7(4)) |
| 8–11 | 12 Apr 2001 (RA) |
| Schs 1, 2 | 12 Apr 2001 (RA) |

### Mortgage Rights (Scotland) Act 2001 (asp 11)

*RA:* 25 Jul 2001

*Commencement provisions:* s 7(1); Mortgage Rights (Scotland) Act 2001 (Commencement and Transitional Provision) Order 2001, SSI 2001/418[1]

| | |
|---|---|
| 1–6 | 3 Dec 2001 (SSI 2001/418) |
| 7 | 25 Jul 2001 (RA) |
| Schedule | 3 Dec 2001 (SSI 2001/418) |

[1]   For a transitional provision, see SSI 2001/418, art 3

### Police and Fire Services (Finance) (Scotland) Act 2001 (asp 15)

*RA:* 5 Dec 2001

*Commencement provisions:* s 3(2); Police and Fire Services (Finance) (Scotland) Act 2001 (Commencement) Order 2002, SSI 2002/84

| | |
|---|---|
| 1, 2 | 11 Mar 2002 (SSI 2002/84) |
| 3 | 5 Dec 2001 (RA) |

### Private Security Industry Act 2001 (c 12)

*RA:* 11 May 2001

*Commencement provisions:* s 26(2); Private Security Industry Act 2001 (Commencement No 1) Order 2002, SI 2002/3125; Private Security Industry Act 2001 (Commencement No 2) Order 2003, SI 2003/2710; Private Security Industry Act 2001 (Commencement No 3) Order 2004, SI 2004/1431; Private Security Industry Act 2001 (Commencement No 4) Order 2004, SI 2004/2191; Private Security Industry Act 2001 (Commencement No 5) Order 2004,

**Private Security Industry Act 2001 (c 12)**—*contd*
    SI 2004/2591; Private Security Industry Act 2001 (Commencement No 6) Order 2004,
SI 2004/3141; Private Security Industry Act 2001 (Commencement No 7) Order 2004,
SI 2004/3230; Private Security Industry Act 2001 (Commencement No 8) Order 2005, SI 2005/243,
as amended by SI 2005/362; Private Security Industry Act 2001 (Commencement No 9) Order 2005,
SI 2005/1104; Private Security Industry Act 2001 (Commencement No 10) Order 2006,
SI 2006/392; Private Security Industry Act 2001 (Commencement No 1) (Scotland) Order 2006,
SSI 2006/382; Private Security Industry Act 2001 (Commencement No 2) (Scotland) Order 2007,
SSI 2007/242; Private Security Industry Act 2001 (Commencement No 1) (Northern Ireland)
Order 2009, SI 2009/644; Private Security Industry Act 2001 (Commencement No 2) (Northern
Ireland) Order 2009, SI 2009/1058

| | | |
|---|---|---|
| 1 | (1)–(5) | 1 Apr 2003 (E) (W) (SI 2002/3125) |
| | | 6 Jul 2006 (S) (SSI 2006/382) |
| | | 11 Mar 2009 (NI) (for the purpose of making regulations or orders) (SI 2009/644) |
| | | 1 May 2009 (NI) (otherwise) (SI 2009/1058) |
| | (6) | See Sch 1 below |
| 2 | | 1 Apr 2003 (E) (W) (SI 2002/3125) |
| | | 6 Jul 2006 (S) (SSI 2006/382) |
| | | 1 May 2009 (NI) (SI 2009/1058) |
| 3 | (1) | 4 Jun 2004 (in the police area of Hampshire) (SI 2004/1431) |
| | | 13 Sep 2004 (in the police areas of Avon and Somerset; Devon and Cornwall; Dorset; Gloucestershire; and Wiltshire) (SI 2004/2191) |
| | | 27 Sep 2004 (in the police areas of Dyfed Powys; Gwent; North Wales; and South Wales) (SI 2004/2191) |
| | | 18 Oct 2004 (in the police areas of Leicestershire; Northamptonshire; Staffordshire; Warwickshire; West Mercia; and West Midlands) (SI 2004/2591) |
| | | 15 Nov 2004 (in the police areas of Cheshire; Cumbria; Greater Manchester; Lancashire; and Merseyside) (SI 2004/2591) |
| | | 13 Dec 2004 (in the police areas of Cleveland; Durham; Humberside; Northumbria; North Yorkshire; South Yorkshire; and West Yorkshire) (SI 2004/3141) |
| | | 3 Jan 2005 (in the police areas of Cambridgeshire; Derbyshire; Lincolnshire; Norfolk; Nottinghamshire; and Suffolk) (SI 2004/3141) |
| | | 28 Feb 2005 (E) (W) (otherwise) (SI 2005/243) |
| | | 6 Jul 2006 (S) (SSI 2006/382) |
| | | 11 Mar 2009 (NI) (for the purpose of making regulations or orders) (SI 2009/644) |
| | | 1 May 2009 (NI) (otherwise) (SI 2009/1058) |
| | (2)(a)–(i) | 24 May 2004 (in the police area of Hampshire) (SI 2004/1431) |
| | | 1 Jun 2004 (in the police areas of Avon and Somerset; Devon and Cornwall; Dorset; Gloucestershire; and Wiltshire) (SI 2004/1431) |
| | | 27 Sep 2004 (in the police areas of Dyfed Powys; Gwent; North Wales; and South Wales) (SI 2004/2191) |
| | | 18 Oct 2004 (in the police areas of Leicestershire; Northamptonshire; Staffordshire; Warwickshire; West Mercia; and West Midlands) (SI 2004/2591) |
| | | 15 Nov 2004 (in the police areas of Cheshire; Cumbria; Greater Manchester; Lancashire; and Merseyside) (SI 2004/2591) |
| | | 13 Dec 2004 (in the police areas of Cleveland; Durham; Humberside; Northumbria; North Yorkshire; South Yorkshire; and West Yorkshire) (SI 2004/3141) |
| | | 3 Jan 2005 (in the police areas of Cambridgeshire; Derbyshire; Lincolnshire; Norfolk; Nottinghamshire; and Suffolk) (SI 2004/3141) |

**Private Security Industry Act 2001 (c 12)**—*contd*

|  |  |  |
|---|---|---|
|  |  | 28 Feb 2005 (in the police areas of Bedfordshire; Essex; Hertfordshire; Kent; Surrey; Sussex; and Thames Valley) (SI 2005/243) |
|  |  | 11 Apr 2005 (E) (W) (otherwise) (SI 2005/243) |
|  |  | 6 Jul 2006 (S) (SSI 2006/382) |
|  |  | 11 Mar 2009 (NI) (for the purpose of making regulations or orders) (SI 2009/644) |
|  |  | 1 May 2009 (NI) (otherwise) (SI 2009/1058) |
|  | (2)(j) | 28 Feb 2005 (E) (W) (SI 2005/243) |
|  |  | 6 Jul 2006 (S) (SSI 2006/382) |
|  |  | 11 Mar 2009 (NI) (for the purpose of making regulations or orders) (SI 2009/644) |
|  |  | 1 May 2009 (NI) (otherwise) (SI 2009/1058) |
|  | (3) | 1 Apr 2003 (E) (W) (for the purpose of making regulations or orders) (SI 2002/3125) |
|  |  | 1 Feb 2004 (E) (W) (otherwise) (SI 2003/2710) |
|  |  | 6 Jul 2006 (S) (SSI 2006/382) |
|  |  | 11 Mar 2009 (NI) (for the purpose of making regulations or orders) (SI 2009/644) |
|  |  | 1 May 2009 (NI) (otherwise) (SI 2009/1058) |
|  | (4)–(6) | 1 Feb 2004 (E) (W) (SI 2003/2710) |
|  |  | 6 Jul 2006 (S) (SSI 2006/382) |
|  |  | 11 Mar 2009 (NI) (for the purpose of making regulations or orders) (SI 2009/644) |
|  |  | 1 May 2009 (NI) (otherwise) (SI 2009/1058) |
| 4 | (1)–(3) | 1 Apr 2003 (E) (W) (for the purpose of making regulations or orders) (SI 2002/3125) |
|  |  | 1 Feb 2004 (E) (W) (otherwise) (SI 2003/2710) |
|  |  | 6 Jul 2006 (S) (SSI 2006/382) |
|  |  | 11 Mar 2009 (NI) (for the purpose of making regulations or orders) (SI 2009/644) |
|  |  | 1 May 2009 (NI) (otherwise) (SI 2009/1058) |
|  | (4), (5) | 1 Feb 2004 (E) (W) (SI 2003/2710) |
|  |  | 6 Jul 2006 (S) (SSI 2006/382) |
|  |  | 11 Mar 2009 (NI) (for the purpose of making regulations or orders) (SI 2009/644) |
|  |  | 1 May 2009 (NI) (otherwise) (SI 2009/1058) |
| 5 |  | 1 Dec 2004 (in the police areas of Avon and Somerset; Cheshire; Cumbria; Devon and Cornwall; Dorset; Dyfed Powys; Gloucestershire; Greater Manchester; Gwent; Hampshire; Lancashire; Leicestershire; Merseyside; North Wales; South Wales; Staffordshire; Warwickshire; West Mercia; West Midlands; and Wiltshire) (SI 2004/3141) |
|  |  | 13 Dec 2004 (in the police areas of Cleveland; Durham; Humberside; Northumbria; North Yorkshire; South Yorkshire; and West Yorkshire) (SI 2004/3141) |
|  |  | 13 Dec 2004 (in the police area of Northamptonshire) (SI 2004/3230) |
|  |  | 3 Jan 2005 (in the police areas of Cambridgeshire; Derbyshire; Lincolnshire; Norfolk; Nottinghamshire; and Suffolk) (SI 2004/3141) |
|  |  | 28 Feb 2005 (in the police areas of Bedfordshire; Essex; Hertfordshire; Kent; Surrey; Sussex; and Thames Valley) (SI 2005/243) |
|  |  | 11 Apr 2005 (E) (W) (otherwise) (SI 2005/243) |
|  |  | 6 Jul 2006 (S) (SSI 2006/382) |
|  |  | 1 May 2009 (NI) (SI 2009/1058) |
| 6 |  | 3 May 2005 (E) (W) (SI 2005/1104) |
|  |  | 1 May 2009 (NI) (SI 2009/1058) |
|  |  | *Never in force* (S) (repealed) |

**Private Security Industry Act 2001 (c 12)**—*contd*

| | | |
|---|---|---|
| 7 | | 1 Nov 2003 (E) (W) (SI 2003/2710) |
| | | 6 Jul 2006 (S) (SSI 2006/382) |
| | | 11 Mar 2009 (NI) (for the purpose of making regulations or orders) (SI 2009/644) |
| | | 1 May 2009 (NI) (otherwise) (SI 2009/1058) |
| 8 | (1) | 1 Feb 2004 (E) (W) (SI 2003/2710) |
| | | 6 Jul 2006 (S) (SSI 2006/382) |
| | | 11 Mar 2009 (NI) (for the purpose of making regulations or orders) (SI 2009/644) |
| | | 1 May 2009 (NI) (otherwise) (SI 2009/1058) |
| | (2) | 1 Apr 2003 (E) (W) (for the purpose of making regulations or orders) (SI 2002/3125) |
| | | 1 Feb 2004 (E) (W) (otherwise) (SI 2003/2710) |
| | | 6 Jul 2006 (S) (SSI 2006/382) |
| | | 11 Mar 2009 (NI) (for the purpose of making regulations or orders) (SI 2009/644) |
| | | 1 May 2009 (NI) (otherwise) (SI 2009/1058) |
| | (3) | 1 Feb 2004 (E) (W) (SI 2003/2710) |
| | | 6 Jul 2006 (S) (SSI 2006/382) |
| | | 11 Mar 2009 (NI) (for the purpose of making regulations or orders) (SI 2009/644) |
| | | 1 May 2009 (NI) (otherwise) (SI 2009/1058) |
| | (4)(a) | 1 Nov 2003 (E) (W) (for the purpose of making regulations) (SI 2003/2710) |
| | | 1 Feb 2004 (E) (W) (otherwise) (SI 2003/2710) |
| | | 6 Jul 2006 (S) (SSI 2006/382) |
| | | 11 Mar 2009 (NI) (for the purpose of making regulations or orders) (SI 2009/644) |
| | | 1 May 2009 (NI) (otherwise) (SI 2009/1058) |
| | (4)(b), (c) | 1 Feb 2004 (E) (W) (SI 2003/2710) |
| | | 6 Jul 2006 (S) (SSI 2006/382) |
| | | 11 Mar 2009 (NI) (for the purpose of making regulations or orders) (SI 2009/644) |
| | | 1 May 2009 (NI) (otherwise) (SI 2009/1058) |
| | (5) | 1 Apr 2003 (E) (W) (for the purpose of making regulations or orders) (SI 2002/3125) |
| | | 1 Feb 2004 (E) (W) (otherwise) (SI 2003/2710) |
| | | 6 Jul 2006 (S) (SSI 2006/382) |
| | | 11 Mar 2009 (NI) (for the purpose of making regulations or orders) (SI 2009/644) |
| | | 1 May 2009 (NI) (otherwise) (SI 2009/1058) |
| | (6) | 1 Feb 2004 (E) (W) (SI 2003/2710) |
| | | 6 Jul 2006 (S) (SSI 2006/382) |
| | | 11 Mar 2009 (NI) (for the purpose of making regulations or orders) (SI 2009/644) |
| | | 1 May 2009 (NI) (otherwise) (SI 2009/1058) |
| | (7), (8) | 1 Apr 2003 (E) (W) (for the purpose of making regulations or orders) (SI 2002/3125) |
| | | 1 Feb 2004 (E) (W) (otherwise) (SI 2003/2710) |
| | | 6 Jul 2006 (S) (SSI 2006/382) |
| | | 11 Mar 2009 (NI) (for the purpose of making regulations or orders) (SI 2009/644) |
| | | 1 May 2009 (NI) (otherwise) (SI 2009/1058) |
| 9 | (1)–(3) | 1 Apr 2003 (E) (W) (for the purpose of making regulations or orders) (SI 2002/3125) |
| | | 1 Feb 2004 (E) (W) (otherwise) (SI 2003/2710) |
| | | 6 Jul 2006 (S) (SSI 2006/382) |
| | | 11 Mar 2009 (NI) (for the purpose of making regulations or orders) (SI 2009/644) |
| | | 1 May 2009 (NI) (otherwise) (SI 2009/1058) |

**Private Security Industry Act 2001 (c 12)**—*contd*

| | | |
|---|---|---|
| | (4), (5) | 1 Feb 2004 (E) (W) (SI 2003/2710) |
| | | 6 Jul 2006 (S) (SSI 2006/382) |
| | | 11 Mar 2009 (NI) (for the purpose of making regulations or orders) (SI 2009/644) |
| | | 1 May 2009 (NI) (otherwise) (SI 2009/1058) |
| 10–12 | | 1 Feb 2004 (E) (W) (SI 2003/2710) |
| | | 6 Jul 2006 (S) (SSI 2006/382) |
| | | 1 May 2009 (NI) (SI 2009/1058) |
| 13 | (1)–(4) | 1 Feb 2004 (SI 2003/2710) |
| | (5), (6) | 1 Apr 2003 (for the purpose of making regulations or orders) (SI 2002/3125) |
| | | 1 Feb 2004 (otherwise) (SI 2003/2710) |
| | (7) | 1 Feb 2004 (SI 2003/2710) |
| 14 | | 20 Mar 2006 (E) (W) (SI 2006/392) |
| | | 6 Apr 2007 (S) (SSI 2007/242) |
| | | 1 May 2009 (NI) (SI 2009/1058) |
| 15 | (1) | 20 Mar 2006 (E) (W) (SI 2006/392) |
| | | 6 Apr 2007 (S) (SSI 2007/242) |
| | | 1 May 2009 (NI) (SI 2009/1058) |
| | (2)(a)–(e), | 20 Mar 2006 (E) (W) (SI 2006/392) |
| | | 6 Apr 2007 (S) (SSI 2007/242) |
| | | 1 May 2009 (NI) (SI 2009/1058) |
| | (2)(f)(i) | 20 Mar 2006 (E) (W) (SI 2006/392) |
| | | 6 Apr 2007 (S) (SSI 2007/242) |
| | | 1 May 2009 (NI) (SI 2009/1058) |
| | (2)(f)(ii) | 1 Apr 2003 (E) (W) (for the purpose of making orders) (SI 2002/3125) |
| | | 20 Mar 2006 (E) (W) (otherwise) (SI 2006/392) |
| | | 6 Jul 2006 (S) (for the purpose of making orders) (SSI 2006/382) |
| | | 6 Apr 2007 (S) (otherwise) (SSI 2007/242) |
| | | 11 Mar 2009 (NI) (for the purpose of making orders) (SI 2009/644) |
| | | 1 May 2009 (NI) (otherwise) (SI 2009/1058) |
| | (2)(g) | 20 Mar 2006 (E) (W) (SI 2006/392) |
| | | 6 Apr 2007 (S) (SSI 2007/242) |
| | | 1 May 2009 (NI) (SI 2009/1058) |
| | (3)(a), (b) | 1 Apr 2003 (E) (W) (for the purpose of making regulations) (SI 2002/3125) |
| | | 20 Mar 2006 (E) (W) (otherwise) (SI 2006/392) |
| | | 6 Jul 2006 (S) (for the purpose of making regulations) (SSI 2006/382) |
| | | 6 Apr 2007 (S) (otherwise) (SSI 2007/242) |
| | | 11 Mar 2009 (NI) (for the purpose of making regulations) (SI 2009/644) |
| | | 1 May 2009 (NI) (otherwise) (SI 2009/1058) |
| | (3)(c), (d) | 20 Mar 2006 (E) (W) (SI 2006/392) |
| | | 6 Apr 2007 (S) (SSI 2007/242) |
| | | 1 May 2009 (NI) (SI 2009/1058) |
| | (4) | 1 Apr 2003 (E) (W) (for the purpose of making regulations) (SI 2002/3125) |
| | | 20 Mar 2006 (E) (W) (otherwise) (SI 2006/392) |
| | | 6 Jul 2006 (S) (for the purpose of making regulations) (SSI 2006/382) |
| | | 6 Apr 2007 (S) (otherwise) (SSI 2007/242) |
| | | 11 Mar 2009 (NI) (for the purpose of making regulations) (SI 2009/644) |
| | | 1 May 2009 (NI) (otherwise) (SI 2009/1058) |
| | (5)–(7) | 20 Mar 2006 (E) (W) (SI 2006/392) |
| | | 6 Apr 2007 (S) (SSI 2007/242) |

**Private Security Industry Act 2001 (c 12)**—*contd*

| | | |
|---|---|---|
| | | 1 May 2009 (NI) (SI 2009/1058) |
| | (8) | 1 Apr 2003 (E) (W) (for the purpose of making regulations) (SI 2002/3125) |
| | | 20 Mar 2006 (E) (W) (otherwise) (SI 2006/392) |
| | | 6 Jul 2006 (S) (for the purpose of making regulations) (SSI 2006/382) |
| | | 6 Apr 2007 (S) (otherwise) (SSI 2007/242) |
| | | 11 Mar 2009 (NI) (for the purpose of making regulations) (SI 2009/644) |
| | | 1 May 2009 (NI) (otherwise) (SI 2009/1058) |
| 16 | | 20 Mar 2006 (E) (W) (SI 2006/392) |
| | | 6 Apr 2007 (S) (SSI 2007/242) |
| | | 1 May 2009 (NI) (SI 2009/1058) |
| 17 | (1) | 1 Apr 2003 (E) (W) (for the purpose of making regulations) (SI 2002/3125) |
| | | 6 Jul 2006 (S) (for the purpose of making regulations) (SSI 2006/382) |
| | | 1 May 2009 (NI) (SI 2009/1058) |
| | | *Not yet in force* (S) (otherwise) |
| | (2)–(4) | *Not yet in force* |
| | (5) | 1 Apr 2003 (E) (W) (for the purpose of making regulations) (SI 2002/3125) |
| | | 6 Jul 2006 (S) (for the purpose of making regulations) (SSI 2006/382) |
| | | 1 May 2009 (NI) (SI 2009/1058) |
| | | *Not yet in force* (S) (otherwise) |
| 18 | | 20 Mar 2006 (E) (W) (SI 2006/392) |
| | | 6 Apr 2007 (S) (SSI 2007/242) |
| | | 1 May 2009 (NI) (SI 2009/1058) |
| 19 | | 1 Feb 2004 (E) (W) (SI 2003/2710) |
| | | 6 Jul 2006 (S) (SSI 2006/382) |
| | | 19 Dec 2009 (NI) (SI 2009/1058) |
| 20 | | 1 Nov 2003 (E) (W) (SI 2003/2710) |
| | | 6 Jul 2006 (S) (SSI 2006/382) |
| | | 19 Dec 2009 (NI) (SI 2009/1058) |
| 21 | | *Never in force* (repealed) |
| 22, 23 | | 1 Feb 2004 (E) (W) (SI 2003/2710) |
| | | 6 Jul 2006 (S) (SSI 2006/382) |
| | | 1 May 2009 (NI) (SI 2009/1058) |
| 24 | | 1 Apr 2003 (E) (W) (SI 2002/3125) |
| | | 6 Jul 2006 (S) (SSI 2006/382) |
| | | 11 Mar 2009 (NI) (for the purpose of making regulations or orders) (SI 2009/644) |
| | | 1 May 2009 (NI) (otherwise) (SI 2009/1058) |
| 25 | | 1 Jan 2003 (E) (W) (SI 2002/3125) |
| | | 6 Jul 2006 (S) (SSI 2006/382) |
| | | 11 Mar 2009 (NI) (for the purpose of making regulations or orders) (SI 2009/644) |
| | | 1 May 2009 (NI) (otherwise) (SI 2009/1058) |
| 26 | | 11 May 2001 (RA) |
| Sch 1 | paras 1–3 | 1 Jan 2003 (E) (W) (SI 2002/3125) |
| | | 6 Jul 2006 (S) (SSI 2006/382) |
| | | 1 May 2009 (NI) (SI 2009/1058) |
| | paras 4, 5 | 1 Apr 2003 (E) (W) (SI 2002/3125) |
| | | 6 Jul 2006 (S) (SSI 2006/382) |
| | | 1 May 2009 (NI) (SI 2009/1058) |
| | para 6(1)(a) | 1 Jan 2003 (E) (W) (SI 2002/3125) |
| | | 6 Jul 2006 (S) (SSI 2006/382) |
| | | 1 May 2009 (NI) (SI 2009/1058) |

**Private Security Industry Act 2001 (c 12)**—*contd*

| | | |
|---|---|---|
| | para 6(1)(b) | 1 Apr 2003 (E) (W) (SI 2002/3125) |
| | | 6 Jul 2006 (S) (SSI 2006/382) |
| | | 1 May 2009 (NI) (SI 2009/1058) |
| | para 6(2) | 1 Jan 2003 (E) (W) (SI 2002/3125) |
| | | 6 Jul 2006 (S) (SSI 2006/382) |
| | | 1 May 2009 (NI) (SI 2009/1058) |
| | para 6(3) | 1 Apr 2003 (E) (W) (SI 2002/3125) |
| | | 6 Jul 2006 (S) (SSI 2006/382) |
| | | 1 May 2009 (NI) (SI 2009/1058) |
| | paras 7–24 | 1 Apr 2003 (E) (W) (SI 2002/3125) |
| | | 6 Jul 2006 (S) (SSI 2006/382) |
| | | 1 May 2009 (NI) (SI 2009/1058) |
| Sch 2 | para 1 | 1 Apr 2003 (E) (W) (for the purpose of making orders) (SI 2002/3125) |
| | | 1 Feb 2004 (E) (W) (otherwise) (SI 2003/2710) |
| | | 6 Jul 2006 (S) (SSI 2006/382) |
| | | 11 Mar 2009 (NI) (for the purpose of making orders) (SI 2009/644) |
| | | 1 May 2009 (NI) (otherwise) (SI 2009/1058) |
| | para 2 | 1 Feb 2004 (E) (W) (SI 2003/2710) |
| | | 6 Jul 2006 (S) (SSI 2006/382) |
| | | 1 May 2009 (NI) (SI 2009/1058) |
| | para 3 | 1 Feb 2004 (E) (W) (SI 2003/2710) |
| | | 1 May 2009 (NI) (SI 2009/1058) |
| | paras 4–6 | 1 Feb 2004 (E) (W) (SI 2003/2710) |
| | | 6 Jul 2006 (S) (SSI 2006/382) |
| | | 1 May 2009 (NI) (SI 2009/1058) |
| | para 7 | 1 Apr 2003 (E) (W) (for the purpose of making orders) (SI 2002/3125) |
| | | 1 Feb 2004 (E) (W) (otherwise) (SI 2003/2710) |
| | | 6 Jul 2006 (S) (SSI 2006/382) |
| | | 11 Mar 2009 (NI) (for the purpose of making orders) (SI 2009/644) |
| | | 1 May 2009 (NI) (otherwise) (SI 2009/1058) |
| | paras 8, 9 | 1 Feb 2004 (E) (W) (SI 2003/2710) |
| | | 6 Jul 2006 (S) (SSI 2006/382) |
| | | 11 Mar 2009 (NI) (for the purpose of making regulations) (SI 2009/644) |
| | | 1 May 2009 (NI) (otherwise) (SI 2009/1058) |

---

## Rating (Former Agricultural Premises and Rural Shops) Act 2001 (c 14)

*RA:* 11 May 2001

*Commencement provisions:* s 6(2); Rating (Former Agricultural Premises and Rural Shops) Act 2001 (Commencement No 1) Order 2001, SI 2001/2580

| | | |
|---|---|---|
| 1 | (1), (2) | 15 Aug 2001 (E) (SI 2001/2580) |
| | | *Not yet in force* (W) |
| | (3) | 17 Jul 2001 (E) (so far as it confers power on the Secretary of State to make an order under Local Government Finance Act 1988, s 43(6F)) (SI 2001/2580) |
| | | 15 Aug 2001 (E) (otherwise) (SI 2001/2580) |
| | | *Not yet in force* (W) |
| | (4) | 15 Aug 2001 (E) (SI 2001/2580) |
| | | *Not yet in force* (W) (otherwise) |
| 2–5 | | 15 Aug 2001 (E) (SI 2001/2580) |
| | | *Not yet in force* (W) (s 2 repealed) |
| 6 | | 11 May 2001 (RA) |

---

### Regulation of Care (Scotland) Act 2001 (asp 8)

*RA:* 5 Jul 2001

*Commencement provisions:* s 81(2), (3); Regulation of Care (Scotland) Act 2001 (Commencement No 1) Order 2001, SSI 2001/304; Regulation of Care (Scotland) Act 2001 (Commencement No 2 and Transitional Provisions) Order 2002, SSI 2002/162[1]; Regulation of Care (Scotland) Act 2001 (Commencement No 3 and Transitional Provisions) Order 2003, SSI 2003/205; Regulation of Care (Scotland) Act 2001 (Commencement No 4) Order 2003, SSI 2003/596; Regulation of Care (Scotland) Act 2001 (Commencement No 5 and Transitional Provisions) Order 2004, SSI 2004/100, as amended by SSI 2004/377; Regulation of Care (Scotland) Act 2001 (Commencement No 6) Order 2005, SSI 2005/426; Regulation of Care (Scotland) Act 2001 (Commencement No 7 and Transitional Provisions) Order 2006, SSI 2006/275, amended by SSI 2007/67

| | | |
|---|---|---|
| 1 | | 19 Jul 2001 (s 81(2)) |
| 2 | (1)(a)–(h) | 1 Apr 2002 (SSI 2002/162) |
| | (1)(i), (j) | 1 Apr 2004 (SSI 2004/100)[6] |
| | (1)(k) | 20 Jun 2006 (SSI 2006/275)[7] |
| | (1)(l), (m) | 1 Apr 2002 (SSI 2002/162) |
| | (1)(n) | 1 Apr 2003 (SSI 2003/205)[5] |
| | (2)–(4) | 1 Apr 2002 (SSI 2002/162) |
| | (5)(a), (b) | 1 Apr 2002 (SSI 2002/162) |
| | (5)(c) | 1 Apr 2002 (so far as relates to certain independent clinics)[2] (SSI 2002/162) |
| | | *Never in force* (otherwise) (repealed) |
| | (5)(d) | *Never in force* (repealed) |
| | (6) | 1 Apr 2002 (SSI 2002/162) |
| | (7) | 1 Apr 2002 (so far as relates to certain child care agencies)[3] (SSI 2002/162) |
| | | 1 Apr 2003 (otherwise) (SSI 2003/205)[5] |
| | (8) | 1 Apr 2003 (SSI 2003/205)[5] |
| | (9) | 1 Apr 2002 (SSI 2002/162) |
| | (10) | 1 Apr 2002 (so far as relates to certain offender accommodation services)[4] (SSI 2002/162) |
| | | 1 Apr 2004 (otherwise) (SSI 2004/100)[6] |
| | (11)–(15) | 1 Apr 2004 (SSI 2004/100)[6] |
| | (16) | 20 Jun 2006 (SSI 2006/275)[7] |
| | (17)–(26) | 1 Apr 2002 (SSI 2002/162) |
| | (27) | 1 Apr 2003 (SSI 2003/205)[5] |
| | (28) | 1 Apr 2002 (SSI 2002/162) |
| 3 | | 1 Apr 2002 (SSI 2002/162) |
| 4 | | 19 Jul 2001 (s 81(2)) |
| 5 | (1), (2) | 1 Oct 2001 (SSI 2001/304) |
| | (3) | 1 Apr 2002 (SSI 2002/162) |
| | (4) | 1 Apr 2004 (SSI 2004/100)[6] |
| 6 | | 1 Oct 2001 (SSI 2001/304) |
| 7 | | 1 Apr 2002 (SSI 2002/162) |
| 8 | | 1 Apr 2003 (SSI 2003/205)[5] |
| 9–23 | | 1 Apr 2002 (SSI 2002/162) |
| 24 | (1) | 1 Oct 2001 (SSI 2001/304) |
| | (2), (3) | 1 Apr 2002 (SSI 2002/162) |
| 25–27 | | 1 Apr 2002 (SSI 2002/162) |
| 28 | | 19 Jul 2001 (s 81(2)) |
| 29, 30 | | 1 Oct 2001 (SSI 2001/304) |
| 31, 32 | | 1 Apr 2002 (SSI 2002/162) |
| 33 | (1)(a), (b) | 1 Apr 2004 (SSI 2004/100)[6] |
| | (1)(c) | 1 Apr 2002 (SSI 2002/162) |
| | (2)–(4) | 1 Apr 2002 (SSI 2002/162) |
| 34–42 | | 1 Apr 2002 (SSI 2002/162) |
| 43 | | 19 Jul 2001 (s 81(2)) |
| 44–51 | | 1 Apr 2002 (SSI 2002/162) |
| 52 | (1)(a) | 1 Sep 2005 (SSI 2005/426) |

**Regulation of Care (Scotland) Act 2001 (asp 8)**—*contd*

|  |  |  |
|---|---|---|
|  | (1)(b) | *Not yet in force* |
|  | (2) | 1 Sep 2005 (SSI 2005/426) |
| 53–55 |  | 1 Oct 2001 (SSI 2001/304) |
| 56–62 |  | 19 Jul 2001 (s 81(2)) |
| 63–65 |  | 1 Oct 2001 (SSI 2001/304) |
| 66 |  | 19 Jul 2001 (s 81(2)) |
| 67 |  | 1 Oct 2001 (SSI 2001/304) |
| 68, 69 |  | 19 Jul 2001 (s 81(2)) |
| 70 |  | 20 Dec 2001 (SSI 2001/304) |
| 71 |  | 1 Oct 2001 (SSI 2001/304) |
| 72 |  | 1 Apr 2002 (SSI 2002/162) |
| 73 | (1)(a) | 5 Dec 2003 (SSI 2003/596) |
|  | (1)(b) | 1 Apr 2004 (SSI 2003/596) |
|  | (2)–(4) | 5 Dec 2003 (SSI 2003/596) |
| 74–78 |  | 19 Jul 2001 (s 81(2)) |
| 79 |  | See Sch 3 below |
| 80 | (1) | See Sch 4 below |
|  | (2) | 19 Jul 2001 (s 81(2)) |
|  | (3), (4) | 1 Oct 2001 (SSI 2001/304) |
| 81 |  | 5 Jul 2001 (RA) |
| Schs 1, 2 |  | 19 Jul 2001 (s 81(2)) |
| Sch 3 | paras 1–3 | 1 Apr 2002 (SSI 2002/162) |
|  | para 4(1) | 1 Apr 2002 (SSI 2002/162) |
|  | para 4(2) | 1 Apr 2004 (SSI 2004/100)[6] |
|  | para 4(3) | 1 Apr 2002 (SSI 2002/162) |
|  | paras 5, 6 | 1 Apr 2002 (SSI 2002/162) |
|  | para 7(1)–(10) | 1 Apr 2004 (SSI 2004/100)[6] |
|  | para 7(11)(a) | 1 Apr 2004 (SSI 2004/100)[6] |
|  | para 7(11)(b) | 1 Apr 2002 (SSI 2002/162) |
|  | para 7(11)(c) | 1 Apr 2004 (SSI 2004/100)[6] |
|  | paras 8–19 | 1 Apr 2002 (SSI 2002/162) |
|  | para 20 | 1 Oct 2001 (SSI 2001/304) |
|  | para 21 | 1 Apr 2002 (SSI 2002/162) |
|  | para 22(a) | *Not yet in force* |
|  | para 22(b), (c) | 1 Apr 2004 (SSI 2004/100)[6] |
|  | para 23(1)–(6) | 1 Apr 2002 (SSI 2002/162) |
|  | para 23(7) | 1 Oct 2001 (SSI 2001/304) |
|  | para 24 | *Never in force* (repealed) |
|  | para 25 | 1 Apr 2002 (SSI 2002/162) |
| Sch 4 |  | 1 Apr 2002 (except repeals of or in Children (Scotland) Act 1995, s 94, Sch 2) (SSI 2002/162) |
|  |  | 1 Apr 2004 (exception noted above) (SSI 2004/100)[6] |

[1] For transitional provisions, see SSI 2002/162, arts 3–13

[2] "Certain independent clinics" means an independent health care service, being an independent clinic, which is substantially the same as a nursing home in respect of which the person providing the independent health care service was, immediately before 1 Apr 2002, registered under the Nursing Homes Registration (Scotland) Act 1938

[3] "Certain child care agencies" means a child care agency, which is substantially the same as a service in respect of which the person providing the child care agency was, immediately before 1 Apr 2002, registered as a child minder under Part X of the Children Act 1989

[4] "Certain accommodation services" means an offender accommodation service which provides accommodation wholly or mainly in—

(a) an establishment in respect of which the person providing the offender accommodation service was, immediately before 1 Apr 2002, registered under the Social Work (Scotland) Act 1968; or

(b) other premises which have at any time been inspected by a person authorised to do so by a local authority as if they were, or formed a part of, an establishment which was required to be registered under that Act

**Regulation of Care (Scotland) Act 2001 (asp 8)**—*contd*

5    For transitional provisions, see SSI 2003/205, art 3

6    For transitional provisions, see SSI 2004/100, arts 3, 4

7    For transitional provisions, see SSI 2006/275, art 3

**Regulatory Reform Act 2001 (c 6)**

*RA:* 10 Apr 2001

Whole Act in force 10 Apr 2001 (RA)

**Salmon Conservation (Scotland) Act 2001 (asp 3)**

*RA:* 14 Feb 2001

*Commencement provisions:* s 3; Salmon Conservation (Scotland) Act 2001 (Commencement) Order 2001, SSI 2001/116

| | |
|---|---|
| 1, 2 | 15 Apr 2001 (SSI 2001/116) |
| 3 | 14 Feb 2001 (RA) |

**Scottish Local Authorities (Tendering) Act 2001 (asp 9)**

*RA:* 6 Jul 2001

*Commencement provisions:* s 2(2)

Whole Act in force 6 Aug 2001 (s 2(2))

**Social Security Contributions (Share Options) Act 2001 (c 20)**

*RA:* 11 May 2001

Whole Act in force 11 May 2001 (RA)

**Social Security Fraud Act 2001 (c 11)**

*RA:* 11 May 2001

*Commencement provisions:* s 20; Social Security Fraud Act 2001 (Commencement No 1) Order 2001, SI 2001/3251; Social Security Fraud Act 2001 (Commencement No 2) Order 2001, SI 2001/3689; Social Security Fraud Act 2001 (Commencement No 3) Order 2002, SI 2002/117; Social Security Fraud Act 2001 (Commencement No 4) Order 2002, SI 2002/403; Social Security Fraud Act 2001 (Commencement No 5) Order 2002, SI 2002/1222; Social Security Fraud Act 2001 (Commencement No 6) Order 2003, SI 2003/273

| | | |
|---|---|---|
| 1 | (1)–(3) | 30 Apr 2002 (SI 2002/1222) |
| | (4) | 26 Feb 2002 (SI 2002/403) |
| | (5)–(8) | 30 Apr 2002 (SI 2002/1222) |
| | (9) | 26 Feb 2002 (SI 2002/403) |
| 2 | | 30 Apr 2002 (SI 2002/1222) |
| 3 | | 28 Jan 2002 (SI 2002/117) |
| 4 | | 30 Apr 2002 (SI 2002/1222) |
| 5 | | 14 Feb 2003 (SI 2003/273) |
| 6 | | 30 Apr 2002 (SI 2002/1222) |
| 7–11 | | 17 Nov 2001 (for the purpose of authorising the making of regulations) (SI 2001/3689) |
| | | 1 Apr 2002 (otherwise) (SI 2001/3689) |
| 12 | | 1 Apr 2002 (SI 2001/3689) |

**Social Security Fraud Act 2001 (c 11)**—*contd*

| | |
|---|---|
| 13 | 17 Nov 2001 (for the purpose of authorising the making of regulations) (SI 2001/3689) |
| | 1 Apr 2002 (otherwise) (SI 2001/3689) |
| 14, 15 | 30 Apr 2002 (SI 2002/1222) |
| 16 | 26 Sep 2001 (for the purpose of authorising the making of regulations) (SI 2001/3251) |
| | 18 Oct 2001 (otherwise) (SI 2001/3251) |
| 17–19 | 30 Apr 2002 (SI 2002/1222) |
| 20, 21 | 11 May 2001 (RA) |
| Schedule | 30 Apr 2002 (SI 2002/1222)[1] |

[1] SI 2002/1222 does not specifically bring the Schedule to this Act into force, however, it does bring into force s 19 of the Act which introduces the Schedule; it is thought that the intention was to bring the Schedule into force on the same date as s 19

## Special Educational Needs and Disability Act 2001 (c 10)

*RA:* 11 May 2001

*Commencement provisions:* s 43; Special Educational Needs and Disability Act 2001 (Commencement No 1) Order 2001, SI 2001/2217, as amended by SI 2001/2614[1]; Special Educational Needs and Disability Act 2001 (Commencement No 2) (Wales) Order 2001, SI 2001/3992; Special Educational Needs and Disability Act 2001 (Commencement) (Wales) Order 2002, SI 2002/74; Special Educational Needs and Disability Act 2001 (Commencement No 3) Order 2002, SI 2002/1647; Special Educational Needs and Disability Act 2001 (Commencement No 4) Order 2002, SI 2002/1721; Special Educational Needs and Disability Act 2001 (Commencement No 5) Order 2002, SI 2002/2217; Special Educational Needs and Disability Act 2001 (Commencement No 2) (Wales) Order 2003, SI 2003/2532

| | | |
|---|---|---|
| 1 | | 15 Jun 2001 (E) (so far as necessary for the purpose of making regulations) (SI 2001/2217) |
| | | 1 Jan 2002 (E) (otherwise) (SI 2001/2217) |
| | | 21 Jan 2002 (W) (so far as necessary for the purpose of making regulations) (SI 2002/74) |
| | | 1 Apr 2002 (W) (otherwise) (SI 2002/74) |
| 2, 3 | | 1 Jan 2002 (E) (SI 2001/2217) |
| | | 1 Apr 2002 (W) (SI 2002/74) |
| 4, 5 | | 11 May 2001 (so far as necessary for enabling the making of regulations) (RA) |
| | | 1 Jan 2002 (E) (otherwise) (SI 2001/2217) |
| | | 1 Apr 2002 (W) (otherwise) (SI 2001/3992) |
| 6 | | 1 Jan 2002 (E) (SI 2001/2217) |
| | | 1 Apr 2002 (W) (SI 2001/3992) |
| 7 | | 1 Jan 2002 (E) (SI 2001/2217) |
| | | 1 Apr 2002 (W) (SI 2002/74) |
| 8 | | 15 Jun 2001 (E) (so far as necessary for the purpose of making regulations) (SI 2001/2217) |
| | | 1 Jan 2002 (E) (otherwise) (SI 2001/2217) |
| | | 21 Jan 2002 (W) (so far as necessary for the purpose of making regulations) (SI 2002/74) |
| | | 1 Apr 2002 (W) (otherwise) (SI 2002/74) |
| 9 | | 11 May 2001 (so far as necessary for enabling the making of regulations) (RA) |
| | | 1 Jan 2002 (E) (otherwise) (SI 2001/2217) |
| | | 1 Apr 2002 (W) (otherwise) (SI 2002/74) |
| 10 | | See Sch 1 below |
| 11–13 | | 1 Sep 2002 (SI 2002/2217) |
| 14 | (1) | 1 Jul 2002 (E) (S) (so far as necessary for enabling the making of regulations) (SI 2002/1721) |
| | | 1 Sep 2002 (E) (S) (otherwise) (SI 2002/2217) |

**Special Educational Needs and Disability Act 2001 (c 10)**—*contd*

| | | |
|---|---|---|
| | | 8 Oct 2003 (W) (SI 2003/2532) |
| | (2) | 1 Sep 2002 (E) (SI 2002/2217) |
| | | *Never in force* (W) (repealed) |
| 15 | | 1 Jul 2002 (E) (S) (so far as necessary for the Secretary of State to issue guidance) (SI 2002/1721) |
| | | 1 Sep 2002 (E) (S) (otherwise) (SI 2002/2217) |
| | | 8 Oct 2003 (W) (SI 2003/2532) |
| 16–18 | | 1 Sep 2002 (SI 2002/2217) |
| 19 | (1) | 1 Jul 2002 (E) (W) (so far as necessary for enabling the making of regulations) (SI 2002/1721) |
| | | 1 Sep 2002 (otherwise) (SI 2002/2217) |
| | (2) | 1 Sep 2002 (SI 2002/2217) |
| 20, 21 | | 1 Sep 2002 (SI 2002/2217) |
| 22 | | 1 Sep 2002 (save in so far as it gives the National Assembly for Wales power to give directions under s 28M(1) or (3) of the Disability Discrimination Act 1995 or makes provision in relation to such a direction) (SI 2002/2217) |
| | | 8 Oct 2003 (exception noted above) (SI 2003/2532) |
| 23–25 | | 1 Sep 2002 (SI 2002/2217) |
| 26 | | 30 May 2002 (for the purpose of allowing the designation of educational institutions pursuant to Disability Discrimination Act 1995, s 28R(6)(c), (7)(e)) (SI 2002/1647) |
| | | 1 Sep 2002 (otherwise) (SI 2002/2217) |
| 27 | | 1 Sep 2002 (SI 2002/2217) |
| 28 | | 1 Sep 2002 (subject to modifications to the duty imposed by s 28T(1) of the Disability Discrimination Act 1995, as inserted by this section) (SI 2002/2217) |
| 29, 30 | | 1 Sep 2002 (SI 2002/2217) |
| 31 | | 30 May 2002 (SI 2002/1647) |
| 32–35 | | 1 Sep 2002 (SI 2002/2217) |
| 36 | (1) | 1 Jul 2002 (E) (W) (so far as relates to s 36(2)) (SI 2002/1721) |
| | | 1 Sep 2002 (otherwise) (SI 2002/2217) |
| | (2) | 1 Jul 2002 (E) (W) (SI 2002/1721) |
| | | 1 Sep 2002 (otherwise) (SI 2002/2217) |
| | (3)–(5) | 1 Sep 2002 (SI 2002/2217) |
| 37–40 | | 1 Sep 2002 (SI 2002/2217) |
| 41 | | 1 Jan 2002 (E) (SI 2001/2217) |
| | | 1 Apr 2002 (W) (SI 2001/3992) |
| | | 1 Sep 2002 (otherwise) (SI 2002/2217) |
| 42 | (1) | See Sch 8 below |
| | (2)–(4) | 11 May 2001 (so far as necessary for enabling the making of regulations) (RA) |
| | | 1 Jan 2002 (E) (otherwise) (SI 2001/2217) |
| | | 1 Apr 2002 (W) (otherwise) (SI 2001/3992) |
| | | 1 Sep 2002 (otherwise) (SI 2002/2217) |
| | (5) | 1 Jan 2002 (E) (SI 2001/2217) |
| | | 1 Sep 2002 (otherwise) (SI 2002/2217) |
| | (6) | See Sch 9 below |
| 43 | | 11 May 2001 (RA) |
| Sch 1 | paras 1, 2 | 1 Jan 2002 (E) (SI 2001/2217) |
| | | 1 Apr 2002 (W) (SI 2001/3992) |
| | para 3 | 15 Jun 2001 (E) (so far as necessary for the purpose of making regulations) (SI 2001/2217) |
| | | 8 Dec 2001 (W) (so far as necessary for the purpose of making regulations) (SI 2001/3992) |
| | | 1 Jan 2002 (E) (otherwise) (SI 2001/2217) |
| | | 1 Apr 2002 (W) (otherwise) (SI 2001/3992) |
| | paras 4–13 | 1 Jan 2002 (E) (SI 2001/2217) |
| | | 1 Apr 2002 (W) (SI 2001/3992) |

**Special Educational Needs and Disability Act 2001 (c 10)**—*contd*

| | | |
|---|---|---|
| | para 14 | 15 Jun 2001 (E) (so far as necessary for the purpose of making regulations) (SI 2001/2217) |
| | | 8 Dec 2001 (W) (so far as necessary for the purpose of making regulations) (SI 2001/3992) |
| | | 1 Jan 2002 (E) (otherwise) (SI 2001/2217) |
| | | 1 Apr 2002 (W) (otherwise) (SI 2001/3992) |
| | paras 15–20 | 1 Jan 2002 (E) (SI 2001/2217) |
| | | 1 Apr 2002 (W) (SI 2001/3992) |
| Schs 2–7 | | 1 Sep 2002 (SI 2002/2217) |
| Sch 8 | para 1 | 1 Jan 2002 (E) (SI 2001/2217) |
| | | 1 Apr 2002 (W) (SI 2002/74) |
| | paras 2–4 | 1 Sep 2002 (SI 2002/2217) |
| | para 5 | 1 Jan 2002 (E) (SI 2001/2217) |
| | | 1 Apr 2002 (W) (SI 2002/74) |
| | paras 6–10 | 11 May 2001 (so far as necessary for enabling the making of regulations) (RA) |
| | | 1 Jan 2002 (E) (otherwise) (SI 2001/2217) |
| | | 1 Apr 2002 (W) (otherwise) (SI 2002/74) |
| | paras 11, 12 | 1 Jan 2002 (E) (SI 2001/2217) |
| | | 1 Apr 2002 (W) (SI 2002/74) |
| | para 13(1)–(4) | 11 May 2001 (so far as necessary for enabling the making of regulations) (RA) |
| | | 1 Jan 2002 (E) (otherwise) (SI 2001/2217) |
| | | 1 Apr 2002 (W) (otherwise) (SI 2001/3992) |
| | para 13(5) | 1 Jul 2002 (SI 2002/1721) |
| | para 14(1), (2) | 1 Jan 2002 (E) (SI 2001/2217) |
| | | 1 Apr 2002 (W) (SI 2002/74) |
| | para 14(3) | 11 May 2001 (so far as necessary for enabling the making of regulations) (RA) |
| | | 1 Jan 2002 (E) (otherwise) (SI 2001/2217) |
| | | 1 Apr 2002 (W) (otherwise) (SI 2002/74) |
| | para 15 | 1 Jan 2002 (E) (SI 2001/2217) |
| | | 1 Apr 2002 (W) (SI 2001/3992) |
| | para 16 | 1 Jan 2002 (E) (SI 2001/2217) |
| | | 1 Apr 2002 (W) (SI 2002/74) |
| | paras 17, 18 | 15 Jun 2001 (E) (so far as necessary for the purpose of making regulations) (SI 2001/2217) |
| | | 1 Jan 2002 (E) (otherwise) (SI 2001/2217) |
| | | 21 Jan 2002 (W) (so far as necessary for the purpose of making regulations) (SI 2002/74) |
| | | 1 Apr 2002 (W) (otherwise) (SI 2002/74) |
| | paras 19–23 | 1 Sep 2002 (SI 2002/2217) |
| Sch 9 | | 1 Jan 2002 (E) (SI 2001/2217), repeals of or in— |
| | | Disabled Persons (Services, Consultation and Representation) Act 1986; |
| | | Education Act 1996, ss 325(1), 336(2), 441(3)(a), Sch 27; |
| | | School Standards and Framework Act 1998, Sch 30 |
| | | 1 Apr 2002 (W) (SI 2001/3992), repeals of or in— |
| | | Education Act 1996, ss 336(2)(d), 441(3)(a); |
| | | School Standards and Framework Act 1998, Sch 30, para 186(2)(b) |
| | | 1 Apr 2002 (W) (SI 2002/74), repeals of or in— |
| | | Disabled Persons (Services, Consultation and Representation) Act 1986, s 5(1); |
| | | Education Act 1996, s 325(1), Sch 27, paras 3(4), 8(1)(b)(iii), 9(1), 10 |
| | | 1 Sep 2002 (otherwise) (SI 2002/2217) |

[1]    SI 2001/2217 is amended by SI 2001/2614 with the effect that 1 Jan 2002 substitutes 1 Sep 2001 as

**Special Educational Needs and Disability Act 2001 (c 10)**—*contd*
the day appointed for the coming into force of the provisions specified in SI 2001/2217, art 5,
Schedule, Pt II

---

**Transport (Scotland) Act 2001 (asp 2)**

*RA:* 25 Jan 2001

*Commencement provisions:* s 84; Transport (Scotland) Act 2001 (Commencement No 1, Transitional
Provisions and Savings) Order 2001, SSI 2001/132; Transport (Scotland) Act 2001 (Commencement
No 2) Order 2001, SSI 2001/167; Transport (Scotland) Act 2001 (Commencement No 3 and
Transitional Provisions) Order 2002, SSI 2002/291[3]; Transport (Scotland) Act 2001 (Commencement
No 4) Order 2003, SSI 2003/588

| | | |
|---|---|---|
| 1, 2 | | 1 Apr 2001 (SSI 2001/132) |
| 3 | | 1 Jul 2001 (SSI 2001/132) |
| 4 | | 1 Apr 2001 (SSI 2001/132) |
| 5–10 | | 1 Jul 2001 (SSI 2001/132) |
| 11 | | 1 Apr 2001 (SSI 2001/132) |
| 12–25 | | 1 Jul 2001 (SSI 2001/132) |
| 26 | | 1 Apr 2001 (SSI 2001/132) |
| 27–35 | | 1 Jul 2001 (SSI 2001/132) |
| 36 | | 1 Apr 2001 (SSI 2001/132)[1] |
| 37 | | 1 Jul 2001 (SSI 2001/132) |
| 38 | (1) | 1 Jul 2002 (SSI 2002/291) |
| | (2) | 1 Apr 2001 (SSI 2001/132) |
| | (3)–(6) | 1 Jul 2002 (SSI 2002/291) |
| 39 | | 1 Jul 2002 (SSI 2002/291)[3] |
| 40 | (1) | 1 Apr 2001 (SSI 2001/132)[2] |
| | (2) | 1 Jul 2001 (SSI 2001/132) |
| | (3), (4) | 1 Apr 2001 (SSI 2001/132)[2] |
| 41–44 | | 1 Apr 2001 (SSI 2001/132) |
| 45 | | 1 Jul 2001 (SSI 2001/132) |
| 46 | | 1 Apr 2001 (SSI 2001/132) |
| 47 | | 1 Jul 2001 (SSI 2001/132) |
| 48–59 | | 1 Apr 2001 (SSI 2001/132) |
| 60 | | See Sch 1 below |
| 61–67 | | 1 Apr 2001 (SSI 2001/132) |
| 68 | | *Not yet in force* |
| 69–72 | | 1 Apr 2001 (SSI 2001/132) |
| 73 | (a), (b) | 1 Jan 2004 (SSI 2003/588) |
| | (c), (d) | 1 Apr 2001 (SSI 2001/132) |
| | (e) | 1 Jan 2004 (SSI 2003/588) |
| 74 | (1)–(3) | 1 Apr 2002 (SSI 2001/132) |
| | (4) | 1 Apr 2001 (SSI 2001/132) |
| | (5) | 1 Apr 2002 (SSI 2001/132) |
| 75–79 | | 1 Apr 2001 (SSI 2001/132) |
| 80 | | 1 May 2001 (SSI 2001/167) |
| 81, 82 | | 1 Apr 2001 (SSI 2001/132) |
| 83 | | See Sch 2 below |
| 84 | | 25 Jan 2001 (RA) |
| Sch 1 | | 1 Apr 2001 (SSI 2001/132) |
| Sch 2 | paras 1–3 | 1 Jul 2001 (SSI 2001/132) |
| | para 4(1)–(3) | 1 Apr 2001 (SSI 2001/132) |
| | para 4(4) | 1 Jul 2001 (SSI 2001/132) |
| | para 4(5) | 1 Apr 2001 (SSI 2001/132) |
| | para 4(6)–(8) | *Not yet in force* |

[1]  For transitional provisions and savings, see SSI 2001/132, art 3

[2]  For transitional provisions and savings, see SSI 2001/132, art 4

**Transport (Scotland) Act 2001 (asp 2)**—*contd*
3   For transitional provisions, see SSI 2002/291, art 3

---

### Vehicles (Crime) Act 2001 (c 3)

*RA:* 10 Apr 2001

*Commencement provisions:* s 44; Vehicles (Crime) Act 2001 (Commencement No 1) Order 2001, SI 2001/3215; Vehicles (Crime) Act 2001 (Commencement No 2) Order 2001, SI 2001/4059; Vehicles (Crime) Act 2001 (Commencement No 3) Order 2002, SI 2002/1914; Vehicles (Crime) Act 2001 (Commencement No 4) Order 2002, SI 2002/2377; Vehicles (Crime) Act 2001 (Commencement No 5) Order 2002, SI 2002/2957

| | | |
|---|---|---|
| 1–7 | | 21 Oct 2002 (SI 2002/1914) |
| 8 | | *Never in force* (repealed) |
| 9–16 | | 21 Oct 2002 (SI 2002/1914) |
| 17 | (1) | 1 Mar 2003 (SI 2002/2957) |
| | (2)–(4) | 1 Dec 2002 (to the extent necessary to enable the Secretary of State to make regulations) (SI 2002/2957) |
| | | 1 Jan 2003 (otherwise) (SI 2002/2957) |
| 18–23 | | 1 Dec 2002 (to the extent necessary to enable the Secretary of State to make regulations) (SI 2002/2957) |
| | | 1 Jan 2003 (otherwise) (SI 2002/2957) |
| 24 | (1)–(3) | 1 Dec 2002 (to the extent necessary to enable the Secretary of State to make regulations) (SI 2002/2957) |
| | | 1 Jan 2003 (otherwise) (SI 2002/2957) |
| | (4), (5) | 1 Mar 2003 (SI 2002/2957) |
| 25 | (1), (2) | 1 Dec 2002 (to the extent necessary to enable the Secretary of State to make regulations) (SI 2002/2957) |
| | | 1 Jan 2003 (otherwise) (SI 2002/2957) |
| | (3), (4) | 1 Mar 2003 (SI 2002/2957) |
| 26 | | 1 Mar 2003 (SI 2002/2957) |
| 27, 28 | | 1 Dec 2002 (to the extent necessary to enable the Secretary of State to make regulations) (SI 2002/2957) |
| | | 1 Jan 2003 (otherwise) (SI 2002/2957) |
| 29 | | 1 Mar 2003 (SI 2002/2957) |
| 30, 31 | | 1 Dec 2002 (to the extent necessary to enable the Secretary of State to make regulations) (SI 2002/2957) |
| | | 1 Jan 2003 (otherwise) (SI 2002/2957) |
| 32, 33 | | 17 Sep 2002 (SI 2002/2377) |
| 34–36 | | *Not yet in force* (ss 35, 36 repealed) |
| 37 | | 1 Oct 2001 (SI 2001/3215) |
| 38 | | 2 Jan 2002 (SI 2001/4059) |
| 39–42 | | 10 Apr 2001 (RA) |
| 43 | | See Schedule below |
| 44–46 | | 10 Apr 2001 (RA) |
| Schedule | paras 1, 2 | *Never in force* (repealed) |
| | paras 3–6 | 17 Sep 2002 (SI 2002/2377) |
| | paras 7–10 | 2 Jan 2002 (SI 2001/4059) |

---

# 2002 Acts

## Adoption and Children Act 2002 (c 38)

*RA:* 7 Nov 2002

*Commencement provisions:* s 148; Adoption and Children Act 2002 (Commencement No 1) (Wales) Order 2003, SI 2003/181; Adoption and Children Act 2002 (Commencement No 2) Order 2003, SI 2003/288; Adoption and Children Act 2002 (Commencement No 3) Order 2003, SI 2003/366; Adoption and Children Act 2002 (Commencement No 4) Order 2003, SI 2003/3079; Adoption and Children Act 2002 (Commencement No 5) (Wales) Order 2004, SI 2004/252; Adoption and Children Act 2002 (Commencement No 6) Order 2004, SI 2004/1403; Adoption and Children Act 2002 (Commencement No 7) Order 2004, SI 2004/3203; Adoption and Children Act 2002 (Commencement No 8) (Wales) Order 2005, SI 2005/1206; Adoption and Children Act 2002 (Commencement No 9) Order 2005, SI 2005/2213, as amended by SI 2005/2897; Adoption and Children Act 2002 (Commencement No 10 Transitional and Savings Provisions) Order 2005, SI 2005/2897, as amended by SI 2005/3504; Adoption and Children Act 2002 (Commencement No 11) (Wales) Order 2005, SI 2005/3112; Adoption and Children Act 2002 (Commencement No 1) (Scotland) Order 2005, SSI 2005/643; Adoption and Children Act 2002 (Commencement No 12) Order 2014 Order 2014, SI 2014/1961

| | | |
|---|---|---|
| 1 | | 30 Dec 2005 (SI 2005/2213) |
| 2 | (1)–(5) | 7 Dec 2004 (SI 2004/3203) |
| | (6) | 10 Mar 2003 (E) (for the purposes of Sch 4, para 3, in relation to the making of regulations) (SI 2003/366) |
| | | 6 Oct 2003 (E) (for the purposes of Sch 4, para 3, otherwise) (SI 2003/366) |
| | | 7 Feb 2004 (W) (SI 2004/252) |
| | | 7 Dec 2004 (E) (otherwise) (SI 2004/3203) |
| | (7), (8) | 10 Mar 2003 (E) (for the purposes of Sch 4, para 3, in relation to the making of regulations) (SI 2003/366) |
| | | 6 Oct 2003 (E) (for the purposes of Sch 4, para 3, otherwise) (SI 2003/366) |
| | | 28 Nov 2003 (W) (for the purposes of Sch 4, para 3) (SI 2003/3079) |
| | | 7 Dec 2004 (otherwise) (SI 2004/3203) |
| 3 | (1), (2) | 30 Dec 2005 (SI 2005/2213) |
| | (3), (4) | 7 Dec 2004 (E) (for the purposes of making regulations) (SI 2004/3203) |
| | | 6 Jun 2005 (W) (SI 2005/1206) |
| | | 30 Dec 2005 (E) (otherwise) (SI 2005/2213) |
| | (5), (6) | 30 Dec 2005 (SI 2005/2213) |
| 4 | (1)(a) | 30 Dec 2005 (SI 2005/2213; SI 2005/3112) |
| | (1)(b) | 7 Feb 2004 (W) (for the purposes of making regulations) (SI 2004/252) |
| | | 7 Dec 2004 (E) (for the purposes of making regulations) (SI 2004/3203) |
| | | 30 Dec 2005 (otherwise) (SI 2005/2213; SI 2005/3112) |
| | (2)–(4) | 30 Dec 2005 (SI 2005/2213; SI 2005/3112) |
| | (5) | 7 Feb 2004 (W) (for the purposes of making regulations) (SI 2004/252) |
| | | 7 Dec 2004 (E) (for the purposes of making regulations) (SI 2004/3203) |

**Adoption and Children Act 2002 (c 38)**—*contd*

|  |  |  |
|---|---|---|
|  |  | 30 Dec 2005 (otherwise) (SI 2005/2213; SI 2005/3112) |
|  | (6) | 10 Mar 2003 (E) (for the purposes of Sch 4, para 3, in relation to the making of regulations) (SI 2003/366) |
|  |  | 6 Oct 2003 (E) (for the purposes of Sch 4, para 3, otherwise) (SI 2003/366) |
|  |  | 7 Feb 2004 (W) (SI 2004/252) |
|  |  | 7 Dec 2004 (E) (otherwise) (SI 2004/3203) |
|  | (7)(a) | 7 Feb 2004 (W) (SI 2004/252) |
|  |  | 7 Dec 2004 (E) (SI 2004/3203) |
|  | (7)(b)–(i) | 10 Mar 2003 (E) (for the purposes of Sch 4, para 3, in relation to the making of regulations) (SI 2003/366) |
|  |  | 6 Oct 2003 (E) (for the purposes of Sch 4, para 3, otherwise) (SI 2003/366) |
|  |  | 7 Feb 2004 (W) (SI 2004/252) |
|  |  | 7 Dec 2004 (E) (otherwise) (SI 2004/3203) |
|  | (8)–(11) | 30 Dec 2005 (SI 2005/2213; SI 2005/3112) |
| 5 |  | *Never in force* (repealed) |
| 6, 7 |  | 30 Dec 2005 (SI 2005/2213; SI 2005/3112) |
| 8 |  | 7 Dec 2004 (E) (for the purposes of making regulations) (SI 2004/3203) |
|  |  | 30 Dec 2005 (otherwise) (SI 2005/2213; SI 2005/3112) |
| 9–11 |  | 7 Feb 2004 (W) (SI 2004/252) |
|  |  | 7 Dec 2004 (E) (SI 2004/3203) |
| 12 | (1)–(3) | 7 Feb 2004 (W) (SI 2004/252) |
|  |  | 7 Dec 2004 (E) (for the purposes of making regulations) (SI 2004/3203) |
|  |  | 30 Dec 2005 (E) (otherwise) (SI 2005/2213) |
|  | (4)–(8) | 30 Dec 2005 (SI 2005/2213; SI 2005/3112) |
| 13–15 |  | 30 Dec 2005 (SI 2005/2213; SI 2005/3112) |
| 16 |  | 1 Feb 2003 (W) (SI 2003/181) |
|  |  | 25 Feb 2003 (E) (so far as inserts Care Standards Act 2000, s 36A(1)–(4), in relation to functions conferred under the Care Standards Act 2000, Pt II and the Adoption Act 1976) (SI 2003/366) |
|  |  | 30 Apr 2003 (E) (otherwise, in relation to functions conferred under the Care Standards Act 2000, Pt II and the Adoption Act 1976) (SI 2003/366) |
|  |  | 30 Dec 2005 (E) (otherwise) (SI 2005/2213) |
| 17 |  | *Never in force* (repealed) |
| 18–26 |  | 30 Dec 2005 (SI 2005/2213) |
| 27 | (1), (2) | 30 Dec 2005 (SI 2005/2213) |
|  | (3) | 7 Feb 2004 (W) (SI 2004/252) |
|  |  | 7 Dec 2004 (E) (SI 2004/3203) |
|  | (4), (5) | 30 Dec 2005 (SI 2005/2213) |
| 28–40 |  | 30 Dec 2005 (SI 2005/2213) |
| 41 | (1)–(4) | 30 Dec 2005 (SI 2005/2213) |
|  | (5)–(9) | 30 Dec 2005 (SI 2005/2213; SSI 2005/643) |
| 42, 43 |  | 30 Dec 2005 (SI 2005/2213) |
| 44 |  | 7 Dec 2004 (for the purposes of making regulations) (SI 2004/3203) |
|  |  | 30 Dec 2005 (otherwise) (SI 2005/2213) |
| 45 |  | 7 Dec 2004 (SI 2004/3203) |
| 46–52 |  | 30 Dec 2005 (SI 2005/2213) |
| 53 | (1)–(3) | 7 Feb 2004 (W) (SI 2004/252) |
|  |  | 7 Dec 2004 (E) (SI 2004/3203) |
|  | (4)–(6) | 30 Dec 2005 (SI 2005/2213) |
| 54 |  | 7 Feb 2004 (W) (SI 2004/252) |
|  |  | 7 Dec 2004 (E) (SI 2004/3203) |
| 55 |  | 30 Dec 2005 (SI 2005/2213) |
| 56 | (1) | 7 Feb 2004 (W) (SI 2004/252) |

**Adoption and Children Act 2002 (c 38)**—*contd*

| | | |
|---|---|---|
| | | 7 Dec 2004 (E) (for the purposes of making regulations) (SI 2004/3203) |
| | | 30 Dec 2005 (E) (otherwise) (SI 2005/2213) |
| | (2) | 7 Dec 2004 (E) (for the purposes of making regulations) (SI 2004/3203) |
| | | 30 Dec 2005 (otherwise) (SI 2005/2213; SI 2005/3112) |
| | (3) | 7 Feb 2004 (W) (SI 2004/252) |
| | | 7 Dec 2004 (E) (for the purposes of making regulations) (SI 2004/3203) |
| | | 30 Dec 2005 (E) (otherwise) (SI 2005/2213) |
| 57 | (1)–(4) | 7 Dec 2004 (E) (for the purposes of making regulations) (SI 2004/3203) |
| | | 30 Dec 2005 (otherwise) (SI 2005/2213; SI 2005/3112) |
| | (5) | 7 Feb 2004 (W) (for the purposes of making regulations) (SI 2004/252) |
| | | 7 Dec 2004 (E) (for the purposes of making regulations) (SI 2004/3203) |
| | | 30 Dec 2005 (otherwise) (SI 2005/2213; SI 2005/3112) |
| | (6) | 7 Feb 2004 (W) (SI 2004/252) |
| | | 7 Dec 2004 (E) (for the purposes of making regulations) (SI 2004/3203) |
| | | 30 Dec 2005 (E) (otherwise) (SI 2005/2213) |
| 58 | (1) | 7 Dec 2004 (E) (for the purposes of making regulations) (SI 2004/3203) |
| | | 30 Dec 2005 (otherwise) (SI 2005/2213; SI 2005/3112) |
| | (2), (3) | 7 Feb 2004 (W) (for the purposes of making regulations) (SI 2004/252) |
| | | 7 Dec 2004 (E) (for the purposes of making regulations) (SI 2004/3203) |
| | | 30 Dec 2005 (otherwise) (SI 2005/2213; SI 2005/3112) |
| 59 | | 7 Feb 2004 (W) (SI 2004/252) |
| | | 7 Dec 2004 (E) (for the purposes of making regulations) (SI 2004/3203) |
| | | 30 Dec 2005 (E) (otherwise) (SI 2005/2213) |
| 60 | (1) | 30 Dec 2005 (SI 2005/2213; SI 2005/3112) |
| | (2) | 7 Feb 2004 (W) (for the purposes of making regulations) (SI 2004/252) |
| | | 7 Dec 2004 (E) (for the purposes of making regulations) (SI 2004/3203) |
| | | 30 Dec 2005 (otherwise) (SI 2005/2213; SI 2005/3112) |
| | (3) | 30 Dec 2005 (SI 2005/2213; SI 2005/3112) |
| | (4) | 7 Feb 2004 (W) (for the purposes of making regulations) (SI 2004/252) |
| | | 7 Dec 2004 (E) (for the purposes of making regulations) (SI 2004/3203) |
| | | 30 Dec 2005 (otherwise) (SI 2005/2213; SI 2005/3112) |
| | (5) | 30 Dec 2005 (SI 2005/2213; SI 2005/3112) |
| 61 | (1)–(4) | 30 Dec 2005 (SI 2005/2213; SI 2005/3112) |
| | (5)(a), (b) | 7 Dec 2004 (E) (for the purposes of making regulations) (SI 2004/3203) |
| | | 30 Dec 2005 (otherwise) (SI 2005/2213; SI 2005/3112) |
| | (5)(c) | 7 Feb 2004 (W) (for the purposes of making regulations) (SI 2004/252) |
| | | 7 Dec 2004 (E) (for the purposes of making regulations) (SI 2004/3203) |
| | | 30 Dec 2005 (otherwise) (SI 2005/2213; SI 2005/3112) |
| | (6) | 30 Dec 2005 (SI 2005/2213; SI 2005/3112) |
| 62 | (1)–(6) | 30 Dec 2005 (SI 2005/2213; SI 2005/3112) |
| | (7)(a), (b) | 7 Dec 2004 (E) (for the purposes of making regulations) (SI 2004/3203) |

**Adoption and Children Act 2002 (c 38)**—*contd*

|        |          |                                                                                      |
|--------|----------|--------------------------------------------------------------------------------------|
|        |          | 30 Dec 2005 (otherwise) (SI 2005/2213; SI 2005/3112)                                 |
|        | (7)(c)   | 7 Feb 2004 (W) (for the purposes of making regulations) (SI 2004/252)                |
|        |          | 7 Dec 2004 (E) (for the purposes of making regulations) (SI 2004/3203)               |
|        |          | 30 Dec 2005 (otherwise) (SI 2005/2213; SI 2005/3112)                                 |
|        | (8)      | 30 Dec 2005 (SI 2005/2213; SI 2005/3112)                                             |
| 63     | (1)      | 7 Feb 2004 (W) (SI 2004/252)                                                         |
|        |          | 7 Dec 2004 (E) (SI 2004/3203)                                                        |
|        | (2)–(5)  | 7 Feb 2004 (W) (SI 2004/252)                                                         |
|        |          | 7 Dec 2004 (E) (S) (NI) (SI 2004/3203)                                               |
| 64     |          | 7 Feb 2004 (W) (SI 2004/252)                                                         |
|        |          | 7 Dec 2004 (E) (SI 2004/3203)                                                        |
| 65     | (1)      | 7 Feb 2004 (W) (SI 2004/252)                                                         |
|        |          | 7 Dec 2004 (E) (SI 2004/3203)                                                        |
|        | (2)(a)   | 7 Feb 2004 (W) (SI 2004/252)                                                         |
|        |          | 7 Dec 2004 (E) (S) (SI 2004/3203)                                                    |
|        | (2)(b)   | 7 Feb 2004 (W) (SI 2004/252)                                                         |
|        |          | 7 Dec 2004 (E) (NI) (SI 2004/3203)                                                   |
|        | (3)      | 7 Feb 2004 (W) (SI 2004/252)                                                         |
|        |          | 7 Dec 2004 (E) (S) (NI) (SI 2004/3203)                                               |
|        | (4), (5) | 7 Feb 2004 (W) (SI 2004/252)                                                         |
|        |          | 7 Dec 2004 (E) (SI 2004/3203)                                                        |
| 66–76  |          | 30 Dec 2005 (SI 2005/2213)                                                           |
| 77     | (1), (2) | 30 Dec 2005 (SI 2005/2213)                                                           |
|        | (3)      | 7 Dec 2004 (for the purposes of making regulations) (SI 2004/3203)                   |
|        |          | 30 Dec 2005 (otherwise) (SI 2005/2213)                                               |
|        | (4), (5) | 30 Dec 2005 (SI 2005/2213)                                                           |
|        | (6)      | See Sch 1 below                                                                      |
| 78     | (1), (2) | 30 Dec 2005 (SI 2005/2213)                                                           |
|        | (3)      | 7 Dec 2004 (for the purposes of making regulations) (SI 2004/3203)                   |
|        |          | 30 Dec 2005 (otherwise) (SI 2005/2213)                                               |
|        | (4)      | 30 Dec 2005 (SI 2005/2213)                                                           |
| 79     | (1)–(4)  | 30 Dec 2005 (SI 2005/2213)                                                           |
|        | (5)      | 7 Dec 2004 (for the purposes of making regulations) (SI 2004/3203)                   |
|        |          | 30 Dec 2005 (otherwise) (SI 2005/2213)                                               |
|        | (6)      | See Sch 2 below                                                                      |
|        | (7)–(9)  | 7 Dec 2004 (for the purposes of making regulations) (SI 2004/3203)                   |
|        |          | 30 Dec 2005 (otherwise) (SI 2005/2213)                                               |
| 80     | (1)      | 30 Dec 2005 (SI 2005/2213)                                                           |
|        | (2)      | 7 Dec 2004 (for the purposes of making regulations) (SI 2004/3203)                   |
|        |          | 30 Dec 2005 (otherwise) (SI 2005/2213)                                               |
|        | (3)      | 30 Dec 2005 (SI 2005/2213)                                                           |
|        | (4)      | 7 Dec 2004 (for the purposes of making regulations) (SI 2004/3203)                   |
|        |          | 30 Dec 2005 (otherwise) (SI 2005/2213)                                               |
|        | (5)      | 30 Dec 2005 (SI 2005/2213)                                                           |
|        | (6)      | 7 Dec 2004 (for the purposes of making regulations) (SI 2004/3203)                   |
|        |          | 30 Dec 2005 (otherwise) (SI 2005/2213)                                               |
| 81     | (1)–(3)  | 30 Dec 2005 (SI 2005/2213)                                                           |
|        | (4)      | 7 Dec 2004 (for the purposes of making regulations) (SI 2004/3203)                   |
|        |          | 30 Dec 2005 (otherwise) (SI 2005/2213)                                               |

**Adoption and Children Act 2002 (c 38)**—*contd*

| | | |
|---|---|---|
| 82 | | 30 Dec 2005 (SI 2005/2213) |
| 83 | (1)–(7) | 7 Dec 2004 (for the purposes of making regulations) (SI 2004/3203) |
| | | 30 Dec 2005 (otherwise) (SI 2005/2213) |
| | (8) | 30 Dec 2005 (SI 2005/2213) |
| | (9) | 7 Dec 2004 (for the purposes of making regulations) (SI 2004/3203) |
| | | 30 Dec 2005 (otherwise) (SI 2005/2213) |
| 84 | | 7 Dec 2004 (for the purposes of making regulations) (SI 2004/3203) |
| | | 30 Dec 2005 (otherwise) (SI 2005/2213) |
| 85 | | 30 Dec 2005 (SI 2005/2213) |
| 86 | | 7 Dec 2004 (for the purposes of making regulations) (SI 2004/3203) |
| | | 30 Dec 2005 (otherwise) (SI 2005/2213) |
| 87 | (1)(a) | 7 Dec 2004 (for the purposes of making regulations) (SI 2004/3203) |
| | | 30 Dec 2005 (otherwise) (SI 2005/2213) |
| | (1)(b) | 1 Jun 2003 (SI 2003/366) |
| | (2) | 7 Dec 2004 (for the purposes of making regulations) (SI 2004/3203) |
| | | 30 Dec 2005 (otherwise) (SI 2005/2213) |
| | (3) | 30 Dec 2005 (SI 2005/2213) |
| | (4) | 1 Jun 2003 (SI 2003/366) |
| | (5), (6) | 7 Dec 2004 (for the purposes of making regulations) (SI 2004/3203) |
| | | 30 Dec 2005 (otherwise) (SI 2005/2213) |
| 88–91 | | 30 Dec 2005 (SI 2005/2213) |
| 92 | | 7 Dec 2004 (for the purposes of making regulations) (SI 2004/3203) |
| | | 30 Dec 2005 (otherwise) (SI 2005/2213) |
| 93 | | 30 Dec 2005 (SI 2005/2213) |
| 94 | (1) | 7 Dec 2004 (for the purposes of making regulations) (SI 2004/3203) |
| | | 30 Dec 2005 (otherwise) (SI 2005/2213) |
| | (2)–(5) | 30 Dec 2005 (SI 2005/2213) |
| 95–97 | | 30 Dec 2005 (SI 2005/2213) |
| 98 | | 7 Feb 2004 (W) (SI 2004/252) |
| | | 7 Dec 2004 (E) (SI 2004/3203) |
| 99–107 | | 30 Dec 2005 (SI 2005/2213) |
| 108 | | 7 Dec 2004 (SI 2004/3203) |
| 109, 110 | | 30 Dec 2005 (SI 2005/2213) |
| 111 | | 1 Dec 2003 (SI 2003/3079) |
| 112–114 | | 30 Dec 2005 (SI 2005/2213) |
| 115 | | 7 Dec 2004 (for the purposes of making regulations) (except in so far as it relates to the insertion of Children Act 1989, s 14G) (SI 2004/3203) |
| | | 30 Dec 2005 (otherwise) (SI 2005/2213) |
| 116 | | 7 Nov 2002 (RA) |
| 117 | | 7 Dec 2004 (for the purposes of making regulations) (SI 2004/3203) |
| | | 30 Dec 2005 (otherwise) (SI 2005/2213) |
| 118 | | 21 May 2004 (SI 2004/1403) |
| 119 | | 30 Jan 2004 (for the purpose of making regulations) (SI 2003/3079) |
| | | 1 Apr 2004 (otherwise) (SI 2003/3079) |
| 120 | | 31 Jan 2005 (SI 2004/3203) |
| 121 | | 7 Dec 2004 (for the purposes of making regulations) (SI 2004/3203) |
| | | 30 Dec 2005 (otherwise) (SI 2005/2213) |

**Adoption and Children Act 2002 (c 38)**—*contd*

| | | |
|---|---|---|
| 122 | (1)(a) | 30 Dec 2005 (SI 2005/2213) |
| | (1)(b) | 7 Dec 2004 (SI 2004/3203) |
| | (2) | 7 Dec 2004 (SI 2004/3203) |
| 123, 124 | | 30 Dec 2005 (SI 2005/2213) |
| 125–129 | | 25 Jul 2014 (SI 2014/1961) |
| 130 | | *Never in force* (repealed) |
| 131 | | 25 Jul 2014 (SI 2014/1961) |
| 132 | | 30 Dec 2005 (SSI 2005/643) |
| 133, 134 | | *Never in force* (repealed) |
| 135 | | 1 Jun 2003 (E) (W) (SI 2003/366) |
| | | *Never in force* (S) (NI) (repealed) |
| 136 | | 7 Nov 2002 (RA) |
| 137, 138 | | 30 Dec 2005 (SI 2005/2213) |
| 139 | (1) | See Sch 3 below |
| | (2) | See Sch 4 below |
| | (3) | See Sch 5 below |
| 140–146 | | 7 Nov 2002 (RA) |
| 147 | | See Sch 6 below |
| 148–150 | | 7 Nov 2002 (RA) |
| Sch 1 | para 1 | 7 Dec 2004 (for the purposes of making regulations) (SI 2004/3203) |
| | | 30 Dec 2005 (otherwise) (SI 2005/2213) |
| | para 2 | 30 Dec 2005 (SI 2005/2213) |
| | para 3 | 7 Dec 2004 (for the purposes of making regulations) (SI 2004/3203) |
| | | 30 Dec 2005 (otherwise) (SI 2005/2213) |
| | paras 4–6 | 30 Dec 2005 (SI 2005/2213) |
| Sch 2 | para 1 | 7 Dec 2004 (for the purposes of making regulations) (SI 2004/3203) |
| | | 30 Dec 2005 (otherwise) (SI 2005/2213) |
| | paras 2–4 | 30 Dec 2005 (SI 2005/2213) |
| Sch 3 | paras 1–5 | 30 Dec 2005 (SI 2005/2213) |
| | paras 6, 7 | 1 Dec 2003 (SI 2003/3079) |
| | para 8 | *Not yet in force* |
| | paras 9–12 | 30 Dec 2005 (SI 2005/2213) |
| | para 13 | 30 Dec 2005 (SI 2005/2213; SI 2005/3112) |
| | paras 14–20 | 30 Dec 2005 (SI 2005/2213) |
| | paras 21–35 | 30 Dec 2005 (SSI 2005/643) |
| | paras 36–43 | 30 Dec 2005 (SI 2005/2213) |
| | para 44 | *Never in force* (repealed) |
| | paras 45–52 | 30 Dec 2005 (SI 2005/2213) |
| | para 53 | 3 Feb 2003 (SI 2003/288) |
| | paras 54–59 | 30 Dec 2005 (SI 2005/2213) |
| | para 60 | 7 Dec 2004 (for the purposes of making regulations) (SI 2004/3203) |
| | | 30 Dec 2005 (otherwise) (SI 2005/2213) |
| | paras 61–64 | 30 Dec 2005 (SI 2005/2213) |
| | para 65 | 30 Dec 2005 (SI 2005/2213; SI 2005/3112) |
| | para 66 | *Not yet in force* |
| | paras 67–78 | 30 Dec 2005 (SI 2005/2213) |
| | para 79 | *Not yet in force* |
| | paras 80, 81 | 30 Dec 2005 (SI 2005/2213) |
| | paras 82–84 | 30 Dec 2005 (SSI 2005/643) |
| | paras 85–93 | 30 Dec 2005 (SI 2005/2213) |
| | para 94 | *Not yet in force* |
| | paras 95–99 | 30 Dec 2005 (SI 2005/2213) |
| | para 100 | *Not yet in force* |
| | paras 101, 102 | 30 Dec 2005 (SI 2005/2213) |
| | para 103 | See paras 104–117 below |

**Adoption and Children Act 2002 (c 38)**—*contd*

| | | |
|---|---|---|
| | para 104 | 30 Dec 2005 (SI 2005/2213) |
| | paras 105, 106 | 25 Feb 2003 (E) (for the purposes of s 16 of this Act, in so far as that section is brought into force on 25 Feb 2003 by SI 2003/366) (SI 2003/366) |
| | | 30 Apr 2003 (E) (otherwise) (SI 2003/366) |
| | | 28 Nov 2003 (W) (SI 2003/3079) |
| | paras 107–109 | 30 Dec 2005 (SI 2005/2213) |
| | para 110 | 30 Apr 2003 (E) (in so far as relates to the Adoption Act 1976) (SI 2003/366) |
| | | 28 Nov 2003 (W) (in so far as relates to the Adoption Act 1976) (SI 2003/3079) |
| | | 30 Dec 2005 (otherwise) (SI 2005/2213) |
| | paras 111–113 | 30 Dec 2005 (SI 2005/2213; SI 2005/3112) |
| | paras 114–117 | 30 Dec 2005 (SI 2005/2213) |
| | para 118 | 28 Nov 2003 (SI 2003/3079) |
| Sch 4 | paras 1, 2 | 30 Dec 2005 (SI 2005/2897)[1] |
| | para 3 | 10 Mar 2003 (E) (for the purpose of making regulations) (SI 2003/366) |
| | | 6 Oct 2003 (E) (otherwise) (SI 2003/366) |
| | | 7 Feb 2004 (W) (SI 2004/252) |
| | para 4(1) | 3 Feb 2003 (SI 2003/288) |
| | para 4(2) | 25 Feb 2003 (SI 2003/366) |
| | para 5 | 1 Dec 2003 (E) (for the purpose of making regulations) (SI 2003/3079) |
| | | 1 Apr 2004 (E) (otherwise) (SI 2003/3079) |
| | | 7 Feb 2004 (W) (SI 2004/252) |
| | paras 6–8 | 30 Dec 2005 (SI 2005/2897) |
| | para 9 | *Not yet in force* |
| | para 10 | 1 Jun 2003 (SI 2003/366) |
| | para 11(a) | 1 Jun 2003 (SI 2003/366) |
| | para 11(b) | *Never in force* (repealed) |
| | para 12 | 1 Apr 2003 (for the purpose of making regulations, except in so far as inserts Adoption Act 1976, s 56A(9), (10)) (SI 2003/366) |
| | | 1 Jun 2003 (otherwise, except in so far as inserts Adoption Act 1976, s 56A(9), (10)) (SI 2003/366) |
| | | *Never in force* (exceptions noted above) (repealed) |
| | paras 13, 14 | 1 Jun 2003 (SI 2003/366) |
| | paras 15, 16 | *Never in force* (repealed) |
| | paras 17–22 | 30 Dec 2005 (SI 2005/2897)[1] |
| | para 23 | 30 Dec 2005 (SSI 2005/643) |
| Sch 5 | | 28 Nov 2003 (repeal in Criminal Justice and Court Services Act 2000, s 12) (SI 2003/3079) |
| | | 30 Dec 2005 (otherwise) (SI 2005/2897)[1], except repeals of or in— |
| | | Adoption (Scotland) Act 1978, ss 50, 52, 53, 65; |
| | | Matrimonial and Family Proceedings Act 1984, s 40; |
| | | Adoption (Intercountry Aspects) Act 1999, s 14 |
| | | 30 Dec 2005 (repeals of or in Adoption (Scotland) Act 1978, ss 52, 53, 65) (SSI 2005/643) |
| | | *Not yet in force,* repeals of or in— |
| | | Adoption (Scotland) Act 1978, s 50; |
| | | Matrimonial and Family Proceedings Act 1984, s 40; |
| | | Adoption (Intercountry Aspects) Act 1999, s 14 |
| Sch 6 | | 7 Nov 2002 (RA) |

---

[1] For transitional provisions and savings, see SI 2005/2897, arts 3–16

## Animal Health Act 2002 (c 42)

*RA:* 7 Nov 2002

*Commencement provisions:* s 19(1); Animal Health Act 2002 (Commencement) Order 2002, SI 2002/3044

| | |
|---|---|
| 1–15 | 14 Jan 2003 (SI 2002/3044) |
| 16 | 1 Jul 2003 (SI 2002/3044) |
| 17 | 14 Jan 2003 (SI 2002/3044) |
| 18 | 24 Mar 2003 (SI 2002/3044) |
| 19–22 | 7 Nov 2002 (RA) |
| Schedule | 14 Jan 2003 (SI 2002/3044) |

## Appropriation Act 2002 (c 18)

*RA:* 8 Jul 2002

Whole Act in force 8 Jul 2002 (RA)

## Appropriation (No 2) Act 2002 (c 44)

*RA:* 17 Dec 2002

Whole Act in force 17 Dec 2002 (RA)

## British Overseas Territories Act 2002 (c 8)

*RA:* 26 Feb 2002

*Commencement provisions:* s 8(2); British Overseas Territories Act 2002 (Commencement) Order 2002, SI 2002/1252

| | |
|---|---|
| 1, 2 | 26 Feb 2002 (RA) |
| 3–6 | 21 May 2002 (SI 2002/1252) |
| 7 | See Sch 2 below |
| 8 | 26 Feb 2002 (RA) |
| Sch 1 | 21 May 2002 (SI 2002/1252) |
| Sch 2 | 26 Feb 2002 (except repeals of or in British Nationality (Falkland Islands) Act 1983) (RA) |
| | 21 May 2002 (so far as relates to British Nationality (Falkland Islands) Act 1983) (SI 2002/1252) |

## Budget (Scotland) Act 2002 (asp 7)

*RA:* 15 Mar 2002

Whole Act in force 15 Mar 2002 (RA)

## Civil Defence (Grant) Act 2002 (c 5)

*RA:* 26 Feb 2002

This Act has effect in relation to the financial year ending 31 Mar 2003 and later financial years (s 2(2))

## Commonhold and Leasehold Reform Act 2002 (c 15)

*RA:* 1 May 2002

*Commencement provisions:* s 181(1); Commonhold and Leasehold Reform Act 2002 (Commencement No 1, Savings and Transitional Provisions) (England) Order 2002, SI 2002/1912; Commonhold and

**Commonhold and Leasehold Reform Act 2002 (c 15)**—*contd*
  Leasehold Reform Act 2002 (Commencement No 1, Savings and Transitional Provisions) (Wales)
  Order 2002, SI 2002/3012; Commonhold and Leasehold Reform Act 2002 (Commencement No 2
  and Savings) (England) Order 2003, SI 2003/1986; Commonhold and Leasehold Reform Act 2002
  (Commencement No 3) Order 2003, SI 2003/2377; Commonhold and Leasehold Reform Act 2002
  (Commencement No 2 and Savings) (Wales) Order 2004, SI 2004/669; Commonhold and Leasehold
  Reform Act 2002 (Commencement No 4) Order 2004, SI 2004/1832; Commonhold and Leasehold
  Reform Act 2002 (Commencement No 5 and Saving and Transitional Provision) Order 2004,
  SI 2004/3056, as amended by SI 2005/193; Commonhold and Leasehold Reform Act 2002
  (Commencement No 3 and Saving and Transitional Provision) (Wales) Order 2005, SI 2005/1353;
  Commonhold and Leasehold Reform Act 2002 (Commencement No 6) (England) Order 2007,
  SI 2007/1256; Commonhold and Leasehold Reform Act 2002 (Commencement No 4) (Wales)
  Order 2007, SI 2007/3161

| | | |
|---|---|---|
| 1–20 | | 27 Sep 2004 (SI 2004/1832) |
| 21 | (1)–(3) | 27 Sep 2004 (SI 2004/1832) |
| | (4), (5) | *Not yet in force* |
| | (6)–(10) | 27 Sep 2004 (SI 2004/1832) |
| 22–41 | | 27 Sep 2004 (SI 2004/1832) |
| 42 | | 29 Sep 2003 (SI 2003/2377) |
| 43–61 | | 27 Sep 2004 (SI 2004/1832) |
| 62 | | 29 Sep 2003 (SI 2003/2377) |
| 63 | | 27 Sep 2004 (SI 2004/1832) |
| 64–67 | | 29 Sep 2003 (SI 2003/2377) |
| 68 | | 27 Sep 2004 (SI 2004/1832) |
| 69, 70 | | 29 Sep 2003 (in so far as relating to ss 42, 62, 64–67) (SI 2003/2377) |
| | | 27 Sep 2004 (otherwise) (SI 2004/1832) |
| 71–73 | | 30 Sep 2003 (E) (SI 2003/1986) |
| | | 30 Mar 2004 (W) (SI 2004/669) |
| 74 | | 26 Jul 2002 (E) (in so far as conferring any power to make regulations) (SI 2002/1912) |
| | | 1 Jan 2003 (W) (in so far as conferring any power to make regulations) (SI 2002/3012) |
| | | 30 Sep 2003 (E) (otherwise) (SI 2003/1986) |
| | | 30 Mar 2004 (W) (otherwise) (SI 2004/669) |
| 75–77 | | 30 Sep 2003 (E) (SI 2003/1986) |
| | | 30 Mar 2004 (W) (SI 2004/669) |
| 78 | | 26 Jul 2002 (E) (in so far as conferring any power to make regulations) (SI 2002/1912) |
| | | 1 Jan 2003 (W) (in so far as conferring any power to make regulations) (SI 2002/3012) |
| | | 30 Sep 2003 (E) (otherwise) (SI 2003/1986) |
| | | 30 Mar 2004 (W) (otherwise) (SI 2004/669) |
| 79 | | 30 Sep 2003 (E) (SI 2003/1986) |
| | | 30 Mar 2004 (W) (SI 2004/669) |
| 80 | | 26 Jul 2002 (E) (in so far as conferring any power to make regulations) (SI 2002/1912) |
| | | 1 Jan 2003 (W) (in so far as conferring any power to make regulations) (SI 2002/3012) |
| | | 30 Sep 2003 (E) (otherwise) (SI 2003/1986) |
| | | 30 Mar 2004 (W) (otherwise) (SI 2004/669) |
| 81–83 | | 30 Sep 2003 (E) (SI 2003/1986) |
| | | 30 Mar 2004 (W) (SI 2004/669) |
| 84 | | 26 Jul 2002 (E) (in so far as conferring any power to make regulations) (SI 2002/1912) |
| | | 1 Jan 2003 (W) (in so far as conferring any power to make regulations) (SI 2002/3012) |
| | | 30 Sep 2003 (E) (otherwise) (SI 2003/1986) |
| | | 30 Mar 2004 (W) (otherwise) (SI 2004/669) |
| 85–91 | | 30 Sep 2003 (E) (SI 2003/1986) |

**Commonhold and Leasehold Reform Act 2002 (c 15)**—*contd*

|  |  |
|---|---|
|  | 30 Mar 2004 (W) (SI 2004/669) |
| 92 | 26 Jul 2002 (E) (in so far as conferring any power to make regulations) (SI 2002/1912) |
|  | 1 Jan 2003 (W) (in so far as conferring any power to make regulations) (SI 2002/3012) |
|  | 30 Sep 2003 (E) (otherwise) (SI 2003/1986) |
|  | 30 Mar 2004 (W) (otherwise) (SI 2004/669) |
| 93–103 | 30 Sep 2003 (E) (SI 2003/1986) |
|  | 30 Mar 2004 (W) (SI 2004/669) |
| 104 | 1 May 2002 (RA) |
| 105–109 | 30 Sep 2003 (E) (SI 2003/1986) |
|  | 30 Mar 2004 (W) (SI 2004/669) |
| 110 | 26 Jul 2002 (E) (in so far as conferring any power to make regulations) (SI 2002/1912) |
|  | 1 Jan 2003 (W) (in so far as conferring any power to make regulations) (SI 2002/3012) |
|  | 30 Sep 2003 (E) (otherwise) (SI 2003/1986) |
|  | 30 Mar 2004 (W) (otherwise) (SI 2004/669) |
| 111–113 | 30 Sep 2003 (E) (SI 2003/1986) |
|  | 30 Mar 2004 (W) (SI 2004/669) |
| 114 | 26 Jul 2002 (E) (SI 2002/1912) |
|  | 1 Jan 2003 (W) (SI 2002/3012) |
| 115–120 | 26 Jul 2002 (E) (SI 2002/1912)[1] |
|  | 1 Jan 2003 (W) (SI 2002/3012)[2] |
| 121 | *Not yet in force* |
| 122 | 26 Jul 2002 (E) (in so far as conferring any power to make regulations) (SI 2002/1912) |
|  | 1 Jan 2003 (W) (in so far as conferring any power to make regulations) (SI 2002/3012) |
|  | *Not yet in force* (otherwise) |
| 123, 124 | *Not yet in force* |
| 125 | 26 Jul 2002 (E) (SI 2002/1912)[1] |
|  | 1 Jan 2003 (W) (SI 2002/3012)[2] |
| 126 | 28 Feb 2005 (E) (SI 2004/3056)[5] |
|  | 31 May 2005 (W) (SI 2005/1353)[6] |
| 127, 128 | 26 Jul 2002 (E) (SI 2002/1912)[1] |
|  | 1 Jan 2003 (W) (SI 2002/3012)[2] |
| 129 | 26 Jul 2002 (E) (SI 2002/1912) |
|  | 1 Jan 2003 (W) (SI 2002/3012) |
| 130, 131 | 26 Jul 2002 (E) (SI 2002/1912)[1] |
|  | 1 Jan 2003 (W) (SI 2002/3012)[2] |
| 132, 133 | 26 Jul 2002 (E) (SI 2002/1912) |
|  | 1 Jan 2003 (W) (SI 2002/3012) |
| 134–136 | 26 Jul 2002 (E) (SI 2002/1912)[1] |
|  | 1 Jan 2003 (W) (SI 2002/3012)[2] |
| 137 | 26 Jul 2002 (E) (SI 2002/1912) |
|  | 1 Jan 2003 (W) (SI 2002/3012) |
| 138–141 | 26 Jul 2002 (E) (SI 2002/1912)[1] |
|  | 1 Jan 2003 (W) (SI 2002/3012)[2] |
| 142 | 26 Jul 2002 (E) (SI 2002/1912) |
|  | 1 Jan 2003 (W) (SI 2002/3012) |
| 143–147 | 26 Jul 2002 (E) (SI 2002/1912)[1] |
|  | 1 Jan 2003 (W) (SI 2002/3012)[2] |
| 148–150 | 30 Sep 2003 (E) (SI 2003/1986)[3] |
|  | 30 Mar 2004 (W) (SI 2004/669)[4] |
| 151 | 26 Jul 2002 (E) (in so far as conferring any power to make regulations) (SI 2002/1912) |
|  | 1 Jan 2003 (W) (in so far as conferring any power to make regulations) (SI 2002/3012) |

**Commonhold and Leasehold Reform Act 2002 (c 15)**—*contd*

|  |  |
|---|---|
|  | 31 Oct 2003 (E) (otherwise) (SI 2003/1986)[3] |
|  | 30 Mar 2004 (W) (otherwise) (SI 2004/669)[4] |
| 152 | 26 Jul 2002 (E) (in so far as conferring any power to make regulations) (SI 2002/1912) |
|  | 1 Jan 2003 (W) (in so far as conferring any power to make regulations) (SI 2002/3012) |
|  | *Not yet in force* (otherwise) |
| 153 | 26 Jul 2002 (E) (in so far as conferring any power to make regulations) (SI 2002/1912) |
|  | 1 Jan 2003 (W) (in so far as conferring any power to make regulations) (SI 2002/3012) |
|  | 1 Oct 2007 (E) (otherwise) (SI 2007/1256) |
|  | 30 Nov 2007 (W) (otherwise) (SI 2007/3161) |
| 154 | *Not yet in force* |
| 155 | 30 Sep 2003 (E) (SI 2003/1986)[3] |
|  | 30 Mar 2004 (W) (SI 2004/669)[4] |
| 156 | 26 Jul 2002 (E) (in so far as conferring any power to make regulations) (SI 2002/1912) |
|  | 1 Jan 2003 (W) (in so far as conferring any power to make regulations) (SI 2002/3012) |
|  | *Not yet in force* (otherwise) |
| 157 | See Sch 10 below |
| 158 | 30 Sep 2003 (E) (SI 2003/1986)[3] |
|  | 30 Mar 2004 (W) (SI 2004/669)[4] |
| 159 | 30 Sep 2003 (E) (SI 2003/1986) |
|  | 30 Mar 2004 (W) (SI 2004/669) |
| 160–162 | 26 Jul 2002 (E) (SI 2002/1912)[1] |
|  | 1 Jan 2003 (W) (SI 2002/3012)[2] |
| 163 | 30 Sep 2003 (E) (SI 2003/1986) |
|  | 30 Mar 2004 (W) (SI 2004/669) |
| 164 | 26 Jul 2002 (E) (in so far as conferring any power to make regulations) (SI 2002/1912) |
|  | 1 Jan 2003 (W) (in so far as conferring any power to make regulations) (SI 2002/3012) |
|  | 28 Feb 2005 (E) (otherwise) (SI 2004/3056) |
|  | 31 May 2005 (W) (otherwise) (SI 2005/1353) |
| 165 | 28 Feb 2005 (E) (SI 2004/3056) |
|  | 31 May 2005 (W) (SI 2005/1353) |
| 166, 167 | 26 Jul 2002 (E) (in so far as conferring any power to make regulations) (SI 2002/1912) |
|  | 1 Jan 2003 (W) (in so far as conferring any power to make regulations) (SI 2002/3012) |
|  | 28 Feb 2005 (E) (otherwise) (SI 2004/3056) |
|  | 31 May 2005 (W) (otherwise) (SI 2005/1353) |
| 168 | 28 Feb 2005 (E) (SI 2004/3056)[5] |
|  | 31 May 2005 (W) (SI 2005/1353)[6] |
| 169 | 28 Feb 2005 (E) (SI 2004/3056) |
|  | 31 May 2005 (W) (SI 2005/1353) |
| 170 | 28 Feb 2005 (E) (SI 2004/3056)[5] |
|  | 31 May 2005 (W) (SI 2005/1353)[6] |
| 171 | 26 Jul 2002 (E) (in so far as conferring any power to make regulations) (SI 2002/1912) |
|  | 1 Jan 2003 (W) (in so far as conferring any power to make regulations) (SI 2002/3012) |
|  | 28 Feb 2005 (E) (otherwise) (SI 2004/3056) |
|  | 31 May 2005 (W) (otherwise) (SI 2005/1353) |
| 172 (1)–(5) | 30 Sep 2003 (E) (except so far as relating to the application to the Crown of ss 152–154, 164–171, Sch 10, paras 1–7 and Sch 13, para 16) (SI 2003/1986)[3] |

**See Halsbury's Statutes Citator for amendments to these Acts** 1307

**Commonhold and Leasehold Reform Act 2002 (c 15)**—*contd*

|  |  |  |
|---|---|---|
|  |  | 30 Mar 2004 (W) (except so far as relating to the application to the Crown of ss 152–154, 164–171, Sch 10, paras 1–7 and Sch 13, para 16) (SI 2004/669)[4] |
|  |  | 28 Feb 2005 (E) (except so far as relating to the application to the Crown of ss 21–22 of the Landlord and Tenant Act 1985, as substituted or inserted by ss 152–154) (SI 2004/3056) |
|  |  | 31 May 2005 (W) (except so far as relating to the application to the Crown of ss 21–22 of the Landlord and Tenant Act 1985, as substituted or inserted by ss 152–154) (SI 2005/1353) |
|  |  | *Not yet in force* (so far as relating to the application to the Crown of ss 21–22 of the Landlord and Tenant Act 1985, as substituted or inserted by ss 152–154) |
|  | (6) | 30 Sep 2003 (E) (except so far as relating to ss 42A and 42B of the Landlord and Tenant Act 1987) (SI 2003/1986)[3] |
|  |  | 30 Mar 2004 (W) (except so far as relating to ss 42A and 42B of the Landlord and Tenant Act 1987) (SI 2004/669)[4] |
|  |  | *Not yet in force* (so far as relating to ss 42A and 42B of the Landlord and Tenant Act 1987) |
| 173 |  | 30 Sep 2003 (E) (SI 2003/1986) |
|  |  | 30 Mar 2004 (W) (SI 2004/669) |
| 174 |  | See Sch 12 below |
| 175 |  | 30 Sep 2003 (E) (SI 2003/1986)[3] |
|  |  | 30 Mar 2004 (W) (SI 2004/669)[4] |
| 176 |  | See Sch 13 below |
| 177–179 |  | 1 May 2002 (RA) |
| 180 |  | See Sch 14 below |
| 181–183 |  | 1 May 2002 (RA) |
| Schs 1–5 |  | 27 Sep 2004 (SI 2004/1832) |
| Schs 6, 7 |  | 30 Sep 2003 (E) (SI 2003/1986) |
|  |  | 30 Mar 2004 (W) (SI 2004/669) |
| Sch 8 |  | *Not yet in force* |
| Sch 9 |  | 30 Sep 2003 (E) (SI 2003/1986)[3] |
|  |  | 30 Mar 2004 (W) (SI 2004/669)[4] |
| Sch 10 | paras 1–7 | *Not yet in force* |
|  | paras 8–13 | 30 Sep 2003 (E) (SI 2003/1986)[3] |
|  |  | 30 Mar 2004 (W) (SI 2004/669)[4] |
|  | para 14 | *Not yet in force* |
|  | para 15 | 28 Feb 2005 (E) (SI 2004/3056) |
|  |  | 31 May 2005 (W) (SI 2005/1353) |
|  | paras 16–19 | *Not yet in force* |
| Sch 11 |  | 30 Sep 2003 (E) (SI 2003/1986)[3] |
|  |  | 30 Mar 2004 (W) (SI 2004/669)[4] |
| Sch 12 |  | 26 Jul 2002 (E) (in so far as conferring any power to make regulations) (SI 2002/1912) |
|  |  | 1 Jan 2003 (W) (in so far as conferring any power to make regulations) (SI 2002/3012) |
|  |  | 30 Sep 2003 (E) (otherwise) (SI 2003/1986) |
|  |  | 30 Mar 2004 (W) (otherwise) (SI 2004/669) |
| Sch 13 | paras 1–15 | 30 Sep 2003 (E) (SI 2003/1986)[3] |
|  |  | 30 Mar 2004 (W) (SI 2004/669)[4] |
|  | para 16 | 28 Feb 2005 (E) (SI 2004/3056) |
|  |  | 31 May 2005 (W) (SI 2005/1353) |
| Sch 14 |  | 26 Jul 2002 (E) (SI 2002/1912)[1], repeals of or in— |
|  |  | Leasehold Reform Act 1967, ss 1, 1AA, 2, 3, 6(2), (5) (the words "or statutory owners, as the case may be,", "or them"), 7, 9, 16, 37, Schs 3, 4A; |
|  |  | Housing Act 1980, Sch 21, para 1; |
|  |  | Local Government and Housing Act 1989, Sch 11, para 10; |
|  |  | Leasehold Reform, Housing and Urban Development Act 1993, ss 5–8, 8A, 10, 13, 39, 42, 45, 62, 94(3), (4), (12), Sch 13; |

**Commonhold and Leasehold Reform Act 2002 (c 15)**—*contd*

Housing Act 1996, ss 105, 111, 112, Sch 9, paras 3, 4, 5(2), (3), Sch 10, para 4

1 Jan 2003 (W) (SI 2002/3012)[2], repeals of or in—

Leasehold Reform Act 1967, ss 1, 1AA, 2, 3(3), 6(2), (5) (the words "or statutory owners, as the case may be,", "or them"), 7, 9, 16, 37, Sch 3, Sch 4A;

Housing Act 1980, Sch 21;

Local Government and Housing Act 1989, Sch 11, para 10;

Leasehold Reform, Housing and Urban Development Act 1993, ss 5–8, 8A, 10, 13, 39, 42, 45, 62, 94(3), (4), (12), Sch 13;

Housing Act 1996, ss 105(3), 111, 112, Sch 9, paras 3, 4, 5(2), (3), Sch 10, para 4

30 Sep 2003 (E) (SI 2003/1986)[3], repeals of or in—

Leasehold Reform Act 1967, s 21;

Housing Act 1980, s 142, Sch 22;

Landlord and Tenant Act 1985;

Landlord and Tenant Act 1987, ss 23(2), 24A, 24B, 29(2)(a), 38, 52A, 53(2) (words "under section 52A(3) or"), 56(2), Sch 2, paras 3, 7;

Tribunals and Inquiries Act 1992;

Leasehold Reform, Housing and Urban Development Act 1993, ss 75(4), (5), 88, 91, 94(10), 101(1);

Housing Act 1996, ss 83, 86, 119, Sch 6, Sch 9, para 2(3), (7)

30 Mar 2004 (W) (SI 2004/669)[4], repeals of or in—

Leasehold Reform Act 1967, s 21;

Housing Act 1980, s 142, Sch 22;

Landlord and Tenant Act 1985;

Landlord and Tenant Act 1987, ss 23(2), 24A, 24B, 29(2)(a), 38, 52A, 53(2) (words "under section 52A(3) or"), 56(2), Sch 2, paras 3, 7;

Tribunals and Enquiries Act 1992;

Leasehold Reform, Housing and Urban Development Act 1993, ss 75(4), (5), 88, 91, 94(10), 101(1);

Housing Act 1996, ss 83, 86, 119, Sch 6, Sch 9, para 2(3), (7)

17 Nov 2004 (repeal of s 104 of this Act) (SI 2004/3056)

28 Feb 2005 (E) (SI 2004/3056), repeals of or in—

Leasehold Reform, Housing and Urban Development Act 1993, Sch 6;

Housing Act 1996, s 82, Sch 10, para 18

31 May 2005 (W) (SI 2005/1353), repeals of or in—

Leasehold Reform, Housing and Urban Development Act 1993, Sch 6;

Housing Act 1996, s 82, Sch 10, para 18

*Not yet in force* (E), repeals of or in—

Leasehold Reform Act 1967, s 6(3), (5) (the words "or (3)");

Land Compensation Act 1973, s 12A(9);

Housing and Planning Act 1986, Sch 5, para 9(2);

Landlord and Tenant Act 1987, s 42(2), (5), (8), Sch 2, paras 5, 6;

Local Government and Housing Act 1989, Sch 11, para 91;

Leasehold Reform, Housing and Urban Development Act 1993, ss 2(3), 11(6), 12(1)(a), (2), (4), (6), 14–16, 18(1), (2), 28(3), (4), 29(5)(a), (b), (7), 33(1), (6), (7), 37A(7), (8)(a), 38(1), 93(2)(b), 99(5)(a), Sch 3, Sch 5, para 5(2)(a)–(c);

Housing Grants, Construction and Regeneration Act 1996, Sch 1, para 12

*Not yet in force* (W), repeals of or in—

Leasehold Reform Act 1967, s 6(3), (5) (words "or 3");

Land Compensation Act 1973, s 12A(9);

Housing and Planning Act 1986, Sch 5;

**Commonhold and Leasehold Reform Act 2002 (c 15)**—*contd*

> Landlord and Tenant Act 1987, ss 42, 53(2) (words ", 42(5)");
> Local Government and Housing Act 1989, Sch 11, para 91;
> Leasehold Reform, Housing and Urban Development Act 1993,
>   ss 2(3), 11(6), 12, 14–16, 18, 38, 93, 99(5)(a), Schs 3, 5;
> Housing Grants, Construction and Regeneration Act 1996,
>   Sch 1, para 12

[1]   For transitional provisions and savings, see SI 2002/1912, art 2(b), Sch 2
[2]   For transitional provisions and savings, see SI 2002/3012, art 2(b), Sch 2
[3]   For savings, see SI 2003/1986, arts 2(c), 3, Sch 2
[4]   For savings, see SI 2004/669, art 2(c), (d), Sch 2
[5]   For savings, see SI 2004/3056, art 4(1A)–(3)
[6]   For transitional provisions and savings, see SI 2005/1353, art 3

---

**Commonwealth Act 2002 (c 39)**

*RA:* 7 Nov 2002

*Commencement provisions:* s 4(2)

| | |
|---|---|
| 1–4 | 7 Jan 2003 (s 4(2)) |
| Schs 1–3 | 7 Jan 2003 (s 4(2)) |

---

**Community Care and Health (Scotland) Act 2002 (asp 5)**

*RA:* 12 Mar 2002

*Commencement provisions:* s 27(2); Community Care and Health (Scotland) Act 2002 (Commencement No 1) Order 2002, SSI 2002/170; Community Care and Health (Scotland) Act 2002 (Commencement No 2) Order 2003, SSI 2003/62; Community Care and Health (Scotland) Act 2002 (Commencement No 3) Order 2004, SSI 2004/33; Community Care and Health (Scotland) Act 2002 (Commencement No 4) Order 2015, SSI 2015/179

| | | |
|---|---|---|
| 1 | (1) | 1 Jul 2002 (SSI 2002/170) |
| | (2) | 1 Apr 2002 (SSI 2002/170) |
| | (3)–(6) | 1 Jul 2002 (SSI 2002/170) |
| | (7) | 1 Apr 2002 (SSI 2002/170) |
| 2 | | 1 Apr 2002 (SSI 2002/170) |
| 3 | | 1 Jul 2002 (SSI 2002/170) |
| 4 | | 13 May 2002 (SSI 2002/170) |
| 5 | (1), (2) | 11 May 2015 (for the purpose of enabling regulations to be made) (SSI 2015/179) |
| | | 24 Jun 2015 (otherwise) (SSI 2015/179) |
| | (3)–(5) | 24 Jun 2015 (SSI 2015/179) |
| | (6) | *Never in force* (substituted) |
| 6 | | 13 May 2002 (SSI 2002/170) |
| 7 | | 1 Jun 2003 (SSI 2002/170) |
| 8–17 | | 1 Sep 2002 (SSI 2002/170) |
| 18 | | *Never in force* (repealed) |
| 19 | | 4 Mar 2004 (SSI 2004/33) |
| 20, 21 | | 13 May 2002 (SSI 2002/170) |
| 22 | | 1 Apr 2002 (SSI 2002/170) |
| 23 | | 12 Mar 2002 (RA) |
| 24 | | 13 May 2002 (SSI 2002/170) |
| 25 | | See Sch 2 below |
| 26 | | 1 Apr 2002 (SSI 2002/170) |
| 27 | | 12 Mar 2002 (RA) |
| Sch 1 | | 1 Jul 2002 (SSI 2002/170) |

**Community Care and Health (Scotland) Act 2002 (asp 5)**—*contd*

| | | |
|---|---|---|
| Sch 2 | para 1(1) | 1 Apr 2002 (SSI 2002/170) |
| | para 1(2), (3) | 1 Jun 2003 (SSI 2002/170) |
| | para 1(4) | 1 Apr 2002 (SSI 2002/170) |
| | para 1(5) | 1 Jul 2002 (SSI 2002/170) |
| | para 2(1), (2) | *Not yet in force* |
| | para 2(3) | 28 Feb 2003 (SSI 2003/62) |
| | para 2(4)(a) | 4 Mar 2004 (for the purpose of applying the first condition of disqualification to lists of persons approved to assist in providing services) (SSI 2004/33) |
| | | 1 Apr 2004 (otherwise) (SSI 2004/33) |
| | para 2(4)(b)(i) | 4 Mar 2004 (SSI 2004/33) |
| | para 2(4)(b)(ii) | 1 Apr 2004 (SSI 2004/33) |
| | para 2(4)(b)(iii) | 4 Mar 2004 (for the purpose of defining "list" to include one prepared by virtue of Pt II of the 1978 Act) (SSI 2004/33) |
| | | 1 Apr 2004 (otherwise) (SSI 2004/33) |
| | para 2(5)(a) | 1 Apr 2004 (SSI 2004/33) |
| | para 2(5)(b) | 4 Mar 2004 (SSI 2004/33) |
| | para 2(6)(a) | 4 Mar 2004 (for the purposes of providing that a local disqualification: |
| | | (a) in the case of a medical practitioner other than one mentioned in s 29(8)(b) of the 1978 Act, shall be disqualification of that practitioner from inclusion in any Health Board's lists under s 29(8)(a) of the 1978 Act (whether or not including the list to which the case relates); and |
| | | (b) in any other case, shall be disqualification in the list to which the case relates) (SSI 2004/33) |
| | | 1 Apr 2004 (otherwise) (SSI 2004/33) |
| | para 2(6)(b) | 4 Mar 2004 (for the purposes of providing that a national disqualification: |
| | | (a) in the case of a medical practitioner other than one mentioned in s 29(8)(b) of the 1978 Act, shall be disqualification of that practitioner from inclusion in all lists within s 29(8)(a); and |
| | | (b) in any other case, shall be disqualification for inclusion in all lists within the same paragraph of s 29(8) as the list to which the case relates) (SSI 2004/33) |
| | | 1 Apr 2004 (otherwise) (SSI 2004/33) |
| | para 2(6)(c) | 1 Apr 2004 (SSI 2004/33) |
| | para 2(7) | 4 Mar 2004 (SSI 2004/33) |
| | para 2(8)(a) | 4 Mar 2004 (SSI 2004/33) |
| | para 2(8)(b)(i) | 4 Mar 2004 (for the purposes of allowing the Scottish Ministers to impose conditions, imposed under the conditional disqualification provisions in England and Wales or Northern Ireland in relation to assistance in provision or performance of services by any person, in relation to the assistance in provision by that person of those services) (SSI 2004/33) |
| | | 1 Apr 2004 (otherwise) (SSI 2004/33) |
| | para 2(8)(b)(ii) | 1 Apr 2004 (SSI 2004/33) |
| | para 2(9)(a), (b) | 1 Apr 2004 (SSI 2004/33) |
| | para 2(9)(c) | 4 Mar 2004 (for the purpose of defining a relevant list so as to include a list of persons approved to assist in providing services) (SSI 2004/33) |
| | para 2(10) | 4 Mar 2004 (SSI 2004/33) |
| | para 2(11)(a) | 4 Mar 2004 (SSI 2004/33) |
| | para 2(11)(b) | 4 Mar 2004 (for the purpose of disqualifying a practitioner for inclusion in any list prepared by virtue of Pt II of the 1978 Act) (SSI 2004/33) |
| | | 1 Apr 2004 (otherwise) (SSI 2004/33) |
| | para 2(11)(c) | 4 Mar 2004 (for the purposes of: |

**Community Care and Health (Scotland) Act 2002 (asp 5)**—*contd*

(a) providing that, where a person is disqualified for inclusion in all lists of persons approved to assist in providing or approved to perform services in England and Wales or in Northern Ireland, s 32D of the 1978 Act applies; and

(b) providing that such a person shall be disqualified for inclusion in any list of persons approved to assist in providing services) (SSI 2004/33)

1 Apr 2004 (otherwise) (SSI 2004/33)

| | |
|---|---|
| para 2(12) | 28 Feb 2003 (SSI 2003/62) |
| para 2(13) | *Not yet in force* |
| para 3 | 28 Feb 2003 (SSI 2003/62) |
| para 4 | 4 Mar 2004 (SSI 2004/33) |

---

**Consolidated Fund Act 2002 (c 10)**

*RA:* 19 Mar 2002

Whole Act in force 19 Mar 2002 (RA)

---

**Consolidated Fund (No 2) Act 2002 (c 43)**

*RA:* 17 Dec 2002

Whole Act in force 17 Dec 2002 (RA)

---

**Copyright, etc and Trade Marks (Offences and Enforcement) Act 2002 (c 25)**

*RA:* 24 Jul 2002

*Commencement provisions:* s 7(2); Copyright, etc and Trade Marks (Offences and Enforcement) Act 2002 (Commencement) Order 2002, SI 2002/2749

| | |
|---|---|
| 1–6 | 20 Nov 2002 (SI 2002/2749) |
| 7 | 24 Jul 2002 (RA) |

---

**Copyright (Visually Impaired Persons) Act 2002 (c 33)**

*RA:* 7 Nov 2002

*Commencement provisions:* s 8(2); Copyright (Visually Impaired Persons) Act 2002 (Commencement) Order 2003, SI 2003/2499

| | |
|---|---|
| 1–7 | 31 Oct 2003 (SI 2003/2499) |
| 8 | 7 Nov 2002 (RA) |

---

**Criminal Procedure (Amendment) (Scotland) Act 2002 (asp 4)**

*RA:* 8 Mar 2002

*Commencement provisions:* s 2(2)

| | |
|---|---|
| 1 | 9 Mar 2002 (s 2(2)) |
| 2 | 8 Mar 2002 (RA) |

---

## Debt Arrangement and Attachment (Scotland) Act 2002 (asp 17)

*RA:* 17 Dec 2002

*Commencement provisions:* s 64(2)–(5); Debt Arrangement and Attachment (Scotland) Act 2002 (Commencement) Order 2004, SSI 2004/401 (revoked by SSI 2004/416, never in force); Debt Arrangement and Attachment (Scotland) Act 2002 (Commencement No 2 and Revocation) Order 2004, SSI 2004/416

| | | |
|---|---|---|
| 1 | | 30 Nov 2004 (SSI 2004/416) |
| 2 | (1), (2) | 30 Nov 2004 (SSI 2004/416) |
| | (3), (4) | 24 Sep 2004 (for the purpose of prescribing forms) (SSI 2004/416) |
| | | 30 Nov 2004 (otherwise) (SSI 2004/416) |
| | (5) | 30 Nov 2004 (SSI 2004/416) |
| 3 | | 30 Nov 2004 (SSI 2004/416) |
| 4 | (1)–(4) | 30 Nov 2004 (SSI 2004/416) |
| | (5) | 24 Sep 2004 (for the purpose of prescribing forms) (SSI 2004/416) |
| | | 30 Nov 2004 (otherwise) (SSI 2004/416) |
| 5 | (1)–(3) | 30 Nov 2004 (SSI 2004/416) |
| | (4) | 24 Sep 2004 (for the purpose of prescribing forms) (SSI 2004/416) |
| | | 30 Nov 2004 (otherwise) (SSI 2004/416) |
| 6 | (1) | 24 Sep 2004 (for the purpose of prescribing forms) (SSI 2004/416) |
| | | 30 Nov 2004 (otherwise) (SSI 2004/416) |
| | (2) | 30 Nov 2004 (SSI 2004/416) |
| 7, 8 | | 24 Sep 2004 (SSI 2004/416) |
| 9 | (1) | 24 Sep 2004 (for the purpose of prescribing forms) (SSI 2004/416) |
| | | 30 Nov 2004 (otherwise) (SSI 2004/416) |
| | (2) | 30 Nov 2004 (SSI 2004/416) |
| 10–42 | | 30 Dec 2002 (s 64(2))[1] |
| 43 | | 17 Dec 2002 (RA) |
| 44–61 | | 30 Dec 2002 (s 64(2))[1] |
| 62 | | 17 Dec 2002 (RA) |
| 63 | | 30 Dec 2002 (s 64(2)) |
| 64 | | 17 Dec 2002 (RA) |
| Schs 1–3 | | 30 Dec 2002 (s 64(2))[1] |

[1] Any power conferred by this Act to make provision by Act of Sederunt is exercisable from Royal Assent

---

## Divorce (Religious Marriages) Act 2002 (c 27)

*RA:* 24 Jul 2002

*Commencement provisions:* s 2(2); Divorce (Religious Marriages) Act 2002 (Commencement) Order 2003, SI 2003/186

| | |
|---|---|
| 1 | 24 Feb 2003 (SI 2003/186) |
| 2 | 24 Jul 2002 (RA) |

---

## Education Act 2002 (c 32)

*RA:* 24 Jul 2002

*Commencement provisions:* s 216; Education Act 2002 (Commencement No 1) Order 2002, SI 2002/2002, as amended by SI 2002/2018; Education Act 2002 (Commencement No 2 and Savings and Transitional Provisions) Order 2002, SI 2002/2439[1], as amended by SI 2003/606 (revoked), SI 2003/2992; Education Act 2002 (Commencement No 3 and Savings and Transitional Provisions) Order 2002, SI 2002/2952[2]; Education Act 2002 (Commencement No 1) (Wales) Order 2002, SI 2002/3185[3]; Education Act 2002 (Commencement No 4 and Transitional and Saving Provisions) Order 2003, SI 2003/124[4]; Education Act 2002 (Commencement No 5 and Transitional and Saving Provisions) Order 2003, SI 2003/1115[5]; Education Act 2002 (Commencement No 6 and Transitional and Saving Provisions) Order 2003, SI 2003/1667[6], as amended by SI 2004/571, SI 2005/2570;

**Education Act 2002 (c 32)**—*contd*
Education Act 2002 (Commencement No 2) (Wales) Order 2003, SI 2003/1718; Education Act 2002 (Commencement No 7 and Transitional Provision) Order 2003, SI 2003/2071; Education Act 2002 (Commencement No 3) (Wales) Order 2003, SI 2003/2961; Education Act 2002 (Commencement No 4 and Transitional Provisions) (Wales) Order 2004, SI 2004/912; Education Act 2002 (Commencement No 8) Order 2004, SI 2004/1318; Education Act 2002 (Commencement No 5) (Wales) Order 2004, SI 2004/1728; Education Act 2002 (Commencement No 6 and Transitional Provisions) (Wales) Order 2005, SI 2005/1395; Education Act 2002 (Commencement No 7) (Wales) Order 2005, SI 2005/2910; Education Act 2002 (Commencement No 8) (Wales) Order 2006, SI 2006/172; Education Act 2002 (Commencement No 9 and Transitional Provisions) (Wales) Order 2006, SI 2006/879; Education Act 2002 (Commencement No 10 and Transitional Provisions) (Wales) Order 2006, SI 2006/1336; Education Act 2002 (Commencement No 9 and Savings) Order 2006, SI 2006/2895; Education Act 2002 (Commencement No 11 and Transitional and Savings Provisions) (Wales) Order 2007, SI 2007/3611; Education Act 2002 (Commencement No 12) (Wales) Order 2008, SI 2008/1728; Education Act 2002 (Commencement No 13) (Wales) Order 2010, SI 2010/707; Education Act 2002 (Commencement No 14) (Wales) Order 2011, SI 2011/1952; Education Act 2002 (Commencement No 15) (Wales) Order 2015, SI 2015/381

| | | |
|---|---|---|
| 1 | (1), (2) | 1 Oct 2002 (E) (SI 2002/2439) |
| | | 27 Feb 2015 (W) (SI 2015/381) |
| | (3) | 1 Oct 2002 (E) (except para (b) in definition "qualifying school") (SI 2002/2439) |
| | | 1 Sep 2003 (E) (exception noted above) (SI 2003/1667) |
| | | 27 Feb 2015 (W) (SI 2015/381) |
| 2 | (1)–(6) | 1 Oct 2002 (E) (SI 2002/2439) |
| | | 27 Feb 2015 (W) (SI 2015/381) |
| | (7)–(9) | 1 Oct 2002 (E) (SI 2002/2439) |
| | | *Never in force* (W) (repealed) |
| 3–5 | | 1 Oct 2002 (E) (SI 2002/2439) |
| | | 27 Feb 2015 (W) (SI 2015/381) |
| 6–10 | | *Not yet in force* |
| 11, 12 | | 20 Jan 2003 (E) (SI 2002/2952) |
| | | *Not yet in force* (W) |
| 13 | | 24 Jul 2002 (RA) |
| 14–17 | | 1 Oct 2002 (E) (SI 2002/2439) |
| | | 31 Mar 2003 (W) (SI 2002/3185) |
| 18 | (1)(a)–(f) | 1 Apr 2003 (E) (SI 2003/124) |
| | | 2 Jan 2008 (W) (SI 2007/3611) |
| | (1)(g) | 1 Apr 2003 (E) (except repeal of Education Act 1996, s 486) (SI 2003/124) |
| | | 6 Nov 2006 (E) (otherwise) (SI 2006/2895) |
| | | 2 Jan 2008 (W) (SI 2007/3611) |
| | (1)(h), (i) | 1 Apr 2003 (E) (SI 2003/124) |
| | | 2 Jan 2008 (W) (SI 2007/3611) |
| | (2) | 31 Mar 2003 (W) (SI 2002/3185) |
| | | 1 Apr 2003 (E) (SI 2003/124)[4] |
| 19 | (1) | 1 Sep 2003 (E) (SI 2003/1667)[6] |
| | | 31 Oct 2005 (W) (SI 2005/2910) |
| | (2)–(5) | 1 Mar 2003 (E) (SI 2003/124) |
| | | 31 Oct 2005 (W) (SI 2005/2910) |
| | (6) | See Sch 1 below |
| | (7) | 1 Mar 2003 (E) (SI 2003/124) |
| | | 31 Oct 2005 (W) (SI 2005/2910) |
| | (8) | 1 Apr 2003 (E) (words "regulations under this section may include provision with respect to the governing bodies of federations") (SI 2003/124) |
| | | 1 Sep 2003 (E) (otherwise) (SI 2003/1667) |
| | | 12 Apr 2010 (W) (SI 2010/707) |
| 20 | (1) | 1 Sep 2003 (E) (SI 2003/1667) |
| | | 31 Oct 2005 (W) (SI 2005/2910) |
| | (2), (3) | 1 Mar 2003 (E) (SI 2003/124) |

**Education Act 2002 (c 32)**—*contd*

| | | |
|---|---|---|
| | | 31 Oct 2005 (W) (SI 2005/2910) |
| | (4) | 1 Apr 2003 (E) (words "regulations under subsection (2) may include provision with respect to instruments of government for federations") (SI 2003/124) |
| | | 1 Sep 2003 (E) (otherwise) (SI 2003/1667) |
| | | 12 Apr 2010 (W) (SI 2010/707) |
| | (5) | 1 Sep 2003 (E) (SI 2003/1667) |
| | | 31 Oct 2005 (W) (SI 2005/2910) |
| 21 | (1), (2) | 1 Sep 2003 (E) (SI 2003/1667) |
| | | 1 Sep 2004 (W) (SI 2004/1728) |
| | (3) | 1 Mar 2003 (E) (SI 2003/124) |
| | | 1 Sep 2004 (W) (SI 2004/1728) |
| | (4) | 1 Sep 2003 (E) (SI 2003/1667) |
| | | 1 Sep 2004 (W) (SI 2004/1728) |
| 22 | | 1 Sep 2003 (E) (SI 2003/1667) |
| | | 1 Sep 2004 (W) (SI 2004/1728) |
| 23 | | 1 Mar 2003 (E) (SI 2003/124) |
| | | 31 Oct 2005 (W) (SI 2005/2910) |
| 24 | (1) | 1 Apr 2003 (E) (for the purpose of making regulations) (SI 2003/124) |
| | | 1 Sep 2003 (E) (otherwise) (SI 2003/1667) |
| | | 12 Apr 2010 (W) (SI 2010/707) |
| | (2)–(6) | 1 Apr 2003 (E) (SI 2003/124) |
| | | 12 Apr 2010 (W) (SI 2010/707) |
| 25 | | 1 Apr 2003 (E) (SI 2003/124) |
| | | 12 Apr 2010 (W) (SI 2010/707) |
| 26 | | 1 Mar 2003 (E) (SI 2003/124) |
| | | 2 Jan 2008 (W) (SI 2007/3611) |
| 27, 28 | | 2 Sep 2002 (E) (SI 2002/2002) |
| | | 1 Sep 2003 (W) (SI 2003/1718) |
| 29 | | 1 Sep 2003 (E) (SI 2003/1667) |
| | | 1 Sep 2003 (W) (SI 2003/1718) |
| 30 | | 1 Oct 2002 (E) (SI 2002/2439) |
| | | 1 Sep 2004 (W) (SI 2004/1728) |
| 31 | | 2 Jan 2008 (W) (for the purpose of making regulations) (SI 2007/3611) |
| | | 31 Mar 2008 (W) (otherwise) (SI 2007/3611) |
| | | *Not yet in force* (E) |
| 32 | | 1 Sep 2003 (E) (SI 2003/1667) |
| | | 1 Sep 2004 (W) (SI 2004/1728) |
| 33 | (1), (2) | 1 Sep 2003 (E) (SI 2003/1667) |
| | | 31 Oct 2005 (W) (SI 2005/2910) |
| | (3) | 1 Mar 2003 (E) (SI 2003/124) |
| | | 31 Oct 2005 (W) (SI 2005/2910) |
| 34 | | 1 Apr 2003 (E) (SI 2003/124) |
| | | 31 Oct 2005 (W) (SI 2005/2910) |
| 35 | (1)–(3) | 1 Sep 2003 (E) (SI 2003/1667) |
| | | 1 Apr 2006 (W) (SI 2006/879) |
| | (4), (5) | 1 Apr 2003 (E) (SI 2003/124) |
| | | 1 Apr 2006 (W) (SI 2006/879) |
| | (6)–(8) | 1 Sep 2003 (E) (SI 2003/1667) |
| | | 1 Apr 2006 (W) (SI 2006/879) |
| 36 | (1)–(3) | 1 Sep 2003 (E) (SI 2003/1667) |
| | | 1 Apr 2006 (W) (SI 2006/879) |
| | (4), (5) | 1 Apr 2003 (E) (SI 2003/124) |
| | | 1 Apr 2006 (W) (SI 2006/879) |
| | (6)–(8) | 1 Sep 2003 (E) (SI 2003/1667) |
| | | 1 Apr 2006 (W) (SI 2006/879) |
| 37 | | 1 Oct 2002 (E) (SI 2002/2439) |

**Education Act 2002 (c 32)**—*contd*

|  |  |  |
|---|---|---|
|  |  | 1 Apr 2006 (W) (SI 2006/879) |
| 38 | (1) | 1 Oct 2003 (E) (SI 2003/1667) |
|  |  | 2 Jan 2008 (W) (SI 2007/3611) |
|  | (2) | 1 Oct 2003 (SI 2003/1667)[6] |
|  | (3) | 2 Jan 2008 (SI 2007/3611)[12] |
|  | (4)–(7) | 1 Oct 2003 (E) (SI 2003/1667) |
|  |  | 2 Jan 2008 (W) (SI 2007/3611) |
| 39 | (1) | 1 Oct 2002 (E) (definition "budget share") (SI 2002/2439) |
|  |  | 1 Apr 2003 (E) (definitions "federation" and "federated school") (SI 2003/124) |
|  |  | 1 Sep 2003 (E) (otherwise) (SI 2003/1667) |
|  |  | 1 Sep 2004 (W) (definition "statutory provision") (SI 2004/1728) |
|  |  | 31 Oct 2005 (W) (otherwise) (SI 2005/2910) |
|  | (2) | 1 Oct 2002 (E) (SI 2002/2439) |
|  |  | 31 Oct 2005 (W) (SI 2005/2910) |
| 40 |  | See Sch 3 below |
| 41 | (1) | 1 Oct 2002 (E) (SI 2002/2439) |
|  |  | 4 Dec 2003 (W) (SI 2003/2961) |
|  | (2) | 4 Dec 2003 (W) (SI 2003/2961) |
|  |  | *Never in force* (E) (repealed) |
|  | (3) | 1 Oct 2002 (E) (SI 2002/2439) |
|  |  | 4 Dec 2003 (W) (SI 2003/2961) |
| 42 |  | 1 Oct 2002 (E) (SI 2002/2439) |
|  |  | 4 Dec 2003 (W) (SI 2003/2961) |
| 43 |  | 2 Sep 2002 (E) (SI 2002/2002) |
|  |  | 1 Nov 2003 (W) (SI 2003/1718) |
| 44 | (1)–(6) | 1 Apr 2003 (E) (SI 2003/124) |
|  |  | *Not yet in force* (W) |
|  | (7) | 1 Sep 2003 (E) (SI 2003/1667) |
|  |  | *Not yet in force* (W) |
| 45 |  | 1 Apr 2003 (E) (SI 2003/124) |
|  |  | *Not yet in force* (W) |
| 46 |  | 20 Jan 2003 (E) (SI 2002/2952) |
|  |  | 1 Dec 2003 (W) (SI 2003/2961) |
| 47, 48 |  | 1 Oct 2002 (E) (SI 2002/2439) |
|  |  | 1 Feb 2006 (W) (SI 2006/172) |
| 49 |  | 1 Oct 2002 (E) (SI 2002/2439) |
|  |  | 19 Dec 2002 (W) (SI 2002/3185)[3] |
| 50 |  | 20 Jan 2003 (E) (SI 2002/2952)[2] |
|  |  | 31 May 2005 (W) (SI 2005/1395) |
| 51 |  | See Sch 4 below |
| 52 | (1)–(6) | 20 Jan 2003 (E) (SI 2002/2952)[2] |
|  |  | 9 Jan 2004 (W) (SI 2003/2961) |
|  | (7)–(10) | 24 Jul 2002 (RA) |
|  | (11) | 1 Sep 2003 (E) (SI 2003/1667) |
|  |  | 31 Oct 2005 (W) (SI 2005/2910) |
| 53 |  | 1 Jun 2004 (E) (SI 2004/1318) |
|  |  | 31 Oct 2005 (W) (SI 2005/2910) |
| 54–56 |  | 2 Sep 2002 (E) (SI 2002/2002) |
|  |  | 19 Dec 2002 (W) (SI 2002/3185) |
| 57–59 |  | 2 Sep 2002 (E) (SI 2002/2002) |
|  |  | 2 Jan 2008 (W) (SI 2007/3611) |
| 60, 61 |  | 26 Jul 2002 (E) (SI 2002/2002) |
|  |  | 1 Aug 2003 (W) (SI 2003/1718) |
| 62–64 |  | 1 Oct 2002 (E) (SI 2002/2439) |
|  |  | 1 Aug 2003 (W) (SI 2003/1718) |
| 65 |  | 26 Jul 2002 (SI 2002/2002) |
| 66 |  | 20 Jan 2003 (E) (SI 2002/2952) |
| 67–69 |  | 26 Jul 2002 (SI 2002/2002) |

**Education Act 2002 (c 32)**—*contd*

| | | |
|---|---|---|
| 70, 71 | | 1 Jun 2003 (SI 2003/1115) |
| 72 | | 1 Apr 2003 (E) (SI 2003/124) |
| | | 1 Aug 2004 (W) (SI 2004/1728) |
| 73 | | 1 Jun 2003 (SI 2003/1115) |
| 74 | (1) | 1 Jun 2003 (E) (SI 2003/1115) |
| | | *Never in force* (W) (repealed) |
| | (2), (3) | 1 Apr 2003 (E) (SI 2003/124) |
| | | *Never in force* (W) (repealed) |
| 75 | | See Sch 10 below |
| 76, 77 | | 1 Oct 2002 (SI 2002/2439) |
| 78 | | 26 Jul 2002 (for the purposes only of the reference to it in s 65) (SI 2002/2002) |
| | | 1 Oct 2002 (otherwise) (SI 2002/2439) |
| 79–96 | | 1 Oct 2002 (SI 2002/2439) |
| 97, 98 | | 19 Dec 2002 (SI 2002/3185) |
| 99 | (1) | 19 Dec 2002 (SI 2002/3185) |
| | (2) | 1 Aug 2008 (SI 2008/1728) |
| 100 | (1)(a) | 19 Dec 2002 (SI 2002/3185) |
| | (1)(b) | 1 Aug 2008 (SI 2008/1728) |
| | (2)(a) | 19 Dec 2002 (SI 2002/3185) |
| | (2)(b) | 1 Aug 2008 (SI 2008/1728) |
| | (3), (4) | 19 Dec 2002 (SI 2002/3185) |
| | (5) | 1 Aug 2008 (SI 2008/1728) |
| | (6)–(8) | 19 Dec 2002 (SI 2002/3185) |
| 101 | (1), (2) | 19 Dec 2002 (SI 2002/3185) |
| | (3)(a) | 19 Dec 2002 (SI 2002/3185) |
| | (3)(b) | 1 Aug 2008 (SI 2008/1728) |
| | (3)(c) | 19 Dec 2002 (SI 2002/3185) |
| 102 | | 1 Aug 2008 (SI 2008/1728) |
| 103 | | 19 Dec 2002 (SI 2002/3185) |
| 104 | | 1 Aug 2008 (SI 2008/1728) |
| 105–107 | | 19 Dec 2002 (SI 2002/3185) |
| 108 | (1)(a) | 1 Aug 2008 (SI 2008/1728) |
| | (1)(b) | 19 Dec 2002 (SI 2002/3185) |
| | (2) | 1 Aug 2008 (SI 2008/1728) |
| | (3)–(5) | 19 Dec 2002 (SI 2002/3185) |
| | (6) | 1 Aug 2008 (SI 2008/1728) |
| | (7)–(11) | 19 Dec 2002 (SI 2002/3185) |
| 109 | | 19 Dec 2002 (SI 2002/3185) |
| 110 | | 1 Aug 2008 (SI 2008/1728) |
| 111–118 | | 19 Dec 2002 (SI 2002/3185) |
| 119 | | 1 Oct 2002 (SI 2002/2439) |
| 120 | (1) | 1 Oct 2002 (SI 2002/2439) |
| | (2) | 1 Aug 2003 (SI 2003/1667) |
| | (3)–(5) | 1 Oct 2002 (SI 2002/2439) |
| 121 | | 1 Oct 2002 (SI 2002/2439) |
| 122–129 | | 1 Aug 2003 (SI 2003/1667) |
| 130 | | 1 Oct 2002 (repeals of or in School Teachers' Pay and Conditions Act 1991, s 1, Schedule) (SI 2002/2439) |
| | | 1 Aug 2003 (otherwise) (SI 2003/1667) |
| 131 | | 1 Oct 2002 (E) (SI 2002/2439) |
| | | 19 Dec 2002 (W) (SI 2002/3185) |
| 132, 133 | | 19 Dec 2002 (W) (SI 2002/3185) |
| | | 1 Aug 2003 (E) (SI 2003/1667) |
| 134 | (1) | 19 Dec 2002 (W) (SI 2002/3185) |
| | | 1 Aug 2003 (E) (SI 2003/1667) |
| | (2), (3) | 6 Nov 2006 (E) (SI 2006/2895) |
| | | *Never in force* (W) (repealed) |
| | (4), (5) | 19 Dec 2002 (W) (SI 2002/3185) |

**Education Act 2002 (c 32)**—*contd*

| | | |
|---|---|---|
| | | 1 Aug 2003 (E) (SI 2003/1667) |
| 135 | | 19 Dec 2002 (W) (SI 2002/3185) |
| | | 1 Oct 2003 (E) (SI 2003/1667) |
| 136–138 | | 1 Sep 2003 (W) (SI 2003/1718) |
| | | 6 Nov 2006 (E) (SI 2006/2895) |
| 139 | | 1 Sep 2003 (SI 2003/1718) |
| 140 | | 1 Sep 2003 (W) (SI 2003/1718) |
| | | 6 Nov 2006 (E) (SI 2006/2895) |
| 141 | | 19 Dec 2002 (W) (SI 2002/3185) |
| | | 1 Aug 2003 (E) (SI 2003/1667) |
| 142–144 | | 31 Mar 2003 (W) (SI 2002/3185) |
| | | 1 Jun 2003 (E) (SI 2003/1115) |
| 145 | | 19 Dec 2002 (W) (SI 2002/3185) |
| | | 1 Aug 2003 (E) (SI 2003/1667) |
| 146 | | 31 Mar 2003 (W) (repeals of or in Education Reform Act 1988, ss 218(2B), (6), (6ZA), (6A), (6B), (7), 218A) (SI 2002/3185) |
| | | 1 Jun 2003 (E) (repeals of or in Education Reform Act 1988, ss 218(6), (6ZA), (6A), (6B), 218A) (SI 2003/1115) |
| | | 1 Aug 2003 (E) (repeals of or in Education Reform Act 1988, s 218(1)(a), (aa), (e), (f), (2), (2A), (2AA), (2B), (3)–(5)) (SI 2003/1667)[6] |
| | | 1 Sep 2003 (E) (repeals of or in Education Reform Act 1988, s 218(1)(d)) (SI 2003/1667) |
| | | 1 Oct 2003 (E) (repeals of or in Education Reform Act 1988 s 218(1)(ab), (2C)–(2F), (9)(b) (words "or course leading to a professional headship qualification for the purposes of subsection (1)(ab) above"), (12), (14)) (SI 2003/1667) |
| | | 6 Nov 2006 (E) (otherwise) (SI 2006/2895) |
| | | 2 Jan 2008 (W) (so far as it repeals Education Reform Act 1988, s 218(1), (2), (2A), (2AA), (2C)–(2F), (3)–(5), (9)–(14)) (SI 2007/3611) |
| 147 | | 24 Jul 2002 (RA) |
| 148 | | See Sch 12 below |
| 149, 150 | | 1 Oct 2002 (E) (SI 2002/2439) |
| | | 31 Mar 2003 (W) (SI 2002/3185) |
| 151 | (1) | 1 Oct 2002 (E) (SI 2002/2439) |
| | | 2 Jan 2008 (W) (SI 2007/3611) |
| | (2) | 19 Dec 2002 (W) (SI 2002/3185) |
| 152 | | See Sch 13 below |
| 153 | | 1 Apr 2003 (E) (SI 2003/124) |
| | | *Not yet in force* (W) |
| 154 | (1), (2) | 1 Jun 2003 (E) (SI 2003/1115)[5] |
| | | 31 Mar 2004 (W) (SI 2004/912)[8] |
| | (3) | 31 Mar 2004 (W) (SI 2004/912)[8] |
| 155 | | See Sch 14 below |
| 156 | | 1 Oct 2002 (E) (SI 2002/2439) |
| | | 31 Mar 2004 (W) (SI 2004/912) |
| 157 | | 1 Sep 2003 (E) (SI 2003/1667) |
| | | 1 Jan 2004 (W) (SI 2003/2961) |
| 158 | (1), (2) | 1 Sep 2003 (E) (SI 2003/1667) |
| | | 1 Jan 2004 (W) (SI 2003/2961) |
| | (3) | 1 Jan 2004 (W) (SI 2003/2961) |
| | | 6 Nov 2006 (E) (SI 2006/2895) |
| 159–164 | | 1 Sep 2003 (E) (SI 2003/1667) |
| | | 1 Jan 2004 (W) (SI 2003/2961) |
| 165 | | 1 Sep 2003 (E) (SI 2003/1667)[6] |
| | | 1 Jan 2004 (W) (SI 2003/2961) |
| 166–174 | | 1 Sep 2003 (E) (SI 2003/1667) |
| | | 1 Jan 2004 (W) (SI 2003/2961) |

**Education Act 2002 (c 32)**—*contd*

| | | |
|---|---|---|
| 175 | | 1 Jun 2004 (E) (SI 2004/1318) |
| | | 1 Sep 2006 (W) (SI 2006/172) |
| 176 | | 1 Sep 2003 (E) (SI 2003/1667) |
| | | 1 Sep 2004 (W) (SI 2004/1728) |
| 177 | | 1 Oct 2002 (E) (SI 2002/2439) |
| | | 1 Aug 2004 (W) (SI 2004/912) |
| 178 | (1) | 1 Oct 2002 (E) (SI 2002/2439) |
| | | 1 Aug 2003 (W) (SI 2003/1718) |
| | (2) | 1 Oct 2002 (E) (SI 2002/2439) |
| | | 2 Jan 2008 (W) (SI 2007/3611) |
| | (3) | 20 Jan 2003 (E) (SI 2002/2952) |
| | (4) | 1 Aug 2003 (W) (SI 2003/1718) |
| 179 | (1) | 1 Oct 2002 (E) (SI 2002/2439) |
| | | 19 Dec 2002 (W) (SI 2002/3185) |
| | (2), (3) | 1 Oct 2002 (E) (SI 2002/2439) |
| | (4)–(6) | 1 Oct 2002 (E) (SI 2002/2439) |
| | | 19 Dec 2002 (W) (SI 2002/3185) |
| 180 | | 1 Oct 2002 (E) (SI 2002/2439) |
| | | 19 Dec 2002 (W) (SI 2002/3185) |
| 181–185 | | 1 Sep 2003 (E) (SI 2003/1667) |
| | | 1 Sep 2003 (W) (SI 2003/1718) |
| 186 | | 24 Jul 2002 (RA) |
| 187 | | See Sch 15 below |
| 188 | | See Sch 16 below |
| 189 | | See Sch 17 below |
| 190 | | 24 Jul 2002 (RA) |
| 191–194 | | 19 Dec 2002 (SI 2002/3185) |
| 195 | | See Sch 18 below |
| 196 | | 19 Dec 2002 (SI 2002/3185) |
| 197 | | 1 Sep 2003 (SI 2003/1718) |
| 198 | | 31 Mar 2004 (SI 2004/912) |
| 199 | | See Sch 19 below |
| 200 | | 31 Mar 2003 (W) (SI 2002/3185) |
| | | 6 Apr 2003 (E) (SI 2003/124) |
| 201 | (1) | 31 Mar 2003 (W) (except in so far as it relates to sub-s (1)(c) of the new s 512) (SI 2002/3185) |
| | | 6 Apr 2003 (E) (except in so far as it relates to sub-ss (1)(c), (2)(b), in sub-s (3) words "or (c)", in sub-s (6) definition "relevant funded nursery education" of the new s 512 and in the new s 512ZB(3) words "or (c)") (SI 2003/124)[4] |
| | | *Not yet in force* (exceptions noted above) |
| | (2), (3) | 31 Mar 2003 (W) (SI 2002/3185) |
| | | 6 Apr 2003 (E) (SI 2003/124)[4] |
| 202, 203 | | 1 Aug 2003 (E) (SI 2003/1667) |
| | | 1 Sep 2003 (W) (SI 2003/1718) |
| 204 | | 2 Sep 2002 (E) (SI 2002/2002) |
| | | 1 Sep 2011 (W) (SI 2011/1952) |
| 205 | | 1 Oct 2002 (E) (SI 2002/2439) |
| | | 1 Aug 2008 (W) (SI 2008/1728) |
| 206 | | See Sch 20 below |
| 207 | | 1 Apr 2003 (E) (SI 2003/124) |
| | | 9 Jan 2004 (W) (SI 2003/2961) |
| 208 | | 1 Apr 2003 (E) (S) (SI 2003/124) |
| | | 9 Jan 2004 (W) (SI 2003/2961) |
| 209 | | 1 Apr 2003 (SI 2003/124) |
| 210–214 | | 24 Jul 2002 (RA) |
| 215 | (1) | See Sch 21 below |
| | (2) | See Sch 22 below |
| 216, 217 | | 24 Jul 2002 (RA) |

**Education Act 2002 (c 32)**—*contd*

| Sch 1 | paras 1, 2 | 1 Oct 2002 (E) (SI 2002/2439) |
| | | 31 Oct 2005 (W) (SI 2005/2910) |
| | para 3(1)(a) | 1 Oct 2002 (E) (SI 2002/2439) |
| | | 31 Oct 2005 (W) (SI 2005/2910) |
| | para 3(1)(b) | 2 Sep 2002 (E) (SI 2002/2002) |
| | | 1 Sep 2003 (W) (SI 2003/1718) |
| | para 3(2) | 1 Oct 2002 (E) (SI 2002/2439) |
| | | 31 Oct 2005 (W) (SI 2005/2910) |
| | para 3(3)–(8) | 2 Sep 2002 (E) (so far as necessary for the purposes of sub-para (1)) (SI 2002/2002) |
| | | 1 Oct 2002 (E) (otherwise) (SI 2002/2439) |
| | | 1 Sep 2003 (W) (so far as relating to the power conferred by sub-para (1)(b)) (SI 2003/1718) |
| | | 31 Oct 2005 (W) (otherwise) (SI 2005/2910) |
| | paras 4, 5 | 1 Oct 2002 (E) (SI 2002/2439) |
| | | 31 Oct 2005 (W) (SI 2005/2910) |
| Sch 2 | | 1 Sep 2003 (E) (SI 2003/1667) |
| | | 1 Apr 2006 (W) (SI 2006/879) |
| Sch 3 | paras 1–5 | 2 Sep 2002 (E) (SI 2002/2002) |
| | | 1 Sep 2003 (W) (SI 2003/1718) |
| | paras 6–8 | 1 Sep 2003 (E) (SI 2003/1667) |
| | | 1 Apr 2006 (W) (SI 2006/879) |
| Sch 4 | para 1 | 1 Oct 2002 (E) (SI 2002/2439) |
| | | 9 Jan 2004 (W) (SI 2003/2961) |
| | para 2 | 20 Jan 2003 (E) (SI 2002/2952)[2] |
| | | 31 May 2005 (W) (SI 2005/1395)[9] |
| | para 3(1)–(5) | 1 Oct 2002 (E) (SI 2002/2439) |
| | | 31 May 2005 (W) (SI 2005/1395)[9] |
| | para 3(6) | 1 Oct 2002 (E) (SI 2002/2439) |
| | | 1 Feb 2006 (W) (SI 2006/172) |
| | para 3(7), (8) | 1 Oct 2002 (E) (SI 2002/2439) |
| | | 31 May 2005 (W) (SI 2005/1395)[9] |
| | para 4 | 20 Jan 2003 (E) (SI 2002/2952) |
| | | 9 Jan 2004 (W) (SI 2003/2961) |
| | paras 5–7 | 1 Oct 2002 (E) (SI 2002/2439) |
| | | 1 Feb 2006 (W) (SI 2006/172) |
| | paras 8, 9 | 20 Jan 2003 (E) (SI 2002/2952)[2] |
| | | 31 May 2005 (W) (SI 2005/1395)[9] |
| | paras 10, 11 | 1 Oct 2002 (E) (SI 2002/2439) |
| | | 31 May 2005 (W) (SI 2005/1395)[9] |
| | para 12(1) | 20 Jan 2003 (E) (SI 2002/2952)[2] |
| | | 31 Mar 2004 (W) (SI 2004/912) |
| | para 12(2) | 20 Jan 2003 (E) (SI 2002/2952)[2] |
| | | 1 Feb 2006 (W) (SI 2006/172) |
| | para 12(3)–(5) | 20 Jan 2003 (E) (SI 2002/2952)[2] |
| | | 31 Mar 2004 (W) (SI 2004/912)[8] |
| | para 12(6) | 20 Jan 2003 (E) (SI 2002/2952)[2] |
| | | 1 Feb 2006 (W) (SI 2006/172) |
| | paras 13, 14 | 1 Oct 2002 (E) (SI 2002/2439) |
| | | 1 Feb 2006 (W) (SI 2006/172) |
| Sch 5 | | 2 Sep 2002 (E) (SI 2002/2002) |
| | | 19 Dec 2002 (W) (SI 2002/3185) |
| Sch 6 | | 2 Sep 2002 (E) (SI 2002/2002) |
| | | 2 Jan 2008 (W) (SI 2007/3611) |
| Sch 7 | | 26 Jul 2002 (SI 2002/2002) |
| Sch 8 | | 1 Jun 2003 (SI 2003/1115) |
| Sch 9 | | 1 Apr 2003 (E) (SI 2003/124) |
| | | 1 Aug 2004 (W) (SI 2004/1728) |
| Sch 10 | para 1 | 19 Dec 2002 (W) (SI 2002/3185) |

**Education Act 2002 (c 32)**—*contd*

| | | |
|---|---|---|
| | | 1 Apr 2003 (E) (SI 2003/124) |
| | paras 2–5 | 1 Jun 2003 (E) (SI 2003/1115)[5] |
| | | 2 Jan 2008 (W) (SI 2007/3611) |
| | para 6 | 19 Dec 2002 (W) (SI 2002/3185) |
| | | 1 Apr 2003 (E) (SI 2003/124) |
| | paras 7–10 | 1 Jun 2003 (E) (SI 2003/1115)[5] |
| | | 2 Jan 2008 (W) (SI 2007/3611) |
| | para 11 | 19 Dec 2002 (W) (SI 2002/3185) |
| | | 1 Apr 2003 (E) (SI 2003/124) |
| | paras 12–14 | 1 Apr 2003 (E) (SI 2003/124) |
| | | 2 Jan 2008 (W) (SI 2007/3611) |
| | para 15 | 19 Dec 2002 (W) (SI 2002/3185) |
| | | 1 Apr 2003 (E) (SI 2003/124) |
| Sch 11 | | 1 Oct 2002 (SI 2002/2439) |
| Sch 12 | paras 1, 2 | 1 Oct 2002 (E) (SI 2002/2439) |
| | | 19 Dec 2002 (W) (SI 2002/3185) |
| | para 3(1) | 1 Aug 2003 (E) (SI 2003/1667) |
| | | 31 May 2006 (W) (SI 2006/1336) |
| | para 3(2) | 1 Aug 2003 (E) (SI 2003/1667) |
| | | *Not yet in force* (W) |
| | para 3(3) | 1 Aug 2003 (E) (except for words "or provisional") (SI 2003/1667) |
| | | 6 Nov 2006 (E) (otherwise) (SI 2006/2895) |
| | | *Not yet in force* (W) |
| | para 3(4) | 1 Aug 2003 (E) (SI 2003/1667) |
| | | *Not yet in force* (W) |
| | para 3(5) | 31 May 2006 (W) (in so far as inserts Teaching and Higher Education Act 1998, s 3(3B), (3D)) (SI 2006/1336)[10] |
| | | 6 Nov 2006 (E) (SI 2006/2895) |
| | | *Not yet in force* (W) (otherwise) |
| | para 3(6) | 1 Aug 2003 (E) (SI 2003/1667) |
| | | *Not yet in force* (W) |
| | para 4(1) | 1 Oct 2002 (E) (SI 2002/2439) |
| | | 19 Dec 2002 (W) (SI 2002/3185) |
| | para 4(2) | 31 May 2006 (W) (SI 2006/1336) |
| | | 6 Nov 2006 (E) (SI 2006/2895) |
| | para 4(3) | 1 Oct 2002 (E) (SI 2002/2439) |
| | | 19 Dec 2002 (W) (SI 2002/3185) |
| | para 4(4) | 1 Aug 2003 (E) (except words "or provisional registration") (SI 2003/1667) |
| | | 6 Nov 2006 (E) (otherwise) (SI 2006/2895) |
| | | *Not yet in force* (W) |
| | para 5 | 31 May 2006 (W) (SI 2006/1336) |
| | | 6 Nov 2006 (E) (SI 2006/2895) |
| | para 6 | 1 Oct 2002 (E) (SI 2002/2439) |
| | | 19 Dec 2002 (W) (SI 2002/3185) |
| | para 7 | 19 Dec 2002 (W) (SI 2002/3185) |
| | para 8 | 1 Aug 2003 (E) (except words "or provisional registration") (SI 2003/1667) |
| | | 6 Nov 2006 (E) (otherwise) (SI 2006/2895) |
| | | *Not yet in force* (W) |
| | para 9 | 1 Oct 2002 (E) (SI 2002/2439) |
| | para 10 | 1 Aug 2003 (E) (except for words "or provisional") (SI 2003/1667) |
| | | 6 Nov 2006 (E) (otherwise) (SI 2006/2895) |
| | | *Not yet in force* (W) |
| | para 11 | 1 Oct 2002 (E) (SI 2002/2439) |
| | para 12(1), (2) | 1 Oct 2002 (E) (SI 2002/2439) |
| | | 31 Mar 2003 (W) (SI 2002/3185) |
| | para 12(3) | 1 Aug 2003 (E) (except for words "or provisional") (SI 2003/1667) |
| | | 6 Nov 2006 (E) (otherwise) (SI 2006/2895) |

**Education Act 2002 (c 32)**—*contd*

|  |  |  |
|---|---|---|
|  |  | *Not yet in force* (W) |
|  | paras 13–15 | 6 Nov 2006 (E) (SI 2006/2895) |
|  |  | *Never in force* (W) (repealed) |
| Sch 13 | paras 1–3 | 1 Oct 2002 (E) (SI 2002/2439) |
|  |  | 19 Dec 2002 (W) (SI 2002/3185) |
|  | para 4 | 2 Sep 2002 (E) (SI 2002/2002) |
|  |  | 2 Jan 2008 (W) (SI 2007/3611) |
|  | para 5 | 2 Sep 2002 (E) (SI 2002/2002) |
|  |  | 19 Dec 2002 (W) (SI 2002/3185) |
|  | para 6 | 1 Oct 2002 (E) (SI 2002/2439) |
|  |  | 19 Dec 2002 (W) (SI 2002/3185) |
|  | para 7(1) | 1 Oct 2002 (E) (W) (NI) (SI 2002/2439) |
|  |  | 19 Dec 2002 (W) (SI 2002/3185) |
|  | para 7(2) | *Never in force* (repealed) |
|  | para 7(3) | 1 Oct 2002 (E) (SI 2002/2439) |
|  |  | 19 Dec 2002 (W) (SI 2002/3185) |
|  | para 8 | 1 Oct 2002 (E) (SI 2002/2439) |
|  |  | 19 Dec 2002 (W) (SI 2002/3185) |
| Sch 14 | paras 1–4 | 2 Sep 2002 (E) (SI 2002/2002) |
|  |  | 1 Sep 2004 (W) (SI 2004/1728) |
|  | paras 5–7 | 1 Oct 2002 (E) (SI 2002/2439) |
|  |  | 1 Sep 2004 (W) (SI 2004/1728) |
| Sch 15 | para 1 | 1 Oct 2002 (E) (SI 2002/2439) |
|  |  | 2 Jan 2008 (W) (SI 2007/3611) |
|  | para 2(1) | 1 Oct 2002 (E) (SI 2002/2439) |
|  |  | 2 Jan 2008 (W) (SI 2007/3611) |
|  | para 2(2) | 1 Oct 2002 (E) (except for the purposes of inserting School Standards and Framework Act 1998, s 10(1A)(b)) (SI 2002/2439) |
|  |  | 1 Sep 2003 (E) (exception noted above) (SI 2003/1667) |
|  |  | 2 Jan 2008 (W) (SI 2007/3611) |
|  | para 2(3)–(6) | 1 Oct 2002 (E) (SI 2002/2439) |
|  |  | 2 Jan 2008 (W) (SI 2007/3611) |
|  | paras 3–8 | 1 Oct 2002 (E) (SI 2002/2439) |
|  |  | 2 Jan 2008 (W) (SI 2007/3611) |
| Sch 16 | para 1 | 1 Sep 2003 (E) (SI 2003/1667) |
|  |  | 1 Dec 2003 (W) (SI 2003/2961) |
|  | para 2 | 1 Dec 2003 (W) (SI 2003/2961) |
|  | para 3 | 1 Sep 2003 (E) (SI 2003/1667) |
|  |  | 1 Dec 2003 (W) (SI 2003/2961) |
|  | paras 4–6 | 19 Dec 2002 (W) (SI 2002/3185) |
|  |  | 1 Sep 2003 (E) (SI 2003/1667) |
|  | paras 7–9 | 1 Oct 2002 (E) (SI 2002/2439) |
|  |  | 19 Dec 2002 (W) (SI 2002/3185) |
| Sch 17 | paras 1–4 | 1 Oct 2002 (SI 2002/2439) |
|  | para 5(1)–(4) | 19 Dec 2002 (SI 2002/3185) |
|  | para 5(5) | *Not yet in force* |
|  | para 5(6) | 19 Dec 2002 (SI 2002/3185) |
|  | paras 6–8 | 19 Dec 2002 (SI 2002/3185) |
|  | para 9 | 1 Oct 2002 (SI 2002/2439) |
| Sch 18 | para 1 | 31 Mar 2003 (SI 2002/3185) |
|  | paras 2, 3 | 1 Sep 2003 (SI 2002/3185) |
|  | paras 4, 5 | 31 Mar 2003 (SI 2002/3185) |
|  | para 6 | 1 Sep 2003 (SI 2002/3185) |
|  | para 7 | 31 Mar 2003 (SI 2002/3185) |
|  | para 8 | 31 Mar 2003 (in so far as it inserts a new s 28H(2)) (SI 2002/3185) |
|  |  | 1 Sep 2003 (otherwise) (SI 2002/3185) |
|  | paras 9–12 | 1 Sep 2003 (SI 2002/3185) |
|  | paras 13–15 | 31 Mar 2003 (SI 2002/3185) |

**Education Act 2002 (c 32)**—*contd*

|  |  |  |
|---|---|---|
|  | paras 16–18 | 1 Sep 2003 (SI 2002/3185) |
| Sch 19 |  | 20 Jan 2003 (E) (SI 2002/2952) |
|  |  | 1 Sep 2003 (W) (SI 2003/1718) |
| Sch 20 |  | 1 Oct 2002 (E) (SI 2002/2439) |
|  |  | 1 Sep 2003 (W) (SI 2003/1718) |
| Sch 21 | para 1 | 20 Jan 2003 (E) (SI 2002/2952) |
|  |  | 9 Jan 2004 (W) (so far as relates to allowances for exclusion appeal panels) (SI 2003/2961) |
|  |  | 31 May 2005 (W) (otherwise) (SI 2005/1395) |
|  | para 2(a) | 20 Jan 2003 (E) (SI 2002/2952) |
|  |  | 31 May 2005 (W) (SI 2005/1395)[9] |
|  | para 2(b) | 20 Jan 2003 (E) (SI 2002/2952) |
|  |  | 9 Jan 2004 (W) (SI 2003/2961) |
|  | para 3(a) | 2 Jan 2008 (W) (SI 2007/3611) |
|  |  | *Never in force* (E) (repealed) |
|  | para 3(b) | 1 Apr 2003 (E) (S) (SI 2003/124) |
|  |  | 2 Jan 2008 (W) (SI 2007/3611) |
|  | para 4 | 20 Jan 2003 (E) (S) (SI 2002/2952) |
|  |  | 1 Sep 2003 (W) (SI 2003/1718) |
|  | paras 5, 6 | 6 Nov 2006 (E) (SI 2006/2895) |
|  |  | 2 Jan 2008 (W) (SI 2007/3611) |
|  | para 7 | 1 Apr 2003 (E) (SI 2003/124) |
|  |  | 2 Jan 2008 (W) (SI 2007/3611) |
|  | para 8 | 1 Oct 2002 (E) (SI 2002/2439) |
|  |  | 19 Dec 2002 (W) (SI 2002/3185) |
|  | para 9 | 31 Mar 2003 (W) (SI 2002/3185) |
|  |  | 1 Jun 2003 (E) (SI 2003/1115) |
|  | para 10 | 6 Nov 2006 (E) (SI 2006/2895) |
|  |  | 2 Jan 2008 (W) (SI 2007/3611) |
|  | para 11 | 1 Oct 2002 (E) (SI 2002/2439) |
|  |  | 19 Dec 2002 (W) (SI 2002/3185) |
|  | para 12 | 1 Sep 2003 (E) (SI 2003/1667) |
|  |  | 31 Oct 2005 (W) (SI 2005/2910) |
|  | para 13 | 1 Oct 2002 (E) (SI 2002/2439) |
|  |  | 19 Dec 2002 (W) (SI 2002/3185) |
|  | para 14 | 1 Oct 2002 (SI 2002/2439) |
|  | para 15 | 6 Nov 2006 (E) (SI 2006/2895) |
|  |  | 2 Jan 2008 (W) (SI 2007/3611) |
|  | para 16 | 1 Oct 2002 (E) (SI 2002/2439) |
|  |  | 19 Dec 2002 (W) (SI 2002/3185) |
|  | para 17 | 1 Aug 2003 (SI 2003/1667) |
|  | para 18 | 1 Oct 2002 (SI 2002/2439) |
|  | paras 19–21 | 1 Oct 2002 (E) (SI 2002/2439) |
|  |  | 19 Dec 2002 (W) (SI 2002/3185) |
|  | para 22 | 20 Jan 2003 (E) (S) (NI) (SI 2002/2952) |
|  |  | 9 Jan 2004 (W) (so far as substitutes Tribunals and Inquiries Act 1992, Sch 1, para 15(b)) (SI 2003/2961) |
|  |  | 31 May 2005 (W) (otherwise) (SI 2005/1395) |
|  | para 23 | 1 Sep 2003 (E) (SI 2003/1667) |
|  |  | 31 Oct 2005 (W) (SI 2005/2910) |
|  | para 24 | 1 Aug 2003 (E) (SI 2003/1667) |
|  |  | *Not yet in force* (W) |
|  | paras 25, 26 | 1 Sep 2003 (E) (SI 2003/1667) |
|  |  | 31 Oct 2005 (W) (SI 2005/2910) |
|  | para 27(1), (2) | 20 Jan 2003 (E) (S) (SI 2002/2952) |
|  |  | 9 Jan 2004 (W) (SI 2003/2961) |
|  | para 27(3) | 1 Sep 2003 (E) (SI 2003/1667) |
|  |  | 31 Oct 2005 (W) (SI 2005/2910) |
|  | paras 28, 29 | 1 Sep 2003 (E) (S) (SI 2003/1667) |

**Education Act 2002 (c 32)**—*contd*

|  |  |
|---|---|
|  | 31 Oct 2005 (W) (SI 2005/2910) |
| para 30 | 1 Sep 2003 (E) (S) (SI 2003/1667) |
|  | 1 Apr 2006 (W) (SI 2006/879) |
| paras 31–33 | 1 Oct 2002 (E) (SI 2002/2439) |
|  | 19 Dec 2002 (W) (SI 2002/3185) |
| para 34 | 2 Sep 2002 (E) (SI 2002/2002) |
|  | 1 Sep 2003 (W) (SI 2003/1718) |
| paras 35–38 | 1 Sep 2003 (E) (SI 2003/1667) |
|  | 31 Oct 2005 (W) (SI 2005/2910) |
| para 39(1) | 1 Sep 2003 (E) (SI 2003/1667) |
|  | 1 Sep 2004 (W) (SI 2004/1728) |
| para 39(2)–(4) | 1 Sep 2003 (E) (SI 2003/1667) |
|  | 31 Oct 2005 (W) (SI 2005/2910) |
| para 39(5) | 1 Oct 2002 (E) (SI 2002/2439) |
|  | 19 Dec 2002 (W) (SI 2002/3185) |
| paras 40–44 | 1 Sep 2003 (E) (SI 2003/1667) |
|  | 31 Oct 2005 (W) (SI 2005/2910) |
| para 45 | 1 Oct 2002 (E) (except for the purposes of substituting para (aa)(ii)) (SI 2002/2439) |
|  | 19 Dec 2002 (W) (SI 2002/3185) |
|  | 1 Mar 2003 (E) (exception noted above) (SI 2003/124) |
| para 46(1)–(3) | 1 Oct 2002 (E) (SI 2002/2439) |
|  | 19 Dec 2002 (W) (SI 2002/3185) |
| para 46(4) | 1 Oct 2002 (E) (except for the purposes of inserting sub-s (4A)(b)) (SI 2002/2439) |
|  | 19 Dec 2002 (W) (SI 2002/3185) |
|  | 1 Mar 2003 (E) (exception noted above) (SI 2003/124) |
| para 46(5) | 1 Oct 2002 (E) (except the words "or 7") (SI 2002/2439) |
|  | 19 Dec 2002 (W) (SI 2002/3185) |
|  | 1 Mar 2003 (E) (exception noted above) (SI 2003/124) |
| para 46(6) | 1 Sep 2003 (E) (SI 2003/1667) |
|  | 1 Aug 2008 (W) (SI 2008/1728) |
| para 47(1), (2) | 1 Oct 2002 (E) (SI 2002/2439) |
|  | 19 Dec 2002 (W) (SI 2002/3185) |
| para 47(3) | 1 Sep 2003 (E) (SI 2003/1667) |
|  | *Not yet in force* (W) |
| para 47(4) | 1 Oct 2002 (E) (SI 2002/2439) |
|  | 19 Dec 2002 (W) (SI 2002/3185) |
| para 48 | 1 Oct 2002 (E) (except the words "or 109" in sub-paras (2) and (3) and the words "or National Curriculum for Wales" in sub-para (2)) (SI 2002/2439) |
|  | 19 Dec 2002 (W) (SI 2002/3185) |
|  | 1 Mar 2003 (E) (exception noted above) (SI 2003/124) |
| para 49 | 31 Mar 2003 (W) (SI 2002/3185) |
|  | 1 Apr 2003 (E) (SI 2003/124)[4] |
| para 50 | 1 Sep 2003 (E) (SI 2003/2071)[7] |
|  | 31 Oct 2005 (W) (SI 2005/2910) |
| para 51 | 1 Oct 2002 (E) (SI 2002/2439) |
|  | 19 Dec 2002 (W) (SI 2002/3185) |
| para 52 | 1 Sep 2003 (E) (SI 2003/1667) |
|  | 31 Oct 2005 (W) (SI 2005/2910) |
| para 53 | 19 Dec 2002 (W) (SI 2002/3185) |
|  | 1 Apr 2003 (E) (SI 2003/124) |
| para 54 | 31 Mar 2003 (W) (SI 2002/3185) |
|  | 1 Jun 2003 (E) (SI 2003/1115) |
| para 55 | 6 Nov 2006 (E) (SI 2006/2895) |
|  | 2 Jan 2008 (W) (SI 2007/3611) |
| para 56 | 1 Aug 2003 (SI 2003/1667) |
| para 57(a) | 1 Sep 2003 (E) (SI 2003/1667) |

**Education Act 2002 (c 32)**—*contd*

| | |
|---|---|
| | 31 Oct 2005 (W) (SI 2005/2910) |
| para 57(b), (c) | 1 Oct 2002 (E) (SI 2002/2439) |
| | 19 Dec 2002 (W) (SI 2002/3185) |
| para 58 | 1 Sep 2003 (E) (SI 2003/1667) |
| | 31 Oct 2005 (W) (SI 2005/2910) |
| para 59(a) | 1 Sep 2003 (E) (SI 2003/1667) |
| | 31 Oct 2005 (W) (SI 2005/2910) |
| para 59(b) | 19 Dec 2002 (W) (SI 2002/3185) |
| | 1 Apr 2003 (E) (SI 2003/124) |
| paras 60–62 | 1 Sep 2003 (E) (SI 2003/1667) |
| | 31 Oct 2005 (W) (SI 2005/2910) |
| para 63(a) | 1 Sep 2003 (E) (SI 2003/1667) |
| | 31 Oct 2005 (W) (SI 2005/2910) |
| para 63(b) | 1 Sep 2003 (E) (SI 2003/1667) |
| | 1 Oct 2002 (W) (SI 2002/2439) |
| paras 64, 65 | 1 Sep 2003 (E) (SI 2003/1667) |
| | 31 Oct 2005 (W) (SI 2005/2910) |
| para 66 | 1 Oct 2002 (E) (except the words "or 101(1)(a)") (SI 2002/2439) |
| | 19 Dec 2002 (W) (SI 2002/3185) |
| | 1 Mar 2003 (E) (exception noted above) (SI 2003/124) |
| para 67 | 1 Sep 2003 (E) (SI 2003/1667) |
| | 31 Oct 2005 (W) (SI 2005/2910) |
| para 68 | 1 Oct 2002 (E) (SI 2002/2439) |
| | 1 Sep 2004 (W) (SI 2004/1728) |
| para 69 | 1 Oct 2002 (E) (SI 2002/2439) |
| | 2 Jan 2008 (W) (SI 2007/3611) |
| para 70 | 19 Dec 2002 (W) (SI 2002/3185) |
| | 1 Mar 2003 (E) (SI 2003/124) |
| para 71 | 31 Mar 2003 (W) (in so far as it relates to s 49(2), (3)) (SI 2002/3185) |
| | 1 Jun 2003 (E) (SI 2003/1115) |
| | 2 Jan 2008 (W) (so far as relates to s 49(1), (4)) (SI 2007/3611) |
| paras 72, 73 | 31 Mar 2003 (W) (SI 2002/3185) |
| | 1 Jun 2003 (E) (SI 2003/1115) |
| para 74 | 19 Dec 2002 (W) (SI 2002/3185) |
| | 1 Aug 2003 (E) (SI 2003/1667) |
| para 75 | 31 Mar 2003 (W) (SI 2002/3185) |
| | 1 Jun 2003 (E) (SI 2003/1115) |
| para 76(a) | 19 Dec 2002 (W) (SI 2002/3185) |
| | 1 Aug 2003 (E) (SI 2003/1667) |
| para 76(b) | 31 Mar 2003 (W) (SI 2002/3185) |
| | 1 Jun 2003 (E) (SI 2003/1115) |
| para 77 | 31 Mar 2003 (W) (SI 2002/3185) |
| | 1 Jun 2003 (E) (SI 2003/1115) |
| para 78 | 19 Dec 2002 (W) (SI 2002/3185) |
| | 1 Aug 2003 (E) (SI 2003/1667) |
| para 79 | 6 Nov 2006 (E) (SI 2006/2895) |
| | 2 Jan 2008 (W) (SI 2007/3611) |
| para 80 | 1 Aug 2003 (E) (SI 2003/1667) |
| | 2 Jan 2008 (W) (SI 2007/3611) |
| para 81 | 19 Dec 2002 (W) (SI 2002/3185) |
| | 1 Aug 2003 (E) (SI 2003/1667) |
| para 82 | 1 Aug 2003 (E) (SI 2003/1667) |
| | 2 Jan 2008 (W) (SI 2007/3611) |
| para 83 | 31 Mar 2003 (W) (SI 2002/3185) |
| | 1 Jun 2003 (E) (SI 2003/1115) |
| para 84 | 1 Oct 2003 (E) (SI 2003/1667) |
| | 2 Jan 2008 (W) (SI 2007/3611) |
| para 85(a) | 1 Oct 2002 (E) (SI 2002/2439) |

**Education Act 2002 (c 32)**—*contd*

|  |  |
|---|---|
|  | 19 Dec 2002 (W) (SI 2002/3185) |
| para 85(b) | 31 Mar 2003 (W) (SI 2002/3185) |
|  | 1 Apr 2003 (E) (SI 2003/124) |
| para 85(c) | 19 Dec 2002 (W) (SI 2002/3185) |
|  | 1 Aug 2003 (E) (SI 2003/1667) |
| para 86 | 31 Mar 2003 (W) (SI 2002/3185) |
|  | 1 Jun 2003 (E) (SI 2003/1115) |
| paras 87, 88 | 19 Dec 2002 (W) (SI 2002/3185) |
|  | 1 Aug 2003 (E) (SI 2003/1667) |
| para 89 | 1 Apr 2003 (E) (SI 2003/124) |
|  | *Not yet in force* (W) |
| para 90 | 1 Sep 2003 (E) (SI 2003/1667) |
|  | 2 Jan 2008 (W) (SI 2007/3611) |
| para 91 | 1 Oct 2002 (SI 2002/2439) |
| paras 92–94 | 1 Sep 2003 (E) (SI 2003/1667) |
|  | 31 Oct 2005 (W) (SI 2005/2910) |
| paras 95, 96 | 19 Dec 2002 (W) (SI 2002/3185) |
|  | 1 Apr 2003 (E) (SI 2003/124) |
| para 97 | 1 Jun 2003 (E) (SI 2003/1115)[5] |
|  | *Never in force* (W) (repealed) |
| para 98(1) | 19 Dec 2002 (W) (SI 2002/3185) |
|  | 1 Apr 2003 (E) (SI 2003/124) |
| para 98(2)(a) | 19 Dec 2002 (W) (SI 2002/3185) |
|  | 1 Apr 2003 (E) (SI 2003/124) |
| para 98(2)(b) | 1 Jun 2003 (E) (SI 2003/1115) |
|  | 31 Mar 2004 (W) (SI 2004/912) |
| para 98(2)(c) | 31 Mar 2004 (W) (SI 2004/912) |
| para 98(3) | 1 Apr 2003 (E) (SI 2003/124) |
|  | 31 Oct 2005 (W) (SI 2005/2910) |
| para 99(1) | 19 Dec 2002 (W) (SI 2002/3185) |
|  | 1 Apr 2003 (E) (SI 2003/124) |
| para 99(2) | 1 Sep 2003 (E) (SI 2003/1667)[6] |
|  | 31 Oct 2005 (W) (SI 2005/2910) |
| para 99(3)(a) | 1 Sep 2003 (E) (SI 2003/1667)[6] |
|  | 31 Oct 2005 (W) (SI 2005/2910) |
| para 99(3)(b) | 19 Dec 2002 (W) (SI 2002/3185) |
|  | 1 Apr 2003 (E) (SI 2003/124) |
| para 100(1), (2) | 1 Oct 2002 (E) (SI 2002/2439) |
|  | 4 Dec 2003 (W) (SI 2003/2961) |
| para 100(3) | 1 Apr 2003 (E) (SI 2003/124) |
|  | 1 Aug 2004 (W) (SI 2004/1728) |
| paras 101–103 | 1 Sep 2003 (E) (SI 2003/1667) |
|  | 31 Oct 2005 (W) (SI 2005/2910) |
| paras 104, 105 | 1 Oct 2002 (E) (except the words "or 101(1)(a)") (SI 2002/2439) |
|  | 19 Dec 2002 (W) (SI 2002/3185) |
|  | 1 Mar 2003 (E) (exception noted above) (SI 2003/124) |
| para 106 | 1 Apr 2003 (E) (SI 2003/124) |
|  | 31 Oct 2005 (W) (SI 2005/2910) |
| para 107 | 1 Aug 2003 (E) (SI 2003/1667) |
|  | 1 Apr 2006 (W) (SI 2006/879) |
| para 108 | 1 Oct 2002 (E) (SI 2002/2439) |
|  | 19 Dec 2002 (W) (SI 2002/3185) |
| para 109 | 19 Dec 2002 (W) (SI 2002/3185) |
|  | 1 Apr 2003 (E) (SI 2003/124) |
| para 110(1) | 1 Apr 2003 (E) (SI 2003/124) |
|  | 1 Sep 2004 (W) (SI 2004/1728) |
| para 110(2) | 1 Sep 2003 (E) (SI 2003/1667) |
|  | 31 Oct 2005 (W) (SI 2005/2910) |
| para 110(3)(a) | 1 Apr 2003 (E) (SI 2003/124) |

**Education Act 2002 (c 32)**—*contd*

|  |  |
|---|---|
|  | *Never in force* (W) (repealed) |
| para 110(3)(b) | 1 Apr 2003 (E) (repeals of or in School Standards and Framework Act 1998, s 127(6)(e)) (SI 2003/124) |
|  | 1 Sep 2003 (E) (repeals of or in School Standards and Framework Act 1998, s 127(6)(f), (h), (k)) (SI 2003/1667) |
|  | 1 Sep 2004 (W) (repeals of or in School Standards and Framework Act 1998, s 127(6)(e)) (SI 2004/1728) |
|  | 31 Oct 2005 (W) (repeals of or in School Standards and Framework Act 1998, s 127(6)(h)) (SI 2005/2910) |
|  | 1 Apr 2006 (W) (repeals of or in School Standards and Framework Act 1998, s 127(6)(f), (k)) (SI 2006/879) |
|  | *Never in force* (so far as repeals School Standards and Framework Act 1998, s 127(6)(i)) (repealed) |
| para 110(3)(c) | 1 Apr 2003 (E) (so far as inserts School Standards and Framework Act 1998, s 127(6)(m)) (SI 2003/124) |
|  | 1 Sep 2003 (E) (so far as inserts School Standards and Framework Act 1998, s 127(6)(p), (q)) (SI 2003/1667) |
|  | 31 Oct 2005 (W) (so far as inserts School Standards and Framework Act 1998, s 127(6)(m)) (SI 2005/2910) |
|  | 1 Apr 2006 (W) (so far as inserts School Standards and Framework Act 1998, s 127(6)(p), (q)) (SI 2006/879) |
|  | *Never in force* (so far as inserts School Standards and Framework Act 1998, s 127(6)(n), (o)) (repealed) |
| para 111 | 1 Oct 2002 (E) (SI 2002/2439) |
|  | 2 Jan 2008 (W) (SI 2007/3611) |
| para 112 | 1 Apr 2003 (E) (so far as inserts definition "exclude" into School Standards and Framework Act 1998, s 142(1)) (SI 2003/124) |
|  | 1 Sep 2003 (E) (otherwise) (SI 2003/1667) |
|  | 9 Jan 2004 (W) (so far as inserts definition "exclude" into School Standards and Framework Act 1998, s 142(1)) (SI 2003/2961) |
|  | 31 Oct 2005 (W) (otherwise) (SI 2005/2910) |
| para 113(a) | 1 Apr 2003 (E) (SI 2003/124) |
|  | 9 Jan 2004 (W) (SI 2003/2961) |
| para 113(b) | 1 Sep 2003 (E) (SI 2003/1667) |
|  | 31 Oct 2005 (W) (SI 2005/2910) |
| para 113(c), (d) | 1 Oct 2002 (E) (SI 2002/2439) |
|  | 4 Dec 2003 (W) (SI 2003/2961) |
| para 113(e) | 19 Dec 2002 (W) (SI 2002/3185) |
|  | 1 Aug 2003 (E) (SI 2003/1667) |
| para 113(f) | 1 Apr 2003 (E) (SI 2003/124) |
|  | 31 Oct 2005 (W) (SI 2005/2910) |
| para 113(g) | 1 Oct 2002 (E) (SI 2002/2439) |
|  | 4 Dec 2003 (W) (SI 2003/2961) |
| para 114 | 19 Dec 2002 (W) (SI 2002/3185) |
|  | 1 Apr 2003 (E) (SI 2003/124) |
| para 115(1), (2) | 1 Apr 2003 (SI 2003/124) |
| para 115(3)(a) | 1 Jun 2003 (SI 2003/1115) |
| para 115(3)(b) | 1 Apr 2003 (SI 2003/124) |
| para 115(4) | 1 Apr 2003 (SI 2003/124) |
| para 115(5)(a) | 1 Jun 2003 (E) (SI 2003/1115) |
|  | 31 Mar 2004 (W) (SI 2004/912) |
| para 115(5)(b) | 1 Jun 2003 (E) (SI 2003/1115) |
|  | 2 Jan 2008 (W) (SI 2007/3611) |
| para 116 | 1 Jun 2003 (SI 2003/1115) |
| para 117 | 1 Oct 2002 (E) (except the words "or 101(1)(a)") (SI 2002/2439) |
|  | 19 Dec 2002 (W) (SI 2002/3185) |
|  | 1 Mar 2003 (E) (exception noted above) (SI 2003/124) |
| para 118(1), (2) | 19 Dec 2002 (W) (SI 2002/3185) |
|  | 1 Apr 2003 (E) (SI 2003/124) |
| para 118(3)(a) | 19 Dec 2002 (W) (SI 2002/3185) |

**Education Act 2002 (c 32)**—*contd*

|  |  |  |
|---|---|---|
|  |  | 1 Apr 2003 (E) (SI 2003/124) |
|  | para 118(3)(b) | 1 Apr 2003 (E) (SI 2003/124) |
|  |  | *Never in force* (W) (repealed) |
|  | para 118(4)(a)(i) | 19 Dec 2002 (W) (SI 2002/3185) |
|  |  | 1 Apr 2003 (E) (SI 2003/124) |
|  | para 118(4)(a)(ii) | 1 Apr 2003 (E) (SI 2003/124) |
|  |  | *Never in force* (W) (repealed) |
|  | para 118(4)(b) | 19 Dec 2002 (W) (SI 2002/3185) |
|  |  | 1 Apr 2003 (E) (SI 2003/124) |
|  | para 118(5) | 19 Dec 2002 (W) (SI 2002/3185) |
|  |  | 1 Apr 2003 (E) (SI 2003/124) |
|  | para 118(6) | 1 Oct 2002 (E) (SI 2002/2439) |
|  |  | 31 Oct 2005 (W) (SI 2005/2910) |
|  | para 119 | 1 Aug 2003 (SI 2003/1667) |
|  | paras 120, 121 | 31 Mar 2003 (W) (SI 2002/3185) |
|  |  | 1 Jun 2003 (E) (SI 2003/1115) |
|  | para 122(a) | 31 Mar 2003 (W) (SI 2002/3185) |
|  |  | 1 Jun 2003 (E) (SI 2003/1115) |
|  | para 122(b) | 1 Jun 2003 (E) (SI 2003/1115) |
|  |  | 1 Jan 2004 (W) (SI 2003/2961) |
|  | para 123 | 31 Mar 2003 (W) (SI 2002/3185) |
|  |  | 1 Jun 2003 (E) (SI 2003/1115) |
|  | para 124(1), (2) | 1 Oct 2002 (E) (SI 2002/2439) |
|  |  | 2 Jan 2008 (W) (SI 2007/3611) |
|  | para 124(3) | 1 Oct 2002 (E) (SI 2002/2439) |
|  |  | *Never in force* (W) (repealed) |
|  | para 125 | 4 Dec 2003 (W) (SI 2003/2961) |
|  | para 126(1), (2) | 19 Dec 2002 (W) (in so far as amends Learning and Skills Act 2000, Sch 7, paras 21, 29) (SI 2002/3185) |
|  |  | 1 Apr 2003 (E) (SI 2003/124) |
|  |  | *Never in force* (W) (in so far as amends paras 17, 25 of that Schedule) (repealed) |
|  | para 126(3) | 19 Dec 2002 (W) (in so far as amends Learning and Skills Act 2000, Sch 7, para 39) (SI 2002/3185) |
|  |  | 1 Apr 2003 (E) (SI 2003/124) |
|  |  | 2 Jan 2008 (W) (otherwise) (SI 2007/3611) |
|  | para 127 | 1 Sep 2003 (E) (S) (NI) (SI 2003/1667) |
|  |  | 31 Oct 2005 (W) (SI 2005/2910) |
|  | para 128 | 31 Mar 2003 (W) (SI 2002/3185) |
|  |  | 1 Jun 2003 (otherwise) (SI 2003/1115) |
| Sch 22 | Pt 1 | 1 Oct 2002 (SI 2002/2439), repeals of or in— |
|  |  | School Teachers' Pay and Conditions Act 1991, s 1, Schedule; |
|  |  | Further and Higher Education Act 1992; |
|  |  | Education Act 1997; |
|  |  | School Standards and Framework Act 1998, Sch 30, paras 25, 44, 214(a) |
|  |  | 1 Aug 2003 (otherwise) (SI 2003/1667) |
|  | Pt 2 | 19 Dec 2002 (repeals of or in Education Act 1997, ss 29(2), 32(3)) (SI 2002/3185) |
|  |  | 1 Sep 2003 (SI 2002/3185), repeals of or in— |
|  |  | Disability Discrimination Act 1995; |
|  |  | Special Educational Needs and Disability Act 2001 |
|  |  | *Not yet in force*, repeals of or in— |
|  |  | Education Act 1997, s 29(3), (4); |
|  |  | School Standards and Framework Act 1998, Sch 30, para 215 |
|  | Pt 3 | 26 Jul 2002 (E) (SI 2002/2002), repeals of or in— |
|  |  | Education Act 1996, s 580, entries relating to "city academy", "city college for the technology of the arts" and "city technology college"; |

**Education Act 2002 (c 32)**—*contd*

Learning and Skills Act 2000, ss 130–132, Sch 8

26 Jul 2002 (E) (S) (NI) (repeals of or in Disability Discrimination
Act 1995, s 28Q(12)) (SI 2002/2002)

2 Sep 2002 (E) (SI 2002/2002), repeals of or in—

Children Act 1989, s 79U;

Education Act 1997, Pt 4, Chapter 1;

School Standards and Framework Act 1998, s 16(4), (13)

1 Oct 2002 (E) (SI 2002/2439), repeals of or in—

Local Government (Miscellaneous Provisions) Act 1982;

Education (No 2) Act 1986, s 49;

Children Act 1989, ss 19(1), (2), (4), 79M(1);

Further and Higher Education Act 1992, ss 23(4), 39–42, 60;

Education Act 1996, ss 2(3)(a), 4(1), 5(1), 350–369, 408(4)(a),
409(1), 410, 483(3A), 483A(7), 497A(3), 548(8)(c), 568(3), (4),
Sch 37, para 55;

School Inspections Act 1996, ss 3(3), 6(3), 16(3);

Education Act 1997, Sch 7, paras 9(3), 27(a), 28(b);

School Standards and Framework Act 1998, ss 10(3), (7),
11(2), (3), 36(2), 42, 46, 57, 84(6), 86(3)(b), (6), 91, 93,
119(5), 120(2), 121(1), (9), 138(2)(b), (4)(b), (5)(b)(ii), 143,
Schs 4, 10, 23, Sch 26, paras 8(9), 15, Sch 28, para 4(1),
Sch 30, paras 14, 85–90, 194(3)(a)(ii), 204(b);

Learning and Skills Act 2000, s 148(2), Sch 9, paras 26, 30, 35

19 Dec 2002 (W) (SI 2002/3185), repeals of or in—

Education (No 2) Act 1986, s 49;

Children Act 1989, ss 79M(1), 79U;

Further and Higher Education Act 1992, ss 23(4), 39–42, 60;

Education Act 1996, ss 350–369, 408, 409;

School Inspections Act 1996, ss 6(3), 16(3);

School Standards and Framework Act 1998, ss 16(4), (13), 22(1),
86(3)(b), 91, Sch 6, para 10(6), Sch 28, para 4(1);

Teaching and Higher Education Act 1998, ss 1(8), 3 (words
"within the meaning of section 218(2) of the Education
Reform Act 1988");

Learning and Skills Act 2000, ss 130–132, 148(2), Sch 9,
paras 26, 30, 35, 59(6)(b)

20 Jan 2003 (E) (SI 2002/2952), repeals of—

Local Government Act 1974, s 25(5)(b);

Further and Higher Education Act 1992, Sch 8, para 90;

Education Act 1996, s 509(6);

Education Act 1997, Sch 7, paras 27, 28;

School Standards and Framework Act 1998, ss 64–68, Schs 18,
24, 25, Sch 30, paras 3(3), 47(a), 133(b)[2];

Learning and Skills Act 2000, Sch 9, para 59(6)(b), (7)(b), (c),
(8)

31 Mar 2003 (W) (SI 2002/3185), repeals of or in—

Education Reform Act 1988, ss 218(2B), (6), (6ZA), (6A), (6B),
(7), 218A;

Children Act 1989, s 19;

Education Act 1997, s 49(2), (3);

Police Act 1997;

School Standards and Framework Act 1998, ss 115, 119(5),
120(2)(a), 121(1), (9);

Teaching and Higher Education Act 1998, Sch 2, para 1(5);

Immigration and Asylum Act 1999;

Protection of Children Act 1999;

Criminal Justice and Court Services Act 2000

1 Apr 2003 (E) (S) (NI) (SI 2003/124), repeals of or in—

Education Act 1967;

Education Act 1986;

**Education Act 2002 (c 32)**—*contd*

Education (No 2) Act 1986, s 50;

Education Reform Act 1988, ss 160, 210, 211;

Further and Higher Education Act 1992, Sch 8, paras 46, 47;

Education Act 1996, ss 318, 484, 487–488, 490–492, 509A, 548(8)(b)(ii), 578, Sch 37, paras 13, 65(2)(b), 131;

Nursery Education and Grant-Maintained Schools Act 1996;

Education Act 1997, Sch 7, paras 8, 36;

School Standards and Framework Act 1998, ss 3, 7(10), 22, 44, 52(2), 115, 127(6)(e), 138(5)(a)(ii), (iii), Sch 6, paras 4(3)(d), 10(6), Sch 26, para 1(1)(c), Sch 28, Pt 2;

Learning and Skills Act 2000, Sch 7, para 35(1), Sch 9, paras 58, 91

6 Apr 2003 (E) (S) (NI) (repeal of Immigration and Asylum Act 1999, Sch 14, para 117) (SI 2003/124)

1 Jun 2003 (E) (S) (NI) (SI 2003/1115), repeals of or in—

Education Reform Act 1988, ss 218(6), (6ZA), (6A), (6B), 218A;

Education Act 1997, s 49;

Police Act 1997;

Teaching and Higher Education Act 1998, Sch 2, para 1(5);

School Standards and Framework Act 1998, Sch 6, paras 3(2), 4(5), 5(9);

Protection of Children Act 1999;

Criminal Justice and Court Services Act 2000

1 Aug 2003 (E) (SI 2003/1667)[6], repeals of or in—

Education Reform Act 1988, s 218(1)(a), (aa), (e), (f), (2), (2A), (2AA), (2B), (3)–(5);

Education Act 1994, s 14, Sch 2;

Teaching and Higher Education Act 1998, ss 1, 3 (words "within the meaning of section 218(2) of the Education Reform Act 1988"), 11, 13;

Learning and Skills Act 2000, Sch 9, para 18

1 Aug 2003 (W) (SI 2003/1718), repeals of or in—

Disability Discrimination Act 1995, s 28Q;

Education Act 1996, ss 483, 483A, 490, 497A, 580 (entries relating to city academy, city college for the technology of the arts, city technology college);

Learning and Skills Act 2000, Sch 8

1 Sep 2003 (E) (S) (NI) (SI 2003/1667)[6], repeals of or in—

Education Reform Act 1988, s 218(1)(d);

Judicial Pensions and Retirement Act 1993;

Education Act 1994, s 4;

Disability Discrimination Act 1995, Sch 4A;

Education Act 1996, ss 29, 316A, 317, 329A, 464–478, 537, 568(2), 580 (entries relating to register, registration, registered school, Registrar of Independent Schools), Sch 34;

School Inspections Act 1996, ss 10, 11, 15, 20, 21, Sch 3;

Education Act 1997, Sch 7, para 14;

School Standards and Framework 1998, ss 36 (in so far as not already repealed), 37–39, 41, 43, 54–56, 127(6)(f), (h), (k), Schs 9, 11, 12, 16, 17, Sch 30, paras 56, 74;

Teaching and Higher Education Act 1998, s 3(3)(c);

Employment Relations Act 1999;

Care Standards Act 2000

1 Sep 2003 (W) (SI 2003/1718), repeals of or in—

Local Government (Miscellaneous Provisions) Act 1982;

Further and Higher Education Act 1992, Sch 8, para 90;

Education Act 1996, s 509, Sch 37, para 55;

Education Act 1997, Sch 7, para 9;

School Standards and Framework Act 1998, Sch 30, para 133

**Education Act 2002 (c 32)**—*contd*

1 Oct 2003 (E) (SI 2003/1667), repeals of or in—
Education Reform Act 1988, s 218(1)(ab), (2C)–(2F), (9)(b)
(words "or course leading to a professional headship
qualification for the purposes of subsection (1)(ab) above"),
(12), (14);
School Standards and Framework Act 1998, Sch 30, para 17;
Teaching and Higher Education Act 1998, s 18

4 Dec 2003 (W) (repeals of or in School Standards and Framework
Act 1998, ss 46, 143 (entry relating to local schools budget))
(SI 2003/2961)

1 Jan 2004 (W) (SI 2003/2961), repeals of or in—
Judicial Pensions and Retirement Act 1993;
Education Act 1996, ss 464–478, 537, 568, 580 (entries relating
to register, registration, registered school and Registrar of
Independent Schools), Sch 34;
School Inspections Act 1996, ss 10, 11(5)(a), 20, 21(4)(b), Sch 3,
para 1(c);
Teaching and Higher Education Act 1998, s 3(3)(c);
Care Standards Act 2000

9 Jan 2004 (W) (SI 2003/2961), repeals of or in—
Local Government Act 1974;
Education Act 1996, s 492, Sch 1, para 7;
Education Act 1997, Sch 7, para 36;
School Standards and Framework Act 1998, ss 64–68, Sch 18

31 Mar 2004 (W) (SI 2004/912), repeals of or in—
Education Act 1996, ss 4(1), 5(1), 548(8)(c);
School Standards and Framework Act 1998, ss 33(1), 39

1 Aug 2004 (W) (repeal in Education Act 1996, s 2(3)(a))
(SI 2004/912)

1 Sep 2004 (W) (SI 2004/1728), repeals of or in—
Children Act 1989, s 79P(4)(d);
School Standards and Framework Act 1998, ss 38, 41, 42,
127(6)(e), 138(4)(b), (5), Sch 11, Pt II, para 7, Sch 30,
para 204(b)

31 May 2005 (W) (repeals of or in School Standards and
Framework Act 1998, Schs 24, 25, Sch 26, paras 6(4), 8(9), 15,
Sch 28, Pt 2, Sch 30, paras 3(3), 47(a)) (SI 2005/1395)[9]

31 Oct 2005 (W) (SI 2005/2910), repeals of or in—
Education Act 1994, s 4;
Disability Discrimination Act 1995, Sch 4A;
Education Act 1996, ss 29, 316A, 317, 329A;
School Inspections Act 1996, ss 11(5)(b), 15; 21(3)(b), Sch 3,
para 1, definition "appropriate authority", para (b);
School Standards and Framework Act 1998, ss 36, 37, 43, 44,
63, 127(6)(h), 138(2)(b), Schs 9, 10, Sch 11 (so far as not
already repealed), Sch 12

1 Feb 2006 (W) (repeals of or in School Standards and Framework
Act 1998, ss 84, 86(6), 93, 143 (entry relating to "relevant
standard number"), Sch 23) (SI 2006/172)

1 Apr 2006 (W) (SI 2006/879), repeals of or in—
Education Reform Act 1988, s 218(1)(d);
School Standards and Framework Act 1998, ss 54–57, 127(6)(f),
(k), Schs 16, 17;
Employment Relations Act 1999

6 Nov 2006 (E) (SI 2006/2895), repeals of or in—
Sex Discrimination Act 1975, Sch 2, para 4;
Education (Fees and Awards) Act 1983, s 1(6);
Education Reform Act 1988, s 218 (so far as not already
repealed)[11];
Environmental Protection Act 1990, s 98(2)(c)(ii);

**Education Act 2002 (c 32)**—*contd*

> Further and Higher Education Act 1992, s 37(1), (8)(a), (9);
> Education Act 1996, s 545(2)(a);
> School Standards and Framework Act 1998, s 63(1), (3), (4);
> Teaching and Higher Education Act 1998, Sch 3, para 5
> 2 Jan 2008 (W) (SI 2007/3611), repeals of or in—
> Education Act 1967;
> Sex Discrimination Act 1975;
> Education (Fees and Awards) Act 1983;
> Education Act 1986;
> Education Reform Act 1988, ss 160, 210, 211, 218 (so far as not already repealed)[12];
> Environmental Protection Act 1990;
> Further and Higher Education Act 1992, s 37, Sch 8, paras 46, 47, 49, 83;
> Education Act 1994, Sch 2, para 8(4);
> Education Act 1996, ss 318, 484, 486–488, 491, 509A, 545, 548(8)(b), 578, Sch 37, paras 13, 76, 131;
> Nursery Education and Grant-Maintained Schools Act 1996;
> Education Act 1997, s 49 (so far as not already repealed), Sch 7, paras 8, 14, 27, 28;
> School Standards and Framework Act 1998, ss 3, 10, 11, Sch 4, Sch 26, para 1, Sch 30, paras 14, 17, 56, 74(2)–(4), 85–90;
> Teaching and Higher Education Act 1998, ss 10, 11, 13, 18, Sch 3, para 5;
> Learning and Skills Act 2000, Sch 9, paras 18, 58, 59(7)(b), (c), (8), 91
> 31 Mar 2008 (W) (repeals of School Standards and Framework Act 1998, s 40, Sch 13) (SI 2007/3611)
> 1 Aug 2008 (W) (repeal of Education Act 1996, s 410) (SI 2008/1728)
> 1 Sep 2011 (W) (repeal of Education Act 1997, Pt IV, Chapter I) (SI 2011/1952)
> *Not yet in force* (E) (and (S) (NI) if applicable), repeals of or in—
> Children Act 1989, s 79P(4);
> Further and Higher Education Act 1992, Sch 8, paras 49, 83;
> Education Act 1996, s 486, Sch 37, para 76;
> School Standards and Framework Act 1998, ss 33(1), 40, Sch 13, Sch 26, para 6(4);
> Teaching and Higher Education Act 1998, s 10
> *Not yet in force* (W), repeals of or in—
> Education (No 2) Act 1986, s 50(1), (3A);
> Education Act 1994, s 14;
> Education Act 1996, Sch 37, para 65(2);
> School Inspections Act 1996, s 3(3);
> School Standards and Framework Act 1998, ss 7(10), 52(2), 93, 127(6)(i), Sch 30, para 194(3)(a)(ii)
> *Not yet in force* (E), repeals of or in—
> Education Act 1996, Sch 1, para 7

[1]   For transitional and saving provisions, see SI 2002/2439, art 4, Schedule

[2]   For transitional and saving provisions, see SI 2002/2952, art 3, Schedule

[3]   For transitional and saving provisions, see SI 2002/3185, art 7

[4]   For transitional and saving provisions, see SI 2003/124, arts 6, 7

[5]   For transitional and saving provisions, see SI 2003/1115, arts 4–6

[6]   For transitional and saving provisions, see SI 2003/1667, art 6, Schedule

[7]   For a transitional provision, see SI 2003/2071, art 2(2)

[8]   For transitional provisions, see SI 2004/912, arts 6, 7

**Education Act 2002 (c 32)**—*contd*

⁹    For transitional provisions, see SI 2005/1395, art 5

¹⁰    For transitional provisions, see SI 2006/1336, art 4, Schedule, Pt 2

¹¹    For saving provisions, see SI 2006/2895, art 3

¹²    For transitional and saving provisions, see SI 2007/3611, art 5, Schedule, Pt 3

**Education (Disability Strategies and Pupils' Educational Records) (Scotland) Act 2002 (asp 12)**

*RA:* 30 Apr 2002

*Commencement provisions:* s 7(2); Education (Disability Strategies and Pupils' Educational Records) (Scotland) Act 2002 (Commencement) Order 2002, SSI 2002/367

| | |
|---|---|
| 1–3 | 15 Aug 2002 (SSI 2002/367) |
| 4–7 | 30 Apr 2002 (RA) |

**Electoral Fraud (Northern Ireland) Act 2002 (c 13)**

*RA:* 1 May 2002

*Commencement provisions:* s 8(3); Electoral Fraud (Northern Ireland) Act 2002 (Commencement) Order 2002, SI 2002/1648

| | |
|---|---|
| 1 | 1 Sep 2002 (SI 2002/1648) |
| 2 | 1 Dec 2002 (SI 2002/1648) |
| 3 | 1 Dec 2002 (SI 2002/1648)¹ |
| 4 | 1 Dec 2002 (SI 2002/1648) |
| 5 | 1 May 2002 (RA) |
| 6 | 1 Jul 2002 (SI 2002/1648) |
| 7 | 1 Sep 2002 (SI 2002/1648) |
| 8 | 1 May 2002 (RA) |

¹    For transitional provisions, see SI 2002/1648, art 4(2)

**Employee Share Schemes Act 2002 (c 34)**

*RA:* 7 Nov 2002

*Commencement provisions:* s 5

Whole Act in force 6 Apr 2003 (s 5)

**Employment Act 2002 (c 22)**

*RA:* 8 Jul 2002

*Commencement provisions:* s 55(2); Employment Act 2002 (Commencement No 1) Order 2002, SI 2002/1989; Employment Act 2002 (Commencement No 2) Order 2002, SI 2002/2256; Employment Act 2002 (Commencement No 3 and Transitional and Saving Provisions) Order 2002, SI 2002/2866; Employment Act 2002 (Commencement No 4 and Transitional Provisions) Order 2003, SI 2003/1190; Employment Act 2002 (Commencement No 5) Order 2003, SI 2003/1666; Employment Act 2002 (Commencement No 6 and Transitional Provision) Order 2004, SI 2004/1717; Employment Act 2002 (Commencement No 7) Order 2004, SI 2004/2185; Employment Act 2002 (Commencement No 8) Order 2004, SI 2004/2822

| | |
|---|---|
| 1–16 | 8 Dec 2002 (SI 2002/2866)¹ |
| 17, 18 | 24 Nov 2002 (SI 2002/2866)¹ |
| 19 | 6 Apr 2003 (SI 2002/2866)¹ |
| 20 | 24 Nov 2002 (SI 2002/2866)¹ |

**Employment Act 2002 (c 22)**—*contd*

| | | |
|---|---|---|
| 21 | | 6 Apr 2003 (SI 2002/2866) |
| 22–27 | | 9 Jul 2004 (SI 2004/1717) |
| 28 | (1) | 9 Jul 2004 (SI 2004/1717) |
| | (2) | *Not yet in force* |
| | (3) | 9 Jul 2004 (SI 2004/1717) |
| 29 | (1) | See Sch 2 below |
| | (2), (3) | 27 Apr 2003 (SI 2003/1190) |
| 30 | (1), (2) | *Never in force* (repealed) |
| | (3) | 27 Apr 2003 (SI 2003/1190) |
| | (4) | *Never in force* (repealed) |
| 31 | (1)–(5) | 1 Oct 2004 (SI 2004/1717)[3] |
| | (6), (7) | 27 Apr 2003 (SI 2003/1190) |
| 32 | (1)–(6) | 1 Oct 2004 (SI 2004/1717)[3] |
| | (7)–(10) | 27 Apr 2003 (SI 2003/1190) |
| 33 | | 27 Apr 2003 (SI 2003/1190) |
| 34–40 | | 1 Oct 2004 (SI 2004/1717) |
| 41, 42 | | 6 Apr 2003 (SI 2002/2866) |
| 43 | | 27 Apr 2003 (subject to a transitional provision) (SI 2003/1190) |
| 44 | | *Not yet in force* |
| 45, 46 | | 8 Jul 2002 (RA) |
| 47 | | 6 Apr 2003 (SI 2002/2866)[1] |
| 48 | (1)(a) | 6 Apr 2003 (SI 2002/2866)[1] |
| | (1)(b) | 24 Nov 2002 (SI 2002/2866)[1] |
| | (1)(c) | 6 Apr 2003 (SI 2002/2866) |
| | (2) | 24 Nov 2002 (SI 2002/2866)[1] |
| 49 | | 5 Jul 2003 (SI 2003/1666) |
| 50 | | See Sch 6 below |
| 51, 52 | | 8 Jul 2002 (RA) |
| 53 | | See Sch 7 below |
| 54 | | See Sch 8 below |
| 55 | | 8 Jul 2002 (RA) |
| Sch 1 | | 8 Dec 2002 (SI 2002/2866) |
| Sch 2 | | 1 Oct 2004 (SI 2004/1717)[3] |
| Schs 3–5 | | 1 Oct 2004 (SI 2004/1717) |
| Sch 6 | | 9 Sep 2002 (SI 2002/2256) |
| Sch 7 | para 1 | 8 Dec 2002 (SI 2002/2866) |
| | para 2 | See paras 3–7 below |
| | para 3 | 8 Dec 2002 (SI 2002/2866) |
| | paras 4–6 | 6 Apr 2003 (SI 2002/2866) |
| | para 7 | 8 Dec 2002 (SI 2002/2866) |
| | para 8 | See paras 9–16 below |
| | paras 9, 10 | 5 Jul 2003 (SI 2003/1666) |
| | para 11 | 8 Dec 2002 (SI 2002/2866) |
| | para 12 | 24 Nov 2002 (SI 2002/2866) |
| | para 13 | 8 Dec 2002 (SI 2002/2866) |
| | para 14 | 6 Apr 2003 (SI 2002/2866) |
| | para 15 | 5 Jul 2003 (SI 2003/1666) |
| | paras 16, 17 | 9 Sep 2002 (SI 2002/2256) |
| | para 18 | See paras 19–22 below |
| | paras 19–21 | 27 Apr 2003 (SI 2003/1190) |
| | para 22 | 6 Apr 2003 (SI 2002/2866)[2] |
| | para 23(1) | See sub-paras (2), (3) below |
| | para 23(2)(a) | 27 Apr 2003 (SI 2003/1190) |
| | para 23(2)(b), (c) | 6 Apr 2003 (SI 2002/2866) |
| | para 23(3) | 1 Oct 2004 (SI 2004/2185) |
| | para 24 | See paras 25–49 below |
| | paras 25, 26 | 8 Dec 2002 (SI 2002/2866) |
| | para 27 | 6 Apr 2003 (SI 2002/2866) |
| | para 28 | 24 Nov 2002 (SI 2002/2866) |

**Employment Act 2002 (c 22)**—*contd*

| | | |
|---|---|---|
| | paras 29–31 | 8 Dec 2002 (SI 2002/2866) |
| | para 32 | 1 Oct 2004 (SI 2004/2185) |
| | para 33 | 8 Dec 2002 (SI 2002/2866) |
| | para 34 | 27 Apr 2003 (SI 2003/1190) |
| | para 35 | 8 Dec 2002 (SI 2002/2866) |
| | paras 36–40 | 1 Oct 2004 (SI 2004/2185) |
| | paras 41–45 | 6 Apr 2003 (SI 2002/2866) |
| | para 46 | 1 Oct 2004 (SI 2004/2185) |
| | para 47(1), (2) | 6 Apr 2003 (SI 2002/2866) |
| | para 47(3) | 1 Nov 2004 (SI 2004/2822) |
| | para 48 | 8 Dec 2002 (SI 2002/2866) |
| | para 49 | 8 Dec 2002 (except so far as relates to the Employment Rights Act 1996, s 80G) (SI 2002/2866) |
| | | 6 Apr 2003 (so far as relates to the Employment Rights Act 1996, s 80G) (SI 2002/2866) |
| | para 50 | 31 Jul 2002 (SI 2002/1989) |
| | para 51 | 5 Jul 2003 (SI 2003/1666) |
| | paras 52, 53 | 24 Nov 2002 (SI 2002/2866) |
| | para 54 | 6 Apr 2003 (SI 2002/2866) |
| | para 55 | 5 Jul 2003 (SI 2003/1666) |
| Sch 8 | | 9 Sep 2002 (SI 2002/2256), repeals of or in— |
| | | Social Security Administration Act 1992, s 122; |
| | | Social Security Administration (Northern Ireland) Act 1992; |
| | | Social Security Administration (Fraud) Act 1997; |
| | | Social Security Act 1998 |
| | | 9 Sep 2002 (revocation of or in Social Security Administration (Fraud) (Northern Ireland) Order 1997, SI 1997/1182) (SI 2002/2256) |
| | | 24 Nov 2002 (SI 2002/2866)[1], repeals of or in— |
| | | Social Security Contributions and Benefits Act 1992, s 164; |
| | | Social Security Administration Act 1992, s 2B |
| | | 6 Apr 2003 (SI 2002/2866), repeals of or in— |
| | | Employment Tribunals Act 1996, s 19; |
| | | Social Security Contributions (Transfer of Functions, etc) Act 1999, Sch 1; |
| | | Welfare Reform and Pensions Act 1999, s 53 |
| | | 6 Apr 2003 (revocation of or in Social Security Contributions (Transfer of Functions, etc) (Northern Ireland) Order 1999, SI 1999/671) (SI 2002/2866) |
| | | 1 Nov 2004 (SI 2004/2822), repeals of or in— |
| | | Employment Rights Act 1996; |
| | | Employment Rights (Dispute Resolution) Act 1998; |
| | | Employment Relations Act 1999 |

[1]    For transitional and saving provisions, see SI 2002/2866, art 3, Sch 3

[2]    SI 2003/1190 also purports to bring Sch 7, para 22 into force on 27 Apr 2003

[3]    For transitional provisions, see SI 2004/1717, art 3

---

**Enterprise Act 2002 (c 40)**

*RA:* 7 Nov 2002

*Commencement provisions:* s 279; Enterprise Act 2002 (Commencement No 1) Order 2003, SI 2003/765; Enterprise Act 2002 (Commencement No 2, Transitional and Transitory Provisions) Order 2003, SI 2003/766[1], as amended by SI 2007/1846; Enterprise Act 2002 (Commencement No 3, Transitional and Transitory Provisions and Savings) Order 2003, SI 2003/1397[3]; Enterprise Act 2002 (Commencement No 4 and Transitional Provisions and Savings) Order 2003, SI 2003/2093, as amended by SI 2003/2332, SI 2003/3340; Enterprise Act 2002 (Commencement No 5 and

**Enterprise Act 2002 (c 40)**—*contd*
Amendment) Order 2003, SI 2003/3340; Enterprise Act 2002 (Commencement No 6) Order 2004, SI 2004/1866; Enterprise Act 2002 (Commencement No 7 and Transitional Provisions and Savings) Order 2004, SI 2004/3233

| | | |
|---|---|---|
| 1–4 | | 1 Apr 2003 (SI 2003/766) |
| 5–7 | | 20 Jun 2003 (SI 2003/1397) |
| 8–10 | | 1 Apr 2003 (SI 2003/766) |
| 11 | | 20 Jun 2003 (SI 2003/1397) |
| 12 | | 1 Apr 2003 (SI 2003/766) |
| 13 | (1)–(5) | 1 Apr 2003 (SI 2003/766) |
| | (6) | See Sch 3 below |
| 14 | (1)–(5) | 1 Apr 2003 (SI 2003/766) |
| | (6) | See Sch 4 below |
| 15 | | 1 Apr 2003 (SI 2003/766) |
| 16 | | 20 Jun 2003 (SI 2003/1397) |
| 17 | | 20 Jun 2003 (SI 2003/1397)[3] |
| 18–20 | | 20 Jun 2003 (SI 2003/1397) |
| 21 | | 1 Apr 2003 (SI 2003/766) |
| 22–69 | | 20 Jun 2003 (SI 2003/1397) |
| 70 | | 29 Dec 2004 (SI 2004/3233)[6] |
| 71–184 | | 20 Jun 2003 (SI 2003/1397) |
| 185 | | See Sch 11 below |
| 186 | | 1 Apr 2003 (SI 2003/766) |
| 187–206 | | 20 Jun 2003 (SI 2003/1397) |
| 207 | | 1 Apr 2003 (SI 2003/766) |
| 208–247 | | 20 Jun 2003 (SI 2003/1397) |
| 248, 249 | | 15 Sep 2003 (SI 2003/2093)[5] |
| 250 | (1) | 18 Mar 2003 (in so far as inserts Insolvency Act 1986, s 72H(2)–(5)) (SI 2003/765) |
| | | 15 Sep 2003 (otherwise) (SI 2003/2093) |
| | (2) | See Sch 18 below |
| 251–255 | | 15 Sep 2003 (SI 2003/2093)[5] |
| 256–261 | | 1 Apr 2004 (SI 2003/2093)[5] |
| 262 | | 15 Sep 2003 (SI 2003/2093)[5] |
| 263–269 | | 1 Apr 2004 (SI 2003/2093)[5] |
| 270 | (1), (2) | 18 Dec 2003 (SI 2003/3340) |
| | (3) | 1 Apr 2004 (SI 2003/2093)[5] |
| | (4) | 18 Dec 2003 (SI 2003/3340) |
| 271 | | 18 Dec 2003 (SI 2003/3340) |
| 272 | | 1 Apr 2004 (SI 2003/2093)[5] |
| 273 | | 18 Mar 2003 (SI 2003/765) |
| 274 | | 1 Apr 2003 (SI 2003/766) |
| 275 | | 18 Mar 2003 (SI 2003/765) |
| 276 | (1) | See Sch 24 below |
| | (2)–(4) | 18 Mar 2003 (SI 2003/765) |
| 277 | | 18 Mar 2003 (SI 2003/765) |
| 278 | (1) | See Sch 25 below |
| | (2) | See Sch 26 below |
| 279–281 | | 7 Nov 2002 (RA) |
| Schs 1, 2 | | 1 Apr 2003 (SI 2003/766) |
| Sch 3 | Pt 1 | 1 Apr 2003 (SI 2003/766) |
| | Pt 2 | 18 Mar 2003 (SI 2003/765) |
| | Pt 3 | 1 Apr 2003 (SI 2003/766) |
| Sch 4 | para 1 | 1 Apr 2003 (SI 2003/766) |
| | paras 2–26 | 20 Jun 2003 (SI 2003/1397) |
| Sch 5 | para 1 | 1 Apr 2003 (SI 2003/766) |
| | para 2(a), (b) | 1 Apr 2003 (SI 2003/766) |
| | para 2(c) | *Not yet in force* |
| | para 3 | 1 Apr 2003 (SI 2003/766) |

**Enterprise Act 2002 (c 40)**—*contd*

|  |  |  |
|---|---|---|
| | para 4 | 1 Apr 2003 (except in relation to decisions of the Competition Appeal Tribunal referred to in s 49(1)(b) as substituted) (SI 2003/766) |
| | | 18 Jul 2004 (otherwise) (SI 2004/1866) |
| | paras 5–8 | 1 Apr 2003 (SI 2003/766)[1, 4] |
| Sch 6 | | 29 Dec 2004 (SI 2004/3233)[6] |
| Schs 7, 8 | | 20 Jun 2003 (SI 2003/1397) |
| Sch 9 | paras 1–6 | 20 Jun 2003 (SI 2003/1397) |
| | para 7 | 20 Jun 2003 (except for purposes relating to the making by the Secretary of State of references under the Water Industry Act 1991, s 32, or any references so made) (SI 2003/1397) |
| | | 29 Dec 2004 (otherwise) (SI 2004/3233)[6] |
| | para 8(a) | 29 Dec 2004 (SI 2004/3233)[6] |
| | para 8(b) | 20 Jun 2003 (SI 2003/1397) |
| | paras 9–26 | 20 Jun 2003 (SI 2003/1397) |
| Sch 10 | | 20 Jun 2003 (SI 2003/1397) |
| Sch 11 | para 1 | See paras 2–12 below |
| | para 2 | 1 Apr 2003 (SI 2003/766) |
| | para 3(a), (b) | 1 Apr 2003 (SI 2003/766) |
| | para 3(c) | 20 Jun 2003 (SI 2003/1397)[3] |
| | para 3(d), (e) | 1 Apr 2003 (SI 2003/766) |
| | para 4(a)–(c) | 1 Apr 2003 (SI 2003/766) |
| | para 4(d) | 20 Jun 2003 (SI 2003/1397)[3] |
| | para 5 | 1 Apr 2003 (except for the re-appointment as a member of any person who is a member on the commencement date) (SI 2003/766) |
| | | *Never in force* (exception noted above) (repealed) |
| | paras 6–8 | 1 Apr 2003 (SI 2003/766) |
| | para 9 | 20 Jun 2003 (SI 2003/1397)[3] |
| | para 10(1) | See sub-paras (2)–(5) below |
| | para 10(2) | 20 Jun 2003 (SI 2003/1397)[3] |
| | para 10(3) | 1 Apr 2003 (SI 2003/766) |
| | para 10(4) | 20 Jun 2003 (except for purposes relating to the making by the Secretary of State of references under the Water Industry Act 1991, s 32, or any references so made) (SI 2003/1397)[3] |
| | | 29 Dec 2004 (otherwise) (SI 2004/3233)[6] |
| | para 10(5) | 20 Jun 2003 (SI 2003/1397)[3] |
| | para 11 | 20 Jun 2003 (except for purposes relating to the making by the Secretary of State of references under the Water Industry Act 1991, s 32, or any references so made) (SI 2003/1397)[3] |
| | | 29 Dec 2004 (otherwise) (SI 2004/3233)[6] |
| | para 12 | 1 Apr 2003 (SI 2003/766) |
| Schs 12–15 | | 20 Jun 2003 (SI 2003/1397) |
| Sch 16 | | 15 Sep 2003 (SI 2003/2093)[5] |
| Sch 17 | paras 1–13 | 15 Sep 2003 (SI 2003/2093)[5] |
| | para 14 | *Not yet in force* |
| | paras 15–58 | 15 Sep 2003 (SI 2003/2093)[5] |
| | para 59 | *Not yet in force* |
| Sch 18 | | 15 Sep 2003 (SI 2003/2093) |
| Sch 19 | paras 1–7 | 1 Apr 2004 (SI 2003/2093)[5] |
| | para 8 | *Not yet in force* |
| Schs 20–23 | | 1 Apr 2004 (SI 2003/2093)[5] |
| Sch 24 | para 1 | 18 Mar 2003 (SI 2003/765) |
| | paras 2–12 | 1 Apr 2003 (SI 2003/766) |
| | para 13 | 20 Jun 2003 (SI 2003/1397)[3] |
| | paras 14–19 | 20 Jun 2003 (SI 2003/1397) |
| | para 20 | 1 Apr 2003 (SI 2003/766) |
| | para 21 | 20 Jun 2003 (SI 2003/1397) |
| | para 22 | 1 Apr 2003 (SI 2003/766) |

**Enterprise Act 2002 (c 40)**—*contd*

| | | |
|---|---|---|
| Sch 25 | para 1(1) | See sub-paras (2), (3) below |
| | para 1(2) | 20 Jun 2003 (except the repeal of para (b) for purposes relating to the making by the Secretary of State of references under the Water Industry Act 1991, s 32, or any references so made) (SI 2003/1397)[3] |
| | | 29 Dec 2004 (otherwise) (SI 2004/3233)[6] |
| | para 1(3) | 20 Jun 2003 (SI 2003/1397)[3] |
| | para 2(1) | See sub-paras (2)–(4) below |
| | para 2(2), (3) | 20 Jun 2003 (SI 2003/1397)[3] |
| | para 2(4) | 1 Apr 2003 (SI 2003/766) |
| | paras 3, 4 | 1 Apr 2003 (SI 2003/766) |
| | para 5(1) | See sub-paras (2)–(4) below |
| | para 5(2) | 1 Apr 2003 (SI 2003/766) |
| | para 5(3) | 20 Jun 2003 (SI 2003/1397)[3] |
| | para 5(4)(a)(i) | 1 Apr 2003 (SI 2003/766) |
| | para 5(4)(a)(ii), (iii) | 20 Jun 2003 (SI 2003/1397)[3] |
| | para 5(4)(b) | 20 Jun 2003 (SI 2003/1397)[3] |
| | paras 6, 7 | 1 Apr 2003 (SI 2003/766) |
| | para 8(1) | See sub-paras (2)–(4) below |
| | para 8(2) | 20 Jun 2003 (SI 2003/1397)[3] |
| | para 8(3) | 20 Jun 2003 (except the repeal of para (b) for purposes relating to the making by the Secretary of State of references under the Water Industry Act 1991, s 32, or any references so made) (SI 2003/1397)[3] |
| | | 29 Dec 2004 (otherwise) (SI 2004/3233)[6] |
| | para 8(4) | 20 Jun 2003 (SI 2003/1397)[3] |
| | para 9 | 1 Apr 2003 (SI 2003/766) |
| | para 10 | 20 Jun 2003 (SI 2003/1397)[3] |
| | para 11 | 1 Apr 2003 (SI 2003/766) |
| | para 12 | 20 Jun 2003 (SI 2003/1397)[3] |
| | para 13(1) | See sub-paras (2)–(10) below |
| | para 13(2) | 1 Apr 2003 (SI 2003/766) |
| | para 13(3)–(5) | 20 Jun 2003 (SI 2003/1397)[3] |
| | para 13(6) | 1 Apr 2003 (SI 2003/766) |
| | para 13(7) | 20 Jun 2003 (SI 2003/1397)[3] |
| | para 13(8)(a) | 20 Jun 2003 (SI 2003/1397)[3] |
| | para 13(8)(b)–(d) | 1 Apr 2003 (SI 2003/766) |
| | para 13(9)(a), (b) | 1 Apr 2003 (SI 2003/766) |
| | para 13(9)(c)(i) | 1 Apr 2003 (SI 2003/766) |
| | para 13(9)(c)(ii) | 20 Jun 2003 (SI 2003/1397)[3] |
| | para 13(10) | 20 Jun 2003 (SI 2003/1397)[3] |
| | para 14(1) | See sub-paras (2)–(6) below |
| | para 14(2)–(4) | 20 Jun 2003 (SI 2003/1397)[3] |
| | para 14(5), (6) | 1 Apr 2003 (SI 2003/766) |
| | para 15(1) | See sub-paras (2)–(14) below |
| | para 15(2) | 1 Apr 2003 (SI 2003/766) |
| | para 15(3)–(6) | 20 Jun 2003 (SI 2003/1397)[2, 3] |
| | para 15(7)–(10) | 1 Apr 2003 (SI 2003/766) |
| | para 15(11)–(13) | 20 Jun 2003 (SI 2003/1397)[3] |
| | para 15(14) | 1 Apr 2003 (SI 2003/766)[2] |
| | paras 16, 17 | 1 Apr 2003 (SI 2003/766) |
| | para 18(1) | See sub-paras (2)–(5) below |
| | para 18(2)–(5) | 20 Jun 2003 (except for purposes relating to the making by the Secretary of State of references under the Water Industry Act 1991, s 32, or any references so made) (SI 2003/1397)[3] |
| | | 29 Dec 2004 (otherwise) (SI 2004/3233)[6] |
| | para 19 | 1 Apr 2003 (SI 2003/766) |
| | para 20(1) | See sub-paras (2)–(13) below |
| | para 20(2) | 1 Apr 2003 (SI 2003/766) |

**Enterprise Act 2002 (c 40)**—*contd*

| | |
|---|---|
| para 20(3)–(6) | 20 Jun 2003 (SI 2003/1397)[3] |
| para 20(7)–(9) | 1 Apr 2003 (SI 2003/766) |
| para 20(10)(a) | 1 Apr 2003 (SI 2003/766) |
| para 20(10)(b) | 20 Jun 2003 (SI 2003/1397)[3] |
| para 20(11)–(13) | 20 Jun 2003 (SI 2003/1397)[3] |
| para 21(1) | See sub-paras (2)–(4) below |
| para 21(2), (3) | 1 Apr 2003 (SI 2003/766) |
| para 21(4)(a)–(f) | 1 Apr 2003 (SI 2003/766) |
| para 21(4)(g) | 20 Jun 2003 (SI 2003/1397)[3] |
| para 22 | 1 Apr 2003 (SI 2003/766) |
| para 23 | 1 Apr 2003 (SI 2003/766) |
| para 24(1) | See sub-paras (2)–(9) below |
| para 24(2)–(8) | 1 Apr 2003 (SI 2003/766) |
| para 24(9)(a)–(c) | 1 Apr 2003 (SI 2003/766) |
| para 24(9)(d)(i) | 1 Apr 2003 (SI 2003/766) |
| para 24(9)(d)(ii), (e) | 20 Jun 2003 (SI 2003/1397)[3] |
| para 24(9)(f)(i) | 1 Apr 2003 (SI 2003/766) |
| para 24(9)(f)(ii), (iii) | 20 Jun 2003 (SI 2003/1397)[3] |
| para 24(9)(g)–(i) | 1 Apr 2003 (SI 2003/766) |
| para 24(9)(j) | 20 Jun 2003 (SI 2003/1397)[3] |
| para 24(9)(k), (l) | 1 Apr 2003 (SI 2003/766) |
| para 25(1) | See sub-paras (2)–(12) below |
| para 25(2) | 1 Apr 2003 (SI 2003/766) |
| para 25(3)–(6) | 20 Jun 2003 (SI 2003/1397)[3] |
| para 25(7), (8) | 1 Apr 2003 (SI 2003/766) |
| para 25(9) | 20 Jun 2003 (SI 2003/1397)[3] |
| para 25(10)(a) | 1 Apr 2003 (SI 2003/766) |
| para 25(10)(b) | 20 Jun 2003 (SI 2003/1397)[3] |
| para 25(11), (12) | 1 Apr 2003 (SI 2003/766) |
| paras 26, 27 | 1 Apr 2003 (SI 2003/766) |
| para 28(1) | See sub-paras (2)–(7) below |
| para 28(2)–(4) | 20 Jun 2003 (SI 2003/1397)[3] |
| para 28(5), (6) | 1 Apr 2003 (SI 2003/766) |
| para 28(7)(a) | 1 Apr 2003 (SI 2003/766) |
| para 28(7)(b) | 20 Jun 2003 (SI 2003/1397)[3] |
| para 29 | 20 Jun 2003 (SI 2003/1397)[3] |
| para 30(1) | See sub-paras (2)–(15) below |
| para 30(2)(a) | 20 Jun 2003 (SI 2003/1397)[3] |
| para 30(2)(b) | 1 Apr 2003 (SI 2003/766) |
| para 30(2)(c) | 20 Jun 2003 (SI 2003/1397)[3] |
| para 30(3)–(6) | 20 Jun 2003 (SI 2003/1397)[3] |
| para 30(7) | 1 Apr 2003 (SI 2003/766) |
| para 30(8) | 20 Jun 2003 (SI 2003/1397)[3] |
| para 30(9), (10) | 1 Apr 2003 (SI 2003/766) |
| para 30(11)(a) | 1 Apr 2003 (SI 2003/766) |
| para 30(11)(b) | 20 Jun 2003 (SI 2003/1397)[3] |
| para 30(12)–(14) | 1 Apr 2003 (SI 2003/766) |
| para 30(15) | 20 Jun 2003 (SI 2003/1397)[3] |
| para 31 | 20 Jun 2003 (SI 2003/1397)[3] |
| para 32 | 1 Apr 2003 (SI 2003/766) |
| para 33(1) | See sub-paras (2)–(6) below |
| para 33(2)–(4) | 20 Jun 2003 (SI 2003/1397)[3] |
| para 33(5), (6) | 1 Apr 2003 (SI 2003/766) |
| paras 34, 35 | 1 Apr 2003 (SI 2003/766) |
| para 36(1) | See sub-paras (2)–(8) below |
| para 36(2)–(4) | 20 Jun 2003 (SI 2003/1397)[3] |
| para 36(5), (6) | 1 Apr 2003 (SI 2003/766) |
| para 36(7) | 20 Jun 2003 (SI 2003/1397)[3] |
| para 36(8) | 1 Apr 2003 (SI 2003/766)[4] |

**Enterprise Act 2002 (c 40)**—*contd*

| | |
|---|---|
| para 37 | 1 Apr 2003 (SI 2003/766) |
| para 38(1) | See sub-paras (2)–(55) below |
| para 38(2) | 20 Jun 2003 (except for purposes relating to the making by the Secretary of State of references under the Water Industry Act 1991, s 32, or any references so made) (SI 2003/1397)[3] |
| | 29 Dec 2004 (otherwise) (SI 2004/3233)[6] |
| para 38(3)–(34) | 1 Apr 2003 (SI 2003/766) |
| para 38(35) | 20 Jun 2003 (SI 2003/1397)[3] |
| para 38(36)–(48) | 1 Apr 2003 (SI 2003/766) |
| para 38(49) | 20 Jun 2003 (SI 2003/1397)[3] |
| para 38(50)(a)–(c) | 20 Jun 2003 (except for purposes relating to the making by the Secretary of State of references under the Water Industry Act 1991, s 32, or any references so made) (SI 2003/1397)[3] |
| | 29 Dec 2004 (otherwise) (SI 2004/3233) |
| para 38(50)(d) | 20 Jun 2003 (SI 2003/1397)[3] |
| para 38(51)–(55) | 1 Apr 2003 (SI 2003/766) |
| para 39 | 1 Apr 2003 (SI 2003/766) |
| para 40(1) | See sub-paras (2)–(21) below |
| para 40(2)–(19) | 1 Apr 2003 (SI 2003/766) |
| para 40(20)(a) | 1 Apr 2003 (SI 2003/766) |
| para 40(20)(b), (c) | 20 Jun 2003 (SI 2003/1397)[3] |
| para 40(21) | 1 Apr 2003 (SI 2003/766) |
| para 41 | 1 Apr 2003 (SI 2003/766) |
| para 42(1) | See sub-paras (2)–(7) below |
| para 42(2)–(5) | 20 Jun 2003 (SI 2003/1397)[3] |
| para 42(6), (7) | 1 Apr 2003 (SI 2003/766) |
| para 43(1) | See sub-paras (2), (3) below |
| para 43(2) | 1 Apr 2003 (SI 2003/766) |
| para 43(3)(a), (b) | 1 Apr 2003 (SI 2003/766) |
| para 43(3)(c)(i) | 1 Apr 2003 (SI 2003/766) |
| para 43(3)(c)(ii) | 20 Jun 2003 (SI 2003/1397)[3] |
| para 44(1) | See sub-paras (2)–(12) below |
| para 44(2)–(5) | 20 Jun 2003 (SI 2003/1397)[3] |
| para 44(6)–(12) | 1 Apr 2003 (SI 2003/766) |
| Sch 26 | 1 Apr 2003 (SI 2003/766), repeals of or in— |
| | Public Records Act 1958; |
| | Parliamentary Commissioner Act 1967; |
| | Fair Trading Act 1973, ss 1, 12–22, Schs 1, 2; |
| | Consumer Credit Act 1974, s 189(1); |
| | House of Commons Disqualification Act 1975; |
| | Northern Ireland Assembly Disqualification Act 1975; |
| | Estate Agents Act 1979, s 33(1); |
| | Competition Act 1980, s 13; |
| | Gas Act 1986, s 36A(1); |
| | Companies Act 1989, Sch 14, para 4(5); |
| | Electricity Act 1989, s 43(1); |
| | Courts and Legal Services Act 1990, ss 46(3), 119(1); |
| | Broadcasting Act 1990, ss 187(3), 194A(9); |
| | Electricity (Northern Ireland) Order 1992, SI 1992/231 (NI 1), art 46, para (1); |
| | Railways Act 1993, s 83(1); |
| | Gas (Northern Ireland) Order 1996, SI 1996/275 (NI 2), art 23(1); |
| | Competition Act 1998, ss 3(1), 48, 59(1), 61(1), Schs 4–6, Sch 7, paras 1, 2, 4–7, 9, Sch 8 |
| | 20 Jun 2003 (SI 2003/1397)[3], repeals of or in— |
| | Registered Designs Act 1949, s 11A(1)(a); |
| | Agricultural Marketing Act 1958; |
| | Trade Descriptions Act 1968; |

**Enterprise Act 2002 (c 40)**—*contd*

Fair Trading Act 1973, ss 2, 3, 5–11, 30, 34–42, 44–56G, 93B,
124, 125, 130, 131, 133, 137(2), definition "the Advisory
Committee", Schs 4–7, 12;

Consumer Credit Act 1974, ss 5, 161(2), 174, Sch 4;

Prices Act 1974;

Patents Act 1977, s 51(1)(a);

Estate Agents Act 1979, ss 9(5), 10, 26(2);

Competition Act 1980, ss 11, 16–21, 24, 31;

Telecommunications Act 1984;

Weights and Measures Act 1985;

Airports Act 1986;

Gas Act 1986, ss 24, 26A, 27, 41E, Sch 7;

Consumer Protection Act 1987;

Consumer Protection (Northern Ireland) Order 1987;

Copyright, Designs and Patents Act 1988;

Control of Misleading Advertisements Regulations 1988;

Companies Act 1989, Sch 14;

Electricity Act 1989, ss 12, 14A, 43(6), (7), 56C, Sch 16;

Water Act 1989;

Courts and Legal Services Act 1990, Sch 18;

Broadcasting Act 1990, s 192, Schs 4, 20;

Property Misdescriptions Act 1991;

Water Industry Act 1991, ss 14, 31;

Water Consolidation (Consequential Provisions) Act 1991, Sch 1,
paras 24, 26, 33, 34;

Timeshare Act 1992;

Electricity (Northern Ireland) Order 1992, arts 15, 46(6), (7),
Sch 12;

Railways Act 1993, ss 4, 13, 66, 67, Sch 12;

Coal Industry Act 1994;

Deregulation and Contracting Out Act 1994, s 7(1), Schs 2, 4,
Sch 11, para 2(4);

Airports (Northern Ireland) Order 1994;

Channel Tunnel Rail Link Act 1996;

Gas (Northern Ireland) Order 1996;

Competition Act 1998, ss 46(3)(h), 55, 56, 66, 67, Sch 7,
paras 10, 23–27, Schs 10, 11, Sch 12, paras 1(4)–(7), (14),
4(3), (4), (9), (10), (12), (15)(a), 10;

Competition Act 1998 (Competition Commission) Transitional,
Consequential and Supplemental Provisions Order 1999;

Financial Services and Markets Act 2000;

Insolvency Act 2000, Sch 4, para 13(3);

Postal Services Act 2000;

Regulation of Investigatory Powers Act 2000;

Transport Act 2000;

Utilities Act 2000;

Competition Act 1998 (Transitional, Consequential and
Supplemental Provisions) Order 2000;

Anti-terrorism, Crime and Security Act 2001;

Stop Now Orders (EC Directive) Regulations 2001;

EC Competition Law (Articles 84 and 85) Enforcement
Regulations 2001

20 Jun 2003 (except for purposes relating to the making by the
Secretary of State of references under the Water Industry
Act 1991, s 32, or any references so made) (SI 2003/1397)[3],
repeals of or in—

Registered Designs Act 1949, s 11A(1)(b);

Fair Trading Act 1973, ss 63–84, 86, 88–93A, 129, 132, 138,
Schs 8, 9;

Patents Act 1977, s 51(1)(b);

**Enterprise Act 2002 (c 40)**—*contd*

Companies Consolidation (Consequential Provisions) Act 1985;
Companies Act 1989, ss 146–150, Sch 20;
EEC Merger Control (Consequential Provisions)
  Regulations 1990;
Deregulation and Contracting Out Act 1994, s 9, Sch 11,
  para 2(3);
Deregulation (Fair Trading Act 1973) (Amendment) (Merger
  Reference Time Limits) Order 1996;
Competition Act 1998, Sch 7, para 15(7)
15 Sep 2003 (SI 2003/2093)[5], repeals of or in—
Bankruptcy (Scotland) Act 1985;
Insolvency Act 1986, ss 212, 230(1), 231, 232, 240(1), 245(3),
  Sch 10 (except entries relating to ss 31, 361, 362);
Criminal Justice Act 1988;
Income and Corporation Taxes Act 1988;
Finance Act 1991;
Social Security (Consequential Provisions) Act 1992;
Finance Act 1993;
Finance Act 1994;
Value Added Tax Act 1994;
Finance Act 1995;
Employment Rights Act 1996;
Finance Act 1996;
Finance Act 1997;
Finance Act 2000;
Finance Act 2001
1 Apr 2004 (SI 2003/2093)[5], repeals of or in—
Local Government Act 1972;
Insolvency Act 1985;
Insolvency Act 1986, ss 275, 282(5), 292(1)(a), 293(1), 294(1),
  297, 298(3), 300, 310(1), 361, 362, 405, 427, Sch 10 (entries
  relating to ss 31, 361, 362);
Justices of the Peace Act 1997
29 Dec 2004 (in so far as not already in force) (SI 2004/3233)[6],
  repeals of or in—
Registered Designs Act 1949, s 11A(1)(b);
Fair Trading Act 1973, ss 63–84, 86, 88–93A, 129, 132, 138,
  Schs 8, 9;
Patents Act 1977, s 51(1)(b);
Companies Consolidation (Consequential Provisions) Act 1985;
Companies Act 1989, ss 146–150, Sch 20;
EEC Merger Control (Consequential Provisions)
  Regulations 1990;
Deregulation and Contracting Out Act 1994, s 9, Sch 11,
  para 2(3);
Deregulation (Fair Trading Act 1973) (Amendment) (Merger
  Reference Time Limits) Order 1996;
Competition Act 1998, Sch 7, para 15(7)
29 Dec 2004 (repeal of Companies Act 1989, s 152)
  (SI 2004/3233)[6]
*Not yet in force*, repeals or revocations of or in—
Fair Trading Act 1973, s 137(2), definition "the Director";
Patents Act 1977, Sch 5, para 7;
Dentists Act 1984, Sch 5, para 6;
Administration of Justice Act 1985, s 60(6);
Gas Act 1986, s 36A(9);
Insolvency Act 1986, Sch 6, paras 1–7;
Water Industry Act 1991, s 36(1);
Water Consolidation (Consequential Provisions) Act 1991, Sch 1,
  para 52;

**Enterprise Act 2002 (c 40)**—*contd*

> Deregulation and Contracting Out Act 1994, Sch 11, para 4(6);
> Value Added Tax Act 1994, Sch 14, para 8;
> Competition Act 1998, Sch 12, para 3;
> Insolvency Act 2000, s 9

[1] For transitional provisions, see SI 2003/766, art 3

[2] The Queen's Printer's copy of SI 2003/766, purports to bring Sch 25, para 15(4) into force, however, this is an error and the intention was to bring Sch 25, para 15(14) into force

[3] For transitional provisions and savings, see SI 2003/1397, arts 4–12

[4] SI 2003/1397 also purports to bring this provision into force on 20 Jun 2003

[5] For transitional provisions and savings, see SI 2003/2093, arts 3–8

[6] For transitional provisions and savings, see SI 2004/3233, arts 3–5

---

**European Communities (Amendment) Act 2002 (c 3)**

*RA:* 26 Feb 2002

Whole Act in force 26 Feb 2002 (RA)

---

**European Parliamentary Elections Act 2002 (c 24)**

*RA:* 24 Jul 2002

*Commencement provisions:* s 18(2)

Whole Act in force 24 Oct 2002 (s 18(2))

---

**Export Control Act 2002 (c 28)**

*RA:* 24 Jul 2002

*Commencement provisions:* s 16(2); Export Control Act 2002 (Commencement & Transitional Provisions) Order 2003, SI 2003/2629

| | | |
|---|---|---|
| 1–12 | | 30 Oct 2003 (SI 2003/2629) |
| 13 | (1) | 24 Jul 2002 (in so far as it applies to orders under s 16) (RA) |
| | | 30 Oct 2003 (otherwise) (SI 2003/2629) |
| | (2)–(4) | 30 Oct 2003 (SI 2003/2629) |
| | (5)(a) | 30 Oct 2003 (SI 2003/2629) |
| | (5)(b) | 24 Jul 2002 (in so far as it applies to orders under s 16) (RA) |
| | | 30 Oct 2003 (otherwise) (SI 2003/2629) |
| 14 | | 30 Oct 2003 (SI 2003/2629) |
| 15 | | 1 May 2004 (SI 2003/2629)[1] |
| 16 | | 24 Jul 2002 (RA) |
| Schedule | | 30 Oct 2003 (SI 2003/2629) |

[1] For transitional provisions, see SI 2003/2629, art 3

---

**Finance Act 2002 (c 23)**

*Budget Day:* 17 Apr 2002

*RA:* 24 Jul 2002

The commencement details of Finance Acts are not set out, as the dates from which their provisions take effect are usually stated clearly and unambiguously in the text of the Act, and charging provisions will normally state for which year or years of assessment they are to have effect.

## Football (Disorder) (Amendment) Act 2002 (c 12)

*RA:* 1 May 2002

*Commencement provisions:* s 3(2); Football (Disorder) (Amendment) Act 2002 (Commencement) Order 2002, SI 2002/2200

| | |
|---|---|
| 1 | 28 Aug 2002 (SI 2002/2200) |
| 2, 3 | 1 May 2002 (RA) |

## Freedom of Information (Scotland) Act 2002 (asp 13)

*RA:* 28 May 2002

*Commencement provisions:* s 75(1); Freedom of Information (Scotland) Act 2002 (Commencement No 1) Order 2002, SSI 2002/437; Freedom of Information (Scotland) Act 2002 (Commencement No 2) Order 2003, SSI 2003/477; Freedom of Information (Scotland) Act 2002 (Commencement No 3) Order 2004, SSI 2004/203

| | | |
|---|---|---|
| 1, 2 | | 1 Jan 2005 (SSI 2004/203) |
| 3 | (1) | 30 Sep 2002 (SSI 2002/437) |
| | (2)–(5) | 1 Jan 2005 (SSI 2004/203) |
| 4–7 | | 30 Sep 2002 (SSI 2002/437) |
| 8 | | 1 Jan 2005 (SSI 2004/203) |
| 9 | | 31 Oct 2003 (for the purpose of making regulations) (SSI 2003/477) |
| | | 1 Jan 2005 (otherwise) (SSI 2004/203) |
| 10, 11 | | 1 Jan 2005 (SSI 2004/203) |
| 12 | | 30 Apr 2004 (for the purpose of making regulations under s 9(4)) (SSI 2004/203) |
| | | 1 Jan 2005 (otherwise) (SSI 2004/203) |
| 13–22 | | 1 Jan 2005 (SSI 2004/203) |
| 23 | (1)–(4) | 31 Oct 2003 (except so far as they relate to those public authorities listed in Sch 1, Pts 4, 5, 7) (SSI 2003/477) |
| | | 1 Dec 2003 (so far as they relate to those public authorities listed in Sch 1, Pts 4, 5) (SSI 2003/477) |
| | | 1 Mar 2004 (so far as they relate to those public authorities listed in Sch 1, Pt 7) (SSI 2003/477) |
| | (5), (6) | 31 Oct 2003 (SSI 2003/477) |
| 24 | | 30 Sep 2002 (SSI 2002/437) |
| 25–41 | | 1 Jan 2005 (SSI 2004/203) |
| 42, 43 | | 30 Sep 2002 (SSI 2002/437) |
| 44 | | 30 Apr 2004 (SSI 2004/203) |
| 45 | | 30 Sep 2002 (SSI 2002/437) |
| 46 | | 30 Apr 2004 (SSI 2004/203) |
| 47–49 | | 1 Jan 2005 (SSI 2004/203) |
| 50, 51 | | 31 Oct 2003 (for the purpose of processing publication schemes required under s 23) (SSI 2003/477) |
| | | 30 Apr 2004 (otherwise) (SSI 2004/203) |
| 52 | | 1 Jan 2005 (SSI 2004/203) |
| 53, 54 | | 31 Oct 2003 (for the purpose of processing publication schemes required under s 23) (SSI 2003/477) |
| | | 30 Apr 2004 (otherwise) (SSI 2004/203) |
| 55, 56 | | 31 Oct 2003 (SSI 2003/477) |
| 57–59 | | 1 Jan 2005 (SSI 2004/203) |
| 60–62 | | 30 Sep 2002 (SSI 2002/437) |
| 63 | | 31 Oct 2003 (SSI 2003/477) |
| 64 | | 30 Sep 2002 (SSI 2002/437) |
| 65 | | 1 Jan 2005 (SSI 2004/203) |
| 66 | | 31 Oct 2003 (SSI 2003/477) |
| 67 | | 1 Jan 2005 (SSI 2004/203) |
| 68 | | 31 Oct 2003 (SSI 2003/477) |

## Freedom of Information (Scotland) Act 2002 (asp 13)—*contd*

| | | |
|---|---|---|
| 69 | | 1 Jan 2005 (SSI 2004/203) |
| 70 | (1), (2) | 30 Sep 2002 (SSI 2002/437) |
| | (3) | 1 Jan 2005 (SSI 2004/203) |
| 71 | | 30 Sep 2002 (SSI 2002/437) |
| 72 | | 28 May 2002 (RA) |
| 73 | | 30 Sep 2002 (SSI 2002/437) |
| 74 | | 30 Apr 2004 (SSI 2004/203) |
| 75, 76 | | 28 May 2002 (RA) |
| Schs 1, 2 | | 30 Sep 2002 (SSI 2002/437) |
| Schs 3, 4 | | 1 Jan 2005 (SSI 2004/203) |

## Fur Farming (Prohibition) (Scotland) Act 2002 (asp 10)

*RA:* 11 Apr 2002

*Commencement provisions:* s 6(1); Fur Farming (Prohibition) (Scotland) Act 2002 (Commencement) Order 2002, SSI 2002/519

| | |
|---|---|
| 1–5 | 1 Jan 2003 (SSI 2002/519) |
| 6 | 11 Apr 2002 (RA) |

## Homelessness Act 2002 (c 7)

*RA:* 26 Feb 2002

*Commencement provisions:* s 20(1); Homelessness Act 2002 (Commencement) (Wales) Order 2002, SI 2002/1736; Homelessness Act 2002 (Commencement No 1) (England) Order 2002, SI 2002/1799; Homelessness Act 2002 (Commencement No 2 and Transitional Provisions) (England) Order 2002, SI 2002/2324; Homelessness Act 2002 (Commencement No 3) (England) Order 2002, SI 2002/3114

| | | |
|---|---|---|
| 1–7 | | 31 Jul 2002 (E) (SI 2002/1799) |
| | | 30 Sep 2002 (W) (SI 2002/1736) |
| 8 | | 26 Feb 2002 (RA) |
| 9, 10 | | 31 Jul 2002 (E) (SI 2002/1799) |
| | | 30 Sep 2002 (W) (SI 2002/1736) |
| 11 | | 30 Sep 2002 (W) (SI 2002/1736) |
| | | 30 Sep 2002 (E) (SI 2002/2324)[1] |
| 12 | | 30 Sep 2002 (W) (SI 2002/1736) |
| | | 1 Oct 2002 (E) (SI 2002/1799) |
| 13 | | 27 Jan 2003 (W) (SI 2002/1736) |
| | | 31 Jan 2003 (E) (SI 2002/3114) |
| 14 | | 27 Jan 2003 (W) (SI 2002/1736) |
| | | 5 Dec 2002 (E) (for the purpose of making regulations) (SI 2002/3114) |
| | | 31 Jan 2003 (E) (otherwise) (SI 2002/3114) |
| 15, 16 | | 27 Jan 2003 (W) (SI 2002/1736) |
| | | 31 Jan 2003 (E) (SI 2002/3114) |
| 17 | | 30 Sep 2002 (W) (SI 2002/1736) |
| 18 | | See Schs 1, 2 below |
| 19 | | 31 Jul 2002 (E) (SI 2002/1799) |
| | | 30 Sep 2002 (W) (SI 2002/1736) |
| 20, 21 | | 26 Feb 2002 (RA) |
| Sch 1 | paras 1, 2 | 27 Jan 2003 (W) (SI 2002/1736) |
| | | 31 Jan 2003 (E) (SI 2002/3114) |
| | para 3 | 26 Feb 2002 (RA) |
| | paras 4–6 | 27 Jan 2003 (W) (SI 2002/1736) |
| | | 31 Jan 2003 (E) (SI 2002/3114) |
| | para 7 | 26 Feb 2002 (RA) |
| | paras 8–12 | 31 Jul 2002 (E) (SI 2002/1799) |
| | | 30 Sep 2002 (W) (SI 2002/1736) |

**Homelessness Act 2002 (c 7)**—*contd*

| | | |
|---|---|---|
| para 13 | 30 Sep 2002 (W) (SI 2002/1736) | |
| | 31 Jan 2003 (E) (SI 2002/3114) | |
| para 14(a) | 30 Sep 2002 (W) (SI 2002/1736) | |
| | 31 Jan 2003 (E) (SI 2002/3114) | |
| para 14(b)–(d) | 31 Jul 2002 (E) (SI 2002/1799) | |
| | 30 Sep 2002 (W) (SI 2002/1736) | |
| paras 15, 16 | 31 Jul 2002 (E) (SI 2002/1799) | |
| | 30 Sep 2002 (W) (SI 2002/1736) | |
| para 17(a) | 30 Sep 2002 (W) (SI 2002/1736) | |
| | 30 Sep 2002 (E) (SI 2002/2324)[1] | |
| para 17(b) | 31 Jul 2002 (E) (SI 2002/1799) | |
| | 30 Sep 2002 (W) (SI 2002/1736) | |
| paras 18–21 | 31 Jul 2002 (E) (SI 2002/1799) | |
| | 30 Sep 2002 (W) (SI 2002/1736) | |

Sch 2      31 Jul 2002 (E) (SI 2002/1799), repeals of or in—
Housing Act 1996, ss 191, 193–198, 200, 205, 207, 218;
Immigration and Asylum Act 1999
30 Sep 2002 (W) (SI 2002/1736), repeals of or in—
Housing Act 1996, ss 191, 193–198, 200, 205, 207, 218;
Immigration and Asylum Act 1999, s 117(4)
27 Jan 2003 (W) (otherwise) (SI 2002/1736)
31 Jan 2003 (E) (SI 2002/3114)

[1]  For transitional provisions, see SI 2002/2324, art 4

---

**Industrial and Provident Societies Act 2002 (c 20)**

*RA:* 8 Jul 2002

*Commencement provisions:* s 4(2)

Whole Act in force 8 Sep 2002 (s 4(2))

---

**International Development Act 2002 (c 1)**

*RA:* 26 Feb 2002

*Commencement provisions:* s 20(2); International Development Act 2002 (Commencement) Order 2002, SI 2002/1408

Whole Act in force 17 Jun 2002 (SI 2002/1408)

---

**Justice (Northern Ireland) Act 2002 (c 26)**

*RA:* 24 Jul 2002

*Commencement provisions:* s 87; Justice (Northern Ireland) Act 2002 (Commencement No 1) Order 2002, SR 2002/319; Justice (Northern Ireland) Act 2002 (Commencement No 2) Order 2002, SR 2002/405; Justice (Northern Ireland) Act 2002 (Commencement No 3) Order 2003, SR 2003/265; Justice (Northern Ireland) Act 2002 (Commencement No 4) Order 2003, SR 2003/416; Justice (Northern Ireland) Act 2002 (Commencement No 5) Order 2003, SR 2003/488; Justice (Northern Ireland) Act 2002 (Commencement No 6) Order 2004, SR 2004/301; Justice (Northern Ireland) Act 2002 (Commencement No 7) Order 2004, SR 2004/502; Justice (Northern Ireland) Act 2002 (Commencement No 8) Order 2005, SR 2005/109; Justice (Northern Ireland) Act 2002 (Commencement No 9 and Transitional Provisions) Order 2005, SR 2005/281; Justice (Northern Ireland) Act 2002 (Commencement No 10) Order 2005, SR 2005/391; Justice (Northern Ireland) Act 2002 (Commencement No 11) Order 2006, SR 2006/124; Justice (Northern Ireland) Act 2002 (Commencement No 12) Order 2007, SR 2007/237; Justice (Northern Ireland) Act 2002

**Justice (Northern Ireland) Act 2002 (c 26)**—*contd*
    (Commencement No 13) Order 2010, SR 2010/52; Justice (Northern Ireland) Act 2002
    (Commencement No 14) Order 2010, SR 2010/113

| | | |
|---|---|---|
| 1 | | 30 Aug 2005 (SR 2005/391) |
| 2, 3 | | 15 Jun 2005 (SR 2005/281) |
| 4 | | *Never in force* (repealed) |
| 5 | (1) | *Never in force* (substituted) |
| | (2)–(9) | 15 Jun 2005 (except in relation to the appointment of lay magistrates) (subject to a saving) (SR 2005/281) |
| | | 10 Dec 2005 (in relation to the appointment of lay magistrates) (SR 2005/281) |
| 6 | | *Never in force* (repealed) |
| 7 | (1)–(4) | 12 Apr 2010 (SR 2010/113) |
| | (5) | *Never in force* (repealed) |
| | (6)–(8) | 12 Apr 2010 (SR 2010/113) |
| 8 | | *Never in force* (substituted) |
| 9 | (1)–(3) | 1 Sep 2004 (SR 2004/301) |
| | (4)–(6) | 15 Oct 2002 (SR 2002/319) |
| | (7)–(11) | 1 Sep 2004 (SR 2004/301) |
| | (12) | 1 Apr 2005 (SR 2005/109) |
| | (13) | 1 Sep 2004 (SR 2004/301) |
| | (14) | 15 Oct 2002 (SR 2002/319) |
| 10 | (1)–(5) | 1 Apr 2005 (SR 2005/109) |
| | (6) | See Sch 4 below |
| | (7) | 1 Apr 2005 (SR 2005/109) |
| 11 | | 1 Apr 2005 (SR 2005/109) |
| 12–16 | | 3 Apr 2006 (SR 2006/124) |
| 17 | | 15 Oct 2002 (SR 2002/319) |
| 18 | (1)–(9) | 15 Oct 2002 (SR 2002/319) |
| | (10) | 3 Apr 2006 (SR 2006/124) |
| 19 | | 15 Oct 2002 (SR 2002/319) |
| 20 | | 3 Apr 2006 (SR 2006/124) |
| 21 | | 15 Oct 2002 (SR 2002/319) |
| 22–27 | | 12 Apr 2010 (SR 2010/113) |
| 28 | (1) | See Sch 7 below |
| | (2) | 12 Apr 2010 (SR 2010/113) |
| 29 | | 13 Jun 2005 (SR 2005/281) |
| 30 | (1)–(10) | 13 Jun 2005 (SR 2005/281) |
| | (11) | 12 Apr 2010 (SR 2010/113) |
| 31, 32 | | 13 Jun 2005 (SR 2005/281) |
| 33 | | 12 Apr 2010 (SR 2010/113) |
| 34–37 | | 13 Jun 2005 (SR 2005/281) |
| 38 | | 1 Jun 2006 (SR 2005/281) |
| 39 | | 1 Sep 2005 (SR 2005/281) |
| 40 | | 13 Jun 2005 (SR 2005/281) |
| 41–43 | | 12 Apr 2010 (SR 2010/113) |
| 44 | | 13 Jun 2005 (SR 2005/281) |
| 45 | (1), (2) | 26 May 2003 (SR 2003/265) |
| | (3) | See Sch 8 below |
| 46 | (1)–(5) | 18 Dec 2003 (SR 2003/488) |
| | (6), (7) | 15 Oct 2002 (SR 2002/319) |
| 47 | | 26 May 2003 (SR 2003/265) |
| 48, 49 | | 18 Dec 2003 (SR 2003/488) |
| 50–52 | | 16 Apr 2007 (SR 2007/237) |
| 53 | (1)–(5) | 1 Dec 2003 (SR 2003/488) |
| | (6) | 30 Aug 2005 (SR 2005/391) |
| 54, 55 | | 1 Dec 2003 (SR 2003/488) |
| 56 | | *Not yet in force* |
| 57–62 | | 1 Dec 2003 (SR 2003/488) |
| 63 | (1) | See Sch 11 below |

**Justice (Northern Ireland) Act 2002 (c 26)**—*contd*

| | | |
|---|---|---|
| | (2) | 30 Aug 2005 (SR 2005/391) |
| 64 | | 30 Aug 2005 (SR 2005/391) |
| 65 | | *Not yet in force* |
| 66 | | 6 Jan 2003 (SR 2002/405) |
| 67 | | 12 Apr 2010 (SR 2010/113) |
| 68–70 | | 26 May 2003 (SR 2003/265) |
| 71 | | 18 Dec 2003 (SR 2003/488) |
| 72, 73 | | *Not yet in force* (s 72 repealed) |
| 74, 75 | | 19 Apr 2004 (SR 2003/416) |
| 76 | | *Never in force* (repealed) |
| 77 | | 1 Nov 2003 (SR 2003/416) |
| 78 | | 1 Mar 2010 (SR 2010/52) |
| 79–81 | | 15 Oct 2002 (SR 2002/319) |
| 82, 83 | | 1 Mar 2010 (SR 2010/52) |
| 84 | (1) | 16 Apr 2007 (SR 2007/237) |
| | (2)–(4) | 12 Apr 2010 (SR 2010/113) |
| 85 | (1) | See Sch 12 below |
| | (2) | 1 Dec 2003 (SR 2003/488) |
| 86 | | See Sch 13 below |
| 87–93 | | 24 Jul 2002 (RA) |
| Schs 1, 2 | | 15 Jun 2005 (SR 2005/281) |
| Sch 3 | | *Not yet in force* (substituted) |
| Sch 4 | paras 1–13 | 1 Apr 2005 (SR 2005/109) |
| | para 14 | *Never in force* (repealed) |
| | paras 15, 16 | 1 Apr 2005 (SR 2005/109) |
| | para 17(1) | 1 Apr 2005 (SR 2005/109) |
| | para 17(2) | *Never in force* (repealed) |
| | para 17(3), (4) | 1 Apr 2005 (SR 2005/109) |
| | paras 18–40 | 1 Apr 2005 (SR 2005/109) |
| Sch 5 | | *Never in force* (repealed) |
| Sch 6 | | 15 Oct 2002 (SR 2002/319) |
| Sch 7 | paras 1, 2 | 12 Apr 2010 (SR 2010/113) |
| | para 3 | *Never in force* (repealed) |
| | paras 4, 5 | 12 Apr 2010 (SR 2010/113) |
| | para 6 | *Never in force* (repealed) |
| | paras 7, 8 | 12 Apr 2010 (SR 2010/113) |
| | para 9 | *Never in force* (repealed) |
| | para 10 | 12 Apr 2010 (SR 2010/113) |
| | para 11 | *Not yet in force* |
| | paras 12–17 | 12 Apr 2010 (SR 2010/113) |
| | para 18 | *Never in force* (repealed) |
| | paras 19–24 | 12 Apr 2010 (SR 2010/113) |
| | para 25 | *Never in force* (repealed) |
| | paras 26–34 | 12 Apr 2010 (SR 2010/113) |
| | para 35 | *Never in force* (repealed) |
| | paras 36, 37 | 12 Apr 2010 (SR 2010/113) |
| Sch 8 | | 26 May 2003 (SR 2003/265) |
| Sch 9 | | 16 Apr 2007 (SR 2007/237) |
| Sch 10 | | 1 Dec 2003 (SR 2003/488) |
| Sch 11 | para 1 | 30 Aug 2005 (SR 2005/391) |
| | para 2 | *Not yet in force* |
| | paras 3, 4 | 30 Aug 2005 (SR 2005/391) |
| | para 5 | *Not yet in force* |
| | paras 6–24 | 30 Aug 2005 (SR 2005/391) |
| Sch 12 | paras 1, 2 | 13 Jun 2005 (SR 2005/281) |
| | paras 3–5 | 16 Apr 2007 (SR 2007/237) |
| | para 6 | 13 Jun 2005 (SR 2005/281) |
| | paras 7–9 | 16 Apr 2007 (SR 2007/237) |
| | paras 10–12 | 12 Apr 2010 (SR 2010/113) |

**Justice (Northern Ireland) Act 2002 (c 26)**—*contd*

| | |
|---|---|
| paras 13, 14 | *Not yet in force* (para 13 repealed) |
| paras 15, 16 | 1 Dec 2003 (SR 2003/488) |
| para 17 | 1 Nov 2003 (SR 2003/416) |
| paras 18–22 | *Never in force* (repealed) |
| para 23 | 1 Sep 2004 (SR 2004/301) |
| paras 24–26 | 1 Dec 2003 (SR 2003/488) |
| para 27(a) | 1 Dec 2003 (in so far as it inserts definition "court-ordered youth conference") (SR 2003/488) |
| | 30 Aug 2005 (in so far as it inserts definition "child") (SR 2005/391) |
| para 27(b), (c) | 1 Dec 2003 (SR 2003/488) |
| para 28 | *Never in force* (repealed) |
| para 29 | 1 Dec 2003 (SR 2003/488) |
| para 30 | *Not yet in force* |
| para 31 | 1 Dec 2003 (except in so far as it relates to Criminal Justice (Children) (Northern Ireland) Order 1998, arts 44C, 44F) (SR 2003/488) |
| | *Not yet in force* (exception noted above) |
| paras 32–40 | *Not yet in force* |
| para 41 | 12 Apr 2010 (SR 2010/113) |
| paras 42–46 | *Not yet in force* |
| para 47 | 3 Apr 2006 (SR 2006/124) |
| para 48 | *Not yet in force* |
| para 49 | 13 Jun 2005 (SR 2005/281) |
| paras 50–52 | *Not yet in force* |
| para 53(1) | See sub-paras (2), (3) below |
| para 53(2) | 15 Oct 2002 (SR 2002/319) |
| para 53(3) | 13 Jun 2005 (so far as it relates to the Director of Public Prosecutions for Northern Ireland, the Deputy Director of Public Prosecutions for Northern Ireland and the members of staff of the Public Prosecution Service for Northern Ireland) (SR 2005/281) |
| | 3 Apr 2006 (otherwise) (SR 2006/124) |
| para 54 | 1 Dec 2003 (SR 2003/488) |
| para 55(1)–(3) | 1 Dec 2003 (SR 2003/488) |
| para 55(4) | *Not yet in force* |
| para 55(5), (6) | 1 Dec 2003 (SR 2003/488) |
| para 56 | 1 Dec 2003 (SR 2003/488) |
| para 57 | *Not yet in force* |
| para 58 | 1 Dec 2003 (SR 2003/488) |
| para 59 | *Not yet in force* |
| para 60 | 30 Aug 2005 (in so far as it substitutes Sex Offenders Act 1997, s 4(1)(c)) (SR 2005/391) |
| | *Not yet in force* (so far as it substitutes Sex Offenders Act 1997, s 4(1)(ca)) |
| paras 61, 62 | *Not yet in force* |
| paras 63, 64 | 1 Jan 2005 (so far as relate to the Chief Inspector of Criminal Justice in Northern Ireland) (SR 2004/502) |
| | 16 Apr 2007 (otherwise) (SR 2007/237) |
| para 65 | 12 Apr 2010 (SR 2010/113) |
| para 66 | 1 Dec 2003 (SR 2003/488) |
| para 67(1), (2) | 1 Dec 2003 (SR 2003/488) |
| para 67(3) | 1 Dec 2003 (except in so far as it inserts definition "custody care order") (SR 2003/488) |
| | *Not yet in force* (exception noted above) |
| para 67(4)–(9) | 1 Dec 2003 (SR 2003/488) |
| para 68 | *Not yet in force* |
| para 69(1) | See sub-paras (2), (3) below |
| para 69(2) | *Not yet in force* |
| para 69(3) | 30 Aug 2005 (SR 2005/391) |

**Justice (Northern Ireland) Act 2002 (c 26)**—*contd*

|  |  |  |
|---|---|---|
| | paras 70, 71 | 1 Dec 2003 (SR 2003/488) |
| | para 72(a) | *Not yet in force* |
| | para 72(b) | 30 Aug 2005 (SR 2005/391) |
| | para 73(1) | See sub-paras (2), (3) below |
| | para 73(2)(a), (b) | *Not yet in force* |
| | para 73(2)(c) | 30 Aug 2005 (SR 2005/391) |
| | para 73(3) | 30 Aug 2005 (SR 2005/391) |
| | para 74 | 15 Oct 2002 (SR 2002/319) |
| | para 75 | 1 Dec 2003 (SR 2003/488) |
| | paras 76–79 | *Not yet in force* |
| | para 80 | 13 Jun 2005 (SR 2005/281) |
| | para 81 | *Never in force* (repealed) |

Sch 13        15 Oct 2002 (SR 2002/319), repeals and revocations of or in—
Promissory Oaths Act 1868;
County Courts Act (Northern Ireland) 1959, s 105(3);
Magistrates' Courts Act (Northern Ireland) 1964, ss 7, 9(2);
Children and Young Persons Act (Northern Ireland) 1968, Sch 2, para 2;
Judicature Act (Northern Ireland) Act 1978, ss 13(2)–(5), 99(1), Schs 2, 3, Sch 5 (to the extent that it relates to Coroners Act (Northern Ireland) 1959, s 2(3), County Courts Act (Northern Ireland) 1959, Magistrates' Courts Act (Northern Ireland) 1964, s 7, Children and Young Persons Act (Northern Ireland) 1968, Sch 2, para 2(2));
Welfare Reform and Pensions Order 1999, SI 1999/3147 (NI 11)
1 Oct 2003 (repeal of Judicature (Northern Ireland) Act 1978, s 75(3)) (SR 2003/416)
1 Dec 2003 (revocation of Criminal Justice (Children) (Northern Ireland) Order 1998, SI 1998/1504 (NI 9), art 4) (SR 2003/488)
1 Apr 2005 (SR 2005/109), repeals and revocations of or in—
Interpretation Act (Northern Ireland) 1954;
Children and Young Persons Act (Northern Ireland) 1968;
Interpretation Act 1978;
Judicature (Northern Ireland) Act 1978, s 51(5);
Magistrates' Courts (Northern Ireland) Order 1981, SI 1981/1675 (NI 26), arts 18, 34, 152, 158A(3), Sch 1;
Courts and Legal Services Act 1990;
Food Safety (Northern Ireland) Order 1991, SI 1991/762 (NI 7);
Juries (Northern Ireland) Order 1996, SI 1996/1141 (NI 6);
Access to Justice Act 1999;
Criminal Evidence (Northern Ireland) Order 1999, SI 1999/2789 (NI 8);
Freedom of Information Act 2000, Sch 1, Pt 7 (entry relating to the Advisory Committee of the Juvenile Court Lay Panel (Northern Ireland));
Justice (Northern Ireland) Act 2002, Sch 6 (entry relating to members of panels formed under the Children and Young Persons Act (Northern Ireland) 1968, Sch 2)
13 Jun 2005 (SR 2005/281), repeals and revocations of or in—
Prosecution of Offences (Northern Ireland) Order 1972, SI 1972/538 (NI 1), arts 1, 2(2) (definitions "deputy Director" and "Director"), (3), 3–6, 8–10;
Northern Ireland Constitution Act 1973, s 34;
Criminal Justice (Northern Ireland) Order 1980, SI 1980/704 (NI 6);
Criminal Justice Act 1987, Sch 1, para 5(2);
Police (Northern Ireland) Act 1998

**Justice (Northern Ireland) Act 2002 (c 26)**—*contd*

15 Jun 2005 (repeal of Judicature (Northern Ireland) Act 1978,
Sch 5, to the extent that it relates to the Children and Young
Persons Act (Northern Ireland) 1968, s 178, Sch 2,
paras 1(1)–(4), 3(2), 6) (SR 2005/281)

30 Aug 2005 (revocation of Criminal Justice (Children) (Northern
Ireland) Order 1998, SI 1998/1504 (NI 9), art 54(3)(b))
(SR 2005/391)

3 Apr 2006 (SR 2006/124), repeals and revocations of or in—
Coroners Act (Northern Ireland) 1959;
County Courts Act (Northern Ireland) 1959, s 105(1), (1A);
Magistrates' Courts Act (Northern Ireland) 1964, ss 1(3), 11;
Lands Tribunal and Compensation Act (Northern Ireland) 1964;
Northern Ireland (Modification of Enactments No 1)
Order 1973, SI 1973/2163, Sch 2;
Judicature (Northern Ireland) Act 1978, ss 2–4, 13(1), 71, Sch 5
(to the extent that it relates to Coroners Act (Northern Ireland)
1959, s 2(2), County Courts Act (Northern Ireland) 1959,
Magistrates' Courts Act (Northern Ireland) 1964, s 11, Lands
Tribunal Compensation Act (Northern Ireland) 1964);
Magistrates' Courts (Northern Ireland) Order 1981,
SI 1981/1675 (NI 26), art 2(3);
Administration of Justice Act 1982, Sch 8;
Social Security Administration (Northern Ireland) Act 1992;
Education (Northern Ireland) Order 1996, SI 1996/274 (NI 1);
Social Security (Northern Ireland) Order 1998, SI 1998/1506
(NI 10);
Fair Employment and Treatment (Northern Ireland) Order 1998,
SI 1998/3162 (NI 21);
Justice (Northern Ireland) Act 2002, s 9(10)

16 Apr 2007 (SR 2007/237), repeals and revocations of or in—
Law Commissions Act 1965;
Northern Ireland Assembly Disqualification Act 1975;
Legal Aid, Advice and Assistance (Northern Ireland) Order 1981,
SI 1981/228 (NI 8), art 34

1 Mar 2010 (SR 2010/52), repeals of or in—
Northern Ireland Act 1998, Sch 2, para 11, Sch 10, paras 6, 12,
14, 22, 24, 36;
Justice (Northern Ireland) Act 2002, s 9(13)

12 Apr 2010 (SR 2010/113), repeals and revocations of or in—
Criminal Justice Act (Northern Ireland) 1945;
County Courts Act (Northern Ireland) 1959, s 136(a);
Grand Jury (Abolition) Act (Northern Ireland) 1969;
Prosecution of Offences (Northern Ireland) Order 1972,
SI 1972/538 (NI 1);
Northern Ireland Constitution Act 1973, s 10(1);
Northern Ireland (Modification of Enactments No 1)
Order 1973, SI 1973/2163, Sch 5;
Energy Act 1976;
Internationally Protected Persons Act 1978;
Judicature (Northern Ireland) Act 1978, Sch 5 (to the extent that
it relates to Coroners Act (Northern Ireland) 1959, ss 2(1), 3,
6(2), Magistrates' Courts Act (Northern Ireland) 1964, s 10(1));
Suppression of Terrorism Act 1978;
Administration of Justice Act 1982;
Civil Aviation Act 1982;
Probation Board (Northern Ireland) Order 1982, SI 1982/713
(NI 10);
Criminal Justice Act 1987, Sch 2, para 6;
Criminal Justice (Northern Ireland) Order 1991, SI 1991/1711
(NI 16);

**Justice (Northern Ireland) Act 2002 (c 26)**—*contd*

> Radioactive Substances Act 1993;
> Criminal Procedure and Investigations Act 1996;
> Northern Ireland Act 1998, s 7(1)
> *Not yet in force*, repeals of or in—
> County Courts Act (Northern Ireland) 1959, s 107(7);
> Magistrates' Courts Act (Northern Ireland) 1964, ss 10(1), 12A(1);
> Judicature (Northern Ireland) Act 1978, ss 51A(6), 119(5), Sch 5 (to the extent that it relates to Treatment of Offenders Act (Northern Ireland) 1968, Prosecution of Offences (Northern Ireland) Order 1972);
> Rehabilitation of Offenders (Northern Ireland) Order 1978, SI 1978/1908 (NI 27);
> County Courts (Northern Ireland) Order 1980, SI 1980/397 (NI 3);
> Legal Aid, Advice and Assistance (Northern Ireland) Order 1981, SI 1981/228 (NI 8), arts 4, 10, Sch 1;
> Magistrates' Courts (Northern Ireland) Order 1981, SI 1981/1675 (NI 26), arts 44(5), 90(4), 168;
> Criminal Justice (Children) (Northern Ireland) Order 1998, SI 1998/1504 (NI 9), art 55, Sch 5;
> Freedom of Information Act 2000, Sch 1, Pt 7 (entry relating to the Law Reform Advisory Committee for Northern Ireland);
> Justice (Northern Ireland) Act 2002, s 90(4), Sch 6 (entry relating to Justice of the Peace)

## Land Registration Act 2002 (c 9)

*RA:* 26 Feb 2002

*Commencement provisions:* s 136(2); Land Registration Act 2002 (Commencement No 1) Order 2003, SI 2003/935; Land Registration Act 2002 (Commencement No 2) Order 2003, SI 2003/1028; Land Registration Act 2002 (Commencement No 3) Order 2003, SI 2003/1612; Land Registration Act 2002 (Commencement No 4) Order 2003, SI 2003/1725

| | | |
|---|---|---|
| 1–96 | | 13 Oct 2003 (SI 2003/1725) |
| 97 | | See Sch 6 below |
| 98 | (1) | 13 Oct 2004 (SI 2003/1725) |
| | (2)–(7) | 13 Oct 2003 (SI 2003/1725) |
| 99–101 | | 13 Oct 2003 (SI 2003/1725) |
| 102 | | 27 Jun 2003 (SI 2003/1612) |
| 103–106 | | 13 Oct 2003 (SI 2003/1725) |
| 107 | (1), (2) | 28 Apr 2003 (SI 2003/1028) |
| | (3) | See Sch 9 below |
| 108–127 | | 13 Oct 2003 (SI 2003/1725) |
| 128–132 | | 4 Apr 2003 (SI 2003/935) |
| 133 | | See Sch 11 below |
| 134 | (1) | 4 Apr 2003 (SI 2003/935) |
| | (2) | See Sch 12 below |
| | (3) | 13 Oct 2003 (SI 2003/1725) |
| 135 | | See Sch 13 below |
| 136 | | 4 Apr 2003 (SI 2003/935) |
| Schs 1–5 | | 13 Oct 2003 (SI 2003/1725) |
| Sch 6 | paras 1–4 | 13 Oct 2003 (SI 2003/1725) |
| | para 5(1)–(3) | 13 Oct 2003 (SI 2003/1725) |
| | para 5(4), (5) | 13 Oct 2004 (SI 2003/1725) |
| | paras 6–15 | 13 Oct 2003 (SI 2003/1725) |
| Schs 7, 8 | | 13 Oct 2003 (SI 2003/1725) |
| Sch 9 | | 28 Apr 2003 (SI 2003/1028) |
| Sch 10 | | 13 Oct 2003 (SI 2003/1725) |

**Land Registration Act 2002 (c 9)**—*contd*

| | | |
|---|---|---|
| Sch 11 | paras 1–27 | 13 Oct 2003 (SI 2003/1725) |
| | para 28 | 28 Apr 2003 (SI 2003/1028) |
| | paras 29–40 | 13 Oct 2003 (SI 2003/1725) |
| Schs 12, 13 | | 13 Oct 2003 (SI 2003/1725) |

## Marriage (Scotland) Act 2002 (asp 8)

*RA:* 4 Apr 2002

*Commencement provisions:* s 2(2); Marriage (Scotland) Act 2002 (Commencement) Order 2002, SSI 2002/184

| | | |
|---|---|---|
| 1 | | 25 Apr 2002 (SSI 2002/184) |
| 2 | | 4 Apr 2002 (RA) |

## Mobile Telephones (Re-programming) Act 2002 (c 31)

*RA:* 24 Jul 2002

*Commencement provisions:* s 3(2); Mobile Telephones (Re-programming) Act 2002 (Commencement) Order 2002, SI 2002/2294

| | | |
|---|---|---|
| 1, 2 | | 4 Oct 2002 (SI 2002/2294) |
| 3 | | 24 Jul 2002 (RA) |

## National Health Service Reform and Health Care Professions Act 2002 (c 17)

*RA:* 25 Jun 2002

*Commencement provisions:* s 42(3); National Health Service Reform and Health Care Professions Act 2002 (Commencement No 1) Order 2002, SI 2002/2202; National Health Service Reform and Health Care Professions Act 2002 (Commencement No 2) Order 2002, SI 2002/2478[1]; National Health Service Reform and Health Care Professions Act 2002 (Commencement) (Wales) Order 2002, SI 2002/2532; National Health Service Reform and Health Care Professions Act 2002 (Commencement No 3) Order 2002, SI 2002/3190; National Health Service Reform and Health Care Professions Act 2002 (Commencement No 4) Order 2003, SI 2003/833; National Health Service Reform and Health Care Professions Act 2002 (Commencement No 5) Order 2003, SI 2003/1580; National Health Service Reform and Health Care Professions Act 2002 (Commencement No 6) Order 2003, SI 2003/2246; National Health Service Reform and Health Care Professions Act 2002 (Commencement No 7) Order 2003, SI 2003/3083; National Health Service (Pre-consolidation Amendments) Order 2006, SI 2006/1407

| | | |
|---|---|---|
| 1 | (1), (2) | 1 Oct 2002 (SI 2002/2478) |
| | (3) | See Sch 1 below |
| 2 | (1)–(4) | 1 Oct 2002 (SI 2002/2478) |
| | (5) | See Sch 2 below |
| 3 | (1) | See sub-ss (2)–(5) below |
| | (2) | 2 Sep 2002 (E) (SI 2002/2202) |
| | | *Never in force* (W) (repealed) |
| | (3) | 2 Sep 2002 (E) (for the purpose of enabling the Secretary of State to make directions under the National Health Service Act 1977, s 17A(3), (4)) (SI 2002/2202) |
| | | 1 Oct 2002 (otherwise) (SI 2002/2478) |
| | (4) | 1 Oct 2002 (SI 2002/2478) |
| | (5)(a), (b) | 2 Sep 2002 (E) (SI 2002/2202) |
| | | *Never in force* (W) (repealed) |
| | (5)(c) | *Never in force* (repealed) |
| 4 | (1), (2) | 1 Oct 2002 (SI 2002/2478) |
| | (3) | See Sch 3 below |
| 5 | | 1 Oct 2002 (SI 2002/2478) |
| 6 | (1) | 10 Oct 2002 (W) (SI 2002/2532) |

**National Health Service Reform and Health Care Professions Act 2002 (c 17)**—*contd*

|  |  |  |
|---|---|---|
| | (2) | See Schs 4, 5 below |
| | (3), (4) | 10 Oct 2002 (W) (SI 2002/2532) |
| 7, 8 | | 1 Oct 2002 (E) (with effect in relation to the period beginning 1 Oct 2002 and ending 31 Mar 2003 as if that period were a financial year and in relation to the financial year ending with 31 Mar 2004 and subsequent financial years) (SI 2002/2478)[1] |
| | | 1 Oct 2002 (W) (SI 2002/2478) |
| 9 | | 10 Oct 2002 (W) (SI 2002/2532) |
| 10 | (1) | See sub-ss (2)–(10) below |
| | (2) | 10 Oct 2002 (W) (SI 2002/2532) |
| | | *Never in force* (E) (repealed) |
| | (3) | 1 Oct 2002 (E) (with effect in relation to the period beginning 1 Oct 2002 and ending 31 Mar 2003 as if that period were a financial year and in relation to the financial year ending with 31 Mar 2004 and subsequent financial years) (SI 2002/2478) |
| | | 10 Oct 2002 (W) (SI 2002/2532) |
| | (4) | 10 Oct 2002 (W) (SI 2002/2532) |
| | (5)–(8) | 1 Oct 2002 (E) (with effect in relation to the period beginning 1 Oct 2002 and ending 31 Mar 2003 as if that period were a financial year and in relation to the financial year ending with 31 Mar 2004 and subsequent financial years) (SI 2002/2478) |
| | | 10 Oct 2002 (W) (SI 2002/2532) |
| | (9) | 10 Oct 2002 (W) (SI 2002/2532) |
| | (10)(a)(i) | 10 Oct 2002 (W) (SI 2002/2532) |
| | (10)(a)(ii) | 1 Oct 2002 (E) (with effect in relation to the period beginning 1 Oct 2002 and ending 31 Mar 2003 as if that period were a financial year and in relation to the financial year ending with 31 Mar 2004 and subsequent financial years) (SI 2002/2478) |
| | | 10 Oct 2002 (W) (SI 2002/2532) |
| | (10)(b) | 1 Oct 2002 (E) (with effect in relation to the period beginning 1 Oct 2002 and ending 31 Mar 2003 as if that period were a financial year and in relation to the financial year ending with 31 Mar 2004 and subsequent financial years) (SI 2002/2478) |
| | | 10 Oct 2002 (W) (SI 2002/2532) |
| | (10)(c)(i), (ii) | 1 Oct 2002 (E) (with effect in relation to the period beginning 1 Oct 2002 and ending 31 Mar 2003 as if that period were a financial year and in relation to the financial year ending with 31 Mar 2004 and subsequent financial years) (SI 2002/2478) |
| | | 10 Oct 2002 (W) (SI 2002/2532) |
| | (10)(c)(iii) | 10 Oct 2002 (W) (SI 2002/2532) |
| 11–14 | | 25 Jun 2002 (for the purposes of making orders or regulations under this Act) (RA) |
| | | *Never in force* (otherwise) (repealed) |
| 15–19 | | 25 Jun 2002 (for the purposes of making orders or regulations under this Act) (RA) |
| | | 1 Sep 2003 (otherwise) (SI 2003/2246) |
| 20 | (1)–(10) | 25 Jun 2002 (for the purposes of making orders or regulations under this Act) (RA) |
| | | 1 Jan 2003 (E) (otherwise) (SI 2002/3190) |
| | (11) | See Sch 6 below |
| | (12) | 25 Jun 2002 (for the purposes of making orders or regulations under this Act) (RA) |
| | | 1 Jan 2003 (E) (otherwise) (SI 2002/3190) |
| 21 | | 25 Jun 2002 (for the purposes of making orders or regulations under this Act) (RA) |
| | | 1 Jan 2003 (E) (otherwise) (SI 2002/3190) |
| | | In force (otherwise) immediately before the National Health Service Act 2006 comes into force (SI 2006/1407)[4] |

**National Health Service Reform and Health Care Professions Act 2002
(c 17)**—*contd*

| | | |
|---|---|---|
| 22 | | 25 Jun 2002 (for the purposes of making orders or regulations under this Act) (RA) |
| | | 1 Dec 2003 (otherwise) (SI 2003/3083) |
| 23 | (1) | 25 Jun 2002 (for the purposes of making orders or regulations under this Act) (RA) |
| | | 10 Oct 2002 (W) (otherwise) (SI 2002/2532) |
| | | 18 Jun 2003 (E) (otherwise) (SI 2003/1580) |
| | (2)–(5) | 25 Jun 2002 (for the purposes of making orders or regulations under this Act) (RA) |
| | | 10 Oct 2002 (W) (SI 2002/2532) |
| | | In force (otherwise) immediately before the National Health Service Act 2006 comes into force (SI 2006/1407)[4] |
| 24 | | 25 Jun 2002 (for the purposes of making orders or regulations under this Act) (RA) |
| | | 10 Oct 2002 (W) (SI 2002/2532) |
| 25 | (1)–(3) | 1 Dec 2002 (for the purpose of enabling the Council for the Regulation of Health Care Professionals to prepare for the exercise of any functions which may be exercisable under ss 26, 27, 29, Sch 7) (SI 2002/2202) |
| | | 1 Apr 2003 (otherwise) (SI 2002/2202) |
| | (4) | See Sch 7 below |
| | (5), (6) | 1 Dec 2002 (for the purpose of enabling the Council for the Regulation of Health Care Professionals to prepare for the exercise of any functions which may be exercisable under ss 26, 27, 29, Sch 7) (SI 2002/2202) |
| | | 1 Apr 2003 (otherwise) (SI 2002/2202) |
| 26, 27 | | 25 Jun 2002 (for the purposes of making orders or regulations under this Act) (RA) |
| | | 1 Apr 2003 (otherwise) (SI 2002/2202) |
| 28 | | 25 Jun 2002 (for the purposes of making orders or regulations under this Act) (RA) |
| 29 | | 1 Apr 2003 (SI 2002/2202) |
| 30–34 | | 1 Apr 2003 (SI 2003/833)[3] |
| 35 | | 1 Oct 2002 (SI 2002/2478) |
| 36 | | 25 Jun 2002 (for the purposes of making orders or regulations under this Act) (RA) |
| | | *Never in force* (otherwise) (repealed) |
| 37 | (1) | See Sch 8 below |
| | (2) | See Sch 9 below |
| 38–42 | | 25 Jun 2002 (RA) |
| Sch 1 | para 1 | See paras 2–35 below |
| | para 2 | 1 Oct 2002 (SI 2002/2478) |
| | paras 3, 4 | 2 Sep 2002 (E) (SI 2002/2202) |
| | | 1 Oct 2002 (otherwise) (SI 2002/2478) |
| | para 5 | 1 Oct 2002 (SI 2002/2478) |
| | paras 6, 7 | 2 Sep 2002 (E) (SI 2002/2202) |
| | | 1 Oct 2002 (otherwise) (SI 2002/2478) |
| | paras 8–18 | 1 Oct 2002 (SI 2002/2478) |
| | para 19 | 2 Sep 2002 (E) (SI 2002/2202) |
| | | 1 Oct 2002 (otherwise) (SI 2002/2478) |
| | paras 20–55 | 1 Oct 2002 (SI 2002/2478) |
| Sch 2 | para 1 | See paras 2–37 below |
| | paras 2–15 | 1 Oct 2002 (SI 2002/2478) |
| | para 16(1)–(5) | 1 Oct 2002 (SI 2002/2478) |
| | para 16(6) | 1 Apr 2003 (SI 2003/833) |
| | para 17(1)–(3) | 1 Oct 2002 (SI 2002/2478) |
| | para 17(4), (5) | In force immediately before the National Health Service Act 2006 comes into force (SI 2006/1407)[4] |
| | paras 18–30 | 1 Oct 2002 (SI 2002/2478) |

**National Health Service Reform and Health Care Professions Act 2002 (c 17)**—*contd*

| | | |
|---|---|---|
| | paras 31, 32 | 2 Sep 2002 (E) (SI 2002/2202) |
| | | 1 Oct 2002 (otherwise) (SI 2002/2478) |
| | paras 33–82 | 1 Oct 2002 (SI 2002/2478) |
| Sch 3 | | 1 Oct 2002 (SI 2002/2478) |
| Sch 4 | | 25 Jun 2002 (for the purposes of making orders or regulations under this Act) (RA) |
| | | 10 Oct 2002 (W) (SI 2002/2532) |
| Sch 5 | | 25 Jun 2002 (for the purposes of making orders or regulations under this Act) (RA) |
| | | 10 Oct 2002 (W) (SI 2002/2532) |
| | | In force (otherwise) immediately before the National Health Service Act 2006 comes into force (SI 2006/1407)[4] |
| Sch 6 | | 25 Jun 2002 (for the purposes of making orders or regulations under this Act) (RA) |
| | | 1 Jan 2003 (otherwise) (SI 2002/3190) |
| Sch 7 | paras 1–3 | 1 Dec 2002 (SI 2002/2202) |
| | paras 4, 5 | 27 Aug 2002 (SI 2002/2202) |
| | para 6 | 25 Jun 2002 (for the purposes of making orders or regulations under this Act) (RA) |
| | | 27 Aug 2002 (otherwise) (SI 2002/2202) |
| | paras 7–15 | 1 Dec 2002 (SI 2002/2202) |
| | para 16(1), (2) | 1 Dec 2002 (SI 2002/2202) |
| | para 16(3), (4) | 1 Apr 2003 (SI 2002/2202) |
| | paras 17–21 | 1 Dec 2002 (SI 2002/2202) |
| | paras 22, 23 | 27 Aug 2002 (SI 2002/2202) |
| | para 24 | 1 Dec 2002 (SI 2002/2202) |
| Sch 8[2] | para 1 | See paras 2–12 below |
| | para 2 | 10 Oct 2002 (W) (SI 2002/2532) |
| | | 1 Jan 2003 (E) (SI 2002/3190) |
| | para 3 | 1 Oct 2002 (E) (SI 2002/2478) |
| | | 10 Oct 2002 (W) (SI 2002/2532) |
| | para 4(1) | 1 Oct 2002 (E) (W) (SI 2002/2478) |
| | | 10 Oct 2002 (W) (SI 2002/2532)[2] |
| | para 4(2)(a) | 1 Oct 2002 (E) (W) (SI 2002/2478) |
| | para 4(2)(b), (c) | 1 Oct 2002 (E) (W) (SI 2002/2478) |
| | | 10 Oct 2002 (W) (SI 2002/2532)[2] |
| | para 4(3), (4) | 1 Oct 2002 (E) (W) (SI 2002/2478) |
| | paras 5–7 | 1 Oct 2002 (E) (W) (SI 2002/2478) |
| | paras 8, 9 | 1 Oct 2002 (E) (SI 2002/2478) |
| | | 10 Oct 2002 (W) (SI 2002/2532) |
| | paras 10, 11 | 10 Oct 2002 (W) (SI 2002/2532)[2] |
| | | 1 Sep 2003 (otherwise) (SI 2003/2246) |
| | para 12 | 1 Oct 2002 (E) (W) (SI 2002/2478) |
| | paras 13–17 | 1 Apr 2003 (SI 2003/833)[3] |
| | para 18 | 1 Oct 2002 (E) (W) (SI 2002/2478) |
| | | 10 Oct 2002 (W) (SI 2002/2532)[2] |
| | para 19 | 10 Oct 2002 (W) (SI 2002/2532)[2] |
| | para 20 | See paras 21, 22 below |
| | para 21 | 1 Oct 2002 (E) (W) (SI 2002/2202) |
| | | 10 Oct 2002 (W) (SI 2002/2532)[2] |
| | para 22 | 1 Oct 2002 (E) (W) (repeals of or in Health Authorities Act 1995, Sch 1, paras 32, 107) (SI 2002/2478) |
| | | 1 Oct 2002 (E) (repeals of or in Health Authorities Act 1995, Sch 1, para 53) (SI 2002/2478) |
| | | 10 Oct 2002 (W) (SI 2002/2532)[2] |
| | paras 23–27 | 1 Oct 2002 (E) (W) (SI 2002/2478) |
| | | 10 Oct 2002 (W) (SI 2002/2532)[2] |
| | para 28 | See paras 29–31 below |

**National Health Service Reform and Health Care Professions Act 2002 (c 17)**—*contd*

| | | |
|---|---|---|
| | para 29 | 1 Oct 2002 (E) (W) (SI 2002/2478) |
| | para 30 | 10 Oct 2002 (W) (SI 2002/2532) |
| | | 11 Jul 2003 (SI 2003/1580) |
| | paras 31–34 | 1 Oct 2002 (E) (W) (SI 2002/2478) |
| | | 10 Oct 2002 (W) (SI 2002/2532)[2] |
| | para 35 | 1 Oct 2002 (E) (W) (SI 2002/2478) |
| | paras 36, 37 | 1 Oct 2002 (E) (W) (SI 2002/2478) |
| | | 10 Oct 2002 (W) (SI 2002/2532)[2] |
| Sch 9 | Pt 1 | 1 Oct 2002 (SI 2002/2478), repeals of or in— |

        National Health Service Act 1977, ss 17B, 18, 29B, 33, 97, 103;
        Health Service Commissioners Act 1993;
        Government of Wales Act 1998;
        Health Act 1999, s 6;
        Health and Social Care Act 2001
      1 Oct 2002 (E) (repeals of or in National Health Service Act 1977, s 44, Sch 12A) (SI 2002/2478)
      10 Oct 2002 (W) (SI 2002/2532)[2], repeals of or in—
        National Health Service Act 1977, ss 22, 28A, 29B, 33, 44, 51, 97, 125, 126, Sch 12A;
        Health Service Commissioners Act 1993, s 2(2)(a);
        Government of Wales Act 1998
      11 Jul 2003 (repeals of or in Health Act 1999, ss 20, 23, Sch 2) (SI 2003/1580)
      In force (otherwise) immediately before the National Health Service Act 2006 comes into force (SI 2006/1407)[4], repeals of or in—
        National Health Service Act 1977;
        National Health Service Reform and Health Care Professions Act 2002, Sch 2, para 2
      *Not yet in force*, repeals of or in—
        Health Services and Public Health Act 1968;
        Acquisition of Land Act 1981;
        National Health Service Reform and Health Care Professions Act 2002, Sch 2, para 55

| | | |
|---|---|---|
| | Pt 2 | 1 Apr 2003 (SI 2003/833)[3] |
| | Pt 3 | 1 Oct 2002 (E) (repeals of or in Health Authorities Act 1995, Sch 1, para 53) (SI 2002/2478) |

      1 Oct 2002 (SI 2002/2478), repeals of or in—
        National Health Service Act 1977;
        National Health Service and Community Care Act 1990;
        Health Authorities Act 1995, s 1, Sch 1, paras 32(b), 107(12)(b);
        Government of Wales Act 1998;
        Health Act 1999;
        Health and Social Care Act 2001
      10 Oct 2002 (W) (SI 2002/2532)[2]
      1 Jan 2003 (repeals of or in National Health Service (Primary Care) Act 1997) (SI 2002/3190)

---

[1]   For transitional provisions, see SI 2002/2478, art 4

[2]   It is thought that the Schedule to SI 2002/2532 contains drafting errors, specifically in relation to paras 4(1), (2)(b), (c), 18, 20–27, 31–34, 36, 37 of Schedule 8 to this Act and the repeals relating to the National Health Service Act 1977, ss 29B(3), 33(1A)(b), 97(6)(bb), (c), (8), 97D(1)(b), the Health Service Commissioners Act 1993, the Government of Wales Act 1998, the National Health Service and Community Care Act 1990, the Health Authorities Act 1995 (except Sch 1, para 53), the Health Act 1999 and the Health and Social Care Act 2001. These provisions were previously brought into force on 1 Oct 2002 by SI 2002/2478. In addition, paras 10, 11, 19 and 30 of Sch 8 above should not have been commenced by that Order. The Government Departments responsible for drafting SI 2002/2532 and SI 2002/2478 have been notified and are taking steps to redress these errors

**National Health Service Reform and Health Care Professions Act 2002 (c 17)**—*contd*
[3]    For saving provisions, see SI 2003/833, art 4

[4]    For a saving, see SI 2006/1407

---

**National Heritage Act 2002 (c 14)**

*RA:* 1 May 2002

*Commencement provisions:* s 8(2)

Whole Act in force 1 Jul 2002 (s 8(2))

---

**National Insurance Contributions Act 2002 (c 19)**

*RA:* 8 Jul 2002

Whole Act in force 8 Jul 2002 (RA); with effect in relation to the tax year 2003–04 and subsequent tax
    years (s 8(2))

---

**Nationality, Immigration and Asylum Act 2002 (c 41)**

*RA:* 7 Nov 2002

*Commencement provisions:* s 162; Nationality, Immigration and Asylum Act 2002 (Commencement No 1)
    Order 2002, SI 2002/2811; Nationality, Immigration and Asylum Act 2002 (Commencement No 2)
    Order 2003, SI 2003/1; Nationality, Immigration and Asylum Act 2002 (Commencement No 3)
    Order 2003, SI 2003/249; Nationality, Immigration and Asylum Act 2002 (Commencement No 4)
    Order 2003, SI 2003/754[3], as amended by SI 2003/1040, SI 2003/1339, SI 2003/2993; Nationality,
    Immigration and Asylum Act 2002 (Commencement No 5) Order 2003, SI 2003/1747; Nationality,
    Immigration and Asylum Act 2002 (Commencement No 6) Order 2003, SI 2003/3156; Nationality,
    Immigration and Asylum Act 2002 (Commencement No 7) Order 2004, SI 2004/1201; Nationality,
    Immigration and Asylum Act 2002 (Commencement No 8) Order 2004, SI 2004/1707; Nationality,
    Immigration and Asylum Act 2002 (Commencement No 9) Order 2004, SI 2004/2998; Nationality,
    Immigration and Asylum Act 2002 (Commencement No 10) Order 2005, SI 2005/2782; Nationality,
    Immigration and Asylum Act 2002 (Commencement No 11) Order 2006, SI 2006/1498; Nationality,
    Immigration and Asylum Act 2002 (Commencement No 12) Order 2006, SI 2006/3144; Nationality,
    Immigration and Asylum Act 2002 (Commencement No 13) Order 2012, SI 2012/1263; Nationality,
    Immigration and Asylum Act 2002 (Commencement No 14) Order 2012, SI 2012/1887

| | | |
|---|---|---|
| 1 | (1), (2) | 1 Nov 2005 (except in the Channel Islands and the Isle of Man) (SI 2005/2782) |
| | | 1 May 2006 (in the Channel Islands and the Isle of Man) (SI 2005/2782) |
| | (3), (4) | 6 Jul 2004 (SI 2004/1707) |
| 2 | | 28 Jul 2004 (SI 2004/1707) |
| 3 | | See Sch 1 below |
| 4 | | 1 Apr 2003 (SI 2003/754) |
| 5 | | 7 Nov 2002 (with effect in relation to an application made after 7 Nov 2002 and an application made but not determined before that date) (s 162(2)) |
| 6, 7 | | 7 Nov 2002 (s 162(2)) |
| 8 | | 1 Apr 2003 (with effect in relation to an application made on or after 1 Apr 2003 and an application made but not determined before that date) (SI 2003/754) |
| 9 | | 5 Jun 2006 (for the purpose of enabling regulations to be made under the British Nationality Act 1981, s 50(9A), (9B)) (SI 2006/1498) |
| | | 1 Jul 2006 (otherwise) (with effect in relation to a child born on or after 1 Jul 2006) (SI 2006/1498) |
| 10 | (1)–(4) | 7 Nov 2002 (s 162(2)) |

**Nationality, Immigration and Asylum Act 2002 (c 41)**—*contd*

| | | |
|---|---|---|
| | (5)(a) | *Not yet in force* |
| | (5)(b) | 21 Dec 2006 (SI 2006/3144) |
| | (6) | 7 Nov 2002 (s 162(2)) |
| 11 | | 7 Nov 2002 (s 162(2)) |
| 12, 13 | | 30 Apr 2003 (SI 2003/754) |
| 14 | | 1 Jan 2004 (SI 2003/3156)[4] |
| 15 | | See Sch 2 below |
| 16 | | 7 Nov 2002 (s 162(2)) |
| 17 | | *Not yet in force* |
| 18 | | 8 Jan 2003 (for the purpose of ss 55(9), 70(3), Sch 3, para 17(1)(b)) (SI 2003/1) |
| | | 10 Feb 2003 (for the purpose of s 71(5), and the Immigration Act 1971, s 26A(2)) (SI 2003/1) |
| | | *Not yet in force (otherwise)* |
| 19–34 | | *Not yet in force (s 34 repealed)* |
| 35 | (1)(a)–(g) | *Not yet in force* |
| | (1)(h) | 7 Nov 2002 (s 162(2)) |
| | (1)(i) | *Not yet in force* |
| | (2), (3) | *Not yet in force* |
| 36, 37 | | *Not yet in force* |
| 38 | | 7 Nov 2002 (s 162(2)) |
| 39 | | *Not yet in force* |
| 40 | (1) | 7 Nov 2002 (s 162(2)) |
| | (2), (3) | *Not yet in force* |
| 41 | (1) | 7 Nov 2002 (s 162(2)) |
| | (2), (3) | *Not yet in force* |
| 42, 43 | | 7 Nov 2002 (s 162(2)) |
| 44–47 | | *Not yet in force* |
| 48–50 | | 7 Nov 2002 (s 162(2)) |
| 51 | | *Not yet in force* |
| 52 | | *Never in force (repealed)* |
| 53 | | *Not yet in force* |
| 54 | | See Sch 3 below |
| 55 | | 8 Jan 2003 (SI 2002/2811) |
| 56 | | 7 Nov 2002 (s 162(2)) |
| 57 | | 8 Dec 2002 (SI 2002/2811) |
| 58, 59 | | 7 Nov 2002 (s 162(2)) |
| 60 | | 10 Feb 2003 (SI 2003/1) |
| 61 | | 7 Nov 2002 (s 162(2)) |
| 62–66 | | 10 Feb 2003 (SI 2003/1) |
| 67 | | 7 Nov 2002 (s 162(2)) |
| 68 | (1)–(5) | 1 Apr 2003 (SI 2003/754) |
| | (6) | 10 Feb 2003 (SI 2003/1) |
| 69, 70 | | 7 Nov 2002 (s 162(2)) |
| 71 | | 10 Feb 2003 (SI 2003/1) |
| 72 | (1)–(8) | 10 Feb 2003 (SI 2003/1) |
| | (9), (10) | 1 Apr 2003 (SI 2003/754) |
| | (11) | 10 Feb 2003 (SI 2003/1) |
| 73–76 | | 10 Feb 2003 (SI 2003/1) |
| 77–79 | | 1 Apr 2003 (SI 2003/754)[3] |
| 80 | | 8 Dec 2002 (except the substitution of Immigration and Asylum Act 1999, s 11(2)–(4), for original s 11(2), (3)) (SI 2002/2811) |
| | | 1 Apr 2003 (exception noted above) (SI 2003/754) |
| 81 | (1)–(7) | 1 Apr 2003 (SI 2003/754) |
| | (8) | See Sch 4 below |
| 82–93 | | 1 Apr 2003 (SI 2003/754)[3] |
| 94 | (1)–(4) | 1 Apr 2003 (SI 2003/754)[3] |

**Nationality, Immigration and Asylum Act 2002 (c 41)**—*contd*

|          |          |                                                                                                                                 |
|----------|----------|---------------------------------------------------------------------------------------------------------------------------------|
|          | (5)      | 10 Feb 2003 (for the purpose of enabling the Secretary of State to exercise the power to make subordinate legislation) (SI 2003/249) |
|          |          | 1 Apr 2003 (otherwise) (SI 2003/754)[3]                                                                                          |
|          | (6)–(9)  | 1 Apr 2003 (SI 2003/754)[3]                                                                                                      |
| 95–99    |          | 1 Apr 2003 (SI 2003/754)[3]                                                                                                      |
| 100      | (1)      | 1 Apr 2003 (SI 2003/754)[3]                                                                                                      |
|          | (2)      | See Sch 5 below                                                                                                                  |
| 101–111  |          | 1 Apr 2003 (SI 2003/754)[3]                                                                                                      |
| 112, 113 |          | 10 Feb 2003 (SI 2003/249)                                                                                                        |
| 114      | (1)      | 1 Apr 2003 (SI 2003/754)                                                                                                         |
|          | (2)      | See Sch 6 below                                                                                                                  |
|          | (3)      | See Sch 7 below                                                                                                                  |
| 115      |          | 7 Nov 2002 (s 162(2))[3]                                                                                                         |
| 116–118  |          | 1 Apr 2003 (SI 2003/754)                                                                                                         |
| 119      |          | 8 Jan 2003 (SI 2002/2811)                                                                                                        |
| 120      |          | 1 Apr 2003 (SI 2003/754)                                                                                                         |
| 121, 122 |          | 10 Feb 2003 (SI 2003/1)                                                                                                          |
| 123      |          | 1 Apr 2004 (SI 2003/754)                                                                                                         |
| 124      |          | 18 Jul 2012 (SI 2012/1887)                                                                                                       |
| 125      |          | See Sch 8 below                                                                                                                  |
| 126      |          | 1 Apr 2003 (SI 2003/754)                                                                                                         |
| 127      |          | 10 Dec 2004 (SI 2004/2998)                                                                                                       |
| 128      |          | 10 Feb 2003 (SI 2003/1)                                                                                                          |
| 129      |          | 30 Jul 2003 (SI 2003/1747)                                                                                                       |
| 130      |          | 1 Apr 2003 (SI 2003/754)                                                                                                         |
| 131–133  |          | 10 Feb 2003 (SI 2003/1)                                                                                                          |
| 134–139  |          | 30 Jul 2003 (SI 2003/1747)                                                                                                       |
| 140      | (1)      | 8 Jan 2003 (SI 2002/2811)[1]                                                                                                     |
|          | (2), (3) | 8 Jan 2003 (SI 2002/2811)                                                                                                        |
| 141      |          | 8 Jan 2003 (SI 2002/2811)                                                                                                        |
| 142      |          | 1 Apr 2003 (SI 2003/754)                                                                                                         |
| 143–146  |          | 10 Feb 2003 (SI 2003/1)                                                                                                          |
| 147      | (1)      | 1 Apr 2003 (SI 2003/754)                                                                                                         |
|          | (2)      | 1 Apr 2003 (for the purpose of enabling the Secretary of State to exercise the power to make subordinate legislation) (SI 2003/754) |
|          |          | 1 May 2004 (otherwise) (SI 2004/1201)                                                                                            |
|          | (3), (4) | 1 Apr 2003 (SI 2003/754)                                                                                                         |
| 148–151  |          | 10 Feb 2003 (SI 2003/1)                                                                                                          |
| 152, 153 |          | 8 Jan 2003 (SI 2002/2811)                                                                                                        |
| 154      |          | 8 Jan 2003 (SI 2002/2811)[1]                                                                                                     |
| 155      |          | 8 Jan 2003 (SI 2002/2811)                                                                                                        |
| 156      |          | 10 Feb 2003 (SI 2003/1)                                                                                                          |
| 157      |          | 7 Nov 2002 (s 162(2))[2]                                                                                                         |
| 158, 159 |          | 10 Feb 2003 (SI 2003/1)                                                                                                          |
| 160      |          | 7 Nov 2002 (s 162(2))                                                                                                            |
| 161      |          | See Sch 9 below                                                                                                                  |
| 162–164  |          | 7 Nov 2002 (s 162(2)) (RA)                                                                                                       |
| Sch 1    |          | 1 Jan 2004 (SI 2003/3156)[4]                                                                                                     |
| Sch 2    |          | 7 Nov 2002 (s 162(2))                                                                                                            |
| Sch 3    | para 1   | 8 Jan 2003 (SI 2002/2811)                                                                                                        |
|          | para 2   | 8 Dec 2002 (for the purpose of enabling the Secretary of State to exercise the power to make subordinate legislation) (SI 2002/2811) |
|          |          | 8 Jan 2003 (otherwise) (SI 2002/2811)                                                                                            |
|          | paras 3–7| 8 Jan 2003 (SI 2002/2811)                                                                                                        |

**Nationality, Immigration and Asylum Act 2002 (c 41)**—*contd*

| | | |
|---|---|---|
| | paras 8–12 | 8 Dec 2002 (for the purpose of enabling the Secretary of State to exercise the power to make subordinate legislation) (SI 2002/2811) |
| | | 8 Jan 2003 (otherwise) (SI 2002/2811) |
| | paras 13, 14 | 8 Jan 2003 (SI 2002/2811) |
| | paras 15, 16 | 8 Dec 2002 (for the purpose of enabling the Secretary of State to exercise the power to make subordinate legislation) (SI 2002/2811) |
| | | 8 Jan 2003 (otherwise) (SI 2002/2811) |
| | para 17 | 8 Jan 2003 (SI 2002/2811) |
| Schs 4–6 | | 1 Apr 2003 (SI 2003/754) |
| Sch 7 | paras 1–28 | 1 Apr 2003 (SI 2003/754) |
| | para 29 | 7 Nov 2002 (s 162(2)) |
| | para 30 | 1 Apr 2003 (SI 2003/754) |
| | paras 31–33 | 10 Feb 2003 (SI 2003/1) |
| Sch 8 | paras 1, 2 | 14 Nov 2002 (for the purpose of enabling the Secretary of State to exercise the power to make subordinate legislation under Immigration and Asylum Act 1999, ss 32(2A), 35(5), (7), (9), (12), (13), 37(5B), (7), 40A(4), (6)) (SI 2002/2811)[1] |
| | | 8 Dec 2002 (for the purpose of clandestine entrants (within the meaning of Immigration and Asylum Act 1999, s 32(1)) who arrive in the United Kingdom concealed in a vehicle or a rail freight wagon) (SI 2002/2811)[1] |
| | | 11 May 2012 (for the purpose of clandestine entrants (within the meaning of Immigration and Asylum Act 1999, s 32(1)) who pass, or attempt to pass, through immigration control concealed in a vehicle) (SI 2012/1263) |
| | | *Not yet in force* (otherwise) |
| | para 3 | 14 Nov 2002 (for the purpose of enabling the Secretary of State to exercise the power under Immigration and Asylum Act 1999, s 32A(1), (3), (4) to lay a draft code of practice before Parliament and bring the code of practice into force) (SI 2002/2811)[1] |
| | | 8 Dec 2002 (for the purpose of clandestine entrants (within the meaning of Immigration and Asylum Act 1999, s 32(1)) who arrive in the United Kingdom concealed in a vehicle or a rail freight wagon) (SI 2002/2811)[1] |
| | | 11 May 2012 (for the purpose of clandestine entrants (within the meaning of Immigration and Asylum Act 1999, s 32(1)) who pass, or attempt to pass, through immigration control concealed in a vehicle) (SI 2012/1263) |
| | | *Not yet in force* (otherwise) |
| | paras 4–6 | 8 Dec 2002 (for the purpose of clandestine entrants (within the meaning of Immigration and Asylum Act 1999, s 32(1)) who arrive in the United Kingdom concealed in a vehicle or a rail freight wagon) (SI 2002/2811)[1] |
| | | 11 May 2012 (for the purpose of clandestine entrants (within the meaning of Immigration and Asylum Act 1999, s 32(1)) who pass, or attempt to pass, through immigration control concealed in a vehicle) (SI 2012/1263) |
| | | *Not yet in force* (otherwise) |
| | para 7 | 14 Nov 2002 (for the purpose of enabling the Secretary of State to exercise the power to make subordinate legislation under Immigration and Asylum Act 1999, ss 32(2A), 35(5), (7), (9), (12), (13), 37(5B), (7), 40A(4), (6)) (SI 2002/2811)[1] |
| | | 8 Dec 2002 (for the purpose of clandestine entrants (within the meaning of Immigration and Asylum Act 1999, s 32(1)) who arrive in the United Kingdom concealed in a vehicle or a rail freight wagon) (SI 2002/2811)[1] |

**Nationality, Immigration and Asylum Act 2002 (c 41)**—*contd*

|  |  |
|---|---|
|  | 11 May 2012 (for the purpose of clandestine entrants (within the meaning of Immigration and Asylum Act 1999, s 32(1)) who pass, or attempt to pass, through immigration control concealed in a vehicle) (SI 2012/1263) |
|  | *Not yet in force* (otherwise) |
| paras 8–10 | 8 Dec 2002 (for the purpose of clandestine entrants (within the meaning of Immigration and Asylum Act 1999, s 32(1)) who arrive in the United Kingdom concealed in a vehicle or a rail freight wagon) (SI 2002/2811)[1] |
|  | 11 May 2012 (for the purpose of clandestine entrants (within the meaning of Immigration and Asylum Act 1999, s 32(1)) who pass, or attempt to pass, through immigration control concealed in a vehicle) (SI 2012/1263) |
|  | *Not yet in force* (otherwise) |
| para 11 | 14 Nov 2002 (for the purpose of enabling the Secretary of State to exercise the power to make subordinate legislation under Immigration and Asylum Act 1999, ss 32(2A), 35(5), (7), (9), (12), (13), 37(5B), (7), 40A(4), (6)) (SI 2002/2811)[1] |
|  | 8 Dec 2002 (for the purpose of clandestine entrants (within the meaning of Immigration and Asylum Act 1999, s 32(1)) who arrive in the United Kingdom concealed in a vehicle or a rail freight wagon) (SI 2002/2811)[1] |
|  | 11 May 2012 (for the purpose of clandestine entrants (within the meaning of Immigration and Asylum Act 1999, s 32(1)) who pass, or attempt to pass, through immigration control concealed in a vehicle) (SI 2012/1263) |
|  | *Not yet in force* (otherwise) |
| para 12 | 8 Dec 2002 (for the purpose of clandestine entrants (within the meaning of Immigration and Asylum Act 1999, s 32(1)) who arrive in the United Kingdom concealed in a vehicle or a rail freight wagon) (SI 2002/2811)[1] |
| para 13 | 14 Nov 2002 (for the purpose of enabling the Secretary of State to exercise the power to make subordinate legislation under Immigration and Asylum Act 1999, ss 32(2A), 35(5), (7), (9), (12), (13), 37(5B), (7), 40A(4), (6)) (SI 2002/2811) |
|  | 8 Dec 2002 (otherwise) (SI 2002/2811) |
| para 14 | 8 Dec 2002 (SI 2002/2811) |
| para 15 | 8 Dec 2002 (SI 2002/2811)[1] |
| para 16(1) | 8 Dec 2002 (for the purpose of clandestine entrants (within the meaning of Immigration and Asylum Act 1999, s 32(1)) who arrive in the United Kingdom concealed in a vehicle or a rail freight wagon) (SI 2002/2811)[1] |
|  | 11 May 2012 (for the purpose of clandestine entrants (within the meaning of Immigration and Asylum Act 1999, s 32(1)) who pass, or attempt to pass, through immigration control concealed in a vehicle) (SI 2012/1263) |
|  | *Not yet in force* (otherwise) |
| para 16(2) | 8 Dec 2002 (for the purpose of clandestine entrants (within the meaning of Immigration and Asylum Act 1999, s 32(1)) who arrive in the United Kingdom concealed in a vehicle or a rail freight wagon) (SI 2002/2811)[1] |
|  | *Not yet in force* (otherwise) |
| para 16(3) | 8 Dec 2002 (for the purpose of clandestine entrants (within the meaning of Immigration and Asylum Act 1999, s 32(1)) who arrive in the United Kingdom concealed in a vehicle or a rail freight wagon) (SI 2002/2811)[1] |
|  | 11 May 2012 (for the purpose of clandestine entrants (within the meaning of Immigration and Asylum Act 1999, s 32(1)) who pass, or attempt to pass, through immigration control concealed in a vehicle) (SI 2012/1263) |
|  | *Not yet in force* (otherwise) |

## Nationality, Immigration and Asylum Act 2002 (c 41)—*contd*

| | |
|---|---|
| para 16(4), (5) | 8 Dec 2002 (for the purpose of clandestine entrants (within the meaning of Immigration and Asylum Act 1999, s 32(1)) who arrive in the United Kingdom concealed in a vehicle or a rail freight wagon) (SI 2002/2811)[1] |
| | *Not yet in force* (otherwise) |
| para 17 | 8 Dec 2002 (for the purpose of clandestine entrants (within the meaning of Immigration and Asylum Act 1999, s 32(1)) who arrive in the United Kingdom concealed in a vehicle or a rail freight wagon) (SI 2002/2811)[1] |
| | *Not yet in force* (otherwise) |
| Sch 9 | 7 Nov 2002 (repeals of or in Immigration and Asylum Act 1999, Sch 4, para 9(1)(a), (4), (5)) (s 162(2)) |
| | 8 Dec 2002 (repeals of or in Immigration and Asylum Act 1999, ss 33(2)(b), 34(3)(c), (5), 36(1), 37(3)(c), 39, 42, 43) (SI 2002/2811) |
| | 10 Feb 2003 (SI 2003/1), repeals of or in— |
| | Immigration Act 1971, ss 7(1)(a), 24A(4), 25A(7), 26(3), 28(1), 28A; |
| | Immigration and Asylum Act 1999, ss 10(1)(c), 44–52, 53(5), 55, 147 |
| | 1 Apr 2003 (SI 2003/754)[3], repeals of or in— |
| | Immigration Act 1971, ss 3(9)(b), 29, 31(d); |
| | Race Relations Act 1976; |
| | British Nationality Act 1981, ss 7–10, 19–22, 27(2), 28, 33, 44(2), (3), Sch 2, para 3(1)(b), Sch 4; |
| | British Nationality (Falkland Islands) Act 1983; |
| | British Nationality (Hong Kong) Act 1990; |
| | Special Immigration Appeals Commission Act 1997; |
| | Immigration and Asylum Act 1999, ss 15, 56–81, Schs 2–4, 14; |
| | Race Relations Amendment Act 2000 |
| | *Not yet in force*, repeals of or in— |
| | British Nationality Act 1981, ss 3(6), 17(6), 47, Sch 1, paras 4(c), 8(c), Sch 2, paras 1(1)(b), 2(1)(b); |
| | Asylum and Immigration Act 1996; |
| | Immigration and Asylum Act 1999, ss 29, 38(1), (3), 94(5), (6), 96(4)–(6), Sch 1, paras 1(2)(a), 5(1), (2)(d), Sch 8, paras 2, 6 |

[1]  For transitional provisions, see SI 2002/2811, arts 3–6

[2]  Note that SI 2002/2811 also purports to bring s 157 into force on 8 Jan 2003

[3]  For transitional provisions, see SI 2003/754, arts 3, 4, Sch 2

[4]  For transitional provisions, see SI 2003/3156, arts 3, 4

---

## Northern Ireland Arms Decommissioning (Amendment) Act 2002 (c 6)

*RA:* 26 Feb 2002

Whole Act in force 26 Feb 2002 (RA)

---

## Office of Communications Act 2002 (c 11)

*RA:* 19 Mar 2002

*Commencement provisions:* s 7(2); Office of Communications Act 2002 (Commencement No 1) Order 2002, SI 2002/1483; Office of Communications Act 2002 (Commencement No 2) Order 2002, SI 2002/2955; Office of Communications Act 2002 (Commencement No 3) and Communications Act 2003 (Commencement No 2) Order 2003, SI 2003/3142, as amended by SI 2004/545, SI 2004/697, SI 2004/1492

**See Halsbury's Statutes Citator for amendments to these Acts**    1363

**Office of Communications Act 2002 (c 11)**—*contd*

| | | |
|---|---|---|
| 1 | (1)–(6) | 1 Jul 2002 (SI 2002/1483) |
| | (7), (8) | 29 Nov 2002 (SI 2002/2955) |
| | (9) | 1 Jul 2002 (SI 2002/1483) |
| | (10) | See Schedule below |
| 2, 3 | | 1 Jul 2002 (SI 2002/1483) |
| 4–7 | | 19 Mar 2002 (RA) |
| Schedule | paras 1–11 | 1 Jul 2002 (SI 2002/1483) |
| | para 12 | 29 Dec 2003 (SI 2003/3142) |
| | paras 13–24 | 1 Jul 2002 (SI 2002/1483) |

**Police Reform Act 2002 (c 30)**

*RA:* 24 Jul 2002

*Commencement provisions:* s 108(2)–(5); Police Reform Act 2002 (Commencement No 1) Order 2002, SI 2002/2306; Police Reform Act 2002 (Commencement No 2) (Scotland) Order 2002, SSI 2002/420; Police Reform Act 2002 (Commencement No 3) Order 2002, SI 2002/2750; Police Reform Act 2002 (Commencement) (Wales) Order 2003, SI 2003/525; Police Reform Act 2002 (Commencement No 4) Order 2003, SI 2003/808; Police Reform Act 2002 (Commencement No 5) Order 2003, SI 2003/2593; Police Reform Act 2002 (Commencement No 6) Order 2004, SI 2004/119; Police Reform Act 2002 (Commencement No 7) Order 2004, SI 2004/636; Police Reform Act 2002 (Commencement No 8) Order 2004, SI 2004/913; Police Reform Act 2002 (Commencement No 9) Order 2004, SI 2004/1319; Police Reform Act 2002 (Commencement No 10) Order 2004, SI 2004/3338

| | | |
|---|---|---|
| 1–8 | | 1 Oct 2002 (SI 2002/2306) |
| 9 | (1) | 1 Apr 2003 (SI 2003/808) |
| | (2)–(4) | 1 Oct 2002 (for the purpose of making appointments) (SI 2002/2306) |
| | | 1 Apr 2003 (otherwise) (SI 2003/808) |
| | (5) | 1 Apr 2003 (SI 2003/808) |
| | (6) | See Sch 2 below |
| | (7) | 1 Apr 2003 (SI 2003/808) |
| 10–12 | | 1 Apr 2004 (SI 2004/913) |
| 13 | | See Sch 3 below |
| 14 | (1) | 1 Apr 2004 (SI 2004/913) |
| | (2), (3) | 1 Oct 2002 (SI 2002/2306) |
| 15, 16 | | 1 Apr 2004 (SI 2004/913) |
| 17 | (1) | 1 Oct 2002 (for the purpose of making regulations or orders) (SI 2002/2306) |
| | | 1 Apr 2004 (otherwise) (SI 2004/913) |
| | (2)–(4) | 1 Apr 2004 (SI 2004/913) |
| | (5) | 1 Oct 2002 (for the purpose of making regulations or orders) (SI 2002/2306) |
| | | 1 Apr 2004 (otherwise) (SI 2004/913) |
| 18 | | 1 Apr 2004 (SI 2004/913) |
| 19 | | 1 Oct 2002 (SI 2002/2306) |
| 20 | (1)–(4) | 1 Apr 2004 (SI 2004/913) |
| | (5)–(8) | 1 Oct 2002 (for the purpose of making regulations or orders) (SI 2002/2306) |
| | | 1 Apr 2004 (otherwise) (SI 2004/913) |
| | (9) | 1 Apr 2004 (SI 2004/913) |
| 21 | (1)–(9) | 1 Apr 2004 (SI 2004/913) |
| | (10)–(12) | 1 Oct 2002 (for the purpose of making regulations or orders) (SI 2002/2306) |
| | | 1 Apr 2004 (otherwise) (SI 2004/913) |
| 22 | | 1 Apr 2004 (SI 2004/913) |
| 23 | | 1 Oct 2002 (SI 2002/2306) |
| 24 | (a) | 15 Nov 2003 (SI 2003/2593) |
| | (b)–(d) | 1 Oct 2002 (SI 2002/2306) |

**Police Reform Act 2002 (c 30)**—*contd*

| | | |
|---|---|---|
| 25 | (1)–(3) | 1 Oct 2002 (SI 2002/2306) |
| | (4) | 1 Apr 2004 (SI 2004/913) |
| | (5) | 1 Oct 2002 (SI 2002/2306) |
| 26, 27 | | 1 Apr 2004 (SI 2004/913) |
| 28, 29 | | 1 Oct 2002 (SI 2002/2306) |
| 30–33 | | 1 Jun 2004 (SI 2004/1319) |
| 34–36 | | 1 Oct 2002 (SI 2002/2306) |
| 37 | | 1 Apr 2004 (SI 2004/913) |
| 38 | | 2 Dec 2002 (SI 2002/2750) |
| 39 | (1)–(8) | 1 Apr 2003 (SI 2003/808) |
| | (9), (10) | 1 Oct 2002 (SI 2002/2306) |
| | (11)(a), (b) | 1 Oct 2002 (SI 2002/2306) |
| | (11)(c) | 1 Apr 2003 (SI 2003/808) |
| | (11)(d) | 1 Oct 2002 (SI 2002/2306) |
| | (12), (13) | 1 Apr 2003 (SI 2003/808) |
| 40, 41 | | 2 Dec 2002 (SI 2002/2750) |
| 42 | | 1 Apr 2003 (SI 2003/808) |
| 43 | | 1 Oct 2002 (SI 2002/2306) |
| 44 | | 2 Dec 2002 (SI 2002/2750) |
| 45 | | *Not yet in force* (sub-s (3)(a), (b), (d), (e) repealed) |
| 46 | | 2 Dec 2002 (SI 2002/2750) |
| 47–49 | | 1 Oct 2002 (SI 2002/2306) |
| 50 | | 2 Dec 2002 (SI 2002/2750) |
| 51–53 | | 1 Apr 2003 (SI 2003/808) |
| 54 | (1) | 1 Apr 2003 (SI 2003/808) |
| | (2), (3) | 1 Oct 2002 (for the purpose of making regulations or orders) (SI 2002/2306) |
| | | 1 Apr 2003 (otherwise) (SI 2003/808) |
| 55 | (1), (2) | 1 Apr 2003 (SI 2003/808) |
| | (3), (4) | 1 Oct 2002 (for the purpose of making regulations or orders) (SI 2002/2306) |
| | | 1 Apr 2003 (otherwise) (SI 2003/808) |
| | (5) | 1 Apr 2003 (SI 2003/808) |
| 56 | | 1 Oct 2002 (SI 2002/2306) |
| 57 | (1), (2) | 1 Oct 2002 (SI 2002/2306) |
| | (3) | 1 Oct 2002 (except for the words "or a registered health care professional") (SI 2002/2306) |
| | | 1 Apr 2003 (exception noted above) (SI 2003/808) |
| | (4), (5) | 1 Oct 2002 (SI 2002/2306) |
| | (6) | 1 Apr 2003 (SI 2003/808) |
| 58 | (1), (2) | 1 Apr 2003 (SI 2003/808) |
| | (3) | 1 Oct 2002 (for the purpose of making regulations or orders) (SI 2002/2306) |
| | | 1 Apr 2003 (otherwise) (SI 2003/808) |
| | (4)–(8) | 1 Oct 2002 (SI 2002/2306) |
| | (9) | 1 Apr 2003 (SI 2003/808) |
| | (10) | 1 Oct 2002 (for the purpose of making regulations or orders) (SI 2002/2306) |
| | | 1 Apr 2003 (otherwise) (SI 2003/808) |
| | (11) | 1 Apr 2003 (SI 2003/808) |
| 59 | | 1 Jan 2003 (SI 2002/2750) |
| 60 | | 1 Oct 2002 (SI 2002/2306) |
| 61, 62 | | 2 Dec 2002 (SI 2002/2750) |
| 63 | | 1 Apr 2003 (SI 2003/808) |
| 64 | | 2 Dec 2002 (SI 2002/2750) |
| 65 | (1) | 2 Dec 2002 (except for the purposes of inserting Crime and Disorder Act 1998, s 1D(1)(b)) (SI 2002/2750) |
| | | 1 Apr 2003 (exception noted above) (SI 2003/808) |
| | (2) | 2 Dec 2002 (SI 2002/2750) |

**Police Reform Act 2002 (c 30)**—*contd*

| | | |
|---|---|---|
| 66 | | 2 Dec 2002 (except for the purposes of inserting Crime and Disorder Act 1998, s 1E(1)(b)) (SI 2002/2750) |
| | | 1 Apr 2003 (exception noted above) (SI 2003/808) |
| 67–69 | | 2 Dec 2002 (SI 2002/2750) |
| 70, 71 | | 1 Oct 2002 (S) (SSI 2002/420) |
| 72–74 | | 2 Dec 2002 (SI 2002/2750) |
| 75–78 | | 1 Oct 2002 (SI 2002/2306) |
| 79 | | 9 Mar 2004 (SI 2004/636) |
| 80, 81 | | 1 Oct 2002 (SI 2002/2306) |
| 82 | (1)–(3) | 3 Feb 2003 (SI 2002/2750) |
| | (4) | 1 Oct 2002 (SI 2002/2306) |
| | (5) | 3 Feb 2003 (SI 2002/2750) |
| 83 | | 1 Oct 2002 (SI 2002/2306) |
| 84 | | 1 Nov 2002 (SI 2002/2306) |
| 85 | | 1 Oct 2002 (SI 2002/2306) |
| 86 | (1) | 1 Apr 2003 (SI 2003/808) |
| | (2)(a) | *Never in force* (repealed) |
| | (2)(b) | 1 Apr 2003 (SI 2003/808) |
| | (3), (4) | *Never in force* (repealed) |
| | (5) | 1 Apr 2003 (SI 2003/808) |
| 87 | (1) | 1 Apr 2003 (SI 2003/808) |
| | (2)(a) | 15 Nov 2003 (SI 2003/2593) |
| | (2)(b) | 1 Apr 2003 (SI 2003/808) |
| | (3), (4) | 15 Nov 2003 (SI 2003/2593) |
| | (5) | 1 Apr 2003 (SI 2003/808) |
| 88, 89 | | 1 Oct 2002 (SI 2002/2306) |
| 90 | (1), (2) | *Never in force* (repealed) |
| | (3) | 1 Oct 2002 (SI 2002/2306) |
| | (4) | *Never in force* (repealed) |
| | (5)–(7) | 1 Oct 2002 (SI 2002/2306) |
| 91 | (1), (2) | 15 Nov 2003 (SI 2003/2593) |
| | (3) | 1 Oct 2002 (SI 2002/2306) |
| | (4) | 15 Nov 2003 (SI 2003/2593) |
| | (5)–(7) | 1 Oct 2002 (SI 2002/2306) |
| 92 | (1) | 1 Oct 2002 (so far as it relates to the insertion of s 6A(14), (15) of the Police Act 1996) (SI 2002/2306) |
| | | 1 Nov 2002 (otherwise) (SI 2002/2306) |
| | (2), (3) | 1 Nov 2002 (SI 2002/2306) |
| 93, 94 | | 1 Oct 2002 (SI 2002/2306) |
| 95 | | *Never in force* (repealed) |
| 96 | | 1 Apr 2003 (SI 2003/808) |
| 97 | (1) | 1 Oct 2002 (E) (SI 2002/2306) |
| | | 1 Apr 2003 (W) (SI 2003/525) |
| | (2) | 1 Apr 2003 (W) (SI 2003/525) |
| | | 1 Apr 2003 (E) (so far as it relates to Crime and Disorder Act 1998, s 5(1)(c), (d)) (SI 2003/808) |
| | | 30 Apr 2004 (E) (otherwise) (SI 2004/913) |
| | (3), (4) | 1 Oct 2002 (E) (SI 2002/2306) |
| | | 1 Apr 2003 (W) (SI 2003/525) |
| | (5) | 1 Apr 2003 (W) (SI 2003/525) |
| | | 23 Feb 2004 (E) (SI 2004/119) |
| | (6) | 1 Apr 2003 (W) (SI 2003/525) |
| | | 1 Apr 2003 (E) (SI 2003/808) |
| | (7) | 1 Oct 2002 (E) (SI 2002/2306) |
| | | 1 Apr 2003 (W) (SI 2003/525) |
| | (8) | 1 Apr 2003 (W) (SI 2003/525) |
| | | 23 Feb 2004 (E) (SI 2004/119) |
| | (9) | 1 Oct 2002 (E) (SI 2002/2306) |
| | | 1 Apr 2003 (W) (SI 2003/525) |

**Police Reform Act 2002 (c 30)**—*contd*

| | | |
|---|---|---|
| | (10), (11) | 1 Oct 2002 (E) (SI 2002/2306) |
| | | 1 Apr 2003 (W) (SI 2003/525) |
| | (12) | 1 Apr 2003 (W) (SI 2003/525) |
| | | 1 Apr 2003 (E) (SI 2003/808) |
| | (13), (14) | 1 Oct 2002 (E) (SI 2002/2306) |
| | | 1 Apr 2003 (W) (SI 2003/525) |
| | (15) | 1 Apr 2003 (W) (SI 2003/525) |
| | | 30 Apr 2004 (E) (SI 2004/913) |
| 98 | | 1 Oct 2002 (E) (SI 2002/2306) |
| | | 1 Apr 2003 (W) (SI 2003/525) |
| 99 | | 1 Oct 2002 (SI 2002/2306) |
| 100 | | 24 Jul 2002 (RA) |
| 101 | | 1 Oct 2002 (SI 2002/2306) |
| 102 | (1)–(6) | 1 Oct 2002 (SI 2002/2306) |
| | (7), (8) | 1 Oct 2002 (S) (SSI 2002/420) |
| 103 | (1)–(3) | 1 Oct 2002 (SI 2002/2306) |
| | (4) | 1 Oct 2002 (S) (SSI 2002/420) |
| | (5)–(7) | 1 Oct 2002 (SI 2002/2306) |
| 104 | (1) | 1 Oct 2002 (SI 2002/2306) |
| | (2) | 1 Oct 2002 (S) (SSI 2002/420) |
| | (3) | 1 Oct 2002 (SI 2002/2306) |
| 105, 106 | | 24 Jul 2002 (RA) |
| 107 | (1) | See Sch 7 below |
| | (2) | See Sch 8 below |
| 108 | | 24 Jul 2002 (RA) |
| Sch 1 | | 1 Oct 2002 (SI 2002/2306) |
| Sch 2 | paras 1–4 | 1 Apr 2003 (SI 2003/808) |
| | para 5(1)–(4) | 1 Apr 2003 (SI 2003/808) |
| | para 5(5) | 1 Oct 2002 (SI 2002/2306) |
| | paras 6–18 | 1 Apr 2003 (SI 2003/808) |
| Sch 3 | | 1 Oct 2002 (for the purpose of making regulations or orders) (SI 2002/2306) |
| | | 1 Apr 2004 (otherwise) (SI 2004/913) |
| Sch 4 | para 1(1) | 2 Dec 2002 (SI 2002/2750) |
| | para 1(2)(a) | 15 Nov 2003 (SI 2003/2593) |
| | para 1(2)(b)–(d) | 2 Dec 2002 (SI 2002/2750) |
| | para 1(3) | 2 Dec 2002 (SI 2002/2750) |
| | para 2(1), (2) | 2 Dec 2002 (SI 2002/2750) |
| | para 2(3), (4) | 2 Dec 2002 (within the following police areas only: Devon and Cornwall, Gwent, Lancashire, Northamptonshire, West Yorkshire, the metropolitan police district) (SI 2002/2750) |
| | | 23 Dec 2004 (otherwise) (SI 2004/3338) |
| | para 2(5)(a) | 2 Dec 2002 (SI 2002/2750) |
| | para 2(5)(b), (c) | 2 Dec 2002 (within the following police areas only: Devon and Cornwall, Gwent, Lancashire, Northamptonshire, West Yorkshire, the metropolitan police district) (SI 2002/2750) |
| | | 23 Dec 2004 (otherwise) (SI 2004/3338) |
| | para 2(6) | 2 Dec 2002 (SI 2002/2750) |
| | para 2(7) | 23 Dec 2004 (SI 2004/3338) |
| | para 3(1) | 2 Dec 2002 (SI 2002/2750) |
| | para 3(2) | 2 Dec 2002 (within the following police areas only: Devon and Cornwall, Gwent, Lancashire, Northamptonshire, West Yorkshire, the metropolitan police district) (SI 2002/2750) |
| | | 23 Dec 2004 (otherwise) (SI 2004/3338) |
| | para 4 | 2 Dec 2002 (within the following police areas only: Devon and Cornwall, Gwent, Lancashire, Northamptonshire, West Yorkshire, the metropolitan police district) (SI 2002/2750) |
| | | 23 Dec 2004 (otherwise) (SI 2004/3338) |
| | paras 5–8 | 2 Dec 2002 (SI 2002/2750) |

**Police Reform Act 2002 (c 30)**—*contd*

|  |  |  |
|---|---|---|
|  | para 9 | 1 Jan 2003 (SI 2002/2750) |
|  | paras 10–36 | 2 Dec 2002 (SI 2002/2750) |
| Sch 5 |  | 2 Dec 2002 (SI 2002/2750) |
| Sch 6 |  | 1 Oct 2002 (SI 2002/2306) |
| Sch 7 | paras 1–3 | 1 Apr 2004 (SI 2004/913) |
|  | para 4 | 2 Dec 2002 (SI 2002/2750) |
|  | paras 5, 6 | 1 Apr 2004 (SI 2004/913) |
|  | para 7(1)–(3) | 1 Apr 2004 (SI 2004/913) |
|  | para 7(4) | 1 Oct 2002 (SI 2002/2306) |
|  | paras 8, 9 | 2 Dec 2002 (SI 2002/2750) |
|  | para 10 | 1 Apr 2004 (SI 2004/913) |
|  | paras 11, 12 | 1 Oct 2002 (SI 2002/2306) |
|  | para 13 | 1 Apr 2004 (SI 2004/913) |
|  | para 14 | 1 Oct 2002 (SI 2002/2306) |
|  | para 15 | 1 Apr 2004 (SI 2004/913) |
|  | paras 16, 17 | 1 Oct 2002 (SI 2002/2306) |
|  | paras 18–20 | 1 Apr 2004 (SI 2004/913) |
|  | para 21(1), (2) | 1 Oct 2002 (SI 2002/2306) |
|  | para 21(3) | 23 Dec 2004 (SI 2004/3338) |
|  | paras 22–24 | 1 Apr 2004 (SI 2004/913) |

Sch 8        24 Jul 2002 (RA), repeals of or in—
       Housing Act 1985;
       Housing Act 1988;
       Greater London Authority Act 1999, Sch 27, paras 51, 59;
       Criminal Justice and Police Act 2001, Sch 6, para 74
     1 Oct 2002 (SI 2002/2306), repeals of or in—
       Road Traffic Act 1988;
       Official Secrets Act 1989;
       Police Act 1996, s 62(1B);
       Police Act 1997, ss 6, 9A, 55A;
       Protection from Harassment Act 1997;
       Crime and Disorder Act 1998, ss 32, 84;
       Football (Offences and Disorder) Act 1999;
       Countryside and Rights of Way Act 2000;
       Criminal Justice and Court Services Act 2000;
       Anti-terrorism, Crime and Security Act 2001;
       Criminal Justice and Police Act 2001, ss 12, 46, 71
     2 Dec 2002 (SI 2002/2750), repeals of or in—
       Police and Criminal Evidence Act 1984;
       Road Traffic Regulation Act 1984;
       Crime and Disorder Act 1998, s 1
     1 Apr 2003 (SI 2002/808), repeals of or in—
       Criminal Justice and Public Order Act 1994;
       Police Act 1996, Schs 2, 2A;
       Police Act 1997, ss 9, 55;
       Criminal Justice and Police Act 2001, s 80(2)
     1 Apr 2004 (SI 2004/913), repeals of or in—
       Superannuation Act 1972;
       House of Commons Disqualification Act 1975;
       Northern Ireland Assembly Disqualification Act 1975;
       Employment Rights Act 1996;
       Police Act 1996, ss 63(3)(b), 65–83, 86, 105(2), Sch 5;
       Police Act 1997, s 39(3);
       Public Interest Disclosure Act 1998;
       Greater London Authority Act 1999, Sch 27, paras 97–99;
       Freedom of Information Act 2000;
       Criminal Justice and Police Act 2001, s 125(4)(b)
    30 Apr 2004 (E) (repeal in Crime and Disorder Act 1998, s 5)
       (SI 2004/913)

**Police Reform Act 2002 (c 30)**—*contd*

    1 Jun 2004 (repeal of Police Act 1996, s 42(5)) (SI 2004/1319)

    23 Dec 2004 (SI 2004/3338), repeals of or in—

        Road Traffic Offenders Act 1988;

        Police Act 1997, s 42(6)(a);

        Police (Northern Ireland) Act 1998, Sch 4, para 22(2), (3), (9);

        Greater London Authority Act 1999, Sch 27, para 90;

        Local Government Act 1999;

        Criminal Justice and Police Act 2001, ss 122(3), 123(3)

    *Not yet in force*, repeals of or in—

        Crime and Disorder Act 1998, s 5(1) (W);

        Police (Northern Ireland) Act 1998, Sch 4, para 22(4);

        Police (Northern Ireland) Act 2000

    *Never in force* (repealed) (entry relating to Police (Health and Safety) Act 1997, s 5)

---

**Private Hire Vehicles (Carriage of Guide Dogs etc) Act 2002 (c 37)**

*RA:* 7 Nov 2002

*Commencement provisions:* s 6(2); Private Hire Vehicles (Carriage of Guide Dogs etc) Act 2002 (Commencement No 1) Order 2003, SI 2003/3123; Private Hire Vehicles (Carriage of Guide Dogs etc) Act 2002 (Commencement No 1) (Scotland) Order 2004, SSI 2004/57; Private Hire Vehicles (Carriage of Guide Dogs etc) Act 2002 (Commencement No 1) (Northern Ireland) Order 2007, SI 2007/3477

| | | |
|---|---|---|
| 1 | (1) | 31 Dec 2003 (E) (W) (in so far as it relates to: |
| | | (a) the Disability Discrimination Act 1995, s 37A(5)–(7), (9); |
| | | (b) the power to make regulations under the Disability Discrimination Act 1995, s 37A(8); and |
| | | (c) ss 3, 4 and 5) (SI 2003/3123) |
| | | 31 Mar 2004 (E) (W) (otherwise) (SI 2003/3123) |
| | | 1 Jan 2008 (NI) (in so far as it relates to: |
| | | (a) the Disability Discrimination Act 1995, s 37A(5)–(7), (9); |
| | | (b) the power to make regulations under the Disability Discrimination Act 1995, s 37A(8); and |
| | | (c) ss 3 and 4) (SI 2007/3477) |
| | | 1 Jun 2008 (NI) (otherwise) (SI 2007/3477) |
| | | *Never in force* (S) (repealed) |
| | (2) | *Never in force* (repealed) |
| 2 | | 31 Mar 2004 (SSI 2004/57) |
| 3–5 | | 31 Mar 2003 (SI 2003/3123) |
| 6 | | 7 Nov 2002 (RA) |

---

**Proceeds of Crime Act 2002 (c 29)**

*RA:* 24 Jul 2002

*Commencement provisions:* s 458; Proceeds of Crime Act 2002 (Commencement No 1 and Savings) Order 2002, SI 2002/3015[1]; Proceeds of Crime Act 2002 (Commencement No 2) Order 2002, SI 2002/3055; Proceeds of Crime Act 2002 (Commencement No 3) Order 2002, SI 2002/3145; Proceeds of Crime Act 2002 (Commencement No 4, Transitional Provisions and Savings) Order 2003, SI 2003/120[2], as amended by SI 2003/333; Proceeds of Crime Act 2002 (Commencement No 5, Transitional Provisions, Savings and Amendment) Order 2003, SI 2003/333[3], as amended by SI 2003/531; Proceeds of Crime Act 2002 (Commencement No 6, Transitional Provisions and Savings) (Scotland) Order 2003, SSI 2003/210

| | | |
|---|---|---|
| 1 | (1)–(6) | 13 Jan 2003 (SI 2002/3055) |
| | (7) | See Sch 1 below |
| 2–5 | | 13 Jan 2003 (SI 2002/3055) |
| 6–88 | | 24 Mar 2003 (SI 2003/333)[3] |

**Proceeds of Crime Act 2002 (c 29)**—*contd*

| | | |
|---|---|---|
| 89, 90 | | 30 Dec 2002 (for the purposes of making secondary legislation) (SI 2002/3015) |
| | | 24 Mar 2003 (otherwise) (SI 2003/333) |
| 91 | | 24 Mar 2003 (SI 2003/333) |
| 92–155 | | 24 Mar 2003 (SSI 2003/210)[5] |
| 156–239 | | 24 Mar 2003 (SI 2003/333)[3] |
| 240–242 | | 30 Dec 2002 (SI 2002/3015) |
| 243–269 | | 24 Feb 2003 (SI 2003/120) |
| 270 | (1)–(3) | 24 Feb 2003 (SI 2003/120) |
| | (4), (5) | 30 Dec 2002 (SI 2002/3015) |
| 271–288 | | 24 Feb 2003 (SI 2003/120) |
| 289–311 | | 30 Dec 2002 (SI 2002/3015) |
| 312, 313 | | 24 Feb 2003 (SI 2003/120) |
| 314–316 | | 30 Dec 2002 (SI 2002/3015) |
| 317–326 | | 24 Feb 2003 (SI 2003/120) |
| 327–332 | | 24 Feb 2003 (SI 2003/120)[2] |
| 333–341 | | 24 Feb 2003 (SI 2003/120) |
| 342 | | 24 Feb 2003 (SI 2003/120)[2] |
| 343–416 | | 24 Feb 2003 (SI 2003/120) |
| 417–434 | | 24 Mar 2003 (SI 2003/333) |
| 435–442 | | 24 Feb 2003 (except so far as they relate to disclosure of information to and by the Lord Advocate in connection with the exercise of any of his functions under Pt 3 of this Act) (SI 2003/120) |
| | | 24 Mar 2003 (otherwise) (SI 2003/333) |
| 443 | | 24 Feb 2003 (SI 2003/120) |
| 444, 445 | | 24 Mar 2003 (SI 2003/333) |
| 446 | | 24 Feb 2003 (SI 2003/120) |
| 447 | | 24 Mar 2003 (SI 2003/333) |
| 448–453 | | 24 Feb 2003 (SI 2003/120) |
| 454, 455 | | 30 Dec 2002 (SI 2002/3015) |
| 456 | | See Sch 11 below |
| 457 | | See Sch 12 below |
| 458–462 | | 24 Jul 2002 (RA) |
| Sch 1 | | 13 Jan 2003 (SI 2002/3055) |
| Sch 2 | | 24 Mar 2003 (SI 2003/333) |
| Schs 3, 4 | | 24 Mar 2003 (SSI 2003/210) |
| Sch 5 | | 24 Mar 2003 (SI 2003/333) |
| Schs 6–10 | | 24 Feb 2003 (SI 2003/120) |
| Sch 11 | para 1 | 24 Mar 2003 (SI 2003/333) |
| | paras 2, 3 | 24 Feb 2003 (SI 2003/120) |
| | paras 4, 5 | 24 Mar 2003 (SI 2003/333) |
| | para 6 | 24 Feb 2003 (SI 2003/120) |
| | para 7 | 24 Mar 2003 (except so far as relates to Pt 3 of this Act) (SI 2003/333) |
| | | 24 Mar 2003 (exception noted above) (SSI 2003/210) |
| | paras 8, 9 | 24 Mar 2003 (SI 2003/333) |
| | para 10(1) | 30 Dec 2002 (SI 2002/3145) |
| | para 10(2) | 24 Feb 2003 (SI 2003/120) |
| | para 10(3), (4) | 30 Dec 2002 (SI 2002/3145) |
| | para 11 | 24 Mar 2003 (except so far as relates to Pt 3 of this Act) (SI 2003/333) |
| | | 24 Mar 2003 (exception noted above) (SSI 2003/210) |
| | para 12 | 24 Mar 2003 (in so far as relates to Pt 3 of this Act) (SSI 2003/210)[5] |
| | para 13 | 24 Feb 2003 (SI 2003/120) |
| | para 14(1) | 24 Feb 2003 (SI 2003/120) |
| | para 14(2), (3) | 24 Mar 2003 (SI 2003/333) |
| | para 14(4) | 24 Feb 2003 (SI 2003/120) |

**Proceeds of Crime Act 2002 (c 29)**—*contd*

| | |
|---|---|
| paras 15, 16 | 24 Mar 2003 (except so far as they relate to Pt 3 of this Act) (SI 2003/333) |
| | 24 Mar 2003 (exception noted above) (SSI 2003/210)[5] |
| para 17(1) | 24 Feb 2003 (SI 2003/120) |
| para 17(2) | 24 Feb 2003 (repeals of or in Criminal Justice Act 1988, ss 93A–93J) (SI 2003/120)[2] |
| | 24 Mar 2003 (repeals of or in Criminal Justice Act 1988, ss 71–89, 94, 99–102, Sch 4) (SI 2003/333) |
| | *Not yet in force* (repeals of Criminal Justice Act 1988, ss 90–93, 95–98) |
| para 17(3) | 24 Feb 2003 (SI 2003/120) |
| para 17(4) | 24 Mar 2003 (SI 2003/333) |
| para 17(5) | 24 Feb 2003 (SI 2003/120) |
| para 17(6) | 24 Mar 2003 (SI 2003/333) |
| para 18 | 24 Feb 2003 (SI 2003/120)[5] |
| para 19(1) | 24 Feb 2003 (SI 2003/120) |
| para 19(2), (3) | 24 Mar 2003 (SI 2003/333) |
| para 19(4) | 24 Feb 2003 (SI 2003/120) |
| paras 20, 21 | 24 Mar 2003 (except so far as they relate to Pt 3 of this Act) (SI 2003/333) |
| | 24 Mar 2003 (exception noted above) (SSI 2003/210)[5] |
| paras 22–24 | 24 Feb 2003 (SI 2003/120) |
| para 25(1) | See sub-paras (2)–(7) below |
| para 25(2)(a) | 30 Dec 2002 (repeals of Drug Trafficking Act 1994, ss 42–48) (SI 2002/3015)[1] |
| | 24 Feb 2003 (repeals of Drug Trafficking Act 1994, ss 49–54) (SI 2003/120) |
| | 24 Mar 2003 (repeals of Drug Trafficking Act 1994, ss 1–38, 41) (SI 2003/333) |
| | *Not yet in force* (repeals of Drug Trafficking Act 1994, ss 39, 40) |
| para 25(2)(b)–(g) | 24 Feb 2003 (SI 2003/120)[2] |
| para 25(2)(h)–(j) | 24 Mar 2003 (SI 2003/333) |
| para 25(3)–(7) | 24 Feb 2003 (SI 2003/120) |
| para 26 | 24 Mar 2003 (SI 2003/333) |
| para 27 | 24 Feb 2003 (repeals of or in Proceeds of Crime Act 1995, s 15(2)) (SI 2003/120) |
| | 24 Mar 2003 (otherwise) (SI 2003/333) |
| para 28(1) | See sub-ss (2)–(6) below |
| para 28(2)(a) | 24 Feb 2003 (repeals of or in Proceeds of Crime (Scotland) Act 1995, ss 18–20) (SI 2003/120) |
| | 24 Mar 2003 (otherwise) (SSI 2003/210)[5] |
| para 28(2)(b)–(d) | 24 Mar 2003 (SSI 2003/210)[5] |
| para 28(2)(e) | 24 Mar 2003 (SI 2003/333) |
| para 28(2)(f) | 24 Mar 2003 (SSI 2003/210)[5] |
| para 28(2)(g) | 24 Mar 2003 (SI 2003/333) |
| para 28(2)(h)–(k) | 24 Mar 2003 (SSI 2003/210)[5] |
| para 28(3)–(6) | 24 Mar 2003 (SSI 2003/210)[5] |
| para 29 | 24 Mar 2003 (SSI 2003/210)[5] |
| para 30 | 24 Feb 2003 (SI 2003/120) |
| para 31(1) | 24 Feb 2003 (SI 2003/120) |
| para 31(2) | 24 Feb 2003 (repeals of or in Proceeds of Crime (Northern Ireland) Order 1996, SI 1996/1299 (NI 9), Part III) (SI 2003/120) |
| | 24 Mar 2003 (repeals of or in Proceeds of Crime (Northern Ireland) Order 1996, SI 1996/1299 (NI 9), arts 4–41) (SI 2003/333) |
| | *Not yet in force* (repeals of Proceeds of Crime (Northern Ireland) Order 1996, SI 1996/1299 (NI 9), Pt II, arts 42, 43) |
| para 31(3)(a), (b) | 24 Mar 2003 (SI 2003/333) |
| para 31(3)(c) | 24 Feb 2003 (SI 2003/120)[2, 4] |

**Proceeds of Crime Act 2002 (c 29)**—*contd*

|  |  |
|---|---|
| para 31(3)(d)–(h) | 24 Feb 2003 (SI 2003/120)[2] |
| para 31(4)–(18) | 24 Feb 2003 (SI 2003/120) |
| para 32 | 24 Mar 2003 (SI 2003/333) |
| para 33 | 24 Mar 2003 (SSI 2003/210)[5] |
| paras 34, 35 | 24 Feb 2003 (SI 2003/120) |
| para 36 | 30 Dec 2002 (SI 2002/3015) |
| para 37 | 24 Mar 2003 (SI 2003/333) |
| para 38 | 24 Feb 2003 (SI 2003/120) |
| para 39 | 24 Mar 2003 (except so far as relates to Pt 3 of this Act) (SI 2003/333) |
|  | 24 Mar 2003 (exception noted above) (SSI 2003/210) |
| para 40 | 24 Feb 2003 (SI 2003/120) |
| Sch 12 | 30 Dec 2002 (repeals of or in Drug Trafficking Act 1994, ss 42–48) (SI 2002/3015)[1] |

24 Feb 2003 (SI 2003/120)[2], repeals of or in—
Misuse of Drugs Act 1971;
Criminal Justice Act 1988, ss 93A–93J;
Extradition Act 1989;
Criminal Justice (International Co-operation) Act 1990, s 14;
Criminal Justice Act 1993, ss 29–33, 35, Schs 4, 5;
Drug Trafficking Act 1994, ss 49–56, 59–61;
Criminal Law (Consolidation) Scotland Act 1995, ss 31–40, 42;
Proceeds of Crime Act 1995, ss 11–13, 15(2);
Proceeds of Crime (Scotland) Act 1995, ss 18–20;
Proceeds of Crime (Northern Ireland) Order 1996,
  SI 1996/1299 (NI 9), Pt III, arts 49, 52, 54–56, Sch 2;
Access to Justice Act 1999, Sch 2;
Financial Investigations (Northern Ireland) Order 2001,
  SI 2001/1866 (NI 1)

24 Mar 2003 (SI 2003/333)[3], repeals of or in—
Criminal Appeal (Northern Ireland) Act 1980;
Police and Criminal Evidence Act 1984;
Criminal Justice Act 1988, ss 71–89, 94, 99–102;
Housing Act 1988;
Police and Criminal Evidence (Northern Ireland) Order 1989,
  SI 1989/1341 (NI 12);
Criminal Justice (International Co-operation Act 1990, s 13;
Criminal Justice (Confiscation) (Northern Ireland) Order 1990,
  SI 1990/2588 (NI 17);
Criminal Justice Act 1993, ss 21, 27, 28, 34;
Drug Trafficking Act 1994, ss 1–38, 41, 62–64, 68, Sch 1;
Criminal Procedure (Consequential Provisions) (Scotland)
  Act 1995, Sch 4;
Proceeds of Crime Act 1995, ss 15(1), (3), 16, Sch 1;
Private International Law (Miscellaneous Provisions) Act 1995;
Proceeds of Crime (Scotland) Act 1995, ss 35–39, 40, 42;
Proceeds of Crime (Northern Ireland) Order 1996,
  SI 1996/1299 (NI 9), arts 4–41;
Justices of the Peace Act 1997;
Crime and Disorder Act 1998, s 83, Schs 8, 9;
Access to Justice Act 1999, Sch 13;
Powers of Criminal Courts (Sentencing) Act 2000;
Terrorism Act 2000, Sch 15, paras 6, 10;
Criminal Justice and Police Act 2001
24 Mar 2003 (SSI 2003/210)[5], repeals of or in—
Criminal Justice (International Co-operation) Act 1990, Sch 4;
Criminal Law (Consolidation) (Scotland) Act 1995, ss 41, 43;
Criminal Procedure (Consequential Provisions) (Scotland)
  Act 1995, Sch 3;

**Proceeds of Crime Act 2002 (c 29)**—*contd*

> Proceeds of Crime (Scotland) Act 1995;
> Crime and Punishment (Scotland) Act 1997;
> Terrorism Act 2000, Sch 15, para 11(2)
> *Not yet in force*, repeals of or in—
> Criminal Justice Act 1988, ss 96, 97, 172;
> Criminal Justice and Public Order Act 1994;
> Drug Trafficking Act 1994, ss 39, 40;
> Proceeds of Crime (Northern Ireland) Order 1996,
>   SI 1996/1299 (NI 9), Pt II, arts 42, 43, Sch 3, paras 1–3, 18;
> Land Registration Act 2002;
> Proceeds of Crime Act 2002

[1]   For savings, see SI 2002/3015, art 3

[2]   For transitional provisions and savings, see SI 2003/120, arts 3–7

[3]   For transitional provisions and savings, see SI 2003/333, arts 3–13

[4]   SI 2003/333 also purports to bring this provision into force on 24 Mar 2003

[5]   For transitional provisions and savings, see SSI 2003/210, arts 3–7

**Protection of Wild Mammals (Scotland) Act 2002 (asp 6)**

*RA:* 15 Mar 2002

*Commencement provisions:* s 12; Protection of Wild Mammals (Scotland) Act 2002 (Commencement) Order 2002, SSI 2002/181

| | |
|---|---|
| 1–11 | 1 Aug 2002 (SSI 2002/181) |
| 12 | 15 Mar 2002 (RA) |
| Schedule | 1 Aug 2002 (SSI 2002/181) |

**Public Trustee (Liability and Fees) Act 2002 (c 35)**

*RA:* 7 Nov 2002

Whole Act in force 7 Nov 2002 (RA)

**School Education (Amendment) (Scotland) Act 2002 (asp 2)**

*RA:* 22 Jan 2002

*Commencement provisions:* s 3(2); School Education (Amendment) (Scotland) Act 2002 (Commencement) Order 2002, SSI 2002/74

| | |
|---|---|
| 1 | 26 Feb 2002 (SSI 2002/74) |
| 2 | 22 Mar 2002 (SSI 2002/74) |
| 3 | 22 Jan 2002 (RA) |

**Scottish Local Government (Elections) Act 2002 (asp 1)**

*RA:* 22 Jan 2002

Whole Act in force 22 Jan 2002 (RA)

## Scottish Parliamentary Standards Commissioner Act 2002 (asp 16)

*RA:* 30 Jul 2002

*Commencement provisions:* s 21(2)

| | |
|---|---|
| 1 | 31 Jul 2002 (s 21(2)(a)) |
| 2–19 | 30 Dec 2002 (s 21(2)(b)) |
| 20, 21 | 31 Jul 2002 (s 21(2)(a)) |
| Schedule | 31 Jul 2002 (s 21(2)(a)) |

## Scottish Public Services Ombudsman Act 2002 (asp 11)

*RA:* 23 Apr 2002

*Commencement provisions:* s 27(1); Scottish Public Services Ombudsman Act 2002 (Commencement and Revocation of Transitory and Transitional Provisions) Order 2002, SSI 2002/467

| | | |
|---|---|---|
| 1 | | 23 Apr 2002 (RA) |
| 2–22 | | 23 Oct 2002 (SSI 2002/467) |
| 23, 24 | | 23 Apr 2002 (RA) |
| 25 | | 23 Oct 2002 (SSI 2002/467) |
| 26 | (1) | 23 Oct 2002 (SSI 2002/467) |
| | (2) | 23 Apr 2002 (RA) |
| 27 | | 23 Apr 2002 (RA) |
| Sch 1 | | 23 Apr 2002 (RA) |
| Schs 2–7 | | 23 Oct 2002 (SSI 2002/467) |

## Scottish Qualifications Authority Act 2002 (asp 14)

*RA:* 6 Jun 2002

*Commencement provisions:* s 6(2); Scottish Qualifications Authority Act 2002 (Commencement No 1) Order 2002, SSI 2002/355; Scottish Qualifications Authority Act 2002 (Commencement No 2) Order 2004, SSI 2004/347

| | | |
|---|---|---|
| 1 | (1)–(6) | 19 Aug 2002 (SSI 2002/355) |
| | (7)(a) | 19 Aug 2002 (SSI 2002/355) |
| | (7)(b) | 31 Aug 2004 (SSI 2004/347) |
| | (8), (9) | 19 Aug 2002 (SSI 2002/355) |
| 2–5 | | 7 Aug 2002 (SSI 2002/355) |
| 6 | | 6 Jun 2002 (RA) |

## Sex Discrimination (Election Candidates) Act 2002 (c 2)

*RA:* 26 Feb 2002

Whole Act in force 26 Feb 2002 (RA)

## Sexual Offences (Procedure and Evidence) (Scotland) Act 2002 (asp 9)

*RA:* 11 Apr 2002

*Commencement provisions:* s 11(2); Sexual Offences (Procedure and Evidence) (Scotland) Act 2002 (Commencement and Transitional Provisions) Order 2002, SSI 2002/443

| | |
|---|---|
| 1–10 | 1 Nov 2002 (SSI 2002/443)[1] |
| 11 | 11 Apr 2002 (RA) |
| Schedule | 1 Nov 2002 (SSI 2002/443)[1] |

[1]  For transitional provisions and savings, see SSI 2002/443, art 4

## State Pension Credit Act 2002 (c 16)

*RA:* 25 Jun 2002

*Commencement provisions:* s 22(2), (3); State Pension Credit Act 2002 (Commencement No 1) Order 2002, SI 2002/1691; State Pension Credit Act (Commencement No 2) Order 2002, SI 2002/2248; State Pension Credit Act 2002 (Commencement No 3) Order 2003, SI 2003/83; State Pension Credit Act 2002 (Commencement No 4) Order 2003, SI 2003/966; State Pension Credit Act 2002 (Commencement No 5) and Appointed Day Order 2003, SI 2003/1766

| | | |
|---|---|---|
| 1–7 | | 2 Jul 2002 (for the purposes of making regulations or orders) (SI 2002/1691) |
| | | 6 Oct 2003 (otherwise) (SI 2003/1766) |
| 8 | | 6 Oct 2003 (SI 2003/1766) |
| 9 | | 2 Jul 2002 (for the purposes of making regulations or orders) (SI 2002/1691) |
| | | 6 Oct 2003 (otherwise) (SI 2003/1766) |
| 10 | | 6 Oct 2003 (SI 2003/1766) |
| 11 | | See Sch 1 below |
| 12, 13 | | 2 Jul 2002 (for the purposes of making regulations or orders) (SI 2002/1691) |
| | | 6 Oct 2003 (otherwise) (SI 2003/1766) |
| 14 | | See Sch 2 below |
| 15–17 | | 2 Jul 2002 (for the purposes of making regulations or orders) (SI 2002/1691) |
| | | 6 Oct 2003 (otherwise) (SI 2003/1766) |
| 18 | | 3 Sep 2002 (SI 2002/2248) |
| 19, 20 | | 25 Jun 2002 (RA) |
| 21 | | See Sch 3 below |
| 22 | | 25 Jun 2002 (RA) |
| Sch 1 | paras 1–7 | 2 Jul 2002 (for the purposes of making regulations or orders) (SI 2002/1691) |
| | | 7 Apr 2003 (otherwise) (SI 2003/966) |
| | paras 8, 9 | 2 Jul 2002 (for the purposes of making regulations or orders) (SI 2002/1691) |
| | | 6 Oct 2003 (otherwise) (SI 2003/1766) |
| | para 10 | 2 Jul 2002 (for the purposes of making regulations or orders) (SI 2002/1691) |
| | | 7 Apr 2003 (otherwise) (SI 2003/966) |
| | para 11 | 2 Jul 2002 (for the purposes of making regulations or orders) (SI 2002/1691) |
| | | 6 Oct 2003 (otherwise) (SI 2003/1766) |
| | para 12 | 2 Jul 2002 (for the purposes of making regulations or orders) (SI 2002/1691) |
| | | 7 Apr 2003 (otherwise) (SI 2003/966) |
| Sch 2 | paras 1, 2 | 2 Jul 2002 (for the purposes of making regulations or orders) (SI 2002/1691) |
| | | 6 Oct 2003 (otherwise) (SI 2003/1766) |
| | para 3 | 27 Jan 2003 (for the purpose of making regulations) (SI 2003/83) |
| | | 6 Oct 2003 (otherwise) (SI 2003/1766) |
| | paras 4–49 | 2 Jul 2002 (for the purposes of making regulations or orders) (SI 2002/1691) |
| | | 6 Oct 2003 (otherwise) (SI 2003/1766) |
| Sch 3 | | 7 Apr 2003 (repeals in Social Security Act 1998, ss 2(2), 11(3), 28(3)) (SI 2003/966) |
| | | 6 Oct 2003 (otherwise) (SI 2003/1766) |

## Tax Credits Act 2002 (c 21)

*RA:* 8 Jul 2002

*Commencement provisions:* s 61; Tax Credits Act 2002 (Commencement No 1) Order 2002, SI 2002/1727, as amended by SI 2002/2158; Tax Credits Act 2002 (Commencement No 2) Order 2003,

**Tax Credits Act 2002 (c 21)**—*contd*

SI 2003/392; Tax Credits Act 2002 (Commencement No 3 and Transitional Provisions and Savings) Order 2003, SI 2003/938; Tax Credits Act 2002 (Commencement No 4, Transitional Provisions and Savings) Order 2003, SI 2003/962, as amended by SI 2006/3369, SI 2008/3151, SI 2011/2910, SI 2014/1848

| | | |
|---|---|---|
| 1 | (1), (2) | 9 Jul 2002 (for all purposes of Pt 1 and, as respects tax credits, Pt 3) (SI 2002/1727) |
| | | *Not yet in force* (otherwise) |
| | (3)(a) | 6 Apr 2003 (SI 2003/962)[4] |
| | (3)(b), (c) | 8 Apr 2003 (SI 2003/962)[4] |
| | (3)(d) | *Not yet in force* |
| | (3)(e) | 6 Apr 2003 (SI 2003/938) |
| | (3)(f) | 6 Apr 2003 (SI 2003/962)[4] |
| 2 | | 9 Jul 2002 (for all purposes of Pt I and, as respects tax credits, Pt 3) (SI 2002/1727) |
| 3 | (1) | 9 Jul 2002 (for the purposes of making regulations about claims) (SI 2002/1727) |
| | | 1 Aug 2002 (for the purposes of making claims) (SI 2002/1727) |
| | | 1 Jan 2003 (for the purposes of making decisions on claims) (SI 2002/1727) |
| | | 6 Apr 2003 (for all other purposes of Pt 1 and, as respects tax credits, Pt 3) (SI 2002/1727) |
| | (2) | 1 Jan 2003 (for all purposes of Pt 1 and, as respects tax credits, Pt 3) (SI 2002/1727) |
| | (3) | 9 Jul 2002 (for the purposes of making regulations about claims) (SI 2002/1727) |
| | | 1 Aug 2002 (for the purposes of making claims) (SI 2002/1727) |
| | | 1 Jan 2003 (for the purposes of making decisions on claims) (SI 2002/1727) |
| | | 6 Apr 2003 (for all other purposes of Pt 1 and, as respects tax credits, Pt 3) (SI 2002/1727) |
| | (4) | 1 Aug 2002 (for the purposes of entitlement to make a claim) (SI 2002/1727) |
| | (5)–(8) | 9 Jul 2002 (for all purposes of Pt 1 and, as respects tax credits, Pt 3) (SI 2002/1727) |
| 4 | (1) | 9 Jul 2002 (SI 2002/1727) |
| | (2) | 1 Aug 2002 (SI 2002/1727) |
| 5 | (1) | 1 Jan 2003 (for the purposes of making regulations) (SI 2002/1727) |
| | (2) | 6 Apr 2003 (SI 2002/1727) |
| | (3) | 1 Jan 2003 (for the purposes of making decisions on claims made before the beginning of the tax year) (SI 2002/1727) |
| | | 6 Apr 2003 (for the purposes of making decisions on other claims) (SI 2002/1727) |
| 6 | | 9 Jul 2002 (SI 2002/1727) |
| 7 | (1)–(5) | 9 Jul 2002 (for the purposes of making regulations) (SI 2002/1727)[1] |
| | | 1 Aug 2002 (for the purposes of making claims) (SI 2002/1727)[1] |
| | | 1 Jan 2003 (for the purposes of making decisions on claims) (SI 2002/1727)[1] |
| | | 6 Apr 2003 (for the purposes of entitlement to payment of an award) (SI 2002/1727)[1] |
| | (6)–(9) | 9 Jul 2002 (for the purposes of making regulations) (SI 2002/1727) |
| | (10) | 1 Aug 2002 (for the purposes of estimating income for the purposes of making, amending or terminating awards) (SI 2002/1727) |
| 8–11 | | 9 Jul 2002 (for the purposes of making regulations) (SI 2002/1727) |
| | | 1 Aug 2002 (for the purposes of making claims) (SI 2002/1727) |
| | | 1 Jan 2003 (for the purposes of making decisions on claims) (SI 2002/1727) |
| | | 6 Apr 2003 (for the purposes of entitlement to payment of an award) (SI 2002/1727) |

**Tax Credits Act 2002 (c 21)**—*contd*

| | | |
|---|---|---|
| 12 | (1)–(4) | 9 Jul 2002 (for the purposes of making regulations) (SI 2002/1727) |
| | | 1 Aug 2002 (for the purposes of making claims) (SI 2002/1727) |
| | | 1 Jan 2003 (for the purposes of making decisions on claims) (SI 2002/1727) |
| | | 6 Apr 2003 (for the purposes of entitlement to payment of award) (SI 2002/1727) |
| | (5) | 9 Jul 2002 (for the purposes of making regulations and schemes) (SI 2002/1727) |
| | | 1 Aug 2002 (for the purposes of making claims) (SI 2002/1727) |
| | | 1 Jan 2003 (for the purposes of making decisions on claims) (SI 2002/1727) |
| | | 6 Apr 2003 (for the purposes of entitlement to payment of an award) (SI 2002/1727) |
| | (6)–(8) | 9 Jul 2002 (for the purposes of making schemes) (SI 2002/1727) |
| 13 | | 9 Jul 2002 (for the purposes of making regulations) (SI 2002/1727) |
| | | 1 Aug 2002 (for the purposes of making claims) (SI 2002/1727) |
| | | 1 Jan 2003 (for the purposes of making decisions on claims) (SI 2002/1727) |
| | | 6 Apr 2003 (for the purposes of entitlement to payment of an award) (SI 2002/1727) |
| 14 | (1) | 1 Jan 2003 (for the purposes of making decisions on claims) (SI 2002/1727) |
| | (2) | 9 Jul 2002 (for the purposes of making regulations) (SI 2002/1727) |
| | | 1 Aug 2002 (for the purposes of dealing with claims) (SI 2002/1727) |
| | (3) | 1 Jan 2003 (for the purposes of making decisions on claims) (SI 2002/1727) |
| 15 | (1) | 1 Jan 2003 (for the purposes of making decisions on whether to amend awards) (SI 2002/1727) |
| | (2) | 9 Jul 2002 (for the purposes of making regulations) (SI 2002/1727) |
| | | 1 Aug 2002 (for the purposes of dealing with notifications of change of circumstances) (SI 2002/1727) |
| 16 | (1) | 1 Jan 2003 (SI 2002/1727) |
| | (2) | 1 Jan 2003 (for the purposes of giving notice under sub-ss (2), (3)) (SI 2002/1727) |
| | (3) | 9 Jul 2002 (for the purposes of making regulations) (SI 2002/1727) |
| | | 1 Jan 2003 (for the purposes of giving notice under sub-ss (2), (3)) (SI 2002/1727) |
| 17 | (1)–(9) | 6 Apr 2003 (for the purposes of giving final notice on an award) (SI 2002/1727) |
| | (10) | 9 Jul 2002 (for the purposes of making regulations) (SI 2002/1727) |
| 18 | | 6 Apr 2003 (for the purposes of making decisions after final notice) (SI 2002/1727) |
| 19 | (1) | 6 Apr 2003 (for the purposes of enquiring into awards) (SI 2002/1727) |
| | (2) | 9 Jul 2002 (for the purposes of making regulations) (SI 2002/1727) |
| | | 6 Apr 2003 (for the purposes of enquiring into awards) (SI 2002/1727) |
| | (3)–(12) | 6 Apr 2003 (for the purposes of enquiring into awards) (SI 2002/1727) |
| 20 | | 6 Apr 2003 (for the purposes of making decisions under sub-ss (1), (4)) (SI 2002/1727) |
| 21, 22 | | 9 Jul 2002 (SI 2002/1727) |
| 23 | | 1 Jan 2003 (for the purposes of giving notices of decisions under ss 14(1), 15(1), 16(1), and of revised decisions under those sections by virtue of regulations under s 21) (SI 2002/1727) |
| | | 6 Apr 2003 (for the purposes of giving notices of decisions under ss 18(1), (5), (6), (9), 19(3), 20(1), (4), and of revised decisions under those sections by virtue of regulations under s 21) (SI 2002/1727) |

See Halsbury's Statutes Citator for amendments to these Acts     1377

**Tax Credits Act 2002 (c 21)**—*contd*

| | | |
|---|---|---|
| 24 | | 9 Jul 2002 (for the purposes of making regulations) (SI 2002/1727) |
| | | 1 Aug 2002 (for the purposes of making claims) (SI 2002/1727) |
| | | 1 Jan 2003 (for the purposes of making decisions on claims) (SI 2002/1727) |
| | | 6 Apr 2003 (for the purposes of entitlement to payment of an award) (SI 2002/1727) |
| 25 | (1), (2) | 9 Jul 2002 (for the purposes of making regulations) (SI 2002/1727) |
| | | *Not yet in force* (otherwise) |
| | (3), (4) | 6 Apr 2003 (for the purposes of the power to call for documents etc in relation to employer's compliance with regulations under s 25) (SI 2002/1727) |
| | (5) | 9 Jul 2002 (for the purposes of making regulations) (SI 2002/1727) |
| | | 6 Apr 2003 (for the purposes of power to call for documents etc in relation to employer's compliance with regulations under s 25) (SI 2002/1727) |
| | (6), (7) | 9 Jul 2002 (for the purposes of making regulations) (SI 2002/1727) |
| | | *Never in force* (otherwise) (repealed) |
| 26 | | 1 Jan 2003 (SI 2002/1727) |
| 27 | | See Sch 1 below |
| 28, 29 | | 6 Apr 2003 (SI 2002/1727) |
| 30 | | 1 Jan 2003 (for the purposes of making regulations) (SI 2002/1727) |
| | | 6 Apr 2003 (for the purposes of liability to repay overpayments or to be paid full entitlement where underpayment) (SI 2002/1727) |
| 31 | | 1 Aug 2002 (for the purposes of imposition of penalties for incorrect statement or declaration in or in connection with a claim for a tax credit or a notification given in accordance with regulations under s 6, or for incorrect information or evidence in response to a requirement imposed by virtue of regulations under s 25) (SI 2002/1727) |
| | | 1 Jan 2003 (for the purposes of the imposition of penalties for incorrect information or evidence in response to a requirement imposed by virtue of ss 14(2), 15(2) or 16(3)) (SI 2002/1727) |
| | | 6 Apr 2003 (for the purposes of imposition of penalties for incorrect information or evidence in response to a requirement imposed by virtue of ss 18(10) or 19(2), or for incorrect statement or declaration in response to a notice under s 17) (SI 2002/1727) |
| 32 | | 1 Aug 2002 (for the purposes of the imposition of penalty for failure to provide information or evidence required by regulations under s 25, or for failure to give notification required by regulations under s 6(3)) (SI 2002/1727) |
| | | 1 Jan 2003 (for the purposes of the imposition of penalty for failure to provide information or evidence under ss 14(2), 15(2) or 16(3)) (SI 2002/1727) |
| | | 6 Apr 2003 (for the purposes of imposition of penalty for failure to provide information or evidence under ss 18(10) or 19(2), or to comply with requirement imposed by notice under s 17 by virtue of s 17(2)(a), (4)(a) or (6)(a)) (SI 2002/1727) |
| 33 | | 6 Apr 2003 (SI 2002/1727) |
| 34 | | See Sch 2 below |
| 35 | | 1 Aug 2002 (for the purposes of instituting criminal proceedings for fraud in connection with obtaining payments of a tax credit) (SI 2002/1727) |
| 36 | | 1 Aug 2002 (for the purposes of the obtaining of documents in relation to offences involving fraud or serious fraud in connection with, or in relation to, tax credits) (SI 2002/1727) |
| 37 | (1) | 6 Apr 2003 (SI 2002/1727) |
| | (2) | 9 Jul 2002 (for the purposes of making regulations to prescribe rates of interest) (SI 2002/1727) |

**Tax Credits Act 2002 (c 21)**—*contd*

6 Apr 2003 (for the purposes of interest on overpayment of a tax credit) (SI 2002/1727)

(3), (4)    6 Apr 2003 (SI 2002/1727)

(5)    9 Jul 2002 (for the purposes of making regulations to prescribe rates of interest) (SI 2002/1727)

1 Aug 2002 (for the purposes of interest on penalties under s 31 for incorrect statement or declaration in or in connection with a claim for a tax credit or a notification given in accordance with regulations under s 6, or for incorrect information or evidence in response to a requirement imposed by virtue of regulations under s 25 and for the purposes of interest on penalties under s 32 for failure to provide information or evidence required by regulations under s 25, or for failure to give notification required by regulations under s 6(3)) (SI 2002/1727)

1 Jan 2003 (for the purposes of interest on penalties under s 31 for incorrect information or evidence in response to a requirement imposed by virtue of ss 14(2), 15(2), or 16(3), and for the purposes of interest on penalties under s 32 for failure to provide information or evidence under ss 14(2), 15(2) or 16(3)) (SI 2002/1727)

6 Apr 2003 (for the purposes of interest on penalties under s 31 for incorrect information or evidence in response to a requirement imposed by virtue of ss 18(10) or 19(2), or for incorrect statement or declaration in response to a notice under s 17 and for the purposes of interest on penalties under s 32 for failure to provide information or evidence under ss 18(10) or 19(2), or to comply with requirement imposed by notice under s 17 by virtue of sub-ss (2)(a), (4)(a) or (6)(a) of that section, and for the purposes of interest on penalties under s 33 for failure by employer to make correct payment to employee) (SI 2002/1727)

(6)    1 Aug 2002 (for the purposes of interest on penalties under s 31 for incorrect statement or declaration in or in connection with a claim for a tax credit or a notification given in accordance with regulations under s 6, or for incorrect information or evidence in response to a requirement imposed by virtue of regulations under s 25 and for the purposes of interest on penalties under s 32 for failure to provide information or evidence required by regulations under s 25, or for failure to give notification required by regulations under s 6(3)) (SI 2002/1727)

1 Jan 2003 (for the purposes of interest on penalties under s 31 for incorrect information or evidence in response to a requirement imposed by virtue of ss 14(2), 15(2), or 16(3), and for the purposes of interest on penalties under s 32 for failure to provide information or evidence under ss 14(2), 15(2) or 16(3)) (SI 2002/1727)

6 Apr 2003 (for the purposes of interest on overpayment of a tax credit, for the purposes of interest on penalties under s 31 for incorrect information or evidence in response to a requirement imposed by virtue of ss 18(10) or 19(2), or for incorrect statement or declaration in response to a notice under s 17 and for the purposes of interest on penalties under s 32 for failure to provide information or evidence under ss 18(10) or 19(2), or to comply with requirement imposed by notice under s 17 by virtue of sub-ss (2)(a), (4)(a) or (6)(a) of that section, and for the purposes of interest on penalties under s 33 for failure by employer to make correct payment to employee) (SI 2002/1727)

**Tax Credits Act 2002 (c 21)**—*contd*

| | |
|---|---|
| 38, 39 | 1 Sep 2002 (for the purposes of appeal against determination of penalty under Sch 2, para 1 where the penalty is imposed under s 31 for incorrect statement or declaration in or in connection with a claim for a tax credit or a notification given in accordance with regulations under s 6, or for incorrect information or evidence in response to a requirement imposed by virtue of regulations under s 25 and for the purposes of appeal against determination of penalty under Sch 2, para 1 where the penalty is imposed under s 32(2)(b) or (3) for failure to provide information or evidence required by regulations under s 25, or for failure to give notification required by regulations under s 6(3)) (SI 2002/1727) |
| | 1 Jan 2003 (for the purposes of appeal against determination of penalty under Sch 2, para 1 where the penalty is imposed under s 31 for incorrect information or evidence in response to a requirement imposed by virtue of ss 14(2), 15(2) or 16(3) and for the purposes of appeal against determination of penalty under Sch 2, para 1 where the penalty is imposed under s 32(2)(b) for failure to provide information or evidence under ss 14(2), 15(2) or 16(3) and for the purposes of appeal against a decision under ss 14(1), 15(1) or 16(1), or under regulations under s 21) (SI 2002/1727) |
| | 6 Apr 2003 (otherwise) (SI 2002/1727) |
| 40 | 6 Apr 2004 (for the purposes of making of annual report by the Board to the Treasury) (SI 2002/1727) |
| 41 | 6 Apr 2003 (for the purposes of the review of prescribed monetary amounts) (SI 2002/1727) |
| 42–44 | 9 Jul 2002 (SI 2002/1727) |
| 45 | 1 Jan 2003 (for all purposes of Pt 1 and, as respects tax credits, Pt 3) (SI 2002/1727) |
| 46 | 1 Aug 2002 (for all purposes of Pt 1 and, as respects tax credits, Pt 3) (SI 2002/1727) |
| 47 | See Sch 3 below |
| 48 | 9 Jul 2002 (for all purposes of Pt 1) (SI 2002/1727) |
| 49, 50 | 1 Apr 2003 (for the purposes of the transfer of functions etc in relation to child benefit and guardian's allowance, other than functions of making subordinate legislation, and minor amendments) (SI 2003/392) |
| | 7 Apr 2003 (for the purposes of entitlement to payment of child benefit and guardian's allowance) (SI 2003/392) |
| 51 | See Sch 4 below |
| 52, 53 | 26 Feb 2003 (for the purposes of making subordinate legislation in relation to child benefit and guardian's allowance) (SI 2003/392) |
| | 1 Apr 2003 (for the purposes of the transfer of functions etc in relation to child benefit and guardian's allowance, other than functions of making subordinate legislation, and minor amendments) (SI 2003/392) |
| | 7 Apr 2003 (for the purposes of entitlement to payment of child benefit and guardian's allowance) (SI 2003/392) |
| 54 (1), (2) | 8 Jul 2002 (RA) |
| (3)–(10) | 26 Feb 2003 (for the purposes of making subordinate legislation in relation to child benefit and guardian's allowance) (SI 2003/392) |
| | 1 Apr 2003 (for the purposes of the transfer of functions etc in relation to child benefit and guardian's allowance, other than functions of making subordinate legislation, and minor amendments) (SI 2003/392) |
| | 7 Apr 2003 (for the purposes of entitlement to payment of child benefit and guardian's allowance) (SI 2003/392) |

**Tax Credits Act 2002 (c 21)**—*contd*

| | |
|---|---|
| 55–57 | 26 Feb 2003 (for the purposes of making subordinate legislation in relation to child benefit and guardian's allowance) (SI 2003/392)[2] |
| | 1 Apr 2003 (for the purposes of the transfer of functions etc in relation to child benefit and guardian's allowance, other than functions of making subordinate legislation, and minor amendments) (SI 2003/392) |
| | 7 Apr 2003 (for the purposes of entitlement to payment of child benefit and guardian's allowance) (SI 2003/392) |
| 58 | 9 Jul 2002 (for the purposes of making regulations in relation to tax credits only) (SI 2002/1727) |
| | 26 Feb 2003 (for the purposes of making regulations in relation to child benefit and guardian's allowance) (SI 2003/392) |
| 59 | See Sch 5 below |
| 60 | See Sch 6 below |
| 61–70 | 8 Jul 2002 (RA) |
| Sch 1 | 1 Sep 2002 (for the purposes of rights conferred on employees by virtue of regulations under s 25) (SI 2002/1727) |
| Sch 2 | 1 Aug 2002 (for the purposes of imposition of penalties under s 31 for incorrect statement or declaration in or in connection with a claim for a tax credit or a notification given in accordance with regulations under s 6, or for incorrect information or evidence in response to a requirement imposed by regulations under s 25; mitigation of such penalties, appeals against such penalties and recovery of such penalties and for the purposes of the imposition of penalties under s 32(2)(b) or (3) for failure to provide information or evidence required by regulations under s 25, or for failure to give notification required by regulations under s 6(3); bringing of proceedings for penalties under s 32(2)(a) before Commissioners for failure to provide information or evidence required by regulations under s 25; mitigation of such penalties, appeals against such penalties and recovery of such penalties) (SI 2002/1727) |
| | 1 Jan 2003 (for the purposes of imposition of penalties under s 31 for incorrect information or evidence in response to a requirement imposed by virtue of ss 14(2), 15(2) or 16(3); mitigation of such penalties, appeals against such penalties and recovery of such penalties and for the purposes of imposition of penalties under s 32(2)(b) for failure to provide information or evidence under ss 14(2), 15(2) or 16(3); bringing of proceedings for such penalties under s 32(2)(a) before Commissioners; mitigation of such penalties, appeals against such penalties and recovery of such penalties) (SI 2002/1727) |
| | 6 Apr 2003 (for the purposes of imposition of penalties under s 31 for incorrect information or evidence in response to a requirement imposed by virtue of ss 18(10) or 19(2), or for incorrect statement or declaration in response to a notice under s 17; mitigation of such penalties, appeals against such penalties and recovery of such penalties and for the purposes of imposition of penalties under s 32(2)(b) for failure to provide information or evidence under ss 18(10) or 19(2), or for failure to comply with requirement imposed by notice under s 17 of the Act by virtue of sub-ss (2)(a), (4)(a) or (6)(a) of that section; bringing of proceedings for such penalties under s 32(2)(a) before Commissioners; mitigation of such penalties, appeals against such penalties and recovery of such penalties and for the purposes of imposition of penalties under s 33 for failure by employer to make correct payment to employee; mitigation of such penalties, appeals against such penalties and recovery of such penalties) (SI 2002/1727) |
| Sch 3   paras 1–3 | 6 Apr 2003 (SI 2003/962)[4] |

**Tax Credits Act 2002 (c 21)**—*contd*

|  | paras 4–7 | 1 Apr 2003 (SI 2003/962)[4] |
|  | paras 8, 9 | 6 Apr 2003 (SI 2003/962)[4] |
|  | paras 10–12 | 8 Apr 2003 (SI 2003/962)[4] |
|  | paras 13–59 | 6 Apr 2003 (SI 2003/962)[4] |

Sch 4      26 Feb 2003 (for the purposes of making subordinate legislation in relation to child benefit and guardian's allowance) (SI 2003/392)

1 Apr 2003 (for the purposes of the transfer of functions etc in relation to child benefit and guardian's allowance, other than functions of making subordinate legislation, and minor amendments) (SI 2003/392)

7 Apr 2003 (for the purposes of entitlement to payment of child benefit and guardian's allowance) (SI 2003/392)

Sch 5      1 Aug 2002 (for all purposes of Pt 1 and, as respects tax credits, Pt 3) (SI 2002/1727)

26 Feb 2003 (for the purposes of making regulations in relation to the use and disclosure of information in connection with child benefit and guardian's allowance) (SI 2003/392)

1 Apr 2003 (for the purposes of the use and disclosure of information relating to child benefit and guardian's allowance) (SI 2003/392)

Sch 6      27 Aug 2002 (repeals of or in Tax Credits Act 1999, s 6 (and regulations made thereunder) for the purposes of awards of working families' tax credit and disabled person's tax credit commencing on or after 27 Aug 2002) (SI 2002/1727)

The day immediately following the expiry of the period of 26 weeks from the date of commencement of an award of a tax credit for a period commencing on or after 6 Apr 2003 (repeals of or in Tax Credits Act 1999, s 6 (and regulations made thereunder) for the purposes of awards of working families' tax credit and disabled person's tax credit that commence on or after 4 Jun 2002 but before 27 Aug 2002 and are existing on 27 Aug 2002) (SI 2002/1727)

26 Feb 2003 (repeal in Social Security Administration Act 1992, s 189(1)) (SI 2003/392)

1 Apr 2003 (SI 2003/392), repeals of or in—

Social Security Contributions and Benefits Act 1992, ss 145(5), 175(1A);

Social Security Administration Act 1992, s 154(2)(b), (c);

Social Security Contributions and Benefits (Northern Ireland) Act 1992, ss 141(5), 172;

Social Security Administration (Northern Ireland) Act 1992, s 134(2)(b), (c)

6 Apr 2003 (SI 2003/938)[3], repeals of or in—

Social Security Contributions and Benefits Act 1992, ss 20(1), 30B(3), 56(1), 60(6), 61(1), (2), 63(c), (f)(i), 77(1), 78(4)(d), 80, 81, 89, 90, 91(1)(b), Sch 4, Pt 4, Sch 5, para 2(5)(b);

Social Security Administration Act 1992, ss 3(3), 150(1)(f)

6 Apr 2003 (SI 2003/962)[4], repeals of or in—

Taxes Management Act 1970;

Income and Corporation Taxes Act 1988;

Children Act 1989;

Education Reform (Northern Ireland) Order 1989;

Child Support Act 1991;

Disability Living Allowance and Disability Working Allowance Act 1991;

Disability Living Allowance and Disability Working Allowance (Northern Ireland) Order 1991;

Child Support (Northern Ireland) Order 1991;

Local Government Finance Act 1992;

**Tax Credits Act 2002 (c 21)**—*contd*

Social Security Administration Act 1992, ss 3, 189;

Social Security Administration (Northern Ireland) Act 1992, s 3;

Social Security Contributions and Benefits Act 1992, ss 21, 45A;

Social Security Contributions and Benefits (Northern Ireland)
Act 1992, ss 20, 21, 30B, 45A, 56, 60, 61, 63, 77, 78, 80, 81,
89–91, Schs 4, 5;

Finance Act 1994;

Social Security (Incapacity for Work) Act 1994;

Social Security (Incapacity for Work) (Northern Ireland)
Order 1994;

Pensions Act 1995;

Pensions (Northern Ireland) Order 1995;

Employment Tribunals Act 1996;

Employment Rights (Northern Ireland) Order 1996;

Access to Justice Act 1999;

Finance Act 1999;

Welfare Reform and Pensions Act 1999;

Welfare Reform and Pensions (Northern Ireland) Order 1999;

Finance Act 2000;

Finance Act 2001

7 Apr 2003 (SI 2003/392), repeals of or in—

Social Security Contributions and Benefits Act 1992, Sch 9,
para 4;

Social Security Contributions and Benefits (Northern Ireland)
Act 1992, Sch 9, para 4

8 Apr 2003 (SI 2003/962)[4], repeals of or in—

Social Security Administration Act 1992, ss 5, 11, 71, 121DA,
124, 163, 179, 191;

Social Security Administration (Northern Ireland) Act 1992, ss 5,
9, 69, 115CA, 134, 155, 167;

Social Security Contributions and Benefits Act 1992, ss 122,
123, 128, 129, 135;

Social Security Contributions and Benefits (Northern Ireland)
Act 1992, ss 121, 122, 127, 128, 131;

Jobseekers Act 1995;

Jobseekers (Northern Ireland) Order 1995;

Finance Act 1997;

Social Security Act 1998;

Tax Credits (Initial Expenditure) Act 1998;

Social Security (Northern Ireland) Order 1998;

Employment Relations Act 1999;

Immigration and Asylum Act 1999;

Tax Credits Act 1999 (otherwise);

Employment Relations (Northern Ireland) Order 1999;

Government Resources and Accounts Act 2000;

Social Security Fraud Act 2001;

Social Security Fraud Act (Northern Ireland) 2001;

Criminal Injuries Compensation (Northern Ireland) Order 2002;

Employment Act 2002

*Not yet in force*, repeals of or in—

Social Security Act 1986;

Social Security Administration Act 1992, s 150(1)(h), (10)(b)(i),
(ii);

Children (Scotland) Act 1995;

Children (Northern Ireland) Order 1995, SI 1995/755 (NI 2);

Employment Rights Act 1996

---

[1]  For transitional provisions, see SI 2002/1727, art 3

[2]  For savings in relation to s 56, see SI 2003/392, art 3

**Tax Credits Act 2002 (c 21)**—*contd*

3   For transitional provisions and savings, see SI 2003/938, arts 3–5

4   For transitional provisions and savings, see SI 2003/962, arts 3–5

---

**Tobacco Advertising and Promotion Act 2002 (c 36)**

*RA:* 7 Nov 2002

*Commencement provisions:* s 22(1); Tobacco Advertising and Promotion Act 2002 (Commencement) Order 2002, SI 2002/2865[1], as amended by SI 2003/258; Tobacco Advertising and Promotion Act 2002 (Commencement) (Scotland) Order 2002, SSI 2002/512, as amended by SSI 2003/80; Tobacco Advertising and Promotion Act 2002 (Commencement No 5) (Scotland) Order 2003, SSI 2003/113; Tobacco Advertising and Promotion Act 2002 (Commencement No 6) Order 2003, SI 2003/396; Tobacco Advertising and Promotion Act 2002 (Commencement No 7) Order 2004, SI 2004/3138; Tobacco Advertising and Promotion Act 2002 (Commencement No 8) (Scotland) Order 2004, SSI 2004/546; Tobacco Advertising and Promotion Act 2002 (Commencement No 9) Order 2006, SI 2006/2372; Tobacco Advertising and Promotion Act 2002 (Commencement No 10) (Scotland) Order 2006, SSI 2006/473

| | | |
|---|---|---|
| 1 | | 20 Nov 2002 (for purpose of making regulations) (SI 2002/2865; SSI 2002/512) |
| | | 14 Feb 2003 (otherwise) (SI 2002/2865; SSI 2002/512)[1] |
| 2 | | 14 Feb 2003 (except in the case of a tobacco advertisement which is, or is to be, published, printed, devised or distributed solely: |
| | | (i) for the purposes of a distribution that is restricted to those members of the public who before 8 Oct 1999 requested their inclusion in such distributions; or |
| | | (ii) for the purposes of the promotion of a tobacco product in a place or on a website where tobacco products are offered for sale) (SI 2002/2865; SSI 2002/512)[1, 2] |
| | | 14 May 2003 (in so far as it relates to a tobacco advertisement which is, or is to be, published, printed, devised or distributed solely for the purposes of a distribution that is restricted to those members of the public who before 8 Oct 1999 requested their inclusion in such distributions) (SI 2002/2865; SSI 2002/512) |
| | | 21 Dec 2004 (in the case of a tobacco advertisement which is, or is to be, published, printed, devised or distributed solely for the purposes of the promotion of a tobacco product in a place where tobacco products are offered for sale) (SI 2004/3138; SSI 2004/546) |
| | | 31 Jul 2005 (otherwise) (except in the case of a tobacco advertisement which is, or is to be, published, devised or distributed solely for the purposes of the promotion of a tobacco product on a website where tobacco products are offered for sale) (SI 2004/3138; SSI 2004/546) |
| | | 26 Sep 2006 (E) (W) (NI) (otherwise) (SI 2006/2372) |
| | | 28 Sep 2006 (S) (otherwise) (SSI 2006/473) |
| 3 | | 14 Feb 2003 (SI 2002/2865[1]; SSI 2002/512[2]) |
| | | 31 Jul 2005 (otherwise) (SI 2004/3138; SSI 2004/546) |
| 4 | (1), (2) | 14 Feb 2003 (SI 2002/2865[1]; SSI 2002/512) |
| | (3), (4) | 20 Nov 2002 (for purpose of making regulations) (SI 2002/2865; SSI 2002/512) |
| | | 25 Feb 2003 (S) (otherwise) (SSI 2003/113) |
| | | 26 Feb 2003 (E) (W) (NI) (otherwise) (SI 2003/396) |
| 5–8 | | 14 Feb 2003 (SI 2002/2865[1]; SSI 2002/512) |
| 9 | | 14 Feb 2003 (except in relation to any case where a free distribution consists solely of the distribution of a coupon which: |
| | | (i) is enclosed within a pack or part of a pack containing a tobacco product; |

## Tobacco Advertising and Promotion Act 2002 (c 36)—*contd*

|        |          |                                                                                 |
|--------|----------|---------------------------------------------------------------------------------|
|        |          | (ii) has a nominal cash value not exceeding one penny; and                      |
|        |          | (iii) is capable of being exchanged for goods but not other products, services or benefits) (SI 2002/2865[1]; SSI 2002/512[2]) |
|        |          | 14 May 2003 (otherwise) (SI 2002/2865[1]; SSI 2002/512[2])                       |
|        |          | 31 Jul 2005 (otherwise) (SI 2004/3138; SSI 2004/546)                             |
| 10     |          | 14 Feb 2003 (SI 2002/2865[1]; SSI 2002/512[2])                                   |
|        |          | 31 Jul 2005 (otherwise) (SI 2004/3138; SSI 2004/546)                             |
| 11     | (1)–(3)  | 20 Nov 2002 (for purpose of making regulations) (SI 2002/2865; SSI 2002/512)     |
|        |          | 25 Feb 2003 (S) (otherwise) (SSI 2003/113)                                       |
|        |          | 26 Feb 2003 (E) (W) (NI) (otherwise) (SI 2003/396)                               |
|        | (4)      | 14 Feb 2003 (SI 2002/2865[1]; SSI 2002/512)                                      |
| 12–18  |          | 14 Feb 2003 (SI 2002/2865[1]; SSI 2002/512)                                      |
| 19     |          | 20 Nov 2002 (for purpose of making regulations) (SI 2002/2865; SSI 2002/512)     |
|        |          | 11 Feb 2003 (E) (W) (NI) (otherwise) (SI 2002/2865)                              |
|        |          | 12 Feb 2003 (S) (SSI 2002/512)                                                   |
| 20     |          | 20 Nov 2002 (for purpose of making regulations) (SI 2002/2865; SSI 2002/512)     |
|        |          | 25 Feb 2003 (S) (otherwise) (SSI 2003/113)                                       |
|        |          | 26 Feb 2003 (E) (W) (NI) (otherwise) (SI 2003/396)                               |
| 21     |          | 20 Nov 2002 (for purpose of making regulations) (SI 2002/2865; SSI 2002/512)     |
|        |          | 14 Feb 2003 (otherwise) (SI 2002/2865[1]; SSI 2002/512)                          |
| 22     |          | 7 Nov 2002 (RA)                                                                  |

[1] For transitional provisions, see SI 2002/2865, art 3

[2] For transitional provisions, see SSI 2002/512, art 3

## Travel Concessions (Eligibility) Act 2002 (c 4)

*RA:* 26 Feb 2002

*Commencement provisions:* s 2(1); Travel Concessions (Eligibility) Act 2002 (Commencement) (England) Order 2002, SI 2002/673; Travel Concessions (Eligibility) Act 2002 (Commencement) (Wales) Order 2002, SI 2002/3014

|       |                                    |
|-------|------------------------------------|
| 1     | 1 Apr 2003 (E) (SI 2002/673)       |
|       | 1 Apr 2003 (W) (SI 2002/3014)      |
| 2, 3  | 26 Feb 2002 (RA)                   |

## University of St Andrews (Postgraduate Medical Degrees) Act 2002 (asp 15)

*RA:* 30 Jul 2002

Whole Act in force 30 Jul 2002 (RA)

## Water Industry (Scotland) Act 2002 (asp 3)

*RA:* 1 Mar 2002

*Commencement provisions:* s 72(1); Water Industry (Scotland) Act 2002 (Commencement and Savings) Order 2002, SSI 2002/118[1]

|        |                                                                                            |
|--------|--------------------------------------------------------------------------------------------|
| 1–19   | 1 Apr 2002 (SSI 2002/118)                                                                   |
| 20     | 8 Mar 2002 (SSI 2002/118)                                                                   |
| 21–55  | 1 Apr 2002 (SSI 2002/118)                                                                   |
| 56     | 8 Mar 2002 (for the purpose of enabling consultation in accordance with sub-s (4)) (SSI 2002/118) |

**See Halsbury's Statutes Citator for amendments to these Acts** 1385

**Water Industry (Scotland) Act 2002 (asp 3)**—*contd*

|  |  |  |
|---|---|---|
|  |  | 1 Apr 2002 (otherwise) (SSI 2002/118) |
| 57–65 |  | 1 Apr 2002 (SSI 2002/118) |
| 66–70 |  | 1 Mar 2002 (RA) |
| 71 |  | 1 Apr 2002 (SSI 2002/118) |
| 72 |  | 1 Mar 2002 (RA) |
| Schs 1, 2 |  | 1 Apr 2002 (SSI 2002/118) |
| Sch 3 |  | 8 Mar 2002 (SSI 2002/118) |
| Schs 4–6 |  | 1 Apr 2002 (SSI 2002/118) |
| Sch 7 | paras 1–22 | 1 Apr 2002 (SSI 2002/118) |
|  | para 23(a)–(c) | 1 Apr 2002 (SSI 2002/118) |
|  | para 23(d) | 1 Apr 2002 (subject to savings) (SSI 2002/118)[1] |
|  | para 23(e)–(g) | 1 Apr 2002 (SSI 2002/118) |
|  | paras 24–28 | 1 Apr 2002 (SSI 2002/118) |

[1]   For savings, see SSI 2002/118, art 3

# 2003 Acts

## Agricultural Holdings (Scotland) Act 2003 (asp 11)

*RA:* 22 Apr 2003

*Commencement provisions:* s 95(3), (4); Agricultural Holdings (Scotland) Act 2003 (Commencement No 1) Order 2003, SSI 2003/248; Agricultural Holdings (Scotland) Act 2003 (Commencement No 2) Order 2003, SSI 2003/305; Agricultural Holdings (Scotland) Act 2003 (Commencement No 3, Transitional and Savings Provisions) Order 2003, SSI 2003/548[1]; Agricultural Holdings (Scotland) Act 2003 (Commencement No 4) Order 2004, SSI 2004/511

| | | |
|---|---|---|
| 1–23 | | 27 Nov 2003 (SSI 2003/548) |
| 24 | | 15 Dec 2004 (SSI 2004/511) |
| 25 | (1), (2) | 15 Dec 2004 (SSI 2004/511) |
| | (3) | 27 Nov 2003 (SSI 2003/548) |
| | (4)–(6) | 15 Dec 2004 (SSI 2004/511) |
| | (7) | 27 Nov 2003 (SSI 2003/548) |
| | (8)–(15) | 15 Dec 2004 (SSI 2004/511) |
| 26 | (1) | 15 Dec 2004 (SSI 2004/511) |
| | (2) | 27 Nov 2003 (SSI 2003/548) |
| 27 | (1)–(4) | 15 Dec 2004 (SSI 2004/511) |
| | (5) | 27 Nov 2003 (SSI 2003/548) |
| 28 | (1)–(4) | 15 Dec 2004 (SSI 2004/511) |
| | (5) | 27 Nov 2003 (SSI 2003/548) |
| 29–33 | | 15 Dec 2004 (SSI 2004/511) |
| 34 | (1)–(5) | 15 Dec 2004 (SSI 2004/511) |
| | (6) | 27 Nov 2003 (SSI 2003/548) |
| | (7), (8) | 15 Dec 2004 (SSI 2004/511) |
| 35 | | 15 Dec 2004 (SSI 2004/511) |
| 36 | (1)–(6) | 15 Dec 2004 (SSI 2004/511) |
| | (7) | 27 Nov 2003 (SSI 2003/548) |
| 37, 38 | | 15 Dec 2004 (SSI 2004/511) |
| 39–69 | | 27 Nov 2003 (SSI 2003/548) |
| 70 | (1)–(6) | 27 Nov 2003 (SSI 2003/548) |
| | (7), (8) | 22 May 2003 (for the purposes of s 72(1), (3)–(9), (11), (12)) (SSI 2003/248) |
| | | 1 Jul 2003 (for the purposes of s 72(10)) (SSI 2003/305) |
| | | 27 Nov 2003 (otherwise) (SSI 2003/548) |
| | (9) | 27 Nov 2003 (SSI 2003/548) |
| 71 | | 27 Nov 2003 (SSI 2003/548) |
| 72 | (1) | 22 May 2003 (SSI 2003/248) |
| | (2) | 27 Nov 2003 (SSI 2003/548) |
| | (3)–(9) | 22 May 2003 (SSI 2003/248) |
| | (10) | 1 Jul 2003 (SSI 2003/305) |
| | (11), (12) | 22 May 2003 (SSI 2003/248) |
| 73 | | 1 Jul 2003 (SSI 2003/305) |
| 74–90 | | 27 Nov 2003 (SSI 2003/548) |
| 91–93 | | 22 Apr 2003 (RA) |
| 94 | | See Schedule below |
| 95 | | 22 Apr 2003 (RA) |

**Agricultural Holdings (Scotland) Act 2003 (asp 11)**—*contd*
Schedule                                          27 Nov 2003 (SSI 2003/548)

---

¹   For transitional provisions and savings, see SSI 2003/548, art 3, and the Schedule

---

**Anti-social Behaviour Act 2003 (c 38)**

*RA:* 20 Nov 2003

*Commencement provisions:* s 93; Anti-social Behaviour Act 2003 (Commencement No 1 and Transitional
   Provisions) Order 2003, SI 2003/3300; Anti-social Behaviour Act 2003 (Commencement No 2)
   Order 2004, SI 2004/690; Anti-social Behaviour Act 2003 (Commencement No 1) (Wales)
   Order 2004, SI 2004/999; Anti-social Behaviour Act 2003 (Commencement No 3 and Savings)
   Order 2004, SI 2004/1502; Anti-social Behaviour Act 2003 (Commencement No 4) Order 2004,
   SI 2004/2168, as amended by SI 2006/835; Anti-social Behaviour Act 2003 (Commencement No 2
   and Savings) (Wales) Order 2004, SI 2004/2557; Anti-social Behaviour Act 2003 (Commencement
   No 3) (Wales) Order 2004, SI 2004/3238; Anti-social Behaviour Act 2003 (Commencement No 5)
   (England) Order 2005, SI 2005/710; Anti-social Behaviour Act 2003 (Commencement No 4) (Wales)
   Order 2005, SI 2005/1225; Anti-social Behaviour Act 2003 (Commencement No 6) (England)
   Order 2006, SI 2006/393; Anti-social Behaviour Act 2003 (Commencement No 5) (Wales)
   Order 2006, SI 2006/1278

| | | |
|---|---|---|
| 1–11 | | 20 Jan 2004 (SI 2003/3300) |
| 12 | | 30 Jun 2004 (E) (SI 2004/1502) |
| | | 30 Apr 2005 (W) (SI 2005/1225) |
| 13 | | 30 Jun 2004 (E) (SI 2004/1502)⁴ |
| | | 30 Sep 2004 (W) (SI 2004/2557)⁷ |
| 14 | (1)–(4) | 30 Jun 2004 (E) (SI 2004/1502) |
| | | 30 Sep 2004 (W) (in so far as they confer the power to make regulations) (SI 2004/2557) |
| | | 30 Apr 2005 (W) (otherwise) (SI 2005/1225) |
| | (5) | See Sch 1 below |
| 15 | | 30 Jun 2004 (E) (SI 2004/1502) |
| | | 30 Apr 2005 (W) (SI 2005/1225) |
| 16 | | 30 Jun 2004 (E) (SI 2004/1502)⁴ |
| | | 30 Sep 2004 (W) (SI 2004/2557)⁷ |
| 17 | | 30 Jun 2004 (E) (SI 2004/1502) |
| | | 30 Sep 2004 (W) (SI 2004/2557) |
| 18 | | 27 Feb 2004 (SI 2003/3300) |
| 19–22 | | 27 Feb 2004 (E) (SI 2003/3300) |
| | | 11 May 2006 (W) (SI 2006/1278) |
| 23 | | 27 Feb 2004 (SI 2003/3300) |
| 24 | | 27 Feb 2004 (E) (SI 2003/3300) |
| | | 11 May 2006 (W) (SI 2006/1278) |
| 25–29 | | 27 Feb 2004 (SI 2003/3300) |
| 30–38 | | 20 Jan 2004 (SI 2003/3300) |
| 39 | (1), (2) | 20 Jan 2004 (SI 2003/3300) |
| | (3) | 20 Jan 2004 (in so far as relating to the purchase, acquisition, manufacture, sale or transfer of the prohibited weapon) (SI 2003/3300) |
| | | 30 Apr 2004 (otherwise) (SI 2003/3300)¹ |
| | (4)–(6) | 20 Jan 2004 (SI 2003/3300) |
| 40–45 | | 31 Mar 2004 (SI 2004/690; SI 2004/999) |
| 46 | | 31 Mar 2004 (SI 2004/690) |
| 47 | | 31 Mar 2004 (SI 2004/690; SI 2004/999) |
| 48–52 | | 31 Mar 2004 (E) (in the specified local authority areas³) (SI 2004/690) |
| | | 31 Mar 2004 (W) (SI 2004/999) |
| | | 6 Apr 2006 (E) (otherwise) (SI 2006/393) |
| 53 | | 20 Jan 2004 (SI 2003/3300) |
| 54 | | 31 Mar 2004 (SI 2004/690) |

**Anti-social Behaviour Act 2003 (c 38)**—*contd*

| | | |
|---|---|---|
| 55, 56 | | 31 Mar 2004 (SI 2004/690; SI 2004/999) |
| 57–59 | | 20 Jan 2004 (SI 2003/3300) |
| 60–64 | | 27 Feb 2004 (SI 2003/3300) |
| 65–70 | | 31 Dec 2004 (W) (SI 2004/3238) |
| | | 1 Jun 2005 (E) (SI 2005/710) |
| 71 | (1)–(6) | 31 Dec 2004 (W) (SI 2004/3238) |
| | | 1 Jun 2005 (E) (SI 2005/710) |
| | (7) | 1 Oct 2004 (E) (SI 2004/2168) |
| | | 31 Dec 2004 (W) (SI 2004/3238) |
| 72 | | 1 Oct 2004 (E) (SI 2004/2168) |
| | | 31 Dec 2004 (W) (SI 2004/3238) |
| 73–84 | | 31 Dec 2004 (W) (SI 2004/3238) |
| | | 1 Jun 2005 (E) (SI 2005/710) |
| 85 | (1)–(3) | 20 Jan 2004 (SI 2003/3300) |
| | (4) | 20 Jan 2004 (in so far as relating to the Crime and Disorder Act 1998, s 1(10B)) (SI 2003/3300) |
| | | 31 Mar 2004 (otherwise) (SI 2004/690) |
| | (5) | 31 Mar 2004 (in so far as relating to persons aged 18 and over) (SI 2004/690) |
| | | 1 Oct 2004 (otherwise) (for a period of two years in relation to applications for anti-social behaviour orders in specified county courts[6]) (SI 2004/2168) |
| | | *Never in force* (in relation to persons aged under 18 except for a period of eighteen months in relation to applications for anti-social behaviour orders in specified county courts[6]) (repealed) |
| | (6) | 31 Mar 2004 (in so far as relating to persons aged 18 and over) (SI 2004/690) |
| | | 30 Sep 2004 (otherwise) (SI 2004/2168) |
| | (7) | 20 Jan 2004 (SI 2003/3300) |
| | (8) | 27 Feb 2004 (SI 2003/3300) |
| | (9)–(11) | 20 Nov 2003 (RA)[2] |
| 86 | (1), (2) | 31 Mar 2004 (SI 2004/690) |
| | (3) | 20 Jan 2004 (in so far as relating to the Crime and Disorder Act 1998, s 1C(9A), (9B)) (SI 2003/3300) |
| | | 31 Mar 2004 (otherwise) (SI 2004/690) |
| | (4)–(6) | 20 Jan 2004 (SI 2003/3300) |
| 87 | | 20 Jan 2004 (SI 2003/3300) |
| 88 | | See Sch 2 below |
| 89 | (1)–(4) | 20 Jan 2004 (SI 2003/3300) |
| | (5) | 31 Mar 2004 (SI 2004/690) |
| | (6), (7) | 20 Jan 2004 (SI 2003/3300) |
| 90 | | 31 Jul 2004 (SI 2004/1502) |
| 91 | | 30 Jun 2004 (E) (SI 2004/1502)[4] |
| | | 30 Sep 2004 (W) (SI 2004/2557)[7] |
| 92 | | See Sch 3 below |
| 93–97 | | 20 Nov 2003 (RA) |
| Sch 1 | | 30 Jun 2004 (E) (SI 2004/1502) |
| | | 30 Sep 2004 (W) (in so far as it confers the power to make regulations) (SI 2004/2557) |
| | | 30 Apr 2005 (W) (otherwise) (SI 2005/1225) |
| Sch 2 | para 1 | 30 Sep 2004 (SI 2004/2168) |
| | para 2(1) | 30 Sep 2004 (SI 2004/2168) |
| | para 2(2) | 30 Sep 2004 (in specified local authority areas[5]) (SI 2004/2168) |
| | | *Never in force* (except in specified local authority areas[5]) (repealed) |
| | para 2(3) | 30 Sep 2004 (SI 2004/2168) |
| | paras 3–6 | 30 Sep 2004 (SI 2004/2168) |
| Sch 3 | | 20 Jan 2004 (SI 2003/3300), repeals of or in— |
| | | Firearms Act 1968; |

**Anti-social Behaviour Act 2003 (c 38)**—*contd*

Prosecution of Offences Act 1985;

Firearms (Amendment) Act 1988;

Criminal Justice and Public Order Act 1994;

Crime and Disorder Act 1998;

Police Reform Act 2002

31 Mar 2004 (repeal in Noise Act 1996) (SI 2004/690)

30 Jun 2004 (E) (repeals of or in Housing Act 1996) (SI 2004/1502)[4]

30 Sep 2004 (repeals in Powers of Criminal Courts (Sentencing) Act 2000, Schs 6, 7) (SI 2004/2168)

30 Sep 2004 (repeal of Powers of Criminal Courts (Sentencing) Act 2000, s 37(4) in specified local authority areas[5]) (SI 2004/2168)

*Not yet in force* (repeal of Powers of Criminal Courts (Sentencing) Act 2000, s 37(4) except in specified local authority areas[5])

*Not yet in force* (W) (repeals of or in Housing Act 1996)

[1]   For transitional provisions, see SI 2003/3300, art 5(2)

[2]   Note that SI 2004/690 also purports to bring these provisions into force on 31 Mar 2004

[3]   The areas of the following local authorities are specified:

(a)   Barnsley Metropolitan Borough Council;

(b)   Bristol City Council;

(c)   Cambridge City Council;

(d)   Dartford Borough Council;

(e)   Doncaster Metropolitan Borough Council;

(f)   Epping Forest District Council;

(g)   Kirklees Metropolitan Borough Council;

(h)   London Borough of Merton;

(i)   London Borough of Westminster;

(j)   Northampton Borough Council;

(k)   Southampton City Council; and

(l)   Wansbeck District Council

[4]   For savings, see SI 2004/1502, Schedule

[5]   The areas of the following local authorities are specified:

(a)   Birmingham City Council;

(b)   Bolton Metropolitan Borough Council;

(c)   Bridgend County Borough Council;

(d)   Calderdale Metropolitan Borough Council;

(e)   Cardiff County Council;

(f)   City and County of Swansea Council;

(g)   Coventry City Council;

(h)   Kirklees Metropolitan Council;

(i)   Leeds City Council;

(j)   Liverpool City Council;

(k)   London Borough of Barking and Dagenham;

(l)   London Borough of Bexley;

(m)   London Borough of Bromley;

(n)   London Borough of Croydon;

**Anti-social Behaviour Act 2003 (c 38)**—*contd*

 (o) London Borough of Greenwich;

 (p) London Borough of Havering;

 (q) London Borough of Lewisham;

 (r) London Borough of Merton;

 (s) London Borough of Redbridge;

 (t) London Borough of Richmond upon Thames;

 (u) London Borough of Southwark;

 (v) London Borough of Sutton;

 (w) London Borough of Waltham Forest;

 (x) Merthyr Tydfil County Borough Council;

 (y) Neath Port Talbot County Borough Council;

 (z) Nottingham City Council;

 (aa) Oldham Metropolitan Borough Council;

 (bb) Rhonda Cynon Taf County Borough Council;

 (cc) Royal Borough of Kingston upon Thames;

 (dd) Solihull Metropolitan Borough Council;

 (ee) Stockport Metropolitan Borough Council;

 (ff) Tameside Metropolitan Borough Council; and

 (gg) Vale of Glamorgan Council

6 The following county courts are specified:

 (a) Bristol;

 (b) Central London;

 (c) Clerkenwell;

 (d) Dewsbury;

 (e) Huddersfield;

 (f) Leicester;

 (g) Manchester;

 (h) Oxford;

 (i) Tameside;

 (j) Wigan; and

 (k) Wrexham

7 For savings, see SI 2004/2557, Schedule

---

**Appropriation Act 2003 (c 13)**

*RA:* 10 Jul 2003

Whole Act in force 10 Jul 2003 (RA)

---

**Arms Control and Disarmament (Inspections) Act 2003 (c 34)**

*RA:* 13 Nov 2003

*Commencement provisions:* s 3(2)

1   (1)   See Sch 1 below

    (2)   See Sch 2 below

**Arms Control and Disarmament (Inspections) Act 2003 (c 34)**—*contd*
2, 3                                               *Not yet in force*
Schs 1, 2                                          *Not yet in force*

---

**Aviation (Offences) Act 2003 (c 19)**

*RA:* 10 Jul 2003

*Commencement provisions:* s 3

Whole Act in force 10 Sep 2003 (s 3)

---

**Budget (Scotland) Act 2003 (asp 6)**

*RA:* 19 Mar 2003

Whole Act in force 19 Mar 2003 (RA)

---

**Building (Scotland) Act 2003 (asp 8)**

*RA:* 26 Mar 2003

*Commencement provisions:* s 59(1); Building (Scotland) Act 2003 (Commencement No 1, Transitional Provisions and Savings) Order 2004, SSI 2004/404; Building (Scotland) Act 2003 (Commencement No 2 and Transitional Provisions) Order 2009, SSI 2009/150

| | | |
|---|---|---|
| 1 | (1), (2) | 22 Sep 2004 (for the purpose of enabling regulations to be made to come into force on 1 May 2005) (SSI 2004/404) |
| | | 1 May 2005 (otherwise) (SSI 2004/404) |
| | (3) | See Sch 1 below |
| | (4), (5) | 1 May 2005 (SSI 2004/404) |
| 2 | | 22 Sep 2004 (for the purpose of enabling regulations to be made to come into force on 1 May 2005) (SSI 2004/404) |
| | | 1 May 2005 (otherwise) (SSI 2004/404) |
| 3 | | 1 May 2005 (SSI 2004/404) |
| 4 | | 22 Sep 2004 (for the purpose of enabling guidance documents and notices to be issued to take effect on 1 May 2005) (SSI 2004/404) |
| | | 1 May 2005 (otherwise) (SSI 2004/404) |
| 5 | | 1 May 2005 (SSI 2004/404) |
| 6 | | *Never in force* (repealed) |
| 7 | (1)–(3) | 4 Nov 2004 (SSI 2004/404) |
| | (4)–(9) | 1 May 2005 (SSI 2004/404) |
| | (10) | 4 Nov 2004 (SSI 2004/404) |
| | (11) | 1 May 2005 (SSI 2004/404) |
| | (12) | See Sch 2 below |
| 8–30 | | 1 May 2005 (SSI 2004/404) |
| 31 | (1), (2) | 1 Jan 2005 (SSI 2004/404)[1] |
| | (3) | 22 Sep 2004 (for the purpose of enabling regulations to be made to come into force on 1 Jan 2005) (SSI 2004/404) |
| | | 1 Jan 2005 (otherwise) (SSI 2004/404)[1] |
| | (4) | 1 Jan 2005 (SSI 2004/404)[1] |
| 32 | | 1 May 2005 (SSI 2004/404) |
| 33 | (1) | 22 Sep 2004 (for the purpose of enabling regulations to be made to come into force not later than 1 May 2005) (SSI 2004/404) |
| | | 1 May 2005 (otherwise) (SSI 2004/404) |
| | (2) | See Sch 3 below |
| | (3), (4) | 22 Sep 2004 (for the purpose of enabling regulations to be made to come into force not later than 1 May 2005) (SSI 2004/404) |
| | | 1 May 2005 (otherwise) (SSI 2004/404) |

**Building (Scotland) Act 2003 (asp 8)**—*contd*

| | | |
|---|---|---|
| 34, 35 | | 1 May 2005 (SSI 2004/404) |
| 36 | | 22 Sep 2004 (for the purpose of enabling regulations to be made to come into force on 1 May 2005) (SSI 2004/404) |
| | | 1 May 2005 (otherwise) (SSI 2004/404) |
| 37 | | 1 May 2005 (SSI 2004/404) |
| 38 | | 22 Sep 2004 (for the purpose of enabling regulations to be made to come into force on 1 May 2005) (SSI 2004/404) |
| | | 1 May 2005 (otherwise) (SSI 2004/404) |
| 39 | (1)–(6) | 1 May 2005 (SSI 2004/404) |
| | (7) | See Sch 4 below |
| | (8) | 1 May 2005 (SSI 2004/404) |
| 40, 41 | | 1 May 2005 (SSI 2004/404) |
| 42 | (1)–(7) | 1 May 2005 (SSI 2004/404) |
| | (8) | See Sch 5 below |
| 43–52 | | 1 May 2005 (SSI 2004/404) |
| 53 | | 1 May 2009 (SSI 2009/150)[2] |
| 54 | | 26 Mar 2003 (RA) |
| 55, 56 | | 22 Sep 2004 (SSI 2004/404) |
| 57 | | 26 Mar 2003 (RA) |
| 58 | | See Sch 6 below |
| 59 | | 26 Mar 2003 (RA) |
| Sch 1 | | 22 Sep 2004 (for the purpose of enabling regulations to be made to come into force on 1 May 2005) (SSI 2004/404) |
| | | 1 May 2005 (otherwise) (SSI 2004/404) |
| Sch 2 | paras 1, 2 | 4 Nov 2004 (SSI 2004/404) |
| | para 3 | 22 Sep 2004 (for the purpose of enabling regulations to be made to come into force not later than 1 May 2005) (SSI 2004/404) |
| | | 4 Nov 2004 (otherwise) (SSI 2004/404) |
| | para 4 | 4 Nov 2004 (SSI 2004/404) |
| | paras 5–10 | 1 May 2005 (SSI 2004/404) |
| | paras 11, 12 | 22 Sep 2004 (for the purpose of enabling regulations to be made to come into force not later than 1 May 2005) (SSI 2004/404) |
| | | 1 May 2005 (otherwise) (SSI 2004/404) |
| Sch 3 | | 22 Sep 2004 (for the purpose of enabling regulations to be made to come into force not later than 1 May 2005) (SSI 2004/404) |
| | | 1 May 2005 (otherwise) (SSI 2004/404) |
| Schs 4–6 | | 1 May 2005 (SSI 2004/404)[1] |

[1]  For transitional provisions and savings, see SSI 2004/404, arts 3, 4

[2]  For transitional provisions, see SSI 2009/150, art 3

---

## Church of England (Pensions) Measure 2003 (No 2)

*RA:* 6 Mar 2003

*Commencement provisions:* s 7(2)

This Measure was brought into force on 1 May 2003 by an instrument made by the Archbishops of Canterbury and York and dated 13 Apr 2003 (made under s 7(2))

---

## Clergy Discipline Measure 2003 (No 3)

*RA:* 10 Jul 2003

*Commencement provisions:* s 48(2)

Provisions of this Measure were brought into force on the following dates by instruments made by the Archbishops of Canterbury and York, and dated 30 Sep 2003, 26 May 2005, 7 Sep 2005 and 7 Dec 2005 (made under s 48(2))

**Clergy Discipline Measure 2003 (No 3)**—*contd*

| | | |
|---|---|---|
| 1, 2 | | 1 Jan 2006 |
| 3 | | 1 Oct 2003 |
| 4, 5 | | 8 Sep 2005 |
| 6–20 | | 1 Jan 2006 |
| 21 | | 8 Sep 2005 |
| 22–38 | | 1 Jan 2006 |
| 39 | | 1 Oct 2003 |
| 40–43 | | 1 Jan 2006 |
| 44 | (1), (2) | 1 Jan 2006 |
| | (3), (4) | 1 Jun 2005 |
| | (5) | 1 Jan 2006 |
| 45 | | 1 Oct 2003 |
| 46, 47 | | 1 Jan 2006 |
| 48 | | 1 Oct 2003 |
| Schs 1, 2 | | 1 Jan 2006 |

---

**Commissioner for Children and Young People (Scotland) Act 2003 (asp 17)**

*RA:* 1 May 2003

*Commencement provisions:* s 17(1)

| | |
|---|---|
| 1–3 | 1 May 2003 (RA) |
| 4–15 | 1 Nov 2003 (s 17(1)) |
| 16, 17 | 1 May 2003 (RA) |
| Sch 1 | 1 May 2003 (RA) |
| Sch 2 | 1 Nov 2003 (s 17(1)) |

---

**Communications Act 2003 (c 21)**

*RA:* 17 Jul 2003

*Commencement provisions:* s 411(2), (3); Communications Act 2003 (Commencement No 1) Order 2003, SI 2003/1900, as amended by SI 2003/3142; Office of Communications Act 2002 (Commencement No 3) and Communications Act 2003 (Commencement No 2) Order 2003, SI 2003/3142, as amended by SI 2004/545, SI 2004/697, SI 2004/1492; Communications Act 2003 (Commencement No 3) Order 2004, SI 2004/3309; Communications Act 2003 (Commencement No 4) Order 2009, SI 2009/2130; Communications Act 2003 (Commencement No 5) Order 2017, SI 2017/1063

| | | |
|---|---|---|
| 1 | (1), (2) | 29 Dec 2003 (SI 2003/3142) |
| | (3) | 25 Jul 2003 (except words "including borrowing money") (to the extent only that this provision is to be taken for the purposes of s 408(3) to be brought into force for the purpose of enabling networks and services functions to be carried out) (for a specified transitional purpose[1]) (SI 2003/1900) |
| | | 29 Dec 2003 (otherwise) (SI 2003/3142) |
| | (4) | 29 Dec 2003 (SI 2003/3142) |
| | (5)(a), (b) | 29 Dec 2003 (SI 2003/3142) |
| | (5)(c) | 25 Jul 2003 (to the extent only that this provision is to be taken for the purposes of s 408(3) to be brought into force for the purpose of enabling networks and services functions to be carried out) (for a specified transitional purpose[1]) (SI 2003/1900) |
| | | 29 Dec 2003 (otherwise) (SI 2003/3142) |
| | (5)(d) | 29 Dec 2003 (SI 2003/3142) |
| | (6)–(8) | 29 Dec 2003 (SI 2003/3142) |
| 2 | (1) | See Sch 1 below |
| | (2)–(4) | 29 Dec 2003 (except to the extent that the Wireless Telegraphy Act 1949 applies in respect of television licences and television receivers) (SI 2003/3142)[3] |

**Communications Act 2003 (c 21)**—*contd*

|  |  |  |
|---|---|---|
|  |  | 1 Apr 2004 (otherwise) (SI 2003/3142) |
| 3 |  | 29 Dec 2003 (SI 2003/3142) |
| 4 |  | 25 Jul 2003 (for a specified transitional purpose[1]) (SI 2003/1900) |
|  |  | 29 Dec 2003 (for the purpose of transferring the networks and services functions and the spectrum functions on OFCOM) (SI 2003/3142) |
| 5 |  | 25 Jul 2003 (to the extent only that this provision is to be taken for the purposes of s 408(3) to be brought into force for the purpose of enabling networks and services functions to be carried out) (for a specified transitional purpose[1]) (SI 2003/1900) |
|  |  | 18 Sep 2003 (otherwise) (SI 2003/1900) |
| 6–23 |  | 29 Dec 2003 (SI 2003/3142) |
| 24, 25 |  | 25 Jul 2003 (for a specified transitional purpose[1]) (SI 2003/1900) |
|  |  | 29 Dec 2003 (for the purpose of transferring the networks and services functions and the spectrum functions on OFCOM) (SI 2003/3142) |
| 26 | (1) | 25 Jul 2003 (for a specified transitional purpose[1]) (SI 2003/1900) |
|  |  | 29 Dec 2003 (otherwise) (SI 2003/3142) |
|  | (2)(a)–(c) | 25 Jul 2003 (for a specified transitional purpose[1]) (SI 2003/1900) |
|  |  | 29 Dec 2003 (otherwise) (SI 2003/3142) |
|  | (2)(d) | 29 Dec 2003 (SI 2003/3142) |
|  | (3)–(6) | 25 Jul 2003 (for a specified transitional purpose[1]) (SI 2003/1900) |
|  |  | 29 Dec 2003 (otherwise) (SI 2003/3142) |
| 27 |  | 29 Dec 2003 (SI 2003/3142) |
| 28, 29 |  | 18 Sep 2003 (SI 2003/1900) |
| 30 | (1)–(11) | 18 Sep 2003 (SI 2003/1900) |
|  | (12) | See Sch 2 below |
| 31 | (1)–(4) | 17 Jul 2003 (s 411(2), (3)) |
|  | (5) | 29 Dec 2003 (SI 2003/3142)[4] |
|  | (6) | 17 Jul 2003 (s 411(2), (3)) |
| 32–55 |  | 25 Jul 2003 (for a specified transitional purpose[1]) (SI 2003/1900) |
|  |  | 29 Dec 2003 (for the purpose of transferring the networks and services functions and the spectrum functions on OFCOM) (SI 2003/3142) |
| 56–63 |  | 25 Jul 2003 (except in respect of any number which is used as an internet domain name, an internet address or an address or identifier incorporating either an internet domain name or an internet address, including an email address) (for a specified transitional purpose[1]) (SI 2003/1900) |
|  |  | 29 Dec 2003 (otherwise) (SI 2003/3142) |
| 64–105 |  | 25 Jul 2003 (for a specified transitional purpose[1]) (SI 2003/1900) |
|  |  | 29 Dec 2003 (for the purpose of transferring the networks and services functions and the spectrum functions on OFCOM) (SI 2003/3142) |
| 106 | (1) | 25 Jul 2003 (for a specified transitional purpose[1]) (SI 2003/1900) |
|  |  | 29 Dec 2003 (for the purpose of transferring the networks and services functions and the spectrum functions on OFCOM) (SI 2003/3142) |
|  | (2) | See Sch 3 below |
|  | (3)–(7) | 25 Jul 2003 (for a specified transitional purpose[1]) (SI 2003/1900) |
|  |  | 29 Dec 2003 (for the purpose of transferring the networks and services functions and the spectrum functions on OFCOM) (SI 2003/3142) |
| 107–117 |  | 25 Jul 2003 (for a specified transitional purpose[1]) (SI 2003/1900) |
|  |  | 29 Dec 2003 (for the purpose of transferring the networks and services functions and the spectrum functions on OFCOM) (SI 2003/3142) |
| 118 |  | See Sch 4 below |
| 119 |  | 25 Jul 2003 (for a specified transitional purpose[1]) (SI 2003/1900) |

**Communications Act 2003 (c 21)**—*contd*

|  |  |  |
|---|---|---|
| | | 29 Dec 2003 (for the purpose of transferring the networks and services functions and the spectrum functions on OFCOM) (SI 2003/3142) |
| 120–124 | | 29 Dec 2003 (SI 2003/3142) |
| 125–151 | | 25 Jul 2003 (for a specified transitional purpose[1]) (SI 2003/1900) |
| | | 29 Dec 2003 (for the purpose of transferring the networks and services functions and the spectrum functions on OFCOM) (SI 2003/3142) |
| 152 | (1) | 18 Sep 2003 (for a specified transitional purpose[1]) (SI 2003/1900) |
| | | 29 Dec 2003 (otherwise) (SI 2003/3142) |
| | (2) | 29 Dec 2003 (SI 2003/3142) |
| | (3) | 18 Sep 2003 (for a specified transitional purpose[1]) (SI 2003/1900) |
| | | 29 Dec 2003 (otherwise) (SI 2003/3142) |
| | (4)–(8) | 29 Dec 2003 (SI 2003/3142) |
| | (9) | 18 Sep 2003 (for a specified transitional purpose[1]) (SI 2003/1900) |
| | | 29 Dec 2003 (otherwise) (SI 2003/3142) |
| 153, 154 | | 25 Jul 2003 (for a specified transitional purpose[1]) (SI 2003/1900) |
| | | 29 Dec 2003 (for the purpose of transferring the networks and services functions and the spectrum functions on OFCOM) (SI 2003/3142) |
| 155–158 | | 29 Dec 2003 (SI 2003/3142) |
| 159 | (1)–(7) | 29 Dec 2003 (SI 2003/3142) |
| | (8) | See Sch 5 below |
| | (9), (10) | 29 Dec 2003 (SI 2003/3142) |
| 160–163 | | 29 Dec 2003 (SI 2003/3142) |
| 164–166 | | 25 Jul 2003 (for a specified transitional purpose[1]) (SI 2003/1900) |
| | | 29 Dec 2003 (for the purpose of transferring the networks and services functions and the spectrum functions on OFCOM) (SI 2003/3142) |
| 167 | | 18 Sep 2003 (for a specified transitional purpose[1]) (SI 2003/1900) |
| | | 29 Dec 2003 (for the purpose of transferring the networks and services functions and the spectrum functions on OFCOM) (SI 2003/3142) |
| 168 | | 29 Dec 2003 (SI 2003/3142) |
| 169 | | 25 Jul 2003 (for a specified transitional purpose[1]) (SI 2003/1900) |
| | | 29 Dec 2003 (for the purpose of transferring the networks and services functions and the spectrum functions on OFCOM) (SI 2003/3142) |
| 170, 171 | | 29 Dec 2003 (SI 2003/3142) |
| 172–174 | | 25 Jul 2003 (for a specified transitional purpose[1]) (SI 2003/1900) |
| | | 29 Dec 2003 (for the purpose of transferring the networks and services functions and the spectrum functions on OFCOM) (SI 2003/3142) |
| 175–177 | | 29 Dec 2003 (SI 2003/3142) |
| 178 | | 25 Jul 2003 (for a specified transitional purpose[1]) (SI 2003/1900) |
| | | 29 Dec 2003 (for the purpose of transferring the networks and services functions and the spectrum functions on OFCOM) (SI 2003/3142) |
| 179 | | 18 Sep 2003 (SI 2003/1900) |
| 180 | | See Sch 6 below |
| 181 | | 18 Sep 2003 (SI 2003/1900) |
| 182 | (1)–(3) | 29 Dec 2003 (SI 2003/3142) |
| | (4) | See Sch 7 below |
| | (5)–(7) | 29 Dec 2003 (SI 2003/3142) |
| 183 | | 25 Jul 2003 (for a specified transitional purpose[1]) (SI 2003/1900) |
| | | 29 Dec 2003 (for the purpose of transferring the networks and services functions and the spectrum functions on OFCOM) (SI 2003/3142) |
| 184 | | 18 Sep 2003 (SI 2003/1900) |
| 185–197 | | 25 Jul 2003 (for a specified transitional purpose[1]) (SI 2003/1900) |

**Communications Act 2003 (c 21)**—*contd*

|  |  |  |
|---|---|---|
|  |  | 29 Dec 2003 (for the purpose of transferring the networks and services functions and the spectrum functions on OFCOM) (SI 2003/3142) |
| 198 |  | 29 Dec 2003 (SI 2003/3142) |
| 199 | (1)–(4) | 29 Dec 2003 (SI 2003/3142)[4] |
|  | (5) | See Sch 9 below |
| 200–218 |  | 29 Dec 2003 (SI 2003/3142) |
| 219 | (1)–(7) | 29 Dec 2003 (SI 2003/3142)[4] |
|  | (8) | See Sch 10 below |
| 220, 221 |  | 29 Dec 2003 (SI 2003/3142)[4] |
| 222–230 |  | 29 Dec 2003 (SI 2003/3142) |
| 231 | (1) | 28 Dec 2004 (SI 2004/3309) |
|  | (2)(a), (b) | 29 Dec 2003 (SI 2003/3142) |
|  | (2)(c) | 10 Dec 2004 (SI 2004/3309) |
|  | (3)–(10) | 29 Dec 2003 (SI 2003/3142) |
| 232–236 |  | 29 Dec 2003 (SI 2003/3142) |
| 237 |  | 29 Dec 2003 (SI 2003/3142)[4] |
| 238–252 |  | 29 Dec 2003 (SI 2003/3142) |
| 253 |  | 2 Jan 2004 (SI 2003/3142) |
| 254–263 |  | 29 Dec 2003 (SI 2003/3142) |
| 264 |  | 25 Jul 2003 (SI 2003/1900)[2] |
| 265–270 |  | 28 Dec 2004 (SI 2004/3309) |
| 271 |  | 29 Dec 2003 (SI 2003/3142) |
| 272, 273 |  | 31 Jan 2010 (SI 2009/2130) |
| 274 |  | *Not yet in force* |
| 275 |  | 29 Dec 2003 (SI 2003/3142) |
| 276 |  | 29 Dec 2003 (SI 2003/3142)[4] |
| 277 |  | 29 Dec 2003 (SI 2003/3142) |
| 278 |  | 1 Jul 2004 (SI 2003/3142) |
| 279–281 |  | 29 Dec 2003 (SI 2003/3142) |
| 282 |  | 12 Dec 2003 (SI 2003/3142) |
| 283–293 |  | 29 Dec 2003 (SI 2003/3142) |
| 294 | (1) | See Sch 11 below |
|  | (2) | 29 Dec 2003 (SI 2003/3142) |
| 295–297 |  | 29 Dec 2003 (SI 2003/3142) |
| 298 |  | 29 Dec 2003 (SI 2003/3142)[4] |
| 299 | (1) | *Not yet in force* |
|  | (2) | 29 Dec 2003 (SI 2003/3142) |
|  | (3), (4) | *Not yet in force* |
| 300 |  | *Not yet in force* |
| 301–307 |  | 29 Dec 2003 (SI 2003/3142) |
| 308 |  | 29 Dec 2003 (SI 2003/3142)[4] |
| 309–324 |  | 29 Dec 2003 (SI 2003/3142) |
| 325 |  | 29 Dec 2003 (SI 2003/3142)[4] |
| 326–337 |  | 29 Dec 2003 (SI 2003/3142) |
| 338 |  | See Sch 12 below |
| 339–344 |  | 29 Dec 2003 (SI 2003/3142) |
| 345 |  | See Sch 13 below |
| 346, 347 |  | 29 Dec 2003 (SI 2003/3142) |
| 348 | (1) | 29 Dec 2003 (SI 2003/3142) |
|  | (2), (3) | 18 Sep 2003 (SI 2003/1900) |
|  | (4) | 29 Dec 2003 (SI 2003/3142) |
|  | (5)–(7) | 18 Sep 2003 (SI 2003/1900) |
| 349 |  | 29 Dec 2003 (SI 2003/3142) |
| 350 | (1), (2) | 29 Dec 2003 (SI 2003/3142)[2] |
|  | (3) | See Sch 14 below |
|  | (4)–(6) | 29 Dec 2003 (SI 2003/3142) |
| 351 | (1)–(3) | 29 Dec 2003 (SI 2003/3142) |
|  | (4)(a)(i) | 1 Jul 2004 (SI 2003/3142) |

**Communications Act 2003 (c 21)**—*contd*

| | | |
|---|---|---|
| | (4)(a)(ii), (iii) | 29 Dec 2003 (SI 2003/3142) |
| | (4)(b) | 29 Dec 2003 (SI 2003/3142) |
| | (5)–(9) | 29 Dec 2003 (SI 2003/3142) |
| | (10) | 29 Dec 2003 (except definition "original production" and para (a) in definition "peak viewing time") (SI 2003/3142) |
| | | 1 Jul 2004 (otherwise) (SI 2003/3142) |
| | (11) | 29 Dec 2003 (SI 2003/3142) |
| 352 | | 29 Dec 2003 (SI 2003/3142) |
| 353 | (1)–(3) | 29 Dec 2003 (SI 2003/3142) |
| | (4)(a)(i) | 1 Jul 2004 (SI 2003/3142) |
| | (4)(a)(ii), (iii) | 29 Dec 2003 (SI 2003/3142) |
| | (4)(b) | 29 Dec 2003 (SI 2003/3142) |
| | (5), (6) | 29 Dec 2003 (SI 2003/3142) |
| | (7) | 29 Dec 2003 (except definition "original production" and para (a) in definition "peak viewing time") (SI 2003/3142) |
| | | 1 Jul 2004 (otherwise) (SI 2003/3142) |
| | (8) | 29 Dec 2003 (SI 2003/3142) |
| 354–359 | | 29 Dec 2003 (SI 2003/3142) |
| 360 | (1), (2) | 29 Dec 2003 (SI 2003/3142) |
| | (3) | See Sch 15 below |
| 361 | | 25 Jul 2003 (SI 2003/1900) |
| 362 | | 25 Jul 2003 (SI 2003/1900)[2] |
| 363–366 | | 1 Apr 2004 (SI 2003/3142) |
| 367 | | 9 Mar 2004 (for the purpose of enabling regulations to be made under Wireless Telegraphy Act 1967, s 6(1)) (SI 2003/3142) |
| | | 1 Apr 2004 (otherwise) (SI 2003/3142) |
| 368 | | 1 Apr 2004 (SI 2003/3142) |
| 369 | (1)(a)–(d) | 25 Jul 2003 (for a specified transitional purpose[1]) (SI 2003/1900) |
| | | 29 Dec 2003 (otherwise) (SI 2003/3142) |
| | (1)(e) | 29 Dec 2003 (SI 2003/3142) |
| | (2), (3) | 25 Jul 2003 (for a specified transitional purpose[1]) (SI 2003/1900) |
| | | 29 Dec 2003 (otherwise) (SI 2003/3142) |
| 370, 371 | | 25 Jul 2003 (for a specified transitional purpose[1]) (SI 2003/1900) |
| | | 29 Dec 2003 (for the purpose of transferring the networks and services functions and the spectrum functions on OFCOM) (SI 2003/3142) |
| 372–388 | | 29 Dec 2003 (SI 2003/3142) |
| 389 | (1) | See Sch 16 below |
| | (2)–(4) | 29 Dec 2003 (SI 2003/3142) |
| 390–392 | | 29 Dec 2003 (SI 2003/3142) |
| 393 | (1)(a), (b) | 25 Jul 2003 (for a specified transitional purpose[1]) (SI 2003/1900) |
| | | 29 Dec 2003 (otherwise) (SI 2003/3142) |
| | (1)(c), (d) | 29 Dec 2003 (SI 2003/3142) |
| | (2)–(4) | 25 Jul 2003 (for a specified transitional purpose[1]) (SI 2003/1900) |
| | | 29 Dec 2003 (otherwise) (SI 2003/3142) |
| | (5)(a)–(i) | 25 Jul 2003 (for a specified transitional purpose[1]) (SI 2003/1900) |
| | | 29 Dec 2003 (otherwise) (SI 2003/3142) |
| | (5)(j), (k) | 29 Dec 2003 (SI 2003/3142) |
| | (5)(l)–(p) | 25 Jul 2003 (for a specified transitional purpose[1]) (SI 2003/1900) |
| | | 29 Dec 2003 (otherwise) (SI 2003/3142) |
| | (6)(a) | 25 Jul 2003 (except in its application to ss 15, 390) (for a specified transitional purpose[1]) (SI 2003/1900) |
| | | 29 Dec 2003 (otherwise) (SI 2003/3142) |
| | (6)(b)–(d) | 25 Jul 2003 (for a specified transitional purpose[1]) (SI 2003/1900) |
| | | 29 Dec 2003 (otherwise) (SI 2003/3142) |
| | (7) | 29 Dec 2003 (SI 2003/3142) |
| | (8)–(12) | 25 Jul 2003 (for a specified transitional purpose[1]) (SI 2003/1900) |
| | | 29 Dec 2003 (otherwise) (SI 2003/3142) |
| 394 | (1) | 25 Jul 2003 (for a specified transitional purpose[1]) (SI 2003/1900) |

**Communications Act 2003 (c 21)**—*contd*

|  |  |  |
|---|---|---|
|  |  | 29 Dec 2003 (otherwise) (SI 2003/3142) |
|  | (2)(a)–(d) | 25 Jul 2003 (for a specified transitional purpose[1]) (SI 2003/1900) |
|  |  | 29 Dec 2003 (otherwise) (SI 2003/3142) |
|  | (2)(e), (f) | 29 Dec 2003 (SI 2003/3142) |
|  | (3)–(10) | 25 Jul 2003 (for a specified transitional purpose[1]) (SI 2003/1900) |
|  |  | 29 Dec 2003 (otherwise) (SI 2003/3142) |
| 395–399 |  | 25 Jul 2003 (for a specified transitional purpose[1]) (SI 2003/1900) |
|  |  | 29 Dec 2003 (for the purpose of transferring the networks and services functions and the spectrum functions on OFCOM) (SI 2003/3142) |
| 400 |  | 29 Dec 2003 (SI 2003/3142) |
| 401 |  | 3 Nov 2017 (SI 2017/1063) |
| 402–404 |  | 25 Jul 2003 (for a specified transitional purpose[1]) (SI 2003/1900) |
|  |  | 29 Dec 2003 (for the purpose of transferring the networks and services functions and the spectrum functions on OFCOM) (SI 2003/3142) |
| 405 |  | 17 Jul 2003 (s 411(2), (3)) |
| 406 | (1) | See Sch 17 below |
|  | (2)–(5) | 25 Jul 2003 (for a specified transitional purpose[1]) (SI 2003/1900) |
|  |  | 29 Dec 2003 (for the purpose of transferring the networks and services functions and the spectrum functions on OFCOM) (SI 2003/3142) |
|  | (6) | See Sch 18 below |
|  | (7) | See Sch 19 below |
|  | (8)–(10) | 25 Jul 2003 (for a specified transitional purpose[1]) (SI 2003/1900) |
|  |  | 29 Dec 2003 (for the purpose of transferring the networks and services functions and the spectrum functions on OFCOM) (SI 2003/3142) |
| 407 |  | 18 Sep 2003 (SI 2003/1900) |
| 408 |  | 25 Jul 2003 (for a specified transitional purpose[1]) (SI 2003/1900) |
|  |  | 29 Dec 2003 (for the purpose of transferring the networks and services functions and the spectrum functions on OFCOM) (SI 2003/3142) |
| 409 |  | *Not yet in force* |
| 410 |  | 25 Jul 2003 (for a specified transitional purpose[1]) (SI 2003/1900) |
|  |  | 29 Dec 2003 (for the purpose of transferring the networks and services functions and the spectrum functions on OFCOM) (SI 2003/3142) |
| 411 |  | 17 Jul 2003 (s 411(2), (3)) |
| Sch 1 | para 1(1)(a) | 29 Dec 2003 (except to the extent that the Wireless Telegraphy Act 1949 applies in respect of television licences and television receivers) (SI 2003/3142)[3] |
|  |  | 1 Apr 2004 (otherwise) (SI 2003/3142) |
|  | para 1(1)(b)–(d) | 29 Dec 2003 (SI 2003/3142) |
|  | para 1(2), (3) | 29 Dec 2003 (SI 2003/3142) |
|  | paras 2–14 | 29 Dec 2003 (SI 2003/3142) |
| Sch 2 |  | 18 Sep 2003 (SI 2003/1900) |
| Schs 3, 4 |  | 25 Jul 2003 (for a specified transitional purpose[1]) (SI 2003/1900) |
|  |  | 29 Dec 2003 (for the purpose of transferring the networks and services functions and the spectrum functions on OFCOM) (SI 2003/3142) |
| Sch 5 |  | 29 Dec 2003 (SI 2003/3142) |
| Sch 6 |  | *Never in force* (repealed) |
| Sch 7 |  | 29 Dec 2003 (SI 2003/3142) |
| Sch 8 |  | 25 Jul 2003 (for a specified transitional purpose[1]) (SI 2003/1900) |
|  |  | 29 Dec 2003 (for the purpose of transferring the networks and services functions and the spectrum functions on OFCOM) (SI 2003/3142) |
| Sch 9 |  | 29 Dec 2003 (SI 2003/3142) |
| Sch 10 |  | 29 Dec 2003 (SI 2003/3142)[4] |

**Communications Act 2003 (c 21)**—*contd*

| | | |
|---|---|---|
| Sch 11 | | 29 Dec 2003 (SI 2003/3142) |
| Sch 12 | paras 1–4 | 29 Dec 2003 (SI 2003/3142) |
| | paras 5, 6 | *Not yet in force* |
| | para 7 | 29 Dec 2003 (SI 2003/3142) |
| | para 8 | 1 Jul 2004 (SI 2003/3142) |
| | paras 9–24 | 29 Dec 2003 (SI 2003/3142) |
| Sch 13 | | 29 Dec 2003 (SI 2003/3142) |
| Sch 14 | paras 1–9 | 29 Dec 2003 (SI 2003/3142) |
| | para 10 | 12 Dec 2003 (SI 2003/3142) |
| | paras 11–14 | 29 Dec 2003 (SI 2003/3142) |
| | paras 15, 16 | 18 Sep 2003 (SI 2003/1900)[2] |
| | para 17 | 18 Sep 2003 (so far as relates to para 16) (SI 2003/1900) |
| | | 12 Dec 2003 (otherwise) (SI 2003/3142) |
| | para 18 | 29 Dec 2003 (SI 2003/3142) |
| Sch 15 | paras 1–19 | 29 Dec 2003 (SI 2003/3142)[2] |
| | para 20(1) | 25 Jul 2003 (SI 2003/1900) |
| | para 20(2)(a) | 25 Jul 2003 (SI 2003/1900) |
| | para 20(2)(b) | 29 Dec 2003 (SI 2003/3142) |
| | para 20(3)–(8) | 29 Dec 2003 (SI 2003/3142) |
| | para 21 | 29 Dec 2003 (SI 2003/3142)[4] |
| | paras 22–51 | 29 Dec 2003 (SI 2003/3142)[2] |
| | para 52(1) | 25 Jul 2003 (SI 2003/1900) |
| | para 52(2)(a) | 25 Jul 2003 (SI 2003/1900) |
| | para 52(2)(b) | 29 Dec 2003 (SI 2003/3142) |
| | para 52(3)–(7) | 29 Dec 2003 (SI 2003/3142) |
| | para 53(1) | 18 Sep 2003 (SI 2003/1900) |
| | para 53(2), (3) | 29 Dec 2003 (SI 2003/3142) |
| | para 53(4) | 18 Sep 2003 (SI 2003/1900) |
| | para 53(5) | 29 Dec 2003 (SI 2003/3142) |
| | paras 54–142 | 29 Dec 2003 (SI 2003/3142)[2] |
| Sch 16 | | 29 Dec 2003 (SI 2003/3142) |
| Sch 17 | paras 1–5 | 25 Jul 2003 (for a specified transitional purpose[1]) (SI 2003/1900) |
| | | 29 Dec 2003 (for the purpose of transferring the networks and services functions and the spectrum functions on OFCOM) (SI 2003/3142) |
| | para 6(1), (2) | 29 Dec 2003 (except to the extent that the Wireless Telegraphy Act 1949 applies in respect of television licences and television receivers) (SI 2003/3142)[3] |
| | | 1 Apr 2004 (otherwise) (SI 2003/3142) |
| | para 6(3) | 1 Apr 2004 (SI 2003/3142) |
| | para 6(4)–(7) | 29 Dec 2003 (except to the extent that the Wireless Telegraphy Act 1949 applies in respect of television licences and television receivers) (SI 2003/3142)[3] |
| | | 1 Apr 2004 (otherwise) (SI 2003/3142) |
| | para 7 | 18 Sep 2003 (SI 2003/1900) |
| | para 8(1) | 25 Jul 2003 (for a specified transitional purpose[1]) (SI 2003/1900) |
| | | 29 Dec 2003 (otherwise) (SI 2003/3142) |
| | para 8(2) | 29 Dec 2003 (SI 2003/3142) |
| | para 8(3) | 25 Jul 2003 (for a specified transitional purpose[1]) (SI 2003/1900) |
| | | 29 Dec 2003 (otherwise) (SI 2003/3142) |
| | para 8(4), (5) | 29 Dec 2003 (SI 2003/3142) |
| | para 8(6) | 25 Jul 2003 (for a specified transitional purpose[1]) (SI 2003/1900) |
| | | 29 Dec 2003 (otherwise) (SI 2003/3142) |
| | para 8(7) | 29 Dec 2003 (SI 2003/3142) |
| | para 8(8) | 25 Jul 2003 (for a specified transitional purpose[1]) (SI 2003/1900) |
| | | 29 Dec 2003 (otherwise) (SI 2003/3142) |

## Communications Act 2003 (c 21)—*contd*

| | |
|---|---|
| para 8(9) | 25 Jul 2003 (except the repeal in the Wireless Telegraphy Act 1949, s 1D(8) of the words from "A notice under this section" to "affected by them") (for a specified transitional purpose[1]) (SI 2003/1900) |
| | 29 Dec 2003 (otherwise) (SI 2003/3142) |
| para 8(10) | 25 Jul 2003 (for a specified transitional purpose[1]) (SI 2003/1900) |
| | 29 Dec 2003 (otherwise) (SI 2003/3142) |
| para 9(1), (2) | 25 Jul 2003 (for a specified transitional purpose[1]) (SI 2003/1900) |
| | 29 Dec 2003 (otherwise) (SI 2003/3142) |
| para 9(3) | 25 Jul 2003 (except so far as inserts Wireless Telegraphy Act 1949, s 3(2A)) (for a specified transitional purpose[1]) (SI 2003/1900) |
| | 29 Dec 2003 (otherwise) (SI 2003/3142) |
| para 10 | 25 Jul 2003 (for a specified transitional purpose[1]) (SI 2003/1900) |
| | 29 Dec 2003 (for the purpose of transferring the networks and services functions and the spectrum functions on OFCOM) (SI 2003/3142) |
| para 11(1)–(3) | 25 Jul 2003 (for a specified transitional purpose[1]) (SI 2003/1900) |
| | 29 Dec 2003 (otherwise) (SI 2003/3142) |
| para 11(4) | 25 Jul 2003 (except so far as inserts Wireless Telegraphy Act 1949, s 10(4A)) (for a specified transitional purpose[1]) (SI 2003/1900) |
| | 29 Dec 2003 (otherwise) (SI 2003/3142) |
| paras 12, 13 | 29 Dec 2003 (SI 2003/3142) |
| para 14(1), (2) | 25 Jul 2003 (for a specified transitional purpose[1]) (SI 2003/1900) |
| | 29 Dec 2003 (otherwise) (SI 2003/3142) |
| para 14(3)(a) | 29 Dec 2003 (SI 2003/3142) |
| para 14(3)(b) | 25 Jul 2003 (for a specified transitional purpose[1]) (SI 2003/1900) |
| | 29 Dec 2003 (otherwise) (SI 2003/3142) |
| para 14(4)(a) | 25 Jul 2003 (for a specified transitional purpose[1]) (SI 2003/1900) |
| | 29 Dec 2003 (otherwise) (SI 2003/3142) |
| para 14(4)(b) | 29 Dec 2003 (SI 2003/3142) |
| para 14(5)–(8) | 29 Dec 2003 (SI 2003/3142) |
| para 15 | 29 Dec 2003 (except to the extent that the Wireless Telegraphy Act 1949 applies in respect of television licences and television receivers) (SI 2003/3142)[3] |
| | 1 Apr 2004 (otherwise) (SI 2003/3142) |
| para 16 | 25 Jul 2003 (for a specified transitional purpose[1]) (SI 2003/1900) |
| | 29 Dec 2003 (for the purpose of transferring the networks and services functions and the spectrum functions on OFCOM) (SI 2003/3142) |
| para 17 | 29 Dec 2003 (SI 2003/3142) |
| para 18 | 18 Sep 2003 (for a specified transitional purpose[1]) (SI 2003/1900) |
| | 29 Dec 2003 (for the purpose of transferring the networks and services functions and the spectrum functions on OFCOM) (SI 2003/3142) |
| paras 19–31 | 25 Jul 2003 (for a specified transitional purpose[1]) (SI 2003/1900) |
| | 29 Dec 2003 (for the purpose of transferring the networks and services functions and the spectrum functions on OFCOM) (SI 2003/3142) |
| paras 32, 33 | 18 Sep 2003 (SI 2003/1900) |
| paras 34–36 | 29 Dec 2003 (SI 2003/3142) |
| para 37(1)–(4) | 25 Jul 2003 (for a specified transitional purpose[1]) (SI 2003/1900) |
| | 29 Dec 2003 (otherwise) (SI 2003/3142) |
| para 37(5) | 25 Jul 2003 (except so far as inserts Wireless Telegraphy Act 1967, s 7(11B)) (for a specified transitional purpose[1]) (SI 2003/1900) |
| | 29 Dec 2003 (otherwise) (SI 2003/3142) |
| para 38 | 25 Jul 2003 (for a specified transitional purpose[1]) (SI 2003/1900) |
| | 29 Dec 2003 (for the purpose of transferring the networks and services functions and the spectrum functions on OFCOM) (SI 2003/3142) |
| para 39 | 29 Dec 2003 (SI 2003/3142) |

**Communications Act 2003 (c 21)**—*contd*

| | |
|---|---|
| paras 40–47 | 25 Jul 2003 (for a specified transitional purpose[1]) (SI 2003/1900) |
| | 29 Dec 2003 (for the purpose of transferring the networks and services functions and the spectrum functions on OFCOM) (SI 2003/3142) |
| paras 48–50 | 29 Dec 2003 (SI 2003/3142) |
| paras 51–60 | 25 Jul 2003 (for a specified transitional purpose[1]) (SI 2003/1900) |
| | 29 Dec 2003 (for the purpose of transferring the networks and services functions and the spectrum functions on OFCOM) (SI 2003/3142) |
| paras 61, 62 | 29 Dec 2003 (SI 2003/3142) |
| para 63 | 25 Jul 2003 (for a specified transitional purpose[1]) (SI 2003/1900) |
| | 29 Dec 2003 (for the purpose of transferring the networks and services functions and the spectrum functions on OFCOM) (SI 2003/3142) |
| paras 64–69 | 29 Dec 2003 (SI 2003/3142) |
| para 70 | 25 Jul 2003 (except for the purpose of the giving of directions to any person to whom directions could not be given on 24 Jul 2003) (for a specified transitional purpose[1]) (SI 2003/1900) |
| | 18 Sep 2003 (otherwise) (SI 2003/1900) |
| para 71 | 25 Jul 2003 (for a specified transitional purpose[1]) (SI 2003/1900) |
| | 29 Dec 2003 (for the purpose of transferring the networks and services functions and the spectrum functions on OFCOM) (SI 2003/3142) |
| para 72(1)–(3) | 25 Jul 2003 (for a specified transitional purpose[1]) (SI 2003/1900) |
| | 29 Dec 2003 (otherwise) (SI 2003/3142) |
| para 72(4) | 29 Dec 2003 (SI 2003/3142) |
| para 72(5), (6) | 25 Jul 2003 (for a specified transitional purpose[1]) (SI 2003/1900) |
| | 29 Dec 2003 (otherwise) (SI 2003/3142) |
| para 72(7) | 29 Dec 2003 (SI 2003/3142) |
| para 73 | 25 Jul 2003 (except so far as inserts Telecommunications Act 1984, s 104(1B)) (for a specified transitional purpose[1]) (SI 2003/1900) |
| | 29 Dec 2003 (otherwise) (SI 2003/3142) |
| para 74 | 29 Dec 2003 (SI 2003/3142) |
| para 75 | 25 Jul 2003 (for a specified transitional purpose[1]) (SI 2003/1900) |
| | 29 Dec 2003 (for the purpose of transferring the networks and services functions and the spectrum functions on OFCOM) (SI 2003/3142) |
| para 76 | 29 Dec 2003 (SI 2003/3142) |
| paras 77–82 | 25 Jul 2003 (for a specified transitional purpose[1]) (SI 2003/1900) |
| | 29 Dec 2003 (for the purpose of transferring the networks and services functions and the spectrum functions on OFCOM) (SI 2003/3142) |
| para 83 | 29 Dec 2003 (SI 2003/3142) |
| paras 84–90 | 25 Jul 2003 (for a specified transitional purpose[1]) (SI 2003/1900) |
| | 29 Dec 2003 (for the purpose of transferring the networks and services functions and the spectrum functions on OFCOM) (SI 2003/3142) |
| paras 91–93 | 29 Dec 2003 (SI 2003/3142) |
| paras 94–128 | 25 Jul 2003 (for a specified transitional purpose[1]) (SI 2003/1900) |
| | 29 Dec 2003 (for the purpose of transferring the networks and services functions and the spectrum functions on OFCOM) (SI 2003/3142) |
| para 129(1) | 25 Jul 2003 (for a specified transitional purpose[1]) (SI 2003/1900) |
| | 29 Dec 2003 (otherwise) (SI 2003/3142) |
| para 129(2) | 29 Dec 2003 (SI 2003/3142) |
| para 129(3) | 25 Jul 2003 (for a specified transitional purpose[1]) (SI 2003/1900) |
| | 29 Dec 2003 (otherwise) (SI 2003/3142) |
| paras 130, 131 | 25 Jul 2003 (for a specified transitional purpose[1]) (SI 2003/1900) |

**Communications Act 2003 (c 21)**—*contd*

| | |
|---|---|
| | 29 Dec 2003 (for the purpose of transferring the networks and services functions and the spectrum functions on OFCOM) (SI 2003/3142) |
| para 132 | 29 Dec 2003 (SI 2003/3142) |
| para 133(1) | 1 Apr 2004 (SI 2003/3142) |
| para 133(2) | *Not yet in force* |
| para 133(3) | 1 Apr 2004 (SI 2003/3142) |
| paras 134–144 | 25 Jul 2003 (for a specified transitional purpose[1]) (SI 2003/1900) |
| | 29 Dec 2003 (for the purpose of transferring the networks and services functions and the spectrum functions on OFCOM) (SI 2003/3142) |
| paras 145, 146 | 29 Dec 2003 (SI 2003/3142) |
| para 147 | 25 Jul 2003 (except for (i) the words "or of grant recognised spectrum access" in the new s 2(1) of the Wireless Telegraphy Act 1998, and (ii) the new s 2(1)(b) of that Act, and the word "or" preceding that paragraph) (for a specified transitional purpose[1]) (SI 2003/1900) |
| | 29 Dec 2003 (otherwise) (SI 2003/3142) |
| para 148 | 29 Dec 2003 (SI 2003/3142) |
| para 149 | 18 Sep 2003 (for a specified transitional purpose[1]) (SI 2003/1900) |
| | 29 Dec 2003 (for the purpose of transferring the networks and services functions and the spectrum functions on OFCOM) (SI 2003/3142) |
| para 150 | 25 Jul 2003 (except so far as inserts Wireless Telegraphy Act 1998, s 6(3)) (for a specified transitional purpose[1]) (SI 2003/1900) |
| | 18 Sep 2003 (so far as inserts Wireless Telegraphy Act 1998, s 6(3) (except the words "or 3A")) (for a specified transitional purpose[1]) (SI 2003/1900) |
| | 29 Dec 2003 (otherwise) (SI 2003/3142) |
| para 151 | 29 Dec 2003 (SI 2003/3142) |
| paras 152–158 | 25 Jul 2003 (for a specified transitional purpose[1]) (SI 2003/1900) |
| | 29 Dec 2003 (for the purpose of transferring the networks and services functions and the spectrum functions on OFCOM) (SI 2003/3142) |
| para 159 | 1 Apr 2004 (SI 2003/3142) |
| para 160 | 25 Jul 2003 (for a specified transitional purpose[1]) (SI 2003/1900) |
| | 29 Dec 2003 (for the purpose of transferring the networks and services functions and the spectrum functions on OFCOM) (SI 2003/3142) |
| para 161(1) | 29 Dec 2003 (SI 2003/3142) |
| para 161(2) | 1 Apr 2004 (SI 2003/3142) |
| para 161(3) | 29 Dec 2003 (SI 2003/3142) |
| paras 162, 163 | 25 Jul 2003 (for a specified transitional purpose[1]) (SI 2003/1900) |
| | 29 Dec 2003 (for the purpose of transferring the networks and services functions and the spectrum functions on OFCOM) (SI 2003/3142) |
| para 164 | 29 Dec 2003 (SI 2003/3142) |
| para 165 | 25 Jul 2003 (for a specified transitional purpose[1]) (SI 2003/1900) |
| | 29 Dec 2003 (for the purpose of transferring the networks and services functions and the spectrum functions on OFCOM) (SI 2003/3142) |
| para 166(1), (2) | 25 Jul 2003 (for a specified transitional purpose[1]) (SI 2003/1900) |
| | 29 Dec 2003 (otherwise) (SI 2003/3142) |
| para 166(3)(a) | 29 Dec 2003 (SI 2003/3142) |
| para 166(3)(b) | 25 Jul 2003 (for a specified transitional purpose[1]) (SI 2003/1900) |
| | 29 Dec 2003 (otherwise) (SI 2003/3142) |
| para 167 | 29 Dec 2003 (SI 2003/3142) |
| paras 168–170 | 25 Jul 2003 (for a specified transitional purpose[1]) (SI 2003/1900) |

**Communications Act 2003 (c 21)**—*contd*

|  |  |  |
|---|---|---|
|  |  | 29 Dec 2003 (for the purpose of transferring the networks and services functions and the spectrum functions on OFCOM) (SI 2003/3142) |
|  | paras 171–173 | 29 Dec 2003 (SI 2003/3142) |
|  | para 174(1), (2) | 25 Jul 2003 (for a specified transitional purpose[1]) (SI 2003/1900) |
|  |  | 29 Dec 2003 (otherwise) (SI 2003/3142) |
|  | para 174(3) | 29 Dec 2003 (SI 2003/3142) |
|  | para 174(4) | 25 Jul 2003 (for a specified transitional purpose[1]) (SI 2003/1900) |
|  |  | 29 Dec 2003 (otherwise) (SI 2003/3142) |
|  | para 174(5) | 29 Dec 2003 (SI 2003/3142) |
|  | para 174(6), (7) | 25 Jul 2003 (for a specified transitional purpose[1]) (SI 2003/1900) |
|  |  | 29 Dec 2003 (otherwise) (SI 2003/3142) |
|  | para 175 | 25 Jul 2003 (for a specified transitional purpose[1]) (SI 2003/1900) |
|  |  | 29 Dec 2003 (for the purpose of transferring the networks and services functions and the spectrum functions on OFCOM) (SI 2003/3142) |
| Sch 18 | paras 1–4 | 25 Jul 2003 (for a specified transitional purpose[1]) (SI 2003/1900) |
|  |  | 29 Dec 2003 (for the purpose of transferring the networks and services functions and the spectrum functions on OFCOM) (SI 2003/3142) |
|  | paras 5, 6 | 29 Dec 2003 (SI 2003/3142) |
|  | paras 7–19 | 25 Jul 2003 (for a specified transitional purpose[1]) (SI 2003/1900) |
|  |  | 29 Dec 2003 (for the purpose of transferring the networks and services functions and the spectrum functions on OFCOM) (SI 2003/3142) |
|  | para 20 | 29 Dec 2003 (SI 2003/3142) |
|  | para 21 | 18 Sep 2003 (for a specified transitional purpose[1]) (SI 2003/1900) |
|  |  | 29 Dec 2003 (for the purpose of transferring the networks and services functions and the spectrum functions on OFCOM) (SI 2003/3142) |
|  | paras 22–26 | 25 Jul 2003 (for a specified transitional purpose[1]) (SI 2003/1900) |
|  |  | 29 Dec 2003 (for the purpose of transferring the networks and services functions and the spectrum functions on OFCOM) (SI 2003/3142) |
|  | paras 27–29 | 29 Dec 2003 (SI 2003/3142) |
|  | para 30 | 25 Jul 2003 (SI 2003/1900) |
|  | paras 31–53 | 29 Dec 2003 (SI 2003/3142) |
|  | para 54(1)–(4) | 18 Sep 2003 (SI 2003/1900) |
|  | para 54(5)–(7) | 29 Dec 2003 (SI 2003/3142) |
|  | para 55 | 1 Apr 2004 (SI 2003/3142) |
|  | paras 56–58 | 25 Jul 2003 (for a specified transitional purpose[1]) (SI 2003/1900) |
|  |  | 29 Dec 2003 (for the purpose of transferring the networks and services functions and the spectrum functions on OFCOM) (SI 2003/3142) |
|  | paras 59–62 | 29 Dec 2003 (SI 2003/3142) |
|  | paras 63, 64 | 25 Jul 2003 (for a specified transitional purpose[1]) (SI 2003/1900) |
|  |  | 29 Dec 2003 (for the purpose of transferring the networks and services functions and the spectrum functions on OFCOM) (SI 2003/3142) |
| Sch 19 | (1) | 25 Jul 2003 (for a specified transitional purpose[1]) (SI 2003/1900), repeals of or in— |

Telegraph Act 1899;

Wireless Telegraphy Act 1949, s 1D(1), (2), (7), s 1D(8) (words "and a reference to such notice shall also be published in the London, Edinburgh and Belfast Gazettes"), ss 1F, 3(1), 9, 10(2), 11(1), 14, 15(4)(c), 19(9), Sch 2;

Army Act 1955;

Air Force Act 1955;

Naval Discipline Act 1957;

Opencast Coal Act 1958;

**Communications Act 2003 (c 21)**—*contd*

    Continental Shelf Act 1964;

    Marine, &c, Broadcasting (Offences) Act 1967;

    Acquisition of Land Act 1981;

    British Telecommunications Act 1981;

    Telecommunications Act 1984, ss 2–53, 60–73, 92–98, 101(2)(a), 102, 104, s 106(1) (except definition "the Director"), ss 107, 109, Schs 2–6;

    Companies Consolidation (Consequential Provisions) Act 1985;

    Housing Act 1985;

    Interception of Communications Act 1985;

    Surrogacy Arrangements Act 1985;

    Airports Act 1986;

    Insolvency Act 1986;

    Channel Tunnel Act 1987;

    Consumer Protection Act 1987;

    Income and Corporation Taxes Act 1988;

    Copyright, Designs and Patents Act 1988, Sch 7;

    Housing Act 1988;

    Legal Aid Act 1988;

    Electricity Act 1989;

    Companies Act 1989, Sch 18;

    Planning (Consequential Provisions) Act 1990;

    Courts and Legal Services Act 1990;

    New Roads and Street Works Act 1991;

    Carriage of Goods by Sea Act 1992;

    Charities Act 1992;

    Competition and Service (Utilities) Act 1992, ss 1–10, 49, Sch 1, paras 1, 2, 4;

    Taxation of Chargeable Gains Act 1992;

    Tribunals and Inquiries Act 1992;

    Cardiff Bay Barrage Act 1993;

    Judicial Pensions and Retirement Act 1993;

    Leasehold Reform, Housing and Urban Development Act 1993;

    Local Government (Wales) Act 1994;

    Criminal Justice and Public Order Act 1994;

    Deregulation and Contracting Out Act 1994, Sch 4;

    Vehicle Excise and Registration Act 1994;

    Arbitration Act 1996;

    Channel Tunnel Rail Link Act 1996;

    Telecommunications (Fraud) Act 1997;

    Competition Act 1998, Sch 7, para 2, Schs 10, 13;

    Petroleum Act 1998;

    Regional Development Agencies Act 1998;

    Wireless Telegraphy Act 1998, s 1(3), Sch 1, paras 2, 3;

    Access to Justice Act 1999;

    Electronic Communications Act 2000;

    Regulation of Investigatory Powers Act 2000;

    Countryside and Rights of Way Act 2000;

    Transport Act 2000, Sch 8;

    Criminal Justice and Police Act 2001;

    Enterprise Act 2002, ss 136, 168, Sch 9, Sch 25, para 13;

    Income Tax (Earnings and Pensions) Act 2003

18 Sep 2003 (repeals of or in Wireless Telegraphy Act 1998, s 3) (for a specified transitional purpose[1]) (SI 2003/1900)

29 Dec 2003 (for the purpose of transferring the networks and services functions and the spectrum functions on OFCOM) (SI 2003/3142), repeals of or in—

    Telegraph Act 1899;

**Communications Act 2003 (c 21)**—*contd*

Wireless Telegraphy Act 1949, s 1D(1), (2), (7), s 1D(8) (words "and a reference to such notice shall also be published in the London, Edinburgh and Belfast Gazettes"), ss 1F, 3(1), 9, 10(2), 11(1), 14, 15(4)(c), 19(9), Sch 2;
Army Act 1955;
Air Force Act 1955;
Naval Discipline Act 1957;
Opencast Coal Act 1958;
Continental Shelf Act 1964;
Marine, &c, Broadcasting (Offences) Act 1967;
Acquisition of Land Act 1981;
British Telecommunications Act 1981;
Companies Consolidation (Consequential Provisions) Act 1985;
Housing Act 1985;
Interception of Communications Act 1985;
Surrogacy Arrangements Act 1985;
Airports Act 1986;
Insolvency Act 1986;
Channel Tunnel Act 1987;
Consumer Protection Act 1987;
Income and Corporation Taxes Act 1988;
Legal Aid Act 1988;
Housing Act 1988;
Electricity Act 1989;
Courts and Legal Services Act 1990;
Planning (Consequential Provisions) Act 1990;
New Roads and Street Works Act 1991;
Taxation of Chargeable Gains Act 1992;
Charities Act 1992;
Carriage of Goods by Sea Act 1992;
Tribunals and Inquiries Act 1992;
Cardiff Bay Barrage Act 1993;
Judicial Pensions and Retirement Act 1993;
Leasehold Reform, Housing and Urban Development Act 1993;
Criminal Justice and Public Order Act 1994;
Local Government (Wales) Act 1994;
Vehicle Excise and Registration Act 1994;
Arbitration Act 1996;
Channel Tunnel Rail Link Act 1996;
Telecommunications (Fraud) Act 1997;
Petroleum Act 1998;
Regional Development Agencies Act 1998;
Wireless Telegraphy Act 1998, ss 1(3), 3, Sch 1, paras 2, 3;
Access to Justice Act 1999;
Electronic Communications Act 2000;
Regulation of Investigatory Powers Act 2000;
Countryside and Rights of Way Act 2000;
Criminal Justice and Police Act 2001;
Income Tax (Earnings and Pensions) Act 2003
29 Dec 2003 (SI 2003/3142), repeals of or in—
Wireless Telegraphy Act 1949, s 1D(8) (so far as not already in force);
Parliamentary Commissioner Act 1967;
Wireless Telegraphy Act 1967, s 7(5);
Fair Trading Act 1973;
House of Commons Disqualification Act 1975;
Northern Ireland Assembly Disqualification Act 1975;
Welsh Development Agency Act 1975;
Telecommunications Act 1984 (except ss 1, 55, Sch 1)[4];

**Communications Act 2003 (c 21)**—*contd*

Copyright, Designs and Patents Act 1988 (so far as not already in force);

Companies Act 1989 (so far as not already in force);

Broadcasting Act 1990 (except ss 180, 181, Sch 18)[4];

Competition and Service (Utilities) Act 1992 (so far as not already in force);

Deregulation and Contracting Out Act 1994 (so far as not already in force);

Criminal Procedure (Consequential Provisions) (Scotland) Act 1995;

Broadcasting Act 1996[4];

Planning (Consequential Provisions) (Scotland) Act 1997;

Wireless Telegraphy Act 1998, ss 3, 5;

Competition Act 1998 (so far as not already in force);

Freedom of Information Act 2000 (except the entries relating to the Broadcasting Standards Commission, the Independent Television Commission and the Radio Authority);

Political Parties, Elections and Referendums Act 2000;

Transport Act 2000 (so far as not already in force);

Anti-terrorism, Crime and Security Act 2001;

Enterprise Act 2002 (so far as not already in force);

Office of Communications Act 2002;

Tobacco Advertising and Promotion Act 2002;

European Parliament (Representation) Act 2003

1 Apr 2004 (SI 2003/3142), repeals of or in—

Wireless Telegraphy Act 1949 (so far as not already in force);

Wireless Telegraphy Act 1967 (so far as not already in force);

Broadcasting Act 1990 (so far as not already in force);

Criminal Procedure (Scotland) Act 1995;

Wireless Telegraphy Act 1998 (so far as not already in force)

*Not yet in force*, repeals of or in—

Telecommunications Act 1984, ss 1, 55, Sch 1;

Freedom of Information Act 2000, Sch 1, Pt 6 (entries relating to the Broadcasting Standards Commission, the Independent Television Commission and the Radio Authority);

Postal Services Act 2000

|  |  |
|---|---|
| (1), Notes 1, 2 | 25 Jul 2003 (for a specified transitional purpose[1]) (SI 2003/1900) |
|  | 29 Dec 2003 (for the purpose of transferring the networks and services functions and the spectrum functions on OFCOM) (SI 2003/3142) |
| (1), Note 3 | 29 Dec 2003 (SI 2003/3142) |
| (1), Notes 4, 5 | 25 Jul 2003 (for a specified transitional purpose[1]) (SI 2003/1900) |
|  | 29 Dec 2003 (for the purpose of transferring the networks and services functions and the spectrum functions on OFCOM) (SI 2003/3142) |
| (1), Note 6 | *Not yet in force* |
| (2) | 25 Jul 2003 (except revocations in Race Relations (Northern Ireland) Order 1997) (for a specified transitional purpose[1]) (SI 2003/1900) |
|  | 29 Dec 2003 (except revocations in Race Relations (Northern Ireland) Order 1997) (for the purpose of transferring the networks and services functions and the spectrum functions on OFCOM) (SI 2003/3142) |
|  | 29 Dec 2003 (revocations in Race Relations (Northern Ireland) Order 1997) (SI 2003/3142) |

---

[1]  The specified transitional purpose is that of enabling the networks and services functions and the spectrum functions to be carried out during the transitional period provided for by s 408(6) of the Act by the Director General of Telecommunications and the Secretary of State respectively

[2]  For transitional provisions, see SI 2003/1900, arts 3–6

**Communications Act 2003 (c 21)**—*contd*

[3]     For transitional provisions, see SI 2003/3142, art 3(3)

[4]     For transitional provisions, see SI 2003/3142, arts 5–11

---

## Community Care (Delayed Discharges etc) Act 2003 (c 5)

*RA:* 8 Apr 2003

*Commencement provisions:* s 20(2); Community Care (Delayed Discharges etc) Act 2003 (Commencement No 1) (England) Order 2003, SI 2003/2280

| | | |
|---|---|---|
| 1 | (1), (2) | 4 Sep 2003 (E) (SI 2003/2280) |
| | | *Not yet in force* (W) |
| | (3)–(5) | 1 Oct 2003 (E) (SI 2003/2280) |
| | | *Not yet in force* (W) |
| 2 | | 1 Oct 2003 (E) (SI 2003/2280) |
| | | *Not yet in force* (W) |
| 3 | (1), (2) | 1 Oct 2003 (E) (SI 2003/2280) |
| | | *Not yet in force* (W) |
| | (3) | 4 Sep 2003 (E) (SI 2003/2280) |
| | | *Not yet in force* (W) |
| | (4) | 1 Oct 2003 (E) (SI 2003/2280) |
| | | *Not yet in force* (W) |
| | (5) | 4 Sep 2003 (E) (SI 2003/2280) |
| | | *Not yet in force* (W) |
| 4 | | 1 Oct 2003 (E) (SI 2003/2280) |
| | | *Not yet in force* (W) |
| 5 | (1)–(6) | 1 Oct 2003 (E) (SI 2003/2280) |
| | | *Not yet in force* (W) |
| | (7), (8) | 4 Sep 2003 (E) (SI 2003/2280) |
| | | *Not yet in force* (W) |
| | (9) | 1 Oct 2003 (E) (SI 2003/2280) |
| | | *Not yet in force* (W) |
| | (10) | 4 Sep 2003 (E) (SI 2003/2280) |
| | | *Not yet in force* (W) |
| 6 | (1) | 5 Jan 2004 (E) (SI 2003/2280) |
| | | *Not yet in force* (W) |
| | (2) | 4 Sep 2003 (E) (in so far as conferring any power to make regulations) (SI 2003/2280) |
| | | 5 Jan 2004 (E) (otherwise) (SI 2003/2280) |
| | | *Not yet in force* (W) |
| | (3)–(6) | 5 Jan 2004 (E) (SI 2003/2280) |
| | | *Not yet in force* (W) |
| | (7) | 4 Sep 2003 (E) (SI 2003/2280) |
| | | *Not yet in force* (W) |
| 7 | (1) | 4 Sep 2003 (E) (SI 2003/2280) |
| | | *Not yet in force* (W) |
| | (2) | 5 Jan 2004 (E) (SI 2003/2280) |
| | | *Not yet in force* (W) |
| | (3) | 4 Sep 2003 (E) (SI 2003/2280) |
| | | *Not yet in force* (W) |
| 8 | | 1 Oct 2003 (E) (SI 2003/2280) |
| | | *Not yet in force* (W) |
| 9 | (1) | 4 Sep 2003 (E) (SI 2003/2280) |
| | | *Not yet in force* (W) |
| | (2) | 4 Sep 2003 (E) (in so far as conferring any power to make regulations) (SI 2003/2280) |
| | | 1 Oct 2003 (E) (otherwise) (SI 2003/2280) |
| | | *Not yet in force* (W) |
| | (3)–(6) | 4 Sep 2003 (E) (SI 2003/2280) |

**Community Care (Delayed Discharges etc) Act 2003 (c 5)**—*contd*

|  |  |
|---|---|
| | *Not yet in force* (W) |
| 10–12 | 4 Sep 2003 (E) (SI 2003/2280) |
| | *Not yet in force* (W) |
| 13 | 1 Oct 2003 (E) (SI 2003/2280) |
| | *Not yet in force* (W) |
| 14 | *Not yet in force* |
| 15–20 | 8 Apr 2003 (RA) |

---

**Consolidated Fund Act 2003 (c 2)**

*RA:* 20 Mar 2003

Whole Act in force 20 Mar 2003 (RA)

---

**Consolidated Fund (No 2) Act 2003 (c 45)**

*RA:* 17 Dec 2003

Whole Act in force 17 Dec 2003 (RA)

---

**Co-operatives and Community Benefit Societies Act 2003 (c 15)**

*RA:* 10 Jul 2003

*Commencement provisions:* s 7; Co-operatives and Community Benefit Societies Act 2003 (Commencement No 1) Order 2003, SI 2003/2678; Cooperatives and Community Benefit Societies Act 2003 (Commencement No 2) Order 2004, SI 2004/3257

|  |  |  |
|---|---|---|
| 1 | | 13 Dec 2004 (SI 2004/3257) |
| 2, 3 | | 1 Apr 2004 (SI 2003/2678) |
| 4 | | 20 Oct 2003 (with effect in relation to contracts or deeds made, and obligations undertaken, on or after 20 Oct 2003) (SI 2003/2678) |
| 5 | (1)–(8) | 20 Oct 2003 (SI 2003/2678) |
| | (9) | See Schedule below |
| 6 | | 20 Oct 2003 (SI 2003/2678) |
| 7–9 | | 10 Jul 2003 (RA) |
| Schedule | | 20 Oct 2003 (SI 2003/2678) |

---

**Council of the Law Society of Scotland Act 2003 (asp 14)**

*RA:* 1 May 2003

*Commencement provisions:* s 3(2)

Whole Act in force 1 Jun 2003 (s 3(2))

---

**Courts Act 2003 (c 39)**

*RA:* 20 Nov 2003

*Commencement provisions:* s 110; Courts Act 2003 (Commencement No 1) Order 2003, SI 2003/3345; Courts Act 2003 (Commencement No 2) Order 2004, SI 2004/174; Courts Act 2003 (Commencement No 3 and Transitional Provisions) Order 2004, SI 2004/401; Courts Act 2003 (Commencement No 4) Order 2004, SI 2004/798; Courts Act 2003 (Commencement No 5) Order 2004, SI 2004/1104; Courts Act 2003 (Commencement No 6 and Savings) Order 2004, SI 2004/2066; Courts Act 2003 (Commencement No 7) Order 2004, SI 2004/2195; Courts Act 2003 (Commencement No 8, Savings and Consequential Provisions) Order 2004, SI 2004/3123; Courts Act 2003 (Commencement No 9, Savings, Consequential and Transitional Provisions) Order 2005,

**Courts Act 2003 (c 39)**—*contd*

SI 2005/547, revoked by SI 2005/910; Courts Act 2003 (Commencement No 10) Order 2005,
SI 2005/910; Courts Act 2003 (Commencement No 11 and Transitional Provision) Order 2005,
SI 2005/2744; Courts Act 2003 (Commencement No 12 and Transitional Provision) Order 2005,
SI 2005/3518; Courts Act 2003 (Commencement No 13) Order 2007, SI 2007/2706, as amended by
SI 2010/2921; Courts Act 2003 (Commencement No 14) Order 2010, SI 2010/2921

| | | |
|---|---|---|
| 1–3 | | 1 Apr 2005 (SI 2005/910) |
| 4 | | 1 Jun 2004 (SI 2004/798) |
| 5 | | 1 Apr 2005 (SI 2005/910) |
| 6 | (1), (2) | 1 Apr 2005 (SI 2005/910) |
| | (3) | See Sch 2 below |
| | (4) | 1 Apr 2005 (SI 2005/910) |
| 7–41 | | 1 Apr 2005 (SI 2005/910) |
| 42 | | 20 Nov 2003 (RA) |
| 43–49 | | 1 Apr 2005 (SI 2005/910) |
| 50 | (1) | 1 Apr 2005 (SI 2005/910) |
| | (2), (3) | 5 Sep 2007 (SI 2007/2706) |
| | (4) | 1 Apr 2005 (SI 2005/910) |
| 51–61 | | 1 Apr 2005 (SI 2005/910) |
| 62–64 | | 26 Jan 2004 (SI 2003/3345) |
| 65 | | 1 Apr 2005 (SI 2005/910) |
| 66 | (1)(a) | 26 Jan 2004 (SI 2003/3345) |
| | (1)(b) | *Never in force* (repealed) |
| | (2), (3) | 26 Jan 2004 (SI 2003/3345) |
| | (4) | *Never in force* (repealed) |
| 67, 68 | | 26 Jan 2004 (SI 2003/3345) |
| 69 | | 1 Sep 2004 (SI 2004/2066) |
| 70, 71 | | 26 Jan 2004 (SI 2003/3345) |
| 72, 73 | | 1 Sep 2004 (SI 2004/2066) |
| 74 | | 26 Jan 2004 (SI 2003/3345) |
| 75, 76 | | 7 Oct 2005 (for a specified purpose only[5]) (SI 2005/2744) |
| | | 12 Dec 2010 (otherwise) (SI 2010/2921) |
| 77, 78 | | 26 Jan 2004 (SI 2003/3345) |
| 79, 80 | | 7 Oct 2005 (for a specified purpose only[5]) (SI 2005/2744) |
| | | 12 Dec 2010 (otherwise) (SI 2010/2921) |
| 81 | | 26 Jan 2004 (SI 2003/3345) |
| 82 | | *Not yet in force* |
| 83, 84 | | 26 Jan 2004 (SI 2003/3345) |
| 85 | | *Not yet in force* |
| 86, 87 | | 1 May 2004 (SI 2004/1104) |
| 88–91 | | 1 Apr 2005 (SI 2005/910) |
| 92 | | 4 Jan 2005 (SI 2004/3123) |
| 93 | | 1 Feb 2004 (SI 2004/174) |
| 94 | | 20 Nov 2003 (RA) |
| 95, 96 | | 5 Apr 2004 (SI 2004/174) |
| 97 | | See Schs 5, 6 below |
| 98 | (1)(a)–(c) | 6 Apr 2006 (SI 2005/3518) |
| | (1)(d) | *Not yet in force* |
| | (1)(e) | 26 Jan 2004 (SI 2003/3345) |
| | (2) | 26 Jan 2004 (SI 2003/3345) |
| | (3)(a), (b) | 6 Apr 2006 (SI 2005/3518) |
| | (3)(c), (d) | 26 Jan 2004 (SI 2003/3345) |
| | (4)–(8) | 26 Jan 2004 (SI 2003/3345) |
| 99 | (1) | See Sch 7 below |
| | (2) | 15 Mar 2004 (SI 2004/401) |
| 100, 101 | | 1 Apr 2005 (SI 2005/910) |
| 102 | | 26 Jan 2004 (SI 2003/3345) |
| 103, 104 | | 1 May 2004 (SI 2004/1104) |
| 105 | | 1 Apr 2005 (SI 2005/910) |
| 106 | | 1 May 2004 (SI 2004/1104) |

**Courts Act 2003 (c 39)**—*contd*

| | | |
|---|---|---|
| 107, 108 | | 20 Nov 2003 (RA) |
| 109 | (1) | See Sch 8 below |
| | (2) | See Sch 9 below |
| | (3) | See Sch 10 below |
| | (4)–(6) | 20 Nov 2003 (RA) |
| 110–112 | | 20 Nov 2003 (RA) |
| Sch 1 | | 1 Jun 2004 (SI 2004/798) |
| Sch 2 | | 1 Sep 2004 (SI 2004/2066) |
| Sch 3 | | 1 Apr 2005 (SI 2005/910) |
| Sch 4 | | *Not yet in force*[4] (para 7 repealed) |
| Sch 5 | | 23 Feb 2004 (in respect of the petty sessions areas specified in columns 1 and 3 of Pt I of the Schedule to the Collection of Fines (Pilot Schemes) Order 2004, SI 2004/175) (SI 2004/174) |
| | | 29 Mar 2004 (in respect of the petty sessions areas specified in columns 1 and 3 of Pt II of the Schedule to the Collection of Fines (Pilot Schemes) Order 2004, SI 2004/175) (SI 2004/174) |
| | | 5 Apr 2004 (in respect of all other petty sessions areas in England and Wales) (SI 2004/174) |
| Sch 6 | para 1(1) | 21 Sep 2004 (SI 2004/2195) |
| | para 1(2) | 1 May 2004 (the entries relating to "the prescribed hourly sum" and "regulations") (SI 2004/1104) |
| | | 21 Sep 2004 (otherwise) (SI 2004/2195) |
| | paras 2–13 | 21 Sep 2004 (SI 2004/2195) |
| Sch 7 | | 15 Mar 2004 (SI 2004/401)[1] |
| Sch 8 | paras 1–4 | 1 Apr 2005 (SI 2005/910) |
| | para 5 | 15 Mar 2004 (SI 2004/401) |
| | paras 6–8 | 1 Apr 2005 (SI 2005/910) |
| | para 9 | 15 Mar 2004 (SI 2004/401) |
| | paras 10–60 | 1 Apr 2005 (SI 2005/910) |
| | para 61(1), (2) | 15 Mar 2004 (SI 2004/401) |
| | para 61(3) | 1 Apr 2005 (SI 2005/910) |
| | para 61(4) | 15 Mar 2004 (SI 2004/401) |
| | para 62 | 15 Mar 2004 (SI 2004/401) |
| | para 63 | 15 Mar 2004 (in so far as inserts definition "enforcement officer") (SI 2004/401) |
| | | 1 Apr 2005 (otherwise) (SI 2005/910) |
| | paras 64–66 | 1 Apr 2005 (SI 2005/910) |
| | para 67 | 1 Sep 2004 (SI 2004/2066)[2] |
| | paras 68–70 | 1 Apr 2005 (SI 2005/910) |
| | para 71 | 1 Sep 2004 (SI 2004/2066)[2] |
| | paras 72–82 | 1 Apr 2005 (SI 2005/910) |
| | para 83 | 1 Sep 2004 (SI 2004/2066)[2] |
| | paras 84–90 | 1 Apr 2005 (SI 2005/910) |
| | para 91(1) | 1 Apr 2005 (SI 2005/910) |
| | para 91(2) | 6 Apr 2011 (SI 2010/2921) |
| | para 91(3), (4) | 1 Apr 2005 (SI 2005/910) |
| | paras 92–106 | 1 Apr 2005 (SI 2005/910) |
| | para 107 | 1 Sep 2004 (SI 2004/2066)[2] |
| | paras 108–121 | 1 Apr 2005 (SI 2005/910) |
| | para 122 | 1 Sep 2004 (for the purpose of amending the Backing of Warrants (Republic of Ireland) Act 1965 so far as it has effect by virtue of the Extradition Act 2003 (Commencement and Savings) Order 2003, SI 2003/3103) (SI 2004/2066)[2] |
| | paras 123–125 | 1 Apr 2005 (SI 2005/910) |
| | para 126 | 1 Sep 2004 (SI 2004/2066)[2] |
| | paras 127–144 | 1 Apr 2005 (SI 2005/910) |
| | para 145 | 1 Sep 2004 (SI 2004/2066)[2] |
| | paras 146–171 | 1 Apr 2005 (SI 2005/910) |
| | paras 172, 173 | 1 Sep 2004 (SI 2004/2066)[2] |

**Courts Act 2003 (c 39)**—*contd*

| | |
|---|---|
| paras 174–181 | 1 Apr 2005 (SI 2005/910) |
| para 182 | 1 Sep 2004 (SI 2004/2066)[2] |
| para 183(1) | 1 Sep 2004 (SI 2004/2066)[2] |
| para 183(2) | 1 Apr 2005 (SI 2005/910) |
| para 183(3) | 1 Sep 2004 (SI 2004/2066)[2] |
| paras 184, 185 | 1 Apr 2005 (SI 2005/910) |
| para 186(1), (2) | 1 Sep 2004 (SI 2004/2066)[2] |
| para 186(3) | 1 Apr 2005 (SI 2005/910) |
| paras 187, 188 | 1 Apr 2005 (SI 2005/910) |
| para 189 | 15 Mar 2004 (SI 2004/401) |
| para 190 | 1 Sep 2004 (SI 2004/2066)[2] |
| paras 191–206 | 1 Apr 2005 (SI 2005/910) |
| para 207 | 1 Sep 2004 (SI 2004/2066)[2] |
| paras 208–218 | 1 Apr 2005 (SI 2005/910) |
| para 219 | 1 Sep 2004 (SI 2004/2066)[2] |
| paras 220–232 | 1 Apr 2005 (SI 2005/910) |
| paras 233, 234 | 1 Sep 2004 (SI 2004/2066)[2] |
| paras 235–237 | 1 Apr 2005 (SI 2005/910) |
| para 238 | 1 Sep 2004 (SI 2004/2066)[2] |
| paras 239–241 | 1 Apr 2005 (SI 2005/910) |
| para 242 | 10 Jan 2006 (subject to a transitional provision) (SI 2005/3518) |
| paras 243, 244 | 1 Apr 2005 (SI 2005/910) |
| para 245(1) | See sub-paras (2)–(5) below |
| para 245(2) | 1 Sep 2004 (for the purpose of creating an exception in relation to "any criminal cause or matter") (SI 2004/2066)[2] |
| | 1 Apr 2005 (so far as not already in force, except so far as creates an exception in relation to "family proceedings") (SI 2005/910) |
| | 7 Oct 2005 (in relation to "family proceedings" as defined by the Magistrates' Courts Act 1980, s 65(1)(h) (as substituted by the Adoption and Children Act 2002)) (SI 2005/2744) |
| | 6 Apr 2011 (in so far as creates an exception in relation to "family proceedings" as defined by the Magistrates' Courts Act 1980, s 65(1)(a)–(ca), (ee), (ef), (f), (i)–(ja), (l), (m), (nm)–(s)) (SI 2010/2921) |
| para 245(3) | 1 Apr 2005 (except to the extent that it omits the reference to "the President of the Family Division of the High Court") (SI 2005/910) |
| | 6 Apr 2011 (exception noted above) (SI 2010/2921) |
| para 245(4), (5) | 1 Apr 2005 (SI 2005/910) |
| para 246 | 1 Sep 2004 (SI 2004/2066)[2] |
| paras 247–249 | 1 Apr 2005 (SI 2005/910) |
| para 250 | 1 Sep 2004 (in so far as it relates to the definitions "the rules" and "prescribed") (SI 2004/2066)[2] |
| | 1 Apr 2005 (otherwise) (SI 2005/910) |
| para 251 | 1 Sep 2004 (SI 2004/2066)[2] |
| paras 252, 253 | 1 Apr 2005 (SI 2005/910) |
| para 254 | 10 Jan 2006 (subject to a transitional provision) (SI 2005/3518) |
| paras 255–262 | 1 Apr 2005 (SI 2005/910) |
| para 263 | 4 Jan 2005 (SI 2004/3123) |
| para 264 | 15 Mar 2004 (SI 2004/401) |
| paras 265–271 | 1 Apr 2005 (SI 2005/910) |
| para 272 | 6 Apr 2011 (SI 2010/2921) |
| para 273 | 1 Apr 2005 (SI 2005/910) |
| paras 274, 275 | 15 Mar 2004 (SI 2004/401) |
| paras 276, 277 | 4 Jan 2005 (SI 2004/3123) |
| para 278(a) | 6 Apr 2011 (SI 2010/2921) |
| para 278(b) | 4 Jan 2005 (SI 2004/3123) |
| paras 279–285 | 1 Apr 2005 (SI 2005/910) |
| para 286 | 1 Sep 2004 (SI 2004/2066)[2] |

**Courts Act 2003 (c 39)**—*contd*

| | |
|---|---|
| para 287 | 1 Apr 2005 (SI 2005/910) |
| para 288(1) | 1 Feb 2004 (SI 2004/174) |
| para 288(2) | 1 Apr 2005 (SI 2005/910) |
| para 288(3)–(5) | 1 Feb 2004 (SI 2004/174) |
| para 289 | 1 Feb 2004 (SI 2004/174) |
| para 290(1) | 1 Sep 2004 (SI 2004/2066)[2] |
| para 290(2) | 1 Apr 2005 (SI 2005/910) |
| para 290(3) | 1 Sep 2004 (SI 2004/2066)[2] |
| paras 291–294 | 1 Apr 2005 (SI 2005/910) |
| paras 295–298 | 15 Mar 2004 (SI 2004/401)[2] |
| paras 299–323 | 1 Apr 2005 (SI 2005/910) |
| para 324 | 1 Sep 2004 (for the purpose of amending the Extradition Act 1989 so far as it has effect by virtue of the Extradition Act 2003 (Commencement and Savings) Order 2003, SI 2003/3103) (SI 2004/2066)[2] |
| paras 325, 326 | 1 Apr 2005 (SI 2005/910) |
| paras 327, 328 | 1 Sep 2004 (for the purpose of amending the Extradition Act 1989 so far as it has effect by virtue of the Extradition Act 2003 (Commencement and Savings) Order 2003, SI 2003/3103) (SI 2004/2066)[2] |
| para 329(1) | 1 Sep 2004 (for the purpose of amending the Extradition Act 1989 so far as it has effect by virtue of the Extradition Act 2003 (Commencement and Savings) Order 2003, SI 2003/3103) (SI 2004/2066)[2] |
| para 329(2), (3) | 1 Apr 2005 (SI 2005/910) |
| para 329(4) | 1 Sep 2004 (for the purpose of amending the Extradition Act 1989 so far as it has effect by virtue of the Extradition Act 2003 (Commencement and Savings) Order 2003, SI 2003/3103) (SI 2004/2066)[2] |
| para 329(5) | 1 Apr 2005 (SI 2005/910) |
| para 330(1), (2) | 1 Sep 2004 (for the purpose of amending the Extradition Act 1989 so far as it has effect by virtue of the Extradition Act 2003 (Commencement and Savings) Order 2003, SI 2003/3103) (SI 2004/2066)[2] |
| para 330(3)(a) | 1 Sep 2004 (for the purpose of amending the Extradition Act 1989 so far as it has effect by virtue of the Extradition Act 2003 (Commencement and Savings) Order 2003, SI 2003/3103) (SI 2004/2066)[2] |
| para 330(3)(b) | 1 Apr 2005 (SI 2005/910) |
| paras 331–336 | 1 Apr 2005 (SI 2005/910) |
| para 337 | 6 Apr 2011 (SI 2010/2921) |
| paras 338–348 | 1 Apr 2005 (SI 2005/910) |
| para 349 | 6 Apr 2011 (SI 2010/2921) |
| paras 350–354 | 1 Apr 2005 (SI 2005/910) |
| para 355(a) | 1 Sep 2004 (SI 2004/2066)[2] |
| para 355(b) | 1 Apr 2005 (SI 2005/910) |
| paras 356–361 | 1 Apr 2005 (SI 2005/910) |
| para 362 | 1 Sep 2004 (SI 2004/2066)[2] |
| para 363 | 1 Apr 2005 (SI 2005/910) |
| para 364 | 1 Sep 2004 (SI 2004/2066)[2] |
| paras 365–376 | 1 Apr 2005 (SI 2005/910) |
| paras 377–381 | 1 Sep 2004 (SI 2004/2066)[2] |
| paras 382, 383 | 1 Apr 2005 (SI 2005/910) |
| para 384 | 1 Sep 2004 (SI 2004/2066)[2] |
| para 385 | 1 Apr 2005 (SI 2005/910) |
| paras 386, 387 | 1 Sep 2004 (SI 2004/2066)[2] |
| para 388 | 1 Apr 2005 (SI 2005/910) |
| paras 389, 390 | 1 Sep 2004 (SI 2004/2066)[2] |
| paras 391–402 | 1 Apr 2005 (SI 2005/910) |
| para 403 | 1 Sep 2004 (SI 2004/2066)[2] |

**Courts Act 2003 (c 39)**—*contd*

|  | para 404 | 1 Apr 2005 (SI 2005/910) |
|  | para 405 | 1 Sep 2004 (SI 2004/2066)[2] |
|  | paras 406–409 | 1 Apr 2005 (SI 2005/910) |
|  | para 410 | 1 Sep 2004 (SI 2004/2066)[2] |
|  | paras 411–414 | 1 Apr 2005 (SI 2005/910) |
| Sch 9 | paras 1–14 | 1 Apr 2005 (SI 2005/910) |

para 15
: 23 Feb 2004 (in respect of the petty sessions areas specified in columns 1 and 3 of Pt I of the Schedule to the Collection of Fines (Pilot Schemes) Order 2004, SI 2004/175) (SI 2004/174)

: 29 Mar 2004 (in respect of the petty sessions areas specified in columns 1 and 3 of Pt II of the Schedule to the Collection of Fines (Pilot Schemes) Order 2004, SI 2004/175) (SI 2004/174)

: 5 Apr 2004 (in respect of all other petty sessions areas in England and Wales) (SI 2004/174)

para 16
: 6 Apr 2006 (SI 2005/3518)

Sch 10
: 26 Jan 2004 (SI 2003/3345), repeals of or in—
Supreme Court Act 1981, s 56A;
Criminal Justice and Public Order Act 1994

: 15 Mar 2004 (SI 2004/401), repeals of or in—
Supreme Court Act 1981, ss 138, 138A, 138B;
County Courts Act 1984, s 99(4)(b)

: 1 May 2004 (SI 2004/1104), repeals of or in—
Judicature (Northern Ireland) Act 1978, ss 48, 70, 73, Sch 3;
Supreme Court Act 1981, s 76;
Judicial Pensions and Retirement Act 1993, Schs 1, 5;
Justice (Northern Ireland) Act 2002

: 1 Sep 2004 (SI 2004/2066)[2], repeals of or in—
Criminal Justice Act 1925;
Attachment of Earnings Act 1971;
Bail Act 1976 s 2;
Magistrates' Courts Act 1980, ss 145, 150(1) (in so far as it relates to the definition "the rules"), Sch 7, paras 5, 101(a), 151;
Supreme Court Act 1981, Sch 5 (in so far as it relates to the Criminal Justice Act 1948);
Access to Justice Act 1999, s 80(2);
Youth Justice and Criminal Evidence Act 1999, s 65(2)

: 4 Jan 2005 (SI 2004/3123), repeals of or in—
Supreme Court Act 1981, s 130[3];
County Courts Act 1984, ss 128[3], 147(1);
Matrimonial and Family Proceedings Act 1984, s 41[3]

: 1 Apr 2005 (otherwise) (SI 2005/910), except repeals of or in—
Maintenance Orders Act 1950, s 25(1);
Magistrates' Courts Act 1980, ss 137, 138, 144(2) (words "the President of the Family Division of the High Court"), Sch 6, Sch 7, para 8;
County Courts Act 1984, ss 73, 73A;
Matrimonial and Family Proceedings Act 1984, s 40;
Children Act 1989, s 97(7)(a);
Courts and Legal Services Act 1990, Sch 18, para 50;
Maintenance Enforcement Act 1991;
Civil Procedure Act 1997

: 10 Jan 2006 (repeal of Magistrates' Courts Act 1980, ss 137, 138, Sch 6) (subject to a transitional provision) (SI 2005/3518)

: 6 Apr 2006 (repeal of County Courts Act 1984, ss 73, 73A) (SI 2005/3518)

: 6 Apr 2011 (otherwise, except repeal of Civil Procedure Act 1997, s 2(6)–(8)) (SI 2010/2921)

## Courts Act 2003 (c 39)—*contd*

*Not yet in force* (exception noted above)

[1] For transitional provisions, see SI 2004/401, art 3

[2] For savings, see SI 2004/2066, art 3

[3] For savings, see SI 2004/3123, art 3

[4] Note that although s 65, which introduces Sch 4, has been brought into force by SI 2005/910, it has been stated that the intention was not to bring Sch 4 into force on the same date

[5] The specified purpose is that of making Family Procedure Rules in respect of all causes and matters (whether at first instance or appeal) relating to adoption including the exercise of the inherent jurisdiction of the High Court with respect to minors, and all proceedings for the purpose of enforcing an order made in proceedings described above

---

## Crime (International Co-operation) Act 2003 (c 32)

*RA:* 30 Oct 2003

*Commencement provisions:* s 94; Crime (International Co-operation) Act 2003 (Commencement No 1) Order 2004, SI 2004/786; Crime (International Co-operation) Act 2003 (Commencement No 2) Order 2004, SI 2004/2624; Crime (International Co-operation) Act 2003 (Commencement No 2) (Scotland) Order 2006, SSI 2006/281; Crime (International Co-operation) Act 2003 (Commencement No 3) Order 2006, SI 2006/2811; Crime (International Co-operation) Act 2003 (Commencement No 4) Order 2008, SI 2008/3009; Crime (International Co-operation) Act 2003 (Commencement No 5) Order 2009, SI 2009/2605; Crime (International Co-operation) Act 2003 (Commencement No 6) Order 2014, SI 2014/3192

| | | |
|---|---|---|
| 1–9 | | 26 Apr 2004 (SI 2004/786) |
| 10–12 | | 19 Oct 2009 (SI 2009/2605) |
| 13–19 | | 26 Apr 2004 (SI 2004/786) |
| 20–25 | | 19 Oct 2009 (SI 2009/2605) |
| 26–31 | | 26 Apr 2004 (SI 2004/786) |
| 32–36 | | 1 Nov 2006 (SI 2006/2811) |
| 37–41 | | 11 Jun 2006 (SSI 2006/281) |
| 42–46 | | 1 Nov 2006 (SI 2006/2811) |
| 47, 48 | | 26 Apr 2004 (SI 2004/786) |
| 49–51 | | 26 Mar 2004 (SI 2004/786) |
| 52, 53 | | 26 Apr 2004 (SI 2004/786) |
| 54, 55 | | 28 Jan 2010[1] (in relation to an offender who is normally resident in Ireland) (SI 2008/3009) |
| | | *Not yet in force* (otherwise) |
| 56–70 | | 28 Jan 2010[1] (in relation to an offence of which an offender has been convicted in Ireland) (SI 2008/3009) |
| | | *Not yet in force* (otherwise) |
| 71–75 | | 28 Jan 2010[1] (SI 2008/3009) |
| 76–79 | | 11 Oct 2004 (SI 2004/2624) |
| 80–85 | | 26 Apr 2004 (SI 2004/786) |
| 86, 87 | | *Never in force* (repealed) |
| 88 | | 26 Apr 2004 (SI 2004/786) |
| 89 | | *Not yet in force* |
| 90 | | See Sch 4 below |
| 91 | (1) | See Sch 5 below |
| | (2) | See Sch 6 below |
| 92–96 | | 30 Oct 2003 (RA) |
| Schs 1, 2 | | 26 Apr 2004 (SI 2004/786) |
| Sch 3 | | 28 Jan 2010[1] (in relation to an offender who is normally resident in Ireland) (SI 2008/3009) |
| | | *Not yet in force* (otherwise) |
| Sch 4 | | 3 Dec 2014 (SI 2014/3192) |
| Sch 5 | paras 1–4 | 26 Apr 2004 (SI 2004/786) |

## Crime (International Co-operation) Act 2003 (c 32)—*contd*

| | | |
|---|---|---|
| paras 5, 6 | 28 Jan 2010[1] (SI 2008/3009) | |
| paras 7–16 | 26 Apr 2004 (SI 2004/786) | |
| para 17 | 11 Oct 2004 (SI 2004/2624) | |
| para 18(a) | 11 Oct 2004 (SI 2004/2624) | |
| para 18(b) | 28 Jan 2010[1] (SI 2008/3009) | |
| paras 19–26 | 11 Oct 2004 (SI 2004/2624) | |
| para 27(a)(i) | 28 Jan 2010[1] (SI 2008/3009) | |
| para 27(a)(ii) | 11 Oct 2004 (SI 2004/2624) | |
| para 27(a)(iii) | 11 Oct 2004 (words "in paragraph (b), after "99C" there is inserted ", 109B"") (SI 2004/2624) | |
| | 28 Jan 2010[1] (otherwise) (SI 2008/3009) | |
| para 27(b) | 11 Oct 2004 (SI 2004/2624) | |
| paras 28–37 | 11 Oct 2004 (SI 2004/2624) | |
| paras 38–44 | 26 Apr 2004 (SI 2004/786) | |
| paras 45–60 | 11 Oct 2004 (SI 2004/2624) | |
| paras 61–71 | 26 Apr 2004 (SI 2004/786) | |
| paras 72–74 | 11 Oct 2004 (SI 2004/2624) | |
| paras 75–83 | 26 Apr 2004 (SI 2004/786) | |
| Sch 6 | 26 Apr 2004 (SI 2004/786), repeals of or in— | |
| | Criminal Justice Act 1987; | |
| | Criminal Justice (International Co-operation) Act 1990; | |
| | Criminal Justice and Public Order Act 1994; | |
| | Criminal Law (Consolidation) (Scotland) Act 1995; | |
| | Criminal Justice and Police Act 2001; | |
| | Proceeds of Crime Act 2002 | |
| | 11 Oct 2004 (SI 2004/2624), repeals of or in— | |
| | Road Traffic Act 1988; | |
| | Road Traffic Offenders Act 1988 | |
| | 17 Dec 2008 (SI 2008/3009), repeals of or in— | |
| | Powers of Criminal Courts (Sentencing) Act 2000 | |

[1]    This date was notified in the *London Gazette* on 26 Jan 2010

## Criminal Justice Act 2003 (c 44)

*RA:* 20 Nov 2003

*Commencement provisions:* s 336; Criminal Justice Act 2003 (Commencement No 1) Order 2003, SI 2003/3282; Criminal Justice Act 2003 (Commencement No 2 and Saving Provisions) Order 2004, SI 2004/81; Criminal Justice Act 2003 (Commencement No 3 and Transitional Provisions) Order 2004, SI 2004/829; Criminal Justice Act 2003 (Commencement No 4 and Saving Provisions) Order 2004, SI 2004/1629; Criminal Justice Act 2003 (Commencement No 5) Order 2004, SI 2004/1867; Criminal Justice Act 2003 (Commencement No 8 and Transitional and Saving Provisions) Order 2005 (Supplementary Provisions) Order 2005, SI 2005/2122; Criminal Justice Act 2003 (Commencement No 6 and Transitional Provisions) Order 2004, SI 2004/3033; Criminal Justice Act 2003 (Commencement No 7) Order 2005, SI 2005/373; Criminal Justice Act 2003 (Commencement No 8 and Transitional and Saving Provisions) Order 2005, SI 2005/950, as amended by Criminal Justice and Immigration Act 2008, s 149, Sch 28, Pt 2, SI 2009/3111; Legal Aid, Sentencing and Punishment of Offenders Act 2012, ss 111(2), 121(3)(b), Sch 14, para 17, SI 2012/2905; Criminal Justice Act 2003 (Commencement No 9) Order 2005, SI 2005/1267; Criminal Justice Act 2003 (Commencement No 10 and Saving Provisions) Order 2005, SI 2005/1817; Criminal Justice Act 2003 (Commencement No 11) Order 2005, SI 2005/3055; Criminal Justice Act 2003 (Commencement No 12) Order 2006, SI 2006/751; Criminal Justice Act 2003 (Commencement No 13 and Transitional Provision) Order 2006, SI 2006/1835; Criminal Justice Act 2003 (Commencement No 14 and Transitional Provision) Order 2006, SI 2006/3217; Criminal Justice Act 2003 (Commencement No 15) Order 2006, SI 2006/3422; Criminal Justice Act 2003 (Commencement No 16) Order 2007, SI 2007/1999; Criminal Justice Act 2003 (Commencement No 17) Order 2007, SI 2007/2874; Criminal Justice Act 2003 (Commencement No 18) Order 2007, SI 2007/3340; Criminal Justice Act 2003 (Commencement No 19 and Transitional Provisions) Order 2007, SI 2007/3451; Criminal Justice Act 2003 (Commencement No 19) Order 2008,

**Criminal Justice Act 2003 (c 44)**—*contd*

SI 2008/694; Criminal Justice Act 2003 (Commencement No 21) Order 2008, SI 2008/1424; Criminal Justice Act 2003 (Commencement No 22) Order 2009, SI 2009/2775; Criminal Justice Act 2003 (Commencement Order No 23) Order 2009, SI 2009/2879; Criminal Justice Act 2003 (Commencement No 24 and Transitional Provisions) Order 2010, SI 2010/1183; Criminal Justice Act 2003 (Commencement No 25) Order 2010, SI 2010/3005; Criminal Justice Act 2003 (Commencement No 26) Order 2011, SI 2011/2188, as amended by SI 2016/992; Criminal Justice Act 2003 (Commencement No 27) Order 2012, SI 2012/825; Criminal Justice Act 2003 (Commencement No 28 and Saving Provisions) Order 2012, SI 2012/1320; Criminal Justice Act 2003 (Commencement No 29 and Saving Provisions) Order 2012, SI 2012/2574, as amended by SI 2012/2761; Criminal Justice Act 2003 (Commencement No 30 and Consequential Amendment) Order 2012, SI 2012/2905; Criminal Justice Act 2003 (Commencement No 31 and Saving Provisions) Order 2013, SI 2013/1103; Criminal Justice Act 2003 (Commencement No 32) Order 2014, SI 2014/633; Criminal Justice Act 2003 (Commencement No 33) and Sentencing Act 2020 (Commencement No 2) Regulations 2022, SI 2022/500; Criminal Justice Act 2003 (Commencement No. 34) and Judicial Review and Courts Act 2022 (Commencement No 1) Regulations 2022, SI 2022/816

| | | |
|---|---|---|
| 1, 2 | | 20 Jan 2004 (SI 2004/81) |
| 3 | | 29 Jan 2004 (SI 2004/81) |
| 4 | | 20 Jan 2004 (SI 2004/81) |
| 5 | | 1 Aug 2004 (within the police areas of Cleveland, Greater Manchester, Humberside, Merseyside, metropolitan police district, Nottinghamshire and West Yorkshire) (SI 2004/1867) |
| | | 1 Dec 2005 (otherwise) (SI 2005/3055) |
| 6–8 | | 20 Jan 2004 (SI 2004/81) |
| 9, 10 | | 5 Apr 2004 (SI 2004/829) |
| 11, 12 | | 20 Jan 2004 (SI 2004/81) |
| 13 | | 5 Apr 2004 (SI 2004/829) |
| 14 | | 1 Jan 2007 (for the purposes only of an offence to which the Bail Act 1976, Sch 1, Pt 1, para 2A(2)(b), 6(2)(b), 9AA(1)(b) or 9AB(1)(b) applies, and in relation to which the defendant is liable on conviction to a sentence of imprisonment for life, detention during Her Majesty's pleasure or custody for life) (SI 2006/3217)[9] |
| | | *Not yet in force* (otherwise) |
| 15 | (1), (2) | 1 Jan 2007 (for the purposes only of an offence to which the Bail Act 1976, Sch 1, Pt 1, para 2A(2)(b), 6(2)(b), 9AA(1)(b) or 9AB(1)(b) applies, and in relation to which the defendant is liable on conviction to a sentence of imprisonment for life, detention during Her Majesty's pleasure or custody for life) (SI 2006/3217)[9] |
| | | *Not yet in force* (otherwise) |
| | (3) | 5 Apr 2004 (SI 2004/829) |
| 16, 17 | | 5 Apr 2004 (SI 2004/829)[2] |
| 18 | | 4 Apr 2005 (SI 2005/950)[5] |
| 19–21 | | 5 Apr 2004 (SI 2004/829) |
| 22–24 | | 3 Jul 2004 (SI 2004/1629) |
| 25 | | 29 Jan 2004 (SI 2004/81) |
| 26 | | 3 Jul 2004 (SI 2004/1629) |
| 27 | | 3 Jul 2004 (except paras (b), (d)–(g) in definition "relevant prosecutor") (SI 2004/1629) |
| | | 16 Nov 2009 (exceptions noted above) (SI 2009/2775) |
| 28 | | See Sch 2 below |
| 29 | (1)–(3) | 25 Jul 2007 (for certain purposes[9]) (SI 2007/1999) |
| | | 9 Jun 2008 (for certain purposes[12]) (SI 2008/1424) |
| | | 1 Nov 2009 (for certain purposes[13]) (SI 2009/2879) |
| | | 1 Jan 2011 (for certain purposes[15]) (SI 2010/3005) |
| | | 6 Sep 2011 (for certain purposes[16]) (SI 2011/2188) |
| | | 3 Oct 2011 (for certain purposes[17]) (SI 2011/2188) |
| | | 19 Mar 2012 (for certain purposes[18]) (SI 2012/825) |
| | | 1 Apr 2014 (for certain purposes[24]) (SI 2014/633) |

**Criminal Justice Act 2003 (c 44)**—*contd*

|  |  |  |
|---|---|---|
|  |  | *Not yet in force* (otherwise) |
|  | (4) | *Not yet in force* |
|  | (5) | 25 Jul 2007 (for certain purposes[9]) (SI 2007/1999) |
|  |  | 9 Jun 2008 (for certain purposes[12]) (SI 2008/1424) |
|  |  | 1 Nov 2009 (for certain purposes[13]) (SI 2009/2879) |
|  |  | 1 Jan 2011 (for certain purposes[15]) (SI 2010/3005) |
|  |  | 6 Sep 2011 (for certain purposes[16]) (SI 2011/2188) |
|  |  | 3 Oct 2011 (for certain purposes[17]) (SI 2011/2188) |
|  |  | 19 Mar 2012 (for certain purposes[18]) (SI 2012/825) |
|  |  | 1 Apr 2014 (for certain purposes[24]) (SI 2014/633) |
|  |  | *Not yet in force* (otherwise) |
|  | (6) | 25 Jul 2007 (for certain purposes[9]) (SI 2007/1999) |
|  |  | 9 Jun 2008 (for certain purposes[12]) (SI 2008/1424) |
|  |  | 1 Nov 2009 (for certain purposes[13]) (SI 2009/2879) |
|  |  | 1 Jan 2011 (for certain purposes[15]) (SI 2010/3005) |
|  |  | 6 Sep 2011 (for certain purposes[16]) (SI 2011/2188) |
|  |  | 3 Oct 2011 (for certain purposes[17]) (SI 2011/2188) |
|  |  | 1 Apr 2014 (for certain purposes[24]) (SI 2014/633) |
|  |  | *Not yet in force* (otherwise) |
| 30 |  | 25 Jul 2007 (for certain purposes[9]) (SI 2007/1999) |
|  |  | 9 Jun 2008 (for certain purposes[12]) (SI 2008/1424) |
|  |  | 1 Nov 2009 (for certain purposes[13]) (SI 2009/2879) |
|  |  | 1 Jan 2011 (for certain purposes[15]) (SI 2010/3005) |
|  |  | 19 Mar 2012 (for certain purposes[18]) (SI 2012/825) |
|  |  | 1 Apr 2014 (for certain purposes[24]) (SI 2014/633) |
|  |  | *Not yet in force* (otherwise) (sub-s (3) repealed) |
| 31 |  | 29 Jan 2004 (SI 2004/81) |
| 32 |  | 4 Apr 2005 (E) (W) (SI 2005/950)[5] |
|  |  | 15 Jul 2005 (NI) (SI 2005/1817)[7] |
| 33 | (1) | 24 Jul 2006 (in so far as inserts Criminal Procedure and Investigations Act 1996, s 5(5C)) (SI 2006/1835)[8] |
|  |  | *Not yet in force* (in so far as inserts Criminal Procedure and Investigations Act 1996, s 5(5A), (5B), (5D)) |
|  | (2) | 4 Apr 2005 (E) (W) (SI 2005/950)[5] |
|  |  | 15 Jul 2005 (NI) (SI 2005/1817)[6] |
|  | (3) | *Not yet in force* |
| 34 |  | 1 May 2010 (E) (W) (SI 2010/1183)[14] |
|  |  | *Not yet in force* (NI) |
| 35 |  | *Not yet in force* |
| 36–38 |  | 4 Apr 2005 (E) (W) (SI 2005/950)[5] |
|  |  | 15 Jul 2005 (NI) (SI 2005/1817)[6] |
| 39 |  | 4 Apr 2005 (E) (W) (except in so far as inserts Criminal Procedure and Investigations Act 1996, s 11(4), (7), (11)) (SI 2005/950)[5] |
|  |  | 15 Jul 2005 (NI) (except in so far as inserts Criminal Procedure and Investigations Act 1996, s 11(4), (7), (11)) (SI 2005/1817)[6] |
|  |  | 1 May 2010 (E) (W) (in so far as inserts Criminal Procedure and Investigations Act 1996, s 11(4), (7)) (SI 2010/1183)[14] |
|  |  | *Not yet in force* (E) (W) (in so far as inserts Criminal Procedure and Investigations Act 1996, s 11(11)) |
|  |  | *Not yet in force* (NI) (exceptions noted above) |
| 40 |  | 5 Apr 2004 (SI 2004/829) |
| 41 |  | See Sch 3 below |
| 42 |  | 22 Jan 2004 (SI 2004/81) |
| 43 |  | *Never in force* (repealed) |
| 44 |  | 24 Jul 2006 (SI 2006/1835) |
| 45 |  | 24 Jul 2006 (in so far as it applies to applications under s 44) (SI 2006/1835) |
|  |  | *Never in force* (in so far as it applies to applications under s 43 (s 43 repealed)) |

**Criminal Justice Act 2003 (c 44)**—*contd*

| | | |
|---|---|---|
| 46, 47 | | 24 Jul 2006 (SI 2006/1835) |
| 48 | | 24 Jul 2006 (in so far as it applies to trials ordered under ss 44, 46) (SI 2006/1835) |
| | | *Not yet in force* (in so far as it applies to trials ordered under s 43) |
| 49 | | 29 Jan 2004 (SI 2004/81) |
| 50 | | 8 Jan 2007 (in so far as it applies to applications under s 44 and trials ordered under s 44 or 46 of this Act) (SI 2006/3422) |
| | | *Not yet in force* (otherwise) |
| 51, 52 | | 7 Dec 2007 (in so far as they apply to proceedings in the Crown Court for a specified offence[10]) (SI 2007/3451)[11] |
| | | 26 Apr 2010 (otherwise) (SI 2010/1183)[14] |
| 53 | | 26 Apr 2010 (SI 2010/1183)[14] |
| 54 | | 7 Dec 2007 (in so far as it applies to proceedings in the Crown Court for a specified offence[10]) (SI 2007/3451)[11] |
| | | 26 Apr 2010 (otherwise) (SI 2010/1183)[14] |
| 55 | | 29 Jan 2004 (SI 2004/81) |
| 56 | | 7 Dec 2007 (in so far as it applies to proceedings in the Crown Court for a specified offence[10]) (SI 2007/3451)[11] |
| | | 26 Apr 2010 (otherwise) (SI 2010/1183)[14] |
| 57–61 | | 4 Apr 2005 (SI 2005/950)[5] |
| 62–66 | | *Not yet in force* |
| 67–72 | | 4 Apr 2005 (SI 2005/950)[5] |
| 73 | | 29 Jan 2004 (SI 2004/81) |
| 74–92 | | 4 Apr 2005 (SI 2005/950)[5] |
| 93 | | 29 Jan 2004 (SI 2004/81) |
| 94, 95 | | 4 Apr 2005 (SI 2005/950) |
| 96 | | 18 Apr 2005 (SI 2005/950) |
| 97 | | 7 Mar 2005 (SI 2005/373) |
| 98–110 | | 15 Dec 2004 (SI 2004/3033) |
| 111 | | 29 Jan 2004 (SI 2004/81) |
| 112 | | 15 Dec 2004 (SI 2004/3033) |
| 113 | | See Sch 6 below |
| 114–131 | | 4 Apr 2005 (SI 2005/950) |
| 132 | | 29 Jan 2004 (SI 2004/81) |
| 133–136 | | 4 Apr 2005 (SI 2005/950) |
| 137, 138 | | *Not yet in force* |
| 139–141 | | 5 Apr 2004 (SI 2004/829) |
| 142–150 | | 4 Apr 2005 (SI 2005/950)[5] |
| 151 | | *Not yet in force* |
| 152, 153 | | 4 Apr 2005 (SI 2005/950)[5] |
| 154, 155 | | *Not yet in force* |
| 156, 157 | | 4 Apr 2005 (SI 2005/950)[5] |
| 158 | (1)(a) | 4 Apr 2005 (SI 2005/950) |
| | (1)(b) | 7 Mar 2005 (SI 2005/373) |
| | (2) | 4 Apr 2005 (SI 2005/950) |
| 159 | (1)–(3) | 4 Apr 2005 (SI 2005/950) |
| | (4) | 7 Mar 2005 (SI 2005/373) |
| | (5)–(7) | 4 Apr 2005 (SI 2005/950) |
| 160 | | 4 Apr 2005 (SI 2005/950) |
| 161 | | *Not yet in force* (sub-s (7) repealed) |
| 162–166 | | 4 Apr 2005 (SI 2005/950)[5] |
| 167 | | 27 Feb 2004 (SI 2004/81) |
| 168 | (1), (2) | 20 Nov 2003 (s 336(1)) |
| | (3)–(5) | 27 Feb 2004 (SI 2004/81) |
| 169–173 | | 27 Feb 2004 (SI 2004/81) |
| 174 | (1)–(3) | 4 Apr 2005 (SI 2005/950)[5] |
| | (4) | 5 Apr 2004 (SI 2004/829) |
| | (5), (6) | 4 Apr 2005 (SI 2005/950)[5] |
| 175 | | 4 Apr 2005 (SI 2005/950) |

**Criminal Justice Act 2003 (c 44)**—*contd*

| | | |
|---|---|---|
| 176 | | 5 Apr 2004 (SI 2004/829) |
| 177 | | 4 Apr 2005 (SI 2005/950)[5] |
| 178 | | 7 Mar 2005 (SI 2005/373) |
| 179 | | See Sch 8 below |
| 180 | | See Sch 9 below |
| 181 | | *Never in force* (repealed) |
| 182 | (1) | 26 Jan 2004 (for the purposes of the passing of a sentence of imprisonment to which an intermittent custody order relates and the release on licence of a person serving such a sentence) (SI 2003/3282) |
| | (2) | *Never in force* (repealed) |
| | (3)–(5) | 26 Jan 2004 (for the purposes of the passing of a sentence of imprisonment to which an intermittent custody order relates and the release on licence of a person serving such a sentence) (SI 2003/3282) |
| 183 | (1)–(7) | 26 Jan 2004 (for the purposes of the passing of a sentence of imprisonment to which an intermittent custody order relates and the release on licence of a person serving such a sentence) (SI 2003/3282) |
| | (8) | 20 Nov 2003 (s 336(1)) |
| | (9) | 26 Jan 2004 (for the purposes of the passing of a sentence of imprisonment to which an intermittent custody order relates and the release on licence of a person serving such a sentence) (SI 2003/3282) |
| 184–186 | | 26 Jan 2004 (for the purposes of the passing of a sentence of imprisonment to which an intermittent custody order relates and the release on licence of a person serving such a sentence) (SI 2003/3282) |
| 187 | | See Sch 10 below |
| 188 | | See Sch 11 below |
| 189–194 | | 4 Apr 2005 (SI 2005/950)[5] |
| 195 | | 26 Jan 2004 (for the purposes of the passing of a sentence of imprisonment to which an intermittent custody order relates and the release on licence of a person serving such a sentence) (SI 2003/3282) |
| | | 4 Apr 2005 (otherwise) (SI 2005/950) |
| 196 | (1)(a) | 4 Apr 2005 (SI 2005/950) |
| | (1)(b) | *Never in force* (repealed) |
| | (1)(c) | 4 Apr 2005 (SI 2005/950) |
| | (1)(d) | 26 Jan 2004 (for the purposes of the passing of a sentence of imprisonment to which an intermittent custody order relates and the release on licence of a person serving such a sentence) (SI 2003/3282) |
| | (2) | 26 Jan 2004 (for the purposes of the passing of a sentence of imprisonment to which an intermittent custody order relates and the release on licence of a person serving such a sentence) (SI 2003/3282) |
| 197 | (1), (2) | 26 Jan 2004 (for the purposes of the passing of a sentence of imprisonment to which an intermittent custody order relates and the release on licence of a person serving such a sentence) (SI 2003/3282) |
| | | 4 Apr 2005 (otherwise) (SI 2005/950) |
| | (3), (4) | 26 Jan 2004 (for the purposes of the passing of a sentence of imprisonment to which an intermittent custody order relates and the release on licence of a person serving such a sentence) (SI 2003/3282) |
| | | 7 Mar 2005 (otherwise) (SI 2005/373) |
| 198, 199 | | 26 Jan 2004 (for the purposes of the passing of a sentence of imprisonment to which an intermittent custody order relates and the release on licence of a person serving such a sentence) (SI 2003/3282) |

**Criminal Justice Act 2003 (c 44)**—*contd*

|  |  |  |
|---|---|---|
|  |  | 4 Apr 2005 (otherwise) (SI 2005/950) |
| 200 | (1) | 26 Jan 2004 (for the purposes of the passing of a sentence of imprisonment to which an intermittent custody order relates and the release on licence of a person serving such a sentence) (SI 2003/3282) |
|  |  | 4 Apr 2005 (otherwise) (SI 2005/950) |
|  | (2)–(4) | 4 Apr 2005 (SI 2005/950) |
| 201 |  | 26 Jan 2004 (for the purposes of the passing of a sentence of imprisonment to which an intermittent custody order relates and the release on licence of a person serving such a sentence) (SI 2003/3282) |
|  |  | 4 Apr 2005 (otherwise) (SI 2005/950) |
| 202 | (1), (2) | 26 Jan 2004 (for the purposes of the passing of a sentence of imprisonment to which an intermittent custody order relates and the release on licence of a person serving such a sentence) (SI 2003/3282) |
|  |  | 4 Apr 2005 (otherwise) (SI 2005/950) |
|  | (3)(a) | 26 Jan 2004 (for the purposes of the passing of a sentence of imprisonment to which an intermittent custody order relates and the release on licence of a person serving such a sentence) (SI 2003/3282) |
|  |  | 4 Apr 2005 (otherwise) (SI 2005/950) |
|  | (3)(b) | 26 Jan 2004 (for the purposes of the passing of a sentence of imprisonment to which an intermittent custody order relates and the release on licence of a person serving such a sentence) (SI 2003/3282) |
|  |  | 7 Mar 2005 (otherwise) (SI 2005/373) |
|  | (4)–(7) | 26 Jan 2004 (for the purposes of the passing of a sentence of imprisonment to which an intermittent custody order relates and the release on licence of a person serving such a sentence) (SI 2003/3282) |
|  |  | 4 Apr 2005 (otherwise) (SI 2005/950) |
| 203 |  | 26 Jan 2004 (for the purposes of the passing of a sentence of imprisonment to which an intermittent custody order relates and the release on licence of a person serving such a sentence) (SI 2003/3282) |
|  |  | 4 Apr 2005 (otherwise) (SI 2005/950) |
| 204 | (1), (2) | 26 Jan 2004 (for the purposes of the passing of a sentence of imprisonment to which an intermittent custody order relates and the release on licence of a person serving such a sentence) (SI 2003/3282) |
|  |  | 4 Apr 2005 (otherwise) (SI 2005/950) |
|  | (3) | 4 Apr 2005 (SI 2005/950) |
|  | (4) | *Never in force* (repealed) |
|  | (5) | 26 Jan 2004 (for the purposes of the passing of a sentence of imprisonment to which an intermittent custody order relates and the release on licence of a person serving such a sentence) (SI 2003/3282) |
|  |  | *Never in force* (otherwise) (repealed) |
|  | (6) | 26 Jan 2004 (for the purposes of the passing of a sentence of imprisonment to which an intermittent custody order relates and the release on licence of a person serving such a sentence) (SI 2003/3282) |
|  |  | 4 Apr 2005 (otherwise) (SI 2005/950) |
| 205 | (1) | 26 Jan 2004 (for the purposes of the passing of a sentence of imprisonment to which an intermittent custody order relates and the release on licence of a person serving such a sentence) (SI 2003/3282) |
|  |  | 4 Apr 2005 (otherwise) (SI 2005/950) |
|  | (2) | 4 Apr 2005 (SI 2005/950) |

**Criminal Justice Act 2003 (c 44)**—*contd*

|  |  |  |
|---|---|---|
| | (3), (4) | 26 Jan 2004 (for the purposes of the passing of a sentence of imprisonment to which an intermittent custody order relates and the release on licence of a person serving such a sentence) (SI 2003/3282) |
| | | 4 Apr 2005 (otherwise) (SI 2005/950) |
| 206–212 | | 4 Apr 2005 (SI 2005/950) |
| 213 | (1), (2) | 26 Jan 2004 (for the purposes of the passing of a sentence of imprisonment to which an intermittent custody order relates and the release on licence of a person serving such a sentence) (SI 2003/3282) |
| | | 4 Apr 2005 (otherwise) (SI 2005/950) |
| | (3)(a) | 4 Apr 2005 (SI 2005/950) |
| | (3)(b) | *Never in force* (repealed) |
| | (3)(c) | 26 Jan 2004 (for the purposes of the passing of a sentence of imprisonment to which an intermittent custody order relates and the release on licence of a person serving such a sentence) (SI 2003/3282) |
| | | *Never in force* (otherwise) (repealed) |
| | (3)(d) | 4 Apr 2005 (SI 2005/950) |
| 214 | | 26 Jan 2004 (for the purposes of the passing of a sentence of imprisonment to which an intermittent custody order relates and the release on licence of a person serving such a sentence) (SI 2003/3282) |
| | | 4 Apr 2005 (otherwise) (SI 2005/950) |
| 215 | (1), (2) | 26 Jan 2004 (for the purposes of the passing of a sentence of imprisonment to which an intermittent custody order relates and the release on licence of a person serving such a sentence) (SI 2003/3282) |
| | | 4 Apr 2005 (otherwise) (SI 2005/950) |
| | (3) | 26 Jan 2004 (for the purposes of the passing of a sentence of imprisonment to which an intermittent custody order relates and the release on licence of a person serving such a sentence) (SI 2003/3282) |
| | | 7 Mar 2005 (otherwise) (SI 2005/373) |
| | (4) | 26 Jan 2004 (for the purposes of the passing of a sentence of imprisonment to which an intermittent custody order relates and the release on licence of a person serving such a sentence) (SI 2003/3282) |
| | | 4 Apr 2005 (otherwise) (SI 2005/950) |
| 216 | (1) | 4 Apr 2005 (SI 2005/950) |
| | (2)(a) | *Never in force* (repealed) |
| | (2)(b) | 26 Jan 2004 (for the purposes of the passing of a sentence of imprisonment to which an intermittent custody order relates and the release on licence of a person serving such a sentence) (SI 2003/3282) |
| | | *Never in force* (otherwise) (repealed) |
| 217 | (1), (2) | 26 Jan 2004 (for the purposes of the passing of a sentence of imprisonment to which an intermittent custody order relates and the release on licence of a person serving such a sentence) (SI 2003/3282) |
| | | 4 Apr 2005 (otherwise) (SI 2005/950) |
| | (3) | 26 Jan 2004 (for the purposes of the passing of a sentence of imprisonment to which an intermittent custody order relates and the release on licence of a person serving such a sentence) (SI 2003/3282) |
| | | 7 Mar 2005 (otherwise) (SI 2005/373) |
| 218 | | 26 Jan 2004 (for the purposes of the passing of a sentence of imprisonment to which an intermittent custody order relates and the release on licence of a person serving such a sentence) (SI 2003/3282) |
| | | 4 Apr 2005 (otherwise) (SI 2005/950) |

**Criminal Justice Act 2003 (c 44)**—*contd*

| | | |
|---|---|---|
| 219 | (1)(a), (b) | 26 Jan 2004 (for the purposes of the passing of a sentence of imprisonment to which an intermittent custody order relates and the release on licence of a person serving such a sentence) (SI 2003/3282) |
| | | 4 Apr 2005 (otherwise) (SI 2005/950) |
| | (1)(c) | 4 Apr 2005 (SI 2005/950) |
| | (1)(d) | 26 Jan 2004 (for the purposes of the passing of a sentence of imprisonment to which an intermittent custody order relates and the release on licence of a person serving such a sentence) (SI 2003/3282) |
| | | 4 Apr 2005 (otherwise) (SI 2005/950) |
| | (2), (3) | 26 Jan 2004 (for the purposes of the passing of a sentence of imprisonment to which an intermittent custody order relates and the release on licence of a person serving such a sentence) (SI 2003/3282) |
| | | 4 Apr 2005 (otherwise) (SI 2005/950) |
| 220 | | 4 Apr 2005 (SI 2005/950) |
| 221 | | 26 Jan 2004 (for the purposes of the passing of a sentence of imprisonment to which an intermittent custody order relates and the release on licence of a person serving such a sentence) (SI 2003/3282) |
| | | 4 Apr 2005 (otherwise) (SI 2005/950) |
| 222 | | 26 Jan 2004 (for the purposes of the passing of a sentence of imprisonment to which an intermittent custody order relates and the release on licence of a person serving such a sentence) (SI 2003/3282) |
| | | 7 Mar 2005 (otherwise) (SI 2005/373) |
| 223 | (1), (2) | 26 Jan 2004 (for the purposes of the passing of a sentence of imprisonment to which an intermittent custody order relates and the release on licence of a person serving such a sentence) (SI 2003/3282) |
| | | 7 Mar 2005 (otherwise) (SI 2005/373) |
| | (3)(a), (b) | 26 Jan 2004 (for the purposes of the passing of a sentence of imprisonment to which an intermittent custody order relates and the release on licence of a person serving such a sentence) (SI 2003/3282) |
| | | 7 Mar 2005 (otherwise) (SI 2005/373) |
| | (3)(c), (d) | 7 Mar 2005 (SI 2005/373) |
| 224–236 | | 4 Apr 2005 (SI 2005/950) |
| 237 | | 26 Jan 2004 (for the purposes of the passing of a sentence of imprisonment to which an intermittent custody order relates and the release on licence of a person serving such a sentence) (SI 2003/3282) |
| | | 4 Apr 2005 (otherwise) (SI 2005/950) |
| 238 | | 4 Apr 2005 (SI 2005/950)[5] |
| 239 | (1)–(4) | 26 Jan 2004 (for the purposes of the passing of a sentence of imprisonment to which an intermittent custody order relates and the release on licence of a person serving such a sentence) (SI 2003/3282) |
| | | 4 Apr 2005 (otherwise) (SI 2005/950)[5] |
| | (5), (6) | 26 Jan 2004 (for the purposes of the passing of a sentence of imprisonment to which an intermittent custody order relates and the release on licence of a person serving such a sentence) (SI 2003/3282) |
| | | 7 Mar 2005 (otherwise) (SI 2005/373) |
| | (7) | See Sch 19 below |
| 240 | (1)–(3) | 4 Apr 2005 (SI 2005/950) |
| | (4)(a) | 7 Mar 2005 (SI 2005/373) |
| | (4)(b) | 4 Apr 2005 (SI 2005/950) |
| | (5)–(10) | 4 Apr 2005 (SI 2005/950) |

**Criminal Justice Act 2003 (c 44)**—*contd*

| | | |
|---|---|---|
| 241 | | 26 Jan 2004 (for the purposes of the passing of a sentence of imprisonment to which an intermittent custody order relates and the release on licence of a person serving such a sentence) (SI 2003/3282) |
| | | 4 Apr 2005 (otherwise) (SI 2005/950) |
| 242 | | 4 Apr 2005 (SI 2005/950) |
| 243 | | 4 Apr 2005 (SI 2005/950)[5] |
| 244 | (1), (2) | 26 Jan 2004 (for the purposes of the passing of a sentence of imprisonment to which an intermittent custody order relates and the release on licence of a person serving such a sentence) (SI 2003/3282) |
| | | 4 Apr 2005 (otherwise) (SI 2005/950)[5] |
| | (3)(a) | 4 Apr 2005 (SI 2005/950)[5] |
| | (3)(b) | *Never in force* (repealed) |
| | (3)(c) | 26 Jan 2004 (for the purposes of the passing of a sentence of imprisonment to which an intermittent custody order relates and the release on licence of a person serving such a sentence) (SI 2003/3282) |
| | | *Never in force* (otherwise) (repealed) |
| | (3)(d) | 26 Jan 2004 (for the purposes of the passing of a sentence of imprisonment to which an intermittent custody order relates and the release on licence of a person serving such a sentence) (SI 2003/3282) |
| | | 4 Apr 2005 (otherwise) (SI 2005/950)[5] |
| 245 | | 26 Jan 2004 (for the purposes of the passing of a sentence of imprisonment to which an intermittent custody order relates and the release on licence of a person serving such a sentence) (SI 2003/3282) |
| | | *Never in force* (otherwise) (repealed) |
| 246 | (1)(a) | 4 Apr 2005 (SI 2005/950)[5] |
| | (1)(b) | 26 Jan 2004 (for the purposes of the passing of a sentence of imprisonment to which an intermittent custody order relates and the release on licence of a person serving such a sentence) (SI 2003/3282) |
| | | 4 Apr 2005 (otherwise) (SI 2005/950)[5] |
| | (2) | 4 Apr 2005 (SI 2005/950)[5] |
| | (3) | 26 Jan 2004 (for the purposes of the passing of a sentence of imprisonment to which an intermittent custody order relates and the release on licence of a person serving such a sentence) (SI 2003/3282) |
| | | 4 Apr 2005 (otherwise) (SI 2005/950)[5] |
| | (4)(a) | 4 Apr 2005 (SI 2005/950)[5] |
| | (4)(b)–(i) | 26 Jan 2004 (for the purposes of the passing of a sentence of imprisonment to which an intermittent custody order relates and the release on licence of a person serving such a sentence) (SI 2003/3282) |
| | | 4 Apr 2005 (otherwise) (SI 2005/950)[5] |
| | (5) | 26 Jan 2004 (for the purposes of the passing of a sentence of imprisonment to which an intermittent custody order relates and the release on licence of a person serving such a sentence) (SI 2003/3282) |
| | | 7 Mar 2005 (otherwise) (SI 2005/373) |
| | (6) | 26 Jan 2004 (for the purposes of the passing of a sentence of imprisonment to which an intermittent custody order relates and the release on licence of a person serving such a sentence) (SI 2003/3282) |
| | | 4 Apr 2005 (otherwise) (SI 2005/950)[5] |
| 247 | | 4 Apr 2005 (SI 2005/950)[5] |

**Criminal Justice Act 2003 (c 44)**—*contd*

| | | |
|---|---|---|
| 248 | (1) | 26 Jan 2004 (for the purposes of the passing of a sentence of imprisonment to which an intermittent custody order relates and the release on licence of a person serving such a sentence) (SI 2003/3282) |
| | | 4 Apr 2005 (otherwise) (SI 2005/950)[5] |
| | (2) | 4 Apr 2005 (SI 2005/950)[5] |
| 249 | | 26 Jan 2004 (for the purposes of the passing of a sentence of imprisonment to which an intermittent custody order relates and the release on licence of a person serving such a sentence) (SI 2003/3282) |
| | | 4 Apr 2005 (otherwise) (SI 2005/950)[5] |
| 250 | (1) | 26 Jan 2004 (for the purposes of the passing of a sentence of imprisonment to which an intermittent custody order relates and the release on licence of a person serving such a sentence) (SI 2003/3282) |
| | | 7 Mar 2005 (otherwise) (SI 2005/373) |
| | (2)(a) | 26 Jan 2004 (for the purposes of the passing of a sentence of imprisonment to which an intermittent custody order relates and the release on licence of a person serving such a sentence) (SI 2003/3282) |
| | | *Never in force* (otherwise) (repealed) |
| | (2)(b)(i) | 26 Jan 2004 (for the purposes of the passing of a sentence of imprisonment to which an intermittent custody order relates and the release on licence of a person serving such a sentence) (SI 2003/3282) |
| | | *Never in force* (otherwise) (repealed) |
| | (2)(b)(ii) | 26 Jan 2004 (for the purposes of the passing of a sentence of imprisonment to which an intermittent custody order relates and the release on licence of a person serving such a sentence) (SI 2003/3282) |
| | | 7 Mar 2005 (otherwise) (SI 2005/373) |
| | (3) | 26 Jan 2004 (for the purposes of the passing of a sentence of imprisonment to which an intermittent custody order relates and the release on licence of a person serving such a sentence) (SI 2003/3282) |
| | | *Never in force* (otherwise) (repealed) |
| | (4)(a) | 4 Apr 2005 (SI 2005/950)[5] |
| | (4)(b)(i) | 4 Apr 2005 (SI 2005/950)[5] |
| | (4)(b)(ii) | 7 Mar 2005 (SI 2005/373) |
| | (5)–(7) | 26 Jan 2004 (for the purposes of the passing of a sentence of imprisonment to which an intermittent custody order relates and the release on licence of a person serving such a sentence) (SI 2003/3282) |
| | | 4 Apr 2005 (otherwise) (SI 2005/950)[5] |
| | (8) | 26 Jan 2004 (for the purposes of the passing of a sentence of imprisonment to which an intermittent custody order relates and the release on licence of a person serving such a sentence) (SI 2003/3282) |
| | | 7 Mar 2005 (otherwise) (SI 2005/373) |
| 251 | | 26 Jan 2004 (for the purposes of the passing of a sentence of imprisonment to which an intermittent custody order relates and the release on licence of a person serving such a sentence) (SI 2003/3282) |
| | | *Never in force* (otherwise) (repealed) |
| 252 | | 26 Jan 2004 (for the purposes of the passing of a sentence of imprisonment to which an intermittent custody order relates and the release on licence of a person serving such a sentence) (SI 2003/3282) |
| | | 4 Apr 2005 (otherwise) (SI 2005/950)[5] |

**Criminal Justice Act 2003 (c 44)**—*contd*

| | | |
|---|---|---|
| 253 | (1)–(4) | 26 Jan 2004 (for the purposes of the passing of a sentence of imprisonment to which an intermittent custody order relates and the release on licence of a person serving such a sentence) (SI 2003/3282) |
| | | 4 Apr 2005 (otherwise) (SI 2005/950)[5] |
| | (5) | 26 Jan 2004 (for the purposes of the passing of a sentence of imprisonment to which an intermittent custody order relates and the release on licence of a person serving such a sentence) (SI 2003/3282) |
| | | 7 Mar 2005 (otherwise) (SI 2005/373) |
| | (6) | 26 Jan 2004 (for the purposes of the passing of a sentence of imprisonment to which an intermittent custody order relates and the release on licence of a person serving such a sentence) (SI 2003/3282) |
| | | 4 Apr 2005 (otherwise) (SI 2005/950)[5] |
| 254–256 | | 26 Jan 2004 (for the purposes of the passing of a sentence of imprisonment to which an intermittent custody order relates and the release on licence of a person serving such a sentence) (SI 2003/3282) |
| | | 4 Apr 2005 (otherwise) (SI 2005/950)[5] |
| 257 | (1) | 26 Jan 2004 (for the purposes of the passing of a sentence of imprisonment to which an intermittent custody order relates and the release on licence of a person serving such a sentence) (SI 2003/3282) |
| | | 7 Mar 2005 (otherwise) (SI 2005/373) |
| | (2)(a), (b) | 26 Jan 2004 (for the purposes of the passing of a sentence of imprisonment to which an intermittent custody order relates and the release on licence of a person serving such a sentence) (SI 2003/3282) |
| | | 4 Apr 2005 (otherwise) (SI 2005/950)[5] |
| | (2)(c) | 26 Jan 2004 (for the purposes of the passing of a sentence of imprisonment to which an intermittent custody order relates and the release on licence of a person serving such a sentence) (SI 2003/3282) |
| | | 3 Dec 2012 (in so far as relates to Sch 20B, paras 17, 19(2) and 26) (SI 2012/2905) |
| | | *Not yet in force* (otherwise) |
| 258 | | 4 Apr 2005 (SI 2005/950)[5] |
| 259 | | 26 Jan 2004 (for the purposes of the passing of a sentence of imprisonment to which an intermittent custody order relates and the release on licence of a person serving such a sentence) (SI 2003/3282) |
| | | 4 Apr 2005 (otherwise) (SI 2005/950)[5] |
| 260 | (1)–(5) | 4 Apr 2005 (SI 2005/950)[5] |
| | (6) | 7 Mar 2005 (SI 2005/373) |
| | (7) | 4 Apr 2005 (SI 2005/950)[5] |
| 261 | | 4 Apr 2005 (SI 2005/950)[5] |
| 262 | | See Sch 20 below |
| 263 | | 26 Jan 2004 (for the purposes of the passing of a sentence of imprisonment to which an intermittent custody order relates and the release on licence of a person serving such a sentence) (SI 2003/3282) |
| | | 4 Apr 2005 (otherwise) (SI 2005/950)[5] |
| 264 | (1)–(3) | 26 Jan 2004 (for the purposes of the passing of a sentence of imprisonment to which an intermittent custody order relates and the release on licence of a person serving such a sentence) (SI 2003/3282) |
| | | 4 Apr 2005 (otherwise) (SI 2005/950)[5] |

**Criminal Justice Act 2003 (c 44)**—*contd*

|  |  |  |
|---|---|---|
| | (4), (5) | 26 Jan 2004 (for the purposes of the passing of a sentence of imprisonment to which an intermittent custody order relates and the release on licence of a person serving such a sentence) (SI 2003/3282) |
| | | *Never in force* (otherwise) (repealed) |
| | (6), (7) | 26 Jan 2004 (for the purposes of the passing of a sentence of imprisonment to which an intermittent custody order relates and the release on licence of a person serving such a sentence) (SI 2003/3282) |
| | | 4 Apr 2005 (otherwise) (SI 2005/950)[5] |
| 265 | | 26 Jan 2004 (for the purposes of the passing of a sentence of imprisonment to which an intermittent custody order relates and the release on licence of a person serving such a sentence) (SI 2003/3282) |
| | | 4 Apr 2005 (otherwise) (SI 2005/950)[5] |
| 266 | | *Never in force* (repealed) |
| 267 | | 7 Mar 2005 (SI 2005/373) |
| 268 | | 26 Jan 2004 (for the purposes of the passing of a sentence of imprisonment to which an intermittent custody order relates and the release on licence of a person serving such a sentence) (SI 2003/3282) |
| | | 4 Apr 2005 (otherwise) (SI 2005/950)[5] |
| 269–277 | | 18 Dec 2003 (s 336(2)) |
| 278 | | See Sch 23 below |
| 279 | | See Sch 24 below |
| 280 | (1) | *Not yet in force* |
| | (2) | See Sch 26 below |
| | (3) | *Not yet in force* |
| 281 | (1)–(6) | *Not yet in force* |
| | (7), (8) | 14 July 2022 (only in so far as relate to s 282 of this Act) (SI 2022/816) |
| | | *Not yet in force* (otherwise) |
| 282 | | 2 May 2022 (SI 2022/500) |
| 283 | (1)(a) | *Not yet in force* |
| | (1)(b) | 2 May 2022 (SI 2022/500) |
| | (2) | *Not yet in force* |
| | (3) | 2 May 2022 (SI 2022/500) |
| | (4) | See Sch 27 below |
| | (5), (6) | *Not yet in force* |
| | (7) | 2 May 2022 (in so far as relates to Sch 27, paras 6, 7) (SI 2022/500) |
| | | *Not yet in force* (otherwise) |
| | (8), (9) | *Not yet in force* |
| 284 | (1) | See Sch 28 below |
| | (2) | 29 Jan 2004 (SI 2004/81) |
| 285 | | 27 Feb 2004 (SI 2004/81) |
| 286 | | 29 Jan 2004 (SI 2004/81) |
| 287–293 | | 22 Jan 2004 (SI 2004/81) |
| 294–297 | | 20 Jan 2004 (SI 2004/81) |
| 298 | | *Not yet in force* |
| 299 | | See Sch 30 below |
| 300 | (1)–(5) | *Not yet in force* |
| | (6) | See Sch 31 below |
| | (7), (8) | *Not yet in force* |
| 301 | (1)–(4) | *Not yet in force* |
| | (5) | 7 Mar 2005 (SI 2005/373) |
| | (6), (7) | *Not yet in force* |

**Criminal Justice Act 2003 (c 44)**—*contd*

| | | |
|---|---|---|
| 302 | | 26 Jan 2004 (for the purposes of the passing of a sentence of imprisonment to which an intermittent custody order relates and the release on licence of a person serving such a sentence) (SI 2003/3282) |
| | | 4 Apr 2005 (otherwise) (SI 2005/950) |
| 303 | (a) | 4 Apr 2005 (SI 2005/950) |
| | (b)(i), (ii) | 18 Dec 2003 (s 336(2)) |
| | (b)(iii) | *Not yet in force* |
| | (c), (d) | 4 Apr 2005 (SI 2005/950)[5] |
| 304 | | See Sch 32 below |
| 305 | (1)–(3) | 26 Jan 2004 (for the purposes of the passing of a sentence of imprisonment to which an intermittent custody order relates and the release on licence of a person serving such a sentence) (SI 2003/3282) |
| | | 4 Apr 2005 (otherwise) (SI 2005/950)[5] |
| | (4) | 4 Apr 2005 (SI 2005/950)[5] |
| 306 | | 20 Jan 2004 (SI 2004/81)[1] |
| 307 | (1)–(3) | 20 Nov 2003 (s 336(1)) |
| | (4) | 21 Jul 2005 (SI 2005/1817) |
| | (5), (6) | 20 Nov 2003 (s 336(1)) |
| 308–312 | | 4 Apr 2005 (SI 2005/950)[5] |
| 313, 314 | | 1 Sep 2004 (SI 2004/1629)[3] |
| 315 | | 4 Apr 2005 (SI 2005/950) |
| 316–318 | | 1 Sep 2004 (SI 2004/1629) |
| 319 | | 4 Apr 2005 (SI 2005/950) |
| 320 | | 20 Jan 2004 (SI 2004/81) |
| 321 | | 5 Apr 2004 (SI 2004/829) |
| 322, 323 | | 1 May 2004 (SI 2004/829) |
| 324 | | See Sch 34 below |
| 325–327 | | 5 Apr 2004 (SI 2004/829)[2] |
| 328 | | See Sch 35 below |
| 329 | | 20 Jan 2004 (SI 2004/81) |
| 330 | | 20 Nov 2003 (s 336(1)) |
| 331 | | See Sch 36 below |
| 332 | | See Sch 37 below |
| 333 | (1)–(5) | 20 Nov 2003 (s 336(1)) |
| | (6) | See Sch 38 below |
| 334–339 | | 20 Nov 2003 (s 336(1)) |
| Sch 1 | | 20 Jan 2004 (SI 2004/81) |
| Sch 2 | paras 1, 2 | 29 Jan 2004 (SI 2004/81) |
| | para 3 | 29 Jan 2004 (except in so far as inserts Police and Criminal Evidence Act 1984, s 37B(8), (9)(a)) (SI 2004/81) |
| | | 3 Jul 2004 (in so far as inserts s 37B(9)(a)) (SI 2004/1629) |
| | | 1 Oct 2007 (in so far as inserts s 37B(8)) (SI 2007/2874) |
| | paras 4–6 | 29 Jan 2004 (SI 2004/81) |
| Sch 3 | para 1 | 18 Jun 2012 (SI 2012/1320) |
| | paras 2–12 | 18 Jun 2012 (in relation to the relevant local justice areas)[19] (SI 2012/1320) |
| | | 5 Nov 2012 (in relation to the relevant local justice areas)[22] (SI 2012/2574) |
| | | 28 May 2013 (in relation to the relevant local justice areas)[23] (SI 2013/1103) |
| | para 13 | *Never in force* (repealed) |
| | para 14 | 18 Jun 2012 (SI 2012/1320) |
| | para 15 | 18 May 2012 (SI 2012/1320)[20] |
| | paras 16, 17 | 18 Jun 2012 (in relation to the relevant local justice areas)[19] (SI 2012/1320) |
| | | 5 Nov 2012 (in relation to the relevant local justice areas)[22] (SI 2012/2574) |

**Criminal Justice Act 2003 (c 44)**—*contd*

|  |  |
|---|---|
|  | 28 May 2013 (in relation to the relevant local justice areas)[23] (SI 2013/1103) |
| para 18 | 4 Apr 2005 (in so far as inserts Crime and Disorder Act 1988, s 51A, except sub-s (3)(a)–(c) of that section and in so far as inserts ss 51D, 51E of the 1998 Act, in relation to cases sent for trial under s 51A(3)(d)) (SI 2005/950) |
|  | 18 Jun 2012 (in relation to the relevant local justice areas)[19] (SI 2012/1320) |
|  | 5 Nov 2012 (in relation to the relevant local justice areas)[22] (SI 2012/2574) |
|  | 28 May 2013 (in relation to the relevant local justice areas)[23] (SI 2013/1103) |
| para 19(1) | 18 Jun 2012 (except in so far as inserts Crime and Disorder Act 1998, s 52B(4)) (SI 2012/1320) |
|  | *Not yet in force* (exception noted above) |
| para 19(2)(a) | 18 Jun 2012 (SI 2012/1320) |
| para 19(2)(b) | *Not yet in force* |
| para 20(1), (2) | 18 May 2012 (SI 2012/1320)[20] |
| para 20(3)–(14) | 18 Jun 2012 (in relation to the relevant local justice areas)[19] (SI 2012/1320) |
|  | 5 Nov 2012 (in relation to the relevant local justice areas)[22] (SI 2012/2574) |
|  | 28 May 2013 (in relation to the relevant local justice areas)[23] (SI 2013/1103) |
| para 21 | See paras 22–28 below |
| para 22 | *Never in force* (repealed) |
| para 23 | 4 Apr 2005 (in so far as inserts Powers of Criminal Courts (Sentencing) Act 2000, s 3C) (SI 2005/950) |
|  | 18 Jun 2012 (in relation to the relevant local justice areas)[19] (SI 2012/1320) |
|  | 5 Nov 2012 (in relation to the relevant local justice areas)[22] (SI 2012/2574) |
|  | 28 May 2013 (in relation to the relevant local justice areas)[23] (SI 2013/1103) |
| paras 24–26 | 18 Jun 2012 (in relation to the relevant local justice areas)[19] (SI 2012/1320) |
|  | 5 Nov 2012 (in relation to the relevant local justice areas)[22] (SI 2012/2574) |
|  | 28 May 2013 (in relation to the relevant local justice areas)[23] (SI 2013/1103) |
| paras 27, 28 | 4 Apr 2005 (in relation to cases committed under the Powers of Criminal Courts (Sentencing) Act 2000, s 3C) (SI 2005/950) |
|  | 18 Jun 2012 (in relation to cases committed under the Powers of Criminal Courts (Sentencing) Act 2000, s 3B or 4A) (in relation to the relevant local justice areas)[19] (SI 2012/1320) |
|  | 5 Nov 2012 (in relation to the relevant local justice areas)[22] (SI 2012/2574) |
|  | 28 May 2013 (in relation to the relevant local justice areas)[23] (SI 2013/1103) |
| paras 29–32 | 18 Jun 2012 (in relation to the relevant local justice areas)[19] (SI 2012/1320) |
|  | 5 Nov 2012 (in relation to the relevant local justice areas)[22] (SI 2012/2574) |
|  | 28 May 2013 (in relation to the relevant local justice areas)[23] (SI 2013/1103) |
| para 33 | 9 May 2005 (in relation to cases sent for trial under the Crime and Disorder Act 1998, ss 51 or 51A(3)(d)) (SI 2005/1267) |
|  | 18 Jun 2012 (in relation to the relevant local justice areas)[19] (SI 2012/1320) |

**Criminal Justice Act 2003 (c 44)**—*contd*

|  |  |
|---|---|
|  | 5 Nov 2012 (in relation to the relevant local justice areas)[22] (SI 2012/2574) |
|  | 28 May 2013 (in relation to the relevant local justice areas)[23] (SI 2013/1103) |
| para 34(1) | See sub-paras (2), (3) below |
| para 34(2)(a) | 9 May 2005 (in relation to cases sent for trial under the Crime and Disorder Act 1998, s 51A(3)(d)) (SI 2005/1267) |
|  | 18 Jun 2012 (in relation to the relevant local justice areas)[19] (SI 2012/1320) |
|  | 5 Nov 2012 (in relation to the relevant local justice areas)[22] (SI 2012/2574) |
|  | 28 May 2013 (in relation to the relevant local justice areas)[23] (SI 2013/1103) |
| para 34(2)(b) | 18 Jun 2012 (in relation to the relevant local justice areas)[19] (SI 2012/1320) |
|  | 5 Nov 2012 (in relation to the relevant local justice areas)[22] (SI 2012/2574) |
|  | 28 May 2013 (in relation to the relevant local justice areas)[23] (SI 2013/1103) |
| para 34(2)(c) | 9 May 2005 (in relation to cases sent for trial under the Crime and Disorder Act 1998, s 51A(3)(d)) (SI 2005/1267[7]) |
|  | 18 Jun 2012 (in relation to the relevant local justice areas)[19] (SI 2012/1320) |
|  | 5 Nov 2012 (in relation to the relevant local justice areas)[22] (SI 2012/2574) |
|  | 28 May 2013 (in relation to the relevant local justice areas)[23] (SI 2013/1103) |
| para 34(2)(d) | 18 Jun 2012 (in relation to the relevant local justice areas)[19] (SI 2012/1320) |
|  | 5 Nov 2012 (in relation to the relevant local justice areas)[22] (SI 2012/2574) |
|  | 28 May 2013 (in relation to the relevant local justice areas)[23] (SI 2013/1103) |
| para 34(2)(e) | 9 May 2005 (in relation to cases sent for trial under the Crime and Disorder Act 1998, ss 51 or 51A(3)(d)) (SI 2005/1267) |
|  | 18 Jun 2012 (in relation to the relevant local justice areas)[19] (SI 2012/1320) |
|  | 5 Nov 2012 (in relation to the relevant local justice areas)[22] (SI 2012/2574) |
|  | 28 May 2013 (in relation to the relevant local justice areas)[23] (SI 2013/1103) |
| para 34(2)(f) | 18 Jun 2012 (in relation to the relevant local justice areas)[19] (SI 2012/1320) |
|  | 5 Nov 2012 (in relation to the relevant local justice areas)[22] (SI 2012/2574) |
|  | 28 May 2013 (in relation to the relevant local justice areas)[23] (SI 2013/1103) |
| para 34(3) | 9 May 2005 (in relation to cases sent for trial under the Crime and Disorder Act 1998, ss 51 or 51A(3)(d)) (SI 2005/1267) |
|  | 18 Jun 2012 (in relation to the relevant local justice areas)[19] (SI 2012/1320) |
|  | 5 Nov 2012 (in relation to the relevant local justice areas)[22] (SI 2012/2574) |
|  | 28 May 2013 (in relation to the relevant local justice areas)[23] (SI 2013/1103) |
| para 35(1) | See sub-paras (2)–(4) below |
| para 35(2) | 9 May 2005 (in relation to cases sent for trial under the Crime and Disorder Act 1998, ss 51 or 51A(3)(d)) (SI 2005/1267) |
|  | 18 Jun 2012 (in relation to the relevant local justice areas)[19] (SI 2012/1320) |

**Criminal Justice Act 2003 (c 44)**—*contd*

|  |  |
|---|---|
|  | 5 Nov 2012 (in relation to the relevant local justice areas)[22] (SI 2012/2574) |
|  | 28 May 2013 (in relation to the relevant local justice areas)[23] (SI 2013/1103) |
| para 35(3), (4) | 18 Jun 2012 (in relation to the relevant local justice areas)[19] (SI 2012/1320) |
|  | 5 Nov 2012 (in relation to the relevant local justice areas)[22] (SI 2012/2574) |
|  | 28 May 2013 (in relation to the relevant local justice areas)[23] (SI 2013/1103) |
| para 36 | 9 May 2005 (in relation to cases sent for trial under the Crime and Disorder Act 1998, ss 51 or 51A(3)(d)) (SI 2005/1267) |
|  | 18 Jun 2012 (in relation to the relevant local justice areas)[19] (SI 2012/1320) |
|  | 5 Nov 2012 (in relation to the relevant local justice areas)[22] (SI 2012/2574) |
|  | 28 May 2013 (in relation to the relevant local justice areas)[23] (SI 2013/1103) |
| paras 37, 38 | *Never in force* (repealed) |
| para 39 | 9 May 2005 (in relation to cases sent for trial under the Crime and Disorder Act 1998, ss 51 or 51A(3)(d)) (SI 2005/1267) |
|  | 18 Jun 2012 (in relation to the relevant local justice areas)[19] (SI 2012/1320) |
|  | 5 Nov 2012 (in relation to the relevant local justice areas)[22] (SI 2012/2574) |
|  | 28 May 2013 (in relation to the relevant local justice areas)[23] (SI 2013/1103) |
| para 40 | *Never in force* (repealed) |
| para 41 | 18 Jun 2012 (in relation to the relevant local justice areas)[19] (SI 2012/1320) |
|  | 5 Nov 2012 (in relation to the relevant local justice areas)[22] (SI 2012/2574) |
|  | 28 May 2013 (in relation to the relevant local justice areas)[23] (SI 2013/1103) |
| para 42(a) | 9 May 2005 (in relation to cases sent for trial under the Crime and Disorder Act 1998, s 51A(3)(d)) (SI 2005/1267) |
|  | 18 Jun 2012 (in relation to the relevant local justice areas)[19] (SI 2012/1320) |
|  | 5 Nov 2012 (in relation to the relevant local justice areas)[22] (SI 2012/2574) |
|  | 28 May 2013 (in relation to the relevant local justice areas)[23] (SI 2013/1103) |
| para 42(b) | 18 Jun 2012 (in relation to the relevant local justice areas)[19] (SI 2012/1320) |
|  | 5 Nov 2012 (in relation to the relevant local justice areas)[22] (SI 2012/2574) |
|  | 28 May 2013 (in relation to the relevant local justice areas)[23] (SI 2013/1103) |
| para 43 | 18 Jun 2012 (in relation to the relevant local justice areas)[19] (SI 2012/1320) |
|  | 5 Nov 2012 (in relation to the relevant local justice areas)[22] (SI 2012/2574) |
|  | 28 May 2013 (in relation to the relevant local justice areas)[23] (SI 2013/1103) |
| para 44(1) | See sub-paras (2), (3) below |
| para 44(2) | 9 May 2005 (in relation to cases sent for trial under the Crime and Disorder Act 1998, ss 51 or 51A(3)(d)) (SI 2005/1267) |
|  | 18 Jun 2012 (in relation to the relevant local justice areas)[19] (SI 2012/1320) |

**Criminal Justice Act 2003 (c 44)**—*contd*

|  |  |
|---|---|
|  | 5 Nov 2012 (in relation to the relevant local justice areas)[22] (SI 2012/2574) |
|  | 28 May 2013 (in relation to the relevant local justice areas)[23] (SI 2013/1103) |
| para 44(3) | 18 Jun 2012 (in relation to the relevant local justice areas)[19] (SI 2012/1320) |
|  | 5 Nov 2012 (in relation to the relevant local justice areas)[22] (SI 2012/2574) |
|  | 28 May 2013 (in relation to the relevant local justice areas)[23] (SI 2013/1103) |
| paras 45–47 | 18 Jun 2012 (in relation to the relevant local justice areas)[19] (SI 2012/1320) |
|  | 5 Nov 2012 (in relation to the relevant local justice areas)[22] (SI 2012/2574) |
|  | 28 May 2013 (in relation to the relevant local justice areas)[23] (SI 2013/1103) |
| para 48(1) | See sub-paras (2)–(5) below |
| para 48(2)(a)(i) | 9 May 2005 (in relation to cases sent for trial under the Crime and Disorder Act 1998, s 51A(3)(d)) (SI 2005/1267) |
|  | 18 Jun 2012 (in relation to the relevant local justice areas)[19] (SI 2012/1320) |
|  | 5 Nov 2012 (in relation to the relevant local justice areas)[22] (SI 2012/2574) |
|  | 28 May 2013 (in relation to the relevant local justice areas)[23] (SI 2013/1103) |
| para 48(2)(a)(ii), (b) | 18 Jun 2012 (in relation to the relevant local justice areas)[19] (SI 2012/1320) |
|  | 5 Nov 2012 (in relation to the relevant local justice areas)[22] (SI 2012/2574) |
|  | 28 May 2013 (in relation to the relevant local justice areas)[23] (SI 2013/1103) |
| para 48(3)(a) | 9 May 2005 (in relation to cases sent for trial under the Crime and Disorder Act 1998, ss 51 or 51A(3)(d)) (SI 2005/1267) |
|  | 18 Jun 2012 (in relation to the relevant local justice areas)[19] (SI 2012/1320) |
|  | 5 Nov 2012 (in relation to the relevant local justice areas)[22] (SI 2012/2574) |
|  | 28 May 2013 (in relation to the relevant local justice areas)[23] (SI 2013/1103) |
| para 48(3)(b)(i) | 9 May 2005 (in relation to cases sent for trial under the Crime and Disorder Act 1998, ss 51 or 51A(3)(d)) (SI 2005/1267) |
|  | 18 Jun 2012 (in relation to the relevant local justice areas)[19] (SI 2012/1320) |
|  | 5 Nov 2012 (in relation to the relevant local justice areas)[22] (SI 2012/2574) |
|  | 28 May 2013 (in relation to the relevant local justice areas)[23] (SI 2013/1103) |
| para 48(3)(b)(ii)–(iv) | 18 Jun 2012 (in relation to the relevant local justice areas)[19] (SI 2012/1320) |
|  | 5 Nov 2012 (in relation to the relevant local justice areas)[22] (SI 2012/2574) |
|  | 28 May 2013 (in relation to the relevant local justice areas)[23] (SI 2013/1103) |
| para 48(4), (5) | 9 May 2005 (in relation to cases sent for trial under the Crime and Disorder Act 1998, ss 51 or 51A(3)(d)) (SI 2005/1267) |
|  | 18 Jun 2012 (in relation to the relevant local justice areas)[19] (SI 2012/1320) |
|  | 5 Nov 2012 (in relation to the relevant local justice areas)[22] (SI 2012/2574) |
|  | 28 May 2013 (in relation to the relevant local justice areas)[23] (SI 2013/1103) |

**Criminal Justice Act 2003 (c 44)**—*contd*

| | |
|---|---|
| para 49(a) | 18 Jun 2012 (in relation to the relevant local justice areas)[19] (SI 2012/1320) |
| | 5 Nov 2012 (in relation to the relevant local justice areas)[22] (SI 2012/2574) |
| para 49(b) | 9 May 2005 (in relation to cases sent for trial under the Crime and Disorder Act 1998, ss 51 or 51A(3)(d)) (SI 2005/1267) |
| | 18 Jun 2012 (in relation to the relevant local justice areas)[19] (SI 2012/1320) |
| | 5 Nov 2012 (in relation to the relevant local justice areas)[22] (SI 2012/2574) |
| | 28 May 2013 (in relation to the relevant local justice areas)[23] (SI 2013/1103) |
| para 50 | 18 Jun 2012 (in relation to the relevant local justice areas)[19] (SI 2012/1320) |
| | 5 Nov 2012 (in relation to the relevant local justice areas)[22] (SI 2012/2574) |
| | 28 May 2013 (in relation to the relevant local justice areas)[23] (SI 2013/1103) |
| para 51(1) | See sub-paras (2)–(14) below |
| para 51(2) | 9 May 2005 (in relation to cases sent for trial under the Crime and Disorder Act 1998, ss 51 or 51A(3)(d)) (SI 2005/1267) |
| | 18 Jun 2012 (in relation to the relevant local justice areas)[19] (SI 2012/1320) |
| | 5 Nov 2012 (in relation to the relevant local justice areas)[22] (SI 2012/2574) |
| | 28 May 2013 (in relation to the relevant local justice areas)[23] (SI 2013/1103) |
| para 51(3), (4) | 18 Jun 2012 (in relation to the relevant local justice areas)[19] (SI 2012/1320) |
| | 5 Nov 2012 (in relation to the relevant local justice areas)[22] (SI 2012/2574) |
| | 28 May 2013 (in relation to the relevant local justice areas)[23] (SI 2013/1103) |
| para 51(5) | 9 May 2005 (in relation to cases sent for trial under the Crime and Disorder Act 1998, ss 51 or 51A(3)(d)) (SI 2005/1267) |
| | 18 Jun 2012 (in relation to the relevant local justice areas)[19] (SI 2012/1320) |
| | 5 Nov 2012 (in relation to the relevant local justice areas)[22] (SI 2012/2574) |
| | 28 May 2013 (in relation to the relevant local justice areas)[23] (SI 2013/1103) |
| para 51(6), (7) | 18 Jun 2012 (in relation to the relevant local justice areas)[19] (SI 2012/1320) |
| | 5 Nov 2012 (in relation to the relevant local justice areas)[22] (SI 2012/2574) |
| | 28 May 2013 (in relation to the relevant local justice areas)[23] (SI 2013/1103) |
| para 51(8) | 9 May 2005 (in relation to cases sent for trial under the Crime and Disorder Act 1998, ss 51 or 51A(3)(d)) (SI 2005/1267) |
| | 18 Jun 2012 (in relation to the relevant local justice areas)[19] (SI 2012/1320) |
| | 5 Nov 2012 (in relation to the relevant local justice areas)[22] (SI 2012/2574) |
| | 28 May 2013 (in relation to the relevant local justice areas)[23] (SI 2013/1103) |
| para 51(9)–(14) | 18 Jun 2012 (in relation to the relevant local justice areas)[19] (SI 2012/1320) |
| | 5 Nov 2012 (in relation to the relevant local justice areas)[22] (SI 2012/2574) |
| | 28 May 2013 (in relation to the relevant local justice areas)[23] (SI 2013/1103) |

**Criminal Justice Act 2003 (c 44)**—*contd*

| | |
|---|---|
| para 52 | 18 Jun 2012 (in relation to the relevant local justice areas)[19] (SI 2012/1320) |
| | 5 Nov 2012 (in relation to the relevant local justice areas)[22] (SI 2012/2574) |
| | 28 May 2013 (in relation to the relevant local justice areas)[23] (SI 2013/1103) |
| para 53 | 18 Jun 2012 (SI 2012/1320)[20] |
| para 54(1) | See sub-paras (2)–(5) below |
| para 54(2) | 18 Jun 2012 (in relation to the relevant local justice areas)[19] (SI 2012/1320) |
| | 5 Nov 2012 (in relation to the relevant local justice areas)[22] (SI 2012/2574) |
| | 28 May 2013 (in relation to the relevant local justice areas)[23] (SI 2013/1103) |
| para 54(3)(a)–(c) | 9 May 2005 (in relation to cases sent for trial under the Crime and Disorder Act 1998, ss 51 or 51A(3)(d)) (SI 2005/1267) |
| | 18 Jun 2012 (in relation to the relevant local justice areas)[19] (SI 2012/1320) |
| | 5 Nov 2012 (in relation to the relevant local justice areas)[22] (SI 2012/2574) |
| | 28 May 2013 (in relation to the relevant local justice areas)[23] (SI 2013/1103) |
| para 54(3)(d), (e) | 18 Jun 2012 (in relation to the relevant local justice areas)[19] (SI 2012/1320) |
| | 5 Nov 2012 (in relation to the relevant local justice areas)[22] (SI 2012/2574) |
| | 28 May 2013 (in relation to the relevant local justice areas)[23] (SI 2013/1103) |
| para 54(4) | 9 May 2005 (in relation to cases sent for trial under the Crime and Disorder Act 1998, ss 51 or 51A(3)(d)) (SI 2005/1267) |
| | 18 Jun 2012 (in relation to the relevant local justice areas)[19] (SI 2012/1320) |
| | 5 Nov 2012 (in relation to the relevant local justice areas)[22] (SI 2012/2574) |
| | 28 May 2013 (in relation to the relevant local justice areas)[23] (SI 2013/1103) |
| para 54(5)(a)(i)(a) | 18 Jun 2012 (in relation to the relevant local justice areas)[19] (SI 2012/1320) |
| | 5 Nov 2012 (in relation to the relevant local justice areas)[22] (SI 2012/2574) |
| | 28 May 2013 (in relation to the relevant local justice areas)[23] (SI 2013/1103) |
| para 54(5)(a)(i)(b) | 9 May 2005 (in relation to cases sent for trial under the Crime and Disorder Act 1998, s 51A(3)(d)) (SI 2005/1267) |
| | 18 Jun 2012 (in relation to the relevant local justice areas)[19] (SI 2012/1320) |
| | 5 Nov 2012 (in relation to the relevant local justice areas)[22] (SI 2012/2574) |
| | 28 May 2013 (in relation to the relevant local justice areas)[23] (SI 2013/1103) |
| para 54(5)(a)(ii) | 18 Jun 2012 (in relation to the relevant local justice areas)[19] (SI 2012/1320) |
| | 5 Nov 2012 (in relation to the relevant local justice areas)[22] (SI 2012/2574) |
| | 28 May 2013 (in relation to the relevant local justice areas)[23] (SI 2013/1103) |
| para 54(5)(b) | 18 Jun 2012 (in relation to the relevant local justice areas)[19] (SI 2012/1320) |
| | 5 Nov 2012 (in relation to the relevant local justice areas)[22] (SI 2012/2574) |

**Criminal Justice Act 2003 (c 44)**—*contd*

|  | 28 May 2013 (in relation to the relevant local justice areas)[23] (SI 2013/1103) |
|---|---|
| para 55(1) | See sub-paras (2), (3) below |
| para 55(2) | 18 Jun 2012 (in relation to the relevant local justice areas)[19] (SI 2012/1320) |
|  | 5 Nov 2012 (in relation to the relevant local justice areas)[22] (SI 2012/2574) |
|  | 28 May 2013 (in relation to remaining local justice areas)[23] (SI 2013/1103) |
| para 55(3) | 9 May 2005 (in relation to cases sent for trial under the Crime and Disorder Act 1998, ss 51 or 51A(3)(d)) (SI 2005/1267) |
|  | 18 Jun 2012 (in relation to the relevant local justice areas)[19] (SI 2012/1320) |
|  | 5 Nov 2012 (in relation to the relevant local justice areas)[22] (SI 2012/2574) |
|  | 28 May 2013 (in relation to remaining local justice areas)[23] (SI 2013/1103) |
| para 56(1) | See sub-paras (2)–(5) below |
| para 56(2)(a) | 18 Jun 2012 (in relation to the relevant local justice areas and in the Crown Court for certain purposes)[19] (SI 2012/1320) |
|  | 5 Nov 2012 (in relation to the relevant local justice areas and in the Crown Court for certain purposes)[22] (SI 2012/2574) |
|  | 28 May 2013 (in relation to the relevant local justice areas and in the Crown Court for certain purposes)[23] (SI 2013/1103) |
| para 56(2)(b) | 9 May 2005 (in relation to cases sent for trial under the Crime and Disorder Act 1998, ss 51 or 51A(3)(d)) (SI 2005/1267) |
|  | 18 Jun 2012 (in relation to the relevant local justice areas)[19] (SI 2012/1320) |
|  | 5 Nov 2012 (in relation to the relevant local justice areas)[22] (SI 2012/2574) |
|  | 28 May 2013 (in relation to the relevant local justice areas)[23] (SI 2013/1103) |
| para 56(3)–(5) | 18 Jun 2012 (in relation to the relevant local justice areas)[19] (SI 2012/1320) |
|  | 5 Nov 2012 (in relation to the relevant local justice areas)[22] (SI 2012/2574) |
|  | 28 May 2013 (in relation to the relevant local justice areas)[23] (SI 2013/1103) |
| para 57(1) | See sub-paras (2)–(7) below |
| para 57(2) | 9 May 2005 (in relation to cases sent for trial under the Crime and Disorder Act 1998, ss 51 or 51A(3)(d)) (SI 2005/1267) |
|  | *Not yet in force* (otherwise) |
| para 57(3)(a) | 18 Jun 2012 (in relation to the relevant local justice areas)[19] (SI 2012/1320) |
|  | 5 Nov 2012 (in relation to the relevant local justice areas)[22] (SI 2012/2574) |
|  | 28 May 2013 (in relation to the relevant local justice areas)[23] (SI 2013/1103) |
| para 57(3)(b)(i) | 9 May 2005 (in relation to cases sent for trial under the Crime and Disorder Act 1998, ss 51 or 51A(3)(d)) (SI 2005/1267) |
|  | 18 Jun 2012 (in relation to the relevant local justice areas)[19] (SI 2012/1320) |
|  | 5 Nov 2012 (in relation to the relevant local justice areas)[22] (SI 2012/2574) |
|  | 28 May 2013 (in relation to the relevant local justice areas)[23] (SI 2013/1103) |
| para 57(3)(b)(ii), (c) | 18 Jun 2012 (in relation to the relevant local justice areas)[19] (SI 2012/1320) |
|  | 5 Nov 2012 (in relation to the relevant local justice areas)[22] (SI 2012/2574) |

**Criminal Justice Act 2003 (c 44)**—*contd*

|  |  |
|---|---|
|  | 28 May 2013 (in relation to the relevant local justice areas)[23] (SI 2013/1103) |
| para 57(4) | 9 May 2005 (in relation to cases sent for trial under the Crime and Disorder Act 1998, ss 51 or 51A(3)(d)) (SI 2005/1267) |
|  | 18 Jun 2012 (in relation to the relevant local justice areas)[19] (SI 2012/1320) |
|  | 5 Nov 2012 (in relation to the relevant local justice areas)[22] (SI 2012/2574) |
|  | 28 May 2013 (in relation to the relevant local justice areas)[23] (SI 2013/1103) |
| para 57(5)(a) | 9 May 2005 (in relation to cases sent for trial under the Crime and Disorder Act 1998, s 51A(3)(d)) (SI 2005/1267) |
|  | 18 Jun 2012 (in relation to the relevant local justice areas)[19] (SI 2012/1320) |
|  | 5 Nov 2012 (in relation to the relevant local justice areas)[22] (SI 2012/2574) |
|  | 28 May 2013 (in relation to the relevant local justice areas)[23] (SI 2013/1103) |
| para 57(5)(b) | 9 May 2005 (in relation to cases sent for trial under the Crime and Disorder Act 1998, ss 51 or 51A(3)(d)) (SI 2005/1267) |
|  | 18 Jun 2012 (in relation to the relevant local justice areas)[19] (SI 2012/1320) |
|  | 5 Nov 2012 (in relation to the relevant local justice areas)[22] (SI 2012/2574) |
|  | 28 May 2013 (in relation to the relevant local justice areas)[23] (SI 2013/1103) |
| para 57(6) | 9 May 2005 (in relation to cases sent for trial under the Crime and Disorder Act 1998, s 51A(3)(d)) (SI 2005/1267) |
|  | 18 Jun 2012 (in relation to the relevant local justice areas)[19] (SI 2012/1320) |
|  | 5 Nov 2012 (in relation to the relevant local justice areas)[22] (SI 2012/2574) |
|  | 28 May 2013 (in relation to the relevant local justice areas)[23] (SI 2013/1103) |
| para 57(7)(a) | 9 May 2005 (in relation to cases sent for trial under the Crime and Disorder Act 1998, ss 51 or 51A(3)(d)) (SI 2005/1267) |
|  | 18 Jun 2012 (in relation to the relevant local justice areas)[19] (SI 2012/1320) |
|  | 5 Nov 2012 (in relation to the relevant local justice areas)[22] (SI 2012/2574) |
|  | 28 May 2013 (in relation to the relevant local justice areas)[23] (SI 2013/1103) |
| para 57(7)(b) | 9 May 2005 (in relation to cases sent for trial under the Crime and Disorder Act 1998, s 51A(3)(d)) (SI 2005/1267) |
|  | 18 Jun 2012 (in relation to the relevant local justice areas)[19] (SI 2012/1320) |
|  | 5 Nov 2012 (in relation to the relevant local justice areas)[22] (SI 2012/2574) |
|  | 28 May 2013 (in relation to the relevant local justice areas)[23] (SI 2013/1103) |
| para 58 | 18 Jun 2012 (in relation to the relevant local justice areas)[19] (SI 2012/1320) |
|  | 5 Nov 2012 (in relation to the relevant local justice areas)[22] (SI 2012/2574) |
|  | 28 May 2013 (in relation to the relevant local justice areas)[23] (SI 2013/1103) |
| para 59 | 9 May 2005 (in relation to cases sent for trial under the Crime and Disorder Act 1998, ss 51 or 51A(3)(d)) (SI 2005/1267) |
|  | 18 Jun 2012 (in relation to the relevant local justice areas)[19] (SI 2012/1320) |

**Criminal Justice Act 2003 (c 44)**—*contd*

|  |  |
|---|---|
|  | 5 Nov 2012 (in relation to the relevant local justice areas)[22] (SI 2012/2574) |
|  | 28 May 2013 (in relation to the relevant local justice areas)[23] (SI 2013/1103) |
| para 60(1) | See sub-paras (2)–(8) below |
| para 60(2)–(6) | 18 Jun 2012 (in relation to the relevant local justice areas)[19] (SI 2012/1320) |
|  | 5 Nov 2012 (in relation to the relevant local justice areas)[22] (SI 2012/2574) |
|  | 28 May 2013 (in relation to the relevant local justice areas)[23] (SI 2013/1103) |
| para 60(7)(a) | 18 Jun 2012 (in relation to the relevant local justice areas)[19] (SI 2012/1320) |
|  | 5 Nov 2012 (in relation to the relevant local justice areas)[22] (SI 2012/2574) |
|  | 28 May 2013 (in relation to the relevant local justice areas)[23] (SI 2013/1103) |
| para 60(7)(b) | 9 May 2005 (in relation to cases sent for trial under the Crime and Disorder Act 1998, s 51A(3)(d)) (SI 2005/1267) |
|  | 18 Jun 2012 (in relation to the relevant local justice areas)[19] (SI 2012/1320) |
|  | 5 Nov 2012 (in relation to the relevant local justice areas)[22] (SI 2012/2574) |
|  | 28 May 2013 (in relation to the relevant local justice areas)[23] (SI 2013/1103) |
| para 60(8) | 18 Jun 2012 (in relation to the relevant local justice areas)[19] (SI 2012/1320) |
|  | 5 Nov 2012 (in relation to the relevant local justice areas)[22] (SI 2012/2574) |
|  | 28 May 2013 (in relation to the relevant local justice areas)[23] (SI 2013/1103) |
| paras 61, 62 | 18 Jun 2012 (in relation to the relevant local justice areas)[19] (SI 2012/1320) |
|  | 5 Nov 2012 (in relation to the relevant local justice areas)[22] (SI 2012/2574) |
|  | 28 May 2013 (in relation to the relevant local justice areas)[23] (SI 2013/1103) |
| para 63 | 9 May 2005 (in relation to cases sent for trial under the Crime and Disorder Act 1998, ss 51 or 51A(3)(d)) (SI 2005/1267) |
|  | 18 Jun 2012 (in relation to the relevant local justice areas)[19] (SI 2012/1320) |
|  | 5 Nov 2012 (in relation to the relevant local justice areas)[22] (SI 2012/2574) |
|  | 28 May 2013 (in relation to the relevant local justice areas)[23] (SI 2013/1103) |
| para 64(1) | See sub-paras (2)–(4) below |
| para 64(2)(a) | 18 Jun 2012 (in relation to the relevant local justice areas)[19] (SI 2012/1320) |
|  | 5 Nov 2012 (in relation to the relevant local justice areas)[22] (SI 2012/2574) |
|  | 28 May 2013 (in relation to the relevant local justice areas)[23] (SI 2013/1103) |
| para 64(2)(b) | 9 May 2005 (in relation to cases sent for trial under the Crime and Disorder Act 1998, ss 51 or 51A(3)(d)) (SI 2005/1267) |
|  | 18 Jun 2012 (in relation to the relevant local justice areas)[19] (SI 2012/1320) |
|  | 5 Nov 2012 (in relation to the relevant local justice areas)[22] (SI 2012/2574) |
|  | 28 May 2013 (in relation to the relevant local justice areas)[23] (SI 2013/1103) |

**Criminal Justice Act 2003 (c 44)**—*contd*

| | |
|---|---|
| para 64(3)(a) | 18 Jun 2012 (in relation to the relevant local justice areas)[19] (SI 2012/1320) |
| | 5 Nov 2012 (in relation to the relevant local justice areas)[22] (SI 2012/2574) |
| | 28 May 2013 (in relation to the relevant local justice areas)[23] (SI 2013/1103) |
| para 64(3)(b) | 9 May 2005 (in relation to cases sent for trial under the Crime and Disorder Act 1998, ss 51 or 51A(3)(d)) (SI 2005/1267) |
| | 18 Jun 2012 (in relation to the relevant local justice areas)[19] (SI 2012/1320) |
| | 5 Nov 2012 (in relation to the relevant local justice areas)[22] (SI 2012/2574) |
| | 28 May 2013 (in relation to the relevant local justice areas)[23] (SI 2013/1103) |
| para 64(4)(a) | 18 Jun 2012 (in relation to the relevant local justice areas)[19] (SI 2012/1320) |
| | 5 Nov 2012 (in relation to the relevant local justice areas)[22] (SI 2012/2574) |
| | 28 May 2013 (in relation to the relevant local justice areas)[23] (SI 2013/1103) |
| para 64(4)(b) | 9 May 2005 (in relation to cases sent for trial under the Crime and Disorder Act 1998, ss 51 or 51A(3)(d)) (SI 2005/1267) |
| | 18 Jun 2012 (in relation to the relevant local justice areas)[19] (SI 2012/1320) |
| | 5 Nov 2012 (in relation to the relevant local justice areas)[22] (SI 2012/2574) |
| | 28 May 2013 (in relation to the relevant local justice areas)[23] (SI 2013/1103) |
| para 65 | *Never in force* (repealed) |
| para 66(1) | See sub-paras (2)–(8) below |
| para 66(2)(a) | 18 Jun 2012 (in relation to the relevant local justice areas)[19] (SI 2012/1320) |
| | 5 Nov 2012 (in relation to the relevant local justice areas)[22] (SI 2012/2574) |
| | 28 May 2013 (in relation to the relevant local justice areas)[23] (SI 2013/1103) |
| para 66(2)(b) | 9 May 2005 (in relation to cases sent for trial under the Crime and Disorder Act 1998, ss 51 or 51A(3)(d)) (SI 2005/1267) |
| | 18 Jun 2012 (in relation to the relevant local justice areas)[19] (SI 2012/1320) |
| | 5 Nov 2012 (in relation to the relevant local justice areas)[22] (SI 2012/2574) |
| | 28 May 2013 (in relation to the relevant local justice areas)[23] (SI 2013/1103) |
| para 66(3)(a), (b) | 18 Jun 2012 (in relation to the relevant local justice areas)[19] (SI 2012/1320) |
| | 5 Nov 2012 (in relation to the relevant local justice areas)[22] (SI 2012/2574) |
| | 28 May 2013 (in relation to the relevant local justice areas)[23] (SI 2013/1103) |
| para 66(3)(c) | 9 May 2005 (in relation to cases sent for trial under the Crime and Disorder Act 1998, s 51A(3)(d)) (SI 2005/1267) |
| | 18 Jun 2012 (in relation to the relevant local justice areas)[19] (SI 2012/1320) |
| | 5 Nov 2012 (in relation to the relevant local justice areas)[22] (SI 2012/2574) |
| | 28 May 2013 (in relation to the relevant local justice areas)[23] (SI 2013/1103) |
| para 66(4) | 18 Jun 2012 (in relation to the relevant local justice areas)[19] (except in so far as omits the modified Criminal Procedure and Investigations Act 1996, s 3(8)(a)) (SI 2012/1320) |

**Criminal Justice Act 2003 (c 44)**—*contd*

|  |  |
|---|---|
|  | 5 Nov 2012 (in relation to the relevant local justice areas)[22] (except in so far as omits that modified para) (SI 2012/2574) |
|  | *Not yet in force* (otherwise) |
| para 66(5) | 18 Jun 2012 (in relation to the relevant local justice areas)[19] (SI 2012/1320) |
|  | 5 Nov 2012 (in relation to the relevant local justice areas)[22] (SI 2012/2574) |
|  | 28 May 2013 (in relation to the relevant local justice areas)[23] (SI 2013/1103) |
| para 66(6)(a) | 9 May 2005 (in relation to cases sent for trial under the Crime and Disorder Act 1998, ss 51 or 51A(3)(d)) (SI 2005/1267) |
|  | 18 Jun 2012 (in relation to the relevant local justice areas)[19] (SI 2012/1320) |
|  | 5 Nov 2012 (in relation to the relevant local justice areas)[22] (SI 2012/2574) |
|  | 28 May 2013 (in relation to the relevant local justice areas)[23] (SI 2013/1103) |
| para 66(6)(b) | 18 Jun 2012 (in relation to the relevant local justice areas)[19] (SI 2012/1320) |
|  | 5 Nov 2012 (in relation to the relevant local justice areas)[22] (SI 2012/2574) |
|  | 28 May 2013 (in relation to the relevant local justice areas)[23] (SI 2013/1103) |
| para 66(7) | 9 May 2005 (in relation to cases sent for trial under the Crime and Disorder Act 1998, ss 51 or 51A(3)(d)) (SI 2005/1267) |
|  | 18 Jun 2012 (in relation to the relevant local justice areas)[19] (SI 2012/1320) |
|  | 5 Nov 2012 (in relation to the relevant local justice areas)[22] (SI 2012/2574) |
|  | 28 May 2013 (in relation to the relevant local justice areas)[23] (SI 2013/1103) |
| para 66(8) | 18 Jun 2012 (in relation to the relevant local justice areas)[19] (SI 2012/1320) |
|  | 5 Nov 2012 (in relation to the relevant local justice areas)[22] (SI 2012/2574) |
|  | 28 May 2013 (in relation to the relevant local justice areas)[23] (SI 2013/1103) |
| para 67 | 18 Jun 2012 (in relation to the relevant local justice areas)[19] (SI 2012/1320) |
|  | 5 Nov 2012 (in relation to the relevant local justice areas)[22] (SI 2012/2574) |
|  | 28 May 2013 (in relation to the relevant local justice areas)[23] (SI 2013/1103) |
| paras 68, 69 | 9 May 2005 (in relation to cases sent for trial under the Crime and Disorder Act 1998, s 51A(3)(d)) (SI 2005/1267) |
|  | 18 Jun 2012 (in relation to the relevant local justice areas)[19] (SI 2012/1320) |
|  | 5 Nov 2012 (in relation to the relevant local justice areas)[22] (SI 2012/2574) |
|  | 28 May 2013 (in relation to the relevant local justice areas)[23] (SI 2013/1103) |
| para 70 | *Not yet in force* |
| para 71(a)–(c) | 18 Jun 2012 (in relation to the relevant local justice areas)[19] (SI 2012/1320) |
|  | 5 Nov 2012 (in relation to the relevant local justice areas)[22] (SI 2012/2574) |
|  | 28 May 2013 (in relation to the relevant local justice areas)[23] (SI 2013/1103) |
| para 71(d) | *Not yet in force* |

**Criminal Justice Act 2003 (c 44)**—*contd*

| | |
|---|---|
| para 72 | 18 Jun 2012 (in relation to the relevant local justice areas)[19] (SI 2012/1320) |
| | 5 Nov 2012 (in relation to the relevant local justice areas)[22] (SI 2012/2574) |
| | 28 May 2013 (in relation to the relevant local justice areas)[23] (SI 2013/1103) |
| para 73(1) | See sub-paras (2), (3) below |
| para 73(2) | 18 Jun 2012 (in relation to the relevant local justice areas)[19] (SI 2012/1320) |
| | 5 Nov 2012 (in relation to the relevant local justice areas)[22] (SI 2012/2574) |
| | 28 May 2013 (in relation to the relevant local justice areas)[23] (SI 2013/1103) |
| para 73(3)(a) | 18 Jun 2012 (in relation to the relevant local justice areas)[19] (SI 2012/1320) |
| | 5 Nov 2012 (in relation to the relevant local justice areas)[22] (SI 2012/2574) |
| | 28 May 2013 (in relation to the relevant local justice areas)[23] (SI 2013/1103) |
| para 73(3)(b) | 9 May 2005 (in relation to cases sent for trial under the Crime and Disorder Act 1998, s 51A(3)(d)) (SI 2005/1267) |
| | 18 Jun 2012 (in relation to the relevant local justice areas)[19] (SI 2012/1320) |
| | 5 Nov 2012 (in relation to the relevant local justice areas)[22] (SI 2012/2574) |
| | 28 May 2013 (in relation to the relevant local justice areas)[23] (SI 2013/1103) |
| para 74(1) | See sub-paras (2)–(6) below |
| para 74(2) | 9 May 2005 (in relation to cases sent for trial under the Crime and Disorder Act 1998, ss 51 or 51A(3)(d)) (SI 2005/1267) |
| | 18 Jun 2012 (in relation to the relevant local justice areas)[19] (SI 2012/1320) |
| | 5 Nov 2012 (in relation to the relevant local justice areas)[22] (SI 2012/2574) |
| | 28 May 2013 (in relation to the relevant local justice areas)[23] (SI 2013/1103) |
| para 74(3)(a) | 18 Jun 2012 (in relation to the relevant local justice areas)[19] (SI 2012/1320) |
| | 5 Nov 2012 (in relation to the relevant local justice areas)[22] (SI 2012/2574) |
| | 28 May 2013 (in relation to the relevant local justice areas)[23] (SI 2013/1103) |
| para 74(3)(b) | 9 May 2005 (in relation to cases sent for trial under the Crime and Disorder Act 1998, s 51A(3)(d)) (SI 2005/1267) |
| | 18 Jun 2012 (in relation to the relevant local justice areas)[19] (SI 2012/1320) |
| | 5 Nov 2012 (in relation to the relevant local justice areas)[22] (SI 2012/2574) |
| | 28 May 2013 (in relation to the relevant local justice areas)[23] (SI 2013/1103) |
| para 74(4)(a) | 18 Jun 2012 (in relation to the relevant local justice areas)[19] (SI 2012/1320) |
| | 5 Nov 2012 (in relation to the relevant local justice areas)[22] (SI 2012/2574) |
| | 28 May 2013 (in relation to the relevant local justice areas)[23] (SI 2013/1103) |
| para 74(4)(b) | 9 May 2005 (in relation to cases sent for trial under the Crime and Disorder Act 1998, s 51A(3)(d)) (SI 2005/1267) |
| | 18 Jun 2012 (in relation to the relevant local justice areas)[19] (SI 2012/1320) |

**Criminal Justice Act 2003 (c 44)**—*contd*

|  |  |  |
|---|---|---|
|  |  | 5 Nov 2012 (in relation to the relevant local justice areas)[22] (SI 2012/2574) |
|  |  | 28 May 2013 (in relation to the relevant local justice areas)[23] (SI 2013/1103) |
|  | para 74(5) | 9 May 2005 (in relation to cases sent for trial under the Crime and Disorder Act 1998, ss 51 or 51A(3)(d)) (SI 2005/1267) |
|  |  | 18 Jun 2012 (in relation to the relevant local justice areas)[19] (SI 2012/1320) |
|  |  | 5 Nov 2012 (in relation to the relevant local justice areas)[22] (SI 2012/2574) |
|  |  | 28 May 2013 (in relation to the relevant local justice areas)[23] (SI 2013/1103) |
|  | para 74(6) | 18 Jun 2012 (in relation to the relevant local justice areas)[19] (SI 2012/1320) |
|  |  | 5 Nov 2012 (in relation to the relevant local justice areas)[22] (SI 2012/2574) |
|  |  | 28 May 2013 (in relation to the relevant local justice areas)[23] (SI 2013/1103) |
|  | para 75(1) | See sub-paras (2)–(4) below |
|  | para 75(2) | 18 Jun 2012 (in relation to the relevant local justice areas)[19] (SI 2012/1320) |
|  |  | 5 Nov 2012 (in relation to the relevant local justice areas)[22] (SI 2012/2574) |
|  |  | 28 May 2013 (in relation to the relevant local justice areas)[23] (SI 2013/1103) |
|  | para 75(3) | 9 May 2005 (in relation to cases committed for sentence under Powers of Criminal Courts (Sentencing) Act 2000, s 3C) (SI 2005/1267) |
|  |  | 18 Jun 2012 (in relation to the relevant local justice areas)[19] (SI 2012/1320) |
|  |  | 5 Nov 2012 (in relation to the relevant local justice areas)[22] (SI 2012/2574) |
|  |  | 28 May 2013 (in relation to the relevant local justice areas)[23] (SI 2013/1103) |
|  | para 75(4) | 18 Jun 2012 (in relation to the relevant local justice areas)[19] (SI 2012/1320) |
|  |  | 5 Nov 2012 (in relation to the relevant local justice areas)[22] (SI 2012/2574) |
|  |  | 28 May 2013 (in relation to the relevant local justice areas)[23] (SI 2013/1103) |
| Sch 4 |  | *Not yet in force* |
| Sch 5 | Pt 1 | 4 Apr 2005 (SI 2005/950) |
|  | Pt 2 | 18 Apr 2005 (SI 2005/950) |
|  | Pt 3 | 4 Apr 2005 (SI 2005/950) |
| Sch 6 |  | 1 Jan 2005 (SI 2004/3033) |
| Sch 7 |  | 4 Apr 2005 (SI 2005/950) |
| Schs 8, 9 |  | 4 Apr 2005 (SI 2005/950)[5] |
| Sch 10 |  | 26 Jan 2004 (for the purposes of the passing of a sentence of imprisonment to which an intermittent custody order relates and the release on licence of a person serving such a sentence) (SI 2003/3282) |
|  |  | *Never in force* (otherwise) (repealed) |
| Sch 11 |  | *Never in force* (repealed) |
| Schs 12, 13 |  | 4 Apr 2005 (SI 2005/950)[5] |
| Sch 14 |  | 26 Jan 2004 (for the purposes of the passing of a sentence of imprisonment to which an intermittent custody order relates and the release on licence of a person serving such a sentence) (SI 2003/3282) |
|  |  | 4 Apr 2005 (otherwise) (SI 2005/950)[5] |
| Schs 15–18 |  | 4 Apr 2005 (SI 2005/950) |

**Criminal Justice Act 2003 (c 44)**—*contd*

| | | |
|---|---|---|
| Sch 19 | | 26 Jan 2004 (for the purposes of the passing of a sentence of imprisonment to which an intermittent custody order relates and the release on licence of a person serving such a sentence) (SI 2003/3282) |
| | | 4 Apr 2005 (otherwise) (SI 2005/950) |
| Sch 20 | | 14 Jun 2004 (SI 2004/829) |
| Schs 21, 22 | | 18 Dec 2003 (s 336(2)) |
| Sch 23 | | 4 Apr 2005 (SI 2005/950) |
| Sch 24 | | 1 Dec 2004 (for the purpose of sentencing persons resident in the following petty sessions areas: Bradford, Calderdale, Keighley, Manchester and Newham, and that part of Teesside petty sessions area that is coterminous with the borough of Middlesbrough) (SI 2004/3033)[4] |
| | | *Never in force* (otherwise) (repealed) |
| Sch 25 | | *Not yet in force* (paras 12–14, 28, 29, 36–51, 54, 60, 61, 70, 74 repealed) |
| Sch 26 | | *Not yet in force* (paras 19, 27, 41, 50, 51, 59 repealed) |
| Sch 27 | paras 1–5 | *Not yet in force* (para 2 repealed) |
| | paras 6, 7 | 22 May 2022 (SI 2022/500) |
| | para 8 | *Never in force* (repealed) |
| Sch 28 | | 29 Jan 2004 (SI 2004/81) |
| Sch 29 | | 22 Jan 2004 (SI 2004/81) |
| Sch 30 | | 1 May 2004 (SI 2004/829) |
| Sch 31 | paras 1–4 | *Not yet in force* |
| | para 5 | 7 Mar 2005 (SI 2005/373) |
| | paras 6–8 | *Not yet in force* |
| Sch 32 | paras 1–10 | 4 Apr 2005 (SI 2005/950)[5] |
| | para 11 | 26 Jan 2004 (for the purposes of the passing of a sentence of imprisonment to which an intermittent custody order relates and the release on licence of a person serving such a sentence) (SI 2003/3282) |
| | | *Not yet in force* (otherwise) |
| | para 12(1)–(3) | 26 Jan 2004 (for the purposes of the passing of a sentence of imprisonment to which an intermittent custody order relates and the release on licence of a person serving such a sentence) (SI 2003/3282) |
| | | 4 Apr 2005 (otherwise) (SI 2005/950)[5] |
| | para 12(4), (5) | 4 Apr 2005 (SI 2005/950)[5] |
| | para 12(6) | 26 Jan 2004 (for the purposes of the passing of a sentence of imprisonment to which an intermittent custody order relates and the release on licence of a person serving such a sentence) (SI 2003/3282) |
| | paras 13–16 | 4 Apr 2005 (SI 2005/950)[5] |
| | para 17 | *Not yet in force* |
| | para 18 | 4 Apr 2005 (SI 2005/950)[5] |
| | para 19 | *Never in force* (repealed) |
| | paras 20–26 | 4 Apr 2005 (SI 2005/950)[5] |
| | paras 27, 28 | *Not yet in force* |
| | para 29 | 26 Jan 2004 (for the purposes of the passing of a sentence of imprisonment to which an intermittent custody order relates and the release on licence of a person serving such a sentence) (SI 2003/3282) |
| | | 4 Apr 2005 (otherwise) (SI 2005/950)[5] |
| | paras 30–32 | 4 Apr 2005 (SI 2005/950)[5] |
| | para 33 | *Not yet in force* |
| | paras 34–41 | 4 Apr 2005 (SI 2005/950)[5] |
| | para 42 | 18 Dec 2003 (s 336(2)) |
| | para 43(1), (2) | 4 Apr 2005 (SI 2005/950)[5] |
| | para 43(3) | 18 Dec 2003 (s 336(2)) |
| | paras 44–47 | 4 Apr 2005 (SI 2005/950)[5] |

**Criminal Justice Act 2003 (c 44)**—*contd*

| | | |
|---|---|---|
| paras 48–50 | 22 Jan 2004 (SI 2004/81) | |
| para 51 | *Not yet in force* | |
| para 52 | See paras 53, 54 below | |
| para 53 | *Not yet in force* | |
| paras 54–56 | 4 Apr 2005 (SI 2005/950)[5] | |
| paras 57, 58 | 26 Jan 2004 (for the purposes of the passing of a sentence of imprisonment to which an intermittent custody order relates and the release on licence of a person serving such a sentence) (SI 2003/3282) | |
| paras 59–61 | 4 Apr 2005 (SI 2005/950)[5] | |
| para 62 | See paras 63, 64 below | |
| para 63 | *Not yet in force* | |
| paras 64, 65 | 4 Apr 2005 (SI 2005/950)[5] | |
| para 66 | 18 Dec 2003 (s 336(2)) | |
| para 67 | 4 Apr 2005 (SI 2005/950)[5] | |
| para 68(1) | 4 Apr 2005 (SI 2005/950)[5] | |
| para 68(2) | *Never in force* (repealed) | |
| para 68(3), (4) | 4 Apr 2005 (SI 2005/950)[5] | |
| paras 69–82 | 4 Apr 2005 (SI 2005/950)[5] | |
| para 83(1)–(3) | 18 Dec 2003 (s 336(2)) | |
| para 83(4) | 4 Apr 2005 (SI 2005/950) | |
| para 84 | 18 Dec 2003 (s 336(2)) | |
| paras 85–89 | 4 Apr 2005 (SI 2005/950)[5] | |
| para 90 | See paras 91–129 below | |
| paras 91–98 | 4 Apr 2005 (SI 2005/950)[5] | |
| para 99 | *Never in force* (repealed) | |
| paras 100, 101 | 4 Apr 2005 (SI 2005/950) | |
| para 102(1) | 4 Apr 2005 (SI 2005/950)[5] | |
| para 102(2)(a) | 4 Apr 2005 (except in so far as it substitutes "16" for "21", in relation to a person aged 16 or 17 convicted of an offence) (SI 2005/950)[5] | |
| | 4 Apr 2009 (otherwise) (SI 2005/950)[5] | |
| para 102(2)(b), (c) | *Not yet in force* | |
| para 102(3) | *Not yet in force* | |
| para 102(4) | 4 Apr 2005 (SI 2005/950)[5] | |
| paras 103–108 | 4 Apr 2005 (SI 2005/950)[5] | |
| para 109(1) | See sub-paras (2)–(5) below | |
| para 109(2) | 18 Dec 2003 (s 336(2)) | |
| para 109(3)(a) | 4 Apr 2005 (SI 2005/950) | |
| para 109(3)(b) | 18 Dec 2003 (s 336(2)) | |
| para 109(4), (5) | 18 Dec 2003 (s 336(2)) | |
| paras 110–121 | 4 Apr 2005 (SI 2005/950)[5] | |
| para 122 | *Never in force* (repealed) | |
| para 123(1), (2) | 4 Apr 2005 (SI 2005/950)[5] | |
| para 123(3) | *Not yet in force* | |
| para 123(4) | 4 Apr 2005 (SI 2005/950)[5] | |
| para 123(5) | 4 Apr 2005 (except words "paragraph 7 of Schedule 3 or" and "paragraph 4(2)(a) or 5(2)(a) of Schedule 3 or") (SI 2005/950)[5] | |
| | *Never in force* (repealed) (otherwise) | |
| para 123(6)–(8) | 4 Apr 2005 (SI 2005/950)[5] | |
| para 124 | 4 Apr 2005 (SI 2005/950)[5] | |
| para 125 | *Never in force* (repealed) | |
| paras 126–139 | 4 Apr 2005 (SI 2005/950)[5] | |
| para 140 | *Never in force* (repealed) | |
| paras 141–144 | 4 Apr 2005 (SI 2005/950)[5] | |
| paras 145–162 | *Not yet in force* (paras 152, 155–157, 162 repealed) | |
| Sch 33 | | 5 Apr 2004 (SI 2004/829)[2] |
| Sch 34 | | 27 Feb 2004 (SI 2004/81) |
| Sch 35 | para 1 | 29 Jan 2004 (E) (W) (SI 2004/81) |

**Criminal Justice Act 2003 (c 44)**—*contd*

|  |  |  |
|---|---|---|
|  |  | 3 Dec 2007 (NI) (SI 2007/3340) |
|  | para 2 | 29 Jan 2004 (SI 2004/81) |
|  | para 3(1) | 29 Jan 2004 (SI 2004/81) |
|  | para 3(2)(a) | *Never in force* (repealed) |
|  | para 3(2)(b), (c) | 29 Jan 2004 (SI 2004/81) |
|  | para 3(3) | *Never in force* (repealed) |
|  | para 4(1) | 29 Jan 2004 (SI 2004/81) |
|  | para 4(2)(a) | *Never in force* (repealed) |
|  | para 4(2)(b), (c) | 29 Jan 2004 (SI 2004/81) |
|  | para 4(3) | 29 Jan 2004 (for the purposes of making regulations only) (SI 2004/81) |
|  |  | *Never in force* (otherwise) (repealed) |
|  | para 4(4), (5) | *Never in force* (repealed) |
|  | para 5 | 29 Jan 2004 (for the purposes of making regulations only) (SI 2004/81) |
|  |  | 6 Apr 2006 (E) (W) (otherwise) (SI 2006/751) |
|  |  | 1 Apr 2008 (NI) (otherwise) (SI 2008/694) |
|  | para 6 | 6 Apr 2006 (E) (W) (SI 2006/751) |
|  |  | 3 Dec 2007 (NI) (SI 2007/3340) |
|  | para 7 | 29 Jan 2004 (SI 2004/81) |
|  |  | 3 Dec 2007 (NI) (SI 2007/3340) |
|  | paras 8, 9 | 6 Apr 2006 (E) (W) (SI 2006/751) |
|  |  | 3 Dec 2007 (NI) (SI 2007/3340) |
|  | paras 10, 11 | 29 Jan 2004 (SI 2004/81) |
|  |  | 3 Dec 2007 (NI) (SI 2007/3340) |
|  | para 12 | 6 Apr 2006 (E) (W) (SI 2006/751) |
|  |  | 3 Dec 2007 (NI) (SI 2007/3340) |
| Sch 36 | para 1 | 5 Apr 2004 (SI 2004/829) |
|  | para 2 | *Not yet in force* |
|  | para 3 | 1 Jan 2007 (SI 2006/3217) |
|  | para 4 | 18 Jun 2012 (SI 2012/1320) |
|  | para 5 | 5 Apr 2004 (SI 2004/829) |
|  | para 6 | 1 Oct 2007 (SI 2007/2874) |
|  | paras 7–9 | *Not yet in force* |
|  | para 10 | 1 Oct 2007 (SI 2007/2874) |
|  | paras 11–14 | *Not yet in force* |
|  | para 15 | 1 Oct 2007 (SI 2007/2874) |
|  | para 16 | *Not yet in force* |
|  | paras 17–39 | 4 Apr 2005 (E) (W) (SI 2005/950)[5] |
|  |  | 15 Jul 2005 (NI) (SI 2005/1817)[6] |
|  | paras 40–78 | 24 Jul 2006 (E) (W) (SI 2006/1835) |
|  |  | 8 Jan 2007 (NI) (SI 2006/3422) |
|  | paras 79, 80 | 15 Dec 2004 (SI 2004/3033) |
|  | paras 81–84 | 1 Jan 2005 (in so far as relating to Sch 6 to this Act) (SI 2004/3033) |
|  |  | 4 Apr 2005 (otherwise) (SI 2005/950) |
|  | para 85 | 15 Dec 2004 (SI 2004/3033) |
|  | para 86 | 1 Sep 2004 (SI 2004/1629) |
|  | paras 87, 88 | 4 Apr 2005 (SI 2005/950) |
|  | para 89 | 1 Sep 2004 (SI 2004/1629) |
|  | para 90 | 4 Apr 2005 (SI 2005/950) |
|  | para 91 | See paras 92–95 below |
|  | para 92(1)–(5) | 8 Jan 2007 (SI 2006/3422) |
|  | para 92(6) | 18 Apr 2005 (SI 2005/950) |
|  | para 92(7) | 8 Jan 2007 (SI 2006/3422) |
|  | para 93 | 8 Jan 2007 (SI 2006/3422) |
|  | para 94 | 18 Apr 2005 (SI 2005/950) |
|  | paras 95, 96 | 4 Apr 2005 (SI 2005/950) |
|  | para 97 | 1 Sep 2004 (SI 2004/1629) |

**Criminal Justice Act 2003 (c 44)**—*contd*

|  | para 98 | *Not yet in force* |
|---|---|---|
| Sch 37 | Pt 1 | 20 Jan 2004 (SI 2004/81), repeals of or in— |

Police and Criminal Evidence Act 1984 (except s 63(3)(a));
Criminal Justice and Public Order Act 1994;
Armed Forces Act 2001;
Police Reform Act 2002

5 Apr 2004 (repeals of or in Police and Criminal Evidence
Act 1984, s 63(3)(a)) (SI 2004/829)

Pt 2    5 Apr 2004 (E) (W) (S) (except repeals of or in Criminal Justice
and Public Order Act 1994) (SI 2004/829)

3 Dec 2007 (NI) (SI 2007/3340)

*Not yet in force* (E) (W) (S) (exception noted above)[21]

Pt 3    4 Apr 2005 (E) (W) (SI 2005/950)[5]

15 Jul 2005 (NI) (SI 2005/1817)[7]

Pt 4    9 May 2005 (in relation to cases sent for trial under the Crime and
Disorder Act 1998, ss 51 or 51A(3)(d)) (SI 2005/1267), repeals
of or in—

Prosecution of Offences Act 1985, s 23A(1)(b);
Criminal Procedure and Investigations Act 1996, s 1(2)(cc)

18 Jun 2012 (repeal of Magistrates' Courts Act 1980, s 42)
(SI 2012/1320)

18 Jun 2012 (in relation to the relevant local justice areas)[19]
(SI 2012/1320), repeals of or in—

Bankers' Books Evidence Act 1879;
Explosive Substances Act 1883;
Criminal Justice Act 1925;
Administration of Justice (Miscellaneous Provisions) Act 1933;
Criminal Justice Act 1948;
Backing of Warrants (Republic of Ireland) Act 1965;
Criminal Procedure (Attendance of Witnesses) Act 1965;
Criminal Justice Act 1967;
Criminal Appeal Act 1968;
Firearms Act 1968;
Theft Act 1968;
Criminal Justice Act 1972;
Bail Act 1976;
Criminal Law Act 1977;
Interpretation Act 1978;
Customs and Excise Management Act 1979;
Magistrates' Courts Act 1980;
Contempt of Court Act 1981;
Criminal Attempts Act 1981;
Criminal Justice (Amendment) Act 1981;
Supreme Court Act 1981;
Criminal Justice Act 1982;
Mental Health Act 1983;
Police and Criminal Evidence Act 1984;
Prosecution of Offences Act 1985 (so far as not already in force);
Criminal Justice Act 1987;
Criminal Justice Act 1988;
Road Traffic Offenders Act 1988;
Broadcasting Act 1990;
Courts and Legal Services Act 1990;
Criminal Justice Act 1991;
Criminal Justice and Public Order Act 1994;
Criminal Procedure and Investigations Act 1996 (so far as not
already in force, except repeal in s 13(1) (para (a) of the
modified s 3(8));
Sexual Offences (Protected Material) Act 1997;

**Criminal Justice Act 2003 (c 44)**—*contd*

          Crime and Disorder Act 1998;

          Access to Justice Act 1999;

          Youth Justice and Criminal Evidence Act 1999;

          Powers of Criminal Courts (Sentencing) Act 2000

          5 Nov 2012 (in relation to the relevant local justice areas, so far as not already in force, except repeal in Criminal Procedure and Investigations Act 1996, s 13(1) (para (a) of the modified s 3(8)))[22] (SI 2012/2574)

          28 May 2013 (in relation to the relevant local justice areas, so far as not already in force, except repeal in Criminal Procedure and Investigations Act 1996, s 13(1) (para (a) of the modified s 3(8)))[23] (SI 2013/1103)

          *Not yet in force* (exception noted above)

| | |
|---|---|
| Pt 5 | 15 Dec 2004 (SI 2004/3033) |
| Pt 6 | 4 Apr 2005 (SI 2005/950) |
| Pt 7 | 27 Feb 2004 (repeal of Crime and Disorder Act 1998, ss 80, 81) (SI 2004/81) |

          5 Apr 2004 (repeal of Powers of Criminal Courts (Sentencing) Act 2000, s 91(2)) (SI 2004/829)

          4 Apr 2005 (SI 2005/950)[5], repeals of or in—

          Piracy Act 1837;

          Criminal Justice Act 1967;

          Criminal Appeal Act 1968;

          Social Work (Scotland) Act 1968;

          Bail Act 1976;

          Magistrates' Courts Act 1980, Sch 6A;

          Mental Health Act 1983;

          Road Traffic Offenders Act 1988;

          Children Act 1989;

          Football Spectators Act 1989, s 7(9);

          Criminal Justice Act 1991, ss 32–51, Sch 5;

          Prisoners and Criminal Proceedings (Scotland) Act 1993;

          Criminal Justice and Public Order Act 1994;

          Criminal Procedure (Scotland) Act 1995;

          Crime (Sentences) Act 1997, Schs 1, 2, 4;

          Crime and Disorder Act 1998, ss 18, 38, 59, 60, 99–101, 103–105, 121;

          Access to Justice Act 1999;

          Criminal Justice and Court Services Act 2000, ss 47–51, 53–55, 63, 78, Sch 7;

          Powers of Criminal Courts (Sentencing) Act 2000, ss 6, 12, 34–36A, 36B, 37, 40A, 41–59, 62, 69, 73, 79–82, 84, 85, 87, 88, 100, 109–129, 151–153, 156–163, 168, Schs 2, 4, 7, 8;

          Terrorism Act 2000;

          Anti-Terrorism, Crime and Security Act 2001

          3 Dec 2012 (SI 2012/2905), repeals of or in—

          Criminal Justice Act 1991, s 65(1);

          Powers of Criminal Courts (Sentencing) Act 2000, ss 85, 116, 117 (so far as they remain in force by virtue of savings in SI 2005/950, Sch 2; repeal of s 85 has no effect in relation to a person convicted before 3 Dec 2012)

          1 May 2013 (repeal of Criminal Justice Act 1991, s 65(1A)–(10)) (SI 2012/2905)

          14 Jul 2022 (repeals in Crime and Disorder Act 1998, Sch 8) (SI 2022/816)

          *Not yet in force,* repeals or revocations of or in—

          Children and Young Persons Act 1933;

          Magistrates' Courts Act 1980, ss 82, 133;

          Forgery and Counterfeiting Act 1981;

          Football Spectators Act 1989, s 7(10);

**Criminal Justice Act 2003 (c 44)**—*contd*

|  |  |
|---|---|
|  | Criminal Justice Act 1991, Sch 12; |
|  | Criminal Justice Act 1993; |
|  | Crime (Sentences) Act 1997, ss 35, 40; |
|  | Crime and Disorder Act 1998, Sch 7; |
|  | Criminal Justice (Children) (Northern Ireland) Order 1998, SI 1998/1504 (NI 9); |
|  | Child Support, Pensions and Social Security Act 2000; |
|  | Criminal Justice and Court Services Act 2000, s 64; |
|  | Powers of Criminal Courts (Sentencing) Act 2000, ss 60, 78, 106, 157, Sch 9; |
|  | Proceeds of Crime Act 2002 |
| Pt 8 | 18 Dec 2003 (s 336(2)) |
| Pt 9 | 20 Nov 2003 (repeal in Countryside and Rights of Way Act 2000) (s 336(1)) |
|  | *Not yet in force*, repeals of or in— |
|  | Vagrancy Act 1824; |
|  | Railway Regulation Act 1842; |
|  | London Hackney Carriages Act 1843; |
|  | Town Police Clauses Act 1847; |
|  | Ecclesiastical Courts Jurisdiction Act 1860; |
|  | Town Gardens Protection Act 1863; |
|  | Public Stores Act 1875; |
|  | North Sea Fisheries Act 1893; |
|  | Children and Young Persons Act 1933; |
|  | Protection of Animals Act 1934; |
|  | Public Health Act 1936; |
|  | Essential Commodities Reserves Act 1938; |
|  | London Building Acts (Amendment) Act 1939; |
|  | Cancer Act 1939; |
|  | Civil Defence Act 1939; |
|  | Hill Farming Act 1946; |
|  | Agriculture Act 1947; |
|  | Agricultural Wages Act 1948; |
|  | Civil Defence Act 1948; |
|  | Coast Protection Act 1949; |
|  | Prevention of Damage by Pests Act 1949; |
|  | Wireless Telegraphy Act 1949; |
|  | Pet Animals Act 1951; |
|  | Cockfighting Act 1952; |
|  | Accommodation Agencies Act 1953; |
|  | Agricultural Land (Removal of Surface Soil) Act 1953; |
|  | Air Force Act 1955; |
|  | Army Act 1955; |
|  | Naval Discipline Act 1957; |
|  | Agricultural Marketing Act 1958; |
|  | Rivers (Prevention of Pollution) Act 1961; |
|  | Animal Boarding Establishments Act 1963; |
|  | Betting, Gaming and Lotteries Act 1963; |
|  | Children and Young Persons Act 1963; |
|  | Agriculture and Horticulture Act 1964; |
|  | Emergency Laws (Re-enactments and Repeals) Act 1964; |
|  | Riding Establishments Act 1964; |
|  | Cereals Marketing Act 1965; |
|  | Gas Act 1965; |
|  | Industrial and Provident Societies Act 1965; |
|  | Armed Forces Act 1966; |
|  | Agriculture Act 1967; |
|  | Criminal Justice Act 1967; |
|  | Sea Fisheries (Shellfish) Act 1967; |

**Criminal Justice Act 2003 (c 44)**—*contd*

|  |  |
|---|---|
|  | Theatres Act 1968; |
|  | Agriculture Act 1970; |
|  | Breeding of Dogs Act 1973; |
|  | Slaughterhouses Act 1974; |
|  | National Health Service Act 1977; |
|  | Magistrates' Courts Act 1980; |
|  | Animal Health Act 1981; |
|  | Fisheries Act 1981; |
|  | Civil Aviation Act 1982; |
|  | Criminal Justice Act 1982; |
|  | Mental Health Act 1983; |
|  | Building Act 1984; |
|  | Surrogacy Arrangements Act 1985; |
|  | Animals (Scientific Procedures) Act 1986; |
|  | Motorcycle Noise Act 1987; |
|  | Human Organ Transplants Act 1989; |
|  | Environmental Protection Act 1990; |
|  | Town and Country Planning Act 1990; |
|  | Criminal Justice Act 1991; |
|  | Deer Act 1991; |
|  | Water Industry Act 1991; |
|  | Local Government Finance Act 1992; |
|  | Social Security Administration Act 1992; |
|  | Trade Union and Labour Relations (Consolidation) Act 1992; |
|  | Merchant Shipping Act 1995; |
|  | Broadcasting Act 1996; |
|  | Housing Act 1996; |
|  | Reserve Forces Act 1996; |
|  | Breeding and Sale of Dogs (Welfare) Act 1999; |
|  | Powers of Criminal Courts (Sentencing) Act 2000; |
|  | Transport Act 2000 |
|  | *Never in force* (repeals in Theft Act 1968) (repealed) |
| Pt 10 | 5 Apr 2004 (SI 2004/829) |
| Pt 11 | 29 Jan 2004 (repeal of Police Act 1997, s 120(3)) (SI 2004/81) |
|  | 6 Apr 2006 (SI 2006/751), repeals of or in— |
|  | Police Act 1997, s 125; |
|  | Criminal Justice and Police Act 2001; |
|  | Private Security Industry Act 2001; |
|  | National Health Service Reform and Health Care Professions Act 2002, s 42 |
|  | *Not yet in force*, repeals of or in— |
|  | Police Act 1997, s 115; |
|  | Care Standards Act 2000; |
|  | Health and Social Care Act 2001; |
|  | National Health Service Reform and Health Care Professions Act 2002, Sch 2; |
|  | Education Act 2002; |
|  | Licensing Act 2003 |
| Pt 12 | 5 Apr 2004 (repeals in Criminal Justice and Court Services Act 2000) (SI 2004/829) |
|  | 15 Dec 2004 (SI 2004/3033), repeals of or in— |
|  | Bail Act 1976; |
|  | Magistrates' Courts Act 1980, ss 1, 13; |
|  | Crime and Disorder Act 1998; |
|  | Youth Justice and Criminal Evidence Act 1999; |
|  | Powers of Criminal Courts (Sentencing) Act 2000 |
|  | 4 Apr 2005 (repeal in Magistrates' Courts Act 1980, s 12) (SI 2005/950) |
|  | *Not yet in force*, repeals of or in— |

**Criminal Justice Act 2003 (c 44)**—*contd*

| | | |
|---|---|---|
| | | Criminal Appeal Act 1968; |
| | | Magistrates' Courts Act 1980, s 12; |
| | | Criminal Appeal (Northern Ireland) Act 1980; |
| | | Criminal Procedure and Investigations Act 1996 |
| Sch 38 | para 1 | 20 Nov 2003 (s 336(1)) |
| | paras 2, 3 | 27 Feb 2004 (SI 2004/81) |
| | paras 4, 5 | *Not yet in force* |
| | para 6 | 20 Nov 2003 (s 336(1)) |
| | para 7 | 4 Apr 2005 (SI 2005/950) |

[1] For savings, see SI 2004/81, art 2(3)

[2] For transitional provisions, see SI 2004/829, art 2(3)–(6)

[3] For savings, see SI 2004/1629, art 3(3), (4)

[4] For transitional provisions, see SI 2004/3033, art 2(3), (4)

[5] For transitional and saving provisions, see SI 2005/950, Sch 2

[6] Note that SI 2005/1267 purports to bring Sch 3, para 34(2)(c)(i) into force; it is thought that this is a reference to the substitution of the Administration of Justice (Miscellaneous Provisions) Act 1933, s 2(2)(i) made by that paragraph

[7] For transitional provision, see SI 2006/1835, art 3

[8] For transitional provisions, see SI 2006/3217, art 3

[9] The certain purposes are as follows: for the purposes of—

(a)  criminal proceedings instituted by a public prosecutor within the meaning of s 29(5)(a) of this Act (a police force, or a person authorised by a police force to institute criminal proceedings), in a magistrates' court sitting in one of the following locations:

  (i)  Barking Magistrates' Court;

  (ii)  Bexley Magistrates' Court;

  (iii)  Brentford Magistrates' Court;

  (iv)  Bromley Magistrates' Court;

  (v)  Coalville Magistrates' Court;

  (vi)  Croydon Magistrates' Court;

  (vii)  Harrow Magistrates' Court;

  (viii)  Hendon Magistrates' Court;

  (ix)  Knowsley Magistrates' Court;

  (x)  Loughborough Magistrates' Court;

  (xi)  Melton Magistrates' Court;

  (xii)  Oakham Magistrates' Court;

  (xiii)  Redbridge Magistrates' Court;

  (xiv)  Richmond Magistrates' Court;

  (xv)  St Helens Magistrates' Court;

  (xvi)  Waltham Forest Magistrates' Court;

  (xvii)  City of Westminster Magistrates' Court; and

  (xviii)  Wimbledon Magistrates' Court; and

(b)  criminal proceedings instituted by a public prosecutor within the meaning of s 29(5)(e) of this Act (a person authorised by a Secretary of State to institute criminal proceedings), who is authorised for the purposes of the Vehicle Excise and Registration Act 1994, s 49 (authorised persons), in a magistrates' court sitting in Portsmouth Magistrates' Court

[10] The specified offences are—

**Criminal Justice Act 2003 (c 44)**—*contd*

    (a)   an offence under Part 1 of the Sexual Offences Act 2003 (rape, assault by penetration, sexual assault etc),

    (b)   rape or burglary with intent to rape,

    (c)   an offence under any of sections 2 to 12 and 14 to 17 of the Sexual Offences Act 1956 (unlawful intercourse, indecent assault, forcible abduction etc),

    (d)   an offence under section 128 of the Mental Health Act 1959 (unlawful intercourse with person receiving treatment for mental disorder by member of hospital staff etc),

    (e)   an offence under section 1 of the Indecency with Children Act 1960 (indecent conduct towards child under 14), and

    (f)   an offence under section 54 of the Criminal Law Act 1977 (incitement of child under 16 to commit incest)

[11]   For a transitional provision, see SI 2007/3451, art 4

[12]   The certain purposes are as follows: for the purposes of criminal proceedings instituted by a public prosecutor within the meaning of s 29(5)(a) of this Act, in a magistrates' court sitting in one of the following locations:

    (a)   Chester;

    (b)   Crewe;

    (c)   Macclesfield;

    (d)   Northwich;

    (e)   Runcorn;

    (f)   Warrington; and

    (g)   Widnes

[13]   The certain purposes are as follows—

    (a)   criminal proceedings instituted by a public prosecutor within the meaning of s 29(5)(a) of this Act (a police force or a person authorised by a police force to institute proceedings), in a magistrates' court sitting in one of the following locations:

        (i)   Brent Magistrates' Court;

        (ii)   Feltham Magistrates' Court;

        (iii)   Havering Magistrates' Court; and

        (iv)   South Western Magistrates' Court;

    (b)   criminal proceedings instituted by a public prosecutor within the meaning of s 29(5)(e) of this Act (a Secretary of State or a person authorised by a Secretary of State to institute criminal proceedings) who is authorised for the purposes of the Vehicle Excise and Registration Act 1994, s 49 (authorised persons) anywhere in England and Wales; and

    (c)   criminal proceedings instituted by a public prosecutor within the meaning of s 29(5)(e) of this Act (a Secretary of State or a person authorised by a Secretary of State to institute criminal proceedings) where they are instituted by the Secretary of State for Work and Pensions or the Secretary of State for Health anywhere in England and Wales

[14]   For transitional provisions, see SI 2010/1183, art 4

[15]   The certain purposes are as follows—

    (a)   criminal proceedings instituted by a police force or a person authorised by a police force to institute proceedings in a magistrates' court sitting in Gloucestershire or Essex; and

    (b)   criminal proceedings instituted by a public prosecutor within the meaning of s 29(5)(e) of this Act (a Secretary of State or a person authorised by one) who is a person authorised to do so on behalf of the Vehicle and Operator Services Agency

[16]   The certain purposes are as follows: for the purposes of criminal proceedings instituted by a public prosecutor specified in an Order made by the Secretary of State under s 29(5)(h) of this Act or a person authorised by such a person (specification of a person as a public prosecutor or a person authorised by such a person for the purposes of issuing a written charge and requisition)

**Criminal Justice Act 2003 (c 44)**—*contd*

17    The certain purposes are as follows: for the purposes of criminal proceedings instituted by a public prosecutor within the meaning of—

(a)   s 29(5)(a) of this Act (a police force or a person authorised by a police force to institute criminal proceedings), so far as not already in force; and

(b)   s 29(5)(e) of this Act (a Secretary of State or a person authorised by a Secretary of State to institute criminal proceedings) where criminal proceedings are instituted by the Secretary of State for Business, Energy and Industrial Strategy or a person authorised by that Secretary of State

18    The certain purposes are as follows: for the purposes of criminal proceedings instituted by—

(a)   the Director of the Serious Fraud Office or a person authorised by the Director to institute criminal proceedings; and

(b)   the Director of Public Prosecutions or a person authorised by the Director to institute criminal proceedings

19    (a)   The relevant local justice areas are: Bath and Wansdyke; Berkshire; Bristol; Liverpool and Knowsley; North Avon; North Hampshire; North Somerset; Ormskirk; Sefton; St Helens; Wigan and Leigh; and Wirral

(b)   These provisions are also to come into force on 18 Jun 2012 in relation to the Crown Court where it deals with—

(i)    a person sent for trial by a magistrates' court in a relevant local justice area;

(ii)   a person committed for sentence by a magistrates' court in a relevant local justice area

(c)   For saving provisions, see SI 2012/1320, art 5

20    For saving provisions, see SI 2012/1320, art 6

21    Note that SI 2012/1320 also purports to bring the repeal in the Senior Courts Act 1981 into force on 18 Jun 2012

22    (a)   The relevant local justice areas are: Birmingham; Bolton; Buckinghamshire; Burnley, Pendle and Rossendale; Bury and Rochdale; Carmarthenshire; Ceredigion and Pembrokeshire; Chorley; Coventry District; Dudley and Halesowen; East Lancashire; Furness and District; Fylde Coast; Gloucestershire; Halton; High Peak; Lancaster; Macclesfield; Manchester and Salford; Mansfield and Worksop; Neath Port Talbot; North Cumbria; North East Derbyshire and Dales; North West Wiltshire; Nottingham and Newark; Oldham; Oxfordshire; Preston; Sandwell; Solihull; South Cheshire; South East Wiltshire; South Lakeland; South Ribble; South Somerset and Mendip; Southern Derbyshire; Stockport; Swansea County; Swindon; Tameside; Taunton Deane, West Somerset and Sedgemoor; Trafford; Walsall and Aldridge; Warrington; Warwickshire; West Cheshire; West Cumbria; West Hampshire; Wolverhampton

(b)   These provisions are also to come into force on 5 Nov 2012 in relation to the Crown Court where it deals with—

(i)    a person sent for trial by a magistrates' court in a relevant local justice area;

(ii)   a person committed for sentence by a magistrates' court in a relevant local justice area

(c)   For saving and transitional provisions, see SI 2012/2574, arts 3, 4

23    (a) The relevant local justice areas are those local justice areas not specified in SI 2012/1320, art 4(2) or SI 2012/2574, art 2(2), Schedule

(b)   These provisions are also to come into force on 28 May 2013 in relation to the Crown Court where it deals with—

(i)    a person sent for trial by a magistrates' court in a relevant local justice area;

(ii)   a person committed for sentence by a magistrates' court in a relevant local justice area

(c)   For saving provisions, see SI 2013/1103, arts 3, 4

24    The certain purposes are as follows: for the purposes of criminal proceedings instituted by a public prosecutor within the meaning of s 29(5)(e) of this Act (a Secretary of State or a person authorised by a Secretary of State to institute criminal proceedings) who is a person authorised to do so on behalf of the Driver and Vehicle Standards Agency

## Criminal Justice (Scotland) Act 2003 (asp 7)

*RA:* 26 Mar 2003

*Commencement provisions:* s 89(2), (3); Criminal Justice (Scotland) Act 2003 (Commencement No 1) Order 2003, SSI 2003/288; Criminal Justice (Scotland) Act 2003 (Commencement No 2) (Scotland) Order 2003, SSI 2003/439 (revoked; never in force); Criminal Justice (Scotland) Act 2003 (Commencement No 3 and Revocation) Order 2003, SSI 2003/475; Criminal Justice (Scotland) Act 2003 (Commencement No 4) Order 2004, SSI 2004/240; Criminal Justice (Scotland) Act 2003 (Commencement No 5) Order 2004, SSI 2004/451; Criminal Justice (Scotland) Act 2003 (Commencement No 6) Order 2005, SSI 2005/433; Criminal Justice (Scotland) Act 2003 (Commencement No 7) Order 2006, SSI 2006/85; Criminal Justice (Scotland) Act 2003 (Commencement No 8) Order 2006, SSI 2006/168; Criminal Justice (Scotland) Act 2003 (Commencement No 9) Order 2006, SSI 2006/332

| | | |
|---|---|---|
| 1 | (1) | 19 Jun 2006 (SSI 2006/332)[2] |
| | (2) | See Sch 1 below |
| 2 | (a) | 4 Oct 2005 (SSI 2005/433) |
| | (b) | 27 Jun 2003 (SSI 2003/288) |
| 3 | (1), (2) | 27 Jun 2003 (SSI 2003/288) |
| | (3) | See Sch 2 below |
| 4–6 | | 1 Jan 2004 (SSI 2003/475) |
| 7–10 | | 4 Oct 2005 (SSI 2005/433) |
| 11, 12 | | 1 Jan 2004 (SSI 2003/475) |
| 13 | | 1 Jan 2004 (SSI 2003/475)[1] |
| 14, 15 | | 25 Nov 2003 (SSI 2003/475) |
| 16, 17 | | 1 Nov 2004 (SSI 2004/451) |
| 18 | | 25 Nov 2003 (SSI 2003/475) |
| 19, 20 | | 27 Jun 2003 (SSI 2003/288) |
| 21 | (1)–(8) | 3 Nov 2003 (so far as they relate to summary proceedings) (SSI 2003/475) |
| | | *Not yet in force* (otherwise) |
| | (9), (10) | 10 Jun 2004 (SSI 2004/240) |
| | (11) | 3 Nov 2003 (so far as relates to summary proceedings) (SSI 2003/475) |
| | | *Not yet in force* (otherwise) |
| 22–25 | | 27 Jun 2003 (SSI 2003/288) |
| 26 | | 1 Dec 2003 (SSI 2003/475) |
| 27–29 | | 27 Jun 2003 (SSI 2003/288) |
| 30 | | 1 Dec 2003 (SSI 2003/475) |
| 31 | | 27 Jun 2003 (SSI 2003/288) |
| 32 | | 2 Apr 2006 (SSI 2006/85) |
| 33–39 | | 27 Jun 2003 (SSI 2003/288) |
| 40 | | 12 Jan 2004 (SSI 2003/475) |
| 41 | | 4 Oct 2005 (SSI 2005/433) |
| 42–50 | | 27 Jun 2003 (SSI 2003/288) |
| 51 | | 27 Oct 2003 (SSI 2003/475) |
| 52–59 | | 27 Jun 2003 (SSI 2003/288) |
| 60 | | 27 Oct 2003 (SSI 2003/475) |
| 61–69 | | 27 Jun 2003 (SSI 2003/288) |
| 70 | (1) | 27 Jun 2003 (SSI 2003/288) |
| | (2) | 1 Apr 2006 (SSI 2006/168) |
| | (3), (4) | 27 Jun 2003 (SSI 2003/288) |
| | (5), (6) | 1 Apr 2006 (SSI 2006/168) |
| | (7) | 27 Jun 2003 (SSI 2003/288) |
| | (8) | 1 Apr 2006 (for the purpose of inserting Police Act 1997, s 124A) (SSI 2006/168) |
| | | *Not yet in force* (for the purpose of inserting Police Act 1997, s 124B) |
| 71–74 | | 27 Jun 2003 (SSI 2003/288) |
| 75 | | 25 Jun 2004 (SSI 2004/240) |
| 76 | | 27 Jun 2003 (SSI 2003/288) |

**Criminal Justice (Scotland) Act 2003 (asp 7)**—*contd*

| | | |
|---|---|---|
| 77 | | See Sch 3 below |
| 78–82 | | 27 Jun 2003 (SSI 2003/288) |
| 83 | | *Never in force* (repealed) |
| 84 | | 26 Mar 2003 (RA) |
| 85 | | See Sch 4 below |
| 86 | | See Sch 5 below |
| 87–89 | | 26 Mar 2003 (RA) |
| Sch 1 | para 1(1), (2) | 19 Jun 2006 (SSI 2006/332)[2] |
| | para 1(3)(a) | 19 Jun 2006 (SSI 2006/332)[2] |
| | para 1(3)(b) | 4 Oct 2005 (SSI 2005/433) |
| | para 2 | 19 Jun 2006 (SSI 2006/332)[2] |
| Sch 2 | | 27 Jun 2003 (SSI 2003/288) |
| Sch 3 | | 26 Mar 2003 (RA) |
| Sch 4 | paras 1, 2 | 27 Jun 2003 (SSI 2003/288) |
| | para 3(1) | 27 Jun 2003 (SSI 2003/288) |
| | para 3(2) | 25 Nov 2003 (SSI 2003/475) |
| | para 3(3) | 27 Jun 2003 (SSI 2003/288) |
| | para 4 | *Not yet in force* |
| | para 5 | 27 Jun 2003 (SSI 2003/288) |
| Sch 5 | | 26 Mar 2003 (repeals of or in Wildlife and Countryside Act 1981) (RA) |
| | | 27 Jun 2003 (otherwise) (SSI 2003/288) |

[1]  For transitional provisions, see SSI 2003/438, art 2 (by virtue of SSI 2003/475, art 3)

[2]  For the purposes of sentences imposed for offences committed on or after 20 Jun 2006, except in respect of sentences imposed for offences for which life imprisonment was the maximum sentence which could be imposed at the time the offence was committed, in relation to which these provisions shall come into force only for the purposes of sentences imposed in cases which are commenced (i e a report is received by the procurator fiscal) on or after 20 Jun 2006; see SSI 2006/332, art 2(2), (3)

---

**Dealing in Cultural Objects (Offences) Act 2003 (c 27)**

*RA:* 30 Oct 2003

*Commencement provisions:* s 6(2)

Whole Act in force 30 Dec 2003 (s 6(2))

---

**Dog Fouling (Scotland) Act 2003 (asp 12)**

*RA:* 22 Apr 2003

*Commencement provisions:* s 18(2)

Whole Act in force 22 Oct 2003 (s 18(2))

---

**Education (School Meals) (Scotland) Act 2003 (asp 18)**

*RA:* 7 Jul 2003

Whole Act in force 7 Jul 2003 (RA)

---

**Electricity (Miscellaneous Provisions) Act 2003 (c 9)**

*RA:* 8 May 2003

Whole Act in force 8 May 2003 (RA)

---

## European Parliament (Representation) Act 2003 (c 7)

*RA:* 8 May 2003

*Commencement provisions:* s 28(3)–(5); European Parliament (Representation) Act 2003 (Commencement No 1) Order 2003, SI 2003/1401; European Parliament (Representation) Act 2003 (Commencement No 2) Order 2003, SI 2003/1402; European Parliament (Representation) Act 2003 (Commencement No 3) Order 2004, SI 2004/24; European Parliament (Representation) Act 2003 (Commencement No 4) Order 2004, SI 2004/320; European Parliament (Representation) Act 2003 (Commencement No 5) Order 2004, SI 2004/700; European Parliament (Representation) Act 2003 (Commencement No 6) Order 2004, SI 2004/1035

| | | |
|---|---|---|
| 1 | | 8 May 2003 (United Kingdom) (s 28(3)) |
| | | 5 Feb 2004 (Gibraltar) (SI 2004/320) |
| 2–6 | | 8 May 2003 (United Kingdom) (s 28(3)) |
| | | 10 Mar 2004 (Gibraltar) (SI 2004/700) |
| 7 | para (1) | 8 May 2003 (United Kingdom) (s 28(3)) |
| | | 10 Mar 2004 (Gibraltar) (SI 2004/700) |
| | para (2) | See Schedule below |
| 8 | | 8 May 2003 (United Kingdom) (s 28(3)) |
| | | 5 Feb 2004 (Gibraltar) (SI 2004/320) |
| 9, 10 | | 8 May 2003 (United Kingdom) (s 28(3)) |
| | | 2 Jun 2003 (Gibraltar) (SI 2003/1402) |
| 11–13 | | 7 Jan 2004 (so far as conferring powers to make subordinate legislation) (SI 2004/24) |
| | | 23 Mar 2004 (otherwise) (SI 2004/1035) |
| 14 | | 7 Jan 2004 (SI 2004/24) |
| 15, 16 | | 7 Jan 2004 (so far as conferring powers to make subordinate legislation) (SI 2004/24) |
| | | 23 Mar 2004 (otherwise) (SI 2004/1035) |
| 17, 18 | | 7 Jan 2004 (so far as conferring powers to make subordinate legislation) (SI 2004/24) |
| | | 23 Mar 2004 (otherwise) (SI 2004/1035) |
| 19 | | 7 Jan 2004 (so far as extending to Gibraltar provisions of the European Parliamentary Elections Act 2002 which confer the power to make subordinate legislation) (SI 2004/24) |
| | | 5 Feb 2004 (otherwise) (except in so far as extending to Gibraltar the European Parliamentary Elections Act 2002, ss 1A, 8, Sch 1A) (SI 2004/320) |
| | | 10 Mar 2004 (in so far as extending to Gibraltar the European Parliamentary Elections Act 2002, s 1A, Sch 1A) (SI 2004/700) |
| | | 23 Mar 2004 (otherwise) (SI 2004/1035) |
| 20, 21 | | 7 Jan 2004 (so far as amending provisions of the European Parliamentary Elections Act 2002 which confer powers to make subordinate legislation) (SI 2004/24) |
| | | 5 Feb 2004 (otherwise) (SI 2004/320) |
| 22 | | 7 Jan 2004 (so far as amending provisions of the European Parliamentary Elections Act 2002 which confer powers to make subordinate legislation) (SI 2004/24) |
| | | 23 Mar 2004 (otherwise) (SI 2004/1035) |
| 23 | | 7 Jan 2004 (so far as conferring powers to make subordinate legislation) (SI 2004/24) |
| | | 23 Mar 2004 (otherwise) (SI 2004/1035) |
| 24 | | 7 Jan 2004 (SI 2004/24) |
| 25 | | 8 May 2003 (United Kingdom) (s 28(3)) |
| | | 7 Jan 2004 (Gibraltar) (SI 2004/24) |
| 26, 27 | | 8 May 2003 (United Kingdom) (s 28(3)) |
| | | 2 Jun 2003 (Gibraltar) (SI 2003/1402) |
| 28 | para (1) | 8 May 2003 (United Kingdom) (s 28(3)) |
| | | 1 Jun 2003 (Gibraltar) (SI 2003/1401) |
| | para (2) | 8 May 2003 (United Kingdom) (s 28(3)) |
| | | 1 Jun 2003 (Gibraltar) (so far as relates to s 28(1), (3)–(5) of this Act) (SI 2003/1401) |

**European Parliament (Representation) Act 2003 (c 7)**—*contd*

|  |  |  |
|---|---|---|
|  |  | 2 Jun 2003 (Gibraltar) (so far as relates to ss 9, 10, 26, 27 of this Act) (SI 2003/1402) |
|  |  | 7 Jan 2004 (Gibraltar) (so far as relates to Pt 2 and s 25 of this Act) (SI 2004/24) |
|  |  | 5 Feb 2004 (Gibraltar) (so far as relates to ss 1, 8, 19–21 of this Act) (SI 2004/320) |
|  |  | 10 Mar 2004 (Gibraltar) (so far as relates to ss 2–7, 19, Schedule) (SI 2004/700) |
|  |  | 23 Mar 2004 (otherwise) (SI 2004/1035) |
|  | paras (3)–(5) | 8 May 2003 (United Kingdom) (s 28(3)) |
|  |  | 1 Jun 2003 (Gibraltar) (SI 2003/1401) |
| Schedule |  | 8 May 2003 (United Kingdom) (s 28(3)) |
|  |  | 10 Mar 2004 (Gibraltar) (SI 2004/700) |

---

**European Union (Accessions) Act 2003 (c 35)**

*RA:* 13 Nov 2003

Whole Act in force 13 Nov 2003 (RA)

---

**Extradition Act 2003 (c 41)**

*RA:* 20 Nov 2003

*Commencement provisions:* s 221; Extradition Act 2003 (Commencement and Savings) Order 2003, SI 2003/3103, as amended by SI 2003/3258, SI 2003/3312

|  |  |  |
|---|---|---|
| 1–217 |  | 1 Jan 2004 (SI 2003/3103)[1] |
| 218 | (a) | 1 Jan 2004 (SI 2003/3103)[1] |
|  | (b) | 1 Jan 2004 (subject to a saving in relation to Jersey, Guernsey, the Isle of Man and any of the British overseas territories except Gibraltar) (SI 2003/3103)[1] |
| 219 | (1) | See Sch 3 below |
|  | (2)–(4) | 1 Jan 2004 (SI 2003/3103)[1] |
| 220 |  | See Sch 4 below |
| 221–227 |  | 20 Nov 2003 (RA) |
| Schs 1–3 |  | 1 Jan 2004 (SI 2003/3103)[1] |
| Sch 4 |  | 1 Jan 2004 (subject to a saving for the repeal of the Extradition Act 1989 in relation to Jersey, Guernsey, the Isle of Man and any of the British overseas territories except Gibraltar) (SI 2003/3103)[1] |

[1]   SI 2003/3103, arts 3–5, as amended, provide that:

(a)   the coming into force of this Act does not apply for the purposes of any request for extradition, whether made under any of the provisions of the Extradition Act 1989 or of the Backing of Warrants (Republic of Ireland) Act 1965 or otherwise, which is received by the relevant authority in the United Kingdom on or before 31 Dec 2003;

(b)   the coming into force of this Act does not apply for the purposes of an extradition made from or to the United Kingdom on or before 31 Dec 2003;

(c)   the coming into force of the repeal of the Extradition Act 1989 by s 218(b) of, and Sch 4 to, this Act does not apply for the purposes of—

(i) the Bailiwick of Jersey;

(ii) the Bailiwick of Guernsey;

(iii) the Isle of Man;

(iv) any of the British overseas territories with the exception of Gibraltar,

**Extradition Act 2003 (c 41)**—*contd*

until such time as any provision which is made for (or by) the dependency or territory in question (whether under s 177, 178 or 222 of this Act or otherwise) and which has the effect of replacing the provisions of the Extradition Act 1989 comes into force

---

**Female Genital Mutilation Act 2003 (c 31)**

*RA:* 30 Oct 2003

*Commencement provisions:* s 8(2); Female Genital Mutilation Act 2003 (Commencement) Order 2004, SI 2004/286

Whole Act in force 3 Mar 2004 (SI 2004/286)

---

**Finance Act 2003 (c 14)**

*Budget Day:* 9 Apr 2003

*RA:* 10 Jul 2003

The commencement details of Finance Acts are not set out, as the dates from which their provisions take effect are usually stated clearly and unambiguously in the text of the Act, and charging provisions will normally state for which year or years of assessment they are to have effect.

---

**Fire Services Act 2003 (c 36)**

*RA:* 13 Nov 2003

Whole Act in force 13 Nov 2003 (RA)

---

**Fireworks Act 2003 (c 22)**

*RA:* 18 Sep 2003

*Commencement provisions:* s 18; Fireworks Act 2003 (Commencement No 1) Order 2003, SI 2003/3084; Fireworks Act 2003 (Commencement No 2) Order 2004, SI 2004/1831

| | |
|---|---|
| 1–3 | 28 Nov 2003 (SI 2003/3084) |
| 4 | 15 Jul 2004 (SI 2004/1831) |
| 5 | 28 Nov 2003 (SI 2003/3084) |
| 6–9 | 15 Jul 2004 (SI 2004/1831) |
| 10 | *Not yet in force* |
| 11–13 | 28 Nov 2003 (for the purposes of fireworks regulations made in exercise of powers conferred by the provisions of the Act brought into force by SI 2003/3084) (SI 2003/3084) |
| | 15 Jul 2004 (for the purposes of fireworks regulations made in exercise of powers conferred by the provisions of the Act brought into force by SI 2004/1831) (SI 2004/1831) |
| | *Not yet in force* (for the purposes of fireworks regulations made in exercise of powers conferred by the provisions of the Act which are not yet in force) |
| 14 | *Not yet in force* |
| 15 | See Schedule below |
| 16 | 28 Nov 2003 (for the purposes of fireworks regulations made in exercise of powers conferred by the provisions of the Act brought into force by SI 2003/3084) (SI 2003/3084) |
| | 15 Jul 2004 (for the purposes of fireworks regulations made in exercise of powers conferred by the provisions of the Act brought into force by SI 2004/1831) (SI 2004/1831) |

**Fireworks Act 2003 (c 22)**—*contd*

|  |  |  |
|---|---|---|
|  | *Not yet in force* (for the purposes of fireworks regulations made in exercise of powers conferred by the provisions of the Act which are not yet in force) |
| 17–19 | 18 Sep 2003 (RA) |
| Schedule | *Not yet in force* |

## Health and Social Care (Community Health and Standards) Act 2003 (c 43)

*RA:* 20 Nov 2003

*Commencement provisions:* s 199; Health and Social Care (Community Health and Standards) Act 2003 Commencement (No 1) Order 2003, SI 2003/3346; Health and Social Care (Community Health and Standards) Act 2003 Commencement (No 2) Order 2004, SI 2004/288[1], as amended by SI 2004/866, SI 2004/1009, SI 2005/2925; Health and Social Care (Community Health and Standards) Act 2003 (Commencement No 1) (Wales) Order 2004, SI 2004/480[3], as amended by SI 2004/1019, SI 2006/345; Health and Social Care (Community Health and Standards) Act 2003 Commencement (No 3) Order 2004, SI 2004/759, as amended by SI 2006/836, SI 2007/1102; Health and Social Care (Community Health and Standards) Act 2003 Commencement (No 2) (Wales) Order 2004, SI 2004/873; Health and Social Care (Community Health and Standards) Act 2003 Commencement (No 4) Order 2004, SI 2004/2626; Health and Social Care (Community Health and Standards) Act 2003 Commencement (No 5) Order 2005, SI 2005/38; Health and Social Care (Community Health and Standards) Act 2003 (Commencement) (No 6) Order 2005, SI 2005/457; Health and Social Care (Community Health and Standards) Act 2003 (Commencement) (No 7) Order 2005, SI 2005/2278; Health and Social Care (Community Health and Standards) Act 2003 Commencement (No 8) Order 2005, SI 2005/2925, as amended by SI 2006/836; Health and Social Care (Community Health and Standards) Act 2003 Commencement (Wales) (No 3) Order 2005, SI 2005/3285; Health and Social Care (Community Health and Standards) Act 2003 Commencement (Wales) (No 4) Order 2006, SI 2006/345; National Health Service (Pre-consolidation Amendments) Order 2006, SI 2006/1407; Health and Social Care (Community Health and Standards) Act 2003 Commencement (No 9) Order 2006, SI 2006/1680; Health and Social Care (Community Health and Standards) Act 2003 (Commencement) (No 10) Order 2006, SI 2006/2817; Health and Social Care (Community Health and Standards) Act 2003 (Commencement) (No 11) Order 2006, SI 2006/3397; Health and Social Care (Community Health and Standards) Act 2003 (Commencement No 1 and Savings) (Scotland) Order 2007, SSI 2007/10; Health and Social Care (Community Health and Standards) Act 2003 (Commencement No 12) Order 2008, SI 2008/1334; Health and Social Care (Community Health and Standards) Act 2003 Commencement (Wales) (No 5) Order 2011, SI 2011/212; Health and Social Care (Community Health and Standards) Act 2003 Commencement (Wales) (No 6) Order 2014, SI 2014/1793

|  |  |  |
|---|---|---|
| 1 | (1) | 20 Nov 2003 (RA)[2] |
|  | (2) | See Sch 1 below |
| 2–4 |  | 1 Jan 2004 (SI 2003/3346) |
| 5–20 |  | 20 Nov 2003 (in so far as conferring any power to make an order or regulations) (RA) |
|  |  | 1 Apr 2004 (otherwise) (SI 2004/759) |
| 21 |  | *Not yet in force* |
| 22–24 |  | 20 Nov 2003 (in so far as conferring any power to make an order or regulations) (RA) |
|  |  | 1 Apr 2004 (otherwise) (SI 2004/759) |
| 25 | (1)–(3) | 20 Nov 2003 (in so far as conferring any power to make an order or regulations) (RA) |
|  |  | 1 Apr 2004 (otherwise) (SI 2004/759) |
|  | (4) | See Sch 3 below |
|  | (5)–(7) | 20 Nov 2003 (in so far as conferring any power to make an order or regulations) (RA) |
|  |  | 1 Apr 2004 (otherwise) (SI 2004/759) |
| 26–33 |  | 20 Nov 2003 (in so far as conferring any power to make an order or regulations) (RA) |
|  |  | 1 Apr 2004 (otherwise) (SI 2004/759) |
| 34 |  | See Sch 4 below |

**Health and Social Care (Community Health and Standards) Act 2003 (c 43)**—*contd*

| | | |
|---|---|---|
| 35 | | 20 Nov 2003 (in so far as conferring any power to make an order or regulations) (RA) |
| | | 1 Apr 2004 (otherwise) (SI 2004/759) |
| 36 | | 1 Jan 2004 (SI 2003/3346) |
| 37 | | 1 Apr 2004 (SI 2004/759) |
| 38 | | See Sch 5 below |
| 39 | | 1 Apr 2004 (SI 2004/759) |
| 40 | | 1 Jan 2004 (SI 2003/3346) |
| 41 | (1) | 8 Jan 2004 (SI 2003/3346) |
| | (2) | See Sch 6 below |
| 42 | (1) | 1 Jan 2004 (E) (SI 2003/3346) |
| | (2) | See Sch 7 below |
| 43 | | See Sch 8 below |
| 44–46 | | 1 Apr 2004 (SI 2004/759) |
| 47 | | 1 Apr 2004 (SI 2004/873) |
| 48, 49 | | 1 Apr 2004 (SI 2004/759) |
| 50 | (1) | 1 Apr 2004 (except as noted below) (SI 2004/759) |
| | | 1 Apr 2006 (in relation to (a) the Oxford Learning Disability National Health Service Trust; (b) the Calderstones National Health Service Trust; (c) the Northgate and Prudhoe National Health Service Trust) (SI 2004/759) |
| | | 1 Apr 2007 (in relation to a Special Health Authority performing functions only or mainly in respect of England, except the NHS Direct Special Health Authority) (SI 2004/759) |
| | | 1 Apr 2008 (in relation to a cross-border SHA, except the Mental Health Act Commission or NHS Blood and Transplant, in so far as it is performing functions in respect of Wales) (SI 2004/759) |
| | | *Never in force* (in relation to (a) the Mental Health Act Commission or NHS Blood and Transplant, in so far as it is performing functions in relation to Wales; and (b) the NHS Direct Special Health Authority) (repealed) |
| | (2), (3) | 1 Apr 2005 (SI 2004/759) |
| | (4) | 1 Apr 2006 (SI 2004/759) |
| | (5) | 1 Apr 2004 (SI 2004/759) |
| | (6) | 20 Nov 2003 (in so far as conferring any power to make an order or regulations) (RA) |
| | | *Never in force* (otherwise) (repealed) |
| 51 | (1)–(3) | 1 Apr 2004 (SI 2004/759) |
| | (4) | 1 Apr 2005 (SI 2004/759) |
| | (5), (6) | 1 Apr 2004 (SI 2004/759) |
| | (7) | 20 Nov 2003 (in so far as conferring any power to make an order or regulations) (RA) |
| | | *Never in force* (otherwise) (repealed) |
| 52 | (1)–(4) | 1 Apr 2004 (SI 2004/759) |
| | (5) | 1 Apr 2005 (SI 2004/759) |
| | (6), (7) | 1 Apr 2004 (SI 2004/759) |
| | (8)–(10) | 20 Nov 2003 (in so far as conferring any power to make an order or regulations) (RA) |
| | | *Never in force* (otherwise) (repealed) |
| 53–57 | | 20 Nov 2003 (in so far as conferring any power to make an order or regulations) (RA) |
| | | 1 Apr 2004 (otherwise) (SI 2004/759) |
| 58, 59 | | 20 Nov 2003 (in so far as conferring any power to make an order or regulations) (RA) |
| | | *Never in force* (otherwise) (repealed) |
| 60, 61 | | 1 Apr 2004 (SI 2004/759) |
| 62, 63 | | 20 Nov 2003 (in so far as conferring any power to make an order or regulations) (RA) |
| | | *Never in force* (otherwise) (repealed) |

**Health and Social Care (Community Health and Standards) Act 2003 (c 43)**—*contd*

| | | |
|---|---|---|
| 64–68 | | 1 Apr 2004 (SI 2004/759) |
| 69 | | 20 Nov 2003 (in so far as conferring any power to make an order or regulations) (RA) |
| | | *Never in force* (otherwise) (repealed) |
| 70–75 | | 20 Nov 2003 (in so far as conferring any power to make an order or regulations) (RA) |
| | | 1 Apr 2004 (otherwise) (SI 2004/873) |
| 76–84 | | 20 Nov 2003 (in so far as conferring any power to make an order or regulations) (RA) |
| | | 1 Apr 2004 (E) (otherwise) (SI 2004/759) |
| 85 | | 20 Nov 2003 (in so far as conferring any power to make an order or regulations) (RA) |
| | | 1 Apr 2005 (E) (otherwise) (SI 2005/457) |
| 86 | | 20 Nov 2003 (in so far as conferring any power to make an order or regulations) (RA) |
| | | 30 Oct 2005 (E) (otherwise) (SI 2005/2925) |
| 87–91 | | 20 Nov 2003 (in so far as conferring any power to make an order or regulations) (RA) |
| | | 1 Apr 2004 (E) (otherwise) (SI 2004/759) |
| 92, 93 | | 20 Nov 2003 (in so far as conferring any power to make an order or regulations) (RA) |
| | | 1 Apr 2004 (otherwise) (SI 2004/873) |
| 94 | (1)–(5) | 20 Nov 2003 (in so far as conferring any power to make an order or regulations) (RA) |
| | | 1 Apr 2004 (otherwise) (SI 2004/873) |
| | (6)–(8) | 20 Nov 2003 (in so far as conferring any power to make an order or regulations) (RA) |
| | | *Not yet in force* (otherwise) |
| 95–101 | | 20 Nov 2003 (in so far as conferring any power to make an order or regulations) (RA) |
| | | 1 Apr 2004 (otherwise) (SI 2004/873) |
| 102, 103 | | 20 Nov 2003 (in so far as conferring any power to make an order or regulations) (RA) |
| | | 1 Apr 2004 (otherwise) (SI 2004/759) |
| 104 | | 20 Nov 2003 (in so far as conferring any power to make an order or regulations) (RA) |
| | | 1 Apr 2004 (E) (otherwise) (SI 2004/759) |
| 105 | (1) | See sub-ss (2)–(7) below |
| | (2) | 20 Nov 2003 (in so far as conferring any power to make an order or regulations) (RA) |
| | | 31 Oct 2005 (in relation only to a determination by the Commission for Healthcare Audit and Inspection of fees payable to it from 1 Apr 2006 and thereafter) (SI 2005/2925) |
| | (3)–(7) | 20 Nov 2003 (in so far as conferring any power to make an order or regulations) (RA) |
| | | 1 Aug 2006 (otherwise) (SI 2006/1680)[7] |
| 106 | | 1 Apr 2004 (SI 2004/759; SI 2004/873) |
| 107 | | 1 Apr 2006 (W) (SI 2005/3285) |
| | | *Not yet in force* (E) |
| 108 | | 1 Apr 2004 (SI 2004/759; SI 2004/873) |
| 109 | | 1 Apr 2004 (SI 2004/873) |
| 110 | | 1 Apr 2004 (E) (SI 2004/759) |
| 111 | | 1 Apr 2004 (SI 2004/759; SI 2004/873) |
| 112 | | 11 Mar 2004 (E) (SI 2004/759) |
| 113 | (1) | 20 Nov 2003 (in so far as conferring any power to make an order or regulations) (RA) |
| | | 1 Sep 2006 (otherwise) (SI 2006/1680) |
| | (2) | 20 Nov 2003 (in so far as conferring any power to make an order or regulations) (RA) |
| | | 7 Feb 2011 (otherwise) (SI 2011/212) |

**Health and Social Care (Community Health and Standards) Act 2003 (c 43)**—_contd_

|  |  |  |
|---|---|---|
|  | (3), (4) | 20 Nov 2003 (in so far as conferring any power to make an order or regulations) (RA) |
|  |  | 1 Sep 2006 (E) (otherwise) (SI 2006/1680) |
|  |  | 7 Feb 2011 (W) (otherwise) (SI 2011/212) |
| 114 | (1), (2) | 20 Nov 2003 (in so far as conferring any power to make an order or regulations) (RA) |
|  |  | 1 Sep 2006 (otherwise) (SI 2006/1680) |
|  | (3), (4) | 20 Nov 2003 (in so far as conferring any power to make an order or regulations) (RA) |
|  |  | 1 Apr 2006 (W) (otherwise) (SI 2005/3285) |
|  | (5) | 20 Nov 2003 (in so far as conferring any power to make an order or regulations) (RA) |
|  |  | 1 Apr 2006 (W) (otherwise) (SI 2005/3285) |
|  |  | 1 Sep 2006 (E) (otherwise) (SI 2006/1680) |
|  | (6) | 20 Nov 2003 (in so far as conferring any power to make an order or regulations) (RA) |
|  |  | 1 Sep 2006 (E) (otherwise) (SI 2006/1680) |
|  |  | _Not yet in force_ (W) (otherwise) |
| 115 | (1), (2) | 20 Nov 2003 (in so far as conferring any power to make an order or regulations) (RA) |
|  |  | 1 Apr 2006 (W) (otherwise) (SI 2005/3285) |
|  |  | 1 Sep 2006 (E) (otherwise) (SI 2006/1680) |
|  | (3) | 20 Nov 2003 (in so far as conferring any power to make an order or regulations) (RA) |
|  |  | 1 Sep 2006 (E) (otherwise) (SI 2006/1680) |
|  |  | 7 Feb 2011 (W) (otherwise) (SI 2011/212) |
|  | (4)–(6) | 20 Nov 2003 (in so far as conferring any power to make an order or regulations) (RA) |
|  |  | 1 Apr 2006 (W) (otherwise) (SI 2005/3285) |
|  |  | 1 Sep 2006 (E) (otherwise) (SI 2006/1680) |
| 116 | (1) | 20 Nov 2003 (in so far as conferring any power to make an order or regulations) (RA) |
|  |  | _Never in force_ (otherwise) (repealed) |
|  | (2) | 1 Apr 2006 (SI 2005/3285) |
|  | (3) | 1 Apr 2006 (W) (SI 2005/3285) |
|  |  | _Not yet in force_ (E) |
| 117 | (1) | 17 Jan 2005 (E) (for the purpose only of the exercise of the power to make regulations) (SI 2005/38) |
|  |  | 30 Dec 2005 (otherwise) (SI 2005/2925; SI 2005/3285) |
|  | (2) | 17 Jan 2005 (E) (SI 2005/38) |
|  |  | 30 Dec 2005 (W) (SI 2005/3285) |
| 118, 119 |  | 20 Nov 2003 (in so far as conferring any power to make an order or regulations) (RA) |
|  |  | 1 Jun 2004 (E) (W) (otherwise) (SI 2004/759) |
| 120, 121 |  | 20 Nov 2003 (in so far as conferring any power to make an order or regulations) (RA) |
|  |  | 1 Apr 2004 (otherwise) (SI 2004/759) |
| 122 |  | 20 Nov 2003 (in so far as conferring any power to make an order or regulations) (RA) |
|  |  | _Never in force_ (otherwise) (repealed) |
| 123 |  | 20 Nov 2003 (in so far as conferring any power to make an order or regulations) (RA) |
|  |  | 1 Apr 2004 (otherwise) (SI 2004/759) |
| 124 |  | 20 Nov 2003 (in so far as conferring any power to make an order or regulations) (RA) |
|  |  | 1 Apr 2004 (E) (W) (otherwise) (SI 2004/759) |
|  |  | 2 Jun 2008 (S) (NI) (SI 2008/1334) |
| 125 |  | 1 Apr 2004 (E) (SI 2004/759) |
|  |  | _Never in force_ (W) (S) (NI) (repealed) |
| 126 |  | 1 Apr 2004 (SI 2004/759) |

**Health and Social Care (Community Health and Standards) Act 2003 (c 43)**—*contd*

| | | |
|---|---|---|
| 127 | | 1 Apr 2004 (E) (SI 2004/759) |
| 128 | | 1 Apr 2004 (SI 2004/759) |
| 129 | | 1 Apr 2004 (E) (SI 2004/759) |
| 130 | | 20 Nov 2003 (in so far as conferring any power to make an order or regulations) (RA) |
| | | 1 Apr 2004 (otherwise) (SI 2004/759) |
| 131 | | 1 Apr 2004 (E) (SI 2004/759) |
| 132 | | 20 Nov 2003 (in so far as conferring any power to make an order or regulations) (RA) |
| | | 1 Apr 2004 (otherwise) (SI 2004/759) |
| 133 | | 1 Apr 2004 (E) (SI 2004/759) |
| 134 | | 1 Apr 2004 (SI 2004/759) |
| 135 | | 1 Apr 2004 (E) (SI 2004/759) |
| 136–138 | | 1 Apr 2004 (SI 2004/759) |
| 139 | | 1 Apr 2004 (E) (SI 2004/759) |
| 140 | | 1 Apr 2004 (SI 2004/759) |
| 141 | | 1 Apr 2004 (E) (SI 2004/759) |
| 142–145 | | 1 Apr 2004 (SI 2004/873) |
| 146 | | 20 Nov 2003 (in so far as conferring any power to make an order or regulations) (RA) |
| | | 1 Apr 2004 (otherwise) (SI 2004/759) |
| 147 | | See Sch 9 below |
| 148 | | 1 Jan 2004 (SI 2003/3346) |
| 149 | | *Not yet in force* |
| 150 | (1)–(7) | 20 Nov 2003 (in so far as conferring any power to make an order or regulations) (RA) |
| | | 28 Jan 2007 (otherwise) (SI 2006/3397; SSI 2007/10[9]) |
| | (8), (9) | 20 Nov 2003 (in so far as conferring any power to make an order or regulations) (RA) |
| | | *Never in force* (otherwise) (spent) |
| | (10)–(14) | 20 Nov 2003 (in so far as conferring any power to make an order or regulations) (RA) |
| | | 28 Jan 2007 (otherwise) (SI 2006/3397; SSI 2007/10[9]) |
| 151–162 | | 20 Nov 2003 (in so far as conferring any power to make an order or regulations) (RA) |
| | | 29 Jan 2007 (otherwise) (SI 2006/3397; SSI 2007/10[9]) |
| 163 | (1), (2) | 20 Nov 2003 (in so far as conferring any power to make an order or regulations) (RA) |
| | | 29 Jan 2007 (otherwise) (SI 2006/3397; SSI 2007/10[9]) |
| | (3) | 20 Nov 2003 (in so far as conferring any power to make an order or regulations) (RA) |
| | | 29 Jan 2007 (E) (W) (otherwise) (SI 2006/3397) |
| | | *Not yet in force* (S) (otherwise) |
| 164 | | 20 Nov 2003 (in so far as conferring any power to make an order or regulations) (RA) |
| | | 29 Jan 2007 (otherwise) (SI 2006/3397; SSI 2007/10[9]) |
| 165 | | 20 Nov 2003 (in so far as conferring any power to make an order or regulations) (RA) |
| | | *Not yet in force* (otherwise) |
| 166 | | 29 Jan 2007 (SI 2006/3397; SSI 2007/10[9]) |
| 167 | | 20 Nov 2003 (RA) |
| 168 | | 20 Nov 2003 (in so far as conferring any power to make an order or regulations) (RA) |
| | | 29 Jan 2007 (otherwise) (SI 2006/3397; SSI 2007/10[9]) |
| 169 | | 29 Jan 2007 (SI 2006/3397[8]; SSI 2007/10[9]) |
| 170 | | 20 Nov 2003 (in so far as conferring any power to make an order or regulations) (RA) |
| | | 1 Jan 2006 (E) (in so far as inserts National Health Service Act 1977, s 16CA(2), (4)) (SI 2005/2925) |

**Health and Social Care (Community Health and Standards) Act 2003 (c 43)**—*contd*

|     |     |     |
| --- | --- | --- |
|     |     | 15 Feb 2006 (W) (in so far as inserts National Health Service Act 1977, s 16CA(2), (4)) (SI 2006/345) |
|     |     | 1 Apr 2006 (otherwise) (SI 2005/2925; SI 2006/345) |
| 171 | (1) | 1 Jan 2006 (E) (in so far as inserts National Health Service Act 1977, s 16CB(1), for the purposes of making regulations) (SI 2005/2925) |
|     |     | 15 Feb 2006 (W) (in so far as inserts National Health Service Act 1977, s 16CB(2), for the purpose of making regulations) (SI 2006/345) |
|     |     | 1 Apr 2006 (E) (in so far as inserts National Health Service Act 1977, s 16CB(1), (4), in so far as not already in force) (SI 2005/2925) |
|     |     | 1 Apr 2006 (W) (in so far as inserts National Health Service Act 1977, s 16CB(2), (3), (5), in so far as not already in force) (SI 2006/345) |
|     | (2) | 1 Apr 2006 (SI 2005/2925; SI 2006/345) |
| 172 | (1) | 1 Dec 2005 (E) (in so far as inserts National Health Service Act 1977, ss 28M, 28O, 28P, for the purposes of making regulations or directions, and in so far as inserts National Health Service Act 1977, ss 28L, 28N) (SI 2005/2925) |
|     |     | 1 Jan 2006 (E) (otherwise) (SI 2005/2925) |
|     |     | 15 Feb 2006 (W) (SI 2006/345) |
|     | (2) | 1 Apr 2006 (SI 2005/2925; SI 2006/345) |
| 173 |     | 20 Nov 2003 (in so far as conferring any power to make an order or regulations) (RA) |
|     |     | 1 Dec 2005 (E) (otherwise) (SI 2005/2925) |
|     |     | 15 Feb 2006 (W) (otherwise) (SI 2006/345) |
| 174 |     | 20 Nov 2003 (in so far as conferring any power to make an order or regulations) (RA) |
|     |     | 28 Feb 2004 (W) (in so far as inserts National Health Service Act 1977, s 16CC(2), (4)) (SI 2004/480) |
|     |     | 1 Mar 2004 (E) (in so far as inserts National Health Service Act 1977, s 16CC(2), (4)) (SI 2004/288) |
|     |     | 1 Apr 2004 (otherwise) (SI 2004/288; SI 2004/480) |
| 175 | (1) | 20 Nov 2003 (in so far as conferring any power to make an order or regulations) (RA) |
|     |     | 3 Feb 2004 (E) (in so far as inserts National Health Service Act 1977, ss 28R, 28T and ss 28S, 28U–28W for the purposes of making regulations or directions) (SI 2004/288) |
|     |     | 28 Feb 2004 (W) (otherwise) (SI 2004/480) |
|     |     | 1 Mar 2004 (E) (otherwise) (SI 2004/288) |
|     | (2) | 20 Nov 2003 (in so far as conferring any power to make an order or regulations) (RA) |
|     |     | 28 Feb 2004 (W) (otherwise) (SI 2004/480) (note that SI 2004/480 also purports to bring this subsection into force on 1 Apr 2004) |
|     |     | 1 Apr 2004 (E) (otherwise) (SI 2004/288) |
| 176 |     | 20 Nov 2003 (in so far as conferring any power to make an order or regulations) (RA) |
|     |     | 3 Feb 2004 (E) (otherwise) (SI 2004/288) |
|     |     | 28 Feb 2004 (W) (otherwise) (SI 2004/480) |
| 177 | (1) | See sub-ss (2)–(6) below |
|     | (2) | 3 Feb 2004 (E) (in so far as inserts National Health Service Act 1977, s 28D(1)(bc), for the purpose of making regulations) (SI 2004/288) |
|     |     | 1 Mar 2004 (E) (otherwise, in so far as relates to primary medical services or personal medical services) (SI 2004/288) |
|     |     | 1 Dec 2005 (E) (otherwise) (SI 2005/2925) |
|     |     | 15 Feb 2006 (W) (in so far as relates to dental services) (SI 2006/345) |

**Health and Social Care (Community Health and Standards) Act 2003 (c 43)**—*contd*

|  |  |  |
|---|---|---|
|  |  | In force (otherwise) immediately before the National Health Service Act 2006 comes into force (SI 2006/1407)[6] |
| | (3)–(11) | 1 Mar 2004 (E) (in so far as they relate to primary medical services or personal medical services) (SI 2004/288) |
| | | 1 Dec 2005 (E) (otherwise) (SI 2005/2925) |
| | | 15 Feb 2006 (W) (in so far as they relate to dental services) (SI 2006/345) |
| | | In force (otherwise) immediately before the National Health Service Act 2006 comes into force (SI 2006/1407)[6] |
| | (12) | 1 Apr 2004 (E) (in so far as repeals National Health Service Act 1977, ss 28F, 28H in relation to primary medical services and personal medical services) (SI 2004/288) |
| | | 1 Apr 2006 (E) (otherwise) (SI 2005/2925) |
| | | 1 Apr 2006 (W) (in so far as relates to dental services) (SI 2006/345) |
| | | In force (otherwise) immediately before the National Health Service Act 2006 comes into force (SI 2006/1407)[6] |
| 178[1, 3] | | 1 Apr 2004 (E) (so far as relates to primary medical services or personal medical services) (SI 2004/288) |
| | | 1 Apr 2006 (E) (otherwise) (SI 2005/2925) |
| | | 1 Apr 2006 (W) (in so far as relates to dental services) (SI 2006/345) |
| | | In force (otherwise) immediately before the National Health Service Act 2006 comes into force (SI 2006/1407)[6] |
| 179 | (1) | 20 Nov 2003 (in so far as conferring any power to make an order or regulations) (RA) |
| | | 3 Feb 2004 (E) (in so far as inserts National Health Service Act 1977, s 28X(1), (3)–(7)) (SI 2004/288) |
| | | 28 Feb 2004 (W) (in so far as inserts National Health Service Act 1977, s 28X(1), (3)–(7)) (SI 2004/480) |
| | | 1 Dec 2005 (E) (otherwise) (SI 2005/2925) |
| | | 15 Feb 2006 (W) (otherwise) (SI 2006/345) |
| | (2) | 20 Nov 2003 (in so far as conferring any power to make an order or regulations) (RA) |
| | | 3 Feb 2004 (E) (otherwise) (SI 2004/288) |
| | | 28 Feb 2004 (W) (otherwise) (SI 2004/480) |
| 180 | | 20 Nov 2003 (in so far as conferring any power to make an order or regulations) (RA) |
| | | 28 Feb 2004 (W) (in so far as inserts National Health Service Act 1977, s 28Y, in its application to primary medical services) (SI 2004/480) |
| | | 1 Mar 2004 (E) (in so far as inserts National Health Service Act 1977, s 28Y, in its application to primary medical services) (SI 2004/288) |
| | | 1 Jan 2006 (E) (otherwise) (SI 2005/2925) |
| | | 15 Feb 2006 (W) (otherwise) (SI 2006/345) |
| 181 | | 1 Apr 2006 (SI 2005/2925) |
| 182 | (1) | 1 Dec 2005 (E) (SI 2005/2925) |
| | (2) | 15 Feb 2006 (W) (SI 2006/345) |
| 183 | | 1 Nov 2005 (E) (for the purposes of making regulations) (SI 2005/2925) |
| | | 15 Feb 2006 (W) (for the purposes of making regulations) (SI 2006/345) |
| | | 1 Apr 2006 (otherwise) (SI 2005/2925; SI 2006/345) |
| 184 | | See Sch 11 below |
| 185 | | 20 Nov 2003 (in so far as conferring any power to make an order or regulations) (RA) |
| | | 12 Aug 2005 (for the purpose of consultation by the Secretary of State of the Scottish Ministers and the National Assembly for Wales before establishing or varying a scheme) (SI 2005/2278) |

**Health and Social Care (Community Health and Standards) Act 2003 (c 43)**—*contd*

|  |  | 7 Oct 2005 (otherwise) (SI 2005/2278), except for the purposes of the Assembly— |
|---|---|---|
|  |  | (a) exercising by regulations the power to prescribe descriptions of food in relation to the operation of a scheme in Wales; |
|  |  | (b) giving directions with the agreement of the Secretary of State— |
|  |  | (i) to a body administering a scheme (or part of a scheme); |
|  |  | (ii) in relation to matters relating to the operation of a scheme (or that part of the scheme) in Wales |
|  |  | 27 Oct 2006 (otherwise) (SI 2006/2817) |
| 186 |  | 20 Nov 2003 (RA) |
| 187, 188 |  | 19 Oct 2004 (SI 2004/2626) |
| 189 | (1) | 20 Nov 2003 (in so far as conferring any power to make an order or regulations) (RA) |
|  |  | 1 Apr 2004 (otherwise) (SI 2004/759) |
|  | (2)–(4) | *Never in force* (repealed) |
| 190 |  | 1 Apr 2005 (SI 2005/457) |
| 191 |  | *Never in force* (repealed) |
| 192–195 |  | 20 Nov 2003 (RA) |
| 196 |  | See Sch 14 below |
| 197–203 |  | 20 Nov 2003 (RA) |
| Sch 1 |  | 20 Nov 2003 (RA)[2] |
| Sch 2 |  | 1 Jan 2004 (SI 2003/3346) |
| Schs 3–5 |  | 20 Nov 2003 (in so far as conferring any power to make an order or regulations) (RA) |
|  |  | 1 Apr 2004 (E) (W) (otherwise) (SI 2004/759) |
| Sch 6 |  | 20 Nov 2003 (in so far as conferring any power to make an order or regulations) (RA) |
|  |  | 8 Jan 2004 (otherwise) (SI 2003/3346) |
| Sch 7 |  | 20 Nov 2003 (in so far as conferring any power to make an order or regulations) (RA) |
|  |  | 1 Jan 2004 (E) (otherwise) (SI 2003/3346) |
| Sch 8 |  | 11 Mar 2004 (SI 2004/759) |
| Sch 9 | para 1 | 20 Nov 2003 (in so far as conferring any power to make an order or regulations) (RA) |
|  |  | 1 Jan 2004 (E) (otherwise) (so far as relates to the Commission for Social Care Inspection) (SI 2003/3346) |
|  |  | 8 Jan 2004 (otherwise) (so far as relates to the Commission for Healthcare Audit and Inspection) (SI 2003/3346) |
|  | para 2 | 20 Nov 2003 (in so far as conferring any power to make an order or regulations) (RA) |
|  |  | 1 Apr 2004 (otherwise) (SI 2004/759) |
|  | para 3 | 20 Nov 2003 (in so far as conferring any power to make an order or regulations) (RA) |
|  |  | 1 Jan 2004 (E) (otherwise) (so far as relates to the Commission for Social Care Inspection) (SI 2003/3346) |
|  |  | 8 Jan 2004 (otherwise) (so far as relates to the Commission for Healthcare Audit and Inspection) (SI 2003/3346) |
|  | para 4 | *Not yet in force* |
|  | paras 5–8 | 20 Nov 2003 (in so far as conferring any power to make an order or regulations) (RA) |
|  |  | 1 Jan 2004 (E) (otherwise) (so far as they relate to the Commission for Social Care Inspection) (SI 2003/3346) |
|  |  | 8 Jan 2004 (otherwise) (so far as they relate to the Commission for Healthcare Audit and Inspection) (SI 2003/3346) |
|  | para 9 | 20 Nov 2003 (in so far as conferring any power to make an order or regulations) (RA) |
|  |  | 1 Jun 2004 (otherwise) (SI 2004/759) |
|  | para 10 | 20 Nov 2003 (in so far as conferring any power to make an order or regulations) (RA) |

**Health and Social Care (Community Health and Standards) Act 2003 (c 43)**—*contd*

| | |
|---|---|
| | 1 Apr 2004 (E) (otherwise) (SI 2004/759) |
| para 11 | 20 Nov 2003 (in so far as conferring any power to make an order or regulations) (RA) |
| | 1 Jun 2004 (E) (W) (otherwise) (SI 2004/759) |
| para 12 | 20 Nov 2003 (in so far as conferring any power to make an order or regulations) (RA) |
| | 1 Apr 2004 (otherwise) (SI 2004/759) |
| para 13 | 20 Nov 2003 (in so far as conferring any power to make an order or regulations) (RA) |
| | 8 Jan 2004 (otherwise) (so far as relates to the Commission for Healthcare Audit and Inspection) (SI 2003/3346) |
| para 14 | 20 Nov 2003 (in so far as conferring any power to make an order or regulations) (RA) |
| | 1 Apr 2004 (otherwise) (SI 2004/759) |
| para 15 | 20 Nov 2003 (in so far as conferring any power to make an order or regulations) (RA) |
| | 15 Jan 2007 (otherwise) (SI 2006/3397) |
| para 16 | See paras 17–30 below |
| paras 17–20 | 20 Nov 2003 (in so far as conferring any power to make an order or regulations) (RA) |
| | 1 Apr 2004 (otherwise) (SI 2004/759) |
| para 21 | 20 Nov 2003 (in so far as conferring any power to make an order or regulations) (RA) |
| | 1 Apr 2004 (E) (otherwise) (SI 2004/759) |
| | *Not yet in force* (W) |
| para 22 | 20 Nov 2003 (in so far as conferring any power to make an order or regulations) (RA) |
| | 1 Apr 2004 (otherwise) (SI 2004/759) |
| para 23(a) | 20 Nov 2003 (in so far as conferring any power to make an order or regulations) (RA) |
| | 1 Apr 2004 (otherwise) (SI 2004/759) |
| para 23(b) | 20 Nov 2003 (in so far as conferring any power to make an order or regulations) (RA) |
| | 11 Mar 2004 (for the purpose of making regulations under Care Standards Act 2000, ss 31(7), 51(1)) (SI 2004/759) |
| | *Not yet in force* (otherwise) |
| para 24 | 20 Nov 2003 (in so far as conferring any power to make an order or regulations) (RA) |
| | 1 Apr 2004 (E) (otherwise) (SI 2004/759) |
| para 25 | 20 Nov 2003 (in so far as conferring any power to make an order or regulations) (RA) |
| | 1 Apr 2004 (otherwise) (SI 2004/759) |
| para 26 | 20 Nov 2003 (in so far as conferring any power to make an order or regulations) (RA) |
| | 1 Apr 2004 (E) (otherwise) (SI 2004/759) |
| para 27 | 20 Nov 2003 (in so far as conferring any power to make an order or regulations) (RA) |
| | 11 Mar 2004 (E) (SI 2004/759) |
| | *Never in force* (W) (repealed) |
| para 28 | 20 Nov 2003 (in so far as conferring any power to make an order or regulations) (RA) |
| | 1 Apr 2004 (E) (otherwise) (SI 2004/759) |
| paras 29, 30 | 20 Nov 2003 (in so far as conferring any power to make an order or regulations) (RA) |
| | 1 Apr 2004 (otherwise) (SI 2004/759) |
| para 31 | 20 Nov 2003 (in so far as conferring any power to make an order or regulations) (RA) |
| | 1 Jan 2004 (E) (otherwise) (so far as relates to the Commission for Social Care Inspection) (SI 2003/3346) |

**Health and Social Care (Community Health and Standards) Act 2003 (c 43)**—*contd*

|  |  |  |
|---|---|---|
|  |  | 8 Jan 2004 (otherwise) (so far as relates to the Commission for Healthcare Audit and Inspection) (SI 2003/3346) |
|  |  | *Not yet in force* (S) (NI) (otherwise) |
|  | para 32 | 20 Nov 2003 (in so far as conferring any power to make an order or regulations) (RA) |
|  |  | 1 Apr 2004 (E) (otherwise) (SI 2004/759) |
| Sch 10 |  | 20 Nov 2003 (in so far as conferring any power to make an order or regulations) (RA) |
|  |  | 29 Jan 2007 (otherwise) (SI 2006/3397; SSI 2007/10⁹) |
| Sch 11 | para 1 | 1 Apr 2004 (SI 2004/288; SI 2004/480) |
|  | para 2 | See paras 3–5 below |
|  | para 3(1) | See sub-paras (2)–(5) below |
|  | para 3(2)(a) | 1 Apr 2004 (SI 2004/288; SI 2004/480) |
|  | para 3(2)(b) | 1 Apr 2006 (E) (SI 2005/2925)⁵ |
|  |  | 1 Apr 2006 (W) (in so far as relates to dental services) (SI 2006/345) |
|  | para 3(3)–(5) | 1 Apr 2004 (SI 2004/288; SI 2004/480) |
|  | paras 4–6 | 1 Apr 2004 (SI 2004/288; SI 2004/480) |
|  | para 7 | See paras 8–45 below |
|  | para 8 | 28 Feb 2004 (W) (SI 2004/480) |
|  |  | 1 Mar 2004 (E) (SI 2004/288) |
|  | para 9 | 1 Apr 2004 (SI 2004/288; SI 2004/480) |
|  | para 10 | 1 Apr 2004 (W) (SI 2004/480) |
|  | para 11 | 1 Apr 2006 (W) (in so far as relates to dental services) (SI 2006/345) |
|  |  | In force (otherwise) immediately before the National Health Service Act 2006 comes into force (SI 2006/1407)⁶ |
|  | para 12 | 1 Apr 2004 (SI 2004/288) |
|  | para 13 | 1 Apr 2004 (SI 2004/288; SI 2004/480) |
|  | paras 14, 15 | 1 Mar 2004 (E) (in so far as they relate to primary medical services or personal medical services) (SI 2004/288) |
|  |  | 1 Dec 2005 (E) (otherwise) (SI 2005/2925) |
|  |  | 15 Feb 2006 (W) (in so far as they relate to dental services) (SI 2006/345) |
|  |  | In force (otherwise) immediately before the National Health Service Act 2006 comes into force (SI 2006/1407)⁶ |
|  | para 16 | 1 Mar 2004 (E) (in so far as relates to primary medical services or personal medical services) (SI 2004/288) |
|  |  | *Never in force* (otherwise) (repealed) |
|  | para 17 | 1 Mar 2004 (E) (in so far as relates to primary medical services or personal medical services) (SI 2004/288) |
|  |  | 1 Apr 2006 (E) (otherwise) (SI 2005/2925)⁵ |
|  |  | 1 Apr 2006 (W) (in so far as relates to dental services) (SI 2006/345) |
|  |  | In force (otherwise) immediately before the National Health Service Act 2006 comes into force (SI 2006/1407)⁶ |
|  | paras 18, 19 | 1 Apr 2006 (E) (SI 2005/2925)⁵ |
|  |  | 1 Apr 2006 (W) (in so far as they relate to dental services) (SI 2006/345) |
|  |  | In force (otherwise) immediately before the National Health Service Act 2006 comes into force (SI 2006/1407)⁶ |
|  | para 20(a) | 1 Apr 2004 (in so far as repeals National Health Service Act 1977, s 43D(10)(a)) (SI 2004/288; SI 2004/480) |
|  |  | 1 Apr 2006 (E) (otherwise) (SI 2005/2925)⁵ |
|  |  | 1 Apr 2006 (W) (otherwise, in so far as relates to dental services) (SI 2006/345) |
|  | para 20(b) | 1 Apr 2006 (E) (SI 2005/2925)⁵ |
|  |  | 1 Apr 2006 (W) (in so far as relates to dental services) (SI 2006/345) |

**Health and Social Care (Community Health and Standards) Act 2003 (c 43)**—*contd*

|  |  |
|---|---|
|  | In force (otherwise) immediately before the National Health Service Act 2006 comes into force (SI 2006/1407)[6] |
| para 21(1) | See sub-paras (2)–(5) below |
| para 21(2) | 1 Apr 2004 (W) (SI 2004/480) |
|  | 1 Apr 2006 (E) (SI 2005/2925)[5] |
| para 21(3) | 1 Apr 2004 (E) (in so far as repeals National Health Service Act 1977, s 44(ZA1), (A1)) (SI 2004/288) |
|  | 1 Apr 2004 (W) (in so far as repeals National Health Service Act 1977, s 44(A1), (B1)) (SI 2004/480) |
|  | 1 Apr 2006 (E) (otherwise) (SI 2005/2925)[5] |
|  | *Never in force* (W) (in so far as repeals National Health Service Act 1977, s 44(A2)) (repealed) |
| para 21(4) | 1 Apr 2004 (W) (SI 2004/480) |
| para 21(5) | 1 Apr 2004 (in so far as repeals National Health Service Act 1977, s 44(3)(a), (b)) (SI 2004/288; SI 2004/480) |
|  | 1 Apr 2006 (E) (otherwise) (SI 2005/2925)[5] |
|  | 1 Apr 2006 (W) (in so far as relates to dental services, repeal of National Health Service Act 1977, s 44(3)(c), (d), (5)) (SI 2006/345) |
|  | In force (otherwise) immediately before the National Health Service Act 2006 comes into force (SI 2006/1407)[6] |
| para 22(1) | See sub-paras (2)–(9) below |
| para 22(2) | 1 Apr 2004 (W) (SI 2004/480) |
|  | 1 Apr 2006 (E) (SI 2005/2925)[5] |
| para 22(3)(a) | 1 Apr 2004 (W) (SI 2004/480) |
| para 22(3)(b) | 1 Apr 2006 (W) (in so far as relates to dental services) (SI 2006/345) |
|  | In force (otherwise) immediately before the National Health Service Act 2006 comes into force (SI 2006/1407)[5, 6] |
| para 22(4) | 1 Apr 2006 (E) (SI 2005/2925) |
| para 22(5)(a) | 1 Apr 2006 (E) (SI 2005/2925) |
| para 22(5)(b) | 1 Apr 2004 (W) (SI 2004/480) |
| para 22(6) | 1 Apr 2006 (E) (SI 2005/2925)[5] |
| para 22(7) | 1 Apr 2004 (W) (SI 2004/480) |
| para 22(8)(a) | 1 Apr 2004 (W) (SI 2004/480) |
| para 22(8)(b) | 1 Apr 2004 (SI 2004/288; SI 2004/480) |
| para 22(9) | 1 Apr 2004 (SI 2004/288; SI 2004/480) |
| para 23 | 3 Feb 2004 (E) (in so far as it inserts National Health Service Act 1977, s 45A(9), for the purposes of making regulations) (SI 2004/288) |
|  | 28 Feb 2004 (W) (in so far as it inserts National Health Service Act 1977, s 45A(9), for the purposes of making regulations) (SI 2004/480) |
|  | 1 Apr 2004 (E) (in so far as it inserts National Health Service Act 1977, s 45A, otherwise) (SI 2004/288) |
|  | 1 Apr 2004 (W) (otherwise) (SI 2004/480) |
|  | 1 Dec 2005 (E) (in so far as it inserts National Health Service Act 1977, s 45B, for the purposes of making regulations) (SI 2005/2925) |
|  | 1 Apr 2006 (E) (otherwise) (SI 2005/2925) |
| para 24(a) | 1 Apr 2004 (SI 2004/288; SI 2004/480) |
| para 24(b) | 1 Apr 2006 (E) (SI 2005/2925)[5] |
|  | 1 Apr 2006 (W) (in so far as relates to dental services) (SI 2006/345) |
|  | In force (otherwise) immediately before the National Health Service Act 2006 comes into force (SI 2006/1407)[6] |
| para 25 | 1 Apr 2004 (SI 2004/288; SI 2004/480) |
| para 26 | 11 Mar 2004 (E) (for the purposes of making regulations under National Health Service Act 1977, s 54(1)) (SI 2004/759) |
|  | 1 Apr 2004 (otherwise) (SI 2004/288; SI 2004/480) |

**See Halsbury's Statutes Citator for amendments to these Acts** 1467

**Health and Social Care (Community Health and Standards) Act 2003 (c 43)**—*contd*

| | |
|---|---|
| para 27 | 1 Apr 2004 (otherwise) (SI 2004/288; SI 2004/480) |
| paras 28–31 | 1 Apr 2006 (E) (SI 2005/2925)[5] |
| | 1 Apr 2006 (W) (in so far as they relate to dental services) (SI 2006/345) |
| | In force (otherwise) immediately before the National Health Service Act 2006 comes into force (SI 2006/1407)[6] |
| para 32 | 1 Apr 2006 (E) (SI 2005/2925)[5] |
| | *Never in force* (W) (repealed) |
| para 33 | 1 Apr 2006 (E) (SI 2005/2925)[5] |
| | *Not yet in force* (W) |
| paras 34, 35 | 1 Apr 2006 (E) (SI 2005/2925)[5] |
| | *Never in force* (W) (repealed) |
| para 36(a) | 1 Apr 2004 (SI 2004/288; SI 2004/480) |
| para 36(b) | 1 Apr 2006 (E) (SI 2005/2925)[5] |
| | 1 Apr 2006 (W) (in so far as relates to dental services) (SI 2006/345) |
| | In force (otherwise) immediately before the National Health Service Act 2006 comes into force (SI 2006/1407)[6] |
| para 37 | 1 Apr 2004 (SI 2004/288; SI 2004/480) |
| para 38 | 3 Feb 2004 (E) (SI 2004/288) |
| | 28 Feb 2004 (W) (SI 2004/480) |
| para 39 | 3 Feb 2004 (E) (in so far as inserts definitions "general medical services contract" and "primary medical services" into National Health Service Act 1977, s 128(1)) (SI 2004/288) |
| | 28 Feb 2004 (W) (in so far as inserts definitions "general medical services contract" and "primary medical services" into National Health Service Act 1977, s 128(1)) (SI 2004/480) |
| | 1 Dec 2005 (E) (otherwise) (SI 2005/2925) |
| | 15 Feb 2006 (W) (otherwise) (SI 2006/345) |
| para 40 | 1 Apr 2004 (W) (SI 2004/480) |
| para 41 | 1 Apr 2004 (W) (SI 2004/480) |
| | 1 Apr 2006 (E) (SI 2005/2925)[5] |
| paras 42–44 | 1 Apr 2004 (SI 2004/288; SI 2004/480) |
| para 45 | 1 Apr 2004 (E) (in so far as relates to National Health Service Act 1977, Sch 12A, paras 1(2)(b), 2(2)(a), 4(2)(aa), 5(2)(a)) (SI 2004/288) |
| | 1 Apr 2004 (W) (in so far as relates to National Health Service Act 1977, Sch 12A, paras 1(2)(b), 2(2)(a), 4(2)(aa), 6B(2)(a)) (SI 2004/480) |
| | 1 Apr 2006 (W) (in so far as relates to dental services, in so far as relates to National Health Service Act 1977, Sch 12A, para 6A(2)(b)) (SI 2006/345) |
| | In force (otherwise) immediately before the National Health Service Act 2006 comes into force (SI 2006/1407)[6] |
| para 46(1) | See sub-paras (2), (3) below |
| para 46(2)(a) | 1 Apr 2004 (SI 2004/288; SI 2004/480) |
| para 46(2)(b) | 1 Apr 2006 (SI 2005/2925; SI 2006/345)[5] |
| para 46(3)(a) | 1 Apr 2004 (SI 2004/288; SI 2004/480) |
| para 46(3)(b), (c) | 1 Apr 2006 (SI 2005/2925; SI 2006/345)[5] |
| paras 47–49 | 1 Apr 2004 (SI 2004/288; SI 2004/480) |
| para 50 | 1 Apr 2006 (E) (SI 2005/2925)[5] |
| | 1 Apr 2006 (W) (in so far as relates to dental services) (SI 2006/345) |
| paras 51, 52 | 1 Apr 2004 (SI 2004/288; SI 2004/480) |
| para 53 | See paras 54, 55 below |
| para 54 | 1 Apr 2006 (SI 2005/2925) |
| paras 55–59 | 1 Apr 2004 (SI 2004/288; SI 2004/480) |
| para 60 | See paras 61–64 below |
| para 61 | 1 Apr 2004 (W) (SI 2004/480) |
| | 1 Apr 2006 (E) (SI 2005/2925) |

**Health and Social Care (Community Health and Standards) Act 2003 (c 43)**—*contd*

| | | |
|---|---|---|
| | paras 62, 63 | 1 Apr 2004 (SI 2004/288; SI 2004/480) |
| | para 64 | 1 Apr 2004 (W) (SI 2004/480) |
| | | 1 Apr 2006 (E) (SI 2005/2925) |
| | para 65 | 1 Apr 2004 (SI 2004/288; SI 2004/480) |
| | para 66 | 1 Apr 2006 (E) (SI 2005/2925) |
| | | 1 Apr 2006 (W) (in so far as relates to dental services) (SI 2006/345) |
| | para 67(a) | 1 Apr 2004 (SI 2004/288; SI 2004/480) |
| | para 67(b) | 1 Apr 2006 (E) (SI 2005/2925) |
| | | 1 Apr 2006 (W) (in so far as relates to dental services) (SI 2006/345) |
| | | In force (otherwise) immediately before the National Health Service Act 2006 comes into force (SI 2006/1407)[6] |
| | para 68 | 17 Jan 2005 (E) (SI 2005/38)[4] |
| | | 1 Apr 2006 (W) (in so far as relates to dental services) (SI 2006/345) |
| | | In force (otherwise) immediately before the National Health Service Act 2006 comes into force (SI 2006/1407)[6] |
| | para 69 | See paras 70–73 below |
| | paras 70, 71 | 1 Apr 2004 (SI 2004/288; SI 2004/480) |
| | para 72 | 1 Apr 2006 (E) (SI 2005/2925) |
| | | 1 Apr 2006 (W) (in so far as relates to dental services) (SI 2006/345) |
| | | In force (otherwise) immediately before the National Health Service Act 2006 comes into force (SI 2006/1407)[6] |
| | paras 73, 74 | 1 Apr 2004 (SI 2004/288; SI 2004/480) |
| Sch 12 | | 19 Oct 2004 (SI 2004/2626) |
| Sch 13 | | 1 Apr 2005 (SI 2005/457) |
| Sch 14 | Pt 1 | 1 Apr 2004 (E) (S) (NI) (SI 2004/288), repeals in or of— |
| | | Health Services and Public Health Act 1968; |
| | | Access to Health Records Act 1990 |
| | | 1 Apr 2004 (E) (W) (otherwise) (SI 2004/759) |
| | Pt 2 | 1 Apr 2004 (W) (repeal in Care Standards Act 2000, s 31(6)) (SI 2004/873) |
| | | 1 Apr 2004 (SI 2004/759), except for repeals of or in— |
| | | Local Authority Social Services Act 1970; |
| | | Hospital Complaints Procedure Act 1985; |
| | | Children Act 1989; |
| | | Health Service Commissioners Act 1993; |
| | | Health and Social Care (Community Health and Standards) Act 2003 |
| | | 1 Sep 2006 (E) (repeal in Local Authority Social Services Act 1970) (SI 2006/1680) |
| | | 1 Aug 2014 (W) (repeal in Local Authority Social Services Act 1970) (SI 2014/1793) |
| | | *Not yet in force* (exceptions noted above) |
| | Pt 3 | 29 Jan 2007 (SI 2006/3397[8]; SSI 2007/10[9]) |
| | Pt 4 | 1 Mar 2004 (E) (in so far as relates to primary medical services or personal medical services, repeals of or in National Health Service Act 1977, ss 28C(3)(a), (7), 28D, 28DA, 28E(2), (3)(f), (g), (k), (5)–(7)) (SI 2004/288) |
| | | 1 Apr 2004 (E) (S) (NI) (SI 2004/288), repeals of or in— |
| | | National Health Service (Amendment) Act 1949; |
| | | Health Services and Public Health Act 1968; |
| | | Patents Act 1977; |

**Health and Social Care (Community Health and Standards) Act 2003 (c 43)**—*contd*

National Health Service Act 1977, ss 3, 18A, 26, 28F, 28H,
29–34A, 43ZA(3)(a), 43C, 43D(1), (10)(a), 44(ZA1),
(A1), (3)(a)–(b), 45(3), 49F(1)(a), 52, 53, 56(a), 102(1)(a)(iii),
(2)(b), 126, 128(1) (in so far as it relates to the definitions
"medical list", "personal medical services" and "terms of
service"), Sch 12A, paras 1, 2, 4, 5;

Health and Social Services and Social Security Adjudications
Act 1983, s 14(1), Sch 6, para 2;

Medical Act 1983;

Copyright, Designs and Patents Act 1988;

Health and Medicines Act 1988, ss 2(1)(a), 8(1)(a) and s 17(1) in
so far as relates to the National Health Service Act 1977, s 29;

Access to Health Records Act 1990;

National Health Service and Community Care Act 1990,
ss 18(7), 23;

Trade Union and Labour Relations (Consolidation) Act 1992;

Health Service Commissioners Act 1993, s 6(5);

Health Authorities Act 1995, Sch 1, paras 18–23;

Medical (Professional Performance) Act 1995;

Employment Rights Act 1996, s 43K;

National Health Service (Primary Care) Act 1997, Pt 1 and
s 40(3) (in so far as they relate to personal medical services),
ss 23, 25, 32, Sch 1, Sch 2, paras 6, 8–11, 71, 80, 81;

Health Act 1999, ss 9(2), 11(2) (in so far as it inserted National
Health Service Act 1977, s 44(A1)), Sch 3, Sch 4, paras 2, 17;

Health and Social Care Act 2001, ss 15, 17, 18, 20(2), (3), 23(2),
27(5)(a) (in so far as it relates to personal medical services), (b),
Sch 5, paras 5(4)–(6), 11(3);

National Health Service Reform and Health Care Professions
Act 2002, ss 5(2), (6)(b), Sch 2, paras 3–8, 72, Sch 3, paras 5,
6, 10, Sch 8

1 Apr 2004 (W) (SI 2004/480), repeals of or in—

National Health Service (Amendment) Act 1949;

Health Services and Public Health Act 1968;

National Health Service Act 1977, ss 3(3), 26, 28F, 28H,
29–34A, 43ZA(3)(a), 43C, 43D(1), (10)(a), 44(A1),
(B1), (3)(a)–(b), 45(3), 49F(1)(a), 52, 53, 56(a), 102(1)(a)(iii),
(2)(b), 126, 128(1) (in relation to the definitions "medical list",
"personal medical services" and "terms of service"), Sch 7A,
Sch 12A, paras 1, 2, 6A, 6B;

Patents Act 1977;

Health and Social Services and Social Security Adjudications
Act 1983, s 14(1), Sch 6, para 2;

Medical Act 1983;

Copyright, Designs and Patents Act 1988;

Health and Medicines Act 1988, ss 2(1)(a), 8(1)(a) and s 17(1) (in
so far as relates to the National Health Service Act 1977, s 29);

Access to Health Records Act 1990;

National Health Service and Community Care Act 1990,
ss 18(7), 23;

Trade Union and Labour Relations (Consolidation) Act 1992;

Health Service Commissioners Act 1993, s 6(5);

Health Authorities Act 1995, Sch 1, paras 18–23;

Medical (Professional Performance) Act 1995;

Employment Rights Act 1996, s 43K;

National Health Service (Primary Care) Act 1997, Pt 1 and
s 40(3) (in so far as relating to personal medical services), ss 23,
25, 32, Sch 1, Sch 2, paras 6, 8–11, 71, 80, 81;

Health Act 1999, ss 9(2), 11(2) (in so far as it inserted National
Health Service Act 1977, s 44(A1)), Sch 3, Sch 4, paras 2, 17;

**Health and Social Care (Community Health and Standards) Act 2003 (c 43)**—*contd*

Health and Social Care Act 2001, ss 15, 17, 18, 20(2), (3), 23(2), 27(5), Sch 5, paras 5(4)–(6), 11(3);

National Health Service Reform and Health Care Professions Act 2002, s 5(2), (6)(b), Sch 2, paras 3–8, 72, Sch 3, paras 5, 6, 10, Sch 8

17 Jan 2005 (E) (repeals of or in Freedom of Information Act 2000, Sch 1, para 44 and Sch 1, para 45, in so far as it relates to personal medical services) (SI 2005/38)[4]

1 Dec 2005 (E) (repeals of or in National Health Service Act 1977, ss 28C(3)(b), 28D(2), 28DA, 28E(2), (3)(j), (k), (5)–(8), otherwise) (SI 2005/2925)

15 Feb 2006 (W) (in so far as relates to dental services, repeals of or in National Health Service Act 1977, ss 28C(3)(b), (7), 28D(2), 28DA, 28E(2), (3)(k), (6) (SI 2006/345)

1 Apr 2006 (SI 2005/2925), repeals and revocations of or in—

Parliamentary Commissioner Act 1967;

House of Commons Disqualification Act 1975;

Race Relations Act 1976;

National Health Service Act 1977, ss 37, 45(1ZA), (1A), 85, 98, 99, 100(1)(e), 102(1)(a)(iv), 102(2)(c), Schs 1, 12;

National Health Service (Scotland) Act 1978;

Health and Medicines Act 1988, s 12;

Income and Corporation Taxes Act 1988;

National Health Service and Community Care Act 1990, ss 4, 60;

Health Authorities Act 1995, Sch 1, para 26;

Employment Rights Act 1996, s 218;

Health Act 1999, s 39(2);

National Assembly for Wales (Transfer of Functions) Order 1999, SI 1999/672;

Freedom of Information Act 2000, Sch 1, para 42;

National Health Service Reform and Health Care Professions Act 2002, Sch 1, para 17

1 Apr 2006 (E) (SI 2005/2925), repeals of or in—

National Health Service Act 1977, ss 5, 28G, 35, 36, 43ZA(3)(b), 43D(10)(b), 44(A2), (B1), (3)(c)–(d), (5), 49F(1)(c), 49H, 56(b), 72, 78, 81–83, 103, 128;

Health Services Act 1980;

Health and Social Services and Social Security Adjudications Act 1983, s 15(a);

Dentists Act 1984;

Health and Social Security Act 1984;

Health and Medicines Act 1988, ss 8(1)(b), 17 (so far as relates to s 36), Sch 2;

National Health Service and Community Care Act 1990, s 24;

Health Authorities Act 1995, Sch 1, paras 24, 25;

National Health Service (Primary Care) Act 1997, Pt I, ss 24, 40, Sch 2, paras 12, 16–19, 24, 25, 72;

Health Act 1999, ss 6, 9(3), 10, 11 (so far as not already in force), 39(3), 61, Sch 4, para 88;

Health and Social Care Act 2001, ss 20(4), 22, 23(3), 26, 27(5) (so far as not already in force), 41, Sch 5, paras 5(7), 11(2), 12(2);

National Health Service Reform and Health Care Professions Act 2002, ss 4, 5(3), (6)(a), (c), 17, Sch 1, Sch 2, paras 9, 10, Sch 3, paras 2–4, 15–17

1 Apr 2006 (W) (in so far as relates to dental services) (SI 2006/345), repeals of or in—

**Health and Social Care (Community Health and Standards) Act 2003 (c 43)**—*contd*

National Health Service Act 1977, ss 5(1A), 28G, 35, 36,
43ZA(3)(b), 43D(10)(b), 44(3)(c), (d), (5), 45(1)(b), 49F(1)(c),
49H(1)(a), 56(b), 72(5)(a), 78, 81(b), 82(b), 83(b), 103(1)(a),
128(1);

Health Services Act 1980;

Health and Social Security Adjudications Act 1983, s 15(a);

Dentists Act 1984;

Health and Social Security Act 1984;

Health and Medicines Act 1988, ss 8(1)(b), 17(1) (in so far as
relates to s 36), Sch 2;

National Health Service and Community Care Act 1990, s 24;

Health Authorities Act 1995, Sch 1, paras 24, 25;

National Health Service (Primary Care) Act 1997, Pt 1, ss 24(1),
40(1), (3), Sch 2, paras 12, 16–19, 24, 25, 72;

Health Act 1999, ss 9(3), 10(1), 11(2) (in so far as it inserts
s 44(B1)), 39(3), 61(2);

Freedom of Information Act 2000, Sch 1, paras 44, 45;

Health and Social Care Act 2001, ss 20(4), 22(1)–(3), (5), 23(3),
26, 41(1), Sch 5, paras 5(7), 11(2), 12(2);

National Health Service Reform and Health Care Professions
Act 2002, s 4(1), Sch 2, para 10(1), (2), Sch 3, para 2(1), (3)

In force (otherwise) immediately before the National Health
Service Act 2006 comes into force (SI 2006/1407)[6], repeals of
or in—

National Health Service Act 1977;

National Health Service (Primary Care) Act 1997, Pt 1,
s 40(1), (3), Sch 1, Sch 2, paras 6, 8–12, 16–19, 24, 25, 71–73;

National Health Service Reform and Health Care Professions
Act 2002

27 Oct 2006 (repeal of Health Service Commissioners Act 1993,
s 2(1)(f)) (SI 2006/2817)

*Not yet in force* (W) repeals of or in—

Health Act 1999, s 6, Sch 4, para 88;

Freedom of Information Act 2000, Sch 1, paras 44 (in relation
to general medical services), 45 (in relation to personal medical
services);

Health and Social Care Act 2001, s 26 (in so far as not already
repealed)

*Not yet in force* (E) (in relation to primary dental services or
personal dental services), repeals of or in—

Freedom of Information Act 2000, Sch 1, para 45

| | |
|---|---|
| Pt 5 | 7 Oct 2005 (SI 2005/2278) |
| Pt 6 | *Not yet in force* |
| Pt 7 | 1 Apr 2005 (SI 2005/457) |

[1]   For transitional provisions and savings, see SI 2004/288, arts 7–9

[2]   SI 2004/759 also purports to bring these provisions into force on 1 Apr 2004

[3]   For transitional provisions, see SI 2004/480, arts 6, 7

[4]   For transitional provisions, see SI 2005/38, art 3

[5]   Note that SI 2005/2925 purports to bring the amendments made by these provisions into force to the
same extent as the enactment amended, however by virtue of s 199(1)(a), (2)(e), the Secretary of State
only has the power to bring these provisions into force in relation to England

[6]   For a saving, see SI 2006/1407, art 4

[7]   For transitional provisions, see SI 2006/1680, art 4

[8]   For savings, see SI 2006/3397, art 4

[9]   For savings, see SSI 2007/10, art 3

## Health (Wales) Act 2003 (c 4)

*RA:* 8 Apr 2003

*Commencement provisions:* s 10(2), (3); Health (Wales) Act 2003 (Commencement No 1) Order 2003, SI 2003/2660; Health (Wales) Act 2003 (Commencement No 2) Order 2003, SI 2003/3064

| | | |
|---|---|---|
| 1 | (1), (2) | 20 Oct 2003 (W) (SI 2003/2660) |
| | | 1 Dec 2003 (E) (SI 2003/3064) |
| | (3) | See Sch 1 below |
| | (4) | 20 Oct 2003 (W) (SI 2003/2660) |
| | | 1 Dec 2003 (E) (SI 2003/3064) |
| 2 | (1)–(4) | 1 Apr 2005 (SI 2003/2660) |
| | (5) | See Sch 2 below |
| 3 | | 20 Oct 2003 (for the purposes of making regulations only) (SI 2003/2660) |
| | | 1 Apr 2005 (otherwise) (SI 2003/2660) |
| 4–6 | | 20 Oct 2003 (SI 2003/2660) |
| 7 | (1) | See Sch 3 below |
| | (2) | See Sch 4 below |
| 8–10 | | 8 Apr 2003 (RA) |
| Sch 1 | | 20 Oct 2003 (W) (SI 2003/2660) |
| | | 1 Dec 2003 (E) (SI 2003/3064) |
| Sch 2 | paras 1–9 | 1 Apr 2005 (SI 2003/2660) |
| | para 10 | 20 Oct 2003 (SI 2003/2660) |
| | paras 11–29 | 1 Apr 2005 (SI 2003/2660) |
| Sch 3 | paras 1, 2 | 1 Apr 2005 (SI 2003/2660) |
| | paras 3–5 | 20 Oct 2003 (W) (SI 2003/2660) |
| | | 1 Dec 2003 (E) (SI 2003/3064)[2] |
| | para 6 | 1 Apr 2005 (SI 2003/2660) |
| | para 7 | 20 Oct 2003 (W) (SI 2003/2660) |
| | | 1 Dec 2003 (E) (SI 2003/3064)[2] |
| | paras 8–13 | 1 Apr 2005 (SI 2003/2660) |
| | para 14 | 20 Oct 2003 (W) (SI 2003/2660) |
| | | 1 Dec 2003 (E) (SI 2003/3064)[2] |
| | para 15 | 1 Apr 2005 (SI 2003/2660) |
| | para 16 | *Not yet in force* |
| Sch 4 | | 20 Oct 2003 (W) (except repeals of or in National Health Service Reform and Health Care Professions Act 2002, s 22(4)) (SI 2003/2660)[1] |
| | | 1 Dec 2003 (E) (except repeals of or in National Health Service Reform and Health Care Professions Act 2002, s 22(4)) (SI 2003/3064) |
| | | *Not yet in force* (exceptions noted above) |

[1]   For savings, see SI 2003/2660, art 2(3)

[2]   Note that SI 2003/2660, art 3(2) also purports to bring these provisions into force "for all remaining purposes" on 1 Apr 2005

---

## Homelessness etc (Scotland) Act 2003 (asp 10)

*RA:* 9 Apr 2003

*Commencement provisions:* s 14(1), (2); Homelessness etc (Scotland) Act 2003 (Commencement No 1) Order 2003, SSI 2003/609; Homelessness etc (Scotland) Act 2003 (Commencement No 2) Order 2004, SSI 2004/288; Homelessness etc (Scotland) Act 2003 (Commencement No 3) Order 2008, SSI 2008/313; Homelessness etc (Scotland) Act 2003 (Commencement No 4) Order 2019, SSI 2019/316

| | |
|---|---|
| 1–3 | 30 Jan 2004 (SSI 2003/609) |
| 4 | 7 Nov 2019 (SSI 2019/316) |

**Homelessness etc (Scotland) Act 2003 (asp 10)**—*contd*

| | | |
|---|---|---|
| 5, 6 | | *Never in force*(repealed) |
| 7 | | 30 Jan 2004 (SSI 2003/609) |
| 8 | | 7 Nov 2019 (SSI 2019/316) |
| 9, 10 | | 30 Jan 2004 (SSI 2003/609) |
| 11 | para (1) | 2 Oct 2008 (for the purpose of making regulations) (SSI 2008/313) |
| | | 1 Apr 2009 (otherwise) (SSI 2008/313) |
| | para (2) | See Schedule below |
| | paras (3)–(9) | 2 Oct 2008 (for the purpose of making regulations) (SSI 2008/313) |
| | | 1 Apr 2009 (otherwise) (SSI 2008/313) |
| 12 | | 2 Jul 2004 (SSI 2004/288) |
| 13, 14 | | 9 Apr 2003 (RA) |
| Schedule | | *Not yet in force* (para 5 repealed) |

---

**Household Waste Recycling Act 2003 (c 29)**

*RA:* 30 Oct 2003

*Commencement provisions:* s 5(2)

Whole Act in force 30 Dec 2003 (s 5(2))

---

**Human Fertilisation and Embryology (Deceased Fathers) Act 2003 (c 24)**

*RA:* 18 Sep 2003

*Commencement provisions:* s 4(2), (3); Human Fertilisation and Embryology (Deceased Fathers) Act 2003 (Commencement) Order 2003, SI 2003/3095

| | |
|---|---|
| 1–3 | 1 Dec 2003 (SI 2003/3095) |
| 4 | 18 Sep 2003 (RA) |
| Schedule | 1 Dec 2003 (SI 2003/3095) |

---

**Income Tax (Earnings and Pensions) Act 2003 (c 1)**

*RA:* 6 Mar 2003

*Commencement provisions:* s 723

The Act has effect: (a) for the purposes of income tax, for the tax year 2003–04 and subsequent tax years, and (b) for the purposes of corporation tax, for accounting periods ending after 5 Apr 2003 (subject to transitional provisions and savings in Sch 7).

---

**Industrial Development (Financial Assistance) Act 2003 (c 11)**

*RA:* 8 May 2003

Whole Act in force 8 May 2003 (RA)

---

**Land Reform (Scotland) Act 2003 (asp 2)**

*RA:* 25 Feb 2003

*Commencement provisions:* s 100(3), (4); Land Reform (Scotland) Act (Commencement No 1) Order 2003, SSI 2003/427; Land Reform (Scotland) Act (Commencement No 2) Order 2004, SSI 2004/247; Land Reform (Scotland) Act 2003 (Commencement No 3) Order 2005, SSI 2005/17

| | |
|---|---|
| 1–7 | 9 Feb 2005 (SSI 2005/17) |
| 8 | 30 Sep 2003 (SSI 2003/427) |
| 9 | 9 Feb 2005 (SSI 2005/17) |

**Land Reform (Scotland) Act 2003 (asp 2)**—*contd*

| | | |
|---|---|---|
| 10 | | 30 Sep 2003 (SSI 2003/427) |
| 11–26 | | 9 Feb 2005 (SSI 2005/17) |
| 27 | | 30 Sep 2003 (SSI 2003/427) |
| 28–32 | | 9 Feb 2005 (SSI 2005/17) |
| 33–97 | | 14 Jun 2004 (SSI 2004/247) |
| 98 | | 25 Feb 2003 (RA) |
| 99 | | See Sch 2 below |
| 100 | | 25 Feb 2003 (RA) |
| Sch 1 | | 9 Feb 2005 (SSI 2005/17) |
| Sch 2 | para 1 | 9 Feb 2005 (SSI 2005/17) |
| | para 2 | 14 Jun 2004 (SSI 2004/247) |
| | paras 3–17 | 9 Feb 2005 (SSI 2005/17) |

**Legal Deposit Libraries Act 2003 (c 28)**

*RA:* 30 Oct 2003

*Commencement provisions:* s 16(1), (2); Legal Deposit Libraries Act 2003 (Commencement) Order 2004, SI 2004/130

| | | |
|---|---|---|
| 1, 2 | | 30 Oct 2003 (in so far as conferring power to make regulations) (RA) |
| | | 1 Feb 2004 (otherwise) (SI 2004/130) |
| 3–5 | | 1 Feb 2004 (SI 2004/130) |
| 6–8 | | 30 Oct 2003 (in so far as conferring power to make regulations) (RA) |
| | | 1 Feb 2004 (otherwise) (SI 2004/130) |
| 9 | | 1 Feb 2004 (SI 2004/130) |
| 10–14 | | 30 Oct 2003 (in so far as conferring power to make regulations) (RA) |
| | | 1 Feb 2004 (otherwise) (SI 2004/130) |
| 15 | para (1) | See Schedule below |
| | paras (2)–(5) | 1 Feb 2004 (SI 2004/130) |
| 16, 17 | | 30 Oct 2003 (RA) |
| Schedule | | 1 Feb 2004 (SI 2004/130) |

**Licensing Act 2003 (c 17)**

*RA:* 10 Jul 2003

*Commencement provisions:* s 201(2); Licensing Act 2003 (Commencement) Order 2003, SI 2003/1911; Licensing Act 2003 (Commencement No 2) Order 2003, SI 2003/2100; Licensing Act 2003 (Commencement No 3) Order 2003, SI 2003/3222; Licensing Act 2003 (Commencement No 4) Order 2004, SI 2004/1738; Licensing Act 2003 (Commencement No 5) Order 2004, SI 2004/2360; Licensing Act 2003 (Commencement No 6) Order 2005, SI 2005/2090; Licensing Act 2003 (Commencement No 7 and Transitional Provisions) Order 2005, SI 2005/3056

| | | |
|---|---|---|
| 1 | | 16 Dec 2003 (SI 2003/3222) |
| 2 | | 24 Nov 2005 (SI 2005/3056) |
| 3–5 | | 16 Dec 2003 (SI 2003/3222) |
| 6 | | 10 Sep 2004 (SI 2004/2360) |
| 7 | | 7 Feb 2005 (SI 2004/2360) |
| 8 | | 16 Dec 2003 (SI 2003/3222) |
| 9 | (1) | 10 Sep 2004 (SI 2004/2360) |
| | (2) | 16 Dec 2003 (SI 2003/3222) |
| | (3) | 10 Sep 2004 (SI 2004/2360) |
| 10–12 | | 7 Feb 2005 (SI 2004/2360) |
| 13 | (1) | 7 Feb 2005 (SI 2004/2360) |
| | (2)(a)–(e) | 7 Feb 2005 (SI 2004/2360) |
| | (2)(f) | 16 Dec 2003 (SI 2003/3222) |

**Licensing Act 2003 (c 17)**—*contd*

|        |            |                                                                                                                      |
|--------|------------|----------------------------------------------------------------------------------------------------------------------|
|        | (3)        | 7 Feb 2005 (SI 2004/2360)                                                                                             |
|        | (4)(a)–(h) | 7 Feb 2005 (SI 2004/2360)                                                                                             |
|        | (4)(i)     | 16 Dec 2003 (SI 2003/3222)                                                                                            |
|        | (5)        | 7 Feb 2005 (SI 2004/2360)                                                                                             |
| 14, 15 |            | 7 Feb 2005 (SI 2004/2360)                                                                                             |
| 16     | (1)(a)–(h) | 7 Feb 2005 (SI 2004/2360)                                                                                             |
|        | (1)(i)     | 16 Dec 2003 (SI 2003/3222)                                                                                            |
|        | (2), (3)   | 7 Feb 2005 (SI 2004/2360)                                                                                             |
| 17     | (1), (2)   | 7 Feb 2005 (SI 2004/2360)                                                                                             |
|        | (3)(a)     | 7 Feb 2005 (SI 2004/2360)                                                                                             |
|        | (3)(b), (c)| 16 Dec 2003 (SI 2003/3222)                                                                                            |
|        | (4), (5)   | 16 Dec 2003 (SI 2003/3222)                                                                                            |
| 18–23  |            | 7 Feb 2005 (SI 2004/2360)                                                                                             |
| 24     |            | 16 Dec 2003 (SI 2003/3222)                                                                                            |
| 25     |            | 7 Feb 2005 (SI 2004/2360)                                                                                             |
| 26–28  |            | 24 Nov 2005 (SI 2005/3056)                                                                                            |
| 29     | (1)–(5)    | 7 Feb 2005 (SI 2004/2360)                                                                                             |
|        | (6)        | 16 Dec 2003 (SI 2003/3222)                                                                                            |
|        | (7)        | 7 Feb 2005 (SI 2004/2360)                                                                                             |
| 30     |            | 16 Dec 2003 (SI 2003/3222)                                                                                            |
| 31     | (1)–(5)    | 7 Feb 2005 (SI 2004/2360)                                                                                             |
|        | (6)(a)     | 16 Dec 2003 (SI 2003/3222)                                                                                            |
|        | (6)(b), (c)| 7 Feb 2005 (SI 2004/2360)                                                                                             |
|        | (7), (8)   | 7 Feb 2005 (SI 2004/2360)                                                                                             |
| 32, 33 |            | 7 Feb 2005 (SI 2004/2360)                                                                                             |
| 34     | (1)–(4)    | 7 Feb 2005 (in so far as they relate to the provisions of Sch 8 brought into force by SI 2004/2360) (SI 2004/2360)    |
|        |            | 7 Aug 2005 (otherwise) (SI 2005/2090)                                                                                 |
|        | (5)        | 16 Dec 2003 (SI 2003/3222)                                                                                            |
| 35, 36 |            | 7 Feb 2005 (in so far as they relate to the provisions of Sch 8 brought into force by SI 2004/2360) (SI 2004/2360)    |
|        |            | 7 Aug 2005 (otherwise) (SI 2005/2090)                                                                                 |
| 37     | (1), (2)   | 7 Feb 2005 (in so far as they relate to the provisions of Sch 8 brought into force by SI 2004/2360) (SI 2004/2360)    |
|        |            | 7 Aug 2005 (otherwise) (SI 2005/2090)                                                                                 |
|        | (3)(a)     | 16 Dec 2003 (SI 2003/3222)                                                                                            |
|        | (3)(b)     | 7 Feb 2005 (in so far as relates to the provisions of Sch 8 brought into force by SI 2004/2360) (SI 2004/2360)        |
|        |            | 7 Aug 2005 (otherwise) (SI 2005/2090)                                                                                 |
|        | (4)–(6)    | 7 Feb 2005 (in so far as they relate to the provisions of Sch 8 brought into force by SI 2004/2360) (SI 2004/2360)    |
|        |            | 7 Aug 2005 (otherwise) (SI 2005/2090)                                                                                 |
| 38     |            | 7 Aug 2005 (SI 2005/2090)                                                                                             |
| 39     |            | 7 Feb 2005 (in so far as relates to the provisions of Sch 8 brought into force by SI 2004/2360) (SI 2004/2360)        |
|        |            | 7 Aug 2005 (otherwise) (SI 2005/2090)                                                                                 |
| 40     |            | 7 Aug 2005 (SI 2005/2090)                                                                                             |
| 41     |            | 24 Nov 2005 (SI 2005/3056)                                                                                            |
| 42     |            | 7 Aug 2005 (SI 2005/2090)                                                                                             |
| 43     | (1), (2)   | 7 Aug 2005 (SI 2005/2090)                                                                                             |
|        | (3)        | 7 Aug 2005 (except the reference to sub-s (4)) (SI 2005/2090)                                                         |
|        |            | 24 Nov 2005 (exception noted above) (SI 2005/3056)                                                                    |
|        | (4)        | 24 Nov 2005 (SI 2005/3056)                                                                                            |
|        | (5), (6)   | 7 Aug 2005 (SI 2005/2090)                                                                                             |
| 44–46  |            | 7 Aug 2005 (SI 2005/2090)                                                                                             |
| 47     | (1)        | 24 Nov 2005 (SI 2005/3056)                                                                                            |
|        | (2)(a)     | 16 Dec 2003 (SI 2003/3222)                                                                                            |
|        | (2)(b)     | 24 Nov 2005 (SI 2005/3056)                                                                                            |
|        | (3)–(10)   | 24 Nov 2005 (SI 2005/3056)                                                                                            |

**Licensing Act 2003 (c 17)**—*contd*

| | | |
|---|---|---|
| 48–50 | | 24 Nov 2005 (SI 2005/3056) |
| 51 | (1), (2) | 24 Nov 2005 (SI 2005/3056) |
| | (3) | 16 Dec 2003 (SI 2003/3222) |
| | (4)–(7) | 24 Nov 2005 (SI 2005/3056) |
| 52, 53 | | 24 Nov 2005 (SI 2005/3056) |
| 54, 55 | | 16 Dec 2003 (SI 2003/3222) |
| 56, 57 | | 24 Nov 2005 (SI 2005/3056) |
| 58 | (1)(a), (b) | 24 Nov 2005 (SI 2005/3056) |
| | (1)(c) | 16 Dec 2003 (SI 2003/3222) |
| | (2), (3) | 24 Nov 2005 (SI 2005/3056) |
| 59 | (1)(a), (b) | 7 Feb 2005 (SI 2004/2360) |
| | (1)(c) | 7 Feb 2005 (in so far as relates to the provisions of Sch 8 brought into force by SI 2004/2360) (SI 2004/2360) |
| | | 24 Nov 2005 (otherwise) (SI 2005/3056) |
| | (1)(d) | 24 Nov 2005 (SI 2005/3056) |
| | (2)(a) | 7 Feb 2005 (SI 2004/2360) |
| | (2)(b) | 24 Nov 2005 (SI 2005/3056) |
| | (3)–(6) | 7 Feb 2005 (SI 2004/2360) |
| 60–66 | | 7 Feb 2005 (SI 2004/2360) |
| 67 | | 24 Nov 2005 (SI 2005/3056) |
| 68 | | 7 Feb 2005 (SI 2004/2360) |
| 69 | (1) | 7 Feb 2005 (SI 2004/2360) |
| | (2)(a)–(e) | 7 Feb 2005 (SI 2004/2360) |
| | (2)(f) | 16 Dec 2003 (SI 2003/3222) |
| | (3) | 7 Feb 2005 (SI 2004/2360) |
| | (4)(a)–(h) | 7 Feb 2005 (SI 2004/2360) |
| | (4)(i) | 16 Dec 2003 (SI 2003/3222) |
| | (5) | 7 Feb 2005 (SI 2004/2360) |
| 70 | | 7 Feb 2005 (SI 2004/2360) |
| 71 | (1)–(3) | 7 Feb 2005 (SI 2004/2360) |
| | (4)(a) | 7 Feb 2005 (SI 2004/2360) |
| | (4)(b) | 16 Dec 2003 (SI 2003/3222) |
| | (4)(c) | 7 Feb 2005 (SI 2004/2360) |
| | (5), (6) | 16 Dec 2003 (SI 2003/3222) |
| 72–77 | | 7 Feb 2005 (SI 2004/2360) |
| 78 | | 16 Dec 2003 (SI 2003/3222) |
| 79 | | 7 Feb 2005 (SI 2004/2360) |
| 80, 81 | | 24 Nov 2005 (SI 2005/3056) |
| 82, 83 | | 7 Feb 2005 (SI 2004/2360) |
| 84 | (1)–(3) | 7 Feb 2005 (in so far as they relate to the provisions of Sch 8 brought into force by SI 2004/2360) (SI 2004/2360) |
| | | 7 Aug 2005 (otherwise) (SI 2005/2090) |
| | (4) | 16 Dec 2003 (SI 2003/3222) |
| 85, 86 | | 7 Feb 2005 (in so far as they relate to the provisions of Sch 8 brought into force by SI 2004/2360) (SI 2004/2360) |
| | | 7 Aug 2005 (otherwise) (SI 2005/2090) |
| 87 | (1), (2) | 24 Nov 2005 (SI 2005/3056) |
| | (3) | 16 Dec 2003 (SI 2003/3222) |
| | (4)–(7) | 24 Nov 2005 (SI 2005/3056) |
| 88, 89 | | 24 Nov 2005 (SI 2005/3056) |
| 90 | | 7 Feb 2005 (SI 2004/2360) |
| 91, 92 | | 16 Dec 2003 (SI 2003/3222) |
| 93, 94 | | 24 Nov 2005 (SI 2005/3056) |
| 95 | (1)(a), (b) | 24 Nov 2005 (SI 2005/3056) |
| | (1)(c) | 16 Dec 2003 (SI 2003/3222) |
| | (2), (3) | 24 Nov 2005 (SI 2005/3056) |
| 96 | (1)(a) | 7 Feb 2005 (SI 2004/2360) |
| | (1)(b) | 7 Feb 2005 (in so far as relates to the provisions of Sch 8 brought into force by SI 2004/2360) (SI 2004/2360) |

**Licensing Act 2003 (c 17)**—*contd*

|  |  |  |
|---|---|---|
|  |  | 24 Nov 2005 (otherwise) (SI 2005/3056) |
|  | (1)(c) | 24 Nov 2005 (SI 2005/3056) |
|  | (2)–(8) | 7 Feb 2005 (SI 2004/2360) |
| 97 |  | 24 Nov 2005 (SI 2005/3056) |
| 98, 99 |  | 10 Nov 2005 (SI 2005/3056) |
| 100 | (1)–(3) | 10 Nov 2005 (SI 2005/3056) |
|  | (4) | 16 Dec 2003 (SI 2003/3222) |
|  | (5)(a)–(e) | 10 Nov 2005 (SI 2005/3056) |
|  | (5)(f) | 16 Dec 2003 (SI 2003/3222) |
|  | (6) | 10 Nov 2005 (SI 2005/3056) |
|  | (7)(a) | 10 Nov 2005 (SI 2005/3056) |
|  | (7)(b) | 16 Dec 2003 (SI 2003/3222) |
|  | (8) | 16 Dec 2003 (SI 2003/3222) |
|  | (9) | 10 Nov 2005 (SI 2005/3056) |
| 101 |  | 10 Nov 2005 (SI 2005/3056) |
| 102 | (1) | 10 Nov 2005 (SI 2005/3056) |
|  | (2) | 16 Dec 2003 (SI 2003/3222) |
|  | (3) | 10 Nov 2005 (SI 2005/3056) |
| 103–106 |  | 10 Nov 2005 (SI 2005/3056) |
| 107 | (1)–(6) | 10 Nov 2005 (SI 2005/3056) |
|  | (7) | 16 Dec 2003 (SI 2003/3222) |
|  | (8)–(11) | 10 Nov 2005 (SI 2005/3056) |
|  | (12) | 16 Dec 2003 (SI 2003/3222) |
|  | (13) | 10 Nov 2005 (SI 2005/3056) |
| 108, 109 |  | 10 Nov 2005 (SI 2005/3056) |
| 110 | (1), (2) | 10 Nov 2005 (SI 2005/3056) |
|  | (3) | 16 Dec 2003 (SI 2003/3222) |
|  | (4)–(6) | 10 Nov 2005 (SI 2005/3056) |
| 111, 112 |  | 7 Feb 2005 (SI 2004/2360) |
| 113 | (1) | See Sch 4 below |
|  | (2) | 16 Dec 2003 (SI 2003/3222) |
|  | (3) | 7 Feb 2005 (SI 2004/2360) |
| 114–118 |  | 7 Feb 2005 (SI 2004/2360) |
| 119 |  | 24 Nov 2005 (SI 2005/3056) |
| 120 | (1) | 7 Feb 2005 (SI 2004/2360) |
|  | (2)(a) | 7 Feb 2005 (SI 2004/2360) |
|  | (2)(b) | 16 Dec 2003 (SI 2003/3222) |
|  | (2)(c), (d) | 7 Feb 2005 (SI 2004/2360) |
|  | (3)–(9) | 7 Feb 2005 (SI 2004/2360) |
| 121 |  | 24 Nov 2005 (SI 2005/3056) |
| 122–124 |  | 7 Feb 2005 (SI 2004/2360) |
| 125 | (1)–(3) | 7 Feb 2005 (SI 2004/2360) |
|  | (4) | 16 Dec 2003 (SI 2003/3222) |
| 126–132 |  | 7 Feb 2005 (SI 2004/2360) |
| 133 |  | 16 Dec 2003 (SI 2003/3222) |
| 134, 135 |  | 7 Feb 2005 (SI 2004/2360) |
| 136–154 |  | 24 Nov 2005 (SI 2005/3056) |
| 155 |  | 10 Sep 2003 (SI 2003/2100) |
| 156, 157 |  | 24 Nov 2005 (SI 2005/3056) |
| 158 |  | 7 Feb 2005 (SI 2004/2360) |
| 159–166 |  | 24 Nov 2005 (SI 2005/3056) |
| 167 | (1)–(3) | 24 Nov 2005 (SI 2005/3056) |
|  | (4) | 16 Dec 2003 (SI 2003/3222) |
|  | (5)–(14) | 24 Nov 2005 (SI 2005/3056) |
| 168–172 |  | 24 Nov 2005 (SI 2005/3056) |
| 173 | (1)(a)–(g) | 24 Nov 2005 (SI 2005/3056) |
|  | (1)(h) | 16 Dec 2003 (SI 2003/3222) |
|  | (2) | 24 Nov 2005 (SI 2005/3056) |
|  | (3) | 16 Dec 2003 (SI 2003/3222) |

**Licensing Act 2003 (c 17)**—*contd*

| | | |
|---|---|---|
| | (4) | 24 Nov 2005 (SI 2005/3056) |
| | (5) | 16 Dec 2003 (SI 2003/3222) |
| | (6) | 24 Nov 2005 (SI 2005/3056) |
| 174, 175 | | 24 Nov 2005 (SI 2005/3056) |
| 176 | (1), (2) | 24 Nov 2005 (SI 2005/3056) |
| | (3) | 16 Dec 2003 (SI 2003/3222) |
| | (4) | 24 Nov 2005 (SI 2005/3056) |
| 177 | | 24 Nov 2005 (SI 2005/3056) |
| 178 | (1)(a) | 7 Feb 2005 (SI 2004/2360) |
| | (1)(b) | 16 Dec 2003 (SI 2003/3222) |
| | (2), (3) | 7 Feb 2005 (SI 2004/2360) |
| | (4)(a)–(c) | 7 Feb 2005 (SI 2004/2360) |
| | (4)(d) | 16 Dec 2003 (SI 2003/3222) |
| | (5) | 7 Feb 2005 (SI 2004/2360) |
| 179, 180 | | 24 Nov 2005 (SI 2005/3056) |
| 181 | (1) | See Sch 5 below |
| | (2) | 7 Feb 2005 (in so far as relates to the provisions of Sch 5 brought into force by SI 2004/2360) (SI 2004/2360) |
| | | 7 Aug 2005 (in so far as relates to the provisions of Sch 5 brought into force by SI 2005/2090) (SI 2005/2090) |
| | | 24 Nov 2005 (otherwise) (SI 2005/3056) |
| 182 | | 16 Dec 2003 (SI 2003/3222) |
| 183 | (1) | 16 Dec 2003 (SI 2003/3222) |
| | (2) | 7 Feb 2005 (SI 2004/2360) |
| 184–186 | | 7 Feb 2005 (SI 2004/2360) |
| 187 | (1)–(6) | 7 Feb 2005 (SI 2004/2360) |
| | (7) | 16 Dec 2003 (SI 2003/3222) |
| | (8) | 7 Feb 2005 (SI 2004/2360) |
| 188–190 | | 7 Feb 2005 (SI 2004/2360) |
| 191–194 | | 16 Dec 2003 (SI 2003/3222) |
| 195 | | 7 Feb 2005 (SI 2004/2360) |
| 196 | | 24 Nov 2005 (SI 2005/3056) |
| 197 | | 16 Dec 2003 (SI 2003/3222) |
| 198 | (1) | See Sch 6 below |
| | (2) | 16 Dec 2003 (SI 2003/3222) |
| 199 | | See Sch 7 below |
| 200 | | See Sch 8 below |
| 201 | | 10 Jul 2003 (RA) |
| Schs 1–3 | | 16 Dec 2003 (SI 2003/3222) |
| Sch 4 | | 7 Feb 2005 (SI 2004/2360) |
| Sch 5 | para 1(a) | 7 Feb 2005 (SI 2004/2360) |
| | para 1(b), (c) | 7 Feb 2005 (in so far as they relate to the transitional provisions in Sch 8) (SI 2004/2360) |
| | | 7 Aug 2005 (otherwise) (SI 2005/2090) |
| | para 1(d) | 7 Feb 2005 (SI 2004/2360) |
| | paras 2, 3 | 7 Feb 2005 (SI 2004/2360) |
| | paras 4, 5 | 7 Feb 2005 (in so far as they relate to the transitional provisions in Sch 8) (SI 2004/2360) |
| | | 7 Aug 2005 (otherwise) (SI 2005/2090) |
| | para 6 | 7 Aug 2005 (SI 2005/2090) |
| | paras 7, 8 | 24 Nov 2005 (SI 2005/3056) |
| | para 9 | 7 Feb 2005 (SI 2004/2360) (note that SI 2005/2090 also purports to bring this provision into force on 7 Aug 2005) |
| | para 10(a) | 7 Feb 2005 (SI 2004/2360) |
| | para 10(b) | 7 Feb 2005 (in so far as relates to the transitional provisions in Sch 8) (SI 2004/2360) |
| | | 7 Aug 2005 (otherwise) (SI 2005/2090) |
| | para 11 | 7 Feb 2005 (SI 2004/2360) |

**Licensing Act 2003 (c 17)**—*contd*

| | | |
|---|---|---|
| | para 12 | 7 Feb 2005 (in so far as relates to the transitional provisions in Sch 8) (SI 2004/2360) |
| | | 7 Aug 2005 (otherwise) (SI 2005/2090) |
| | paras 13, 14 | 24 Nov 2005 (SI 2005/3056) |
| | para 15 | 7 Feb 2005 (SI 2004/2360) |
| | para 16 | 24 Nov 2005 (SI 2005/3056) |
| | para 17(1)(a) | 7 Feb 2005 (SI 2004/2360) |
| | para 17(1)(b) | 24 Nov 2005 (SI 2005/3056) |
| | para 17(2)–(8) | 7 Feb 2005 (SI 2004/2360) |
| | para 17(9), (10) | 24 Nov 2005 (SI 2005/3056) |
| | para 17(11) | 7 Feb 2005 (SI 2004/2360) |
| | para 18 | 24 Nov 2005 (SI 2005/3056) |
| Sch 6 | paras 1–48 | 24 Nov 2005 (SI 2005/3056) |
| | para 49 | 24 Nov 2005 (SI 2005/3056)[1] |
| | paras 50, 51 | 24 Nov 2005 (SI 2005/3056) |
| | para 52 | 24 Nov 2005 (SI 2005/3056)[1] |
| | paras 53–61 | 24 Nov 2005 (SI 2005/3056) |
| | paras 62–66 | 24 Nov 2005 (SI 2005/3056)[1] |
| | paras 67–97 | 24 Nov 2005 (SI 2005/3056) |
| | para 98 | *Not yet in force* |
| | para 99(a), (b) | 24 Nov 2005 (SI 2005/3056) |
| | para 99(c) | *Not yet in force* |
| | para 99(d)–(h) | 24 Nov 2005 (SI 2005/3056) |
| | paras 100–128 | 24 Nov 2005 (SI 2005/3056) |
| Sch 7 | | 17 Jul 2003 (repeals of or in Licensing Act 1964, ss 66, 67, Sch 8) (SI 2003/1911) |
| | | 10 Sep 2003 (SI 2003/2100), repeals of or in— |
| | |   Confiscation of Alcohol (Young Persons) Act 1997; |
| | |   Criminal Justice and Police Act 2001, s 12 |
| | | 24 Nov 2005 (otherwise, except repeal of Sporting Events (Control of Alcohol etc) Act 1985, ss 2(1A), 5A)[1] (SI 2005/3056) |
| | | *Not yet in force* (exception noted above) |
| Sch 8 | para 1(1) | 16 Dec 2003 (definitions "first appointed day" and "second appointed day") (SI 2003/3222) |
| | | 7 Feb 2005 (otherwise) (SI 2004/2360) |
| | para 1(2), (3) | 7 Feb 2005 (SI 2004/2360) |
| | para 2(1)–(3) | 7 Feb 2005 (SI 2004/2360) |
| | para 2(4)(a) | 7 Feb 2005 (SI 2004/2360) |
| | para 2(4)(b), (c) | 16 Dec 2003 (SI 2003/3222) |
| | para 2(5) | 7 Feb 2005 (SI 2004/2360) |
| | para 2(6)(a) | 7 Feb 2005 (SI 2004/2360) |
| | para 2(6)(b) | 16 Dec 2003 (SI 2003/3222) |
| | para 2(6)(c) | 7 Feb 2005 (SI 2004/2360) |
| | para 2(6)(d)–(f) | 16 Dec 2003 (SI 2003/3222) |
| | para 2(7)(a)–(c) | 7 Feb 2005 (SI 2004/2360) |
| | para 2(7)(d) | 16 Dec 2003 (SI 2003/3222) |
| | para 2(8) | 7 Feb 2005 (SI 2004/2360) |
| | paras 3–5 | 7 Feb 2005 (SI 2004/2360) |
| | para 6(1)–(7) | 7 Feb 2005 (SI 2004/2360) |
| | para 6(8) | 16 Dec 2003 (SI 2003/3222) |
| | para 6(9)–(11) | 7 Feb 2005 (SI 2004/2360) |
| | paras 7–10 | 7 Feb 2005 (SI 2004/2360) |
| | para 11(1)(a) | 16 Dec 2003 (SI 2003/3222) |
| | para 11(1)(b) | 7 Feb 2005 (SI 2004/2360) |
| | para 11(2)–(4) | 7 Feb 2005 (SI 2004/2360) |
| | para 12(1)(a) | 16 Dec 2003 (SI 2003/3222) |
| | para 12(1)(b), (c) | 7 Feb 2005 (SI 2004/2360) |
| | para 12(2) | 7 Feb 2005 (SI 2004/2360) |

**Licensing Act 2003 (c 17)**—*contd*

| | | |
|---|---|---|
| para 13(1) | | 16 Dec 2003 (definitions "first appointed day" and "second appointed day") (SI 2003/3222) |
| | | 7 Feb 2005 (otherwise) (SI 2004/2360) |
| para 13(2) | | 7 Feb 2005 (SI 2004/2360) |
| para 14(1), (2) | | 7 Feb 2005 (SI 2004/2360) |
| para 14(3)–(5) | | 16 Dec 2003 (SI 2003/3222) |
| para 14(6)(a), (b) | | 7 Feb 2005 (SI 2004/2360) |
| para 14(6)(c) | | 16 Dec 2003 (SI 2003/3222) |
| para 14(7) | | 7 Feb 2005 (SI 2004/2360) |
| paras 15–17 | | 7 Feb 2005 (SI 2004/2360) |
| para 18(1)–(4) | | 7 Feb 2005 (SI 2004/2360) |
| para 18(5) | | 16 Dec 2003 (SI 2003/3222) |
| para 18(6) | | 7 Feb 2005 (SI 2004/2360) |
| paras 19–22 | | 7 Feb 2005 (SI 2004/2360) |
| para 23(1) | | 7 Feb 2005 (SI 2004/2360) |
| para 23(2) | | 16 Dec 2003 (SI 2003/3222) |
| para 23(3)(a) | | 7 Feb 2005 (SI 2004/2360) |
| para 23(3)(b) | | 16 Dec 2003 (SI 2003/3222) |
| para 23(3)(c) | | 7 Feb 2005 (SI 2004/2360) |
| para 23(4)(a), (b) | | 7 Feb 2005 (SI 2004/2360) |
| para 23(4)(c) | | 16 Dec 2003 (SI 2003/3222) |
| para 23(5) | | 7 Feb 2005 (SI 2004/2360) |
| paras 24–28 | | 7 Feb 2005 (SI 2004/2360) |
| para 29 | | 16 Dec 2003 (SI 2003/3222) |
| para 30 | | 7 Feb 2005 (SI 2004/2360) |
| paras 31–33 | | 24 Nov 2005 (SI 2005/3056) |
| para 34 | | 7 Jul 2004 (SI 2004/1738) |

[1]  For transitional provisions and savings, see SI 2005/3056, arts 3, 4, Schedule

---

**Local Government Act 2003 (c 26)**

*RA:* 18 Sep 2003

*Commencement provisions:* s 128; Local Government Act 2003 (Commencement No 1 and Transitional Provisions and Savings) Order 2003, SI 2003/2938; Local Government Act 2003 (Commencement) (Wales) Order 2003, SI 2003/3034[2]; Local Government Act 2003 (Commencement No 2 and Savings) Order 2004, SI 2004/3132; Local Government Act 2003 (Commencement No 1 and Savings) (Wales) Order 2006, SI 2006/3339

| | | |
|---|---|---|
| 1, 2 | | 27 Nov 2003 (W) (SI 2003/3034)[3] |
| | | 1 Apr 2004 (E) (SI 2003/2938, art 7) |
| 3 | (1), (2) | 27 Nov 2003 (W) (SI 2003/3034)[3] |
| | | 1 Jan 2004 (E) (SI 2003/2938, art 5)[1] |
| | (3), (4) | 27 Nov 2003 (W) (SI 2003/3034)[3] |
| | | 1 Jan 2004 (E) (SI 2003/2938, art 5) |
| | (5)–(7) | 18 Nov 2003 (E) (SI 2003/2938, art 3) |
| | | 27 Nov 2003 (W) (SI 2003/3034)[3] |
| | (8), (9) | 27 Nov 2003 (W) (SI 2003/3034)[3] |
| | | 1 Jan 2004 (E) (SI 2003/2938, art 5) |
| | (10) | 18 Nov 2003 (E) (SI 2003/2938, art 3) |
| | | 27 Nov 2003 (W) (SI 2003/3034)[3] |
| | (11) | 27 Nov 2003 (W) (SI 2003/3034)[3] |
| | | 1 Jan 2004 (E) (SI 2003/2938, art 5) |
| 4 | (1)–(3) | 18 Nov 2003 (E) (SI 2003/2938, art 3)[1] |
| | | 27 Nov 2003 (W) (SI 2003/3034)[3] |
| | (4) | 27 Nov 2003 (W) (SI 2003/3034)[3] |
| | | 1 Apr 2004 (E) (SI 2003/2938, art 7)[1] |
| | (5) | 18 Nov 2003 (E) (SI 2003/2938, art 3)[1] |

**Local Government Act 2003 (c 26)**—*contd*

| | | |
|---|---|---|
| | | 27 Nov 2003 (W) (SI 2003/3034)[3] |
| | (6) | 27 Nov 2003 (W) (SI 2003/3034)[3] |
| | | 1 Apr 2004 (E) (SI 2003/2938, art 7)[1] |
| 5, 6 | | 27 Nov 2003 (W) (SI 2003/3034)[3] |
| | | 1 Apr 2004 (E) (SI 2003/2938, art 7) |
| 7 | (1) | 27 Nov 2003 (W) (SI 2003/3034)[3] |
| | | 1 Apr 2004 (E) (SI 2003/2938, art 7)[1] |
| | (2)(a) | 27 Nov 2003 (W) (SI 2003/3034)[3] |
| | | 1 Apr 2004 (E) (SI 2003/2938, art 7)[1] |
| | (2)(b) | 18 Nov 2003 (E) (SI 2003/2938, art 3)[1] |
| | | 27 Nov 2003 (W) (SI 2003/3034)[3] |
| | (3)(a), (b) | 27 Nov 2003 (W) (SI 2003/3034)[3] |
| | | 1 Apr 2004 (E) (SI 2003/2938, art 7)[1] |
| | (3)(c) | 18 Nov 2003 (E) (SI 2003/2938, art 3)[1] |
| | | 27 Nov 2003 (W) (SI 2003/3034)[3] |
| 8 | (1), (2) | 27 Nov 2003 (W) (SI 2003/3034)[3] |
| | | 1 Apr 2004 (E) (SI 2003/2938, art 7) |
| | (3) | 18 Nov 2003 (E) (SI 2003/2938, art 3) |
| | | 27 Nov 2003 (W) (SI 2003/3034)[3] |
| 9 | (1), (2) | 27 Nov 2003 (W) (SI 2003/3034)[3] |
| | | 1 Apr 2004 (E) (SI 2003/2938, art 7) |
| | (3) | 18 Nov 2003 (E) (SI 2003/2938, art 3) |
| | | 27 Nov 2003 (W) (SI 2003/3034)[3] |
| | (4) | 27 Nov 2003 (W) (SI 2003/3034)[3] |
| | | 1 Apr 2004 (E) (SI 2003/2938, art 7) |
| 10, 11 | | 18 Nov 2003 (E) (SI 2003/2938, art 3) |
| | | 27 Nov 2003 (W) (SI 2003/3034)[3] |
| 12, 13 | | 27 Nov 2003 (W) (SI 2003/3034)[3] |
| | | 1 Apr 2004 (E) (SI 2003/2938, art 7) |
| 14 | | 18 Nov 2003 (E) (SI 2003/2938, art 3)[1] |
| | | 27 Nov 2003 (W) (SI 2003/3034)[3] |
| 15 | | 18 Nov 2003 (E) (SI 2003/2938, art 3) |
| | | 27 Nov 2003 (W) (SI 2003/3034)[3] |
| 16 | (1) | 27 Nov 2003 (W) (SI 2003/3034)[3] |
| | | 1 Apr 2004 (E) (SI 2003/2938, art 7) |
| | (2) | 18 Nov 2003 (E) (SI 2003/2938, art 3) |
| | | 27 Nov 2003 (W) (SI 2003/3034)[3] |
| 17 | | 27 Nov 2003 (W) (SI 2003/3034)[3] |
| | | 1 Apr 2004 (E) (SI 2003/2938, art 7) |
| 18 | | 18 Nov 2003 (E) (SI 2003/2938, art 3) |
| | | 27 Nov 2003 (W) (SI 2003/3034)[3] |
| 19 | (1) | 18 Nov 2003 (E) (so far as relates to ss 9(3), 10, 11, 15, 16(2), 18) (SI 2003/2938, art 3) |
| | | 27 Nov 2003 (W) (SI 2003/3034)[3] |
| | | 1 Apr 2004 (E) (otherwise) (SI 2003/2938, art 7) |
| | (2) | See Sch 1 below |
| | (3) | 18 Nov 2003 (E) (SI 2003/2938, art 3) |
| | | 27 Nov 2003 (W) (SI 2003/3034)[3] |
| 20 | | 18 Nov 2003 (E) (SI 2003/2938, art 3) |
| | | 27 Nov 2003 (W) (SI 2003/3034)[3] |
| 21 | (1) | 18 Nov 2003 (E) (SI 2003/2938, art 3) |
| | | 27 Nov 2003 (W) (SI 2003/3034)[3] |
| | (2)(a) | 27 Nov 2003 (W) (SI 2003/3034)[3] |
| | | 1 Apr 2004 (E) (SI 2003/2938, art 7) |
| | (2)(b) | 18 Nov 2003 (E) (so far as enables regulations to be made) (SI 2003/2938, art 3) |
| | | 27 Nov 2003 (W) (SI 2003/3034)[3] |
| | | 1 Apr 2004 (E) (otherwise) (SI 2003/2938, art 7) |
| | (3), (4) | 27 Nov 2003 (W) (SI 2003/3034)[3] |

**Local Government Act 2003 (c 26)**—*contd*

| | | |
|---|---|---|
| | | 1 Apr 2004 (E) (SI 2003/2938, art 7) |
| | (5), (6) | 18 Nov 2003 (E) (SI 2003/2938, art 3) |
| | | 27 Nov 2003 (W) (SI 2003/3034)[3] |
| 22 | | 27 Nov 2003 (W) (SI 2003/3034)[3] |
| | | 1 Apr 2004 (E) (SI 2003/2938, art 7) |
| 23 | | 18 Nov 2003 (E) (SI 2003/2938, art 3) |
| | | 27 Nov 2003 (W) (SI 2003/3034)[3] |
| 24 | | 27 Nov 2003 (W) (SI 2003/3034)[3] |
| 25, 26 | | 18 Nov 2003 (E) (SI 2003/2938, art 3)[1] |
| | | 27 Nov 2003 (W) (SI 2003/3034)[3] |
| 27 | | 27 Nov 2003 (W) (SI 2003/3034)[3] |
| | | 1 Apr 2004 (E) (SI 2003/2938, art 7)[1] |
| 28 | | 27 Nov 2003 (W) (SI 2003/3034)[3] |
| | | 1 Apr 2004 (E) (SI 2003/2938, art 7) |
| 29 | | 1 Apr 2004 (E) (SI 2003/2938, art 7) |
| 30 | | 18 Sep 2003 (s 128(1)) |
| 31–33 | | 18 Nov 2003 (s 128(2)) |
| 34, 35 | | 18 Sep 2003 (s 128(1)) |
| 36 | | 18 Nov 2003 (E) (SI 2003/2938, art 3) |
| | | 27 Nov 2003 (W) (SI 2003/3034) |
| 37 | | 27 Nov 2003 (W) (SI 2003/3034)[3] |
| | | 1 Apr 2004 (E) (SI 2003/2938, art 7) |
| 38, 39 | | 18 Nov 2003 (E) (s 128(2)) |
| | | 27 Nov 2003 (W) (SI 2003/3034) |
| 40 | (1) | See Sch 2 below |
| | (2) | 27 Nov 2003 (SI 2003/3034) |
| 41–57 | | 18 Nov 2003 (E) (SI 2003/2938, art 3) |
| | | 27 Nov 2003 (W) (SI 2003/3034) |
| 58 | | 27 Nov 2003 (W) (SI 2003/3034) |
| 59, 60 | | 18 Nov 2003 (E) (SI 2003/2938, art 3) |
| | | 27 Nov 2003 (W) (SI 2003/3034) |
| 61 | (1), (2) | 27 Nov 2003 (W) (SI 2003/3034) |
| | | 1 Apr 2005 (E) (SI 2004/3132) |
| | (3) | 27 Nov 2003 (W) (SI 2003/3034) |
| | | 25 Nov 2004 (E) (so far as enables an order to be made) (SI 2004/3132) |
| | | 1 Apr 2005 (E) (otherwise) (SI 2004/3132) |
| | (4) | 27 Nov 2003 (W) (SI 2003/3034) |
| | | 1 Apr 2005 (E) (SI 2004/3132) |
| | (5) | 27 Nov 2003 (W) (SI 2003/3034) |
| | | 25 Nov 2004 (E) (so far as enables an order to be made) (SI 2004/3132) |
| | | 1 Apr 2005 (E) (otherwise) (SI 2004/3132) |
| | (6), (7) | 27 Nov 2003 (SI 2003/3034) |
| 62 | (1) | 27 Nov 2003 (W) (SI 2003/3034) |
| | | 25 Nov 2004 (E) (SI 2004/3132)[4] |
| | (2) | 25 Nov 2004 (SI 2004/3132)[4] |
| | (3)–(10) | 27 Nov 2003 (W) (SI 2003/3034) |
| | | 25 Nov 2004 (E) (SI 2004/3132)[4] |
| | (11) | 25 Nov 2004 (SI 2004/3132)[4] |
| 63 | | 1 Apr 2007 (SI 2006/3339)[5] |
| 64 | | 1 Apr 2004 (SI 2003/2938, art 7; SI 2003/3034) |
| 65 | | 25 Nov 2004 (E) (SI 2004/3132)[4] |
| 66 | | 27 Nov 2003 (W) (SI 2003/3034) |
| | | 1 Apr 2005 (E) (SI 2004/3132) |
| 67 | (1) | 18 Nov 2003 (E) (SI 2003/2938, art 3) |
| | | 27 Nov 2003 (W) (SI 2003/3034) |
| | (2) | 1 Apr 2004 (SI 2003/2938, art 7; SI 2003/3034) |
| | (3)–(5) | 18 Nov 2003 (E) (SI 2003/2938, art 3) |

**Local Government Act 2003 (c 26)**—*contd*

| | | |
|---|---|---|
| | | 27 Nov 2003 (W) (SI 2003/3034) |
| 68, 69 | | *Not yet in force* |
| 70 | (1) | 18 Nov 2003 (E) (SI 2003/2938, art 3) |
| | | 27 Nov 2003 (W) (SI 2003/3034) |
| | (2), (3) | 18 Nov 2003 (E) (SI 2003/2938, art 3)[1] |
| | | 27 Nov 2003 (W) (SI 2003/3034) |
| | (4)–(6) | 18 Nov 2003 (SI 2003/2938, art 2) |
| | (7)–(9) | 27 Nov 2003 (SI 2003/3034) |
| 71 | | 18 Nov 2003 (E) (SI 2003/2938, art 3) |
| | | 27 Nov 2003 (W) (SI 2003/3034) |
| 72, 73 | | 18 Sep 2003 (s 128(1)) |
| 74 | | 18 Nov 2003 (s 128(2)) |
| 75 | (1) | 18 Nov 2003 (s 128(2)) |
| | (2)–(5) | 27 Nov 2003 (SI 2003/3034) |
| 76–82 | | 18 Nov 2003 (s 128(2)) |
| 83 | | 18 Nov 2003 (SI 2003/2938, art 2)[1] |
| 84–88 | | 18 Nov 2003 (s 128(2)) |
| 89 | | 18 Nov 2003 (E) (SI 2003/2938, art 3)[1] |
| | | 27 Nov 2003 (W) (SI 2003/3034)[3] |
| 90 | (1) | 18 Nov 2003 (E) (SI 2003/2938, art 3)[1] |
| | | 27 Nov 2003 (W) (SI 2003/3034)[3] |
| | (2), (3) | 27 Nov 2003 (W) (SI 2003/3034)[3] |
| | | 1 Apr 2004 (E) (SI 2003/2938, art 7)[1] |
| | (4) | *Not yet in force* |
| 91 | | 18 Nov 2003 (s 128(2)) |
| 92 | (1) | 18 Nov 2003 (SI 2003/2938, art 2)[1] |
| | (2) | 1 Apr 2004 (SI 2003/3034) |
| 93–98 | | 18 Nov 2003 (s 128(2)) |
| 99 | | 18 Nov 2003 (SI 2003/2938, art 2) |
| 100 | (1), (2) | 18 Nov 2003 (SI 2003/2938, art 2) |
| | (3) | See Sch 3 below |
| | (4)–(8) | 18 Nov 2003 (SI 2003/2938, art 2) |
| 101 | | 18 Nov 2003 (so far as relating to England and to a best value authority in Wales mentioned in s 101(7)) (SI 2003/2938, art 2) |
| | | 27 Nov 2003 (so far as relating to a best value authority in Wales, other than one mentioned in s 101(7)) (SI 2003/3034) |
| | | *Not yet in force* (S) (sub-s (7) repealed) |
| 102 | | 1 Apr 2004 (E) (SI 2003/2938, art 7) |
| | | 27 Nov 2003 (W) (SI 2003/3034) |
| | | *Not yet in force* (S) |
| 103, 104 | | 18 Sep 2003 (s 128(1)) |
| 105 | (1)–(8) | 1 Apr 2004 (SI 2003/2938, art 6) |
| | (9) | See Sch 4 below |
| 106 | (1), (2) | 18 Nov 2003 (SI 2003/2938, art 2) |
| | (3) | See Sch 5 below |
| 107, 108 | | 18 Nov 2003 (SI 2003/2938, art 2) |
| 109 | (1) | 18 Nov 2003 (for the purpose of the application of the Audit Commission Act 1998, s 41A to registered social landlords for which the Housing Corporation is the Relevant Authority for the purposes of the Housing Act 1996, Pt I) (SI 2003/2938, art 2) |
| | | 27 Nov 2003 (in relation to registered social landlords for which the National Assembly for Wales is the Relevant Authority for the purposes of the Housing Act 1996, Pt I) (SI 2003/3034) |
| | | 1 Apr 2004 (for the purpose of the application of the Audit Commission Act 1998, s 41B to registered social landlords for which the Housing Corporation is the Relevant Authority for the purposes of the Housing Act 1996, Pt I) (SI 2003/2938, art 6) |

**Local Government Act 2003 (c 26)**—*contd*

| | | |
|---|---|---|
| | (2) | 27 Nov 2003 (SI 2003/3034) |
| | (3), (4) | 18 Nov 2003 (SI 2003/2938, art 2) |
| 110 | | 18 Sep 2003 (s 128(1)) |
| 111, 112 | | 18 Nov 2003 (SI 2003/2938, art 2) |
| 113 | | 18 Nov 2003 (s 128(2)) |
| 114 | | 18 Sep 2003 (s 128(1)) |
| 115 | | 18 Nov 2003 (SI 2003/2938, art 2) |
| 116 | | 18 Nov 2003 (s 128(2)) |
| 117 | | 18 Nov 2003 (E) (SI 2003/2938, art 3) |
| | | 27 Nov 2003 (W) (SI 2003/3034)[3] |
| 118 | | 27 Nov 2003 (W) (SI 2003/3034) |
| | | 1 Apr 2004 (E) (SI 2003/2938, art 7) |
| 119 | | 18 Nov 2003 (E) (SI 2003/2938, art 3) |
| | | 27 Nov 2003 (W) (SI 2003/3034) |
| 120 | (1)–(5) | 1 Apr 2004 (SI 2003/2938, art 7; SI 2003/3034) |
| | (6) | See Sch 6 below |
| 121 | | 18 Sep 2003 (s 128(1)) |
| 122 | | 18 Nov 2003 (s 128(2)) |
| 123, 124 | | 18 Sep 2003 (s 128(1)) |
| 125 | | 18 Nov 2003 (so far as it enables an order to be made and so far as it applies to the Isles of Scilly the provisions of Pts 1, 2 of the Act brought into force by art 3 of SI 2003/2938) (SI 2003/2938, art 2) |
| | | 1 Jan 2004 (so far as it applies to the Isles of Scilly the provisions of Pt 1 of the Act brought into force by art 5 of SI 2003/2938) (SI 2003/2938, art 4) |
| | | 1 Apr 2004 (otherwise) (SI 2003/2938, art 6) |
| 126 | | 18 Nov 2003 (E) (SI 2003/2938, art 3) |
| | | *Not yet in force* (W) |
| 127 | (1) | See Sch 7 below |
| | (2) | See Sch 8 below |
| | (3), (4) | 18 Nov 2003 (E) (SI 2003/2938, art 3) |
| | | 27 Nov 2003 (W) (SI 2003/3034) |
| 128, 129 | | 18 Sep 2003 (s 128(1)) |
| Sch 1 | paras 1–3 | 27 Nov 2003 (W) (SI 2003/3034)[3] |
| | | 1 Apr 2004 (E) (SI 2003/2938, art 7) |
| | para 4(1) | 27 Nov 2003 (W) (SI 2003/3034)[3] |
| | | 1 Apr 2004 (E) (SI 2003/2938, art 7) |
| | para 4(2) | 18 Nov 2003 (E) (so far as enables regulations to be made) (SI 2003/2938, art 3) |
| | | 27 Nov 2003 (W) (SI 2003/3034)[3] |
| | | 1 Apr 2004 (E) (otherwise) (SI 2003/2938, art 7) |
| | para 5 | 27 Nov 2003 (W) (SI 2003/3034)[3] |
| | | 1 Apr 2004 (E) (SI 2003/2938, art 7) |
| Sch 2 | | 27 Nov 2003 (SI 2003/3034)[3] |
| Sch 3 | | 18 Nov 2003 (E) (SI 2003/2938, art 3) |
| | | 27 Nov 2003 (W) (SI 2003/3034) |
| Sch 4 | paras 1–6 | 1 Apr 2004 (SI 2003/2938, art 6) |
| | para 7(1) | 1 Apr 2004 (SI 2003/2938, art 6) |
| | para 7(2)(a) | 18 Nov 2003 (SI 2003/2938, art 2) |
| | para 7(2)(b) | 1 Apr 2004 (SI 2003/2938, art 6) |
| | para 7(3) | 18 Nov 2003 (SI 2003/2938, art 2) |
| | para 7(4), (5) | 1 Apr 2004 (SI 2003/2938, art 6) |
| | paras 8–17 | 1 Apr 2004 (SI 2003/2938, art 6) |
| | para 18(1) | 18 Nov 2003 (SI 2003/2938, art 2) |
| | para 18(2) | 1 Apr 2004 (SI 2003/2938, art 6) |
| | paras 19–27 | 1 Apr 2004 (SI 2003/2938, art 6) |
| Sch 5 | | 18 Nov 2003 (SI 2003/2938, art 2) |
| Sch 6 | | 1 Apr 2004 (SI 2003/2938, art 7; SI 2003/3034) |

**Local Government Act 2003 (c 26)**—*contd*

| | | |
|---|---|---|
| Sch 7 | para 1 | 18 Nov 2003 (SI 2003/2938, art 2)[1] |
| | paras 2, 3 | 27 Nov 2003 (W) (SI 2003/3034)[3] |
| | | 1 Apr 2004 (E) (SI 2003/2938) |
| | para 4 | 1 Apr 2004 (SI 2003/2938, art 7; SI 2003/3034) |
| | para 5 | 27 Nov 2003 (SI 2003/3034) |
| | para 6 | 27 Nov 2003 (W) (SI 2003/3034)[3] |
| | | 1 Apr 2004 (E) (SI 2003/2938) |
| | para 7 | 18 Sep 2003 (s 128(1)) |
| | para 8 | 18 Nov 2003 (E) (SI 2003/2938, art 3) |
| | | 27 Nov 2003 (W) (SI 2003/3034) |
| | para 9(1) | 18 Sep 2003 (s 128(1)) |
| | para 9(2) | 27 Nov 2003 (SI 2003/3034) |
| | paras 10, 11 | 25 Nov 2004 (E) (SI 2004/3132)[4] |
| | paras 12–17 | 27 Nov 2003 (SI 2003/3034) |
| | para 18 | 27 Nov 2003 (W) (SI 2003/3034)[3] |
| | | 1 Apr 2004 (E) (SI 2003/2938, art 7) |
| | para 19 | 18 Nov 2003 (E) (SI 2003/2938, art 3) |
| | | 27 Nov 2003 (W) (SI 2003/3034) |
| | paras 20, 21 | 25 Nov 2004 (SI 2004/3132)[4] |
| | para 22 | 27 Nov 2003 (SI 2003/3034) |
| | para 23 | 18 Nov 2003 (E) (SI 2003/2938, art 3) |
| | | 27 Nov 2003 (W) (SI 2003/3034) |
| | para 24(1), (2) | 18 Sep 2003 (s 128(1)) |
| | para 24(3) | 25 Nov 2004 (E) (SI 2004/3132)[4] |
| | para 24(4) | 27 Nov 2003 (SI 2003/3034) |
| | para 24(5) | 18 Sep 2003 (s 128(1)) |
| | para 25(1) | 18 Sep 2003 (s 128(1)) |
| | para 25(2), (3) | 27 Nov 2003 (SI 2003/3034) |
| | para 25(4)–(6) | 25 Nov 2004 (SI 2004/3132)[4] |
| | para 26(1), (2) | 18 Nov 2003 (E) (SI 2003/2938) |
| | | 27 Nov 2003 (W) (SI 2003/3034) |
| | para 26(3) | 25 Nov 2004 (SI 2004/3132)[4] |
| | para 27 | 1 Apr 2004 (SI 2003/2938) |
| | para 28 | 18 Sep 2003 (s 128(1)) |
| | para 29 | 18 Nov 2003 (E) (so far as relates to the Local Government and Housing Act 1989, ss 45, 53) (SI 2003/2938)[1] |
| | | 27 Nov 2003 (W) (SI 2003/3034)[3] |
| | | 1 Apr 2004 (E) (otherwise) (SI 2003/2938)[1] |
| | para 30 | 18 Nov 2003 (E) (SI 2003/2938) |
| | | 27 Nov 2003 (W) (SI 2003/3034) |
| | para 31 | 18 Nov 2003 (SI 2003/2938)[1] |
| | para 32 | 27 Nov 2003 (W) (SI 2003/3034)[3] |
| | | 1 Apr 2004 (E) (SI 2003/2938) |
| | para 33(1) | 18 Sep 2003 (s 128(1)) |
| | para 33(2) | 1 Apr 2004 (SI 2003/2938)[1] |
| | para 33(3) | 18 Nov 2003 (E) (SI 2003/2938)[1] |
| | | 27 Nov 2003 (W) (SI 2003/3034)[3] |
| | para 33(4) | 1 Apr 2004 (SI 2003/2938)[1] |
| | para 33(5) | 18 Nov 2003 (E) (SI 2003/2938)[1] |
| | | 27 Nov 2003 (W) (SI 2003/3034)[3] |
| | paras 34, 35 | 18 Sep 2003 (s 128(1)) |
| | paras 36–39 | 18 Nov 2003 (SI 2003/2938)[1] |
| | para 40 | 18 Sep 2003 (s 128(1)) |
| | paras 41–48 | 18 Nov 2003 (s 128(2)) |
| | para 49(a) | 18 Nov 2003 (s 128(2)) |
| | para 49(b) | 27 Nov 2003 (SI 2003/3034) |
| | para 50(a) | 18 Nov 2003 (s 128(2)) |
| | para 50(b) | 27 Nov 2003 (SI 2003/3034) |
| | para 51(1) | 18 Sep 2003 (s 128(1)) |

**Local Government Act 2003 (c 26)**—*contd*

|  |  |  |
|---|---|---|
| | para 51(2) | 27 Nov 2003 (SI 2003/3034) |
| | para 51(3) | 27 Nov 2003 (W) (SI 2003/3034)[3] |
| | | 1 Apr 2004 (E) (SI 2003/2938) |
| | paras 52–54 | 18 Nov 2003 (s 128(2)) |
| | para 55 | 18 Sep 2003 (s 128(1)) |
| | para 56 | 27 Nov 2003 (SI 2003/3034) |
| | para 57 | 27 Nov 2003 (SI 2003/3034)[3] |
| | para 58 | 27 Nov 2003 (SI 2003/3034) |
| | para 59 | 18 Nov 2003 (E) (SI 2003/2938) |
| | | 27 Nov 2003 (W) (SI 2003/3034) |
| | para 60 | 18 Sep 2003 (s 128(1)) |
| | paras 61, 62 | 18 Nov 2003 (E) (SI 2003/2938) |
| | | 27 Nov 2003 (W) (SI 2003/3034) |
| | paras 63, 64 | 27 Nov 2003 (W) (SI 2003/3034)[3] |
| | | 1 Apr 2004 (E) (SI 2003/2938) |
| | para 65 | 18 Nov 2003 (SI 2003/2938) |
| | para 66(1) | 18 Nov 2003 (E) (SI 2003/2938) |
| | | 27 Nov 2003 (W) (SI 2003/3034) |
| | para 66(2) | 27 Nov 2003 (SI 2003/3034) |
| | para 66(3)–(6) | 18 Nov 2003 (E) (SI 2003/2938) |
| | | 27 Nov 2003 (W) (SI 2003/3034) |
| | para 67 | 27 Nov 2003 (SI 2003/3034)[3] |
| | paras 68, 69 | 18 Nov 2003 (SI 2003/2938) |
| | para 70 | 1 Apr 2004 (SI 2003/2938) |
| | para 71 | 1 Jan 2004 (so far as relates to the Greater London Authority Act 1999, ss 113, 115(2)) (SI 2003/2938)[1] |
| | | 1 Apr 2004 (otherwise) (SI 2003/2938)[1] |
| | paras 72–74 | 1 Apr 2004 (SI 2003/2938) |
| | paras 75–77 | 1 Jan 2004 (SI 2003/2938) |
| | para 78 | 1 Apr 2004 (SI 2003/2938)[1] |
| | para 79 | 27 Nov 2003 (SI 2003/3034)[3] |
| | para 80 | 18 Nov 2003 (SI 2003/2938) |
| | para 81 | 18 Nov 2003 (s 128(2)) |
| Sch 8 | Pt 1 | 18 Sep 2003 (s 128(1)), repeals of or in— |
| | | Fire Services Act 1947; |
| | | Fire Services Act 1959; |
| | | Local Government Finance Act 1988, Sch 9; |
| | | Local Government Finance Act 1992, Sch 13, para 80(1) |
| | | 18 Nov 2003 (s 128(2)), repeals of or in— |
| | | Local Government Act 1986; |
| | | Local Government Act 1988, s 28; |
| | | Local Government and Housing Act 1989, Sch 4, Pt 4; |
| | | Local Government Finance Act 1992, s 25; |
| | | Local Government (Wales) Act 1994, Sch 16, paras 96, 97; |
| | | Education Act 1996; |
| | | School Standards and Framework Act 1998; |
| | | Greater London Authority Act 1999, s 136(1); |
| | | Local Government Act 1999, s 31; |
| | | Local Government Act 2000 |
| | | 18 Nov 2003 (SI 2003/2938, art 2)[1], repeals of or in— |
| | | Social Security Administration Act 1992; |
| | | Social Security Administration (Fraud) Act 1997; |
| | | Greater London Authority Act 1999, s 52(7); |
| | | Local Government Act 1999, s 22(2); |
| | | Child Support, Pensions and Social Security Act 2000 |
| | | 18 Nov 2003 (E) (SI 2003/2938, art 3)[1], repeals of or in— |
| | | Housing Act 1985; |
| | | Local Government Act 1988, s 33; |

**Local Government Act 2003 (c 26)**—*contd*

    Local Government and Housing Act 1989, ss 45, 53, 80(3),
      Sch 5, para 37(2), Sch 11, para 97;

    Environmental Protection Act 1990;

    Local Government Finance Act 1992, s 11(3);

    Environment Act 1995, Sch 8, para 8(5);

    Greater London Authority Act 1999, s 108(2)

27 Nov 2003 (SI 2003/3034), repeals of or in—

    Local Government Act 1972, s 137(4C);

    Local Government Finance Act 1988, s 140(2);

    Local Government Finance Act 1992, s 69(1);

    Local Government (Wales) Act 1994, s 51(2)[3], Sch 15, para 30

27 Nov 2003 (W) (SI 2003/3034), repeals of or in—

    Local Government Act 1972, s 137(4AA);

    Stock Transfer Act 1982[3];

    Housing Act 1985;

    Local Government Act 1988, s 33;

    Local Government and Housing Act 1989, ss 39–66[3], 80[3],
      155(4)[3], Sch 3[3], Sch 5, paras 37(2), 60[3], Sch 11, paras 6[3], 7[3],
      59[3], 97;

    Environmental Protection Act 1990;

    Local Government Finance Act 1992, ss 11(3), 32(11)[3], 43(8)[3],
      50(6)[3], 52Z(3), Sch 13, para 90[3];

    Local Government (Wales) Act 1994, Sch 16, para 88[3];

    Police and Magistrates' Courts Act 1994[3];

    Environment Act 1995, s 73[3], Sch 8, para 8(5), Sch 10,
      para 31(2)[3];

    Police Act 1996[3];

    Local Government Finance (Supplementary Credit Approvals)
      Act 1997[3];

    Government of Wales Act 1998, s 81(4)[3];

    Access to Justice Act 1999[3];

    Criminal Justice and Police Act 2001[3];

    Rating (Former Agricultural Premises and Rural Shops)
      Act 2001

1 Jan 2004 (repeals of or in Greater London Authority Act 1999,
    ss 113, 115(2), 122(3)(b), (6)(b), 124(4)(b)) (SI 2003/2938,
    art 4)[1]

1 Apr 2004 (SI 2003/2938, art 6)[1], repeals of or in—

    Local Government and Housing Act 1989, Sch 4, Pt 1, item 5,
      Pt 2, item 4;

    Greater London Authority Act 1999, ss 111, 112, 114,
      115(1), (3), 116–118, 119(1), (3)(b)

1 Apr 2004 (E) (SI 2003/2938, art 7)[1], repeals of or in—

    Local Government Act 1972, s 137(4AA);

    Stock Transfer Act 1982;

    Local Government and Housing Act 1989, ss 39–44, 46–52,
      54–66, 80(2), 155(4), Sch 3, Sch 5, para 60, Sch 11, paras 6, 7,
      59;

    Local Government Finance Act 1992, ss 32(11), 43(8), 50(6),
      Sch 13, para 90;

    Police and Magistrates' Courts Act 1994;

    Environment Act 1995, s 73, Sch 10, para 31(2);

    Police Act 1996;

    Local Government Finance (Supplementary Credit Approvals)
      Act 1997;

    Access to Justice Act 1999;

    Criminal Justice and Police Act 2001

25 Nov 2004 (repeals in Local Government Finance Act 1992,
    Sch 10, Sch 13, para 84) (SI 2004/3132)[4]

**Local Government Act 2003 (c 26)**—*contd*

|  |  |
|--|--|
|  | 1 Apr 2005 (E) (repeal in Rating (Former Agricultural Premises and Rural Shops) Act 2001) (SI 2004/3132) |
|  | *Not yet in force*, repeals of or in— |
|  | Local Government Finance Act 1988, ss 53(4A), 143, Sch 6; |
|  | Local Government and Housing Act 1989, Sch 5, para 38; |
|  | Ports Act 1991; |
|  | Local Government and Rating Act 1997 |
| Pt 2 | 18 Nov 2003 (except revocation in National Assembly for Wales (Transfer of Functions) Order 1999, SI 1999/672) (SI 2003/2938, art 2)[1] |
|  | 27 Nov 2003 (revocation in National Assembly for Wales (Transfer of Functions) Order 1999, SI 1999/672) (SI 2003/3034)[3] |

[1]   For transitional provisions and savings, see SI 2003/2938, art 8, Schedule

[2]   For transitional provisions and savings, see SI 2003/3034, art 3, Sch 2

[3]   For the purpose of and in relation to financial years beginning on or after 1 Apr 2004

[4]   For savings, see SI 2004/3132, art 4

[5]   For savings, see SI 2006/3339, art 3

---

**Local Government in Scotland Act 2003 (asp 1)**

*RA:* 11 Feb 2003

*Commencement provisions:* s 62(2); Local Government in Scotland Act 2003 (Commencement No 1) Order 2003, SSI 2003/134; Local Government in Scotland Act 2003 (Commencement No 2) Order 2004, SSI 2004/28; Local Government in Scotland Act 2003 (Commencement No 3) Order 2006, SSI 2006/89; Local Government in Scotland Act 2003 (Commencement No 4) Order 2009, SSI 2009/275; Local Government in Scotland Act 2003 (Commencement No 5 and Saving) Order 2010, SSI 2010/119

| | | |
|--|--|--|
| 1–7 | | 1 Apr 2003 (SSI 2003/134) |
| 8 | (1) | 1 Apr 2003 (SSI 2003/134) |
| | (2)(a)(i)–(iv) | 1 Apr 2003 (SSI 2003/134) |
| | (2)(a)(v) | 1 Apr 2003 (in so far as it repeals words following s 1(1)(d) of the Local Authorities (Goods and Services) Act 1970) (SSI 2003/134) |
| | | *Not yet in force* (in so far as it repeals Local Authorities (Goods and Services) Act 1970, s 1(1)(d)) |
| | (2)(b) | 1 Apr 2003 (SSI 2003/134) |
| | (2)(c)(i) | 1 Apr 2003 (SSI 2003/134) |
| | (2)(c)(ii) | *Not yet in force* |
| | (2)(c)(iii), (iv) | 1 Apr 2003 (SSI 2003/134) |
| | (2)(d)(i) | 1 Apr 2003 (in so far as it repeals definition "public body" in s 1(4) of the Local Authorities (Goods and Services Act 1970)) (SSI 2003/134) |
| | | *Not yet in force* (in so far as it repeals definition "works of maintenance" in the Local Authorities (Goods and Services) Act 1970, s 1(4)) |
| | (2)(d)(ii) | 1 Apr 2003 (SSI 2003/134) |
| | (2)(e) | 1 Apr 2003 (SSI 2003/134) |
| | (3) | 1 Apr 2003 (SSI 2003/134) |
| 9 | | *Not yet in force* |
| 10 | | 1 Apr 2003 (SSI 2003/134) |
| 11 | | 20 Apr 2010 (for the purpose of conferring power to make regulations) (SI 2010/119) |
| | | 1 Jun 2010 (otherwise) (SI 2010/119)[1] |
| 12–34 | | 1 Apr 2003 (SSI 2003/134) |
| 35 | (1) | 1 Apr 2003 (SSI 2003/134) |

**Local Government in Scotland Act 2003 (asp 1)**—*contd*

|        |         |                                |
|--------|---------|--------------------------------|
|        | (2)–(4) | 30 Jan 2004 (SSI 2004/28)      |
| 36     |         | 30 Jan 2004 (SSI 2004/28)      |
| 37–39  |         | 1 Apr 2003 (SSI 2003/134)      |
| 40     |         | 8 Sep 2009 (SSI 2009/275)      |
| 41     |         | 1 Apr 2003 (SSI 2003/134)      |
| 42     | (1)     | 16 Feb 2001 (s 42(2))          |
|        | (2)     | 11 Feb 2003 (RA)               |
|        | (3)     | 1 Apr 2003 (SSI 2003/134)      |
| 43–46  |         | 1 Apr 2003 (SSI 2003/134)      |
| 47     | (1)     | 3 Jul 2006 (SSI 2006/89)       |
|        | (2)–(6) | 20 Mar 2006 (SSI 2006/89)      |
|        | (7)     | 3 Jul 2006 (SSI 2006/89)       |
| 48, 49 |         | 1 Apr 2003 (SSI 2003/134)      |
| 50     |         | 11 Feb 2003 (RA)               |
| 51–59  |         | 1 Apr 2003 (SSI 2003/134)      |
| 60     | (1)(a)  | 1 Apr 2003 (SSI 2003/134)      |
|        | (1)(b)  | 1 Apr 2004 (SSI 2004/28)       |
|        | (1)(c)–(f) | 1 Apr 2003 (SSI 2003/134)   |
|        | (1)(g)  | 1 May 2003 (SSI 2003/134)      |
|        | (1)(h)–(j) | 1 Apr 2003 (SSI 2003/134)   |
|        | (2), (3) | 1 Apr 2003 (SSI 2003/134)     |
| 61     |         | 1 Apr 2003 (SSI 2003/134)      |
| 62     |         | 11 Feb 2003 (RA)               |

[1]   For a saving, see SI 2010/119, art 4

**Marine Safety Act 2003 (c 16)**

*RA:* 10 Jul 2003

*Commencement provisions:* s 4

Whole Act in force 10 Sep 2003 (s 4)

**Mental Health (Care and Treatment) (Scotland) Act 2003 (asp 13)**

*RA:* 25 Apr 2003

*Commencement provisions:* s 333(2)–(4); Mental Health (Care and Treatment) (Scotland) Act 2003 (Commencement No 1) Order 2003, SSI 2003/316; Mental Health (Care and Treatment) (Scotland) Act 2003 (Commencement No 2) Order 2004, SSI 2004/153; Mental Health (Care and Treatment) (Scotland) Act 2003 (Commencement No 3) Order 2004, SSI 2004/367; Mental Health (Care and Treatment) (Scotland) Act 2003 (Commencement No 4) Order 2005, SSI 2005/161, as amended by SSI 2005/375, SSI 2005/459

|        |          |                                                                            |
|--------|----------|----------------------------------------------------------------------------|
| 1–3    |          | 5 Oct 2005 (SSI 2005/161)                                                  |
| 4      | (1), (2) | 5 Oct 2005 (SSI 2005/161)                                                  |
|        | (3)      | See Sch 1 below                                                            |
| 5–14   |          | 5 Oct 2005 (SSI 2005/161)                                                  |
| 15     |          | 21 Mar 2005 (for the purpose of enabling regulations to be made) (SSI 2005/161) |
|        |          | 5 Oct 2005 (otherwise) (SSI 2005/161)                                      |
| 16     |          | 5 Oct 2005 (SSI 2005/161)                                                  |
| 17     |          | 21 Mar 2005 (for the purpose of enabling regulations to be made) (SSI 2005/161) |
|        |          | 5 Oct 2005 (otherwise) (SSI 2005/161)                                      |
| 18–20  |          | 5 Oct 2005 (SSI 2005/161)                                                  |
| 21     | (1)      | 3 May 2004 (SSI 2004/153)                                                  |
|        | (2)      | 5 Oct 2005 (SSI 2005/161)                                                  |

**Mental Health (Care and Treatment) (Scotland) Act 2003 (asp 13)**—*contd*

| | | |
|---|---|---|
| | (3) | 3 May 2004 (SSI 2004/153) |
| | (4) | See Sch 2 below |
| 22 | | 21 Mar 2005 (for the purpose of enabling directions to be made and medical practitioners to be approved) (SSI 2005/161) |
| | | 5 Oct 2005 (otherwise) (SSI 2005/161) |
| 23–31 | | 5 Oct 2005 (SSI 2005/161) |
| 32 | | 21 Mar 2005 (for the purpose of enabling directions to be made) (SSI 2005/161) |
| | | 5 Oct 2005 (otherwise) (SSI 2005/161) |
| 33–35 | | 5 Oct 2005 (SSI 2005/161) |
| 36 | | 21 Mar 2005 (for the purpose of enabling regulations to be made) (SSI 2005/161) |
| | | 5 Oct 2005 (otherwise) (SSI 2005/161) |
| 37–43 | | 5 Oct 2005 (SSI 2005/161) |
| 44 | | 21 Mar 2005 (for the purpose of enabling regulations to be made) (SSI 2005/161) |
| | | 5 Oct 2005 (otherwise) (SSI 2005/161) |
| 45, 46 | | 5 Oct 2005 (SSI 2005/161) |
| 47 | | 21 Mar 2005 (for the purpose of enabling regulations to be made) (SSI 2005/161) |
| | | 5 Oct 2005 (otherwise) (SSI 2005/161) |
| 48–57 | | 5 Oct 2005 (SSI 2005/161) |
| 58 | | 21 Mar 2005 (for the purpose of enabling regulations to be made) (SSI 2005/161) |
| | | 5 Oct 2005 (otherwise) (SSI 2005/161) |
| 59–63 | | 5 Oct 2005 (SSI 2005/161) |
| 64 | | 21 Mar 2005 (for the purpose of enabling regulations to be made) (SSI 2005/161) |
| | | 5 Oct 2005 (otherwise) (SSI 2005/161) |
| 65 | | 5 Oct 2005 (SSI 2005/161) |
| 66 | | 21 Mar 2005 (for the purpose of enabling regulations to be made) (SSI 2005/161) |
| | | 5 Oct 2005 (otherwise) (SSI 2005/161) |
| 67–75 | | 5 Oct 2005 (SSI 2005/161) |
| 76 | | 21 Mar 2005 (for the purpose of enabling regulations to be made) (SSI 2005/161) |
| | | 5 Oct 2005 (otherwise) (SSI 2005/161) |
| 77–86 | | 5 Oct 2005 (SSI 2005/161) |
| 87 | | 21 Mar 2005 (for the purpose of enabling regulations to be made) (SSI 2005/161) |
| | | 5 Oct 2005 (otherwise) (SSI 2005/161) |
| 88–91 | | 5 Oct 2005 (SSI 2005/161) |
| 92 | | 21 Mar 2005 (for the purpose of enabling regulations to be made) (SSI 2005/161) |
| | | 5 Oct 2005 (otherwise) (SSI 2005/161) |
| 93, 94 | | 5 Oct 2005 (SSI 2005/161) |
| 95, 96 | | 21 Mar 2005 (for the purpose of enabling regulations to be made) (SSI 2005/161) |
| | | 5 Oct 2005 (otherwise) (SSI 2005/161) |
| 97–100 | | 5 Oct 2005 (SSI 2005/161) |
| 101 | (1) | 5 Oct 2005 (SSI 2005/161) |
| | (2)(a) | 5 Oct 2005 (SSI 2005/161) |
| | (2)(b) | *Never in force* (substituted) |
| 102–108 | | 5 Oct 2005 (SSI 2005/161) |
| 109 | | 21 Mar 2005 (for the purpose of enabling regulations to be made) (SSI 2005/161) |
| | | 5 Oct 2005 (otherwise) (SSI 2005/161) |
| 110–132 | | 5 Oct 2005 (SSI 2005/161) |
| 133, 134 | | 21 Mar 2005 (for the purpose of enabling regulations to be made) (SSI 2005/161) |

**Mental Health (Care and Treatment) (Scotland) Act 2003 (asp 13)**—*contd*

|  |  |
|---|---|
|  | 5 Oct 2005 (otherwise) (SSI 2005/161) |
| 135, 136 | 5 Oct 2005 (SSI 2005/161) |
| 137 | 21 Mar 2005 (for the purpose of enabling regulations to be made) (SSI 2005/161) |
|  | 5 Oct 2005 (otherwise) (SSI 2005/161) |
| 138–148 | 5 Oct 2005 (SSI 2005/161) |
| 149 | 21 Mar 2005 (for the purpose of enabling regulations to be made) (SSI 2005/161) |
|  | 5 Oct 2005 (otherwise) (SSI 2005/161) |
| 150–152 | 5 Oct 2005 (SSI 2005/161) |
| 153 | 21 Mar 2005 (for the purpose of enabling regulations to be made) (SSI 2005/161) |
|  | 5 Oct 2005 (otherwise) (SSI 2005/161) |
| 154–157 | 5 Oct 2005 (SSI 2005/161) |
| 158 | 21 Mar 2005 (for the purpose of enabling regulations to be made) (SSI 2005/161) |
|  | 5 Oct 2005 (otherwise) (SSI 2005/161) |
| 159, 160 | 5 Oct 2005 (SSI 2005/161) |
| 161 | 21 Mar 2005 (for the purpose of enabling regulations to be made) (SSI 2005/161) |
|  | 5 Oct 2005 (otherwise) (SSI 2005/161) |
| 162–172 | 5 Oct 2005 (SSI 2005/161) |
| 173 | 21 Mar 2005 (for the purpose of enabling regulations to be made) (SSI 2005/161) |
|  | 5 Oct 2005 (otherwise) (SSI 2005/161) |
| 174–190 | 5 Oct 2005 (SSI 2005/161) |
| 191 | 21 Mar 2005 (for the purpose of enabling regulations to be made) (SSI 2005/161) |
|  | 5 Oct 2005 (otherwise) (SSI 2005/161) |
| 192–230 | 5 Oct 2005 (SSI 2005/161) |
| 231 | 21 Mar 2005 (for the purpose of enabling regulations to be made) (SSI 2005/161) |
|  | 5 Oct 2005 (otherwise) (SSI 2005/161) |
| 232 | 5 Oct 2005 (SSI 2005/161) |
| 233 | 21 Mar 2005 (for the purpose of enabling regulations to be made, compiling lists of medical practitioners and requiring those medical practitioners to undertake training) (SSI 2005/161) |
|  | 5 Oct 2005 (otherwise) (SSI 2005/161) |
| 234 | 21 Mar 2005 (for the purpose of enabling regulations to be made) (SSI 2005/161) |
|  | 5 Oct 2005 (otherwise) (SSI 2005/161) |
| 235, 236 | 5 Oct 2005 (SSI 2005/161) |
| 237 | 21 Mar 2005 (for the purpose of enabling regulations to be made) (SSI 2005/161) |
|  | 5 Oct 2005 (otherwise) (SSI 2005/161) |
| 238, 239 | 5 Oct 2005 (SSI 2005/161) |
| 240 | 21 Mar 2005 (for the purpose of enabling orders and regulations to be made) (SSI 2005/161) |
|  | 5 Oct 2005 (otherwise) (SSI 2005/161) |
| 241–243 | 5 Oct 2005 (SSI 2005/161) |
| 244–246 | 21 Mar 2005 (for the purpose of enabling regulations to be made) (SSI 2005/161) |
|  | 5 Oct 2005 (otherwise) (SSI 2005/161) |
| 247–249 | 5 Oct 2005 (SSI 2005/161) |
| 250 | 1 Sep 2004 (for the purpose of enabling regulations to be made) (SSI 2004/367) |
|  | 4 Oct 2004 (otherwise) (SSI 2004/367) |
| 251, 252 | 5 Oct 2005 (SSI 2005/161) |
| 253 | 1 Sep 2004 (for the purpose of enabling regulations to be made) (SSI 2004/367) |

**Mental Health (Care and Treatment) (Scotland) Act 2003 (asp 13)**—*contd*

| | |
|---|---|
| | 4 Oct 2004 (otherwise) (SSI 2004/367) |
| 254, 255 | 5 Oct 2005 (SSI 2005/161) |
| 256 | 21 Mar 2005 (for the purpose of enabling regulations to be made) (SSI 2005/161) |
| | 5 Oct 2005 (otherwise) (SSI 2005/161) |
| 257 | 5 Oct 2005 (SSI 2005/161) |
| 258 | 1 Sep 2004 (SSI 2004/367) |
| 259 | 5 Oct 2005 (SSI 2005/161) |
| 260 | 21 Mar 2005 (for the purpose of enabling regulations to be made) (SSI 2005/161) |
| | 5 Oct 2005 (otherwise) (SSI 2005/161) |
| 261–263 | 5 Oct 2005 (SSI 2005/161) |
| 264–267 | 1 May 2006[1] (s 333(2)) |
| 268 | 6 Jan 2006 (for the purpose of enabling regulations to be made) (SSI 2005/161) |
| | 1 May 2006[1] (otherwise) (s 333(2)) |
| 269–272 | 1 May 2006[1] (s 333(2)) |
| 273 | 6 Jan 2006 (for the purpose of enabling regulations to be made) (SSI 2005/161) |
| | 1 May 2006[1] (otherwise) (s 333(2)) |
| 274 | 26 Mar 2004 (SSI 2004/153) |
| 275 | 1 Sep 2004 (for the purpose of enabling regulations to be made) (SSI 2004/367) |
| | 4 Oct 2004 (otherwise) (SSI 2004/367) |
| 276–278 | 5 Oct 2005 (SSI 2005/161) |
| 279 | 21 Mar 2005 (for the purpose of enabling regulations to be made) (SSI 2005/161) |
| | 5 Oct 2005 (otherwise) (SSI 2005/161) |
| 280 | 5 Oct 2005 (SSI 2005/161) |
| 281–284 | 21 Mar 2005 (for the purpose of enabling regulations to be made) (SSI 2005/161) |
| | 5 Oct 2005 (otherwise) (SSI 2005/161) |
| 285 | 21 Mar 2005 (for the purpose of enabling directions to be made) (SSI 2005/161) |
| | 5 Oct 2005 (otherwise) (SSI 2005/161) |
| 286 | 21 Mar 2005 (for the purpose of enabling directions and regulations to be made) (SSI 2005/161) |
| | 5 Oct 2005 (otherwise) (SSI 2005/161) |
| 287, 288 | 5 Oct 2005 (SSI 2005/161) |
| 289, 290 | 21 Mar 2005 (for the purpose of enabling regulations to be made) (SSI 2005/161) |
| | 5 Oct 2005 (otherwise) (SSI 2005/161) |
| 291, 292 | 5 Oct 2005 (SSI 2005/161) |
| 293 | 21 Mar 2005 (for the purpose of enabling regulations to be made) (SSI 2005/161) |
| | 5 Oct 2005 (otherwise) (SSI 2005/161) |
| 294 | 5 Oct 2005 (SSI 2005/161) |
| 295 | 21 Mar 2005 (for the purpose of enabling regulations to be made) (SSI 2005/161) |
| | 5 Oct 2005 (otherwise) (SSI 2005/161) |
| 296, 297 | 5 Oct 2005 (SSI 2005/161) |
| 298, 299 | 21 Mar 2005 (for the purpose of enabling regulations to be made) (SSI 2005/161) |
| | 5 Oct 2005 (otherwise) (SSI 2005/161) |
| 300–308 | 5 Oct 2005 (SSI 2005/161) |
| 309, 310 | 21 Mar 2005 (for the purpose of enabling regulations to be made) (SSI 2005/161) |
| | 5 Oct 2005 (otherwise) (SSI 2005/161) |
| 311, 312 | 5 Oct 2005 (SSI 2005/161) |

**Mental Health (Care and Treatment) (Scotland) Act 2003 (asp 13)**—*contd*

| | | |
|---|---|---|
| 313 | | 21 Mar 2005 (for the purpose of enabling regulations to be made) (SSI 2005/161) |
| | | 5 Oct 2005 (otherwise) (SSI 2005/161) |
| 314–323 | | 5 Oct 2005 (SSI 2005/161) |
| 324 | | 21 Mar 2005 (for the purpose of enabling regulations to be made) (SSI 2005/161) |
| | | 5 Oct 2005 (otherwise) (SSI 2005/161) |
| 325, 326 | | 25 Apr 2003 (RA) |
| 327 | | 21 Mar 2005 (SSI 2005/161) |
| 328 | | 5 Oct 2005 (SSI 2005/161) |
| 329 | | 26 Mar 2004 (SSI 2004/153) |
| 330 | | 25 Apr 2003 (RA) |
| 331 | (1) | See Sch 4 below |
| | (2) | See Sch 5, Pt 1 below |
| | (3) | See Sch 5, Pt 2 below |
| 332, 333 | | 25 Apr 2003 (RA) |
| Sch 1 | paras 1, 2 | 5 Oct 2005 (SSI 2005/161) |
| | para 3 | 21 Mar 2005 (for the purpose of enabling orders and regulations to be made) (SSI 2005/161) |
| | | 5 Oct 2005 (otherwise) (SSI 2005/161) |
| | paras 4–7 | 5 Oct 2005 (SSI 2005/161) |
| | para 8 | 21 Mar 2005 (for the purpose of enabling regulations to be made) (SSI 2005/161) |
| | | 5 Oct 2005 (otherwise) (SSI 2005/161) |
| | para 9 | 5 Oct 2005 (SSI 2005/161) |
| | para 10 | 1 Jul 2003 (SSI 2003/316) |
| Sch 2 | para 1(1) | 26 Mar 2004 (for the purpose of enabling regulations to be made) (SSI 2004/153) |
| | | 1 Sep 2004 (otherwise) (SSI 2004/367) |
| | para 1(2)(a), (b) | 3 May 2004 (SSI 2004/153) |
| | para 1(2)(c) | 26 Mar 2004 (for the purpose of enabling regulations to be made) (SSI 2004/153) |
| | | 3 May 2004 (otherwise) (SSI 2004/153) |
| | para 2 | 5 Oct 2005 (SSI 2005/161) |
| | para 3(1), (2) | 3 May 2004 (SSI 2004/153) |
| | para 3(3) | 26 Mar 2004 (for the purpose of enabling regulations to be made) (SSI 2004/153) |
| | | 3 May 2004 (otherwise) (SSI 2004/153) |
| | para 3(4)–(7) | 3 May 2004 (SSI 2004/153) |
| | paras 4–13 | 3 May 2004 (SSI 2004/153) |
| | para 14 | 5 Oct 2005 (SSI 2005/161) |
| | paras 15, 16 | 3 May 2004 (SSI 2004/153) |
| Sch 3 | | 5 Oct 2005 (SSI 2005/161) |
| Sch 4 | paras 1–9 | 5 Oct 2005 (SSI 2005/161) |
| | para 10(a) | *Not yet in force* |
| | para 10(b) | 5 Oct 2005 (SSI 2005/161) |
| | paras 11–13 | 5 Oct 2005 (SSI 2005/161) |
| Sch 5 | Pt 1 | 5 Oct 2005 (except repeals of or in Regulation of Care (Scotland) Act 2001, ss 2(5)(b), 77) (SSI 2005/161) |
| | | *Not yet in force* (exception noted above) |
| | Pt 2 | 5 Oct 2005 (SSI 2005/161) |
| Sch 6 | | 25 Apr 2003 (RA) |

---

[1]   S 333(2) provides that Chapter 3 of Pt 17 comes into force on 1 May 2006 or on such day or days before then as the Scottish Ministers may by order appoint

---

## National Galleries of Scotland Act 2003 (asp 16)

*RA:* 1 May 2003

*Commencement provisions:* s 3(2)

Whole Act in force 8 May 2003 (s 3(2))

---

## National Lottery (Funding of Endowments) Act 2003 (c 23)

*RA:* 18 Sep 2003

Whole Act in force 18 Sep 2003 (RA)

---

## National Minimum Wage (Enforcement Notices) Act 2003 (c 8)

*RA:* 8 May 2003

*Commencement provisions:* s 2(2)

Whole Act in force 8 Jul 2003 (s 2(2))

---

## Northern Ireland Assembly Elections Act 2003 (c 3)

*RA:* 20 Mar 2003

Whole Act in force 20 Mar 2003 (RA)

---

## Northern Ireland Assembly (Elections and Periods of Suspension) Act 2003 (c 12)

*RA:* 15 May 2003

Whole Act in force 15 May 2003 (RA)

---

## Northern Ireland (Monitoring Commission etc) Act 2003 (c 25)

*RA:* 18 Sep 2003

*Commencement provisions:* s 12(2); Northern Ireland (Monitoring Commission etc) Act 2003 (Commencement No 1) Order 2003, SI 2003/2646; Northern Ireland (Monitoring Commission etc) Act 2003 (Commencement No 2) Order 2004, SI 2004/83

| | |
|---|---|
| 1 | 13 Oct 2003 (SI 2003/2646) |
| 2–11 | 7 Jan 2004 (SI 2004/83) |
| 12 | 18 Sep 2003 (RA) |

---

## Police (Northern Ireland) Act 2003 (c 6)

*RA:* 8 Apr 2003

*Commencement provisions:* ss 4(3), 6(12), 7(8), 8(6), 9(9), 10(5), 11(5), 12(5), 15(6), 16(2), 19(2), 26(4), 29(2), (3), 41(2), 42(6), Sch 4, paras 1, 2; Police (Northern Ireland) Act 2003 (Commencement) Order 2004, SR 2004/501; Police (Northern Ireland) Act 2003 (Commencement No 2) Order 2007, SR 2007/177; Police (Northern Ireland) Act 2003 (Commencement No 3) Order 2007, SR 2007/371

| | | |
|---|---|---|
| 1–3 | | 8 Apr 2003 (RA) |
| 4 | (1) | 8 Apr 2003 (with effect in relation to years ending on or after 8 Apr 2003) (s 4(3)) |
| | (2), (3) | 8 Apr 2003 (RA) |
| 5 | | 8 Apr 2003 (RA) |

**Police (Northern Ireland) Act 2003 (c 6)**—*contd*

| | | |
|---|---|---|
| 6 | (1)–(11) | 8 Apr 2003 (with effect in relation to financial years ending on or after 31 Mar 2004) (s 6(12)) |
| | (12) | 8 Apr 2003 (RA) |
| 7 | (1)–(7) | 8 Apr 2003 (with effect in relation to financial years ending on or after 31 Mar 2004) (s 7(8)) |
| | (8) | 8 Apr 2003 (RA) |
| 8 | (1)–(5) | 8 Apr 2003 (with effect in relation to financial years ending on or after 31 Mar 2004) (s 8(6)) |
| | (6) | 8 Apr 2003 (RA) |
| 9 | (1)–(8) | 8 Apr 2003 (with effect in relation to financial years ending on or after 31 Mar 2004) (s 9(9)) |
| | (9) | 8 Apr 2003 (RA) |
| 10 | (1)–(4) | 8 Apr 2003 (with effect in accordance with s 10(5)) (s 10(5)) |
| | (5) | 8 Apr 2003 (RA) |
| 11 | (1)–(4) | 8 Apr 2003 (with effect in accordance with s 11(5)) (s 11(5)) |
| | (5) | 8 Apr 2003 (RA) |
| 12 | (1)–(4) | 8 Apr 2003 (with effect in relation to meetings under Police (Northern Ireland) Act 2000, Sch 1, para 18 called on or after 8 Apr 2003) (s 12(5)) |
| | (5) | 8 Apr 2003 (RA) |
| 13, 14 | | 8 Apr 2003 (RA) |
| 15 | (1)–(5) | 4 Sep 2007 (SR 2007/371) |
| | (6) | 8 Apr 2003 (RA) |
| 16 | (1) | 4 Sep 2007 (SR 2007/371) |
| | (2) | 8 Apr 2003 (RA) |
| 17, 18 | | 8 Apr 2003 (RA) |
| 19 | (1) | See Sch 1 below |
| | (2) | 8 Apr 2003 (RA) |
| 20–25 | | 8 Apr 2003 (RA) |
| 26 | (1)–(3) | 15 Dec 2004 (SR 2004/501) |
| | (4) | 8 Apr 2003 (RA) |
| 27, 28 | | 8 Apr 2003 (RA) |
| 29 | (1) | 8 Apr 2003 (with effect for the purposes of s 59 of the Police (Northern Ireland) Act 2000 in accordance with s 10(5) of this Act, and, for the purposes of s 60 of the 2000 Act, in accordance with s 11(5) of this Act) (s 29(2), (3)) |
| | (2), (3) | 8 Apr 2003 (RA) |
| 30, 31 | | 8 Apr 2003 (RA) |
| 32 | (1) | See Sch 3 below |
| | (2) | 8 Apr 2003 (RA) |
| 33–40 | | 8 Apr 2003 (RA) |
| 41 | (1) | 1 Mar 2007 (SR 2007/177) |
| | (2) | 8 Apr 2003 (RA) |
| 42 | (1)–(5) | 1 Mar 2007 (SR 2007/177) |
| | (6) | 8 Apr 2003 (RA) |
| 43, 44 | | 8 Apr 2003 (RA) |
| 45 | | See Sch 4 below |
| 46, 47 | | 8 Apr 2003 (RA) |
| Sch 1 | | 4 Sep 2007 (SR 2007/371) |
| Schs 2, 3 | | 8 Apr 2003 (RA) |
| Sch 4 | | 8 Apr 2003 (RA), repeals of or in— Police (Northern Ireland) Act 1998; Police (Northern Ireland) Act 2000, ss 25(2), 32(4), (5), 63(1), Sch 1 |
| | | 8 Apr 2003 (repeals of or in Police (Northern Ireland) Act 2000, s 28(5), with effect in relation to financial years ending on or after 31 Mar 2004) (Sch 24, para 1) |
| | | *Not yet in force*, revocations of or in— Employment Rights (Northern Ireland) Order 1996, SI 1996/1919 (NI 16), art 243(1); |

**Police (Northern Ireland) Act 2003 (c 6)**—*contd*

Public Interest Disclosure (Northern Ireland) Order 1998,
SI 1998/1763 (NI 17), art 16

**Protection of Children (Scotland) Act 2003 (asp 5)**

*RA:* 19 Mar 2003

*Commencement provisions:* s 22(2), (3); Protection of Children (Scotland) Act 2003 (Commencement No 1) Order 2004, SSI 2004/522, as amended by SSI 2004/556

| | | |
|---|---|---|
| 1–10 | | 10 Jan 2005 (SSI 2004/522) |
| 11 | (1), (2) | 10 Jan 2005 (SSI 2004/522) |
| | (3)(a) | 11 Apr 2005 (SSI 2004/522) |
| | (3)(b) | *Never in force* (repealed) |
| | (4)–(7) | 10 Jan 2005 (SSI 2004/522) |
| 12–20 | | 10 Jan 2005 (SSI 2004/522) |
| 21, 22 | | 19 Mar 2003 (RA) |
| Schs 1, 2 | | 10 Jan 2005 (SSI 2004/522) |

**Public Appointments and Public Bodies etc (Scotland) Act 2003 (asp 4)**

*RA:* 11 Mar 2003

*Commencement provisions:* s 21(2), (3); Public Appointments and Public Bodies etc (Scotland) Act 2003 (Commencement No 1) Order 2003, SSI 2003/219; Public Appointments and Public Bodies etc (Scotland) Act 2003 (Commencement No 2) Order 2003, SSI 2003/348; Public Appointments and Public Bodies etc (Scotland) Act 2003 (Commencement No 3) Order 2003, SSI 2003/384; Public Appointments and Public Bodies etc (Scotland) Act 2003 (Commencement No 4) Order 2003, SSI 2003/602, as amended by SSI 2004/45; Public Appointments and Public Bodies etc (Scotland) Act 2003 (Commencement No 5) Order 2004, SSI 2004/148; Public Appointments and Public Bodies etc (Scotland) Act 2003 (Commencement No 6) Order 2004, SSI 2004/198; Public Appointments and Public Bodies etc (Scotland) Act 2003 (Commencement No 3) Order 2004, SSI 2004/232

| | | |
|---|---|---|
| 1 | (1) | 1 Jun 2004 (SSI 2004/232) |
| | (2) | See Sch 1 below |
| 2 | (1)(a) | See Sch 2 below |
| | (1)(b) | 1 Jun 2004 (SSI 2004/232) |
| | (2)–(10) | 1 Jun 2004 (SSI 2004/232) |
| 3 | | 1 Jun 2004 (SSI 2004/232) |
| 4 | (a), (b) | 31 May 2003 (SSI 2003/219) |
| | (c) | 6 May 2004 (SSI 2004/198) |
| | (d) | 1 Apr 2004 (SSI 2004/148) |
| | (e) | 15 Aug 2003 (SSI 2003/384) |
| 5 | (1) | 12 Feb 2004 (for the purpose of the transfer to and vesting in Health Boards of the property comprised in the main transfer of Trust property (as defined in the Scottish Hospital Trust (Transfer of Property) Regulations 2004, SSI 2004/46)) (SSI 2003/602) |
| | | 31 Mar 2004 (otherwise) (SSI 2003/602) |
| | (2)–(6) | 1 Jan 2004 (SSI 2003/602) |
| 6 | | 12 Feb 2004 (SSI 2003/602) |
| 7 | (1)–(7) | 12 Feb 2004 (SSI 2003/602) |
| | (8) | 1 Jan 2004 (SSI 2003/602) |
| 8 | | 1 Jan 2004 (SSI 2003/602) |
| 9, 10 | | 12 Feb 2004 (SSI 2003/602) |
| 11–14 | | 15 Aug 2003 (SSI 2003/384) |
| 15 | (1) | 1 Jun 2003 (SSI 2003/219) |
| | (2) | See Sch 3 below |
| 16 | | 1 Jun 2003 (SSI 2003/219) |

**Public Appointments and Public Bodies etc (Scotland) Act 2003 (asp 4)**—*contd*

| | | |
|---|---|---|
| 17 | | See Sch 4 below |
| 18–21 | | 11 Mar 2003 (RA)[1] |
| Schs 1, 2 | | 1 Jun 2004 (SSI 2004/232) |
| Sch 3 | | 1 Jun 2003 (SSI 2003/219)[2] |
| Sch 4 | para 1 | 15 Aug 2003 (SSI 2003/384) |
| | para 2 | 31 May 2003 (SSI 2003/219) |
| | para 3(a) | 1 Apr 2004 (SSI 2004/148) |
| | para 3(b) | 15 Aug 2003 (SSI 2003/384) |
| | para 4(a), (b) | 31 May 2003 (SSI 2003/219) |
| | para 4(c) | 6 Feb 2004 (SSI 2003/602) |
| | para 4(d) | 1 Apr 2004 (SSI 2004/148) |
| | para 4(e) | 15 Aug 2003 (SSI 2003/384) |
| | para 5(1) | *Not yet in force* |
| | para 5(2) | 1 Apr 2004 (SSI 2004/148) |
| | para 5(3) | 6 May 2004 (SSI 2004/198) |
| | para 5(4)–(9) | *Never in force* (repealed) |
| | para 5(10)–(13) | 1 Apr 2004 (SSI 2004/148) |
| | para 5(14) | 1 Apr 2004 (entry relating to the Medical Practices Committee) (SSI 2004/148) |
| | | *Not yet in force* (entry relating to the Hospital Trust) |
| | para 5(15) | 6 Feb 2004 (SSI 2003/602) |
| | para 5(16) | 1 Apr 2004 (SSI 2004/148) |
| | para 5(17) | 6 May 2004 (SSI 2004/198) |
| | para 5(18) | 1 Apr 2004 (SSI 2004/148) |
| | para 6 | 31 May 2003 (SSI 2003/219) |
| | para 7 | 15 Aug 2003 (SSI 2003/384) |
| | para 8 | *Not yet in force* |
| | para 9 | 15 Aug 2003 (SSI 2003/384) |
| | para 10 | 31 May 2003 (SSI 2003/219) |
| | para 11(a) | 1 Apr 2004 (SSI 2004/148) |
| | para 11(b) | *Not yet in force* |
| | para 12 | 15 Aug 2003 (SSI 2003/384) |
| | para 13 | 31 May 2003 (SSI 2003/219) |
| | para 14 | 1 Apr 2004 (SSI 2004/148) |
| | para 15(a) | 1 Apr 2004 (SSI 2004/148) |
| | para 15(b) | 15 Aug 2003 (SSI 2003/384) |
| | para 16(a) | 1 Apr 2004 (SSI 2004/148) |
| | para 16(b) | *Never in force* (repealed) |
| | para 17(a)(i) | 6 May 2004 (SSI 2004/198) |
| | para 17(a)(ii) | 1 Apr 2004 (SSI 2004/148) |
| | para 17(b)(i), (ii) | 31 May 2003 (SSI 2003/219) |
| | para 17(b)(iii) | 15 Aug 2003 (SSI 2003/384) |
| | para 17(c)(i) | *Not yet in force* |
| | para 17(c)(ii) | 1 Jun 2003 (SSI 2003/219) |

[1]  Note that SSI 2003/384 also purports to bring the definitions of "the 1980 Act" and "the 1990 Act" in s 20 into force on 15 Aug 2003

[2]  Note that SSI 2003/348 (made in error) also purports to bring Sch 3 into force, in this case on 5 Jul 2003

---

**Ragwort Control Act 2003 (c 40)**

*RA*: 20 Nov 2003

*Commencement provisions:* s 3(2)

Whole Act in force 20 Feb 2004 (s 3(2))

---

## Railways and Transport Safety Act 2003 (c 20)

*RA:* 10 Jul 2003

*Commencement provisions:* s 120; Railways and Transport Safety Act 2003 (Commencement No 1) Order 2003, SI 2003/2681; Railways and Transport Safety Act 2003 (Commencement No 2) Order 2004, SI 2004/827; Railways and Transport Safety Act 2003 (Commencement No 3) Order 2004, SI 2004/1572; Railways and Transport Safety Act 2003 (Commencement No 4) Order 2004, SI 2004/2759; Railways and Transport Safety Act 2003 (Commencement No 5) Order 2005, SI 2005/1991

| | | |
|---|---|---|
| 1–14 | | 17 Oct 2005 (SI 2005/1991) |
| 15–17 | | 5 Jul 2004 (SI 2004/827) |
| 18 | (1) | 1 Jul 2004 (SI 2004/1572) |
| | (2) | See Sch 4 below |
| | (3) | 1 Jul 2004 (SI 2004/1572) |
| 19–33 | | 1 Jul 2004 (SI 2004/1572) |
| 34 | (1) | 19 Jun 2004 (SI 2004/1572) |
| | (2)–(4) | 1 Jul 2004 (SI 2004/1572) |
| | (5) | 31 Oct 2004 (SI 2004/2759) |
| 35–72 | | 1 Jul 2004 (SI 2004/1572) |
| 73 | (1) | See Sch 5 below |
| | (2)–(4) | 1 Jul 2004 (SI 2004/1572) |
| 74 | | 19 Jun 2004 (SI 2004/1572) |
| 75–77 | | 1 Jul 2004 (SI 2004/1572) |
| 78, 79 | | 30 Mar 2004 (SI 2004/827) |
| 80 | (1)–(3) | *Not yet in force* |
| | (4), (5) | 30 Mar 2004 (SI 2004/827) |
| 81, 82 | | 30 Mar 2004 (SI 2004/827) |
| 83 | | 29 Mar 2004 (for the purposes of bringing Sch 7, para 1 into force in so far as it substitutes s 6A(1), for the purpose of enabling the Secretary of State to approve a device for indicating whether the proportion of alcohol in a person's breath or blood is likely to exceed the limits prescribed in ss 81(1), 93(2), (3)) (SI 2004/827) |
| | | 30 Mar 2004 (otherwise) (SI 2004/827) |
| 84–95 | | 30 Mar 2004 (SI 2004/827) |
| 96 | | 29 Mar 2004 (for the purposes of bringing Sch 7, para 1 into force in so far as it substitutes s 6A(1), for the purpose of enabling the Secretary of State to approve a device for indicating whether the proportion of alcohol in a person's breath or blood is likely to exceed the limits prescribed in ss 81(1), 93(2), (3)) (SI 2004/827) |
| | | 30 Mar 2004 (otherwise) (SI 2004/827) |
| 97–103 | | 30 Mar 2004 (SI 2004/827) |
| 104 | | 10 Jul 2003 (s 120(5)) |
| 105 | | 10 Sep 2003 (s 120(6)) |
| 106 | | 30 Mar 2004 (SI 2004/827) |
| 107 | | See Sch 7 below |
| 108 | | *Not yet in force* |
| 109 | | 30 Mar 2004 (SI 2004/827) |
| 110 | | 1 Mar 2005 (SI 2004/2759) |
| 111 | | 31 Oct 2003 (SI 2003/2681) |
| 112 | | 10 Sep 2003 (s 120(7)) |
| 113 | | 30 Mar 2004 (SI 2004/827) |
| 114 | | 10 Jul 2003 (s 120(8)) |
| 115 | | 31 Oct 2003 (SI 2003/2681) |
| 116 | | 5 Jul 2004 (for the purposes relating to a person becoming liable to dismissal under Sch 1, para 2(d)) (SI 2004/827) |
| | | 31 Oct 2004 (otherwise) (SI 2004/2759) |
| 117 | | 30 Mar 2004 (SI 2004/827) |
| 118 | | See Sch 8 below |

**Railways and Transport Safety Act 2003 (c 20)**—*contd*

| | | |
|---|---|---|
| 119 | | 30 Mar 2004 (SI 2004/827) |
| 120–122 | | 10 Jul 2003 (RA) |
| Schs 1–3 | | 5 Jul 2004 (SI 2004/827) |
| Schs 4, 5 | | 1 Jul 2004 (SI 2004/1572) |
| Sch 6 | | 30 Mar 2004 (SI 2004/827) |
| Sch 7 | para 1 | 29 Mar 2004 (in so far as it substitutes s 6A(1), for the purpose of enabling the Secretary of State to approve a device for indicating whether the proportion of alcohol in a person's breath or blood is likely to exceed the limits prescribed in ss 81(1), 93(2), (3)) (SI 2004/827) |
| | | 30 Mar 2004 (otherwise) (SI 2004/827) |
| | paras 2–13 | 30 Mar 2004 (SI 2004/827) |
| Sch 8 | | 10 Jul 2003 (s 120(5), (8)), repeals of or in— |
| | | Railways Act 1993, s 4(5)(c); |
| | | Greater London Authority Act 1999 |
| | | 10 Sep 2003 (repeals of or in Merchant Shipping Act 1995, s 311) (s 120(7)) |
| | | 30 Mar 2004 (SI 2004/827), repeals of or in— |
| | | Road Traffic Act 1988; |
| | | Road Traffic Offenders Act 1988; |
| | | Merchant Shipping Act 1995, s 117 |
| | | 1 Jul 2004 (SI 2004/1572), repeals of or in— |
| | | British Transport Commission Act 1949; |
| | | Railways Act 1993, ss 132, 133, Sch 10; |
| | | Transport Act 2000, Sch 18; |
| | | Anti-terrorism, Crime and Security Act 2001 |
| | | 5 Jul 2004 (SI 2004/827), repeals of or in— |
| | | House of Commons Disqualification Act 1975; |
| | | Railways Act 1993, ss 15(4A), 15C(3), 21(5), 57B, 74(8), 151(1), Sch 1; |
| | | Transport Act 2000, s 251(2), Sch 27 |
| | | 5 Jul 2004 (repeal of Railways Act 1993, s 1) (SI 2004/1572) |

---

**Regional Assemblies (Preparations) Act 2003 (c 10)**

*RA:* 8 May 2003

*Commencement provisions:* s 27

| | |
|---|---|
| 1–12 | 8 Jul 2003 (s 27(1)) |
| 13–20 | 8 May 2003 (RA) |
| 21–24 | 8 Jul 2003 (s 27(1)) |
| 25 | 8 May 2003 (RA) |
| 26 | 8 Jul 2003 (s 27(1)) |
| 27–31 | 8 May 2003 (RA) |
| Schedule | 8 May 2003 (RA) |

---

**Robin Rigg Offshore Wind Farm (Navigation and Fishing) (Scotland) Act 2003 (asp 19)**

*RA:* 1 Aug 2003

Whole Act in force 1 Aug 2003 (RA)

---

**Salmon and Freshwater Fisheries (Consolidation) (Scotland) Act 2003 (asp 15)**

*RA:* 1 May 2003

*Commencement provisions:* s 71(2); Salmon and Freshwater Fisheries (Consolidation) (Scotland) Act 2003 (Commencement) Order 2005, SSI 2005/174

**Salmon and Freshwater Fisheries (Consolidation) (Scotland) Act 2003 (asp 15)**—*contd*

| | |
|---|---|
| 1–70 | 1 Apr 2005 (SSI 2005/174) |
| 71 | 1 May 2003 (RA) |
| Schs 1–4 | 1 Apr 2005 (SSI 2005/174) |

## Sexual Offences Act 2003 (c 42)

*RA:* 20 Nov 2003

*Commencement provisions:* s 141; Sexual Offences Act 2003 (Commencement) Order 2004, SI 2004/874; Sexual Offences Act 2003 (Commencement) (Scotland) Order 2004, SSI 2004/138

| | | |
|---|---|---|
| 1–55 | | 1 May 2004 (SI 2004/874) |
| 56 | | See Sch 1 below |
| 57–71 | | 1 May 2004 (SI 2004/874) |
| 72 | (1)–(6) | 1 May 2004 (SI 2004/874) |
| | (7) | See Sch 2 below |
| 73–79 | | 1 May 2004 (SI 2004/874) |
| 80–92 | | 1 May 2004 (SI 2004/874; SSI 2004/138) |
| 93 | | See Sch 4 below |
| 94–122 | | 1 May 2004 (SI 2004/874; SSI 2004/138) |
| 123–129 | | 1 May 2004 (SI 2004/874) |
| 130–136 | | 1 May 2004 (SI 2004/874; SSI 2004/138) |
| 137 | | 1 May 2004 (SI 2004/874) |
| 138 | | 20 Nov 2003 (RA) |
| 139 | | See Sch 6 below |
| 140 | | See Sch 7 below |
| 141–143 | | 20 Nov 2003 (RA) |
| Schs 1, 2 | | 1 May 2004 (SI 2004/874) |
| Sch 3 | | 1 May 2004 (SI 2004/874; SSI 2004/138) |
| Sch 4 | | 1 May 2004 (SI 2004/874) |
| Sch 5 | | 1 May 2004 (SI 2004/874; SSI 2004/138) |
| Schs 6, 7 | | 1 May 2004 (SI 2004/874) |

## Sunday Working (Scotland) Act 2003 (c 18)

*RA:* 10 Jul 2003

*Commencement provisions:* s 3; Sunday Working (Scotland) Act 2003 (Commencement No 1) Order 2004, SI 2004/958

| | |
|---|---|
| 1 | 6 Apr 2004 (SI 2004/958) |
| 2 | *Not yet in force* |
| 3, 4 | 10 Jul 2003 (RA) |

## Sustainable Energy Act 2003 (c 30)

*RA:* 30 Oct 2003

*Commencement provisions:* s 9(5)–(8); Sustainable Energy Act 2003 (Commencement No 1) Order 2003, SI 2003/2986; Sustainable Energy Act 2003 (Commencement No 2) Order 2004, SI 2004/1203

| | |
|---|---|
| 1 | 30 Dec 2003 (s 9(7)) |
| 2 | 25 Apr 2004 (SI 2004/1203) |
| 3, 4 | *Not yet in force* (s 4(13)(b) repealed) |
| 5 | 28 Nov 2003 (SI 2003/2986) |
| 6–9 | 30 Dec 2003 (s 9(7)) |

## Synodical Government (Amendment) Measure 2003 (No 1)

*RA:* 6 Mar 2003

*Commencement provisions:* s 4(2)

The provisions of this Measure were brought into force on 1 Jan 2004 by an instrument made by the Archbishops of Canterbury and York and dated 11 Jul 2003 (made under s 4(2))

---

## Title Conditions (Scotland) Act 2003 (asp 9)

*RA:* 3 Apr 2003

*Commencement provisions:* s 129(2)–(5); Title Conditions (Scotland) Act 2003 (Commencement No 1) Order 2003, SSI 2003/454; Abolition of Feudal Tenure etc (Scotland) Act 2000 (Commencement No 2) (Appointed Day) Order 2003, SSI 2003/456[1]; Title Conditions (Scotland) Act 2003 (Commencement No 2) Order 2009, SSI 2009/190

| | | |
|---|---|---|
| 1–10 | | 4 Apr 2003 (for the purposes of Pt 3 and s 63 of this Act) (s 129(5)) |
| | | 28 Nov 2004 (otherwise) (SSI 2003/456)[1] |
| 11–24 | | 4 Apr 2003 (for the purposes of Pt 3 and s 63 of this Act) (s 129(5)) |
| | | 28 Nov 2004 (otherwise) (SSI 2003/456)[1] |
| 25–37 | | 28 Nov 2004 (SSI 2003/456)[1] |
| 38–42 | | 1 Nov 2003 (SSI 2003/454) |
| 43 | | 28 Nov 2004 (SSI 2003/454) |
| 44–48 | | 1 Nov 2003 (SSI 2003/454) |
| 49–62 | | 28 Nov 2004 (SSI 2003/456)[1] |
| 63 | | 4 Apr 2003 (s 129(3)) |
| 64, 65 | | 28 Nov 2004 (SSI 2003/456)[1] |
| 66, 67 | | 4 Apr 2003 (s 129(3)) |
| 68–70 | | 28 Nov 2004 (SSI 2003/456)[1] |
| 71–74 | | 1 Jun 2009 (SSI 2009/190) |
| 75–85 | | 28 Nov 2004 (SSI 2003/456)[1] |
| 86 | | 4 Apr 2003 (s 129(3)) |
| 87 | | 28 Nov 2004 (SSI 2003/456)[1] |
| 88 | (a) | 4 Apr 2003 (except so far as it inserts Prescription and Limitation (Scotland) Act 1973, Sch 1, para 1(ab)(ii)) (s 129(3)) |
| | | 28 Nov 2004 (exception noted above) (SSI 2003/456)[1] |
| | (b) | 4 Apr 2003 (s 129(3)) |
| 89 | | 28 Nov 2004 (SSI 2003/456)[1] |
| 90–104 | | 4 Apr 2003 (for the purposes of any application under s 107(5) of this Act) (s 129(3)) |
| | | 28 Nov 2004 (otherwise) (SSI 2003/456)[1] |
| 105 | | 28 Nov 2004 (SSI 2003/456)[1] |
| 106, 107 | | 1 Nov 2003 (SSI 2003/454) |
| 108 | | 28 Nov 2004 (SSI 2003/454) |
| 109, 110 | | 1 Nov 2003 (SSI 2003/454) |
| 111 | | 4 Apr 2003 (s 129(3)) |
| 112 | | 28 Nov 2004 (SSI 2003/456)[1] |
| 113 | | 4 Apr 2003 (s 129(3)) |
| 114 | (1)–(5) | 4 Apr 2003 (s 129(3)) |
| | (6) | See Sch 13 below |
| 115, 116 | | 28 Nov 2004 (SSI 2003/456)[1] |
| 117, 118 | | 4 Apr 2003 (s 129(3)) |
| 119–121 | | 28 Nov 2004 (SSI 2003/456)[1] |
| 122–124 | | 4 Apr 2003 (s 129(3)) |
| 125 | | 28 Nov 2004 (SSI 2003/456)[1] |
| 126, 127 | | 4 Apr 2003 (s 129(3)) |
| 128 | (1) | See Sch 14 below |
| | (2) | See Sch 15 below |

**Title Conditions (Scotland) Act 2003 (asp 9)**—*contd*

| | | |
|---|---|---|
| | (3)–(5) | 4 Apr 2003 (s 129(3)) |
| 129 | | 3 Apr 2003 (RA) |
| Sch 1 | | 4 Apr 2003 (for the purposes of Pt 3 and s 63 of this Act) (s 129(5)) |
| | | 28 Nov 2004 (otherwise) (SSI 2003/456)[1] |
| Schs 2, 3 | | 4 Apr 2003 (for the purposes of Pt 3 and s 63 of this Act) (s 129(5)) |
| | | 28 Nov 2004 (otherwise) (SSI 2003/456)[1] |
| Schs 4–10 | | 28 Nov 2004 (SSI 2003/456)[1] |
| Sch 11 | | 4 Apr 2003 (for the purposes of any application under s 107(5) of this Act) (s 129(3)) |
| | | 28 Nov 2004 (otherwise) (SSI 2003/456)[1] |
| Schs 12, 13 | | 4 Apr 2003 (s 129(3)) |
| Sch 14 | paras 1–6 | 28 Nov 2004 (SSI 2003/456)[1] |
| | para 7(1) | 4 Apr 2003 (s 129(3)) |
| | para 7(2) | 28 Nov 2004 (SSI 2003/456)[1] |
| | para 7(3) | 4 Apr 2003 (s 129(3)) |
| | para 7(4), (5) | 28 Nov 2004 (SSI 2003/456)[1] |
| | para 7(6) | 4 Apr 2003 (s 129(3)) |
| | para 7(7) | 28 Nov 2004 (SSI 2003/456)[1] |
| | paras 8–13 | 28 Nov 2004 (SSI 2003/456)[1] |
| Sch 15 | | 4 Apr 2003 (repeals of or in Abolition of Feudal Tenure etc (Scotland) Act 2000) (s 129(5)) |
| | | 28 Nov 2004 (otherwise) (SSI 2003/456)[1] |

[1] By virtue of ss 122(1), 129(2) of this Act, SSI 2003/456 (made under the Abolition of Feudal Tenure etc (Scotland) Act 2000, s 71) specifies the appointed day for the purposes of the entry into force of this Act

**Waste and Emissions Trading Act 2003 (c 33)**

*RA:* 13 Nov 2003

*Commencement provisions:* s 40; Waste and Emissions Trading Act 2003 (Commencement No 1) Order 2004, SI 2004/1163; Waste and Emissions Trading Act 2003 (Commencement) (Wales) Order 2004, SI 2004/1488; Waste and Emissions Trading Act 2003 (Commencement No 2) Order 2004, SI 2004/1874; Waste and Emissions Trading Act 2003 (Commencement No 1) Order (Northern Ireland) 2004, SR 2004/399; Waste and Emissions Trading Act 2003 (Commencement No 1) (England) Order 2004, SI 2004/3181; Waste and Emissions Trading Act 2003 (Commencement No 3) Order 2004, SI 2004/3192; Waste and Emissions Trading Act 2003 (Commencement No 1) (England and Wales) Order 2004, SI 2004/3319; Waste and Emissions Trading Act 2003 (Commencement No 1) (Great Britain) Order 2004, SI 2004/3320; Waste and Emissions Trading Act 2003 (Commencement No 2) (England) Order 2004, SI 2004/3321; Waste and Emissions Trading Act 2003 (Commencement) (Scotland) Order 2005, SSI 2005/52

| | | |
|---|---|---|
| 1 | | 20 Jul 2004 (SI 2004/1874) |
| 2 | | 20 Apr 2004 (SI 2004/1163) |
| 3 | | 3 Dec 2004 (SI 2004/3192) |
| 4, 5 | | 25 Jun 2004 (W) (SI 2004/1488) |
| | | 17 Sep 2004 (NI) (SR 2004/399) |
| | | 3 Dec 2004 (E) (SI 2004/3181) |
| | | 3 Feb 2005 (S) (SSI 2005/52) |
| 6–8 | | 13 Nov 2003 (RA) |
| 9 | | 25 Jun 2004 (W) (SI 2004/1488) |
| | | 17 Sep 2004 (NI) (SR 2004/399) |
| | | 1 Apr 2005 (E) (SI 2004/3181) |
| | | 1 Apr 2005 (S) (SSI 2005/52) |
| 10 | (1) | 25 Jun 2004 (W) (SI 2004/1488) |
| | | 17 Sep 2004 (NI) (SR 2004/399) |
| | | 3 Dec 2004 (E) (SI 2004/3181) |

**Waste and Emissions Trading Act 2003 (c 33)**—*contd*

| | | |
|---|---|---|
| | | 3 Feb 2005 (S) (SSI 2005/52) |
| | (2) | 25 Jun 2004 (W) (SI 2004/1488) |
| | | 17 Sep 2004 (NI) (SR 2004/399) |
| | | 1 Apr 2005 (E) (SI 2004/3181) |
| | | 1 Apr 2005 (S) (SSI 2005/52) |
| 11–16 | | 13 Nov 2003 (RA) |
| 17 | | 20 Jul 2004 (SI 2004/1874) |
| 18 | | 1 Apr 2005 (S) (SSI 2005/52) |
| 19 | | 25 Jun 2004 (SI 2004/1488) |
| 20 | | 17 Sep 2004 (SR 2004/399) |
| 21–30 | | 13 Nov 2003 (RA) |
| 31 | | 1 Jan 2005 (SI 2004/3319) |
| 32 | (1)–(9) | 13 Jan 2004 (s 40(6)) |
| | (10), (11) | 13 Nov 2003 (RA) |
| | (12) | 1 Jan 2005 (SI 2004/3320) |
| 33, 34 | | 13 Nov 2003 (RA) |
| 35 | (a) | 25 Jun 2004 (W) (SI 2004/1488) |
| | | 1 Jan 2005 (E) (SI 2004/3321) |
| | (b) | 1 Jan 2005 (SI 2004/3320) |
| | (c) | 25 Jun 2004 (SI 2004/1488) |
| 36–38 | | 13 Nov 2003 (RA) |
| 39 | | 20 Apr 2004 (SI 2004/1163) |
| 40–42 | | 13 Nov 2003 (RA) |

**Water Act 2003 (c 37)**

*RA:* 20 Nov 2003

*Commencement provisions:* s 105(3)–(6); Water Act 2003 (Commencement No 1 and Transitional Provisions) Order 2004, SI 2004/641[1]; Water Act 2003 (Commencement) (Wales) Order 2004, SI 2004/910; Water Act 2003 (Commencement No 2, Transitional Provisions and Savings) Order 2004, SI 2004/2528[3], as amended by SI 2005/968, SI 2007/1021; Water Act 2003 (Commencement No 2) (Wales) Order 2004, SI 2004/2916; Water Act 2003 (Commencement No 3) (England) Order 2005, SI 2005/344; Water Act 2003 (Commencement No 4, Transitional Provisions and Savings) Order 2005, SI 2005/968, as amended by SI 2005/2714; Water Act 2003 (Commencement No 5, Transitional Provisions and Savings) Order 2005, SI 2005/2714[7], as amended by SI 2007/1021; Water Act 2003 (Commencement No 6, Transitional Provisions and Savings) Order 2006, SI 2006/984[8], as amended by SI 2007/1021; Water Act 2003 (Commencement No 7 and Transitional Provisions) Order 2007, SI 2007/1021; Water Act 2003 (Commencement No 8) Order 2008, SI 2008/1922; Water Act 2003 (Commencement No 9 and Saving Provisions) (England) Order 2009, SI 2009/359[9]; Water Act 2003 (Commencement No 10) Order 2010, SI 2010/975; Water Act 2003 (Commencement No 11) Order 2012, SI 2012/264; Water Act 2003 (Commencement No 3) (Wales) Order 2012, SI 2012/284; Water Act 2003 (Commencement No 4) (Wales) Order 2017, SI 2017/88; Water Act 2003 (Commencement No 12) Order 2017, SI 2017/1043

| | | |
|---|---|---|
| 1–4 | | 1 Apr 2006 (SI 2006/984)[8] |
| 5 | | 1 Jan 2018 (SI 2017/1043) |
| 6 | (1) | 1 Apr 2004 (in so far as inserts Water Resources Act 1991, s 27A) (SI 2004/641) |
| | | 1 Apr 2005 (otherwise) (SI 2005/968) |
| | (2) | 1 Apr 2005 (SI 2005/968) |
| 7 | | 1 Jan 2018 (SI 2017/1043) |
| 8 | (1) | See sub-ss (2)–(7) below |
| | (2) | 1 Jan 2018 (SI 2017/1043) |
| | (3)–(7) | 1 Apr 2006 (SI 2006/984)[8] |
| 9 | | 1 Apr 2004 (SI 2004/641) |
| 10 | (1)–(10) | 1 Apr 2005 (SI 2005/968) |
| | (11) | 1 Apr 2004 (SI 2004/641) |
| | (12) | 1 Apr 2005 (SI 2005/968) |
| 11–14 | | 1 Apr 2006 (SI 2006/984)[8] |

**Water Act 2003 (c 37)**—*contd*

| | | |
|---|---|---|
| 15 | | 1 Apr 2004 (SI 2004/641) |
| 16 | (1)–(3) | 1 Apr 2004 (SI 2004/641) |
| | (4), (5) | 1 Apr 2005 (SI 2005/968) |
| | (6), (7) | 1 Apr 2004 (SI 2004/641) |
| 17 | | 1 Apr 2005 (SI 2005/968) |
| 18 | | 1 Apr 2004 (SI 2004/641) |
| 19 | (1)–(3) | 1 Apr 2006 (SI 2006/984)[8] |
| | (4) | 1 Apr 2004 (SI 2004/641) |
| | (5), (6) | 1 Apr 2006 (SI 2006/984)[8] |
| 20 | | 1 Apr 2004 (SI 2004/641) |
| 21–23 | | 1 Apr 2006 (SI 2006/984)[8] |
| 24 | | 1 Apr 2005 (SI 2004/641) |
| 25 | (1) | See sub-ss (2), (3) below |
| | (2) | 1 Apr 2004 (SI 2004/641) |
| | (3) | 1 Apr 2006 (SI 2006/984)[8] |
| | (4) | 1 Apr 2004 (SI 2004/641) |
| 26 | | 1 Oct 2004 (SI 2004/2528) |
| 27 | | 1 Apr 2004 (SI 2004/641) |
| 28, 29 | | 1 Oct 2004 (SI 2004/2528) |
| 30 | | 1 Apr 2006 (SI 2006/984)[8] |
| 31 | | 1 Oct 2004 (SI 2004/2528) |
| 32 | | 1 Jan 2018 (SI 2017/1043) |
| 33 | | 1 Apr 2006 (SI 2006/984)[8] |
| 34 | (1) | 1 Apr 2006 (SI 2005/2714) |
| | (2) | See Sch 1 below |
| | (3), (4) | 1 Apr 2006 (SI 2005/2714) |
| 35 | (1) | 1 Aug 2005 (in so far as inserts s 27A(5), (6) and s 27A(4) in so far as that provision has effect for the purpose of enabling the Assembly and the Secretary of State to give directions) (SI 2005/968) |
| | | 1 Oct 2005 (in so far as inserts s 27A for all remaining purposes) (SI 2005/2714) |
| | | 1 Apr 2006 (otherwise) (SI 2005/2714) |
| | (2)–(4) | 1 Oct 2005 (SI 2005/2714) |
| 36 | (1), (2) | 1 Apr 2006 (SI 2005/2714) |
| | (3)–(5) | 1 Apr 2005 (SI 2005/968) |
| | (6) | See Sch 3 below |
| 37 | | 1 Apr 2004 (SI 2004/641) |
| 38 | (1) | 1 Oct 2004 (SI 2004/2528) |
| | (2) | 1 Oct 2004 (in so far as it repeals Water Industry Act 1991, s 193) (SI 2004/2528) |
| | | 1 Oct 2005 (otherwise) (SI 2005/2714) |
| 39–42 | | 1 Apr 2005 (SI 2005/968) |
| 43–47 | | 1 Oct 2005 (SI 2005/2714) |
| 48 | (1) | 1 Oct 2004 (in so far as inserts following provisions of the Water Industry Act 1991: s 22A(4) (for the purpose of defining "enforcement authority"); s 22A(11) (for the purpose of enabling the Secretary of State to make an order); and s 22B) (SI 2004/2528) |
| | | 1 Apr 2005 (for remaining purposes) (SI 2005/968) |
| | (2) | 1 Apr 2005 (SI 2005/968) |
| 49, 50 | | 1 Oct 2004 (SI 2004/2528) |
| 51 | | 1 Apr 2005 (SI 2005/968) |
| 52 | | 1 Apr 2006 (SI 2005/2714) |
| 53 | | 1 Apr 2004 (SI 2004/641) |
| 54, 55 | | 1 Oct 2004 (SI 2004/2528) |
| 56 | | See Sch 4 below |
| 57 | | 1 Apr 2004 (SI 2004/641) |
| 58 | (1) | See sub-ss (2)–(14) below |

**Water Act 2003 (c 37)**—*contd*

|  |  |
|---|---|
| (2) | 1 Aug 2008 (E) (in so far as inserts Water Industry Act 1991, s 87(1) (for the purposes of s 89(2)(a) thereof), (3)(a)(i) (in relation to the definition of "relevant authority" for the purposes of s 87(11) thereof and for the purposes of s 89 thereof, in relation to the provisions of that section commenced by SI 2008/1922), and (11)) (SI 2008/1922) |
|  | 25 Feb 2009 (E) (otherwise) (SI 2009/359) |
|  | *Not yet in force* (W) |
| (3), (4) | 25 Feb 2009 (E) (SI 2009/359) |
|  | *Not yet in force* (W) |
| (5) | 18 Feb 2005 (E) (in so far as inserts Water Industry Act 1991, s 89(1)(a), (b), (2)(b), (d), (3), (5)(b), for the purpose of enabling the Secretary of State to make regulations) (SI 2005/344) |
|  | 1 Aug 2008 (E) (in so far as inserts Water Industry Act 1991, s 89(2)(a), and in so far as inserts s 89(1), (3) and (5)(b) for remaining purposes) (SI 2008/1922) |
|  | 25 Feb 2009 (E) (otherwise) (SI 2009/359) |
|  | *Not yet in force* (W) |
| (6) | 18 Feb 2005 (E) (in so far as inserts Water Industry Act 1991, s 90(3), for the purpose of enabling the Secretary of State to make regulations) (SI 2005/344) |
|  | 25 Feb 2009 (E) (otherwise) (SI 2009/359) |
|  | *Not yet in force* (W) |
| (7) | 26 Mar 2010 (E) (SI 2010/975) |
|  | *Not yet in force* (W) |
| (8) | 18 Feb 2005 (E) (in so far as it relates to the Water Industry Act 1991, ss 89(1)(a), (b), (2)(b), (d), (3), (5)(b), 90(3), for the purpose of enabling the Secretary of State to make regulations) (SI 2005/344) |
|  | 25 Feb 2009 (E) (otherwise) (SI 2009/359) |
|  | 1 Feb 2017 (W) (SI 2017/88) |
| (9) | 26 Mar 2010 (E) (SI 2010/975) |
|  | *Not yet in force* (W) |
| (10) | 25 Feb 2009 (SI 2009/359) |
| (11)–(14) | 25 Feb 2009 (E) (except in relation to pre-1985 arrangements (as defined by SI 2009/359, art 1(3)) (SI 2009/359) |
|  | 26 Mar 2010 (E) (otherwise) (SI 2010/975) |
|  | *Not yet in force* (W) |
| 59 | 1 Oct 2004 (SI 2004/2528) |
| 60, 61 | 1 Apr 2004 (SI 2004/641) |
| 62 | 1 Oct 2004 (in so far as it has effect for the purpose of enabling the Secretary of State to make regulations and give directions in relation to drought plans under Water Industry Act 1991, s 37B as applied by s 39B(5) thereof) (SI 2004/2528) |
|  | 1 Oct 2005 (otherwise, in so far as inserts Water Industry Act 1991, s 37B as applied by s 39B(5) thereof) (SI 2005/2714) |
|  | 1 Apr 2006 (in so far as inserts Water Industry Act 1991, ss 37A, 37D and for all remaining purposes in so far as inserts Water Industry Act 1991, s 37B) (SI 2006/984)[8] |
|  | 1 Apr 2007 (in so far as inserts Water Industry Act 1991, s 37C) (SI 2007/1021) |
| 63 | 1 Oct 2004 (in so far as it has effect for the purpose of enabling the Secretary of State to make regulations and give directions in relation to drought plans under Water Industry Act 1991, s 39B or s 37B as applied by s 39B(5) of that Act) (SI 2004/2528) |
|  | 1 Oct 2005 (otherwise) (SI 2005/2714) |
| 64–66 | 1 Apr 2004 (SI 2004/641) |
| 67 | 1 Apr 2004 (SI 2004/910) |
| 68 | 1 Apr 2004 (SI 2004/641) |

**Water Act 2003 (c 37)**—*contd*

| | | |
|---|---|---|
| 69 | | 17 Mar 2004 (E) (SI 2004/641) |
| | | 1 Apr 2004 (W) (SI 2004/910) |
| 70 | | 1 Apr 2005 (SI 2005/968) |
| 71, 72 | | 1 Apr 2004 (SI 2004/641) |
| 73 | | 1 Jan 2018 (SI 2017/1043) |
| 74 | | 1 Oct 2004 (SI 2004/2528) |
| 75 | | 1 Apr 2004 (SI 2004/641; SI 2004/910) |
| 76 | | 1 Oct 2004 (SI 2004/2528) |
| 77, 78 | | 1 Oct 2004 (E) (SI 2004/2528) |
| | | 11 Nov 2004 (W) (SI 2004/2916) |
| 79 | | 1 Oct 2004 (SI 2004/2528) |
| 80 | | 1 Oct 2004 (E) (SI 2004/2528) |
| | | 11 Nov 2004 (W) (SI 2004/2916) |
| 81 | | 1 Apr 2004 (E) (SI 2004/641) |
| | | 11 Nov 2004 (W) (SI 2004/2916) |
| 82–85 | | 1 Apr 2004 (SI 2004/641) |
| 86 | (1) | See sub-ss (2)–(7) below |
| | (2)(a)–(e) | 6 Apr 2012 (E) (SI 2012/264) |
| | | 6 Apr 2012 (W) (SI 2012/284) |
| | (2)(f) | 1 Oct 2004 (E) (SI 2004/2528) |
| | | 11 Nov 2004 (W) (SI 2004/2916) |
| | (3)–(7) | 6 Apr 2012 (E) (SI 2012/264) |
| | | 6 Apr 2012 (W) (SI 2012/284) |
| 87 | | 1 Oct 2004 (SI 2004/2528) |
| 88, 89 | | *Not yet in force* |
| 90–97 | | 28 May 2004 (SI 2004/641) |
| 98 | | 1 Apr 2007 (SI 2007/1021) |
| 99 | | 28 May 2004 (SI 2004/641) |
| 100 | (1) | 1 Oct 2004 (SI 2004/2528) |
| | (2)(a)(i) | 1 Apr 2005 (SI 2005/968) |
| | (2)(a)(ii) | 1 Apr 2004 (in so far as it relates to provisions brought into force by virtue of SI 2004/641) (SI 2004/641) |
| | | 1 Oct 2004 (in so far as it relates to provisions amended or introduced by any provision brought into force by virtue of SI 2004/2528, art 2) (SI 2004/2528) |
| | | 1 Apr 2005 (in so far as it relates to provisions amended or introduced by any provision brought into force by virtue of SI 2005/968, art 2) (SI 2005/968) |
| | | 1 Aug 2005 (in so far as it relates to provisions amended or introduced by any provision brought into force by virtue of SI 2005/968, art 3) (SI 2005/968) |
| | | 1 Dec 2005 (in so far as it relates to provisions amended or introduced by any provision brought into force by virtue of SI 2005/2714, art 3) (SI 2005/2714) |
| | (2)(a)(iii) | 1 Aug 2005 (in so far as it relates to provisions amended or introduced by any provision brought into force by virtue of SI 2005/968, art 3) (SI 2005/968) |
| | | 1 Oct 2005 (in so far as it relates to provisions amended or introduced by any provision brought into force by virtue of SI 2005/2714, art 2) (SI 2005/2714) |
| | | 1 Apr 2006 (otherwise) (SI 2005/2714) |
| | (2)(a)(iv) | 1 Apr 2004 (in so far as it relates to provisions brought into force by virtue of SI 2004/641) (SI 2004/641) |
| | | 1 Oct 2005 (in so far as it relates to provisions amended or introduced by any provision brought into force by virtue of SI 2005/2714, art 2) (SI 2005/2714) |
| | | 1 Dec 2005 (in so far as it relates to provisions amended or introduced by any provision brought into force by virtue of SI 2005/2714, art 3) (SI 2005/2714) |
| | | 1 Apr 2006 (otherwise) (SI 2005/2714) |

**Water Act 2003 (c 37)**—*contd*

| | |
|---|---|
| (2)(a)(v) | 1 Oct 2005 (in so far as it relates to provisions amended or introduced by any provision brought into force by virtue of SI 2005/2714, art 2) (SI 2005/2714) |
| (2)(a)(vi) | 1 Oct 2004 (in so far as it relates to provisions amended or introduced by any provision brought into force by virtue of SI 2004/2528, art 2) (SI 2004/2528) |
| | 1 Oct 2005 (in so far as it relates to provisions amended or introduced by any provision brought into force by virtue of SI 2005/2714, art 2) (SI 2005/2714) |
| (2)(a)(vii) | 1 Apr 2005 (SI 2005/968) |
| (2)(a)(viii) | 1 Oct 2005 (in so far as it relates to provisions amended or introduced by any provision brought into force by virtue of SI 2005/2714, art 2) (SI 2005/2714) |
| | 1 Apr 2006 (otherwise) (SI 2005/2714) |
| (2)(a)(ix) | 1 Apr 2004 (in so far as it relates to provisions brought into force by virtue of SI 2004/641) (SI 2004/641) |
| | 1 Oct 2004 (in so far as it relates to provisions amended or introduced by any provision brought into force by virtue of SI 2004/2528, art 2) (SI 2004/2528) |
| | 1 Apr 2005 (in so far as it relates to provisions amended or introduced by any provision brought into force by virtue of SI 2005/968, art 2) (SI 2005/968) |
| | 1 Aug 2005 (in so far as it relates to provisions amended or introduced by any provision brought into force by virtue of SI 2005/968, art 3) (SI 2005/968) |
| | 1 Oct 2005 (in so far as it relates to provisions amended or introduced by any provision brought into force by virtue of SI 2005/2714, art 2) (SI 2005/2714) |
| | 1 Dec 2005 (in so far as it relates to provisions amended or introduced by any provision brought into force by virtue of SI 2005/2714, art 3) (SI 2005/2714) |
| | 1 Apr 2006 (otherwise) (SI 2005/2714) |
| (2)(b)(i) | 1 Apr 2005 (in so far as it relates to provisions amended or introduced by any provision brought into force by virtue of SI 2005/968, art 2) (SI 2005/968) |
| | 1 Dec 2005 (in so far as it relates to provisions amended or introduced by any provision brought into force by virtue of SI 2005/2714, art 3) (SI 2005/2714) |
| (2)(b)(ii) | 1 Oct 2004 (in so far as it relates to provisions amended or introduced by any provision brought into force by virtue of SI 2004/2528, art 2) (SI 2004/2528) |
| | 1 Dec 2005 (in so far as it relates to provisions amended or introduced by any provision brought into force by virtue of SI 2005/2714, art 3) (SI 2005/2714) |
| (2)(b)(iii) | 28 May 2004 (SI 2004/641)[5] |
| (2)(b)(iv) | 1 Apr 2004 (in so far as it relates to provisions brought into force by virtue of SI 2004/641) (SI 2004/641) |
| | 1 Oct 2004 (in so far as it relates to provisions amended or introduced by any provision brought into force by virtue of SI 2004/2528, art 2) (SI 2004/2528) |
| | 1 Dec 2005 (in so far as it relates to provisions amended or introduced by any provision brought into force by virtue of SI 2005/2714, art 3) (SI 2005/2714) |
| (2)(b)(v) | 1 Dec 2005 (in so far as it relates to provisions amended or introduced by any provision brought into force by virtue of SI 2005/2714, art 3) (SI 2005/2714) |
| (2)(b)(vi) | 1 Apr 2005 (in so far as it relates to provisions amended or introduced by any provision brought into force by virtue of SI 2005/968, art 2) (SI 2005/968) |

**Water Act 2003 (c 37)**—*contd*

|  |  |
|---|---|
|  | 1 Oct 2005 (in so far as it relates to provisions amended or introduced by any provision brought into force by virtue of SI 2005/2714, art 2) (SI 2005/2714) |
|  | 1 Apr 2007 (otherwise) (SI 2007/1021) |
| (2)(b)(vii) | 1 Apr 2007 (SI 2007/1021) |
| (2)(b)(viii) | 1 Apr 2004 (in so far as it relates to provisions brought into force by virtue of SI 2004/641) (SI 2004/641) |
|  | 1 Dec 2005 (in so far as it relates to provisions amended or introduced by any provision brought into force by virtue of SI 2005/2714, art 3) (SI 2005/2714) |
| (2)(b)(ix) | 1 Dec 2005 (in so far as it relates to provisions amended or introduced by any provision brought into force by virtue of SI 2005/2714, art 3) (SI 2005/2714) |
| (2)(b)(x) | 1 Apr 2004 (in so far as it relates to provisions brought into force by virtue of SI 2004/641) (SI 2004/641) |
|  | 1 Oct 2004 (in so far as it relates to provisions amended or introduced by any provision brought into force by virtue of SI 2004/2528, art 2) (SI 2004/2528) |
|  | 1 Apr 2005 (in so far as it relates to provisions amended or introduced by any provision brought into force by virtue of SI 2005/968, art 2) (SI 2005/968) |
|  | 1 Oct 2005 (in so far as it relates to provisions amended or introduced by any provision brought into force by virtue of SI 2005/2714, art 2) (SI 2005/2714) |
|  | 1 Dec 2005 (in so far as it relates to provisions amended or introduced by any provision brought into force by virtue of SI 2005/2714, art 3) (SI 2005/2714) |
|  | 1 Apr 2007 (otherwise) (SI 2007/1021) |
| (2)(c) | 1 Apr 2006 (SI 2006/984)[8] |
| (2)(d) | 1 Apr 2004 (in so far as it relates to provisions brought into force by virtue of SI 2004/641) (SI 2004/641) |
|  | 1 Oct 2004 (in so far as it relates to provisions brought into force by virtue of SI 2004/2528, art 2) (SI 2004/2528) |
|  | 1 Apr 2005 (in so far as it relates to provisions amended or introduced by any provision brought into force by virtue of SI 2005/968, art 2) (SI 2005/968) |
|  | 1 Dec 2005 (in so far as it relates to provisions amended or introduced by any provision brought into force by virtue of SI 2005/2714, art 3) (SI 2005/2714) |
| (2)(e) | 1 Apr 2004 (in so far as it relates to provisions brought into force by virtue of SI 2004/641) (SI 2004/641) |
|  | 1 Dec 2005 (in so far as it relates to provisions amended or introduced by any provision brought into force by virtue of SI 2005/2714, art 3) (SI 2005/2714) |
|  | 1 Apr 2007 (otherwise) (SI 2007/1021) |
| (2)(f) | 1 Apr 2004 (in so far as it relates to provisions brought into force by virtue of SI 2004/641) (SI 2004/641) |
|  | 1 Apr 2007 (otherwise) (SI 2007/1021) |
| (2)(g) | 1 Oct 2004 (in so far as it relates to provisions amended or introduced by any provision brought into force by virtue of SI 2004/2528, art 2) (SI 2004/2528) |
|  | 1 Oct 2005 (in so far as it relates to provisions amended or introduced by any provision brought into force by virtue of SI 2005/2714, art 2) (SI 2005/2714) |
|  | 1 Apr 2006 (in so far as relates to provisions amended or introduced by any provision brought into force by virtue of SI 2006/984, art 2) (SI 2006/984)[8] |
|  | 1 Apr 2007 (otherwise) (SI 2007/1021) |
| (2)(h) | 1 Dec 2005 (in so far as it relates to provisions amended or introduced by any provision brought into force by virtue of SI 2005/2714, art 3) (SI 2005/2714) |

**Water Act 2003 (c 37)**—*contd*

| | | |
|---|---|---|
| (2)(i) | | 1 Apr 2004 (in so far as they relate to provisions brought into force by virtue of SI 2004/641) (SI 2004/641) |
| | | 1 Dec 2005 (in so far as it relates to provisions amended or introduced by any provision brought into force by virtue of SI 2005/2714, art 3) (SI 2005/2714) |
| (2)(j) | | 1 Apr 2004 (in so far as they relate to provisions brought into force by virtue of SI 2004/641) (SI 2004/641) |
| | | 1 Aug 2005 (in so far as it relates to provisions amended or introduced by any provision brought into force by virtue of SI 2005/968, art 3) (SI 2005/968) |
| | | 1 Dec 2005 (in so far as it relates to provisions amended or introduced by any provision brought into force by virtue of SI 2005/2714, art 3) (SI 2005/2714) |
| | | 1 Apr 2007 (otherwise) (SI 2007/1021) |
| (3) | | 1 Oct 2004 (in so far as it relates to provisions amended or introduced by any provision brought into force by virtue of SI 2004/2528, art 2) (SI 2004/2528) |
| | | 1 Oct 2005 (in so far as it relates to provisions amended or introduced by any provision brought into force by virtue of SI 2005/2714, art 2) (SI 2005/2714) |
| | | 1 Apr 2007 (otherwise) (SI 2007/1021) |
| (4)(a) | | 1 Oct 2004 (SI 2004/2528) |
| (4)(b)(i), (ii) | | 1 Apr 2004 (SI 2004/641) |
| (4)(b)(iii) | | 1 Apr 2006 (SI 2006/984)[8] |
| (5) | | 1 Apr 2004 (SI 2004/641) |
| (6) | | 17 Mar 2004 (in so far as it relates to references to provisions amended by any provision of this Act which comes into force by virtue of SI 2004/641, art 2) (SI 2004/641) |
| | | 1 Apr 2004 (in so far as it relates to references to provisions amended by any provision of this Act which comes into force by virtue of SI 2004/641, art 3 or SI 2004/910) (SI 2004/641) |
| | | 28 May 2004 (in so far as it relates to references to provisions amended by any provision of this Act which comes into force by virtue of SI 2004/641, art 4) (SI 2004/641) |
| | | 1 Oct 2004 (in so far as it relates to any Act generally or to references to provisions amended or introduced by any provision of the Act which is brought into force by virtue of SI 2004/2528, art 2) (SI 2004/2528) |
| | | 1 Apr 2005 (in so far as it relates to references to provisions amended or introduced by any provision brought into force by virtue of SI 2005/968, art 2) (SI 2005/968) |
| | | 1 Aug 2005 (in so far as it relates to references to provisions amended or introduced by any provision brought into force by virtue of SI 2005/968, art 3) (SI 2005/968) |
| | | 1 Oct 2005 (in so far as it relates to references to provisions amended or introduced by any provision brought into force by virtue of SI 2005/2714, art 2) (SI 2005/2714) |
| | | 1 Dec 2005 (in so far as it relates to references to provisions amended or introduced by any provision brought into force by virtue of SI 2005/2714, art 3) (SI 2005/2714) |
| | | 1 Apr 2006 (in so far as it relates to references to provisions amended or introduced by any provision brought into force by virtue of SI 2005/2714, art 4) (SI 2005/2714) |
| | | 1 Apr 2006 (in so far as it relates to references to provisions amended or introduced by any provision brought into force by virtue of SI 2006/984, art 2) (SI 2006/984)[8] |
| | | 1 Apr 2007 (otherwise) (SI 2007/1021) |
| (7) | | See sub-ss (1)–(6) above |
| 101 | (1) | See Schs 7, 8 below |
| | (2) | See Sch 9 below |
| 102–105 | | 20 Nov 2003 (RA) |

**Water Act 2003 (c 37)**—*contd*

| | | |
|---|---|---|
| Sch 1 | | 1 Apr 2006 (except in so far as inserts Water Industry Act 1991, Sch 1A, para 11) (SI 2005/2714) |
| | | *Not yet in force* (exception noted above) |
| Sch 2 | | 1 Oct 2005 (SI 2005/2714) |
| Sch 3 | | 1 Apr 2005 (SI 2005/968)[6] |
| Sch 4 | para 1 | See paras 2–4 below |
| | para 2 | 1 Apr 2004 (in so far as inserts following provisions of the Water Industry Act 1991— |

s 17A(1), (2), (4)–(6) (for the purpose of enabling the Secretary of State to give a general authorisation to the Water Services Regulation Authority);

s 17A(3) (for the purposes of enabling the Authority to issue guidance under ss 17A(9), 17D(3) and of enabling the Secretary of State and the Assembly to make regulations under s 17C(3), (4));

ss 17A(9), (10), 17B, 17C, 17D(1)–(7);

s 17D(12) (for the purpose of enabling the Secretary of State to make regulations under s 17D(7));

s 17F(1)–(3) (for the purposes of enabling the Secretary of State to make regulations under s 17F(1)–(3), (5));

s 17F(5);

s 17G (for the purpose of enabling the Secretary of State to determine standard licence conditions pursuant to s 17H);

s 17H(1)–(4);

s 17J(6), (7), (9)–(11) (for the purpose of enabling the Secretary of State to make an order under s 17J(6)) (SI 2004/641)

1 Aug 2005 (for the purpose of giving effect to the Water Industry Act 1991, s 17F(1)–(3) for all remaining purposes; inserting s 17F(4), (8) thereof; and giving effect to s 17A thereof in so far as relevant for the purposes of s 17F in so far as brought into force by virtue of SI 2005/968, art 3) (SI 2005/968)

1 Oct 2005 (for the purposes of inserting the Water Industry Act 1991, ss 17K, 17M, 17P, 17Q) (SI 2005/2714)

1 Dec 2005 (for all remaining purposes) (SI 2005/2714)

| | | |
|---|---|---|
| | para 3 | 1 Apr 2004 (in so far as inserts following provisions of the Water Industry Act 1991— |

s 66A(6) (for the purpose of enabling the Secretary of State to make regulations prescribing which requirements of regulations under s 74 are relevant);

ss 66B(8)–(10), (12), 66D(4)–(6), 66E, 66F(5)–(8), 66I(3);

s 66I(8) (for the purpose of enabling the Secretary of State and the Assembly to make regulations under s 66I(3));

s 66J(3);

s 66J(9) (for the purpose of enabling the Secretary of State and the Assembly to make regulations under s 66J(3));

ss 66K, 66L (SI 2004/641)

1 Dec 2005 (for all remaining purposes) (SI 2005/2714)

| | | |
|---|---|---|
| | para 4 | 1 Dec 2005 (SI 2005/2714)[2] |
| Schs 5, 6 | | 1 Apr 2004 (SI 2004/641) |
| Sch 7 | para 1 | See paras 2–14 below |
| | para 2 | 1 Oct 2004 (SI 2004/2528) |
| | para 3 | 1 Jan 2018 (SI 2017/1043) |
| | para 4 | 1 Apr 2006 (SI 2006/984)[8] |
| | para 5 | 1 Jan 2018 (SI 2017/1043) |
| | para 6 | 1 Apr 2004 (SI 2004/641) |
| | paras 7, 8 | 1 Apr 2006 (SI 2006/984)[8] |
| | para 9 | 1 Jan 2018 (SI 2017/1043) |
| | paras 10–13 | 1 Apr 2006 (SI 2006/984)[8] |
| | para 14 | 1 Apr 2004 (SI 2004/641) |
| | para 15 | 1 Apr 2006 (SI 2006/984)[8] |

**Water Act 2003 (c 37)**—*contd*

| | |
|---|---|
| paras 16, 17 | 1 Oct 2005 (SI 2005/2714) |
| para 18(a) | 1 Oct 2005 (in so far as has effect for the purposes of inserting the entry relating to the Council) (SI 2005/2714) |
| | 1 Apr 2006 (otherwise) (SI 2005/2714) |
| para 18(b) | 1 Apr 2006 (SI 2005/2714) |
| para 19 | 1 Oct 2005 (SI 2005/2714) |
| para 20(1) | See sub-paras (2), (3) below |
| para 20(2) | 1 Oct 2005 (in so far as has effect for the purposes of inserting the entry relating to the Council and the regional committees of the Council) (SI 2005/2714) |
| | 1 Apr 2006 (otherwise) (SI 2005/2714) |
| para 20(3)(a) | 1 Oct 2005 (SI 2005/2714) |
| para 20(3)(b) | 1 Apr 2006 (SI 2005/2714) |
| para 21(1) | See sub-paras (2), (3) below |
| para 21(2) | 1 Oct 2005 (in so far as has effect for the purposes of inserting the entry relating to the Council and the regional committees of the Council) (SI 2005/2714) |
| | 1 Apr 2006 (otherwise) (SI 2005/2714) |
| para 21(3)(a) | 1 Oct 2005 (SI 2005/2714) |
| para 21(3)(b) | 1 Apr 2006 (SI 2005/2714) |
| para 22 | 1 Oct 2005 (SI 2005/2714) |
| para 23(a) | 1 Apr 2006 (SI 2005/2714) |
| para 23(b) | 1 Apr 2004 (SI 2004/641) |
| para 24(a) | 1 Apr 2006 (SI 2005/2714) |
| para 24(b) | 1 Apr 2004 (SI 2004/641) |
| para 25 | 1 Apr 2006 (SI 2005/2714) |
| para 26(1) | See sub-paras (2)–(6) below |
| para 26(2)(a)(i)(a) | 1 Oct 2005 (in so far as has effect for the purposes of inserting the entry relating to the Council) (SI 2005/2714) |
| | 1 Apr 2006 (otherwise) (SI 2005/2714) |
| para 26(2)(a)(i)(b) | 1 Apr 2004 (SI 2004/641) |
| para 26(2)(a)(ii) | 1 Oct 2005 (SI 2005/2714) |
| para 26(2)(a)(iii) | 1 Apr 2004 (SI 2004/641) |
| para 26(2)(b)(i) | 1 Apr 2006 (SI 2005/2714) |
| para 26(2)(b)(ii) | 1 Oct 2005 (SI 2005/2714) |
| para 26(3), (4) | 1 Apr 2006 (SI 2005/2714) |
| para 26(5) | 1 Oct 2005 (SI 2005/2714) |
| para 26(6) | 1 Apr 2006 (SI 2005/2714) |
| para 27(1) | See sub-paras (2)–(7) below |
| para 27(2) | 29 Dec 2004 (SI 2004/2528) |
| para 27(3), (4) | 1 Oct 2005 (SI 2005/2714) |
| para 27(5)(a)(i) | 1 Oct 2005 (SI 2005/2714) |
| para 27(5)(a)(ii), (iii) | 1 Apr 2004 (SI 2004/641) |
| para 27(5)(a)(iv) | 1 Oct 2005 (SI 2005/2714) |
| para 27(5)(a)(v) | 1 Apr 2004 (SI 2004/641) |
| para 27(5)(b)(i) | 1 Oct 2005 (SI 2005/2714) |
| para 27(5)(b)(ii) | 1 Apr 2004 (SI 2004/641) |
| para 27(6) | 1 Oct 2005 (SI 2005/2714) |
| para 27(7)(a) | 1 Apr 2004 (SI 2004/641) |
| para 27(7)(b) | 1 Aug 2005 (SI 2005/968) |
| para 27(7)(c) | 1 Apr 2006 (SI 2005/2714) |
| para 27(7)(d) | 1 Oct 2005 (SI 2005/2714) |
| para 28(1) | See sub-paras (2)–(4) below |
| para 28(2) | 1 Apr 2006 (SI 2005/2714) |
| para 28(3)(a)(i) | 1 Oct 2005 (SI 2005/2714) |
| para 28(3)(a)(ii), (iii) | 1 Apr 2004 (SI 2004/641) |
| para 28(3)(a)(iv) | 1 Oct 2005 (SI 2005/2714) |

**Water Act 2003 (c 37)**—*contd*

| | | |
|---|---|---|
| para 28(3)(a)(v) | 1 Apr 2004 (SI 2004/641) | |
| para 28(3)(b)(i) | 1 Apr 2006 (SI 2005/2714) | |
| para 28(3)(b)(ii) | 1 Oct 2005 (SI 2005/2714) | |
| para 28(3)(b)(iii) | 1 Apr 2004 (SI 2004/641) | |
| para 28(4) | 1 Apr 2006 (SI 2005/2714) | |
| para 29(1) | See sub-paras (2), (3) below | |
| para 29(2) | 1 Oct 2005 (SI 2005/2714) | |
| para 29(3) | 1 Apr 2006 (SI 2005/2714) | |
| para 30 | 1 Apr 2005 (SI 2005/968) | |
| para 31 | 1 Apr 2004 (SI 2004/641) | |
| para 32(1) | See sub-paras (2)–(5) below | |
| para 32(2) | 1 Apr 2006 (SI 2005/2714) | |
| para 32(3) | 1 Apr 2004 (SI 2004/641) | |
| para 32(4)(a) | 1 Apr 2005 (SI 2005/968) | |
| para 32(4)(b) | 1 Apr 2004 (in so far as relates to para 13(3)) (SI 2004/641) | |
| | 1 Oct 2004 (otherwise) (SI 2004/2528) | |
| para 32(5) | 1 Apr 2006 (SI 2005/2714) | |
| para 33(a) | 1 Apr 2006 (SI 2005/2714) | |
| para 33(b) | 1 Apr 2004 (SI 2004/641) | |
| para 34(a) | 1 Apr 2006 (SI 2005/2714) | |
| para 34(b) | 1 Apr 2004 (SI 2004/641) | |
| para 35(a) | 1 Apr 2006 (SI 2005/2714) | |
| para 35(b) | 1 Apr 2004 (SI 2004/641) | |
| para 36(1) | See sub-paras (2)–(4) below | |
| para 36(2), (3) | 1 Apr 2006 (SI 2005/2714) | |
| para 36(4) | 1 Apr 2004 (SI 2004/641) | |
| para 37 | 1 Apr 2004 (SI 2004/641) | |
| para 38 | 1 Oct 2004 (E) (SI 2004/2528) | |
| | 11 Nov 2004 (W) (SI 2004/2916) | |
| para 39 | 1 Apr 2007 (SI 2007/1021) | |
| para 40 | 1 Apr 2004 (SI 2004/641) | |
| para 41 | 1 Aug 2008 (E) (SI 2008/1922) | |
| | *Not yet in force* (W) | |
| para 42 | 17 Mar 2004 (E) (SI 2004/641) | |
| | 1 Apr 2004 (W) (SI 2004/910) | |
| Sch 8 | para 1(1) | See sub-paras (2)–(4) below |
| | para 1(2), (3) | 1 Dec 2005 (SI 2005/2714) |
| | para 1(4) | 1 Apr 2004 (SI 2004/641) |
| | para 2 | See paras 3–52 below |
| | paras 3–18 | 1 Dec 2005 (SI 2005/2714) |
| | para 19 | 1 Apr 2004 (SI 2004/641) |
| | para 20 | 1 Oct 2004 (SI 2004/2528) |
| | paras 21, 22 | 1 Dec 2005 (SI 2005/2714) |
| | para 23 | 1 Apr 2004 (SI 2004/641) |
| | paras 24–42 | 1 Dec 2005 (SI 2005/2714) |
| | paras 43, 44 | 1 Apr 2004 (SI 2004/641) |
| | paras 45, 46 | 1 Dec 2005 (SI 2005/2714) |
| | para 47(1) | See sub-paras (2)–(4) below |
| | para 47(2), (3) | 1 Dec 2005 (SI 2005/2714) |
| | para 47(4) | 1 Apr 2004 (SI 2004/641) |
| | para 48 | 1 Apr 2004 (SI 2004/641) |
| | para 49(1) | See sub-paras (2), (3) below |
| | para 49(2) | 1 Dec 2005 (SI 2005/2714) |
| | para 49(3) | 1 Apr 2004 (SI 2004/641) |
| | para 50(1), (2) | 1 Apr 2004 (in so far as the definitions they amend have effect for the purposes of the provisions of the Water Industry Act 1991 amended or introduced by virtue of a provision brought into force by SI 2004/641) (SI 2004/641) |
| | | 1 Dec 2005 (otherwise) (SI 2005/2714) |

**Water Act 2003 (c 37)**—*contd*

|  |  |  |
|---|---|---|
| | para 50(3) | 1 Apr 2004 (in so far as the definitions it amends have effect for the purposes of the provisions of the Water Industry Act 1991 amended or introduced by virtue of a provision brought into force by SI 2004/641) (SI 2004/641) |
| | | 1 Oct 2004 (in so far as the provision it introduces has effect for the purposes of the provisions of the Water Industry Act 1991 amended or introduced by a provision brought into force by SI 2004/2528, art 2) (SI 2004/2528) |
| | | 1 Dec 2005 (otherwise) (SI 2005/2714) |
| | paras 51, 52 | 1 Dec 2005 (SI 2005/2714) |
| | para 53(1) | See sub-paras (2), (3) below |
| | para 53(2) | 1 Dec 2005 (SI 2005/2714) |
| | para 53(3)(a), (b) | 1 Dec 2005 (SI 2005/2714) |
| | para 53(3)(c) | 1 Apr 2004 (SI 2004/641) |
| | paras 54, 55 | 1 Dec 2005 (SI 2005/2714) |
| Sch 9 | Pt 1 | 1 Apr 2004 (repeal of Water Resources Act 1991, s 33) (SI 2004/641) |
| | | 1 Apr 2005 (repeals of Water Resources Act 1991, ss 28, 39(3)) (SI 2005/968) |
| | | 1 Apr 2006 (repeals of or in Water Resources Act 1991, ss 25(2), 30, 31, 36, 49, 50, 52(8)) (SI 2006/984)[8] |
| | | 1 Jan 2018 (repeals of or in Water Resources Act 1991, ss 21, 29, 47, 49, 50, 223) (SI 2017/1043) |
| | Pt 2 | 1 Apr 2004 (SI 2004/641), repeals of or in— |
| | | Water Industry Act 1991, s 14(8), (8A); |
| | | Utilities Act 2000 |
| | | 1 Oct 2004 (repeals of or in Water Industry Act 1991, ss 12, 193) (SI 2004/2528) |
| | | 1 Apr 2005 (repeals in Water Industry Act 1991, ss 39, 96, 195) (SI 2005/968) |
| | | 1 Oct 2005 (repeals of Water Industry Act 1991, ss 28, 30, 194, Sch 4) (SI 2005/2714) |
| | | 1 Apr 2006 (repeals of Water Industry Act 1991, s 1, Sch 1) (SI 2005/2714) |
| | Pt 3 | 17 Mar 2004 (E) (SI 2004/641), repeals of or in— |
| | | Water Resources Act 1991, ss 147–149, 221(1); |
| | | Environment Act 1995, s 101 |
| | | 1 Apr 2004 (SI 2004/641), repeals of or in— |
| | | Metropolis Water Act 1852; |
| | | Water Industry Act 1991, s 86(1); |
| | | Water Resources Act 1991, ss 77, 79A; |
| | | Environment Act 1995, Sch 4; |
| | | Competition Act 1998, Sch 7, Sch 10, para 13(3); |
| | | National Assembly for Wales (Transfer of Functions) Order 1999, SI 1999/672, Sch 1 (entry relating to Water Industry Act 1991, ss 68–70 in so far as they relate to provisions brought into force by SI 2004/641) |
| | | 1 Apr 2004 (W) (SI 2004/910), repeals of or in— |
| | | Water Resources Act 1991, s 222(1) (it is thought that this should be a reference to s 221(1))[4]; |
| | | Environment Act 1995, s 101(1)[4] |
| | | 28 May 2004 (repeals of or in Water Industry Act 1991, ss 98(5), 101A(2), 102(1)(a), 103(1)(a), 104(6)) (SI 2004/641) |
| | | 1 Oct 2004 (SI 2004/2528), repeals or revocations of or in— |
| | | Reservoirs Act 1975; |
| | | Water Resources Act 1991, Sch 10; |
| | | Competition Act 1998, Sch 10, para 13(2); |

**Water Act 2003 (c 37)**—*contd*

National Assembly for Wales (Transfer of Functions) Order 1999, SI 1999/672, Sch 1 (entry relating to Water Industry Act 1991, ss 18–22, in so far as it relates to provisions brought into force by SI 2004/2528, art 2, and ss 68–70, in so far as it relates to s 70 of that Act)

11 Nov 2004 (W) (repeal of Water Resources Act 1991, ss 147–149) (SI 2004/2916)

1 Apr 2005 (SI 2005/968), repeals or revocations of or in—

Water Industry Act 1991, s 44(5);

Competition and Service (Utilities) Act 1992, s 50;

Competition Act 1998, Sch 10, para 5(3);

National Assembly for Wales (Transfer of Functions) Order 1999, Sch 1 (entry relating to Water Industry Act 1991, s 2, in so far as it relates to provisions amended or introduced by SI 2005/968, art 2)

1 Oct 2005 (SI 2005/2714), repeals or revocations of or in—

House of Commons Disqualification Act 1975, Sch 1, Pt 3 (entry relating to the Chairman of a customer service committee);

Northern Ireland Assembly Disqualification Act 1975, Sch 1, Pt 3 (entry relating to the Chairman of a customer service committee);

Water Act 1989, Sch 4, para 6;

Water Consolidation (Consequential Provisions) Act 1991;

National Assembly for Wales (Transfer of Functions) Order 1999, Sch 1 (entry relating to Water Industry Act 1991, s 28(4))

1 Dec 2005 (revocations in National Assembly for Wales (Transfer of Functions) Order 1999, SI 1999/672, for all remaining purposes) (SI 2005/2714)

1 Apr 2006 (SI 2005/2714), repeals of or in—

Parliamentary Commissioner Act 1967;

House of Commons Disqualification Act 1975, Sch 1, Pt 3 (entry relating to the Director);

Northern Ireland Assembly Disqualification Act 1975, Sch 1, Pt 3 (entry relating to the Director);

Water Act 1989, s 185, Schs 3, 25;

Water Industry Act 1991, s 219(1)

1 Apr 2006 (repeal of Water Resources Act 1991, s 125(2)) (SI 2006/984)[8]

1 Aug 2008 (E) (repeal in Health Authorities Act 1995) (SI 2008/1922)

26 Mar 2010 (E) (repeal of Water Industry Act 1991, Sch 7) (SI 2010/975)

*Not yet in force*, repeals of or in—

Environmental Protection Act 1990;

Water Industry Act 1991, ss 69, 138(5), and Sch 7 (W);

Water Resources Act 1991, ss 66(2)(a), 71(4);

Environment Act 1995, Sch 22;

Health Authorities Act 1995 (W)

[1]    For transitional provisions, see SI 2004/461, art 6, Sch 3

[2]    SI 2004/641 purports to bring Sch 4, para 4 into force for certain purposes, however, it is thought that the intention was to bring para 3 of that Schedule into force as noted above

[3]    For transitional provisions and savings, see SI 2004/2528, art 4, Schedule

[4]    Note that SI 2004/2916 also purports to bring these repeals into force on 11 Nov 2004

[5]    Note that SI 2005/968 also purports to bring this provision into force for certain purposes on 1 Apr 2005

**Water Act 2003 (c 37)**—*contd*

6    It is unclear whether the intention was for Sch 3 to be brought into force on the same date as
     s 36(3)–(6)

7    For transitional provisions and savings, see SI 2005/2714, art 5, Schedule

8    For transitional provisions and savings, see SI 2006/984, art 3(1), Schedule

9    For saving provisions, see SI 2009/359, art 3(1), Schedule

---

## Water Environment and Water Services (Scotland) Act 2003 (asp 3)

*RA:* 5 Mar 2003

*Commencement provisions:* s 38(1); Water Environment and Water Services (Scotland) Act 2003
(Commencement No 1) Order 2003, SSI 2003/562; Water Environment and Water Services
(Scotland) Act 2003 (Commencement No 2) Order 2005, SSI 2005/235; Water Environment and
Water Services (Scotland) Act 2003 (Commencement No 3) Order 2005, SSI 2005/256; Water
Environment and Water Services (Scotland) Act 2003 (Commencement No 4) Order 2006,
SSI 2006/55; Water Environment and Water Services (Scotland) Act 2003 (Commencement No 5)
Order 2007, SSI 2007/50; Water Environment and Water Services (Scotland) Act 2003
(Commencement No 6) Order 2007, SSI 2007/512; Water Environment and Water Services
(Scotland) Act 2003 (Commencement No 7) Order 2007, SSI 2007/530; Water Environment and
Water Services (Scotland) Act 2003 (Commencement No 8) Order 2008, SSI 2008/269; Water
Environment and Water Services (Scotland) Act 2003 (Commencement Order No 9) Order 2013,
SSI 2013/252

| | | |
|---|---|---|
| 1–7 | | 15 Dec 2003 (SSI 2003/562) |
| 8–11 | | 1 Jun 2005 (SSI 2005/235) |
| 12–14 | | 14 Dec 2007 (SSI 2007/530) |
| 15 | | 1 Jun 2005 (SSI 2005/235) |
| 16 | | 14 Dec 2007 (SSI 2007/530) |
| 17 | | 1 Jun 2005 (SSI 2005/235) |
| 18 | | 15 Dec 2003 (SSI 2003/562) |
| 19 | | 14 Dec 2007 (SSI 2007/530) |
| 20, 21 | | 15 Dec 2003 (SSI 2003/562) |
| 22 | | 10 Jul 2008 (SSI 2008/269) |
| 23 | | 21 Sep 2013 (SSI 2013/252) |
| 24 | (1)–(4) | 6 Feb 2007 (for the purpose of enabling provision to be made by order) (SSI 2007/50) |
| | | 31 Mar 2007 (otherwise) (SSI 2007/50) |
| | (5)–(7) | *Never in force* (repealed) |
| 25 | | 20 May 2005 (SSI 2005/256) |
| 26–28 | | 15 Dec 2003 (SSI 2003/562) |
| 29 | | 6 Mar 2006 (SSI 2006/55) |
| 30 | | *Not yet in force* |
| 31 | | 10 Jul 2008 (SSI 2008/269) |
| 32 | | 6 Mar 2006 (SSI 2006/55) |
| 33 | (1) | 6 Mar 2006 (in so far as inserts definitions "public SUD system", "road water", "SUD system" and "sustainable urban drainage system") (SSI 2006/55) |
| | | 30 Nov 2007 (in so far as inserts definition "private SUD system") (SSI 2007/512) |
| | (2) | See Sch 3 below |
| 34 | | See Sch 4 below |
| 35–38 | | 5 Mar 2003 (RA) |
| Schs 1, 2 | | 20 May 2005 (SSI 2005/256) |
| Sch 3 | | 30 Nov 2007 (SSI 2007/512) |
| Sch 4 | para 1 | 10 Jul 2008 (SSI 2008/269) |
| | para 2 | 10 Jul 2008 (SSI 2008/269) (in so far as inserts Water (Scotland) Act 1980, s 23(2B)) |
| | | *Not yet in force* (in so far as inserts s 23(2A) of that Act) |
| | paras 3–5 | *Not yet in force* |

# 2004 Acts

## Age-Related Payments Act 2004 (c 10)

*RA:* 8 Jul 2004

Whole Act in force 8 Jul 2004 (RA)

---

## Antisocial Behaviour etc (Scotland) Act 2004 (asp 8)

*RA:* 26 Jul 2004

*Commencement provisions:* s 145; Antisocial Behaviour etc (Scotland) Act 2004 (Commencement and Savings) Order 2004, SSI 2004/420[1], as amended by SSI 2005/553, SSI 2006/104

| | | |
|---|---|---|
| 1–12 | | 28 Oct 2004 (SSI 2004/420) |
| 13 | | 4 Apr 2005 (SSI 2004/420) |
| 14–40 | | 28 Oct 2004 (SSI 2004/420) |
| 41–54 | | 1 Dec 2004 (SSI 2004/420) |
| 55 | | 5 Nov 2004 (SSI 2004/420) |
| 56–67 | | 28 Oct 2004 (SSI 2004/420) |
| 68 | | 9 Nov 2005 (for the purpose of enabling orders to be made) (SSI 2004/420)[2] |
| | | 30 Apr 2006 (otherwise) (SSI 2004/420) |
| 69–71 | | 30 Apr 2006 (SSI 2004/420) |
| 72 | | 9 Nov 2005 (for the purpose of enabling regulations to be made) (SSI 2004/420)[2] |
| | | 30 Apr 2006 (otherwise) (SSI 2004/420) |
| 73 | | 30 Apr 2006 (SSI 2004/420) |
| 74 | (1)–(4) | 30 Apr 2006 (SSI 2004/420) |
| | (5) | See Sch 3 below |
| 75–77 | | 30 Apr 2006 (SSI 2004/420) |
| 78 | | 9 Nov 2005 (for the purpose of enabling regulations to be made) (SSI 2004/420)[2] |
| | | 30 Apr 2006 (otherwise) (SSI 2004/420) |
| 79 | | 30 Apr 2006 (SSI 2004/420) |
| 80 | | 9 Nov 2005 (for the purpose of enabling regulations to be made) (SSI 2004/420)[2] |
| | | 30 Apr 2006 (otherwise) (SSI 2004/420) |
| 81, 82 | | 30 Apr 2006 (SSI 2004/420) |
| 83 | | 28 Oct 2004 (for the purpose of enabling applications for registration to be made, and fees to be determined by the local authority) (SSI 2004/420) |
| | | 9 Nov 2005 (for the purpose of enabling orders and regulations to be made) (SSI 2004/420)[2] |
| | | 30 Apr 2006 (otherwise) (SSI 2004/420) |
| 84–86 | | 30 Apr 2006 (SSI 2004/420) |
| 87 | | 9 Nov 2005 (for the purpose of enabling regulations to be made) (SSI 2004/420)[2] |
| | | 30 Apr 2006 (otherwise) (SSI 2004/420) |
| 88–96 | | 30 Apr 2006 (SSI 2004/420) |

**Antisocial Behaviour etc (Scotland) Act 2004 (asp 8)**—*contd*

| | | |
|---|---|---|
| 97 | | 9 Nov 2005 (for the purpose of enabling regulations to be made) (SSI 2004/420)[2] |
| | | 30 Apr 2006 (otherwise) (SSI 2004/420) |
| 98 | | 4 Apr 2005 (SSI 2004/420) |
| 99 | | 9 Nov 2005 (for the purpose of enabling regulations to be made) (SSI 2004/420)[2] |
| | | 30 Apr 2006 (otherwise) (SSI 2004/420) |
| 100 | | 28 Oct 2004 (SSI 2004/420) |
| 101 | | 30 Apr 2006 (SSI 2004/420) |
| 102–117 | | 4 Apr 2005 (SSI 2004/420) |
| 118–120 | | 28 Oct 2004 (SSI 2004/420) |
| 121 | | 4 Apr 2005 (SSI 2004/420) |
| 122–125 | | 5 Nov 2004 (SSI 2004/420) |
| 126–134 | | 28 Oct 2004 (SSI 2004/420) |
| 135–137 | | 31 Jan 2005 (SSI 2004/420) |
| 138–140 | | 28 Oct 2004 (SSI 2004/420) |
| 141 | | 26 Jul 2004 (RA) |
| 142, 143 | | 28 Oct 2004 (SSI 2004/420) |
| 144 | (1) | See Sch 4 below |
| | (2) | See Sch 5 below |
| 145 | | 26 Jul 2004 (RA) |
| Sch 1 | | 1 Dec 2004 (SSI 2004/420) |
| Sch 2 | | 28 Oct 2004 (SSI 2004/420) |
| Sch 3 | | 9 Nov 2005 (for the purpose of enabling regulations to be made) (SSI 2004/420)[2] |
| | | 30 Apr 2006 (otherwise) (SSI 2004/420) |
| Sch 4 | para 1(a)(i) | 4 Apr 2005 (SSI 2004/420) |
| | para 1(a)(ii) | 28 Oct 2004 (for the purpose of bringing into force Social Work (Scotland) Act 1968, s 27(1)(b)(va)) (SSI 2004/420) |
| | | 4 Apr 2005 (otherwise) (SSI 2004/420) |
| | para 1(b), (c) | 28 Oct 2004 (SSI 2004/420) |
| | para 2 | 28 Oct 2004 (SSI 2004/420) |
| | para 3 | 1 Dec 2004 (SSI 2004/420) |
| | para 4(1) | 28 Oct 2004 (SSI 2004/420) |
| | para 4(2)–(5) | 31 Jan 2005 (SSI 2004/420) |
| | para 4(6) | 28 Oct 2004 (SSI 2004/420) |
| | para 5(1)–(3) | 28 Oct 2004 (SSI 2004/420) |
| | para 5(4), (5) | 4 Apr 2005 (SSI 2004/420) |
| | para 5(6) | 28 Oct 2004 (SSI 2004/420) |
| | para 5(7)–(10) | 4 Apr 2005 (SSI 2004/420) |
| | para 5(11) | 28 Oct 2004 (SSI 2004/420) |
| | para 5(12) | 1 Dec 2004 (SSI 2004/420) |
| | para 6 | 28 Oct 2004 (SSI 2004/420) |
| Sch 5 | | 28 Oct 2004 (SSI 2004/420), repeals of or in— |
| | | Social Work (Scotland) Act 1968; |
| | | Law Reform (Miscellaneous Provisions) (Scotland) Act 1990; |
| | | Criminal Procedure (Consequential Provisions) (Scotland) Act 1995; |
| | | Crime and Disorder Act 1998; |
| | | Criminal Justice (Scotland) Act 2003 |
| | | 4 Apr 2005 (otherwise) (SSI 2004/420) |

[1]  For savings, see SSI 2004/420, art 4

[2]  Note that SSI 2004/420, Sch 1 originally provided for these provisions to be brought into force on 28 Oct 2004, for the purpose of making orders and/or regulations to come into force on 15 Nov 2005 (ie the date originally appointed for these provisions to come fully into force). Following the amendment of SSI 2004/420 by SSI 2005/553, it is thought that the relevant entries in SSI 2004/420,

**Antisocial Behaviour etc (Scotland) Act 2004 (asp 8)**—*contd*

Sch 1, have been superseded by entries in the inserted Sch 6, which provide for these provisions to be brought into force on 9 Nov 2005 for the purposes of making orders and/or regulations

## Appropriation Act 2004 (c 9)

*RA:* 8 Jul 2004

Whole Act in force 8 Jul 2004 (RA)

## Armed Forces (Pensions and Compensation) Act 2004 (c 32)

*RA:* 18 Nov 2004

*Commencement provisions:* s 8; Armed Forces (Pensions and Compensation) Act 2004 (Commencement No 1) Order 2005, SI 2005/116; Armed Forces (Pensions and Compensation) Act 2004 (Commencement No 2) Order 2005, SI 2005/356; Armed Forces (Pensions and Compensation) Act 2004 (Commencement No 3) Order 2005, SI 2005/3107

| | | |
|---|---|---|
| 1 | | 22 Feb 2005 (SI 2005/356) |
| 2 | | 6 Apr 2005 (SI 2005/356) |
| 3 | | 22 Feb 2005 (SI 2005/356) |
| 4 | | 21 Jan 2005 (SI 2005/116) |
| 5 | | See Sch 1 below |
| 6 | | 11 Nov 2005 (SI 2005/3107) |
| 7 | (1), (2) | 6 Apr 2005 (SI 2005/356) |
| | (3) | 21 Jan 2005 (SI 2005/116) |
| | (4) | See Sch 3 below |
| 8–12 | | 18 Nov 2004 (RA) |
| Sch 1 | para 1 | See paras 2–10 below |
| | para 2 | 21 Jan 2005 (SI 2005/116) |
| | para 3 | 6 Apr 2005 (SI 2005/356) |
| | para 4 | 22 Feb 2005 (for the purpose of making regulations under Pensions Appeal Tribunals Act 1943, ss 6A, 6C, 6D) (SI 2005/356) |
| | | 6 Apr 2005 (otherwise) (SI 2005/356) |
| | para 5 | 6 Apr 2005 (SI 2005/356) |
| | para 6 | 21 Jan 2005 (for the purposes of regulations made under Pensions Appeal Tribunals Act 1943, s 5A) (SI 2005/116) |
| | | 22 Feb 2005 (for the purpose of making regulations under Pensions Appeal Tribunals Act 1943, ss 6A, 6C, 6D) (SI 2005/356) |
| | | 6 Apr 2005 (otherwise) (SI 2005/356) |
| | paras 7, 8 | 6 Apr 2005 (SI 2005/356) |
| | para 9 | 22 Feb 2005 (for the purpose of the Lord Chancellor making regulations under Pensions Appeal Tribunals Act 1943, ss 6A, 6C, 6D) (SI 2005/356) |
| | | 6 Apr 2005 (otherwise) (SI 2005/356) |
| | para 10 | 6 Apr 2005 (SI 2005/356) |
| Sch 2 | | 11 Nov 2005 (SI 2005/3107) |
| Sch 3 | | 21 Jan 2005 (repeals of or in Pensions Appeal Tribunals Act 1943, s 5A(2), (3)) (SI 2005/116) |
| | | 6 Apr 2005 (otherwise) (SI 2005/356), except repeals of or in— |
| | | Patriotic Fund Reorganisation Act 1903; |
| | | Naval and Military War Pensions etc Act 1915; |
| | | War Pensions (Administrative Provisions) Act 1918; |
| | | Royal Patriotic Fund Corporation Act 1950 |
| | | 1 Jan 2006 (exceptions noted above) (SI 2005/3107) |

**Asylum and Immigration (Treatment of Claimants, etc) Act 2004 (c 19)**

*RA:* 22 Jul 2004

*Commencement provisions:* s 48; Asylum and Immigration (Treatment of Claimants, etc) Act 2004 (Commencement No 1) Order 2004, SI 2004/2523; Asylum and Immigration (Treatment of Claimants etc) Act 2004 (Commencement) (Scotland) Order 2004, SSI 2004/494; Asylum and Immigration (Treatment of Claimants, etc) Act 2004 (Commencement No 2) Order 2004, SI 2004/2999; Asylum and Immigration (Treatment of Claimants, etc) Act 2004 (Commencement No 3) Order 2004, SI 2004/3398; Asylum and Immigration (Treatment of Claimants, etc) Act 2004 (Commencement No 4) Order 2005, SI 2005/372; Asylum and Immigration (Treatment of Claimants, etc) Act 2004 (Commencement No 5 and Transitional Provisions) Order 2005, SI 2005/565; Asylum and Immigration (Treatment of Claimants, etc) Act 2004 (Commencement No 6) Order 2006, SI 2006/1517; Asylum and Immigration (Treatment of Claimants, etc) Act 2004 (Commencement No 1) (Northern Ireland) Order 2007, SI 2007/845; Asylum and Immigration (Treatment of Claimants, etc) Act 2004 (Commencement No 7 and Transitional Provisions) Order 2007, SI 2007/1602

| | | |
|---|---|---|
| 1 | | 1 Oct 2004 (SI 2004/2523) |
| 2 | | 22 Sep 2004 (s 48(1)) |
| 3 | | 1 Oct 2004 (SI 2004/2523) |
| 4, 5 | | 1 Dec 2004 (SI 2004/2999; SSI 2004/494) |
| 6 | | 1 Oct 2004 (SI 2004/2523) |
| 7 | | 1 Dec 2004 (SI 2004/2999) |
| 8 | (1)–(6) | 1 Jan 2005 (SI 2004/3398) |
| | (7) | 1 Oct 2004 (for the purpose of enabling the Secretary of State to exercise the power to make subordinate legislation under s 8(7)) (SI 2004/2523) |
| | | 1 Jan 2005 (otherwise) (SI 2004/3398) |
| | (8), (9) | 1 Jan 2005 (SI 2004/3398) |
| | (10), (11) | 1 Oct 2004 (for the purpose of enabling the Secretary of State to exercise the power to make subordinate legislation under s 8(7)) (SI 2004/2523) |
| | | 1 Jan 2005 (otherwise) (SI 2004/3398) |
| | (12), (13) | 1 Jan 2005 (SI 2004/3398) |
| 9 | | 1 Dec 2004 (SI 2004/2999)[2] |
| 10 | (1), (2) | 1 Dec 2004 (SI 2004/2999) |
| | (3)–(5) | 31 Mar 2005 (SI 2005/372) |
| | (6), (7) | 1 Dec 2004 (SI 2004/2999) |
| 11 | | 4 Jan 2005 (SI 2004/2999) |
| 12 | | 14 Jun 2007 (SI 2007/1602)[4] |
| 13 | | 29 Jun 2006 (SI 2006/1517) |
| 14 | | 1 Dec 2004 (SI 2004/2999) |
| 15 | | 1 Oct 2004 (SI 2004/2523) |
| 16 | | *Not yet in force* |
| 17 | | 1 Dec 2004 (SI 2004/2999) |
| 18 | | 1 Oct 2004 (SI 2004/2523) |
| 19 | (1) | 1 Feb 2005 (SI 2004/3398) |
| | (2), (3) | 1 Dec 2004 (for the purpose of enabling the Secretary of State to exercise the powers to make subordinate legislation under s 19(2)(a), (3)(c)) (SI 2004/2999) |
| | | 1 Feb 2005 (otherwise) (SI 2004/3398) |
| | (4) | 1 Dec 2004 (for the purpose of enabling the Registrar General to issue guidance under s 19(4)(d)) (SI 2004/2999) |
| | | 1 Feb 2005 (otherwise) (SI 2004/3398) |
| 20 | (1), (2) | 1 Feb 2005 (SI 2004/3398) |
| | (3), (4) | 1 Dec 2004 (for the purpose of enabling the Secretary of State to exercise the powers to make subordinate legislation under s 19(2)(a), (3)(c)) (SI 2004/2999) |
| | | 1 Feb 2005 (otherwise) (SI 2004/3398) |
| | (5), (6) | 1 Feb 2005 (SI 2004/3398) |
| 21 | (1) | 1 Feb 2005 (SI 2004/3398) |

**Asylum and Immigration (Treatment of Claimants, etc) Act 2004 (c 19)**—*contd*

| | | |
|---|---|---|
| | (2), (3) | 1 Dec 2004 (for the purpose of enabling the Secretary of State to exercise the powers to make subordinate legislation under s 21(2)(a), (3)(c)) (SI 2004/2999) |
| | | 1 Feb 2005 (otherwise) (SI 2004/3398) |
| | (4) | 1 Feb 2005 (SI 2004/3398) |
| | (5) | 1 Dec 2004 (for the purpose of enabling the Secretary of State to issue guidance under s 21(5) and to consult with the Registrar General for Scotland for that purpose) (SI 2004/2999) |
| | | 1 Feb 2005 (otherwise) (SI 2004/3398) |
| 22 | (1) | 1 Feb 2005 (SI 2004/3398) |
| | (2), (3) | 1 Dec 2004 (for the purpose of enabling the Secretary of State to exercise the powers to make subordinate legislation under s 21(2)(a), (3)(c)) (SI 2004/2999) |
| | | 1 Feb 2005 (otherwise) (SI 2004/3398) |
| 23 | (1) | 1 Feb 2005 (SI 2004/3398) |
| | (2), (3) | 1 Dec 2004 (for the purpose of enabling the Secretary of State to exercise the powers to make subordinate legislation under s 23(2)(a), (b), (3)(c)) (SI 2004/2999) |
| | | 1 Feb 2005 (otherwise) (SI 2004/3398) |
| | (4), (5) | 1 Feb 2005 (SI 2004/3398) |
| | (6) | 1 Dec 2004 (for the purpose of enabling the Secretary of State to issue guidance under s 23(6)(d) and to consult with the Registrar General for Northern Ireland for that purpose) (SI 2004/2999) |
| | | 1 Feb 2005 (otherwise) (SI 2004/3398) |
| 24 | (1) | 1 Feb 2005 (SI 2004/3398) |
| | (2) | 1 Dec 2004 (for the purpose of enabling the Secretary of State to exercise the powers to make subordinate legislation under s 23(2)(a), (b), (3)(c)) (SI 2004/2999) |
| | | 1 Feb 2005 (otherwise) (SI 2004/3398) |
| | (3) | 1 Feb 2005 (SI 2004/3398) |
| | (4) | 1 Dec 2004 (for the purpose of enabling the Secretary of State to exercise the powers to make subordinate legislation under s 23(2)(a), (b), (3)(c)) (SI 2004/2999) |
| | | 1 Feb 2005 (otherwise) (SI 2004/3398) |
| 25 | | 1 Dec 2004 (SI 2004/2999) |
| 26 | (1)–(5) | 4 Apr 2005 (SI 2005/565)[3] |
| | (6) | 4 Apr 2005 (except the insertion of s 103D in relation to Northern Ireland) (SI 2005/565)[3] |
| | | 30 Apr 2007 (exception noted above) (SI 2007/845) |
| | (7)–(10) | 4 Apr 2005 (SI 2005/565) |
| 27–31 | | 1 Oct 2004 (SI 2004/2523) |
| 32 | (1) | 22 Sep 2004 (in relation to determinations of the Special Immigration Appeals Commission made after that date) (s 48(2)) |
| | (2) | 22 Sep 2004 (s 48(1)) |
| 33 | | 1 Oct 2004 (SI 2004/2523)[1] |
| 34 | | 1 Oct 2004 (SI 2004/2523) |
| 35 | | 22 Sep 2004 (s 48(1)) |
| 36–46 | | 1 Oct 2004 (SI 2004/2523) |
| 47 | | See Sch 4 below |
| 48–50 | | 22 Jul 2004 (RA) |
| Schs 1, 2 | | 4 Apr 2005 (SI 2005/565)[3] |
| Sch 3 | | 1 Oct 2004 (SI 2004/2523) |
| Sch 4 | | 1 Oct 2004 (SI 2004/2523), repeals of or in— |
| | | Asylum and Immigration Act 1996; |
| | | Immigration and Asylum Act 1999, ss 11, 12, 85, 87, Sch 6; |
| | | Nationality, Immigration and Asylum Act 2002, ss 80, 93, 94 |
| | | 14 Jun 2007 (SI 2007/1602)[4], repeals of or in— |
| | | Immigration and Asylum Act 1999, s 123; |

**Asylum and Immigration (Treatment of Claimants, etc) Act 2004 (c 19)**—*contd*
Nationality, Immigration and Asylum Act 2002, s 52;
State Pension Credit Act 2002;
State Pension Credit Act (Northern Ireland) 2002 (NI);
Tax Credits Act 2002
*Not yet in force*, repeals of or in—
Immigration Act 1971;
House of Commons Disqualification Act 1975;
Northern Ireland Assembly Disqualification Act 1975;
British Nationality Act 1981, s 40A(6)–(8);
Tribunals and Inquiries Act 1992;
Asylum and Immigration Appeals Act 1993, s 9A;
Immigration and Asylum Act 1999, s 72;
Nationality, Immigration and Asylum Act 2002, ss 87, 100–104,
106, 107, Sch 5

[1]   For transitional provisions, see SI 2004/2523, art 3

[2]   For modifications and transitional provisions, see SI 2004/2999, arts 3, 4

[3]   For transitional provisions, see SI 2005/565, arts 3–9

[4]   For transitional provisions, see SI 2007/1602, art 2(3), (4)

---

**Budget (Scotland) Act 2004 (asp 2)**

*RA:* 23 Mar 2004

Whole Act in force 23 Mar 2004 (RA)

---

**Carers (Equal Opportunities) Act 2004 (c 15)**

*RA:* 22 Jul 2004

*Commencement provisions:* s 6; Carers (Equal Opportunities) Act 2004 (Commencement) (England) Order 2005, SI 2005/876; Carers (Equal Opportunities) Act 2004 (Commencement) (Wales) Order 2005, SI 2005/1153

| | | |
|---|---|---|
| 1–5 | | 1 Apr 2005 (E) (SI 2005/876) |
| | | 18 Apr 2005 (W) (SI 2005/1153) |
| 6 | | 22 Jul 2004 (RA) |

---

**Child Trust Funds Act 2004 (c 6)**

*RA:* 13 May 2004

*Commencement provisions:* s 27; Child Trust Funds Act 2004 (Commencement No 1) Order 2004, SI 2004/2422; Child Trust Funds Act 2004 (Commencement No 2) Order 2004, SI 2004/3369

| | | |
|---|---|---|
| 1 | (1), (2) | 6 Apr 2005 (SI 2004/3369) |
| | (3) | 1 Jan 2005 (SI 2004/2422) |
| 2 | | 6 Apr 2005 (SI 2004/3369) |
| 3 | (1) | 1 Jan 2005 (save that an account may only be a child trust fund from the day on which ss 8, 9 come into force) (SI 2004/2422) |
| | (2) | 1 Jan 2005 (for the purpose of allowing accounts to be opened, and contracts with an account provider for their management to be signed, save that the account is only to be a child trust fund, or subscribed to and operated, from the day on which ss 8, 9 come into force) (SI 2004/2422) |
| | | 6 Apr 2005 (otherwise) (SI 2004/3369) |
| | (3) | 1 Jan 2005 (save that an account may only be a child trust fund from the day on which ss 8, 9 come into force) (SI 2004/2422) |

**Child Trust Funds Act 2004 (c 6)**—*contd*

| | | |
|---|---|---|
| | (4)–(9) | 1 Jan 2005 (for the purpose of allowing accounts to be opened, and contracts with an account provider for their management to be signed, save that the account is only to be a child trust fund, or subscribed to and operated, from the day on which ss 8, 9 come into force) (SI 2004/2422) |
| | | 6 Apr 2005 (otherwise) (SI 2004/3369) |
| | (10), (11) | 6 Apr 2005 (SI 2004/3369) |
| | (12) | 1 Jan 2005 (for the purpose of allowing accounts to be opened, and contracts with an account provider for their management to be signed, save that the account is only to be a child trust fund, or subscribed to and operated, from the day on which ss 8, 9 come into force) (SI 2004/2422) |
| | | 6 Apr 2005 (otherwise) (SI 2004/3369) |
| 4 | | 6 Apr 2005 (SI 2004/3369) |
| 5 | (1), (2) | 1 Jan 2005 (for the purpose of ensuring an orderly introduction of accounts, by issuing some vouchers before the day on which ss 8, 9 come into force) (SI 2004/2422) |
| | | 6 Apr 2005 (otherwise) (SI 2004/3369) |
| | (3)–(5) | 1 Jan 2005 (for the purpose of allowing accounts to be opened where a voucher has been issued before the day on which ss 8, 9 come into force, under s 5(1), save that the account is only to be a child trust fund, or subscribed to and operated, from that day) (SI 2004/2422) |
| | | 6 Apr 2005 (otherwise) (SI 2004/3369) |
| 6–14 | | 6 Apr 2005 (SI 2004/3369) |
| 15 | (1) | 1 Jan 2005 (so far as relates to the persons referred to in s 15(2)(a)) (SI 2004/2422) |
| | | 6 Apr 2005 (otherwise) (SI 2004/3369) |
| | (2)(a) | 1 Jan 2005 (SI 2004/2422) |
| | (2)(b)–(f) | 6 Apr 2005 (SI 2004/3369) |
| | (3) | 1 Jan 2005 (so far as relates to the persons referred to in s 15(2)(a)) (SI 2004/2422) |
| | | 6 Apr 2005 (otherwise) (SI 2004/3369) |
| 16 | | 6 Apr 2005 (SI 2004/3369) |
| 17, 18 | | 1 Jan 2005 (SI 2004/2422) |
| 19 | | 6 Apr 2005 (SI 2004/3369) |
| 20 | (1)(a) | 1 Jan 2005 (except for the purposes of ss 6, 7, 9, 10 or 13) (SI 2004/2422) |
| | | 6 Apr 2005 (exception noted above) (SI 2004/3369) |
| | (1)(b), (c) | 6 Apr 2005 (SI 2004/3369) |
| | (2)–(6) | 1 Jan 2005 (except for the purposes of ss 6, 7, 9, 10 or 13) (SI 2004/2422) |
| | | 6 Apr 2005 (exception noted above) (SI 2004/3369) |
| | (7)(a), (b) | 1 Jan 2005 (except for the purposes of ss 6, 7, 9, 10 or 13) (SI 2004/2422) |
| | | 6 Apr 2005 (exception noted above) (SI 2004/3369) |
| | (7)(c) | 6 Apr 2005 (SI 2004/3369) |
| | (8), (9) | 1 Jan 2005 (except for the purposes of ss 6, 7, 9, 10 or 13) (SI 2004/2422) |
| | | 6 Apr 2005 (exception noted above) (SI 2004/3369) |
| 21 | | 1 Jan 2005 (for the purposes of the provisions of s 20 which are commenced by SI 2004/2422) (SI 2004/2422) |
| | | 6 Apr 2005 (otherwise) (SI 2004/3369) |
| 22 | (1) | 1 Jan 2005 (SI 2004/2422) |
| | (2)–(5) | 6 Apr 2005 (SI 2004/3369) |
| | (6) | 1 Jan 2005 (SI 2004/2422) |
| 23 | (1) | 1 Jan 2005 (SI 2004/2422; SI 2004/3369) |
| | (2), (3) | 1 Jan 2005 (for the purposes of s 22(1), (6)) (SI 2004/2422) |
| | | 6 Apr 2005 (otherwise) (SI 2004/3369) |
| | (4)–(7) | 6 Apr 2005 (SI 2004/3369) |

**Child Trust Funds Act 2004 (c 6)**—*contd*

| | | |
|---|---|---|
| 24 | (1)(a), (b) | 1 Jan 2005 (for the purposes of s 22(1), (6)) (SI 2004/2422) |
| | | 6 Apr 2005 (otherwise) (SI 2004/3369) |
| | (1)(c) | 6 Apr 2005 (SI 2004/3369) |
| | (2), (3) | 1 Jan 2005 (for the purposes of s 22(1), (6)) (SI 2004/2422) |
| | | 6 Apr 2005 (otherwise) (SI 2004/3369) |
| | (4) | 6 Apr 2005 (SI 2004/3369) |
| | (5)–(7) | 1 Jan 2005 (SI 2004/2422) |
| 25–31 | | 13 May 2004 (RA) |

**Children Act 2004 (c 31)**

*RA:* 15 Nov 2004

*Commencement provisions:* s 67 (and see also s 18(10)); Children Act 2004 (Commencement No 1) Order 2005, SI 2005/394; Children Act 2004 (Commencement No 2) Order 2005, SI 2005/700; Children Act 2004 (Commencement No 3) Order 2005, SI 2005/847; Children Act 2004 (Commencement No 4 and Savings) Order 2005, SI 2005/2298; Children Act 2004 (Commencement No 5) (Wales) Order 2005, SI 2005/3363; Children Act 2004 (Commencement No 5) Order 2005, SI 2005/3464; Children Act 2004 (Commencement No 6) (Wales) Order 2006, SI 2006/885; Children Act 2004 (Commencement No 8) Order 2006, SI 2006/927; Children Act 2004 (Commencement No 7) (Wales) Order 2006, SI 2006/870; Children Act 2004 (Director of Children's Services) Appointed Day Order 2007, SI 2007/1792; Children Act 2004 (Commencement No 9) Order 2008, SI 2008/752; Children Act 2004 (Commencement No 8) (Wales) Order 2008, SI 2008/1904; Children Act 2004 (Commencement No 9) (Wales) Order 2013, SI 2013/2247

| | | |
|---|---|---|
| 1–9 | | 15 Nov 2004 (s 67(1)) |
| 10 | | 1 Apr 2005 (E) (SI 2005/394) |
| 11 | | 1 Mar 2005 (E) (for the purposes of making an order under s 11(1)(d)) (SI 2005/394) |
| | | 1 Oct 2005 (E) (otherwise) (SI 2005/394) |
| 12 | | 1 Jan 2006 (E) (SI 2005/3464) |
| 13, 14 | | 1 Mar 2005 (E) (for the purposes of making regulations) (SI 2005/394) |
| | | 1 Apr 2006 (otherwise) (SI 2006/927) |
| 15 | | 1 Apr 2006 (SI 2006/927) |
| 16 | | 1 Mar 2005 (E) (for the purposes of making regulations) (SI 2005/394) |
| | | 1 Apr 2006 (otherwise) (SI 2006/927) |
| 17 | | 1 Mar 2005 (E) (SI 2005/394) |
| 18 | | 1 Apr 2005 (E) (SI 2005/394) |
| 19 | | 21 Mar 2008 (SI 2008/752) |
| 20–23 | | 1 Mar 2005 (E) (SI 2005/394) |
| 24 | | 1 Apr 2005 (E) (SI 2005/394) |
| 25 | | 1 Sep 2006 (SI 2006/870) |
| 26 | | 31 Mar 2006 (SI 2006/885) |
| 27 | | 1 Sep 2006 (SI 2006/885) |
| 28 | (1)(a)–(c) | 1 Apr 2006 (SI 2006/885) |
| | (1)(d)–(h) | 9 Sep 2013 (SI 2013/2247) |
| | (1)(i) | 1 Apr 2006 (SI 2006/885) |
| | (2) | 1 Apr 2006 (so far as relating to the persons and bodies referred to in sub-s (1)(a)–(c) and (i)) (SI 2006/885) |
| | | 9 Sep 2013 (so far as relating to the persons and bodies referred to in sub-s (1)(d)–(h)) (SI 2013/2247) |
| | (3), (4) | 1 Apr 2006 (SI 2006/885) |
| | (5) | 9 Sep 2013 (SI 2013/2247) |
| 29 | | *Not yet in force* |
| 30 | | 1 Oct 2006 (SI 2006/885) |
| 31 | | 1 Oct 2006 (SI 2006/870) |
| 32–34 | | 1 Oct 2006 (SI 2006/885) |
| 35–41 | | 1 Apr 2005 (SI 2005/700) |

**Children Act 2004 (c 31)**—*contd*

| | | |
|---|---|---|
| 42, 43 | | 16 Mar 2005 (SI 2005/700) |
| 44 | | 1 Apr 2005 (E) (for the purposes of making regulations) (SI 2005/394) |
| | | 1 Jul 2005 (E) (otherwise) (SI 2005/394) |
| | | 1 Apr 2006 (W) (SI 2006/885) |
| 45–47 | | 15 Jan 2005 (s 67(7)(b)) |
| 48 | | See Sch 4 below |
| 49 | | 15 Jan 2005 (s 67(7)(d)) |
| 50 | | 1 Mar 2005 (E) (SI 2005/394) |
| | | 1 Oct 2006 (W) (SI 2006/885) |
| 51 | | 1 Apr 2005 (E) (SI 2005/394) |
| | | 31 Jul 2008 (W) (SI 2008/1904) |
| 52 | | 1 Jul 2005 (E) (SI 2005/394) |
| | | 1 Oct 2006 (W) (SI 2006/885) |
| 53, 54 | | 1 Mar 2005 (E) (SI 2005/394) |
| | | 1 Apr 2006 (W) (SI 2006/885) |
| 55 | | 1 Apr 2005 (E) (SI 2005/394) |
| | | 1 Apr 2006 (W) (SI 2006/885) |
| 56 | | 1 Apr 2006 (E) (SI 2006/927) |
| | | 1 Oct 2006 (W) (SI 2006/885) |
| 57 | | 1 Mar 2005 (E) (SI 2005/394) |
| | | 30 Dec 2005 (W) (SI 2005/3363) |
| 58 | | 15 Jan 2005 (s 67(7)(f)) |
| 59 | | 15 Nov 2004 (s 67(7)(g)) |
| 60 | | 1 Mar 2005 (SI 2005/394) |
| 61 | | 1 Apr 2006 (SI 2006/885) |
| 62 | | 12 Apr 2005 (SI 2005/847) |
| 63 | | 15 Nov 2004 (s 67(7)(k)) |
| 64–69 | | 15 Nov 2004 (s 67(8)) |
| Sch 1 | | 15 Nov 2004 (s 67(1)) |
| Sch 2 | | In relation to any authority which appoints a director of children's services before the day appointed under s 18(10), this Schedule has effect from the day of his appointment (s 18(9)(a)) |
| | | 1 Jan 2008 (otherwise) (SI 2007/1792)[2] |
| Sch 3 | | 1 Apr 2005 (SI 2005/700) |
| Sch 4 | para 1 | See paras 2–9 below |
| | para 2 | 1 Mar 2005 (E) (SI 2005/394) |
| | | 1 Apr 2006 (W) (SI 2006/885) |
| | paras 3, 4 | 3 Oct 2005 (E) (SI 2005/2298) |
| | | 1 Apr 2006 (W) (SI 2006/885) |
| | para 5 | 1 Mar 2005 (E) (SI 2005/394) |
| | | *Not yet in force* (W) |
| | para 6 | 3 Oct 2005 (E) (SI 2005/2298)[1] |
| | | 1 Apr 2006 (W) (SI 2006/885) |
| | paras 7–9 | 1 Mar 2005 (E) (SI 2005/394) |
| | | 1 Apr 2006 (W) (SI 2006/885) |
| Sch 5 | Pt 1 | 1 Mar 2005 (E) (SI 2005/394) |
| | | 1 Apr 2006 (W) (in so far as it relates to the Adoption and Children Act 2002, s 5) (SI 2006/885) |
| | | 1 Sep 2006 (W) (otherwise, except repeal of the Children Act 1989, Sch 2, para 1A) (SI 2006/885) |
| | | 31 Jul 2008 (W) (exception noted above) (SI 2008/1904) |
| | Pt 2 | 1 Mar 2005 (E) (repeals of or in Children Act 1989, s 79G(2), Sch 9A, para 4(3A)(b)) (SI 2005/394) |
| | | 3 Oct 2005 (E) (otherwise) (SI 2005/2298) |
| | | 1 Apr 2006 (W) (SI 2006/885) |
| | Pt 3 | 1 Apr 2005 (E) (SI 2005/394) |
| | | 31 Jul 2008 (W) (SI 2008/1904) |
| | Pt 4 | 1 Apr 2005 (E) (SI 2005/394) |

**Children Act 2004 (c 31)**—*contd*

|  |  |  |
|---|---|---|
|  |  | 1 Apr 2006 (W) (SI 2006/885) |
|  | Pt 5 | 15 Jan 2005 (Sch 5, Pt 5) |
|  | Pt 6 | 1 Mar 2005 (Sch 5, Pt 6; SI 2005/394) |

[1]   For savings, see SI 2005/2298, art 2(2)

[2]   1 Jan 2008 was the day appointed under the Children Act 2004, s 18(10)

---

**Christmas Day (Trading) Act 2004 (c 26)**

*RA:* 28 Oct 2004

*Commencement provisions:* s 6(3); Christmas Day (Trading) Act 2004 (Commencement) Order 2004, SI 2004/3235

Whole Act in force 9 Dec 2004 (SI 2004/3235)

---

**Civil Contingencies Act 2004 (c 36)**

*RA:* 18 Nov 2004

*Commencement provisions:* s 34; Civil Contingencies Act 2004 (Commencement No 1) Order 2004, SI 2004/3281; Civil Contingencies Act 2004 (Commencement No 2) Order 2005, SI 2005/772; Civil Contingencies Act 2004 (Commencement No 3) Order 2005, SI 2005/2040; Civil Contingencies Act 2004 (Commencement) (Scotland) Order 2005, SSI 2005/493

| | | |
|---|---|---|
| 1 | (1)–(3) | 14 Nov 2005 (SI 2005/2040) |
| | (4) | 14 Nov 2005 (SI 2005/2040; SSI 2005/493) |
| | (5) | 14 Nov 2005 (SI 2005/2040) |
| 2 | (1), (2) | 14 Nov 2005 (SI 2005/2040; SSI 2005/493) |
| | (3) | 22 Jul 2005 (except in so far as it relates to sub-ss (4), (6) of this section) (SI 2005/2040) |
| | | *Not yet in force* (exception noted above) |
| | (4) | 6 Oct 2005 (SSI 2005/493) |
| | (5) | 22 Jul 2005 (except in so far as it relates to sub-ss (4), (6) of this section) (SI 2005/2040) |
| | | 6 Oct 2005 (exception noted above) (SSI 2005/493) |
| | (6) | 6 Oct 2005 (SSI 2005/493) |
| 3 | (1) | 14 Nov 2005 (except in so far as it relates to sub-s (2) of this section) (SI 2005/2040) |
| | (2) | 6 Oct 2005 (SSI 2005/493) |
| | (3) | 14 Nov 2005 (SI 2005/2040; SSI 2005/493) |
| | (4), (5) | 6 Oct 2005 (in so far as they relate to sub-s (2) of this section) (SSI 2005/493) |
| | | 14 Nov 2005 (otherwise) (SI 2005/2040) |
| 4 | (1) | 14 Nov 2005 (only for the purpose of permitting a body specified in Sch 1, paras 1, 2, 13 of this Act to provide advice and assistance of the kind specified in sub-s (1) of this section) (SI 2005/2040; SSI 2005/493) |
| | | 15 May 2006 (otherwise) (SI 2005/2040; SSI 2005/493) |
| | (2) | 22 Jul 2005 (except in so far as it relates to sub-ss (3), (7) of this section and only for the purpose of permitting a body specified in Sch 1, paras 1, 2 of this Act to provide advice and assistance of the kind specified in sub-s (1) of this section) (SI 2005/2040) |
| | | 15 May 2006 (otherwise, except in so far as it relates to sub-ss (3), (7) of this section) (SI 2005/2040) |
| | (3) | 6 Oct 2005 (SSI 2005/493) |

**Civil Contingencies Act 2004 (c 36)**—*contd*

| | | |
|---|---|---|
| | (4), (5) | 22 Jul 2005 (except in so far as they relate to sub-ss (3), (7) of this section and only for the purpose of permitting a body specified in Sch 1, paras 1, 2 of this Act to provide advice and assistance of the kind specified in sub-s (1) of this section) (SI 2005/2040) |
| | | 6 Oct 2005 (in so far as they relate to sub-ss (3), (7) of this section) (SSI 2005/493) |
| | | 15 May 2006 (otherwise) (SI 2005/2040) |
| | (6) | 14 Nov 2005 (except in so far as it relates to sub-ss (3), (7) of this section and only for the purpose of permitting a body specified in Sch 1, paras 1, 2 of this Act to provide advice and assistance of the kind specified in sub-s (1) of this section) (SI 2005/2040) |
| | | 15 May 2006 (otherwise, except in so far as it relates to sub-ss (3), (7) of this section) (SI 2005/2040) |
| | (7) | 6 Oct 2005 (SSI 2005/493) |
| | (8) | 14 Nov 2005 (except in so far as it relates to sub-ss (3), (7) of this section and only for the purpose of permitting a body specified in Sch 1, paras 1, 2 of this Act to provide advice and assistance of the kind specified in sub-s (1) of this section) (SI 2005/2040) |
| | | 14 Nov 2005 (in so far as it relates to sub-ss (3), (7) of this section) (SSI 2005/493) |
| | | 15 May 2006 (otherwise) (SI 2005/2040) |
| 5 | (1) | 14 Nov 2005 (except in so far as it relates to sub-ss (2), (5) of this section) (SI 2005/2040) |
| | (2) | 14 Nov 2005 (SSI 2005/493) |
| | (3), (4) | 14 Nov 2005 (SI 2005/2040; SSI 2005/493) |
| | (5) | 14 Nov 2005 (SSI 2005/493) |
| 6 | (1) | 22 Jul 2005 (except in so far as it relates to sub-ss (2), (5) of this section) (SI 2005/2040) |
| | (2) | 6 Oct 2005 (SSI 2005/493) |
| | (3) | 6 Oct 2005 (in so far as it relates to sub-ss (2), (5) of this section) (SSI 2005/493) |
| | | 14 Nov 2005 (otherwise) (SI 2005/2040) |
| | (4) | 14 Nov 2005 (except in so far as it relates to sub-ss (2), (5) of this section) (SI 2005/2040) |
| | (5) | 6 Oct 2005 (SSI 2005/493) |
| | (6) | 14 Nov 2005 (SI 2005/2040; SSI 2005/493) |
| 7 | | 14 Nov 2005 (SI 2005/2040) |
| 8 | | 14 Nov 2005 (SSI 2005/493) |
| 9 | (1) | 14 Nov 2005 (except in so far as it relates to sub-s (2) of this section) (SI 2005/2040) |
| | (2) | 14 Nov 2005 (SSI 2005/493) |
| | (3), (4) | 14 Nov 2005 (SI 2005/2040; SSI 2005/493) |
| 10 | | 14 Nov 2005 (SI 2005/2040) |
| 11 | | 14 Nov 2005 (SSI 2005/493) |
| 12 | | 22 Jul 2005 (SI 2005/2040) |
| 13 | (1) | 22 Jul 2005 (except in so far as it relates to sub-s (2) of this section) (SI 2005/2040) |
| | (2) | 6 Oct 2005 (SSI 2005/493) |
| | (3) | 22 Jul 2005 (except in so far as it relates to sub-s (2) of this section) (SI 2005/2040) |
| | | 6 Oct 2005 (exception noted above) (SSI 2005/493) |
| 14 | (1) | 14 Nov 2005 (SI 2005/2040) |
| | (2) | 6 Oct 2005 (SSI 2005/493) |
| 15 | | 22 Jul 2005 (SI 2005/2040) |
| 16 | | 14 Nov 2005 (SI 2005/2040) |
| 17 | (1) | 6 Oct 2005 (in so far as it relates to sub-ss (3), (5) of this section) (SSI 2005/493) |

**Civil Contingencies Act 2004 (c 36)**—*contd*

|  |  | 14 Nov 2005 (otherwise) (SI 2005/2040) |
| --- | --- | --- |
|  | (2) | 14 Nov 2005 (except in so far as it relates to sub-ss (3), (5) of this section) (SI 2005/2040) |
|  | (3) | 6 Oct 2005 (SSI 2005/493) |
|  | (4) | 14 Nov 2005 (except in so far as it relates to sub-ss (3), (5) of this section) (SI 2005/2040) |
|  | (5) | 6 Oct 2005 (SSI 2005/493) |
|  | (6) | 22 Jul 2005 (except in so far as it relates to sub-ss (3), (5) of this section) (SI 2005/2040) |
|  |  | 6 Oct 2005 (exception noted above) (SSI 2005/493) |
| 18 |  | 14 Nov 2005 (SI 2005/2040) |
| 19–31 |  | 10 Dec 2004 (SI 2004/3281) |
| 32 | (1) | See Sch 2 below |
|  | (2) | See Sch 3 below |
| 33 |  | 14 Nov 2005 (SI 2005/2040) |
| 34–36 |  | 18 Nov 2004 (RA) |
| Sch 1 |  | 14 Nov 2005 (SI 2005/2040) |
| Sch 2 | Pt 1, paras 1, 2 | 14 Nov 2005 (SI 2005/2040) |
|  | Pt 1, para 3 | 1 Apr 2005 (in so far as it relates to the Civil Defence Act 1948, ss 3, 3A, 3B, in so far as those provisions relate to, or to anything done in, a financial year beginning on or after 1 Apr 2005) (SI 2005/772) |
|  |  | *Not yet in force* (otherwise)[1] |
|  | Pt 1, paras 4–9 | 14 Nov 2005 (SI 2005/2040) |
|  | Pt 1, para 10 | 1 Apr 2005 (SI 2005/772) |
|  | Pt 2 | 10 Dec 2004 (SI 2004/3281) |
|  | Pt 3 | 19 Jan 2005 (SI 2004/3281) |
| Sch 3 |  | 10 Dec 2004 (repeals of Emergency Powers Act 1920; Emergency Powers Act (Northern Ireland) 1926) (SI 2004/3281) |
|  |  | 1 Apr 2005 (repeals of Civil Defence Act 1948, ss 3, 3A, 3B, in so far as those provisions relate to, or to anything done in, a financial year beginning on or after 1 Apr 2005) (SI 2005/772) |
|  |  | 14 Nov 2005 (otherwise, except for remaining repeals of Civil Defence Act 1948, ss 3, 3A, 3B) (SI 2005/2040) |

[1]    Note that the Civil Contingencies Secretariat Legislation Team have confirmed that the intention was to bring the repeal of the Civil Defence Act 1948, ss 1, 2, 4–11 into force on 14 Nov 2005 at the same time as the corresponding repeal in Sch 3

**Civil Partnership Act 2004 (c 33)**

*RA:* 18 Nov 2004

*Commencement provisions:* s 263; Civil Partnership Act 2004 (Commencement No 1) Order 2005, SI 2005/1112; Civil Partnership Act 2004 (Commencement No 1) (Scotland) Order 2005, SSI 2005/428; Civil Partnership Act 2004 (Commencement No 2) (Scotland) Order 2005, SSI 2005/604; Civil Partnership Act 2004 (Commencement No 1) (Northern Ireland) Order 2005, SI 2005/2399; Civil Partnership Act 2004 (Commencement No 2) (Northern Ireland) Order 2005, SI 2005/3058; Civil Partnership Act 2004 (Commencement No 2) Order 2005, SI 2005/3175; Civil Partnership Act 2004 (Commencement No 3) (Northern Ireland) Order 2005, SI 2005/3255; Civil Partnership Act 2004 (Commencement No 3) Order 2006, SI 2006/639; Civil Partnership Act 2004 (Commencement No 4) (Northern Ireland) Order 2006, SI 2006/928

| 1 |  | 5 Dec 2005 (SI 2005/3175) |
| --- | --- | --- |
| 2 | (1)–(3) | 5 Dec 2005 (SI 2005/3175) |
|  | (4)(a) | 5 Dec 2005 (SI 2005/3175) |
|  | (4)(b) | 15 Apr 2005 (for the purpose of the power to prescribe information by regulations) (SI 2005/1112) |
|  |  | 5 Dec 2005 (otherwise) (SI 2005/3175) |
|  | (5)–(7) | 5 Dec 2005 (SI 2005/3175) |

**Civil Partnership Act 2004 (c 33)**—*contd*

| | | |
|---|---|---|
| 3–7 | | 5 Dec 2005 (SI 2005/3175) |
| 8 | (1) | *Never in force* (substituted) |
| | (2) | 15 Apr 2005 (for the purpose of the power to prescribe information by regulations) (SI 2005/1112) |
| | | 5 Dec 2005 (otherwise) (SI 2005/3175) |
| | (3)–(7) | 5 Dec 2005 (SI 2005/3175) |
| 9 | | 5 Dec 2005 (SI 2005/3175) |
| 10 | (1) | 5 Dec 2005 (SI 2005/3175) |
| | (2)(a), (b) | 5 Dec 2005 (SI 2005/3175) |
| | (2)(c) | 15 Apr 2005 (for the purpose of the power to prescribe information by regulations) (SI 2005/1112) |
| | | 5 Dec 2005 (otherwise) (SI 2005/3175) |
| 11 | | 5 Dec 2005 (SI 2005/3175) |
| 12 | (1) | 5 Dec 2005 (SI 2005/3175) |
| | (2) | 15 Apr 2005 (SI 2005/1112) |
| | (3) | 5 Dec 2005 (SI 2005/3175) |
| 13 | | 5 Dec 2005 (SI 2005/3175) |
| 14 | (1) | 5 Dec 2005 (SI 2005/3175) |
| | (2) | 15 Apr 2005 (SI 2005/1112) |
| | (3)–(5) | 5 Dec 2005 (SI 2005/3175) |
| 15–17 | | 5 Dec 2005 (SI 2005/3175) |
| 18 | (1)–(3) | 5 Dec 2005 (SI 2005/3175) |
| | (4) | 15 Apr 2005 (for the purpose of the power to prescribe matters by regulations) (SI 2005/1112) |
| | | 5 Dec 2005 (otherwise) (SI 2005/3175) |
| | (5), (6) | 5 Dec 2005 (SI 2005/3175) |
| 19 | (1)–(4) | 5 Dec 2005 (SI 2005/3175) |
| | (5) | 15 Apr 2005 (for the purpose of the power to prescribe matters by regulations) (SI 2005/1112) |
| | | 5 Dec 2005 (otherwise) (SI 2005/3175) |
| | (6)–(8) | 5 Dec 2005 (SI 2005/3175) |
| 20 | | 5 Dec 2005 (SI 2005/3175) |
| 21 | (1) | 5 Dec 2005 (SI 2005/3175) |
| | (2) | 15 Apr 2005 (for the purpose of the power to prescribe matters by regulations) (SI 2005/1112) |
| | | 5 Dec 2005 (otherwise) (SI 2005/3175) |
| | (3) | 5 Dec 2005 (SI 2005/3175) |
| 22–24 | | 5 Dec 2005 (SI 2005/3175) |
| 25 | (1)–(4) | 5 Dec 2005 (SI 2005/3175) |
| | (5) | 15 Apr 2005 (SI 2005/1112) |
| | (6), (7) | 5 Dec 2005 (SI 2005/3175) |
| 26–33 | | 5 Dec 2005 (SI 2005/3175) |
| 34 | (1) | 15 Apr 2005 (SI 2005/1112) |
| | (2) | 5 Dec 2005 (SI 2005/3175) |
| 35, 36 | | 15 Apr 2005 (SI 2005/1112) |
| 37–41 | | 5 Dec 2005 (SI 2005/3175) |
| 42 | (1) | 15 Apr 2005 (for the purpose of making rules of court under s 42(2)) (SI 2005/1112) |
| | | 5 Dec 2005 (otherwise) (SI 2005/3175) |
| | (2) | 15 Apr 2005 (SI 2005/1112) |
| | (3), (4) | 5 Dec 2005 (SI 2005/3175) |
| 43, 44 | | 5 Dec 2005 (SI 2005/3175) |
| 45 | (1), (2) | 5 Dec 2005 (SI 2005/3175) |
| | (3), (4) | 15 Apr 2005 (SI 2005/1112) |
| | (5)–(8) | 5 Dec 2005 (SI 2005/3175) |
| 46–60 | | 5 Dec 2005 (SI 2005/3175) |
| 61 | (1) | 15 Apr 2005 (for the purpose of making rules of court under s 61(2)) (SI 2005/1112) |
| | | 5 Dec 2005 (otherwise) (SI 2005/3175) |

**See Halsbury's Statutes Citator for amendments to these Acts**

**Civil Partnership Act 2004 (c 33)**—*contd*

| | | |
|---|---|---|
| | (2) | 15 Apr 2005 (SI 2005/1112) |
| 62, 63 | | 5 Dec 2005 (SI 2005/3175) |
| 64 | (1), (2) | 15 Apr 2005 (SI 2005/1112) |
| | (3) | 5 Dec 2005 (SI 2005/3175) |
| 65 | | 5 Dec 2005 (SI 2005/3175) |
| 66 | (1)(a) | 5 Dec 2005 (SI 2005/3175) |
| | (1)(b) | 15 Apr 2005 (for the purpose of making rules of court under s 66(3)) (SI 2005/1112) |
| | | 5 Dec 2005 (otherwise) (SI 2005/3175) |
| | (2) | 5 Dec 2005 (SI 2005/3175) |
| | (3) | 15 Apr 2005 (SI 2005/1112) |
| 67–74 | | 5 Dec 2005 (SI 2005/3175) |
| 75 | (1) | 5 Dec 2005 (SI 2005/3175) |
| | (2) | 30 Dec 2005 (SI 2005/3175) |
| | (3), (4) | 5 Dec 2005 (SI 2005/3175) |
| 76–78 | | 5 Dec 2005 (SI 2005/3175) |
| 79 | | 30 Dec 2005 (SI 2005/3175) |
| 80–84 | | 5 Dec 2005 (SI 2005/3175) |
| 85–87 | | 5 Dec 2005 (SSI 2005/604) |
| 88 | (1) | 14 Sep 2005 (for the purpose of the power to prescribe matters by regulations) (SSI 2005/428) |
| | | 5 Dec 2005 (otherwise) (SSI 2005/604) |
| | (2)–(4) | 5 Dec 2005 (SSI 2005/604) |
| | (5) | 14 Sep 2005 (for the purpose of the power to prescribe matters by regulations) (SSI 2005/428) |
| | | 5 Dec 2005 (otherwise) (SSI 2005/604) |
| | (6) | 5 Dec 2005 (SSI 2005/604) |
| 89 | (1) | 14 Sep 2005 (for the purpose of the power to prescribe particulars by regulations) (SSI 2005/428) |
| | | 5 Dec 2005 (otherwise) (SSI 2005/604) |
| | (2) | 14 Sep 2005 (SSI 2005/428) |
| 90 | (1)–(3) | 5 Dec 2005 (SSI 2005/604) |
| | (4) | 14 Sep 2005 (SSI 2005/428) |
| 91–93 | | 5 Dec 2005 (SSI 2005/604) |
| 94 | | 14 Sep 2005 (for the purpose of the power to prescribe a form by regulations) (SSI 2005/428) |
| | | 5 Dec 2005 (otherwise) (SSI 2005/604) |
| 95 | (1), (2) | 5 Dec 2005 (SSI 2005/604) |
| | (3), (4) | 14 Sep 2005 (SSI 2005/428) |
| 96 | | 5 Dec 2005 (SSI 2005/604) |
| 97 | (1), (2) | 5 Dec 2005 (SSI 2005/604) |
| | (3) | 14 Sep 2005 (for the purpose of the power to prescribe a form by regulations) (SSI 2005/428) |
| | | 5 Dec 2005 (otherwise) (SSI 2005/604) |
| | (4)–(6) | 5 Dec 2005 (SSI 2005/604) |
| 98 | | 5 Dec 2005 (SSI 2005/604) |
| 99 | (1) | 5 Dec 2005 (SSI 2005/604) |
| | (2) | 14 Sep 2005 (for the purpose of the power to prescribe errors by regulations) (SSI 2005/428) |
| | | 5 Dec 2005 (otherwise) (SSI 2005/604) |
| | (3) | 5 Dec 2005 (SSI 2005/604) |
| 100–121 | | 5 Dec 2005 (SSI 2005/604) |
| 122 | (1), (2) | 5 Dec 2005 (SSI 2005/604) |
| | (3) | 14 Sep 2005 (SSI 2005/428) |
| | (4) | 14 Sep 2005 (for the purpose of the power to prescribe fees by regulations) (SSI 2005/428) |
| | | 5 Dec 2005 (otherwise) (SSI 2005/604) |
| | (5), (6) | 5 Dec 2005 (SSI 2005/604) |
| 123–125 | | 5 Dec 2005 (SSI 2005/604) |

**Civil Partnership Act 2004 (c 33)**—*contd*

| | | |
|---|---|---|
| 126 | | 14 Sep 2005 (SSI 2005/428) |
| 127–133 | | 5 Dec 2005 (SSI 2005/604) |
| 134 | | 14 Sep 2005 (for the purpose of the power to prescribe matters by regulations) (SSI 2005/428) |
| | | 5 Dec 2005 (otherwise) (SSI 2005/604) |
| 135, 136 | | 14 Sep 2005 (SSI 2005/428) |
| 137, 138 | | 5 Dec 2005 (SI 2005/3255) |
| 139 | (1) | 5 Dec 2005 (SI 2005/3255) |
| | (2), (3) | 5 Sep 2005 (for the purpose of the power to prescribe matters by regulations) (SI 2005/2399) |
| | | 5 Dec 2005 (otherwise) (SI 2005/3255) |
| 140 | (1)(a) | 5 Sep 2005 (for the purpose of the power to prescribe matters by regulations) (SI 2005/2399) |
| | | 5 Dec 2005 (otherwise) (SI 2005/3255) |
| | (1)(b) | 5 Dec 2005 (SI 2005/3255) |
| | (2)–(5) | 5 Dec 2005 (SI 2005/3255) |
| 141, 142 | | 5 Dec 2005 (SI 2005/3255) |
| 143 | | 5 Sep 2005 (for the purpose of the power to prescribe matters by regulations) (SI 2005/2399) |
| | | 5 Dec 2005 (otherwise) (SI 2005/3255) |
| 144 | (1)–(3) | 5 Dec 2005 (SI 2005/3255) |
| | (4) | 5 Sep 2005 (for the purpose of the power to prescribe matters by regulations) (SI 2005/2399) |
| | | 5 Dec 2005 (otherwise) (SI 2005/3255) |
| | (5) | 5 Dec 2005 (SI 2005/3255) |
| | (6) | 5 Sep 2005 (for the purpose of the power to prescribe matters by regulations) (SI 2005/2399) |
| | | 5 Dec 2005 (otherwise) (SI 2005/3255) |
| | (7) | 5 Dec 2005 (SI 2005/3255) |
| 145 | (1), (2) | 5 Dec 2005 (SI 2005/3255) |
| | (3) | 5 Sep 2005 (for the purpose of the power to prescribe matters by regulations) (SI 2005/2399) |
| | | 5 Dec 2005 (otherwise) (SI 2005/3255) |
| | (4), (5) | 5 Dec 2005 (SI 2005/3255) |
| 146 | | 5 Dec 2005 (SI 2005/3255) |
| 147 | (1) | 5 Sep 2005 (for the purpose of the power to prescribe matters by regulations) (SI 2005/2399) |
| | | 5 Dec 2005 (otherwise) (SI 2005/3255) |
| | (2) | 5 Dec 2005 (SI 2005/3255) |
| 148 | | 5 Dec 2005 (SI 2005/3255) |
| 149 | (1) | 5 Dec 2005 (SI 2005/3255) |
| | (2)(a) | 5 Sep 2005 (for the purpose of the power to prescribe matters by regulations) (SI 2005/2399) |
| | | 5 Dec 2005 (otherwise) (SI 2005/3255) |
| | (2)(b), (c) | 5 Dec 2005 (SI 2005/3255) |
| | (3)–(5) | 5 Dec 2005 (SI 2005/3255) |
| 150, 151 | | 5 Dec 2005 (SI 2005/3255) |
| 152 | (1)–(4) | 5 Dec 2005 (SI 2005/3255) |
| | (5) | 5 Sep 2005 (SI 2005/2399) |
| | (6) | 5 Dec 2005 (SI 2005/3255) |
| 153, 154 | | 5 Dec 2005 (SI 2005/3255) |
| 155 | (1), (2) | 5 Dec 2005 (SI 2005/3255) |
| | (3) | 5 Sep 2005 (for the purpose of the power to prescribe matters by Order) (SI 2005/2399) |
| | | 5 Dec 2005 (otherwise) (SI 2005/3255) |
| | (4), (5) | 5 Dec 2005 (SI 2005/3255) |
| 156 | (1) | 5 Sep 2005 (for the purpose of the power to prescribe matters by regulations or Order) (SI 2005/2399) |
| | | 5 Dec 2005 (otherwise) (SI 2005/3255) |
| | (2) | 5 Dec 2005 (SI 2005/3255) |

**See Halsbury's Statutes Citator for amendments to these Acts**

**Civil Partnership Act 2004 (c 33)**—*contd*

| | | |
|---|---|---|
| | (3) | 5 Sep 2005 (for the purpose of the power to prescribe matters by regulations or Order) (SI 2005/2399) |
| | | 5 Dec 2005 (otherwise) (SI 2005/3255) |
| 157 | | 5 Sep 2005 (SI 2005/2399) |
| 158 | | 5 Dec 2005 (SI 2005/3255) |
| 159, 160 | | 5 Sep 2005 (SI 2005/2399) |
| 161–168 | | 5 Dec 2005 (SI 2005/3255) |
| 169 | (1), (2) | 5 Dec 2005 (SI 2005/3255) |
| | (3), (4) | 5 Sep 2005 (SI 2005/2399) |
| | (5)–(8) | 5 Dec 2005 (SI 2005/3255) |
| 170–183 | | 5 Dec 2005 (SI 2005/3255) |
| 184 | (1) | 5 Sep 2005 (for the purpose of making rules of court under sub-s (2)) (SI 2005/2399) |
| | | 5 Dec 2005 (otherwise) (SI 2005/3255) |
| | (2) | 5 Sep 2005 (SI 2005/2399) |
| | (3)–(5) | 5 Dec 2005 (SI 2005/3255) |
| | (6) | 5 Sep 2005 (SI 2005/2399) |
| | (7) | 5 Dec 2005 (SI 2005/3255) |
| | (8) | 5 Sep 2005 (SI 2005/2399) |
| 185, 186 | | 5 Dec 2005 (SI 2005/3255) |
| 187 | (1), (2) | 5 Sep 2005 (SI 2005/2399) |
| | (3) | 5 Dec 2005 (SI 2005/3255) |
| 188 | | 5 Sep 2005 (SI 2005/2399) |
| 189 | (1) | 5 Sep 2005 (SI 2005/2399) |
| | (2) | 5 Sep 2005 (for the purpose of making rules of court under sub-s (1)) (SI 2005/2399) |
| | | 5 Dec 2005 (otherwise) (SI 2005/3255) |
| | (3) | 5 Dec 2005 (SI 2005/3255) |
| 190 | (1) | 5 Dec 2005 (SI 2005/3255) |
| | (2)–(4) | 5 Sep 2005 (for the purpose of making rules of court under sub-s (2)) (SI 2005/2399) |
| | | 5 Dec 2005 (otherwise) (SI 2005/3255) |
| | (5), (6) | 5 Dec 2005 (SI 2005/3255) |
| 191 | (1), (2) | 5 Dec 2005 (SI 2005/3255) |
| | (3) | 5 Sep 2005 (for the purpose of making rules of court) (SI 2005/2399) |
| | | 5 Dec 2005 (otherwise) (SI 2005/3255) |
| 192–209 | | 5 Dec 2005 (SI 2005/3255) |
| 210 | (1), (2) | 15 Apr 2005 (SI 2005/1112) |
| | (3) | 5 Dec 2005 (SI 2005/3175) |
| | (4), (5) | 15 Apr 2005 (SI 2005/1112) |
| 211 | | 15 Apr 2005 (SI 2005/1112) |
| 212 | | 5 Dec 2005 (SI 2005/3175) |
| 213 | (1) | 5 Dec 2005 (SI 2005/3175) |
| | (2)–(6) | 18 Nov 2004 (s 263(6)) |
| 214–218 | | 5 Dec 2005 (SI 2005/3175) |
| 219 | | 15 Apr 2005 (SI 2005/1112) |
| 220 | | 15 Apr 2005 (for the purpose of making rules of court under s 223) (SI 2005/1112) |
| | | 5 Dec 2005 (otherwise) (SI 2005/3175) |
| 221, 222 | | 5 Dec 2005 (SI 2005/3175) |
| 223 | | 15 Apr 2005 (SI 2005/1112) |
| 224, 225 | | 5 Dec 2005 (SI 2005/3175) |
| 226 | | 15 Apr 2005 (SI 2005/1112) |
| 227 | | 5 Dec 2005 (SI 2005/3175) |
| 228 | | 15 Apr 2005 (for the purpose of making rules of court under s 231) (SI 2005/1112) |
| | | 5 Dec 2005 (otherwise) (SI 2005/3175) |
| 229, 230 | | 5 Dec 2005 (SI 2005/3175) |

**Civil Partnership Act 2004 (c 33)**—*contd*

| | | |
|---|---|---|
| 231 | | 15 Apr 2005 (SI 2005/1112) |
| 232–236 | | 5 Dec 2005 (SI 2005/3175) |
| 237 | (1) | 5 Dec 2005 (SI 2005/3175) |
| | (2)–(5) | 15 Apr 2005 (SI 2005/1112) |
| | (6) | 5 Dec 2005 (SI 2005/3175) |
| 238 | | 5 Dec 2005 (SI 2005/3175) |
| 239–244 | | 15 Apr 2005 (SI 2005/1112) |
| 245 | | 15 Apr 2005 (for the purpose of the provisions of Pt 5 of the Act brought into force by this order) (SI 2005/1112) |
| | | 5 Dec 2005 (otherwise) (SI 2005/3175) |
| 246 | | 5 Dec 2005 (SI 2005/3175) |
| 247 | (1) | 5 Dec 2005 (SI 2005/3175) |
| | (2)–(7) | 18 Nov 2004 (s 263(7)(c)) |
| | (8), (9) | 18 Nov 2004 (RA) |
| 248 | (1) | 5 Dec 2005 (SI 2005/3255) |
| | (2)–(5) | 18 Nov 2004 (s 263(7)(c)) |
| 249–251 | | 5 Dec 2005 (SI 2005/3175) |
| 252 | | 5 Dec 2005 (SI 2005/3255) |
| 253 | | 5 Dec 2005 (SI 2005/3175) |
| 254 | (1) | See Sch 24 below |
| | (2)–(6) | 18 Nov 2004 (s 263(8)(f)) |
| 255 | | 18 Nov 2004 (s 263(8)(f)) |
| 256, 257 | | 5 Dec 2005 (SI 2005/3175) |
| 258–260 | | 18 Nov 2004 (s 263(10)(a)) |
| 261 | (1) | 5 Dec 2005 (SI 2005/3175) |
| | (2) | See Sch 28 below |
| | (3) | See Sch 29 below |
| | (4) | See Sch 30 below |
| 262–264 | | 18 Nov 2004 (s 263(10)(a)) |
| Sch 1 | paras 1, 2 | 5 Dec 2005 (SI 2005/3175) |
| | para 3 | *Not yet in force* |
| | para 4 | 5 Dec 2005 (SI 2005/3175) |
| | para 5(1), (2) | 5 Dec 2005 (SI 2005/3175) |
| | para 5(3) | 15 Apr 2005 (for the purpose of the power to prescribe matters by regulations) (SI 2005/1112) |
| | | 5 Dec 2005 (otherwise) (SI 2005/3175) |
| | para 5(4), (5) | 5 Dec 2005 (SI 2005/3175) |
| | paras 6–8 | 5 Dec 2005 (SI 2005/3175) |
| | para 9 | *Not yet in force* |
| Sch 2 | paras 1–14 | 5 Dec 2005 (SI 2005/3175) |
| | para 15(1) | 5 Dec 2005 (SI 2005/3175) |
| | para 15(2), (3) | 15 Apr 2005 (SI 2005/1112) |
| Schs 3, 4 | | 5 Dec 2005 (SI 2005/3175) |
| Sch 5 | paras 1–14 | 5 Dec 2005 (SI 2005/3175) |
| | para 15(1) | 5 Dec 2005 (SI 2005/3175) |
| | para 15(2) | 15 Apr 2005 (for the purpose of the power to prescribe matters by regulations) (SI 2005/1112) |
| | | 5 Dec 2005 (otherwise) (SI 2005/3175) |
| | paras 16–18 | 5 Dec 2005 (SI 2005/3175) |
| | para 19(1) | 5 Dec 2005 (SI 2005/3175) |
| | para 19(2), (3) | 15 Apr 2005 (for the purpose of the power to prescribe matters by regulations) (SI 2005/1112) |
| | | 5 Dec 2005 (otherwise) (SI 2005/3175) |
| | paras 20–26 | 5 Dec 2005 (SI 2005/3175) |
| | para 27(a), (b) | 5 Dec 2005 (SI 2005/3175) |
| | para 27(c) | 15 Apr 2005 (for the purpose of the power to prescribe matters by regulations) (SI 2005/1112) |
| | | 5 Dec 2005 (otherwise) (SI 2005/3175) |

**Civil Partnership Act 2004 (c 33)**—*contd*

| | | |
|---|---|---|
| | para 28 | 15 Apr 2005 (for the purpose of the power to prescribe matters by regulations) (SI 2005/1112) |
| | | 5 Dec 2005 (otherwise) (SI 2005/3175) |
| | para 29(1) | 5 Dec 2005 (SI 2005/3175) |
| | para 29(2), (3) | 15 Apr 2005 (for the purpose of the power to prescribe matters by regulations) (SI 2005/1112) |
| | | 5 Dec 2005 (otherwise) (SI 2005/3175) |
| | paras 30–37 | 6 Apr 2006 (SI 2006/639) |
| | paras 38–45 | 5 Dec 2005 (SI 2005/3175) |
| | para 46(1) | 5 Dec 2005 (SI 2005/3175) |
| | para 46(2) | 15 Apr 2005 (for the purpose of making rules of court under para 46(3)) (SI 2005/1112) |
| | | 5 Dec 2005 (otherwise) (SI 2005/3175) |
| | para 46(3) | 15 Apr 2005 (SI 2005/1112) |
| | paras 47–56 | 5 Dec 2005 (SI 2005/3175) |
| | para 57(1), (2) | 5 Dec 2005 (SI 2005/3175) |
| | para 57(3), (4) | 15 Apr 2005 (for the purpose of the power to prescribe matters by regulations) (SI 2005/1112) |
| | | 5 Dec 2005 (otherwise) (SI 2005/3175) |
| | paras 58–79 | 5 Dec 2005 (SI 2005/3175) |
| | para 80(1), (2) | 5 Dec 2005 (SI 2005/3175) |
| | para 80(3) | 15 Apr 2005 (for the purpose of making rules of court and the powers to make regulations under the provisions of Sch 5 brought into force by this order) (SI 2005/1112) |
| | | 5 Dec 2005 (otherwise) (SI 2005/3175) |
| | para 80(4), (5) | 5 Dec 2005 (SI 2005/3175) |
| Sch 6 | paras 1–9 | 5 Dec 2005 (SI 2005/3175) |
| | para 10 | 15 Apr 2005 (for the purpose of making rules of court under para 11(2)) (SI 2005/1112) |
| | | 5 Dec 2005 (otherwise) (SI 2005/3175) |
| | para 11(1) | 5 Dec 2005 (SI 2005/3175) |
| | para 11(2) | 15 Apr 2005 (for the purpose of making rules of court) (SI 2005/1112) |
| | | 5 Dec 2005 (otherwise) (SI 2005/3175) |
| | paras 12–48 | 5 Dec 2005 (SI 2005/3175) |
| Sch 7 | para 1 | 5 Dec 2005 (SI 2005/3175) |
| | para 2(1), (2) | 5 Dec 2005 (SI 2005/3175) |
| | para 2(3) | 15 Apr 2005 (for the purpose of making rules of court) (SI 2005/1112) |
| | | 5 Dec 2005 (otherwise) (SI 2005/3175) |
| | para 3 | 5 Dec 2005 (SI 2005/3175) |
| | para 4(1) | 15 Apr 2005 (for the purpose of making rules of court) (SI 2005/1112) |
| | | 5 Dec 2005 (otherwise) (SI 2005/3175) |
| | para 4(2)–(4) | 5 Dec 2005 (SI 2005/3175) |
| | paras 5–9 | 5 Dec 2005 (SI 2005/3175) |
| | para 10(1)–(3) | 5 Dec 2005 (SI 2005/3175) |
| | para 10(4)(a) | 5 Dec 2005 (SI 2005/3175) |
| | para 10(4)(b) | 6 Apr 2006 (SI 2006/639) |
| | para 10(5)(a) | 5 Dec 2005 (SI 2005/3175) |
| | para 10(5)(b) | 6 Apr 2006 (SI 2006/639) |
| | para 10(6)–(8) | 5 Dec 2005 (SI 2005/3175) |
| | para 10(9)(a), (b) | 5 Dec 2005 (SI 2005/3175) |
| | para 10(9)(c) | 6 Apr 2006 (SI 2006/639) |
| | para 11 | 5 Dec 2005 (SI 2005/3175) |
| | para 12(1) | 15 Apr 2005 (for the purpose of making rules of court) (SI 2005/1112) |
| | | 5 Dec 2005 (otherwise) (SI 2005/3175) |
| | para 12(2)–(4) | 5 Dec 2005 (SI 2005/3175) |

**Civil Partnership Act 2004 (c 33)**—*contd*

| | | |
|---|---|---|
| | para 12(5) | 15 Apr 2005 (for the purpose of making rules of court) (SI 2005/1112) |
| | | 5 Dec 2005 (otherwise) (SI 2005/3175) |
| | para 13 | 5 Dec 2005 (SI 2005/3175) |
| | para 14(1)–(3) | 5 Dec 2005 (SI 2005/3175) |
| | para 14(4), (5) | 15 Apr 2005 (SI 2005/1112) |
| | paras 15–19 | 5 Dec 2005 (SI 2005/3175) |
| Sch 8 | | 5 Dec 2005 (SI 2005/3175) |
| Sch 9 | paras 1–12 | 5 Dec 2005 (SI 2005/3175) |
| | para 13(1) | 5 Dec 2005 (SI 2005/3175) |
| | para 13(2)(a) | 5 Dec 2005 (immediately after the Domestic Violence, Crime and Victims Act 2004, s 3 has come into force) (SI 2005/3175) |
| | para 13(2)(b) | 5 Dec 2005 (SI 2005/3175) |
| | para 13(3), (4) | 5 Dec 2005 (SI 2005/3175) |
| | paras 14–25 | 5 Dec 2005 (SI 2005/3175) |
| Sch 10 | paras 1, 2 | 5 Dec 2005 (SSI 2005/604) |
| | para 3 | *Never in force* (repealed) |
| Sch 11 | | 5 Dec 2005 (SSI 2005/604) |
| Sch 12 | paras 1, 2 | 5 Dec 2005 (SI 2005/3255) |
| | para 3 | *Not yet in force* (repealed (NI)) |
| Sch 13 | paras 1–5 | 5 Dec 2005 (SI 2005/3255) |
| | para 6 | 5 Sep 2005 (for the purpose of the powers in these provisions to prescribe matters by regulations) (SI 2005/2399) |
| | | 5 Dec 2005 (otherwise) (SI 2005/3255) |
| | para 7 | 5 Dec 2005 (SI 2005/3255) |
| Sch 14 | | 5 Dec 2005 (SI 2005/3255) |
| Sch 15 | paras 1–9 | 5 Dec 2005 (SI 2005/3255) |
| | para 10(1) | 5 Dec 2005 (SI 2005/3255) |
| | para 10(2) | 7 Nov 2005 (for the purpose of the power to prescribe matters by regulations) (SI 2005/3058) |
| | | 5 Dec 2005 (otherwise) (SI 2005/3255) |
| | paras 11–13 | 5 Dec 2005 (SI 2005/3255) |
| | para 14(1) | 5 Dec 2005 (SI 2005/3255) |
| | para 14(2)–(4) | 7 Nov 2005 (for the purpose of the power to prescribe matters by regulations) (SI 2005/3058) |
| | | 5 Dec 2005 (otherwise) (SI 2005/3255) |
| | paras 15–21 | 5 Dec 2005 (SI 2005/3255) |
| | para 22(a), (b) | 5 Dec 2005 (SI 2005/3255) |
| | para 22(c) | 7 Nov 2005 (for the purpose of the power to prescribe matters by regulations) (SI 2005/3058) |
| | | 5 Dec 2005 (otherwise) (SI 2005/3255) |
| | para 23 | 7 Nov 2005 (for the purpose of the power to prescribe matters by regulations) (SI 2005/3058) |
| | | 5 Dec 2005 (otherwise) (SI 2005/3255) |
| | para 24(1) | 5 Dec 2005 (SI 2005/3255) |
| | para 24(2), (3) | 7 Nov 2005 (for the purpose of the power to prescribe matters by regulations) (SI 2005/3058) |
| | | 5 Dec 2005 (otherwise) (SI 2005/3255) |
| | paras 25–32 | 6 Apr 2006 (SI 2006/928) |
| | paras 33–40 | 5 Dec 2005 (SI 2005/3255) |
| | para 41(1) | 5 Dec 2005 (SI 2005/3255) |
| | para 41(2) | 5 Sep 2005 (for the purpose of making rules of court under para 41(3)) (SI 2005/2399) |
| | | 5 Dec 2005 (otherwise) (SI 2005/3255) |
| | para 41(3) | 5 Sep 2005 (SI 2005/2399) |
| | paras 42–49 | 5 Dec 2005 (SI 2005/3255) |
| | para 50(1), (2) | 5 Dec 2005 (SI 2005/3255) |
| | para 50(3)–(5) | 5 Sep 2005 (for the purpose of the power to prescribe matters by regulations) (SI 2005/2399) |

**Civil Partnership Act 2004 (c 33)**—*contd*

|  |  |  |
|---|---|---|
|  |  | 5 Dec 2005 (otherwise) (SI 2005/3255) |
|  | paras 51–74 | 5 Dec 2005 (SI 2005/3255) |
|  | para 75(1)–(3) | 5 Dec 2005 (SI 2005/3255) |
|  | para 75(4) | 5 Sep 2005 (for the purpose of making rules of court and the powers to make regulations under the other provisions of Sch 15 brought into force by SI 2005/2399) (SI 2005/2399) |
|  |  | 5 Dec 2005 (otherwise) (SI 2005/3255) |
|  | para 75(5), (6) | 5 Dec 2005 (SI 2005/3255) |
| Sch 16 | paras 1–9 | 5 Dec 2005 (SI 2005/3255) |
|  | para 10 | 5 Sep 2005 (for the purpose of making rules of court under para 11(2)) (SI 2005/2399) |
|  |  | 5 Dec 2005 (otherwise) (SI 2005/3255) |
|  | para 11(1) | 5 Dec 2005 (SI 2005/3255) |
|  | para 11(2) | 5 Sep 2005 (for the purpose of making rules of court under para 11(2)) (SI 2005/2399) |
|  |  | 5 Dec 2005 (otherwise) (SI 2005/3255) |
|  | paras 12–47 | 5 Dec 2005 (SI 2005/3255) |
| Sch 17 | para 1 | 5 Dec 2005 (SI 2005/3255) |
|  | para 2(1), (2) | 5 Dec 2005 (SI 2005/3255) |
|  | para 2(3) | 5 Sep 2005 (for the purpose of making rules of court) (SI 2005/2399) |
|  |  | 5 Dec 2005 (otherwise) (SI 2005/3255) |
|  | para 3 | 5 Dec 2005 (SI 2005/3255) |
|  | para 4(1) | 5 Sep 2005 (for the purpose of making rules of court) (SI 2005/2399) |
|  |  | 5 Dec 2005 (otherwise) (SI 2005/3255) |
|  | para 4(2)–(4) | 5 Dec 2005 (SI 2005/3255) |
|  | paras 5–9 | *Not yet in force* |
|  | para 10(1)–(3) | 5 Dec 2005 (SI 2005/3255) |
|  | para 10(4)(a) | 5 Dec 2005 (SI 2005/3255) |
|  | para 10(4)(b) | 6 Apr 2006 (SI 2006/928) |
|  | para 10(5)(a) | 5 Dec 2005 (SI 2005/3255) |
|  | para 10(5)(b) | 6 Apr 2006 (SI 2006/928) |
|  | para 10(6)–(8) | 5 Dec 2005 (SI 2005/3255) |
|  | para 10(9)(a), (b) | 5 Dec 2005 (SI 2005/3255) |
|  | para 10(9)(c) | 6 Apr 2006 (SI 2006/928) |
|  | para 11 | 5 Dec 2005 (SI 2005/3255) |
|  | para 12(1) | 5 Sep 2005 (for the purpose of making rules of court) (SI 2005/2399) |
|  |  | 5 Dec 2005 (otherwise) (SI 2005/3255) |
|  | para 12(2)–(4) | 5 Dec 2005 (SI 2005/3255) |
|  | para 12(5) | 5 Sep 2005 (for the purpose of making rules of court) (SI 2005/2399) |
|  |  | 5 Dec 2005 (otherwise) (SI 2005/3255) |
|  | para 13 | 5 Dec 2005 (SI 2005/3255) |
|  | para 14(1)–(3) | 5 Dec 2005 (SI 2005/3255) |
|  | para 14(4)–(6) | 5 Sep 2005 (SI 2005/2399) |
|  | paras 15–19 | 5 Dec 2005 (SI 2005/3255) |
| Schs 18–21 |  | 5 Dec 2005 (SI 2005/3175; SI 2005/3255) |
| Sch 22 | paras 1–18 | 5 Dec 2005 (SI 2005/3255) |
|  | para 19 | *Not yet in force* |
|  | paras 20–24 | 5 Dec 2005 (SI 2005/3255) |
| Sch 23 | para 1 | 5 Dec 2005 (SI 2005/3175) |
|  | para 2(1) | 15 Apr 2005 (for the purpose of the powers to make regulations) (SI 2005/1112) |
|  |  | 5 Dec 2005 (otherwise) (SI 2005/3175) |
|  | para 2(2) | 5 Dec 2005 (SI 2005/3175) |
|  | para 2(3) | 15 Apr 2005 (for the purpose of the powers to make regulations) (SI 2005/1112) |

**Civil Partnership Act 2004 (c 33)**—*contd*

| | | |
|---|---|---|
| | | 5 Dec 2005 (otherwise) (SI 2005/3175) |
| | para 3 | 5 Dec 2005 (SI 2005/3175) |
| | para 4 | 15 Apr 2005 (for the purpose of the powers to make regulations) (SI 2005/1112) |
| | | 5 Dec 2005 (otherwise) (SI 2005/3175) |
| | para 5 | 5 Dec 2005 (SI 2005/3175) |
| | para 6 | 15 Apr 2005 (for the purpose of the powers to issue guidance) (SI 2005/1112) |
| | | 5 Dec 2005 (otherwise) (SI 2005/3175) |
| | paras 7, 8 | 5 Dec 2005 (SI 2005/3175) |
| | para 9 | 15 Apr 2005 (for the purpose of the powers to make regulations) (SI 2005/1112) |
| | | 5 Dec 2005 (otherwise) (SI 2005/3175) |
| | para 10(1) | 15 Apr 2005 (for the purpose of the powers to issue guidance) (SI 2005/1112) |
| | | 5 Dec 2005 (otherwise) (SI 2005/3175) |
| | para 10(2) | 5 Dec 2005 (SI 2005/3175) |
| | para 10(3) | 15 Apr 2005 (for the purpose of the powers to issue guidance) (SI 2005/1112) |
| | | 5 Dec 2005 (otherwise) (SI 2005/3175) |
| | paras 11, 12 | 5 Dec 2005 (SI 2005/3175) |
| | para 13 | 15 Apr 2005 (for the purpose of the powers to make regulations) (SI 2005/1112) |
| | | 5 Dec 2005 (otherwise) (SI 2005/3175) |
| | para 14 | 5 Dec 2005 (SI 2005/3175) |
| | para 15(1) | 15 Apr 2005 (for the purpose of the powers to issue guidance) (SI 2005/1112) |
| | | 5 Dec 2005 (otherwise) (SI 2005/3175) |
| | para 15(2) | 5 Dec 2005 (SI 2005/3175) |
| | para 15(3) | 15 Apr 2005 (for the purpose of the powers to issue guidance) (SI 2005/1112) |
| | | 5 Dec 2005 (otherwise) (SI 2005/3175) |
| | para 16(1), (2) | 5 Dec 2005 (SI 2005/3175) |
| | para 16(3)(a) | 15 Apr 2005 (for the purpose of the powers to make regulations) (SI 2005/1112) |
| | | 5 Dec 2005 (otherwise) (SI 2005/3175) |
| | para 16(3)(b), (c) | 5 Dec 2005 (SI 2005/3175) |
| | para 16(4) | 5 Dec 2005 (SI 2005/3175) |
| | para 17 | 15 Apr 2005 (SI 2005/1112) |
| Sch 24 | | 5 Dec 2005 (SI 2005/3175; SI 2005/3255) |
| Sch 25 | | 5 Dec 2005 (SI 2005/3175) |
| Sch 26 | paras 1–3 | 5 Dec 2005 (SI 2005/3175) |
| | paras 4, 5 | 15 Apr 2005 (for the purpose of amending the powers to make regulations) (SI 2005/1112) |
| | | 5 Dec 2005 (otherwise) (SI 2005/3175) |
| | paras 6, 7 | 5 Dec 2005 (SI 2005/3175) |
| | para 8 | 15 Apr 2005 (for the purpose of amending the powers to make regulations) (SI 2005/1112) |
| | | 5 Dec 2005 (otherwise) (SI 2005/3175) |
| | paras 9–16 | 5 Dec 2005 (SI 2005/3175) |
| | para 17 | 15 Apr 2005 (for the purpose of amending the powers to make regulations) (SI 2005/1112) |
| | | 5 Dec 2005 (otherwise) (SI 2005/3175) |
| | paras 18–33 | 5 Dec 2005 (SI 2005/3175) |
| Sch 27 | paras 1–11 | 5 Dec 2005 (SI 2005/3175) |
| | para 12 | 15 Apr 2005 (SI 2005/1112) |
| | para 13(1)–(3) | 5 Dec 2005 (SI 2005/3175) |
| | para 13(4), (5) | *Never in force* (repealed) |

**Civil Partnership Act 2004 (c 33)**—*contd*

| | | |
|---|---|---|
| | para 13(6) | 5 Dec 2005 (repeal of Marriage Act 1949, s 1(6), (7), only in so far as those subsections apply to Sch 1, Pt 2 to that Act) (SI 2005/3175) |
| | | *Never in force* (otherwise) (repealed) |
| | para 14 | 15 Apr 2005 (for the purpose of amending the power to make regulations in the Marriage Act 1949, s 27(1)) (SI 2005/1112) |
| | | 5 Dec 2005 (otherwise) (SI 2005/3175) |
| | paras 15, 16 | 5 Dec 2005 (SI 2005/3175) |
| | para 17 | 5 Dec 2005 (so far as substitutes Marriage Act 1949, Sch 1, Pts 1, 2) (SI 2005/3175) |
| | | *Not yet in force* (in so far as substitutes Marriage Act 1949, Sch 1, Pt 3) |
| | paras 18–20 | 5 Dec 2005 (SI 2005/3175) |
| | para 21 | 15 Apr 2005 (for the purpose of the amendments to the power to make an Order in Council) (SI 2005/1112) |
| | | 5 Dec 2005 (otherwise) (SI 2005/3175) |
| | paras 22–69 | 5 Dec 2005 (SI 2005/3175) |
| | para 70 | 15 Apr 2005 (for the purpose of exercising the power in the Matrimonial and Family Proceedings Act 1984, s 40 to make family proceedings rules) (SI 2005/1112) |
| | | 5 Dec 2005 (otherwise) (SI 2005/3175) |
| | paras 71–136 | 5 Dec 2005 (SI 2005/3175) |
| | para 137 | 15 Apr 2005 (SI 2005/1112) |
| | paras 138, 139 | 5 Dec 2005 (SI 2005/3175) |
| | para 140(1), (2) | 5 Dec 2005 (SI 2005/3175) |
| | para 140(3) | 15 Apr 2005 (for the purpose of the amendments to the powers to make regulations) (SI 2005/1112) |
| | | 5 Dec 2005 (otherwise) (SI 2005/3175) |
| | paras 141–161 | 5 Dec 2005 (SI 2005/3175) |
| | para 162 | 15 Apr 2005 (for the purpose of the power to make regulations) (SI 2005/1112) |
| | | 5 Dec 2005 (otherwise) (SI 2005/3175) |
| | para 163 | 15 Apr 2005 (SI 2005/1112) |
| | paras 164–171 | 5 Dec 2005 (SI 2005/3175) |
| | para 172 | 15 Apr 2005 (SI 2005/1112) |
| | paras 173–175 | 5 Dec 2005 (SI 2005/3175) |
| Sch 28 | paras 1–41 | 5 Dec 2005 (SSI 2005/604) |
| | para 42 | *Not yet in force* |
| | paras 43–59 | 5 Dec 2005 (SSI 2005/604) |
| | para 60(1), (2) | 5 Dec 2005 (SSI 2005/604) |
| | para 60(3) | *Not yet in force* |
| | paras 61–70 | 5 Dec 2005 (SSI 2005/604) |
| Sch 29 | paras 1–63 | 5 Dec 2005 (SI 2005/3255) |
| | para 64(1), (2) | 5 Dec 2005 (SI 2005/3255) |
| | para 64(3) | 5 Dec 2005 (in so far as substitutes Pts 1, 2 of the table) (SI 2005/3255) |
| | | *Not yet in force* (in so far as substitutes Pt 3 of the table) |
| | para 64(4), (5) | 5 Dec 2005 (SI 2005/3255) |
| | para 64(6), (7) | *Not yet in force* |
| | paras 65–92 | 5 Dec 2005 (SI 2005/3255) |
| | para 93 | *Not yet in force* |
| | para 94 | 5 Sep 2005 (for the purpose of exercising the power in the Family Law (Northern Ireland) Order 1993, art 12, to make family proceedings rules) (SI 2005/2399) |
| | | 5 Dec 2005 (otherwise) (SI 2005/3255) |
| | paras 95–117 | 5 Dec 2005 (SI 2005/3255) |
| Sch 30 | | 5 Dec 2005 (except repeal of Marriage Act 1949, s 1(8), and s 1(6), (7), in so far as those subsections apply to s 1(5) of, Sch 1, Pt 3 to that Act) (SI 2005/3175; SI 2005/3255; SSI 2005/604) |

**Civil Partnership Act 2004 (c 33)**—*contd*

*Not yet in force* (exceptions noted above)

---

## Companies (Audit, Investigations and Community Enterprise) Act 2004 (c 27)

*RA:* 28 Oct 2004

*Commencement provisions:* s 65(1); Companies (Audit, Investigations and Community Enterprise) Act 2004 (Commencement) and Companies Act 1989 (Commencement No 18) Order 2004, SI 2004/3322

| | | |
|---|---|---|
| 1, 2 | | 6 Apr 2005 (SI 2004/3322)[1] |
| 3–5 | | 1 Jan 2005 (SI 2004/3322) |
| 6 | | 6 Apr 2005 (SI 2004/3322)[1] |
| 7 | | 1 Oct 2005 (SI 2004/3322)[1] |
| 8, 9 | | 6 Apr 2005 (SI 2004/3322)[1] |
| 10 | | 1 Jan 2005 (SI 2004/3322) |
| 11, 12 | | 6 Apr 2005 (SI 2004/3322)[1] |
| 13, 14 | | 1 Jan 2005 (SI 2004/3322) |
| 15 | | 6 Apr 2005 (SI 2004/3322)[1] |
| 16–18 | | 1 Jan 2005 (SI 2004/3322) |
| 19–24 | | 6 Apr 2005 (SI 2004/3322)[1] |
| 25 | | See Sch 2 below |
| 26 | | 1 Jul 2005 (SI 2004/3322) |
| 27 | | 1 Jan 2005 (SI 2004/3322) |
| 28–63 | | 1 Jul 2005 (SI 2004/3322) |
| 64 | | See Sch 8 below |
| 65–67 | | 28 Oct 2004 (RA) |
| Sch 1 | | 6 Apr 2005 (SI 2004/3322)[1] |
| Sch 2 | para 1 | 1 Jan 2005 (SI 2004/3322) |
| | para 2 | 6 Apr 2005 (SI 2004/3322)[1] |
| | paras 3, 4 | 1 Jan 2005 (SI 2004/3322) |
| | paras 5–24 | 6 Apr 2005 (SI 2004/3322)[1] |
| | para 25 | 6 Apr 2005 (except in respect of Companies Act 1985, Sch 15D, paras 40, 45) (SI 2004/3322)[1] |
| | | 1 Jul 2005 (otherwise) (SI 2004/3322) |
| | paras 26–28 | 6 Apr 2005 (SI 2004/3322)[1] |
| | para 29 | 1 Jul 2005 (SI 2004/3322) |
| | paras 30, 31 | 6 Apr 2005 (SI 2004/3322)[1] |
| Sch 3 | | 1 Jan 2005 (SI 2004/3322) |
| Schs 4–7 | | 1 Jul 2005 (SI 2004/3322) |
| Sch 8 | | 1 Jan 2005 (SI 2004/3322), repeals of or in— |
| | |   Companies Act 1985, ss 245C(6), 256(3); |
| | |   Companies Act 1989, s 48(3); |
| | |   Companies (Northern Ireland) Order 1990; |
| | |   Competition Act 1998; |
| | |   Competition Act 1998 (Competition Commission) Transitional, Consequential and Supplemental Provisions Order 1999; |
| | |   Enterprise Act 2002 |
| | | 6 Apr 2005 (SI 2004/3322)[1], repeals of or in— |
| | |   Companies Act 1985, ss 310, 734(1), Sch 24; |
| | |   Insolvency Act 1985; |
| | |   Insolvency Act 1986; |
| | |   Companies Act 1989, ss 63, 65, 67, 69, 120; |
| | |   Friendly Societies Act 1992; |
| | |   Pensions Act 1995; |
| | |   Bank of England Act 1998; |
| | |   Youth Justice and Criminal Evidence Act 1999 |
| | | 1 Jul 2005 (repeal in Companies Act 1985, s 27(4)) (SI 2004/3322) |
| | | 1 Oct 2005 (otherwise) (SI 2004/3322)[1] |

**Companies (Audit, Investigations and Community Enterprise) Act 2004 (c 27)**—*contd*

1    For transitional provisions and savings, see SI 2004/3322, arts 3–13

---

**Consolidated Fund Act 2004 (c 1)**

*RA:* 22 Mar 2004

Whole Act in force 22 Mar 2004 (RA)

---

**Consolidated Fund (No 2) Act 2004 (c 38)**

*RA:* 16 Dec 2004

Whole Act in force 16 Dec 2004 (RA)

---

**Criminal Procedure (Amendment) (Scotland) Act 2004 (asp 5)**

*RA:* 4 Jun 2004

*Commencement provisions:* s 27(1), (2); Criminal Procedure (Amendment) (Scotland) Act 2004 (Commencement, Transitional Provisions and Savings) Order 2004, SSI 2004/405[1]

| | | |
|---|---|---|
| 1 | (1), (2) | 1 Feb 2005 (SSI 2004/405) |
| | (3) | 1 Feb 2005 (except for the purpose of inserting Criminal Procedure (Scotland) Act 1995, ss 72(6)(b)(ii), (6)(e), (7), 72B(1)(c)) (SSI 2004/405) |
| | | In force for remaining purposes as from the day on which the insertion of ss 271A, 271C, 271D into the 1995 Act by the Vulnerable Witnesses (Scotland) Act 2004, s 1 comes into force[2] (SSI 2004/405) |
| 2, 3 | | 1 Feb 2005 (SSI 2004/405) |
| 4 | (1), (2) | 1 Feb 2005 (SSI 2004/405) |
| | (3), (4) | In force as from the day on which the insertion of ss 288E, 288F into the 1995 Act by the Vulnerable Witnesses (Scotland) Act 2004, s 6 comes into force[2] (SSI 2004/405) |
| 5–7 | | 1 Feb 2005 (SSI 2004/405) |
| 8 | | 4 Dec 2004 (SSI 2004/405) |
| 9, 10 | | 1 Feb 2005 (SSI 2004/405) |
| 11 | | 1 Feb 2005 (except for the purpose of inserting Criminal Procedure (Scotland) Act 1995, ss 90B(7)–(9), (11)(b), 90C(3)–(9)) (SSI 2004/405) |
| | | *Not yet in force* (exception noted above) |
| 12 | | 4 Dec 2004 (SSI 2004/405) |
| 13–16 | | 1 Feb 2005 (SSI 2004/405) |
| 17 | | 4 Oct 2004 (SSI 2004/405) |
| 18, 19 | | 1 Feb 2005 (SSI 2004/405) |
| 20–24 | | 4 Oct 2004 (SSI 2004/405) |
| 25 | | See Schedule below |
| 26, 27 | | 4 Jun 2004 (RA) |
| Schedule | para 1 | See paras 2–58 below |
| | para 2 | 1 Feb 2005 (SSI 2004/405) |
| | para 3 | 4 Dec 2004 (SSI 2004/405) |
| | paras 4, 5 | 1 Feb 2005 (SSI 2004/405) |
| | para 6 | 4 Oct 2004 (SSI 2004/405) |
| | paras 7–11 | 1 Feb 2005 (SSI 2004/405) |
| | para 12 | 4 Dec 2004 (SSI 2004/405) |
| | paras 13–16 | 1 Feb 2005 (SSI 2004/405) |
| | para 17 | 4 Oct 2004 (SSI 2004/405) |
| | paras 18–20 | 1 Feb 2005 (SSI 2004/405) |

**Criminal Procedure (Amendment) (Scotland) Act 2004 (asp 5)**—*contd*

| | |
|---|---|
| para 21 | 4 Dec 2004 (SSI 2004/405) |
| paras 22–32 | 1 Feb 2005 (SSI 2004/405) |
| para 33 | 4 Oct 2004 (SSI 2004/405) |
| para 34 | 1 Feb 2005 (SSI 2004/405) |
| paras 35–37 | 4 Oct 2004 (SSI 2004/405) |
| paras 38–42 | 1 Feb 2005 (SSI 2004/405) |
| paras 43, 44 | In force as from the day on which the insertion of ss 271A, 271C, 271D into the 1995 Act by the Vulnerable Witnesses (Scotland) Act 2004, s 1 comes into force[2] (SSI 2004/405) |
| paras 45–49 | 1 Feb 2005 (SSI 2004/405) |
| para 50 | 1 Apr 2005 (SSI 2004/405; SSI 2005/168) |
| paras 51–58 | 1 Feb 2005 (SSI 2004/405) |

[1]   For transitional provisions and savings, see SSI 2004/405, arts 3–5

[2]   As to the extent to which those sections have been brought into force, see the Vulnerable Witnesses (Scotland) Act 2004

---

**Domestic Violence, Crime and Victims Act 2004 (c 28)**

*RA:* 15 Nov 2004

*Commencement provisions:* s 60; Domestic Violence, Crime and Victims Act 2004 (Commencement No 1) Order 2005, SI 2005/579; Domestic Violence, Crime and Victims Act 2004 (Commencement No 2) Order 2005, SI 2005/1705; Domestic Violence, Crime and Victims Act 2004 (Commencement No 3) Order 2005, SI 2005/1821; Domestic Violence, Crime and Victims Act 2004 (Commencement No 4) Order 2005, SI 2005/2848; Domestic Violence, Crime and Victims Act 2004 (Commencement No 5) Order 2005, SI 2005/3196; Domestic Violence, Crime and Victims Act 2004 (Commencement No 6) Order 2006, SI 2006/2662; Domestic Violence, Crime and Victims Act 2004 (Commencement No 7 and Transitional Provisions) Order 2006, SI 2006/3423; Domestic Violence, Crime and Victims Act 2004 (Commencement No 8) Order 2007, SI 2007/602; Domestic Violence, Crime and Victims Act 2004 (Commencement No 9 and Transitional Provisions) Order 2007, SI 2007/1845; Domestic Violence, Crime and Victims Act 2004 (Commencement No 10) Order 2008, SI 2008/3065; Domestic Violence, Crime and Victims Act 2004 (Commencement No 11) Order 2009, SI 2009/2501; Domestic Violence, Crime and Victims Act 2004 (Commencement No 12) Order 2009, SI 2009/2616; Domestic Violence, Crime and Victims Act 2004 (Commencement No 13) Order 2010, SI 2010/129; Domestic Violence, Crime and Victims Act 2004 (Commencement No 14) Order 2011, SI 2011/1008; Domestic Violence, Crime and Victims Act 2004 (Commencement No 15) Order 2012, SI 2012/1697; Domestic Violence, Crime and Victims Act 2004 (Commencement No 1) Order (Northern Ireland) 2020

| | | |
|---|---|---|
| 1 | | 1 Jul 2007 (SI 2007/1845)[2] |
| 2, 3 | | 5 Dec 2005 (SI 2005/3196) |
| 4 | | 1 Jul 2007 (SI 2007/1845) |
| 5–8 | | 21 Mar 2005 (SI 2005/579) |
| 9 | | 13 Apr 2011 (E) (W) (SI 2011/1008) |
| | | 10 Dec 2020 (NI) (SI 2020/1465) |
| 10 | (1) | *Never in force* (repealed) |
| | (2) | 1 Jul 2005 (SI 2005/1705) |
| 11 | | 31 Mar 2005 (SI 2005/579) |
| 12, 13 | | 30 Sep 2009 (SI 2009/2501) |
| 14 | | 1 Apr 2007 (SI 2007/602) |
| 15 | | 1 Oct 2012 (SI 2012/1697) |
| 16 | | *Not yet in force* (sub-s (2) repealed) |
| 17–20 | | 8 Jan 2007 (SI 2006/3423)[1] |
| 21 | (1) | See Sch 1 below |
| | (2) | 8 Jan 2007 (SI 2006/3423) |
| 22–26 | | 31 Mar 2005 (SI 2005/579) |
| 27 | (1) | 18 Jul 2005 (SI 2005/1821) |
| | (2) | See Sch 4 below |
| 28, 29 | | 31 Mar 2005 (SI 2005/579) |

**Domestic Violence, Crime and Victims Act 2004 (c 28)**—*contd*

| | | |
|---|---|---|
| 30 | | 8 Jan 2007 (SI 2006/3423) |
| 31 | | 31 Mar 2005 (SI 2005/579) |
| 32–34 | | 18 Oct 2005 (SI 2005/2848) |
| 35–45 | | 1 Jul 2005 (SI 2005/1705) |
| 46 | | 14 Dec 2008 (SI 2008/3065) |
| 47 | | 18 Oct 2005 (SI 2005/2848) |
| 48 | (1)–(5) | 1 Feb 2010 (SI 2010/129) |
| | (6) | See Sch 8 below |
| 49–53 | | 1 Feb 2010 (SI 2010/129) |
| 54 | (1) | 18 Oct 2005 (SI 2005/2848) |
| | (2)(a), (b) | 18 Oct 2005 (SI 2005/2848) |
| | (2)(c) | 1 Feb 2010 (SI 2010/129) |
| | (3)(a), (b) | 18 Oct 2005 (SI 2005/2848) |
| | (3)(c), (d) | 1 Feb 2010 (SI 2010/129) |
| | (4)–(8) | 18 Oct 2005 (SI 2005/2848) |
| 55 | | 4 Oct 2006 (SI 2006/2662) |
| 56 | | 8 Jan 2007 (SI 2006/3423) |
| 57 | | *Not yet in force* |
| 58 | (1) | See Sch 10 below |
| | (2) | See Sch 11 below |
| 59 | | See Sch 12 below |
| 60–63 | | 15 Nov 2004 (RA) |
| Sch 1 | | 8 Jan 2007 (SI 2006/3423) |
| Schs 2, 3 | | 31 Mar 2005 (SI 2005/579) |
| Sch 4 | | 18 Jul 2005 (SI 2005/1821) |
| Schs 5, 6 | | 31 Mar 2005 (SI 2005/579) |
| Sch 7 | | 18 Oct 2005 (SI 2005/2848) |
| Sch 8 | | *Never in force* (repealed) |
| Sch 9 | | 1 Feb 2010 (SI 2010/129) |
| Sch 10 | para 1 | 31 Mar 2005 (SI 2005/579) |
| | para 2 | 21 Mar 2005 (SI 2005/579) |
| | paras 3–6 | 31 Mar 2005 (SI 2005/579) |
| | para 7 | 21 Mar 2005 (SI 2005/579) |
| | para 8 | 31 Mar 2005 (SI 2005/579) |
| | paras 9–11 | 1 Apr 2007 (SI 2007/602) |
| | para 12 | 31 Mar 2005 (SI 2005/579) |
| | para 13 | *Not yet in force* |
| | para 14 | 31 Mar 2005 (SI 2005/579) |
| | para 15 | *Not yet in force* |
| | para 16 | 21 Mar 2005 (SI 2005/579) |
| | paras 17–23 | 31 Mar 2005 (SI 2005/579) |
| | para 24 | 21 Mar 2005 (SI 2005/579) |
| | para 25 | 31 Mar 2005 (SI 2005/579) |
| | paras 26, 27 | 21 Mar 2005 (SI 2005/579) |
| | para 28 | *Not yet in force* |
| | para 29 | 21 Mar 2005 (SI 2005/579) |
| | para 30 | 1 Apr 2007 (SI 2007/602) |
| | paras 31, 32 | 31 Mar 2005 (SI 2005/579) |
| | para 33 | 21 Mar 2005 (SI 2005/579) |
| | paras 34, 35 | 5 Dec 2005 (SI 2005/3196) |
| | paras 36–39 | 1 Jul 2007 (SI 2007/1845)[2] |
| | paras 40–42 | 5 Dec 2005 (SI 2005/3196) |
| | paras 43, 44 | 30 Sep 2009 (SI 2009/2501) |
| | paras 45, 46 | 31 Mar 2005 (SI 2005/579) |
| | para 47 | 30 Sep 2009 (SI 2009/2501) |
| | para 48 | 30 Sep 2009 (SI 2009/2616) |
| | paras 49–53 | 1 Apr 2007 (SI 2007/602) |
| | para 54 | 21 Mar 2005 (SI 2005/579) |
| | para 55 | 1 Jul 2005 (SI 2005/1705) |

**Domestic Violence, Crime and Victims Act 2004 (c 28)**—*contd*

|  |  |  |
|---|---|---|
|  | para 56 | 21 Mar 2005 (SI 2005/579) |
|  | paras 57, 58 | 31 Mar 2005 (SI 2005/579) |
|  | para 59 | 21 Mar 2005 (SI 2005/579) |
|  | paras 60, 61 | 31 Mar 2005 (SI 2005/579) |
|  | para 62 | 8 Jan 2007 (SI 2006/3423) |
|  | para 63 | 1 Apr 2007 (SI 2007/602) |
|  | para 64 | *Not yet in force* |
|  | paras 65, 66 | 21 Mar 2005 (SI 2005/579) |
| Sch 11 |  | 21 Mar 2005 (SI 2005/579), repeals of or in— |

       Coroners Act 1988;
       Law Reform (Year and a Day Rule) Act 1996
  31 Mar 2005 (SI 2005/579), repeals of or in—
       Criminal Procedure (Insanity) Act 1964;
       Courts-Martial (Appeals) Act 1968;
       Criminal Appeal Act 1968;
       Juries Act 1974;
       Supreme Court Act 1981;
       Mental Health Act 1983;
       Prosecution of Offences Act 1985;
       Criminal Procedure (Insanity and Unfitness to Plead) Act 1991;
       Armed Forces Act 1996;
       Crime (Sentences) Act 1997;
       Sexual Offences Act 2003
  1 Jul 2005 (repeals in Criminal Justice and Court Services Act 2000) (SI 2005/1705)
  5 Dec 2005 (repeal of Family Law Act 1996, s 41) (SI 2005/3196)
  1 Jul 2007 (repeals in Family Law Act 1996, ss 42, 47, 49) (SI 2007/1845)[2]
  30 Sep 2009 (SI 2009/2501), repeals of or in—
       Protection from Harassment Act 1997;
       Protection from Harassment (Northern Ireland) Order 1997, SI 1997/1180
  30 Sep 2009 (SI 2009/2616), repeals of or in—
       Crime and Disorder Act 1998
  *Not yet in force*, repeals of or in—
       Access to Justice Act 1999;
       Care Standards Act 2000;
       Powers of Criminal Courts (Sentencing) Act 2000;
       Criminal Justice Act 2003

|  |  |  |
|---|---|---|
| Sch 12 | para 1 | 1 Jul 2007 (SI 2007/1845)[2] |
|  | para 2 | 21 Mar 2005 (SI 2005/579) |
|  | para 3 | *Not yet in force* |
|  | para 4 | 1 Jul 2005 (so far as relates to s 10(2)) (SI 2005/1705) |
|  |  | *Not yet in force* (so far as relates to s 10(1)) |
|  | paras 5, 6 | 30 Sep 2009 (SI 2009/2616) |
|  | para 7 | 1 Apr 2007 (SI 2007/602) |
|  | paras 8, 9 | 31 Mar 2005 (SI 2005/579) |
|  | para 10 | *Not yet in force* |

[1]   For transitional provisions, see SI 2006/3423, art 3

[2]   For transitional provisions, see SI 2007/1845, art 3

---

**Education (Additional Support for Learning) (Scotland) Act 2004 (asp 4)**

*RA:* 7 May 2004

*Commencement provisions:* s 35(1); Education (Additional Support for Learning) (Scotland) Act 2004 (Commencement No 1) Order 2005, SSI 2005/154; Education (Additional Support for Learning)

**Education (Additional Support for Learning) (Scotland) Act 2004 (asp 4)**—*contd*
(Scotland) Act 2004 (Commencement No 2) Order 2005, SSI 2005/263; Education (Additional
Support for Learning) (Scotland) Act 2004 (Commencement No 3) Order 2005, SSI 2005/564

| | | |
|---|---|---|
| 1–10 | | 14 Nov 2005 (SSI 2005/564) |
| 11 | (1)–(7) | 14 Nov 2005 (SSI 2005/564) |
| | (8) | 18 May 2005 (for the purpose of enabling regulations to be made) (SSI 2005/263) |
| | | 14 Nov 2005 (otherwise) (SSI 2005/564) |
| 12 | | 14 Nov 2005 (SSI 2005/564) |
| 13 | (1)–(5) | 14 Nov 2005 (SSI 2005/564) |
| | (6) | 18 May 2005 (for the purpose of enabling regulations to be made) (SSI 2005/263) |
| | | 14 Nov 2005 (otherwise) (SSI 2005/564) |
| | (7), (8) | 14 Nov 2005 (SSI 2005/564) |
| 14, 15 | | 14 Nov 2005 (SSI 2005/564) |
| 16 | | 18 May 2005 (for the purpose of enabling regulations to be made) (SSI 2005/263) |
| | | 14 Nov 2005 (otherwise) (SSI 2005/564) |
| 17 | | 3 May 2005 (SSI 2005/154) |
| 18, 19 | | 14 Nov 2005 (SSI 2005/564) |
| 20 | | *Not yet in force* |
| 21 | | 14 Nov 2005 (SSI 2005/564) |
| 22 | | See Sch 2 below |
| 23 | (1) | 14 Nov 2005 (SSI 2005/564) |
| | (2)(a), (b) | 14 Nov 2005 (SSI 2005/564) |
| | (2)(c) | 18 May 2005 (for the purpose of enabling orders to be made) (SSI 2005/263) |
| | | 14 Nov 2005 (otherwise) (SSI 2005/564) |
| | (3) | 14 Nov 2005 (SSI 2005/564) |
| | (4) | 18 May 2005 (for the purpose of enabling orders to be made) (SSI 2005/263) |
| | | 14 Nov 2005 (otherwise) (SSI 2005/564) |
| | (5) | 14 Nov 2005 (SSI 2005/564) |
| 24 | | *Not yet in force* |
| 25 | | 14 Nov 2005 (SSI 2005/564) |
| 26 | (1), (2) | 14 Nov 2005 (SSI 2005/564) |
| | (3) | 18 May 2005 (for the purpose of enabling regulations to be made) (SSI 2005/263) |
| | | 14 Nov 2005 (otherwise) (SSI 2005/564) |
| 27 | | 18 May 2005 (SSI 2005/263) |
| 28 | | 14 Nov 2005 (SSI 2005/564) |
| 29 | | 7 May 2004 (RA) |
| 30, 31 | | 14 Nov 2005 (SSI 2005/564) |
| 32 | | 7 May 2004 (RA) |
| 33 | | See Sch 3 below |
| 34, 35 | | 7 May 2004 (RA) |
| Sch 1 | | 3 May 2005 (SSI 2005/154) |
| Sch 2 | paras 1, 2 | 14 Nov 2005 (SSI 2005/564) |
| | para 3(1)–(4) | 14 Nov 2005 (SSI 2005/564) |
| | para 3(5) | 14 Nov 2005 (except for the power to make regulations) (SSI 2005/564) |
| | | *Not yet in force* (exception noted above) |
| | para 3(6) | 14 Nov 2005 (SSI 2005/564) |
| | para 4(1), (2) | 14 Nov 2005 (SSI 2005/564) |
| | para 4(3) | 18 May 2005 (for the purpose of enabling regulations to be made) (SSI 2005/263) |
| | | 14 Nov 2005 (otherwise) (SSI 2005/564) |
| | para 5 | 14 Nov 2005 (SSI 2005/564) |
| | para 6(1)–(5) | 14 Nov 2005 (SSI 2005/564) |

**Education (Additional Support for Learning) (Scotland) Act 2004 (asp 4)**—*contd*

|         | para 6(6)         | 18 May 2005 (for the purpose of enabling regulations to be made) (SSI 2005/263) |
|---------|-------------------|--------------------------------------------------------------------------------|
|         |                   | 14 Nov 2005 (otherwise) (SSI 2005/564)                                          |
|         | paras 7, 8        | 14 Nov 2005 (SSI 2005/564)                                                      |
| Sch 3   | paras 1, 2        | 14 Nov 2005 (SSI 2005/564)                                                      |
|         | para 3(1)–(6)     | 14 Nov 2005 (SSI 2005/564)                                                      |
|         | para 3(7)(a)      | *Not yet in force*                                                             |
|         | para 3(7)(b)      | 14 Nov 2005 (SSI 2005/564)                                                      |
|         | para 3(8)–(14)    | 14 Nov 2005 (SSI 2005/564)                                                      |
|         | paras 4–11        | 14 Nov 2005 (SSI 2005/564)                                                      |

## Employment Relations Act 2004 (c 24)

*RA:* 16 Sep 2004

*Commencement provisions:* s 59(2)–(4); Employment Relations Act 2004 (Commencement No 1 and Transitional Provisions) Order 2004, SI 2004/2566[1]; Employment Relations Act 2004 (Commencement No 2 and Transitional Provisions) Order 2004, SI 2004/3342[2]; Employment Relations Act 2004 (Commencement No 3 and Transitional Provisions) Order 2005, SI 2005/872; Employment Relations Act 2004 (Commencement No 4 and Transitional Provisions) Order 2005, SI 2005/2419

| 1–8 |  | 6 Apr 2005 (SI 2005/872)[3] |
|------|--|------------------------------|
| 9, 10 |  | 1 Oct 2005 (SI 2005/2419)[4] |
| 11, 12 |  | 6 Apr 2005 (SI 2005/872)[3] |
| 13 |  | 1 Oct 2005 (SI 2005/2419)[4] |
| 14 |  | 6 Apr 2005 (SI 2005/872)[3] |
| 15 |  | 31 Dec 2004 (SI 2004/3342)[2] |
| 16, 17 |  | 6 Apr 2005 (SI 2005/872) |
| 18 |  | 31 Dec 2004 (SI 2004/3342) |
| 19–21 |  | 6 Apr 2005 (SI 2005/872) |
| 22 |  | 1 Oct 2005 (SI 2005/2419)[4] |
| 23, 24 |  | 6 Apr 2005 (SI 2005/872) |
| 25 |  | 1 Oct 2005 (SI 2005/2419)[4] |
| 26–28 |  | 6 Apr 2005 (SI 2005/872)[3] |
| 29–32 |  | 1 Oct 2004 (SI 2004/2566) |
| 33, 34 |  | 31 Dec 2004 (SI 2004/3342)[2] |
| 35 |  | 6 Apr 2005 (SI 2005/872)[3] |
| 36 |  | 31 Dec 2004 (SI 2004/3342) |
| 37, 38 |  | 1 Oct 2004 (SI 2004/2566) |
| 39 |  | 31 Dec 2004 (SI 2004/3342) |
| 40, 41 |  | 6 Apr 2005 (SI 2005/872)[3] |
| 42, 43 |  | 16 Sep 2004 (s 59(2)) |
| 44–53 |  | 6 Apr 2005 (SI 2005/872)[3] |
| 54 |  | 31 Dec 2004 (SI 2004/3342)[1] |
| 55 |  | 6 Apr 2005 (SI 2005/872) |
| 56 |  | 16 Sep 2004 (s 59(2)) |
| 57 | (1) | See Sch 1 below |
|    | (2) | See Sch 2 below |
| 58, 59 |  | 16 Sep 2004 (s 59(2)) |
| Sch 1 | paras 1–7 | 6 Apr 2005 (SI 2005/872)[3] |
|       | paras 8–12 | 1 Oct 2004 (SI 2004/2566) |
|       | paras 13–15 | 6 Apr 2005 (SI 2005/872) |
|       | paras 16–18 | 1 Oct 2004 (SI 2004/2566) |
|       | para 19 | 6 Apr 2005 (SI 2005/872) |
|       | paras 20, 21 | 1 Oct 2004 (SI 2004/2566) |
|       | para 22 | 6 Apr 2005 (SI 2005/872) |
|       | para 23(1)–(21) | 6 Apr 2005 (SI 2005/872)[3] |
|       | para 23(22), (23) | 1 Oct 2005 (SI 2005/2419)[4] |
|       | para 23(24)–(27) | 6 Apr 2005 (SI 2005/872)[3] |

**Employment Relations Act 2004 (c 24)**—*contd*

| | | |
|---|---|---|
| | paras 24, 25 | 1 Oct 2004 (SI 2004/2566) |
| | paras 26, 27 | 31 Dec 2004 (SI 2004/3342)[2] |
| | paras 28–30 | 6 Apr 2005 (SI 2005/872) |
| | para 31 | 1 Oct 2004 (SI 2004/2566) |
| | paras 32–41 | 6 Apr 2005 (SI 2005/872) |
| | para 42(1), (2) | 1 Oct 2004 (SI 2004/2566) |
| | para 42(3) | 31 Dec 2004 (SI 2004/3342) |
| | para 42(4) | 1 Oct 2004 (SI 2004/2566) |
| | para 43 | 1 Oct 2004 (SI 2004/2566) |
| Sch 2 | | 1 Oct 2004 (SI 2004/2566), repeals of or in— |

Trade Union and Labour Relations (Consolidation) Act 1992,
ss 146, 148, 151(1), 152, 155;
Employment Relations Act 1999, s 17
31 Dec 2004 (SI 2004/3342), repeals of or in—
Trade Union and Labour Relations (Consolidation) Act 1992,
ss 67, 176;
Employment Relations Act 1999, s 23(5)
6 Apr 2005 (SI 2005/872), repeals of or in—
Agricultural Wages Act 1948;
Trade Union and Labour Relations (Consolidation) Act 1992 (all
remaining entries except ss 226A, 234A, Sch A1, para 119(3))[3];
Employment Rights Act 1996;
Employment Tribunals Act 1996;
Employment Act 2002
1 Oct 2005 (repeals of or in Trade Union and Labour Relations
(Consolidation) Act 1992, ss 226A, 234A, Sch A1, para 119(3))
(SI 2005/2419)

[1]   For transitional provisions, see SI 2004/2566, arts 4–8

[2]   For transitional provisions, see SI 2004/3342, arts 5–12

[3]   For transitional provisions, see SI 2005/872, arts 5–21

[4]   For transitional provisions, see SI 2005/2419, arts 5–7

**Energy Act 2004 (c 20)**

*RA:* 22 Jul 2004

*Commencement provisions:* s 198; Energy Act 2004 (Commencement No 1) Order 2004, SI 2004/1973;
Energy Act 2004 (Commencement No 2) Order 2004, SI 2004/2184; Energy Act 2004
(Commencement No 3) Order 2004, SI 2004/2575; Energy Act 2004 (Commencement No 4)
Order 2005, SI 2005/442; Energy Act 2004 (Commencement No 5) Order 2005, SI 2005/877;
Energy Act 2004 (Commencement No 6) Order 2005, SI 2005/2965; Energy Act 2004
(Commencement No 7) Order 2006, SI 2006/1964; Energy Act 2004 (Commencement No 8)
Order 2007, SI 2007/1091; Energy Act 2004 (Commencement No 9) Order 2009, SI 2009/1269;
Energy Act 2004 (Commencement No 10) Order 2010, SI 2010/1889; Energy Act 2004
(Commencement No 11) Order 2014, SI 2014/1460

| | | |
|---|---|---|
| 1 | | 27 Jul 2004 (SI 2004/1973) |
| 2 | (1)–(9) | 27 Jul 2004 (SI 2004/1973) |
| | (10) | See Sch 1 below |
| 3, 4 | | 24 Aug 2004 (SI 2004/2184) |
| 5 | (1) | 24 Aug 2004 (SI 2004/2184) |
| | (2)–(9) | 5 Oct 2004 (SI 2004/2575) |
| 6 | | 24 Aug 2004 (SI 2004/2184) |
| 7, 8 | | 5 Oct 2004 (SI 2004/2575) |
| 9 | | 24 Aug 2004 (SI 2004/2184) |
| 10 | | 27 Jul 2004 (SI 2004/1973) |
| 11 | (1), (2) | 31 Mar 2005 (SI 2005/442) |

**Energy Act 2004 (c 20)**—*contd*

| | | |
|---|---|---|
| | (3) | See Sch 2 below |
| 12 | | 31 Mar 2005 (SI 2005/442) |
| 13 | (1)–(7) | 24 Aug 2004 (SI 2004/2184) |
| | (8) | See Sch 3 below |
| 14–21 | | 5 Oct 2004 (SI 2004/2575) |
| 22 | | 24 Aug 2004 (SI 2004/2184) |
| 23–35 | | 5 Oct 2004 (SI 2004/2575) |
| 36, 37 | | 24 Aug 2004 (in so far as they relate to provisions in Pt 1, Chapter 1 of the Act already in force) (SI 2004/2184) |
| | | 5 Oct 2004 (otherwise) (SI 2004/2575) |
| 38–50 | | 5 Oct 2004 (SI 2004/2575) |
| 51 | (1) | 1 Mar 2005 (SI 2005/442) |
| | (2) | See Sch 10 below |
| 52 | (1) | 1 Mar 2005 (SI 2005/442) |
| | (2)–(5) | 1 Apr 2005 (SI 2005/877) |
| | (6) | 1 Mar 2005 (SI 2005/442) |
| | (7) | 1 Apr 2005 (SI 2005/877) |
| 53 | (1), (2) | 1 Mar 2005 (SI 2005/442) |
| | (3) | 1 Apr 2005 (SI 2005/877) |
| | (4) | 1 Mar 2005 (SI 2005/442) |
| | (5) | See Sch 11 below |
| 54–60 | | 1 Apr 2005 (SI 2005/877) |
| 61 | | See Sch 12 below |
| 62 | | 1 Apr 2005 (SI 2005/877) |
| 63 | | 1 Mar 2005 (SI 2005/442) |
| 64–68 | | 1 Apr 2005 (SI 2005/877) |
| 69 | (1) | See Sch 14 below |
| | (2), (3) | 1 Mar 2005 (SI 2005/442) |
| 70 | | 1 Apr 2005 (SI 2005/877) |
| 71 | | 1 Mar 2005 (SI 2005/442) |
| 72–74 | | 27 Jul 2004 (SI 2004/1973) |
| 75 | | See Sch 15 below |
| 76–88 | | 5 Oct 2004 (SI 2004/2575) |
| 89 | | 1 Mar 2005 (for the purpose of defining "relevant place" where that term is used in s 93) (SI 2005/442) |
| | | 29 Jul 2010 (for specified purposes[2]) (SI 2010/1889) |
| | | 10 Jun 2014 (for the purposes of defining "relevant place" (other than where that term is used in s 93), "generate", "system" and "premises" in the Electricity Act 1989) (SI 2014/1460) |
| 90, 91 | | 19 Jun 2009 (SI 2009/1269) |
| 92 | | 20 May 2009 (SI 2009/1269) |
| 93 | | 1 Mar 2005 (SI 2005/442) |
| 94 | | 5 Oct 2004 (SI 2004/2575) |
| 95 | (1)–(8) | 1 Oct 2005 (SI 2005/877) |
| | (9) | See Sch 16 below |
| | (10) | 1 Oct 2005 (SI 2005/877) |
| 96–98 | | 1 Oct 2005 (SI 2005/877) |
| 99 | (1) | 1 Mar 2005 (apart from the obligation upon the Secretary of State or the Scottish Ministers, arising under the Electricity Act 1989, s 36B(3), (4), to have regard to how powers under ss 95, 96, 100 and Pt 2, Chapter 3 of this Act have been or will be exercised) (SI 2005/442) |
| | | 1 Sep 2005 (in so far as it obliges the Secretary of State and the Scottish Ministers, by virtue of the Electricity Act 1989, s 36B(4)(a) to have regard to how their powers under s 100 of this Act have been or will be exercised) (SI 2005/442) |
| | | 1 Oct 2005 (otherwise) (SI 2005/877) |
| | (2)–(5) | 1 Mar 2005 (SI 2005/442) |
| 100 | | 1 Sep 2005 (SI 2005/442) |
| 101 | | 5 Oct 2004 (SI 2004/2575) |

**Energy Act 2004 (c 20)**—*contd*

| | | |
|---|---|---|
| 102 | (1) | 5 Oct 2004 (SI 2004/2575) |
| | (2), (3) | 1 Oct 2005 (SI 2005/877) |
| | (4) | 5 Oct 2004 (SI 2004/2575) |
| | (5) | 1 Apr 2005 (SI 2005/877) |
| 103 | (1) | 1 Jan 2006 (SI 2005/877) |
| | (2) | 5 Oct 2004 (SI 2004/2575) |
| | (3) | 1 Apr 2005 (SI 2005/877) |
| | (4) | 5 Oct 2004 (SI 2004/2575) |
| 104 | | 5 Oct 2004 (SI 2004/2575) |
| 105–114 | | 1 Oct 2005 (SI 2005/877) |
| 115–132 | | 5 Oct 2004 (SI 2004/2575) |
| 133, 134 | | 24 Aug 2004 (SI 2004/2184) |
| 135 | | 24 Aug 2004 (for the purpose of defining "transmission" and "transmission system" in s 133) (SI 2004/2184) |
| | | 1 Sep 2004 (otherwise) (SI 2004/2184) |
| 136 | | 1 Sep 2004 (SI 2004/2184) |
| 137 | (1)–(4) | 24 Aug 2004 (SI 2004/2184) |
| | (5), (6) | 1 Sep 2004 (SI 2004/2184) |
| | (7) | 24 Aug 2004 (SI 2004/2184) |
| 138 | | See Sch 17 below |
| 139 | | *Not yet in force* |
| 140 | (1) | *Not yet in force* |
| | (2)–(4) | 24 Aug 2004 (SI 2004/2184) |
| 141 | | See Sch 18 below |
| 142 | | 24 Aug 2004 (SI 2004/2184) |
| 143 | (1) | See Sch 19 below |
| | (2) | 1 Sep 2004 (SI 2004/2184) |
| 144 | | 24 Aug 2004 (SI 2004/2184) |
| 145 | (1) | 1 Dec 2004 (SI 2004/2575) |
| | (2) | 14 Aug 2006 (SI 2006/1964) |
| | (3) | 1 Dec 2004 (SI 2004/2575) |
| | (4) | 14 Aug 2006 (SI 2006/1964) |
| | (5)–(7) | 1 Dec 2004 (SI 2004/2575) |
| 146 | (1)–(5) | 1 Dec 2004 (SI 2004/2575) |
| | (6) | 1 Apr 2005 (SI 2005/877) |
| | (7) | 1 Dec 2004 (SI 2004/2575) |
| 147 | (1)–(4) | 1 Dec 2004 (SI 2004/2575) |
| | (5) | 14 Aug 2006 (SI 2006/1964) |
| | (6)–(8) | 1 Dec 2004 (SI 2004/2575) |
| 148 | | 1 Dec 2004 (SI 2004/2575) |
| 149 | (1) | 1 Dec 2004 (SI 2004/2575) |
| | (2) | 14 Aug 2006 (SI 2006/1964) |
| | (3) | 1 Dec 2004 (SI 2004/2575) |
| | (4) | 14 Aug 2006 (SI 2006/1964) |
| | (5)–(9) | 1 Dec 2004 (SI 2004/2575) |
| | (10) | 14 Aug 2006 (SI 2006/1964) |
| | (11) | 1 Dec 2004 (SI 2004/2575) |
| 150 | (1)–(5) | 1 Dec 2004 (SI 2004/2575) |
| | (6) | 1 Apr 2005 (SI 2005/877) |
| | (7)–(10) | 1 Dec 2004 (SI 2004/2575) |
| 151 | | 14 Aug 2006 (SI 2006/1964) |
| 152 | | 1 Dec 2004 (SI 2004/2575) |
| 153 | | 14 Aug 2006 (SI 2006/1964) |
| 154–176 | | 5 Oct 2004 (SI 2004/2575) |
| 177 | | 1 Nov 2005 (SI 2005/2965) |
| 178 | | 5 Oct 2004 (SI 2004/2575) |
| 179 | | 1 Apr 2006 (except for specified purposes[1]) (SI 2005/2965) |
| | | 1 Apr 2010 (otherwise) (SI 2005/2965) |
| 180 | (1) | 29 Jul 2010 (for specified purposes[2]) (SI 2010/1889) |

**Energy Act 2004 (c 20)**—*contd*

| | | |
|---|---|---|
| | | 10 Jun 2014 (otherwise) (SI 2014/1460) |
| | (2) | *Never in force* |
| 181 | | 5 Oct 2004 (SI 2004/2575) |
| 182 | | 6 Apr 2007 (SI 2007/1091) |
| 183–189 | | 5 Oct 2004 (SI 2004/2575) |
| 190–196 | | 24 Aug 2004 (in so far as relate to Pt 3, Chapter 1 of the Act) (SI 2004/2184) |
| | | 5 Oct 2004 (otherwise) (SI 2004/2575) |
| 197 | (1)–(7) | 5 Oct 2004 (SI 2004/2575) |
| | (8) | 1 Sep 2004 (SI 2004/2184) |
| | (9), (10) | See Sch 23 below |
| 198 | | 22 Jul 2004 (RA) |
| Sch 1 | | 27 Jul 2004 (SI 2004/1973) |
| Sch 2 | | 31 Mar 2005 (SI 2005/442) |
| Sch 3 | | 24 Aug 2004 (SI 2004/2184) |
| Schs 4–9 | | 5 Oct 2004 (SI 2004/2575) |
| Sch 10 | paras 1–5 | 1 Mar 2005 (SI 2005/442) |
| | paras 6–9 | 1 Apr 2005 (SI 2005/877) |
| | paras 10–18 | 1 Mar 2005 (SI 2005/442) |
| Sch 11 | | 1 Mar 2005 (SI 2005/442) |
| Sch 12 | | 1 Apr 2005 (SI 2005/877) |
| Sch 13 | | 1 Mar 2005 (SI 2005/442) |
| Sch 14 | paras 1, 2 | 1 Mar 2005 (SI 2005/442) |
| | para 3 | 1 Apr 2005 (SI 2005/877) |
| | para 4 | 1 Mar 2005 (SI 2005/442) |
| | para 5 | 1 Apr 2005 (SI 2005/877) |
| | paras 6, 7 | 1 Mar 2005 (SI 2005/442) |
| | paras 8–11 | 1 Apr 2005 (SI 2005/877) |
| Sch 15 | | 27 Jul 2004 (SI 2004/1973) |
| Sch 16 | paras 1–6 | 1 Oct 2005 (SI 2005/877) |
| | para 7 | 6 Apr 2007 (SI 2007/1091) |
| | paras 8, 9 | 1 Oct 2005 (SI 2005/877) |
| Sch 17 | | 24 Aug 2004 (SI 2004/2184) |
| Schs 18, 19 | | 1 Sep 2004 (SI 2004/2184) |
| Schs 20–22 | | 5 Oct 2004 (SI 2004/2575) |
| Sch 23 | Pt 1 | 1 Sep 2004 (SI 2004/2184), repeals of or in— |
| | |   Electricity Act 1989, ss 6(9), 11A(10), 64(1); |
| | |   Utilities Act 2000, ss 33(1), 53(5), Sch 6, para 31(2)(a) |
| | | 5 Oct 2004 (SI 2004/2575), repeals of or in— |
| | |   Atomic Energy Act 1954, s 2, Sch 1; |
| | |   Nuclear Installations Act 1965, s 27; |
| | |   Atomic Energy Authority Act 1971, ss 4, 11, 20; |
| | |   Nuclear Industry Finance Act 1977; |
| | |   Atomic Energy (Miscellaneous Provisions) Act 1981; |
| | |   Police and Criminal Evidence Act 1984, s 23; |
| | |   Atomic Energy Authority Act 1995 |
| | | 1 Dec 2004 (repeals of or in Electricity Act 1989, s 6(1)(c)) (SI 2004/2575) |
| | | 1 Apr 2005 (SI 2005/877), repeals of or in— |
| | |   Atomic Energy Authority Act 1954, s 9, Sch 3; |
| | |   Nuclear Installations Act 1965, Sch 1; |
| | |   Atomic Energy Authority Act 1971, s 19; |
| | |   Atomic Energy Authority (Special Constables) Act 1976; |
| | |   Police and Criminal Evidence Act 1984, s 6; |
| | |   Ministry of Defence Police Act 1987; |
| | |   Terrorism Act 2000; |
| | |   Anti-terrorism, Crime and Security Act 2001; |
| | |   Criminal Justice and Police Act 2001; |
| | |   Police Reform Act 2002 |

**Energy Act 2004 (c 20)**—*contd*

|  |  |  |
|---|---|---|
|  |  | 1 Jan 2006 (repeal in Continental Shelf Act 1964) (SI 2005/877) |
|  |  | 1 Apr 2006 (repeal of Utilities Act 2000, s 28(3)(b), except for specified purposes[1]) (SI 2005/2965) |
|  |  | 1 Apr 2010 (repeal of Utilities Act 2000, s 28(3)(b), otherwise) (SI 2005/2965) |
|  |  | *Not yet in force*, repeals of or in— |
|  |  | Pipe-lines Act 1962; |
|  |  | Gas Act 1986; |
|  |  | Electricity Act 1989, s 4; |
|  |  | Petroleum Act 1998 |
|  | Pt 2, para 1 | 1 Apr 2005 (SI 2005/877) |
|  | Pt 2, para 2 | 5 Oct 2004 (SI 2004/2575) |
|  | Pt 2, para 3 | 1 Apr 2005 (SI 2005/877) |

[1]   The specified purposes are: (1) for the purposes of the Electricity Act 1989, ss 32–32C, in respect of any electricity which (without being conveyed to the premises wholly or partly by means of a distribution system) is supplied to premises occupied by a high electricity user (as defined by SI 2005/2965, art 1(2)) from a substation to which it has been conveyed by means of a transmission system; and (2) in respect of any electricity which, being stand-by electricity (as defined by SI 2005/2965, art 1(2)), is supplied (without being conveyed to the premises wholly or partly by means of a distribution system) to premises occupied by a body corporate from a substation to which it has been conveyed by means of a transmission system

[2]   The specified purposes are: (a) in relation to assets which: (i) have been the subject of a tender exercise; (ii) have been transferred to the person who was the successful bidder in relation to that tender exercise; and (iii) were not constructed or installed by that person; (b) in relation to any electric line and associated electrical plant which (i) is located partly in an area of offshore waters; and (ii) is used in the conveyance of electricity generated only by a generating station located otherwise than in an area of offshore waters

---

**European Parliamentary and Local Elections (Pilots) Act 2004 (c 2)**

*RA:* 1 Apr 2004

Whole Act in force 1 Apr 2004 (RA)

---

**Finance Act 2004 (c 12)**

*Budget Day:* 17 Mar 2004

*RA:* 22 Jul 2004

The commencement details of Finance Acts are not set out, as the dates from which their provisions take effect are usually stated clearly and unambiguously in the text of the Act, and charging provisions will normally state for which year or years of assessment they are to have effect.

---

**Fire and Rescue Services Act 2004 (c 21)**

*RA:* 22 Jul 2004

*Commencement provisions:* s 61; Fire and Rescue Services Act 2004 (Commencement) (England and Scotland) Order 2004, SI 2004/2304; Fire and Rescue Services Act 2004 (Commencement) (Wales) Order 2004, SI 2004/2917

|  |  |  |
|---|---|---|
| 1–52 |  | 7 Sep 2004 (E) (S) (so far as they enable an order to be made under ss 19, 21, 36) (SI 2004/2304) |
|  |  | 1 Oct 2004 (E) (S) (otherwise) (SI 2004/2304)[1] |
|  |  | 10 Nov 2004 (W) (SI 2004/2917) |
| 53 | (1) | See Sch 1 below |

**Fire and Rescue Services Act 2004 (c 21)**—*contd*

|  |  |  |
|---|---|---|
| | (2)–(4) | 7 Sep 2004 (E) (S) (so far as they enable an order to be made under ss 19, 21, 36) (SI 2004/2304) |
| | | 1 Oct 2004 (E) (S) (otherwise) (SI 2004/2304)[1] |
| | | 10 Nov 2004 (W) (SI 2004/2917) |
| 54 | | See Sch 2 below |
| 55–64 | | 22 Jul 2004 (RA) |
| Schs 1, 2 | | 7 Sep 2004 (E) (S) (so far as they enable an order to be made under ss 19, 21, 36) (SI 2004/2304) |
| | | 1 Oct 2004 (E) (S) (otherwise) (SI 2004/2304)[1] |
| | | 10 Nov 2004 (W) (SI 2004/2917) |

---

[1] For savings, see SI 2004/2304, art 3

---

**Gangmasters (Licensing) Act 2004 (c 11)**

*RA:* 8 Jul 2004

*Commencement provisions:* s 29; Gangmasters (Licensing) Act 2004 (Commencement No 1) Order 2004, SI 2004/2857; Gangmasters (Licensing) Act 2004 (Commencement No 2) Order 2005, SI 2005/447; Gangmasters (Licensing) Act 2004 (Commencement No 3) Order 2006, SI 2006/2406; Gangmasters (Licensing) Act 2004 (Commencement No 4) Order 2006, SI 2006/2906; Gangmasters (Licensing) Act 2004 (Commencement No 5) Order 2007, SI 2007/695

|  |  |  |
|---|---|---|
| 1–5 | | 1 Dec 2004 (SI 2004/2857) |
| 6 | (1) | 1 Oct 2006 (for purposes related to work falling within s 3(1)(a) and (c)) (SI 2006/2406) |
| | | 6 Apr 2007 (for purposes related to work falling within s 3(1)(b)) (SI 2007/695) |
| | (2) | 1 Dec 2004 (SI 2004/2857) |
| 7–9 | | 1 Apr 2005 (SI 2005/447) |
| 10 | | 1 Dec 2004 (SI 2004/2857) |
| 11 | | 1 Oct 2006 (SI 2006/2406) |
| 12 | | 1 Oct 2006 (for purposes related to work falling within s 3(1)(a) and (c)) (SI 2006/2406) |
| | | 6 Apr 2007 (for purposes related to work falling within s 3(1)(b)) (SI 2007/695) |
| 13 | (1), (2) | 1 Dec 2006 (for purposes related to work falling within s 3(1)(a) and (c)) (SI 2006/2906) |
| | | 6 Apr 2007 (for purposes related to work falling within s 3(1)(b)) (SI 2007/695) |
| | (3) | 1 Oct 2006 (SI 2006/2406) |
| | (4) | 1 Dec 2006 (for purposes related to work falling within s 3(1)(a) and (c)) (SI 2006/2906) |
| | | 6 Apr 2007 (for purposes related to work falling within s 3(1)(b)) (SI 2007/695) |
| 14 | | 1 Oct 2006 (SI 2006/2406) |
| 15–24 | | 1 Apr 2005 (SI 2005/447) |
| 25, 26 | | 1 Dec 2004 (SI 2004/2857) |
| 27 | | 1 Oct 2006 (for purposes related to work falling within s 3(1)(a) and (c)) (SI 2006/2406) |
| | | 6 Apr 2007 (for purposes related to work falling within s 3(1)(b)) (SI 2007/695) |
| 28 | | See Sch 2 below |
| 29 | | 8 Jul 2004 (RA) |
| 30 | | 1 Dec 2004 (SI 2004/2857) |
| Sch 1 | | 1 Dec 2004 (SI 2004/2857) |
| Sch 2 | paras 1–8 | 1 Dec 2004 (SI 2004/2857) |
| | paras 9, 10 | 1 Apr 2005 (SI 2005/447) |
| | para 11 | 1 Dec 2004 (SI 2004/2857) |
| | paras 12–14 | 1 Oct 2006 (SI 2006/2406) |

## Gangmasters (Licensing) Act 2004 (c 11)—*contd*

| | | |
|---|---|---|
| paras 15–18 | 1 Apr 2005 (SI 2005/447) | |
| para 19 | 1 Dec 2004 (SI 2004/2857) | |
| para 20 | 1 Oct 2006 (for purposes related to work falling within s 3(1)(a) and (c)) (SI 2006/2406) | |
| | 6 Apr 2007 (for purposes related to work falling within s 3(1)(b)) (SI 2007/695) | |
| para 21 | 1 Dec 2004 (SI 2004/2857) | |

## Gender Recognition Act 2004 (c 7)

*RA:* 1 Jul 2004

*Commencement provisions:* s 26; Gender Recognition Act 2004 (Commencement) Order 2005, SI 2005/54

| | |
|---|---|
| 1–22 | 4 Apr 2005 (SI 2005/54) |
| 23–26 | 1 Jul 2004 (RA) |
| 27 | 4 Apr 2005 (SI 2005/54) |
| 28, 29 | 1 Jul 2004 (RA) |
| Schs 1–6 | 4 Apr 2005 (SI 2005/54) |

## Health Protection Agency Act 2004 (c 17)

*RA:* 22 Jul 2004

*Commencement provisions:* s 12; Health Protection Agency Act 2004 (Commencement) Order 2005, SI 2005/121

| | | |
|---|---|---|
| 1 | (1) | 1 Apr 2005 (SI 2005/121) |
| | (2) | See Sch 1 below |
| 2 | (1) | 1 Apr 2005 (SI 2005/121) |
| | (2)(a) | 31 Jan 2005 (for the purposes of making regulations giving directions (after consultation with the National Assembly for Wales)) (SI 2005/121) |
| | | 1 Apr 2005 (otherwise) (SI 2005/121) |
| | (2)(b) | 1 Apr 2005 (SI 2005/121) |
| | (3) | 31 Jan 2005 (for the purposes of making regulations giving directions (after consultation with the National Assembly for Wales)) (SI 2005/121) |
| | | 1 Apr 2005 (otherwise) (SI 2005/121) |
| | (4)–(12) | 1 Apr 2005 (SI 2005/121) |
| 3 | (1) | 1 Apr 2005 (SI 2005/121) |
| | (2), (3) | 31 Jan 2005 (for the purposes of enabling the appropriate authority to give directions) (SI 2005/121) |
| | | 1 Apr 2005 (otherwise) (SI 2005/121) |
| | (4), (5) | 1 Apr 2005 (SI 2005/121) |
| | (6) | 31 Jan 2005 (for the purposes of enabling the appropriate authority to give directions) (SI 2005/121) |
| | | 1 Apr 2005 (otherwise) (SI 2005/121) |
| | (7), (8) | 1 Apr 2005 (SI 2005/121) |
| 4, 5 | | 1 Apr 2005 (SI 2005/121) |
| 6 | | 31 Jan 2005 (for the purposes of enabling the appropriate authority to give directions) (SI 2005/121) |
| | | 1 Apr 2005 (otherwise) (SI 2005/121) |
| 7 | | 1 Apr 2005 (SI 2005/121) |
| 8 | (1)–(4) | 31 Jan 2005 (SI 2005/121) |
| | (5)–(11) | 1 Apr 2005 (SI 2005/121) |
| | (12) | See Sch 2 below |
| | (13) | 1 Apr 2005 (SI 2005/121) |
| 9 | | 31 Jan 2005 (SI 2005/121) |
| 10 | | 1 Apr 2005 (SI 2005/121) |

**Health Protection Agency Act 2004 (c 17)**—*contd*

| | | |
|---|---|---|
| 11 | (1) | See Sch 3 below |
| | (2) | See Sch 4 below |
| | (3) | 1 Apr 2005 (SI 2005/121) |
| 12, 13 | | 22 Jul 2004 (RA) |
| Sch 1 | para 1(1)–(5) | 1 Apr 2005 (SI 2005/121) |
| | para 1(6), (7) | 31 Jan 2005 (so far as relating to the making of regulations) (SI 2005/121) |
| | | 1 Apr 2005 (otherwise) (SI 2005/121) |
| | para 2 | 1 Apr 2005 (SI 2005/121) |
| | para 3 | 31 Jan 2005 (so far as relating to the making of regulations) (SI 2005/121) |
| | | 1 Apr 2005 (otherwise) (SI 2005/121) |
| | paras 4–7 | 1 Apr 2005 (SI 2005/121) |
| | para 8(1), (2) | 31 Jan 2005 (so far as relating to the making of regulations) (SI 2005/121) |
| | | 1 Apr 2005 (otherwise) (SI 2005/121) |
| | para 8(3) | 1 Apr 2005 (SI 2005/121) |
| | para 8(4) | 31 Jan 2005 (so far as relating to the making of regulations) (SI 2005/121) |
| | | 1 Apr 2005 (otherwise) (SI 2005/121) |
| | para 9 | 1 Apr 2005 (SI 2005/121) |
| | para 10 | 31 Jan 2005 (so far as relating to the making of regulations) (SI 2005/121) |
| | | 1 Apr 2005 (otherwise) (SI 2005/121) |
| | paras 11–28 | 1 Apr 2005 (SI 2005/121) |
| | paras 29, 30 | 31 Jan 2005 (so far as relating to the making of regulations) (SI 2005/121) |
| | | 1 Apr 2005 (otherwise) (SI 2005/121) |
| Sch 2 | | 31 Jan 2005 (SI 2005/121) |
| Sch 3 | para 1 | *Never in force* (superseded) |
| | para 2 | 1 Apr 2005 (SI 2005/121) |
| | para 3 | 22 Sep 2004 (s 12(3)) |
| | paras 4–20 | 1 Apr 2005 (SI 2005/121) |
| Sch 4 | | 1 Apr 2005 (SI 2005/121) |

**Higher Education Act 2004 (c 8)**

*RA:* 1 Jul 2004

*Commencement provisions:* s 52; Higher Education Act 2004 (Commencement No 1 and Transitional Provisions) Order 2004, SI 2004/2781; Higher Education Act 2004 (Commencement No 1 and Transitional Provision) (Wales) Order 2004, SI 2004/3144; Higher Education Act 2004 (Commencement No 2) Order 2004, SI 2004/3255; Higher Education Act 2004 (Commencement No 1) (Scotland) Order 2005, SSI 2005/33; Higher Education Act 2004 (Commencement No 3) Order 2005, SI 2005/767; Higher Education Act 2004 (Commencement No 2 and Transitional Provision) (Wales) Order 2005, SI 2005/1833, as amended by SI 2006/1660; Higher Education Act 2004 (Commencement No 4) Order 2006, SI 2006/51; Higher Education Act 2004 (Commencement No 3) (Wales) Order 2011, SI 2011/297

| | | |
|---|---|---|
| 1 | | 16 Dec 2004 (SI 2004/3255) |
| 2 | | 1 Apr 2005 (SI 2005/767) |
| 3–9 | | 16 Dec 2004 (SI 2004/3255) |
| 10 | (1) | 16 Dec 2004 (SI 2004/3255) |
| | (2) | 7 Jul 2005 (SI 2005/1833) |
| | (3) | 31 Jan 2005 (S) (SSI 2005/33) |
| | (4) | 16 Dec 2004 (SI 2004/3255) |
| 11–18 | | 1 Nov 2004 (E) (SI 2004/2781) |
| | | 1 Dec 2004 (W) (SI 2004/3144) |
| 19 | | 1 Nov 2004 (SI 2004/2781) |
| 20 | | 1 Jan 2005 (SI 2004/2781[1]; SI 2004/3144[2]) |

**Higher Education Act 2004 (c 8)**—*contd*

| | | |
|---|---|---|
| 21 | | 1 Nov 2004 (E) (SI 2004/2781) |
| | | 1 Dec 2004 (W) (SI 2004/3144) |
| 22 | | 1 Jul 2004 (E) (s 52(1)) |
| | | 11 Feb 2011 (W) (SI 2011/297) |
| 23 | | 14 Jan 2006 (SI 2006/51) |
| 24 | (1)–(5) | 14 Jan 2006 (SI 2006/51) |
| | (6) | 1 Jul 2004 (for the purpose of making regulations) (s 52(1)) |
| | | 14 Jan 2006 (otherwise) (SI 2006/51) |
| 25 | | 14 Jan 2006 (SI 2006/51) |
| 26 | | 1 Jul 2004 (s 52(1)) |
| 27 | | *Never in force* (substituted)[4] |
| 28 | (1)–(5) | 31 Mar 2011 (SI 2011/297) |
| | (6) | 11 Feb 2011 (for the purpose of making regulations) (SI 2011/297) |
| | | 31 Mar 2011 (otherwise) (SI 2011/297) |
| 29 | | 1 Jul 2004 (E) (s 52(1)) |
| | | 31 Mar 2011 (W) (SI 2011/297) |
| 30 | (1) | 1 Jul 2004 (E) (s 52(1)) |
| | | 31 Mar 2011 (W) (SI 2011/297) |
| | (2), (3) | 31 Mar 2011 (SI 2011/297) |
| 31 | | 1 Jul 2004 (s 52(1)) |
| 32 | (1) | 1 Jul 2004 (s 52(1)) |
| | (2), (3) | 1 Nov 2004 (SI 2004/2781) |
| | (4) | 31 Mar 2011 (SI 2011/297) |
| 33, 34 | | 1 Jul 2004 (E) (s 52(1)) |
| | | 11 Feb 2011 (W) (for the purpose of making regulations) (SI 2011/297) |
| | | 31 Mar 2011 (W) (otherwise) (SI 2011/297) |
| 35, 36 | | 1 Jul 2004 (E) (for the purpose of making regulations) (s 52(1)) |
| | | 1 Nov 2004 (E) (otherwise) (SI 2004/2781) |
| | | 11 Feb 2011 (W) (for the purpose of making regulations) (SI 2011/297) |
| | | 31 Mar 2011 (W) (otherwise) (SI 2011/297) |
| 37 | | 1 Jul 2004 (for the purpose of making regulations) (s 52(1)) |
| | | 1 Nov 2004 (otherwise) (SI 2004/2781) |
| 38 | | 11 Feb 2011 (for the purpose of making regulations) (SI 2011/297) |
| | | 31 Mar 2011 (otherwise) (SI 2011/297) |
| 39 | | 1 Jul 2004 (E) (s 52(1)) |
| | | 11 Feb 2011 (W) (for the purpose of making regulations) (SI 2011/297) |
| | | 31 Mar 2011 (W) (otherwise) (SI 2011/297) |
| 40 | | 1 Jul 2004 (s 52(1)) |
| 41 | | 1 Jul 2004 (E) (s 52(1)) |
| | | 11 Feb 2011 (W) (SI 2011/297) |
| 42 | | 1 Jul 2004 (s 52(1)) |
| 43 | | 14 Jan 2006 (SI 2006/51) |
| 44 | (1), (2) | 7 Jul 2005 (SI 2005/1833)[3] |
| | (3) | 1 Sep 2006 (SI 2005/1833) |
| | (4) | 23 Jun 2006 (SI 2005/1833) |
| | (5), (6) | 7 Jul 2005 (SI 2005/1833) |
| 45 | | 14 Jan 2006 (SI 2006/51) |
| 46 | | 1 Jan 2005 (SI 2004/2781[1]; SI 2004/3144[2]) |
| 47, 48 | | 1 Jul 2004 (s 52(1)) |
| 49 | | See Sch 6 below |
| 50 | | See Sch 7 below |
| 51–54 | | 1 Jul 2004 (s 52(1)) |
| Schs 1–4 | | 1 Nov 2004 (E) (SI 2004/2781) |
| | | 1 Dec 2004 (W) (SI 2004/3144) |
| Sch 5 | | 1 Jul 2004 (s 52(1)) |
| Sch 6 | para 1 | 1 Jul 2004 (s 52(1)) |

**Higher Education Act 2004 (c 8)**—*contd*

| | | |
|---|---|---|
| | para 2 | *Never in force* (superseded) |
| | para 3 | 1 Apr 2005 (SI 2005/767) |
| | para 4 | 1 Jul 2004 (so far as relating to the Director of Fair Access to Higher Education) (s 52(1)) |
| | | 16 Dec 2004 (otherwise) (SI 2004/3255) |
| | paras 5, 6 | 16 Dec 2004 (SI 2004/3255) |
| | para 7 | 7 Jul 2005 (W) (in so far as repeals Teaching and Higher Education Act 1998, s 26(5)) (SI 2005/1833) |
| | | 14 Jan 2006 (E) (SI 2006/51) |
| | | 31 Mar 2011 (W) (otherwise) (SI 2011/297) |
| | para 8 | 14 Jan 2006 (E) (SI 2006/51) |
| | | 31 Mar 2011 (W) (SI 2011/297) |
| | para 9 | 14 Jan 2006 (SI 2006/51) |
| | | *Not yet in force* (W) (S) |
| | para 10 | 1 Jul 2004 (so far as relating to the Director of Fair Access to Higher Education) (s 52(1)) |
| | | 16 Dec 2004 (otherwise) (SI 2004/3255) |
| Sch 7 | | 1 Jan 2005 (repeals in Education Reform Act 1988) (SI 2004/2781; SI 2004/3144) |
| | | 1 Apr 2005 (repeal in Superannuation Act 1972) (SI 2005/767) |
| | | 7 Jul 2005 (W) (repeal of Teaching and Higher Education Act 1998, s 26(5)) (SI 2005/1833) |
| | | 14 Jan 2006 (repeals in Teaching and Higher Education Act 1998, s 22) (SI 2006/51) |
| | | 14 Jan 2006 (E) (repeals of or in Teaching and Higher Education Act 1998, ss 26, 28(1)) (SI 2006/51) |
| | | 31 Mar 2011 (W) (repeals of or in Teaching and Higher Education Act 1998, ss 26(3), (4), (6)–(11), 28(1)) (SI 2011/297) |
| | | *Not yet in force*, repeals of or in— |
| | | Learning and Skills Act 2000 |

[1]    For transitional provisions, see SI 2004/2781, art 5

[2]    For transitional provisions, see SI 2004/3144, art 6

[3]    For a transitional and saving provision, see SI 2005/1833, art 6

[4]    This section was substituted by the Education Act 2005, s 98, Sch 14, para 27, as from 1 Sep 2005. Note however that SI 2011/297 purports to bring this section into force on 31 Mar 2011

---

**Highways (Obstruction by Body Corporate) Act 2004 (c 29)**

*RA:* 15 Nov 2004

*Commencement provisions:* s 2(1)

Whole Act in force 15 Jan 2005 (s 2(1))

---

**Horserace Betting and Olympic Lottery Act 2004 (c 25)**

*RA:* 28 Oct 2004

*Commencement provisions:* s 40; Horserace Betting and Olympic Lottery Act 2004 (Commencement No 1) Order 2004, SI 2004/3283; Horserace Betting and Olympic Lottery Act 2004 (Commencement No 2) Order 2005, SI 2005/1134; Horserace Betting and Olympic Lottery Act 2004 (Commencement No 3) Order 2005, SI 2005/1831; Horserace Betting and Olympic Lottery Act 2004 (Commencement No 4) Order 2011, SI 2011/462; Horserace Betting and Olympic Lottery Act 2004 (Commencement No 5) Order 2011, SI 2011/1704

| | | |
|---|---|---|
| 1–8 | | 25 Feb 2011 (SI 2011/462) |
| 9 | (1) | 25 Feb 2011 (SI 2011/462) |
| | (2), (3) | *Not yet in force* |

**Horserace Betting and Olympic Lottery Act 2004 (c 25)**—*contd*

|        |            |                                                                 |
|--------|------------|-----------------------------------------------------------------|
|        | (4)        | 25 Feb 2011 (SI 2011/462)                                       |
|        | (5)        | *Not yet in force*                                             |
|        | (6), (7)   | 25 Feb 2011 (SI 2011/462)                                       |
| 10     | (1)        | *Not yet in force*                                             |
|        | (2)        | See Sch 1 below                                                 |
|        | (3)        | *Not yet in force*                                             |
| 11     |            | 1 Jan 2005 (SI 2004/3283)                                       |
| 12     |            | 1 Jan 2005 (for the purposes of s 11) (SI 2004/3283)           |
|        |            | 25 Feb 2011 (for the purposes of ss 1–8, 9(1), (4), (6), (7)) (SI 2011/462) |
|        |            | *Not yet in force* (for the purposes of ss 9(2), (3), (5), 10, 13, 14) |
| 13     |            | See Sch 2 below                                                 |
| 14     |            | 8 Apr 2005 (SI 2005/1134)                                       |
| 15     |            | *Not yet in force*                                             |
| 16     | (1)–(6)    | *Not yet in force*                                             |
|        | (7)        | See Sch 3 below                                                 |
| 17     | (1)        | *Not yet in force*                                             |
|        | (2)        | See Sch 4 below                                                 |
|        | (3)        | *Not yet in force*                                             |
| 18, 19 |            | *Not yet in force*                                             |
| 20–24  |            | 8 Apr 2005 (SI 2005/1134)                                       |
| 25–27  |            | 8 Jul 2005 (SI 2005/1831)                                       |
| 28     |            | 8 Apr 2005 (SI 2005/1134)                                       |
| 29–32  |            | 8 Jul 2005 (SI 2005/1831)                                       |
| 33     |            | 8 Apr 2005 (SI 2005/1134)                                       |
| 34     | (1)–(5)    | 8 Apr 2005 (SI 2005/1134)                                       |
|        | (6)        | 8 Jul 2005 (SI 2005/1831)                                       |
|        | (7), (8)   | 8 Apr 2005 (SI 2005/1134)                                       |
|        | (9)(a), (b)| 8 Apr 2005 (SI 2005/1134)                                       |
|        | (9)(c)     | 8 Jul 2005 (SI 2005/1831)                                       |
|        | (10), (11) | 8 Apr 2005 (SI 2005/1134)                                       |
| 35–37  |            | 8 Apr 2005 (SI 2005/1134)                                       |
| 38     |            | See Sch 6 below                                                 |
| 39     |            | 8 Apr 2005 (SI 2005/1134)                                       |
| 40–42  |            | 28 Oct 2004 (RA)                                                |
| Sch 1  |            | *Not yet in force*                                             |
| Sch 2  | paras 1–11 | *Not yet in force*                                             |
|        | paras 12, 13 | 13 Jul 2011 (SI 2011/1704)                                    |
|        | paras 14–18 | *Not yet in force*                                            |
|        | para 19    | 13 Jul 2011 (SI 2011/1704)                                      |
|        | para 20    | *Not yet in force*                                             |
|        | paras 21, 22 | 13 Jul 2011 (SI 2011/1704)                                    |
| Schs 3, 4 |         | *Not yet in force*                                             |
| Sch 5  |            | 8 Jul 2005 (SI 2005/1831)                                       |
| Sch 6  |            | 8 Apr 2005 (repeals of or in National Lottery etc Act 1993, ss 21(2), 22(3)(e), 30) (SI 2005/1134) |
|        |            | 13 Jul 2011 (SI 2011/1704), repeals of or in—                  |
|        |            | National Lottery etc Act 1993, s 17;                           |
|        |            | Horserace Totalisator Board Act 1997;                          |
|        |            | Freedom of Information Act 2000                                 |
|        |            | *Not yet in force*, repeals of or in—                         |
|        |            | Betting, Gaming and Lotteries Act 1963;                        |
|        |            | Horserace Totalisator and Betting Levy Boards Act 1972;        |
|        |            | Race Relations Act 1976;                                       |
|        |            | Trustee Act 2000                                               |

## Housing Act 2004 (c 34)

*RA:* 18 Nov 2004

*Commencement provisions:* s 270(2)–(8); Housing Act 2004 (Commencement No 1) (England) Order 2005, SI 2005/326; Housing Act 2004 (Commencement No 2) (England) Order 2005, SI 2005/1120; Housing Act 2004 (Commencement No 3) (England) Order 2005, SI 2005/1451; Housing Act 2004 (Commencement No 4 and Transitional Provisions) (England) Order 2005, SI 2005/1729; Housing Act 2004 (Commencement No 1) (Wales) Order 2005, SI 2005/1814; Housing Act 2004 (Commencement No 2) (Wales) Order 2005, SI 2005/3237; Housing Act 2004 (Commencement No 5 and Transitional Provisions and Savings) (England) Order 2006, SI 2006/1060; Housing Act 2004 (Commencement No 3 and Transitional Provisions and Savings) (Wales) Order 2006, SI 2006/1535; Housing Act 2004 (Commencement No 6) (England) Order 2006, SI 2006/3191; Housing Act 2004 (Commencement No 4) (Wales) Order 2007, SI 2007/305; Housing Act 2004 (Commencement No 7) (England) Order 2007, SI 2007/1068; Housing Act 2004 (Commencement No 8) (England and Wales) Order 2007, SI 2007/1668; Housing Act 2004 (Commencement No 9) (England and Wales) Order 2007, SI 2007/2471; Housing Act 2004 (Commencement No 5) (Wales) Order 2007, SI 2007/3232; Housing Act 2004 (Commencement No 10) (England and Wales) Order 2007, SI 2007/3308; Housing Act 2004 (Commencement No 11) (England and Wales) Order 2008, SI 2008/898

| | |
|---|---|
| 1 | 6 Apr 2006 (E) (SI 2006/1060)[2] |
| | 16 Jun 2006 (W) (SI 2006/1535)[3] |
| 2 | 18 Nov 2004 (s 270(2)(a)) |
| 3 | 6 Apr 2006 (E) (SI 2006/1060)[2] |
| | 16 Jun 2006 (W) (SI 2006/1535)[3] |
| 4 | 18 Nov 2004 (so far as confers any power to make an order or regulations which is exercisable by the Secretary of State or the National Assembly for Wales) (s 270(2)(b)) |
| | 25 Nov 2005 (W) (otherwise) (SI 2005/3237) |
| | 6 Apr 2006 (E) (otherwise) (SI 2006/1060)[2] |
| 5–8 | 6 Apr 2006 (E) (SI 2006/1060)[2] |
| | 16 Jun 2006 (W) (SI 2006/1535)[3] |
| 9 | 18 Nov 2004 (s 270(2)(a)) |
| 10–17 | 6 Apr 2006 (E) (SI 2006/1060)[2] |
| | 16 Jun 2006 (W) (SI 2006/1535)[3] |
| 18 | See Sch 1 below |
| 19–26 | 6 Apr 2006 (E) (SI 2006/1060)[2] |
| | 16 Jun 2006 (W) (SI 2006/1535)[3] |
| 27 | See Sch 2 below |
| 28–30 | 6 Apr 2006 (E) (SI 2006/1060)[2] |
| | 16 Jun 2006 (W) (SI 2006/1535)[3] |
| 31 | See Sch 3 below |
| 32–45 | 6 Apr 2006 (E) (SI 2006/1060)[2] |
| | 16 Jun 2006 (W) (SI 2006/1535)[3] |
| 46, 47 | 18 Nov 2004 (so far as they confer any power to make an order or regulations which is exercisable by the Secretary of State or the National Assembly for Wales) (s 270(2)(b)) |
| | 6 Apr 2006 (E) (otherwise) (SI 2006/1060)[2] |
| | 16 Jun 2006 (W) (otherwise) (SI 2006/1535)[3] |
| 48 | 6 Apr 2006 (E) (SI 2006/1060)[2] |
| | 16 Jun 2006 (W) (SI 2006/1535)[3] |
| 49, 50 | 18 Nov 2004 (so far as they confer any power to make an order or regulations which is exercisable by the Secretary of State or the National Assembly for Wales) (s 270(2)(b)) |
| | 6 Apr 2006 (E) (otherwise) (SI 2006/1060)[2] |
| | 16 Jun 2006 (W) (otherwise) (SI 2006/1535)[3] |
| 51, 52 | 6 Apr 2006 (E) (SI 2006/1060)[2] |
| | 16 Jun 2006 (W) (SI 2006/1535)[3] |
| 53 | 6 Apr 2007 (E) (SI 2007/1068) |
| | *Not yet in force* (W) |
| 54 | 6 Apr 2006 (E) (SI 2006/1060)[2] |

**Housing Act 2004 (c 34)**—*contd*

|        |            |                                                                                                 |
|--------|------------|-------------------------------------------------------------------------------------------------|
|        |            | 16 Jun 2006 (W) (SI 2006/1535)[3]                                                               |
| 55     | (1), (2)   | 15 Jun 2005 (E) (SI 2005/1451)                                                                  |
|        |            | 25 Nov 2005 (W) (SI 2005/3237)                                                                  |
|        | (3), (4)   | 18 Nov 2004 (so far as they confer any power to make an order or regulations which is exercisable by the Secretary of State or the National Assembly for Wales) (s 270(2)(b)) |
|        |            | 6 Apr 2006 (E) (otherwise) (SI 2006/1060)[2]                                                    |
|        |            | 16 Jun 2006 (W) (otherwise) (SI 2006/1535)[3]                                                   |
|        | (5)(a), (b)| 15 Jun 2005 (E) (SI 2005/1451)                                                                  |
|        |            | 25 Nov 2005 (W) (SI 2005/3237)                                                                  |
|        | (5)(c)     | 6 Apr 2006 (E) (SI 2006/1060)[2]                                                                |
|        |            | 16 Jun 2006 (W) (SI 2006/1535)[3]                                                               |
|        | (6)        | 6 Apr 2006 (E) (SI 2006/1060)[2]                                                                |
|        |            | 16 Jun 2006 (W) (SI 2006/1535)[3]                                                               |
| 56, 57 |            | 15 Jun 2005 (E) (SI 2005/1451)                                                                  |
|        |            | 25 Nov 2005 (W) (SI 2005/3237)                                                                  |
| 58     |            | 6 Apr 2006 (E) (SI 2006/1060)[2]                                                                |
|        |            | 16 Jun 2006 (W) (SI 2006/1535)[3]                                                               |
| 59–61  |            | 18 Nov 2004 (so far as they confer any power to make an order or regulations which is exercisable by the Secretary of State or the National Assembly for Wales) (s 270(2)(b)) |
|        |            | 6 Apr 2006 (E) (otherwise) (SI 2006/1060)[2]                                                    |
|        |            | 16 Jun 2006 (W) (otherwise) (SI 2006/1535)[3]                                                   |
| 62     |            | 6 Apr 2006 (E) (SI 2006/1060)[2]                                                                |
|        |            | 16 Jun 2006 (W) (SI 2006/1535)[3]                                                               |
| 63     |            | 18 Nov 2004 (so far as confers any power to make an order or regulations which is exercisable by the Secretary of State or the National Assembly for Wales) (s 270(2)(b)) |
|        |            | 6 Apr 2006 (E) (otherwise) (SI 2006/1060)[2]                                                    |
|        |            | 16 Jun 2006 (W) (otherwise) (SI 2006/1535)[3]                                                   |
| 64     |            | 6 Apr 2006 (E) (SI 2006/1060)[2]                                                                |
|        |            | 16 Jun 2006 (W) (SI 2006/1535)[3]                                                               |
| 65     |            | 18 Nov 2004 (so far as confers any power to make an order or regulations which is exercisable by the Secretary of State or the National Assembly for Wales) (s 270(2)(b)) |
|        |            | 6 Apr 2006 (E) (otherwise) (SI 2006/1060)[2]                                                    |
|        |            | 16 Jun 2006 (W) (otherwise) (SI 2006/1535)[3]                                                   |
| 66     |            | 6 Apr 2006 (E) (SI 2006/1060)[2]                                                                |
|        |            | 16 Jun 2006 (W) (SI 2006/1535)[3]                                                               |
| 67     | (1), (2)   | 6 Apr 2006 (E) (SI 2006/1060)[2]                                                                |
|        |            | 16 Jun 2006 (W) (SI 2006/1535)[3]                                                               |
|        | (3)        | See Sch 4 below                                                                                 |
|        | (4)–(6)    | 6 Apr 2006 (E) (SI 2006/1060)[2]                                                                |
|        |            | 16 Jun 2006 (W) (SI 2006/1535)[3]                                                               |
| 68, 69 |            | 6 Apr 2006 (E) (SI 2006/1060)[2]                                                                |
|        |            | 16 Jun 2006 (W) (SI 2006/1535)[3]                                                               |
| 70     |            | 18 Nov 2004 (so far as confers any power to make an order or regulations which is exercisable by the Secretary of State or the National Assembly for Wales) (s 270(2)(b)) |
|        |            | 6 Apr 2006 (E) (otherwise) (SI 2006/1060)[2]                                                    |
|        |            | 16 Jun 2006 (W) (otherwise) (SI 2006/1535)[3]                                                   |
| 71     |            | See Sch 5 below                                                                                 |
| 72     | (1)        | 16 Jun 2006 (W) (SI 2006/1535)[3]                                                               |
|        |            | 6 Jul 2006 (E) (SI 2006/1060)[2]                                                                |
|        | (2), (3)   | 6 Apr 2006 (E) (SI 2006/1060)[2]                                                                |
|        |            | 16 Jun 2006 (W) (SI 2006/1535)[3]                                                               |
|        | (4)        | 16 Jun 2006 (W) (SI 2006/1535)[3]                                                               |
|        |            | 6 Jul 2006 (E) (SI 2006/1060)[2]                                                                |
|        | (5)–(7)    | 6 Apr 2006 (E) (SI 2006/1060)[2]                                                                |

**Housing Act 2004 (c 34)**—*contd*

|  |  |  |
|---|---|---|
|  |  | 16 Jun 2006 (W) (SI 2006/1535)[3] |
|  | (8)–(10) | 16 Jun 2006 (W) (SI 2006/1535)[3] |
|  |  | 6 Jul 2006 (E) (SI 2006/1060)[2] |
| 73 |  | 16 Jun 2006 (W) (SI 2006/1535)[3] |
|  |  | 6 Jul 2006 (E) (SI 2006/1060)[2] |
| 74 |  | 18 Nov 2004 (so far as confers any power to make an order or regulations which is exercisable by the Secretary of State or the National Assembly for Wales) (s 270(2)(b)) |
|  |  | 16 Jun 2006 (W) (otherwise) (SI 2006/1535)[3] |
|  |  | 6 Jul 2006 (E) (otherwise) (SI 2006/1060)[2] |
| 75–78 |  | 6 Apr 2006 (E) (SI 2006/1060)[2] |
|  |  | 16 Jun 2006 (W) (SI 2006/1535)[3] |
| 79, 80 |  | 18 Nov 2004 (so far as they confer any power to make an order or regulations which is exercisable by the Secretary of State or the National Assembly for Wales) (s 270(2)(b)) |
|  |  | 15 Jun 2005 (E) (otherwise) (SI 2005/1451) |
|  |  | 25 Nov 2005 (W) (otherwise) (SI 2005/3237) |
| 81 |  | 15 Jun 2005 (E) (SI 2005/1451) |
|  |  | 25 Nov 2005 (W) (SI 2005/3237) |
| 82 |  | 6 Apr 2006 (E) (SI 2006/1060)[2] |
|  |  | 16 Jun 2006 (W) (SI 2006/1535)[3] |
| 83, 84 |  | 18 Nov 2004 (so far as they confer any power to make an order or regulations which is exercisable by the Secretary of State or the National Assembly for Wales) (s 270(2)(b)) |
|  |  | 6 Apr 2006 (E) (otherwise) (SI 2006/1060)[2] |
|  |  | 16 Jun 2006 (W) (otherwise) (SI 2006/1535)[3] |
| 85, 86 |  | 6 Apr 2006 (E) (SI 2006/1060)[2] |
|  |  | 16 Jun 2006 (W) (SI 2006/1535)[3] |
| 87 |  | 18 Nov 2004 (so far as confers any power to make an order or regulations which is exercisable by the Secretary of State or the National Assembly for Wales) (s 270(2)(b)) |
|  |  | 6 Apr 2006 (E) (otherwise) (SI 2006/1060)[2] |
|  |  | 16 Jun 2006 (W) (otherwise) (SI 2006/1535)[3] |
| 88, 89 |  | 6 Apr 2006 (E) (SI 2006/1060)[2] |
|  |  | 16 Jun 2006 (W) (SI 2006/1535)[3] |
| 90 | (1)–(3) | 18 Nov 2004 (so far as they confer any power to make an order or regulations which is exercisable by the Secretary of State or the National Assembly for Wales) (s 270(2)(b)) |
|  |  | 6 Apr 2006 (E) (otherwise) (SI 2006/1060)[2] |
|  |  | 16 Jun 2006 (W) (otherwise) (SI 2006/1535)[3] |
|  | (4) | See Sch 4 below |
|  | (5)–(7) | 6 Apr 2006 (E) (SI 2006/1060)[2] |
|  |  | 16 Jun 2006 (W) (SI 2006/1535)[3] |
| 91, 92 |  | 6 Apr 2006 (E) (SI 2006/1060)[2] |
|  |  | 16 Jun 2006 (W) (SI 2006/1535)[3] |
| 93 |  | 18 Nov 2004 (so far as confers any power to make an order or regulations which is exercisable by the Secretary of State or the National Assembly for Wales) (s 270(2)(b)) |
|  |  | 6 Apr 2006 (E) (otherwise) (SI 2006/1060)[2] |
|  |  | 16 Jun 2006 (W) (otherwise) (SI 2006/1535)[3] |
| 94 |  | See Sch 5 below |
| 95 | (1) | 16 Jun 2006 (W) (SI 2006/1535)[3] |
|  |  | 6 Jul 2006 (E) (SI 2006/1060)[2] |
|  | (2) | 6 Apr 2006 (E) (SI 2006/1060)[2] |
|  |  | 16 Jun 2006 (W) (SI 2006/1535)[3] |
|  | (3) | 16 Jun 2006 (W) (SI 2006/1535)[3] |
|  |  | 6 Jul 2006 (E) (SI 2006/1060)[2] |
|  | (4) | 6 Apr 2006 (E) (SI 2006/1060)[2] |
|  |  | 16 Jun 2006 (W) (SI 2006/1535)[3] |
|  | (5) | 16 Jun 2006 (W) (SI 2006/1535)[3] |

**See Halsbury's Statutes Citator for amendments to these Acts**

**Housing Act 2004 (c 34)**—*contd*

| | | |
|---|---|---|
| | | 6 Jul 2006 (E) (SI 2006/1060)[2] |
| | (6) | 6 Apr 2006 (E) (SI 2006/1060)[2] |
| | | 16 Jun 2006 (W) (SI 2006/1535)[3] |
| | (7)–(9) | 16 Jun 2006 (W) (SI 2006/1535)[3] |
| | | 6 Jul 2006 (E) (SI 2006/1060)[2] |
| 96 | | 16 Jun 2006 (W) (SI 2006/1535)[3] |
| | | 6 Jul 2006 (E) (SI 2006/1060)[2] |
| 97 | | 18 Nov 2004 (so far as confers any power to make an order or regulations which is exercisable by the Secretary of State or the National Assembly for Wales) (s 270(2)(b)) |
| | | 16 Jun 2006 (W) (otherwise) (SI 2006/1535)[3] |
| | | 6 Jul 2006 (E) (otherwise) (SI 2006/1060)[2] |
| 98–102 | | 6 Apr 2006 (E) (SI 2006/1060)[2] |
| | | 16 Jun 2006 (W) (SI 2006/1535)[3] |
| 103 | | 18 Nov 2004 (so far as confers any power to make an order or regulations which is exercisable by the Secretary of State or the National Assembly for Wales) (s 270(2)(b)) |
| | | 6 Apr 2006 (E) (otherwise) (SI 2006/1060)[2] |
| | | 16 Jun 2006 (W) (otherwise) (SI 2006/1535)[3] |
| 104–107 | | 6 Apr 2006 (E) (SI 2006/1060)[2] |
| | | 16 Jun 2006 (W) (SI 2006/1535)[3] |
| 108 | | 18 Nov 2004 (so far as confers any power to make an order or regulations which is exercisable by the Secretary of State or the National Assembly for Wales) (s 270(2)(b)) |
| | | 6 Apr 2006 (E) (otherwise) (SI 2006/1060)[2] |
| | | 16 Jun 2006 (W) (otherwise) (SI 2006/1535)[3] |
| 109–116 | | 6 Apr 2006 (E) (SI 2006/1060)[2] |
| | | 16 Jun 2006 (W) (SI 2006/1535)[3] |
| 117 | | 18 Nov 2004 (so far as confers any power to make an order or regulations which is exercisable by the Secretary of State or the National Assembly for Wales) (s 270(2)(b)) |
| | | 6 Apr 2006 (E) (otherwise) (SI 2006/1060)[2] |
| | | 16 Jun 2006 (W) (otherwise) (SI 2006/1535)[3] |
| 118–122 | | 6 Apr 2006 (E) (SI 2006/1060)[2] |
| | | 16 Jun 2006 (W) (SI 2006/1535)[3] |
| 123 | | See Sch 6 below |
| 124–131 | | 6 Apr 2006 (E) (SI 2006/1060)[2] |
| | | 16 Jun 2006 (W) (SI 2006/1535)[3] |
| 132 | (1)–(5) | 6 Apr 2006 (E) (SI 2006/1060)[2] |
| | | 16 Jun 2006 (W) (SI 2006/1535)[3] |
| | (6) | See Sch 7 below |
| 133 | | 6 Apr 2006 (E) (SI 2006/1060)[2] |
| | | 16 Jun 2006 (W) (SI 2006/1535)[3] |
| 134 | | 18 Nov 2004 (so far as confers any power to make an order or regulations which is exercisable by the Secretary of State or the National Assembly for Wales) (s 270(2)(b)) |
| | | 16 Jun 2006 (W) (otherwise) (SI 2006/1535)[3] |
| | | 6 Jul 2006 (E) (otherwise) (SI 2006/1060)[2] |
| 135–144 | | 6 Apr 2006 (E) (SI 2006/1060)[2] |
| | | 16 Jun 2006 (W) (SI 2006/1535)[3] |
| 145, 146 | | 18 Nov 2004 (so far as they confer any power to make an order or regulations which is exercisable by the Secretary of State or the National Assembly for Wales) (s 270(2)(b)) |
| | | 6 Apr 2006 (E) (otherwise) (SI 2006/1060)[2] |
| | | 16 Jun 2006 (W) (otherwise) (SI 2006/1535)[3] |
| 147 | | 6 Apr 2006 (E) (SI 2006/1060)[2] |
| | | 16 Jun 2006 (W) (SI 2006/1535)[3] |
| 148–160 | | 1 Aug 2007 (in so far as they relate to the types of property described in SI 2007/1668, art 3(1), and to the extent specified in art 3(2) thereof) (SI 2007/1668) |

**Housing Act 2004 (c 34)**—*contd*

|  |  |  |
|---|---|---|
|  |  | 10 Sep 2007 (in so far as they relate to the types of property described in SI 2007/2471, art 3(1), and to the extent specified in art 3(2) thereof) (SI 2007/2471) |
|  |  | 14 Dec 2007 (in so far as they relate to the types of property described in SI 2007/3308, art 3(1), and to the extent specified in art 3(2) thereof) (SI 2007/3308) |
|  |  | 6 Apr 2008 (otherwise) (SI 2008/898) |
| 161–164 |  | 18 Nov 2004 (s 270(2)(a)) |
| 165–167 |  | 1 Aug 2007 (in so far as it relates to the types of property described in SI 2007/1668, art 3(1), and to the extent specified in art 3(2) thereof) (SI 2007/1668) |
|  |  | 10 Sep 2007 (in so far as it relates to the types of property described in SI 2007/2471, art 3(1), and to the extent specified in art 3(2) thereof) (SI 2007/2471) |
|  |  | 14 Dec 2007 (in so far as it relates to the types of property described in SI 2007/3308, art 3(1), and to the extent specified in art 3(2) thereof) (SI 2007/3308) |
|  |  | 6 Apr 2008 (otherwise) (SI 2008/898) |
| 168 | (1), (2) | 1 Aug 2007 (in so far as they relate to the types of property described in SI 2007/1668, art 3(1), and to the extent specified in art 3(2) thereof) (SI 2007/1668) |
|  |  | 10 Sep 2007 (in so far as they relate to the types of property described in SI 2007/2471, art 3(1), and to the extent specified in art 3(2) thereof) (SI 2007/2471) |
|  |  | 14 Dec 2007 (in so far as they relate to the types of property described in SI 2007/3308, art 3(1), and to the extent specified in art 3(2) thereof) (SI 2007/3308) |
|  |  | 6 Apr 2008 (otherwise) (SI 2008/898) |
|  | (3) | See Sch 8 below |
| 169 |  | 1 Aug 2007 (in so far as it relates to the types of property described in SI 2007/1668, art 3(1), and to the extent specified in art 3(2) thereof) (SI 2007/1668) |
|  |  | 10 Sep 2007 (in so far as it relates to the types of property described in SI 2007/2471, art 3(1), and to the extent specified in art 3(2) thereof) (SI 2007/2471) |
|  |  | 14 Dec 2007 (in so far as it relates to the types of property described in SI 2007/3308, art 3(1), and to the extent specified in art 3(2) thereof) (SI 2007/3308) |
|  |  | 6 Apr 2008 (otherwise) (SI 2008/898) |
| 170 |  | 18 Nov 2004 (so far as confers any power to make an order or regulations which is exercisable by the Secretary of State or the National Assembly for Wales) (s 270(2)(b)) |
|  |  | 1 Aug 2007 (in so far as it relates to the types of property described in SI 2007/1668, art 3(1), and to the extent specified in art 3(2) thereof) (SI 2007/1668) |
|  |  | 10 Sep 2007 (in so far as it relates to the types of property described in SI 2007/2471, art 3(1), and to the extent specified in art 3(2) thereof) (SI 2007/2471) |
|  |  | 14 Dec 2007 (in so far as it relates to the types of property described in SI 2007/3308, art 3(1), and to the extent specified in art 3(2) thereof) (SI 2007/3308) |
|  |  | 6 Apr 2008 (otherwise) (SI 2008/898) |
| 171 |  | 1 Aug 2007 (in so far as it relates to the types of property described in SI 2007/1668, art 3(1), and to the extent specified in art 3(2) thereof) (SI 2007/1668) |
|  |  | 10 Sep 2007 (in so far as it relates to the types of property described in SI 2007/2471, art 3(1), and to the extent specified in art 3(2) thereof) (SI 2007/2471) |
|  |  | 14 Dec 2007 (in so far as it relates to the types of property described in SI 2007/3308, art 3(1), and to the extent specified in art 3(2) thereof) (SI 2007/3308) |

**Housing Act 2004 (c 34)**—*contd*

|  |  |
|---|---|
|  | 6 Apr 2008 (otherwise) (SI 2008/898) |
| 172 | 18 Nov 2004 (so far as confers any power to make an order or regulations which is exercisable by the Secretary of State or the National Assembly for Wales) (s 270(2)(b)) |
|  | 1 Aug 2007 (in so far as it relates to the types of property described in SI 2007/1668, art 3(1), and to the extent specified in art 3(2) thereof) (SI 2007/1668) |
|  | 10 Sep 2007 (in so far as it relates to the types of property described in SI 2007/2471, art 3(1), and to the extent specified in art 3(2) thereof) (SI 2007/2471) |
|  | 14 Dec 2007 (in so far as it relates to the types of property described in SI 2007/3308, art 3(1), and to the extent specified in art 3(2) thereof) (SI 2007/3308) |
|  | 6 Apr 2008 (otherwise) (SI 2008/898) |
| 173–175 | 1 Aug 2007 (in so far as they relate to the types of property described in SI 2007/1668, art 3(1), and to the extent specified in art 3(2) thereof) (SI 2007/1668) |
|  | 10 Sep 2007 (in so far as they relate to the types of property described in SI 2007/2471, art 3(1), and to the extent specified in art 3(2) thereof) (SI 2007/2471) |
|  | 14 Dec 2007 (in so far as they relate to the types of property described in SI 2007/3308, art 3(1), and to the extent specified in art 3(2) thereof) (SI 2007/3308) |
|  | 6 Apr 2008 (otherwise) (SI 2008/898) |
| 176 | 18 Nov 2004 (s 270(2)(a)) |
| 177, 178 | 1 Aug 2007 (in so far as they relate to the types of property described in SI 2007/1668, art 3(1), and to the extent specified in art 3(2) thereof) (SI 2007/1668) |
|  | 10 Sep 2007 (in so far as they relate to the types of property described in SI 2007/2471, art 3(1), and to the extent specified in art 3(2) thereof) (SI 2007/2471) |
|  | 14 Dec 2007 (in so far as they relate to the types of property described in SI 2007/3308, art 3(1), and to the extent specified in art 3(2) thereof) (SI 2007/3308) |
|  | 6 Apr 2008 (otherwise) (SI 2008/898) |
| 179 | 6 Jun 2005 (E) (SI 2005/1451) |
|  | 25 Nov 2005 (W) (SI 2005/3237) |
| 180 | 18 Jan 2005 (s 270(3)(a)) |
| 181 | 4 Jul 2005 (E) (SI 2005/1729)[1] |
|  | *Not yet in force* (W) |
| 182–186 | 18 Jan 2005 (s 270(3)(a)) |
| 187–189 | 18 Nov 2004 (so far as they confer any power to make an order or regulations which is exercisable by the Secretary of State or the National Assembly for Wales) (s 270(2)(b)) |
|  | 18 Jan 2005 (otherwise) (s 270(3)(a)) |
| 190 | 18 Nov 2004 (s 270(2)(a)) |
| 191 | 6 Jun 2005 (E) (SI 2005/1451) |
|  | 14 Jul 2005 (W) (SI 2005/1814) |
| 192–194 | 6 Jun 2005 (E) (SI 2005/1451) |
|  | 25 Nov 2005 (W) (SI 2005/3237) |
| 195, 196 | 18 Jan 2005 (s 270(3)(a)) |
| 197, 198 | 18 Nov 2004 (so far as they confer any power to make an order or regulations which is exercisable by the Secretary of State or the National Assembly for Wales) (s 270(2)(b)) |
|  | 18 Jan 2005 (otherwise) (s 270(3)(a)) |
| 199 | 18 Jan 2005 (s 270(3)(a)) |
| 200, 201 | 18 Nov 2004 (so far as they confer any power to make an order or regulations which is exercisable by the Secretary of State or the National Assembly for Wales) (s 270(2)(b)) |
|  | 18 Jan 2005 (otherwise) (s 270(3)(a)) |

**Housing Act 2004 (c 34)**—*contd*

| | |
|---|---|
| 202, 203 | 18 Jan 2005 (s 270(3)(a)) |
| 204–206 | 18 Nov 2004 (so far as they confer any power to make an order or regulations which is exercisable by the Secretary of State or the National Assembly for Wales) (s 270(2)(b)) |
| | 18 Jan 2005 (otherwise) (s 270(3)(a)) |
| 207 | 18 Jan 2005 (s 270(3)(a)) |
| 208 | 18 Nov 2004 (s 270(2)(a)) |
| 209–211 | 18 Jan 2005 (s 270(3)(a)) |
| 212, 213 | 18 Nov 2004 (so far as they confer any power to make an order or regulations which is exercisable by the Secretary of State or the National Assembly for Wales) (s 270(2)(b)) |
| | 6 Apr 2007 (otherwise) (SI 2007/305; SI 2007/1068) |
| 214, 215 | 6 Apr 2007 (SI 2007/305; SI 2007/1068) |
| 216 | 18 Nov 2004 (s 270(2)(a)) |
| 217 | 18 Jan 2005 (s 270(3)(a)) |
| 218 | See Sch 11 below |
| 219 | 18 Jan 2005 (s 270(3)(a)) |
| 220 | 18 Nov 2004 (so far as confers any power to make an order or regulations which is exercisable by the Secretary of State or the National Assembly for Wales) (s 270(2)(b)) |
| | 17 Feb 2005 (E) (otherwise) (SI 2005/326) |
| | *Not yet in force* (W) (otherwise) |
| 221 | 17 Feb 2005 (E) (SI 2005/326) |
| | *Not yet in force* (W) |
| 222 | 18 Jan 2005 (s 270(3)(a)) |
| 223 | 27 Apr 2005 (E) (SI 2005/1120) |
| | *Not yet in force* (W) |
| 224 | 18 Jan 2005 (s 270(3)(a)) |
| 225 | 18 Nov 2004 (so far as confers any power to make an order or regulations which is exercisable by the Secretary of State or the National Assembly for Wales) (s 270(2)(b)) |
| | 2 Jan 2007 (E) (otherwise) (SI 2006/3191) |
| | 13 Dec 2007 (W) (otherwise) (SI 2007/3232) |
| 226 | 2 Jan 2007 (E) (SI 2006/3191) |
| | 13 Dec 2007 (W) (SI 2007/3232) |
| 227 | 17 Feb 2005 (E) (SI 2005/326) |
| | 14 Jul 2005 (W) (SI 2005/1814) |
| 228 | 18 Nov 2004 (so far as confers any power to make an order or regulations which is exercisable by the Secretary of State or the National Assembly for Wales) (s 270(2)(b)) |
| | 14 Jul 2005 (otherwise) (SI 2005/1814) |
| 229 | 18 Nov 2004 (so far as confers any power to make an order or regulations which is exercisable by the Secretary of State or the National Assembly for Wales) (s 270(2)(b)) |
| | 4 Jul 2005 (E) (otherwise) (SI 2005/1729) |
| | 16 Jun 2006 (W) (otherwise) (SI 2006/1535)[3] |
| 230, 231 | 4 Jul 2005 (E) (SI 2005/1729) |
| | 16 Jun 2006 (W) (SI 2006/1535)[3] |
| 232 | 18 Nov 2004 (so far as confers any power to make an order or regulations which is exercisable by the Secretary of State or the National Assembly for Wales) (s 270(2)(b)) |
| | 6 Apr 2006 (E) (otherwise) (SI 2006/1060)[2] |
| | 16 Jun 2006 (W) (otherwise) (SI 2006/1535)[3] |
| 233, 234 | 18 Nov 2004 (s 270(2)(a)) |
| 235, 236 | 6 Apr 2006 (E) (SI 2006/1060)[2] |
| | 16 Jun 2006 (W) (SI 2006/1535)[3] |
| 237 | 15 Jun 2005 (E) (SI 2005/1451) |
| | 25 Nov 2005 (W) (SI 2005/3237) |
| 238–243 | 6 Apr 2006 (E) (SI 2006/1060)[2] |
| | 16 Jun 2006 (W) (SI 2006/1535)[3] |

**Housing Act 2004 (c 34)**—*contd*

| | | |
|---|---|---|
| 244 | | 18 Nov 2004 (s 270(2)(a)) |
| 245–247 | | 18 Jan 2005 (s 270(3)(a)) |
| 248 | | 18 Nov 2004 (s 270(2)(a)) |
| 249 | | 18 Jan 2005 (s 270(3)(a)) |
| 250 | | 18 Nov 2004 (s 270(2)(a)) |
| 251 | | 18 Jan 2005 (s 270(3)(a)) |
| 252 | | 18 Nov 2004 (s 270(2)(a)) |
| 253 | | 18 Jan 2005 (s 270(3)(a)) |
| 254 | | 18 Nov 2004 (so far as confers any power to make an order or regulations which is exercisable by the Secretary of State or the National Assembly for Wales) (s 270(2)(b)) |
| | | 18 Jan 2005 (otherwise) (s 270(3)(a)) |
| 255–257 | | 18 Jan 2005 (s 270(3)(a)) |
| 258, 259 | | 18 Nov 2004 (so far as they confer any power to make an order or regulations which is exercisable by the Secretary of State or the National Assembly for Wales) (s 270(2)(b)) |
| | | 18 Jan 2005 (otherwise) (s 270(3)(a)) |
| 260–263 | | 18 Jan 2005 (s 270(3)(a)) |
| 264 | | 18 Nov 2004 (s 270(2)(a)) |
| 265 | (1) | See Sch 15 below |
| | (2)–(5) | 18 Nov 2004 (s 270(2)(a)) |
| 266 | | See Sch 16 below |
| 267–270 | | 18 Nov 2004 (s 270(2)(a)) |
| Schs 1–3 | | 6 Apr 2006 (E) (SI 2006/1060)[2] |
| | | 16 Jun 2006 (W) (SI 2006/1535)[3] |
| Sch 4 | | 18 Nov 2004 (so far as confers any power to make an order or regulations which is exercisable by the Secretary of State or the National Assembly for Wales) (s 270(2)(b)) |
| | | 6 Apr 2006 (E) (otherwise) (SI 2006/1060)[2] |
| | | 16 Jun 2006 (W) (otherwise) (SI 2006/1535)[3] |
| Schs 5, 6 | | 6 Apr 2006 (E) (SI 2006/1060)[2] |
| | | 16 Jun 2006 (W) (SI 2006/1535)[3] |
| Sch 7 | | 18 Nov 2004 (so far as confers any power to make an order or regulations which is exercisable by the Secretary of State or the National Assembly for Wales) (s 270(2)(b)) |
| | | 6 Apr 2006 (E) (otherwise) (SI 2006/1060)[2] |
| | | 16 Jun 2006 (W) (otherwise) (SI 2006/1535)[3] |
| Sch 8 | | 18 Nov 2004 (so far as confers any power to make an order or regulations which is exercisable by the Secretary of State or the National Assembly for Wales) (s 270(2)(b)) |
| | | 1 Aug 2007 (in so far as it relates to the types of property described in SI 2007/1668, art 3(1), and to the extent specified in art 3(2) thereof) (SI 2007/1668) |
| | | 10 Sep 2007 (in so far as it relates to the types of property described in SI 2007/2471, art 3(1), and to the extent specified in art 3(2) thereof) (SI 2007/2471) |
| | | 14 Dec 2007 (in so far as it relates to the types of property described in SI 2007/3308, art 3(1), and to the extent specified in art 3(2) thereof) (SI 2007/3308) |
| | | 6 Apr 2008 (otherwise) (SI 2008/898) |
| Sch 9 | | 18 Jan 2005 (s 270(3)(a)) |
| Sch 10 | | 18 Nov 2004 (so far as confers any power to make an order or regulations which is exercisable by the Secretary of State or the National Assembly for Wales) (s 270(2)(b)) |
| | | 6 Apr 2007 (otherwise) (SI 2007/305; SI 2007/1068) |
| Sch 11 | paras 1–14 | 18 Jan 2005 (s 270(3)(c)) |
| | paras 15, 16 | 18 Nov 2004 (so far as they confer any power to make an order or regulations which is exercisable by the Secretary of State or the National Assembly for Wales) (s 270(2)(b)) |
| | | *Not yet in force* (otherwise) |

**Housing Act 2004 (c 34)**—*contd*

| | | |
|---|---|---|
| | paras 17–26 | 18 Jan 2005 (s 270(3)(c)) |
| Sch 12 | | 14 Jul 2005 (SI 2005/1814) |
| Sch 13 | | 18 Nov 2004 (so far as confers any power to make an order or regulations which is exercisable by the Secretary of State or the National Assembly for Wales) (s 270(2)(b)) |
| | | 4 Jul 2005 (E) (otherwise) (SI 2005/1729) |
| | | 16 Jun 2006 (W) (otherwise) (SI 2006/1535)[3] |
| Sch 14 | | 18 Nov 2004 (so far as confers any power to make an order or regulations which is exercisable by the Secretary of State or the National Assembly for Wales) (s 270(2)(b)) |
| | | 18 Jan 2005 (otherwise) (s 270(3)(d)) |
| Sch 15 | para 1 | 14 Jul 2005 (W) (SI 2005/1814) |
| | paras 2–6 | 6 Apr 2006 (E) (SI 2006/1060)[2] |
| | | 16 Jun 2006 (W) (SI 2006/1535)[3] |
| | para 7(1), (2) | 14 Jul 2005 (W) (SI 2005/1814) |
| | para 7(3)(a) | 14 Jul 2005 (W) (SI 2005/1814) |
| | para 7(3)(b) | *Never in force* (repealed) |
| | para 7(3)(c) | 14 Jul 2005 (W) (SI 2005/1814) |
| | para 7(4)(a) | 14 Jul 2005 (W) (SI 2005/1814) |
| | para 7(4)(b) | *Never in force* (repealed) |
| | para 7(5) | 14 Jul 2005 (W) (SI 2005/1814) |
| | para 8 | 6 Apr 2006 (E) (SI 2006/1060)[2] |
| | paras 9–15 | 6 Apr 2006 (E) (SI 2006/1060)[2] |
| | | 16 Jun 2006 (W) (SI 2006/1535)[3] |
| | para 16 | 18 Nov 2004 (so far as confers any power to make an order or regulations which is exercisable by the Secretary of State or the National Assembly for Wales) (s 270(2)(b)) |
| | | 6 Apr 2006 (E) (otherwise) (SI 2006/1060)[2] |
| | | 16 Jun 2006 (W) (otherwise) (SI 2006/1535)[3] |
| | paras 17–34 | 6 Apr 2006 (E) (SI 2006/1060)[2] |
| | | 16 Jun 2006 (W) (SI 2006/1535)[3] |
| | para 35 | 14 Jul 2005 (W) (SI 2005/1814) |
| | | 6 Apr 2006 (E) (SI 2006/1060)[2] |
| | para 36 | 6 Apr 2006 (E) (SI 2006/1060)[2] |
| | | 16 Jun 2006 (W) (SI 2006/1535)[3] |
| | para 37(1) | 14 Jul 2005 (W) (SI 2005/1814) |
| | para 37(2)(a), (b) | 14 Jul 2005 (W) (SI 2005/1814) |
| | para 37(2)(c), (d) | *Never in force* (repealed) |
| | para 37(3) | 14 Jul 2005 (W) (SI 2005/1814) |
| | paras 38–44 | 6 Apr 2006 (E) (SI 2006/1060)[2] |
| | | 16 Jun 2006 (W) (SI 2006/1535)[3] |
| | para 45(1) | 14 Jul 2005 (W) (SI 2005/1814) |
| | para 45(2)(a) | *Never in force* (repealed) |
| | para 45(2)(b)–(d) | 14 Jul 2005 (W) (SI 2005/1814) |
| | para 45(3) | 14 Jul 2005 (W) (SI 2005/1814) |
| | para 46 | 14 Jul 2005 (W) (SI 2005/1814) |
| | para 47 | 2 Jan 2007 (E) (SI 2006/3191) |
| | | 13 Dec 2007 (W) (SI 2007/3232) |
| Sch 16 | | 6 Apr 2006 (E), 16 Jun 2006 (W) (SI 2006/1060[2]; SI 2006/1535[3]), repeals of or in— |
| | | Friendly and Industrial and Provident Societies Act 1968; |
| | | Land Compensation Act 1973; |
| | | Civil Aviation Act 1982; |
| | | Mobile Homes Act 1983; |
| | | Housing Act 1985; |
| | | Housing Associations Act 1985; |
| | | Housing (Consequential Provisions) Act 1985; |
| | | Airports Act 1986; |
| | | Housing Act 1988; |

**Housing Act 2004 (c 34)**—*contd*

Electricity Act 1989;
Local Government and Housing Act 1989;
Housing Act 1996;
Housing Grants, Construction and Regeneration Act 1996;
Transport Act 2000
6 Apr 2007 (SI 2007/1068), repeals of or in—
London Building Acts (Amendment) Act 1939;
County of Merseyside Act 1980;
Building Act 1984 (E);
Leicestershire Act 1985
*Not yet in force*, repeals of or in—
Local Government Act 1974;
Building Act 1984 (W);
Health Service Commissioners Act 1993;
Government of Wales Act 1998

[1]   For transitional provisions, see SI 2005/1729, art 3

[2]   For transitional provisions and savings, see SI 2006/1060, art 2

[3]   For transitional provisions and savings, see SI 2006/1535, art 3, Schedule

**Human Tissue Act 2004 (c 30)**

*RA:* 15 Nov 2004

*Commencement provisions:* s 60; Human Tissue Act 2004 (Commencement No 1) Order 2005, SI 2005/919;
Human Tissue Act 2004 (Commencement No 2) Order 2005, SI 2005/2632; Human Tissue Act 2004
(Commencement No 3 and Transitional Provisions) Order 2005, SI 2005/2792; Human Tissue
Act 2004 (Commencement No 4 and Transitional Provisions) Order 2006, SI 2006/404; Human
Tissue Act 2004 (Commencement No 5 and Transitional Provisions) Order 2006, SI 2006/1997, as
amended by SI 2006/2169

| | | |
|---|---|---|
| 1 | | 20 Oct 2005 (for the purpose of conferring power to make orders and regulations) (SI 2005/2792) |
| | | 1 Sep 2006 (otherwise) (SI 2006/1997)[5] |
| 2, 3 | | 1 Sep 2006 (SI 2006/1997)[5] |
| 4 | | 20 Oct 2005 (for the purpose of conferring power to make orders and regulations) (SI 2005/2792) |
| | | 1 Sep 2006 (otherwise) (SI 2006/1997)[5] |
| 5 | | 1 Sep 2006 (SI 2006/1997)[5] |
| 6, 7 | | 20 Oct 2005 (for the purpose of conferring power to make orders and regulations) (SI 2005/2792) |
| | | 1 Sep 2006 (otherwise) (SI 2006/1997)[5] |
| 8 | | 20 Oct 2005 (for the purpose of conferring power to make orders and regulations) (SI 2005/2792) |
| | | 1 Dec 2006 (otherwise) (SI 2006/1997)[5] |
| 9 | | 1 Sep 2006 (SI 2006/1997)[5] |
| 10 | | 20 Oct 2005 (for the purpose of conferring power to make orders and regulations) (SI 2005/2792) |
| | | 1 Sep 2006 (otherwise) (SI 2006/1997)[5] |
| 11, 12 | | 1 Sep 2006 (SI 2006/1997)[5] |
| 13–15 | | 1 Apr 2005 (SI 2005/919)[1] |
| 16 | (1) | 1 Mar 2006 (for specified purposes[3], except in so far as requires the authority of a licence for: (a) storage of relevant material for 48 hours or less; (b) storage of relevant material for scheduled purposes other than transplantation; (c) storage of relevant material for the purpose of organ transplantation) (SI 2006/404)[4] |

**Human Tissue Act 2004 (c 30)**—*contd*

|  |  |
|---|---|
|  | 7 Apr 2006 (otherwise, except in so far as requires the authority of a licence for: (a) storage of relevant material for 48 hours or less; (b) storage of relevant material for scheduled purposes other than transplantation; (c) storage of relevant material for the purpose of organ transplantation) (SI 2006/404)[4] |
|  | 31 Jul 2006 (otherwise, for specified purposes[3]) (SI 2006/1997)[5] |
|  | 1 Sep 2006 (otherwise) (SI 2006/1997)[5] |
| (2)(a)–(d), (e)(i) | 31 Jul 2006 (for specified purposes[3]) (SI 2006/1997)[5] |
|  | 1 Sep 2006 (otherwise) (SI 2006/1997)[5] |
| (2)(e)(ii) | 1 Mar 2006 (for specified purposes[3], except in so far as requires the authority of a licence for: (a) storage of relevant material for 48 hours or less; (b) storage of relevant material for scheduled purposes other than transplantation; (c) storage of relevant material for the purpose of organ transplantation) (SI 2006/404)[4] |
|  | 7 Apr 2006 (otherwise, except in so far as requires the authority of a licence for: (a) storage of relevant material for 48 hours or less; (b) storage of relevant material for scheduled purposes other than transplantation; (c) storage of relevant material for the purpose of organ transplantation) (SI 2006/404)[4] |
|  | 31 Jul 2006 (otherwise, for specified purposes[3]) (SI 2006/1997)[5] |
|  | 1 Sep 2006 (otherwise) (SI 2006/1997)[5] |
| (2)(f) | 31 Jul 2006 (for specified purposes[3]) (SI 2006/1997)[5] |
|  | 1 Sep 2006 (otherwise) (SI 2006/1997)[5] |
| (3) | 20 Oct 2005 (for the purpose of conferring power to make orders and regulations) (SI 2005/2792) |
|  | 31 Jul 2006 (otherwise, for specified purposes[3]) (SI 2006/1997)[5] |
|  | 1 Sep 2006 (otherwise) (SI 2006/1997)[5] |
| (4) | 31 Jul 2006 (for specified purposes[3]) (SI 2006/1997)[5] |
|  | 1 Sep 2006 (otherwise) (SI 2006/1997)[5] |
| (5) | 20 Oct 2005 (for the purpose of conferring power to make orders and regulations) (SI 2005/2792) |
|  | 31 Jul 2006 (otherwise, for specified purposes[3]) (SI 2006/1997)[5] |
|  | 1 Sep 2006 (otherwise) (SI 2006/1997)[5] |
| (6) | See Sch 3 below |
| (7) | 31 Jul 2006 (for specified purposes[3]) (SI 2006/1997)[5] |
|  | 1 Sep 2006 (otherwise) (SI 2006/1997)[5] |
| 17–20 | 1 Mar 2006 (for specified purposes[3]) (SI 2006/404)[4] |
|  | 7 Apr 2006 (otherwise, in so far as relevant to s 16 as brought into force by SI 2006/404 or to provisions of the Act brought into force by previous Orders) (SI 2006/404)[4] |
|  | 31 Jul 2006 (otherwise, for specified purposes[3]) (SI 2006/1997)[5] |
|  | 1 Sep 2006 (otherwise) (SI 2006/1997)[5] |
| 21 | 20 Oct 2005 (for the purpose of conferring power to make orders and regulations) (SI 2005/2792) |
|  | 1 Mar 2006 (for specified purposes[3]) (SI 2006/404)[4] |
|  | 7 Apr 2006 (otherwise, in so far as relevant to s 16 as brought into force by SI 2006/404 or to provisions of the Act brought into force by previous Orders) (SI 2006/404)[4] |
|  | 31 Jul 2006 (otherwise, for specified purposes[3]) (SI 2006/1997)[5] |
|  | 1 Sep 2006 (otherwise) (SI 2006/1997)[5] |
| 22–24 | 1 Mar 2006 (for specified purposes[3]) (SI 2006/404)[4] |
|  | 7 Apr 2006 (otherwise, in so far as relevant to s 16 as brought into force by SI 2006/404 or to provisions of the Act brought into force by previous Orders) (SI 2006/404)[4] |
|  | 31 Jul 2006 (otherwise, for specified purposes[3]) (SI 2006/1997)[5] |
|  | 1 Sep 2006 (otherwise) (SI 2006/1997)[5] |
| 25 | 1 Mar 2006 (for specified purposes[3]) (SI 2006/404)[4] |

**Human Tissue Act 2004 (c 30)**—*contd*

|  |  |  |
|---|---|---|
|  |  | 7 Apr 2006 (otherwise, in so far as relevant to s 16 as brought into force by SI 2006/404 or to provisions of the Act brought into force by previous Orders) (SI 2006/404)[4] |
|  |  | 1 Sep 2006 (otherwise) (SI 2006/1997)[5] |
| 26–29 |  | 1 Apr 2005 (SI 2005/919)[1] |
| 30, 31 |  | 1 Sep 2006 (SI 2006/1997)[5] |
| 32 |  | 20 Oct 2005 (SI 2005/2792) |
| 33, 34 |  | 20 Oct 2005 (for the purpose of conferring power to make orders and regulations) (SI 2005/2792) |
|  |  | 1 Sep 2006 (otherwise) (SI 2006/1997)[5] |
| 35, 36 |  | 1 Apr 2005 (SI 2005/919)[1] |
| 37 |  | 20 Oct 2005 (for the purpose of conferring power to make orders and regulations) (SI 2005/2792) |
|  |  | 1 Mar 2006 (for specified purposes[3]) (SI 2006/404)[4] |
|  |  | 7 Apr 2006 (otherwise, in so far as relevant to s 16 as brought into force by SI 2006/404 or to provisions of the Act brought into force by previous Orders) (SI 2006/404)[4] |
|  |  | 31 Jul 2006 (otherwise, for specified purposes[3]) (SI 2006/1997)[5] |
|  |  | 1 Sep 2006 (otherwise) (SI 2006/1997)[5] |
| 38 |  | 1 Apr 2005 (SI 2005/919)[1] |
| 39 |  | 1 Apr 2005 (so far as it relates to s 14) (SI 2005/919)[1] |
|  |  | 1 Mar 2006 (for specified purposes[3]) (SI 2006/404)[4] |
|  |  | 7 Apr 2006 (otherwise, in so far as relevant to s 16 as brought into force by SI 2006/404 or to provisions of the Act brought into force by previous Orders) (SI 2006/404)[4] |
|  |  | 31 Jul 2006 (otherwise, for specified purposes[3]) (SI 2006/1997)[5] |
|  |  | 1 Sep 2006 (otherwise) (SI 2006/1997)[5] |
| 40 |  | 1 Apr 2005 (so far as it relates to s 14) (SI 2005/919)[1] |
|  |  | 31 Jul 2006 (otherwise, for specified purposes[3]) (SI 2006/1997)[5] |
|  |  | 1 Sep 2006 (otherwise) (SI 2006/1997)[5] |
| 41 |  | 1 Apr 2005 (so far as relevant to the provisions brought into force by SI 2005/919) (SI 2005/919)[1] |
|  |  | 1 Mar 2006 (for specified purposes[3]) (SI 2006/404)[4] |
|  |  | 7 Apr 2006 (otherwise, in so far as relevant to s 16 as brought into force by SI 2006/404 or to provisions of the Act brought into force by previous Orders) (SI 2006/404)[4] |
|  |  | 31 Jul 2006 (otherwise, for specified purposes[3]) (SI 2006/1997)[5] |
|  |  | 1 Sep 2006 (otherwise) (SI 2006/1997)[5] |
| 42 |  | 1 Apr 2005 (SI 2005/919)[1] |
| 43 |  | 1 Sep 2006 (SI 2006/1997)[5] |
| 44 |  | 1 Mar 2006 (for specified purposes[3]) (SI 2006/404)[4] |
|  |  | 7 Apr 2006 (otherwise, in so far as relevant to s 16 as brought into force by SI 2006/404 or to provisions of the Act brought into force by previous Orders) (SI 2006/404)[4] |
|  |  | 31 Jul 2006 (otherwise, for specified purposes[3]) (SI 2006/1997)[5] |
|  |  | 1 Sep 2006 (otherwise) (SI 2006/1997)[5] |
| 45 | (1)–(3) | 1 Sep 2006 (SI 2006/1997)[5] |
|  | (4) | See Sch 4 below |
|  | (5) | 1 Sep 2006 (SI 2006/1997)[5] |
| 46 |  | 20 Oct 2005 (for the purpose of conferring power to make orders and regulations) (SI 2005/2792) |
|  |  | 1 Sep 2006 (otherwise) (SI 2006/1997)[5] |
| 47 |  | 3 Oct 2005 (SI 2005/2632) |
| 48 |  | See Sch 5 below |
| 49, 50 |  | 1 Mar 2006 (for specified purposes[3]) (SI 2006/404)[4] |
|  |  | 7 Apr 2006 (otherwise, in so far as relevant to s 16 as brought into force by SI 2006/404 or to provisions of the Act brought into force by previous Orders) (SI 2006/404)[4] |
|  |  | 1 Sep 2006 (otherwise) (SI 2006/1997)[5] |

**Human Tissue Act 2004 (c 30)**—*contd*

| | | |
|---|---|---|
| 51 | | 20 Oct 2005 (except modification made to s 33(6)(a) by s 51(2)) (SI 2005/2792) |
| | | 1 Mar 2006 (modification made to s 33(6)(a) by s 51(2), for specified purposes[3]) (SI 2006/404)[4] |
| | | 7 Apr 2006 (modification made to s 33(6)(a) by s 51(2), in so far as not already in force and so far as relevant to s 16 as brought into force by SI 2006/404 or to provisions of the Act brought into force by previous Orders) (SI 2006/404)[4] |
| | | 1 Sep 2006 (otherwise) (SI 2006/1997)[5] |
| 52 | | 1 Apr 2005 (so far as relevant to the provisions brought into force by SI 2005/919) (SI 2005/919)[1] |
| | | 20 Oct 2005 (so far as relevant to the provisions brought into force by SI 2005/2792) (SI 2005/2792) |
| | | 1 Mar 2006 (for specified purposes[3]) (SI 2006/404)[4] |
| | | 7 Apr 2006 (otherwise, in so far as relevant to s 16 as brought into force by SI 2006/404 or to provisions of the Act brought into force by previous Orders) (SI 2006/404)[4] |
| | | 31 Jul 2006 (otherwise, for specified purposes[3]) (SI 2006/1997)[5] |
| | | 1 Sep 2006 (otherwise) (SI 2006/1997)[5] |
| 53 | | 1 Apr 2005 (so far as relevant to the provisions brought into force by SI 2005/919) (SI 2005/919)[1] |
| | | 1 Mar 2006 (for specified purposes[3]) (SI 2006/404)[4] |
| | | 7 Apr 2006 (otherwise, in so far as relevant to s 16 as brought into force by SI 2006/404 or to provisions of the Act brought into force by previous Orders) (SI 2006/404)[4] |
| | | 31 Jul 2006 (otherwise, for specified purposes[3]) (SI 2006/1997)[5] |
| | | 1 Sep 2006 (otherwise) (SI 2006/1997)[5] |
| 54 | | 1 Apr 2005 (so far as relevant to the provisions brought into force by SI 2005/919) (SI 2005/919)[1] |
| | | 20 Oct 2005 (so far as relevant to the provisions brought into force by SI 2005/2792 and also for the purpose of conferring power to make orders and regulations) (SI 2005/2792) |
| | | 1 Mar 2006 (for specified purposes[3]) (SI 2006/404)[4] |
| | | 7 Apr 2006 (otherwise, in so far as relevant to s 16 as brought into force by SI 2006/404 or to provisions of the Act brought into force by previous Orders) (SI 2006/404)[4] |
| | | 31 Jul 2006 (otherwise, for specified purposes[3]) (SI 2006/1997)[5] |
| | | 1 Sep 2006 (otherwise) (SI 2006/1997)[5] |
| 55 | | 1 Apr 2005 (SI 2005/919)[1] |
| 56 | | See Sch 6 below |
| 57 | | See Sch 7 below |
| 58 | (1), (2) | 1 Mar 2006 (for specified purposes[3]) (SI 2006/404)[4] |
| | | 7 Apr 2006 (otherwise, in so far as relevant to s 16 as brought into force by SI 2006/404 or to provisions of the Act brought into force by previous Orders) (SI 2006/404)[4] |
| | | 31 Jul 2006 (otherwise, for specified purposes[3]) (SI 2006/1997)[5] |
| | | 1 Sep 2006 (otherwise) (SI 2006/1997)[5] |
| | (3)–(7) | 15 Nov 2004 (s 60(1)) |
| 59–61 | | 15 Nov 2004 (s 60(1)) |
| Schs 1, 2 | | 1 Apr 2005 (SI 2005/919)[1] |
| Sch 3 | | 20 Oct 2005 (for the purpose of conferring power to make orders and regulations) (SI 2005/2792) |
| | | 1 Mar 2006 (for specified purposes[3]) (SI 2006/404)[4] |
| | | 7 Apr 2006 (otherwise, in so far as relevant to s 16 as brought into force by SI 2006/404 or to provisions of the Act brought into force by previous Orders) (SI 2006/404)[4] |
| | | 31 Jul 2006 (otherwise, for specified purposes[3]) (SI 2006/1997)[5] |
| | | 1 Sep 2006 (otherwise) (SI 2006/1997)[5] |
| Sch 4 | | 20 Oct 2005 (for the purpose of conferring power to make orders and regulations) (SI 2005/2792) |

**Human Tissue Act 2004 (c 30)**—*contd*

|  |  |  |
|---|---|---|
| | | 1 Sep 2006 (otherwise) (SI 2006/1997)[5] |
| Sch 5 | | 20 Oct 2005 (for the purpose of conferring power to make orders and regulations) (SI 2005/2792) |
| | | 1 Mar 2006 (for specified purposes[3]) (SI 2006/404)[4] |
| | | 7 Apr 2006 (otherwise, in so far as relevant to s 16 as brought into force by SI 2006/404 or to provisions of the Act brought into force by previous Orders) (SI 2006/404)[4] |
| | | 1 Sep 2006 (otherwise) (SI 2006/1997)[5] |
| Sch 6 | paras 1–3 | 1 Sep 2006 (SI 2006/1997)[5] |
| | para 4 | 20 Oct 2005 (SI 2005/2792) |
| | para 5 | 20 Oct 2005 (for the purpose of conferring power to make orders and regulations) (SI 2005/2792) |
| | | 1 Mar 2006 (for specified purposes[3]) (SI 2006/404)[4] |
| | | 7 Apr 2006 (otherwise, in so far as relevant to s 16 as brought into force by SI 2006/404 or to provisions of the Act brought into force by previous Orders) (SI 2006/404)[4] |
| | | 1 Sep 2006 (otherwise) (SI 2006/1997)[5] |
| | para 6 | 1 Apr 2005 (SI 2005/919)[1] |
| | para 7 | 20 Oct 2005 (SI 2005/2792)[2] |
| Sch 7 | Pt 1 | 20 Oct 2005 (repeals of Human Organ Transplants Act 1989, s 1 and the reference to that section in s 5 of that Act) (SI 2005/2792) |
| | | 1 Sep 2006 (otherwise) (SI 2006/1997)[5] |
| | Pt 2 | 20 Oct 2005 (revocation of SI 1989/2408, art 3, and the reference to that article in art 6 of that order) (SI 2005/2792) |
| | | 1 Sep 2006 (otherwise) (SI 2006/1997)[5] |

[1]   For transitional provisions, see SI 2005/919, art 2

[2]   For transitional provisions, see SI 2005/2792, art 3

[3]   The specified purposes are: (a) to enable the Authority to grant or refuse licences; (b) to require that applications for licences are accompanied by such fee as the Authority shall determine in accordance with Sch 3, para 13(2) to the Act; (c) to enable the Authority to impose conditions on licences; (d) to enable the Authority to vary, revoke or suspend licences; (e) to enable the Authority to give directions under ss 23 and 24 of the Act and under Sch 3, para 2(4) to the Act; (f) to require the Authority to give notice of its decisions in accordance with Sch 3, paras 10 and 11 to the Act; (g) to enable a person to whom notice is given in accordance with Sch 3, para 10 to the Act to require the Authority to give him an opportunity to make representations in accordance with that paragraph; (h) to enable applicants to require the Authority to reconsider decisions to revoke or vary licences; (i) to enable the Authority to reconsider decisions to revoke or vary licences; (j) to enable persons aggrieved by a decision on reconsideration to appeal on a point of law to the High Court

[4]   For transitional provisions, see SI 2006/404, arts 5, 6

[5]   For transitional provisions, see SI 2006/1997, arts 4–8

---

**Hunting Act 2004 (c 37)**

*RA:* 18 Nov 2004

*Commencement provisions:* s 15

Whole Act in force 18 Feb 2005 (s 15)

---

**Justice (Northern Ireland) Act 2004 (c 4)**

*RA:* 13 May 2004

*Commencement provisions:* s 19; Justice (Northern Ireland) Act 2004 (Commencement) Order 2004, SR 2004/267; Justice (Northern Ireland) Act 2004 (Commencement No 2) Order 2004, SR

**Justice (Northern Ireland) Act 2004 (c 4)**—*contd*
2004/432; Justice (Northern Ireland) Act 2004 (Commencement No 3) Order 2005, SR 2005/282;
Justice (Northern Ireland) Act 2004 (Commencement No 4) Order 2010, SR 2010/114

| | | |
|---|---|---|
| 1–3 | | 15 Jun 2005 (SR 2005/282) |
| 4, 5 | | *Never in force* (repealed) |
| 6, 7 | | 13 Jun 2005 (SR 2005/282) |
| 8 | (1)–(8) | 1 Feb 2006 (SR 2005/282) |
| | (9) | 12 Apr 2010 (SR 2010/114) |
| 9 | | 14 Jul 2004 (SR 2004/267) |
| 10 | | 29 Oct 2004 (SR 2004/432) |
| 11–15 | | 14 Jul 2004 (SR 2004/267) |
| 16 | | See Sch 3 below |
| 17 | | 14 Jul 2004 (SR 2004/267) |
| 18 | | See Sch 4 below |
| 19–23 | | 13 May 2004 (RA) |
| Sch 1 | | 15 Jun 2005 (SR 2005/282) |
| Sch 2 | | 14 Jul 2004 (SR 2004/267) |
| Sch 3 | | 25 Jul 2005 (SR 2005/282) |
| Sch 4 | | 14 Jul 2004 (SR 2004/267), repeals and revocations of or in— |
| | | Prisons Act (Northern Ireland) 1953; |
| | | Malone and Whiteabbey Training Schools Act (Northern Ireland) 1956; |
| | | Criminal Justice (Children) (Northern Ireland) Order 1998; |
| | | Justice (Northern Ireland) Act 2002, s 46(1)(h); |
| | | Commissioner for Children and Young People (Northern Ireland) Order 2003; |
| | | Criminal Justice (Northern Ireland) Order 2003 |
| | | 13 Jun 2005 (repeals in Police (Northern Ireland) Act 1998) (SR 2005/282) |
| | | 12 Apr 2010 (SR 2010/114), repeals and revocations of or in— |
| | | Justice (Northern Ireland) Act 2002, ss 34(4), 79–81, 90(2), (3), Sch 12, para 75 |

**Local Governance (Scotland) Act 2004 (asp 9)**

*RA:* 29 Jul 2004

*Commencement provisions:* s 17; Local Governance (Scotland) Act 2004 (Commencement No 1 and
Transitional Provisions) Order 2004, SSI 2004/351; Local Governance (Scotland) Act 2004
(Commencement No 2) Order 2004, SSI 2004/558; Local Governance (Scotland) Act 2004
(Commencement No 3) Order 2006, SSI 2006/470; Local Governance (Scotland) Act 2004
(Commencement No 4) Order 2007, SSI 2007/25

| | | |
|---|---|---|
| 1, 2 | | 2 May 2007 (SSI 2007/25) |
| 3 | | 14 Sep 2006 (SSI 2006/470) |
| 4 | (1)–(4) | 20 Aug 2004 (SSI 2004/351) |
| | (5)(a)–(c) | 20 Aug 2004 (SSI 2004/351) |
| | (5)(d), (e) | 2 May 2007 (SSI 2007/25) |
| | (5)(f) | 20 Aug 2004 (SSI 2004/351) |
| | (5)(g), (h) | 2 May 2007 (SSI 2007/25) |
| 5 | | 2 May 2007 (SSI 2007/25) |
| 6 | | 20 Aug 2004 (SSI 2004/351) |
| 7, 8 | | 20 Jan 2005 (SSI 2004/558) |
| 9 | | 28 Feb 2007 (SSI 2007/25) |
| 10 | | 2 May 2007 (SSI 2007/25) |
| 11, 12 | | 14 Sep 2006 (SSI 2006/470) |
| 13 | (1)–(5) | 20 Jan 2005 (SSI 2004/558) |
| | (6) | See Schedule below |
| 14 | | 20 Jan 2005 (SSI 2004/558) |
| 15–17 | | 29 Jul 2004 (RA) |

**Local Governance (Scotland) Act 2004 (asp 9)**—*contd*

| | |
|---|---|
| Schedule | 20 Jan 2005 (SSI 2004/558) |

---

## National Health Service Reform (Scotland) Act 2004 (asp 7)

*RA:* 11 Jun 2004

*Commencement provisions:* s 12; National Health Service Reform (Scotland) Act 2004 (Commencement No 1) Order 2004, SSI 2004/335; National Health Service Reform (Scotland) Act 2004 (Commencement No 2) Order 2004, SSI 2004/361

| | | |
|---|---|---|
| 1 | (1) | 1 Sep 2004 (for the purpose of providing that the National Health Service (Scotland) Act 1978 be referred to as "the 1978 Act") (SSI 2004/361) |
| | | *Not yet in force* (repeals of National Health Service (Scotland) Act 1978, s 12A, Sch 7A) |
| | (2), (3) | 30 Sep 2004 (SSI 2004/361) |
| 2 | | 1 Sep 2004 (for the purpose of enabling the Scottish Ministers to make regulations under s 4B(6) of the 1978 Act) (SSI 2004/361) |
| | | 30 Sep 2004 (otherwise) (SSI 2004/361) |
| 3–7 | | 30 Sep 2004 (SSI 2004/361) |
| 8 | | 1 Feb 2005 (SSI 2004/361) |
| 9 | | 1 Jan 2005 (SSI 2004/361) |
| 10 | | 11 Jun 2004 (RA) |
| 11 | (1) | See Sch 1 below |
| | (2) | See Sch 2 below |
| 12 | | 11 Jun 2004 (RA) |
| Sch 1 | para 1(1)–(3) | 30 Sep 2004 (SSI 2004/361) |
| | para 1(4), (5) | *Not yet in force* |
| | para 1(6) | 30 Sep 2004 (SSI 2004/361) |
| | para 1(7)–(11) | *Not yet in force* |
| | para 2 | 30 Jul 2004 (SSI 2004/335) |
| | paras 3, 4 | *Not yet in force* |
| Sch 2 | | *Not yet in force* |

---

## National Insurance Contributions and Statutory Payments Act 2004 (c 3)

*RA:* 13 May 2004

*Commencement provisions:* s 13, National Insurance Contributions and Statutory Payments Act 2004 (Commencement) Order 2004, SI 2004/1943

| | | |
|---|---|---|
| 1–6 | | 1 Sep 2004 (SI 2004/1943) |
| 7, 8 | | 6 Apr 2005 (SI 2004/1943) |
| 9 | (1)–(3) | 1 Jan 2005 (SI 2004/1943) |
| | (4), (5) | 6 Apr 2005 (SI 2004/1943) |
| 10 | (1)–(3) | 1 Jan 2005 (SI 2004/1943) |
| | (4), (5) | 6 Apr 2005 (SI 2004/1943) |
| 11 | | See Sch 1 below |
| 12 | | See Sch 2 below |
| 13–15 | | 13 May 2004 (RA) |
| Sch 1 | paras 1, 2 | 1 Sep 2004 (SI 2004/1943) |
| | para 3(1) | See sub-paras (2), (3) below |
| | para 3(2) | 6 Apr 2005 (SI 2004/1943) |
| | para 3(3) | 1 Sep 2004 (SI 2004/1943) |
| | para 4(1) | See sub-paras (2), (3) below |
| | para 4(2) | 6 Apr 2005 (SI 2004/1943) |
| | para 4(3) | 1 Sep 2004 (SI 2004/1943) |
| | para 5 | 1 Sep 2004 (SI 2004/1943) |
| Sch 2 | Pt 1 | 1 Sep 2004 (SI 2004/1943), repeals of or in— |

**National Insurance Contributions and Statutory Payments Act 2004 (c 3)**—*contd*

|  |  |  |
|---|---|---|
|  |  | Social Security Contributions and Benefits Act 1992; |
|  |  | Social Security Contributions and Benefits (Northern Ireland) Act 1992; |
|  |  | Social Security Contributions (Transfer of Functions, etc) Act 1999, s 4, Sch 3; |
|  |  | Welfare Reform and Pensions Act 1999 |
|  |  | 6 Apr 2005 (SI 2004/1943), repeals of or in— |
|  |  | Taxes Management Act 1970; |
|  |  | Social Security Administration Act 1992; |
|  |  | Social Security Administration (Northern Ireland) Act 1992; |
|  |  | Social Security Contributions (Transfer of Functions, etc) Act 1999, Sch 5; |
|  |  | Child Support Pensions and Social Security Act 2000; |
|  |  | Child Support, Pensions and Social Security Act (Northern Ireland) 2000 |
|  | Pt 2 | 1 Sep 2004 (SI 2004/1943), revocations of or in— |
|  |  | Social Security (Northern Ireland) Order 1998; |
|  |  | Social Security Contributions (Transfer of Functions, etc) (Northern Ireland) Order 1999, SI 1999/671, Sch 3, Sch 4, para 8 |
|  |  | 6 Apr 2005 (revocations of or in Social Security Contributions (Transfer of Functions, etc) (Northern Ireland) Order 1999, Sch 4, paras 1, 3) (SI 2004/1943) |

---

**Nature Conservation (Scotland) Act 2004 (asp 6)**

*RA:* 11 Jun 2004

*Commencement provisions:* s 59; Nature Conservation (Scotland) Act 2004 (Commencement) Order 2004, SSI 2004/407; Nature Conservation (Scotland) Act 2004 (Commencement No 2) Order 2004, SSI 2004/495; Nature Conservation (Scotland) Act 2004 (Commencement No 3) Order 2008, SSI 2008/193

| | | |
|---|---|---|
| 1–14 | | 29 Nov 2004 (SSI 2004/495) |
| 15 | (1) | 29 Nov 2004 (SSI 2004/495) |
| | (2) | 1 Oct 2004 (SSI 2004/407) |
| | (3)–(10) | 29 Nov 2004 (SSI 2004/495) |
| 16–21 | | 29 Nov 2004 (SSI 2004/495) |
| 22 | (1), (2) | 30 Jun 2008 (SSI 2008/193) |
| | (3) | 2 Jun 2008 (SSI 2008/193) |
| 23–49 | | 29 Nov 2004 (SSI 2004/495) |
| 50 | | See Sch 6 below |
| 51 | | 1 Oct 2004 (SSI 2004/407) |
| 52 | | 29 Nov 2004 (SSI 2004/495) |
| 53 | | 11 Jun 2004 (RA) |
| 54 | | 1 Oct 2004 (SSI 2004/407) |
| 55 | | 29 Nov 2004 (SSI 2004/495) |
| 56 | | 11 Jun 2004 (RA) |
| 57, 58 | | 29 Nov 2004 (SSI 2004/495) |
| 59 | | 11 Jun 2004 (RA) |
| Schs 1–5 | | 29 Nov 2004 (SSI 2004/495) |
| Sch 6 | | 1 Oct 2004 (SSI 2004/407) |
| Sch 7 | | 29 Nov 2004 (SSI 2004/495) |

---

**Patents Act 2004 (c 16)**

*RA:* 22 Jul 2004

*Commencement provisions:* s 17; Patents Act 2004 (Commencement No 1 and Consequential and Transitional Provisions) Order 2004, SI 2004/2177, as amended by SI 2007/3291; Patents Act 2004

**Patents Act 2004 (c 16)**—*contd*
(Commencement No 2 and Consequential, etc and Transitional Provisions) Order 2004,
SI 2004/3205, as amended by SI 2007/3291; Patents Act 2004 (Commencement No 3 and
Transitional Provisions) Order 2005, SI 2005/2471; Patents Act 2004 (Commencement No 4 and
Transitional Provisions) Order 2007, SI 2007/3396

| | | |
|---|---|---|
| 1 | | 13 Dec 2007 (SI 2007/3396) |
| 2 | (1), (2) | 13 Dec 2007 (SI 2007/3396) |
| | (3), (4) | *Never in force* (repealed) |
| | (5) | 13 Dec 2007 (SI 2007/3396) |
| 3, 4 | | 13 Dec 2007 (SI 2007/3396) |
| 5 | | See Sch 1 below |
| 6, 7 | | 1 Jan 2005 (SI 2004/3205)[2] |
| 8 | | 1 Oct 2005 (SI 2005/2471)[3] |
| 9 | | 1 Oct 2005 (SI 2005/2471) |
| 10–12 | | 1 Jan 2005 (SI 2004/3205)[2] |
| 13 | | 1 Oct 2005 (SI 2005/2471) |
| 14 | | 1 Jan 2005 (SI 2004/3205)[2] |
| 15 | | 1 Oct 2005 (SI 2005/2471)[3] |
| 16 | (1) | See Sch 2 below |
| | (2) | See Sch 3 below |
| | (3) | 1 Jan 2005 (SI 2004/3205)[2] |
| 17, 18 | | 22 Jul 2004 (RA) |
| Sch 1 | para 1 | 1 Jan 2005 (SI 2004/3205)[2] |
| | paras 2–5 | 13 Dec 2007 (SI 2007/3396)[4] |
| | paras 6–8 | 1 Jan 2005 (SI 2004/3205)[2] |
| | para 9(1) | 1 Jan 2005 (SI 2004/3205)[2] |
| | para 9(2)(a) | 1 Jan 2005 (SI 2004/3205)[2] |
| | para 9(2)(b) | 1 Jan 2005 (for the purposes of the Patent Co-operation Treaty) (SI 2004/3205)[2] |
| | | 13 Dec 2007 (for the purposes of the European Patent Convention) (SI 2007/3396) |
| | para 9(3) | 1 Jan 2005 (SI 2004/3205)[2] |
| | para 9(4) | 13 Dec 2007 (SI 2007/3396) |
| Sch 2 | para 1 | 1 Jan 2005 (SI 2004/3205)[2] |
| | paras 2–4 | 13 Dec 2007 (SI 2007/3396) |
| | para 5 | 1 Jan 2005 (SI 2004/3205)[2] |
| | para 6 | 1 Oct 2005 (SI 2005/2471) |
| | para 7 | 1 Jan 2005 (s 17(2)) |
| | para 8 | 1 Jan 2005 (SI 2004/3205)[2] |
| | para 9 | 1 Oct 2005 (SI 2005/2471) |
| | paras 10–14 | 1 Jan 2005 (SI 2004/3205)[2] |
| | para 15 | 1 Oct 2005 (SI 2005/2471) |
| | paras 16, 17 | 1 Jan 2005 (SI 2004/3205)[2] |
| | para 18 | 1 Oct 2005 (SI 2005/2471) |
| | paras 19–22 | 1 Jan 2005 (SI 2004/3205)[2] |
| | para 23 | 1 Jan 2005 (s 17(2)) |
| | para 24 | 22 Sep 2004 (SI 2004/2177)[1] |
| | para 25 | 1 Jan 2005 (SI 2004/3205)[2] |
| | para 26(1) | 22 Sep 2004 (SI 2004/2177)[1] |
| | para 26(2) | 1 Oct 2005 (SI 2005/2471) |
| | para 26(3), (4) | 22 Sep 2004 (SI 2004/2177)[1] |
| | paras 27, 28 | 1 Jan 2005 (SI 2004/3205)[2] |
| Sch 3 | | 22 Sep 2004 (repeal of Patents Act 1977, s 123(4), (5)) (SI 2004/2177)[1] |
| | | 1 Jan 2005 (repeals of or in Patents Act 1977, ss 41, 53, 60, 86, 87, 89, 95, 103, 105, 106, 121, 130) (SI 2004/3205)[2] |
| | | 1 Oct 2005 (repeal in Patents Act 1977, s 72(1)) (SI 2005/2471) |
| | | 13 Dec 2007 (otherwise) (SI 2007/3396) |

---

[1]   For transitional provisions, see SI 2004/2177, arts 6–8

**Patents Act 2004 (c 16)**—*contd*

² For transitional provisions, see SI 2004/3205, art 9

³ For transitional provisions, see SI 2005/2471, arts 3, 4

⁴ For transitional provisions, see SI 2007/3396, art 3

**Pensions Act 2004 (c 35)**

*RA:* 18 Nov 2004

*Commencement provisions:* s 322; Pensions Act 2004 (Commencement No 1 and Consequential and Transitional Provisions) Order 2004, SI 2004/3350; Pensions Act 2004 (Commencement No 2, Transitional Provisions and Consequential Amendments) Order 2005, SI 2005/275, as amended by SI 2005/695; Pensions Act 2004 (Commencement No 3, Transitional Provisions and Amendment) Order 2005, SI 2005/695, as amended by SI 2005/1108; Pensions Act 2004 (Commencement No 4 and Amendment) Order 2005, SI 2005/1108; Pensions Act 2004 (Commencement No 5) Order 2005, SI 2005/1436; Pensions Act 2004 (Commencement No 6, Transitional Provisions and Savings) Order 2005, SI 2005/1720, as amended by SI 2009/1583; Pensions Act 2004 (Commencement No 7) Order 2005, SI 2005/2447; Pensions Act 2004 (Commencement No 8) Order 2005, SI 2005/3331; Pensions Act 2004 (Commencement No 9) Order 2006, SI 2006/560; Pensions Act 2004 (Commencement No 10 and Saving Provision) Order 2006, SI 2006/2272; Pensions Act 2004 (Commencement No 11) Order 2008, SI 2008/627; Pensions Act 2004 (Commencement No 12) Order 2009, SI 2009/325; Pensions Act 2004 (Commencement No 13) Order 2009, SI 2009/1542; Pensions Act 2004 (Commencement No 14) Order 2010, SI 2010/443; Pensions Act 2004 (Commencement No 15) Order 2014, SI 2014/1636

| | | |
|---|---|---|
| 1 | | 17 Dec 2004 (SI 2004/3350) |
| 2 | (1), (2) | 17 Dec 2004 (SI 2004/3350) |
| | (3) | 6 Apr 2005 (SI 2005/275) |
| | (4)–(6) | 17 Dec 2004 (SI 2004/3350) |
| 3 | | See Sch 1 below |
| 4 | (1)(a) | 6 Apr 2005 (SI 2005/275) |
| | (1)(b) | 17 Dec 2004 (SI 2004/3350) |
| | (2), (3) | 6 Apr 2005 (SI 2005/275) |
| 5 | (1), (2) | 6 Apr 2005 (SI 2005/275) |
| | (3) | 17 Dec 2004 (SI 2004/3350) |
| 6 | | 17 Dec 2004 (SI 2004/3350) |
| 7 | | 6 Apr 2005 (SI 2005/275) |
| 8 | (1) | 6 Apr 2005 (SI 2005/275) |
| | (2), (3) | 17 Dec 2004 (SI 2004/3350) |
| | (4)–(6) | 6 Apr 2005 (SI 2005/275) |
| | (7) | 17 Dec 2004 (SI 2004/3350) |
| | (8)(a) | 17 Dec 2004 (SI 2004/3350) |
| | (8)(b) | 6 Apr 2005 (SI 2005/275) |
| | (9), (10) | 6 Apr 2005 (SI 2005/275) |
| 9 | | 17 Dec 2004 (SI 2004/3350) |
| 10 | (1)–(3) | 6 Apr 2005 (SI 2005/695)³ |
| | (4) | See Sch 2 below |
| | (5)(a) | 10 Feb 2005 (for the purpose of conferring power to make regulations, orders or rules) (SI 2005/275) |
| | | 6 Apr 2005 (otherwise) (SI 2005/275) |
| | (5)(b), (c) | 6 Apr 2005 (SI 2005/695)³ |
| | (6)–(8) | 6 Apr 2005 (SI 2005/695)³ |
| | (9)(a) | 6 Apr 2005 (SI 2005/695)³ |
| | (9)(b) | 17 Dec 2004 (in so far as it relates to Sch 1, para 18(2)) (SI 2004/3350) |
| | | 6 Apr 2005 (otherwise) (SI 2005/695)³ |
| | (10) | 6 Apr 2005 (SI 2005/695)³ |
| 11 | | 10 Feb 2005 (SI 2005/275) |
| 12 | (1) | 17 Dec 2004 (SI 2004/3350) |
| | (2)(a), (b) | 17 Dec 2004 (SI 2004/3350) |

**Pensions Act 2004 (c 35)**—*contd*

|  |  |  |
|---|---|---|
|  | (2)(c) | *Not yet in force* |
|  | (3), (4) | 17 Dec 2004 (SI 2004/3350) |
| 13–17 |  | 6 Apr 2005 (SI 2005/275) |
| 18 | (1), (2) | 6 Apr 2005 (SI 2005/275) |
|  | (3)(a) | 6 Apr 2005 (SI 2005/275) |
|  | (3)(b) | 6 Apr 2006 (SI 2006/560) |
|  | (3)(c) | 6 Apr 2005 (SI 2005/275) |
|  | (4)(a) | 6 Apr 2005 (SI 2005/275) |
|  | (4)(b) | 6 Apr 2006 (SI 2006/560) |
|  | (4)(c), (d) | 6 Apr 2005 (SI 2005/275) |
|  | (5) | 6 Apr 2005 (SI 2005/275) |
| 19 | (1)–(6) | 6 Apr 2005 (SI 2005/275) |
|  | (7) | 10 Feb 2005 (for the purpose of conferring power to make regulations, orders or rules) (SI 2005/275) |
|  |  | 6 Apr 2005 (otherwise) (SI 2005/275) |
|  | (8)–(10) | 6 Apr 2005 (SI 2005/275) |
| 20 | (1), (2) | 6 Apr 2005 (SI 2005/275) |
|  | (3)(a), (b) | 6 Apr 2005 (SI 2005/275) |
|  | (3)(c) | *Not yet in force* |
|  | (4)–(11) | 6 Apr 2005 (SI 2005/275) |
| 21 | (1)–(3) | 6 Apr 2005 (SI 2005/275) |
|  | (4) | 10 Feb 2005 (for the purpose of conferring power to make regulations, orders or rules) (SI 2005/275) |
|  |  | 6 Apr 2005 (otherwise) (SI 2005/275) |
|  | (5)–(7) | 6 Apr 2005 (SI 2005/275) |
| 22 |  | 6 Apr 2005 (SI 2005/275) |
| 23 | (1)–(9) | 6 Apr 2005 (SI 2005/275) |
|  | (10) | 10 Feb 2005 (definition "the actuary", para (b)(i), for the purpose of conferring power to make regulations, orders or rules) (SI 2005/275) |
|  |  | 6 Apr 2005 (otherwise) (SI 2005/275) |
|  | (11) | 6 Apr 2005 (SI 2005/275) |
| 24 | (1)–(6) | 6 Apr 2005 (SI 2005/275) |
|  | (7)(a) | 10 Feb 2005 (for the purpose of conferring power to make regulations, orders or rules) (SI 2005/275) |
|  |  | 6 Apr 2005 (otherwise) (SI 2005/275) |
|  | (7)(b) | 6 Apr 2005 (SI 2005/275) |
|  | (8)–(10) | 6 Apr 2005 (SI 2005/275) |
| 25–29 |  | 6 Apr 2005 (SI 2005/275) |
| 30 | (1)–(6) | 6 Apr 2005 (SI 2005/275) |
|  | (7)(a), (b) | 6 Apr 2005 (SI 2005/275) |
|  | (7)(c) | 10 Feb 2005 (for the purpose of conferring power to make regulations, orders or rules) (SI 2005/275) |
|  |  | 6 Apr 2005 (otherwise) (SI 2005/275) |
|  | (8), (9) | 6 Apr 2005 (SI 2005/275) |
| 31–35 |  | 6 Apr 2005 (SI 2005/275) |
| 36 | (1) | 6 Apr 2005 (SI 2005/275) |
|  | (2), (3) | 10 Feb 2005 (for the purpose of conferring power to make regulations, orders or rules) (SI 2005/275) |
|  |  | 6 Apr 2005 (otherwise) (SI 2005/275) |
|  | (4) | 6 Apr 2005 (SI 2005/275) |
| 37 |  | 6 Apr 2005 (SI 2005/275) |
| 38 | (1)(a) | 6 Apr 2005 (SI 2005/275) |
|  | (1)(b) | 10 Feb 2005 (for the purpose of conferring power to make regulations, orders or rules) (SI 2005/275) |
|  |  | 6 Apr 2005 (otherwise) (SI 2005/275) |
|  | (2), (3) | 6 Apr 2005 (SI 2005/275) |
|  | (4) | *Not yet in force* |
|  | (5), (6) | 6 Apr 2005 (SI 2005/275) |

**Enquiry Bureau   legislation.direct@lexisnexis.co.uk**

**Pensions Act 2004 (c 35)**—*contd*

| | | |
|---|---|---|
| | (7)(a)–(f) | 6 Apr 2005 (SI 2005/275) |
| | (7)(g) | *Not yet in force* |
| | (8)–(11) | 6 Apr 2005 (SI 2005/275) |
| 39, 40 | | 6 Apr 2005 (SI 2005/275) |
| 41 | (1)–(9) | 6 Apr 2005 (SI 2005/275) |
| | (10)(a)–(e) | 6 Apr 2005 (SI 2005/275) |
| | (10)(f) | *Not yet in force* |
| | (11), (12) | 6 Apr 2005 (SI 2005/275) |
| 42 | (1) | 6 Apr 2005 (SI 2005/275) |
| | (2)(a), (b) | 6 Apr 2005 (SI 2005/275) |
| | (2)(c) | *Not yet in force* |
| | (3)–(5) | 6 Apr 2005 (SI 2005/275) |
| 43 | (1)(a) | 6 Apr 2005 (SI 2005/275) |
| | (1)(b) | 10 Feb 2005 (for the purpose of conferring power to make regulations, orders or rules) (SI 2005/275) |
| | | 6 Apr 2005 (otherwise) (SI 2005/275) |
| | (2) | 6 Apr 2005 (SI 2005/275) |
| | (3)(a), (b) | 6 Apr 2005 (SI 2005/275) |
| | (3)(c) | 10 Feb 2005 (for the purpose of conferring power to make regulations, orders or rules) (SI 2005/275) |
| | | 6 Apr 2005 (otherwise) (SI 2005/275) |
| | (4)–(6) | 6 Apr 2005 (SI 2005/275) |
| | (7)(a)–(d) | 6 Apr 2005 (SI 2005/275) |
| | (7)(e) | *Not yet in force* |
| | (8) | 6 Apr 2005 (SI 2005/275) |
| | (9) | 10 Feb 2005 (for the purpose of conferring power to make regulations, orders or rules) (SI 2005/275) |
| | | 6 Apr 2005 (otherwise) (SI 2005/275) |
| | (10), (11) | 6 Apr 2005 (SI 2005/275) |
| 44 | (1), (2) | 6 Apr 2005 (SI 2005/275) |
| | (3)(a) | 10 Feb 2005 (for the purpose of conferring power to make regulations, orders or rules) (SI 2005/275) |
| | | 6 Apr 2005 (otherwise) (SI 2005/275) |
| | (3)(b) | 6 Apr 2005 (SI 2005/275) |
| | (4) | 10 Feb 2005 (for the purpose of conferring power to make regulations, orders or rules) (SI 2005/275) |
| | | 6 Apr 2005 (otherwise) (SI 2005/275) |
| | (5)–(7) | 6 Apr 2005 (SI 2005/275) |
| 45 | (1) | 6 Apr 2005 (SI 2005/275) |
| | (2)(a) | 6 Apr 2005 (SI 2005/275) |
| | (2)(b) | 10 Feb 2005 (for the purpose of conferring power to make regulations, orders or rules) (SI 2005/275) |
| | | 6 Apr 2005 (otherwise) (SI 2005/275) |
| | (2)(c), (d) | 6 Apr 2005 (SI 2005/275) |
| | (3), (4) | 6 Apr 2005 (SI 2005/275) |
| 46 | | 6 Apr 2005 (SI 2005/275) |
| 47 | (1)–(3) | 6 Apr 2005 (SI 2005/275) |
| | (4)(a)–(f) | 6 Apr 2005 (SI 2005/275) |
| | (4)(g) | *Not yet in force* |
| | (5) | 6 Apr 2005 (SI 2005/275) |
| 48, 49 | | 6 Apr 2005 (SI 2005/275) |
| 50 | (1)–(9) | 6 Apr 2005 (SI 2005/275) |
| | (10)(a)–(e) | 6 Apr 2005 (SI 2005/275) |
| | (10)(f) | *Not yet in force* |
| | (11) | 6 Apr 2005 (SI 2005/275) |
| 51 | | 6 Apr 2005 (SI 2005/275) |
| 52 | (1)(a) | 6 Apr 2005 (SI 2005/275) |
| | (1)(b) | 10 Feb 2005 (for the purpose of conferring power to make regulations, orders or rules) (SI 2005/275) |

**Pensions Act 2004 (c 35)**—*contd*

| | | |
|---|---|---|
| | | 6 Apr 2005 (otherwise) (SI 2005/275) |
| | (2)–(6) | 6 Apr 2005 (SI 2005/275) |
| | (7)(a) | 10 Feb 2005 (for the purpose of conferring power to make regulations, orders or rules) (SI 2005/275) |
| | | 6 Apr 2005 (otherwise) (SI 2005/275) |
| | (7)(b) | 6 Apr 2005 (SI 2005/275) |
| | (8), (9) | 6 Apr 2005 (SI 2005/275) |
| 53–56 | | 6 Apr 2005 (SI 2005/275) |
| 57 | (1)–(4) | 10 Feb 2005 (for the purpose of conferring power to make regulations, orders or rules) (SI 2005/275) |
| | | 6 Apr 2005 (otherwise) (SI 2005/275) |
| | (5)–(7) | 6 Apr 2005 (SI 2005/275) |
| 58 | | 6 Apr 2005 (SI 2005/275) |
| 59 | (1) | 6 Apr 2005 (SI 2005/275) |
| | (2) | 10 Feb 2005 (for the purpose of conferring power to make regulations) (SI 2005/275) |
| | | 1 Apr 2005 (otherwise) (SI 2005/275) |
| | (3)–(7) | 6 Apr 2005 (SI 2005/275) |
| 60 | (1) | 6 Apr 2005 (SI 2005/275) |
| | (2)(a)–(g) | 6 Apr 2005 (SI 2005/275) |
| | (2)(h) | 10 Feb 2005 (for the purpose of conferring power to make regulations, orders or rules) (SI 2005/275) |
| | | 6 Apr 2005 (otherwise) (SI 2005/275) |
| | (3) | 10 Feb 2005 (for the purpose of conferring power to make regulations, orders or rules) (SI 2005/275) |
| | | 6 Apr 2005 (otherwise) (SI 2005/275) |
| | (4) | 6 Apr 2005 (SI 2005/275) |
| 61 | (1)–(3) | 10 Feb 2005 (for the purpose of conferring power to make regulations, orders or rules) (SI 2005/275) |
| | | 6 Apr 2005 (otherwise) (SI 2005/275) |
| | (4)–(6) | 6 Apr 2005 (SI 2005/275) |
| 62–68 | | 6 Apr 2005 (SI 2005/275) |
| 69 | (1) | 6 Apr 2005 (SI 2005/275) |
| | (2) | 10 Feb 2005 (for the purpose of conferring power to make regulations, orders or rules) (SI 2005/275) |
| | | 6 Apr 2005 (otherwise) (SI 2005/275) |
| | (3)(a)(i) | 6 Apr 2005 (SI 2005/275) |
| | (3)(a)(ii) | 10 Feb 2005 (for the purpose of conferring power to make regulations, orders or rules) (SI 2005/275) |
| | | 6 Apr 2005 (otherwise) (SI 2005/275) |
| | (3)(b)(i) | 6 Apr 2005 (SI 2005/275) |
| | (3)(b)(ii) | 10 Feb 2005 (for the purpose of conferring power to make regulations, orders or rules) (SI 2005/275) |
| | | 6 Apr 2005 (otherwise) (SI 2005/275) |
| | (4) | 6 Apr 2005 (SI 2005/275) |
| | (5) | 10 Feb 2005 (for the purpose of conferring power to make regulations, orders or rules) (SI 2005/275) |
| | | 6 Apr 2005 (otherwise) (SI 2005/275) |
| | (6)–(9) | 6 Apr 2005 (SI 2005/275) |
| 70–85 | | 6 Apr 2005 (SI 2005/275) |
| 86 | (1) | See Sch 3 below |
| | (2) | 6 Apr 2006 (SI 2006/560) |
| 87–89 | | 6 Apr 2005 (SI 2005/275) |
| 90 | (1) | 6 Apr 2005 (SI 2005/275) |
| | (2)(a)–(j) | 6 Apr 2005 (SI 2005/275) |
| | (2)(k) | 14 Nov 2005 (SI 2005/2447) |
| | (3)–(7) | 6 Apr 2005 (SI 2005/275) |
| 91 | (1)–(9) | 17 Dec 2004 (SI 2004/3350) |
| | (10)–(12) | 6 Apr 2005 (SI 2005/275) |

**Pensions Act 2004 (c 35)**—*contd*

| | | |
|---|---|---|
| 92 | | 6 Apr 2005 (SI 2005/275) |
| 93 | (1) | 6 Apr 2005 (SI 2005/275) |
| | (2)(a)–(p) | 6 Apr 2005 (SI 2005/275) |
| | (2)(q) | 10 Feb 2005 (for the purpose of conferring power to make regulations, orders or rules) (SI 2005/275) |
| | | 6 Apr 2005 (otherwise) (SI 2005/275) |
| | (3)–(5) | 6 Apr 2005 (SI 2005/275) |
| 94 | | 6 Apr 2005 (SI 2005/275) |
| 95 | (1)(a) | 6 Apr 2005 (SI 2005/275) |
| | (1)(b)(i) | 6 Apr 2005 (SI 2005/275) |
| | (1)(b)(ii) | *Not yet in force* |
| | (2), (3) | 6 Apr 2005 (SI 2005/275) |
| 96 | (1)–(5) | 6 Apr 2005 (SI 2005/275) |
| | (6)(a)–(t) | 6 Apr 2005 (SI 2005/275) |
| | (6)(u) | *Not yet in force* |
| | (6)(v) | 6 Apr 2005 (SI 2005/275) |
| 97 | (1)–(4) | 6 Apr 2005 (SI 2005/275) |
| | (5)(a)–(t) | 6 Apr 2005 (SI 2005/275) |
| | (5)(u) | 10 Feb 2005 (for the purpose of conferring power to make regulations, orders or rules) (SI 2005/275) |
| | | 6 Apr 2005 (otherwise) (SI 2005/275) |
| | (5)(v) | 6 Apr 2005 (SI 2005/275) |
| 98–100 | | 6 Apr 2005 (SI 2005/275) |
| 101 | (1) | 6 Apr 2005 (SI 2005/275) |
| | (2)(a)–(c) | 6 Apr 2005 (SI 2005/275) |
| | (2)(d) | *Not yet in force* |
| | (3)–(5) | 6 Apr 2005 (SI 2005/275) |
| 102 | (1) | 17 Dec 2004 (SI 2004/3350) |
| | (2) | 6 Apr 2005 (SI 2005/275) |
| | (3) | 10 Feb 2005 (for the purpose of conferring power to make regulations, orders or rules) (SI 2005/275) |
| | | 6 Apr 2005 (otherwise) (SI 2005/275) |
| | (4) | See Sch 4 below |
| | (5) | 6 Apr 2005 (SI 2005/275) |
| 103 | (1)(a), (b) | 6 Apr 2005 (SI 2005/275) |
| | (1)(c) | 10 Feb 2005 (for the purpose of conferring power to make regulations, orders or rules) (SI 2005/275) |
| | | 6 Apr 2005 (otherwise) (SI 2005/275) |
| | (2)–(9) | 6 Apr 2005 (SI 2005/275) |
| 104 | (1)–(5) | 6 Apr 2005 (SI 2005/275) |
| | (6) | 10 Feb 2005 (for the purpose of conferring power to make regulations, orders or rules) (SI 2005/275) |
| | | 6 Apr 2005 (otherwise) (SI 2005/275) |
| 105 | | 6 Apr 2005 (SI 2005/275) |
| 106 | (1)–(4) | 10 Feb 2005 (for the purpose of conferring power to make regulations, orders or rules) (SI 2005/275) |
| | | 6 Apr 2005 (otherwise) (SI 2005/275) |
| | (5), (6) | 6 Apr 2005 (SI 2005/275) |
| 107 | | 17 Dec 2004 (SI 2004/3350) |
| 108 | (1), (2) | 17 Dec 2004 (SI 2004/3350) |
| | (3) | *Not yet in force* |
| | (4) | 6 Apr 2005 (SI 2005/275) |
| | (5)–(7) | 17 Dec 2004 (SI 2004/3350) |
| 109 | | See Sch 5 below |
| 110 | (1)(a) | 6 Apr 2005 (SI 2005/275) |
| | (1)(b) | 1 Sep 2005 (SI 2005/1720)[4] |
| | (2) | 9 Dec 2005 (SI 2005/3331) |
| | (3) | 17 Dec 2004 (SI 2004/3350) |
| 111 | | 17 Dec 2004 (SI 2004/3350) |

**Pensions Act 2004 (c 35)**—*contd*

| | | |
|---|---|---|
| 112 | (1)–(3) | 17 Dec 2004 (SI 2004/3350) |
| | (4)(a) | 10 Feb 2005 (SI 2005/275) |
| | (4)(b)–(d) | 17 Dec 2004 (SI 2004/3350) |
| | (5), (6) | 6 Apr 2005 (SI 2005/275) |
| | (7), (8) | 10 Feb 2005 (SI 2005/275) |
| 113 | | 6 Apr 2005 (SI 2005/275) |
| 114 | (1)(a) | 6 Apr 2005 (SI 2005/275) |
| | (1)(b) | 10 Feb 2005 (for the purpose of conferring power to make regulations, orders or rules) (SI 2005/275) |
| | | 6 Apr 2005 (otherwise) (SI 2005/275) |
| | (2) | 6 Apr 2005 (SI 2005/275) |
| | (3), (4) | 10 Feb 2005 (for the purpose of conferring power to make regulations, orders or rules) (SI 2005/275) |
| | | 6 Apr 2005 (otherwise) (SI 2005/275) |
| 115 | (1), (2) | 8 Mar 2005 (SI 2005/275) |
| | (3) | 10 Feb 2005 (definition "borrowing limit", for the purpose of conferring power to make regulations or orders) (SI 2005/275) |
| | | 8 Mar 2005 (otherwise) (SI 2005/275) |
| | (4) | 8 Mar 2005 (SI 2005/275) |
| 116 | | 17 Dec 2004 (SI 2004/3350) |
| 117 | (1) | 10 Feb 2005 (for the purpose of conferring power to make regulations) (SI 2005/275) |
| | | 1 Apr 2005 (otherwise) (SI 2005/275) |
| | (2)(a) | 1 Apr 2005 (SI 2005/275) |
| | (2)(b) | *Not yet in force* |
| | (3) | 10 Feb 2005 (for the purpose of conferring power to make regulations) (SI 2005/275) |
| | | 1 Apr 2005 (otherwise) (SI 2005/275) |
| | (4) | 10 Feb 2005 (SI 2005/275) |
| | (5), (6) | 1 Apr 2005 (SI 2005/275) |
| | (7)(a) | 10 Feb 2005 (for the purpose of conferring power to make regulations) (SI 2005/275) |
| | | 1 Apr 2005 (otherwise) (SI 2005/275) |
| | (7)(b) | 1 Jan 2007 (for the purpose of conferring power to make regulations) (SI 2006/2272) |
| | | 1 Mar 2007 (otherwise) (SI 2006/2272) |
| 118 | | *Not yet in force* |
| 119 | | 6 Apr 2005 (SI 2005/275) |
| 120 | (1), (2) | 6 Apr 2005 (SI 2005/275) |
| | (3), (4) | 10 Feb 2005 (for the purpose of conferring power to make regulations, orders or rules) (SI 2005/275) |
| | | 6 Apr 2005 (otherwise) (SI 2005/275) |
| 121 | (1)–(4) | 6 Apr 2005 (SI 2005/275) |
| | (5) | 10 Feb 2005 (for the purpose of conferring power to make regulations, orders or rules) (SI 2005/275) |
| | | 6 Apr 2005 (otherwise) (SI 2005/275) |
| | (6) | 6 Apr 2005 (SI 2005/275) |
| | (7) | 30 Jun 2005 (SI 2005/1720) |
| | (8) | 6 Apr 2005 (SI 2005/275) |
| | (9)(a) | 6 Apr 2005 (SI 2005/275) |
| | (9)(b) | 25 Jun 2014 (SI 2014/1636) |
| | (10), (11) | 6 Apr 2005 (SI 2005/275) |
| 122 | (1), (2) | 6 Apr 2005 (SI 2005/275) |
| | (3) | 10 Feb 2005 (for the purpose of conferring power to make regulations, orders or rules) (SI 2005/275) |
| | | 6 Apr 2005 (otherwise) (SI 2005/275) |
| | (4) | 6 Apr 2005 (SI 2005/275) |
| | (5) | 10 Feb 2005 (for the purpose of conferring power to make regulations, orders or rules) (SI 2005/275) |
| | | 6 Apr 2005 (otherwise) (SI 2005/275) |

**Pensions Act 2004 (c 35)**—*contd*

| | | |
|---|---|---|
| | (6), (7) | 6 Apr 2005 (SI 2005/275) |
| | (8) | 10 Feb 2005 (for the purpose of conferring power to make regulations, orders or rules) (SI 2005/275) |
| | | 6 Apr 2005 (otherwise) (SI 2005/275) |
| 123 | (1)–(4) | 6 Apr 2005 (SI 2005/275) |
| | (5) | 10 Feb 2005 (for the purpose of conferring power to make regulations, orders or rules) (SI 2005/275) |
| | | 6 Apr 2005 (otherwise) (SI 2005/275) |
| 124 | | 6 Apr 2005 (SI 2005/275) |
| 125 | (1)–(3) | 6 Apr 2005 (SI 2005/275) |
| | (4)(a) | 10 Feb 2005 (for the purpose of conferring power to make regulations, orders or rules) (SI 2005/275) |
| | | 6 Apr 2005 (otherwise) (SI 2005/275) |
| | (4)(b) | 6 Apr 2005 (SI 2005/275) |
| 126 | (1)(a) | 1 Apr 2005 (SI 2005/275) |
| | (1)(b) | 10 Feb 2005 (for the purpose of conferring power to make regulations) (SI 2005/275) |
| | | 1 Apr 2005 (otherwise) (SI 2005/275) |
| | (2) | 10 Feb 2005 (for the purpose of conferring power to make regulations or orders) (SI 2005/275) |
| | | 8 Mar 2005 (otherwise) (SI 2005/275) |
| | (3) | 10 Feb 2005 (for the purpose of conferring power to make regulations, orders or rules) (SI 2005/275) |
| | | 6 Apr 2005 (otherwise) (SI 2005/275) |
| | (4) | 6 Apr 2005 (SI 2005/275) |
| | (5) | 10 Feb 2005 (for the purpose of conferring power to make regulations) (SI 2005/275) |
| | | 1 Apr 2005 (otherwise) (SI 2005/275) |
| 127, 128 | | 6 Apr 2005 (SI 2005/275) |
| 129 | (1)(a) | 6 Apr 2005 (SI 2005/275) |
| | (1)(b) | 10 Feb 2005 (for the purpose of conferring power to make regulations, orders or rules) (SI 2005/275) |
| | | 6 Apr 2005 (otherwise) (SI 2005/275) |
| | (2) | 6 Apr 2005 (SI 2005/275) |
| | (3) | 10 Feb 2005 (for the purpose of conferring power to make regulations, orders or rules) (SI 2005/275) |
| | | 6 Apr 2005 (otherwise) (SI 2005/275) |
| | (4)–(7) | 6 Apr 2005 (SI 2005/275) |
| | (8) | 10 Feb 2005 (for the purpose of conferring power to make regulations, orders or rules) (SI 2005/275) |
| | | 6 Apr 2005 (otherwise) (SI 2005/275) |
| 130 | (1)–(4) | 6 Apr 2005 (SI 2005/275) |
| | (5) | 10 Feb 2005 (for the purpose of conferring power to make regulations, orders or rules) (SI 2005/275) |
| | | 6 Apr 2005 (otherwise) (SI 2005/275) |
| | (6), (7) | 6 Apr 2005 (SI 2005/275) |
| | (8) | 10 Feb 2005 (for the purpose of conferring power to make regulations, orders or rules) (SI 2005/275) |
| | | 6 Apr 2005 (otherwise) (SI 2005/275) |
| | (9) | 6 Apr 2005 (SI 2005/275) |
| 131 | | 6 Apr 2005 (SI 2005/275) |
| 132 | (1)–(5) | 6 Apr 2005 (SI 2005/275) |
| | (6) | 6 Apr 2007 (SI 2006/2272) |
| 133 | (1), (2) | 6 Apr 2005 (SI 2005/275) |
| | (3) | 10 Feb 2005 (for the purpose of conferring power to make regulations, orders or rules) (SI 2005/275) |
| | | 6 Apr 2005 (otherwise) (SI 2005/275) |
| | (4)–(11) | 6 Apr 2005 (SI 2005/275) |
| 134 | (1) | 6 Apr 2005 (SI 2005/275) |
| | (2)(a)–(c) | 6 Apr 2005 (SI 2005/275) |

**Pensions Act 2004 (c 35)**—*contd*

|     |     |     |
| --- | --- | --- |
|     | (2)(d) | 23 Jun 2009 (for the purpose of conferring power to make regulations) (SI 2009/1542) |
|     |     | 21 Jul 2009 (otherwise) (SI 2009/1542) |
|     | (3)(a)(i), (ii) | 6 Apr 2005 (SI 2005/275) |
|     | (3)(a)(iii) | 10 Feb 2005 (for the purpose of conferring power to make regulations, orders or rules) (SI 2005/275) |
|     |     | 6 Apr 2005 (otherwise) (SI 2005/275) |
|     | (3)(b) | 6 Apr 2005 (SI 2005/275) |
|     | (4)–(6) | 6 Apr 2005 (SI 2005/275) |
| 135 | (1)–(3) | 6 Apr 2005 (SI 2005/275) |
|     | (4) | 10 Feb 2005 (for the purpose of conferring power to make regulations, orders or rules) (SI 2005/275) |
|     |     | 6 Apr 2005 (otherwise) (SI 2005/275) |
|     | (5)–(11) | 6 Apr 2005 (SI 2005/275) |
| 136, 137 |     | 6 Apr 2005 (SI 2005/275) |
| 138 | (1)–(9) | 6 Apr 2005 (SI 2005/275) |
|     | (10)(a) | 25 Jun 2014 (SI 2014/1636) |
|     | (10)(b) | 10 Feb 2005 (for the purpose of conferring power to make regulations, orders or rules) (SI 2005/275) |
|     |     | 6 Apr 2005 (otherwise) (SI 2005/275) |
|     | (11) | 6 Apr 2005 (SI 2005/275) |
|     | (12) | 10 Feb 2005 (for the purpose of conferring power to make regulations, orders or rules) (SI 2005/275) |
|     |     | 6 Apr 2005 (otherwise) (SI 2005/275) |
|     | (13) | 6 Apr 2005 (SI 2005/275) |
| 139 | (1)–(5) | 6 Apr 2005 (SI 2005/275) |
|     | (6) | 10 Feb 2005 (for the purpose of conferring power to make regulations, orders or rules) (SI 2005/275) |
|     |     | 6 Apr 2005 (otherwise) (SI 2005/275) |
|     | (7) | 6 Apr 2005 (SI 2005/275) |
| 140 | (1), (2) | 6 Apr 2005 (SI 2005/275) |
|     | (3)(a) | 6 Apr 2005 (SI 2005/275) |
|     | (3)(b) | 10 Feb 2005 (for the purpose of conferring power to make regulations, orders or rules) (SI 2005/275) |
|     |     | 6 Apr 2005 (otherwise) (SI 2005/275) |
|     | (4), (5) | 6 Apr 2005 (SI 2005/275) |
|     | (6) | 10 Feb 2005 (for the purpose of conferring power to make regulations, orders or rules) (SI 2005/275) |
|     |     | 6 Apr 2005 (otherwise) (SI 2005/275) |
| 141 | (1) | 6 Apr 2005 (SI 2005/275) |
|     | (2) | 10 Feb 2005 (for the purpose of conferring power to make regulations, orders or rules) (SI 2005/275) |
|     |     | 6 Apr 2005 (otherwise) (SI 2005/275) |
|     | (3)–(5) | 6 Apr 2005 (SI 2005/275) |
|     | (6) | 10 Feb 2005 (for the purpose of conferring power to make regulations, orders or rules) (SI 2005/275) |
|     |     | 6 Apr 2005 (otherwise) (SI 2005/275) |
| 142 |     | 6 Apr 2005 (SI 2005/275) |
| 143 | (1), (2) | 6 Apr 2005 (SI 2005/275) |
|     | (3)–(5) | 10 Feb 2005 (for the purpose of conferring power to make regulations, orders or rules) (SI 2005/275) |
|     |     | 6 Apr 2005 (otherwise) (SI 2005/275) |
|     | (6)–(10) | 6 Apr 2005 (SI 2005/275) |
|     | (11)(a)(i) | 10 Feb 2005 (for the purpose of conferring power to make regulations, orders or rules) (SI 2005/275) |
|     |     | 6 Apr 2005 (otherwise) (SI 2005/275) |
|     | (11)(a)(ii)(a) | 10 Feb 2005 (for the purpose of conferring power to make regulations, orders or rules) (SI 2005/275) |
|     |     | 6 Apr 2005 (otherwise) (SI 2005/275) |
|     | (11)(a)(ii)(b) | 6 Apr 2005 (SI 2005/275) |

**Pensions Act 2004 (c 35)**—*contd*

| | | |
|---|---|---|
| | (11)(b)–(d) | 6 Apr 2005 (SI 2005/275) |
| 144 | | 6 Apr 2005 (SI 2005/275) |
| 145 | (1)–(3) | 6 Apr 2005 (SI 2005/275) |
| | (4) | 10 Feb 2005 (for the purpose of conferring power to make regulations, orders or rules) (SI 2005/275) |
| | | 6 Apr 2005 (otherwise) (SI 2005/275) |
| 146 | (1) | 10 Feb 2005 (for the purpose of conferring power to make regulations, orders or rules) (SI 2005/275) |
| | | 6 Apr 2005 (otherwise) (SI 2005/275) |
| | (2)–(4) | 6 Apr 2005 (SI 2005/275) |
| | (5) | 10 Feb 2005 (for the purpose of conferring power to make regulations, orders or rules) (SI 2005/275) |
| | | 6 Apr 2005 (otherwise) (SI 2005/275) |
| | (6) | 6 Apr 2005 (SI 2005/275) |
| 147 | (1)(a) | 10 Feb 2005 (for the purpose of conferring power to make regulations, orders or rules) (SI 2005/275) |
| | | 6 Apr 2005 (otherwise) (SI 2005/275) |
| | (1)(b)–(d) | 6 Apr 2005 (SI 2005/275) |
| | (2)–(4) | 6 Apr 2005 (SI 2005/275) |
| | (5) | 10 Feb 2005 (for the purpose of conferring power to make regulations, orders or rules) (SI 2005/275) |
| | | 6 Apr 2005 (otherwise) (SI 2005/275) |
| | (6) | 6 Apr 2005 (SI 2005/275) |
| 148 | (1)–(7) | 6 Apr 2005 (SI 2005/275) |
| | (8) | 10 Feb 2005 (for the purpose of conferring power to make regulations, orders or rules) (SI 2005/275) |
| | | 6 Apr 2005 (otherwise) (SI 2005/275) |
| | (9) | 6 Apr 2005 (SI 2005/275) |
| 149 | | 6 Apr 2005 (SI 2005/275) |
| 150 | (1)–(4) | 6 Apr 2005 (SI 2005/275) |
| | (5) | 10 Feb 2005 (for the purpose of conferring power to make regulations, orders or rules) (SI 2005/275) |
| | | 6 Apr 2005 (otherwise) (SI 2005/275) |
| | (6)(a)–(c) | 10 Feb 2005 (for the purpose of conferring power to make regulations, orders or rules) (SI 2005/275) |
| | | 6 Apr 2005 (otherwise) (SI 2005/275) |
| | (6)(d) | *Not yet in force* |
| | (7) | 6 Apr 2005 (SI 2005/275) |
| 151 | (1)–(3) | 6 Apr 2005 (SI 2005/275) |
| | (4) | 10 Feb 2005 (for the purpose of conferring power to make regulations, orders or rules) (SI 2005/275) |
| | | 6 Apr 2005 (otherwise) (SI 2005/275) |
| | (5) | 6 Apr 2005 (SI 2005/275) |
| | (6) | 10 Feb 2005 (for the purpose of conferring power to make regulations, orders or rules) (SI 2005/275) |
| | | 6 Apr 2005 (otherwise) (SI 2005/275) |
| | (7) | 6 Apr 2005 (SI 2005/275) |
| | (8) | 10 Feb 2005 (definition "audited scheme accounts", para (b), for the purpose of conferring power to make regulations, orders or rules) (SI 2005/275) |
| | | 6 Apr 2005 (otherwise) (except definition "audited scheme accounts", para (a)) (SI 2005/275) |
| | | 1 Apr 2006 (exception noted above) (SI 2006/560) |
| | (9)(a) | 6 Apr 2005 (SI 2005/275) |
| | (9)(b) | 10 Feb 2005 (for the purpose of conferring power to make regulations, orders or rules) (SI 2005/275) |
| | | 6 Apr 2005 (otherwise) (SI 2005/275) |
| | (10), (11) | 6 Apr 2005 (SI 2005/275) |
| | (12)(a) | *Not yet in force* |
| | (12)(b) | 6 Apr 2005 (SI 2005/275) |

**Pensions Act 2004 (c 35)**—*contd*

| | | |
|---|---|---|
| | (13) | 6 Apr 2005 (SI 2005/275) |
| 152 | (1)–(3) | 6 Apr 2005 (SI 2005/275) |
| | (4) | 10 Feb 2005 (for the purpose of conferring power to make regulations, orders or rules) (SI 2005/275) |
| | | 6 Apr 2005 (otherwise) (SI 2005/275) |
| | (5)–(7) | 6 Apr 2005 (SI 2005/275) |
| | (8) | 10 Feb 2005 (for the purpose of conferring power to make regulations, orders or rules) (SI 2005/275) |
| | | 6 Apr 2005 (otherwise) (SI 2005/275) |
| | (9)–(12) | 6 Apr 2005 (SI 2005/275) |
| 153 | (1)–(3) | 6 Apr 2007 (SI 2006/2272) |
| | (4) | 1 Nov 2006 (for the purpose of conferring power to make regulations) (SI 2006/2272) |
| | | 6 Apr 2007 (otherwise) (SI 2006/2272) |
| | (5), (6) | 6 Apr 2007 (SI 2006/2272) |
| | (7) | 1 Nov 2006 (for the purpose of conferring power to make regulations) (SI 2006/2272) |
| | | 6 Apr 2007 (otherwise) (SI 2006/2272) |
| | (8) | 6 Apr 2007 (SI 2006/2272) |
| 154 | (1) | 6 Apr 2005 (SI 2005/275) |
| | (2)(a) | 6 Apr 2005 (SI 2005/275) |
| | (2)(b) | 6 Apr 2007 (SI 2006/2272) |
| | (2)(c) | 6 Apr 2005 (SI 2005/275) |
| | (3)–(5) | 6 Apr 2007 (SI 2006/2272) |
| | (6)–(15) | 6 Apr 2005 (SI 2005/275) |
| 155 | (1) | 1 Nov 2006 (for the purpose of conferring power to make regulations) (SI 2006/2272) |
| | | 6 Apr 2007 (otherwise) (SI 2006/2272) |
| | (2), (3) | 6 Apr 2007 (SI 2006/2272) |
| | (4) | 1 Nov 2006 (for the purpose of conferring power to make regulations) (SI 2006/2272) |
| | | 6 Apr 2007 (otherwise) (SI 2006/2272) |
| 156 | (1), (2) | 1 Nov 2006 (for the purpose of conferring power to make regulations) (SI 2006/2272) |
| | | 6 Apr 2007 (otherwise) (SI 2006/2272) |
| | (3), (4) | 6 Apr 2007 (SI 2006/2272) |
| | (5), (6) | 1 Nov 2006 (for the purpose of conferring power to make regulations) (SI 2006/2272) |
| | | 6 Apr 2007 (otherwise) (SI 2006/2272) |
| 157 | (1) | 1 Nov 2006 (for the purpose of conferring power to make regulations) (SI 2006/2272) |
| | | 6 Apr 2007 (otherwise) (SI 2006/2272) |
| | (2)–(6) | 6 Apr 2007 (SI 2006/2272) |
| | (7) | 1 Nov 2006 (for the purpose of conferring power to make regulations) (SI 2006/2272) |
| | | 6 Apr 2007 (otherwise) (SI 2006/2272) |
| | (8) | 6 Apr 2007 (SI 2006/2272) |
| | (9) | 1 Nov 2006 (for the purpose of conferring power to make regulations) (SI 2006/2272) |
| | | 6 Apr 2007 (otherwise) (SI 2006/2272) |
| 158, 159 | | 6 Apr 2007 (SI 2006/2272) |
| 160 | (1)–(3) | 6 Apr 2005 (SI 2005/275) |
| | (4) | 6 Apr 2007 (SI 2006/2272) |
| | (5), (6) | 6 Apr 2005 (SI 2005/275) |
| | (7) | 6 Apr 2005 (in so far as it relates to s 172(1)) (SI 2005/275) |
| | | 6 Apr 2006 (otherwise) (SI 2006/560) |
| 161 | (1) | 1 Jan 2006 (for the purpose of conferring power to make regulations) (SI 2005/3331) |
| | | 6 Apr 2006 (otherwise) (SI 2005/3331) |

**Pensions Act 2004 (c 35)**—*contd*

|  |  |  |
|---|---|---|
|  | (2)(a), (b) | 1 Jan 2006 (for the purpose of conferring power to make regulations) (SI 2005/3331) |
|  |  | 6 Apr 2006 (otherwise) (SI 2005/3331) |
|  | (2)(c) | 6 Apr 2005 (SI 2005/275) |
|  | (3)(a) | 1 Jan 2006 (for the purpose of conferring power to make regulations) (SI 2005/3331) |
|  |  | 6 Apr 2006 (otherwise) (SI 2005/3331) |
|  | (3)(b) | 25 Jun 2014 (SI 2014/1636) |
|  | (4) | 1 Jan 2006 (for the purpose of conferring power to make regulations) (SI 2005/3331) |
|  |  | 6 Apr 2006 (otherwise) (SI 2005/3331) |
|  | (5) | 6 Apr 2006 (SI 2005/3331) |
|  | (6)–(8) | 1 Jan 2006 (for the purpose of conferring power to make regulations) (SI 2005/3331) |
|  |  | 6 Apr 2006 (otherwise) (SI 2005/3331) |
| 162 | (1) | See Sch 7 below |
|  | (2) | *Not yet in force* |
| 163 | (1)–(4) | 1 Jan 2006 (for the purpose of conferring power to make regulations) (SI 2005/3331) |
|  |  | 6 Apr 2006 (otherwise) (SI 2005/3331) |
|  | (5)(a) | 1 Jan 2006 (for the purpose of conferring power to make regulations) (SI 2005/3331) |
|  |  | 6 Apr 2006 (otherwise) (SI 2005/3331) |
|  | (5)(b) | *Not yet in force* |
|  | (6), (7) | 1 Jan 2006 (for the purpose of conferring power to make regulations) (SI 2005/3331) |
|  |  | 6 Apr 2006 (otherwise) (SI 2005/3331) |
| 164 |  | 6 Apr 2005 (SI 2005/1108) |
| 165 |  | 6 Apr 2006 (SI 2006/560) |
| 166 | (1)–(5) | 1 Jan 2006 (for the purpose of conferring power to make regulations) (SI 2005/3331) |
|  |  | 6 Apr 2006 (otherwise) (SI 2005/3331) |
|  | (6), (7) | 1 Mar 2009 (SI 2009/325) |
|  | (8) | 1 Jan 2006 (for the purpose of conferring power to make regulations) (SI 2005/3331) |
|  |  | 6 Apr 2006 (otherwise) (SI 2005/3331) |
| 167 | (1) | 10 Feb 2005 (for the purpose of conferring power to make regulations, orders or rules) (SI 2005/275) |
|  |  | 6 Apr 2005 (otherwise) (SI 2005/275) |
|  | (2) | 6 Apr 2005 (SI 2005/275) |
| 168 |  | 20 Jul 2005 (as modified by regulations made under s 286(3)(j)) (SI 2005/1436) |
|  | (1) | 1 Jan 2006 (SI 2005/3331) |
|  | (2)(a)–(c) | 1 Jan 2006 (SI 2005/3331) |
|  | (2)(d) | *Not yet in force* |
|  | (2)(e), (f) | 1 Jan 2006 (SI 2005/3331) |
|  | (3) | 1 Jan 2006 (SI 2005/3331) |
| 169 | (1) | 6 Apr 2006 (SI 2006/560) |
|  | (2)(a)–(c) | 6 Apr 2006 (SI 2006/560) |
|  | (2)(d) | *Not yet in force* |
| 170, 171 |  | 1 Jan 2006 (for the purpose of conferring power to make regulations) (SI 2005/3331) |
|  |  | 6 Apr 2006 (otherwise) (SI 2005/3331) |
| 172 | (1) | 6 Apr 2005 (SI 2005/275) |
|  | (2)–(4) | 1 Sep 2005 (SI 2005/1720)[4] |
|  | (5)(a)–(c) | 1 Sep 2005 (SI 2005/1720)[4] |
|  | (5)(d) | 6 Apr 2007 (SI 2006/2272) |
|  | (6) | 1 Sep 2005 (SI 2005/1720)[4] |
| 173 | (1)(a) | 6 Apr 2006 (SI 2006/560) |
|  | (1)(b) | 20 Jun 2005 (so far as relates to s 174) (SI 2005/1436) |

**Pensions Act 2004 (c 35)**—*contd*

|  |  |  |
|---|---|---|
|  |  | 1 Apr 2006 (otherwise) (SI 2006/560) |
|  | (1)(c)–(e) | 6 Apr 2005 (SI 2005/275) |
|  | (1)(f) | 6 Apr 2006 (SI 2006/560) |
|  | (1)(g)–(i) | 6 Apr 2005 (SI 2005/275) |
|  | (1)(j) | 6 Apr 2010 (SI 2010/443) |
|  | (1)(k) | *Not yet in force* |
|  | (2) | 20 Jun 2005 (SI 2005/1436) |
|  | (3)(a) | 6 Apr 2006 (SI 2006/560) |
|  | (3)(b)–(d) | 6 Apr 2005 (SI 2005/275) |
|  | (3)(e)–(g) | 6 Apr 2006 (SI 2006/560) |
|  | (3)(h), (i) | 6 Apr 2005 (SI 2005/275) |
|  | (3)(j) | 6 Apr 2006 (SI 2006/560) |
|  | (3)(k) | 1 Jun 2005 (for the purpose of conferring power to make regulations) (SI 2005/1436) |
|  |  | 30 Jun 2005 (otherwise) (SI 2005/1436) |
|  | (4), (5) | 20 Jun 2005 (SI 2005/1436) |
| 174 |  | 10 Feb 2005 (for the purpose of conferring power to make regulations) (SI 2005/275) |
|  |  | 1 Apr 2005 (otherwise) (SI 2005/275) |
| 175 | (1) | 20 Jun 2005 (so far as relates to a consultation by the Board under s 176) (SI 2005/1436) |
|  |  | 9 Dec 2005 (otherwise) (SI 2005/3331) |
|  | (2)(a)(i) | 6 Apr 2005 (SI 2005/275) |
|  | (2)(a)(ii) | 20 Jun 2005 (so far as relates to a consultation by the Board under s 176) (SI 2005/1436) |
|  |  | 9 Dec 2005 (otherwise) (SI 2005/3331) |
|  | (2)(a)(iii) | 6 Apr 2005 (SI 2005/275) |
|  | (2)(b) | 20 Jun 2005 (so far as relates to a consultation by the Board under s 176) (SI 2005/1436) |
|  |  | 9 Dec 2005 (otherwise) (SI 2005/3331) |
|  | (3)(a) | 6 Apr 2005 (SI 2005/275) |
|  | (3)(b) | 20 Jun 2005 (so far as relates to a consultation by the Board under s 176) (SI 2005/1436) |
|  |  | 9 Dec 2005 (otherwise) (SI 2005/3331) |
|  | (4)(a), (b) | 20 Jun 2005 (so far as they relate to a consultation by the Board under s 176) (SI 2005/1436) |
|  |  | 9 Dec 2005 (otherwise) (SI 2005/3331) |
|  | (4)(c) | 20 Jun 2005 (so far as relates to a consultation by the Board under s 176) (SI 2005/1436) |
|  |  | *Not yet in force* (otherwise) |
|  | (5)–(10) | 20 Jun 2005 (so far as they relate to a consultation by the Board under s 176) (SI 2005/1436) |
|  |  | 9 Dec 2005 (otherwise) (SI 2005/3331) |
| 176 |  | 27 May 2005 (for the purpose of conferring power to make regulations) (SI 2005/1436) |
|  |  | 20 Jun 2005 (otherwise) (SI 2005/1436) |
| 177 | (1)–(3) | 9 Dec 2005 (SI 2005/3331) |
|  | (4) | 1 Sep 2006 (for the purpose of conferring power to make regulations) (SI 2006/2272) |
|  |  | 1 Oct 2006 (otherwise) (SI 2006/2272) |
|  | (5) | 1 Sep 2006 (SI 2006/2272) |
|  | (6), (7) | *Not yet in force* |
|  | (8) | 1 Sep 2006 (SI 2006/2272) |
|  | (9)(a) | 9 Dec 2005 (SI 2005/3331) |
|  | (9)(b) | 1 Apr 2006 (SI 2006/560) |
| 178 | (1), (2) | 9 Dec 2005 (SI 2005/3331) |
|  | (3) | 1 Jan 2007 (for the purpose of conferring power to make orders) (SI 2006/2272) |
|  |  | 1 Mar 2007 (otherwise) (SI 2006/2272) |

**Pensions Act 2004 (c 35)**—*contd*

|  |  |  |
|---|---|---|
| | (4) | 1 Sep 2006 (for the purpose of conferring power to make regulations) (SI 2006/2272) |
| | | 1 Oct 2006 (otherwise) (SI 2006/2272) |
| | (5) | 1 Sep 2006 (SI 2006/2272) |
| | (6) | 1 Oct 2006 (for the purpose of conferring power to make orders) (SI 2006/2272) |
| | | 1 Dec 2006 (otherwise) (SI 2006/2272) |
| | (7) | 1 Sep 2006 (for the purpose of conferring power to make regulations) (SI 2006/2272) |
| | | 1 Oct 2006 (otherwise) (SI 2006/2272) |
| | (8) | 1 Jan 2007 (for the purpose of conferring power to make orders) (SI 2006/2272) |
| | | 1 Mar 2007 (otherwise) (SI 2006/2272) |
| | (9) | 1 Sep 2006 (for the purpose of conferring power to make regulations) (SI 2006/2272) |
| | | 1 Oct 2006 (otherwise) (SI 2006/2272) |
| 179 | (1)(a) | 10 Feb 2005 (for the purpose of conferring power to make regulations, orders or rules) (SI 2005/275) |
| | | 6 Apr 2005 (otherwise) (SI 2005/275) |
| | (1)(b) | *Not yet in force* |
| | (2) | 10 Feb 2005 (definition "the actuary", para (b)(i), for the purpose of conferring power to make regulations, orders or rules) (SI 2005/275) |
| | | 6 Apr 2005 (otherwise) (SI 2005/275) |
| | (3) | 10 Feb 2005 (for the purpose of conferring power to make regulations, orders or rules) (SI 2005/275) |
| | | 6 Apr 2005 (otherwise) (SI 2005/275) |
| | (4)–(6) | 6 Apr 2005 (SI 2005/275) |
| 180 | (1)–(3) | 9 Dec 2005 (SI 2005/3331) |
| | (4) | *Not yet in force* |
| 181 | (1)(a) | 1 Apr 2005 (SI 2005/275) |
| | (1)(b) | 9 Dec 2005 (SI 2005/3331) |
| | (2)(a) | 1 Apr 2005 (SI 2005/275) |
| | (2)(b) | *Not yet in force* |
| | (3), (4) | 1 Apr 2005 (SI 2005/275) |
| | (5) | 10 Feb 2005 (for the purpose of conferring power to make regulations) (SI 2005/275) |
| | | 1 Apr 2005 (otherwise) (SI 2005/275) |
| | (6), (7) | 1 Apr 2005 (SI 2005/275) |
| | (8) | 10 Feb 2005 (for the purpose of conferring power to make regulations) (SI 2005/275) |
| | | 1 Apr 2005 (otherwise) (SI 2005/275) |
| 182, 183 | | 12 Jul 2005 (for the purpose of conferring power to make regulations) (SI 2005/1720)[4] |
| | | 1 Sep 2005 (otherwise) (SI 2005/1720)[4] |
| 184 | | 1 Sep 2005 (SI 2005/1720)[4] |
| 185, 186 | | 12 Jul 2005 (for the purpose of conferring power to make regulations) (SI 2005/1720)[4] |
| | | 1 Sep 2005 (otherwise) (SI 2005/1720)[4] |
| 187 | | 25 Feb 2010 (for the purpose of conferring power to make regulations) (SI 2010/443) |
| | | 6 Apr 2010 (otherwise) (SI 2010/443) |
| 188 | (1), (2) | 1 Sep 2005 (SI 2005/1720)[4] |
| | (3)(a)–(c) | 1 Sep 2005 (SI 2005/1720)[4] |
| | (3)(d) | 6 Apr 2010 (SI 2010/443) |
| | (3)(e) | 1 Sep 2005 (SI 2005/1720)[4] |
| | (4), (5) | 1 Sep 2005 (SI 2005/1720)[4] |
| 189 | (1), (2) | 1 Jan 2006 (for the purpose of conferring power to make regulations) (SI 2005/3331) |
| | | 1 Apr 2006 (otherwise) (SI 2005/3331) |

**Pensions Act 2004 (c 35)**—*contd*

|  |  |  |
|---|---|---|
| | (3)(a) | 1 Jan 2006 (for the purpose of conferring power to make regulations) (SI 2005/3331) |
| | | 1 Apr 2006 (otherwise) (SI 2005/3331) |
| | (3)(b) | *Not yet in force* |
| | (4)–(10) | 1 Jan 2006 (for the purpose of conferring power to make regulations) (SI 2005/3331) |
| | | 1 Apr 2006 (otherwise) (SI 2005/3331) |
| | (11)(a) | 10 Feb 2005 (for the purpose of conferring power to make regulations) (SI 2005/275) |
| | | 1 Apr 2005 (otherwise) (SI 2005/275) |
| | (11)(b) | 1 Jan 2006 (for the purpose of conferring power to make regulations) (SI 2005/3331) |
| | | 1 Apr 2006 (otherwise) (SI 2005/3331) |
| 190 | | 10 Feb 2005 (for the purpose of conferring power to make regulations, orders or rules) (SI 2005/275) |
| | | 6 Apr 2005 (otherwise) (SI 2005/275) |
| 191 | | 17 Dec 2004 (SI 2004/3350) |
| 192 | | 6 Apr 2005 (SI 2005/275) |
| 193 | (1) | 17 Dec 2004 (SI 2004/3350) |
| | (2), (3) | 6 Apr 2005 (SI 2005/275) |
| | (4)–(7) | 17 Dec 2004 (so far as they relate to s 191) (SI 2004/3350) |
| | | 6 Apr 2005 (so far as they relate to s 192) (SI 2005/275) |
| 194–199 | | 6 Apr 2005 (SI 2005/275) |
| 200 | (1) | See Sch 8 below |
| | (2) | 6 Apr 2005 (SI 2005/275) |
| 201, 202 | | 6 Apr 2005 (SI 2005/275) |
| 203 | (1) | 10 Feb 2005 (for the purpose of conferring power to make regulations, orders or rules) (SI 2005/275) |
| | | 6 Apr 2005 (otherwise) (SI 2005/275) |
| | (2)–(6) | 6 Apr 2005 (SI 2005/275) |
| 204 | (1), (2) | 6 Apr 2005 (SI 2005/275) |
| | (3) | 6 Apr 2006 (SI 2006/560) |
| 205 | | 6 Apr 2005 (SI 2005/275) |
| 206 | (1) | See Sch 9 below |
| | (2)–(4) | 10 Feb 2005 (for the purpose of conferring power to make regulations, orders or rules) (SI 2005/275) |
| | | 6 Apr 2005 (otherwise) (SI 2005/275) |
| | (5) | 1 Sep 2005 (SI 2005/2447) |
| 207 | | 10 Feb 2005 (for the purpose of conferring power to make regulations, orders or rules) (SI 2005/275) |
| | | 6 Apr 2005 (otherwise) (SI 2005/275) |
| 208 | (1) | 10 Feb 2005 (for the purpose of conferring power to make regulations, orders or rules) (SI 2005/275) |
| | | 6 Apr 2005 (otherwise) (SI 2005/275) |
| | (2) | 6 Apr 2005 (SI 2005/275) |
| | (3)–(6) | 10 Feb 2005 (for the purpose of conferring power to make regulations, orders or rules) (SI 2005/275) |
| | | 6 Apr 2005 (otherwise) (SI 2005/275) |
| 209 | (1)–(3) | 17 Dec 2004 (SI 2004/3350) |
| | (4)(a)–(d) | 10 Feb 2005 (for the purpose of conferring power to make regulations, orders or rules) (SI 2005/275) |
| | | 6 Apr 2005 (otherwise) (SI 2005/275) |
| | (4)(e) | *Not yet in force* |
| | (4)(f), (g) | 10 Feb 2005 (for the purpose of conferring power to make regulations, orders or rules) (SI 2005/275) |
| | | 6 Apr 2005 (otherwise) (SI 2005/275) |
| | (5) | *Not yet in force* |
| | (6) | 6 Apr 2005 (SI 2005/275) |
| | (7), (8) | 10 Feb 2005 (for the purpose of conferring power to make regulations) (SI 2005/275) |

**Pensions Act 2004 (c 35)**—*contd*

|  |  |  |
|---|---|---|
|  |  | 1 Apr 2005 (otherwise) (SI 2005/275) |
| 210 | (1)–(3) | 17 Dec 2004 (SI 2004/3350) |
|  | (4), (5) | 6 Apr 2005 (SI 2005/275) |
|  | (6) | 10 Feb 2005 (for the purpose of conferring power to make regulations, orders or rules) (SI 2005/275) |
|  |  | 6 Apr 2005 (otherwise) (SI 2005/275) |
| 211 |  | 6 Apr 2005 (SI 2005/275) |
| 212 |  | In force as from the first day after the day on which the first regulations made under s 213 or 214 of this Act come into force, whichever is the earlier (SI 2005/1720) |
| 213 | (1)–(3) | 1 Jul 2005 (for the purpose of conferring power to make regulations) (SI 2005/1720) |
|  |  | 21 Jul 2005 (otherwise) (SI 2005/1720) |
|  | (4)(a)–(d) | 1 Jul 2005 (for the purpose of conferring power to make regulations) (SI 2005/1720) |
|  |  | 21 Jul 2005 (otherwise) (SI 2005/1720) |
|  | (4)(e) | *Not yet in force* |
|  | (4)(f) | 1 Jul 2005 (for the purpose of conferring power to make regulations) (SI 2005/1720) |
|  |  | 21 Jul 2005 (otherwise) (SI 2005/1720) |
|  | (5)(a)–(d) | 1 Jul 2005 (for the purpose of conferring power to make regulations) (SI 2005/1720) |
|  |  | 21 Jul 2005 (otherwise) (SI 2005/1720) |
|  | (5)(e) | *Not yet in force* |
|  | (5)(f) | 1 Jul 2005 (for the purpose of conferring power to make regulations) (SI 2005/1720) |
|  |  | 21 Jul 2005 (otherwise) (SI 2005/1720) |
| 214 | (1) | 1 Jul 2005 (for the purpose of conferring power to make regulations) (SI 2005/1720) |
|  |  | 21 Jul 2005 (otherwise) (SI 2005/1720) |
|  | (2)(a)–(j) | 1 Jul 2005 (for the purpose of conferring power to make regulations) (SI 2005/1720) |
|  |  | 21 Jul 2005 (otherwise) (SI 2005/1720) |
|  | (2)(k) | *Not yet in force* |
|  | (2)(l) | 1 Jul 2005 (for the purpose of conferring power to make regulations) (SI 2005/1720) |
|  |  | 21 Jul 2005 (otherwise) (SI 2005/1720) |
| 215–218 |  | 21 Jul 2005 (otherwise) (SI 2005/1720) |
| 219 |  | 6 Apr 2005 (SI 2005/275) |
| 220 |  | 1 Jan 2006 (SI 2005/3331) |
| 221–233 |  | 4 Dec 2005 (for the purpose of conferring power to make regulations) (SI 2005/3331) |
|  |  | 30 Dec 2005 (otherwise) (SI 2005/3331) |
| 234–236 |  | 18 Nov 2004 (s 322(2)(a)) |
| 237, 238 |  | *Not yet in force* |
| 239 |  | 1 Jul 2005 (for the purpose of conferring power to make regulations) (SI 2005/1720) |
|  |  | 22 Sep 2005 (in the case of an occupational pension scheme that has its main administration in the United Kingdom) (SI 2005/1720) |
|  |  | 6 Apr 2006 (otherwise) (SI 2005/1720) |
| 240 |  | *Not yet in force* |
| 241, 242 |  | 1 Nov 2005 (for the purpose of conferring power to make regulations) (SI 2005/2447) |
|  |  | 6 Apr 2006 (otherwise) (SI 2005/2447) |
| 243 |  | 1 Nov 2005 (SI 2005/2447) |
| 244–246 |  | 4 Dec 2005 (for the purpose of conferring power to make regulations) (SI 2005/3331) |
|  |  | 30 Dec 2005 (otherwise) (SI 2005/3331) |
| 247, 248 |  | 6 Apr 2006 (SI 2006/560) |

**Pensions Act 2004 (c 35)**—*contd*

| | | |
|---|---|---|
| 249 | (1) | 6 Apr 2006 (SI 2006/560) |
| | (2) | 9 Mar 2006 (for the purpose of conferring power to make regulations) (SI 2006/560) |
| | | 6 Apr 2006 (otherwise) (SI 2006/560) |
| | (3) | 6 Apr 2006 (SI 2006/560) |
| 250, 251 | | 9 Mar 2006 (for the purpose of conferring power to make regulations) (SI 2006/560) |
| | | 6 Apr 2006 (otherwise) (SI 2006/560) |
| 252 | | 1 Jul 2005 (for the purpose of conferring power to make regulations) (SI 2005/1720) |
| | | 22 Sep 2005 (otherwise) (SI 2005/1720) |
| 253 | | 1 Jan 2006 (for the purpose of conferring power to make regulations) (SI 2005/3331) |
| | | 6 Apr 2006 (otherwise) (SI 2005/3331) |
| 254 | | 6 Apr 2006 (SI 2006/560) |
| 255 | | 1 Jul 2005 (for the purpose of conferring power to make regulations) (SI 2005/1720) |
| | | 22 Sep 2005 (otherwise) (SI 2005/1720) |
| 256 | | 30 Jun 2005 (SI 2005/1720) |
| 257 | | 6 Apr 2005 (SI 2005/275) |
| 258 | (1) | 6 Apr 2005 (SI 2005/275) |
| | (2)(a), (b) | 6 Apr 2005 (SI 2005/275) |
| | (2)(c)(i) | 6 Apr 2005 (SI 2005/275) |
| | (2)(c)(ii) | 10 Feb 2005 (for the purpose of conferring power to make regulations, orders or rules) (SI 2005/275) |
| | | 6 Apr 2005 (otherwise) (SI 2005/275) |
| | (3)–(6) | 6 Apr 2005 (SI 2005/275) |
| | (7) | 10 Feb 2005 (definition "relevant contributions", for the purpose of conferring power to make regulations, orders or rules) (SI 2005/275) |
| | | 6 Apr 2005 (otherwise) (SI 2005/275) |
| 259–261 | | 1 Jan 2006 (for the purpose of conferring power to make regulations) (SI 2005/3331) |
| | | 6 Apr 2006 (otherwise) (SI 2005/3331) |
| 262 | | 1 Nov 2005 (for the purpose of conferring power to make regulations) (SI 2005/2447) |
| | | 6 Apr 2006 (otherwise) (SI 2005/2447) |
| 263 | | 6 Apr 2005 (SI 2005/275) |
| 264 | | 1 Jan 2006 (for the purpose of conferring power to make regulations) (SI 2005/3331) |
| | | 6 Apr 2006 (otherwise) (SI 2005/3331) |
| 265 | | 6 Apr 2005 (SI 2005/275)[2] |
| 266 | | 6 Apr 2005 (SI 2005/275) |
| 267, 268 | | 6 Apr 2006 (SI 2006/560) |
| 269 | | 1 Jul 2005 (for the purpose of conferring power to make regulations) (SI 2005/1720) |
| | | 6 Apr 2006 (otherwise) (SI 2005/1720) |
| 270, 271 | | 10 Feb 2005 (for the purpose of conferring power to make regulations, orders or rules) (SI 2005/275)[2] |
| | | 6 Apr 2005 (otherwise) (SI 2005/275)[2] |
| 272 | : s 75A(1)–(4) | 10 Feb 2005 (for the purpose of conferring power to make regulations, orders or rules) (SI 2005/275) |
| | | 6 Apr 2005 (otherwise) (SI 2005/275) |
| | : s 75A(5)–(14) | 15 Mar 2005 (SI 2005/695)[3] |
| 273 | | 5 Mar 2008 (for the purposes of conferring power to make regulations) (SI 2008/627) |
| | | 6 Apr 2008 (otherwise) (SI 2008/627) |
| 274 | | 17 Dec 2004 (SI 2004/3350) |
| 275, 276 | | 6 Apr 2005 (SI 2005/275) |
| 277 | | 17 Dec 2004 (SI 2004/3350)[1] |

**Pensions Act 2004 (c 35)**—*contd*

| | | |
|---|---|---|
| 278 | | 15 Mar 2005 (for the purpose of conferring power to make regulations) (SI 2005/695)[3] |
| | | 6 Apr 2005 (otherwise) (SI 2005/275) |
| 279 | | 6 Apr 2005 (SI 2005/275) |
| 280 | | 15 Mar 2005 (for the purpose of conferring power to make regulations) (SI 2005/695)[3] |
| | | 6 Apr 2005 (otherwise) (SI 2005/275) |
| 281 | | 18 Nov 2004 (s 322(2)(b)) |
| 282 | | 6 Apr 2005 (SI 2005/275) |
| 283 | | 1 Jul 2005 (SI 2005/1720) |
| 284 | | 1 Jul 2005 (for the purpose of conferring power to make regulations) (SI 2005/1720) |
| | | 6 Apr 2006 (otherwise) (SI 2005/1720) |
| 285 | | 6 Apr 2005 (SI 2005/275) |
| 286 | | 1 Jun 2005 (SI 2005/1436) |
| 287 | | 4 Dec 2005 (in so far as relates to an occupational pension scheme with its main administration in the United Kingdom which is not a pay-as-you-go scheme, for the purpose of conferring power to make regulations) (SI 2005/3331) |
| | | 30 Dec 2005 (in so far as relates to an occupational pension scheme with its main administration in the United Kingdom which is not a pay-as-you-go scheme, otherwise) (SI 2005/3331) |
| | | In force the day after the expiry of the period of 5 months beginning with the application date, in so far as relates to a "pre-23 Sep 2005 scheme" (ie certain occupational pension schemes with their main administration in the United Kingdom which are not pay-as-you-go schemes) where both an application for authorisation under s 288 and an application for approval under s 289 have been made on or before 29 Mar 2006 (SI 2005/3331) |
| | | 30 Mar 2006 (in so far as relates to a "pre-23 Sep 2005 scheme" (as defined above) where both an application for authorisation under s 288 and an application for approval under s 289 have not been made on or before 29 Mar 2006) (SI 2005/3331) |
| 288–295 | | 4 Dec 2005 (in so far as they relate to an occupational pension scheme with its main administration in the United Kingdom which is not a pay-as-you-go scheme, for the purpose of conferring power to make regulations) (SI 2005/3331) |
| | | 30 Dec 2005 (in so far as they relate to an occupational pension scheme with its main administration in the United Kingdom which is not a pay-as-you-go scheme, otherwise) (SI 2005/3331) |
| | | *Not yet in force* (otherwise) |
| 296 | | 18 Nov 2004 (s 322(2)(c)(i)) |
| 297 | (1), (2) | 18 Nov 2004 (so far as is necessary for enabling the making of any regulations for which this section provides) (s 322(3)(a)) |
| | | 6 Apr 2005 (otherwise) (s 322(3)(b)) |
| | (3) | 18 Nov 2004 (s 322(2)(c)(ii)) |
| | (4) | See Sch 11 below |
| 298 | (1)–(3) | 18 Nov 2004 (s 322(2)(c)(iii)) |
| | (4) | 6 Apr 2005 (SI 2005/275) |
| | (5)(a) | 18 Nov 2004 (s 322(2)(c)(iii)) |
| | (5)(b) | 6 Apr 2005 (SI 2005/275) |
| | (5)(c) | 18 Nov 2004 (s 322(2)(c)(iii)) |
| 299 | | 18 Nov 2004 (s 322(2)(c)(iv)) |
| 300 | (1) | 6 Apr 2005 (SI 2005/695)[3] |
| | (2) | 10 Feb 2005 (for the purpose of conferring power to make regulations or orders) (SI 2005/275) |
| | | 8 Mar 2005 (otherwise) (SI 2005/275) |

**Pensions Act 2004 (c 35)**—*contd*

| | | |
|---|---|---|
| | (3)–(5) | 6 Apr 2005 (SI 2005/275) |
| 301 | | 6 Apr 2005 (SI 2005/275) |
| 302 | (1) | 1 Sep 2005 (SI 2005/1720)[4] |
| | (2) | 27 May 2005 (SI 2005/1436) |
| | (3)–(5) | 1 Sep 2005 (SI 2005/2447) |
| 303–305 | | 18 Nov 2004 (s 322(2)(d)(i)) |
| 306 | (1) | 1 Sep 2005 (SI 2005/2447) |
| | (2)(a)–(g) | 1 Sep 2005 (SI 2005/2447) |
| | (2)(h) | 4 Dec 2005 (for the purpose of conferring power to make regulations) (SI 2005/3331) |
| | | 30 Dec 2005 (otherwise) (SI 2005/3331) |
| | (2)(i) | *Not yet in force* |
| | (2)(j), (k) | 6 Apr 2006 (SI 2006/560) |
| | (2)(l) | 1 Sep 2005 (SI 2005/2447) |
| | (2)(m) | 4 Dec 2005 (for the purpose of conferring power to make regulations) (SI 2005/3331) |
| | | 30 Dec 2005 (otherwise) (SI 2005/3331) |
| | (2)(n) | 1 Sep 2005 (SI 2005/2447) |
| | (3) | 1 Sep 2005 (SI 2005/2447) |
| | (4), (5) | 6 Apr 2006 (SI 2006/560) |
| 307 | (1)(a) | 10 Feb 2005 (for the purpose of conferring power to make regulations, orders or rules) (SI 2005/275) |
| | | 6 Apr 2005 (otherwise) (SI 2005/275) |
| | (1)(b) | 10 Feb 2005 (for the purpose of conferring power to make regulations or orders) (SI 2005/275) |
| | | 8 Mar 2005 (otherwise) (SI 2005/275) |
| | (1)(c) | 10 Feb 2005 (for the purpose of conferring power to make regulations, orders or rules) (SI 2005/275) |
| | | 6 Apr 2005 (otherwise) (SI 2005/275) |
| | (2) | 8 Mar 2005 (SI 2005/275) |
| | (3) | 10 Feb 2005 (for the purpose of conferring power to make regulations or orders) (SI 2005/275) |
| | | 8 Mar 2005 (otherwise) (SI 2005/275) |
| | (4) | 8 Mar 2005 (SI 2005/275) |
| 308 | | *Not yet in force* |
| 309–312 | | 1 Sep 2005 (SI 2005/2447) |
| 313 | | 18 Nov 2004 (s 322(2)(d)(ii)) |
| 314 | | 1 Sep 2005 (SI 2005/2447) |
| 315 | (1)–(5) | 18 Nov 2004 (s 322(2)(d)(ii)) |
| | (6) | 4 Dec 2005 (for the purpose of conferring power to make regulations) (SI 2005/3331) |
| | | 30 Dec 2005 (otherwise) (SI 2005/3331) |
| 316, 317 | | 18 Nov 2004 (s 322(2)(d)(ii)) |
| 318 | (1)–(3) | 18 Nov 2004 (s 322(2)(d)(ii)) |
| | (4)(a) | 10 Feb 2005 (for the purpose of conferring power to make regulations, orders or rules) (SI 2005/275) |
| | | 6 Apr 2005 (otherwise) (SI 2005/275) |
| | (4)(b) | *Not yet in force* |
| | (5) | 1 Jun 2005 (SI 2005/1436) |
| 319 | (1) | See Sch 12 below |
| | (2)(a) | 1 Sep 2005 (SI 2005/2447) |
| | (2)(b) | 9 Dec 2005 (SI 2005/3331) |
| 320 | | See Sch 13 below |
| 321 | | 6 Apr 2006 (SI 2006/560) |
| 322–325 | | 18 Nov 2004 (s 322(2)(d)(ii)) |
| Sch 1 | paras 1–18 | 17 Dec 2004 (SI 2004/3350) |
| | para 19 | *Not yet in force* |
| | para 20(1), (2) | 6 Apr 2005 (SI 2005/275) |
| | para 20(3) | 17 Dec 2004 (SI 2004/3350) |

**Pensions Act 2004 (c 35)**—*contd*

|  |  |  |
|---|---|---|
| | para 20(4)–(7) | 6 Apr 2005 (SI 2005/275) |
| | para 21 | 15 Mar 2005 (for the purpose of conferring power to make regulations) (SI 2005/695)[3] |
| | | 6 Apr 2005 (otherwise) (SI 2005/695)[3] |
| | paras 22–24 | 17 Dec 2004 (SI 2004/3350) (note that SI 2005/275 also purports to bring para 24 into force on 6 Apr 2005) |
| | para 25 | 6 Apr 2005 (SI 2005/275) |
| | para 26 | 10 Feb 2005 (for the purpose of conferring power to make regulations) (SI 2005/275) |
| | | 1 Apr 2005 (otherwise) (SI 2005/275) |
| | para 27 | 10 Feb 2005 (SI 2005/275) |
| | para 28 | 6 Apr 2005 (SI 2005/275) |
| | paras 29–32 | 17 Dec 2004 (SI 2004/3350) |
| | para 33 | 6 Apr 2005 (SI 2005/275) |
| | para 34 | 17 Dec 2004 (SI 2004/3350) |
| | para 35(1)–(3) | 17 Dec 2004 (SI 2004/3350) |
| | para 35(4)(a), (b) | 6 Apr 2005 (SI 2005/275) |
| | para 35(4)(c) | 17 Dec 2004 (SI 2004/3350) |
| | para 35(5) | 17 Dec 2004 (in so far as relates to sub-paras (1)–(3), (4)(c)) (SI 2004/3350) |
| | | 6 Apr 2005 (in so far as relates to sub-para (4)(a), (b)) (SI 2005/275) |
| Sch 2 | | 6 Apr 2005 (SI 2005/695)[3] |
| Sch 3 | | 6 Apr 2005 (SI 2005/275) |
| Sch 4 | paras 1–7 | 17 Dec 2004 (SI 2004/3350) |
| | para 8 | 6 Apr 2005 (SI 2005/275) |
| | para 9 | 10 Feb 2005 (for the purpose of conferring power to make regulations, orders or rules) (SI 2005/275) |
| | | 6 Apr 2005 (otherwise) (SI 2005/275) |
| | paras 10–16 | 6 Apr 2005 (SI 2005/275) |
| | para 17 | 17 Dec 2004 (SI 2004/3350) |
| | para 18 | 6 Apr 2006 (SI 2006/560) |
| | paras 19–21 | 6 Apr 2005 (SI 2005/275) |
| Sch 5 | paras 1–12 | 17 Dec 2004 (SI 2004/3350) |
| | para 13(1), (2) | 17 Dec 2004 (SI 2004/3350) |
| | para 13(3)(a) | 17 Dec 2004 (SI 2004/3350) |
| | para 13(3)(b) | *Not yet in force* |
| | para 13(4) | 17 Dec 2004 (SI 2004/3350) |
| | paras 14–17 | 17 Dec 2004 (SI 2004/3350) |
| | para 18(1) | 1 Sep 2005 (SI 2005/2447) |
| | para 18(2)(a)–(e) | 6 Apr 2006 (SI 2006/560) |
| | para 18(2)(f)–(h) | 6 Apr 2005 (SI 2005/275) |
| | para 18(3) | 1 Sep 2005 (SI 2005/2447) |
| | para 19 | 6 Apr 2005 (SI 2005/275) |
| | paras 20, 21 | 17 Dec 2004 (SI 2004/3350) |
| | para 22(1)–(3) | 6 Apr 2005 (SI 2005/275) |
| | para 22(4) | 1 Jan 2006 (for the purpose of conferring power to make regulations) (SI 2005/3331) |
| | | 1 Apr 2006 (otherwise) (SI 2005/3331) |
| | para 22(5)–(7) | 6 Apr 2005 (SI 2005/275) |
| | para 23(a) | 6 Apr 2005 (SI 2005/275) |
| | para 23(b) | 17 Dec 2004 (SI 2004/3350) |
| | paras 24–28 | 17 Dec 2004 (SI 2004/3350) |
| | para 29(1)–(4) | 17 Dec 2004 (SI 2004/3350) |
| | para 29(5) | In force as from the first day after the day on which the first regulations made under s 213 or 214 of this Act come into force, whichever is the earlier (SI 2005/1720) |
| Sch 6 | | 6 Apr 2006 (SI 2005/3331) |
| Sch 7 | paras 1–3 | 6 Apr 2005 (SI 2005/275) |

**See Halsbury's Statutes Citator for amendments to these Acts**

**Pensions Act 2004 (c 35)**—*contd*

| | |
|---|---|
| para 4(1)–(3) | 6 Apr 2005 (SI 2005/275) |
| para 4(4) | 10 Feb 2005 (for the purpose of conferring power to make regulations, orders or rules) (SI 2005/275) |
| | 6 Apr 2005 (otherwise) (SI 2005/275) |
| para 4(5) | 6 Apr 2005 (SI 2005/275) |
| para 5 | 6 Apr 2005 (SI 2005/275) |
| para 6(1)–(3) | 6 Apr 2005 (SI 2005/275) |
| para 6(4) | 10 Feb 2005 (for the purpose of conferring power to make regulations, orders or rules) (SI 2005/275) |
| | 6 Apr 2005 (otherwise) (SI 2005/275) |
| para 6(5) | 6 Apr 2005 (SI 2005/275) |
| paras 7, 8 | 6 Apr 2005 (SI 2005/275) |
| para 9(1)–(3) | 6 Apr 2005 (SI 2005/275) |
| para 9(4) | 10 Feb 2005 (for the purpose of conferring power to make regulations, orders or rules) (SI 2005/275) |
| | 6 Apr 2005 (otherwise) (SI 2005/275) |
| para 9(5) | 6 Apr 2005 (SI 2005/275) |
| paras 10, 11 | 6 Apr 2005 (SI 2005/275) |
| para 12(1)–(3) | 6 Apr 2005 (SI 2005/275) |
| para 12(4)(a) | 10 Feb 2005 (for the purpose of conferring power to make regulations, orders or rules) (SI 2005/275) |
| | 6 Apr 2005 (otherwise) (SI 2005/275) |
| para 12(4)(b) | 6 Apr 2005 (SI 2005/275) |
| para 12(5), (6) | 6 Apr 2005 (SI 2005/275) |
| para 13(1)–(3) | 6 Apr 2005 (SI 2005/275) |
| para 13(4) | 10 Feb 2005 (for the purpose of conferring power to make regulations, orders or rules) (SI 2005/275) |
| | 6 Apr 2005 (otherwise) (SI 2005/275) |
| para 13(5) | 6 Apr 2005 (SI 2005/275) |
| paras 14, 15 | 6 Apr 2005 (SI 2005/275) |
| para 16(1), (2) | 6 Apr 2005 (SI 2005/275) |
| para 16(3)(a) | 6 Apr 2005 (SI 2005/275) |
| para 16(3)(b) | 10 Feb 2005 (for the purpose of conferring power to make regulations, orders or rules) (SI 2005/275) |
| | 6 Apr 2005 (otherwise) (SI 2005/275) |
| para 16(4) | 6 Apr 2005 (SI 2005/275) |
| para 17(1)–(3) | 6 Apr 2005 (SI 2005/275) |
| para 17(4)(a) | 10 Feb 2005 (for the purpose of conferring power to make regulations, orders or rules) (SI 2005/275) |
| | 6 Apr 2005 (otherwise) (SI 2005/275) |
| para 17(4)(b) | 6 Apr 2005 (SI 2005/275) |
| para 17(5), (6) | 6 Apr 2005 (SI 2005/275) |
| para 18(1)–(3) | 6 Apr 2005 (SI 2005/275) |
| para 18(4) | 10 Feb 2005 (for the purpose of conferring power to make regulations, orders or rules) (SI 2005/275) |
| | 6 Apr 2005 (otherwise) (SI 2005/275) |
| para 18(5) | 6 Apr 2005 (SI 2005/275) |
| para 19 | 6 Apr 2005 (SI 2005/275) |
| para 20(1)–(3) | 6 Apr 2005 (SI 2005/275) |
| para 20(4) | 10 Feb 2005 (for the purpose of conferring power to make regulations, orders or rules) (SI 2005/275) |
| | 6 Apr 2005 (otherwise) (SI 2005/275) |
| para 20(5), (6) | 6 Apr 2005 (SI 2005/275) |
| para 20(7), (8) | 10 Feb 2005 (for the purpose of conferring power to make regulations, orders or rules) (SI 2005/275) |
| | 6 Apr 2005 (otherwise) (SI 2005/275) |
| paras 21, 22 | 6 Apr 2005 (SI 2005/275) |
| para 23 | 10 Feb 2005 (for the purpose of conferring power to make regulations, orders or rules) (SI 2005/275) |
| | 6 Apr 2005 (otherwise) (SI 2005/275) |

**Pensions Act 2004 (c 35)**—*contd*

| | | |
|---|---|---|
| | para 24(1), (2) | 10 Feb 2005 (for the purpose of conferring power to make regulations, orders or rules) (SI 2005/275) |
| | | 6 Apr 2005 (otherwise) (SI 2005/275) |
| | para 24(3)–(5) | 6 Apr 2005 (SI 2005/275) |
| | para 24(6) | 10 Feb 2005 (for the purpose of conferring power to make regulations, orders or rules) (SI 2005/275) |
| | | 6 Apr 2005 (otherwise) (SI 2005/275) |
| | para 24(7), (8) | 6 Apr 2005 (SI 2005/275) |
| | para 25(1) | 10 Feb 2005 (for the purpose of conferring power to make regulations, orders or rules) (SI 2005/275) |
| | | 6 Apr 2005 (otherwise) (SI 2005/275) |
| | para 25(2), (3) | 6 Apr 2005 (SI 2005/275) |
| | para 26(1)–(6) | 6 Apr 2005 (SI 2005/275) |
| | para 26(7) | 10 Feb 2005 (definition "the compensation cap", para (a), for the purpose of conferring power to make regulations, orders or rules) (SI 2005/275) |
| | | 6 Apr 2005 (otherwise) (SI 2005/275) |
| | para 26(8) | 6 Apr 2005 (SI 2005/275) |
| | para 26(9), (10) | 10 Feb 2005 (for the purpose of conferring power to make regulations, orders or rules) (SI 2005/275) |
| | | 6 Apr 2005 (otherwise) (SI 2005/275) |
| | para 27 | 6 Apr 2005 (SI 2005/275) |
| | para 28(1)–(5) | 6 Apr 2005 (SI 2005/275) |
| | para 28(6), (7) | 10 Feb 2005 (for the purpose of conferring power to make regulations, orders or rules) (SI 2005/275) |
| | | 6 Apr 2005 (otherwise) (SI 2005/275) |
| | para 28(8), (9) | 6 Apr 2005 (SI 2005/275) |
| | paras 29, 30 | 6 Apr 2005 (SI 2005/275) |
| | para 31(1) | 6 Apr 2005 (SI 2005/275) |
| | para 31(2), (3) | 10 Feb 2005 (for the purpose of conferring power to make regulations, orders or rules) (SI 2005/275) |
| | | 6 Apr 2005 (otherwise) (SI 2005/275) |
| | para 32 | 6 Apr 2005 (SI 2005/275) |
| | para 33 | 10 Feb 2005 (for the purpose of conferring power to make regulations, orders or rules) (SI 2005/275) |
| | | 6 Apr 2005 (otherwise) (SI 2005/275) |
| | paras 34–36 | 6 Apr 2005 (SI 2005/275) |
| | para 37(1)–(3) | 6 Apr 2005 (SI 2005/275) |
| | para 37(4) | 10 Feb 2005 (for the purpose of conferring power to make regulations, orders or rules) (SI 2005/275) |
| | | 6 Apr 2005 (otherwise) (SI 2005/275) |
| Sch 8 | | 9 Dec 2005 (SI 2005/3331) |
| Sch 9 | paras 1–19 | 6 Apr 2005 (SI 2005/275) |
| | paras 20–26 | 1 Sep 2005 (SI 2005/1720)[4] |
| | paras 27, 28 | 6 Apr 2010 (SI 2010/443) |
| | paras 29, 30 | 1 Sep 2005 (SI 2005/1720)[4] |
| Sch 10 | | 18 Nov 2004 (s 322(2)(a)) |
| Sch 11 | paras 1–23 | 18 Nov 2004 (so far as is necessary for enabling the making of any regulations for which this Schedule provides) (s 322(3)(a)) |
| | | 6 Apr 2005 (otherwise) (s 322(3)(b)) |
| | para 24 | 18 Nov 2004 (s 322(2)(e)) |
| | paras 25–27 | 18 Nov 2004 (so far as is necessary for enabling the making of any regulations for which this Schedule provides) (s 322(3)(a)) |
| | | 6 Apr 2005 (otherwise) (s 322(3)(b)) |
| Sch 12 | para 1 | 6 Apr 2005 (SI 2005/275) |
| | para 2 | 10 Feb 2005 (SI 2005/275) |
| | paras 3, 4 | 1 Jan 2006 (SI 2005/3331) |
| | para 5(1) | 6 Apr 2005 (SI 2005/275) |
| | para 5(2) | 6 Apr 2006 (SI 2006/560) |
| | para 5(3) | 6 Apr 2005 (SI 2005/275) |

**Pensions Act 2004 (c 35)**—*contd*

| | |
|---|---|
| para 6 | 6 Apr 2005 (SI 2005/275) |
| para 7 | 6 Apr 2005 (SI 2005/695)[3] |
| para 8 | 10 Feb 2005 (SI 2005/275) |
| para 9 | 6 Apr 2005 (SI 2005/1108) |
| para 10 | 6 Apr 2006 (SI 2006/560) |
| para 11(1) | See sub-paras (2), (3) below |
| para 11(2) | 6 Apr 2006 (SI 2006/560) |
| para 11(3) | 1 Oct 2006 (for the purpose of conferring power to make regulations) (SI 2006/2272) |
| | 1 Jan 2007 (otherwise) (SI 2006/2272) |
| paras 12, 13 | 6 Apr 2006 (SI 2005/3331) |
| paras 14–17 | 6 Apr 2006 (SI 2006/560) |
| para 18 | 1 Jan 2006 (for the purpose of conferring power to make regulations) (SI 2005/3331) |
| | 6 Apr 2006 (otherwise) (SI 2005/3331) |
| paras 19, 20 | 22 Sep 2005 (SI 2005/2447) |
| paras 21, 22 | 6 Apr 2006 (SI 2006/560) |
| para 23 | *Not yet in force* |
| para 24(a) | 6 Apr 2005 (SI 2005/275) |
| para 24(b) | *Not yet in force* |
| para 24(c) | 6 Apr 2005 (SI 2005/275) |
| paras 25, 26 | 6 Apr 2005 (SI 2005/275)[2] |
| para 27 | 6 Apr 2006 (SI 2006/560) |
| para 28 | 10 Feb 2005 (for the purpose of conferring power to make regulations) (SI 2005/275) |
| | 1 Apr 2005 (otherwise) (SI 2005/275)[2] |
| para 29 | 6 Apr 2006 (SI 2006/560) |
| paras 30–32 | 6 Apr 2006 (SI 2005/3331) |
| para 33 | 6 Apr 2006 (SI 2006/560) |
| para 34 | 6 Apr 2005 (SI 2005/1108) |
| paras 35–43 | 6 Apr 2005 (SI 2005/695)[3] |
| para 44 | 6 Apr 2005 (SI 2005/1108) |
| para 45 | 9 Dec 2005 (SI 2005/3331) |
| para 46(a) | 9 Dec 2005 (SI 2005/3331) |
| para 46(b) | 6 Apr 2005 (SI 2005/1108) |
| para 47 | 6 Apr 2005 (SI 2005/695)[3] |
| para 48 | 6 Apr 2006 (SI 2006/560) |
| para 49 | 4 Dec 2005 (for the purpose of conferring power to make regulations) (SI 2005/3331) |
| | 30 Dec 2005 (otherwise) (SI 2005/3331) |
| para 50 | 9 Dec 2005 (SI 2005/3331) |
| paras 51, 52 | 4 Dec 2005 (for the purpose of conferring power to make regulations) (SI 2005/3331) |
| | 30 Dec 2005 (otherwise) (SI 2005/3331) |
| para 53 | 6 Apr 2006 (SI 2005/3331) |
| paras 54, 55 | 9 Dec 2005 (SI 2005/3331) |
| para 56(a) | 6 Apr 2006 (SI 2005/3331) |
| para 56(b) | 1 Sep 2005 (SI 2005/1720)[4] |
| paras 57, 58 | 6 Apr 2006 (SI 2006/560) |
| paras 59, 60 | 6 Apr 2005 (SI 2005/1108) |
| para 61 | *Not yet in force* |
| para 62(a), (b) | 6 Apr 2006 (SI 2006/560) |
| para 62(c) | 6 Apr 2006 (SI 2005/3331) |
| para 63(a), (b) | *Never in force* (repealed) |
| para 63(c) | 6 Apr 2006 (SI 2005/3331) |
| paras 64, 65 | 6 Apr 2006 (SI 2006/560) |
| para 66 | 6 Apr 2005 (SI 2005/695)[3] |
| para 67 | 6 Apr 2005 (SI 2005/1108) |
| para 68 | 6 Apr 2005 (SI 2005/695)[3] |

**Pensions Act 2004 (c 35)**—*contd*

| | | |
|---|---|---|
| | para 69 | 6 Apr 2006 (SI 2005/3331) |
| | para 70 | 6 Apr 2005 (SI 2005/695)³ |
| | para 71 | 6 Apr 2005 (SI 2005/1108) |
| | para 72 | *Not yet in force* |
| | para 73 | 6 Apr 2005 (SI 2005/695)³ |
| | para 74 | 22 Sep 2005 (SI 2005/1720) |
| | para 75 | 4 Dec 2005 (for the purpose of conferring power to make regulations) (SI 2005/3331) |
| | | 30 Dec 2005 (otherwise) (SI 2005/3331) |
| | para 76(1) | 4 Dec 2005 (for the purpose of conferring power to make regulations) (SI 2005/3331) |
| | | 30 Dec 2005 (otherwise) (SI 2005/3331) |
| | para 76(2)(a) | 6 Apr 2005 (SI 2005/275) |
| | para 76(2)(b) | 9 Dec 2005 (SI 2005/3331) |
| | para 76(2)(c) | 4 Dec 2005 (for the purpose of conferring power to make regulations) (SI 2005/3331) |
| | | 30 Dec 2005 (otherwise) (SI 2005/3331) |
| | para 76(2)(d) | 9 Dec 2005 (SI 2005/3331) |
| | para 76(2)(e) | *Not yet in force* |
| | para 76(3) | 30 Jun 2005 (in so far as relates to ss 67, 318 of this Act) (SI 2005/1720) |
| | | 1 Sep 2005 (in so far as relates to Pt 2, Chapter 4 of this Act) (SI 2005/1720)⁴ |
| | | 1 Sep 2005 (in so far as relates to Pt 2, Chapter 5 of this Act) (SI 2005/2447) |
| | | 6 Apr 2006 (otherwise) (SI 2006/560) |
| | para 76(4) | 6 Apr 2005 (SI 2005/275) |
| | para 76(5) | 12 Jul 2005 (in so far as relates to Pt 2, Chapter 4 of this Act, for the purpose of conferring power to make regulations) (SI 2005/1720) |
| | | 1 Sep 2005 (in so far as relates to Pt 2, Chapter 4 of this Act, otherwise) (SI 2005/1720) |
| | | 9 Dec 2005 (otherwise) (SI 2005/3331) |
| | para 77(1) | 6 Apr 2005 (SI 2005/695)³ |
| | para 77(2) | 4 Dec 2005 (for the purpose of conferring power to make regulations) (SI 2005/3331) |
| | | 30 Dec 2005 (otherwise) (SI 2005/3331) |
| | para 77(3) | 6 Apr 2005 (SI 2005/695)³ |
| | para 78 | 6 Apr 2005 (SI 2005/695)³ |
| | para 79 | 6 Apr 2005 (SI 2005/275) |
| | para 80 | 6 Apr 2005 (SI 2005/695)³ |
| Sch 13 | Pt 1 | 18 Nov 2004 (repeal of Welfare Reform and Pensions Act 1999, s 50(2)) (s 322(2)(e)) |
| | | 1 Apr 2005 (repeal of Pension Schemes Act 1993, s 175) (SI 2005/275) |
| | | 1 Apr 2005 (repeal of Welfare Reform and Pensions Act 1999, Sch 1, para 1(2)(a)) (SI 2005/695)³ |
| | | 6 Apr 2005 (repeals of Pensions Act 1995, s 134(3), Sch 4, para 21(14)) (s 322(4)) |
| | | 6 Apr 2005 (SI 2005/275), repeals of or in— |
| | | Parliamentary Commissioner Act 1967, Sch 2, entry relating to the Occupational Pensions Regulatory Authority; |
| | | House of Commons Disqualification Act 1975, Sch 1, Pt 2, entry relating to the Occupational Pensions Regulatory Authority; |
| | | Northern Ireland Assembly Disqualification Act 1975, Sch 1, Pt 2, entry relating to the Occupational Pensions Regulatory Authority; |
| | | Tribunals and Inquiries Act 1992, Sch 1, Pt 1, para 35(g); |

**Pensions Act 2004 (c 35)**—*contd*

Pensions Act 1995, ss 51(1), 54(3), 162(1), Sch 3, para 21, Sch 4, para 21(13);

Child Support, Pensions and Social Security Act 2000, s 54;

Freedom of Information Act 2000, Sch 1, Pt 6, entries relating to the Occupational Pensions Regulatory Authority and the Registrar of Occupational and Personal Pension Schemes

6 Apr 2005 (SI 2005/695)[3], repeals of or in—

Pension Schemes Act 1993, ss 6, 99(6), 101J(3), 129, 168A, 181 (except the definition "voluntary contributions requirements" in sub-s (1)), 192(2);

Pensions Act 1995, ss 1, 2, 5, 7(1), (4), 10(5)(a), 11(3), 13, 22(1)(b), 25(2), 26A–26C, 28(4), 29, 30, 30A, 31, 48, 72A(9), 72C(2), 74, 75(9), 96–114, Sch 1, Sch 3, para 23, Sch 5, para 20;

Welfare Reform and Pensions Act 1999, ss 2(5), (6), 4, 5, 38(1), Sch 1, paras 1(2)(b)(i), (xi)–(xiii), 2, 3, Sch 2, para 9, Sch 12, para 55;

Anti-terrorism, Crime and Security Act 2001

6 Apr 2005 (SI 2005/1108), repeals of or in—

Social Security Contributions (Transfer of Functions, etc) Act 1999;

Welfare Reform and Pensions Act 1999, Sch 12, para 60;

Child Support, Pensions and Social Security Act 2000, s 47, Sch 5, para 10

1 Sep 2005 (SI 2005/1720)[4], repeals of or in—

Parliamentary Commissioner Act 1967 (otherwise);

House of Commons Disqualification Act 1975 (otherwise);

Northern Ireland Assembly Disqualification Act 1975 (otherwise);

Tribunals and Inquiries Act 1992 (otherwise);

Pensions Act 1995, ss 78–86;

Welfare Reform and Pensions Act 1999, s 17, Sch 1, para 1(2)(b)(ix), Sch 2, para 16;

Freedom of Information Act 2000 (otherwise)

1 Sep 2005 (repeal of Child Support, Pensions and Social Security Act 2000, Sch 5, para 3(3), (4)) (SI 2005/2447)

22 Sep 2005 (repeals of or in Pension Schemes Act 1993, s 123(3), (4)) (SI 2005/2447)

9 Dec 2005 (repeals of or in Pensions Act 1995, ss 49, 49A(4)) (SI 2005/3331)

30 Dec 2005 (SI 2005/3331), repeals of or in—

Pensions Act 1995, ss 36(2), 41(2)(c), 56–61;

Welfare Reform and Pensions Act 1999, Sch 1, para 1(2)(b)(iii), Sch 2, para 14

6 Apr 2006 (repeals of or in Pension Schemes Act 1993, ss 28, 29) (SI 2005/1720)

6 Apr 2006 (SI 2005/3331), repeals of or in—

Pensions Act 1995, ss 16–21, 89(2), 117(2);

Welfare Reform and Pensions Act 1999, Sch 12, paras 44–49, 53;

Child Support, Pensions and Social Security Act 2000, ss 43–46

6 Apr 2006 (SI 2006/560), repeals of or in—

Pension Schemes Act 1993, ss 111, 111A, 111B, 132, 148, 149, 151, 158, 177, 181(1) (definition "voluntary contributions requirements"), Sch 9;

Pensions Act 1995, ss 38, 69, 71A, 72B, 76, 87, 88, 118, 119, 124(1) (definitions "member-nominated director" and "member-nominated trustee"), 142, 178, Sch 2, Sch 3, paras 12, 44(a)(ii), Sch 6;

**Pensions Act 2004 (c 35)**—*contd*

> Criminal Procedure (Consequential Provisions) (Scotland)
> Act 1995;
> Bank of England Act 1998;
> Welfare Reform and Pensions Act 1999, Sch 2, paras 3(1)(a), 13,
> Sch 12 (note that certain repeals in Sch 12 had already been
> brought into force);
> Child Support, Pensions and Social Security Act 2000 (note that
> certain repeals in this Act had already been brought into force);
> Employment Act 2002
> 6 Apr 2007 (repeal of Pensions Act 1995, s 124(1), definition
> "minimum funding requirement") (SI 2006/2272)[5]
> *Not yet in force*, repeals of or in—
> Pension Schemes Act 1993, ss 34, 131;
> Pensions Act 1995, ss 63, 73, 124 (definitions "employer",
> "pensionable service"), 175, Sch 5, para 77;
> Employment Rights Act 1996;
> Welfare Reform and Pensions Act 1999, s 46, Sch 2, paras 14,
> 15

|      |                   |
|------|-------------------|
| Pt 2 | *Not yet in force* |

[1] For transitional provisions, see SI 2004/3350, art 4

[2] For savings and transitional provisions, see SI 2005/275, arts 2(8)–(12), 3, 4

[3] For savings and transitional provisions, see SI 2005/695, arts 5, 6, 6A, Schs 2, 3

[4] For savings and transitional provisions, see SI 2005/1720, arts 4, 5

[5] For savings, see SI 2006/2272, art 3

---

**Planning and Compulsory Purchase Act 2004 (c 5)**

*RA:* 13 May 2004

*Commencement provisions:* s 121; Planning and Compulsory Purchase Act 2004 (Commencement No 1 and Transitional Provision) (Wales) Order 2004, SI 2004/1814; Planning and Compulsory Purchase Act 2004 (Commencement No 2) (Wales) Order 2004, SI 2004/1813; Planning and Compulsory Purchase Act 2004 (Commencement No 1) Order 2004, SI 2004/2097; Planning and Compulsory Purchase Act 2004 (Commencement No 2, Transitional Provisions and Savings) Order 2004, SI 2004/2202; Planning and Compulsory Purchase Act 2004 (Commencement No 3) Order 2004, SI 2004/2593; Planning and Compulsory Purchase Act 2004 (Commencement No 4 and Savings) Order 2005, SI 2005/204; Planning and Compulsory Purchase Act 2004 (Commencement No 3 and Consequential and Transitional Provisions) (Wales) Order 2005, SI 2005/1229, as amended by SI 2005/2722; Planning and Compulsory Purchase Act 2004 (Commencement No 5 and Savings) Order 2005, SI 2005/2081; Planning and Compulsory Purchase Act 2004 (Commencement No 4 and Consequential, Transitional and Savings Provisions) (Wales) Order 2005, SI 2005/2722, as amended by SI 2006/842, SI 2006/1700, SI 2006/3119, SI 2007/546, SI 2007/1023, SI 2007/2371, SI 2007/2447, SI 2007/2449, SI 2008/10, SI 2008/2162, SI 2009/2645, SI 2010/2002, SI 2011/101, SI 2012/1664; Planning and Compulsory Purchase Act 2004 (Commencement No 6, Transitional Provisions and Savings) Order 2005, SI 2005/2847; Planning and Compulsory Purchase Act 2004 (Commencement No 1) (Scotland) Order 2006, SSI 2006/101; Planning and Compulsory Purchase Act 2004 (Commencement No 7) Order 2006, SI 2006/931; Planning and Compulsory Purchase Act 2004 (Commencement No 8 and Saving) Order 2006, SI 2006/1061, as amended by SI 2010/321; Planning and Compulsory Purchase Act 2004 (Commencement No 2 and Consequential Provisions) (Scotland) Order 2006, SSI 2006/243; Planning and Compulsory Purchase Act 2004 (Commencement No 9 and Consequential Provisions) Order 2006, SI 2006/1281; Planning and Compulsory Purchase Act 2004 (Commencement No 3) (Scotland) Order 2006, SSI 2006/268; Planning and Compulsory Purchase Act 2004 (Commencement No 10 and Saving) Order 2007, SI 2007/1369, as amended by SI 2010/321, the Planning (Wales) Act 2015, s 30; Planning and Compulsory Purchase Act 2004 (Commencement No 11) Order 2009, SI 2009/384; Planning and Compulsory Purchase Act 2004 (Commencement No 12, Revocation and Amendment) Order 2010,

**Planning and Compulsory Purchase Act 2004 (c 5)**—*contd*
  SI 2010/321; Planning and Compulsory Purchase Act 2004 (Commencement No 13) Order 2012,
  SI 2012/1100; Planning and Compulsory Purchase Act 2004 (Commencement No 14 and Saving)
  Order 2015, SI 2015/340

| | | |
|---|---|---|
| 1–3 | | 6 Aug 2004 (in so far as they confer certain powers and duties[1]) (SI 2004/2097) |
| | | 28 Sep 2004 (E) (otherwise) (SI 2004/2202) |
| 4 | | 28 Sep 2004 (E) (SI 2004/2202) |
| 5 | | 6 Aug 2004 (in so far as confers certain powers and duties[1]) (SI 2004/2097) |
| | | 28 Sep 2004 (E) (otherwise) (SI 2004/2202) |
| 6, 7 | | 28 Sep 2004 (E) (SI 2004/2202) |
| 8 | | 6 Aug 2004 (in so far as confers certain powers and duties[1]) (SI 2004/2097) |
| | | 28 Sep 2004 (E) (otherwise) (SI 2004/2202) |
| 9 | | 28 Sep 2004 (E) (SI 2004/2202) |
| 10–17 | | 6 Aug 2004 (in so far as they confer certain powers and duties[1]) (SI 2004/2097) |
| | | 28 Sep 2004 (E) (otherwise) (SI 2004/2202) |
| 18 | | 28 Sep 2004 (E) (SI 2004/2202) |
| 19–22 | | 6 Aug 2004 (in so far as they confer certain powers and duties[1]) (SI 2004/2097) |
| | | 28 Sep 2004 (E) (otherwise) (SI 2004/2202) |
| 23 | | 28 Sep 2004 (E) (SI 2004/2202) |
| 24–26 | | 6 Aug 2004 (in so far as they confer certain powers and duties[1]) (SI 2004/2097) |
| | | 28 Sep 2004 (E) (otherwise) (SI 2004/2202) |
| 27 | | 28 Sep 2004 (E) (SI 2004/2202) |
| 28, 29 | | 6 Aug 2004 (in so far as they confer certain powers and duties[1]) (SI 2004/2097) |
| | | 28 Sep 2004 (E) (otherwise) (SI 2004/2202) |
| 30 | | 28 Sep 2004 (E) (SI 2004/2202) |
| 31 | | 6 Aug 2004 (in so far as confers certain powers and duties[1]) (SI 2004/2097) |
| | | 28 Sep 2004 (E) (otherwise) (SI 2004/2202) |
| 32–34 | | 28 Sep 2004 (E) (SI 2004/2202) |
| 35, 36 | | 6 Aug 2004 (in so far as they confer certain powers and duties[1]) (SI 2004/2097) |
| | | 28 Sep 2004 (E) (otherwise) (SI 2004/2202) |
| 37 | | 28 Sep 2004 (E) (SI 2004/2202) |
| 38, 39 | | 28 Sep 2004 (E) (SI 2004/2202) |
| | | 15 Oct 2005 (W) (SI 2005/2847)[7] |
| 40, 41 | | 6 Aug 2004 (in so far as confers certain powers and duties[1]) (SI 2004/2097) |
| | | 10 May 2006 (E) (otherwise) (SI 2006/1061) |
| | | 30 Apr 2012 (W) (otherwise) (SI 2012/1100) |
| 42 | (1) | 6 Aug 2004 (in so far as confers certain powers and duties[1]) (SI 2004/2097) |
| | | 10 Aug 2006 (E) (otherwise) (SI 2006/1061) |
| | | 30 Jun 2007 (W) (otherwise) (SI 2007/1369)[8] |
| | (2)–(4) | 6 Aug 2004 (in so far as they confer certain powers and duties[1]) (SI 2004/2097) |
| | | *Not yet in force* (W) (otherwise) |
| | (5)–(9) | 6 Aug 2004 (in so far as they confer certain powers and duties[1]) (SI 2004/2097) |
| | | 10 Aug 2006 (E) (otherwise) (SI 2006/1061) |
| | | 30 Jun 2007 (W) (otherwise) (SI 2007/1369)[8] |
| 43 | (1) | 24 Aug 2005 (E) (except in so far as the substitution made by this subsection relates to Town and Country Planning Act 1990, s 70B) (SI 2005/2081) |

**Planning and Compulsory Purchase Act 2004 (c 5)**—*contd*

|  |  |  |
|---|---|---|
|  |  | 6 Apr 2009 (E) (exception noted above) (SI 2009/384) |
|  |  | *Not yet in force* (W) |
|  | (2) | 6 Apr 2009 (E) (SI 2009/384) |
|  |  | *Not yet in force* (W) |
|  | (3) | 24 Aug 2005 (E) (except in so far as the substitution made by this subsection relates to Planning (Listed Buildings and Conservation Areas) Act 1990, s 81B) (SI 2005/2081) |
|  |  | 6 Apr 2009 (E) (exception noted above) (SI 2009/384) |
|  |  | *Not yet in force* (W) |
|  | (4)(a) | 24 Aug 2005 (E) (SI 2005/2081) |
|  |  | *Not yet in force* (W) |
|  | (4)(b) | 24 Aug 2005 (E) (except in so far as the substitution made by this paragraph relates to Planning (Listed Buildings and Conservation Areas) Act 1990, s 81B) (SI 2005/2081) |
|  |  | 6 Apr 2009 (E) (exception noted above) (SI 2009/384) |
|  |  | *Not yet in force* (W) |
|  | (5) | 24 Aug 2005 (E) (SI 2005/2081) |
|  |  | *Not yet in force* (W) |
| 44 |  | 6 Aug 2004 (in so far as confers certain powers and duties[1]) (SI 2004/2097) |
|  |  | 24 Aug 2005 (E) (otherwise) (SI 2005/2081)[6] |
| 45 |  | *Not yet in force* |
| 46–48 |  | 6 Aug 2004 (in so far as they confer certain powers and duties[1]) (SI 2004/2097) |
|  |  | *Never in force* (otherwise) (repealed) |
| 49 |  | 6 Aug 2004 (in so far as confers certain powers and duties[1]) (SI 2004/2097) |
|  |  | 10 May 2006 (E) (otherwise) (SI 2006/1061) |
|  |  | 22 Jun 2015 (W) (otherwise) (SI 2015/340) |
| 50 |  | 6 Aug 2004 (in so far as confers certain powers and duties[1]) (SI 2004/2097) |
|  |  | 22 Jun 2015 (W) (otherwise) (SI 2015/340) |
|  |  | *Not yet in force* (E) (otherwise) |
| 51 |  | 24 Aug 2005 (E) (SI 2005/2081)[6] |
|  |  | 22 Jun 2015 (W) (in so far as inserts Town and Country Planning Act 1990, s 91(3C)) (SI 2015/340) |
|  |  | *Not yet in force* (W) (otherwise) |
| 52 |  | 6 Aug 2004 (in so far as confers certain powers and duties[1]) (SI 2004/2097) |
|  |  | 7 Mar 2005 (E) (otherwise) (SI 2005/204) |
|  |  | 22 Jun 2015 (W) (otherwise) (SI 2015/340) |
| 53 |  | 6 Aug 2004 (in so far as confers certain powers and duties[1]) (SI 2004/2097) |
|  |  | 7 Mar 2005 (E) (otherwise) (SI 2005/204) |
|  |  | 1 Apr 2006 (W) (otherwise) (SI 2006/931) |
| 54 |  | 6 Aug 2004 (in so far as confers certain powers and duties[1]) (SI 2004/2097) |
|  |  | 24 Aug 2005 (E) (otherwise) (SI 2005/2081)[6] |
|  |  | 22 Jun 2015 (W) (otherwise) (SI 2015/340)[9] |
| 55 |  | See Sch 2 below |
| 56 |  | 28 Sep 2004 (SI 2004/2202) |
| 57 |  | 6 Aug 2004 (in so far as confers certain powers and duties[1]) (SI 2004/2097) |
|  |  | 28 Sep 2004 (otherwise) (SI 2004/2202) |
| 58 |  | 28 Sep 2004 (SI 2004/2202) |
| 59 |  | 6 Aug 2004 (in so far as confers certain powers and duties[1]) (SI 2004/2097) |
|  |  | 28 Sep 2004 (otherwise) (SI 2004/2202) |
| 60 |  | 14 Jul 2004 (SI 2004/1814)[4] |
| 61 |  | 5 Oct 2005 (for the purpose of making regulations) (SI 2005/2722) |

**Planning and Compulsory Purchase Act 2004 (c 5)**—*contd*

|   |   |   |
|---|---|---|
|  |  | 15 Oct 2005 (otherwise) (SI 2005/2722) |
| 62 | (1)–(3) | 30 Apr 2005 (SI 2005/1229)[5] |
|  | (4) | 1 Aug 2004 (SI 2004/1813) |
|  | (5)(a)–(f) | 30 Apr 2005 (SI 2005/1229)[5] |
|  | (5)(g) | 1 Aug 2004 (SI 2004/1813) |
|  | (6)–(8) | 30 Apr 2005 (SI 2005/1229)[5] |
| 63 | (1), (2) | 30 Apr 2005 (SI 2005/1229)[5] |
|  | (3)(a) | 1 Aug 2004 (SI 2004/1813) |
|  | (3)(b) | 30 Apr 2005 (SI 2005/1229)[5] |
|  | (4)–(6) | 30 Apr 2005 (SI 2005/1229)[5] |
|  | (7) | 1 Aug 2004 (SI 2004/1813) |
| 64–71 |  | 5 Oct 2005 (for the purpose of making regulations) (SI 2005/2722) |
|  |  | 15 Oct 2005 (otherwise) (SI 2005/2722) |
| 72, 73 |  | 30 Apr 2005 (SI 2005/1229)[5] |
| 74 |  | 5 Oct 2005 (for the purpose of making regulations) (SI 2005/2722) |
|  |  | 15 Oct 2005 (otherwise) (SI 2005/2722) |
| 75 |  | 1 Aug 2004 (SI 2004/1813) |
| 76 | (1) | 5 Oct 2005 (for the purpose of making regulations) (SI 2005/2722) |
|  |  | 15 Oct 2005 (otherwise) (SI 2005/2722) |
|  | (2), (3) | 1 Aug 2004 (for the purpose of empowering the National Assembly for Wales to make regulations prescribing the matters referred to in s 76(2), (3)) (SI 2004/1813) |
|  |  | 15 Oct 2005 (otherwise) (SI 2005/2722) |
| 77, 78 |  | 1 Aug 2004 (SI 2004/1813) |
| 79 | (1)–(3) | 6 Aug 2004 (in so far as they confer certain powers and duties[1]) (SI 2004/2097) |
|  |  | 7 Jun 2006 (otherwise) (SI 2006/1281) |
|  | (4) | See Sch 3 below |
| 80–83 |  | 6 Aug 2004 (in so far as they confer certain powers and duties[1]) (SI 2004/2097) |
|  |  | 7 Jun 2006 (otherwise) (SI 2006/1281) |
| 84–87 |  | 7 Jun 2006 (SI 2006/1281) |
| 88 |  | 6 Aug 2004 (in so far as confers certain powers and duties[1]) (SI 2004/2097) |
|  |  | 7 Jun 2006 (otherwise) (SI 2006/1281) |
| 89 |  | See Sch 4 below |
| 90 |  | 12 Jun 2006 (SSI 2006/268) |
| 91 |  | 6 Aug 2004 (in so far as confers certain powers and duties[1]) (SI 2004/2097) |
|  |  | 7 Jun 2006 (otherwise) (SI 2006/1281) |
| 92 | (1) | 20 Mar 2006 (for the purpose of enabling provision to be made by development order) (SSI 2006/101) |
|  |  | 11 May 2006 (otherwise) (SSI 2006/243) |
|  | (2) | 11 May 2006 (SSI 2006/243) |
| 93 | (1) | 20 Mar 2006 (for the purpose of enabling regulations to be made) (SSI 2006/101) |
|  |  | 11 May 2006 (otherwise) (SSI 2006/243) |
|  | (2) | 11 May 2006 (SSI 2006/243) |
| 94 | (1)–(3) | 12 Jun 2006 (SSI 2006/268) |
|  | (4) | 11 May 2006 (SSI 2006/243) |
|  | (5) | 12 Jun 2006 (SSI 2006/268) |
| 95–97 |  | 12 Jun 2006 (SSI 2006/268) |
| 98 |  | 20 Mar 2006 (SSI 2006/101) |
| 99 |  | 31 Oct 2004 (SI 2004/2593) |
| 100, 101 |  | 6 Aug 2004 (in so far as they confer certain powers and duties[1]) (SI 2004/2097) |
|  |  | 31 Oct 2004 (otherwise) (SI 2004/2593) |
| 102–110 |  | 31 Oct 2004 (SI 2004/2593) |
| 111 | (1) | 7 Jun 2006 (SI 2006/1281) |

**Planning and Compulsory Purchase Act 2004 (c 5)**—*contd*

| | | |
|---|---|---|
| | (2) | 31 Oct 2004 (SI 2004/2593) |
| 112 | | 7 Jun 2006 (SI 2006/1281) |
| 113 | | 28 Sep 2004 (E) (SI 2004/2202) |
| | | 15 Oct 2005 (W) (SI 2005/2847) |
| 114 | | 28 Sep 2004 (E) (in so far as relates to Pt 2 of the Act) (SI 2004/2202) |
| | | 15 Oct 2005 (W) (SI 2005/2847) |
| 115 | | 13 May 2004 (RA) |
| 116 | | 6 Aug 2004 (in so far as confers certain powers and duties[1]) (SI 2004/2097) |
| | | 24 Aug 2005 (otherwise) (SI 2005/2081) |
| 117 | (1)–(7) | 6 Aug 2004 (in so far as they confer certain powers and duties[1]) (SI 2004/2097) |
| | | 28 Sep 2004 (otherwise) (SI 2004/2202) |
| | (8) | 12 Jun 2006 (SSI 2006/268) |
| 118 | (1) | See Sch 6 below |
| | (2) | See Sch 7 below |
| | (3), (4) | 6 Aug 2004 (in so far as they confer certain powers and duties[1]) (SI 2004/2097) |
| | | 28 Sep 2004 (otherwise) (SI 2004/2202) |
| 119 | (1) | See Sch 8 below |
| | (2) | 20 Mar 2006 (SSI 2006/101) |
| 120 | | See Sch 9 below |
| 121–125 | | 13 May 2004 (RA) |
| Sch 1 | | 6 Aug 2004 (in so far as confers certain powers and duties[1]) (SI 2004/2097) |
| | | 10 May 2006 (E) (otherwise) (SI 2006/1061) |
| | | 30 Apr 2012 (W) (otherwise) (SI 2012/1100) |
| Sch 2 | paras 1, 2 | 1 Apr 2005 (E) (subject to savings[3]) (SI 2005/204) |
| | | *Not yet in force* (W) |
| | para 3 | 6 Aug 2004 (in so far as confers certain powers and duties[1]) (SI 2004/2097) |
| | | 1 Apr 2005 (E) (otherwise) (subject to savings[3]) (SI 2005/204) |
| | | *Not yet in force* (W) (otherwise) |
| | paras 4–8 | 1 Apr 2005 (E) (subject to savings[3]) (SI 2005/204) |
| | | *Not yet in force* (W) |
| Sch 3 | paras 1–5 | 7 Jun 2006 (SI 2006/1281) |
| | paras 6–8 | 6 Aug 2004 (in so far as they confer certain powers and duties[1]) (SI 2004/2097) |
| | | 7 Jun 2006 (otherwise) (SI 2006/1281) |
| | para 9 | 7 Jun 2006 (SI 2006/1281) |
| | paras 10–12 | 6 Aug 2004 (in so far as they confer certain powers and duties[1]) (SI 2004/2097) |
| | | 7 Jun 2006 (otherwise) (SI 2006/1281) |
| | paras 13–27 | 7 Jun 2006 (SI 2006/1281) |
| Sch 4 | | 7 Jun 2006 (SI 2006/1281) |
| Sch 5 | paras 1–5 | 12 Jun 2006 (SSI 2006/268) |
| | paras 6–8 | 20 Mar 2006 (for the purposes of enabling rules, regulations, development orders or other orders to be made) (SSI 2006/101) |
| | | 12 Jun 2006 (otherwise) (SSI 2006/268) |
| | para 9 | 12 Jun 2006 (SSI 2006/268) |
| | paras 10, 11 | 20 Mar 2006 (for the purposes of enabling rules, regulations, development orders or other orders to be made) (SSI 2006/101) |
| | | 12 Jun 2006 (otherwise) (SSI 2006/268) |
| | para 12 | 12 Jun 2006 (SSI 2006/268) |
| | para 13 | 20 Mar 2006 (for the purposes of enabling rules, regulations, development orders or other orders to be made) (SSI 2006/101) |

**Planning and Compulsory Purchase Act 2004 (c 5)**—*contd*

| | | |
|---|---|---|
| | | 12 Jun 2006 (otherwise) (SSI 2006/268) |
| | paras 14–26 | 12 Jun 2006 (SSI 2006/268) |
| Sch 6 | para 1 | See paras 2–18 below |
| | para 2 | 7 Jun 2006 (SI 2006/1281) |
| | para 3 | 6 Aug 2004 (in so far as confers certain powers and duties[1]) (SI 2004/2097) |
| | | 22 Feb 2010 (otherwise) (SI 2010/321) |
| | paras 4–6 | *Not yet in force* (para 5 repealed) |
| | para 7 | 31 Oct 2004 (SI 2004/2593) |
| | paras 8–13 | 28 Sep 2004 (E) (SI 2004/2202)[2] |
| | | 15 Oct 2005 (W) (SI 2005/2847) |
| | para 14 | 6 Aug 2004 (in so far as confers certain powers and duties[1]) (SI 2004/2097) |
| | | *Not yet in force* (otherwise) |
| | para 15 | 28 Sep 2004 (E) (SI 2004/2202) |
| | | 15 Oct 2005 (W) (SI 2005/2847) |
| | para 16(1) | See sub-paras (2)–(4) below |
| | para 16(2) | 6 Aug 2004 (in so far as confers certain powers and duties[1]) (SI 2004/2097) |
| | | 28 Sep 2004 (E) (otherwise) (SI 2004/2202)[2] |
| | | *Not yet in force* (W) (otherwise) |
| | para 16(3) | 6 Aug 2004 (in so far as confers certain powers and duties[1]) (SI 2004/2097) |
| | | *Not yet in force* (otherwise) |
| | para 16(4) | 6 Aug 2004 (in so far as confers certain powers and duties[1]) (SI 2004/2097) |
| | | 24 Aug 2005 (E) (otherwise) (SI 2005/2081)[6] |
| | | *Not yet in force* (W) (otherwise) |
| | paras 17, 18 | 28 Sep 2004 (E) (SI 2004/2202)[2] |
| | | 15 Oct 2005 (W) (SI 2005/2847) |
| | para 19 | See paras 20–26 below |
| | para 20 | 6 Aug 2004 (in so far as confers certain powers and duties[1]) (SI 2004/2097) |
| | | 28 Sep 2004 (otherwise) (SI 2004/2202) |
| | paras 21, 22 | 28 Sep 2004 (E) (SI 2004/2202) |
| | | 15 Oct 2005 (W) (SI 2005/2847) |
| | paras 23, 24 | 6 Aug 2004 (in so far as they confer certain powers and duties[1]) (SI 2004/2097) |
| | | 28 Sep 2004 (otherwise) (SI 2004/2202) |
| | para 25 | 28 Sep 2004 (E) (SI 2004/2202) |
| | | 15 Oct 2005 (W) (SI 2005/2847) |
| | para 26 | 6 Aug 2004 (in so far as confers certain powers and duties[1]) (SI 2004/2097) |
| | | 28 Sep 2004 (otherwise) (SI 2004/2202) |
| | para 27 | 6 Aug 2004 (in so far as confers certain powers and duties[1]) (SI 2004/2097) |
| | | *Not yet in force* (otherwise) |
| Sch 7 | para 1 | *Not yet in force* |
| | paras 2, 3 | 28 Sep 2004 (E) (SI 2004/2202) |
| | | 15 Oct 2005 (W) (SI 2005/2847) |
| | paras 4, 5 | 31 Oct 2004 (SI 2004/2593) |
| | para 6 | 28 Sep 2004 (E) (SI 2004/2202) |
| | para 7 | 31 Oct 2004 (SI 2004/2593) |
| | para 8 | 28 Sep 2004 (E) (SI 2004/2202) |
| | para 9 | 31 Oct 2004 (SI 2004/2593) |
| | para 10(1)–(6) | 31 Oct 2004 (SI 2004/2593) |
| | para 10(7) | 13 Jul 2004 (s 121(6)) |
| | para 11(1)–(3) | 28 Sep 2004 (E) (SI 2004/2202) |
| | | 15 Oct 2005 (W) (SI 2005/2847) |

**Planning and Compulsory Purchase Act 2004 (c 5)**—*contd*

| | | |
|---|---|---|
| | para 11(4), (5) | 31 Oct 2004 (SI 2004/2593) |
| | paras 12–15 | 31 Oct 2004 (SI 2004/2593) |
| | paras 16, 17 | 28 Sep 2004 (E) (SI 2004/2202)[2] |
| | | 15 Oct 2005 (W) (SI 2005/2847) |
| | para 18 | 31 Oct 2004 (SI 2004/2593) |
| | para 19(1) | See sub-paras (2)–(4) below |
| | para 19(2) | 6 Aug 2004 (in so far as confers certain powers and duties[1]) (SI 2004/2097) |
| | | 28 Sep 2004 (E) (otherwise) (SI 2004/2202) |
| | | 15 Oct 2005 (W) (otherwise) (SI 2005/2847) |
| | para 19(3), (4) | 6 Aug 2004 (in so far as they confer certain powers and duties[1]) (SI 2004/2097) |
| | | *Not yet in force* (otherwise) |
| | para 20 | 12 Jun 2006 (SSI 2006/268) |
| | para 21 | 31 Oct 2004 (SI 2004/2593) |
| | para 22 | 28 Sep 2004 (E) (SI 2004/2202) |
| | para 23 | 28 Sep 2004 (E) (SI 2004/2202) |
| | | 15 Oct 2005 (W) (SI 2005/2847) |
| Sch 8 | paras 1–3 | 28 Sep 2004 (E) (SI 2004/2202) |
| | | *Not yet in force* (W) |
| | para 4 | 6 Aug 2004 (in so far as confers certain powers and duties[1]) (SI 2004/2097) |
| | | 28 Sep 2004 (E) (otherwise) (SI 2004/2202) |
| | | *Not yet in force* (W) (otherwise) |
| | paras 5–8 | 28 Sep 2004 (E) (SI 2004/2202) |
| | | *Not yet in force* (W) |
| | para 9 | 6 Aug 2004 (in so far as confers certain powers and duties[1]) (SI 2004/2097) |
| | | 28 Sep 2004 (E) (otherwise) (SI 2004/2202) |
| | | *Not yet in force* (W) (otherwise) |
| | paras 10–16 | 28 Sep 2004 (E) (SI 2004/2202) |
| | | *Not yet in force* (W) |
| | paras 17, 18 | 6 Aug 2004 (in so far as they confer certain powers and duties[1]) (SI 2004/2097) |
| | | 28 Sep 2004 (E) (otherwise) (SI 2004/2202) |
| | | *Not yet in force* (W) (otherwise) |
| | para 19 | 28 Sep 2004 (E) (SI 2004/2202) |
| | | *Not yet in force* (W) |
| Sch 9 | | 6 Aug 2004 (in so far as confers certain powers and duties[1]) (SI 2004/2097), except repeals of or in— |
| | | Planning (Hazardous Substances) (Scotland) Act 1997; |
| | | Planning (Listed Buildings and Conservation Areas) (Scotland) Act 1997; |
| | | Town and Country Planning (Scotland) Act 1997 |
| | | 28 Sep 2004 (repeals of or in Planning (Listed Buildings and Conservation Areas) Act 1990, ss 10(3), 67, 91) (SI 2004/2202) |
| | | 28 Sep 2004 (E) (SI 2004/2202), repeals of or in— |
| | | Greater London Council (General Powers) Act 1973; |
| | | Town and Country Planning Act 1990, Pt 2 (ie ss 10–54A, Sch 2), ss 284, 287, 303, 303A, Schs 1, 2, 13[2]; |
| | | Planning and Compensation Act 1991, Sch 4[2]; |
| | | Local Government Act 1992; |
| | | Environment Act 1995; |
| | | Countryside and Rights of Way Act 2000 |
| | | 31 Oct 2004 (SI 2004/2593), repeals of or in— |
| | | Land Compensation Act 1973; |
| | | Welsh Development Agency Act 1975; |
| | | Highways Act 1980; |
| | | Local Government, Planning and Land Act 1980; |

**Planning and Compulsory Purchase Act 2004 (c 5)**—*contd*

Housing Act 1988;

Town and Country Planning Act 1990, ss 226, 245;

Planning and Compensation Act 1991, Sch 18;

Leasehold Reform, Housing and Urban Development Act 1993;

Regional Development Agencies Act 1998

15 Oct 2005 (W) (SI 2005/2847), repeals of or in—

Town and Country Planning Act 1990, Pt 2 (ie ss 10–54A,
Sch 2), ss 284(1)(a), 287, 303(6), 303A, Sch 2, Pt 3, Sch 13[7];

Planning and Compensation Act 1991, Sch 4;

Local Government Act 1992;

Environment Act 1995;

Countryside and Rights of Way Act 2000

7 Jun 2006 (SI 2006/1281), repeals of or in—

Planning (Listed Buildings and Conservation Areas) Act 1990,
ss 83, 84, 92(2)(a);

Planning (Hazardous Substances) Act 1990;

Town and Country Planning Act 1990, ss 55(2)(b), 293(4),
294–297, 298(1), (2), 299–301

12 Jun 2006 (SSI 2006/268), repeals of or in—

Planning (Listed Buildings and Conservation Areas) (Scotland)
Act 1997;

Planning (Hazardous Substances) (Scotland) Act 1997;

Town and Country Planning (Scotland) Act 1997

10 Aug 2006 (E); 30 Jun 2007 (W) (repeal of Town and Country
Planning Act 1990, s 76) (SI 2006/1061; SI 2007/1369)

*Not yet in force* (except in so far as confers certain powers and
duties[1]) repeals of or in—

Planning (Listed Buildings and Conservation Areas) Act 1990,
s 10(2);

Planning and Compensation Act 1991, s 17;

Town and Country Planning Act 1990, ss 73, 83, 106–106B,
220, Sch 1 (W), Sch 7

*Never in force* (superseded) (W) (repeals of Town and Country
Planning Act 1990, ss 12, 21, 23B)

[1]  These provisions are brought into force in so far as they confer on the Secretary of State, the
Lord Chancellor, the National Assembly for Wales or the Scottish Ministers a power or impose a duty
to make or to make provision by rules, regulations, development order or other order or to give
directions, or make provision with respect to the exercise of any such power or performance of such
duty

[2]  For savings and transitional provisions, see SI 2004/2202, art 4

[3]  For savings, see SI 2005/204, art 4

[4]  For transitional provisions, see SI 2004/1814, art 3

[5]  For transitional provisions, see SI 2005/1229, art 4 (revoked by SI 2005/2722, art 4)

[6]  For savings, see SI 2005/2081, art 4

[7]  For transitional provisions and savings, see SI 2005/2722, arts 5–7 and SI 2005/2847, art 3

[8]  For a saving, see SI 2007/1369, art 3

[9]  For a saving, see SI 2015/340, art 4

---

**Primary Medical Services (Scotland) Act 2004 (asp 1)**

*RA:* 27 Jan 2004

*Commencement provisions:* s 9(1), (2); Primary Medical Services (Scotland) Act 2004 (Commencement)
Order 2004, SSI 2004/58

**Primary Medical Services (Scotland) Act 2004 (asp 1)**—*contd*

| | | |
|---|---|---|
| 1 | (1), (2) | 13 Feb 2004 (for the purpose of enabling arrangements and regulations to be made under s 2C(2), (3), (5)–(7) of the National Health Service (Scotland) Act 1978) (SSI 2004/58) |
| | | 1 Apr 2004 (otherwise) (SSI 2004/58) |
| | (3) | 1 Apr 2004 (SSI 2004/58) |
| 2 | (1)–(4) | 13 Feb 2004 (for the purpose of making an agreement under s 17C of the National Health Service (Scotland) Act 1978 and regulations under ss 17D(1)(b)(i) and (ii), (1A), (1B), (3) and 17E of that Act) (SSI 2004/58) |
| | | 1 Apr 2004 (otherwise) (SSI 2004/58) |
| | (5) | 1 Apr 2004 (SSI 2004/58) |
| 3 | | 1 Apr 2004 (SSI 2004/58) |
| 4 | | 13 Feb 2004 (for the purpose of enabling a Health Board to make and enter into a general medical services contract under s 17J of the National Health Service (Scotland) Act 1978, giving directions under s 17M and making regulations under ss 17K, 17L and 17O and giving directions and making regulations under s 17N of that Act) (SSI 2004/58) |
| | | 1 Apr 2004 (otherwise) (SSI 2004/58) |
| 5 | | 13 Feb 2004 (for the purpose of making regulations under ss 17P and 29(8)(a) of the National Health Service (Scotland) Act 1978) (SSI 2004/58) |
| | | 1 Apr 2004 (otherwise) (SSI 2004/58) |
| 6 | | 1 Apr 2004 (SSI 2004/58) |
| 7 | | 27 Jan 2004 (RA) |
| 8 | | See Schedule below |
| 9 | | 27 Jan 2004 (RA) |
| Schedule | para 1(1) | 13 Feb 2004 (for the purpose of making regulations under s 35 of the National Health Service (Scotland) Act 1978) (SSI 2004/58) |
| | | 1 Apr 2004 (otherwise) (SSI 2004/58) |
| | para 1(2)–(13) | 1 Apr 2004 (SSI 2004/58) |
| | para 1(14) | 13 Feb 2004 (for the purpose of making regulations under s 35 of the National Health Service (Scotland) Act 1978) (SSI 2004/58) |
| | | 1 Apr 2004 (otherwise) (SSI 2004/58) |
| | para 1(15)–(17) | 1 Apr 2004 (SSI 2004/58) |
| | paras 2–5 | 1 Apr 2004 (SSI 2004/58) |

**Public Audit (Wales) Act 2004 (c 23)**

*RA:* 16 Sep 2004

*Commencement provisions:* s 73; Public Audit (Wales) Act 2004 (Commencement No 1) Order 2005, SI 2005/71; Public Audit (Wales) Act 2004 (Commencement No 2 and Transitional Provisions and Savings) Order 2005, SI 2005/558; Public Audit (Wales) Act 2004 (Commencement No 3) Order 2005, SI 2005/1911

| | | |
|---|---|---|
| 1–6 | | 1 Apr 2005 (SI 2005/558) |
| 7 | | 1 Apr 2005 (SI 2005/558)[1] |
| 8–11 | | 1 Apr 2005 (SI 2005/558) |
| 12 | | 31 Jan 2005 (SI 2005/71) |
| 13–15 | | 1 Apr 2005 (SI 2005/558) |
| 16 | | 31 Jan 2005 (SI 2005/71) |
| 17–19 | | 1 Apr 2005 (SI 2005/558) |
| 20 | (1)–(3) | 31 Jan 2005 (for the purpose of the prescription of scales of fees for the audit of accounts prepared in respect of financial years beginning on or after 1 Apr 2005) (SI 2005/71) |
| | (4)–(6) | 1 Apr 2005 (SI 2005/558) |
| 21 | (1), (2) | 31 Jan 2005 (SI 2005/71) |

**Public Audit (Wales) Act 2004 (c 23)**—*contd*

|  |  |  |
|---|---|---|
|  | (3), (4) | 1 Apr 2005 (SI 2005/558) |
|  | (5) | 31 Jan 2005 (SI 2005/71) |
| 22–38 |  | 1 Apr 2005 (SI 2005/558) |
| 39 |  | 31 Jan 2005 (for the purpose of consulting on, and making, regulations in relation to accounts or statements of accounts prepared in respect of financial years beginning on or after 1 Apr 2005) (SI 2005/71) |
|  |  | 1 Apr 2005 (otherwise, in relation to accounts or statements of accounts prepared in respect of a financial year beginning on or after 1 Apr 2005) (SI 2005/558) |
| 40–49 |  | 1 Apr 2005 (SI 2005/558) |
| 50 |  | See Sch 1 below |
| 51–53 |  | 1 Apr 2005 (SI 2005/558) |
| 54 | (1)–(5) | 20 Jul 2005 (SI 2005/1911) |
|  | (6)–(8) | 31 Jan 2005 (SI 2005/71) |
| 55–57 |  | 1 Apr 2005 (SI 2005/558) |
| 58, 59 |  | 31 Jan 2005 (SI 2005/71) |
| 60–67 |  | 1 Apr 2005 (SI 2005/558) |
| 68 |  | 31 Jan 2005 (SI 2005/71) |
| 69 |  | 1 Apr 2005 (SI 2005/558)[1] |
| 70 |  | 1 Apr 2005 (SI 2005/558) |
| 71 |  | 16 Sep 2004 (RA) |
| 72 |  | See Sch 4 below |
| 73–75 |  | 16 Sep 2004 (RA) |
| Sch 1 | para 1 | See paras 2–17 below |
|  | paras 2–6 | 1 Apr 2005 (SI 2005/558) |
|  | para 7 | 31 Jan 2005 (in so far as it inserts Local Government Act 1999, s 8A) (SI 2005/71) |
|  |  | 1 Apr 2005 (otherwise) (SI 2005/558) |
|  | paras 8–17 | 1 Apr 2005 (SI 2005/558) |
| Sch 2 |  | 1 Apr 2005 (SI 2005/558)[1] |
| Sch 3 |  | 31 Jan 2005 (SI 2005/71) |
| Sch 4 |  | 1 Apr 2005 (SI 2005/558)[1] |

[1]  For savings and transitional provisions, see SI 2005/558, art 3, Sch 2

---

**School Education (Ministerial Powers and Independent Schools) (Scotland) Act 2004 (asp 12)**

*RA:* 12 Nov 2004

*Commencement provisions:* s 9; School Education (Ministerial Powers and Independent Schools) (Scotland) Act 2004 (Commencement No 1) Order 2005, SSI 2005/10; School Education (Ministerial Powers and Independent Schools) (Scotland) Act 2004 (Commencement No 2 and Transitional Provisions) Order 2005, SSI 2005/570[1]

|  |  |  |
|---|---|---|
| 1, 2 |  | 31 Jan 2005 (SSI 2005/10) |
| 3–7 |  | 31 Dec 2005 (SSI 2005/570) |
| 8 | (1) | See Sch 1 below |
|  | (2) | 31 Dec 2005 (SSI 2005/570) |
| 9 |  | 12 Nov 2004 (RA) |
| Sch 1 | para 1(1)–(7) | 31 Dec 2005 (SSI 2005/570) |
|  | para 1(8)(a) | 31 Dec 2005 (SSI 2005/570) |
|  | para 1(8)(b), (c) | 31 Jan 2005 (SSI 2005/10) |
|  | para 1(8)(d) | 31 Dec 2005 (SSI 2005/570) |
|  | para 2 | 31 Jan 2005 (SSI 2005/10) |
| Sch 2 |  | 31 Dec 2005 (SSI 2005/570) |

**School Education (Ministerial Powers and Independent Schools) (Scotland) Act 2004 (asp 12)**—*contd*

1    For transitional provisions, see SSI 2005/570, art 3

---

**Scottish Parliament (Constituencies) Act 2004 (c 13)**

*RA:* 22 Jul 2004

Whole Act in force 22 Jul 2004 (RA)

---

**Statute Law (Repeals) Act 2004 (c 14)**

*RA:* 22 Jul 2004

Whole Act in force 22 Jul 2004 (RA)

---

**Stirling-Alloa-Kincardine Railway and Linked Improvements (Scotland) Act 2004 (asp 10)**

*RA:* 10 Aug 2004

Whole Act in force 10 Aug 2004 (RA)

---

**Sustainable and Secure Buildings Act 2004 (c 22)**

*RA:* 16 Sep 2004

*Commencement provisions:* s 11; Sustainable and Secure Buildings Act 2004 (Commencement No 1) Order 2006, SI 2006/224

| | | |
|---|---|---|
| 1 | | 16 Nov 2004 (s 11(4)) |
| 2 | | 1 Feb 2006 (SI 2006/224) |
| 3 | (1)–(7) | 16 Nov 2004 (s 11(4)) |
| | (8), (9) | *Not yet in force* |
| 4 | (1)–(3) | 16 Nov 2004 (s 11(4)) |
| | (4) | *Not yet in force* |
| | (5) | 16 Nov 2004 (s 11(4)) |
| 5 | | *Not yet in force* |
| 6 | | 16 Nov 2004 (s 11(4)) |
| 7 | | 1 Feb 2006 (for the purpose only of conferring power to make regulations) (SI 2006/224) |
| | | *Not yet in force* (otherwise) |
| 8, 9 | | 1 Feb 2006 (SI 2006/224) |
| 10 | | 16 Nov 2004 (s 11(4)) |
| 11 | (1) | 16 Nov 2004 (s 11(4)) |
| | (2) | See Schedule below |
| | (3)–(5) | 16 Nov 2004 (s 11(4)) |
| Schedule | | *Not yet in force* |

---

**Tenements (Scotland) Act 2004 (asp 11)**

*RA:* 22 Oct 2004

*Commencement provisions:* s 34; Tenements (Scotland) Act 2004 (Commencement No 1) Order 2004, SSI 2004/487; Tenements (Scotland) Act 2004 (Commencement No 2) Order 2007, SSI 2007/17

| | | |
|---|---|---|
| 1–12 | | 28 Nov 2004 (SSI 2004/487) |
| 13 | (1)–(5) | 28 Nov 2004 (SSI 2004/487) |
| | (6) | 10 Nov 2004 (SSI 2004/487) |

**Tenements (Scotland) Act 2004 (asp 11)**—*contd*

|          | (7)        | 28 Nov 2004 (SSI 2004/487)  |
|----------|------------|------------------------------|
| 14–17    |            | 28 Nov 2004 (SSI 2004/487)  |
| 18       |            | 24 Jan 2007 (SSI 2007/17)   |
| 19–24    |            | 28 Nov 2004 (SSI 2004/487)  |
| 25       |            | 23 Oct 2004 (s 34(3))       |
| 26–30    |            | 28 Nov 2004 (SSI 2004/487)  |
| 31, 32   |            | 10 Nov 2004 (SSI 2004/487)  |
| 33       |            | 28 Nov 2004 (SSI 2004/487)  |
| 34       |            | 22 Oct 2004 (RA)            |
| Schs 1–3 |            | 28 Nov 2004 (SSI 2004/487)  |
| Sch 4    |            | 23 Oct 2004 (s 34(3))       |

---

**Traffic Management Act 2004 (c 18)**

*RA:* 22 Jul 2004

*Commencement provisions:* s 99; Traffic Management Act 2004 (Commencement No 1 and Transitional Provision) (England) Order 2004, SI 2004/2380; Traffic Management Act 2004 (Commencement No 2) (England) Order 2004, SI 2004/3110; Traffic Management Act 2004 (Commencement No 3) (England) Order 2006, SI 2006/1736; Traffic Management Act 2004 (Commencement No 1) (Wales) Order 2006, SI 2006/2826; Traffic Management Act 2004 (Commencement No 4 and Transitional Provisions) (England) Order 2007, SI 2007/1890; Traffic Management Act 2004 (Commencement No 5 and Transitional Provisions) (England) Order 2007, SI 2007/2053, as amended by SI 2008/757, SI 2011/2938, SI 2022/66; Traffic Management Act 2004 (Commencement No 2 and Transitional Provisions) (Wales) Order 2007, SI 2007/3174; Traffic Management Act 2004 (Commencement No 6) (England) Order 2007, SI 2007/3184; Traffic Management Act 2004 (Commencement No 3) (Wales) Order 2009, SI 2009/1095; Traffic Management Act 2004 (Commencement No 7) (England) Order 2013, SI 2013/2408; Traffic Management Act 2004 (Commencement No 8) (England) Order 2015, SI 2015/199; Traffic Management Act 2004 (Commencement No 9) (England) Order 2020, SI 2020/659; Traffic Management Act 2004 (Commencement No 10 and Savings and Transitional Provisions) (England) Order 2022, SI 2022/66; Traffic Management Act 2004 (Commencement No 11) (England) Order 2022, SI 2022/649

| 1–4    |           | 4 Oct 2004 (E) (SI 2004/2380)   |
|--------|-----------|----------------------------------|
|        |           | 1 May 2009 (W) (SI 2009/1095)   |
| 5      | (1)–(3)   | 4 Oct 2004 (E) (SI 2004/2380)   |
|        |           | 1 May 2009 (W) (SI 2009/1095)   |
|        | (4), (5)  | 4 Oct 2004 (E) (SI 2004/2380)   |
|        |           | 26 Oct 2006 (W) (SI 2006/2826)  |
|        | (6)       | 4 Oct 2004 (E) (SI 2004/2380)   |
|        |           | 1 May 2009 (W) (SI 2009/1095)   |
| 6–9    |           | 4 Oct 2004 (E) (SI 2004/2380)   |
|        |           | 1 May 2009 (W) (SI 2009/1095)   |
| 10     |           | 4 Oct 2004 (E) (SI 2004/2380)   |
|        |           | 26 Oct 2006 (W) (SI 2006/2826)  |
| 11–15  |           | 4 Oct 2004 (E) (SI 2004/2380)   |
|        |           | 1 May 2009 (W) (SI 2009/1095)   |
| 16–31  |           | 4 Jan 2005 (E) (SI 2004/3110)   |
|        |           | 26 Oct 2006 (W) (SI 2006/2826)  |
| 32     |           | 1 Dec 2007 (E) (SI 2007/3184)   |
|        |           | 31 Mar 2008 (W) (SI 2007/3174)  |
| 33–36  |           | 1 Apr 2008 (E) (SI 2007/3184)   |
|        |           | 31 Mar 2008 (W) (SI 2007/3174)  |
| 37     |           | 1 Dec 2007 (E) (SI 2007/3184)   |
|        |           | 31 Mar 2008 (W) (SI 2007/3174)  |
| 38     |           | 1 Apr 2008 (E) (SI 2007/3184)   |
|        |           | 31 Mar 2008 (W) (SI 2007/3174)  |
| 39     |           | 1 Dec 2007 (E) (SI 2007/3184)   |
|        |           | 31 Mar 2008 (W) (SI 2007/3174)  |
| 40     | (1), (2)  | 4 Oct 2004 (E) (SI 2004/2380)[1] |

**Traffic Management Act 2004 (c 18)**—*contd*

|   |   |   |
|---|---|---|
| | | 26 Nov 2007 (W) (SI 2007/3174)[4] |
| | (3) | 4 Oct 2004 (E) (except words "or (4A)" in the substituted New Roads and Street Works Act 1991, s 70(6)(a)) (SI 2004/2380)[1] |
| | | 26 Nov 2007 (W) (except words "or (4A)" in the substituted New Roads and Street Works Act 1991, s 70(6)(a)) (SI 2007/3174)[4] |
| | | 1 Apr 2008 (otherwise) (SI 2007/1890; SI 2007/3174) |
| | (4), (5) | 4 Oct 2004 (E) (SI 2004/2380)[1] |
| | | 26 Nov 2007 (W) (SI 2007/3174) |
| 41 | (1) | 29 Jun 2007 (E) (in so far as confers power to make orders) (SI 2007/1890) |
| | | 26 Nov 2007 (W) (in so far as confers power to make orders) (SI 2007/3174) |
| | | 12 May 2008 (otherwise) (SI 2007/1890; SI 2007/3174)[2, 4] |
| | (2) | 12 May 2008 (SI 2007/1890; SI 2007/3174) |
| | (3) | See Schs 2, 3 below |
| 42 | | 29 Jun 2007 (E) (in so far as confers power to make regulations) (SI 2007/1890) |
| | | 26 Nov 2007 (W) (in so far as confers power to make regulations) (SI 2007/3174) |
| | | *Not yet in force* (otherwise) |
| 43 | (1) | 4 Jan 2005 (E) (SI 2004/3110) |
| | | 26 Nov 2007 (W) (SI 2007/3174) |
| | (2) | 4 Jan 2005 (E) (SI 2004/3110) |
| | | 1 Apr 2008 (W) (SI 2007/3174) |
| | (3) | 1 Apr 2008 (E) (SI 2007/1890)[2] |
| | | 1 Apr 2008 (W) (SI 2007/3174)[4] |
| | (4) | 4 Jan 2005 (E) (SI 2004/3110) |
| | | 1 Apr 2008 (W) (SI 2007/3174) |
| 44 | | 29 Jun 2007 (E) (in so far as confers power (a) to make regulations under the New Roads and Street Works Act 1991, s 56A(4), and (b) to issue or approve, under s 56A(8), a code of practice for the purposes of s 56A) (SI 2007/1890) |
| | | 26 Nov 2007 (W) (in so far as confers power (a) to make regulations under the New Roads and Street Works Act 1991, s 56A(4), and (b) to issue or approve, under s 56A(8), a code of practice for the purposes of s 56A) (SI 2007/3174) |
| | | 1 Apr 2008 (otherwise) (SI 2007/1890; SI 2007/3174)[2, 4] |
| 45 | (1) | 29 Jun 2020 (E) (SI 2020/659) |
| | | *Not yet in force* (W) |
| | (2) | *Not yet in force* |
| | (3), (4) | 29 Jun 2020 (E) (SI 2020/659) |
| | | *Not yet in force* (W) |
| 46–48 | | *Not yet in force* |
| 49 | | 29 Jun 2007 (E) (in so far as confers power to make regulations) (SI 2007/1890) |
| | | 26 Nov 2007 (W) (in so far as confers power to make regulations) (SI 2007/3174) |
| | | 1 Apr 2008 (otherwise) (SI 2007/1890; SI 2007/3174)[2, 4] |
| 50 | | *Not yet in force* |
| 51 | (1)–(3) | 29 Jun 2007 (E) (in so far as they confer power to make regulations) (SI 2007/1890)[2] |
| | | 26 Nov 2007 (W) (in so far as they confer power to make regulations) (SI 2007/3174)[4] |
| | | 1 Apr 2008 (otherwise) (SI 2007/1890; SI 2007/3174)[2, 4] |
| | (4) | 29 Jun 2007 (E) (SI 2007/1890)[2] |
| | | 26 Nov 2007 (W) (SI 2007/3174)[4] |
| | (5) | 29 Jun 2007 (E) (in so far as confers power to make regulations) (SI 2007/1890) |
| | | 26 Nov 2007 (W) (in so far as confers power to make regulations) (SI 2007/3174) |

**Traffic Management Act 2004 (c 18)**—*contd*

|  |  |  |
|---|---|---|
|  |  | 1 Apr 2008 (otherwise) (SI 2007/1890; SI 2007/3174)[2, 4] |
|  | (6) | 1 Apr 2008 (SI 2007/1890; SI 2007/3174)[2, 4] |
|  | (7)–(9) | 29 Jun 2007 (E) (in so far as they confer power to make regulations) (SI 2007/1890) |
|  |  | 26 Nov 2007 (W) (in so far as they confer power to make regulations) (SI 2007/3174) |
|  |  | 1 Apr 2008 (otherwise) (SI 2007/1890; SI 2007/3174)[2, 4] |
| 52 | (1) | 29 Jun 2007 (E) (in so far as confers power to make regulations) (SI 2007/1890) |
|  |  | 26 Nov 2007 (W) (in so far as confers power to make regulations) (SI 2007/3174) |
|  |  | 1 Apr 2008 (otherwise) (SI 2007/1890; SI 2007/3174)[2, 4] |
|  | (2) | See Sch 4 below |
|  | (3) | 1 Apr 2008 (SI 2007/1890; SI 2007/3174) |
|  | (4), (5) | 29 Jun 2007 (in so far as they confer power to make regulations) (SI 2007/1890) |
|  |  | 26 Nov 2007 (W) (in so far as they confer power to make regulations) (SI 2007/3174) |
|  |  | 1 Apr 2008 (otherwise) (SI 2007/1890; SI 2007/3174) |
|  | (6), (7) | 1 Apr 2008 (SI 2007/1890; SI 2007/3174) |
| 53 |  | *Not yet in force* |
| 54 |  | 29 Jun 2007 (E) (in so far as confers power to make regulations) (SI 2007/1890) |
|  |  | 26 Nov 2007 (W) (in so far as confers power to make regulations) (SI 2007/3174) |
|  |  | 1 Apr 2008 (otherwise) (SI 2007/1890; SI 2007/3174)[2, 4] |
| 55–57 |  | *Not yet in force* |
| 58 | (1) | *Not yet in force* |
|  | (2) | 17 Jun 2022 (except words ", or pay the prescribed fee," in New Roads and Street Works Act 1991, s 75(6)) (E) (SI 2022/649) |
|  |  | *Not yet in force* (exception noted above) (E) |
|  |  | *Not yet in force* (W) |
| 59 |  | 6 Apr 2015 (E) (SI 2015/199) |
|  |  | *Not yet in force* (W) |
| 60–63 |  | 4 Oct 2004 (E) (SI 2004/2380) |
| 64 | (1), (2) | *Not yet in force* |
|  | (3) | See Schs 5, 6 below |
|  | (4), (5) | *Not yet in force* |
| 65–70 |  | *Not yet in force* |
| 71 |  | 26 Nov 2007 (W) (SI 2007/3174) |
|  |  | 1 Oct 2013 (E) (SI 2013/2408) |
| 72, 73 |  | 26 Oct 2006 (W) (SI 2006/2826) |
|  |  | 23 Jul 2007 (E) (SI 2007/2053)[3] |
| 74 |  | See Sch 8 below |
| 75 |  | 26 Oct 2006 (W) (SI 2006/2826) |
|  |  | 31 Mar 2008 (E) (SI 2007/2053)[3] |
| 76 |  | 26 Oct 2006 (W) (SI 2006/2826) |
|  |  | 23 Jul 2007 (E) (SI 2007/2053)[3] |
| 77 |  | See Sch 9 below |
| 78–83 |  | 26 Oct 2006 (W) (SI 2006/2826) |
|  |  | 23 Jul 2007 (E) (SI 2007/2053)[3] |
| 84 |  | See Sch 10 below |
| 85, 86 |  | 26 Oct 2006 (W) (SI 2006/2826) |
|  |  | 31 Mar 2008 (E) (SI 2007/2053)[3] |
| 87–90 |  | 26 Oct 2006 (W) (SI 2006/2826) |
|  |  | 23 Jul 2007 (E) (SI 2007/2053)[3] |
| 91 |  | See Sch 11 below |
| 92, 93 |  | 26 Oct 2006 (W) (SI 2006/2826) |
|  |  | 23 Jul 2007 (E) (SI 2007/2053)[3] |

**Traffic Management Act 2004 (c 18)**—*contd*

| | | |
|---|---|---|
| 94 | | 29 Sep 2006 (E) (SI 2006/1736) |
| | | 26 Oct 2006 (W) (SI 2006/2826) |
| 95 | | 4 Oct 2004 (E) (SI 2004/2380) |
| | | 26 Oct 2006 (W) (SI 2006/2826) |
| 96 | | 26 Oct 2006 (W) (SI 2006/2826) |
| | | 29 Jun 2007 (E) (SI 2007/1890) |
| 97 | | 4 Oct 2004 (E) (SI 2004/2380) |
| | | *Not yet in force* (W) |
| 98 | | See Sch 12 below |
| 99, 100 | | 22 Jul 2004 (RA) |
| Sch 1 | | 4 Oct 2004 (E) (SI 2004/2380) |
| | | 26 Nov 2007 (W) (SI 2007/3174)[4] |
| Sch 2 | | 12 May 2008 (SI 2007/1890; SI 2007/3174)[2, 4] |
| Sch 3 | | 29 Jun 2007 (E) (in so far as confers power to make regulations) (SI 2007/1890) |
| | | 26 Nov 2007 (W) (in so far as confers power to make orders) (SI 2007/3174) |
| | | 12 May 2008 (otherwise) (SI 2007/1890; SI 2007/3174) |
| Sch 4 | | 29 Jun 2007 (E) (in so far as confers power to make regulations) (SI 2007/1890) |
| | | 26 Nov 2007 (W) (in so far as confers power to make orders) (SI 2007/3174) |
| | | 1 Apr 2008 (otherwise) (SI 2007/1890; SI 2007/3174)[2, 4] |
| Schs 5, 6 | | *Not yet in force* |
| Sch 7[5] | para 1 | 23 Jul 2007 (E) (SI 2007/2053)[3] |
| | | 31 Mar 2008 (W) (SI 2007/3174) |
| | paras 2, 3 | 23 Jul 2007 (SI 2007/2053)[3] |
| | paras 4, 5(1) | 23 Jul 2007 (E) (SI 2007/2053)[3] |
| | | 31 Mar 2008 (W) (SI 2007/3174) |
| | para 5(2) | 23 Jul 2007 (SI 2007/2053)[3] |
| | paras 5(3), 6 | 23 Jul 2007 (E) (SI 2007/2053)[3] |
| | | 31 Mar 2008 (W) (SI 2007/3174) |
| | para 7 | 23 Jul 2007 (SI 2007/2053)[3] |
| | para 8(1), (2) | 23 Jul 2007 (E) (SI 2007/2053)[3] |
| | | 31 Mar 2008 (W) (SI 2007/3174) |
| | para 8(3) | 23 Jul 2007 (SI 2007/2053)[3] |
| | paras 8(4), 9, 10 | 23 Jul 2007 (E) (SI 2007/2053)[3] |
| | | 31 Mar 2008 (W) (SI 2007/3174) |
| Sch 8[5] | paras 1–3 | 31 Mar 2008 (SI 2007/2053)[3] |
| | paras 4–7 | *Not yet in force* |
| | para 8(1) | 31 Mar 2008 (SI 2007/2053[3]; SI 2007/3174) |
| | para 8(2)(a) | 31 Mar 2008 (SI 2007/2053)[3] |
| | para 8(2)(b) | 31 Mar 2008 (SI 2007/2053[3]; SI 2007/3174) |
| | para 8(2)(c)–(e) | 31 Mar 2008 (SI 2007/2053)[3] |
| | para 8(3)–(5) | 31 Mar 2008 (SI 2007/2053[3]; SI 2007/3174) |
| | paras 9, 10(1), (2) | 31 Mar 2008 (W) (SI 2007/3174) |
| | | 31 May 2022 (E) (SI 2022/66)[6] |
| | para 10(3)(a) | 31 May 2022 (SI 2022/66)[6] |
| | para 10(3)(b) | 31 Mar 2008 (SI 2007/3174) |
| | para 10(3)(c)–(e) | 31 May 2022 (E) (SI 2022/66)[6] |
| | | *Not yet in force* (W) |
| | para 10(4), (5) | 31 Mar 2008 (W) (SI 2007/3174) |
| | | 31 May 2022 (E) (SI 2022/66)[6] |
| Sch 9[5] | para 1 | 23 Jul 2007 (E) (SI 2007/2053)[3] |
| | | 26 Nov 2007 (W) (SI 2007/3174) |
| | paras 2–6 | 23 Jul 2007 (SI 2007/2053)[3] |
| | paras 7–9 | 23 Jul 2007 (E) (SI 2007/2053)[3] |
| | | 26 Nov 2007 (W) (SI 2007/3174) |
| Sch 10[5] | paras 1, 2 | 31 Mar 2008 (SI 2007/2053)[3] |

**Traffic Management Act 2004 (c 18)**—*contd*

|  |  |  |
|---|---|---|
| | para 3(1), (2) | 31 Mar 2008 (SI 2007/2053³; SI 2007/3174) |
| | para 3(3)(a) | 31 Mar 2008 (SI 2007/2053)³ |
| | para 3(3)(b) | 31 Mar 2008 (SI 2007/2053³; SI 2007/3174) |
| | para 3(3)(c)–(e) | 31 Mar 2008 (SI 2007/2053)³ |
| | para 3(4), (5) | 31 Mar 2008 (SI 2007/2053³; SI 2007/3174) |
| Sch 11⁵ | paras 1, 2 | 31 Mar 2008 (SI 2007/2053³; SI 2007/3174) |
| | para 3 | 23 Jul 2007 (E) (to the extent that it inserts Road Traffic Regulation Act 1984, s 101B) (SI 2007/2053)³ |
| | | 31 Mar 2008 (E) (otherwise) (SI 2007/2053)³ |
| | | 31 Mar 2008 (W) (SI 2007/3174) |
| | paras 4, 5 | 31 Mar 2008 (SI 2007/2053³; SI 2007/3174) |
| | paras 6, 7 | 31 Mar 2008 (SI 2007/2053)³ |
| Sch 12 | Pt 1 | 31 Mar 2008 (E) (SI 2007/2053), repeals of or in— |

Road Traffic Regulation Act 1984;
Road Traffic Act 1991, ss 43, 65–67, 69–74A, 76–79, Schs 3, 6;
Local Government Wales Act 1994;
London Local Authorities Act 1995, ss 4, 7, 8;
Greater London Authority Act 1999;
London Local Authorities Act 2000, ss 4, 5, 7, 8;
London Local Authorities and Transport for London Act 2003, s 15

31 Mar 2008 (W) (SI 2007/3174)

31 May 2022 (E) (repeal of Transport Act 2000, s 144) (SI 2022/66)⁶

*Not yet in force* (E), repeals of or in—
Road Traffic Act 1988;
Road Traffic Act 1991, s 68;
London Local Authorities Act 1995, s 5;
London Local Authorities Act 2000, ss 3(1), 6, 9–14;
Transport Act 2000;
London Local Authorities and Transport for London Act 2003, ss 4–7, 14, Schs 1–3

|  |  |  |
|---|---|---|
| | Pt 2 | 4 Oct 2004 (E) (SI 2004/2380) |
| | | 26 Oct 2006 (W) (SI 2006/2826) |

¹   For transitional provisions, see SI 2004/2380, art 3

²   For transitional provisions, see SI 2007/1890, arts 3–8

³   For transitional provisions, see SI 2007/2053, art 4

⁴   For transitional provisions, see SI 2007/3174, arts 3–9

⁵   Note that SI 2006/2826 brought the sections which introduce Schs 7–11 into force on 26 Oct 2006, however these Schedules were not intended to be brought into force on that date

⁶   For transitional provisions and savings see SI 2022/66, art 3

---

**Vulnerable Witnesses (Scotland) Act 2004 (asp 3)**

*RA:* 14 Apr 2004

*Commencement provisions:* s 25; Vulnerable Witnesses (Scotland) Act 2004 (Commencement) Order 2005, SSI 2005/168; Vulnerable Witnesses (Scotland) Act 2004 (Commencement No 2, Saving and Transitional Provisions) Order 2005, SSI 2005/590; Vulnerable Witnesses (Scotland) Act 2004 (Commencement No 3, Savings and Transitional Provisions) Order 2006, SSI 2006/59⁵; Vulnerable Witnesses (Scotland) Act 2004 (Commencement No 4, Savings and Transitional Provisions) Order 2007, SSI 2007/101; Vulnerable Witnesses (Scotland) Act 2004 (Commencement No 5, Savings and Transitional Provisions) Order 2007, SSI 2007/329¹¹; Vulnerable Witnesses (Scotland) Act 2004 (Commencement No 6, Savings and Transitional Provisions) Order 2007, SSI 2007/447¹²; Vulnerable Witnesses (Scotland) Act 2004 (Commencement No 7, Savings and Transitional Provisions) Order 2008, SSI 2008/57; Vulnerable Witnesses (Scotland) Act 2004 (Commencement No 8) Order 2015, SSI 2015/244

**Vulnerable Witnesses (Scotland) Act 2004 (asp 3)**—*contd*

| | | |
|---|---|---|
| 1 | (1): s 271(1)–(4) | 1 Apr 2005 (for the first specified purposes[1]) (SSI 2005/168)[2] |
| | | 1 Apr 2006 (in so far as not already in force in respect of solemn proceedings in the High Court and sheriff court) (SSI 2006/59) |
| | | 1 Apr 2007 (for the fourth[7] and fifth[9] specified purposes) (SSI 2007/101)[8] |
| | | 2 Jul 2007 (for the sixth specified purposes)[10] (SSI 2007/329)[11] |
| | | 1 Apr 2008 (otherwise) (SSI 2008/57)[14] |
| | (1): s 271(5), (6) | 1 Apr 2005 (except references to s 271I) (for the first specified purposes[1]) (SSI 2005/168)[2] |
| | | 30 Nov 2005 (references to s 271I) (for the second specified purposes[3]) (SSI 2005/590)[4] |
| | | 1 Apr 2006 (references to ss 271H(1)(a), 271I) (for the third specified purposes[6]) (SSI 2006/59) |
| | | 1 Apr 2007 (for the fourth specified purposes[7] (except reference to s 271I) and for the fifth specified purposes[9]) (SSI 2007/101)[8] |
| | | 2 Jul 2007 (for the sixth specified purposes)[10] (SSI 2007/329)[11] |
| | | 1 Apr 2008 (otherwise) (SSI 2008/57)[14] |
| | (1): ss 271A, 271B | 1 Apr 2005 (for the first specified purposes[1]) (SSI 2005/168)[2] |
| | | 1 Apr 2007 (for the fourth specified purposes[7]) (SSI 2007/101)[8] |
| | | 2 Jul 2007 (for the sixth specified purposes[10]) (SSI 2007/329)[11] |
| | | 1 Apr 2008 (otherwise) (SSI 2008/57)[14] |
| | (1): s 271C | 1 Apr 2006 (in respect of solemn proceedings in the High Court and sheriff court) (SSI 2006/59) |
| | | 2 Jul 2007 (for the sixth specified purposes[10]) (SSI 2007/329)[11] |
| | | 1 Apr 2008 (otherwise) (SSI 2008/57)[14] |
| | (1): s 271D(1) | 1 Apr 2005 (for the first specified purposes[1]) (SSI 2005/168)[2] |
| | | 1 Apr 2006 (in so far as not already in force in respect of solemn proceedings in the High Court and sheriff court) (SSI 2006/59) |
| | | 1 Apr 2007 (for the fourth specified purposes[7]) (SSI 2007/101)[8] |
| | | 2 Jul 2007 (for the sixth specified purposes[10]) (SSI 2007/329)[11] |
| | | 1 Apr 2008 (otherwise) (SSI 2008/57)[14] |
| | (1): s 271D(2)(a) | 1 Apr 2005 (except reference to s 271C) (for specified purposes[1]) (SSI 2005/168)[2] |
| | | 1 Apr 2006 (in so far as not already in force in respect of solemn proceedings in the High Court and sheriff court) (SSI 2006/59) |
| | | 1 Apr 2007 (except reference to s 271C) (for the fourth specified purposes[7]) (SSI 2007/101)[8] |
| | | 2 Jul 2007 (for the sixth specified purposes[10]) (SSI 2007/329)[11] |
| | | 1 Apr 2008 (otherwise) (SSI 2008/57)[14] |
| | (1): s 271D(2)(b) | 1 Apr 2005 (for the first specified purposes[1]) (SSI 2005/168)[2] |
| | | 1 Apr 2006 (in so far as not already in force in respect of solemn proceedings in the High Court and sheriff court) (SSI 2006/59) |
| | | 1 Apr 2007 (for the fourth specified purposes[7]) (SSI 2007/101)[8] |
| | | 2 Jul 2007 (for the sixth specified purposes[10]) (SSI 2007/329)[11] |
| | | 1 Apr 2008 (otherwise) (SSI 2008/57)[14] |
| | (1): s 271D(3), (4) | 1 Apr 2005 (for the first specified purposes[1]) (SSI 2005/168)[2] |
| | | 1 Apr 2006 (in so far as not already in force in respect of solemn proceedings in the High Court and sheriff court) (SSI 2006/59) |
| | | 1 Apr 2007 (for the fourth specified purposes[7]) (SSI 2007/101)[8] |
| | | 2 Jul 2007 (for the sixth specified purposes[10]) (SSI 2007/329)[11] |
| | | 1 Apr 2008 (otherwise) (SSI 2008/57)[14] |
| | (1): s 271D(5) | 1 Apr 2006 (in respect of solemn proceedings in the High Court and sheriff court) (SSI 2006/59) |
| | | 2 Jul 2007 (for the sixth specified purposes[10]) (SSI 2007/329)[11] |
| | | 1 Apr 2008 (otherwise) (SSI 2008/57)[14] |
| | (1): s 271D(6) | 1 Apr 2005 (for the first specified purposes[1]) (SSI 2005/168)[2] |
| | | 1 Apr 2006 (in so far as not already in force in respect of solemn proceedings in the High Court and sheriff court) (SSI 2006/59) |
| | | 1 Apr 2007 (for the fourth specified purposes[7]) (SSI 2007/101)[8] |
| | | 2 Jul 2007 (for the sixth specified purposes[10]) (SSI 2007/329)[11] |

**Vulnerable Witnesses (Scotland) Act 2004 (asp 3)**—*contd*

|  |  |
|---|---|
|  | 1 Apr 2008 (otherwise) (SSI 2008/57)[14] |
| (1): s 271E(1)(a) | 1 Apr 2005 (for the first specified purposes[1]) (SSI 2005/168)[2] |
|  | 1 Apr 2006 (in so far as not already in force in respect of solemn proceedings in the High Court and sheriff court) (SSI 2006/59) |
|  | 1 Apr 2007 (for the fourth specified purposes[7]) (SSI 2007/101)[8] |
|  | 2 Jul 2007 (for the sixth specified purposes[10]) (SSI 2007/329)[11] |
|  | 1 Apr 2008 (otherwise) (SSI 2008/57)[14] |
| (1): s 271E(1)(b) | 1 Apr 2005 (except reference to s 271C) (for the first specified purposes[1]) (SSI 2005/168)[2] |
|  | 1 Apr 2006 (in so far as not already in force in respect of solemn proceedings in the High Court and sheriff court) (SSI 2006/59) |
|  | 1 Apr 2007 (except reference to s 271C) (for the fourth specified purposes[7]) (SSI 2007/101)[8] |
|  | 2 Jul 2007 (for the sixth specified purposes[10]) (SSI 2007/329)[11] |
|  | 1 Apr 2008 (otherwise) (SSI 2008/57)[14] |
| (1): s 271E(2)–(4) | 1 Apr 2005 (for the first specified purposes[1]) (SSI 2005/168)[2] |
|  | 1 Apr 2006 (in so far as not already in force in respect of solemn proceedings in the High Court and sheriff court) (SSI 2006/59) |
|  | 1 Apr 2007 (for the fourth specified purposes[7]) (SSI 2007/101)[8] |
|  | 2 Jul 2007 (for the sixth specified purposes[10]) (SSI 2007/329)[11] |
|  | 1 Apr 2008 (otherwise) (SSI 2008/57)[14] |
| (1): s 271F(1), (2) | 1 Apr 2005 (for the first specified purposes[1]) (SSI 2005/168)[2] |
|  | 1 Apr 2006 (in so far as not already in force in respect of solemn proceedings in the High Court and sheriff court) (SSI 2006/59) |
|  | 1 Apr 2007 (for the fourth specified purposes[7]) (SSI 2007/101)[8] |
|  | 2 Jul 2007 (for the sixth specified purposes[10]) (SSI 2007/329)[11] |
|  | 1 Apr 2008 (otherwise) (SSI 2008/57)[14] |
| (1): s 271F(3), (4) | 1 Apr 2006 (in respect of solemn proceedings in the High Court and sheriff court) (SSI 2006/59) |
|  | 2 Jul 2007 (for the sixth specified purposes[10]) (SSI 2007/329)[11] |
|  | 1 Apr 2008 (otherwise) (SSI 2008/57)[14] |
| (1): s 271F(5)–(7) | 1 Apr 2005 (for the first specified purposes[1]) (SSI 2005/168)[2] |
|  | 1 Apr 2006 (in so far as not already in force in respect of solemn proceedings in the High Court and sheriff court) (SSI 2006/59) |
|  | 1 Apr 2007 (for the fourth specified purposes[7]) (SSI 2007/101)[8] |
|  | 2 Jul 2007 (for the sixth specified purposes[10]) (SSI 2007/329)[11] |
|  | 1 Apr 2008 (otherwise) (SSI 2008/57)[14] |
| (1): s 271F(8)(a) | 1 Apr 2005 (for the first specified purposes[1]) (SSI 2005/168)[2] |
|  | 1 Apr 2006 (in so far as not already in force in respect of solemn proceedings in the High Court and sheriff court) (SSI 2006/59) |
|  | 1 Apr 2007 (for the fourth specified purposes[7]) (SSI 2007/101)[8] |
|  | 2 Jul 2007 (for the sixth specified purposes[10]) (SSI 2007/329)[11] |
|  | 1 Apr 2008 (otherwise) (SSI 2008/57)[14] |
| (1): s 271F(8)(b) | 30 Nov 2005 (for the second specified purposes[3]) (SSI 2005/590)[4] |
|  | 1 Apr 2006 (in so far as not already in force in respect of solemn proceedings in the High Court and sheriff court) (SSI 2006/59) |
|  | 1 Apr 2007 (for the fifth specified purposes[7]) (SSI 2007/101)[9] |
|  | 2 Jul 2007 (for the sixth specified purposes[10]) (SSI 2007/329)[11] |
|  | 1 Apr 2008 (otherwise) (SSI 2008/57)[14] |
| (1): s 271G | 1 Apr 2005 (except in relation to s 271C) (for the first specified purposes[1]) (SSI 2005/168)[2] |
|  | 1 Apr 2006 (in so far as not already in force in respect of solemn proceedings in the High Court and sheriff court) (SSI 2006/59) |
|  | 1 Apr 2007 (other than in respect of s 271C) (for the fourth specified purposes[7]) (SSI 2007/101)[8] |
|  | 2 Jul 2007 (for the sixth specified purposes[10]) (SSI 2007/329)[11] |
|  | 1 Apr 2008 (otherwise) (SSI 2008/57)[14] |
| (1): s 271H(1) | 1 Apr 2005 (except sub-s (1)(a) and reference to s 271C) (for the first specified purposes[1]) (SSI 2005/168)[2] |

**Vulnerable Witnesses (Scotland) Act 2004 (asp 3)**—*contd*

|  |  |
|---|---|
|  | 30 Nov 2005 (sub-s (1)(a)) (for the second specified purposes[3]) (SSI 2005/590)[4] |
|  | 1 Apr 2006 (except sub-s (1)(a)) (in so far as not already in force in respect of solemn proceedings in the High Court and sheriff court) (SSI 2006/59) |
|  | 1 Apr 2007 (except sub-s (1)(a) and reference to s 271C) (for the fourth specified purposes[7]) (SSI 2007/101)[8] |
|  | 1 Apr 2007 (sub-s (1)(a)) (for the fifth specified purposes[9]) (SSI 2007/101)[8] |
|  | 2 Jul 2007 (for the sixth specified purposes[10]) (SSI 2007/329)[11] |
|  | 1 Apr 2008 (otherwise) (SSI 2008/57)[14] |
| (1): s 271H(2) | 1 Apr 2005 (for the first specified purposes[1]) (SSI 2005/168)[2] |
|  | 1 Apr 2006 (in so far as not already in force in respect of solemn proceedings in the High Court and sheriff court) (SSI 2006/59) |
|  | 1 Apr 2007 (for the fourth specified purposes[7]) (SSI 2007/101)[8] |
|  | 2 Jul 2007 (for the sixth specified purposes[10]) (SSI 2007/329)[11] |
|  | 1 Apr 2008 (otherwise) (SSI 2008/57)[14] |
| (1): s 271H(3) | 1 Apr 2005 (except reference to s 271C) (for the first specified purposes[1]) (SSI 2005/168)[2] |
|  | 1 Apr 2006 (in so far as not already in force in respect of solemn proceedings in the High Court and sheriff court) (SSI 2006/59) |
|  | 1 Apr 2007 (except reference to s 271C) (for the fourth specified purposes[7]) (SSI 2007/101)[8] |
|  | 2 Jul 2007 (for the sixth specified purposes[10]) (SSI 2007/329)[11] |
|  | 1 Apr 2008 (otherwise) (SSI 2008/57)[14] |
| (1): s 271I | 30 Nov 2005 (for the second specified purposes[3]) (SSI 2005/590)[4] |
|  | 1 Apr 2007 (for the fifth specified purposes[9]) (SSI 2007/101)[8] |
|  | 2 Jul 2007 (for the sixth specified purposes[10]) (SSI 2007/329)[11] |
|  | 1 Apr 2008 (otherwise) (SSI 2008/57)[14] |
| (1): ss 271J–271M | 1 Apr 2005 (for the first specified purposes[1]) (SSI 2005/168)[2] |
|  | 1 Apr 2006 (in so far as not already in force in respect of solemn proceedings in the High Court and sheriff court) (SSI 2006/59) |
|  | 1 Apr 2007 (for the fourth specified purposes[7]) (SSI 2007/101)[8] |
|  | 2 Jul 2007 (for the sixth specified purposes[10]) (SSI 2007/329)[11] |
|  | 1 Apr 2008 (otherwise) (SSI 2008/57)[14] |
| (2) | 2 Jul 2007 (for the sixth specified purposes[10]) (SSI 2007/329)[11] |
|  | 1 Apr 2008 (otherwise) (SSI 2008/57)[14] |
| 2 (1) | 1 Apr 2005 (for the first specified purposes[1]) (SSI 2005/168)[2] |
|  | 1 Apr 2006 (in so far as not already in force in respect of solemn proceedings in the High Court and sheriff court) (SSI 2006/59) |
|  | 1 Apr 2008 (otherwise) (SSI 2008/57)[14] |
| (2), (3) | *Not yet in force* |
| (4) | 1 Apr 2005 (for the first specified purposes[1]) (SSI 2005/168)[2] |
|  | 1 Apr 2006 (in so far as not already in force in respect of solemn proceedings in the High Court and sheriff court) (SSI 2006/59) |
|  | 1 Apr 2008 (otherwise) (SSI 2008/57)[14] |
| (5) | 1 Apr 2007 (only in respect of child witnesses as referred to in the Criminal Procedure (Scotland) Act 1995, s 27(1)(a)) (SSI 2007/101)[8] |
|  | 1 Apr 2008 (otherwise) (SSI 2008/57)[14] |
| 3 | 1 Apr 2005 (except reference in s 15A(1) to s 271I and reference in s 15A(3)(b) to s 271C) (for the first specified purposes[1]) (SSI 2005/168)[2] |
|  | 30 Nov 2005 (reference in s 15A(1) to s 271I) (for the second specified purposes[3]) (SSI 2005/590)[4] |
|  | 1 Apr 2006 (except reference in s 15A(1) to s 271I) (in so far as not already in force in respect of solemn proceedings in the High Court and sheriff court) (SSI 2006/59) |
|  | 1 Apr 2006 (reference in s 15A(1) to s 271I) (for the third specified purposes[6]) (SSI 2006/59) |

**Vulnerable Witnesses (Scotland) Act 2004 (asp 3)**—*contd*

|   |   |   |
|---|---|---|
| | | 1 Apr 2007 (except reference in s 15A(1) to s 271I and reference in s 15A(3)(b) to s 271C) (for the fourth specified purposes[7]) (SSI 2007/101)[8] |
| | | 1 Apr 2007 (except reference in s 15A(3)(b) to s 271C) (for the fifth specified purposes[9]) (SSI 2007/101)[8] |
| | | 2 Jul 2007 (for the sixth specified purposes[10]) (SSI 2007/329)[11] |
| | | 1 Apr 2008 (otherwise) (SSI 2008/57)[14] |
| 4, 5 | | 1 Apr 2005 (SSI 2005/168) |
| 6 | | 1 Apr 2005 (in so far as inserts Criminal Procedure (Scotland) Act 1995, s 288E, only in respect of solemn proceedings in the High Court and Sheriff Court) (SSI 2005/168)[2] |
| | | 1 Apr 2005 (in so far as inserts Criminal Procedure (Scotland) Act 1995, s 288F, for the first specified purposes[1]) (SSI 2005/168)[2] |
| | | 1 Apr 2006 (in so far as not already in force in respect of solemn proceedings in the High Court and sheriff court) (SSI 2006/59) |
| | | 1 Apr 2007 (in so far as inserts Criminal Procedure (Scotland) Act 1995, s 288E, only in respect of summary proceedings in the sheriff Court) (SSI 2005/101)[8] |
| | | 1 Apr 2007 (in so far as inserts Criminal Procedure (Scotland) Act 1995, s 288F, for the fourth specified purposes[7]) (SSI 2005/101)[8] |
| | | 1 Apr 2008 (otherwise) (SSI 2008/57)[14] |
| 7 | (1) | 1 Apr 2005 (for the first specified purposes[1]) (SSI 2005/168)[2] |
| | | 1 Apr 2006 (in so far as not already in force in respect of solemn proceedings in the High Court and sheriff court) (SSI 2006/59) |
| | | *Not yet in force* (otherwise) |
| | (2) | *Not yet in force* |
| | (3) | 1 Apr 2005 (for the first specified purposes[1]) (SSI 2005/168)[2] |
| | | 1 Apr 2006 (in so far as not already in force in respect of solemn proceedings in the High Court and sheriff court) (SSI 2006/59) |
| | | *Not yet in force* (otherwise) |
| 8 | | 1 Apr 2005 (only in respect of solemn proceedings at the High Court and sheriff court) (SSI 2005/168)[2] |
| | | 1 Apr 2007 (only in respect of summary proceedings in the sheriff court) (SSI 2007/101)[8] |
| | | *Not yet in force* (otherwise) |
| 9 | | 1 Apr 2007 (only in respect of child witnesses as referred to in the Criminal Procedure (Scotland) Act 1995, s 271(1)(a)) (SSI 2007/101)[8] |
| | | 1 Apr 2008 (otherwise) (SSI 2008/57)[14] |
| 10 | | 1 Jul 2015 (SSI 2015/244) |
| 11 | (1)(a) | 1 Apr 2005 (only in respect of proceedings in the sheriff court under Pt II of the Children (Scotland) Act 1995 in respect of appeals under s 51(1) and applications under ss 68, 85 of that Act, and only in respect of child witnesses) (SSI 2005/168)[2] |
| | | 30 Nov 2005 (only in respect of proceedings in the sheriff court under Pt II of the Children (Scotland) Act 1995 in respect of applications under s 65(7), (9) of that Act, and only in respect of child witnesses) (SSI 2005/590)[4] |
| | | 1 Apr 2006 (in so far as not already in force in respect of proceedings in the sheriff court under Pt II of the Children (Scotland) Act 1995 in respect of appeals under s 51(1) and applications under ss 65(7), (9), 85 of that Act) (SSI 2006/59) |
| | | 1 Nov 2007 (otherwise) (SSI 2007/447)[12] |
| | (1)(b) | 1 Apr 2006 (only in respect of proceedings in the sheriff court under Pt II of the Children (Scotland) Act 1995 in respect of appeals under s 51(1) and applications under ss 65(7), (9), 85 of that Act) (SSI 2006/59) |
| | | 1 Nov 2007 (otherwise) (SSI 2007/447)[12] |

**Vulnerable Witnesses (Scotland) Act 2004 (asp 3)**—*contd*

(2)     1 Apr 2006 (only in respect of proceedings in the sheriff court under Pt II of the Children (Scotland) Act 1995 in respect of appeals under s 51(1) and applications under ss 65(7), (9), 85 of that Act) (SSI 2006/59)

1 Nov 2007 (otherwise) (SSI 2007/447)[12]

(3)     1 Apr 2005 (only in respect of proceedings in the sheriff court under Pt II of the Children (Scotland) Act 1995 in respect of appeals under s 51(1) and applications under ss 68, 85 of that Act, and only in respect of child witnesses) (SSI 2005/168)[2]

30 Nov 2005 (only in respect of proceedings in the sheriff court under Pt II of the Children (Scotland) Act 1995 in respect of applications under s 65(7), (9) of that Act, and only in respect of child witnesses) (SSI 2005/590)[4]

1 Apr 2006 (in so far as not already in force in respect of proceedings in the sheriff court under Pt II of the Children (Scotland) Act 1995 in respect of appeals under s 51(1) and applications under ss 65(7), (9), 85 of that Act) (SSI 2006/59)

1 Nov 2007 (otherwise) (SSI 2007/447)[12]

(4)     1 Apr 2006 (only in respect of proceedings in the sheriff court under Pt II of the Children (Scotland) Act 1995 in respect of appeals under section 51(1) and applications under ss 65(7), (9), 85 of that Act) (SSI 2006/59)

1 Nov 2007 (otherwise) (SSI 2007/447)[12]

(5)     1 Apr 2005 (except definition "vulnerable witness application", and the reference to s 18 does not include s 18(1)(a)) (only in respect of proceedings in the sheriff court under Pt II of the Children (Scotland) Act 1995 in respect of appeals under s 51(1) and applications under ss 68, 85 of that Act, and only in respect of child witnesses) (SSI 2005/168)[2]

30 Nov 2005 (otherwise, except definition "vulnerable witness application") (only in respect of child witnesses and only in respect of proceedings in the sheriff court under Pt II of the Children (Scotland) Act 1995 in respect of: (a) appeals under s 51(1) of that Act; (b) applications under s 65(7), (9) of that Act, other than applications to which s 68A(1)(a) applies; or (c) applications under s 85 of that Act, other than applications to which s 68A(1)(b) applies) (SSI 2005/590)[4]

1 Apr 2006 (except in so far as the reference to s 18 includes s 18(1)(a)) (in so far as not already in force in respect of proceedings in the sheriff court under Pt II of the Children (Scotland) Act 1995 in respect of appeals under s 51(1) and applications under ss 65(7), (9), 85 of that Act) (SSI 2006/59)

1 Apr 2006 (in so far as the reference to s 18 includes s 18(1)(a)) (only in respect of proceedings in the sheriff court under Pt II of the Children (Scotland) Act 1995 in respect of: (a) appeals under s 51(1) of that Act; (b) applications under s 65(7), (9) of that Act, other than applications to which s 68A(1)(a) applies; or (c) applications under s 85 of that Act, other than applications to which s 68A(1)(b) applies) (SSI 2006/59)

1 Nov 2007 (otherwise) (SSI 2007/447)[12]

12     (1)–(4)     1 Apr 2005 (only in respect of proceedings in the sheriff court under Pt II of the Children (Scotland) Act 1995 in respect of appeals under s 51(1) and applications under ss 68, 85 of that Act) (SSI 2005/168)[2]

30 Nov 2005 (only in respect of proceedings in the sheriff court under Pt II of the Children (Scotland) Act 1995 in respect of applications under s 65(7), (9) of that Act, and only in respect of child witnesses) (SSI 2005/590)[4]

**Vulnerable Witnesses (Scotland) Act 2004 (asp 3)**—*contd*

|  |  |  |
|---|---|---|
|  |  | 1 Apr 2006 (in so far as not already in force in respect of proceedings in the sheriff court under Pt II of the Children (Scotland) Act 1995 in respect of appeals under s 51(1) and applications under ss 65(7), (9), 85 of that Act) (SSI 2006/59) |
|  |  | 1 Nov 2007 (otherwise) (SSI 2007/447)[12] |
|  | (5)–(7) | 1 Apr 2006 (only in respect of proceedings in the sheriff court under Pt II of the Children (Scotland) Act 1995 in respect of appeals under s 51(1) and applications under ss 65(7), (9), 85 of that Act) (SSI 2006/59) |
|  |  | 1 Nov 2007 (otherwise) (SSI 2007/447)[12] |
| 13, 14 |  | 1 Apr 2005 (only in respect of proceedings in the sheriff court under Pt II of the Children (Scotland) Act 1995 in respect of appeals under s 51(1) and applications under ss 68, 85 of that Act, and only in respect of child witnesses) (SSI 2005/168)[2] |
|  |  | 30 Nov 2005 (only in respect of proceedings in the sheriff court under Pt II of the Children (Scotland) Act 1995 in respect of applications under s 65(7), (9) of that Act, and only in respect of child witnesses) (SSI 2005/590)[4] |
|  |  | 1 Apr 2006 (in so far as not already in force in respect of proceedings in the sheriff court under Pt II of the Children (Scotland) Act 1995 in respect of appeals under s 51(1) and applications under ss 65(7), (9), 85 of that Act) (SSI 2006/59) |
|  |  | 1 Nov 2007 (otherwise) (SSI 2007/447)[12] |
| 15 | (1)(a) | 1 Apr 2005 (except words "or a vulnerable witness application") (only in respect of proceedings in the sheriff court under Pt II of the Children (Scotland) Act 1995 in respect of appeals under s 51(1) and applications under ss 68, 85 of that Act) (SSI 2005/168)[2] |
|  |  | 30 Nov 2005 (except words "or a vulnerable witness application") (only in respect of proceedings in the sheriff court under Pt II of the Children (Scotland) Act 1995 in respect of applications under s 65(7), (9) of that Act, and only in respect of child witnesses) (SSI 2005/590)[4] |
|  |  | 1 Apr 2006 (in so far as not already in force in respect of proceedings in the sheriff court under Pt II of the Children (Scotland) Act 1995 in respect of appeals under s 51(1) and applications under ss 65(7), (9), 85 of that Act) (SSI 2006/59) |
|  |  | 1 Nov 2007 (otherwise) (SSI 2007/447)[12] |
|  | (1)(b) | 1 Apr 2005 (only in respect of proceedings in the sheriff court under Pt II of the Children (Scotland) Act 1995 in respect of appeals under s 51(1) and applications under ss 68, 85 of that Act) (SSI 2005/168)[2] |
|  |  | 30 Nov 2005 (only in respect of proceedings in the sheriff court under Pt II of the Children (Scotland) Act 1995 in respect of applications under s 65(7), (9) of that Act, and only in respect of child witnesses) (SSI 2005/590)[4] |
|  |  | 1 Apr 2006 (in so far as not already in force in respect of proceedings in the sheriff court under Pt II of the Children (Scotland) Act 1995 in respect of appeals under s 51(1) and applications under ss 65(7), (9), 85 of that Act) (SSI 2006/59) |
|  |  | 1 Nov 2007 (otherwise) (SSI 2007/447)[12] |
|  | (2), (3) | 1 Apr 2005 (only in respect of proceedings in the sheriff court under Pt II of the Children (Scotland) Act 1995 in respect of appeals under s 51(1) and applications under ss 68, 85 of that Act) (SSI 2005/168)[2] |
|  |  | 30 Nov 2005 (only in respect of proceedings in the sheriff court under Pt II of the Children (Scotland) Act 1995 in respect of applications under s 65(7), (9) of that Act, and only in respect of child witnesses) (SSI 2005/590)[4] |

**Vulnerable Witnesses (Scotland) Act 2004 (asp 3)**—*contd*

1 Apr 2006 (in so far as not already in force in respect of proceedings in the sheriff court under Pt II of the Children (Scotland) Act 1995 in respect of appeals under s 51(1) and applications under ss 65(7), (9), 85 of that Act) (SSI 2006/59)

1 Nov 2007 (otherwise) (SSI 2007/447)[12]

(4)     1 Apr 2005 (except words "or vulnerable witness application") (only in respect of proceedings in the sheriff court under Pt II of the Children (Scotland) Act 1995 in respect of appeals under s 51(1) and applications under ss 68, 85 of that Act) (SSI 2005/168)[2]

30 Nov 2005 (except words "or vulnerable witness application") (only in respect of proceedings in the sheriff court under Pt II of the Children (Scotland) Act 1995 in respect of applications under s 65(7), (9) of that Act, and only in respect of child witnesses) (SSI 2005/590)[4]

1 Apr 2006 (in so far as not already in force in respect of proceedings in the sheriff court under Pt II of the Children (Scotland) Act 1995 in respect of appeals under s 51(1) and applications under ss 65(7), (9), 85 of that Act) (SSI 2006/59)

1 Nov 2007 (otherwise) (SSI 2007/447)[12]

16      1 Apr 2005 (except words "or other person") (only in respect of proceedings in the sheriff court under Pt II of the Children (Scotland) Act 1995 in respect of appeals under s 51(1) and applications under ss 68, 85 of that Act) (SSI 2005/168)[2]

30 Nov 2005 (except words "or other person") (only in respect of proceedings in the sheriff court under Pt II of the Children (Scotland) Act 1995 in respect of applications under s 65(7), (9) of that Act, and only in respect of child witnesses) (SSI 2005/590)[4]

1 Apr 2006 (in so far as not already in force in respect of proceedings in the sheriff court under Pt II of the Children (Scotland) Act 1995 in respect of appeals under s 51(1) and applications under ss 65(7), (9), 85 of that Act) (SSI 2006/59)

1 Nov 2007 (otherwise) (SSI 2007/447)[12]

17      (1)     1 Apr 2005 (only in so far as the sections mentioned therein have been commenced) (SSI 2005/168)[2]

1 Nov 2007 (otherwise) (SSI 2007/447)[12]

(2)     1 Apr 2005 (only in respect of proceedings in the sheriff court under Pt II of the Children (Scotland) Act 1995 in respect of appeals under s 51(1) and applications under ss 68, 85 of that Act, and only in respect of child witnesses) (SSI 2005/168)[2]

30 Nov 2005 (only in respect of proceedings in the sheriff court under Pt II of the Children (Scotland) Act 1995 in respect of applications under s 65(7), (9) of that Act, and only in respect of child witnesses) (SSI 2005/590)[4]

1 Apr 2006 (in so far as not already in force in respect of proceedings in the sheriff court under Pt II of the Children (Scotland) Act 1995 in respect of appeals under s 51(1) and applications under ss 65(7), (9), 85 of that Act) (SSI 2006/59)

1 Nov 2007 (otherwise) (SSI 2007/447)[12]

18      (1)(a)  30 Nov 2005 (only in respect of child witnesses and only in respect of proceedings in the sheriff court under Pt II of the Children (Scotland) Act 1995 in respect of: (a) appeals under s 51(1) of that Act; (b) applications under s 65(7), (9) of that Act, other than applications to which s 68A(1)(a) applies; or (c) applications under s 85 of that Act, other than applications to which s 68A(1)(b) applies) (SSI 2005/590)[4]

**Vulnerable Witnesses (Scotland) Act 2004 (asp 3)**—*contd*

1 Apr 2006 (in so far as not already in force in respect of proceedings in the sheriff court under Pt II of the Children (Scotland) Act 1995 in respect of: (a) appeals under s 51(1) of that Act; (b) applications under s 65(7), (9) of that Act, other than applications to which s 68A(1)(a) applies; or (c) applications under s 85 of that Act, other than applications to which s 68A(1)(b) applies) (SSI 2006/59)

1 Nov 2007 (for the seventh specified purposes[13]) (SSI 2007/447)[12]

*Not yet in force* (otherwise)

(1)(b)–(e)      1 Apr 2005 (only in respect of proceedings in the sheriff court under Pt II of the Children (Scotland) Act 1995 in respect of appeals under s 51(1) and applications under ss 68, 85 of that Act, and only in respect of child witnesses) (SSI 2005/168)[2]

30 Nov 2005 (only in respect of proceedings in the sheriff court under Pt II of the Children (Scotland) Act 1995 in respect of applications under s 65(7), (9) of that Act, and only in respect of child witnesses) (SSI 2005/590)[4]

1 Apr 2006 (in so far as not already in force in respect of proceedings in the sheriff court under Pt II of the Children (Scotland) Act 1995 in respect of appeals under s 51(1) and applications under ss 65(7), (9), 85 of that Act) (SSI 2006/59)

1 Nov 2007 (otherwise) (SSI 2007/447)[12]

(2)      1 Apr 2005 (only in respect of proceedings in the sheriff court under Pt II of the Children (Scotland) Act 1995 in respect of appeals under s 51(1) and applications under ss 68, 85 of that Act, and only in respect of child witnesses) (SSI 2005/168)[2]

30 Nov 2005 (only in respect of proceedings in the sheriff court under Pt II of the Children (Scotland) Act 1995 in respect of applications under s 65(7), (9) of that Act, and only in respect of child witnesses) (SSI 2005/590)[4]

1 Apr 2006 (in so far as not already in force in respect of proceedings in the sheriff court under Pt II of the Children (Scotland) Act 1995 in respect of appeals under s 51(1) and applications under ss 65(7), (9), 85 of that Act) (SSI 2006/59)

1 Nov 2007 (otherwise) (SSI 2007/447)[12]

19      30 Nov 2005 (only in respect of child witnesses and only in respect of proceedings in the sheriff court under Pt II of the Children (Scotland) Act 1995 in respect of: (a) appeals under s 51(1) of that Act; (b) applications under s 65(7), (9) of that Act, other than applications to which s 68A(1)(a) applies; or (c) applications under s 85 of that Act, other than applications to which s 68A(1)(b) applies) (SSI 2005/590)[4]

1 Apr 2006 (in so far as not already in force in respect of proceedings in the sheriff court under Pt II of the Children (Scotland) Act 1995 in respect of: (a) appeals under s 51(1) of that Act; (b) applications under s 65(7), (9) of that Act, other than applications to which s 68A(1)(a) applies; or (c) applications under s 85 of that Act, other than applications to which s 68A(1)(b) applies) (SSI 2006/59)

1 Nov 2007 (for the seventh specified purposes[13]) (SSI 2007/447)[12]

*Not yet in force* (otherwise)

20–22      1 Apr 2005 (only in respect of proceedings in the sheriff court under Pt II of the Children (Scotland) Act 1995 in respect of appeals under s 51(1) and applications under ss 68, 85 of that Act, and only in respect of child witnesses) (SSI 2005/168)[2]

30 Nov 2005 (only in respect of proceedings in the sheriff court under Pt II of the Children (Scotland) Act 1995 in respect of applications under s 65(7), (9) of that Act, and only in respect of child witnesses) (SSI 2005/590)[4]

**Vulnerable Witnesses (Scotland) Act 2004 (asp 3)**—*contd*

|  |  |
|---|---|
|  | 1 Apr 2006 (in so far as not already in force in respect of proceedings in the sheriff court under Pt II of the Children (Scotland) Act 1995 in respect of appeals under s 51(1) and applications under ss 65(7), (9), 85 of that Act) (SSI 2006/59) |
|  | 1 Nov 2007 (otherwise) (SSI 2007/447)[12] |
| 23, 24 | 1 Apr 2005 (SSI 2005/168) |
| 25 | 14 Apr 2004 (RA) |

<sup>1</sup> The first specified purposes are: (a) in respect of solemn proceedings in the High Court and sheriff court; and (b) in respect of child witnesses as referred to in the Criminal Procedure (Scotland) Act 1995, s 271(1)(a)

<sup>2</sup> For transitional provisions and savings, see SSI 2005/168, art 4

<sup>3</sup> The second specified purposes are: (a) in respect of child witnesses as referred to in the Criminal Procedure (Scotland) Act 1995, s 271(1)(a); and (b) in respect of solemn proceedings in the High Court and sheriff court, other than those in which, at the time the court is considering a child witness notice under s 271A(5) or (9) of that Act, or is reviewing the current arrangements for taking a child witness's evidence under s 271D(1) of that Act—

(a) the accused is charged with a sexual offence to which s 288C of the 1995 Act applies;

(b) the accused is charged with an offence in respect of which the court has made an order under s 288C(4) of the 1995 Act;

(c) s 288E of the 1995 Act applies to the proceedings in respect of which the child witness notice under consideration has been lodged or is being reviewed; or

(d) an order has been made under s 288F(2) in the proceedings in respect of which the child witness notice under consideration has been lodged or is being reviewed

<sup>4</sup> For transitional provisions and savings, see SSI 2005/590, art 4

<sup>5</sup> For transitional provisions and savings, see SSI 2006/59, art 4

<sup>6</sup> The third specified purposes are in respect of solemn proceedings in the High Court and sheriff court, other than those in which, at the time the court is considering a vulnerable witness application under Criminal Procedure (Scotland) Act 1995, s 271C(5) or 271C(7), or is reviewing the current arrangements for taking a vulnerable witness's evidence under s 271D(1) of the 1995 Act—

(a) the accused is charged with a sexual offence to which section 288C of the 1995 Act applies;

(b) the accused is charged with an offence in respect of which the court has made an order under s 288C(4) of the 1995 Act;

(c) s 288E of the 1995 Act applies to the proceedings in respect of which the vulnerable witness application under consideration has been lodged or is being reviewed; or

(d) an order has been made under s 288F(2) in the proceedings in respect of which the vulnerable witness notice under consideration has been lodged or is being reviewed

<sup>7</sup> The fourth specified purposes are (a) in respect of summary proceedings in the sheriff court; and (b) in respect of child witnesses as referred to in the Criminal Procedure (Scotland) Act 1995, s 271(1)(a)

<sup>8</sup> For transitional provisions and savings, see SSI 2007/101, art 4

<sup>9</sup> The fifth specified purposes are in respect of child witnesses as referred to in the Criminal Procedure (Scotland) Act, s 271(1)(a) and only in respect of summary proceedings in the sheriff court, other than those in which, at the time the court is considering a child witness notice under s 271A(5) or 271A(9) of that Act, or is reviewing the current arrangements for taking a child witness's evidence under s 271D(1) of that Act—

(a) the accused is charged with a sexual offence to which s 288C of the 1995 Act applies;

(b) the accused is charged with an offence in respect of which the court has made an order under s 288C(4) of the 1995 Act;

(c) s 288E of the 1995 Act applies to the proceedings in respect of which the child witness notice under consideration has been lodged or is being reviewed; or

(d) an order has been made under s 288F(2) in the proceedings in respect of which the child witness notice under consideration has been lodged or is being reviewed

<sup>10</sup> The sixth specified purposes are (a) in respect of child witnesses as referred to in the Criminal

**Vulnerable Witnesses (Scotland) Act 2004 (asp 3)**—*contd*

Procedure (Scotland) Act 1995, s 271(1)(a) in relation to solemn proceedings in the High Court and the sheriff court and summary proceedings in the sheriff court; and (b) in respect of vulnerable witnesses other than child witnesses as referred to s 271(1)(b) of the 1995 Act, only in relation to solemn proceedings in the High Court and the sheriff court

[11]    For transitional provisions and savings, see SSI 2007/329, art 4

[12]    For transitional provisions and savings, see SSI 2007/447, art 4

[13]    The seventh specified purposes are in respect of proceedings other than proceedings in respect of (a) applications under the Children (Scotland) Act 1995, s 65(7) or 65(9) to which s 68A(1)(a) of that Act applies; and (b) applications under s 85 of the 1995 Act to which s 68A(1)(b) of that Act applies

[14]    For transitional provisions and savings, see SSI 2008/57, art 3

# 2005 Acts

## Appropriation Act 2005 (c 3)

*RA:* 17 Mar 2005

Whole Act in force 17 Mar 2005 (RA)

---

## Appropriation (No 2) Act 2005 (c 8)

*RA:* 7 Apr 2005

Whole Act in force 7 Apr 2005 (RA)

---

## Appropriation (No 3) Act 2005 (c 21)

*RA:* 20 Jul 2005

Whole Act in force 20 Jul 2005 (RA)

---

## Baird Trust Reorganisation Act 2005 (asp 11)

*RA:* 19 Jul 2005

*Commencement provisions:* s 6(2), (3)

| | |
|---|---|
| 1, 2 | 18 Jul 2005 (s 6(2)) |
| 3 | 19 Jul 2006 (s 6(3)) |
| 4, 5 | 18 Jul 2005 (s 6(2)) |
| 6 | 19 Jul 2005 (RA) |

---

## Breastfeeding etc (Scotland) Act 2005 (asp 1)

*RA:* 18 Jan 2005

*Commencement provisions:* s 5

| | |
|---|---|
| 1–4 | 18 Mar 2005 (s 5(1)) |
| 5 | 18 Jan 2005 (RA) |

---

## Budget (Scotland) Act 2005 (asp 4)

*RA:* 17 Mar 2005

Whole Act in force 17 Mar 2005 (RA)

---

## Care of Cathedrals (Amendment) Measure 2005 (No 2)

*RA:* 24 Mar 2005

*Commencement provisions:* s 20(3)

Provisions of this Measure were brought into force on the following dates by instruments made by the Archbishops of Canterbury and York, and dated 2 Jun 2005, 6 Feb 2006 and 20 Dec 2007 (made under s 20(3))

| | | |
|---|---|---|
| 1–7 | | 1 Jan 2008 |
| 8 | (1)–(3) | 1 Jan 2008 |
| | (4)(a) | 7 Feb 2006 |
| | (4)(b)–(d) | 1 Jan 2008 |
| 9–11 | | 1 Jan 2008 |
| 12 | (1) | 7 Feb 2006 |
| | (2), (3) | 1 Jan 2008 |
| 13–16 | | 1 Jan 2008 |
| 17 | | See Sch 1 below |
| 18 | | 7 Feb 2006 |
| 19 | | See Sch 3 below |
| 20 | | 6 Jun 2005 |
| Sch 1 | paras 1–8 | 7 Feb 2006 |
| | paras 9–11 | 1 Jan 2008 |
| | para 12 | 7 Feb 2006 |
| Sch 2 | | 7 Feb 2006 |
| Sch 3 | paras 1–3 | 1 Jan 2008 |
| | para 4(a) | 1 Jan 2008 |
| | para 4(b) | 7 Feb 2006 |
| | para 4(c), (d) | 1 Jan 2008 |
| | para 4(e) | 7 Feb 2006 |
| | para 4(f) | 1 Jan 2008 |
| | para 4(g) | 7 Feb 2006 |
| | para 4(h) | 1 Jan 2008 |
| | para 4(i) | 7 Feb 2006 |
| | para 4(j), (k) | 1 Jan 2008 |
| | para 5 | 1 Jan 2008 |
| | para 6 | 6 Jun 2005 |
| | para 7 | 7 Feb 2006 |
| | paras 8–10 | 1 Jan 2008 |

## Charities and Trustee Investment (Scotland) Act 2005 (asp 10)

*RA:* 14 Jul 2005

*Commencement provisions:* s 107(2); Charities and Trustee Investment (Scotland) Act 2005 (Commencement No 1) Order 2005, SSI 2005/644; Charities and Trustee Investment (Scotland) Act 2005 (Commencement No 2) Order 2006, SSI 2006/74; Charities and Trustee Investment (Scotland) Act 2005 (Commencement No 3, Transitional and Savings Provision) Order 2006, SSI 2006/189; Charities and Trustee Investment (Scotland) Act 2005 (Commencement No 4) Order 2007, SSI 2007/117; Charities and Trustee Investment (Scotland) Act 2005 (Commencement No 5) Order 2011, SSI 2011/20

| | | |
|---|---|---|
| 1 | (1)–(4) | 24 Feb 2006 (SSI 2006/74) |
| | (5)(a) | 24 Apr 2006 (SSI 2006/189) |
| | (5)(b)–(e) | 1 Apr 2006 (SSI 2006/189) |
| | (6)–(9) | 24 Feb 2006 (SSI 2006/74) |
| | (10) | See Sch 1 below |
| 2 | | 24 Apr 2006 (SSI 2006/189) |
| 3 | | 1 Jan 2006 (only for the purpose of enabling regulations to be made) (SSI 2005/644) |
| | | 1 Apr 2006 (otherwise) (SSI 2006/189) |

**Charities and Trustee Investment (Scotland) Act 2005 (asp 10)**—*contd*

| | |
|---|---|
| 4, 5 | 24 Apr 2006 (SSI 2006/189) |
| 6 | 1 Jan 2006 (only for the purpose of enabling regulations to be made) (SSI 2005/644) |
| | 24 Apr 2006 (otherwise) (SSI 2006/189) |
| 7 | 1 Jan 2006 (only for the purpose of enabling orders to be made) (SSI 2005/644) |
| | 24 Apr 2006 (otherwise) (SSI 2006/189) |
| 8 | 24 Apr 2006 (SSI 2006/189) |
| 9 | 24 Feb 2006 (SSI 2006/74) |
| 10–12 | 24 Apr 2006 (SSI 2006/189) |
| 13, 14 | 1 Apr 2006 (SSI 2006/189) |
| 15 | 1 Jan 2006 (only for the purpose of enabling regulations to be made) (SSI 2005/644) |
| | 24 Apr 2006 (otherwise) (SSI 2006/189) |
| 16, 17 | 1 Apr 2006 (SSI 2006/189)[1] |
| 18 | 24 Apr 2006 (SSI 2006/189) |
| 19 | 1 Jan 2006 (only for the purpose of enabling orders and regulations to be made) (SSI 2005/644) |
| | 24 Apr 2006 (otherwise) (SSI 2006/189) |
| 20, 21 | 24 Apr 2006 (SSI 2006/189) |
| 22 | 1 Apr 2006 (SSI 2006/189) |
| 23 | 1 Jan 2006 (only for the purpose of enabling orders to be made) (SSI 2005/644) |
| | 24 Apr 2006 (otherwise) (SSI 2006/189) |
| 24 | 24 Apr 2006 (SSI 2006/189) |
| 25 | 1 Jan 2006 (only for the purpose of enabling orders to be made) (SSI 2005/644) |
| | 24 Apr 2006 (otherwise) (SSI 2006/189) |
| 26, 27 | 24 Apr 2006 (SSI 2006/189) |
| 28, 29 | 1 Apr 2006 (SSI 2006/189)[1] |
| 30 | 24 Apr 2006 (SSI 2006/189) |
| 31–34 | 1 Apr 2006 (SSI 2006/189)[1] |
| 35 | 1 Jan 2006 (only for the purpose of enabling regulations to be made) (SSI 2005/644) |
| | 1 Apr 2006 (otherwise) (SSI 2006/189) |
| 36–38 | 1 Apr 2006 (SSI 2006/189) |
| 39 | 1 Jan 2006 (only for the purpose of enabling regulations to be made) (SSI 2005/644) |
| | 31 May 2007 (otherwise) (SSI 2007/117) |
| 40–42 | 31 May 2007 (SSI 2007/117) |
| 43 | 1 Apr 2006 (SSI 2006/189) |
| 44 | 1 Jan 2006 (only for the purpose of enabling regulations to be made) (SSI 2005/644) |
| | 1 Apr 2006 (otherwise) (SSI 2006/189) |
| 45–47 | 1 Apr 2006 (SSI 2006/189) |
| 48 | 1 Jan 2006 (only for the purpose of enabling regulations to be made) (SSI 2005/644) |
| | 1 Apr 2006 (otherwise) (SSI 2006/189) |
| 49 | 1 Apr 2011 (SSI 2011/20) |
| 50 | 21 Jan 2011 (only for the purpose of enabling regulations to be made) (SSI 2011/20) |
| | 1 Apr 2011 (otherwise) (SSI 2011/20) |
| 51 | 1 Apr 2011 (SSI 2011/20) |
| 52 | 21 Jan 2011 (only for the purpose of enabling regulations to be made) (SSI 2011/20) |
| | 1 Apr 2011 (otherwise) (SSI 2011/20) |
| 53–55 | 1 Apr 2011 (SSI 2011/20) |
| 56–61 | 1 Jan 2012 (SSI 2011/20) |
| 62, 63 | 1 Apr 2011 (SSI 2011/20) |
| 64 | 21 Jan 2011 (SSI 2011/20) |

**Charities and Trustee Investment (Scotland) Act 2005 (asp 10)**—*contd*

| | | |
|---|---|---|
| 65–74 | | 1 Apr 2006 (SSI 2006/189)[1] |
| 75 | (1) | 24 Feb 2006 (SSI 2006/74) |
| | (2) | See Sch 2 below |
| 76–78 | | 1 Apr 2006 (SSI 2006/189) |
| 79 | | 1 Jan 2006 (SSI 2005/644) |
| 80–82 | | 24 Apr 2006 (SSI 2006/189) |
| 83 | | 1 Jan 2006 (only for the purpose of enabling regulations to be made) (SSI 2005/644) |
| | | 24 Apr 2006 (otherwise) (SSI 2006/189) |
| 84, 85 | | *Not yet in force* |
| 86 | | 1 Jan 2006 (only for the purpose of enabling regulations to be made) (SSI 2005/644) |
| | | *Not yet in force (otherwise)* |
| 87–89 | | *Not yet in force* |
| 90, 91 | | 1 Jan 2006 (only for the purpose of enabling regulations to be made) (SSI 2005/644) |
| | | *Not yet in force (otherwise)* |
| 92 | | *Not yet in force* |
| 93, 94 | | 1 Jan 2006 (SSI 2005/644) |
| 95 | | See Sch 3 below |
| 96 | | 27 Feb 2007 (SSI 2007/117) |
| 97 | | 1 Jan 2006 (SSI 2005/644) |
| 98 | | 1 Apr 2006 (SSI 2005/644) |
| 99 | (1), (2) | 1 Apr 2006 (SSI 2006/189) |
| | (3), (4) | 24 Feb 2006 (SSI 2006/74) |
| 100, 101 | | 24 Apr 2006 (SSI 2006/189) |
| 102, 103 | | 14 Jul 2005 (RA) |
| 104 | | See Sch 4 below |
| 105 | | 1 Apr 2006 (SSI 2006/189) |
| 106 | | 1 Jan 2006 (SSI 2005/644) |
| 107 | | 14 Jul 2005 (RA) |
| Sch 1 | | 1 Jan 2006 (only for the purpose of enabling orders to be made) (SSI 2005/644) |
| | | 24 Feb 2006 (otherwise) (SSI 2006/74) |
| Sch 2 | | 1 Jan 2006 (only for the purpose of enabling orders and rules to be made) (SSI 2005/644) |
| | | 24 Feb 2006 (otherwise) (SSI 2006/74) |
| Sch 3 | | 1 Jan 2006 (SSI 2005/644) |
| Sch 4 | paras 1–4 | 1 Apr 2006 (SSI 2006/189) |
| | para 5(a) | 1 Apr 2006 (SSI 2006/189) |
| | para 5(b), (c) | *Not yet in force* |
| | paras 6, 7 | 1 Apr 2006 (SSI 2006/189)[1] |
| | para 8 | *Not yet in force* |
| | para 9 | 24 Apr 2006 (SSI 2006/189) |
| | para 10 | 1 Apr 2006 (SSI 2006/189) |
| | para 11 | *Not yet in force* |
| | paras 12–19 | 1 Apr 2006 (SSI 2006/189) |

[1]    For transitional and savings provisions, see SSI 2006/189, art 3

---

**Child Benefit Act 2005 (c 6)**

*RA*: 24 Mar 2005

*Commencement provisions*: s 6

Whole Act in force 24 Mar 2005 (so far as any power to make regulations is conferred on the treasury by virtue of this Act); 10 Apr 2006 (otherwise) (s 6)

---

## Church of England (Miscellaneous Provisions) Measure 2005 (No 3)

*RA:* 24 Mar 2005

*Commencement provisions:* s 11(2)

Provisions of this Measure were brought into force on 1 Jun 2005 and 1 Sep 2005 by an instrument made by the Archbishops of Canterbury and York, and dated 26 May 2005 (made under s 11(2))

| | |
|---|---|
| 1–8 | 1 Jun 2005 |
| 9 | 1 Sep 2005 |
| 10, 11 | 1 Jun 2005 |
| Schs 1–5 | 1 Jun 2005 |

## Clean Neighbourhoods and Environment Act 2005 (c 16)

*RA:* 7 Apr 2005

*Commencement provisions:* s 108; Clean Neighbourhoods and Environment Act 2005 (Commencement No 1) Order 2005, SI 2005/1675; Clean Neighbourhoods and Environment Act 2005 (Commencement No 2, Transitional Provisions and Savings) (England and Wales) Order 2005, SI 2005/2896, as amended by SI 2006/1002; Clean Neighbourhoods and Environment Act 2005 (Commencement No 3) Order 2005, SI 2005/3439; Clean Neighbourhoods and Environment Act 2005 (Commencement No 4) Order 2006, SI 2006/656; Clean Neighbourhoods and Environment Act 2005 (Commencement No 1 and Savings) (Wales) Order 2006, SI 2006/768, as amended by SI 2006/2797; Clean Neighbourhoods and Environment Act 2005 (Commencement No 1, Transitional and Savings Provisions) (England) Order 2006, SI 2006/795; Clean Neighbourhoods and Environment Act 2005 (Commencement No 2) (England) Order 2006, SI 2006/1361; Clean Neighbourhoods and Environment Act 2005 (Commencement No 3) (England) Order 2006, SI 2006/2006; Clean Neighbourhoods and Environment Act 2005 (Commencement No 2, Transitional Provisions and Savings) (Wales) Order 2006, SI 2006/2797, as amended by SI 2007/120; Clean Neighbourhoods and Environment Act 2005 (Commencement No 4) (England) Order 2007, SI 2007/390; Clean Neighbourhoods and Environment Act 2005 (Commencement No 3) (Wales) Order 2007, SI 2007/3371; Clean Neighbourhoods and Environment Act 2005 (Commencement No 5) Order 2008, SI 2008/956; Clean Neighbourhoods and Environment Act 2005 (Commencement No 6 and Saving) (England and Wales) Order 2015, SI 2015/425

*See also:* Contaminated Land (Wales) Regulations 2006, SI 2006/2989

| | |
|---|---|
| 1 | *Never in force* (repealed) |
| 2 | 16 Mar 2006 (W) (for specified purposes[3]) (SI 2006/768) |
| | 1 Apr 2006 (E) (SI 2006/795) |
| | 19 Feb 2007 (the date on which the Highways Act 1980 (Gating Orders) (Wales) Regulations 2007 came into force) (W) (otherwise) (SI 2006/2797) |
| 3–5 | 7 Jun 2005 (s 108(4)(a)) |
| 6 | 14 Mar 2006 (E) (for the purposes of enabling regulations to be made by the Secretary of State under s 6(11)) (SI 2006/795) |
| | 16 Mar 2006 (W) (for specified purposes[3]) (SI 2006/768) |
| | 6 Apr 2006 (E) (otherwise) (SI 2006/795) |
| | 15 Mar 2007 (the date on which the Environmental Offences (Fixed Penalties) (Miscellaneous Provisions) (Wales) Regulations 2007 came into force) (W) (otherwise) (SI 2006/2797) |
| 7 | 6 Apr 2006 (E) (SI 2006/795) |
| | 15 Mar 2007 (the date on which the Environmental Offences (Fixed Penalties) (Miscellaneous Provisions) (Wales) Regulations 2007 came into force) (W) (SI 2006/2797) |
| 8 | 14 Mar 2006 (E) (for the purposes of enabling regulations to be made by the Secretary of State under s 8(2)(d)) (SI 2006/795) |
| | 16 Mar 2006 (W) (for specified purposes[3]) (SI 2006/768) |
| | 6 Apr 2006 (E) (otherwise) (SI 2006/795) |

**Clean Neighbourhoods and Environment Act 2005 (c 16)**—*contd*

|  |  |  |
|---|---|---|
| | | 15 Mar 2007 (the date on which the Environmental Offences (Fixed Penalties) (Miscellaneous Provisions) (Wales) Regulations 2007 came into force) (W) (otherwise) (SI 2006/2797) |
| 9 | | 14 Mar 2006 (E) (SI 2006/795) |
| | | 15 Mar 2007 (the date on which the Environmental Offences (Fixed Penalties) (Miscellaneous Provisions) (Wales) Regulations 2007 came into force) (W) (SI 2006/2797) |
| 10 | | 16 Mar 2006 (W) (for specified purposes³) (SI 2006/768) |
| | | 6 Apr 2006 (E) (SI 2006/795) |
| | | 15 Mar 2007 (the date on which the Environmental Offences (Fixed Penalties) (Miscellaneous Provisions) (Wales) Regulations 2007 came into force) (W) (otherwise) (SI 2006/2797) |
| 11, 12 | | 18 Oct 2005 (E) (SI 2005/2896)¹ |
| | | 27 Oct 2006 (W) (SI 2006/2797)⁵ |
| 13 | | 18 Oct 2005 (E) (SI 2005/2896)¹ |
| | | 16 Mar 2006 (W) (for specified purposes³) (SI 2006/768) |
| | | 27 Oct 2006 (W) (otherwise) (SI 2006/2797)⁵ |
| 14 | | 7 Apr 2005 (RA) |
| 15, 16 | | 18 Oct 2005 (E) (SI 2005/2896)¹ |
| | | 27 Oct 2006 (W) (SI 2006/2797)⁵ |
| 17 | | 18 Oct 2005 (E) (SI 2005/2896)¹ |
| | | 16 Mar 2006 (W) (for specified purposes³) (SI 2006/768) |
| | | 27 Oct 2006 (W) (otherwise) (SI 2006/2797)⁵ |
| 18 | | 7 Jun 2005 (s 108(4)(b)) |
| 19 | (1) | See sub-ss (2)–(6) below |
| | (2)–(5) | 16 Mar 2006 (W) (for specified purposes³) (SI 2006/768) |
| | | 6 Apr 2006 (E) (SI 2006/795)² |
| | | 15 Mar 2007 (the date on which the Environmental Offences (Fixed Penalties) (Miscellaneous Provisions) (Wales) Regulations 2007 came into force) (W) (otherwise) (SI 2006/2797) |
| | (6) | 14 Mar 2006 (E) (SI 2006/795)² |
| | | 16 Mar 2006 (W) (for specified purposes³) (SI 2006/768) |
| | | 15 Mar 2007 (the date on which the Environmental Offences (Fixed Penalties) (Miscellaneous Provisions) (Wales) Regulations 2007 came into force) (W) (otherwise) (SI 2006/2797) |
| 20 | | 16 Mar 2006 (W) (for specified purposes³) (SI 2006/768) |
| | | 6 Apr 2006 (E) (SI 2006/795)² |
| | | 15 Mar 2007 (the date on which the Environmental Offences (Fixed Penalties) (Miscellaneous Provisions) (Wales) Regulations 2007 came into force) (W) (otherwise) (SI 2006/2797) |
| 21–23 | | 6 Apr 2006 (E) (SI 2006/795)² |
| | | 15 Mar 2007 (the date on which the Environmental Offences (Fixed Penalties) (Miscellaneous Provisions) (Wales) Regulations 2007 came into force) (W) (SI 2006/2797) |
| 24 | | 16 Mar 2006 (W) (for specified purposes³) (SI 2006/768) |
| | | 6 Apr 2006 (E) (SI 2006/795)² |
| | | 15 Mar 2007 (the date on which the Environmental Offences (Fixed Penalties) (Miscellaneous Provisions) (Wales) Regulations 2007 came into force) (W) (otherwise) (SI 2006/2797) |
| 25 | | 6 Apr 2006 (E) (SI 2006/795)² |
| | | 15 Mar 2007 (the date on which the Environmental Offences (Fixed Penalties) (Miscellaneous Provisions) (Wales) Regulations 2007 came into force) (W) (SI 2006/2797) |
| 26 | | 7 Apr 2005 (RA) |

**Clean Neighbourhoods and Environment Act 2005 (c 16)**—*contd*

| | | |
|---|---|---|
| 27 | | 7 Jun 2005 (s 108(4)(c)) |
| 28 | | 16 Mar 2006 (W) (for specified purposes[3]) (SI 2006/768) |
| | | 6 Apr 2006 (E) (SI 2006/795) |
| | | 15 Mar 2007 (the date on which the Environmental Offences (Fixed Penalties) (Miscellaneous Provisions) (Wales) Regulations 2007 came into force) (W) (otherwise) (SI 2006/2797) |
| 29 | | 6 Apr 2006 (E) (SI 2006/795) |
| | | 15 Mar 2007 (the date on which the Environmental Offences (Fixed Penalties) (Miscellaneous Provisions) (Wales) Regulations 2007 came into force) (W) (SI 2006/2797) |
| 30 | (1) | 16 Mar 2006 (W) (for specified purposes[3]) (SI 2006/768) |
| | | 6 Apr 2006 (E) (SI 2006/795) |
| | | 15 Mar 2007 (the date on which the Environmental Offences (Fixed Penalties) (Miscellaneous Provisions) (Wales) Regulations 2007 came into force) (W) (otherwise) (SI 2006/2797) |
| | (2) | 14 Mar 2006 (E) (SI 2006/795) |
| | | 16 Mar 2006 (W) (for specified purposes[3]) (SI 2006/768) |
| | | 15 Mar 2007 (the date on which the Environmental Offences (Fixed Penalties) (Miscellaneous Provisions) (Wales) Regulations 2007 came into force) (W) (otherwise) (SI 2006/2797) |
| 31 | | 6 Apr 2006 (E) (SI 2006/795) |
| | | 15 Mar 2007 (the date on which the Environmental Offences (Fixed Penalties) (Miscellaneous Provisions) (Wales) Regulations 2007 came into force) (W) (SI 2006/2797) |
| 32 | | 1 Jul 2005 (SI 2005/1675) |
| 33 | | 7 Jun 2005 (s 108(4)(d)) |
| 34 | | 6 Apr 2006 (E) (SI 2006/795) |
| | | 27 Oct 2006 (W) (SI 2006/2797) |
| 35, 36 | | 7 Jun 2005 (s 108(4)(e)) |
| 37 | | 16 Mar 2006 (W) (for specified purposes[3]) (SI 2006/768) |
| | | 6 Apr 2006 (E) (for the purposes of substituting s 5 (but excluding s 5(2)(d)) of the Control of Pollution (Amendment) Act 1989) (SI 2006/795) |
| | | 27 Oct 2006 (W) (for the purposes of substituting s 5 (but excluding s 5(2)(d)) of the Control of Pollution (Amendment) Act 1989) (SI 2006/2797) |
| | | 3 Mar 2015 (E) (for the purpose of making regulations and issuing guidance) (SI 2015/425) |
| | | 6 Apr 2015 (for the purposes of substituting s 5(2)(d)) (SI 2015/425) |
| 38 | | 16 Mar 2006 (W) (for specified purposes[3]) (SI 2006/768) |
| | | 6 Apr 2006 (E) (SI 2006/795) |
| | | 15 Mar 2007 (the date on which the Environmental Offences (Fixed Penalties) (Miscellaneous Provisions) (Wales) Regulations 2007 came into force) (W) (otherwise) (SI 2006/2797) |
| 39 | | 7 Apr 2005 (RA) |
| 40, 41 | | 7 Jun 2005 (s 108(4)(f), (g)) |
| 42–44 | | 18 Oct 2005 (SI 2005/2896) |
| 45 | | 16 Mar 2006 (W) (for specified purposes[3]) (SI 2006/768) |
| | | 6 Apr 2006 (E) (SI 2006/795) |
| | | 15 Mar 2007 (the date on which the Environmental Offences (Fixed Penalties) (Miscellaneous Provisions) (Wales) Regulations 2007 came into force) (W) (otherwise) (SI 2006/2797) |
| 46 | | 16 Mar 2006 (W) (for specified purposes[3]) (SI 2006/768) |

**Clean Neighbourhoods and Environment Act 2005 (c 16)**—*contd*

|  |  |  |
|---|---|---|
|  |  | 3 Mar 2015 (E) (for the purpose of making regulations and issuing guidance) (SI 2015/425) |
|  |  | 6 Apr 2015 (otherwise) (SI 2015/425) |
| 47 |  | 18 Oct 2005 (E) (SI 2005/2896)[1] |
|  |  | 16 Mar 2006 (W) (SI 2006/768)[4] |
| 48 |  | 16 Mar 2006 (W) (for specified purposes[3]) (SI 2006/768) |
|  |  | 6 Apr 2006 (E) (SI 2006/795) |
|  |  | 15 Mar 2007 (the date on which the Environmental Offences (Fixed Penalties) (Miscellaneous Provisions) (Wales) Regulations 2007 came into force) (W) (otherwise) (SI 2006/2797) |
| 49 | (1) | 7 Mar 2006 (SI 2006/656) |
|  | (2) | 7 Mar 2006 (for the purpose of enabling regulations to be made by the Secretary of State) (SI 2006/656) |
|  |  | 6 Apr 2006 (otherwise) (SI 2006/656) |
|  | (3) | 7 Mar 2006 (SI 2006/656) |
|  | (4) | 6 Apr 2006 (SI 2006/656) |
|  | (5) | *Not yet in force* |
|  | (6) | 7 Mar 2006 (for the purpose of enabling regulations to be made by the Secretary of State) (SI 2006/656) |
|  |  | 6 Apr 2006 (otherwise) (SI 2006/656) |
|  | (7) | *Not yet in force* |
|  | (8) | 6 Apr 2006 (for the purpose of enabling guidance to be given by the Secretary of State under s 52(8A)(a)) (SI 2006/656) |
|  |  | *Not yet in force* (otherwise) |
|  | (9) | 6 Apr 2006 (SI 2006/656) |
| 50 |  | 6 Apr 2006 (E) (SI 2006/795) |
|  |  | 27 Oct 2006 (W) (SI 2006/2797) |
| 51 |  | 7 Apr 2005 (RA) |
| 52 |  | 16 Mar 2006 (W) (for specified purposes[3]) (SI 2006/768) |
|  |  | 6 Apr 2006 (E) (SI 2006/795) |
|  |  | 15 Mar 2007 (the date on which the Environmental Offences (Fixed Penalties) (Miscellaneous Provisions) (Wales) Regulations 2007 came into force) (W) (otherwise) (SI 2006/2797) |
| 53 |  | 18 Oct 2005 (E) (SI 2005/2896) |
|  |  | 16 Mar 2006 (W) (SI 2006/768) |
| 54 |  | 7 Jun 2005 (s 108(4)(h)) |
| 55 |  | 14 Mar 2006 (E) (for the purposes of enabling regulations to be made by the Secretary of State under s 55(4), (5)) (SI 2006/795) |
|  |  | 16 Mar 2006 (W) (for specified purposes[3]) (SI 2006/768) |
|  |  | 6 Apr 2006 (E) (otherwise) (SI 2006/795) |
|  |  | 15 Mar 2007 (the date on which the Dog Control Orders (Miscellaneous Provisions) (Wales) Regulations 2007 came into force) (W) (otherwise) (SI 2006/2797) |
| 56 |  | 14 Mar 2006 (E) (SI 2006/795) |
|  |  | 16 Mar 2006 (W) (for specified purposes[3]) (SI 2006/768) |
|  |  | 27 Oct 2006 (W) (otherwise) (SI 2006/2797) |
| 57 |  | 14 Mar 2006 (E) (for the purposes of enabling an order to be made by the Secretary of State under s 57(3)) (SI 2006/795) |
|  |  | 16 Mar 2006 (W) (for specified purposes[3]) (SI 2006/768) |
|  |  | 6 Apr 2006 (E) (otherwise) (SI 2006/795) |
|  |  | 15 Mar 2007 (the date on which the Dog Control Orders (Miscellaneous Provisions) (Wales) Regulations 2007 came into force) (W) (otherwise) (SI 2006/2797) |
| 58 |  | 16 Mar 2006 (W) (for specified purposes[3]) (SI 2006/768) |
|  |  | 6 Apr 2006 (E) (SI 2006/795) |

**Clean Neighbourhoods and Environment Act 2005 (c 16)**—*contd*

|  |  |
|---|---|
|  | 15 Mar 2007 (the date on which the Dog Control Orders (Miscellaneous Provisions) (Wales) Regulations 2007 came into force) (W) (otherwise) (SI 2006/2797) |
| 59 | 14 Mar 2006 (E) (for the purposes of enabling regulations to be made by the Secretary of State under s 59(12)) (SI 2006/795) |
|  | 16 Mar 2006 (W) (for specified purposes[3]) (SI 2006/768) |
|  | 6 Apr 2006 (E) (otherwise) (SI 2006/795) |
|  | 15 Mar 2007 (the date on which the Environmental Offences (Fixed Penalties) (Miscellaneous Provisions) (Wales) Regulations 2007 came into force) (W) (otherwise) (SI 2006/2797) |
| 60 | 14 Mar 2006 (E) (for the purposes of enabling regulations to be made by the Secretary of State under s 60(4), (5)) (SI 2006/795) |
|  | 16 Mar 2006 (W) (for specified purposes[3]) (SI 2006/768) |
|  | 6 Apr 2006 (E) (otherwise) (SI 2006/795) |
|  | 15 Mar 2007 (the date on which the Environmental Offences (Fixed Penalties) (Miscellaneous Provisions) (Wales) Regulations 2007 came into force) (W) (otherwise) (SI 2006/2797) |
| 61, 62 | 6 Apr 2006 (E) (SI 2006/795)[2] |
|  | 15 Mar 2007 (the date on which the Environmental Offences (Fixed Penalties) (Miscellaneous Provisions) (Wales) Regulations 2007 came into force) (W) (otherwise) (SI 2006/2797) |
| 63–65 | 6 Apr 2006 (E) (SI 2006/795)[2] |
|  | 15 Mar 2007 (W) (the date on which the Dog Control Orders (Miscellaneous Provisions) (Wales) Regulations 2007 came into force) (SI 2006/2797)[5] |
| 66 | 14 Mar 2006 (E) (SI 2006/795) |
|  | 27 Oct 2006 (W) (SI 2006/2797) |
| 67 | 14 Mar 2006 (E) (SI 2006/795) |
|  | 16 Mar 2006 (W) (for specified purposes[3]) (SI 2006/768) |
|  | 27 Oct 2006 (W) (otherwise) (SI 2006/2797) |
| 68 | 6 Apr 2008 (SI 2008/956) |
| 69–72 | 6 Apr 2006 (E) (SI 2006/795) |
|  | 15 Mar 2007 (the date on which the Environmental Offences (Fixed Penalties) (Miscellaneous Provisions) (Wales) Regulations 2007 came into force) (W) (SI 2006/2797) |
| 73 | 16 Mar 2006 (W) (for specified purposes[3]) (SI 2006/768) |
|  | 6 Apr 2006 (E) (SI 2006/795) |
|  | 15 Mar 2007 (the date on which the Environmental Offences (Fixed Penalties) (Miscellaneous Provisions) (Wales) Regulations 2007 came into force) (W) (otherwise) (SI 2006/2797) |
| 74 | 14 Mar 2006 (E) (for the purposes of enabling regulations to be made by the Secretary of State under s 74(4), (5)) (SI 2006/795) |
|  | 16 Mar 2006 (W) (for specified purposes[3]) (SI 2006/768) |
|  | 6 Apr 2006 (E) (otherwise) (SI 2006/795) |
|  | 15 Mar 2007 (the date on which the Environmental Offences (Fixed Penalties) (Miscellaneous Provisions) (Wales) Regulations 2007 came into force) (W) (otherwise) (SI 2006/2797) |
| 75 | 14 Mar 2006 (E) (for the purposes of enabling regulations to be made by the Secretary of State under s 75(2)(d), (3)) (SI 2006/795) |
|  | 16 Mar 2006 (W) (for specified purposes[3]) (SI 2006/768) |
|  | 6 Apr 2006 (E) (otherwise) (SI 2006/795) |

**Clean Neighbourhoods and Environment Act 2005 (c 16)**—*contd*

|  |  |  |
|---|---|---|
|  |  | 15 Mar 2007 (the date on which the Environmental Offences (Fixed Penalties) (Miscellaneous Provisions) (Wales) Regulations 2007 came into force) (W) (otherwise) (SI 2006/2797) |
| 76–79 |  | 6 Apr 2006 (E) (SI 2006/795) |
|  |  | 15 Mar 2007 (the date on which the Environmental Offences (Fixed Penalties) (Miscellaneous Provisions) (Wales) Regulations 2007 came into force) (W) (SI 2006/2797) |
| 80, 81 |  | 14 Mar 2006 (E) (SI 2006/795) |
|  |  | 27 Oct 2006 (W) (SI 2006/2797) |
| 82 |  | 16 Mar 2006 (W) (for specified purposes[3]) (SI 2006/768) |
|  |  | 6 Apr 2006 (E) (SI 2006/795) |
|  |  | 15 Mar 2007 (the date on which the Environmental Offences (Fixed Penalties) (Miscellaneous Provisions) (Wales) Regulations 2007 came into force) (W) (otherwise) (SI 2006/2797) |
| 83 | (1) | 14 Mar 2006 (E) (SI 2006/795) |
|  |  | 27 Oct 2006 (W) (SI 2006/2797) |
|  | (2) | 7 Jun 2005 (s 108(4)(i)) |
|  | (3) | 14 Mar 2006 (E) (SI 2006/795) |
|  |  | 27 Oct 2006 (W) (SI 2006/2797) |
| 84 |  | See Sch 1 below |
| 85 |  | 7 Apr 2005 (RA) |
| 86 |  | 6 Apr 2006 (E) (SI 2006/795) |
|  |  | 27 Oct 2006 (W) (SI 2006/2797) |
| 87 | (1) | 1 Jan 2006 (SI 2005/3439) |
|  | (2) | See Sch 2 below |
| 88–91 |  | 1 Jan 2006 (SI 2005/3439) |
| 92 |  | See Sch 3 below |
| 93–95 |  | 1 Jan 2006 (SI 2005/3439) |
| 96 |  | 14 Mar 2006 (E) (for the purposes of enabling regulations to be made by the Secretary of State under s 96(4)(d), (5)) (SI 2006/795) |
|  |  | 16 Mar 2006 (W) (for specified purposes[3]) (SI 2006/768) |
|  |  | 6 Apr 2006 (E) (otherwise) (SI 2006/795) |
|  |  | 15 Mar 2007 (the date on which the Environmental Offences (Fixed Penalties) (Miscellaneous Provisions) (Wales) Regulations 2007 came into force) (W) (otherwise) (SI 2006/2797) |
| 97, 98 |  | 14 Mar 2006 (E) (SI 2006/795) |
|  |  | 16 Mar 2006 (W) (for specified purposes[3]) (SI 2006/768) |
|  |  | 15 Mar 2007 (the date on which the Environmental Offences (Fixed Penalties) (Miscellaneous Provisions) (Wales) Regulations 2007 came into force) (W) (otherwise) (SI 2006/2797) |
| 99, 100 |  | 6 Apr 2006 (E) (SI 2006/795) |
|  |  | 27 Oct 2006 (W) (SI 2006/2797) |
| 101 |  | 16 Mar 2006 (W) (for specified purposes[3]) (SI 2006/768) |
|  |  | 6 Apr 2006 (E) (SI 2006/795) |
|  |  | 31 Jan 2007 (the date on which the Statutory Nuisance (Miscellaneous Provisions) (Wales) Regulations 2007 came into force) (W) (otherwise) (SI 2006/2797) |
| 102 |  | 6 Apr 2006 (E) (SI 2006/795) |
|  |  | 31 Jan 2007 (the date on which the Statutory Nuisance (Miscellaneous Provisions) (Wales) Regulations 2007 came into force) (W) (SI 2006/2797) |
| 103 | (1) | 16 Mar 2006 (W) (for specified purposes[3]) (SI 2006/768) |
|  |  | 6 Apr 2006 (E) (SI 2006/795) |

**Clean Neighbourhoods and Environment Act 2005 (c 16)**—*contd*

|  |  |  |
|---|---|---|
|  |  | 31 Jan 2007 (the date on which the Statutory Nuisance (Miscellaneous Provisions) (Wales) Regulations 2007 came into force) (W) (otherwise) (SI 2006/2797) |
| | (2)(a), (b) | 16 Mar 2006 (W) (for specified purposes[3]) (SI 2006/768) |
| | | 6 Apr 2006 (E) (SI 2006/795) |
| | | 31 Jan 2007 (the date on which the Statutory Nuisance (Miscellaneous Provisions) (Wales) Regulations 2007 came into force) (W) (otherwise) (SI 2006/2797) |
| | (3) | 16 Mar 2006 (W) (for specified purposes[3]) (SI 2006/768) |
| | | 6 Apr 2006 (E) (SI 2006/795) |
| | | 31 Jan 2007 (the date on which the Statutory Nuisance (Miscellaneous Provisions) (Wales) Regulations 2007 came into force) (W) (otherwise) (SI 2006/2797) |
| | (4)(a) | 16 Mar 2006 (W) (for specified purposes[3]) (SI 2006/768) |
| | | 6 Apr 2006 (E) (SI 2006/795) |
| | | 31 Jan 2007 (the date on which the Statutory Nuisance (Miscellaneous Provisions) (Wales) Regulations 2007 came into force) (W) (otherwise) (SI 2006/2797) |
| | (4)(b) | 16 Mar 2006 (W) (for specified purposes[3]) (SI 2006/768) |
| | | 6 Apr 2006 (E) (SI 2006/795) |
| | | 31 Jan 2007 (the date on which the Statutory Nuisance (Miscellaneous Provisions) (Wales) Regulations 2007 came into force) (W) (otherwise) (SI 2006/2797) |
| | (5) | 16 Mar 2006 (W) (for specified purposes[3]) (SI 2006/768) |
| | | 6 Apr 2006 (E) (SI 2006/795) |
| | | 31 Jan 2007 (the date on which the Statutory Nuisance (Miscellaneous Provisions) (Wales) Regulations 2007 came into force) (W) (otherwise) (SI 2006/2797) |
| 104 | | 16 Mar 2006 (W) (for specified purposes[3]) (SI 2006/768) |
| | | 4 Aug 2006 (E) (in so far as makes amendments to the Environmental Protection Act 1990, s 78L which relate to appeals against remediation notices served by a local authority in England or by the Environment Agency in relation to land in England) (SI 2006/1361) |
| | | 10 Dec 2006 (W) (for remaining purposes) (SI 2006/768; SI 2006/2989) |
| 105 | | 7 Jun 2005 (s 108(4)(j)) |
| 106 | | See Sch 4 below |
| 107 | | See Sch 5 below |
| 108–111 | | 7 Apr 2005 (RA) |
| Sch 1 | para 1 | 1 Oct 2006 (E) (SI 2006/2006) |
| | | 15 Mar 2007 (the date on which the Environmental Offences (Fixed Penalties) (Miscellaneous Provisions) (Wales) Regulations 2007 came into force) (W) (SI 2006/2797) |
| | para 2 | 6 Apr 2006 (E) (SI 2006/795) |
| | | 27 Oct 2006 (W) (SI 2006/2797) |
| | paras 3–6 | 1 Oct 2006 (E) (SI 2006/2006) |
| | | 15 Mar 2007 (the date on which the Environmental Offences (Fixed Penalties) (Miscellaneous Provisions) (Wales) Regulations 2007 came into force) (W) (SI 2006/2797) |
| | para 7(1) | 1 Oct 2006 (E) (SI 2006/2006) |
| | | 15 Mar 2007 (the date on which the Environmental Offences (Fixed Penalties) (Miscellaneous Provisions) (Wales) Regulations 2007 came into force) (W) (SI 2006/2797) |
| | para 7(2)(a) | 6 Apr 2006 (E) (SI 2006/795) |
| | | 27 Oct 2006 (W) (SI 2006/2797) |
| | para 7(2)(b) | 1 Oct 2006 (E) (SI 2006/2006) |
| | | 15 Mar 2007 (the date on which the Environmental Offences (Fixed Penalties) (Miscellaneous Provisions) (Wales) Regulations 2007 came into force) (W) (SI 2006/2797) |

**See Halsbury's Statutes Citator for amendments to these Acts**     

**Clean Neighbourhoods and Environment Act 2005 (c 16)**—*contd*

| | | |
|---|---|---|
| | para 7(3) | 6 Apr 2006 (E) (SI 2006/795) |
| | | 27 Oct 2006 (W) (SI 2006/2797) |
| | para 8(1) | 1 Oct 2006 (E) (SI 2006/2006) |
| | | 15 Mar 2007 (the date on which the Environmental Offences (Fixed Penalties) (Miscellaneous Provisions) (Wales) Regulations 2007 came into force) (W) (SI 2006/2797) |
| | para 8(2) | 6 Apr 2006 (E) (SI 2006/795) |
| | | 27 Oct 2006 (W) (SI 2006/2797) |
| | para 8(3) | 1 Oct 2006 (E) (SI 2006/2006) |
| | | 15 Mar 2007 (the date on which the Environmental Offences (Fixed Penalties) (Miscellaneous Provisions) (Wales) Regulations 2007 came into force) (W) (SI 2006/2797) |
| | paras 9–11 | 1 Oct 2006 (E) (SI 2006/2006) |
| | | 15 Mar 2007 (the date on which the Environmental Offences (Fixed Penalties) (Miscellaneous Provisions) (Wales) Regulations 2007 came into force) (W) (SI 2006/2797) |
| | para 12(1) | 1 Oct 2006 (E) (SI 2006/2006) |
| | | 15 Mar 2007 (the date on which the Environmental Offences (Fixed Penalties) (Miscellaneous Provisions) (Wales) Regulations 2007 came into force) (W) (SI 2006/2797) |
| | para 12(2) | 6 Apr 2006 (E) (SI 2006/795) |
| | | 27 Oct 2006 (W) (SI 2006/2797) |
| | para 12(3) | 1 Oct 2006 (E) (SI 2006/2006) |
| | | 15 Mar 2007 (the date on which the Environmental Offences (Fixed Penalties) (Miscellaneous Provisions) (Wales) Regulations 2007 came into force) (W) (SI 2006/2797) |
| | para 12(4) | 14 Mar 2006 (E) (SI 2006/795) |
| | | 15 Mar 2007 (the date on which the Environmental Offences (Fixed Penalties) (Miscellaneous Provisions) (Wales) Regulations 2007 came into force) (W) (SI 2006/2797) |
| | para 12(5), (6) | 6 Apr 2006 (E) (SI 2006/795) |
| | | 27 Oct 2006 (W) (SI 2006/2797) |
| | para 12(7) | 1 Oct 2006 (E) (SI 2006/2006) |
| | | 15 Mar 2007 (the date on which the Environmental Offences (Fixed Penalties) (Miscellaneous Provisions) (Wales) Regulations 2007 came into force) (W) (SI 2006/2797) |
| | paras 13, 14 | 1 Oct 2006 (E) (SI 2006/2006) |
| | | 15 Mar 2007 (the date on which the Environmental Offences (Fixed Penalties) (Miscellaneous Provisions) (Wales) Regulations 2007 came into force) (W) (SI 2006/2797) |
| Schs 2, 3 | | 1 Jan 2006 (SI 2005/3439) |
| Sch 4 | paras 1, 2 | 7 Apr 2005 (RA) |
| | para 3(1)–(4) | 6 Apr 2006 (SI 2006/656) |
| | para 3(5) | *Not yet in force* |
| | para 3(6) | 6 Apr 2006 (for the purposes of amendments to s 52(1), (3)) (SI 2006/656) |
| | | *Not yet in force* (for the purposes of amendments to s 52(2), (4)) |
| | para 4 | 18 Oct 2005 (E) (SI 2005/2896) |
| | | 16 Mar 2006 (W) (SI 2006/768) |
| | paras 5–9 | 6 Mar 2007 (E) (SI 2007/390) |
| | | 18 Jan 2008 (W) (SI 2007/3371) |
| | paras 10–13 | 7 Apr 2005 (RA) |
| | paras 14–19 | 6 Mar 2007 (E) (SI 2007/390) |
| | | 18 Jan 2008 (W) (SI 2007/3371) |
| Sch 5 | Pt 1 | 7 Jun 2005 (s 108(4)(a)), repeals of or in— |
| | | Greater London Council (General Powers) Act 1982; |
| | | London Local Authorities Act 2004, s 11 |
| | | 18 Oct 2005 (SI 2005/2896), repeals of or in— |
| | | Refuse Disposal (Amenity) Act 1978 (E); |
| | | Road Traffic Regulation Act 1984 (E); |

**Clean Neighbourhoods and Environment Act 2005 (c 16)**—*contd*

| | |
|---|---|
| | London Local Authorities Act 2004, s 3 |
| | 27 Oct 2006 (SI 2006/2797), repeals of or in— |
| | Refuse Disposal (Amenity) Act 1978 (W); |
| | Road Traffic Regulation Act 1984 (W) |
| Pt 2 | 6 Apr 2006 (SI 2006/795)², repeals of or in— |
| | Local London Authorities Act 1994; |
| | City of Newcastle upon Tyne Act 2000 |
| | 6 Mar 2007 (E) (repeals in Environmental Protection Act 1990) (SI 2007/390) |
| | 15 Mar 2007 (the date on which the Environmental Offences (Fixed Penalties) (Miscellaneous Provisions) (Wales) Regulations 2007 came into force) (W) (repeals in Environmental Protection Act 1990) (SI 2006/2797) |
| Pt 3 | 7 Jun 2005 (repeal in London Local Authorities Act 2004) (s 108(4)(d)) |
| | 6 Apr 2006 (E) (otherwise) (SI 2006/795) |
| | 18 Jan 2008 (W) (SI 2007/3371) |
| Pt 4 | 7 Jun 2005 (repeals in Control of Pollution (Amendment) Act 1989, ss 1, 2) (s 108(4)(e)) |
| | 7 Jun 2005 (repeal in Environmental Protection Act 1990, s 33) (s 108(4)(f)) |
| | 18 Oct 2005 (E) (remaining repeals in Environmental Protection Act 1990) (SI 2005/2896)¹ |
| | 16 Mar 2006 (W) (remaining repeals in Environmental Protection Act 1990) (SI 2006/768)⁴ |
| | 6 Apr 2015 (repeal of Control of Pollution (Amendment) Act 1989, s 6) (SI 2015/425)⁶ |
| Pt 5 | 6 Apr 2006 (E) (SI 2006/795)² |
| | 15 Mar 2007 (W) (the date on which the Dog Control Orders (Miscellaneous Provisions) (Wales) Regulations 2007 came into force) (SI 2006/2797)⁵ |
| Pt 6 | 6 Apr 2008 (SI 2008/956) |
| Pt 7 | 6 Apr 2006 (E) (SI 2006/795) |
| | 18 Jan 2008 (W) (SI 2007/3371) |
| Pt 8 | 1 Jan 2006 (SI 2005/3439) |
| Pt 9 | 6 Apr 2006 (E) (repeal of Local Government Act 2003, s 119) (SI 2006/795)² |
| | 6 Mar 2007 (E) (otherwise) (SI 2007/390) |
| | 15 Mar 2007 (the date on which the Environmental Offences (Fixed Penalties) (Miscellaneous Provisions) (Wales) Regulations 2007 came into force) (W) (repeal of Local Government Act 2003, s 119) (SI 2006/2797) |
| | 18 Jan 2008 (W) (repeal in Anti-social Behaviour Act 2003) (SI 2007/3371) |
| | 3 Mar 2015 (W) (repeal of Local Government Act 2003, s 100(2)(f)) (SI 2015/425) |
| Pt 10 | 4 Aug 2006 (E) (in so far as makes amendments to the Environmental Protection Act 1990, s 78L which relate to appeals against remediation notices served by a local authority in England or by the Environment Agency in relation to land in England) (SI 2006/1361) |
| | 10 Dec 2006 (W) (SI 2006/768; SI 2006/2989) |

¹ For savings and transitional provisions, see SI 2005/2896, arts 4–6

² For transitional provisions and savings, see SI 2006/795, arts 3, 4

³ The specified purposes are to confer on the National Assembly a power or impose a duty to make or make provision by regulations or orders, or to give directions or give or issue guidance, or make provision with respect to the exercise of any such power or performance of any such duty

⁴ For savings, see SI 2006/768, art 5

**Clean Neighbourhoods and Environment Act 2005 (c 16)**—*contd*

[5]    For transitional provisions and savings, see SI 2006/2797, arts 8–10

[6]    For a saving, see SI 2015/425, art 5

---

**Commissioners for Revenue and Customs Act 2005 (c 11)**

*RA:* 7 Apr 2005

*Commencement provisions:* s 53; Commissioners for Revenue and Customs Act 2005 (Commencement) Order 2005, SI 2005/1126

| | | |
|---|---|---|
| 1–4 | | 7 Apr 2005 (SI 2005/1126) |
| 5–8 | | 18 Apr 2005 (SI 2005/1126) |
| 9–15 | | 7 Apr 2005 (SI 2005/1126) |
| 16 | | 18 Apr 2005 (SI 2005/1126) |
| 17–34 | | 7 Apr 2005 (SI 2005/1126) |
| 35, 36 | | 18 Apr 2005 (SI 2005/1126) |
| 37–49 | | 7 Apr 2005 (SI 2005/1126) |
| 50 | | 18 Apr 2005 (SI 2005/1126) |
| 51 | | 7 Apr 2005 (SI 2005/1126) |
| 52 | | 18 Apr 2005 (SI 2005/1126) |
| 53 | | 7 Apr 2005 (SI 2005/1126) |
| 54 | | 18 Apr 2005 (SI 2005/1126) |
| 55–57 | | 7 Apr 2005 (SI 2005/1126) |
| Sch 1 | | 18 Apr 2005 (SI 2005/1126) |
| Sch 2 | paras 1–14 | 18 Apr 2005 (SI 2005/1126) |
| | paras 15–20 | 7 Apr 2005 (SI 2005/1126) |
| Sch 3 | | 7 Apr 2005 (SI 2005/1126) |
| Schs 4, 5 | | 18 Apr 2005 (SI 2005/1126) |

---

**Consolidated Fund Act 2005 (c 23)**

*RA:* 19 Dec 2005

Whole Act in force 19 Dec 2005 (RA)

---

**Constitutional Reform Act 2005 (c 4)**

*RA:* 24 Mar 2005

*Commencement provisions:* s 148; Constitutional Reform Act 2005 (Commencement No 1) Order 2005, SI 2005/1431; Constitutional Reform Act 2005 (Commencement No 2) Order 2005, SI 2005/2284; Constitutional Reform Act 2005 (Commencement No 3) Order 2005, SI 2005/2505; Constitutional Reform Act 2005 (Commencement No 4) Order 2006, SI 2006/228; Constitutional Reform Act 2005 (Commencement No 5) Order 2006, SI 2006/1014; Constitutional Reform Act 2005 (Commencement No 6) Order 2006, SI 2006/1537; Constitutional Reform Act 2005 (Commencement No 7) Order 2007, SI 2007/967; Constitutional Reform Act 2005 (Commencement No 8) Order 2007, SI 2007/1121; Constitutional Reform Act 2005 (Commencement No 9) Order 2007, SI 2007/1252; Constitutional Reform Act 2005 (Commencement No 10) Order 2008, SI 2008/2597; Constitutional Reform Act 2005 (Commencement No 11) Order 2009, SI 2009/1604; Constitutional Reform Act 2005 (Commencement No 12) Order 2010, SI 2010/883

| | | |
|---|---|---|
| 1–3 | | 3 Apr 2006 (SI 2006/1014) |
| 4 | | 8 May 2007 (SI 2007/1121) |
| 5 | (1), (2) | 3 Apr 2006 (SI 2006/1014) |
| | (3), (4) | 8 May 2007 (SI 2007/1252) |
| | (5) | 3 Apr 2006 (SI 2006/1014) |
| 6 | | 8 May 2007 (SI 2007/1252) |
| 7 | | 3 Apr 2006 (SI 2006/1014) |

**Constitutional Reform Act 2005 (c 4)**—*contd*

| | | |
|---|---|---|
| 8 | | 2 Oct 2008 (SI 2008/2597) |
| 9, 10 | | 3 Apr 2006 (SI 2006/1014) |
| 11 | | 3 Apr 2006 (except in so far as it inserts Justice (Northern Ireland) Act 2002, s 12(1B)(b)) (SI 2006/1014) |
| | | 8 May 2007 (otherwise) (SI 2007/1252) |
| 12, 13 | | 3 Apr 2006 (SI 2006/1014) |
| 14 | | See Sch 3 below |
| 15 | (1) | See Sch 4 below |
| | (2) | See Sch 5 below |
| 16, 17 | | 3 Apr 2006 (SI 2006/1014) |
| 18–22 | | 24 Mar 2005 (RA) |
| 23–44 | | 1 Oct 2009 (SI 2009/1604) |
| 45, 46 | | 27 Feb 2006 (SI 2006/228) |
| 47–60 | | 1 Oct 2009 (SI 2009/1604) |
| 61 | (1) | 3 Apr 2006 (SI 2006/1014) |
| | (2) | See Sch 12 below |
| 62–64 | | 3 Apr 2006 (SI 2006/1014) |
| 65 | (1)–(3) | 1 Oct 2005 (SI 2005/2505) |
| | (4) | 3 Apr 2006 (SI 2006/1014) |
| 66 | | 1 Oct 2005 (SI 2005/2505) |
| 67–84 | | 2 Oct 2006 (SI 2006/1014) |
| 85 | (1)(a) | 2 Apr 2007 (SI 2006/1014) |
| | (1)(b), (c) | See Sch 14 below |
| | (2) | 3 Apr 2006 (SI 2006/1014) |
| | (3) | 1 Oct 2005 (SI 2005/2505) |
| 86–114 | | 3 Apr 2006 (SI 2006/1014) |
| 115–118 | | 1 Oct 2005 (for the purpose of making regulations or rules) (SI 2005/2505) |
| | | 3 Apr 2006 (otherwise) (SI 2006/1014) |
| 119–122 | | 3 Apr 2006 (SI 2006/1014) |
| 123 | | 15 Jun 2005 (except so far as inserts Justice (Northern Ireland) Act 2002, s 5A(6)) (SI 2005/1431) |
| | | 12 Apr 2010 (otherwise) (SI 2010/883) |
| 124 | | 25 Sep 2006 (SI 2006/1537) |
| 125 | | 25 Sep 2006 (except in so far as inserts Justice (Northern Ireland) Act 2002, s 9B(3)(b)) (SI 2006/1537) |
| | | *Not yet in force* (exception noted above) |
| 126–131 | | 25 Sep 2006 (SI 2006/1537) |
| 132 | | 15 Jun 2005 (SI 2005/1431) |
| 133–136 | | 3 Apr 2006 (SI 2006/1014) |
| 137 | | 1 Oct 2009 (SI 2009/1604) |
| 138 | | See Sch 16 below |
| 139 | | 3 Apr 2006 (SI 2006/1014) |
| 140–144 | | 24 Mar 2005 (RA) |
| 145 | | See Sch 17 below |
| 146 | | See Sch 18 below |
| 147–149 | | 24 Mar 2005 (RA) |
| Schs 1, 2 | | 3 Apr 2006 (SI 2006/1014) |
| Sch 3 | paras 1, 2 | 3 Apr 2006 (SI 2006/1014) |
| | para 3(1) | 3 Apr 2006 (SI 2006/1014) |
| | para 3(2), (3) | 3 Apr 2006 (except in respect of appointments to the offices in the Supreme Court listed in the Supreme Court Act 1981, Sch 2, Pt III, column 1) (SI 2006/1014) |
| | | *Not yet in force* (exceptions noted above) |
| | para 3(4) | 3 Apr 2006 (SI 2006/1014) |
| | para 3(5) | 3 Apr 2006 (except in respect of appointments to the offices in the Supreme Court listed in the Supreme Court Act 1981, Sch 2, Pt III, column 1) (SI 2006/1014) |
| | | *Not yet in force* (exceptions noted above) |

**Constitutional Reform Act 2005 (c 4)**—*contd*

|  | paras 4–6 | 3 Apr 2006 (SI 2006/1014) |
|---|---|---|
| Sch 4 | paras 1–6 | 3 Apr 2006 (SI 2006/1014) |
|  | paras 7–12 | *Not yet in force* |
|  | para 13 | 3 Apr 2006 (SI 2006/1014) |
|  | para 14 | *Not yet in force* |
|  | paras 15–17 | 3 Apr 2006 (SI 2006/1014) |
|  | para 18 | *Not yet in force* |
|  | paras 19–41 | 3 Apr 2006 (SI 2006/1014) |
|  | para 42 | *Not yet in force* |
|  | paras 43–114 | 3 Apr 2006 (SI 2006/1014) |
|  | para 115(1) | 3 Apr 2006 (SI 2006/1014) |
|  | para 115(2)(a), (b) | 3 Apr 2006 (SI 2006/1014) |
|  | para 115(2)(c) | 1 Oct 2005 (SI 2005/2505) |
|  | para 115(2)(d) | 3 Apr 2006 (SI 2006/1014) |
|  | para 115(3), (4) | 3 Apr 2006 (SI 2006/1014) |
|  | para 115(5)(a) | 3 Apr 2006 (SI 2006/1014) |
|  | para 115(5)(b) | 1 Oct 2005 (SI 2005/2505) |
|  | para 116 | 3 Apr 2006 (SI 2006/1014) |
|  | para 117(1) | 3 Apr 2006 (SI 2006/1014) |
|  | para 117(2)(a) | 3 Apr 2006 (SI 2006/1014) |
|  | para 117(2)(b) | 1 Oct 2005 (SI 2005/2505) |
|  | para 117(3) | 3 Apr 2006 (SI 2006/1014) |
|  | para 117(4)(a) | 3 Apr 2006 (SI 2006/1014) |
|  | para 117(4)(b) | 1 Oct 2005 (SI 2005/2505) |
|  | para 118(1), (2) | 3 Apr 2006 (SI 2006/1014) |
|  | para 118(3) | 1 Oct 2005 (SI 2005/2505) |
|  | para 118(4)–(6) | 3 Apr 2006 (SI 2006/1014) |
|  | para 119 | 3 Apr 2006 (SI 2006/1014) |
|  | para 120(1), (2) | 3 Apr 2006 (SI 2006/1014) |
|  | para 120(3)(a) | 3 Apr 2006 (SI 2006/1014) |
|  | para 120(3)(b) | 1 Oct 2005 (SI 2005/2505) |
|  | para 121 | 3 Apr 2006 (SI 2006/1014) |
|  | para 122(1) | 3 Apr 2006 (SI 2006/1014) |
|  | para 122(2)(a) | 1 Oct 2005 (SI 2005/2505) |
|  | para 122(2)(b) | 3 Apr 2006 (SI 2006/1014) |
|  | para 122(3) | 3 Apr 2006 (SI 2006/1014) |
|  | para 122(4) | 1 Oct 2005 (SI 2005/2505) |
|  | para 122(5) | 3 Apr 2006 (SI 2006/1014) |
|  | para 123(1)–(3) | 3 Apr 2006 (SI 2006/1014) |
|  | para 123(4) | 1 Oct 2005 (SI 2005/2505) |
|  | para 124 | 3 Apr 2006 (SI 2006/1014) |
|  | para 125 | 1 Oct 2005 (SI 2005/2505) |
|  | paras 126–141 | 3 Apr 2006 (SI 2006/1014) |
|  | para 142 | 1 Oct 2005 (SI 2005/2505) |
|  | paras 143–158 | 3 Apr 2006 (SI 2006/1014) |
|  | para 159 | *Not yet in force* |
|  | paras 160–211 | 3 Apr 2006 (SI 2006/1014) |
|  | para 212(1), (2) | 3 Apr 2006 (SI 2006/1014) |
|  | para 212(3) | 1 Oct 2005 (SI 2005/2505) |
|  | para 212(4) | 3 Apr 2006 (SI 2006/1014) |
|  | paras 213–215 | 3 Apr 2006 (SI 2006/1014) |
|  | para 216 | 1 Oct 2005 (SI 2005/2505) |
|  | paras 217–228 | 3 Apr 2006 (SI 2006/1014) |
|  | para 229 | 1 Oct 2005 (SI 2005/2505) |
|  | paras 230–279 | 3 Apr 2006 (SI 2006/1014) |
|  | para 280(1) | 3 Apr 2006 (SI 2006/1014) |
|  | para 280(2) | 1 Oct 2005 (SI 2005/2505) |
|  | para 280(3) | 3 Apr 2006 (SI 2006/1014) |
|  | paras 281–308 | 3 Apr 2006 (SI 2006/1014) |

**Constitutional Reform Act 2005 (c 4)**—*contd*

| | para 309 | 1 Oct 2005 (SI 2005/2505) |
|---|---|---|
| | paras 310–330 | 3 Apr 2006 (SI 2006/1014) |
| | para 331(1) | 3 Apr 2006 (SI 2006/1014) |
| | para 331(2)(a) | 3 Apr 2006 (SI 2006/1014) |
| | para 331(2)(b)(i), (ii) | 3 Apr 2006 (SI 2006/1014) |
| | para 331(2)(b)(iii) | *Not yet in force* |
| | para 331(2)(b)(iv), (v) | 3 Apr 2006 (SI 2006/1014) |
| | para 331(2)(b)(vi) | *Not yet in force* |
| | para 331(2)(b) (vii)–(ix) | 3 Apr 2006 (SI 2006/1014) |
| | para 331(3)–(5) | 3 Apr 2006 (SI 2006/1014) |
| | paras 332–344 | 3 Apr 2006 (SI 2006/1014) |
| | para 345 | 1 Oct 2005 (SI 2005/2505) |
| | paras 346–350 | 3 Apr 2006 (SI 2006/1014) |
| | para 351 | 1 Oct 2005 (SI 2005/2505) |
| | paras 352–407 | 3 Apr 2006 (SI 2006/1014) |
| Sch 5 | paras 1–87 | 3 Apr 2006 (SI 2006/1014) |
| | para 88 | *Not yet in force* |
| | paras 89–114 | 3 Apr 2006 (SI 2006/1014) |
| | para 115(1) | 3 Apr 2006 (SI 2006/1014) |
| | para 115(2) | *Not yet in force* |
| | para 116 | *Never in force* (repealed) |
| | paras 117–119 | 3 Apr 2006 (SI 2006/1014) |
| | paras 120, 121 | 12 Apr 2010 (SI 2010/883) |
| | para 122(1)–(3) | 3 Apr 2006 (SI 2006/1014) |
| | para 122(4) | 31 Aug 2005 (SI 2005/2284) |
| | para 122(5) | 3 Apr 2006 (only in so far as providing for the office of General Commissioner for a division in Northern Ireland to be a listed judicial office for the purposes of the Justice (Northern Ireland) Act 2002, s 16, and the Constitutional Reform Act 2005, ss 134–136) (SI 2006/1014) |
| | | 15 Jun 2006 (otherwise) (except in so far as it makes the office of General Commissioner for a division in Northern Ireland a listed judicial office for the purposes of the Justice (Northern Ireland) Act 2002, ss 5, 9B) (SI 2006/1537) |
| | | *Not yet in force* (exception noted above) |
| | para 123 | *Never in force* (repealed) |
| | paras 124, 125 | 3 Apr 2006 (SI 2006/1014) |
| | para 126(1), (2) | 3 Apr 2006 (SI 2006/1014) |
| | para 126(3) | *Not yet in force* |
| | para 126(4) | 31 Aug 2005 (SI 2005/2284) |
| | para 126(5) | 3 Apr 2006 (except in relation to the office of General Commissioner for a division in Northern Ireland) (SI 2006/1014) |
| | | *Not yet in force* (exception noted above) |
| | para 127 | 12 Apr 2010 (SI 2010/883) |
| | para 128(1), (2) | 3 Apr 2006 (SI 2006/1014) |
| | para 128(3) | 12 Apr 2010 (SI 2010/883) |
| | para 129 | 3 Apr 2006 (SI 2006/1014) |
| | para 130 | *Not yet in force* |
| | para 131 | 3 Apr 2006 (SI 2006/1014) |
| | para 132 | *Not yet in force* |
| | paras 133, 134 | 3 Apr 2006 (SI 2006/1014) |
| Schs 6, 7 | | 24 Mar 2005 (RA) |
| Schs 8–11 | | 1 Oct 2009 (SI 2009/1604) |
| Sch 12 | paras 1–25 | 3 Apr 2006 (SI 2006/1014) |
| | para 26 | 1 Oct 2005 (for the purpose of making regulations or rules) (SI 2005/2505) |

**Constitutional Reform Act 2005 (c 4)**—*contd*

|  |  |  |
|---|---|---|
|  |  | 3 Apr 2006 (otherwise) (SI 2006/1014) |
|  | paras 27–36 | 3 Apr 2006 (SI 2006/1014) |
| Sch 13 |  | 3 Apr 2006 (SI 2006/1014) |
| Sch 14 | Pt 1 | 3 Apr 2006 (SI 2006/1014)[1] |
|  | Pt 2 | 3 Apr 2006 (except for entries relating to General Commissioner for a division in England and Wales, Justice of the peace, and Justice of the peace who is not a District Judge (Magistrates' Courts)) (SI 2006/1014)[1] |
|  |  | *Not yet in force* (exceptions noted above) |
|  |  | *Never in force* (entries relating to General Commissioner for a division in England and Wales) (repealed) |
|  | Pt 3 | 3 Apr 2006 (except for entries relating to Member of panel appointed under the Rent Act 1977, Sch 10, para 2(a), Member of the Mental Health Review Tribunal, and Member of panel of persons to act as Members of appeal tribunals appointed under the Social Security Act 1998, s 6(2), where it is a requirement that the Member be a medical practitioner) (SI 2006/1014)[1] |
|  |  | 21 Mar 2007 (otherwise) (SI 2007/967) |
| Sch 15 |  | 25 Sep 2006 (SI 2006/1537) |
| Sch 16 |  | 1 Oct 2009 (SI 2009/1604) |
| Sch 17 | paras 1–6 | 3 Apr 2006 (SI 2006/1014) |
|  | paras 7, 8 | *Not yet in force* |
|  | paras 9–35 | 1 Oct 2009 (SI 2009/1604) |
|  | paras 36–39 | *Never in force* (repealed) |
| Sch 18 | Pt 1 | 3 Apr 2006 (SI 2006/1014) |
|  | Pt 2 | 3 Apr 2006 (except repeals in Pluralities Act 1838, and Ecclesiastical Leasing Act 1842) (SI 2006/1014) |
|  |  | *Not yet in force* (exceptions noted above) |
|  | Pt 3 | 3 Apr 2006 (except repeals and revocations of or in Justice (Northern Ireland) Act 2002, Sch 3, para 33, and Health and Personal Social Services (Quality, Improvement and Regulation) (Northern Ireland) Order 2003, SI 2003/431 (NI 9), Sch 4) (SI 2006/1014) |
|  |  | *Not yet in force* (exceptions noted above) |
|  | Pt 4 | 3 Apr 2006 (except repeals in Patronage (Benefices) Measure 1986, and Priests (Ordination of Women) Measure 1993) (SI 2006/1014) |
|  |  | *Not yet in force* (exceptions noted above) |
|  | Pts 5, 6 | 1 Oct 2009 (SI 2009/1604) |

[1] For transitional provisions, see SI 2006/1014, art 2(a), Sch 1, para 20(2), (3)

---

**Disability Discrimination Act 2005 (c 13)**

*RA:* 7 Apr 2005

*Commencement provisions:* s 20(3)–(6), (10); Disability Discrimination Act 2005 (Commencement No 1) Order 2005, SI 2005/1676; Disability Discrimination Act 2005 (Commencement No 2) Order 2005, SI 2005/2774; Disability Discrimination Act 2005 (Commencement No 3) Order 2007, SI 2007/1555; Disability Discrimination Act 2005 (Commencement No 1) (Wales) Order 2007, SI 2007/3285; Disability Discrimination Act 2005 (Commencement No 4) Order 2010, SI 2010/341

|  |  |  |
|---|---|---|
| 1 | : s 15A | 5 Dec 2005 (so far as relates to s 15B) (SI 2005/2774) |
|  |  | 4 Dec 2006 (otherwise) (SI 2005/2774) |
|  | : s 15B | 5 Dec 2005 (SI 2005/2774) |
|  | : s 15C | 4 Dec 2006 (SI 2005/2774) |
| 2 | : ss 21B, 21C | 4 Dec 2006 (SI 2005/2774) |
|  | : ss 21D, 21E | 30 Jun 2005 (for the purpose of exercising any power to make regulations, orders or rules of court) (SI 2005/1676) |

**Disability Discrimination Act 2005 (c 13)**—*contd*

| | | |
|---|---|---|
| | | 4 Dec 2006 (otherwise) (SI 2005/2774) |
| 3 | : s 49A(1) | 5 Dec 2005 (for the purpose only of regulations under s 49D) (SI 2005/2774) |
| | | 4 Dec 2006 (otherwise) (SI 2005/2774) |
| | : s 49A(2) | 4 Dec 2006 (SI 2005/2774) |
| | : ss 49B, 49C | 5 Dec 2005 (SI 2005/2774) |
| | : s 49D | 30 Jun 2005 (for the purpose of exercising any power to make regulations, orders or rules of court) (SI 2005/1676) |
| | | 5 Dec 2005 (otherwise) (SI 2005/2774) |
| | : ss 49E, 49F | 5 Dec 2005 (SI 2005/2774) |
| 4 | | 5 Dec 2005 (SI 2005/2774) |
| 5 | | 30 Jun 2005 (SI 2005/1676) |
| 6 | (1), (2) | 22 Feb 2010 (for the purpose of exercising any power to make regulations or orders) (SI 2010/341) |
| | | 6 Apr 2010 (otherwise) (SI 2010/341) |
| | (3)–(5) | 5 Dec 2005 (SI 2005/2774) |
| 7, 8 | | *Never in force* (repealed) |
| 9 | | 30 Jun 2005 (E) (SI 2005/1676) |
| | | 30 Mar 2008 (W) (SI 2007/3285) |
| 10, 11 | | 5 Dec 2005 (SI 2005/2774) |
| 12 | : s 21F | 10 Oct 2005 (for the purpose of exercising any power to make regulations) (SI 2005/2774) |
| | | 5 Dec 2005 (otherwise) (SI 2005/2774) |
| | : ss 21G, 21H | 30 Jun 2005 (for the purpose of exercising any power to make regulations, orders or rules of court) (SI 2005/1676) |
| | | 5 Dec 2005 (otherwise) (SI 2005/2774) |
| | : s 21J | 5 Dec 2005 (SI 2005/2774) |
| 13 | : ss 24A–24J | 4 Dec 2006 (SI 2005/2774) |
| | : ss 24K, 24L | 30 Jun 2005 (for the purpose of exercising any power to make regulations, orders or rules of court) (SI 2005/1676) |
| | | 4 Dec 2006 (otherwise) (SI 2005/2774) |
| 14 | | 4 Dec 2006 (SI 2005/2774) |
| 15 | : s 31AA | 11 Jun 2007 (for the purpose of exercising any power to make regulations) (SI 2007/1555) |
| | | 1 Sep 2007 (otherwise) (SI 2007/1555) |
| | : ss 31AB, 31AC | 1 Sep 2007 (SI 2007/1555) |
| | : ss 31AD, 31AE | 11 Jun 2007 (for the purpose of exercising any power to make regulations) (SI 2007/1555) |
| | | 1 Sep 2007 (otherwise) (SI 2007/1555) |
| | : s 31AF | 11 Jun 2007 (SI 2007/1555) |
| 16 | (1) | 4 Dec 2006 (SI 2005/2774) |
| | (2) | 30 Jun 2005 (SI 2005/1676) |
| | (3) | 4 Dec 2006 (SI 2005/2774) |
| 17 | : s 56(1)–(5) | 30 Jun 2005 (for the purpose of exercising any power to make regulations, orders or rules of court) (SI 2005/1676) |
| | | 5 Dec 2005 (otherwise) (SI 2005/2774) |
| | : s 56(6), (7) | 30 Jun 2005 (for the purpose of exercising any power to make regulations, orders or rules of court) (SI 2005/1676) |
| | | 4 Dec 2006 (otherwise) (SI 2005/2774) |
| | : s 56(8) | 5 Dec 2005 (SI 2005/2774) |
| | : s 56(9) | 4 Dec 2006 (SI 2005/2774) |
| 18 | | 30 Jun 2005 (for the purpose of exercising any power to make regulations, orders or rules of court) (SI 2005/1676) |
| | | 5 Dec 2005 (otherwise) (SI 2005/2774) |
| 19 | (1) | See Sch 1 below |
| | (2) | See Sch 2 below |
| 20 | | 7 Apr 2005 (RA) |
| Sch 1 | para 1 | 30 Jun 2005 (SI 2005/1676) |
| | para 2(1) | 30 Jun 2005 (SI 2005/1676) |
| | para 2(2) | 5 Dec 2005 (SI 2005/2774) |

**See Halsbury's Statutes Citator for amendments to these Acts**

**Disability Discrimination Act 2005 (c 13)**—*contd*

| | |
|---|---|
| para 2(3) | 30 Jun 2005 (SI 2005/1676) |
| para 2(4) | 4 Dec 2006 (SI 2005/2774) |
| para 3(1)–(4) | 30 Jun 2005 (SI 2005/1676) |
| para 3(5) | 5 Dec 2005 (SI 2005/2774) |
| paras 4–6 | 5 Dec 2005 (SI 2005/2774) |
| para 7(a) | 5 Dec 2005 (so far as relates to s 15B) (SI 2005/2774) |
| | 4 Dec 2006 (otherwise) (SI 2005/2774) |
| para 7(b) | 5 Dec 2005 (SI 2005/2774) |
| para 8(1) | 5 Dec 2005 (SI 2005/2774) |
| para 8(2) | 5 Dec 2005 (so far as relates to s 15B) (SI 2005/2774) |
| | 4 Dec 2006 (otherwise) (SI 2005/2774) |
| para 8(3) | 5 Dec 2005 (SI 2005/2774) |
| para 9 | 30 Jun 2005 (SI 2005/1676) |
| para 10 | 5 Dec 2005 (SI 2005/2774) |
| paras 11, 12 | 4 Dec 2006 (SI 2005/2774) |
| para 13(1)–(3) | 30 Jun 2005 (SI 2005/1676) |
| para 13(4) | 4 Dec 2006 (SI 2005/2774) |
| paras 14–16 | 30 Jun 2005 (SI 2005/1676) |
| para 17 | 30 Jun 2005 (for the purpose of exercising any power to make regulations, orders or rules of court) (SI 2005/1676) |
| | 4 Dec 2006 (otherwise) (SI 2005/2774) |
| para 18 | 30 Jun 2005 (SI 2005/1676) |
| para 19(1) | 30 Jun 2005 (SI 2005/1676) |
| para 19(2)–(4) | 4 Dec 2006 (SI 2005/2774) |
| para 19(5) | 30 Jun 2005 (SI 2005/1676) |
| para 20 | 4 Dec 2006 (SI 2005/2774) |
| paras 21, 22 | 5 Dec 2005 (SI 2005/2774) |
| para 23 | 30 Jun 2005 (for the purpose of exercising any power to make regulations, orders or rules of court) (SI 2005/1676) |
| | 4 Dec 2006 (otherwise) (SI 2005/2774) |
| para 24 | 30 Jun 2005 (SI 2005/1676) |
| para 25 | 1 Sep 2007 (SI 2007/1555) |
| para 26 | 5 Dec 2005 (SI 2005/2774) |
| para 27 | 22 Feb 2010 (for the purpose of exercising any power to make regulations) (SI 2010/341) |
| | 6 Apr 2010 (otherwise) (SI 2010/341) |
| para 28(1)–(5) | 30 Jun 2005 (SI 2005/1676) |
| para 28(6) | 4 Dec 2006 (SI 2005/2774) |
| para 28(7) | 30 Jun 2005 (SI 2005/1676) |
| para 29(1) | 5 Dec 2005 (SI 2005/2774) |
| para 29(2) | 4 Dec 2006 (SI 2005/2774) |
| para 29(3)–(5) | 5 Dec 2005 (SI 2005/2774) |
| para 30 | 30 Jun 2005 (SI 2005/1676) |
| para 31 | 5 Dec 2005 (so far as relates to Pt 5A) (SI 2005/2774) |
| | 4 Dec 2006 (otherwise) (SI 2005/2774) |
| para 32 | 5 Dec 2005 (SI 2005/2774) |
| para 33(1)–(3) | 30 Jun 2005 (SI 2005/1676) |
| para 33(4), (5) | 30 Jun 2005 (for the purpose of exercising any power to make regulations, orders or rules of court) (SI 2005/1676) |
| | 5 Dec 2005 (otherwise) (SI 2005/2774) |
| para 34(1) | 30 Jun 2005 (SI 2005/1676) |
| para 34(2) | 5 Dec 2005 (so far as inserts definition "employment services") (SI 2005/2774) |
| | 4 Dec 2006 (otherwise) (SI 2005/2774) |
| para 34(3), (4) | 5 Dec 2005 (SI 2005/2774) |
| para 34(5) | 30 Jun 2005 (SI 2005/1676) |
| para 34(6) | 10 Oct 2005 (SI 2005/2774) |
| para 34(7) | 4 Dec 2006 (SI 2005/2774) |
| para 35 | 4 Dec 2006 (SI 2005/2774) |

**Disability Discrimination Act 2005 (c 13)**—*contd*

| | | |
|---|---|---|
| para 36 | 5 Dec 2005 (SI 2005/2774) | |
| para 37(1), (2) | 5 Dec 2005 (SI 2005/2774) | |
| para 37(3) | 1 Sep 2007 (SI 2007/1555) | |
| para 37(4)(a) | 4 Dec 2006 (SI 2005/2774) | |
| para 37(4)(b) | 1 Sep 2007 (SI 2007/1555) | |
| para 37(5)(a) | 4 Dec 2006 (SI 2005/2774) | |
| para 37(5)(b) | 1 Sep 2007 (SI 2007/1555) | |
| para 37(6) | 4 Dec 2006 (SI 2005/2774) | |
| para 38(1) | 30 Jun 2005 (SI 2005/1676) | |
| para 38(2) | 5 Dec 2005 (SI 2005/2774) | |
| para 38(3), (4) | 30 Jun 2005 (SI 2005/1676) | |
| para 38(5) | 4 Dec 2006 (SI 2005/2774) | |
| para 38(6)–(13) | 30 Jun 2005 (SI 2005/1676) | |
| para 39(1), (2) | 30 Jun 2005 (SI 2005/1676) | |
| para 39(3) | 5 Dec 2005 (SI 2005/2774) | |
| para 40(1), (2) | 5 Dec 2005 (SI 2005/2774) | |
| para 40(3), (4) | 4 Dec 2006 (SI 2005/2774) | |
| para 40(5), (6) | 5 Dec 2005 (SI 2005/2774) | |
| paras 41–48 | 30 Jun 2005 (E) (SI 2005/1676) | |
| | 30 Mar 2008 (W) (SI 2007/3285) | |
| para 49 | 5 Dec 2005 (SI 2005/2774) | |
| para 50(1) | 5 Dec 2005 (SI 2005/2774) | |
| para 50(2), (3) | 4 Dec 2006 (SI 2005/2774) | |
| para 50(4)(a) | 1 Sep 2007 (SI 2007/1555) | |
| para 50(4)(b) | 4 Dec 2006 (SI 2005/2774) | |
| para 50(5) | 1 Sep 2007 (SI 2007/1555) | |
| para 50(6) | 5 Dec 2005 (SI 2005/2774) | |
| para 50(7) | 4 Dec 2006 (SI 2005/2774) | |

Sch 2    30 Jun 2005 (repeals of or in Disability Discrimination Act 1995, s 17A(1B), Sch 3A) (SI 2005/1676)

30 Jun 2005 (E) (SI 2005/1676), repeals of or in—
Road Traffic Regulation Act 1984;
Traffic Management Act 2004

5 Dec 2005 (SI 2005/2774), repeals and revocations of or in—
Disability Discrimination Act 1995, ss 16A, 16B, 18, 55, 68, Sch 1;
Disability Rights Commission Act 1999;
Scotland Act 1998 (Transfer of Functions to the Scottish Ministers etc) Order 1999

4 Dec 2006 (repeals in Special Educational Needs and Disability Act 2001) (SI 2005/2774)

30 Mar 2008 (W) (SI 2007/3285), repeals of or in—
Road Traffic Regulation Act 1984;
Traffic Management Act 2004

22 Feb 2010 (repeals of or in Disability Discrimination Act 1995, ss 46, 48, for the purpose of exercising any power to make regulations or orders) (SI 2010/341)

6 Apr 2010 (repeals and revocations of or in Disability Discrimination Act 1995, ss 46, 48, otherwise) (SI 2010/341)

*Never in force,* (repealed) repeals of or in—
Disability Discrimination Act 1995, s 49

---

**Drugs Act 2005 (c 17)**

*RA:* 7 Apr 2005

*Commencement provisions:* s 24(2)–(5); Drugs Act 2005 (Commencement No 1) Order 2005, SI 2005/1650; Drugs Act 2005 (Commencement No 2) Order 2005, SI 2005/2223; Drugs Act 2005

**Drugs Act 2005 (c 17)**—*contd*
(Commencement No 3) Order 2005, SI 2005/3053; Drugs Act 2005 (Commencement No 4) Order 2006, SI 2006/2136; Drugs Act 2005 (Commencement No 5) Order 2007, SI 2007/562

| | | |
|---|---|---|
| 1 | | 1 Jan 2006 (SI 2005/3053) |
| 2 | | *Never in force* (repealed) |
| 3 | | 1 Jan 2006 (SI 2005/3053) |
| 4 | | 1 Apr 2007 (SI 2007/562) |
| 5 | | 1 Jan 2006 (SI 2005/3053) |
| 6 | | 1 Apr 2007 (SI 2007/562) |
| 7 | | 1 Dec 2005 (SI 2005/3053) |
| 8 | | 1 Jan 2006 (SI 2005/3053) |
| 9 | | 1 Dec 2005 (SI 2005/3053) |
| 10 | | 1 Apr 2007 (SI 2007/562) |
| 11 | | 1 Dec 2005 (in so far as relates to an initial assessment required under s 9) (SI 2005/3053) |
| | | 1 Apr 2007 (otherwise) (SI 2007/562) |
| 12 | | 1 Dec 2005 (SI 2005/3053) |
| 13, 14 | | 1 Apr 2007 (SI 2007/562) |
| 15–17 | | 1 Dec 2005 (in so far as relates to an initial assessment required under s 9) (SI 2005/3053) |
| | | 1 Apr 2007 (otherwise) (SI 2007/562) |
| 18, 19 | | 1 Dec 2005 (SI 2005/3053) |
| 20 | | 1 Oct 2006 (SI 2006/2136) |
| 21 | | 18 Jul 2005 (SI 2005/1650) |
| 22 | | 7 Apr 2005 (s 24(2)) |
| 23 | (1) | See Sch 1 below |
| | (2) | See Sch 2 below |
| 24 | | 7 Apr 2005 (s 24(2)) |
| Sch 1 | paras 1–5 | 1 Dec 2005 (SI 2005/3053) |
| | paras 6, 7 | 1 Sep 2005 (SI 2005/2223) |
| | para 8 | 1 Dec 2005 (SI 2005/3053) |
| Sch 2 | | 1 Sep 2005 (repeal in Criminal Justice and Police Act 2001) (SI 2005/2223) |
| | | 1 Dec 2005 (otherwise) (SI 2005/3053) |

**Education Act 2005 (c 18)**

*RA:* 7 Apr 2005

*Commencement provisions:* s 125; Education Act 2005 (Commencement No 1 and Savings and Transitional Provisions) Order 2005, SI 2005/2034; Education Act 2005 (Commencement No 1 and Transitional Provisions) (Wales) Order 2006, SI 2006/1338; Education Act 2005 (Commencement No 2 and Transitional Provisions) (Wales) Order 2006, SI 2006/2129; Education Act 2005 (Commencement No 2) (Wales) Order 2010, SI 2010/735

| | |
|---|---|
| 1–18 | 1 Sep 2005 (SI 2005/2034) |
| 19–26 | 1 Sep 2006 (SI 2006/1338) |
| 27 | 1 Sep 2006 (SI 2006/1338)[2] |
| 28–40 | 1 Sep 2006 (SI 2006/1338) |
| 41, 42 | 1 Sep 2006 (in relation to special schools as described in s 28(2)(d)) (SI 2006/1338) |
| | *Not yet in force* (in relation to schools described in s 28(2)(a)–(c)) |
| 43 | 1 Sep 2006 (SI 2006/1338) |
| 44, 45 | 1 Sep 2005 (E) (SI 2005/2034) |
| | 1 Sep 2006 (W) (SI 2006/1338) |
| 46 | See Sch 5 below |
| 47 | 1 Sep 2005 (E) (SI 2005/2034) |
| | 1 Sep 2006 (W) (SI 2006/1338) |
| 48, 49 | 1 Sep 2005 (SI 2005/2034) |
| 50 | 1 Sep 2006 (SI 2006/1338) |

**Education Act 2005 (c 18)**—*contd*

| | | |
|---|---|---|
| 51 | | 1 Sep 2005 (E) (SI 2005/2034) |
| | | 1 Sep 2006 (W) (SI 2006/1338) |
| 52 | | 1 Sep 2006 (SI 2006/1338) |
| 53 | | See Sch 7 below |
| 54 | | See Sch 8 below |
| 55–57 | | 1 Apr 2007 (SI 2006/1338) |
| 58 | | 1 Sep 2005 (E) (SI 2005/2034) |
| | | 1 Sep 2006 (W) (SI 2006/1338) |
| 59 | | 3 Oct 2005 (E) (SI 2005/2034) |
| | | 1 Sep 2006 (W) (SI 2006/1338) |
| 60 | | 1 Sep 2005 (E) (SI 2005/2034)[1] |
| | | 1 Sep 2006 (W) (SI 2006/1338)[2] |
| 61 | | See Sch 9 below |
| 62, 63 | | 7 Apr 2005 (s 125(1)(a)) |
| 64 | | 1 Sep 2006 (SI 2006/2129)[3] |
| 65 | | 1 Aug 2006 (in so far as inserts s 28A(8)) (SI 2006/2129)[3] |
| | | 1 Sep 2006 (otherwise) (SI 2006/2129)[3] |
| 66 | (1)–(5) | 1 Sep 2006 (SI 2006/2129)[3] |
| | (6) | 1 Aug 2006 (SI 2006/2129)[3] |
| | (7)–(9) | 1 Sep 2006 (SI 2006/2129)[3] |
| | (10) | 1 Aug 2006 (SI 2006/2129)[3] |
| | (11) | 1 Sep 2006 (SI 2006/2129)[3] |
| | (12) | See Sch 10 below |
| | (13) | 1 Aug 2006 (SI 2006/2129)[3] |
| | (14) | 1 Sep 2006 (SI 2006/2129)[3] |
| 67 | | 1 Sep 2006 (SI 2006/2129) |
| 68 | | 1 Sep 2006 (SI 2006/2129)[3] |
| 69 | | 1 Sep 2006 (SI 2006/2129) |
| 70 | | 1 Sep 2006 (E) (SI 2006/2129) |
| | | *Never in force* (W) (repealed) |
| 71 | | 1 Sep 2006 (SI 2006/1338; SI 2006/2129) |
| 72 | | See Sch 12 below |
| 73 | | 1 Sep 2006 (SI 2006/2129) |
| 74 | | 1 Sep 2005 (s 125(3)(a)) |
| 75 | (1)–(4) | 1 Sep 2005 (s 125(3)(a)) |
| | (5) | 7 Apr 2005 (s 125(1)(b)) |
| 76 | | 1 Sep 2005 (s 125(3)(a)) |
| 77 | (1) | 1 Sep 2005 (s 125(3)(a)) |
| | (2) | See Sch 13 below |
| 78 | (1), (2) | 1 Sep 2005 (s 125(3)(a)) |
| | (3) | 7 Apr 2005 (s 125(1)(b)) |
| 79–95 | | 1 Sep 2005 (s 125(3)(a)) |
| 96, 97 | | 7 Apr 2005 (s 125(1)(b)) |
| 98 | | See Sch 14 below |
| 99 | | See Sch 15 below |
| 100 | | 7 Apr 2005 (s 125(1)(b)) |
| 101 | | See Sch 16 below |
| 102 | | 7 Jun 2005 (s 125(2)) |
| 103, 104 | | 1 Sep 2005 (SI 2005/2034)[1] |
| 105 | | 1 Sep 2005 (E) (in so far as inserts Education Act 2002, s 28A(1), (2), (5)) (SI 2005/2034) |
| | | 1 Sep 2006 (W) (SI 2006/1338) |
| 106 | | 3 Oct 2005 (E) (SI 2005/2034) |
| | | 1 Sep 2006 (W) (SI 2006/1338) |
| 107 | | See Sch 17 below |
| 108–114 | | 7 Jun 2005 (s 125(2)) |
| 115, 116 | | 1 Sep 2005 (E) (SI 2005/2034) |
| | | 1 Sep 2006 (W) (SI 2006/1338) |
| 117 | | See Sch 18 below |

**Education Act 2005 (c 18)**—*contd*

| | | |
|---|---|---|
| 118 | | 1 Sep 2005 (E) (SI 2005/2034) |
| | | 1 Sep 2006 (W) (SI 2006/1338) |
| 119–122 | | 7 Apr 2005 (s 125(1)(c)) |
| 123 | | See Sch 19 below |
| 124–128 | | 7 Apr 2005 (s 125(1)(c)) |
| Sch 1 | | 1 Sep 2005 (SI 2005/2034) |
| Sch 2 | | 1 Sep 2006 (SI 2006/1338) |
| Sch 3 | | 1 Sep 2006 (SI 2006/1338)[2] |
| Sch 4 | | 1 Sep 2006 (SI 2006/1338) |
| Sch 5 | | 1 Sep 2005 (E) (SI 2005/2034) |
| | | 1 Sep 2006 (W) (SI 2006/1338) |
| Sch 6 | | 1 Sep 2006 (SI 2006/1338) |
| Sch 7 | paras 1, 2 | 3 Oct 2005 (SI 2005/2034) |
| | para 3(1)–(5) | 3 Oct 2005 (SI 2005/2034) |
| | para 3(6) | 1 Aug 2005 (SI 2005/2034) |
| | para 3(7), (8) | 3 Oct 2005 (SI 2005/2034) |
| | para 4(1)–(3) | 3 Oct 2005 (SI 2005/2034) |
| | para 4(4) | 1 Aug 2005 (SI 2005/2034) |
| | para 4(5) | 3 Oct 2005 (SI 2005/2034) |
| | para 5 | 1 Sep 2006 (SI 2006/1338) |
| | paras 6–8 | 3 Oct 2005 (E) (SI 2005/2034) |
| | | 1 Sep 2006 (W) (SI 2006/1338) |
| | para 9 | 1 Sep 2006 (W) (SI 2006/1338) |
| | | *Not yet in force* (E) |
| | paras 10, 11 | 3 Oct 2005 (E) (SI 2005/2034) |
| | | 1 Sep 2006 (W) (SI 2006/1338) |
| | para 12 | 1 Aug 2005 (E) (for the purpose of making regulations under School Standards and Framework Act 1998, Sch 26, para 6A(4)) (SI 2005/2034) |
| | | 3 Oct 2005 (E) (otherwise) (SI 2005/2034) |
| | | 1 Sep 2006 (W) (SI 2006/1338) |
| | paras 13–19 | 3 Oct 2005 (E) (SI 2005/2034) |
| | | 1 Sep 2006 (W) (SI 2006/1338) |
| | para 20 | 1 Aug 2005 (E) (for the purpose of making regulations under School Standards and Framework Act 1998, Sch 26, para 13A(2)) (SI 2005/2034) |
| | | 3 Oct 2005 (E) (otherwise) (SI 2005/2034) |
| | | 1 Sep 2006 (W) (SI 2006/1338) |
| | paras 21–24 | 3 Oct 2005 (E) (SI 2005/2034) |
| | | 1 Sep 2006 (W) (SI 2006/1338) |
| Sch 8 | | 1 Sep 2005 (E) (SI 2005/2034) |
| | | 1 Sep 2006 (W) (SI 2006/1338) |
| Sch 9 | paras 1–5 | 1 Sep 2005 (SI 2005/2034) |
| | paras 6, 7 | 1 Sep 2006 (SI 2006/1338) |
| | paras 8–21 | 1 Sep 2005 (E) (SI 2005/2034) |
| | | 1 Sep 2006 (W) (SI 2006/1338) |
| | para 22 | 1 Sep 2006 (SI 2006/1338) |
| | para 23 | 1 Sep 2005 (SI 2005/2034) |
| | paras 24, 25 | 1 Sep 2006 (SI 2006/1338) |
| | para 26 | 1 Sep 2005 (SI 2005/2034) |
| | para 27 | 1 Sep 2006 (SI 2006/1338) |
| | paras 28–30 | 1 Sep 2005 (E) (SI 2005/2034) |
| | | 1 Sep 2006 (W) (SI 2006/1338) |
| Sch 10 | paras 1–3 | 1 Sep 2006 (SI 2006/2129) |
| | para 4(1)–(3) | 1 Sep 2006 (SI 2006/2129) |
| | para 4(4) | 1 Aug 2006 (SI 2006/2129) |
| | para 4(5)–(7) | 1 Sep 2006 (SI 2006/2129) |
| | paras 5–7 | 1 Sep 2006 (SI 2006/2129) |
| | para 8 | 1 Aug 2006 (SI 2006/2129) |

**Education Act 2005 (c 18)**—*contd*

|            | paras 9–15   | 1 Sep 2006 (SI 2006/2129) |
|------------|--------------|---------------------------|
| Sch 11     |              | 1 Sep 2006 (SI 2006/2129) |
| Sch 12     | paras 1–8    | 1 Sep 2006 (SI 2006/2129) |
|            | para 9       | 1 Sep 2006 (E) (SI 2006/2129) |
|            |              | *Never in force* (W) (repealed) |
|            | paras 10–13  | 1 Sep 2006 (SI 2006/2129) |
|            | para 14      | 1 Sep 2006 (except in so far as para 14(14) repeals Sch 7, para 16(6)) (SI 2006/2129) |
|            |              | *Never in force* (exception noted above) (repealed) |
|            | paras 15, 16 | 1 Sep 2006 (SI 2006/2129) |
| Schs 13, 14|              | 1 Sep 2005 (s 125(3)(a)) |
| Sch 15     | paras 1, 2   | 1 Sep 2005 (s 125(3)(a)) |
|            | para 3       | 7 Apr 2005 (s 125(1)(b)) |
|            | paras 4–6    | 1 Sep 2005 (s 125(3)(a)) |
| Sch 16     | paras 1–4    | 1 Nov 2005 (E) (SI 2005/2034) |
|            |              | 1 Apr 2010 (W) (SI 2010/735) |
|            | paras 5–7    | 1 Nov 2005 (E) (SI 2005/2034)[1] |
|            |              | 1 Apr 2010 (W) (SI 2010/735) |
|            | para 8       | 1 Nov 2005 (SI 2005/2034) |
| Sch 17     |              | 7 Jun 2005 (s 125(2)) |
| Sch 18     | para 1       | 1 Sep 2005 (E) (SI 2005/2034) |
|            |              | 1 Sep 2006 (W) (SI 2006/1338) |
|            | paras 2–4    | 1 Sep 2005 (SI 2005/2034)[1] |
|            | para 5       | 1 Nov 2005 (E) (SI 2005/2034) |
|            |              | 1 Apr 2010 (W) (SI 2010/735) |
|            | para 6       | 1 Sep 2005 (E) (SI 2005/2034) |
|            |              | 1 Sep 2006 (W) (SI 2006/1338) |
|            | paras 7–9    | 1 Nov 2005 (E) (SI 2005/2034) |
|            |              | 1 Apr 2010 (W) (SI 2010/735) |
|            | para 10      | 1 Nov 2005 (E) (SI 2005/2034) |
|            |              | *Not yet in force* (W) |
|            | para 11      | 1 Nov 2005 (E) (SI 2005/2034) |
|            |              | 1 Apr 2010 (W) (SI 2010/735) |
|            | para 12      | 1 Nov 2005 (E) (SI 2005/2034) |
|            |              | *Not yet in force* (W) |
|            | para 13      | 1 Apr 2010 (SI 2010/735) |
|            | para 14      | 1 Nov 2005 (E) (SI 2005/2034) |
|            |              | 1 Apr 2010 (W) (SI 2010/735) |
|            | para 15      | 1 Sep 2005 (E) (SI 2005/2034) |
|            |              | 1 Sep 2006 (W) (SI 2006/1338) |
| Sch 19     | Pt 1         | 1 Sep 2005 (SI 2005/2034), repeals of or in— |
|            |              | Parliamentary Commissioner Act 1967; |
|            |              | Education Act 1996 (E); |
|            |              | School Inspections Act 1996 (E)[1]; |
|            |              | Education Act 1997 (E); |
|            |              | School Standards and Framework Act 1998, ss 15, 127, 134, 135, Sch 28, 30 (E); |
|            |              | Protection of Children Act 1999; |
|            |              | Learning and Skills Act 2000, Schs 7, 9 (E); |
|            |              | Education Act 2002 (E) |
|            |              | 3 Oct 2005 (E) (repeals in School Standards and Framework Act 1998, Sch 26) (SI 2005/2034) |
|            |              | 1 Sep 2006 (SI 2006/1338), repeals of or in— |
|            |              | Children Act 1989, s 79T; |
|            |              | Education Act 1996 (W); |
|            |              | School Inspections Act 1996 (W)[2]; |
|            |              | Education Act 1997 (W); |
|            |              | School Standards and Framework Act 1998 (W); |
|            |              | Learning and Skills Act 2000, Schs 7, 9 (W); |

**Education Act 2005 (c 18)**—*contd*

>                         Education Act 2002 (W)
>                         1 Apr 2007 (SI 2006/1338) repeals of or in—
>                             Teaching and Higher Education Act 1998;
>                             Learning and Skills Act 2000, s 81
>                         *Never in force* (repeals of or in Children Act 1989, ss 79P–79R)

| Pt 2 | 1 Sep 2006 (except in so far as repeals School Standards and Framework Act 1998, Sch 7, para 16(6)) (SI 2006/2129)[3] |

>                         *Not yet in force* (exception noted above)

| Pt 3 | 1 Sep 2005 (s 125(3)(b)) |
| Pt 4 | 1 Sep 2005 (SI 2005/2034), repeals of or in— |

>                             Special Educational Needs and Disability Act 2001[1];
>                             Education Act 2002, Sch 21, para 39(5)[1]
>                         1 Nov 2005 (E) (SI 2005/2034), repeals of or in—
>                             School Standards and Framework Act 1998;
>                             Education Act 2002, ss 41(2), 42, Sch 21, para 124(3);
>                             Local Government Act 2003
>                         1 Apr 2010 (W) (SI 2010/735), repeals of or in—
>                             School Standards and Framework Act 1998;
>                             Education Act 2002, ss 41(2), 42, Sch 21, para 124(3), 125(3);
>                             Local Government Act 2003
>                         *Not yet in force*, repeal of—
>                             Education Act 2002, Sch 21, para 125(3) (E)

[1]    For transitional provisions and savings, see SI 2005/2034, art 10, Schedule

[2]    For transitional provisions and savings, see SI 2006/1338, art 6, Sch 4

[3]    For transitional provisions and savings, see SI 2006/2129, art 6

---

**Electoral Registration (Northern Ireland) Act 2005 (c 1)**

*RA:* 24 Feb 2005

Whole Act in force 24 Feb 2005 (RA)

---

**Emergency Workers (Scotland) Act 2005 (asp 2)**

*RA:* 1 Feb 2005

*Commencement provisions:* s 9(2); Emergency Workers (Scotland) Act 2005 (Commencement) Order 2005, SSI 2005/229

| 1–8 | 9 May 2005 (SSI 2005/229) |
| 9 | 1 Feb 2005 (RA) |

---

**Environmental Assessment (Scotland) Act 2005 (asp 15)**

*RA:* 14 Dec 2005

*Commencement provisions:* s 26(1), (2); Environmental Assessment (Scotland) Act 2005 (Commencement and Savings) Order 2006, SSI 2006/19

| 1–20 | 20 Feb 2006 (SSI 2006/19) |
| 21–23 | 14 Dec 2005 (RA) |
| 24 | 20 Feb 2006 (SSI 2006/19)[1] |
| 25, 26 | 14 Dec 2005 (RA) |
| Schs 1–3 | 20 Feb 2006 (SSI 2006/19) |

[1]    For a saving, see SSI 2006/19, art 3

---

## Finance Act 2005 (c 7)

*Budget Day:* 16 Mar 2005

*RA:* 7 Apr 2005

The commencement details of Finance Acts are not set out, as the dates from which their provisions take effect are usually stated clearly and unambiguously in the text of the Act, and charging provisions will normally state for which year or years of assessment they are to have effect.

## Finance (No 2) Act 2005 (c 22)

*RA:* 20 Jul 2005

The commencement details of Finance Acts are not set out, as the dates from which their provisions take effect are usually stated clearly and unambiguously in the text of the Act, and charging provisions will normally state for which year or years of assessment they are to have effect.

## Fire (Scotland) Act 2005 (asp 5)

*RA:* 1 Apr 2005

*Commencement provisions:* s 90; Fire (Scotland) Act 2005 (Commencement No 1) Order 2005, SSI 2005/207; Fire (Scotland) Act 2005 (Commencement No 2) Order 2005, SSI 2005/392; Fire (Scotland) Act 2005 (Commencement No 3 and Savings) Order 2006, SSI 2006/458

| | |
|---|---|
| 1–10 | 2 Aug 2005 (SSI 2005/392) |
| 11 | 6 Apr 2005 (so far as enables orders to be made) (SSI 2005/207) |
| | 2 Aug 2005 (otherwise) (SSI 2005/392) |
| 12–15 | 2 Aug 2005 (SSI 2005/392) |
| 16 | 6 Apr 2005 (so far as enables orders to be made) (SSI 2005/207) |
| | 2 Aug 2005 (otherwise) (SSI 2005/392) |
| 17–39 | 2 Aug 2005 (SSI 2005/392) |
| 40 | 6 Apr 2005 (so far as enables orders to be made) (SSI 2005/207) |
| | 2 Aug 2005 (otherwise) (SSI 2005/392) |
| 41–52 | 2 Aug 2005 (SSI 2005/392) |
| 53–56 | 1 Oct 2006 (SSI 2006/458) |
| 57, 58 | 6 Apr 2005 (so far as they enable regulations to be made) (SSI 2005/207) |
| | 1 Oct 2006 (otherwise) (SSI 2006/458) |
| 59–77 | 1 Oct 2006 (SSI 2006/458)[1] |
| 78 | 6 Apr 2005 (so far as enables regulations to be made) (SSI 2005/207) |
| | 1 Oct 2006 (otherwise) (SSI 2006/458) |
| 79 | 1 Oct 2006 (SSI 2006/458) |
| 80, 81 | 2 Aug 2005 (SSI 2005/392) |
| 82 | 6 Apr 2005 (SSI 2005/207) |
| 83–86 | 2 Aug 2005 (SSI 2005/392) |
| 87 | 6 Apr 2005 (SSI 2005/207) |
| 88 | 1 Apr 2005 (RA) |
| 89 | 2 Aug 2005 (SSI 2005/392) |
| 90 | 1 Apr 2005 (RA) |
| 91 | 2 Aug 2005 (SSI 2005/392) |
| Sch 1 | 2 Aug 2005 (SSI 2005/392) |
| Sch 2 | 1 Oct 2006 (SSI 2006/458) |
| Schs 3, 4 | 2 Aug 2005 (SSI 2005/392) |

[1] For a saving, see SSI 2006/458, art 3. S 77A was inserted by the Fire (Scotland) Act 2005 (Consequential Provisions and Modifications) Order 2005, SI 2005/2060, art 2(7)

## Further and Higher Education (Scotland) Act 2005 (asp 6)

*RA:* 1 Jun 2005

*Commencement provisions:* s 36(2), (3); Further and Higher Education (Scotland) Act 2005 (Commencement) Order 2005, SSI 2005/419

| | |
|---|---|
| 1 | 3 Oct 2005 (SSI 2005/419) |
| 2 | 8 Sep 2005 (SSI 2005/419) |
| 3–32 | 3 Oct 2005 (SSI 2005/419) |
| 33–36 | 1 Jun 2005 (RA) |
| Schs 1–3 | 3 Oct 2005 (SSI 2005/419) |

## Gaelic Language (Scotland) Act 2005 (asp 7)

*RA:* 1 Jun 2005

*Commencement provisions:* s 13(2); Gaelic Language (Scotland) Act 2005 Commencement Order 2006, SSI 2006/31

| | |
|---|---|
| 1–10 | 13 Feb 2006 (SSI 2006/31) |
| 11 | 1 Jun 2005 (RA) |
| 12 | See Sch 2 below |
| 13 | 1 Jun 2005 (RA) |
| Schs 1, 2 | 13 Feb 2006 (SSI 2006/31) |

## Gambling Act 2005 (c 19)

*RA:* 7 Apr 2005

*Commencement provisions:* s 358; Gambling Act 2005 (Commencement No 1) Order 2005, SI 2005/2425; Gambling Act 2005 (Commencement No 2 and Transitional Provisions) Order 2005, SI 2005/2455; Gambling Act 2005 (Commencement No 3) Order 2006, SI 2006/631; Gambling Act 2005 (Commencement No 4) Order 2006, SI 2006/2964; Gambling Act 2005 (Commencement No 5) Order 2006, SI 2006/3220; Gambling Act 2005 (Commencement No 6 and Transitional Provisions) Order 2006, SI 2006/3272, as amended by SI 2006/3361, SI 2007/1157, SI 2007/1527, SI 2007/2169; Gambling Act 2005 (Commencement No 7) Order 2007, SI 2007/3155; Gambling Act 2005 (Commencement No 8) Order 2008, SI 2008/1326

| | | |
|---|---|---|
| 1–6 | | 1 Oct 2005 (SI 2005/2455) |
| 7 | (1)–(4) | 1 Oct 2005 (SI 2005/2455) |
| | (5)(a) | *Not yet in force* |
| | (5)(b)–(d), (6), (7) | 20 May 2008 (SI 2008/1326) |
| 8, 9 | | 1 Oct 2005 (SI 2005/2455) |
| 10 | (1), (2) | 1 Oct 2005 (SI 2005/2455) |
| | (3) | 1 Sep 2007 (SI 2006/3272) |
| 11–14 | | 1 Oct 2005 (SI 2005/2455) |
| 15 | (1)–(4) | 1 Oct 2005 (SI 2005/2455) |
| | (5) | See Sch 3 below |
| 16–20 | | 1 Oct 2005 (SI 2005/2455) |
| 21 | | 1 Oct 2005 (SI 2005/2455)[1] |
| 22, 23 | | 1 Oct 2005 (SI 2005/2455) |
| 24 | (1)–(8) | 1 Oct 2005 (SI 2005/2455) |
| | (9) | 1 Sep 2007 (SI 2006/3272) |
| | (10), (11) | 1 Oct 2005 (SI 2005/2455) |
| 25, 26 | | 1 Oct 2005 (SI 2005/2455) |
| 27 | | 1 Sep 2007 (SI 2006/3272) |
| 28 | | 1 Jan 2007 (in so far as relates to an offence under s 342) (SI 2006/3272) |
| | | 1 Sep 2007 (otherwise) (SI 2006/3272) |
| 29 | | 1 Sep 2007 (SI 2006/3272) |
| 30–32 | | 1 Oct 2005 (SI 2005/2455) |

**Gambling Act 2005 (c 19)**—*contd*

| | | |
|---|---|---|
| 33–64 | | 1 Sep 2007 (SI 2006/3272) |
| 65 | (1) | 1 Jan 2007 (for the purpose of enabling advance applications for operating licences to be made, considered and determined and of enabling such licences to be issued before 1 Sep 2007) (SI 2006/3272) |
| | | 1 Sep 2007 (otherwise) (SI 2006/3272) |
| | (2) | 1 Oct 2005 (SI 2005/2455) |
| | (3)–(5) | 1 Jan 2007 (for the purpose of enabling advance applications for operating licences to be made, considered and determined and of enabling such licences to be issued before 1 Sep 2007) (SI 2006/3272) |
| | | 1 Sep 2007 (otherwise) (SI 2006/3272) |
| 66–74 | | 1 Jan 2007 (for the purpose of enabling advance applications for operating licences to be made, considered and determined and of enabling such licences to be issued before 1 Sep 2007) (SI 2006/3272) |
| | | 1 Sep 2007 (otherwise) (SI 2006/3272) |
| 75 | (1), (2) | 1 Oct 2005 (SI 2005/2455) |
| | (3) | 1 Jan 2007 (SI 2006/3272) |
| 76 | (1)–(3) | 1 Oct 2005 (SI 2005/2455) |
| | (4)–(6) | 1 Jan 2007 (SI 2006/3272) |
| 77, 78 | | 1 Jan 2007 (SI 2006/3272) |
| 79 | | 1 Oct 2005 (in so far as relates to ss 75(1), (2), 76(1)–(3) of this Act) (SI 2005/2455) |
| | | 1 Jan 2007 (in so far as relates to ss 75(3), 76(4)–(6), 77, 78 of this Act) (SI 2006/3272) |
| 80 | | 1 Oct 2005 (in so far as has effect to define "management office" and "operational function" for the purposes of s 127 of this Act) (SI 2005/2455) |
| | | 1 Jan 2007 (otherwise) (SI 2006/3272) |
| 81 | | 1 Jan 2007 (SI 2006/3272) |
| 82, 83 | | 1 Sep 2007 (SI 2006/3272) |
| 84–88 | | 1 Jan 2007 (SI 2006/3272) |
| 89 | (1) | 1 Jan 2007 (SI 2006/3272) |
| | (2), (3) | *Never in force* (repealed) |
| | (4)–(7) | 1 Jan 2007 (SI 2006/3272) |
| 90–107 | | 1 Jan 2007 (SI 2006/3272) |
| 108 | | 1 Sep 2007 (SI 2006/3272) |
| 109 | | 1 Jan 2007 (SI 2006/3272) |
| 110–112 | | 1 Sep 2007 (SI 2006/3272) |
| 113–115 | | 1 Jan 2007 (SI 2006/3272) |
| 116 | (1) | 1 Sep 2007 (SI 2006/3272) |
| | (2)(a) | 1 Sep 2007 (SI 2006/3272) |
| | (2)(b), (c) | 1 Jan 2007 (SI 2006/3272) |
| | (3)–(5) | 1 Jan 2007 (SI 2006/3272) |
| 117–120 | | 1 Jan 2007 (in so far as they relate to a review under s 116(2)(b) or (c)) (SI 2006/3272) |
| | | 1 Sep 2007 (otherwise) (SI 2006/3272) |
| 121 | | 1 Sep 2007 (SI 2006/3272) |
| 122 | | 1 Jan 2007 (SI 2006/3272) |
| 123 | | 1 Sep 2007 (SI 2006/3272) |
| 124, 125 | | 1 Jan 2007 (SI 2006/3272) |
| 126 | (1) | 1 Jan 2007 (SI 2006/3272) |
| | (2)(a) | See Sch 7 below |
| | (2)(b) | 1 Jan 2007 (SI 2006/3272) |
| | (3) | 1 Jan 2007 (SI 2006/3272) |
| 127 | | 1 Oct 2005 (SI 2005/2455) |
| 128 | | 1 Oct 2005 (in so far as applies to ss 75(1), (2), 76(1)–(3), 79 of this Act) (SI 2005/2455) |

**Gambling Act 2005 (c 19)**—*contd*

|  |  |  |
|---|---|---|
| | | 1 Jan 2007 (for the purpose of applying provisions of Pt 5 listed in SI 2006/3272, Sch 1, Column 1 to the making, consideration and determination of advance applications for personal licences, and the provisional licences issued on the grant of such applications) (SI 2006/3272) |
| | | 1 Sep 2007 (otherwise) (SI 2006/3272) |
| 129 | | 1 Jan 2007 (SI 2006/3272) |
| 130 | | 1 Jan 2007 (for the purpose of applying provisions of Pt 5 listed in SI 2006/3272, Sch 1, Column 1 to the making, consideration and determination of advance applications for personal licences, and the provisional licences issued on the grant of such applications) (SI 2006/3272) |
| | | 1 Sep 2007 (otherwise) (SI 2006/3272) |
| 131 | | 1 Sep 2007 (SI 2006/3272) |
| 132, 133 | | 1 Jan 2007 (SI 2006/3272) |
| 134, 135 | | 1 Sep 2007 (SI 2006/3272) |
| 136 | | 1 Jan 2007 (SI 2006/3272) |
| 137–139 | | 1 Sep 2007 (SI 2006/3272) |
| 140–149 | | 1 Jan 2007 (SI 2006/3272) |
| 150–153 | | 21 May 2007 (SI 2006/3272) |
| 154 | (1) | 13 Nov 2006 (for the purpose of enabling a licensing authority to delegate their functions under s 212) (SI 2006/2964) |
| | | 21 May 2007 (otherwise) (SI 2006/3272) |
| | (2)(a) | 21 May 2007 (SI 2006/3272) |
| | (2)(b) | 13 Nov 2006 (SI 2006/2964) |
| | (2)(c) | 21 May 2007 (SI 2006/3272) |
| | (3)–(5) | 21 May 2007 (SI 2006/3272) |
| 155–158 | | 21 May 2007 (SI 2006/3272) |
| 159–165 | | 21 May 2007 (for specified purposes[3]) (SI 2006/3272) |
| | | 1 Sep 2007 (otherwise, except for the purposes of enabling a non-conversion application for a casino premises licence to be made, considered and determined; and enabling a regional, large or small casino premises licence to be issued on such an application) (SI 2006/3272) |
| | | 20 May 2008 (for the purposes of enabling an application for a large or small casino premises licences to be made, considered and determined; and enabling such a licence to be issued on such an application) (SI 2008/1326) |
| | | *Not yet in force* (otherwise) |
| 166 | | 31 Mar 2006 (SI 2006/631) |
| 167–171 | | 21 May 2007 (SI 2006/3272) |
| 172, 173 | | 1 Sep 2007 (SI 2006/3272) |
| 174 | (1) | 21 May 2007 (SI 2006/3272) |
| | (2)–(8) | 1 Sep 2007 (SI 2006/3272) |
| 175 | (1) | *Not yet in force* |
| | (2)–(8) | 20 May 2008 (in so far as relating to large and small casino premises licences and provisional statements in respect of large and small casinos) (SI 2008/1326) |
| | | *Not yet in force* (otherwise) |
| 176 | (1), (2) | 21 May 2007 (SI 2006/3272) |
| | (3) | 1 Sep 2007 (SI 2006/3272) |
| 177–180 | | 1 Sep 2007 (SI 2006/3272) |
| 181 | | 21 May 2007 (SI 2006/3272) |
| 182 | (1)–(3) | 1 Sep 2007 (SI 2006/3272) |
| | (4) | 30 Apr 2007 (SI 2006/3272) |
| 183 | | 1 Sep 2007 (SI 2006/3272) |
| 184 | | 21 May 2007 (SI 2006/3272) |
| 185 | | 1 Sep 2007 (SI 2006/3272) |
| 186–190 | | 21 May 2007 (SI 2006/3272) |
| 191 | | 1 Sep 2007 (SI 2006/3272) |

**Gambling Act 2005 (c 19)**—*contd*

| | | |
|---|---|---|
| 192 | | 21 May 2007 (SI 2006/3272) |
| 193 | | 1 Sep 2007 (SI 2006/3272) |
| 194–196 | | 21 May 2007 (SI 2006/3272) |
| 197–203 | | 1 Sep 2007 (SI 2006/3272) |
| 204 | | 21 May 2007 (for specified purposes[4]) (SI 2006/3272) |
| | | 1 Sep 2007 (otherwise, except for the purposes of enabling applications for a provisional statement with respect to a casino to be made, considered and determined; and enabling such statements to be issued) (SI 2006/3272) |
| | | 20 May 2008 (for the purposes of enabling an application for a provisional statement to be made in respect of a large or small casino; and enabling a provisional statement to be issued on such an application) (SI 2008/1326) |
| | | *Not yet in force* (otherwise) |
| 205–213 | | 21 May 2007 (SI 2006/3272) |
| 214–234 | | 1 Dec 2007 (SI 2007/3155) |
| 235 | (1) | 1 Jan 2007 (SI 2006/3272) |
| | (2)(a) | 1 Sep 2007 (SI 2006/3272) |
| | (2)(b)–(i) | 1 Jan 2007 (SI 2006/3272) |
| | (3)(a)–(e) | 1 Jan 2007 (SI 2006/3272) |
| | (3)(f) | 1 Sep 2007 (SI 2006/3272) |
| | (4) | 1 Sep 2007 (SI 2006/3272) |
| | (5) | 1 Jan 2007 (SI 2006/3272) |
| 236 | | 1 Sep 2007 (SI 2006/3272) |
| 237–241 | | 1 Jan 2007 (SI 2006/3272) |
| 242–244 | | 1 Sep 2007 (SI 2006/3272) |
| 245 | | *Never in force* (repealed) |
| 246 | | 1 Sep 2007 (SI 2006/3272) |
| 247 | (1) | 1 Sep 2007 (SI 2006/3272) |
| | (2) | 13 Nov 2006 (SI 2006/2964) |
| | (3) | See Sch 10 below |
| 248 | (1) | 1 Sep 2007 (SI 2006/3272) |
| | (2) | 1 Jan 2007 (SI 2006/3272) |
| 249, 250 | | 1 Sep 2007 (SI 2006/3272) |
| 251–257 | | 1 Jan 2007 (SI 2006/3272) |
| 258 | (1)–(4) | 1 Sep 2007 (SI 2006/3272) |
| | (5) | See Sch 11 below |
| 259–265 | | 1 Sep 2007 (SI 2006/3272) |
| 266–268 | | 1 Aug 2007 (SI 2006/3272) |
| 269, 270 | | 1 Sep 2007 (SI 2006/3272) |
| 271 | (1) | 1 Sep 2007 (SI 2006/3272) |
| | (2) | 1 Aug 2007 (SI 2006/3272) |
| | (3)–(7) | 1 Sep 2007 (SI 2006/3272) |
| 272 | | 1 Sep 2007 (SI 2006/3272) |
| 273 | (1) | 1 Sep 2007 (SI 2006/3272) |
| | (2) | 1 Aug 2007 (SI 2006/3272) |
| | (3)–(5) | 1 Sep 2007 (SI 2006/3272) |
| 274 | (1) | See Sch 12 below |
| | (2) | 1 Sep 2007 (SI 2006/3272) |
| 275 | | 1 Sep 2007 (SI 2006/3272) |
| 276–278 | | 1 Aug 2007 (SI 2006/3272) |
| 279–281 | | 1 Sep 2007 (SI 2006/3272) |
| 282 | (1) | 1 Sep 2007 (SI 2006/3272) |
| | (2) | 1 Aug 2007 (for the purposes of enabling a person to comply with the condition in this subsection before 1 Sep 2007) (SI 2006/3272) |
| | | 1 Sep 2007 (otherwise) (SI 2006/3272) |
| | (3)–(5) | 1 Sep 2007 (SI 2006/3272) |
| 283 | (1) | 1 Sep 2007 (SI 2006/3272) |

**Gambling Act 2005 (c 19)**—*contd*

| | | |
|---|---|---|
| | (2) | 1 Aug 2007 (SI 2006/3272) |
| | (3), (4) | 1 Sep 2007 (SI 2006/3272) |
| | (5) | See Sch 13 below |
| 284 | | 1 Aug 2007 (SI 2006/3272) |
| 285 | | 1 Jan 2007 (SI 2006/3272) |
| 286, 287 | | 1 Sep 2007 (SI 2006/3272) |
| 288 | | 1 Jan 2007 (SI 2006/3272) |
| 289 | (1) | 1 Sep 2007 (SI 2006/3272) |
| | (2) | 13 Nov 2006 (SI 2006/2964) |
| | (3) | See Sch 14 below |
| 290 | | 1 Sep 2007 (SI 2006/3272) |
| 291 | | 1 Jan 2007 (for the purposes of enabling conditions to be attached to an operating licence under s 75 or s 78 in connection with any of the matters referred to in s 291(2), (3)) (SI 2006/3272) |
| | | 1 Sep 2007 (otherwise) (SI 2006/3272) |
| 292–302 | | 1 Sep 2007 (SI 2006/3272) |
| 303, 304 | | 21 May 2007 (SI 2006/3272) |
| 305–308 | | 1 Sep 2007 (SI 2006/3272) |
| 309 | (1) | 21 May 2007 (SI 2006/3272) |
| | (2) | 1 Sep 2007 (SI 2006/3272) |
| 310 | (1) | 1 Aug 2007 (SI 2006/3272) |
| | (2) | 1 Sep 2007 (SI 2006/3272) |
| 311 | (1) | 21 May 2007 (SI 2006/3272) |
| | (2) | 1 Sep 2007 (SI 2006/3272) |
| 312 | (1)–(3) | 1 Sep 2007 (SI 2006/3272) |
| | (4) | 1 Aug 2007 (SI 2006/3272) |
| 313 | (1) | 21 May 2007 (SI 2006/3272) |
| | (2) | 1 Sep 2007 (SI 2006/3272) |
| 314–316 | | 1 Sep 2007 (SI 2006/3272) |
| 317–326 | | 21 May 2007 (SI 2006/3272) |
| 327–340 | | 1 Sep 2007 (SI 2006/3272) |
| 341 | | 1 Jan 2007 (in so far as it relates to an offence under s 342) (SI 2006/3272) |
| | | 1 Sep 2007 (otherwise) (SI 2006/3272) |
| 342 | | 1 Jan 2007 (in so far as it relates to the provision of information to the Gambling Commission) (SI 2006/3272) |
| | | 21 May 2007 (otherwise) (SI 2006/3272) |
| 343 | | 21 May 2007 (SI 2006/3272) |
| 344 | | 1 Sep 2007 (SI 2006/3272) |
| 345 | | 1 Jan 2007 (in so far as it relates to an offence under s 342) (SI 2006/3272) |
| | | 1 Sep 2007 (otherwise) (SI 2006/3272) |
| 346 | (1)(a)–(k) | 1 Sep 2007 (SI 2006/3272) |
| | (1)(l) | 21 May 2007 (SI 2006/3272) |
| | (1)(m)–(o) | 1 Sep 2007 (SI 2006/3272) |
| | (2), (3) | 21 May 2007 (SI 2006/3272) |
| 347 | | 21 May 2007 (SI 2006/3272) |
| 348 | | 1 Sep 2007 (SI 2006/3272) |
| 349 | | 31 Mar 2006 (SI 2006/631) |
| 350, 351 | | 1 Jan 2007 (SI 2006/3272) |
| 352 | | 1 Oct 2005 (SI 2005/2455) |
| 353 | | 1 Jan 2007 (SI 2006/3272) |
| 354 | | 1 Oct 2005 (SI 2005/2455) |
| 355 | | 28 Aug 2005 (SI 2005/2425) |
| 356 | (1), (2) | See Sch 16 below |
| | (3)(a)–(e) | 1 Sep 2007 (SI 2006/3272) |
| | (3)(f) | 1 Sep 2007 (SI 2006/3272)[8] |
| | (3)(g) | 1 Sep 2007 (SI 2006/3272)[9] |
| | (3)(h) | 1 Sep 2007 (SI 2006/3272) |

**Gambling Act 2005 (c 19)**—*contd*

| | | |
|---|---|---|
| | (3)(i) | 1 Sep 2007 (SI 2006/3272)[10] |
| | (4), (5) | See Sch 17 below |
| 357 | | 1 Oct 2005 (SI 2005/2455) |
| 358 | (1), (2) | 7 Apr 2005 (RA) |
| | (3) | See Sch 18 below |
| | (4)–(6) | 7 Apr 2005 (RA) |
| 359–362 | | 7 Apr 2005 (RA) |
| Schs 1, 2 | | 1 Oct 2005 (SI 2005/2455) |
| Sch 3 | para 1 | 1 Sep 2007 (SI 2006/3272) |
| | para 2 | 1 Oct 2005 (SI 2005/2455) |
| | para 3 | 1 Sep 2007 (SI 2006/3272) |
| Schs 4–6 | | 1 Oct 2005 (SI 2005/2455) |
| Sch 7 | paras 1–22 | 1 Jan 2007 (SI 2006/3272) |
| | para 23 | 5 Dec 2006 (SI 2006/3220) |
| Sch 8 | | 1 Jan 2007 (SI 2006/3272) |
| Sch 9 | | 20 May 2008 (in so far as it relates to applications for large and small casino premises licences and provisional statements in respect of large and small casinos) (SI 2008/1326) |
| | | *Not yet in force* (otherwise) |
| Sch 10 | para 1 | 13 Nov 2006 (SI 2006/2964) |
| | paras 2–5 | 21 May 2007 (for specified purposes[5]) (SI 2006/3272) |
| | | 1 Sep 2007 (otherwise) (SI 2006/3272) |
| | para 6 | 21 May 2007 (SI 2006/3272) |
| | para 7(1), (2) | 13 Nov 2006 (SI 2006/2964) |
| | para 7(3) | 13 Nov 2006 (for the purpose of enabling a licensing authority to carry out their functions under para 7(1), (2) of this Schedule) (SI 2006/2964) |
| | | 21 May 2007 (otherwise) (SI 2006/3272) |
| | paras 8–11 | 21 May 2007 (for specified purposes[5]) (SI 2006/3272) |
| | | 1 Sep 2007 (otherwise) (SI 2006/3272) |
| | para 12(a) | 21 May 2007 (SI 2006/3272) |
| | para 12(b) | 1 Sep 2007 (SI 2006/3272) |
| | para 13 | 21 May 2007 (SI 2006/3272) |
| | para 14 | 1 Sep 2007 (SI 2006/3272) |
| | paras 15–17 | 21 May 2007 (SI 2006/3272) |
| | paras 18–20 | 1 Sep 2007 (SI 2006/3272) |
| | para 21 | 21 May 2007 (SI 2006/3272) |
| | para 22 | 21 May 2007 (for specified purposes[5]) (SI 2006/3272) |
| | | 1 Sep 2007 (otherwise) (SI 2006/3272) |
| | paras 23, 24 | 21 May 2007 (SI 2006/3272) |
| Sch 11 | paras 1–8 | 1 Oct 2005 (for the purposes of ss 17, 18 of this Act) (SI 2005/2455) |
| | | 1 Sep 2007 (otherwise) (SI 2006/3272) |
| | para 9 | 1 Sep 2007 (SI 2006/3272) |
| | paras 10–12 | 1 Oct 2005 (for the purposes of ss 17, 18 of this Act) (SI 2005/2455) |
| | | 1 Sep 2007 (otherwise) (SI 2006/3272) |
| | paras 13–19 | 1 Sep 2007 (SI 2006/3272) |
| | para 20 | 1 Oct 2005 (for the purposes of ss 17, 18 of this Act) (SI 2005/2455) |
| | | 1 Sep 2007 (otherwise) (SI 2006/3272) |
| | paras 21–29 | 1 Sep 2007 (SI 2006/3272) |
| | paras 30, 31 | 1 Oct 2005 (for the purposes of ss 17, 18 of this Act) (SI 2005/2455) |
| | | 1 Sep 2007 (otherwise) (SI 2006/3272) |
| | paras 32–63 | 1 Sep 2007 (SI 2006/3272) |
| Sch 12 | paras 1–11 | 1 Aug 2007 (for specified purposes[7]) (SI 2006/3272) |
| | | 1 Sep 2007 (otherwise) (SI 2006/3272) |
| | paras 12, 13 | 1 Sep 2007 (SI 2006/3272) |

**Gambling Act 2005 (c 19)**—*contd*

| | | |
|---|---|---|
| | paras 14–21 | 1 Aug 2007 (SI 2006/3272) |
| | para 22 | 1 Sep 2007 (SI 2006/3272) |
| | para 23 | 1 Aug 2007 (SI 2006/3272) |
| | para 24 | 1 Sep 2007 (SI 2006/3272) |
| | para 25 | 1 Aug 2007 (for specified purposes[7]) (SI 2006/3272) |
| | | 1 Sep 2007 (otherwise) (SI 2006/3272) |
| | paras 26–31 | 1 Aug 2007 (SI 2006/3272) |
| Sch 13 | paras 1, 2 | 1 Aug 2007 (for specified purposes[11]) (SI 2006/3272) |
| | | 1 Sep 2007 (otherwise) (SI 2006/3272) |
| | para 3 | 1 Aug 2007 (SI 2006/3272) |
| | paras 4–7 | 1 Aug 2007 (for specified purposes[11]) (SI 2006/3272) |
| | | 1 Sep 2007 (otherwise) (SI 2006/3272) |
| | para 8 | 1 Sep 2007 (SI 2006/3272) |
| | para 9 | 1 Aug 2007 (SI 2006/3272) |
| | para 10 | 1 Sep 2007 (SI 2006/3272) |
| | paras 11–20 | 1 Aug 2007 (SI 2006/3272) |
| | para 21 | 1 Aug 2007 (for specified purposes[11]) (SI 2006/3272) |
| | | 1 Sep 2007 (otherwise) (SI 2006/3272) |
| | paras 22, 23 | 1 Aug 2007 (SI 2006/3272) |
| Sch 14 | para 1 | 13 Nov 2006 (SI 2006/2964) |
| | para 2 | 21 May 2007 (SI 2006/3272) |
| | paras 3–6 | 21 May 2007 (for specified purposes[6]) (SI 2006/3272) |
| | | 1 Sep 2007 (otherwise) (SI 2006/3272) |
| | para 7 | 21 May 2007 (SI 2006/3272) |
| | para 8(1), (2) | 13 Nov 2006 (SI 2006/2964) |
| | para 8(3) | 13 Nov 2006 (for the purpose of enabling a licensing authority to carry out their functions under para 8(1), (2) of this Schedule) (SI 2006/2964) |
| | | 21 May 2007 (otherwise) (SI 2006/3272) |
| | paras 9–12 | 21 May 2007 (for specified purposes[6]) (SI 2006/3272) |
| | | 1 Sep 2007 (otherwise) (SI 2006/3272) |
| | para 13(a) | 21 May 2007 (SI 2006/3272) |
| | para 13(b) | 1 Sep 2007 (SI 2006/3272) |
| | paras 14–17 | 21 May 2007 (SI 2006/3272) |
| | paras 18–20 | 1 Sep 2007 (SI 2006/3272) |
| | para 21 | 21 May 2007 (SI 2006/3272) |
| | para 22 | 21 May 2007 (for specified purposes[6]) (SI 2006/3272) |
| | | 1 Sep 2007 (otherwise) (SI 2006/3272) |
| | paras 23, 24 | 21 May 2007 (SI 2006/3272) |
| Sch 15 | | 1 Sep 2007 (SI 2006/3272) |
| Sch 16 | paras 1, 2 | 1 Sep 2007 (SI 2006/3272) |
| | para 3(1) | 1 Oct 2005 (SI 2005/2455) |
| | para 3(2) | 24 Nov 2005 (SI 2005/2455) |
| | para 3(3)–(6) | 1 Oct 2005 (SI 2005/2455) |
| | para 3(7), (8) | 25 Nov 2005 (SI 2005/2455) |
| | para 4 | 1 Sep 2007 (SI 2006/3272) |
| | paras 5–7 | 1 Oct 2005 (SI 2005/2455) |
| | para 8 | 1 Sep 2007 (SI 2006/3272) |
| | para 9 | 1 Oct 2005 (SI 2005/2455) |
| | paras 10, 11 | 1 Sep 2007 (SI 2006/3272) |
| | para 12 | 1 Jan 2007 (for specified purposes[2]) (SI 2006/3272) |
| | | 1 Sep 2007 (otherwise) (SI 2006/3272) |
| | paras 13, 14 | 1 Oct 2005 (SI 2005/2455) |
| | para 15 | 1 Sep 2007 (SI 2006/3272) |
| | para 16 | 1 Oct 2005 (SI 2005/2455) |
| | para 17 | *Never in force* (repealed) |
| | para 18 | 1 Sep 2007 (SI 2006/3272) |
| | para 19 | 1 Oct 2005 (SI 2005/2455) |
| | para 20 | 1 Sep 2007 (SI 2006/3272) |

**Gambling Act 2005 (c 19)**—*contd*

| | |
|---|---|
| para 21 | 1 Oct 2005 (SI 2005/2455) |
| Sch 17 | 1 Oct 2005 (repeal of Gaming Act 1968, s 10, Sch 1) (SI 2005/2455) |
| | 1 Jan 2007 (SI 2006/3272), repeals of— |
| | Betting, Gaming and Lotteries Act 1963, Sch 2, para 10; |
| | Gaming (Bingo) Act 1985, Schedule, para 5(b) |
| | 1 Sep 2007 (SI 2006/3272), repeals of or in— |
| | Gaming Act 1710; |
| | Gaming Act 1738; |
| | Gaming Act 1835; |
| | Metropolitan Police Act 1839; |
| | Gaming Act 1845; |
| | Gaming Act 1892; |
| | Libraries Offences Act 1898; |
| | Betting, Gaming and Lotteries Act 1963 (in so far as not already in force)[8]; |
| | Police Act 1964; |
| | Local Government Act 1966; |
| | Gaming Act 1968 (in so far as not already in force)[9]; |
| | Theft Act 1968; |
| | Decimal Currency Act 1969; |
| | Family Law Reform Act 1969; |
| | Chronically Sick and Disabled Persons Act 1970; |
| | Courts Act 1971; |
| | Local Government Act 1972; |
| | Gaming (Amendment) Act 1973; |
| | Lotteries Act 1975; |
| | Licensing (Scotland) Act 1976; |
| | Lotteries and Amusements Act 1976[10]; |
| | Criminal Law Act 1977; |
| | Gaming (Amendment) Act 1980; |
| | Local Government, Planning and Land Act 1980; |
| | Betting and Gaming Duties Act 1981; |
| | Supreme Court Act 1981; |
| | Criminal Justice Act 1982; |
| | Gaming (Amendment) Act 1982; |
| | Betting, Gaming and Lotteries (Amendment) Act 1984; |
| | Lotteries (Amendment) Act 1984; |
| | Police and Criminal Evidence Act 1984; |
| | Betting, Gaming and Lotteries (Amendment) Act 1985; |
| | Companies Consolidation (Consequential Provisions) Act 1985; |
| | Gaming (Bingo) Act 1985 (in so far as not already in force); |
| | Local Government Act 1985; |
| | Social Security Act 1985; |
| | Gaming (Amendment) Act 1986; |
| | Gaming (Amendment) Act 1987; |
| | Companies Act 1989; |
| | Gaming (Amendment) Act 1990; |
| | Bingo Act 1992; |
| | National Lottery etc Act 1993; |
| | Coal Industry Act 1994; |
| | Deregulation and Contracting Out Act 1994; |
| | Local Government (Wales) Act 1994; |
| | Civil Evidence Act 1995; |
| | Employment Rights Act 1996; |
| | Access to Justice Act 1999; |
| | Financial Services and Markets Act 2000; |
| | Criminal Justice and Police Act 2001; |
| | Licensing Act 2003; |

**Gambling Act 2005 (c 19)**—*contd*

|         | Courts Act 2003; |
|---------|------------------|
|         | Criminal Justice Act 2003 |
| Sch 18  | 7 Apr 2005 (RA) |

[1]   For transitional provisions, see SI 2005/2455, art 3

[2]   The specified purposes are: enabling a person to obtain an enhanced criminal records certificate under the Police Act 1997, s 115 in respect of an advance application for an operating or a personal licence. This is to be without prejudice to paras (a) to (c) of s 115 of that Act continuing to have effect without the amendment made by Sch 16, para 2 for the purposes of the matters referred to in those paragraphs

[3]   (1) Subject to para (3) below, ss 159–165 are to have effect for the purpose of enabling advance applications for premises licences under Part 8 of this Act to be made, considered and determined; and for enabling such licences to be issued before 1 Sep 2007

(2) Ss 159–165 are also to have effect for the purposes of applications under s 187 (applications to vary a premises licence), s 188 (applications to transfer a premises licence), s 195 (applications for the reinstatement of a premises licence) and s 204 (applications for a provisional statement) of this Act

(3) The reference in para (1) to applications for premises licences is not to include non-conversion applications for casino premises licences

[4]   (1) Subject to para (2) below, s 204 is to have effect for the purposes of enabling applications for a provisional statement to be made, considered and determined; and for enabling such statements to be issued

(2) The reference in para (1) to applications for a provisional statement is not to include applications for a provisional statement in respect of a casino

[5]   The specified purposes are: enabling advance applications for family entertainment centre gaming machine permits and appeals in connection with such applications to be made, considered and determined and enabling such permits to be issued before 1 Sep 2007

[6]   The specified purposes are: enabling advance applications for prize gaming permits and appeals in connection with such applications to be made, considered and determined and enabling such permits to be issued before 1 Sep 2007

[7]   The specified purposes are: enabling advance applications for club gaming permits and club machine permits and appeals in connection with such applications to be made, considered and determined and enabling such permits to be issued before 1 Sep 2007

[8]   For transitional provisions and savings, see SI 2006/3272, arts 3, 6, Sch 4, Pt 2, paras 2–4

[9]   For transitional provisions and savings, see SI 2006/3272, arts 4, 6, Sch 4, Pt 2, paras 5–12

[10]  For transitional provisions and savings, see SI 2006/3272, arts 5, 6, Sch 4, Pt 2, paras 13–16

[11]  The specified purposes are: enabling advance applications for licensed premises gaming machine permits and appeals in connection with such applications to be made, considered and determined and enabling such permits to be issued before 1 Sep 2007

---

**Income Tax (Trading and Other Income) Act 2005 (c 5)**

*RA:* 24 Mar 2005

*Commencement provisions:* s 883(1)–(3)

| | |
|---|---|
| 1–872 | 6 Apr 2005 (has effect: (a) for income tax purposes, for the tax year 2005–06 and subsequent tax years, and (b) for corporation tax purposes, for accounting periods ending after 5 Apr 2005) (s 883(1)) |
| 873 | 24 Mar 2005 (s 883(3)) |
| 874 | 6 Apr 2005 (has effect: (a) for income tax purposes, for the tax year 2005–06 and subsequent tax years, and (b) for corporation tax purposes, for accounting periods ending after 5 Apr 2005) (s 883(1)) |
| 875–881 | 24 Mar 2005 (s 883(3)) |

**Income Tax (Trading and Other Income) Act 2005 (c 5)**—*contd*

| | | |
|---|---|---|
| 882 | (1) | 6 Apr 2005 (has effect: (a) for income tax purposes, for the tax year 2005–06 and subsequent tax years, and (b) for corporation tax purposes, for accounting periods ending after 5 Apr 2005) (s 883(1)) |
| | (2)–(5) | 24 Mar 2005 (s 883(3)) |
| 883 | (1)–(3) | 24 Mar 2005 (s 883(3)) |
| | (4) | See Sch 2 below |
| | (5) | 24 Mar 2005 (s 883(3)) |
| 884 | | 6 Apr 2005 (has effect: (a) for income tax purposes, for the tax year 2005–06 and subsequent tax years, and (b) for corporation tax purposes, for accounting periods ending after 5 Apr 2005) (s 883(1)) |
| 885, 886 | | 24 Mar 2005 (s 883(3)) |
| Sch 1 | | 6 Apr 2005 (has effect: (a) for income tax purposes, for the tax year 2005–06 and subsequent tax years, and (b) for corporation tax purposes, for accounting periods ending after 5 Apr 2005) (s 883(1)) |
| Sch 2 | paras 1–77 | 6 Apr 2005 (has effect: (a) for income tax purposes, for the tax year 2005–06 and subsequent tax years, and (b) for corporation tax purposes, for accounting periods ending after 5 Apr 2005) (s 883(1)) |
| | para 78 | 24 Mar 2005 (s 883(3)) |
| | paras 79–147 | 6 Apr 2005 (has effect: (a) for income tax purposes, for the tax year 2005–06 and subsequent tax years, and (b) for corporation tax purposes, for accounting periods ending after 5 Apr 2005) (s 883(1)) |
| | para 148(1)–(4) | 6 Apr 2005 (has effect: (a) for income tax purposes, for the tax year 2005–06 and subsequent tax years, and (b) for corporation tax purposes, for accounting periods ending after 5 Apr 2005) (s 883(1)) |
| | para 148(5) | 24 Mar 2005 (s 883(3)) |
| | paras 149–161 | 6 Apr 2005 (has effect: (a) for income tax purposes, for the tax year 2005–06 and subsequent tax years, and (b) for corporation tax purposes, for accounting periods ending after 5 Apr 2005) (s 883(1)) |
| Sch 3 | | 6 Apr 2005 (has effect: (a) for income tax purposes, for the tax year 2005–06 and subsequent tax years, and (b) for corporation tax purposes, for accounting periods ending after 5 Apr 2005) (s 883(1)) |
| Sch 4 | | 24 Mar 2005 (s 883(3)) |

---

## Inquiries Act 2005 (c 12)

*RA:* 7 Apr 2005

*Commencement provisions:* s 51; Inquiries Act 2005 (Commencement) Order 2005, SI 2005/1432

| | |
|---|---|
| 1–50 | 7 Jun 2005 (SI 2005/1432) |
| 51–53 | 7 Apr 2005 (s 51(1)) |
| Schs 1–3 | 7 Jun 2005 (SI 2005/1432) |

---

## International Organisations Act 2005 (c 20)

*RA:* 7 Apr 2005

*Commencement provisions:* s 11(3), (4); International Organisations Act 2005 (Commencement) Order 2005, SI 2005/1870

| | |
|---|---|
| 1, 2 | 11 Jul 2005 (SI 2005/1870) |
| 3 | 6 Apr 2006 (SI 2005/1870) |
| 4–11 | 7 Jun 2005 (s 11(3)) |

**International Organisations Act 2005 (c 20)**—*contd*
Schedule                                        7 Jun 2005 (s 11(3))

**Licensing (Scotland) Act 2005 (asp 16)**

*RA:* 21 Dec 2005

*Commencement provisions:* s 150(2); Licensing (Scotland) Act 2005 (Commencement No 1 and Transitional
Provisions) Order 2006, SSI 2006/239 (revoked by SSI 2006/286); Licensing (Scotland) Act 2005
(Commencement No 2 and Transitional Provisions) Order 2006, SSI 2006/286; Licensing (Scotland)
Act 2005 (Commencement No 3) Order 2007, SSI 2007/129; Licensing (Scotland) Act 2005
(Commencement No 4) Order 2007, SSI 2007/472; Licensing (Scotland) Act 2005 (Commencement
No 5) Order 2008, SSI 2008/292

| | | |
|---|---|---|
| 1 | | 1 Sep 2009 (at 0500 hrs) (SSI 2007/472) |
| 2–6 | | 1 May 2007 (SSI 2007/129) |
| 7 | (1) | 1 Sep 2009 (at 0500 hrs) (SSI 2007/472) |
| | (2) | 1 May 2007 (SSI 2007/129) |
| | (3)–(5) | 1 Sep 2009 (at 0500 hrs) (SSI 2007/472) |
| 8 | | 1 May 2007 (SSI 2007/129) |
| 9 | | 1 Feb 2008 (SSI 2007/472) |
| 10–14 | | 1 May 2007 (SSI 2007/129) |
| 15 | | 1 Sep 2009 (at 0500 hrs) (SSI 2007/472) |
| 16, 17 | | 1 May 2007 (SSI 2007/129) |
| 18 | | 1 Feb 2008 (SSI 2007/472) |
| 19 | (1) | 1 May 2007 (SSI 2007/129) |
| | (2) | 1 Feb 2008 (SSI 2007/472) |
| 20–26 | | 1 Feb 2008 (SSI 2007/472) |
| 27 | (1) | See Sch 3 below |
| | (2)–(10) | 1 Feb 2008 (SSI 2007/472) |
| 28–51 | | 1 Feb 2008 (SSI 2007/472) |
| 52 | | 1 Sep 2009 (at 0500 hrs) (SSI 2007/472) |
| 53 | | 1 Feb 2008 (SSI 2007/472) |
| 54 | | 1 Sep 2009 (at 0500 hrs) (SSI 2007/472) |
| 55–59 | | 1 Feb 2008 (SSI 2007/472) |
| 60 | (1) | See Sch 4 below |
| | (2)–(7) | 1 Feb 2008 (SSI 2007/472) |
| 61 | | 1 Feb 2008 (SSI 2007/472) |
| 62 | | 1 May 2007 (SSI 2007/129) |
| 63 | | 1 Sep 2009 (at 0500 hrs) (SSI 2007/472) |
| 64, 65 | | 1 Feb 2008 (SSI 2007/472) |
| 66 | | 1 May 2007 (SSI 2007/129) |
| 67–70 | | 1 Feb 2008 (SSI 2007/472) |
| 71 | | 1 May 2007 (SSI 2007/129) |
| 72–83 | | 1 Feb 2008 (SSI 2007/472) |
| 84 | | 1 Sep 2009 (at 0500 hrs) (SSI 2007/472) |
| 85–89 | | 1 Feb 2008 (SSI 2007/472) |
| 90, 91 | | 1 May 2007 (SSI 2007/129) |
| 92 | | 1 Feb 2008 (SSI 2007/472) |
| 93 | | 1 Sep 2009 (at 0500 hrs) (SSI 2007/472) |
| 94–96 | | 1 Feb 2008 (SSI 2007/472) |
| 97–104 | | 1 Sep 2009 (at 0500 hrs) (SSI 2007/472) |
| 105 | (1), (2) | 1 Jun 2006 (SSI 2006/286)[1] |
| | (3) | 1 Jun 2006 (SSI 2006/286) |
| | (4), (5) | 1 Sep 2009 (at 0500 hrs) (SSI 2007/472) |
| | (6) | 1 Jun 2006 (SSI 2006/286) |
| | (7) | 1 Sep 2009 (at 0500 hrs) (SSI 2007/472) |
| 106–122 | | 1 Sep 2009 (at 0500 hrs) (SSI 2007/472) |
| 123 | | 5 Sep 2008 (SSI 2008/292) |
| 124 | | 1 Sep 2009 (at 0500 hrs) (SSI 2007/472) |

**Licensing (Scotland) Act 2005 (asp 16)**—*contd*

| | | |
|---|---|---|
| 125, 126 | | 1 Feb 2008 (SSI 2007/472) |
| 127, 128 | | 1 Sep 2009 (at 0500 hrs) (SSI 2007/472) |
| 129 | | 1 May 2007 (SSI 2007/129) |
| 130 | | 1 Feb 2008 (SSI 2007/472) |
| 131 | (1) | See Sch 5 below |
| | (2)–(6) | 1 Feb 2008 (SSI 2007/472) |
| 132, 133 | | 1 Feb 2008 (SSI 2007/472) |
| 134 | | 1 May 2007 (SSI 2007/129) |
| 135 | | 1 Feb 2008 (SSI 2007/472) |
| 136 | | 1 May 2007 (SSI 2007/129) |
| 137 | | 1 Feb 2008 (SSI 2007/472) |
| 138 | | 1 Sep 2009 (at 0500 hrs) (SSI 2007/472) |
| 139 | | 1 May 2007 (SSI 2007/129) |
| 140 | | 1 Sep 2009 (at 0500 hrs) (SSI 2007/472) |
| 141 | | 1 May 2007 (SSI 2007/129) |
| 142 | | 19 Mar 2007 (SSI 2007/129) |
| 143 | | 1 May 2007 (SSI 2007/129) |
| 144 | | See Sch 6 below |
| 145–148 | | 21 Dec 2005 (RA) |
| 149 | | See Sch 7 below |
| 150 | | 21 Dec 2005 (RA) |
| Schs 1–5 | | 1 Sep 2009 (at 0500 hrs) (SSI 2007/472)[2] |
| Sch 6 | paras 1–8 | 1 Sep 2009 (at 0500 hrs) (SSI 2007/472) |
| | paras 9, 10 | 1 May 2007 (SSI 2007/129) |
| Sch 7 | | 1 Jun 2006 (repeal in Licensing (Scotland) Act 1976, s 68(2), words "in licensed premises buy or attempt to buy alcoholic liquor nor") (SSI 2006/286) |

Sch 7 (continued):

1 May 2007 (SSI 2007/129), repeals of or in—

Licensing (Scotland) Act 1976, ss 1, 2(1), (3), 3, 6, 7;

Law Reform (Miscellaneous Provisions) (Scotland) Act 1990, Sch 8, para 4;

Local Government etc (Scotland) Act 1994, s 46, Sch 13, para 106(2), (3), (5);

Licensing (Amendment) (Scotland) Act 1996, s 2

1 Feb 2008 (SSI 2007/472), repeals of or in—

Licensing (Scotland) Act 1976, ss 4, 5(2)(a) (words ", including the provisional grant,"), (b)–(e), (m), (6), 9(5), 10(1) (words from "not later" to the end), 12, 13(1), 25(4B), 26(2)(b) (and word "but" immediately preceding it), (3), (8), (9), 30(2)–(5), 35(1) (words from "at a" to "by the board"), 39(7) (words from "and any" to the end);

Licensed Premises (Exclusion of Certain Persons) Act 1980;

Law Reform (Miscellaneous Provisions) (Scotland) Act 1990, ss 46(3), 51(1), Sch 8, Pt I, para 3;

Access to Justice Act 1999;

Powers of Criminal Courts (Sentencing) Act 2000;

Courts Act 2003;

Licensing Act 2003

1 Sep 2009 (at 0500 hrs) (otherwise) (SSI 2007/472)

---

[1]   For transitional provisions, see SSI 2006/286, arts 3–5

[2]   Note that ss 5, 10, 27, 60 and 131, which introduce these Schedules, are brought into force on 1 May 2007 and 1 Feb 2008 by SSI 2007/129 and SSI 2007/472 respectively, but these Schedules are not specified as coming into force on those dates

## Management of Offenders etc (Scotland) Act 2005 (asp 14)

*RA:* 8 Dec 2005

*Commencement provisions:* s 24; Management of Offenders etc (Scotland) Act 2005 (Commencement No 1) Order 2006, SSI 2006/48; Management of Offenders etc (Scotland) Act 2005 (Commencement No 2) Order 2006, SSI 2006/331; Management of Offenders etc (Scotland) Act 2005 (Commencement No 3) Order 2006, SSI 2006/545; Management of Offenders etc (Scotland) Act 2005 (Commencement No 4) Order 2008, SSI 2008/21; Management of Offenders etc (Scotland) Act 2005 (Commencement No 5) Order 2008, SSI 2008/149; Management of Offenders etc (Scotland) Act 2005 (Commencement No 6) Order 2009, SSI 2009/240; Management of Offenders etc (Scotland) Act 2005 (Commencement No 7) Order 2009, SSI 2009/269; Management of Offenders etc. (Scotland) Act 2005 (Commencement No 8 and Consequential Provisions) Order 2015, SSI 2015/397; Management of Offenders etc. (Scotland) Act 2005 (Commencement No 8) Order 2015, SSI 2015/429

| | | |
|---|---|---|
| 1, 2 | | 3 Apr 2006 (SSI 2006/48) |
| 3 | (1) | 8 Feb 2006 (SSI 2006/48) |
| | (2) | 3 Apr 2006 (SSI 2006/48) |
| | (3), (4) | 8 Feb 2006 (SSI 2006/48) |
| | (5)(a) | 3 Apr 2006 (SSI 2006/48) |
| | (5)(b), (c) | 2 Apr 2007 (SSI 2006/545) |
| | (5)(d) | 3 Apr 2006 (SSI 2006/48) |
| | (5)(e) | 2 Apr 2007 (SSI 2006/545) |
| | (5)(f)–(h) | 3 Apr 2006 (SSI 2006/48) |
| | (6), (7) | 2 Apr 2007 (SSI 2006/545) |
| | (8), (9) | 3 Apr 2006 (SSI 2006/48) |
| | (10) | 2 Apr 2007 (SSI 2006/545) |
| | (11), (12) | 8 Feb 2006 (SSI 2006/48) |
| | (13)–(17) | 3 Apr 2006 (SSI 2006/48) |
| | (18), (19) | 2 Apr 2007 (SSI 2006/545) |
| | (20)(a) | 2 Apr 2007 (SSI 2006/545) |
| | (20)(b) | 3 Apr 2006 (SSI 2006/48) |
| | (21), (22) | 3 Apr 2006 (SSI 2006/48) |
| | (23)–(25) | 8 Feb 2006 (SSI 2006/48) |
| 4 | | 3 Apr 2006 (SSI 2006/48) |
| 5 | (1)(a) | 3 Apr 2006 (SSI 2006/48) |
| | (1)(b) | 2 Apr 2007 (SSI 2006/545) |
| | (2)–(4) | 3 Apr 2006 (SSI 2006/48) |
| 6–9 | | 3 Apr 2006 (SSI 2006/48) |
| 10 | (1)(a) | 2 Apr 2007 (SSI 2006/545) |
| | (1)(b) | *Not yet in force* |
| | (1)(c) | 30 Apr 2008 (SSI 2008/149) |
| | (1)(d) | 30 Apr 2008 (in so far as it relates to a person mentioned in sub-s (11)(a) below) (SSI 2008/149) |
| | | *Not yet in force* (in so far as it relates to persons mentioned in sub-s (11)(b)–(d) below) |
| | (1)(e) | 26 Jun 2009 (in so far as it relates to persons mentioned in sub-s (11)(b)–(d) below) (SSI 2009/240) |
| | | 31 Mar 2016 (in so far as it relates to a person mentioned in sub-s (11)(a) below) (SSI 2015/397) |
| | | 31 Mar 2016 (otherwise) (SSI 2015/429) |
| | (2)(a) | 2 Apr 2007 (SSI 2006/545) |
| | (2)(b) | 26 Jun 2009 (for the purposes of sub-s (1)(e) above, in so far as that para relates to persons subject to (a) the order referred to in sub-s (11)(b) below and (b) the directions referred to in sub-s (11)(c) and (d) below) (SSI 2009/269) |
| | | 31 Mar 2016 (otherwise) (SSI 2015/397, SSI 2015/429) |
| | (2)(c) | 30 Apr 2008 (SSI 2008/149) |
| | (3) | 1 Dec 2006 (for the purpose of enabling the Scottish Ministers to specify such persons as described in this section) (SSI 2006/545) |

**Management of Offenders etc (Scotland) Act 2005 (asp 14)**—*contd*

|  |  |  |
|---|---|---|
|  |  | 2 Apr 2007 (otherwise) (SSI 2006/545) |
|  | (4)–(10) | 2 Apr 2007 (SSI 2006/545) |
|  | (11)(a), (b) | 30 Apr 2008 (SSI 2008/149) |
|  | (11)(c), (d) | 2 Apr 2007 (SSI 2006/545) |
|  | (12)–(14) | 2 Apr 2007 (SSI 2006/545) |
| 11 |  | 2 Apr 2007 (SSI 2006/545) |
| 12 |  | 8 Feb 2006 (SSI 2006/48) |
| 13 |  | 8 Dec 2005 (s 24(1)) |
| 14 |  | 20 Jun 2006 (SSI 2006/331)[1] |
| 15 | (1)–(3) | 8 Feb 2006 (SSI 2006/48) |
|  | (4) | 3 Jul 2006 (in relation to prisoners to whom the Prisoners and Criminal Proceedings (Scotland) Act 1993, s 3AA(1)(a), applies) (SSI 2006/331) |
|  |  | 21 Mar 2008 (otherwise) (SSI 2008/21) |
|  | (5) | 3 Jul 2006 (in relation to prisoners to whom the Prisoners and Criminal Proceedings (Scotland) Act 1993, s 3AA(1)(a), applies) (SSI 2006/331) |
|  |  | 11 Feb 2008 (in so far as inserts Prisoners and Criminal Proceedings (Scotland) Act 1993, s 3AA(6)) (SSI 2008/21) |
|  |  | 21 Mar 2008 (otherwise) (SSI 2008/21) |
|  | (6) | 3 Jul 2006 (in relation to prisoners to whom the Prisoners and Criminal Proceedings (Scotland) Act 1993, s 3AA(1)(a), applies) (SSI 2006/331) |
|  |  | 21 Mar 2008 (otherwise) (SSI 2008/21) |
|  | (7) | 8 Feb 2006 (SSI 2006/48) |
|  | (8), (9) | 3 Jul 2006 (in relation to prisoners to whom the Prisoners and Criminal Proceedings (Scotland) Act 1993, s 3AA(1)(a), applies) (SSI 2006/331) |
|  |  | 21 Mar 2008 (otherwise) (SSI 2008/21) |
|  | (10) | 8 Feb 2006 (only for the purpose of enabling the Scottish Ministers to prescribe conditions as "standard conditions" for the purpose of the Prisoners and Criminal Proceedings (Scotland) Act 1993, s 12AA) (SSI 2006/48) |
|  |  | 3 Jul 2006 (in relation to prisoners to whom the Prisoners and Criminal Proceedings (Scotland) Act 1993, s 3AA(1)(a), applies) (SSI 2006/331) |
|  |  | 11 Feb 2008 (in so far as inserts Prisoners and Criminal Proceedings (Scotland) Act 1993, s 12AA(3)–(5)) (SSI 2008/21) |
|  |  | 21 Mar 2008 (otherwise) (SSI 2008/21) |
|  | (11)–(13) | 3 Jul 2006 (in relation to prisoners to whom the Prisoners and Criminal Proceedings (Scotland) Act 1993, s 3AA(1)(a), applies) (SSI 2006/331) |
|  |  | 21 Mar 2008 (otherwise) (SSI 2008/21) |
|  | (14) | 8 Feb 2006 (SSI 2006/48) |
| 16 |  | 8 Feb 2006 (SSI 2006/48) |
| 17 |  | 8 Dec 2005 (s 24(1)) |
| 18 |  | 8 Feb 2006 (SSI 2006/48) |
| 19 |  | 20 Jun 2006 (SSI 2006/331)[1] |
| 20 |  | 8 Dec 2005 (s 24(1)) |
| 21 | (1)(a)(i) | 3 Apr 2006 (SSI 2006/48) |
|  | (1)(a)(ii) | 8 Feb 2006 (SSI 2006/48) |
|  | (1)(b), (c) | 8 Feb 2006 (SSI 2006/48) |
|  | (2), (3) | 3 Apr 2006 (SSI 2006/48) |
|  | (4), (5) | 8 Feb 2006 (SSI 2006/48) |
|  | (6) | 2 Apr 2007 (SSI 2006/545) |
|  | (7) | 3 Apr 2006 (SSI 2006/48) |
|  | (8) | 8 Feb 2006 (SSI 2006/48) |
|  | (9) | 3 Apr 2006 (SSI 2006/48) |
|  | (10) | 8 Feb 2006 (SSI 2006/48) |
|  | (11), (12) | 3 Apr 2006 (SSI 2006/48) |

**Management of Offenders etc (Scotland) Act 2005 (asp 14)**—*contd*

|  | (13) | 1 Dec 2006 (SSI 2006/545) |
|---|---|---|
| 22–25 | | 8 Dec 2005 (s 24(1)) |

[1] For the purposes of sentences imposed for offences committed on or after 20 Jun 2006, except in respect of sentences imposed for offences for which life imprisonment was the maximum sentence which could be imposed at the time the offence was committed, in relation to which these provisions come into force only for the purposes of sentences imposed in cases which are commenced (ie a report is received by the procurator fiscal) on or after 20 Jun 2006

## Mental Capacity Act 2005 (c 9)

*RA:* 7 Apr 2005

*Commencement provisions:* s 68(1)–(3); Mental Capacity Act 2005 (Commencement No 1) Order 2006, SI 2006/2814, as amended by SI 2006/3473; Mental Capacity Act 2005 (Commencement No 1) (England and Wales) Order 2007, SI 2007/563; Mental Capacity Act 2005 (Commencement) (Wales) Order 2007, SI 2007/856; Mental Capacity Act 2005 (Commencement No 2) Order 2007, SI 2007/1897

| | | |
|---|---|---|
| 1–4 | | 1 Apr 2007 (for the purposes of s 44 of this Act) (SI 2007/563) |
| | | 1 Apr 2007 (E) (for purposes relating to the independent mental capacity advocate service) (SI 2007/563) |
| | | 1 Oct 2007 (otherwise) (SI 2007/1897) |
| 5–29 | | 1 Oct 2007 (SI 2007/1897) |
| 30–34 | | 1 Jul 2007 (for the purpose of enabling applications for approval in relation to research to be made to, and determined by, an appropriate body) (SI 2006/2814; SI 2007/856) |
| | | 1 Oct 2007 (otherwise, except for the purposes noted below) (SI 2006/2814; SI 2007/856) |
| | | 1 Oct 2008 (for the purposes of any research carried out as part of a research project begun before 1 Oct 2007 and approved before 1 Oct 2007 by a committee established to advise on, or on matters which include, the ethics of research in relation to people who lack capacity to consent to it) (SI 2006/2814; SI 2007/856) |
| 35–41 | | 1 Nov 2006 (E) (for the purposes of enabling the Secretary of State to make arrangements under s 35 of this Act and enabling local authorities to approve independent mental capacity advocates in accordance with the Mental Capacity Act 2005 (Independent Mental Capacity Advocates) (General) Regulations 2006, SI 2006/1832) (SI 2006/2814) |
| | | 1 Apr 2007 (E) (otherwise) (SI 2006/2814) |
| | | 1 Oct 2007 (W) (SI 2007/856) |
| 42 | (1)–(3) | 1 Apr 2007 (SI 2007/563) |
| | (4), (5) | 1 Apr 2007 (for the purposes of s 44 of this Act) (SI 2007/563) |
| | | 1 Apr 2007 (E) (for purposes relating to the independent mental capacity advocate service) (SI 2007/563) |
| | | 1 Oct 2007 (otherwise) (SI 2007/1897) |
| | (6), (7) | 1 Apr 2007 (SI 2007/563) |
| 43, 44 | | 1 Apr 2007 (SI 2007/563) |
| 45–63 | | 1 Oct 2007 (SI 2007/1897) |
| 64 | | 1 Apr 2007 (for the purposes of SI 2007/563, art 2(1), (3)) (SI 2007/563) |
| | | 1 Apr 2007 (E) (for the purposes of SI 2007/563, art 2(2)) (SI 2007/563) |
| | | 1 Oct 2007 (otherwise) (SI 2007/1897) |
| 65–69 | | 1 Oct 2007 (SI 2007/1897) |
| Schs 1–7 | | 1 Oct 2007 (SI 2007/1897) |

## Prevention of Terrorism Act 2005 (c 2)

*RA:* 11 Mar 2005

*Continuance orders*: Prevention of Terrorism Act 2005 (Continuance in force of sections 1 to 9) Order 2006, SI 2006/512; Prevention of Terrorism Act 2005 (Continuance in force of sections 1 to 9) Order 2007, SI 2007/706

Whole Act in force 11 Mar 2005 (RA) (except s 16(2) which comes into force on 14 Mar 2005 by virtue of s 16(3))

Ss 1–9 are continued in force for a period of one year beginning with 11 Mar 2010 (SI 2010/645)

## Prohibition of Female Genital Mutilation (Scotland) Act 2005 (asp 8)

*RA:* 1 Jul 2005

*Commencement provisions:* s 8(2)

Whole Act in force 1 Sep 2005 (s 8(2))

## Protection of Children and Prevention of Sexual Offences (Scotland) Act 2005 (asp 9)

*RA:* 12 Jul 2005

*Commencement provisions:* s 20(2); Protection of Children and Prevention of Sexual Offences (Scotland) Act 2005 (Commencement and Savings) Order 2005, SSI 2005/480[1]

| | |
|---|---|
| 1–17 | 7 Oct 2005 (SSI 2005/480) |
| 18 | See Schedule below |
| 19 | 7 Oct 2005 (SSI 2005/480) |
| 20 | 12 Jul 2005 (RA) |
| Schedule | 7 Oct 2005 (SSI 2005/480) |

[1] For savings, see SSI 2005/480, art 3

## Public Services Ombudsman (Wales) Act 2005 (c 10)

*RA:* 7 Apr 2005

*Commencement provisions:* s 40; Public Services Ombudsman (Wales) Act 2005 (Commencement No 1 and Transitional Provisions and Savings) Order 2005, SI 2005/2800

| | | |
|---|---|---|
| 1 | (1) | 12 Oct 2005 (for the purpose of appointing the Ombudsman) (SI 2005/2800) |
| | | 1 Apr 2006 (otherwise) (SI 2005/2800) |
| | (2) | See Sch 1 below |
| 2–9 | | 1 Apr 2006 (SI 2005/2800)[1] |
| 10 | | 12 Oct 2005 (SI 2005/2800) |
| 11–19 | | 1 Apr 2006 (SI 2005/2800) |
| 20 | | *Not yet in force* |
| 21–24 | | 1 Apr 2006 (SI 2005/2800) |
| 25 | (1)–(6) | 1 Apr 2006 (SI 2005/2800) |
| | (7)–(9) | 12 Oct 2005 (SI 2005/2800) |
| 26, 27 | | 1 Apr 2006 (SI 2005/2800) |
| 28–30 | | 12 Oct 2005 (SI 2005/2800) |
| 31–34 | | 1 Apr 2006 (SI 2005/2800) |
| 35 | | See Sch 4 below |
| 36–38 | | 1 Apr 2006 (SI 2005/2800) |
| 39 | (1) | See Sch 6 below |
| | (2) | See Sch 7 below |

**Public Services Ombudsman (Wales) Act 2005 (c 10)**—*contd*

| | | |
|---|---|---|
| 40–46 | | 7 Apr 2005 (RA) |
| Sch 1 | paras 1–3 | 12 Oct 2005 (for the purpose of appointing the Ombudsman) (SI 2005/2800) |
| | | 1 Apr 2006 (otherwise) (SI 2005/2800) |
| | para 4 | 1 Apr 2006 (SI 2005/2800) |
| | para 5(1)–(3) | 12 Oct 2005 (for the purpose of appointing the Ombudsman) (SI 2005/2800) |
| | | 1 Apr 2006 (otherwise) (SI 2005/2800) |
| | para 5(4) | 1 Apr 2006 (SI 2005/2800) |
| | para 6 | 12 Oct 2005 (for the purpose of appointing the Ombudsman) (SI 2005/2800) |
| | | 1 Apr 2006 (otherwise) (SI 2005/2800) |
| | para 7 | 1 Apr 2006 (SI 2005/2800) |
| | para 8 | 12 Oct 2005 (for the purpose of appointing the Ombudsman) (SI 2005/2800) |
| | | 1 Apr 2006 (otherwise) (SI 2005/2800) |
| | paras 9–14 | 1 Apr 2006 (SI 2005/2800) |
| | para 15(1)–(4) | 1 Apr 2006 (SI 2005/2800)[1] |
| | para 15(5) | *Not yet in force* |
| | paras 16–21 | 1 Apr 2006 (SI 2005/2800) |
| Schs 2, 3 | | 12 Oct 2005 (SI 2005/2800) |
| Sch 4 | paras 1, 2 | 12 Oct 2005 (for the purpose of making orders and regulations relating to the functions of the Ombudsman under the Local Government Act 2000, Pt 3) (SI 2005/2800)[1] |
| | | 1 Apr 2006 (otherwise) (SI 2005/2800) |
| | para 3 | 1 Apr 2006 (SI 2005/2800) |
| | para 4 | 12 Oct 2005 (for the purpose of making orders and regulations relating to the functions of the Ombudsman under the Local Government Act 2000, Pt 3) (SI 2005/2800)[1] |
| | | 1 Apr 2006 (otherwise) (SI 2005/2800) |
| | paras 5–10 | 1 Apr 2006 (SI 2005/2800) |
| | para 11(a) | 12 Oct 2005 (for the purpose of making orders and regulations relating to the functions of the Ombudsman under the Local Government Act 2000, Pt 3) (SI 2005/2800)[1] |
| | | 1 Apr 2006 (otherwise) (SI 2005/2800) |
| | para 11(b) | 1 Apr 2006 (SI 2005/2800) |
| | para 11(c)–(e) | 12 Oct 2005 (for the purpose of making orders and regulations relating to the functions of the Ombudsman under the Local Government Act 2000, Pt 3) (SI 2005/2800)[1] |
| | | 1 Apr 2006 (otherwise) (SI 2005/2800) |
| | paras 12, 13 | 1 Apr 2006 (SI 2005/2800) |
| | para 14(a) | 12 Oct 2005 (for the purpose of making orders and regulations relating to the functions of the Ombudsman under the Local Government Act 2000, Pt 3) (SI 2005/2800)[1] |
| | | 1 Apr 2006 (otherwise) (SI 2005/2800) |
| | para 14(b), (c) | 1 Apr 2006 (SI 2005/2800) |
| | paras 15–22 | 1 Apr 2006 (SI 2005/2800) |
| | para 23 | 12 Oct 2005 (for the purpose of making orders and regulations relating to the functions of the Ombudsman under the Local Government Act 2000, Pt 3) (SI 2005/2800)[1] |
| | | 1 Apr 2006 (otherwise) (SI 2005/2800) |
| | para 24 | 1 Apr 2006 (SI 2005/2800) |
| Sch 5 | | 1 Apr 2006 (SI 2005/2800) |
| Sch 6 | paras 1–17 | 1 Apr 2006 (SI 2005/2800) |
| | para 18(1)–(10) | 1 Apr 2006 (SI 2005/2800) |
| | para 18(11) | 12 Oct 2005 (for the purpose of removing the duty on the Commission for Local Administration in Wales to prepare and submit an estimate of the expenses it will incur in the financial year ending 31 Mar 2007) (SI 2005/2800) |
| | | 1 Apr 2006 (otherwise) (SI 2005/2800) |

### Public Services Ombudsman (Wales) Act 2005 (c 10)—*contd*

|  |  |  |
|--|--|--|
| | para 18(12) | 1 Apr 2006 (SI 2005/2800) |
| | para 18(13) | 12 Oct 2005 (for the purpose of removing the duty on the Commission for Local Administration in Wales to prepare and submit an estimate of the expenses it will incur in the financial year ending 31 Mar 2007) (SI 2005/2800) |
| | | 1 Apr 2006 (otherwise) (SI 2005/2800) |
| | paras 19–60 | 1 Apr 2006 (SI 2005/2800) |
| | paras 61–63 | 12 Oct 2005 (for the purpose of appointing the Ombudsman) (SI 2005/2800) |
| | | 1 Apr 2006 (otherwise) (SI 2005/2800) |
| | paras 64–77 | 1 Apr 2006 (SI 2005/2800) |
| Sch 7 | | 12 Oct 2005 (repeal of Health Service Commissioners Act 1993, Sch 1A, para 9, for the purpose of removing the duty on the Health Service Commissioner for Wales to prepare and submit an estimate of the income and expenses of his office for financial year ending 31 Mar 2007) (SI 2005/2800) |
| | | 12 Oct 2005 (repeal of Government of Wales Act 1998, Sch 9, para 8, for the purpose of removing the duty on the Welsh Administration Ombudsman to prepare and submit an estimate of the income and expenses of his office for the financial year ending 31 Mar 2007) (SI 2005/2800) |
| | | 1 Apr 2006 (otherwise) (SI 2005/2800)[1] |

[1]   For transitional provisions and savings, see SI 2005/2800, arts 4(3), 5(2), 6, 7, Sch 2

---

### Railways Act 2005 (c 14)

*RA:* 7 Apr 2005

*Commencement provisions:* s 60(2)–(4); Railways Act 2005 (Commencement No 1) Order 2005, SI 2005/1444; Railways Act 2005 (Commencement No 2) Order 2005, SI 2005/1909; Railways Act 2005 (Commencement No 3) Order 2005, SI 2005/2252; Railways Act 2005 (Commencement No 4) Order 2005, SI 2005/2812; Railways Act 2005 (Commencement No 5) Order 2006, SI 2006/266; Railways Act 2005 (Commencement No 6) Order 2006, SI 2006/1951; Railways Act 2005 (Commencement No 7, Transitional and Saving Provisions) Order 2006, SI 2006/2911; Railways Act 2005 (Commencement No 8) Order 2007, SI 2007/62; Railways Act 2005 (Commencement No 9) Order 2007, SI 2007/1993

|  |  |  |
|--|--|--|
| 1 | (1) | See Sch 1 below |
| | (2) | 8 Jun 2005 (SI 2005/1444) |
| | (3)(a)–(d) | 8 Jun 2005 (SI 2005/1444) |
| | (3)(e) | 24 Jul 2005 (SI 2005/1909) |
| | (3)(f) | 8 Jun 2005 (SI 2005/1444) |
| | (4)–(9) | 8 Jun 2005 (SI 2005/1444) |
| | (10) | 1 Aug 2006 (SI 2006/1951) |
| 2 | | See Sch 3 below |
| 3 | (1) | See sub-ss (2)–(11) below |
| | (2) | 8 Jun 2005 (except in so far as it inserts words "that are not safety functions") (SI 2005/1444) |
| | | 1 Apr 2006 (otherwise) (SI 2006/266) |
| | (3) | 26 Jun 2005 (SI 2005/1444) |
| | (4) | 1 Apr 2006 (SI 2006/266) |
| | (5) | 1 Dec 2006 (SI 2006/2911) |
| | (6) | 16 Oct 2005 (so far as the inserted Railways Act 1993, s 4(3B) relates to functions transferred or assigned to the Scottish Ministers under or by virtue of Part 1 of that Act) (SI 2005/2812) |
| | | 1 Dec 2006 (so far as inserts Railways Act 1993, s 4(3B), in relation to functions transferred or assigned to the Scottish Ministers under or by virtue of the Railways Act 2005, or so far as inserts s 4(3C)) (SI 2006/2911) |

**Railways Act 2005 (c 14)**—*contd*

| | | |
|---|---|---|
| | (7) | 26 Jun 2005 (SI 2005/1444) |
| | (8)(a) | 8 Jun 2005 (except in so far as it inserts words "that are not safety functions") (SI 2005/1444) |
| | | 1 Apr 2006 (otherwise) (SI 2006/266) |
| | (8)(b) | 16 Oct 2005 (SI 2005/2812) |
| | (8)(c) | 8 Jun 2005 (SI 2005/1444) |
| | (8)(d) | 24 Jul 2005 (SI 2005/1909) |
| | (9) | 8 Jun 2005 (to the extent that it inserts sub-s (5A)) (SI 2005/1444) |
| | | 1 Apr 2006 (to the extent that it inserts sub-s (5B)) (SI 2006/266) |
| | | 29 Jan 2007 (otherwise) (SI 2007/62) |
| | (10) | 16 Oct 2005 (except the words "or (5B)" in the substituted Railways Act 1993, s 4(7ZA)) (SI 2005/2812) |
| | | 1 Apr 2006 (otherwise) (SI 2006/266) |
| | (11)(a) | 24 Jul 2005 (SI 2005/1909) |
| | (11)(b) | 26 Jun 2005 (in so far as inserts definition "railway service performance") (SI 2005/1444) |
| | | 1 Apr 2006 (otherwise) (SI 2006/266) |
| 4 | | See Sch 4 below |
| 5 | | 21 Aug 2005 (SI 2005/2252) |
| 6 | (1)–(3) | 8 Jun 2005 (SI 2005/1444) |
| | (4) | 8 Jun 2005 (except para (a) and the words "9 or" in the final line) (SI 2005/1444) |
| | | 16 Oct 2005 (otherwise) (SI 2005/2812) |
| | (5)–(8) | 8 Jun 2005 (SI 2005/1444) |
| 7 | | 8 Jun 2005 (SI 2005/1444) |
| 8, 9 | | 16 Oct 2005 (SI 2005/2812) |
| 10 | (1)–(5) | 8 Jun 2005 (SI 2005/1444) |
| | (6) | 24 Jul 2005 (except the words "or the Scottish Ministers" and "or their") (SI 2005/1909) |
| | | 16 Oct 2005 (otherwise) (SI 2005/2812) |
| | (7)–(12) | 8 Jun 2005 (SI 2005/1444) |
| 11 | | 8 Jun 2005 (SI 2005/1444) |
| 12 | (1)–(6) | 24 Jul 2005 (SI 2005/1909) |
| | (7) | See Sch 2 below |
| | (8) | 24 Jul 2005 (except definition "appropriate national authority", para (b) and word "and" immediately preceding it) (SI 2005/1909) |
| | | 16 Oct 2005 (otherwise) (SI 2005/2812) |
| 13 | | 24 Jul 2005 (SI 2005/1909) |
| 14 | | 24 Jul 2005 (E) (W) (SI 2005/1909) |
| | | *Not yet in force* (S) |
| 15, 16 | | 24 Jul 2005 (SI 2005/1909) |
| 17 | | 8 Aug 2007 (SI 2007/1993) |
| 18–21 | | 24 Jul 2005 (SI 2005/1909) |
| 22–39 | | 1 Dec 2006 (SI 2006/2911) |
| 40 | (1)–(3) | 24 Jul 2005 (SI 2005/1909) |
| | (4)(a) | 24 Jul 2005 (SI 2005/1909) |
| | (4)(b) | 16 Oct 2005 (SI 2005/2812) |
| | (4)(c) | 24 Jul 2005 (SI 2005/1909) |
| | (5) | 16 Oct 2005 (SI 2005/2812) |
| | (6), (7) | 24 Jul 2005 (SI 2005/1909) |
| 41 | | 1 Dec 2006 (SI 2006/2911) |
| 42, 43 | | 1 Aug 2006 (SI 2006/1951) |
| 44 | | 1 Dec 2006 (SI 2006/2911) |
| 45 | (1) | 1 Aug 2006 (definitions "closure", "closures guidance" and "railway funding authority") (SI 2006/1951) |
| | | 1 Dec 2006 (definitions "closure non-ratification notice", "closure ratification notice", "the end of the interim period", "excluded proposal", "experimental passenger service", "proposal date", "secured service" and "secured") (SI 2006/2911) |

**Railways Act 2005 (c 14)**—*contd*

| | | |
|---|---|---|
| | (2) | 1 Aug 2006 (SI 2006/1951) |
| | (3)–(9) | 1 Dec 2006 (SI 2006/2911) |
| 46 | (1), (2) | 24 Jul 2005 (SI 2005/1909) |
| | (3) | See Sch 9 below |
| | (4)–(6) | 16 Oct 2005 (SI 2005/2812) |
| | (7), (8) | 24 Jul 2005 (SI 2005/1909) |
| 47–50 | | 16 Oct 2005 (SI 2005/2812) |
| 51 | (1)(a) | 8 Jun 2005 (SI 2005/1444) |
| | (1)(b) | 1 Apr 2006 (SI 2006/266) |
| | (1)(c) | 8 Jun 2005 (SI 2005/1444) |
| | (2) | 16 Oct 2005 (SI 2005/2812) |
| | (3), (4) | 8 Jun 2005 (SI 2005/1444) |
| | (5) | 1 Apr 2006 (SI 2006/266) |
| 52 | | 24 Jul 2005 (SI 2005/1909) |
| 53 | | See Sch 10 below |
| 54 | (1)–(3) | 8 Jun 2005 (SI 2005/1444) |
| | (4) | See Sch 11 below |
| 55 | | 8 Jun 2005 (SI 2005/1444) |
| 56 | (1) | 7 Apr 2005 (RA) |
| | (2) | 8 Jun 2005 (except the words "or of the Scottish Parliament" in para (b)) (SI 2005/1444) |
| | | 1 Aug 2006 (exception noted above) (SI 2006/1951) |
| | (3)(a) | 8 Jun 2005 (SI 2005/1444) |
| | (3)(b), (c) | 1 Aug 2006 (SI 2006/1951) |
| | (4) | 8 Jun 2005 (SI 2005/1444) |
| | (5) | 8 Jun 2005 (except the words "or Scottish Ministers") (SI 2005/1444) |
| | | 16 Oct 2005 (otherwise) (SI 2005/2812) |
| | (6) | 8 Jun 2005 (SI 2005/1444) |
| 57, 58 | | 8 Jun 2005 (SI 2005/1444) |
| 59 | (1) | See Sch 12 below |
| | (2)–(5) | 8 Jun 2005 (SI 2005/1444) |
| | (6), (7) | See Sch 13 below |
| 60 | | 7 Apr 2005 (RA) |
| Sch 1 | paras 1–10 | 24 Jul 2005 (SI 2005/1909) |
| | para 11 | 16 Oct 2005 (SI 2005/2812) |
| | para 12 | 1 Dec 2006 (SI 2006/2911) |
| | para 13(1) | 24 Jul 2005 (SI 2005/1909) |
| | para 13(2) | 16 Oct 2005 (SI 2005/2812) |
| | para 13(3) | 24 Jul 2005 (SI 2005/1909) |
| | para 13(4)(a) | 24 Jul 2005 (in so far as relates to the Secretary of State) (SI 2005/1909) |
| | | 16 Oct 2005 (otherwise) (SI 2005/2812) |
| | para 13(4)(b) | 24 Jul 2005 (in so far as relates to an agreement to which either the Secretary of State is party or the Secretary of State and the National Assembly for Wales are jointly party) (SI 2005/1909) |
| | | 16 Oct 2005 (otherwise) (SI 2005/2812) |
| | para 13(5) | 24 Jul 2005 (in so far as relates to a designation which is to have effect as a designation by the Secretary of State) (SI 2005/1909) |
| | | 16 Oct 2005 (otherwise) (SI 2005/2812) |
| | para 14 | 16 Oct 2005 (SI 2005/2812) |
| | paras 15–19 | 24 Jul 2005 (in so far as they relate to the Secretary of State) (SI 2005/1909) |
| | | 16 Oct 2005 (otherwise) (SI 2005/2812) |
| | para 20(1) | 24 Jul 2005 (in so far as relates to services for which the Secretary of State is the relevant franchising authority) (SI 2005/1909) |
| | | 16 Oct 2005 (otherwise) (SI 2005/2812) |
| | para 20(2), (3) | 24 Jul 2005 (SI 2005/1909) |

**Railways Act 2005 (c 14)**—*contd*

| | |
|---|---|
| para 20(4) | 24 Jul 2005 (except in so far as the inserted Railways Act 1993, s 30(3A) relates to the Scottish Ministers) (SI 2005/1909) |
| | 16 Oct 2005 (otherwise) (SI 2005/2812) |
| para 20(5) | 24 Jul 2005 (in so far as relates to services for which the Secretary of State is to be treated as the relevant franchising authority) (SI 2005/1909) |
| | 16 Oct 2005 (otherwise) (SI 2005/2812) |
| para 21(1) | See sub-paras (2)–(8) below |
| para 21(2) | 24 Jul 2005 (SI 2005/1909) |
| para 21(3) | 1 Dec 2006 (SI 2006/2911) |
| para 21(4)–(8) | 24 Jul 2005 (SI 2005/1909), except in so far as they relate— |

(1) to the transfer of functions relating to the enforcement of relevant conditions or requirements which are closure restrictions or closure conditions from the Strategic Rail Authority to the Secretary of State and to the Scottish Ministers, and

(2) to the transfer of functions relating to the enforcement of relevant conditions or requirements which are terms of franchise agreements from the Strategic Rail Authority to the Scottish Ministers

| | |
|---|---|
| | 16 Oct 2005 (exception (2) noted above) (SI 2005/2812) |
| | 1 Dec 2006 (exception (1) noted above) (SI 2006/2911) |
| para 22 | 24 Jul 2005 (SI 2005/1909), except in so far as relates— |

(1) to the transfer of functions relating to the enforcement of relevant conditions or requirements which are closure restrictions or closure conditions from the Strategic Rail Authority to the Secretary of State and to the Scottish Ministers, and

(2) to the transfer of functions relating to the enforcement of relevant conditions or requirements which are terms of franchise agreements from the Strategic Rail Authority to the Scottish Ministers

| | |
|---|---|
| | 16 Oct 2005 (exception (2) noted above) (SI 2005/2812) |
| | 1 Dec 2006 (exception (1) noted above) (SI 2006/2911) |
| para 23(1) | See sub-paras (2), (3) below |
| para 23(2), (3) | 24 Jul 2005 (SI 2005/1909), except in so far as they relate— |

(1) to the transfer of functions relating to the enforcement of relevant conditions or requirements which are closure restrictions or closure conditions from the Strategic Rail Authority to the Secretary of State and to the Scottish Ministers, and

(2) to the transfer of functions relating to the enforcement of relevant conditions or requirements which are terms of franchise agreements from the Strategic Rail Authority to the Scottish Ministers

| | |
|---|---|
| | 16 Oct 2005 (exception (2) noted above) (SI 2005/2812) |
| | 1 Dec 2006 (exception (1) noted above) (SI 2006/2911) |
| para 24(1) | 24 Jul 2005 (SI 2005/1909), except in so far as relates— |

(1) to the transfer of functions relating to the enforcement of relevant conditions or requirements which are closure restrictions or closure conditions from the Strategic Rail Authority to the Secretary of State and to the Scottish Ministers, and

(2) to the transfer of functions relating to the enforcement of relevant conditions or requirements which are terms of franchise agreements from the Strategic Rail Authority to the Scottish Ministers

| | |
|---|---|
| | 16 Oct 2005 (exception (2) noted above) (SI 2005/2812) |
| | 1 Dec 2006 (exception (1) noted above) (SI 2006/2911) |
| para 24(2) | 24 Jul 2005 (except the words ", by the Scottish Ministers") (SI 2005/1909) |

**Railways Act 2005 (c 14)**—*contd*

|  |  |  |
|---|---|---|
|  |  | 16 Oct 2005 (otherwise) (SI 2005/2812) |
|  | paras 25, 26 | 24 Jul 2005 (SI 2005/1909), except in so far as they relate— |
|  |  | (1) to the transfer of functions relating to the enforcement of relevant conditions or requirements which are closure restrictions or closure conditions from the Strategic Rail Authority to the Secretary of State and to the Scottish Ministers, and |
|  |  | (2) to the transfer of functions relating to the enforcement of relevant conditions or requirements which are terms of franchise agreements from the Strategic Rail Authority to the Scottish Ministers |
|  |  | 16 Oct 2005 (exception (2) noted above) (SI 2005/2812) |
|  |  | 1 Dec 2006 (exception (1) noted above) (SI 2006/2911) |
|  | paras 27, 28 | 24 Jul 2005 (SI 2005/1909) |
|  | para 29 | 26 Jun 2005 (SI 2005/1444) |
|  | para 30(1), (2) | 24 Jul 2005 (SI 2005/1909) |
|  | para 30(3)(a) | 24 Jul 2005 (SI 2005/1909) |
|  | para 30(3)(b) | 16 Oct 2005 (SI 2005/2812) |
|  | para 30(3)(c), (d) | 24 Jul 2005 (SI 2005/1909) |
|  | para 30(4)–(7) | 24 Jul 2005 (SI 2005/1909) |
|  | para 31 | 16 Oct 2005 (SI 2005/2812) |
|  | para 32(1) | 24 Jul 2005 (SI 2005/1909) |
|  | para 32(2) | 1 Dec 2006 (in so far as it relates to the Railways Act 1993, s 76(4)(b)) (SI 2006/2911) |
|  |  | *Not yet in force* (so far as relates to the Railways Act 1993, s 76(4), (4)(a)) |
|  | para 32(3)–(5) | 24 Jul 2005 (SI 2005/1909) |
|  | para 33 | 24 Jul 2005 (SI 2005/1909) |
|  | para 34 | 1 Dec 2006 (SI 2006/2911) |
|  | para 35 | 24 Jul 2005 (except in so far as relates to a transfer of functions from the Strategic Rail Authority to the Scottish Ministers) (SI 2005/1909) |
|  |  | 16 Oct 2005 (otherwise) (SI 2005/2812) |
|  | para 36(a) | 24 Jul 2005 (SI 2005/1909) |
|  | para 36(b) | 1 Dec 2006 (SI 2006/2911) |
|  | para 36(c) | 16 Oct 2005 (SI 2005/2812) |
|  | para 37 | 8 Jun 2005 (SI 2005/1444) |
| Sch 2 |  | 8 Jun 2005 (in so far as it makes provision in relation to transfer schemes made under s 1(2)) (SI 2005/1444) |
|  |  | 24 Jul 2005 (otherwise) (SI 2005/1909) |
| Sch 3 | para 1 | 7 Feb 2006 (SI 2006/266) |
|  | paras 2–11 | 1 Apr 2006 (SI 2006/266) |
|  | para 12 | 7 Feb 2006 (SI 2006/266) |
|  | paras 13–15 | 1 Apr 2006 (SI 2006/266) |
| Sch 4 |  | 29 Jan 2007 (SI 2007/62) |
| Schs 5, 6 |  | 24 Jul 2005 (SI 2005/1909) |
| Schs 7, 8 |  | 1 Dec 2006 (SI 2006/2911) |
| Sch 9 |  | 24 Jul 2005 (in so far as relates to bye-laws in relation to which the Secretary of State acting alone is the appropriate national authority by virtue of para 1(1)) (SI 2005/1909) |
|  |  | 16 Oct 2005 (otherwise) (SI 2005/2812) |
| Sch 10 | Pts 1, 2 | 8 Jun 2005 (SI 2005/1444) |
|  | Pt 3 | 24 Jul 2005 (SI 2005/1909) |
|  | Pts 4, 5 | 8 Jun 2005 (in so far as they make provision in relation to transfer schemes made under s 1(2)) (SI 2005/1444) |
|  |  | 24 Jul 2005 (otherwise) (SI 2005/1909) |
| Sch 11 | para 1 | See paras 2–16 below |
|  | paras 2–5 | 1 Dec 2006 (SI 2006/2911) |
|  | para 6 | 24 Jul 2005 (SI 2005/1909), except in so far as relates to— |

**Railways Act 2005 (c 14)**—*contd*

|  |  |  |
|---|---|---|
|  |  | (1) the transfer of functions from the Strategic Rail Authority to the Scottish Ministers, and |
|  |  | (2) the repeal of functions of Passenger Transport Authorities and Executives in Scotland |
|  |  | 16 Oct 2005 (exception (1) noted above) (SI 2005/2812) |
|  |  | *Not yet in force* (exception (2) noted above) |
|  | para 7(1) | 1 Dec 2006 (SI 2006/2911) |
|  | para 7(2) | 24 Jul 2005 (SI 2005/1909) |
|  | para 7(3)–(6) | 1 Dec 2006 (SI 2006/2911) |
|  | paras 8, 9 | 24 Jul 2005 (SI 2005/1909) |
|  | paras 10, 11 | 1 Dec 2006 (SI 2006/2911) |
|  | para 12 | 24 Jul 2005 (SI 2005/1909) |
|  | para 13 | 1 Dec 2006 (SI 2006/2911) |
|  | para 14(1)–(5) | 8 Jun 2005 (SI 2005/1444) |
|  | para 14(6), (7) | 24 Jul 2005 (E) (W) (SI 2005/1909) |
|  |  | *Not yet in force* (S) |
|  | para 15 | 24 Jul 2005 (except in so far as each of sub-paras (a)–(c) insert the words "or the Scottish Ministers") (SI 2005/1909) |
|  |  | 16 Oct 2005 (otherwise) (SI 2005/2812) |
|  | para 16(1) | 8 Jun 2005 (SI 2005/1444) |
|  | para 16(2) | 24 Jul 2005 (SI 2005/1909) |
| Sch 12 | para 1(1) | See sub-paras (2), (3) below |
|  | para 1(2) | 1 Dec 2006 (SI 2006/2911) |
|  | para 1(3) | 24 Jul 2005 (SI 2005/1909) |
|  | para 2(1) | See sub-paras (2)–(4) below |
|  | para 2(2), (3) | 24 Jul 2005 (SI 2005/1909) |
|  | para 2(4)(a) | 24 Jul 2005 (SI 2005/1909) |
|  | para 2(4)(b) | 24 Jul 2005 (except words ", the Scottish Ministers") (SI 2005/1909) |
|  |  | 16 Oct 2005 (otherwise) (SI 2005/2812) |
|  | para 3 | 24 Jul 2005 (SI 2005/1909) |
|  | para 4 | 1 Apr 2006 (SI 2006/266) |
|  | para 5 | 24 Jul 2005 (SI 2005/1909) |
|  | para 6 | 1 Apr 2006 (SI 2006/266) |
|  | para 7 | 8 Jun 2005 (SI 2005/1444) |
|  | para 8 | 24 Jul 2005 (except in so far as relates to the transfer of functions from the Strategic Rail Authority to the Scottish Ministers) (SI 2005/1909) |
|  |  | 16 Oct 2005 (otherwise) (SI 2005/2812) |
|  | paras 9–11 | 8 Jun 2005 (SI 2005/1444) |
|  | para 12 | 1 Apr 2006 (SI 2006/266) |
|  | para 13 | 21 Nov 2005 (SI 2005/2812) |
|  | para 14(1) | See sub-paras (2)–(9) below |
|  | para 14(2) | 1 Dec 2006 (SI 2006/2911) |
|  | para 14(3), (4) | 24 Jul 2005 (SI 2005/1909) |
|  | para 14(5)(a) | 1 Dec 2006 (SI 2006/2911) |
|  | para 14(5)(b) | 8 Jun 2005 (SI 2005/1444) |
|  | para 14(6)–(9) | 24 Jul 2005 (SI 2005/1909) |
|  | paras 15, 16 | 8 Jun 2005 (SI 2005/1444) |
|  | para 17(1) | See sub-paras (2)–(9) below |
|  | para 17(2), (3) | 24 Jul 2005 (SI 2005/1909) |
|  | para 17(4)–(6) | 1 Aug 2006 (SI 2006/1951) |
|  | para 17(7) | 8 Jun 2005 (SI 2005/1444) |
|  | para 17(8), (9) | 24 Jul 2005 (SI 2005/1909) |
|  | para 18(1) | See sub-paras (2)–(4) below |
|  | para 18(2)(a), (b) | 24 Jul 2005 (SI 2005/1909) |
|  | para 18(2)(c) | 24 Jul 2005 (except in so far as relates to the transfer of functions from the Strategic Rail Authority to the Scottish Ministers) (SI 2005/1909) |

**Railways Act 2005 (c 14)**—*contd*

|  |  |  |
|---|---|---|
|  |  | 16 Oct 2005 (otherwise) (SI 2005/2812) |
|  | para 18(3) | 24 Jul 2005 (except in so far as relates to the transfer of functions from the Strategic Rail Authority to the Scottish Ministers) (SI 2005/1909) |
|  |  | 16 Oct 2005 (otherwise) (SI 2005/2812) |
|  | para 18(4) | 8 Jun 2005 (SI 2005/1444) |
| Sch 13 | Pt 1 | 8 Jun 2005 (SI 2005/1444), repeals of or in— |

Ministry of Transport Act 1919;

Health and Safety at Work etc Act 1974, s 18(5);

Railways Act 1993, s 4(5)(d);

Transport Act 2000, Sch 27, para 41(2)

26 Jun 2005 (SI 2005/1444), repeals of or in—

Railways Act 1993, s 4(3A)(a);

Transport Act 2000, s 206, Sch 28, para 15

24 Jul 2005 (SI 2005/1909), repeals of or in—

Transport Act 1962, s 56;

Parliamentary Commissioner Act 1967, Sch 2 (entry relating to Rail Passengers' Committees);

Transport Act 1968 (E) (W);

House of Commons Disqualification Act 1975, Sch 1, Pt 3;

Transport Act 1985 (E) (W);

Channel Tunnel Act 1987;

Railways Act 1993, ss 2, 3, 7, 7A, 8 (except words "and to the Health and Safety Executive" in sub-s (7)(a), (b)), 10–15, 15A, 15B (except words "and the Health and Safety Executive" in sub-s (5)), 15C, 16(3) (except words "and to the Health and Safety Executive"), 30, 34 (E) (W), 35 (E) (W), 43(4), 47(6), 54 (E) (W), 55(10) (definition "the appropriate authority"), 61–63, 68, 71A, 72, 73, 76, 77, 79, 83(3), 144 (E) (W), 145(7), Schs 2, 3, 6;

Channel Tunnel Rail Link Act 1996, s 19;

Greater London Authority Act 1999, ss 175, 197, 199, 201, 252, Sch 19;

Freedom of Information Act 2000, Sch 1, Pt 6 (entry relating to any Rail Passengers' Committee established under the Railways Act 1993, s 2(2));

Transport Act 2000, ss 212, 213, 224, 226–228, 251, Sch 16, paras 2–7, 9, 10, 40, 41, 44, 47, 48, 59, 62, 64, Sch 17, paras 2–4, 6–11, 13, 14, 16, 18–24, Sch 22, paras 2, 3, 7–13, 15, 18, 22, 23, Sch 23, Sch 27, paras 30, 39(5), Sch 28, paras 5, 14;

Enterprise Act 2002, s 168(4);

Scottish Public Services Ombudsman Act 2002;

Railways and Transport Safety Act 2003, s 104, Sch 2, paras 3 (entries relating to ss 7A, 77, 79, Schs 2, 3), 16

16 Oct 2005 (SI 2005/2812), repeals of or in—

Railways Act 1993, ss 23, 24, 26, 59;

Transport Act 2000, s 219, Sch 16, paras 14–19, 39, 50, 51(4), (5), Sch 20, Sch 28, para 4;

Enterprise Act 2002, s 168(5)

21 Nov 2005 (repeals of or in Railway Heritage Act 1996; Transport Act 2000, Sch 31) (SI 2005/2812)

1 Apr 2006 (SI 2006/266), repeals of or in—

Health and Safety at Work etc Act 1974, s 78(7)(c);

Railways Act 1993, ss 4(3)(a), 8, 15B, 16(3) (to the extent that each has not already come into force), Sch 4A (in so far as it repeals words "and the Health and Safety Executive" in para 7(4)(b));

Railways and Transport Safety Act 2003, s 62(1)(m), (n)

1 Aug 2006 (repeal in Transport Act 2000, s 248) (SI 2006/1951)

**Railways Act 2005 (c 14)**—*contd*

                1 Dec 2006 (SI 2006/2911), repeals of or in—

                Transport Act 1962, s 43;

                Parliamentary Commissioner Act 1967, Sch 2 (entry relating to the Strategic Rail Authority);

                Superannuation Act 1972;

                House of Commons Disqualification Act 1975, Sch 1, Pt 2;

                Northern Ireland Assembly Disqualification Act 1975;

                Race Relations Act 1976;

                Railways Act 1993, ss 4(3A)(b), 37–42, 43(1)–(3), (5)–(13), 44–46B, 47(1)–(5), 47A, 48, 49, 50, 55(5), (10) (definition "relevant condition or requirement"), 67(6), 69(4), 75, 83(1), 118, 130, 136, 145 (words "the Authority", wherever occurring), 151, Sch 4A, para 7(4)(b) (words "the Authority"), Schs 5, 11[1];

                Channel Tunnel Rail Link Act 1996, s 42A;

                Greater London Authority Act 1999, ss 196, 203, 204, 235;

                Freedom of Information Act 2000, Sch 1, Pt 6 (entry relating to the Strategic Rail Authority);

                Transport Act 2000, ss 201–205, 207–211, 214, 217(2), 218, 220–222, 234–239, 249, 278, Schs 14, 15, Sch 16, paras 11–13, 22–33, 35, 42, 45, 46, 49, 51(2), 52, 53, 61, 66, Sch 17, paras 25–27, 29, 30, Pt 3, Schs 18, 19, 21, Sch 22, paras 4, 5, 14, Sch 25, Sch 27, paras 1, 2–5, 14, 24–29, 35, 39(3), 43, 46, 47, 55, 58, 60–62, Sch 28, paras 1, 6–9, 12–13, 16;

                Railways and Transport Safety Act 2003, ss 62(1)(j), 73(3), Sch 2, paras 3 (entries relating to ss 43, 46, 46A, 46B, 75), 11, Sch 4

                29 Jan 2007 (SI 2007/62), repeals of or in—

                Railways Act 1993, Sch 4A, paras 3, 10;

                Transport Act 2000, Sch 28, para 11

                *Not yet in force,* repeals of or in—

                Transport Act 1968 (S);

                Transport Act 1985 (S);

                Railways Act 1993 (S), ss 34, 35, 54, 144;

                Transport Act 2000, s 246, Sch 16, paras 20, 21, 34

| | | |
|---|---|---|
| Pt 2, para 1 | 1 Dec 2006 (SI 2006/2911) | |
| Pt 2, para 2 | 16 Oct 2005 (SI 2005/2812) | |
| Pt 2, paras 3, 4 | 1 Dec 2006 (SI 2006/2911) | |

[1]    For transitional provisions and savings, see SI 2006/2911, arts 3–7

---

**Regulation of Financial Services (Land Transactions) Act 2005 (c 24)**

*RA:* 19 Dec 2005

*Commencement provisions:* s 2(2)

Whole Act in force 19 Feb 2006 (s 2(2))

---

**Serious Organised Crime and Police Act 2005 (c 15)**

*RA:* 7 Apr 2005

*Commencement provisions:* s 178; Serious Organised Crime and Police Act 2005 (Commencement No 1, Transitional and Transitory Provisions) Order 2005, SI 2005/1521; Serious Organised Crime and Police Act 2005 (Commencement No 1) (Scotland) Order 2005, SSI 2005/358; Serious Organised Crime and Police Act 2005 (Commencement No 2) Order 2005, SI 2005/2026; Serious Organised Crime and Police Act 2005 (Commencement No 3) Order 2005, SI 2005/3136; Serious Organised Crime and Police Act 2005 (Commencement No 4 and Transitory Provisions) Order 2005, SI 2005/3495; Serious Organised Crime and Police Act 2005 (Commencement No 5 and Transitional

**Serious Organised Crime and Police Act 2005 (c 15)**—*contd*
and Transitory Provisions and Savings) Order 2006, SI 2006/378; Serious Organised Crime and Police
Act 2005 (Commencement No 6 and Appointed Day) Order 2006, SI 2006/1085; Serious Organised
Crime and Police Act 2005 (Commencement No 2) (Scotland) Order 2006, SSI 2006/166; Serious
Organised Crime and Police Act 2005 (Commencement No 7) Order 2006, SSI 2006/381; Serious
Organised Crime and Police Act 2005 (Commencement) (No 8) Order 2006, SI 2006/1871, as
amended by SI 2006/2182; Serious Organised Crime and Police Act 2005 (Commencement No 9
and Amendment) Order 2006, SI 2006/2182; Serious Organised Crime and Police Act 2005
(Commencement No 10) Order 2007, SSI 2007/241; Serious Organised Crime and Police Act 2005
(Commencement No 10) Order 2007, SI 2007/3064; Serious Organised Crime and Police Act 2005
(Commencement No 11) Order 2007, SI 2007/3341; Serious Organised Crime and Police Act 2005
(Commencement No 12) Order 2008, SI 2008/306; Serious Organised Crime and Police Act 2005
(Commencement No 12) Order 2008, SI 2008/697; Serious Organised Crime and Police Act 2005
(Commencement No 13) Order 2008, SI 2008/1325; Serious Organised Crime and Police Act 2005
(Commencement No 14) Order 2011, SI 2011/410; Serious Organised Crime and Police Act 2005
(Commencement No 15) Order 2015, SI 2015/188; Serious Organised Crime and Police Act 2005
(Commencement No 16) Order 2020, SI 2020/357

| | | |
|---|---|---|
| 1 | (1) | 1 Mar 2006 (for specified purposes[2]) (SI 2006/378)[3] |
| | | 1 Apr 2006 (otherwise) (SI 2006/378)[3] |
| | (2) | See Sch 1 below |
| | (3) | 1 Jan 2006 (SI 2005/3495) |
| 2–5 | | 1 Apr 2006 (SI 2006/378)[3] |
| 6 | | 1 Mar 2006 (SI 2006/378)[3] |
| 7 | | 1 Apr 2006 (SI 2006/378)[3] |
| 8–10 | | 1 Jan 2006 (s 9(2)(a) is brought into force subject to a transitional provision) (SI 2005/3495) |
| 11–16 | | 1 Apr 2006 (SI 2006/378)[3] |
| 17, 18 | | 1 Jan 2006 (SI 2005/3495) |
| 19–26 | | 1 Apr 2006 (SI 2006/378)[3] |
| 27 | | 1 Jan 2006 (SI 2005/3495) |
| 28–38 | | 1 Apr 2006 (SI 2006/378)[3] |
| 39 | | 1 Jan 2006 (SI 2005/3495) |
| 40, 41 | | 1 Apr 2006 (SI 2006/378)[3] |
| 42 | | 1 Jan 2006 (SI 2005/3495) |
| 43 | | 1 Mar 2006 (SI 2006/378)[3] |
| 44 | (1) | 1 Mar 2006 (SI 2006/378)[3] |
| | (2) | 1 Jan 2006 (SI 2005/3495) |
| 45–51 | | 1 Apr 2006 (SI 2006/378)[3] |
| 52 | | 1 Jan 2006 (SI 2005/3495) |
| 53 | | 1 Apr 2006 (SI 2006/378)[3] |
| 54 | | 1 Jan 2006 (SI 2005/3495) |
| 55 | (1) | See Sch 2 below |
| | (2) | 1 Mar 2006 (SI 2006/378)[3] |
| 56, 57 | | 1 Apr 2006 (SI 2006/378)[3] |
| 58 | | 1 Jan 2006 (SI 2005/3495) |
| 59 | | See Sch 4 below |
| 60–68 | | 1 Apr 2006 (SI 2005/1521; SSI 2006/166) |
| 69 | | 1 Apr 2006 (E) (W) (NI) (SI 2005/1521) |
| 70 | | 1 Apr 2006 (SI 2005/1521; SSI 2006/166) |
| 71–76 | | 1 Apr 2006 (SI 2006/378)[3] |
| 77 | | 1 May 2006 (SSI 2006/166) |
| 78 | | 1 Apr 2006 (SI 2006/378)[3] |
| 79 | | 1 Apr 2006 (E) (W) (NI) (SI 2006/378) |
| | | 1 May 2006 (S) (SSI 2006/166) |
| 80 | (1), (2) | 1 Apr 2006 (E) (W) (NI) (SI 2006/378) |
| | | 1 May 2006 (S) (SSI 2006/166) |
| | (3)–(5) | 1 Apr 2006 (E) (W) (NI) (SI 2006/378) |
| 81 | | 1 Apr 2006 (E) (W) (NI) (SI 2006/378) |
| | | 1 May 2006 (S) (SSI 2006/166) |
| 82–94 | | 1 Apr 2006 (SI 2005/1521; SSI 2006/166) |

**Serious Organised Crime and Police Act 2005 (c 15)**—*contd*

| | | |
|---|---|---|
| 95 | | 1 Jul 2005 (SI 2005/1521) |
| 96 | | 1 Jul 2005 (SI 2005/1521; SSI 2005/358) |
| 97 | | 1 Jul 2005 (SI 2005/1521) |
| 98 | | 1 Jan 2006 (SI 2005/3136) |
| 99, 100 | | 1 Jul 2005 (SI 2005/1521) |
| 101 | | 1 Jul 2005 (SI 2005/1521)[1] |
| 102 | | 15 May 2006 (SI 2006/1085) |
| 103, 104 | | 1 Jul 2005 (SI 2005/1521)[1] |
| 105–108 | | 1 Jul 2005 (SI 2005/1521) |
| 109 | | See Sch 6 below |
| 110, 111 | | 1 Jan 2006 (SI 2005/3495) |
| 112 | | 1 Jul 2005 (SI 2005/1521) |
| 113 | | 1 Jan 2006 (SI 2005/3495) |
| 114 | (1)–(8) | 1 Jan 2006 (SI 2005/3495) |
| | (9) | *Not yet in force* |
| 115 | | 1 Jul 2005 (SI 2005/1521) |
| 116 | (1) | 1 Aug 2005 (SI 2005/2026) |
| | (2) | 1 Jan 2006 (SI 2005/3495) |
| | (3)–(5) | 1 Aug 2005 (SI 2005/2026) |
| 117 | (1), (2) | 7 Mar 2011 (SI 2011/410) |
| | (3) | *Not yet in force* |
| | (4)(a) | 7 Mar 2011 (SI 2011/410) |
| | (4)(b) | *Not yet in force* |
| | (5) | 7 Mar 2011 (SI 2011/410) |
| | (6) | See sub-ss (7)–(10) below |
| | (7) | 7 Apr 2005 (s 178(1)(a)) |
| | (8)–(10) | 7 Mar 2011 (SI 2011/410) |
| 118 | | 1 Jan 2006 (SI 2005/3495) |
| 119 | | 1 Jul 2005 (SI 2005/1521) |
| 120 | | *Never in force* (repealed) |
| 121 | | 7 Mar 2011 (so far as relates to sub-s (5)(a)) (SI 2011/410) |
| | | *Never in force* (repealed) (otherwise) |
| 122 | (1)–(6) | 1 Jul 2005 (in so far as they relate to the provisions of Schs 8, 9 brought into force on that date by SI 2005/1521) (SI 2005/1521) |
| | | 1 Aug 2005 (otherwise) (SI 2005/2026) |
| | (7) | See Schs 8, 9 below |
| 123–131 | | 1 Jul 2005 (SI 2005/1521) |
| 132 | (1)–(6) | 1 Aug 2005 (SI 2005/1521)[1] |
| | (7) | 1 Jul 2005 (SI 2005/1521) |
| 133 | | 1 Jul 2005 (for the purpose of giving notice of a demonstration in the designated area which is due to start or continue on or after 1 Aug 2005) (SI 2005/1521)[1] |
| | | 1 Aug 2005 (otherwise) (SI 2005/1521)[1] |
| 134 | (1)–(6) | 1 Jul 2005 (SI 2005/1521) |
| | (7), (8) | 1 Aug 2005 (SI 2005/1521) |
| | (9), (10) | 1 Jul 2005 (SI 2005/1521) |
| 135–137 | | 1 Aug 2005 (SI 2005/1521) |
| 138–143 | | 1 Jul 2005 (SI 2005/1521) |
| 144 | | See Sch 10 below |
| 145–155 | | 1 Jul 2005 (SI 2005/1521) |
| 156 | | 1 Jul 2005 (SSI 2005/358) |
| 157 | | 1 Apr 2006 (SI 2005/1521) |
| 158 | | 7 Apr 2005 (s 178(1)(a)) |
| 159 | | See Sch 11 below |
| 160 | | See Sch 12 below |
| 161 | (1) | 8 May 2006 (SI 2006/1085) |
| | (2)–(4) | 1 Jul 2005 (in so far as they relate to the provisions of Sch 13 brought into force by SI 2005/1521) (SI 2005/1521) |

**Serious Organised Crime and Police Act 2005 (c 15)**—*contd*

| | | |
|---|---|---|
| | | 1 Aug 2005 (otherwise) (SI 2005/2026) |
| | (5) | See Sch 13 below |
| 162 | (1), (2) | 1 Jul 2005 (SI 2005/1521) |
| | (3) | *Not yet in force* |
| | (4) | 1 Jul 2005 (SI 2005/1521) |
| 163 | (1) | 1 Apr 2006 (S) (SSI 2006/166) |
| | | 6 Apr 2006 (E) (W) (SI 2006/378) |
| | | *Not yet in force* (NI) |
| | (2) | 1 Apr 2006 (S) (except for the purpose of inserting the Police Act 1997, s 113E) (SSI 2006/166)[4] |
| | | 6 Apr 2006 (E) (W) (except for the purpose of inserting the Police Act 1997, ss 113B(10)(a)–(i), (m), 113C(3)(b)–(d), 113D(3)(b), 113E(1), (2)) (SI 2006/378) |
| | | 25 Sep 2006 (E) (W) (for the purpose of inserting the Police Act 1997, s 113B(10)(h)) (SI 2006/2182) |
| | | 12 Nov 2007 (E) (W) (for the purpose of inserting the Police Act 1997, s 113B(10)(a)–(d)) (SI 2007/3064) |
| | | 29 Feb 2008 (E) (W) (for the purpose of inserting the Police Act 1997, s 113B(10)(e)) (SI 2008/306) |
| | | 1 Apr 2008 (NI) (SI 2008/697) |
| | | 9 Mar 2015 (E) (W) (for the purpose of inserting the Police Act 1997, s 113B(10)(i), (m)) (SI 2015/188) |
| | | 27 Mar 2020 (for the purpose of inserting the Police Act 1997, s 113E(1), (2), so far as relate to applications for an enhanced criminal record certificate under s 113B of the 1996 Act for specified purposes[5]) (SI 2020/357) |
| | | *Not yet in force* (exception noted above) (E) (W) |
| | (3) | See Sch 14 below |
| | (4) | 7 Jul 2005 (s 178(2)) |
| 164 | | 1 Jul 2005 (SI 2005/1521; SSI 2005/358) |
| | | 1 Apr 2008 (NI) (SI 2008/697) |
| 165 | (1)(a) | 1 Jul 2005 (E) (W) (NI) (SI 2005/1521) |
| | | 1 Apr 2006 (S) (SSI 2006/166) |
| | | 1 Apr 2008 (NI) (SI 2008/697) |
| | (1)(b) | 1 Apr 2006 (S) (SSI 2006/166) |
| | | 6 Apr 2006 (E) (W) (SI 2006/378) |
| | | 1 Apr 2008 (NI) (SI 2008/697) |
| | (2), (3) | 1 Apr 2006 (S) (SSI 2006/166) |
| | | 6 Apr 2006 (E) (W) (SI 2006/378) |
| | | 3 Dec 2007 (NI) (SI 2007/3341) |
| 166 | (1) | 1 Apr 2006 (S) (SSI 2006/166) |
| | (2) | 1 Jul 2005 (E) (W) (S) (SI 2005/1521; SSI 2005/358) |
| | | 3 Dec 2007 (NI) (SI 2007/3341) |
| 167 | | 7 Apr 2005 (s 178(1)(a)) |
| 168, 169 | | 1 Jul 2005 (SI 2005/1521) |
| 170 | | 1 Jun 2008 (SI 2008/1325) |
| 171 | (1) | See Sch 15 below |
| | (2) | 6 Jul 2006 (SSI 2006/381) |
| 172, 173 | | 7 Apr 2005 (s 178(1)(a)) |
| 174 | (1) | 1 Jan 2006 (SI 2005/3495) |
| | (2) | See Sch 17 below |
| 175 | | 1 Jul 2005 (SI 2005/1521) |
| 176–179 | | 7 Apr 2005 (s 178(1)(a)) |
| Sch 1 | paras 1–8 | 1 Mar 2006 (for specified purposes[2]) (SI 2006/378)[3] |
| | | 1 Apr 2006 (otherwise) (SI 2006/378)[3] |
| | para 9(1)–(3) | 1 Mar 2006 (for specified purposes[2]) (SI 2006/378)[3] |
| | | 1 Apr 2006 (otherwise) (SI 2006/378)[3] |
| | para 9(4) | 1 Apr 2006 (SI 2006/378)[3] |
| | paras 10, 11 | 1 Mar 2006 (for specified purposes[2]) (SI 2006/378)[3] |

**Serious Organised Crime and Police Act 2005 (c 15)**—*contd*

|  |  |  |
|---|---|---|
|  |  | 1 Apr 2006 (otherwise) (SI 2006/378)[3] |
|  | paras 12, 13 | 1 Apr 2006 (SI 2006/378)[3] |
|  | para 14 | 1 Mar 2006 (for specified purposes[2]) (SI 2006/378)[3] |
|  |  | 1 Apr 2006 (otherwise) (SI 2006/378)[3] |
|  | para 15(1)–(4) | 1 Mar 2006 (for specified purposes[2]) (SI 2006/378)[3] |
|  |  | 1 Apr 2006 (otherwise) (SI 2006/378)[3] |
|  | para 15(5) | 1 Apr 2006 (SI 2006/378)[3] |
|  | paras 16–21 | 1 Mar 2006 (for specified purposes[2]) (SI 2006/378)[3] |
|  |  | 1 Apr 2006 (otherwise) (SI 2006/378)[3] |
| Sch 2 | paras 1–7 | 1 Apr 2006 (SI 2006/378)[3] |
|  | para 8 | 1 Mar 2006 (SI 2006/378)[3] |
|  | paras 9–11 | 1 Apr 2006 (SI 2006/378)[3] |
| Sch 3 |  | 1 Jan 2006 (SI 2005/3495) |
| Sch 4 | paras 1–41 | 1 Apr 2006 (SI 2006/378)[3] |
|  | para 42 | 1 Jan 2006 (SI 2005/3495) |
|  | paras 43–169 | 1 Apr 2006 (SI 2006/378)[3] |
|  | paras 170–172 | *Never in force* (repealed) |
|  | paras 173–200 | 1 Apr 2006 (SI 2006/378)[3] |
| Sch 5 |  | 1 Apr 2006 (SI 2005/1521; SSI 2006/166) |
| Sch 6 | paras 1–3 | 1 Jan 2006 (SI 2005/3136) |
|  | para 4 | 1 Aug 2005 (SI 2005/2026) |
|  | paras 5–19 | 1 Jan 2006 (SI 2005/3136) |
|  | para 20 | 1 Aug 2005 (SI 2005/2026) |
|  | paras 21–23 | 1 Jan 2006 (SI 2005/3136) |
| Sch 7 |  | 1 Jan 2006 (SI 2005/3495) |
| Sch 8 | para 1 | 1 Jul 2005 (SI 2005/1521) |
|  | para 2 | 1 Jul 2005 (except so far as relates to relevant licensing offences) (SI 2005/1521) |
|  |  | 1 Jan 2006 (exception noted above) (SI 2005/3495) |
|  | para 3(1), (2) | 1 Jul 2005 (SI 2005/1521) |
|  | para 3(3)(a) | 1 Jul 2005 (SI 2005/1521) |
|  | para 3(3)(b) | 1 Jan 2006 (SI 2005/3495) |
|  | para 3(4)–(7) | 1 Jul 2005 (SI 2005/1521) |
|  | para 3(8) | 1 Jul 2005 (except in so far as inserts Police Reform Act 2002, Sch 4, para 2(6A)) (SI 2005/1521) |
|  |  | 1 Jan 2006 (exception noted above) (SI 2005/3495) |
|  | para 3(9), (10) | 1 Jul 2005 (SI 2005/1521) |
|  | para 4 | 1 Jan 2006 (SI 2005/3495) |
|  | paras 5–7 | 1 Jul 2005 (SI 2005/1521) |
|  | paras 8, 9 | 1 Jan 2006 (SI 2005/3495) |
|  | paras 10, 11 | 1 Jul 2005 (SI 2005/1521) |
|  | para 12 | 1 Jan 2006 (SI 2005/3495) |
|  | paras 13–15 | 1 Jul 2005 (SI 2005/1521) |
|  | para 16 | 1 Jan 2006 (SI 2005/3495) |
|  | paras 17–20 | 1 Jul 2005 (SI 2005/1521) |
|  | para 21 | 1 Jan 2006 (SI 2005/3495) |
| Sch 9 | paras 1–9 | 1 Jul 2005 (SI 2005/1521) |
|  | para 10 | *Never in force* (repealed) |
| Sch 10 |  | 20 Jul 2006 (in the counties of Hampshire, Hertfordshire, Nottinghamshire and Worcestershire; the cities of Leicester and York; the metropolitan boroughs of Gateshead and South Tyneside; and the London boroughs of Southwark and Wandsworth) (SI 2006/1871) |
|  |  | *Not yet in force* (otherwise) |
| Schs 11, 12 |  | 1 Jul 2005 (SI 2005/1521) |
| Sch 13 | paras 1–8 | 1 Jul 2005 (SI 2005/1521) |
|  | paras 9, 10 | 8 May 2006 (SI 2006/1085) |
|  | para 11 | 1 Jul 2005 (SI 2005/1521) |
|  | para 12 | 8 May 2006 (SI 2006/1085) |

**Serious Organised Crime and Police Act 2005 (c 15)**—*contd*

|  |  |  |
|---|---|---|
|  | para 13 | 1 Jul 2005 (SI 2005/1521) |
| Sch 14 | para 1 | 1 Apr 2006 (S) (SSI 2006/166) |
|  |  | 6 Apr 2006 (E) (W) (SI 2006/378) |
|  |  | 3 Dec 2007 (NI) (SI 2007/3341) |
|  | paras 2, 3 | 1 Apr 2006 (S) (SSI 2006/166) |
|  |  | 6 Apr 2006 (E) (W) (SI 2006/378) |
|  |  | 1 Apr 2008 (NI) (SI 2008/697) |
|  | para 4 | 1 Apr 2006 (S) (SSI 2006/166) |
|  |  | 6 Apr 2006 (E) (W) (SI 2006/378) |
|  |  | *Not yet in force* (NI) |
|  | para 5 | 1 Apr 2006 (S) (SSI 2006/166) |
|  | para 6(a) | 1 Apr 2006 (S) (SSI 2006/166) |
|  |  | 3 Dec 2007 (NI) (SI 2007/3341) |
|  | para 6(b), (c) | 1 Apr 2006 (S) (SSI 2006/166) |
|  |  | 6 Apr 2006 (E) (W) (SI 2006/378) |
|  |  | 3 Dec 2007 (NI) (SI 2007/3341) |
|  | paras 7, 8 | 1 Apr 2006 (S) (SSI 2006/166) |
|  |  | 6 Apr 2006 (E) (W) (SI 2006/378) |
|  |  | 3 Dec 2007 (NI) (SI 2007/3341) |
|  | para 9 | 1 Apr 2006 (S) (SSI 2006/166) |
|  | para 10 | 1 Apr 2006 (S) (SSI 2006/166) |
|  |  | 6 Apr 2006 (E) (W) (SI 2006/378) |
|  |  | *Not yet in force* (NI) |
|  | paras 11, 12 | 1 Apr 2006 (S) (SSI 2006/166) |
|  |  | 6 Apr 2006 (E) (W) (SI 2006/378) |
|  |  | 3 Dec 2007 (NI) (SI 2007/3341) |
|  | para 13 | *Not yet in force* |
|  | para 14 | 1 Apr 2006 (S) (SSI 2006/166) |
|  |  | 6 Apr 2006 (E) (W) (SI 2006/378) |
|  |  | 3 Dec 2007 (NI) (SI 2007/3341) |
| Sch 15 | paras 1–6 | 30 Jun 2006 (S) (SSI 2006/381) |
|  |  | 6 Jul 2006 (E) (W) (SSI 2006/381) |
|  | para 7 | 6 Jul 2006 (E) (W) (SSI 2006/381) |
|  | para 8 | 30 Jun 2006 (S) (SSI 2006/381) |
|  |  | 6 Jul 2006 (E) (W) (for the purpose of making regulations) (SSI 2006/381) |
|  |  | 6 Apr 2007 (E) (W) (otherwise) (SSI 2007/241) |
|  | para 9 | 30 Jun 2006 (S) (SSI 2006/381) |
|  |  | 6 Apr 2007 (E) (W) (SSI 2007/241) |
|  | paras 10–14 | 30 Jun 2006 (S) (SSI 2006/381) |
|  |  | 6 Jul 2006 (E) (W) (SSI 2006/381) |
| Sch 16 |  | 1 Jan 2006 (SI 2005/3495) |
| Sch 17 | Pt 1 | 7 Apr 2005 (s 178(1)(b)) |
|  | Pt 2 | 1 Jul 2005 (SI 2005/1521), repeals of or in— |

Pt 2 (continued):
Criminal Justice Act 1988, s 140;
Local Government Finance Act 1992;
Drug Trafficking Act 1994, Sch 1, para 25;
Criminal Procedure (Consequential Provisions) (Scotland) Act 1995;
Crime and Disorder Act 1998, s 1C;
Police Reform Act 2002, Sch 4, para 2, Sch 5;
Proceeds of Crime Act 2002, ss 330(9)(b), 337–339, 447;
Anti-social Behaviour Act 2003, s 23(5)
1 Jan 2006 (SI 2005/3495), repeals of or in—
Unlawful Drilling Act 1819;
Vagrancy Act 1824;
Railway Regulation Act 1842;
Companies Clauses Consolidation Act 1845;
Railway Clauses Consolidation Act 1845;

**Serious Organised Crime and Police Act 2005 (c 15)**—*contd*

Licensing Act 1872;
Public Stores Act 1875;
London County Council (General Powers) Act 1894;
London County Council (General Powers) Act 1900;
Licensing Act 1902;
Official Secrets Act 1911;
Protection of Animals Act 1911;
Public Order Act 1936;
Street Offences Act 1959;
Criminal Justice Act 1967;
Ministry of Housing and Local Government Provisional Order
  (Greater London Parks and Open Spaces) Act 1967;
Port of London Act 1968;
Theft Act 1968;
Criminal Law Act 1977;
Theft Act 1978;
Animal Health Act 1981;
Aviation Security Act 1982;
Local Government (Miscellaneous Provisions) Act 1982;
Police and Criminal Evidence Act 1984, ss 15, 25, 66, 116, 118,
  Schs 1, 1A, 2, 5, 6;
Sporting Events (Control of Alcohol etc) Act 1985;
Public Order Act 1986;
Criminal Justice Act 1988, Sch 15;
Road Traffic Act 1988, ss 4, 163;
Road Traffic (Consequential Provisions) Act 1988;
Football Spectators Act 1989;
Aviation and Maritime Security Act 1990, Sch 3;
Football (Offences) Act 1991;
Road Traffic Act 1991;
Trade Union and Labour Relations (Consolidation) Act 1992;
Transport and Works Act 1992;
Criminal Justice and Public Order Act 1994;
Drug Trafficking Act 1994, Sch 1, para 9;
Offensive Weapons Act 1996;
Reserve Forces Act 1996;
Public Order (Amendment) Act 1996;
Confiscation of Alcohol (Young Persons) Act 1997;
Crime and Disorder Act 1998, ss 27, 31;
Criminal Justice and Court Services Act 2000;
Football (Disorder) Act 2000, Sch 2;
Terrorism Act 2000;
Criminal Justice and Police Act 2001, ss 42, 47;
Anti-terrorism, Crime and Security Act 2001;
Police Reform Act 2002, ss 48, 49, Sch 6;
Proceeds of Crime Act 2002, Sch 11, para 14;
Anti-social Behaviour Act 2003, ss 4, 32, 37;
Aviation (Offences) Act 2003;
Communications Act 2003;
Courts Act 2003;
Crime (International Co-operation) Act 2003, s 17;
Criminal Justice Act 2003, s 3;
Licensing Act 2003, Sch 6, para 93;
Sexual Offences Act 2003;
Domestic Violence, Crime and Victims Act 2004;
Hunting Act 2004;
Prevention of Terrorism Act 2005;
Serious Organised Crime and Police Act 2005
1 Apr 2006 (SI 2006/378)[3], repeals and revocations of or in—

**Serious Organised Crime and Police Act 2005 (c 15)**—*contd*

Army Act 1955;
Air Force Act 1955;
Naval Discipline Act 1957;
Public Records Act 1958;
Trustee Investments Act 1961;
Leasehold Reform Act 1967;
Parliamentary Commissioner Act 1967;
Police (Scotland) Act 1967;
Employment Agencies Act 1973;
House of Commons Disqualification Act 1975;
Northern Ireland Assembly Disqualification Act 1975;
Sex Discrimination Act 1975;
Police Pensions Act 1976;
Race Relations Act 1976;
Health and Safety at Work (Northern Ireland) Order 1978;
Stock Transfer Act 1982;
Police and Criminal Evidence Act 1984, ss 5, 55;
Prosecution of Offences Act 1985;
Ministry of Defence Police Act 1987;
Road Traffic Act 1988, ss 124, 144;
Aviation and Maritime Security Act 1990, s 22(4);
Tribunals and Inquiries Act 1992;
Criminal Appeal Act 1995;
Disability Discrimination Act 1995;
Employment Rights Act 1996;
Police Act 1996;
Juries (Northern Ireland) Order 1996;
Employment Rights (Northern Ireland) Order 1996;
Police (Health and Safety) Act 1997;
Police Act 1997, ss 1–87, 89, 90, 93, 94, 111, 137, Schs 1–2A, 9;
Police (Health and Safety) (Northern Ireland) Order 1997;
Crime and Disorder Act 1998, s 113;
Police (Northern Ireland) Act 1998;
Regulation of Investigatory Powers Act 2000, ss 33, 34, 45, 56, 75, 76A, Sch 4;
Football (Disorder) Act 2000, s 2;
Freedom of Information Act 2000;
Police (Northern Ireland) Act 2000;
Criminal Justice and Police Act 2001, ss 104, 107–121, 138, Schs 4–6;
International Development Act 2002;
Police Reform Act 2002, ss 8–10, 15, 25, 38, 42, 45, 47, 82(1)(c), (2), (3)(d), 85–91, 93, 102, 103, 108; Sch 1, Sch 4, para 36, Sch 7;
Proceeds of Crime Act 2002, s 313, Sch 11, paras 30, 34;
Crime (International Co-operation) Act 2003, s 85;
Energy Act 2004
1 Apr 2006 (S) (SSI 2006/166), repeals of or in—
Police Act 1997, ss 113, 115, 125;
Regulation of Care (Scotland) Act 2001;
Criminal Justice (Scotland) Act 2003;
Protection of Children (Scotland) Act 2003
6 Apr 2006 (E) (W) (SI 2006/378), repeals of or in—
Police Act 1997, ss 113, 115;
Protection of Children Act 1999;
Care Standards Act 2000;
Health and Social Care Act 2001;
Adoption and Children Act 2002;

**Serious Organised Crime and Police Act 2005 (c 15)**—*contd*
>Education Act 2002;
>National Health Service Reform and Health Care Professions
>   Act 2002;
>Criminal Justice Act 2003, Sch 35;
>Licensing Act 2003, Sch 6, para 116
>8 May 2006 (SI 2006/1085), repeals of or in—
>Regulation of Investigatory Powers Act 2000, Sch 1;
>Police Reform Act 2002, s 82(1)(f), (5)
>1 Apr 2008 (NI) (repeals of or in Police Act 1997) (SI 2008/697)
>*Not yet in force*, repeals of or in—
>Protection of Children Act 1999 (S);
>Care Standards Act 2000 (S);
>Health and Social Care Act 2001 (S);
>National Health Service Reform and Health Care Professions
>   Act 2002 (S);
>Licensing Act 2003, Sch 6, para 116 (S);
>Protection of Children and Vulnerable Adults (Northern Ireland)
>   Order 2003, SI 2003/417 (NI 4);
>Criminal Justice Act 2003, Sch 35 (S)
>*Never in force* (repealed) repeals of or in Proceeds of Crime
>   Act 2002, ss 330(5)(b), 331, 332, Sch 11, para 3

[1]   For transitional provisions and savings, see SI 2005/1521, arts 2(2), 3(4), (5), 4(2)

[2]   The specified purposes are:

(a) making appointments which take effect before 1 Apr 2006 of the chairman and other members of SOCA;

(b) SOCA exercising the powers in s 6 of the Act;

(c) SOCA exercising the powers in Sch 1, para 8(1)(b) and (2) to the Act in respect of appointments or secondments to take effect on or after 1 Apr 2006;

(d) SOCA exercising its power under Sch 1, paras 15(1) and 16(1) to the Act in respect of committees and delegation to take effect on or after 1 Apr 2006;

(e) making determinations under Sch 1, para 17 to the Act;

(f) SOCA exercising functions under Sch 1, para 21 to the Act, the Police Reform Act 2002, s 26A or the Police (Northern Ireland) Act 1998, s 60ZA;

(g) the Director General of SOCA exercising the powers in s 44(1) of, and Sch 1, para 11 to, the Act;

(h) the Director General of SOCA, or any employee of SOCA to whom functions under s 43 of the Act have been delegated, exercising the functions in that section to take effect on or after 1 Apr 2006

[3]   For transitional provisions and savings, see SI 2006/378, arts 2(2)–(5), 3(3), (4), 4(2)–(7), 5(2)

[4]   Note that s 113E of the 1997 Act is repealed in relation to Scotland

[5]   The specified purposes are:

(i) by a person who is registered, or who the Registrar is considering registering, as a nurse, midwife or nursing associate (individually or as part of a specified group) under article 9A of the Nursing and Midwifery Order 2001 (temporary registration in emergencies involving loss of human life or human illness etc)(e);

(ii) by a person who is registered, or who the Registrar is considering registering, as a member of a relevant profession (individually or as part of a specified group) under article 9A of the Health Professions Order 2001 (temporary registration in emergencies involving loss of human life or human illness etc)(f);

(iii) by a person who is registered, or who the regulator is considering registering, as a social worker (individually or as part of a specified group) under regulation 12A of the Social Workers Regulations 2018 (temporary registration in emergencies involving loss of human life or human illness etc)(g);

(iv) by a person who is registered, or who the registrar is considering registering, as a social worker

**Serious Organised Crime and Police Act 2005 (c 15)**—*contd*

(individually or as part of a specified group) under section 83A of the Regulation and Inspection of Social Care (Wales) Act 2016 (temporary registration in emergencies involving loss of human life or human illness etc)(h);

(v) by a person who is registered, or who the Registrar is considering registering, as a fully registered medical practitioner (individually or as part of a specified group) under section 18A of the Medical Act 1983 (temporary registration with regard to emergencies involving loss of human life or human illness etc)(a);

(vi) by a person who is registered, or who the Registrar is considering registering, as a pharmacist or a pharmacy technician (individually or as part of a specified group) under article 34 of the Pharmacy Order 2010 (temporary entry with regard to emergencies involving loss of human life or human illness etc)(b);

(vii) for the purposes of considering the applicant's suitability for employment for the purposes of providing, or being engaged to provide, NHS health services or social care services in connection with, or in consequence of, the provision of care or treatment to a person who has, or is suspected of having, coronavirus disease as defined by section 1 of the Coronavirus Act 2020(c), whether or not in respect of that disease.

---

**Smoking, Health and Social Care (Scotland) Act 2005 (asp 13)**

*RA:* 5 Aug 2005

*Commencement provisions:* s 43(2)–(4); Smoking, Health and Social Care (Scotland) Act 2005 (Commencement No 1) Order 2005, SSI 2005/492; Smoking, Health and Social Care (Scotland) Act 2005 (Commencement No 2) Order 2005, SSI 2005/642; Smoking, Health and Social Care (Scotland) Act 2005 (Commencement No 3) Order 2006, SSI 2006/47; Smoking, Health and Social Care (Scotland) Act 2005 (Commencement No 4) Order 2006, SSI 2006/121; Smoking, Health and Social Care (Scotland) Act 2005 (Commencement No 5) Order 2007, SSI 2007/218; Smoking, Health and Social Care (Scotland) Act 2005 (Commencement No 6) Order 2010, SSI 2010/185

| | | |
|---|---|---|
| 1, 2 | | 26 Mar 2006 (at 0600 hours) (SSI 2005/492) |
| 3 | (1), (2) | 26 Mar 2006 (at 0600 hours) (SSI 2005/492) |
| | (3) | 1 Nov 2005 (SSI 2005/492) |
| | (4) | 26 Mar 2006 (at 0600 hours) (SSI 2005/492) |
| 4 | (1) | 7 Feb 2006 (SSI 2006/47) |
| | (2), (3) | 1 Nov 2005 (SSI 2005/492) |
| | (4), (5) | 7 Feb 2006 (SSI 2006/47) |
| | (6) | 16 Dec 2005 (SSI 2005/642) |
| | (7) | 1 Nov 2005 (SSI 2005/492) |
| | (8), (9) | 16 Dec 2005 (SSI 2005/642) |
| 5 | | 26 Mar 2006 (at 0600 hours) (SSI 2005/492) |
| 6 | | See Sch 1 below |
| 7–10 | | 26 Mar 2006 (at 0600 hours) (SSI 2005/492) |
| 11 | | 17 Oct 2005 (SSI 2005/492) |
| 12 | | 7 Mar 2006 (for the purpose of enabling the Scottish Ministers to make regulations under the National Health Service (Scotland) Act 1978, ss 70A(1), 71 and the National Health Service (Primary Care) Act 1997, s 20, to come into force not earlier than 1 Apr 2006) (SSI 2006/121) |
| | | 1 Apr 2006 (otherwise) (SSI 2005/492) |
| 13 | | 7 Mar 2006 (for the purpose of enabling the Scottish Ministers to make regulations under the National Health Service (Scotland) Act 1978, ss 26, 70, to come into force not earlier than 1 Apr 2006) (SSI 2006/121) |
| | | 1 Apr 2006 (otherwise) (SSI 2005/492) |
| 14 | | *Not yet in force* |
| 15 | | 20 May 2010 (for the purpose of enabling the Scottish Ministers to make regulations under the National Health Service (Scotland) Act 1978, s 25(1), (2), (2A) and (2B)) (SSI 2010/185) |
| | | 2 Jul 2010 (otherwise) (SSI 2010/185) |

**Smoking, Health and Social Care (Scotland) Act 2005 (asp 13)**—*contd*

| | | |
|---|---|---|
| 16 | | 17 Oct 2005 (SSI 2005/492) |
| 17 | | 20 May 2010 (for the purpose of enabling the Scottish Ministers to make regulations under the National Health Service (Scotland) Act 1978, s 25(1), (2), (2A), (2B) (SSI 2010/185) |
| | | 2 Jul 2010 (otherwise) (SSI 2010/185) |
| 18 | | *Not yet in force* |
| 19 | | 7 Mar 2006 (for the purpose of enabling the Scottish Ministers to make regulations under the National Health Service (Scotland) Act 1978, s 26(2), (2A), (2B), to come into force not earlier than 1 Apr 2006) (SSI 2006/121) |
| | | 1 Apr 2006 (otherwise) (SSI 2006/121) |
| 20–25 | | *Not yet in force* |
| 26 | (1) | 7 Mar 2006 (for the purpose of enabling the Scottish Ministers to make regulations under the National Health Service (Scotland) Act 1978, ss 29(4)(b), 29A(5), 32, 32A, to come into force not earlier than 1 Apr 2006) (SSI 2006/121) |
| | | 1 Apr 2006 (otherwise) (SSI 2006/121) |
| | (2)(a), (b) | 7 Mar 2006 (for the purpose of enabling the Scottish Ministers to make regulations under the National Health Service (Scotland) Act 1978, ss 29(4)(b), 29A(5), 32, 32A, to come into force not earlier than 1 Apr 2006) (SSI 2006/121) |
| | | 1 Apr 2006 (otherwise) (SSI 2006/121) |
| | (2)(c)(i) | 7 Mar 2006 (for the purpose of enabling the Scottish Ministers to make regulations under the National Health Service (Scotland) Act 1978, ss 29(4)(b), 29A(5), 32, 32A, to come into force not earlier than 1 Apr 2006) (SSI 2006/121) |
| | | 1 Apr 2006 (otherwise) (SSI 2006/121) |
| | (2)(c)(ii) | 7 Mar 2006 (for the purpose of enabling the Scottish Ministers to make regulations under the National Health Service (Scotland) Act 1978, ss 29(4)(b), 29A(5), 32, 32A, to come into force not earlier than 1 Apr 2006) (SSI 2006/121) |
| | | 1 Apr 2006 (for the purpose of substituting words from "list" to the end and word "list", (a) in relation to a list referred to in sub-s (8)(a), "perform"; and (b) in relation to the list referred to in sub-s (8)(d), "undertake to provide or are approved to assist in providing") (SSI 2006/121) |
| | | 2 Jul 2010 (for the purpose of substituting sub-s (6)(b)) (SSI 2010/185) |
| | | *Not yet in force* (otherwise) |
| | (2)(d) | 7 Mar 2006 (for the purpose of enabling the Scottish Ministers to make regulations under the National Health Service (Scotland) Act 1978, ss 29(4)(b), 29A(5), 32, 32A, to come into force not earlier than 1 Apr 2006) (SSI 2006/121) |
| | | 1 Apr 2006 (otherwise) (SSI 2006/121) |
| | (2)(e)(i) | 7 Mar 2006 (for the purpose of enabling the Scottish Ministers to make regulations under the National Health Service (Scotland) Act 1978, ss 29(4)(b), 29A(5), 32, 32A, to come into force not earlier than 1 Apr 2006) (SSI 2006/121) |
| | | 1 Apr 2006 (otherwise) (SSI 2006/121) |
| | (2)(e)(ii) | 7 Mar 2006 (for the purpose of enabling the Scottish Ministers to make regulations under the National Health Service (Scotland) Act 1978, ss 29(4)(b), 29A(5), 32, 32A, to come into force not earlier than 1 Apr 2006) (SSI 2006/121) |
| | | 1 Apr 2006 (for the purpose of substituting para (d) for existing paras (c)–(e)) (SSI 2006/121) |
| | | 2 Jul 2010 (for the purpose of substituting the new para (c)) (SSI 2010/185) |
| | | *Not yet in force* (otherwise) |

**Smoking, Health and Social Care (Scotland) Act 2005 (asp 13)**—*contd*

| | |
|---|---|
| (2)(f) | 7 Mar 2006 (for the purpose of enabling the Scottish Ministers to make regulations under the National Health Service (Scotland) Act 1978, ss 29(4)(b), 29A(5), 32, 32A, to come into force not earlier than 1 Apr 2006) (SSI 2006/121) |
| | 1 Apr 2006 (otherwise) (SSI 2006/121) |
| (3)(a) | 7 Mar 2006 (for the purpose of enabling the Scottish Ministers to make regulations under the National Health Service (Scotland) Act 1978, ss 29(4)(b), 29A(5), 32, 32A, to come into force not earlier than 1 Apr 2006) (SSI 2006/121) |
| | 1 Apr 2006 (otherwise) (SSI 2006/121) |
| (3)(b) | 7 Mar 2006 (for the purpose of enabling the Scottish Ministers to make regulations under the National Health Service (Scotland) Act 1978, ss 29(4)(b), 29A(5), 32, 32A, to come into force not earlier than 1 Apr 2006) (SSI 2006/121) |
| | 2 Jul 2010 (otherwise) (SSI 2010/185) |
| (3)(c) | 7 Mar 2006 (for the purpose of enabling the Scottish Ministers to make regulations under the National Health Service (Scotland) Act 1978, ss 29(4)(b), 29A(5), 32, 32A, to come into force not earlier than 1 Apr 2006) (SSI 2006/121) |
| | 1 Apr 2006 (for the purpose of applying in relation to the list referred to in the National Health Service (Scotland) Act 1978, s 29(8)(d)) (SSI 2006/121) |
| | 2 Jul 2010 (for the purpose of applying in relation to the list referred to in s 29(8)(c) of the 1978 Act) (SSI 2010/185) |
| | *Not yet in force* (otherwise) |
| (3)(d), (e) | 7 Mar 2006 (for the purpose of enabling the Scottish Ministers to make regulations under the National Health Service (Scotland) Act 1978, ss 29(4)(b), 29A(5), 32, 32A, to come into force not earlier than 1 Apr 2006) (SSI 2006/121) |
| | 1 Apr 2006 (otherwise) (SSI 2006/121) |
| (4)(a) | 7 Mar 2006 (for the purpose of enabling the Scottish Ministers to make regulations under the National Health Service (Scotland) Act 1978, ss 29(4)(b), 29A(5), 32, 32A, to come into force not earlier than 1 Apr 2006) (SSI 2006/121) |
| | 1 Apr 2006 (otherwise) (SSI 2006/121) |
| (4)(b) | 7 Mar 2006 (for the purpose of enabling the Scottish Ministers to make regulations under the National Health Service (Scotland) Act 1978, ss 29(4)(b), 29A(5), 32, 32A, to come into force not earlier than 1 Apr 2006) (SSI 2006/121) |
| | 1 Apr 2006 (for the purpose of substituting sub-s (2)(a), (b) for existing sub-s (2)) (SSI 2006/121) |
| | *Not yet in force* (otherwise) |
| (4)(c) | 7 Mar 2006 (for the purpose of enabling the Scottish Ministers to make regulations under the National Health Service (Scotland) Act 1978, ss 29(4)(b), 29A(5), 32, 32A, to come into force not earlier than 1 Apr 2006) (SSI 2006/121) |
| | 1 Apr 2006 (otherwise) (SSI 2006/121) |
| (5)(a) | 7 Mar 2006 (for the purpose of enabling the Scottish Ministers to make regulations under the National Health Service (Scotland) Act 1978, ss 29(4)(b), 29A(5), 32, 32A, to come into force not earlier than 1 Apr 2006) (SSI 2006/121) |
| | 1 Apr 2006 (otherwise) (SSI 2006/121) |
| (5)(b) | 7 Mar 2006 (for the purpose of enabling the Scottish Ministers to make regulations under the National Health Service (Scotland) Act 1978, ss 29(4)(b), 29A(5), 32, 32A, to come into force not earlier than 1 Apr 2006) (SSI 2006/121) |
| | *Not yet in force* (otherwise) |
| (6) | 7 Mar 2006 (for the purpose of enabling the Scottish Ministers to make regulations under the National Health Service (Scotland) Act 1978, ss 29(4)(b), 29A(5), 32, 32A, to come into force not earlier than 1 Apr 2006) (SSI 2006/121) |

**Smoking, Health and Social Care (Scotland) Act 2005 (asp 13)**—*contd*

|  |  |  |
|---|---|---|
|  |  | 1 Apr 2006 (otherwise) (SSI 2006/121) |
|  | (7)(a) | 7 Mar 2006 (for the purpose of enabling the Scottish Ministers to make regulations under the National Health Service (Scotland) Act 1978, ss 29(4)(b), 29A(5), 32, 32A, to come into force not earlier than 1 Apr 2006) (SSI 2006/121) |
|  |  | *Not yet in force* (otherwise) |
|  | (7)(b)(i) | 7 Mar 2006 (for the purpose of enabling the Scottish Ministers to make regulations under the National Health Service (Scotland) Act 1978, ss 29(4)(b), 29A(5), 32, 32A, to come into force not earlier than 1 Apr 2006) (SSI 2006/121) |
|  |  | *Not yet in force* (otherwise) |
|  | (7)(b)(ii) | 7 Mar 2006 (for the purpose of enabling the Scottish Ministers to make regulations under the National Health Service (Scotland) Act 1978, ss 29(4)(b), 29A(5), 32, 32A, to come into force not earlier than 1 Apr 2006) (SSI 2006/121) |
|  |  | 1 Apr 2006 (otherwise) (SSI 2006/121) |
|  | (7)(c) | 7 Mar 2006 (for the purpose of enabling the Scottish Ministers to make regulations under the National Health Service (Scotland) Act 1978, ss 29(4)(b), 29A(5), 32, 32A, to come into force not earlier than 1 Apr 2006) (SSI 2006/121) |
|  |  | 1 Apr 2006 (otherwise) (SSI 2006/121) |
|  | (7)(d) | 7 Mar 2006 (for the purpose of enabling the Scottish Ministers to make regulations under the National Health Service (Scotland) Act 1978, ss 29(4)(b), 29A(5), 32, 32A, to come into force not earlier than 1 Apr 2006) (SSI 2006/121) |
|  |  | 1 Apr 2006 (for the purpose of inserting the National Health Service (Scotland) Act 1978, s 26(7), enabling regulations to be made regarding s 26(2) thereof) (SSI 2006/121) |
|  |  | *Not yet in force* (otherwise) |
| 27 |  | 7 Mar 2006 (for the purpose of enabling the Scottish Ministers to make regulations under the National Health Service (Scotland) Act 1978, s 32D(3), to come into force not earlier than 1 Apr 2006) (SSI 2006/121) |
|  |  | 1 Apr 2006 (otherwise) (SSI 2006/121) |
| 28–32 |  | 17 Oct 2005 (SSI 2005/492) |
| 33, 34 |  | 6 Aug 2005 (s 43(2)) |
| 35 |  | 19 Dec 2005 (SSI 2005/492) |
| 36, 37 |  | 17 Oct 2005 (SSI 2005/492) |
| 38 |  | 1 Nov 2005 (SSI 2005/492) |
| 39, 40 |  | 5 Aug 2005 (RA) |
| 41 |  | 6 Aug 2005 (s 43(2)) |
| 42 | (1) | See Sch 2 below |
|  | (2) | See Sch 3 below |
| 43 |  | 5 Aug 2005 (RA) |
| Sch 1 | para 1 | 26 Mar 2006 (at 0600 hours) (SSI 2005/492) |
|  | para 2 | 1 Nov 2005 (for the purpose of enabling the Scottish Ministers to make regulations to come into force not earlier than 0600 hours on 26 Mar 2006) (SSI 2005/492) |
|  |  | 26 Mar 2006 (at 0600 hours) (otherwise) (SSI 2005/492) |
|  | para 3 | 26 Mar 2006 (at 0600 hours) (SSI 2005/492) |
|  | para 4(1) | 1 Nov 2005 (for the purpose of enabling the Scottish Ministers to make regulations to come into force not earlier than 0600 hours on 26 Mar 2006) (SSI 2005/492) |
|  |  | 26 Mar 2006 (at 0600 hours) (otherwise) (SSI 2005/492) |
|  | para 4(2), (3) | 26 Mar 2006 (at 0600 hours) (SSI 2005/492) |
|  | para 5(1) | 26 Mar 2006 (at 0600 hours) (SSI 2005/492) |
|  | para 5(2) | 1 Nov 2005 (for the purpose of enabling the Scottish Ministers to make regulations to come into force not earlier than 0600 hours on 26 Mar 2006) (SSI 2005/492) |
|  |  | 26 Mar 2006 (at 0600 hours) (otherwise) (SSI 2005/492) |

**Smoking, Health and Social Care (Scotland) Act 2005 (asp 13)**—*contd*

| | | |
|---|---|---|
| | para 5(3) | 26 Mar 2006 (at 0600 hours) (SSI 2005/492) |
| | paras 6–11 | 26 Mar 2006 (at 0600 hours) (SSI 2005/492) |
| | para 12 | 1 Nov 2005 (for the purpose of enabling the Scottish Ministers to make regulations to come into force not earlier than 0600 hours on 26 Mar 2006) (SSI 2005/492) |
| | | 26 Mar 2006 (at 0600 hours) (otherwise) (SSI 2005/492) |
| | para 13 | 26 Mar 2006 (at 0600 hours) (SSI 2005/492) |
| Sch 2 | para 1 | 17 Oct 2005 (SSI 2005/492) |
| | para 2(1) | 17 Oct 2005 (SSI 2005/492) |
| | para 2(2) | 6 Aug 2005 (s 43(2)) |
| | para 2(3) | 2 Jul 2010 (SSI 2010/185) |
| | para 2(4) | 6 Aug 2005 (s 43(2)) |
| | para 2(5) | 1 Apr 2006 (SSI 2006/121) |
| | para 2(6)–(9) | *Not yet in force* |
| | para 2(10)–(14) | 1 Apr 2006 (SSI 2006/121) |
| | para 2(15) | 2 Jul 2010 (for the purpose of substituting words from "any list" to the end of para (c) in the National Health Service (Scotland) Act 1978, s 33) (SSI 2010/185) |
| | | *Not yet in force* (otherwise) |
| | para 2(16) | 2 Jul 2010 (SSI 2010/185) |
| | para 2(17), (18) | *Not yet in force* |
| | para 2(19)(a)(i) | *Not yet in force* |
| | para 2(19)(a)(ii) | 1 Apr 2006 (SSI 2005/492) |
| | para 2(19)(a)(iii) | *Not yet in force* |
| | para 2(19)(a)(iv) | 1 Nov 2005 (SSI 2005/492) |
| | para 2(19)(b) | 2 Jul 2010 (SSI 2010/185) |
| | para 2(20) | 1 Apr 2006 (SSI 2006/121) |
| | para 3(a), (b) | *Not yet in force* |
| | para 3(c) | 2 Jul 2010 (SSI 2010/185) |
| | paras 4–6 | *Not yet in force* |
| Sch 3 | | 17 Oct 2005 (repeal in Mental Health (Care and Treatment) (Scotland) Act 2003) (SSI 2005/492) |
| | | 1 Nov 2005 (SSI 2005/492), repeals of or in— |
| | | Ethical Standards in Public Life etc (Scotland) Act 2000; |
| | | Public Finance and Accountability (Scotland) Act 2000; |
| | | Freedom of Information (Scotland) Act 2002 |
| | | 1 Apr 2006 (SSI 2006/121), repeals of or in— |
| | | National Health Service (Scotland) Act 1978, ss 29A(5), 29B, 30, 31, 32A, 32B; |
| | | Health and Social Security Act 1984; |
| | | Health Act 1999; |
| | | Community Care and Health (Scotland) Act 2002; |
| | | Primary Medical Services (Scotland) Act 2004, s 5(3)(a), Schedule, para 1(11)(a), (13) |
| | | 1 Apr 2007 (repeal of Health and Medicines Act 1988, s 8) (SSI 2007/218) |
| | | 2 Jul 2010 (SSI 2010/185), repeals of or in— |
| | | National Health Service (Scotland) Act 1978, Sch 8, para 8; |
| | | National Health Service and Community Care Act 1990, s 40, Sch 9, para 19(6) |
| | | *Not yet in force*, repeals of or in— |
| | | National Health Service (Scotland) Act 1978, ss 17C(6), 25(3)–(5), 27, 28, 28B(6), 29A(2), 85AA(11), 85AB(6); |
| | | Health Services Act 1980; |
| | | Health and Social Services and Social Security Adjudications Act 1983; |
| | | Dentists Act 1984; |
| | | National Health Service (Amendment) Act 1986; |
| | | Health and Medicines Act 1988 (except s 8); |

**Smoking, Health and Social Care (Scotland) Act 2005 (asp 13)**—*contd*

National Health Service and Community Care Act 1990, Sch 9,
para 19(7), (8);
National Health Service (Primary Care) Act 1997;
Primary Medical Services (Scotland) Act 2004, Schedule,
para 1(8), (10), (16)(a)

---

**Stipends (Cessation of Special Payments) Measure 2005 (No 1)**

*RA:* 24 Mar 2005

*Commencement provisions:* s 5(2)

Provisions of this Measure were brought into force on 1 Jul 2005 and 31 Dec 2005 by an instrument made
by the Archbishops of Canterbury and York, and dated 2 Jun 2005 (made under s 5(2))

| | |
|---|---|
| 1 | 1 Jul 2005 |
| 2 | 31 Dec 2005 |
| 3–5 | 1 Jul 2005 |

---

**Transport (Scotland) Act 2005 (asp 12)**

*RA:* 5 Aug 2005

*Commencement provisions:* s 54(2); Transport (Scotland) Act 2005 (Commencement No 1) Order 2005,
SSI 2005/454; Transport (Scotland) Act 2005 (Commencement No 2) Order 2007, SSI 2007/161;
Transport (Scotland) Act 2005 (Commencement No 3) Order 2007, SSI 2007/409; Transport
(Scotland) Act 2005 (Commencement No 4) Order 2008, SSI 2008/15, as amended by SSI 2008/90

| | | |
|---|---|---|
| 1 | | 14 Sep 2005 (SSI 2005/454) |
| 2, 3 | | 10 Oct 2005 (SSI 2005/454) |
| 4 | | See Sch 1 below |
| 5–12 | | 10 Oct 2005 (SSI 2005/454) |
| 13 | | 14 Sep 2005 (SSI 2005/454) |
| 14–17 | | 10 Oct 2005 (SSI 2005/454) |
| 18 | | 1 Apr 2008 (SSI 2008/15) |
| 19 | (1) | 29 Feb 2008 (for the purpose of enabling regulations under the New Roads and Street Works Act 1991, s 112A(4) to be made so as to come into force on or after that day and to provide definitions of "the Commissioner" and "the SRWR" for that purpose) (SSI 2008/15) |
| | | 1 Apr 2008 (otherwise) (SSI 2008/15)[1] |
| | (2) | 1 Apr 2008 (SSI 2008/15) |
| | (3), (4) | 1 Apr 2008 (SSI 2008/15)[1] |
| | (5), (6) | 1 Apr 2008 (SSI 2008/15) |
| | (7) | 29 Feb 2008 (for the purpose of enabling regulations under the New Roads and Street Works Act 1991, s 112A(4) to be made so as to come into force on or after that day and to provide definitions of "the Commissioner" and "the SRWR" for that purpose) (SSI 2008/15) |
| | | 1 Apr 2008 (otherwise) (SSI 2008/15) |
| 20, 21 | | 1 Apr 2008 (SSI 2008/15) |
| 22 | | 1 Apr 2008 (except sub-s (1)(a)) (SSI 2008/15)[1] |
| | | *Not yet in force* (exception noted above) |
| 23, 24 | | 1 Apr 2008 (SSI 2008/15) |
| 25 | | 1 Oct 2007 (SSI 2007/409) |
| 26–29 | | 1 Apr 2008 (SSI 2008/15) |
| 30–32 | | *Not yet in force* |
| 33 | | See Sch 3 below |
| 34 | (1), (2) | 1 Oct 2008 (SSI 2008/15) |
| | (3) | See Schs 4, 5 below |
| 35 | | *Not yet in force* |

**Transport (Scotland) Act 2005 (asp 12)**—*contd*

| | | |
|---|---|---|
| 36 | | 1 Apr 2008 (SSI 2008/15) |
| 37 | | 1 Oct 2008 (SSI 2008/15) |
| 38 | | *Not yet in force* |
| 39 | | 1 Oct 2007 (SSI 2007/409) |
| 40 | | 10 Oct 2005 (SSI 2005/454) |
| 41–43 | | 3 Apr 2006 (SSI 2005/454) |
| 44–48 | | 10 Oct 2005 (SSI 2005/454) |
| 49 | | 1 Apr 2007 (SSI 2007/161) |
| 50, 51 | | 10 Oct 2005 (SSI 2005/454) |
| 52 | | 5 Aug 2005 (RA) |
| 53 | | 10 Oct 2005 (SSI 2005/454) |
| 54 | | 5 Aug 2005 (RA) |
| Sch 1 | paras 1–10 | 10 Oct 2005 (SSI 2005/454) |
| | para 11 | 3 Apr 2006 (SSI 2005/454) |
| | paras 12–19 | 10 Oct 2005 (SSI 2005/454) |
| | para 20 | 3 Apr 2006 (SSI 2005/454) |
| Sch 2 | | 10 Oct 2005 (SSI 2005/454) |
| Sch 3 | | 1 Apr 2008 (SSI 2008/15)[1] |
| Schs 4–7 | | 1 Oct 2008 (SSI 2008/15) |

[1]    For transitional provisions, see SSI 2008/15, art 3

---

## Water Services etc (Scotland) Act 2005 (asp 3)

*RA:* 17 Mar 2005

*Commencement provisions:* s 37(2), (3); Water Services etc (Scotland) Act 2005 (Commencement No 1 and Savings) Order 2005, SSI 2005/351; Water Services etc (Scotland) Act 2005 (Commencement No 2) Order 2006, SSI 2006/40; Water Services etc (Scotland) Act 2005 (Commencement No 3 and Savings) Order 2006, SSI 2006/167; Water Services etc (Scotland) Act 2005 (Commencement No 4) Order 2006, SSI 2006/445; Water Services etc (Scotland) Act 2005 (Commencement No 5) Order 2006, SSI 2006/599; Water Services etc (Scotland) Act 2005 (Commencement No 6) Order 2012, SSI 2012/192

| | | |
|---|---|---|
| 1 | (1) | 20 Jun 2005 (for the purpose of bringing into force the substituted s 1(1) of the 2002 Act) (SSI 2005/351) |
| | | 1 Jul 2005 (otherwise) (SSI 2005/351) |
| | (2), (3) | 1 Jul 2005 (SSI 2005/351) |
| | (4) | See Sch 1 below |
| 2 | | 1 Jul 2005 (SSI 2005/351)[2] |
| 3 | | 1 Apr 2006 (SSI 2006/167) |
| 4 | (1)–(5) | 20 Jun 2005 (SSI 2005/351) |
| | (6) | 7 Sep 2006 (SSI 2006/445) |
| | (7)–(12) | 20 Jun 2005 (SSI 2005/351) |
| 5 | (1)–(5) | 20 Jun 2005 (SSI 2005/351) |
| | (6) | 7 Sep 2006 (SSI 2006/445) |
| | (7)–(13) | 20 Jun 2005 (SSI 2005/351) |
| 6, 7 | | 7 Sep 2006 (in relation to applications for licences submitted in respect of the business undertaking established under s 13) (SSI 2006/445) |
| | | 8 Jan 2007 (otherwise) (SSI 2006/599) |
| 8 | | 7 Sep 2006 (SSI 2006/445) |
| 9 | | 20 Jun 2005 (only for the purpose of any water sewerage services licence applied for or held by any undertaking established under s 13 of this Act) (SSI 2005/351) |
| | | 8 Jan 2007 (otherwise) (SSI 2006/599) |
| 10, 11 | | 7 Sep 2006 (SSI 2006/445) |
| 12 | | See Sch 2 below |
| 13–20 | | 7 Sep 2006 (SSI 2006/445) |

**Water Services etc (Scotland) Act 2005 (asp 3)**—*contd*

| | | |
|---|---|---|
| 21 | (1)–(3) | 1 Jul 2005 (SSI 2005/351) |
| | (4), (5) | 7 Sep 2006 (SSI 2006/445) |
| | (6) | See Sch 3 below |
| 22 | | 1 Jul 2005 (SSI 2005/351) |
| 23 | | 1 Apr 2006 (SSI 2006/167)[1] |
| 24 | | 1 Jul 2005 (SSI 2005/351) |
| 25 | | 10 Feb 2006 (SSI 2006/40) |
| 26 | (1)–(9) | 22 Apr 2006 (SSI 2006/167) |
| | (10) | 22 Apr 2006 (in relation to any sewerage nuisance to which the Sewerage Nuisance (Code of Practice) (Scotland) Order 2006, SSI 2006/155, applies) (SSI 2006/167) |
| | | *Not yet in force* (otherwise) |
| | (11) | 22 Apr 2006 (SSI 2006/167) |
| | (12) | 10 Feb 2006 (in so far as it applies to s 25) (SSI 2006/40) |
| | | 22 Apr 2006 (otherwise) (SSI 2006/167) |
| 27 | | 7 Sep 2006 (SSI 2006/445) |
| 28–31 | | 20 Jun 2005 (SSI 2005/351) |
| 32 | | See Sch 5 below |
| 33–37 | | 17 Mar 2005 (RA) |
| Sch 1 | | 20 Jun 2005 (only for the purpose of bringing into force Sch A1, paras 1–7 of the 2002 Act) (SSI 2005/351) |
| | | 1 Jul 2005 (otherwise) (SSI 2005/351) |
| Sch 2 | paras 1–3 | 7 Sep 2006 (SSI 2006/445) |
| | para 4 | 8 Jan 2007 (SSI 2006/599) |
| | paras 5–12 | 7 Sep 2006 (SSI 2006/445) |
| Sch 3 | | 1 Jul 2005 (SSI 2005/351) |
| Sch 4 | | 20 Jun 2005 (SSI 2005/351) |
| Sch 5 | paras 1–6 | 1 Jul 2005 (SSI 2005/351) |
| | para 7(1), (2) | 1 Jul 2005 (SSI 2005/351) |
| | para 7(3) | 1 Apr 2006 (SSI 2006/167) |
| | para 7(4) | 1 Jul 2005 (SSI 2005/351) |
| | para 7(5) | 22 Jul 2012 (SSI 2012/192) |
| | para 7(6) | 1 Jul 2005 (SSI 2005/351) |
| | para 7(7) | 7 Sep 2006 (SSI 2006/445) |
| | para 7(8), (9) | 1 Jul 2005 (SSI 2005/351) |
| | para 7(10) | 8 Jan 2007 (SSI 2006/599) |
| | para 8(a) | 1 Apr 2006 (SSI 2006/167) |
| | para 8(b) | 1 Jul 2005 (SSI 2005/351) |
| | para 9(a) | 1 Apr 2006 (SSI 2006/167) |
| | para 9(b) | 1 Jul 2005 (SSI 2005/351) |
| | para 10 | 1 Jul 2005 (SSI 2005/351) |

---

[1]  For savings, see SSI 2006/167, art 3

[2]  Note that SSI 2006/599 also purports to bring s 2 into force on 8 Jan 2007

# 2006 Acts

## Animal Health and Welfare (Scotland) Act 2006 (asp 11)

*RA:* 11 Jul 2006

*Commencement provisions:* s 55; Animal Health and Welfare (Scotland) Act 2006 (Commencement No 1, Savings and Transitional Provisions) Order 2006, SSI 2006/482; Animal Health and Welfare (Scotland) Act 2006 (Commencement No 2) Order 2007, SSI 2007/257; Animal Health and Welfare (Scotland) Act 2006 (Commencement No 3 and Saving Provisions) Order 2020, SSI 2020/464

| | | |
|---|---|---|
| 1–19 | | 6 Oct 2006 (SSI 2006/482) |
| 20 | (1)–(3) | 30 Apr 2007 (SSI 2007/257) |
| | (4)–(6) | 6 Oct 2006 (SSI 2006/482) |
| 21–36 | | 6 Oct 2006 (SSI 2006/482) |
| 37 | | 6 Oct 2006 (SSI 2006/482)[1] |
| 38 | | 6 Oct 2006 (SSI 2006/482) |
| 39–42 | | 6 Oct 2006 (SSI 2006/482)[1] |
| 43–51 | | 6 Oct 2006 (SSI 2006/482) |
| 52 | | See Sch 2 below |
| 53–55 | | 11 Jul 2006 (RA) |
| Sch 1 | | 6 Oct 2006 (SSI 2006/482) |
| Sch 2 | paras 1–5 | 6 Oct 2006 (SSI 2006/482) |
| | para 6 | *Not yet in force* |
| | para 7 | 6 Oct 2006 (SSI 2006/482) |
| | para 8(1) | 6 Oct 2006 (SSI 2006/482)[1] |
| | para 8(2) | 6 Oct 2006 (SSI 2006/482) |
| | para 9(a) | 6 Oct 2006 (SSI 2006/482) |
| | para 9(b) | *Not yet in force* |
| | para 9(c) | 6 Oct 2006 (SSI 2006/482) |
| | para 9(d) | 6 Oct 2006 (repeal of Pet Animals Act 1951, s 3) (SSI 2006/482) |
| | | 1 Sep 2021 (repeal of Pet Animals Act 1951, ss 1, 2, 4–8) (SSI 2020/464)[2] |
| | para 9(e)–(g) | 6 Oct 2006 (SSI 2006/482) |
| | para 9(h)–(j) | *Not yet in force* |
| | para 9(k), (l) | 1 Sep 2021 (SSI 2020/464)[2] |
| | para 9(m) | 6 Oct 2006 (SSI 2006/482) |
| | para 9(n) | 1 Sep 2021 (SSI 2020/464)[2] |
| | para 9(o) | 6 Oct 2006 (SSI 2006/482) |
| | para 9(p) | 1 Sep 2021 (SSI 2020/464)[2] |

[1] For savings and transitional provisions, see SSI 2006/482, art 4

[2] For savings, see SSI 2020/464, art 3

## Animal Welfare Act 2006 (c 45)

*RA:* 8 Nov 2006

*Commencement provisions:* s 68; Animal Welfare Act 2006 (Commencement No 1) (England) Order 2007, SI 2007/499; Animal Welfare Act 2006 (Commencement No 1) (Wales) Order 2007, SI 2007/1030;

**Animal Welfare Act 2006 (c 45)**—*contd*

Animal Welfare Act 2006 (Commencement No 2 and Saving and Transitional Provisions) (England) Order 2007, SI 2007/2711; Animal Welfare Act 2006 (Commencement No 2 and Saving and Transitional Provisions) (Wales) Order 2007, SI 2007/3065; Animal Welfare Act 2006 (Commencement No 1) (Scotland) Order 2007, SSI 2007/519

| | | |
|---|---|---|
| 1–4 | | 27 Mar 2007 (W) (SI 2007/1030) |
| | | 6 Apr 2007 (E) (SI 2007/499) |
| 5 | (1)–(3) | 27 Mar 2007 (W) (SI 2007/1030) |
| | | 6 Apr 2007 (E) (SI 2007/499) |
| | (4), (5) | 23 Mar 2007 (E) (for the purpose of making regulations) (SI 2007/499) |
| | | 27 Mar 2007 (W) (SI 2007/1030) |
| | | 6 Apr 2007 (E) (otherwise) (SI 2007/499) |
| | (6) | 27 Mar 2007 (W) (SI 2007/1030) |
| | | 6 Apr 2007 (E) (SI 2007/499) |
| 6 | (1)–(3) | 27 Mar 2007 (W) (SI 2007/1030) |
| | | 6 Apr 2007 (E) (SI 2007/499) |
| | (4)–(6) | 23 Mar 2007 (E) (for the purpose of making regulations) (SI 2007/499) |
| | | 27 Mar 2007 (W) (SI 2007/1030) |
| | | 6 Apr 2007 (E) (otherwise) (SI 2007/499) |
| | (7) | 27 Mar 2007 (W) (SI 2007/1030) |
| | | 6 Apr 2007 (E) (SI 2007/499) |
| | (8)(a) | 27 Mar 2007 (W) (SI 2007/1030) |
| | | 6 Apr 2007 (E) (SI 2007/499) |
| | (8)(b) | 23 Mar 2007 (E) (for the purpose of making regulations) (SI 2007/499) |
| | | 27 Mar 2007 (W) (SI 2007/1030) |
| | | 6 Apr 2007 (E) (otherwise) (SI 2007/499) |
| | (9)–(13) | 27 Mar 2007 (W) (SI 2007/1030) |
| | | 6 Apr 2007 (E) (SI 2007/499) |
| | (14) | 23 Mar 2007 (E) (for the purpose of making regulations) (SI 2007/499) |
| | | 27 Mar 2007 (W) (SI 2007/1030) |
| | | 6 Apr 2007 (E) (otherwise) (SI 2007/499) |
| | (15), (16) | 27 Mar 2007 (W) (SI 2007/1030) |
| | | 6 Apr 2007 (E) (SI 2007/499) |
| 7 | | 27 Mar 2007 (W) (SI 2007/1030) |
| | | 6 Apr 2007 (E) (SI 2007/499) |
| 8 | (1), (2) | 27 Mar 2007 (W) (SI 2007/1030) |
| | | 6 Apr 2007 (E) (SI 2007/499) |
| | (3)–(6) | *Not yet in force* (sub-s (6) repealed) |
| | (7), (8) | 27 Mar 2007 (W) (SI 2007/1030) |
| | | 6 Apr 2007 (E) (SI 2007/499) |
| 9–13 | | 27 Mar 2007 (W) (SI 2007/1030) |
| | | 6 Apr 2007 (E) (SI 2007/499) |
| 14 | | 1 Oct 2007 (E) (SI 2007/2711) |
| | | 24 Oct 2007 (W) (SI 2007/3065) |
| 15 | | 1 Oct 2007 (SI 2007/2711) |
| 16 | | 24 Oct 2007 (SI 2007/3065) |
| 17–45 | | 27 Mar 2007 (W) (SI 2007/1030) |
| | | 6 Apr 2007 (E) (SI 2007/499) |
| 46–50 | | 12 Dec 2007 (SSI 2007/519) |
| 51–60 | | 27 Mar 2007 (W) (SI 2007/1030) |
| | | 6 Apr 2007 (E) (SI 2007/499) |
| 61 | | 8 Nov 2006 (s 68(1)) |
| 62, 63 | | 27 Mar 2007 (W) (SI 2007/1030) |
| | | 6 Apr 2007 (E) (SI 2007/499) |
| 64 | | See Sch 3 below |
| 65 | | See Sch 4 below |

**Animal Welfare Act 2006 (c 45)**—*contd*

| | |
|---|---|
| 66 | 27 Mar 2007 (W) (SI 2007/1030) |
| | 6 Apr 2007 (E) (SI 2007/499) |
| 67–69 | 8 Nov 2006 (s 68(1)) |
| Schs 1, 2 | 27 Mar 2007 (W) (SI 2007/1030) |
| | 6 Apr 2007 (E) (SI 2007/499) |
| Sch 3 | 27 Mar 2007 (W) (except in so far as it relates to para 3(1) of this Schedule) (SI 2007/1030) |
| | 6 Apr 2007 (E) (except in so far as it relates to para 3(1) of this Schedule) (SI 2007/499) |
| | *Not yet in force* (E) (W) (exceptions noted above) |
| Sch 4 | 27 Mar 2007 (W), 6 Apr 2007 (E) (SI 2007/1030; SI 2007/499), repeals of or in— |

Metropolitan Police Act 1839;
Town Police Clauses Act 1847;
Protection of Animals Act 1911;
Protection of Animals (1911) Amendment Act 1921;
Protection of Animals Act 1934;
Docking and Nicking of Horses Act 1949;
Pet Animals Act 1951, s 3;
Cockfighting Act 1952;
Protection of Animals (Amendment) Act 1954;
Protection of Animals (Anaesthetics) Act 1954;
Abandonment of Animals Act 1960;
Animals (Cruel Poisons Act) 1962;
Protection of Animals (Anaesthetics) Act 1964;
Agriculture (Miscellaneous Provisions) Act 1968, ss 1, 4, 5;
Animals (Scientific Procedures) Act 1986;
Protection of Animals (Penalties) Act 1987;
Protection against Cruel Tethering Act 1988;
Protection of Animals (Amendment) Act 1988;
Protection of Animals (Amendment) Act 2000

1 Oct 2007 (E), 24 Oct 2007 (W) (SI 2007/2711; SI 2007/3065), repeals of or in—
Agriculture (Miscellaneous Provisions) Act 1968, ss 2, 3[1], 6–8;
Animal Health Act 1981, Sch 5, para 8

*Not yet in force*, repeals of or in—
Pet Animals Act 1951, s 2;
Animal Health Act 1981, ss 37–39

[1]    For transitional provisions and savings, see SI 2007/2711, art 3, SI 2007/3065, art 3

---

**Appropriation Act 2006 (c 6)**

*RA:* 30 Mar 2006

Whole Act in force 30 Mar 2006 (RA)

---

**Appropriation (No 2) Act 2006 (c 24)**

*RA:* 19 Jul 2006

Whole Act in force 19 Jul 2006 (RA)

---

**Armed Forces Act 2006 (c 52)**

*RA:* 8 Nov 2006

*Commencement provisions:* s 383; Armed Forces Act 2006 (Commencement No 1) Order 2007, SI 2007/1442; Armed Forces Act 2006 (Commencement No 2) Order 2007, SI 2007/2913; Armed

**Armed Forces Act 2006 (c 52)**—*contd*

Forces Act 2006 (Commencement No 3) Order 2008, SI 2008/1650; Armed Forces Act 2006 (Commencement No 4) Order 2009, SI 2009/812; Armed Forces Act 2006 (Commencement No 5) Order 2009, SI 2009/1167

| | | |
|---|---|---|
| 1–211 | | 28 Mar 2009 (for certain purposes)[3] (SI 2009/812) |
| | | 31 Oct 2009 (otherwise) (SI 2009/1167) |
| 212 | (1) | 28 Mar 2009 (for certain purposes)[3] (SI 2009/812) |
| | | 31 Oct 2009 (otherwise) (SI 2009/1167) |
| | (2) | 28 Mar 2009 (for certain purposes)[3] (SI 2009/812) |
| | | *Not yet in force* (otherwise) |
| 213–271 | | 28 Mar 2009 (for certain purposes)[3] (SI 2009/812) |
| | | 31 Oct 2009 (otherwise) (SI 2009/1167) |
| 272 | (1) | 28 Mar 2009 (for certain purposes)[3] (SI 2009/812) |
| | | 31 Oct 2009 (otherwise) (SI 2009/1167) |
| | (2) | See Sch 8 below |
| 273–333 | | 28 Mar 2009 (for certain purposes)[3] (SI 2009/812) |
| | | 31 Oct 2009 (otherwise) (SI 2009/1167) |
| 334–339 | | 1 Jan 2008 (SI 2007/2913) |
| 340–342 | | 28 Mar 2009 (for certain purposes)[3] (SI 2009/812) |
| | | 31 Oct 2009 (otherwise) (SI 2009/1167) |
| 343 | | 1 Oct 2008 (SI 2008/1650) |
| 344–350 | | 28 Mar 2009 (for certain purposes)[3] (SI 2009/812) |
| | | 31 Oct 2009 (otherwise) (SI 2009/1167) |
| 351 | | See Sch 12 below |
| 352 | | 28 Mar 2009 (for certain purposes)[3] (SI 2009/812) |
| | | 31 Oct 2009 (otherwise) (SI 2009/1167) |
| 353 | | See Sch 13 below |
| 354–357 | | 28 Mar 2009 (for certain purposes)[3] (SI 2009/812) |
| | | 31 Oct 2009 (otherwise) (SI 2009/1167) |
| 358 | | See Sch 14 below |
| 359 | | 8 Nov 2006 (s 383(1)) |
| 360 | | 15 Oct 2007 (SI 2007/2913) |
| 361–363 | | 28 Mar 2009 (for certain purposes)[3] (SI 2009/812) |
| | | 31 Oct 2009 (otherwise) (SI 2009/1167) |
| 364 | | 24 Jun 2008 (SI 2008/1650) |
| 365 | | 28 Mar 2009 (for certain purposes)[3] (SI 2009/812) |
| | | 6 May 2009 (so far as is necessary to enable the Director of Service Prosecutions to appoint prosecuting officers) (SI 2009/1167) |
| | | 31 Oct 2009 (otherwise) (SI 2009/1167) |
| 366 | | 1 Jan 2008 (SI 2007/2913) |
| 367 | | 1 Jan 2008 (so far as it relates to ss 334–338) (SI 2007/2913) |
| | | 1 Oct 2008 (so far as it relates to s 343) (SI 2008/1650) |
| | | 28 Mar 2009 (for certain purposes)[3] (SI 2009/812) |
| | | 31 Oct 2009 (otherwise) (SI 2009/1167) |
| 368, 369 | | 1 Jan 2008 (SI 2007/2913) |
| 370 | (1) | 28 Mar 2009 (for certain purposes)[3, 4] (SI 2009/812) |
| | | 31 Oct 2009 (otherwise) (SI 2009/1167) |
| | (2) | See Sch 15, Pt 2 below |
| 371, 372 | | 28 Mar 2009 (for certain purposes)[3] (SI 2009/812) |
| | | 31 Oct 2009 (otherwise) (SI 2009/1167) |
| 373 | | 8 Nov 2006 (s 383(1)) |
| 374 | | 1 Jan 2008 (so far as is necessary to bring into force the definitions of "officer", "service police force", "service policeman", "subject to service law", "the regular forces" and "the reserve forces") (SI 2007/2913) |
| | | 1 Oct 2008 (so far as is necessary to bring into force the definitions of "civilian court", "Her Majesty's forces", "British overseas territory police force", "overseas police force" and "UK police force") (SI 2008/1650) |
| | | 28 Mar 2009 (for certain purposes)[3] (SI 2009/812) |

**Armed Forces Act 2006 (c 52)**—*contd*

| | | |
|---|---|---|
| | | 31 Oct 2009 (otherwise) (SI 2009/1167) |
| 375 | (1) | 1 Jan 2008 (SI 2007/2913) |
| | (2)–(4) | 1 Oct 2008 (SI 2008/1650) |
| | (5) | 1 Jan 2008 (SI 2007/2913) |
| 376, 377 | | 28 Mar 2009 (for certain purposes)[3] (SI 2009/812) |
| | | 31 Oct 2009 (otherwise) (SI 2009/1167) |
| 378 | (1) | See Sch 16 below |
| | (2) | See Sch 17 below |
| 379 | | 4 Jun 2007 (SI 2007/1442) |
| 380 | | 28 Mar 2009 (for certain purposes)[3] (SI 2009/812) |
| | | 31 Oct 2009 (otherwise) (SI 2009/1167) |
| 381 | | 4 Jun 2007 (SI 2007/1442) |
| 382–384 | | 8 Nov 2006 (s 383(1)) |
| 385 | | 28 Mar 2009 (for certain purposes)[3] (SI 2009/812) |
| | | 31 Oct 2009 (otherwise) (SI 2009/1167) |
| 386 | | 8 Nov 2006 (s 383(1)) |
| Schs 1–7 | | 28 Mar 2009 (for certain purposes)[3] (SI 2009/812) |
| | | 31 Oct 2009 (otherwise) (SI 2009/1167) |
| Sch 8 | paras 1–8 | 28 Mar 2009 (for certain purposes)[3] (SI 2009/812) |
| | | 31 Oct 2009 (otherwise) (SI 2009/1167) |
| | para 9 | 1 Jan 2008 (SI 2007/2913) |
| | paras 10–20 | 28 Mar 2009 (for certain purposes)[3] (SI 2009/812) |
| | | 31 Oct 2009 (otherwise) (SI 2009/1167) |
| | para 21(a), (b) | 28 Mar 2009 (for certain purposes)[3] (SI 2009/812) |
| | | 31 Oct 2009 (otherwise) (SI 2009/1167) |
| | para 21(c) | 24 Jun 2008 (SI 2008/1650) |
| | para 21(d)–(g) | 28 Mar 2009 (for certain purposes)[3] (SI 2009/812) |
| | | 31 Oct 2009 (otherwise) (SI 2009/1167) |
| | paras 22–35 | 28 Mar 2009 (for certain purposes)[3] (SI 2009/812) |
| | | 31 Oct 2009 (otherwise) (SI 2009/1167) |
| | para 36(a)(i) | 28 Mar 2009 (for certain purposes)[3] (SI 2009/812) |
| | | 31 Oct 2009 (otherwise) (SI 2009/1167) |
| | para 36(a)(ii), (iii) | 1 Jan 2008 (SI 2007/2913) |
| | para 36(b), (c) | 28 Mar 2009 (for certain purposes)[3] (SI 2009/812) |
| | | 31 Oct 2009 (otherwise) (SI 2009/1167) |
| | para 37(a) | 24 Jun 2008 (SI 2008/1650) |
| | para 37(b)–(e) | 28 Mar 2009 (for certain purposes)[3] (SI 2009/812) |
| | | 31 Oct 2009 (otherwise) (SI 2009/1167) |
| | paras 38–42 | 28 Mar 2009 (for certain purposes)[3] (SI 2009/812) |
| | | 31 Oct 2009 (otherwise) (SI 2009/1167) |
| | para 43(a) | 28 Mar 2009 (for certain purposes)[3] (SI 2009/812) |
| | | 31 Oct 2009 (otherwise) (SI 2009/1167) |
| | para 43(b) | 24 Jun 2008 (SI 2008/1650) |
| | paras 44–56 | 28 Mar 2009 (for certain purposes)[3] (SI 2009/812) |
| | | 31 Oct 2009 (otherwise) (SI 2009/1167) |
| Schs 9–11 | | 28 Mar 2009 (for certain purposes)[3] (SI 2009/812) |
| | | 31 Oct 2009 (otherwise) (SI 2009/1167) |
| Sch 12 | | 28 Mar 2009 (so far as is necessary for enabling the Defence Council to make appointments under this Act) (SI 2009/812) |
| | | *Not yet in force* (otherwise) |
| Sch 13 | | 28 Mar 2009 (for certain purposes)[3] (SI 2009/812) |
| | | 31 Oct 2009 (otherwise) (SI 2009/1167) |
| Sch 14 | paras 1–32 | 28 Mar 2009 (for certain purposes)[3] (SI 2009/812) |
| | | 31 Oct 2009 (otherwise) (SI 2009/1167) |
| | paras 33–36 | 15 Oct 2007 (SI 2007/2913) |
| | paras 37–59 | 28 Mar 2009 (for certain purposes)[3] (SI 2009/812) |
| | | 31 Oct 2009 (otherwise) (SI 2009/1167) |
| Sch 15 | | 28 Mar 2009 (for certain purposes)[3, 4] (SI 2009/812) |
| | | 31 Oct 2009 (otherwise) (SI 2009/1167) |

**Armed Forces Act 2006 (c 52)**—*contd*

| | | |
|---|---|---|
| Sch 16 | paras 1–9 | 28 Mar 2009 (for certain purposes)[3] (SI 2009/812) |
| | | 31 Oct 2009 (otherwise) (SI 2009/1167) |
| | para 10 | 28 Mar 2009 (for certain purposes)[3] (SI 2009/812) |
| | | 6 May 2009 (otherwise) (SI 2009/1167) |
| | paras 11–15 | 28 Mar 2009 (for certain purposes)[3] (SI 2009/812) |
| | | 31 Oct 2009 (otherwise) (SI 2009/1167) |
| | para 16 | 1 Jan 2008 (SI 2007/2913) |
| | paras 17–19 | 28 Mar 2009 (for certain purposes)[3] (SI 2009/812) |
| | | 31 Oct 2009 (otherwise) (SI 2009/1167) |
| | paras 20, 21 | 1 Jan 2008 (SI 2007/2913) |
| | para 22 | 15 Oct 2007 (SI 2007/2913) |
| | paras 23, 24 | 1 Jan 2008 (SI 2007/2913) |
| | para 25 | 15 Oct 2007 (SI 2007/2913) |
| | paras 26, 27 | 1 Jan 2008 (SI 2007/2913) |
| | para 28 | 4 Jun 2007 (SI 2007/1442) |
| | paras 29–38 | 1 Jan 2008 (SI 2007/2913) |
| | paras 39–53 | 28 Mar 2009 (for certain purposes)[3] (SI 2009/812) |
| | | 31 Oct 2009 (otherwise) (SI 2009/1167) |
| | paras 54–58 | 1 Jan 2008 (SI 2007/2913) |
| | paras 59–70 | 28 Mar 2009 (for certain purposes)[3] (SI 2009/812) |
| | | 31 Oct 2009 (otherwise) (SI 2009/1167) |
| | para 71 | 1 Jan 2008 (SI 2007/2913) |
| | paras 72–79 | 28 Mar 2009 (for certain purposes)[3] (SI 2009/812) |
| | | 31 Oct 2009 (otherwise) (SI 2009/1167) |
| | para 80 | 1 Jan 2008 (SI 2007/2913) |
| | para 81 | 28 Mar 2009 (for certain purposes)[3] (SI 2009/812) |
| | | 31 Oct 2009 (otherwise) (SI 2009/1167) |
| | para 82 | 1 Jan 2008 (SI 2007/2913) |
| | paras 83–99 | 28 Mar 2009 (for certain purposes)[3] (SI 2009/812) |
| | | 31 Oct 2009 (otherwise) (SI 2009/1167) |
| | para 100(a) | 4 Jun 2007 (SI 2007/1442) |
| | para 100(b) | 1 Jan 2008 (SI 2007/2913) |
| | paras 101–120 | 28 Mar 2009 (for certain purposes)[3] (SI 2009/812) |
| | | 31 Oct 2009 (otherwise) (SI 2009/1167) |
| | para 121 | 28 Mar 2009 (for certain purposes)[3] (SI 2009/812) |
| | | *Not yet in force* (otherwise) |
| | paras 122–135 | 28 Mar 2009 (for certain purposes)[3] (SI 2009/812) |
| | | 31 Oct 2009 (otherwise) (SI 2009/1167) |
| | para 136 | 1 Jan 2008 (SI 2007/2913) |
| | paras 137–145 | 28 Mar 2009 (for certain purposes)[3] (SI 2009/812) |
| | | 31 Oct 2009 (otherwise) (SI 2009/1167) |
| | para 146(1) | See sub-paras (2)–(5) below |
| | para 146(2), (3) | 4 Jun 2007 (SI 2007/1442) |
| | para 146(4), (5) | 28 Mar 2009 (for certain purposes)[3] (SI 2009/812) |
| | | 31 Oct 2009 (otherwise) (SI 2009/1167) |
| | para 147 | 4 Jun 2007 (SI 2007/1442) |
| | para 148 | 28 Mar 2009 (for certain purposes)[3] (SI 2009/812) |
| | | 31 Oct 2009 (otherwise) (SI 2009/1167) |
| | para 149 | 4 Jun 2007 (SI 2007/1442) |
| | para 150 | 1 Jan 2008 (SI 2007/2913) |
| | paras 151–169 | 28 Mar 2009 (for certain purposes)[3] (SI 2009/812) |
| | | 31 Oct 2009 (otherwise) (SI 2009/1167) |
| | para 170 | 4 Jun 2007 (SI 2007/1442) |
| | para 171(1) | See sub-paras (2), (3) below |
| | para 171(2)(a) | 4 Jun 2007 (SI 2007/1442) |
| | para 171(2)(b) | 28 Mar 2009 (for certain purposes)[3] (SI 2009/812) |
| | | 31 Oct 2009 (otherwise) (SI 2009/1167) |
| | para 171(3) | 28 Mar 2009 (for certain purposes)[3] (SI 2009/812) |
| | | 31 Oct 2009 (otherwise) (SI 2009/1167) |

**Armed Forces Act 2006 (c 52)**—*contd*

| | |
|---|---|
| paras 172–174 | 4 Jun 2007 (SI 2007/1442) |
| para 175(1) | See sub-paras (2)–(4) below |
| para 175(2)(a), (b) | 28 Mar 2009 (for certain purposes)[3] (SI 2009/812) |
| | 31 Oct 2009 (otherwise) (SI 2009/1167) |
| para 175(2)(c) | 4 Jun 2007 (SI 2007/1442) |
| para 175(3) | 28 Mar 2009 (for certain purposes)[3] (SI 2009/812) |
| | 31 Oct 2009 (otherwise) (SI 2009/1167) |
| para 175(4) | 4 Jun 2007 (SI 2007/1442) |
| paras 176, 177 | 28 Mar 2009 (for certain purposes)[3] (SI 2009/812) |
| | 31 Oct 2009 (otherwise) (SI 2009/1167) |
| para 178 | 1 Jan 2008 (SI 2007/2913) |
| paras 179–186 | 28 Mar 2009 (for certain purposes)[3] (SI 2009/812) |
| | 31 Oct 2009 (otherwise) (SI 2009/1167) |
| para 187(a) | 4 Jun 2007 (SI 2007/1442) |
| para 187(b) | 1 Jan 2008 (SI 2007/2913) |
| paras 188–224 | 28 Mar 2009 (for certain purposes)[3] (SI 2009/812) |
| | 31 Oct 2009 (otherwise) (SI 2009/1167) |
| para 225 | 28 Mar 2009 (for certain purposes)[3] (SI 2009/812) |
| | *Never in force* (otherwise) (repealed) |
| paras 226–246 | 28 Mar 2009 (for certain purposes)[3] (SI 2009/812) |
| | 31 Oct 2009 (otherwise) (SI 2009/1167) |
| Sch 17 | 8 Nov 2006 (repeal of Armed Forces Act 2001, s 1) (s 383(1)) |
| | 1 Jan 2008 (SI 2007/2913), repeals of or in— |
| | Courts-Martial (Appeals) Act 1951; |
| | Army Act 1955, s 180[1]; |
| | Air Force Act 1955, s 180[1]; |
| | Naval Discipline Act 1957, s 130[1]; |
| | Courts-Martial (Appeals) Act 1968, ss 11, 34(1)(a); |
| | House of Commons Disqualification Act 1975, Sch 1, Pt 3; |
| | Northern Ireland Assembly Disqualification Act 1975, Sch 1, Pt 3; |
| | Judicial Pensions and Retirement Act 1993[1]; |
| | Criminal Justice and Police Act 2001; |
| | Constitutional Reform Act 2005, Sch 14, Pt 1 |
| | 24 Jun 2008 (SI 2008/1650), repeals of or in— |
| | Criminal Justice Act 1967, s 11 |
| | 1 Oct 2008 (SI 2008/1650), repeals of or in— |
| | Army Act 1955, ss 135–137[2]; |
| | Air Force Act 1955, ss 135–137[2] |
| | 28 Mar 2009 (otherwise, for certain purposes)[3] (SI 2009/812) |
| | 31 Oct 2009 (otherwise) (SI 2009/1167) |

[1] For savings, see SI 2007/2913, art 4

[2] For savings, see SI 2008/1650, art 3

[3] The certain purposes are as follows:

(a) so far as is necessary for the purpose of enabling—

(i) the Defence Council to make regulations,

(ii) the Secretary of State to make orders, regulations and rules,

(iii) Royal Warrants to be made, and

(iv) Orders in Council to be made,

under this Act or under any other Act modified or amended by this Act;

(b) so far as is necessary for the purpose of enabling the Defence Council to make appointments under this Act

[4] S 370 and Sch 15 are also brought into force so far as is necessary for enabling the Defence Council,

**Armed Forces Act 2006 (c 52)**—*contd*
or an officer authorised by the Defence Council, to make designations for the purposes of Sch 15, para 7

---

**Budget (Scotland) Act 2006 (asp 5)**

*RA:* 21 Mar 2006

Whole Act in force 21 Mar 2006 (RA)

---

**Charities Act 2006 (c 50)**

*RA:* 8 Nov 2006

*Commencement provisions:* s 79; Charities Act 2006 (Commencement No 1, Transitional Provisions and Savings) Order 2007, SI 2007/309; Charities Act 2006 (Commencement No 2, Transitional Provisions and Savings) Order 2007, SI 2007/3286; Charities Act 2006 (Commencement No 3, Transitional Provisions and Savings) Order 2008, SI 2008/751; Charities Act 2006 (Commencement No 4, Transitional Provisions and Savings) Order 2008, SI 2008/945, as amended by SI 2009/841; Charities Act 2006 (Commencement No 5, Transitional and Transitory Provisions and Savings) Order 2008, SI 2008/3267[5], as amended by SI 2009/2648, SI 2010/1942, SI 2011/1725; Charities Act 2006 (Commencement No 6 and Commencement No 5, Transitional and Transitory Provisions and Savings) Order 2009, SI 2009/2648; Charities Act 2006 (Commencement No 7, Transitional and Transitory Provisions and Savings) Order 2010, SI 2010/503; Charities Act 2006 (Commencement No 8, Transitional Provisions and Savings) Order 2011, SI 2011/1728

| | | |
|---|---|---|
| 1 | | 1 Apr 2008 (SI 2008/945)[4] |
| 2 | (1)(a) | 1 Apr 2008 (SI 2008/945)[4] |
| | (1)(b) | 27 Feb 2007 (for the purposes of the definition of the Charity Commission's public benefit objective (as defined by the Charities Act 1993, s 1B(3), (4)) and to enable the Charity Commission to issue guidance in pursuance of that objective) (SI 2007/309) |
| | | 1 Apr 2008 (otherwise) (SI 2008/945)[4] |
| | (2)–(8) | 1 Apr 2008 (SI 2008/945)[4] |
| 3 | (1) | 27 Feb 2007 (for the purpose of enabling the Charity Commission to issue guidance under s 4 in pursuance of its public benefit objective) (SI 2007/309) |
| | | 1 Apr 2008 (otherwise) (SI 2008/945)[4] |
| | (2)–(4) | 1 Apr 2008 (SI 2008/945)[4] |
| 4 | (1)–(5) | 27 Feb 2007 (SI 2007/309) |
| | (6) | 1 Apr 2008 (SI 2008/945)[4] |
| 5 | (1) | See sub-ss (2)–(5) below |
| | (2) | 1 Apr 2008 (SI 2008/945)[4] |
| | (3) | 1 Apr 2010 (SI 2008/945)[4] |
| | (4), (5) | 1 Apr 2009 (SI 2008/945)[4] |
| 6 | | 27 Feb 2007 (SI 2007/309) |
| 7 | | 27 Feb 2007 (except in so far as it inserts Charities Act 1993, ss 1C(2), para 4, 1C(5), 1E(3)) (SI 2007/309) |
| | | 18 Mar 2008 (in so far as inserts s 1E(3) of that Act) (SI 2008/751) |
| | | *Never in force* (exceptions noted above) (repealed) |
| 8 | (1) | 27 Feb 2007 (in so far as inserts Charities Act 1993, ss 2B(1)–(4), (8), (9), 2C(5)(b) for the purpose of enabling the Lord Chancellor to exercise the power to make subordinate legislation) (SI 2007/309) |
| | | 18 Mar 2008 (otherwise) (SI 2008/751) |
| | (2) | See Sch 3 below |
| | (3) | See Sch 4 below |

**Charities Act 2006 (c 50)**—*contd*

| | | |
|---|---|---|
| 9 | | 27 Feb 2007 (in so far as inserts Charities Act 1993, ss 3A(2)(c), (4)(b), (5), 3B(2)(b) for the purpose of enabling the Minister to exercise the power to make subordinate legislation) (SI 2007/309) |
| | | 31 Jan 2009 (otherwise, except in so far as inserts Charities Act 1993, s 3A(6) (SI 2008/3267) |
| | | *Never in force* (exception noted above) (repealed) |
| 10 | | 27 Feb 2007 (SI 2007/309) |
| 11 | (1) | See sub-ss (2)–(10) below |
| | (2), (3) | 1 Jun 2010 (SI 2010/503)[7] |
| | (4), (5) | 31 Jan 2009 (SI 2008/3267) |
| | (6), (7) | 1 Jun 2010 (SI 2010/503)[7] |
| | (8) | *Never in force* (repealed) |
| | (9) | 1 Jun 2010 (in so far as inserts Charities Act 1993, Sch 2, Notes 1(c), 2) (SI 2010/503)[7] |
| | | *Never in force* (in so far as inserts Note 1(a), (b) to that Schedule) (repealed) |
| | (10) | *Never in force* (repealed) |
| | (11)–(14) | 27 Feb 2007 (SI 2007/309) |
| 12 | | See Sch 5 below |
| 13 | (1)–(3) | 1 Jun 2010 (in relation to specified exempt charities)[6] (SI 2010/503) |
| | | 1 Aug 2011 (in relation to specified exempt charities)[8, 9] (SI 2011/1728) |
| | | *Never in force* (otherwise) (repealed) |
| | (4), (5) | 8 Nov 2006 (s 79(1)(a)) |
| 14 | | 1 Jun 2010 (in relation to specified exempt charities)[6] (SI 2010/503) |
| | | 1 Aug 2011 (in relation to specified exempt charities)[8, 9] (SI 2011/1728) |
| | | *Never in force* (otherwise) (repealed) |
| 15, 16 | | 18 Mar 2008 (SI 2008/751)[3] |
| 17 | | 27 Feb 2007 (in so far as inserts Charities Act 1993, s 14A(9)) (SI 2007/309) |
| | | 18 Mar 2008 (otherwise) (SI 2008/751)[3] |
| 18–21 | | 18 Mar 2008 (SI 2008/751) |
| 22–28 | | 27 Feb 2007 (SI 2007/309) |
| 29 | (1) | 1 Apr 2008 (SI 2008/945) |
| | (2) | 1 Jun 2010 (in relation to specified exempt charities)[6] (SI 2010/503) |
| | | 1 Aug 2011 (in relation to specified exempt charities)[8, 9] (SI 2011/1728) |
| | | *Never in force* (otherwise) (repealed) |
| 30 | (1) | 1 Apr 2008 (SI 2008/945) |
| | (2) | See Sch 6 below |
| 31 | | 18 Mar 2008 (SI 2008/751)[3] |
| 32 | | 27 Feb 2007 (SI 2007/309) |
| 33 | | 1 Apr 2008 (SI 2008/945) |
| 34 | | See Sch 7 below |
| 35 | | 27 Feb 2007 (SI 2007/309) |
| 36, 37 | | 18 Mar 2008 (SI 2008/751) |
| 38 | | 27 Feb 2007 (except in so far as inserts Charities Act 1993, s 73E(2)(b) and refers to group accounts as required to be prepared under Sch 5A to that Act) (SI 2007/309) |
| | | 1 Apr 2008 (in so far as refers to group accounts as required to be prepared under Charities Act 1993, Sch 5A) (SI 2008/945) |
| | | *Never in force* (in so far as inserts Charities Act 1993, s 73E(2)(b)) (repealed) |
| 39 | | 27 Feb 2007 (SI 2007/309) |
| 40, 41 | | 18 Mar 2008 (SI 2008/751)[3] |

**Charities Act 2006 (c 50)**—*contd*

| | | |
|---|---|---|
| 42 | | 27 Feb 2007 (SI 2007/309) |
| 43 | | 18 Mar 2008 (SI 2008/751)[3] |
| 44 | | 28 Nov 2007 (except in so far as inserts Charities Act 1993, s 75C(11)) (SI 2007/3286) |
| | | *Never in force* (exception noted above) (repealed) |
| 45 | (1) | *Never in force* (repealed) |
| | (2)–(6) | 1 Apr 2008 (for the purposes of Charities Act 1992, Pt 2, definition "professional fund-raiser" (as amended by Sch 8, para 90(3) below) and of s 60A of that Act to the extent that it is brought into force by this order) (SI 2007/3286)[2] |
| | | *Not yet in force* (otherwise) |
| 46 | | 1 Apr 2008 (for the purposes of s 45 of this Act, in so far as that section is brought into force by this order) (SI 2007/3286)[2] |
| | | *Not yet in force* (otherwise) |
| 47 | (1) | 1 Apr 2008 (definitions "collector", "proceeds", "promoter", for the purposes of Charities Act 1992, Pt 2, definition "professional fund-raiser" (as amended by Sch 8, para 90(3) below) and of s 60A of that Act to the extent that it is brought into force by this order) (SI 2007/3286)[2] |
| | | *Not yet in force* (otherwise) |
| | (2), (3) | *Not yet in force* |
| 48–66 | | *Not yet in force* |
| 67 | | 1 Apr 2008 (SI 2007/3286)[2] |
| 68 | | 27 Feb 2007 (in so far as inserts Charities Act 1992, s 60B(6) for the purpose of enabling the Minister to exercise the power to make subordinate legislation) (SI 2007/309) |
| | | 1 Apr 2008 (in so far as inserts Charities Act 1992, ss 60A(4)–(10) (except sub-s (8)(a) and definition "public charitable collection" in sub-s (10)), 60B(4), (5)) (SI 2007/3286)[2] |
| | | *Not yet in force* (otherwise) |
| 69 | | 27 Feb 2007 (SI 2007/309) |
| 70 | | 1 Apr 2007 (SI 2007/309) |
| 71, 72 | | 27 Feb 2007 (SI 2007/309) |
| 73 | | 31 Jan 2009 (SI 2008/3267) |
| 74 | | 8 Nov 2006 (s 79(1)(b)) |
| 75 | (1) | See Sch 8 below |
| | (2) | See Sch 9 below |
| | (3) | See Sch 10 below |
| | (4), (5) | 8 Nov 2006 (s 79(1)(c)) |
| | (6) | 27 Feb 2007 (SI 2007/309) |
| 76 | | 27 Feb 2007 (SI 2007/309) |
| 77 | | 8 Nov 2006 (s 79(1)(e)) |
| 78 | | 8 Nov 2006 (s 79(1)(d)) |
| 79, 80 | | 8 Nov 2006 (s 79(1)(f)) |
| Schs 1, 2 | | 27 Feb 2007 (SI 2007/309) |
| Sch 3 | | 18 Mar 2008 (SI 2008/751) |
| Sch 4 | | 27 Feb 2007 (in so far as inserts Charities Act 1993, Sch 1C, para 6 for the purpose of enabling the Minister to exercise the power to make subordinate legislation) (SI 2007/309) |
| | | 18 Mar 2008 (SI 2008/751)— |
| | | (a) in so far as inserts para 1 of that Schedule, in relation to all decisions, directions and orders mentioned in column 1 of the Table other than the decisions of the Commission under ss 3A, 69E, 69H, 69K or 69M of, or Sch 5B, para 15 to, the 1993 Act mentioned in that column of the Table; |
| | | (b) in so far as inserts paras 2–5 of that Schedule; |
| | | (c) in so far as inserts para 6 of that Schedule (for all remaining purposes); |
| | | (d) in so far as inserts Sch 1D to the 1993 Act |

**Charities Act 2006 (c 50)**—*contd*

|  |  |  |
|---|---|---|
|  |  | 31 Jan 2009 (in so far as inserts Charities Act 1993, Sch 1C, para 1, in relation to decisions of the Commission under s 3A of that Act) (SI 2008/3267) |
|  |  | *Never in force* (otherwise) (repealed) |
| Sch 5 |  | 1 Jun 2010 (in relation to specified exempt charities)[6] (SI 2010/503)[7] |
|  |  | 1 Aug 2011 (in relation to specified exempt charities)[8, 9] (SI 2011/1728) |
|  |  | *Never in force* (otherwise) (repealed) |
| Sch 6 |  | 27 Feb 2007 (in so far as inserts Charities Act 1993, Sch 5A, paras 3(3)(b), (4), (5), 4(2), (3), 6(2), 8, 10(2), (3), 15 for the purpose of enabling the Minister to exercise the power to make subordinate legislation) (SI 2007/309) |
|  |  | 1 Apr 2008 (otherwise) (SI 2008/945) |
| Sch 7 | para 1 | 27 Feb 2007 (in so far as inserts Charities Act 1993, Pt 8A, ss 69B(3), (5), 69E(2)(b), 69G(5)(d), 69H(4), 69J, 69N, 69Q for the purpose of enabling the Minister (and the Charity Commission in relation to s 69B(5)) to exercise the power to make subordinate legislation) (SI 2007/309) |
|  |  | *Never in force* (otherwise) (repealed) |
|  | para 2 | 27 Feb 2007 (in so far as inserts Charities Act 1993, Sch 5B, paras 10(2), (3), 13 for the purpose of enabling the Minister to exercise the power to make subordinate legislation) (SI 2007/309) |
|  |  | *Never in force* (otherwise) (repealed) |
|  | paras 3–5 | *Never in force* (repealed) |
|  | para 6 | 27 Feb 2007 (SI 2007/309) |
|  | para 7 | *Never in force* (repealed) |
| Sch 8 | para 1 | 27 Feb 2007 (SI 2007/309) |
|  | para 2(a) | 31 Jan 2009 (SI 2008/3267) |
|  | para 2(b) | 27 Feb 2007 (SI 2007/309) |
|  | paras 3–14 | 27 Feb 2007 (SI 2007/309) |
|  | para 15 | *Not yet in force* |
|  | paras 16–38 | 27 Feb 2007 (SI 2007/309) |
|  | para 39 | 1 Apr 2008 (SI 2008/945) |
|  | para 40 | *Not yet in force* |
|  | paras 41–50 | 27 Feb 2007 (SI 2007/309) |
|  | para 51(1)–(4) | 27 Feb 2007 (SI 2007/309) |
|  | para 51(5) | 18 Mar 2008 (SI 2008/751)[3] |
|  | paras 52–65 | 27 Feb 2007 (SI 2007/309) |
|  | para 66 | *Not yet in force* |
|  | paras 67–72 | 27 Feb 2007 (SI 2007/309) |
|  | para 73 | *Never in force* (repealed) |
|  | para 74 | 27 Feb 2007 (SI 2007/309) |
|  | para 75 | *Never in force* (repealed) |
|  | para 76 | 27 Feb 2007 (SI 2007/309) |
|  | para 77(1), (2) | 27 Feb 2007 (SI 2007/309) |
|  | para 77(3) | 31 Jan 2009 (SI 2008/3267) |
|  | paras 78, 79 | 27 Feb 2007 (SI 2007/309) |
|  | para 80(1)–(5) | 27 Feb 2007 (SI 2007/309) |
|  | para 80(6)(a) | 18 Mar 2008 (SI 2008/751)[3] |
|  | para 80(6)(b)–(d) | 27 Feb 2007 (SI 2007/309) |
|  | para 80(6)(e) | 18 Mar 2008 (SI 2008/751)[3] |
|  | para 80(7) | 27 Feb 2007 (SI 2007/309) |
|  | para 80(8) | 18 Mar 2008 (SI 2008/751)[3] |
|  | para 80(9), (10) | 27 Feb 2007 (SI 2007/309) |
|  | para 81 | 27 Feb 2007 (SI 2007/309) |
|  | para 82(1), (2) | 27 Feb 2007 (SI 2007/309) |
|  | para 82(3) | 18 Mar 2008 (SI 2008/751)[3] |
|  | para 82(4)–(7) | 27 Feb 2007 (SI 2007/309) |

**Charities Act 2006 (c 50)**—*contd*

| | |
|---|---|
| para 83(1), (2) | 27 Feb 2007 (SI 2007/309) |
| para 83(3), (4) | 18 Mar 2008 (SI 2008/751)[3] |
| para 84 | 27 Feb 2007 (SI 2007/309) |
| para 85 | 31 Jan 2009 (SI 2008/3267) |
| para 86 | 27 Feb 2007 (SI 2007/309) |
| paras 87, 88 | 31 Jan 2009 (SI 2008/3267) |
| para 89 | 27 Feb 2007 (SI 2007/309) |
| para 90(1) | 1 Apr 2008 (SI 2007/3286)[2] |
| para 90(2) | 8 Nov 2006 (s 79(1)(g)) |
| para 90(3) | 1 Apr 2008 (SI 2007/3286)[2] |
| para 90(4) | 1 Apr 2008 (SI 2008/945) |
| paras 91–93 | 27 Feb 2007 (SI 2007/309) |
| paras 94, 95 | *Not yet in force* |
| paras 96–98 | 27 Feb 2007 (SI 2007/309)[1] |
| para 99(1), (2) | 27 Feb 2007 (SI 2007/309) |
| para 99(3), (4)(a) | 18 Mar 2008 (SI 2008/751)[3] |
| para 99(4)(b), (c) | 27 Feb 2007 (SI 2007/309) |
| para 99(5)(a) | 18 Mar 2008 (SI 2008/751)[3] |
| para 99(5)(b) | 27 Feb 2007 (SI 2007/309) |
| para 99(5)(c) | 18 Mar 2008 (SI 2008/751)[3] |
| para 100(1), (2) | 27 Feb 2007 (SI 2007/309) |
| para 100(3) | 31 Jan 2009 (SI 2008/3267) |
| paras 101–103 | 27 Feb 2007 (SI 2007/309) |
| para 104 | 8 Nov 2006 (in so far as it confers power to make regulations) (s 79(1)(g)) |
| | 27 Feb 2007 (otherwise, except in so far as inserts Charities Act 1993, s 10B or refers thereto) (SI 2007/309)[1] |
| | 1 Jun 2010 (in so far as inserts Charities Act 1993, s 10B or refers thereto for the purpose of enabling disclosure of information to and by the principal regulators of specified exempt charities)[6] (SI 2010/503) |
| | 1 Aug 2011 (in so far as inserts Charities Act 1993, s 10B or refers thereto for the purpose of enabling disclosure of information to and by the principal regulators of specified exempt charities)[8, 9] (SI 2011/1728) |
| | *Never in force* (otherwise) (repealed) |
| paras 105–108 | 27 Feb 2007 (SI 2007/309) |
| para 109(1)–(11) | 27 Feb 2007 (SI 2007/309) |
| para 109(12) | 18 Mar 2008 (SI 2008/751)[3] |
| para 109(13) | 27 Feb 2007 (SI 2007/309) |
| para 110 | 27 Feb 2007 (SI 2007/309) |
| para 111(1)–(6) | 27 Feb 2007 (SI 2007/309) |
| para 111(7) | 18 Mar 2008 (SI 2008/751)[3] |
| para 111(8)–(10) | 27 Feb 2007 (SI 2007/309) |
| para 112 | 27 Feb 2007 (SI 2007/309) |
| para 113 | 27 Feb 2007 (except in so far as refers to Charities Act 1993, ss 18A, 19A, 19B) (SI 2007/309) |
| | 18 Mar 2008 (exception noted above) (SI 2008/751) |
| paras 114–132 | 27 Feb 2007 (SI 2007/309)[1] |
| para 133 | 1 Apr 2008 (SI 2008/945)[4] |
| paras 134–138 | 27 Feb 2007 (SI 2007/309)[1] |
| para 139(1), (2) | 27 Feb 2007 (SI 2007/309) |
| para 139(3) | 31 Jan 2009 (in so far as inserts Charities Act 1993, s 46(3), (3B) (SI 2008/3267) |
| | 1 Jun 2010 (in so far as inserts Charities Act 1993, s 46(3A)) (SI 2010/503)[7] |
| para 139(4) | 31 Jan 2009 (SI 2008/3267) |
| para 139(5) | 27 Feb 2007 (SI 2007/309) |
| para 139(6) | 1 Apr 2008 (SI 2008/945)[4] |
| para 139(7) | 31 Jan 2009 (SI 2008/3267) |

**Charities Act 2006 (c 50)**—*contd*

| | |
|---|---|
| paras 140–142 | 27 Feb 2007 (SI 2007/309)[1] |
| para 143(1), (2) | 27 Feb 2007 (SI 2007/309) |
| para 143(3)(a), (b) | 27 Feb 2007 (SI 2007/309) |
| para 143(3)(c) | 30 Sep 2009 (SI 2009/2648) |
| paras 144–161 | 27 Feb 2007 (SI 2007/309) |
| para 162 | 27 Feb 2007 (except in so far as sub-para (2) inserts Charities Act 1993, s 80(1)(c)) (SI 2007/309) |
| | 18 Mar 2008 (exception noted above) (SI 2008/751) |
| para 163(1)–(3) | 27 Feb 2007 (SI 2007/309) |
| para 163(4) | 18 Mar 2008 (SI 2008/751) |
| para 163(5) | 27 Feb 2007 (SI 2007/309) |
| para 164 | 27 Feb 2007 (SI 2007/309) |
| para 165(1) | 27 Feb 2007 (SI 2007/309) |
| para 165(2)(a) | 27 Feb 2007 (SI 2007/309) |
| para 165(2)(b) | 18 Mar 2008 (SI 2008/751) |
| para 165(3), (4) | 27 Feb 2007 (SI 2007/309) |
| para 166 | 27 Feb 2007 (SI 2007/309) |
| para 167(1) | 27 Feb 2007 (SI 2007/309) |
| para 167(2) | 18 Mar 2008 (SI 2008/751) |
| para 167(3)–(5) | 27 Feb 2007 (SI 2007/309) |
| paras 168–170 | 27 Feb 2007 (SI 2007/309) |
| para 171 | 18 Mar 2008 (SI 2008/751)[3] |
| para 172 | 27 Feb 2007 (SI 2007/309) |
| para 173(1) | 27 Feb 2007 (SI 2007/309) |
| para 173(2) | 1 Apr 2008 (SI 2008/945) |
| para 173(3)(a) | *Never in force* (repealed) |
| para 173(3)(b) | 1 Apr 2008 (SI 2008/945) |
| para 173(4) | 27 Feb 2007 (SI 2007/309) |
| para 174(a) | 1 Apr 2008 (SI 2008/945) |
| para 174(b), (c) | 27 Feb 2007 (SI 2007/309) |
| para 174(d) | 8 Nov 2006 (s 79(1)(g)) |
| para 175 | 27 Feb 2007 (except in so far as refers to Charities Act 1993, Pt 8A) (SI 2007/309) |
| | *Never in force* (exception noted above) (repealed) |
| para 176 | 27 Feb 2007 (except in so far as refers to Charities Act 1993, s 10B) (SI 2007/309) |
| | 1 Jun 2010 (in so far as refers to the said s 10B for the purposes for which para 104 above has been commenced by SI 2010/503) (SI 2010/503) |
| | 1 Aug 2011 (in so far as refers to the said s 10B for the purposes for which para 104 above has been commenced by SI 2011/1728) (SI 2011/1728)[9] |
| | *Never in force* (otherwise) (repealed) |
| paras 177–190 | 27 Feb 2007 (SI 2007/309)[1] |
| para 191 | 31 Jan 2009 (SI 2008/3267) |
| para 192 | 27 Feb 2007 (SI 2007/309)[1] |
| paras 193–195 | 31 Jan 2009 (SI 2008/3267) |
| paras 196–198 | 27 Feb 2007 (SI 2007/309) |
| para 199 | 31 Jan 2009 (SI 2008/3267) |
| paras 200–207 | 27 Feb 2007 (SI 2007/309) |
| para 208 | 18 Mar 2008 (SI 2008/751) |
| para 209 | 27 Feb 2007 (SI 2007/309) |
| para 210(a) | 27 Feb 2007 (SI 2007/309) |
| para 210(b), (c) | 31 Jan 2009 (SI 2008/3267) |
| para 211 | 27 Feb 2007 (SI 2007/309) |
| para 212(1), (2) | 27 Feb 2007 (SI 2007/309) |
| para 212(3) | 1 Apr 2008 (SI 2008/945) |
| Sch 9 | 27 Feb 2007 (SI 2007/309), repeals of or in— Charities Act 1992, Pt 3, ss 76, 77, Sch 6; |

**Charities Act 2006 (c 50)**—*contd*

Charities Act 1993, ss 1, 2, 23, 44, 61, Sch 1;
Local Government (Wales) Act 1994
28 Nov 2007 (repeals of or in Intervention Board for Agricultural
Produce (Abolition) Regulations 2001, SI 2001/3686)
(SI 2007/3286)
18 Mar 2008 (SI 2008/751)[3], repeals of or in—
Reverter of Sites Act 1987;
Charities Act 1993, ss 4, 16(11)–(14), 18, 92
1 Apr 2008 (SI 2008/945)[4], repeals of or in—
Charities Act 1992, Pt 1, Sch 5;
Charities Act 1993, s 96(4);
Deregulation and Contracting Out Act 1994
31 Jan 2009 (SI 2008/3267), repeals of or in—
Charities Act 1960;
Housing Act 1985;
Charities Act 1993, Sch 6;
Housing Act 1996;
School Standards and Framework Act 1998;
Teaching and Higher Education Act 1998;
Regulatory Reform (National Health Service Charitable and
Non-Charitable Trust Accounts and Audit) Order 2005,
SI 2005/1074
30 Sep 2009 (SI 2009/2648), repeals of or in—
Charities Act 1993, s 46
1 Apr 2010 (SI 2008/945), repeals of or in—
Recreational Charities Act 1958
1 Jun 2010 (SI 2010/503), repeals of or in—
Charities Act 1993, ss 6(9), 9(4), 16(4)(c), (5), 17(7), 28(10),
33(2), (7), 73(4) (in so far as they relate to specified exempt
charities)[6];
Charities Act 1993, Sch 2, paras (b), (x)
1 Aug 2011 (SI 2011/1728), repeals of or in—
Charities Act 1993, ss 6(9), 9(4), 16(4)(c), (5), 17(7), 28(10),
33(2), (7), 73(4) (in so far as they relate to specified exempt
charities)[8, 9]
*Not yet in force*, repeals of or in—
Police, Factories, &c (Miscellaneous Provisions) Act 1916;
Church Funds Investment Measure 1958;
Charities Act 1992, s 79, Sch 7;
Charities Act 1993, ss 6, 9, 16(4)(c), (5), 17, 24, 28, 33, 73,
96(1) (so far as not already repealed);
National Lottery etc Act 1993

| | | |
|---|---|---|
| Sch 10 | para 1 | 27 Feb 2007 (SI 2007/309) |
| | para 2 | 1 Apr 2010 (SI 2008/945) |
| | paras 3–5 | 18 Mar 2008 (SI 2008/751) |
| | paras 6, 7 | 27 Feb 2007 (SI 2007/309) |
| | para 8 | 1 Apr 2008 (in so far as it relates to amendments made by s 29(1) and the duty imposed by the Charities Act 1993, s 44A(2)) (SI 2008/945) |
| | | 1 Jun 2010 (in so far as relates to amendments made by s 29(2) and to the duty imposed by s 46(2A) of the 1993 Act in relation to specified exempt charities)[6] (SI 2010/503) |
| | | 1 Aug 2011 (in so far as relates to amendments made by s 29(2) and to the duty imposed by s 46(2A) of the 1993 Act in relation to specified exempt charities)[8, 9] (SI 2011/1728) |
| | | *Never in force* (otherwise) (repealed) |
| | para 9 | 27 Feb 2007 (SI 2007/309) |
| | para 10 | 1 Apr 2008 (SI 2008/945) |
| | para 11 | 27 Feb 2007 (SI 2007/309) |
| | para 12 | 18 Mar 2008 (SI 2008/751) |

**Charities Act 2006 (c 50)**—*contd*

|  |  |
|---|---|
| para 13 | 27 Feb 2007 (SI 2007/309) |
| para 14 | 28 Nov 2007 (SI 2007/3286) |
| para 15 | 1 Apr 2008 (SI 2007/3286)[2] |
| para 16 | 27 Feb 2007 (SI 2007/309) |
| para 17 | 1 Apr 2008 (SI 2008/945) |
| para 18 | 18 Mar 2008 (SI 2008/751) |
| paras 19, 20 | 27 Feb 2007 (SI 2007/309) |
| paras 21–27 | 31 Jan 2009 (SI 2008/3267) |
| para 28 | 1 Apr 2008 (SI 2008/945) |
| para 29(1) | 1 Apr 2008 (SI 2008/945) |
| para 29(2)(a) | 31 Jan 2009 (SI 2008/3267) |
| para 29(2)(b), (c) | 1 Apr 2008 (SI 2008/945) |

[1]  For transitional provisions and savings, see SI 2007/309, arts 4–13

[2]  For transitional provisions and savings, see SI 2007/3286, art 4

[3]  For transitional provisions and savings, see SI 2008/751, arts 3–12

[4]  For transitional provisions and savings, see SI 2008/945, arts 4–11

[5]  For transitional and transitory provisions and savings, see SI 2008/3267, arts 3–27

[6]  A "specified exempt charity" means an exempt charity:

(a)  included in paragraph (a) of Sch 2 to the Charities Act 1993 other than an excluded fund;

(b)  included in paragraphs (b), (c), (h), (i), (k), (l), (m), (n), (o), (p), (q), (r), (s), (t), (u), (v) or (za) of that Schedule to that Act; or

(c)  falling within paragraph (w) of that Schedule to that Act and administered by or on behalf of an institution included—

(i)  in paragraph (a) of that Schedule other than an excluded fund; or

(ii)  in paragraphs (b), (c), (h), (i) or (k) to (v) of that Schedule

[7]  For transitional provisions and savings, see SI 2010/503, art 3, Sch 2

[8]  A "specified exempt charity" means an exempt charity which—

(a)  is a foundation or voluntary school charity; or

(b)  is an academy or sixth form college charity

[9]  For transitional provisions and savings, see SI 2011/1728, art 3, Sch 2

---

**Childcare Act 2006 (c 21)**

*RA:* 11 Jul 2006

*Commencement provisions:* s 109; Childcare Act 2006 (Commencement No 1) Order 2006, SI 2006/3360; Childcare Act 2006 (Commencement No 2 and Savings and Transitional Provisions) Order 2007, SI 2007/1019; Childcare Act 2006 (Commencement No 3 and Transitional Provision) Order 2007, SI 2007/2717; Childcare Act 2006 (Commencement No 1) (Wales) Order 2008, SI 2008/17; Childcare Act 2006 (Commencement No 4) Order 2008, SI 2008/785; Childcare Act 2006 (Commencement No 5 and Savings and Transitional Provisions) Order 2008, SI 2008/2261

| | |
|---|---|
| 1 | 20 Dec 2006 (for the purposes of making regulations) (SI 2006/3360) |
| | 1 Apr 2008 (otherwise) (SI 2008/785) |
| 2–4 | 1 Apr 2008 (SI 2008/785) |
| 5 | *Not yet in force* |
| 6 | 1 Apr 2008 (SI 2008/785) |
| 7 | 1 Apr 2008 (for the purposes of making regulations) (SI 2008/785) |
| | 1 Sep 2008 (otherwise) (SI 2008/2261) |
| 8–10 | 1 Oct 2007 (SI 2007/2717) |
| 11 | 20 Dec 2006 (for the purposes of making regulations) (SI 2006/3360) |

**Childcare Act 2006 (c 21)**—*contd*

|  |  |
|---|---|
|  | 1 Apr 2007 (otherwise) (SI 2007/1019) |
| 12 | 20 Dec 2006 (for the purposes of making regulations) (SI 2006/3360) |
|  | 1 May 2007 (in so far as it requires an English local authority to establish and maintain a service providing information relating to the provision of childcare in the area of the local authority by persons registered under Part 3, Chapter 4) (SI 2007/1019) |
|  | 1 Apr 2008 (otherwise) (SI 2008/785) |
| 13 | 20 Dec 2006 (for the purposes of making regulations) (SI 2006/3360) |
|  | 1 Oct 2007 (otherwise) (SI 2007/2717) |
| 14 | *Never in force* (repealed) |
| 15, 16 | 1 Apr 2007 (SI 2007/1019) |
| 17 | 1 Oct 2007 (SI 2007/2717) |
| 18–21 | 20 Dec 2006 (SI 2006/3360) |
| 22–30 | 31 Jan 2008 (SI 2008/17) |
| 31 | *Never in force* (repealed) |
| 32 | 6 Apr 2007 (in so far as it requires the Chief Inspector to maintain Part B of the second register) (SI 2007/1019) |
|  | 1 Sep 2008 (in so far as it requires the Chief Inspector to maintain the first register and Part A of the second register) (SI 2008/2261) |
| 33–37 | 1 Oct 2007 (for the purposes of making an order or regulations) (SI 2007/2717) |
|  | 1 Sep 2008 (otherwise) (SI 2008/2261) |
| 38 | 1 Sep 2008 (SI 2008/2261) |
| 39 | 20 Dec 2006 (SI 2006/3360) |
| 40 | 1 Sep 2008 (SI 2008/2261) |
| 41–46 | 20 Dec 2006 (SI 2006/3360) |
| 47 | 1 Sep 2008 (SI 2008/2261) |
| 48 | See Sch 1 below |
| 49, 50 | 1 Oct 2007 (for the purposes of making an order or regulations) (SI 2007/2717) |
|  | 1 Sep 2008 (otherwise) (SI 2008/2261) |
| 51 | 1 Oct 2007 (SI 2007/2717) |
| 52–56 | 1 Oct 2007 (for the purposes of making an order or regulations) (SI 2007/2717) |
|  | 1 Sep 2008 (otherwise) (SI 2008/2261) |
| 57, 58 | 1 Sep 2008 (SI 2008/2261) |
| 59–61 | 1 Oct 2007 (for the purposes of making an order or regulations) (SI 2007/2717) |
|  | 1 Sep 2008 (otherwise) (SI 2008/2261) |
| 62, 63 | 20 Dec 2006 (for the purposes of making regulations) (SI 2006/3360) |
|  | 6 Apr 2007 (otherwise, except sub-s (1)(b) of each section) (SI 2007/1019) |
|  | 1 Sep 2008 (exceptions noted above) (SI 2008/2261) |
| 64 | 20 Dec 2006 (for the purposes of making regulations) (SI 2006/3360) |
|  | 6 Apr 2007 (otherwise) (SI 2007/1019) |
| 65 | 1 Sep 2008 (SI 2008/2261) |
| 66 | 6 Apr 2007 (SI 2007/1019) |
| 67 | 20 Dec 2006 (for the purposes of making regulations) (SI 2006/3360) |
|  | 6 Apr 2007 (otherwise) (SI 2007/1019) |
| 68 | 6 Apr 2007 (SI 2007/1019) |
| 69 | 20 Dec 2006 (for the purposes of making regulations) (SI 2006/3360) |
|  | 6 Apr 2007 (otherwise) (SI 2007/1019) |
| 70 | 6 Apr 2007 (SI 2007/1019) |

**Childcare Act 2006 (c 21)**—*contd*

| | | |
|---|---|---|
| 71 | | 20 Dec 2006 (SI 2006/3360) |
| 72, 73 | | 6 Apr 2007 (SI 2007/1019) |
| 74 | | 20 Dec 2006 (for the purposes of making regulations) (SI 2006/3360) |
| | | 6 Apr 2007 (otherwise) (SI 2007/1019) |
| 75 | | 20 Dec 2006 (SI 2006/3360) |
| 76 | | 1 Sep 2008 (SI 2008/2261) |
| 77–79 | | 6 Apr 2007 (SI 2007/1019) |
| 80, 81 | | *Never in force* (repealed) |
| 82 | | 6 Apr 2007 (SI 2007/1019) |
| 83, 84 | | 20 Dec 2006 (for the purposes of making regulations) (SI 2006/3360) |
| | | 6 Apr 2007 (otherwise) (SI 2007/1019) |
| 85–88 | | 6 Apr 2007 (SI 2007/1019) |
| 89 | | 20 Dec 2006 (SI 2006/3360) |
| 90 | | 20 Dec 2006 (for the purposes of making regulations) (SI 2006/3360) |
| | | 6 Apr 2007 (otherwise) (SI 2007/1019) |
| 91 | | 6 Apr 2007 (SI 2007/1019) |
| 92 | | 20 Dec 2006 (for the purposes of making regulations) (SI 2006/3360) |
| | | 1 Sep 2008 (otherwise) (SI 2008/2261) |
| 93, 94 | | 6 Apr 2007 (SI 2007/1019) |
| 95 | | 1 Sep 2008 (SI 2008/2261) |
| 96 | | 20 Dec 2006 (for the purposes of making regulations) (SI 2006/3360) |
| | | 6 Apr 2007 (otherwise) (SI 2007/1019) |
| 97 | | 6 Apr 2007 (SI 2007/1019) |
| 98 | | 20 Dec 2006 (SI 2006/3360) |
| 99 | | 20 Dec 2006 (for the purposes of making regulations) (SI 2006/3360) |
| | | 30 Mar 2007 (otherwise) (SI 2007/1019) |
| 100 | | 20 Dec 2006 (SI 2006/3360) |
| 101 | | 31 Jan 2008 (SI 2008/17) |
| 102 | | 20 Dec 2006 (E) (SI 2006/3360) |
| | | 31 Jan 2008 (W) (SI 2008/17) |
| 103 | (1) | See Sch 2 below |
| | (2) | See Sch 3 below |
| 104–111 | | 11 Jul 2006 (s 109(1)) |
| Sch 1 | para 1 | 1 Sep 2008 (SI 2008/2261)[3] |
| | para 2(1) | 1 Oct 2007 (SI 2007/2717) |
| | para 2(2) | 1 Sep 2008 (SI 2008/2261)[3] |
| | para 2(3) | 1 Oct 2007 (SI 2007/2717) |
| | para 2(4) | 1 Sep 2008 (SI 2008/2261)[3] |
| | para 2(5) | 1 Oct 2007 (SI 2007/2717)[2] |
| | paras 3–16 | 1 Sep 2008 (SI 2008/2261)[3] |
| Sch 2 | para 1 | 11 Jul 2006 (s 109(1)) |
| | paras 2, 3 | 6 Apr 2007 (SI 2007/1019) |
| | para 4 | 1 Oct 2007 (SI 2007/2717) |
| | paras 5–17 | 1 Sep 2008 (SI 2008/2261)[3] |
| | para 18(1)–(4) | 1 Sep 2008 (SI 2008/2261)[3] |
| | para 18(5)(a) | 1 Sep 2008 (SI 2008/2261)[3] |
| | para 18(5)(b), (c) | 1 Sep 2008 (E) (SI 2008/2261)[3] |
| | | *Never in force* (W) (repealed) |
| | para 18(6), (7) | 1 Sep 2008 (SI 2008/2261)[3] |
| | para 19 | 6 Apr 2007 (SI 2007/1019)[1] |
| | paras 20–24 | 1 Sep 2008 (E) (SI 2008/2261)[3] |
| | | *Not yet in force* (W) (paras 21, 22(4) repealed)[4] |
| | paras 25, 26 | 1 Sep 2008 (SI 2008/2261)[3] |

**Childcare Act 2006 (c 21)**—*contd*

| | | |
|---|---|---|
| | para 27 | 1 Sep 2008 (E) (SI 2008/2261)[3] |
| | | *Not yet in force* (W) |
| | para 28 | 1 Apr 2008 (SI 2008/17) |
| | para 29(a) | 6 Apr 2007 (SI 2007/1019) |
| | para 29(b), (c) | 1 Sep 2008 (SI 2008/2261)[3] |
| | para 30 | 1 Sep 2008 (SI 2008/2261)[3] |
| | para 31 | 1 Apr 2007 (E) (SI 2007/1019) |
| | | *Not yet in force* (W) |
| | para 32(1)–(3) | 1 Oct 2007 (SI 2007/2717) |
| | para 32(4) | 1 Oct 2007 (E) (SI 2007/2717) |
| | | *Not yet in force* (W) |
| | para 32(5) | 1 Oct 2007 (SI 2007/2717) |
| | para 33 | 1 Sep 2008 (SI 2008/2261)[3] |
| | para 34 | 1 Sep 2008 (E) (SI 2008/2261)[3] |
| | | *Not yet in force* (W) |
| | paras 35, 36 | 1 Sep 2008 (SI 2008/2261)[3] |
| | paras 37, 38 | 6 Apr 2007 (SI 2007/1019) |
| | paras 39, 40 | 6 Apr 2007 (SI 2007/1019)[1] |
| | para 41 | 1 Sep 2008 (SI 2008/2261)[3] |
| | para 42 | *Never in force* (repealed) |
| | para 43 | 6 Apr 2007 (SI 2007/1019)[1] |
| | para 44 | 1 Sep 2008 (SI 2008/2261)[3] |
| Sch 3 | Pt 1 | 1 Sep 2008 (E) (SI 2008/2261)[3] |
| | Pt 2 | 1 Apr 2007 (E) (SI 2007/1019), repeals of or in— |
| | | School Standards and Framework Act 1998, s 118A[1]; |
| | | Education Act 2002, s 149(1) |
| | | 1 Apr 2007 (repeals in Children Act 2004) (SI 2007/1019) |
| | | 6 Apr 2007 (repeal in Protection of Children Act 1999, s 9(2)) (SI 2007/1019) |
| | | 1 Oct 2007 (E) (repeal in School Standards and Framework Act 1998, s 119) (SI 2007/2717) |
| | | 1 Sep 2008 (E) (SI 2008/2261)[3], repeals of or in— |
| | | Children Act 1989; |
| | | Police Act 1997; |
| | | School Standards and Framework Act 1998, Sch 26; |
| | | Education Act 2002, ss 150, 153; |
| | | Education Act 2005, s 59, Sch 7 |
| | | *Not yet in force* (W), repeals of or in— |
| | | School Standards and Framework Act 1998, ss 118A, 119; |
| | | Education Act 2002, ss 149(1), 150(1) |

[1]　For transitional provisions and savings, see SI 2007/1019, art 6, Schedule

[2]　For a transitional provision, see SI 2007/2717, art 3

[3]　For transitional provisions and savings, see SI 2008/2261, arts 3, 4, Schs 1, 2

[4]　It is thought to be unlikely that Sch 2, para 23 will ever be commenced in relation to Wales. That paragraph amends the Education Act 1996, s 509A and, as a consequence of the amendments made by the Apprenticeships, Skills, Children and Learning Act 2009 and the Learner Travel (Wales) Measure 2008, that section only applies in relation to England

---

**Children and Adoption Act 2006 (c 20)**

*RA:* 21 Jun 2006

*Commencement provisions:* s 17(2)–(5); Children and Adoption Act 2006 (Commencement No 1) (Wales) Order 2007, SI 2007/733; Children and Adoption Act 2006 (Commencement No 1) Order 2007, SI 2007/2287; Children and Adoption Act 2006 (Commencement No 2) Order 2008, SI 2008/1798; Children and Adoption Act 2006 (Commencement No 3) Order 2008, SI 2008/2870; Children and Adoption Act 2006 (Commencement No 4) Order 2010, SI 2010/2612

## Children and Adoption Act 2006 (c 20)—*contd*

| | | |
|---|---|---|
| 1 | | 7 Nov 2008 (in so far as inserts Children Act 1989, s 11F) (SI 2008/2870) |
| | | 8 Dec 2008 (otherwise) (SI 2008/2870) |
| 2, 3 | | 8 Dec 2008 (SI 2008/2870) |
| 4 | (1) | 8 Dec 2008 (SI 2008/2870) |
| | (2) | See Sch 1 below |
| 5 | | 8 Dec 2008 (SI 2008/2870) |
| 6, 7 | | 1 Oct 2007 (SI 2007/2287) |
| 8 | | 8 Dec 2008 (SI 2008/2870) |
| 9 | (1)–(3) | 1 Aug 2008 (SI 2008/1798) |
| | (4) | 7 Jul 2008 (SI 2008/1798) |
| | (5)–(10) | 1 Aug 2008 (SI 2008/1798) |
| 10 | | 1 Aug 2008 (SI 2008/1798) |
| 11 | | 2 Aug 2007 (for the purposes of making regulations) (SI 2007/2287) |
| | | 1 Aug 2008 (otherwise) (SI 2008/1798) |
| 12 | (1) | 2 Aug 2007 (for the purposes of making regulations) (SI 2007/2287) |
| | | 1 Aug 2008 (otherwise) (SI 2008/1798) |
| | (2)–(6) | 1 Aug 2008 (SI 2008/1798) |
| | (7) | 2 Aug 2007 (for the purposes of making regulations) (SI 2007/2287) |
| | | 1 Aug 2008 (otherwise) (SI 2008/1798) |
| 13 | | 2 Apr 2007 (W) (so far as it relates to adoptions and prospective adoptions in respect of which the National Assembly for Wales may charge a fee under the Adoption and Children Act 2002, s 91A) (SI 2007/733) |
| | | 28 Oct 2010 (otherwise) (SI 2010/2612) |
| 14 | (1), (2) | 1 Oct 2007 (SI 2007/2287) |
| | (3) | 2 Aug 2007 (SI 2007/2287) |
| 15 | (1) | See Sch 2 below |
| | (2) | See Sch 3 below |
| 16 | | 7 Jul 2008 (SI 2008/1798) |
| 17 | | 21 Jun 2006 (RA) |
| Schs 1, 2 | | 8 Dec 2008 (SI 2008/2870) |
| Sch 3 | | 1 Oct 2007 (repeal of Children Act 1989, s 16(3)(a)) (SI 2007/2287) |
| | | 8 Dec 2008 (otherwise) (SI 2008/2870) |

---

## Church of England (Miscellaneous Provisions) Measure 2006 (No 1)

*RA:* 11 Jul 2006

This Measure was brought into force on 1 Oct 2006 by an instrument made by the Archbishops of Canterbury and York, and dated 11 Sep 2006 and brought into force on 2 Dec 2007 by an instrument made by the Archbishops of Canterbury and York, and dated 29 Nov 2007 (made under s 16(2))

| | |
|---|---|
| 1 | 2 Dec 2007 |
| 2–16 | 1 Oct 2006 |
| Sch 1 | 2 Dec 2007 |
| Schs 2–6 | 1 Oct 2006 |

---

## Civil Aviation Act 2006 (c 34)

*RA:* 8 Nov 2006

*Commencement provisions:* s 14(2)–(5); Civil Aviation Act 2006 (Commencement No 1) Order 2007, SI 2007/598

| | |
|---|---|
| 1–5 | 1 Mar 2007 (SI 2007/598) |

**Civil Aviation Act 2006 (c 34)**—*contd*

| | |
|---|---|
| 6 | 8 Nov 2006 (s 14(2)) |
| 7, 8 | 1 Mar 2007 (SI 2007/598) |
| 9 | *Not yet in force* |
| 10–12 | 1 Mar 2007 (SI 2007/598) |
| 13 | See Sch 2 below |
| 14 | 8 Nov 2006 (s 14(2)) |
| Sch 1 | 8 Nov 2006 (s 14(2)) |
| Sch 2 | 1 Mar 2007 (SI 2007/598) |

**Climate Change and Sustainable Energy Act 2006 (c 19)**

*RA:* 21 Jun 2006

*Commencement provisions:* s 28; Climate Change and Sustainable Energy Act 2006 (Commencement) Order 2007, SI 2007/538

| | |
|---|---|
| 1 | 21 Aug 2006 (s 28(1)) |
| 2 | 1 Jan 2007 (s 28(2)) |
| 3–5 | 21 Aug 2006 (s 28(1)) |
| 6 | 1 Jan 2007 (s 28(2)) |
| 7–11 | 21 Aug 2006 (s 28(1)) |
| 12 | 1 Jan 2007 (s 28(2)) |
| 13, 14 | 21 Aug 2006 (s 28(1)) |
| 15–17 | 28 Feb 2007 (SI 2007/538) |
| 18–21 | 21 Aug 2006 (s 28(1)) |
| 22 | 1 Jan 2007 (s 28(2)) |
| 23–25 | 21 Aug 2006 (s 28(1)) |
| 26–29 | 21 Jun 2006 (RA) |
| Schedule | 28 Feb 2007 (SI 2007/538) |

**Commissioner for Older People (Wales) Act 2006 (c 30)**

*RA:* 25 Jul 2006

*Commencement provisions:* s 23; Commissioner for Older People (Wales) Act 2006 (Commencement) Order 2006, SI 2006/2699

| | |
|---|---|
| 1–22 | 14 Oct 2006 (SI 2006/2699) |
| 23–30 | 25 Jul 2006 (RA) |
| Schs 1–4 | 14 Oct 2006 (SI 2006/2699) |

**Commons Act 2006 (c 26)**

*RA:* 19 Jul 2006

*Commencement provisions:* s 56; Commons Act 2006 (Commencement No 1, Transitional Provisions and Savings) (England) Order 2006, SI 2006/2504; Commons Act 2006 (Commencement No 2, Transitional Provisions and Savings) (England) Order 2007, SI 2007/456; Commons Act 2006 (Commencement No 1, Transitional Provisions and Savings) (Wales) Order 2007, SI 2007/2386; Commons Act 2006 (Commencement No 3, Transitional Provisions and Savings) (England) Order 2007, SI 2007/2584; Commons Act 2006 (Commencement No 4 and Savings) (England) Order 2008, SI 2008/1960; Commons Act 2006 (Commencement No 5) (England) Order 2010, SI 2010/61, as amended by SI 2010/2356; Commons Act 2006 (Commencement No 1 and Savings (England and Wales) and Commencement No 5 (England) (Amendment)) Order 2010, SI 2010/2356; Commons Act 2006 (Commencement No 6) (England) Order 2011, SI 2011/2460; Commons Act 2006 (Commencement No 2, Transitional Provisions and Savings) (Wales) Order 2012, SI 2012/739; Commons Act 2006 (Commencement No 2) (Wales) Order 2012, SI 2012/806; Commons Act 2006 (Commencement No 7, Transitional and Savings Provisions) (England) Order 2014, SI 2014/3026; Commons Act 2006 (Commencement No 4) (Wales) Order 2017, SI 2017/564, as amended by SI 2017/933; Commons Act 2006 (Commencement No 5 and

**Commons Act 2006 (c 26)**—*contd*
Transitional Provisions (Wales) and Commencement No 4 (Wales) (Amendment)) Order 2017, SI 2017/933; Commons Act 2006 (Commencement No 6) (Wales) Order 2021, SI 2021/1015

| | | |
|---|---|---|
| 1, 2 | | 1 Oct 2008 (E) (in relation to the pilot areas[6]) (SI 2008/1960)[7] |
| | | 12 Nov 2014 (E) (in relation to the 2014 pilot areas[12], in so far as is required for the making of regulations) (SI 2014/3026)[14] |
| | | 15 Dec 2014 (E) (in relation to the 2014 pilot areas[12]) (otherwise) (SI 2014/3026)[14] |
| | | *Not yet in force* (otherwise) |
| 3 | (1)–(4) | 1 Oct 2008 (E) (in relation to the pilot areas[6]) (SI 2008/1960)[7] |
| | | 12 Nov 2014 (E) (in relation to the 2014 pilot areas[12], in so far as is required for the making of regulations) (SI 2014/3026)[14] |
| | | 15 Dec 2014 (E) (in relation to the 2014 pilot areas[12]) (otherwise) (SI 2014/3026)[14] |
| | | 12 Nov 2014 (in relation to the other registration areas[13], in so far as is required for the making of regulations and only to the extent that they enable an application to any of the other registration areas to amend its register of common land or its register of town or village greens under s 19 or Sch 2, para 6, 7, 8 or 9) (SI 2014/3026)[14] |
| | | 15 Dec 2014 (E) (in relation to the other registration areas[13]) (otherwise) (SI 2014/3026)[14] |
| | | *Not yet in force* (otherwise) |
| | (5) | 12 Aug 2007 (W) (in so far as it confers a power, or imposes a duty, on the Welsh Ministers to make, or make provision by, regulations; give guidance or directions; or make provision with respect to the exercise of any such power or performance of such duty) (SI 2007/2386) |
| | | 1 Oct 2008 (E) (in relation to the pilot areas[6]) (SI 2008/1960)[7] |
| | | 12 Nov 2014 (E) (in relation to the 2014 pilot areas[12], in so far as is required for the making of regulations) (SI 2014/3026)[14] |
| | | 15 Dec 2014 (E) (in relation to the 2014 pilot areas[12]) (otherwise) (SI 2014/3026)[14] |
| | | 12 Nov 2014 (in relation to the other registration areas[13], in so far as is required for the making of regulations and only to the extent that they enable an application to any of the other registration areas to amend its register of common land or its register of town or village greens under s 19 or Sch 2, para 6, 7, 8 or 9) (SI 2014/3026)[14] |
| | | 15 Dec 2014 (E) (in relation to the other registration areas) (otherwise) (SI 2014/3026)[14] |
| | | *Not yet in force* (otherwise) |
| | (6), (7) | 1 Oct 2008 (E) (in relation to the pilot areas[6]) (SI 2008/1960)[7] |
| | | 12 Nov 2014 (E) (in relation to the 2014 pilot areas[12], in so far as is required for the making of regulations) (SI 2014/3026)[14] |
| | | 15 Dec 2014 (E) (in relation to the 2014 pilot areas[12]) (otherwise) (SI 2014/3026)[14] |
| | | 12 Nov 2014 (in relation to the other registration areas[13], in so far as is required for the making of regulations and only to the extent that they enable an application to any of the other registration areas to amend its register of common land or its register of town or village greens under s 19 or Sch 2, para 6, 7, 8 or 9) (SI 2014/3026)[14] |
| | | 15 Dec 2014 (E) (in relation to the other registration areas[13]) (otherwise) (SI 2014/3026)[14] |
| | | *Not yet in force* (otherwise) |
| 4, 5 | | 6 Apr 2007 (E) (SI 2007/456) |
| | | 6 Sep 2007 (W) (SI 2007/2386) |
| 6 | (1)–(3) | 1 Oct 2008 (E) (in relation to the pilot areas[6]) (SI 2008/1960)[7] |
| | | 12 Nov 2014 (E) (in relation to the 2014 pilot areas[12], in so far as is required for the making of regulations) (SI 2014/3026)[14] |

**Commons Act 2006 (c 26)**—*contd*

|  |  |  |
|--|--|--|
|  |  | 15 Dec 2014 (E) (in relation to the 2014 pilot areas[12]) (otherwise) (SI 2014/3026)[14] |
|  |  | *Not yet in force* (otherwise) |
|  | (4) | 12 Aug 2007 (W) (in so far as it confers a power, or imposes a duty, on the Welsh Ministers to make, or make provision by, regulations; give guidance or directions; or make provision with respect to the exercise of any such power or performance of such duty) (SI 2007/2386) |
|  |  | 1 Oct 2008 (E) (in relation to the pilot areas[6]) (SI 2008/1960)[7] |
|  |  | 12 Nov 2014 (E) (in relation to the 2014 pilot areas[12], in so far as is required for the making of regulations) (SI 2014/3026)[14] |
|  |  | 15 Dec 2014 (E) (in relation to the 2014 pilot areas[12]) (otherwise) (SI 2014/3026)[14] |
|  |  | *Not yet in force* (otherwise) |
|  | (5), (6) | 1 Oct 2008 (E) (in relation to the pilot areas[6]) (SI 2008/1960)[7] |
|  |  | 12 Nov 2014 (E) (in relation to the 2014 pilot areas[12], in so far as is required for the making of regulations) (SI 2014/3026) |
|  |  | 15 Dec 2014 (E) (in relation to the 2014 pilot areas[12]) (otherwise) (SI 2014/3026)[14] |
|  |  | *Not yet in force* (W) |
| 7 | (1)–(3) | 1 Oct 2008 (E) (in relation to the pilot areas[6]) (SI 2008/1960)[7] |
|  |  | 12 Nov 2014 (E) (in relation to the 2014 pilot areas, in so far as is required for the making of regulations) (SI 2014/3026)[14] |
|  |  | 15 Dec 2014 (E) (in relation to the 2014 pilot areas) (otherwise) (SI 2014/3026)[14] |
|  |  | *Not yet in force* (W) |
|  | (4) | 12 Aug 2007 (W) (in so far as it confers a power, or imposes a duty, on the Welsh Ministers to make, or make provision by, regulations; give guidance or directions; or make provision with respect to the exercise of any such power or performance of such duty) (SI 2007/2386) |
|  |  | 1 Oct 2008 (E) (in relation to the pilot areas[6]) (SI 2008/1960)[7] |
|  |  | 12 Nov 2014 (E) (in relation to the 2014 pilot areas[12], in so far as is required for the making of regulations) (SI 2014/3026)[14] |
|  |  | 15 Dec 2014 (E) (in relation to the 2014 pilot areas[12]) (otherwise) (SI 2014/3026)[14] |
|  |  | *Not yet in force* (otherwise) |
|  | (5) | 1 Oct 2008 (E) (in relation to the pilot areas[6]) (SI 2008/1960)[7] |
|  |  | 12 Nov 2014 (E) (in relation to the 2014 pilot areas[12], in so far as is required for the making of regulations) (SI 2014/3026)[14] |
|  |  | 15 Dec 2014 (E) (in relation to the 2014 pilot areas[12]) (otherwise) (SI 2014/3026)[14] |
|  |  | *Not yet in force* (otherwise) |
| 8 | (1), (2) | 12 Aug 2007 (W) (in so far as they confer a power, or impose a duty, on the Welsh Ministers to make, or make provision by, regulations; give guidance or directions; or make provision with respect to the exercise of any such power or performance of such duty) (SI 2007/2386) |
|  |  | 1 Oct 2008 (E) (in relation to the pilot areas[6]) (SI 2008/1960)[7] |
|  |  | 12 Nov 2014 (E) (in relation to the 2014 pilot areas[12], in so far as is required for the making of regulations) (SI 2014/3026)[14] |
|  |  | 15 Dec 2014 (E) (in relation to the 2014 pilot areas) (otherwise) (SI 2014/3026)[14] |
|  |  | *Not yet in force* (otherwise) |
|  | (3) | 1 Oct 2008 (E) (in relation to the pilot areas[6]) (SI 2008/1960)[7] |
|  |  | 12 Nov 2014 (E) (in relation to the 2014 pilot areas[12], in so far as is required for the making of regulations) (SI 2014/3026)[14] |
|  |  | 15 Dec 2014 (E) (in relation to the 2014 pilot areas[12]) (otherwise) (SI 2014/3026)[14] |
|  |  | *Not yet in force* (otherwise) |

**Commons Act 2006 (c 26)**—*contd*

| | | |
|---|---|---|
| 9 | | 28 Jun 2005 (s 9(7)) |
| 10 | | 1 Oct 2008 (E) (in relation to the pilot areas[6]) (SI 2008/1960)[7] |
| | | 12 Nov 2014 (E) (in relation to the 2014 pilot areas[12], in so far as is required for the making of regulations) (SI 2014/3026)[14] |
| | | 15 Dec 2014 (E) (in relation to the 2014 pilot areas) (otherwise) (SI 2014/3026)[14] |
| | | *Not yet in force* (otherwise) |
| 11 | (1)–(4) | 1 Oct 2008 (E) (in relation to the pilot areas[6]) (SI 2008/1960)[7] |
| | | 12 Nov 2014 (E) (in relation to the 2014 pilot areas[12], in so far as is required for the making of regulations) (SI 2014/3026)[14] |
| | | 15 Dec 2014 (E) (in relation to the 2014 pilot areas[12]) (otherwise) (SI 2014/3026)[14] |
| | | *Not yet in force* (otherwise) |
| | (5), (6) | 12 Aug 2007 (W) (in so far as they confer a power, or impose a duty, on the Welsh Ministers to make, or make provision by, regulations; give guidance or directions; or make provision with respect to the exercise of any such power or performance of such duty) (SI 2007/2386) |
| | | 1 Oct 2008 (E) (in relation to the pilot areas[6]) (SI 2008/1960)[7] |
| | | 12 Nov 2014 (E) (in relation to the 2014 pilot areas[12], in so far as is required for the making of regulations) (SI 2014/3026)[14] |
| | | 15 Dec 2014 (E) (in relation to the 2014 pilot areas[12]) (otherwise) (SI 2014/3026)[14] |
| | | *Not yet in force* (otherwise) |
| 12 | (a) | 12 Aug 2007 (W) (in so far as it confers a power, or imposes a duty, on the Welsh Ministers to make, or make provision by, regulations; give guidance or directions; or make provision with respect to the exercise of any such power or performance of such duty) (SI 2007/2386) |
| | | 1 Oct 2008 (E) (in relation to the pilot areas[6]) (SI 2008/1960)[7] |
| | | 12 Nov 2014 (E) (in relation to the 2014 pilot areas[12], in so far as is required for the making of regulations) (SI 2014/3026)[14] |
| | | 15 Dec 2014 (E) (in relation to the 2014 pilot areas[12]) (otherwise) (SI 2014/3026)[14] |
| | | *Not yet in force* (otherwise) |
| | (b) | 1 Oct 2008 (E) (in relation to the pilot areas[6]) (SI 2008/1960)[7] |
| | | 12 Nov 2014 (E) (in relation to the 2014 pilot areas[12], in so far as is required for the making of regulations) (SI 2014/3026)[14] |
| | | 15 Dec 2014 (E) (in relation to the 2014 pilot areas[12]) (otherwise) (SI 2014/3026)[14] |
| | | *Not yet in force* (otherwise) |
| 13 | (1)(a) | 12 Aug 2007 (W) (in so far as it confers a power, or imposes a duty, on the Welsh Ministers to make, or make provision by, regulations; give guidance or directions; or make provision with respect to the exercise of any such power or performance of such duty) (SI 2007/2386) |
| | | 1 Oct 2008 (E) (in relation to the pilot areas[6]) (SI 2008/1960)[7] |
| | | 12 Nov 2014 (E) (in relation to the 2014 pilot areas[12], in so far as is required for the making of regulations) (SI 2014/3026)[14] |
| | | 15 Dec 2014 (E) (in relation to the 2014 pilot areas[12]) (otherwise) (SI 2014/3026)[14] |
| | | *Not yet in force* (otherwise) |
| | (1)(b) | 1 Oct 2008 (E) (in relation to the pilot areas[6]) (SI 2008/1960)[7] |
| | | 12 Nov 2014 (E) (in relation to the 2014 pilot areas[12], in so far as is required for the making of regulations) (SI 2014/3026)[14] |
| | | 15 Dec 2014 (E) (in relation to the 2014 pilot areas[12]) (otherwise) (SI 2014/3026)[14] |
| | | *Not yet in force* (otherwise) |
| | (2), (3) | 1 Oct 2008 (E) (in relation to the pilot areas6) (SI 2008/1960)7 |

**Commons Act 2006 (c 26)**—*contd*

|  |  |  |
|---|---|---|
|  |  | 12 Nov 2014 (E) (in relation to the 2014 pilot areas12, in so far as is required for the making of regulations) (SI 2014/3026)14 |
|  |  | 15 Dec 2014 (E) (in relation to the 2014 pilot areas12) (otherwise) (SI 2014/3026)14 |
|  |  | Not yet in force (otherwise) |
| 14 |  | 12 Aug 2007 (W) (in so far as it confers a power, or imposes a duty, on the Welsh Ministers to make, or make provision by, regulations; give guidance or directions; or make provision with respect to the exercise of any such power or performance of such duty) (SI 2007/2386) |
|  |  | 1 Oct 2008 (E) (in relation to the pilot areas[6]) (SI 2008/1960)[7] |
|  |  | 12 Nov 2014 (E) (in relation to the 2014 pilot areas[12], in so far as is required for the making of regulations) (SI 2014/3026)[14] |
|  |  | 15 Dec 2014 (E) (in relation to the 2014 pilot areas[12]) (otherwise) (SI 2014/3026)[14] |
|  |  | *Not yet in force (otherwise)* |
| 15 |  | 6 Apr 2007 (E) (SI 2007/456)[2] |
|  |  | 6 Sep 2007 (W) (SI 2007/2386)[3] |
| 16 |  | 1 Oct 2007 (E) (SI 2007/2584)[4] |
|  |  | 1 Apr 2012 (W) (SI 2012/739)[10] |
| 17 | (1), (2) | 1 Oct 2007 (E) (SI 2007/2584)[4] |
|  |  | 1 Apr 2012 (W) (SI 2012/739)[10] |
|  | (3) | 12 Aug 2007 (W) (in so far as it confers a power, or imposes a duty, on the Welsh Ministers to make, or make provision by, regulations; give guidance or directions; or make provision with respect to the exercise of any such power or performance of such duty) (SI 2007/2386) |
|  |  | 1 Oct 2007 (E) (SI 2007/2584)[4] |
|  |  | 1 Apr 2012 (W) (otherwise) (SI 2012/739)[10] |
|  | (4)–(9) | 1 Oct 2007 (E) (SI 2007/2584)[4] |
|  |  | 1 Apr 2012 (W) (SI 2012/739)[10] |
|  | (10) | 12 Aug 2007 (W) (in so far as it confers a power, or imposes a duty, on the Welsh Ministers to make, or make provision by, regulations; give guidance or directions; or make provision with respect to the exercise of any such power or performance of such duty) (SI 2007/2386) |
|  |  | 1 Oct 2007 (E) (SI 2007/2584)[4] |
|  |  | 1 Apr 2012 (W) (otherwise) (SI 2012/739)[10] |
| 18 |  | 1 Oct 2008 (E) (in relation to the pilot areas[6]) (SI 2008/1960)[7] |
|  |  | 12 Nov 2014 (E) (in relation to the 2014 pilot areas[12], in so far as is required for the making of regulations) (SI 2014/3026)[14] |
|  |  | 15 Dec 2014 (E) (in relation to the 2014 pilot areas[12]) (otherwise) (SI 2014/3026)[14] |
|  |  | *Not yet in force (otherwise)* |
| 19 | (1), (2)(a) | 1 Oct 2008 (E) (in relation to the pilot areas[6]) (SI 2008/1960)[7] |
|  |  | 12 Nov 2014 (E) (in relation to the 2014 pilot areas12, in so far as is required for the making of regulations) (SI 2014/3026)14 |
|  |  | 15 Dec 2014 (E) (in relation to the 2014 pilot areas[12]) (otherwise) (SI 2014/3026)[14] |
|  |  | 12 Nov 2014 (in relation to the other registration areas[13], in so far as is required for the making of regulations and only to the extent that they enable an application to any of the other registration areas to amend its register of common land or its register of town or village greens under s 19 or Sch 2, para 6, 7, 8 or 9) (SI 2014/3026)[14] |
|  |  | 15 Dec 2014 (E) (in relation to the other registration areas[13]) (otherwise) (SI 2014/3026)[14] |
|  |  | 10 Apr 2017 (otherwise) (W) (SI 2017/564) |
|  | (2)(b)–(e) | 1 Oct 2008 (E) (in relation to the pilot areas[6]) (SI 2008/1960)[7] |

**Commons Act 2006 (c 26)**—*contd*

            12 Nov 2014 (E) (in relation to the 2014 pilot areas[12], in so far as is required for the making of regulations) (SI 2014/3026)[14]

            15 Dec 2014 (E) (in relation to the 2014 pilot areas[12]) (otherwise) (SI 2014/3026)[14]

            10 Apr 2017 (otherwise) (W) (SI 2017/564)

(3)        1 Oct 2008 (E) (in relation to the pilot areas[6]) (SI 2008/1960)[7]

            12 Nov 2014 (E) (in relation to the 2014 pilot areas[12], in so far as is required for the making of regulations) (SI 2014/3026)[14]

            15 Dec 2014 (in relation to the 2014 pilot areas[12]) (otherwise) (E) (SI 2014/3026)[14]

            12 Nov 2014 (in relation to the other registration areas[13], in so far as is required for the making of regulations and only to the extent that they enable an application to any of the other registration areas to amend its register of common land or its register of town or village greens under s 19 or Sch 2, para 6, 7, 8 or 9) (SI 2014/3026)[14]

            15 Dec 2014 (in relation to the other registration areas[13]) (otherwise) (E) (SI 2014/3026)[14]

            10 Apr 2017 (otherwise) (W) (SI 2017/564)

(4)(a)      1 Oct 2008 (E) (in relation to the pilot areas[6]) (SI 2008/1960)[7]

            12 Nov 2014 (E) (in relation to the 2014 pilot areas[12], in so far as is required for the making of regulations) (SI 2014/3026)[14]

            15 Dec 2014 (E) (in relation to the 2014 pilot areas[12]) (otherwise) (SI 2014/3026)[14]

            10 Apr 2017 (otherwise) (W) (SI 2017/564)

(4)(b), (5)   1 Oct 2008 (E) (in relation to the pilot areas[6]) (SI 2008/1960)[7]

            12 Nov 2014 (E) (in relation to the 2014 pilot areas[12], in so far as is required for the making of regulations) (SI 2014/3026)[14]

            15 Dec 2014 (E) (in relation to the 2014 pilot areas[12]) (otherwise) (SI 2014/3026)[14]

            12 Nov 2014 (in relation to the other registration areas[13], in so far as is required for the making of regulations and only to the extent that they enable an application to any of the other registration areas to amend its register of common land or its register of town or village greens under s 19 or Sch 2, para 6, 7, 8 or 9) (SI 2014/3026)[14]

            15 Dec 2014 (in relation to the other registration areas[13]) (otherwise) (E) (SI 2014/3026)[14]

            10 Apr 2017 (otherwise) (W) (SI 2017/564)

(6)        12 Aug 2007 (W) (in so far as it confers a power, or imposes a duty, on the Welsh Ministers to make, or make provision by, regulations; give guidance or directions; or make provision with respect to the exercise of any such power or performance of such duty) (SI 2007/2386)

            1 Oct 2008 (E) (in relation to the pilot areas[6]) (SI 2008/1960)[7]

            12 Nov 2014 (E) (in relation to the 2014 pilot areas[12], in so far as is required for the making of regulations) (SI 2014/3026)[14]

            15 Dec 2014 (E) (in relation to the 2014 pilot areas12) (otherwise) (SI 2014/3026)[14]

            12 Nov 2014 (in relation to the other registration areas, in so far as is required for the making of regulations and only to the extent that they enable an application to any of the other registration areas to amend its register of common land or its register of town or village greens under s 19 or Sch 2, para 6, 7, 8 or 9) (SI 2014/3026)[14]

            15 Dec 2014 (in relation to the other registration areas) (otherwise) (E) (SI 2014/3026)[14]

            10 Apr 2017 (otherwise) (W) (SI 2017/564)

(7)        1 Oct 2008 (E) (in relation to the pilot areas[6]) (SI 2008/1960)[7]

            12 Nov 2014 (E) (in relation to the 2014 pilot areas[12], in so far as is required for the making of regulations) (SI 2014/3026)[14]

Commons Act 2006 (c 26)—*contd*

|  |  |  |
|---|---|---|
|  |  | 15 Dec 2014 (E) (in relation to the 2014 pilot areas12) (otherwise) (SI 2014/3026)[14] |
|  |  | 12 Nov 2014 (in relation to the other registration areas[13], in so far as is required for the making of regulations and only to the extent that they enable an application to any of the other registration areas to amend its register of common land or its register of town or village greens under s 19 or Sch 2, para 6, 7, 8 or 9) (SI 2014/3026)[14] |
|  |  | 15 Dec 2014 (in relation to the other registration areas[13]) (otherwise) (E) (SI 2014/3026)[14] |
|  |  | 10 Apr 2017 (otherwise) (W) (SI 2017/564) |
| 20 | (1) | 1 Oct 2008 (E) (in relation to the pilot areas[6]) (SI 2008/1960)[7] |
|  |  | 12 Nov 2014 (E) (in relation to the 2014 pilot areas[12], in so far as is required for the making of regulations) (SI 2014/3026) |
|  |  | 15 Dec 2014 (E) (in relation to the 2014 pilot areas[12]) (otherwise) (SI 2014/3026) |
|  |  | 12 Nov 2014 (in relation to the other registration areas[13], in so far as is required for the making of regulations and only to the extent that they enable an application to any of the other registration areas to amend its register of common land or its register of town or village greens under s 19 or Sch 2, para 6, 7, 8 or 9) (SI 2014/3026)[14] |
|  |  | 15 Dec 2014 (in relation to the other registration areas[13]) (otherwise) (E) (SI 2014/3026)[14] |
|  |  | 20 Sep 2017 (otherwise) (W) (SI 2017/933)[15] |
|  | (2), (3) | 12 Aug 2007 (W) (in so far as they confer a power, or impose a duty, on the Welsh Ministers to make, or make provision by, regulations; give guidance or directions; or make provision with respect to the exercise of any such power or performance of such duty) (SI 2007/2386) |
|  |  | 1 Oct 2008 (E) (in relation to the pilot areas[6]) (SI 2008/1960)[7] |
|  |  | 12 Nov 2014 (E) (in relation to the 2014 pilot areas, in so far as is required for the making of regulations) (SI 2014/3026)[14] |
|  |  | 15 Dec 2014 (in relation to the 2014 pilot areas) (otherwise) (E) (SI 2014/3026)[14] |
|  |  | 12 Nov 2014 (in relation to the other registration areas[13], in so far as is required for the making of regulations and only to the extent that they enable an application to any of the other registration areas to amend its register of common land or its register of town or village greens under s 19 or Sch 2, para 6, 7, 8 or 9) (SI 2014/3026)[14] |
|  |  | 15 Dec 2014 (in relation to the other registration areas[13]) (otherwise) (E) (SI 2014/3026)[14] |
|  |  | 20 Sep 2017 (otherwise) (W) (SI 2017/933)[15] |
| 21 | (1) | 1 Oct 2008 (E) (in relation to the pilot areas[6]) (SI 2008/1960)[7] |
|  |  | 12 Nov 2014 (E) (in relation to the 2014 pilot areas[12], in so far as is required for the making of regulations) (SI 2014/3026)[14] |
|  |  | 15 Dec 2014 (E) (in relation to the 2014 pilot areas[12]) (otherwise) (SI 2014/3026)[14] |
|  |  | 12 Nov 2014 (in relation to the other registration areas, in so far as is required for the making of regulations and only to the extent that they enable an application to any of the other registration areas to amend its register of common land or its register of town or village greens under s 19 or Sch 2, para 6, 7, 8 or 9) (SI 2014/3026)[14] |
|  |  | 15 Dec 2014 (in relation to the other registration areas[13]) (otherwise) (E) (SI 2014/3026)[14] |
|  |  | 20 Sep 2017 (otherwise) (W) (SI 2017/933)[15] |

**Commons Act 2006 (c 26)**—*contd*

|  |  |  |
|---|---|---|
| | (2), (3) | 12 Aug 2007 (W) (in so far as they confer a power, or impose a duty, on the Welsh Ministers to make, or make provision by, regulations; give guidance or directions; or make provision with respect to the exercise of any such power or performance of such duty) (SI 2007/2386) |
| | | 1 Oct 2008 (E) (in relation to the pilot areas[6]) (SI 2008/1960)[7] |
| | | 12 Nov 2014 (E) (in relation to the 2014 pilot areas[12], in so far as is required for the making of regulations) (SI 2014/3026)[14] |
| | | 15 Dec 2014 (E) (in relation to the 2014 pilot areas[12]) (otherwise) (SI 2014/3026)[14] |
| | | 12 Nov 2014 (in relation to the other registration areas[13], in so far as is required for the making of regulations and only to the extent that they enable an application to any of the other registration areas to amend its register of common land or its register of town or village greens under s 19 or Sch 2, para 6, 7, 8 or 9) (SI 2014/3026)[14] |
| | | 15 Dec 2014 (in relation to the other registration areas[13]) (otherwise) (E) (SI 2014/3026)[14] |
| | | 20 Sep 2017 (otherwise) (W) (SI 2017/933)[15] |
| 22 | | See Sch 2 below |
| 23 | | See Sch 3 below |
| 24 | | 6 Apr 2007 (E) (SI 2007/456)[2] |
| | | 12 Aug 2007 (W) (in so far as it confers a power, or imposes a duty, on the Welsh Ministers to make, or make provision by, regulations; give guidance or directions; or make provision with respect to the exercise of any such power or performance of such duty) (SI 2007/2386) |
| | | 6 Sep 2007 (W) (otherwise) (SI 2007/2386)[3] |
| 25 | | 12 Aug 2007 (W) (in so far as it confers a power, or imposes a duty, on the Welsh Ministers to make, or make provision by, regulations; give guidance or directions; or make provision with respect to the exercise of any such power or performance of such duty) (SI 2007/2386) |
| | | *Not yet in force* (otherwise) |
| 26–28 | | 20 Jan 2010 (E) (SI 2010/61) |
| | | *Not yet in force* (W) |
| 29 | (1) | 12 Aug 2007 (W) (in so far as it confers a power, or imposes a duty, on the Welsh Ministers to make, or make provision by, regulations; give guidance or directions; or make provision with respect to the exercise of any such power or performance of such duty) (SI 2007/2386) |
| | | 20 Jan 2010 (E) (SI 2010/61) |
| | | *Not yet in force* (W) (otherwise) |
| | (2)–(5) | 20 Jan 2010 (E) (SI 2010/61) |
| | | *Not yet in force* (W) |
| | (6) | 12 Aug 2007 (W) (in so far as it confers a power, or imposes a duty, on the Welsh Ministers to make, or make provision by, regulations; give guidance or directions; or make provision with respect to the exercise of any such power or performance of such duty) (SI 2007/2386) |
| | | 20 Jan 2010 (E) (SI 2010/61) |
| | | *Not yet in force* (W) (otherwise) |
| 30 | | 20 Jan 2010 (E) (SI 2010/61) |
| | | *Not yet in force* (W) |
| 31 | (1)–(5) | 20 Jan 2010 (E) (SI 2010/61) |
| | | *Not yet in force* (W) |
| | (6)(a) | 12 Aug 2007 (W) (in so far as it confers a power, or imposes a duty, on the Welsh Ministers to make, or make provision by, regulations; give guidance or directions; or make provision with respect to the exercise of any such power or performance of such duty) (SI 2007/2386) |

**Commons Act 2006 (c 26)**—*contd*

|  |  |  |
|---|---|---|
|  |  | 20 Jan 2010 (E) (SI 2010/61) |
|  |  | *Not yet in force* (W) (otherwise) |
|  | (6)(b), (7) | 20 Jan 2010 (E) (SI 2010/61) |
|  |  | *Not yet in force* (W) |
| 32–37 |  | 20 Jan 2010 (E) (SI 2010/61) |
|  |  | *Not yet in force* (W) |
| 38 |  | 1 Oct 2007 (E) (SI 2007/2584)[4] |
|  |  | 1 Apr 2012 (W) (SI 2012/739)[10] |
| 39 | (1)–(5) | 1 Oct 2007 (E) (SI 2007/2584) |
|  |  | 1 Apr 2012 (W) (SI 2012/739) |
|  | (6) | 12 Aug 2007 (W) (in so far as it confers a power, or imposes a duty, on the Welsh Ministers to make, or make provision by, regulations; give guidance or directions; or make provision with respect to the exercise of any such power or performance of such duty) (SI 2007/2386) |
|  |  | 1 Apr 2012 (W) (otherwise) (SI 2012/739) |
|  |  | 1 Oct 2007 (E) (SI 2007/2584) |
|  | (7) | 1 Oct 2007 (E) (SI 2007/2584) |
|  |  | 1 Apr 2012 (W) (SI 2012/739) |
| 40 |  | 12 Aug 2007 (W) (in so far as it confers a power, or imposes a duty, on the Welsh Ministers to make, or make provision by, regulations; give guidance or directions; or make provision with respect to the exercise of any such power or performance of such duty) (SI 2007/2386) |
|  |  | 1 Oct 2007 (E) (SI 2007/2584) |
|  |  | 1 Apr 2012 (W) (otherwise) (SI 2012/739) |
| 41 |  | 1 Oct 2007 (E) (SI 2007/2584) |
|  |  | 1 Apr 2012 (W) (SI 2012/739) |
| 42 | (1)–(3) | 1 Oct 2007 (E) (SI 2007/2584) |
|  |  | 1 Apr 2012 (W) (SI 2012/739) |
|  | (4) | 12 Aug 2007 (W) (in so far as it confers a power, or imposes a duty, on the Welsh Ministers to make, or make provision by, regulations; give guidance or directions; or make provision with respect to the exercise of any such power or performance of such duty) (SI 2007/2386) |
|  |  | 1 Oct 2007 (E) (SI 2007/2584) |
|  |  | 1 Apr 2012 (W) (otherwise) (SI 2012/739) |
|  | (5) | 1 Oct 2007 (E) (SI 2007/2584) |
|  |  | 1 Apr 2012 (W) (SI 2012/739) |
| 43 |  | 12 Aug 2007 (W) (in so far as it confers a power, or imposes a duty, on the Welsh Ministers to make, or make provision by, regulations; give guidance or directions; or make provision with respect to the exercise of any such power or performance of such duty) (SI 2007/2386) |
|  |  | 1 Oct 2007 (E) (SI 2007/2584) |
|  |  | 1 Apr 2012 (W) (otherwise) (SI 2012/739) |
| 44 | (1) | See Sch 4 below |
|  | (2)–(4) | 12 Aug 2007 (W) (in so far as they confer a power, or impose a duty, on the Welsh Ministers to make, or make provision by, regulations; give guidance or directions; or make provision with respect to the exercise of any such power or performance of such duty) (SI 2007/2386) |
|  |  | 1 Oct 2007 (E) (SI 2007/2584)[4] |
|  |  | 1 Apr 2012 (W) (otherwise) (SI 2012/739)[10] |
| 45 |  | 1 Oct 2006 (E) (SI 2006/2504)[1] |
|  |  | 6 Sep 2007 (W) (SI 2007/2386)[3] |
| 46 |  | 1 Oct 2008 (E) (SI 2008/1960)[7] |
|  |  | 1 Apr 2012 (W) (SI 2012/806) |
| 47 |  | 1 Oct 2006 (E) (SI 2006/2504) |
|  |  | 6 Sep 2007 (W) (SI 2007/2386) |

**Commons Act 2006 (c 26)**—*contd*

| | | |
|---|---|---|
| 48 | | 1 Oct 2007 (E) (SI 2007/2584) |
| | | 1 Apr 2012 (W) (SI 2012/739) |
| 49 | | 1 Oct 2006 (E) (SI 2006/2504) |
| | | 6 Sep 2007 (W) (SI 2007/2386) |
| 50 | (1) | 12 Aug 2007 (W) (in so far as it confers a power, or imposes a duty, on the Welsh Ministers to make, or make provision by, regulations; give guidance or directions; or make provision with respect to the exercise of any such power or performance of such duty) (SI 2007/2386) |
| | | *Not yet in force* (otherwise) |
| | (2), (3) | *Not yet in force* |
| | (4)–(6) | 12 Aug 2007 (W) (in so far as they confer a power, or impose a duty, on the Welsh Ministers to make, or make provision by, regulations; give guidance or directions; or make provision with respect to the exercise of any such power or performance of such duty) (SI 2007/2386) |
| | | *Not yet in force* (otherwise) |
| | (7) | *Not yet in force* |
| 51 | | 1 Oct 2006 (E) (SI 2006/2504)[5] |
| | | 6 Sep 2007 (W) (SI 2007/2386) |
| 52 | | See Sch 5 below |
| 53 | | See Sch 6 below |
| 54, 55 | | 19 Sep 2006 (s 56(2)) |
| 56 | | 19 Jul 2006 (RA) |
| 57 | | 28 Jun 2005 (s 57(4)) |
| 58–63 | | 19 Jul 2006 (RA) |
| Sch 1 | | 28 Jun 2005 (s 9(7)) |
| Sch 2 | para 1 | 1 Oct 2008 (E) (in relation to the pilot areas[6]) (SI 2008/1960)[7] |
| | | 12 Nov 2014 (E) (in relation to the 2014 pilot areas[12], in so far as is required for the making of regulations) (SI 2014/3026)[14] |
| | | 15 Dec 2014 (E) (in relation to the 2014 pilot areas[12]) (otherwise) (SI 2014/3026)[14] |
| | | 12 Nov 2014 (in relation to the other registration areas[13], in so far as is required for the making of regulations and only to the extent that they enable an application to any of the other registration areas to amend its register of common land or its register of town or village greens under s 19 or Sch 2, para 6, 7, 8 or 9) (SI 2014/3026)[14] |
| | | 15 Dec 2014 (E) (in relation to the other registration areas[13]) (otherwise) (SI 2014/3026)[14] |
| | | 10 Apr 2017 (W) (otherwise) (SI 2017/564) |
| | para 2(1) | 1 Oct 2008 (E) (in relation to the pilot areas[6]) (SI 2008/1960)[7] |
| | | 12 Nov 2014 (E) (in relation to the 2014 pilot areas[12], in so far as is required for the making of regulations) (SI 2014/3026)[14] |
| | | 15 Dec 2014 (E) (in relation to the 2014 pilot areas[12]) (otherwise) (SI 2014/3026)[14] |
| | | 10 Apr 2017 (W) (otherwise) (SI 2017/564) |
| | para 2(2)(a)–(c) | 1 Oct 2008 (E) (in relation to the pilot areas[6]) (SI 2008/1960)[7] |
| | | 12 Nov 2014 (E) (in relation to the 2014 pilot areas[12], in so far as is required for the making of regulations) (SI 2014/3026)[14] |
| | | 15 Dec 2014 (E) (in relation to the 2014 pilot areas[12]) (otherwise) (SI 2014/3026)[14] |
| | | 10 Apr 2017 (W) (otherwise) (SI 2017/564) |
| | para 2(2)(d) | 12 Aug 2007 (W) (in so far as it confers a power, or imposes a duty, on the Welsh Ministers to make, or make provision by, regulations; give guidance or directions; or make provision with respect to the exercise of any such power or performance of such duty) (SI 2007/2386) |
| | | 1 Oct 2008 (E) (in relation to the pilot areas[6]) (SI 2008/1960)[7] |

**Commons Act 2006 (c 26)**—*contd*

12 Nov 2014 (E) (in relation to the 2014 pilot areas[12], in so far as is required for the making of regulations) (SI 2014/3026)[14]

15 Dec 2014 (E) (in relation to the 2014 pilot areas[12]) (otherwise) (SI 2014/3026)[14]

10 Apr 2017 (W) (otherwise) (SI 2017/564)

para 2(3)    12 Aug 2007 (W) (in so far as it confers a power, or imposes a duty, on the Welsh Ministers to make, or make provision by, regulations; give guidance or directions; or make provision with respect to the exercise of any such power or performance of such duty) (SI 2007/2386)

1 Oct 2008 (E) (in relation to the pilot areas[6]) (SI 2008/1960)[7]

12 Nov 2014 (E) (in relation to the 2014 pilot areas[12], in so far as is required for the making of regulations) (SI 2014/3026)[14]

15 Dec 2014 (E) (in relation to the 2014 pilot areas[12]) (otherwise) (SI 2014/3026)[14]

10 Apr 2017 (W) (otherwise) (SI 2017/564)

para 3(1)    1 Oct 2008 (E) (in relation to the pilot areas[6]) (SI 2008/1960)[7]

12 Nov 2014 (E) (in relation to the 2014 pilot areas[12], in so far as is required for the making of regulations) (SI 2014/3026)[14]

15 Dec 2014 (E) (in relation to the 2014 pilot areas[12]) (otherwise) (SI 2014/3026)[14]

10 Apr 2017 (W) (otherwise) (SI 2017/564)

para 3(2)(a)–(d)    1 Oct 2008 (E) (in relation to the pilot areas[6]) (SI 2008/1960)[7]

12 Nov 2014 (E) (in relation to the 2014 pilot areas[12], in so far as is required for the making of regulations) (SI 2014/3026)[14]

15 Dec 2014 (E) (in relation to the 2014 pilot areas12) (otherwise) (SI 2014/3026)[14]

10 Apr 2017 (W) (otherwise) (SI 2017/564)

para 3(2)(e)    12 Aug 2007 (W) (in so far as it confers a power, or imposes a duty, on the Welsh Ministers to make, or make provision by, regulations; give guidance or directions; or make provision with respect to the exercise of any such power or performance of such duty) (SI 2007/2386)

1 Oct 2008 (E) (in relation to the pilot areas[6]) (SI 2008/1960)[7]

12 Nov 2014 (E) (in relation to the 2014 pilot areas[12], in so far as is required for the making of regulations) (SI 2014/3026)[14]

15 Dec 2014 (E) (in relation to the 2014 pilot areas[12]) (otherwise) (SI 2014/3026)[14]

10 Apr 2017 (W) (otherwise) (SI 2017/564)

para 3(3)    12 Aug 2007 (W) (in so far as it confers a power, or imposes a duty, on the Welsh Ministers to make, or make provision by, regulations; give guidance or directions; or make provision with respect to the exercise of any such power or performance of such duty) (SI 2007/2386)

1 Oct 2008 (E) (in relation to the pilot areas[6]) (SI 2008/1960)[7]

12 Nov 2014 (E) (in relation to the 2014 pilot areas[12], in so far as is required for the making of regulations) (SI 2014/3026)[14]

15 Dec 2014 (E) (in relation to the 2014 pilot areas12) (otherwise) (SI 2014/3026)[14]

10 Apr 2017 (W) (otherwise) (SI 2017/564)

para 4(1)–(5)    1 Oct 2008 (E) (in relation to the pilot areas[6]) (SI 2008/1960)[7]

12 Nov 2014 (E) (in relation to the 2014 pilot areas[12], in so far as is required for the making of regulations) (SI 2014/3026)[14]

15 Dec 2014 (E) (in relation to the 2014 pilot areas[12]) (otherwise) (SI 2014/3026)[14]

10 Apr 2017 (W) (otherwise) (SI 2017/564)

para 4(6)    12 Aug 2007 (W) (in so far as it confers a power, or imposes a duty, on the Welsh Ministers to make, or make provision by, regulations; give guidance or directions; or make provision with respect to the exercise of any such power or performance of such duty) (SI 2007/2386)

**Commons Act 2006 (c 26)**—*contd*

        1 Oct 2008 (E) (in relation to the pilot areas[6]) (SI 2008/1960)[7]

        12 Nov 2014 (E) (in relation to the 2014 pilot areas[12], in so far as is required for the making of regulations) (SI 2014/3026)[14]

        15 Dec 2014 (E) (in relation to the 2014 pilot areas[12]) (otherwise) (SI 2014/3026)[14]

        10 Apr 2017 (W) (otherwise) (SI 2017/564)

para 5(1), (2)    1 Oct 2008 (E) (in relation to the pilot areas[6]) (SI 2008/1960)[7]

        12 Nov 2014 (E) (in relation to the 2014 pilot areas[12], in so far as is required for the making of regulations) (SI 2014/3026)[14]

        15 Dec 2014 (E) (in relation to the 2014 pilot areas[12]) (otherwise) (SI 2014/3026)[14]

        10 Apr 2017 (W) (otherwise) (SI 2017/564)

para 5(3)    12 Aug 2007 (W) (in so far as it confers a power, or imposes a duty, on the Welsh Ministers to make, or make provision by, regulations; give guidance or directions; or make provision with respect to the exercise of any such power or performance of such duty) (SI 2007/2386)

        1 Oct 2008 (E) (in relation to the pilot areas[6]) (SI 2008/1960)[7]

        12 Nov 2014 (E) (in relation to the 2014 pilot areas[12], in so far as is required for the making of regulations) (SI 2014/3026)[14]

        15 Dec 2014 (E) (in relation to the 2014 pilot areas[12]) (otherwise) (SI 2014/3026)[14]

        10 Apr 2017 (W) (otherwise) (SI 2017/564)

para 6(1), (2)    1 Oct 2008 (E) (in relation to the pilot areas[6]) (SI 2008/1960)[7]

        12 Nov 2014 (E) (in relation to the 2014 pilot areas[12], in so far as is required for the making of regulations) (SI 2014/3026)[14]

        15 Dec 2014 (E) (in relation to the 2014 pilot areas[12]) (otherwise) (SI 2014/3026)[14]

        12 Nov 2014 (in relation to the other registration areas[13], in so far as is required for the making of regulations and only to the extent that they enable an application to any of the other registration areas to amend its register of common land or its register of town or village greens under s 19 or Sch 2, para 6, 7, 8 or 9) (SI 2014/3026)[14]

        15 Dec 2014 (in relation to the other registration areas[13]) (otherwise) (E) (SI 2014/3026)[14]

        10 Apr 2017 (W) (otherwise) (SI 2017/564)

para 6(3)    12 Aug 2007 (W) (in so far as it confers a power, or imposes a duty, on the Welsh Ministers to make, or make provision by, regulations; give guidance or directions; or make provision with respect to the exercise of any such power or performance of such duty) (SI 2007/2386)

        1 Oct 2008 (E) (in relation to the pilot areas[6]) (SI 2008/1960)[7]

        12 Nov 2014 (E) (in relation to the 2014 pilot areas[12], in so far as is required for the making of regulations) (SI 2014/3026)[14]

        15 Dec 2014 (E) (in relation to the 2014 pilot areas[12]) (otherwise) (SI 2014/3026)[14]

        12 Nov 2014 (in relation to the other registration areas[13], in so far as is required for the making of regulations and only to the extent that they enable an application to any of the other registration areas to amend its register of common land or its register of town or village greens under s 19 or Sch 2, para 6, 7, 8 or 9) (SI 2014/3026)[14]

        15 Dec 2014 (in relation to the other registration areas[13]) (otherwise) (E) (SI 2014/3026)[14]

        10 Apr 2017 (W) (otherwise) (SI 2017/564)

para 7(1), (2)    1 Oct 2008 (E) (in relation to the pilot areas[6]) (SI 2008/1960)[7]

        12 Nov 2014 (E) (in relation to the 2014 pilot areas[12], in so far as is required for the making of regulations) (SI 2014/3026)[14]

        15 Dec 2014 (E) (in relation to the 2014 pilot areas[12]) (otherwise) (SI 2014/3026)[14]

**Commons Act 2006 (c 26)**—*contd*

<table>
<tr><td></td><td>12 Nov 2014 (in relation to the other registration areas[13], in so far as is required for the making of regulations and only to the extent that they enable an application to any of the other registration areas to amend its register of common land or its register of town or village greens under s 19 or Sch 2, para 6, 7, 8 or 9) (SI 2014/3026)[14]</td></tr>
<tr><td></td><td>15 Dec 2014 (in relation to the other registration areas[13]) (otherwise) (E) (SI 2014/3026)[14]</td></tr>
<tr><td></td><td>10 Apr 2017 (W) (otherwise) (SI 2017/564)</td></tr>
<tr><td>para 7(3)</td><td>12 Aug 2007 (W) (in so far as it confers a power, or imposes a duty, on the Welsh Ministers to make, or make provision by, regulations; give guidance or directions; or make provision with respect to the exercise of any such power or performance of such duty) (SI 2007/2386)</td></tr>
<tr><td></td><td>1 Oct 2008 (E) (in relation to the pilot areas[6]) (SI 2008/1960)[7]</td></tr>
<tr><td></td><td>12 Nov 2014 (E) (in relation to the 2014 pilot areas[12], in so far as is required for the making of regulations) (SI 2014/3026)[14]</td></tr>
<tr><td></td><td>15 Dec 2014 (E) (in relation to the 2014 pilot areas[12]) (otherwise) (SI 2014/3026)[14]</td></tr>
<tr><td></td><td>12 Nov 2014 (in relation to the other registration areas[13], in so far as is required for the making of regulations and only to the extent that they enable an application to any of the other registration areas to amend its register of common land or its register of town or village greens under s 19 or Sch 2, para 6, 7, 8 or 9) (SI 2014/3026)[14]</td></tr>
<tr><td></td><td>15 Dec 2014 (E) (in relation to the other registration areas[13]) (otherwise) (SI 2014/3026)[14]</td></tr>
<tr><td></td><td>10 Apr 2017 (W) (otherwise) (SI 2017/564)</td></tr>
<tr><td>para 8(1), (2)</td><td>1 Oct 2008 (E) (in relation to the pilot areas[6]) (SI 2008/1960)[7]</td></tr>
<tr><td></td><td>12 Nov 2014 (E) (in relation to the 2014 pilot areas[12], in so far as is required for the making of regulations) (SI 2014/3026)[14]</td></tr>
<tr><td></td><td>15 Dec 2014 (E) (in relation to the 2014 pilot areas12) (otherwise) (SI 2014/3026)[14]</td></tr>
<tr><td></td><td>12 Nov 2014 (in relation to the other registration areas[13], in so far as is required for the making of regulations and only to the extent that they enable an application to any of the other registration areas to amend its register of common land or its register of town or village greens under s 19 or Sch 2, para 6, 7, 8 or 9) (SI 2014/3026)[14]</td></tr>
<tr><td></td><td>15 Dec 2014 (E) (in relation to the other registration areas[13]) (otherwise) (SI 2014/3026)[14]</td></tr>
<tr><td></td><td>10 Apr 2017 (W) (otherwise) (SI 2017/564)</td></tr>
<tr><td>para 8(3)</td><td>12 Aug 2007 (W) (in so far as it confers a power, or imposes a duty, on the Welsh Ministers to make, or make provision by, regulations; give guidance or directions; or make provision with respect to the exercise of any such power or performance of such duty) (SI 2007/2386)</td></tr>
<tr><td></td><td>1 Oct 2008 (E) (in relation to the pilot areas[6]) (SI 2008/1960)[7]</td></tr>
<tr><td></td><td>12 Nov 2014 (E) (in relation to the 2014 pilot areas[12], in so far as is required for the making of regulations) (SI 2014/3026)[14]</td></tr>
<tr><td></td><td>15 Dec 2014 (E) (in relation to the 2014 pilot areas[12]) (otherwise) (SI 2014/3026)[14]</td></tr>
<tr><td></td><td>12 Nov 2014 (in relation to the other registration areas[13], in so far as is required for the making of regulations and only to the extent that they enable an application to any of the other registration areas to amend its register of common land or its register of town or village greens under s 19 or Sch 2, para 6, 7, 8 or 9) (SI 2014/3026)[14]</td></tr>
<tr><td></td><td>15 Dec 2014 (E) (in relation to the other registration areas[13]) (otherwise) (SI 2014/3026)[14]</td></tr>
<tr><td></td><td>10 Apr 2017 (W) (otherwise) (SI 2017/564)</td></tr>
</table>

**Commons Act 2006 (c 26)**—*contd*

| | | |
|---|---|---|
| para 9(1)–(3) | | 1 Oct 2008 (E) (in relation to the pilot areas[6]) (SI 2008/1960)[7] |

        12 Nov 2014 (E) (in relation to the 2014 pilot areas[12], in so far as is required for the making of regulations) (SI 2014/3026)[14]

        15 Dec 2014 (E) (in relation to the 2014 pilot areas[12]) (otherwise) (SI 2014/3026)[14]

        12 Nov 2014 (in relation to the other registration areas[13], in so far as is required for the making of regulations and only to the extent that they enable an application to any of the other registration areas to amend its register of common land or its register of town or village greens under s 19 or Sch 2, para 6, 7, 8 or 9) (SI 2014/3026)[14]

        15 Dec 2014 (E) (in relation to the other registration areas[13]) (otherwise) (SI 2014/3026)[14]

        10 Apr 2017 (W) (otherwise) (SI 2017/564)

    para 9(4)    12 Aug 2007 (W) (in so far as it confers a power, or imposes a duty, on the Welsh Ministers to make, or make provision by, regulations; give guidance or directions; or make provision with respect to the exercise of any such power or performance of such duty) (SI 2007/2386)

        1 Oct 2008 (E) (in relation to the pilot areas[6]) (SI 2008/1960)[7]

        12 Nov 2014 (E) (in relation to the 2014 pilot areas[12], in so far as is required for the making of regulations) (SI 2014/3026)[14]

        15 Dec 2014 (E) (in relation to the 2014 pilot areas[12]) (otherwise) (SI 2014/3026)[14]

        12 Nov 2014 (in relation to the other registration areas[13], in so far as is required for the making of regulations and only to the extent that they enable an application to any of the other registration areas to amend its register of common land or its register of town or village greens under s 19 or Sch 2, para 6, 7, 8 or 9) (SI 2014/3026)[14]

        15 Dec 2014 (in relation to the other registration areas[13]) (otherwise) (E) (SI 2014/3026)[14]

        10 Apr 2017 (W) (otherwise) (SI 2017/564)

    para 10    12 Aug 2007 (W) (in so far as it confers a power, or imposes a duty, on the Welsh Ministers to make, or make provision by, regulations; give guidance or directions; or make provision with respect to the exercise of any such power or performance of such duty) (SI 2007/2386)

        1 Oct 2008 (E) (in relation to the pilot areas[6]) (SI 2008/1960)[7]

        12 Nov 2014 (E) (in relation to the 2014 pilot areas[12], in so far as is required for the making of regulations) (SI 2014/3026)[14]

        15 Dec 2014 (E) (in relation to the 2014 pilot areas[12]) (otherwise) (SI 2014/3026)[14]

        12 Nov 2014 (in relation to the other registration areas[13], in so far as is required for the making of regulations and only to the extent that they enable an application to any of the other registration areas to amend its register of common land or its register of town or village greens under s 19 or Sch 2, para 6, 7, 8 or 9) (SI 2014/3026)[14]

        15 Dec 2014 (in relation to the other registration areas[13]) (otherwise) (E) (SI 2014/3026)[14]

        10 Apr 2017 (W) (otherwise) (SI 2017/564)

Sch 3    para 1    1 Oct 2008 (E) (in relation to the pilot areas[6]) (SI 2008/1960)[7]

        12 Nov 2014 (E) (in relation to the 2014 pilot areas[12], in so far as is required for the making of regulations) (SI 2014/3026)[14]

        15 Dec 2014 (E) (in relation to the 2014 pilot areas[12]) (otherwise) (SI 2014/3026)[14]

        *Not yet in force* (otherwise)

**Commons Act 2006 (c 26)**—*contd*

<table>
<tr><td>para 2(1)</td><td>12 Aug 2007 (W) (in so far as it confers a power, or imposes a duty, on the Welsh Ministers to make, or make provision by, regulations; give guidance or directions; or make provision with respect to the exercise of any such power or performance of such duty) (SI 2007/2386)</td></tr>
<tr><td></td><td>1 Oct 2008 (E) (in relation to the pilot areas[6]) (SI 2008/1960)[7]</td></tr>
<tr><td></td><td>12 Nov 2014 (E) (in relation to the 2014 pilot areas[12], in so far as is required for the making of regulations) (SI 2014/3026)[14]</td></tr>
<tr><td></td><td>15 Dec 2014 (E) (in relation to the 2014 pilot areas[12]) (otherwise) (SI 2014/3026)[14]</td></tr>
<tr><td></td><td>*Not yet in force* (otherwise)</td></tr>
<tr><td>para 2(2)–(4)</td><td>1 Oct 2008 (E) (in relation to the pilot areas[6]) (SI 2008/1960)[7]</td></tr>
<tr><td></td><td>12 Nov 2014 (E) (in relation to the 2014 pilot areas[12], in so far as is required for the making of regulations) (SI 2014/3026)[14]</td></tr>
<tr><td></td><td>15 Dec 2014 (E) (in relation to the 2014 pilot areas[12]) (otherwise) (SI 2014/3026)[14]</td></tr>
<tr><td></td><td>*Not yet in force* (otherwise)</td></tr>
<tr><td>para 2(5), (6)</td><td>12 Aug 2007 (W) (in so far as they confer a power, or impose a duty, on the Welsh Ministers to make, or make provision by, regulations; give guidance or directions; or make provision with respect to the exercise of any such power or performance of such duty) (SI 2007/2386)</td></tr>
<tr><td></td><td>1 Oct 2008 (E) (in relation to the pilot areas[6]) (SI 2008/1960)[7]</td></tr>
<tr><td></td><td>12 Nov 2014 (E) (in relation to the 2014 pilot areas[12], in so far as is required for the making of regulations) (SI 2014/3026)[14]</td></tr>
<tr><td></td><td>15 Dec 2014 (E) (in relation to the 2014 pilot areas[12]) (otherwise) (SI 2014/3026)[14]</td></tr>
<tr><td></td><td>*Not yet in force* (otherwise)</td></tr>
<tr><td>para 3</td><td>1 Oct 2008 (E) (in relation to the pilot areas[6]) (SI 2008/1960)[7]</td></tr>
<tr><td></td><td>12 Nov 2014 (E) (in relation to the 2014 pilot areas[12], in so far as is required for the making of regulations) (SI 2014/3026)[14]</td></tr>
<tr><td></td><td>15 Dec 2014 (E) (in relation to the 2014 pilot areas[12]) (otherwise) (SI 2014/3026)[14]</td></tr>
<tr><td></td><td>*Not yet in force* (otherwise)</td></tr>
<tr><td>paras 4, 5</td><td>12 Aug 2007 (W) (in so far as they confer a power, or impose a duty, on the Welsh Ministers to make, or make provision by, regulations; give guidance or directions; or make provision with respect to the exercise of any such power or performance of such duty) (SI 2007/2386)</td></tr>
<tr><td></td><td>1 Oct 2008 (E) (in relation to the pilot areas[6]) (SI 2008/1960)[7]</td></tr>
<tr><td></td><td>12 Nov 2014 (E) (in relation to the 2014 pilot areas[12], in so far as is required for the making of regulations) (SI 2014/3026)[14]</td></tr>
<tr><td></td><td>15 Dec 2014 (E) (in relation to the 2014 pilot areas[12]) (otherwise) (SI 2014/3026)[14]</td></tr>
<tr><td></td><td>*Not yet in force* (otherwise)</td></tr>
<tr><td>paras 6, 7, 8(1)</td><td>1 Oct 2008 (E) (in relation to the pilot areas[6]) (SI 2008/1960)[7]</td></tr>
<tr><td></td><td>12 Nov 2014 (E) (in relation to the 2014 pilot areas[12], in so far as is required for the making of regulations) (SI 2014/3026)[14]</td></tr>
<tr><td></td><td>15 Dec 2014 (E) (in relation to the 2014 pilot areas[12]) (otherwise) (SI 2014/3026)[14]</td></tr>
<tr><td></td><td>*Not yet in force* (otherwise)</td></tr>
<tr><td>para 8(2), (3)</td><td>12 Aug 2007 (W) (in so far as they confer a power, or impose a duty, on the Welsh Ministers to make, or make provision by, regulations; give guidance or directions; or make provision with respect to the exercise of any such power or performance of such duty) (SI 2007/2386)</td></tr>
<tr><td></td><td>1 Oct 2008 (E) (in relation to the pilot areas[6]) (SI 2008/1960)[7]</td></tr>
<tr><td></td><td>12 Nov 2014 (E) (in relation to the 2014 pilot areas[12], in so far as is required for the making of regulations) (SI 2014/3026)[14]</td></tr>
<tr><td></td><td>15 Dec 2014 (E) (in relation to the 2014 pilot areas[12]) (otherwise) (SI 2014/3026)[14]</td></tr>
</table>

**Commons Act 2006 (c 26)**—*contd*

|  |  |  |
|---|---|---|
|  |  | *Not yet in force* (otherwise) |
|  | para 9 | 1 Oct 2006 (E) (SI 2006/2504) |
|  |  | 6 Sep 2007 (W) (SI 2007/2386) |
| Sch 4 | paras 1, 2 | 1 Oct 2007 (SI 2007/2584)[4] |
|  | paras 3–5 | 1 Oct 2007 (E) (SI 2007/2584)[4] |
|  |  | 1 Apr 2012 (W) (SI 2012/739)[10] |
|  | para 6 | 1 Oct 2006 (E) (SI 2006/2504) |
|  |  | 6 Sep 2007 (W) (SI 2007/2386) |
|  | para 7 | 1 Oct 2007 (E) (SI 2007/2584) |
|  |  | 1 Apr 2012 (W) (SI 2012/739) |
| Sch 5 | paras 1, 2 | 31 Oct 2011 (E) (SI 2011/2460)[9] |
|  |  | *Not yet in force* (W) |
|  | para 3 | 31 Oct 2011 (E) (in relation to the pilot areas[6]) (SI 2011/2460) |
|  |  | 12 Nov 2014 (E) (in relation to the 2014 pilot areas[12], in so far as is required for the making of regulations) (SI 2014/3026)[14] |
|  |  | 15 Dec 2014 (E) (in relation to the 2014 pilot areas[12]) (otherwise) (SI 2014/3026)[14] |
|  |  | *Not yet in force* (otherwise) |
|  | para 4 | 20 Feb 2007 (E) (SI 2007/456) |
|  |  | 6 Sep 2007 (W) (SI 2007/2386) |
|  | para 5(a), (b) | 31 Oct 2011 (E) (SI 2011/2460)[9] |
|  |  | *Not yet in force* (W) |
|  | para 5(c) | 31 Oct 2011 (E) (SI 2011/2460)[9] |
|  |  | 30 Sep 2021 (W) (SI 2021/1015) |
|  | para 6(a) | 20 Feb 2007 (E) (SI 2007/456) |
|  |  | 6 Sep 2007 (W) (SI 2007/2386) |
|  | para 6(b) | 31 Oct 2011 (E) (in relation to the pilot areas[6]) (SI 2011/2460) |
|  |  | 12 Nov 2014 (E) (in relation to the 2014 pilot areas[12], in so far as is required for the making of regulations) (SI 2014/3026)[14] |
|  |  | 15 Dec 2014 (E) (in relation to the 2014 pilot areas[12]) (otherwise) (SI 2014/3026)[14] |
|  |  | *Not yet in force* (otherwise) |
|  | para 7(1) | See sub-paras (2)–(5) below |
|  | para 7(2)–(4) | 31 Oct 2011 (E) (in relation to the pilot areas[6]) (SI 2011/2460) |
|  |  | 12 Nov 2014 (E) (in relation to the 2014 pilot areas[12], in so far as is required for the making of regulations) (SI 2014/3026)[14] |
|  |  | 15 Dec 2014 (E) (in relation to the 2014 pilot areas[12]) (otherwise) (SI 2014/3026)[14] |
|  |  | *Not yet in force* (otherwise) |
|  | para 7(5) | 1 Oct 2006 (E) (SI 2006/2504) |
|  |  | 6 Sep 2007 (W) (SI 2007/2386) |
|  | para 8 | 31 Oct 2011 (E) (in relation to the pilot areas[6]) (SI 2011/2460) |
|  |  | 12 Nov 2014 (E) (in relation to the 2014 pilot areas[12], in so far as is required for the making of regulations) (SI 2014/3026)[14] |
|  |  | 15 Dec 2014 (E) (in relation to the 2014 pilot areas[12]) (otherwise) (SI 2014/3026)[14] |
|  |  | *Not yet in force* (otherwise) |
| Sch 6 | Pt 1 | 1 Oct 2006 (E) (SI 2006/2504), repeals of or in— |
|  |  | Commons Registration Act 1965, ss 8, 9, 13(a)[1]; |
|  |  | Local Government Act 1972; |
|  |  | Local Government Act 1985; |
|  |  | Dartmoor Commons Act 1985; |
|  |  | Common Land (Rectification of Registers) Act 1989; |
|  |  | Countryside and Rights of Way Act 2000, s 46(1); |
|  |  | Greenham and Crookham Commons Act 2002 |
|  |  | 6 Apr 2007 (E) (SI 2007/456), repeals of or in— |
|  |  | Commons Registration Act 1965, s 13(b)[2]; |
|  |  | Countryside and Rights of Way Act 2000, s 98 |
|  |  | 6 Sep 2007 (W) (SI 2007/2386), repeals of or in— |

**Commons Act 2006 (c 26)**—*contd*

          Commons Registration Act 1965[3], ss 8, 9, 13(a), (b);
          Local Government Act 1972;
          Local Government Act 1985;
          Dartmoor Commons Act 1985;
          Common Land (Rectification of Registers) Act 1989;
          Countryside and Rights of Way Act 2000, ss 46(1), 98;
          Greenham and Crookham Commons Act 2002
       1 Oct 2008 (E) (in relation to the pilot areas[6]) (SI 2008/1960)[7], repeals of or in—
          Commons Registration Act 1965, ss 1–7, 10–12, 13(c), 14–16, 19
       1 Dec 2010 (SI 2010/2356)[8], repeals of or in—
          Commons Registration Act 1965, ss 4–7, 17, 18, 19(1)(c), (e), (f), (h), (i) (in so far as the repeal of these provisions has not already been commenced), and s 19(1)(k) (in so far as it relates to the making of regulations which prescribe anything required or authorised to be prescribed by ss 4–7 of the 1965 Act);
          Parliamentary Commissioner Act 1967;
          Tribunals and Inquiries Act 1992;
          Judicial Pensions and Retirement Act 1993;
          Constitutional Reform Act 2005
       12 Nov 2014 (E) (in relation to the 2014 pilot areas[12], in so far as is required for the making of regulations) (SI 2014/3026)[14] repeals of or in—
          Commons Registration Act 1965, ss 1–3, 10–12, 13(c), 14–16 and 19 (all except as noted above), and ss 20–25
       15 Dec 2014 (E) (in relation to the 2014 pilot areas[12]) (otherwise) (SI 2014/3026)[14]
       *Not yet in force* (otherwise)
       *Not yet in force*, repeals of or in—
          Courts and Legal Services Act 1990;
          Countryside and Rights of Way Act 2000, s 1;
          Land Registration Act 2002

Pt 2     1 Oct 2006 (E) (SI 2006/2504), repeals of or in—
          Metropolitan Commons Act 1866;
          Commons Act 1876, s 30;
          Commons Act 1899;
          Compulsory Purchase Act 1965
       6 Sep 2007 (W) (SI 2007/2386), repeals of or in—
          Metropolitan Commons Act 1866;
          Commons Act 1876, s 30;
          Commons Act 1899;
          Compulsory Purchase Act 1965
       1 Oct 2007 (E) (otherwise) (SI 2007/2584)[4]
       1 Apr 2012 (W) (otherwise) (SI 2012/739)[10]

Pt 3     1 Oct 2006 (E) (SI 2006/2504), repeals of or in—
          Commons Act 1285;
          Law of Commons Amendment Act 1893
       6 Sep 2007 (W) (SI 2007/2386), repeals of or in—
          Commons Act 1285;
          Commons Act 1876;
          Law of Commons Amendment Act 1893
       1 Oct 2007 (E) (otherwise) (SI 2007/2584)[4]
       1 Apr 2012 (W) (otherwise) (SI 2012/739)[10]

Pt 4     *Not yet in force*

Pt 5     6 Sep 2007 (W) (SI 2007/2386)[11]
       1 Oct 2007 (E) (SI 2007/2584)[5]

---

[1]   For transitional provisions and savings, see SI 2006/2504, art 3

## Commons Act 2006 (c 26)—*contd*

[2]   For transitional provisions and savings, see SI 2007/456, art 4

[3]   For transitional provisions and savings, see SI 2007/2386, art 4

[4]   For transitional provisions and savings, see SI 2007/2584, art 3

[5]   Note that s 51 and Sch 6, Pt 5 both make the same repeal, but come into force on different days in relation to England

[6]   The pilot areas are: Blackburn with Darwen Borough Council, Cornwall County Council, Devon County Council, County of Herefordshire District Council, Hertfordshire County Council, Kent County Council and Lancashire County Council; see SI 2008/1960, art 2(a), Schedule

[7]   For transitional provisions and savings, see SI 2008/1960, art 3

[8]   For transitional provisions and savings, see SI 2010/2356, arts 4, 5

[9]   For transitional provisions, see SI 2011/2460, art 3

[10]   For transitional provisions and savings, see SI 2012/739, art 4

[11]   Note that SI 2012/739, art 2(h)(ii) purports to bring this Part of this Schedule into force in relation to Wales, in so far as not already in force, on 1 Apr 2012

[12]   The 2014 pilot areas are: Cumbria County Council and North Yorkshire County Council; see SI 2014/3026, art 2

[13]   The other registration areas are the registration areas in England of all commons registration authorities that are neither part of the pilot areas nor part of the 2014 pilot areas; see SI 2014/3026, art 2

[14]   For transitional provisions and savings, see SI 2014/3026, arts 4, 5

[15]   For transitional provisions, see SI 2017/933, art 4

## Companies Act 2006 (c 46)

*RA:* 8 Nov 2006

*Commencement provisions:* s 1300; Companies Act 2006 (Commencement No 1, Transitional Provisions and Savings) Order 2006, SI 2006/3428[1], as amended by SI 2007/2194, SI 2007/3495, SI 2008/2860, SI 2009/2392; Companies Act 2006 (Commencement No 2, Consequential Amendments, Transitional Provisions and Savings) Order 2007, SI 2007/1093[2], as amended by SI 2007/2194, SI 2008/948, SI 2008/2860, SI 2009/1941; Companies Act 2006 (Commencement No 3, Consequential Amendments, Transitional Provisions and Savings) Order 2007, SI 2007/2194[3], as amended by SI 2007/2607, SI 2007/2974, SI 2007/3495, SI 2008/674, SI 2008/948, SI 2008/2860, Housing and Regeneration Act 2008, s 321(1), Sch 16, SI 2009/1632, SI 2009/1941, Charities Act 2011, s 354(4), Sch 10, Co-operative and Community Benefit Societies Act 2014, s 151(4), Sch 7; Companies Act 2006 (Commencement No 4 and Commencement No 3 (Amendment)) Order 2007, SI 2007/2607; Companies Act 2006 (Commencement No 5, Transitional Provisions and Savings) Order 2007, SI 2007/3495[5], as amended by SI 2008/674, SI 2008/1886[7], SI 2008/2860; Companies Act 2006 (Commencement No 6, Saving and Commencement Nos 3 and 5 (Amendment)) Order 2008, SI 2008/674[6], as amended by SI 2008/2860; Companies Act 2006 (Commencement No 7, Transitional Provisions and Savings) Order 2008, SI 2008/1886[7], as amended by SI 2008/2860; Companies Act 2006 (Commencement No 8, Transitional Provisions and Savings) Order 2008, SI 2008/2860[8], as amended by SI 2009/1802, SI 2009/1941, SI 2009/2476, SI 2011/1265, SI 2013/1947

| | |
|---|---|
| 1 | 1 Oct 2009 (SI 2008/2860) |
| 2 | 1 Jan 2007 (in so far as necessary for the purposes of ss 1068(5), 1077–1080, 1085–1092, 1102–1107, 1111 of this Act) (SI 2006/3428) |
| | 20 Jan 2007 (in so far as necessary for the purposes of ss 308, 333, 463, 791–810, 811(1)–(3), 813, 815–828, 1143–1148, Schs 4, 5 of this Act) (SI 2006/3428) |
| | 6 Apr 2007 (otherwise) (SI 2007/1093)[2] |
| 3–6 | 1 Oct 2009 (SI 2008/2860) |
| 7 | 1 Oct 2009 (SI 2008/2860)[8] |

**Companies Act 2006 (c 46)**—*contd*

| | | |
|---|---|---|
| 8 | | 20 Jan 2007 (for the purpose of enabling the exercise of powers to make orders or regulations by statutory instrument) (SI 2006/3428) |
| | | 1 Oct 2009 (otherwise) (SI 2008/2860)[8] |
| 9 | | 1 Oct 2009 (SI 2008/2860)[8] |
| 10, 11 | | 20 Jan 2007 (for the purpose of enabling the exercise of powers to make orders or regulations by statutory instrument) (SI 2006/3428) |
| | | 1 Oct 2009 (otherwise) (SI 2008/2860)[8] |
| 12–16 | | 1 Oct 2009 (SI 2008/2860)[8] |
| 17 | | 1 Oct 2007 (in so far as necessary for the purposes of the provisions mentioned in SI 2007/2194, art 2(1), (2)) (SI 2007/2194)[3] |
| | | 6 Apr 2008 (in so far as necessary for the purposes of the provisions mentioned in SI 2007/3495, art 3(1)(a)–(t), (2)) (SI 2007/3495) |
| | | 1 Oct 2009 (otherwise) (SI 2008/2860) |
| 18 | | 1 Oct 2009 (SI 2008/2860)[8] |
| 19 | | 20 Jan 2007 (for the purpose of enabling the exercise of powers to make orders or regulations by statutory instrument) (SI 2006/3428) |
| | | 1 Oct 2009 (otherwise) (SI 2008/2860)[8] |
| 20, 21 | | 1 Oct 2009 (SI 2008/2860)[8] |
| 22 | (1) | 1 Oct 2009 (SI 2008/2860)[8] |
| | (2) | *Not yet in force* |
| | (3), (4) | 1 Oct 2009 (SI 2008/2860)[8] |
| 23–28 | | 1 Oct 2009 (SI 2008/2860)[8] |
| 29, 30 | | 1 Oct 2007 (SI 2007/2194)[3] |
| 31 | | 1 Oct 2009 (SI 2008/2860) |
| 32 | | 20 Jan 2007 (for the purpose of enabling the exercise of powers to make orders or regulations by statutory instrument) (SI 2006/3428) |
| | | 1 Oct 2009 (otherwise) (SI 2008/2860)[8] |
| 33–43 | | 1 Oct 2009 (SI 2008/2860)[8] |
| 44 | | 6 Apr 2008 (SI 2007/3495)[5] |
| 45–53 | | 1 Oct 2009 (SI 2008/2860)[8] |
| 54–57 | | 20 Jan 2007 (for the purpose of enabling the exercise of powers to make orders or regulations by statutory instrument) (SI 2006/3428) |
| | | 1 Oct 2009 (otherwise) (SI 2008/2860)[8] |
| 58, 59 | | 1 Oct 2009 (SI 2008/2860) |
| 60 | | 20 Jan 2007 (for the purpose of enabling the exercise of powers to make orders or regulations by statutory instrument) (SI 2006/3428) |
| | | 1 Oct 2009 (otherwise) (SI 2008/2860) |
| 61–64 | | 1 Oct 2009 (SI 2008/2860) |
| 65–67 | | 20 Jan 2007 (for the purpose of enabling the exercise of powers to make orders or regulations by statutory instrument) (SI 2006/3428) |
| | | 1 Oct 2009 (otherwise) (SI 2008/2860)[8] |
| 68 | | 1 Oct 2009 (SI 2008/2860) |
| 69–74 | | 1 Oct 2008 (SI 2007/3495) |
| 75–81 | | 1 Oct 2009 (SI 2008/2860)[8] |
| 82 | | 20 Jan 2007 (for the purpose of enabling the exercise of powers to make orders or regulations by statutory instrument) (SI 2006/3428) |
| | | 1 Oct 2008 (otherwise) (SI 2007/3495) |
| 83–85 | | 1 Oct 2008 (SI 2007/3495) |
| 86–102 | | 1 Oct 2009 (SI 2008/2860)[8] |

**Companies Act 2006 (c 46)**—*contd*

| | |
|---|---|
| 103 | 20 Jan 2007 (for the purpose of enabling the exercise of powers to make orders or regulations by statutory instrument) (SI 2006/3428) |
| | 1 Oct 2009 (otherwise) (SI 2008/2860)[8] |
| 104–107 | 1 Oct 2009 (SI 2008/2860)[8] |
| 108 | 20 Jan 2007 (for the purpose of enabling the exercise of powers to make orders or regulations by statutory instrument) (SI 2006/3428) |
| | 1 Oct 2009 (otherwise) (SI 2008/2860)[8] |
| 109 | 1 Oct 2009 (SI 2008/2860) |
| 110 | 20 Jan 2007 (for the purpose of enabling the exercise of powers to make orders or regulations by statutory instrument) (SI 2006/3428) |
| | 1 Oct 2009 (otherwise) (SI 2008/2860) |
| 111–115 | 1 Oct 2009 (SI 2008/2860) |
| 116 | 20 Jan 2007 (for the purpose of enabling the exercise of powers to make orders or regulations by statutory instrument) (SI 2006/3428) |
| | 1 Oct 2007 (otherwise) (SI 2007/2194)[3] |
| 117–119 | 1 Oct 2007 (SI 2007/2194)[3] |
| 120 | 1 Oct 2009 (SI 2008/2860)[8] |
| 121 | 6 Apr 2008 (SI 2007/3495)[5] |
| 122–127 | 1 Oct 2009 (SI 2008/2860) |
| 128 | 6 Apr 2008 (SI 2007/3495)[5] |
| 129 | 20 Jan 2007 (for the purpose of enabling the exercise of powers to make orders or regulations by statutory instrument) (SI 2006/3428) |
| | 1 Oct 2009 (otherwise) (SI 2008/2860) |
| 130 | 1 Oct 2009 (SI 2008/2860) |
| 131 | 20 Jan 2007 (for the purpose of enabling the exercise of powers to make orders or regulations by statutory instrument) (SI 2006/3428) |
| | 1 Oct 2009 (otherwise) (SI 2008/2860) |
| 132–144 | 1 Oct 2009 (SI 2008/2860) |
| 145–150 | 1 Oct 2007 (SI 2007/2194)[3] |
| 151 | 20 Jan 2007 (for the purpose of enabling the exercise of powers to make orders or regulations by statutory instrument) (SI 2006/3428) |
| | 1 Oct 2007 (otherwise) (SI 2007/2194)[3] |
| 152–154 | 1 Oct 2007 (SI 2007/2194)[3] |
| 155–157 | 1 Oct 2008 (SI 2007/3495)[5] |
| 158 | 20 Jan 2007 (for the purpose of enabling the exercise of powers to make orders or regulations by statutory instrument) (SI 2006/3428) |
| | 1 Oct 2008 (otherwise) (SI 2007/3495) |
| 159 | 1 Oct 2008 (SI 2007/3495) |
| 160, 161 | 1 Oct 2007 (SI 2007/2194)[3] |
| 162 | 20 Jan 2007 (for the purpose of enabling the exercise of powers to make orders or regulations by statutory instrument) (SI 2006/3428) |
| | 1 Oct 2009 (otherwise) (SI 2008/2860)[8] |
| 163–165 | 1 Oct 2009 (SI 2008/2860)[8] |
| 166 | 20 Jan 2007 (for the purpose of enabling the exercise of powers to make orders or regulations by statutory instrument) (SI 2006/3428) |
| | 1 Oct 2009 (otherwise) (SI 2008/2860)[8] |
| 167 | 1 Oct 2009 (SI 2008/2860)[8] |
| 168–174 | 1 Oct 2007 (SI 2007/2194)[3] |
| 175–177 | 1 Oct 2008 (SI 2007/3495)[5] |
| 178–181 | 1 Oct 2007 (SI 2007/2194)[3] |

**Companies Act 2006 (c 46)**—*contd*

| | | |
|---|---|---|
| 182–187 | | 1 Oct 2008 (SI 2007/3495)[5] |
| 188–228 | | 1 Oct 2007 (SI 2007/2194)[3] |
| 229 | | 20 Jan 2007 (for the purpose of enabling the exercise of powers to make orders or regulations by statutory instrument) (SI 2006/3428) |
| | | 1 Oct 2007 (otherwise) (SI 2007/2194)[3] |
| 230–237 | | 1 Oct 2007 (SI 2007/2194)[3] |
| 238 | | 20 Jan 2007 (for the purpose of enabling the exercise of powers to make orders or regulations by statutory instrument) (SI 2006/3428) |
| | | 1 Oct 2007 (otherwise) (SI 2007/2194)[3] |
| 239 | | 1 Oct 2007 (SI 2007/2194)[3] |
| 240–242 | | 1 Oct 2009 (SI 2008/2860)[8] |
| 243 | | 20 Jan 2007 (for the purpose of enabling the exercise of powers to make orders or regulations by statutory instrument) (SI 2006/3428) |
| | | 1 Oct 2009 (otherwise) (SI 2008/2860)[8] |
| 244–247 | | 1 Oct 2009 (SI 2008/2860)[8] |
| 248–257 | | 1 Oct 2007 (SI 2007/2194)[3] |
| 258 | | 20 Jan 2007 (for the purpose of enabling the exercise of powers to make orders or regulations by statutory instrument) (SI 2006/3428) |
| | | 1 Oct 2007 (otherwise) (SI 2007/2194) |
| 259–262 | | 1 Oct 2007 (SI 2007/2194)[3] |
| 263 | | 20 Jan 2007 (for the purpose of enabling the exercise of powers to make orders or regulations by statutory instrument) (SI 2006/3428) |
| | | 1 Oct 2007 (otherwise) (SI 2007/2194)[3] |
| 264–267 | | 1 Oct 2007 (SI 2007/2194)[3] |
| 268 | | 20 Jan 2007 (for the purpose of enabling the exercise of powers to make orders or regulations by statutory instrument) (SI 2006/3428) |
| | | 1 Oct 2007 (otherwise) (SI 2007/2194)[3] |
| 269 | | 1 Oct 2007 (SI 2007/2194)[3] |
| 270–274 | | 6 Apr 2008 (SI 2007/3495)[5] |
| 275 | | 20 Jan 2007 (for the purpose of enabling the exercise of powers to make orders or regulations by statutory instrument) (SI 2006/3428) |
| | | 1 Oct 2009 (otherwise) (SI 2008/2860)[8] |
| 276–278 | | 1 Oct 2009 (SI 2008/2860)[8] |
| 279 | | 20 Jan 2007 (for the purpose of enabling the exercise of powers to make orders or regulations by statutory instrument) (SI 2006/3428) |
| | | 1 Oct 2009 (otherwise) (SI 2008/2860)[8] |
| 280 | | 6 Apr 2008 (SI 2007/3495) |
| 281–307 | | 1 Oct 2007 (SI 2007/2194)[3] |
| 308, 309 | | 20 Jan 2007 (SI 2006/3428) |
| 310–326 | | 1 Oct 2007 (SI 2007/2194)[3] |
| 327 | (1) | 1 Oct 2007 (SI 2007/2194)[3] |
| | (2)(a), (b) | 1 Oct 2007 (SI 2007/2194)[3] |
| | (2)(c) | *Never in force* (repealed) |
| | (3) | 1 Oct 2007 (SI 2007/2194)[3] |
| 328, 329 | | 1 Oct 2007 (SI 2007/2194)[3] |
| 330 | (1)–(5) | 1 Oct 2007 (SI 2007/2194)[3] |
| | (6)(a), (b) | 1 Oct 2007 (SI 2007/2194)[3] |
| | (6)(c) | *Never in force* (repealed) |
| | (7) | 1 Oct 2007 (SI 2007/2194)[3] |
| 331, 332 | | 1 Oct 2007 (SI 2007/2194)[3] |
| 333 | | 20 Jan 2007 (SI 2006/3428) |
| 334–343 | | 1 Oct 2007 (SI 2007/2194)[3] |

**Companies Act 2006 (c 46)**—*contd*

| | | |
|---|---|---|
| 344 | | 20 Jan 2007 (for the purpose of enabling the exercise of powers to make orders or regulations by statutory instrument) (SI 2006/3428) |
| | | 1 Oct 2007 (otherwise) (SI 2007/2194)[3] |
| 345–353 | | 1 Oct 2007 (SI 2007/2194)[3] |
| 354 | | 20 Jan 2007 (for the purpose of enabling the exercise of powers to make orders or regulations by statutory instrument) (SI 2006/3428) |
| | | 1 Oct 2007 (otherwise) (SI 2007/2194)[3] |
| 355–357 | | 1 Oct 2007 (SI 2007/2194)[3] |
| 358 | | 20 Jan 2007 (for the purpose of enabling the exercise of powers to make orders or regulations by statutory instrument) (SI 2006/3428) |
| | | 1 Oct 2007 (otherwise) (SI 2007/2194)[3] |
| 359–361 | | 1 Oct 2007 (SI 2007/2194)[3] |
| 362 | (a) | 1 Oct 2007 (except words "and to independent election candidates") (SI 2007/2194) |
| | | 1 Oct 2008 (exception noted above) (SI 2007/2194)[3] |
| | (b) | 1 Oct 2007 (E) (W) (S) (SI 2007/2194) |
| | | 1 Nov 2007 (NI) (SI 2007/2194)[3] |
| 363 | (1) | 1 Oct 2007 (E) (W) (S) (SI 2007/2194) |
| | | 1 Nov 2007 (NI) (SI 2007/2194)[3] |
| | (2)(a) | 1 Oct 2007 (except words "or an independent election candidate to whom") (SI 2007/2194) |
| | | 1 Oct 2008 (exception noted above) (SI 2007/2194)[3] |
| | (2)(b) | 1 Oct 2007 (E) (W) (S) (SI 2007/2194) |
| | | 1 Nov 2007 (NI) (SI 2007/2194)[3] |
| | (3) | 1 Oct 2008 (SI 2007/2194)[3] |
| | (4) | 1 Oct 2007 (except words "or independent election candidate" and "independent candidate") (SI 2007/2194) |
| | | 1 Oct 2008 (exceptions noted above) (SI 2007/2194)[3] |
| 364 | (1), (2) | 1 Oct 2007 (E) (W) (S) (SI 2007/2194) |
| | | 1 Nov 2007 (NI) (SI 2007/2194)[3] |
| | (3) | 1 Oct 2008 (SI 2007/2194)[3] |
| | (4) | 1 Oct 2007 (E) (W) (S) (SI 2007/2194) |
| | | 1 Nov 2007 (NI) (SI 2007/2194)[3] |
| 365 | (1)(a) | 1 Oct 2007 (except words "or an independent election candidate") (SI 2007/2194) |
| | | 1 Oct 2008 (exception noted above) (SI 2007/2194)[3] |
| | (1)(b)(i) | 1 Oct 2007 (except words "or an independent election candidate") (SI 2007/2194) |
| | | 1 Oct 2008 (exception noted above) (SI 2007/2194)[3] |
| | (1)(b)(ii) | 1 Oct 2007 (E) (W) (S) (SI 2007/2194) |
| | | 1 Nov 2007 (NI) (SI 2007/2194)[3] |
| | (2) | 1 Oct 2007 (E) (W) (S) (SI 2007/2194) |
| | | 1 Nov 2007 (NI) (SI 2007/2194)[3] |
| 366 | (1)(a) | 1 Oct 2007 (except words "or to an independent election candidate") (SI 2007/2194) |
| | | 1 Oct 2008 (exception noted above) (SI 2007/2194)[3] |
| | (1)(b) | 1 Oct 2007 (E) (W) (S) (SI 2007/2194) |
| | | 1 Nov 2007 (NI) (SI 2007/2194)[3] |
| | (2)–(6) | 1 Oct 2007 (E) (W) (S) (SI 2007/2194) |
| | | 1 Nov 2007 (NI) (SI 2007/2194)[3] |
| 367 | (1), (2) | 1 Oct 2007 (E) (W) (S) (SI 2007/2194) |
| | | 1 Nov 2007 (NI) (SI 2007/2194)[3] |
| | (3)(a) | 1 Oct 2007 (except words "or independent election candidates") (SI 2007/2194) |
| | | 1 Oct 2008 (exception noted above) (SI 2007/2194)[3] |
| | (3)(b), (c) | 1 Oct 2007 (E) (W) (S) (SI 2007/2194) |
| | | 1 Nov 2007 (NI) (SI 2007/2194)[3] |

**Companies Act 2006 (c 46)**—*contd*

| | | |
|---|---|---|
| | (4)–(7) | 1 Oct 2007 (E) (W) (S) (SI 2007/2194) |
| | | 1 Nov 2007 (NI) (SI 2007/2194)[3] |
| 368 | | 1 Oct 2007 (E) (W) (S) (SI 2007/2194) |
| | | 1 Nov 2007 (NI) (SI 2007/2194)[3] |
| 369 | | 20 Jan 2007 (for the purpose of enabling the exercise of powers to make orders or regulations by statutory instrument) (SI 2006/3428) |
| | | 1 Oct 2007 (E) (W) (S) (otherwise) (SI 2007/2194) |
| | | 1 Nov 2007 (NI) (otherwise) (SI 2007/2194)[3] |
| 370–376 | | 1 Oct 2007 (E) (W) (S) (SI 2007/2194) |
| | | 1 Nov 2007 (NI) (SI 2007/2194)[3] |
| 377 | | 20 Jan 2007 (for the purpose of enabling the exercise of powers to make orders or regulations by statutory instrument) (SI 2006/3428) |
| | | 1 Oct 2007 (E) (W) (S) (otherwise) (SI 2007/2194) |
| | | 1 Nov 2007 (NI) (otherwise) (SI 2007/2194)[3] |
| 378 | (1) | 1 Oct 2007 (E) (W) (S) (SI 2007/2194) |
| | | 1 Nov 2007 (NI) (SI 2007/2194)[3] |
| | (2) | 1 Oct 2007 (except words "or to an independent election candidate") (SI 2007/2194) |
| | | 1 Oct 2008 (exception noted above) (SI 2007/2194)[3] |
| | (3) | 1 Oct 2007 (E) (W) (S) (SI 2007/2194) |
| | | 1 Nov 2007 (NI) (SI 2007/2194)[3] |
| 379 | | 1 Oct 2007 (E) (W) (S) (SI 2007/2194) |
| | | 1 Nov 2007 (NI) (SI 2007/2194)[3] |
| 380–384 | | 6 Apr 2008 (SI 2007/3495)[5] |
| 385 | | 20 Jan 2007 (for the purpose of enabling the exercise of powers to make orders or regulations by statutory instrument) (SI 2006/3428) |
| | | 1 Oct 2007 (in so far as necessary for the purposes of the provisions mentioned in SI 2007/2194, art 2(1), (2)) (SI 2007/2194) |
| | | 6 Apr 2008 (otherwise) (SI 2007/3495)[5] |
| 386–395 | | 6 Apr 2008 (SI 2007/3495)[5] |
| 396 | | 20 Jan 2007 (for the purpose of enabling the exercise of powers to make orders or regulations by statutory instrument) (SI 2006/3428) |
| | | 6 Apr 2008 (otherwise) (SI 2007/3495) |
| 397–403 | | 6 Apr 2008 (SI 2007/3495) |
| 404 | | 20 Jan 2007 (for the purpose of enabling the exercise of powers to make orders or regulations by statutory instrument) (SI 2006/3428) |
| | | 6 Apr 2008 (otherwise) (SI 2007/3495) |
| 405–408 | | 6 Apr 2008 (SI 2007/3495) |
| 409 | | 20 Jan 2007 (for the purpose of enabling the exercise of powers to make orders or regulations by statutory instrument) (SI 2006/3428) |
| | | 6 Apr 2008 (otherwise) (SI 2007/3495) |
| 410, 411 | | 6 Apr 2008 (SI 2007/3495) |
| 412 | | 20 Jan 2007 (for the purpose of enabling the exercise of powers to make orders or regulations by statutory instrument) (SI 2006/3428) |
| | | 6 Apr 2008 (otherwise) (SI 2007/3495) |
| 413–415 | | 6 Apr 2008 (SI 2007/3495) |
| 416 | | 20 Jan 2007 (for the purpose of enabling the exercise of powers to make orders or regulations by statutory instrument) (SI 2006/3428) |
| | | 6 Apr 2008 (otherwise) (SI 2007/3495) |
| 417 | | 1 Oct 2007 (SI 2007/2194)[3] |
| 418–420 | | 6 Apr 2008 (SI 2007/3495) |

**Companies Act 2006 (c 46)**—*contd*

| | |
|---|---|
| 421 | 20 Jan 2007 (for the purpose of enabling the exercise of powers to make orders or regulations by statutory instrument) (SI 2006/3428) |
| | 6 Apr 2008 (otherwise) (SI 2007/3495) |
| 422–425 | 6 Apr 2008 (SI 2007/3495) |
| 426–428 | 20 Jan 2007 (for the purpose of enabling the exercise of powers to make orders or regulations by statutory instrument) (SI 2006/3428) |
| | 6 Apr 2008 (otherwise) (SI 2007/3495) |
| 429–443 | 6 Apr 2008 (SI 2007/3495) |
| 444, 445 | 20 Jan 2007 (for the purpose of enabling the exercise of powers to make orders or regulations by statutory instrument) (SI 2006/3428) |
| | 6 Apr 2008 (otherwise) (SI 2007/3495) |
| 446–452 | 6 Apr 2008 (SI 2007/3495) |
| 453, 454 | 20 Jan 2007 (for the purpose of enabling the exercise of powers to make orders or regulations by statutory instrument) (SI 2006/3428) |
| | 6 Apr 2008 (otherwise) (SI 2007/3495) |
| 455, 456 | 6 Apr 2008 (SI 2007/3495) |
| 457 | 20 Jan 2007 (for the purpose of enabling the exercise of powers to make orders or regulations by statutory instrument) (SI 2006/3428) |
| | 6 Apr 2008 (otherwise) (SI 2007/3495) |
| 458–461 | 6 Apr 2008 (SI 2007/3495) |
| 462 | 20 Jan 2007 (for the purpose of enabling the exercise of powers to make orders or regulations by statutory instrument) (SI 2006/3428) |
| | 6 Apr 2008 (otherwise) (SI 2007/3495) |
| 463 | 20 Jan 2007 (SI 2006/3428)[1] |
| 464 | 20 Jan 2007 (for the purpose of enabling the exercise of powers to make orders or regulations by statutory instrument) (SI 2006/3428) |
| | 6 Apr 2008 (otherwise) (SI 2007/3495) |
| 465–467 | 6 Apr 2008 (SI 2007/3495) |
| 468 | 20 Jan 2007 (for the purpose of enabling the exercise of powers to make orders or regulations by statutory instrument) (SI 2006/3428) |
| | 6 Apr 2008 (otherwise) (SI 2007/3495) |
| 469 | 6 Apr 2008 (SI 2007/3495) |
| 470 | 20 Jan 2007 (for the purpose of enabling the exercise of powers to make orders or regulations by statutory instrument) (SI 2006/3428) |
| | 6 Apr 2008 (otherwise) (SI 2007/3495) |
| 471, 472 | 6 Apr 2008 (SI 2007/3495)[5] |
| 473 | 20 Jan 2007 (for the purpose of enabling the exercise of powers to make orders or regulations by statutory instrument) (SI 2006/3428) |
| | 6 Apr 2008 (otherwise) (SI 2007/3495)[5] |
| 474–482 | 6 Apr 2008 (SI 2007/3495)[5] |
| 483, 484 | 20 Jan 2007 (for the purpose of enabling the exercise of powers to make orders or regulations by statutory instrument) (SI 2006/3428) |
| | 6 Apr 2008 (otherwise) (SI 2007/3495)[5] |
| 485–488 | 1 Oct 2007 (SI 2007/2194)[3] |
| 489–492 | 6 Apr 2008 (SI 2007/3495)[5] |
| 493, 494 | 20 Jan 2007 (for the purpose of enabling the exercise of powers to make orders or regulations by statutory instrument) (SI 2006/3428) |
| | 6 Apr 2008 (otherwise) (SI 2007/3495)[5] |

Companies Act 2006 (c 46)—*contd*

| | | |
|---|---|---|
| 495–503 | | 6 Apr 2008 (SI 2007/3495)[5] |
| 504 | | 20 Jan 2007 (for the purpose of enabling the exercise of powers to make orders or regulations by statutory instrument) (SI 2006/3428) |
| | | 6 Apr 2008 (otherwise) (SI 2007/3495)[5] |
| 505–534 | | 6 Apr 2008 (SI 2007/3495)[5] |
| 535 | | 20 Jan 2007 (for the purpose of enabling the exercise of powers to make orders or regulations by statutory instrument) (SI 2006/3428) |
| | | 6 Apr 2008 (otherwise) (SI 2007/3495) |
| 536, 537 | | 6 Apr 2008 (SI 2007/3495) |
| 538 | | 20 Jan 2007 (for the purpose of enabling the exercise of powers to make orders or regulations by statutory instrument) (SI 2006/3428) |
| | | 6 Apr 2008 (otherwise) (SI 2007/3495) |
| 539 | | 6 Apr 2008 (SI 2007/3495) |
| 540 | (1) | 1 Oct 2007 (in so far as necessary for the purposes of the provisions mentioned in SI 2007/2194, art 2(1), (2)) (SI 2007/2194) |
| | | 6 Apr 2008 (in so far as necessary for the purposes of the provisions mentioned in SI 2007/3495, art 3(1)(a)–(t), (2)) (SI 2007/3495) |
| | | 1 Oct 2009 (otherwise) (SI 2008/2860) |
| | (2), (3) | 1 Oct 2009 (SI 2008/2860)[8] |
| | (4) | 1 Oct 2007 (in so far as necessary for the purposes of the provisions mentioned in SI 2007/2194, art 2(1), (2)) (SI 2007/2194) |
| | | 6 Apr 2008 (in so far as necessary for the purposes of the provisions mentioned in SI 2007/3495, art 3(1)(a)–(t), (2)) (SI 2007/3495) |
| | | 1 Oct 2009 (otherwise) (SI 2008/2860) |
| 541–543 | | 1 Oct 2009 (SI 2008/2860) |
| 544 | | 6 Apr 2008 (SI 2007/3495) |
| 545 | | 1 Oct 2007 (in so far as necessary for the purposes of the provisions mentioned in SI 2007/2194, art 2(1), (2)) (SI 2007/2194) |
| | | 6 Apr 2008 (in so far as necessary for the purposes of the provisions mentioned in SI 2007/3495, art 3(1)(a)–(t), (2)) (SI 2007/3495) |
| | | 1 Oct 2009 (otherwise) (SI 2008/2860) |
| 546 | | 6 Apr 2007 (in so far as necessary for the purposes of ss 2, 942–992, 1043, 1170, 1284(1), Sch 2 of this Act) (SI 2007/1093) |
| | | 1 Oct 2007 (in so far as necessary for the purposes of the provisions mentioned in SI 2007/2194, art 2(1), (2)) (SI 2007/2194) |
| | | 1 Nov 2007 (in so far as necessary for the purposes of the provisions mentioned in SI 2007/2194, art 3(1)) (SI 2007/2194) |
| | | 6 Apr 2008 (in so far as necessary for the purposes of the provisions mentioned in SI 2007/3495, art 3(1)(a)–(t), (2)) (SI 2007/3495) |
| | | 1 Oct 2009 (otherwise) (SI 2008/2860) |
| 547 | | 1 Oct 2009 (SI 2008/2860) |
| 548 | | 1 Oct 2007 (in so far as necessary for the purposes of the provisions mentioned in SI 2007/2194, art 2(1), (2)) (SI 2007/2194) |
| | | 6 Apr 2008 (in so far as necessary for the purposes of the provisions mentioned in SI 2007/3495, art 3(1)(a)–(t), (2)) (SI 2007/3495) |
| | | 1 Oct 2009 (otherwise) (SI 2008/2860) |

**Companies Act 2006 (c 46)**—*contd*

| | | |
|---|---|---|
| 549–554 | | 1 Oct 2009 (SI 2008/2860)[8] |
| 555, 556 | | 20 Jan 2007 (for the purpose of enabling the exercise of powers to make orders or regulations by statutory instrument) (SI 2006/3428) |
| | | 1 Oct 2009 (otherwise) (SI 2008/2860)[8] |
| 557 | | 1 Oct 2009 (SI 2008/2860) |
| 558 | | 6 Apr 2007 (in so far as necessary for the purposes of ss 2, 942–992, 1043, 1170, 1284(1), Sch 2 of this Act) (SI 2007/1093) |
| | | 1 Oct 2009 (otherwise) (SI 2008/2860) |
| 559–561 | | 1 Oct 2009 (SI 2008/2860)[8] |
| 562 | | 20 Jan 2007 (for the purpose of enabling the exercise of powers to make orders or regulations by statutory instrument) (SI 2006/3428) |
| | | 1 Oct 2009 (otherwise) (SI 2008/2860)[8] |
| 563–582 | | 1 Oct 2009 (SI 2008/2860)[8] |
| 583 | | 20 Jan 2007 (for the purpose of enabling the exercise of powers to make orders or regulations by statutory instrument) (SI 2006/3428) |
| | | 1 Oct 2009 (otherwise) (SI 2008/2860)[8] |
| 584–591 | | 1 Oct 2009 (SI 2008/2860)[8] |
| 592 | | 20 Jan 2007 (for the purpose of enabling the exercise of powers to make orders or regulations by statutory instrument) (SI 2006/3428) |
| | | 1 Oct 2009 (otherwise) (SI 2008/2860) |
| 593–608 | | 1 Oct 2009 (SI 2008/2860)[8] |
| 609 | | 20 Jan 2007 (for the purpose of enabling the exercise of powers to make orders or regulations by statutory instrument) (SI 2006/3428) |
| | | 1 Oct 2009 (otherwise) (SI 2008/2860) |
| 610 | (1) | 1 Oct 2009 (SI 2008/2860) |
| | (2)–(4) | 1 Oct 2008 (so far as relating to a reduction of capital under ss 641(1)(a), (2)–(6), 642–644 of this Act) (SI 2008/1886) |
| | | 1 Oct 2009 (otherwise) (SI 2008/2860) |
| | (5), (6) | 1 Oct 2009 (SI 2008/2860) |
| 611–613 | | 1 Oct 2009 (SI 2008/2860) |
| 614 | | 20 Jan 2007 (for the purpose of enabling the exercise of powers to make orders or regulations by statutory instrument) (SI 2006/3428) |
| | | 1 Oct 2009 (otherwise) (SI 2008/2860) |
| 615–618 | | 1 Oct 2009 (SI 2008/2860) |
| 619 | | 20 Jan 2007 (for the purpose of enabling the exercise of powers to make orders or regulations by statutory instrument) (SI 2006/3428) |
| | | 1 Oct 2009 (otherwise) (SI 2008/2860) |
| 620 | | 1 Oct 2009 (SI 2008/2860) |
| 621 | | 20 Jan 2007 (for the purpose of enabling the exercise of powers to make orders or regulations by statutory instrument) (SI 2006/3428) |
| | | 1 Oct 2009 (otherwise) (SI 2008/2860) |
| 622–624 | | 1 Oct 2009 (SI 2008/2860) |
| 625 | | 20 Jan 2007 (for the purpose of enabling the exercise of powers to make orders or regulations by statutory instrument) (SI 2006/3428) |
| | | 1 Oct 2009 (otherwise) (SI 2008/2860) |
| 626 | | 1 Oct 2009 (SI 2008/2860) |
| 627 | | 20 Jan 2007 (for the purpose of enabling the exercise of powers to make orders or regulations by statutory instrument) (SI 2006/3428) |
| | | 1 Oct 2009 (otherwise) (SI 2008/2860) |

**Companies Act 2006 (c 46)**—*contd*

| | | |
|---|---|---|
| 628 | | 1 Oct 2009 (SI 2008/2860) |
| 629 | | 1 Oct 2007 (in so far as necessary for the purposes of the provisions mentioned in SI 2007/2194, art 2(1), (2)) (SI 2007/2194) |
| | | 6 Apr 2008 (in so far as necessary for the purposes of the provisions mentioned in SI 2007/3495, art 3(1)(a)–(t), (2)) (SI 2007/3495) |
| | | 1 Oct 2009 (otherwise) (SI 2008/2860) |
| 630–640 | | 1 Oct 2009 (SI 2008/2860)[8] |
| 641 | (1)(a) | 1 Oct 2008 (SI 2008/1886) |
| | (1)(b) | 1 Oct 2009 (SI 2008/2860) |
| | (2)–(6) | 1 Oct 2008 (SI 2008/1886) |
| 642 | | 1 Oct 2008 (SI 2008/1886) |
| 643, 644 | | 20 Jan 2007 (for the purpose of enabling the exercise of powers to make orders or regulations by statutory instrument) (SI 2006/3428) |
| | | 1 Oct 2008 (otherwise) (SI 2008/1886) |
| 645–648 | | 1 Oct 2009 (SI 2008/2860)[8] |
| 649 | | 20 Jan 2007 (for the purpose of enabling the exercise of powers to make orders or regulations by statutory instrument) (SI 2006/3428) |
| | | 1 Oct 2009 (otherwise) (SI 2008/2860) |
| 650, 651 | | 1 Oct 2009 (SI 2008/2860) |
| 652 | (1) | 1 Oct 2008 (so far as relating to a reduction of capital under ss 641(1)(a), (2)–(6), 642–644 of this Act) (SI 2008/1886) |
| | | 1 Oct 2009 (otherwise) (SI 2008/2860) |
| | (2) | 1 Oct 2009 (SI 2008/2860) |
| | (3) | 1 Oct 2008 (so far as relating to a reduction of capital under ss 641(1)(a), (2)–(6), 642–644 of this Act) (SI 2008/1886) |
| | | 1 Oct 2009 (otherwise) (SI 2008/2860) |
| 653 | | 1 Oct 2009 (SI 2008/2860) |
| 654 | | 20 Jan 2007 (for the purpose of enabling the exercise of powers to make orders or regulations by statutory instrument) (SI 2006/3428) |
| | | 1 Oct 2008 (otherwise) (SI 2008/1886)[7] |
| 655, 656 | | 1 Oct 2009 (SI 2008/2860) |
| 657 | | 20 Jan 2007 (for the purpose of enabling the exercise of powers to make orders or regulations by statutory instrument) (SI 2006/3428) |
| | | 1 Oct 2009 (otherwise) (SI 2008/2860) |
| 658–662 | | 1 Oct 2009 (SI 2008/2860)[8] |
| 663 | | 20 Jan 2007 (for the purpose of enabling the exercise of powers to make orders or regulations by statutory instrument) (SI 2006/3428) |
| | | 1 Oct 2009 (otherwise) (SI 2008/2860)[8] |
| 664–688 | | 1 Oct 2009 (SI 2008/2860)[8] |
| 689 | | 20 Jan 2007 (for the purpose of enabling the exercise of powers to make orders or regulations by statutory instrument) (SI 2006/3428) |
| | | 1 Oct 2009 (otherwise) (SI 2008/2860)[8] |
| 690–707 | | 1 Oct 2009 (SI 2008/2860)[8] |
| 708 | | 20 Jan 2007 (for the purpose of enabling the exercise of powers to make orders or regulations by statutory instrument) (SI 2006/3428) |
| | | 1 Oct 2009 (otherwise) (SI 2008/2860)[8] |
| 709–713 | | 1 Oct 2009 (SI 2008/2860)[8] |
| 714 | | 20 Jan 2007 (for the purpose of enabling the exercise of powers to make orders or regulations by statutory instrument) (SI 2006/3428) |
| | | 1 Oct 2009 (otherwise) (SI 2008/2860)[8] |

**Companies Act 2006 (c 46)**—*contd*

| | | |
|---|---|---|
| 715–726 | | 1 Oct 2009 (SI 2008/2860)[8] |
| 727 | | 20 Jan 2007 (for the purpose of enabling the exercise of powers to make orders or regulations by statutory instrument) (SI 2006/3428) |
| | | 1 Oct 2009 (otherwise) (SI 2008/2860)[8] |
| 728, 729 | | 1 Oct 2009 (SI 2008/2860) |
| 730 | | 20 Jan 2007 (for the purpose of enabling the exercise of powers to make orders or regulations by statutory instrument) (SI 2006/3428) |
| | | 1 Oct 2009 (otherwise) (SI 2008/2860)[8] |
| 731, 732 | | 1 Oct 2009 (SI 2008/2860) |
| 733 | (1)–(4) | 1 Oct 2009 (SI 2008/2860) |
| | (5), (6) | 1 Oct 2008 (so far as relating to a reduction of capital under ss 641(1)(a), (2)–(6), 642–644 of this Act) (SI 2008/1886) |
| | | 1 Oct 2009 (otherwise) (SI 2008/2860) |
| 734–736 | | 1 Oct 2009 (SI 2008/2860) |
| 737 | | 20 Jan 2007 (for the purpose of enabling the exercise of powers to make orders or regulations by statutory instrument) (SI 2006/3428) |
| | | 1 Oct 2009 (otherwise) (SI 2008/2860) |
| 738–743 | | 6 Apr 2008 (SI 2007/3495)[5] |
| 744 | | 20 Jan 2007 (for the purpose of enabling the exercise of powers to make orders or regulations by statutory instrument) (SI 2006/3428) |
| | | 6 Apr 2008 (otherwise) (SI 2007/3495)[5] |
| 745–748 | | 6 Apr 2008 (SI 2007/3495)[5] |
| 749 | | 20 Jan 2007 (for the purpose of enabling the exercise of powers to make orders or regulations by statutory instrument) (SI 2006/3428) |
| | | 6 Apr 2008 (otherwise) (SI 2007/3495) |
| 750–762 | | 6 Apr 2008 (SI 2007/3495)[5] |
| 763, 764 | | 20 Jan 2007 (for the purpose of enabling the exercise of powers to make orders or regulations by statutory instrument) (SI 2006/3428) |
| | | 6 Apr 2008 (otherwise) (SI 2007/3495) |
| 765 | | 6 Apr 2008 (SI 2007/3495) |
| 766 | | 20 Jan 2007 (for the purpose of enabling the exercise of powers to make orders or regulations by statutory instrument) (SI 2006/3428) |
| | | 6 Apr 2008 (otherwise) (SI 2007/3495) |
| 767–783 | | 6 Apr 2008 (SI 2007/3495)[5] |
| 784–789 | | 20 Jan 2007 (for the purpose of enabling the exercise of powers to make orders or regulations by statutory instrument) (SI 2006/3428) |
| | | 6 Apr 2008 (otherwise) (SI 2007/3495) |
| 790 | | 6 Apr 2008 (SI 2007/3495) |
| 791–810 | | 20 Jan 2007 (SI 2006/3428)[1] |
| 811 | (1)–(3) | 20 Jan 2007 (SI 2006/3428) |
| | (4) | 6 Apr 2008 (SI 2007/3495)[5] |
| 812 | | 6 Apr 2008 (SI 2007/3495)[5] |
| 813 | | 20 Jan 2007 (SI 2006/3428)[1] |
| 814 | | 6 Apr 2008 (SI 2007/3495)[5] |
| 815–828 | | 20 Jan 2007 (SI 2006/3428)[1] |
| 829–834 | | 6 Apr 2008 (SI 2007/3495)[5] |
| 835 | | 20 Jan 2007 (for the purpose of enabling the exercise of powers to make orders or regulations by statutory instrument) (SI 2006/3428) |
| | | 6 Apr 2008 (otherwise) (SI 2007/3495)[5] |
| 836–853 | | 6 Apr 2008 (SI 2007/3495)[5] |
| 854 | | 1 Oct 2009 (SI 2008/2860)[8] |

**Companies Act 2006 (c 46)**—*contd*

| | |
|---|---|
| 855–857 | 20 Jan 2007 (for the purpose of enabling the exercise of powers to make orders or regulations by statutory instrument) (SI 2006/3428) |
| | 1 Oct 2009 (otherwise) (SI 2008/2860)[8] |
| 858, 859 | 1 Oct 2009 (SI 2008/2860)[8] |
| 860 | 20 Jan 2007 (for the purpose of enabling the exercise of powers to make orders or regulations by statutory instrument) (SI 2006/3428) |
| | 1 Oct 2009 (otherwise) (SI 2008/2860)[8] |
| 861 | 1 Oct 2009 (SI 2008/2860)[8] |
| 862 | 20 Jan 2007 (for the purpose of enabling the exercise of powers to make orders or regulations by statutory instrument) (SI 2006/3428) |
| | 1 Oct 2009 (otherwise) (SI 2008/2860)[8] |
| 863–876 | 1 Oct 2009 (SI 2008/2860)[8] |
| 877, 878 | 20 Jan 2007 (for the purpose of enabling the exercise of powers to make orders or regulations by statutory instrument) (SI 2006/3428) |
| | 1 Oct 2009 (otherwise) (SI 2008/2860)[8] |
| 879 | 1 Oct 2009 (SI 2008/2860) |
| 880 | 20 Jan 2007 (for the purpose of enabling the exercise of powers to make orders or regulations by statutory instrument) (SI 2006/3428) |
| | 1 Oct 2009 (otherwise) (SI 2008/2860)[8] |
| 881–891 | 1 Oct 2009 (SI 2008/2860)[8] |
| 892–894 | 20 Jan 2007 (for the purpose of enabling the exercise of powers to make orders or regulations by statutory instrument) (SI 2006/3428) |
| | 1 Oct 2009 (otherwise) (SI 2008/2860) |
| 895–935 | 6 Apr 2008 (SI 2007/3495)[5] |
| 936 | 20 Jan 2007 (for the purpose of enabling the exercise of powers to make orders or regulations by statutory instrument) (SI 2006/3428) |
| | 6 Apr 2008 (otherwise) (SI 2007/3495) |
| 937–941 | 6 Apr 2008 (SI 2007/3495) |
| 942–947 | 6 Apr 2007 (SI 2007/1093)[2] |
| 948 | 20 Jan 2007 (for the purpose of enabling the exercise of powers to make orders or regulations by statutory instrument) (SI 2006/3428) |
| | 6 Apr 2007 (otherwise) (SI 2007/1093) |
| 949–957 | 6 Apr 2007 (SI 2007/1093)[2] |
| 958 | 20 Jan 2007 (for the purpose of enabling the exercise of powers to make orders or regulations by statutory instrument) (SI 2006/3428) |
| | 6 Apr 2007 (otherwise) (SI 2007/1093) |
| 959–964 | 6 Apr 2007 (SI 2007/1093) |
| 965, 966 | 20 Jan 2007 (for the purpose of enabling the exercise of powers to make orders or regulations by statutory instrument) (SI 2006/3428) |
| | 6 Apr 2007 (otherwise) (SI 2007/1093) |
| 967–972 | 6 Apr 2007 (SI 2007/1093)[2] |
| 973 | 20 Jan 2007 (for the purpose of enabling the exercise of powers to make orders or regulations by statutory instrument) (SI 2006/3428) |
| | 6 Apr 2007 (otherwise) (SI 2007/1093) |
| 974–979 | 6 Apr 2007 (SI 2007/1093) |
| 980 | 20 Jan 2007 (for the purpose of enabling the exercise of powers to make orders or regulations by statutory instrument) (SI 2006/3428) |
| | 6 Apr 2007 (otherwise) (SI 2007/1093) |

**Companies Act 2006 (c 46)**—*contd*

| | |
|---|---|
| 981–983 | 6 Apr 2007 (SI 2007/1093) |
| 984 | 20 Jan 2007 (for the purpose of enabling the exercise of powers to make orders or regulations by statutory instrument) (SI 2006/3428) |
| | 6 Apr 2007 (otherwise) (SI 2007/1093) |
| 985–992 | 6 Apr 2007 (SI 2007/1093) |
| 993–999 | 1 Oct 2007 (SI 2007/2194)[3] |
| 1000–1002 | 1 Oct 2008 (SI 2008/2860) |
| 1003, 1004 | 20 Jan 2007 (for the purpose of enabling the exercise of powers to make orders or regulations by statutory instrument) (SI 2006/3428) |
| | 1 Oct 2009 (otherwise) (SI 2008/2860) |
| 1005 | 1 Oct 2009 (SI 2008/2860) |
| 1006, 1007 | 20 Jan 2007 (for the purpose of enabling the exercise of powers to make orders or regulations by statutory instrument) (SI 2006/3428) |
| | 1 Oct 2009 (otherwise) (SI 2008/2860) |
| 1008 | 1 Oct 2009 (SI 2008/2860) |
| 1009 | 20 Jan 2007 (for the purpose of enabling the exercise of powers to make orders or regulations by statutory instrument) (SI 2006/3428) |
| | 1 Oct 2009 (otherwise) (SI 2008/2860) |
| 1010–1034 | 1 Oct 2009 (SI 2008/2860)[8] |
| 1035–1039 | 1 Oct 2007 (SI 2007/2194)[3] |
| 1040, 1041 | 1 Oct 2009 (SI 2008/2860)[8] |
| 1042 | 20 Jan 2007 (for the purpose of enabling the exercise of powers to make orders or regulations by statutory instrument) (SI 2006/3428) |
| | 1 Oct 2009 (otherwise) (SI 2008/2860)[8] |
| 1043 | 20 Jan 2007 (for the purpose of enabling the exercise of powers to make orders or regulations by statutory instrument) (SI 2006/3428) |
| | 6 Apr 2007 (otherwise) (SI 2007/1093) |
| 1044 | 1 Oct 2009 (SI 2008/2860) |
| 1045, 1046 | 20 Jan 2007 (for the purpose of enabling the exercise of powers to make orders or regulations by statutory instrument) (SI 2006/3428) |
| | 1 Oct 2009 (otherwise) (SI 2008/2860) |
| 1047, 1048 | 1 Oct 2009 (SI 2008/2860) |
| 1049–1058 | 20 Jan 2007 (for the purpose of enabling the exercise of powers to make orders or regulations by statutory instrument) (SI 2006/3428) |
| | 1 Oct 2009 (otherwise) (SI 2008/2860) |
| 1059 | 1 Oct 2009 (SI 2008/2860) |
| 1060, 1061 | 6 Apr 2007 (in so far as necessary for the purposes of ss 1063, 1176–1179, 1281, and s 1295, Sch 16 of this Act (so far as relate to the repeal of the provisions of SI 1986/1032, corresponding to the repeal of the Companies Act 1985, ss 1176–1179; the Companies Act 1985, ss 41, 293, 294; SI 1986/1032, arts 51, 301, 302) (SI 2006/3428) |
| | 1 Oct 2009 (otherwise) (SI 2008/2860) |
| 1062 | 1 Oct 2009 (SI 2008/2860) |
| 1063 | 20 Jan 2007 (for the purpose of enabling the exercise of powers to make orders or regulations by statutory instrument) (SI 2006/3428) |
| | 6 Apr 2007 (otherwise, see exception below) (SI 2006/3428)[1] |
| | 1 Oct 2009 (NI) (otherwise) (SI 2008/2860)[8] |
| 1064–1067 | 1 Oct 2009 (SI 2008/2860)[8] |

**Companies Act 2006 (c 46)**—*contd*

| | | |
|---|---|---|
| 1068 | (1)–(4) | 1 Jan 2007 (in so far as necessary for the purposes of ss 1068(5), 1077–1080, 1085–1092, 1102–1107, 1111 of this Act) (SI 2006/3428) |
| | | 15 Dec 2007 (so far as necessary for the purposes of any regulations made before that date in implementation of Directive 2005/56/EC of the European Parliament and of the Council of 26 Oct 2005 on cross-border mergers of limited liability companies) (SI 2007/2194) |
| | | 1 Oct 2009 (otherwise) (SI 2008/2860)[8] |
| | (5) | 1 Jan 2007 (SI 2006/3428) |
| | (6), (7) | 1 Jan 2007 (in so far as necessary for the purposes of ss 1068(5), 1077–1080, 1085–1092, 1102–1107, 1111 of this Act) (SI 2006/3428) |
| | | 15 Dec 2007 (so far as necessary for the purposes of any regulations made before that date in implementation of Directive 2005/56/EC of the European Parliament and of the Council of 26 Oct 2005 on cross-border mergers of limited liability companies) (SI 2007/2194) |
| | | 1 Oct 2009 (otherwise) (SI 2008/2860)[8] |
| 1069 | | 20 Jan 2007 (for the purpose of enabling the exercise of powers to make orders or regulations by statutory instrument) (SI 2006/3428) |
| | | 1 Oct 2009 (otherwise) (SI 2008/2860)[8] |
| 1070–1076 | | 1 Oct 2009 (SI 2008/2860)[8] |
| 1077–1080 | | 1 Jan 2007 (SI 2006/3428)[1] |
| 1081, 1082 | | 20 Jan 2007 (for the purpose of enabling the exercise of powers to make orders or regulations by statutory instrument) (SI 2006/3428) |
| | | 1 Oct 2009 (otherwise) (SI 2008/2860)[8] |
| 1083, 1084 | | 1 Oct 2009 (SI 2008/2860) |
| 1085–1092 | | 1 Jan 2007 (SI 2006/3428)[1] |
| 1093, 1094 | | 1 Oct 2009 (SI 2008/2860)[8] |
| 1095 | | 20 Jan 2007 (for the purpose of enabling the exercise of powers to make orders or regulations by statutory instrument) (SI 2006/3428) |
| | | 1 Oct 2009 (otherwise) (SI 2008/2860)[8] |
| 1096–1098 | | 1 Oct 2009 (SI 2008/2860)[8] |
| 1099 | | 20 Jan 2007 (for the purpose of enabling the exercise of powers to make orders or regulations by statutory instrument) (SI 2006/3428) |
| | | 1 Oct 2009 (otherwise) (SI 2008/2860) |
| 1100 | | 1 Oct 2009 (SI 2008/2860) |
| 1101 | | 20 Jan 2007 (for the purpose of enabling the exercise of powers to make orders or regulations by statutory instrument) (SI 2006/3428) |
| | | 1 Oct 2009 (otherwise) (SI 2008/2860) |
| 1102–1107 | | 1 Jan 2007 (SI 2006/3428)[1] |
| 1108 | | 20 Jan 2007 (for the purpose of enabling the exercise of powers to make orders or regulations by statutory instrument) (SI 2006/3428) |
| | | 1 Oct 2009 (otherwise) (SI 2008/2860)[8] |
| 1109 | | 1 Oct 2009 (SI 2008/2860)[8] |
| 1110 | | 20 Jan 2007 (for the purpose of enabling the exercise of powers to make orders or regulations by statutory instrument) (SI 2006/3428) |
| | | 1 Oct 2009 (otherwise) (SI 2008/2860)[8] |
| 1111 | | 1 Jan 2007 (SI 2006/3428) |
| 1112, 1113 | | 1 Oct 2009 (SI 2008/2860)[8] |

**Companies Act 2006 (c 46)**—*contd*

| | |
|---|---|
| 1114 | 1 Jan 2007 (in so far as necessary for the purposes of ss 1068(5), 1077–1080, 1085–1092, 1102–1107, 1111 of this Act) (SI 2006/3428) |
| | 1 Oct 2009 (otherwise) (SI 2008/2860) |
| 1115 | 1 Oct 2009 (SI 2008/2860)[8] |
| 1116 | 20 Jan 2007 (for the purpose of enabling the exercise of powers to make orders or regulations by statutory instrument) (SI 2006/3428) |
| | 1 Oct 2009 (otherwise) (SI 2008/2860) |
| 1117 | 1 Jan 2007 (in so far as necessary for the purposes of ss 1068(5), 1077–1080, 1085–1092, 1102–1107, 1111 of this Act) (SI 2006/3428) |
| | 6 Apr 2008 (in so far as necessary for the purpose of enabling rules to be made before the date on which this section is brought generally into force) (SI 2007/3495) |
| | 1 Oct 2009 (otherwise) (SI 2008/2860) |
| 1118, 1119 | 1 Oct 2009 (SI 2008/2860) |
| 1120 | 1 Jan 2007 (in so far as necessary for the purposes of ss 1068(5), 1077–1080, 1085–1092, 1102–1107, 1111 of this Act) (SI 2006/3428)[1] |
| | 1 Oct 2009 (otherwise) (SI 2008/2860) |
| 1121, 1122 | 20 Jan 2007 (in so far as necessary for the purposes of ss 308, 333, 463, 791–810, 811(1)–(3), 813, 815–828, 1143–1148, Schs 4, 5 of this Act) (SI 2006/3428) |
| | 6 Apr 2007 (in so far as necessary for the purposes of ss 2, 942–992, 1043, 1170, 1284(1), Sch 2 of this Act) (SI 2007/1093) |
| | 1 Oct 2007 (in so far as apply to offences under the Companies Act 1985, Part 14 or 15; and in so far as necessary for the purposes of the provisions mentioned in SI 2007/2194, art 2(1), (2)) (SI 2007/2194) |
| | 6 Apr 2008 (in so far as necessary for the purposes of the provisions mentioned in SI 2007/3495, art 3(1)(a)–(t), (2)) (SI 2007/3495) |
| | 1 Oct 2008 (in so far as necessary for the purposes of the provisions mentioned in SI 2007/3495, art 5(1)(a)–(f)) (SI 2007/3495) |
| | 1 Oct 2009 (otherwise) (SI 2008/2860) |
| 1123 | 6 Apr 2007 (in so far as necessary for the purposes of ss 2, 942–992, 1043, 1170, 1284(1), Sch 2 of this Act) (SI 2007/1093) |
| | 1 Oct 2007 (in so far as applies to offences under the Companies Act 1985, Part 14 or 15) (SI 2007/2194) |
| | 6 Apr 2008 (in so far as necessary for the purposes of the provisions mentioned in SI 2007/3495, art 3(1)(a)–(t), (2)) (SI 2007/3495) |
| | 1 Oct 2008 (in so far as necessary for the purposes of the provisions mentioned in SI 2007/3495, art 5(1)(a)–(f)) (SI 2007/3495) |
| | 1 Oct 2009 (otherwise) (SI 2008/2860) |
| 1124 | See Sch 3 below |
| 1125 | 20 Jan 2007 (in so far as necessary for the purposes of ss 308, 333, 463, 791–810, 811(1)–(3), 813, 815–828, 1143–1148, Schs 4, 5 of this Act) (SI 2006/3428) |
| | 6 Apr 2007 (in so far as necessary for the purposes of ss 2, 942–992, 1043, 1170, 1284(1), Sch 2 of this Act) (SI 2007/1093) |
| | 1 Oct 2007 (in so far as applies to offences under the Companies Act 1985, Part 14 or 15; and in so far as necessary for the purposes of the provisions mentioned in SI 2007/2194, art 2(1), (2)) (SI 2007/2194) |

**Companies Act 2006 (c 46)**—*contd*

|  | |
|---|---|
| | 6 Apr 2008 (in so far as necessary for the purposes of the provisions mentioned in SI 2007/3495, art 3(1)(a)–(t), (2)) (SI 2007/3495) |
| | 1 Oct 2008 (in so far as necessary for the purposes of the provisions mentioned in SI 2007/3495, art 5(1)(a)–(f)) (SI 2007/3495) |
| | 1 Oct 2009 (otherwise) (SI 2008/2860) |
| 1126 | 20 Jan 2007 (in so far as necessary for the purposes of ss 308, 333, 463, 791–810, 811(1)–(3), 813, 815–828, 1143–1148, Schs 4, 5 of this Act) (SI 2006/3428) |
| | 6 Apr 2007 (in so far as necessary for the purposes of ss 2, 942–992, 1043, 1170, 1284(1), Sch 2 of this Act) (SI 2007/1093) |
| | 1 Oct 2007 (in so far as applies to offences under the Companies Act 1985, Part 14 or 15) (SI 2007/2194) |
| | 6 Apr 2008 (otherwise) (SI 2007/3495) |
| 1127–1131 | 20 Jan 2007 (in so far as necessary for the purposes of ss 308, 333, 463, 791–810, 811(1)–(3), 813, 815–828, 1143–1148, Schs 4, 5 of this Act) (SI 2006/3428) |
| | 6 Apr 2007 (in so far as necessary for the purposes of ss 2, 942–992, 1043, 1170, 1284(1), Sch 2 of this Act) (SI 2007/1093) |
| | 1 Oct 2007 (in so far as apply to offences under the Companies Act 1985, Part 14 or 15; and in so far as necessary for the purposes of the provisions mentioned in SI 2007/2194, art 2(1), (2)) (SI 2007/2194) |
| | 6 Apr 2008 (in so far as necessary for the purposes of the provisions mentioned in SI 2007/3495, art 3(1)(a)–(t), (2)) (SI 2007/3495) |
| | 1 Oct 2008 (in so far as necessary for the purposes of the provisions mentioned in SI 2007/3495, art 5(1)(a)–(f)) (SI 2007/3495) |
| | 1 Oct 2009 (otherwise) (SI 2008/2860) |
| 1132 | 6 Apr 2007 (in so far as necessary for the purposes of ss 2, 942–992, 1043, 1170, 1284(1), Sch 2 of this Act) (SI 2007/1093) |
| | 1 Oct 2007 (in so far as applies to offences under the Companies Act 1985, Part 14 or 15; and in so far as necessary for the purposes of the provisions mentioned in SI 2007/2194, art 2(1), (2)) (SI 2007/2194) |
| | 6 Apr 2008 (in so far as necessary for the purposes of the provisions mentioned in SI 2007/3495, art 3(1)(a)–(t), (2)) (SI 2007/3495) |
| | 1 Oct 2008 (in so far as necessary for the purposes of the provisions mentioned in SI 2007/3495, art 5(1)(a)–(f)) (SI 2007/3495) |
| | 1 Oct 2009 (otherwise) (SI 2008/2860) |
| 1133 | 20 Jan 2007 (in so far as necessary for the purposes of ss 308, 333, 463, 791–810, 811(1)–(3), 813, 815–828, 1143–1148, Schs 4, 5 of this Act) (SI 2006/3428) |
| | 6 Apr 2007 (in so far as necessary for the purposes of ss 2, 942–992, 1043, 1170, 1284(1), Sch 2 of this Act) (SI 2007/1093) |
| | 1 Oct 2007 (in so far as applies to offences under the Companies Act 1985, Part 14 or 15; and in so far as necessary for the purposes of the provisions mentioned in SI 2007/2194, art 2(1), (2)) (SI 2007/2194) |
| | 6 Apr 2008 (in so far as necessary for the purposes of the provisions mentioned in SI 2007/3495, art 3(1)(a)–(t), (2)) (SI 2007/3495) |

**Companies Act 2006 (c 46)**—*contd*

|  |  |  |
|---|---|---|
|  |  | 1 Oct 2008 (in so far as necessary for the purposes of the provisions mentioned in SI 2007/3495, art 5(1)(a)–(f)) (SI 2007/3495) |
|  |  | 1 Oct 2009 (otherwise) (SI 2008/2860) |
| 1134, 1135 |  | 6 Apr 2007 (in so far as necessary for the purposes of ss 2, 942–992, 1043, 1170, 1284(1), Sch 2 of this Act) (SI 2007/1093) |
|  |  | 1 Oct 2009 (otherwise) (SI 2008/2860) |
| 1136 |  | 20 Jan 2007 (for the purpose of enabling the exercise of powers to make orders or regulations by statutory instrument) (SI 2006/3428) |
|  |  | 1 Oct 2009 (otherwise) (SI 2008/2860) |
| 1137 | (1) | 20 Jan 2007 (for the purpose of enabling the exercise of powers to make orders or regulations by statutory instrument) (SI 2006/3428) |
|  |  | 30 Sep 2007 (otherwise) (SI 2007/2607) |
|  | (2), (3) | 20 Jan 2007 (for the purpose of enabling the exercise of powers to make orders or regulations by statutory instrument) (SI 2006/3428) |
|  |  | 1 Oct 2009 (otherwise) (SI 2008/2860) |
|  | (4) | 20 Jan 2007 (for the purpose of enabling the exercise of powers to make orders or regulations by statutory instrument) (SI 2006/3428) |
|  |  | 30 Sep 2007 (otherwise) (SI 2007/2607) |
|  | (5)(a) | 20 Jan 2007 (for the purpose of enabling the exercise of powers to make orders or regulations by statutory instrument) (SI 2006/3428) |
|  |  | 1 Oct 2009 (otherwise) (SI 2008/2860) |
|  | (5)(b) | 20 Jan 2007 (for the purpose of enabling the exercise of powers to make orders or regulations by statutory instrument) (SI 2006/3428) |
|  |  | 30 Sep 2007 (otherwise) (SI 2007/2607) |
|  | (6) | 20 Jan 2007 (for the purpose of enabling the exercise of powers to make orders or regulations by statutory instrument) (SI 2006/3428) |
|  |  | 30 Sep 2007 (otherwise) (SI 2007/2607) |
| 1138 |  | 6 Apr 2007 (in so far as necessary for the purposes of ss 2, 942–992, 1043, 1170, 1284(1), Sch 2 of this Act) (SI 2007/1093)[2] |
|  |  | 1 Oct 2009 (otherwise) (SI 2008/2860) |
| 1139, 1140 |  | 6 Apr 2007 (in so far as necessary for the purposes of ss 2, 942–992, 1043, 1170, 1284(1), Sch 2 of this Act) (SI 2007/1093)[2] |
|  |  | 6 Apr 2008 (in so far as necessary for the purposes of the provisions mentioned in SI 2007/3495, art 3(1)(a)–(t), (2)) (SI 2007/3495) |
|  |  | 1 Oct 2009 (otherwise) (SI 2008/2860) |
| 1141 |  | 20 Jan 2007 (for the purpose of enabling the exercise of powers to make orders or regulations by statutory instrument) (SI 2006/3428) |
|  |  | 1 Oct 2009 (otherwise) (SI 2008/2860) |
| 1142 |  | 1 Oct 2009 (SI 2008/2860) |
| 1143 |  | 20 Jan 2007 (SI 2006/3428)[1] |
| 1144 | (1) | See Sch 4 below |
|  | (2) | See Sch 5 below |
|  | (3) | 20 Jan 2007 (SI 2006/3428) |
| 1145–1148 |  | 20 Jan 2007 (SI 2006/3428) |
| 1149, 1150 |  | 1 Oct 2009 (SI 2008/2860) |

**Companies Act 2006 (c 46)**—*contd*

| | | |
|---|---|---|
| 1151 | | 20 Jan 2007 (for the purpose of enabling the exercise of powers to make orders or regulations by statutory instrument) (SI 2006/3428) |
| | | 1 Oct 2009 (otherwise) (SI 2008/2860) |
| 1152–1155 | | 1 Oct 2009 (SI 2008/2860)[8] |
| 1156 | | 20 Jan 2007 (for the purpose of enabling the exercise of powers to make orders or regulations by statutory instrument) (SI 2006/3428) |
| | | 1 Oct 2009 (otherwise) (SI 2008/2860) |
| 1157 | | 1 Oct 2008 (SI 2007/3495) |
| 1158 | | 1 Oct 2007 (in so far as necessary for the purposes of the provisions mentioned in SI 2007/2194, art 2(1), (2)) (SI 2007/2194) |
| | | 1 Nov 2007 (in so far as necessary for the purposes of the provisions mentioned in SI 2007/2194, art 3(1)) (SI 2007/2194)[3] |
| | | 1 Oct 2009 (otherwise) (SI 2008/2860) |
| 1159 | (1), (2) | 6 Apr 2008 (in so far as necessary for the purposes of ss 1209–1241, 1245–1264, Schs 10, 11, 13, 14 of this Act) (SI 2007/3495) |
| | | 1 Oct 2009 (otherwise) (SI 2008/2860) |
| | (3) | See Sch 6 below |
| | (4) | 6 Apr 2008 (in so far as necessary for the purposes of ss 1209–1241, 1245–1264, Schs 10, 11, 13, 14 of this Act) (SI 2007/3495) |
| | | 1 Oct 2009 (otherwise) (SI 2008/2860) |
| 1160 | | 20 Jan 2007 (for the purpose of enabling the exercise of powers to make orders or regulations by statutory instrument) (SI 2006/3428) |
| | | 6 Apr 2008 (in so far as necessary for the purposes of ss 1209–1241, 1245–1264, Schs 10, 11, 13, 14 of this Act) (SI 2007/3495) |
| | | 1 Oct 2009 (otherwise) (SI 2008/2860) |
| 1161, 1162 | | 6 Apr 2008 (SI 2007/3495) |
| 1163 | | 1 Oct 2009 (SI 2008/2860) |
| 1164, 1165 | | 6 Apr 2008 (SI 2007/3495) |
| 1166 | | 1 Oct 2009 (SI 2008/2860) |
| 1167 | | 20 Jan 2007 (for the purpose of enabling the exercise of powers to make orders or regulations by statutory instrument) (SI 2006/3428) |
| | | 30 Sep 2007 (otherwise) (SI 2007/2607) |
| 1168 | | 1 Jan 2007 (in so far as necessary for the purposes of ss 1068(5), 1077–1080, 1085–1092, 1102–1107, 1111 of this Act) (SI 2006/3428) |
| | | 20 Jan 2007 (in so far as necessary for the purposes of ss 308, 333, 463, 791–810, 811(1)–(3), 813, 815–828, 1143–1148, Schs 4, 5 of this Act) (SI 2006/3428) |
| | | 6 Apr 2007 (in so far as necessary for the purposes of ss 2, 942–992, 1043, 1170, 1284(1), Sch 2 of this Act) (SI 2007/1093) |
| | | 1 Oct 2007 (in so far as necessary for the purposes of the provisions mentioned in SI 2007/2194, art 2(1), (2)) (SI 2007/2194) |
| | | 15 Dec 2007 (in so far as necessary for the purposes of the provisions mentioned in SI 2007/2194, art 4(1)) (SI 2007/2194) |
| | | 6 Apr 2008 (in so far as necessary for the purposes of the provisions mentioned in SI 2007/3495, art 3(1)(a)–(t), (2)) (SI 2007/3495) |

**Companies Act 2006 (c 46)**—*contd*

|  |  |
|---|---|
|  | 1 Oct 2008 (in so far as necessary for the purposes of the provisions mentioned in SI 2007/3495, art 5(1)(a)–(f)) (SI 2007/3495) |
|  | 1 Oct 2009 (otherwise) (SI 2008/2860) |
| 1169 | 6 Apr 2008 (SI 2007/3495) |
| 1170 | 6 Apr 2007 (SI 2007/1093) |
| 1171 | 1 Oct 2009 (SI 2008/2860) |
| 1172 | 6 Apr 2008 (SI 2007/3495) |
| 1173 | 1 Jan 2007 (the definitions "Gazette" and "working day" in so far as necessary for the purposes of ss 1068(5), 1077–1080, 1085–1092, 1102–1107, 1111 of this Act) (SI 2006/3428) |
|  | 20 Jan 2007 (the definition "working day" in so far as necessary for the purposes of ss 308, 333, 463, 791–810, 811(1)–(3), 813, 815–828, 1143–1148, Schs 4, 5 of this Act) (SI 2006/3428) |
|  | 6 Apr 2007 (the definitions "body corporate", "the Gazette" and "regulated market" in so far as necessary for the purposes of ss 2, 942–992, 1043, 1170, 1284(1), Sch 2 of this Act) (SI 2007/1093) |
|  | 1 Oct 2007 (the definitions "body corporate", "firm" and "working day", in so far as necessary for the purposes of the provisions mentioned in SI 2007/2194, art 2(1), (2)) (SI 2007/2194) |
|  | 1 Nov 2007 (the definition "body corporate", in so far as necessary for the purposes of the provisions mentioned in SI 2007/2194, art 3(1)) (SI 2007/2194) |
|  | 6 Apr 2008 (the definitions "credit institution" and "working day" (in so far as not already in force)) (SI 2007/3495) |
|  | 6 Apr 2008 (the definitions "body corporate", "corporation", "firm", "the Gazette", "parent company" and "regulated market", in so far as necessary for the purposes of the provisions mentioned in SI 2007/3495, art 3(1)(a)–(t), (2)) (SI 2007/3495) |
|  | 1 Oct 2008 (the definitions "body corporate", "corporation", "firm" and "officer", in so far as necessary for the purposes of the provisions mentioned in SI 2007/3495, art 5(1)(a)–(f)) (SI 2007/3495) |
|  | 1 Oct 2009 (otherwise) (SI 2008/2860) |
| 1174 | See Sch 8 below |
| 1175 | See Sch 9 below |
| 1176–1179 | 6 Apr 2007 (SI 2006/3428) |
| 1180 | 1 Oct 2009 (SI 2008/2860) |
| 1181 | 20 Jan 2007 (for the purpose of enabling the exercise of powers to make orders or regulations by statutory instrument) (SI 2006/3428) |
|  | 1 Oct 2009 (otherwise) (SI 2008/2860) |
| 1182, 1183 | 1 Oct 2009 (SI 2008/2860) |
| 1184–1189 | 20 Jan 2007 (for the purpose of enabling the exercise of powers to make orders or regulations by statutory instrument) (SI 2006/3428) |
|  | 1 Oct 2009 (otherwise) (SI 2008/2860) |
| 1190 | 1 Oct 2009 (SI 2008/2860) |
| 1191 | 20 Jan 2007 (for the purpose of enabling the exercise of powers to make orders or regulations by statutory instrument) (SI 2006/3428) |
|  | 1 Oct 2009 (otherwise) (SI 2008/2860) |
| 1192 | 1 Oct 2009 (SI 2008/2860) |
| 1193–1195 | 20 Jan 2007 (for the purpose of enabling the exercise of powers to make orders or regulations by statutory instrument) (SI 2006/3428) |
|  | 1 Oct 2009 (otherwise) (SI 2008/2860) |
| 1196 | 1 Oct 2009 (SI 2008/2860) |

**Companies Act 2006 (c 46)**—*contd*

| | | |
|---|---|---|
| 1197 | | 20 Jan 2007 (for the purpose of enabling the exercise of powers to make orders or regulations by statutory instrument) (SI 2006/3428) |
| | | 1 Oct 2009 (otherwise) (SI 2008/2860) |
| 1198–1201 | | 1 Oct 2009 (SI 2008/2860) |
| 1202 | | 20 Jan 2007 (for the purpose of enabling the exercise of powers to make orders or regulations by statutory instrument) (SI 2006/3428) |
| | | 1 Oct 2009 (otherwise) (SI 2008/2860) |
| 1203 | | 1 Oct 2009 (SI 2008/2860) |
| 1204 | | 20 Jan 2007 (for the purpose of enabling the exercise of powers to make orders or regulations by statutory instrument) (SI 2006/3428) |
| | | 1 Oct 2009 (otherwise) (SI 2008/2860) |
| 1205–1208 | | 1 Oct 2009 (SI 2008/2860) |
| 1209 | | 6 Apr 2008 (SI 2007/3495) |
| 1210 | | 20 Jan 2007 (for the purpose of enabling the exercise of powers to make orders or regulations by statutory instrument) (SI 2006/3428) |
| | | 6 Apr 2008 (otherwise) (SI 2007/3495) |
| 1211–1213 | | 6 Apr 2008 (SI 2007/3495)[5] |
| 1214 | | 20 Jan 2007 (for the purpose of enabling the exercise of powers to make orders or regulations by statutory instrument) (SI 2006/3428) |
| | | 6 Apr 2008 (otherwise) (SI 2007/3495)[5] |
| 1215–1219 | | 6 Apr 2008 (SI 2007/3495)[5] |
| 1220 | (1), (2) | 6 Apr 2008 (SI 2007/3495)[5] |
| | (3) | See Sch 11 below |
| 1221–1227 | | 6 Apr 2008 (SI 2007/3495)[5] |
| 1228 | | 20 Jan 2007 (for the purpose of enabling the exercise of powers to make orders or regulations by statutory instrument) (SI 2006/3428) |
| | | 6 Apr 2008 (otherwise) (SI 2007/3495) |
| 1229, 1230 | | 6 Apr 2008 (SI 2007/3495)[5] |
| 1231 | | 20 Jan 2007 (for the purpose of enabling the exercise of powers to make orders or regulations by statutory instrument) (SI 2006/3428) |
| | | 6 Apr 2008 (SI 2007/3495)[5] |
| 1232–1236 | | 6 Apr 2008 (SI 2007/3495)[5] |
| 1237 | | 20 Jan 2007 (for the purpose of enabling the exercise of powers to make orders or regulations by statutory instrument) (SI 2006/3428) |
| | | 6 Apr 2008 (SI 2007/3495)[5] |
| 1238 | | 6 Apr 2008 (SI 2007/3495)[5] |
| 1239–1241 | | 20 Jan 2007 (for the purpose of enabling the exercise of powers to make orders or regulations by statutory instrument) (SI 2006/3428) |
| | | 6 Apr 2008 (otherwise) (SI 2007/3495) |
| 1242 | (1), (2) | 29 Jun 2008 (SI 2007/3495)[5] |
| | (3) | See Sch 12 below |
| | (4) | 29 Jun 2008 (SI 2007/3495)[5] |
| 1243, 1244 | | 29 Jun 2008 (SI 2007/3495)[5] |
| 1245 | | 6 Apr 2008 (SI 2007/3495) |
| 1246 | | 20 Jan 2007 (for the purpose of enabling the exercise of powers to make orders or regulations by statutory instrument) (SI 2006/3428) |
| | | 6 Apr 2008 (otherwise) (SI 2007/3495) |
| 1247–1250 | | 6 Apr 2008 (SI 2007/3495)[5] |

**Companies Act 2006 (c 46)**—*contd*

| | |
|---|---|
| 1251–1253 | 20 Jan 2007 (for the purpose of enabling the exercise of powers to make orders or regulations by statutory instrument) (SI 2006/3428) |
| | 6 Apr 2008 (otherwise) (SI 2007/3495)[5] |
| 1254–1260 | 6 Apr 2008 (SI 2007/3495)[5] |
| 1261 | 20 Jan 2007 (for the purpose of enabling the exercise of powers to make orders or regulations by statutory instrument) (SI 2006/3428) |
| | 6 Apr 2008 (otherwise) (SI 2007/3495) |
| 1262 | 6 Apr 2008 (SI 2007/3495) |
| 1263 | 20 Jan 2007 (for the purpose of enabling the exercise of powers to make orders or regulations by statutory instrument) (SI 2006/3428) |
| | 6 Apr 2008 (otherwise) (SI 2007/3495) |
| 1264 | See Sch 14 below |
| 1265–1271 | 8 Nov 2006 (s 1300(1)(a)) |
| 1272 | See Sch 15 below |
| 1273 | 8 Nov 2006 (s 1300(1)(a)) |
| 1274 | 8 Nov 2006 (s 1300(1)(b)) |
| 1275 | 1 Oct 2009 (SI 2008/2860) |
| 1276 | 8 Nov 2006 (s 1300(1)(b)) |
| 1277–1280 | 20 Jan 2007 (for the purpose of enabling the exercise of powers to make orders or regulations by statutory instrument) (SI 2006/3428) |
| | 1 Oct 2008 (otherwise) (SI 2007/3495) |
| 1281 | 20 Jan 2007 (for the purpose of enabling the exercise of powers to make orders or regulations by statutory instrument) (SI 2006/3428) |
| | 6 Apr 2007 (otherwise) (SI 2006/3428) |
| 1282 | 6 Apr 2008 (SI 2007/3495)[5] |
| 1283 | 1 Oct 2009 (SI 2008/2860)[8] |
| 1284      (1) | 1 Jan 2007 (in so far as necessary for the purposes of ss 1068(5), 1077–1080, 1085–1092, 1102–1107, 1111 of this Act) (SI 2006/3428) |
| | 20 Jan 2007 (in so far as necessary for the purposes of ss 308, 333, 463, 791–810, 811(1)–(3), 813, 815–828, 1143–1148, Schs 4, 5 of this Act) (SI 2006/3428) |
| | 6 Apr 2007 (in so far as necessary for the purposes of ss 1063, 1176–1179, 1281, 1295, Sch 16 of this Act (so far as relating to the repeal of the provisions of SI 1986/1032, corresponding to the repeal of the Companies Act 1985, ss 1176–1179; the Companies Act 1985, ss 41, 293, 294; SI 1986/1032, arts 51, 301, 302)) (SI 2006/3428) |
| | 6 Apr 2007 (in so far as it relates to ss 2, 942–992, 1043, Sch 2 of this Act and Companies (Audit, Investigations and Community Enterprise) Act 2004, Pt 2) (SI 2007/1093) |
| | 30 Sep 2007 (in so far as necessary for the purposes of the provisions mentioned in SI 2007/2607, art 2(1)) (SI 2007/2607) |
| | 1 Oct 2007 (in so far as necessary for the purposes of the provisions mentioned in SI 2007/2194, art 2(1)(a)–(j)) (SI 2007/2194) |
| | 1 Nov 2007 (in so far as necessary for the purposes of the provisions mentioned in SI 2007/2194, art 3(1)) (SI 2007/2194) |
| | 15 Dec 2007 (in so far as necessary for the purposes of the provisions mentioned in SI 2007/2194, art 4(1)) (SI 2007/2194) |
| | 6 Apr 2008 (in so far as necessary for the purposes of the provisions mentioned in SI 2007/3495, art 3(1)(a)–(t), (2), (3)) (SI 2007/3495) |

**Companies Act 2006 (c 46)**—*contd*

| | | |
|---|---|---|
| | | 1 Oct 2008 (in so far as necessary for the purposes of the provisions mentioned in SI 2007/2194, art 5(1)) (SI 2007/2194) |
| | | 1 Oct 2008 (in so far as necessary for the purposes of the provisions mentioned in SI 2007/3495, art 5(1)–(3)) (SI 2007/3495) |
| | | 1 Oct 2008 (in so far as necessary for the purposes of the provisions mentioned in SI 2008/1886, art 2(a)–(c)) (SI 2008/1886) |
| | | 1 Oct 2009 (otherwise) (SI 2008/2860)[1, 8] |
| | (2) | 6 Apr 2007 (in so far as relates to repeals of or in the Companies (Northern Ireland) Order 1986, SI 1986/1032, arts 2, 421–423F, Sch 7, paras 2, 2A, 2B, and the Companies (Audit, Investigations and Community Enterprise) (Northern Ireland) Order 2005, SI 2005/1967, Pt III) (SI 2007/1093)[2] |
| | | 1 Oct 2007 (in so far as relates to the repeals of or in the provisions specified in SI 2007/2194, Sch 2, Pt 2) (SI 2007/2194) |
| | | 6 Apr 2008 (in so far as relates to the repeals of or in the provisions specified in SI 2007/3495, Sch 2, Pt 2) (SI 2007/3495) |
| | | 1 Oct 2008 (in so far as relates to the repeals of or in the provisions specified in SI 2007/3495, Sch 3, Pt 2) (SI 2007/3495) |
| | | 1 Oct 2009 (otherwise) (SI 2008/2860) |
| 1285 | | 1 Oct 2009 (SI 2008/2860) |
| 1286 | (1)(a) | 1 Oct 2008 (so far as relating to the application to limited liability partnerships of the subject matter of Parts 15, 16 and 42 of this Act) (SI 2008/1886)[7] |
| | | 1 Oct 2009 (otherwise) (SI 2008/2860) |
| | (1)(b)–(d) | 1 Oct 2009 (SI 2008/2860) |
| | (2)(a) | 1 Oct 2008 (so far as relating to the application to limited liability partnerships of the subject matter of Parts 15, 16 and 42 of this Act) (SI 2008/1886)[7] |
| | | 1 Oct 2009 (otherwise) (SI 2008/2860) |
| | (2)(b)–(d) | 1 Oct 2009 (SI 2008/2860) |
| 1287 | | 1 Oct 2009 (SI 2008/2860) |
| 1288–1294 | | 8 Nov 2006 (s 1300(1)(c)) |
| 1295 | | See Sch 16 below |
| 1296, 1297 | | 8 Nov 2006 (s 1300(1)(c)) |
| 1298–1300 | | 8 Nov 2006 (s 1300(1)(d)) |
| Sch 1 | | 1 Oct 2007 (SI 2007/2194)[4] |
| Sch 2 | | 20 Jan 2007 (for the purpose of enabling the exercise of powers to make orders or regulations by statutory instrument) (SI 2006/3428) |
| | | 6 Apr 2007 (otherwise) (SI 2007/1093) |
| Sch 3 | | 1 Oct 2007 (SI 2007/2194)[3] |
| Schs 4, 5 | | 20 Jan 2007 (SI 2006/3428)[1] |
| Sch 6 | | 6 Apr 2008 (in so far as necessary for the purposes of ss 1209–1241, 1245–1264, Schs 10, 11, 13, 14 of this Act) (SI 2007/3495) |
| | | 1 Oct 2009 (otherwise) (SI 2008/2860) |
| Sch 7 | | 6 Apr 2008 (SI 2007/3495) |
| Sch 8 | | 1 Oct 2009 (SI 2008/2860) |
| Sch 9 | Pt 1 | 1 Apr 2008 (SI 2008/674)[6] |
| | Pt 2 | *Never in force* (repealed) |
| Sch 10 | | 6 Apr 2008 (SI 2007/3495) |
| Sch 11 | | 20 Jan 2007 (for the purpose of enabling the exercise of powers to make orders or regulations by statutory instrument) (SI 2006/3428) |
| | | 6 Apr 2008 (otherwise) (SI 2007/3495) |

**Companies Act 2006 (c 46)**—*contd*

| | | |
|---|---|---|
| Sch 12 | | 20 Jan 2007 (for the purpose of enabling the exercise of powers to make orders or regulations by statutory instrument) (SI 2006/3428) |
| | | 29 Jun 2008 (otherwise) (SI 2007/3495)[5] |
| Sch 13 | | 20 Jan 2007 (for the purpose of enabling the exercise of powers to make orders or regulations by statutory instrument) (SI 2006/3428) |
| | | 6 Apr 2008 (otherwise) (SI 2007/3495) |
| Sch 14 | | 6 Apr 2008 (SI 2007/3495) |
| Sch 15 | paras 1–10, 11(1) | 8 Nov 2006 (s 1300(1)(a)) |
| | para 11(2) | 1 Oct 2008 (SI 2008/1886) |
| | paras 11(3), 12–15 | 8 Nov 2006 (s 1300(1)(a)) |
| Sch 16 | | 1 Jan 2007 (SI 2006/3428), repeals and revocations of or in— |

Companies Act 1985, ss 29(4), 42; 228(2)(f) and 228A(2)(g) (words from "subject to" to "without a translation)" in both provisions); 242(1), 272(5) and 273(7) (words from "then, subject to" to "without a translation)" in each provision); 707A(1), 709, 710B, 711, 723C(1)(a), Sch 9, Pt 2, para 7(3) (words from "then, subject to" to "without a translation)");

Insolvency Act 1986, Sch 13 (entry relating to the Companies Act 1985, s 711(2));

Welsh Language Act 1993, s 30;

Companies (Northern Ireland) Order 1986 (SI 1986/1032) (NI 6), arts 39(4), 52, 656A(1), 658, 660;

Insolvency (Northern Ireland) Order 1989 (SI 1989/2405) (NI 19), Sch 9, para 22;

Companies (Northern Ireland) Order 1990 (SI 1990/593) (NI 5), Sch 10, para 19

20 Jan 2007 (SI 2006/3428), repeals and revocations of or in—
Companies Act 1985, ss 198–220, 238(4A)–(4E), 239(2A), (2B), 251(2A)–(2E), 253(2A), 262(1) (definition "address"), 262A (entry "address"), 366A(3A), (5A), 369(4A)–(4G), 372(2A), (2B), (6A), 379A(2B)–(2F), (5A);

Companies Act 1989, ss 134, 143(5), Sch 10, paras 3, 6, 14;

Criminal Justice and Police Act 2001, s 45(4);

Civil Partnership Act 2004, Sch 27, para 99;

Companies (Northern Ireland) Order 1986 (SI 1986/1032) (NI 6), arts 206–228, 246(4A)–(4E), 247(2A), (2B), 259(2A)–(2E), 261(2A), 270, 270A, 374A(3A), (6), 377(5)–(11), 380(2A), (2B), (6A), 387A(2B)–(2F), (6);

Companies (Northern Ireland) Order 1990 (SI 1990/593) (NI 5), Sch 10, paras 4, 5, 8, 19;

Companies (No 2) (Northern Ireland) Order 1990 (SI 1990/1504) (NI 10), arts 6, 69, 77(10)

6 Apr 2007 (SI 2006/3428), repeals and revocations of or in—
Limited Partnerships Act 1907;

Companies Act 1985, ss 41, 293, 294, 311, 323–329, 343, 344, 438, 439, 453(1A)(b), 708(5), 720, 729, Sch 13, Pts 2–4, Sch 23;

Companies Act 1989, ss 58, 143(10), Sch 17, para 4;

Age of Legal Capacity (Scotland) Act 1991, Sch 1, para 39;

Civil Partnership Act 2004, Sch 27, paras 100, 101;

Companies (Northern Ireland) Order 1986 (SI 1986/1032) (NI 6), arts 51, 301, 302, 319, 331–337, 351, 352, 432(2), (3), (7), (8), 446(2)(b), 669, 677, Sch 13, Pts 2–4, Sch 22; and so far as corresponds to repeals of the Companies Act 1985, ss 1176–1179;

Companies (Northern Ireland) Order 1990 (SI 1990/593) (NI 5), Sch 10, para 14;

**Companies Act 2006 (c 46)**—*contd*

Companies (No 2) (Northern Ireland) Order 1990
(SI 1990/1504) (NI 10), Sch 4, para 4

6 Apr 2007 (SI 2007/1093)[2], repeals and revocations of or in—

Companies Act 1985, ss 428–430F, 744 (definition "EEA State"),
Sch 7, paras 2, 2A, 2B;

Companies (Northern Ireland) Order 1986, SI 1986/1032
(NI 6), arts 2 (definition "EEA State"), 421–423F, Sch 7,
paras 2, 2A, 2B;

Companies (Audit, Investigations and Community Enterprise)
(Northern Ireland) Order 2005, SI 2005/1967 (NI 17), Pt III

1 Oct 2007 (SI 2007/2194)[3], repeals and revocations of or in—

Companies Act 1985, ss 125(6), 234(1)(a), 234ZZB, 241 (as it
applies to private companies)[3], 246(4)(a) (words "and 234ZZB
(directors' report: business review)"), 246A(2A), 252[3], 253[3],
282, 285, 292, 303, 304, 309–309C, 312–316, 318–322, 322B,
330–347[3], 347A–347K, 356, 357 (words "section 356
(inspection)" and words from "and the power of the court" to
the end), 366–379, 379A(1)(b)–(e), 380(4)(a), (c)–(m),
381–383, 384 and 385 (as they apply to private companies),
385A, 386, 387–388A (as they apply to private companies),
393, 437, 442, 446, 448, 449, 450, 451, 453(1A)(d) (and word
"and" preceding it), 453A, 458–461, 730(5), 741, Sch 13,
Pt I[3], Sch 15A;

Companies Act 1985, Sch 24[3], entries relating to: ss 210, 211,
214–219, 241(2) (as it applies to private companies), 314, 318,
322B, 323, 324, 326, 328, 329, 342, 343, 356, 366, 367, 372,
376, 381B, 382, 382B, 383, 387 (as it applies to private
companies), 429, 430A, 444, 448–451, 453A, 455, 458, 461,
720;

Insolvency Act 1986, Sch 13, Pt 1, entries relating to the
Companies Act 1985, ss 380(4), 461(6);

Water Act 1989;

Companies Act 1989, ss 16, 113, 114(1), 115(2), (3), 138,
143(8), (9), Sch 10, para 10, Sch 18, paras 34–36, Sch 19,
paras 8, 9, 17;

Political Parties, Elections and Referendums Act 2000, s 139(1),
Sch 19, Sch 23, para 12;

Companies (Audit, Investigations and Community Enterprise)
Act 2004, ss 19(1), 20, Sch 2, paras 7–9, 22, 23;

Civil Partnership Act 2004, Sch 27, para 102;

Companies (Northern Ireland) Order 1986 (SI 1986/1032)
(NI 6), arts 9, 135(6), 242(1) (words from "and containing the
business review" to the end), 242ZZB, 249 (as it applies to
private companies), 254(4)(a) (words "and 242ZZB (directors'
report: business review)"), 254A(2A), 260[3], 261[3], 290, 293,
300, 311, 312, 317, 318 (as it applies to directors), 320–324,
326–330, 330B, 338–355[3], 364, 365 (words "Article 364
(inspection)" and words from "and the power of the court" to
the end), 374–387, 387A(1)(b)–(e), 388(4)(a), (c)–(m),
389–391, 392 and 393 (as they apply to private companies),
393A, 394, 395–396A (as they apply to private companies),
401, 451–454, Sch 13, Pt I[3], Sch 15A;

Companies (Northern Ireland) Order 1986 (SI 1986/1032)
(NI 6), Sch 23[3], entries relating to: arts 218(3), 219(10),
222(5), 223(8), 224(3), 225(7), 226(3), 227(3), 249(2) (as it
applies to private companies), 322(3), 326(8), 330B(4), 331(2),
332(7), 334(2)–(5), 336(6), 337(3), 350(1)–(3), 351(8), 364(5),
374(4), 375(3), (5), 380(4), (6), 384(7), 389B(2), 390(5),
390B(2), 391(4), 395(2) (as it applies to private companies),
422(6), 423A(6), 451, 454(5), 669(4);

**Companies Act 2006 (c 46)**—*contd*

Companies (Northern Ireland) Order 1990 (SI 1990/593) (NI 5),
art 18;

Companies (No 2) (Northern Ireland) Order 1990
(SI 1990/1504) (NI 10), arts 48, 49(1), 50(2), (3), 73, Sch 3,
paras 14–16, Sch 5, para 11;

Companies (Audit, Investigations and Community Enterprise)
(Northern Ireland) Order 2005 (SI 2005/1967) (NI 17), art 19

1 Apr 2008 (SI 2008/674)[6], repeals of or in—

Companies Act 1985, ss 240(1) (words from "or, as the case may
be," to "section 249A(2)"), (3)(c) (words from "and, if no such
report" to "any financial year"), (3)(e) (and word "; and"
preceding it), (3) (words from "or any report" to
"section 249A(2)"), 245(4)(b) (words "or reporting
accountant"), 249A(2), (3A), (4), (6A) (words "or (2)"), (7)
(definition "gross income" and word ", and" preceding it),
249B(1) (words "or (2)"), (1C)(b) (words from "where the
company referred to" to "is not a charity"), (3) (words "or
(2)"), (4) (words "or (2)"), (4)(a) (words "or (2)"), 249C, 249D,
249E(2), 262A (entry "reporting accountant")

6 Apr 2008 (SI 2007/3495)[5], repeals and revocations of or in—

Companies Act 1985, ss 36A(2), (3) (words from "however" to
the end), (4)–(8), 58, 81, 117, 118, 182(1)(b), 183–197,
221–251 (in so far as not already repealed), 254–281 (in so far
as not already repealed), 283, 284, 286, 310, 352(6), (7),
380(4)(b), 384, 385, 387–388A, 389A–392A, 394, 394A,
425–427A, 732–734, 742A–742C, 744 (definitions "authorised
minimum", "debenture", "insurance market activity",
"prescribed" and "undistributable reserves"), Schs 4–11, 15B;

Companies Act 1985, Sch 24, entries relating to: ss 81, 117, 183,
185, 189, 191, 221(5) or 222(4), 222(6), 231–234, 234ZA,
234A, 234AA, 234AB, 234B, 234C, 236, 238–240, 241(2) or
242(2), 241A, 245, 245E, 245G, 251, 255, 384, 387, 389B,
390, 391, 392(3), 392A, 394A, 425–427;

Insolvency Act 1985, Sch 6, paras 11, 12;

Insolvency Act 1986, Sch 13, Pt 1, entry relating to the
Companies Act 1985, s 196;

Finance Act 1988;

Companies Act 1989, ss 1–15, 17–22, 24–54, 114(2), 118–122,
123(1)–(4), 137, 143(4), 207, Schs 1–9, Sch 10, paras 2, 4, 5,
7, 8, 19–23, Schs 11–13, Sch 17, paras 5, 6, Sch 19, para 18;

Trade Marks Act 1994, Sch 4, para 1(2), entries relating to the
Companies Act 1985, Schs 4, 9;

Requirements of Writing (Scotland) Act 1995, Sch 4, paras 55,
56;

Criminal Procedure (Consequential Provisions) (Scotland)
Act 1995, Sch 4, paras 56(4), 74(2);

Disability Discrimination Act 1995;

Political Parties, Elections and Referendums Act 2000, ss 139(2),
140, Sch 23, para 13;

Enterprise Act 2002, Sch 17, paras 4–6;

Companies (Audit, Investigations and Community Enterprise)
Act 2004, ss 1–13, 19(2), Sch 1, Sch 2, paras 1–3, 5, 10, 24;

Civil Partnership Act 2004, Sch 27, paras 104, 105, 128;

Companies (Northern Ireland) Order 1986 (SI 1986/1032)
(NI 6), arts 2 (definitions "authorised minimum", "debenture",
"insurance market activity", "prescribed" and "undistributable
reserves"), 10A–10C, 46A(2), (3) (words from "however" to the
end), (4)–(6), 68, 91, 127, 128, 192(1)(b), 193–205,
229–242ZZA, 242ZA–259, 262–289, 291, 292, 294, 318,
360(6), (7), 388(4)(b), 392, 393, 395–396A, 397A–400A, 401A,
401B, 418–420A, 680–680B, Schs 4–11, 15B;

**Companies Act 2006 (c 46)**—*contd*

Companies (Northern Ireland) Order 1986 (SI 1986/1032)
(NI 6), Sch 23, entries relating to: arts 91(2), 127(7), (7A),
193(6), 195(5), 199(5), (6), 200(4), 229(5) or 230(4), 230(6),
239(7), 240(4), 241(5), (6), 242(5), 242A(4), 242AA(5),
242AB(4), 242B(3), (6), 242C(4), 244(4), 246(5), 247(3),
248(6), 249(2) or 250(2), 249A(9), (10), 253(1), (2), 253E(3),
259(5), 395(2), 397A(2), (3), 399(2), 400(3), 400A(5),
401B(1), (4), 418(4), 419(6), (7), 420(5);

Industrial Relations (Northern Ireland) Order 1987, SI 1987/936
(NI 9);

Finance Act 1988, s 117(3) (NI);

Insolvency (Northern Ireland) Order 1989, SI 1989/2405
(NI 19), Sch 9, paras 11–13, 16, 17;

Companies (Northern Ireland) Order 1990, SI 1990/593 (NI 5),
arts 3–17, 19–24, 27–56, Schs 1–10, paras 6–10, Schs 11–13;

Companies (No 2) (Northern Ireland) Order 1990, SI 1990/1504
(NI 10), arts 54–58, 72, Sch 4, paras 5, 6;

Companies (Audit, Investigations and Community Enterprise)
Act 2004, s 11(2), Sch 2, paras 11–15;

Law Reform (Miscellaneous Provisions) (Northern Ireland)
Order 2005, SI 2005/1452 (NI 7);

Companies (Audit, Investigations and Community Enterprise)
(Northern Ireland) Order 2005, SI 2005/1967 (NI 17),
arts 3–14, Sch 1, Sch 2, paras 1–9, 16–18

1 Oct 2008 (SI 2007/3495)[5], repeals and revocations of or in—

Companies Act 1985, ss 151–153 and 155–158 (so far as they
apply to the giving of financial assistance by a private company
for the purposes of the acquisition of shares in itself or another
private company), ss 305, 317, 348, 349, 351, 727;

Companies Act 1985, Sch 24, entries relating to ss 317, 348, 349,
351;

Business Names Act 1985, s 4 (as it applies to companies);

Companies (Audit, Investigations and Community Enterprise)
Act 2004, Sch 6, para 8;

Companies (Northern Ireland) Order 1986 (SI 1986/1032)
(NI 6), arts 161–163 and 165–168 (so far as they apply to the
giving of financial assistance by a private company for the
purposes of the acquisition of shares in itself or another private
company), arts 313, 325, 356, 357, 359, 675;

Companies (Northern Ireland) Order 1986 (SI 1986/1032)
(NI 6), Sch 23, entries relating to: arts 325(7), 356(2),
357(2), (3), (4), 359(3)(a), (b);

Business Names (Northern Ireland) Order 1986, SI 1986/1033
(NI 7), art 6 (as it applies to companies);

Companies (Audit, Investigations and Community Enterprise)
(Northern Ireland) Order 2005, SI 2005/1967 (NI 17), Sch 7,
para 6

1 Oct 2008 (SI 2008/1886), repeals and revocations of or in—

Companies Act 1989, s 141(4) (second sentence only);

Companies (No 2) (Northern Ireland) Order 1990,
SI 1990/1504 (NI 10), art 75(4) (second sentence only)

1 Oct 2009 (SI 2008/2860), repeals and revocations of or in—

Companies Act 1985[8] (so far as not already in force, except for
ss 726(2), 746, note that repeals of provisions which had
previously been repealed by earlier Acts have not been
commenced);

Business Names Act 1985 (so far as not already in force);

Insolvency Act 1985 (so far as not already in force);

Insolvency Act 1986, Sch 13, Pt 1 (entries relating to ss 13(4),
44(7), 103(7), 131(7), 140(2), 173(4), 657(2), 658(1);

Building Societies Act 1986;

**Companies Act 2006 (c 46)**—*contd*

Companies Act 1989, ss 92–110, 115(1), 116(1), (2), 117, 123(5), 125(1), 126–129, 130(1)–(5), (7), 131–133, 136, 139(1)–(3), 141–143, 144(1), (3), Sch 10, paras 1, 9–18, 24, Schs 15–17, Sch 18, paras 32–38, Sch 19, paras 1–7, 11–17, 19–21;

Charities Act 1993;

Criminal Justice Act 1993;

Pension Schemes Act 1993;

Trade Marks Act 1994 (so far as not already in force) (note that although SI 2008/2860 refers to an entry relating to s 392 of the 1985 Act, it is thought that this should refer to the entry relating to s 396 thereof);

Deregulation and Contracting Out Act 1994;

Requirements of Writing (Scotland) Act 1995 (so far as not already in force);

Criminal Procedure (Consequential Provisions) (Scotland) Act 1995, Sch 4, para 56(4) (note that this repeal was previously brought into force by SI 2007/3495);

Limited Liability Partnerships Act 2000;

Political Parties, Elections and Referendums Act 2000, s 139(2) (note that this repeal was previously brought into force by SI 2007/3495);

Criminal Justice and Police Act 2001 (so far as not already in force);

Enterprise Act 2002 (so far as not already in force);

Companies (Audit, Investigations and Community Enterprise) Act 2004, ss 19(1), 20, Sch 6, paras 1–9 (note that repeals of ss 19(1), 20 were previously brought into force by SI 2007/2194);

Civil Partnership Act 2004, Sch 27, para 104 (note that this repeal was previously brought into force by SI 2007/1093);

Companies (Northern Ireland) Order 1986 (SI 1986/1032) (NI 6)[8], arts 1–8, 10–38, 39(1)–(3), (5), (6), 40–46, 46A(1), (3), 46B–50, 53–65, 72 (so far as not already revoked), 90, 90A, 92–126, 129–134, 135(1)–(5), (7), (8), 136–192, 295–299, 314–316, 330A, 358, 360–363, 365–373, 387A, 388, 402–417J, 424–450, 602–655, 656A(2)–(4), 656B, 657, 659, 659A, 662, 663, 664A, 667, 668, 670–673, 676, 678, 679, 681, Schs 1, 2, Sch 3, para 2 (so far as not already revoked), Schs 14, 20–21, 23, 24;

Business Names (Northern Ireland) Order 1986, SI 1986/1033 (NI 7) (so far as not already in force);

Companies Consolidation (Consequential Provisions) (Northern Ireland) Order 1986, SI 1986/1035 (NI 9);

Companies (Northern Ireland) Order 1989, SI 1989/2404 (NI 18), arts 1–2A, 26, 35, 36, Schs 4, 5;

Insolvency (Northern Ireland) Order 1989, SI 1989/2405 (NI 19), Sch 9, Pt I (so far as not already in force);

European Economic Interest Groupings Regulations (Northern Ireland) 1989, SR 1989/216;

Companies (Northern Ireland) Order 1990, SI 1990/593 (NI 5), arts 1, 2, 25, 26, 57, Schs 10, 15;

Companies (No 2) (Northern Ireland) Order 1990, SI 1990/1504 (NI 10), arts 3–5, 7–20, 28–42, 44–46, 49–53, 59–61, 62(1)–(3), (5), 63–68, 70, 71, 74–78, Sch 1, Sch 2, paras 1, 2, Schs 4–6;

Criminal Justice Act 1993, Sch 5, Pt 2;

Financial Provisions (Northern Ireland) Order 1993, SI 1993/1252 (NI 5);

Pensions (Northern Ireland) Order 1995, SI 1995/3213 (NI 22);

**Companies Act 2006 (c 46)**—*contd*

> Deregulation and Contracting Out (Northern Ireland)
>   Order 1996, SI 1996/1632 (NI 11), Sch 5, para 4;
> Youth Justice and Criminal Evidence Act 1999, Sch 4, para 18;
> Limited Liability Partnerships Act (Northern Ireland) 2002;
> Open-Ended Investment Companies Act (Northern Ireland)
>   2002;
> Company Directors Disqualification (Northern Ireland)
>   Order 2002, SI 2002/3150 (NI 4);
> Companies (Audit, Investigations and Community Enterprise)
>   (Northern Ireland) Order 2005, SI 2005/1967 (NI 17) (so far
>   as not already revoked)
>
> *Not yet in force*, repeals of or in—
> Companies Act 1985, ss 726(2), 746 (and previously repealed
>   provisions, as noted above);
> Insolvency Act 1986, Sch 13, Pt 1 (entries relating to ss 156(3),
>   462(5), 463(2), 463(3), 464(6));
> Companies Act 1989, ss 56(5), 57, 64(2), 66(3), 71, 116(3),
>   125(2), 130(6), 135, 144(2), (6);
> Water Consolidation (Consequential Provisions) Act 1991;
> Charities Act 1992;
> Criminal Procedure (Consequential Provisions) (Scotland)
>   Act 1995, Sch 4, para 56(3) (it is thought that the intention of
>   SI 2008/2860 was to repeal this paragraph rather than
>   para 56(4) as stated);
> Financial Services and Markets Act 2000;
> Companies (Audit, Investigations and Community Enterprise)
>   Act 2004, Sch 2, paras 4, 6, 26;
> Civil Partnership Act 2004, Sch 27, para 103 (it is thought that
>   the intention of SI 2008/2860 was to repeal this paragraph
>   rather than para 104 as stated);
> Constitutional Reform Act 2005
>
> *Not yet in force* (NI), repeals of or in—
> Companies (Northern Ireland) Order 1986, SI 1986/1032
>   (NI 6) (except as previously noted);
> Companies (Northern Ireland) Order 1989, SI 1989/2404
>   (NI 18) (except as previously noted);
> Insolvency (Northern Ireland) Order 1989, SI 1989/2405
>   (NI 19), Sch 7;
> Companies (Northern Ireland) Order 1990, SI 1990/593 (NI 5)
>   (except as previously noted);
> Companies (No 2) (Northern Ireland) Order 1990,
>   SI 1990/1504 (NI 10) (except as previously noted);
> Criminal Justice Act 1993, Sch 6;
> Deregulation and Contracting Out (Northern Ireland)
>   Order 1996, SI 1996/1632 (NI 11), art 11, Sch 2

[1]  For transitional provisions and savings, see SI 2006/3428, arts 5, 8, Schs 1, 5

[2]  For transitional provisions and savings, see SI 2007/1093, arts 3, 8–11, Sch 1, Sch 6, paras 1, 5

[3]  For transitional provisions and savings, see SI 2007/2194, arts 6, 9, 12, Schs 1, 3

[4]  It is thought that the intention in SI 2007/2194, art 2(1)(d), is for Sch 1 to be brought into force
     together with ss 254, 255

[5]  For transitional provisions and savings, see SI 2007/3495, arts 6, 9, 12, Schs 1, 4

[6]  For savings, see SI 2008/674, arts 3, 4, 6, Sch 2

[7]  For transitional provisions and savings, see SI 2008/1886, art 7

[8]  For transitional provisions and savings, see SI 2008/2860, arts 5, 7, 8, Sch 2

## Compensation Act 2006 (c 29)

*RA:* 25 Jul 2006

*Commencement provisions:* s 16; Compensation Act 2006 (Commencement No 1) Order 2006, SI 2006/3005; Compensation Act 2006 (Commencement No 2) Order 2007, SI 2007/94; Compensation Act 2006 (Commencement No 3) Order 2007, SI 2007/922

| | | |
|---|---|---|
| 1, 2 | | 25 Jul 2006 (RA) |
| 3 | | 25 Jul 2006 (deemed always to have had effect, subject to a saving) (s 16(3), (4)) |
| 4 | (1) | 23 Apr 2007 (SI 2007/922) |
| | (2), (3) | 1 Dec 2006 (SI 2006/3005) |
| | (4) | 23 Apr 2007 (SI 2007/922) |
| | (5), (6) | 1 Dec 2006 (SI 2006/3005) |
| 5, 6 | | 1 Dec 2006 (SI 2006/3005) |
| 7 | | 23 Apr 2007 (SI 2007/922) |
| 8 | (1)–(7) | 23 Apr 2007 (SI 2007/922) |
| | (8) | 1 Dec 2006 (SI 2006/3005) |
| 9 | | 1 Dec 2006 (SI 2006/3005) |
| 10, 11 | | 23 Apr 2007 (SI 2007/922) |
| 12 | | 23 Jan 2007 (SI 2007/94) |
| 13 | (1) | 23 Jan 2007 (SI 2007/94) |
| | (2) | *Not yet in force* |
| | (3), (4) | 23 Jan 2007 (SI 2007/94) |
| 14, 15 | | 1 Dec 2006 (SI 2006/3005) |
| 16–18 | | 25 Jul 2006 (RA) |
| Schedule | | 1 Dec 2006 (SI 2006/3005) |

## Consolidated Fund Act 2006 (c 54)

*RA:* 19 Dec 2006

Whole Act in force 19 Dec 2006 (RA)

## Consumer Credit Act 2006 (c 14)

*RA:* 30 Mar 2006

*Commencement provisions:* s 71(2); Consumer Credit Act 2006 (Commencement No 1) Order 2006, SI 2006/1508; Consumer Credit Act 2006 (Commencement No 2 and Transitional Provisions and Savings) Order 2007, SI 2007/123, as amended by SI 2007/387; Consumer Credit Act 2006 (Commencement No 3) Order 2007, SI 2007/3300; Consumer Credit Act 2006 (Commencement No 4 and Transitional Provisions) Order 2008, SI 2008/831, as amended by SI 2008/2444

| | | |
|---|---|---|
| 1 | | 6 Apr 2007 (SI 2007/123)[1] |
| 2 | (1) | 6 Apr 2008 (in so far as it applies to agreements other than relevant agreements[2]) (SI 2008/831)[3] |
| | | 31 Oct 2008 (in so far as it applies to relevant agreements[2]) (SI 2008/831)[3] |
| | (2), (3) | 6 Apr 2008 (SI 2008/831) |
| 3 | | 16 Jun 2006 (in so far as inserts Consumer Credit Act 1974, s 16A(1)–(7)) (SI 2006/1508) |
| | | 6 Apr 2008 (in so far as inserts s 16A(8) of that Act) (SI 2007/3300) |
| 4 | | 16 Jun 2006 (in so far as inserts Consumer Credit Act 1974, s 16B(4)) (SI 2006/1508) |
| | | 6 Apr 2008 (s 16B(1)–(3), (5), (6) of that Act) (SI 2007/3300) |
| 5 | (1)–(4) | 6 Apr 2008 (SI 2007/3300) |
| | (5), (6) | 6 Apr 2007 (SI 2007/123) |
| | (7) | 6 Apr 2008 (SI 2007/3300) |
| | (8), (9) | 6 Apr 2007 (SI 2007/123) |

**Consumer Credit Act 2006 (c 14)**—*contd*

| | | |
|---|---|---|
| | (10) | 6 Apr 2008 (SI 2007/3300) |
| 6 | | 16 Jun 2006 (in so far as inserts Consumer Credit Act 1974, s 77A(2)) (SI 2006/1508) |
| | | 1 Oct 2008 (in so far as inserts s 77A(1), (3)–(8) of that Act) (SI 2007/3300) |
| 7 | (1), (2) | 16 Jun 2006 (SI 2006/1508) |
| | (3) | 1 Oct 2008 (SI 2007/3300) |
| 8 | | 31 Jan 2007 (SI 2007/123) |
| 9 | | 16 Jun 2006 (in so far as inserts Consumer Credit Act 1974, s 86B(8)) (SI 2006/1508) |
| | | 1 Oct 2008 (in so far as inserts s 86B(1)–(7), (9)–(12) of that Act) (SI 2007/3300) |
| 10 | | 16 Jun 2006 (in so far as inserts Consumer Credit Act 1974, s 86C(6)) (SI 2006/1508) |
| | | 1 Oct 2008 (in so far as inserts s 86C(1)–(5), (7) of that Act) (SI 2007/3300) |
| 11 | | 1 Oct 2008 (SI 2007/3300) |
| 12 | | 16 Jun 2006 (in so far as inserts Consumer Credit Act 1974, s 86E(2) (for the purpose of prescribing the period referred to therein) and s 86E(7)) (SI 2006/1508) |
| | | 1 Oct 2008 (in so far as inserts s 86E(1), (2) (except for the purpose of prescribing the period referred to therein), (3)–(6), (8) of that Act) (SI 2007/3300) |
| 13 | | 1 Oct 2008 (SI 2007/3300) |
| 14 | (1) | 1 Oct 2006 (SI 2006/1508) |
| | (2) | 16 Jun 2006 (SI 2006/1508) |
| | (3) | 1 Oct 2008 (SI 2007/3300) |
| 15 | | 6 Apr 2007 (SI 2007/123) |
| 16 | | 1 Oct 2008 (SI 2007/3300) |
| 17 | | 16 Jun 2006 (in so far as inserts Consumer Credit Act 1974, s 130A(6), (9)) (SI 2006/1508) |
| | | 1 Oct 2008 (in so far as inserts s 130A(1)–(5), (7), (8) of that Act) (SI 2007/3300) |
| 18 | | 16 Jun 2006 (SI 2006/1508) |
| 19–22 | | 6 Apr 2007 (SI 2007/123) |
| 23 | | 6 Apr 2008 (SI 2007/3300) |
| 24 | (1) | 1 Oct 2008 (SI 2007/3300) |
| | (2) | 16 Jun 2006 (SI 2006/1508) |
| | (3) | 1 Oct 2008 (SI 2007/3300) |
| | (4) | 16 Jun 2006 (SI 2006/1508) |
| | (5) | 1 Oct 2008 (SI 2007/3300) |
| | (6) | 16 Jun 2006 (SI 2006/1508) |
| 25 | (1) | 1 Oct 2008 (SI 2007/3300) |
| | (2) | 16 Jun 2006 (SI 2006/1508) |
| | (3), (4) | 1 Oct 2008 (SI 2007/3300) |
| | (5) | 16 Jun 2006 (SI 2006/1508) |
| 26 | | 6 Apr 2008 (SI 2007/3300) |
| 27 | (1) | 16 Jun 2006 (in so far as inserts Consumer Credit Act 1974, s 6A(2)–(4)) (SI 2006/1508) |
| | | 6 Apr 2008 (in so far as inserts s 6A(1) of that Act) (SI 2007/3300) |
| | (2)–(4) | 6 Apr 2008 (SI 2007/3300) |
| 28 | | 16 Jun 2006 (in so far as inserts s 24A(5), (6) of that Act) (SI 2006/1508) |
| | | 6 Apr 2008 (in so far as inserts s 24A(1)–(4) of that Act) (SI 2007/3300) |
| 29 | | 6 Apr 2008 (SI 2007/3300) |
| 30 | | 1 Dec 2007 (SI 2007/3300) |
| 31, 32 | | 6 Apr 2008 (SI 2007/3300) |
| 33 | (1)–(3) | 6 Apr 2008 (SI 2007/3300) |
| | (4) | 1 Dec 2007 (SI 2007/3300) |

**Consumer Credit Act 2006 (c 14)**—*contd*

| | | |
|---|---|---|
| | (5)–(12) | 6 Apr 2008 (SI 2007/3300) |
| 34 | (1) | 6 Apr 2008 (SI 2007/3300) |
| | (2) | 16 Jun 2006 (in so far as inserts Consumer Credit Act 1974, s 22(1B), (1E) for the purpose of prescribing the period referred to) (SI 2006/1508) |
| | | 6 Apr 2008 (in so far as inserts s 22(1A), (1C), (1D), and s 22(1B), (1E) (except for the purpose noted above) of that Act) (SI 2007/3300) |
| | (3)–(7) | 6 Apr 2008 (SI 2007/3300) |
| | (8) | 16 Jun 2006 (in so far as inserts Consumer Credit Act 1974, s 37(1B)(a), (b) for the purpose of specifying the form and content of a notice) (SI 2006/1508) |
| | | 6 Apr 2008 (in so far as inserts s 37(1A), (1B)(c), (d), and s 37(1B)(a), (b) (otherwise) of that Act) (SI 2007/3300) |
| | (9) | 6 Apr 2008 (SI 2007/3300) |
| 35 | | 16 Jun 2006 (in so far as inserts Consumer Credit Act 1974, s 28A(3)–(6)) (SI 2006/1508) |
| | | 6 Apr 2008 (in so far as inserts s 28A(1), (2) of that Act) (SI 2007/3300) |
| 36 | | 16 Jun 2006 (in so far as inserts Consumer Credit Act 1974, s 28B(2) for the purpose of determining the day before which an application under s 28B(1) shall be made) (SI 2006/1508) |
| | | 6 Apr 2008 (in so far as inserts s 28B(1), (3), (4), and s 28B(2) (except for the purpose noted above) of that Act) (SI 2007/3300) |
| 37–41 | | 6 Apr 2008 (SI 2007/3300) |
| 42 | | 1 Dec 2007 (SI 2007/3300) |
| 43 | | 6 Apr 2008 (SI 2007/3300) |
| 44 | (1) | 1 Dec 2007 (SI 2007/3300) |
| | (2) | 6 Apr 2008 (SI 2007/3300) |
| | (3) | 1 Dec 2007 (in so far as inserts Consumer Credit Act 1974, s 6(6) for the purpose of specifying the period referred to in that section) (SI 2007/3300) |
| | | 6 Apr 2008 (otherwise) (SI 2007/3300) |
| 45 | | 1 Dec 2007 (in so far as inserts Consumer Credit Act 1974, s 36A(6), (7)) (SI 2007/3300) |
| | | 6 Apr 2008 (otherwise) (SI 2007/3300) |
| 46–53 | | 6 Apr 2008 (SI 2007/3300) |
| 54 | | 1 Dec 2007 (SI 2007/3300) |
| 55 | (1) | 1 Dec 2007 (in so far as inserts Consumer Credit Act 1974, s 40A(3), (4) (in so far as it relates to Sch A1, paras 9(2), 10), (5)) (SI 2007/3300) |
| | | 6 Apr 2008 (in so far as inserts Consumer Credit Act 1974, s 40A(1), (2), (4) (in so far as it relates to Sch A1, paras 1–9(1), 12–16)) (SI 2007/3300) |
| | | *Never in force* (otherwise) (repealed) |
| | (2) | See Sch 1 below |
| 56 | (1) | 6 Apr 2008 (SI 2007/3300) |
| | (2) | 1 Dec 2007 (in so far as inserts Consumer Credit Act 1974, s 41(1D)) (SI 2007/3300) |
| | | 6 Apr 2008 (otherwise) (SI 2007/3300) |
| | (3) | 6 Apr 2008 (SI 2007/3300) |
| 57 | | 1 Dec 2007 (in so far as inserts Consumer Credit Act 1974, s 41A(6)) (SI 2007/3300) |
| | | 6 Apr 2008 (otherwise) (SI 2007/3300) |
| 58 | (1) | 6 Apr 2008 (SI 2007/3300) |
| | (2), (3) | 1 Dec 2007 (SI 2007/3300) |
| | (4) | 6 Apr 2008 (SI 2007/3300) |
| | (5) | *Never in force* (repealed) |
| 59–61 | | 16 Jun 2006 (SI 2006/1508) |

**Consumer Credit Act 2006 (c 14)**—*contd*

| | | |
|---|---|---|
| 62 | | 6 Apr 2008 (SI 2007/3300) |
| 63 | | 16 Jun 2006 (SI 2006/1508) |
| 64 | | 6 Apr 2008 (SI 2007/3300) |
| 65–68 | | 16 Jun 2006 (SI 2006/1508) |
| 69 | (1) | See Sch 3 below |
| | (2)–(5) | 16 Jun 2006 (SI 2006/1508) |
| 70 | | See Sch 4 below |
| 71 | | 30 Mar 2006 (RA) |
| Sch 1 | | 1 Dec 2007 (in so far as inserts Consumer Credit Act 1974, Sch A1, paras 9(2), 10) (SI 2007/3300) |
| | | 6 Apr 2008 (in so far as inserts paras 1–9(1), 12–16 of that Schedule) (SI 2007/3300) |
| | | *Never in force* (in so far as inserts para 11 of that Schedule) (repealed) |
| Sch 2 | | 16 Jun 2006 (SI 2006/1508) |
| Sch 3 | para 1(1) | 16 Jun 2006 (SI 2006/1508) |
| | para 1(2) | 6 Apr 2007 (SI 2007/123) |
| | paras 2–4 | 1 Oct 2008 (SI 2007/3300) |
| | para 5 | 31 Jan 2007 (SI 2007/123) |
| | paras 6–9 | 1 Oct 2008 (SI 2007/3300) |
| | para 10 | 1 Oct 2006 (SI 2006/1508) |
| | para 11 | 6 Apr 2007 (SI 2007/123) |
| | paras 12, 13 | 1 Oct 2008 (SI 2007/3300) |
| | paras 14–16 | 6 Apr 2007 (SI 2007/123) |
| | para 17 | *Not yet in force* |
| | para 18 | 6 Apr 2008 (SI 2007/3300) |
| | para 19 | 1 Dec 2007 (SI 2007/3300) |
| | paras 20, 21 | 6 Apr 2008 (SI 2007/3300) |
| | paras 22–25 | 1 Dec 2007 (SI 2007/3300) |
| | paras 26–28 | 6 Apr 2008 (SI 2007/3300) |
| | para 29 | 6 Apr 2007 (SI 2007/123) |

Sch 4      6 Apr 2007 (SI 2007/123), repeals of or in—

         Consumer Credit Act 1974, ss 16, 127, 137–140, 143, 171, 181(1), (2) (words "139(5) and (7)", and "or 139(5) or (7)" respectively), 185;

         Bankruptcy (Scotland) Act 1985;

         Insolvency Act 1986;

         Insolvency (Northern Ireland) Order 1989, SI 1989/2405 (NI 19)

     6 Apr 2008 (SI 2007/3300), repeals of or in—

         Consumer Credit Act 1974, ss 2, 6, 15, 22, 23, 25, 29, 32, 36, 40, 41, 43, 147, 150, 162, 181(1), (2) (word "43(3)(a)," in each case), 189(1), (definitions "cost" and "licence");

         Tribunals and Inquiries Act 1992;

         Enterprise Act 2002

     6 Apr 2008 (SI 2008/831), repeals of or in—

         Consumer Credit Act 1974, ss 8, 189 (definition "personal credit agreement"), Sch 2 (in so far as they relate to agreements other than relevant agreements[2])

     31 Oct 2008 (SI 2008/831), repeals of or in—

         Consumer Credit Act 1974, ss 8, 189 (definition "personal credit agreement"), Sch 2 (in so far as they relate to relevant agreements[2])

---

[1]    For transitional provisions and savings, see SI 2007/123, arts 4, 5

[2]    For the meaning of "relevant agreement" in SI 2008/831, see art 2(1), Sch 1 thereto

[3]    For transitional provisions, see SI 2008/831, art 4

## Council Tax (New Valuation Lists for England) Act 2006 (c 7)

*RA:* 30 Mar 2006

Whole Act in force 30 Mar 2006 (RA)

## Criminal Defence Service Act 2006 (c 9)

*RA:* 30 Mar 2006

*Commencement provisions:* s 5(2); Criminal Defence Service Act 2006 (Commencement) Order 2006, SI 2006/2491

| | |
|---|---|
| 1–4 | 2 Oct 2006 (SI 2006/2491) |
| 5 | 30 Mar 2006 (RA) |

## Edinburgh Tram (Line One) Act 2006 (asp 7)

*RA:* 8 May 2006

*Commencement provisions:* s 44

| | |
|---|---|
| 1–44 | 8 May 2006 (RA) |
| 45–48 | *Not yet in force* |
| 49–85 | 8 May 2006 (RA) |
| Schs 1–10 | 8 May 2006 (RA) |

## Edinburgh Tram (Line Two) Act 2006 (asp 6)

*RA:* 27 Apr 2006

*Commencement provisions:* s 44

| | |
|---|---|
| 1–44 | 27 Apr 2006 (RA) |
| 45–48 | *Not yet in force* |
| 49–83 | 27 Apr 2006 (RA) |
| Schs 1–10 | 27 Apr 2006 (RA) |

## Education and Inspections Act 2006 (c 40)

*RA:* 8 Nov 2006

*Commencement provisions:* s 188; Education and Inspections Act 2006 (Commencement No 1 and Savings Provisions) Order 2006, SI 2006/2990, as amended by SI 2008/54; Education and Inspections Act 2006 (Commencement No 2) Order 2006, SI 2006/3400; Education and Inspections Act 2006 (Commencement No 3 and Transitional Provisions and Savings) Order 2007, SI 2007/935[2], as amended by SI 2007/1271; Education and Inspections Act 2006 (Commencement No 4 and Transitional Provisions and Amendment) Order 2007, SI 2007/1271[3]; Education and Inspections Act 2006 (Commencement No 5 and Saving Provisions) Order 2007, SI 2007/1801; Education and Inspections Act 2006 (Commencement No 6) Order 2007, SI 2007/3074; Education and Inspections Act 2006 (Commencement No 1 and Saving Provisions) (Wales) Order 2008, SI 2008/1429; Education and Inspections Act 2006 (Commencement No 7 and Transitional Provisions) Order 2008, SI 2008/1971; Education and Inspections Act 2006 (Commencement No 2) (Wales) Order 2009, SI 2009/49; Education and Inspections Act 2006 (Commencement No 3) (Wales) Order 2009, SI 2009/1027; Education and Inspections Act 2006 (Commencement No 4 and Transitional Provisions) (Wales) Order 2009, SI 2009/2545; Education and Inspections Act 2006 (Commencement No 5 and Transitional Provision) (Wales) Order 2010, SI 2010/736; Education and Inspections Act 2006 (Commencement No 6) (Wales) Order 2010, SI 2010/2543; Education and Inspections Act 2006 (Commencement No 8) Order 2014, SI 2014/2380

| | |
|---|---|
| 1 | 25 May 2007 (E) (SI 2007/935) |
| | 30 Jun 2008 (W) (SI 2008/1429) |
| 2, 3 | 25 May 2007 (SI 2007/935) |

**Education and Inspections Act 2006 (c 40)**—*contd*

| | | |
|---|---|---|
| 4 | | 27 Feb 2007 (E) (SI 2006/3400) |
| | | 1 Sep 2009 (W) (SI 2009/1027) |
| 5 | | 8 Feb 2007 (in relation to secondary schools which are not special schools and in relation to primary schools which are not special, only in relation to the local education authorities listed in SI 2006/3400, Schedule) (SI 2006/3400) |
| | | 1 Apr 2007 (in relation to primary schools which are not special schools, only in relation to the local education authorities listed in SI 2007/935, Schedule) (SI 2007/935) |
| | | 1 Sep 2007 (in relation to primary schools which are not special schools, only in relation to the local education authorities listed in SI 2007/1801, Schedule, Pt 1) (SI 2007/1801) |
| | | 1 Sep 2007 (in relation to special schools, only in relation to the local education authorities listed in SI 2007/1801, Schedule, Pt 2) (SI 2007/1801) |
| | | 1 Jan 2008 (in relation to special schools, only in relation to the local education authorities listed in SI 2007/3074, Schedule, Pt 1) (SI 2007/3074) |
| | | 1 Apr 2008 (in relation to special schools, only in relation to the local education authorities listed in SI 2007/3074, Schedule, Pt 2A) (SI 2007/3074) |
| | | 1 Apr 2008 (in relation to primary schools, only in relation to the local education authorities listed in SI 2007/3074, Schedule, Pt 2B) (SI 2007/3074) |
| | | *Never in force* (otherwise) (repealed) |
| 6 | | 8 Jan 2007 (s 188(2)) |
| 7–17 | | 25 May 2007 (SI 2007/935) |
| 18 | (1)–(3) | 1 Apr 2007 (SI 2007/935) |
| | (4), (5) | 25 May 2007 (SI 2007/935) |
| 19, 20 | | 25 May 2007 (SI 2007/935) |
| 21–24 | | 1 Apr 2007 (SI 2007/935) |
| 25 | (1)–(4) | 25 May 2007 (SI 2007/935) |
| | (5)–(7) | 1 Apr 2007 (SI 2007/935) |
| | (8) | 25 May 2007 (SI 2007/935) |
| 26 | | 1 Apr 2007 (SI 2007/935) |
| 27 | (1)–(6) | 1 Apr 2007 (SI 2007/935) |
| | (7) | 25 May 2007 (SI 2007/935) |
| | (8) | 1 Apr 2007 (SI 2007/935) |
| 28–30 | | 25 May 2007 (SI 2007/935) |
| 31, 32 | | 1 Apr 2007 (SI 2007/935) |
| 33 | | 1 Apr 2007 (to the extent that it inserts School Standards and Framework Act 1998, ss 23A(9), (10), 23B) (SI 2007/935) |
| | | 25 May 2007 (otherwise) (SI 2007/935) |
| 34 | | 25 May 2007 (SI 2007/935) |
| 35 | | 1 Apr 2007 (to the extent that it inserts School Standards and Framework Act 1998, Sch 3, para 9A(3)) (SI 2007/935) |
| | | 25 May 2007 (otherwise) (SI 2007/935) |
| 36 | | See Sch 4 below |
| 37 | (1) | 30 Jun 2008 (W) (SI 2008/1429) |
| | | 1 Sep 2008 (E) (SI 2008/1971)[6] |
| | (2)(a) | 30 Jun 2008 (W) (SI 2008/1429) |
| | | 1 Sep 2008 (E) (SI 2008/1971)[6] |
| | (2)(b) | 1 Sep 2008 (E) (SI 2008/1971)[6] |
| | | *Not yet in force* (W) |
| 38 | (1) | 25 May 2007 (E) (except so far as inserts Education Act 2002, s 21(5)(a), (b), (8), (9)(b)) (SI 2007/1271) |
| | | 1 Sep 2007 (E) (exceptions noted above) (SI 2007/1801) |
| | | 1 Sep 2008 (W) (SI 2008/1429) |
| | (2) | 25 May 2007 (E) (SI 2007/1271) |
| | | 1 Sep 2008 (W) (SI 2008/1429) |

**Education and Inspections Act 2006 (c 40)**—*contd*

| | | |
|---|---|---|
| 39 | | 27 Feb 2007 (E) (SI 2006/3400) |
| | | 30 Jun 2008 (W) (SI 2008/1429) |
| 40 | | 12 Dec 2006 (E) (SI 2006/2990)[1] |
| | | 1 Sep 2008 (W) (SI 2008/1429)[5] |
| 41, 42 | | 27 Feb 2007 (SI 2006/3400) |
| 43 | | 8 Jan 2007 (E) (SI 2006/3400) |
| | | 30 Jun 2008 (W) (SI 2008/1429) |
| 44 | | 27 Feb 2007 (E) (SI 2006/3400) |
| | | 30 Jun 2008 (W) (SI 2008/1429) |
| 45 | | 8 Jan 2007 (E) (SI 2006/3400) |
| | | 30 Jun 2008 (W) (SI 2008/1429) |
| 46 | | 27 Feb 2007 (E) (SI 2006/3400) |
| 47 | | 27 Feb 2007 (E) (SI 2006/3400) |
| | | 30 Jun 2008 (W) (SI 2008/1429) |
| 48–51 | | 8 Jan 2007 (SI 2006/3400) |
| 52 | | 8 Jan 2007 (s 188(2)) |
| 53 | | 27 Feb 2007 (E) (SI 2006/3400) |
| | | 30 Jun 2008 (W) (SI 2008/1429) |
| 54 | (1), (2) | 8 Jan 2007 (SI 2006/3400) |
| | (3)(a) | 25 May 2007 (SI 2007/935) |
| | (3)(b) | 8 Jan 2007 (SI 2006/3400) |
| 55 | (1)–(7) | 1 Sep 2007 (E) (SI 2007/1801) |
| | | 9 Feb 2009 (W) (SI 2009/49) |
| | (8), (9) | 25 Jun 2007 (E) (SI 2007/1801) |
| | | 9 Feb 2009 (W) (SI 2009/49) |
| 56 | | 25 May 2007 (E) (SI 2007/935) |
| | | *Not yet in force* (W) |
| 57 | | See Sch 5 below |
| 58 | | 8 Jan 2007 (s 188(2)) |
| 59–73 | | 1 Apr 2007 (SI 2007/935) |
| 74 | (1)–(3) | *Not yet in force* (sub-s (3) repealed) |
| | (4) | 1 Apr 2007 (SI 2007/935) |
| | (5) | *Not yet in force* |
| 75 | | *Never in force* (repealed) |
| 76 | | 1 Apr 2007 (SI 2007/935) |
| 77 | (1) | 1 Apr 2007 (to the extent that it inserts Education Act 1996, ss 508B(11), 508D) (SI 2007/935) |
| | | 1 Sep 2007 (otherwise) (SI 2007/1801) |
| | (2) | See Sch 8 below |
| 78–80 | | 1 Apr 2007 (SI 2007/935) |
| 81 | | *Never in force* (repealed) |
| 82 | | 1 Sep 2007 (SI 2007/1801) |
| 83 | | 1 Apr 2007 (SI 2007/935)[2] |
| 84 | | 1 Apr 2007 (to the extent that it relates to travel functions under the Education Act 1996, ss 508A, 509AA) (SI 2007/935) |
| | | 1 Sep 2007 (otherwise, except in relation to travel functions under the Education Act 1996, s 508F) (SI 2007/1801) |
| | | *Not yet in force* (exception noted above) |
| 85 | | See Sch 10 below |
| 86, 87 | | 8 Nov 2006 (s 188(1)) |
| 88 | | 1 Apr 2007 (E) (SI 2007/935) |
| | | 31 Oct 2010 (W) (SI 2010/2543) |
| 89 | (1)–(3) | 1 Apr 2007 (E) (SI 2007/935) |
| | | 1 Jan 2010 (W) (SI 2009/2545)[7] |
| | (4) | 1 Apr 2007 (E) (SI 2007/935) |
| | | 31 Oct 2010 (W) (SI 2010/2543) |
| | (5), (6) | 1 Apr 2007 (E) (SI 2007/935) |
| | | 1 Jan 2010 (W) (SI 2009/2545) |
| 90, 91 | | 1 Apr 2007 (E) (SI 2007/935) |

**Education and Inspections Act 2006 (c 40)**—*contd*

| | | |
|---|---|---|
| | | 31 Oct 2010 (W) (SI 2010/2543) |
| 92 | (1)–(7) | 1 Apr 2007 (E) (SI 2007/935) |
| | | 31 Oct 2010 (W) (SI 2010/2543) |
| | (8)(a) | 1 Apr 2007 (E) (SI 2007/935) |
| | | 31 Oct 2010 (W) (SI 2010/2543) |
| | (8)(b) | 1 Apr 2007 (E) (SI 2007/935) |
| | | *Not yet in force* (W) |
| | (8)(c) | 1 Apr 2007 (E) (SI 2007/935) |
| | | 31 Oct 2010 (W) (SI 2010/2543) |
| 93–95 | | 1 Apr 2007 (E) (SI 2007/935) |
| | | 31 Oct 2010 (W) (SI 2010/2543) |
| 96 | (a) | 1 Apr 2007 (E) (SI 2007/935) |
| | | 31 Oct 2010 (W) (SI 2010/2543) |
| | (b) | 1 Apr 2007 (E) (SI 2007/935) |
| | | 1 Jan 2010 (W) (in so far as relates to repeal of the School Standards and Framework Act 1998, s 61(4)–(7)) (SI 2009/2545) |
| | | 31 Oct 2010 (W) (in so far as relates to repeals of the Education Act 1996, ss 550A, 550B, and s 61(1)–(3), (8) of the 1998 Act) (SI 2010/2543) |
| 97 | | 1 Sep 2007 (E) (SI 2007/1801)[4] |
| | | 31 Oct 2010 (W) (SI 2010/2543) |
| 98, 99 | | 1 Sep 2007 (E) (SI 2007/1801)[4] |
| | | 31 Oct 2010 (W) (for the purposes of making regulations under the Anti-social Behaviour Act 2003, ss 20(2A), 22A) (SI 2010/2543) |
| | | 5 Jan 2011 (W) (otherwise) (SI 2010/2543) |
| 100, 101 | | 1 Sep 2007 (SI 2007/1801) |
| 102 | | 1 Sep 2007 (E) (SI 2007/1801) |
| | | 31 Oct 2010 (W) (for the purposes of making regulations) (SI 2010/2543) |
| | | 5 Jan 2011 (W) (otherwise) (SI 2010/2543) |
| 103–107 | | 1 Sep 2007 (SI 2007/1801) |
| 108 | | 1 Sep 2007 (E) (SI 2007/1801) |
| | | 31 Oct 2010 (W) (SI 2010/2543) |
| 109 | (1)–(7) | 8 Nov 2006 (s 188(1)) |
| | (8) | 1 Sep 2007 (SI 2007/1801) |
| | (9)–(11) | 8 Nov 2006 (s 188(1)) |
| 110 | | 1 Sep 2007 (SI 2007/1801) |
| 111 | | 8 Nov 2006 (s 188(1)) |
| 112 | (1)–(3) | 8 Nov 2006 (so far as they confer power to make subordinate legislation) (s 188(1)) |
| | | 12 Dec 2006 (otherwise) (SI 2006/2990) |
| | (4) | See Sch 11 below |
| 113, 114 | | 8 Nov 2006 (so far as they confer power to make subordinate legislation) (s 188(1)) |
| | | 1 Apr 2007 (otherwise) (SI 2007/935) |
| 115 | | See Sch 12 below |
| 116 | (1)(a), (b) | 8 Nov 2006 (so far as they confer power to make subordinate legislation) (s 188(1)) |
| | | 12 Dec 2006 (otherwise) (SI 2006/2990) |
| | (1)(c) | 8 Nov 2006 (so far as confers power to make subordinate legislation) (s 188(1)) |
| | | 1 Apr 2007 (otherwise) (SI 2007/935) |
| | (2) | 8 Nov 2006 (so far as confers power to make subordinate legislation) (s 188(1)) |
| | | 1 Apr 2007 (otherwise) (SI 2007/935) |
| 117 | | 8 Nov 2006 (so far as confers power to make subordinate legislation) (s 188(1)) |
| | | 12 Dec 2006 (otherwise) (SI 2006/2990) |

**Education and Inspections Act 2006 (c 40)**—*contd*

| | | |
|---|---|---|
| 118–148 | | 8 Nov 2006 (so far as they confer power to make subordinate legislation) (s 188(1)) |
| | | 1 Apr 2007 (otherwise) (SI 2007/935) |
| 149 | | See Sch 13 below |
| 150–153 | | 8 Nov 2006 (so far as they confer power to make subordinate legislation) (s 188(1)) |
| | | 1 Apr 2007 (otherwise) (SI 2007/935) |
| 154 | | 8 Nov 2006 (so far as confers power to make subordinate legislation) (s 188(1)) |
| | | 1 Sep 2008 (otherwise) (SI 2008/1971) |
| 155 | | 8 Nov 2006 (so far as confers power to make subordinate legislation) (s 188(1)) |
| | | 1 Apr 2007 (otherwise) (SI 2007/935) |
| 156 | | 8 Nov 2006 (so far as confers power to make subordinate legislation) (s 188(1)) |
| | | 30 Jun 2008 (otherwise) (SI 2008/1429) |
| 157 | | See Sch 14 below |
| 158 | | See Sch 15 below |
| 159 | | 8 Nov 2006 (so far as confers power to make subordinate legislation) (s 188(1)) |
| | | 12 Dec 2006 (otherwise) (SI 2006/2990) |
| 160 | | 28 Mar 2007 (SI 2007/935) |
| 161 | | 8 Nov 2006 (s 188(1)) |
| 162 | | 8 Jan 2007 (s 188(2)) |
| 163 | | 8 Jan 2007 (SI 2006/3400) |
| 164 | | 28 Mar 2007 (E) (SI 2007/935) |
| | | 1 Sep 2009 (W) (SI 2009/1027) |
| 165 | | 1 Apr 2007 (E) (SI 2007/935) |
| | | *Not yet in force* (W) |
| 166 | | 1 Apr 2007 (E) (SI 2007/935) |
| | | 30 Jun 2008 (W) (SI 2008/1429) |
| 167 | | 1 Sep 2007 (E) (SI 2007/1801) |
| | | 31 Oct 2010 (W) (SI 2010/2543) |
| 168 | | 8 Jan 2007 (s 188(2)) |
| 169 | | 12 Oct 2009 (W) (SI 2009/2545) |
| | | *Not yet in force* (E) |
| 170 | (1) | 12 Oct 2009 (W) (SI 2009/2545) |
| | | *Not yet in force* (E) |
| | (2) | 12 Oct 2009 (W) (SI 2009/2545) |
| | | 8 Sep 2014 (E) (SI 2014/2380) |
| | (3) | 12 Oct 2009 (W) (SI 2009/2545) |
| | | *Not yet in force* (E) |
| 171 | | 12 Oct 2009 (W) (SI 2009/2545) |
| | | *Not yet in force* (E) |
| 172 | | 8 Jan 2007 (s 188(2)) |
| 173 | | 8 Jan 2007 (E) (SI 2006/3400) |
| | | *Not yet in force* (W) |
| 174 | | 8 Jan 2007 (s 188(2)) |
| 175 | | See Sch 17 below |
| 176 | | 1 Apr 2007 (SI 2007/935) |
| 177–179 | | 8 Jan 2007 (s 188(2)) |
| 180–183 | | 8 Nov 2006 (s 188(1)) |
| 184 | | See Sch 18 below |
| 185–191 | | 8 Nov 2006 (s 188(1)) |
| Sch 1 | | 8 Jan 2007 (s 188(2)) |
| Sch 2 | paras 1–4 | 25 May 2007 (SI 2007/935) |
| | para 5 | 1 Apr 2007 (SI 2007/935) |
| | paras 6–10 | 25 May 2007 (SI 2007/935) |
| | para 11 | 1 Apr 2007 (SI 2007/935) |

**Education and Inspections Act 2006 (c 40)**—*contd*

| | | |
|---|---|---|
| | para 12 | 25 May 2007 (SI 2007/935) |
| | paras 13–15 | 1 Apr 2007 (SI 2007/935) |
| | para 16 | 25 May 2007 (SI 2007/935) |
| | para 17 | *Not yet in force* |
| | para 18(1) | 1 Apr 2007 (SI 2007/935) |
| | para 18(2)–(5) | 25 May 2007 (SI 2007/935) |
| | paras 19, 20 | 1 Apr 2007 (SI 2007/935) |
| | paras 21–31 | 25 May 2007 (SI 2007/935) |
| Sch 3 | | 25 May 2007 (SI 2007/935) |
| Sch 4 | | 25 May 2007 (SI 2007/935)[2] |
| Sch 5 | paras 1, 2 | 8 Feb 2007 (E) (SI 2006/3400) |
| | | 2 Apr 2010 (W) (SI 2010/736) |
| | paras 3–5 | 8 Feb 2007 (E) (SI 2006/3400) |
| | | 15 Mar 2010 (W) (for the purpose of making regulations) (SI 2010/736) |
| | | 2 Apr 2010 (W) (otherwise) (SI 2010/736)[8] |
| | para 6 | 8 Feb 2007 (E) (SI 2006/3400) |
| | | 2 Apr 2010 (W) (SI 2010/736) |
| Sch 6 | | 1 Apr 2007 (SI 2007/935) |
| Sch 7 | | 1 Apr 2007 (SI 2007/935)[2] |
| Sch 8 | | 1 Sep 2007 (to the extent that it inserts Education Act 1996, Sch 35B, paras 1 (but only in relation to paras 2–7 or 9, 10), 2–10, 14, 15) (SI 2007/1801) |
| | | 1 Sep 2008 (otherwise) (SI 2008/1971) |
| Sch 9 | | 1 Apr 2007 (SI 2007/935) |
| Sch 10 | paras 1–4 | 1 Sep 2007 (except for words "section 508F(1)" in paras 1(a), 2(3) and words "section 508F(3)" in para 3) (SI 2007/1801)[4] |
| | | *Not yet in force* (exceptions noted above) (para 4 repealed) |
| | para 5 | 1 Apr 2007 (SI 2007/935) |
| Sch 11 | para 1 | 12 Dec 2006 (SI 2006/2990) |
| | para 2(1) | 12 Dec 2006 (SI 2006/2990) |
| | para 2(2) | 12 Dec 2006 (in so far as it relates to provisions of this Schedule below brought into force by SI 2006/2990) (SI 2006/2990) |
| | | 1 Apr 2007 (otherwise) (SI 2007/935) |
| | para 2(3) | 1 Apr 2007 (SI 2007/935) |
| | para 3 | 12 Dec 2006 (SI 2006/2990) |
| | para 4 | 1 Apr 2007 (SI 2007/935) |
| | para 5(1) | 12 Dec 2006 (SI 2006/2990) |
| | para 5(2)–(4) | 1 Apr 2007 (SI 2007/935) |
| | para 6(1)–(4) | 12 Dec 2006 (SI 2006/2990) |
| | para 6(5) | 1 Apr 2007 (SI 2007/935) |
| | para 7(1) | 12 Dec 2006 (SI 2006/2990) |
| | para 7(2), (3) | 1 Apr 2007 (SI 2007/935) |
| | paras 8–11 | 12 Dec 2006 (SI 2006/2990) |
| | para 12(1)–(3) | 12 Dec 2006 (SI 2006/2990) |
| | para 12(4) | 1 Apr 2007 (SI 2007/935) |
| | para 13 | 12 Dec 2006 (SI 2006/2990) |
| Schs 12–14 | | 1 Apr 2007 (SI 2007/935) |
| Sch 15 | paras 1–6 | 1 Apr 2007 (SI 2007/935) |
| | para 7 | 12 Dec 2006 (SI 2006/2990) |
| | para 8 | 1 Apr 2007 (SI 2007/935) |
| | para 9 | 12 Dec 2006 (in so far as it relates to para 7 of this Schedule) (SI 2006/2990) |
| | | 1 Apr 2007 (in so far as it relates to paras 1–6 and 8 of this Schedule) (SI 2007/935)[2] |
| Sch 16 | | 8 Nov 2006 (s 188(1)) |
| Sch 17 | | 30 Jun 2008 (SI 2008/1429) |
| Sch 18 | Pt 1 | 8 Nov 2006 (s 188(1)) |
| | Pt 2 | 8 Jan 2007 (s 188(2)) |

**Education and Inspections Act 2006 (c 40)**—*contd*

| | |
|---|---|
| Pt 3 | 25 May 2007 (SI 2007/935) |
| Pt 4 | 1 Apr 2007 (SI 2007/935) |
| Pt 5 | 1 Apr 2007 (except repeal of Children Act 2004, s 38) (SI 2007/935) |
| | 30 Jun 2008 (otherwise) (SI 2008/1429) |
| Pt 6 | 12 Dec 2006 (E) (repeals of or in School Standards and Framework Act 1998, ss 84, 85) (SI 2006/2990) |

8 Jan 2007 (E) (repeals of or in School Standards and Framework Act 1998, s 89(2)) (SI 2006/3400)

8 Jan 2007 (repeals of or in School Standards and Framework Act 1998, s 89(1A)) (SI 2006/3400)

8 Feb 2007 (E) (repeals of or in School Standards and Framework Act 1998, ss 17, 47A, 48, Schs 14, 15) (SI 2006/3400)

27 Feb 2007 (repeals of or in School Standards and Framework Act 1998, s 85A) (SI 2006/3400)

27 Feb 2007 (E) (SI 2006/3400), repeals of or in—
Education Act 1996, s 437;
School Standards and Framework Act 1998, ss 90, 99

1 Apr 2007 (E) (SI 2007/935), repeals of or in—
Education Act 1996, ss 550A, 550B;
Education Act 1997;
School Standards and Framework Act 1998, s 61

25 May 2007 (E) (repeals of School Standards and Framework Act 1998, s 5) (SI 2007/935)

25 May 2007 (SI 2007/935), repeals of or in—
School Standards and Framework Act 1998, s 77, Schs 3, 22;
Education Act 2002, Sch 21;
Education Act 2005

1 Sep 2007 (E) (SI 2007/1801), repeals of or in—
Education Act 2002, s 176;
Anti-social Behaviour Act 2003[4];
Childcare Act 2006

1 Sep 2007 (repeals of or in Education Act 1996, s 509) (SI 2007/1801)[4]

30 Jun 2008 (W) (repeals of or in School Standards and Framework Act 1998, ss 5, 58(4), 89(2)(c), 90, 99) (SI 2008/1429)

1 Sep 2008 (W) (repeals of or in School Standards and Framework Act 1998, ss 84, 85) (SI 2008/1429)

1 Sep 2009 (W) (repeal in Education Act 1996, s 437) (SI 2009/1027)

1 Jan 2010 (W) (repeal of School Standards and Framework Act 1998, s 61(4)–(7)) (SI 2009/2545)

2 Apr 2010 (W) (repeals of or in School Standards and Framework Act 1998, ss 17, 47A, 48, Schs 14, 15) (SI 2010/736)[8]

31 Oct 2010 (W) (2010/2543), repeals of or in—
Education Act 1996, ss 550A, 550B;
Education Act 1997, ss 4, 5;
School Standards and Framework Act 1998, s 61 (so far as not already repealed);
Education Act 2002, s 176;
Childcare Act 2006, Sch 2, para 42

*Not yet in force* (E), repeal of—
School Standards and Framework Act 1998, s 58(4)

*Not yet in force* (W), repeal of—
Anti-social Behaviour Act 2003, s 21(4)

---

[1]   For savings, see SI 2006/2990, arts 3, 4

[2]   For transitional provisions and savings, see SI 2007/935, art 8

[3]   For transitional provisions and savings, see SI 2007/1271, art 5

**Education and Inspections Act 2006 (c 40)**—*contd*

[4] For savings, see SI 2007/1801, art 5

[5] For savings, see SI 2008/1429, art 4

[6] For transitional provisions and savings, see SI 2008/1971, art 3

[7] For a transitional provision, see SI 2009/2545, art 4

[8] For a transitional provision, see SI 2010/736, art 4

---

**Electoral Administration Act 2006 (c 22)**

*RA:* 11 Jul 2006

*Commencement provisions:* s 77; Electoral Administration Act 2006 (Commencement No 1 and Transitional Provisions) Order 2006, SI 2006/1972, as amended by SI 2006/2268; Electoral Administration Act 2006 (Commencement No 2, Transitional and Savings Provisions) Order 2006, SI 2006/3412[2]; Electoral Administration Act 2006 (Commencement No 3) Order 2007, SI 2007/230; Electoral Administration Act 2006 (Commencement No 4 and Transitional Provision) Order 2007, SI 2007/1847; Electoral Administration Act 2006 (Commencement No 5) Order 2007, SI 2007/3376; Electoral Administration Act 2006 (Commencement No 6) Order 2008, SI 2008/610; Electoral Administration Act 2006 (Commencement No 7) Order 2008, SI 2008/1316; Electoral Administration Act 2006 (Commencement No 1 and Transitional Provisions) (Northern Ireland) Order 2008, SI 2008/1656; Electoral Administration Act 2006 (Commencement No 8 and Transitional Provision) Order 2009, SI 2009/1509; Electoral Administration Act 2006 (Commencement No 1 and Saving Provision) (Scotland) Order 2010, SI 2010/275; Electoral Administration Act 2006 (Commencement No 2) (Northern Ireland) Order 2014, SI 2014/1809; Electoral Administration Act 2006 (Commencement No 9) Order 2016, SI 2016/538; Electoral Administration Act 2006 (Commencement No 10 and Transitional Provision) Order 2016, SI 2016/551

| | | |
|---|---|---|
| 1 | (1) | 11 Jul 2006 (s 77(1)) |
| | (2) | *Never in force* (repealed) |
| | (3), (4) | 11 Jul 2006 (s 77(1)) |
| | (5) | *Never in force* (repealed) |
| | (6)–(11) | 11 Jul 2006 (s 77(1)) |
| 2 | (1) | 11 Jul 2006 (s 77(1)) |
| | (2) | *Never in force* (repealed) |
| | (3) | 11 Jul 2006 (s 77(1)) |
| | (4)–(9) | *Never in force* (repealed) |
| | (10), (11) | 11 Jul 2006 (s 77(1)) |
| | (12) | *Never in force* (repealed) |
| | (13) | 11 Jul 2006 (s 77(1)) |
| 3, 4 | | 11 Jul 2006 (s 77(1)) |
| 5 | (1)–(9) | 11 Jul 2006 (s 77(1)) |
| | (10) | *Never in force* (repealed) |
| 6 | | 11 Jul 2006 (s 77(1)) |
| 7 | | *Never in force* (repealed) |
| 8 | | 11 Jul 2006 (s 77(1)) |
| 9 | | 11 Sep 2006 (SI 2006/1972) |
| 10, 11 | | 1 Jan 2007 (SI 2006/3412) |
| 12 | | 1 Jan 2007 (E) (W) (S) (SI 2006/3412) |
| | | 14 May 2008 (NI) (SI 2008/1316) |
| 13 | (1) | 1 Jan 2007 (E) (W) (S) (SI 2006/3412) |
| | | 14 May 2008 (NI) (SI 2008/1316) |
| | (2), (3) | 30 Nov 2007 (SI 2007/3376) |
| 14 | | 1 Jan 2007 (SI 2006/3412) |
| 15 | | 11 Sep 2006 (SI 2006/1972) |
| 16 | | 1 Jan 2007 (E) (W) (S) (SI 2006/3412) |
| | | 1 Jul 2008 (NI) (SI 2008/1316) |
| 17 | | 1 Jan 2007 (E) (W) (S) (SI 2006/3412) |
| | | 7 Feb 2007 (NI) (SI 2007/230) |

**Electoral Administration Act 2006 (c 22)**—*contd*

| | | |
|---|---|---|
| 18 | (1)–(5) | 1 Jan 2007 (E) (W) (S) (SI 2006/3412) |
| | | 1 Jul 2008 (NI) (SI 2008/1316) |
| | (6) | See Sch 1, Pt 3 below |
| | (7) | 1 Jan 2007 (E) (W) (S) (SI 2006/3412) |
| | | 1 Jul 2008 (NI) (SI 2008/1316) |
| 19 | | 1 Jan 2007 (E) (W) (S) (SI 2006/3412) |
| | | 1 Jul 2008 (NI) (SI 2008/1316) |
| 20 | | See Sch 1, Pt 4 below |
| 21, 22 | | 1 Jan 2007 (E) (W) (S) (SI 2006/3412) |
| | | 1 Jul 2008 (NI) (SI 2008/1316) |
| 23 | (1) | 11 Sep 2006 (SI 2006/1972) |
| | (2) | 1 Jan 2007 (E) (W) (S) (SI 2006/3412) |
| | | 1 Jul 2008 (NI) (SI 2008/1316) |
| | (3) | 11 Sep 2006 (except so far as inserts Representation of the People Act 1983, s 65A(1A)(c) and word "or" preceding it) (SI 2006/1972) |
| | | 1 Jan 2007 (E) (W) (S) (otherwise) (SI 2006/3412) |
| | | 1 Jul 2008 (NI) (otherwise) (SI 2008/1316) |
| | (4) | 1 Jan 2007 (E) (W) (S) (SI 2006/3412) |
| | | 1 Jul 2008 (NI) (SI 2008/1316) |
| 24 | | 1 Jan 2007 (E) (W) (S) (SI 2006/3412) |
| | | 1 Jul 2008 (NI) (SI 2008/1316) |
| 25 | | 11 Sep 2006 (SI 2006/1972)[1] |
| 26 | | 1 Jan 2007 (E) (W) (S) (SI 2006/3412) |
| | | 1 Jul 2008 (NI) (SI 2008/1316) |
| 27 | | 11 Sep 2006 (SI 2006/1972)[1] |
| 28 | | 1 Jan 2007 (E) (W) (S) (SI 2006/3412) |
| | | 1 Jul 2008 (NI) (SI 2008/1316) |
| 29 | | 31 Jan 2007 (E) (W) (S) (SI 2006/3412) |
| | | 1 Jul 2008 (NI) (SI 2008/1316) |
| 30 | | 1 Jan 2007 (E) (W) (S) (SI 2006/3412) |
| | | 1 Jul 2008 (NI) (SI 2008/1316) |
| 31 | (1) | 1 Jan 2007 (E) (W) (S) (SI 2006/3412) |
| | | 1 Jul 2008 (NI) (SI 2008/1316) |
| | (2) | 1 Jan 2007 (E) (W) (S) (SI 2006/3412) |
| | | 14 May 2008 (NI) (SI 2008/1316) |
| | (3) | 1 Jan 2007 (E) (W) (S) (SI 2006/3412) |
| | | 1 Jul 2008 (NI) (SI 2008/1316) |
| | (4)(a) | 1 Jan 2007 (E) (W) (S) (except to the extent that it relates to Representation of the People Act 1983, Sch 1, r 37(1)(d)) (SI 2006/3412) |
| | | *Not yet in force* (exception noted above) |
| | (4)(b), (c) | 1 Jan 2007 (E) (W) (S) (except to the extent that it relates to Representation of the People Act 1983, Sch 1, r 37(1)(d)) (SI 2006/3412) |
| | | 1 Jul 2008 (NI) (in so far as relates to paras (b), (c)) (SI 2008/1316) |
| | | *Not yet in force* (exception noted above) |
| | (5)–(9) | 1 Jan 2007 (E) (W) (S) (SI 2006/3412) |
| | | 1 Jul 2008 (NI) (SI 2008/1316) |
| 32–35 | | 1 Jan 2007 (SI 2006/3412) |
| 36 | | 1 Jan 2007 (E) (W) (S) (SI 2006/3412) |
| | | 1 Jul 2008 (NI) (SI 2008/1316) |
| 37 | | 1 Jan 2007 (E) (W) (S) (SI 2006/3412) |
| | | 14 May 2008 (NI) (SI 2008/1316) |
| 38 | (1)–(3) | 1 Jan 2007 (E) (W) (S) (SI 2006/3412) |
| | | 1 Jul 2008 (NI) (SI 2008/1316) |
| | (4), (5) | 1 Jul 2008 (SI 2008/1316) |
| | (6) | 1 Jan 2007 (E) (W) (S) (SI 2006/3412) |
| | | 1 Jul 2008 (NI) (SI 2008/1316) |

**Electoral Administration Act 2006 (c 22)**—*contd*

| | | |
|---|---|---|
| 39, 40 | | 11 Sep 2006 (SI 2006/1972) |
| 41 | (1)–(6) | 1 Jan 2007 (E) (W) (S) (SI 2006/3412) |
| | | 14 May 2008 (NI) (SI 2008/1316) |
| | (7) | 1 Jul 2008 (SI 2008/1316) |
| | (8), (9) | 1 Jan 2007 (E) (W) (S) (SI 2006/3412) |
| | | 14 May 2008 (NI) (SI 2008/1316) |

42      1 Jan 2007 (E) (W) (for the purposes of: any local government election (as defined by Representation of the People Act 1983, s 203(1)) other than an Authority Election (as defined by that section); any referendum held under, or by virtue of regulations or an order made under, any provision of Local Government Act 2000, Pt 2; any election for the return of an elected mayor held in accordance with regulations made under Local Government Act 2000, Pt 2; any election to the National Assembly for Wales under Government of Wales Act 1998, Pt 1 or Government of Wales Act 2006, Pt 1) (SI 2006/3412)

     1 Jan 2008 (E) (W) (for the purposes of Authority elections (as defined by Representation of the People Act 1983, s 203(1)) (SI 2007/3376)

     14 May 2008 (NI) (for the purposes of Sch 1, paras 70, 109 of this Act) (SI 2008/1316)

     *Not yet in force* (otherwise)

43, 44      1 Jan 2007 (E) (W) (for the purposes of: any local government election (as defined by Representation of the People Act 1983, s 203(1))) other than an Authority Election (as defined by that section); any referendum held under, or by virtue of regulations or an order made under, any provision of Local Government Act 2000, Pt 2; any election for the return of an elected mayor held in accordance with regulations made under Local Government Act 2000, Pt 2; any election to the National Assembly for Wales under Government of Wales Act 1998, Pt 1 or Government of Wales Act 2006, Pt 1) (SI 2006/3412)

     1 Jan 2008 (E) (W) (for the purposes of Authority elections (as defined by Representation of the People Act 1983, s 203(1))) (SI 2007/3376)

     1 Jul 2008 (NI) (for the purposes of general elections to the Northern Ireland Assembly) (SI 2008/1316)

     *Not yet in force* (otherwise)

| | | |
|---|---|---|
| 45, 46 | | 1 Jan 2007 (E) (W) (S) (SI 2006/3412) |
| | | 1 Jul 2008 (NI) (SI 2008/1316) |
| 47 | | See Sch 1, Pt 5 below |
| 48 | | 11 Sep 2006 (SI 2006/1972) |
| 49 | | 1 Jan 2007 (SI 2006/3412) |
| 50, 51 | | 11 Sep 2006 (SI 2006/1972) |
| 52 | (1)–(3) | 11 Sep 2006 (SI 2006/1972) |

           (4)–(6)      11 Sep 2006 (for the purposes of the parliamentary elections and elections to the Northern Ireland Assembly within the meaning of the Political Parties, Elections and Referendums Act 2000, s 22(5)(a), (e)) (SI 2006/1972)

                 1 Jan 2007 (for the purposes of elections to the Scottish Parliament and the National Assembly for Wales within the meaning of the Political Parties, Elections and Referendums Act 2000, s 22(5)(c), (d)) (SI 2006/3412)

                 7 Feb 2007 (for the purposes of local government elections within the meaning of the Political Parties, Elections and Referendums Act 2000, s 22(5)(f)) (SI 2007/230)

                 1 Jul 2008 (NI) (for the purposes of local elections in Northern Ireland within the meaning of the Political Parties, Elections and Referendums Act 2000, s 22(5)(g)) (SI 2008/1316)

                 *Not yet in force* (otherwise)

| | | |
|---|---|---|
| 53–57 | | 11 Sep 2006 (SI 2006/1972) |

**Electoral Administration Act 2006 (c 22)**—*contd*

| | | |
|---|---|---|
| 58 | | 30 Jun 2007 (SI 2007/1847)[3] |
| 59 | (1)–(3) | 1 Jul 2009 (so far as relates to a Member of the House of Commons) (SI 2009/1509)[6] |
| | | 4 May 2016 (so far as relates to a member of the Scottish Parliament) (SI 2016/551)[8] |
| | | *Not yet in force* (otherwise) |
| | (4), (5) | 1 Jul 2009 (so far as relates to a Member of the House of Commons) (SI 2009/1509)[6] |
| | | 27 Apr 2016 (otherwise) (SI 2016/538) |
| 60 | | 11 Sep 2006 (SI 2006/1972) |
| 61 | (1) | 11 Sep 2006 (E) (W) (S) (except so far as applies to minor parties within the meaning of the Political Parties, Elections and Referendums Act 2000, s 160(1), and except so far as inserts s 71S(3) thereof) (SI 2006/1972) |
| | | 1 Jan 2007 (E) (W) (S) (except so far as applies to minor parties within the meaning of the Political Parties, Elections and Referendums Act 2000, s 160(1), so far as inserts s 71S(3) thereof) (SI 2006/3412) |
| | | 1 Jul 2008 (NI) (except so far as inserts Political Parties, Elections and Referendums Act 2000, s 71S(3)) (SI 2008/1656)[5] |
| | | 15 Sep 2014 (NI) (exception noted above) (SI 2014/1809) |
| | | *Not yet in force* (exceptions noted above) (otherwise) |
| | (2)–(4) | 11 Sep 2006 (E) (W) (S) (except so far as they apply to minor parties within the meaning of the Political Parties, Elections and Referendums Act 2000, s 160(1)) (SI 2006/1972) |
| | | 1 Jul 2008 (NI) (SI 2008/1656)[5] |
| | | *Not yet in force* (E) (W) (S) (otherwise) |
| | (5) | 11 Sep 2006 (E) (W) (S) (except so far as applies to minor parties within the meaning of the Political Parties, Elections and Referendums Act 2000, s 160(1), and except so far as inserts Sch 6A, paras 2(3), 3(2) thereto) (SI 2006/1972) |
| | | 1 Jan 2007 (E) (W) (S) (except so far as applies to minor parties within the meaning of the Political Parties, Elections and Referendums Act 2000, s 160(1), so far as inserts Sch 6A, paras 2(3), 3(2) thereto) (SI 2006/3412) |
| | | 1 Jul 2008 (NI) (except so far as inserts Political Parties, Elections and Referendums Act 2000, Sch 6A, paras 2(3), 3(2)) (SI 2008/1656)[5] |
| | | 15 Sep 2014 (NI) (exception noted above) (SI 2014/1809) |
| | | *Not yet in force* (exceptions noted above) (otherwise) |
| | (6) | 11 Sep 2006 (E) (W) (S) (except so far as applies to minor parties within the meaning of the Political Parties, Elections and Referendums Act 2000, s 160(1)) (SI 2006/1972) |
| | | 1 Jul 2008 (NI) (SI 2008/1656)[5] |
| | | *Not yet in force* (E) (W) (S) (otherwise) |
| | (7) | See Sch 1, Pt 6 below |
| 62 | | 11 Sep 2006 (E) (W) (S) (SI 2006/1972) |
| | | 1 Jul 2008 (NI) (SI 2008/1656)[5] |
| 63 | | 10 Mar 2008 (SI 2008/610) |
| 64, 65 | | 11 Sep 2006 (SI 2006/1972) |
| 66 | | 1 Jan 2007 (E) (W) (S) (SI 2006/3412) |
| | | 1 Jul 2008 (NI) (SI 2008/1316) |
| 67 | | 11 Sep 2006 (SI 2006/1972) |
| 68 | | 1 Jan 2007 (E) (W) (SI 2006/3412) |
| | | 1 Jul 2008 (NI) (SI 2008/1316) |
| | | 10 Feb 2010 (S) (SI 2010/275)[7] |
| 69 | | 1 Jan 2007 (E) (W) (S) (SI 2006/3412) |
| | | *Not yet in force* (otherwise) |
| 70–72 | | 1 Jan 2007 (SI 2006/3412) |
| 73 | (1), (2) | 1 Jan 2007 (E) (W) (S) (SI 2006/3412) |

**Electoral Administration Act 2006 (c 22)**—*contd*

|  |  | 1 Jul 2008 (NI) (SI 2008/1316) |
|---|---|---|
|  | (3) | 1 Jul 2008 (SI 2008/1316) |
| 74 | (1) | See Sch 1, Pt 7 below |
|  | (2) | See Sch 2 below |
| 75–79 |  | 11 Jul 2006 (s 77(1)) |
| Sch 1 | paras 1–40 | 1 Jan 2007 (SI 2006/3412) |
|  | paras 41–46 | 1 Jan 2007 (E) (W) (S) (SI 2006/3412) |
|  |  | 1 Jul 2008 (NI) (SI 2008/1316) |
|  | paras 47, 48 | 1 Jul 2008 (SI 2008/1316) |
|  | paras 49–52 | 1 Jan 2007 (E) (W) (S) (SI 2006/3412) |
|  |  | 1 Jul 2008 (NI) (SI 2008/1316) |
|  | para 53 | 1 Jan 2007 (SI 2006/3412) |
|  | para 54 | 1 Jan 2007 (E) (W) (S) (SI 2006/3412) |
|  |  | 1 Jul 2008 (NI) (SI 2008/1316) |
|  | paras 55–68 | 1 Jul 2008 (SI 2008/1316) |
|  | para 69 | 1 Jan 2007 (E) (W) (S) (SI 2006/3412) |
|  |  | 1 Jul 2008 (NI) (SI 2008/1316) |
|  | para 70 | 1 Jan 2007 (E) (W) (S) (SI 2006/3412) |
|  |  | 14 May 2008 (NI) (SI 2008/1316) |
|  | para 71 | 11 Sep 2006 (SI 2006/1972) |
|  | paras 72, 73 | 1 Jan 2007 (E) (W) (S) (SI 2006/3412) |
|  |  | 1 Jul 2008 (NI) (SI 2008/1316) |
|  | para 74 | 1 Jan 2007 (E) (W) (S) (SI 2006/3412) |
|  |  | 1 Jul 2008 (NI) (except in so far as relates to the substituted Registration of the People Act 1983, r 35(1), Table, question 3) (SI 2008/1316) |
|  |  | *Not yet in force* (NI) (exception noted above) |
|  | para 75 | 1 Jan 2007 (except in so far as relates to the insertion of Representation of the People Act 1983, Sch 1, para 37(1)(d), (4)) (SI 2006/3412) |
|  |  | *Not yet in force* (otherwise) |
|  | paras 76–81 | 1 Jan 2007 (E) (W) (S) (SI 2006/3412) |
|  |  | 1 Jul 2008 (NI) (SI 2008/1316) |
|  | paras 82–85 | 31 Jan 2007 (E) (W) (S) (SI 2006/3412) |
|  |  | 1 Jul 2008 (NI) (SI 2008/1316) |
|  | paras 86–89 | 1 Jan 2007 (E) (W) (S) (SI 2006/3412) |
|  |  | 1 Jul 2008 (NI) (SI 2008/1316) |
|  | para 90 | 1 Jul 2008 (SI 2008/1316) |
|  | paras 91–94 | 1 Jan 2007 (E) (W) (S) (SI 2006/3412) |
|  |  | 1 Jul 2008 (NI) (SI 2008/1316) |
|  | para 95 | 1 Jul 2008 (SI 2008/1316) |
|  | para 96 | 1 Jan 2007 (E) (W) (S) (SI 2006/3412) |
|  |  | 1 Jul 2008 (NI) (SI 2008/1316) |
|  | paras 97, 98 | 11 Sep 2006 (E) (W) (S) (except so far as they apply to minor parties within the meaning of the Political Parties, Elections and Referendums Act 2000, s 160(1), or the members or members' associations of such parties) (SI 2006/1972) |
|  |  | 1 Jul 2008 (NI) (SI 2008/1656)[5] |
|  |  | *Not yet in force* (E) (W) (S) (otherwise) |
|  | para 99 | 11 Sep 2006 (E) (W) (S) (except so far as applies to minor parties within the meaning of the Political Parties, Elections and Referendums Act 2000, s 160(1), or the members or members' associations of such parties, and except so far as inserts Sch 7A, para 16 thereto) (SI 2006/1972) |
|  |  | 1 Jul 2008 (NI) (except so far as inserts Political Parties, Elections and Referendums Act 2000, Sch 7A, para 16) (SI 2008/1656)[5] |
|  |  | 1 Jul 2009 (so far as inserts Political Parties, Elections and Referendums Act 2000, Sch 7A, para 16, in relation to a Member of House of Commons) (SI 2009/1509)[6] |

**Electoral Administration Act 2006 (c 22)**—*contd*

|  |  |
|---|---|
|  | 4 May 2016 (so far as inserts Political Parties, Elections and Referendums Act 2000, Sch 7A, para 16, in relation to a Member of the Scottish Parliament) (SI 2016/551)[8] |
|  | *Not yet in force* (so far as applies to minor parties within the meaning of the Political Parties, Elections and Referendums Act 2000, s 160(1), or the members or members' associations of such parties (E) (W) (S)) |
| paras 100–102 | 11 Sep 2006 (E) (W) (S) (except so far as they apply to minor parties within the meaning of the Political Parties, Elections and Referendums Act 2000, s 160(1), or the members or members' associations of such parties) (SI 2006/1972) |
|  | 1 Jul 2008 (NI) (SI 2008/1656)[5] |
|  | *Not yet in force* (E) (W) (S) (otherwise) |
| para 103 | 1 Jan 2007 (E) (W) (S) (SI 2006/3412) |
|  | 7 Feb 2007 (NI) (SI 2007/230) |
| para 104 | 11 Sep 2006 (SI 2006/1972) |
| paras 105, 106 | 1 Jan 2007 (E) (W) (S) (SI 2006/3412) |
|  | 1 Jul 2008 (NI) (SI 2008/1316) |
| para 107 | *Not yet in force* |
| para 108 | 1 Jan 2007 (E) (W) (S) (SI 2006/3412) |
|  | 1 Jul 2008 (NI) (SI 2008/1316) |
| para 109 | 1 Jan 2007 (E) (W) (S) (SI 2006/3412) |
|  | 14 May 2008 (NI) (SI 2008/1316)[4] |
| para 110 | 1 Jul 2008 (SI 2008/1316) |
| paras 111, 112 | 11 Sep 2006 (SI 2006/1972)[1] |
| paras 113–115 | 1 Jan 2007 (E) (W) (S) (SI 2006/3412) |
|  | 1 Jul 2008 (NI) (SI 2008/1316) |
| paras 116–119 | 11 Sep 2006 (SI 2006/1972)[1] |
| paras 120–127 | 11 Sep 2006 (SI 2006/1972) |
| paras 128–132 | 1 Jan 2007 (E) (W) (S) (SI 2006/3412) |
|  | 1 Jul 2008 (NI) (SI 2008/1316) |
| para 133 | 11 Sep 2006 (SI 2006/1972) |
| paras 134, 135 | 1 Jul 2008 (SI 2008/1316) |
| para 136 | 1 Jan 2007 (E) (W) (S) (SI 2006/3412) |
|  | 1 Jul 2008 (NI) (SI 2008/1316) |
| para 137 | 1 Jan 2007 (SI 2006/3412) |
| paras 138, 139 | 11 Sep 2006 (SI 2006/1972) |
| paras 140, 141 | 11 Sep 2006 (E) (W) (S) (except so far as they apply to minor parties within the meaning of the Political Parties, Elections and Referendums Act 2000, s 160(1), or the members or members' associations of such parties) (SI 2006/1972) |
|  | 1 Jul 2008 (NI) (SI 2008/1656)[5] |
|  | *Not yet in force* (E) (W) (S) (otherwise) |
| para 142 | 11 Sep 2006 (SI 2006/1972) |
| para 143(1), (2) | 11 Sep 2006 (SI 2006/1972) |
| para 143(3) | *Not yet in force* |
| para 144 | 11 Sep 2006 (E) (W) (S) (except so far as applies to minor parties within the meaning of the Political Parties, Elections and Referendums Act 2000, s 160(1), or the members or members' associations of such parties) (SI 2006/1972) |
|  | 1 Jul 2008 (NI) (SI 2008/1656)[5] |
|  | *Not yet in force* (E) (W) (S) (otherwise) |
| para 145 | 11 Sep 2006 (SI 2006/1972) |
| para 146 | 11 Sep 2006 (E) (W) (S) (except so far as applies to minor parties within the meaning of the Political Parties, Elections and Referendums Act 2000, s 160(1), or the members or members' associations of such parties) (SI 2006/1972) |
|  | 1 Jul 2008 (NI) (SI 2008/1656)[5] |
|  | *Not yet in force* (E) (W) (S) (otherwise) |
| para 147 | 11 Sep 2006 (SI 2006/1972) |

**Electoral Administration Act 2006 (c 22)**—*contd*

| | |
|---|---|
| para 148 | 11 Sep 2006 (E) (W) (S) (except so far as applies to minor parties within the meaning of the Political Parties, Elections and Referendums Act 2000, s 160(1), or the members or members' associations of such parties) (SI 2006/1972) |
| | 1 Jul 2008 (NI) (SI 2008/1656)[5] |
| | *Not yet in force* (E) (W) (S) (otherwise) |
| para 149 | 11 Sep 2006 (SI 2006/1972) |
| paras 150, 151 | 11 Sep 2006 (E) (W) (S) (except so far as they apply to minor parties within the meaning of the Political Parties, Elections and Referendums Act 2000, s 160(1), or the members or members' associations of such parties) (SI 2006/1972) |
| | 1 Jul 2008 (NI) (SI 2008/1656)[5] |
| | *Not yet in force* (E) (W) (S) (otherwise) |
| para 152 | 11 Sep 2006 (SI 2006/1972) |
| para 153 | 11 Sep 2006 (E) (W) (S) (except so far as applies to minor parties within the meaning of the Political Parties, Elections and Referendums Act 2000, s 160(1), or the members or members' associations of such parties) (SI 2006/1972) |
| | 1 Jul 2008 (NI) (SI 2008/1656)[5] |
| | *Not yet in force* (E) (W) (S) (otherwise) |
| para 154(1), (2) | 11 Sep 2006 (E) (W) (S) (except so far as they apply to minor parties within the meaning of the Political Parties, Elections and Referendums Act 2000, s 160(1), or the members or members' associations of such parties) (SI 2006/1972) |
| | 1 Jul 2008 (NI) (SI 2008/1656)[5] |
| | *Not yet in force* (E) (W) (S) (otherwise) |
| para 154(3) | 11 Sep 2006 (SI 2006/1972) |
| para 154(4)–(7) | 11 Sep 2006 (E) (W) (S) (except so far as they apply to minor parties within the meaning of the Political Parties, Elections and Referendums Act 2000, s 160(1), or the members or members' associations of such parties) (SI 2006/1972) |
| | 1 Jul 2008 (NI) (SI 2008/1656)[5] |
| | *Not yet in force* (E) (W) (S) (otherwise) |
| para 154(8), (9) | 11 Sep 2006 (SI 2006/1972) |
| paras 155, 156 | 11 Sep 2006 (SI 2006/1972) |
| Sch 2 | 11 Sep 2006 (SI 2006/1972), repeals of or in— Representation of the People Act 1983, ss 9, 74A, 75, 90A, 90B; Political Parties, Elections and Referendums Act 2000, ss 52(2)(b), 68, 69, Sch 7, paras 4, 14, 15, Sch 20 |
| | 11 Sep 2006 (E) (W) (S) (SI 2006/1972), repeals of or in— Political Parties, Elections and Referendums Act 2000, ss 50, 53, Sch 7, paras 2, 5 |
| | 1 Jan 2007 (SI 2006/3412), repeals of or in— Representation of the People Act 1983, s 10A(5); Police and Criminal Evidence Act 1984; Representation of the People Act 1985, s 19(6)(b); Representation of the People Act 2000, Sch 4 |
| | 1 Jan 2007 (E) (W) (S) (SI 2006/3412), repeals of or in— Parliamentary Elections Act 1695; Election Act 1707; Family Law Reform Act 1969; British Nationality Act 1981; Representation of the People Act 1983, ss 29 (E) (W), 40(1), 81, 119(2), 202(1), Sch 1, rr 2, 6, 19, 29, 43, 45, 55, Appendix; Political Parties, Elections and Referendums Act 2000, s 77, Sch 18; Civil Partnership Act 2004, Sch 27, para 85(2), (3), (5) |
| | 7 Feb 2007 (SI 2007/230), repeals of or in— Parliamentary Elections Act 1695 (NI); Election Act 1707 (NI); |

**Electoral Administration Act 2006 (c 22)**—*contd*

> Parliamentary Elections (Ireland) Act 1823;
> Family Law Reform Act 1969 (NI)
> 1 Jul 2008 (SI 2008/1316), repeals of or in—
> Electoral Law (Northern Ireland) Act 1962;
> Representation of the People Act 1985, Sch 1;
> Elected Authorities (Northern Ireland) Act 1989;
> Electoral Fraud (Northern Ireland) Act 2002
> 1 Jul 2008 (NI) (SI 2008/1316), repeals of or in—
> British Nationality Act 1981;
> Representation of the People Act 1983, ss 29, 40, 81, 119, 202,
>   Sch 1, rr 2, 6, 19, 29, 43, 45, 55, Appendix;
> Political Parties, Elections and Referendums Act 2000, s 77,
>   Sch 18;
> Civil Partnership Act 2004, Sch 27, para 85(2), (3), (5)
> 1 Jul 2008 (NI) (SI 2008/1656), repeals of or in—
> Political Parties, Elections and Referendums Act 2000,
>   ss 50(2)(e), (4), 53(4)(a), Sch 7, paras 2, 5(4)(a)
> *Not yet in force*, repeals of or in—
> Representation of the People Act 1983, ss 18, 29 (S), Sch 1,
>   rr 37(1)(a), 40(1B)(a);
> Representation of the People Act 1985, s 25, Sch 4;
> Political Parties, Elections and Referendums Act 2000, s 52(1)(a);
> Civil Partnership Act 2004, Sch 27, para 85(4);
> Electoral Administration Act 2006

[1] For transitional provisions, see SI 2006/1972, art 4, Sch 2

[2] For transitional provisions, see SI 2006/3412, art 6, Sch 2

[3] For a transitional provision, see SI 2007/1847, art 3

[4] Note that SI 2008/1316 also purports to bring this paragraph into force on 1 Jul 2008 in relation to Northern Ireland

[5] For transitional provisions, see SI 2008/1656, art 3, Sch 1

[6] For a transitional provision, see SI 2009/1509, art 3

[7] For a saving, see SI 2010/275, art 4

[8] For a transitional provision, see SI 2016/551, art 3

---

**Emergency Workers (Obstruction) Act 2006 (c 39)**

*RA:* 8 Nov 2006

*Commencement provisions:* s 7(2); Emergency Workers (Obstruction) Act 2006 (Commencement) Order 2007, SI 2007/153

| | |
|---|---|
| 1–6 | 20 Feb 2007 (SI 2007/153) |
| 7 | 8 Nov 2006 (s 7(2)) |

---

**Equality Act 2006 (c 3)**

*RA:* 16 Feb 2006

*Commencement provisions:* s 93; Equality Act 2006 (Commencement No 1) Order 2006, SI 2006/1082; Equality Act 2006 (Commencement No 2) Order 2007, SI 2007/1092; Equality Act 2006 (Commencement No 3 and Savings) Order 2007, SI 2007/2603

| | |
|---|---|
| 1–5 | 18 Apr 2006 (SI 2006/1082) |
| 6–32 | 1 Oct 2007 (SI 2007/2603) |
| 33–39 | 18 Apr 2006 (SI 2006/1082) |
| 40 | See Sch 3 below |

**Equality Act 2006 (c 3)**—*contd*

| | | |
|---|---|---|
| 41, 42 | | 16 Feb 2006 (RA) |
| 43 | (1) | 4 Dec 2006 (SI 2006/1082) |
| | (2) | 18 Apr 2006 (SI 2006/1082) |
| | (3) | 4 Dec 2006 (SI 2006/1082) |
| 44–51 | | 30 Apr 2007 (SI 2007/1092) |
| 52 | (1)–(5) | 30 Apr 2007 (SI 2007/1092) |
| | (6) | 18 Apr 2006 (SI 2006/1082) |
| | (7)–(9) | 30 Apr 2007 (SI 2007/1092) |
| 53–69 | | 30 Apr 2007 (SI 2007/1092) |
| 70, 71 | | 18 Apr 2006 (SI 2006/1082) |
| 72–80 | | 30 Apr 2007 (SI 2007/1092) |
| 81, 82 | | 18 Apr 2006 (SI 2006/1082) |
| 83 | | 6 Apr 2007 (SI 2006/1082) |
| 84 | | 18 Apr 2006 (in so far as inserts Sex Discrimination Act 1975, s 76A, for the purpose only of exercising any power to make orders, ss 76B, 76C of that Act) (SI 2006/1082) |
| | | 6 Apr 2007 (otherwise) (SI 2006/1082) |
| 85 | | 18 Apr 2006 (in so far as inserts Sex Discrimination Act 1975, ss 76B, 76C, for the purpose only of exercising any power to make orders) (SI 2006/1082) |
| | | 6 Apr 2007 (otherwise) (SI 2006/1082) |
| 86 | | 16 Feb 2006 (RA) |
| 87–90 | | 18 Apr 2006 (SI 2006/1082) |
| 91 | | See Sch 4 below |
| 92 | | 18 Apr 2006 (SI 2006/1082) |
| 93–95 | | 16 Feb 2006 (RA) |
| Sch 1 | | 18 Apr 2006 (SI 2006/1082) |
| Sch 2 | | 1 Oct 2007 (SI 2007/2603) |
| Sch 3 | paras 1–34 | 1 Oct 2007 (SI 2007/2603) |
| | para 35(a) | 1 Oct 2007 (SI 2007/2603) |
| | para 35(b) | 18 Apr 2006 (SI 2006/1082) |
| | paras 36–56 | 1 Oct 2007 (SI 2007/2603) |
| | para 57 | 30 Apr 2007 (SI 2007/1092) |
| | paras 58–63 | 1 Oct 2007 (SI 2007/2603) |
| Sch 4 | | 1 Oct 2007 (SI 2007/2603) |

**European Union (Accessions) Act 2006 (c 2)**

*RA:* 16 Feb 2006

Whole Act in force 16 Feb 2006 (RA)

**Family Law (Scotland) Act 2006 (asp 2)**

*RA:* 20 Jan 2006

*Commencement provisions:* s 46(2), (3); Family Law (Scotland) Act 2006 (Commencement, Transitional Provisions and Savings) Order 2006, SSI 2006/212

| | |
|---|---|
| 1–45 | 4 May 2006 (SSI 2006/212)[1] |
| 46 | 20 Jan 2006 (RA) |
| Schs 1–3 | 4 May 2006 (SSI 2006/212)[1] |

[1]    For transitional provisions and savings, see SSI 2006/212, arts 3–13

## Finance Act 2006 (c 25)

*Budget Day:* 22 Mar 2006

*RA:* 19 Jul 2006

The commencement details of Finance Acts are not set out, as the dates from which their provisions take effect are usually stated clearly and unambiguously in the text of the Act, and charging provisions will normally state for which year or years of assessment they are to have effect.

## Fraud Act 2006 (c 35)

*RA:* 8 Nov 2006

*Commencement provisions:* s 15(1); Fraud Act 2006 (Commencement) Order 2006, SI 2006/3200

| | |
|---|---|
| 1–14 | 15 Jan 2007 (SI 2006/3200) |
| 15, 16 | 8 Nov 2006 (s 15(1)) |
| Schs 1–3 | 15 Jan 2007 (SI 2006/3200) |

## Government of Wales Act 2006 (c 32)

*RA:* 25 Jul 2006

*Commencement provisions:* ss 105, 161; Government of Wales Act 2006 (Commencement of Assembly Act Provisions, Transitional and Saving Provisions and Modifications) Order 2011, SI 2011/1011

| | | |
|---|---|---|
| 1–94 | | In force immediately after the 2007 election (except for specified purposes[1]) (s 161(1), (4)) |
| | | In force (otherwise) on the day on which the first appointment is made under s 46 (s 161(4), (5)) |
| 95, 96 | | 25 Jul 2006 (s 161(2)) |
| 97–106 | | In force immediately after the 2007 election (except for specified purposes[1]) (s 161(1), (4)) |
| | | In force (otherwise) on the day on which the first appointment is made under s 46 (s 161(4), (5)) |
| 107, 108 | | 5 May 2011 (SI 2011/1011) |
| 109 | | 25 Jul 2006 (s 161(2)) |
| 110–115 | | 5 May 2011 (SI 2011/1011) |
| 116 | | In force immediately after the 2007 election (except for specified purposes[1]) (s 161(1), (4)) |
| | | In force (otherwise) on the day on which the first appointment is made under s 46 (s 161(4), (5)) |
| 117, 118 | | 1 Apr 2007 (s 161(3)) |
| 119 | | 25 Jul 2006 (s 161(2)) |
| 120 | (1), (2) | 1 Apr 2007 (s 161(3)) |
| | (3) | 25 Jul 2006 (s 161(2)) |
| | (4)–(6) | 1 Apr 2007 (s 161(3)) |
| | (7) | 25 Jul 2006 (s 161(2)) |
| | (8) | 1 Apr 2007 (s 161(3)) |
| 121, 122 | | 1 Apr 2007 (s 161(3)) |
| 123 | | In force immediately after the 2007 election (except for specified purposes[1]) (s 161(1), (4)) |
| | | In force (otherwise) on the day on which the first appointment is made under s 46 (s 161(4), (5)) |
| 124 | | 1 Apr 2007 (s 161(3)) |
| 125 | | 25 Jul 2006 (s 161(2)) |
| 126 | | 1 Apr 2007 (s 161(3)) |
| 127 | | In force immediately after the 2007 election (except for specified purposes[1]) (s 161(1), (4)) |
| | | In force (otherwise) on the day on which the first appointment is made under s 46 (s 161(4), (5)) |

**Government of Wales Act 2006 (c 32)**—*contd*

| | | |
|---|---|---|
| 128, 129 | | 1 Apr 2007 (s 161(3)) |
| 130–156 | | In force immediately after the 2007 election (except for specified purposes[1]) (s 161(1), (4)) |
| | | In force (otherwise) on the day on which the first appointment is made under s 46 (s 161(4), (5)) |
| 157–159 | | 25 Jul 2006 (s 161(2)) |
| 160 | (1) | In force immediately after the 2007 election (except for specified purposes[1]) (s 161(1), (4)) |
| | | In force (otherwise) on the day on which the first appointment is made under s 46 (s 161(4), (5)) |
| | (2)–(4) | 25 Jul 2006 (s 161(2)) |
| 161, 162 | | 25 Jul 2006 (s 161(2)) |
| 163 | | In force immediately after the 2007 election (except for specified purposes[1]) (s 161(1), (4)) |
| | | In force (otherwise) on the day on which the first appointment is made under s 46 (s 161(4), (5)) |
| 164–166 | | 25 Jul 2006 (s 161(2)) |
| Sch 1 | | In force immediately after the 2007 election (except for specified purposes[1]) (s 161(1), (4)) |
| | | In force (otherwise) on the day on which the first appointment is made under s 46 (s 161(4), (5)) |
| Sch 2 | paras 1–4 | In force immediately after the 2007 election (except for specified purposes[1]) (s 161(1), (4)) |
| | | In force (otherwise) on the day on which the first appointment is made under s 46 (s 161(4), (5)) |
| | paras 5, 6 | 25 Jul 2006 (s 161(2)) |
| | paras 7–11 | In force immediately after the 2007 election (except for specified purposes[1]) (s 161(1), (4)) |
| | | In force (otherwise) on the day on which the first appointment is made under s 46 (s 161(4), (5)) |
| | para 12 | 25 Jul 2006 (s 161(2)) |
| Schs 3, 4 | | In force immediately after the 2007 election (except for specified purposes[1]) (s 161(1), (4)) |
| | | In force (otherwise) on the day on which the first appointment is made under s 46 (s 161(4), (5)) |
| Sch 5 | | 25 Jul 2006 (s 161(2)) |
| Sch 6 | | In force immediately after the 2007 election (except for specified purposes[1]) (s 161(1), (4)) |
| | | In force (otherwise) on the day on which the first appointment is made under s 46 (s 161(4), (5)) |
| Sch 7 | | 25 Jul 2006 (s 161(2)) |
| Schs 8, 9 | | In force immediately after the 2007 election (except for specified purposes[1]) (s 161(1), (4)) |
| | | In force (otherwise) on the day on which the first appointment is made under s 46 (s 161(4), (5)) |
| Sch 10 | paras 1–11 | In force immediately after the 2007 election (except for specified purposes[1]) (s 161(1), (4)) |
| | | In force (otherwise) on the day on which the first appointment is made under s 46 (s 161(4), (5)) |
| | para 12 | 1 Apr 2007 (s 161(3)) |
| | paras 13–20 | In force immediately after the 2007 election (except for specified purposes[1]) (s 161(1), (4)) |
| | | In force (otherwise) on the day on which the first appointment is made under s 46 (s 161(4), (5)) |
| | para 21 | 1 Apr 2007 (s 161(3)) |
| | paras 22–32 | In force immediately after the 2007 election (except for specified purposes[1]) (s 161(1), (4)) |
| | | In force (otherwise) on the day on which the first appointment is made under s 46 (s 161(4), (5)) |
| | para 33 | 1 Apr 2007 (s 161(3)) |

**Government of Wales Act 2006 (c 32)**—*contd*

| | |
|---|---|
| paras 34–40 | In force immediately after the 2007 election (except for specified purposes[1]) (s 161(1), (4)) |
| | In force (otherwise) on the day on which the first appointment is made under s 46 (s 161(4), (5)) |
| paras 41–55 | In force on the day on which the first appointment is made under s 46 (s 161(4), (5)) |
| paras 56–60 | In force immediately after the 2007 election (except for specified purposes[1]) (s 161(1), (4)) |
| | In force (otherwise) on the day on which the first appointment is made under s 46 (s 161(4), (5)) |
| para 61 | 25 Jul 2006 (s 161(2)) |
| paras 62–97 | In force immediately after the 2007 election (except for specified purposes[1]) (s 161(1), (4)) |
| | In force (otherwise) on the day on which the first appointment is made under s 46 (s 161(4), (5)) |
| Sch 11 | 25 Jul 2006 (s 161(2)) |
| Sch 12 | 25 Jul 2006 (repeals of Government of Wales Act 1998, ss 12(1)(d), 81, 86) (s 161(2)) |
| | 1 Apr 2007 (repeals of Government of Wales Act 1998, ss 80, 82, 84, 85(1), 89) (s 161(3)) |
| | Repeals of Government of Wales Act 1998, ss 83, 88, 93(8), 97, 101A (and other provisions of that Act so far as relating thereto) come into force when each section has been complied with for the financial year ending 31 Mar 2007 (s 161(6)) |
| | Remaining repeals in force immediately after the 2007 election (except in so far as consequential upon: (a) any provision of this Act relating to the Auditor General or the Comptroller and Auditor General or functions of the Welsh Ministers, the First Minister, the Counsel General or the Assembly Commission; or (b) amendments made by Sch 10, paras 41–55) (s 161(1), (4)) |
| | In force (otherwise) on the day on which the first appointment is made under s 46 (s 161(4), (5)) |

[1]   The specified purposes are, in so far as relating to the Auditor General or the Comptroller and Auditor General or functions of the Welsh Ministers, the First Minister, the Counsel General or the Assembly Commission

---

**Health Act 2006 (c 28)**

*RA:* 19 Jul 2006

*Commencement provisions:* s 83; Health Act 2006 (Commencement No 1 and Transitional Provisions) Order 2006, SI 2006/2603; Health Act 2006 (Commencement No 2) Order 2006, SI 2006/3125; Health Act 2006 (Commencement No 1) (Scotland) Order 2007, SSI 2007/9; Health Act 2006 (Commencement No 1 and Transitional Provisions) (Wales) Order 2007, SI 2007/204; Health Act 2006 (Commencement No 3) Order 2007, SI 2007/1375; Health Act 2006 (Commencement No 4) Order 2008, SI 2008/1147; Health Act 2006 (Commencement No 5) Order 2008, SI 2008/1972; Health Act 2006 (Commencement No 6) Order 2008, SI 2008/2714; Health Act 2006 (Commencement No 2) (Wales) Order 2008, SI 2008/3171; Health (2006 Act) (Commencement) Order (Northern Ireland) 2012, SR 2012/307; Health Act 2006 (Commencement No 3) (Wales) Order 2013, SI 2013/1112

| | |
|---|---|
| 1–3 | 19 Jul 2006 (in so far as confer power to make an order or regulations or define any expression relevant to the exercise of any such power) (s 83(1)) |
| | 2 Apr 2007 (W) (otherwise) (SI 2007/204) |
| | 1 Jul 2007 (E) (otherwise) (SI 2007/1375) |
| 4 | 19 Jul 2006 (in so far as confers power to make an order or regulations or defines any expression relevant to the exercise of any such power) (s 83(1)) |
| | 1 Jul 2007 (E) (otherwise) (SI 2007/1375) |

**Health Act 2006 (c 28)**—*contd*

|  |  | *Not yet in force* (otherwise) |
|---|---|---|
| 5 | (1)–(3) | 19 Jul 2006 (in so far as confer power to make an order or regulations or define any expression relevant to the exercise of any such power) (s 83(1)) |
|  |  | 2 Apr 2007 (W) (otherwise) (SI 2007/204) |
|  |  | 1 Jul 2007 (E) (otherwise) (SI 2007/1375) |
|  | (4) | 19 Jul 2006 (in so far as confers power to make an order or regulations or defines any expression relevant to the exercise of any such power) (s 83(1)) |
|  |  | 2 Apr 2007 (W) (otherwise) (SI 2007/204) |
|  |  | 1 Jul 2007 (E) (S) (NI) (otherwise) (SI 2007/1375) |
|  | (5) | 19 Jul 2006 (in so far as confers power to make an order or regulations or defines any expression relevant to the exercise of any such power) (s 83(1)) |
|  |  | 2 Apr 2007 (W) (otherwise) (SI 2007/204) |
|  |  | 1 Jul 2007 (E) (otherwise) (SI 2007/1375) |
| 6–12 |  | 19 Jul 2006 (in so far as confer power to make an order or regulations or define any expression relevant to the exercise of any such power) (s 83(1)) |
|  |  | 2 Apr 2007 (W) (otherwise) (SI 2007/204) |
|  |  | 1 Jul 2007 (E) (otherwise) (SI 2007/1375) |
| 13 |  | 19 Jul 2006 (in so far as confers power to make an order or regulations or defines any expression relevant to the exercise of any such power) (s 83(1)) |
|  |  | 1 Jul 2007 (E) (W) (otherwise) (SI 2007/1375) |
| 14–16 |  | 1 Oct 2006 (SI 2006/2603) |
| 17, 18 |  | 19 Jul 2006 (in so far as confer power to make an order or regulations or define any expression relevant to the exercise of any such power) (s 83(1)) |
|  |  | 1 Jan 2007 (E) (otherwise) (SI 2006/3125) |
|  |  | 1 Mar 2007 (S) (otherwise) (SI 2006/3125) |
|  |  | 13 Dec 2008 (W) (otherwise) (SI 2008/3171) |
|  |  | 1 Aug 2012 (NI) (otherwise) (SR 2012/307) |
| 19 |  | 1 Jan 2007 (E) (SI 2006/3125) |
|  |  | 1 Mar 2007 (S) (SI 2006/3125) |
|  |  | 13 Dec 2008 (W) (SI 2008/3171) |
|  |  | 1 Aug 2012 (NI) (SR 2012/307) |
| 20 |  | 19 Jul 2006 (in so far as confers power to make an order or regulations or defines any expression relevant to the exercise of any such power) (s 83(1)) |
|  |  | 1 Jan 2007 (E) (otherwise) (SI 2006/3125) |
|  |  | 1 Mar 2007 (S) (otherwise) (SI 2006/3125) |
|  |  | 13 Dec 2008 (W) (otherwise) (SI 2008/3171) |
|  |  | 1 Aug 2012 (NI) (otherwise) (SR 2012/307) |
| 21–25 |  | 1 Jan 2007 (E) (SI 2006/3125) |
|  |  | 1 Mar 2007 (S) (SI 2006/3125) |
|  |  | 13 Dec 2008 (W) (SI 2008/3171) |
|  |  | 1 Aug 2012 (NI) (SR 2012/307) |
| 26 |  | 19 Jul 2006 (in so far as confers power to make an order or regulations or defines any expression relevant to the exercise of any such power) (s 83(1)) |
|  |  | *Not yet in force* (otherwise) |
| 27–29 |  | 1 Oct 2009 (SI 2008/2714) |
| 30 |  | 19 Jul 2006 (in so far as confers power to make an order or regulations or defines any expression relevant to the exercise of any such power) (s 83(1)) |
|  |  | 1 Oct 2009 (otherwise) (SI 2008/2714) |
| 31 |  | 1 Oct 2009 (SI 2008/2714) |

**Health Act 2006 (c 28)**—*contd*

| | |
|---|---|
| 32 | 19 Jul 2006 (in so far as confers power to make an order or regulations or defines any expression relevant to the exercise of any such power) (s 83(1)) |
| | *Not yet in force* (otherwise) |
| 33 | 1 Oct 2006 (SI 2006/2603) |
| 34 | 19 Jul 2006 (in so far as confers power to make an order or regulations or defines any expression relevant to the exercise of any such power) (s 83(1)) |
| | 28 Feb 2007 (except in so far as it relates to the Assembly's functions under the National Health Service Act 1977, s 42B) (SI 2006/3125) |
| | 9 May 2013 (exception noted above) (SI 2013/1112) |
| 35 | 19 Jul 2006 (in so far as confers power to make an order or regulations or defines any expression relevant to the exercise of any such power) (s 83(1)) |
| | 28 Feb 2007 (except in so far as it relates to the Assembly's functions under the National Health Service Act 1977, s 42) (SI 2006/3125) |
| | *Not yet in force* (exception noted above) |
| 36 (1) | 19 Jul 2006 (in so far as confers power to make an order or regulations or defines any expression relevant to the exercise of any such power) (s 83(1)) |
| | *Not yet in force* (otherwise) |
| (2) | *Not yet in force* |
| 37–42 | 19 Jul 2006 (in so far as confer power to make an order or regulations or define any expression relevant to the exercise of any such power) (s 83(1)) |
| | 1 Aug 2008 (otherwise) (SI 2008/1972) |
| 43 | 19 Jul 2006 (in so far as confers power to make an order or regulations or defines any expression relevant to the exercise of any such power) (s 83(1)) |
| | 1 May 2008 (otherwise) (SI 2008/1147) |
| 44–55 | 19 Jul 2006 (in so far as confer power to make an order or regulations or define any expression relevant to the exercise of any such power) (s 83(1)) |
| | 1 Feb 2007 (so far as they relate to the National Assembly for Wales' counter fraud functions in relation to the health service in Wales or to offences committed in relation to those functions) (SI 2007/204) |
| | 22 Apr 2008 (E) (otherwise) (SI 2008/1147) |
| 56 | 1 Oct 2006 (except so far as relating to Welsh NHS bodies) (SI 2006/2603)[1] |
| | 1 Feb 2007 (so far as relating to Welsh NHS bodies) (SI 2007/204)[2] |
| 57 | 19 Jul 2006 (in so far as confers power to make an order or regulations or defines any expression relevant to the exercise of any such power) (s 83(1)) |
| | 1 Oct 2006 (otherwise) (SI 2006/2603) |
| 58–62 | 28 Sep 2006 (for the purpose of conferring power to make a direction) (SI 2006/2603) |
| | 1 Oct 2006 (otherwise) (SI 2006/2603) |
| 63, 64 | 1 Oct 2006 (SI 2006/2603) |
| 65 | 19 Jul 2006 (in so far as confers power to make an order or regulations or defines any expression relevant to the exercise of any such power) (s 83(1)) |
| | 1 Oct 2006 (otherwise) (SI 2006/2603) |
| 66–69 | 1 Oct 2006 (SI 2006/2603) |
| 70 | 28 Sep 2006 (for the purpose of conferring power to make a direction) (SI 2006/2603) |
| | 1 Oct 2006 (otherwise) (SI 2006/2603) |

**Health Act 2006 (c 28)**—*contd*

| | | |
|---|---|---|
| 71 | | 19 Jul 2006 (in so far as confers power to make an order or regulations or defines any expression relevant to the exercise of any such power) (s 83(1)) |
| | | 28 Sep 2006 (for the purpose of defining any expression relevant to the exercise of the power to make a direction) (SI 2006/2603) |
| | | 1 Oct 2006 (otherwise) (SI 2006/2603) |
| 72 | | 19 Jul 2006 (in so far as confers power to make an order or regulations or defines any expression relevant to the exercise of any such power) (s 83(1)) |
| | | 28 Apr 2008 (otherwise) (SI 2008/1147) |
| 73 | | 19 Jul 2006 (in so far as confers power to make an order or regulations or defines any expression relevant to the exercise of any such power) (s 83(1)) |
| | | 29 Jan 2007 (otherwise) (SI 2006/3125; SSI 2007/9) |
| 74, 75 | | 19 Jul 2006 (s 83(1)) |
| 76, 77 | | 1 Feb 2007 (W) (so far as they relate to offences under Chapter 3 of Part 4) (SI 2007/204) |
| | | 2 Apr 2007 (W) (so far as they relate to offences under Chapter 1 of Part 1) (SI 2007/204) |
| | | 1 Jul 2007 (E) (so far as they relate to offences under Part 1) (SI 2007/1375) |
| | | 22 Apr 2008 (E) (so far as they relate to offences under Chapter 3 of Part 4) (SI 2008/1147) |
| | | 22 Apr 2008 (E) (S) (so far they relate to offences under Chapter 1 of Part 3) (SI 2008/1147) |
| | | 13 Dec 2008 (W) (so far as they relate to offences under Chapter 1 of Part 3) (SI 2008/3171) |
| | | 1 Aug 2012 (NI) (so far as they relate to offences under Chapter 1 of Part 3) (SR 2012/307) |
| | | *Not yet in force* (otherwise) |
| 78 | | 1 Feb 2007 (W) (so far as relates to offences under Chapter 3 of Part 4) (SI 2007/204) |
| | | 2 Apr 2007 (W) (so far as relates to offences under Chapter 1 of Part 1) (SI 2007/204) |
| | | 22 Apr 2008 (E) (so far as relates to offences under Chapter 3 of Part 4) (SI 2008/1147) |
| | | 22 Apr 2008 (E) (so far as relates to offences under Chapter 1 of Part 3) (SI 2008/1147) |
| | | 13 Dec 2008 (W) (so far as relates to offences under Chapter 1 of Part 3) (SI 2008/3171) |
| | | *Not yet in force* (otherwise) |
| 79 | | 19 Jul 2006 (s 83(1)) |
| 80 | (1) | See Sch 8 below |
| | (2) | See Sch 9 below |
| | (3)–(8) | 19 Jul 2006 (s 83(1)) |
| 81–84 | | 19 Jul 2006 (s 83(1)) |
| Sch 1 | | 19 Jul 2006 (in so far as confers power to make an order or regulations or defines any expression relevant to the exercise of any such power) (s 83(1)) |
| | | 2 Apr 2007 (W) (otherwise) (SI 2007/204) |
| | | 1 Jul 2007 (E) (otherwise) (SI 2007/1375) |
| Sch 2 | | 2 Apr 2007 (W) (SI 2007/204) |
| | | 1 Jul 2007 (E) (SI 2007/1375) |
| Sch 3 | | 1 Oct 2006 (except so far as relates to Welsh NHS bodies) (SI 2006/2603)[1] |
| | | 1 Feb 2007 (so far as relates to Welsh NHS bodies) (SI 2007/204)[2] |
| Sch 4 | | 19 Jul 2006 (in so far as confers power to make an order or regulations or defines any expression relevant to the exercise of any such power) (s 83(1)) |
| | | 1 Oct 2006 (otherwise) (SI 2006/2603) |

**Health Act 2006 (c 28)**—*contd*

| | | |
|---|---|---|
| Schs 5, 6 | | 28 Sep 2006 (for the purpose of conferring power to make a direction) (SI 2006/2603) |
| | | 1 Oct 2006 (otherwise) (SI 2006/2603) |
| Sch 7 | | 1 Oct 2006 (SI 2006/2603) |
| Sch 8 | paras 1–5 | 1 Oct 2006 (SI 2006/2603) |
| | paras 6–23 | 19 Jul 2006 (in so far as confer power to make an order or regulations or define any expression relevant to the exercise of any such power) (s 83(1)) |
| | | 1 Aug 2008 (otherwise) (SI 2008/1972) |
| | para 24(a) | 1 Oct 2006 (except so far as relates to Welsh NHS bodies) (SI 2006/2603) |
| | | 1 Feb 2007 (so far as relates to Welsh NHS bodies) (SI 2007/204) |
| | para 24(b) | 19 Jul 2006 (in so far as confers power to make an order or regulations or defines any expression relevant to the exercise of any such power) (s 83(1)) |
| | | 1 Aug 2008 (otherwise) (SI 2008/1972) |
| | para 25 | 19 Jul 2006 (in so far as confers power to make an order or regulations or defines any expression relevant to the exercise of any such power) (s 83(1)) |
| | | 1 Aug 2008 (otherwise) (SI 2008/1972) |
| | paras 26–28 | 1 Oct 2006 (SI 2006/2603) |
| | para 29 | 19 Jul 2006 (in so far as confers power to make an order or regulations or defines any expression relevant to the exercise of any such power) (s 83(1)) |
| | | 1 Aug 2008 (otherwise) (SI 2008/1972) |
| | para 30 | 19 Jul 2006 (in so far as confers power to make an order or regulations or defines any expression relevant to the exercise of any such power) (s 83(1)) |
| | | *Not yet in force* (otherwise) |
| | para 31 | 1 Oct 2006 (SI 2006/2603) |
| | paras 32–34 | 19 Jul 2006 (in so far as confer power to make an order or regulations or define any expression relevant to the exercise of any such power) (s 83(1)) |
| | | 1 Aug 2008 (otherwise) (SI 2008/1972) |
| | para 35 | 1 Oct 2006 (SI 2006/2603) |
| | para 36 | 19 Jul 2006 (s 83(1)) |
| | paras 37, 38 | 19 Jul 2006 (in so far as confer power to make an order or regulations or define any expression relevant to the exercise of any such power) (s 83(1)) |
| | | *Not yet in force* (otherwise) |
| | paras 39–42 | 1 Oct 2006 (except so far as relating to Welsh NHS bodies) (SI 2006/2603)[1] |
| | | *Never in force* (so far as relating to Welsh NHS bodies) (repealed) |
| | para 43 | 19 Jul 2006 (in so far as confers power to make an order or regulations or defines any expression relevant to the exercise of any such power) (s 83(1)) |
| | | 1 Feb 2007 (otherwise) (SI 2007/204) |
| | para 44 | 1 Oct 2006 (except so far as relates to Welsh NHS bodies) (SI 2006/2603)[1] |
| | | 1 Feb 2007 (so far as relates to Welsh NHS bodies) (SI 2007/204) |
| | para 45(1) | See sub-paras (2), (3) below |
| | para 45(2) | 19 Jul 2006 (in so far as confers power to make an order or regulations or defines any expression relevant to the exercise of any such power) (s 83(1)) |
| | | 1 Aug 2008 (otherwise) (SI 2008/1972) |
| | para 45(3) | 1 Oct 2006 (SI 2006/2603) |
| | para 46 | 19 Jul 2006 (in so far as confers power to make an order or regulations or defines any expression relevant to the exercise of any such power) (s 83(1)) |
| | | 1 Aug 2008 (otherwise) (SI 2008/1972) |

**Health Act 2006 (c 28)**—*contd*

|  |  |  |
|--|--|--|
| | paras 47, 48 | 1 Oct 2006 (SI 2006/2603) |
| | para 49 | See paras 50–52 below |
| | para 50 | 19 Jul 2006 (in so far as confers power to make an order or regulations or defines any expression relevant to the exercise of any such power) (s 83(1)) |
| | | 1 Aug 2008 (otherwise) (SI 2008/1972) |
| | paras 51, 52 | 1 Oct 2006 (SI 2006/2603) |
| | paras 53, 54 | 19 Jul 2006 (s 83(1)) |
| | para 55 | 19 Jul 2006 (in so far as confers power to make an order or regulations or defines any expression relevant to the exercise of any such power) (s 83(1)) |
| | | 29 Jan 2007 (otherwise) (SSI 2007/9) |
| | paras 56–61 | 1 Oct 2006 (SI 2006/2603) |
| | para 62 | 19 Jul 2006 (in so far as confers power to make an order or regulations or defines any expression relevant to the exercise of any such power) (s 83(1)) |
| | | 1 Feb 2007 (otherwise) (SI 2007/204) |

Sch 9       1 Oct 2006 (SI 2006/2603), repeals and revocations of or in—
Pharmacy Act 1954;
Medical Act 1983;
Dentists Act 1984;
Opticians Act 1989;
Osteopaths Act 1993;
Chiropractors Act 1994;
National Health Service Appointments Commission (Establishment and Constitution) Order 2001, SI 2001/793;
Nursing and Midwifery Order 2001, SI 2002/253;
Health Professions Order 2001, SI 2002/254;
National Health Service Reform and Health Care Professions Act 2002, Schs 6, 7;
Health and Social Care (Community Health and Standards) Act 2003 (except Sch 11, para 33);
General and Specialist Medical Practice (Education, Training and Qualifications) Order 2003, SI 2003/1250;
Health Protection Agency Act 2004

1 Oct 2006 (except so far as relating to Welsh NHS bodies) (SI 2006/2603), repeals and revocations of or in—
Audit Commission Act 1998[1];
Government Resources and Accounts Act 2000 (Audit of Health Service Bodies) Order 2003, SI 2003/1324;
Government Resources and Accounts Act 2000 (Audit of Health Service Bodies) Order 2004, SI 2004/1714;
Regulatory Reform (National Health Service Charitable and Non-Charitable Trusts Accounts and Audit) Order 2005, SI 2005/1074;
Special Health Authorities (Audit) Order 2006, SI 2006/960[1]

1 Feb 2007 (so far as relating to Welsh NHS bodies) (SI 2007/204), repeals and revocations of or in—
National Health Service Reform and Health Care Professions Act 2002, Sch 5, para 21;
Public Audit (Wales) Act 2004, Sch 2, para 2;
Regulatory Reform (National Health Service Charitable and Non-Charitable Trusts Accounts and Audit) Order 2005, SI 2005/1074, art 2

1 Aug 2008 (repeals of or in National Health Service Act 1977) (SI 2008/1972)

1 Oct 2009 (repeals of or in Medicines Act 1968) (SI 2008/2714)

*Not yet in force*, repeals of or in—
Health and Social Services and Social Security Adjudications Act 1983;

**Health Act 2006 (c 28)**—*contd*

National Health Service and Community Care Act 1990;
Health Service Commissioners Act 1993;
Health Authorities Act 1995;
Pharmacists (Fitness to Practise) Act 1997;
Audit Commission Act 1998 (so far as relating to Welsh NHS
  bodies);
Health Act 1999;
Health Act 1999 (Supplementary, Consequential etc Provisions)
  Order 2000, SI 2000/90;
National Health Service Reform and Health Care Professions
  Act 2002, s 35, Schs 1, 2, and 5 (except so far as Sch 5 relates
  to Welsh NHS bodies);
Health and Social Care (Community Health and Standards)
  Act 2003, Sch 11, para 33;
Government Resources and Accounts Act 2000 (Audit of Health
  Service Bodies) Order 2003, SI 2003/1324 (so far as relating to
  Welsh NHS bodies);
Public Audit (Wales) Act 2004, Sch 2, paras 2 (except so far as
  relates to Welsh NHS bodies), 38(2);
Government Resources and Accounts Act 2000 (Audit of Health
  Service Bodies) Order 2004, SI 2004/1714 (so far as relating to
  Welsh NHS bodies);
Regulatory Reform (National Health Service Charitable and
  Non-Charitable Trusts Accounts and Audit) Order 2005,
  SI 2005/1074, art 4 (so far as relating to Welsh NHS bodies);
Special Health Authorities (Audit) Order 2006, SI 2006/960 (so
  far as relating to Welsh NHS bodies)

[1]   For transitional provisions, see SI 2006/2603, art 6

[2]   For transitional provisions, see SI 2007/204, art 5

---

**Housing Corporation (Delegation) etc Act 2006 (c 27)**

*RA:* 19 Jul 2006

Whole Act in force 19 Jul 2006 (RA)

---

**Housing (Scotland) Act 2006 (asp 1)**

*RA:* 5 Jan 2006

*Commencement provisions:* s 195(2), (3); Housing (Scotland) Act 2006 (Commencement No 1) Order 2006,
  SSI 2006/14; Housing (Scotland) Act 2006 (Commencement No 2) Order 2006, SSI 2006/252;
  Housing (Scotland) Act 2006 (Commencement No 3) Order 2006, SSI 2006/395; Housing (Scotland)
  Act 2006 (Commencement No 4) Order 2006, SSI 2006/569; Housing (Scotland) Act 2006
  (Commencement No 5, Savings and Transitional Provisions) Order 2007, SSI 2007/270; Housing
  (Scotland) Act 2006 (Commencement No 6 and Transitional Provision) Order 2008, SSI 2008/308;
  Housing (Scotland) Act 2006 (Commencement No 7, Savings and Transitional Provisions)
  Order 2009, SSI 2009/122, as amended by SSI 2010/114; Housing (Scotland) Act 2006
  (Commencement No 8, Transitional Provisions and Savings) Order 2010, SSI 2010/159; Housing
  (Scotland) Act 2006 (Commencement No 9) Order 2010, SSI 2010/436

| | | |
|---|---|---|
| 1–11 | | 1 Apr 2009 (SSI 2009/122) |
| 12–21 | | 3 Sep 2007 (SSI 2007/270) |
| 22 | (1)–(4) | 3 Sep 2007 (SSI 2007/270) |
| | (5) | See Sch 2 below |
| | (6) | 3 Sep 2007 (SSI 2007/270) |
| 23–29 | | 3 Sep 2007 (SSI 2007/270) |
| 30–35 | | 1 Apr 2009 (SSI 2009/122) |

**Housing (Scotland) Act 2006 (asp 1)**—*contd*

| | | |
|---|---|---|
| 36–39 | | 3 Sep 2007 (SSI 2007/270) |
| 40–51 | | 1 Apr 2009 (SSI 2009/122) |
| 52–54 | | 4 Dec 2006 (SSI 2006/395) |
| 55–57 | | 4 Dec 2006 (SSI 2006/569) |
| 58 | | 3 Sep 2007 (SSI 2007/270) |
| 59 | (1) | 1 Apr 2009 (SSI 2009/122) |
| | (2)–(5) | 3 Sep 2007 (SSI 2007/270) |
| | (6) | 1 Apr 2009 (SSI 2009/122) |
| 60, 61 | | 3 Sep 2007 (SSI 2007/270) |
| 62 | | 1 Apr 2009 (SSI 2009/122) |
| 63 | (1) | 4 Dec 2006 (SSI 2006/569) |
| | (2)–(9) | 3 Sep 2007 (SSI 2007/270) |
| 64 | (1)–(5) | 3 Sep 2007 (SSI 2007/270) |
| | (6) | 4 Dec 2006 (SSI 2006/395) |
| | (7) | 4 Dec 2006 (only for the purpose of an appeal under Housing (Scotland) Act 2006, s 64(6)) (SSI 2006/395) |
| | | 3 Sep 2007 (otherwise) (SSI 2007/270) |
| 65 | (1), (2) | 3 Sep 2007 (SSI 2007/270) |
| | (3), (4) | 4 Dec 2006 (SSI 2006/395) |
| | (5) | 4 Dec 2006 (only for the purpose of an appeal under Housing (Scotland) Act 2006, s 64(6)) (SSI 2006/395) |
| | | 3 Sep 2007 (otherwise) (SSI 2007/270) |
| | (6) | 1 Apr 2009 (SSI 2009/122) |
| 66 | (1) | 4 Dec 2006 (only for the purpose of an appeal under Housing (Scotland) Act 2006, s 64(6)) (SSI 2006/395) |
| | | 3 Sep 2007 (otherwise) (SSI 2007/270) |
| | (2), (3) | 3 Sep 2007 (SSI 2007/270) |
| | (4) | 4 Dec 2006 (only for the purpose of an appeal under Housing (Scotland) Act 2006, s 64(6)) (SSI 2006/395) |
| | | 3 Sep 2007 (otherwise) (SSI 2007/270) |
| 67 | | 3 Sep 2007 (SSI 2007/270) |
| 68, 69 | | 1 Apr 2009 (SSI 2009/122) |
| 70 | | 5 Jul 2006 (SSI 2006/395) |
| 71, 72 | | 1 Apr 2009 (SSI 2009/122) |
| 73 | | 29 Sep 2008 (for the purpose of enabling regulations to be made) (SSI 2008/308) |
| | | 1 Apr 2009 (otherwise) (SSI 2009/122) |
| 74–76 | | 1 Apr 2009 (SSI 2009/122) |
| 77 | | 29 Sep 2008 (for the purpose of enabling regulations to be made) (SSI 2008/308) |
| | | 1 Apr 2009 (otherwise) (SSI 2009/122) |
| 78 | | 1 Apr 2009 (SSI 2009/122) |
| 79 | | 29 Sep 2008 (for the purpose of enabling regulations to be made) (SSI 2008/308) |
| | | 1 Apr 2009 (otherwise) (SSI 2009/122) |
| 80–97 | | 1 Apr 2009 (SSI 2009/122) |
| 98 | | 1 Dec 2008 (SSI 2008/308)[2] |
| 99 | | 4 Dec 2006 (for the purpose of enabling regulations to be made) (SSI 2006/569) |
| | | 1 Dec 2008 (otherwise) (SSI 2008/308)[2] |
| 100–103 | | 1 Dec 2008 (SSI 2008/308)[2] |
| 104, 105 | | 4 Dec 2006 (for the purpose of enabling regulations to be made) (SSI 2006/569) |
| | | 1 Dec 2008 (otherwise) (SSI 2008/308)[2] |
| 106–110 | | 1 Dec 2008 (SSI 2008/308)[2] |
| 111 | (1), (2) | 1 Dec 2008 (SSI 2008/308)[2] |
| | (3) | See Sch 3 below |
| | (4), (5) | 1 Dec 2008 (SSI 2008/308)[2] |
| 112–118 | | 1 Dec 2008 (SSI 2008/308)[2] |

**Housing (Scotland) Act 2006 (asp 1)**—*contd*

| | | |
|---|---|---|
| 119 | | 1 Dec 2008 (SSI 2008/308) |
| 120–123 | | 21 Dec 2010 (SSI 2010/436) |
| 124–166 | | 31 Aug 2011 (SSI 2010/159)[5] |
| 167–171 | | 28 May 2007 (SSI 2007/270) |
| 172–174 | | 3 Sep 2007 (SSI 2007/270) |
| 175 | | 5 Jul 2006 (SSI 2006/395) |
| 176, 177 | | 29 Jan 2006 (SSI 2006/14) |
| 178 | | 17 May 2006 (SSI 2006/252) |
| 179 | | 28 May 2007 (SSI 2007/270) |
| 180 | | 17 May 2006 (SSI 2006/252) |
| 181 | (1)(a), (b) | 1 Apr 2009 (SSI 2009/122) |
| | (1)(c) | 4 Dec 2006 (SSI 2006/569) |
| | (1)(d), (e) | 1 Apr 2009 (SSI 2009/122) |
| | (2) | 3 Sep 2007 (SSI 2007/270) |
| | (3) | 1 Apr 2009 (SSI 2009/122) |
| | (4) | 3 Sep 2007 (SSI 2007/270) |
| | (5) | 4 Dec 2006 (SSI 2006/569) |
| | (6) | 3 Sep 2007 (SSI 2007/270) |
| 182 | | 4 Dec 2006 (SSI 2006/569) |
| 183 | | 3 Sep 2007 (SSI 2007/270) |
| 184 | | 4 Dec 2006 (SSI 2006/569) |
| 185 | | 5 Jul 2006 (SSI 2006/395) |
| 186–189 | | 4 Dec 2006 (SSI 2006/569) |
| 190, 191 | | 5 Jan 2006 (RA) |
| 192 | (1) | See Sch 6 below |
| | (2) | See Sch 7 below |
| 193, 194 | | 5 Jul 2006 (SSI 2006/395) |
| 195 | | 5 Jan 2006 (RA) |
| Sch 1 | | 1 Apr 2009 (SSI 2009/122) |
| Sch 2 | paras 1–7 | 3 Sep 2007 (SSI 2007/270) |
| | para 8 | 4 Dec 2006 (for the purpose of enabling regulations to be made) (SSI 2006/569) |
| | | 3 Sep 2007 (otherwise) (SSI 2007/270) |
| Sch 3 | para 1 | *Not yet in force*[3] |
| | para 2 | 4 Dec 2006 (for the purpose of enabling regulations to be made) (SSI 2006/569) |
| | | *Not yet in force* (otherwise)[3] |
| | paras 3–8 | *Not yet in force*[3] |
| Schs 4, 5 | | 31 Aug 2011 (SSI 2010/159)[5] |
| Sch 6 | paras 1–3 | 1 Apr 2009 (SSI 2009/122)[4] |
| | paras 4, 5 | 3 Sep 2007 (SSI 2007/270) |
| | para 6 | 1 Apr 2009 (SSI 2009/122)[4] |
| | paras 7, 8 | 3 Sep 2007 (SSI 2007/270) |
| | paras 9, 10 | 1 Apr 2009 (SSI 2009/122) |
| | para 11 | 1 Apr 2010 (SSI 2009/122) |
| | para 12 | 1 Apr 2009 (SSI 2009/122)[4] |
| | para 13 | *Not yet in force* |
| | para 14 | 1 Apr 2009 (SSI 2009/122) |
| | para 15 | *Not yet in force* |
| | paras 16, 17 | 3 Sep 2007 (SSI 2007/270) |
| | para 18 | 31 Aug 2011 (SSI 2010/159)[5] |
| | para 19 | 3 Sep 2007 (SSI 2007/270) |
| | paras 20–22 | 1 Apr 2009 (SSI 2009/122) |
| | paras 23, 24 | 31 Aug 2011 (SSI 2010/159)[5] |
| Sch 7 | | 3 Sep 2007 (repeals of Housing (Scotland) Act 1987, s 113, Sch 10) (SSI 2007/270)[1] |
| | | 1 Apr 2009 (SSI 2009/122), repeals of or in— |
| | | Caravan Sites and Control of Development Act 1960; |

**Housing (Scotland) Act 2006 (asp 1)**—*contd*

Housing (Scotland) Act 1987, ss 244(1)–(5), (9), (10), (13), 338(1) (definition "standard amenities"), Sch 23;

Housing Act 2004

1 Apr 2010 (SSI 2009/122)[4], repeals of or in—

Land Compensation (Scotland) Act 1973;

Civic Government (Scotland) Act 1982;

Housing (Scotland) Act 1987, ss 85(3), 88–106, 108–112, 120(6), 124(4), 214, 215, 217, 218, 219(1)(a), 236–243, 244(7), (12), (14), 245–256A, 309(1), 310, 311(1)(e), 313(4), 319(1) (words from second "any" to "Part V or" in para (a)), 338 (so far as not already repealed), Schs 7, 8, 17, 19;

Housing (Scotland) Act 1988;

Local Government Act 1988;

Local Government and Housing Act 1989;

Agricultural Holdings (Scotland) Act 1991;

Clean Air Act 1993;

Leasehold Reform, Housing and Urban Development Act 1993;

Housing (Scotland) Act 2001

31 Aug 2011 (SSI 2010/159)[5], repeals of or in—

Housing (Scotland) Act 1987, Pt 8, Sch 11;

Fire (Scotland) Act 2005

*Not yet in force*, repeals of or in—

Housing (Scotland) Act 1987, s 244(6), (8), (11), s 319(1) (words from "or" following para (a) to the end of para (c), and words from "or, in a case falling under paragraph (c)" to the end);

Abolition of Feudal Tenure etc (Scotland) Act 2000;

Antisocial Behaviour etc (Scotland) Act 2004

[1]   For savings and transitional provisions, see SSI 2007/270, arts 4–6

[2]   For a transitional provision, see SSI 2008/308, art 4

[3]   Note that s 111(3), which introduces this Schedule, is brought into force on 1 Dec 2008 by SSI 2008/308, but that Order does not explicitly bring this Schedule into force on that date

[4]   For savings and transitional provisions, see SSI 2009/122, arts 4–7

[5]   For savings and transitional provisions, see SSI 2010/159, arts 4–6

---

**Human Tissue (Scotland) Act 2006 (asp 4)**

*RA*: 16 Mar 2006

*Commencement provisions*: s 62(2), (3); Human Tissue (Scotland) Act 2006 (Commencement) Order 2006, SSI 2006/251

| | | |
|---|---|---|
| 1–10 | | 1 Sep 2006 (SSI 2006/251) |
| 11 | (1)(a) | 1 Sep 2006 (SSI 2006/251) |
| | (1)(b) | 12 May 2006 (only for the purpose of enabling regulations to be made to come into force on or after 1 Sep 2006) (SSI 2006/251) |
| | | 1 Sep 2006 (otherwise) (SSI 2006/251) |
| | (2) | 12 May 2006 (only for the purpose of enabling regulations to be made to come into force on or after 1 Sep 2006) (SSI 2006/251) |
| | | 1 Sep 2006 (otherwise) (SSI 2006/251) |
| | (3)–(5) | 1 Sep 2006 (SSI 2006/251) |
| 12–16 | | 1 Sep 2006 (SSI 2006/251) |
| 17 | (1)–(2) | 1 Sep 2006 (SSI 2006/251) |
| | (3)–(5) | 12 May 2006 (only for the purpose of enabling regulations to be made to come into force on or after 1 Sep 2006) (SSI 2006/251) |

**Human Tissue (Scotland) Act 2006 (asp 4)**—*contd*

|  |  |  |
|---|---|---|
|  |  | 1 Sep 2006 (otherwise) (SSI 2006/251) |
|  | (6)–(10) | 1 Sep 2006 (SSI 2006/251) |
| 18 | (1) | 1 Sep 2006 (SSI 2006/251) |
|  | (2) | 12 May 2006 (only for the purpose of enabling regulations to be made to come into force on or after 1 Sep 2006) (SSI 2006/251) |
|  |  | 1 Sep 2006 (otherwise) (SSI 2006/251) |
|  | (3) | 1 Sep 2006 (SSI 2006/251) |
| 19 | (1) | 12 May 2006 (only for the purpose of enabling regulations to be made to come into force on or after 1 Sep 2006) (SSI 2006/251) |
|  |  | 1 Sep 2006 (otherwise) (SSI 2006/251) |
|  | (2)–(5) | 1 Sep 2006 (SSI 2006/251) |
| 20–39 |  | 1 Sep 2006 (SSI 2006/251) |
| 40 | (1) | 1 Sep 2006 (SSI 2006/251) |
|  | (2)(a), (b) | 1 Sep 2006 (SSI 2006/251) |
|  | (2)(c) | 12 May 2006 (only for the purpose of enabling orders to be made to come into force on or after 1 Sep 2006) (SSI 2006/251) |
|  |  | 1 Sep 2006 (otherwise) (SSI 2006/251) |
| 41 | (1) | 1 Sep 2006 (SSI 2006/251) |
|  | (2)(a) | 1 Sep 2006 (SSI 2006/251) |
|  | (2)(b) | 12 May 2006 (only for the purpose of enabling orders to be made to come into force on or after 1 Sep 2006) (SSI 2006/251) |
|  |  | 1 Sep 2006 (otherwise) (SSI 2006/251) |
|  | (3) | 1 Sep 2006 (SSI 2006/251) |
| 42–47 |  | 1 Sep 2006 (SSI 2006/251) |
| 48 | (1) | 1 Sep 2006 (SSI 2006/251) |
|  | (2) | 12 May 2006 (only for the purpose of enabling orders to be made to come into force on or after 1 Sep 2006) (SSI 2006/251) |
|  |  | 1 Sep 2006 (otherwise) (SSI 2006/251) |
| 49–51 |  | 1 Sep 2006 (SSI 2006/251) |
| 52 |  | 16 Mar 2006 (RA) |
| 53 | (1)–(5) | 1 Sep 2006 (SSI 2006/251) |
|  | (6) | 12 May 2006 (only for the purpose of enabling orders under Anatomy Act 1984, s 4B(3) to be made to come into force on or after 1 Sep 2006) (SSI 2006/251) |
|  |  | 1 Sep 2006 (otherwise) (SSI 2006/251) |
|  | (7)(a)–(d) | 1 Sep 2006 (SSI 2006/251) |
|  | (7)(e) | 12 May 2006 (only for the purpose of enabling regulations under Anatomy Act 1984, s 5(6)(a) to be made to come into force on or after 1 Sep 2006) (SSI 2006/251) |
|  |  | 1 Sep 2006 (otherwise) (SSI 2006/251) |
|  | (8) | 1 Sep 2006 (SSI 2006/251) |
|  | (9) | 12 May 2006 (only for the purposes of enabling orders and regulations under Anatomy Act 1984, s 6A(2), (12), and applications for licences under s 6A(9) of that Act to be made and determined to come into force on or after 1 Sep 2006) (SSI 2006/251) |
|  |  | 1 Sep 2006 (otherwise) (SSI 2006/251) |
|  | (10), (11) | 1 Sep 2006 (SSI 2006/251) |
|  | (12) | 12 May 2006 (only for the purpose of enabling regulations under Anatomy Act 1984, s 8(1) to be made to come into force on or after 1 Sep 2006) (SSI 2006/251) |
|  |  | 1 Sep 2006 (otherwise) (SSI 2006/251) |
|  | (13) | 12 May 2006 (only for the purposes of enabling the Scottish Ministers to prepare, consult and publish a code of practice under Anatomy Act 1984, s 8A(1), (3), (4), and orders under s 8A(2)(a), (b) of that Act to be made to come into force on or after 1 Sep 2006) (SSI 2006/251) |
|  |  | 1 Sep 2006 (otherwise) (SSI 2006/251) |

**Human Tissue (Scotland) Act 2006 (asp 4)**—*contd*

|              |                                                                 |
|--------------|-----------------------------------------------------------------|
| (14)–(17)    | 1 Sep 2006 (SSI 2006/251)                                       |
| 54           | 1 Sep 2006 (SSI 2006/251)                                       |
| 55           | 12 May 2006 (only for the purpose of enabling regulations to be made to come into force on or after 1 Sep 2006) (SSI 2006/251) |
|              | 1 Sep 2006 (otherwise) (SSI 2006/251)                           |
| 56, 57       | 1 Sep 2006 (SSI 2006/251)                                       |
| 58           | 12 May 2006 (only for the purpose of enabling orders to be made to come into force on or after 1 Sep 2006) (SSI 2006/251) |
|              | 1 Sep 2006 (otherwise) (SSI 2006/251)                           |
| 59, 60       | 16 Mar 2006 (RA)                                                |
| 61           | See Schedule below                                              |
| 62           | 16 Mar 2006 (RA)                                                |
| Schedule     | 1 Sep 2006 (SSI 2006/251)                                       |

## Identity Cards Act 2006 (c 15)

*RA:* 30 Mar 2006

*Commencement provisions:* s 44(3)–(5); Identity Cards Act 2006 (Commencement No 1) Order 2006, SI 2006/1439; Identity Cards Act 2006 (Commencement No 2) Order 2006, SI 2006/2602; Identity Cards Act 2006 (Commencement No 3) Order 2009, SI 2009/2303; Identity Cards Act 2006 (Commencement No 4) Order 2009, SI 2009/2565; Identity Cards Act 2006 (Commencement No 5) Order 2009, SI 2009/3032; Identity Cards Act 2006 (Commencement No 6) Order 2009, SI 2009/3323; Identity Cards Act 2006 (Commencement No 7) Order 2010, SI 2010/126

|          |           |                                                                 |
|----------|-----------|-----------------------------------------------------------------|
| 1        | (1)–(4)   | 20 Oct 2009 (SI 2009/2565)                                      |
|          | (5)–(8)   | 7 Jun 2006 (in so far as necessary for the interpretation of provisions brought into force by SI 2006/1439) (SI 2006/1439) |
|          |           | 20 Oct 2009 (otherwise) (SI 2009/2565)                          |
| 2        | (1), (2)  | 20 Oct 2009 (in relation to specified persons[1]) (SI 2009/2565) |
|          |           | 10 Nov 2009 (in relation to specified persons[2]) (SI 2009/2565) |
|          |           | 24 Nov 2009 (in relation to specified persons[3]) (SI 2009/2565) |
|          |           | 30 Nov 2009 (in relation to specified persons, in so far as not already in force in respect of such persons[4]) (SI 2009/3032) |
|          |           | 4 Jan 2010 (in relation to specified persons, in so far as not already in force in respect of such persons[5]) (SI 2009/3323) |
|          |           | 8 Feb 2010 (in relation to specified persons, in so far as not already in force in respect of such persons[6]) (SI 2010/126) |
|          |           | *Never in force* (otherwise) (repealed)                         |
|          | (3)–(7)   | 20 Oct 2009 (SI 2009/2565)                                      |
| 3, 4     |           | 20 Oct 2009 (SI 2009/2565)                                      |
| 5        | (1)(a)    | *Never in force* (repealed)                                     |
|          | (1)(b)    | 20 Oct 2009 (in relation to specified persons[1]) (SI 2009/2565) |
|          |           | 10 Nov 2009 (in relation to specified persons[2]) (SI 2009/2565) |
|          |           | 24 Nov 2009 (in relation to specified persons[3]) (SI 2009/2565) |
|          |           | 30 Nov 2009 (in relation to specified persons, in so far as not already in force in respect of such persons[4]) (SI 2009/3032) |
|          |           | 4 Jan 2010 (in relation to specified persons, in so far as not already in force in respect of such persons[5]) (SI 2009/3323) |
|          |           | 8 Feb 2010 (in relation to specified persons, in so far as not already in force in respect of such persons[6]) (SI 2010/126) |
|          |           | *Never in force* (otherwise) (repealed)                         |
|          | (2)–(7)   | 20 Oct 2009 (SI 2009/2565)                                      |
| 6        |           | 20 Oct 2009 (SI 2009/2565)                                      |
| 7        |           | *Never in force* (repealed)                                     |
| 8–21     |           | 20 Oct 2009 (SI 2009/2565)                                      |
| 22–24    |           | 1 Oct 2009 (SI 2009/2303)                                       |
| 25, 26   |           | 7 Jun 2006 (SI 2006/1439)                                       |
| 27–29    |           | 20 Oct 2009 (SI 2009/2565)                                      |

**Identity Cards Act 2006 (c 15)**—*contd*

| | | |
|---|---|---|
| 30 | (1)–(3) | 7 Jun 2006 (SI 2006/1439) |
| | (4) | 7 Jun 2006 (except for the purposes of references to Identity Cards Act 2006, ss 27, 28) (SI 2006/1439) |
| | | 20 Oct 2009 (exception noted above) (SI 2009/2565) |
| | (5) | 7 Jun 2006 (SI 2006/1439) |
| 31–35 | | 20 Oct 2009 (SI 2009/2565) |
| 36 | | 30 May 2006 (s 44(5)) |
| 37 | | 30 Sep 2006 (SI 2006/2602) |
| 38 | | 30 May 2006 (s 44(5)) |
| 39 | | 20 Oct 2009 (SI 2009/2565) |
| 40 | | 7 Jun 2006 (SI 2006/1439) |
| 41 | | 20 Oct 2009 (SI 2009/2565) |
| 42 | | 7 Jun 2006 (in so far as necessary for the interpretation of provisions brought into force by SI 2006/1439) (SI 2006/1439) |
| | | 1 Oct 2009 (in so far as necessary for the interpretation of provisions brought into force by SI 2009/2303) (SI 2009/2303) |
| | | 20 Oct 2009 (otherwise) (SI 2009/2565) |
| 43 | | 20 Oct 2009 (SI 2009/2565) |
| 44 | | 30 Mar 2006 (RA) |
| Sch 1 | | 20 Oct 2009 (SI 2009/2565) |
| Sch 2 | | 7 Jun 2006 (SI 2006/1439) |

[1] The specified persons are British citizens and EEA nationals—

(a) employed by the Identity and Passport Service who work at premises located in the counties of Greater Manchester, Merseyside or Durham, or in a London borough;

(b) who work under a contract for services for the Identity and Passport Service in connection with the operation of this Act at premises located at the following addresses, and hold a pass allowing unaccompanied access to those premises:

(i) Gorse Street, Chadderton, Oldham, Lancashire OL9 9QH

(ii) Dolphin House, Ashurst Drive, Bird Hall Lane, Cheadle Heath, Stockport, Cheshire SK3 0XB

(iii) Poseidon House, Ashurst Drive, Bird Hall Lane, Cheadle Heath, Stockport, Cheshire SK3 0XB;

(c) who work under a contract for services for the Identity and Passport Service in connection with the operation of this Act at premises occupied by the Identity and Passport Service in a London borough, and hold a pass allowing unaccompanied access to those premises;

(d) who are employees or office-holders and work in connection with the operation of this Act, and hold a pass allowing unaccompanied access to the premises occupied by the Secretary of State located at 2 Marsham Street, London SW1P 4DF

[2] The specified persons are British citizens and EEA nationals employed by Manchester Airport Group plc and holding an airside pass in respect of Manchester Airport, or who hold employment or have been offered employment for which such a pass is required

[3] The specified persons are British citizens and EEA nationals employed by London City Airport Limited and holding a pass allowing unaccompanied access to London City Airport, or who hold employment or have been offered employment for which such a pass is required

[4] The specified persons are British citizens or EEA nationals who—

(a) are employed by, or are working under a contract for services for, the Identity and Passport Service;

(b) are employed by, or are working under a contract for services for, the Home Office and whose place of work is permanently or temporarily at premises located in a London borough, in the City of London, or in the Inner Temple or the Middle Temple;

(c) hold, or have at any time on or after 1 Jan 2009 held, a United Kingdom passport (within the meaning of the Immigration Act 1971) which provides evidence of their British citizenship, and either—

**Identity Cards Act 2006 (c 15)**—*contd*

(i)   the address of their place of residence is located in an area to which one of the postcodes listed in the Schedule to SI 2009/3032 corresponds; or

(ii)   are employed and their place of work is permanently or temporarily at premises located in an area to which one of the postcodes listed in that Schedule corresponds;

(d)  hold an airside pass in respect of Manchester Airport or London City Airport, hold employment for which such a pass is required, or have been offered employment for which such a pass is required;

(e)  are members of the Public Panel or the Experts Group established by the Identity and Passport Service

5     The specified persons are British citizens who—

(a)   hold, or have at any time on or after 1 Jan 2009 held, a United Kingdom passport (within the meaning of the Immigration Act 1971) which provides evidence of their British citizenship; and

(b)   either—

(i)   the address of their place of residence is located in an area in England to which one of the postcodes listed in the Schedule to SI 2009/3323 corresponds; or

(ii)   are employed and their place of work is permanently or temporarily at premises located in an area in England to which one of the postcodes listed in the Schedule to SI 2009/3323 corresponds

6     The specified persons are as follows:

(a)   British citizens who—

(i)   are under the age of 25 at the time they submit their application to be entered in the Register;

(ii)   hold, or have at any time on or after 1 Jan 2009 held, a passport which provides evidence of their British citizenship; and

(iii)   the address of their place of residence is located in an area to which one of the postcodes listed in the Schedule to SI 2010/126 corresponds; or

(b)   British citizens who—

(i)   hold, or have at any time on or after 1 Jan 2009 held, a passport which provides evidence of their British citizenship; and

(ii)   have registered their interest in identity cards on the website established for this purpose by the Identity and Passport Service, such registration has been confirmed by the Identity and Passport Service on that website before 30 Jun 2010, and they have not cancelled such registration on that website at the time they submit their application to be entered in the Register

---

## Immigration, Asylum and Nationality Act 2006 (c 13)

*RA:* 30 Mar 2006

*Commencement provisions:* s 62; Immigration, Asylum and Nationality Act 2006 (Commencement No 1) Order 2006, SI 2006/1497; Immigration, Asylum and Nationality Act 2006 (Commencement No 2) Order 2006, SI 2006/2226; Immigration, Asylum and Nationality Act 2006 (Commencement No 3) Order 2006, SI 2006/2838; Immigration, Asylum and Nationality Act 2006 (Commencement No 4) Order 2007, SI 2007/182; Immigration, Asylum and Nationality Act 2006 (Commencement No 5) Order 2007, SI 2007/467; Immigration, Asylum and Nationality Act 2006 (Commencement No 6) Order 2007, SI 2007/1109, as amended by SI 2011/1158; Immigration, Asylum and Nationality Act 2006 (Commencement No 7) Order 2007, SI 2007/3138, as amended by SI 2007/3580; Immigration, Asylum and Nationality Act 2006 (Commencement No 8 and Transitional and Saving Provisions) Order 2008, SI 2008/310, as amended by SI 2012/1531

| | |
|---|---|
| 1–3 | 31 Aug 2006 (SI 2006/2226)[1] |
| 4 | 1 Apr 2008 (but s 4(1), (2) only apply so far as they relate to applications of a kind identified in rules made under the Immigration Act 1971, s 3(2) as requiring to be considered under a "Points Based System") (SI 2008/310)[4] |
| 5, 6 | 31 Aug 2006 (SI 2006/2226)[1] |
| 7 | 31 Aug 2006 (SI 2006/2226) |
| 8 | 30 Apr 2007 (SI 2007/1109) |

**Immigration, Asylum and Nationality Act 2006 (c 13)**—*contd*

| | | |
|---|---|---|
| 9 | | 13 Nov 2006 (SI 2006/2838) |
| 10 | | 16 Jun 2006 (SI 2006/1497) |
| 11 | | 31 Aug 2006 (SI 2006/2226)[1] |
| 12, 13 | | *Not yet in force* |
| 14 | | See Sch 1 below |
| 15 | | 5 Nov 2007 (for the purposes of making an order under sub-ss (2), (3), (7)) (SI 2007/3138) |
| | | 29 Feb 2008 (otherwise) (SI 2008/310)[4] |
| 16 | | 5 Nov 2007 (for the purposes of making an order under sub-ss (3), (5)) (SI 2007/3138) |
| | | 29 Feb 2008 (otherwise) (SI 2008/310)[4] |
| 17, 18 | | 29 Feb 2008 (SI 2008/310)[4] |
| 19 | | 31 Aug 2006 (SI 2006/2226) |
| 20 | | 5 Nov 2007 (SI 2007/3138) |
| 21, 22 | | 29 Feb 2008 (SI 2008/310)[4] |
| 23 | | 31 Aug 2006 (SI 2006/2226) |
| 24 | | 29 Feb 2008 (SI 2008/310)[4] |
| 25 | | 5 Nov 2007 (SI 2007/3138) |
| 26 | | 29 Feb 2008 (SI 2008/310)[4] |
| 27 | | 31 Aug 2006 (SI 2006/2226)[1] |
| 28, 29 | | 31 Aug 2006 (SI 2006/2226) |
| 30 | | 16 Jun 2006 (SI 2006/1497) |
| 31 | | 5 Nov 2007 (for the purposes of making an order under the Immigration Act 1971, Sch 2, paras 27(2), 27B as amended by this section) (SI 2007/3138) |
| | | 1 Mar 2008 (otherwise) (SI 2007/3138) |
| 32 | | 5 Nov 2007 (for the purposes of making an order under sub-s (5)(a)) (SI 2007/3138) |
| | | 1 Mar 2008 (otherwise) (SI 2007/3138) |
| 33 | | 1 Apr 2008 (for the purposes of making an order under sub-s (5)(a)) (SI 2008/310) |
| | | *Not yet in force* (otherwise) |
| 34, 35 | | 1 Mar 2008 (SI 2007/3138) |
| 36 | | 5 Nov 2007 (for the purposes of making an order under sub-s (4)) (SI 2007/3138) |
| | | 1 Mar 2008 (otherwise) (SI 2007/3138) |
| 37 | | 5 Nov 2007 (for the purposes of laying a draft code before Parliament and making an order under sub-s (2)) (SI 2007/3138) |
| | | 1 Mar 2008 (otherwise) (SI 2007/3138) |
| 38 | | 5 Nov 2007 (for the purposes of making an order under sub-s (4)) (SI 2007/3138) |
| | | 1 Mar 2008 (otherwise) (SI 2007/3138) |
| 39 | | 1 Mar 2008 (SI 2007/3138) |
| 40–42 | | 31 Aug 2006 (SI 2006/2226) |
| 43 | | 16 Jun 2006 (SI 2006/1497) |
| 44 | | *Not yet in force* |
| 45 | | 30 Jun 2006 (SI 2006/1497) |
| 46 | | 31 Aug 2006 (SI 2006/2226) |
| 47 | | 1 Apr 2008 (SI 2008/310) |
| 48 | | 16 Jun 2006 (SI 2006/1497) |
| 49 | | 31 Aug 2006 (SI 2006/2226) |
| 50 | (1), (2) | 31 Jan 2007 (SI 2007/182) |
| | (3)(a) | 29 Feb 2008 (SI 2008/310) |
| | (3)(b) | *Not yet in force* |
| | (4), (5) | 5 Nov 2007 (SI 2007/3138) |
| | (6) | *Not yet in force* |
| 51 | | 31 Jan 2007 (SI 2007/182) |
| 52 | (1)–(6) | 31 Jan 2007 (SI 2007/182) |

**Immigration, Asylum and Nationality Act 2006 (c 13)**—*contd*

|        |              |                                                                                 |
|--------|--------------|---------------------------------------------------------------------------------|
|        | (7)          | See Sch 2 below                                                                 |
| 53, 54 |              | 31 Aug 2006 (SI 2006/2226)                                                      |
| 55     |              | 31 Aug 2006 (SI 2006/2226)[1]                                                   |
| 56, 57 |              | 16 Jun 2006 (SI 2006/1497)                                                      |
| 58     |              | 4 Dec 2006 (SI 2006/2838)[2]                                                    |
| 59     |              | 31 Aug 2006 (SI 2006/2226)                                                      |
| 60     |              | 16 Jun 2006 (SI 2006/1497)                                                      |
| 61     |              | See Sch 3 below                                                                 |
| 62–64  |              | 30 Mar 2006 (RA)                                                                |
| Sch 1  | paras 1–10   | 31 Aug 2006 (SI 2006/2226)                                                      |
|        | para 11      | *Not yet in force*                                                              |
|        | paras 12–14  | 31 Aug 2006 (SI 2006/2226)                                                      |
| Sch 2  | paras 1–5    | 2 Apr 2007 (SI 2007/1109)                                                       |
|        | para 6       | 7 Mar 2007 (SI 2007/467)                                                        |
| Sch 3  |              | 16 Jun 2006 (repeal in British Nationality Act 1981, s 40A(3)) (SI 2006/1497)   |

31 Aug 2006 (SI 2006/2226)[1], repeals of or in—
Prison Act 1952;
Immigration Act 1971, Sch 2;
Anti-terrorism, Crime and Security Act 2001;
Nationality, Immigration and Asylum Act 2002, s 82(3)

2 Apr 2007 (SI 2007/1109)[3], repeals of or in—
British Nationality Act 1981, ss 41, 42A;
Immigration and Asylum Act 1999, ss 5, 27;
Nationality, Immigration and Asylum Act 2002, ss 10, 122;
Asylum and Immigration (Treatment of Claimants, etc)
    Act 2004, ss 25, 42

1 Mar 2008 (repeal in Immigration Act 1971, s 27) (SI 2007/3138)

29 Feb 2008 (SI 2008/310)[4], repeals of or in—
Immigration Act 1971, s 31A;
Asylum and Immigration Act 1996

*Not yet in force*[5], repeals of or in—
Immigration Act 1971, s 32;
Immigration and Asylum Act 1999, s 167;
Nationality, Immigration and Asylum Act 2002, ss 110, 158;
Asylum and Immigration (Treatment of Claimants, etc)
    Act 2004, s 44;
Civil Partnership Act 2004

---

[1]  For transitional provisions, see SI 2006/2226, art 4

[2]  For transitional provisions, see SI 2006/2838, art 4

[3]  For transitional provisions, see SI 2007/1109, arts 5, 6, Schedule

[4]  For transitional and saving provisions, see SI 2008/310, arts 4, 5

[5]  It is thought that the intention was to bring these repeals, except the repeal in the Civil Partnership Act 2004, into force at the same time as s 64 (ie 30 Mar 2006) or, in the case of the repeal of s 110 of the 2002 Act, at the same time as s 10 (ie 16 Jun 2006)

---

**Interests of Members of the Scottish Parliament Act 2006 (asp 12)**

*RA:* 13 Jul 2006

*Commencement provisions:* s 21

Whole Act in force 4 Apr 2007 (that is, the day after the date of the first dissolution of the Parliament following 13 Jul 2006 (except that ss 4(1), (2), 11(1), 13(2), 19, 21 and Schedule, para 8(2)(b) came into force on 14 Jul 2006 for the purpose of enabling the Parliament to make determinations to come into force when the remaining provisions of this Act come into force))

## International Development (Reporting and Transparency) Act 2006 (c 31)

*RA:* 25 Jul 2006

*Commencement provisions:* s 9(2)

| | |
|---|---|
| 1–6 | 25 Oct 2006 (s 9(2)) |
| 7–9 | 25 Jul 2006 (RA) |
| Schedule | 25 Oct 2006 (s 9(2)) |

## Investment Exchanges and Clearing Houses Act 2006 (c 55)

*RA:* 19 Dec 2006

*Commencement provisions:* s 5(2)

Whole Act in force 20 Dec 2006 (s 5(2))

## Joint Inspection of Children's Services and Inspection of Social Work Services (Scotland) Act 2006 (asp 3)

*RA:* 22 Feb 2006

*Commencement provisions:* s 10(2)

Whole Act in force 23 Feb 2006 (s 10(2))

## Legislative and Regulatory Reform Act 2006 (c 51)

*RA:* 8 Nov 2006

*Commencement provisions:* s 33

Whole Act in force 8 Jan 2007 (s 33)

## Local Electoral Administration and Registration Services (Scotland) Act 2006 (asp 14)

*RA:* 1 Aug 2006

*Commencement provisions:* s 63; Local Electoral Administration and Registration Services (Scotland) Act 2006 (Commencement No 1 and Transitional Provision) Order 2006, SSI 2006/469; Local Electoral Administration and Registration Services (Scotland) Act 2006 (Commencement No 2 and Transitional Provisions) Order 2007, SSI 2007/26; Local Electoral Administration and Registration Services (Scotland) Act 2006 (Commencement No 3 and Transitional Provisions) Order 2007, SSI 2007/566; Local Electoral Administration and Registration Services (Scotland) Act 2006 (Commencement No 4) Order 2008, SSI 2008/405; Local Electoral Administration and Registration Services (Scotland) Act 2006 (Commencement No 5 and Transitional Provision) Order 2009, SSI 2009/2; Local Electoral Administration and Registration Services (Scotland) Act 2006 (Commencement No. 6 and Transitional Provision) Order 2021, SSI 2021/314; Local Electoral Administration and Registration Services (Scotland) Act 2006 (Commencement No 7) Order 2022, SSI 2022/266

| | | |
|---|---|---|
| 1–4 | | 17 Feb 2007 (SSI 2007/26)[2] |
| 5 | (1) | 17 Feb 2007 (SSI 2007/26)[2] |
| | (2)(a) | 17 Feb 2007 (for the purpose of inspection of paper documents only) (SSI 2007/26)[2] |
| | | *Not yet in force* (otherwise) |
| | (2)(b) | 17 Feb 2007 (SSI 2007/26)[2] |
| | (3)–(8) | 17 Feb 2007 (SSI 2007/26)[2] |
| 6–11 | | 17 Feb 2007 (SSI 2007/26)[2] |
| 12–16 | | 29 Jan 2007 (SSI 2007/26) |

**Local Electoral Administration and Registration Services (Scotland) Act 2006 (asp 14)**—*contd*

| | | |
|---|---|---|
| 17 | (1)–(3) | *Not yet in force* |
| | (4) | See Sch 1 below |
| 18 | | 29 Jan 2007 (SSI 2007/26) |
| 19 | | *Not yet in force* |
| 20 | | 29 Jan 2007 (SSI 2007/26) |
| 21–24 | | 22 Jan 2009 (SSI 2009/2)[4] |
| 25 | | 29 Jan 2007 (SSI 2007/26) |
| 26, 27 | | 17 Feb 2007 (SSI 2007/26)[2] |
| 28 | | 29 Jan 2007 (SSI 2007/26) |
| 29 | | 29 Jan 2007 (SSI 2007/26)[2] |
| 30 | | 29 Jan 2007 (SSI 2007/26) |
| 31, 32 | | 17 Feb 2007 (SSI 2007/26)[2] |
| 33 | | 29 Jan 2007 (SSI 2007/26) |
| 34 | (1) | 17 Feb 2007 (SSI 2007/26)[2] |
| | (2), (3) | 29 Jan 2007 (SSI 2007/26) |
| | (4), (5) | 17 Feb 2007 (SSI 2007/26)[2] |
| | (6) | 29 Jan 2007 (SSI 2007/26) |
| 35 | | See Sch 2 below |
| 36 | | 29 Jan 2007 (SSI 2007/26) |
| 37 | | 1 Jan 2007 (SSI 2006/469)[1] |
| 38 | | 1 Jan 2007 (SSI 2006/469) |
| 39 | (1) | See sub-ss (2)–(8) below |
| | (2) | 1 Oct 2006 (for the purpose of prescribing by regulations: (a) particulars of births and still-births; (b) forms concerning births and still-births; (c) means of submission; and (d) manners of attestation) (SSI 2006/469) |
| | | 1 Jan 2007 (otherwise) (SSI 2006/469) |
| | (3)(a), (b) | 1 Oct 2006 (for the purpose of prescribing by regulations: (a) particulars of births and still-births; (b) forms concerning births and still-births; (c) means of submission; and (d) manners of attestation) (SSI 2006/469) |
| | | 24 Sep 2022 (otherwise) (SSI 2022/266) |
| | (3)(c) | 1 Oct 2006 (for the purpose of prescribing by regulations: (a) particulars of births and still-births; (b) forms concerning births and still-births; (c) means of submission; and (d) manners of attestation) (SSI 2006/469) |
| | | 1 Jan 2007 (otherwise) (SSI 2006/469) |
| | (4), (5) | 1 Oct 2006 (for the purpose of prescribing by regulations: (a) particulars of births and still-births; (b) forms concerning births and still-births; (c) means of submission; and (d) manners of attestation) (SSI 2006/469) |
| | | 1 Jan 2007 (otherwise) (SSI 2006/469) |
| | (6) | 1 Oct 2006 (for the purpose of prescribing by regulations: (a) particulars of births and still-births; (b) forms concerning births and still-births; (c) means of submission; and (d) manners of attestation) (SSI 2006/469) |
| | | 24 Sep 2022 (for the purpose of inserting Registration of Births, Deaths and Marriages (Scotland) Act 1965, s 16B) (SSI 2022/266) |
| | | *Not yet in force* (otherwise) |
| | (7), (8) | 1 Oct 2006 (for the purpose of prescribing by regulations: (a) particulars of births and still-births; (b) forms concerning births and still-births; (c) means of submission; and (d) manners of attestation) (SSI 2006/469) |
| | | 1 Jan 2007 (otherwise) (SSI 2006/469) |
| 40 | | 1 Oct 2006 (for the purpose of prescribing by regulations: (a) particulars of births and still-births; (b) forms concerning births and still-births; (c) means of submission; and (d) manners of attestation) (SSI 2006/469) |

**Local Electoral Administration and Registration Services (Scotland) Act 2006 (asp 14)**—*contd*

|    |    |    |
|----|----|----|
|    |    | 1 Jan 2007 (otherwise) (SSI 2006/469) |
| 41 | (1) | See sub-ss (2), (3) below |
|    | (2)(a) | 1 Oct 2006 (SSI 2006/469) |
|    | (2)(b) | 1 Jan 2007 (SSI 2006/469) |
|    | (3) | 1 Oct 2006 (SSI 2006/469) |
| 42 | (1) | See sub-ss (2)–(8) below |
|    | (2) | 1 Oct 2006 (for the purpose of prescribing by regulations: (a) particulars of deaths; (b) forms concerning deaths; (c) means of submission; and (d) manners of attestation) (SSI 2006/469) |
|    |    | 1 Jan 2007 (otherwise) (SSI 2006/469) |
|    | (3)(a)(i), (ii) | 1 Oct 2006 (for the purpose of prescribing by regulations: (a) particulars of deaths; (b) forms concerning deaths; (c) means of submission; and (d) manners of attestation) (SSI 2006/469) |
|    |    | 24 Sep 2022 (otherwise) (SSI 2022/266) |
|    | (3)(a)(iii), (iv) | 1 Oct 2006 (for the purpose of prescribing by regulations: (a) particulars of deaths; (b) forms concerning deaths; (c) means of submission; and (d) manners of attestation) (SSI 2006/469) |
|    |    | 1 Jan 2007 (otherwise) (SSI 2006/469) |
|    | (3)(b) | 1 Oct 2006 (for the purpose of prescribing by regulations: (a) particulars of deaths; (b) forms concerning deaths; (c) means of submission; and (d) manners of attestation) (SSI 2006/469) |
|    |    | 14 Jan 2008 (for the purpose of inserting the Registration of Births, Deaths and Marriages (Scotland) Act 1965, s 23(1A)(a)) (SSI 2007/566)[3] |
|    |    | 24 Sep 2022 (otherwise) (SSI 2022/266) |
|    | (3)(c) | 1 Oct 2006 (for the purpose of prescribing by regulations: (a) particulars of deaths; (b) forms concerning deaths; (c) means of submission; and (d) manners of attestation) (SSI 2006/469) |
|    |    | 1 Jan 2007 (otherwise) (SSI 2006/469) |
|    | (4), (5) | 1 Oct 2006 (for the purpose of prescribing by regulations: (a) particulars of deaths; (b) forms concerning deaths; (c) means of submission; and (d) manners of attestation) (SSI 2006/469) |
|    |    | 1 Jan 2007 (otherwise) (SSI 2006/469) |
|    | (6) | 1 Oct 2006 (for the purpose of prescribing by regulations: (a) particulars of deaths; (b) forms concerning deaths; (c) means of submission; and (d) manners of attestation) (SSI 2006/469) |
|    |    | 14 Jan 2008 (for the purpose of inserting the Registration of Births, Deaths and Marriages (Scotland) Act 1965, s 25B) (SSI 2007/566)[3] |
|    |    | *Not yet in force* (otherwise) |
|    | (7), (8) | 1 Oct 2006 (for the purpose of prescribing by regulations: (a) particulars of deaths; (b) forms concerning deaths; (c) means of submission; and (d) manners of attestation) (SSI 2006/469) |
|    |    | 1 Jan 2007 (otherwise) (SSI 2006/469) |
| 43 |    | 1 Oct 2006 (SSI 2006/469) |
| 44 | (1) | See sub-ss (2)–(8) below |
|    | (2) | 1 Jan 2007 (SSI 2006/469) |
|    | (3), (4) | 1 Oct 2006 (SSI 2006/469) |
|    | (5) | 1 Oct 2006 ((a) for the purpose of prescribing by regulations: (i) the form of applications for notice of registration events and deaths in Scotland; (ii) the means of giving such notice; (iii) the form of such notice; and (iv) particulars contained in abbreviated extracts of births or deaths; and (b) for the purpose of prescribing fees by regulations for: (i) applications for notice of registration events and deaths in Scotland; and (ii) abbreviated extracts of births or deaths) (SSI 2006/469) |
|    |    | 1 Jan 2007 (for the purpose of substituting ss 39B–39E of the 1965 Act for ss 39, 40 of that Act) (SSI 2006/469) |

**Local Electoral Administration and Registration Services (Scotland) Act 2006 (asp 14)**—*contd*

|  |  |  |
|---|---|---|
|  |  | *Not yet in force* (for the purpose of substituting s 39A of the 1965 Act for ss 39, 40 of that Act) |
|  | (6) | 1 Oct 2006 (for the purpose of prescribing by regulations: (a) the form of extracts and notices; and (b) the manner of authentication of extracts and notices) (SSI 2006/469) |
|  |  | 1 Jan 2007 (otherwise) (SSI 2006/469) |
|  | (7), (8) | 1 Jan 2007 (SSI 2006/469) |
| 45 |  | 1 Oct 2006 (SSI 2006/469) |
| 46 |  | 1 Oct 2006 (for the purpose of prescribing by regulations the form of applications for change of name or surname) (SSI 2006/469) |
|  |  | 1 Jan 2007 (otherwise) (SSI 2006/469) |
| 47 | (1) | See sub-ss (2), (3) below |
|  | (2) | 1 Jan 2007 (SSI 2006/469) |
|  | (3) | 1 Oct 2006 (SSI 2006/469) |
| 48 | (1) | See sub-ss (2)–(9) below |
|  | (2)–(6) | 1 Jan 2007 (SSI 2006/469) |
|  | (7) | 1 Oct 2006 (SSI 2006/469) |
|  | (8) | 1 Jan 2007 (SSI 2006/469) |
|  | (9)(a) | 1 Oct 2006 (SSI 2006/469) |
|  | (9)(b)(i) | 1 Jan 2007 (SSI 2006/469) |
|  | (9)(b)(ii) | 1 Oct 2006 (SSI 2006/469) |
|  | (9)(c) | 1 Oct 2006 (SSI 2006/469) |
| 49 |  | 1 Oct 2006 (for the purpose of prescribing by regulations the relevant particulars of the intended marriage) (SSI 2006/469) |
|  |  | 1 Jan 2007 (otherwise) (SSI 2006/469) |
| 50 | (1) | See sub-ss (2)–(10) below |
|  | (2)–(9) | 1 Oct 2006 (for the purpose of prescribing manners of attestation by regulations) (SSI 2006/469) |
|  |  | 1 Jan 2007 (otherwise) (SSI 2006/469) |
|  | (10) | 1 Oct 2006 (SSI 2006/469) |
| 51 |  | 1 Jan 2007 (SSI 2006/469) |
| 52 | (1) | See sub-ss (2)–(7) below |
|  | (2)(a)–(c) | 1 Oct 2006 (for the purpose of prescribing by regulations: (a) fees for registration as civil partners; and (b) manners of attestation) (SSI 2006/469) |
|  |  | 1 Jan 2007 (otherwise) (SSI 2006/469) |
|  | (2)(d) | 1 Oct 2006 (SSI 2006/469) |
|  | (3) | 1 Oct 2006 (SSI 2006/469) |
|  | (4) | 1 Oct 2006 (for the purpose of prescribing manners of attestation by regulations) (SSI 2006/469) |
|  |  | 1 Jan 2007 (otherwise) (SSI 2006/469) |
|  | (5) | 1 Oct 2006 (SSI 2006/469) |
|  | (6) | 1 Oct 2006 (for the purpose of prescribing by regulations: (a) the form of applications for notice of registration of civil partnerships in Scotland; (b) the means of giving such notice; (c) the form of such notice; and (d) fees for search and issue of an extract of an entry in the civil partnership register) (SSI 2006/469) |
|  |  | 1 Jan 2007 (for the purpose of substituting s 98(1) of the 2004 Act for s 98 of that Act) (SSI 2006/469) |
|  |  | *Not yet in force* (for the purpose of substituting s 98(2), (3) of the 2004 Act for s 98 of that Act) |
|  | (7) | 1 Oct 2006 (SSI 2006/469) |
| 53 |  | 1 Oct 2006 (SSI 2006/469) |
| 54, 55 |  | 1 Oct 2006 (for the purpose of prescribing by regulations: (a) the form of an application to have a qualifying event registered; (b) fees for such an application; (c) documents to be submitted; and (d) the form of an entry) (SSI 2006/469) |
|  |  | 5 Jan 2009 (otherwise) (SSI 2008/405) |

**Local Electoral Administration and Registration Services (Scotland) Act 2006 (asp 14)**—*contd*

| | | |
|---|---|---|
| 56–58 | | 1 Oct 2006 (SSI 2006/469) |
| 59 | (1)(a) | 1 Jan 2007 (SSI 2006/469) |
| | (1)(b) | 1 Oct 2006 (SSI 2006/469) |
| | (2)–(5) | 1 Jan 2007 (SSI 2006/469) |
| 60 | | 1 Oct 2006 (SSI 2006/469) |
| 61–63 | | 1 Aug 2006 (RA) |
| Sch 1 | | 28 Sep 2021 (SSI 2021/314)[5] |
| Sch 2 | paras 1, 2 | 17 Feb 2007 (SSI 2007/26)[2] |
| | paras 3, 4 | *Not yet in force* |
| | para 5 | 17 Feb 2007 (SSI 2007/26)[2] |
| | para 6 | 29 Jan 2007 (SSI 2007/26) |
| | para 7 | 17 Feb 2007 (SSI 2007/26)[2] |
| | para 8 | 29 Jan 2007 (SSI 2007/26) |
| | para 9 | *Not yet in force* |
| | para 10 | 17 Feb 2007 (SSI 2007/26)[2] |
| | para 11 | 29 Jan 2007 (SSI 2007/26) |
| | paras 12–14 | 17 Feb 2007 (SSI 2007/26)[2] |

[1]  For transitional provisions, see SSI 2006/469, art 4

[2]  For transitional provisions, see SSI 2007/26, arts 2(2), 3(2)

[3]  For a transitional provision, see SSI 2007/566, art 3

[4]  For a transitional provision, see SSI 2009/2, art 3

[5]  For a transitional provision, see SSI 2021/314, art 3

---

**London Olympic Games and Paralympic Games Act 2006 (c 12)**

*RA:* 30 Mar 2006

*Commencement provisions:* s 40(1)–(4); London Olympic Games and Paralympic Games Act 2006 (Commencement No 1) Order 2006, SI 2006/1118; London Olympic Games and Paralympic Games Act 2006 (Commencement) (Scotland) Order 2006, SSI 2006/611; London Olympic Games and Paralympic Games Act 2006 (Commencement No 2) Order 2007, SI 2007/1064; London Olympic Games and Paralympic Games Act 2006 (Commencement No 3) Order 2009, SI 2009/2577

| | | |
|---|---|---|
| 1 | | 30 Mar 2006 (s 40(1)(a)) |
| 2 | | 30 May 2006 (SI 2006/1118) |
| 3–5 | | 30 Mar 2006 (s 40(1)(b)) |
| 6–12 | | 30 May 2006 (SI 2006/1118) |
| 13–16 | | 5 Oct 2009 (SI 2009/2577) |
| 17, 18 | | 30 May 2006 (SI 2006/1118) |
| 19–31 | | 30 May 2006 (E) (W) (NI) (SI 2006/1118) |
| | | 31 Dec 2006 (S) (SSI 2006/611) |
| 32 | | See Sch 3 below |
| 33 | | See Sch 4 below |
| 34 | | 30 Mar 2006 (s 40(1)(e)) |
| 35 | (1), (2) | 30 Mar 2006 (s 40(1)(e)) |
| | (3)–(5) | 30 May 2006 (SI 2006/1118) |
| 36 | (1), (2) | 30 May 2006 (SI 2006/1118) |
| | (3)(a) | 30 Mar 2006 (with effect in relation to compulsory purchase orders made on or after 1 Oct 2005) (s 40(1)(f), (9)(a)) |
| | (3)(b) | 30 May 2006 (with effect in relation to purchases completed before, on or after that date) (SI 2006/1118) |
| | (3)(c) | 30 May 2006 (with effect in relation to purchases completed on or after 1 Oct 2005) (SI 2006/1118) |
| | (3)(d) | 30 Mar 2006 (with retrospective effect from 1 Oct 2005) (s 40(1)(f), (9)(d)) |
| | (4), (5) | 30 May 2006 (SI 2006/1118) |

**London Olympic Games and Paralympic Games Act 2006 (c 12)**—*contd*

| | | |
|---|---|---|
| 37, 38 | | 30 Mar 2006 (s 40(1)(g), (h)) |
| 39 | (1) | *Not yet in force* |
| | (2), (3) | 30 May 2006 (E) (W) (NI) (SI 2006/1118) |
| | | 31 Dec 2006 (S) (SSI 2006/611) |
| 40–42 | | 30 Mar 2006 (RA) |
| Sch 1 | | 30 Mar 2006 (s 40(1)(b)) |
| Sch 2 | | 30 May 2006 (SI 2006/1118) |
| Sch 3 | paras 1–11 | 30 Mar 2006 (s 40(1)(c)) |
| | para 12 | 2 Apr 2007 (SI 2007/1064) |
| | para 13 | 2 Apr 2007 (except to the extent that it inserts the Olympic Symbol etc (Protection) Act 1995, s 8B(1)) (SI 2007/1064) |
| | | *Not yet in force* (exception noted above) |
| | para 14 | 2 Apr 2007 (SI 2007/1064) |
| Sch 4 | | 30 Mar 2006 (s 40(1)(d)) |

---

**Merchant Shipping (Pollution) Act 2006 (c 8)**

*RA:* 30 Mar 2006

*Commencement provisions:* s 4(2)

| | | |
|---|---|---|
| 1 | (1) | 30 Mar 2006 (RA) |
| | (2)(a) | 30 Mar 2006 (RA) |
| | (2)(b) | 30 May 2006 (s 4(2)) |
| | (3)–(8) | 30 Mar 2006 (RA) |
| 2 | | 30 Mar 2006 (RA) |
| 3 | | 30 May 2006 (s 4(2)) |
| 4 | | 30 Mar 2006 (RA) |

---

**National Health Service Act 2006 (c 41)**

*RA:* 8 Nov 2006

*Commencement provisions:* s 277

| | | |
|---|---|---|
| 1, 2 | | 1 Mar 2007 (s 277) |
| 3 | | 1 Mar 2007 (except in relation to primary ophthalmic services) (s 277) |
| | | In force immediately after, and to the extent that, the Health Act 2006, s 80, Sch 8, para 7 comes into force (in relation to primary ophthalmic services) (s 277(3)(j), (4), (5)) |
| 4–10 | | 1 Mar 2007 (s 277) |
| 11 | (1)(a)–(c) | 1 Mar 2007 (except in relation to primary ophthalmic services) (s 277) |
| | | In force immediately after, and to the extent that, the Health Act 2006, s 80, Sch 8, para 29 comes into force (in relation to primary ophthalmic services) (s 277(3)(j), (4), (5)) |
| | (1)(d) | In force immediately after, and to the extent that, the Smoking, Health and Social Care (Scotland) Act 2005, s 20 comes into force (s 277(3)(e), (f), (4), (5)) |
| | (2)–(5) | 1 Mar 2007 (except in relation to primary ophthalmic services) (s 277) |
| | | In force immediately after, and to the extent that, the Health Act 2006, s 80, Sch 8, para 29 comes into force (in relation to primary ophthalmic services) (s 277(3)(j), (4), (5)) |
| | (6) | In force immediately after, and to the extent that, the Smoking, Health and Social Care (Scotland) Act 2005, s 20 comes into force (s 277(3)(e), (f), (4), (5)) |
| | (7) | 1 Mar 2007 (except in relation to primary ophthalmic services) (s 277) |

**National Health Service Act 2006 (c 41)**—*contd*

|  |  |  |
|---|---|---|
|  |  | In force immediately after, and to the extent that, the Health Act 2006, s 80, Sch 8, para 29 comes into force (in relation to primary ophthalmic services) (s 277(3)(j), (4), (5)) |
| 12–20 |  | 1 Mar 2007 (s 277) |
| 21 |  | 1 Mar 2007 (except in so far as sub-s (3) relates to primary ophthalmic services) (s 277) |
|  |  | In force immediately after, and to the extent that, the Health Act 2006, s 80, Sch 8, para 9 comes into force (in so far as sub-s (3) relates to primary ophthalmic services) (s 277(3)(j), (4), (5)) |
| 22 |  | 1 Mar 2007 (except in relation to primary ophthalmic services) (s 277) |
|  |  | In force immediately after, and to the extent that, the Health Act 2006, s 80, Sch 8, para 8 comes into force (in relation to primary ophthalmic services) (s 277(3)(j), (4), (5)) |
| 23–49 |  | 1 Mar 2007 (s 277) |
| 50 |  | In force immediately after, and to the extent that, the Health and Social Care (Community Health and Standards) Act 2003, s 21 comes into force (s 277(3)(c), (4), (5)) |
| 51–79 |  | 1 Mar 2007 (s 277) |
| 80 | (1)–(4) | 1 Mar 2007 (s 277) |
|  | (5)(a) | 1 Mar 2007 (s 277) |
|  | (5)(b) | 1 Mar 2007 (except in relation to primary ophthalmic services) (s 277) |
|  |  | In force immediately after, and to the extent that, the Health Act 2006, s 80, Sch 8, para 11 comes into force (in relation to primary ophthalmic services) (s 277(3)(j), (4), (5)) |
|  | (5)(c), (d) | 1 Mar 2007 (s 277) |
|  | (6) | 1 Mar 2007 (s 277) |
|  | (7)(a) | 1 Mar 2007 (s 277) |
|  | (7)(b) | 1 Mar 2007 (except in relation to primary ophthalmic services) (s 277) |
|  |  | In force immediately after, and to the extent that, the Health Act 2006, s 80, Sch 8, para 11 comes into force (in relation to primary ophthalmic services) (s 277(3)(j), (4), (5)) |
|  | (7)(c)–(e) | 1 Mar 2007 (s 277) |
| 81–96 |  | 1 Mar 2007 (s 277) |
| 97 | (1) | 1 Mar 2007 (s 277) |
|  | (2), (3) | 1 Mar 2007 (except in relation to primary ophthalmic services) (s 277) |
|  |  | In force immediately after, and to the extent that, the Health Act 2006, s 80, Sch 8, para 17 comes into force (in relation to primary ophthalmic services) (s 277(3)(j), (4), (5)) |
|  | (4)–(12) | 1 Mar 2007 (s 277) |
| 98–114 |  | 1 Mar 2007 (s 277) |
| 115, 116 |  | In force immediately after, and to the extent that, the Health Act 2006, s 37 comes into force (s 277(3)(j), (4), (5)) |
| 117–122 |  | In force immediately after, and to the extent that, the Health Act 2006, s 38 comes into force (s 277(3)(j), (4), (5)) |
| 123 |  | In force immediately after, and to the extent that, the Health Act 2006, s 39 comes into force (s 277(3)(j), (4), (5)) |
| 124 |  | In force immediately after, and to the extent that, the Health Act 2006, s 40 comes into force (s 277(3)(j), (4), (5)) |
| 125 |  | In force immediately after, and to the extent that, the Health Act 2006, s 41 comes into force (s 277(3)(j), (4), (5)) |
| 126 | (1)–(3) | 1 Mar 2007 (s 277) |
|  | (4)(a)–(c) | 1 Mar 2007 (s 277) |
|  | (4)(d) | 1 Mar 2007 (except in so far as the word "optometrist" replaces the words "ophthalmic optician") (s 277) |

**National Health Service Act 2006 (c 41)**—*contd*

|  |  |  |
|---|---|---|
|  |  | In force immediately after, and to the extent that, the Health Act 2006, s 80, Sch 8, para 14 comes into force (in so far as the word "optometrist" replaces the words "ophthalmic optician") (s 277(3)(o), (4), (5)) |
| 127 |  | 1 Mar 2007 (s 277) |
| 128 | (1) | 1 Mar 2007 (s 277) |
|  | (2)(a) | 1 Mar 2007 (s 277) |
|  | (2)(b) | In force immediately after, and to the extent that, the Smoking, Health and Social Care (Scotland) Act 2005, s 20 (s 277(3)(d), (4), (5) comes into force) |
|  | (3)–(6) | 1 Mar 2007 (s 277) |
| 129–131 |  | 1 Mar 2007 (s 277) |
| 132 | (1) | 1 Mar 2007 (s 277) |
|  | (2) | In force immediately after, and to the extent that, the Health Act 2006, s 36(1) comes into force (s 277(3)(i), (4), (5)) |
|  | (3)–(9) | 1 Mar 2007 (s 277) |
| 133–168 |  | 1 Mar 2007 (s 277) |
| 169 |  | See Sch 13 below |
| 170–179 |  | 1 Mar 2007 (s 277) |
| 180 | (1) | 1 Mar 2007 (s 277) |
|  | (2)(a), (b) | 1 Mar 2007 (s 277) |
|  | (2)(c) | In force immediately after, and to the extent that, the Health Act 2006, s 42(2) comes into force (s 277(3)(k), (4), (5)) |
|  | (2)(d) | 1 Mar 2007 (s 277) |
|  | (3)–(12) | 1 Mar 2007 (s 277) |
| 181 |  | In force immediately after, and to the extent that, the Health Act 2006, s 42(3) comes into force (s 277(3)(l), (4), (5)) |
| 182–194 |  | 1 Mar 2007 (s 277) |
| 195–207 |  | In force immediately after, and to the extent that, the Health Act 2006, ss 44–55 come into force (s 277(3)(m), (4), (5)) |
| 208, 209 |  | In force immediately after, and to the extent that, the Health Act 2006, ss 76–78 (in so far as they relate to ss 44–55 of that Act) come into force (s 277(3)(m), (4), (5)) |
| 210 |  | In force immediately after, and to the extent that, the Health Act 2006, ss 44–55 come into force (s 277(3)(m), (4), (5)) |
| 211–233 |  | 1 Mar 2007 (s 277) |
| 234 | (1)(a) | 1 Mar 2007 (except in relation to primary ophthalmic services) (s 277) |
|  |  | In force immediately after, and to the extent that, the Health Act 2006, s 80, Sch 8, para 22 comes into force (in relation to primary ophthalmic services) (s 277(3)(j), (4), (5)) |
|  | (1)(b) | 1 Mar 2007 (s 277) |
|  | (2)–(4) | 1 Mar 2007 (s 277) |
| 235–238 |  | 1 Mar 2007 (s 277) |
| 239 | (1)(a)–(g) | 1 Mar 2007 (s 277) |
|  | (1)(h) | In force immediately after, and to the extent that, the Health Act 2006, s 80, Sch 8, para 50 comes into force (s 277(3)(j), (4), (5)) |
|  | (1)(i), (j) | 1 Mar 2007 (s 277) |
| 240–245 |  | 1 Mar 2007 (s 277) |
| 246 |  | See Sch 17 below |
| 247–253 |  | 1 Mar 2007 (s 277) |
| 254 |  | See Sch 20 below |
| 255–260 |  | 1 Mar 2007 (s 277) |
| 261 |  | In force immediately after, and to the extent that, the Health Act 1999, s 33 comes into force (s 277(3)(a), (4), (5)) |
| 262 |  | 1 Mar 2007 (s 277) |
| 263 |  | In force immediately after, and to the extent that, the Health Act 1999, s 35 comes into force (s 277(3)(a), (4), (5)) |

**National Health Service Act 2006 (c 41)**—*contd*

| | | |
|---|---|---|
| 264 | | In force immediately after, and to the extent that, the Health Act 1999, s 36 comes into force (s 277(a), (4), (5)) |
| 265 | | In force immediately after, and to the extent that, the Health Act 1999, s 37 comes into force (s 277(3)(a), (4), (5)) |
| 266 | | In force immediately after, and to the extent that, the Health Act 1999, s 38 comes into force (s 277(3)(a), (4), (5)) |
| 267 | (1)–(4) | 1 Mar 2007 (s 277) |
| | (5)(a), (b) | 1 Mar 2007 (s 277) |
| | (5)(c) | 1 Mar 2007 (except in relation to primary ophthalmic services) (s 277) |
| | | In force immediately after, and to the extent that, the Health Act 2006, s 80, Sch 8, para 21(b) comes into force (in relation to primary ophthalmic services) (s 277(3)(j), (4), (5)) |
| | (6) | 1 Mar 2007 (s 277) |
| 268–274 | | 1 Mar 2007 (s 277) |
| 275 | (1) | 1 Mar 2007 (except in so far as the word "optometrist" replaces the words "ophthalmic optician") (s 277) |
| | | In force immediately after, and to the extent that, the Health Act 2006, s 80, Sch 8, para 24(b) comes into force (in so far as the word "optometrist" replaces the words "ophthalmic optician") (s 277(3)(o), (4), (5)) |
| | (2)–(4) | 1 Mar 2007 (s 277) |
| 276–278 | | 1 Mar 2007 (s 277) |
| Schs 1–12 | | 1 Mar 2007 (s 277) |
| Sch 13 | paras 1–5 | 1 Mar 2007 (s 277) |
| | para 6(1)(a) | 1 Mar 2007 (s 277) |
| | para 6(1)(b) | 1 Mar 2007 (except in so far as the word "optometrist" replaces the words "ophthalmic optician") (s 277) |
| | | In force immediately after, and to the extent that, the Health Act 2006, s 80, Sch 8, para 25 comes into force (in so far as the word "optometrist" replaces the words "ophthalmic optician") (s 277(3)(o), (4), (5)) |
| | para 6(1)(c) | 1 Mar 2007 (s 277) |
| | para 6(2) | 1 Mar 2007 (s 277) |
| | paras 7–22 | 1 Mar 2007 (s 277) |
| Schs 14–16 | | 1 Mar 2007 (s 277) |
| Sch 17 | paras 1–11 | 1 Mar 2007 (s 277) |
| | paras 12, 13 | 1 Mar 2007 (except in relation to primary ophthalmic services) (s 277) |
| | | In force immediately after, and to the extent that, the Health Act 2006, s 80, Sch 8, para 46 comes into force (in relation to primary ophthalmic services) (s 277(3)(j), (4), (5)) |
| | paras 14–20 | 1 Mar 2007 (s 277) |
| Schs 18, 19 | | 1 Mar 2007 (s 277) |
| Sch 20 | para 1 | 1 Mar 2007 (s 277) |
| | para 2(1)–(6) | 1 Mar 2007 (s 277) |
| | para 2(7) | In force immediately after, and to the extent that, the Nationality, Immigration and Asylum Act 2002, s 45(7) comes into force (s 277(3)(b), (4), (5)) |
| | para 2(8)–(11) | 1 Mar 2007 (s 277) |
| | paras 3, 4 | 1 Mar 2007 (s 277) |
| Schs 21, 22 | | 1 Mar 2007 (s 277) |

---

**National Health Service (Consequential Provisions) Act 2006 (c 43)**

*RA:* 8 Nov 2006

*Commencement provisions:* s 8

| | |
|---|---|
| 1–5 | 1 Mar 2007 (s 8) |

**National Health Service (Consequential Provisions) Act 2006 (c 43)**—*contd*

| | |
|---|---|
| 6 | See Sch 4 below |
| 7, 8 | 1 Mar 2007 (s 8) |
| Schs 1–3 | 1 Mar 2007 (s 8) |
| Sch 4 | 1 Mar 2007 (s 8), repeals of or in— |

      National Health Service Act 1977[1];

      Public Health Laboratory Act 1979;

      Health Services Act 1980;

      Acquisition of Land Act 1981;

      British Nationality Act 1981;

      New Towns Act 1981;

      Mental Health (Amendment) Act 1982;

      Health and Social Services and Social Security Adjudications Act 1983;

      Medical Act 1983;

      Mental Health Act 1983;

      Dentists Act 1984;

      Health and Social Security Act 1984;

      Housing (Consequential Provisions) Act 1985;

      Family Practitioner Committees (Consequential Modifications) Order 1985, SI 1985/39;

      National Health Service (Amendment) Act 1986;

      AIDS (Control) Act 1987;

      Pharmaceutical Qualifications (EEC Recognition) Order 1987, SI 1987/2202;

      Community Health Councils (Access to Information) Act 1988;

      Health and Medicines Act 1988;

      Social Security Act 1988;

      Children Act 1989;

      Access to Health Records Act 1990;

      National Health Service and Community Care Act 1990;

      Planning (Consequential Provisions) Act 1990;

      Health and Personal Social Services (Northern Ireland Consequential Amendments) Order 1991, SI 1991/195;

      Local Government (Wales) Act 1994;

      Vehicle Excise and Registration Act 1994;

      Health Authorities Act 1995;

      Education Act 1996;

      Employment Rights Act 1996;

      National Health Service (Residual Liabilities) Act 1996;

      Housing Act 1996 (Consequential Provisions) Order 1996, SI 1996/2325;

      National Health Service (Primary Care) Act 1997;

      National Health Service (Private Finance) Act 1997;

      Pharmacists (Fitness to Practice) Act 1997;

      Audit Commission Act 1998;

      Government of Wales Act 1998;

      School Standards and Framework Act 1998;

      Health Act 1999 (except for repeals of or in ss 33, 35–38, 62(2), (8) (see below));

      Immigration and Asylum Act 1999;

      Health Act 1999 (Supplementary and Consequential Provisions) Order 1999, SI 1999/2795;

      National Assembly for Wales (Transfer of Functions) Order 1999, SI 1999/672;

      Freedom of Information Act 2000;

      Government Resources and Accounts Act 2000;

      Local Government Act 2000;

      Health Act 1999 (Supplementary, Consequential etc Provisions) Order 2000, SI 2000/90;

**National Health Service (Consequential Provisions) Act 2006 (c 43)**—*contd*

Anti-Terrorism, Crime and Security Act 2001;

Health and Social Care Act 2001 (except for repeal of or in s 40(1), (2) (see below));

Financial Services and Markets Act 2000 (Consequential Amendments and Repeals) Order 2001, SI 2001/3649;

Adoption and Children Act 2002;

National Health Service Reform and Health Care Professions Act 2002;

National Health Service Act 1977 and National Health Service and Community Care Act 1990 (Amendment) Regulations 2002, SI 2002/2759;

National Health Service Reform and Health Care Professions Act 2002 (Supplementary, Consequential etc Provisions) Regulations 2002, 2002/2469;

Nursing and Midwifery Order 2001, SI 2002/253;

Health and Social Care (Community Health and Standards) Act 2003 (except for repeal of or in s 21);

Health (Wales) Act 2003;

General and Specialist Medical Practice (Education, Training and Qualifications) Order 2003, SI 2003/1250;

Health Professions Order 2001 (Consequential Amendments) Order 2003, SI 2003/1590;

Health, Social Care and Well-being Strategies (Wales) Regulations 2003, SI 2003/154;

National Health Service Reform and Health Care Professions Act 2002 (Supplementary, Consequential etc Provisions) Regulations 2003, SI 2003/1937;

Health Protection Agency Act 2004;

Public Audit (Wales) Act 2004;

Freedom of Information (Removal and Relaxation of Statutory Prohibitions on Disclosure of Information) Order 2004, SI 2004/3363;

Health Act 1999 (Consequential Amendments) (Nursing and Midwifery) Order 2004, SI 2004/1771;

Health and Social Care (Community Health and Standards) Act 2003 (Commission for Healthcare Audit and Inspection and Commission for Social Care Inspection) (Consequential Provisions) Order 2004, SI 2004/2987;

Primary Medical Services (Scotland) Act 2004 (Consequential Modifications) Order 2004, SI 2004/957;

Constitutional Reform Act 2005;

Public Services Ombudsman (Wales) Act 2005;

Dentists Act 1984 (Amendment) Order 2005, SI 2005/2011;

Opticians Act 1989 (Amendment) Order 2005, SI 2005/848;

Health Act 2006 (except for repeals of or in ss 34, 35, 36(1), 42, 44–56, 78(3), Sch 8, paras 10, 12(b), 13(3), (4), 14, 18, 19, 21(a), 24, 25, and, except in relation to primary ophthalmic services, ss 37–41, Sch 8, paras 7–9, 11, 12(a), 13(2), (5), (6), 15–17, 21(b), 22, 29, 46, 50);

National Health Service (Pre-consolidation Amendments) Order 2006, SI 2006/1407

*Not yet in force,* (in force immediately after, and to the extent that, the provision which is repealed or revoked comes into force; see s 8(4), (5)) repeals of or in—

Health Act 1999, ss 33, 35–38;

Health and Social Care Act 2001, s 40(1), (2);

Nationality, Immigration and Asylum Act 2002;

Health and Social Care (Community Health and Standards) Act 2003, s 21;

**National Health Service (Consequential Provisions) Act 2006 (c 43)**—*contd*

        Smoking, Health and Social Care (Scotland) Act 2005
        (Consequential Modifications) (England, Wales and Northern
        Ireland) Order 2006, SI 2006/1056;

        Health Act 2006, ss 34, 35, 36(1), 42, 44–56, 78(3), Sch 8,
        paras 10, 12(b), 13(3), (4), 14, 18, 19, 21(a), 24, 25, and, in
        relation to primary ophthalmic services, ss 37–41, Sch 8,
        paras 7–9, 11, 12(a), 13(2), (5), (6), 15–17, 21(b), 22, 29, 46,
        50

        *Not yet in force*, (s 8(7), (8)) repeals of or in—

        Health Act 1999, s 62(2) (in force immediately, after and to the
        extent that, the Health Act 1999, s 38(1)(b) comes into force);

        Health Act 1999, s 62(8) (in force immediately, after and to the
        extent that, the Health Act 1999, s 37 comes into force)

[1]   Subject to transitory modifications, see Sch 3, Pt 1, para 1 to this Act

---

**NHS Redress Act 2006 (c 44)**

*RA:* 8 Nov 2006

*Commencement provisions:* s 19(2)–(4)

| | |
|---|---|
| 1–16 | *Not yet in force* |
| 17 | *Never in force* (repealed) |
| 18, 19 | 8 Nov 2006 (s 19(2)) |

---

**National Health Service (Wales) Act 2006 (c 42)**

*RA:* 8 Nov 2006

*Commencement provisions:* s 208

| | | |
|---|---|---|
| 1, 2 | | 1 Mar 2007 (s 208) |
| 3 | (1)(a), (b) | 1 Mar 2007 (s 208) |
| | (1)(c) | 1 Mar 2007 (except in relation to primary ophthalmic services) (s 208) |
| | | In force immediately after, and to the extent that, the Health Act 2006, s 80, Sch 8, para 7(2), (3) comes into force (in relation to primary ophthalmic services) (s 208(3)(l), (4), (5)) |
| | (1)(d)–(f) | 1 Mar 2007 (s 208) |
| | (2), (3) | 1 Mar 2007 (s 208) |
| 4–8 | | 1 Mar 2007 (s 208) |
| 9 | (1)(a) | 1 Mar 2007 (except in relation to primary ophthalmic services) (s 208) |
| | | In force immediately after, and to the extent that, the Health Act 2006, s 80, Sch 8, para 29 comes into force (in relation to primary ophthalmic services) (s 208(3)(l), (4), (5)) |
| | (1)(b), (c) | 1 Mar 2007 (s 208) |
| | (1)(d) | In force immediately after, and to the extent that, the Smoking, Health and Social Care (Scotland) Act 2005, s 20 comes into force (s 208(3)(d), (4), (5)) |
| | (2) | 1 Mar 2007 (except in relation to primary ophthalmic services) (s 208) |
| | | In force immediately after, and to the extent that, the Health Act 2006, s 80, Sch 8, para 29 comes into force (in relation to primary ophthalmic services) (s 208(3)(l), (4), (5)) |
| | (3) | 1 Mar 2007 (s 208) |
| | (4) | 1 Mar 2007 (except in relation to primary ophthalmic services) (s 208) |

**National Health Service (Wales) Act 2006 (c 42)**—*contd*

|  |  |  |
|---|---|---|
|  |  | In force immediately after, and to the extent that, the Health Act 2006, s 80, Sch 8, para 29 comes into force (in relation to primary ophthalmic services) (s 208(3)(l), (4), (5)) |
|  | (5) | 1 Mar 2007 (s 208) |
| 10–70 |  | 1 Mar 2007 (s 208) |
| 71 | (1)(a) | 1 Mar 2007 (s 208) |
|  | (1)(b) | 1 Mar 2007 (except in so far as the word "optometrist" replaces the words "ophthalmic optician") (s 208) |
|  |  | In force immediately after, and to the extent that, the Health Act 2006, s 80, Sch 8, para 12(b) comes into force (in so far as the word "optometrist" replaces the words "ophthalmic optician") (s 208(3)(m), (4), (5)) |
|  | (2)–(10) | 1 Mar 2007 (s 208) |
| 72 | (1)(a)–(c) | 1 Mar 2007 (except in so far as the word "optometrist" replaces the words "ophthalmic optician") (s 208) |
|  |  | In force immediately after, and to the extent that, the Health Act 2006, s 80, Sch 8, para 13(3), (4) comes into force (in so far as the word "optometrist" replaces the words "ophthalmic optician") (s 208(3)(m), (4), (5)) |
|  | (1)(d) | 1 Mar 2007 (s 208) |
|  | (2) | 1 Mar 2007 (s 208) |
|  | (3)(a) | 1 Mar 2007 (except in so far as the word "optometrist" replaces the words "ophthalmic optician") (s 208) |
|  |  | In force immediately after, and to the extent that, the Health Act 2006, s 80, Sch 8, para 13(3), (4) comes into force (in so far as the word "optometrist" replaces the words "ophthalmic optician") (s 208(3)(m), (4), (5)) |
|  | (3)(b)–(f) | 1 Mar 2007 (s 208) |
|  | (4)–(7) | 1 Mar 2007 (s 208) |
| 73–79 |  | 1 Mar 2007 (s 208) |
| 80 | (1)–(3) | 1 Mar 2007 (s 208) |
|  | (4)(a)–(c) | 1 Mar 2007 (s 208) |
|  | (4)(d) | 1 Mar 2007 (except in so far as the word "optometrist" replaces the words "ophthalmic optician") (s 208) |
|  |  | In force immediately after, and to the extent that, the Health Act 2006, s 80, Sch 8, para 14 comes into force (in so far as the word "optometrist" replaces the words "ophthalmic optician") (s 208(3)(m), (4), (5)) |
|  | (4)(e)–(i) | 1 Mar 2007 (s 208) |
|  | (5)–(9) | 1 Mar 2007 (s 208) |
| 81 |  | 1 Mar 2007 (s 208) |
| 82 | (1) | 1 Mar 2007 (s 208) |
|  | (2)(a) | 1 Mar 2007 (s 208) |
|  | (2)(b) | In force immediately after, and to the extent that, the Smoking, Health and Social Care (Scotland) Act 2005, s 20 comes into force (s 208(3)(c), (4), (5)) |
|  | (3)–(6) | 1 Mar 2007 (s 208) |
| 83 | (1)–(3) | 1 Mar 2007 (s 208) |
|  | (4), (5) | In force immediately after, and to the extent that, the Health Act 2006, s 35 comes into force (s 208(3)(g), (4), (5)) |
|  | (6)–(11) | 1 Mar 2007 (s 208) |
| 84 |  | 1 Mar 2007 (s 208) |
| 85 |  | In force immediately after, and to the extent that, the Health Act 2006, s 34 comes into force (s 208(3)(f), (4), (5)) |
| 86 | (1) | 1 Mar 2007 (s 208) |
|  | (2) | In force immediately after, and to the extent that, the Health Act 2006, s 36(1) comes into force (s 208(3)(h), (4), (5)) |
|  | (3)–(9) | 1 Mar 2007 (s 208) |
| 87–101 |  | 1 Mar 2007 (s 208) |

**National Health Service (Wales) Act 2006 (c 42)**—*contd*

| | | |
|---|---|---|
| 102 | | In force immediately after, and to the extent that, the Health and Social Care Act 2001, s 40(1) comes into force (s 208(3)(a), (4), (5)) |
| 103–108 | | 1 Mar 2007 (s 208) |
| 109 | (1) | 1 Mar 2007 (except in so far as the word "optometrist" replaces the words "ophthalmic optician") (s 208) |
| | | In force immediately after, and to the extent that, the Health Act 2006, s 80, Sch 8, para 19 comes into force (in so far as the word "optometrist" replaces the words "ophthalmic optician") (s 208(3)(m), (4), (5)) |
| | (2) | 1 Mar 2007 (s 208) |
| 110–128 | | 1 Mar 2007 (s 208) |
| 129 | (1) | 1 Mar 2007 (s 208) |
| | (2)(a) | 1 Mar 2007 (s 208) |
| | (2)(b) | In force immediately after, and to the extent that, the Health Act 2006, s 42(2) comes into force (s 208(3)(i), (4), (5)) |
| | (2)(c) | 1 Mar 2007 (s 208) |
| | (3)–(12) | 1 Mar 2007 (s 208) |
| 130–142 | | 1 Mar 2007 (s 208) |
| 143 | | In force immediately after, and to the extent that, the Health Act 2006, s 44 comes into force (s 208(3)(j), (4), (5)) |
| 144 | | In force immediately after, and to the extent that, the Health Act 2006, s 45 comes into force (s 208(3)(j), (4), (5)) |
| 145 | | In force immediately after, and to the extent that, the Health Act 2006, s 46 comes into force (s 208(3)(j), (4), (5)) |
| 146 | | In force immediately after, and to the extent that, the Health Act 2006, s 47 comes into force (s 208(3)(j), (4), (5)) |
| 147 | | In force immediately after, and to the extent that, the Health Act 2006, s 48 comes into force (s 208(3)(j), (4), (5)) |
| 148 | | In force immediately after, and to the extent that, the Health Act 2006, s 49 comes into force (s 208(3)(j), (4), (5)) |
| 149 | | In force immediately after, and to the extent that, the Health Act 2006, s 50 comes into force (s 208(3)(j), (4), (5)) |
| 150 | | In force immediately after, and to the extent that, the Health Act 2006, s 51 comes into force (s 208(3)(j), (4), (5)) |
| 151 | | In force immediately after, and to the extent that, the Health Act 2006, s 54 comes into force (s 208(3)(j), (4), (5)) |
| 152 | | In force immediately after, and to the extent that, the Health Act 2006, s 52 comes into force (s 208(3)(j), (4), (5)) |
| 153 | | In force immediately after, and to the extent that, the Health Act 2006, s 53 comes into force (s 208(3)(j), (4), (5)) |
| 154 | | In force immediately after, and to the extent that, the Health Act 2006, s 76 comes into force (s 208(3)(j), (4), (5)) |
| 155 | | In force immediately after, and to the extent that, the Health Act 2006, s 77 comes into force (s 208(3)(j), (4), (5)) |
| 156 | | In force immediately after, and to the extent that, the Health Act 2006, s 78 comes into force (s 208(3)(j), (4), (5)) |
| 157 | | 1 Mar 2007 (s 208) |
| 158 | | In force immediately after, and to the extent that, the Health Act 2006, s 55 comes into force (s 208(3)(j), (4), (5)) |
| 159–177 | | 1 Mar 2007 (s 208) |
| 178 | | In force immediately after, and to the extent that, the Health Act 2006, s 56(1) comes into force (s 208(3)(k), (4), (5)) |
| 179–189 | | 1 Mar 2007 (s 208) |
| 190 | (1) | 1 Mar 2007 (s 208) |
| | (2)(a)–(d) | 1 Mar 2007 (s 208) |
| | (2)(e) | 1 Mar 2007 (except in so far as the word "optometrist" replaces the words "ophthalmic optician") (s 208) |

**National Health Service (Wales) Act 2006 (c 42)**—*contd*

| | | |
|---|---|---|
| | | In force immediately after, and to the extent that, the Health Act 2006, s 80, Sch 8, para 10 comes into force (in so far as the word "optometrist" replaces the words "ophthalmic optician") (s 208(3)(m), (4), (5)) |
| | (3)–(5) | 1 Mar 2007 (s 208) |
| 191–197 | | 1 Mar 2007 (s 208) |
| 198 | (1)–(4) | 1 Mar 2007 (s 208) |
| | (5)(a) | 1 Mar 2007 (except in so far as the word "optometrist" replaces the words "ophthalmic optician") (s 208) |
| | | In force immediately after, and to the extent that, the Health Act 2006, s 80, Sch 8, para 21(a) comes into force (in so far as the word "optometrist" replaces the words "ophthalmic optician") (s 208(3)(m), (4), (5)) |
| | (5)(b)–(d) | 1 Mar 2007 (s 208) |
| | (6) | 1 Mar 2007 (s 208) |
| 199–205 | | 1 Mar 2007 (s 208) |
| 206 | (1) | 1 Mar 2007 (except in relation to definitions of "financial year" and "optometrist") (s 208) |
| | | In force immediately after, and to the extent that, the Health Act 2006, s 80, Sch 8, para 24 comes into force (in relation to definitions of "financial year" and "optometrist") (s 208(3)(k), (m), (4), (5)) |
| | (2), (3) | 1 Mar 2007 (s 208) |
| 207–209 | | 1 Mar 2007 (s 208) |
| Schs 1–6 | | 1 Mar 2007 (s 208) |
| Sch 7 | | In force immediately after, and to the extent that, the Health and Social Care Act 2001, s 40(2) comes into force (s 208(3)(a), (4), (5)) |
| Sch 8 | | 1 Mar 2007 (s 208) |
| Sch 9 | | In force immediately after, and to the extent that, the Health Act 2006, s 56(2) comes into force (s 208(3)(k), (4), (5)) |
| Sch 10 | | 1 Mar 2007 (s 208) |
| Sch 11 | paras 1–11 | 1 Mar 2007 (s 208) |
| | paras 12, 13 | 1 Mar 2007 (except in relation to primary ophthalmic services) (s 208) |
| | | In force immediately after, and to the extent that, the Health Act 2006, s 80, Sch 8, para 46 comes into force (in relation to primary ophthalmic services) (s 208(3)(l), (4), (5)) |
| | paras 14–20 | 1 Mar 2007 (s 208) |
| Schs 12–14 | | 1 Mar 2007 (s 208) |
| Sch 15 | para 1 | 1 Mar 2007 (s 208) |
| | para 2(1)–(6) | 1 Mar 2007 (s 208) |
| | para 2(7) | In force immediately after, and to the extent that, the Nationality, Immigration and Asylum Act 2002, s 45(7) comes into force (s 208(3)(b), (4), (5)) |
| | para 2(8)–(11) | 1 Mar 2007 (s 208) |
| | para 3 | 1 Mar 2007 (s 208) |

---

**National Insurance Contributions Act 2006 (c 10)**

*RA:* 30 Mar 2006

*Commencement provisions:* s 9

Whole Act in force 30 Mar 2006 (s 9)

---

**National Lottery Act 2006 (c 23)**

*RA:* 11 Jul 2006

*Commencement provisions:* s 22(1); National Lottery Act 2006 (Commencement No 1) Order 2006, SI 2006/2177; National Lottery Act 2006 (Commencement No 2 and Transitional Provisions)

**National Lottery Act 2006 (c 23)**—*contd*

Order 2006, SI 2006/2630; National Lottery Act 2006 (Commencement No 3) Order 2006, SI 2006/3201; National Lottery Act 2006 (Commencement No 4) Order 2007, SI 2007/539; National Lottery Act 2006 (Commencement No 5) Order 2010, SI 2010/2

| | | |
|---|---|---|
| 1–4 | | 1 Oct 2006 (SI 2006/2630)[1] |
| 5 | | 6 Jan 2010 (SI 2010/2) |
| 6 | | 11 Jul 2006 (RA) |
| 7 | (1), (2) | 1 Dec 2006 (SI 2006/3201) |
| | (3) | 1 Dec 2006 (except in so far as it relates to the insertion of the National Lottery etc Act 1993, s 22(3B)(e)) (SI 2006/3201) |
| | | *Not yet in force* (exception noted above) |
| 8 | | 1 Oct 2006 (SI 2006/2630)[1] |
| 9 | | 1 Apr 2007 (SI 2007/539) |
| 10–12 | | 1 Oct 2006 (SI 2006/2630)[1] |
| 13 | (1) | 1 Dec 2006 (except in so far as it relates to the insertion of the National Lottery etc Act 1993, s 25(6)(b)) (SI 2006/3201) |
| | | *Not yet in force* (exception noted above) |
| | (2) | 1 Dec 2006 (except in so far as it relates to the insertion of the National Lottery etc Act 1993, s 25A(13)) (SI 2006/3201) |
| | | *Not yet in force* (exception noted above) |
| 14 | | 1 Aug 2006 (SI 2006/2177) |
| 15 | | 1 Dec 2006 (SI 2006/3201) |
| 16 | | 11 Jul 2006 (RA) |
| 17–21 | | 1 Dec 2006 (SI 2006/3201) |
| 22–24 | | 11 Jul 2006 (RA) |
| Sch 1 | | *Not yet in force* |
| Sch 2 | | 1 Aug 2006 (SI 2006/2177) |
| Sch 3 | | 1 Dec 2006 (SI 2006/3201) |

[1]   For transitional provisions, see SI 2006/2630, arts 3, 4

---

**Natural Environment and Rural Communities Act 2006 (c 16)**

*RA:* 30 Mar 2006

*Commencement provisions*: s 107; Natural Environment and Rural Communities Act 2006 (Commencement No 1) Order 2006, SI 2006/1176; Natural Environment and Rural Communities Act 2006 (Commencement No 2) Order 2006, SI 2006/1382; Natural Environment and Rural Communities Act 2006 (Commencement No 3 and Transitional Provisions) Order 2006, SI 2006/2541; Natural Environment and Rural Communities Act 2006 (Commencement) (Wales) Order 2006, SI 2006/2992; Natural Environment and Rural Communities Act 2006 (Commencement No 4) Order 2007, SI 2007/816; Natural Environment and Rural Communities Act 2006 (Commencement No 1) (England) Order 2007, SI 2007/2540

| | | |
|---|---|---|
| 1 | (1)–(3) | 2 May 2006 (SI 2006/1176) |
| | (4) | 1 Oct 2006 (SI 2006/2541) |
| | (5) | 2 May 2006 (SI 2006/1176) |
| 2 | | 2 May 2006 (SI 2006/1176) |
| 3, 4 | | 1 Oct 2006 (SI 2006/2541) |
| 5 | | 2 May 2006 (SI 2006/1176) |
| 6–8 | | 1 Oct 2006 (SI 2006/2541) |
| 9 | | 2 May 2006 (SI 2006/1176) |
| 10 | | 1 Oct 2006 (SI 2006/2541) |
| 11 | (1) | 2 May 2006 (SI 2006/1176) |
| | (2)(a) | 1 Oct 2006 (SI 2006/2541) |
| | (2)(b) | 2 May 2006 (SI 2006/1176) |
| | (2)(c) | 1 Oct 2006 (SI 2006/2541) |
| | (3)–(7) | 1 Oct 2006 (SI 2006/2541) |
| 12 | | 1 Oct 2006 (SI 2006/2541) |
| 13, 14 | | 2 May 2006 (SI 2006/1176) |

**Natural Environment and Rural Communities Act 2006 (c 16)**—*contd*

| | | |
|---|---|---|
| 15 | (1) | 1 Oct 2006 (SI 2006/2541) |
| | (2)–(6) | 2 May 2006 (SI 2006/1176) |
| 16 | | 2 May 2006 (SI 2006/1176) |
| 17–28 | | 1 Oct 2006 (SI 2006/2541) |
| 29 | | 2 May 2006 (SI 2006/1176) |
| 30–46 | | 1 Oct 2006 (SI 2006/2541) |
| 47 | | 31 May 2006 (SI 2006/1382) |
| 48–51 | | 1 Oct 2006 (SI 2006/2541) |
| 52 | | See Sch 5 below |
| 53 | | See Sch 6 below |
| 54, 55 | | 1 Oct 2006 (SI 2006/2541) |
| 56, 57 | | 31 May 2006 (SI 2006/1382) |
| 58 | | 1 Oct 2006 (SI 2006/2541) |
| 59 | | 30 May 2006 (s 107(3)(a)) |
| 60 | | 1 Oct 2006 (SI 2006/2541) |
| 61 | (1) | See sub-ss (2)–(6) below |
| | (2)–(5) | 10 May 2007 (SI 2007/816) |
| | (6) | 1 Oct 2006 (SI 2006/2541) |
| 62–65 | | 1 Oct 2006 (SI 2006/2541) |
| 66–71 | | 2 May 2006 (E) (SI 2006/1176) |
| | | 16 Nov 2006 (W) (SI 2006/2992) |
| 72 | | 16 Nov 2006 (W) (SI 2006/2992) |
| | | 1 Oct 2007 (E) (SI 2007/2540) |
| 73–77 | | 1 Apr 2007 (SI 2007/816) |
| 78, 79 | | 31 May 2006 (SI 2006/1382) |
| 80 | (1) | See Sch 7 below |
| | (2)–(6) | 31 May 2006 (SI 2006/1382) |
| 81–86 | | 31 May 2006 (SI 2006/1382) |
| 87–97 | | 1 Oct 2006 (SI 2006/2541) |
| 98 | | 2 May 2006 (SI 2006/1176) |
| 99 | | 30 May 2006 (s 107(7)(a)) |
| 100 | | 30 Mar 2006 (RA) (however note that SI 2006/2541 purports to bring s 100 into force on 1 Oct 2006) |
| 101 | | 1 Oct 2006 (SI 2006/2541) |
| 102–104 | | 30 Mar 2006 (RA) |
| 105 | (1) | See Sch 11 below |
| | (2) | See Sch 12 below |
| 106–109 | | 30 Mar 2006 (RA) |
| Sch 1 | | 2 May 2006 (SI 2006/1176) |
| Schs 2–4 | | 1 Oct 2006 (SI 2006/2541) |
| Schs 5–7 | | 31 May 2006 (SI 2006/1382) |
| Schs 8–10 | | 1 Oct 2006 (SI 2006/2541) |
| Sch 11 | paras 1–13 | 1 Oct 2006 (SI 2006/2541) |
| | para 14 | 1 Oct 2006 (SI 2006/2541)[1] |
| | paras 15–33 | 1 Oct 2006 (SI 2006/2541) |
| | para 34(1), (2) | 2 May 2006 (in so far as they insert words "Natural England") (SI 2006/1176) |
| | | 1 Oct 2006 (otherwise) (SI 2006/2541) |
| | para 34(3) | 1 Oct 2006 (SI 2006/2541) |
| | paras 35–38 | 1 Oct 2006 (SI 2006/2541) |
| | para 39(1), (2) | 2 May 2006 (in so far as they insert words "Natural England") (SI 2006/1176) |
| | | 1 Oct 2006 (otherwise) (SI 2006/2541) |
| | para 39(3) | 1 Oct 2006 (SI 2006/2541) |
| | paras 40–48 | 1 Oct 2006 (SI 2006/2541) |
| | para 49 | 1 Oct 2006 (SI 2006/2541)[1] |
| | paras 50–57 | 1 Oct 2006 (SI 2006/2541) |
| | para 58(1), (2) | 2 May 2006 (in so far as they insert words "Natural England") (SI 2006/1176) |

**Natural Environment and Rural Communities Act 2006 (c 16)**—*contd*

| | | |
|---|---|---|
| | | 1 Oct 2006 (otherwise) (SI 2006/2541) |
| | para 58(3) | 1 Oct 2006 (E) (SI 2006/2541) |
| | para 59 | 1 Oct 2006 (SI 2006/2541) |
| | para 60(1), (2) | 2 May 2006 (in so far as they insert words "Natural England") (SI 2006/1176) |
| | | 1 Oct 2006 (otherwise) (SI 2006/2541) |
| | para 60(3) | 1 Oct 2006 (SI 2006/2541) |
| | para 61(1) | See sub-paras (2)–(5) below |
| | para 61(2) | 1 Oct 2006 (SI 2006/2541) |
| | para 61(3) | 2 May 2006 (in so far as inserts words "Natural England") (SI 2006/1176) |
| | | 1 Oct 2006 (otherwise) (SI 2006/2541) |
| | para 61(4), (5) | 1 Oct 2006 (SI 2006/2541) |
| | paras 62–86 | 1 Oct 2006 (SI 2006/2541) |
| | para 87 | 1 Oct 2006 (SI 2006/2541)[1] |
| | paras 88–104 | 1 Oct 2006 (SI 2006/2541) |
| | para 105 | 2 May 2006 (in so far as inserts words "Natural England") (SI 2006/1176) |
| | | 1 Oct 2006 (otherwise) (SI 2006/2541) |
| | paras 106–152 | 1 Oct 2006 (SI 2006/2541) |
| | para 153(1), (2) | 2 May 2006 (in so far as they insert words "Natural England") (SI 2006/1176) |
| | | 1 Oct 2006 (otherwise) (SI 2006/2541) |
| | para 153(3) | 1 Oct 2006 (SI 2006/2541) |
| | paras 154–161 | 1 Oct 2006 (SI 2006/2541) |
| | para 162 | 1 Oct 2006 (SI 2006/2541)[1] |
| | paras 163–173 | 1 Oct 2006 (SI 2006/2541) |
| | para 174 | *Never in force* (repealed) |
| | paras 175, 176 | 1 Apr 2007 (SI 2007/816) |
| Sch 12 | | 2 May 2006 (E) (SI 2006/1176), repeals of or in— Road Traffic Act 1988; Countryside and Rights of Way Act 2000, Sch 7 |
| | | 1 Oct 2006 (otherwise, except repeal in Transport Act 1968) (SI 2006/2541) |
| | | 1 Apr 2007 (exception noted above) (SI 2007/816) |

[1]   For transitional provisions, see SI 2006/2541, art 3, Schedule

---

**Northern Ireland Act 2006 (c 17)**

*RA:* 8 May 2006

Whole Act in force 8 May 2006 (RA) (however Schs 2, 3 only have effect in accordance with s 2)

---

**Northern Ireland (Miscellaneous Provisions) Act 2006 (c 33)**

*RA:* 25 Jul 2006

*Commencement provisions:* ss 10(2), 31; Northern Ireland (Miscellaneous Provisions) Act 2006 (Commencement No 1) Order 2006, SI 2006/2688; Northern Ireland (Miscellaneous Provisions) Act 2006 (Commencement No 2) Order 2006, SI 2006/2966; Northern Ireland (Miscellaneous Provisions) Act 2006 (Commencement No 3) Order 2006, SI 2006/3263; Northern Ireland (Miscellaneous Provisions) Act 2006 (Commencement No 4) Order 2008, SI 2008/1318; Northern Ireland (Miscellaneous Provisions) Act 2006 (Commencement No 5) Order 2009, SI 2009/448

| | |
|---|---|
| 1 | 25 Jul 2006 (s 31(1)) |
| 2–5 | 1 Dec 2006 (SI 2006/2688) |
| 6 | 14 May 2008 (SI 2008/1318) |
| 7–9 | 16 Oct 2006 (SI 2006/2688) |

**Northern Ireland (Miscellaneous Provisions) Act 2006 (c 33)**—*contd*

| | | |
|---|---|---|
| 10 | | 25 Jul 2006 (s 31(1)) |
| 11 | | 25 Sep 2006 (s 10(2)) |
| 12–14 | | 1 Nov 2007 (s 10(2)) |
| 15 | | 25 Sep 2006 (s 10(2)) |
| 16–20 | | 11 Mar 2009 (SI 2009/448) |
| 21 | | 10 Dec 2006 (SI 2006/3263) |
| 22–24 | | 25 Jul 2006 (s 31(1)) |
| 25 | | 31 Mar 2007 (SI 2006/2966) |
| 26 | (1) | 1 Dec 2006 (SI 2006/2966) |
| | (2) | See Sch 3 below |
| 27–29 | | 25 Jul 2006 (s 31(1)) |
| 30 | (1) | See Sch 4 below |
| | (2) | See Sch 5 below |
| | (3)–(6) | 25 Jul 2006 (s 31(1)) |
| 31–33 | | 25 Jul 2006 (s 31(1)) |
| Sch 1 | | 1 Nov 2007 (s 10(2)) |
| Sch 2 | | 11 Mar 2009 (SI 2009/448) |
| Sch 3 | | 1 Dec 2006 (SI 2006/2966) |
| Sch 4 | paras 1–6 | 14 May 2008 (SI 2008/1318) |
| | para 7(1) | 1 Dec 2006 (SI 2006/2688) |
| | para 7(2)(a) | 1 Dec 2006 (SI 2006/2688) |
| | para 7(2)(b) | 14 May 2008 (SI 2008/1318) |
| | para 7(3)–(5) | 14 May 2008 (SI 2008/1318) |
| | para 8 | 1 Dec 2006 (SI 2006/2688) |
| | para 9 | 16 Oct 2006 (SI 2006/2688) |
| | paras 10–14 | 11 Mar 2009 (SI 2009/448) |
| | para 15 | *Not yet in force* |
| Sch 5 | | 25 Jul 2006 (s 31(4)), repeals and revocations of or in— |
| | | Northern Ireland (Loans) Act 1975; |
| | | Northern Ireland (Loans) Act 1985; |
| | | Northern Ireland (Loans) (Increase of Limit) Order 1995, SI 1995/675 |
| | | 25 Sep 2006 (s 31(4)), repeals of or in— |
| | | Representation of the People Act 1983, Sch 2A; |
| | | Political Parties, Elections and Referendums Act 2000; |
| | | Electoral Administration Act 2006, s 60 |
| | | 16 Oct 2006 (s 31(4)), repeals of or in— |
| | | Electoral Law (Northern Ireland) Act 1962; |
| | | *Not yet in force*, repeals of or in— |
| | | Representation of the People Act 1983, s 13B; |
| | | Northern Ireland Act 1998; |
| | | Serious Organised Crime and Police Act 2005; |
| | | Electoral Administration Act 2006, Sch 1, para 110 |

**Northern Ireland (St Andrews Agreement) Act 2006 (c 53)**

*RA*: 22 Nov 2006

*Commencement provisions*: s 27; Northern Ireland (St Andrews Agreement) Act 2006 (Commencement No 1) Order 2007, SI 2007/92; Northern Ireland (St Andrews Agreement) Act 2006 (Commencement No 2) Order 2007, SI 2007/2491

See also: Northern Ireland (St Andrews Agreement) Act 2007, which modifies certain commencement information in this Act; Northern Ireland Act 2000 (Restoration of Devolved Government) Order 2007, SI 2007/1397, the making of which affects the commencement of this Act; Police (Northern Ireland) Act 2003 (Commencement No 3) Order 2007, SR 2007/371, which brings Sch 9 to this Act into force by virtue of s 27(6) of this Act

| | | |
|---|---|---|
| 1, 2 | | 22 Nov 2006 (s 27(8)) |
| 3 | (1) | 26 Jan 2007 (s 27(2)) |

**Northern Ireland (St Andrews Agreement) Act 2006 (c 53)**—*contd*

|  |  |  |
|---|---|---|
| (2), (3) |  | 22 Nov 2006 (s 27(8)) |
| 4 |  | 26 Jan 2007 (SI 2007/92) |
| 5–19 |  | 8 May 2007 (s 27(4), (5)) |
| 20 | (1) | See Sch 8 below |
|  | (2) | See Sch 9 below |
| 21 | (1) | 22 Nov 2006 (s 27(8)) |
|  | (2) | 10 May 2007 (ss 21(3), (4), 27(7)) |
|  | (3)–(5) | 22 Nov 2006 (s 27(8)) |
| 22–28 |  | 22 Nov 2006 (s 27(8)) |
| Sch 1 |  | 22 Nov 2006 (s 27(8)) |
| Sch 2 |  | 8 May 2007 (ss 2(2), 27(1)) |
| Sch 3 |  | *Never in force* (repealed) |
| Sch 4 |  | 10 May 2007 (ss 2(5), 27(1)) |
| Schs 5–7 |  | 8 May 2007 (s 27(4), (5)) |
| Sch 8 |  | 4 Sep 2007 (SI 2007/2491) |
| Sch 9 |  | 4 Sep 2007 (brought into force by SR 2003/371, made under the Police (Northern Ireland) Act 2003, s 19(2)) (s 27(6)) |

**Parliamentary Costs Act 2006 (c 37)**

*RA:* 8 Nov 2006

*Commencement provisions:* s 19(1)

Whole Act in force 1 Apr 2007 (s 19(1))

**Pastoral (Amendment) Measure 2006 (No 2)**

*RA:* 11 Jul 2006

*Commencement provisions:* s 2(2); instrument made by the Archbishops of Canterbury and York, and dated 22 Dec 2006 (made under s 2(2))

Whole Act in force 1 Jan 2007

**Planning etc (Scotland) Act 2006 (asp 17)**

*RA:* 20 Dec 2006

*Commencement provisions:* s 59; Planning etc (Scotland) Act 2006 (Commencement No 1) Order 2007, SSI 2007/49; Planning etc (Scotland) Act 2006 (Commencement No 2) Order 2007, SSI 2007/130; Planning etc (Scotland) Act 2006 (Commencement No 3) Order 2008, SSI 2008/164, as amended by SSI 2008/191; Planning etc (Scotland) Act 2006 (Commencement No 4) Order 2008, SSI 2008/191; Planning etc (Scotland) Act 2006 (Commencement No 5) Order 2008, SSI 2008/411; Planning etc (Scotland) Act 2006 (Commencement No 6) Order 2009, SSI 2009/70; Planning etc (Scotland) Act 2006 (Commencement No 7) Order 2009, SSI 2009/100; Planning etc (Scotland) Act 2006 (Commencement No 8) Order 2009, SSI 2009/179; Planning etc (Scotland) Act 2006 (Commencement No 9) Order 2009, SSI 2009/219; Planning etc (Scotland) Act 2006 (Commencement No 10) Order 2010, SSI 2010/400, as amended by SSI 2010/430; Planning etc (Scotland) Act 2006 (Commencement No 11) Order 2010, SSI 2010/430; Planning etc (Scotland) Act 2006 (Commencement No 12) Order 2011, SSI 2011/382

|  |  |
|---|---|
| 1 | 1 Apr 2007 (SSI 2007/130) |
| 2 | 19 May 2008 (for the purposes of enabling orders and regulations to be made and guidance to be issued) (SSI 2008/164) |

**Planning etc (Scotland) Act 2006 (asp 17)**—*contd*

|   |   |   |
|---|---|---|
|   |   | 25 Jun 2008 (for the purposes of (a) the determination and re-determination of the boundary of a strategic development plan area and procedures relating thereto; (b) requiring a strategic development planning authority to have regard to guidance issued by the Scottish Ministers; and (c) the definitions "strategic development plan", "strategic development plan area" and "strategic development planning authority") (SSI 2008/164) |
|   |   | 28 Feb 2009 (otherwise) (SSI 2009/70) |
| 3 | (1)(a) | 6 Feb 2007 (for the purpose of enabling provision to be made by order, direction or regulations) (SSI 2007/49) |
|   |   | 1 Apr 2007 (otherwise) (SSI 2007/130) |
|   | (1)(b) | 6 Feb 2007 (for the purpose of enabling provision to be made by order, direction or regulations) (SSI 2007/49) |
|   |   | 12 Dec 2008 (for the purpose of enabling orders or regulations to be made) (SSI 2008/411) |
|   |   | *Not yet in force* (otherwise) |
|   | (1)(c)–(e) | 6 Feb 2007 (for the purpose of enabling provision to be made by order, direction or regulations) (SSI 2007/49) |
|   |   | 1 Apr 2007 (otherwise) (SSI 2007/130) |
|   | (2), (3) | 6 Feb 2007 (for the purpose of enabling provision to be made by order, direction or regulations) (SSI 2007/49) |
|   |   | 12 Dec 2008 (for the purpose of enabling orders or regulations to be made) (SSI 2008/411) |
|   |   | *Not yet in force* (otherwise) |
|   | (4) | 6 Feb 2007 (for the purpose of enabling provision to be made by order, direction or regulations) (SSI 2007/49) |
|   |   | 1 Apr 2007 (otherwise) (SSI 2007/130) |
| 4 |   | 1 Apr 2007 (SSI 2007/130) |
| 5 |   | 12 Dec 2008 (for the purpose of enabling orders or regulations to be made) (SSI 2008/411) |
|   |   | 6 Apr 2009 (otherwise) (SSI 2009/100) |
| 6 |   | 12 Dec 2008 (for the purpose of enabling orders or regulations to be made) (SSI 2008/411) |
|   |   | 3 Aug 2009 (otherwise) (SSI 2009/219) |
| 7 | (1), (2) | 12 Dec 2008 (for the purpose of enabling orders or regulations to be made) (SSI 2008/411) |
|   |   | 3 Aug 2009 (otherwise) (SSI 2009/219) |
|   | (3) | 12 Dec 2008 (for the purpose of enabling orders or regulations to be made) (SSI 2008/411) |
|   |   | *Not yet in force* (otherwise) |
| 8–10 |   | 12 Dec 2008 (for the purpose of enabling orders or regulations to be made) (SSI 2008/411) |
|   |   | 3 Aug 2009 (otherwise) (SSI 2009/219) |
| 11 |   | 12 Dec 2008 (for the purpose of enabling orders or regulations to be made) (SSI 2008/411) |
|   |   | 6 Apr 2009 (otherwise) (SSI 2009/100) |
| 12 | (a)(i), (ii) | 12 Dec 2008 (for the purpose of enabling orders or regulations to be made) (SSI 2008/411) |
|   |   | 3 Aug 2009 (otherwise) (SSI 2009/219) |
|   | (a)(iii), (iv) | 1 Apr 2007 (SSI 2007/130) |
|   | (a)(v), (b) | 12 Dec 2008 (for the purpose of enabling orders or regulations to be made) (SSI 2008/411) |
|   |   | 3 Aug 2009 (otherwise) (SSI 2009/219) |
| 13–15 |   | 12 Dec 2008 (for the purpose of enabling orders or regulations to be made) (SSI 2008/411) |
|   |   | 3 Aug 2009 (otherwise) (SSI 2009/219) |
| 16 | (a) | 1 Mar 2007 (SSI 2007/130) |
|   | (b) | 12 Dec 2008 (for the purpose of enabling orders or regulations to be made) (SSI 2008/411) |

**Planning etc (Scotland) Act 2006 (asp 17)**—*contd*

| | | |
|---|---|---|
| | | 3 Aug 2009 (otherwise) (SSI 2009/219) |
| | (c) | 12 Dec 2008 (for the purpose of enabling orders or regulations to be made) (SSI 2008/411) |
| | | 1 Feb 2011 (otherwise) (SSI 2010/400) |
| 17 | | 12 Dec 2008 (for the purpose of enabling orders or regulations to be made) (SSI 2008/411) |
| | | 6 Apr 2009 (for the purpose of enabling and requiring the preparation and adoption of a scheme of delegation under the Town and Country Planning (Scotland) Act 1997, s 43A(1)) (SSI 2009/100) |
| | | 3 Aug 2009 (otherwise) (SSI 2009/219) |
| 18 | | 1 Apr 2007 (SSI 2007/130) |
| 19 | | 12 Dec 2008 (for the purpose of enabling orders or regulations to be made) (SSI 2008/411) |
| | | 3 Aug 2009 (otherwise) (SSI 2009/219) |
| 20 | (1), (2) | 3 Aug 2009 (SSI 2009/219) |
| | (3) | 1 Dec 2011 (SSI 2011/382) |
| 21, 22 | | 12 Dec 2008 (for the purpose of enabling orders or regulations to be made) (SSI 2008/411) |
| | | 3 Aug 2009 (otherwise) (SSI 2009/219) |
| 23, 24 | | 12 Dec 2008 (for the purpose of enabling orders or regulations to be made) (SSI 2008/411) |
| | | 1 Feb 2011 (SSI 2010/400) (otherwise) |
| 25, 26 | | 12 Dec 2008 (for the purpose of enabling orders or regulations to be made) (SSI 2008/411) |
| | | 3 Aug 2009 (otherwise) (SSI 2009/219) |
| 27 | | 1 Apr 2007 (SSI 2007/130) |
| 28 | (1)(a)–(c) | 1 Apr 2007 (SSI 2007/130) |
| | (1)(d) | 1 Feb 2011 (SSI 2010/400) |
| | (2)(a), (b) | 1 Feb 2011 (SSI 2010/400) |
| | (2)(c) | 26 Nov 2010 (SSI 2010/400) |
| | (3)–(6) | 1 Feb 2011 (SSI 2010/400) |
| 29, 30 | | *Not yet in force* |
| 31 | | 14 May 2009 (SSI 2009/179) |
| 32 | | 1 Apr 2007 (SSI 2007/130) |
| 33–49 | | 6 Feb 2007 (for the purpose of enabling regulations to be made) (SSI 2007/49) |
| | | 1 Apr 2007 (otherwise) (SSI 2007/130) |
| 50 | | 1 Apr 2007 (for the purpose of enabling regulations to be made and guidance to be issued) (SSI 2007/130) |
| | | 26 Nov 2010 (otherwise) (SSI 2010/400) |
| 51 | | 1 Apr 2007 (SSI 2007/130) |
| 52 | | *Not yet in force* |
| 53 | | 28 Feb 2009 (SSI 2009/70) |
| 54 | (1), (2) | 1 Apr 2007 (SSI 2007/130) |
| | (3)–(10) | 3 Aug 2009 (SSI 2009/219) |
| | (11)(a) | 28 Feb 2009 (SSI 2009/70) |
| | (11)(b)(i) | 1 Apr 2007 (SSI 2007/130) |
| | (11)(b)(ii) | 1 Feb 2011 (SSI 2010/400) |
| | (11)(b)(iii) | 1 Apr 2007 (SSI 2007/130) |
| | (12) | 28 Feb 2009 (SSI 2009/70) |
| | (13) | 3 Aug 2009 (SSI 2009/219) |
| | (14), (15) | 28 Feb 2009 (SSI 2009/70) |
| | (16)(a) | 6 Feb 2007 (SSI 2007/49) |
| | (16)(b)(i) | 19 May 2008 (for the purposes of enabling orders and regulations to be made and guidance to be issued) (SSI 2008/164) |
| | | 28 Feb 2009 (otherwise) (SSI 2009/70) |
| | (16)(b)(ii) | *Not yet in force* |
| | (16)(c) | 19 May 2008 (for the purposes of enabling orders and regulations to be made and guidance to be issued) (SSI 2008/164) |

**Planning etc (Scotland) Act 2006 (asp 17)**—*contd*

| | | |
|---|---|---|
| | | *Not yet in force* (otherwise) |
| | (16)(d), (e) | 1 Apr 2007 (SSI 2007/130) |
| | (16)(f) | 19 May 2008 (for the purposes of enabling orders and regulations to be made and guidance to be issued) (SSI 2008/164) |
| | | 28 Feb 2009 (otherwise) (SSI 2009/70) |
| | (17)(a)(i) | 1 Apr 2007 (for the purpose of inserting the definitions "national developments" and "National Planning Framework" into the Town and Country Planning (Scotland) Act 1997, s 277(1)) (SSI 2007/130) |
| | | 25 Jun 2008 (for the purposes of inserting the definitions "strategic development plan", "strategic development plan area" and "strategic development planning authority" into the Town and Country Planning (Scotland) Act 1997, s 277(1)) (SSI 2008/164) |
| | | 12 Dec 2008 (for the purpose of enabling orders or regulations to be made) (SSI 2008/411) |
| | | 28 Feb 2009 (for the purpose of inserting the definition "local development plan" into the Town and Country Planning (Scotland) Act 1997, s 277(1)) (SSI 2009/70) |
| | | 6 Apr 2009 (for the purpose of inserting the definitions "local developments" and "major developments" into the Town and Country Planning (Scotland) Act 1997, s 277(1)) (SSI 2009/100) |
| | | 3 Aug 2009 (for the remaining purpose of inserting the definition "temporary stop notice" into the Town and Country Planning (Scotland) Act 1997, s 277(1)) (SSI 2009/219) |
| | (17)(a)(ii), (iii) | 1 Apr 2007 (SSI 2007/130) |
| | (17)(a)(iv), (b) | 12 Dec 2008 (for the purpose of enabling orders or regulations to be made) (SSI 2008/411) |
| | | 1 Feb 2011 (otherwise) (SSI 2010/400) |
| | (18)(a) | 16 Dec 2010 (SSI 2010/430) |
| | (18)(b)(i) | 1 Feb 2011 (SSI 2010/400) |
| | (18)(b)(ii) | *Not yet in force* |
| | (19) | 6 Apr 2009 (SSI 2009/100) |
| 55 | (1) | 1 Apr 2007 (SSI 2007/130) |
| | (2) | 1 Jun 2008 (SSI 2008/191) |
| | (3) | 1 Apr 2007 (SSI 2007/130) |
| | (4), (5) | *Not yet in force* |
| 56 | | See Schedule below |
| 57, 58 | | 6 Feb 2007 (SSI 2007/49) |
| 59 | | *Not yet in force* |
| 60 | | 20 Dec 2006 (s 59(1)) |
| Schedule | | 1 Apr 2007 (SSI 2007/130), repeals of or in— |
| | | Town and Country Planning (Scotland) Act 1997, s 263, Sch 18, Pt 2; |
| | | Water Environment and Water Services (Scotland) Act 2003 |
| | | 3 Aug 2009 (SSI 2009/219), repeals of or in— |
| | | Town and Country Planning (Scotland) Act 1997, ss 41, 42, 45, 46, 48, 130, 131, 133, 143, 155, 169, 277, Schs 3, 4 |
| | | 1 Feb 2011 (SSI 2010/400), repeals of or in— |
| | | Town and Country Planning (Scotland) Act 1997, ss 163, 252 |
| | | 1 Dec 2011 (SSI 2011/382), repeals of or in— |
| | | Planning (Listed Buildings and Conservation Areas) (Scotland) Act 1997 |
| | | *Not yet in force*, repeals of or in— |
| | | Town and Country Planning (Scotland) Act 1997, ss 67, 182 |

## Police and Justice Act 2006 (c 48)

*RA:* 8 Nov 2006

*Commencement provisions:* s 53; Police and Justice Act 2006 (Commencement No 1, Transitional and Saving Provisions) Order 2006, SI 2006/3364, as amended by SI 2007/29, SI 2008/617; Police and Justice Act 2006 (Commencement No 2, Transitional and Saving Provisions) Order 2007, SI 2007/709; Police and Justice Act 2006 (Commencement No 3) Order 2007, SI 2007/1614 (amended by correction slip); Police and Justice Act 2006 (Commencement No 1) (Northern Ireland) Order 2007, SI 2007/2052; Police and Justice Act 2006 (Commencement No 4) Order 2007, SI 2007/2754; Police and Justice Act 2006 (Commencement) (Scotland) Order 2007, SSI 2007/434; Police and Justice Act 2006 (Commencement No 5) Order 2007, SI 2007/3073; Police and Justice Act 2006 (Commencement No 6) Order 2007, SI 2007/3203; Police and Justice Act 2006 (Commencement No 1) (Wales) Order 2007, SI 2007/3251; Police and Justice Act 2006 (Commencement No 7 and Savings Provision) Order 2008, SI 2008/311; Police and Justice Act 2006 (Commencement No 8) Order 2008, SI 2008/790; Police and Justice Act 2006 (Commencement No 9) Order 2008, SI 2008/2503; Police and Justice Act 2006 (Commencement No 10) Order 2008, SI 2008/2785[9]; Police and Justice Act 2006 (Commencement No 1) (England) Order 2009, SI 2009/936; Police and Justice Act 2006 (Commencement No 11) Order 2009, SI 2009/1679; Police and Justice Act 2006 (Commencement No 2) (Wales) Order 2009, SI 2009/2540; Police and Justice Act 2006 (Commencement No 12) Order 2009, SI 2009/2774; Police and Justice Act 2006 (Commencement No 13) Order 2010, SI 2010/414; Police and Justice Act 2006 (Commencement No 14) Order 2011, SI 2011/2144; Police and Justice Act 2006 (Commencement No 15) Order 2012, SI 2012/2373; Police and Justice Act 2006 (Commencement No 16) Order 2013, SI 2013/592

| | | |
|---|---|---|
| 1 | (1) | 1 Apr 2007 (SI 2007/709)[4] |
| | (2)(a) | 1 Apr 2007 (SI 2007/709)[4] |
| | (2)(b) | 1 Apr 2007 (E) (W) (SI 2007/709)[4] |
| | | *Never in force* (S) (NI) (repealed) |
| | (3) | See Sch 1 below |
| 2 | | See Sch 2 below |
| 3 | | 29 Jun 2007 (SI 2007/1614) |
| 4 | | 31 Mar 2007 (SI 2007/709)[4] |
| 5 | | See Sch 3 below |
| 6 | | 1 Apr 2007 (E) (W) (SI 2007/709) |
| | | *Not yet in force* (NI) |
| 7 | (1) | 1 Dec 2007 (SI 2007/3203) |
| | (2) | 1 Apr 2007 (SI 2007/709) |
| 8 | | 1 Apr 2007 (SI 2007/709) |
| 9 | | See Sch 5 below |
| 10 | | See Sch 6 below |
| 11 | | 15 Jan 2007 (SI 2006/3364) |
| 12 | | 1 Apr 2007 (SI 2007/709) |
| 13 | | 29 Jun 2007 (E) (W) (SI 2007/1614) |
| | | 30 Jul 2007 (NI) (SI 2007/2052) |
| 14 | | *Not yet in force* |
| 15, 16 | | 1 Apr 2007 (SI 2007/709) |
| 17 | (1), (2) | Immediately before 8 Jul 2009 (in relation to the police areas of Cambridgeshire, Merseyside and Norfolk) (SI 2009/1679) |
| | | 16 Nov 2009 (in relation to the police areas of Hampshire and Humberside) (SI 2009/2774) |
| | | 8 Apr 2013 (otherwise) (SI 2013/592) |
| | (3) | Immediately before 8 Jul 2009 (in relation to the police areas of Cambridgeshire, Merseyside and Norfolk) (in so far as it inserts the Criminal Justice Act 2003, s 22(3A)(a)) (SI 2009/1679) |
| | | 16 Nov 2009 (in relation to the police areas of Hampshire and Humberside) (in so far as it inserts the Criminal Justice Act 2003, s 22(3A)(a)) (SI 2009/2774) |
| | | 8 Apr 2013 (otherwise, in so far as inserts s 22(3A)(a) of that Act) (SI 2013/592) |
| | | *Not yet in force* (in so far as inserts s 22(3A)(b), (3B), (3C) of that Act) |

**Police and Justice Act 2006 (c 48)**—*contd*

|  |  |  |
|---|---|---|
| | (4) | Immediately before 8 Jul 2009 (in relation to the police areas of Cambridgeshire, Merseyside and Norfolk) (SI 2009/1679) |
| | | 16 Nov 2009 (in relation to the police areas of Hampshire and Humberside) (SI 2009/2774) |
| | | 8 Apr 2013 (otherwise) (SI 2013/592) |
| | (5) | Immediately before 8 Jul 2009 (in relation to the police areas of Cambridgeshire, Merseyside and Norfolk) (in so far as it inserts the Criminal Justice Act 2003, s 330(5)(aa)) (SI 2009/1679) |
| | | 16 Nov 2009 (in relation to remaining police areas) (in so far as it inserts the Criminal Justice Act 2003, s 330(5)(aa)) (SI 2009/2774) |
| | | *Not yet in force* (in so far as amends s 330(5)(a) of that Act) |
| 18 | | 29 Jun 2007 (SI 2007/1614) |
| 19, 20 | | 30 Apr 2009 (E) (SI 2009/936) |
| | | 1 Oct 2009 (W) (SI 2009/2540) |
| 21 | | 30 Apr 2009 (E) (SI 2009/936) |
| | | *Not yet in force* (W) |
| 22 | | See Sch 9 below |
| 23–25 | | 1 Aug 2007 (E) (SI 2007/1614) |
| | | *Not yet in force* (W) |
| 26 | | 6 Apr 2007 (E) (SI 2007/709)[4] |
| | | *Never in force* (W) (repealed) |
| 27 | | 6 Apr 2007 (E) (SI 2007/709) |
| | | *Not yet in force* (W) |
| 28–33 | | 1 Apr 2007 (SI 2007/709) |
| 34 | | *Never in force* (repealed) |
| 35–38 | | 1 Oct 2007 (S) (SSI 2007/434) |
| | | 1 Oct 2008 (E) (W) (NI) (SI 2008/2503) |
| 39, 40 | | 1 Apr 2008 (SI 2008/790) |
| 41 | | 29 Jun 2007 (E) (W) (SI 2007/1614) |
| | | 10 Oct 2007 (S) (NI) (SI 2007/2754) |
| 42 | | See Sch 13 below |
| 43 | (1) | *Not yet in force* |
| | (2)–(6) | 8 Nov 2006 (s 53(2)(a)) |
| 44 | | 15 Jan 2007 (SI 2006/3364) |
| 45 | | 15 Jan 2007 (other than to the extent it substitutes Crime and Disorder Act 1998, s 57C) (SI 2006/3364)[2] |
| | | 1 Apr 2007 (otherwise, in the local justice area of Lambeth and Southwark) (SI 2007/709) |
| | | 14 Nov 2008 (SI 2008/2785), otherwise, in the following local justice areas— |
| | | in London: Barking and Dagenham, Barnet, Bexley, Brent, Bromley, Camden and Islington, City of London, City of Westminster, Croydon, Ealing, Enfield, Greenwich and Lewisham, Hackney and Tower Hamlets, Hammersmith and Fulham and Kensington and Chelsea, Haringey, Harrow Gore, Havering, Hillingdon, Hounslow, Kingston-upon-Thames, Merton, Newham, Redbridge, Richmond-upon-Thames, Sutton, Waltham Forest, and Wandsworth; |
| | | in Kent: Central Kent, East Kent and North Kent |
| | | 3 Oct 2011 (SI 2011/2144), otherwise, in the following local justice areas—Central Hertfordshire; Chester, Ellesmere Port and Neston; East Hertfordshire; Halton; Macclesfield; North Hertfordshire; South Cheshire; Vale Royal; Warrington; and West Hertfordshire |
| | | 8 Oct 2012 (otherwise) (SI 2012/2373) |
| 46 | | 1 Apr 2007 (in the local justice area of Lambeth and Southwark) (SI 2007/709) |
| | | 14 Nov 2008 (SI 2008/2785), in the following local justice areas— |

**Police and Justice Act 2006 (c 48)**—*contd*

|  |  |  |
|---|---|---|
|  |  | in London: Barking and Dagenham, Barnet, Bexley, Brent, Bromley, Camden and Islington, City of London, City of Westminster, Croydon, Ealing, Enfield, Greenwich and Lewisham, Hackney and Tower Hamlets, Hammersmith and Fulham and Kensington and Chelsea, Haringey, Harrow Gore, Havering, Hillingdon, Hounslow, Kingston-upon-Thames, Merton, Newham, Redbridge, Richmond-upon-Thames, Sutton, Waltham Forest, and Wandsworth; |
|  |  | in Kent: Central Kent, East Kent and North Kent |
|  |  | 3 Oct 2011 (SI 2011/2144), in the following local justice areas—Central Hertfordshire; Chester, Ellesmere Port and Neston; East Hertfordshire; Halton; Macclesfield; North Hertfordshire; South Cheshire; Vale Royal; Warrington; and West Hertfordshire |
|  |  | 8 Oct 2012 (otherwise) (SI 2012/2373) |
| 47, 48 |  | 15 Jan 2007 (SI 2006/3364) |
| 49–51 |  | 8 Nov 2006 (s 53(1)) |
| 52 |  | See Schs 14, 15 below |
| 53–55 |  | 8 Nov 2006 (s 53(1)) |
| Sch 1 | Pts 1, 2 | 1 Apr 2007 (SI 2007/709)[4] |
|  | Pt 3 | 1 Apr 2007 (except para 30(3)) (SI 2007/709)[4] |
|  |  | *Never in force* (exception noted above) (repealed) |
|  | Pt 4 | 1 Apr 2007 (SI 2007/709)[4] |
|  | Pts 5, 6 | 1 Apr 2007 (E) (W) (SI 2007/709)[4] |
|  |  | *Never in force* (S) (NI) (repealed) |
|  | Pt 7 | 1 Apr 2007 (SI 2007/709)[4] |
| Sch 2 | paras 1–6 | 15 Jan 2007 (SI 2006/3364)[1] |
|  | para 7(1), (2) | 29 Jun 2007 (SI 2007/1614) |
|  | para 7(3)(a) | 8 Nov 2006 (s 53(2)(c)) |
|  | para 7(3)(b), (c) | 1 Apr 2008 (SI 2008/790) |
|  | para 7(4) | 1 Apr 2008 (SI 2008/790) |
|  | para 8 | 15 Jan 2007 (SI 2006/3364)[1] |
|  | paras 9, 10 | 14 Mar 2008 (SI 2008/311)[7] |
|  | paras 11–13 | 1 Apr 2008 (SI 2008/790) |
|  | paras 14, 15 | 8 Nov 2006 (s 53(2)(c)) |
|  | paras 16–23 | 1 Apr 2007 (SI 2007/709) |
|  | paras 24–26 | 8 Nov 2006 (s 53(2)(c)) |
|  | paras 27–29 | 1 Apr 2007 (SI 2007/709) |
|  | para 30 | 15 Mar 2010 (SI 2010/414) |
| Sch 3 |  | 31 Dec 2007 (SI 2007/3203) |
| Sch 4 |  | 1 Apr 2007 (SI 2007/709) |
| Sch 5 | paras 1–3 | 1 Dec 2007 (SI 2007/3203) |
|  | para 4 | 1 Apr 2007 (SI 2007/709) |
|  | para 5(1) | See sub-paras (2)–(13) below |
|  | para 5(2)(a) | 1 Apr 2007 (SI 2007/709) |
|  | para 5(2)(b), (3)–(10) | 1 Dec 2007 (SI 2007/3203) |
|  | para 5(11) | *Never in force* (repealed) |
|  | para 5(12), (13) | 1 Dec 2007 (SI 2007/3203) |
|  | para 6 | 1 Dec 2007 (SI 2007/3203) |
| Schs 6, 7 |  | 1 Apr 2007 (SI 2007/709) |
| Sch 8 |  | 30 Apr 2009 (E) (SI 2009/936) |
|  |  | 1 Oct 2009 (W) (SI 2009/2540) |
| Sch 9 | paras 1–6 | 1 Aug 2007 (E) (SI 2007/1614) |
|  |  | 19 Nov 2007 (W) (SI 2007/3073) |
|  | para 7(1) | 1 Aug 2007 (E) (SI 2007/1614) |
|  |  | 19 Nov 2007 (W) (SI 2007/3073) |
|  | para 7(2) | 1 Aug 2007 (E) (SI 2007/1614) |
|  |  | 19 Nov 2007 (W) (SI 2007/3251)[6] |
|  | para 7(3) | 1 Aug 2007 (E) (SI 2007/1614) |

**Police and Justice Act 2006 (c 48)**—*contd*

|  |  |  |
|---|---|---|
|  |  | 19 Nov 2007 (W) (SI 2007/3073) |
| Sch 10 |  | 6 Apr 2007 (E) (SI 2007/709) |
|  |  | *Not yet in force* (W) |
| Schs 11, 12 |  | 1 Apr 2008 (SI 2008/790) |
| Sch 13 | paras 1–3 | 15 Jan 2007 (SI 2006/3364) |
|  | paras 4, 5 | *Never in force* (repealed) |
|  | para 6 | 8 Nov 2006 (s 53(2)(b)) |
|  | paras 7–35 | 15 Jan 2007 (SI 2006/3364) |
| Sch 14 | para 1 | 1 Apr 2007 (SI 2007/709) |
|  | para 2 | 1 Oct 2008 (SI 2008/2503) |
|  | paras 3, 4 | 15 Jan 2007 (SI 2006/3364) |
|  | para 5 | 1 Apr 2007 (SI 2007/709) |
|  | para 6 | 1 Oct 2008 (SI 2008/2503) |
|  | para 7 | *Not yet in force* |
|  | para 8 | 1 Apr 2007 (SI 2007/709) |
|  | paras 9, 10 | 15 Jan 2007 (SI 2006/3364) |
|  | para 11 | 1 Apr 2007 (SI 2007/709) |
|  | paras 12, 13 | 6 Apr 2007 (E) (SI 2007/709)[4] |
|  |  | *Not yet in force* (W) (paras 12(3), 13(3) repealed) |
|  | para 14 | 1 Apr 2007 (SI 2007/709) |
|  | para 15 | *Never in force* (repealed) |
|  | para 16 | 1 Apr 2007 (SI 2007/709) |
|  | paras 17–19 | 1 Oct 2007 (S) (SSI 2007/434) |
|  |  | 1 Oct 2008 (E) (W) (NI) (SI 2008/2503) |
|  | paras 20–24 | 1 Oct 2008 (SI 2008/2503) |
|  | para 25 | 1 Oct 2007 (S) (SSI 2007/434) |
|  | paras 26, 27 | 1 Oct 2008 (SI 2008/2503) |
|  | para 28 | 1 Oct 2008 (NI) (SI 2008/2503) |
|  | para 29 | 1 Oct 2007 (S) (SSI 2007/434) |
|  |  | 1 Oct 2008 (E) (W) (NI) (SI 2008/2503) |
|  | paras 30, 31 | 1 Apr 2007 (SI 2007/709) |
|  | paras 32, 33 | 6 Apr 2007 (E) (SI 2007/709)[4] |
|  |  | *Not yet in force* (W) |
|  | para 34 | 8 Nov 2006 (s 53(2)(d)) |
|  | para 35 | 1 Apr 2007 (SI 2007/709) |
|  | para 36 | *Not yet in force* |
|  | para 37 | 1 Apr 2007 (SI 2007/709) |
|  | para 38 | *Not yet in force* |
|  | para 39 | 8 Nov 2006 (s 53(2)(d)) |
|  | para 40 | 1 Apr 2007 (SI 2007/709) |
|  | para 41 | *Not yet in force* |
|  | paras 42–46 | 1 Apr 2007 (SI 2007/709) |
|  | para 47 | 8 Nov 2006 (s 53(2)(d)) |
|  | para 48 | 1 Apr 2007 (SI 2007/709) |
|  | para 49 | 8 Nov 2006 (s 53(2)(d)) |
|  | paras 50, 51 | 14 Nov 2008 (SI 2008/2785) |
|  | para 52 | 1 Apr 2007 (SI 2007/709) |
|  | paras 53–57 | 29 Jun 2007 (E) (SI 2007/1614)[8] |
|  |  | *Not yet in force* (W) (para 55(5) repealed) |
|  | para 58 | 1 Apr 2007 (SI 2007/709)[5] |
|  | para 59 | 8 Nov 2006 (s 53(2)(d)) |
|  | para 60 | 1 Apr 2007 (SI 2007/709) |
|  | paras 61, 62 | 15 Jan 2007 (SI 2006/3364) |
| Sch 15 | Pt 1(A) | 1 Apr 2007 (SI 2007/709)[4] |
|  | Pt 1(B) | 8 Nov 2006 (s 53(2)(e)), repeals of or in— |
|  |  | Police Act 1996, ss 36A, 37; |
|  |  | Railways and Transport Safety Act 2003 |
|  |  | 15 Jan 2007 (repeals of or in Police Act 1996, Schs 3, 3A[1, 3]) |
|  |  | (SI 2006/3364) |

**Police and Justice Act 2006 (c 48)**—*contd*

        1 Apr 2007 (SI 2007/709)[4], repeals of or in—
        Criminal Procedure and Investigations Act 1996;
        Employment Rights Act 1996;
        Police Act 1996, ss 6, 15, 30, 41A, 41B;
        Greater London Authority Act 1999;
        Insolvency Act 2000;
        Police Reform Act 2002, ss 5, 94, 96;
        Courts Act 2003
        1 Dec 2007 (repeal in Police Reform Act 2002, Sch 4)
        (SI 2007/3203)
        14 Mar 2008 (repeals of Police Act 1996, ss 6A, 7–9)
        (SI 2008/311)[7]
        *Not yet in force*, repeals of or in—
        Local Government Act 1972;
        Police Act 1996, s 96B;
        Local Government Act 1999;
        Criminal Justice and Police Act 2001;
        Police Reform Act 2002, ss 1, 40, 92, Sch 7

Pt 2     1 Apr 2007 (E) (SI 2007/709), repeals of or in—
        Aviation Security Act 1982;
        Police and Criminal Evidence Act 1984
        29 Jun 2007 (repeals of or in Criminal Justice Act 2003)
        (SI 2007/1614)
        *Not yet in force*, repeals of or in—
        Immigration, Asylum and Nationality Act 2006

Pt 3     6 Apr 2007 (E) (repeals of or in Anti-social Behaviour Act 2003)
        (SI 2007/709)[4]
        1 Aug 2007 (E) (SI 2007/1614), repeals of or in—
        Crime and Disorder Act 1998;
        Police Reform Act 2002;
        Clean Neighbourhoods and Environment Act 2005
        19 Nov 2007 (W) (SI 2007/3073), repeals of or in—
        Crime and Disorder Act 1998;
        Police Reform Act 2002;
        Clean Neighbourhoods and Environment Act 2005
        *Not yet in force*, repeals of or in—
        Powers of Criminal Courts (Sentencing) Act 2000;
        Anti-social Behaviour Act 2003 (W)

Pt 4     1 Oct 2007 (S) (SSI 2007/434), repeals of or in—
        Computer Misuse Act 1990, ss 13, 17(7);
        Criminal Procedure (Consequential Provisions) (Scotland)
        Act 1995
        1 Apr 2008 (SI 2008/790), repeals of or in—
        Protection of Children Act 1978;
        Criminal Justice Act 1988;
        Criminal Justice (Evidence, etc) (Northern Ireland) Order 1988
        (SI 1988/1847 (NI 17));
        Criminal Justice and Public Order Act 1994;
        Criminal Justice and Police Act 2001 (NI);
        Justice (Northern Ireland) Act 2002;
        Courts Act 2003, Sch 8, paras 199, 200
        1 Oct 2008 (SI 2008/2503), repeals of or in—
        Computer Misuse Act 1990, ss 11, 12, 14, 16, 17 (E) (W);
        Courts Act 2003, Sch 4, Sch 8, para 347;
        Serious Organised Crime and Police Act 2005
        *Not yet in force*, repeals of or in—
        Magistrates' Courts (Northern Ireland) Order 1981
        (SI 1981/1675 (NI 26));
        Criminal Justice and Police Act 2001 (E) (W) (spent);

## Police and Justice Act 2006 (c 48)—*contd*
Justice (Northern Ireland) Act 2004

1   For transitional provisions, see SI 2006/3364, art 3

2   For transitional provisions, see SI 2006/3364, art 4

3   Note that SI 2006/3364, art 2(l) purports to bring into force the repeal of Schs 3, 3A to the 1996 Act in "Part II of Schedule 15". Those repeals are in fact contained in Sch 15, Pt 1(B)

4   For transitional and saving provisions, see SI 2007/709, arts 5–8

5   Note that SI 2007/1614 also purports to bring this paragraph into force on 29 Jun 2007

6   Note that SI 2007/3073, made by the Secretary of State, also brought this sub-paragraph into force in relation to Wales, however s 53(5) requires that this sub-paragraph be brought into force by order made by the Welsh Ministers

7   For a saving, see SI 2008/311, art 3

8   It is thought that the intention of the correction slip for SI 2007/1614 is to clarify that paras 53–57 were brought into force on 29 Jun 2007 in relation to England only

9   SI 2008/2785 also purports to bring s 45 and Sch 14, paras 47 and 49 into force on 14 Nov 2008, even though they appear to already be in force

---

## Police, Public Order and Criminal Justice (Scotland) Act 2006 (asp 10)

*RA:* 4 Jul 2006

*Commencement provisions:* s 104; Police, Public Order and Criminal Justice (Scotland) Act 2006 (Commencement No 1) Order 2006, SSI 2006/432; Police, Public Order and Criminal Justice (Scotland) Act 2006 (Commencement No 2) Order 2006, SSI 2006/607; Police, Public Order and Criminal Justice (Scotland) Act 2006 (Commencement No 3, Transitional and Savings Provisions) Order 2007, SSI 2007/84

| | | |
|---|---|---|
| 1 | (1) | 1 Jan 2007 (SSI 2006/607) |
| | (2) | See Sch 1 below |
| 2 | (1) | 1 Jan 2007 (SSI 2006/607) |
| | (2), (3) | 1 Apr 2007 (SSI 2007/84) |
| 3 | (1) | 1 Apr 2007 (SSI 2007/84) |
| | (2)(a)–(c) | 1 Apr 2007 (SSI 2007/84) |
| | (2)(d) | *Never in force* (repealed) |
| | (2)(e), (f) | 1 Apr 2007 (SSI 2007/84) |
| | (3)–(7) | 1 Apr 2007 (SSI 2007/84) |
| | (8) | *Never in force* (repealed) |
| 4 | | 1 Jan 2007 (SSI 2006/607) |
| 5–7 | | 1 Apr 2007 (SSI 2007/84) |
| 8 | | 1 Jan 2007 (SSI 2006/607) |
| 9 | | 1 Apr 2007 (SSI 2007/84) |
| 10 | | 1 Jan 2007 (SSI 2006/607) |
| 11 | | 1 Apr 2007 (SSI 2007/84) |
| 12 | (1)(a), (b) | 1 Jan 2007 (SSI 2006/607) |
| | (1)(c) | 1 Apr 2007 (SSI 2007/84) |
| | (1)(d) | 1 Jan 2007 (SSI 2006/607) |
| | (2) | See Sch 2 below |
| 13 | | 1 Jan 2007 (SSI 2006/607) |
| 14, 15 | | 1 Apr 2007 (SSI 2007/84) |
| 16 | (1) | 1 Jan 2007 (SSI 2006/607) |
| | (2) | 1 Apr 2007 (SSI 2007/84) |
| 17 | | 1 Apr 2007 (SSI 2007/84) |
| 18 | | 1 Jan 2007 (SSI 2006/607) |
| 19–22 | | 1 Apr 2007 (SSI 2007/84) |
| 23–25 | | 1 Jan 2007 (SSI 2006/607) |
| 26–29 | | 1 Apr 2007 (SSI 2007/84) |

**Police, Public Order and Criminal Justice (Scotland) Act 2006 (asp 10)**—*contd*

| | | |
|---|---|---|
| 30 | | 1 Jan 2007 (SSI 2006/607) |
| 31 | | See Sch 3 below |
| 32 | | 1 Jan 2007 (SSI 2006/607) |
| 33 | (1), (2) | 1 Jan 2007 (SSI 2006/607) |
| | (3) | See Sch 4 below |
| 34 | | 1 Jan 2007 (SSI 2006/607) |
| 35, 36 | | 1 Jan 2007 (for the purpose of making enabling regulations) (SSI 2006/607) |
| | | 1 Apr 2007 (otherwise) (SSI 2007/84) |
| 37 | | 1 Apr 2007 (SSI 2007/84) |
| 38 | (1)–(3) | 1 Apr 2007 (SSI 2007/84) |
| | (4) | 1 Jan 2007 (SSI 2006/607) |
| | (5), (6) | 1 Apr 2007 (SSI 2007/84) |
| 39 | | 1 Jan 2007 (for the purpose of enabling regulations to be made) (SSI 2006/607) |
| | | 1 Apr 2007 (otherwise) (SSI 2007/84) |
| 40 | | 1 Apr 2007 (SSI 2007/84) |
| 41 | | 1 Jan 2007 (SSI 2006/607) |
| 42, 43 | | 1 Apr 2007 (SSI 2007/84) |
| 44 | | 1 Jan 2007 (for the purpose of making enabling regulations) (SSI 2006/607) |
| | | 1 Apr 2007 (otherwise) (SSI 2007/84) |
| 45, 46 | | 1 Apr 2007 (SSI 2007/84) |
| 47 | | 1 Jan 2007 (SSI 2006/607) |
| 48–69 | | 1 Sep 2006 (SSI 2006/432) |
| 70–72 | | 1 Apr 2007 (SSI 2007/84)[1] |
| 73–81 | | 1 Sep 2006 (SSI 2006/432) |
| 82 | | *Not yet in force* |
| 83 | | 1 Jan 2007 (SSI 2006/607) |
| 84 | | 1 Jan 2007 (for the purpose of making an enabling order under the Criminal Procedure (Scotland) Act 1995, s 20A(3)(c)) (SSI 2006/607) |
| | | 25 Feb 2007 (for the purpose of commencing the Criminal Procedure (Scotland) Act 1995, s 20B(3)) (SSI 2007/84) |
| | | 12 Jun 2007 (otherwise) (SSI 2007/84) |
| 85 | (1), (2) | 12 Jun 2007 (SSI 2007/84) |
| | (3) | 1 Jan 2007 (SSI 2006/607) |
| 86–88 | | 12 Jun 2007 (SSI 2007/84) |
| 89 | | 1 Apr 2007 (SSI 2007/84) |
| 90 | | 1 Jan 2007 (for the purpose of making enabling regulations to prescribe the qualifications and experience which a suitably qualified person must have) (SSI 2006/607) |
| | | 25 Feb 2007 (otherwise) (SSI 2007/84) |
| 91–97 | | 1 Mar 2007 (SSI 2007/84) |
| 98 | | 1 Sep 2006 (SSI 2006/432) |
| 99, 100 | | 4 Jul 2006 (RA) |
| 101 | | See Sch 6 below |
| 102–105 | | 4 Jul 2006 (RA) |
| Sch 1 | paras 1–9 | 1 Jan 2007 (SSI 2006/607) |
| | para 10(1) | 1 Jan 2007 (SSI 2006/607) |
| | para 10(2)–(11) | 1 Apr 2007 (SSI 2007/84) |
| | para 11(1) | 1 Jan 2007 (SSI 2006/607) |
| | para 11(2)–(4) | 1 Apr 2007 (SSI 2007/84) |
| | para 11(5)–(8) | 1 Jan 2007 (SSI 2006/607) |
| | paras 12, 13 | 1 Jan 2007 (SSI 2006/607) |
| | para 14(1) | 1 Jan 2007 (SSI 2006/607) |
| | para 14(2) | *Never in force* (repealed) |
| | para 14(3) | 1 Jan 2007 (SSI 2006/607) |
| | paras 15, 16 | 1 Jan 2007 (SSI 2006/607) |

**Police, Public Order and Criminal Justice (Scotland) Act 2006 (asp 10)**—*contd*

| | | |
|---|---|---|
| Sch 2 | paras 1–6 | 1 Jan 2007 (SSI 2006/607) |
| | para 7 | 1 Apr 2007 (SSI 2007/84) |
| | paras 8, 9 | 1 Jan 2007 (SSI 2006/607) |
| Schs 3, 4 | | 1 Jan 2007 (SSI 2006/607) |
| Sch 5 | | 1 Sep 2006 (SSI 2006/432) |
| Sch 6 | para 1(1), (2) | 1 Sep 2006 (SSI 2006/432) |
| | para 1(3) | 1 Apr 2007 (SSI 2007/84) |
| | para 1(4)(a) | 1 Sep 2006 (SSI 2006/432) |
| | para 1(4)(b) | 1 Apr 2007 (SSI 2007/84) |
| | para 1(5)(a) | 1 Sep 2006 (SSI 2006/432) |
| | para 1(5)(b) | 1 Apr 2007 (SSI 2007/84) |
| | para 1(5)(c), (d) | 1 Sep 2006 (SSI 2006/432) |
| | para 1(6) | 1 Apr 2007 (SSI 2007/84) |
| | para 1(7) | 1 Apr 2007 (SSI 2007/84)[1] |
| | para 1(8) | 1 Sep 2006 (SSI 2006/432) |
| | paras 2–4 | 1 Sep 2006 (SSI 2006/432) |
| | para 5(1)–(3) | 1 Apr 2007 (SSI 2007/84) |
| | para 5(4), (5) | 1 Jan 2007 (SSI 2006/607) |
| | para 6 | 1 Apr 2007 (SSI 2007/84) |
| | para 7 | 1 Jan 2007 (SSI 2006/607) |
| | paras 8–11 | 1 Apr 2007 (SSI 2007/84) |
| | para 12 | 1 Jan 2007 (SSI 2006/607) |
| | paras 13, 14 | 1 Apr 2007 (SSI 2007/84) |

[1] For transitional provisions and savings, see SSI 2007/84, arts 4–6

---

**Racial and Religious Hatred Act 2006 (c 1)**

*RA:* 16 Feb 2006

*Commencement provisions:* s 3(2), (3); Racial and Religious Hatred Act 2006 (Commencement No 1) Order 2007, SI 2007/2490

| | |
|---|---|
| 1 | See Schedule below |
| 2, 3 | 1 Oct 2007 (SI 2007/2490) |
| Schedule | 1 Oct 2007 (except so far as inserts Public Order Act 1986, ss 29B(3), 29H(2), 29I(2)(b), (4)) (SI 2007/2490) |
| | *Not yet in force* (exceptions noted above) |

---

**Road Safety Act 2006 (c 49)**

*RA:* 8 Nov 2006

*Commencement provisions:* s 61; Road Safety Act 2006 (Commencement No 1) Order 2007, SI 2007/237; Road Safety Act 2006 (Commencement No 1) (England and Wales) Order 2007, SI 2007/466; Road Safety Act 2006 (Commencement No 2) Order 2007, SI 2007/2472; Road Safety Act 2006 (Commencement No 2) (England and Wales) Order 2007, SI 2007/3492; Road Safety Act 2006 (Commencement No 3) (England and Wales) Order 2008, SI 2008/1862; Road Safety Act 2006 (Commencement No 3) Order 2008, SI 2008/1864; Road Safety Act 2006 (Commencement No 4) Order 2008, SI 2008/1918; Road Safety Act 2006 (Commencement No 5) Order 2008, SI 2008/3164; Road Safety Act 2006 (Commencement No 6) Order 2011, SI 2011/19; Road Safety Act 2006 (Commencement No 7) Order 2011, SI 2011/1119; Road Safety Act 2006 (Commencement No 8) Order 2012, SI 2012/1357; Road Safety Act 2006 (Commencement No 9 and Transitional Provisions) Order 2012, SI 2012/2938; Road Safety Act 2006 (Commencement No 10) Order 2013, SI 2013/1012; Road Safety Act 2006 (Commencement No 11 and Transitional Provisions) Order 2015, SI 2015/560

| | |
|---|---|
| 1 | 8 Jan 2007 (s 61(7)(a)) |
| 2 | 8 Nov 2006 (so far as confers any power to make orders or regulations) (s 61(10)) |

**Road Safety Act 2006 (c 49)**—*contd*

|  |  |  |
|---|---|---|
|  |  | *Not yet in force* (otherwise) |
| 3 |  | 8 Nov 2006 (so far as confers any power to make orders or regulations) (s 61(10)) |
|  |  | 5 Jan 2009 (otherwise) (SI 2008/3164) |
| 4 |  | 8 Nov 2006 (so far as confers any power to make orders or regulations) (s 61(10)) |
|  |  | 31 Mar 2009 (otherwise) (SI 2008/3164) |
| 5 |  | See Sch 1 below |
| 6 |  | 31 Mar 2009 (SI 2008/3164) |
| 7 |  | 8 Nov 2006 (so far as confers any power to make orders or regulations) (s 61(10)) |
|  |  | 31 Mar 2009 (otherwise) (SI 2008/3164) |
| 8 |  | 8 Nov 2006 (so far as confers any power to make orders or regulations) (s 61(10)) |
|  |  | 1 Apr 2009 (otherwise) (SI 2008/3164) |
| 9 | (1)–(5) | 1 Apr 2009 (SI 2008/3164) |
|  | (6) | See Sch 2 below |
| 10 | (1)–(11) | 8 Jun 2015 (SI 2015/560)[2] |
|  | (12) | See Sch 3 below |
| 11 | (1), (2) | 8 Nov 2006 (so far as confer any power to make orders or regulations) (s 61(10)) |
|  |  | 5 Jan 2009 (otherwise) (SI 2008/3164) |
|  | (3) | See Sch 4 below |
| 12 |  | 5 Jan 2009 (SI 2008/3164) |
| 13 |  | 1 Jun 2013 (SI 2013/1012) |
| 14 |  | 24 Sep 2007 (SI 2007/2472) |
| 15, 16 |  | 8 Nov 2006 (so far as confer any power to make orders or regulations) (s 61(10)) |
|  |  | *Not yet in force* (otherwise) |
| 17, 18 |  | *Not yet in force* |
| 19 |  | 8 Nov 2006 (so far as confers any power to make orders or regulations) (s 61(10)) |
|  |  | *Not yet in force* (otherwise) |
| 20, 21 |  | 18 Aug 2008 (SI 2008/1918) |
| 22 | (1), (2) | 8 Nov 2006 (so far as confer any power to make orders or regulations) (s 61(10)) |
|  |  | 4 Feb 2011 (otherwise) (SI 2011/19) |
|  | (3) | See Sch 5 below |
|  | (4) | 16 May 2011 (SI 2011/1119) |
|  | (5) | 4 Feb 2011 (SI 2011/19) |
|  | (6) | See sub-ss (7), (8) below |
|  | (7) | 4 Feb 2011 (SI 2011/19) |
|  | (8) | 16 May 2011 (in so far as relates to the Road Traffic Act 1998, Sch 2A, para 2(1)–(3)) (SI 2011/1119) |
|  |  | *Not yet in force* (otherwise) |
| 23–25 |  | 24 Sep 2007 (SI 2007/2472) |
| 26 |  | 27 Feb 2007 (SI 2007/237) |
| 27–29 |  | 24 Sep 2007 (SI 2007/2472) |
| 30 |  | 24 Sep 2007 (so far as the inserted Road Traffic Act 1988, s 3ZA has effect for the purposes of ss 3, 3A of that Act) (SI 2007/2472) |
|  |  | 18 Aug 2008 (so far as the inserted Road Traffic Act 1988, s 3ZA has effect for the purposes of s 2B of that Act) (SI 2008/1918) |
| 31–33 |  | 24 Sep 2007 (SI 2007/2472) |
| 34 |  | 8 Nov 2006 (so far as confers any power to make orders or regulations) (s 61(10)) |
|  |  | *Not yet in force* (otherwise) |
| 35 |  | 8 Nov 2006 (so far as confers any power to make orders or regulations) (s 61(10)) |

**Road Safety Act 2006 (c 49)**—*contd*

|  |  |  |
|---|---|---|
|  |  | 21 Dec 2012 (for the purposes of the making of applications for approval, the approval, and the appeal against refusal of approval or conditional approval of courses for persons convicted of a relevant drink offence) (SI 2012/2938)[1] |
|  |  | 24 Jun 2013 (for all purposes having application where a person is convicted of a relevant drink offence) (SI 2012/2938)[1] |
|  |  | *Not yet in force* (otherwise) |
| 36 |  | 8 Nov 2006 (so far as confers any power to make orders or regulations) (s 61(10)) |
|  |  | 27 Feb 2007 (otherwise) (SI 2007/237) |
| 37–39 |  | 8 Nov 2006 (so far as confer any power to make orders or regulations) (s 61(10)) |
|  |  | *Not yet in force* (otherwise) |
| 40 |  | 8 Nov 2006 (so far as confers any power to make orders or regulations) (s 61(10)) |
|  |  | 27 Feb 2007 (otherwise) (SI 2007/237) |
| 41 |  | 24 Sep 2007 (SI 2007/2472) |
| 42 |  | See Sch 6 below |
| 43 |  | 8 Nov 2006 (so far as confers any power to make orders or regulations) (s 61(10)) |
|  |  | 24 Sep 2007 (otherwise) (SI 2007/2472) |
| 44 |  | 16 Mar 2007 (SI 2007/466) |
| 45 | (1) | 8 Nov 2006 (so far as confers any power to make orders or regulations) (s 61(10)) |
|  |  | 30 Jul 2008 (otherwise) (SI 2008/1862) |
|  | (2) | 8 Nov 2006 (so far as confers any power to make orders or regulations) (s 61(10)) |
|  |  | 30 Jul 2008 (except for the purposes of the Vehicles (Crime) Act 2001, s 28(1)) (SI 2008/1862) |
|  |  | 1 Nov 2008 (exception noted above) (SI 2008/1862) |
|  | (3)–(7) | 8 Nov 2006 (so far as confer any power to make orders or regulations) (s 61(10)) |
|  |  | 1 Nov 2008 (otherwise) (SI 2008/1862) |
| 46 |  | 31 Jul 2008 (except for the purposes of extending the Vehicles (Crime) Act 2001, ss 17(1), 28 to Scotland and Northern Ireland) (SI 2008/1864) |
|  |  | 1 Nov 2008 (exception noted above) (SI 2008/1864) |
| 47 |  | 8 Nov 2006 (so far as confers any power to make orders or regulations) (s 61(10)) |
|  |  | *Not yet in force* (otherwise) |
| 48 |  | *Not yet in force* |
| 49 |  | 8 Jan 2007 (s 61(7)(b)) |
| 50 |  | 8 Nov 2006 (so far as confers any power to make orders or regulations) (s 61(10)) |
|  |  | 27 Feb 2007 (otherwise) (SI 2007/237) |
| 51 |  | 8 Nov 2006 (s 61(9)(a)) |
| 52 |  | 16 Mar 2007 (SI 2007/466) |
| 53 |  | 28 Jan 2008 (SI 2007/3492) |
| 54 |  | 31 Mar 2008 (SI 2007/3492) |
| 55 |  | 28 Jan 2008 (SI 2007/3492) |
| 56 |  | 8 Nov 2006 (so far as confers any power to make orders or regulations) (s 61(10)) |
|  |  | *Not yet in force* (otherwise) |
| 57 |  | *Never in force* (repealed) |
| 58 |  | 8 Nov 2006 (s 61(9)(b)) |
| 59 |  | See Sch 7 below |
| 60 |  | 8 Nov 2006 (s 61(9)) |
| 61–63 |  | 8 Nov 2006 (s 61(1)) |
| Sch 1 |  | 31 Mar 2009 (SI 2008/3164) |
| Sch 2 |  | 1 Apr 2009 (SI 2008/3164) |

**Road Safety Act 2006 (c 49)**—*contd*

| | | |
|---|---|---|
| Sch 3 | paras 1–5 | 8 Jun 2015 (SI 2015/560)[2] |
| | para 6(1), (2)(a) | 8 Jun 2015 (SI 2015/560)[2] |
| | para 6(2)(b) | *Not yet in force* |
| | para 6(2)(c) | 8 Jun 2015 (SI 2015/560)[2] |
| | para 6(3) | *Not yet in force* |
| | para 7 | 8 Jun 2015 (SI 2015/560)[2] |
| | para 8 | *Not yet in force* |
| | para 9 | 8 Jun 2015 (SI 2015/560)[2] |
| | para 10 | *Not yet in force* |
| | paras 11–23 | 8 Jun 2015 (SI 2015/560)[2] |
| | paras 24, 25 | *Not yet in force* |
| | paras 26, 27 | 8 Jun 2015 (SI 2015/560)[2] |
| | para 28(1), (2) | 8 Jun 2015 (SI 2015/560)[2] |
| | para 28(3) | *Not yet in force* |
| | paras 29–58 | 8 Jun 2015 (SI 2015/560)[2] |
| | para 59(1) | 8 Jun 2015 (SI 2015/560)[2] |
| | para 59(2) | *Not yet in force* |
| | para 59(3)–(7) | 8 Jun 2015 (SI 2015/560)[2] |
| | paras 60–75 | 8 Jun 2015 (SI 2015/560)[2] |
| | para 76 | *Not yet in force* |
| | para 77(1), (2) | 8 Jun 2015 (SI 2015/560)[2] |
| | para 77(3) | *Not yet in force* |
| | paras 78, 79 | *Not yet in force* |
| | para 80 | 8 Jun 2015 (SI 2015/560)[2] |
| Sch 4 | | 8 Nov 2006 (so far as confers any power to make orders or regulations) (s 61(10)) |
| | | 5 Jan 2009 (otherwise) (SI 2008/3164) |
| Sch 5 | | 8 Nov 2006 (so far as confers any power to make orders or regulations) (s 61(10)) |
| | | 4 Feb 2011 (otherwise) (SI 2011/19) |
| Sch 6 | para 1 | See paras 2–30 below |
| | paras 2–23 | 8 Nov 2006 (so far as confer any power to make orders or regulations) (s 61(10)) |
| | | *Not yet in force (otherwise)* (paras 6, 7 repealed) |
| | para 24 | 8 Nov 2006 (so far as confers any power to make orders or regulations) (s 61(10)) |
| | | 21 May 2012 (otherwise) (SI 2012/1357) |
| | paras 25–33 | 8 Nov 2006 (so far as confer any power to make orders or regulations) (s 61(10)) |
| | | *Not yet in force (otherwise)* |
| Sch 7 | (1) | 5 Jan 2009 (SI 2008/3164) |
| | (2) | 31 Mar 2009 (SI 2008/3164) |
| | (3) | 1 Apr 2009 (SI 2008/3164) |
| | (4) | 8 Jun 2015 (except entries relating to Road Traffic Act 1988, ss 97(1)(c)(ia), (1AA), 98A, 99A, 105(2)(b)(iii), 141A(5), 142; Road Traffic (Driver Licensing and Information Systems) Act 1989, Sch 3, para 25; Crime (International Co-operation) Act 2003, ss 64, 74(1)) (SI 2015/560)[2] |
| | | *Not yet in force* (exceptions noted above) |
| | (5) | 24 Sep 2007 (SI 2007/2472) |
| | (6), (7) | *Not yet in force* |
| | (8) | 21 Dec 2012 (to the extent it relates to the purposes of the making of applications for approval, the approval, and the appeal against refusal of approval or conditional approval of courses for persons convicted of a relevant drink offence) (SI 2012/2938) |
| | | 24 Jun 2013 (to the extent it relates to all purposes having application where a person is convicted of a relevant drink offence) (SI 2012/2938) |
| | | *Not yet in force (otherwise)* |
| | (9) | 27 Feb 2007 (SI 2007/237) |

**Road Safety Act 2006 (c 49)**—*contd*

| | |
|---|---|
| (10), (11) | *Not yet in force* |
| (12) | 27 Feb 2007 (SI 2007/237) |
| (13) | 24 Sep 2007 (SI 2007/2472) |
| (14), (15) | *Not yet in force* |
| (16) | 27 Feb 2007 (SI 2007/237) |
| (17), (18) | *Not yet in force* |
| (19) | 8 Nov 2006 (s 61(9)) |

1    For transitional provisions, see SI 2012/2938, art 3

2    For transitional provisions, see SI 2015/560, arts 4–9

---

### Safeguarding Vulnerable Groups Act 2006 (c 47)

*RA:* 8 Nov 2006

*Commencement provisions:* s 65; Safeguarding Vulnerable Groups Act 2006 (Commencement No 1) Order 2007, SI 2007/3545; Safeguarding Vulnerable Groups Act 2006 (Commencement No 1) (Northern Ireland) Order 2008, SI 2008/930; Safeguarding Vulnerable Groups Act 2006 (Commencement No 2) Order 2008, SI 2008/1320; Safeguarding Vulnerable Groups Act 2006 (Commencement No 1) (England) Order 2008, SI 2008/3204; Safeguarding Vulnerable Groups Act 2006 (Commencement No 3) Order 2009, SI 2009/39; Safeguarding Vulnerable Groups Act 2006 (Commencement No 4) Order 2009, SI 2009/1503; Safeguarding Vulnerable Groups Act 2006 (Regulated Activity, Miscellaneous and Transitional Provisions and Commencement No 5) Order 2009, SI 2009/2610; Safeguarding Vulnerable Groups Act 2006 (Commencement No 6, Transitional Provisions and Savings) Order 2009, SI 2009/2611, as amended by SI 2010/1101, SI 2012/3006; Safeguarding Vulnerable Groups Act 2006 (Commencement No 6, Transitional Provisions and Savings (Amendment)) and (Commencement No 7) Order 2010, SI 2010/1101, as amended by SI 2012/3006; Safeguarding Vulnerable Groups Act 2006 (Commencement No 8 and Saving) Order 2012, SI 2012/2231

| | | |
|---|---|---|
| 1 | | 2 Jan 2008 (E) (W) (SI 2007/3545) |
| | | 31 Mar 2008 (NI) (SI 2008/930) |
| 2 | (1) | 11 Feb 2008 (in so far as necessary for the exercise of functions to be conferred on the Independent Barring Board under Sch 8) (SI 2007/3545) |
| | | 20 Jan 2009 (for the purposes of the Safeguarding Vulnerable Groups Act 2006 (Transitory Provisions) Order 2009, SI 2009/12) (SI 2009/39) |
| | | 12 Oct 2009 (otherwise) (SI 2009/2611) |
| | (2)–(4) | See Sch 3 below |
| | (5) | 31 Dec 2007 (for the purposes of making regulations) (SI 2007/3545) |
| | | 11 Feb 2008 (in so far as necessary for the exercise of functions to be conferred on the Independent Barring Board under Sch 8) (SI 2007/3545) |
| | | 20 Jan 2009 (for the purposes of the Safeguarding Vulnerable Groups Act 2006 (Transitory Provisions) Order 2009, SI 2009/12) (SI 2009/39) |
| | | 12 Oct 2009 (otherwise) (SI 2009/2611) |
| 3 | (1), (2)(a) | 19 May 2008 (for the purposes of regulations made under the Childcare Act 2006, s 75) (SI 2008/1320) |
| | | 12 Oct 2009 (otherwise) (SI 2009/2611) |
| | (2)(b) | 19 May 2008 (for the purposes of making orders) (SI 2008/1320) |
| | | 12 Oct 2009 (otherwise) (SI 2009/2611) |
| | (3)(a) | 12 Oct 2009 (SI 2009/2611) |
| | (3)(b) | 19 May 2008 (for the purposes of making orders) (SI 2008/1320) |
| | | 12 Oct 2009 (otherwise) (SI 2009/2611) |
| 4 | (1)–(7) | 19 May 2008 (SI 2008/1320) |
| | (8) | 31 Dec 2007 (SI 2007/3545) |
| | (9)–(11) | 19 May 2008 (SI 2008/1320) |

**Safeguarding Vulnerable Groups Act 2006 (c 47)**—*contd*

| | | |
|---|---|---|
| 5 | (1), (2) | See Sch 4 below |
| | (3), (4) | 19 May 2008 (for the purposes of making orders) (SI 2008/1320) |
| | | 20 Jan 2009 (otherwise) (SI 2009/39) |
| 6 | (1)–(11) | 11 Feb 2008 (in so far as necessary for the exercise of functions to be conferred on the Independent Barring Board under Sch 8) (SI 2007/3545) |
| | | 20 Jan 2009 (in so far as relates to s 37 of this Act) (SI 2009/39) |
| | | 12 Oct 2009 (otherwise) (SI 2009/2611) |
| | (12) | 11 Feb 2008 (in so far as necessary for the exercise of functions to be conferred on the Independent Barring Board under Sch 8) (SI 2007/3545) |
| | | 19 May 2008 (for the purposes of making orders) (SI 2008/1320) |
| | | 20 Jan 2009 (in so far as relates to s 37 of this Act) (SI 2009/39) |
| | | 12 Oct 2009 (otherwise) (SI 2009/2611) |
| 7 | | 12 Oct 2009 (SI 2009/2611) |
| 8 | | *Never in force* (repealed) |
| 9 | | 12 Oct 2009 (SI 2009/2611) |
| 10 | | *Never in force* (repealed) |
| 11 | (1) | *Never in force* (repealed) |
| | (2) | 19 May 2008 (for the purposes of making regulations) (SI 2008/1320) |
| | | *Never in force* (otherwise) (repealed) |
| | (3)–(10) | *Never in force* (repealed) |
| 12 | (1) | See Sch 6 below |
| | (2) | 19 May 2008 (for the purposes of making orders) (SI 2008/1320) |
| | | *Never in force* (otherwise) (repealed) |
| 13 | (1) | 19 May 2008 (for the purposes of making regulations) (SI 2008/1320) |
| | | *Never in force* (otherwise) (repealed) |
| | (2)–(4) | *Never in force* (repealed) |
| | (5) | 19 May 2008 (for the purposes of making regulations) (SI 2008/1320) |
| | | *Never in force* (otherwise) (repealed) |
| 14 | (1)–(3) | 19 May 2008 (for the purposes of making regulations) (SI 2008/1320) |
| | | *Never in force* (otherwise) (repealed) |
| | (4) | *Never in force* (repealed) |
| 15–17 | | *Never in force* (repealed) |
| 18 | | 12 Oct 2009 (in so far as relates to an offence under ss 9 or 38 of this Act) (SI 2009/2611) |
| | | *Not yet in force* (in so far as relates to an offence under s 10, 11, 23, 27 or Sch 6) |
| 19 | (1) | *Never in force* (repealed) |
| | (2) | 12 Oct 2009 (SI 2009/2611) |
| | (3), (4) | *Never in force* (repealed) |
| | (5) | 12 Oct 2009 (SI 2009/2611) |
| | (6), (7) | *Never in force* (repealed) |
| | (8) | 12 Oct 2009 (in so far as relates to sub-s (2) above) (SI 2009/2611) |
| | | *Not yet in force* (in so far as relates to sub-s (3) above) |
| | (9) | *Never in force* (repealed) |
| | (10) | 12 Oct 2009 (SI 2009/2611) |
| 20 | (1) | 12 Oct 2009 (in so far as relates to an offence under s 19(2) of this Act) (SI 2009/2611) |
| | | *Not yet in force* (in so far as relates to an offence under s 19(1) or (3)) |
| | (2)–(7) | *Never in force* (repealed) |
| 21 | | 20 Jan 2009 (in so far as relates to s 37 of this Act) (SI 2009/39) |
| | | 12 Oct 2009 (in so far as relates to ss 35, 36, 39, 41, 45 of this Act) (SI 2009/2611) |
| | | 30 Mar 2010 (otherwise) (SI 2010/1101) |

**Safeguarding Vulnerable Groups Act 2006 (c 47)**—*contd*

| | | |
|---|---|---|
| 22 | (1)–(4) | 20 Jan 2009 (in so far as they relate to s 37 of this Act) (SI 2009/39) |
| | | 12 Oct 2009 (in so far as they relate to ss 35, 36, 39, 41, 45 of this Act) (SI 2009/2611) |
| | | 30 Mar 2010 (otherwise) (SI 2010/1101) |
| | (5)(a), (b) | 20 Jan 2009 (in so far as they relate to s 37 of this Act) (SI 2009/39) |
| | | 12 Oct 2009 (in so far as they relate to ss 35, 36, 39, 41, 45 of this Act) (SI 2009/2611) |
| | | 30 Mar 2010 (otherwise) (SI 2010/1101) |
| | (5)(c) | 12 Oct 2009 (in so far as relates to ss 35, 36, 39, 41, 45 of this Act) (SI 2009/2611) |
| | | 30 Mar 2010 (otherwise) (SI 2010/1101) |
| | (6) | 20 Jan 2009 (in so far as relates to s 37 of this Act) (SI 2009/39) |
| | | 12 Oct 2009 (in so far as relates to ss 35, 36, 39, 41, 45 of this Act) (SI 2009/2611) |
| | | 30 Mar 2010 (otherwise) (SI 2010/1101) |
| 23 | (1), (2) | 12 Oct 2009 (SI 2009/2611) |
| | (3) | 20 Jan 2009 (in so far as relates to s 37 of this Act) (SI 2009/39) |
| | | 12 Oct 2009 (in so far as relates to s 35 of this Act) (SI 2009/2611) |
| | | 30 Mar 2010 (otherwise) (SI 2010/1101) |
| 24 | (1)(a), (b) | *Never in force* (repealed) |
| | (1)(c), (d) | 19 May 2008 (for the purposes of making regulations) (SI 2008/1320) |
| | | *Never in force* (otherwise) (repealed) |
| | (2)–(7) | *Never in force* (otherwise) (repealed) |
| | (8)(a) | 19 May 2008 (for the purposes of making regulations) (SI 2008/1320) |
| | | *Never in force* (otherwise) (repealed) |
| | (8)(b) | *Never in force* (otherwise) (repealed) |
| | (8)(c) | 19 May 2008 (for the purposes of making regulations) (SI 2008/1320) |
| | | *Never in force* (otherwise) (repealed) |
| | (9) | *Never in force* (otherwise) (repealed) |
| | (10), (11) | 19 May 2008 (for the purposes of making regulations) (SI 2008/1320) |
| | | *Never in force* (otherwise) (repealed) |
| | (12)(a)–(c) | *Never in force* (otherwise) (repealed) |
| | (12)(d) | 19 May 2008 (for the purposes of making regulations) (SI 2008/1320) |
| | | *Never in force* (otherwise) (repealed) |
| | (13), (14) | *Never in force* (otherwise) (repealed) |
| 25 | | 19 May 2008 (SI 2008/1320) |
| 26 | (1) | 19 May 2008 (for the purposes of making regulations) (SI 2008/1320) |
| | | *Never in force* (otherwise) (repealed) |
| | (2) | *Never in force* (otherwise) (repealed) |
| 27 | | *Never in force* (otherwise) (repealed) |
| 28, 29 | | 20 Jan 2009 (SI 2009/39) |
| 30 | (1)–(6) | *Not yet in force* |
| | (7), (8) | 19 May 2008 (for the purposes of making regulations) (SI 2008/1320) |
| | | *Not yet in force* (otherwise) |
| 31 | (1)–(5) | *Not yet in force* |
| | (6) | 19 May 2008 (for the purposes of making orders) (SI 2008/1320) |
| | | *Not yet in force* (otherwise) |
| 32 | (1)–(9) | *Not yet in force* |
| | (10) | 19 May 2008 (for the purposes of making regulations) (SI 2008/1320) |
| | | *Not yet in force* (otherwise) |

**Safeguarding Vulnerable Groups Act 2006 (c 47)**—*contd*

| | | |
|---|---|---|
| 33 | (1), (2) | *Not yet in force* |
| | (3) | 19 May 2008 (for the purposes of making regulations) (SI 2008/1320) |
| | | *Not yet in force* (otherwise) |
| | (4)(a) | *Not yet in force* |
| | (4)(b) | 19 May 2008 (for the purposes of making regulations) (SI 2008/1320) |
| | | *Not yet in force* (otherwise) |
| | (5), (6) | *Not yet in force* |
| 34 | | *Not yet in force* |
| 35 | (1) | 19 May 2008 (for the purposes of making regulations) (SI 2008/1320) |
| | | 12 Oct 2009 (otherwise) (SI 2009/2611) |
| | (2)–(7) | 12 Oct 2009 (SI 2009/2611) |
| 36 | (1)–(3) | 19 May 2008 (for the purposes of making regulations) (SI 2008/1320) |
| | | 12 Oct 2009 (otherwise) (SI 2009/2611) |
| | (4)–(10) | 12 Oct 2009 (SI 2009/2611) |
| 37 | (1) | 11 Feb 2008 (in so far as necessary for the exercise of functions to be conferred on the Independent Barring Board under Sch 8) (SI 2007/3545) |
| | | 20 Jan 2009 (otherwise) (SI 2009/39) |
| | (2) | 11 Feb 2008 (in so far as necessary for the exercise of functions to be conferred on the Independent Barring Board under Sch 8) (SI 2007/3545) |
| | | 19 May 2008 (for the purposes of making regulations) (SI 2008/1320) |
| | | 20 Jan 2009 (otherwise) (SI 2009/39) |
| | (3)–(6) | 11 Feb 2008 (in so far as necessary for the exercise of functions to be conferred on the Independent Barring Board under Sch 8) (SI 2007/3545) |
| | | 20 Jan 2009 (otherwise) (SI 2009/39) |
| 38 | | 11 Feb 2008 (in so far as necessary for the exercise of functions to be conferred on the Independent Barring Board under Sch 8) (SI 2007/3545) |
| | | 20 Jan 2009 (in so far as relates to s 37 of this Act) (SI 2009/39) |
| | | 12 Oct 2009 (otherwise) (SI 2009/2611) |
| 39 | (1) | 19 May 2008 (for the purposes of making regulations) (SI 2008/1320) |
| | | 12 Oct 2009 (otherwise) (SI 2009/2611) |
| | (2)–(4) | 12 Oct 2009 (SI 2009/2611) |
| | (5) | 19 May 2008 (for the purposes of making regulations) (SI 2008/1320) |
| | | 12 Oct 2009 (otherwise) (SI 2009/2611) |
| | (6), (7) | 12 Oct 2009 (SI 2009/2611) |
| 40 | (1) | 11 Feb 2008 (in so far as necessary for the exercise of functions to be conferred on the Independent Barring Board under Sch 8) (SI 2007/3545) |
| | | 20 Jan 2009 (otherwise) (SI 2009/39) |
| | (2) | 11 Feb 2008 (in so far as necessary for the exercise of functions to be conferred on the Independent Barring Board under Sch 8) (SI 2007/3545) |
| | | 19 May 2008 (for the purposes of making regulations) (SI 2008/1320) |
| | | 20 Jan 2009 (otherwise) (SI 2009/39) |
| | (3), (4) | 11 Feb 2008 (in so far as necessary for the exercise of functions to be conferred on the Independent Barring Board under Sch 8) (SI 2007/3545) |
| | | 20 Jan 2009 (otherwise) (SI 2009/39) |

**Safeguarding Vulnerable Groups Act 2006 (c 47)**—*contd*

| | | |
|---|---|---|
| 41 | (1) | 19 May 2008 (for the purposes of making regulations) (SI 2008/1320) |
| | | 12 Oct 2009 (otherwise) (SI 2009/2611) |
| | (2)–(4) | 12 Oct 2009 (SI 2009/2611) |
| | (5) | 19 May 2008 (for the purposes of making regulations) (SI 2008/1320) |
| | | 12 Oct 2009 (otherwise) (SI 2009/2611) |
| | (6) | 12 Oct 2009 (SI 2009/2611) |
| | (7) | 20 Jan 2009 (in so far as relates to s 42 of this Act) (SI 2009/39) |
| | | 12 Oct 2009 (otherwise) (SI 2009/2611) |
| | (8) | 19 May 2008 (for the purposes of making orders) (SI 2008/1320) |
| | | 12 Oct 2009 (otherwise) (SI 2009/2611) |
| 42 | (1) | 11 Feb 2008 (in so far as necessary for the exercise of functions to be conferred on the Independent Barring Board under Sch 8) (SI 2007/3545) |
| | | 20 Jan 2009 (otherwise) (SI 2009/39) |
| | (2) | 11 Feb 2008 (in so far as necessary for the exercise of functions to be conferred on the Independent Barring Board under Sch 8) (SI 2007/3545) |
| | | 19 May 2008 (for the purposes of making regulations) (SI 2008/1320) |
| | | 20 Jan 2009 (otherwise) (SI 2009/39) |
| | (3), (4) | 11 Feb 2008 (in so far as necessary for the exercise of functions to be conferred on the Independent Barring Board under Sch 8) (SI 2007/3545) |
| | | 20 Jan 2009 (otherwise) (SI 2009/39) |
| 43 | (1), (2) | *Not yet in force* |
| | (3)–(5) | 11 Feb 2008 (in so far as necessary for the exercise of functions to be conferred on the Independent Barring Board under Sch 8) (SI 2007/3545) |
| | | *Never in force* (otherwise) (substituted) |
| | (6) | 10 Sep 2012 (SI 2012/2231) |
| | (7) | 19 May 2008 (for the purposes of making orders) (SI 2008/1320) |
| | | 10 Sep 2012 (otherwise) (SI 2012/2231) |
| 44 | (1)–(5) | *Never in force* (repealed) |
| | (6) | 19 May 2008 (for the purposes of making orders) (SI 2008/1320) |
| | | *Never in force* (otherwise) (repealed) |
| | (7) | 19 May 2008 (for the purposes of making regulations) (SI 2008/1320) |
| | | *Never in force* (otherwise) (repealed) |
| 45 | (1) | 19 May 2008 (for the purposes of making regulations) (SI 2008/1320) |
| | | 12 Oct 2009 (otherwise) (SI 2009/2611) |
| | (2)–(4) | 12 Oct 2009 (SI 2009/2611) |
| | (5) | 19 May 2008 (for the purposes of making regulations) (SI 2008/1320) |
| | | 12 Oct 2009 (otherwise) (SI 2009/2611) |
| | (6) | 12 Oct 2009 (SI 2009/2611) |
| | (7) | 20 Jan 2009 (in so far as relates to s 46 of this Act) (SI 2009/39) |
| | | 12 Oct 2009 (otherwise) (SI 2009/2611) |
| | (8) | 12 Oct 2009 (SI 2009/2611) |
| | (9) | 19 May 2008 (for the purposes of making orders) (SI 2008/1320) |
| | | 12 Oct 2009 (otherwise) (SI 2009/2611) |
| | (10) | 12 Oct 2009 (SI 2009/2611) |
| 46 | (1)(a) | 11 Feb 2008 (in so far as necessary for the exercise of functions to be conferred on the Independent Barring Board under Sch 8) (SI 2007/3545) |
| | | 19 May 2008 (for the purposes of making regulations) (SI 2008/1320) |
| | | 20 Jan 2009 (otherwise) (SI 2009/39) |

**Safeguarding Vulnerable Groups Act 2006 (c 47)**—*contd*

|       |         |                                                                                                                                                                                 |
|-------|---------|---------------------------------------------------------------------------------------------------------------------------------------------------------------------------------|
|       | (1)(b)  | 11 Feb 2008 (in so far as necessary for the exercise of functions to be conferred on the Independent Barring Board under Sch 8) (SI 2007/3545)                                  |
|       |         | 20 Jan 2009 (otherwise) (SI 2009/39)                                                                                                                                            |
|       | (2)     | 11 Feb 2008 (in so far as necessary for the exercise of functions to be conferred on the Independent Barring Board under Sch 8) (SI 2007/3545)                                  |
|       |         | 19 May 2008 (for the purposes of making regulations) (SI 2008/1320)                                                                                                             |
|       |         | 20 Jan 2009 (otherwise) (SI 2009/39)                                                                                                                                            |
|       | (3)     | 11 Feb 2008 (in so far as necessary for the exercise of functions to be conferred on the Independent Barring Board under Sch 8) (SI 2007/3545)                                  |
|       |         | 20 Jan 2009 (otherwise) (SI 2009/39)                                                                                                                                            |
| 47    | (1)–(4) | 10 Sep 2012 (SI 2012/2231)                                                                                                                                                      |
|       | (5)     | *Never in force* (repealed)                                                                                                                                                     |
|       | (6)     | 19 May 2008 (for the purposes of making orders) (SI 2008/1320)                                                                                                                  |
|       |         | *Not yet in force* (otherwise)                                                                                                                                                  |
|       | (7)     | 19 May 2008 (for the purposes of making regulations) (SI 2008/1320)                                                                                                             |
|       |         | 10 Sep 2012 (otherwise) (SI 2012/2231)                                                                                                                                          |
| 48    | (1)–(5) | *Not yet in force*                                                                                                                                                              |
|       | (6)     | 19 May 2008 (for the purposes of making orders) (SI 2008/1320)                                                                                                                  |
|       |         | *Not yet in force* (otherwise)                                                                                                                                                  |
|       | (7), (8)| 19 May 2008 (for the purposes of making regulations) (SI 2008/1320)                                                                                                             |
|       |         | *Not yet in force* (otherwise)                                                                                                                                                  |
| 49    | (1)–(5) | *Not yet in force*                                                                                                                                                              |
|       | (6)     | 19 May 2008 (for the purposes of making orders) (SI 2008/1320)                                                                                                                  |
|       |         | *Not yet in force* (otherwise)                                                                                                                                                  |
|       | (7), (8)| 19 May 2008 (for the purposes of making regulations) (SI 2008/1320)                                                                                                             |
|       |         | *Not yet in force* (otherwise)                                                                                                                                                  |
| 50    |         | 11 Feb 2008 (in so far as necessary for the exercise of functions to be conferred on the Independent Barring Board under Sch 8) (SI 2007/3545)                                  |
|       |         | 22 Jun 2009 (in so far as necessary for the provision of information to Her Majesty's Chief Inspector of Schools in England relating to non-maintained special schools in England and independent schools in England) (SI 2009/1503) |
|       |         | 22 Apr 2010 (for the purposes of the provision of information to the Secretary of State in the exercise of the Secretary of State's functions under the Education Act 2002, Pt 10, Chapter 1) (SI 2010/1101) |
|       |         | 10 Sep 2012 (otherwise) (SI 2012/2231)                                                                                                                                          |
| 51    |         | 11 Feb 2008 (in so far as necessary for the exercise of functions to be conferred on the Independent Barring Board under Sch 8) (SI 2007/3545)                                  |
|       |         | 12 Oct 2009 (otherwise) (SI 2009/2611)                                                                                                                                          |
| 52    |         | 12 Oct 2009 (SI 2009/2611)                                                                                                                                                      |
| 53    |         | 11 Feb 2008 (in so far as necessary for the exercise of functions to be conferred on the Independent Barring Board under Sch 8) (SI 2007/3545)                                  |
|       |         | 20 Jan 2009 (otherwise) (SI 2009/39)                                                                                                                                            |
| 54    | (1), (2)| 19 May 2008 (for the purposes of making orders) (SI 2008/1320)                                                                                                                  |
|       |         | 12 Oct 2009 (otherwise) (SI 2009/2611)                                                                                                                                          |
|       | (3)–(5) | 12 Oct 2009 (SI 2009/2611)                                                                                                                                                      |
| 55    |         | 8 Nov 2006 (s 65)                                                                                                                                                               |
| 56    |         | 31 Dec 2007 (SI 2007/3545)                                                                                                                                                      |

**Safeguarding Vulnerable Groups Act 2006 (c 47)**—*contd*

| | | |
|---|---|---|
| 57 | | 11 Feb 2008 (in so far as necessary for the exercise of functions to be conferred on the Independent Barring Board under Sch 8) (SI 2007/3545) |
| | | 20 Jan 2009 (otherwise) (SI 2009/39) |
| 58 | (1)–(5) | 11 Feb 2008 (in so far as necessary for the exercise of functions to be conferred on the Independent Barring Board under Sch 8) (SI 2007/3545) |
| | | 12 Oct 2009 (otherwise) (SI 2009/2611) |
| | (6) | 11 Feb 2008 (in so far as necessary for the exercise of functions to be conferred on the Independent Barring Board under Sch 8) (SI 2007/3545) |
| | | 19 May 2008 (for the purposes of making orders) (SI 2008/1320) |
| | | 12 Oct 2009 (otherwise) (SI 2009/2611) |
| 59 | | 11 Feb 2008 (in so far as necessary for the exercise of functions to be conferred on the Independent Barring Board under Sch 8) (SI 2007/3545) |
| | | 31 Mar 2008 (NI) (in so far as it relates to s 1 of and Sch 1 to this Act) (SI 2008/930) |
| | | 12 Oct 2009 (otherwise) (SI 2009/2611) |
| 60 | (1) | 31 Dec 2007 (for the purposes of making orders and regulations) (SI 2007/3545) |
| | | 11 Feb 2008 (in so far as necessary for the exercise of functions to be conferred on the Independent Barring Board under Sch 8) (SI 2007/3545) |
| | | 31 Mar 2008 (NI) (in so far as it relates to s 1 of and Sch 1 to this Act) (SI 2008/930) |
| | | 12 Oct 2009 (otherwise) (SI 2009/2611) |
| | (2), (3) | 31 Mar 2008 (NI) (in so far as they relate to s 1 of and Sch 1 to this Act) (SI 2008/930) |
| | | 12 Oct 2009 (otherwise) (SI 2009/2611) |
| | (4) | 11 Feb 2008 (in so far as necessary for the exercise of functions to be conferred on the Independent Barring Board under Sch 8) (SI 2007/3545) |
| | | 31 Mar 2008 (NI) (in so far as it relates to s 1 of and Sch 1 to this Act) (SI 2008/930) |
| | | 12 Oct 2009 (otherwise) (SI 2009/2611) |
| 61 | | 31 Dec 2007 (E) (W) (SI 2007/3545) |
| | | 31 Mar 2008 (NI) (in so far as it relates to s 1 of and Sch 1 to this Act) (SI 2008/930) |
| | | 12 Oct 2009 (otherwise) (SI 2009/2611) |
| 62 | | See Sch 8 below |
| 63 | (1) | See Sch 9 below |
| | (2) | See Sch 10 below |
| 64 | | 31 Dec 2007 (SI 2007/3545) |
| 65 | | 8 Nov 2006 (s 65) |
| 66, 67 | | 31 Dec 2007 (SI 2007/3545) |
| Sch 1 | | 2 Jan 2008 (E) (W) (SI 2007/3545) |
| | | 31 Mar 2008 (NI) (SI 2008/930) |
| Sch 2 | | 2 Jan 2008 (E) (W) (SI 2007/3545) |
| | | *Never in force* (NI) (repealed) |
| Sch 3 | para 1(1) | 31 Dec 2007 (for the purposes of making regulations) (SI 2007/3545) |
| | | 11 Feb 2008 (in so far as necessary for the exercise of functions to be conferred on the Independent Barring Board under Sch 8) (SI 2007/3545) |
| | | 20 Jan 2009 (otherwise) (SI 2009/39) |
| | para 1(2), (3) | 11 Feb 2008 (in so far as necessary for the exercise of functions to be conferred on the Independent Barring Board under Sch 8) (SI 2007/3545) |
| | | 20 Jan 2009 (otherwise) (SI 2009/39) |

**Safeguarding Vulnerable Groups Act 2006 (c 47)**—*contd*

| | |
|---|---|
| para 2(1) | 31 Dec 2007 (for the purposes of making regulations) (SI 2007/3545) |
| | 11 Feb 2008 (in so far as necessary for the exercise of functions to be conferred on the Independent Barring Board under Sch 8) (SI 2007/3545) |
| | 20 Jan 2009 (otherwise) (SI 2009/39) |
| para 2(2)–(4) | 11 Feb 2008 (in so far as necessary for the exercise of functions to be conferred on the Independent Barring Board under Sch 8) (SI 2007/3545) |
| | 20 Jan 2009 (otherwise) (SI 2009/39) |
| para 3 | 11 Feb 2008 (in so far as necessary for the exercise of functions to be conferred on the Independent Barring Board under Sch 8) (SI 2007/3545) |
| | 20 Jan 2009 (otherwise) (SI 2009/39) |
| para 4(1)–(4) | 11 Feb 2008 (in so far as necessary for the exercise of functions to be conferred on the Independent Barring Board under Sch 8) (SI 2007/3545) |
| | 20 Jan 2009 (otherwise) (SI 2009/39) |
| para 4(5) | 11 Feb 2008 (in so far as necessary for the exercise of functions to be conferred on the Independent Barring Board under Sch 8) (SI 2007/3545) |
| | 12 Oct 2009 (otherwise) (SI 2009/2611) |
| paras 4(6), 5 | 11 Feb 2008 (in so far as necessary for the exercise of functions to be conferred on the Independent Barring Board under Sch 8) (SI 2007/3545) |
| | 20 Jan 2009 (otherwise) (SI 2009/39) |
| para 6(1)(a) | 11 Feb 2008 (in so far as necessary for the exercise of functions to be conferred on the Independent Barring Board under Sch 8) (SI 2007/3545) |
| | 12 Oct 2009 (otherwise) (SI 2009/2611) |
| para 6(1)(b) | 11 Feb 2008 (in so far as necessary for the exercise of functions to be conferred on the Independent Barring Board under Sch 8) (SI 2007/3545) |
| | 19 May 2008 (for the purposes of making orders) (SI 2008/1320) |
| | 12 Oct 2009 (otherwise) (SI 2009/2611) |
| para 6(2) | 11 Feb 2008 (in so far as necessary for the exercise of functions to be conferred on the Independent Barring Board under Sch 8) (SI 2007/3545) |
| | 19 May 2008 (for the purposes of making orders) (SI 2008/1320) |
| | 12 Oct 2009 (otherwise) (SI 2009/2611) |
| para 6(3) | 11 Feb 2008 (in so far as necessary for the exercise of functions to be conferred on the Independent Barring Board under Sch 8) (SI 2007/3545) |
| | 19 May 2008 (for the purposes of making orders) (SI 2008/1320) |
| | 12 Oct 2009 (otherwise) (SI 2009/2611) |
| para 7(1) | 31 Dec 2007 (for the purposes of making regulations) (SI 2007/3545) |
| | 11 Feb 2008 (in so far as necessary for the exercise of functions to be conferred on the Independent Barring Board under Sch 8) (SI 2007/3545) |
| | 20 Jan 2009 (otherwise) (SI 2009/39) |
| para 7(2), (3) | 11 Feb 2008 (in so far as necessary for the exercise of functions to be conferred on the Independent Barring Board under Sch 8) (SI 2007/3545) |
| | 20 Jan 2009 (otherwise) (SI 2009/39) |
| para 8(1) | 31 Dec 2007 (for the purposes of making regulations) (SI 2007/3545) |
| | 11 Feb 2008 (in so far as necessary for the exercise of functions to be conferred on the Independent Barring Board under Sch 8) (SI 2007/3545) |

**Safeguarding Vulnerable Groups Act 2006 (c 47)**—*contd*

|  |  |
|---|---|
|  | 20 Jan 2009 (otherwise) (SI 2009/39) |
| para 8(2)–(4) | 11 Feb 2008 (in so far as necessary for the exercise of functions to be conferred on the Independent Barring Board under Sch 8) (SI 2007/3545) |
|  | 20 Jan 2009 (otherwise) (SI 2009/39) |
| para 9 | 11 Feb 2008 (in so far as necessary for the exercise of functions to be conferred on the Independent Barring Board under Sch 8) (SI 2007/3545) |
|  | 20 Jan 2009 (otherwise) (SI 2009/39) |
| para 10(1)–(4) | 11 Feb 2008 (in so far as necessary for the exercise of functions to be conferred on the Independent Barring Board under Sch 8) (SI 2007/3545) |
|  | 20 Jan 2009 (otherwise) (SI 2009/39) |
| para 10(5) | 11 Feb 2008 (in so far as necessary for the exercise of functions to be conferred on the Independent Barring Board under Sch 8) (SI 2007/3545) |
|  | 12 Oct 2009 (otherwise) (SI 2009/2611) |
| paras 10(6) | 11 Feb 2008 (in so far as necessary for the exercise of functions to be conferred on the Independent Barring Board under Sch 8) (SI 2007/3545) |
|  | 20 Jan 2009 (otherwise) (SI 2009/39) |
| para 11 | 11 Feb 2008 (in so far as necessary for the exercise of functions to be conferred on the Independent Barring Board under Sch 8) (SI 2007/3545) |
|  | 20 Jan 2009 (otherwise) (SI 2009/39) |
| para 12(1)(a) | 11 Feb 2008 (in so far as necessary for the exercise of functions to be conferred on the Independent Barring Board under Sch 8) (SI 2007/3545) |
|  | 12 Oct 2009 (otherwise) (SI 2009/2611) |
| para 12(1)(b) | 11 Feb 2008 (in so far as necessary for the exercise of functions to be conferred on the Independent Barring Board under Sch 8) (SI 2007/3545) |
|  | 19 May 2008 (for the purposes of making orders) (SI 2008/1320) |
|  | 12 Oct 2009 (otherwise) (SI 2009/2611) |
| para 12(2), (3) | 11 Feb 2008 (in so far as necessary for the exercise of functions to be conferred on the Independent Barring Board under Sch 8) (SI 2007/3545) |
|  | 19 May 2008 (for the purposes of making orders) (SI 2008/1320) |
|  | 12 Oct 2009 (otherwise) (SI 2009/2611) |
| para 13 | 11 Feb 2008 (in so far as necessary for the exercise of functions to be conferred on the Independent Barring Board under Sch 8) (SI 2007/3545) |
|  | 12 Oct 2009 (otherwise) (SI 2009/2611) |
| para 14 | 11 Feb 2008 (in so far as necessary for the exercise of functions to be conferred on the Independent Barring Board under Sch 8) (SI 2007/3545) |
|  | 20 Jan 2009 (otherwise) (SI 2009/39) |
| para 15 | 31 Dec 2007 (SI 2007/3545) |
| para 16(1)–(4) | 11 Feb 2008 (in so far as necessary for the exercise of functions to be conferred on the Independent Barring Board under Sch 8) (SI 2007/3545) |
|  | 20 Jan 2009 (otherwise) (SI 2009/39) |
| para 16(5) | 11 Feb 2008 (in so far as necessary for the exercise of functions to be conferred on the Independent Barring Board under Sch 8) (SI 2007/3545) |
|  | 19 May 2008 (for the purposes of making orders) (SI 2008/1320) |
|  | 20 Jan 2009 (otherwise) (SI 2009/39) |
| para 17 | 11 Feb 2008 (in so far as necessary for the exercise of functions to be conferred on the Independent Barring Board under Sch 8) (SI 2007/3545) |

**Safeguarding Vulnerable Groups Act 2006 (c 47)**—*contd*

|  |  |
|---|---|
|  | 20 Jan 2009 (otherwise) (SI 2009/39) |
| para 18(1), (2) | 11 Feb 2008 (in so far as necessary for the exercise of functions to be conferred on the Independent Barring Board under Sch 8) (SI 2007/3545) |
|  | 20 Jan 2009 (otherwise) (SI 2009/39) |
| para 18(3)(a) | 11 Feb 2008 (in so far as necessary for the exercise of functions to be conferred on the Independent Barring Board under Sch 8) (SI 2007/3545) |
|  | 20 Jan 2009 (otherwise) (SI 2009/39) |
| para 18(3)(b) | 31 Dec 2007 (SI 2007/3545) |
| para 18(4), (5) | 11 Feb 2008 (in so far as necessary for the exercise of functions to be conferred on the Independent Barring Board under Sch 8) (SI 2007/3545) |
|  | 20 Jan 2009 (otherwise) (SI 2009/39) |
| para 18(6) | 31 Dec 2007 (SI 2007/3545) |
| para 19(1)(a) | 11 Feb 2008 (in so far as necessary for the exercise of functions to be conferred on the Independent Barring Board under Sch 8) (SI 2007/3545) |
|  | 20 Jan 2009 (otherwise) (SI 2009/39) |
| para 19(1)(b) | 1 Feb 2008 (in so far as necessary for the exercise of functions to be conferred on the Independent Barring Board under Sch 8) (SI 2007/3545) |
|  | 19 May 2008 (for the purposes of making regulations) (SI 2008/1320) |
|  | 20 Jan 2009 (otherwise) (SI 2009/39) |
| para 19(1)(c), (d) | 11 Feb 2008 (in so far as necessary for the exercise of functions to be conferred on the Independent Barring Board under Sch 8) (SI 2007/3545) |
|  | 20 Jan 2009 (otherwise) (SI 2009/39) |
| para 19(2)–(8) | 11 Feb 2008 (in so far as necessary for the exercise of functions to be conferred on the Independent Barring Board under Sch 8) (SI 2007/3545) |
|  | 20 Jan 2009 (otherwise) (SI 2009/39) |
| para 20 | 11 Feb 2008 (in so far as necessary for the exercise of functions to be conferred on the Independent Barring Board under Sch 8) (SI 2007/3545) |
|  | 20 Jan 2009 (otherwise) (SI 2009/39) |
| para 21(a) | 11 Feb 2008 (in so far as necessary for the exercise of functions to be conferred on the Independent Barring Board under Sch 8) (SI 2007/3545) |
|  | 19 May 2008 (for the purposes of making regulations) (SI 2008/1320) |
|  | 12 Oct 2009 (otherwise) (SI 2009/2611) |
| para 21(b), (c) | 11 Feb 2008 (in so far as necessary for the exercise of functions to be conferred on the Independent Barring Board under Sch 8) (SI 2007/3545) |
|  | 19 May 2008 (for the purposes of making regulations) (SI 2008/1320) |
|  | *Not yet in force* (otherwise) |
| paras 22, 23 | 11 Feb 2008 (in so far as necessary for the exercise of functions to be conferred on the Independent Barring Board under Sch 8) (SI 2007/3545) |
|  | 20 Jan 2009 (otherwise) (SI 2009/39) |
| para 24(1), (2) | 31 Dec 2007 (SI 2007/3545) |
| para 24(3)–(7) | 11 Feb 2008 (in so far as necessary for the exercise of functions to be conferred on the Independent Barring Board under Sch 8) (SI 2007/3545) |
|  | 20 Jan 2009 (otherwise) (SI 2009/39) |

**Safeguarding Vulnerable Groups Act 2006 (c 47)**—*contd*

| | | |
|---|---|---|
| | para 24(8) | 11 Feb 2008 (in so far as necessary for the exercise of functions to be conferred on the Independent Barring Board under Sch 8) (SI 2007/3545) |
| | | *Never in force* (otherwise) (repealed) |
| | para 24(9) | 31 Dec 2007 (SI 2007/3545) |
| | para 25 | 11 Feb 2008 (in so far as necessary for the exercise of functions to be conferred on the Independent Barring Board under Sch 8) (SI 2007/3545) |
| | | 20 Jan 2009 (otherwise) (SI 2009/39) |
| Sch 4 | para 1 | 11 Feb 2008 (in so far as necessary for the exercise of functions to be conferred on the Independent Barring Board under Sch 8) (SI 2007/3545) |
| | | 19 May 2008 (for the purposes of regulations made under the Childcare Act 2006, s 75) (SI 2008/1320) |
| | | 20 Jan 2009 (otherwise) (SI 2009/39) |
| | para 2(1)(a)–(e) | 11 Feb 2008 (in so far as necessary for the exercise of functions to be conferred on the Independent Barring Board under Sch 8) (SI 2007/3545) |
| | | 19 May 2008 (for the purposes of regulations made under the Childcare Act 2006, s 75) (SI 2008/1320) |
| | | 20 Jan 2009 (otherwise) (SI 2009/39) |
| | para 2(1)(f) | 11 Feb 2008 (in so far as necessary for the exercise of functions to be conferred on the Independent Barring Board under Sch 8) (SI 2007/3545) |
| | | 19 May 2008 (for the purposes of regulations made under the Childcare Act 2006, s 75 and for the purposes of making regulations hereunder) (SI 2008/1320) |
| | | 20 Jan 2009 (otherwise) (SI 2009/39) |
| | para 2(2)–(6) | 11 Feb 2008 (in so far as necessary for the exercise of functions to be conferred on the Independent Barring Board under Sch 8) (SI 2007/3545) |
| | | 19 May 2008 (for the purposes of regulations made under the Childcare Act 2006, s 75) (SI 2008/1320) |
| | | 20 Jan 2009 (otherwise) (SI 2009/39) |
| | paras 3–5 | 11 Feb 2008 (in so far as necessary for the exercise of functions to be conferred on the Independent Barring Board under Sch 8) (SI 2007/3545) |
| | | 19 May 2008 (for the purposes of regulations made under the Childcare Act 2006, s 75) (SI 2008/1320) |
| | | 20 Jan 2009 (otherwise) (SI 2009/39) |
| | para 6 | 11 Feb 2008 (in so far as necessary for the exercise of functions to be conferred on the Independent Barring Board under Sch 8) (SI 2007/3545) |
| | | 19 May 2008 (for the purposes of regulations made under the Childcare Act 2006, s 75 and for the purposes of making orders hereunder) (SI 2008/1320) |
| | | 20 Jan 2009 (otherwise) (SI 2009/39) |
| | para 7(1)(a)–(e) | 11 Feb 2008 (in so far as necessary for the exercise of functions to be conferred on the Independent Barring Board under Sch 8) (SI 2007/3545) |
| | | 19 May 2008 (for the purposes of regulations made under the Childcare Act 2006, s 75) (SI 2008/1320) |
| | | 20 Jan 2009 (otherwise) (SI 2009/39) |
| | para 7(1)(f) | 11 Feb 2008 (in so far as necessary for the exercise of functions to be conferred on the Independent Barring Board under Sch 8) (SI 2007/3545) |
| | | 19 May 2008 (for the purposes of regulations made under the Childcare Act 2006, s 75 and for the purposes of making regulations hereunder) (SI 2008/1320) |
| | | 20 Jan 2009 (otherwise) (SI 2009/39) |

**Safeguarding Vulnerable Groups Act 2006 (c 47)**—*contd*

| | | |
|---|---|---|
| | para 7(1)(g) | 11 Feb 2008 (in so far as necessary for the exercise of functions to be conferred on the Independent Barring Board under Sch 8) (SI 2007/3545) |
| | | 19 May 2008 (for the purposes of regulations made under the Childcare Act 2006, s 75) (SI 2008/1320) |
| | | 20 Jan 2009 (otherwise) (SI 2009/39) |
| | para 7(2)–(10) | 11 Feb 2008 (in so far as necessary for the exercise of functions to be conferred on the Independent Barring Board under Sch 8) (SI 2007/3545) |
| | | 19 May 2008 (for the purposes of regulations made under the Childcare Act 2006, s 75) (SI 2008/1320) |
| | | 20 Jan 2009 (otherwise) (SI 2009/39) |
| | para 8 | 11 Feb 2008 (in so far as necessary for the exercise of functions to be conferred on the Independent Barring Board under Sch 8) (SI 2007/3545) |
| | | 19 May 2008 (for the purposes of regulations made under the Childcare Act 2006, s 75) (SI 2008/1320) |
| | | 20 Jan 2009 (otherwise) (SI 2009/39) |
| | para 9 | 11 Feb 2008 (in so far as necessary for the exercise of functions to be conferred on the Independent Barring Board under Sch 8) (SI 2007/3545) |
| | | 19 May 2008 (for the purposes of regulations made under the Childcare Act 2006, s 75 and for the purposes of making orders hereunder) (SI 2008/1320) |
| | | 20 Jan 2009 (otherwise) (SI 2009/39) |
| | para 10 | 11 Feb 2008 (in so far as necessary for the exercise of functions to be conferred on the Independent Barring Board under Sch 8) (SI 2007/3545) |
| | | 19 May 2008 (for the purposes of regulations made under the Childcare Act 2006, s 75) (SI 2008/1320) |
| | | 20 Jan 2009 (otherwise) (SI 2009/39) |
| Sch 5 | para 1(1) | 19 May 2008 (for the purposes of making regulations) (SI 2008/1320) |
| | | *Never in force* (otherwise) (repealed) |
| | para 1(2) | *Never in force* (otherwise) (repealed) |
| | para 2(1)(a) | 19 May 2008 (for the purposes of making regulations) (SI 2008/1320) |
| | | *Never in force* (otherwise) (repealed) |
| | para 2(1)(b), (c) | *Never in force* (otherwise) (repealed) |
| | para 2(2) | *Never in force* (otherwise) (repealed) |
| | para 3(1)(a), (b) | *Never in force* (otherwise) (repealed) |
| | para 3(1)(c) | 19 May 2008 (for the purposes of making regulations) (SI 2008/1320) |
| | | *Never in force* (otherwise) (repealed) |
| | para 3(2) | 19 May 2008 (for the purposes of making regulations) (SI 2008/1320) |
| | | *Never in force* (otherwise) (repealed) |
| | para 4(1)(a), (b) | *Never in force* (repealed) |
| | para 4(1)(c) | 19 May 2008 (for the purposes of making regulations) (SI 2008/1320) |
| | | *Never in force* (repealed) |
| | para 4(2) | 19 May 2008 (for the purposes of making regulations) (SI 2008/1320) |
| | | *Never in force* (repealed) |
| | para 5 | 19 May 2008 (for the purposes of making regulations) (SI 2008/1320) |
| | | *Never in force* (repealed) |
| | para 6(1)(a), (b) | *Never in force* (repealed) |
| | para 6(1)(c), (2) | 19 May 2008 (for the purposes of making regulations) (SI 2008/1320) |

**Safeguarding Vulnerable Groups Act 2006 (c 47)**—*contd*

|         |                      |                                                                                      |
|---------|----------------------|--------------------------------------------------------------------------------------|
|         |                      | *Never in force* (otherwise) (repealed)                                               |
|         | para 6(3)            | *Never in force* (repealed)                                                           |
|         | para 7(1)(a), (b)    | *Never in force* (repealed)                                                           |
|         | para 7(1)(c), (2)    | 19 May 2008 (for the purposes of making regulations) (SI 2008/1320)                  |
|         |                      | *Never in force* (otherwise) (repealed)                                               |
|         | para 7(3)            | *Never in force* (repealed)                                                           |
|         | para 8               | 19 May 2008 (for the purposes of making regulations) (SI 2008/1320)                  |
|         |                      | *Never in force* (otherwise) (repealed)                                               |
|         | para 9(1)(a), (b)    | *Never in force* (repealed)                                                           |
|         | para 9(1)(c)         | 19 May 2008 (for the purposes of making regulations) (SI 2008/1320)                  |
|         |                      | *Never in force* (otherwise) (repealed)                                               |
|         | para 9(2)            | 19 May 2008 (for the purposes of making regulations) (SI 2008/1320)                  |
|         |                      | *Never in force* (otherwise) (repealed)                                               |
|         | para 9(3)            | *Never in force* (repealed)                                                           |
|         | para 10(1)(a), (b)   | *Never in force* (repealed)                                                           |
|         | para 10(1)(c), (2)   | 19 May 2008 (for the purposes of making regulations) (SI 2008/1320)                  |
|         |                      | *Never in force* (otherwise) (repealed)                                               |
|         | para 10(3)           | *Never in force* (repealed)                                                           |
|         | paras 11–13          | *Never in force* (repealed)                                                           |
|         | para 14              | 19 May 2008 (for the purposes of making orders) (SI 2008/1320)                       |
|         |                      | *Never in force* (otherwise) (repealed)                                               |
| Sch 6   | para 1               | *Never in force* (repealed)                                                           |
|         | para 2(1)            | 19 May 2008 (for the purposes of making regulations) (SI 2008/1320)                  |
|         |                      | *Never in force* (otherwise) (repealed)                                               |
|         | para 2(2)–(4)        | *Never in force* (repealed)                                                           |
|         | paras 3, 4           | *Never in force* (repealed)                                                           |
|         | para 5               | 19 May 2008 (for the purposes of making orders) (SI 2008/1320)                       |
|         |                      | *Never in force* (otherwise) (repealed)                                               |
|         | para 6               | *Never in force* (repealed)                                                           |
| Sch 7   | para 1               | 19 May 2008 (for the purposes of making regulations) (SI 2008/1320)                  |
|         |                      | In force on the day on which the Protection of Freedoms Act 2012, s 72 comes into force for the purposes of inserting s 30A of this Act (otherwise) (SI 2012/2231) |
|         | para 2               | 19 May 2008 (for the purposes of making orders) (SI 2008/1320)                       |
|         |                      | In force on the day on which the Protection of Freedoms Act 2012, s 72 comes into force for the purposes of inserting s 30A of this Act (otherwise) (SI 2012/2231) |
|         | paras 3–6            | In force on the day on which the Protection of Freedoms Act 2012, s 72 comes into force for the purposes of inserting s 30A of this Act (SI 2012/2231) |
| Sch 8   | para 1               | 11 Feb 2008 (in so far as necessary for the exercise of functions to be conferred on the Independent Barring Board under Sch 8) (SI 2007/3545) |
|         |                      | *Not yet in force* (otherwise)                                                        |
|         | paras 2–4            | 31 Dec 2007 (for the purposes of making orders) (SI 2007/3545)                       |
|         |                      | 11 Feb 2008 (in so far as necessary for the exercise of functions to be conferred on the Independent Barring Board under Sch 8) (SI 2007/3545) |
|         |                      | *Not yet in force* (otherwise)                                                        |
|         | para 5               | 11 Feb 2008 (in so far as necessary for the exercise of functions to be conferred on the Independent Barring Board under Sch 8) (SI 2007/3545) |
|         |                      | *Never in force* (otherwise) (repealed)                                               |

**Safeguarding Vulnerable Groups Act 2006 (c 47)**—*contd*

| | | |
|---|---|---|
| Sch 9 | para 1 | 12 Oct 2009 (SI 2009/2611) |
| | para 2 | See paras 3–7 below |
| | paras 3, 4 | 12 Oct 2009 (SI 2009/2611) |
| | para 5(1) | See sub-paras (2)–(7) below |
| | para 5(2), (3) | 17 Dec 2008 (E) (for the purposes of making regulations) (SI 2008/3204) |
| | | 20 Jan 2009 (E) (otherwise) (SI 2009/39) |
| | | 12 Oct 2009 (W) (SI 2009/2611) |
| | para 5(4) | 17 Dec 2008 (for the purposes of making regulations) (SI 2008/3204) |
| | | 20 Jan 2009 (otherwise) (SI 2009/39) |
| | para 5(5) | 12 Oct 2009 (SI 2009/2611) |
| | para 5(6), (7) | 17 Dec 2008 (E) (for the purposes of making regulations) (SI 2008/3204) |
| | | 20 Jan 2009 (E) (otherwise) (SI 2009/39) |
| | | 12 Oct 2009 (W) (SI 2009/2611) |
| | para 6(1) | See sub-paras (2)–(6) below |
| | para 6(2), (3) | 17 Dec 2008 (E) (for the purposes of making regulations) (SI 2008/3204) |
| | | 20 Jan 2009 (E) (otherwise) (SI 2009/39) |
| | | 12 Oct 2009 (W) (SI 2009/2611) |
| | para 6(4) | 17 Dec 2008 (for the purposes of making regulations) (SI 2008/3204) |
| | | 20 Jan 2009 (otherwise) (SI 2009/39) |
| | para 6(5) | 12 Oct 2009 (SI 2009/2611) |
| | para 6(6) | 17 Dec 2008 (E) (for the purposes of making regulations) (SI 2008/3204) |
| | | 20 Jan 2009 (E) (otherwise) (SI 2009/39) |
| | | 12 Oct 2009 (W) (SI 2009/2611) |
| | para 7 | 17 Dec 2008 (E) (for the purposes of making regulations) (SI 2008/3204) |
| | | 20 Jan 2009 (E) (otherwise) (SI 2009/39) |
| | | 12 Oct 2009 (W) (SI 2009/2611) |
| | paras 8, 9 | 12 Oct 2009 (SI 2009/2611) |
| | para 10 | 19 May 2008 (SI 2008/1320) |
| | paras 11–13 | 12 Oct 2009 (SI 2009/2611) |
| | para 14(1) | 22 Jun 2009 (for the purposes of making regulations) (SI 2009/1503) |
| | | 12 Oct 2009 (otherwise) (SI 2009/2610; SI 2009/2611) |
| | para 14(2), (3) | 12 Oct 2009 (SI 2009/2610; SI 2009/2611) |
| | para 14(4) | 22 Jun 2009 (for the purposes of making regulations) (SI 2009/1503) |
| | | 12 Oct 2009 (otherwise) (SI 2009/2610; SI 2009/2611) |
| | para 14(5)–(7) | 12 Oct 2009 (SI 2009/2610; SI 2009/2611) |
| | para 15 | 19 May 2008 (SI 2008/1320) |
| | para 16 | 12 Oct 2009 (SI 2009/2611) |
| Sch 10 | | 12 Oct 2009 (repeals of Police Act 1997, ss 113C, 113D, 113F) (SI 2009/2610) |
| | | 12 Oct 2009 (SI 2009/2611)[3], repeals of or in— |
| | | Teaching and Higher Education Act 1998, s 15(4); |
| | | Protection of Children Act 1999 (except s 9(2)(e)); |
| | | Care Standards Act 2000; |
| | | Criminal Justice and Court Services Act 2000, repeals of Sch 7, paras 155, 157 (in so far as relates to the Protection of Children Act 1999, s 9(2)(a)–(d)), 158 are brought completely into force, repeals of or in ss 24, 26–38, 42, Sch 4, Sch 7, para 157 (except as noted above) are brought into force for certain purposes only[1]; |

**Safeguarding Vulnerable Groups Act 2006 (c 47)**—*contd*

> Education Act 2002, repeals of Sch 21, paras 121, 122(a), 123
> are brought completely into force, repeals of or in ss 142–144,
> Sch 21, paras 75, 76, 86, 128 are brought into force for certain
> purposes only[2];
> Health and Social Care (Community Health and Standards)
> Act 2003;
> Inquiries Act 2005
> 30 Mar 2010 (SI 2010/1101), repeals of or in—
> Criminal Justice and Court Services Act 2000, in so far as not
> already repealed, for certain purposes only[4]
> In force on the day on which the Protection of Freedoms
> Act 2012, s 83 comes into force (SI 2012/2231), repeals of or
> in—
> Criminal Justice and Court Services Act 2000, in so far as not
> already repealed, for remaining purposes (except repeal of s 38)[5]
> *Not yet in force*, repeals of or in—
> Children Act 1989;
> Police Act 1997, s 113E;
> Teaching and Higher Education Act 1998, ss 2, 3;
> Protection of Children Act 1999, s 9(2)(e);
> Criminal Justice and Court Services Act 2000, s 38, except as
> noted above;
> Education Act 2002, ss 142–144, Sch 21, paras 75, 76, 86, 128,
> except as noted above;
> Adoption and Children Act 2002;
> Criminal Justice Act 2003;
> Children Act 2004;
> Civil Partnership Act 2004;
> Constitutional Reform Act 2005;
> Serious Organised Crime and Police Act 2005;
> Childcare Act 2006

[1] These provisions shall cease to have effect for the purposes of enabling a disqualification order to be made in relation to a person who is barred from regulated activity by virtue of section 3(2) of the 2006 Act

Section 35 of the 2000 Act shall cease to have effect for the purpose of making it an offence for a person knowingly to apply for, to offer to do, to accept or to do any work in a regulated position (within the meaning of section 36 of that Act) where—

(a) the person ("P")—
  (i) is or has at any time been barred from regulated activity by virtue of section 3(2) of the 2006 Act; or
  (ii) has been included in the children's barred list pursuant to article 2(2)(a) of the Safeguarding Vulnerable Groups Act 2006 (Transitional Provisions) Order 2008, SI 2008/473, but is removed from that list by IBB in accordance with paragraph 2(4) of that Order; and

(b) P is disqualified from working with children only by reason of a disqualification order, P was subject to the disqualification order immediately before IBB (as defined by s 1 of the 2006 Act) included P in the children's barred list, and at that time IBB was aware that P was subject to the disqualification order

[2] These provisions shall be repealed for all purposes, except that they shall continue to have effect for the purpose of enabling the Secretary of State to make a direction under section 142(1)(a) of the 2002 Act where—

(a) the effect of the direction is to prevent a person from taking part in the management of an independent school, and

(b) the direction is made on grounds relating to a person's misconduct pursuant to section 142(4)(c) of that Act

[3] For transitional provisions and savings, see SI 2009/2611, arts 5–7

[4] These provisions shall cease to have effect for the following purposes—

**Safeguarding Vulnerable Groups Act 2006 (c 47)**—*contd*

Section 35 of the 2000 Act shall cease to have effect for the purpose of making it an offence for a person knowingly to—
    (i)  offer work in a regulated position to,
    (ii)  procure work in a position for, or
    (iii)  fail to remove from a regulated position
a person falling within paragraph (a)

(a)  A person ("P") falls within this paragraph if P is disqualified from working with children only by reason of a disqualification order falling within paragraph (b) and P—
    (i)  is or has at any time been barred from regulated activity relating to children by virtue of section 3(2) of this Act, or
    (ii)  has been included in the children's barred list pursuant to article 2(2)(a) of the Safeguarding Vulnerable Groups Act 2006 (Transitional Provisions) Order 2008, SI 2008/473, but is removed from that list by the ISA in accordance with article 2(4) of that Order

(b)  A disqualification order falls within this paragraph if—
    (i)  P was subject to the disqualification order immediately before ISA included P in the children's barred list, and
    (ii)  at that time ISA was aware that P was subject to the disqualification order

[5]  For savings, see SI 2012/2231, art 5

---

## Scottish Commission for Human Rights Act 2006 (asp 16)

*RA:* 8 Dec 2006

*Commencement provisions:* s 22(3); Scottish Commission for Human Rights Act 2006 (Commencement No 1) Order 2007, SSI 2007/448; Scottish Commission for Human Rights Act 2006 (Commencement No 2) Order 2008, SSI 2008/112

| | | |
|---|---|---|
| 1 | (1) | 1 Apr 2008 (SSI 2008/112) |
| | (2) | See Sch 1 below |
| 2–6 | | 1 Apr 2008 (SSI 2008/112) |
| 7 | | 8 Nov 2007 (SSI 2007/448) |
| 8–20 | | 1 Apr 2008 (SSI 2008/112) |
| 21, 22 | | 8 Dec 2006 (s 22(3)) |
| Sch 1 | paras 1–15 | 8 Nov 2007 (SSI 2007/448) |
| | paras 16, 17 | 1 Apr 2008 (SSI 2008/112) |
| Schs 2, 3 | | 1 Apr 2008 (SSI 2008/112) |

---

## Scottish Schools (Parental Involvement) Act 2006 (asp 8)

*RA:* 14 Jun 2006

*Commencement provisions:* s 24(2); Scottish Schools (Parental Involvement) Act 2006 (Commencement No 1) Order 2006, SSI 2006/454; Scottish Schools (Parental Involvement) Act 2006 (Commencement No 2) Order 2007, SSI 2007/31

| | | |
|---|---|---|
| 1 | | 12 Sep 2006 (SSI 2006/454) |
| 2–4 | | 1 Aug 2007 (SSI 2007/31) |
| 5 | | 12 Sep 2006 (SSI 2006/454) |
| 6 | (1)–(6) | 12 Sep 2006 (SSI 2006/454) |
| | (7)–(10) | 1 Aug 2007 (SSI 2007/31) |
| 7 | | 12 Sep 2006 (SSI 2006/454) |
| 8–11 | | 1 Aug 2007 (SSI 2007/31) |
| 12 | | 12 Sep 2006 (SSI 2006/454) |
| 13 | | 1 Aug 2007 (SSI 2007/31) |
| 14 | | 5 Feb 2007 (for the purpose of enabling regulations to be made to come into force not earlier than 1 Aug 2007) (SSI 2007/31) |
| | | 1 Aug 2007 (otherwise) (SSI 2007/31) |
| 15 | | 1 Aug 2007 (SSI 2007/31) |
| 16 | (1)–(7) | 12 Sep 2006 (SSI 2006/454) |

### Scottish Schools (Parental Involvement) Act 2006 (asp 8)—*contd*

|  |  |  |
|---|---|---|
| | (8)–(12) | 1 Aug 2007 (SSI 2007/31) |
| | (13), (14) | 12 Sep 2006 (SSI 2006/454) |
| | (15), (16) | 1 Aug 2007 (SSI 2007/31) |
| 17, 18 | | 1 Aug 2007 (SSI 2007/31) |
| 19–22 | | 12 Sep 2006 (SSI 2006/454) |
| 23 | | See Schedule below |
| 24 | | 14 Jun 2006 (RA) |
| Schedule | | 5 Feb 2007 (repeals of or in Education (Scotland) Act 1980, ss 87A, 87B) (SSI 2007/31) |
| | | 1 Aug 2007 (otherwise) (SSI 2007/31) |

### Senior Judiciary (Vacancies and Incapacity) (Scotland) Act 2006 (asp 9)

*RA:* 27 Jun 2006

Whole Act in force 27 Jun 2006 (RA)

### Terrorism Act 2006 (c 11)

*RA:* 30 Mar 2006

*Commencement provisions:* s 39(2); Terrorism Act 2006 (Commencement No 1) Order 2006, SI 2006/1013; Terrorism Act 2006 (Commencement No 2) Order 2006, SI 2006/1936

|  |  |  |
|---|---|---|
| 1–22 | | 13 Apr 2006 (SI 2006/1013) |
| 23–25 | | 25 Jul 2006 (SI 2006/1936) |
| 26–36 | | 13 Apr 2006 (SI 2006/1013) |
| 37 | (1)–(4) | 13 Apr 2006 (SI 2006/1013) |
| | (5) | See Sch 3 below |
| 38 | | 13 Apr 2006 (SI 2006/1013) |
| 39 | | 30 Mar 2006 (RA) |
| Schs 1, 2 | | 13 Apr 2006 (SI 2006/1013) |
| Sch 3 | | 13 Apr 2006 (except repeals of or in Terrorism Act 2000, Sch 8, para 36(1); Criminal Justice Act 2003, s 306(2), (3)) (SI 2006/1013) |
| | | 25 Jul 2006 (exceptions noted above) (SI 2006/1936) |

### Terrorism (Northern Ireland) Act 2006 (c 4)

*RA:* 16 Feb 2006

*Commencement provisions:* s 5(3)

Whole Act in force 18 Feb 2006 (s 5(3))

### Tourist Boards (Scotland) Act 2006 (asp 15)

*RA:* 30 Nov 2006

*Commencement provisions:* s 5(1); Tourist Boards (Scotland) Act 2006 (Commencement) Order 2007, SSI 2007/47

|  |  |  |
|---|---|---|
| 1, 2 | | 1 Apr 2007 (SSI 2007/47) |
| 3 | (1), (2) | 1 Apr 2007 (SSI 2007/47) |
| | (3) | See Sch 1 below |
| 4 | | See Sch 2 below |
| 5 | | 30 Nov 2006 (s 5(1)) |
| Schs 1, 2 | | 1 Apr 2007 (SSI 2007/47) |

## Transport (Wales) Act 2006 (c 5)

*RA:* 16 Feb 2006

*Commencement provisions:* s 12; Transport (Wales) Act 2006 (Commencement) Order 2006, SI 2006/1403

| | |
|---|---|
| 1–11 | 26 May 2006 (SI 2006/1403) |
| 12–17 | 16 Feb 2006 (RA) |
| Schedule | 26 May 2006 (SI 2006/1403) |

## Violent Crime Reduction Act 2006 (c 38)

*RA:* 8 Nov 2006

*Commencement provisions:* s 66(2), (3); Violent Crime Reduction Act 2006 (Commencement No 1) Order 2007, SI 2007/74; Violent Crime Reduction Act 2006 (Commencement No 2) Order 2007, SI 2007/858; Violent Crime Reduction Act 2006 (Commencement No 3) Order 2007, SI 2007/2180; Violent Crime Reduction Act 2006 (Commencement No 4) Order 2007, SI 2007/2518; Violent Crime Reduction Act 2006 (Commencement No 5) Order 2008, SI 2008/791; Violent Crime Reduction Act 2006 (Commencement No 6) Order 2008, SI 2008/1407; Violent Crime Reduction Act 2006 (Commencement No 7) Order 2009, SI 2009/1840; Violent Crime Reduction Act 2006 (Commencement No 8) Order 2010, SI 2010/469; Violent Crime Reduction Act 2006 (Commencement No 1) (Wales) Order 2010, SI 2010/2426; Violent Crime Reduction Act 2006 (Commencement No 9) Order 2010, SI 2010/2541

| | | |
|---|---|---|
| 1–5 | | 31 Aug 2009 (SI 2009/1840) |
| 6–8 | | 1 Apr 2010 (in relation to proceedings in magistrates' courts in specified local justice areas[1]) (SI 2010/469) |
| | | 1 Nov 2010 (in relation to proceedings in magistrates' courts in the specified local justice areas[2]) (SI 2010/2541) |
| | | *Never in force* (otherwise) |
| 9–14 | | 31 Aug 2009 (so far as they relate to a drinking banning order under s 3 or 4 of this Act) (SI 2009/1840) |
| | | 1 Apr 2010 (in relation to proceedings in magistrates' courts in specified local justice areas[1]) (SI 2010/469) |
| | | 1 Nov 2010 (in relation to proceedings in magistrates' courts in the specified local justice areas[2]) (SI 2010/2541) |
| | | *Never in force* (otherwise) |
| 15–20 | | 5 Jun 2008 (SI 2008/1407) |
| 21, 22 | | 1 Oct 2007 (SI 2007/2180) |
| 23, 24 | | 6 Apr 2007 (SI 2007/858) |
| 25 | | 8 Nov 2006 (s 66(2)(b)) |
| 26 | | 6 Apr 2007 (SI 2007/858) |
| 27 | | 22 Aug 2007 (SI 2007/2180) |
| 28–30 | | 6 Apr 2007 (SI 2007/858) |
| 31 | (1), (2) | 1 Oct 2007 (SI 2007/2180) |
| | (3) | 6 Apr 2007 (in so far as it makes provisions for the interpretation of the Firearms Act 1968, ss 33–39, 45, 56 (in so far as it applies to a notice required or authorised by s 36 or 38 of that Act), Sch 5, and s 57(4) (definition "registered" as that term applies to those provisions)) (SI 2007/858) |
| | | 1 Oct 2007 (otherwise) (SI 2007/2180) |
| 32–34 | | 1 Oct 2007 (SI 2007/2180) |
| 35 | | 6 Apr 2007 (SI 2007/858) |
| 36–40 | | 1 Oct 2007 (SI 2007/2180) |
| 41 | | 1 Oct 2007 (SI 2007/2518) |
| 42 | | 12 Feb 2007 (SI 2007/74) |
| 43 | (1), (2) | 1 Oct 2007 (SI 2007/2180) |
| | (3) | 6 Apr 2008 (SI 2008/791) |
| | (4) | 1 Apr 2008 (in so far as inserts the Criminal Justice Act 1988, s 141(11D), (11E)) (SI 2008/791) |

**Violent Crime Reduction Act 2006 (c 38)**—*contd*

|  |  |  |
|---|---|---|
|  |  | 6 Apr 2008 (in so far as inserts s 141(11A)–(11C) of that Act) (SI 2008/791) |
|  | (5) | 6 Apr 2008 (SI 2008/791) |
| 44 |  | 1 Oct 2007 (SI 2007/2180) |
| 45, 46 |  | 31 May 2007 (E) (SI 2007/858) |
|  |  | 31 Oct 2010 (W) (SI 2010/2426) |
| 47 |  | 1 Oct 2007 (SI 2007/2180) |
| 48 |  | 31 May 2007 (SI 2007/858) |
| 49 |  | See Sch 1 below |
| 50 | (1), (2) | 6 Apr 2007 (SI 2007/858) |
|  | (3) | 6 Apr 2007 (in so far as it makes provision for the Firearms Act 1968, ss 46, 51(4), 52, 58 to apply as if ss 28, 29, 35 of this Act were contained in that Act) (SI 2007/858) |
|  |  | 1 Oct 2007 (otherwise) (SI 2007/2180) |
|  | (4)(a), (b) | 6 Apr 2007 (SI 2007/858) |
|  | (4)(c) | 1 Oct 2007 (SI 2007/2180) |
|  | (4)(d) | 6 Apr 2007 (in so far as it relates to ss 28, 29 of this Act) (SI 2007/858) |
|  |  | 1 Oct 2007 (otherwise) (SI 2007/2180) |
|  | (5) | 6 Apr 2007 (SI 2007/858) |
| 51 |  | See Sch 2 below |
| 52, 53 |  | 6 Apr 2007 (SI 2007/858) |
| 54 |  | See Sch 4 below |
| 55 |  | 12 Feb 2007 (SI 2007/74) |
| 56 |  | 8 Nov 2006 (s 66(2)(c)) |
| 57 |  | 12 Feb 2007 (SI 2007/74) |
| 58 |  | 31 May 2007 (SI 2007/858) |
| 59 |  | 6 Apr 2008 (SI 2008/791) |
| 60 |  | 8 Nov 2006 (s 66(2)(d)) |
| 61 |  | *Never in force* (repealed) |
| 62 |  | 6 Apr 2007 (SI 2007/858) |
| 63 |  | 8 Nov 2006 (s 66(2)(e)) |
| 64 |  | 1 Oct 2007 (SI 2007/2180) |
| 65 |  | See Sch 5 below |
| 66 |  | 8 Nov 2006 (s 66(2)(a)) |
| Sch 1 |  | 6 Apr 2007 (SI 2007/858) |
| Sch 2 | paras 1–3 | 6 Apr 2007 (SI 2007/858) |
|  | paras 4–8 | 1 Oct 2007 (SI 2007/2180) |
|  | para 9 | 1 Oct 2007 (SI 2007/2518) |
|  | para 10 | 1 Oct 2007 (SI 2007/2180) |
|  | para 11(1) | 1 Apr 2008 (SI 2008/791) |
|  | para 11(2) | 6 Apr 2008 (SI 2008/791) |
|  | para 11(3) | 1 Apr 2008 (in so far as inserts the Criminal Justice Act 1988, s 141(11D), (11E)) (SI 2008/791) |
|  |  | 6 Apr 2008 (in so far as inserts s 141(11A)–(11C) of that Act) (SI 2008/791) |
|  | para 11(4) | 6 Apr 2008 (SI 2008/791) |
|  | para 12 | 1 Oct 2007 (SI 2007/2180) |
|  | para 13 | 31 May 2007 (SI 2007/858) |
|  | para 14(1), (2) | 6 Apr 2007 (SI 2007/858) |
|  | para 14(3) | 6 Apr 2007 (in so far as it makes provision for the Firearms (Northern Ireland) Order 2004, arts 52, 69(4), 72, 81 to apply as if Sch 2, paras 1, 2 of this Act were contained in that Order) (SI 2007/858) |
|  |  | 1 Oct 2007 (otherwise) (SI 2007/2180) |
|  | para 14(4)(a) | 1 Oct 2007 (SI 2007/2180) |
|  | para 14(4)(b) | 6 Apr 2007 (in so far as it relates to Sch 2, paras 1, 2 of this Act) (SI 2007/858) |
|  |  | 1 Oct 2007 (otherwise) (SI 2007/2180) |

**Violent Crime Reduction Act 2006 (c 38)**—*contd*

| | |
|---|---|
| Sch 3 | 6 Apr 2007 (SI 2007/858) |
| Sch 4 | 12 Feb 2007 (SI 2007/74) |
| Sch 5 | 8 Nov 2006 (repeal in Crime and Disorder Act 1998, s 18) (s 66(2)(d)) |

6 Apr 2007 (SI 2007/858), repeals of or in—
Firearms Act 1968, s 51A;
Magistrates' Courts Act 1980;
Mental Health Act 1983;
Criminal Justice Act 1988, s 36;
Football Spectators Act 1989;
Criminal Justice and Public Order Act 1994, s 166;
Data Protection Act 1998;
Crime and Disorder Act 1998, s 51A;
Football (Offences and Disorder) Act 1999;
Access to Justice Act 1999, Sch 13, para 158;
Powers of Criminal Courts (Sentencing) Act 2000, s 164;
Football (Disorder) Act 2000;
Football (Disorder) (Amendment) Act 2002;
Mobile Telephones (Reprogramming) Act 2002;
Anti-social Behaviour Act 2003, s 37;
Courts Act 2003, Sch 8, para 331;
Criminal Justice Act 2003, s 150, Sch 26, para 41

1 Oct 2007 (SI 2007/2180), repeals of or in—
Firearms Act 1968 (in so far as not already in force);
Anti-social Behaviour Act 2003, s 38

1 Oct 2007 (repeals of or in Criminal Justice and Public Order Act 1994, Sch 8, Pt 3) (SI 2007/2518)

1 Apr 2008 (repeals of or in Criminal Justice Act 1988, s 141) (SI 2008/791)

*Not yet in force*, repeals of or in—
Licensed Premises (Exclusion of Certain Persons) Act 1980;
Criminal Justice Act 1991;
Criminal Procedure (Consequential Provisions) (Scotland) Act 1995;
Access to Justice Act 1999, Sch 13, para 94;
Powers of Criminal Courts (Sentencing) Act 2000, Sch 9;
Licensing Act 2003;
Courts Act 2003, Sch 8, unnumbered para after para 200;
Criminal Justice Act 2003, Sch 26, para 27

[1]    The specified local justice areas are: Cardiff; Central and South West Staffordshire; City of London; City of Salford; Corby; Coventry District; Doncaster; East Dorset; East Kent; Fylde Coast; Hackney and Tower Hamlets; Halton; Hull and Holderness; Leicester; Lincoln District; North Staffordshire; Nottingham; Reading; South Devon; South East Hampshire; Southampton; Southern Derbyshire; Sussex (Central); Teesside; Wakefield

[2]    The specified local justice areas are: Birmingham; Bristol; Burnley, Pendle and Rossendale; City of Westminster; Denbighshire; East Berkshire; Fenland; Grimsby and Cleethorpes; Gwent; Hammersmith and Fulham and Kensington and Chelsea; Hartlepool; Lambeth and Southwark; Manchester City; Mansfield; Merthyr Tydfil; Newcastle-upon-Tyne District; North East Derbyshire and Dales; North East Suffolk; North Kent; North Tyneside District; Northampton; Plymouth District; Sedgemoor; West Cornwall; West Hertfordshire

---

**Waverley Railway (Scotland) Act 2006 (asp 13)**

*RA:* 24 Jul 2006

Whole Act in force 24 Jul 2006 (RA)

---

## Wireless Telegraphy Act 2006 (c 36)

*RA:* 8 Nov 2006

*Commencement provisions:* s 126(2)

Whole Act in force 8 Feb 2007 (s 126(2))

---

## Work and Families Act 2006 (c 18)

*RA:* 21 Jun 2006

*Commencement provisions:* s 19; Work and Families Act 2006 (Commencement No 1) Order 2006, SI 2006/1682; Work and Families Act 2006 (Commencement No 2) Order 2006, SI 2006/2232; Work and Families Act 2006 (Commencement No 3) Order 2010, SI 2010/128 (revoked by SI 2010/495); Work and Families Act 2006 (Commencement No 4) Order 2010, SI 2010/495

| | | |
|---|---|---|
| 1 | | 27 Jun 2006 (for the purpose of the power in Social Security Contributions and Benefits Act 1992, s 165(1) to prescribe the maternity pay period) (SI 2006/1682) |
| | | 1 Oct 2006 (otherwise) (SI 2006/1682) |
| 2 | | 27 Jun 2006 (for the purpose of the power in Social Security Contributions and Benefits Act 1992, s 171ZN(2) to prescribe the adoption pay period) (SI 2006/1682) |
| | | 1 Oct 2006 (otherwise) (SI 2006/1682) |
| 3–10 | | 3 Mar 2010 (SI 2010/495) |
| 11 | (1) | See Sch 1 below |
| | (2), (3) | 6 Apr 2010 (SI 2010/495) |
| 12 | | 6 Apr 2007 (SI 2006/1682) |
| 13, 14 | | 1 Oct 2006 (SI 2006/1682) |
| 15 | | See Sch 2 below |
| 16–20 | | 21 Jun 2006 (s 19(1)) |
| Sch 1 | paras 1–5 | 6 Apr 2010 (SI 2010/495) |
| | paras 6, 7 | 27 Jun 2006 (for the purpose of the powers to prescribe matters by regulations) (SI 2006/1682) |
| | | 1 Oct 2006 (otherwise) (SI 2006/1682) |
| | para 8 | 1 Oct 2006 (SI 2006/1682) |
| | para 9 | 27 Jun 2006 (for the purpose of the powers to prescribe matters by regulations) (SI 2006/1682) |
| | | 1 Oct 2006 (otherwise) (SI 2006/1682) |
| | paras 10–15 | 6 Apr 2010 (SI 2010/495) |
| | para 16(1) | See sub-paras (2), (3) below |
| | para 16(2) | 6 Apr 2010 (SI 2010/495) |
| | para 16(3) | 1 Oct 2006 (SI 2006/2232) |
| | paras 17, 18 | 6 Apr 2010 (SI 2010/495) |
| | paras 19, 20 | 3 Mar 2010 (SI 2010/495) |
| | para 21 | 27 Jun 2006 (for the purpose of the powers to prescribe matters by regulations) (SI 2006/1682) |
| | | 1 Oct 2006 (otherwise) (SI 2006/1682) |
| | para 22 | 3 Mar 2010 (SI 2010/495) |
| | para 23 | 1 Oct 2006 (SI 2006/1682) |
| | para 24 | 3 Mar 2010 (SI 2010/495) |
| | paras 25–29 | 6 Apr 2010 (SI 2010/495) |
| | para 30 | 3 Mar 2010 (SI 2010/495) |
| | paras 31–34 | 27 Jun 2006 (for the purpose of the powers to prescribe matters by regulations) (SI 2006/1682) |
| | | 1 Oct 2006 (otherwise) (SI 2006/1682) |
| | paras 35, 36 | 6 Apr 2010 (SI 2010/495) |
| | paras 37, 38 | 3 Mar 2010 (SI 2010/495) |
| | paras 39, 40 | 6 Apr 2010 (SI 2010/495 |
| | para 41 | 3 Mar 2010 (SI 2010/495) |
| | para 42 | 6 Apr 2010 (SI 2010/495) |

**Work and Families Act 2006 (c 18)**—*contd*

| | | |
|---|---|---|
| | paras 43, 44 | 3 Mar 2010 (SI 2010/495) |
| | para 45 | 6 Apr 2010 (SI 2010/495) |
| | paras 46 | 3 Mar 2010 (SI 2010/495) |
| | paras 47–49 | 6 Apr 2010 (SI 2010/495) |
| | paras 50–52 | 3 Mar 2010 (SI 2010/495) |
| | paras 53–61 | 6 Apr 2010 (SI 2010/495) |
| Sch 2 | | 1 Oct 2006 (SI 2006/1682), repeals of or in— |
| | | Social Security Contributions and Benefits Act 1992; |
| | | Employment Act 2002, s 18 |
| | | 6 Apr 2007 (repeals in Employment Rights Act 1996) |
| | | (SI 2006/1682) |
| | | 6 Apr 2010 (SI 2010/495), repeals of or in— |
| | | Employment Act 2002, s 6, Sch 7; |
| | | Income Tax (Earnings and Pensions) Act 2003 |

# 2007 Acts

## Adoption and Children (Scotland) Act 2007 (asp 4)

*RA:* 15 Jan 2007

*Commencement provisions:* s 121(2), (3); Adoption and Children (Scotland) Act 2007 (Commencement No 1) Order 2008, SSI 2008/130; Adoption and Children (Scotland) Act 2007 (Commencement No 2) Order 2008, SSI 2008/282; Adoption and Children (Scotland) Act 2007 (Commencement No 3) Order 2009, SSI 2009/147; Adoption and Children (Scotland) Act 2007 (Commencement No 4, Transitional and Savings Provisions) Order 2009, SSI 2009/267[1], as amended by SSI 2012/99

| | | |
|---|---|---|
| 1 | | 28 Sep 2009 (SSI 2009/267) |
| 2 | (1), (2) | 28 Sep 2009 (SSI 2009/267) |
| | (3) | 7 Apr 2008 (in so far as relates to the definition of "registered adoption service" in s 119(1) of this Act) (SSI 2008/130) |
| | | 28 Sep 2009 (otherwise) (SSI 2009/267) |
| 3 | (a) | 28 Sep 2009 (SSI 2009/267) |
| | (b) | 20 Apr 2009 (for the purpose of enabling regulations, orders or rules to be made) (SSI 2009/147) |
| | | 28 Sep 2009 (otherwise) (SSI 2009/267) |
| 4–7 | | 28 Sep 2009 (SSI 2009/267) |
| 8 | | 20 Apr 2009 (for the purpose of enabling regulations, orders or rules to be made) (SSI 2009/147) |
| | | 28 Sep 2009 (otherwise) (SSI 2009/267) |
| 9 | (1), (2) | 28 Sep 2009 (SSI 2009/267) |
| | (3) | 20 Apr 2009 (for the purpose of enabling regulations, orders or rules to be made) (SSI 2009/147) |
| | | 28 Sep 2009 (otherwise) (SSI 2009/267) |
| 10–12 | | 28 Sep 2009 (SSI 2009/267) |
| 13 | | 20 Apr 2009 (for the purpose of enabling regulations, orders or rules to be made) (SSI 2009/147) |
| | | 28 Sep 2009 (otherwise) (SSI 2009/267) |
| 14–19 | | 28 Sep 2009 (SSI 2009/267) |
| 20 | (1) | 20 Apr 2009 (for the purpose of enabling regulations, orders or rules to be made) (SSI 2009/147) |
| | | 28 Sep 2009 (otherwise) (SSI 2009/267) |
| | (2), (3) | 28 Sep 2009 (SSI 2009/267) |
| 21–36 | | 28 Sep 2009 (SSI 2009/267) |
| 37, 38 | | 20 Apr 2009 (for the purpose of enabling regulations, orders or rules to be made) (SSI 2009/147) |
| | | 28 Sep 2009 (otherwise) (SSI 2009/267) |
| 39–48 | | 28 Sep 2009 (SSI 2009/267) |
| 49 | (1)–(6) | 28 Sep 2009 (SSI 2009/267) |
| | (7) | 20 Apr 2009 (for the purpose of enabling regulations, orders or rules to be made) (SSI 2009/147) |
| | | 28 Sep 2009 (otherwise) (SSI 2009/267) |
| | (8) | 28 Sep 2009 (SSI 2009/267) |
| 50–52 | | 28 Sep 2009 (SSI 2009/267) |
| 53 | (1)–(3) | 28 Sep 2009 (SSI 2009/267) |
| | (4) | See Sch 1 below |
| 54–57 | | 28 Sep 2009 (SSI 2009/267) |

**Adoption and Children (Scotland) Act 2007 (asp 4)**—*contd*

| | | |
|---|---|---|
| 58 | (1)–(4) | 28 Sep 2009 (SSI 2009/267) |
| | (5)–(7) | 20 Apr 2009 (for the purpose of enabling regulations, orders or rules to be made) (SSI 2009/147) |
| | | 28 Sep 2009 (otherwise) (SSI 2009/267) |
| | (8), (9) | 28 Sep 2009 (SSI 2009/267) |
| | (10) | 20 Apr 2009 (for the purpose of enabling regulations, orders or rules to be made) (SSI 2009/147) |
| | | 28 Sep 2009 (otherwise) (SSI 2009/267) |
| 59 | (1), (2) | 28 Sep 2009 (SSI 2009/267) |
| | (3) | 20 Apr 2009 (for the purpose of enabling regulations, orders or rules to be made) (SSI 2009/147) |
| | | 28 Sep 2009 (otherwise) (SSI 2009/267) |
| | (4), (5) | 28 Sep 2009 (SSI 2009/267) |
| | (6) | 20 Apr 2009 (for the purpose of enabling regulations, orders or rules to be made) (SSI 2009/147) |
| | | 28 Sep 2009 (otherwise) (SSI 2009/267) |
| 60 | | 28 Sep 2009 (SSI 2009/267) |
| 61 | (1) | 20 Apr 2009 (for the purpose of enabling regulations, orders or rules to be made) (SSI 2009/147) |
| | | 28 Sep 2009 (otherwise) (SSI 2009/267) |
| | (2) | 28 Sep 2009 (SSI 2009/267) |
| 62–65 | | 1 Sep 2008 (SSI 2008/282) |
| 66–68 | | 28 Sep 2009 (SSI 2009/267) |
| 69 | (1) | 20 Apr 2009 (for the purpose of enabling regulations, orders or rules to be made) (SSI 2009/147) |
| | | 28 Sep 2009 (otherwise) (SSI 2009/267) |
| | (2), (3) | 28 Sep 2009 (SSI 2009/267) |
| 70 | | 28 Sep 2009 (SSI 2009/267) |
| 71 | (1)(a) | 20 Apr 2009 (for the purpose of enabling regulations, orders or rules to be made) (SSI 2009/147) |
| | | 28 Sep 2009 (otherwise) (SSI 2009/267) |
| | (1)(b) | 28 Sep 2009 (SSI 2009/267) |
| | (2) | 28 Sep 2009 (SSI 2009/267) |
| | (3), (4) | 20 Apr 2009 (for the purpose of enabling regulations, orders or rules to be made) (SSI 2009/147) |
| | | 28 Sep 2009 (otherwise) (SSI 2009/267) |
| 72, 73 | | 28 Sep 2009 (SSI 2009/267) |
| 74 | | 20 Apr 2009 (for the purpose of enabling regulations, orders or rules to be made) (SSI 2009/147) |
| | | 28 Sep 2009 (otherwise) (SSI 2009/267) |
| 75–94 | | 28 Sep 2009 (SSI 2009/267) |
| 95 | (1) | 28 Sep 2009 (SSI 2009/267) |
| | (2) | 20 Apr 2009 (for the purpose of enabling regulations, orders or rules to be made) (SSI 2009/147) |
| | | 28 Sep 2009 (otherwise) (SSI 2009/267) |
| | (3) | 28 Sep 2009 (SSI 2009/267) |
| 96–103 | | 28 Sep 2009 (SSI 2009/267) |
| 104 | | 20 Apr 2009 (for the purpose of enabling regulations, orders or rules to be made) (SSI 2009/147) |
| | | 28 Sep 2009 (otherwise) (SSI 2009/267) |
| 105 | | 28 Sep 2009 (SSI 2009/267) |
| 106 | (1), (2) | 28 Sep 2009 (SSI 2009/267) |
| | (3) | 20 Apr 2009 (for the purpose of enabling regulations, orders or rules to be made) (SSI 2009/147) |
| | | 28 Sep 2009 (otherwise) (SSI 2009/267) |
| | (4) | 28 Sep 2009 (SSI 2009/267) |
| 107 | | 28 Sep 2009 (SSI 2009/267) |
| 108 | | 20 Apr 2009 (for the purpose of enabling regulations, orders or rules to be made) (SSI 2009/147) |
| | | 28 Sep 2009 (SSI 2009/267) |

**Adoption and Children (Scotland) Act 2007 (asp 4)**—*contd*

| | | |
|---|---|---|
| 109–113 | | 28 Sep 2009 (SSI 2009/267) |
| 114 | | 20 Apr 2009 (for the purpose of enabling regulations, orders or rules to be made) (SSI 2009/147) |
| | | 28 Sep 2009 (otherwise) (SSI 2009/267) |
| 115 | | 28 Sep 2009 (SSI 2009/267) |
| 116, 117 | | 15 Jan 2007 (s 121(2)) |
| 118 | | 28 Sep 2009 (SSI 2009/267) |
| 119 | (1) | 7 Apr 2008 (SSI 2008/130) |
| | (2)–(7) | 28 Sep 2009 (SSI 2009/267) |
| 120 | (1) | See Sch 2 below |
| | (2) | See Sch 3 below |
| 121 | | 15 Jan 2007 (s 121(2)) |
| Sch 1 | para 1(1) | 20 Apr 2009 (for the purpose of enabling regulations, orders or rules to be made) (SSI 2009/147) |
| | | 28 Sep 2009 (otherwise) (SSI 2009/267) |
| | para 1(2) | 28 Sep 2009 (SSI 2009/267) |
| | paras 2–5 | 28 Sep 2009 (SSI 2009/267) |
| | para 6(1), (2) | 28 Sep 2009 (SSI 2009/267) |
| | para 6(3)–(5) | 20 Apr 2009 (for the purpose of enabling regulations, orders or rules to be made) (SSI 2009/147) |
| | | 28 Sep 2009 (otherwise) (SSI 2009/267) |
| | para 7(1)–(3) | 28 Sep 2009 (SSI 2009/267) |
| | para 7(4) | 20 Apr 2009 (for the purpose of enabling regulations, orders or rules to be made) (SSI 2009/147) |
| | | 28 Sep 2009 (otherwise) (SSI 2009/267) |
| | para 7(5)–(10) | 28 Sep 2009 (SSI 2009/267) |
| | para 7(11) | 20 Apr 2009 (for the purpose of enabling regulations, orders or rules to be made) (SSI 2009/147) |
| | | 28 Sep 2009 (otherwise) (SSI 2009/267) |
| | para 8 | 28 Sep 2009 (SSI 2009/267) |
| Sch 2 | paras 1–8 | 28 Sep 2009 (SSI 2009/267) |
| | para 9(1) | 7 Apr 2008 (SSI 2008/130) |
| | para 9(2)–(4) | 28 Sep 2009 (SSI 2009/267) |
| | para 9(5) | 7 Apr 2008 (SSI 2008/130) |
| | para 9(6)–(10) | 28 Sep 2009 (SSI 2009/267) |
| | paras 10–14 | 28 Sep 2009 (SSI 2009/267) |
| Sch 3 | | 28 Sep 2009 (SSI 2009/267) |

[1]    For transitional provisions and savings, see SSI 2009/267, arts 3–21

---

**Adult Support and Protection (Scotland) Act 2007 (asp 10)**

*RA:* 21 Mar 2007

*Commencement provisions:* s 79; Adult Support and Protection (Scotland) Act 2007 (Commencement No 1, Transitional Provisions and Savings) Order 2007, SSI 2007/334; Adult Support and Protection (Scotland) Act 2007 (Commencement No 2 and Transitional Provisions) Order 2008, SSI 2008/49, as amended by SSI 2008/116, SSI 2008/314; Adult Support and Protection (Scotland) Act 2007 (Commencement No 3 and Related Amendments) Order 2008, SSI 2008/314

| | | |
|---|---|---|
| 1–47 | | 29 Oct 2008 (SSI 2008/314) |
| 48 | | 5 Oct 2007 (SSI 2007/334) |
| 49–51 | | 29 Oct 2008 (SSI 2008/314) |
| 52–56 | | 5 Oct 2007 (SSI 2007/334) |
| 57 | (1)(a) | 5 Oct 2007 (SSI 2007/334)[1] |
| | (1)(b)(i) | 5 Oct 2007 (SSI 2007/334) |
| | (1)(b)(ii), (iii) | 1 Apr 2008 (SSI 2008/49) |
| | (1)(c), (d) | 5 Oct 2007 (SSI 2007/334) |
| | (2)(a) | 5 Oct 2007 (SSI 2007/334)[1] |

**Adult Support and Protection (Scotland) Act 2007 (asp 10)**—*contd*

|        |                |                                                     |
|--------|----------------|-----------------------------------------------------|
|        | (2)(b)(i)      | 5 Oct 2007 (SSI 2007/334)                           |
|        | (2)(b)(ii), (iii) | 1 Apr 2008 (SSI 2008/49)                         |
|        | (2)(c), (d)    | 5 Oct 2007 (SSI 2007/334)                           |
|        | (3)            | 1 Apr 2008 (SSI 2008/49)                            |
|        | (4)–(6)        | 5 Oct 2007 (SSI 2007/334)                           |
|        | (7)            | 1 Apr 2008 (SSI 2008/49)                            |
|        | (8), (9)       | 5 Oct 2007 (SSI 2007/334)                           |
| 58     |                | 1 Apr 2008 (SSI 2008/49)[2]                         |
| 59     | (1)            | 1 Apr 2008 (SSI 2008/49)                            |
|        | (2), (3)       | 5 Oct 2007 (SSI 2007/334)                           |
| 60     | (1)–(6)        | 1 Apr 2008 (SSI 2008/49)                            |
|        | (7), (8)       | 5 Oct 2007 (SSI 2007/334)[1]                        |
|        | (9)            | 1 Apr 2008 (SSI 2008/49)                            |
|        | (10)           | 5 Oct 2007 (SSI 2007/334)                           |
|        | (11)–(14)      | 1 Apr 2008 (SSI 2008/49)                            |
|        | (15)           | 5 Oct 2007 (SSI 2007/334)                           |
|        | (16)           | 1 Apr 2008 (SSI 2008/49)                            |
|        | (17)           | 5 Oct 2007 (SSI 2007/334)                           |
| 61–63  |                | 5 Oct 2007 (SSI 2007/334)[1]                        |
| 64     |                | 22 Mar 2007 (s 79(2))                               |
| 65     |                | 5 Oct 2007 (SSI 2007/334)                           |
| 66     |                | *Not yet in force*                                  |
| 67, 68 |                | 5 Oct 2007 (SSI 2007/334)                           |
| 69, 70 |                | 22 Mar 2007 (s 79(2))                               |
| 71–73  |                | 30 Jun 2007 (SSI 2007/334)                          |
| 74     |                | 3 Nov 2008 (SSI 2008/49)                            |
| 75     |                | 30 Jun 2007 (SSI 2007/334)                          |
| 76     |                | 21 Mar 2007 (RA)                                    |
| 77     | (1)            | See Sch 1 below                                     |
|        | (2)            | See Sch 2 below                                     |
| 78–80  |                | 21 Mar 2007 (RA)                                    |
| Sch 1  | para 1         | 5 Oct 2007 (SSI 2007/334)                           |
|        | para 2         | 30 Jun 2007 (SSI 2007/334)                          |
|        | para 3(a)      | 29 Oct 2008 (SSI 2008/314)                          |
|        | para 3(b)      | 5 Oct 2007 (SSI 2007/334)                           |
|        | paras 4, 5     | 5 Oct 2007 (SSI 2007/334)                           |
|        | para 6         | 30 Jun 2007 (SSI 2007/334)                          |
| Sch 2  |                | 5 Oct 2007 (SSI 2007/334)[1], repeals of or in—     |

Sch 2 (continued):

5 Oct 2007 (SSI 2007/334)[1], repeals of or in—
National Assistance Act 1948, ss 48, 50, 51;
Solicitors (Scotland) Act 1980;
Mental Health Act 1983, s 142;
Law Reform (Parent and Child) (Scotland) Act 1986;
Courts Act 2003
29 Oct 2008 (SSI 2008/314), repeals of or in—
National Assistance Act 1948, s 47;
National Assistance (Amendment) Act 1951;
Mental Health Act 1983, s 1461;
Adults with Incapacity (Scotland) Act 2000
3 Nov 2008 (SSI 2008/49), repeal in—
Mental Health Act 1983, s 146

---

[1]   For transitional provisions and savings, see SSI 2007/334, arts 3–6

[2]   For transitional provisions, see SSI 2008/49, arts 3, 4

**Airdrie-Bathgate Railway and Linked Improvements Act 2007 (asp 19)**

*RA:* 8 May 2007

Whole Act in force 8 May 2007 (RA)

---

**Appropriation Act 2007 (c 1)**

*RA:* 20 Mar 2007

Whole Act in force 20 Mar 2007 (RA)

---

**Appropriation (No 2) Act 2007 (c 10)**

*RA:* 19 Jul 2007

Whole Act in force 19 Jul 2007 (RA)

---

**Aquaculture and Fisheries (Scotland) Act 2007 (asp 12)**

*RA:* 5 Apr 2007

*Commencement provisions:* s 45(2), (3); Aquaculture and Fisheries (Scotland) Act 2007 (Commencement and Transitional Provisions) Order 2007, SSI 2007/333

| | |
|---|---|
| 1–11 | 1 Aug 2007 (SSI 2007/333) |
| 12 | 5 Apr 2007 (s 45(2)) |
| 13–31 | 1 Aug 2007 (SSI 2007/333) |
| 32 | 1 Aug 2007 (SSI 2007/333)[1] |
| 33, 34 | 1 Aug 2007 (SSI 2007/333) |
| 35 | 1 Aug 2008 (SSI 2007/333) |
| 36–41 | 1 Aug 2007 (SSI 2007/333) |
| 42–45 | 5 Apr 2007 (s 45(2)) |
| Schedule | 1 Aug 2007 (SSI 2007/333)[1] |

[1]   For transitional provisions, see SSI 2007/333, arts 3, 4

---

**Bankruptcy and Diligence etc (Scotland) Act 2007 (asp 3)**

*RA:* 15 Jan 2007

*Commencement provisions:* s 227(2)–(4); Bankruptcy and Diligence etc (Scotland) Act 2007 (Commencement No 1) Order 2007, SSI 2007/82; Bankruptcy and Diligence etc (Scotland) Act 2007 (Commencement No 2 and Saving) Order 2008, SSI 2008/45; Bankruptcy and Diligence etc (Scotland) Act 2007 (Commencement No 3, Savings and Transitionals) Order 2008, SSI 2008/115[2] as amended by SSI 2009/67, SSI 2011/31, SSI 2014/173; Bankruptcy and Diligence etc (Scotland) Act 2007 (Commencement No 4, Savings and Transitionals) Order 2009, SSI 2009/67[3], as amended by SSI 2011/31; Bankruptcy and Diligence etc (Scotland) Act 2007 (Commencement No 5 and Transitional) Order 2009, SSI 2009/369[4], as amended by SSI 2011/31; Bankruptcy and Diligence etc (Scotland) Act 2007 (Commencement No 6 and Savings) Order 2010, SSI 2010/249[5]; Bankruptcy and Diligence etc (Scotland) Act 2007 (Commencement No 7 and Transitionals) Order 2011, SSI 2011/31; Bankruptcy and Diligence etc (Scotland) Act 2007 (Commencement No 8 and Transitionals) Order 2011, SSI 2011/179; Bankruptcy and Diligence etc (Scotland) Act 2007 (Commencement No 9 and Savings Amendment) Order 2014, SSI 2014/173

| | | |
|---|---|---|
| 1–17 | | 1 Apr 2008 (SSI 2008/115) |
| 18 | (1)–(4) | 1 Apr 2008 (SSI 2008/115) |
| | (5) | *Not yet in force* |
| 19 | | 1 Apr 2008 (SSI 2008/115) |
| 20 | | 19 Feb 2008 (SSI 2008/45)[1] |
| 21 | (1), (2) | *Not yet in force* |

**Bankruptcy and Diligence etc (Scotland) Act 2007 (asp 3)**—*contd*

| | | |
|---|---|---|
| | (3), (4) | 1 Apr 2008 (in so far as inserts Bankruptcy (Scotland) Act 1985, Sch 4, paras 4(c), 5, 8A for the purposes of making regulations or orders) (SSI 2008/115) |
| | | *Not yet in force* (otherwise) |
| | (5), (6) | *Not yet in force* |
| | (7) | 1 Apr 2008 (in so far as inserts Bankruptcy (Scotland) Act 1985, Sch 4, para 11(3) for the purposes of making regulations or orders) (SSI 2008/115) |
| | | *Not yet in force* (otherwise) |
| | (8)–(13) | *Not yet in force* |
| 22–24 | | 1 Apr 2008 (SSI 2008/115) |
| 25 | (a) | 1 Apr 2008 (in so far as substitutes words in the Bankruptcy (Scotland) Act 1985, s 5(2B)(a) for the purposes of making regulations or orders) (SSI 2008/115) |
| | | 1 Apr 2015 (otherwise) (SSI 2014/173) |
| | (b) | 1 Apr 2008 (except in so far as it applies to debtor applications) (SSI 2008/115) |
| | | 1 Apr 2015 (exception noted above) (SSI 2014/173) |
| 26–34 | | 1 Apr 2008 (SSI 2008/115) |
| 35 | | 19 Feb 2008 (SSI 2008/45) |
| 36 | | See Sch 1 below |
| 37 | (1)–(6) | *Not yet in force* |
| | (7), (8) | 1 Apr 2008 (for the purposes of making regulations or orders) (SSI 2008/115) |
| | | *Not yet in force* (otherwise) |
| | (9) | *Not yet in force* |
| 38–49 | | *Not yet in force* |
| 50 | (1)–(3) | *Never in force* (repealed) |
| | (4), (5) | 1 Apr 2008 (for the purposes of making regulations or orders) (SSI 2008/115) |
| | | *Never in force* (otherwise) (repealed) |
| | (6) | *Never in force* (repealed) |
| | (7) | See Sch 2 below |
| 51 | (1) | *Never in force* (repealed) |
| | (2) | 31 Jan 2011 (SSI 2011/31) |
| | (3)(a) | *Never in force* (repealed) |
| | (3)(b), (4), (5) | 31 Jan 2011 (SSI 2011/31) |
| | (6) | *Never in force* (repealed) |
| 52 | | *Never in force* (repealed) |
| 53 | | 31 Jan 2011 (SSI 2011/31) |
| 54–57 | | *Never in force* (repealed) |
| 58 | (1)–(4) | *Never in force* (repealed) |
| | (5)(a), (b) | *Never in force* (repealed) |
| | (5)(c) | 1 Apr 2008 (for the purposes of making regulations or orders) (SSI 2008/115) |
| | | *Never in force* (otherwise) (repealed) |
| | (5)(d), (e) | *Never in force* (repealed) |
| 59, 60 | | *Never in force* (repealed) |
| 61 | (1)–(3) | 1 Apr 2008 (for the purposes of making regulations or orders) (SSI 2008/115) |
| | | 31 Jan 2011 (otherwise) (SSI 2011/31) |
| | (4)–(7) | *Never in force* (repealed) |
| 62 | | 1 Apr 2011 (SSI 2011/31) |
| 63 | (1), (2) | 1 Apr 2008 (for the purposes of making regulations or orders) (SSI 2008/115) |
| | | 31 Jan 2011 (for the purposes of making regulations) (SSI 2011/31) |
| | | 1 Apr 2011 (otherwise) (SSI 2011/31) |
| | (3) | 1 Apr 2011 (SSI 2011/31) |
| 64, 65 | | 1 Apr 2011 (SSI 2011/31) |
| 66 | | 31 Jan 2011 (SSI 2011/31) |

**Bankruptcy and Diligence etc (Scotland) Act 2007 (asp 3)**—*contd*

| | | |
|---|---|---|
| 67–74 | | *Never in force* (repealed) |
| 75 | (1)–(6) | 31 Jan 2011 (SSI 2011/31) |
| | (7) | 1 Apr 2008 (for the purposes of making regulations or orders) (SSI 2008/115) |
| | | 31 Jan 2011 (otherwise) (SSI 2011/31) |
| 76 | | *Never in force* (repealed) |
| 77, 78 | | 31 Jan 2011 (SSI 2011/31) |
| 79, 80 | | *Not yet in force* |
| 81 | (1)–(6) | *Not yet in force* |
| | (7) | 1 Apr 2008 (for the purposes of making regulations or orders) (SSI 2008/115) |
| | | *Not yet in force* (otherwise) |
| | (8) | *Not yet in force* |
| 82 | | *Not yet in force* |
| 83 | (1)(a) | 1 Apr 2008 (for the purposes of making regulations or orders) (SSI 2008/115) |
| | | *Not yet in force* (otherwise) |
| | (1)(b), (c), (2), (3)(a) | *Not yet in force* |
| | (3)(b) | 1 Apr 2008 (for the purposes of making regulations or orders) (SSI 2008/115) |
| | | *Not yet in force* (otherwise) |
| 84–87 | | *Not yet in force* |
| 88 | (1), (2) | *Not yet in force* |
| | (3)(a) | 1 Apr 2008 (for the purposes of making regulations or orders) (SSI 2008/115) |
| | | *Not yet in force* (otherwise) |
| | (3)(b), (4) | *Not yet in force* |
| 89, 90 | | *Not yet in force* |
| 91 | (1) | *Not yet in force* |
| | (2) | 1 Apr 2008 (for the purposes of making regulations or orders) (SSI 2008/115) |
| | | *Not yet in force* (otherwise) |
| 92 | (1) | *Not yet in force* |
| | (2) | 1 Apr 2008 (for the purposes of making regulations or orders) (SSI 2008/115) |
| | | *Not yet in force* (otherwise) |
| | (3)(a) | *Not yet in force* |
| | (3)(b), (4)(a) | 1 Apr 2008 (for the purposes of making regulations or orders) (SSI 2008/115) |
| | | *Not yet in force* (otherwise) |
| | (4)(b), (c)(i)–(v) | *Not yet in force* |
| | (4)(c)(vi) | 1 Apr 2008 (for the purposes of making regulations or orders) (SSI 2008/115) |
| | | *Not yet in force* (otherwise) |
| | (5)(a)–(e) | *Not yet in force* |
| | (5)(f) | 1 Apr 2008 (for the purposes of making regulations or orders) (SSI 2008/115) |
| | | *Not yet in force* (otherwise) |
| | (6) | *Not yet in force* |
| | (7) | 1 Apr 2008 (for the purposes of making regulations or orders) (SSI 2008/115) |
| | | *Not yet in force* (otherwise) |
| | (8), (9) | *Not yet in force* |
| 93–95 | | *Not yet in force* |
| 96 | (1)–(4) | *Not yet in force* |
| | (5) | 1 Apr 2008 (for the purposes of making regulations or orders) (SSI 2008/115) |
| | | *Not yet in force* (otherwise) |
| 97 | (1)–(6) | *Not yet in force* |

**Bankruptcy and Diligence etc (Scotland) Act 2007 (asp 3)**—*contd*

|        |                   |                                                                                 |
|--------|-------------------|---------------------------------------------------------------------------------|
|        | (7)               | 1 Apr 2008 (for the purposes of making regulations or orders) (SSI 2008/115)    |
|        |                   | *Not yet in force* (otherwise)                                                  |
|        | (8)               | *Not yet in force*                                                              |
| 98     | (1)–(5)           | *Not yet in force*                                                              |
|        | (6)               | 1 Apr 2008 (for the purposes of making regulations or orders) (SSI 2008/115)    |
|        |                   | *Not yet in force* (otherwise)                                                  |
|        | (7)–(9)           | *Not yet in force*                                                              |
| 99–105 |                   | *Not yet in force*                                                              |
| 106    | (1)               | *Not yet in force*                                                              |
|        | (2)               | 1 Apr 2008 (for the purposes of making regulations or orders) (SSI 2008/115)    |
|        |                   | *Not yet in force* (otherwise)                                                  |
|        | (3)               | *Not yet in force*                                                              |
|        | (4)               | 1 Apr 2008 (for the purposes of making regulations or orders) (SSI 2008/115)    |
|        |                   | *Not yet in force* (otherwise)                                                  |
| 107    |                   | *Not yet in force*                                                              |
| 108    | (1)               | *Not yet in force*                                                              |
|        | (2)               | 1 Apr 2008 (for the purposes of making regulations or orders) (SSI 2008/115)    |
|        |                   | *Not yet in force* (otherwise)                                                  |
|        | (3)–(7)           | *Not yet in force*                                                              |
|        | (8)               | 1 Apr 2008 (for the purposes of making regulations or orders) (SSI 2008/115)    |
|        |                   | *Not yet in force* (otherwise)                                                  |
| 109, 110 |                 | *Not yet in force*                                                              |
| 111    | (1), (2)(a)       | *Not yet in force*                                                              |
|        | (2)(b)            | 1 Apr 2008 (for the purposes of making regulations or orders) (SSI 2008/115)    |
|        |                   | *Not yet in force* (otherwise)                                                  |
|        | (3)               | *Not yet in force*                                                              |
| 112    |                   | *Not yet in force*                                                              |
| 113    | (1)               | *Not yet in force*                                                              |
|        | (2)(a)            | 1 Apr 2008 (for the purposes of making regulations or orders) (SSI 2008/115)    |
|        |                   | *Not yet in force* (otherwise)                                                  |
|        | (2)(b), (3)       | *Not yet in force*                                                              |
| 114    | (1)–(3)           | *Not yet in force*                                                              |
|        | (4)               | 1 Apr 2008 (for the purposes of making regulations or orders) (SSI 2008/115)    |
|        |                   | *Not yet in force* (otherwise)                                                  |
| 115, 116 |                 | *Not yet in force*                                                              |
| 117    | (1)               | *Not yet in force*                                                              |
|        | (2)               | 1 Apr 2008 (for the purposes of making regulations or orders) (SSI 2008/115)    |
|        |                   | *Not yet in force* (otherwise)                                                  |
|        | (3)–(6), (7)(a)   | *Not yet in force*                                                              |
|        | (7)(b), (8)(a)    | 1 Apr 2008 (for the purposes of making regulations or orders) (SSI 2008/115)    |
|        |                   | *Not yet in force* (otherwise)                                                  |
|        | (8)(b), (c), (9)  | *Not yet in force*                                                              |
| 118, 119 |                 | *Not yet in force*                                                              |
| 120    | (1)–(4)           | *Not yet in force*                                                              |
|        | (5)               | 1 Apr 2008 (for the purposes of making regulations or orders) (SSI 2008/115)    |
|        |                   | *Not yet in force* (otherwise)                                                  |
| 121, 122 |                 | *Not yet in force*                                                              |
| 123    | (1)               | *Not yet in force*                                                              |

**Bankruptcy and Diligence etc (Scotland) Act 2007 (asp 3)**—*contd*

|         | (2)(a)           | 1 Apr 2008 (for the purposes of making regulations or orders) (SSI 2008/115) |
|---------|------------------|-----------------------------------------------------------------------------|
|         |                  | *Not yet in force (otherwise)*                                              |
|         | (2)(b), (3), (4) | *Not yet in force*                                                         |
|         | (5)              | 1 Apr 2008 (for the purposes of making regulations or orders) (SSI 2008/115) |
|         |                  | *Not yet in force (otherwise)*                                             |
|         | (6)              | *Not yet in force*                                                         |
| 124     | (1)              | *Not yet in force*                                                         |
|         | (2)              | 1 Apr 2008 (for the purposes of making regulations or orders) (SSI 2008/115) |
|         |                  | *Not yet in force (otherwise)*                                             |
|         | (3), (4)         | *Not yet in force*                                                         |
| 125–127 |                  | *Not yet in force*                                                         |
| 128     | (1), (2)         | *Not yet in force*                                                         |
|         | (3)              | 1 Apr 2008 (for the purposes of making regulations or orders) (SSI 2008/115) |
|         |                  | *Not yet in force (otherwise)*                                             |
| 129     |                  | 1 Apr 2008 (for the purposes of making regulations or orders) (SSI 2008/115) |
|         |                  | *Not yet in force (otherwise)*                                             |
| 130     | (1)              | *Not yet in force*                                                         |
|         | (2)(a)           | 1 Apr 2008 (for the purposes of making regulations or orders) (SSI 2008/115) |
|         |                  | *Not yet in force (otherwise)*                                             |
|         | (2)(b)–(d), (3)  | *Not yet in force*                                                         |
| 131, 132|                  | *Not yet in force*                                                         |
| 133     | (1)              | *Not yet in force*                                                         |
|         | (2)(a)           | 1 Apr 2008 (for the purposes of making regulations or orders) (SSI 2008/115) |
|         |                  | *Not yet in force (otherwise)*                                             |
|         | (2)(b), (c)      | *Not yet in force*                                                         |
| 134     |                  | *Not yet in force*                                                         |
| 135     | (1)              | *Not yet in force*                                                         |
|         | (2)(a)           | 1 Apr 2008 (for the purposes of making regulations or orders) (SSI 2008/115) |
|         |                  | *Not yet in force (otherwise)*                                             |
|         | (2)(b)–(d)(i)    | *Not yet in force*                                                         |
|         | (2)(d)(ii)       | 1 Apr 2008 (for the purposes of making regulations or orders) (SSI 2008/115) |
|         |                  | *Not yet in force (otherwise)*                                             |
|         | (3)–(5)          | *Not yet in force*                                                         |
| 136–139 |                  | *Not yet in force*                                                         |
| 140     | (1)              | *Not yet in force*                                                         |
|         | (2)(a)           | 1 Apr 2008 (for the purposes of making regulations or orders) (SSI 2008/115) |
|         |                  | *Not yet in force (otherwise)*                                             |
|         | (2)(b), (3), (4) | *Not yet in force*                                                         |
|         | (5)              | 1 Apr 2008 (for the purposes of making regulations or orders) (SSI 2008/115) |
|         |                  | *Not yet in force (otherwise)*                                             |
| 141, 142|                  | *Not yet in force*                                                         |
| 143     | (1)–(4)          | *Not yet in force*                                                         |
|         | (5)              | 1 Apr 2008 (for the purposes of making regulations or orders) (SSI 2008/115) |
|         |                  | *Not yet in force (otherwise)*                                             |
| 144     |                  | *Not yet in force*                                                         |
| 145     | (1)              | *Not yet in force*                                                         |
|         | (2)              | 1 Apr 2008 (for the purposes of making regulations or orders) (SSI 2008/115) |

**Bankruptcy and Diligence etc (Scotland) Act 2007 (asp 3)**—*contd*

| | | |
|---|---|---|
| | | *Not yet in force* (otherwise) |
| 146 | (1)–(8) | 22 Apr 2009 (SSI 2009/67) |
| | (9) | 1 Apr 2008 (for the purposes of making regulations or orders) (SSI 2008/115) |
| | | 22 Apr 2009 (otherwise) (SSI 2009/67) |
| 147 | | 22 Apr 2009 (SSI 2009/67) |
| 148 | (1), (2) | 22 Apr 2009 (SSI 2009/67) |
| | (3) | 1 Apr 2008 (for the purposes of making regulations or orders) (SSI 2008/115) |
| | | 22 Apr 2009 (otherwise) (SSI 2009/67) |
| 149 | | 1 Apr 2008 (in so far as inserts Titles to Land Consolidation (Scotland) Act 1868, s 155(4) for the purposes of making regulations or orders) (SSI 2008/115) |
| | | 22 Apr 2009 (otherwise) (SSI 2009/67) |
| 150–161 | | 22 Apr 2009 (SSI 2009/67) |
| 162 | | 1 Apr 2008 (in so far as inserts Titles to Land Consolidation (Scotland) Act 1868, s 159A(3) for the purposes of making regulations or orders) (SSI 2008/115) |
| | | 22 Apr 2009 (otherwise) (SSI 2009/67) |
| 163 | | 22 Apr 2009 (SSI 2009/67) |
| 164 | | 1 Apr 2008 (in so far as substitutes s 159 of the Titles to Land Consolidation (Scotland) Act 1868 and inserts s 159B thereof for the purposes of making regulations or orders) (SSI 2008/115) |
| | | 22 Apr 2009 (otherwise) (SSI 2009/67) |
| 165 | (1) | 22 Apr 2009 (SSI 2009/67) |
| | (2) | *Not yet in force* |
| | (3), (4) | 22 Apr 2009 (SSI 2009/67) |
| 166–168 | | 22 Apr 2009 (SSI 2009/67) |
| 169 | | 1 Apr 2008 (except for the insertion of the Debtors (Scotland) Act 1987, s 15H(4)) (SSI 2008/115) |
| | | 22 Apr 2009 (exception noted above) (SSI 2009/67) |
| 170, 171 | | 1 Apr 2008 (SSI 2008/115) |
| 172 | | *Not yet in force* |
| 173 | | 1 Apr 2008 (SSI 2008/115) |
| 174 | | 23 Nov 2009 (SSI 2009/369) |
| 175 | (1), (2) | 23 Nov 2009 (SSI 2009/369) |
| | (3) | 1 Apr 2008 (for the purposes of making regulations or orders) (SSI 2008/115) |
| | | 23 Nov 2009 (otherwise) (SSI 2009/369) |
| 176 | (1)(a), (b) | 23 Nov 2009 (SSI 2009/369) |
| | (1)(c) | 1 Apr 2008 (for the purposes of making regulations or orders) (SSI 2008/115) |
| | | 23 Nov 2009 (otherwise) (SSI 2009/369) |
| | (2)–(4) | 23 Nov 2009 (SSI 2009/369) |
| 177, 178 | | 23 Nov 2009 (SSI 2009/369) |
| 179 | (1) | 23 Nov 2009 (SSI 2009/369) |
| | (2)(a)(i) | 1 Apr 2008 (for the purposes of making regulations or orders) (SSI 2008/115) |
| | | 23 Nov 2009 (otherwise) (SSI 2009/369) |
| | (2)(a)(ii), (b), (3), (4) | 23 Nov 2009 (SSI 2009/369) |
| 180, 181 | | 23 Nov 2009 (SSI 2009/369) |
| 182 | (1) | 23 Nov 2009 (SSI 2009/369) |
| | (2)(a) | 1 Apr 2008 (for the purposes of making regulations or orders) (SSI 2008/115) |
| | | 23 Nov 2009 (otherwise) (SSI 2009/369) |
| | (2)(b), (3)–(7) | 23 Nov 2009 (SSI 2009/369) |
| 183 | (1), (2) | 23 Nov 2009 (SSI 2009/369) |

**Bankruptcy and Diligence etc (Scotland) Act 2007 (asp 3)**—*contd*

| | | |
|---|---|---|
| | (3)(a) | 1 Apr 2008 (for the purposes of making regulations or orders) (SSI 2008/115) |
| | | 23 Nov 2009 (otherwise) (SSI 2009/369) |
| | (3)(b), (4)–(6) | 23 Nov 2009 (SSI 2009/369) |
| | (7)(a) | 1 Apr 2008 (for the purposes of making regulations or orders) (SSI 2008/115) |
| | | 23 Nov 2009 (otherwise) (SSI 2009/369) |
| | (7)(b), (8)–(12) | 23 Nov 2009 (SSI 2009/369) |
| 184 | | 23 Nov 2009 (SSI 2009/369) |
| 185 | (1)–(3) | 23 Nov 2009 (SSI 2009/369) |
| | (4) | 1 Apr 2008 (for the purposes of making regulations or orders) (SSI 2008/115) |
| | | 23 Nov 2009 (otherwise) (SSI 2009/369) |
| | (5)–(7) | 23 Nov 2009 (SSI 2009/369) |
| 186, 187 | | 23 Nov 2009 (SSI 2009/369) |
| 188 | (1)–(3) | 23 Nov 2009 (SSI 2009/369) |
| | (4)(a) | 1 Apr 2008 (for the purposes of making regulations or orders) (SSI 2008/115) |
| | | 23 Nov 2009 (otherwise) (SSI 2009/369) |
| | (4)(b), (5) | 23 Nov 2009 (SSI 2009/369) |
| 189 | (1), (2) | 23 Nov 2009 (SSI 2009/369) |
| | (3)(a) | 1 Apr 2008 (for the purposes of making regulations or orders) (SSI 2008/115) |
| | | 23 Nov 2009 (otherwise) (SSI 2009/369) |
| | (3)(b), (4)–(7) | 23 Nov 2009 (SSI 2009/369) |
| 190–195 | | 23 Nov 2009 (SSI 2009/369) |
| 196 | (1) | See Sch 3 below |
| | (2) | 1 Apr 2008 (for the purposes of making regulations or orders) (SSI 2008/115) |
| | | 23 Nov 2009 (otherwise) (SSI 2009/369) |
| 197 | | 23 Nov 2009 (SSI 2009/369) |
| 198 | (1) | 23 Nov 2009 (SSI 2009/369) |
| | (2) | 1 Apr 2008 (for the purposes of making regulations or orders) (SSI 2008/115) |
| | | 23 Nov 2009 (otherwise) (SSI 2009/369) |
| | (3) | 23 Nov 2009 (SSI 2009/369) |
| 199–205 | | 1 Apr 2008 (SSI 2008/115) |
| 206 | | 1 Apr 2008 (for the purposes of the insertion of the Debtors (Scotland) Act 1987, s 73A(2)) (SSI 2008/115) |
| | | 1 Apr 2008 (for the purposes of the insertion of the Debtors (Scotland) Act 1987, ss 73A(5), 73B(2), 73C(2), 73E(3), 73F(6), 73G(2), 73H(1), (2), 73M(2)(a), 73Q(3)(a), 73S(1), (2) for the purposes of making regulations or orders) (SSI 2008/115) |
| | | 22 Apr 2009 (otherwise, except for the purpose of the insertion of the Debtors (Scotland) Act 1987, s 73D) (SSI 2009/67) |
| | | *Not yet in force* (exception noted above) |
| 207 | | *Not yet in force* |
| 208–210 | | 1 Apr 2008 (SSI 2008/115) |
| 211 | | 8 Mar 2007 (SSI 2007/82) |
| 212 | (1) | See sub-ss (2)–(16) below |
| | (2)–(6) | 8 Mar 2007 (SSI 2007/82) |
| | (7) | *Never in force* (repealed) |
| | (8)–(16) | 31 Mar 2007 (SSI 2007/82) |
| 213 | | See Sch 4 below |
| 214 | (1)–(3) | 4 Apr 2011 (SSI 2011/179)[6] |
| | (4) | 1 Apr 2008 (for the purposes of making regulations or orders) (SSI 2008/115) |
| | | 4 Apr 2011 (otherwise) (SSI 2011/179)[6] |
| 215 | | 1 Apr 2008 (for the purposes of making regulations or orders) (SSI 2008/115) |

**Bankruptcy and Diligence etc (Scotland) Act 2007 (asp 3)**—*contd*

|  |  |  |
|---|---|---|
|  |  | 4 Apr 2011 (otherwise) (SSI 2011/179)[6] |
| 216 | (1)–(5) | 4 Apr 2011 (SSI 2011/179)[6] |
|  | (6) | 1 Apr 2008 (for the purposes of making regulations or orders) (SSI 2008/115) |
|  |  | 4 Apr 2011 (otherwise) (SSI 2011/179)[6] |
| 217 | (1)(a), (b) | 4 Apr 2011 (SSI 2011/179)[6] |
|  | (1)(c) | 1 Apr 2008 (for the purposes of making regulations or orders) (SSI 2008/115) |
|  |  | 4 Apr 2011 (otherwise) (SSI 2011/179)[6] |
|  | (2) | 4 Apr 2011 (SSI 2011/179)[6] |
| 218, 219 |  | 4 Apr 2011 (SSI 2011/179)[6] |
| 220 |  | 1 Apr 2008 (for the purposes of making regulations or orders) (SSI 2008/115) |
|  |  | *Not yet in force* (otherwise) |
| 221 |  | 8 Mar 2007 (SSI 2007/82) |
| 222 |  | 16 Jan 2007 (s 227(2)) |
| 223 |  | 8 Mar 2007 (SSI 2007/82) |
| 224, 225 |  | 15 Jan 2007 (s 227(3)) |
| 226 | (1) | See Sch 5 below |
|  | (2) | See Sch 6 below |
|  | (3) | 1 Apr 2008 (SSI 2008/115) |
| Sch 1 | paras 1–40 | 1 Apr 2008 (SSI 2008/115) |
|  | para 41(a) | *Never in force* (repealed) |
|  | para 41(b) | 1 Apr 2008 (SSI 2008/115) |
|  | para 42(a) | 31 Mar 2007 (SSI 2007/82) |
|  | para 42(b), (c) | 1 Apr 2008 (SSI 2008/115) |
|  | para 43 | 1 Apr 2008 (SSI 2008/115) |
|  | para 44(1), (2)(a) | 1 Apr 2008 (except in so far as they apply to company insolvencies) (SSI 2008/115) |
|  |  | *Not yet in force* (exception noted above) |
|  | para 44(2)(b), (3) | 1 Apr 2008 (SSI 2008/115) |
|  | paras 45–62 | 1 Apr 2008 (SSI 2008/115) |
| Sch 2 | paras 1–21 | *Never in force* (repealed) |
|  | para 22 | 1 Apr 2008 (for the purposes of making regulations or orders) (SSI 2008/115) |
|  |  | *Never in force* (otherwise) (repealed) |
|  | paras 23–35 | *Never in force* (repealed) |
| Sch 3 | paras 1–3 | 23 Nov 2009 (SSI 2009/369) |
|  | para 4 | 1 Apr 2008 (for the purposes of making regulations or orders) (SSI 2008/115) |
|  |  | 23 Nov 2009 (otherwise) (SSI 2009/369) |
|  | para 5 | 23 Nov 2009 (SSI 2009/369) |
| Sch 4 |  | 1 Jul 2010 (SSI 2010/249) |
| Sch 5 | paras 1, 2 | 23 Nov 2009 (SSI 2009/369) |
|  | para 3 | *Not yet in force* |
|  | para 4 | 23 Nov 2009 (SSI 2009/369) |
|  | para 5 | 22 Apr 2009 (SSI 2009/67) |
|  | para 6(1) | See sub-paras (2)–(4) below |
|  | para 6(2) | 23 Nov 2009 (SSI 2009/369) |
|  | para 6(3) | 4 Apr 2011 (SSI 2011/179)[6] |
|  | para 6(4) | *Never in force* (repealed) |
|  | para 7(1) | See sub-paras (2)–(4) below |
|  | para 7(2)(a) | *Never in force* (repealed) |
|  | para 7(2)(b)(i), (ii) | *Never in force* (repealed) |
|  | para 7(2)(b)(iii) | 22 Apr 2009 (SSI 2009/67) |
|  | para 7(2)(c) | 22 Apr 2009 (for the purposes of the substitution of the term "solicitor" for "law agent") (SSI 2009/67) |
|  |  | 31 Jan 2011 (otherwise) (SSI 2011/31) |
|  | para 7(2)(d) | 22 Apr 2009 (SSI 2009/67) |

**Bankruptcy and Diligence etc (Scotland) Act 2007 (asp 3)**—*contd*

| | |
|---|---|
| para 7(3)(a) | *Never in force* (repealed) |
| para 7(3)(b) | 22 Apr 2009 (SSI 2009/67) |
| para 7(4) | *Never in force* (repealed) |
| paras 8, 9 | 23 Nov 2009 (SSI 2009/369) |
| para 10 | 1 Apr 2008 (for the purpose of substituting "an interim attachment, an attachment") (SSI 2008/115) |
| | 23 Nov 2009 (for the purpose of substituting "a money attachment") (SSI 2009/369) |
| | *Not yet in force* (for the purpose of substituting "a land attachment or a residual attachment") |
| para 11 | *Not yet in force* |
| para 12 | 1 Apr 2008 (SSI 2008/115) |
| para 13(1) | See sub-paras (2), (3) below |
| para 13(2), (3)(a) | 1 Apr 2008 (SSI 2008/115) |
| para 13(3)(b) | 22 Apr 2009 (SSI 2009/67) |
| para 13(3)(c)(i) | 1 Apr 2008 (for the purpose of inserting ", interim attachment") (SSI 2008/115) |
| | 23 Nov 2009 (for the purpose of inserting ", money attachment") (SSI 2009/369) |
| para 13(3)(c)(ii) | 1 Apr 2008 (SSI 2008/115) |
| para 13(3)(d)(i) | 1 Apr 2008 (for the purpose of inserting ", interim attachment") (SSI 2008/115) |
| | 23 Nov 2009 (for the purpose of inserting ", money attachment") (SSI 2009/369) |
| para 13(3)(d)(ii) | 1 Apr 2008 (SSI 2008/115) |
| para 13(3)(d)(iii) | 23 Nov 2009 (SSI 2009/369) |
| para 13(3)(d)(iv) | 1 Apr 2008 (for the purpose of inserting ", interim attachment") (SSI 2008/115) |
| | 23 Nov 2009 (for the purpose of inserting ", money attachment") (SSI 2009/369) |
| para 13(3)(e) | *Not yet in force* |
| para 13(3)(f), (g) | 1 Apr 2008 (in so far as they insert the Bankruptcy (Scotland) Act 1985, s 37(8F), (10) for the purposes of making regulations or orders) (SSI 2008/115) |
| | *Not yet in force* (otherwise) |
| para 14 | *Not yet in force* |
| para 15 | 23 Nov 2009 (SSI 2009/369) |
| para 16(1) | See sub-paras (2)–(14) below |
| para 16(2)(a) | 23 Nov 2009 (for the purpose of inserting the Debtors (Scotland) Act 1987, s 2(1)(b)(v)) (SSI 2009/369) |
| | *Not yet in force* (for the purposes of inserting s 2(1)(b)(vi), (vii) thereof) |
| para 16(2)(b) | *Not yet in force* |
| para 16(2)(c) | 1 Apr 2008 (for the purposes of the insertion of the Debtors (Scotland) Act 1987, s 2(2B)) (SSI 2008/115) |
| | 22 Apr 2009 (for the purposes of the insertion of s 2(2A) of that Act) (SSI 2009/67) |
| para 16(2)(d), (e) | 1 Apr 2008 (SSI 2008/115) |
| para 16(2)(f) | 22 Apr 2009 (SSI 2009/67) |
| para 16(3) | 1 Apr 2008 (SSI 2008/115) |
| para 16(4)(a) | 1 Apr 2008 (for the purposes of the substitution of the Debtors (Scotland) Act 1987, s 5(5)(a)) (SSI 2008/115) |
| | 23 Nov 2009 (for the purposes of the substitution of s 5(5)(aa) of that Act) (SSI 2009/369) |
| para 16(4)(b) | *Not yet in force* |
| para 16(4)(c) | 22 Apr 2009 (SSI 2009/67) |
| para 16(5), (6) | 22 Apr 2009 (SSI 2009/67) |
| para 16(7)(a)(i) | 1 Apr 2008 (SSI 2008/115) |
| para 16(7)(a)(ii) | 22 Apr 2009 (SSI 2009/67) |
| para 16(7)(a)(iii) | 23 Nov 2009 (SSI 2009/369) |

**Bankruptcy and Diligence etc (Scotland) Act 2007 (asp 3)**—*contd*

| | |
|---|---|
| para 16(7)(a)(iv) | 22 Apr 2009 (SSI 2009/67) |
| para 16(7)(a)(v) | *Not yet in force* |
| para 16(7)(b) | 22 Apr 2009 (SSI 2009/67) |
| para 16(8)(a) | 23 Nov 2009 (for the purpose of inserting the Debtors (Scotland) Act 1987, s 9(1)(b)(v)) (SSI 2009/369) |
| | *Not yet in force* (for the purposes of inserting s 9(1)(b)(vi), (vii) thereof) |
| para 16(8)(b) | 1 Apr 2008 (for the purposes of the insertion of the Debtors (Scotland) Act 1987, s 9(2)(cb)) (SSI 2008/115) |
| | *Not yet in force* (otherwise) |
| para 16(8)(c) | *Not yet in force* |
| para 16(8)(d) | 1 Apr 2008 (SSI 2008/115) |
| para 16(8)(e)(i) | 22 Apr 2009 (SSI 2009/67) |
| para 16(8)(e)(ii) | 1 Apr 2008 (SSI 2008/115) |
| para 16(8)(f) | 22 Apr 2009 (SSI 2009/67) |
| para 16(8)(g) | 1 Apr 2008 (SSI 2008/115) |
| para 16(8)(h) | 22 Apr 2009 (SSI 2009/67) |
| para 16(8)(i) | 1 Apr 2008 (SSI 2008/115) |
| para 16(9), (10) | 1 Apr 2008 (SSI 2008/115) |
| para 16(11) | 23 Nov 2009 (for the purpose of inserting words ", a money attachment", in both places) (SSI 2009/369) |
| | *Not yet in force* (for the purposes of inserting words "land attachment" and "residual attachment", in both places) |
| para 16(12), (13) | 1 Apr 2008 (SSI 2008/115) |
| para 16(14)(a), (b) | 1 Apr 2008 (SSI 2008/115) |
| para 16(14)(c) | *Never in force* (repealed) |
| para 17 | 23 Nov 2009 (SSI 2009/369) |
| para 18(a)(i) | *Not yet in force* |
| para 18(a)(ii) | 22 Apr 2009 (except for the purposes of substituting the reference to an action of adjudication) (SSI 2009/67) |
| | *Not yet in force* (exception noted above) |
| para 18(b) | *Not yet in force* |
| paras 19, 20 | 23 Nov 2009 (SSI 2009/369) |
| para 21 | *Never in force* (repealed) |
| para 22 | 22 Apr 2009 (SSI 2009/67) |
| paras 23, 24 | 23 Nov 2009 (SSI 2009/369) |
| para 25 | *Never in force* (repealed) |
| para 26(1) | See sub-paras (2), (3) below |
| para 26(2) | 23 Nov 2009 (SSI 2009/369) |
| para 26(3) | 1 Apr 2008 (for the purposes of the insertion of the reference to the Debt Arrangement and Attachment (Scotland) Act 2002, s 39(1)) (SSI 2008/115) |
| | 23 Nov 2009 (for the purposes of the insertion of the reference to the Bankruptcy and Diligence etc (Scotland) Act 2007, s 196(1)) (SSI 2009/369) |
| paras 27, 28 | *Never in force* (repealed) |
| para 29 | 22 Apr 2009 (SSI 2009/67) |
| para 30(1) | See sub-paras (2)–(15) below |
| para 30(2) | 1 Apr 2008 (SSI 2008/115) |
| para 30(3) | 23 Nov 2009 (SSI 2009/369) |
| para 30(4) | 1 Apr 2008 (in so far as inserts Debt Arrangement and Attachment (Scotland) Act 2002, s 13A(2)(a) for the purposes of making regulations or orders) (SSI 2008/115) |
| | 22 Apr 2009 (otherwise) (SSI 2009/67) |
| para 30(5)–(7) | 31 Mar 2007 (in so far as it relates to attachments executed on or after 31 Mar 2007) (SSI 2007/82) |
| | *Not yet in force* (otherwise) |
| para 30(8)(a) | 31 Mar 2007 (in so far as it relates to attachments executed on or after 31 Mar 2007) (SSI 2007/82) |
| | *Not yet in force* (otherwise) |

**Bankruptcy and Diligence etc (Scotland) Act 2007 (asp 3)**—*contd*

|  |  |  |
|---|---|---|
| | para 30(8)(b) | *Never in force* (repealed) |
| | para 30(9) | 22 Apr 2009 (SSI 2009/67) |
| | para 30(10) | 31 Mar 2007 (SSI 2007/82) |
| | para 30(11)(a)(i) | 22 Apr 2009 (SSI 2009/67) |
| | para 30(11)(a)(ii) | 31 Mar 2007 (SSI 2007/82) |
| | para 30(11)(b) | 31 Mar 2007 (SSI 2007/82) |
| | para 30(12) | 1 Apr 2008 (SSI 2008/115) |
| | para 30(13) | *Never in force* (repealed) |
| | para 30(14) | 1 Apr 2008 (SSI 2008/115) |
| | para 30(15) | 31 Mar 2007 (in so far as it relates to attachments executed on or after 31 Mar 2007) (SSI 2007/82) |
| | | *Not yet in force* (otherwise) |
| | para 31 | *Never in force* (repealed) |
| | para 32 | 23 Nov 2009 (SSI 2009/369) |
| | para 33 | *Never in force* (repealed) |
| Sch 6 | Pt 1 | 1 Apr 2008 (SSI 2008/115), repeals of or in— |

> Debtors (Scotland) Act 1838, s 17, s 22 (for the purpose of diligence on the dependence);
> Hypothec Amendment (Scotland) Act 1867;
> Hypothec Abolition (Scotland) Act 1880;
> Judicial Factors (Scotland) Act 1889;
> Sheriff Courts (Scotland) Act 1971;
> Sale of Goods Act 1979;
> Family Law (Scotland) Act 1985 (for the purpose of diligence on the dependence);
> Bankruptcy (Scotland) Act 1985 (except repeals of or in ss 7(1)(c)(iv), 14(1)(a), (2), (3)(a), (4) (words "and adjudications"), (5), 15(5), 17(8)(a), 31(2) (words "(reserving the effect of such inhibition on ranking)"), 37(1), (2) (words "which" and "shall be effectual to create a preference for the inhibitor and"), (8), 54(7), Sch 5, para 2);
> Insolvency Act 1986;
> Debtors (Scotland) Act 1987, ss 8, 9(8), Sch 6 (for the purpose of diligence on the dependence);
> Proceeds of Crime Act 2002, s 285 (for the purpose of the abolition of sequestrian for rent);
> Debt Arrangement and Attachment (Scotland) Act 2002, ss 4, 60

> 22 Apr 2009 (SSI 2009/67), repeals of or in—
> Arrestments Act 1617;
> Debtors (Scotland) Act 1838, s 22 (otherwise);
> Titles to Land Consolidation (Scotland) Act 1868, Sch PP, Sch RR (for the purpose of notice of Summons for breach of inhibition);
> Sheriff Courts (Scotland) Act 1907, s 29;
> Taxes Management Act 1970;
> Rent (Scotland) Act 1984;
> Family Law (Scotland) Act 1985 (otherwise);
> Bankruptcy (Scotland) Act 1985, ss 14(5), 31(2) (words "(reserving any effect of such inhibition on ranking)"), 37(2) (word "which" and words "shall be effectual to create a preference for the inhibitor and");
> Debtors (Scotland) Act 1987, Sch 6 (otherwise);
> Proceeds of Crime (Scotland) Act 1995, s 32(2), (3);
> Proceeds of Crime Act 2002, s 123(4)

> 4 Apr 2011 (repeal of Ejection Caution Act 1594) (SSI 2011/179)[6]
> *Not yet in force*, repeals of or in—
> Decrees in Absence Act 1584;
> Diligence Act 1621;
> Adjudication Act 1621;
> Diligence Act 1661;

**Bankruptcy and Diligence etc (Scotland) Act 2007 (asp 3)**—*contd*

Minority Act 1663;

Adjudications Act 1672;

Titles to Land Consolidation (Scotland) Act 1868, ss 3, 62, 129, 159, Sch RR (except as noted above);

Heritable Securities (Scotland) Act 1894;

Sheriff Courts (Scotland) Act 1907, ss 5, 40;

Conveyancing (Scotland) Act 1924;

Execution of Diligence (Scotland) Act 1926;

Public Registers and Records (Scotland) Act 1948;

Reserve and Auxiliary Forces (Protection of Civil Interests) Act 1951;

Prescription and Limitation (Scotland) Act 1973;

Land Registration (Scotland) Act 1979;

Bankruptcy (Scotland) Act 1985 (exceptions noted above);

Law Reform (Miscellaneous Provisions) (Scotland) Act 1985;

Debtors (Scotland) Act 1987, ss 2, 5, 9(1), 15, Pt V, s 101;

Proceeds of Crime (Scotland) Act 1995, s 32(5)(b), Sch 1;

Terrorism Act 2000;

Mortgage Rights (Scotland) Act 2001;

International Criminal Court (Scotland) Act 2001;

Proceeds of Crime Act 2002, ss 123(7)(b), 285 (except for the purpose of the abolition of sequestrian for rent), Sch 3;

Debt Arrangement and Attachment (Scotland) Act 2002, s 15, Sch 1

| Pt 2 | 1 Apr 2008 (SSI 2008/115) |
|---|---|

[1]   For a saving, see SSI 2008/45, art 3

[2]   For transitional provisions, see SSI 2008/115, arts 4–15

[3]   For transitional modifications and savings, see SSI 2009/67, arts 4–6

[4]   For a transitional modification, see SSI 2009/369, art 4

[5]   For savings, see SSI 2010/249, art 3

[6]   For transitional provisions, see SSI 2011/179, art 4

---

**Budget (Scotland) Act 2007 (asp 9)**

*RA:* 20 Mar 2007

Whole Act in force 20 Mar 2007 (RA)

---

**Building Societies (Funding) and Mutual Societies (Transfers) Act 2007 (c 26)**

*RA:* 23 Oct 2007

*Commencement provisions:* s 6(2); Building Societies (Funding) and Mutual Societies (Transfers) Act 2007 (Commencement No 1) Order 2009, SI 2009/36; Building Societies (Funding) and Mutual Societies (Transfers) Act 2007 (Commencement No 2) Order 2014, SI 2014/2796

| 1 | *Not yet in force* |
|---|---|
| 2 | 20 Nov 2014 (SI 2014/2796) |
| 3–5 | 16 Jan 2009 (SI 2009/36) |
| 6 | 23 Oct 2007 (RA) |

---

**Christmas Day and New Year's Day Trading (Scotland) Act 2007 (asp 13)**

*RA:* 13 Apr 2007

Whole Act in force 13 Apr 2007 (RA)

---

## Concessionary Bus Travel Act 2007 (c 13)

*RA:* 19 Jul 2007

*Commencement provisions:* s 15(1); Concessionary Bus Travel Act 2007 (Commencement and Transitional Provisions) Order 2007, SI 2007/2799

Whole Act in force as follows—

17 Oct 2007 (for specified purposes[1]) (SI 2007/2799)

1 Apr 2008 (otherwise) (SI 2007/2799) (subject to transitional provisions; see art 4)

[1]   The specified purposes are—

(a)   permitting the Secretary of State to issue guidance pursuant to the Transport Act 2000, s 145A(6), (8) and the Greater London Authority Act 1999, s 240(5C);

(b)   permitting the Secretary of State to make regulations under—

(i)   the Transport Act 2000, s 145A(5);

(ii)   the Greater London Authority Act 1999, s 243(7);

(c)   permitting a travel concession authority in England, any London authority and the Council of the Isles of Scilly to issue statutory travel concession permits in accordance with the provisions made by this Act on or before 1 Apr 2008 to those persons who will be entitled to make use of such permits from that date;

(d)   pursuant to the Transport Act 2000, ss 149, 150, permitting—

(i)   a travel concession authority in England, any London authority and the Council of the Isles of Scilly to determine the arrangements or variations to apply with respect to the re-imbursement of operators in relation to concessions exercised on or after 1 Apr 2008 as a consequence of the issue and use of statutory travel concession permits;

(ii)   an operator affected by such arrangements or variations to apply for the modification of them;

(iii)   the Secretary of State to take such steps as are necessary to determine any such application; and

(iv)   for any direction to be given in relation to the application pursuant to the Transport Act 2000, s 150(8); and

(e)   pursuant to the Greater London Authority Act 1999—

(i)   requiring Transport for London to take into account, when forming its view pursuant to the Greater London Authority Act 1999, s 241(1), the requirement that from 1 Apr 2008 travel concessions be provided for all eligible England residents and that additional travel concessions be provided for all eligible London residents;

(ii)   permitting any London authority and Transport for London to make all arrangements necessary to enable the travel concession specified in the Greater London Authority Act 1999, s 242(8) and the additional travel concession mentioned in s 242(8A) of that Act to be provided to those entitled to those concessions from 1 Apr 2008;

(iii)   permitting London authorities to make arrangements pursuant to the Greater London Authority Act 1999, s 244 for the joint discharge of their functions under the Transport Act 2000, ss 148–150; and

(iv)   requiring Transport for London, when notifying each London authority of the charge to be paid by the authority pursuant to the Greater London Authority Act 1999, Sch 16, para 5, to take into account any service outside Greater London which, but for s 179(2) of that Act, would be part of the London bus network

## Consolidated Fund Act 2007 (c 31)

*RA:* 13 Dec 2007

Whole Act in force 13 Dec 2007 (RA)

## Consumers, Estate Agents and Redress Act 2007 (c 17)

*RA:* 19 Jul 2007

*Commencement provisions:* s 66; Consumers, Estate Agents and Redress Act 2007 (Commencement No 1) Order, SI 2007/2934; Consumers, Estate Agents and Redress Act 2007 (Commencement No 2) Order 2007, SI 2007/3546; Consumers, Estate Agents and Redress Act 2007 (Commencement No 3 and Supplementary Provision) Order 2008, SI 2008/1262; Consumers, Estate Agents and Redress Act 2007 (Commencement No 4) Order 2008, SI 2008/905; Consumers, Estate Agents and Redress Act 2007 (Commencement No 5 and Savings and Transitional Provisions) Order 2008, SI 2008/2550

| | | |
|---|---|---|
| 1 | (1) | 21 Dec 2007 (SI 2007/3546) |
| | (2)(a), (b) | 21 Dec 2007 (SI 2007/3546) |
| | (2)(c) | 1 Oct 2008 (SI 2008/2550) |
| | (3) | 21 Dec 2007 (SI 2007/3546) |
| | (4) | See Sch 1 below |
| 2 | (1)(a), (b) | 21 Dec 2007 (in so far as they relate to ss 9, 10(1)(a) and (2)) (SI 2007/3546) |
| | | 1 Oct 2008 (otherwise) (SI 2008/2550) |
| | (1)(c) | 1 Oct 2008 (SI 2008/2550) |
| | (2)–(4) | 21 Dec 2007 (SI 2007/3546) |
| 3, 4 | | 21 Dec 2007 (SI 2007/3546) |
| 5 | | 7 May 2008 (SI 2008/1262) |
| 6 | (1) | 21 Dec 2007 (SI 2007/3546) |
| | (2) | 1 Oct 2008 (SI 2008/2550) |
| | (3)–(10) | 21 Dec 2007 (SI 2007/3546) |
| 7, 8 | | 1 Oct 2008 (SI 2008/2550) |
| 9 | | 21 Dec 2007 (SI 2007/3546) |
| 10 | (1)(a) | 21 Dec 2007 (SI 2007/3546) |
| | (1)(b), (c) | 1 Oct 2008 (SI 2008/2550) |
| | (2) | 21 Dec 2007 (SI 2007/3546) |
| 11–19 | | 1 Oct 2008 (SI 2008/2550) |
| 20 | | 21 Dec 2007 (SI 2007/3546) |
| 21 | | 1 Oct 2008 (SI 2008/2550) |
| 22, 23 | | 21 Dec 2007 (SI 2007/3546) |
| 24–29 | | 1 Oct 2008 (SI 2008/2550) |
| 30 | (1)–(3) | 1 Oct 2008 (SI 2008/2550) |
| | (4)(a), (b) | 1 Oct 2008 (SI 2008/2550) |
| | (4)(c) | 21 Dec 2007 (for the purposes of the Postal Services Act 2000, s 39A) (SI 2007/3546) |
| | | 1 Oct 2008 (otherwise) (SI 2008/2550) |
| | (4)(d) | 21 Dec 2007 (for the purposes of the Utilities Act 2000, s 8) (SI 2007/3546) |
| | | 1 Oct 2008 (otherwise) (SI 2008/2550) |
| | (5) | See Sch 3 below |
| 31–34 | | 1 Oct 2008 (SI 2008/2550) |
| 35, 36 | | 21 Dec 2007 (SI 2007/3546) |
| 37, 38 | | 1 Oct 2008 (SI 2008/2550) |
| 39–44 | | 21 Dec 2007 (SI 2007/3546) |
| 45 | | 1 Oct 2008 (SI 2008/2550) |
| 46–51 | | 21 Dec 2007 (SI 2007/3546) |
| 52 | | 1 Oct 2008 (SI 2008/2550) |
| 53 | (1) | See Sch 6 below |
| | (2) | 1 Oct 2008 (SI 2008/905) |
| | (3) | 1 Oct 2008 (SI 2008/2550) |
| 54 | | *Not yet in force* |
| 55–58 | | 1 Oct 2008 (SI 2008/905) |
| 59 | | 21 Dec 2007 (SI 2007/3546) |
| 60–62 | | 19 Jul 2007 (s 66(1)) |
| 63 | (1) | See Sch 7 below |
| | (2)–(5) | 21 Dec 2007 (SI 2007/3546) |
| 64 | | See Sch 8 below |

**Consumers, Estate Agents and Redress Act 2007 (c 17)**—*contd*

| | | |
|---|---|---|
| 65–67 | | 19 Jul 2007 (s 66(1)) |
| Sch 1 | paras 1–26 | 21 Dec 2007 (SI 2007/3546) |
| | para 27 | 1 Oct 2008 (SI 2008/2550) |
| | paras 28–31 | 21 Dec 2007 (SI 2007/3546) |
| | para 32 | 1 Apr 2008 (SI 2008/905) |
| | paras 33–38 | 21 Dec 2007 (SI 2007/3546) |
| Schs 2, 3 | | 1 Oct 2008 (SI 2008/2550) |
| Sch 4 | | 21 Dec 2007 (SI 2007/3546) |
| Sch 5 | | 1 Oct 2008 (SI 2008/2550) |
| Sch 6 | | 12 Oct 2007 (SI 2007/2934) |
| Sch 7 | paras 1, 2 | 1 Oct 2008 (SI 2008/905) |
| | para 3 | *Not yet in force* |
| | paras 4–10 | 1 Oct 2008 (SI 2008/2550) |
| | para 11 | 21 Dec 2007 (SI 2007/3546) |
| | paras 12–23 | 1 Oct 2008 (SI 2008/2550) |
| Sch 8 | | 21 Dec 2007 (SI 2007/3546), repeals of or in— |

Postal Services Act 2000, ss 2 (words "(in this Act referred to as "the Council")" in sub-s (1), for the purposes of s 39A), 39; Utilities Act 2000, s 8

1 Oct 2008 (SI 2008/905)1, repeals of or in—
Estate Agents Act 1979

1 Oct 2008 (SI 2008/2550), repeals of or in—
Public Records Act 1958;
Parliamentary Commissioner Act 1967;
House of Commons Disqualification Act 1975;
Race Relations Act 1976;
Gas Act 1986;
Electricity Act 1989;
Freedom of Information Act 2000;
Postal Services Act 2000, ss 2 (otherwise), 51–59, 61, Schs 2, 7, 8;
Utilities Act 2000, ss 2–4, 17–27, 105, Schs 2, 6, 7;
Warm Homes and Energy Conservation Act 2000;
Enterprise Act 2002;
Energy Act 2004;
Housing Act 2004

[1] For savings and transitional provisions, see SI 2008/2550, art 3

## Corporate Manslaughter and Corporate Homicide Act 2007 (c 19)

*RA:* 26 Jul 2007

*Commencement provisions:* s 27; Corporate Manslaughter and Corporate Homicide Act 2007 (Commencement No 1) Order 2008, SI 2008/401; Corporate Manslaughter and Corporate Homicide Act 2007 (Commencement No 2) Order 2010, SI 2010/276; Corporate Manslaughter and Corporate Homicide Act 2007 (Commencement No 3) Order 2011, SI 2011/1867; Corporate Manslaughter and Corporate Homicide (2007 Act) (Commencement) Order (Northern Ireland) 2012, SR 2012/286

| | | |
|---|---|---|
| 1 | | 6 Apr 2008 (SI 2008/401) |
| 2 | (1)(a)–(c) | 6 Apr 2008 (SI 2008/401) |
| | (1)(d) | 1 Sep 2011 (E) (W) (S) (SI 2011/1867) |
| | | 3 Sep 2012 (NI) (SR 2012/286) |
| | (2)–(7) | 6 Apr 2008 (SI 2008/401)1 |
| 3 | | 6 Apr 2008 (SI 2008/401)1 |
| 4 | | 6 Apr 2008 (SI 2008/401) |
| 5 | | 6 Apr 2008 (SI 2008/401)1 |
| 6 | | 6 Apr 2008 (SI 2008/401) |

**Corporate Manslaughter and Corporate Homicide Act 2007 (c 19)**—*contd*

| | |
|---|---|
| 7 | 6 Apr 2008 (SI 2008/401)[1] |
| 8, 9 | 6 Apr 2008 (SI 2008/401) |
| 10 | 15 Feb 2010 (SI 2010/276)[2] |
| 11–19 | 6 Apr 2008 (SI 2008/401) |
| 20 | 6 Apr 2008 (SI 2008/401)[1] |
| 21–26 | 6 Apr 2008 (SI 2008/401) |
| 27–29 | 26 Jul 2007 (RA) |
| Schs 1, 2 | 6 Apr 2008 (SI 2008/401) |

[1]   For transitional provisions, see SI 2008/401, art 2(3)

[2]   For transitional provisions, see SI 2010/276, art 3

**Criminal Proceedings etc (Reform) (Scotland) Act 2007 (asp 6)**

*RA:* 22 Feb 2007

*Commencement provisions:* s 84(1), (2); Criminal Proceedings etc (Reform) (Scotland) Act 2007 (Commencement and Savings) Order 2007, SSI 2007/250; Criminal Proceedings etc (Reform) (Scotland) Act 2007 (Commencement No 2 and Transitional Provisions and Savings) Order 2007, SSI 2007/479, as amended by SSI 2007/527; Criminal Proceedings etc (Reform) (Scotland) Act 2007 (Commencement No 3 and Savings) Order 2008, SSI 2008/42; Criminal Proceedings etc (Reform) (Scotland) Act 2007 (Commencement No 4) Order 2008, SSI 2008/192; Criminal Proceedings etc (Reform) (Scotland) Act 2007 (Commencement No 5) Order 2008, SSI 2008/329; Criminal Proceedings etc (Reform) (Scotland) Act 2007 (Commencement No 6) Order 2008, SSI 2008/362; Criminal Proceedings etc (Reform) (Scotland) Act 2007 (Commencement No 7) Order 2009, SSI 2009/116 (revoked by SSI 2009/238); Criminal Proceedings etc (Reform) (Scotland) Act 2007 (Commencement No 8) Order 2009, SSI 2009/432; Criminal Proceedings etc (Reform) (Scotland) Act 2007 (Commencement No 9) Order 2011, SSI 2011/188; Criminal Proceedings etc (Reform) (Scotland) Act 2007 (Commencement No 10) Order 2012, SSI 2012/274

| | | |
|---|---|---|
| 1 | | 10 Dec 2007 (SSI 2007/479) |
| 2–4 | | 10 Dec 2007 (SSI 2007/479)[2] |
| 5, 6 | | 10 Dec 2007 (SSI 2007/479) |
| 7 | (1) | 10 Mar 2008 (SSI 2008/42)[3] |
| | (2)(a), (b) | 10 Mar 2008 (SSI 2008/42)[3] |
| | (2)(c) | 10 Dec 2007 (SSI 2007/479)[2] |
| | (2)(d)–(f) | 10 Mar 2008 (SSI 2008/42)[3] |
| | (2)(g) | *Never in force* (repealed) |
| | (3) | 10 Mar 2008 (SSI 2008/42)[3] |
| 8–10 | | 10 Dec 2007 (SSI 2007/479) |
| 11 | | 10 Mar 2008 (SSI 2008/42) |
| 12 | (1) | 10 Dec 2007 (SSI 2007/479) |
| | (2) | 10 Dec 2007 (for the purpose of bringing the Criminal Procedure (Scotland) Act 1995, s 166B into force) (SSI 2007/479) |
| | | 10 Mar 2008 (for the purpose of bringing the Criminal Procedure (Scotland) Act 1995, s 166A into force) (SSI 2008/42)[3] |
| 13, 14 | | 10 Dec 2007 (SSI 2007/479) |
| 15 | | 10 Dec 2007 (SSI 2007/479)[2] |
| 16, 17 | | 10 Mar 2008 (SSI 2008/42) |
| 18 | | 10 Dec 2007 (SSI 2007/479) |
| 19–21 | | 10 Dec 2007 (SSI 2007/479)[2] |
| 22, 23 | | 10 Mar 2008 (SSI 2008/42) |
| 24–26 | | 10 Dec 2007 (SSI 2007/479) |
| 27 | | 10 Dec 2007 (SSI 2007/479)[2] |
| 28 | | 10 Mar 2008 (SSI 2008/42) |
| 29 | | 1 Nov 2012 (SSI 2012/274) |
| 30 | | 10 Dec 2007 (SSI 2007/479) |
| 31 | | 10 Mar 2008 (SSI 2008/42) |
| 32–34 | | 10 Dec 2007 (SSI 2007/479) |

**Criminal Proceedings etc (Reform) (Scotland) Act 2007 (asp 6)**—*contd*

| | | |
|---|---|---|
| 35, 36 | | 23 Apr 2007 (SSI 2007/250) |
| 37 | | 10 Dec 2007 (SSI 2007/479)[2] |
| 38, 39 | | 10 Dec 2007 (SSI 2007/479) |
| 40 | | 10 Dec 2007 (SSI 2007/479)[2] |
| 41 | (1) | 10 Dec 2007 (for the purpose of bringing the Criminal Procedure (Scotland) Act 1995, s 303B(6) into force) (SSI 2007/479) |
| | | 1 Nov 2012 (for the purpose of bringing the Criminal Procedure (Scotland) Act 1995, s 303B(1)–(5), (7)–(10) into force) (SSI 2012/274) |
| | (2) | 10 Dec 2007 (for the purpose of bringing the Criminal Procedure (Scotland) Act 1995, s 308A(2)–(4) into force) (SSI 2007/479) |
| | | 1 Nov 2012 (for the purpose of bringing the Criminal Procedure (Scotland) Act 1995, s 308A(1) into force) (SSI 2012/274) |
| 42 | | 1 Nov 2012 (SSI 2012/274) |
| 43 | | 10 Dec 2007 (SSI 2007/479)[2] |
| 44 | (1) | 10 Dec 2007 (SSI 2007/479) |
| | (2) | 23 Apr 2007 (SSI 2007/250) |
| | (3)–(6) | 10 Dec 2007 (SSI 2007/479) |
| 45 | | 10 Dec 2007 (SSI 2007/479)[2] |
| 46 | | *Not yet in force* |
| 47, 48 | | 10 Dec 2007 (SSI 2007/479)[2] |
| 49, 50 | | 10 Mar 2008 (SSI 2008/42)[3] |
| 51 | | 2 Jun 2008 (for the purpose only of making a work order where one or more of the alleged offences in relation to which the work order is to be made was committed in any of the local authority areas of Highland, South Lanarkshire, West Dunbartonshire or West Lothian and in respect of which arrangements have been made by a local authority within those areas for the supervision of any such work order) (SSI 2008/192) |
| | | 1 Apr 2011 (for the purpose only of making a work order where one or more of the alleged offences in relation to which the work order is to be made was committed in a local authority area where arrangements have been made by that local authority for the supervision of any such work order) (SSI 2011/188) |
| | | *Not yet in force* (otherwise) |
| 52–54 | | 10 Mar 2008 (SSI 2008/42)[3] |
| 55 | | 10 Mar 2008 (except for the purposes of any relevant penalty which requires to be paid in any district court) (SSI 2008/42) |
| | | *Not yet in force* (exception noted above) |
| 56 | | 23 Apr 2007 (SSI 2007/250) |
| 57 | | 10 Dec 2007 (SSI 2007/479) |
| 58 | | 10 Dec 2007 (SSI 2007/479)[2] |
| 59 | (1) | 10 Dec 2007 (for the purpose of enabling orders to be made under sub-s (2)) (SSI 2007/479) |
| | | 10 Mar 2008 (for the Sheriffdom of Lothian and Borders) (SSI 2008/42) |
| | | 2 Jun 2008 (for the Sheriffdom of Grampian, Highland and Islands) (SSI 2008/192) |
| | | 8 Dec 2008 (for the Sheriffdom of Glasgow and Strathkelvin) (SSI 2008/329) |
| | | 23 Feb 2009 (for the Sheriffdom of Tayside, Central and Fife) (SSI 2008/362) |
| | | 14 Dec 2009 (for the Sheriffdom of North Strathclyde) (SSI 2009/432) |
| | | 22 Feb 2010 (otherwise) (SSI 2009/432) |
| | (2) | 10 Dec 2007 (for the purpose of enabling orders to be made under sub-s (2)) (SSI 2007/479) |
| | | 22 Feb 2010 (otherwise) (SSI 2009/432) |

**Criminal Proceedings etc (Reform) (Scotland) Act 2007 (asp 6)**—*contd*

| | |
|---|---|
| (3)–(5) | 10 Dec 2007 (for the purpose of enabling orders to be made under sub-s (2)) (SSI 2007/479) |
| | 10 Mar 2008 (for the Sheriffdom of Lothian and Borders) (SSI 2008/42) |
| | 2 Jun 2008 (for the Sheriffdom of Grampian, Highland and Islands) (SSI 2008/192) |
| | 8 Dec 2008 (for the Sheriffdom of Glasgow and Strathkelvin) (SSI 2008/329) |
| | 23 Feb 2009 (for the Sheriffdom of Tayside, Central and Fife) (SSI 2008/362) |
| | 14 Dec 2009 (for the Sheriffdom of North Strathclyde) (SSI 2009/432) |
| | 22 Feb 2010 (otherwise) (SSI 2009/432) |
| (6) | 10 Dec 2007 (for the purpose of enabling orders to be made under sub-s (2)) (SSI 2007/479) |
| | 10 Mar 2008 (otherwise) (SSI 2008/42) |
| (7) | 10 Dec 2007 (for the purpose of enabling orders to be made under sub-s (2)) (SSI 2007/479) |
| | 10 Mar 2008 (for the Sheriffdom of Lothian and Borders) (SSI 2008/42) |
| | 2 Jun 2008 (for the Sheriffdom of Grampian, Highland and Islands) (SSI 2008/192) |
| | 8 Dec 2008 (for the Sheriffdom of Glasgow and Strathkelvin) (SSI 2008/329) |
| | 23 Feb 2009 (for the Sheriffdom of Tayside, Central and Fife) (SSI 2008/362) |
| | 14 Dec 2009 (for the Sheriffdom of North Strathclyde) (SSI 2009/432) |
| | 22 Feb 2010 (otherwise) (SSI 2009/432) |
| (8), (9) | 10 Dec 2007 (for the purpose of enabling orders to be made under sub-s (2)) (SSI 2007/479) |
| | 10 Mar 2008 (otherwise) (SSI 2008/42) |
| 60 | 10 Dec 2007 (SSI 2007/479) |
| 61 | 10 Mar 2008 (SSI 2008/42) |
| 62 (1)–(3) | 10 Mar 2008 (for the Sheriffdom of Lothian and Borders) (SSI 2008/42) |
| | 2 Jun 2008 (for the Sheriffdom of Grampian, Highland and Islands) (SSI 2008/192) |
| | 8 Dec 2008 (for the Sheriffdom of Glasgow and Strathkelvin) (SSI 2008/329) |
| | 23 Feb 2009 (for the Sheriffdom of Tayside, Central and Fife) (SSI 2008/362) |
| | 14 Dec 2009 (for the Sheriffdom of North Strathclyde) (SSI 2009/432) |
| | 22 Feb 2010 (otherwise) (SSI 2009/432) |
| (4)–(7) | 10 Dec 2007 (except so far as they apply to stipendiary magistrates) (SSI 2007/479) |
| | 10 Mar 2008 (otherwise, for the Sheriffdom of Lothian and Borders) (SSI 2008/42) |
| | 2 Jun 2008 (otherwise, for the Sheriffdom of Grampian, Highland and Islands) (SSI 2008/192) |
| | 8 Dec 2008 (otherwise) (SSI 2008/329) |
| (8) | 10 Mar 2008 (for the Sheriffdom of Lothian and Borders) (SSI 2008/42) |
| | 2 Jun 2008 (for the Sheriffdom of Grampian, Highland and Islands) (SSI 2008/192) |
| | 8 Dec 2008 (for the Sheriffdom of Glasgow and Strathkelvin) (SSI 2008/329) |
| | 23 Feb 2009 (for the Sheriffdom of Tayside, Central and Fife) (SSI 2008/362) |

**Criminal Proceedings etc (Reform) (Scotland) Act 2007 (asp 6)**—*contd*

|  |  |  |
|---|---|---|
|  |  | 14 Dec 2009 (for the Sheriffdom of North Strathclyde) (SSI 2009/432) |
|  |  | 22 Feb 2010 (otherwise) (SSI 2009/432) |
| 63 | (1) | 10 Mar 2008 (SSI 2008/42) |
|  | (2) | *Not yet in force* |
|  | (3)–(6) | 10 Mar 2008 (SSI 2008/42) |
| 64–66 |  | 10 Dec 2007 (SSI 2007/479) |
| 67 | (1)–(4) | 10 Dec 2007 (SSI 2007/479) |
|  | (5), (6) | 23 Apr 2007 (SSI 2007/250) |
|  | (7), (8) | 10 Dec 2007 (SSI 2007/479) |
| 68 | (1)–(3) | 10 Dec 2007 (SSI 2007/479) |
|  | (4), (5) | 10 Mar 2008 (for the Sheriffdom of Lothian and Borders) (SSI 2008/42) |
|  |  | 2 Jun 2008 (for the Sheriffdom of Grampian, Highland and Islands) (SSI 2008/192) |
|  |  | 8 Dec 2008 (for the Sheriffdom of Glasgow and Strathkelvin) (SSI 2008/329) |
|  |  | 23 Feb 2009 (for the Sheriffdom of Tayside, Central and Fife) (SSI 2008/362) |
|  |  | 14 Dec 2009 (for the Sheriffdom of North Strathclyde) (SSI 2009/432) |
|  |  | 22 Feb 2010 (otherwise) (SSI 2009/432) |
| 69 |  | 23 Apr 2007 (SSI 2007/250) |
| 70–73 |  | 10 Dec 2007 (SSI 2007/479) |
| 74, 75 |  | 10 Mar 2008 (for the Sheriffdom of Lothian and Borders) (SSI 2008/42) |
|  |  | 2 Jun 2008 (for the Sheriffdom of Grampian, Highland and Islands) (SSI 2008/192) |
|  |  | 8 Dec 2008 (for the Sheriffdom of Glasgow and Strathkelvin) (SSI 2008/329) |
|  |  | 23 Feb 2009 (for the Sheriffdom of Tayside, Central and Fife) (SSI 2008/362) |
|  |  | 14 Dec 2009 (for the Sheriffdom of North Strathclyde) (SSI 2009/432) |
|  |  | 22 Feb 2010 (otherwise) (SSI 2009/432) |
| 76 |  | 10 Dec 2007 (SSI 2007/479) |
| 77 | (1) | 10 Dec 2007 (SSI 2007/479) |
|  | (2), (3) | 10 Mar 2008 (for the Sheriffdom of Lothian and Borders) (SSI 2008/42) |
|  |  | 2 Jun 2008 (for the Sheriffdom of Grampian, Highland and Islands) (SSI 2008/192) |
|  |  | 8 Dec 2008 (for the Sheriffdom of Glasgow and Strathkelvin) (SSI 2008/329) |
|  |  | 23 Feb 2009 (for the Sheriffdom of Tayside, Central and Fife) (SSI 2008/362) |
|  |  | 14 Dec 2009 (for the Sheriffdom of North Strathclyde) (SSI 2009/432) |
|  |  | 22 Feb 2010 (otherwise) (SSI 2009/432) |
|  | (4) | 10 Dec 2007 (SSI 2007/479) |
|  | (5) | 10 Mar 2008 (for the Sheriffdom of Lothian and Borders) (SSI 2008/42) |
|  |  | 2 Jun 2008 (for the Sheriffdom of Grampian, Highland and Islands) (SSI 2008/192) |
|  |  | 8 Dec 2008 (for the Sheriffdom of Glasgow and Strathkelvin) (SSI 2008/329) |
|  |  | 23 Feb 2009 (for the Sheriffdom of Tayside, Central and Fife) (SSI 2008/362) |
|  |  | 14 Dec 2009 (for the Sheriffdom of North Strathclyde) (SSI 2009/432) |
|  |  | 22 Feb 2010 (otherwise) (SSI 2009/432) |

**Criminal Proceedings etc (Reform) (Scotland) Act 2007 (asp 6)**—*contd*

| | | |
|---|---|---|
| 78, 79 | | 23 Apr 2007 (SSI 2007/250) |
| 80 | | See Schedule below |
| 81–84 | | 22 Feb 2007 (s 84(1)) |
| Schedule | para 1 | 10 Dec 2007 (SSI 2007/479) |
| | para 2 | 10 Mar 2008 (SSI 2008/42) |
| | para 3(a) | 2 Jun 2008 (only in the local authority areas of Highland, South Lanarkshire, West Dunbartonshire and West Lothian) (SSI 2008/192) |
| | | 1 Apr 2011 (for the purpose only of making a work order where one or more of the alleged offences in relation to which the work order is to be made was committed in a local authority area where arrangements have been made by that local authority for the supervision of any such work order) (SSI 2011/188) |
| | | *Not yet in force* (otherwise) |
| | para 3(b) | *Not yet in force* |
| | para 3(c) | 2 Jun 2008 (only in the local authority areas of Highland, South Lanarkshire, West Dunbartonshire and West Lothian) (SSI 2008/192) |
| | | 1 Apr 2011 (for the purpose only of making a work order where one or more of the alleged offences in relation to which the work order is to be made was committed in a local authority area where arrangements have been made by that local authority for the supervision of any such work order) (SSI 2011/188) |
| | | *Not yet in force* (otherwise) |
| | para 4 | 10 Mar 2008 (for the Sheriffdom of Lothian and Borders) (SSI 2008/42) |
| | | 2 Jun 2008 (for the Sheriffdom of Grampian, Highland and Islands) (SSI 2008/192) |
| | | 8 Dec 2008 (for the Sheriffdom of Glasgow and Strathkelvin) (SSI 2008/329) |
| | | 23 Feb 2009 (for the Sheriffdom of Tayside, Central and Fife) (SSI 2008/362) |
| | | 14 Dec 2009 (for the Sheriffdom of North Strathclyde) (SSI 2009/432) |
| | | 22 Feb 2010 (otherwise) (SSI 2009/432) |
| | para 5 | 10 Dec 2007 (SSI 2007/479) |
| | para 6 | 23 Apr 2007 (SSI 2007/250) |
| | para 7 | 10 Mar 2008 (for the Sheriffdom of Lothian and Borders) (SSI 2008/42) |
| | | 2 Jun 2008 (for the Sheriffdom of Grampian, Highland and Islands) (SSI 2008/192) |
| | | 8 Dec 2008 (for the Sheriffdom of Glasgow and Strathkelvin) (SSI 2008/329) |
| | | 23 Feb 2009 (for the Sheriffdom of Tayside, Central and Fife) (SSI 2008/362) |
| | | 14 Dec 2009 (for the Sheriffdom of North Strathclyde) (SSI 2009/432) |
| | | 22 Feb 2010 (otherwise) (SSI 2009/432) |
| | para 8 | 10 Mar 2008 (SSI 2008/42) |
| | para 9(1)–(6) | 10 Mar 2008 (for the Sheriffdom of Lothian and Borders) (SSI 2008/42) |
| | | 2 Jun 2008 (for the Sheriffdom of Grampian, Highland and Islands) (SSI 2008/192) |
| | | 8 Dec 2008 (for the Sheriffdom of Glasgow and Strathkelvin) (SSI 2008/329) |
| | | 23 Feb 2009 (for the Sheriffdom of Tayside, Central and Fife) (SSI 2008/362) |

**Criminal Proceedings etc (Reform) (Scotland) Act 2007 (asp 6)**—*contd*

|  |  |
|---|---|
|  | 14 Dec 2009 (for the Sheriffdom of North Strathclyde) (SSI 2009/432) |
|  | 22 Feb 2010 (otherwise) (SSI 2009/432) |
| para 9(7) | 10 Dec 2007 (in so far as it applies to justices of the peace) (SSI 2007/479) |
|  | 8 Dec 2008 (in so far as it applies to stipendiary magistrates, for the Sheriffdoms of Glasgow and Strathkelvin, Grampian, Highland and Islands and Lothian and Borders) (SSI 2008/329) |
|  | 23 Feb 2009 (in so far as it applies to stipendiary magistrates, for the Sheriffdom of Tayside, Central and Fife) (SSI 2008/362) |
|  | 14 Dec 2009 (in so far as it applies to stipendiary magistrates, for the Sheriffdom of North Strathclyde) (SSI 2009/432) |
|  | 22 Feb 2010 (in so far as it applies to stipendiary magistrates, otherwise) (SSI 2009/432) |
|  | *Not yet in force* (except in so far as applies to stipendiary magistrates)[4] |
| paras 10, 11 | 10 Mar 2008 (SSI 2008/42) |
| paras 12, 13 | 10 Dec 2007 (SSI 2007/479) |
| para 14 | 10 Dec 2007 (SSI 2007/479)[2] |
| para 15 | 10 Dec 2007 (SSI 2007/479) |
| para 16(1) | 23 Apr 2007 (SSI 2007/250)[1] |
| para 16(2)–(5) | 10 Dec 2007 (SSI 2007/479) |
| para 16(6) | 10 Dec 2007 (SSI 2007/479)[2] |
| para 17 | 10 Dec 2007 (SSI 2007/479) |
| para 18(1) | 10 Dec 2007 (SSI 2007/479) |
| para 18(2), (3) | 23 Apr 2007 (SSI 2007/250)[1] |
| para 18(4) | 10 Dec 2007 (SSI 2007/479) |
| para 19 | 23 Apr 2007 (SSI 2007/250)[1] |
| para 20(1)(a), (b)(i) | 10 Mar 2008 (SSI 2008/42) |
| para 20(1)(b)(ii) | 10 Mar 2008 (except for the purposes of any fines or expenses which require to be paid to the clerk of any district court) (SSI 2008/42) |
|  | *Not yet in force* (exception noted above) |
| para 20(1)(b)(iii) | 10 Mar 2008 (SSI 2008/42) |
| para 20(2) | 10 Mar 2008 (SSI 2008/42) |
| para 20(3)(a) | 10 Mar 2008 (SSI 2008/42) |
| para 20(3)(b) | 10 Mar 2008 (for the Sheriffdom of Lothian and Borders) (SSI 2008/42) |
|  | 2 Jun 2008 (for the Sheriffdom of Grampian, Highland and Islands) (SSI 2008/192) |
|  | 8 Dec 2008 (for the Sheriffdom of Glasgow and Strathkelvin) (SSI 2008/329) |
|  | 23 Feb 2009 (for the Sheriffdom of Tayside, Central and Fife) (SSI 2008/362) |
|  | 14 Dec 2009 (for the Sheriffdom of North Strathclyde) (SSI 2009/432) |
|  | 22 Feb 2010 (otherwise) (SSI 2009/432) |
| para 20(3)(c), (d) | 10 Mar 2008 (SSI 2008/42) |
| para 20(4) | 10 Mar 2008 (SSI 2008/42) |
| para 21 | 10 Dec 2007 (SSI 2007/479) |
| para 22 | 10 Mar 2008 (for the Sheriffdom of Lothian and Borders) (SSI 2008/42) |
|  | 2 Jun 2008 (for the Sheriffdom of Grampian, Highland and Islands) (SSI 2008/192) |
|  | 8 Dec 2008 (for the Sheriffdom of Glasgow and Strathkelvin) (SSI 2008/329) |
|  | 23 Feb 2009 (for the Sheriffdom of Tayside, Central and Fife) (SSI 2008/362) |
|  | 14 Dec 2009 (for the Sheriffdom of North Strathclyde) (SSI 2009/432) |

**Criminal Proceedings etc (Reform) (Scotland) Act 2007 (asp 6)**—*contd*

|  |  |
|---|---|
|  | 22 Feb 2010 (otherwise) (SSI 2009/432) |
| paras 23, 24 | 10 Dec 2007 (SSI 2007/479) |
| para 25(a) | 10 Mar 2008 (for the Sheriffdom of Lothian and Borders) (SSI 2008/42) |
|  | 2 Jun 2008 (for the Sheriffdom of Grampian, Highland and Islands) (SSI 2008/192) |
|  | 8 Dec 2008 (for the Sheriffdom of Glasgow and Strathkelvin) (SSI 2008/329) |
|  | 23 Feb 2009 (for the Sheriffdom of Tayside, Central and Fife) (SSI 2008/362) |
|  | 14 Dec 2009 (for the Sheriffdom of North Strathclyde) (SSI 2009/432) |
|  | 22 Feb 2010 (otherwise) (SSI 2009/432) |
| para 25(b) | 10 Dec 2007 (SSI 2007/479) |
| para 25(c) | 10 Mar 2008 (SSI 2008/42) |
| para 25(d) | 10 Mar 2008 (for the Sheriffdom of Lothian and Borders) (SSI 2008/42) |
|  | 2 Jun 2008 (for the Sheriffdom of Grampian, Highland and Islands) (SSI 2008/192) |
|  | 8 Dec 2008 (for the Sheriffdom of Glasgow and Strathkelvin) (SSI 2008/329) |
|  | 23 Feb 2009 (for the Sheriffdom of Tayside, Central and Fife) (SSI 2008/362) |
|  | 14 Dec 2009 (for the Sheriffdom of North Strathclyde) (SSI 2009/432) |
|  | 22 Feb 2010 (otherwise) (SSI 2009/432) |
| para 26(a)–(s) | 10 Mar 2008 (for the Sheriffdom of Lothian and Borders) (SSI 2008/42) |
|  | 2 Jun 2008 (for the Sheriffdom of Grampian, Highland and Islands) (SSI 2008/192) |
|  | 8 Dec 2008 (for the Sheriffdom of Glasgow and Strathkelvin) (SSI 2008/329) |
|  | 23 Feb 2009 (for the Sheriffdom of Tayside, Central and Fife) (SSI 2008/362) |
|  | 14 Dec 2009 (for the Sheriffdom of North Strathclyde) (SSI 2009/432) |
|  | 22 Feb 2010 (otherwise) (SSI 2009/432) |
| para 26(t) | 10 Mar 2008 (for the Sheriffdom of Lothian and Borders) (SSI 2008/42) |
|  | 2 Jun 2008 (for the Sheriffdom of Grampian, Highland and Islands) (SSI 2008/192) |
|  | 8 Dec 2008 (otherwise) (SSI 2008/329) |
| para 26(u)–(v) | 10 Mar 2008 (for the Sheriffdom of Lothian and Borders) (SSI 2008/42) |
|  | 2 Jun 2008 (for the Sheriffdom of Grampian, Highland and Islands) (SSI 2008/192) |
|  | 8 Dec 2008 (for the Sheriffdom of Glasgow and Strathkelvin) (SSI 2008/329) |
|  | 23 Feb 2009 (for the Sheriffdom of Tayside, Central and Fife) (SSI 2008/362) |
|  | 14 Dec 2009 (for the Sheriffdom of North Strathclyde) (SSI 2009/432) |
|  | 22 Feb 2010 (otherwise) (SSI 2009/432) |
| para 27(a), (b) | 10 Mar 2008 (for the Sheriffdom of Lothian and Borders) (SSI 2008/42) |
|  | 2 Jun 2008 (for the Sheriffdom of Grampian, Highland and Islands) (SSI 2008/192) |
|  | 8 Dec 2008 (for the Sheriffdom of Glasgow and Strathkelvin) (SSI 2008/329) |

**Criminal Proceedings etc (Reform) (Scotland) Act 2007 (asp 6)**—*contd*

|  |  |
|---|---|
|  | 23 Feb 2009 (for the Sheriffdom of Tayside, Central and Fife) (SSI 2008/362) |
|  | 14 Dec 2009 (for the Sheriffdom of North Strathclyde) (SSI 2009/432) |
|  | 22 Feb 2010 (otherwise) (SSI 2009/432) |
| para 27(c) | 10 Dec 2007 (in so far as repeals Bail, Judicial Appointments etc (Scotland) Act 2000, Schedule, para 2) (SSI 2007/479) |
|  | 10 Mar 2008 (for the Sheriffdom of Lothian and Borders) (SSI 2008/42) |
|  | 2 Jun 2008 (for the Sheriffdom of Grampian, Highland and Islands) (SSI 2008/192) |
|  | 8 Dec 2008 (for the Sheriffdom of Glasgow and Strathkelvin) (SSI 2008/329) |
|  | 23 Feb 2009 (for the Sheriffdom of Tayside, Central and Fife) (SSI 2008/362) |
|  | 14 Dec 2009 (for the Sheriffdom of North Strathclyde) (SSI 2009/432) |
|  | 22 Feb 2010 (otherwise) (SSI 2009/432) |
| para 28 | 10 Dec 2007 (SSI 2007/479)[2] |
| para 29 | 10 Dec 2007 (SSI 2007/479) |
| para 30(a) | 10 Mar 2008 (for the Sheriffdom of Lothian and Borders) (SSI 2008/42) |
|  | 2 Jun 2008 (for the Sheriffdom of Grampian, Highland and Islands) (SSI 2008/192) |
|  | 8 Dec 2008 (for the Sheriffdom of Glasgow and Strathkelvin) (SSI 2008/329) |
|  | 23 Feb 2009 (for the Sheriffdom of Tayside, Central and Fife) (SSI 2008/362) |
|  | 14 Dec 2009 (for the Sheriffdom of North Strathclyde) (SSI 2009/432) |
|  | 22 Feb 2010 (otherwise) (SSI 2009/432) |
| para 30(b) | *Not yet in force* |
| para 31 | 10 Mar 2008 (SSI 2008/42) |
| para 32(a) | 10 Mar 2008 (SSI 2008/42) |
| para 32(b), (c) | 10 Mar 2008 (for the Sheriffdom of Lothian and Borders) (SSI 2008/42) |
|  | 2 Jun 2008 (for the Sheriffdom of Grampian, Highland and Islands) (SSI 2008/192) |
|  | 8 Dec 2008 (for the Sheriffdom of Glasgow and Strathkelvin) (SSI 2008/329) |
|  | 23 Feb 2009 (for the Sheriffdom of Tayside, Central and Fife) (SSI 2008/362) |
|  | 14 Dec 2009 (for the Sheriffdom of North Strathclyde) (SSI 2009/432) |
|  | 22 Feb 2010 (otherwise) (SSI 2009/432) |
| para 33(1), (2) | 10 Mar 2008 (for the Sheriffdom of Lothian and Borders, except for the purposes of any statutory instrument made under this Act) (SSI 2008/42) |
|  | 2 Jun 2008 (for the Sheriffdom of Grampian, Highland and Islands, except for the purposes of any statutory instrument made under this Act) (SSI 2008/192) |
|  | 8 Dec 2008 (for the Sheriffdom of Glasgow and Strathkelvin, except for the purposes of any statutory instrument made under this Act) (SSI 2008/329) |
|  | 23 Feb 2009 (for the Sheriffdom of Tayside, Central and Fife, except for the purposes of any statutory instrument made under this Act) (SSI 2008/362) |
|  | 14 Dec 2009 (for the Sheriffdom of North Strathclyde, except for the purposes of any statutory instrument made under this Act) (SSI 2009/432) |

**Criminal Proceedings etc (Reform) (Scotland) Act 2007 (asp 6)**—*contd*

|  |  | 22 Feb 2010 (otherwise, except for the purposes of any statutory instrument made under this Act) (SSI 2009/432) |
|--|--|--|
|  |  | *Not yet in force* (exception noted above)[4] |
|  | para 33(3), (4) | 10 Dec 2007 (SSI 2007/479) |

[1]    For savings, see SSI 2007/250, art 4

[2]    For transitional provisions and savings, see SSI 2007/479, arts 4–14

[3]    For savings, see SSI 2008/42, arts 4–6

[4]    Note that before its revocation SSI 2009/116 was originally intended to bring this provision into force for further purposes

---

**Crofting Reform etc Act 2007 (asp 7)**

*RA:* 1 Mar 2007

*Commencement provisions:* s 43(3), (4); Crofting Reform etc Act 2007 (Commencement No 1) Order 2007, SSI 2007/269; Crofting Reform etc Act 2007 (Commencement No 2) Order 2007, SSI 2007/568

| 1, 2 |  | 25 Jun 2007 (SSI 2007/269) |
|--|--|--|
| 3–5 |  | 28 Jan 2008 (SSI 2007/568) |
| 6 |  | 25 Jun 2007 (SSI 2007/269) |
| 7 | (1)(a), (b) | 28 Jan 2008 (SSI 2007/568) |
|  | (1)(c) | 25 Jun 2007 (only for the purpose of bringing Crofters (Scotland) Act 1993, s 5(3)–(6) into force) (SSI 2007/269) |
|  |  | 28 Jan 2008 (SSI 2007/568) (for the purpose of bringing Crofters (Scotland) Act 1993, s 5(7)–(10) into force) |
|  | (2)(a)–(d) | 28 Jan 2008 (SSI 2007/568) |
|  | (2)(e)–(h) | 25 Jun 2007 (SSI 2007/269) |
|  | (2)(i), (3) | 28 Jan 2008 (SSI 2007/568) |
| 8 |  | 25 Jun 2007 (SSI 2007/269) |
| 9, 10 |  | 28 Jan 2008 (SSI 2007/568) |
| 11 | (1) | 28 Jan 2008 (SSI 2007/568) |
|  | (2), (3) | 25 Jun 2007 (SSI 2007/269) |
| 12–17 |  | 28 Jan 2008 (SSI 2007/568) |
| 18–23 |  | 25 Jun 2007 (SSI 2007/269) |
| 24, 25 |  | 28 Jan 2008 (SSI 2007/568) |
| 26 | (1)(a)–(d) | 25 Jun 2007 (SSI 2007/269) |
|  | (1)(e) | 28 Jan 2008 (SSI 2007/568) |
|  | (1)(f), (g) | 25 Jun 2007 (SSI 2007/269) |
|  | (2) | 25 Jun 2007 (only for the purpose of bringing Crofters (Scotland) Act 1993, s 50A into force) (SSI 2007/269) |
|  |  | 28 Jan 2008 (SSI 2007/568) (for the purpose of bringing Crofters (Scotland) Act 1993, s 50B into force) |
| 27 |  | 25 Jun 2007 (SSI 2007/269) |
| 28 |  | 28 Jan 2008 (SSI 2007/568) |
| 29–37 |  | 25 Jun 2007 (SSI 2007/269) |
| 38 |  | 1 Mar 2007 (s 43(3)) |
| 39 |  | See Sch 1 below |
| 40, 41 |  | 1 Mar 2007 (s 43(3)) |
| 42 |  | See Sch 2 below |
| 43 |  | 1 Mar 2007 (s 43(3)) |
| Sch 1 |  | 25 Jun 2007 (SSI 2007/269) |
| Sch 2 |  | 25 Jun 2007 (SSI 2007/269), repeals in— Crofters (Scotland) Act 1993 |
|  |  | 28 Jan 2008 (SSI 2007/568), repeals in— Succession (Scotland) Act 1964 |

## Custodial Sentences and Weapons (Scotland) Act 2007 (asp 17)

*RA:* 19 Apr 2007

*Commencement provisions:* s 67(2), (3); Custodial Sentences and Weapons (Scotland) Act 2007 (Commencement No 1) Order 2007, SSI 2007/431; Custodial Sentences and Weapons (Scotland) Act 2007 (Commencement No 2 and Transitional Provisions) Order 2009, SSI 2009/197

| | | |
|---|---|---|
| 1 | (1)–(4) | *Not yet in force* |
| | (5) | See Sch 1 below |
| 2–51 | | *Not yet in force* |
| 52 | | See Sch 2 below |
| 53 | | See Sch 3 below |
| 54–57 | | *Not yet in force* |
| 58 | | 1 Nov 2007 (for the purposes of enabling the Scottish Ministers to make orders under the Civic Government (Scotland) Act 1982, ss 27A(7), (8), 27C(1)(a), 27K(7), 27R, and to enable the High Court to make an Act of Adjournal to be made under s 27K(4) of that Act) (SSI 2007/431) |
| | | 1 Jun 2009 (for the purposes of inserting s 27S of the 1982 Act) (SSI 2009/197) |
| | | 1 Sep 2009 (for the purposes of inserting ss 27A(1) (for the purposes of definition "knife dealer's licence"), (2)–(6), 27B, 27C (so far as not already in force), 27L (for the purposes of offences specified in paras (a), (b) thereof), 27M–27Q, and 27R (so far as not already in force) of the 1982 Act) (SSI 2009/197) |
| | | 1 Jun 2010 (otherwise) (SSI 2009/197) |
| 59 | (1) | 1 Sep 2009 (SSI 2009/197) |
| | (2) | 1 Jun 2010 (SSI 2009/197) |
| | (3)(a)–(c) | 1 Jun 2010 (SSI 2009/197) |
| | (3)(d) | 1 Sep 2009 (SSI 2009/197) |
| 60 | (1)(a) | 1 Nov 2007 (SSI 2007/431) |
| | (1)(b) | 1 Nov 2007 (for the purpose of inserting sub-ss (11F)–(11J) into the Criminal Justice Act 1988, s 141) (SSI 2007/431) |
| | | *Not yet in force* (for the purposes of inserting s 141(11A)–(11E) of that Act) |
| | (2) | *Not yet in force* |
| 61 | | 1 Nov 2007 (SSI 2007/431) |
| 62 | | 1 Oct 2007 (SSI 2007/431) |
| 63 | | 1 Nov 2007 (SSI 2007/431) |
| 64 | | *Not yet in force* |
| 65 | | 19 Apr 2007 (s 67(2)) |
| 66 | (1) | See Sch 4 below |
| | (2) | See Sch 5 below |
| | (3) | See Sch 6 below |
| 67 | | 19 Apr 2007 (s 67(2)) |
| Schs 1–4 | | *Not yet in force* |
| Sch 5 | | 1 Nov 2007 (SSI 2007/431), repeals of or in— Criminal Justice Act 1988 |
| | | *Not yet in force*, repeals of or in— Prisons (Scotland) Act 1989; Prisoners and Criminal Proceedings (Scotland) Act 1993; Criminal Procedure (Scotland) Act 1995; Crime and Disorder Act 1998 |
| Sch 6 | | *Never in force* (substituted) |

## Digital Switchover (Disclosure of Information) Act 2007 (c 8)

*RA:* 18 Jun 2007

Whole Act in force 18 Jun 2007 (RA)

## Dioceses, Pastoral and Mission Measure 2007 (No 1)

*RA:* 30 Oct 2007

*Commencement provisions:* s 66

Provisions of this Measure were brought into force on the following dates by instruments made by the Archbishops of Canterbury and York, and dated 20 Dec 2007, 19 Mar 2008, 7 Aug 2008, 5 Dec 2008 and 10 Jun 2010 (made under s 66(2))

| | | |
|---|---|---|
| 1 | | 1 Jan 2008 |
| 2 | | 1 Sep 2008 |
| 3 | (1)–(4) | 1 Feb 2009 |
| | (5), (6) | 1 Sep 2008 |
| 4, 5 | | 1 Sep 2008 |
| 6 | (1), (2) | 1 Sep 2008 |
| | (3) | 1 Feb 2009 |
| | (4)–(8) | 1 Sep 2008 |
| 7–11 | | 1 Sep 2008 |
| 12 | | 1 Jan 2011 |
| 13–16 | | 1 May 2008 |
| 17 | | 1 Jan 2011 |
| 18–21 | | 1 Sep 2008 |
| 22 | | 1 May 2008 |
| 23–46 | | 11 Jun 2008 |
| 47–50 | | 31 Mar 2008 |
| 51 | | 1 Jan 2008 |
| 52 | | 1 Feb 2008 |
| 53–60 | | 11 Jun 2008 |
| 61 | | 1 Feb 2008 |
| 62 | (1)–(3) | 1 Jan 2008 |
| | (4) | 11 Jun 2008 |
| | (5) | 1 Feb 2008 |
| | (6) | 11 Jun 2008 |
| 63 | (1) | See Sch 5 below |
| | (2), (3) | 11 Jun 2008 |
| | (4) | 31 Mar 2008 |
| | (5) | 1 Jan 2008 |
| | (6) | 1 Sep 2008 |
| | (7) | 1 May 2008 |
| 64 | | See Sch 6 below |
| 65 | | See Sch 7 below |
| 66 | | 1 Jan 2008 |
| Schs 1, 2 | | 1 Sep 2008 |
| Sch 3 | | 1 Feb 2008 |
| Sch 4 | | 11 Jun 2008 |
| Sch 5 | paras 1–6 | 11 Jun 2008 |
| | para 7(a) | 11 Jun 2008 |
| | para 7(b) | 1 Jan 2008 |
| | para 7(c) | 11 Jun 2008 |
| | paras 8–23 | 11 Jun 2008 |
| Sch 6 | | 1 Feb 2008 |
| Sch 7 | | 1 Feb 2008, repeals of or in— |

Pastoral Measure 1983, s 1, Sch 1, Sch 5, paras 5–12;
Church of England (Miscellaneous Provisions) Measure 1995, s 11(e);
Synodical Government (Amendment) Measure 2003, s 2(4), (5)
1 May 2008, repeals of or in—
Dioceses Measure 1978, ss 10–15;
Church of England (Miscellaneous Provisions) Measure 1983;
Bishops (Retirement) Measure 1986;
Clergy (Ordination) Measure 1990;

## Dioceses, Pastoral and Mission Measure 2007 (No 1)—*contd*

Church of England (Miscellaneous Provisions) Measure 1995, s 12

11 Jun 2008, repeals of or in—
Faculty Jurisdiction Measure 1964;
Pastoral Measure 1983, ss 2, 41, 45, 87(1), Sch 5, paras 1–4;
Care of Cathedrals Measure 1990;
Care of Churches and Ecclesiastical Jurisdiction Measure 1991;
Pastoral (Amendment) Measure 1994;
Care of Places of Worship Measure 1999;
Synodical Government (Amendment) Measure 2003, s 2(3);
Church of England (Miscellaneous Provisions) Measure 2005

1 Sep 2008, repeals of or in—
Synodical Government Measure 1969;
Dioceses Measure 1978, ss 1–9, 16, 17, 18(1)(a), (2)–(4), (5) and (7) (words "and of the report of the Commission thereon" in both cases), 19–25, Schedule;
Church of England (Legal Aid and Miscellaneous Provisions) Measure 1988;
Church of England (Miscellaneous Provisions) Measure 1992;
Cathedrals Measure 1999;
Church of England (Miscellaneous Provisions) Measure 2000

1 Jan 2011, repeals of or in—
Dioceses Measure 1978, s 18(1)(b), (5) (except words noted above), (6), (7) (except words noted above)

## Edinburgh Airport Rail Link Act 2007 (asp 16)

*RA:* 19 Apr 2007

Whole Act in force 19 Apr 2007 (RA)

## Finance Act 2007 (c 11)

*Budget Day:* 21 Mar 2007

*RA:* 19 Jul 2007

The commencement details of Finance Acts are not set out, as the dates from which their provisions take effect are usually stated clearly and unambiguously in the text of the Act, and charging provisions will normally state for which year or years of assessment they are to have effect.

## Forced Marriage (Civil Protection) Act 2007 (c 20)

*RA:* 26 Jul 2007

*Commencement provisions:* s 4(2)–(5); Forced Marriage (Civil Protection) Act 2007 (Commencement No 1) Order 2008, SI 2008/2779; Forced Marriage (Civil Protection) Act 2007 (Commencement No 1) Order (Northern Ireland) 2008, SR 2008/446

| | | |
|---|---|---|
| 1 | | 25 Nov 2008 (except in so far as it inserts Family Law Act 1996, s 63N) (SI 2008/2779) |
| | | *Not yet in force* (exception noted above) |
| 2 | | See Sch 1 below |
| 3 | (1) | See Sch 2 below |
| | (2)–(10) | 26 Jul 2007 (RA) |
| 4 | | 26 Jul 2007 (RA) |
| Sch 1 | paras 1, 2, 3(1), (2)(a) | 25 Nov 2008 (SR 2008/446) |
| | para 3(2)(b) | *Not yet in force* |

**Forced Marriage (Civil Protection) Act 2007 (c 20)**—*contd*

|  | para 3(3)–(6) | 25 Nov 2008 (SR 2008/446) |
|---|---|---|
|  | para 3(7) | 25 Nov 2008 (except insofar as sets out the definition of "relevant third party") (SR 2008/446) |
|  |  | *Not yet in force* (exception noted above) |
|  | para 3(8) | *Not yet in force* |
|  | paras 4–8 | 25 Nov 2008 (SR 2008/446) |
|  | para 9 | *Not yet in force* |
|  | paras 10–13 | 25 Nov 2008 (SR 2008/446) |
|  | para 14(1) | *Not yet in force* |
|  | paras 14(2), (3), 15, 16 | 25 Nov 2008 (SR 2008/446) |
| Sch 2 | paras 1, 2 | 25 Nov 2008 (SI 2008/2779) |
|  | para 3(1), (2) | 25 Nov 2008 (SI 2008/2779) |
|  | para 3(3) | *Never in force* (repealed) |
|  | paras 4, 5 | 25 Nov 2008 (SR 2008/446) |

---

**Further Education and Training Act 2007 (c 25)**

*RA:* 23 Oct 2007

*Commencement provisions:* s 32; Further Education and Training Act 2007 (Commencement No 1 and Transitional Provisions) Order 2007, SI 2007/3505; Further Education and Training Act 2007 (Commencement No 1) (Wales) Order 2007, SI 2007/3565; Further Education and Training Act 2007 (Commencement No 1) (England) Order 2008, SI 2008/313; Further Education and Training Act 2007 (Commencement No 2) (Wales) Order 2008, SI 2008/983; Further Education and Training Act 2007 (Commencement No 1) (England and Wales) Order 2008, SI 2008/1065

| | | |
|---|---|---|
| 1 |  | 21 Feb 2008 (SI 2008/313) |
| 2 |  | 31 Jan 2008 (to the extent that it inserts Learning and Skills Act 2000, s 18A(2)–(4)) (SI 2007/3505) |
|  |  | 1 Sep 2008 (otherwise) (SI 2008/313) |
| 3–5 |  | 21 Feb 2008 (SI 2008/313) |
| 6–8 |  | 23 Dec 2007 (SI 2007/3505) |
| 9 |  | 23 Oct 2007 (s 32(1)) |
| 10 |  | *Never in force* (repealed) |
| 11–13 |  | 23 Dec 2007 (SI 2007/3505) |
| 14–16 |  | *Never in force* (repealed) |
| 17 |  | 23 Dec 2007 (to the extent that it inserts Further and Higher Education Act 1992, s 56B) (SI 2007/3505) |
|  |  | 18 Apr 2008 (otherwise) (SI 2007/3505) |
| 18 | (1)–(4) | 18 Apr 2008 (SI 2008/983) |
|  | (5) | 23 Dec 2007 (SI 2007/3565) |
| 19, 20 |  | 1 May 2008 (SI 2007/3505) |
| 21 |  | 23 Oct 2007 (s 32(1)) |
| 22, 23 |  | 23 Dec 2007 (E) (SI 2007/3505) |
|  |  | *Not yet in force* (otherwise) (s 22 repealed) |
| 24, 25 |  | 2 Mar 2008 (SI 2007/3505)[1] |
| 26 |  | 23 Oct 2007 (s 32(1)) |
| 27 |  | 23 Dec 2007 (s 32(2)) |
| 28 |  | 23 Oct 2007 (s 32(1)) |
| 29 |  | See Sch 1 below |
| 30 |  | See Sch 2 below |
| 31–34 |  | 23 Oct 2007 (s 32(1)) |
| Sch 1 | paras 1–5 | 2 Mar 2008 (SI 2007/3505)[1] |
|  | para 6 | See paras 7–11 below |
|  | paras 7, 8 | 23 Dec 2007 (SI 2007/3505) |
|  | para 9 | 18 Apr 2008 (SI 2008/1065) |
|  | paras 10, 11 | 23 Dec 2007 (SI 2007/3505) |
|  | para 12 | See paras 13–16 below |
|  | para 13 | 23 Dec 2007 (SI 2007/3505) |

**Further Education and Training Act 2007 (c 25)**—*contd*

| | | |
|---|---|---|
| | para 14 | 21 Feb 2008 (SI 2008/313) |
| | para 15 | 31 Jan 2008 (SI 2007/3505) |
| | para 16 | 21 Feb 2008 (SI 2008/313) |
| Sch 2 | | 23 Dec 2007 (repeal of Learning and Skills Act 2000, s 15(2)) (SI 2007/3505) |
| | | 2 Mar 2008 (repeals in Industrial Training Act 1982) (SI 2007/3505)[1] |
| | | 21 Feb 2008 (SI 2008/313), repeals of or in— |
| | | Learning and Skills Act 2000, ss 19–24, Schs 2, 3; |
| | | Education Act 2002; |
| | | Children Act 2004 |
| | | 18 Apr 2008 (SI 2008/1065), repeals of or in— |
| | | Further and Higher Education Act 1992, s 57; |
| | | Education and Inspections Act 2006 |
| | | *Not yet in force*, repeals of or in— |
| | | Further and Higher Education Act 1992, ss 17, 27 |

[1] For a transitional provision, see SI 2007/3505, art 7

---

**Glasgow Airport Rail Link Act 2007 (asp 1)**

*RA:* 15 Jan 2007

Whole Act in force 15 Jan 2007 (RA)

---

**Greater London Authority Act 2007 (c 24)**

*RA:* 23 Oct 2007

*Commencement provisions:* s 59(4)–(9); Greater London Authority Act 2007 (Commencement No 1 and Appointed Day) Order 2007, SI 2007/3107; Greater London Authority Act 2007 (Commencement No 2) Order 2008, SI 2008/113; Greater London Authority Act 2007 (Commencement No 3) Order 2008, SI 2008/582; Greater London Authority Act 2007 (Commencement No 4 and Saving) Order 2008, SI 2008/1372; Greater London Authority Act 2007 (Commencement No 5) Order 2008, SI 2008/2037

| | | |
|---|---|---|
| 1–3 | | 21 Jan 2008 (SI 2008/113) |
| 4 | (1) | 23 Oct 2007 (so far as confers power to make orders) (s 59(4)(b)) |
| | | 21 Jan 2008 (otherwise) (SI 2008/113) |
| | (2) | See Sch 1 below |
| | (3) | 21 Jan 2008 (SI 2008/113) |
| 5–11 | | 21 Jan 2008 (SI 2008/113) |
| 12–14 | | 30 Oct 2007 (SI 2007/3107)[1] |
| 15, 16 | | 30 Oct 2007 (SI 2007/3107) |
| 17–27 | | 21 Jan 2008 (SI 2008/113) |
| 28 | | 23 Dec 2007 (s 59(5)) |
| 29 | | 21 Jan 2008 (SI 2008/113) |
| 30 | | 23 Oct 2007 (so far as confers power to make orders or regulations) (s 59(4)(b)) |
| | | 27 Jun 2008 (otherwise) (SI 2008/1372)[2] |
| 31 | | 23 Oct 2007 (so far as confers power to make orders or regulations) (s 59(4)(b)) |
| | | 6 Apr 2008 (otherwise) (SI 2008/582) |
| 32–34 | | 6 Apr 2008 (SI 2008/582) |
| 35, 36 | | 23 Oct 2007 (so far as they confer power to make orders or regulations) (s 59(4)(b)) |
| | | 6 Apr 2008 (otherwise) (SI 2008/582) |
| 37 | | 21 Jan 2008 (SI 2008/113) |
| 38 | | 23 Oct 2007 (so far as confers power to make orders) (s 59(4)(b)) |

**Greater London Authority Act 2007 (c 24)**—*contd*

|  |  |
|---|---|
|  | 24 Jul 2008 (otherwise) (SI 2008/2037) |
| 39–42 | 21 Jan 2008 (SI 2008/113) |
| 43 | 23 Oct 2007 (so far as confers power to make orders) (s 59(4)(b)) |
|  | 21 Jan 2008 (otherwise) (SI 2008/113) |
| 44 | 21 Jan 2008 (SI 2008/113) |
| 45 | 6 Apr 2008 (SI 2008/582) |
| 46 | 23 Dec 2007 (s 59(5)) |
| 47–49 | 6 Apr 2008 (SI 2008/582) |
| 50 | 23 Oct 2007 (so far as confers power to make orders) (s 59(4)(b)) |
|  | 21 Jan 2008 (otherwise) (SI 2008/113) |
| 51 | 23 Oct 2007 (so far as confers power to make orders) (s 59(4)(b)) |
|  | 6 Apr 2008 (otherwise) (SI 2008/582) |
| 52 | 23 Oct 2007 (so far as confers power to make orders) (s 59(4)(b)) |
|  | 21 Jan 2008 (otherwise) (SI 2008/113) |
| 53–56 | 23 Oct 2007 (s 59(4)(a)) |
| 57 | See Sch 2 below |
| 58, 59 | 23 Oct 2007 (s 59(4)(a)) |
| Sch 1 | 23 Oct 2007 (so far as confers power to make orders) (s 59(4)(b)) |
|  | 21 Jan 2008 (otherwise) (SI 2008/113) |
| Sch 2 | 30 Oct 2007 (repeal in Greater London Authority Act 1999, Sch 4) (SI 2007/3107) |
|  | 21 Jan 2008 (SI 2008/113), repeals of or in— |
|  | Greater London Authority Act 1999 (in so far as not already repealed); |
|  | Railways Act 2005 |
|  | 6 Apr 2008 (SI 2008/582), repeals in— |
|  | Museum of London Act 1986 |

[1]    Ss 12–14 have effect in relation to financial years beginning on or after this date; see s 59(6)

[2]    For a saving, see SI 2008/1372, art 3

# Income Tax Act 2007 (c 3)

*RA:* 20 Mar 2007

*Commencement provisions:* s 1034

|  |  |
|---|---|
| 1–155 | 6 Apr 2007 (with effect (a) for income tax purposes, for the tax year 2007–08 and subsequent tax years, and (b) for corporation tax purposes, for accounting periods ending after 5 Apr 2007) (s 1034(1)) |
| 156–257 | 6 Apr 2007 (with effect (a) for income tax purposes, for the tax year 2007–08 and subsequent tax years, and (b) for corporation tax purposes, for accounting periods ending after 5 Apr 2007; do not have effect in relation to shares issued before 6 Apr 2007) (s 1034(1), (3)) |
| 258–851 | 6 Apr 2007 (with effect (a) for income tax purposes, for the tax year 2007–08 and subsequent tax years, and (b) for corporation tax purposes, for accounting periods ending after 5 Apr 2007) (s 1034(1)) |
| 852 | 20 Mar 2007 (s 1034(4)) |
| 853–1016 | 6 Apr 2007 (with effect (a) for income tax purposes, for the tax year 2007–08 and subsequent tax years, and (b) for corporation tax purposes, for accounting periods ending after 5 Apr 2007) (s 1034(1)) |
| 1017, 1018 | 20 Mar 2007 (s 1034(4)) |
| 1019–1026 | 6 Apr 2007 (with effect (a) for income tax purposes, for the tax year 2007–08 and subsequent tax years, and (b) for corporation tax purposes, for accounting periods ending after 5 Apr 2007) (s 1034(1)) |

**Income Tax Act 2007 (c 3)**—*contd*

| | | |
|---|---|---|
| 1027 | | See Sch 1 below |
| 1028, 1029 | | 20 Mar 2007 (s 1034(4)) |
| 1030 | (1) | See Sch 2 below |
| | (2)–(4) | 20 Mar 2007 (s 1034(4)) |
| 1031 | | See Sch 3 below |
| 1032 | | See Sch 4 below |
| 1033–1035 | | 20 Mar 2007 (s 1034(4)) |
| Sch 1 | Pts 1, 2 | 6 Apr 2007 (with effect (a) for income tax purposes, for the tax year 2007–08 and subsequent tax years, and (b) for corporation tax purposes, for accounting periods ending after 5 Apr 2007) (s 1034(1)) |
| | Pt 3 | 6 Apr 2007 (with effect (a) for income tax purposes, for the tax year 2007–08 and subsequent tax years, and (b) for corporation tax purposes, for accounting periods ending after 5 Apr 2007; does not have effect in relation to shares issued before 6 Apr 2007) (s 1034(1), (3)) |
| Sch 2 | | 6 Apr 2007 (with effect (a) for income tax purposes, for the tax year 2007–08 and subsequent tax years, and (b) for corporation tax purposes, for accounting periods ending after 5 Apr 2007) (s 1034(1)) |
| Sch 3 | Pt 1 | 6 Apr 2007 (with effect (a) for income tax purposes, for the tax year 2007–08 and subsequent tax years, and (b) for corporation tax purposes, for accounting periods ending after 5 Apr 2007) (s 1034(1)) |
| | Pt 2 | 6 Apr 2007 (with effect (a) for income tax purposes, for the tax year 2007–08 and subsequent tax years, and (b) for corporation tax purposes, for accounting periods ending after 5 Apr 2007; does not have effect in relation to shares issued before 6 Apr 2007) (s 1034(1), (3)) |
| Sch 4 | | 6 Apr 2007 (with effect (a) for income tax purposes, for the tax year 2007–08 and subsequent tax years, and (b) for corporation tax purposes, for accounting periods ending after 5 Apr 2007) (s 1034(1)) |

---

**International Tribunals (Sierra Leone) Act 2007 (c 7)**

*RA: 18 Jun 2007*

Whole Act in force 18 Jun 2007 (RA)

---

**Justice and Security (Northern Ireland) Act 2007 (c 6)**

*RA: 24 May 2007*

*Commencement provisions:* s 53; Justice and Security (Northern Ireland) Act 2007 (Commencement No 1 and Transitional Provisions) Order 2007, SI 2007/2045; Justice and Security (Northern Ireland) Act 2007 (Commencement No 2) Order 2007, SI 2007/3069; Justice and Security (Northern Ireland) Act 2007 (Commencement No 3) Order 2009, SI 2009/446

| | | |
|---|---|---|
| 1–7 | | 1 Aug 2007 (SI 2007/2045) |
| 8 | (1)–(3) | 1 Aug 2007 (SI 2007/2045) |
| | (4) | 19 Jul 2007 (SI 2007/2045) |
| 9 | | 24 May 2007 (s 53(3)(a)) |
| 10–20 | | 1 Aug 2007 (SI 2007/2045) |
| 21–40 | | 1 Aug 2007 (s 53(2)) |
| 41–43 | | 1 Aug 2007 (SI 2007/2045) |
| 44 | | 11 Mar 2009 (SI 2009/446) |
| 45 | | 7 Nov 2007 (SI 2007/3069) |
| 46, 47 | | 1 Aug 2007 (SI 2007/2045) |
| 48 | (1), (2) | 1 Aug 2007 (SI 2007/2045) |

**Justice and Security (Northern Ireland) Act 2007 (c 6)**—*contd*

| | | |
|---|---|---|
| | (3)–(5) | 8 Mar 2009 (SI 2009/446) |
| | (6), (7) | 1 Aug 2007 (SI 2007/2045) |
| 49 | | 8 Mar 2009 (SI 2009/446) |
| 50 | | See Sch 7 below |
| 51–54 | | 24 May 2007 (s 53(3)(b)–(d)) |
| Schs 1, 2 | | 1 Aug 2007 (SI 2007/2045) |
| Schs 3, 4 | | 1 Aug 2007 (s 53(2)) |
| Sch 5 | | 11 Mar 2009 (SI 2009/446) |
| Sch 6 | | 1 Aug 2007 (SI 2007/2045)[1] |
| Sch 7 | | *Not yet in force* |

[1]   For transitional provisions, see SI 2007/2045, art 3

---

**Legal Profession and Legal Aid (Scotland) Act 2007 (asp 5)**

*RA:* 19 Jan 2007

*Commencement provisions:* s 82(2), (3); Legal Profession and Legal Aid (Scotland) Act 2007 (Commencement No 1) Order 2007, SSI 2007/57; Legal Profession and Legal Aid (Scotland) Act 2007 (Commencement No 2) Order 2007, SSI 2007/140; Legal Profession and Legal Aid (Scotland) Act 2007 (Commencement No 3) Order 2007, SSI 2007/335; Legal Profession and Legal Aid (Scotland) Act 2007 (Commencement No 4) Order 2007, SSI 2007/497; Legal Profession and Legal Aid (Scotland) Act 2007 (Commencement No 5) Order 2008, SSI 2008/311; Legal Profession and Legal Aid (Scotland) Act 2007 (Commencement No 6) Order 2010, SSI 2010/376

| | | |
|---|---|---|
| 1 | | See Sch 1 below |
| 2–26 | | 1 Oct 2008 (SSI 2008/311) |
| 27 | | 23 Nov 2007 (SSI 2007/497) |
| 28 | | 1 Oct 2008 (SSI 2008/311) |
| 29–32 | | 23 Nov 2007 (SSI 2007/497) |
| 33 | | 1 Oct 2008 (SSI 2008/311) |
| 34 | | 23 Nov 2007 (SSI 2007/497) |
| 35–38 | | 1 Oct 2008 (SSI 2008/311) |
| 39 | | 23 Nov 2007 (SSI 2007/497) |
| 40 | | 1 Oct 2008 (SSI 2008/311) |
| 41 | | 23 Nov 2007 (SSI 2007/497) |
| 42, 43 | | 1 Oct 2008 (SSI 2008/311) |
| 44 | | 19 Mar 2007 (SSI 2007/140) |
| 45 | | 1 Oct 2008 (SSI 2008/311) |
| 46 | | 19 Jan 2007 (s 82(2)) |
| 47–57 | | 1 Oct 2008 (SSI 2008/311) |
| 58–60 | | 23 Nov 2007 (SSI 2007/497) |
| 61 | | 19 Mar 2007 (SSI 2007/140) |
| 62, 63 | | 23 Nov 2007 (SSI 2007/497) |
| 64, 65 | | 25 Nov 2010 (SSI 2010/376) |
| 66 | | 1 Oct 2008 (SSI 2008/311) |
| 67, 68 | | 30 Jul 2007 (SSI 2007/335) |
| 69 | (1) | 8 Feb 2007 (SSI 2007/57) |
| | (2)(a) | 8 Feb 2007 (SSI 2007/57) |
| | (2)(b) | *Not yet in force* |
| | (3) | *Not yet in force* |
| | (4) | 8 Feb 2007 (SSI 2007/57) |
| 70 | | *Not yet in force* |
| 71 | | 8 Feb 2007 (SSI 2007/57) |
| 72 | | 25 Nov 2010 (SSI 2010/376) |
| 73 | | 8 Feb 2007 (SSI 2007/57) |
| 74 | | 30 Jul 2007 (SSI 2007/335) |
| 75 | | *Not yet in force* |
| 76 | | 8 Feb 2007 (SSI 2007/57) |

## Legal Profession and Legal Aid (Scotland) Act 2007 (asp 5)—*contd*

| | | |
|---|---|---|
| 77 | | 1 Oct 2008 (SSI 2008/311) |
| 78 | | 23 Nov 2007 (SSI 2007/497) |
| 79, 80 | | 19 Jan 2007 (s 82(2)) |
| 81 | | See Sch 5 below |
| 82 | | 19 Jan 2007 (s 82(2)) |
| Sch 1 | paras 1–7 | 19 Mar 2007 (SSI 2007/140) |
| | paras 8–11 | 23 Nov 2007 (SSI 2007/497) |
| | para 12 | 19 Mar 2007 (SSI 2007/140) |
| | para 13 | 23 Nov 2007 (SSI 2007/497) |
| | para 14 | 19 Mar 2007 (SSI 2007/140) |
| | paras 15, 16 | 23 Nov 2007 (SSI 2007/497) |
| Sch 2 | | 1 Oct 2008 (SSI 2008/311) |
| Sch 3 | | 23 Nov 2007 (SSI 2007/497) |
| Sch 4 | | 1 Oct 2008 (SSI 2008/311) |
| Sch 5 | para 1(1)–(14) | 1 Oct 2008 (SSI 2008/311) |
| | para 1(15), (16) | 23 Nov 2007 (SSI 2007/497) |
| | para 1(17)–(26) | 1 Oct 2008 (SSI 2008/311) |
| | para 2 | 1 Oct 2008 (SSI 2008/311) |
| | para 3(1)–(6) | 1 Oct 2008 (SSI 2008/311) |
| | para 3(7)(a)(i), (ii) | 1 Oct 2008 (SSI 2008/311) |
| | para 3(7)(a)(iii) | *Not yet in force* |
| | para 3(7)(b) | 1 Oct 2008 (SSI 2008/311) |
| | para 3(8), (9) | 1 Oct 2008 (SSI 2008/311) |
| | para 3(10) | 19 Mar 2007 (SSI 2007/140) |
| | para 3(11), (12) | 1 Oct 2008 (SSI 2008/311) |
| | paras 4, 5 | 1 Oct 2008 (SSI 2008/311) |
| | para 6 | 23 Nov 2007 (SSI 2007/497) |

## Legal Services Act 2007 (c 29)

*RA:* 30 Oct 2007

*Commencement provisions:* s 211; Legal Services Act 2007 (Commencement No 1 and Transitory Provisions) Order 2008, SI 2008/222; Legal Services Act 2007 (Commencement No 2 and Transitory Provisions) Order 2008, SI 2008/1436, as amended by SI 2008/1591; Legal Services Act 2007 (Commencement No 3 and Transitory Provisions) Order 2008, SI 2008/3149; Legal Services Act 2007 (Commencement No 4, Transitory and Transitional Provisions and Appointed Day) Order 2009, SI 2009/503; Legal Services Act 2007 (Commencement No 5, Transitory and Transitional Provisions) Order 2009, SI 2009/1365; Legal Services Act 2007 (Commencement No 6, Transitory, Transitional and Saving Provisions) Order 2009, SI 2009/3250, as amended by SI 2011/2196; Legal Services Act 2007 (Commencement No 7) Order 2010, SI 2010/1118; Legal Services Act 2007 (Commencement No 8, Transitory and Transitional Provisions) Order 2010, SI 2010/2089, as amended by SI 2011/2196; Legal Services Act 2007 (Commencement No 9) Order 2010, SI 2010/2842; Legal Services Act 2007 (Commencement No 10) Order 2011, SI 2011/720; Legal Services Act 2007 (Commencement No 11, Transitory and Transitional Provisions and Related Amendments) Order 2011, SI 2011/2196; Legal Services Act 2007 (Commencement No 12, Supplementary and Transitory Provision) Order 2014, SI 2014/3307

| | | |
|---|---|---|
| 1 | | 7 Mar 2008 (SI 2008/222)[1] |
| 2, 3 | | 7 Mar 2008 (SI 2008/222) |
| 4 | | 1 Jan 2010 (SI 2009/3250) |
| 5–7 | | 7 Mar 2008 (SI 2008/222) |
| 8 | | 1 Jan 2009 (SI 2008/3149)[4] |
| 9–11 | | 1 Jan 2009 (SI 2008/3149) |
| 12 | (1) | 7 Mar 2008 (in so far as defines the term "reserved legal activity" for the purposes of ss 1, 207 (definition "consumers"), 69(4) (as modified by this order), Sch 1 para 2(3)–(5), Sch 15, para 2(3), (4), Sch 22, para 2(6), (7)(b)) (SI 2008/222) |
| | | 31 Mar 2009 (in so far as defines that term for the purposes of the Administration of Justice Act 1985, ss 9, 32A) (SI 2009/503) |

**Legal Services Act 2007 (c 29)**—*contd*

| | | |
|---|---|---|
| | | 1 Jan 2010 (otherwise) (SI 2009/3250) |
| | (2) | See Sch 2 below |
| | (3)–(6) | 1 Jan 2010 (SI 2009/3250) |
| 13–17 | | 1 Jan 2010 (SI 2009/3250) |
| 18 | (1)(a) | 1 Jan 2010 (SI 2009/3250)[7] |
| | (1)(b) | 6 Oct 2011 (SI 2011/2196) |
| | (2)–(4) | 1 Oct 2011 (SI 2011/2196) |
| | (5), (6) | 6 Oct 2011 (SI 2011/2196) |
| 19 | | 1 Jan 2010 (SI 2009/3250) |
| 20 | (1) | 1 Jan 2010 (SI 2009/3250) |
| | (2) | 7 Mar 2008 (in so far as defines the term "approved regulator" for the purposes of ss 69(4) (as modified by this order), 69(7), 172(1)(a), Sch 22, paras 2(6), (7)(b), 5) (SI 2008/222) |
| | | 1 Jan 2010 (otherwise) (SI 2009/3250) |
| | (3), (4) | 1 Jan 2010 (SI 2009/3250) |
| | (5) | See Sch 4 below |
| | (6) | 1 Jan 2010 (SI 2009/3250) |
| 21 | (1)(a)–(i) | 1 Jan 2010 (SI 2009/3250) |
| | (1)(j) | 1 Oct 2011 (SI 2011/2196) |
| | (2)–(4) | 1 Jan 2010 (SI 2009/3250) |
| 22 | | See Sch 5 below |
| 23 | | 1 Jan 2010 (SI 2009/3250) |
| 24 | (1), (2) | 1 Jan 2010 (SI 2009/3250) |
| | (3) | See Sch 6 below |
| | (4), (5) | 1 Jan 2010 (SI 2009/3250) |
| 25 | | 1 Jan 2010 (except in so far as relates to Sch 10) (SI 2009/3250)[7] |
| | | 2 Aug 2010 (exception noted above) (SI 2010/1118) |
| 26 | (1) | 1 Jan 2010 (SI 2009/3250) |
| | (2) | See Sch 6 below |
| | (3), (4) | 1 Jan 2010 (SI 2009/3250) |
| 27 | | 1 Jan 2009 (SI 2008/3149) |
| 28 | | 1 Jan 2010 (SI 2009/3250) |
| 29, 30 | | 1 Jan 2009 (SI 2008/3149) |
| 31, 32 | | 1 Jan 2010 (SI 2009/3250) |
| 33 | | See Sch 7 below |
| 34–36 | | 1 Jan 2010 (SI 2009/3250) |
| 37 | (1)–(3) | 1 Jan 2010 (SI 2009/3250) |
| | (4), (5) | 1 Jan 2009 (SI 2008/3149) |
| | (6), (7) | 1 Jan 2010 (SI 2009/3250) |
| 38–40 | | 1 Jan 2010 (SI 2009/3250) |
| 41 | (1)–(3) | 1 Jan 2010 (SI 2009/3250) |
| | (4) | See Sch 8, Pt 1 below |
| | (5) | 1 Jan 2009 (SI 2008/3149) |
| 42 | (1)–(5) | 1 Jan 2010 (SI 2009/3250) |
| | (6)–(10) | 1 Jan 2009 (SI 2008/3149) |
| 43 | | 1 Jan 2010 (SI 2009/3250) |
| 44 | (1) | 1 Jan 2010 (SI 2009/3250) |
| | (2) | See Sch 8, Pt 2 below |
| 45 | (1), (2) | 1 Jan 2010 (SI 2009/3250) |
| | (3)(a) | 1 Jan 2010 (SI 2009/3250) |
| | (3)(b), (c) | 1 Jan 2009 (SI 2008/3149) |
| | (4) | 1 Jan 2009 (SI 2008/3149) |
| | (5), (6) | 1 Jan 2010 (SI 2009/3250) |
| | (7) | See Sch 9 below |
| | (8)–(10) | 1 Jan 2010 (SI 2009/3250) |
| 46, 47 | | 1 Jan 2010 (SI 2009/3250) |
| 48 | (1)–(5) | 1 Jan 2010 (SI 2009/3250) |
| | (6)–(9) | 1 Jan 2009 (SI 2008/3149) |
| | (10) | 1 Jan 2010 (SI 2009/3250) |

**Legal Services Act 2007 (c 29)**—*contd*

| | | |
|---|---|---|
| 49, 50 | | 1 Jan 2009 (SI 2008/3149) |
| 51 | (1) | 1 Jan 2009 (SI 2008/3149) |
| | (2) | 1 Jan 2010 (SI 2009/3250) |
| | (3), (4) | 1 Jan 2009 (SI 2008/3149) |
| | (5) | 1 Jan 2010 (SI 2009/3250) |
| | (6)–(8) | 1 Jan 2009 (SI 2008/3149) |
| 52–63 | | 1 Jan 2010 (SI 2009/3250) |
| 64 | (1), (2) | 1 Jan 2010 (SI 2009/3250) |
| | (3) | 1 Oct 2011 (SI 2011/2196) |
| | (4)–(6) | 1 Jan 2010 (SI 2009/3250)[7] |
| 65–68 | | 1 Jan 2010 (SI 2009/3250) |
| 69, 70 | | 7 Mar 2008 (SI 2008/222)[2] |
| 71 | | 1 Oct 2011 (SI 2011/2196) |
| 72 | | 31 Mar 2009 (in so far as defines the term "an interest in a body" for the purposes of the Solicitors Act 1974, ss 43, 44, 44B, and the Administration of Justice Act 1985, ss 9, 32A, Sch 2, paras 9, 10, 14, 18A; and in so far as defines the term "shares" for the purposes of s 9A of the 1985 Act) (SI 2009/503) |
| | | 1 Oct 2011 (otherwise) (SI 2011/2196) |
| 73 | (1) | 7 Mar 2008 (in so far as defines the term "licensing authority" for the purposes of ss 69(7)(a), 172(1)(a), Sch 1, Sch 22, para 2(7)(b)) (SI 2008/222) |
| | | 1 Oct 2011 (so far as relates to para (b)) (SI 2011/2196) |
| | | *Not yet in force* (otherwise) |
| | (2)(a) | *Not yet in force* |
| | (2)(b) | 1 Oct 2011 (SI 2011/2196) |
| | (3) | *Not yet in force* |
| | (4) | 1 Oct 2011 (SI 2011/2196) |
| 74 | | See Sch 10, Pt 1 below |
| 75 | | 2 Aug 2010 (SI 2010/1118) |
| 76 | (1), (2) | 2 Aug 2010 (SI 2010/1118) |
| | (3)(a) | 2 Aug 2010 (SI 2010/1118) |
| | (3)(b), (c) | 1 Jan 2009 (SI 2008/3149) |
| | (4) | 1 Jan 2009 (SI 2008/3149) |
| | (5), (6) | 2 Aug 2010 (SI 2010/1118) |
| | (7) | See Sch 10, Pt 2 below |
| | (8), (9) | 2 Aug 2010 (SI 2010/1118) |
| 77, 78 | | 2 Aug 2010 (SI 2010/1118) |
| 79 | (1)–(5) | 2 Aug 2010 (SI 2010/1118) |
| | (6)–(10) | 1 Jan 2009 (SI 2008/3149) |
| 80, 81 | | 30 Nov 2010 (SI 2010/2842) |
| 82 | | 1 Oct 2011 (SI 2011/2196)[10] |
| 83 | (1), (2) | *Not yet in force* |
| | (3)–(7) | 2 Aug 2010 (SI 2010/1118) |
| | (8), (9) | *Not yet in force* |
| 84 | (1) | 1 Oct 2011 (SI 2011/2196)[10] |
| | (2) | 1 Jan 2009 (in so far as introduces Sch 12) (SI 2008/3149) |
| | | *Not yet in force* (otherwise) |
| | (3)–(6) | 1 Oct 2011 (SI 2011/2196)[10] |
| 85 | | 1 Oct 2011 (SI 2011/2196)[10] |
| 86 | (1) | 1 Oct 2011 (SI 2011/2196) |
| | (2) | *Not yet in force* |
| | (3), (4) | 1 Oct 2011 (SI 2011/2196) |
| 87 | (1)–(3) | 1 Oct 2011 (SI 2011/2196) |
| | (4), (5) | 1 Jan 2009 (SI 2008/3149) |
| 88 | | 1 Oct 2011 (SI 2011/2196) |
| 89 | | See Sch 13 below |
| 90–94 | | 1 Oct 2011 (SI 2011/2196) |
| 95 | (1), (2) | 1 Oct 2011 (SI 2011/2196) |

**Legal Services Act 2007 (c 29)**—*contd*

|  |  |  |
|---|---|---|
|  | (3), (4) | 1 Jan 2009 (SI 2008/3149) |
|  | (5)–(7) | 1 Oct 2011 (SI 2011/2196) |
| 96 | (1) | 1 Jan 2009 (SI 2008/3149) |
|  | (2)–(8) | 1 Oct 2011 (SI 2011/2196) |
| 97–101 |  | 1 Oct 2011 (SI 2011/2196) |
| 102 |  | See Sch 14 below |
| 103 |  | *Not yet in force* |
| 104 |  | 1 Oct 2011 (SI 2011/2196) |
| 105–108 |  | *Not yet in force* |
| 109 |  | 31 Mar 2009 (in so far as defines the term "an interest in a body" for the purposes of the Solicitors Act 1974, ss 43, 44, 44B, and the Administration of Justice Act 1985, ss 9, 32A, Sch 2, paras 9, 10, 14, 18A) (SI 2009/503) |
|  |  | *Not yet in force* (otherwise) |
| 110, 111 |  | 1 Oct 2011 (SI 2011/2196) |
| 112 | (1) | 6 Oct 2010 (SI 2010/2089) |
|  | (2) | 1 Jan 2009 (SI 2008/3149) |
|  | (3) | 6 Oct 2010 (SI 2010/2089) |
|  | (4) | 1 Jan 2009 (SI 2008/3149) |
|  | (5) | *Not yet in force* |
| 113 |  | 6 Oct 2010 (SI 2010/2089)[8] |
| 114 | (1) | 7 Mar 2008 (SI 2008/222) |
|  | (2) | See Sch 15 below |
| 115–124 |  | 1 Jan 2009 (SI 2008/3149) |
| 125 |  | 6 Oct 2010 (SI 2010/2089) |
| 126 | (1), (2) | 6 Oct 2010 (SI 2010/2089)[8] |
|  | (3) | 1 Jan 2009 (SI 2008/3149) |
| 127 |  | 1 Jan 2009 (SI 2008/3149) |
| 128 | (1), (2) | 6 Oct 2010 (SI 2010/2089) |
|  | (3)(a) | 6 Oct 2010 (SI 2010/2089) |
|  | (3)(b) | 1 Jan 2009 (SI 2008/3149) |
|  | (4)(a)–(c) | 6 Oct 2010 (SI 2010/2089) |
|  | (4)(d) | 1 Jan 2009 (SI 2008/3149) |
|  | (5)(a), (b) | 6 Oct 2010 (SI 2010/2089) |
|  | (5)(c) | 1 Jan 2009 (SI 2008/3149) |
|  | (6), (7) | 6 Oct 2010 (SI 2010/2089) |
| 129 |  | 6 Oct 2010 (SI 2010/2089) |
| 130 |  | 1 Jan 2009 (SI 2008/3149) |
| 131 |  | 6 Oct 2010 (SI 2010/2089) |
| 132, 133 |  | 1 Jan 2009 (SI 2008/3149) |
| 134, 135 |  | 6 Oct 2010 (SI 2010/2089) |
| 136 |  | 1 Jan 2009 (SI 2008/3149) |
| 137 | (1)–(3) | 6 Oct 2010 (SI 2010/2089) |
|  | (4) | 1 Jan 2009 (SI 2008/3149) |
|  | (5) | 6 Oct 2010 (SI 2010/2089) |
| 138, 139 |  | 6 Oct 2010 (SI 2010/2089) |
| 140 | (1)–(5) | 6 Oct 2010 (SI 2010/2089) |
|  | (6)(a), (b) | 6 Oct 2010 (SI 2010/2089) |
|  | (6)(c) | 1 Jan 2009 (SI 2008/3149) |
|  | (7)–(11) | 6 Oct 2010 (SI 2010/2089) |
| 141 | (1)–(4) | 6 Oct 2010 (SI 2010/2089) |
|  | (5)–(7) | 1 Jan 2009 (SI 2008/3149) |
| 142, 143 |  | 6 Oct 2010 (SI 2010/2089) |
| 144 | (1) | 1 Jan 2009 (SI 2008/3149) |
|  | (2) | 6 Oct 2010 (SI 2010/2089)[8] |
|  | (3)–(7) | 1 Jan 2009 (SI 2008/3149)[4] |
|  | (8), (9) | 6 Oct 2010 (SI 2010/2089)[8] |
| 145 | (1) | 6 Oct 2010 (SI 2010/2089)[8] |
|  | (2), (3) | 1 Jan 2009 (SI 2008/3149) |

**Legal Services Act 2007 (c 29)**—*contd*

| | | |
|---|---|---|
| | (4) | 6 Oct 2010 (SI 2010/2089)[8] |
| 146–150 | | 6 Oct 2010 (SI 2010/2089) |
| 151, 152 | | 1 Jan 2010 (for the purpose only of enabling the Lord Chancellor to make orders under s 152(3)(g), (5)) (SI 2009/3250) |
| | | 6 Oct 2010 (otherwise) (SI 2010/2089) |
| 153, 154 | | 6 Oct 2010 (SI 2010/2089) |
| 155, 156 | | 1 Jan 2009 (SI 2008/3149) |
| 157 | (1), (2) | 6 Oct 2010 (SI 2010/2089)[8] |
| | (3) | 2 Aug 2010 (SI 2010/1118) |
| | (4)–(7) | 6 Oct 2010 (SI 2010/2089)[8] |
| 158 | | 6 Oct 2010 (SI 2010/2089)[8] |
| 159 | (1) | 6 Oct 2010 (in so far as it relates to the Legal Services Complaints Commissioner) (SI 2010/2089) |
| | | 31 Dec 2011 (otherwise) (save in relation to, and so far as is required to give effect to: (a) the Legal Services Ombudsman's duty (set out in the Courts and Legal Services Act 1990, Sch 3, paras 5, 6) to produce an annual report and accounts for the period 1 Apr 2011 to 31 Mar 2012 and (b) the power of the Secretary of State set out in the Courts and Legal Services Act 1990, Sch 3, para 7, until 30 Apr 2012) (SI 2010/2089) |
| | (2)(a) | 6 Oct 2010 (SI 2010/2089) |
| | (2)(b) | 6 Oct 2010 (in so far as it relates to s 22(8)(a) of the 1990 Act) (SI 2010/2089) |
| | | 1 Jan 2011 (in so far as it relates to s 23(2)(a) of the 1990 Act) (SI 2010/2089) |
| | | 31 Dec 2011 (otherwise) (save in relation to, and so far as is required to give effect to: (a) the Legal Services Ombudsman's duty (set out in the Courts and Legal Services Act 1990, Sch 3, paras 5, 6) to produce an annual report and accounts for the period 1 Apr 2011 to 31 Mar 2012 and (b) the power of the Secretary of State set out in the Courts and Legal Services Act 1990, Sch 3, para 7, until 30 Apr 2012) (SI 2010/2089) |
| 160 | | 1 Jan 2009 (SI 2008/3149) |
| 161 | (1), (2) | 28 Jan 2015 (SI 2014/3307) |
| | (3) | 20 Jan 2015 (SI 2014/3307) |
| | (4) | 28 Jan 2015 (SI 2014/3307) |
| 162 | | 1 Jan 2009 (SI 2008/3149) |
| 163 | | 1 Jan 2010 (SI 2009/3250) |
| 164–166 | | 6 Oct 2010 (SI 2010/2089) |
| 167–171 | | 1 Jan 2010 (SI 2009/3250)[7] |
| 172 | | 7 Mar 2008 (SI 2008/222) |
| 173 | (1) | 1 Jan 2009 (SI 2008/3149)[4] |
| | (2) | 1 Jan 2010 (SI 2009/3250) |
| | (3)–(11) | 1 Jan 2009 (SI 2008/3149)[4] |
| 174 | (1) | 1 Jan 2009 (SI 2008/3149)[4] |
| | (2) | 1 Jan 2010 (SI 2009/3250) |
| | (3), (4) | 1 Jan 2009 (SI 2008/3149)[4] |
| | (5) | 1 Jan 2010 (SI 2009/3250) |
| | (6), (7) | 1 Jan 2009 (SI 2008/3149)[4] |
| 175 | (1)(a), (b) | 1 Jan 2010 (SI 2009/3250) |
| | (1)(c) | 1 Jan 2009 (SI 2008/3149) |
| | (1)(d) | 1 Jan 2010 (SI 2009/3250) |
| | (1)(e), (f) | *Not yet in force* |
| | (1)(g)–(i) | 6 Oct 2010 (SI 2010/2089) |
| | (1)(j) | 1 Jan 2010 (SI 2009/3250) |
| | (1)(k) | 1 Jan 2009 (SI 2008/3149) |
| | (1)(l) | 1 Jan 2010 (SI 2009/3250) |
| | (1)(m), (n) | 1 Jan 2009 (SI 2008/3149) |
| | (2)(a), (b) | 1 Jan 2010 (SI 2009/3250) |
| | (2)(c), (d) | 2 Aug 2010 (SI 2010/1118) |

**Legal Services Act 2007 (c 29)**—*contd*

| | | |
|---|---|---|
| | (2)(e) | 1 Apr 2011 (SI 2011/720) |
| 176 | (1), (2) | 1 Jan 2010 (SI 2009/3250) |
| | (3) | *Not yet in force* |
| 177 | | See Sch 16 below |
| 178, 179 | | 1 Jan 2010 (SI 2009/3250) |
| 180 | | 7 Mar 2008 (SI 2008/222)[2] |
| 181 | | 1 Jan 2010 (SI 2009/3250) |
| 182 | | See Sch 17 below |
| 183–185 | | 1 Jan 2010 (SI 2009/3250) |
| 186 | | See Sch 18 below |
| 187 | | See Sch 19 below |
| 188–190 | | 1 Jan 2010 (SI 2009/3250) |
| 191 | | *Not yet in force* |
| 192, 193 | | 1 Jan 2010 (SI 2009/3250) |
| 194 | (1)–(7) | 1 Oct 2008 (SI 2008/1436) |
| | (8), (9) | 30 Jun 2008 (SI 2008/1436) |
| | (10) | 30 Jun 2008 (definition "free of charge") (SI 2008/1436) |
| | | 1 Oct 2008 (otherwise) (SI 2008/1436) |
| | (11) | 1 Oct 2008 (SI 2008/1436) |
| 195, 196 | | 1 Oct 2008 (SI 2008/1436) |
| 197, 198 | | 1 Jan 2010 (SI 2009/3250) |
| 199 | (1), (2) | 7 Mar 2008 (SI 2008/222) |
| | (3) | 31 Mar 2009 (SI 2009/503) |
| | (4) | 30 Jun 2008 (SI 2008/1436) |
| | (5) | 30 Jun 2008 (in so far as relates to the Administration of Justice Act 1985, s 9(7)) (SI 2008/1436) |
| | | 31 Mar 2009 (otherwise) (SI 2009/503) |
| | (6)(a) | 31 Mar 2009 (in so far as it relates to the Courts and Legal Services Act 1990, s 53) (SI 2009/503) |
| | | 1 Jan 2010 (otherwise) (SI 2009/3250) |
| | (6)(b) | 30 Jun 2008 (in so far as relates to the Courts and Legal Services Act 1990, s 89) (SI 2008/1436) |
| | | 31 Mar 2009 (otherwise) (SI 2009/503) |
| | (7) | 1 Jan 2010 (SI 2009/3250) |
| 200 | (1) | 7 Mar 2008 (SI 2008/222) |
| | (2)–(4) | 1 Jan 2009 (SI 2008/3149) |
| 201–203 | | 1 Jan 2009 (SI 2008/3149) |
| 204 | (1) | 7 Mar 2008 (SI 2008/222) |
| | (2) | 1 Jan 2009 (SI 2008/3149) |
| | (3), (4)(a) | 7 Mar 2008 (SI 2008/222) |
| | (4)(b), (c) | 1 Jan 2009 (SI 2008/3149) |
| 205 | | 1 Jan 2009 (SI 2008/3149) |
| 206 | | 7 Mar 2008 (SI 2008/222) |
| 207 | | 7 Mar 2008 (definitions "barrister", "consumers", "court", "functions", "immigration advice", "immigration services", "modify" and "solicitor") (SI 2008/222) |
| | | 7 Mar 2008 (in so far as defines the term "non-commercial legal services" for the purposes of Sch 1, Sch 15, para 4(g)) (SI 2008/222) |
| | | 30 Jun 2008 (definition "manager" in sub-ss (1), (5)) (SI 2008/1436) |
| | | 31 Mar 2009 (definition "conveyancing services") (SI 2009/503) |
| | | 1 Jan 2010 (otherwise) (SI 2009/3250) |
| 208 | (1) | See Sch 21 below |
| | (2)–(5) | 30 Oct 2007 (s 211(1)) |
| 209 | | See Sch 22 below |
| 210 | | See Sch 23 below |
| 211, 212 | | 30 Oct 2007 (s 211(1)) |
| 213 | | See Sch 24 below |

**Legal Services Act 2007 (c 29)**—*contd*

| | | |
|---|---|---|
| 214 | | 30 Oct 2007 (s 211(1)) |
| Sch 1 | | 7 Mar 2008 (SI 2008/222) |
| Sch 2 | | 7 Mar 2008 (in so far as defines the term "reserved legal activity" for the purposes of ss 1, 20 (definition "consumers"), 69(4) (as modified by this order), Sch 1, para 2(3)–(5), Sch 15, para 2(3), (4), Sch 22, para 2(6), (7)(b)) (SI 2008/222) |
| | | 31 Mar 2009 (in so far as defines that term for the purposes of the Administration of Justice Act 1985, ss 9, 32A) (SI 2009/503) |
| | | 1 Jan 2010 (otherwise) (SI 2009/3250) |
| Sch 3 | | 1 Jan 2010 (SI 2009/3250) |
| Sch 4 | paras 1, 2 | 1 Jan 2010 (SI 2009/3250) |
| | para 3(1) | 1 Jan 2009 (SI 2008/3149) |
| | para 3(2) | 1 Jan 2010 (SI 2009/3250) |
| | para 3(3), (4) | 1 Jan 2009 (SI 2008/3149) |
| | paras 3(5), (6), 4(1) | 1 Jan 2010 (SI 2009/3250) |
| | para 4(2) | 1 Jan 2009 (SI 2008/3149) |
| | paras 4(3), (4), 5–10, 11(1), (2) | 1 Jan 2010 (SI 2009/3250) |
| | para 11(3) | 1 Jan 2009 (SI 2008/3149) |
| | paras 11(4)–(6), 12 | 1 Jan 2010 (SI 2009/3250) |
| | para 13 | 1 Jan 2009 (SI 2008/3149) |
| | paras 14–18 | 1 Jan 2010 (SI 2009/3250) |
| | para 19(1)–(2)(e) | 1 Jan 2010 (SI 2009/3250) |
| | para 19(2)(f) | 1 Apr 2011 (SI 2011/720) |
| | para 19(3)–(7) | 1 Jan 2010 (SI 2009/3250) |
| | para 20 | 1 Jan 2009 (SI 2008/3149) |
| | paras 21, 22, 23(1), (2) | 1 Jan 2010 (SI 2009/3250) |
| | para 23(3) | 1 Jan 2009 (SI 2008/3149) |
| | paras 23(4)–(6), 24–27 | 1 Jan 2010 (SI 2009/3250) |
| Sch 5 | paras 1–6, 7(1)–(3) | 1 Jan 2010 (SI 2009/3250)[7] |
| | para 7(4) | 31 Mar 2009 (in so far as defines the term "legal partnership" for the purposes of Sch 22, para 13) (SI 2009/503) |
| | | 1 Jan 2010 (otherwise) (SI 2009/3250)[7] |
| | paras 8–11, 12(1)–(3) | 1 Jan 2010 (SI 2009/3250)[7] |
| | para 12(4) | 31 Mar 2009 (in so far as defines the term "duly certificated notary" for the purposes of Sch 22, para 15(1)(h)) (SI 2009/503) |
| | | 1 Jan 2010 (otherwise) (SI 2009/3250)[7] |
| | paras 13, 14(1)–(6) | 1 Jan 2010 (SI 2009/3250)[7] |
| | para 14(7) | 31 Mar 2009 (in so far as defines the term "patent attorney body" for the purposes of Sch 22, para 15(1)(k)) (SI 2009/503) |
| | | 1 Jan 2010 (otherwise) (SI 2009/3250)[7] |
| | paras 15, 16(1)–(6) | 1 Jan 2010 (SI 2009/3250)[7] |
| | para 16(7) | 31 Mar 2009 (in so far as defines the term "trade mark attorney body" for the purposes of Sch 22, para 15(1)(m)) (SI 2009/503) |
| | | 1 Jan 2010 (otherwise) (SI 2009/3250)[7] |
| | para 17(1) | 1 Jan 2010 (SI 2009/3250)[7] |
| | para 17(2) | 31 Mar 2009 (in so far as defines the term "authorised member of the Association of Law Costs Draftsmen" for the purposes of Sch 22, para 15(1)(n)) (SI 2009/503) |
| | | 1 Jan 2010 (otherwise) (SI 2009/3250)[7] |
| | paras 17(3), 18(1) | 1 Jan 2010 (SI 2009/3250)[7] |
| | para 18(2) | 31 Mar 2009 (in so far as defines the term "carries on an activity which is a reserved legal activity within Sch 5, para 18(2)" for the purposes of Sch 22, para 15(1)(o)) (SI 2009/503) |
| | | 1 Jan 2010 (otherwise) (SI 2009/3250)[7] |

**Legal Services Act 2007 (c 29)**—*contd*

|        | paras 18(3), 19 | 1 Jan 2010 (SI 2009/3250)[7] |
|--------|-----------------|------------------------------|
| Sch 6  | paras 1–11 | 1 Jan 2010 (SI 2009/3250) |
|        | para 12(1)–(3) | 1 Jan 2009 (SI 2008/3149) |
|        | para 12(4), (5) | 1 Jan 2010 (SI 2009/3250) |
|        | paras 13, 14 | 1 Jan 2009 (SI 2008/3149) |
|        | paras 15–18 | 1 Jan 2010 (SI 2009/3250) |
| Sch 7  | para 1 | 1 Jan 2009 (SI 2008/3149) |
|        | para 2(1)–(4) | 1 Jan 2010 (SI 2009/3250) |
|        | para 2(5) | 1 Jan 2009 (SI 2008/3149) |
|        | paras 2(6)–(8), 3–9, 10(1), (2) | 1 Jan 2010 (SI 2009/3250) |
|        | para 10(3) | 1 Jan 2009 (SI 2008/3149) |
|        | paras 10(4)–(6), 11, 12 | 1 Jan 2010 (SI 2009/3250) |
| Sch 8  | para 1 | 1 Jan 2009 (SI 2008/3149) |
|        | para 2(1)–(4) | 1 Jan 2010 (SI 2009/3250) |
|        | para 2(5) | 1 Jan 2009 (SI 2008/3149) |
|        | paras 2(6)–(8), 3–9, 10(1)–(4) | 1 Jan 2010 (SI 2009/3250) |
|        | para 10(5) | 1 Jan 2009 (SI 2008/3149) |
|        | paras 10(6)–(9), 11, 12, 13(1) | 1 Jan 2010 (SI 2009/3250) |
|        | para 13(2)(a) | 1 Jan 2009 (SI 2008/3149) |
|        | paras 13(2)(b), 14–20, 21(1)–(4) | 1 Jan 2010 (SI 2009/3250) |
|        | para 21(5) | 1 Jan 2009 (SI 2008/3149) |
|        | paras 21(6)–(9), 22, 23 | 1 Jan 2010 (SI 2009/3250) |
| Sch 9  | para 1 | 1 Jan 2009 (SI 2008/3149) |
|        | para 2(1)–(4) | 1 Jan 2010 (SI 2009/3250) |
|        | para 2(5) | 1 Jan 2009 (SI 2008/3149) |
|        | paras 2(6)–(9), 3–8, 9(1)–(4) | 1 Jan 2010 (SI 2009/3250) |
|        | para 9(5) | 1 Jan 2009 (SI 2008/3149) |
|        | para 9(6)–(9) | 1 Jan 2010 (SI 2009/3250) |
|        | paras 10, 11 | 1 Jan 2010 (SI 2009/3250) |
| Sch 10 | para 1(1) | 1 Jan 2009 (SI 2008/3149) |
|        | para 1(2), (3) | 2 Aug 2010 (SI 2010/1118) |
|        | para 1(4), (5) | 1 Jan 2009 (SI 2008/3149) |
|        | paras 1(6), 2(1) | 2 Aug 2010 (SI 2010/1118) |
|        | para 2(2) | 1 Jan 2009 (SI 2008/3149) |
|        | paras 2(3), (4), 3–8, 9(1), (2) | 2 Aug 2010 (SI 2010/1118) |
|        | para 9(3) | 1 Jan 2009 (SI 2008/3149) |
|        | paras 9(4)–(6), 10 | 2 Aug 2010 (SI 2010/1118) |
|        | para 11 | 1 Jan 2009 (SI 2008/3149) |
|        | paras 12–16 | 2 Aug 2010 (SI 2010/1118) |
|        | para 17 | 1 Jan 2009 (SI 2008/3149) |
|        | para 18(1)–(4) | 2 Aug 2010 (SI 2010/1118) |
|        | para 18(5) | 1 Jan 2009 (SI 2008/3149) |
|        | paras 18(6)–(9), 19–24, 25(1)–(4) | 2 Aug 2010 (SI 2010/1118) |
|        | para 25(5) | 1 Jan 2009 (SI 2008/3149) |
|        | para 25(6)–(9) | 2 Aug 2010 (SI 2010/1118) |
|        | paras 26, 27 | 2 Aug 2010 (SI 2010/1118) |
| Sch 11 |  | 2 Aug 2010 (SI 2010/1118) |
| Sch 12 | paras 1, 2(1)–(3) | *Not yet in force* |
|        | para 2(4), (5) | 1 Jan 2009 (SI 2008/3149) |
|        | para 3 | *Not yet in force* |

**Legal Services Act 2007 (c 29)**—*contd*

| | | |
|---|---|---|
| | para 4 | 1 Jan 2009 (SI 2008/3149) |
| | paras 5–7 | *Not yet in force* |
| Sch 13 | paras 1–7 | 1 Oct 2011 (SI 2011/2196) |
| | para 8 | 1 Jan 2009 (SI 2008/3149) |
| | paras 9–16, 17(1)–(3), (4)(a) | 1 Oct 2011 (SI 2011/2196) |
| | para 17(4)(b), (5) | 1 Jan 2009 (in so far as they relate to the exercise of powers by virtue of para 8) (SI 2008/3149) |
| | | 1 Oct 2011 (otherwise) (SI 2011/2196) |
| | para 17(6), (7) | 1 Oct 2011 (SI 2011/2196) |
| | para 18(1) | 1 Jan 2009 (in so far as relates to the exercise of powers by virtue of para 8) (SI 2008/3149) |
| | | 1 Oct 2011 (otherwise) (SI 2011/2196) |
| | para 18(2) | 1 Oct 2011 (SI 2011/2196) |
| | para 18(3) | 1 Jan 2009 (in so far as relates to the exercise of powers by virtue of para 8) (SI 2008/3149) |
| | | 1 Oct 2011 (otherwise) (SI 2011/2196) |
| | paras 18(4), (5), 19(1), (2), (3)(a) | 1 Oct 2011 (SI 2011/2196) |
| | para 19(3)(b), (4) | 1 Jan 2009 (in so far as they relate to the exercise of powers by virtue of para 8) (SI 2008/3149) |
| | | 1 Oct 2011 (otherwise) (SI 2011/2196) |
| | para 19(5), (6) | 1 Oct 2011 (SI 2011/2196) |
| | para 20(1) | 1 Jan 2009 (in so far as relates to the exercise of powers by virtue of para 8) (SI 2008/3149) |
| | | 1 Oct 2011 (otherwise) (SI 2011/2196) |
| | para 20(2) | 1 Oct 2011 (SI 2011/2196) |
| | para 20(3) | 1 Jan 2009 (in so far as relates to the exercise of powers by virtue of para 8) (SI 2008/3149) |
| | | 1 Oct 2011 (otherwise) (SI 2011/2196) |
| | paras 20(4), (5), 21–24, 25(1) | 1 Oct 2011 (SI 2011/2196) |
| | para 25(2) | 1 Jan 2009 (in so far as relates to the exercise of powers by virtue of para 8) (SI 2008/3149) |
| | | 1 Oct 2011 (otherwise) (SI 2011/2196) |
| | paras 25(3), 26, 27, 28(1)–(4), (5)(a) | 1 Oct 2011 (SI 2011/2196) |
| | para 28(5)(b), (6) | 1 Jan 2009 (in so far as they relate to the exercise of powers by virtue of para 8) (SI 2008/3149) |
| | | 1 Oct 2011 (otherwise) (SI 2011/2196) |
| | para 28(7), (8) | 1 Oct 2011 (SI 2011/2196) |
| | para 29(1) | 1 Jan 2009 (in so far as relates to the exercise of powers by virtue of para 8) (SI 2008/3149) |
| | | 1 Oct 2011 (otherwise) (SI 2011/2196) |
| | para 29(2) | 1 Oct 2011 (SI 2011/2196) |
| | para 29(3) | 1 Jan 2009 (in so far as relates to the exercise of powers by virtue of para 8) (SI 2008/3149) |
| | | 1 Oct 2011 (otherwise) (SI 2011/2196) |
| | paras 29(4), (5), 30, 31(1)–(3), (4)(a) | 1 Oct 2011 (SI 2011/2196) |
| | para 31(4)(b), (5) | 1 Jan 2009 (in so far as they relate to the exercise of powers by virtue of para 8) (SI 2008/3149) |
| | | 1 Oct 2011 (otherwise) (SI 2011/2196) |
| | para 31(6), (7) | 1 Oct 2011 (SI 2011/2196) |
| | para 32(1) | 1 Jan 2009 (in so far as relates to the exercise of powers by virtue of para 8) (SI 2008/3149) |
| | | 1 Oct 2011 (otherwise) (SI 2011/2196) |
| | para 32(2) | 1 Oct 2011 (SI 2011/2196) |
| | para 32(3) | 1 Jan 2009 (in so far as relates to the exercise of powers by virtue of para 8) (SI 2008/3149) |

**Legal Services Act 2007 (c 29)**—*contd*

|  |  |
|---|---|
|  | 1 Oct 2011 (otherwise) (SI 2011/2196) |
| paras 32(4), (5), 33(1), (2)(a) | 1 Oct 2011 (SI 2011/2196) |
| para 33(2)(b) | 1 Jan 2009 (in so far as relates to the exercise of powers by virtue of para 8) (SI 2008/3149) |
|  | 1 Oct 2011 (otherwise) (SI 2011/2196) |
| para 33(3), (4), (5)(a) | 1 Oct 2011 (SI 2011/2196) |
| para 33(5)(b), (6) | 1 Jan 2009 (in so far as they relate to the exercise of powers by virtue of para 8) (SI 2008/3149) |
|  | 1 Oct 2011 (otherwise) (SI 2011/2196) |
| para 33(7), (8) | 1 Oct 2011 (SI 2011/2196) |
| para 34(1) | 1 Jan 2009 (in so far as relates to the exercise of powers by virtue of para 8) (SI 2008/3149) |
|  | 1 Oct 2011 (otherwise) (SI 2011/2196) |
| para 34(2) | 1 Oct 2011 (SI 2011/2196) |
| para 34(3) | 1 Jan 2009 (in so far as relates to the exercise of powers by virtue of para 8) (SI 2008/3149) |
|  | 1 Oct 2011 (otherwise) (SI 2011/2196) |
| paras 34(4), (5), 35, 36(1) | 1 Oct 2011 (SI 2011/2196) |
| para 36(2) | 1 Jan 2009 (in so far as relates to the exercise of powers by virtue of para 8) (SI 2008/3149) |
|  | 1 Oct 2011 (otherwise) (SI 2011/2196) |
| para 36(3), (4), (5)(a) | 1 Oct 2011 (SI 2011/2196) |
| para 36(5)(b), (6) | 1 Jan 2009 (in so far as they relate to the exercise of powers by virtue of para 8) (SI 2008/3149) |
|  | 1 Oct 2011 (otherwise) (SI 2011/2196) |
| para 36(7), (8) | 1 Oct 2011 (SI 2011/2196) |
| para 37(1) | 1 Jan 2009 (in so far as relates to the exercise of powers by virtue of para 8) (SI 2008/3149) |
|  | 1 Oct 2011 (otherwise) (SI 2011/2196) |
| para 37(2), (3) | 1 Oct 2011 (SI 2011/2196) |
| para 37(4) | 1 Jan 2009 (in so far as relates to the exercise of powers by virtue of para 8) (SI 2008/3149) |
|  | 1 Oct 2011 (otherwise) (SI 2011/2196) |
| paras 37(5), (6), 38–42, 43(1), (2) | 1 Oct 2011 (SI 2011/2196) |
| para 43(3) | 1 Jan 2009 (in so far as relates to the exercise of powers by virtue of para 8) (SI 2008/3149) |
|  | 1 Oct 2011 (otherwise) (SI 2011/2196) |
| para 44(1)–(3) | 1 Oct 2011 (SI 2011/2196) |
| para 44(4)(a) | 1 Oct 2011 (SI 2011/2196) |
| para 44(4)(b) | 1 Jan 2009 (in so far as relates to the exercise of powers by virtue of para 8) (SI 2008/3149) |
|  | 1 Oct 2011 (otherwise) (SI 2011/2196) |
| paras 44(4)(c), 45, 46(1), (2) | 1 Oct 2011 (SI 2011/2196) |
| para 46(3) | 1 Jan 2009 (in so far as relates to the exercise of powers by virtue of para 8) (SI 2008/3149) |
|  | 1 Oct 2011 (otherwise) (SI 2011/2196) |
| paras 46(4), (5), 47, 48, 49(1)–(3), (4)(a) | 1 Oct 2011 (SI 2011/2196) |
| para 49(4)(b), (5) | 1 Jan 2009 (in so far as they relate to the exercise of powers by virtue of para 8) (SI 2008/3149) |
|  | 1 Oct 2011 (otherwise) (SI 2011/2196) |
| para 49(6), (7) | 1 Oct 2011 (SI 2011/2196) |

**Legal Services Act 2007 (c 29)**—*contd*

|  |  |  |
|---|---|---|
| | para 50(1) | 1 Jan 2009 (in so far as relates to the exercise of powers by virtue of para 8) (SI 2008/3149) |
| | | 1 Oct 2011 (otherwise) (SI 2011/2196) |
| | para 50(2) | 1 Oct 2011 (SI 2011/2196) |
| | para 50(3) | 1 Jan 2009 (in so far as relates to the exercise of powers by virtue of para 8) (SI 2008/3149) |
| | | 1 Oct 2011 (otherwise) (SI 2011/2196) |
| | paras 50(4)–(6), 51 | 1 Oct 2011 (SI 2011/2196) |
| Sch 14 | | 1 Oct 2011 (SI 2011/2196) |
| Sch 15 | paras 1–12 | 7 Mar 2008 (SI 2008/222) |
| | paras 13–34 | 1 Jan 2009 (SI 2008/3149) |
| Sch 16 | para 1 | 7 Mar 2008 (SI 2008/222) |
| | para 2(a) | 1 Jan 2010 (SI 2009/3250) |
| | para 2(b) | 7 Mar 2008 (SI 2008/222) |
| | para 2(c) | 1 Jan 2010 (SI 2009/3250) |
| | para 3 | 1 Jul 2009 (SI 2009/1365) |
| | para 4(a) | 1 Jan 2010 (SI 2009/3250) |
| | para 4(b) | 7 Mar 2008 (SI 2008/222) |
| | para 4(c) | 1 Jan 2010 (SI 2009/3250) |
| | paras 5, 6, 7(a) | 1 Jul 2009 (SI 2009/1365) |
| | paras 7(b), 8(1), (2) | 7 Mar 2008 (SI 2008/222) |
| | para 8(3)–(5) | 1 Jul 2009 (SI 2009/1365)[6] |
| | paras 9–20 | 1 Jul 2009 (SI 2009/1365)[6] |
| | para 21 | 7 Mar 2008 (SI 2008/222) |
| | paras 22, 23 | 1 Jul 2009 (SI 2009/1365) |
| | paras 24–29 | 1 Jan 2010 (SI 2009/3250)[7] |
| | para 30 | 1 Jul 2009 (SI 2009/1365)[6] |
| | para 31(1), (2)(a) | 7 Mar 2008 (SI 2008/222) |
| | para 31(2)(b) | 1 Jan 2010 (SI 2009/3250) |
| | para 31(2)(c) | 31 Mar 2009 (SI 2009/503) |
| | para 31(2)(d) | 7 Mar 2008 (SI 2008/222) |
| | para 31(2)(e) | 31 Mar 2009 (SI 2009/503) |
| | para 31(3), (4) | 1 Jan 2010 (SI 2009/3250) |
| | para 32(1), (2)(a) | 31 Mar 2009 (SI 2009/503) |
| | para 32(2)(b) | 1 Jan 2010 (SI 2009/3250) |
| | paras 32(2)(c)–(e), (3)–(7), 33 | 31 Mar 2009 (SI 2009/503) |
| | para 34(1), (2)(a) | 7 Mar 2008 (SI 2008/222) |
| | para 34(2)(b) | 1 Jan 2010 (SI 2009/3250) |
| | para 34(3) | 7 Mar 2008 (SI 2008/222) |
| | paras 35–37 | 31 Mar 2009 (SI 2009/503)[5] |
| | para 38(a) | 7 Mar 2008 (in so far as it substitutes word "Society" for the word "Council") (SI 2008/222) |
| | | 1 Jan 2010 (otherwise) (SI 2009/3250) |
| | para 38(b)(i), (ii) | 7 Mar 2008 (SI 2008/222) |
| | para 38(b)(iii) | 30 Jun 2008 (SI 2008/1436) |
| | para 39 | 6 Oct 2010 (SI 2010/2089)[8] |
| | para 40 | 1 Jul 2009 (SI 2009/1365) |
| | para 41(1), (2) | 31 Mar 2009 (SI 2009/503) |
| | para 41(3)–(6) | 1 Jul 2009 (SI 2009/1365)[6] |
| | paras 42–46 | 31 Mar 2009 (SI 2009/503)[5] |
| | paras 47, 48 | 30 Jun 2008 (SI 2008/1436)[3] |
| | para 49(a) | 1 Jul 2009 (SI 2009/1365) |
| | para 49(b) | 31 Mar 2009 (SI 2009/503) |
| | para 49(c) | 1 Jul 2009 (SI 2009/1365) |
| | para 49(d) | 31 Mar 2009 (SI 2009/503) |
| | para 49(e) | 1 Jul 2009 (SI 2009/1365) |

**Legal Services Act 2007 (c 29)**—*contd*

|  |  |
|---|---|
| para 49(f) | 31 Mar 2009 (SI 2009/503)[5] |
| para 49(g) | 1 Oct 2011 (SI 2011/2196) |
| para 49(h) | 31 Mar 2009 (SI 2009/503) |
| para 50(a)(i) | 1 Jul 2009 (SI 2009/1365) |
| para 50(a)(ii) | 7 Mar 2008 (SI 2008/222) |
| para 50(b), (c) | 31 Mar 2009 (SI 2009/503) |
| paras 51, 52 | 1 Jul 2009 (SI 2009/1365)[6] |
| paras 53, 54(1) | 7 Mar 2008 (SI 2008/222) |
| para 54(2)(a) | 30 Jun 2008 (SI 2008/1436) |
| para 54(2)(b) | 1 Jul 2009 (SI 2009/1365) |
| para 54(2)(c), (3), (4)(a) | 30 Jun 2008 (SI 2008/1436) |
| para 54(4)(b) | 7 Mar 2008 (SI 2008/222) |
| para 54(5), (6)(a) | 30 Jun 2008 (SI 2008/1436) |
| para 54(6)(b), (7) | 31 Mar 2009 (SI 2009/503)[5] |
| para 54(8), (9)(a) | 1 Jan 2010 (SI 2009/3250) |
| para 54(9)(b) | 30 Jun 2008 (SI 2008/1436) |
| paras 55, 56(a), (b) | 1 Jan 2010 (SI 2009/3250) |
| para 56(c) | 30 Jun 2008 (SI 2008/1436) |
| paras 57, 58, 59(a), (b)(i), (ii) | 1 Jan 2010 (SI 2009/3250) |
| para 59(b)(iii) | 31 Mar 2009 (SI 2009/503) |
| paras 60, 61, 62(a)–(c) | 1 Jan 2010 (SI 2009/3250) |
| para 62(d), (e) | 31 Mar 2009 (SI 2009/503)[5] |
| para 63 | 1 Jan 2010 (SI 2009/3250) |
| para 64(1) | 7 Mar 2008 (SI 2008/222) |
| para 64(2) | 1 Jan 2010 (SI 2009/3250) |
| para 64(3), (4) | 7 Mar 2008 (SI 2008/222) |
| paras 65–69 | 1 Jan 2010 (SI 2009/3250) |
| para 70 | 31 Mar 2009 (SI 2009/503) |
| para 71 | 7 Mar 2008 (SI 2008/222)[1] |
| para 72(a) | 7 Mar 2008 (SI 2008/222) |
| para 72(b) | 31 Mar 2009 (SI 2009/503) |
| para 73 | 1 Jan 2010 (SI 2009/3250)[7] |
| paras 74, 75(a) | 31 Mar 2009 (SI 2009/503) |
| para 75(b) | 1 Jul 2009 (SI 2009/1365) |
| para 75(c) | 7 Mar 2008 (in so far as repeals definitions "articles", "employee") (SI 2008/222) |
|  | 31 Mar 2009 (in so far as repeals definition "controlled trust") (SI 2009/503) |
|  | 1 Jul 2009 (in so far as repeals definitions "indemnity conditions", "replacement date" and "training conditions") (SI 2009/1365) |
|  | 1 Jan 2010 (in so far as repeals definition "duly certificated notary public") (SI 2009/3250) |
| para 76 | 1 Jan 2010 (SI 2009/3250) |
| para 77 | 31 Mar 2009 (SI 2009/503)[5] |
| para 78 | 6 Oct 2010 (SI 2010/2089)[8] |
| para 79 | 31 Mar 2009 (SI 2009/503)[5] |
| para 80 | 7 Mar 2008 (SI 2008/222) |
| para 81(1) | 30 Jun 2008 (SI 2008/1436) |
| para 81(2)–(8) | 31 Mar 2009 (SI 2009/503)[5] |
| para 81(9) | 30 Jun 2008 (SI 2008/1436) |
| para 81(10), (11) | 31 Mar 2009 (SI 2009/503)[5] |
| paras 82, 83, 84(1), (2) | 31 Mar 2009 (SI 2009/503) |
| para 84(3) | 1 Oct 2011 (SI 2011/2196) |
| paras 84(4), 85, 86(a)–(f) | 31 Mar 2009 (SI 2009/503) |

**Legal Services Act 2007 (c 29)**—*contd*

| | | |
|---|---|---|
| | para 86(g) | 30 Jun 2008 (in so far as relates to definition "manager") (SI 2008/1436) |
| | | 31 Mar 2009 (otherwise) (SI 2009/503) |
| | paras 87–99 | 31 Mar 2009 (SI 2009/503)[5] |
| | para 100 | 6 Oct 2010 (SI 2010/2089)[8] |
| | paras 101–104, 105(a), (b)(i) | 31 Mar 2009 (SI 2009/503)[5] |
| | para 105(b)(ii) | 6 Oct 2010 (SI 2010/2089)[8] |
| | paras 105(b)(iii), (c), 106(a), (b) | 31 Mar 2009 (SI 2009/503) |
| | para 106(c) | 6 Oct 2010 (SI 2010/2089)[8] |
| | para 106(d) | 31 Mar 2009 (SI 2009/503) |
| | para 106(e) | 31 Mar 2009 (in so far as repeals Administration of Justice Act 1985, Sch 2, para 18(4)) (SI 2009/503) |
| | | 1 Oct 2011 (otherwise) (SI 2011/2196) |
| | paras 107–110 | 31 Mar 2009 (SI 2009/503)[5] |
| | paras 111, 112(a) | 30 Jun 2008 (SI 2008/1436) |
| | para 112(b) | 1 Jan 2010 (SI 2009/3250) |
| | para 112(c), (d) | 30 Jun 2008 (SI 2008/1436) |
| | para 113(a), (b)(i), (ii) | 1 Jan 2010 (SI 2009/3250) |
| | para 113(b)(iii) | 30 Jun 2008 (SI 2008/1436) |
| | paras 113(b)(iv), (c), 114 | 31 Mar 2009 (SI 2009/503) |
| | para 115 | 7 Mar 2008 (SI 2008/222) |
| | paras 116–123 | 31 Mar 2009 (SI 2009/503) |
| | para 124 | 7 Mar 2008 (SI 2008/222) |
| | para 125(a), (b) | 31 Mar 2009 (SI 2009/503)[5] |
| | para 125(c)–(g) | 30 Jun 2008 (SI 2008/1436) |
| | para 125(h)–(j) | 31 Mar 2009 (SI 2009/503)[5] |
| | para 126 | 7 Mar 2008 (SI 2008/222) |
| | para 127 | 31 Mar 2009 (SI 2009/503) |
| | para 128(a) | 7 Mar 2008 (SI 2008/222) |
| | para 128(b) | 1 Jan 2010 (SI 2009/3250) |
| | para 128(c)(i) | 7 Mar 2008 (SI 2008/222) |
| | para 128(c)(ii) | 30 Jun 2008 (SI 2008/1436) |
| | para 128(d) | 1 Jul 2009 (SI 2009/1365) |
| | para 128(e)(i) | 1 Jan 2010 (SI 2009/3250) |
| | paras 128(e)(ii), (f), (g), 129 | 1 Jul 2009 (SI 2009/1365) |
| | para 130 | 7 Mar 2008 (SI 2008/222) |
| | paras 131–134 | 31 Mar 2009 (SI 2009/503)[5] |
| | para 135 | 1 Jul 2009 (SI 2009/1365)[6] |
| | para 136 | 31 Mar 2009 (SI 2009/503) |
| | para 137 | 1 Jan 2010 (SI 2009/3250) |
| | para 138 | 1 Jul 2009 (SI 2009/1365)[6] |
| Sch 17 | para 1 | 7 Mar 2008 (SI 2008/222) |
| | para 2(a) | 31 Mar 2009 (SI 2009/503) |
| | paras 2(b), (c), 3 | 1 Jan 2010 (SI 2009/3250) |
| | paras 4, 5(1), (2)(a) | 31 Mar 2009 (SI 2009/503) |
| | para 5(2)(b) | 31 Mar 2009 (in so far as inserts Administration of Justice Act 1985, s 16(1)(ea)) (SI 2009/503) |
| | | 1 Oct 2011 (SI 2011/2196) (in so far as inserts paras (eb), (ec) of that subsection) |
| | para 5(3)(a) | 31 Mar 2009 (SI 2009/503) |
| | para 5(3)(b) | 31 Mar 2009 (in so far as inserts reference to "(ea)," into the Administration of Justice Act 1985, s 16(4)) (SI 2009/503) |
| | | 1 Oct 2011 (SI 2011/2196) (in so far as inserts references to "(eb), (ec)," into that subsection) |

**Legal Services Act 2007 (c 29)**—*contd*

| | | |
|---|---|---|
| para 5(4), (5) | 1 Oct 2011 (SI 2011/2196) | |
| paras 6, 7(1), (2)(a) | 31 Mar 2009 (SI 2009/503) | |
| para 7(2)(b) | 31 Mar 2009 (in so far as inserts reference to "(ea)," into the Administration of Justice Act 1985, s 17(2)(a)) (SI 2009/503) | |
| | 1 Oct 2011 (SI 2011/2196) (in so far as inserts references to "(eb), (ec)," into that paragraph) | |
| para 7(3), (4) | 1 Oct 2011 (SI 2011/2196) | |
| paras 8, 9 | 31 Mar 2009 (SI 2009/503) | |
| para 10 | 1 Jan 2010 (SI 2009/3250) | |
| para 11 | 7 Mar 2008 (SI 2008/222) | |
| paras 12–22 | 31 Mar 2009 (SI 2009/503)[5] | |
| para 23 | 1 Jan 2010 (SI 2009/3250) | |
| paras 24–26 | 31 Mar 2009 (SI 2009/503) | |
| para 27 | 1 Jan 2010 (SI 2009/3250) | |
| paras 28, 29, 30(1) | 31 Mar 2009 (SI 2009/503) | |
| para 30(2)(a) | 1 Jan 2010 (SI 2009/3250) | |
| paras 30(2)(b), (3), 31, 32(1)–(6)(f) | 31 Mar 2009 (SI 2009/503)[5] | |
| para 32(6)(g) | 31 Mar 2009 (in so far as repeals Administration of Justice Act 1985, Sch 6, para 4(4)) (SI 2009/503) | |
| | 6 Oct 2010 (in so far as repeals para 4(3), (3A) of that Schedule) (SI 2010/2089) | |
| paras 32(7)–(18), 33, 34(1) | 31 Mar 2009 (SI 2009/503) | |
| para 34(2)–(4) | 1 Jan 2010 (SI 2009/3250) | |
| para 34(5), (6) | 31 Mar 2009 (SI 2009/503) | |
| para 34(7) | 1 Jan 2010 (SI 2009/3250) | |
| para 35(1) | 31 Mar 2009 (SI 2009/503) | |
| para 35(2)–(4) | 1 Jan 2010 (SI 2009/3250) | |
| para 35(5) | 31 Mar 2009 (SI 2009/503) | |
| para 35(6) | 1 Jan 2010 (SI 2009/3250) | |
| para 35(7)–(11) | 31 Mar 2009 (SI 2009/503) | |
| Sch 18 | paras 1–17 | 1 Apr 2011 (SI 2011/720) |
| | paras 18–23 | *Not yet in force* |
| Sch 19 | para 1 | 7 Mar 2008 (SI 2008/222) |
| | paras 2–4 | *Not yet in force* |
| | para 5 | 7 Mar 2008 (SI 2008/222) |
| | para 6(1), (2) | 30 Jun 2008 (SI 2008/1436) |
| | para 6(3) | *Not yet in force* |
| | para 7 | *Not yet in force* |
| | paras 8, 9 | 7 Mar 2008 (SI 2008/222) |
| | para 10 | *Not yet in force* |
| | para 11(1) | 30 Jun 2008 (SI 2008/1436) |
| | para 11(2)–(5) | *Not yet in force* |
| | para 11(6) | 30 Jun 2008 (SI 2008/1436) |
| Sch 20 | | 1 Oct 2008 (SI 2008/1436) |
| Sch 21 | paras 1–64 | 1 Jan 2010 (SI 2009/3250) |
| | para 65 | 31 Mar 2009 (SI 2009/503) |
| | para 66 | 1 Jan 2010 (SI 2009/3250) |
| | para 67 | 31 Mar 2009 (SI 2009/503) |
| | paras 68–82 | 1 Jan 2010 (SI 2009/3250) |
| | para 83 | 31 Mar 2009 (SI 2009/503) |
| | paras 84–86 | 1 Jan 2010 (SI 2009/3250)[7] |
| | para 87 | 31 Mar 2009 (SI 2009/503) |
| | paras 88–98 | 1 Jan 2010 (SI 2009/3250)[7] |
| | para 99 | 31 Mar 2009 (SI 2009/503) |
| | para 100(a) | 1 Jan 2010 (SI 2009/3250)[7] |

**Legal Services Act 2007 (c 29)**—*contd*

|   |   |   |
|---|---|---|
| | para 100(b)–(d) | 31 Mar 2009 (SI 2009/503) |
| | para 100(e) | 1 Jan 2010 (SI 2009/3250)[9] |
| | para 100(f) | 1 Jan 2010 (SI 2009/3250)[7] |
| | para 101 | 31 Mar 2009 (SI 2009/503) |
| | paras 102–118 | 1 Jan 2010 (SI 2009/3250) |
| | para 119 | *Never in force* (repealed) |
| | paras 120–162 | 1 Jan 2010 (SI 2009/3250) |
| Sch 22 | paras 1–5 | 7 Mar 2008 (SI 2008/222) |
| | paras 6–8 | 31 Mar 2009 (SI 2009/503) |
| | para 9 | 7 Mar 2008 (in so far as allows the exercise of the powers in Sch 1, paras 13, 15, 16 and Sch 15, paras 1–9, 11) (SI 2008/222) |
| | | *Not yet in force* (otherwise) |
| | para 10 | *Not yet in force* |
| | para 11(1) | 31 Mar 2009 (SI 2009/503) |
| | paras 11(2), 12 | *Not yet in force* |
| | paras 13–17 | 31 Mar 2009 (SI 2009/503)[5] |
| | para 18 | 30 Jun 2008 (SI 2008/1436) |
| Sch 23 | | 7 Mar 2008 (SI 2008/222), repeals of or in— |

Solicitors Act 1974, ss 1A(c), 2(3), 17, 48, 87(1) (definitions "articles" and "employee");
Administration of Justice Act 1985, s 22

30 Jun 2008 (repeals of or in Solicitors Act 1974, s 46) (SI 2008/1436)

1 Oct 2008 (SI 2008/1436), repeals of or in—
Solicitors (Scotland) Act 1980;
Law Reform (Miscellaneous Provisions) (Scotland) Act 1990;
Legal Profession and Legal Aid (Scotland) Act 2007

31 Mar 2009 (SI 2009/503), repeals of or in—
Parliamentary Commissioner Act 1967, Sch 2, entry "Authorised Conveyancing Practitioners Board";
Solicitors Act 1974, ss 32(1) (words from "and the rules" to the end), (2), (4), (6), 33, 34, 43, 47, 76–78, 80, 87(1) (definition "controlled trust"), Schs 1, 2;
House of Commons Disqualification Act 1975, Sch 1, Pt II;
Northern Ireland Assembly Disqualification Act 1975, Sch 1, Pt II;
Administration of Justice Act 1985, ss 2, 9, 10, 15, 24, 26, 29, 31, 32, 34, 35, 39, Sch 2, paras 1, 4, 11, 12, 16, 17(a) (words "11(1), 15(2) or"), 18(2), (4), 20, 31, 32, 34, 35, Sch 3, Sch 4, para 3, Sch 5, Sch 6, paras 1, 3, 4(2), (4), 7, 8, 10, 12, 13, 15, Sch 9, para 2;
Courts and Legal Services Act 1990, ss 34–52, 53(9)(e), 120(4) (words "37(10), 40(1)"), Schs 5–7, Sch 8, paras 11, 13, 23, Sch 14, paras 1, 5, 15, Sch 18, para 1;
Freedom of Information Act 2000, Sch 1, Pt 6, entry "The Authorised Conveyancing Practitioners Board"

1 Jul 2009 (SI 2009/1365), repeals of or in—
Solicitors Act 1974, ss 6(2)–(4), 8(5), 12, 12A, 14, 28, 40, 41(5), 49(4), (7), 87(1) (definitions "indemnity conditions", "replacement date" and "training conditions");
Courts and Legal Services Act 1990, Sch 14, paras 2(3), (5), 14(2), (3), 17(2), (4)

1 Jan 2010 (SI 2009/3250), repeals of or in—
Public Notaries Act 1801;
Public Notaries Act 1843;
Commissioners for Oaths Act 1889;
Children and Young Persons Act 1933;
Poisons Act 1972;
Solicitors Act 1974, ss 1A(b), 2(1), (4), (5), 19, 22–23, 26, 27, 31, 33A, 46, 70, 81, 81A, 89, Sch 3[7];

**Legal Services Act 2007 (c 29)**—*contd*

>                    Race Relations Act 1976;
>                    Patents Act 1977;
>                    Mental Health Act 1983;
>                    County Courts Act 1984;
>                    Administration of Justice Act 1985, ss 4, 6, 7, 11, 12, 20, 22, 38,
>                       Sch 1, Sch 4, para 1(3), (4), Sch 6, para 9(2), Sch 9, paras 4, 6;
>                    Insolvency Act 1985;
>                    Prosecution of Offences Act 1985;
>                    Building Societies Act 1986;
>                    Social Security Act 1986;
>                    Copyright, Designs and Patents Act 1988, s 292;
>                    Law of Property (Miscellaneous Provisions) Act 1989;
>                    Courts and Legal Services Act 1990, ss 17, 18, 18A, 27–29, 31,
>                       31A, 53(5), 54, 55, 68–70, 73, 86–88, 90, 93, 96, 113, 119,
>                       120(5), Sch 4, Sch 8, para 7, Schs 9, 10, 17, Sch 18,
>                       paras 9–12, 18, 20, 56[7];
>                    Environmental Protection Act 1990;
>                    Friendly Societies Act 1992;
>                    Trade Union and Labour Relations (Consolidation) Act 1992;
>                    Statute Law (Repeals) Act 1993;
>                    Trade Marks Act 1994;
>                    Agricultural Tenancies Act 1995;
>                    Environment Act 1995;
>                    Bank of England Act 1998;
>                    Access to Justice Act 1999, ss 35, 36, 37, 40–42, 44, 46, 47,
>                       Schs 4–7, 14;
>                    Immigration and Asylum Act 1999, s 86(1)(a), (d), (e), (5)(a),
>                       (6)(a), Sch 5;
>                    National Minimum Wage Act 1999;
>                    Trustee Act 2000;
>                    Enterprise Act 2002;
>                    Pensions Act 2004;
>                    Constitutional Reform Act 2005;
>                    Mental Capacity Act 2005;
>                    Serious Organised Crime and Police Act 2005;
>                    Compensation Act 2006;
>                    National Health Service Act 2006;
>                    National Health Service (Wales) Act 2006;
>                    Natural Environment and Rural Communities Act 2006
>                6 Oct 2010 (SI 2010/2089)[8], repeals of or in—
>                    Parliamentary Commissioner Act 1967, Sch 2, entry "The Legal
>                       Services Complaints Commissioner";
>                    Solicitors Act 1974, s 37A, Sch 1A;
>                    House of Commons Disqualification Act 1975, Sch 1, Pt 3,
>                       entry "The Legal Services Complaints Commissioner";
>                    Northern Ireland Assembly Disqualification Act 1975, Sch 1,
>                       Pt 3, entry "The Legal Services Complaints Commissioner";
>                    Administration of Justice Act 1985, Sch 2, paras 13, 17(a),
>                       18(1)(d), Sch 6, paras 4(3), (3A), 9(2) (note that repeal of
>                       para 9(2) was already brought into force by SI 2009/3250);
>                    Courts and Legal Services Act 1990, s 22(8)(a), Sch 8,
>                       paras 14–21, Sch 15;
>                    Access to Justice Act 1999, ss 49–52, Sch 8;
>                    Freedom of Information Act 2000, Sch 1, Pt 6, entries "The
>                       Legal Services Complaints Commissioner" and "The Legal
>                       Services Consultative Panel"
>                1 Jan 2011 (SI 2010/2089), repeal of—
>                    Courts and Legal Services Act 1990, s 23(2)(a)
>                1 Oct 2011 (SI 2011/2196), repeals of or in—

**Legal Services Act 2007 (c 29)**—*contd*

Solicitors Act 1974, ss 32(1) (words "with the concurrence of the Master of the Rolls,"), 87(1) (definition "duly certificated notary public");

Administration of Justice Act 1985, Sch 2, para 18(3);

Copyright, Designs and Patents Act 1988, ss 279, 280;

Courts and Legal Services Act 1990, ss 63, 94, 120(4) (words "26(1)" and from "paragraph 24" to "Schedule 9")

31 Dec 2011 (SI 2010/2089), repeals of or in—

Public Records Act 1958;

Superannuation Act 1972;

House of Commons Disqualification Act 1975, Sch 1, Pt 3, entry "The Legal Services Ombudsman";

Northern Ireland Assembly Disqualification Act 1975, Sch 1, Pt 3, entry "The Legal Services Ombudsman";

Courts and Legal Services Act 1990, ss 21–26 (so far as not already repealed), Sch 3 (for savings, see the entry for s 159 above);

Immigration and Asylum Act 1999, s 86(4)(b);

Freedom of Information Act 2000, Sch 1, Pt 6, entry "The Legal Services Ombudsman"

*Not yet in force,* repeal of—

Freedom of Information Act 2000, Sch 1, Pt 6, entry "The Authorised Conveyancing Practitioners Board"

Sch 24          1 Jan 2010 (SI 2009/3250)

[1]   For transitory provisions, see SI 2008/222, arts 7, 8

[2]   For transitory modifications, see SI 2008/222, arts 4–6

[3]   For transitory provisions, see SI 2008/1436, art 4

[4]   For transitory provisions, see SI 2008/3149, art 3

[5]   For transitory and transitional provisions, see SI 2009/503, arts 4, 5

[6]   For transitory and transitional provisions, see SI 2009/1365, arts 3, 4

[7]   For transitory and transitional provisions and savings, see SI 2009/3250, arts 3–6, 9

[8]   For transitory and transitional provisions, see SI 2010/2089, arts 5–8

[9]   Note that SI 2010/2089 also purports to bring this sub-paragraph into force on 6 Oct 2010

[10]  For transitory and transitional provisions, see SI 2011/2196, arts 3, 4

---

## Local Government and Public Involvement in Health Act 2007 (c 28)

*RA:* 30 Oct 2007

*Commencement provisions:* s 245; Local Government and Public Involvement in Health Act 2007 (Commencement No 1 and Savings) Order 2007, SI 2007/3136; Local Government and Public Involvement in Health Act 2007 (Commencement No 2 and Savings) Order 2008, SI 2008/172, as amended by SI 2008/337; Local Government and Public Involvement in Health Act 2007 (Commencement No 3, Transitional and Saving Provisions and Commencement No 2 (Amendment)) Order 2008, SI 2008/337; Local Government and Public Involvement in Health Act 2007 (Commencement No 4) Order 2008, SI 2008/461; Local Government and Public Involvement in Health Act 2007 (Commencement) (Wales) Order 2008, SI 2008/591; Local Government and Public Involvement in Health Act 2007 (Commencement No 5 and Transitional, Saving and Transitory Provision) Order 2008, SI 2008/917; Local Government and Public Involvement in Health Act 2007 (Commencement No 6 and Transitional and Saving Provision) Order 2008, SI 2008/1265; Local Government and Public Involvement in Health Act 2007 (Commencement No 7) Order 2008, SI 2008/2434; Local Government and Public Involvement in Health Act 2007 (Commencement No 8) Order 2008, SI 2008/3110; Local Government and Public Involvement in Health Act 2007 (Commencement No 1) (England) Order 2009, SI 2009/959; Local Government and Public

**Local Government and Public Involvement in Health Act 2007 (c 28)**—*contd*
Involvement in Health Act 2007 (Commencement No 2) (Wales) Order 2009, SI 2009/2539; Local Government and Public Involvement in Health Act 2007 (Commencement No 9) Order 2010, SI 2010/112

| | | |
|---|---|---|
| 1–30 | | 1 Nov 2007 (SI 2007/3136) |
| 31–73 | | 30 Dec 2007 (s 245(2)) |
| 74 | (1) | See Sch 3 below |
| | (2) | See Sch 4 below |
| 75 | | 13 Feb 2008 (SI 2008/337) |
| 76 | | 1 Apr 2008 (in so far as it confers powers to make regulations under the Local Government Act 1972, s 16A) (SI 2008/917) |
| | | *Not yet in force* (otherwise) |
| 77 | | 1 Apr 2008 (in so far as it confers powers to make an order under the Local Government Act 2000, s 1(2)) (SI 2008/917) |
| | | 31 Dec 2008 (otherwise) (SI 2008/3110) |
| 78 | | 31 Dec 2008 (SI 2008/3110) |
| 79–100 | | 13 Feb 2008 (SI 2008/337) |
| 101 | | See Sch 5 below |
| 102 | | 13 Feb 2008 (SI 2008/337) |
| 103–115 | | 30 Dec 2007 (s 245(2)) |
| 116 | | 1 Apr 2008 (SI 2008/461) |
| 117, 118 | | 30 Dec 2007 (s 245(2)) |
| 119 | | 12 Dec 2008 (for the purpose of conferring power on the Secretary of State to make an order specifying what is an excluded matter for the purposes of the Local Government Act 2000, s 21A) (SI 2008/3110) |
| | | 1 Apr 2009 (otherwise) (SI 2008/3110) |
| 120–124 | | 1 Apr 2009 (SI 2008/3110) |
| 125 | | 12 Dec 2008 (SI 2008/3110) |
| 126 | | 30 Apr 2009 (E) (SI 2009/959) |
| | | 1 Oct 2009 (W) (SI 2009/2539) |
| 127, 128 | | 1 Apr 2009 (SI 2008/3110) |
| 129–135 | | 27 Jan 2010 (SI 2010/112) |
| 136 | | 1 Apr 2008 (SI 2008/917) |
| 137 | | 1 Apr 2008 (W) (except in relation to a police authority for a police area in Wales) (SI 2008/591) |
| | | 1 Apr 2008 (otherwise) (SI 2008/917) |
| 138 | | 1 Apr 2009 (SI 2008/3110) |
| 139 | | 1 Apr 2008 (SI 2008/917)[4] |
| 140 | | 1 Apr 2008 (W) (except in relation to a police authority for a police area in Wales) (SI 2008/591) |
| | | 1 Apr 2008 (E) (SI 2008/917) |
| | | *Not yet in force* (W) (otherwise) |
| 141–143 | | 30 Dec 2007 (s 245(2)) |
| 144 | | 1 Apr 2008 (SI 2008/917) |
| 145 | | 1 Aug 2009 (SI 2008/3110) |
| 146, 147 | | 1 Apr 2008 (SI 2008/172) |
| 148 | | 31 Mar 2008 (SI 2008/172) |
| 149 | | 31 Jan 2008 (SI 2008/172) |
| 150 | | 1 Apr 2008 (SI 2008/172) |
| 151 | | 31 Jan 2008 (SI 2008/172) |
| 152 | | 1 Apr 2008 (SI 2008/172) |
| 153–155 | | 31 Jan 2008 (SI 2008/172) |
| 156, 157 | | 1 Apr 2008 (SI 2008/172) |
| 158 | | 1 Aug 2009 (SI 2008/3110) |
| 159–163 | | 1 Apr 2008 (SI 2008/172) |
| 164 | | 31 Jan 2008 (SI 2008/172) |
| 165 | | 1 Apr 2008 (SI 2008/172) |
| 166, 167 | | 31 Jan 2008 (SI 2008/172) |

**Local Government and Public Involvement in Health Act 2007 (c 28)**—*contd*

| | | |
|---|---|---|
| 168 | | 1 Apr 2008 (in so far as it relates to appointments of Local Commissioners made on or after that date) (SI 2008/917)[4] |
| 169 | | 1 Apr 2008 (SI 2008/917) |
| 170 | | 1 Apr 2008 (in relation to any report submitted on or after that date) (SI 2008/917)[4] |
| 171–176 | | 1 Apr 2008 (in relation to matters coming to the attention of the Commission on or after that date) (SI 2008/917)[4] |
| 177–179 | | 1 Apr 2008 (SI 2008/917) |
| 180 | | 1 Apr 2009 (SI 2008/917) |
| 181 | | 1 Apr 2008 (in relation to matters coming to the attention of the Commission on or after that date) (SI 2008/917)[4] |
| 182 | | See Sch 12 below |
| 183 | (1) | 31 Jan 2008 (in so far as it inserts Local Government Act 2000, s 49(2C), (2D)) (SI 2008/172) |
| | | *Never in force* (in so far as inserts s 49(2A), (2B) of that Act) (repealed) |
| | (2) | 31 Jan 2008 (in so far as it inserts Local Government Act 2000, s 50(4C)–(4E)) (SI 2008/172) |
| | | *Never in force* (in so far as inserts s 50(4A), (4B) of that Act) (repealed) |
| | (3) | 31 Jan 2008 (in so far as it inserts Local Government Act 2000, s 51(4C)) (SI 2008/172) |
| | | *Never in force* (in so far as inserts s 51(4A), (4B) of that Act) (repealed) |
| | (4)–(6) | 31 Jan 2008 (W) (SI 2008/172) |
| | | *Not yet in force* (E) |
| | (7)–(11) | 31 Jan 2008 (SI 2008/172) |
| 184 | | 31 Jan 2008 (SI 2008/172) |
| 185 | | 31 Jan 2008 (in so far as it confers powers to make regulations under the Local Government Act 2000, ss 57C, 57D) (SI 2008/172) |
| | | 8 May 2008 (otherwise) (SI 2008/1265)[5] |
| 186 | | 8 May 2008 (SI 2008/1265) |
| 187 | | 1 Apr 2008 (SI 2008/172) |
| 188–190 | | 31 Jan 2008 (SI 2008/172) |
| 191 | (1), (2) | 1 Apr 2008 (in relation to any case referred to the Standards Board for England under the Local Government Act 2000, s 58, on or after 1 Apr 2008) (SI 2008/172)[2] |
| | (3) | 31 Jan 2008 (SI 2008/172)[2] |
| | (4), (5) | 1 Apr 2008 (in relation to any case referred to the Standards Board for England under the Local Government Act 2000, s 58, on or after 1 Apr 2008) (SI 2008/172)[2] |
| 192 | (1)–(6) | 31 Jan 2008 (SI 2008/172) |
| | (7) | 12 Dec 2008 (SI 2008/3110) |
| | (8)–(10) | 31 Jan 2008 (SI 2008/172) |
| 193–195 | | 31 Jan 2008 (SI 2008/172) |
| 196 | | 1 Apr 2008 (SI 2008/172) |
| 197 | | 12 Dec 2008 (SI 2008/3110) |
| 198 | | 31 Jan 2008 (in so far as it confers powers to make regulations under the Local Government Act 2000, s 78A(4)–(7)) (SI 2008/172) |
| | | 12 Dec 2008 (otherwise) (SI 2008/3110) |
| 199 | | 12 Dec 2008 (SI 2008/3110) |
| 200, 201 | | 1 Apr 2008 (SI 2008/172) |
| 202 | (1) | 1 Apr 2008 (SI 2008/172) |
| | (2) | 31 Jan 2008 (in so far as it confers power to make regulations under the Local Government and Housing Act 1989, s 3A(8), and inserts s 3B thereof) (SI 2008/172) |
| | | 1 Apr 2008 (otherwise) (SI 2008/172) |
| 203 | | 1 Apr 2008 (SI 2008/172) |

**Local Government and Public Involvement in Health Act 2007 (c 28)**—*contd*

| | | |
|---|---|---|
| 204 | | 31 Jan 2008 (SI 2008/172) |
| 205–209 | | 1 Apr 2008 (SI 2008/917) |
| 210 | | 1 Apr 2008 (except in relation to a police authority for a police area in Wales) (SI 2008/591) |
| | | *Not yet in force* (otherwise) |
| 211 | | 1 Apr 2008 (SI 2008/917) |
| 212–215 | | 30 Dec 2007 (s 245(2)) |
| 216 | (1) | *Not yet in force* |
| | (2) | See Sch 14 below |
| | (3)–(5) | 30 Dec 2007 (s 245(2)) |
| 217, 218 | | 30 Dec 2007 (s 245(2)) |
| 219 | (1) | See Sch 15 below |
| | (2)–(4) | 1 Oct 2009 (SI 2008/3110) |
| 220 | (1) | See Sch 16 below |
| | (2)–(4) | 1 Apr 2008 (SI 2008/917) |
| 221, 222 | | 1 Apr 2008 (SI 2008/461) |
| 223, 224 | | 21 Feb 2008 (SI 2008/461) |
| 225 | | 31 Jan 2008 (SI 2008/172) |
| 226 | (1)–(5) | 1 Apr 2008 (SI 2008/461) |
| | (6) | 21 Feb 2008 (SI 2008/461) |
| | (7), (8) | 1 Apr 2008 (SI 2008/461) |
| 227 | | 10 Mar 2008 (for the purpose of giving directions) (SI 2008/461) |
| | | 1 Apr 2008 (otherwise) (SI 2008/461) |
| 228 | (1), (2) | 1 Apr 2008 (SI 2008/461) |
| | (3)–(8) | 21 Feb 2008 (SI 2008/461) |
| 229 | | 31 Jan 2008 (SI 2008/172) |
| 230, 231 | | 1 Apr 2008 (SI 2008/461) |
| 232 | (1) | 1 Apr 2008 (in so far as omits the National Health Service Act 2006, s 243(2)(d), (f)(i)) (SI 2008/461) |
| | | 30 Jun 2008 (otherwise) (SI 2008/461) |
| | (2)–(9) | 30 Jun 2008 (SI 2008/461) |
| 233 | (1)–(4) | 3 Nov 2008 (SI 2008/2434) |
| | (5) | 26 Sep 2008 (in so far as inserts National Health Service Act 2006, s 242B, for the purposes of making regulations) (SI 2008/2434) |
| | | 3 Nov 2008 (in so far as inserts s 242B of the 2006 Act, for remaining purposes) (SI 2008/2434) |
| | | 22 Feb 2010 (otherwise) (SI 2010/112) |
| 234 | | 3 Nov 2008 (SI 2008/2434) |
| 235 | | 30 Dec 2007 (s 245(2)) |
| 236 | | 12 Dec 2008 (in so far as confers power for the Secretary of State to make an order under sub-s (4)) (SI 2008/3110) |
| | | 1 Apr 2009 (otherwise) (SI 2008/3110) |
| 237 | | 12 Dec 2008 (SI 2008/3110) |
| 238 | | 31 Jan 2008 (SI 2008/172) |
| 239 | | 1 Apr 2008 (SI 2008/917)[4] |
| 240 | | 30 Oct 2007 (s 245(1)) |
| 241 | | See Sch 18 below |
| 242 | | 30 Oct 2007 (s 245(1)) |
| 243 | | 21 Feb 2008 (SI 2008/461) |
| 244–246 | | 30 Oct 2007 (s 245(1)) |
| Sch 1 | | 1 Nov 2007 (SI 2007/3136)[1] |
| Schs 2, 3 | | 30 Dec 2007 (s 245(2)) |
| Sch 4 | paras 1–12 | 30 Dec 2007 (s 245(2)) |
| | para 13 | 30 Oct 2007 (s 245(1)) |
| Sch 5 | | 13 Feb 2008 (except para 7) (SI 2008/337) |
| | | 31 Dec 2008 (exception noted above) (SI 2008/3110) |
| Sch 6 | | *Not yet in force*[7] |
| Schs 7, 8 | | 1 Apr 2008 (SI 2008/917) |
| Sch 9 | | 1 Apr 2008 (SI 2008/172) |

**Local Government and Public Involvement in Health Act 2007 (c 28)**—*contd*

| | | |
|---|---|---|
| Sch 10 | | 31 Mar 2008 (SI 2008/172) |
| Sch 11 | | 31 Jan 2008 (SI 2008/172) |
| Sch 12 | | 1 Apr 2008 (SI 2008/917)[4] |
| Sch 13 | | 1 Apr 2008 (SI 2008/917) |
| Sch 14 | | *Not yet in force* (paras 1, 5(6) repealed)[6] |
| Sch 15 | paras 1, 2 | 1 Apr 2008 (in so far as they relate to the Local Government Finance Act 1988, Sch 11, Pt 1, paras A1, A4–A17, A19, A20) (SI 2008/917) |
| | | 12 Dec 2008 (in so far as they relate to the Local Government Finance Act 1988, Sch 11, Pt 1, para A3) (SI 2008/3110) |
| | | 1 Oct 2009 (in so far as they relate to the Local Government Finance Act 1988, Sch 11, Pt 1, paras A2, A18) (SI 2008/3110) |
| | paras 3–19 | 1 Oct 2009 (SI 2008/3110) |
| Sch 16 | para 1 | 1 Apr 2008 (SI 2008/917) |
| | paras 2–9 | 1 Oct 2009 (SI 2008/3110) |
| | para 10 | See paras 11–13 below |
| | para 11(1) | See sub-paras (2)–(4) below |
| | para 11(2)(a)–(d) | 1 Oct 2009 (SI 2008/3110) |
| | para 11(2)(e) | 1 Apr 2008 (SI 2008/917) |
| | para 11(2)(f), (3), (4) | 1 Oct 2009 (SI 2008/3110) |
| | para 12 | 1 Oct 2009 (SI 2008/3110) |
| | para 13(1) | See sub-paras (2)–(6) below |
| | para 13(2)(a) | 1 Apr 2008 (SI 2008/917) |
| | para 13(2)(b) | 1 Oct 2009 (SI 2008/3110) |
| | para 13(3) | 1 Apr 2008 (SI 2008/917) |
| | para 13(4)–(6) | 1 Oct 2009 (SI 2008/3110) |
| | paras 14–16 | 1 Apr 2008 (in so far as they relate to the office of President or the office of Vice-President) (SI 2008/917) |
| | | 1 Oct 2009 (otherwise) (SI 2008/3110) |
| Sch 17 | | 30 Dec 2007 (s 245(2)) |
| Sch 18 | Pt 1 | 1 Nov 2007 (SI 2007/3136)[1] |
| | Pts 2, 3 | *Not yet in force* |
| | Pt 4 | 13 Feb 2008 (SI 2008/337)[3] |
| | Pt 5 | 30 Dec 2007 (s 245(2)) |
| | Pt 6 | 30 Apr 2009 (E) (SI 2009/959), repeals of or in— Police and Justice Act 2006 |
| | | 1 Oct 2009 (W) (SI 2009/2539), repeals of or in— Police and Justice Act 2006 |
| | | *Not yet in force*, repeals of or in— Local Government Act 2000; National Health Service (Consequential Provisions) Act 2006 |
| | Pt 7 | *Not yet in force* |
| | Pt 8 | 30 Dec 2007 (repeal of Local Government Act 1999, s 29(3)) (s 245(2)) |
| | | 1 Apr 2008 (W) (except in relation to a police authority for a police area in Wales) (SI 2008/591), repeals of or in— Local Government Act 1999, ss 5, 6, 28; Local Government Act 2000 |
| | | 1 Apr 2008 (otherwise) (SI 2008/917)[6] |
| | Pt 9 | 1 Apr 2008 (SI 2008/172) |
| | Pts 10–13 | 31 Jan 2008 (SI 2008/172) |
| | Pt 14 | 1 Apr 2008 (SI 2008/917) |
| | Pt 15 | 31 Jan 2008 (repeals in Local Government Act 2000, ss 52 (W), 54A(2), 55, 62(1), Sch 4) (SI 2008/172)[2] |
| | | 1 Apr 2008 (repeal in Local Government and Housing Act 1989) (SI 2008/172) |
| | | *Not yet in force* (E) (repeal of Local Government Act 2000, s 52)[9] |
| | Pts 16, 17 | *Not yet in force* |

**Local Government and Public Involvement in Health Act 2007 (c 28)**—*contd*

| | |
|---|---|
| Pt 18 | 1 Apr 2008 (SI 2008/461), repeals of or in— |
| | House of Commons Disqualification Act 1975, Sch 1, Pt 2, entry in respect of Patients' Forums established under the National Health Service Act 2006, s 237; |
| | Mental Health Act 1983; |
| | Freedom of Information Act 2000, Sch 1, Pt 3, para 41A; |
| | National Health Service Reform and Health Care Professions Act 2002, s 19(6), (7); |
| | National Health Service Reform and Health Care Professions Act (Commencement No 6) Order 2003, SI 2003/2246; |
| | National Health Service Act 2006, ss 35, 56, 237–241, 243(2)(d), (f)(i), 271(3)(e); |
| | National Health Service (Consequential Provisions) Act 2006 |
| | 30 Jun 2008 (otherwise) (SI 2008/461) |
| Pt 19 | *Not yet in force* |

1  For savings, see SI 2007/3136, art 3

2  For savings, see SI 2008/172, arts 2(2), 7(3)

3  For transitional provisions and savings, see SI 2008/337, art 2(d), Schedule

4  For transitional and saving provisions, see SI 2008/917, art 6

5  For transitional and saving provisions, see SI 2008/1265, art 3

6  Note however the repeal relating to the Local Government Act 1999, s 5 is duplicated in s 140 and that section has not been brought into force in relation to police authorities in police areas in Wales. It is thought therefore that the corresponding repeal in Sch 18, Pt 8 is still to be brought into force for those purposes

7  S 135, which introduces Sch 6, was brought into force on 27 Jan 2010 by SI 2010/112, however that order does not specifically bring Sch 6 into force

8  In light of the amendments made to this section and to the Local Government Act 2000, Pt III by the Localism Act 2011, it is unlikely that sub-ss (1)–(6) will be further commenced. That Part applies now only to Welsh authorities (see definition "relevant authority" in s 49(6) thereof), so sub-ss (1)–(6) are now considered spent in so far as they relate to England

9  In light of the amendments made to the Local Government Act 2000, Pt III by the Localism Act 2011, that Part applies now only to Welsh authorities (see definition "relevant authority" in s 49(6) thereof). It is therefore unlikely that this repeal will be brought into force in England and is now considered spent in so far as it relates to England

**Mental Health Act 2007 (c 12)**

*RA:* 19 Jul 2007

*Commencement provisions:* ss 56, 57; Mental Health Act 2007 (Commencement No 1) Order 2007, SI 2007/2156; Mental Health Act 2007 (Commencement No 2) Order 2007, SI 2007/2635; Mental Health Act 2007 (Commencement No 3) Order 2007, SI 2007/2798; Mental Health Act 2007 (Commencement No 4) Order 2008, SI 2008/745; Mental Health Act 2007 (Commencement No 5 and Transitional Provisions) Order 2008, SI 2008/800; Mental Health Act 2007 (Commencement No 6 and After-care under Supervision: Savings, Modifications and Transitional Provisions) Order 2008, SI 2008/1210; Mental Health Act 2007 (Commencement No 7 and Transitional Provisions) Order 2008, SI 2008/1900; Mental Health Act 2007 (Commencement No 8 and Transitional Provisions) Order 2008, SI 2008/2561; Mental Health Act 2007 (Commencement No 9) Order 2008, SI 2008/2788; Mental Health Act 2007 (Commencement No 10 and Transitional Provisions) Order 2009, SI 2009/139; Mental Health Act 2007 (Commencement No 11) Order 2010, SI 2010/143; Mental Health Act 2007 (Commencement No 12 and Transitional Provisions) Order 2017, SI 2017/1038

| | | |
|---|---|---|
| 1 | (1)–(3) | 3 Nov 2008 (SI 2008/1900)[3] |
| | (4) | See Sch 1 below |
| 2–16 | | 3 Nov 2008 (SI 2008/1900)[3] |

**Mental Health Act 2007 (c 12)**—*contd*

| | | |
|---|---|---|
| 17 | | 1 Apr 2008 (SI 2008/745) |
| 18 | | 1 Apr 2008 (in so far as substitutes Mental Health Act 1983, s 114(9), (10), and for the purposes of making regulations under that substituted section) (SI 2008/745) |
| | | 3 Nov 2008 (otherwise) (SI 2008/1900; SI 2008/2561)[3, 4] |
| 19, 20 | | 1 Oct 2007 (SI 2007/2798) |
| 21 | | See Sch 2 below |
| 22 | (1)–(4) | 3 Nov 2008 (SI 2008/1900)[3] |
| | (5) | 1 Apr 2008 (SI 2008/745) |
| | (6) | 3 Nov 2008 (SI 2008/1900)[3] |
| 23–25 | | 3 Nov 2008 (SI 2008/1900)[3] |
| 26 | | 1 Dec 2007 (SI 2007/2798) |
| 27–29 | | 3 Nov 2008 (SI 2008/1900)[3] |
| 30 | (1) | 3 Nov 2008 (W) (SI 2008/2561)[4] |
| | | 1 Apr 2009 (E) (SI 2009/139) |
| | (2) | 1 Apr 2008 (in so far as inserts Mental Health Act 1983, s 130C(5), and in so far as inserts Mental Health Act 1983, s 130A for the purposes of making regulations) (SI 2008/745) |
| | | 3 Nov 2008 (W) (otherwise) (SI 2008/2561)[4] |
| | | 1 Apr 2009 (E) (otherwise) (SI 2009/139) |
| | (3) | 1 Apr 2008 (for the purposes of making regulations) (SI 2008/745) |
| | | 3 Nov 2008 (W) (otherwise) (SI 2008/2561)[4] |
| | | 1 Apr 2009 (E) (otherwise) (SI 2009/139) |
| 31 | (1), (2) | 3 Nov 2008 (SI 2008/1900)[3] |
| | (3) | 1 Apr 2010 (SI 2010/143) |
| | (4) | 3 Nov 2008 (SI 2008/1900)[3] |
| 32 | (1) | 3 Nov 2008 (SI 2008/1900)[3] |
| | (2) | 1 Apr 2008 (in so far as inserts Mental Health Act 1983, s 17F, for the purposes of making regulations) (SI 2008/745) |
| | | 3 Nov 2008 (otherwise) (SI 2008/1900)[3] |
| | (3) | 3 Nov 2008 (SI 2008/1900)[3] |
| | (4) | See Schs 3, 4 below |
| 33, 34 | | 3 Nov 2008 (SI 2008/1900)[3] |
| 35 | | 1 Apr 2008 (in so far as inserts Mental Health Act 1983, s 64H(9), and for the purposes of making regulations under that inserted section) (SI 2008/745) |
| | | 3 Nov 2008 (otherwise) (SI 2008/1900)[3] |
| 36 | | 3 Nov 2008 (SI 2008/1210)[2] |
| 37 | | 3 Nov 2008 (SI 2008/1900)[3] |
| 38 | (1), (2) | 3 Nov 2008 (SI 2008/1900)[3] |
| | (3)(a) | 1 Dec 2017 (SI 2017/1038) |
| | (3)(b), (c) | *Never in force* (repealed) |
| | (3)(d) | 1 Dec 2017 (SI 2017/1038) |
| | (3)(e) | 3 Nov 2008 (SI 2008/1900)[3] |
| | (4) | *Never in force* (repealed) |
| | (5) | See sub-ss (6)–(9) below |
| | (6) | 1 Dec 2017 (SI 2017/1038)[6] |
| | (7)(a) | 1 Dec 2017 (SI 2017/1038) |
| | (7)(b) | 3 Nov 2008 (SI 2008/1900)[3] |
| | (8) | *Never in force* (repealed) |
| | (9) | 1 Dec 2017 (SI 2017/1038)[6] |
| 39 | (1) | 1 Oct 2007 (SI 2007/2798) |
| | (2) | See Sch 5 below |
| 40–42 | | 1 Oct 2007 (SI 2007/2798) |
| 43 | | 1 Jan 2008 (SI 2007/2798) |
| 44 | | 30 Apr 2008 (SI 2008/800)[1] |
| 45 | | 24 Jul 2007 (SI 2007/2156) |
| 46 | | 1 Oct 2007 (SI 2007/2798) |
| 47 | | 1 Apr 2008 (SI 2008/745) |

**Mental Health Act 2007 (c 12)**—*contd*

| | | |
|---|---|---|
| 48 | | See Sch 6 below |
| 49 | | 1 Oct 2007 (SI 2007/2798) |
| 50 | (1)–(4) | 1 Apr 2009 (SI 2009/139) |
| | (5) | See Sch 7 below |
| | (6) | See Sch 8 below |
| | (7) | See Sch 9 below |
| | (8)–(13) | 1 Apr 2008 (SI 2008/745) |
| 51 | | 1 Oct 2007 (SI 2007/2635) |
| 52 | | 19 Jul 2007 (RA) |
| 53 | | See Sch 10 below |
| 54 | | 1 Apr 2008 (SI 2008/745) |
| 55 | | See Sch 11 below |
| 56–59 | | 19 Jul 2007 (RA) |
| Sch 1 | paras 1–12 | 3 Nov 2008 (SI 2008/1900)[3] |
| | para 13 | 3 Nov 2008 (SI 2008/1210) |
| | paras 14–26 | 3 Nov 2008 (SI 2008/1900)[3] |
| Sch 2 | | 3 Nov 2008 (SI 2008/1900; SI 2008/2561)[3, 4] |
| Sch 3 | paras 1–3 | 3 Nov 2008 (SI 2008/1900)[3] |
| | para 4 | 1 Apr 2008 (for the purposes of making regulations) (SI 2008/745) |
| | | 3 Nov 2008 (otherwise) (SI 2008/1900)[3] |
| | paras 5–15 | 3 Nov 2008 (SI 2008/1900)[3] |
| | paras 16, 17 | 3 Nov 2008 (SI 2008/1210) |
| | paras 18–20 | 3 Nov 2008 (SI 2008/1900)[3] |
| | para 21(1)–(3) | 3 Nov 2008 (SI 2008/1900)[3] |
| | para 21(4) | 3 Nov 2008 (SI 2008/1210) |
| | para 22 | 3 Nov 2008 (SI 2008/1900)[3] |
| | paras 23–25 | 3 Nov 2008 (SI 2008/1210) |
| | paras 26–37 | 3 Nov 2008 (SI 2008/1900)[3] |
| Sch 4 | | 3 Nov 2008 (SI 2008/1900)[3] |
| Sch 5 | para 1 | 3 Nov 2008 (SI 2008/1900)[3] |
| | para 2 | 1 Apr 2008 (SI 2008/745) |
| | para 3 | 3 Nov 2008 (SI 2008/1900)[3] |
| | para 4 | 1 Oct 2007 (in so far as inserts Mental Health Act 1983, s 80D) (SI 2007/2798) |
| | | 3 Nov 2008 (otherwise) (SI 2008/1900)[3] |
| | para 5 | 1 Apr 2008 (SI 2008/745) |
| | para 6 | 3 Nov 2008 (SI 2008/1900)[3] |
| | paras 7–9 | 1 Oct 2007 (SI 2007/2798) |
| | para 10 | 3 Nov 2008 (SI 2008/1900)[3] |
| | para 11 | 1 Oct 2007 (SI 2007/2798) |
| | para 12 | 3 Nov 2008 (SI 2008/1900)[3] |
| | para 13 | 1 Oct 2007 (SI 2007/2798) |
| | para 14 | 28 Oct 2008 (SI 2008/2788) |
| | paras 15–17 | 3 Nov 2008 (SI 2008/1900)[3] |
| | para 18(a) | 1 Oct 2007 (SI 2007/2798) |
| | para 18(b) | 3 Nov 2008 (SI 2008/1900)[3] |
| | para 19 | 1 Oct 2007 (SI 2007/2798) |
| | para 20 | 28 Oct 2008 (SI 2008/2788) |
| | para 21(1), (2)(a), (b) | 3 Nov 2008 (SI 2008/1900)[3] |
| | para 21(2)(c) | 1 Oct 2007 (SI 2007/2798) |
| | para 21(3), (4) | 3 Nov 2008 (SI 2008/1900)[3] |
| Sch 6 | | 3 Nov 2008 (SI 2008/1900)[3] |
| Sch 7 | | 1 Apr 2008 (for the purposes of making regulations or directions and inserting any definition relevant to those regulations or directions) (SI 2008/745) |
| | | 1 Apr 2009 (otherwise) (SI 2009/139)[5] |
| Sch 8 | | 1 Apr 2009 (SI 2009/139) |
| Sch 9 | paras 1–7 | 1 Apr 2009 (SI 2009/139) |

**Mental Health Act 2007 (c 12)**—*contd*

|  |  |  |
|---|---|---|
|  | para 8 | 1 Apr 2008 (SI 2008/745) |
|  | para 9 | 1 Apr 2009 (SI 2009/139) |
|  | paras 10, 11 | 1 Apr 2008 (SI 2008/745) |
|  | paras 12, 13 | 1 Apr 2009 (SI 2009/139) |
| Sch 10 |  | 19 Jul 2007 (RA) |
| Sch 11 | Pts 1–4 | 3 Nov 2008 (SI 2008/1900)[3] |
|  | Pt 5 | 3 Nov 2008 (SI 2008/1210)[2] |
|  | Pt 6 | 3 Nov 2008 (SI 2008/1900)[3] |
|  | Pt 7 | 28 Oct 2008 (SI 2008/2788) |
|  | Pts 8, 9 | 3 Nov 2008 (SI 2008/1900)[3] |
|  | Pt 10 | 1 Apr 2009 (SI 2009/139) |

[1]   For transitional provisions, see SI 2008/800, art 3

[2]   For savings, see SI 2008/1210, art 4

[3]   For transitional provisions and savings, see SI 2008/1900, art 3, Schedule

[4]   For transitional provisions and savings, see SI 2008/2561, art 3, Schedule

[5]   For transitional provisions, see SI 2009/139, art 3, Schedule

[6]   For transitional provisions, see SI 2017/1038, arts 3, 4

---

**Northern Ireland (St Andrews Agreement) Act 2007 (c 4)**

*RA:* 27 Mar 2007

Whole Act in force 27 Mar 2007 (RA)

---

**Offender Management Act 2007 (c 21)**

*RA:* 26 Jul 2007

*Commencement provisions:* s 41; Offender Management Act 2007 (Commencement No 1 and Transitional Provisions) Order 2007, SI 2007/3001[1]; Offender Management Act 2007 (Commencement No 2 and Transitional Provision) Order 2008, SI 2008/504; Offender Management Act 2007 (Commencement No 3) Order 2009, SI 2009/32; Offender Management Act 2007 (Commencement No 4) Order 2009, SI 2009/547; Offender Management Act 2007 (Commencement No 5) Order 2010, SI 2010/191; Offender Management Act 2007 (Commencement No 6) Order 2013, SI 2013/1963

| | | |
|---|---|---|
| 1, 2 |  | 1 Apr 2008 (in relation to the police areas of Humberside, Leicestershire, Merseyside, West Mercia, Dyfed Powys, South Wales) (SI 2008/504)[2] |
|  |  | 1 Apr 2009 (in relation to the police areas of Greater Manchester and Lancashire) (SI 2009/547) |
|  |  | 1 Apr 2010 (otherwise) (SI 2010/191) |
| 3 | (1)–(5) | 1 Apr 2008 (in relation to the police areas of Humberside, Leicestershire, Merseyside, West Mercia, Dyfed Powys, South Wales) (SI 2008/504) |
|  |  | 1 Apr 2009 (in relation to the police areas of Greater Manchester and Lancashire) (SI 2009/547) |
|  |  | 1 Apr 2010 (otherwise) (SI 2010/191) |
|  | (6) | 1 Apr 2008 (SI 2008/504) |
|  | (7) | 1 Apr 2008 (in relation to the police areas of Humberside, Leicestershire, Merseyside, West Mercia, Dyfed Powys, South Wales) (SI 2008/504) |
|  |  | 1 Apr 2009 (in relation to the police areas of Greater Manchester and Lancashire) (SI 2009/547) |
|  |  | 1 Apr 2010 (otherwise) (SI 2010/191) |

**Offender Management Act 2007 (c 21)**—*contd*

| | | |
|---|---|---|
| 4 | | 1 Apr 2008 (in relation to the police areas of Humberside, Leicestershire, Merseyside, West Mercia, Dyfed Powys, South Wales) (SI 2008/504) |
| | | 1 Apr 2009 (in relation to the police areas of Greater Manchester and Lancashire) (SI 2009/547) |
| | | 1 Apr 2010 (otherwise) (SI 2010/191) |
| 5 | | 1 Mar 2008 (SI 2008/504) |
| 6 | | 1 Apr 2008 (in relation to the police areas of Humberside, Leicestershire, Merseyside, West Mercia, Dyfed Powys, South Wales) (SI 2008/504) |
| | | 1 Apr 2009 (in relation to the police areas of Greater Manchester and Lancashire) (SI 2009/547) |
| | | 1 Apr 2010 (otherwise) (SI 2010/191) |
| 7 | (1), (2) | 1 Apr 2008 (SI 2008/504) |
| | (3) | 1 Apr 2008 (in relation to the police areas of Humberside, Leicestershire, Merseyside, West Mercia, Dyfed Powys, South Wales) (SI 2008/504) |
| | | 1 Apr 2009 (in relation to the police areas of Greater Manchester and Lancashire) (SI 2009/547) |
| | | 1 Apr 2010 (otherwise) (SI 2010/191) |
| 8 | | 1 Apr 2008 (in relation to the police areas of Humberside, Leicestershire, Merseyside, West Mercia, Dyfed Powys, South Wales) (SI 2008/504) |
| | | 1 Apr 2009 (in relation to the police areas of Greater Manchester and Lancashire) (SI 2009/547) |
| | | 1 Apr 2010 (otherwise) (SI 2010/191) |
| 9 | | 1 Apr 2008 (SI 2008/504) |
| 10 | | 1 Apr 2008 (in relation to the police areas of Humberside, Leicestershire, Merseyside, West Mercia, Dyfed Powys, South Wales) (SI 2008/504) |
| | | 1 Apr 2009 (in relation to the police areas of Greater Manchester and Lancashire) (SI 2009/547) |
| | | 1 Apr 2010 (otherwise) (SI 2010/191) |
| 11 | (1) | 1 Apr 2008 (in relation to the police areas of Humberside, Leicestershire, Merseyside, West Mercia, Dyfed Powys, South Wales) (SI 2008/504) |
| | | 1 Apr 2009 (in relation to the police areas of Greater Manchester and Lancashire) (SI 2009/547) |
| | | 1 Apr 2010 (otherwise) (SI 2010/191) |
| | (2) | See Sch 2 below |
| 12 | (1), (2) | 1 Apr 2008 (SI 2008/504) |
| | (3) | 1 Apr 2008 (in relation to the police areas of Humberside, Leicestershire, Merseyside, West Mercia, Dyfed Powys, South Wales) (SI 2008/504) |
| | | 1 Apr 2009 (in relation to the police areas of Greater Manchester and Lancashire) (SI 2009/547) |
| | | 1 Apr 2010 (otherwise) (SI 2010/191) |
| 13, 14 | | 1 Apr 2008 (SI 2008/504) |
| 15 | | 1 Apr 2008 (in relation to the police areas of Humberside, Leicestershire, Merseyside, West Mercia, Dyfed Powys, South Wales) (SI 2008/504) |
| | | 1 Apr 2009 (in relation to the police areas of Greater Manchester and Lancashire) (SI 2009/547) |
| | | 1 Apr 2010 (otherwise) (SI 2010/191) |
| 16–20 | | 1 Nov 2007 (SI 2007/3001) |
| 21–24 | | 1 Apr 2008 (SI 2008/504) |
| 25–27 | | 1 Nov 2007 (SI 2007/3001) |

**Offender Management Act 2007 (c 21)**—*contd*

| | | |
|---|---|---|
| 28, 29 | | 19 Jan 2009 (in relation to the police areas of Derbyshire, Leicestershire, Lincolnshire, Northamptonshire, Nottinghamshire, Staffordshire, Warwickshire, West Mercia, West Midlands, for a period beginning on 19 Jan 2009 and ending on 31 Mar 2012) (SI 2009/32) |
| | | 6 Jan 2014 (otherwise) (SI 2013/1963) |
| 30 | | 19 Jan 2009 (SI 2009/32) |
| 31 | | 1 May 2008 (SI 2007/3001) |
| 32–38 | | 1 Nov 2007 (SI 2007/3001) |
| 39 | | See Schs 3–5 below |
| 40 | | 1 Nov 2007 (SI 2007/3001) |
| 41, 42 | | 26 Jul 2007 (RA) |
| Schs 1, 2 | | 1 Mar 2008 (SI 2008/504) |
| Sch 3 | Pt 1 | 1 Apr 2008 (SI 2008/504) |
| | Pts 2–4 | 1 Nov 2007 (SI 2007/3001) |
| Sch 4 | Pts 1, 2 | 1 Apr 2008 (SI 2008/504) |
| | Pt 3 | 1 Nov 2007 (SI 2007/3001) |
| Sch 5 | Pt 1 | 1 Apr 2008 (SI 2008/504), repeals of or in— |
| | | Criminal Justice and Court Services Act 2000, ss 6, 9, 25; |
| | | Local Government and Public Involvement in Health Act 2007 |
| | | 1 Apr 2008 (repeal of or in Criminal Justice and Court Services Act 2000, ss 1–5, 8, 10, 18, 20–22, Sch 1, in relation to the police areas of Humberside, Leicestershire, Merseyside, West Mercia, Dyfed Powys, South Wales) (SI 2008/504) |
| | | 1 Apr 2009 (repeals of or in Criminal Justice and Court Services Act 2000, ss 1–5, 8, 10, 18, 20–22, Sch 1, in relation to the police areas of Greater Manchester and Lancashire) (SI 2009/547) |
| | | 1 Apr 2010 (repeals of or in Criminal Justice and Court Services Act 2000, ss 1–5, 8, 10, 18, 20–22, 78, Sch 1, in so far as not already in force) (SI 2010/191) |
| | | *Not yet in force*, repeals of or in— |
| | | Criminal Justice and Court Services Act 2000, s 23 |
| | Pt 2 | 1 Nov 2007 (except repeal of Prison Act 1952, s 41) (SI 2007/3001) |
| | | 1 Apr 2008 (repeal of Prison Act 1952, s 41) (SI 2008/504) |
| | Pt 3 | 1 Nov 2007 (except repeal of Criminal Justice Act 2003, s 202(3)(b)) (SI 2007/3001) |
| | | 1 May 2008 (otherwise) (SI 2007/3001) |

¹   For transitional provisions, see SI 2007/3001, art 2(2)

²   For a transitional provision, see SI 2008/504, art 5

---

**Parliament (Joint Departments) Act 2007 (c 16)**

*RA:* 19 Jul 2007

Whole Act in force 19 Jul 2007 (RA)

---

**Pensions Act 2007 (c 22)**

*RA:* 26 Jul 2007

*Commencement provisions:* s 30; Pensions Act 2007 (Commencement No 1) Order 2007, SI 2007/3063; Pensions Act 2007 (Commencement No 2) Order 2007, SI 2007/3512; Pensions Act 2007 (Commencement No 3) Order 2009, SI 2009/406; Pensions Act 2007 (Commencement No 4) Order 2011, SI 2011/1267, as amended by SI 2012/911

| | | |
|---|---|---|
| 1 | (1)–(3) | 26 Sep 2007 (s 30(3)) |

**Pensions Act 2007 (c 22)**—*contd*

| | | |
|---|---|---|
| | (4) | See Sch 1, Pt 1 below |
| 2 | (1)–(3) | 26 Sep 2007 (s 30(3)) |
| | (4) | See Sch 1, Pt 2 below |
| | (5), (6) | 26 Sep 2007 (s 30(3)) |
| 3 | (1), (2) | 26 Sep 2007 (s 30(3)) |
| | (3) | See Sch 1, Pt 3 below |
| 4 | (1), (2) | 26 Sep 2007 (s 30(3)) |
| | (3) | See Sch 1, Pt 4 below |
| | (4)–(8) | 26 Sep 2007 (s 30(3)) |
| 5 | (1) | 26 Jul 2007 (so far as relates to the amounts mentioned in the Social Security Administration Act 1992, s 150A(1)(d), as inserted by this section) (s 30(1)(a)) |
| | | 26 Sep 2007 (otherwise) (s 30(3)) |
| | (2) | See Sch 1, Pt 5 below |
| | (3)–(7) | 26 Jul 2007 (so far as relates to the amounts mentioned in the Social Security Administration Act 1992, s 150A(1)(d), as inserted by this section) (s 30(1)(a)) |
| | | 26 Sep 2007 (otherwise) (s 30(3)) |
| 6 | | 26 Jul 2007 (so far as relates to the amounts mentioned in the Social Security Administration Act 1992, s 150A(1)(d), as inserted by s 5 of this Act) (s 30(1)(a)) |
| | | 26 Sep 2007 (otherwise) (s 30(3)) |
| 7, 8 | | 26 Sep 2007 (s 30(3)) |
| 9 | (1) | 26 Sep 2007 (s 30(3)) |
| | (2) | See Sch 1, Pt 6 below |
| 10 | | 26 Sep 2007 (s 30(3)) |
| 11 | (1)–(4) | 26 Sep 2007 (s 30(3)) |
| | (5) | See Sch 2 below |
| 12 | (1)–(3) | 26 Sep 2007 (s 30(3)) |
| | (4) | See Sch 1, Pt 7 below |
| | (5)–(10) | 26 Sep 2007 (s 30(3)) |
| 13 | (1) | See Sch 3 below |
| | (2) | See Sch 1, Pt 8 below |
| | (3) | 26 Sep 2007 (s 30(3)) |
| 14 | | 1 Mar 2009 (for the purpose of conferring power to make regulations) (SI 2009/406) |
| | | 6 Apr 2009 (otherwise) (SI 2009/406) |
| 15 | (1) | 6 Apr 2012 (SI 2011/1267) |
| | (2) | 26 Sep 2007 (s 30(3)) |
| | (3) | See Sch 4 below |
| | (4)–(8) | 26 Sep 2007 (s 30(3)) |
| 16 | | 26 Sep 2007 (s 30(3)) |
| 17 | | See Sch 5 below |
| 18 | (1)–(3) | 14 Dec 2007 (SI 2007/3512) |
| | (4)–(11) | 26 Jul 2007 (s 30(1)(b)) |
| 19 | | 26 Jul 2007 (s 30(1)(b)) |
| 20–23 | | 26 Jul 2007 (s 30(1)(c)) |
| 24–26 | | 26 Jul 2007 (s 30(1)(d)) |
| 27 | | 26 Jul 2007 (s 30(1)(d)) (but see Sch 7 below) |
| 28–31 | | 26 Jul 2007 (s 30(1)(d)) |
| Sch 1 | Pts 1–4 | 26 Sep 2007 (s 30(3)) |
| | Pt 5 | 26 Jul 2007 (so far as relates to the amounts mentioned in the Social Security Administration Act 1992, s 150A(1)(d), as inserted by s 5 of this Act) (s 30(1)(a)) |
| | | 26 Sep 2007 (otherwise) (s 30(3)) |
| | Pts 6–8 | 26 Sep 2007 (s 30(3)) |
| Schs 2, 3 | | 26 Sep 2007 (s 30(3)) |
| Sch 4 | Pt 1 | 26 Sep 2007 (s 30(3)) |
| | Pt 2, para 42(1) | See sub-paras (2), (3) below |

**Pensions Act 2007 (c 22)**—*contd*

|  |  |  |
|---|---|---|
| | Pt 2, para 42(2) | 6 Apr 2015 (SI 2011/1267) |
| | Pt 2, para 42(3)(a) | *Not yet in force* |
| | Pt 2, para 42(3)(b) | 6 Apr 2015 (SI 2011/1267) |
| | Pt 2, para 42(3)(c) | *Not yet in force* |
| | Pt 2, paras 43–45 | *Not yet in force* |
| | Pt 2, para 46 | See paras 47–60 below |
| | Pt 2, para 47 | 6 Apr 2015 (SI 2011/1267) |
| | Pt 2, para 48 | *Not yet in force* |
| | Pt 2, para 49 | 6 Apr 2015 (SI 2011/1267) |
| | Pt 2, paras 50–53 | *Not yet in force* |
| | Pt 2, para 54 | 6 Apr 2015 (SI 2011/1267) |
| | Pt 2, paras 55–58 | *Not yet in force* (para 55 repealed) |
| | Pt 2, para 59(1) | See sub-paras (2)–(4) below |
| | Pt 2, para 59(2)–(4) | 6 Apr 2012 (SI 2011/1267) |
| | Pt 2, para 59(3) | 6 Apr 2015 (SI 2011/1267) |
| | Pt 2, para 59(4) | 6 Apr 2012 (SI 2011/1267) |
| | Pt 2, para 60 | 6 Apr 2012 (SI 2011/1267) |
| | Pt 3 | 26 Sep 2007 (s 30(3)) |
| Sch 5 | | 1 Nov 2007 (SI 2007/3063) |
| Sch 6 | | 26 Jul 2007 (s 30(1)(c)) |
| Sch 7 | Pts 1–6 | 26 Jul 2007 (s 30(1)(d)) |
| | Pt 7 | 6 Apr 2012 (SI 2011/1267), repeals of or in— |

Pt 7 (continued):

6 Apr 2012 (SI 2011/1267), repeals of or in—
Pension Schemes Act 1993, Sch 4, para 2;
Pensions Act 1995, s 137(7)(a)

6 Apr 2015 (SI 2011/1267), repeals of or in—
Social Security Contributions and Benefits Act 1992, s 4C(2)(d), (5)(g), (h);
Pension Schemes Act 1993, ss 8(3), 31, 45B;
Pensions Act 1995, s 139, Sch 5, para 36;
Social Security Contributions (Transfer of Functions, etc) Act 1999, Sch 1, paras 34(b), 43, 50

*Not yet in force*, repeals of or in—
Social Security Contributions and Benefits Act 1992, s 4C(5)(b), (i), (j), Sch 1, para 1;
Pension Schemes Act 1993, ss 20(3), 40(b), 42A, 43, 45, 164(2)(b), 177, 181;
Pensions Act 1995, ss 137(1), (5), (6), (7)(b), 138(1)–(4), Sch 5, paras 42, 43;
Social Security Act 1998;
Social Security Contributions (Transfer of Functions, etc) Act 1999, Sch 1, paras 46, 47, 49, 61(3)(a);
Welfare Reform and Pensions Act 1999;
National Insurance Contributions Act 2002

Pt 8          1 Nov 2007 (SI 2007/3063)

---

**Planning-gain Supplement (Preparations) Act 2007 (c 2)**

*RA:* 20 Mar 2007

Whole Act in force 20 Mar 2007 (RA)

---

**Prostitution (Public Places) (Scotland) Act 2007 (asp 11)**

*RA:* 5 Apr 2007

*Commencement provisions:* s 3(2); Prostitution (Public Places) (Scotland) Act 2007 (Commencement) Order 2007, SSI 2007/382

1, 2                          15 Oct 2007 (SSI 2007/382)

**See Halsbury's Statutes Citator for amendments to these Acts**          1917

**Prostitution (Public Places) (Scotland) Act 2007 (asp 11)**—*contd*
3                                          5 Apr 2007 (s 3(2))

---

**Protection of Vulnerable Groups (Scotland) Act 2007 (asp 14)**

*RA:* 18 Apr 2007

*Commencement provisions:* s 101; Protection of Vulnerable Groups (Scotland) Act 2007 (Commencement No 1) Order 2007, SSI 2007/385; Protection of Vulnerable Groups (Scotland) Act 2007 (Commencement No 2) Order 2007, SSI 2007/564; Protection of Vulnerable Groups (Scotland) Act 2007 (Commencement No 3) Order 2010, SSI 2010/133; Protection of Vulnerable Groups (Scotland) Act 2007 (Commencement No 4) and the Criminal Justice and Licensing (Scotland) Act 2010 (Commencement No 3) Order 2010, SSI 2010/344; Protection of Vulnerable Groups (Scotland) Act 2007 (Commencement No 5, Savings, Transitional and Consequential Provisions) and the Criminal Justice and Licensing (Scotland) Act 2010 (Commencement No 7, Savings and Transitional Provisions) Order 2011, SSI 2011/157

| | | |
|---|---|---|
| 1, 2 | | 28 Feb 2011 (SSI 2011/157) |
| 3 | (1), (2) | 18 Apr 2010 (for the purpose of making regulations or orders) (SSI 2010/133) |
| | | 28 Feb 2011 (otherwise) (SSI 2011/157) |
| | (3), (4) | 28 Feb 2011 (SSI 2011/157) |
| 4, 5 | | 18 Apr 2010 (for the purpose of making regulations or orders) (SSI 2010/133) |
| | | 28 Feb 2011 (otherwise) (SSI 2011/157) |
| 6 | (1) | 28 Feb 2011 (SSI 2011/157) |
| | (2) | 18 Apr 2010 (for the purpose of making regulations or orders) (SSI 2010/133) |
| | | 28 Feb 2011 (otherwise) (SSI 2011/157) |
| 7 | (1) | 18 Apr 2010 (for the purpose of making regulations or orders) (SSI 2010/133) |
| | | 28 Feb 2011 (otherwise) (SSI 2011/157) |
| | (2) | 28 Feb 2011 (SSI 2011/157) |
| | (3) | 18 Apr 2010 (for the purpose of making regulations or orders) (SSI 2010/133) |
| | | 28 Feb 2011 (otherwise) (SSI 2011/157) |
| | (4) | 28 Feb 2011 (SSI 2011/157) |
| 8 | (1), (2) | 18 Apr 2010 (for the purpose of making regulations or orders) (SSI 2010/133) |
| | | 28 Feb 2011 (otherwise) (SSI 2011/157) |
| | (3)(a)–(c) | 28 Feb 2011 (SSI 2011/157) |
| | (3)(d) | 12 Oct 2010 (SSI 2010/344) |
| 9–13 | | 28 Feb 2011 (SSI 2011/157) |
| 14 | (1), (2) | 28 Feb 2011 (SSI 2011/157) |
| | (3), (4) | 18 Apr 2010 (for the purpose of making regulations or orders) (SSI 2010/133) |
| | | 28 Feb 2011 (otherwise) (SSI 2011/157) |
| 15, 16 | | 28 Feb 2011 (SSI 2011/157) |
| 17 | (1)–(4), (5)(a)–(c) | 28 Feb 2011 (SSI 2011/157) |
| | (5)(d) | 18 Apr 2010 (for the purpose of making regulations or orders) (SSI 2010/133) |
| | | 28 Feb 2011 (otherwise) (SSI 2011/157) |
| | (6) | 28 Feb 2011 (SSI 2011/157) |
| 18 | | 28 Feb 2011 (SSI 2011/157) |
| 19 | (1), (2) | 28 Feb 2011 (SSI 2011/157) |
| | (3) | 12 Oct 2010 (SSI 2010/344) |
| 20–24 | | 28 Feb 2011 (SSI 2011/157) |
| 25 | (1), (2) | 28 Feb 2011 (SSI 2011/157) |
| | (3)(a) | 18 Apr 2010 (for the purpose of making regulations or orders) (SSI 2010/133) |
| | | 28 Feb 2011 (otherwise) (SSI 2011/157) |

**Protection of Vulnerable Groups (Scotland) Act 2007 (asp 14)**—*contd*

|  |  |  |
|---|---|---|
|  | (3)(b), (4)–(6) | 28 Feb 2011 (SSI 2011/157) |
| 26–31 |  | 28 Feb 2011 (SSI 2011/157) |
| 32 | (1) | 28 Feb 2011 (SSI 2011/157) |
|  | (2) | 18 Apr 2010 (for the purpose of making regulations or orders) (SSI 2010/133) |
|  |  | 28 Feb 2011 (otherwise) (SSI 2011/157) |
|  | (3), (4) | 28 Feb 2011 (SSI 2011/157) |
| 33, 34 |  | 28 Feb 2011 (SSI 2011/157) |
| 35 | (1) | 28 Feb 2011 (SSI 2011/157) |
|  | (2), (3) | 18 Apr 2010 (for the purpose of making regulations or orders) (SSI 2010/133) |
|  |  | 28 Feb 2011 (otherwise) (SSI 2011/157) |
|  | (4)–(7) | 28 Feb 2011 (SSI 2011/157) |
| 36–41 |  | 28 Feb 2011 (SSI 2011/157) |
| 42 | (1)(a), (b) | 28 Feb 2011 (SSI 2011/157) |
|  | (1)(c), (2) | 18 Apr 2010 (for the purpose of making regulations or orders) (SSI 2010/133) |
|  |  | 28 Feb 2011 (otherwise) (SSI 2011/157) |
| 43 |  | 28 Feb 2011 (SSI 2011/157) |
| 44 |  | 28 Feb 2011 (SSI 2011/157)[1] |
| 45–48 |  | 28 Feb 2011 (SSI 2011/157) |
| 49 | (1)(a)–(c) | 28 Feb 2011 (SSI 2011/157) |
|  | (1)(d) | 18 Apr 2010 (for the purpose of making regulations or orders) (SSI 2010/133) |
|  |  | 28 Feb 2011 (otherwise) (SSI 2011/157) |
|  | (2) | 28 Feb 2011 (SSI 2011/157) |
| 50–62 |  | 28 Feb 2011 (SSI 2011/157) |
| 63 | (1) | 18 Apr 2010 (for the purpose of making regulations or orders) (SSI 2010/133) |
|  |  | 28 Feb 2011 (otherwise) (SSI 2011/157) |
|  | (2)–(5) | 28 Feb 2011 (SSI 2011/157) |
| 64 | (1) | 28 Feb 2011 (SSI 2011/157) |
|  | (2) | 18 Apr 2010 (for the purpose of making regulations or orders) (SSI 2010/133) |
|  |  | 28 Feb 2011 (otherwise) (SSI 2011/157) |
| 65, 66 |  | 28 Feb 2011 (SSI 2011/157) |
| 67 | (1), (2), (3)(a) | 28 Feb 2011 (SSI 2011/157) |
|  | (3)(b) | 18 Apr 2010 (for the purpose of making regulations or orders) (SSI 2010/133) |
|  |  | 28 Feb 2011 (otherwise) (SSI 2011/157) |
|  | (4) | 28 Feb 2011 (SSI 2011/157) |
| 68, 69 |  | 28 Feb 2011 (SSI 2011/157) |
| 70 | (1)–(3) | 18 Apr 2010 (for the purpose of making regulations or orders) (SSI 2010/133) |
|  |  | 28 Feb 2011 (otherwise) (SSI 2011/157) |
|  | (4) | 28 Feb 2011 (SSI 2011/157) |
| 71 |  | 12 Oct 2010 (SSI 2010/344) |
| 72 |  | 18 Apr 2010 (for the purpose of making regulations or orders) (SSI 2010/133) |
|  |  | 28 Feb 2011 (otherwise) (SSI 2011/157) |
| 73 | (a)–(f) | 28 Feb 2011 (SSI 2011/157) |
|  | (g) | 18 Apr 2010 (for the purpose of making regulations or orders) (SSI 2010/133) |
|  |  | 28 Feb 2011 (otherwise) (SSI 2011/157) |
| 74–77 |  | 28 Feb 2011 (SSI 2011/157) |
| 78 | (1) | *Not yet in force* |
|  | (2)–(4) | 28 Feb 2011 (SSI 2011/157)[1] |
| 79, 80 |  | 11 Jan 2008 (SSI 2007/564) |
| 81 | (1) | 28 Feb 2011 (SSI 2011/157)[1] |

**Protection of Vulnerable Groups (Scotland) Act 2007 (asp 14)**—*contd*

| | | |
|---|---|---|
| | (2) | 12 Oct 2010 (SSI 2010/344) |
| | (3) | 28 Feb 2011 (SSI 2011/157)[1] |
| 82, 83 | | 1 Sep 2007 (SSI 2007/385) |
| 84, 85 | | 28 Feb 2011 (SSI 2011/157) |
| 86 | | 1 Sep 2007 (SSI 2007/385) |
| 87 | | 11 Jan 2008 (SSI 2007/564) |
| 88 | | See Sch 4 below |
| 89, 90 | | 28 Feb 2011 (SSI 2011/157)[1] |
| 91 | (1) | 28 Feb 2011 (SSI 2011/157) |
| | (2) | See Sch 2 below |
| | (3) | See Sch 3 below |
| | (4) | 28 Feb 2011 (SSI 2011/157)[1] |
| 92 | (1), (2) | 28 Feb 2011 (SSI 2011/157) |
| | (3)–(6) | 18 Apr 2010 (for the purpose of making regulations or orders) (SSI 2010/133) |
| | | 28 Feb 2011 (otherwise) (SSI 2011/157) |
| 93 | | 28 Feb 2011 (SSI 2011/157) |
| 94 | (1)(a) | 28 Feb 2011 (SSI 2011/157) |
| | (1)(b) | 18 Apr 2010 (for the purpose of making regulations or orders) (SSI 2010/133) |
| | | 28 Feb 2011 (otherwise) (SSI 2011/157) |
| | (1)(c) | 28 Feb 2011 (SSI 2011/157) |
| | (1)(d) | 18 Apr 2010 (for the purpose of making regulations or orders) (SSI 2010/133) |
| | | 28 Feb 2011 (otherwise) (SSI 2011/157) |
| | (2)–(5) | 28 Feb 2011 (SSI 2011/157) |
| 95, 96 | | 28 Feb 2011 (SSI 2011/157) |
| 97 | (1) | 1 Sep 2007 (SSI 2007/385) |
| | (2)–(5) | 28 Feb 2011 (SSI 2011/157) |
| | (6) | See Sch 5 below |
| 98–102 | | 18 Apr 2007 (RA) |
| Sch 1 | | 28 Feb 2011 (SSI 2011/157) |
| Sch 2 | paras 1–27 | 28 Feb 2011 (SSI 2011/157) |
| | paras 28, 29 | 18 Apr 2010 (for the purpose of making regulations or orders) (SSI 2010/133) |
| | | 28 Feb 2011 (otherwise) (SSI 2011/157) |
| Sch 3 | paras 1–12 | 28 Feb 2011 (SSI 2011/157) |
| | para 13 | 18 Apr 2010 (for the purpose of making regulations or orders) (SSI 2010/133) |
| | | 28 Feb 2011 (otherwise) (SSI 2011/157) |
| | para 14 | 28 Feb 2011 (SSI 2011/157) |
| Sch 4 | para 1 | 1 Sep 2007 (SSI 2007/385) |
| | para 2 | 28 Feb 2011 (SSI 2011/157) |
| | paras 3, 4 | 1 Sep 2007 (SSI 2007/385) |
| | paras 5–12 | 28 Feb 2011 (SSI 2011/157) |
| | paras 13–26 | 28 Feb 2011 (SSI 2011/157)[1] |
| | para 27 | See paras 28–41 below |
| | para 28 | 28 Feb 2011 (SSI 2011/157)[1] |
| | para 29 | 18 Apr 2010 (for the purpose of making regulations or orders) (SSI 2010/133) |
| | | 28 Feb 2011 (otherwise) (SSI 2011/157)[1] |
| | paras 30–32 | 28 Feb 2011 (SSI 2011/157)[1] |
| | paras 33, 34 | 11 Jan 2008 (SSI 2007/564) |
| | paras 35–37 | 28 Feb 2011 (SSI 2011/157)[1] |
| | para 38 | 11 Jan 2008 (SSI 2007/564) |
| | para 39 | 28 Feb 2011 (SSI 2011/157)[1] |
| | para 40 | 11 Jan 2008 (SSI 2007/564) |
| | para 41 | 28 Feb 2011 (SSI 2011/157)[1] |
| | para 42 | 28 Feb 2011 (SSI 2011/157) |

**Protection of Vulnerable Groups (Scotland) Act 2007 (asp 14)**—*contd*

|  | paras 43–45 | 28 Feb 2011 (SSI 2011/157)[1] |
|---|---|---|
|  | para 46 | 11 Jan 2008 (SSI 2007/564) |
| Sch 5 |  | 28 Feb 2011 (SSI 2011/157) |

[1]   For transitional provisions and savings, see SSI 2011/157, arts 3–5

---

**Rating (Empty Properties) Act 2007 (c 9)**

*RA:* 19 Jul 2007

*Commencement provisions:* s 3(2)

Whole Act in force 19 Jul 2007 (s 3(2))

---

**Rights of Relatives to Damages (Mesothelioma) (Scotland) Act 2007 (asp 18)**

*RA:* 26 Apr 2007

*Commencement provisions:* s 2(2)

Whole Act in force 27 Apr 2007 (s 2(2))

---

**St Andrew's Day Bank Holiday (Scotland) Act 2007 (asp 2)**

*RA:* 15 Jan 2007

*Commencement provisions:* s 2(2)

Whole Act in force 16 Jan 2007 (s 2(2))

---

**Schools (Health Promotion and Nutrition) (Scotland) Act 2007 (asp 15)**

*RA:* 19 Apr 2007

*Commencement provisions:* s 11; Schools (Health Promotion and Nutrition) (Scotland) Act 2007 (Commencement No 1) Order 2007, SSI 2007/372; Schools (Health Promotion and Nutrition) (Scotland) Act 2007 (Commencement No 2) Order 2008, SSI 2008/171

| | |
|---|---|
| 1, 2 | 3 Jan 2008 (SSI 2007/372) |
| 3 | 12 May 2008 (for the purpose of making regulations under the Education (Scotland) Act 1980, ss 56A, 56B, 56D) (SSI 2008/171) |
| | 4 Aug 2008 (otherwise) (SSI 2008/171) |
| 4 | 12 May 2008 (SSI 2008/171) |
| 5 | 4 Aug 2008 (SSI 2008/171) |
| 6 | 10 Aug 2007 (SSI 2007/372) |
| 7–9 | 4 Aug 2008 (SSI 2008/171) |
| 10 | 10 Aug 2007 (SSI 2007/372) |
| 11 | 19 Apr 2007 (s 11(2)) |

---

**Serious Crime Act 2007 (c 27)**

*RA:* 30 Oct 2007

*Commencement provisions:* s 94; Serious Crime Act 2007 (Commencement No 1) Order 2008, SI 2008/219; Serious Crime Act 2007 (Commencement No 2 and Transitional and Transitory Provisions and Savings) Order 2008, SI 2008/755; Serious Crime Act 2007 (Commencement No 1) (Scotland)

**Serious Crime Act 2007 (c 27)**—*contd*
>    Order 2008, SSI 2008/152; Serious Crime Act 2007 (Commencement No 3) Order 2008,
>    SI 2008/2504; Serious Crime Act 2007 (Commencement No 2) (Scotland) Order 2009,
>    SSI 2009/224

| | | |
|---|---|---|
| 1–23 | | 6 Apr 2008 (SI 2008/755) |
| 24 | (1)–(8) | 6 Apr 2008 (SI 2008/755)[1] |
| | (9), (10) | 1 Mar 2008 (SI 2008/219) |
| | (11), (12) | 6 Apr 2008 (SI 2008/755)[1] |
| 25–36 | | 6 Apr 2008 (SI 2008/755) |
| 37 | | See Sch 2 below |
| 38, 39 | | 6 Apr 2008 (SI 2008/755) |
| 40 | (1), (2) | 1 Mar 2008 (SI 2008/219) |
| | (3) | 6 Apr 2008 (SI 2008/755) |
| | (4) | 1 Mar 2008 (SI 2008/219) |
| | (5)–(8) | 6 Apr 2008 (SI 2008/755) |
| 41–43 | | 6 Apr 2008 (SI 2008/755) |
| 44–67 | | 1 Oct 2008 (SI 2008/2504) |
| 68 | (1)–(7) | 1 Oct 2008 (SI 2008/2504) |
| | (8) | 1 Mar 2008 (SI 2008/219) |
| 69, 70 | | 1 Oct 2008 (SI 2008/2504) |
| 71 | (1), (2) | 1 Mar 2008 (SI 2008/219) |
| | (3) | 1 Oct 2008 (SI 2008/2504) |
| | (4), (5) | 1 Mar 2008 (SI 2008/219) |
| | (6) | 1 Oct 2008 (SI 2008/2504) |
| 72 | | 1 Oct 2008 (SI 2008/2504) |
| 73 | | See Sch 7 below |
| 74 | (1) | 1 Mar 2008 (SI 2008/219) |
| | (2) | See Sch 8 below |
| | (3) | See Sch 9 below |
| | (4) | 1 Apr 2008 (SI 2008/755) |
| 75 | (1)–(3) | 6 Apr 2008 (SI 2008/755) |
| | (4), (5) | 18 Jun 2009 (SSI 2009/224) |
| 76 | (1)–(3) | 6 Apr 2008 (SI 2008/755) |
| | (4)–(6) | 18 Jun 2009 (SSI 2009/224) |
| 77 | | See Sch 10 below |
| 78–84 | | 6 Apr 2008 (SI 2008/755)[1] |
| 85 | | 15 Feb 2008 (SI 2008/219) |
| 86 | | 28 Apr 2008 (SSI 2008/152) |
| 87 | | 6 Apr 2008 (SI 2008/755) |
| 88 | | See Sch 12 below |
| 89, 90 | | 30 Oct 2007 (RA) |
| 91 | (1) | See Sch 13 below |
| | (2), (3) | 30 Oct 2007 (RA) |
| 92 | | See Sch 14 below |
| 93, 94 | | 30 Oct 2007 (RA) |
| Sch 1 | | 6 Apr 2008 (SI 2008/755) |
| Sch 2 | paras 1–3 | 6 Apr 2008 (SI 2008/755) |
| | para 4 | 1 Mar 2008 (SI 2008/219) |
| | paras 5–17 | 6 Apr 2008 (SI 2008/755) |
| | para 18 | 1 Mar 2008 (SI 2008/219) |
| | paras 19–21 | 6 Apr 2008 (SI 2008/755) |
| Schs 3–6 | | 1 Oct 2008 (SI 2008/2504) |
| Sch 7 | para 1 | See paras 2, 3 below |
| | para 2 | 1 Mar 2008 (in so far as inserts Audit Commission Act 1998, s 32G(1), (3), (4)) (SI 2008/219) |
| | | 6 Apr 2008 (in so far as inserts ss 32A–32F, 32G(2), 32H of that Act) (SI 2008/755) |
| | para 3 | 6 Apr 2008 (SI 2008/755) |
| | para 4 | 1 Mar 2008 (in so far as inserts Public Audit (Wales) Act 2004, s 64G(1), (3), (4)) (SI 2008/219) |

**Serious Crime Act 2007 (c 27)**—*contd*

|  |  |  |
|---|---|---|
|  |  | 6 Apr 2008 (in so far as inserts ss 64A–64F, 64G(2), 64H of that Act) (SI 2008/755) |
|  | para 5 | 6 Apr 2008 (SI 2008/755) |
|  | para 6 | 1 Mar 2008 (in so far as inserts Audit and Accountability (Northern Ireland) Order 2003, SI 2003/418, art 4G(1), (3), (4)) (SI 2008/219) |
|  |  | 6 Apr 2008 (in so far as inserts arts 4A–4F, 4G(2), 4H of that order) (SI 2008/755) |
|  | para 7 | 6 Apr 2008 (SI 2008/755) |
| Sch 8 | paras 1–114 | 1 Apr 2008 (SI 2008/755)[1] |
|  | para 115 | 1 Mar 2008 (in so far as inserts Proceeds of Crime Act 2002, s 377A(1)–(5), (10)) (SI 2008/219) |
|  |  | 1 Apr 2008 (in so far as inserts s 377A(6)–(9) of that Act) (SI 2008/755)[1] |
|  | paras 116–168 | 1 Apr 2008 (SI 2008/755)[1] |
|  | para 169 | 1 Mar 2008 (for the purpose of the preparation of the Serious Organised Crime Agency's annual plan under the Serious Organised Crime and Police Act 2005, s 6 for the financial year commencing 1 Apr 2008) (SI 2008/219) |
|  |  | 1 Apr 2008 (otherwise) (SI 2008/755)[1] |
|  | paras 170–178 | 1 Apr 2008 (SI 2008/755)[1] |
| Sch 9 |  | 1 Mar 2008 (SI 2008/219) |
| Sch 10 | para 1 | See paras 2–28 below |
|  | paras 2–8 | 6 Apr 2008 (SI 2008/755) |
|  | para 9(1) | See sub-paras (2)–(6) below |
|  | para 9(2)–(4) | 6 Apr 2008 (SI 2008/755) |
|  | para 9(5), (6) | 1 Apr 2008 (for the purpose of civil recovery investigations and the amendment made by Sch 8, para 107(3) of this Act) (SI 2008/755) |
|  |  | 6 Apr 2008 (otherwise) (SI 2008/755) |
|  | paras 10–13 | 6 Apr 2008 (SI 2008/755) |
|  | paras 14–23 | 18 Jun 2009 (SSI 2009/224) |
|  | para 24 | 6 Apr 2008 (SI 2008/755) |
|  | para 25 | 6 Apr 2008 (in so far as it does not extend to Scotland) (SI 2008/755) |
|  |  | 18 Jun 2009 (in so far as it extends to Scotland) (SSI 2009/224) |
|  | paras 26–28 | 6 Apr 2008 (SI 2008/755) |
| Sch 11 |  | 6 Apr 2008 (SI 2008/755) |
| Sch 12 |  | 15 Feb 2008 (SI 2008/219) |
| Sch 13 | paras 1–4 | 6 Apr 2008 (SI 2008/755) |
|  | paras 5, 6 | 1 Oct 2008 (SI 2008/2504) |
|  | para 7 | *Not yet in force* |
|  | para 8 | 1 Oct 2008 (SI 2008/2504) |
|  | para 9 | 6 Apr 2008 (SI 2008/755) |
| Sch 14 |  | 15 Feb 2008 (SI 2008/219), repeals of or in— Police Act 1997; Regulation of Investigatory Powers Act 2000; Commissioners for Revenue and Customs Act 2005, Sch 2 |
|  |  | 1 Apr 2008 (SI 2008/755), repeals of or in— Parliamentary Commissioner Act 1967; Criminal Appeal Act 1968; Criminal Appeal (Northern Ireland) Act 1980; Legal Aid, Advice and Assistance (Northern Ireland) Order 1981, SI 1981/228 (NI 8); Bankruptcy (Scotland) Act 1985; Insolvency Act 1986; Insolvency (Northern Ireland) Order 1989, SI 1989/2405 (NI 19); Police Act 1996; Police (Northern Ireland) Act 1998; |

**Serious Crime Act 2007 (c 27)**—*contd*

> Access to Justice Act 1999;
> Proceeds of Crime Act 2002;
> Crime (International Co-operation) Act 2003;
> Access to Justice (Northern Ireland) Order 2003, SI 2003/435 (NI 10);
> Commissioners for Revenue and Customs Act 2005, s 21, Sch 4;
> Gambling Act 2005;
> Serious Organised Crime and Police Act 2005;
> Tribunals, Courts and Enforcement Act 2007;
> Corporate Manslaughter and Corporate Homicide Act 2007
> 1 Oct 2008 (SI 2008/2504), repeals of or in—
> Criminal Law Act 1977;
> Magistrates' Courts Act 1980;
> Magistrates' Courts (Northern Ireland) Order 1981, SI 1981/1675 (NI 26);
> Criminal Attempts and Conspiracy (Northern Ireland) Order 1983, SI 1983/1120 (NI 13);
> Public Order Act 1986;
> Computer Misuse Act 1990;
> International Criminal Court Act 2001;
> Police and Justice Act 2006
> *Not yet in force*, repeals of or in—
> Wireless Telegraphy Act 2006

[1]   For transitional and savings provisions, see SI 2008/755, arts 3–12, 15(2), (3), 17(2), (3)

---

**Statistics and Registration Service Act 2007 (c 18)**

*RA:* 26 Jul 2007

*Commencement provisions:* s 74; Statistics and Registration Service Act 2007 (Commencement No 1) Order 2007, SI 2007/3388; Statistics and Registration Service Act 2007 (Commencement No 2 and Transitional Provisions) Order 2008, SI 2008/839

| | |
|---|---|
| 1–7 | 1 Dec 2007 (SI 2007/3388) |
| 8, 9 | 1 Apr 2008 (SI 2008/839) |
| 10, 11 | 1 Dec 2007 (SI 2007/3388) |
| 12–23 | 1 Apr 2008 (SI 2008/839) |
| 24 | 1 Dec 2007 (SI 2007/3388) |
| 25 | 1 Apr 2008 (SI 2008/839) |
| 26 | 1 Dec 2007 (SI 2007/3388) |
| 27 | 1 Apr 2008 (SI 2008/839)[1] |
| 28 | 1 Dec 2007 (SI 2007/3388) |
| 29–38 | 1 Apr 2008 (SI 2008/839) |
| 39, 40 | 1 Dec 2007 (SI 2007/3388) |
| 41–46 | 1 Apr 2008 (SI 2008/839) |
| 47–54 | 1 Dec 2007 (SI 2007/3388) |
| 55–64 | 1 Apr 2008 (SI 2008/839) |
| 65–67 | 1 Dec 2007 (SI 2007/3388) |
| 68 | 1 Apr 2008 (SI 2008/839) |
| 69–72 | 1 Dec 2007 (SI 2007/3388) |
| 73 | 1 Apr 2008 (SI 2008/839) |
| 74–76 | 26 Jul 2007 (RA) |
| Schs 1–4 | 1 Apr 2008 (SI 2008/839) |

[1]   For a transitional provision, see SI 2008/839, art 3

---

## Sustainable Communities Act 2007 (c 23)

*RA:* 23 Oct 2007

Whole Act in force 23 Oct 2007 (RA)

---

## Transport and Works (Scotland) Act 2007 (asp 8)

*RA:* 14 Mar 2007

*Commencement provisions:* s 30(2)–(4); Transport and Works (Scotland) Act 2007 (Commencement) Order 2007, SSI 2007/516

| | | |
|---|---|---|
| 1–24 | | 28 Dec 2007 (SSI 2007/516) |
| 25 | (1) | 28 Dec 2007 (SSI 2007/516) |
| | (2) | 14 May 2007 (s 30(3)) |
| | (3), (4) | 28 Dec 2007 (SSI 2007/516) |
| | (5)(a)–(g) | 14 May 2007 (s 30(3)) |
| | (5)(h) | 28 Dec 2007 (SSI 2007/516) |
| | (5)(i), (j) | 14 May 2007 (s 30(3)) |
| | (5)(k)–(p), (6) | 28 Dec 2007 (SSI 2007/516) |
| 26 | | 28 Dec 2007 (SSI 2007/516) |
| 27 | | 14 May 2007 (s 30(3)) |
| 28 | | 15 Mar 2007 (s 30(2)) |
| 29 | | 28 Dec 2007 (SSI 2007/516) |
| 30 | | 15 Mar 2007 (s 30(2)) |
| Schs 1–3 | | 28 Dec 2007 (SSI 2007/516) |

---

## Tribunals, Courts and Enforcement Act 2007 (c 15)

*RA:* 19 Jul 2007

*Commencement provisions:* s 148; Tribunals, Courts and Enforcement Act 2007 (Commencement No 1) Order 2007, SI 2007/2709; Tribunals, Courts and Enforcement Act 2007 (Commencement No 2) Order 2007, SI 2007/3613; Tribunals, Courts and Enforcement Act 2007 (Commencement No 3) Order 2008, SI 2008/749; Tribunals, Courts and Enforcement Act 2007 (Commencement) (Scotland) Order 2008, SSI 2008/150; Tribunals, Courts and Enforcement Act 2007 (Commencement No 4) Order 2008, SI 2008/1158; Tribunals, Courts and Enforcement Act 2007 (Commencement No 5 and Transitional Provisions) Order 2008, SI 2008/1653; Tribunals, Courts and Enforcement Act 2007 (Commencement No 6 and Transitional Provisions) Order 2008, SI 2008/2696[2]; Tribunals, Courts and Enforcement Act 2007 (Commencement No 7) Order 2009, SI 2009/382; Tribunals, Courts and Enforcement Act 2007 (Commencement No 8) Order 2012, SI 2012/1312; Tribunals, Courts and Enforcement Act 2007 (Commencement No 9) Order 2013, SI 2013/1739; Tribunals, Courts and Enforcement Act 2007 (Commencement No 10) Order 2013, SI 2013/2043; Tribunals, Courts and Enforcement Act 2007 (Commencement No 11) Order 2014, SI 2014/768

It is thought that the reforms in Pt 4 of this Act which are not yet in force (ie ss 91, 92, 95–105 and Sch 15) concerning attachment of earnings fixed tables and tracing, charging orders and information requests and orders will not be implemented.

| | | |
|---|---|---|
| 1 | | 19 Sep 2007 (SI 2007/2709) |
| 2 | (1) | 19 Sep 2007 (SI 2007/2709) |
| | (2) | See Sch 1 below |
| | (3), (4) | 19 Sep 2007 (SI 2007/2709) |
| 3–6 | | 3 Nov 2008 (SI 2008/2696) |
| 7 | (1) | 19 Sep 2007 (SI 2007/2709) |
| | (2)–(7) | 3 Nov 2008 (SI 2008/2696) |
| | (8) | See Sch 4 below |
| | (9) | 19 Sep 2007 (SI 2007/2709) |
| 8 | | 3 Nov 2008 (SI 2008/2696) |
| 9 | (1), (2) | 3 Nov 2008 (SI 2008/2696) |
| | (3) | 19 Sep 2007 (SI 2007/2709) |

**Tribunals, Courts and Enforcement Act 2007 (c 15)**—*contd*

| | | |
|---|---|---|
| | (4)–(11) | 3 Nov 2008 (SI 2008/2696) |
| 10 | (1), (2) | 3 Nov 2008 (SI 2008/2696) |
| | (3) | 19 Sep 2007 (SI 2007/2709) |
| | (4)–(9) | 3 Nov 2008 (SI 2008/2696) |
| 11 | (1)–(4) | 3 Nov 2008 (SI 2008/2696) |
| | (5)(a)–(e) | 3 Nov 2008 (SI 2008/2696) |
| | (5)(f) | 19 Sep 2007 (SI 2007/2709) |
| | (6)–(8) | 19 Sep 2007 (SI 2007/2709) |
| 12 | | 3 Nov 2008 (SI 2008/2696) |
| 13 | (1)–(5) | 3 Nov 2008 (SI 2008/2696) |
| | (6) | 19 Sep 2007 (SI 2007/2709) |
| | (7) | 3 Nov 2008 (SI 2008/2696) |
| | (8)(a)–(e) | 3 Nov 2008 (SI 2008/2696) |
| | (8)(f) | 19 Sep 2007 (SI 2007/2709) |
| | (9), (10) | 19 Sep 2007 (SI 2007/2709) |
| | (11)–(13) | 3 Nov 2008 (SI 2008/2696) |
| | (14), (15) | 19 Sep 2007 (SI 2007/2709) |
| 14–17 | | 3 Nov 2008 (SI 2008/2696) |
| 18 | (1)–(9) | 3 Nov 2008 (SI 2008/2696) |
| | (10), (11) | 19 Sep 2007 (SI 2007/2709) |
| | (12) | 3 Nov 2008 (SI 2008/2696) |
| 19 | | 3 Nov 2008 (SI 2008/2696) |
| 20 | (1), (2) | 3 Nov 2008 (SI 2008/2696) |
| | (3) | 19 Sep 2007 (SI 2007/2709) |
| | (4), (5) | 3 Nov 2008 (SI 2008/2696) |
| | (6), (7) | 19 Sep 2007 (SI 2007/2709) |
| | (8) | 3 Nov 2008 (SI 2008/2696) |
| 21 | (1)–(5) | 3 Nov 2008 (SI 2008/2696) |
| | (6) | 19 Sep 2007 (SI 2007/2709) |
| 22 | | 19 Sep 2007 (SI 2007/2709) |
| 23–26 | | 3 Nov 2008 (SI 2008/2696) |
| 27 | (1)–(4) | 1 Apr 2009 (SI 2008/2696) |
| | (5), (6) | 19 Sep 2007 (SI 2007/2709) |
| 28, 29 | | 3 Nov 2008 (SI 2008/2696) |
| 30–42 | | 19 Sep 2007 (SI 2007/2709) |
| 43 | | 3 Nov 2008 (SI 2008/2696) |
| 44 | (1) | 1 Nov 2007 (SI 2007/2709) |
| | (2) | See Sch 7 below |
| 45 | (1), (2) | 1 Nov 2007 (SI 2007/2709) |
| | (3) | 19 Sep 2007 (SI 2007/2709) |
| 46 | | 19 Sep 2007 (in so far as relates to Sch 5 of this Act) (SI 2007/2709) |
| | | 3 Nov 2008 (otherwise) (SI 2008/2696) |
| 47 | | 3 Nov 2008 (SI 2008/2696) |
| 48 | (1) | See Sch 8 below |
| | (2) | See Sch 9 below |
| 49 | | 19 Sep 2007 (SI 2007/2709) |
| 50 | (1)–(5) | 19 Sep 2007 (for the purposes of Sch 1, para 3 of this Act) (SI 2007/2709) |
| | | 21 Jul 2008 (otherwise) (SI 2008/1653)[1] |
| | (6) | See Sch 10 below |
| | (7) | 19 Sep 2007 (for the purposes of Sch 1, para 3 of this Act) (SI 2007/2709) |
| | | 21 Jul 2008 (otherwise) (SI 2008/1653)[1] |
| 51, 52 | | 19 Sep 2007 (for the purposes of Sch 1, para 3 of this Act) (SI 2007/2709) |
| | | 21 Jul 2008 (otherwise) (SI 2008/1653)[1] |
| 53 | | 19 Jul 2007 (RA) |
| 54 | | 19 Sep 2007 (SI 2007/2709) |

**Tribunals, Courts and Enforcement Act 2007 (c 15)**—*contd*

| | | |
|---|---|---|
| 55–57 | | 19 Jul 2007 (RA) |
| 58, 59 | | 19 Sep 2007 (SI 2007/2709) |
| 60 | | 19 Sep 2007 (s 148(1)) |
| 61 | | 19 Sep 2007 (SI 2007/2709) |
| 62 | (1) | See Sch 12 below |
| | (2) | 6 Apr 2014 (SI 2014/768) |
| | (3) | See Sch 13 below |
| | (4) | 6 Apr 2014 (SI 2014/768) |
| 63 | | 6 Apr 2014 (SI 2014/768) |
| 64 | (1) | 6 Apr 2014 (SI 2014/768) |
| | (2)–(4) | 15 Jul 2013 (for the purpose of exercising and power to make regulations) (SI 2013/1739) |
| | | 6 Apr 2014 (otherwise) (SI 2014/768) |
| 65–72 | | 6 Apr 2014 (SI 2014/768) |
| 73 | (1)–(7) | 6 Apr 2014 (SI 2014/768) |
| | (8) | 15 Jul 2013 (for the purpose of exercising and power to make regulations) (SI 2013/1739) |
| | | 6 Apr 2014 (otherwise) (SI 2014/768) |
| | (9) | 6 Apr 2014 (SI 2014/768) |
| 74–76 | | 6 Apr 2014 (SI 2014/768) |
| 77 | (1)–(3) | 6 Apr 2014 (SI 2014/768) |
| | (4) | 15 Jul 2013 (for the purpose of exercising and power to make regulations) (SI 2013/1739) |
| | | 6 Apr 2014 (otherwise) (SI 2014/768) |
| | (5) | 6 Apr 2014 (SI 2014/768) |
| | (6) | 15 Jul 2013 (for the purpose of exercising and power to make regulations) (SI 2013/1739) |
| | | 6 Apr 2014 (otherwise) (SI 2014/768) |
| | (7) | 6 Apr 2014 (SI 2014/768) |
| 78 | (1) | 6 Apr 2014 (SI 2014/768) |
| | (2) | 15 Jul 2013 (for the purpose of exercising and power to make regulations) (SI 2013/1739) |
| | | 6 Apr 2014 (otherwise) (SI 2014/768) |
| | (3) | 6 Apr 2014 (SI 2014/768) |
| 79, 80 | | 6 Apr 2014 (SI 2014/768) |
| 81 | (1)–(4) | 6 Apr 2014 (SI 2014/768) |
| | (5), (6) | 15 Jul 2013 (for the purpose of exercising and power to make regulations) (SI 2013/1739) |
| | | 6 Apr 2014 (SI 2014/768) |
| | (7), (8) | 6 Apr 2014 (SI 2014/768) |
| 82–84 | | 6 Apr 2014 (SI 2014/768) |
| 85 | | 6 Apr 2014 (except in relation to licences to occupy land as commercial premises)[3] (SI 2014/768) |
| | | *Not yet in force* (exception noted above) |
| 86 | | See Sch 14 below |
| 87–89 | | 6 Apr 2014 (SI 2014/768) |
| 90 | | 15 Jul 2013 (SI 2013/1739) |
| 91, 92 | | *Not yet in force* |
| 93 | | 1 Oct 2012 (SI 2012/1312) |
| 94 | | 17 May 2012 (SI 2012/1312) |
| 95–105 | | *Not yet in force* |
| 106 | (1) | *Not yet in force* |
| | (2) | See Sch 16 below |
| | (3) | *Not yet in force* |
| 107 | | *Not yet in force* |
| 108 | (1) | See Sch 17 below |
| | (2) | See Schs 18, 19 below |
| | (3) | See Sch 20 below |
| 109–133 | | *Not yet in force* |

**Tribunals, Courts and Enforcement Act 2007 (c 15)**—*contd*

| | | |
|---|---|---|
| 134–138 | | 31 Dec 2007 (E) (SI 2007/3613) |
| | | 21 Apr 2008 (S) (SSI 2008/150) |
| | | 22 Apr 2008 (W) (NI) (SI 2008/1158) |
| 139, 140 | | 1 Apr 2008 (SI 2007/2709) |
| 141 | | 6 Apr 2008 (SI 2008/749) |
| 142 | | 1 Apr 2009 (SI 2008/2696) |
| 143 | | *Never in force* (repealed) |
| 144 | (1) | 19 Sep 2007 (SI 2007/2709) |
| | (2)–(4) | *Not yet in force* |
| | (5) | 19 Sep 2007 (SI 2007/2709) |
| | (6) | *Not yet in force* |
| | (7) | 19 Sep 2007 (SI 2007/2709) |
| | (8)–(10) | *Not yet in force* |
| | (11) | 19 Sep 2007 (in so far as relates to Pt 1 and s 51 of this Act) (SI 2007/2709) |
| | | *Not yet in force (otherwise)* |
| 145 | | 19 Jul 2007 (RA) |
| 146 | | See Sch 23 below |
| 147–149 | | 19 Jul 2007 (RA) |
| Sch 1 | paras 1–11 | 19 Sep 2007 (SI 2007/2709) |
| | paras 12–14 | 3 Nov 2008 (SI 2008/2696) |
| Schs 2, 3 | | 3 Nov 2008 (SI 2008/2696) |
| Sch 4 | paras 1–14 | 3 Nov 2008 (SI 2008/2696) |
| | para 15 | 19 Sep 2007 (SI 2007/2709) |
| Schs 5, 6 | | 19 Sep 2007 (SI 2007/2709) |
| Sch 7 | paras 1–6 | 1 Nov 2007 (SI 2007/2709) |
| | paras 7–9 | 1 Jun 2008 (SI 2007/2709) |
| | para 10(1)(a), (b) | 1 Nov 2007 (SI 2007/2709) |
| | para 10(1)(c) | 1 Jun 2008 (SI 2007/2709) |
| | para 10(2)(a), (b) | 1 Nov 2007 (SI 2007/2709) |
| | para 10(2)(c) | 1 Jun 2008 (SI 2007/2709) |
| | para 10(3)(a), (b) | 1 Nov 2007 (SI 2007/2709) |
| | para 10(3)(c) | 1 Jun 2008 (SI 2007/2709) |
| | para 10(4) | 1 Nov 2007 (SI 2007/2709) |
| | para 11 | 1 Nov 2007 (in so far as relates to the Administrative Justice and Tribunals Council and to the Scottish Committee of the Administrative Justice and Tribunals Council) (SI 2007/2709) |
| | | 1 Jun 2008 (otherwise) (SI 2007/2709) |
| | paras 12, 13 | 1 Nov 2007 (SI 2007/2709) |
| | para 14(1), (2) | 1 Nov 2007 (SI 2007/2709) |
| | para 14(3)(a) | 1 Nov 2007 (SI 2007/2709) |
| | para 14(3)(b) | 1 Jun 2008 (SI 2007/2709) |
| | para 14(4) | 1 Nov 2007 (SI 2007/2709) |
| | paras 15–18 | 1 Nov 2007 (SI 2007/2709) |
| | para 19 | 1 Jun 2008 (SI 2007/2709) |
| | para 20 | 1 Nov 2007 (SI 2007/2709) |
| | para 21(1), (2) | 1 Nov 2007 (SI 2007/2709) |
| | para 21(3) | 1 Jun 2008 (SI 2007/2709) |
| | para 21(4), (5) | 1 Nov 2007 (SI 2007/2709) |
| | para 21(6) | 1 Nov 2007 (in so far as relates to reports made by the Administrative Justice and Tribunals Council) (SI 2007/2709) |
| | | 1 Jun 2008 (otherwise) (SI 2007/2709) |
| | para 22(1)(a), (b) | 1 Nov 2007 (SI 2007/2709) |
| | para 22(1)(c) | 1 Jun 2008 (SI 2007/2709) |
| | para 22(2) | 1 Nov 2007 (SI 2007/2709) |
| | para 22(3) | 1 Nov 2007 (in so far as relates to the Administrative Justice and Tribunals Council and to the Scottish Committee of the Administrative Justice and Tribunals Council) (SI 2007/2709) |
| | | 1 Jun 2008 (otherwise) (SI 2007/2709) |

**Tribunals, Courts and Enforcement Act 2007 (c 15)**—*contd*

|  |  |  |
|--|--|--|
| | para 23 | 1 Nov 2007 (SI 2007/2709) |
| | para 24 | 21 Jul 2008 (SI 2008/1653)[1] |
| | para 25(1) | 1 Nov 2007 (SI 2007/2709) |
| | paras 25(2)–(7), 26–28 | 19 Sep 2007 (SI 2007/2709) |
| Sch 8 | para 1 | 1 Apr 2009 (SI 2008/2696)[2] |
| | paras 2, 3 | 1 Nov 2007 (SI 2007/2709) |
| | paras 4, 5 | 1 Nov 2007 (in so far as they relate to the Administrative Justice and Tribunals Council and to the Scottish Committee of the Administrative Justice and Tribunals Council) (SI 2007/2709) |
| | | 1 Jun 2008 (in so far as they relate to the Welsh Committee of the Administrative Justice and Tribunals Council) (SI 2007/2709) |
| | | 3 Nov 2008 (otherwise) (SI 2008/2696) |
| | para 6 | 3 Nov 2008 (SI 2008/2696) |
| | para 7 | 1 Nov 2007 (in so far as relates to the Administrative Justice and Tribunals Council and to the Scottish Committee of the Administrative Justice and Tribunals Council) (SI 2007/2709) |
| | | 1 Jun 2008 (otherwise) (SI 2007/2709) |
| | paras 8–12 | 1 Nov 2007 (SI 2007/2709) |
| | para 13 | *Not yet in force* |
| | paras 14, 15 | 1 Nov 2007 (SI 2007/2709) |
| | para 16 | 3 Nov 2008 (SI 2008/2696) |
| | para 17 | 1 Nov 2007 (SI 2007/2709) |
| | para 18 | 1 Nov 2007 (in so far as relates to the Administrative Justice and Tribunals Council) (SI 2007/2709) |
| | | 1 Jun 2008 (otherwise) (SI 2007/2709) |
| | paras 19–23 | 1 Nov 2007 (SI 2007/2709) |
| | para 24 | 19 Aug 2013 (SI 2013/2043) |
| | para 25 | 3 Nov 2008 (so far as it relates to the Tribunals and Inquiries Act 1992, Sch 1, para 7(b)) (SI 2008/2696) |
| | | *Not yet in force* (otherwise) |
| | para 26 | *Never in force* (repealed) |
| | para 27 | 21 Jul 2008 (in so far as it applies to the powers of a Minister) (SI 2008/1653)[1] |
| | | 19 Aug 2013 (otherwise) (SI 2013/2043) |
| | para 28 | 3 Nov 2008 (SI 2008/2696) |
| | para 29 | *Not yet in force* |
| | para 30(a)–(c) | 1 Nov 2007 (SI 2007/2709) |
| | para 30(d) | 1 Jun 2008 (SI 2007/2709) |
| | para 31(1)–(3) | 19 Sep 2007 (SI 2007/2709) |
| | para 31(4)–(6) | 3 Nov 2008 (SI 2008/2696) |
| | para 32 | 1 Nov 2007 (SI 2007/2709) |
| | para 33(1), (2) | 1 Nov 2007 (SI 2007/2709) |
| | para 33(3) | 3 Nov 2008 (SI 2008/2696) |
| | para 34 | *Not yet in force* |
| | paras 35–39 | 1 Dec 2007 (SI 2007/2709) |
| | paras 40–42 | 3 Nov 2008 (SI 2008/2696) |
| | para 43 | 1 Apr 2009 (SI 2008/2696) |
| | paras 44–48 | 3 Nov 2008 (SI 2008/2696) |
| | paras 49–52 | 1 Nov 2007 (SI 2007/2709) |
| | para 53 | 1 Nov 2007 (in so far as relates to the Administrative Justice and Tribunals Council and to the Scottish Committee of the Administrative Justice and Tribunals Council) (SI 2007/2709) |
| | | 1 Jun 2008 (otherwise) (SI 2007/2709) |
| | para 54 | 3 Nov 2008 (SI 2008/2696) |
| | para 55 | 1 Apr 2009 (SI 2008/2696) |
| | paras 56–61 | 1 Nov 2007 (SI 2007/2709) |
| | paras 62, 63 | 19 Sep 2007 (SI 2007/2709) |
| | para 64(a) | *Not yet in force* |
| | para 64(b) | 3 Nov 2008 (SI 2008/2696) |

**Tribunals, Courts and Enforcement Act 2007 (c 15)**—*contd*

|  | para 65(1), (2) | 19 Sep 2007 (SI 2007/2709) |
|---|---|---|
|  | para 65(3) | 19 Sep 2007 (in so far as relates to the Senior President of Tribunals) (SI 2007/2709) |
|  |  | 3 Nov 2008 (otherwise) (SI 2008/2696) |
|  | para 66 | 3 Nov 2008 (SI 2008/2696) |
| Sch 9 | paras 1, 2 | 19 Sep 2007 (SI 2007/2709) |
|  | paras 3–11 | 3 Nov 2008 (SI 2008/2696) |
|  | para 12(1) | 3 Nov 2008 (SI 2008/2696) |
|  | para 12(2) | 19 Sep 2007 (SI 2007/2709) |
|  | para 12(3)–(7) | 3 Nov 2008 (SI 2008/2696) |
|  | paras 13–19 | 3 Nov 2008 (SI 2008/2696) |
| Sch 10 |  | 21 Jul 2008 (SI 2008/1653)[1] |
| Sch 11 |  | 19 Jul 2007 (RA) |
| Sch 12 | paras 1, 2 | 6 Apr 2014 (SI 2014/768) |
|  | para 3(1) | 15 Jul 2013 (for the purpose of exercising and power to make regulations) (SI 2013/1739) |
|  |  | 6 Apr 2014 (otherwise) (SI 2014/768) |
|  | paras 3(2), 4–6, 7(1) | 6 Apr 2014 (SI 2014/768) |
|  | para 7(2) | 15 Jul 2013 (for the purpose of exercising and power to make regulations) (SI 2013/1739) |
|  |  | 6 Apr 2014 (otherwise) (SI 2014/768) |
|  | para 7(3) | 6 Apr 2014 (SI 2014/768) |
|  | para 7(4) | 15 Jul 2013 (for the purpose of exercising and power to make regulations) (SI 2013/1739) |
|  |  | 6 Apr 2014 (otherwise) (SI 2014/768) |
|  | para 7(5) | 6 Apr 2014 (SI 2014/768) |
|  | para 8 | 15 Jul 2013 (for the purpose of exercising and power to make regulations) (SI 2013/1739) |
|  |  | 6 Apr 2014 (otherwise) (SI 2014/768) |
|  | paras 9, 10, 11(1) | 6 Apr 2014 (SI 2014/768) |
|  | paras 11(2), 12(1) | 15 Jul 2013 (for the purpose of exercising and power to make regulations) (SI 2013/1739) |
|  |  | 6 Apr 2014 (otherwise) (SI 2014/768) |
|  | paras 12(2)–(4), 13(1), (2) | 6 Apr 2014 (SI 2014/768) |
|  | para 13(3) | 15 Jul 2013 (for the purpose of exercising and power to make regulations) (SI 2013/1739) |
|  |  | 6 Apr 2014 (otherwise) (SI 2014/768) |
|  | paras 13(4), 14(1), (2) | 6 Apr 2014 (SI 2014/768) |
|  | para 14(3) | 15 Jul 2013 (for the purpose of exercising and power to make regulations) (SI 2013/1739) |
|  |  | 6 Apr 2014 (otherwise) (SI 2014/768) |
|  | paras 14(4)–(6), 15(1), (2) | 6 Apr 2014 (SI 2014/768) |
|  | para 15(3) | 15 Jul 2013 (for the purpose of exercising and power to make regulations) (SI 2013/1739) |
|  |  | 6 Apr 2014 (otherwise) (SI 2014/768) |
|  | paras 16–21 | 6 Apr 2014 (SI 2014/768) |
|  | para 22(1) | 15 Jul 2013 (for the purpose of exercising and power to make regulations) (SI 2013/1739) |
|  |  | 6 Apr 2014 (otherwise) (SI 2014/768) |
|  | paras 22(2), 23 | 6 Apr 2014 (SI 2014/768) |
|  | para 24(1) | 15 Jul 2013 (for the purpose of exercising and power to make regulations) (SI 2013/1739) |
|  |  | 6 Apr 2014 (otherwise) (SI 2014/768) |
|  | para 24(2) | 6 Apr 2014 (SI 2014/768) |
|  | para 25(1), (2) | 15 Jul 2013 (for the purpose of exercising and power to make regulations) (SI 2013/1739) |

**Tribunals, Courts and Enforcement Act 2007 (c 15)**—*contd*

| | |
|---|---|
| | 6 Apr 2014 (otherwise) (SI 2014/768) |
| paras 25(3), 26, 27, 28(1) | 6 Apr 2014 (SI 2014/768) |
| para 28(2), (3) | 15 Jul 2013 (for the purpose of exercising and power to make regulations) (SI 2013/1739) |
| | 6 Apr 2014 (otherwise) (SI 2014/768) |
| paras 28(4)–(6), 29, 30, 31(1) | 6 Apr 2014 (SI 2014/768) |
| para 31(2) | 15 Jul 2013 (for the purpose of exercising and power to make regulations) (SI 2013/1739) |
| | 6 Apr 2014 (otherwise) (SI 2014/768) |
| para 31(3) | 6 Apr 2014 (SI 2014/768) |
| para 31(4) | 15 Jul 2013 (for the purpose of exercising and power to make regulations) (SI 2013/1739) |
| | 6 Apr 2014 (otherwise) (SI 2014/768) |
| para 31(5) | 6 Apr 2014 (SI 2014/768) |
| para 32(1), (2) | 15 Jul 2013 (for the purpose of exercising and power to make regulations) (SI 2013/1739) |
| | 6 Apr 2014 (otherwise) (SI 2014/768) |
| paras 32(3), 33(1) | 6 Apr 2014 (SI 2014/768) |
| para 33(2) | 15 Jul 2013 (for the purpose of exercising and power to make regulations) (SI 2013/1739) |
| | 6 Apr 2014 (otherwise) (SI 2014/768) |
| paras 33(3), (4), 34(1)–(3) | 6 Apr 2014 (SI 2014/768) |
| para 34(4) | 15 Jul 2013 (for the purpose of exercising and power to make regulations) (SI 2013/1739) |
| | 6 Apr 2014 (otherwise) (SI 2014/768) |
| para 35(1) | 6 Apr 2014 (SI 2014/768) |
| paras 35(2), 36 | 15 Jul 2013 (for the purpose of exercising and power to make regulations) (SI 2013/1739) |
| | 6 Apr 2014 (otherwise) (SI 2014/768) |
| paras 37, 38, 39(1) | 6 Apr 2014 (SI 2014/768) |
| para 39(2) | 15 Jul 2013 (for the purpose of exercising and power to make regulations) (SI 2013/1739) |
| | 6 Apr 2014 (otherwise) (SI 2014/768) |
| para 40(1) | 6 Apr 2014 (SI 2014/768) |
| para 40(2), (3) | 15 Jul 2013 (for the purpose of exercising and power to make regulations) (SI 2013/1739) |
| | 6 Apr 2014 (otherwise) (SI 2014/768) |
| paras 40(4)–(7), 41(1), (2) | 6 Apr 2014 (SI 2014/768) |
| para 41(3) | 15 Jul 2013 (for the purpose of exercising and power to make regulations) (SI 2013/1739) |
| | 6 Apr 2014 (otherwise) (SI 2014/768) |
| para 41(4) | 6 Apr 2014 (SI 2014/768) |
| paras 41(5), 42, 43(1)–(3) | 15 Jul 2013 (for the purpose of exercising and power to make regulations) (SI 2013/1739) |
| | 6 Apr 2014 (otherwise) (SI 2014/768) |
| paras 43(4), 44–47 | 6 Apr 2014 (SI 2014/768) |
| para 48 | 15 Jul 2013 (for the purpose of exercising and power to make regulations) (SI 2013/1739) |
| | 6 Apr 2014 (otherwise) (SI 2014/768) |
| para 49(1), (2) | 6 Apr 2014 (SI 2014/768) |
| para 49(3), (4) | 15 Jul 2013 (for the purpose of exercising and power to make regulations) (SI 2013/1739) |
| | 6 Apr 2014 (otherwise) (SI 2014/768) |
| paras 49(5)–(8), 50(1), (2) | 6 Apr 2014 (SI 2014/768) |

**See Halsbury's Statutes Citator for amendments to these Acts**

**Tribunals, Courts and Enforcement Act 2007 (c 15)**—*contd*

|  |  |  |
|---|---|---|
| | para 50(3), (4) | 15 Jul 2013 (for the purpose of exercising and power to make regulations) (SI 2013/1739) |
| | | 6 Apr 2014 (otherwise) (SI 2014/768) |
| | para 50(5), (6) | 6 Apr 2014 (SI 2014/768) |
| | para 50(7) | 15 Jul 2013 (for the purpose of exercising and power to make regulations) (SI 2013/1739) |
| | | 6 Apr 2014 (otherwise) (SI 2014/768) |
| | paras 51, 52, 53(1), (2) | 6 Apr 2014 (SI 2014/768) |
| | para 53(3) | 15 Jul 2013 (for the purpose of exercising and power to make regulations) (SI 2013/1739) |
| | | 6 Apr 2014 (otherwise) (SI 2014/768) |
| | para 54(1) | 6 Apr 2014 (SI 2014/768) |
| | para 54(2) | 15 Jul 2013 (for the purpose of exercising and power to make regulations) (SI 2013/1739) |
| | | 6 Apr 2014 (otherwise) (SI 2014/768) |
| | paras 54(3), 55, 56(1), (2) | 6 Apr 2014 (SI 2014/768) |
| | para 56(3) | 15 Jul 2013 (for the purpose of exercising and power to make regulations) (SI 2013/1739) |
| | | 6 Apr 2014 (otherwise) (SI 2014/768) |
| | paras 57–59, 60(1)–(3) | 6 Apr 2014 (SI 2014/768) |
| | para 60(4), (5) | 15 Jul 2013 (for the purpose of exercising and power to make regulations) (SI 2013/1739) |
| | | 6 Apr 2014 (otherwise) (SI 2014/768) |
| | paras 60(6)–(8), 61 | 6 Apr 2014 (SI 2014/768) |
| | para 62 | 15 Jul 2013 (for the purpose of exercising and power to make regulations) (SI 2013/1739) |
| | | 6 Apr 2014 (otherwise) (SI 2014/768) |
| | paras 63–69 | 6 Apr 2014 (SI 2014/768) |
| Schs 13, 14 | | 6 Apr 2014 (SI 2014/768) |
| Schs 15, 16 | | *Not yet in force* |
| Schs 17–20 | | 24 Feb 2009 (for the purpose of making rules, regulations and orders) (SI 2009/382) |
| | | 6 Apr 2009 (otherwise) (SI 2009/382) |
| Sch 21 | | *Not yet in force* |
| Sch 22 | | 1 Apr 2008 (SI 2007/2709) |
| Sch 23 | Pt 1 | 1 Nov 2007 (SI 2007/2709), repeals of or in— |

House of Commons Disqualification Act 1975;
Northern Ireland Assembly Disqualification Act 1975;
Race Relations Act 1976;
Estate Agents Act 1979;
Tribunals and Inquiries Act 1992, ss 1–4, 13(5)(c);
Scotland Act 1998 (Cross-Border Public Authorities) (Adaptation of Functions etc) Order 1999, SI 1999/1747, Sch 9 (in so far as applies to the Tribunals and Inquiries Act 1992, ss 2, 4);
Freedom of Information Act 2000;
Scottish Public Services Ombudsman Act 2002 (Consequential Provisions and Modifications) Order 2004, SI 2004/1823
3 Nov 2008 (SI 2008/2696), repeals of or in—
Consumer Credit Act 1974;
Judicial Pensions and Retirement Act 1993;
Employment Tribunals Act 1996;
Justice (Northern Ireland) Act 2002;
Nationality, Immigration and Asylum Act 2002;
Constitutional Reform Act 2005, Sch 4;
Tribunals, Courts and Enforcement Act 2007
1 Apr 2009 (SI 2008/2696), repeals of or in—

**Tribunals, Courts and Enforcement Act 2007 (c 15)**—*contd*

Taxes Management Act 1970[2];
Finance Act 1972;
Superannuation Act 1972;
Finance Act 1988;
Finance (No 2) Act 1992;
Access to Justice Act 1999;
Social Security Contributions (Transfer of Functions, etc) Act 1999;
Social Security Contributions (Transfer of Functions, etc) (Northern Ireland) Order 1999, SI 1999/671;
Scotland Act 1998 (Transfer of Functions to the Scottish Ministers etc) Order 1999, SI 1999/1750;
Constitutional Reform Act 2005, Sch 12, Sch 14, Pt 2
19 Aug 2013 (SI 2013/2043), repeals of or in—
Tribunals and Inquiries Act 1992, ss 5, 8
*Not yet in force*, repeals of or in—
Food Safety Act 1990;
Tribunals and Inquiries Act 1992, ss 6, 13(2), 14, 16, Sch 1;
Social Security Act 1998;
Scotland Act 1998 (Cross-Border Public Authorities) (Adaptation of Functions etc) Order 1999, SI 1999/1747, Sch 9 (in so far as applies to the Tribunals and Inquiries Act 1992, s 5);
Financial Services and Markets Act 2000 (Consequential Amendments and Repeals) Order 2001, SI 2001/3649;
Constitutional Reform Act 2005, Schs 5, 7, Sch 14, Pt 3

| | |
|---|---|
| Pt 2 | 3 Nov 2008 (SI 2008/2696) |
| Pts 3, 4 | 6 Apr 2014 (SI 2014/768) |
| Pts 5, 6 | *Not yet in force* |

[1]    For transitional provisions, see SI 2008/1653, arts 3, 4

[2]    For transitional provisions, see SI 2008/2696, arts 3, 4

[3]    For definition of commercial premises, see SI 2014/768, art 2(3)–6)

---

**UK Borders Act 2007 (c 30)**

*RA:* 30 Oct 2007

*Commencement provisions:* s 59; UK Borders Act 2007 (Commencement No 1 and Transitional Provisions) Order 2008, SI 2008/99; UK Borders Act 2007 (Commencement No 2 and Transitional Provisions) Order 2008, SI 2008/309; UK Borders Act 2007 (Commencement No 3 and Transitional Provisions) Order 2008, SI 2008/1818; UK Borders Act 2007 (Commencement No 4) Order 2008, SI 2008/2822; UK Borders Act 2007 (Commencement No 5) Order 2008, SI 2008/3136; UK Borders Act 2007 (Commencement No 6) Order 2010, SI 2010/606; UK Borders Act 2007 (Commencement No 7 and Transitional Provisions) Order 2011, SI 2011/1293

| | |
|---|---|
| 1–8 | 31 Jan 2008 (SI 2008/99) |
| 9 | 25 Nov 2008 (SI 2008/2822) |
| 10 | 31 Jan 2008 (for the purposes of making an order under sub-ss (2), (4)) (SI 2008/99) |
| | 25 Nov 2008 (otherwise) (SI 2008/2822) |
| 11 | 31 Jan 2008 (for the purposes of making rules under sub-s (6)) (SI 2008/99) |
| | 25 Nov 2008 (otherwise) (SI 2008/2822) |
| 12 | 25 Nov 2008 (SI 2008/2822) |
| 13 | 31 Jan 2008 (for the purposes of issuing a code of practice under sub-s (1) and making an order under sub-s (6)) (SI 2008/99) |
| | 25 Nov 2008 (otherwise) (SI 2008/2822) |
| 14, 15 | 31 Jan 2008 (SI 2008/99) |
| 16 | 31 Jan 2008 (SI 2008/99)[1] |

**UK Borders Act 2007 (c 30)**—*contd*

| | |
|---|---|
| 17 | 30 Oct 2007 (s 59(1)) |
| 18 | 31 Jan 2008 (SI 2008/99) |
| 19 | 23 May 2011 (SI 2011/1293)[4] |
| 20 | 31 Jan 2008 (SI 2008/99) |
| 21 | 6 Jan 2009 (SI 2008/3136) |
| 22, 23 | 31 Jan 2008 (SI 2008/99) |
| 24 | 1 Apr 2010 (SI 2010/606) |
| 25 | 31 Mar 2008 (SI 2008/309)[2] |
| 26 | 31 Jan 2008 (for the purposes of making regulations under sub-s (5)) (SI 2008/99)[1] |
| | 1 Apr 2008 (otherwise) (SI 2008/309)[2] |
| 27, 28 | 29 Feb 2008 (SI 2008/309)[2] |
| 29–31 | 31 Jan 2008 (SI 2008/99) |
| 32–38 | 1 Aug 2008 (in respect of a person to whom Condition 1 applies (within the meaning of s 32)) (SI 2008/1818)[3] |
| | *Not yet in force* (otherwise) |
| 39 | 1 Aug 2008 (SI 2008/1818) |
| 40–43 | 31 Jan 2008 (SI 2008/99) |
| 44–47 | 31 Mar 2008 (SI 2008/309) |
| 48–50 | 1 Apr 2008 (SI 2008/309) |
| 51 | 1 Apr 2008 (for the purposes of making regulations under sub-ss (2)–(6)) (SI 2008/309) |
| | 6 Jan 2009 (otherwise) (SI 2008/3136) |
| 52, 53 | 1 Apr 2008 (for the purposes of making orders) (SI 2008/309) |
| | 6 Jan 2009 (otherwise) (SI 2008/3136) |
| 54–56 | 1 Apr 2008 (SI 2008/309) |
| 57 | *Not yet in force* |
| 58 | See Schedule below |
| 59–61 | 30 Oct 2007 (RA) |
| Schedule | 31 Jan 2008 (SI 2008/99), repeals of or in— |
| | Immigration Act 1971; |
| | Immigration and Asylum Act 1999; |
| | Nationality, Immigration and Asylum Act 2002, s 130; |
| | Commissioners for Revenue and Customs Act 2005; |
| | Immigration, Asylum and Nationality Act 2006 |
| | 1 Apr 2008 (SI 2008/309), repeals of or in— |
| | Race Relations Act 1976; |
| | Nationality, Immigration and Asylum Act 2002, ss 37, 111, 142; |
| | Tribunals, Courts and Enforcement Act 2007 |

[1]   For transitional provisions, see SI 2008/99, arts 3, 4

[2]   For transitional provisions, see SI 2008/309, arts 5–7

[3]   For transitional provisions, see SI 2008/1818, art 3

[4]   For transitional provisions, see SI 2011/1293, art 3

---

**Vehicle Registration Marks Act 2007 (c 14)**

*RA:* 19 Jul 2007

Whole Act in force 19 Jul 2007 (RA)

---

**Welfare Reform Act 2007 (c 5)**

*RA:* 3 May 2007

*Commencement provisions:* s 70; Welfare Reform Act 2007 Commencement (No 1) Order 2007, SI 2007/1721; Welfare Reform Act 2007 Commencement (No 2) Order 2007, SI 2007/1991; Welfare

**Welfare Reform Act 2007 (c 5)**—*contd*
    Reform Act 2007 Commencement (No 3) Order 2007, SI 2007/2819; Welfare Reform Act 2007 (Commencement No 4, and Savings and Transitional Provisions) Order 2007, SI 2007/2872; Welfare Reform Act 2007 (Commencement No 5) Order 2008, SI 2008/411; Welfare Reform Act 2007 (Commencement No 6 and Consequential Provisions) Order 2008, SI 2008/787; Welfare Reform Act 2007 (Commencement No 7, Transitional and Savings Provisions) Order 2008, SI 2008/2101; Welfare Reform Act 2007 (Commencement No 8) Order 2008, SI 2008/2772; Welfare Reform Act 2007 (Commencement No 9) Order 2008, SI 2008/3167; Welfare Reform Act 2007 (Commencement No 10, Transitional and Savings Provisions) Order 2009, SI 2009/775; Welfare Reform Act 2007 (Commencement No 11) Order 2009, SI 2009/1608; Welfare Reform Act 2007 (Commencement No 12) Order 2010, SI 2010/1905; Welfare Reform Act 2007 (Commencement No 13) Order 2011, SI 2011/330

| | | |
|---|---|---|
| 1 | | 27 Oct 2008 (SI 2008/787) |
| 2–5 | | 18 Mar 2008 (for the purpose of making regulations) (SI 2008/787) |
| | | 27 Oct 2008 (otherwise) (SI 2008/787) |
| 6, 7 | | 27 Oct 2008 (SI 2008/787) |
| 8, 9 | | 18 Mar 2008 (for the purpose of making regulations) (SI 2008/787) |
| | | 27 Oct 2008 (otherwise) (SI 2008/787) |
| 10 | | 27 Oct 2008 (SI 2008/787) |
| 11, 12 | | 18 Mar 2008 (for the purpose of making regulations) (SI 2008/787) |
| | | 27 Oct 2008 (otherwise) (SI 2008/787) |
| 13 | (1)–(6) | 11 Feb 2011 (SI 2011/330) |
| | (7) | 27 Oct 2008 (SI 2008/2772) |
| 14 | | 18 Mar 2008 (for the purpose of making regulations) (SI 2008/787) |
| | | 27 Oct 2008 (otherwise) (SI 2008/787) |
| 15 | | 11 Feb 2011 (SI 2011/330) |
| 16–18 | | 18 Mar 2008 (for the purpose of making regulations) (SI 2008/787) |
| | | 27 Oct 2008 (otherwise) (SI 2008/787) |
| 19 | | 27 Oct 2008 (SI 2008/787) |
| 20 | | 18 Mar 2008 (for the purpose of making regulations) (SI 2008/787) |
| | | 27 Oct 2008 (otherwise) (SI 2008/787) |
| 21 | | 27 Oct 2008 (SI 2008/787) |
| 22–24 | | 18 Mar 2008 (for the purpose of making regulations) (SI 2008/787) |
| | | 27 Oct 2008 (otherwise) (SI 2008/787) |
| 25 | (1), (2)(a) | 18 Mar 2008 (for the purpose of making regulations) (SI 2008/787) |
| | | 27 Oct 2008 (otherwise) (SI 2008/787) |
| | (2)(b) | 18 Mar 2008 (for the purpose of making regulations) (SI 2008/787) |
| | | 27 Jul 2008 (otherwise) (SI 2008/787) |
| | (2)(c), (3)–(7) | 18 Mar 2008 (for the purpose of making regulations) (SI 2008/787) |
| | | 27 Oct 2008 (otherwise) (SI 2008/787) |
| 26 | | 18 Mar 2008 (for the purpose of making regulations) (SI 2008/787) |
| | | 27 Oct 2008 (otherwise) (SI 2008/787) |
| 27 | | 27 Oct 2008 (SI 2008/787) |
| 28 | (1) | See Sch 3 below |
| | (2) | 18 Mar 2008 (for the purpose of making regulations) (SI 2008/787) |
| | | 27 Oct 2008 (otherwise) (SI 2008/787) |
| | (3) | 27 Oct 2008 (SI 2008/787) |
| 29 | | See Sch 4 below |
| 30 | (1) | 7 Apr 2008 (SI 2007/2872) |

**Welfare Reform Act 2007 (c 5)**—*contd*

| | | |
|---|---|---|
| | (2), (3) | 1 Oct 2007 (for the purpose of conferring power to make regulations) (SI 2007/2872) |
| | | 7 Apr 2008 (otherwise) (SI 2007/2872) |
| 31 | | 14 Jun 2007 (for the purpose of exercising any power to make regulations) (SI 2007/1721) |
| | | 1 Nov 2007 (otherwise) (SI 2007/1721) |
| 32–34 | | 1 Apr 2008 (for the purpose of conferring power to make regulations) (SI 2008/411) |
| | | 6 Oct 2008 (otherwise) (SI 2008/411) |
| 35 | (1), (2) | 1 Oct 2007 (for the purpose of conferring power to make regulations) (SI 2007/2872) |
| | | 7 Apr 2008 (otherwise) (SI 2007/2872) |
| | (3) | 7 Apr 2008 (SI 2007/2872) |
| 36 | | 27 Mar 2009 (SI 2009/775) |
| 37 | | *Not yet in force* (repealed in part) |
| 38, 39 | | 1 Apr 2008 (SI 2008/411) |
| 40 | | See Sch 5 below |
| 41 | (1) | 1 Oct 2007 (SI 2007/2819) |
| | (2), (3) | 3 Jul 2007 (s 70(1)(a)) |
| 42 | | 5 Aug 2008 (for the purpose of conferring power to make regulations) (SI 2008/2101) |
| | | 1 Sep 2008 (otherwise) (SI 2008/2101) |
| 43 | | 1 Sep 2008 (SI 2008/2101) |
| 44, 45 | | 3 Jul 2007 (s 70(1)(a)) |
| 46, 47 | | 19 Feb 2008 (for the purpose of conferring power to make regulations) (SI 2008/411) |
| | | 7 Apr 2008 (otherwise) (SI 2008/411) |
| 48 | | 2 Jul 2009 (SI 2009/1608) |
| 49 | | 1 Apr 2008 (SI 2008/787) |
| 50, 51 | | 7 Oct 2008 (SI 2008/2101)[2] |
| 52, 53 | | 1 Oct 2007 (SI 2007/2819) |
| 54, 55 | | 3 Jul 2007 (s 70(1)(a)) |
| 56, 57 | | *Not yet in force* |
| 58 | | 12 Jul 2007 (for the purpose of conferring power to make an order) (SI 2007/1991) |
| | | 10 Aug 2007 (otherwise) (SI 2007/1991) |
| 59 | | 3 Jul 2007 (s 70(1)(a)) |
| 60 | | 1 Oct 2007 (for the purpose of exercising any power to make regulations) (SI 2007/2819) |
| | | 29 Oct 2007 (otherwise) (SI 2007/2819) |
| 61 | (1)(a) | *Not yet in force* |
| | (1)(b), (2)–(6) | 3 Jul 2007 (s 70(1)(a)) |
| 62 | | 3 Jul 2007 (s 70(1)(a)) |
| 63 | | See Sch 7 below |
| 64–66 | | 3 May 2007 (s 70(2)) |
| 67 | | See Sch 8 below |
| 68–71 | | 3 May 2007 (s 70(2)) |
| Schs 1, 2 | | 18 Mar 2008 (for the purpose of making regulations) (SI 2008/787) |
| | | 27 Oct 2008 (otherwise) (SI 2008/787) |
| Sch 3 | paras 1–4 | 27 Oct 2008 (SI 2008/787) |
| | para 5 | *Not yet in force* |
| | para 6 | 27 Oct 2008 (SI 2008/787) |
| | para 7(1) | 18 Mar 2008 (for the purpose of making regulations) (SI 2008/787) |
| | | 27 Oct 2008 (otherwise) (SI 2008/787) |
| | para 7(2)–(6) | *Not yet in force* |
| | para 7(7), (8) | 18 Mar 2008 (for the purpose of making regulations) (SI 2008/787) |
| | | 27 Oct 2008 (otherwise) (SI 2008/787) |

**Welfare Reform Act 2007 (c 5)**—*contd*

| | | |
|---|---|---|
| | para 8 | 18 Mar 2008 (for the purpose of making regulations) (SI 2008/787) |
| | | 27 Oct 2008 (otherwise) (SI 2008/787) |
| | para 9(1)–(4) | 18 Mar 2008 (for the purpose of making regulations) (SI 2008/787) |
| | | 27 Oct 2008 (otherwise) (SI 2008/787) |
| | para 9(5) | *Not yet in force* |
| | para 9(6)–(11) | 27 Oct 2008 (SI 2008/787) |
| | para 9(12) | *Not yet in force* |
| | para 9(13) | 27 Oct 2008 (SI 2008/787) |
| | para 10(1), (2) | 18 Mar 2008 (for the purpose of making regulations) (SI 2008/787) |
| | | 27 Jul 2008 (otherwise) (SI 2008/787) |
| | para 10(3)–(31) | 18 Mar 2008 (for the purpose of making regulations) (SI 2008/787) |
| | | 27 Oct 2008 (otherwise) (SI 2008/787) |
| | para 10(32) | 18 Mar 2008 (for the purpose of making regulations) (SI 2008/787) |
| | | 27 Jul 2008 (otherwise) (SI 2008/787) |
| | paras 11–16 | 18 Mar 2008 (for the purpose of making regulations) (SI 2008/787) |
| | | 27 Oct 2008 (otherwise) (SI 2008/787) |
| | para 17(1)–(3) | 18 Mar 2008 (for the purpose of making regulations) (SI 2008/787) |
| | | 27 Jul 2008 (otherwise) (SI 2008/787) |
| | para 17(4), (5) | 27 Oct 2008 (SI 2008/787) |
| | para 17(6) | 18 Mar 2008 (for the purpose of making regulations) (SI 2008/787) |
| | | 27 Jul 2008 (otherwise) (SI 2008/787) |
| | paras 17(7)–(9), 18–20 | 18 Mar 2008 (for the purpose of making regulations) (SI 2008/787) |
| | | 27 Oct 2008 (otherwise) (SI 2008/787) |
| | para 21 | *Not yet in force* |
| | paras 22–24 | 18 Mar 2008 (for the purpose of making regulations) (SI 2008/787) |
| | | 27 Oct 2008 (otherwise) (SI 2008/787) |
| Sch 4 | paras 1, 2 | 18 Mar 2008 (for the purpose of making regulations) (SI 2008/787) |
| | | 27 Jul 2008 (otherwise) (SI 2008/787) |
| | para 3(a) | *Not yet in force* |
| | para 3(b)–(d) | 18 Mar 2008 (for the purpose of making regulations) (SI 2008/787) |
| | | 27 Jul 2008 (otherwise) (SI 2008/787) |
| | paras 4–6 | *Not yet in force* |
| | paras 7, 8 | 27 Jul 2010 (SI 2010/1905) |
| | para 9 | *Not yet in force* |
| | para 10 | 11 Dec 2008 (SI 2008/3167) |
| | para 11 | 27 Jul 2008 (SI 2008/787) |
| Sch 5 | paras 1–4 | 3 Jul 2007 (s 70(1)(b)) |
| | paras 5–7 | 1 Apr 2008 (in so far as they relate to the amendment of the Social Security Administration Act 1992, ss 139E–139G) (SI 2008/411) |
| | para 8 | 3 May 2007 (s 70(2)) |
| | para 9 | 1 Apr 2008 (in so far as it relates to the amendment of the Social Security Administration Act 1992, s 140B(5A)) (SI 2008/411) |
| | paras 10, 11 | 3 Jul 2007 (s 70(1)(b)) |
| | para 12 | 7 Apr 2008 (SI 2007/2872) |
| | para 13 | *Not yet in force* (repealed in part) |
| | para 14 | 3 Jul 2007 (s 70(1)(b)) |

**Welfare Reform Act 2007 (c 5)**—*contd*

| | | |
|---|---|---|
| Sch 6 | | 12 Jul 2007 (for the purpose of conferring power to make an order) (SI 2007/1991) |
| | | 10 Aug 2007 (otherwise) (SI 2007/1991) |
| Sch 7 | para 1 | *Not yet in force* (sub-paras (4)(a), (8), (9) repealed) |
| | para 2(1) | 3 Jul 2007 (s 70(1)(c)) |
| | para 2(2) | 1 Oct 2007 (SI 2007/2819) |
| | paras 2(3), 3, 4 | 3 Jul 2007 (s 70(1)(c)) |

Sch 8
3 Jul 2007 (s 70(1)(d)), repeals of or in—
Pneumoconiosis etc (Workers' Compensation) Act 1979;
Social Security Contributions and Benefits Act 1992, s 140(1A);
Social Security Administration Act 1992, ss 71(5), 71ZA(2), 134(8)(a), 168(3)(d);
Social Security Administration (Northern Ireland) Act 1992;
Local Government etc (Scotland) Act 1994;
Social Security Act 1998, s 38(7)(a)(iii), Sch 7, para 81(2);
Civil Partnership Act 2004, Sch 24, para 65
1 Oct 2007 (repeals of or in Social Security Contributions and Benefits Act 1992, ss 72(6), 73(5)) (SI 2007/2819)
7 Apr 2008 (SI 2007/2872)1, repeals of or in—
Social Security Administration Act 1992, s 5;
Social Security Contributions and Benefits Act 1992, s 130;
Housing Act 1996
1 Sep 2008 (repeals of or in Local Government Act 2000) (SI 2008/2101)[2]
7 Oct 2008 (repeals of or in Tax Credits Act 2002, Sch 3, paras 26, 28) (SI 2008/2101)
27 Oct 2008 (SI 2008/787), repeals of or in—
Social Security Administration Act 1992, s 73;
Social Security Contributions and Benefits Act 1992, ss 6A, 124;
Jobseekers Act 1995, Sch 2, paras 19(2), (3), 40, 53;
Social Security Act 1998, ss 2, 28, Schs 2, 3;
Welfare Reform and Pensions Act 1999, s 72
27 Mar 2009 (repeals in Social Security Contributions and Benefits Act 1992, ss 37, 39A) (SI 2009/775)[3]
*Not yet in force*, repeals of or in—
Vaccine Damage Payments Act 1979;
Income and Corporation Taxes Act 1988;
Criminal Justice Act 1991;
Social Security Administration Act 1992, ss 2A, 2AA, 130, 132, 150;
Social Security Contributions and Benefits Act 1992, ss 20, 21, 30A–30E, 40–42, 44, 47, 61, 61A, 84, 86A, 87, 89, 93, 150, 171ZP, 171A–171G, 176, Schs 3, 4, 11–13;
Disability (Grants) Act 1993;
Pension Schemes Act 1993;
Social Security (Incapacity for Work) Act 1994;
Jobseekers Act 1995, Sch 2, paras 19(5), 25, 26;
Pensions Act 1995;
Social Security Act 1998, ss 31, 77, Sch 7, paras 73, 103;
Welfare Reform and Pensions Act 1999, ss 61–64, Sch 8;
State Pension Credit Act 2002;
National Insurance Contributions Act 2002;
Tax Credits Act 2002, Sch 3, paras 25, 30;
Income Tax (Earnings and Pensions) Act 2003;
Civil Partnership Act 2004, Sch 24, paras 14, 15

[1] For transitional provisions and savings, see SI 2007/2872, arts 3–5

[2] For transitional provisions and savings, see SI 2008/2101, art 3

**Welfare Reform Act 2007 (c 5)**—*contd*

3    For transitional provisions and savings, see SI 2009/775, art 3

# 2008 Acts

## Abolition of Bridge Tolls (Scotland) Act 2008 (asp 1)

*RA:* 24 Jan 2008

*Commencement provisions:* s 4(2); Abolition of Bridge Tolls (Scotland) Act 2008 (Commencement) Order 2008, SSI 2008/22

| | |
|---|---|
| 1–3 | 11 Feb 2008 (SSI 2008/22) |
| 4 | 24 Jan 2008 (RA) |
| Schs 1, 2 | 11 Feb 2008 (SSI 2008/22) |

## Appropriation Act 2008 (c 3)

*RA:* 20 Mar 2008

Whole Act in force 20 Mar 2008 (RA)

## Appropriation (No 2) Act 2008 (c 8)

*RA:* 21 Jul 2008

Whole Act in force 21 Jul 2008 (RA)

## Appropriation (No 3) Act 2008 (c 19)

*RA:* 16 Oct 2008

Whole Act in force 16 Oct 2008 (RA)

## Banking (Special Provisions) Act 2008 (c 2)

*RA:* 21 Feb 2008

*Commencement provisions:* s 17(2)

Whole Act in force 21 Feb 2008 (s 17(2))

## Budget (Scotland) Act 2008 (asp 2)

*RA:* 12 Mar 2008

Whole Act in force 12 Mar 2008 (RA)

**Channel Tunnel Rail Link (Supplementary Provisions) Act 2008 (c 5)**

*RA:* 22 May 2008

*Commencement provisions:* s 6(2)

Whole Act in force 22 Jul 2008 (s 6(2))

---

**Child Maintenance and Other Payments Act 2008 (c 6)**

*RA:* 5 Jun 2008

*Commencement provisions:* s 62; Child Maintenance and Other Payments Act 2008 (Commencement) Order 2008, SI 2008/1476; Child Maintenance and Other Payments Act 2008 (Commencement No 2) Order 2008, SI 2008/2033; Child Maintenance and Other Payments Act 2008 (Commencement No 3 and Transitional and Savings Provisions) Order 2008, SI 2008/2548; Child Maintenance and Other Payments Act 2008 (Commencement No 4 and Transitional Provision) Order 2008, SI 2008/2675[4]; Child Maintenance and Other Payments Act 2008 (Commencement No 5) Order 2009, SI 2009/1314; Child Maintenance and Other Payments Act 2008 (Commencement No 6) Order 2009, SI 2009/3072; Child Maintenance and Other Payments Act 2008 (Commencement No 7) Order 2010, SI 2010/697; Child Maintenance and Other Payments Act 2008 (Commencement No 8) Order 2012, SI 2012/1649; Child Maintenance and Other Payments Act 2008 (Commencement No 9) and the Welfare Reform Act 2009 (Commencement No 9) Order 2012, SI 2012/2523; Child Maintenance and Other Payments Act 2008 (Commencement No 10 and Transitional Provisions) Order 2012, SI 2012/3042, as amended by SI 2013/1860, SI 2014/1635; Child Maintenance and Other Payments Act 2008 (Commencement No 11 and Transitional Provisions) Order 2013, SI 2013/1860, as amended by SI 2014/1635; Child Maintenance and Other Payments Act 2008 (Commencement No 12 and Savings Provisions) and the Welfare Reform Act 2012 (Commencement No 15) Order 2013, SI 2013/2947; Child Maintenance and Other Payments Act 2008 (Commencement No 13) Order 2014, SI 2014/576; Child Maintenance and Other Payments Act 2008 (Commencement No 14 and Transitional Provisions) and the Welfare Reform Act 2012 (Commencement No 18 and Transitional and Savings Provisions) Order 2014, SI 2014/1635; Child Maintenance and Other Payments Act 2008 (Commencement No 15) Order 2015, SI 2015/176; Child Maintenance and Other Payments Act 2008 (Commencement No 16) Order 2018, SI 2018/1261

| | | |
|---|---|---|
| 1 | (1) | 10 Jun 2008 (for the purpose of conferring power to appoint the members of the Commission) (SI 2008/1476) |
| | | 24 Jul 2008 (otherwise) (SI 2008/2033) |
| | (2) | See Sch 1 below |
| 2 | | 24 Jul 2008 (SI 2008/2033) |
| 3 | (1)(a) | 1 Nov 2008 (SI 2008/2675) |
| | (1)(b) | 24 Jul 2008 (SI 2008/2033) |
| | (2), (3) | 24 Jul 2008 (SI 2008/2033) |
| 4–12 | | 24 Jul 2008 (SI 2008/2033) |
| 13 | (1), (2) | 1 Nov 2008 (SI 2008/2675)[4] |
| | (3) | See Sch 2 below |
| | (4) | See Sch 3 below |
| 14 | | 1 Nov 2008 (SI 2008/2675) |
| 15 | (a) | 14 Jul 2008 (except in relation to existing cases[1, 2]) (SI 2008/1476) |
| | | 27 Oct 2008 (exception noted above) (SI 2008/2548)[3] |
| | (b) | 14 Jul 2008 (SI 2008/1476) |
| 16 | | See Sch 4 below |
| 17 | | 8 Oct 2012 (for the purpose of making regulations) (SI 2012/2523) |
| | | 10 Dec 2012 (for the purposes of those types of cases falling within SI 2012/3042, art 3) (SI 2012/3042)[5] |
| | | 29 Jul 2013 (for the purposes of those types of cases falling within SI 2013/1860, art 3) (SI 2013/1860)[6] |
| | | 25 Nov 2013 (otherwise) (SI 2013/2947)[7] |
| 18 | | 10 Dec 2012 (for the purposes of those types of cases falling within SI 2012/3042, art 3) (SI 2012/3042)[5] |
| | | 29 Jul 2013 (for the purposes of those types of cases falling within SI 2013/1860, art 3) (SI 2013/1860)[6] |

**Child Maintenance and Other Payments Act 2008 (c 6)**—*contd*

| | | |
|---|---|---|
| | | 25 Nov 2013 (otherwise) (SI 2013/2947)[7] |
| 19 | | See Sch 5 below |
| 20 | | 26 Sep 2008 (for the purpose of making regulations) (SI 2008/2548) |
| | | 27 Oct 2008 (otherwise) (SI 2008/2548) |
| 21 | | *Not yet in force* |
| 22, 23 | | 1 Jun 2009 (for the purpose of making regulations) (SI 2009/1314) |
| | | 3 Aug 2009 (otherwise) (SI 2009/1314) |
| 24 | | 6 Apr 2010 (SI 2010/697) |
| 25, 26 | | *Not yet in force* |
| 27 | | 29 Nov 2018 (for the purpose of making regulations) (SI 2018/1261) |
| | | 14 Dec 2018 (otherwise) (SI 2018/1261) |
| 28–30 | | *Not yet in force* |
| 31 | | 26 Nov 2009 (for the purpose of making regulations) (SI 2009/3072) |
| | | 25 Jan 2010 (otherwise) (SI 2009/3072) |
| 32, 33 | | 8 Oct 2012 (for the purpose of making regulations) (SI 2012/2523) |
| | | 10 Dec 2012 (otherwise) (SI 2012/3042) |
| 34 | | *Not yet in force* |
| 35 | | 6 Jun 2008 (s 62(2)) |
| 36 | | 26 Sep 2008 (for the purpose of making regulations) (SI 2008/2548) |
| | | 27 Oct 2008 (otherwise) (SI 2008/2548) |
| 37 | | 8 Oct 2012 (SI 2012/2523) |
| 38 | | 26 Nov 2009 (SI 2009/3072) |
| 39 | | *Not yet in force* |
| 40 | | 10 Feb 2015 (for the purpose of making regulations) (SI 2015/176) |
| | | 23 Mar 2015 (otherwise) (SI 2015/176) |
| 41 | | 8 Oct 2012 (SI 2012/2523) |
| 42 | | 8 Oct 2012 (for the purpose of making regulations) (SI 2012/2523) |
| | | 10 Dec 2012 (otherwise) (SI 2012/3042) |
| 43 | | 5 Aug 2008 (SI 2008/2033) |
| 44 | | See Sch 6 below |
| 45 | | 14 Jul 2008 (SI 2008/1476) |
| 46 | (1), (2) | 1 Oct 2008 (SI 2008/1476) |
| | (3) | 10 Jun 2008 (for the purpose of conferring power to make regulations) (SI 2008/1476) |
| | | 1 Oct 2008 (otherwise) (SI 2008/1476) |
| | (4), (5) | 1 Oct 2008 (SI 2008/1476) |
| 47 | (1)(a) | 1 Oct 2008 (SI 2008/1476) |
| | (1)(b), (c) | 10 Jun 2008 (for the purpose of conferring power to make regulations) (SI 2008/1476) |
| | | 1 Oct 2008 (otherwise) (SI 2008/1476) |
| | (2)(a) | 1 Oct 2008 (SI 2008/1476) |
| | (2)(b), (c) | 10 Jun 2008 (for the purpose of conferring power to make regulations) (SI 2008/1476) |
| | | 1 Oct 2008 (otherwise) (SI 2008/1476) |
| | (3)(a)–(d) | 1 Oct 2008 (SI 2008/1476) |
| | (3)(e) | 10 Jun 2008 (for the purpose of conferring power to make regulations) (SI 2008/1476) |
| | | 1 Oct 2008 (otherwise) (SI 2008/1476) |
| | (4)(a)–(c) | 1 Oct 2008 (SI 2008/1476) |
| | (4)(d) | 10 Jun 2008 (for the purpose of conferring power to make regulations) (SI 2008/1476) |
| | | 1 Oct 2008 (otherwise) (SI 2008/1476) |
| | (5) | 1 Oct 2008 (SI 2008/1476) |
| 48 | (1)–(3) | 10 Jun 2008 (for the purpose of conferring power to make regulations) (SI 2008/1476) |

**Child Maintenance and Other Payments Act 2008 (c 6)**—*contd*

|  |  |  |
|---|---|---|
|  |  | 1 Oct 2008 (otherwise) (SI 2008/1476) |
|  | (4) | 1 Oct 2008 (SI 2008/1476) |
| 49 | (1) | 1 Oct 2008 (SI 2008/1476) |
|  | (2) | 10 Jun 2008 (for the purpose of conferring power to make regulations) (SI 2008/1476) |
|  |  | 1 Oct 2008 (otherwise) (SI 2008/1476) |
|  | (3)–(7) | 1 Oct 2008 (SI 2008/1476) |
| 50 | (1)–(3) | 1 Oct 2008 (SI 2008/1476) |
|  | (4)(a), (b) | 1 Oct 2008 (SI 2008/1476) |
|  | (4)(c) | 10 Jun 2008 (for the purpose of conferring power to make regulations) (SI 2008/1476) |
|  |  | 1 Oct 2008 (otherwise) (SI 2008/1476) |
| 51, 52 |  | 1 Oct 2008 (SI 2008/1476) |
| 53 |  | 10 Jun 2008 (for the purpose of conferring power to make regulations) (SI 2008/1476) |
|  |  | 1 Oct 2008 (otherwise) (SI 2008/1476) |
| 54 |  | 10 Jun 2008 (for the purpose of conferring power to make regulations under the Social Security (Recovery of Benefits) Act 1997, s 1A) (SI 2008/1476) |
|  |  | 1 Oct 2008 (otherwise) (SI 2008/1476) |
| 55 |  | 5 Jun 2008 (s 62(1)) |
| 56 |  | 10 Jun 2008 (SI 2008/1476) |
| 57 | (1) | See Sch 7 below |
|  | (2) | 10 Jun 2008 (SI 2008/1476) |
| 58 |  | See Sch 8 below |
| 59 | (1)–(7) | 10 Jun 2008 (SI 2008/1476) |
|  | (8) | 5 Jun 2008 (s 62(1)) |
| 60 | (1) | 10 Jun 2008 (SI 2008/1476) |
|  | (2) | *Not yet in force* |
| 61–63 |  | 5 Jun 2008 (s 62(1)) |
| Sch 1 | para 1(a), (b) | 10 Jun 2008 (for the purpose of conferring power to appoint the members of the Commission) (SI 2008/1476) |
|  |  | 24 Jul 2008 (otherwise) (SI 2008/2033) |
|  | para 1(c) | 24 Jul 2008 (SI 2008/2033) |
|  | para 1(d) | 10 Jun 2008 (for the purpose of conferring power to appoint the members of the Commission) (SI 2008/1476) |
|  |  | 24 Jul 2008 (otherwise) (SI 2008/2033) |
|  | paras 2–32 | 24 Jul 2008 (SI 2008/2033) |
| Sch 2 |  | 1 Nov 2008 (SI 2008/2675) |
| Sch 3 | paras 1–39 | 1 Nov 2008 (SI 2008/2675) |
|  | para 40(a) | 1 Nov 2008 (SI 2008/2675) |
|  | para 40(b) | In force immediately after the Bankruptcy and Diligence etc (Scotland) Act 2007, Sch 5, para 18(a)(i) comes into force (S) (SI 2008/2675) |
|  |  | In force immediately after that paragraph extends to England and Wales (E) (W) (SI 2008/2675) |
|  | para 40(c) | 1 Nov 2008 (SI 2008/2675) |
|  | paras 41–55 | 1 Nov 2008 (SI 2008/2675) |
| Sch 4 | para 1 | See paras 2–10 below |
|  | para 2 | 8 Oct 2012 (for the purpose of making regulations) (SI 2012/2523) |
|  |  | 10 Dec 2012 (for the purposes of those types of cases falling within SI 2012/3042, art 3) (SI 2012/3042)[5] |
|  |  | 29 Jul 2013 (for the purposes of those types of cases falling within SI 2013/1860, art 3) (SI 2013/1860)[6] |
|  |  | 25 Nov 2013 (otherwise) (SI 2013/2947)[7] |
|  | para 3 | 10 Dec 2012 (for the purposes of those types of cases falling within SI 2012/3042, art 3) (SI 2012/3042)[5] |
|  |  | 29 Jul 2013 (for the purposes of those types of cases falling within SI 2013/1860, art 3) (SI 2013/1860)[6] |
|  |  | 25 Nov 2013 (otherwise) (SI 2013/2947)[7] |

**Child Maintenance and Other Payments Act 2008 (c 6)**—*contd*

| | | |
|---|---|---|
| | para 4 | 25 Nov 2013 (SI 2013/2947)[7] |
| | para 5(1) | 10 Dec 2012 (for the purposes of those types of cases falling within SI 2012/3042, art 3) (SI 2012/3042)[5] |
| | | 29 Jul 2013 (for the purposes of those types of cases falling within SI 2013/1860, art 3) (SI 2013/1860)[6] |
| | | 25 Nov 2013 (otherwise) (SI 2013/2947)[7] |
| | para 5(2) | 8 Oct 2012 (for the purpose of making regulations) (SI 2012/2523) |
| | | 10 Dec 2012 (for the purposes of those types of cases falling within SI 2012/3042, art 3) (SI 2012/3042)[5] |
| | | 29 Jul 2013 (for the purposes of those types of cases falling within SI 2013/1860, art 3) (SI 2013/1860)[6] |
| | | 25 Nov 2013 (otherwise) (SI 2013/2947)[7] |
| | para 6 | 10 Dec 2012 (for the purposes of those types of cases falling within SI 2012/3042, art 3) (SI 2012/3042)[5] |
| | | 29 Jul 2013 (for the purposes of those types of cases falling within SI 2013/1860, art 3) (SI 2013/1860)[6] |
| | | 25 Nov 2013 (otherwise) (SI 2013/2947)[7] |
| | paras 7–9 | 8 Oct 2012 (for the purpose of making regulations) (SI 2012/2523) |
| | | 10 Dec 2012 (for the purposes of those types of cases falling within SI 2012/3042, art 3) (SI 2012/3042)[5] |
| | | 29 Jul 2013 (for the purposes of those types of cases falling within SI 2013/1860, art 3) (SI 2013/1860)[6] |
| | | 25 Nov 2013 (otherwise) (SI 2013/2947)[7] |
| | para 10 | 10 Dec 2012 (for the purposes of those types of cases falling within SI 2012/3042, art 3) (SI 2012/3042)[5] |
| | | 29 Jul 2013 (for the purposes of those types of cases falling within SI 2013/1860, art 3) (SI 2013/1860)[6] |
| | | 25 Nov 2013 (otherwise) (SI 2013/2947)[7] |
| Sch 5 | para 1 | 30 Jun 2014 (SI 2014/1635)[8] |
| | paras 2, 3 | 9 Mar 2014 (for the purpose of making regulations) (SI 2014/576) |
| | | 30 Jun 2014 (otherwise) (SI 2014/1635)[8] |
| | para 4 | 30 Jun 2014 (SI 2014/1635)[8] |
| | paras 5–7 | 9 Mar 2014 (for the purpose of making regulations) (SI 2014/576) |
| | | 30 Jun 2014 (otherwise) (SI 2014/1635)[8] |
| Sch 6 | | 1 Nov 2008 (SI 2008/2675) |
| Sch 7 | para 1(1) | See sub-paras (2)–(34) below |
| | para 1(2) | 10 Dec 2012 (for the purposes of those types of cases falling within SI 2012/3042, art 3) (SI 2012/3042)[5] |
| | | 29 Jul 2013 (for the purposes of those types of cases falling within SI 2013/1860, art 3) (SI 2013/1860)[6] |
| | | 25 Nov 2013 (otherwise) (SI 2013/2947)[7] |
| | para 1(3)–(6) | *Not yet in force* |
| | para 1(7) | 1 Jun 2009 (SI 2009/1314) |
| | para 1(8) | *Not yet in force* |
| | para 1(9), (10) | 1 Jun 2009 (SI 2009/1314) |
| | para 1(11)–(18) | *Not yet in force* |
| | para 1(19)–(21) | 1 Nov 2008 (SI 2008/2675) |
| | para 1(22)(a) | 1 Jun 2009 (for the purpose of making regulations) (SI 2009/1314) |
| | | 3 Aug 2009 (otherwise) (SI 2009/1314) |
| | para 1(22)(b) | 27 Jun 2012 (SI 2012/1649) |
| | para 1(23) | 27 Jun 2012 (SI 2012/1649) |
| | para 1(24) | 8 Oct 2012 (SI 2012/2523) |
| | para 1(25)(a) | 1 Jun 2009 (except in relation to the definition of "curfew order") (SI 2009/1314) |
| | | *Not yet in force* (exception noted above) |
| | para 1(25)(b) | *Not yet in force* |
| | para 1(26) | 1 Jun 2009 (SI 2009/1314) |
| | para 1(27) | *Not yet in force* |
| | para 1(28) | 25 Nov 2013 (SI 2013/2947)[7] |

**Child Maintenance and Other Payments Act 2008 (c 6)**—*contd*

| | |
|---|---|
| para 1(29) | 10 Dec 2012 (for the purposes of those types of cases falling within SI 2012/3042, art 3) (SI 2012/3042)[5] |
| | 29 Jul 2013 (for the purposes of those types of cases falling within SI 2013/1860, art 3) (SI 2013/1860)[6] |
| | 25 Nov 2013 (otherwise) (SI 2013/2947)[7] |
| para 1(30), (31) | 8 Oct 2012 (SI 2012/2523) |
| para 1(32) | 1 Jun 2009 (SI 2009/1314) |
| para 1(33) | 1 Nov 2008 (SI 2008/2675) |
| para 1(34) | 14 Jul 2008 (except in relation to existing cases[1]) (SI 2008/1476) |
| | 1 Jun 2009 (exception noted above) (SI 2009/1314) |
| para 2(1), (2) | 27 Oct 2008 (SI 2008/2548) |
| para 2(3)–(6) | 1 Jun 2009 (SI 2009/1314) |
| para 3 | 6 Apr 2010 (SI 2010/697) |
| para 4 | 1 Jun 2009 (SI 2009/1314) |
| paras 5, 6 | *Not yet in force* |
| Sch 8 | 14 Jul 2008 (SI 2008/1476), repeals of or in— |

    Child Support Act 1991, ss 16, 17, 20, 28ZA, 28ZC, 46;
    Social Security Administration Act 1992, s 106;
    Child Support, Pensions and Social Security Act 2000, s 19,
      Sch 3, para 11(11)(a), (13)(d)

14 Jul 2008 (except in relation to existing cases[1, 2]) (SI 2008/1476),
    repeals of or in—
    Child Support Act 1991, ss 4(10), 6, 7

27 Oct 2008 (SI 2008/2548), repeals of or in—
    Child Support Act 1991, ss 4(9), (11), 8, 9, 11, 12, 14, 26, 27,
      27A, 28, 28A, 28F, 28J, 29, 41, 52, Schs 4A, 4B[3];
    Social Security Administration Act 1992, ss 107, 122;
    Child Support, Pensions and Social Security Act 2000, s 3,
      Sch 3, para 11(3)–(6), (8)–(10), (13)(a), (22)

1 Nov 2008 (SI 2008/2675), repeals of or in—
    Child Support Act 1991, s 50(5), Sch 2;
    Welfare Reform and Pensions Act 1999, s 80

1 Jun 2009 (SI 2009/1314), repeals of or in—
    Child Support Act 1991, ss 6, 7 (exception noted above),
      s 36(2);
    Child Support Act 1995, Sch 3, para 9

8 Oct 2012 (SI 2012/2523), repeal in—
    Child Support Act 1991, Sch 1 (for the purpose of making
      regulations)

10 Dec 2012 (SI 2012/3042) (for the purposes of those types of
    cases falling within SI 2012/3042, art 3)[5], repeals in—
    Child Support Act 1991, Sch 1;
    Civil Partnership Act 2004

29 Jul 2013 (for the purposes of those types of cases falling within
    SI 2013/1860, art 3) (SI 2013/1860)[6], repeals in—
    Child Support Act 1991, Sch 1;
    Civil Partnership Act 2004

29 Jul 2013 (SI 2013/1860), repeal of—
    Child Support, Pensions and Social Security Act 2000, s 28

25 Nov 2013 (SI 2013/2947)[7], repeals in—
    Child Support Act 1991, Sch 1 (for remaining purposes);
    Civil Partnership Act 2004 (for remaining purposes)

*Not yet in force*, repeals of or in—
    Debtors (Scotland) Act 1987;
    Child Support Act 1991, ss 32–34, 36(1), 37, 39A, 40A, 40B, 47
      (for remaining purposes), Sch 5;
    Child Support Act 1991, s 4(10) (exception noted above);
    Child Support Act 1995, Sch 3, para 10;
    Child Support, Pensions and Social Security Act 2000, ss 16,
      Sch 3, para 11(17);

## Child Maintenance and Other Payments Act 2008 (c 6)—*contd*

Employment Act 2002;
Welfare Reform Act 2007;
Tribunals, Courts and Enforcement Act 2007

[1] An existing case is one in which, immediately before 14 Jul 2008, the Child Support Act 1991, s 6 applies in relation to a parent with care and—

(a) a maintenance calculation or maintenance assessment is in force as a result of the Secretary of State acting under that section, or

(b) no maintenance calculation or maintenance assessment has been made but the Secretary of State has given notice in accordance with SI 2001/157, reg 5 or SI 1992/1813, reg 5

[2] For a saving, see SI 2008/1476, art 2(4)

[3] For transitional and savings provisions, see SI 2008/2548, art 4

[4] For a transitional provision, see SI 2008/2675, art 4

[5] For transitional provisions, see SI 2012/3042, art 5

[6] For transitional provisions, see SI 2013/1860, art 5

[7] For savings, see SI 2013/2947, arts 3–5

[8] For transitional provisions, see SI 2014/1635, art 3

## Children and Young Persons Act 2008 (c 23)

*RA:* 13 Nov 2008

*Commencement provisions:* s 44; Children and Young Persons Act 2008 (Commencement No 1 and Saving Provision) Order 2009, SI 2009/268; Children and Young Persons Act 2008 (Commencement No 1) (England) Order 2009, SI 2009/323; Children and Young Persons Act 2008 (Commencement No 1) (Wales) Order 2009, SI 2009/728; Children and Young Persons Act 2008 (Commencement No 2) (Wales) Order 2009, SI 2009/1921; Children and Young Persons Act 2008 (Commencement No 2) (England) Order 2009, SI 2009/2273; Children and Young Persons Act 2008 (Commencement No 2) Order 2009, SI 2009/3354; Children and Young Persons Act 2008 (Commencement No 3) (Wales) Order 2010, SI 2010/749; Children and Young Persons Act 2008 (Commencement No 4) (Wales) Order 2010, SI 2010/1329; Children and Young Persons Act 2008 (Commencement No 3) (England) Order 2010, SI 2010/2714; Children and Young Persons Act 2008 (Commencement No 3, Saving and Transitional Provisions) Order 2010, SI 2010/2981; Children and Young Persons Act 2008 (Commencement No 5) (Wales) Order 2011, SI 2011/824; Children and Young Persons Act 2008 (Commencement No 6) (Wales) Order 2011, SI 2011/949; Children and Young Persons Act 2008 (Commencement No 4) (England) Order 2011, SI 2011/2703; Children and Young Persons Act 2008 (Commencement No 7) (Wales) Order 2012, SI 2012/1553; Children and Young Persons Act 2008 (Commencement No 5) (England) Order 2013, SI 2013/2606; Children and Young Persons Act 2008 (Commencement No 8 and Saving Provision) (Wales) Order 2016, SI 2016/452; Children and Young Persons Act 2008 (Commencement No 9) (Wales) Order 2017, SI 2017/948

| | | |
|---|---|---|
| 1 | | 16 Feb 2009 (E) (in so far as relates to specified local authorities)[2] (SI 2009/323) |
| | | 16 Dec 2010 (E) (in so far as relates to specified local authorities)[3] (SI 2010/2981) |
| | | 14 Nov 2011 (E) (in so far as relates to specified local authorities)[5] (SI 2011/2703) |
| | | 12 Nov 2013 (E) (otherwise) (SI 2013/2606) |
| | | *Not yet in force* (W) |
| 2, 3 | | 16 Feb 2009 (E) (SI 2009/323) |
| | | *Not yet in force* (W) |
| 4 | | 12 Nov 2013 (E) (SI 2013/2606) |
| | | *Never in force* (W) (repealed) |
| 5 | | 16 Feb 2009 (E) (SI 2009/323) |
| | | *Not yet in force* (W) |
| 6 | (1) | 16 Feb 2009 (E) (SI 2009/323) |
| | | *Not yet in force* (W) |

**Children and Young Persons Act 2008 (c 23)**—*contd*

| | | |
|---|---|---|
| | (2) | 12 Feb 2009 (E) (SI 2009/268) |
| | | *Not yet in force* (W) |
| | (3)–(6) | 16 Feb 2009 (E) (SI 2009/323) |
| | | *Not yet in force* (W) |
| 7 | | 13 Nov 2008 (s 44(1)) |
| 8 | (1) | 1 Sep 2009 (E) (in so far as substitutes Children Act 1989, ss 22C(11), 22F) (SI 2009/2273) |
| | | 26 Apr 2010 (W) (in so far as substitutes Children Act 1989, ss 22C(11), 22F) (SI 2010/1329) |
| | | 1 Apr 2011 (E) (otherwise) (SI 2010/2981) |
| | | 6 Apr 2016 (W) (otherwise) (SI 2016/452) |
| | (2) | See Sch 1 below |
| | (3) | See Sch 2 below |
| 9 | | 1 Apr 2011 (E) (SI 2010/2981) |
| | | *Not yet in force* (W) |
| 10 | (1) | 1 Sep 2009 (E) (in so far as inserts Children Act 1989, ss 25A(4), 25B(1)(b), (d), (2)(a), for the purpose only of enabling regulations to be made) (SI 2009/2273) |
| | | 26 Apr 2010 (W) (in so far as inserts Children Act 1989, ss 25A(4), 25B(1)(b), (d), (2)(a), for the purpose only of enabling regulations to be made) (SI 2010/1329) |
| | | 1 Apr 2011 (E) (otherwise) (SI 2010/2981) |
| | | 6 Apr 2016 (W) (otherwise) (SI 2016/452) |
| | (2) | 1 Apr 2011 (E) (SI 2010/2981)[4] |
| | | 1 Dec 2017 (W) (SI 2017/948) |
| | (3) | 1 Apr 2011 (E) (SI 2010/2981)[4] |
| | | 6 Apr 2016 (W) (SI 2016/452) |
| 11–14 | | *Not yet in force* |
| 15 | | 1 Sep 2009 (E) (in so far as inserts Children Act 1989, s 23ZA(3)(a) (for the purpose only of enabling regulations to be made) and (4)) (SI 2009/2273) |
| | | 26 Apr 2010 (W) (in so far as inserts Children Act 1989, s 23ZA(3)(a) (for the purpose only of enabling regulations to be made) and (4)) (SI 2010/1329) |
| | | 15 Nov 2010 (E) (in so far as inserts Children Act 1989, s 23ZA(1)(b) (for the purpose only of enabling regulations to be made)) (SI 2010/2714) |
| | | 28 Mar 2011 (W) (otherwise) (SI 2011/949) |
| | | 1 Apr 2011 (E) (otherwise) (SI 2010/2981) |
| 16 | (1) | 1 Sep 2009 (E) (in so far as inserts Children Act 1989, s 23ZB(1)(a) (for the purpose only of enabling regulations to be made) and (9)) (SI 2009/2273) |
| | | 26 Apr 2010 (W) (in so far as inserts Children Act 1989, s 23ZB(1)(a) (for the purpose only of enabling regulations to be made) and (9)) (SI 2010/1329) |
| | | 1 Apr 2011 (E) (otherwise) (SI 2010/2981) |
| | | 6 Apr 2016 (W) (otherwise) (SI 2016/452) |
| | (2) | 1 Apr 2011 (E) (SI 2010/2981) |
| | | 6 Apr 2016 (W) (otherwise) (SI 2016/452) |
| 17 | | 1 Apr 2011 (SI 2010/2981) |
| 18 | | 1 Jan 2010 (in so far as inserts Children Act 1989, s 86A(4), (5)) (SI 2009/3354) |
| | | 1 Apr 2011 (otherwise) (SI 2010/2981) |
| 19 | | 28 Mar 2011 (W) (SI 2011/949) |
| | | 1 Apr 2011 (E) (SI 2010/2981) |
| 20 | (1), (2) | 1 Sep 2009 (E) (SI 2009/2273) |
| | | 1 Sep 2011 (W) (SI 2011/949) |
| | (3) | 12 Feb 2009 (E) (SI 2009/268) |
| | | 26 Apr 2010 (W) (SI 2010/1329) |
| | (4)–(7) | 1 Sep 2009 (E) (SI 2009/2273) |

**Children and Young Persons Act 2008 (c 23)**—*contd*

|  |  |  |
|---|---|---|
|  |  | 1 Sep 2011 (W) (SI 2011/949) |
| 21 | (1) | See sub-ss (2)–(4) below |
|  | (2) | 12 Feb 2009 (E) (in so far as inserts Children Act 1989, s 23C(5B)) (SI 2009/268) |
|  |  | 22 Aug 2009 (E) (otherwise) (SI 2009/2273) |
|  |  | 26 Apr 2010 (W) (in so far as inserts Children Act 1989, s 23C(5B)) (SI 2010/1329) |
|  |  | 18 Mar 2011 (W) (otherwise) (SI 2011/824) |
|  | (3), (4) | 22 Aug 2009 (E) (SI 2009/2273) |
|  |  | 18 Mar 2011 (W) (SI 2011/824) |
| 22 | (1), (2) | 1 Apr 2011 (E) (SI 2010/2981)[4] |
|  |  | 19 Jun 2012 (W) (SI 2012/1553)[6] |
|  | (3) | See sub-ss (4), (5) below |
|  | (4) | 1 Apr 2011 (E) (SI 2010/2981) |
|  |  | 19 Jun 2012 (W) (SI 2012/1553) |
|  | (5) | 1 Sep 2009 (E) (in so far as inserts Children Act 1989, s 23E(1B), (1C)) (SI 2009/2273) |
|  |  | 26 Apr 2010 (W) (in so far as inserts Children Act 1989, s 23E(1B), (1C)) (SI 2010/1329) |
|  |  | 1 Apr 2011 (E) (otherwise) (SI 2010/2981) |
|  |  | 19 Jun 2012 (W) (otherwise) (SI 2012/1553) |
|  | (6) | 1 Apr 2011 (E) (SI 2010/2981) |
|  |  | 19 Jun 2012 (W) (SI 2012/1553) |
| 23 | (1) | 1 Jan 2010 (E) (SI 2009/3354) |
|  |  | 26 Apr 2010 (W) (SI 2010/1329) |
|  | (2) | 1 Apr 2011 (E) (SI 2010/2981) |
|  |  | 19 Jun 2012 (W) (SI 2012/1553) |
| 24 |  | 1 Apr 2011 (E) (SI 2010/2981) |
|  |  | 19 Jun 2012 (W) (SI 2012/1553) |
| 25 | (1)–(3) | 1 Apr 2011 (E) (SI 2010/2981) |
|  |  | 19 Jun 2012 (W) (SI 2012/1553) |
|  | (4) | 1 Sep 2009 (E) (in so far as inserts Children Act 1989, Sch 2, para 6(2), for the purpose only of enabling regulations to be made) (SI 2009/2273) |
|  |  | 26 Apr 2010 (W) (in so far as inserts Children Act 1989, Sch 2, para 6(2), for the purpose only of enabling regulations to be made) (SI 2010/1329) |
|  |  | 1 Apr 2011 (E) (otherwise) (SI 2010/2981) |
|  |  | 19 Jun 2012 (W) (otherwise) (SI 2012/1553) |
| 26 |  | 1 Apr 2010 (E) (SI 2009/3354) |
|  |  | *Not yet in force* (W) |
| 27, 28 |  | 1 Apr 2010 (E) (SI 2009/3354) |
|  |  | 26 Apr 2010 (W) (SI 2010/1329) |
| 29 |  | 1 Sep 2009 (E) (in so far as inserts Care Standards Act 2000, s 30A(3) and (4), for the purpose only of enabling regulations to be made) (SI 2009/2273) |
|  |  | 26 Apr 2010 (W) (in so far as inserts Care Standards Act 2000, s 30A(3) and (4), for the purpose only of enabling regulations to be made) (SI 2010/1239) |
|  |  | 28 Mar 2011 (W) (otherwise) (SI 2011/949) |
|  |  | 1 Apr 2011 (E) (otherwise) (SI 2010/2981) |
| 30 |  | 6 Apr 2009 (SI 2009/268; SI 2009/728) |
| 31, 32 |  | 1 Apr 2009 (SI 2009/268) |
| 33 |  | 12 Feb 2009 (E) (SI 2009/268) |
|  |  | 26 Apr 2010 (W) (SI 2010/1239) |
| 34 | (1) | See sub-ss (2)–(7) below |
|  | (2), (3) | 12 Feb 2009 (E) (SI 2009/268)[1] |
|  |  | 31 Mar 2010 (W) (SI 2010/749) |
|  | (4) | 12 Feb 2009 (E) (in so far as inserts Adoption and Children Act 2002, s 12(3A)) (SI 2009/268)[1] |

**Children and Young Persons Act 2008 (c 23)**—*contd*

|  |  |  |
|---|---|---|
|  |  | 1 Apr 2009 (E) (otherwise) (SI 2009/268)[1] |
|  |  | 31 Mar 2010 (W) (SI 2010/749) |
|  | (5)–(7) | 1 Apr 2009 (E) (SI 2009/268)[1] |
|  |  | 31 Mar 2010 (W) (SI 2010/749) |
| 35 |  | 12 Feb 2009 (E) (SI 2009/268) |
|  |  | 6 Apr 2009 (W) (SI 2009/728) |
| 36–38 |  | 1 Sep 2009 (SI 2009/1921; SI 2009/2273) |
| 39 |  | See Sch 3 below |
| 40, 41 |  | 13 Nov 2008 (s 44(1)) |
| 42 |  | See Sch 4 below |
| 43–45 |  | 13 Nov 2008 (s 44(1)) |
| Sch 1 | para 1 | 1 Apr 2011 (E) (SI 2010/2981) |
|  |  | 6 Apr 2016 (W) (SI 2016/452) |
|  | para 2(1)–(3) | 1 Apr 2011 (E) (SI 2010/2981) |
|  |  | 6 Apr 2016 (W) (SI 2016/452) |
|  | para 2(4)–(7) | 15 Nov 2010 (E) (SI 2010/2714) |
|  |  | 6 Apr 2016 (W) (SI 2016/452) |
|  | para 3(1)–(3) | 1 Apr 2011 (E) (SI 2010/2981) |
|  |  | 6 Apr 2016 (W) (SI 2016/452) |
|  | para 3(4) | 1 Apr 2011 (E) (SI 2010/2981) |
|  |  | *Not yet in force* (W) |
|  | para 4 | 1 Sep 2009 (E) (SI 2009/2273) |
|  |  | 26 Apr 2010 (W) (SI 2010/1329) |
|  | paras 5, 6 | 1 Apr 2011 (E) (SI 2010/2981) |
|  |  | 6 Apr 2016 (W) (SI 2016/452) |
|  | para 7 | 1 Apr 2011 (E) (SI 2010/2981) |
|  |  | *Not yet in force* (W) |
|  | para 8 | 1 Apr 2011 (E) (SI 2010/2981) |
|  |  | *Never in force* (W) (repealed) |
|  | paras 9–14 | 1 Apr 2011 (E) (SI 2010/2981) |
|  |  | *Not yet in force* (W) |
|  | paras 15–18 | 1 Apr 2011 (E) (SI 2010/2981) |
|  |  | 6 Apr 2016 (W) (SI 2016/452) |
|  | para 19 | 1 Apr 2011 (E) (SI 2010/2981) |
|  |  | 1 Dec 2017 (W) (SI 2017/948) |
|  | para 20 | 1 Apr 2011 (E) (SI 2010/2981) |
|  |  | *Not yet in force* (W) |
|  | para 21 | 1 Apr 2011 (E) (SI 2010/2981) |
|  |  | 6 Apr 2016 (W) (SI 2016/452) |
| Sch 2 |  | 12 Feb 2009 (E) (SI 2009/268) |
|  |  | 31 Mar 2010 (W) (SI 2010/749) |
| Sch 3 | paras 1–3 | 13 Nov 2008 (s 44(1)) |
|  | para 4 | Comes into force on the same day as the Carers and Disabled Children Act 2000, s 7(1) comes into force for the purposes of inserting the Children Act 1989, s 17B in relation to Wales (s 44(9)) |
|  | paras 5–28 | 13 Nov 2008 (s 44(1)) |
| Sch 4 |  | 1 Apr 2009 (E) (repeals of or in Adoption and Children Act 2002, s 12) (SI 2009/268) |
|  |  | 6 Apr 2009 (repeals of or in Children Act 1989, s 45) (SI 2009/268; SI 2009/728) |
|  |  | 1 Sep 2009 (repeals of or in Children Act 1989, ss 12, 91) (SI 2009/1921; SI 2009/2273) |
|  |  | 31 Mar 2010 (W) (repeals of or in Adoption and Children Act 2002, s 12) (SI 2010/739) |
|  |  | 1 Apr 2010 (E) (repeals of or in Care Standards Act 2000, s 21) (SI 2009/3354) |
|  |  | 28 Mar 2011 (W) (SI 2011/949), repeals of or in— |
|  |  | Children Act 1989, s 104; |

**Children and Young Persons Act 2008 (c 23)**—*contd*

> Care Standards Act 2000, s 21
> 1 Apr 2011 (E) (SI 2010/2981)[4], otherwise, except repeals of or in—
>> Care Standards Act 2000, s 5;
>> Children and Young Persons Act 2008
> 19 Jun 2012 (W) (SI 2012/1553), repeals of or in—
>> Children Act 1989, ss 17, 23B, Sch 2, para 6
> 6 Apr 2016 (SI 2016/452), repeals of or in—
>> Children Act 1989, s 26[7]
> 1 Dec 2017 (W) (SI 2017/948), repeals of or in—
>> Children Act 1989, ss 59, 105(1);
>> Income Tax (Trading and Other Income) Act 2005, s 806(5);
>> Childcare Act 2006, s 18(8)(a)
> *Not yet in force* (W), repeals of or in—
>> Children Act 1989, Sch 2, para 17;
>> Criminal Justice Act 1991;
>> Care Standards Act 2000, s 5 (also not yet in force in relation to England);
>> Adoption and Children Act 2002, s 118;
>> Education and Inspections Act 2006;
>> Safeguarding Vulnerable Groups Act 2006;
>> Children and Young Persons Act 2008 (also not yet in force in relation to England)

[1]  For a saving, see SI 2009/268, art 4

[2]  The specified local authorities are:

  (a)  Liverpool City Council,

  (b)  Kent County Council,

  (c)  Sandwell Metropolitan Borough Council,

  (d)  Blackburn with Darwen Borough Council,

  (e)  Hillingdon London Borough Council, and

  (f)  Staffordshire County Council

[3]  The specified local authorities are:

  (a)  Bristol City Council,

  (b)  Coventry City Council,

  (c)  Lincolnshire County Council,

  (d)  Norfolk County Council,

  (e)  North Tyneside Council,

  (f)  Northumberland County Council,

  (g)  Peterborough City Council,

  (h)  South Tyneside Council,

  (i)  Wakefield Council, and

  (j)  Warwickshire County Council

[4]  For transitional provisions and savings, see SI 2010/2981, arts 5, 6

[5]  The specified local authorities are:

  (a)  Barnet London Borough Council,

  (b)  Redbridge London Borough Council,

  (c)  Shropshire Council, and

  (d)  Sunderland City Council

[6]  For a transitional provision, see SI 2012/1553, art 3

**Children and Young Persons Act 2008 (c 23)**—*contd*
7   For a saving provision, see SI 2016/452, art 3

---

**Church of England Marriage Measure 2008 (No 1)**

*RA:* 22 May 2008

This Measure is brought into force on 1 Oct 2008 by an instrument made by the Archbishops of Canterbury and York, and dated 22 May 2008 (made under s 5(2))

---

**Climate Change Act 2008 (c 27)**

*RA:* 26 Nov 2008

*Commencement provisions:* s 100

| | | |
|---|---|---|
| 1–43 | | 26 Nov 2008 (s 100(1)) |
| 44–70 | | 26 Jan 2009 (s 100(5)) |
| 71 | (1) | See Sch 5 below |
| | (2), (3) | 26 Jan 2009 (s 100(5)) |
| 72–80 | | 26 Jan 2009 (s 100(5)) |
| 81 | | *Not yet in force* (sub-s (3) repealed) |
| 82 | | 1 Jan 2009 (s 100(4)) |
| 83–88 | | 26 Jan 2009 (s 100(5)) |
| 89–101 | | 26 Nov 2008 (s 100(1)) |
| Schs 1–4 | | 26 Jan 2009 (s 100(5)) |
| Sch 5 | | *Never in force* (repealed) |
| Schs 6–8 | | 26 Jan 2009 (s 100(5)) |

---

**Consolidated Fund Act 2008 (c 33)**

*RA:* 18 Dec 2008

Whole Act in force 18 Dec 2008 (RA)

---

**Counter-Terrorism Act 2008 (c 28)**

*RA:* 26 Nov 2008

*Commencement provisions:* s 100; Counter-Terrorism Act 2008 (Commencement No 1) Order 2008, SI 2008/3296; Counter-Terrorism Act 2008 (Commencement No 2) Order 2008, SI 2009/58; Counter-Terrorism Act 2008 (Commencement No 3) Order 2009, SI 2009/1256; Counter-Terrorism Act 2008 (Commencement No 4) Order 2009, SI 2009/1493; Counter-Terrorism Act 2008 (Commencement No 5) Order 2012, SI 2012/1121; Counter-Terrorism Act 2008 (Commencement No 6) Order 2012, SI 2012/1724; Counter-Terrorism Act 2008 (Commencement No 7) Order 2012, SI 2012/1966

| | |
|---|---|
| 1–18 | *Not yet in force* (ss 1(1)(e), 10–13, 14(4)–(6), 16, 17 repealed) |
| 19–21 | 24 Dec 2008 (SI 2008/3296) |
| 22, 23 | 10 Jul 2012 (SI 2012/1724) |
| 24 | *Not yet in force* |
| 25 | 10 Jul 2012 (E) (W) (S) (SI 2012/1724) |
| | *Not yet in force* (NI) |
| 26 | 30 Apr 2012 (SI 2012/1121) |
| 27 | 26 Jul 2012 (E) (W) (S) (SI 2012/1966) |
| | *Not yet in force* (NI) |
| 28 | 18 Jun 2009 (SI 2009/1256) |
| 29 | 16 Feb 2009 (SI 2009/58) |
| 30–39 | 18 Jun 2009 (SI 2009/1256) |
| 40–61 | 1 Oct 2009 (SI 2009/1493) |

**Counter-Terrorism Act 2008 (c 28)**—*contd*

| | | |
|---|---|---|
| 62–73 | | 27 Nov 2008 (s 100(2)) |
| 74–84 | | 16 Feb 2009 (SI 2009/58) |
| 85–90 | | 26 Jan 2009 (s 100(3)) |
| 91 | | In force when the Justice (Northern Ireland) Act 2002, s 27 comes into force (s 91(3)) |
| 92–98 | | 26 Nov 2008 (s 100(1)) |
| 99 | | See Sch 9 below |
| 100–102 | | 26 Nov 2008 (s 100(1)) |
| Sch 1 | | 24 Dec 2008 (SI 2008/3296) |
| Schs 2, 3 | | 18 Jun 2009 (SI 2009/1256) |
| Schs 4–6 | | 1 Oct 2009 (SI 2009/1493) |
| Sch 7 | | 27 Nov 2008 (s 100(2)) |
| Sch 8 | | 16 Feb 2009 (SI 2009/58) |
| Sch 9 | Pt 1 | *Not yet in force* |
| | Pt 2 | 16 Feb 2009 (SI 2009/58) |
| | Pt 3 | 18 Jun 2009 (SI 2009/1256) |
| | Pts 4–6 | 16 Feb 2009 (SI 2009/58) |

---

**Criminal Evidence (Witness Anonymity) Act 2008 (c 15)**

*RA:* 21 Jul 2008

*Commencement provisions*: s 13

Whole Act in force 21 Jul 2008 (s 13)

---

**Criminal Justice and Immigration Act 2008 (c 4)**

*RA:* 8 May 2008

*Commencement provisions:* s 153; Criminal Justice and Immigration Act 2008 (Commencement No 1 and Transitional Provisions) Order 2008, SI 2008/1466; Criminal Justice and Immigration Act 2008 (Commencement No 2 and Transitional and Saving Provisions) Order 2008, SI 2008/1586[2]; Criminal Justice and Immigration Act 2008 (Commencement No 3 and Transitional Provisions) Order 2008, SI 2008/2712; Criminal Justice and Immigration Act 2008 (Commencement No 4 and Saving Provision) Order 2008, SI 2008/2993; Criminal Justice and Immigration Act 2008 (Commencement No 5) Order 2008, SI 2008/3260; Criminal Justice and Immigration Act 2008 (Commencement No 6 and Transitional Provisions) Order 2009, SI 2009/140; Criminal Justice and Immigration Act 2008 (Commencement No 7) Order 2009, SI 2009/860; Criminal Justice and Immigration Act 2008 (Commencement No 8) Order 2009, SI 2009/1028; Criminal Justice and Immigration Act 2008 (Commencement No 9) Order 2009, SI 2009/1678; Criminal Justice and Immigration (2008 Act) (Commencement No 1) Order (Northern Ireland) 2009, SR 2009/243; Criminal Justice and Immigration Act 2008 (Commencement No 10) Order 2009, SI 2009/1842; Criminal Justice and Immigration Act 2008 (Commencement No 11) Order 2009, SI 2009/2606; Criminal Justice and Immigration Act 2008 (Commencement No 12) Order 2009, SI 2009/2780; Criminal Justice and Immigration Act 2008 (Commencement No 13 and Transitory Provision) Order 2009, SI 2009/3074; Criminal Justice and Immigration Act 2008 (Commencement No 14) Order 2010, SI 2010/712; Criminal Justice and Immigration (2008 Act) (Commencement No 2) Order (Northern Ireland) 2010, SR 2010/349; Criminal Justice and Immigration Act 2008 (Commencement No 15) Order 2013, SI 2013/616

| | | |
|---|---|---|
| 1 | (1)–(4) | 30 Nov 2009 (SI 2009/3074) |
| | (5) | See Sch 1 below |
| | (6) | 30 Nov 2009 (SI 2009/3074) |
| 2–5 | | 30 Nov 2009 (SI 2009/3074) |
| 6 | (1) | 30 Nov 2009 (except to the extent it abolishes attendance centre orders) (SI 2009/3074) |
| | | *Not yet in force* (exception noted above) |
| | (2), (3) | See Sch 4 below |
| 7, 8 | | 30 Nov 2009 (SI 2009/3074) |

**Criminal Justice and Immigration Act 2008 (c 4)**—*contd*

| | | |
|---|---|---|
| 9 | | *Not yet in force* |
| 10 | | 14 Jul 2008 (SI 2008/1586) |
| 11 | (1) | 14 Jul 2008 (SI 2008/1586)[2] |
| | (2)–(8) | *Not yet in force* |
| 12 | | 14 Jul 2008 (SI 2008/1586) |
| 13–18 | | 14 Jul 2008 (SI 2008/1586)[2] |
| 19 | | *Not yet in force* |
| 20 | | 14 Jul 2008 (SI 2008/1586) |
| 21 | (1) | 3 Nov 2008 (SI 2008/2712) |
| | (2) | 31 Oct 2009 (SI 2009/2606) |
| | (3)–(7) | 3 Nov 2008 (SI 2008/2712) |
| 22, 23 | | 3 Nov 2008 (SI 2008/2712) |
| 24 | | 14 Jul 2008 (SI 2008/1586) |
| 25 | | 14 Jul 2008 (SI 2008/1586)[2] |
| 26 | | 9 Jun 2008 (except in so far as sub-s (2) inserts Criminal Justice Act 1991, s 33(1C), (1D)) (SI 2008/1466)[1] |
| | | 31 Oct 2009 (exception noted above) (SI 2009/2606) |
| 27, 28 | | 14 Jul 2008 (SI 2008/1586) |
| 29 | | 14 Jul 2008 (except in so far as sub-s (2) inserts Criminal Justice Act 2003, s 255A(9), (10)) (SI 2008/1586)[2] |
| | | 31 Oct 2009 (exception noted above) (SI 2009/2606) |
| 30 | | 14 Jul 2008 (SI 2008/1586)[2] |
| 31, 32 | | 14 Jul 2008 (SI 2008/1586) |
| 33 | (1) | 3 Nov 2008 (SI 2008/2712) |
| | (2) | *Never in force* (repealed) |
| | (3) | 3 Nov 2008 (SI 2008/2712) |
| | (4) | *Never in force* (repealed) |
| | (5), (6) | 3 Nov 2008 (SI 2008/2712) |
| | (7), (8) | *Never in force* (repealed) |
| 34 | (1) | 3 Nov 2008 (SI 2008/2712) |
| | (2) | *Never in force* (repealed) |
| | (3) | 3 Nov 2008 (SI 2008/2712) |
| | (4)(a) | 3 Nov 2008 (SI 2008/2712) |
| | (4)(b) | *Never in force* (repealed) |
| | (5) | 3 Nov 2008 (SI 2008/2712) |
| | (6) | 3 Nov 2008 (except in so far as it provides that the Criminal Justice Act 2003, s 260(3A) ceases to have effect) (SI 2008/2712) |
| | | *Not yet in force* (exception noted above) |
| | (7) | *Never in force* (repealed) |
| | (8), (9) | 3 Nov 2008 (SI 2008/2712) |
| | (10) | *Never in force* (repealed) |
| 35–37 | | 27 Apr 2009 (SI 2009/860) |
| 38 | | 14 Jul 2008 (SI 2008/1586) |
| 39 | | *Not yet in force* |
| 40 | | 14 Jul 2008 (SI 2008/1586) |
| 41 | | 3 Nov 2008 (SI 2008/2712) |
| 42–45 | | 14 Jul 2008 (SI 2008/1586) |
| 46 | (1) | 14 Jul 2008 (SI 2008/1586) |
| | (2) | *Not yet in force* |
| | (3) | 14 Jul 2008 (SI 2008/1586) |
| 47 | | See Sch 8 below |
| 48 | (1)(a) | 1 Feb 2009 (SI 2009/140) |
| | (1)(b) | 16 Nov 2009 (in relation to the police areas of Cambridgeshire, Hampshire, Humberside, Merseyside and Norfolk) (SI 2009/2780) |
| | | *Never in force* (otherwise) (repealed) |
| | (2) | *Not yet in force* |
| 49, 50 | | 19 Dec 2008 (SI 2008/3260) |

**Criminal Justice and Immigration Act 2008 (c 4)**—*contd*

| | | |
|---|---|---|
| 51 | | See Sch 11 below |
| 52 | | See Sch 12 below |
| 53 | | 8 May 2008 (s 153(1)(a)) |
| 54–59 | | 14 Jul 2008 (SI 2008/1586) |
| 60 | | 3 Nov 2008 (SI 2008/2712)[3] |
| 61 | | 1 Dec 2008 (SI 2008/2993) |
| 62 | | 8 Jul 2008 (s 153(2)(a)) |
| 63–67 | | 26 Jan 2009 (SI 2008/2993) |
| 68 | | See Sch 14 below |
| 69 | | 8 Jul 2008 (s 153(2)(b)) |
| 70 | | 8 Jul 2008 (s 153(2)(c)) |
| 71 | | 26 Jan 2009 (SI 2008/2993) |
| 72 | | 14 Jul 2008 (SI 2008/1586) |
| 73 | | See Sch 15 below |
| 74 | | See Sch 16 below |
| 75 | | See Sch 17 below |
| 76 | | 14 Jul 2008 (SI 2008/1586) |
| 77 | | 8 May 2008 (s 153(1)(b)) |
| 78 | | *Not yet in force* |
| 79 | | 8 Jul 2008 (s 153(2)(d)) |
| 80–92 | | 1 Oct 2009 (SI 2009/2606) |
| 93–97 | | 14 Jul 2008 (SI 2008/1586) |
| 98–117 | | 3 Aug 2009 (SI 2009/1842) |
| 118 | | See Sch 20 below |
| 119 | (1)–(3) | 30 Nov 2009 (in relation to English NHS premises) (SI 2009/3074) |
| | | *Not yet in force (otherwise)* |
| | (4) | 1 Jan 2009 (in relation to English NHS premises) (SI 2008/3260) |
| | | *Not yet in force (otherwise)* |
| 120 | (1)–(4) | 30 Nov 2009 (in relation to English NHS premises) (SI 2009/3074) |
| | | *Not yet in force (otherwise)* |
| | (5), (6) | 1 Jan 2009 (in relation to English NHS premises) (SI 2008/3260) |
| | | *Not yet in force (otherwise)* |
| 121 | (1)–(3) | 1 Jan 2009 (in relation to English NHS premises) (SI 2008/3260) |
| | | *Not yet in force (otherwise)* |
| | (4) | 30 Nov 2009 (in relation to English NHS premises) (SI 2009/3074) |
| | | *Not yet in force (otherwise)* |
| | (5), (6) | 1 Jan 2009 (in relation to English NHS premises) (SI 2008/3260) |
| | | *Not yet in force (otherwise)* |
| 122 | | See Sch 21 below |
| 123, 124 | | 1 Feb 2009 (SI 2009/140) |
| 125 | | 1 Apr 2009 (SI 2009/860) |
| 126 | | See Sch 22 below |
| 127 | | See Sch 23 below |
| 128 | | 8 May 2008 (s 153(1)(c)) |
| 129 | | 3 Nov 2008 (SI 2008/2712) |
| 130–133 | | *Not yet in force* |
| 134 | | *Not yet in force* (s 134(6) repealed) |
| 135 | | *Not yet in force* (s 135(3), (7) repealed) |
| 136, 137 | | *Not yet in force* |
| 138 | (1)–(4) | 8 May 2008 (s 153(1)(d)) |
| | (5) | *Not yet in force* |
| 139 | | 8 May 2008 (s 153(1)(d)) |
| 140–142 | | 14 Jul 2008 (SI 2008/1586) |
| 143 | | 1 Apr 2009 (SI 2009/860) |

**Criminal Justice and Immigration Act 2008 (c 4)**—*contd*

| | | |
|---|---|---|
| 144 | (1) | 1 Oct 2009 (in so far as inserts Data Protection Act 1998, ss 55A(4), (5), (7), (9), 55B(2), (3)(b), (6), 55C and 55E) (SI 2009/2606) |
| | | 6 Apr 2010 (otherwise) (SI 2010/712) |
| | (2) | 1 Oct 2009 (SI 2009/2606) |
| 145 | | See Sch 25 below |
| 146 | | 1 Apr 2009 (SI 2009/860) |
| 147 | | 8 May 2008 (s 153(1)(e)) |
| 148 | (1) | See Sch 26 below |
| | (2) | See Sch 27 below |
| | (3)–(7) | 8 May 2008 (s 153(1)(f)) |
| | (8)–(10) | *Not yet in force* |
| 149 | | See Sch 28 below |
| 150 | | 8 May 2008 (s 153(1)(g)) |
| 151 | | 31 Oct 2009 (SI 2009/2606) |
| 152 | | 8 May 2008 (s 153(1)(g)) |
| 153 | | 8 May 2008 (s 153(1)(h)) |
| 154 | | 8 May 2008 (s 153(1)(i)) |
| Sch 1 | paras 1–25 | 30 Nov 2009 (SI 2009/3074) |
| | para 26(1)–(4) | 30 Nov 2009 (SI 2009/3074) |
| | para 26(5) | 1 Apr 2009 (SI 2009/860) |
| | para 26(6), (7) | 30 Nov 2009 (SI 2009/3074) |
| | paras 27–34 | 30 Nov 2009 (SI 2009/3074) |
| | para 35 | 1 Apr 2009 (SI 2009/860) |
| | para 36 | 30 Nov 2009 (SI 2009/3074) |
| Schs 2, 3 | | 30 Nov 2009 (SI 2009/3074) |
| Sch 4 | paras 1, 2 | 30 Nov 2009 (SI 2009/3074) |
| | para 3(1), (2) | 30 Nov 2009 (SI 2009/3074) |
| | para 3(3) | *Not yet in force* |
| | para 3(4) | 30 Nov 2009 (SI 2009/3074) |
| | para 3(5) | *Not yet in force* |
| | paras 4–23 | 30 Nov 2009 (SI 2009/3074) |
| | para 24 | 30 Nov 2009 (except in so far as repeals entry relating to Sch 5 to the PCCSA 2000 in the Magistrates' Courts Act 1980, Sch 6A) (SI 2009/3074) |
| | | *Not yet in force* (exception noted above) |
| | para 25 | *Not yet in force* |
| | paras 26–53 | 30 Nov 2009 (SI 2009/3074) |
| | para 54 | 30 Nov 2009 (in so far as repeals words "any community order or" in the Powers of Criminal Courts (Sentencing) Act 2000, s 74(3)(a)) (SI 2009/3074) |
| | | *Not yet in force* (otherwise) |
| | paras 55, 56 | 30 Nov 2009 (SI 2009/3074) |
| | para 57 | 30 Nov 2009 (except in so far as repeals Powers of Criminal Courts (Sentencing) Act 2000, s 137(2)(b)) (SI 2009/3074) |
| | | *Not yet in force* (otherwise) |
| | paras 58, 59(a), (b) | 30 Nov 2009 (SI 2009/3074) |
| | para 59(c) | *Not yet in force* |
| | paras 59(d), 60(1) | 30 Nov 2009 (SI 2009/3074) |
| | para 60(2) | 30 Nov 2009 (in so far as repeals words "40(1), 40C(1) or" in sub-s (2)(a) of and words "40(2)(b), 40C(2), 68" in sub-s (2)(b) of the Powers of Criminal Courts (Sentencing) Act 2000, s 160) (SI 2009/3074) |
| | | *Never in force* (in so far as repeals remainder of s 160(2) of the 2000 Act) (repealed) |
| | para 60(3) | 30 Nov 2009 (SI 2009/3074) |
| | para 60(4) | 30 Nov 2009 (in so far as repeals words "37(6), 40(2), 40A(6), 40C(2)" in sub-s (5)(a) of and sub-s (5)(b) of the Powers of Criminal Courts (Sentencing) Act 2000, s 160) (SI 2009/3074) |

**Criminal Justice and Immigration Act 2008 (c 4)**—*contd*

| | | |
|---|---|---|
| | | *Never in force* (in so far as repeals remainder of s 160(5) of the 2000 Act) (repealed) |
| | para 61(a) | 30 Nov 2009 (except in so far as repeals definitions "attendance centre", "attendance centre order" and "youth community order" in the Powers of Criminal Courts (Sentencing) Act 2000, s 163) (SI 2009/3074) |
| | | *Not yet in force* (exceptions noted above) |
| | para 61(b), (c) | 30 Nov 2009 (SI 2009/3074) |
| | paras 62–91 | 30 Nov 2009 (SI 2009/3074) |
| | para 92(a) | *Not yet in force* |
| | para 92(b) | 30 Nov 2009 (SI 2009/3074) |
| | para 92(c) | *Not yet in force* |
| | paras 93–109 | 30 Nov 2009 (SI 2009/3074) |
| Sch 5 | | 14 Jul 2008 (SI 2008/1586)[2] |
| Sch 6 | | 3 Nov 2008 (SI 2008/2712) |
| Sch 7 | | *Not yet in force* |
| Sch 8 | | 14 Jul 2008 (SI 2008/1586)[2] |
| Sch 9 | para 1 | 1 Feb 2009 (SI 2009/140) |
| | para 2 | 16 Nov 2009 (in relation to the police areas of Cambridgeshire, Hampshire, Humberside, Merseyside and Norfolk) (SI 2009/2780) |
| | | *Never in force* (otherwise) (repealed) |
| | para 3 | 1 Feb 2009 (in so far as inserts Crime and Disorder Act 1998, ss 66G, 66H) (SI 2009/140) |
| | | 1 Apr 2009 (in so far as inserts Crime and Disorder Act 1998, s 66C) (SI 2009/860) |
| | | 16 Nov 2009 (in so far as inserts ss 66A, 66B, 66D–66F of that Act, in relation to the police areas of Cambridgeshire, Hampshire, Humberside, Merseyside and Norfolk) (SI 2009/2780) |
| | | 8 Apr 2013 (otherwise) (SI 2013/616) |
| | para 4 | 1 Feb 2009 (SI 2009/140) |
| Sch 10 | | 19 Dec 2008 (SI 2008/3260) |
| Sch 11 | | 3 Nov 2008 (SI 2008/2712) |
| Sch 12 | | 14 Jul 2008 (SI 2008/1586) |
| Sch 13 | | 8 May 2008 (s 153(1)(a)) |
| Sch 14 | | 26 Jan 2009 (SI 2008/2993) |
| Sch 15 | para 1 | 14 Jul 2008 (SI 2008/1586) |
| | paras 2–7 | 8 Jul 2008 (s 153(2)(e)) |
| Sch 16 | paras 1–5 | 23 Mar 2010 (SI 2010/712) |
| | para 6(1), (2) | 23 Mar 2010 (SI 2010/712) |
| | para 6(3) | 8 May 2008 (s 153(1)(j)) |
| | paras 7–11 | 23 Mar 2010 (SI 2010/712) |
| | paras 12–16 | 8 May 2008 (s 153(1)(j)) |
| | para 17 | 23 Mar 2010 (SI 2010/712) |
| Sch 17 | | 30 Nov 2009 (SI 2009/3074) |
| Schs 18, 19 | | 1 Oct 2009 (SI 2009/2606) |
| Sch 20 | | 1 Dec 2008 (SI 2008/2993) |
| Sch 21 | para 1(1)–(3) | 18 Oct 2010 (SR 2010/349) |
| | para 1(4) | 22 Jun 2009 (in relation to HSS premises) (SR 2009/243) |
| | | 18 Oct 2010 (otherwise) (SR 2010/349) |
| | para 2(1)–(4) | 18 Oct 2010 (SR 2010/349) |
| | para 2(5) | 22 Jun 2009 (in relation to HSS premises) (SR 2009/243) |
| | | 18 Oct 2010 (otherwise) (SR 2010/349) |
| | para 3(1)–(3) | 22 Jun 2009 (in relation to HSS premises) (SR 2009/243) |
| | | 18 Oct 2010 (otherwise) (SR 2010/349) |
| | para 3(4) | 18 Oct 2010 (SR 2010/349) |
| | para 3(5) | 22 Jun 2009 (in relation to HSS premises) (SR 2009/243) |
| | | 18 Oct 2010 (otherwise) (SR 2010/349) |
| Sch 22 | paras 1, 2 | 3 Nov 2008 (SI 2008/2712) |

**See Halsbury's Statutes Citator for amendments to these Acts** 1957

**Criminal Justice and Immigration Act 2008 (c 4)**—*contd*

| | | |
|---|---|---|
| | paras 3, 4 | 3 Nov 2008 (for the purposes of making regulations) (SI 2008/2712)[3] |
| | | 1 Dec 2008 (otherwise) (SI 2008/2993)[4] |
| | para 5 | 1 Dec 2008 (SI 2008/2993)[4] |
| | para 6 | 14 Jul 2008 (SI 2008/1586) |
| | para 7 | 3 Nov 2008 (for the purposes of making regulations) (SI 2008/2712)[3] |
| | | 1 Dec 2008 (otherwise) (SI 2008/2993)[4] |
| | para 8 | 3 Nov 2008 (for the purpose of making rules) (SI 2008/2712)[3] |
| | | 1 Dec 2008 (otherwise) (SI 2008/2993)[4] |
| | para 9 | 1 Dec 2008 (SI 2008/2993)[4] |
| | para 10 | *Not yet in force* |
| | para 11 | 1 Dec 2008 (SI 2008/2993)[4] |
| | paras 12–16 | 30 Nov 2009 (SI 2009/3074) |
| | paras 17–21 | 1 Dec 2008 (SI 2008/2993) |
| Sch 23 | paras 1–3 | 3 Nov 2008 (SI 2008/2712) |
| | para 4 | 1 Dec 2008 (SI 2008/2993)[4] |
| | para 5 | 3 Nov 2008 (for the purposes of making regulations) (SI 2008/2712)[3] |
| | | 1 Dec 2008 (otherwise) (SI 2008/2993)[4] |
| | paras 6–11 | 1 Dec 2008 (SI 2008/2993)[4] |
| | para 12(1) | 3 Nov 2008 (SI 2008/2712) |
| | para 12(2), (3) | 1 Dec 2008 (SI 2008/2993)[4] |
| | para 12(4) | 3 Nov 2008 (for the purposes of making regulations) (SI 2008/2712)[3] |
| | | 1 Dec 2008 (otherwise) (SI 2008/2993)[4] |
| | paras 13–18 | 1 Dec 2008 (SI 2008/2993)[4] |
| | para 19 | 3 Nov 2008 (for the purposes of making regulations) (SI 2008/2712)[3] |
| | | 1 Dec 2008 (otherwise) (SI 2008/2993)[4] |
| Sch 24 | | 14 Jul 2008 (SI 2008/1586) |
| Sch 25 | paras 1–23 | 31 Oct 2009 (SI 2009/1028) |
| | paras 24, 25 | *Not yet in force* (para 24 repealed) |
| | para 26(1), (2) | 31 Oct 2009 (SI 2009/1028) |
| | paras 26(3), (4), 27 | *Never in force* (repealed) |
| | paras 28–33 | 31 Oct 2009 (SI 2009/1028) |
| | para 34 | 31 Oct 2009 (SI 2009/2606) |
| Sch 26 | para 1 | *Not yet in force* |
| | para 2(1), (2) | 14 Jul 2008 (SI 2008/1586) |
| | para 2(3) | *Not yet in force* |
| | para 2(4)–(6) | 14 Jul 2008 (SI 2008/1586) |
| | paras 3, 4 | 14 Jul 2008 (SI 2008/1586) |
| | para 5 | 3 Nov 2008 (SI 2008/2712) |
| | paras 6–8 | 14 Jul 2008 (SI 2008/1586) |
| | para 9 | 9 Jun 2008 (SI 2008/1466) |
| | paras 10, 11 | 14 Jul 2008 (SI 2008/1586) |
| | para 12(1) | 9 Jun 2008 (SI 2008/1466) |
| | para 12(2) | 14 Jul 2008 (SI 2008/1586) |
| | para 12(3)(a) | 14 Jul 2008 (SI 2008/1586) |
| | para 12(3)(b) | 9 Jun 2008 (SI 2008/1466) |
| | para 12(4) | 14 Jul 2008 (SI 2008/1586) |
| | paras 13–18 | 14 Jul 2008 (SI 2008/1586) |
| | para 19(1) | 9 Jun 2008 (SI 2008/1466) |
| | para 19(2), (3) | 14 Jul 2008 (SI 2008/1586) |
| | para 19(4) | 9 Jun 2008 (SI 2008/1466)[1] |
| | para 19(5), (6) | 14 Jul 2008 (SI 2008/1586) |
| | para 20 | 16 Nov 2009 (in relation to the police areas of Cambridgeshire, Hampshire, Humberside, Merseyside and Norfolk) (SI 2009/2780) |

**Criminal Justice and Immigration Act 2008 (c 4)**—*contd*

|  |  |  |
|---|---|---|
|  | | *Not yet in force* (otherwise) |
|  | paras 21–23 | 14 Jul 2008 (SI 2008/1586) |
|  | para 24 | 8 Jul 2008 (s 153(2)(b)) |
|  | para 25 | 8 Jul 2008 (s 153(2)(c)) |
|  | paras 26–28 | 14 Jul 2008 (SI 2008/1586) |
|  | para 29(1), (2) | 9 Jun 2008 (SI 2008/1466) |
|  | para 29(3), (4) | 3 Nov 2008 (SI 2008/2712) |
|  | para 29(5) | 9 Jun 2008 (SI 2008/1466) |
|  | para 29(6), (7) | 3 Nov 2008 (SI 2008/2712) |
|  | para 30 | 14 Jul 2008 (SI 2008/1586) |
|  | para 31 | 9 Jun 2008 (SI 2008/1466) |
|  | para 32 | 14 Jul 2008 (SI 2008/1586) |
|  | para 33(1)–(3) | 9 Jun 2008 (SI 2008/1466) |
|  | para 33(4) | 14 Jul 2008 (SI 2008/1586) |
|  | para 34(1), (2) | 16 Nov 2009 (SI 2009/2780) |
|  | para 34(3) | 16 Nov 2009 (in relation to the police areas of Cambridgeshire, Hampshire, Humberside, Merseyside and Norfolk) (SI 2009/2780) |
|  | | *Not yet in force* (otherwise) |
|  | paras 35–39 | 8 May 2008 (s 153(1)(k)) |
|  | para 40 | 27 Apr 2009 (SI 2009/860) |
|  | para 41 | 14 Jul 2008 (SI 2008/1586) |
|  | paras 42, 43 | 27 Apr 2009 (SI 2009/860) |
|  | para 44 | 14 Jul 2008 (SI 2008/1586) |
|  | para 45(a) | 9 Jun 2008 (SI 2008/1466) |
|  | para 45(b) | 14 Jul 2008 (SI 2008/1586) |
|  | paras 46–48 | 14 Jul 2008 (SI 2008/1586) |
|  | para 49 | 27 Apr 2009 (SI 2009/860) |
|  | para 50 | *Not yet in force* |
|  | paras 51–53 | 14 Jul 2008 (SI 2008/1586) |
|  | paras 54, 55 | 31 Oct 2009 (SI 2009/2606) |
|  | para 56(1), (2)(a) | 14 Jul 2008 (SI 2008/1586) |
|  | para 56(2)(b), (3) | 31 Oct 2009 (SI 2009/2606) |
|  | para 56(4) | 14 Jul 2008 (SI 2008/1586) |
|  | para 57 | 14 Jul 2008 (SI 2008/1586) |
|  | para 58 | 26 Jan 2009 (SI 2008/2993) |
|  | para 59 | 14 Jul 2008 (SI 2008/1586) |
|  | para 60 | 8 Jul 2009 (in so far as relates to the amendments to the Criminal Justice Act 2003 made immediately before 8 Jul 2009 by the Police and Justice Act 2006, s 17) (SI 2009/1678) |
|  | | 8 Apr 2013 (otherwise) (SI 2013/616) |
|  | para 61 | 8 Jul 2009 (SI 2009/1678) |
|  | para 62 | 8 Jul 2009 (in so far as relates to the amendments to the Criminal Justice Act 2003 made immediately before 8 Jul 2009 by the Police and Justice Act 2006, s 17) (SI 2009/1678) |
|  | | 8 Apr 2013 (otherwise) (SI 2013/616) |
|  | para 63 | 15 Jul 2008 (SI 2008/1586) |
|  | paras 64–69 | 14 Jul 2008 (SI 2008/1586) |
|  | para 70 | 23 Mar 2010 (SI 2010/712) |
|  | para 71 | 14 Jul 2008 (SI 2008/1586)[2] |
|  | paras 72–76 | 14 Jul 2008 (SI 2008/1586) |
|  | para 77 | 8 May 2008 (s 153(1)(a)) |
|  | para 78 | 14 Jul 2008 (SI 2008/1586) |
|  | para 79 | 30 Nov 2009 (SI 2009/3074) |
|  | paras 80, 81 | 14 Jul 2008 (SI 2008/1586) |
|  | para 82 | 31 Oct 2009 (SI 2009/2606) |
|  | para 83 | 1 Apr 2010 (SI 2010/712) |
| Sch 27 | paras 1–5 | 30 Nov 2009 (SI 2009/3074) |
|  | para 6 | 14 Jul 2008 (SI 2008/1586) |

**Criminal Justice and Immigration Act 2008 (c 4)**—*contd*

|  |  |  |
|---|---|---|
|  | para 7 | 30 Nov 2009 (SI 2009/3074) |
|  | paras 8, 9 | 9 Jun 2008 (SI 2008/1466) |
|  | paras 10–12 | 14 Jul 2008 (SI 2008/1586) |
|  | para 13(1) | *Not yet in force* |
|  | para 13(2) | 14 Jul 2008 (SI 2008/1586) |
|  | paras 14–17 | 14 Jul 2008 (SI 2008/1586) |
|  | para 18 | 16 Nov 2009 (in relation to the police areas of Cambridgeshire, Hampshire, Humberside, Merseyside and Norfolk) (SI 2009/2780) |
|  |  | *Not yet in force* (otherwise) |
|  | paras 19, 20 | 19 Dec 2008 (SI 2008/3260) |
|  | para 21 | 14 Jul 2008 (SI 2008/1586) |
|  | para 22 | 1 Dec 2008 (SI 2008/2993) |
|  | para 23 | 26 Jan 2009 (SI 2008/2993) |
|  | para 24 | 8 Jul 2008 (s 153(2)(f)) |
|  | para 25 | 26 Jan 2009 (SI 2008/2993) |
|  | para 26 | 30 Nov 2009 (SI 2009/3074) |
|  | para 27 | 14 Jul 2008 (SI 2008/1586) |
|  | para 28 | *Not yet in force* |
|  | para 29 | 1 Oct 2009 (SI 2009/2606) |
|  | para 30 | 14 Jul 2008 (SI 2008/1586) |
|  | paras 31, 32 | 3 Aug 2009 (SI 2009/1842) |
|  | paras 33, 34 | 1 Feb 2009 (SI 2009/140) |
|  | para 35(1) | 1 Dec 2008 (SI 2008/2993) |
|  | para 35(2)(a) | 1 Dec 2008 (SI 2008/2993) |
|  | para 35(2)(b) | 30 Nov 2009 (SI 2009/3074) |
|  | para 35(3) | 1 Dec 2008 (SI 2008/2993) |
|  | para 36 | *Not yet in force* |
|  | para 37 | 1 Apr 2009 (SI 2009/860) |
|  | para 38 | 14 Jul 2008 (SI 2008/1586) |
| Sch 28 | Pt 1 | 30 Nov 2009 (SI 2009/3074), repeals of or in— |

        Children and Young Persons Act 1933, s 34(7);

        Social Work (Scotland) Act 1968;

        Children and Young Persons Act 1969;

        Northern Ireland (Modification of Enactments – No 1) Order 1973, SI 1973/2163;

        Transfer of Functions (Local Government, etc) (Northern Ireland) Order 1973, SR & O 1973/256;

        Bail Act 1976;

        Magistrates' Courts Act 1980, Sch 6A (except entry relating to PCCSA 2000, Sch 5);

        Criminal Justice Act 1982, Sch 13;

        Mental Health Act 1983;

        Health and Social Services and Social Security Adjudications Act 1983;

        Children Act 1989;

        Criminal Justice Act 1991;

        Children (Prescribed Orders – Northern Ireland, Guernsey and Isle of Man) Regulations 1991, SI 1991/2032;

        Prisoners (Return to Custody) Act 1995;

        Children (Northern Ireland Consequential Amendments) Order 1995, SI 1995/756;

        Crime and Disorder Act 1998;

        Powers of Criminal Courts (Sentencing) Act 2000, as follows—

         Pt 4, Chapter 1 (except ss 33(1)(c), 36B),

         Pt 4, Chapter 2,

         Pt 4, Chapter 4 (s 60(1)(a) only),

         Pt 4, Chapter 5,

         s 74(3)(a) (words "any community order or"),

**Criminal Justice and Immigration Act 2008 (c 4)**—*contd*

         s 75,

         s 137(2)(a), (c), (d),

         s 159 (except words "paragraph 1(1) of Schedule 5 to this Act"),

         s 160(2) (words "40(1), 40C(1) or" in para (a) and words "40(2)(b), 40C(2), 68" in para (b)),

         s 160(3)(a),

         s 160(5)(a) (words "37(6), 40(2), 40A(6), 40C(2)" only),

         s 160(5)(b),

         s 163 (except definitions "attendance centre", "attendance centre order" and "youth community order"),

         Schs 3, 6–8,

         Sch 9 (except to the extent that para 80 thereof relates to the failure to comply with an attendance centre order or attendance centre rules),

         Schs 10, 11;

         Care Standards Act 2000;

         Criminal Justice and Court Services Act 2000, ss 46, 70, Sch 7 (except paras 196(a), (d), 197(a));

         Anti-social Behaviour Act 2003;

         Criminal Justice Act 2003 (except s 221, Sch 32, paras 8, 95 (in so far as relates to the references to an attendance centre order), 96, 102, 107, 123(3), (8))

     *Not yet in force*, repeals of or in—

         Children and Young Persons Act 1933, s 49;

         Magistrates' Courts Act 1980, Sch 6A (entry relating to PCCSA 2000, Sch 5);

         Contempt of Court Act 1981;

         Criminal Justice Act 1982, Sch 14;

         Powers of Criminal Courts (Sentencing) Act 2000, as follows—

         Pt 4, Chapter 1 (ss 33(1)(c), 36B only),

         Pt 4, Chapter 4 (except s 60(1)(a)),

         s 74(3)(a) (except words "any community order or"),

         s 137(2)(b),

         s 159 (words "paragraph 1(1) of Schedule 5 to this Act"),

         s 160(2) (except words "40(1), 40C(1) or" in para (a) and words "40(2)(b), 40C(2), 68" in para (b)),

         s 160(5)(a) (except words "37(6), 40(2), 40A(6), 40C(2)"),

         s 163 (definitions "attendance centre", "attendance centre order" and "youth community order"),

         Sch 5,

         Sch 9, para 80 (to the extent that it relates to the failure to comply with an attendance centre order or attendance centre rules);

         Criminal Justice and Court Services Act 2000, s 52, Sch 7, paras 196(a), (d), 197(a);

         Criminal Justice Act 2003, s 221, Sch 32, paras 8, 95 (in so far as relates to the references to an attendance centre order), 96, 102, 107, 123(3), (8)

    Pt 2       14 Jul 2008 (SI 2008/1586), repeals of or in—

         Criminal Justice Act 1991, ss 45, 46, 50;

         Crime (Sentences) Act 1997;

         Criminal Justice Act 2003, (except ss 142, 233, 260, 264A, 300)[2];

         SI 2005/950

     3 Nov 2008 (SI 2008/2712), repeals of or in—

         Criminal Justice Act 1991, s 46A;

         Criminal Justice Act 2003, s 260(3), (6)

     27 Apr 2009 (SI 2009/860), repeals of or in—

         Powers of Criminal Courts (Sentencing) Act 2000, s 17

**Criminal Justice and Immigration Act 2008 (c 4)**—*contd*

|  |  |
|---|---|
|  | 31 Oct 2009 (SI 2009/2606), repeals of or in— |
|  | Criminal Justice Act 2003, s 260(3A); |
|  | Armed Forces Act 2006, ss 221, 223, Sch 16 |
|  | 23 Mar 2010 (SI 2010/712), repeals of or in— |
|  | Criminal Justice Act 2003, s 233 |
|  | *Not yet in force*, repeals of or in— |
|  | Powers of Criminal Courts (Sentencing) Act 2000, s 92; |
|  | Criminal Justice Act 2003, ss 142, 264A, 300; |
|  | SI 2003/1605; |
|  | Armed Forces Act 2006, s 270 |
| Pt 3 | 14 Jul 2008 (except repeals in Courts-Martial (Appeals) Act 1968 and Criminal Justice Act 2003) (SI 2008/1586)[2] |
|  | *Not yet in force* (exceptions noted above) |
| Pt 4 | 8 May 2008 (repeals of or in Criminal Justice Act 2003, Sch 3, paras 13, 22, Sch 37, Pt 4) (s 153(1)(a)) |
|  | 8 Jul 2008 (repeals in Criminal Justice (Terrorism and Conspiracy) Act 1998) (s 153(2)(a)) |
|  | 14 Jul 2008 (SI 2008/1586), repeals of or in— |
|  | Magistrates' Courts Act 1980, s 13; |
|  | Prosecution of Offences Act 1985; |
|  | Access to Justice Act 1999; |
|  | Sexual Offences Act 2003; |
|  | Criminal Justice Act 2003, s 23A[5] |
|  | 3 Nov 2008 (SI 2008/2712), repeals of or in— |
|  | Children and Young Persons Act 1969; |
|  | Bail Act 1976 |
|  | *Not yet in force*, repeals of or in— |
|  | Magistrates' Courts Act 1980, s 24; |
|  | Powers of Criminal Courts (Sentencing) Act 2000; |
|  | Criminal Justice Act 2003, Sch 3, para 57, Sch 36 |
| Pt 5 | 8 May 2008 (repeals in Public Order Act 1986) (s 153(1)(j)) |
|  | 8 Jul 2008 (s 153(2)(d)), repeals of or in— |
|  | Criminal Libel Act 1819; |
|  | Law of Libel Amendment Act 1888 |
|  | 14 Jul 2008 (repeals in Sexual Offences Act 2003) (SI 2008/1586) |
|  | 30 Nov 2009 (repeals in Nuclear Material (Offences) Act 1983) (SI 2009/3074) |
|  | *Not yet in force*, repeals of or in— |
|  | Terrorism Act 2006 |
| Pt 6 | 14 Jul 2008 (SI 2008/1586) |
| Pt 7 | 1 Apr 2009 (SI 2009/860) |
| Pt 8 | 14 Jul 2008 (SI 2008/1586), repeals of or in— |
|  | Police Act 1996, s 54; |
|  | Police and Justice Act 2006, s 49, Sch 1 |
|  | 1 Dec 2008 (SI 2008/2993), repeals of or in— |
|  | Police Act 1996, s 50, Sch 6; |
|  | Police Reform Act 2002; |
|  | Legal Services Act 2007, Sch 21, para 119 |
|  | *Not yet in force*, repeals of or in— |
|  | Police Act 1996, s 97; |
|  | Greater London Authority Act 1999; |
|  | Criminal Justice and Police Act 2001; |
|  | Railways and Transport Safety Act 2003; |
|  | Police and Justice Act 2006, Sch 2; |
|  | Legal Services Act 2007, Sch 21, para 73 |

[1]    For transitional provisions, see SI 2008/1466, arts 3, 4

[2]    For transitional provisions, see SI 2008/1586, art 2(3), Sch 2

## Criminal Justice and Immigration Act 2008 (c 4)—*contd*

3     For transitional provisions, see SI 2008/2712, arts 3, 4

4     For savings, see SI 2008/2993, art 3

5     Note that SI 2009/1678, art 3(c) and SI 2013/616, art 2(d) also purport to bring these repeals into force on 8 Jul 2009 (for certain purposes) and 8 Apr 2013 respectively

## Crossrail Act 2008 (c 18)

*RA:* 22 Jul 2008

Whole Act in force 22 Jul 2008 (RA)

## Dormant Bank and Building Society Accounts Act 2008 (c 31)

*RA:* 26 Nov 2008

*Commencement provisions:* s 31; Dormant Bank and Building Society Accounts Act 2008 (Commencement and Transitional Provisions) Order 2009, SI 2009/490

| | |
|---|---|
| 1–27 | 12 Mar 2009 (SI 2009/490)[1] |
| 28–32 | 26 Nov 2008 (RA) |
| Schs 1–3 | 12 Mar 2009 (SI 2009/490)[1] |

1     For transitional provisions, see SI 2009/490, art 3

## Education and Skills Act 2008 (c 25)

*RA:* 26 Nov 2008

*Commencement provisions:* s 173; Education and Skills Act 2008 (Commencement No 1 and Savings) Order 2008, SI 2008/3077; Education and Skills Act 2008 (Commencement No 2 and Savings) Order 2009, SI 2009/387; Education and Skills Act 2008 (Commencement No 1 and Savings) (Wales) Order 2009, SI 2009/784; Education and Skills Act 2008 (Commencement No 3) Order 2009, SI 2009/1513, amended by SI 2009/1606; Education and Skills Act 2008 (Commencement No 4, Commencement No 3 (Amendment), Transitory and Saving Provisions) Order 2009, SI 2009/1606; Education and Skills Act 2008 (Commencement No 5) Order 2009, SI 2009/3316; Education and Skills Act 2008 (Commencement No 6) Order 2010, SI 2010/1093; Education and Skills Act 2008 (Commencement No 7 and Transitory Provisions) Order 2010, SI 2010/2906; Education and Skills Act 2008 (Commencement No 8) Order 2012, SI 2012/2197; Education and Skills Act 2008 (Commencement No 9 and Transitory Provision) Order 2013, SI 2013/1204; Education and Skills Act 2008 (Commencement No 10 and Transitory Provisions) Order 2014, SI 2014/2379; Education and Skills Act 2008 (Commencement No 11 and Saving and Transitory Provisions) Order 2014, SI 2014/3364

| | | |
|---|---|---|
| 1 | | 28 Jun 2013 (para (b) only, and with words "the first anniversary of the date on which the person ceased to be of compulsory school age" substituted for words "the age of 18") (SI 2013/1204) |
| | | 26 Jun 2015 (otherwise) (SI 2013/1204) |
| 2–8 | | 28 Jun 2013 (SI 2013/1204) |
| 9 | | *Never in force* (repealed) |
| 10–14 | | 28 Jun 2013 (SI 2013/1204) |
| 15 | | *Never in force* (repealed) |
| 16–18 | | 28 Jun 2013 (SI 2013/1204) |
| 19–38 | | *Not yet in force* |
| 39 | (1), (2) | 28 Jun 2013 (SI 2013/1204)[6] |
| | (3)–(6) | *Not yet in force* |
| 40–61 | | *Not yet in force* |
| 62 | (1), (2) | 28 Jun 2013 (SI 2013/1204) |
| | (3), (4) | *Not yet in force* |

**Education and Skills Act 2008 (c 25)**—*contd*

|  |  |  |
|---|---|---|
|  | (5), (6) | 28 Jun 2013 (SI 2013/1204) |
| 63 |  | *Not yet in force* |
| 64 | (1), (2) | 28 Jun 2013 (SI 2013/1204) |
|  | (3), (4) | *Not yet in force* |
|  | (5) | 28 Jun 2013 (SI 2013/1204) |
|  | (6) | *Not yet in force* |
| 65 |  | *Not yet in force* |
| 66 |  | 28 Jun 2013 (SI 2013/1204) |
| 67 |  | *Not yet in force* |
| 68–78 |  | 26 Jan 2009 (SI 2008/3077) |
| 79 |  | 26 Jan 2009 (to the extent that it repeals Learning and Skills Act 2000, ss 114(2), (3), (5), 115, 116, 118, 121) (SI 2008/3077) |
|  |  | 12 Jan 2010 (to the extent that it repeals s 114(1), (4), (6)–(10), 117, 119, 120 of that Act) (SI 2009/3316) |
| 80 |  | 26 Nov 2008 (s 173(1)(a)) |
| 81 |  | 1 Sep 2009 (SI 2009/1513) |
| 82 |  | 28 Feb 2009 (SI 2009/387) |
| 83, 84 |  | 7 Mar 2009 (SI 2009/387)[2] |
| 85 |  | 28 Feb 2009 (SI 2009/387) |
| 86 |  | 19 Jun 2009 (for the purposes of exercising any power to make subordinate legislation conferred by the Learning and Skills Act 2000, ss 4A–4C or Sch 1A) (SI 2009/1513) |
|  |  | 1 Aug 2009 (otherwise) (SI 2009/1606) |
| 87–91 |  | 26 Jan 2009 (SI 2008/3077) |
| 92 | (1) | 1 Sep 2009 (SI 2009/1606) |
|  | (2) | *Not yet in force* |
|  | (3) | 19 Jun 2009 (SI 2009/1513) |
|  | (4) | *Not yet in force* |
| 93 |  | 1 Sep 2009 (SI 2009/1606) |
| 94–97 |  | 19 Jun 2009 (for the purposes of making regulations) (SI 2009/1513) |
|  |  | 5 Jan 2015 (otherwise) (SI 2014/3364)[7] |
| 98, 99 |  | 19 Jun 2009 (for the purposes of making regulations) (SI 2009/1513) |
|  |  | 1 Jan 2011 (otherwise) (SI 2010/2906) |
| 100 |  | 19 Jun 2009 (for the purposes of making regulations) (SI 2009/1513) |
|  |  | 5 Jan 2015 (otherwise) (SI 2014/3364)[7] |
| 101–105 |  | 19 Jun 2009 (for the purposes of making regulations) (SI 2009/1513) |
|  |  | *Not yet in force* (otherwise) |
| 106 |  | 19 Jun 2009 (for the purposes of making regulations) (SI 2009/1513) |
|  |  | 8 Sep 2014 (otherwise) (SI 2014/2379) |
| 107 |  | 19 Jun 2009 (for the purposes of making regulations) (SI 2009/1513) |
|  |  | 8 Sep 2014 (otherwise) (SI 2014/2379) |
| 108 |  | 19 Jun 2009 (for the purposes of making regulations) (SI 2009/1513) |
|  |  | *Not yet in force* (otherwise) |
| 109, 110 |  | 19 Jun 2009 (for the purposes of making regulations) (SI 2009/1513) |
|  |  | 5 Jan 2015 (otherwise) (SI 2014/3364)[7] |
| 111 |  | 19 Jun 2009 (for the purposes of making regulations) (SI 2009/1513)[4] |
|  |  | 1 Sep 2009 (otherwise) (SI 2009/1606) |
| 112 | (1), (2) | 1 Sep 2009 (SI 2009/1606) |
|  | (3) | 5 Jan 2015 (SI 2014/3364)[7] |

**Education and Skills Act 2008 (c 25)**—*contd*

| | | |
|---|---|---|
| 113 | (1) | 19 Jun 2009 (for the purposes of making regulations) (SI 2009/1513) |
| | | 5 Jan 2015 (otherwise) (SI 2014/3364)[7] |
| | (2) | 19 Jun 2009 (for the purposes of making regulations) (SI 2009/1513) |
| | | *Not yet in force* (otherwise) |
| 114–116 | | 19 Jun 2009 (for the purposes of making regulations) (SI 2009/1513) |
| | | 5 Jan 2015 (otherwise) (SI 2014/3364)[7] |
| 117 | (1) | 12 Oct 2009 (SI 2009/1606) |
| | (2)(a), (b) | 5 Jan 2015 (SI 2014/3364)[7] |
| | (2)(c) | 12 Oct 2009 (SI 2009/1606) |
| 118 | | 19 Jun 2009 (for the purposes of making regulations) (SI 2009/1513) |
| | | 5 Jan 2015 (otherwise) (SI 2014/3364)[7] |
| 119 | | 19 Jun 2009 (for the purposes of making regulations) (SI 2009/1513) |
| | | 12 Oct 2009 (otherwise) (SI 2009/1606) |
| 120–122 | | 19 Jun 2009 (for the purposes of making regulations) (SI 2009/1513) |
| | | 5 Jan 2015 (otherwise) (SI 2014/3364)[7] |
| 123 | | 19 Jun 2009 (for the purposes of making regulations) (SI 2009/1513) |
| | | 1 Jan 2011 (otherwise) (SI 2010/2906) |
| 124 | (1)(a) | 12 Oct 2009 (for the purposes of appeals to the Tribunal against a decision of the Secretary of State to remove an institution from the register under s 119) (SI 2009/1606) |
| | | 1 Jan 2011 (for the purposes of appeals to the Tribunal against a decision of the Secretary of State to remove an institution from the register by virtue of s 123) (SI 2010/2906) |
| | | 5 Jan 2015 (otherwise) (SI 2014/3364)[7] |
| | (1)(b) | 12 Oct 2009 (for the purposes of appeals to the Tribunal against a decision of the Secretary of State to remove an institution from the register under s 119) (SI 2009/1606) |
| | | 1 Jan 2011 (for the purposes of appeals to the Tribunal against a decision of the Secretary of State to remove an institution from the register by virtue of s 123) (SI 2010/2906) |
| | | *Not yet in force* (otherwise) |
| | (1)(c)–(f) | 12 Oct 2009 (for the purposes of appeals to the Tribunal against a decision of the Secretary of State to remove an institution from the register under s 119) (SI 2009/1606)[5] |
| | | 1 Jan 2011 (for the purposes of appeals to the Tribunal against a decision of the Secretary of State to remove an institution from the register by virtue of s 123) (SI 2010/2906) |
| | | 5 Jan 2015 (otherwise) (SI 2014/3364)[7] |
| | (2)–(5) | 12 Oct 2009 (for the purposes of appeals to the Tribunal against a decision of the Secretary of State to remove an institution from the register under s 119) (SI 2009/1606) |
| | | 1 Jan 2011 (for the purposes of appeals to the Tribunal against a decision of the Secretary of State to remove an institution from the register by virtue of s 123) (SI 2010/2906) |
| | | 5 Jan 2015 (otherwise) (SI 2014/3364)[7] |
| 125 | (1)(a) | 19 Jun 2009 (for the purposes of making regulations) (SI 2009/1513) |
| | | 5 Jan 2015 (otherwise) (SI 2014/3364)[7] |
| | (1)(b) | 19 Jun 2009 (for the purposes of making regulations) (SI 2009/1513) |
| | | *Not yet in force* (otherwise) |
| | (1)(c), (d) | 19 Jun 2009 (for the purposes of making regulations) (SI 2009/1513) |

**Education and Skills Act 2008 (c 25)**—*contd*

|  |  |  |
|---|---|---|
|  |  | 5 Jan 2015 (otherwise) (SI 2014/3364)[7] |
|  | (2)–(7) | 19 Jun 2009 (for the purposes of making regulations) (SI 2009/1513) |
|  |  | 5 Jan 2015 (otherwise) (SI 2014/3364)[7] |
| 126 |  | 19 Jun 2009 (for the purposes of making regulations) (SI 2009/1513) |
|  |  | 5 Jan 2015 (otherwise) (SI 2014/3364)[7] |
| 127 |  | 12 Oct 2009 (SI 2009/1606) |
| 128 |  | 19 Jun 2009 (for the purposes of making regulations) (SI 2009/1513) |
|  |  | 8 Sep 2014 (otherwise) (SI 2014/2379) |
| 129–131 |  | 19 Jun 2009 (for the purposes of making regulations) (SI 2009/1513) |
|  |  | 8 Sep 2014 (otherwise) (SI 2014/2379) |
| 132, 133 |  | 19 Jun 2009 (for the purposes of making regulations) (SI 2009/1513) |
|  |  | *Not yet in force* (otherwise) |
| 134–136 |  | 19 Jun 2009 (for the purposes of making regulations) (SI 2009/1513) |
|  |  | 12 Oct 2009 (otherwise) (SI 2009/1606) |
| 137 |  | 1 Sep 2009 (SI 2009/1606) |
| 138 | (1) | 1 Sep 2009 (so far as necessary for the interpretation of provisions brought into force by SI 2009/1606, art 3 or made under such provisions) (SI 2009/1606) |
|  |  | 12 Oct 2009 (so far as necessary for the interpretation of provisions brought into force by SI 2009/1606, art 4 or made under such provisions) (SI 2009/1606) |
|  |  | 1 Jan 2011 (so far as necessary for the interpretation of provisions brought into force by SI 2010/2906, art 2 or made under such provisions) (SI 2010/2906) |
|  |  | 8 Sep 2014 (so far as necessary for the interpretation of provisions brought into force by SI 2014/2379, art 2 or made under such provisions) (SI 2014/2379) |
|  |  | 5 Jan 2015 (otherwise) (SI 2014/3364)[7] |
|  | (2) | 5 Jan 2015 (SI 2014/3364)[7] |
| 139 |  | 19 Jun 2009 (for the purposes of making regulations) (SI 2009/1513) |
|  |  | 5 Jan 2015 (otherwise) (SI 2014/3364)[7] |
| 140 | (1) | 5 Jan 2015 (SI 2014/3364)[7] |
|  | (2) | 19 Jun 2009 (for the purposes of making regulations) (SI 2009/1513) |
|  |  | 1 Sep 2009 (otherwise) (SI 2009/1606) |
| 141 |  | 19 Jun 2009 (for the purposes of making regulations) (SI 2009/1513) |
|  |  | 5 Jan 2015 (otherwise) (SI 2014/3364)[7] |
| 142–145 |  | 30 Mar 2010 (SI 2010/1093) |
| 146–148 |  | 1 Sep 2009 (SI 2009/1513) |
| 149 |  | 26 Jan 2009 (s 173(2)(a)) |
| 150 |  | 26 Jan 2009 (E) (SI 2008/3077)[1] |
|  |  | 31 Mar 2009 (W) (SI 2009/784) |
| 151 | (1) | See sub-ss (2)–(4) below |
|  | (2), (3) | 26 Jan 2009 (SI 2008/3077) |
|  | (4) | 2 Dec 2008 (in so far as inserts School Standards and Framework Act 1998, ss 88B–88I, 88K, 88L) (SI 2008/3077) |
|  |  | 26 Jan 2009 (in so far as inserts ss 88P, 88Q of that Act) (s 173(2)(b)) |
|  |  | 26 Jan 2009 (in so far as inserts ss 88J, 88M–88O of that Act) (SI 2008/3077) |
| 152 |  | 26 Jan 2009 (E) (SI 2008/3077)[1] |
|  |  | 31 Mar 2009 (W) (SI 2009/784)[3] |

**Education and Skills Act 2008 (c 25)**—*contd*

| | | |
|---|---|---|
| 153 | | 26 Jan 2009 (E) (SI 2008/3077)[1] |
| | | 31 Mar 2009 (W) (SI 2009/784) |
| 154 | | 30 Mar 2010 (for the purposes of making regulations) (SI 2010/1093) |
| | | 1 Sep 2010 (otherwise) (SI 2010/1093) |
| 155 | | 1 Sep 2012 (SI 2012/2197) |
| 156 | | 26 Nov 2008 (s 173(1)(b)) |
| 157, 158 | | *Not yet in force* |
| 159 | | 28 Feb 2009 (SI 2009/387) |
| 160 | | *Never in force* (repealed) |
| 161 | (1), (2), (3)(a) | 28 Feb 2009 (SI 2009/387) |
| | (3)(b), (4) | *Never in force* (repealed) |
| | (5)–(9) | 28 Feb 2009 (SI 2009/387) |
| | (10)–(13) | *Never in force* (repealed) |
| 162 | (1), (2), (3)(a), (b) | 31 Mar 2009 (SI 2009/784) |
| | (3)(c) | 31 Oct 2009 (SI 2009/784) |
| | (4)–(10) | 31 Mar 2009 (SI 2009/784) |
| 163 | | *Never in force* (repealed) |
| 164 | | 26 Jan 2009 (s 173(2)(c)) |
| 165 | | 26 Jan 2009 (E) (SI 2008/3077)[1] |
| | | *Not yet in force* (W) |
| 166–168 | | 26 Nov 2008 (s 173(1)(c)) |
| 169 | (1) | See Sch 1 below |
| | (2) | See Sch 2 below |
| 170–172 | | 26 Nov 2008 (s 173(1)(d)) |
| 173 | | 26 Nov 2008 (s 173(1)(e)) |
| 174 | | 26 Nov 2008 (s 173(1)(f)) |
| Sch 1 | paras 1–11 | *Not yet in force* (paras 1–4 repealed) |
| | para 12 | 8 Sep 2014 (SI 2014/2379) |
| | para 13 | See paras 14–24 below |
| | para 14 | *Not yet in force* |
| | paras 15–17 | 5 Jan 2015 (SI 2014/3364)[7] |
| | para 18 | 1 Sep 2009 (in so far as repeals Education Act 2002, s 162B(6), (7)) (SI 2009/1606)[5] |
| | | 5 Jan 2015 (in so far as repeals ss 162A, 162B(1)–(5) of that Act) (SI 2014/3364)[7] |
| | paras 19–25 | 5 Jan 2015 (SI 2014/3364)[7] |
| | paras 26, 27 | *Not yet in force* |
| | paras 28–38 | 5 Jan 2015 (SI 2014/3364)[7] |
| | para 39 | *Not yet in force* |
| | paras 40, 41 | 5 Jan 2015 (SI 2014/3364)[7] |
| | para 42 | *Not yet in force* |
| | para 43 | 1 Sep 2012 (SI 2012/2197) |
| | paras 44–47 | 26 Jan 2009 (SI 2008/3077) |
| | para 48 | See paras 49–52 below |
| | para 49 | *Not yet in force* |
| | paras 50–52 | 1 Sep 2012 (SI 2012/2197) |
| | para 53 | See paras 54–73 below |
| | para 54(1)–(4) | 26 Jan 2009 (E) (SI 2008/3077)[1] |
| | | 31 Mar 2009 (W) (SI 2009/784)[3] |
| | para 54(5)–(7) | 2 Dec 2008 (E) (SI 2008/3077)[1] |
| | | 31 Mar 2009 (W) (SI 2009/784)[3] |
| | para 54(8), (9) | 26 Jan 2009 (E) (SI 2008/3077)[1] |
| | | 31 Mar 2009 (W) (SI 2009/784)[3] |
| | para 55 | 26 Jan 2009 (E) (SI 2008/3077)[1] |
| | | 31 Mar 2009 (W) (SI 2009/784) |
| | para 56 | 26 Jan 2009 (SI 2008/3077) |
| | paras 57, 58 | 2 Dec 2008 (SI 2008/3077) |
| | para 59(1)–(6) | 26 Jan 2009 (SI 2008/3077) |

**Education and Skills Act 2008 (c 25)**—*contd*

| | |
|---|---|
| para 59(7) | 26 Jan 2009 (E) (SI 2008/3077)[1] |
| | 31 Mar 2009 (W) (SI 2009/784) |
| para 60 | 26 Jan 2009 (SI 2008/3077) |
| paras 61–64 | 2 Dec 2008 (SI 2008/3077) |
| para 65 | 26 Jan 2009 (SI 2008/3077) |
| paras 66, 67 | 26 Jan 2009 (E) (SI 2008/3077)[1] |
| | 31 Mar 2009 (W) (SI 2009/784)[3] |
| paras 68–73 | 2 Dec 2008 (SI 2008/3077) |
| para 74 | 30 Mar 2010 (SI 2010/1093) |
| paras 75–77 | 26 Nov 2008 (s 173(1)(g)) |
| para 78 | 26 Jan 2009 (SI 2008/3077) |
| para 79 | *Not yet in force* |
| para 80 | 1 Sep 2012 (SI 2012/2197) |
| paras 81–85 | 26 Jan 2009 (SI 2008/3077) |
| paras 86–88 | 26 Nov 2008 (s 173(1)(g)) |
| para 89 | 26 Jan 2009 (SI 2008/3077) |
| para 90 | *Not yet in force* |
| Sch 2 | 26 Nov 2008 (repeal of Learning and Skills Act 2000, s 140) (s 173(1)(h)) |
| | 2 Dec 2008 (repeals of School Standards and Framework Act 1998, ss 89, 89D, 90, 90A) (SI 2008/3077) |
| | 26 Jan 2009 (SI 2008/3077), repeals of or in— |
| | School Standards and Framework Act 1998, s 94(7); |
| | Welfare Reform and Pensions Act 1999; |
| | Learning and Skills Act 2000, ss 114(2), (3), (5), 115, 116, 118, 121; |
| | Criminal Justice and Court Services Act 2000; |
| | Tax Credits Act 2002; |
| | Education Act 2005, s 106; |
| | Education and Inspections Act 2006, ss 46, 47(5)(a), 50(3), 52(2); |
| | National Health Service (Consequential Provisions) Act 2006 |
| | 26 Jan 2009 (E) (repeals of or in School Standards and Framework Act 1998, ss 86, 94) (SI 2008/3077)[1] |
| | 31 Mar 2009 (W) (repeals of or in School Standards and Framework Act 1998, ss 86, 94) (SI 2009/784)[3] |
| | 1 Sep 2009 (repeal in Education Act 1996, s 349) (SI 2009/1513) |
| | 1 Sep 2009 (repeal of Education Act 2002, s 162B(6), (7)) (SI 2009/1606)[5] |
| | 30 Mar 2010 (repeal in Education Act 1996, s 342) (SI 2010/1093) |
| | 5 Jan 2015 (SI 2014/3364), repeals of or in— |
| | Education Act 2002 (except s 162B(6), (7)); |
| | Education Act 2005, s 59, Sch 8 |
| | *Not yet in force*, repeals and revocations of or in— |
| | Local Government Act 1972; |
| | School Standards and Framework Act 1998, ss 47A, Sch 30; |
| | Learning and Skills Act 2000, ss 98, 99, 114(1), (4), (6)–(10), 117, 119, 120; |
| | Education Act 2005, Sch 9; |
| | Childcare Act 2006; |
| | Education and Inspections Act 2006, Sch 14; |
| | Qualifications, Curriculum and Assessment Authority for Wales (Transfer of Functions to the National Assembly for Wales and Abolition) Order 2005, SI 2005/3239 |

[1]  For savings, see SI 2008/3077, art 6

[2]  For savings, see SI 2009/387, art 3(2), (3)

[3]  For savings, see SI 2009/784, art 4

[4]  For transitory provisions and a saving, see SI 2009/1513, art 2A

### Education and Skills Act 2008 (c 25)—*contd*

5  For a saving, see SI 2009/1606, art 6

6  For a transitory provision, see SI 2013/1204, art 4

7  For saving and transitory provisions, see SI 2014/3364, arts 3–5

### Employment Act 2008 (c 24)

*RA:* 13 Nov 2008

*Commencement provisions:* s 22; Employment Act 2008 (Commencement No 1, Transitional Provisions and Savings) Order 2008, SI 2008/3232; Employment Act 2008 (Commencement No 2, Transitional Provisions and Savings) Order 2009, SI 2009/603

| | | |
|---|---|---|
| 1–7 | | 6 Apr 2009 (SI 2008/3232)[1] |
| 8, 9 | | 6 Apr 2009 (SI 2009/603)[2] |
| 10 | | 13 Jan 2009 (s 22(1)(b)) |
| 11, 12 | | 6 Apr 2009 (SI 2009/603) |
| 13, 14 | | 13 Jan 2009 (s 22(1)(d)) |
| 15–17 | | 6 Apr 2009 (s 22(1)(e)) |
| 18, 19 | | 6 Apr 2009 (SI 2009/603)[2] |
| 20 | | See Schedule below |
| 21–23 | | 13 Nov 2008 (s 22(1)(g)) |
| Schedule | Pt 1 | 6 Apr 2009 (SI 2008/3232)[1] |
| | Pt 2 | 6 Apr 2009 (SI 2009/603) |
| | Pt 3 | 13 Jan 2009 (s 22(1)(b)) |
| | Pt 4 | 6 Apr 2009 (SI 2009/603) |
| | Pt 5 | 6 Apr 2009 (s 22(1)(e)) |

1  For transitional provisions and savings, see SI 2008/3232, art 3, Schedule

2  For transitional provisions and savings, see SI 2009/603, art 3, Schedule

### Energy Act 2008 (c 32)

*RA:* 26 Nov 2008

*Commencement provisions*: s 110; Energy Act 2008 (Commencement No 1 and Savings) Order 2009, SI 2009/45; Energy Act 2008 (Commencement No 2) Order 2009, SI 2009/559; Energy Act 2008 (Commencement No 3) Order 2009, SI 2009/1270; Energy Act 2008 (Commencement No 4 and Transitional Provisions) Order 2009, SI 2009/2809; Energy Act 2008 (Commencement No 5) Order 2010, SI 2010/1888; Energy Act 2008 (Commencement No 6) Order 2014, SI 2014/1461

| | | |
|---|---|---|
| 1 | | 6 Apr 2009 (SI 2009/45) |
| 2–16 | | 13 Nov 2009 (except in so far as they relate to the use of a controlled place for the unloading of gas to a pipeline, and in so far as they relate to the establishment or maintenance of an installation for that purpose so far as it consists of apparatus, works or services associated with the operations of a pipeline (within the meaning of the Petroleum Act 1998, s 26)) (SI 2009/2809)[2] |
| | | *Not yet in force* (exceptions noted above) (ss 5(1)(e), 13(2) repealed) |
| 17–35 | | 6 Apr 2009 (SI 2009/45) |
| 36 | | See Sch 1 below |
| 37 | | 26 Nov 2008 (so far as is necessary for enabling the exercise on or after that date of any power to make regulations that is conferred by virtue of this section) (s 110(1)(a)) |
| | | 1 Apr 2009 (otherwise) (SI 2009/45)[1] |
| 38 | (1) | 26 Nov 2008 (s 110(1)(a)) |
| | (2) | 26 Jan 2009 (SI 2009/45) |
| | (3) | 7 Mar 2009 (SI 2009/559) |
| 39–43 | | 26 Jan 2009 (SI 2009/45) |

**Energy Act 2008 (c 32)**—*contd*

| | | |
|---|---|---|
| 44 | (1), (2) | 20 May 2009 (SI 2009/1270) |
| | (3) | 29 Jul 2010 (in relation to assets which have been the subject of a tender exercise, have been transferred to the person who was the successful bidder in relation to that tender exercise, and were not constructed or installed by that person; and in relation to any electric line and associated electrical plant which is located partly in an area of offshore waters and is used in the conveyance of electricity generated only by a generating station located otherwise than in an area of offshore waters) (SI 2010/1888) |
| | | 10 Jun 2014 (otherwise) (SI 2014/1461) |
| | (4) | See Sch 2 below |
| 45–71 | | 6 Apr 2009 (SI 2009/45) |
| 72–77 | | 26 Jan 2009 (SI 2009/45) |
| 78–82 | | 6 Apr 2009 (SI 2009/45) |
| 83 | | 26 Jan 2009 (SI 2009/45) |
| 84–86 | | 29 Jul 2010 (SI 2010/1888) |
| 87 | | 26 Jan 2009 (SI 2009/45) |
| 88–91 | | 26 Nov 2008 (s 110(1)(b)) |
| 92, 93 | | 1 Apr 2009 (SI 2009/45) |
| 94 | | 26 Jan 2009 (SI 2009/45) |
| 95, 96 | | 1 Apr 2009 (SI 2009/45) |
| 97, 98 | | 26 Jan 2009 (SI 2009/45) |
| 99 | | *Not yet in force* |
| 100, 101 | | 26 Jan 2009 (SI 2009/45) |
| 102 | | 26 Nov 2008 (s 110(1)(c)) |
| 103 | | 26 Jan 2009 (SI 2009/45) |
| 104, 105 | | 26 Nov 2008 (in so far as they apply in relation to orders made under s 90(3)) (s 110(1)(b)) |
| | | 26 Jan 2009 (otherwise) (SI 2009/45) |
| 106 | | 26 Nov 2008 (s 110(1)(d)) |
| 107 | (1) | See Sch 5 below |
| | (2), (3) | 26 Jan 2009 (SI 2009/45) |
| 108 | | See Sch 6 below |
| 109 | | 26 Jan 2009 (SI 2009/45) |
| 110–113 | | 26 Nov 2008 (s 110(1)(d)) |
| Sch 1 | paras 1–3 | 6 Apr 2009 (SI 2009/45) |
| | paras 4, 5 | 13 Nov 2009 (except in so far as they relate to the use of a controlled place for the unloading of gas to a pipeline, and in so far as they relate to the establishment or maintenance of an installation for that purpose so far as it consists of apparatus, works or services associated with the operations of a pipeline (within the meaning of the Petroleum Act 1998, s 26)) (SI 2009/2809) |
| | | *Not yet in force* (exceptions noted above) |
| | para 6 | 6 Apr 2009 (SI 2009/45) |
| | para 7(a)–(c) | 6 Apr 2009 (SI 2009/45) |
| | para 7(d) | 13 Nov 2009 (except in so far as relates to the use of a controlled place for the unloading of gas to a pipeline, and in so far as relates to the establishment or maintenance of an installation for that purpose so far as it consists of apparatus, works or services associated with the operations of a pipeline (within the meaning of the Petroleum Act 1998, s 26)) (SI 2009/2809) |
| | | *Not yet in force* (exceptions noted above) |
| | para 7(e)–(g) | 6 Apr 2009 (SI 2009/45) |
| | para 7(h) | 6 Apr 2009 (except in so far as relates to the Petroleum Act 1998, s 11(9)(a)) (SI 2009/45) |

**Energy Act 2008 (c 32)**—*contd*

|  |  |  |
|---|---|---|
|  |  | 13 Nov 2009 (otherwise, except in so far as relates to the use of a controlled place for the unloading of gas to a pipeline, and in so far as relates to the establishment or maintenance of an installation for that purpose so far as it consists of apparatus, works or services associated with the operations of a pipeline (within the meaning of the Petroleum Act 1998, s 26)) (SI 2009/2809) |
|  |  | *Not yet in force* (exceptions noted above) |
|  | para 8 | 6 Apr 2009 (SI 2009/45) |
|  | paras 9–11 | 13 Nov 2009 (except in so far as they relate to the use of a controlled place for the unloading of gas to a pipeline, and in so far as they relate to the establishment or maintenance of an installation for that purpose so far as it consists of apparatus, works or services associated with the operations of a pipeline (within the meaning of the Petroleum Act 1998, s 26)) (SI 2009/2809) |
|  |  | *Not yet in force* (exceptions noted above) |
|  | paras 12, 13 | 6 Apr 2009 (SI 2009/45) |
| Sch 2 |  | 20 May 2009 (SI 2009/1270) |
| Sch 3 |  | 26 Jan 2009 (SI 2009/45) |
| Sch 4 |  | 26 Nov 2008 (s 110(1)(b)) |
| Sch 5 | para 1 | 6 Apr 2009 (SI 2009/45) |
|  | para 2 | 26 Jan 2009 (SI 2009/45) |
|  | para 3 | 1 Apr 2009 (SI 2009/45) |
|  | para 4 | 26 Jan 2009 (SI 2009/45) |
|  | para 5 | 26 Nov 2008 (s 110(1)(e)) |
|  | para 6 | 26 Jan 2009 (SI 2009/45) |
|  | paras 7, 8 | 6 Apr 2009 (SI 2009/45) |
|  | para 9–14 | 26 Jan 2009 (SI 2009/45) |
|  | para 15(a), (b) | 26 Jan 2009 (SI 2009/45) |
|  | para 15(c) | 1 Apr 2009 (SI 2009/45) |
|  | para 16 | 26 Jan 2009 (SI 2009/45) |
|  | paras 17, 18 | 6 Apr 2009 (SI 2009/45) |
|  | paras 19, 20 | 1 Apr 2009 (SI 2009/45) |
|  | para 21 | 26 Jan 2009 (SI 2009/45) |
| Sch 6 |  | 26 Jan 2009 (SI 2009/45), repeals of or in— |
|  |  | Gas Act 1986, s 4AA; |
|  |  | Electricity Act 1989; |
|  |  | Petroleum Act 1998, ss 31, 34; |
|  |  | Utilities Act 2000; |
|  |  | Sustainable Energy Act 2003; |
|  |  | Energy Act 2004, s 81; |
|  |  | Climate Change and Sustainable Energy Act 2006, ss 5, 18, 22 |
|  |  | 1 Apr 2009 (SI 2009/45), repeals of or in— |
|  |  | Energy Act 2004, s 116; |
|  |  | Climate Change and Sustainable Energy Act 2006, ss 23, 24 |
|  |  | 6 Apr 2009 (SI 2009/45), repeals of or in— |
|  |  | Pipe-lines Act 1962; |
|  |  | Gas Act 1995; |
|  |  | Petroleum Act 1998, ss 26, 28; |
|  |  | Energy Act 2004, ss 105, 107 |
|  |  | 10 Jun 2014 (SI 2014/1461), repeals of or in— |
|  |  | Energy Act 2004, s 180 |
|  |  | *Not yet in force*, repeals of or in— |
|  |  | Gas Act 1986, s 17 |

---

[1]   For savings, see SI 2009/45, art 5

[2]   For transitional provisions, see SI 2009/2809, arts 3, 4

## European Communities (Finance) Act 2008 (c 1)

*RA:* 19 Feb 2008

Whole Act in force 19 Feb 2008 (RA)

## European Union (Amendment) Act 2008 (c 7)

*RA:* 19 Jun 2008

*Commencement provisions:* s 8; European Union (Amendment) Act 2008 (Commencement No 1) Order 2009, SI 2009/3143

| | |
|---|---|
| 1, 2 | 19 Jun 2008 (s 8(3)) |
| 3 | 1 Dec 2009 (SI 2009/3143) |
| 4–8 | 19 Jun 2008 (s 8(3)) |
| Schedule | 1 Dec 2009 (SI 2009/3143) |

## Finance Act 2008 (c 9)

*Budget Day:* 12 Mar 2008

*RA:* 21 Jul 2008

The commencement details of Finance Acts are not set out, as the dates from which their provisions take effect are usually stated clearly and unambiguously in the text of the Act, and charging provisions will normally state for which year or years of assessment they are to have effect.

## Glasgow Commonwealth Games Act 2008 (asp 4)

*RA:* 10 Jun 2008

*Commencement provisions:* s 49; Glasgow Commonwealth Games Act 2008 (Commencement No 1) Order 2008, SSI 2008/245; Glasgow Commonwealth Games Act 2008 (Commencement No 2) Order 2009, SSI 2009/377; Glasgow Commonwealth Games Act 2008 (Commencement No 3) Order 2012, SSI 2012/261; Glasgow Commonwealth Games Act 2008 (Commencement No 4) Order 2013, SSI 2013/260

| | | |
|---|---|---|
| 1 | | 13 Nov 2009 (SSI 2009/377) |
| 2 | (1), (2) | 1 Oct 2013 (SSI 2013/260) |
| | (3) | 13 Nov 2009 (SSI 2009/377) |
| | (4) | 1 Oct 2013 (SSI 2013/260) |
| 3–6 | | 13 Nov 2009 (SSI 2009/377) |
| 7, 8 | | 1 Oct 2013 (SSI 2013/260) |
| 9 | | 13 Nov 2009 (SSI 2009/377) |
| 10 | (1) | 1 Oct 2013 (SSI 2013/260) |
| | (2) | 13 Nov 2009 (SSI 2009/377) |
| | (3) | 1 Oct 2013 (SSI 2013/260) |
| 11 | (1)–(3) | 1 Oct 2013 (SSI 2013/260) |
| | (4) | 13 Nov 2009 (SSI 2009/377) |
| 12–14 | | 13 Nov 2009 (SSI 2009/377) |
| 15 | | 1 Oct 2013 (SSI 2013/260) |
| 16 | | 13 Nov 2009 (SSI 2009/377) |
| 17, 18 | | 29 Nov 2012 (SSI 2012/261) |
| 19 | | 13 Nov 2009 (SSI 2009/377) |
| 20 | (1)–(3) | 29 Nov 2012 (SSI 2012/261) |
| | (4) | 13 Nov 2009 (SSI 2009/377) |
| 21 | | 13 Nov 2009 (SSI 2009/377) |
| 22–29 | | 29 Nov 2012 (SSI 2012/261) |
| 30 | (1) | 29 Nov 2012 (SSI 2012/261) |
| | (2) | 13 Nov 2009 (SSI 2009/377) |

**Glasgow Commonwealth Games Act 2008 (asp 4)**—*contd*

|  |  |  |
|---|---|---|
|  | (3) | 29 Nov 2012 (SSI 2012/261) |
| 31, 32 |  | 29 Nov 2012 (SSI 2012/261) |
| 33 |  | 13 Nov 2009 (SSI 2009/377) |
| 34 | (1) | 1 Oct 2013 (SSI 2013/260) |
|  | (2) | 29 Nov 2012 (SSI 2012/261) |
| 35 | (1) | 1 Oct 2013 (SSI 2013/260) |
|  | (2) | 29 Nov 2012 (SSI 2012/261) |
| 36 |  | 29 Nov 2012 (SSI 2012/261) |
| 37–40 |  | 13 Nov 2009 (SSI 2009/377) |
| 41, 42 |  | 20 Jun 2008 (SSI 2008/245) |
| 43 |  | 10 Jun 2008 (s 49(1)) |
| 44–46 |  | 13 Nov 2009 (SSI 2009/377) |
| 47–51 |  | 10 Jun 2008 (s 49(1)) |
| Schedule |  | 10 Jun 2008 (s 49(1))[1] |

[1]  The Schedule is introduced by s 48(2) and it is thought that it comes into force together with that subsection, although this is not specified in s 49(1)

---

**Graduate Endowment Abolition (Scotland) Act 2008 (asp 3)**

*RA:* 4 Apr 2008

*Commencement provisions:* s 7(1)

Whole Act in force 5 Apr 2008 (s 7(1))

---

**Health and Safety (Offences) Act 2008 (c 20)**

*RA:* 16 Oct 2008

*Commencement provisions:* s 3(2)

Whole Act in force 16 Jan 2009 (s 3(2))

---

**Health and Social Care Act 2008 (c 14)**

*RA:* 21 Jul 2008

*Commencement provisions:* s 170; Health and Social Care Act 2008 (Commencement No 1) Order 2008, SI 2008/2214; Health and Social Care Act 2008 (Commencement No 2) Order 2008, SI 2008/2497; Health and Social Care Act 2008 (Commencement No 3) Order 2008, SI 2008/2717; Health and Social Care Act 2008 (Commencement No 4) Order 2008, SI 2008/2994; Health and Social Care Act 2008 (Commencement No 5) Order 2008, SI 2008/3137; Health and Social Care Act 2008 (Commencement No 6, Transitory and Transitional Provisions) Order 2008, SI 2008/3168; Health and Social Care Act 2008 (Commencement No 7) Order 2008, SI 2008/3244; Health and Social Care Act 2008 (Commencement No 8) Order 2009, SI 2009/270; Health and Social Care Act 2008 (Commencement No 9, Consequential Amendments and Transitory, Transitional and Saving Provisions) Order 2009, SI 2009/462[3], as amended by SI 2009/580, SI 2010/708, SI 2012/1641; Health and Social Care Act 2008 (Commencement No 1) (Wales) Order 2009, SI 2009/631; Health and Social Care Act 2008 (Commencement No 10) Order 2009, SI 2009/1310; Health and Social Care Act 2008 (Commencement No 11) Order 2009, SI 2009/2567; Health and Social Care Act 2008 (Commencement No 12) Order 2009, SI 2009/2862; Health and Social Care Act 2008 (Commencement No 13, Transitory and Transitional Provisions and Electronic Communications) Order 2009, SI 2009/3023, as amended by SI 2010/47; Health and Social Care Act 2008 (Commencement No 14) Order 2010, SI 2010/23; Health and Social Care Act 2008 (Commencement No 15, Consequential Amendments and Transitional and Savings Provisions) Order 2010, SI 2010/708; Health and Social Care Act 2008 (Commencement No 16, Transitory and Transitional Provisions) Order 2010, SI 2010/807[5]; Health and Social Care Act 2008 (Commencement No 2 and Transitional Provisions) (Wales) Order 2010, SI 2010/989; Health and Social Care Act 2008 (Commencement No 3) (Wales) Order 2010, SI 2010/1457; Health and Social

**Health and Social Care Act 2008 (c 14)**—*contd*

Care Act 2008 (Commencement No 4, Transitional and Savings Provisions) (Wales) Order 2010, SI 2010/1547; Health and Social Care Act 2008 (Commencement No 17) Order 2011, SI 2011/986; Health and Social Care Act 2008 (Commencement No 18) Order 2013, SI 2013/159; Health and Social Care Act 2008 (Commencement No 19) Order 2014, SI 2014/3251

| | | |
|---|---|---|
| 1 | (1) | 1 Oct 2008 (SI 2008/2497) |
| | (2) | 1 Apr 2009 (SI 2009/462) |
| | (3) | See Sch 1 below |
| 2 | (1) | 1 Oct 2008 (SI 2008/2497) |
| | (2)(a) | 12 Jan 2009 (except to the extent that it relates to the registration of managers) (SI 2008/3168) |
| | | 6 Apr 2010 (exception noted above) (SI 2010/807) |
| | (2)(b), (c) | 1 Apr 2009 (SI 2009/462) |
| 3–7 | | 1 Oct 2008 (SI 2008/2497) |
| 8 | | 21 Jul 2008 (in so far as is necessary for enabling the exercise on or after that date of the power to make regulations that is conferred by this section or in so far as it defines any expression relevant to the exercise of such power) (s 170(1)(b)) |
| | | 12 Jan 2009 (otherwise) (except to the extent that it relates to the registration of managers) (SI 2008/3168) |
| | | 6 Apr 2010 (exception noted above) (SI 2010/807) |
| 9 | | 1 Oct 2008 (SI 2008/2497) |
| 10 | (1), (2) | 21 Jul 2008 (in so far as is necessary for enabling the exercise on or after that date of the power to make regulations that is conferred by these provisions or in so far as they define any expression relevant to the exercise of such power) (s 170(1)(b)) |
| | | 1 Apr 2009 (otherwise, except to the extent that they relate to the registration of managers under this Chapter) (SI 2009/462) |
| | | *Not yet in force* (exception noted above) |
| | (3) | 21 Jul 2008 (in so far as is necessary for enabling the exercise on or after that date of the power to make regulations that is conferred by this section or in so far as it defines any expression relevant to the exercise of such power) (s 170(1)(b)) |
| | | 12 Jan 2009 (otherwise) (except to the extent that it relates to the registration of managers) (SI 2008/3168) |
| | | *Not yet in force* (exception noted above) |
| | (4), (5) | 21 Jul 2008 (in so far as is necessary for enabling the exercise on or after that date of the power to make regulations that is conferred by these provisions or in so far as they define any expression relevant to the exercise of such power) (s 170(1)(b)) |
| | | 1 Apr 2009 (otherwise, except to the extent that they relate to the registration of managers under this Chapter) (SI 2009/462) |
| | | *Not yet in force* (exception noted above) |
| 11 | | 12 Jan 2009 (except to the extent that it relates to the registration of managers) (SI 2008/3168)[2] |
| | | *Not yet in force* (exception noted above) |
| 12 | (1)–(5) | 12 Jan 2009 (except to the extent that they relate to the registration of managers) (SI 2008/3168)[2] |
| | | *Not yet in force* (exception noted above) |
| | (6) | 6 Apr 2010 (SI 2010/807) |
| 13 | | 21 Jul 2008 (in so far as is necessary for enabling the exercise on or after that date of the power to make regulations that is conferred by this section or in so far as it defines any expression relevant to the exercise of such power) (s 170(1)(b)) |
| | | 6 Apr 2010 (otherwise) (SI 2010/807) |
| 14, 15 | | 6 Apr 2010 (SI 2010/807) |
| 16 | | 21 Jul 2008 (in so far as is necessary for enabling the exercise on or after that date of the power to make regulations that is conferred by this section or in so far as it defines any expression relevant to the exercise of such power) (s 170(1)(b)) |

**Health and Social Care Act 2008 (c 14)**—*contd*

|  |  |  |
|---|---|---|
|  |  | 1 Apr 2009 (otherwise, except to the extent that it relates to the registration of managers under this Chapter) (SI 2009/462) |
|  |  | 11 Dec 2009 (exception noted above) (SI 2009/3023) |
| 17 | (1) | 21 Jul 2008 (in so far as is necessary for enabling the exercise on or after that date of the power to make regulations that is conferred by this section or in so far as it defines any expression relevant to the exercise of such power) (s 170(1)(b)) |
|  |  | 1 Apr 2009 (otherwise, except to the extent that it relates to the registration of managers under this Chapter) (SI 2009/462) |
|  |  | 1 Oct 2010 (exception noted above) (SI 2010/807) |
|  | (2) | 21 Jul 2008 (in so far as is necessary for enabling the exercise on or after that date of the power to make regulations that is conferred by this section or in so far as it defines any expression relevant to the exercise of such power) (s 170(1)(b)) |
|  |  | 1 Oct 2010 (otherwise) (SI 2010/807) |
|  | (3), (4) | 21 Jul 2008 (in so far as is necessary for enabling the exercise on or after that date of the power to make regulations that is conferred by this section or in so far as it defines any expression relevant to the exercise of such power) (s 170(1)(b)) |
|  |  | 1 Apr 2009 (otherwise, except to the extent that they relate to the registration of managers under this Chapter) (SI 2009/462) |
|  |  | 1 Oct 2010 (exception noted above) (SI 2010/807) |
| 18, 19 |  | 1 Apr 2009 (except to the extent that they relate to the registration of managers under this Chapter) (SI 2009/462) |
|  |  | 1 Oct 2010 (exception noted above) (SI 2010/807) |
| 20 |  | 21 Jul 2008 (in so far as is necessary for enabling the exercise on or after that date of the power to make regulations that is conferred by this section or in so far as it defines any expression relevant to the exercise of such power) (s 170(1)(b)) |
|  |  | 12 Jan 2009 (otherwise) (except to the extent that it relates to the registration of managers) (SI 2008/3168) |
|  |  | 6 Apr 2010 (otherwise) (SI 2010/807) |
| 21, 22 |  | 12 Jan 2009 (except to the extent that they relate to the registration of managers) (SI 2008/3168)[2] |
|  |  | *Not yet in force* (exception noted above) |
| 23, 24 |  | 11 Dec 2009 (SI 2009/3023) |
| 25 |  | 12 Jan 2009 (in so far as relates to a code of practice under s 21) (except to the extent that it relates to the registration of managers) (SI 2008/3168) |
|  |  | 11 Dec 2009 (otherwise) (SI 2009/3023) |
| 26 | (1) | See sub-ss (2), (3) below |
|  | (2) | 6 Apr 2010 (SI 2010/807) |
|  | (3) | 12 Jan 2009 (except to the extent that it relates to the registration of managers) (SI 2008/3168) |
|  |  | 6 Apr 2010 (exception noted above) (SI 2010/807) |
|  | (4), (5) | 1 Apr 2009 (except to the extent that they relate to the registration of managers under this Chapter) (SI 2009/462) |
|  |  | 6 Apr 2010 (exception noted above) (SI 2010/807) |
|  | (6) | 12 Jan 2009 (except to the extent that it relates to the registration of managers) (SI 2008/3168) |
|  |  | 6 Apr 2010 (exception noted above) (SI 2010/807) |
| 27 |  | 12 Jan 2009 (except to the extent that it relates to the registration of managers) (SI 2008/3168) |
|  |  | 6 Apr 2010 (exception noted above) (SI 2010/807) |
| 28 | (1)–(3) | 12 Jan 2009 (except to the extent that they relate to the registration of managers) (SI 2008/3168) |
|  |  | 6 Apr 2010 (exception noted above) (SI 2010/807) |
|  | (4)(a) | 12 Jan 2009 (except to the extent that it relates to the registration of managers) (SI 2008/3168) |
|  |  | 6 Apr 2010 (exception noted above) (SI 2010/807) |

**Health and Social Care Act 2008 (c 14)**—*contd*

| | | |
|---|---|---|
| | (4)(b) | 6 Apr 2010 (SI 2010/807) |
| | (4)(c), (d) | 1 Apr 2009 (except to the extent that they relate to the registration of managers under this Chapter) (SI 2009/462) |
| | | 6 Apr 2010 (exception noted above) (SI 2010/807) |
| | (5)–(7) | 6 Apr 2010 (SI 2010/807) |
| 29 | | 1 Apr 2009 (except to the extent that it relates to the registration of managers under this Chapter) (SI 2009/462) |
| | | 1 Oct 2010 (exception noted above) (SI 2010/807) |
| 30 | | 21 Jul 2008 (in so far as is necessary for enabling the exercise on or after that date of the power to make regulations that is conferred by this section or in so far as it defines any expression relevant to the exercise of such power) (s 170(1)(b)) |
| | | 1 Apr 2009 (otherwise, except to the extent that it relates to the registration of managers under this Chapter) (SI 2009/462) |
| | | 1 Oct 2010 (exception noted above) (SI 2010/807) |
| 31 | | 1 Apr 2009 (except to the extent that it relates to the registration of managers under this Chapter) (SI 2009/462) |
| | | 1 Oct 2010 (exception noted above) (SI 2010/807) |
| 32 | | 12 Jan 2009 (except to the extent that it relates to the registration of managers) (SI 2008/3168)[2] |
| | | 6 Apr 2010 (exception noted above) (SI 2010/807) |
| 33 | | 1 Apr 2009 (except to the extent that it relates to the registration of managers under this Chapter) (SI 2009/462) |
| | | 1 Oct 2010 (exception noted above) (SI 2010/807) |
| 34 | (1) | 1 Apr 2009 (except to the extent that it relates to the registration of managers under this Chapter) (SI 2009/462) |
| | | *Not yet in force* (exception noted above) |
| | (2)–(4) | 1 Oct 2010 (SI 2010/807) |
| | (5) | 1 Apr 2009 (except to the extent that it relates to the registration of managers under this Chapter) (SI 2009/462) |
| | | 1 Oct 2010 (exception noted above) (SI 2010/807) |
| 35 | | 12 Jan 2009 (except to the extent that it relates to the registration of managers) (SI 2008/3168) |
| | | *Not yet in force* (exception noted above) |
| 36 | | 1 Apr 2009 (except to the extent that it relates to the registration of managers under this Chapter) (SI 2009/462) |
| | | *Not yet in force* (exception noted above) |
| 37 | | 12 Jan 2009 (except to the extent that it relates to the registration of managers) (SI 2008/3168) |
| | | 6 Apr 2010 (exception noted above) (SI 2010/807) |
| 38, 39 | | 21 Jul 2008 (in so far as is necessary for enabling the exercise on or after that date of the power to make regulations that is conferred by these sections or in so far as they define any expression relevant to the exercise of such power) (s 170(1)(b)) |
| | | 1 Apr 2009 (otherwise, except to the extent that they relate to the registration of managers under this Chapter) (SI 2009/462) |
| | | 1 Oct 2010 (exception noted above) (SI 2010/807) |
| 40 | | 21 Jul 2008 (in so far as is necessary for enabling the exercise on or after that date of the power to make regulations that is conferred by this section or in so far as it defines any expression relevant to the exercise of such power) (s 170(1)(b)) |
| | | 1 Apr 2009 (otherwise, except to the extent that it relates to the registration of managers under this Chapter) (SI 2009/462) |
| | | *Not yet in force* (exception noted above) |
| 41, 42 | | 21 Jul 2008 (in so far as is necessary for enabling the exercise on or after that date of the power to make regulations that is conferred by these sections or in so far as they define any expression relevant to the exercise of such power) (s 170(1)(b)) |
| | | 11 Dec 2009 (otherwise) (SI 2009/3023) |

**Health and Social Care Act 2008 (c 14)**—*contd*

| | | |
|---|---|---|
| 43 | | 21 Jul 2008 (in so far as is necessary for enabling the exercise on or after that date of the power to make regulations that is conferred by this section or in so far as it defines any expression relevant to the exercise of such power) (s 170(1)(b)) |
| | | 6 Apr 2010 (otherwise) (SI 2010/807) |
| 44 | | 12 Jan 2009 (except to the extent that it relates to the registration of managers) (SI 2008/3168) |
| | | 6 Apr 2010 (exception noted above) (SI 2010/807) |
| 45 | | 1 Apr 2010 (SI 2010/708) |
| 46 | (1)–(3) | 21 Jul 2008 (in so far as is necessary for enabling the exercise on or after that date of the power to make regulations that is conferred by this section or in so far as it defines any expression relevant to the exercise of such power) (s 170(1)(b)) |
| | | 1 Apr 2009 (otherwise) (SI 2009/462) |
| | (4)–(8) | 21 Jul 2008 (in so far as is necessary for enabling the exercise on or after that date of the power to make regulations that is conferred by this section or in so far as it defines any expression relevant to the exercise of such power) (s 170(1)(b)) |
| | | 1 Oct 2008 (otherwise) (SI 2008/2497) |
| | (9) | 21 Jul 2008 (in so far as is necessary for enabling the exercise on or after that date of the power to make regulations that is conferred by this section or in so far as it defines any expression relevant to the exercise of such power) (s 170(1)(b)) |
| | | 1 Apr 2009 (otherwise) (SI 2009/462) |
| 47 | | 1 Oct 2008 (SI 2008/2497) |
| 48 | | 21 Jul 2008 (in so far as is necessary for enabling the exercise on or after that date of the power to make regulations that is conferred by this section or in so far as it defines any expression relevant to the exercise of such power) (s 170(1)(b)) |
| | | 1 Apr 2009 (otherwise) (SI 2009/462) |
| 49 | | 21 Jul 2008 (in so far as is necessary for enabling the exercise on or after that date of the power to make regulations that is conferred by this section or in so far as it defines any expression relevant to the exercise of such power) (s 170(1)(b)) |
| | | 11 Dec 2009 (otherwise) (SI 2009/3023) |
| 50 | | 1 Apr 2009 (SI 2009/462) |
| 51 | | 1 Apr 2009 (except in so far as it relates to a review under s 49) (SI 2009/462) |
| | | 11 Dec 2009 (exception noted above) (SI 2009/3023) |
| 52–54 | | 1 Apr 2009 (SI 2009/462) |
| 55 | | 21 Jul 2008 (in so far as is necessary for enabling the exercise on or after that date of the power to make regulations that is conferred by this section or in so far as it defines any expression relevant to the exercise of such power) (s 170(1)(b)) |
| | | 1 Apr 2009 (otherwise) (SI 2009/462) |
| 56–59 | | 1 Apr 2009 (SI 2009/462) |
| 60 | | 12 Jan 2009 (except to the extent that it relates to the registration of managers) (SI 2008/3168) |
| | | 6 Apr 2010 (exception noted above) (SI 2010/807) |
| 61 | | 21 Jul 2008 (in so far as is necessary for enabling the exercise on or after that date of the power to make regulations that is conferred by this section or in so far as it defines any expression relevant to the exercise of such power) (s 170(1)(b)) |
| | | 12 Jan 2009 (otherwise) (except to the extent that it relates to the registration of managers) (SI 2008/3168) |
| | | 6 Apr 2010 (exception noted above) (SI 2010/807) |
| 62–64 | | 12 Jan 2009 (except to the extent that they relate to the registration of managers) (SI 2008/3168) |
| | | 6 Apr 2010 (exception noted above) (SI 2010/807) |

**Health and Social Care Act 2008 (c 14)**—*contd*

| | |
|---|---|
| 65 | 21 Jul 2008 (in so far as is necessary for enabling the exercise on or after that date of the power to make regulations that is conferred by this section or in so far as it defines any expression relevant to the exercise of such power) (s 170(1)(b)) |
| | 12 Jan 2009 (otherwise) (except to the extent that it relates to the registration of managers) (SI 2008/3168) |
| | 6 Apr 2010 (exception noted above) (SI 2010/807) |
| 66 | See Sch 4 below |
| 67 | 1 Apr 2009 (SI 2009/462) |
| 68 | 21 Jul 2008 (in so far as is necessary for enabling the exercise on or after that date of the power to make regulations that is conferred by this section or in so far as it defines any expression relevant to the exercise of such power) (s 170(1)(b)) |
| | 1 Apr 2009 (otherwise) (SI 2009/462) |
| 69–71 | 1 Apr 2009 (SI 2009/462) |
| 72 | 1 Apr 2009 (except in so far as it relates to a review under s 49) (SI 2009/462) |
| | 11 Dec 2009 (exception noted above) (SI 2009/3023) |
| 73 | 21 Jul 2008 (in so far as is necessary for enabling the exercise on or after that date of the power to make regulations that is conferred by this section or in so far as it defines any expression relevant to the exercise of such power) (s 170(1)(b)) |
| | 1 Apr 2009 (otherwise) (SI 2009/462) |
| 74, 75 | 1 Apr 2009 (SI 2009/462) |
| 76–80 | 1 Oct 2008 (SI 2008/2497) |
| 81 | 21 Jul 2008 (in so far as is necessary for enabling the exercise on or after that date of the power to make orders that is conferred by this section or in so far as it defines any expression relevant to the exercise of such power) (s 170(1)(b)) |
| | 1 Oct 2008 (otherwise) (SI 2008/2497) |
| 82, 83 | 1 Oct 2008 (SI 2008/2497) |
| 84 | 1 Apr 2009 (SI 2009/462) |
| 85 | 21 Jul 2008 (in so far as is necessary for enabling the exercise on or after that date of the power to make regulations that is conferred by this section or in so far as it defines any expression relevant to the exercise of such power) (s 170(1)(b)) |
| | 1 Oct 2008 (otherwise) (SI 2008/2497) |
| 86, 87 | 21 Jul 2008 (in so far as is necessary for enabling the exercise on or after that date of the power to make regulations that is conferred by these sections or in so far as they define any expression relevant to the exercise of such power) (s 170(1)(b)) |
| | 1 Apr 2009 (otherwise) (SI 2009/462) |
| 88 | 21 Jul 2008 (in so far as is necessary for enabling the exercise on or after that date of the power to make regulations that is conferred by this section or in so far as it defines any expression relevant to the exercise of such power) (s 170(1)(b)) |
| | 1 Oct 2008 (otherwise) (SI 2008/2497) |
| 89 | 21 Jul 2008 (in so far as is necessary for enabling the exercise on or after that date of the power to make regulations that is conferred by this section or in so far as it defines any expression relevant to the exercise of such power) (s 170(1)(b)) |
| | 1 Apr 2009 (otherwise) (SI 2009/462) |
| 90 | 12 Jan 2009 (except to the extent that they relate to the registration of managers) (SI 2008/3168) |
| | 6 Apr 2010 (exception noted above) (SI 2010/807) |
| 91, 92 | 12 Jan 2009 (except to the extent that they relate to the registration of managers) (SI 2008/3168) |
| | *Not yet in force* (exception noted above) |
| 93, 94 | 12 Jan 2009 (except to the extent that they relate to the registration of managers) (SI 2008/3168) |

**Health and Social Care Act 2008 (c 14)**—*contd*

| | | |
|---|---|---|
| | | 6 Apr 2010 (exception noted above) (SI 2010/807) |
| 95 | | See Sch 5 below |
| 96 | | 1 Apr 2009 (SI 2009/462) |
| 97 | | 21 Jul 2008 (in so far as this section defines any expression relevant to the exercise on or after that date of any power to make orders or regulations that is conferred by this Act) (s 170(1)(b)) |
| | | 1 Oct 2008 (otherwise) (SI 2008/2497) |
| 98 | (1) | 25 Jan 2010 (SI 2010/23) |
| | (2) | *Never in force* (repealed) |
| | (3) | See Sch 6 below |
| 99 | | See Sch 7 below |
| 100–106 | | *Never in force* (repealed) |
| 107 | (1) | 25 Jan 2010 (SI 2010/23) |
| | (2), (3) | *Never in force* (repealed) |
| | (4) | 25 Jan 2010 (in so far as it relates to sub-s (1)) (SI 2010/23) |
| | | *Never in force* (in so far as it relates to sub-s (2)) (repealed) |
| | (5) | *Never in force* (repealed) |
| 108 | | 25 Jan 2010 (SI 2010/23) |
| 109 | | *Never in force* (repealed) |
| 110 | | 21 Jul 2008 (in so far as is necessary for enabling the exercise on or after that date of the power to make regulations that is conferred by this section or in so far as it defines any expression relevant to the exercise of such power) (s 170(1)(b)) |
| | | *Never in force* (otherwise) (repealed) |
| 111 | | See Sch 8 below |
| 112 | | 3 Nov 2008 (for the purposes of new proceedings[1]) (SI 2008/2717) |
| 113–117 | | 1 Jan 2009 (SI 2008/3244) |
| 118 | (1) | See sub-ss (2)–(6) below |
| | (2)(a) | 1 Jan 2009 (SI 2008/3244) |
| | (2)(b) | *Never in force* (repealed) |
| | (2)(c) | 1 Jan 2009 (SI 2008/3244) |
| | (2)(d) | *Never in force* (repealed) |
| | (2)(e)–(g) | 1 Jan 2009 (SI 2008/3244) |
| | (3)–(6) | 1 Jan 2009 (SI 2008/3244) |
| 119 | | 21 Jul 2008 (in so far as is necessary for enabling the exercise on or after that date of the power to make regulations that is conferred by any amendment made by this section or in so far as any amendment made by this section defines any expression relevant to the exercise of such power) (s 170(1)(b)) |
| | | 1 Apr 2010 (E) (W) (S) (otherwise) (SI 2010/708) |
| | | *Not yet in force* (NI) (otherwise) |
| 120 | | 21 Jul 2008 (in so far as is necessary for enabling the exercise on or after that date of the power to make regulations that is conferred by these sections or in so far as it defines any expression relevant to the exercise of such power) (s 170(1)(b)) |
| | | 1 Apr 2010 (E) (W) (otherwise) (SI 2010/708) |
| | | *Not yet in force* (NI) |
| 121 | | 21 Jul 2008 (in so far as is necessary for enabling the exercise on or after that date of the power to make regulations that is conferred by any amendment made by this section or in so far as any amendment made by this section defines any expression relevant to the exercise of such power) (s 170(1)(b)) |
| | | 1 Apr 2010 (otherwise) (SI 2010/708) |
| 122 | | 1 Apr 2010 (E) (W) (SI 2010/708) |
| | | *Not yet in force* (NI) |
| 123 | (1) | 1 Aug 2010 (SI 2010/708) |
| | (2) | 1 Apr 2010 (except in so far as relating to ss 1(1), (7), 12 and the Schedule of the Hearing Aid Council Act 1968) (SI 2010/708) |
| | | 1 Aug 2010 (otherwise) (SI 2010/708) |

**Health and Social Care Act 2008 (c 14)**—*contd*

|  |  |  |
|---|---|---|
| | (3)–(6) | 21 Jul 2008 (in so far as is necessary for enabling the exercise on or after that date of the power to make orders that is conferred by this section or in so far as it defines any expression relevant to the exercise of such power) (s 170(1)(b)) |
| | | 1 Oct 2008 (otherwise) (SI 2008/2497) |
| 124 | (1) | 21 Jul 2008 (in so far as is necessary for enabling the exercise on or after that date of the power to make regulations that is conferred by this section or in so far as it defines any expression relevant to the exercise of such power) (s 170(1)(b)) |
| | | *Not yet in force* (otherwise) |
| | (2) | See Sch 9 below |
| | (3), (4) | 21 Jul 2008 (in so far as is necessary for enabling the exercise on or after that date of the power to make regulations that is conferred by this section or in so far as it defines any expression relevant to the exercise of such power) (s 170(1)(b)) |
| | | *Not yet in force* (otherwise) |
| 125, 126 | | 21 Jul 2008 (in so far as is necessary for enabling the exercise on or after that date of the power to make regulations that is conferred by these sections or in so far as it defines any expression relevant to the exercise of such power) (s 170(1)(b)) |
| | | *Not yet in force* (otherwise) (s 125(3)(a) repealed) |
| 127 | | See Sch 10 below |
| 128 | | 21 Jul 2008 (in so far as this section defines any expression relevant to the exercise on or after that date of any power to make orders or regulations that is conferred by this Act) (s 170(1)(b)) |
| | | *Not yet in force* (otherwise) |
| 129 | | 21 Jul 2008 (in so far as is necessary for enabling the exercise on or after that date of the power to make regulations that is conferred by any amendment made by this section or in so far as any amendment made by this section defines any expression relevant to the exercise of such power) (s 170(1)(b)) |
| | | 1 Apr 2009 (E) (in so far as inserts Public Health (Control of Disease) Act 1984, ss 45A, 45C–45F, 45P–45T) (SI 2009/462) |
| | | 6 Apr 2010 (E) (otherwise) (SI 2010/708) |
| | | 26 Jul 2010 (W) (otherwise) (SI 2010/1547) |
| 130 | (1) | 6 Apr 2010 (E) (except in so far as relating to ss 13–15, 76 of the Public Health (Control of Disease) Act 1984 ceasing to have effect) (SI 2010/708)[4] |
| | | 26 Jul 2010 (W) (except in so far as it relates to ss 13–15, 76 of the Public Health (Control of Disease) Act 1984 ceasing to have effect) (SI 2010/1547)[7] |
| | | *Not yet in force* (exceptions noted above) |
| | (2) | See Sch 11 below |
| 131 | | 21 Jul 2008 (in so far as is necessary for enabling the exercise on or after that date of the power to make regulations that is conferred by any amendment made by this section or in so far as any amendment made by this section defines any expression relevant to the exercise of such power) (s 170(1)(b)) |
| | | 1 Jan 2009 (otherwise) (SI 2008/3137) |
| 132, 133 | | 1 Jan 2009 (SI 2008/3137) |
| 134–136 | | 21 Jul 2008 (in so far as is necessary for enabling the exercise on or after that date of the power to make regulations that is conferred by any amendment made by these sections or in so far as any amendment made by these sections define any expression relevant to the exercise of such power) (s 170(1)(b)) |
| | | 1 Jan 2009 (otherwise) (SI 2008/3137) |
| 137, 138 | | 1 Jan 2009 (SI 2008/3137) |
| 139 | | 1 Apr 2010 (SI 2010/708) |
| 140 | | See Sch 12 below |
| 141 | (1) | 1 Apr 2013 (SI 2013/159) |
| | (2) | *Not yet in force* |

**Health and Social Care Act 2008 (c 14)**—*contd*

| | | |
|---|---|---|
| 142 | | 1 Oct 2008 (SI 2008/2497) |
| 143 | | 21 Jul 2008 (in so far as is necessary for enabling the exercise on or after that date of the power to make regulations that is conferred by any amendment made by this section or in so far as any amendment made by this section defines any expression relevant to the exercise of such power) (s 170(1)(b)) |
| | | 1 Oct 2008 (otherwise) (SI 2008/2497) |
| 144 | | 21 Jul 2008 (in so far as is necessary for enabling the exercise on or after that date of the power to make regulations that is conferred by any amendment made by this section or in so far as any amendment made by this section defines any expression relevant to the exercise of such power) (s 170(1)(b)) |
| | | 1 Aug 2011 (otherwise) (SI 2011/986) |
| 145 | | 1 Dec 2008 (except in relation to a person who is an adult placement carer within the meaning of the Care Homes (Wales) Regulations 2002, SI 2002/324, reg 46) (SI 2008/2994) |
| | | *Never in force* (exception noted above) (repealed) |
| 146 | (1)–(7) | 21 Jul 2008 (in so far as is necessary for enabling the exercise on or after that date of the power to make regulations that is conferred by any amendment made by this section or in so far as any amendment made by this section defines any expression relevant to the exercise of such power) (s 170(1)(b)) |
| | | 9 Nov 2009 (E) (otherwise) (SI 2009/2567) |
| | | 29 Mar 2011 (W) (otherwise) (SI 2011/986) |
| | (8) | 21 Jul 2008 (in so far as is necessary for enabling the exercise on or after that date of the power to make regulations that is conferred by any amendment made by this section or in so far as any amendment made by this section defines any expression relevant to the exercise of such power) (s 170(1)(b)) |
| | | 29 Mar 2011 (otherwise) (SI 2011/986) |
| 147 | | 6 Apr 2009 (SI 2009/462; SI 2009/631) |
| 148 | | 19 Apr 2010 (SI 2010/708; SI 2010/989)[4, 6] |
| 149, 150 | | 21 Jul 2008 (in so far as is necessary for enabling the exercise on or after that date of the power to make regulations that is conferred by these sections or in so far as they define any expression relevant to the exercise of such power) (s 170(1)(b)) |
| | | 1 Apr 2009 (otherwise) (SI 2008/2994) |
| 151–154 | | 1 Apr 2009 (SI 2008/2994) |
| 155 | | 1 Dec 2008 (SI 2008/2994) |
| 156 | (1) | 1 Dec 2008 (SI 2008/2994) |
| | (2) | 1 Dec 2008 (definition "company") (SI 2008/2994) |
| | | 1 Apr 2009 (otherwise) (SI 2008/2994) |
| 157 | (1) | 21 Jul 2008 (in so far as is necessary for enabling the exercise on or after that date of the power to make regulations that is conferred by any amendment made by this section or in so far as any amendment made by this section defines any expression relevant to the exercise of such power) (s 170(1)(b)) |
| | | 1 Oct 2008 (in so far as inserts National Health Service Act 2006, ss 250A(1), 250C) (SI 2008/2497) |
| | | 1 Jan 2009 (otherwise) (SI 2008/2497) |
| | (2) | 1 Jan 2009 (SI 2008/2497) |
| 158 | | 1 Jan 2009 (SI 2008/2497) |
| 159 | (1)–(4) | 1 Apr 2009 (SI 2009/270) |
| | (5)(a) | 1 Mar 2009 (SI 2009/270) |
| | (5)(b) | 1 Apr 2009 (SI 2009/270) |
| | (6) | 1 Apr 2009 (SI 2009/270) |
| 160 | | See Sch 14 below |
| 161–165 | | 21 Jul 2008 (s 170(1)(a)) |
| 166 | | See Sch 15 below |

**Health and Social Care Act 2008 (c 14)**—*contd*

| | | |
|---|---|---|
| 167–173 | | 21 Jul 2008 (s 170(1)(a)) |
| Sch 1 | paras 1–5 | 21 Jul 2008 (in so far as is necessary for enabling the exercise on or after that date of the power to make regulations that is conferred by this Schedule or in so far as it defines any expression relevant to the exercise of such power) (s 170(1)(b)) |
| | | 1 Oct 2008 (otherwise) (SI 2008/2497) |
| | para 6(1), (2) | 21 Jul 2008 (in so far as is necessary for enabling the exercise on or after that date of the power to make regulations that is conferred by this Schedule or in so far as it defines any expression relevant to the exercise of such power) (s 170(1)(b)) |
| | | 1 Apr 2009 (otherwise) (SI 2009/462) |
| | para 6(3) | 21 Jul 2008 (in so far as is necessary for enabling the exercise on or after that date of the power to make regulations that is conferred by this Schedule or in so far as it defines any expression relevant to the exercise of such power) (s 170(1)(b)) |
| | | 1 Oct 2008 (otherwise) (SI 2008/2497) |
| | para 6(4) | 21 Jul 2008 (in so far as is necessary for enabling the exercise on or after that date of the power to make regulations that is conferred by this Schedule or in so far as it defines any expression relevant to the exercise of such power) (s 170(1)(b)) |
| | | 1 Oct 2008 (otherwise) (except in so far as relates to the advisory committee) (SI 2008/2497) |
| | | 1 Apr 2009 (exception noted above) (SI 2009/462) |
| | para 6(5) | 21 Jul 2008 (in so far as is necessary for enabling the exercise on or after that date of the power to make regulations that is conferred by this Schedule or in so far as it defines any expression relevant to the exercise of such power) (s 170(1)(b)) |
| | | 1 Apr 2009 (otherwise) (SI 2009/462) |
| | para 6(6)–(8) | 1 Oct 2008 (SI 2008/2497) |
| | para 7(1), (2) | 1 Oct 2008 (SI 2008/2497) |
| | para 7(3) | 1 Apr 2009 (SI 2009/462) |
| | paras 8–12 | 1 Oct 2008 (SI 2008/2497) |
| Sch 2 | | 1 Oct 2008 (SI 2008/2497) |
| Sch 3 | | 21 Jul 2008 (in so far as is necessary for enabling the exercise on or after that date of the power to make regulations that is conferred by any amendment made by this Schedule or in so far as any amendment made by this Schedule defines any expression relevant to the exercise of such power) (s 170(1)(b)) |
| | | 1 Apr 2009 (otherwise) (SI 2009/462) |
| Sch 4 | para 1 | 21 Jul 2008 (in so far as is necessary for enabling the exercise on or after that date of the power to make orders that is conferred by this Schedule or in so far as it defines any expression relevant to the exercise of such power) (s 170(1)(b)) |
| | | 1 Oct 2008 (otherwise) (SI 2008/2497) |
| | para 2 | 21 Jul 2008 (in so far as is necessary for enabling the exercise on or after that date of the power to make orders that is conferred by this Schedule or in so far as it defines any expression relevant to the exercise of such power) (s 170(1)(b)) |
| | | 1 Apr 2009 (otherwise) (SI 2009/462) |
| | para 3 | 21 Jul 2008 (in so far as is necessary for enabling the exercise on or after that date of the power to make orders that is conferred by this Schedule or in so far as it defines any expression relevant to the exercise of such power) (s 170(1)(b)) |
| | | 1 Oct 2008 (otherwise) (SI 2008/2497) |
| | para 4 | 1 Apr 2009 (SI 2009/462) |
| | para 5 | 21 Jul 2008 (in so far as is necessary for enabling the exercise on or after that date of the power to make orders that is conferred by this Schedule or in so far as it defines any expression relevant to the exercise of such power) (s 170(1)(b)) |
| | | 1 Oct 2008 (in so far as it relates to the functions of inspecting and reporting under Pt 1 of this Act) (SI 2008/2497) |

**Health and Social Care Act 2008 (c 14)**—*contd*

|  |  |  |
|---|---|---|
|  |  | 1 Oct 2010 (otherwise) (SI 2010/807) |
|  | para 6 | 21 Jul 2008 (in so far as is necessary for enabling the exercise on or after that date of the power to make orders that is conferred by this Schedule or in so far as it defines any expression relevant to the exercise of such power) (s 170(1)(b)) |
|  |  | 1 Apr 2009 (otherwise) (SI 2009/462) |
|  | paras 7, 8 | 21 Jul 2008 (in so far as is necessary for enabling the exercise on or after that date of the power to make orders that is conferred by this Schedule or in so far as it defines any expression relevant to the exercise of such power) (s 170(1)(b)) |
|  |  | 1 Oct 2008 (otherwise) (SI 2008/2497) |
|  | paras 9, 10 | 21 Jul 2008 (in so far as is necessary for enabling the exercise on or after that date of the power to make orders that is conferred by this Schedule or in so far as it defines any expression relevant to the exercise of such power) (s 170(1)(b)) |
|  |  | 1 Apr 2009 (otherwise) (SI 2009/462) |
| Sch 5 | para 1 | 1 Apr 2009 (SI 2009/462) |
|  | paras 2–4 | 21 Jul 2008 (in so far as is necessary for enabling the exercise on or after that date of the power to make regulations that is conferred by any amendment made by this Schedule or in so far as any amendment made by this Schedule defines any expression relevant to the exercise of such power) (s 170(1)(b)) |
|  |  | 1 Oct 2010 (otherwise) (SI 2010/807) |
|  | paras 5, 6 | 1 Oct 2010 (SI 2010/807) |
|  | para 7 | 1 Apr 2009 (SI 2009/462) |
|  | para 8 | 21 Jul 2008 (in so far as is necessary for enabling the exercise on or after that date of the power to make regulations that is conferred by any amendment made by this Schedule or in so far as any amendment made by this Schedule defines any expression relevant to the exercise of such power) (s 170(1)(b)) |
|  |  | 1 Apr 2009 (otherwise) (SI 2009/462) |
|  | para 9 | 1 Apr 2009 (SI 2009/462) |
|  | para 10 | 21 Jul 2008 (in so far as is necessary for enabling the exercise on or after that date of the power to make regulations that is conferred by any amendment made by this Schedule or in so far as any amendment made by this Schedule defines any expression relevant to the exercise of such power) (s 170(1)(b)) |
|  |  | 1 Oct 2010 (otherwise) (SI 2010/807) |
|  | para 11 | 21 Jul 2008 (in so far as is necessary for enabling the exercise on or after that date of the power to make regulations that is conferred by any amendment made by this Schedule or in so far as any amendment made by this Schedule defines any expression relevant to the exercise of such power) (s 170(1)(b)) |
|  |  | 2 Nov 2009 (E) (otherwise) (SI 2009/2862) |
|  |  | 1 Oct 2010 (W) (otherwise) (SI 2010/807) |
|  | para 12 | 21 Jul 2008 (in so far as is necessary for enabling the exercise on or after that date of the power to make regulations that is conferred by any amendment made by this Schedule or in so far as any amendment made by this Schedule defines any expression relevant to the exercise of such power) (s 170(1)(b)) |
|  |  | 1 Oct 2010 (otherwise) (SI 2010/807) |
|  | para 13 | 1 Apr 2009 (except in so far as it relates to notice given under the Care Standards Act 2000, s 20B) (SI 2009/462) |
|  |  | 1 Oct 2010 (exception noted above) (SI 2010/807) |
|  | para 14(a), (b)(i) | 21 Jul 2008 (in so far as is necessary for enabling the exercise on or after that date of the power to make regulations that is conferred by any amendment made by this Schedule or in so far as any amendment made by this Schedule defines any expression relevant to the exercise of such power) (s 170(1)(b)) |
|  |  | 1 Apr 2009 (otherwise) (SI 2009/462) |

**Health and Social Care Act 2008 (c 14)**—*contd*

| | |
|---|---|
| para 14(b)(ii) | 21 Jul 2008 (in so far as is necessary for enabling the exercise on or after that date of the power to make regulations that is conferred by any amendment made by this Schedule or in so far as any amendment made by this Schedule defines any expression relevant to the exercise of such power) (s 170(1)(b)) |
| | 2 Nov 2009 (E) (otherwise) (SI 2009/2862) |
| | 1 Oct 2010 (W) (otherwise) (SI 2010/807) |
| para 14(c) | 21 Jul 2008 (in so far as is necessary for enabling the exercise on or after that date of the power to make regulations that is conferred by any amendment made by this Schedule or in so far as any amendment made by this Schedule defines any expression relevant to the exercise of such power) (s 170(1)(b)) |
| | 1 Apr 2009 (otherwise) (SI 2009/462) |
| para 14(d) | 21 Jul 2008 (in so far as is necessary for enabling the exercise on or after that date of the power to make regulations that is conferred by any amendment made by this Schedule or in so far as any amendment made by this Schedule defines any expression relevant to the exercise of such power) (s 170(1)(b)) |
| | 1 Oct 2010 (otherwise) (SI 2010/807) |
| para 15 | 21 Jul 2008 (in so far as is necessary for enabling the exercise on or after that date of the power to make regulations that is conferred by any amendment made by this Schedule or in so far as any amendment made by this Schedule defines any expression relevant to the exercise of such power) (s 170(1)(b)) |
| | 2 Nov 2009 (E) (otherwise) (SI 2009/2862) |
| | 1 Oct 2010 (W) (otherwise) (SI 2010/807) |
| para 16(a) | 1 Oct 2010 (SI 2010/807) |
| paras 16(b), (c), 17 | 1 Apr 2009 (SI 2009/462) |
| paras 18, 19 | 1 Oct 2010 (SI 2010/807) |
| para 20(1) | See sub-paras (2)–(6) below |
| para 20(2)–(4) | 1 Oct 2010 (SI 2010/807) |
| para 20(5), (6) | 1 Apr 2009 (SI 2009/462) |
| para 21 | 21 Jul 2008 (in so far as is necessary for enabling the exercise on or after that date of the power to make regulations that is conferred by any amendment made by this Schedule or in so far as any amendment made by this Schedule defines any expression relevant to the exercise of such power) (s 170(1)(b)) |
| | 1 Oct 2010 (otherwise) (SI 2010/807) |
| paras 22, 23 | 1 Apr 2009 (SI 2009/462) |
| para 24(a) | 21 Jul 2008 (in so far as is necessary for enabling the exercise on or after that date of the power to make regulations that is conferred by any amendment made by this Schedule or in so far as any amendment made by this Schedule defines any expression relevant to the exercise of such power) (s 170(1)(b)) |
| | 1 Oct 2010 (otherwise) (SI 2010/807) |
| paras 24(b), (c), 25 | 21 Jul 2008 (in so far as is necessary for enabling the exercise on or after that date of the power to make regulations that is conferred by any amendment made by this Schedule or in so far as any amendment made by this Schedule defines any expression relevant to the exercise of such power) (s 170(1)(b)) |
| | 1 Apr 2009 (otherwise) (SI 2009/462) |
| paras 26–28 | 21 Jul 2008 (in so far as is necessary for enabling the exercise on or after that date of the power to make regulations that is conferred by any amendment made by this Schedule or in so far as any amendment made by this Schedule defines any expression relevant to the exercise of such power) (s 170(1)(b)) |
| | 1 Oct 2010 (otherwise) (SI 2010/807) |

**Health and Social Care Act 2008 (c 14)**—*contd*

| | | |
|---|---|---|
| para 29 | | 21 Jul 2008 (in so far as is necessary for enabling the exercise on or after that date of the power to make regulations that is conferred by any amendment made by this Schedule or in so far as any amendment made by this Schedule defines any expression relevant to the exercise of such power) (s 170(1)(b)) |
| | | 1 Apr 2009 (otherwise) (SI 2009/462) |
| para 30 | | 1 Apr 2009 (SI 2009/462) |
| para 31 | | 1 Oct 2010 (otherwise) (SI 2010/807) |
| para 32 | | 21 Jul 2008 (in so far as is necessary for enabling the exercise on or after that date of the power to make regulations that is conferred by any amendment made by this Schedule or in so far as any amendment made by this Schedule defines any expression relevant to the exercise of such power) (s 170(1)(b)) |
| | | 1 Apr 2009 (otherwise) (SI 2009/462) |
| paras 33–36 | | 1 Apr 2009 (SI 2009/462) |
| paras 37, 38 | | 1 Apr 2010 (SI 2010/708) |
| para 39 | | 1 Apr 2009 (SI 2009/462) |
| para 40 | | 1 Apr 2009 (except in so far as it relates to the Health and Social Care (Community Health and Standards) Act 2003, ss 66–69A) (SI 2009/462) |
| | | 6 Apr 2010 (exception noted above) (SI 2010/807) |
| para 41 | | 1 Apr 2009 (except in so far as it relates to the Health and Social Care (Community Health and Standards) Act 2003, ss 88–91) (SI 2009/462) |
| | | 6 Apr 2010 (exception noted above) (SI 2010/807) |
| para 42 | | 21 Jul 2008 (in so far as is necessary for enabling the exercise on or after that date of the power to make regulations that is conferred by any amendment made by this Schedule or in so far as any amendment made by this Schedule defines any expression relevant to the exercise of such power) (s 170(1)(b)) |
| | | 1 Apr 2009 (otherwise) (SI 2009/462) |
| paras 43–46 | | 1 Apr 2009 (SI 2009/462) |
| para 47 | | 1 Apr 2009 (except in so far as it relates to the Health and Social Care (Community Health and Standards) Act 2003, ss 136, 137) (SI 2009/462) |
| | | 6 Apr 2010 (exception noted above) (SI 2010/807) |
| paras 48–53, 54(a) | | 1 Apr 2009 (SI 2009/462) |
| para 54(b) | | 1 Oct 2008 (SI 2008/2497) |
| paras 55, 56(a) | | 1 Apr 2009 (SI 2009/462) |
| para 56(b) | | 1 Oct 2008 (SI 2008/2497) |
| para 57(1) | | See sub-paras (2), (3) below |
| para 57(2)(a) | | 1 Apr 2009 (SI 2009/462) |
| para 57(2)(b) | | 1 Oct 2008 (SI 2008/2497) |
| paras 57(3), 58(a) | | 1 Apr 2009 (SI 2009/462) |
| para 58(b) | | 1 Oct 2008 (SI 2008/2497) |
| para 59(1) | | See sub-paras (2), (3) below |
| para 59(2)(a) | | 1 Apr 2009 (SI 2009/462) |
| para 59(2)(b) | | 1 Oct 2008 (SI 2008/2497) |
| paras 59(3), 60–72, 73(a) | | 1 Apr 2009 (SI 2009/462) |
| para 73(b) | | 1 Oct 2008 (SI 2008/2497) |
| paras 74–79, 80(a) | | 1 Apr 2009 (SI 2009/462) |
| para 80(b) | | 1 Oct 2008 (SI 2008/2497) |
| paras 81–93 | | 1 Apr 2009 (SI 2009/462) |
| para 94 | | 1 Oct 2008 (SI 2008/2497) |
| Sch 6 | paras 1–3 | 21 Jul 2008 (in so far as is necessary for enabling the exercise on or after that date of the power to make regulations that is conferred by this Schedule or in so far as it defines any expression relevant to the exercise of such power) (s 170(1)(b)) |
| | | 25 Jan 2010 (otherwise) (SI 2010/23) |

**Health and Social Care Act 2008 (c 14)**—*contd*

| | | |
|---|---|---|
| | paras 4–10 | 21 Jul 2008 (in so far as is necessary for enabling the exercise on or after that date of the power to make regulations that is conferred by this Schedule or in so far as it defines any expression relevant to the exercise of such power) (s 170(1)(b)) |
| | | 28 Sep 2009 (otherwise) (SI 2009/2567) |
| | paras 11–14 | 21 Jul 2008 (in so far as is necessary for enabling the exercise on or after that date of the power to make regulations that is conferred by this Schedule or in so far as it defines any expression relevant to the exercise of such power) (s 170(1)(b)) |
| | | 25 Jan 2010 (otherwise) (SI 2010/23) |
| | paras 15, 16 | 21 Jul 2008 (in so far as is necessary for enabling the exercise on or after that date of the power to make regulations that is conferred by this Schedule or in so far as it defines any expression relevant to the exercise of such power) (s 170(1)(b)) |
| | | *Never in force* (otherwise) (repealed) |
| | paras 17–23 | 21 Jul 2008 (in so far as is necessary for enabling the exercise on or after that date of the power to make regulations that is conferred by this Schedule or in so far as it defines any expression relevant to the exercise of such power) (s 170(1)(b)) |
| | | 25 Jan 2010 (otherwise) (SI 2010/23) |
| Sch 7 | | *Never in force* (repealed) |
| Sch 8 | paras 1, 2 | 1 Jan 2009 (SI 2008/3244) |
| | para 3 | See paras 4–10 below |
| | paras 4, 5(1)–(3) | 1 Jan 2009 (SI 2008/3244) |
| | para 5(4) | 1 Oct 2008 (SI 2008/2497) |
| | paras 6, 7 | 1 Jan 2009 (SI 2008/3244) |
| | para 8(a) | 1 Oct 2008 (SI 2008/2497) |
| | paras 8(b), 9 | 1 Jan 2009 (SI 2008/3244) |
| | para 10 | 15 Jan 2014 (SI 2014/3251) |
| Sch 9 | | *Not yet in force* (para 9 repealed) |
| Sch 10 | paras 1, 2(a) | 1 Jan 2009 (SI 2008/3244) |
| | para 2(b) | 25 Jan 2010 (SI 2010/23) |
| | para 3 | 1 Jan 2009 (in so far as relates to the Public Bodies (Admission to Meetings) Act 1960, Schedule, paras 1(bca), 2(ca)) (SI 2008/3244) |
| | | 25 Jan 2010 (in so far as relates to paras 1(bcb), 2(cb) of that Schedule) (SI 2010/23) |
| | para 4(a) | 1 Jan 2009 (SI 2008/3244) |
| | para 4(b) | 28 Sep 2009 (SI 2009/2567) |
| | para 5(a) | 1 Jan 2009 (SI 2008/3244) |
| | para 5(b) | 28 Sep 2009 (SI 2009/2567) |
| | para 6(a) | 25 Jan 2010 (SI 2010/23) |
| | para 6(b) | 1 Jan 2009 (SI 2008/3244) |
| | para 7 | *Never in force* (repealed) |
| | para 8 | 1 Jan 2009 (SI 2008/3244) |
| | para 9 | *Never in force* (repealed) |
| | paras 10–12, 13(a) | 1 Jan 2009 (SI 2008/3244) |
| | para 13(b) | 25 Jan 2010 (SI 2010/23) |
| | paras 14, 15 | *Never in force* (repealed) |
| | paras 16, 17 | 1 Jan 2009 (SI 2008/3244) |
| | para 18 | *Never in force* (repealed) |
| | para 19 | 1 Jan 2009 (SI 2008/3244) |
| | para 20 | 25 Aug 2008 (SI 2008/2214) |
| | para 21 | 25 Aug 2008 (in so far as inserts Health Act 2006, s 60(3)(a)) (SI 2008/2214) |
| | | 4 Jun 2009 (in so far as inserts s 60(3)(b) thereof) (SI 2009/1310) |
| | para 22 | 25 Jan 2010 (SI 2010/23) |
| | paras 23–25, 26(a) | 1 Jan 2009 (SI 2008/3244) |
| | para 26(b) | 28 Sep 2009 (SI 2009/2567) |
| | para 27 | *Never in force* (repealed) |

**Health and Social Care Act 2008 (c 14)**—*contd*

| | | |
|---|---|---|
| Sch 11 | | 21 Jul 2008 (in so far as is necessary for enabling the exercise on or after that date of the power to make regulations that is conferred by any amendment made by this Schedule or in so far as any amendment made by this Schedule defines any expression relevant to the exercise of such power) (s 170(1)(b)) |
| | | 6 Apr 2010 (E) (otherwise) (SI 2010/708) |
| | | 26 Jul 2010 (W) (otherwise) (SI 2010/1547)[7] |
| Sch 12 | Pt 1 | 1 Apr 2010 (SI 2010/708) |
| | Pt 2 | 21 May 2010 (SI 2010/1457) |
| Sch 13 | | 6 Apr 2009 (SI 2009/462; SI 2009/631) |
| Sch 14 | para 1 | *Never in force* (repealed) |
| | paras 2–4 | 1 Oct 2008 (SI 2008/2497) |
| | para 5 | 1 Jan 2009 (SI 2008/2497) |
| | paras 6, 7 | 1 Apr 2009 (SI 2009/462) |
| | para 8 | *Not yet in force* |
| Sch 15 | Pt 1 | 1 Apr 2009 (SI 2009/462), except repeals of or in— |
| | |   Care Standards Act 2000, ss 11, 30A, 42, 113A; |
| | |   Health and Social Care (Community Health and Standards) Act 2003, ss 46, 66–69A, 88–91 |
| | | 1 Apr 2010 (SI 2010/708), repeal of— |
| | |   Health and Social Care (Community Health and Standards) Act 2003, s 46 |
| | | 6 Apr 2010 (SI 2010/807), repeals of or in— |
| | |   Care Standards Act 2000, ss 30A, 42, 113A; |
| | |   Health and Social Care (Community Health and Standards) Act 2003, ss 66–69A, 88–91 |
| | | 1 Oct 2010 (SI 2010/807), repeal in— |
| | |   Care Standards Act 2000, s 11 |
| | Pt 2 | 1 Jan 2009 (SI 2008/3244), repeals of or in— |
| | |   National Health Service Reform and Health Care Professions Act 2002, ss 25, 26, 29(1)(e), Sch 7; |
| | |   Health Act 2006 |
| | | 1 Apr 2010 (except in so far as relating to ss 1(1), (7), 12 and the Schedule of the Hearing Aid Council Act 1968) (SI 2010/708), repeals of or in— |
| | |   Hearing Aid Council Act 1968; |
| | |   Hearing Aid Council (Extension) Act 1975; |
| | |   Hearing Aid Council (Amendment) Act 1989 |
| | | 1 Aug 2010 (SI 2010/708), repeals of or in— |
| | |   Hearing Aid Council Act 1968 (otherwise); |
| | |   Hearing Aid Council (Extension) Act 1975 (otherwise); |
| | |   Supreme Court Act 1981; |
| | |   Hearing Aid Council (Amendment) Act 1989 (otherwise); |
| | |   Courts and Legal Services Act 1990; |
| | |   Value Added Tax Act 1994; |
| | |   Freedom of Information Act 2000; |
| | |   Income Tax (Earnings and Pensions) Act 2003; |
| | |   Constitutional Reform Act 2005 |
| | | *Not yet in force*, repeals of or in— |
| | |   Medical Act 1983; |
| | |   Opticians Act 1989; |
| | |   Health Act 1999; |
| | |   National Health Service Reform and Health Care Professions Act 2002, s 29(1)(c), (f) |
| | Pt 3 | 6 Apr 2010 (E) (SI 2010/708)[4], repeals of or in— |
| | |   Local Government, Planning and Land Act 1980; |
| | |   Public Health (Control of Disease) Act 1984 (except ss 13–15, 76); |
| | |   Planning and Compensation Act 1991 |
| | | 26 Jul 2010 (W) (SI 2010/1547)[7], repeals of or in— |

**Health and Social Care Act 2008 (c 14)**—*contd*

|  |  |
|---|---|
|  | Local Government, Planning and Land Act 1980; |
|  | Public Health (Control of Disease) Act 1984 (except ss 13–15, 76); |
|  | Planning and Compensation Act 1991 |
|  | *Not yet in force*, repeals of or in— |
|  | Public Health (Control of Disease) Act 1984 (exceptions noted above) |
| Pt 4 | 1 Apr 2010 (SI 2010/708), repeals of or in— |
|  | National Health Service Act 2006, ss 228–230, Sch 14 |
|  | 21 May 2010 (SI 2010/1457), repeals of or in— |
|  | National Health Service (Wales) Act 2006, ss 174–176, Sch 8 |
|  | 1 Apr 2013 (SI 2013/159), repeals of or in— |
|  | National Health Service Act 2006, s 164 |
|  | *Not yet in force*, repeals of or in— |
|  | National Health Service Act 2006, s 71; |
|  | National Health Service (Wales) Act 2006, s 88 |
| Pt 5 | 6 Apr 2009 (SI 2009/462; SI 2009/631) |
| Pt 6 | 1 Jan 2009 (SI 2008/2497) |
| Pt 7 | 1 Apr 2009 (SI 2009/270) |

[1]  SI 2008/2717, art 2(2) defines "new proceedings" as all proceedings to which the Health Act 1999, s 60A(1) applies, except—

(a)  proceedings under the General Optical Council (Fitness to Practise) Rules 2005 where the Presenting Officer addressed the Fitness to Practise Committee in relation to each allegation in accordance with rule 45 before 3 Nov 2008;

(b)  proceedings under the General Medical Council (Fitness to Practise) Rules 2004—

  (i)  before a Fitness to Practise Panel where the allegation and the alleged facts were read out by the person acting as secretary in accordance with rule 17(2)(c) before 31 May 2008, or

  (ii)  before the Investigation Committee where the Presenting Officer began to outline the allegation and the facts in accordance with rule 11(7) before 31 May 2008;

(c)  proceedings under the Nursing and Midwifery Council (Fitness to Practise) Rules 2004 where the Chair of the Committee asked for the charge to be read out in accordance with rule 24(2)(b) before 3 Nov 2008;

(d)  proceedings under the Nurses, Midwives and Health Visitors (Professional Conduct) Rules 1993 where the charge was read out in accordance with rule 15(2) before 3 Nov 2008;

(e)  proceedings under the General Dental Council Professional Conduct Committee (Procedure) Rules 1984; and

(f)  proceedings under the General Dental Council Health Committee (Procedure) Rules 1984

[2]  For transitory and transitional provisions, see SI 2008/3168, arts 3–8

[3]  For transitory, transitional and saving provisions, see SI 2009/462, arts 7–11, Schs 2–4

[4]  For transitional provisions and savings, see SI 2010/708, arts 9, 12, Sch 2

[5]  For transitory and transitional provisions, see SI 2010/807, arts 3–22

[6]  For transitional provisions, see SI 2010/989, arts 3, 4

[7]  For transitional provisions and savings, see SI 2010/1547, art 3, Sch 1

**Housing and Regeneration Act 2008 (c 17)**

*RA:* 22 Jul 2008

*Commencement provisions*: s 325; Housing and Regeneration Act 2008 (Commencement No 1 and Transitional Provision) Order 2008, SI 2008/2358; Housing and Regeneration Act 2008 (Commencement No 2 and Transitional, Saving and Transitory Provisions) Order 2008, SI 2008/3068[2]; Housing and Regeneration Act 2008 (Commencement No 3) Order 2009, SI 2009/363; Housing and Regeneration Act 2008 (Commencement No 1 and Saving Provisions)

**Housing and Regeneration Act 2008 (c 17)**—*contd*

Order 2009, SI 2009/415; Housing and Regeneration Act 2008 (Commencement No 1) (Wales) Order 2009, SI 2009/773; Housing and Regeneration Act 2008 (Commencement No 4 and Transitory Provisions) Order 2009, SI 2009/803; Housing and Regeneration Act 2008 (Commencement No 5) Order 2009, SI 2009/1261; Housing and Regeneration Act 2008 (Commencement No 6 and Transitional and Savings Provisions) Order 2009, SI 2009/2096; Housing and Regeneration Act 2008 (Commencement No 7 and Transitional and Saving Provisions) Order 2010, SI 2010/862[5]; Housing and Regeneration Act 2008 (Commencement No 8 and Transitional, Transitory and Saving Provisions) Order 2011, SI 2011/1002; Housing and Regeneration Act 2008 (Commencement No 2) (Wales) Order 2011, SI 2011/1863; Housing and Regeneration Act 2008 (Commencement No 3 and Transitional, Transitory and Saving Provisions) (Wales) Order 2013, SI 2013/1469

| | | |
|---|---|---|
| 1–3 | | 8 Sep 2008 (SI 2008/2358) |
| 4 | | 8 Sep 2008 (in relation to the specific powers brought into force by SI 2008/2358) (SI 2008/2358) |
| | | 1 Dec 2008 (in relation to the powers brought into force by SI 2008/3068) (SI 2008/3068)[2] |
| | | 1 Apr 2010 (otherwise) (SI 2010/862) |
| 5–18 | | 1 Dec 2008 (SI 2008/3068)[2] |
| 19 | (1)–(4) | 1 Dec 2008 (except for the purpose of enabling the HCA to give financial assistance on condition that the recipient provides social housing) (SI 2008/3068) |
| | | 1 Apr 2010 (exception noted above) (SI 2010/862) |
| | (5) | 1 Dec 2008 (SI 2008/3068) |
| | (6) | 1 Apr 2010 (SI 2010/862) |
| 20–30 | | 1 Dec 2008 (SI 2008/3068) |
| 31 | | 1 Apr 2010 (SI 2010/862) |
| 32 | | 1 Apr 2009 (for the purposes of enabling the HCA to make a determination under sub-s (1) or (8)) (SI 2009/803) |
| | | 1 Apr 2010 (otherwise) (SI 2010/862) |
| 33 | | 1 Apr 2009 (for the purposes of enabling the HCA to make a determination under sub-s (8)) (SI 2009/803) |
| | | 1 Apr 2010 (otherwise) (SI 2010/862) |
| 34 | | 1 Apr 2009 (SI 2009/803) |
| 35 | | 1 Apr 2010 (SI 2010/862) |
| 36 | | 1 Apr 2009 (SI 2009/803) |
| 37 | | 8 Sep 2008 (SI 2008/2358) |
| 38–43 | | 1 Dec 2008 (SI 2008/3068) |
| 44 | | 8 Sep 2008 (SI 2008/2358) |
| 45 | | 1 Dec 2008 (SI 2008/3068) |
| 46, 47 | | 8 Sep 2008 (SI 2008/2358) |
| 48 | | 1 Dec 2008 (SI 2008/3068) |
| 49 | | 8 Sep 2008 (SI 2008/2358) |
| 50 | (1) | 8 Sep 2008 (SI 2008/2358) |
| | (2) | See Sch 5 below |
| 51–55 | | 8 Sep 2008 (SI 2008/2358) |
| 56 | | See Sch 8 below |
| 57 | | 8 Sep 2008 (so far as required for the interpretation of provisions commenced by SI 2008/2358) (SI 2008/2358) |
| | | 1 Dec 2008 (so far as required for the interpretation of provisions commenced by SI 2008/3068) (SI 2008/3068) |
| | | 1 Apr 2010 (otherwise) (SI 2010/862) |
| 58 | | 8 Sep 2008 (so far as required for the interpretation of provisions commenced by SI 2008/2358) (SI 2008/2358) |
| | | 1 Dec 2008 (so far as required for the interpretation of provisions commenced by SI 2008/3068) (SI 2008/3068) |
| | | 1 Apr 2009 (so far as required for the interpretation of provisions commenced by SI 2009/803, art 2) (SI 2009/803) |
| | | 1 Apr 2010 (otherwise) (SI 2010/862) |
| 59 | | 8 Sep 2008 (SI 2008/2358) |
| 60–63 | | 1 Apr 2010 (SI 2010/862) |

**Housing and Regeneration Act 2008 (c 17)**—*contd*

| | | |
|---|---|---|
| 64 | (1), (2) | 16 Feb 2009 (SI 2009/363) |
| | (3) | 1 Apr 2010 (SI 2010/862) |
| 65, 66 | | 8 Sep 2008 (in so far as they apply in relation to, or make provision about the tax implications of, schemes under s 65) (SI 2008/2358) |
| | | *Not yet in force* (otherwise) |
| 67 | | 8 Sep 2008 (in so far as they apply in relation to, or make provision about the tax implications of, schemes under s 65) (SI 2008/2358) |
| | | 1 Apr 2010 (otherwise) (SI 2010/862) |
| 68–71 | | 8 Sep 2008 (for the purposes of interpretation of, and giving effect to, s 72 and other provisions of Pt 2 commenced by SI 2008/2358) (SI 2008/2358) |
| | | 1 Apr 2010 (otherwise) (SI 2010/862) |
| 72 | | 8 Sep 2008 (SI 2008/2358) |
| 73–80 | | 8 Sep 2008 (for the purposes of interpretation of, and giving effect to, s 72 and other provisions of Pt 2 commenced by SI 2008/2358) (SI 2008/2358) |
| | | 1 Apr 2010 (otherwise) (SI 2010/862) |
| 81–85 | | 8 Sep 2008 (SI 2008/2358) |
| 86 | | 8 Sep 2008 (in relation to the exercise of functions of the regulator commenced by SI 2008/2358) (SI 2008/2358) |
| | | 1 Apr 2010 (otherwise) (SI 2010/862) |
| 87–92 | | 8 Sep 2008 (SI 2008/2358) |
| 93 | | 8 Sep 2008 (in relation only to the exercise of functions of the regulator commenced by SI 2008/2358) (SI 2008/2358) |
| | | 1 Apr 2009 (otherwise) (SI 2009/803) |
| 94 | | 1 Apr 2010 (SI 2010/862) |
| 95 | (1), (2) | 8 Sep 2008 (in relation only to the exercise of functions of the regulator commenced by SI 2008/2358) (SI 2008/2358) |
| | | 1 Apr 2010 (otherwise) (SI 2010/862) |
| | (3), (4) | 1 Apr 2010 (SI 2010/862) |
| | (5) | 8 Sep 2008 (in relation only to the exercise of functions of the regulator commenced by SI 2008/2358) (SI 2008/2358) |
| | | 1 Apr 2010 (otherwise) (SI 2010/862) |
| 96–98 | | 8 Sep 2008 (in relation only to the exercise of functions of the regulator commenced by SI 2008/2358) (SI 2008/2358) |
| | | 1 Apr 2010 (otherwise) (SI 2010/862) |
| 99–105 | | 8 Sep 2008 (SI 2008/2358) |
| 106–111 | | 1 Apr 2010 (SI 2010/862) |
| 112 | (1), (2) | 1 Apr 2010 (SI 2010/862) |
| | (3), (4) | 8 Sep 2008 (for the purpose only of the regulator setting relevant criteria under sub-s (3)) (SI 2008/2358)[1] |
| | | 1 Apr 2010 (otherwise) (SI 2010/862) |
| 113 | (1)–(4) | 1 Apr 2010 (SI 2010/862) |
| | (5), (6) | 8 Sep 2008 (for the purpose only of the Secretary of State making regulations under sub-s (5)) (SI 2008/2358) |
| | | 1 Apr 2010 (otherwise) (SI 2010/862) |
| 114 | | 8 Sep 2008 (for the purpose only of consultation being carried out by the Secretary of State under sub-s (6)) (SI 2008/2358) |
| | | 7 Sep 2009 (otherwise) (SI 2009/2096) |
| 115 | | 1 Apr 2010 (SI 2010/862) |
| 116 | (1) | 1 Apr 2010 (SI 2010/862) |
| | (2) | 8 Sep 2008 (SI 2008/2358) |
| | (3)–(5) | 1 Apr 2010 (SI 2010/862) |
| 117 | | 8 Sep 2008 (for the purpose only of the regulator prescribing the amount of fees and making related provision as described in sub-ss (3)–(8)) (SI 2008/2358) |
| | | 1 Apr 2010 (otherwise) (SI 2010/862) |
| 118 | | 1 Apr 2010 (SI 2010/862) |

**Housing and Regeneration Act 2008 (c 17)**—*contd*

| | | |
|---|---|---|
| 119 | (1) | 1 Apr 2010 (SI 2010/862) |
| | (2) | 8 Sep 2008 (for the purpose only of the regulator setting and publishing criteria for de-registration) (SI 2008/2358) |
| | | 1 Apr 2010 (otherwise) (SI 2010/862) |
| | (3)–(6) | 1 Apr 2010 (SI 2010/862) |
| | (7) | 8 Sep 2008 (for the purpose only of the regulator setting and publishing criteria for de-registration) (SI 2008/2358) |
| | | 1 Apr 2010 (otherwise) (SI 2010/862) |
| 120–126 | | 1 Apr 2010 (SI 2010/862) |
| 127 | (1)–(5) | 1 Apr 2010 (SI 2010/862) |
| | (6) | 8 Sep 2008 (for the purpose only of consultation by the regulator with bodies mentioned herein) (SI 2008/2358)[1] |
| | | 1 Apr 2010 (otherwise) (SI 2010/862) |
| | (7) | 1 Apr 2010 (SI 2010/862) |
| 128–130 | | 1 Apr 2010 (SI 2010/862) |
| 131 | (1)–(4) | 1 Apr 2010 (SI 2010/862) |
| | (5) | 8 Sep 2008 (SI 2008/2358) |
| | (6), (7) | 1 Apr 2010 (SI 2010/862) |
| 132–143 | | 1 Apr 2010 (SI 2010/862) |
| 144 | | 1 Apr 2009 (for the purposes of enabling the Secretary of State to make an order) (SI 2009/803) |
| | | 1 Apr 2010 (otherwise) (SI 2010/862) |
| 145 | (1)–(3) | 1 Apr 2010 (SI 2010/862) |
| | (4) | 1 Apr 2009 (for the purposes of enabling the Secretary of State to make an order) (SI 2009/803) |
| | | 1 Apr 2010 (otherwise) (SI 2010/862) |
| 146–173 | | 1 Apr 2010 (SI 2010/862) |
| 174 | (1)–(4) | 1 Apr 2010 (SI 2010/862) |
| | (5), (6) | 8 Sep 2008 (SI 2008/2358)[1] |
| 175–191 | | 1 Apr 2010 (SI 2010/862) |
| 192–197 | | 8 Sep 2008 (SI 2008/2358)[1] |
| 198 | (1) | 1 Apr 2010 (SI 2010/862) |
| | (2)–(5) | 8 Sep 2008 (SI 2008/2358) |
| 199–201 | | 1 Apr 2010 (SI 2010/862) |
| 202 | (1)–(3) | 1 Apr 2010 (SI 2010/862) |
| | (4) | 8 Sep 2008 (for the purposes only of the Secretary of State authorising the regulator to charge fees for inspections, and of the regulator prescribing a scale of fees for inspections) (SI 2008/2358) |
| | | 1 Apr 2010 (otherwise) (SI 2010/862) |
| | (5) | 1 Apr 2010 (SI 2010/862) |
| | (6), (7) | 8 Sep 2008 (for the purposes only of the Secretary of State authorising the regulator to charge fees for inspections, and of the regulator prescribing a scale of fees for inspections) (SI 2008/2358) |
| | | 1 Apr 2010 (otherwise) (SI 2010/862) |
| 203–211 | | 1 Apr 2010 (SI 2010/862) |
| 212 | (1) | 1 Apr 2010 (SI 2010/862) |
| | (2) | 8 Sep 2008 (SI 2008/2358) |
| | (3)–(7) | 1 Apr 2010 (SI 2010/862) |
| | (8) | 8 Sep 2008 (SI 2008/2358) |
| 213 | | 1 Apr 2010 (SI 2010/862) |
| 214 | (1) | 1 Apr 2010 (SI 2010/862) |
| | (2) | 8 Sep 2008 (SI 2008/2358) |
| | (3)–(6) | 1 Apr 2010 (SI 2010/862) |
| | (7) | 8 Sep 2008 (SI 2008/2358) |
| 215 | (1), (2) | 8 Sep 2008 (SI 2008/2358) |
| | (3) | 1 Apr 2010 (SI 2010/862) |
| 216 | | 8 Sep 2008 (SI 2008/2358)[1] |
| 217–227 | | 1 Apr 2010 (SI 2010/862) |

**Housing and Regeneration Act 2008 (c 17)**—*contd*

| | | |
|---|---|---|
| 228 | (1)–(4) | 1 Apr 2010 (SI 2010/862) |
| | (5) | 1 Apr 2009 (for the purposes of enabling the Secretary of State to make regulations) (SI 2009/803) |
| | | 1 Apr 2010 (otherwise) (SI 2010/862) |
| 229–233 | | 1 Apr 2010 (SI 2010/862) |
| 234 | (1) | 1 Apr 2010 (SI 2010/862) |
| | (2) | 1 Apr 2009 (for the purposes of enabling the Treasury to make regulations) (SI 2009/803) |
| | | 1 Apr 2010 (otherwise) (SI 2010/862) |
| | (3) | 1 Apr 2010 (SI 2010/862) |
| | (4) | 1 Apr 2009 (for the purposes of enabling the Treasury to make regulations) (SI 2009/803) |
| | | 1 Apr 2010 (otherwise) (SI 2010/862) |
| | (5), (6) | 1 Apr 2010 (SI 2010/862) |
| 235–239 | | 1 Apr 2010 (SI 2010/862) |
| 240 | (1)–(4) | 1 Apr 2010 (SI 2010/862) |
| | (5) | 1 Apr 2009 (for the purposes of enabling the Secretary of State to make regulations) (SI 2009/803) |
| | | 1 Apr 2010 (otherwise) (SI 2010/862) |
| 241–243 | | 1 Apr 2010 (SI 2010/862) |
| 244 | (1) | 1 Apr 2010 (SI 2010/862) |
| | (2) | 1 Apr 2009 (for the purposes of enabling the Treasury to make regulations) (SI 2009/803) |
| | | 1 Apr 2010 (otherwise) (SI 2010/862) |
| | (3) | 1 Apr 2010 (SI 2010/862) |
| | (4) | 1 Apr 2009 (for the purposes of enabling the Treasury to make regulations) (SI 2009/803) |
| | | 1 Apr 2010 (otherwise) (SI 2010/862) |
| 245–274 | | 1 Apr 2010 (SI 2010/862) |
| 275, 276 | | 8 Sep 2008 (so far as required for the interpretation of provisions commenced by SI 2008/2358) (SI 2008/2358) |
| | | 1 Apr 2010 (otherwise) (SI 2010/862) |
| 277 | | See Sch 9 below |
| 278 | | 1 Apr 2010 (SI 2010/862) |
| 279–284 | | *Not yet in force* |
| 285 | (1), (2) | *Not yet in force* |
| | (3) | See Sch 10 below |
| 286–293 | | *Not yet in force* |
| 294 | | 22 Sep 2008 (s 325(2)) |
| 295, 296 | | 1 Dec 2008 (E) (SI 2008/3068)[3] |
| | | *Not yet in force* (W) |
| 297 | | 1 Jan 2009 (E) (SI 2008/3068)[3] |
| | | *Not yet in force* (W) |
| 298 | (1)–(4) | 1 Jan 2009 (E) (SI 2008/3068)[3] |
| | | *Not yet in force* (W) |
| | (5), (6) | 1 Dec 2008 (for the purpose of enabling the Secretary of State to make regulations under sub-s (5) or (8)) (SI 2008/3068) |
| | | 1 Jan 2009 (E) (otherwise) (SI 2008/3068)[3] |
| | | *Not yet in force* (W) |
| | (7) | 1 Jan 2009 (E) (SI 2008/3068)[3] |
| | | *Not yet in force* (W) |
| | (8), (9) | 1 Dec 2008 (for the purpose of enabling the Secretary of State to make regulations under sub-s (5) or (8)) (SI 2008/3068) |
| | | 1 Jan 2009 (E) (otherwise) (SI 2008/3068)[3] |
| | | *Not yet in force* (W) |
| | (10) | 1 Jan 2009 (E) (SI 2008/3068)[3] |
| | | *Not yet in force* (W) |
| 299 | | See Sch 11 below |
| 300 | | 7 Sep 2009 (E) (SI 2009/2096)[4] |

**Housing and Regeneration Act 2008 (c 17)**—*contd*

| | | |
|---|---|---|
| | | *Not yet in force* (W) |
| 301, 302 | | 1 Dec 2008 (for the purpose of enabling the Secretary of State to make (a) regulations, prescribing requirements, exemptions, conditions and percentages, for the purposes of the Leasehold Reform Act 1967, Sch 4A, paras 3A or 4A; and (b) orders under para 4A of that Schedule) (SI 2008/3068) |
| | | 7 Sep 2009 (E) (otherwise) (SI 2009/2096)[4] |
| | | *Not yet in force* (W) |
| 303 | | See Sch 12 below |
| 304 | | 22 Sep 2008 (s 325(2)) |
| 305 | | See Sch 13 below |
| 306, 307 | | 22 Sep 2008 (s 325(2)) |
| 308 | | 1 Dec 2008 (in relation to loans in respect of service charges on flats in England only) (SI 2008/3068) |
| | | 19 Aug 2011 (W) (SI 2011/1863) |
| 309 | | 1 Dec 2008 (for the purpose of enabling the Secretary of State to make regulations under the Housing Act 1985, s 450D) (SI 2008/3068) |
| | | 6 Apr 2009 (E) (otherwise) (SI 2009/803) |
| | | 26 Jul 2011 (for the purpose of enabling the Welsh Ministers to make regulations under the Housing Act 1985, s 450D) (SI 2011/1863) |
| | | 19 Aug 2011 (W) (otherwise) (SI 2011/1863) |
| 310 | | 22 Sep 2008 (s 325(2)) |
| 311 | | See Sch 14 below |
| 312, 313 | | 22 Sep 2008 (s 325(2)) |
| 314 | | See Sch 15 below |
| 315 | | 1 Dec 2008 (E) (in relation to applications (a) for an allocation of housing accommodation, to which section 166 of the Housing Act 1996 applies; or (b) to which Part VII, as applied by s 183(1) of that Act, applies, made on or after this date) (SI 2008/3068)[3] |
| | | 30 Mar 2009 (W) (in relation to applications (a) for an allocation of housing accommodation, to which section 166 of the Housing Act 1996 applies; or (b) to which Part VII, as applied by s 183(1) of that Act, applies, made on or after this date) (SI 2009/773) |
| | | *Not yet in force* (otherwise) |
| 316 | | 7 Sep 2009 (SI 2009/2096)[4] |
| 317 | | 22 Sep 2008 (SI 2008/2358) |
| 318 | | 30 Apr 2011 (E) (SI 2011/1002)[6] |
| | | 10 Jul 2013 (W) (SI 2013/1469)[7] |
| 319 | | 22 Sep 2008 (s 325(2)) |
| 320 | | 22 Jul 2008 (s 325(6)) |
| 321 | (1) | See Sch 16 below |
| | (2)–(4) | 22 Jul 2008 (s 325(6)) |
| 322–326 | | 22 Jul 2008 (s 325(6)) |
| Sch 1 | | 8 Sep 2008 (SI 2008/2358) |
| Schs 2–4 | | 1 Dec 2008 (SI 2008/3068)[2] |
| Sch 5 | para 1 | 1 Dec 2008 (SI 2008/3068) |
| | paras 2–4 | 1 Apr 2009 (SI 2009/803) |
| | paras 5–9 | 1 Dec 2008 (SI 2008/3068)[2] |
| | paras 10–24 | 1 Apr 2009 (SI 2009/803) |
| | paras 25, 26 | 1 Dec 2008 (SI 2008/3068) |
| | paras 27, 28 | 1 Apr 2009 (SI 2009/803) |
| | para 29 | 1 Dec 2008 (SI 2008/3068) |
| | para 30 | 1 Apr 2009 (SI 2009/803) |
| | para 31 | 1 Dec 2008 (SI 2008/3068)[2] |
| | para 32 | 1 Apr 2009 (SI 2009/803) |

**Housing and Regeneration Act 2008 (c 17)**—*contd*

| | | |
|---|---|---|
| Schs 6, 7 | | 8 Sep 2008 (in so far as they apply in relation to, or make provision about the tax implications of, schemes under s 65) (SI 2008/2358) |
| | | *Not yet in force* (otherwise) (Sch 7, para 9 repealed) |
| Sch 8 | para 1 | 8 Sep 2008 (SI 2008/2358) |
| | paras 2, 3 | 1 Dec 2008 (SI 2008/3068) |
| | para 4(a), (b) | 8 Sep 2008 (SI 2008/2358)[2] |
| | para 4(c), (d) | 1 Apr 2009 (SI 2009/803) |
| | paras 5–12 | 1 Dec 2008 (SI 2008/3068)[2] |
| | para 13 | 1 Apr 2009 (SI 2009/803) |
| | paras 14–18 | 1 Dec 2008 (SI 2008/3068)[2] |
| | para 19(1), (2) | 8 Sep 2008 (SI 2008/2358) |
| | para 19(3) | 1 Apr 2009 (SI 2009/803) |
| | para 20(1), (2) | 8 Sep 2008 (SI 2008/2358) |
| | para 20(3) | 1 Apr 2009 (SI 2009/803) |
| | para 21(1), (2) | 8 Sep 2008 (SI 2008/2358) |
| | para 21(3) | 1 Apr 2009 (SI 2009/803) |
| | paras 22–34 | 1 Dec 2008 (SI 2008/3068) |
| | para 35 | 1 Apr 2010 (SI 2010/862) |
| | paras 36–43 | 1 Dec 2008 (SI 2008/3068)[2] |
| | paras 44–50 | 1 Apr 2010 (SI 2010/862) |
| | paras 51–62 | 1 Dec 2008 (SI 2008/3068)[2] |
| | para 63 | 1 Dec 2008 (except in so far as relates to repeals of the Leasehold Reform, Housing and Urban Development Act 1993, s 158, Schs 17, 18) (SI 2008/3068)[2] |
| | | 1 Apr 2009 (exception noted above) (SI 2009/803) |
| | para 64 | 1 Dec 2008 (SI 2008/3068)[2] |
| | para 65 | 1 Apr 2010 (SI 2010/862) |
| | paras 66–76 | 1 Dec 2008 (SI 2008/3068)[2] |
| | para 77(1), (2) | 8 Sep 2008 (SI 2008/2358) |
| | para 77(3) | 1 Apr 2009 (SI 2009/803) |
| | paras 78–83 | 1 Dec 2008 (SI 2008/3068)[2] |
| Sch 9 | para 1 | 8 Sep 2008 (SI 2008/2358) |
| | para 2(1), (2) | 8 Sep 2008 (SI 2008/2358) |
| | para 2(3) | 1 Apr 2009 (SI 2009/803) |
| | para 3(1), (2) | 8 Sep 2008 (SI 2008/2358) |
| | para 3(3) | 1 Apr 2009 (SI 2009/803) |
| | para 4 | 1 Dec 2008 (SI 2008/3068) |
| | para 5 | 1 Apr 2010 (SI 2010/862) |
| | para 6 | 1 Dec 2008 (SI 2008/3068) |
| | paras 7–27 | 1 Apr 2010 (SI 2010/862) |
| | para 28(1), (2) | 8 Sep 2008 (SI 2008/2358) |
| | para 28(3) | 1 Apr 2009 (SI 2009/803) |
| | paras 29–34 | 1 Apr 2010 (SI 2010/862) |
| Sch 10 | | *Not yet in force* |
| Sch 11 | Pt 1, paras 1, 2 | 20 May 2009 (SI 2009/1261) |
| | Pt 1, para 3(1), (2) | 20 May 2009 (SI 2009/1261) |
| | Pt 1, para 3(3) | *Not yet in force* |
| | Pt 1, paras 3(4), 4–7, 8(1), (2) | 20 May 2009 (SI 2009/1261) |
| | Pt 1, para 8(3) | *Not yet in force* |
| | Pt 1, paras 8(4), 9–13, 14(1), (2) | 20 May 2009 (SI 2009/1261) |
| | Pt 1, para 14(3) | *Not yet in force* |
| | Pt 1, para 14(4), (5) | 20 May 2009 (SI 2009/1261) |
| | Pt 2, paras 15–26 | 1 Dec 2008 (for the purpose of enabling the appropriate national authority to make orders under this Part of this Schedule) (SI 2008/3068) |

**Housing and Regeneration Act 2008 (c 17)**—*contd*

|  |  |  |
|---|---|---|
|  |  | 20 May 2009 (otherwise) (SI 2009/1261) |
| Sch 12 | paras 1–10 | 1 Dec 2008 (for the purpose of enabling the Secretary of State to make regulations under the Landlord and Tenant Act 1985, s 21) (SI 2008/3068) |
|  |  | *Not yet in force* (otherwise) |
|  | paras 11–13 | 1 Dec 2008 (for the purpose of enabling the Secretary of State to make regulations under the Landlord and Tenant Act 1987, s 42A) (SI 2008/3068) |
|  |  | *Not yet in force* (otherwise) |
|  | paras 14–16 | *Not yet in force* |
| Sch 13 |  | 22 Sep 2008 (s 325(2)) |
| Sch 14 |  | 1 Dec 2008 (SI 2008/3068) |
| Sch 15 | Pt 1, paras 1–8 | 2 Mar 2009 (in relation to applications for an allocation of housing accommodation under the Housing Act 1996, Pt VI or for accommodation or assistance in obtaining accommodation under Pt VII of that Act made on or after that date) (SI 2009/415) |
|  | Pt 2, paras 9–22 | 2 Mar 2009 (in relation to applications for accommodation or assistance in obtaining accommodation under the Housing (Scotland) Act 1987, Pts I or II or for housing assistance under the Housing (Northern Ireland) Order 1988, SI 1988/1990, Pt II made on or after that date) (SI 2009/415) |
|  | Pt 3, paras 23–25 | 2 Mar 2009 (SI 2009/415) |
| Sch 16 |  | 22 Sep 2008 (repeal of or in Housing Act 1985, ss 125D(2), 128(2), 136(2), Sch 5, para 13(5)) (s 325(2)) |
|  |  | 22 Sep 2008 (repeal of Housing Act 1985, s 156(5), (6)) (SI 2008/2358) |
|  |  | 1 Dec 2008 (SI 2008/3068), repeals of or in— |

Leasehold Reform Act 1967, Sch 4 (E)[3];

Local Government Act 1974;

Statutory Corporations (Financial Provisions) Act 1974;

Local Government, Planning and Land Act 1980;

New Towns Act 1981, ss 36–38, 41, 72, 82, Sch 10;

Compulsory Purchase (Vesting Declarations) Act 1981;

New Towns and Urban Development Corporations Act 1985, ss 1, 2, Sch 3, paras 5, 6, 16;

Landlord and Tenant Act 1987, s 58;

Local Government and Housing Act 1989, s 172;

Town and Country Planning Act 1990;

Leasehold Reform, Housing and Urban Development Act 1993, ss 135, 137, 159–173, 175, 177, 181, 183–185, 188, Schs 19, 20, 21;

Finance Act 1996;

Housing Act 1996, s 199 (E)[3], s 202, Sch 13;

Housing Grants, Construction and Regeneration Act 1996, s 129;

Housing Act 1996 (Consequential Provisions) Order 1996, SI 1996/2325, Sch 2, para 21;

Regional Development Agencies Act 1998;

Urban Development Corporations in England (Transfer of Property, Rights and Liabilities) Commission for the New Towns) Order 1998, SI 1998/85;

Greater London Authority Act 1999;

Transport Act 2000;

Armed Forces Act 2001;

Postal Services Act 2000 (Consequential Modifications No 1) Order 2001, SI 2001/1149;

Deregulation (Disposals of Dwelling-houses by Local Authorities) Order 2002, SI 2002/367;

Communications Act 2003;

**Housing and Regeneration Act 2008 (c 17)**—*contd*
  Armed Forces Act 2006;
  Tribunals, Courts and Enforcement Act 2007
 2 Mar 2009 (SI 2009/415), repeals of or in—
  Housing Act 1996, s 202 (already brought into force by
   SI 2008/3068);
  Criminal Justice and Immigration Act 2008
 1 Apr 2009 (SI 2009/803), repeals of or in—
  Parliamentary Commissioner Act 1967;
  National Loans Act 1968;
  House of Commons Disqualification Act 1975;
  Northern Ireland Assembly Disqualification Act 1975;
  Race Relations Act 1976;
  New Towns Act 1981, ss 35, 58, 58A, 59–61, 62B, 63, 67–71,
   77, 80, Schs 9, 11;
  New Towns and Urban Development Corporations Act 1985,
   Sch 3, paras 3, 8, 12;
  Local Government and Housing Act 1989, Sch 11;
  Leasehold Reform, Housing and Urban Development Act 1993,
   s 158, Schs 17, 18;
  New Towns (Amendment) Act 1994;
  Local Government (Wales) Act 1994;
  Housing Act 1996, Sch 18;
  Housing Grants, Construction and Regeneration Act 1996,
   s 145;
  Freedom of Information Act 2000;
  Government Resources and Accounts Act 2000 (Audit of Public
   Bodies) Order 2003, SI 2003/1326;
  Companies Act 2006 (Commencement No 3, Consequential
   Amendments, Transitional Provisions and Savings) Order 2007,
   SI 2007/2194
 20 May 2009 (SI 2009/1261), repeals of or in—
  Anti-social Behaviour Act 2003
 7 Sep 2009 (E) (SI 2009/2096)[4], repeals of or in—
  Leasehold Reform Act 1967 (so far as not already repealed)
 1 Apr 2010 (SI 2010/862), repeals of or in—
  Housing Associations Act 1985;
  Housing Act 1988 (except s 9);
  Local Government and Housing Act 1989, s 173;
  Housing Act 1996, ss 1, 28, 56, Sch 2;
  Housing Act 1996 (Consequential Provisions) Order 1996,
   SI 1996/2325, Sch 2, paras 15, 18, 19;
  Housing Act 1996 (Consequential Provisions) Order 1997,
   SI 1997/74;
  Audit Commission Act 1998;
  Government of Wales Act 1998;
  Local Government Act 2003;
  Public Audit (Wales) Act 2004;
  Charities Act 2006;
  Local Government and Public Involvement in Health Act 2007;
  Housing and Regeneration Act 2008
 30 Apr 2011 (E) (SI 2011/1002)[6], repeals of or in—
  Mobile Homes Act 1983 (E);
  Criminal Justice and Public Order Act 1994 (E)
 10 Jul 2013 (W) (SI 2013/1469)[7], repeals of or in—
  Mobile Homes Act 1983;
  Criminal Justice and Public Order Act 1994
 *Not yet in force*, repeals of or in—
  Leasehold Reform Act 1967 (W);
  Building Act 1984;

**Housing and Regeneration Act 2008 (c 17)**—*contd*

> Housing Act 1985, s 85;
> Landlord and Tenant Act 1985;
> Housing (Scotland) Act 1987;
> Landlord and Tenant Act 1987, s 53, Sch 2;
> Housing Act 1988, s 9;
> Companies Act 1989 (Eligibility for Appointment as Company
>   Auditor) (Consequential Amendments) Regulations 1991,
>   SI 1991/1997;
> Leasehold Reform, Housing and Urban Development Act 1993,
>   s 65;
> Environment Act 1995;
> Family Law Act 1996;
> Housing Act 1996, ss 105, 127, 143D, s 199 (W), Sch 9;
> Commonhold and Leasehold Reform Act 2002;
> Civil Partnership Act 2004

[1]   For a transitional provision, see SI 2008/2358, art 3(3), (4)

[2]   For transitional and saving provisions, see SI 2008/3068, arts 6–13

[3]   It is thought that because SI 2008/3068 was made by the Secretary of State, it brings these provisions into force in relation to England only; see s 325(3), (4) of this Act

[4]   For transitional and saving provisions, see SI 2009/2096, art 3

[5]   For transitional and saving provisions, see SI 2010/862, Schedule

[6]   For transitional and saving provisions, see SI 2011/1002, arts 3–7

[7]   For transitional, transitory and saving provisions, see SI 2013/1469, arts 3–7, Schedule

---

**Human Fertilisation and Embryology Act 2008 (c 22)**

*RA:* 13 Nov 2008

*Commencement provisions:* s 68; Human Fertilisation and Embryology Act 2008 (Commencement No 1 and Transitional Provisions) Order 2009, SI 2009/479, as amended by SI 2009/2232; Human Fertilisation and Embryology Act 2008 (Commencement No 2 and Transitional Provision) and (Commencement No 1 Amendment) Order 2009, SI 2009/2232; Human Fertilisation and Embryology Act 2008 (Commencement No 3) Order 2010, SI 2010/987

| | | |
|---|---|---|
| 1–7 | | 1 Oct 2009 (SI 2009/2232) |
| 8 | | 6 Apr 2009 (in so far as inserts Human Fertilisation and Embryology Act 1990, ss 8B, 8C(1)–(6), 8D, but only for the purpose of enabling the establishment of one or more committees to carry out the Authority's functions under new s 20 of the 1990 Act when it is brought into force) (SI 2009/479) |
| | | 1 Oct 2009 (otherwise) (SI 2009/2232) |
| 9–13 | | 1 Oct 2009 (SI 2009/2232) |
| 14 | (1) | See sub-ss (2)–(4) below |
| | (2) | 1 Oct 2009 (SI 2009/2232) |
| | (3) | 6 Apr 2009 (SI 2009/479)[1] |
| | (4) | 1 Oct 2009 (SI 2009/2232) |
| | (5) | See Sch 4 below |
| | (6) | 1 Oct 2009 (SI 2009/2232) |
| 15 | (1), (2) | 1 Oct 2009 (SI 2009/2232) |
| | (3) | 6 Apr 2009 (for the purpose of making regulations under the Human Fertilisation and Embryology Act 1990, s 14(5)) (SI 2009/479)[2] |
| | | 1 Oct 2009 (otherwise) (SI 2009/2232) |
| | (4) | 1 Oct 2009 (SI 2009/2232) |

**Human Fertilisation and Embryology Act 2008 (c 22)**—*contd*

| | | |
|---|---|---|
| (5) | | 6 Apr 2009 (for the purpose of making regulations under the Human Fertilisation and Embryology Act 1990, s 14(5)) (SI 2009/479)[2] |
| | | 1 Oct 2009 (otherwise) (SI 2009/2232) |
| 16–18 | | 1 Oct 2009 (SI 2009/2232) |
| 19 | | 6 Apr 2009 (for the purpose of enabling regulations to be made under the new Human Fertilisation and Embryology Act 1990, s 19(6) and directions to be made under new s 19B(1) of the 1990 Act) (SI 2009/479)[2] |
| | | 1 Oct 2009 (otherwise) (SI 2009/2232) |
| 20 | | 1 Oct 2009 (SI 2009/2232) |
| 21 | | 6 Apr 2009 (for the purpose of (a) substituting the new Human Fertilisation and Embryology Act 1990, s 20A(1), (2), to enable the establishment of one or more committees to carry out the Authority's functions under new s 20 of the 1990 Act when it is brought into force; and (b) enabling regulations to be made under new ss 20A(3)–(5), 20B(2)–(6) of the 1990 Act) (SI 2009/479)[2] |
| | | 1 Oct 2009 (otherwise) (SI 2009/2232) |
| 22, 23 | | 1 Oct 2009 (SI 2009/2232) |
| 24 | | 6 Apr 2009 (for the purpose of enabling regulations to be made under the new Human Fertilisation and Embryology Act 1990, s 31ZA(2)(a)) (SI 2009/479)[2] |
| | | 1 Oct 2009 (otherwise) (SI 2009/2232) |
| 25 | | 6 Apr 2009 (for the purpose of enabling regulations to be made under the new Human Fertilisation and Embryology Act 1990, s 33D) (SI 2009/479)[2] |
| | | 1 Oct 2009 (otherwise, except in so far as inserts Human Fertilisation and Embryology Act 1990, s 33A(2)(q)) (SI 2009/2232)[4] |
| | | 6 Apr 2010 (otherwise) (SI 2010/987) |
| 26 | | 1 Oct 2009 (except in so far as inserts Human Fertilisation and Embryology Act 1990, s 35A(2)(b)) (SI 2009/2232) |
| | | 6 Apr 2010 (otherwise) (SI 2010/987) |
| 27–29 | | 1 Oct 2009 (SI 2009/2232) |
| 30 | | 6 Apr 2009 (SI 2009/479)[2] |
| 31, 32 | | 1 Oct 2009 (SI 2009/2232) |
| 33–53 | | 6 Apr 2009 (SI 2009/479)[1] |
| 54 | | 1 Oct 2009 (for the purpose of enabling regulations to be made under s 55 in relation to parental orders) (SI 2009/2232) |
| | | 6 Apr 2010 (otherwise) (SI 2010/987) |
| 55 | | 1 Oct 2009 (SI 2009/2232) |
| 56 | | See Sch 6 below |
| 57 | (1), (2) | 6 Apr 2009 (SI 2009/479) |
| | (3), (4) | 6 Apr 2010 (SI 2010/987) |
| 58 | | 6 Apr 2009 (SI 2009/479) |
| 59, 60 | | 1 Oct 2009 (SI 2009/2232) |
| 61–64 | | 13 Nov 2008 (s 68(1)) |
| 65 | | See Sch 7 below |
| 66 | | See Sch 8 below |
| 67–69 | | 13 Nov 2008 (s 68(1)) |
| Schs 1–3 | | 1 Oct 2009 (SI 2009/2232) |
| Sch 4 | | 6 Apr 2009 (SI 2009/479)[1] |
| Sch 5 | | 1 Oct 2009 (SI 2009/2232) |
| Sch 6 | paras 1–12 | 6 Apr 2009 (for the purpose of enabling the exercise of any power to make orders, regulations or other instruments or other documents) (SI 2009/479) |
| | | 1 Sep 2009 (otherwise) (SI 2009/479) |
| | paras 13–15 | 6 Apr 2009 (SI 2009/479) |

**Human Fertilisation and Embryology Act 2008 (c 22)**—*contd*

| | |
|---|---|
| paras 16–19 | 6 Apr 2009 (for the purpose of enabling the exercise of any power to make orders, regulations or other instruments or other documents) (SI 2009/479) |
| | 1 Sep 2009 (otherwise) (SI 2009/479) |
| paras 20, 21 | 6 Apr 2010 (SI 2010/987) |
| para 22 | 6 Apr 2009 (SI 2009/479) |
| para 23 | 6 Apr 2009 (for the purpose of enabling the exercise of any power to make orders, regulations or other instruments or other documents) (SI 2009/479) |
| | 1 Sep 2009 (otherwise) (SI 2009/479) |
| paras 24, 25 | 6 Apr 2009 (SI 2009/479) |
| paras 26–32 | 6 Apr 2009 (for the purpose of enabling the exercise of any power to make orders, regulations or other instruments or other documents) (SI 2009/479) |
| | 1 Sep 2009 (otherwise) (SI 2009/479) |
| paras 33–35 | 6 Apr 2009 (SI 2009/479) |
| para 36 | 6 Apr 2009 (for the purpose of substituting the Child Support Act 1991, s 26(2), case B1 only) (SI 2009/479) |
| | 6 Apr 2010 (otherwise) (SI 2010/987) |
| paras 37, 38 | 6 Apr 2010 (SI 2010/987) |
| para 39 | 6 Apr 2009 (for the purpose of enabling the exercise of any power to make orders, regulations or other instruments or other documents) (SI 2009/479) |
| | 1 Sep 2009 (otherwise) (SI 2009/479) |
| para 40 | 6 Apr 2009 (SI 2009/479) |
| paras 41–51, 52(1) | 6 Apr 2009 (for the purpose of enabling the exercise of any power to make orders, regulations or other instruments or other documents) (SI 2009/479) |
| | 1 Sep 2009 (otherwise) (SI 2009/479) |
| para 52(2) | 6 Apr 2009 (for the purpose of enabling the exercise of any power to make orders, regulations or other instruments or other documents) (SI 2009/479) |
| | 6 Apr 2010 (otherwise) (SI 2010/987) |
| paras 52(3), 53, 54(a) | 6 Apr 2009 (for the purpose of enabling the exercise of any power to make orders, regulations or other instruments or other documents) (SI 2009/479) |
| | 1 Sep 2009 (otherwise) (SI 2009/479) |
| para 54(b) | 6 Apr 2009 (for the purpose of enabling the exercise of any power to make orders, regulations or other instruments or other documents) (SI 2009/479) |
| | 6 Apr 2010 (otherwise) (SI 2010/987) |
| paras 55, 56 | 6 Apr 2009 (for the purpose of enabling the exercise of any power to make orders, regulations or other instruments or other documents) (SI 2009/479) |
| | 1 Sep 2009 (otherwise) (SI 2009/479) |
| paras 57–59 | 6 Apr 2009 (SI 2009/479) |
| paras 60–66 | 6 Apr 2009 (for the purpose of enabling the exercise of any power to make orders, regulations or other instruments or other documents) (SI 2009/479) |
| | 1 Sep 2009 (otherwise) (SI 2009/479) |
| para 67 | 6 Apr 2009 (SI 2009/479) |
| para 68 | 6 Apr 2009 (for the purpose of enabling the exercise of any power to make orders, regulations or other instruments or other documents) (SI 2009/479) |
| | 1 Sep 2009 (otherwise) (SI 2009/479) |
| para 69 | 6 Apr 2009 (for the purpose of substituting the Child Support (Northern Ireland) Order 1991, art 27(2), case B1 only) (SI 2009/479) |
| | 6 Apr 2010 (otherwise) (SI 2010/987) |

**Human Fertilisation and Embryology Act 2008 (c 22)**—*contd*

| | | |
|---|---|---|
| | paras 70–72 | 6 Apr 2009 (for the purpose of enabling the exercise of any power to make orders, regulations or other instruments or other documents) (SI 2009/479) |
| | | 1 Sep 2009 (otherwise) (SI 2009/479) |
| | para 73 | 6 Apr 2010 (SI 2010/987) |
| | paras 74–78 | 6 Apr 2009 (for the purpose of enabling the exercise of any power to make orders, regulations or other instruments or other documents) (SI 2009/479) |
| | | 1 Sep 2009 (otherwise) (SI 2009/479) |
| | para 79 | 6 Apr 2010 (SI 2010/987) |
| Sch 7 | paras 1–14, 15(a), (b) | 1 Oct 2009 (SI 2009/2232) |
| | para 15(c) | 6 Apr 2009 (SI 2009/479)[2] |
| | paras 16–25 | 1 Oct 2009 (SI 2009/2232) |
| Sch 8 | Pt 1 | 6 Apr 2009 (SI 2009/479), repeal in— |

Human Fertilisation and Embryology Act 1990, s 14(5) (for the purpose of making regulations under that subsection)

1 Sep 2009 (SI 2009/479), repeals of or in—
Family Law Act (Northern Ireland) 2001;
Human Fertilisation and Embryology (Deceased Fathers) Act 2003

1 Oct 2009 (SI 2009/2232), repeals of or in—
Surrogacy Arrangements Act 1985;
Human Fertilisation and Embryology Act 1990 (so far as not already repealed, except s 30);
Human Fertilisation and Embryology (Disclosure of Information) Act 1992;
Criminal Justice and Police Act 2001;
Human Reproductive Cloning Act 2001

6 Apr 2010 (SI 2010/987), repeals of or in—
Human Fertilisation and Embryology Act 1990, s 30

| | | |
|---|---|---|
| | Pt 2 | 6 Apr 2009 (SI 2009/479), revocations in— |

Children (Northern Ireland) Order 1995 (for the purpose of enabling the exercise of any power to make orders, regulations or other instruments or other documents)[3]

1 Sep 2009 (SI 2009/479), revocations in—
Children (Northern Ireland) Order 1995 (so far as not already in force)

1 Oct 2009 (SI 2009/2232), revocation of—
Human Fertilisation and Embryology (Research Purposes) Regulations 2001, SI 2001/188

[1]   For transitional provisions, see SI 2009/479, art 7, Sch 1

[2]   By SI 2009/479, art 5(h), any provision of this Act in so far as the provision, or any amendment made by the provision, defines any expression relevant to the exercise of any power to make orders, regulations or directions under this Act or any provision conferred or amended by this Act that is commenced by SI 2009/479, comes into force on 6 Apr 2009

[3]   The drafting of SI 2009/479, art 6(e) is unclear but it is thought the intention is to bring this repeal into force for these purposes on 6 Apr 2009

[4]   For a transitional provision, see SI 2009/2232, art 4

---

## Judiciary and Courts (Scotland) Act 2008 (asp 6)

*RA*: 29 Oct 2008

*Commencement provisions*: s 76(1); Judiciary and Courts (Scotland) Act 2008 (Commencement No 1) Order 2009, SSI 2009/83; Judiciary and Courts (Scotland) Act 2008 (Commencement No 2) Order 2009, SSI 2009/192; Judiciary and Courts (Scotland) Act 2008 (Commencement No 3)

**Judiciary and Courts (Scotland) Act 2008 (asp 6)**—*contd*
    Order 2009, SSI 2009/318; Judiciary and Courts (Scotland) Act 2008 (Commencement No 4, Transitional Provisions and Savings) Order 2010, SSI 2010/39

| | | |
|---|---|---|
| 1 | | 1 Jun 2009 (SSI 2009/192) |
| 2 | (1) | 1 Jun 2009 (for the purposes of sub-s (2)(b), (c)) (SSI 2009/192) |
| | | 1 Apr 2010 (otherwise) (SSI 2010/39) |
| | (2)(a) | 1 Apr 2010 (SSI 2010/39) |
| | (2)(b), (c) | 1 Jun 2009 (SSI 2009/192) |
| | (2)(d), (e) | 1 Apr 2010 (SSI 2010/39) |
| | (3), (4) | 1 Apr 2010 (SSI 2010/39) |
| | (5), (6) | 1 Jun 2009 (for the purposes of sub-s (2)(b), (c)) (SSI 2009/192) |
| | | 1 Apr 2010 (otherwise) (SSI 2010/39) |
| | (7) | 1 Apr 2010 (SSI 2010/39) |
| 3 | | 1 Apr 2010 (SSI 2010/39) |
| 4–26 | | 1 Jun 2009 (SSI 2009/192) |
| 27 | | 1 Oct 2009 (SSI 2009/318) |
| 28–36 | | 1 Apr 2010 (SSI 2010/39)[1] |
| 37 | (1)–(4) | 1 Apr 2010 (SSI 2010/39)[1] |
| | (5) | 20 Feb 2010 (SSI 2010/39)[1] |
| | (6), (7) | 1 Apr 2010 (SSI 2010/39)[1] |
| 38, 39 | | 1 Apr 2010 (SSI 2010/39)[1] |
| 40 | | 20 Feb 2010 (in so far as it inserts Sheriff Courts (Scotland Act) 1971, s 12(C)(5))) (SSI 2010/39)[1] |
| | | 1 Apr 2010 (otherwise) (SSI 2010/39)[1] |
| 41–43 | | 1 Apr 2010 (SSI 2010/39)[1] |
| 44–46 | | 1 Jun 2009 (SSI 2009/192) |
| 47–58 | | 1 Apr 2010 (SSI 2010/39)[1] |
| 59 | | 16 Mar 2009 (SSI 2009/83) |
| 60 | (1) | 1 Oct 2009 (SSI 2009/318) |
| | (2) | See Sch 3 below |
| 61–65 | | 1 Apr 2010 (SSI 2010/39) |
| 66 | | 1 Oct 2009 (SSI 2009/318) |
| 67–70 | | 1 Apr 2010 (SSI 2010/39) |
| 71, 72 | | 29 Oct 2008 (RA) |
| 73 | | See Sch 5 below |
| 74–76 | | 29 Oct 2008 (RA) |
| Schs 1, 2 | | 1 Jun 2009 (SSI 2009/192) |
| Sch 3 | para 1 | *Never in force* (repealed) |
| | paras 2, 3(1) | 1 Jun 2009 (SSI 2009/192) |
| | para 3(2)–(4) | 16 Mar 2009 (SSI 2009/83) |
| | paras 4, 5 | 1 Jun 2009 (SSI 2009/192) |
| | para 6 | 1 Oct 2009 (SSI 2009/318) |
| | paras 7, 8 | 1 Jun 2009 (SSI 2009/192) |
| | paras 9–14 | 1 Oct 2009 (SSI 2009/318) |
| | paras 15–17 | 1 Apr 2010 (SSI 2010/39) |
| | para 18 | 1 Oct 2009 (SSI 2009/318) |
| | para 19 | 1 Apr 2010 (SSI 2010/39) |
| | para 20 | 1 Oct 2009 (SSI 2009/318) |
| Sch 4 | | 1 Apr 2010 (SSI 2010/39) |
| Sch 5 | paras 1–3 | 1 Apr 2010 (SSI 2010/39)[1] |
| | para 4 | 1 Jun 2009 (SSI 2009/192) |
| | para 5 | 1 Apr 2010 (SSI 2010/39) |

---

[1]   For transitional provisions and savings, see SS1 2010/39, arts 3–8

**Learner Travel (Wales) Measure 2008 (nawm 2)**

*Passed by the National Assembly for Wales:* 30 Sep 2008

*Approved by Her Majesty in Council:* 10 Dec 2008

*Commencement provisions:* s 28; Learner Travel (Wales) Measure 2008 (Commencement No 1) Order 2009, SI 2009/371; Learner Travel (Wales) Measure 2008 (Commencement No 2) Order 2009, SI 2009/2819

| | | |
|---|---|---|
| 1 | (1)–(3) | 6 Mar 2009 (SI 2009/371) |
| | (4)(a)–(i) | 6 Mar 2009 (SI 2009/371) |
| | (4)(j) | 30 Oct 2009 (in so far as relates to s 12) (SI 2009/2819) |
| | | *Not yet in force* (otherwise) |
| 2 | | 6 Mar 2009 (SI 2009/371) |
| 3, 4 | | 1 Sep 2009 (SI 2009/371) |
| 5 | | 6 Mar 2009 (in so far as relates to s 2) (SI 2009/371) |
| | | 1 Sep 2009 (in so far as relates to ss 3, 4) (SI 2009/371) |
| 6 | | 6 Mar 2009 (SI 2009/371) |
| 7–9 | | 1 Sep 2009 (SI 2009/371) |
| 10, 11 | | 6 Mar 2009 (SI 2009/371) |
| 12 | | 30 Oct 2009 (SI 2009/2819) |
| 13, 14 | | 4 Jan 2010 (SI 2009/2819) |
| 15, 16 | | 6 Mar 2009 (SI 2009/371) |
| 17 | (1), (2) | 6 Mar 2009 (SI 2009/371) |
| | (3) | 1 Sep 2009 (SI 2009/371) |
| | (4) | 4 Jan 2010 (SI 2009/2819) |
| 18 | | 1 Sep 2009 (SI 2009/371) |
| 19 | | 6 Mar 2009 (SI 2009/371) |
| 20 | | 1 Sep 2009 (SI 2009/371) |
| 21 | | 6 Mar 2009 (SI 2009/371) |
| 22 | | 1 Sep 2009 (SI 2009/371) |
| 23, 24 | | 6 Mar 2009 (SI 2009/371) |
| 25 | | See Sch 1 below |
| 26 | | See Sch 2 below |
| 27–29 | | 10 Feb 2009 (s 28(1)) |
| Sch 1 | para 1 | 1 Sep 2009 (SI 2009/371) |
| | para 2(1) | 1 Sep 2009 (SI 2009/371) |
| | para 2(2)(a), (b) | 1 Sep 2009 (SI 2009/371) |
| | para 2(2)(c) | 6 Mar 2009 (in so far as inserts Transport Act 1985, s 6(1B)(e)) (SI 2009/371) |
| | | 1 Sep 2009 (in so far as inserts Transport Act 1985, s 6(1B)(d)) (SI 2009/371) |
| | para 2(3) | 6 Mar 2009 (except in so far as substitutes reference to the Transport Act 1985, s 6(1C)(d)) (SI 2009/371) |
| | | 1 Sep 2009 (exception noted above) (SI 2009/371) |
| | para 3 | 1 Sep 2009 (SI 2009/371) |
| | para 4(1)–(4) | 6 Mar 2009 (SI 2009/371) |
| | para 4(5) | 1 Sep 2009 (SI 2009/371) |
| | para 5 | 1 Sep 2009 (SI 2009/371) |
| Sch 2 | | 6 Mar 2009 (SI 2009/371), repeals of or in— |
| | | Education Act 1996, ss 509AA, 509AB, 509AC; |
| | | Education and Inspections Act 2006, s 83, Sch 10, para 5 |
| | | 1 Sep 2009 (SI 2009/371), repeals of or in— |
| | | Public Passenger Vehicles Act 1981; |
| | | Transport Act 1985; |
| | | Education Act 1996, ss 444, 455, 509, 509A; |
| | | School Standards and Framework Act 1998; |
| | | Learning and Skills Act 2000; |
| | | Education Act 2002 |
| | | 30 Oct 2009 (SI 2009/2819), repeals of or in— |
| | | Education and Inspections Act 2006, Sch 10, para 4 |

## Local Transport Act 2008 (c 26)

*RA:* 26 Nov 2008

*Commencement provisions:* s 134; Local Transport Act 2008 (Commencement No 1 and Transitional Provisions) Order 2009, SI 2009/107; Local Transport Act 2008 (Commencement No 1 and Transitional Provisions) (Wales) Order 2009, SI 2009/579; Local Transport Act 2008 (Commencement No 2 and Transitional Provision) Order 2009, SI 2009/3242; Local Transport Act 2008 (Commencement No 2) (Wales) Order 2009, SI 2009/3294; Local Transport Act 2008 (Commencement No 3) Order 2013, SI 2013/685

| | | |
|---|---|---|
| 1 | | 26 Nov 2008 (so far as confers power to make an order) (s 134(1)(c)) |
| | | 9 Feb 2009 (otherwise) (SI 2009/107) |
| 2 | | In force on the day after the day on which the Secretary of State first makes an order under s 6 hereof (SI 2013/685) |
| 3 | (1) | 4 Mar 2009 (so far as inserts Public Passenger Vehicles Act 1981, ss 4A, 4C, 4D) (SI 2009/107) |
| | | In force on the day after the day on which the Secretary of State first makes an order under s 6 hereof (otherwise) (SI 2013/685) |
| | (2)–(4) | 4 Mar 2009 (SI 2009/107) |
| 4 | (1) | See sub-ss (2)–(9) below |
| | (2), (3) | 6 Apr 2013 (SI 2013/685) |
| | (4)–(9) | In force on the day after the day on which the Secretary of State first makes an order under s 6 hereof (SI 2013/685) |
| 5 | | In force on the day after the day on which the Secretary of State first makes an order under s 6 hereof (SI 2013/685) |
| 6 | | 26 Nov 2008 (so far as confers the power to make an order) (s 134(1)(c)) |
| | | 9 Feb 2009 (otherwise) (SI 2009/107) |
| 7 | | 9 Feb 2009 (E) (SI 2009/107) |
| | | 1 Apr 2009 (W) (SI 2009/579) |
| 8 | | 9 Feb 2009 (E) (SI 2009/107)[1] |
| | | 1 Apr 2009 (W) (SI 2009/579) |
| 9 | (1) | 1 Apr 2009 (W) (SI 2009/579) |
| | | 1 Apr 2011 (E) (SI 2009/107) |
| | (2) | See sub-ss (3)–(5) below |
| | (3) | 1 Apr 2009 (W) (SI 2009/579) |
| | | 1 Apr 2011 (SI 2009/107)[1] |
| | (4), (5) | 9 Feb 2009 (E) (SI 2009/107) |
| | | 1 Apr 2009 (W) (SI 2009/579) |
| 10–12 | | 9 Feb 2009 (E) (SI 2009/107)[1] |
| | | 1 Apr 2009 (W) (SI 2009/579)[2] |
| 13 | (1) | See sub-ss (2)–(7) below |
| | (2) | 9 Feb 2009 (E) (SI 2009/107) |
| | | 1 Apr 2009 (W) (SI 2009/579) |
| | (3)–(7) | 6 Apr 2009 (E) (SI 2009/107) |
| | | 31 Jan 2010 (W) (SI 2009/3294) |
| 14–18 | | 6 Apr 2009 (E) (SI 2009/107) |
| | | 31 Jan 2010 (W) (SI 2009/3294) |
| 19–22 | | 11 Jan 2010 (E) (SI 2009/3242)[3] |
| | | *Not yet in force* (W) |
| 23 | | 26 Nov 2008 (so far as confers the power to make regulations) (s 134(1)(c)) |
| | | 11 Jan 2010 (E) (otherwise) (SI 2009/3242) |
| | | *Not yet in force* (W) (otherwise) |
| 24 | | 11 Jan 2010 (E) (SI 2009/3242) |
| | | *Not yet in force* (W) |
| 25 | | 26 Nov 2008 (so far as confers the power to make regulations) (s 134(1)(c)) |
| | | 11 Jan 2010 (E) (otherwise) (SI 2009/3242) |
| | | *Not yet in force* (W) (otherwise) |

**Local Transport Act 2008 (c 26)**—*contd*

| | | |
|---|---|---|
| 26 | (1)–(7) | 11 Jan 2010 (E) (SI 2009/3242) |
| | | *Not yet in force* (W) |
| | (8) | 26 Nov 2008 (so far as confers the power to make an order) (s 134(1)(c)) |
| | | 11 Jan 2010 (E) (otherwise) (SI 2009/3242) |
| | | *Not yet in force* (W) (otherwise) |
| | (9) | 11 Jan 2010 (E) (SI 2009/3242) |
| | | *Not yet in force* (W) |
| 27–34 | | 11 Jan 2010 (E) (SI 2009/3242) |
| | | *Not yet in force* (W) |
| 35 | | 26 Nov 2008 (so far as confers the power to make regulations) (s 134(1)(c)) |
| | | 11 Jan 2010 (E) (otherwise) (SI 2009/3242) |
| | | *Not yet in force* (W) (otherwise) |
| 36, 37 | | 11 Jan 2010 (E) (SI 2009/3242) |
| | | *Not yet in force* (W) |
| 38 | | 26 Nov 2008 (so far as confers the power to make regulations) (s 134(1)(c)) |
| | | 11 Jan 2010 (E) (otherwise) (SI 2009/3242) |
| | | *Not yet in force* (W) (otherwise) |
| 39, 40 | | 11 Jan 2010 (E) (SI 2009/3242) |
| | | *Not yet in force* (W) |
| 41 | (1)–(5) | 11 Jan 2010 (E) (SI 2009/3242) |
| | | *Not yet in force* (W) |
| | (6) | 26 Nov 2008 (so far as confers the power to make regulations) (s 134(1)(c)) |
| | | 11 Jan 2010 (E) (otherwise) (SI 2009/3242) |
| | | *Not yet in force* (W) (otherwise) |
| 42, 43 | | 11 Jan 2010 (E) (SI 2009/3242) |
| | | *Not yet in force* (W) |
| 44 | (1) | 26 Nov 2008 (so far as confers the power to make regulations) (s 134(1)(c)) |
| | | 11 Jan 2010 (E) (otherwise) (SI 2009/3242) |
| | | *Not yet in force* (W) (otherwise) |
| | (2), (3) | 11 Jan 2010 (E) (SI 2009/3242) |
| | | *Not yet in force* (W) |
| 45 | | 11 Jan 2010 (E) (SI 2009/3242) |
| | | *Not yet in force* (W) |
| 46 | (1), (2) | 9 Feb 2009 (E) (SI 2009/107) |
| | | 1 Apr 2009 (W) (SI 2009/579) |
| | (3) | See Sch 2 below |
| 47 | (1) | 9 Feb 2009 (SI 2009/107) |
| | (2) | See Sch 3 below |
| 48 | | 26 Nov 2008 (so far as confers the power to make regulations) (s 134(1)(c)) |
| | | 6 Apr 2009 (otherwise) (SI 2009/107) |
| 49 | | 26 Nov 2008 (so far as confers the power to make regulations) (s 134(1)(c)) |
| | | 11 Jan 2010 (otherwise) (SI 2009/3242) |
| 50–52 | | 9 Feb 2009 (SI 2009/107)[1] |
| 53 | | 6 Apr 2009 (SI 2009/107) |
| 54 | (1)–(7) | 6 Apr 2009 (SI 2009/107) |
| | (8) | 26 Nov 2008 (so far as confers the power to make an order) (s 134(1)(c)) |
| | | 6 Apr 2009 (otherwise) (SI 2009/107) |
| 55, 56 | | 26 Jan 2009 (s 134(2)) |
| 57–59 | | 6 Apr 2009 (SI 2009/107)[1] |
| 60 | | 26 Nov 2008 (so far as confers the power to make regulations) (s 134(1)(c)) |

**Local Transport Act 2008 (c 26)**—*contd*

| | | |
|---|---|---|
| | | 6 Apr 2009 (otherwise) (SI 2009/107) |
| 61 | | 6 Apr 2009 (SI 2009/107) |
| 62, 63 | | 9 Feb 2009 (SI 2009/107)[1] |
| 64 | (1), (2) | 9 Feb 2009 (E) (SI 2009/107)[1] |
| | | 1 Apr 2009 (W) (SI 2009/579)[2] |
| | (3) | 26 Nov 2008 (so far as confers the power to make an order) (s 134(1)(c)) |
| | | 9 Feb 2009 (E) (otherwise) (SI 2009/107)[1] |
| | | 1 Apr 2009 (W) (otherwise) (SI 2009/579)[2] |
| | (4)–(14) | 9 Feb 2009 (E) (SI 2009/107)[1] |
| | | 1 Apr 2009 (W) (SI 2009/579)[2] |
| 65 | (1) | 9 Feb 2009 (E) (SI 2009/107) |
| | | 1 Apr 2009 (W) (SI 2009/579) |
| | (2)–(4) | 9 Feb 2009 (SI 2009/107) |
| 66, 67 | | 9 Feb 2009 (SI 2009/107) |
| 68 | (1) | See sub-ss (2), (3) below |
| | (2) | 9 Feb 2009 (E) (S) (SI 2009/107) |
| | | 31 Jan 2010 (W) (SI 2009/3294) |
| | (3) | 9 Feb 2009 (E) (SI 2009/107) |
| | | 1 Apr 2009 (W) (SI 2009/579) |
| 69–71 | | 9 Feb 2009 (E) (SI 2009/107)[1] |
| | | 1 Apr 2009 (W) (SI 2009/579)[2] |
| 72 | | 6 Apr 2009 (SI 2009/107) |
| 73 | (1) | 26 Nov 2008 (so far as confers the power to make an order) (s 134(1)(c)) |
| | | *Not yet in force* (otherwise) |
| | (2) | *Not yet in force* |
| 74 | | 26 Nov 2008 (so far as confers the power to make an order) (s 134(1)(c)) |
| | | 9 Feb 2009 (otherwise) (SI 2009/107) |
| 75 | | 26 Nov 2008 (so far as confers the power to make regulations) (s 134(1)(c)) |
| | | 9 Feb 2009 (E) (otherwise) (SI 2009/107) |
| | | 1 Apr 2009 (W) (otherwise) (SI 2009/579) |
| 76 | | 9 Feb 2009 (SI 2009/107) |
| 77 | (1)–(4) | 9 Feb 2009 (SI 2009/107) |
| | (5) | See Sch 4 below |
| | (6)–(9) | 9 Feb 2009 (SI 2009/107) |
| | (10) | 26 Nov 2008 (s 134(1)(a)) |
| | (11) | 9 Feb 2009 (SI 2009/107) |
| 78 | | 26 Nov 2008 (so far as confers the power to make an order) (s 134(1)(c)) |
| | | 9 Feb 2009 (otherwise) (SI 2009/107) |
| 79–83 | | 9 Feb 2009 (SI 2009/107) |
| 84 | | 26 Nov 2008 (so far as confers the power to make an order) (s 134(1)(c)) |
| | | 9 Feb 2009 (otherwise) (SI 2009/107) |
| 85 | | 9 Feb 2009 (SI 2009/107) |
| 86–88 | | 26 Nov 2008 (so far as confer the power to make an order) (s 134(1)(c)) |
| | | 9 Feb 2009 (otherwise) (SI 2009/107) |
| 89 | | 9 Feb 2009 (SI 2009/107) |
| 90, 91 | | 26 Nov 2008 (so far as confer the power to make an order) (s 134(1)(c)) |
| | | 9 Feb 2009 (otherwise) (SI 2009/107) |
| 92 | | 9 Feb 2009 (SI 2009/107) |
| 93 | | 26 Nov 2008 (so far as confers the power to make an order) (s 134(1)(c)) |
| | | 9 Feb 2009 (otherwise) (SI 2009/107) |

**Local Transport Act 2008 (c 26)**—*contd*

| | | |
|---|---|---|
| 94–99 | | 9 Feb 2009 (SI 2009/107) |
| 100, 101 | | 26 Nov 2008 (so far as confer the power to make an order) (s 134(1)(c)) |
| | | 9 Feb 2009 (otherwise) (SI 2009/107) |
| 102 | | 9 Feb 2009 (SI 2009/107) |
| 103–111 | | 9 Feb 2009 (E) (SI 2009/107)[1] |
| | | 1 Apr 2009 (W) (SI 2009/579) |
| 112 | (1) | 9 Feb 2009 (E) (SI 2009/107) |
| | | 1 Apr 2009 (W) (SI 2009/579) |
| | (2) | 9 Feb 2009 (SI 2009/107) |
| 113 | (1) | 9 Feb 2009 (E) (SI 2009/107) |
| | | 1 Apr 2009 (W) (SI 2009/579) |
| | (2) | 26 Nov 2008 (so far as confers the power to make regulations) (s 134(1)(c)) |
| | | 9 Feb 2009 (E) (otherwise) (SI 2009/107) |
| | | 1 Apr 2009 (W) (otherwise) (SI 2009/579) |
| | (3), (4) | 9 Feb 2009 (E) (SI 2009/107) |
| | | 1 Apr 2009 (W) (SI 2009/579) |
| | (5), (6) | 9 Feb 2009 (SI 2009/107) |
| | (7) | 26 Nov 2008 (so far as confers the power to make regulations) (s 134(1)(c)) |
| | | 9 Feb 2009 (otherwise) (SI 2009/107) |
| 114 | | 9 Feb 2009 (E) (SI 2009/107) |
| | | 1 Apr 2009 (W) (SI 2009/579) |
| 115 | (1), (2) | 9 Feb 2009 (E) (SI 2009/107) |
| | | 1 Apr 2009 (W) (SI 2009/579) |
| | (3)–(5) | 9 Feb 2009 (SI 2009/107) |
| 116 | (1)–(3) | 9 Feb 2009 (E) (SI 2009/107) |
| | | 1 Apr 2009 (W) (SI 2009/579) |
| | (4)–(8) | 9 Feb 2009 (SI 2009/107) |
| 117 | (1) | 9 Feb 2009 (E) (SI 2009/107) |
| | | 1 Apr 2009 (W) (SI 2009/579) |
| | (2) | 9 Feb 2009 (SI 2009/107) |
| 118 | (1)–(5) | 9 Feb 2009 (E) (SI 2009/107) |
| | | 1 Apr 2009 (W) (SI 2009/579) |
| | (6)–(9) | 9 Feb 2009 (SI 2009/107) |
| 119, 120 | | 9 Feb 2009 (SI 2009/107) |
| 121 | | See Sch 6 below |
| 122–124 | | 26 Jan 2009 (s 134(2)) |
| 125 | | 9 Feb 2009 (SI 2009/107) |
| 126 | | 26 Nov 2008 (so far as confers the power to make regulations) (s 134(1)(c)) |
| | | 9 Feb 2009 (otherwise) (SI 2009/107) |
| 127 | | 26 Jan 2009 (s 134(2)) |
| 128–130 | | 9 Feb 2009 (SI 2009/107) |
| 131 | | See Sch 7 below |
| 132–135 | | 26 Nov 2008 (s 134(1)(b)) |
| Sch 1 | | 9 Feb 2009 (E) (SI 2009/107) |
| | | 1 Apr 2009 (W) (SI 2009/579) |
| Sch 2 | paras 1–14 | 9 Feb 2009 (E) (SI 2009/107) |
| | | 1 Apr 2009 (W) (SI 2009/579) |
| | para 15 | 26 Nov 2008 (so far as confers the power to make an order) (s 134(1)(c)) |
| | | 9 Feb 2009 (E) (otherwise) (SI 2009/107) |
| | | 1 Apr 2009 (W) (otherwise) (SI 2009/579) |
| | para 16 | 9 Feb 2009 (E) (SI 2009/107) |
| | | 1 Apr 2009 (W) (SI 2009/579) |
| Sch 3 | | 26 Nov 2008 (so far as confers the power to make regulations) (s 134(1)(c)) |

**Local Transport Act 2008 (c 26)**—*contd*

| | | |
|---|---|---|
| | | 9 Feb 2009 (otherwise) (SI 2009/107) |
| Sch 4 | | 9 Feb 2009 (SI 2009/107) |
| Sch 5 | | 9 Feb 2009 (E) (SI 2009/107) |
| | | 1 Apr 2009 (W) (SI 2009/579) |
| Sch 6 | Pt 1 | 9 Feb 2009 (E) (SI 2009/107) |
| | | 1 Apr 2009 (W) (SI 2009/579) |
| | Pt 2 | 9 Feb 2009 (SI 2009/107) |
| Sch 7 | Pt 1 | 9 Feb 2009 (E) (SI 2009/107), repeals of or in— |
| | | Transport Act 1968; |
| | | Transport Act 1985; |
| | | Transport Act 2000 |
| | | 11 Jan 2010 (E) (SI 2009/3242), repeals of or in— |
| | | Transport (Wales) Act 2006 |
| | | 31 Jan 2010 (W) (SI 2009/3294) |
| | Pt 2 | 9 Feb 2009 (E) (SI 2009/107), repeals of or in— |
| | | Transport Act 2000, Sch 10; |
| | | Enterprise Act 2002 |
| | | 6 Apr 2009 (E) (SI 2009/107), repeals of or in— |
| | | Transport Act 2000, s 116 |
| | | 11 Jan 2010 (E) (SI 2009/3242), repeals of or in— |
| | | Transport Act 2000, ss 125, 126, 129, 162 |
| | | 31 Jan 2010 (W) (SI 2009/3294), repeals of or in— |
| | | Transport Act 2000, s 116(2), Sch 10; |
| | | Enterprise Act 2002 |
| | | *Not yet in force*, repeals of or in— |
| | | Transport Act 2000, ss 125, 126, 129, 162 (W) |
| | Pt 3 | 9 Feb 2009 (SI 2009/107), repeals of or in— |
| | | Transport Act 1968; |
| | | Transport Act 1985, ss 9, 60; |
| | | Constitutional Reform Act 2005 |
| | | 9 Feb 2009 (E) (SI 2009/107), repeals of or in— |
| | | Transport Act 1985, ss 74, 75, 79; |
| | | Transport Act 2000 |
| | | 6 Apr 2009 (SI 2009/107), repeals of or in— |
| | | Transport Act 1985, ss 22, 23 |
| | | 31 Jan 2010 (W) (SI 2009/3294) |
| | Pt 4 | 9 Feb 2009 (SI 2009/107) |
| | Pt 5 | 9 Feb 2009 (SI 2009/107), repeals of or in— |
| | | Greater London Authority Act 1999; |
| | | Transport Act 2000 (E) |
| | | 31 Jan 2010 (W) (SI 2009/3294) |

[1] For transitional provisions, see SI 2009/107, arts 2(1), (2), 4, 5(2), Sch 1, Pt 2, Sch 2, Pt 2, Sch 4, Pt 2

[2] For transitional provisions, see SI 2009/579, art 2, Schedule

[3] For a transitional provision, see SI 2009/3242, art 3

**National Insurance Contributions Act 2008 (c 16)**

*RA:* 21 Jul 2008

*Commencement provisions:* s 6

| | | |
|---|---|---|
| 1–3 | | 21 Sep 2008 (s 6(1)) |
| 4 | (1) | See Sch 1 below |
| | (2) | See Sch 2 below |
| 5–7 | | 21 Sep 2008 (s 6(1)) |
| Sch 1 | paras 1–5 | 21 Sep 2008 (s 6(1)) |
| | para 6(1), (2) | 21 Sep 2008 (s 6(1)) |

**National Insurance Contributions Act 2008 (c 16)**—*contd*

| | | |
|---|---|---|
| | para 6(3) | *Not yet in force* (in force as from the day the Pensions Act 2007, Sch 4, para 45(2) comes into force) |
| | para 6(4), (5) | 21 Sep 2008 (s 6(1)) |
| | paras 7–13 | 21 Sep 2008 (s 6(1)) |
| Sch 2 | | 21 Sep 2008 (s 6(1)), except repeals in— |
| | | Social Security Contributions and Benefits Act 1992, Sch 1 |
| | | *Not yet in force* (exception noted above) (in force as from the day the Pensions Act 2007, Sch 4, para 45(2) comes into force) |

---

**NHS Redress (Wales) Measure 2008 (nawm 1)**

*Passed by the National Assembly for Wales:* 6 May 2008

*Approved by Her Majesty in Council:* 9 Jul 2008

*Commencement provisions:* s 14(2), (3); NHS Redress (Wales) Measure 2008 (Commencement) Order 2011, SI 2011/211

| | |
|---|---|
| 1–13 | 7 Feb 2011 (SI 2011/211) |
| 14 | 9 Jul 2008 (s 14(2)) |

---

**Pensions Act 2008 (c 30)**

*RA:* 26 Nov 2008

*Commencement provisions:* s 149; Pensions Act 2008 (Commencement No 1 and Consequential Provision) Order 2008, SI 2008/3241; Pensions Act 2008 (Commencement No 2) Order 2009, SI 2009/82; Pensions Act 2008 (Commencement No 3 and Consequential Provisions) Order 2009, SI 2009/809; Pensions Act 2008 (Commencement No 4) Order 2009, SI 2009/1566; Pensions Act 2008 (Commencement No 5) Order 2010, SI 2010/10; Pensions Act 2008 (Commencement No 6) Order 2010, SI 2010/467; Pensions Act 2008 (Commencement No 7 and Saving, Consequential and Incidental Provisions) Order 2010, SI 2010/1145; Pensions Act 2008 (Commencement No 8) Order 2010, SI 2010/1221; Pensions Act 2008 (Commencement No 9) Order 2011, SI 2011/664; Pensions Act 2008 (Commencement No 10) Order 2011, SI 2011/1266; Pensions Act 2008 (Commencement No 11) Order 2011, SI 2011/3033; Pensions Act 2008 (Commencement No 12) Order 2012, SI 2012/683[2]; Pensions Act 2008 (Commencement No 13) Order 2012, SI 2012/1682; Pensions Act 2008 (Commencement No 14 and Supplementary Provisions) Order 2012, SI 2012/2480; Pensions Act 2008 (Commencement No 15) Order 2014, SI 2014/463; Pensions Act 2008 (Commencement No 16) Order 2018, SI 2018/63

| | |
|---|---|
| 1 | 30 Jun 2012 (SI 2012/1682) |
| 2, 3 | 26 Nov 2008 (so far as they confer any power to make regulations) (s 149(2)(k)) |
| | 30 Jun 2012 (otherwise) (SI 2012/1682) |
| 4 | 26 Nov 2008 (so far as confers any power to make regulations) (s 149(2)(k)) |
| | *Never in force* (otherwise) (substituted) |
| 5 | 26 Nov 2008 (so far as confers any power to make regulations) (s 149(2)(k)) |
| | 30 Jun 2012 (otherwise) (SI 2012/1682) |
| 6 | 30 Jun 2012 (SI 2012/1682) |
| 7–10 | 26 Nov 2008 (so far as they confer any power to make regulations) (s 149(2)(k)) |
| | 30 Jun 2012 (otherwise) (SI 2012/1682) |
| 11, 12 | 26 Nov 2008 (so far as they confer any power to make regulations) (s 149(2)(k)) |
| | *Not yet in force* (otherwise) |
| 13 | 26 Nov 2008 (so far as confers any power to make regulations) (s 149(2)(k)) |
| | 30 Jun 2012 (otherwise) (SI 2012/1682) |

**Pensions Act 2008 (c 30)**—*contd*

| | | |
|---|---|---|
| 14 | | 26 Nov 2008 (so far as confers any power to make an order) (s 149(2)(k)) |
| | | 6 Mar 2012 (otherwise) (SI 2012/683)[2] |
| 15–18 | | 26 Nov 2008 (so far as they confer any power to make regulations) (s 149(2)(k)) |
| | | 30 Jun 2012 (otherwise) (SI 2012/1682) |
| 19 | | 30 Jun 2012 (SI 2012/1682) |
| 20 | | 26 Nov 2008 (so far as confers any power to make regulations) (s 149(2)(k)) |
| | | 30 Jun 2012 (otherwise) (SI 2012/1682) |
| 21 | | 26 Nov 2008 (so far as confers any power to make an order) (s 149(2)(k)) |
| | | 30 Jun 2012 (otherwise) (SI 2012/1682) |
| 22 | | 26 Nov 2008 (so far as confers any power to make regulations) (s 149(2)(k)) |
| | | 30 Jun 2012 (otherwise) (SI 2012/1682) |
| 23 | | 26 Nov 2008 (so far as confers any power to make regulations) (s 149(2)(k)) |
| | | *Never in force* (otherwise) (substituted) |
| 24 | | 26 Nov 2008 (so far as confers any power to make regulations or rules) (s 149(2)(k)) |
| | | 30 Jun 2012 (otherwise) (SI 2012/1682) |
| 25 | | 26 Nov 2008 (so far as confers any power to make regulations) (s 149(2)(k)) |
| | | *Not yet in force* (otherwise) |
| 26 | | 26 Nov 2008 (so far as confers any power to make regulations) (s 149(2)(k)) |
| | | 30 Jun 2012 (otherwise) (SI 2012/1682) |
| 27 | | 26 Nov 2008 (so far as confers any power to make regulations) (s 149(2)(k)) |
| | | *Not yet in force* (otherwise) |
| 28 | | 26 Nov 2008 (so far as confers any power to make regulations or an order) (s 149(2)(k)) |
| | | 7 Mar 2012 (otherwise) (SI 2012/683) |
| 29, 30 | | 26 Nov 2008 (so far as they confer any power to make regulations) (s 149(2)(k)) |
| | | 30 Jun 2012 (otherwise) (SI 2012/1682) |
| 31 | | 30 Jun 2012 (SI 2012/1682) |
| 32 | | 26 Nov 2008 (so far as confers any power to make regulations) (s 149(2)(k)) |
| | | 30 Jun 2012 (otherwise) (SI 2012/1682) |
| 33–36 | | 30 Jun 2012 (SI 2012/1682) |
| 37, 38 | | 26 Nov 2008 (so far as they confer any power to make regulations) (s 149(2)(k)) |
| | | 30 Jun 2012 (otherwise) (SI 2012/1682) |
| 39 | | 30 Jun 2012 (SI 2012/1682) |
| 40 | (1)(a)–(c) | 30 Jun 2012 (SI 2012/1682) |
| | (1)(d) | 30 Jun 2012 (for the purposes of the exercise of the Regulator's functions under or by virtue of Part 1 hereof) (SI 2012/1682) |
| | | *Not yet in force* (otherwise) |
| | (2)–(5) | 26 Nov 2008 (so far as they confer any power to make regulations) (s 149(2)(k)) |
| | | 30 Jun 2012 (otherwise) (SI 2012/1682) |
| 41 | (1)(a)–(c) | 30 Jun 2012 (SI 2012/1682) |
| | (1)(d) | 30 Jun 2012 (for the purposes of the exercise of the Regulator's functions under or by virtue of Part 1 hereof) (SI 2012/1682) |
| | | *Not yet in force* (otherwise) |
| | (2)–(6) | 26 Nov 2008 (so far as they confer any power to make regulations) (s 149(2)(k)) |
| | | 30 Jun 2012 (otherwise) (SI 2012/1682) |

**Pensions Act 2008 (c 30)**—*contd*

| | | |
|---|---|---|
| 42 | | 30 Jun 2012 (SI 2012/1682) |
| 43 | | 26 Nov 2008 (so far as confers any power to make regulations) (s 149(2)(k)) |
| | | 30 Jun 2012 (otherwise) (SI 2012/1682) |
| 44–48 | | 30 Jun 2012 (SI 2012/1682) |
| 49 | | 3 Jan 2012 (in so far as it relates to the powers to make regulations under the Pension Schemes Act 1993, s 111A, for the purposes only of making regulations) (SI 2011/3033) |
| | | 30 Jun 2012 (otherwise) (SI 2012/1682) |
| 50, 51 | | 30 Jun 2012 (SI 2012/1682) |
| 52 | | 26 Nov 2008 (so far as confers any power to make regulations) (s 149(2)(k)) |
| | | 30 Jun 2012 (otherwise) (SI 2012/1682) |
| 53 | | 30 Jun 2012 (SI 2012/1682) |
| 54 | | 26 Nov 2008 (so far as confers any power to make regulations) (s 149(2)(k)) |
| | | 30 Jun 2012 (otherwise) (SI 2012/1682) |
| 55, 56 | | 30 Jun 2012 (SI 2012/1682) |
| 57 | (1), (2) | 30 Jun 2012 (SI 2012/1682) |
| | (3) | *Not yet in force* |
| | (4)–(7) | 30 Jun 2012 (SI 2012/1682) |
| 58 | | 26 Nov 2008 (so far as confers any power to make an order) (s 149(2)(k)) |
| | | 30 Jun 2012 (otherwise) (SI 2012/1682) |
| 59 | | 30 Jun 2012 (SI 2012/1682) |
| 60 | | 26 Nov 2008 (so far as confers any power to make regulations) (s 149(2)(k)) |
| | | *Not yet in force* (otherwise) |
| 61 | | 30 Jun 2012 (SI 2012/1682) |
| 62–64 | | 26 Jan 2009 (SI 2009/82) |
| 65 | | 16 Mar 2011 (SI 2011/664) |
| 66 | | 30 Jun 2012 (SI 2012/1682) |
| 67–73 | | 26 Nov 2008 (RA) |
| 74 | | 1 Jul 2009 (SI 2009/1566) |
| 75 | | 26 Nov 2008 (so far as confers any power to make an order) (s 149(2)(k)) |
| | | 5 Jul 2010 (otherwise) (SI 2010/10) |
| 76 | | 5 Jul 2010 (SI 2010/10) |
| 77 | | 26 Nov 2008 (so far as confers any power to make regulations) (s 149(2)(k)) |
| | | *Not yet in force* (otherwise) |
| 78–86 | | 26 Nov 2008 (RA) |
| 87 | | 1 Oct 2012 (SI 2012/2480)[3] |
| 88–95 | | 30 Jun 2012 (SI 2012/1682) |
| 96 | | 26 Nov 2008 (so far as confers any power to make regulations) (s 149(2)(k)) |
| | | 30 Jun 2012 (otherwise) (SI 2012/1682) |
| 97 | | 26 Nov 2008 (so far as confers any power to make an Order in Council) (s 149(2)(k)) |
| | | *Not yet in force* (otherwise) |
| 98 | | 26 Nov 2008 (so far as confers any power to make regulations) (s 149(2)(k)) |
| | | *Not yet in force* (otherwise) |
| 99 | | 5 Jul 2010 (SI 2010/10) |
| 100 | | 6 Apr 2009 (SI 2009/82) |
| 101 | | 6 Apr 2009 (SI 2009/82; SI 2009/809) |
| 102 | (1)–(4) | *Never in force* (repealed) |
| | (5) | See Sch 3 below |
| | (6), (7) | *Never in force* (repealed) |
| 103 | (1) | See sub-ss (2)–(5) below |

**Pensions Act 2008 (c 30)**—*contd*

| | | |
|---|---|---|
| | (2) | *Never in force* (repealed) |
| | (3) | 8 Apr 2010 (in so far as inserts Pension Schemes Act 1993, s 46A(5)–(7)) (SI 2010/1221) |
| | | *Never in force* (in so far as inserts sub-ss (1)–(4), (8)–(10) of that section) (repealed) |
| | (4), (5) | *Never in force* (repealed) |
| 104 | | See Sch 4 below |
| 105 | | 6 Apr 2009 (s 149(4)) |
| 106 | | 6 Apr 2012 (SI 2011/1266) |
| 107 | | 26 Nov 2008 (so far as confers any power to make regulations) (s 149(2)(k)) |
| | | 6 Apr 2011 (otherwise) (SI 2011/664) |
| 108 | | 6 Apr 2011 (SI 2011/664) |
| 109 | | 26 Nov 2008 (so far as confers any power to make regulations) (s 149(2)(k)) |
| | | 6 Apr 2011 (otherwise) (SI 2011/664) |
| 110–112 | | 26 Nov 2008 (so far as confers any power to make regulations) (s 149(2)(k)) |
| | | 6 Apr 2011 (otherwise) (SI 2011/664) |
| 113 | | 6 Apr 2011 (SI 2011/664) |
| 114–119 | | 26 Nov 2008 (so far as confers any power to make regulations) (s 149(2)(k)) |
| | | 6 Apr 2011 (otherwise) (SI 2011/664) |
| 120 | | See Schs 6, 7 below |
| 121 | | 6 Mar 2011 (for the purpose of conferring power to make regulations) (SI 2011/664) |
| | | 6 Apr 2011 (otherwise) (SI 2011/664) |
| 122 | | See Sch 8 below |
| 123 | | 6 Apr 2011 (SI 2011/664) |
| 124 | (1) | 26 Nov 2008 (RA) |
| | (2) | 19 Dec 2008 (for the purposes only of the Pensions Act 2004, s 286A) (SI 2008/3241) |
| | | 31 Mar 2010 (otherwise) (SI 2010/1145)[1] |
| | (3) | 26 Nov 2008 (RA) |
| | (4), (5) | *Not yet in force* |
| | (6) | 19 Dec 2008 (for the purposes only of the Pensions Act 2004, s 286A) (SI 2008/3241) |
| | | 31 Mar 2010 (otherwise) (SI 2010/1145)[1] |
| | (7)–(10) | 26 Nov 2008 (RA) |
| 125 | | 26 Nov 2008 (RA) |
| 126 | | See Sch 9 below |
| 127 | | 30 Jun 2012 (SI 2012/1682) |
| 128 | | 26 Jan 2009 (SI 2009/82) |
| 129 | | See Sch 10 below |
| 130 | | 6 Apr 2009 (SI 2009/82) |
| 131 | | 26 Jan 2009 (s 149(5)) |
| 132 | | 26 Jan 2009 (SI 2009/82) |
| 133, 134 | | 26 Nov 2008 (RA) |
| 135, 136 | | 6 Apr 2009 (s 149(4)) |
| 137 | | 13 Mar 2014 (SI 2014/463) |
| 138 | | 26 Jan 2009 (SI 2009/82) |
| 139 | | 6 Apr 2009 (SI 2009/82) |
| 140–147 | | 26 Nov 2008 (RA) |
| 148 | | See Sch 11 below |
| 149–151 | | 26 Nov 2008 (RA) |
| Sch 1 | | 26 Nov 2008 (so far as confers any power to make an order) (s 149(2)(k)) |
| | | 5 Jul 2010 (otherwise) (SI 2010/10) |
| Sch 2 | | 6 Apr 2009 (SI 2009/82; SI 2009/809) |

**Pensions Act 2008 (c 30)**—*contd*

| | | |
|---|---|---|
| Sch 3 | | *Never in force* (repealed) |
| Sch 4 | para 1 | See paras 2–13 below |
| | paras 2, 3 | 3 Jan 2012 (SI 2011/3033) |
| | para 4(1) | See sub-paras (2), (3) below |
| | para 4(2), (3) | 3 Jan 2012 (except sub-paras (2)(b), (3)(b) in so far as they relate to the Social Security Contributions and Benefits Act 1992, Sch 4C) (SI 2011/3033) |
| | | *Not yet in force* (exceptions noted above) (para 4(2)(b), (3)(b) repealed) |
| | para 5 | 3 Jan 2012 (SI 2011/3033) |
| | para 6(1) | See sub-paras (2), (3) below |
| | para 6(2) | 3 Jan 2012 (SI 2011/3033) |
| | paras 6(3), 7(a) | *Never in force* (repealed) |
| | para 7(b) | 3 Jan 2012 (SI 2011/3033) |
| | para 8(a) | *Never in force* (repealed) |
| | para 8(b) | 3 Jan 2012 (SI 2011/3033) |
| | para 9(1) | See sub-paras (2), (3) below |
| | para 9(2)(a), (b) | 3 Jan 2012 (SI 2011/3033) |
| | para 9(2)(c) | *Never in force* (repealed) |
| | para 9(2)(d), (3) | 3 Jan 2012 (SI 2011/3033) |
| | para 10 | *Never in force* (repealed) |
| | paras 11, 12 | 3 Jan 2012 (SI 2011/3033) |
| | paras 13–22 | *Never in force* (repealed) |
| Sch 5 | paras 1–10 | 26 Nov 2008 (so far as they confer any power to make regulations or an order) (s 149(2)(k)) |
| | | 6 Apr 2011 (otherwise) (SI 2011/664) |
| | para 11 | 26 Nov 2008 (so far as confers any power to make regulations or an order) (s 149(2)(k)) |
| | | *Never in force* (otherwise) (repealed) |
| | paras 12–20 | 26 Nov 2008 (so far as they confer any power to make regulations or an order) (s 149(2)(k)) |
| | | 6 Apr 2011 (otherwise) (SI 2011/664) |
| Sch 6 | para 1 | See paras 2–9 below |
| | para 2 | 6 Apr 2011 (SI 2011/664) |
| | para 3 | 6 Mar 2011 (in so far as inserts Matrimonial Causes Act 1973, s 24F, for the purpose of conferring power to make regulations) (SI 2011/664) |
| | | 6 Apr 2011 (otherwise) (SI 2011/664) |
| | paras 4–6 | 6 Apr 2011 (SI 2011/664) |
| | para 7 | 6 Mar 2011 (in so far as inserts Matrimonial Causes Act 1973, s 25G, for the purpose of conferring power to make regulations) (SI 2011/664) |
| | | 6 Apr 2011 (otherwise) (SI 2011/664) |
| | para 8(1) | See sub-paras (2)–(8) below |
| | para 8(2)–(4) | 6 Apr 2011 (SI 2011/664) |
| | para 8(5) | 6 Mar 2011 (for the purpose of conferring power to make regulations) (SI 2011/664) |
| | | 6 Apr 2011 (otherwise) (SI 2011/664) |
| | para 8(6)–(8) | 6 Apr 2011 (SI 2011/664) |
| | paras 9–12 | 6 Apr 2011 (SI 2011/664) |
| | para 13(1) | See sub-paras (2)–(6) below |
| | para 13(2)–(5) | 6 Apr 2011 (SI 2011/664) |
| | para 13(6) | 6 Mar 2011 (for the purpose of conferring power to make regulations) (SI 2011/664) |
| | | 6 Apr 2011 (otherwise) (SI 2011/664) |
| | para 14 | See paras 15–20 below |
| | para 15 | 6 Mar 2011 (in so far as inserts Civil Partnership Act 2004, Sch 5, para 19E, for the purpose of conferring power to make regulations) (SI 2011/664) |
| | | 6 Apr 2011 (otherwise) (SI 2011/664) |

**Pensions Act 2008 (c 30)**—*contd*

| | | |
|---|---|---|
| | para 16 | 6 Apr 2011 (SI 2011/664) |
| | para 17(1) | See sub-paras (2)–(5) below |
| | para 17(2), (3) | 6 Apr 2011 (SI 2011/664) |
| | para 17(4) | 6 Mar 2011 (for the purpose of conferring power to make regulations) (SI 2011/664) |
| | | 6 Apr 2011 (otherwise) (SI 2011/664) |
| | para 17(5) | 6 Apr 2011 (SI 2011/664) |
| | para 18(1) | See sub-paras (2)–(8) below |
| | para 18(2)–(6), (7)(a)–(d) | 6 Apr 2011 (SI 2011/664) |
| | para 18(7)(e) | 6 Mar 2011 (for the purpose of conferring power to make regulations) (SI 2011/664) |
| | | 6 Apr 2011 (otherwise) (SI 2011/664) |
| | paras 18(8), 19 | 6 Apr 2011 (SI 2011/664) |
| | para 20(1)–(3), (4)(a)–(f) | 6 Apr 2011 (SI 2011/664) |
| | para 20(4)(g) | 6 Mar 2011 (for the purpose of conferring power to make regulations) (SI 2011/664) |
| | | 6 Apr 2011 (otherwise) (SI 2011/664) |
| Sch 7 | para 1 | See paras 2–9 below |
| | paras 2, 3 | 6 Apr 2011 (SI 2011/664) |
| | para 4 | 6 Mar 2011 (for the purpose of conferring power to make regulations) (SI 2011/664) |
| | | 6 Apr 2011 (otherwise) (SI 2011/664) |
| | paras 5–9 | 6 Apr 2011 (SI 2011/664) |
| Sch 8 | paras 1–9 | 1 Apr 2009 (SI 2009/809) |
| | paras 10–12 | *Not yet in force* (paras 10, 11 repealed) |
| | para 13 | 1 Apr 2009 (for the purpose only of the insertion by para 14 below of Pensions Act 2004, Sch 7, paras 25B–25F) (SI 2009/809) |
| | | *Not yet in force* (otherwise) |
| | para 14 | 1 Apr 2009 (except for the purpose of the deferral of compensation entitlement in the definition of "relevant age" in the inserted para 25B) (SI 2009/809) |
| | | *Not yet in force* (exception noted above) |
| | para 15 | 22 Jan 2018 (SI 2018/63) |
| | paras 16–18 | 1 Apr 2009 (SI 2009/809) |
| Sch 9 | para 1 | See paras 2–14 below |
| | para 2 | 26 Nov 2008 (so far as necessary for the purposes of para 3) (RA) |
| | | 29 Jun 2009 (otherwise) (SI 2009/1566) |
| | para 3 | 26 Nov 2008 (RA) |
| | para 4 | 29 Jun 2009 (SI 2009/1566) |
| | paras 5–7 | 26 Nov 2008 (RA) |
| | para 8 | 26 Nov 2008 (except for the purposes of the material detriment test) (RA) |
| | | 29 Jun 2009 (exception noted above) (SI 2009/1566) |
| | paras 9–14 | 26 Nov 2008 (RA) |
| | para 15(1) | 26 Nov 2008 (so far as relates to paras 6, 7) (RA) |
| | | 29 Jun 2009 (otherwise) (SI 2009/1566) |
| | para 15(2) | 26 Nov 2008 (except for the purposes of the material detriment test) (RA) |
| | | 29 Jun 2009 (exception noted above) (SI 2009/1566) |
| | para 15(3), (4) | 26 Nov 2008 (RA) |
| | para 16 | 26 Nov 2008 (RA) |
| Sch 10 | para 1 | *Not yet in force* |
| | para 2 | See paras 3–9 below |
| | para 3 | *Not yet in force* |
| | paras 4, 5 | 26 Feb 2010 (SI 2010/467) |
| | paras 6–9 | *Not yet in force* |
| Sch 11 | Pt 1 | *Not yet in force* |
| | Pt 2 | 6 Apr 2009 (SI 2009/82) |

**Pensions Act 2008 (c 30)**—*contd*

|  |  |  |
|---|---|---|
| Pt 3 | | 6 Apr 2012 (SI 2011/1266) |
| Pt 4 | | 6 Apr 2011 (SI 2011/664) |
| Pt 5 | | *Not yet in force* |
| Pt 6 | | 26 Nov 2008 (repeal in Pensions Act 2004, s 38, and the note relating to that repeal) (RA) |
| | | *Not yet in force,* repeals of or in— |
| | | Social Security Pensions Act 1975; |
| | | Pensions Act 1995; |
| | | Pensions Act 2004, s 321, Sch 1 |

[1]    For a saving, see SI 2010/1145, art 3

[2]    S 14 has been substituted by the Pensions Act 2011, s 8(1), which was brought fully into force on 3 Jan 2012. Note that SI 2012/683 also purports to bring s 15A of this Act fully into force on 7 Mar 2012; that section was inserted by s 9 of the 2011 Act, which was brought fully into force on 6 Mar 2012

[3]    For supplementary provisions, see SI 2012/2480, art 3

---

**Planning Act 2008 (c 29)**

*RA:* 26 Nov 2008

*Commencement provisions:* s 241; Planning Act 2008 (Commencement No 1 and Savings) Order 2009, SI 2009/400; Planning Act 2008 (Commencement No 1) (England) Order 2009, SI 2009/1303; Planning Act 2008 (Commencement No 2) Order 2009, SI 2009/2260; Planning Act 2008 (Commencement No 3) Order 2009, SI 2009/2573; Planning Act 2008 (Commencement No 4 and Saving) Order 2010, SI 2010/101; Planning Act 2008 (Commencement No 5 and Saving) Order 2010, SI 2010/566; Planning Act 2008 (Commencement No 6) Order 2011, SI 2011/705; Planning Act 2008 (Commencement No 7) Order 2011, SI 2011/2054; Planning Act 2008 (Commencement No 2) (England) Order 2012, SI 2012/601; Planning Act 2008 (Commencement No 1) (Wales) Order 2012, SI 2012/802; Planning Act 2008 (Commencement No 2) (Wales) Order 2014, SI 2014/1769; Planning Act 2008 (Commencement No 3) (Wales) Order 2014, SI 2014/2780; Planning Act 2008 (Commencement No 3) (England) Order 2017, SI 2017/1078

|  |  |  |
|---|---|---|
| 1–3 | | 1 Oct 2009 (SI 2009/2260) |
| 4 | | 26 Nov 2008 (so far as conferring power to make orders (other than orders granting, or making changes to orders granting, development consent), regulations or rules, or so far as making provision about what is (or is not) permitted to be done, or what is required to be done, in the exercise of any such power) (s 241(1)(a)) |
| | | 1 Oct 2009 (otherwise) (SI 2009/2260) |
| 5, 6 | | 6 Apr 2009 (SI 2009/400) |
| 7 | | 26 Nov 2008 (so far as conferring power to make orders (other than orders granting, or making changes to orders granting, development consent), regulations or rules, or so far as making provision about what is (or is not) permitted to be done, or what is required to be done, in the exercise of any such power) (s 241(1)(a)) |
| | | 6 Apr 2009 (otherwise) (SI 2009/400) |
| 8–13 | | 6 Apr 2009 (SI 2009/400) |
| 14 | (1)(a)–(l) | 26 Nov 2008 (so far as conferring power to make orders (other than orders granting, or making changes to orders granting, development consent), regulations or rules, or so far as making provision about what is (or is not) permitted to be done, or what is required to be done, in the exercise of any such power) (s 241(1)(a)) |
| | | 1 Mar 2010 (otherwise) (SI 2010/101)[3] |
| | (1)(m), (n) | 1 Jan 2018 (E) (SI 2017/1078) |
| | | *Not yet in force* (W) (S) |
| | (1)(o) | 6 Apr 2011 (E) (W) (SI 2011/705) |
| | | *Not yet in force* (S) |

**Planning Act 2008 (c 29)**—*contd*

|        |        |
|--------|--------|
| (1)(p) | 1 Oct 2011 (SI 2011/2054) |
| (2)–(7) | 26 Nov 2008 (so far as conferring power to make orders (other than orders granting, or making changes to orders granting, development consent), regulations or rules, or so far as making provision about what is (or is not) permitted to be done, or what is required to be done, in the exercise of any such power) (s 241(1)(a)) |
|        | 1 Mar 2010 (otherwise) (SI 2010/101)[3] |
| 15–24  | 1 Mar 2010 (SI 2010/101)[3] |
| 25     | 26 Nov 2008 (so far as conferring power to make orders (other than orders granting, or making changes to orders granting, development consent), regulations or rules, or so far as making provision about what is (or is not) permitted to be done, or what is required to be done, in the exercise of any such power) (s 241(1)(a)) |
|        | 1 Mar 2010 (otherwise) (SI 2010/101)[3] |
| 26     | 1 Mar 2010 (SI 2010/101)[3] |
| 27, 28 | 1 Jan 2018 (E) (SI 2017/1078) |
|        | *Not yet in force* (W) |
| 29     | 6 Apr 2011 (SI 2011/705) |
| 30     | 1 Oct 2011 (SI 2011/2054) |
| 31–35  | 1 Mar 2010 (SI 2010/101)[3] |
| 36     | See Sch 2 below |
| 37, 38 | 26 Nov 2008 (so far as conferring power to make orders (other than orders granting, or making changes to orders granting, development consent), regulations or rules, or so far as making provision about what is (or is not) permitted to be done, or what is required to be done, in the exercise of any such power) (s 241(1)(a)) |
|        | 1 Oct 2009 (otherwise) (SI 2009/2260) |
| 39     | 1 Oct 2009 (SI 2009/2260) |
| 40     | 26 Nov 2008 (so far as conferring power to make orders (other than orders granting, or making changes to orders granting, development consent), regulations or rules, or so far as making provision about what is (or is not) permitted to be done, or what is required to be done, in the exercise of any such power) (s 241(1)(a)) |
|        | 1 Oct 2009 (otherwise) (SI 2009/2260) |
| 41     | 1 Oct 2009 (SI 2009/2260) |
| 42     | 26 Nov 2008 (so far as conferring power to make orders (other than orders granting, or making changes to orders granting, development consent), regulations or rules, or so far as making provision about what is (or is not) permitted to be done, or what is required to be done, in the exercise of any such power) (s 241(1)(a)) |
|        | 1 Oct 2009 (otherwise) (SI 2009/2260) |
| 43–46  | 1 Oct 2009 (SI 2009/2260) |
| 47, 48 | 26 Nov 2008 (so far as conferring power to make orders (other than orders granting, or making changes to orders granting, development consent), regulations or rules, or so far as making provision about what is (or is not) permitted to be done, or what is required to be done, in the exercise of any such power) (s 241(1)(a)) |
|        | 1 Oct 2009 (otherwise) (SI 2009/2260) |
| 49, 50 | 1 Oct 2009 (SI 2009/2260) |
| 51     | 26 Nov 2008 (so far as conferring power to make orders (other than orders granting, or making changes to orders granting, development consent), regulations or rules, or so far as making provision about what is (or is not) permitted to be done, or what is required to be done, in the exercise of any such power) (s 241(1)(a)) |

**Planning Act 2008 (c 29)**—*contd*

|  |  |  |
|---|---|---|
|  |  | 1 Oct 2009 (otherwise) (SI 2009/2260) |
| 52–54 |  | 1 Oct 2009 (SI 2009/2260) |
| 55 |  | 1 Mar 2010 (SI 2010/101)[3] |
| 56 |  | 26 Nov 2008 (so far as conferring power to make orders (other than orders granting, or making changes to orders granting, development consent), regulations or rules, or so far as making provision about what is (or is not) permitted to be done, or what is required to be done, in the exercise of any such power) (s 241(1)(a)) |
|  |  | 1 Oct 2009 (otherwise) (SI 2009/2260) |
| 57 |  | 1 Oct 2009 (SI 2009/2260) |
| 58, 59 |  | 26 Nov 2008 (so far as conferring power to make orders (other than orders granting, or making changes to orders granting, development consent), regulations or rules, or so far as making provision about what is (or is not) permitted to be done, or what is required to be done, in the exercise of any such power) (s 241(1)(a)) |
|  |  | 1 Oct 2009 (otherwise) (SI 2009/2260) |
| 60–96 |  | 1 Mar 2010 (SI 2010/101)[3] |
| 97 |  | 26 Nov 2008 (so far as conferring power to make orders (other than orders granting, or making changes to orders granting, development consent), regulations or rules, or so far as making provision about what is (or is not) permitted to be done, or what is required to be done, in the exercise of any such power) (s 241(1)(a)) |
|  |  | 1 Mar 2010 (otherwise) (SI 2010/101)[3] |
| 98–101 |  | 1 Mar 2010 (SI 2010/101)[3] |
| 102 |  | 26 Nov 2008 (so far as conferring power to make orders (other than orders granting, or making changes to orders granting, development consent), regulations or rules, or so far as making provision about what is (or is not) permitted to be done, or what is required to be done, in the exercise of any such power) (s 241(1)(a)) |
|  |  | 1 Mar 2010 (otherwise) (SI 2010/101)[3] |
| 103 |  | 1 Mar 2010 (SI 2010/101)[3] |
| 104, 105 |  | 26 Nov 2008 (so far as conferring power to make orders (other than orders granting, or making changes to orders granting, development consent), regulations or rules, or so far as making provision about what is (or is not) permitted to be done, or what is required to be done, in the exercise of any such power) (s 241(1)(a)) |
|  |  | 1 Mar 2010 (otherwise) (SI 2010/101)[3] |
| 106–110 |  | 1 Mar 2010 (SI 2010/101)[3] |
| 111 |  | 26 Nov 2008 (so far as conferring power to make orders (other than orders granting, or making changes to orders granting, development consent), regulations or rules, or so far as making provision about what is (or is not) permitted to be done, or what is required to be done, in the exercise of any such power) (s 241(1)(a)) |
|  |  | 1 Mar 2010 (otherwise) (SI 2010/101)[3] |
| 112 |  | 1 Mar 2010 (SI 2010/101)[3] |
| 113 | (1)–(3) | 1 Mar 2010 (SI 2010/101)[3] |
|  | (4) | See Sch 3 below |
|  | (5)–(11) | 1 Mar 2010 (SI 2010/101)[3] |
| 114 |  | 26 Nov 2008 (so far as conferring power to make orders (other than orders granting, or making changes to orders granting, development consent), regulations or rules, or so far as making provision about what is (or is not) permitted to be done, or what is required to be done, in the exercise of any such power) (s 241(1)(a)) |
|  |  | 1 Mar 2010 (otherwise) (SI 2010/101)[3] |

**Planning Act 2008 (c 29)**—*contd*

| | |
|---|---|
| 115–118 | 1 Mar 2010 (SI 2010/101)[3] |
| 119 | See Sch 4 below |
| 120–122 | 1 Mar 2010 (SI 2010/101)[3] |
| 123 | 26 Nov 2008 (so far as conferring power to make orders (other than orders granting, or making changes to orders granting, development consent), regulations or rules, or so far as making provision about what is (or is not) permitted to be done, or what is required to be done, in the exercise of any such power) (s 241(1)(a)) |
| | 1 Mar 2010 (otherwise) (SI 2010/101)[3] |
| 124–126 | 1 Mar 2010 (SI 2010/101)[3] |
| 127 | 26 Nov 2008 (so far as conferring power to make orders (other than orders granting, or making changes to orders granting, development consent), regulations or rules, or so far as making provision about what is (or is not) permitted to be done, or what is required to be done, in the exercise of any such power) (s 241(1)(a)) |
| | 1 Mar 2010 (otherwise) (SI 2010/101)[3] |
| 128–130 | 1 Mar 2010 (SI 2010/101)[3] |
| 131, 132 | 26 Nov 2008 (so far as conferring power to make orders (other than orders granting, or making changes to orders granting, development consent), regulations or rules, or so far as making provision about what is (or is not) permitted to be done, or what is required to be done, in the exercise of any such power) (s 241(1)(a)) |
| | 1 Mar 2010 (otherwise) (SI 2010/101)[3] |
| 133 | 1 Mar 2010 (SI 2010/101)[3] |
| 134 | 26 Nov 2008 (so far as conferring power to make orders (other than orders granting, or making changes to orders granting, development consent), regulations or rules, or so far as making provision about what is (or is not) permitted to be done, or what is required to be done, in the exercise of any such power) (s 241(1)(a)) |
| | 1 Mar 2010 (otherwise) (SI 2010/101)[3] |
| 135–149 | 1 Mar 2010 (SI 2010/101)[3] |
| 150 | 26 Nov 2008 (so far as conferring power to make orders (other than orders granting, or making changes to orders granting, development consent), regulations or rules, or so far as making provision about what is (or is not) permitted to be done, or what is required to be done, in the exercise of any such power) (s 241(1)(a)) |
| | 1 Mar 2010 (otherwise) (SI 2010/101)[3] |
| 151, 152 | 1 Mar 2010 (SI 2010/101)[3] |
| 153 | See Sch 6 below |
| 154, 155 | 26 Nov 2008 (so far as conferring power to make orders (other than orders granting, or making changes to orders granting, development consent), regulations or rules, or so far as making provision about what is (or is not) permitted to be done, or what is required to be done, in the exercise of any such power) (s 241(1)(a)) |
| | 1 Mar 2010 (otherwise) (SI 2010/101)[3] |
| 156–159 | 1 Mar 2010 (SI 2010/101)[3] |
| 160, 161 | 26 Nov 2008 (so far as conferring power to make orders (other than orders granting, or making changes to orders granting, development consent), regulations or rules, or so far as making provision about what is (or is not) permitted to be done, or what is required to be done, in the exercise of any such power) (s 241(1)(a)) |
| | 1 Mar 2010 (otherwise) (SI 2010/101)[3] |
| 162–164 | 1 Mar 2010 (SI 2010/101)[3] |

**Planning Act 2008 (c 29)**—*contd*

| | | |
|---|---|---|
| 165 | | 26 Nov 2008 (so far as conferring power to make orders (other than orders granting, or making changes to orders granting, development consent), regulations or rules, or so far as making provision about what is (or is not) permitted to be done, or what is required to be done, in the exercise of any such power) (s 241(1)(a)) |
| | | 1 Mar 2010 (otherwise) (SI 2010/101)[3] |
| 166–168 | | 1 Mar 2010 (SI 2010/101)[3] |
| 169, 170 | | 26 Nov 2008 (so far as conferring power to make orders (other than orders granting, or making changes to orders granting, development consent), regulations or rules, or so far as making provision about what is (or is not) permitted to be done, or what is required to be done, in the exercise of any such power) (s 241(1)(a)) |
| | | 1 Mar 2010 (otherwise) (SI 2010/101)[3] |
| 171 | | 1 Mar 2010 (SI 2010/101)[3] |
| 172 | | 26 Nov 2008 (s 241(1)(a)) |
| 173, 174 | | 1 Mar 2010 (SI 2010/101)[3] |
| 175 | (1), (2) | 6 Apr 2009 (so far as relate to land identified in a national policy statement) (SI 2009/400) |
| | | 1 Mar 2010 (otherwise) (SI 2010/101)[3] |
| | (3) | 1 Mar 2010 (SI 2010/101)[3] |
| | (4)–(8) | 6 Apr 2009 (so far as relate to land identified in a national policy statement) (SI 2009/400) |
| | | 1 Mar 2010 (otherwise) (SI 2010/101)[3] |
| 176 | (1)–(3) | 6 Apr 2009 (so far as relate to land identified in national policy statements) (SI 2009/400) |
| | | 1 Mar 2010 (otherwise) (SI 2010/101)[3] |
| | (4) | 1 Mar 2010 (SI 2010/101)[3] |
| | (5)–(9) | 6 Apr 2009 (so far as relate to land identified in national policy statements) (SI 2009/400) |
| | | 1 Mar 2010 (otherwise) (SI 2010/101)[3] |
| 177–182 | | 6 Apr 2009 (SI 2009/400) |
| 183 | | 6 Apr 2009 (E) (SI 2009/400) |
| | | *Not yet in force* (W) |
| 184 | | 6 Apr 2009 (SI 2009/400) |
| 185 | | 6 Apr 2009 (E) (SI 2009/400) |
| | | 8 Aug 2014 (W) (SI 2014/1769) |
| 186 | | *Not yet in force* |
| 187 | | See Sch 7 below |
| 188 | | 23 Jun 2009 (E) (SI 2009/1303) |
| | | 30 Apr 2012 (W) (SI 2012/802) |
| 189 | | 6 Apr 2010 (SI 2010/566)[4] |
| 190 | (1)–(3) | 1 Oct 2009 (SI 2009/2260) |
| | (4) | 6 Apr 2010 (SI 2010/566) |
| | (5), (6) | 1 Oct 2009 (SI 2009/2260) |
| 191 | (1) | 6 Apr 2009 (E) (SI 2009/400)[1] |
| | | *Not yet in force* (W) |
| | (2) | 6 Apr 2009 (SI 2009/400)[1] |
| | (3) | 6 Apr 2009 (E) (SI 2009/400)[1] |
| | | *Not yet in force* (W) |
| 192 | (1)–(7) | 6 Apr 2012 (E) (SI 2012/601) |
| | | *Not yet in force* (W) |
| | (8) | See Sch 8 below |
| 193 | | 6 Apr 2012 (E) (SI 2012/601) |
| | | *Not yet in force* (W) |
| 194 | (1) | See Sch 9 below |
| | (2)–(5) | 26 Jan 2009 (s 241(6)) |
| 195 | | 6 Apr 2009 (SI 2009/400) |

**Planning Act 2008 (c 29)**—*contd*

| | | |
|---|---|---|
| 196 | (1)–(3) | 6 Apr 2009 (so far as they relate to an appeal under the Town and Country Planning Act 1990, ss 78, 174) (SI 2009/400)[1] |
| | | *Not yet in force* (otherwise) |
| | (4) | See Sch 10 below |
| 197 | | See Sch 11 below |
| 198 | | 6 Apr 2009 (E) (SI 2009/400) |
| | | 28 Nov 2014 (W) (SI 2014/2780) |
| 199 | | 6 Apr 2009 (E) (SI 2009/400) |
| | | 8 Aug 2014 (W) (SI 2014/1769) |
| 200 | | 1 Oct 2009 (E) (SI 2009/2260) |
| | | *Not yet in force* (W) |
| 201–203 | | 26 Jan 2009 (s 241(6)) |
| 204 | | 15 Oct 2005 (s 204(5)) |
| 205 | | 26 Nov 2008 (s 241(1)(b)) |
| 206 | | 6 Apr 2009 (for the purposes of s 211(7)) (SI 2009/400) |
| | | 6 Apr 2010 (otherwise) (SI 2010/566) |
| 207–210 | | 26 Nov 2008 (s 241(1)(b)) |
| 211 | (1)–(6) | 26 Nov 2008 (s 241(1)(b)) |
| | (7) | 6 Apr 2009 (SI 2009/400) |
| | (8)–(10) | 26 Nov 2008 (s 241(1)(b)) |
| 212–223 | | 26 Nov 2008 (s 241(1)(b)) |
| 224 | (1) | 6 Apr 2009 (SI 2009/400) |
| | (2) | *Not yet in force* |
| | (3) | 6 Apr 2010 (SI 2010/566) |
| | (4) | 6 Apr 2009 (SI 2009/400) |
| 225 | | 26 Jan 2009 (s 241(6)) |
| 226–237 | | 26 Nov 2008 (s 241(1)(c)) |
| 238 | | See Sch 13 below |
| 239–242 | | 26 Nov 2008 (s 241(1)(c)) |
| Sch 1 | | 1 Oct 2009 (SI 2009/2260; SI 2009/2573) |
| Sch 2 | | 1 Mar 2010 (SI 2010/101)[3] |
| Schs 3, 4 | | 26 Nov 2008 (so far as conferring power to make orders (other than orders granting, or making changes to orders granting, development consent), regulations or rules, or so far as making provision about what is (or is not) permitted to be done, or what is required to be done, in the exercise of any such power) (s 241(1)(a)) |
| | | 1 Mar 2010 (otherwise) (SI 2010/101)[3] |
| Sch 5 | | 1 Mar 2010 (SI 2010/101)[3] |
| Sch 6 | | 26 Nov 2008 (so far as conferring power to make orders (other than orders granting, or making changes to orders granting, development consent), regulations or rules, or so far as making provision about what is (or is not) permitted to be done, or what is required to be done, in the exercise of any such power) (s 241(1)(a)) |
| | | 1 Oct 2011 (otherwise) (SI 2011/2054) |
| Sch 7 | para 1 | See paras 2, 3 below |
| | para 2(1), (2) | 6 Apr 2009 (E) (SI 2009/400) |
| | | *Not yet in force* (W) |
| | para 2(3), (4) | 6 Apr 2009 (SI 2009/400) |
| | para 3(1), (2) | 6 Apr 2009 (E) (SI 2009/400) |
| | | *Not yet in force* (W) |
| | para 3(3) | 6 Apr 2009 (SI 2009/400) |
| | para 3(4) | 6 Apr 2009 (E) (SI 2009/400) |
| | | *Not yet in force* (W) |
| | paras 4–6 | 6 Apr 2009 (E) (SI 2009/400) |
| | | *Not yet in force* (W) |
| | para 7 | 26 Jan 2009 (s 241(6)) |
| Sch 8 | | 6 Apr 2012 (E) (SI 2012/601) |
| | | *Not yet in force* (W) |

**Planning Act 2008 (c 29)**—*contd*

| | | |
|---|---|---|
| Sch 9 | paras 1–4 | 6 Apr 2009 (SI 2009/400) |
| | para 5 | *Never in force* (spent) |
| | para 6 | 6 Apr 2009 (SI 2009/400) |
| Sch 10 | para 1 | See paras 2–14 below |
| | para 2 | *Not yet in force* |
| | paras 3–6 | 6 Apr 2009 (so far as relate to an appeal under the Town and Country Planning Act 1990, ss 78, 174) (SI 2009/400) |
| | | *Not yet in force* (otherwise) |
| | paras 7–9 | *Not yet in force* |
| | paras 10–14 | 6 Apr 2009 (so far as relate to an appeal under the Town and Country Planning Act 1990, ss 78, 174) (SI 2009/400) |
| | | *Not yet in force* (otherwise) |
| | paras 15–30 | *Not yet in force* |
| Sch 11 | | 26 Nov 2008 (so far as conferring power to make orders (other than orders granting, or making changes to orders granting, development consent), regulations or rules, or so far as making provision about what is (or is not) permitted to be done, or what is required to be done, in the exercise of any such power) (s 241(1)(a)) |
| | | 6 Apr 2009 (E) (otherwise) (SI 2009/400) |
| | | 30 Apr 2012 (W) (otherwise) (SI 2012/802) |
| Sch 12 | | 26 Nov 2008 (s 241(1)(c))[2] |
| Sch 13 | | 26 Jan 2009 (s 241(6)), repeals of or in— |
| | | Planning and Compulsory Purchase Act 2004, ss 46–48, Sch 6, para 5 |
| | | 6 Apr 2009 (SI 2009/400), repeals of or in— |
| | | Planning and Compulsory Purchase Act 2004, ss 15, 17, 18 |
| | | 6 Apr 2009 (E) (SI 2009/400), repeals of or in— |
| | | Town and Country Planning Act 1990, s 284; |
| | | Environmental Protection Act 1990, Sch 13, para 10; |
| | | Planning and Compensation Act 1991, s 6; |
| | | Planning and Compulsory Purchase Act 2004, s 53 |
| | | 23 Jun 2009 (E) (SI 2009/1303), repeals of or in— |
| | | Town and Country Planning Act 1990, s 61A, Sch 4A |
| | | 6 Apr 2010 (SI 2010/566), repeals of or in— |
| | | Planning and Compulsory Purchase Act 2004, s 122 |
| | | 6 Apr 2012 (E) (SI 2012/601), repeals of or in— |
| | | Forestry Act 1967; |
| | | Town and Country Planning Act 1990, ss 198, 199, 201–205, 212, Sch 1; |
| | | Planning and Compensation Act 1991, Sch 18; |
| | | Planning and Compulsory Purchase Act 2004, s 42 |
| | | 30 Apr 2012 (W) (SI 2012/802), repeals of or in— |
| | | Town and Country Planning Act 1990, s 61A, Sch 4A |
| | | *Not yet in force*, repeals of or in— |
| | | Forestry Act 1967 (W); |
| | | Town and Country Planning Act 1990 (except as noted above); |
| | | Environmental Protection Act 1990, Sch 13, para 10 (W); |
| | | Planning and Compensation Act 1991 (W); |
| | | Planning and Compulsory Purchase Act 2004, ss 42, 53 (W); |
| | | Greater London Authority Act 2007 |

[1]   For a saving, see SI 2009/400, art 6

[2]   Note that SI 2009/400 also purports to bring para 1 of this Schedule into force on 6 Apr 2009

[3]   For a saving, see SI 2010/101, art 6

[4]   For a saving, see SI 2010/566, art 4

## Planning and Energy Act 2008 (c 21)

*RA:* 13 Nov 2008

Whole Act in force 13 Nov 2008 (RA)

---

## Public Health etc (Scotland) Act 2008 (asp 5)

*RA:* 16 Jul 2008

*Commencement provisions:* s 128(2); Public Health etc (Scotland) Act 2008 (Commencement No 1) Order 2009, SSI 2009/9; Public Health etc (Scotland) Act 2008 (Commencement No 2, Savings and Consequential Provisions) Order 2009, SSI 2009/319, as amended by SSI 2009/404; Public Health etc (Scotland) Act 2008 (Commencement No 3, Consequential Provisions and Revocation) Order 2009, SSI 2009/404

| | | |
|---|---|---|
| 1, 2 | | 1 Oct 2009 (SSI 2009/319) |
| 3 | | 1 Apr 2009 (so far as confers the power to make regulations) (SSI 2009/9) |
| | | 1 Oct 2009 (otherwise) (SSI 2009/319) |
| 4 | | 1 Oct 2009 (SSI 2009/319) |
| 5 | | 1 Apr 2009 (so far as confers the power to make regulations) (SSI 2009/9) |
| | | 1 Oct 2009 (otherwise) (SSI 2009/319) |
| 6–11 | | 1 Oct 2009 (SSI 2009/319) |
| 12–19 | | 1 Jan 2010 (SSI 2009/404) |
| 20–86 | | 1 Oct 2009 (SSI 2009/319) |
| 87–89 | | 1 Apr 2009 (SSI 2009/9) |
| 90–93 | | 1 Oct 2009 (SSI 2009/319) |
| 94 | | 1 Apr 2009 (SSI 2009/9) |
| 95–99 | | 1 Dec 2009 (SSI 2009/404) |
| 100, 101 | | 1 Apr 2009 (so far as they confer the power to make regulations) (SSI 2009/9) |
| | | 1 Dec 2009 (otherwise) (SSI 2009/404) |
| 102–108 | | 1 Dec 2009 (SSI 2009/404) |
| 109–115 | | 26 Jan 2009 (SSI 2009/9) |
| 116 | | 1 Apr 2009 (SSI 2009/9) |
| 117–120 | | 1 Oct 2009 (SSI 2009/319) |
| 121 | | 1 Apr 2009 (SSI 2009/9) |
| 122 | | 16 Jul 2008 (RA) |
| 123 | | 1 Oct 2009 (SSI 2009/319) |
| 124 | | 1 Apr 2009 (SSI 2009/9) |
| 125 | | See Sch 2 below |
| 126 | (1) | See Sch 3 below |
| | (2) | 1 Oct 2009 (SSI 2009/319) |
| 127 | | 1 Oct 2009 (SSI 2009/319) |
| 128 | | 16 Jul 2008 (RA) |
| Sch 1 | | *Not yet in force* |
| Sch 2 | | 26 Jan 2009 (SSI 2009/9) |
| Sch 3 | Pt 1 | 1 Apr 2009 (SSI 2009/9), repeals of or in— |
| | | Public Health (Scotland) Act 1897, ss 68, 70, 71 |
| | | 1 Oct 2009 (SSI 2009/319), repeals of or in— |
| | | Cleansing of Persons Act 1897; |
| | | Public Health (Scotland) Act 1897 (except ss 32, 73(1), 161, 164)[1]; |
| | | Public Health (Scotland) Amendment Act 1907; |
| | | Small Landholders (Scotland) Act 1911, s 11; |
| | | Land Settlement (Scotland) Act 1919, s 18; |
| | | Local Government (Scotland) Act 1947, s 377; |
| | | Atomic Energy Authority Act 1954, s 5; |
| | | Offices, Shops and Railways Premises Act 1963, s 9; |

**Public Health etc (Scotland) Act 2008 (asp 5)**—*contd*

Criminal Justice Act 1967, s 92, Sch 3;
Health Services and Public Health Act 1968, ss 62, 71, 72, 73;
Sewerage (Scotland) Act 1968, Schs 1, 2;
Transport Act 1968, ss 108, 112;
Post Office Act 1969, Sch 9;
Finance Act 1970, Sch 8;
Local Government (Scotland) Act 1973, s 202, Sch 27;
Control of Pollution Act 1974, ss 47, 106, Sch 4;
National Health Service (Scotland) Act 1978, ss 14, 108;
Slaughter of Animals (Scotland) Act 1980, Sch 3;
Local Government (Miscellaneous Provisions) (Scotland)
  Act 1981, Schs 2, 4;
Civic Government (Scotland) Act 1982, s 87;
Roads (Scotland) Act 1984, Schs 9, 11;
AIDS (Control) Act 1987;
Local Government and Housing Act 1989, s 152;
Food Safety Act 1990, s 5;
Environmental Protection Act 1990, s 79;
National Health Service and Community Care Act 1990, Sch 9,
  para 1;
Local Government Finance Act 1992, Sch 13;
Clean Air Act 1993, ss 61, 64;
Value Added Tax Act 1994, s 33;
Local Government etc (Scotland) Act 1994, Sch 13, para 9,
  Sch 14;
Environment Act 1995, Schs 17, 24;
Debt Arrangement and Attachment (Scotland) Act 2002, Sch 3;
Smoking, Health and Social Care (Scotland) Act 2005, s 36,
  Sch 2;
Housing (Scotland) Act 2006, s 173
1 Jan 2010 (SSI 2009/404), repeals of or in—
Infectious Disease (Notification) Act 1889;
Public Health (Scotland) Act 1897, s 32;
Health Services and Public Health Act 1968, s 71A(a), (c) (it is
  thought that this should be a reference to sub-s (1)(a), (c) of
  this section);
National Health Service (Scotland) Act 1972
*Not yet in force,* repeals of or in—
Public Health (Scotland) Act 1897, ss 73(1), 161, 164;
Public Health (Scotland) Act 1945;
Health Services and Public Health Act 1968, s 71A (except as
  noted above);
National Health Service and Community Care Act 1990, Sch 9,
  para 4;
Local Government etc (Scotland) Act 1994, Sch 13, para 26;
Criminal Procedure (Consequential Provisions) (Scotland)
  Act 1995, Sch 2

Pt 2      1 Jan 2010 (SSI 2009/404), revocations of—
National Health Service (Designated Medical Officers)
  (Scotland) Regulations 1974, SI 1974/470;
Public Health (Notification of Infectious Diseases) (Scotland)
  Regulations 1988, SI 1988/1550
*Not yet in force,* revocations of—
Public Health (Aircraft) (Scotland) Regulations 1971,
  SI 1971/131;
Public Health (Ships) (Scotland) Regulations 1971, SI 1971/132;
Public Health (Ships) (Scotland) Amendment Regulations 1974,
  SI 1974/1008;
Public Health (Aircraft) (Scotland) Amendment
  Regulations 1974, SI 1974/1017;

**Public Health etc (Scotland) Act 2008 (asp 5)**—*contd*

Public Health (Ships) (Scotland) Amendment Regulations 1978,
SI 1978/369;
Public Health (Aircraft) (Scotland) Amendment
Regulations 1978, SI 1978/370

¹  For savings, see SSI 2009/319, art 3

**Regulatory Enforcement and Sanctions Act 2008 (c 13)**

*RA:* 21 Jul 2008

*Commencement provisions*: s 76; Regulatory Enforcement and Sanctions Act 2008 (Commencement No 1)
Order 2008, SI 2008/2371; Regulatory Enforcement and Sanctions Act 2008 (Commencement No 2)
Order 2009, SI 2009/550

| | | |
|---|---|---|
| 1–21 | | 1 Oct 2008 (SI 2008/2371) |
| 22, 23 | | 6 Apr 2009 (SI 2009/550) |
| 24 | (1)(a) | 6 Apr 2009 (SI 2009/550) |
| | (1)(b), (c) | 1 Oct 2008 (SI 2008/2371) |
| | (2)–(6) | 6 Apr 2009 (SI 2009/550) |
| 25–27 | | 6 Apr 2009 (SI 2009/550) |
| 28 | (1)–(5) | 6 Apr 2009 (SI 2009/550) |
| | (6) | 1 Oct 2008 (SI 2008/2371) |
| | (7) | See Sch 4 below |
| | (8)–(10) | 6 Apr 2009 (SI 2009/550) |
| 29–33 | | 6 Apr 2009 (SI 2009/550) |
| 34 | | 1 Oct 2008 (SI 2008/2371) |
| 35 | | 6 Apr 2009 (SI 2009/550) |
| 36–73 | | 1 Oct 2008 (SI 2008/2371) |
| 74–77 | | 21 Jul 2008 (s 76(2)) |
| Schs 1–3 | | 1 Oct 2008 (SI 2008/2371) |
| Sch 4 | paras 1–5 | 6 Apr 2009 (SI 2009/550) |
| | para 6(1) | 6 Apr 2009 (SI 2009/550) |
| | para 6(2) | 1 Oct 2008 (SI 2008/2371) |
| | paras 7, 8 | 6 Apr 2009 (SI 2009/550) |
| Schs 5–7 | | 1 Oct 2008 (SI 2008/2371) |

**Sale of Student Loans Act 2008 (c 10)**

*RA:* 21 Jul 2008

*Commencement provisions*: s 14

Whole Act in force 21 Jul 2008 (s 14)

**Scottish Register of Tartans Act 2008 (asp 7)**

*RA:* 13 Nov 2008

*Commencement provisions*: s 18(2); Scottish Register of Tartans Act 2008 (Commencement) Order 2009,
SSI 2009/5

| | |
|---|---|
| 1–17 | 5 Feb 2009 (SSI 2009/5) |
| 18 | 13 Nov 2008 (RA) |

## Special Educational Needs (Information) Act 2008 (c 11)

*RA:* 21 Jul 2008

*Commencement provisions*: s 2(2), (3); Special Educational Needs (Information) Act 2008 (Commencement)
   Order 2008, SI 2008/2664

| | |
|---|---|
| 1 | 1 Jan 2009 (SI 2008/2664) |
| 2 | 21 Jul 2008 (s 2(2)) |

## Statute Law (Repeals) Act 2008 (c 12)

*RA:* 21 Jul 2008

Whole Act in force 21 Jul 2008 (RA)

# 2009 Acts

## Apprenticeships, Skills, Children and Learning Act 2009 (c 22)

*RA:* 12 Nov 2009

*Commencement provisions:* s 269; Apprenticeships, Skills, Children and Learning Act 2009 (Commencement No 1 and Saving Provision) Order 2009, SI 2009/3317; Apprenticeships, Skills, Children and Learning Act 2009 (Commencement No 1) (Wales) Order 2009, SI 2009/3341; Apprenticeships, Skills, Children and Learning Act 2009 (Commencement No 2 and Transitional and Saving Provisions) Order 2010, SI 2010/303, as amended by SI 2010/1151, SI 2010/1172, SI 2010/1891, SI 2011/882; Apprenticeships, Skills, Children and Learning Act 2009 (Commencement No 3 and Transitional and Transitory Provisions) and (Commencement No 2 (Amendment)) Order 2010, SI 2010/1151[3], as amended by SI 2010/1702; Apprenticeships, Skills, Children and Learning Act 2009 (Commencement No 4) Order 2010, SI 2010/2374; Apprenticeships, Skills, Children and Learning Act 2009 (Commencement No 2 and Transitional Provisions) (Wales) Order 2010, SI 2010/2413; Apprenticeships, Skills, Children and Learning Act 2009 (Commencement No 5) Order 2011, SI 2011/200; Apprenticeships, Skills, Children and Learning Act 2009 (Commencement No 3) (Wales) Order 2011, SI 2011/829; Apprenticeships, Skills, Children and Learning Act 2009 (Commencement No 6) Order 2013, SI 2013/975; Apprenticeships, Skills, Children and Learning Act 2009 (Commencement No 4) (Wales) Order 2013, SI 2013/1100

| | | |
|---|---|---|
| 1 | | 6 Apr 2011 (SI 2011/200) |
| 2 | | 10 May 2013 (SI 2013/1100) |
| 3–6 | | 6 Apr 2011 (SI 2011/200) |
| 7–10 | | 10 May 2013 (SI 2013/1100) |
| 11 | | 6 Apr 2011 (E) (SI 2011/200) |
| | | 10 May 2013 (W) (SI 2013/1100) |
| 12 | | 1 Mar 2011 (E) (SI 2011/200) |
| | | 10 May 2013 (W) (SI 2013/1100) |
| 13–16 | | 1 Mar 2011 (SI 2011/200) |
| 17 | | 6 Apr 2011 (SI 2011/200) |
| 18–22 | | 10 May 2013 (SI 2013/1100) |
| 23–27 | | 30 Sep 2010 (SI 2010/2374) |
| 28–31 | | 10 May 2013 (SI 2013/1100) |
| 32–36 | | 6 Apr 2011 (E) (SI 2011/200) |
| | | 1 Aug 2011 (W) (SI 2011/200) |
| 37 | | 6 Apr 2011 (SI 2011/200) |
| 38 | | 1 Mar 2011 (SI 2011/200) |
| 39 | | 6 Apr 2011 (E) (SI 2011/200) |
| | | 10 May 2013 (W) (SI 2013/1100) |
| 40 | (1)–(4) | 6 Apr 2010 (except in relation to small employers and their employees, as defined by SI 2010/303, Sch 3) (SI 2010/303) |
| | | *Not yet in force* (exception noted above)[6] |
| | (5) | See Sch 1 below |
| 41–44 | | 1 Apr 2010 (SI 2010/303) |
| 45 | | *Not yet in force* |
| 46, 47 | | 1 Apr 2010 (SI 2010/303) |
| 48 | | 1 Sep 2010 (E) (in so far as it inserts Education Act 1996, s 18A(1), (2)(a)–(d), (3), (5)–(8), in relation to persons who are subject to youth detention by virtue of being detained in a relevant young offender institution) (SI 2010/303) |

**Apprenticeships, Skills, Children and Learning Act 2009 (c 22)**—*contd*

| | | |
|---|---|---|
| | | *Not yet in force* (otherwise) |
| 49, 50 | | 1 Sep 2010 (E) (for the purposes specified in SI 2010/303, Sch 5) (SI 2010/303) |
| | | 1 Apr 2011 (W) (for the purposes specified in SI 2011/829, art 2) (SI 2011/829) |
| | | *Not yet in force* (otherwise) |
| 51, 52 | | 1 Sep 2010 (E) (SI 2010/303) |
| | | 1 Apr 2011 (W) (SI 2011/829) |
| 53, 54 | | 1 Apr 2010 (SI 2010/303)[2] |
| 55, 56 | | 12 Jan 2010 (SI 2009/3317)[1] |
| 57 | | 1 Apr 2010 (SI 2010/303)[2] |
| 58 | | 12 Jan 2010 (s 269(2)(a)) |
| 59 | | See Sch 2 below |
| 60 | (1)–(3) | 1 Apr 2010 (SI 2010/303) |
| | (4) | See Sch 3 below |
| 61–90 | | 1 Apr 2010 (SI 2010/303)[2] |
| 91–99 | | *Never in force* (repealed) |
| 100–104 | | 1 Apr 2010 (SI 2010/303) |
| 105 | | 6 Apr 2011 (SI 2011/200) |
| 106–111 | | 1 Apr 2010 (SI 2010/303) |
| 112 | (1)–(3) | 12 Jan 2010 (SI 2009/3317) |
| | (4)–(6) | 1 Apr 2010 (SI 2010/303) |
| 113–124 | | 1 Apr 2010 (SI 2010/303) |
| 125 | | See Sch 8 below |
| 126 | | 12 Jan 2010 (SI 2009/3317) |
| 127–144 | | 1 Apr 2010 (SI 2010/1151) |
| 145, 146 | | 31 May 2013 (SI 2013/975)[7] |
| 147 | | 1 Apr 2010 (SI 2010/1151) |
| 148 | (1)(a), (b) | 1 Apr 2010 (SI 2010/1151) |
| | (1)(c) | *Not yet in force* |
| | (2) | 1 Apr 2010 (SI 2010/1151) |
| 149–154 | | 1 Apr 2010 (SI 2010/1151) |
| 155 | | *Not yet in force* |
| 156, 157 | | 1 Apr 2010 (SI 2010/1151) |
| 158 | (1) | 1 Apr 2010 (except for the definitions "Northern Ireland-only qualification" and "number of hours of guided learning") (SI 2010/1151) |
| | | *Not yet in force* (exceptions noted above) |
| | (2) | 1 Apr 2010 (SI 2010/1151) |
| | (3) | *Not yet in force* |
| 159 | (1), (2) | 1 Apr 2010 (SI 2010/1151) |
| | (3) | 1 Apr 2010 (in relation to an order under the Education Act 2002, s 87(3)(c) made on or after 1 Apr 2010 which includes provision made by virtue of section 87(8) of that Act) (SI 2010/1151) |
| | | *Not yet in force* (otherwise) |
| | (4) | 1 Apr 2010 (in relation to an order under the Education Act 2002, s 87(3)(c) made on or after 1 Apr 2010 which includes provision made by virtue of section 87(11) of that Act) (SI 2010/1151) |
| | | *Not yet in force* (otherwise) |
| 160 | (1), (2) | 1 Apr 2010 (SI 2010/1151) |
| | (3) | 1 Apr 2010 (in relation to an order under the Childcare Act 2006, s 41(2)(c) made on or after 1 Apr 2010 which includes provision made by virtue of s 42(3) of that Act) (SI 2010/1151) |
| | | *Not yet in force* (otherwise) |
| | (4) | 1 Apr 2010 (in relation to an order under the Childcare Act 2006, s 41(2)(c) made on or after 1 Apr 2010 which includes provision made by virtue of section 42(6) of that Act) (SI 2010/1151) |

**Apprenticeships, Skills, Children and Learning Act 2009 (c 22)**—*contd*

|         |             |                                                                                  |
|---------|-------------|----------------------------------------------------------------------------------|
|         |             | *Not yet in force* (otherwise)                                                   |
| 161–173 |             | 1 Apr 2010 (SI 2010/1151)                                                        |
| 174     |             | See Sch 12 below                                                                 |
| 175–177 |             | 1 Apr 2010 (SI 2010/1151)                                                        |
| 178     | (1)         | 1 Apr 2010 (SI 2010/1151)                                                        |
|         | (2)         | 12 Jan 2010 (SI 2009/3317)                                                       |
|         | (3), (4)    | 1 Apr 2010 (SI 2010/1151)                                                        |
| 179     |             | 1 Apr 2010 (SI 2010/1151)                                                        |
| 180     |             | 1 Apr 2010 (except for para (c) of definition of "qualifications criteria" in sub-s (4)) (SI 2010/1151) |
|         |             | *Never in force* (exception noted above) (repealed)                             |
| 181–191 |             | 1 Apr 2010 (SI 2010/1151)                                                        |
| 192     |             | See Sch 12 below                                                                 |
| 193     | (1), (2)(a) | 12 Jan 2010 (SI 2009/3317)                                                       |
|         | (2)(b)      | 1 Apr 2010 (SI 2010/303)                                                         |
|         | (3)–(5)     | 12 Jan 2010 (SI 2009/3317)                                                       |
| 194     | (1)–(3)     | 26 Feb 2010 (for the purpose of making regulations under the Children Act 2004, ss 12A(4), 17(1)) (SI 2010/303) |
|         |             | 1 Apr 2010 (otherwise) (SI 2010/303)[2]                                          |
|         | (4)–(9)     | 1 Apr 2010 (SI 2010/303)[2]                                                      |
| 195     |             | 12 Jan 2010 (SI 2009/3317)                                                       |
| 196, 197|             | 1 Apr 2010 (SI 2010/303)                                                         |
| 198–201 |             | 12 Jan 2010 (s 269(2)(b))                                                        |
| 202     | (1), (2)    | 12 Jan 2010 (SI 2009/3317)                                                       |
|         | (3)         | 28 Feb 2011 (SI 2010/2374)                                                       |
| 203, 204|             | 12 Jan 2010 (SI 2009/3317)                                                       |
| 205     |             | See Sch 14 below                                                                 |
| 206–224 |             | 19 Apr 2010 (in relation to a complaint against a school maintained by Barking and Dagenham London Borough Council, Cambridgeshire County Council, Medway Council or Sefton Council) (SI 2010/303) |
|         |             | 1 Sep 2010 (in relation to a complaint against a school maintained by Bristol City Council, Dorset County Council, Hammersmith and Fulham London Borough Council, Hillingdon London Borough Council, Kent County Council, Kensington and Chelsea London Borough Council, Lincolnshire County Council, Portsmouth City Council, Sheffield City Council or Wolverhampton City Council) (SI 2010/1151) |
|         |             | *Never in force* (otherwise) (repealed)                                          |
| 225     |             | 12 Jan 2010 (except in so far as inserts Education Act 2005, s 14A(3)) (SI 2009/3317) |
|         |             | 1 Apr 2010 (exception noted above) (SI 2010/303)                                 |
| 226–241 |             | 12 Jan 2010 (SI 2009/3317)                                                       |
| 242–245 |             | 1 Sep 2010 (SI 2010/303)                                                         |
| 246–248 |             | *Not yet in force* (s 248 repealed)                                              |
| 249     | (1), (2)    | *Never in force* (repealed)                                                      |
|         | (3)         | 1 Sep 2010 (SI 2010/303)[4]                                                      |
| 250     |             | *Never in force* (repealed)                                                      |
| 251–255 |             | 12 Jan 2010 (SI 2009/3317)                                                       |
| 256     |             | 1 Apr 2010 (SI 2010/303)                                                         |
| 257, 258|             | 12 Jan 2010 (SI 2009/3317)                                                       |
| 259     |             | 1 Oct 2010 (SI 2010/2413)                                                        |
| 260     |             | *Not yet in force*                                                               |
| 261     |             | 12 Jan 2010 (SI 2009/3317)                                                       |
| 262–265 |             | 12 Nov 2009 (s 269(1))                                                           |
| 266     |             | See Sch 16 below                                                                 |
| 267–270 |             | 12 Nov 2009 (s 269(1))                                                           |
| Sch 1   |             | 6 Apr 2010 (except in relation to small employers and their employees, as defined by SI 2010/303, Sch 3) (SI 2010/303) |

**Apprenticeships, Skills, Children and Learning Act 2009 (c 22)**—*contd*

| | | *Not yet in force* (exception noted above)[6] |
|---|---|---|
| Sch 2 | para 1 | See paras 2–14 below |
| | paras 2–5 | 1 Apr 2010 (SI 2010/303) |
| | para 6 | 1 Sep 2010 (SI 2010/303) |
| | para 7 | 12 Jan 2010 (in so far as amends Education Act 1996, s 496 to make it subject to s 509AE of that Act) (SI 2009/3317)[1] |
| | | 1 Apr 2010 (otherwise) (SI 2010/303) |
| | para 8 | 12 Jan 2010 (in so far as amends Education Act 1996, s 497 to make it subject to s 509AE of that Act) (SI 2009/3317)[1] |
| | | 1 Apr 2010 (otherwise) (SI 2010/303) |
| | para 9 | 12 Jan 2010 (in so far as amends Education Act 1996, s 497A to make it subject to s 509AE of that Act) (SI 2009/3317)[1] |
| | | 1 Apr 2010 (otherwise) (SI 2010/303) |
| | para 10 | 12 Jan 2010 (SI 2009/3317) |
| | paras 11–14 | 1 Sep 2010 (SI 2010/303) |
| Sch 3 | paras 1–12 | 1 Apr 2010 (SI 2010/303) |
| | para 13(1) | 1 Apr 2010 (SI 2010/303) |
| | para 13(2) | 1 Apr 2010 (only in relation to the academic year commencing on 1 Sep 2010 and all following academic years) (SI 2010/303) |
| | | *Never in force* (otherwise) (repealed) |
| | para 13(3), (4) | 1 Apr 2010 (SI 2010/303) |
| | paras 14–22 | 1 Apr 2010 (SI 2010/303) |
| Schs 4, 5 | | 1 Apr 2010 (SI 2010/303)[2] |
| Sch 6 | paras 1–53 | 1 Apr 2010 (SI 2010/303)[2] |
| | paras 54–56 | 1 Apr 2010 (except in relation to Wales) (SI 2010/303)[2] |
| | | 1 Apr 2011 (in relation to Wales) (SI 2011/829) |
| | paras 57–62 | 1 Apr 2010 (SI 2010/303)[2] |
| Sch 7 | | 1 Apr 2010 (SI 2010/303)[2] |
| Sch 8 | para 1 | See paras 2–15 below |
| | para 2 | 1 Apr 2010 (SI 2010/303) |
| | para 3 | 12 Jan 2010 (in so far as inserts Further and Higher Education Act 1992, ss 33A–33J, 33M and 33N) (SI 2009/3317) |
| | | 1 Apr 2010 (in so far as inserts ss 33K, 33L of that Act) (SI 2010/303) |
| | paras 4–10 | 1 Apr 2010 (SI 2010/303) |
| | para 11(1) | See sub-paras (2)–(4) below |
| | para 11(2)(a) | 12 Jan 2010 (SI 2009/3317) |
| | para 11(2)(b), (3), (4) | 1 Apr 2010 (SI 2010/303) |
| | paras 12–14 | 12 Jan 2010 (SI 2009/3317) |
| | para 15 | 1 Apr 2010 (SI 2010/303) |
| Schs 9–11 | | 1 Apr 2010 (SI 2010/1151) |
| Sch 12 | paras 1–10 | 1 Apr 2010 (SI 2010/1151) |
| | para 11 | 1 Apr 2010 (except in relation to Wales) (SI 2010/1151) |
| | | 1 Nov 2010 (in relation to Wales) (SI 2010/2413)[5] |
| | para 12 | 1 Apr 2010 (SI 2010/1151) |
| | para 13 | 1 Apr 2010 (except in relation to Wales) (SI 2010/1151) |
| | | 1 Nov 2010 (in relation to Wales) (SI 2010/2413)[5] |
| | paras 14–19 | 1 Nov 2010 (SI 2010/2413)[5] |
| | paras 20–26 | 1 Apr 2010 (SI 2010/1151) |
| | para 27 | 1 Apr 2010 (except in relation to Wales) (SI 2010/1151) |
| | | 1 Nov 2010 (in relation to Wales) (SI 2010/2413)[5] |
| | para 28 | 1 Apr 2010 (SI 2010/1151) |
| | para 29 | 1 Nov 2010 (SI 2010/2413)[5] |
| | paras 30–43 | 1 Apr 2010 (SI 2010/1151) |
| Sch 13 | | 12 Jan 2010 (SI 2009/3317) |
| Sch 14 | | 12 Jan 2010 (SI 2009/3341) |
| Sch 15 | | 12 Jan 2010 (SI 2009/3317) |

## Apprenticeships, Skills, Children and Learning Act 2009 (c 22)—*contd*

| | | |
|---|---|---|
| Sch 16 | Pt 1 | 12 Jan 2010 (repeals in School Standards and Framework Act 1998) (s 129(2)(a)) |
| | | 1 Apr 2010 (SI 2010/303), repeals in— |
| | | Education Act 1996; |
| | | Education and Inspections Act 2006 |
| | Pt 2 | 1 Apr 2010 (SI 2010/303)² |
| | Pt 3 | 12 Jan 2010 (SI 2009/3317) |
| | Pt 4 | 1 Apr 2010 (E) (except repeal of Education and Skills Act 2008, s 9, and repeals to be brought into force by order of the Welsh Ministers as specified by s 269(3)) (SI 2010/1151) |
| | | 1 Nov 2010 (W) (SI 2010/2413)⁵, repeals of or in— |
| | | Education Act 1997, ss 21–26A, 30, 32, 32A; |
| | | School Standards and Framework Act 1998; |
| | | Learning and Skills Act 2000; |
| | | Education Act 2002, s 216(2), Sch 17, paras 1–4, 5(6), Sch 21, para 69; |
| | | Childcare Act 2006, Sch 1, para 2; |
| | | Education and Inspections Act 2006, Sch 14, para 21; |
| | | Education and Skills Act 2008, ss 161, 162(2)–(5), 163 |
| | | 31 May 2013 (repeal of Education and Skills Act 2008, s 9) (SI 2013/975) |
| | Pt 5 | 12 Jan 2010 (repeals of Children Act 2004, s 10(6), (7)) (SI 2009/3317) |
| | | 1 Apr 2010 (repeal of Children Act 2004, s 10(4)(g)) (SI 2010/303) |
| | Pt 6 | 12 Jan 2010 (SI 2009/3317) |
| | Pt 7 | 19 Apr 2010 (in relation to a complaint against a school maintained by Barking and Dagenham London Borough Council, Cambridgeshire County Council, Medway Council or Sefton Council) (SI 2010/303) |
| | | 1 Sep 2010 (in relation to a complaint against a school maintained by Bristol City Council, Dorset County Council, Hammersmith and Fulham London Borough Council, Hillingdon London Borough Council, Kent County Council, Kensington and Chelsea London Borough Council, Lincolnshire County Council, Portsmouth City Council, Sheffield City Council or Wolverhampton City Council) (SI 2010/1151) |
| | | *Never in force* (otherwise) (repealed) |
| | Pts 8–10 | 12 Jan 2010 (SI 2009/3317) |
| | Pt 11 | 1 Oct 2010 (W) (SI 2010/2413) |

¹   For a saving, see SI 2009/3317, art 3

²   For transitional provisions and savings, see SI 2010/303, arts 8–14

³   For transitional and transitory provisions, see SI 2010/1151, arts 5–21

⁴   For a transitional provision, see SI 2010/1891, art 3

⁵   For transitional provisions, see SI 2010/2413, arts 3–5

⁶   SI 2011/882 amends SI 2010/303 with the effect that these provisions will no longer come into force on 6 Apr 2011 in relation to small employers and their employees as specified in that Order

⁷   For a transitional provision, see SI 2013/975, art 3

## Appropriation Act 2009 (c 2)

*RA:* 12 Mar 2009

Whole Act in force 12 Mar 2009 (RA)

## Appropriation (No 2) Act 2009 (c 9)

*RA:* 21 Jul 2009

Whole Act in force 21 Jul 2009 (RA)

---

## Autism Act 2009 (c 15)

*RA:* 12 Nov 2009

Whole Act in force 12 Jan 2010 (s 6(2))

---

## Banking Act 2009 (c 1)

*RA:* 12 Feb 2009

*Commencement provisions:* s 263; Banking Act 2009 (Commencement No 1) Order 2009, SI 2009/296; Banking Act 2009 (Commencement No 2) Order 2009, SI 2009/1296; Banking Act 2009 (Commencement No 3) Order 2009, SI 2009/2038; Banking Act 2009 (Commencement No 4) Order 2009, SI 2009/3000; Banking Act 2009 (Commencement No 5) Order 2016, SI 2016/598

| | |
|---|---|
| 1 | 21 Feb 2009 (SI 2009/296) |
| 2 | 17 Feb 2009 (in so far as confers power to make subordinate legislation, but no such subordinate legislation may come into force before 21 Feb 2009) (SI 2009/296) |
| | 21 Feb 2009 (otherwise) (SI 2009/296) |
| 3, 4 | 21 Feb 2009 (SI 2009/296) |
| 5, 6 | 17 Feb 2009 (in so far as they confer power to make a code of practice, but no such code may come into force before 21 Feb 2009) (SI 2009/296) |
| | 21 Feb 2009 (otherwise) (SI 2009/296) |
| 7–24 | 21 Feb 2009 (SI 2009/296) |
| 25 | 17 Feb 2009 (in so far as confers power to make subordinate legislation, but no such subordinate legislation may come into force before 21 Feb 2009) (SI 2009/296) |
| | 21 Feb 2009 (otherwise) (SI 2009/296) |
| 26–46 | 21 Feb 2009 (SI 2009/296) |
| 47, 48 | 17 Feb 2009 (in so far as confer power to make subordinate legislation, but no such subordinate legislation may come into force before 21 Feb 2009) (SI 2009/296) |
| | 21 Feb 2009 (otherwise) (SI 2009/296) |
| 49–54 | 21 Feb 2009 (SI 2009/296) |
| 55, 56 | 17 Feb 2009 (in so far as confer power to make subordinate legislation, but no such subordinate legislation may come into force before 21 Feb 2009) (SI 2009/296) |
| | 21 Feb 2009 (otherwise) (SI 2009/296) |
| 57–59 | 21 Feb 2009 (SI 2009/296) |
| 60 | 17 Feb 2009 (in so far as confers power to make subordinate legislation, but no such subordinate legislation may come into force before 21 Feb 2009) (SI 2009/296) |
| | 21 Feb 2009 (otherwise) (SI 2009/296) |
| 61 | 21 Feb 2009 (SI 2009/296) |
| 62 | 17 Feb 2009 (in so far as confers power to make subordinate legislation, but no such subordinate legislation may come into force before 21 Feb 2009) (SI 2009/296) |
| | 21 Feb 2009 (otherwise) (SI 2009/296) |
| 63–68 | 21 Feb 2009 (SI 2009/296) |
| 69 | 17 Feb 2009 (in so far as confers power to make subordinate legislation, but no such subordinate legislation may come into force before 21 Feb 2009) (SI 2009/296) |
| | 21 Feb 2009 (otherwise) (SI 2009/296) |

**Banking Act 2009 (c 1)**—*contd*

| | |
|---|---|
| 70, 71 | 21 Feb 2009 (SI 2009/296) |
| 72 | 17 Feb 2009 (in so far as confers power to make subordinate legislation, but no such subordinate legislation may come into force before 21 Feb 2009) (SI 2009/296) |
| | 21 Feb 2009 (otherwise) (SI 2009/296) |
| 73 | 21 Feb 2009 (SI 2009/296) |
| 74, 75 | 17 Feb 2009 (in so far as confer power to make subordinate legislation, but no such subordinate legislation may come into force before 21 Feb 2009) (SI 2009/296) |
| | 21 Feb 2009 (otherwise) (SI 2009/296) |
| 76, 77 | 21 Feb 2009 (SI 2009/296) |
| 78 | 17 Feb 2009 (in so far as confers power to make subordinate legislation, but no such subordinate legislation may come into force before 21 Feb 2009) (SI 2009/296) |
| | 21 Feb 2009 (otherwise) (SI 2009/296) |
| 79–84 | 21 Feb 2009 (SI 2009/296) |
| 85, 86 | 17 Feb 2009 (in so far as confer power to make subordinate legislation, but no such subordinate legislation may come into force before 21 Feb 2009) (SI 2009/296) |
| | 21 Feb 2009 (otherwise) (SI 2009/296) |
| 87 | 21 Feb 2009 (SI 2009/296) |
| 88, 89 | 17 Feb 2009 (in so far as confer power to make subordinate legislation, but no such subordinate legislation may come into force before 21 Feb 2009) (SI 2009/296) |
| | 21 Feb 2009 (otherwise) (SI 2009/296) |
| 90 | 21 Feb 2009 (SI 2009/296) |
| 91 | 17 Feb 2009 (in so far as confers power to make subordinate legislation, but no such subordinate legislation may come into force before 21 Feb 2009) (SI 2009/296) |
| | 21 Feb 2009 (otherwise) (SI 2009/296) |
| 92–121 | 21 Feb 2009 (SI 2009/296) |
| 122 | 17 Feb 2009 (in so far as confers power to make subordinate legislation, but no such subordinate legislation may come into force before 21 Feb 2009) (SI 2009/296) |
| | 21 Feb 2009 (otherwise) (SI 2009/296) |
| 123–129 | 21 Feb 2009 (SI 2009/296) |
| 130–133 | 17 Feb 2009 (in so far as confer power to make subordinate legislation, but no such subordinate legislation may come into force before 21 Feb 2009) (SI 2009/296) |
| | 21 Feb 2009 (otherwise) (SI 2009/296) |
| 134 | 21 Feb 2009 (SI 2009/296) |
| 135 | 17 Feb 2009 (in so far as confers power to make subordinate legislation, but no such subordinate legislation may come into force before 21 Feb 2009) (SI 2009/296) |
| | 21 Feb 2009 (otherwise) (SI 2009/296) |
| 136–147 | 21 Feb 2009 (SI 2009/296) |
| 148, 149 | 17 Feb 2009 (in so far as confer power to make subordinate legislation, but no such subordinate legislation may come into force before 21 Feb 2009) (SI 2009/296) |
| | 21 Feb 2009 (otherwise) (SI 2009/296) |
| 150, 151 | 21 Feb 2009 (SI 2009/296) |
| 152 | 17 Feb 2009 (in so far as confers power to make subordinate legislation, but no such subordinate legislation may come into force before 21 Feb 2009) (SI 2009/296) |
| | 21 Feb 2009 (otherwise) (SI 2009/296) |
| 153–155 | 21 Feb 2009 (SI 2009/296) |
| 156 | 17 Feb 2009 (in so far as confers power to make subordinate legislation, but no such subordinate legislation may come into force before 21 Feb 2009) (SI 2009/296) |
| | 21 Feb 2009 (otherwise) (SI 2009/296) |

**Banking Act 2009 (c 1)**—*contd*

| | | |
|---|---|---|
| 157 | | 21 Feb 2009 (SI 2009/296) |
| 158, 159 | | 17 Feb 2009 (in so far as confer power to make subordinate legislation, but no such subordinate legislation may come into force before 21 Feb 2009) (SI 2009/296) |
| | | 21 Feb 2009 (otherwise) (SI 2009/296) |
| 160–162 | | 21 Feb 2009 (SI 2009/296) |
| 163, 164 | | 17 Feb 2009 (in so far as confer power to make subordinate legislation, but no such subordinate legislation may come into force before 21 Feb 2009) (SI 2009/296) |
| | | 21 Feb 2009 (otherwise) (SI 2009/296) |
| 165–167 | | 21 Feb 2009 (SI 2009/296) |
| 168 | | 17 Feb 2009 (in so far as confer power to make subordinate legislation, but no such subordinate legislation may come into force before 21 Feb 2009) (SI 2009/296) |
| | | 21 Feb 2009 (otherwise) (SI 2009/296) |
| 169 | | 21 Feb 2009 (SI 2009/296) |
| 170 | | *Not yet in force* |
| 171 | | 21 Feb 2009 (SI 2009/296) |
| 172 | | *Not yet in force* |
| 173–180 | | 21 Feb 2009 (SI 2009/296) |
| 181–187 | | 4 Aug 2009 (SI 2009/2038) |
| 188–190 | | 31 Dec 2009 (SI 2009/3000) |
| 191 | | 12 Nov 2009 (for the purpose of enabling subordinate legislation to be made, but no such subordinate legislation may come into force before 31 Dec 2009) (SI 2009/3000) |
| | | 31 Dec 2009 (otherwise) (SI 2009/3000) |
| 192–202 | | 31 Dec 2009 (SI 2009/3000) |
| 203 | | 12 Nov 2009 (for the purpose of enabling subordinate legislation to be made, but no such subordinate legislation may come into force before 31 Dec 2009) (SI 2009/3000) |
| | | 31 Dec 2009 (otherwise) (SI 2009/3000) |
| 204 | (1)(a) | 4 Aug 2009 (SI 2009/2038) |
| | (1)(b) | 31 Dec 2009 (SI 2009/3000) |
| | (2), (3) | 4 Aug 2009 (SI 2009/2038) |
| | (4)(a), (b) | 4 Aug 2009 (SI 2009/2038) |
| | (4)(c)–(e) | 31 Dec 2009 (SI 2009/3000) |
| | (5), (6) | 4 Aug 2009 (SI 2009/2038) |
| | (7) | 31 Dec 2009 (SI 2009/3000) |
| | (8)–(11) | 4 Aug 2009 (SI 2009/2038) |
| 205 | | 4 Aug 2009 (SI 2009/2038) |
| 206 | | 31 Dec 2009 (SI 2009/3000) |
| 207–214 | | 23 Nov 2009 (SI 2009/3000) |
| 215–220 | | 12 Nov 2009 (for the purpose of enabling subordinate legislation to be made, but no such subordinate legislation may come into force before 23 Nov 2009) (SI 2009/3000) |
| | | 23 Nov 2009 (otherwise) (SI 2009/3000) |
| 221 | | 23 Nov 2009 (SI 2009/3000) |
| 222–224 | | 12 Nov 2009 (for the purpose of enabling subordinate legislation to be made, but no such subordinate legislation may come into force before 23 Nov 2009) (SI 2009/3000) |
| | | 23 Nov 2009 (otherwise) (SI 2009/3000) |
| 225 | | 23 Nov 2009 (SI 2009/3000) |
| 226 | | 12 Nov 2009 (for the purpose of enabling subordinate legislation to be made, but no such subordinate legislation may come into force before 23 Nov 2009) (SI 2009/3000) |
| | | 23 Nov 2009 (otherwise) (SI 2009/3000) |
| 227 | | 23 Nov 2009 (SI 2009/3000) |
| 228, 229 | | 21 Feb 2009 (SI 2009/296) |

## Banking Act 2009 (c 1)—*contd*

| | |
|---|---|
| 230 | 17 Feb 2009 (in so far as confers power to make subordinate legislation, but no such subordinate legislation may come into force before 21 Feb 2009) (SI 2009/296) |
| | 21 Feb 2009 (otherwise) (SI 2009/296) |
| 231 | 21 Feb 2009 (SI 2009/296) |
| 232–235 | 17 Feb 2009 (in so far as confer power to make subordinate legislation, but no such subordinate legislation may come into force before 21 Feb 2009) (SI 2009/296) |
| | 21 Feb 2009 (otherwise) (SI 2009/296) |
| 236, 237 | 21 Feb 2009 (SI 2009/296) |
| 238–243 | 1 Jun 2009 (SI 2009/1296) |
| 244–248 | 21 Feb 2009 (SI 2009/296) |
| 249 | 17 Feb 2009 (in so far as confers power to make subordinate legislation, but no such subordinate legislation may come into force before 21 Feb 2009) (SI 2009/296) |
| | 21 Feb 2009 (otherwise) (SI 2009/296) |
| 250 | 21 Feb 2009 (SI 2009/296) |
| 251 | 17 Feb 2009 (in so far as confers power to make subordinate legislation, but no such subordinate legislation may come into force before 21 Feb 2009) (SI 2009/296) |
| | 21 Feb 2009 (otherwise) (SI 2009/296) |
| 252, 253 | 21 Feb 2009 (SI 2009/296) |
| 254 | 12 Apr 2009 (s 263(2)) |
| 255, 256 | 25 May 2016 (SI 2016/598) |
| 257 | 17 Feb 2009 (in so far as confers power to make subordinate legislation, but no such subordinate legislation may come into force before 21 Feb 2009) (SI 2009/296) |
| | 21 Feb 2009 (otherwise) (SI 2009/296) |
| 258–261 | 21 Feb 2009 (SI 2009/296) |
| 262 | 17 Feb 2009 (in so far as confers power to make subordinate legislation, but no such subordinate legislation may come into force before 21 Feb 2009) (SI 2009/296) |
| | 21 Feb 2009 (otherwise) (SI 2009/296) |
| 263–265 | 12 Feb 2009 (RA) |

## Borders, Citizenship and Immigration Act 2009 (c 11)

*RA:* 21 Jul 2009

*Commencement provisions:* s 58; Borders, Citizenship and Immigration Act 2009 (Commencement No 1) Order 2009, SI 2009/2731; Borders, Citizenship and Immigration Act 2009 (Commencement No 2) Order 2011, SI 2011/1741; Borders, Citizenship and Immigration Act 2009 (Commencement No 3) Order 2014, SI 2014/2634

| | | |
|---|---|---|
| 1–38 | | 21 Jul 2009 (s 58(1)) |
| 39–40 | | *Not yet in force* |
| 41 | (1)–(4) | *Not yet in force* |
| | (5) | 27 Oct 2014 (in so far as inserts British Nationality Act 1981, s 41(8)(b), words "under subsection (1)") (SI 2014/2634) |
| | | *Not yet in force* (otherwise) |
| 42–48 | | 13 Jan 2010 (SI 2009/2731) |
| 49 | (1) | 13 Jan 2010 (SI 2009/2731) |
| | (2), (3) | *Not yet in force* |
| 50 | | 21 Jul 2009 (s 58(3)) |
| 51 | | 10 Nov 2009 (SI 2009/2731) |
| 52 | | 27 Oct 2014 (SI 2014/2634) |
| 53 | | 8 Aug 2011 (SI 2011/1741) |
| 54 | | 10 Nov 2009 (SI 2009/2731) |
| 55 | | 2 Nov 2009 (SI 2009/2731) |
| 56 | | See Schedule below |

**Borders, Citizenship and Immigration Act 2009 (c 11)**—*contd*

| | | |
|---|---|---|
| 57–59 | | 21 Jul 2009 (s 58(6)) |
| Schedule | Pt 1 | 21 Jul 2009 (s 58(5)) |
| | Pt 2 | 13 Jan 2010 (except for repeals in British Nationality Act 1981, Sch 1) (SI 2009/2731) |
| | | *Not yet in force* (exceptions noted above) |
| | Pt 3 | *Not yet in force* |
| | Pt 4 | 2 Nov 2009 (SI 2009/2731) |

**Budget (Scotland) Act 2009 (asp 2)**

*RA:* 10 Mar 2009

Whole Act in force 10 Mar 2009 (RA)

**Business Rate Supplements Act 2009 (c 7)**

*RA:* 2 Jul 2009

*Commencement provisions:* s 32; Business Rate Supplements Act 2009 (Commencement No 1) (England) Order 2009, SI 2009/2202; Business Rate Supplements Act 2009 (Commencement No 2) (England) Order 2014, SI 2014/1860; Business Rate Supplements Act 2009 (Commencement No 3) (England) Order 2014, SI 2014/3200

| | | |
|---|---|---|
| 1–15 | | 19 Aug 2009 (E) (SI 2009/2202) |
| | | *Not yet in force* (W) (s 10(7)–(9) repealed in part) |
| 16 | (1)–(4) | 19 Aug 2009 (E) (SI 2009/2202) |
| | | *Not yet in force* (W) |
| | (5) | 16 Jul 2014 (E) (SI 2014/1860) |
| | | *Not yet in force* (W) |
| 23–26 | | 19 Aug 2009 (E) (SI 2009/2202) |
| | | *Not yet in force* (W) |
| 27 | | 19 Aug 2009 (SI 2009/2202) |
| 28–32 | | 2 Jul 2009 (s 32(1)) |
| Sch 1 | | 19 Aug 2009 (E) (SI 2009/2202) |
| | | *Not yet in force* (W) |
| Sch 2 | | 16 Jul 2014 (so far as confers power to make regulations) (SI 2014/1860) |
| | | 2 Dec 2014 (otherwise) (SI 2014/3200) |
| Sch 3 | | 19 Aug 2009 (SI 2009/2202) |
| | | *Not yet in force* (W) |

**Church of England Pensions (Amendment) Measure 2009 (No 2)**

*RA:* 2 Apr 2009

Whole Measure in force 2 Apr 2009 (RA)

**Climate Change (Scotland) Act 2009 (asp 12)**

*RA:* 4 Aug 2009

*Commencement provisions:* ss 26, 100; Climate Change (Scotland) Act 2009 (Commencement No 1) Order 2009, SSI 2009/341

| | | |
|---|---|---|
| 1–24 | | 31 Oct 2009 (SSI 2009/341) |
| 25 | (1), (2) | *Not yet in force* |
| | (3) | See Sch 1 below |
| | (4) | *Not yet in force* |
| 26 | | 31 Oct 2009 (SSI 2009/341) |

**Climate Change (Scotland) Act 2009 (asp 12)**—*contd*

| | | |
|---|---|---|
| 27–32 | | *Not yet in force* |
| 33–43 | | 31 Oct 2009 (SSI 2009/341) |
| 44–52 | | 1 Jan 2011 (SSI 2009/341) |
| 53–55 | | 31 Oct 2009 (SSI 2009/341) |
| 56 | | *Not yet in force* |
| 57–62 | | 31 Oct 2009 (SSI 2009/341) |
| 63–69 | | 1 Apr 2010 (SSI 2009/341) |
| 70 | | 5 Aug 2009 (s 100(4)) |
| 71–73 | | 1 Apr 2010 (SSI 2009/341) |
| 74–95 | | 31 Oct 2009 (SSI 2009/341) |
| 96 | | 4 Aug 2009 (RA) |
| 97, 98 | | 31 Oct 2009 (SSI 2009/341) |
| 99 | | See Sch 2 below |
| 100 | | 4 Aug 2009 (RA) |
| Sch 1 | | *Not yet in force* |
| Sch 2 | paras 1, 2 | 31 Oct 2009 (SSI 2009/341) |
| | paras 3–6 | *Not yet in force* |
| | para 7 | 31 Oct 2009 (SSI 2009/341) |

---

**Consolidated Fund Act 2009 (c 27)**

*RA:* 16 Dec 2009

Whole Act in force 16 Dec 2009 (RA)

---

**Convention Rights Proceedings (Amendment) (Scotland) Act 2009 (asp 11)**

*RA:* 23 Jul 2009

Whole Act in force 24 Jul 2009 (s 2(1))

---

**Coroners and Justice Act 2009 (c 25)**

*RA:* 12 Nov 2009

*Commencement provisions*: s 182; Coroners and Justice Act 2009 (Commencement No 1 and Transitional Provisions) Order 2009, SI 2009/3253; Coroners and Justice Act 2009 (Commencement No 2) Order 2010, SI 2010/28; Coroners and Justice Act 2009 (Commencement No 3 and Transitional Provision) Order 2010, SI 2010/145, as amended by SI 2010/186; Coroners and Justice Act 2009 (Commencement No 4, Transitional and Saving Provisions) Order 2010, SI 2010/816, as amended by SI 2011/722; Coroners and Justice Act 2009 (Commencement No 5) Order 2010, SI 2010/1858; Coroners and Justice Act 2009 (Commencement No 1) (Northern Ireland) Order 2011, SR 2011/182; Coroners and Justice Act 2009 (Commencement No 6) Order 2011, SI 2011/1122; Coroners and Justice Act 2009 (Commencement No 7) Order 2011, SI 2011/1452; Coroners and Justice Act 2009 (Commencement No 8) Order 2011, SI 2011/2148; Coroners and Justice Act 2009 (Commencement No 9) Order 2012, SI 2012/1810; Coroners and Justice Act 2009 (Commencement No 10) Order 2012, SI 2012/2374; Coroners and Justice Act 2009 (Commencement No 11) Order 2013, SI 2013/250; Coroners and Justice Act 2009 (Commencement No 12) Order 2013, SI 2013/705; Coroners and Justice Act 2009 (Commencement No 13) Order 2013, SI 2013/1104; Coroners and Justice Act 2009 (Commencement No 14) Order 2013, SI 2013/1628; Coroners and Justice Act 2009 (Commencement No 15, Consequential and Transitory Provisions) Order 2013, SI 2013/1869; Coroners and Justice Act 2009 (Commencement No 16) Order 2013, SI 2013/2908; Coroners and Justice Act 2009 (Commencement No 17) Order 2015, SI 2015/819; Coroners and Justice Act 2009 (Commencement No 18) Order 2018, SI 2018/733; Coroners and Justice Act 2009 (Commencement No 19) Order 2018, SI 2018/727; Coroners and Justice Act 2009 (Commencement No 20) Order 2019, SI 2019/1105

| | |
|---|---|
| 1–11 | 25 Jul 2013 (SI 2013/1869) |
| 12 | 24 Sep 2012 (SI 2012/2374) |

**See Halsbury's Statutes Citator for amendments to these Acts**    

**Coroners and Justice Act 2009 (c 25)**—*contd*

| | | |
|---|---|---|
| 13–17 | | 25 Jul 2013 (SI 2013/1869) |
| 18 | | 9 Jul 2019 (SI 2019/1105) |
| 19, 20 | | *Not yet in force* |
| 21 | | 18 Jun 2018 (SI 2018/727) |
| 22–24 | | 25 Jul 2013 (SI 2013/1869) |
| 25 | | See Sch 4 below |
| 26–31 | | *Not yet in force* |
| 32 | | See Sch 5 below |
| 33, 34 | | 25 Jul 2013 (SI 2013/1869) |
| 35 | | 1 Feb 2010 (SI 2010/145) |
| 36 | (1)–(3), (4)(a), (b) | 25 Jul 2013 (SI 2013/1869) |
| | (4)(c) | *Not yet in force* |
| | (4)(d), (5)–(7) | 25 Jul 2013 (SI 2013/1869) |
| 37 | | 25 Jul 2013 (SI 2013/1869) |
| 38 | | See Sch 9 below |
| 39, 40 | | *Never in force (repealed)* |
| 41 | | See Sch 10 below |
| 42 | | 25 Jul 2013 (SI 2013/1869) |
| 43 | | 3 Jul 2013 (SI 2013/1628) |
| 44 | | *Not yet in force* |
| 45 | | 3 Jul 2013 (SI 2013/1628) |
| 46 | | 25 Jul 2013 (SI 2013/1869) |
| 47, 48 | | 12 Nov 2009 (s 182(1)(a)) |
| 49 | (1) | *Not yet in force* |
| | (2) | See Sch 11 below |
| 50 | | 24 Sep 2012 (SI 2012/2374) |
| 51 | | *Never in force (repealed)* |
| 52 | | 4 Oct 2010 (SI 2010/816) |
| 53 | | 1 Jun 2011 (SR 2011/182) |
| 54, 55 | | 4 Oct 2010 (E) (W) (SI 2010/816) |
| | | 1 Jun 2011 (NI) (SR 2011/182) |
| 56 | (1) | 4 Oct 2010 (E) (W) (SI 2010/816) |
| | | 1 Jun 2011 (NI) (SR 2011/182) |
| | (2)(a) | 4 Oct 2010 (SI 2010/816) |
| | (2)(b) | 1 Jun 2011 (SR 2011/182) |
| 57 | | 4 Oct 2010 (SI 2010/816) |
| 58 | | 1 Jun 2011 (SR 2011/182) |
| 59–61 | | 1 Feb 2010 (SI 2010/145) |
| 62–71 | | 6 Apr 2010 (SI 2010/816) |
| 72 | | 1 Feb 2010 (SI 2010/145) |
| 73 | | 12 Jan 2010 (s 182(2)(a)) |
| 74 | | 6 Apr 2010 (E) (W) (SI 2010/816) |
| | | 18 Apr 2011 (NI) (SR 2011/182) |
| 75 | (1) | 6 Apr 2010 (E) (W) (SI 2010/816) |
| | | 18 Apr 2011 (NI) (SR 2011/182) |
| | (2)(a), (b) | 6 Apr 2010 (SI 2010/816) |
| | (2)(c) | 6 Apr 2010 (E) (W) (SI 2010/816) |
| | | 2 May 2011 (NI) (SI 2011/1122) |
| | (2)(d) | 18 Apr 2011 (NI) (SR 2011/182) |
| | (3), (4) | 6 Apr 2010 (E) (W) (SI 2010/816) |
| | | 18 Apr 2011 (NI) (SR 2011/182) |
| 76 | (1)–(11) | 6 Apr 2010 (E) (W) (SI 2010/816) |
| | | 18 Apr 2011 (NI) (SR 2011/182) |
| | (12)(a) | 6 Apr 2010 (SI 2010/816) |
| | (12)(b), (13) | 6 Apr 2010 (E) (W) (SI 2010/816) |
| | | 18 Apr 2011 (NI) (SR 2011/182) |
| 77 | (1)(a), (b) | 6 Apr 2010 (SI 2010/816) |
| | (1)(c) | 6 Apr 2010 (E) (W) (SI 2010/816) |
| | | 2 May 2011 (NI) (SI 2011/1122) |

**Coroners and Justice Act 2009 (c 25)**—*contd*

| | | |
|---|---|---|
| | (1)(d) | 6 Apr 2010 (E) (W) (SI 2010/816) |
| | | 18 Apr 2011 (NI) (SR 2011/182) |
| | (1)(e), (f) | 6 Apr 2010 (SI 2010/816) |
| | (1)(g) | 18 Apr 2011 (SR 2011/182) |
| | (2)–(8) | 6 Apr 2010 (E) (W) (SI 2010/816) |
| | | 18 Apr 2011 (NI) (SR 2011/182) |
| 78 | | 6 Apr 2010 (E) (W) (SI 2010/816) |
| | | 18 Apr 2011 (NI) (SR 2011/182) |
| 79 | (1)–(5) | 6 Apr 2010 (E) (W) (SI 2010/816) |
| | | 18 Apr 2011 (NI) (SR 2011/182) |
| | (6)(a) | 6 Apr 2010 (SI 2010/816) |
| | (6)(b) | 18 Apr 2011 (SR 2011/182) |
| 80 | (1), (2)(a) | 6 Apr 2010 (E) (W) (SI 2010/816) |
| | | 18 Apr 2011 (NI) (SR 2011/182) |
| | (2)(b), (c) | 6 Apr 2010 (SI 2010/816) |
| | (2)(d) | 18 Apr 2011 (SR 2011/182) |
| | (2)(e) | 6 Apr 2010 (E) (W) (SI 2010/816) |
| | | 18 Apr 2011 (NI) (SR 2011/182) |
| | (3)–(8) | 6 Apr 2010 (E) (W) (SI 2010/816) |
| | | 18 Apr 2011 (NI) (SR 2011/182) |
| 81 | (1), (2) | 6 Apr 2010 (SI 2010/816) |
| | (3) | 6 Apr 2010 (E) (W) (SI 2010/816) |
| | | 2 May 2011 (NI) (SI 2011/1122) |
| | (4) | 18 Apr 2011 (SR 2011/182) |
| | (5), (6) | 6 Apr 2010 (SI 2010/816) |
| | (7) | 18 Apr 2011 (SR 2011/182) |
| 82 | | 6 Apr 2010 (E) (W) (SI 2010/816) |
| | | 18 Apr 2011 (NI) (SR 2011/182) |
| 83, 84 | | 6 Apr 2010 (SI 2010/816) |
| 85 | | 6 Apr 2010 (E) (W) (SI 2010/816) |
| | | 18 Apr 2011 (NI) (SR 2011/182) |
| 86–97 | | 1 Jan 2010 (s 182(3)(a)) |
| 98–103 | | 27 Jun 2011 (SI 2011/1452) |
| 104 | | *Not yet in force* |
| 105 | | 27 Jun 2011 (SI 2011/1452) |
| 106 | (1) | See sub-ss (2)–(5) below |
| | (2) | 14 Dec 2009 (SI 2009/3253)[1] |
| | (3) | 14 Dec 2009 (in relation to specified local justice areas) (SI 2009/3253)[1, 2] |
| | | 3 Oct 2011 (in relation to specified local justice areas) (SI 2011/2148)[5] |
| | | 8 Oct 2012 (otherwise) (SI 2012/2374) |
| | (4) | 14 Dec 2009 (SI 2009/3253) |
| | (5) | 14 Dec 2009 (SI 2009/3253)[1] |
| 107, 108 | | 14 Dec 2009 (in relation to specified local justice areas) (SI 2009/3253)[1, 2] |
| | | 3 Oct 2011 (in relation to specified local justice areas) (SI 2011/2148)[5] |
| | | 8 Oct 2012 (otherwise) (SI 2012/2374) |
| 109, 110 | | 14 Dec 2009 (SI 2009/3253) |
| 111 | | 27 Jun 2011 (SI 2011/1452) |
| 112 | | 1 Feb 2010 (SI 2010/145) |
| 113 | | 6 Apr 2010 (SI 2010/816) |
| 114, 115 | | 1 Feb 2010 (SI 2010/145) |
| 116 | | 12 Nov 2009 (s 182(1)(b)) |
| 117 | (1)–(3) | 7 Aug 2012 (SI 2012/1810) |
| | (4)–(8) | 22 Apr 2013 (SI 2013/705) |
| 118 | (1) | 6 Apr 2010 (SI 2010/816) |
| | (2) | See Sch 15 below |

**Coroners and Justice Act 2009 (c 25)**—*contd*

| | | |
|---|---|---|
| 119–136 | | 6 Apr 2010 (SI 2010/816)[4] |
| 137 | | See Sch 16 below |
| 138 | | 12 Jan 2010 (s 182(2)(b)) |
| 139 | | 12 Jan 2010 (SI 2010/28) |
| 140, 141 | | 1 Feb 2010 (SI 2010/145) |
| 142 | | Immediately before 1 Feb 2010 (SI 2010/145) |
| 143 | | 12 Nov 2009 (s 182(1)(c)) |
| 144 | | See Sch 17 below |
| 145 | | 2 Aug 2010 (SI 2010/1858) |
| 146, 147 | | 6 Apr 2010 (SI 2010/816) |
| 148 | | 18 Nov 2013 (SI 2013/2908) |
| 149 | | 1 Feb 2010 (SI 2010/145) |
| 150 | | 1 Feb 2010 (SI 2010/145)[3] |
| 151, 152 | | 12 Nov 2009 (s 182(1)(d)) |
| 153 | | 1 Feb 2010 (SI 2010/145) |
| 154 | | 12 Nov 2009 (s 182(1)(e)) |
| 155–172 | | 6 Apr 2010 (SI 2010/816) |
| 173 | | 1 Feb 2010 (so far as inserts Data Protection Act 1998, s 41C) (SI 2010/145) |
| | | 6 Apr 2010 (so far as inserts ss 41A, 41B of that Act) (SI 2010/816) |
| 174 | | 1 Feb 2010 (SI 2010/145) |
| 175 | | See Sch 20 below |
| 176 | | 12 Nov 2009 (s 182(1)(f)) |
| 177 | (1) | See Sch 21 below |
| | (2) | See Sch 22 below |
| | (3)–(10) | 12 Nov 2009 (s 182(1)(f)) |
| 178 | | See Sch 23 below |
| 179 | | 12 Nov 2009 (s 182(1)(f)) |
| 180 | | 1 Feb 2010 (SI 2010/145) |
| 181–183 | | 12 Nov 2009 (s 182(1)(f)) |
| Schs 1–3 | | 25 Jul 2013 (SI 2013/1869) |
| Sch 4 | | *Not yet in force* |
| Sch 5 | paras 1, 2 | 25 Jul 2013 (SI 2013/1869) |
| | paras 3–5 | *Not yet in force* |
| | paras 6, 7 | 25 Jul 2013 (SI 2013/1869) |
| Schs 6, 7 | | 25 Jul 2013 (SI 2013/1869) |
| Sch 8 | | 1 Feb 2010 (SI 2010/145) |
| Sch 9 | | *Not yet in force* |
| Sch 10 | para 1 | 25 Jul 2013 (SI 2013/1869) |
| | para 2 | *Not yet in force* |
| | para 3 | 25 Jul 2013 (SI 2013/1869) |
| | para 4 | *Never in force* (repealed) |
| | para 5 | 25 Jul 2013 (SI 2013/1869) |
| Sch 11 | | *Not yet in force* |
| Sch 12 | | 1 Feb 2010 (SI 2010/145) |
| Sch 13 | | 6 Apr 2010 (SI 2010/816) |
| Sch 14 | | 27 Jun 2011 (SI 2011/1452) |
| Sch 15 | paras 1–4 | 1 Feb 2010 (SI 2010/145) |
| | para 5 | 1 Feb 2010 (for the purposes of making appointments) (SI 2010/145) |
| | | 6 Apr 2010 (otherwise) (SI 2010/816) |
| | para 6 | 1 Feb 2010 (SI 2010/145) |
| | para 7 | 1 Feb 2010 (for the purposes of making appointments) (SI 2010/145) |
| | | 6 Apr 2010 (otherwise) (SI 2010/816) |
| | para 8 | 6 Apr 2010 (SI 2010/816) |
| | para 9 | 1 Feb 2010 (SI 2010/145) |
| | para 10 | 1 Feb 2010 (for the purposes of making appointments) (SI 2010/145) |

**Coroners and Justice Act 2009 (c 25)**—*contd*

| | | |
|---|---|---|
| | | 6 Apr 2010 (otherwise) (SI 2010/816) |
| Sch 16 | para 1 | *Not yet in force* |
| | para 2(1), (2) | 13 Apr 2015 (SI 2015/819) |
| | para 2(3) | 16 Jul 2018 (SI 2018/733) |
| | paras 3, 4 | *Not yet in force* |
| | para 5 | 13 Apr 2015 (SI 2015/819) |
| | para 6 | *Not yet in force* |
| Sch 17 | para 1 | 15 Aug 2010 (SI 2010/1858) |
| | para 2 | 18 Apr 2011 (SR 2011/182) |
| | para 3 | 15 Aug 2010 (SI 2010/1858) |
| | paras 4, 5 | 28 May 2013 (SI 2013/1104) |
| | paras 6, 7 | 15 Aug 2010 (SI 2010/1858) |
| | paras 8, 9 | *Not yet in force* (para 9 repealed) |
| | paras 10–15 | 15 Aug 2010 (SI 2010/1858) |
| | paras 16–18 | 18 Apr 2011 (SR 2011/182) |
| Sch 18 | | 12 Nov 2009 (s 182(1)(g)) |
| Sch 19 | | 6 Apr 2010 (SI 2010/816) |
| Sch 20 | paras 1–3 | 1 Feb 2010 (SI 2010/145) |
| | para 4 | *Not yet in force* |
| | paras 5–14 | 6 Apr 2010 (SI 2010/816) |
| Sch 21 | paras 1–7 | 25 Jul 2013 (SI 2013/1869) |
| | para 8(1)–(3) | *Not yet in force* |
| | para 8(4) | 25 Jul 2013 (SI 2013/1869) |
| | paras 8(5), 9(1), (2), (3)(a)–(c) | *Not yet in force* |
| | para 9(3)(d) | 25 Jul 2013 (SI 2013/1869) |
| | para 9(4), 10, 11(1), (2) | *Not yet in force* |
| | para 11(3) | 25 Jul 2013 (SI 2013/1869) |
| | paras 12–14 | *Not yet in force* |
| | para 15(1) | 25 Jul 2013 (SI 2013/1869) |
| | para 15(2) | 25 Jul 2013 (in so far as substitutes Births and Deaths Registration Act 1953, s 2(2)) (SI 2013/1869) |
| | | *Not yet in force* (in so far as substitutes s 2(2ZA) thereof) |
| | para 15(3), (4) | 25 Jul 2013 (SI 2013/1869) |
| | paras 16, 17 | *Not yet in force* |
| | para 18(1) | See sub-paras (2)–(4) below |
| | para 18(2) | 25 Jul 2013 (in so far as inserts Births and Deaths Registration Act 1953, s 29(3B)) (SI 2013/1869) |
| | | *Not yet in force* (in so far as inserts s 29(3A) thereof) |
| | para 18(3), (4) | 25 Jul 2013 (SI 2013/1869) |
| | paras 19, 20 | *Not yet in force* |
| | para 21(1) | 25 Jul 2013 (in so far as inserts definition "the 2009 Act" into Births and Deaths Registration Act 1953, s 41) (SI 2013/1869) |
| | | *Not yet in force* (otherwise) |
| | para 21(2) | 25 Jul 2013 (in so far as inserts Births and Deaths Registration Act 1953, s 41(3)) (SI 2013/1869) |
| | | *Not yet in force* (in so far as inserts s 41(2) thereof) |
| | paras 22–25 | 25 Jul 2013 (SI 2013/1869) |
| | para 26 | 25 Jul 2013 (except in so far as inserts entry "Coroner for Treasure" into House of Commons Disqualification Act 1975, Sch 1, Pt III) (SI 2013/1869) |
| | | *Not yet in force* (exception noted above) |
| | para 27 | *Not yet in force* |
| | para 28 | 25 Jul 2013 (SI 2013/1869) |
| | para 29 | *Not yet in force* |
| | para 30 | 25 Jul 2013 (SI 2013/1869) |
| | para 31 | *Not yet in force* |
| | paras 32–36 | 25 Jul 2013 (SI 2013/1869) |

**See Halsbury's Statutes Citator for amendments to these Acts**

**Coroners and Justice Act 2009 (c 25)**—*contd*

| | | |
|---|---|---|
| | paras 37–43 | *Not yet in force* |
| | paras 44, 45 | 25 Jul 2013 (SI 2013/1869) |
| | para 46 | *Never in force* (repealed) |
| | paras 47–50 | *Not yet in force* |
| | para 51 | 25 Jul 2013 (in so far as relates to the Deputy Chief Coroner) (SI 2013/1869) |
| | | *Not yet in force* (in so far as relates to the Coroner for Treasure) |
| | para 52 | 4 Oct 2010 (SI 2010/816)[4] |
| | paras 53–61 | 1 Feb 2010 (SI 2010/145) |
| | para 62(1), (2) | 6 Apr 2010 (SI 2010/816) |
| | para 62(3) | 12 Nov 2009 (s 182(1)(h)) |
| | paras 62(4), (5), 63, 64 | 6 Apr 2010 (SI 2010/816) |
| | paras 65–68 | 12 Jan 2010 (s 182(2)(c)) |
| | paras 69–71 | 1 Jan 2010 (s 182(3)(b)) |
| | paras 72, 73 | 27 Jun 2011 (SI 2011/1452) |
| | paras 74–78 | 1 Feb 2010 (SI 2010/145) |
| | paras 79–89 | 6 Apr 2010 (SI 2010/816)[4] |
| | para 90(1), (2) | 16 Jul 2018 (SI 2018/733) |
| | para 90(3)–(5) | *Not yet in force* |
| | para 90(6)–(9) | 16 Jul 2018 (SI 2018/733) |
| | para 91 | 16 Jul 2018 (SI 2018/733) |
| | paras 92, 93 | *Not yet in force* |
| | paras 94–98 | 12 Nov 2009 (s 182(1)(h)) |
| Sch 22 | paras 1–6 | 12 Nov 2009 (s 182(1)(i)) |
| | paras 7–11 | 1 Feb 2010 (SI 2010/145) |
| | paras 12–15 | 6 Apr 2010 (SI 2010/816) |
| | paras 16–22 | 1 Jan 2010 (s 182(3)(c)) |
| | paras 23, 24 | 27 Jun 2011 (SI 2011/1452) |
| | para 25 | 1 Feb 2010 (SI 2010/145) |
| | para 26 | 12 Nov 2009 (s 182(1)(i)) |
| | para 27 | 6 Apr 2010 (SI 2010/816) |
| | para 28 | 1 Feb 2010 (SI 2010/145) |
| | paras 29–34 | 13 Apr 2015 (SI 2015/819) |
| | paras 35, 36 | *Not yet in force* |
| | para 37 | 12 Jan 2010 (s 182(2)(d)) |
| | para 38 | 12 Jan 2010 (SI 2010/28) |
| | para 39 | 1 Feb 2010 (SI 2010/145) |
| | para 40 | 15 Aug 2010 (so far as it relates to Sch 17, paras 1, and 13–15) (SI 2010/1858) |
| | | 18 Apr 2011 (so far as it relates to Sch 17, paras 2 and 16–18) (SR 2011/182) |
| | para 41 | 15 Aug 2010 (so far as it relates to Sch 17, paras 6, 10, 12) (SI 2010/1858) |
| | | *Not yet in force* (so far as it relates to Sch 17, para 8) |
| | para 42 | 15 Aug 2010 (so far as it relates to Sch 17, para 7) (SI 2010/1858) |
| | | *Not yet in force* (so far as it relates to Sch 17, paras 9, 11) |
| | para 43 | 2 Aug 2010 (SI 2010/1858) |
| | paras 44–46 | 6 Apr 2010 (SI 2010/816) |
| | para 47 | 12 Nov 2009 (s 182(1)(i)) |
| Sch 23 | Pt 1 | 12 Feb 2013 (SI 2013/250), repeals of or in— Coroners Act 1988, s 5(2) |
| | | 25 Jul 2013 (SI 2013/1869), repeals of or in— Coroners Act 1988 (otherwise, except ss 4A(8), 13(1), (2))[6] |
| | | *Not yet in force* (otherwise) |
| | Pt 2 | 12 Jan 2010 (s 182(2)(e)), repeals of or in— Libel Act 1792; Criminal Libel Act 1819; Libel Act 1843; |

**Coroners and Justice Act 2009 (c 25)**—*contd*

|  | Newspaper Libel and Registration Act 1881; |
|  | Law of Libel Amendment Act 1888; |
|  | Defamation Act 1952; |
|  | Theatres Act 1968; |
|  | Broadcasting Act 1990; |
|  | Criminal Procedure and Investigations Act 1996; |
|  | Defamation Act 1996; |
|  | Legal Deposit Libraries Act 2003 |
|  | 1 Feb 2010 (SI 2010/145), repeals in— |
|  | Suicide Act 1961 |
|  | 4 Oct 2010 (SI 2010/816)[4], repeals of or in— |
|  | Homicide Act 1957; |
|  | Criminal Justice Act 2003 |
|  | 1 Jun 2011 (SR 2011/182), repeals of or in— |
|  | Criminal Justice Act (Northern Ireland) 1966 |

Pt 3 — 12 Nov 2009 (s 182(1)(j)), repeals in—
Administration of Justice (Miscellaneous Provisions) Act 1933;
Senior Courts Act 1981, s 82(1)

1 Jan 2010 (s 182(3)(d)), repeals in—
Criminal Evidence (Witness Anonymity) Act 2008

6 Apr 2010 (SI 2010/816) (in relation to specified local justice areas)[2], repeals of or in—
Police and Criminal Evidence Act 1984;
Crime and Disorder Act 1998, s 57C

6 Apr 2010 (SI 2010/816), repeals of or in—
Crime and Disorder Act 1998, ss 57D, 57E;
Criminal Justice Act 2003, s 120

27 Jun 2011 (SI 2011/1452), repeals of or in—
Crime and Disorder Act 1998, s 1I(3)(c);
Youth Justice and Criminal Evidence Act 1999;
Criminal Justice Act 2003, s 138

3 Oct 2011 (SI 2011/2148) (in relation to specified local justice areas)[5], repeals of or in—
Police and Criminal Evidence Act 1984;
Crime and Disorder Act 1998, s 57C

8 Oct 2012 (SI 2012/2374), repeals in—
Police and Criminal Evidence Act 1984 (otherwise);
Crime and Disorder Act 1998, s 57C (otherwise)

Pt 4 — 12 Nov 2009 (s 182(1)(j)), repeals in—
Criminal Justice and Immigration Act 2008

6 Apr 2010 (SI 2010/816)[4], repeals of or in—
Parliamentary Commissioner Act 1967;
Race Relations Act 1976;
Freedom of Information Act 2000;
Criminal Justice Act 2003;
Constitutional Reform Act 2005

*Not yet in force*, repeals of or in—
Criminal Procedure (Scotland) Act 1995

Pt 5 — 12 Nov 2009 (s 182(1)(j)), repeal of—
Animal Welfare Act 2006, s 8(6)

Immediately before 1 Feb 2010 (SI 2010/145), repeals of or in—
Superannuation Act 1972;
House of Commons Disqualification Act 1975;
Northern Ireland Assembly Disqualification Act 1975;
Domestic Violence, Crime and Victims Act 2004

2 Aug 2010 (SI 2010/1858), repeals of or in—
Criminal Justice Act 1991;
Criminal Justice and Immigration Act 2008

15 Aug 2010 (SI 2010/1858), repeals of or in—

**Coroners and Justice Act 2009 (c 25)**—*contd*

|            |            | Criminal Justice and Public Order Act 1994; |
|------------|------------|---------------------------------------------|

Criminal Justice and Public Order Act 1994;
Powers of Criminal Courts (Sentencing) Act 2000;
Criminal Justice Act 2003;
Armed Forces Act 2006, s 238
*Not yet in force*, repeals of or in—
Magistrates' Courts Act 1980;
Crime and Disorder Act 1998;
Armed Forces Act 2006, s 270B (repealed)

| Pt 6 | 12 Nov 2009 (s 182(1)(j)), repeals in— |
|------|----------------------------------------|
|      | Access to Justice Act 1999, ss 17, 17A, Sch 3 |
|      | 1 Feb 2010 (SI 2010/145)[3], repeals in— |
|      | Access to Justice Act 1999, s 2, Sch 2 |
| Pt 7 | 6 Apr 2010 (SI 2010/816) |
| Pt 8 | 6 Apr 2010 (SI 2010/816), repeals of or in— |
|      | Data Protection Act 1998, s 16, Sch 9 |
|      | *Not yet in force*, repeals of or in— |
|      | Data Protection Act 1998, s 20 |
| Pt 9 | 12 Nov 2009 (s 182(1)(j)) |

[1]    For transitional provisions, see SI 2009/3253, art 4

[2]    The local justice areas are—

Barking and Dagenham; Barnet; Bexley; Brent; Bromley; Camden and Islington; City of London; City of Westminster; Croydon; Ealing; Enfield; Greenwich and Lewisham; Hackney and Tower Hamlets; Hammersmith and Fulham and Kensington and Chelsea; Haringey; Harrow Gore; Havering; Hillingdon; Hounslow; Kingston-upon-Thames; Lambeth and Southwark; Merton; Newham; Redbridge; Richmond-upon-Thames; Sutton; Waltham Forest; Wandsworth; Central Kent; East Kent; North Kent

[3]    For transitional provisions, see SI 2010/145, art 3

[4]    For transitional and saving provisions, see SI 2010/816, art 7

[5]    The local justice areas are—

Central Hertfordshire; Chester; Ellesmere Port and Neston; East Hertfordshire; Halton; Macclesfield; North Hertfordshire; South Cheshire; Vale Royal; Warrington; West Hertfordshire

[6]    For a transitory provision, see SI 2013/1869, art 3

---

**Corporation Tax Act 2009 (c 4)**

*RA:* 26 Mar 2009

*Commencement provisions:* s 1329

| 1–1309 |          | 1 Apr 2009 (s 1329(1)) |
|--------|----------|------------------------|
| 1310 |            | 26 Mar 2009 (RA) |
| 1311–1322 |         | 1 Apr 2009 (s 1329(1)) |
| 1323, 1324 |        | 26 Mar 2009 (RA) |
| 1325 | (1)        | See Sch 2 below |
|      | (2), (3)   | 26 Mar 2009 (RA) |
| 1326 |            | See Sch 3 below |
| 1327 |            | 1 Apr 2009 (s 1329(1)) |
| 1328–1330 |         | 26 Mar 2009 (RA) |
| Sch 1 |           | 1 Apr 2009 (s 1329(1)) |
| Sch 2 | paras 1–70 | 1 Apr 2009 (s 1329(1)) |
|       | para 71    | *Never in force* (repealed) |
|       | paras 72–98 | 1 Apr 2009 (s 1329(1)) |
|       | para 99    | *Never in force* (repealed) |
|       | paras 100–147 | 1 Apr 2009 (s 1329(1)) |
| Sch 3 | Pt 1       | 1 Apr 2009 (s 1329(1)) |
|       | Pt 2       | *Never in force* (repealed) |

## Corporation Tax Act 2009 (c 4)—*contd*

Sch 4                    1 Apr 2009 (s 1329(1))

---

## Damages (Asbestos-related Conditions) (Scotland) Act 2009 (asp 4)

*RA:* 17 Apr 2009

*Commencement provisions*: s 4; Damages (Asbestos-related Conditions) (Scotland) Act 2009 (Commencement) Order 2009, SSI 2009/172

| | | |
|---|---|---|
| 1, 2 | | 17 Jun 2009 (SSI 2009/172) (but see also s 4(2), (3)) |
| 3 | | 17 Jun 2009 (SSI 2009/172) |
| 4 | (1) | 17 Apr 2009 (RA) |
| | (2), (3) | 17 Jun 2009 (SSI 2009/172) |
| 5 | | 17 Apr 2009 (RA) |

---

## Disabled Persons' Parking Places (Scotland) Act 2009 (asp 3)

*RA:* 1 Apr 2009

*Commencement provisions:* s 15(2)

| | |
|---|---|
| 1–14 | 1 Oct 2009 (s 15(2)) |
| 15 | 1 Apr 2009 (RA) |
| Schedule | 1 Oct 2009 (s 15(2)) |

---

## Driving Instruction (Suspension and Exemption Powers) Act 2009 (c 17)

*RA:* 12 Nov 2009

*Commencement provisions:* s 7(2), (3); Driving Instruction (Suspension and Exemption Powers) Act 2009 (Commencement No 1) Order 2012, SI 2012/1356

| | | |
|---|---|---|
| 1–3 | | *Not yet in force* |
| 4 | (1) | See Sch 1 below |
| | (2) | See Sch 2 below |
| 5–7 | | 12 Nov 2009 (s 7(2)) |
| Sch 1 | paras 1–6 | 6 Jul 2012 (SI 2012/1356) |
| | para 7 | 8 Jun 2012 (for the purpose of making regulations under the Road Traffic Act 1988, s 131A) (SI 2012/1356) |
| | | 6 Jul 2012 (otherwise) (SI 2012/1356) |
| Sch 2 | | *Not yet in force* |

---

## Ecclesiastical Offices (Terms of Service) Measure 2009 (No 1)

*RA:* 2 Apr 2009

*Commencement provisions:* s 13(2)

Provisions of this Measure were brought into force on the following dates by instruments made by the Archbishops of Canterbury and York, and dated 11 Jun 2009, 24 Nov 2009, 13 Sep 2010 and 14 Dec 2010 (made under s 13(2))

| | | |
|---|---|---|
| 1 | | 31 Jan 2011 |
| 2 | | 1 Jul 2009 |
| 3–7 | | 31 Jan 2011 |
| 8 | | 24 Nov 2009 |
| 9 | | 31 Jan 2011 |
| 10 | | 1 Jul 2009 |
| 11 | (1)–(3) | 27 Sep 2010 |
| | (4) | See Sch 2 below |
| | (5)–(8) | 31 Jan 2011 |

**Ecclesiastical Offices (Terms of Service) Measure 2009 (No 1)**—*contd*

| | | |
|---|---|---|
| 12 | | See Sch 3 below |
| 13 | | 1 Jul 2009 |
| Sch 1 | | 31 Jan 2011 |
| Sch 2 | paras 1–5 | 31 Jan 2011 |
| | para 6 | *Never in force* (repealed) |
| | paras 7–9 | 31 Jan 2011 |
| | para 10 | *Never in force* (repealed) |
| | para 11 | 31 Jan 2011 |
| | paras 12, 13 | *Never in force* (repealed) |
| | paras 14–22 | 31 Jan 2011 |
| Sch 3 | | 31 Jan 2011 |

---

## Education (Additional Support for Learning) (Scotland) Act 2009 (asp 7)

*RA:* 25 Jun 2009

*Commencement provisions*: s 26(2), (3); Education (Additional Support for Learning) (Scotland) Act 2009, SSI 2010/129; Education (Additional Support for Learning) (Scotland) Act 2009 (Commencement No 2) Order 2010, SSI 2010/277; Education (Additional Support for Learning) (Scotland) Act 2009 (Commencement No 3) Order 2010, SSI 2010/368

| | | |
|---|---|---|
| 1 | (1)–(4) | 14 Nov 2010 (SSI 2010/277) |
| | (5) | 2 Apr 2010 (SSI 2010/129) |
| | (6)–(9) | 14 Nov 2010 (SSI 2010/277) |
| 2–11 | | 14 Nov 2010 (SSI 2010/277) |
| 12 | | 2 Apr 2010 (SSI 2010/129) |
| 13–15 | | 14 Nov 2010 (SSI 2010/277) |
| 16 | | 2 Apr 2010 (SSI 2010/129) |
| 17–19 | | 14 Nov 2010 (SSI 2010/277) |
| 20 | | 2 Apr 2010 (SSI 2010/129) |
| 21, 22 | | 14 Nov 2010 (SSI 2010/277) |
| 23 | | 14 Nov 2010 (SSI 2010/368) |
| 24–26 | | 25 Jun 2009 (s 26(2)) |

---

## Education (Wales) Measure 2009 (nawm 5)

*Passed by the National Assembly for Wales:* 3 Nov 2009

*Approved by Her Majesty in Council:* 9 Dec 2009

*Commencement provisions:* s 26; Education (Wales) Measure 2009 (Commencement No 1) Order 2011, SI 2011/1468; Education (Wales) Measure 2009 (Commencement No 2) Order 2011, SI 2011/1951; Education (Wales) Measure 2009 (Commencement No 3 and Transitional Provisions) Order 2012, SI 2012/320

| | | |
|---|---|---|
| 1, 2 | | 6 Mar 2012 (SI 2012/320) |
| 3 | | 10 Feb 2012 (SI 2012/320) |
| 4–6 | | 6 Mar 2012 (SI 2012/320) |
| 7, 8 | | 10 Feb 2012 (SI 2012/320) |
| 9, 10 | | 6 Mar 2012 (SI 2012/320) |
| 11, 12 | | 10 Feb 2012 (SI 2012/320) |
| 13–16 | | 6 Mar 2012 (SI 2012/320) |
| 17–19 | | 10 Feb 2012 (SI 2012/320) |
| 20 | | 11 Jun 2011 (SI 2011/1468) |
| 21, 22 | | 1 Sep 2011 (SI 2011/1951) |
| 23 | | See Schedule below |
| 24–27 | | 9 Feb 2010 (s 26(1)) |
| Schedule | para 1 | 10 Feb 2012 (SI 2012/320) |
| | paras 2, 3 | 6 Mar 2012 (SI 2012/320) |
| | para 4 | 10 Feb 2012 (SI 2012/320) |

**Education (Wales) Measure 2009 (nawm 5)**—*contd*

|  |  |  |
|---|---|---|
| | para 5 | 6 Mar 2012 (SI 2012/320) |
| | paras 6–9 | *Never in force* (repealed) |
| | paras 10–12 | 9 Dec 2009 (s 26(2)) |

## Finance Act 2009 (c 10)

*Budget Day:* 22 Apr 2009

*RA:* 21 Jul 2009

The commencement details of Finance Acts are not set out, as the dates from which their provisions take effect are usually stated clearly and unambiguously in the text of the Act, and charging provisions will normally state for which year or years of assessment they are to have effect.

## Flood Risk Management (Scotland) Act 2009 (asp 6)

*RA:* 16 Jun 2009

*Commencement provisions*: s 97(1); Flood Risk Management (Scotland) Act 2009 (Commencement No 1 and Transitional and Savings Provisions) Order 2009, SSI 2009/393; Flood Risk Management (Scotland) Act 2009 (Commencement No 2 and Savings Provisions) Order 2010, SSI 2010/401

|  |  |  |
|---|---|---|
| 1, 2 | | 26 Nov 2009 (SSI 2009/393) |
| 3–6 | | 16 Jun 2009 (RA) |
| 7–41 | | 26 Nov 2009 (SSI 2009/393) |
| 42 | | *Not yet in force* |
| 43–54 | | 26 Nov 2009 (SSI 2009/393) |
| 55 | | 16 Jun 2009 (RA) |
| 56–58 | | 24 Dec 2010 (SSI 2010/401) |
| 59 | | 1 Jun 2011 (SSI 2010/401) |
| 60 | (1), (2) | 29 Nov 2010 (SSI 2010/401) |
| | (3) | See Sch 2 below |
| | (4), (5) | 29 Nov 2010 (SSI 2010/401) |
| 61 | | 24 Dec 2010 (SSI 2010/401) |
| 62–64 | | *Not yet in force* |
| 65–69 | | 24 Dec 2010 (SSI 2010/401) |
| 70 | | 24 Dec 2010 (SSI 2010/401)[2] |
| 71 | | 16 Jun 2009 (RA) |
| 72–78 | | 26 Nov 2009 (SSI 2009/393) |
| 79 | (1) | 26 Nov 2009 (SSI 2009/393) |
| | (2)(a)–(d) | 26 Nov 2009 (SSI 2009/393) |
| | (2)(e)–(g) | 24 Dec 2010 (SSI 2010/401) |
| | (2)(h) | 1 Jun 2011 (SSI 2010/401) |
| | (2)(i) | 24 Dec 2010 (SSI 2010/401) |
| | (3) | 26 Nov 2009 (SSI 2009/393) |
| 80, 81 | | 26 Nov 2009 (SSI 2009/393) |
| 82 | (1) | 26 Nov 2009 (SSI 2009/393) |
| | (2)(a)–(e) | 24 Dec 2010 (SSI 2010/401) |
| | (2)(f) | 26 Nov 2009 (SSI 2009/393) |
| 83 | | 26 Nov 2009 (SSI 2009/393) |
| 84–90 | | *Never in force* (repealed) |
| 91–93 | | 26 Nov 2009 (SSI 2009/393) |
| 94 | | 16 Jun 2009 (RA) |
| 95 | (1), (2) | 16 Jun 2009 (RA) |
| | (3) | See Sch 4 below |
| 96 | | See Sch 3 below |
| 97 | | 16 Jun 2009 (RA) |
| Sch 1 | | 26 Nov 2009 (SSI 2009/393) |
| Sch 2 | paras 1–12 | 24 Dec 2010 (SSI 2010/401) |

## Flood Risk Management (Scotland) Act 2009 (asp 6)—*contd*

|         | paras 13, 14 | 29 Nov 2010 (SSI 2010/401)        |
|---------|--------------|-----------------------------------|
| Sch 3   | para 1       | 24 Dec 2010 (SSI 2010/401)        |
|         | para 2       | 26 Nov 2009 (SSI 2009/393)[1]     |
|         | paras 3–6    | 24 Dec 2010 (SSI 2010/401)        |
|         | para 7       | 26 Nov 2009 (SSI 2009/393)        |
|         | paras 8–13   | 24 Dec 2010 (SSI 2010/401)        |
|         | para 14      | 26 Nov 2009 (SSI 2009/393)        |
| Sch 4   |              | *Not yet in force*                |

[1]  For transitional provisions and savings, see SSI 2009/393, arts 3–5

[2]  For savings, see SSI 2010/401, art 5

## Geneva Conventions and United Nations Personnel (Protocols) Act 2009 (c 6)

*RA:* 2 Jul 2009

*Commencement provisions*: s 3(1); Geneva Conventions and United Nations Personnel (Protocols) Act 2009 (Commencement No 1) Order 2009, SI 2009/2892; Geneva Conventions and United Nations Personnel (Protocols) Act 2009 (Commencement No 2) Order 2010, SI 2010/1779

| 1        | 5 Apr 2010 (SI 2009/2892) |
|----------|---------------------------|
| 2        | 28 Jul 2010 (SI 2010/1779) |
| 3        | 2 Jul 2009 (RA)           |
| Schedule | 5 Apr 2010 (SI 2009/2892) |

## Green Energy (Definition and Promotion) Act 2009 (c 19)

*RA:* 12 Nov 2009

*Commencement provisions:* s 6(2)

Whole Act in force 12 Jan 2010 (s 6(2))

## Health Act 2009 (c 21)

*RA:* 12 Nov 2009

*Commencement provisions*: s 40; Health Act 2009 (Commencement No 1) Order 2010, SI 2010/30; Health Act 2009 (Commencement No 2) Order 2010, SI 2010/779; Health Act 2009 (Commencement No 3) Order 2010, SI 2010/1068, as amended by SI 2011/1255; Health Act 2009 (Commencement No 1) (Wales) Order 2010, SI 2010/930; Health Act 2009 (Commencement No 4) Order 2010, SI 2010/1863; Health Act 2009 (Commencement No 2) (Wales) Order 2011, SI 2011/2362; Health (2009 Act) (Commencement No 1) Order (Northern Ireland) 2012, SR 2012/68; Health Act 2009 (Commencement No 3) (Wales) Order 2012, SI 2012/1288; Health Act 2009 (Commencement No 5) Order 2012, SI 2012/1902; Health Act 2009 (Commencement No 6) Order 2012, SI 2012/2647; Health (2009 Act) (Commencement No 2) Order (Northern Ireland) 2012, SR 2012/389

| 1–7   |           | 19 Jan 2010 (SI 2010/30)                                             |
|-------|-----------|---------------------------------------------------------------------|
| 8     |           | 12 Nov 2009 (for the purposes of making regulations) (s 40(6)(a))   |
|       |           | 1 Apr 2010 (otherwise) (SI 2010/30)                                 |
| 9     | (1)–(4)   | 1 Apr 2010 (SI 2010/30)                                             |
|       | (5)       | 12 Nov 2009 (for the purposes of making regulations) (s 40(6)(a))   |
|       |           | 1 Apr 2010 (otherwise) (SI 2010/30)                                 |
|       | (6)–(9)   | 1 Apr 2010 (SI 2010/30)                                             |
| 10    |           | 12 Nov 2009 (for the purposes of making regulations) (s 40(6)(a))   |
|       |           | 1 Apr 2010 (otherwise) (SI 2010/30)                                 |
| 11–13 |           | 19 Jan 2010 (SI 2010/30)                                            |
| 14    |           | *Not yet in force*                                                  |

**Health Act 2009 (c 21)**—*contd*

| | | |
|---|---|---|
| 15 | (1) | 19 Jan 2010 (for the purposes of the Independent Regulator of the NHS Foundation Trusts consulting and publishing guidance in accordance with the National Health Service Act 2006, s 52C) (SI 2010/30) |
| | | *Never in force* (otherwise) (repealed) |
| | (2) | See Sch 2 below |
| 16, 17 | | 15 Feb 2010 (SI 2010/30) |
| 18 | | 15 Feb 2010 (except in relation to any references to the National Health Services Act 2006, ss 52B, 52C, 52D or s 52E in sub-s (5), (8), (9) or (12)) (SI 2010/30) |
| | | *Not yet in force* (exceptions noted above) (sub-ss (2)–(6), (11) repealed) |
| 19 | | See Sch 3 below |
| 20 | | 12 Nov 2009 (for the purposes of making regulations) (s 40(6)(b)) |
| | | 6 Apr 2015 (E) (otherwise) (SI 2010/1068; SI 2012/1288; SR 2012/389) |
| 21 | | 12 Nov 2009 (for the purposes of making regulations) (s 40(6)(b)) |
| | | 6 Apr 2012 (E) (in so far as inserts Tobacco Advertising and Promotion Act 2002, ss 7A–7C, for the purpose of large shops other than bulk tobacconists and specialist tobacconists) (SI 2010/1068) |
| | | 3 Dec 2012 (W) (in so far as inserts ss 7A–7C of that Act, for the purpose of large shops other than bulk tobacconists and specialist tobacconists) (SI 2012/1288) |
| | | 6 Apr 2015 (in so far as inserts ss 7A–7C of that Act, for remaining purposes) (SI 2010/1068; SI 2012/1288; SR 2012/389) |
| | | 31 Oct 2012 (NI) (in so far as inserts ss 7A–7C of that Act, for the purpose of large shops other than bulk tobacconists and specialist tobacconists) (SR 2012/389) |
| | | *Not yet in force* (in so far as inserts s 7D of that Act) |
| 22 | | 12 Nov 2009 (for the purposes of making regulations) (s 40(6)(b)) |
| | | 1 Oct 2011 (E) (otherwise) (SI 2010/1068) |
| | | 1 Feb 2012 (W) (otherwise) (SI 2011/2362) |
| 23 | | 12 Nov 2009 (for the purposes of making regulations) (s 40(6)(b)) |
| | | 1 Mar 2012 (otherwise) (SR 2012/68) |
| 24 | | See Sch 4 below |
| 25 | | 18 Mar 2010 (for the purposes of making regulations) (SI 2010/779) |
| | | 24 May 2010 (otherwise) (SI 2010/779) |
| 26–29 | | 1 Sep 2012 (SI 2012/1902) |
| 30–32 | | *Not yet in force* |
| 33 | | 19 Jan 2010 (SI 2010/30) |
| 34 | | 12 Jan 2010 (s 40(7)(a)) |
| 35 | | See Sch 5 below |
| 36 | | 19 Jan 2010 (SI 2010/30) |
| 37 | | 12 Nov 2009 (s 40(5)(c)) |
| 38 | | See Sch 6 below |
| 39–41 | | 12 Nov 2009 (s 40(5)(c)) |
| Sch 1 | | 19 Jan 2010 (SI 2010/30) |
| Sch 2 | | 15 Feb 2010 (except in relation to the National Health Service Act 2006, s 52D in paras 1(1) and 4(1)) (SI 2010/30) |
| | | *Not yet in force* (exceptions noted above) |
| Sch 3 | paras 1–13 | 19 Jan 2010 (SI 2010/30) |
| | paras 14–17 | 1 Apr 2010 (SI 2010/930) |
| | paras 18, 19 | 19 Jan 2010 (E) (except in so far as they relate to amendments of the National Health Service (Wales) Act 2006) (SI 2010/30) |
| | | 1 Apr 2010 (W) (except in so far as they relate to amendments of the National Health Service (Wales) Act 2006) (SI 2010/930) |
| | | *Not yet in force* (otherwise) |
| Sch 4 | para 1 | 12 Jan 2010 (s 40(7)(b)) |

**Health Act 2009 (c 21)**—*contd*

| | | |
|---|---|---|
| | para 2 | See paras 3–13 below |
| | para 3 | 6 Apr 2015 (SI 2010/1068; SI 2012/1288; SR 2012/389) |
| | para 4(1) | See sub-paras (2)–(6) below |
| | para 4(2) | 6 Apr 2015 (SI 2010/1068; SI 2012/1288; SR 2012/389) |
| | para 4(3), (4) | 12 Jan 2010 (s 40(7)(b)) |
| | para 4(5) | 6 Apr 2015 (SI 2010/1068; SI 2012/1288; SR 2012/389) |
| | para 4(6) | 12 Jan 2010 (s 40(7)(b)) |
| | para 5 | 12 Jan 2010 (s 40(7)(b)) |
| | para 6(1) | See sub-paras (2), (3) below |
| | para 6(2) | 6 Apr 2012 (E) (SI 2010/1068) |
| | | 3 Dec 2012 (W) (SI 2012/1288) |
| | | 31 Oct 2012 (SR 2012/389) |
| | para 6(3) | 12 Jan 2010 (s 40(7)(b)) |
| | para 7(1) | See sub-paras (2)–(6) below |
| | para 7(2) | 12 Jan 2010 (s 40(7)(b)) |
| | para 7(3), (4) | 31 Oct 2012 (NI) (SR 2012/389) |
| | | *Not yet in force* (E) (W) |
| | para 7(5) | 6 Apr 2012 (E) (SI 2010/1068) |
| | | *Not yet in force* (W) |
| | para 7(6) | 6 Apr 2012 (E) (SI 2010/1068) |
| | | 1 Jun 2012 (W) (SI 2012/1288) |
| | para 8(1) | See sub-paras (2), (3) below |
| | para 8(2) | 31 Oct 2012 (NI) (SR 2012/389) |
| | para 8(3) | 1 Jun 2012 (SI 2012/1288) |
| | para 9(1) | See sub-paras (2)–(4) below |
| | para 9(2) | 12 Nov 2009 (s 40(5)(a)) |
| | para 9(3) | 12 Jan 2010 (s 40(7)(b)) |
| | para 9(4) | 12 Nov 2009 (s 40(5)(c)) |
| | para 10 | 6 Apr 2012 (E) (SI 2010/1068) |
| | | 3 Dec 2012 (W) (SI 2012/1288) |
| | | 31 Oct 2012 (NI) (SR 2012/389) |
| | paras 11, 12 | 12 Nov 2009 (for the purposes of making regulations) (s 40(6)(c)) |
| | | 6 Apr 2012 (E) (otherwise) (SI 2010/1068) |
| | | 3 Dec 2012 (W) (otherwise) (SI 2012/1288) |
| | | 31 Oct 2012 (NI) (otherwise) (SR 2012/389) |
| | para 13 | 12 Jan 2010 (for the purposes of the Tobacco Advertising and Promotion Act 2002, ss 8, 9, 11) (s 40(7)(b)) |
| | | *Not yet in force* (for the purpose of s 7D of that Act) |
| Sch 5 | | 1 Oct 2010 (SI 2010/1863) |
| Sch 6 | | 12 Nov 2009 (s 40(5)(b)), repeals of or in— |
| | | Tobacco Advertising and Promotion Act 2002, s 16(1A); |
| | | Tobacco Advertising and Promotion Act 2002 etc (Amendment) Regulations 2006, SI 2006/2369 |
| | | 1 Oct 2011 (SI 2010/1068), repeals of or in— |
| | | Children and Young Persons Act 1933 |
| | | 6 Apr 2012 (SI 2010/1068), repeal in— |
| | | Tobacco Advertising and Promotion Act 2002, s 14(12) |
| | | 1 Sep 2012 (SI 2012/1902), repeals in— |
| | | National Health Service Act 2006 |
| | | 31 Oct 2012 (SI 2012/2647), repeals of— |
| | | Tobacco Advertising and Promotion Act 2002, ss 13(4), 14(11) |
| | | *Not yet in force*, repeals of or in— |
| | | Health Service Commissioners Act 1993; |
| | | Public Service Ombudsman (Wales) Act 2005; |
| | | National Health Service (Wales) Act 2006; |
| | | Safeguarding Vulnerable Groups Act 2006 |

## Health Boards (Membership and Elections) (Scotland) Act 2009 (asp 5)

*RA:* 22 Apr 2009

*Commencement provisions:* s 11; Health Boards (Membership and Elections) (Scotland) Act 2009 (Commencement No 1) Order 2009, SSI 2009/242; Health Boards (Membership and Elections) (Scotland) Act 2009 (Commencement No 2) Order 2009, SSI 2009/433

| | | |
|---|---|---|
| 1–3 | | 24 Jun 2009 (for the areas for which Fife Health Board and Dumfries and Galloway Health Board are constituted) (SSI 2009/242) |
| | | *Not yet in force* (otherwise) (coming into force in accordance with s 7) |
| 4, 5 | | 22 Apr 2009 (s 11(2)) |
| 6 | (1), (2) | 22 Apr 2009 (s 11(2)) |
| | (3), (4) | *Not yet in force* (coming into force in accordance with s 6(2)) |
| 7 | | 22 Apr 2009 (s 11(2)) |
| 8 | | See Schedule below |
| 9–12 | | 22 Apr 2009 (s 11(2)) |
| Schedule | para 1 | 8 Jan 2010 (SSI 2009/233) |
| | para 2 | *Never in force* (repealed) |

## Healthy Eating in Schools (Wales) Measure 2009 (nawm 3)

*Passed by the National Assembly for Wales:* 8 Jul 2009

*Approved by Her Majesty in Council:* 15 Oct 2009

*Commencement provisions:* s 12(2), (3); Healthy Eating in Schools (Wales) Measure 2009 (Commencement) Order 2013, SI 2013/1985

| | |
|---|---|
| 1–3 | 2 Sep 2013 (SI 2013/1985) |
| 4 | 8 Aug 2013 (SI 2013/1985) |
| 5–11 | 2 Sep 2013 (SI 2013/1985) |
| 12 | 15 Oct 2009 (s 12(2)) |

## Holocaust (Return of Cultural Objects) Act 2009 (c 16)

*RA:* 12 Nov 2009

*Commencement provisions:* s 4(3)–(6); Holocaust (Return of Cultural Objects) Act 2009 (Commencement) Order 2010, SI 2010/50

| | |
|---|---|
| 1–3 | 13 Jan 2010 (SI 2010/50) |
| 4 | 12 Nov 2009 (RA) |

## Industry and Exports (Financial Support) Act 2009 (c 5)

*RA:* 21 May 2009

Whole Act in force 21 May 2009 (s 3(2))

## Law Commission Act 2009 (c 14)

*RA:* 12 Nov 2009

Whole Act in force 12 Jan 2010 (s 3(1))

## Learning and Skills (Wales) Measure 2009 (nawm 1)

*Passed by the National Assembly for Wales:* 17 Mar 2009

*Approved by Her Majesty in Council:* 13 May 2009

*Commencement provisions:* s 49; Learning and Skills (Wales) Measure 2009 (Commencement No 1 and Transitional Provision) Order 2009, SI 2009/3174, as amended by SI 2010/1142; Learning and Skills (Wales) Measure 2009 (Commencement No 2) Order 2011, SI 2011/97

| | |
|---|---|
| 1 | 7 Dec 2009 (SI 2009/3174) |
| 2, 3 | 1 Jan 2010 (SI 2009/3174) |
| 4 | 7 Dec 2009 (for the purpose of carrying out the preparatory work necessary to form the local curriculum in accordance with the provisions of s 4 when it comes fully into force and for the purposes of making regulations under the Education Act 2002, s 116A(5) and giving directions under s 116A(6) of the 2002 Act) (SI 2009/3174) |
| | 1 Jan 2010 (otherwise) (SI 2009/3174) |
| 5, 6 | 1 Jan 2010 (SI 2009/3174)[1] |
| 7 | 7 Dec 2009 (for the purpose of making regulations under the Education Act 2002, s 116D(2)) (SI 2009/3174) |
| | 1 Jan 2010 (otherwise) (SI 2009/3174) |
| 8 | 1 Jan 2010 (SI 2009/3174) |
| 9 | 7 Dec 2009 (for the purpose of making regulations under the Education Act 2002, s 116F(3)) (SI 2009/3174) |
| | 1 Jan 2010 (otherwise) (SI 2009/3174) |
| 10 | 1 Jan 2010 (SI 2009/3174) |
| 11 | 7 Dec 2009 (for the purpose of making regulations under the Education Act 2002, s 116H(3)) (SI 2009/3174) |
| | 1 Jan 2010 (otherwise) (SI 2009/3174) |
| 12–14 | 7 Dec 2009 (SI 2009/3174) |
| 15–17 | 1 Jan 2010 (SI 2009/3174) |
| 18 | 7 Dec 2009 (SI 2009/3174) |
| 19 | 1 Jan 2010 (SI 2009/3174) |
| 20 | 7 Dec 2009 (SI 2009/3174) |
| 21, 22 | 14 Feb 2011 (SI 2011/97) |
| 23 | 19 Jan 2011 (SI 2011/97) |
| 24 | 14 Feb 2011 (SI 2011/97) |
| 25, 26 | 19 Jan 2011 (SI 2011/97) |
| 27 | 14 Feb 2011 (SI 2011/97) |
| 28 | 19 Jan 2011 (for the purpose of making regulations under the Learning and Skills Act 2000, s 33G(3)) (SI 2011/97) |
| | 14 Feb 2011 (otherwise) (SI 2011/97) |
| 29 | 14 Feb 2011 (SI 2011/97) |
| 30 | 19 Jan 2011 (for the purpose of making regulations under the Learning and Skills Act 2000, s 33I(3)) (SI 2011/97) |
| | 14 Feb 2011 (otherwise) (SI 2011/97) |
| 31–39 | 19 Jan 2011 (SI 2011/97) |
| 40–45 | 7 Dec 2009 (SI 2009/3174) |
| 46 | 13 Jul 2009 (s 49(1)) |
| 47 | See Schedule below |
| 48–50 | 13 Jul 2009 (s 49(1)) |
| Schedule | paras 1–10 19 Jan 2011 (SI 2011/97) |
| | paras 11–22 7 Dec 2009 (SI 2009/3174) |

[1] For a transitional provision, see SI 2009/3174, art 3

## Local Democracy, Economic Development and Construction Act 2009 (c 20)

*RA:* 12 Nov 2009

*Commencement provisions:* ss 148, 149; Local Democracy, Economic Development and Construction Act 2009 (Commencement No 1) Order 2009, SI 2009/3087; Local Democracy, Economic

**Local Democracy, Economic Development and Construction Act 2009 (c 20)**—*contd*
Development and Construction Act 2009 (Commencement No 2) Order 2009, SI 2009/3318; Local
Democracy, Economic Development and Construction Act 2009 (Commencement No 3)
Order 2010, SI 2010/881; Local Democracy, Economic Development and Construction Act 2009
(Commencement No 1) (Scotland) Order 2011, SSI 2011/269; Local Democracy, Economic
Development and Construction Act 2009 (Commencement No 1) (Wales) Order 2011,
SI 2011/1514; Local Democracy, Economic Development and Construction Act 2009
(Commencement No 1) (England) Order 2011, SI 2011/1569; Local Democracy, Economic
Development and Construction Act 2009 (Commencement No 2) (England) Order 2011,
SI 2011/1582; Local Democracy, Economic Development and Construction Act 2009
(Commencement No 2) (Wales) Order 2011, SI 2011/1597; Local Democracy, Economic
Development and Construction Act 2009 (Commencement No 2) (Scotland) Order 2011,
SSI 2011/291; Local Democracy, Economic Development and Construction Act 2009
(Commencement No 3) (Scotland) Order 2011, SSI 2011/337

| | | |
|---|---|---|
| 1–9 | | *Never in force* (repealed) |
| 10 | (1), (2) | 15 Dec 2010 (E) (SI 2010/881) |
| | | *Never in force* (W) (repealed) |
| | (3), (4) | 15 Jun 2010 (E) (SI 2010/881) |
| | | *Never in force* (W) (repealed) |
| 11 | | 15 Jun 2010 (E) (SI 2010/881) |
| | | *Never in force* (W) (repealed) |
| 12 | (1)(a)–(c) | 15 Jun 2010 (E) (SI 2010/881) |
| | | *Never in force* (W) (repealed) |
| | (1)(d) | 15 Dec 2010 (E) (SI 2010/881) |
| | | *Never in force* (W) (repealed) |
| | (2), (3)(a) | 15 Jun 2010 (E) (SI 2010/881) |
| | | *Never in force* (W) (repealed) |
| | (3)(b) | 15 Dec 2010 (E) (SI 2010/881) |
| | | *Never in force* (W) (repealed) |
| 13 | | 15 Jun 2010 (E) (SI 2010/881) |
| | | *Never in force* (W) (repealed) |
| 14 | (1)–(3) | 15 Jun 2010 (E) (SI 2010/881) |
| | | *Never in force* (W) (repealed) |
| | (4) | 20 Mar 2010 (E) (for the purpose of enabling the Secretary of State to make orders, give guidance or give directions) (SI 2010/881) |
| | | 15 Jun 2010 (E) (otherwise) (SI 2010/881) |
| | | *Never in force* (W) (repealed) |
| | (5)–(9) | 15 Jun 2010 (E) (SI 2010/881) |
| | | *Never in force* (W) (repealed) |
| 15–18 | | 15 Jun 2010 (E) (SI 2010/881) |
| | | *Never in force* (W) (repealed) |
| 19–22 | | 20 Mar 2010 (E) (for the purpose of enabling the Secretary of State to make orders, give guidance or give directions) (SI 2010/881) |
| | | 15 Jun 2010 (E) (otherwise) (SI 2010/881) |
| | | *Never in force* (W) (repealed) |
| 23, 24 | | 1 Apr 2010 (SI 2009/3318) |
| 25, 26 | | 12 Nov 2009 (s 148(1)(c)) |
| 27–30 | | 12 Jan 2010 (s 148(1)(d)) |
| 31 | | 1 Apr 2010 (SI 2009/3318) |
| 32, 33 | | 12 Jan 2010 (s 148(2)(a)(ii)) |
| 34–51 | | *Not yet in force* (ss 35(2)(q), 36(4), (6)(b), 37(1), 38(4), (7), 42(6), 46(1)–(3), 50(1), (4), (8)–(11) repealed) |
| 52 | | *Never in force* (repealed) |
| 53, 54 | | *Not yet in force* (s 53(4) repealed) |
| 55–61 | | 1 Apr 2010 (SI 2009/3318) |
| 62 | | 12 Nov 2009 (s 148(3)(a)) |
| 63 | | 1 Apr 2010 (SI 2009/3318) |
| 64 | | 12 Nov 2009 (s 148(3)(a)) |

**Local Democracy, Economic Development and Construction Act 2009 (c 20)**—*contd*

| | | |
|---|---|---|
| 65–67 | | 1 Apr 2010 (SI 2009/3318) |
| 68 | | 12 Nov 2009 (s 148(3)(a)) |
| 69 | (1), (2) | 1 Apr 2010 (SI 2009/3318) |
| | (3) | 25 Nov 2009 (SI 2009/3087) |
| | (4), (5) | 1 Apr 2010 (SI 2009/3318) |
| | (6)–(8) | 25 Nov 2009 (SI 2009/3087) |
| 70 | | 1 Apr 2010 (SI 2009/3318) |
| 71 | | 25 Nov 2009 (SI 2009/3087) |
| 72–83 | | 1 Apr 2010 (SI 2009/3318) |
| 84 | | 25 Nov 2009 (SI 2009/3087) |
| 85 | | 1 Apr 2010 (SI 2009/3318) |
| 86, 87 | | 25 Nov 2009 (SI 2009/3087) |
| 88–113 | | 17 Dec 2009 (SI 2009/3318) |
| 114–117 | | 12 Jan 2010 (SI 2009/3318) |
| 118–120 | | 17 Dec 2009 (SI 2009/3318) |
| 121–137 | | 12 Jan 2010 (s 148(7)) |
| 138 | | 18 Jun 2011 (so far as extending to England and Wales, for the purpose of enabling the Welsh Ministers to make orders in relation to construction contracts which relate to the carrying out of construction operations in Wales) (SI 2011/1514) |
| | | 24 Jun 2011 (S) (SSI 2011/269) |
| | | 24 Jun 2011 (so far as extending to England and Wales, in so far as not already in force, for the purpose of enabling the Secretary of State to make orders, but not in relation to construction contracts which relate to the carrying out of construction operations in Wales) (SI 2011/1569) |
| | | 1 Oct 2011 (so far as extending to England and Wales, in so far as not already in force, except in relation to construction contracts which relate to the carrying out of construction operations in Wales) (SI 2011/1582) |
| | | 1 Oct 2011 (all remaining purposes) (SI 2011/1597) |
| 139–145 | | 1 Oct 2011 (so far as extending to England and Wales, except in relation to construction contracts which relate to the carrying out of construction operations in Wales) (SI 2011/1582) |
| | | 1 Oct 2011 (so far as extending to England and Wales, for all remaining purposes) (SI 2011/1597) |
| | | 1 Nov 2011 (S) (SSI 2011/291) |
| 146 | | See Sch 7 below |
| 147–150 | | 12 Nov 2009 (s 148(9)) |
| Schs 1, 2 | | 1 Apr 2010 (SI 2009/3318) |
| Sch 3 | | 12 Nov 2009 (s 148(3)(a)) |
| Schs 4, 5 | | 1 Apr 2010 (SI 2009/3318) |
| Sch 6 | | 17 Dec 2009 (SI 2009/3318) |
| Sch 7 | Pt 1 | 12 Jan 2010 (ss 146(3)(a), 148(1)(d)) |
| | Pt 2 | *Not yet in force* (s 146(3)(b))[1] |
| | Pts 3, 4 | 1 Apr 2010 (SI 2009/3318) |
| | Pt 5 | 1 Oct 2011 (so far as extending to England and Wales, except in relation to construction contracts which relate to the carrying out of construction operations in Wales) (SI 2011/1582)[2] |
| | | 1 Oct 2011 (so far as extending to England and Wales, for all remaining purposes) (SI 2011/1597)[2] |
| | | 1 Nov 2011 (S) (SSI 2011/337) |

[1]   Sch 7, Pt 2 which repeals Audit Commission Act 1998, s 31, no longer has any effect as that Act has been fully repealed

[2]   S 146(3)(e) states that the repeals in Sch 7, Pt 5 are part of Pt 8 (ss 138–145), therefore it is thought that these repeals are intended to come into force at the same time as the corresponding provisions of Pt 8

## Local Government (Wales) Measure 2009 (nawm 2)

*Passed by the National Assembly for Wales:* 28 Apr 2009

*Approved by Her Majesty in Council:* 10 Jun 2009

*Commencement provisions:* s 53; Local Government (Wales) Measure 2009 (Commencement No 1) Order 2009, SI 2009/1796; Local Government (Wales) Measure 2009 (Commencement No 2, Transitional Provisions and Savings) Order 2009, SI 2009/3272, as amended by SI 2010/2237

| | | |
|---|---|---|
| 1 | | 17 Jul 2009 (SI 2009/1796) |
| 2 | (1) | 1 Apr 2010 (SI 2009/3272) |
| | (2), (3) | 17 Jul 2009 (SI 2009/1796) |
| 3 | | 1 Apr 2010 (SI 2009/3272) |
| 4–7 | | 17 Jul 2009 (SI 2009/1796) |
| 8 | (1)–(6) | 17 Jul 2009 (SI 2009/1796) |
| | (7) | 1 Apr 2010 (SI 2009/3272) |
| 9–13 | | 1 Apr 2010 (SI 2009/3272) |
| 14 | | 1 Apr 2011 (SI 2009/3272) |
| 15 | (1) | 1 Apr 2010 (SI 2009/3272) |
| | (2)–(5) | 1 Apr 2011 (SI 2009/3272) |
| | (6) | 1 Apr 2010 (SI 2009/3272) |
| | (7) | 1 Jan 2010 (for the purposes of making orders under para (b)) (SI 2009/3272) |
| | | 1 Apr 2010 (otherwise) (SI 2009/3272) |
| | (8), (9) | 17 Jul 2009 (SI 2009/1796) |
| 16 | | 17 Jul 2009 (SI 2009/1796) |
| 17 | (a) | 1 Apr 2010 (for the purposes of carrying out an audit to determine whether a Welsh improvement authority has discharged its duties under s 15(6) and (7)) (SI 2009/3272) |
| | | 1 Apr 2011 (otherwise) (SI 2009/3272) |
| | (b) | 1 Apr 2011 (SI 2009/3272) |
| 18 | | 1 Apr 2010 (SI 2009/3272) |
| 19 | (1)(a) | 1 Apr 2011 (SI 2009/3272) |
| | (1)(b) | 1 Apr 2010 (for the purposes of issuing a report stating whether a Welsh improvement authority has discharged its duties under s 15(6) and (7)) (SI 2009/3272) |
| | | 1 Apr 2011 (otherwise) (SI 2009/3272) |
| | (1)(c)–(h) | 1 Apr 2010 (SI 2009/3272) |
| | (2)–(4) | 1 Apr 2010 (SI 2009/3272) |
| 20–24 | | 1 Apr 2010 (SI 2009/3272)[1] |
| 25 | | 17 Jul 2009 (SI 2009/1796) |
| 26–30 | | 1 Apr 2010 (SI 2009/3272) |
| 31, 32 | | 17 Jul 2009 (SI 2009/1796) |
| 33, 34 | | 1 Apr 2010 (SI 2009/3272) |
| 35, 36 | | 17 Jul 2009 (SI 2009/1796) |
| 37 | | 1 Jan 2010 (SI 2009/3272) |
| 38 | | 17 Jul 2009 (SI 2009/1796) |
| 39–44 | | 1 Jan 2010 (SI 2009/3272) |
| 45 | | 17 Jul 2009 (SI 2009/1796) |
| 46 | | 1 Jan 2010 (SI 2009/3272) |
| 47 | | 17 Jul 2009 (SI 2009/1796) |
| 48–50 | | 10 Jun 2009 (s 53(1)) |
| 51 | (1) | See Sch 1 below |
| | (2), (3) | 1 Jan 2010 (SI 2009/3272) |
| | (4)–(7) | 10 Jun 2009 (s 53(1)) |
| 52 | | See Sch 4 below |
| 53, 54 | | 10 Jun 2009 (s 53(1)) |
| Sch 1 | | 1 Apr 2010 (SI 2009/3272)[2] |
| Schs 2, 3 | | 1 Jan 2010 (SI 2009/3272) |
| Sch 4 | | 1 Jan 2010 (repeal in Local Government Act 2000) (SI 2009/3272) |
| | | 1 Apr 2010 (SI 2009/3272)[2], repeals in— |

**Local Government (Wales) Measure 2009 (nawm 2)**—*contd*
Audit Commission Act 1998;
Local Government Act 1999

[1]    Note that although SI 2009/3272, Sch 2 brings ss 20–24 into force on 1 Apr 2010, Sch 3 thereto
purports to bring s 24(2)(a) into force on 1 Apr 2011

[2]    For transitional provisions and savings, see SI 2009/3272, art 3(2)–(5)

---

**Marine and Coastal Access Act 2009 (c 23)**

*RA:* 12 Nov 2009

*Commencement provisions:* s 324; Marine and Coastal Access Act 2009 (Commencement No 1 and
Transitional Provisions) Order 2009, SI 2009/3345; Marine and Coastal Access Act 2009
(Commencement No 2 and Transitional Provisions) Order 2010, SI 2010/298; Marine and Coastal
Access Act 2009 (Commencement No 1, Consequential, Transitional and Savings Provisions) (England
and Wales) Order 2010, SI 2010/630, as amended by SI 2011/1988, SI 2012/2571, SI 2015/2076;
Marine and Coastal Access Act 2009 (Commencement No 3) Order 2010, SI 2010/907; Marine and
Coastal Access Act 2009 (Commencement No 4 and Transitional Provisions) Order 2010,
SI 2010/2195; Marine and Coastal Access Act 2009 (Commencement No 5, Consequential and
Transitional Provisions) Order 2011, SI 2011/556; Marine and Coastal Access Act 2009
(Commencement No 6) Order 2013, SI 2013/3055; Marine and Coastal Access Act 2009
(Commencement and Consequential Provisions) (Wales) Order 2014, SI 2014/3088

| | | |
|---|---|---|
| 1–3 | | 12 Jan 2010 (SI 2009/3345) |
| 4–7 | | 1 Apr 2010 (SI 2010/907) |
| 8 | | 12 Nov 2009 (in so far as relating to any power of a Minister of the Crown, the Scottish Ministers, the Welsh Ministers or a Northern Ireland department to make regulations or an order under or by virtue of the Act) (s 324(1)(c)) |
| | | 1 Apr 2010 (otherwise) (SI 2010/907) |
| 9–13 | | 1 Apr 2010 (SI 2010/298)[1] |
| 14, 15 | | 12 Jan 2010 (SI 2009/3345) |
| 16, 17 | | 12 Nov 2009 (in so far as relating to any power of a Minister of the Crown, the Scottish Ministers, the Welsh Ministers or a Northern Ireland department to make regulations or an order under or by virtue of the Act) (s 324(1)(c)) |
| | | 12 Jan 2010 (otherwise) (SI 2009/3345) |
| 18–22 | | 12 Jan 2010 (SI 2009/3345) |
| 23 | | 1 Apr 2010 (SI 2010/298) |
| 24 | | 12 Jan 2010 (SI 2009/3345) |
| 25 | | 1 Apr 2010 (SI 2010/298) |
| 26–28 | | 12 Jan 2010 (SI 2009/3345) |
| 29, 30 | | 1 Apr 2010 (SI 2010/298) |
| 31–33 | | 12 Jan 2010 (SI 2009/3345) |
| 34 | | 12 Nov 2009 (in so far as relating to any power of a Minister of the Crown, the Scottish Ministers, the Welsh Ministers or a Northern Ireland department to make regulations or an order under or by virtue of the Act) (s 324(1)(c)) |
| | | 12 Jan 2010 (otherwise) (SI 2009/3345) |
| 35–40 | | 12 Jan 2010 (SI 2009/3345) |
| 41 | (1)–(7) | 12 Nov 2009 (in so far as relating to any power of a Minister of the Crown, the Scottish Ministers, the Welsh Ministers or a Northern Ireland department to make regulations or an order under or by virtue of the Act) (s 324(1)(c)) |
| | | 31 Mar 2014 (otherwise) (SI 2013/3055) |
| | (8) | See Sch 4, Pt 1 below |
| 42 | | 12 Jan 2010 (SI 2009/3345) |
| 43 | | 12 Nov 2009 (insofar as the amendments made by this section confer any power to make an Order in Council under the Government of Wales Act 2006) (s 324(1)(b)) |

**Marine and Coastal Access Act 2009 (c 23)**—*contd*

| | | |
|---|---|---|
| | | 12 Jan 2010 (otherwise) (SI 2009/3345) |
| 44 | (1)(a) | 12 Jan 2010 (s 324(2)(a)) |
| | (1)(b) | 12 Nov 2009 (in so far as relates to Sch 5, paras 4(1)–(4), 5 and 6 below) (s 324(1)(a)(ii)) |
| | | 12 Jan 2010 (otherwise) (s 324(2)(a)) |
| | (1)(c), (2)–(4) | 12 Jan 2010 (s 324(2)(a)) |
| | (5) | 12 Nov 2009 (in so far as relates to Sch 5, paras 4(1)–(4), 5 and 6 below) (s 324(1)(a)(ii)) |
| | | 12 Jan 2010 (otherwise) (s 324(2)(a)) |
| 45 | (1)–(3) | 12 Jan 2010 (s 324(2)(a)) |
| | (4) | 12 Nov 2009 (in so far as relates to Sch 5, paras 4(1)–(4), 5 and 6 below) (s 324(1)(a)(ii)) |
| | | 12 Jan 2010 (otherwise) (s 324(2)(a)) |
| 46–64 | | 12 Jan 2010 (s 324(2)(a)) |
| 65 | | 6 Apr 2011 (SI 2011/556) |
| 66, 67 | | 12 Nov 2009 (in so far as relating to any power of a Minister of the Crown, the Scottish Ministers, the Welsh Ministers or a Northern Ireland department to make regulations or an order under or by virtue of the Act) (s 324(1)(c)) |
| | | 6 Apr 2011 (otherwise) (SI 2011/556) |
| 68 | | 6 Apr 2011 (SI 2011/556) |
| 69 | | 12 Nov 2009 (in so far as relating to any power of a Minister of the Crown, the Scottish Ministers, the Welsh Ministers or a Northern Ireland department to make regulations or an order under or by virtue of the Act) (s 324(1)(c)) |
| | | 6 Apr 2011 (otherwise) (SI 2011/556) |
| 70–72 | | 6 Apr 2011 (SI 2011/556) |
| 73, 74 | | 12 Nov 2009 (in so far as relating to any power of a Minister of the Crown, the Scottish Ministers, the Welsh Ministers or a Northern Ireland department to make regulations or an order under or by virtue of the Act) (s 324(1)(c)) |
| | | 6 Apr 2011 (otherwise) (SI 2011/556) |
| 75–77 | | 6 Apr 2011 (SI 2011/556) |
| 78, 79 | | 12 Nov 2009 (in so far as relating to any power of a Minister of the Crown, the Scottish Ministers, the Welsh Ministers or a Northern Ireland department to make regulations or an order under or by virtue of the Act) (s 324(1)(c)) |
| | | 6 Apr 2011 (otherwise) (SI 2011/556) |
| 80–87 | | 6 Apr 2011 (SI 2011/556) |
| 88 | | 12 Nov 2009 (in so far as relating to any power of a Minister of the Crown, the Scottish Ministers, the Welsh Ministers or a Northern Ireland department to make regulations or an order under or by virtue of the Act) (s 324(1)(c)) |
| | | 6 Apr 2011 (otherwise) (SI 2011/556) |
| 89–92 | | 6 Apr 2011 (SI 2011/556) |
| 93 | | 12 Nov 2009 (in so far as relating to any power of a Minister of the Crown, the Scottish Ministers, the Welsh Ministers or a Northern Ireland department to make regulations or an order under or by virtue of the Act) (s 324(1)(c)) |
| | | 6 Apr 2011 (otherwise) (SI 2011/556) |
| 94 | | 6 Apr 2011 (SI 2011/556) |
| 95 | | 12 Nov 2009 (in so far as relating to any power of a Minister of the Crown, the Scottish Ministers, the Welsh Ministers or a Northern Ireland department to make regulations or an order under or by virtue of the Act) (s 324(1)(c)) |
| | | 6 Apr 2011 (otherwise) (SI 2011/556) |
| 96 | | 6 Apr 2011 (SI 2011/556) |
| 97 | | See Sch 7 below |

**Marine and Coastal Access Act 2009 (c 23)**—*contd*

| | | |
|---|---|---|
| 98, 99 | | 12 Nov 2009 (in so far as relating to any power of a Minister of the Crown, the Scottish Ministers, the Welsh Ministers or a Northern Ireland department to make regulations or an order under or by virtue of the Act) (s 324(1)(c)) |
| | | 6 Apr 2011 (otherwise) (SI 2011/556) |
| 100 | | 6 Apr 2011 (SI 2011/556) |
| 101 | | 12 Nov 2009 (otherwise, in so far as relating to any power of a Minister of the Crown, the Scottish Ministers, the Welsh Ministers or a Northern Ireland department to make regulations or an order under or by virtue of the Act) (s 324(1)(c)) |
| | | 6 Apr 2011 (otherwise) (SI 2011/556) |
| 102–111 | | 6 Apr 2011 (SI 2011/556) |
| 112 | (1) | See Sch 8 below |
| | (2) | See Sch 9 below |
| 113–115 | | 6 Apr 2011 (SI 2011/556) |
| 116–128 | | 12 Jan 2010 (so far as not relating to MCZs in Wales) (s 324(2)(b)(i)) |
| | | 12 Dec 2014 (exception noted above) (SI 2014/3088) |
| 129–133 | | 12 Jan 2010 (so far as not relating to MCZs in Wales) (s 324(2)(b)(i)) |
| | | *Not yet in force* (exception noted above) |
| 134–137 | | 12 Jan 2010 (so far as not relating to MCZs in Wales) (s 324(2)(b)(i)) |
| | | 12 Dec 2014 (exception noted above) (SI 2014/3088) |
| 138 | | 12 Nov 2009 (in so far as relating to any power of a Minister of the Crown, the Scottish Ministers, the Welsh Ministers or a Northern Ireland department to make regulations or an order under or by virtue of the Act) (s 324(1)(c)) |
| | | 12 Jan 2010 (otherwise, so far as not relating to MCZs in Wales) (s 324(2)(b)(i)) |
| | | 12 Dec 2014 (exception noted above) (SI 2014/3088) |
| 139, 140 | | 12 Jan 2010 (so far as not relating to MCZs in Wales) (s 324(2)(b)(i)) |
| | | 12 Dec 2014 (exception noted above) (SI 2014/3088) |
| 141, 142 | | 12 Nov 2009 (otherwise, in so far as relating to any power of a Minister of the Crown, the Scottish Ministers, the Welsh Ministers or a Northern Ireland department to make regulations or an order under or by virtue of the Act) (s 324(1)(c)) |
| | | 12 Jan 2010 (otherwise, so far as not relating to MCZs in Wales) (s 324(2)(b)(i)) |
| | | 12 Dec 2014 (exception noted above) (SI 2014/3088) |
| 143 | | 12 Jan 2010 (so far as not relating to MCZs in Wales) (s 324(2)(b)(i)) |
| | | 12 Dec 2014 (exception noted above) (SI 2014/3088) |
| 144 | | See Sch 10 below |
| 145 | | 12 Jan 2010 (so far as not relating to MCZs in Wales) (s 324(2)(b)(i)) |
| | | 12 Dec 2014 (exception noted above) (SI 2014/3088) |
| 146 | (1) | See Sch 11 below |
| | (2) | See Sch 12 below |
| 147 | | 12 Jan 2010 (so far as not relating to MCZs in Wales) (s 324(2)(b)(i)) |
| | | 12 Dec 2014 (exception noted above) (SI 2014/3088) |
| 148 | | See Sch 13 below |
| 149 | | 12 Nov 2009 (s 324(1)(c)) |
| 150 | | 1 Oct 2010 (SI 2010/2195) |

**Marine and Coastal Access Act 2009 (c 23)**—*contd*

| | | |
|---|---|---|
| 151 | | 12 Nov 2009 (in so far as relating to any power of a Minister of the Crown, the Scottish Ministers, the Welsh Ministers or a Northern Ireland department to make regulations or an order under or by virtue of the Act) (s 324(1)(c)) |
| | | 1 Oct 2010 (otherwise) (SI 2010/2195) |
| 152 | | 12 Nov 2009 (s 324(1)(c)) |
| 153–158 | | 1 Apr 2011 (SI 2011/556) |
| 159, 160 | | 12 Nov 2009 (in so far as relating to any power of a Minister of the Crown, the Scottish Ministers, the Welsh Ministers or a Northern Ireland department to make regulations or an order under or by virtue of the Act) (s 324(1)(c)) |
| | | 1 Apr 2011 (otherwise) (SI 2011/556) |
| 161–164 | | 1 Apr 2011 (SI 2011/556) |
| 165 | | 1 Oct 2010 (SI 2010/2195) |
| 166 | | 12 Nov 2009 (in so far as relating to any power of a Minister of the Crown, the Scottish Ministers, the Welsh Ministers or a Northern Ireland department to make regulations or an order under or by virtue of the Act) (s 324(1)(c)) |
| | | 1 Apr 2011 (otherwise) (SI 2011/556) |
| 167 | | 1 Apr 2011 (SI 2011/556) |
| 168 | | 12 Nov 2009 (in so far as relating to any power of a Minister of the Crown, the Scottish Ministers, the Welsh Ministers or a Northern Ireland department to make regulations or an order under or by virtue of the Act) (s 324(1)(c)) |
| | | 1 Apr 2011 (otherwise) (SI 2011/556) |
| 169–173 | | 1 Apr 2011 (SI 2011/556) |
| 174 | | 1 Oct 2010 (SI 2010/2195) |
| 175 | | 1 Apr 2011 (SI 2011/556) |
| 176 | (1) | 1 Oct 2010 (SI 2010/2195) |
| | (2) | 1 Apr 2011 (SI 2011/556) |
| 177 | | 1 Oct 2010 (SI 2010/2195) |
| 178 | | 1 Apr 2011 (SI 2011/556) |
| 179 | | 1 Oct 2010 (SI 2010/2195)[3] |
| 180 | | 12 Nov 2009 (in so far as relating to any power of a Minister of the Crown, the Scottish Ministers, the Welsh Ministers or a Northern Ireland department to make regulations or an order under or by virtue of the Act) (s 324(1)(c)) |
| | | 1 Oct 2010 (otherwise) (SI 2010/2195) |
| 181, 182 | | 1 Oct 2010 (SI 2010/2195)[3] |
| 183 | | 1 Apr 2011 (SI 2011/556) |
| 184 | | See Sch 14 below |
| 185 | | 1 Apr 2011 (SI 2011/556) |
| 186 | | 12 Nov 2009 (in so far as relating to any power of a Minister of the Crown, the Scottish Ministers, the Welsh Ministers or a Northern Ireland department to make regulations or an order under or by virtue of the Act) (s 324(1)(c)) |
| | | 1 Oct 2010 (in so far as relating to the definitions "authority for an IFC district", "IFC authority", "IFC district", "local authority area" and "relevant council") (SI 2010/2195) |
| | | 1 Apr 2011 (otherwise) (SI 2011/556) |
| 187 | | 1 Apr 2010 (W) (SI 2010/630)[2] |
| | | 1 Apr 2011 (E) (SI 2011/556) |
| 188, 189 | | 12 Nov 2009 (in so far as relating to any power of a Minister of the Crown, the Scottish Ministers, the Welsh Ministers or a Northern Ireland department to make regulations or an order under or by virtue of the Act) (s 324(1)(c)) |
| | | *Not yet in force* (otherwise) |
| 190–193 | | 12 Jan 2010 (s 324(2)(c)) |

**Marine and Coastal Access Act 2009 (c 23)**—*contd*

| | | |
|---|---|---|
| 194–196 | | 12 Nov 2009 (in so far as relating to any power of a Minister of the Crown, the Scottish Ministers, the Welsh Ministers or a Northern Ireland department to make regulations or an order under or by virtue of the Act) (s 324(1)(c)) |
| | | 12 Jan 2010 (otherwise) (SI 2009/3345) |
| 197 | | 12 Jan 2010 (SI 2009/3345) |
| 198 | | 12 Nov 2009 (in so far as relating to any power of a Minister of the Crown, the Scottish Ministers, the Welsh Ministers or a Northern Ireland department to make regulations or an order under or by virtue of the Act) (s 324(1)(c)) |
| | | 12 Jan 2010 (otherwise) (SI 2009/3345) |
| 199–201 | | 12 Jan 2010 (SI 2009/3345) |
| 202–204 | | 12 Nov 2009 (in so far as relating to any power of a Minister of the Crown, the Scottish Ministers, the Welsh Ministers or a Northern Ireland department to make regulations or an order under or by virtue of the Act) (s 324(1)(c)) |
| | | 12 Jan 2010 (otherwise) (SI 2009/3345) |
| 205–210 | | 12 Jan 2010 (SI 2009/3345) |
| 211 | | 12 Nov 2009 (in so far as relating to any power of a Minister of the Crown, the Scottish Ministers, the Welsh Ministers or a Northern Ireland department to make regulations or an order under or by virtue of the Act) (s 324(1)(c)) |
| | | 12 Jan 2010 (otherwise) (SI 2009/3345) |
| 212 | | 12 Jan 2010 (SI 2009/3345) |
| 213–216 | | 12 Nov 2009 (in so far as relating to any power of a Minister of the Crown, the Scottish Ministers, the Welsh Ministers or a Northern Ireland department to make regulations or an order under or by virtue of the Act) (s 324(1)(c)) |
| | | 12 Jan 2010 (otherwise) (SI 2009/3345) |
| 217 | (1) | 12 Nov 2009 (in so far as relating to any power of a Minister of the Crown, the Scottish Ministers, the Welsh Ministers or a Northern Ireland department to make regulations or an order under or by virtue of the Act) (s 324(1)(c)) |
| | | 12 Jan 2010 (so far as relates to the meaning of "that section" in sub-ss (3), (4) below) (SI 2009/3345) |
| | | 1 Jan 2011 (SI 2010/298) |
| | (2) | 1 Jan 2011 (SI 2010/298) |
| | (3), (4) | 12 Jan 2010 (SI 2009/3345) |
| | (5)–(7) | 1 Jan 2011 (otherwise) (SI 2010/298) |
| 218 | | 12 Nov 2009 (in so far as relating to any power of a Minister of the Crown, the Scottish Ministers, the Welsh Ministers or a Northern Ireland department to make regulations or an order under or by virtue of the Act) (s 324(1)(c)) |
| | | 1 Jan 2011 (otherwise) (SI 2010/298) |
| 219 | | 1 Jan 2011 (SI 2010/298) |
| 220 | | 12 Jan 2010 (SI 2009/3345) |
| 221, 222 | | 12 Nov 2009 (in so far as relating to any power of a Minister of the Crown, the Scottish Ministers, the Welsh Ministers or a Northern Ireland department to make regulations or an order under or by virtue of the Act) (s 324(1)(c)) |
| | | 12 Jan 2010 (otherwise) (SI 2009/3345) |
| 223 | (1) | See sub-ss (2)–(6) below |
| | (2) | 12 Jan 2010 (SI 2009/3345) |
| | (3)–(5) | 1 Jan 2011 (SI 2010/298) |
| | (6) | 12 Jan 2010 (SI 2009/3345) |
| 224 | | 12 Nov 2009 (in so far as relating to any power of a Minister of the Crown, the Scottish Ministers, the Welsh Ministers or a Northern Ireland department to make regulations or an order under or by virtue of the Act) (s 324(1)(c)) |
| | | 12 Jan 2010 (otherwise) (SI 2009/3345) |

**Marine and Coastal Access Act 2009 (c 23)**—*contd*

| | | |
|---|---|---|
| 225–228 | | 12 Jan 2010 (SI 2009/3345) |
| 229–232 | | 12 Nov 2009 (in so far as relating to any power of a Minister of the Crown, the Scottish Ministers, the Welsh Ministers or a Northern Ireland department to make regulations or an order under or by virtue of the Act) (s 324(1)(c)) |
| | | 12 Jan 2010 (otherwise) (SI 2009/3345) |
| 233 | (1) | See Sch 16 below |
| | (2) | 12 Jan 2010 (SI 2009/3345) |
| 234 | | 1 Apr 2010 (SI 2010/298) |
| 235 | | 12 Jan 2010 (SI 2009/3345) |
| 236 | | 6 Apr 2011 (SI 2011/556) |
| 237–239 | | 12 Jan 2010 (SI 2009/3345) |
| 240–242 | | 6 Apr 2011 (SI 2011/556) |
| 243–262 | | 12 Jan 2010 (SI 2009/3345) |
| 263 | | 6 Apr 2011 (SI 2011/556) |
| 264–292 | | 12 Jan 2010 (SI 2009/3345) |
| 293, 294 | | 12 Nov 2009 (in so far as relating to any power of a Minister of the Crown, the Scottish Ministers, the Welsh Ministers or a Northern Ireland department to make regulations or an order under or by virtue of the Act) (s 324(1)(c)) |
| | | 12 Jan 2010 (otherwise) (SI 2009/3345) |
| 295 | | 12 Jan 2010 (SI 2009/3345) |
| 296–299 | | 12 Jan 2010 (s 324(2)(d)) |
| 300 | | 12 Nov 2009 (in so far as relating to any power of a Minister of the Crown, the Scottish Ministers, the Welsh Ministers or a Northern Ireland department to make regulations or an order under or by virtue of the Act) (s 324(1)(c)) |
| | | 12 Jan 2010 (otherwise) (s 324(2)(d)) |
| 301 | | 12 Jan 2010 (s 324(2)(d)) |
| 302–304 | | 12 Nov 2009 (in so far as relating to any power of a Minister of the Crown, the Scottish Ministers, the Welsh Ministers or a Northern Ireland department to make regulations or an order under or by virtue of the Act) (s 324(1)(c)) |
| | | 12 Jan 2010 (otherwise) (s 324(2)(d)) |
| 305, 306 | | 12 Jan 2010 (s 324(2)(d)) |
| 307 | | 12 Nov 2009 (in so far as relating to any power of a Minister of the Crown, the Scottish Ministers, the Welsh Ministers or a Northern Ireland department to make regulations or an order under or by virtue of the Act) (s 324(1)(c)) |
| | | 12 Jan 2010 (otherwise) (s 324(2)(d)) |
| 308–310 | | 12 Jan 2010 (s 324(2)(d)) |
| 311–313 | | 12 Jan 2010 (SI 2009/3345) |
| 314 | | 12 Nov 2009 (in so far as relating to any power of a Minister of the Crown, the Scottish Ministers, the Welsh Ministers or a Northern Ireland department to make regulations or an order under or by virtue of the Act) (s 324(1)(c)) |
| | | 6 Apr 2011 (otherwise) (SI 2011/556) |
| 315 | | See Sch 21 below |
| 316–320 | | 12 Nov 2009 (s 324(1)(b)) |
| 321 | | See Sch 22 below |
| 322–325 | | 12 Nov 2009 (s 324(1)(b)) |
| Sch 1 | | 12 Nov 2009 (in so far as relating to any power of a Minister of the Crown, the Scottish Ministers, the Welsh Ministers or a Northern Ireland department to make regulations or an order under or by virtue of the Act) (s 324(1)(c)) |
| | | 12 Jan 2010 (otherwise) (SI 2009/3345) |
| Schs 2, 3 | | 12 Jan 2010 (SI 2009/3345) |

**Marine and Coastal Access Act 2009 (c 23)**—*contd*

| | | |
|---|---|---|
| Sch 4 | paras 1–5 | 12 Nov 2009 (in so far as relating to any power of a Minister of the Crown, the Scottish Ministers, the Welsh Ministers or a Northern Ireland department to make regulations or an order under or by virtue of the Act) (s 324(1)(c)) |
| | | 31 Mar 2014 (otherwise) (SI 2013/3055) |
| | para 6 | 12 Nov 2009 (in so far as the amendments made by this paragraph confer any power to make an Order in Council under the Government of Wales Act 2006) (s 324(1)(b)) |
| | | 12 Jan 2010 (otherwise) (SI 2009/3345) |
| Sch 5 | paras 1, 2 | 12 Nov 2009 (in so far as they relate to paras 4(1)–(4), 5 and 6 below) (s 324(1)(a)(i)) |
| | | 12 Jan 2010 (otherwise) (s 324(2)(a)) |
| | para 3 | 12 Jan 2010 (s 324(2)(a)) |
| | para 4(1)–(4) | 12 Nov 2009 (s 324(1)(a)(i)) |
| | para 4(5) | 12 Jan 2010 (s 324(2)(a)) |
| | paras 5, 6 | 12 Nov 2009 (s 324(1)(a)(i)) |
| | paras 7–13 | 12 Jan 2010 (s 324(2)(a)) |
| Sch 6 | | 12 Jan 2010 (s 324(2)(a)) |
| Sch 7 | | 6 Apr 2011 (SI 2011/556) |
| Sch 8 | paras 1–6 | 6 Apr 2011 (SI 2011/556) |
| | paras 7, 8 | 12 Nov 2009 (in so far as relating to any power of a Minister of the Crown, the Scottish Ministers, the Welsh Ministers or a Northern Ireland department to make regulations or an order under or by virtue of the Act) (s 324(1)(c)) |
| | | 1 Apr 2010 (otherwise) (SI 2010/298) |
| Sch 9 | | 6 Apr 2011 (SI 2011/556)[4] |
| Schs 10–12 | | 12 Jan 2010 (so far as not relating to MCZs in Wales) (s 324(2)(b)(i)) |
| | | 12 Dec 2014 (exception noted above) (SI 2014/3088) |
| Sch 13 | | 12 Nov 2009 (in so far as relating to any power of a Minister of the Crown, the Scottish Ministers, the Welsh Ministers or a Northern Ireland department to make regulations or an order under or by virtue of the Act) (s 324(1)(c)) |
| | | 12 Jan 2010 (in so far as not relating to Wales) (s 324(2)(b)(ii)) |
| | | 12 Dec 2014 (W) (SI 2014/3088) |
| Sch 14 | paras 1–8 | 1 Apr 2011 (SI 2011/556) |
| | para 9 | 1 Oct 2010 (SI 2010/2195) |
| | paras 10, 11 | 1 Apr 2011 (SI 2011/556) |
| | paras 12–15 | 1 Oct 2010 (SI 2010/2195) |
| | paras 16–18 | 1 Apr 2011 (SI 2011/556) |
| | para 19 | 1 Oct 2010 (SI 2010/2195) |
| | para 20 | 1 Apr 2011 (SI 2011/556) |
| Sch 15 | | 12 Jan 2010 (SI 2009/3345) |
| Sch 16 | para 1 | See paras 2–17 below |
| | para 2 | 1 Jan 2011 (SI 2010/298) |
| | para 3(1) | See sub-paras (2)–(4) below |
| | para 3(2) | 1 Jan 2011 (SI 2010/298) |
| | para 3(3) | 12 Jan 2010 (SI 2009/3345) |
| | paras 3(4), 4–7 | 1 Jan 2011 (SI 2010/298) |
| | para 8 | 12 Jan 2010 (except in so far as repeals Salmon and Freshwater Fisheries Act 1975, s 20) (SI 2009/3345) |
| | | 1 Jan 2011 (otherwise) (SI 2010/298) |
| | paras 9–11 | 1 Jan 2011 (SI 2010/298) |
| | paras 12, 13 | 12 Jan 2010 (SI 2009/3345) |
| | para 14(1) | See sub-paras (2)–(4) below |
| | para 14(2) | 12 Jan 2010 (SI 2009/3345) |
| | para 14(3), (4) | 1 Jan 2011 (SI 2010/298) |
| | para 15 | 12 Jan 2010 (SI 2009/3345) |
| | para 16(1) | See sub-paras (2)–(12) below |
| | para 16(2), (3) | 12 Jan 2010 (SI 2009/3345) |

**Marine and Coastal Access Act 2009 (c 23)**—*contd*

| | | |
|---|---|---|
| | para 16(4) | 1 Jan 2011 (SI 2010/298) |
| | para 16(5), (6) | 12 Jan 2010 (SI 2009/3345) |
| | para 16(7), (8) | 1 Jan 2011 (SI 2010/298) |
| | para 16(9) | 12 Jan 2010 (SI 2009/3345) |
| | para 16(10)–(12) | 1 Jan 2011 (SI 2010/298) |
| | para 17(1) | See sub-paras (2)–(8) below |
| | para 17(2) | 12 Jan 2010 (SI 2009/3345) |
| | para 17(3) | 1 Jan 2011 (SI 2010/298) |
| | para 17(4), (5) | 12 Jan 2010 (SI 2009/3345) |
| | para 17(6)–(8) | 1 Jan 2011 (SI 2010/298) |
| | paras 18–26 | 12 Jan 2010 (SI 2009/3345) |
| Schs 17, 18 | | 12 Jan 2010 (SI 2009/3345) |
| Schs 19, 20 | | 12 Nov 2009 (in so far as relating to any power of a Minister of the Crown, the Scottish Ministers, the Welsh Ministers or a Northern Ireland department to make regulations or an order under or by virtue of the Act) (s 324(1)(c)) |
| | | 12 Jan 2010 (otherwise) (s 324(2)(d)) |
| Sch 21 | | 12 Nov 2010 (in so far as relating to any power of a Minister of the Crown, the Scottish Ministers, the Welsh Ministers or a Northern Ireland department to make regulations or an order under or by virtue of the Act) (s 324(1)(c)) |
| | | 12 Jan 2010 (otherwise) (SI 2009/3345) |
| Sch 22 | Pt 1 | 12 Jan 2010 (repeal in Government of Wales Act 2006) (SI 2009/3345) |
| | | *Not yet in force* (repeals in Fishery Limits Act 1976) |
| | Pt 2 | 6 Apr 2011 (SI 2011/556) |
| | Pt 3 | 12 Jan 2010 (so far as not relating to Wales or MCZs in Wales) (s 324(2)(b)(i), (4)) |
| | | 12 Dec 2014 (exception noted above) (SI 2014/3088) |
| | Pt 4 | 1 Apr 2010 (W) (SI 2010/630)[2] |
| | | 1 Apr 2011 (E) (SI 2011/556) |
| | Pt 5 | 12 Jan 2010 (repeals in Table A) (SI 2009/3345) |
| | | 12 Jan 2010 (repeals in Table B of or in: Theft Act 1968; Salmon and Freshwater Fisheries Act 1975, ss 1, 4, 19, 21–25, 31, 32, 34, 35, Schs 1, 2, 4; Fisheries Act 1981; Salmon Act 1986; Water Act 1989; Water Resources Act 1991; Environment Act 1995; Criminal Justice Act 2003; Serious Crime Act 2007) (SI 2009/3345) |
| | | 1 Apr 2010 (repeals in Table C) (SI 2010/298) |
| | | 1 Jan 2011 (repeals in Table B of or in: Salmon and Freshwater Fisheries Act 1975, ss 3, 6–8, 16, 17, 20; Territorial Sea Act 1987) (SI 2010/298) |
| | Pt 6 | 12 Jan 2010 (SI 2009/3345) |
| | Pt 7 | 12 Jan 2010 (s 324(2)(d), (4)) |
| | Pt 8 | 12 Jan 2010 (SI 2009/3345) |

[1]   For transitional provisions and savings, see SI 2010/298, art 4

[2]   For transitional provisions, see SI 2010/630, arts 8, 12

[3]   For transitional provisions, see SI 2010/2195, art 4

[4]   For transitional provisions, see SI 2011/556, art 4

**National Assembly for Wales Commissioner for Standards Measure 2009 (nawm 4)**

*Passed by the National Assembly for Wales:* 14 Oct 2009

*Approved by Her Majesty in Council:* 9 Dec 2009

*Commencement provisions:* s 21(2), (3)

| | |
|---|---|
| 1 | 10 Dec 2009 (s 21(2)(a)) |
| 2 | *Not yet in force* |
| 3 | See Schedule below |
| 4–19 | *Not yet in force* |
| 20, 21 | 10 Dec 2009 (s 21(2)(a)) |
| Schedule | 10 Dec 2009 (s 21(2)(a)) |

**Northern Ireland Act 2009 (c 3)**

*RA:* 12 Mar 2009

*Commencement provisions:* s 5(6), (7); Northern Ireland Act 2009 (Commencement No 1) Order 2009, SI 2009/2466; Northern Ireland Act 2009 (Commencement No 2) Order 2010, SI 2010/812

| | | |
|---|---|---|
| 1 | | See Sch 1 below |
| 2 | (1), (2) | See Schs 2–6 below |
| | (3) | See Sch 4 below |
| | (4), (5) | See Schs 2–6 below |
| 3 | (1) | 12 Apr 2010 (SI 2010/812) |
| | (2) | 12 Mar 2009 (s 5(6)) |
| 4, 5 | | 12 Mar 2009 (s 5(6)) |
| Sch 1 | | 12 Mar 2009 (s 5(6)) |
| Schs 2, 3 | | 12 Apr 2010 (SI 2010/812) |
| Sch 4 | paras 1–34 | 12 Apr 2010 (SI 2010/812) |
| | para 35(1) | 26 Sep 2009 (in so far as it relates to the President or other member of the Charity Tribunal for Northern Ireland) (SI 2009/2466) |
| | | 12 Apr 2010 (otherwise) (SI 2010/812) |
| | para 35(2) | 12 Apr 2010 (SI 2010/812) |
| | para 35(3) | 26 Sep 2009 (in so far as it relates to the President or other member of the Charity Tribunal for Northern Ireland) (SI 2009/2466) |
| | | 12 Apr 2010 (otherwise) (SI 2010/812) |
| | para 35(4) | 12 Apr 2010 (SI 2010/812) |
| | paras 36–47 | 12 Apr 2010 (SI 2010/812) |
| Schs 5, 6 | | 12 Apr 2010 (SI 2010/812) |

**Offences (Aggravation by Prejudice) (Scotland) Act 2009 (asp 8)**

*RA:* 8 Jul 2009

*Commencement provisions:* s 3(1); Offences (Aggravation by Prejudice) (Scotland) Act 2009 (Commencement) Order 2010, SSI 2010/115

| | |
|---|---|
| 1, 2 | 24 Mar 2010 (in respect of offences committed on or after that date) (SSI 2010/115) |
| 3 | 8 Jul 2009 (RA) |

**Parliamentary Standards Act 2009 (c 13)**

*RA:* 21 Jul 2009

*Commencement provisions:* s 14(2), (3); Parliamentary Standards Act 2009 (Commencement No 1) Order 2009, SI 2009/2500; Parliamentary Standards Act 2009 (Commencement No 2) Order 2009,

## Parliamentary Standards Act 2009 (c 13)—*contd*

SI 2009/2612; Parliamentary Standards Act 2009 (Commencement No 3) Order 2010, SI 2010/1033; Parliamentary Standards Act 2009 (Commencement No 4) Order 2010, SI 2010/1278

| | | |
|---|---|---|
| 1, 2 | | 12 Oct 2009 (SI 2009/2500) |
| 3 | (1) | 12 Oct 2009 (SI 2009/2500) |
| | (2) | See Sch 1 below |
| | (3) | *Never in force* (substituted) |
| | (4) | See Sch 2 below |
| | (5), (6) | 26 Oct 2009 (SI 2009/2612) |
| 4 | | 7 May 2010 (the day after the day on which the poll is taken at a parliamentary general election for the first or only time in 2010) (SI 2010/1033) |
| 5, 6 | | 29 Mar 2010 (SI 2010/1033) |
| 7 | | 7 May 2010 (SI 2010/1278) |
| 8, 9 | | *Never in force* (s 8 repealed; s 9 substituted) |
| 10 | | 7 May 2010 (the day after the day on which the poll is taken at a parliamentary general election for the first or only time in 2010) (SI 2010/1033) |
| 11 | | *Never in force* (repealed) |
| 12–15 | | 21 Jul 2009 (s 14(2)) |
| Sch 1 | paras 1–8 | 26 Oct 2009 (SI 2009/2612) |
| | paras 9–16 | 12 Oct 2009 (SI 2009/2500) |
| | paras 17, 18(1), (2)(a) | 7 May 2010 (the day after the day on which the poll is taken at a parliamentary general election for the first or only time in 2010) (SI 2010/1033) |
| | para 18(2)(b), (c) | *Never in force* (sub-para (2)(b) repealed; sub-para (2)(c) substituted) |
| | paras 19–29 | 12 Oct 2009 (SI 2009/2500) |
| Sch 2 | | *Never in force* (substituted) |
| Sch 3 | | 26 Oct 2009 (SI 2009/2612) |

## Perpetuities and Accumulations Act 2009 (c 18)

*RA:* 12 Nov 2009

*Commencement provisions:* s 22; Perpetuities and Accumulations Act 2009 (Commencement) Order 2010, SI 2010/37

| | |
|---|---|
| 1–21 | 6 Apr 2010 (SI 2010/37) |
| 22–24 | 12 Nov 2009 (s 22(1)) |
| Schedule | 6 Apr 2010 (SI 2010/37) |

## Policing and Crime Act 2009 (c 26)

*RA:* 12 Nov 2009

*Commencement provisions:* s 116; Policing and Crime Act 2009 (Commencement No 1 and Transitional and Saving Provisions) Order 2009, SI 2009/3096; Policing and Crime Act 2009 (Commencement No 2) Order 2010, SI 2010/52; Policing and Crime Act 2009 (Commencement No 3) Order 2010, SI 2010/125; Policing and Crime Act 2009 (Commencement No 4) Order 2010, SI 2010/507; Policing and Crime Act 2009 (Commencement No 1 and Transitional and Saving Provisions) (England) Order 2010, SI 2010/722; Policing and Crime Act 2009 (Commencement No 5) Order 2010, SI 2010/999, as amended by SI 2010/1986; Policing and Crime Act 2009 (Commencement No 1) (Wales) Order 2010, SI 2010/1375; Policing and Crime Act 2009 (Commencement No 6 and Commencement No 5 (Amendment)) Order 2010, SI 2010/1986; Policing and Crime Act 2009 (Commencement No 7) Order 2010, SI 2010/2988; Policing and Crime Act 2009 (Commencement No 8) Order 2012, SI 2012/2235; Policing and Crime Act 2009 (Commencement No 9) Order 2014, SI 2014/3101; Policing and Crime Act 2009 (Commencement No 10, Transitional Provision and Savings) Order 2015, SI 2015/983; Policing and Crime Act 2009 (Commencement No 11 and Transitional Provisions and Savings) Order 2016, SI 2016/147

| | |
|---|---|
| 1 | 15 Mar 2010 (SI 2010/125) |

**Policing and Crime Act 2009 (c 26)**—*contd*

| | | |
|---|---|---|
| 2 | (1) | *Never in force* (repealed) |
| | (2) | 1 Sep 2010 (SI 2010/999) |
| | (3), (4) | *Not yet in force* (sub-s (3) repealed) |
| 3, 4 | | 19 Apr 2010 (SI 2010/999) |
| 5 | | 12 Mar 2010 (SI 2010/507) |
| 6–9 | | 25 Jan 2010 (SI 2009/3096) |
| 10–13 | | 29 Jan 2010 (SI 2010/125) |
| 14–20 | | 1 Apr 2010 (SI 2010/507)[2] |
| 21 | (1) | See Sch 2 below |
| | (2) | 1 Apr 2010 (E) (W) (SI 2010/507) |
| 22–25 | | 1 Apr 2010 (SI 2010/507) |
| 26 | | 25 Jan 2010 (SI 2009/3096) |
| 27 | (1)–(10) | 6 Apr 2010 (E) (SI 2010/722)[3] |
| | | 8 May 2010 (W) (SI 2010/1375) |
| | (11) | See Sch 3 below |
| 28–33 | | 29 Jan 2010 (SI 2010/125) |
| 34–50 | | 31 Jan 2011 (SI 2010/2988) |
| 51 | | 25 Jan 2010 (SI 2009/3096) |
| 52, 53 | | 1 Jun 2015 (SI 2015/983) |
| 54 | | 1 Mar 2016 (SI 2016/147) |
| 55 | (1) | See sub-ss (2)–(4) below |
| | (2) | 22 Nov 2014 (in so far as inserts Proceeds of Crime Act 2002, ss 47A, 47G, 47S(1)–(5), in so far as they confer the power to make subordinate legislation under that Act or for the Lord Advocate to issue guidance under s 127R thereof, and in so far as is necessary for the purpose of making regulations, rules of court, orders, codes of practice or issuing guidance) (SI 2014/3101) |
| | | 1 Jun 2015 (otherwise) (SI 2015/983) |
| | (3) | 1 Jun 2015 (SI 2015/983)[4] |
| | (4) | 1 Jun 2015 (SI 2015/983) |
| 56 | (1) | See sub-ss (2)–(4) below |
| | (2) | 22 Nov 2014 (insertions of Proceeds of Crime Act 2002, ss 127A, 127G, 127R) (for exercising the power to make subordinate legislation under that Act or for the Lord Advocate to issue guidance under s 127R thereof, and in so far as is necessary for the purpose of making regulations, rules of court, orders, codes of practice or issuing guidance) (SI 2014/3101) |
| | | 1 Jun 2015 (otherwise) (SI 2015/983) |
| | (3) | 1 Jun 2015 (SI 2015/983)[4] |
| | (4) | 1 Jun 2015 (SI 2015/983) |
| 57 | (1) | See sub-ss (2)–(4) below |
| | (2) | 22 Nov 2014 (in so far as inserts Proceeds of Crime Act 2002, ss 195S(1)–(5), 195T (1)–(7), in so far as they confer the power to make subordinate legislation under that Act or for the Lord Advocate to issue guidance under s 127R thereof, and in so far as is necessary for the purpose of making regulations, rules of court, orders, codes of practice or issuing guidance) (SI 2014/3101) |
| | | 1 Mar 2016 (otherwise) (SI 2016/147) |
| | (3) | 1 Mar 2016 (SI 2016/147)[5] |
| | (4) | 1 Mar 2016 (SI 2016/147) |
| 58, 59 | | 1 Jun 2015 (SI 2015/983) |
| 60 | | 1 Mar 2016 (SI 2016/147) |
| 61, 62 | | 25 Jan 2010 (SI 2009/3096) |
| 63 | (1)–(3) | 1 Jun 2015 (SI 2015/983) |
| | (4) | 1 Jun 2015 (except in so far as inserts Proceeds of Crime Act 2002, s 289(5)(c) words "or Northern Ireland") (SI 2015/983) |
| | | 1 Mar 2016 (exception noted above) (SI 2016/147) |
| 64 | | 25 Jan 2010 (SI 2009/3096) |

**Policing and Crime Act 2009 (c 26)**—*contd*

| | | |
|---|---|---|
| 65 | (1) | 22 Nov 2014 (in so far as inserts Proceeds of Crime Act 2002, s 297A(3)–(5), in so far as it confers the power to make subordinate legislation under that Act or for the Lord Advocate to issue guidance under s 127R thereof, and in so far as is necessary for the purpose of making regulations, rules of court, orders, codes of practice or issuing guidance) (SI 2014/3101) |
| | | 1 Jun 2015 (otherwise, except words "or Northern Ireland" in the Proceeds of Crime Act 2002, ss 297A(1), 297E(2)) (SI 2015/983) |
| | | 1 Mar 2016 (exception noted above) (SI 2016/147) |
| | (2)–(4) | 1 Jun 2015 (SI 2015/983) |
| 66 | (1) | See sub-ss (2)–(7) below |
| | (2)–(4) | 1 Jun 2015 (SI 2015/983)[6] |
| | (5) | 22 Nov 2014 (for exercising the power to make subordinate legislation under that Act or for the Lord Advocate to issue guidance under s 127R thereof, and in so far as is necessary for the purpose of making regulations, rules of court, orders, codes of practice or issuing guidance) (SI 2014/3101) |
| | | 1 Jun 2015 (otherwise) (SI 2015/983)[6] |
| | (6), (7) | 1 Jun 2015 (SI 2015/983)[6] |
| 67–71 | | 25 Jan 2010 (SI 2009/3096)[1] |
| 72–75 | | 25 Jan 2010 (SI 2009/3096) |
| 76–78 | | 25 Jan 2010 (SI 2009/3096)[1] |
| 79 | | 29 Jan 2010 (E) (W) (S) (SI 2010/125) |
| | | 1 Apr 2010 (NI) (SI 2010/507) |
| 80 | | See Sch 6 below |
| 81 | | 12 Nov 2009 (s 116(5)(a)) |
| 82 | | *Never in force* (repealed) |
| 83 | | 29 Jan 2010 (SI 2010/125) |
| 84 | | 29 Jan 2010 (for the purpose of making regulations) (SI 2010/125) |
| | | *Never in force* (otherwise) (repealed) |
| 85–87 | | *Never in force* (repealed) |
| 88 | | 30 Nov 2009 (SI 2009/3096) |
| 89, 90 | | *Never in force* (repealed) |
| 91 | | 30 Nov 2009 (SI 2009/3096) |
| 92–95 | | *Not yet in force* (ss 92, 93 repealed) |
| 96 | | 10 Sep 2012 (SI 2012/2235) |
| 97 | | 29 Jan 2010 (SI 2010/125) |
| 98, 99 | | 25 Jan 2010 (SI 2010/52) |
| 100 | | 12 Nov 2009 (s 116(5)(b)) |
| 101 | | 25 Jan 2010 (SI 2010/52) |
| 102 | | *Not yet in force* |
| 103–107 | | 1 Apr 2010 (SI 2010/507) |
| 108 | (1)–(3) | 1 Apr 2010 (SI 2010/507) |
| | (4), (5) | 2 Mar 2010 (for the purpose of making regulations under the Crime and Disorder Act 1998, s 6) (SI 2010/507) |
| | | 1 Apr 2010 (otherwise) (SI 2010/507) |
| | (6) | 1 Apr 2010 (SI 2010/507) |
| 109 | | 6 Nov 2010 (SI 2010/1986) |
| 110 | | 29 Jan 2010 (SI 2010/125) |
| 111 | | 12 Nov 2009 (s 116(5)(c)) |
| 112 | (1) | See Sch 7 below |
| | (2) | See Sch 8 below |
| | (3)–(9) | 12 Nov 2009 (s 116(5)(d)) |
| 113–117 | | 12 Nov 2009 (s 116(5)(d)) |
| Sch 1 | | 1 Apr 2010 (SI 2010/507) |
| Sch 2 | | 1 Apr 2010 (E) (W) (SI 2010/507) |
| | | *Not yet in force* (NI) |
| Sch 3 | paras 1, 2 | 6 Apr 2010 (E) (SI 2010/722)[3] |
| | | 8 May 2010 (W) (SI 2010/1375) |

**Policing and Crime Act 2009 (c 26)**—*contd*

|  |  |  |
|---|---|---|
| | para 3 | 2 Mar 2010 (E) (SI 2010/507) |
| | | 1 May 2010 (W) (for the purpose of making orders) (SI 2010/1375) |
| | | 8 May 2010 (W) (otherwise) (SI 2010/1375) |
| | para 4 | 6 Apr 2010 (E) (SI 2010/722)[3] |
| | | 8 May 2010 (W) (SI 2010/1375) |
| | para 5 | 2 Mar 2010 (E) (for the purpose of making orders under para 3 above) (SI 2010/507) |
| | | 6 Apr 2010 (E) (otherwise) (SI 2010/722)[3] |
| | | 1 May 2010 (W) (for the purpose of making orders under para 3 above) (SI 2010/1375) |
| | | 8 May 2010 (W) (otherwise) (SI 2010/1375) |
| Sch 4 | | 29 Jan 2010 (SI 2010/125) |
| Sch 5 | | 31 Jan 2011 (SI 2010/2988) |
| Sch 6 | | 29 Jan 2010 (E) (W) (S) (SI 2010/125) |
| | | 1 Apr 2010 (NI) (SI 2010/507) |
| Sch 7 | paras 1–11 | 12 Mar 2010 (SI 2010/507) |
| | paras 12–17 | 25 Jan 2010 (SI 2009/3096) |
| | paras 18–22 | 1 Apr 2010 (SI 2010/507) |
| | para 23 | 6 Apr 2010 (E) (SI 2010/722)[3] |
| | | 8 May 2010 (W) (SI 2010/999; SI 2010/1375) |
| | para 24 | 1 Apr 2010 (SI 2010/507) |
| | para 25 | 25 Jan 2010 (SI 2009/3096) |
| | para 26 | 1 Apr 2010 (SI 2010/507) |
| | paras 27–44 | 29 Jan 2010 (SI 2010/125) |
| | para 45 | 1 Mar 2016 (SI 2016/147) |
| | para 46 | 1 Jun 2015 (SI 2015/983) |
| | para 47 | 1 Jun 2015 (except in so far as relates to Bankruptcy (Scotland) Act 1985, s 7(1), definition "relevant detention power": words ", 193A, 195J, 195K, 195M or 195P") (SI 2015/983) |
| | | 1 Mar 2016 (exception noted above) (SI 2016/147) |
| | para 48 | 1 Jun 2015 (except in so far as relates to Bankruptcy (Scotland) Act 1985, s 31A(1)(b): words "or 215A", s 31A(1)(d): words ", 193A or 195J") (SI 2015/983) |
| | | 1 Mar 2016 (exception noted above) (SI 2016/147) |
| | paras 49–51 | 1 Jun 2015 (SI 2015/983) |
| | para 52 | 1 Jun 2015 (except in so far as relates to Bankruptcy (Scotland) Act 1985, s 31C(2): words "or 190A") (SI 2015/983) |
| | | 1 Mar 2016 (exception noted above) (SI 2016/147) |
| | para 53 | 1 Jun 2015 (SI 2015/983) |
| | para 54 | 1 Jun 2015 (except in so far as relates to Insolvency Act 1986, s 306A(1)(b): words "or 215A", s 306A(1)(d): words ", 193A or 195J") (SI 2015/983) |
| | | 1 Mar 2016 (exception noted above) (SI 2016/147) |
| | paras 55–57 | 1 Jun 2015 (SI 2015/983) |
| | para 58 | 1 Jun 2015 (except in so far as relates to Insolvency Act 1986, s 306C(2): words "or 190A") (SI 2015/983) |
| | | 1 Mar 2016 (exception noted above) (SI 2016/147) |
| | para 59 | 1 Jun 2015 (SI 2015/983) |
| | para 60 | 1 Jun 2015 (except in so far as relates to Insolvency (Northern Ireland) Order 1989, SI 1989/2405 (NI 19), art 279C(2): words "or 190A") (SI 2015/983) |
| | | 1 Mar 2016 (exception noted above) (SI 2016/147) |
| | paras 61–63 | 1 Jun 2015 (SI 2015/983) |
| | para 64 | 1 Jun 2015 (except in so far as relates to Insolvency (Northern Ireland) Order 1989, SI 1989/2405 (NI 19), art 279A(1)(b): words "or 215A", art 279A(1)(d): words ", 193A or 195J") (SI 2015/983) |
| | | 1 Mar 2016 (exception noted above) (SI 2016/147) |
| | para 65 | *Never in force* (repealed) |

**Policing and Crime Act 2009 (c 26)**—*contd*

| | |
|---|---|
| para 66 | See paras 67–96 below |
| paras 67–73 | 1 Jun 2015 (SI 2015/983) |
| para 74 | 1 Mar 2016 (SI 2016/147) |
| paras 75–77 | 1 Jun 2015 (SI 2015/983) |
| para 78 | 1 Jun 2015 (except in so far as relates to Proceeds of Crime Act 2002, s 308(8A): words ", 193A, 195J, 195K, 195M or 195P") (SI 2015/983) |
| | 1 Mar 2016 (exception noted above) (SI 2016/147) |
| para 79 | 1 Jun 2015 (except in so far as relates to Proceeds of Crime Act 2002, s 417(2): words ", 193A, 195J, 195K, 195M or 195P" and "or 215A") (SI 2015/983) |
| | 1 Mar 2016 (exception noted above) (SI 2016/147) |
| para 80 | 1 Jun 2015 (except word "and" at the end of sub-para (2)(b), sub-para (2)(c), and in so far as relates to Proceeds of Crime Act 2002, s 418(3)(f): words "or 215D(2)(c)") (SI 2015/983) |
| | 1 Mar 2016 (exception noted above) (SI 2016/147) |
| para 81 | 1 Jun 2015 (except in so far as relates to Proceeds of Crime Act 2002, s 419(2)(aa): words ", 193A, 195J, 195K, 195M or 195P", s 419(2)(c): words "or 215A") (SI 2015/983) |
| | 1 Mar 2016 (exception noted above) (SI 2016/147) |
| para 82 | 1 Jun 2015 (except in so far as relates to Proceeds of Crime Act 2002, s 420(2): words ", 193A, 195J, 195K, 195M or 195P" and "or 215A") (SI 2015/983) |
| | 1 Mar 2016 (exception noted above) (SI 2016/147) |
| para 83 | 1 Jun 2015 (except word "and" at the end of sub-para (2)(b), sub-para (2)(c) and in so far as relates to Proceeds of Crime Act 2002, s 421(3)(f): words "or 215D(2)(c)") (SI 2015/983) |
| | 1 Mar 2016 (exception noted above) (SI 2016/147) |
| para 84 | 1 Jun 2015 (except in so far as relates to Proceeds of Crime Act 2002, s 422(2)(aa): words ", 193A, 195J, 195K, 195M or 195P", s (2)(b): words "or 215A") (SI 2015/983) |
| | 1 Mar 2016 (exception noted above) (SI 2016/147) |
| para 85 | 1 Jun 2015 (except in so far as relates to Proceeds of Crime Act 2002, s 423(2): words ", 193A, 195J, 195K, 195M or 195P" and "or 215A") (SI 2015/983) |
| | 1 Mar 2016 (exception noted above) (SI 2016/147) |
| para 86 | 1 Jun 2015 (except word "and" at the end of sub-para (2)(b), sub-para (2)(c) and in so far as relates to Proceeds of Crime Act 2002, s 424(3)(f): words "or 215D(2)(c)") (SI 2015/983) |
| | 1 Mar 2016 (exception noted above) (SI 2016/147) |
| para 87 | 1 Jun 2015 (except in so far as relates to Proceeds of Crime Act 2002, s 425(2)(aa): words ", 193A, 195J, 195K, 195M or 195P", s (2)(b): words "or 215A") (SI 2015/983) |
| | 1 Mar 2016 (exception noted above) (SI 2016/147) |
| para 88 | 1 Jun 2015 (except word "and" at the end of sub-para (3)(b), sub-para (3)(c) and in so far as relates to Proceeds of Crime Act 2002, s 426(2): words ", 193A, 195J, 195K, 195M or 195P" and "or 215A") (SI 2015/983) |
| | 1 Mar 2016 (exception noted above) (SI 2016/147) |
| para 89 | 1 Jun 2015 (except in so far as relates to Proceeds of Crime Act 2002, s 427(3)(aa): words ", 193A, 195J, 195K, 195M or 195P", s (3)(b): words "or 215A") (SI 2015/983) |
| | 1 Mar 2016 (exception noted above) (SI 2016/147) |
| para 90 | 1 Jun 2015 (except word "and" at the end of sub-para (3)(b), sub-para (3)(c) and in so far as relates to Proceeds of Crime Act 2002, s 428(2): words ", 193A, 195J, 195K, 195M or 195P" and "or 215A") (SI 2015/983) |
| | 1 Mar 2016 (exception noted above) (SI 2016/147) |
| para 91 | 1 Jun 2015 (except in so far as relates to Proceeds of Crime Act 2002, s 429(3)(aa): words ", 193A, 195J, 195K, 195M or 195P", s (3)(b): words "or 215A") (SI 2015/983) |

**Policing and Crime Act 2009 (c 26)**—*contd*

|  |  |  |
|---|---|---|
|  |  | 1 Mar 2016 (exception noted above) (SI 2016/147) |
|  | para 92 | 1 Jun 2015 (except word "and" at the end of sub-para (3)(b), sub-para (3)(c) and in so far as relates to Proceeds of Crime Act 2002, s 430(2): words ", 193A, 195J, 195K, 195M or 195P" and "or 215A") (SI 2015/983) |
|  |  | 1 Mar 2016 (exception noted above) (SI 2016/147) |
|  | para 93 | 1 Jun 2015 (except in so far as relates to Proceeds of Crime Act 2002, s 432(6A)(a): words ", 193A, 195J, 195K, 195M or 195P", sub-s (7)(c)) (SI 2015/983) |
|  |  | 1 Mar 2016 (exception noted above) (SI 2016/147) |
|  | para 94 | 1 Jun 2015 (except in so far as relates to Proceeds of Crime Act 2002, s 453A(5)(a): words "or 195C to 195F") (SI 2015/983) |
|  |  | 1 Mar 2016 (exception noted above) (SI 2016/147) |
|  | para 95 | 22 Nov 2014 (SI 2014/3101) |
|  | paras 96, 97 | 1 Mar 2016 (SI 2016/147) |
|  | para 98 | *Never in force* (repealed) |
|  | paras 99–108 | 1 Jun 2015 (SI 2015/983) |
|  | para 109 | 1 Jun 2015 (except in so far as relates to Proceeds of Crime Act 2002, s 302(1): words "or Northern Ireland") (SI 2015/983) |
|  |  | 1 Mar 2016 (exception noted above) (SI 2016/147) |
|  | paras 110, 111 | 1 Jun 2015 (SI 2015/983) |
|  | para 112 | 1 Mar 2016 (SI 2016/147) |
|  | para 113 | 1 Jun 2015 (SI 2015/983) |
|  | paras 114, 115 | 1 Jun 2015 (SI 2015/983)[4] |
|  | para 116 | *Never in force* (repealed) |
|  | para 117 | 25 Jan 2010 (SI 2009/3096) |
|  | para 118 | 10 Sep 2012 (SI 2012/2235) |
|  | paras 119, 120 | *Not yet in force* |
|  | para 121 | 1 Apr 2010 (SI 2010/507) |
|  | paras 122–134 | 12 Jan 2010 (s 116(6)(a)) |
| Sch 8 | Pt 1 | 19 Apr 2010 (SI 2010/999) |
|  | Pt 2 | 1 Apr 2010 (SI 2010/507) |
|  | Pt 3 | 29 Jan 2010 (SI 2010/125) |
|  | Pt 4 | 1 Jun 2015 (except in so far as relates to Proceeds of Crime Act 2002, ss 194, 235, Access to Justice (Northern Ireland) Order 2003, SI 2003/435 (NI 10), Serious Crime Act 2007, s 78(3), (4)) (SI 2015/983) |
|  |  | 1 Mar 2016 (otherwise) (SI 2016/147) |
|  | Pt 5 | 22 Nov 2014 (in so far as relates to Proceeds of Crime Act 2002, s 351(8), in so far as confers power to make subordinate legislation under that Act or for the Lord Advocate to issue guidance under s 127R thereof, and in so far as is necessary for the purpose of making regulations, rules of court, orders, codes of practice or issuing guidance) (SI 2014/3101) |
|  |  | 1 Jun 2015 (otherwise) (SI 2015/983)[4, 6] |
|  | Pt 6 | 25 Jan 2010 (SI 2009/3096)[1] |
|  | Pt 7 | 29 Jan 2010 (SI 2010/125) |
|  | Pt 8 | 29 Jan 2010 (SI 2010/125), repeals of or in— Police Act 1997; Criminal Justice Act 2003 |
|  |  | *Not yet in force*, repeals of or in— Criminal Justice and Police Act 2001; Serious Organised Crime and Police Act 2005; Safeguarding Vulnerable Groups Act 2006; Safeguarding Vulnerable Groups (Northern Ireland) Order 2007, SI 2007/1351 (NI 11) |
|  | Pt 9 | 25 Jan 2010 (SI 2010/52) |
|  | Pt 10 | *Not yet in force* |

### Policing and Crime Act 2009 (c 26)—*contd*

| | | |
|---|---|---|
| Pt 11 | 1 Apr 2010 (SI 2010/507) | |
| Pt 12 | 12 Nov 2009 (s 116(5)(c)) | |
| Pt 13 | 12 Jan 2010 (s 116(6)(a)) | |

[1] For transitional and saving provisions, see SI 2009/3096, art 4

[2] For transitional and saving provisions, see SI 2010/507, art 6

[3] For transitional and saving provisions, see SI 2010/722, arts 4–12

[4] For transitional and saving provisions, see SI 2015/983, arts 4–6

[5] For transitional provisions and savings, see SI 2016/147, arts 4, 5

[6] Note that SI 2016/147 also purports to bring these provisions into force for remaining purposes on 1 Mar 2016

---

### Political Parties and Elections Act 2009 (c 12)

*RA:* 21 Jul 2009

*Commencement provisions:* s 43; Political Parties and Elections Act 2009 (Commencement No 1 and Transitional Provisions) Order 2009, SI 2009/2395; Political Parties and Elections Act 2009 (Commencement No 2 and Transitional Provisions) Order 2009, SI 2009/3084; Political Parties and Elections Act 2009 (Commencement No 3 and Saving Provision) Order 2010, SI 2010/969; Political Parties and Elections Act 2009 (Commencement No 4) Order 2010, SI 2010/2409; Political Parties and Elections Act 2009 (Commencement No 5 and Saving Provisions) Order 2010, SI 2010/2866; Political Parties and Elections Act 2009 (Commencement No 6) Order 2013, SI 2013/99

| | | |
|---|---|---|
| 1 | (1) | 21 Jul 2009 (s 43(5)(a)) |
| | (2) | 1 Dec 2010 (SI 2010/2866) |
| | (3) | 21 Jul 2009 (s 43(5)(a)) |
| 2, 3 | | 1 Dec 2010 (SI 2010/2866)[4] |
| 4, 5 | | 21 Jul 2009 (s 43(5)(b)) |
| 6 | | 1 Oct 2010 (SI 2010/2409) |
| 7 | | 21 Jul 2009 (s 43(5)(b)) |
| 8 | | 1 Jan 2011 (SI 2010/2866) |
| 9 | (1)–(7) | *Not yet in force* |
| | (8) | See Sch 3 below |
| | (9)–(11) | *Not yet in force* |
| 10 | (1)–(7) | *Not yet in force* |
| | (8) | See Sch 4 below |
| 11 | | *Not yet in force* |
| 12–18 | | 1 Jan 2010 (SI 2009/3084)[2] |
| 19 | | 21 Jul 2009 (s 43(5)(c)) |
| 20 | | 1 Jan 2010 (SI 2009/3084) |
| 21 | | 25 Nov 2009 (SI 2009/3084) |
| 22 | | 21 Jul 2009 (s 43(5)(d)) |
| 23, 24 | | 4 Sep 2009 (SI 2009/2395)[1] |
| 25 | | 26 Mar 2010 (SI 2010/969)[3] |
| 26 | | 21 Jul 2009 (s 43(5)(e)) |
| 27 | (1), (2) | 22 Jan 2013 (SI 2013/99) |
| | (3) | 1 Jan 2014 (SI 2013/99) |
| | (4) | 22 Jan 2013 (SI 2013/99) |
| 28–30 | | *Never in force* (repealed) |
| 31 | (1)–(7) | *Never in force* (repealed) |
| | (8) | 1 Jan 2011 (SI 2010/2866) |
| | (9)–(11) | *Never in force* (repealed) |
| 32 | (1)–(5) | *Never in force* (repealed) |
| | (6) | 21 Jul 2009 (s 43(5)(f)) |
| | (7)–(11) | *Never in force* (repealed) |
| 33, 34 | | *Never in force* (repealed) |

**Political Parties and Elections Act 2009 (c 12)**—*contd*

| | | |
|---|---|---|
| 35–37 | | 1 Jan 2011 (SI 2010/2866) |
| 38 | | 21 Jul 2009 (s 43(5)(g)) |
| 39 | | See Schs 6, 7 below |
| 40–44 | | 21 Jul 2009 (s 43(5)(i)) |
| Schs 1, 2 | | 1 Dec 2010 (SI 2010/2866)[4] |
| Schs 3, 4 | | *Not yet in force* |
| Sch 5 | | 21 Jul 2009 (s 43(5)(c)) |
| Sch 6 | paras 1–5 | 4 Sep 2009 (SI 2009/2395)[1] |
| | paras 6, 7 | 25 Nov 2009 (SI 2009/3084) |
| | para 8 | 4 Sep 2009 (SI 2009/2395)[1] |
| | paras 9–11 | 21 Jul 2009 (s 43(5)(b)) |
| | paras 12–21 | *Not yet in force* |
| | paras 22, 23 | 1 Dec 2010 (SI 2010/2866) |
| | para 24 | 1 Jan 2010 (SI 2009/3084) |
| | paras 25, 26 | 1 Dec 2010 (SI 2010/2866) |
| | para 27 | 21 Jul 2009 (s 43(5)(b)) |
| | paras 28–31 | *Not yet in force* |
| Sch 7 | | 21 Jul 2009 (repeals in Political Parties, Elections and Referendums Act 2000, Sch 1) (s 43(5)(b)) |
| | | 4 Sep 2009 (repeals in Representation of the People Act 1983, s 10A(2), Sch 1) (SI 2009/2395)[1] |
| | | 25 Nov 2009 (repeal in Representation of the People Act 1983, s 76A) (SI 2009/3084) |
| | | 1 Jan 2010 (repeals in Political Parties, Elections and Referendums Act 2000, ss 47, 65, 71S, 149, Sch 7, para 12, Sch 7A) (SI 2009/3084) |
| | | 26 Mar 2010 (repeal in Representation of the People Act 1983, s 63) (SI 2010/969)[3] |
| | | 1 Dec 2010 (repeals of or in Political Parties, Elections and Referendums Act 2000, s 145, Sch 20) (SI 2010/2866)[4] |
| | | 1 Jan 2011 (repeals of or in Political Parties, Elections and Referendums Act 2000, s 13) (SI 2010/2866) |
| | | *Not yet in force*, repeals of or in— |
| | | Representation of the People Act 1983, ss 10ZB, 10A(1A), 13A, Sch 2; |
| | | Political Parties, Elections and Referendums Act 2000, s 54, Sch 7, para 6, Schs 11, 15; |
| | | Electoral Fraud (Northern Ireland) Act 2002; |
| | | Northern Ireland (Miscellaneous Provisions) Act 2006 |

[1]    For transitional provisions, see SI 2009/2395, art 3

[2]    For transitional provisions, see SI 2009/3084, arts 5, 6

[3]    For a saving, see SI 2010/969, art 3

[4]    For saving provisions, see SI 2010/2866, arts 5, 6

---

**Saving Gateway Accounts Act 2009 (c 8)**

*RA:* 2 Jul 2009

*Commencement provisions*: s 31; Saving Gateway Accounts Act 2009 (Commencement No 1) Order 2009, SI 2009/3332; Saving Gateway Accounts Act 2009 (Commencement No 2) Order 2010, SI 2010/921 (revoked by SI 2010/1640)

| | | |
|---|---|---|
| 1–3 | | *Never in force (repealed)*[1] |
| 4 | (1) | 1 Jan 2010 (SI 2009/3332) |
| | (2)–(5) | *Never in force (repealed)*[1] |
| 5 | (1) | 1 Jan 2010 (SI 2009/3332) |
| | (2) | *Never in force (repealed)*[1] |

**Saving Gateway Accounts Act 2009 (c 8)**—*contd*

| | | |
|---|---|---|
| 6–17 | | *Never in force* (repealed)[1] |
| 18 | | 1 Jan 2010 (SI 2009/3332) |
| 19–22 | | *Never in force* (repealed)[1] |
| 23 | (1)(a) | 1 Jan 2010 (SI 2009/3332) |
| | (1)(b)–(e), (2)–(4) | *Never in force* (repealed)[1] |
| 24, 25 | | 1 Jan 2010 (in so far as they apply to an appeal under s 23(1)(a)) (SI 2009/3332) |
| | | *Never in force* (repealed)[1] |
| 26–28 | | *Never in force* (repealed)[1] |
| 29 | | 2 Jul 2009 (RA) |
| 30 | | *Never in force* (repealed)[1] |
| 31–33 | | 2 Jul 2009 (RA) |

[1]   These provisions were previously brought into force as from 1 Jul 2010 by SI 2010/921 (revoked)

---

## Scottish Local Government (Elections) Act 2009 (asp 10)

*RA:* 21 Jul 2009

*Commencement provisions:* s 3(2), (3); Scottish Local Government (Elections) Act 2009 (Commencement) Order 2010, SI 2010/132

| | |
|---|---|
| 1, 2 | 30 Apr 2010 (SI 2010/132) |
| 3 | 21 Jul 2009 (s 3(2)) |
| Schedule | 30 Apr 2010 (SI 2010/132) |

## Scottish Parliamentary Pensions Act 2009 (asp 1)

*RA:* 25 Feb 2009

*Commencement provisions:* s 5

| | | |
|---|---|---|
| 1 | (1) | See Sch 1 below |
| | (2) | 1 Sep 2009 (s 5(3)) |
| | (3) | See Sch 3 below |
| 2 | | See Sch 2 below |
| 3 | | 25 Feb 2009 (s 5(2)) |
| 4–6 | | 25 Feb 2009 (s 5(1)) |
| Sch 1 | rr 1–3 | 1 Sep 2009 (s 5(3)) |
| | r 4 | 25 Feb 2009 (s 5(1)) |
| | rr 5–7 | 1 Sep 2009 (s 5(3)) |
| | rr 8–11 | 25 Feb 2009 (s 5(1)) |
| | rr 12–110 | 1 Sep 2009 (s 5(3)) |
| Sch 2 | | 1 Sep 2009 (s 5(3)) |
| Sch 3 | para 1 | 25 Feb 2009 (s 5(1)) |
| | paras 2, 3 | 1 Sep 2009 (s 5(3)) |
| | para 4 | 25 Feb 2009 (s 5(1)) |
| | paras 5–8 | 1 Sep 2009 (s 5(3)) |
| | para 9 | 25 Feb 2009 (s 5(1)) |
| | paras 10–23 | 1 Sep 2009 (s 5(3)) |

---

## Sexual Offences (Scotland) Act 2009 (asp 9)

*RA:* 14 Jul 2009

*Commencement provisions:* s 62(2); Sexual Offences (Scotland) Act 2009 (Commencement No 1) and the Criminal Justice and Licensing (Scotland) Act 2010 (Commencement No 4) Order 2010, SSI 2010/357; Sexual Offences (Scotland) Act 2009 (Commencement No 2) Order 2013, SSI 2013/341

**Sexual Offences (Scotland) Act 2009 (asp 9)**—*contd*

| | | |
|---|---|---|
| 1 | (1)–(3) | 1 Dec 2010 (SSI 2010/357) |
| | (4) | 14 Jul 2009 (s 62(2)) |
| 2–16 | | 1 Dec 2010 (SSI 2010/357) |
| 17 | (1), (2) | 1 Dec 2010 (SSI 2010/357) |
| | (3) | 14 Jul 2009 (s 62(2)) |
| 18–51 | | 1 Dec 2010 (SSI 2010/357) |
| 52 | | 16 Dec 2013 (SSI 2013/341) |
| 53 | (1) | 1 Dec 2010 (SSI 2010/357) |
| | (2)(a)–(d) | 16 Dec 2013 (SSI 2013/341) |
| | (2)(e)–(g) | 1 Dec 2010 (SSI 2010/357) |
| | (3)–(5) | 1 Dec 2010 (SSI 2010/357) |
| 54–57 | | 1 Dec 2010 (SSI 2010/357) |
| 58–60 | | 14 Jul 2009 (s 62(2)) |
| 61 | (1) | See Sch 5 below |
| | (2) | See Sch 6 below |
| 62 | | 14 Jul 2009 (s 62(2)) |
| Schs 1–6 | | 1 Dec 2010 (SSI 2010/357) |

**Welfare Reform Act 2009 (c 24)**

*RA:* 12 Nov 2009

*Commencement provisions*: s 61; Welfare Reform Act 2009 (Commencement No 1) Order 2010, SI 2010/45; Welfare Reform Act 2009 (Commencement No 2 and Transitory Provision) Order 2010, SI 2010/293; Welfare Reform Act 2009 (Commencement No 3) Order 2010, SI 2010/2377; Welfare Reform Act 2009 (Commencement No 4) Order 2011, SI 2011/682; Welfare Reform Act 2009 (Commencement No 5) Order 2011, SI 2011/2427; Welfare Reform Act 2009 (Commencement No 6) Order 2011, SI 2011/2857; Welfare Reform Act 2009 (Commencement No 7) Order 2012, SI 2012/68; Welfare Reform Act 2009 (Commencement No 8) Order 2012, SI 2012/1256; Child Maintenance and Other Payments Act 2008 (Commencement No 9) and the Welfare Reform Act 2009 (Commencement No 9) Order 2012, SI 2012/2523; Welfare Reform Act 2009 (Commencement No 10) Order 2016, SI 2016/913

| | | |
|---|---|---|
| 1, 2 | | 12 Nov 2009 (s 61(1)) |
| 3 | (1) | 21 May 2012 (for the purpose of inserting the Social Security Contributions and Benefits Act 1992, s 124(1A)) (SI 2012/1256) |
| | | *Not yet in force* (in so far as inserts s 124(1B) thereof) |
| | (2) | 6 Oct 2011 (for the purpose of conferring power to make regulations under the Social Security Administration Act 1992, s 2A(2B)) (SI 2011/2427) |
| | | 31 Oct 2011 (otherwise) (SI 2011/2427) |
| | (3) | 31 Oct 2011 (SI 2011/2427) |
| | (4) | *Not yet in force* (repealed in part) |
| | (5) | 6 Oct 2011 (for the purpose of conferring power to make regulations under the Welfare Reform Act 2007, s 24(3B)) (SI 2011/2427) |
| | | 31 Oct 2011 (otherwise) (SI 2011/2427) |
| 4 | (1)–(3) | *Not yet in force* (repealed in part) |
| | (4) | See Sch 1 below |
| 5–7 | | *Not yet in force* (s 5 repealed in part) |
| 8 | | 12 Nov 2009 (s 61(1)) |
| 9 | | *Not yet in force* (repealed in part) |
| 10 | | 10 Feb 2010 (SI 2010/293) |
| 11 | | 12 Nov 2009 (s 61(1)) |
| 12 | (1) | 1 Oct 2010 (SI 2010/2377) |
| | (2) | 1 Nov 2010 (SI 2010/2377) |
| | (3) | 1 Oct 2010 (SI 2010/2377) |
| | (4) | 1 Nov 2010 (SI 2010/2377) |

**Welfare Reform Act 2009 (c 24)**—*contd*

|  |  |  |
|---|---|---|
| | (5) | 29 Nov 2011 (in so far as inserts Jobseekers Act 1995, s 2(3B)(a), (3C)) (SI 2011/2857) |
| | | *Not yet in force* (in so far as inserts s 2(3B)(b) thereof) |
| | (6) | 1 Nov 2010 (SI 2010/2377) |
| 13 | (1) | 1 Oct 2010 (SI 2010/2377) |
| | (2), (3) | 1 Nov 2010 (SI 2010/2377) |
| | (4) | 1 Oct 2010 (for the purpose of conferring power to make regulations) (SI 2010/2377) |
| | | 1 Nov 2010 (otherwise) (SI 2010/2377) |
| | (5)(a), (b) | 29 Nov 2011 (SI 2011/2857) |
| | (5)(c) | *Not yet in force* |
| 14 | | 11 Apr 2010 (for the purpose of making regulations) (SI 2010/293) |
| | | 15 Oct 2010 (for the purposes of assessing claims and making decisions on eligibility) (SI 2010/293) |
| | | 11 Apr 2011 (otherwise) (SI 2010/293) |
| 15 | | 12 Jan 2010 (s 61(2)) |
| 16–22 | | *Never in force* (repealed) |
| 23 | | 12 Nov 2009 (s 61(1)) |
| 24 | | 12 Jan 2010 (for the purposes of making regulations) (SI 2010/45) |
| | | 1 Apr 2010 (otherwise) (SI 2010/45) |
| 25 | | *Never in force* (repealed) |
| 26 | | 22 Mar 2010 (SI 2010/293)[1] |
| 27, 28 | | 12 Nov 2009 (s 61(1)) |
| 29 | | 19 Jan 2012 (SI 2012/68) |
| 30, 31 | | *Not yet in force* |
| 32 | (1) | See sub-ss (2)–(5) below |
| | (2) | 9 Mar 2011 (so far as it confers power to make regulations under the Jobseekers Act 1995, s 20E(3) in relation to the functions of the Secretary of State under regulations under s 17A of that Act; and so far as it inserts s 20E(4)–(12) of that Act, in so far as they apply in connection with or for the purposes of such regulations) (SI 2011/682) |
| | | *Not yet in force* (otherwise) (repealed in part) |
| | (3)–(5) | *Not yet in force* (sub-ss (4), (5) repealed) |
| 33 | | 10 Feb 2010 (for the purpose of making regulations) (SI 2010/293) |
| | | 6 Apr 2010 (otherwise) (SI 2010/293)[2] |
| 34 | | 12 Jan 2010 (s 61(2)) |
| 35 | | 10 Feb 2010 (SI 2010/293) |
| 36 | | *Not yet in force* (repealed in part) |
| 37 | | 12 Nov 2009 (s 61(1)) |
| 38–50 | | 12 Jan 2010 (s 61(2)) |
| 51 | (1)–(5) | *Not yet in force* |
| | (6) | See Sch 5 below |
| 52, 53 | | *Not yet in force* |
| 54 | | 8 Oct 2012 (SI 2012/2523) |
| 55 | (1) | See sub-ss (2), (3) below |
| | (2) | 8 Oct 2012 (SI 2012/2523) |
| | (3) | 14 Jan 2010 (SI 2010/45) |
| 56 | | See Sch 6 below |
| 57 | | 12 Nov 2009 (s 61(1)) |
| 58 | (1) | See Sch 7 below |
| | (2), (3) | 12 Jan 2010 (s 61(2)) |
| 59–62 | | 12 Nov 2009 (s 61(1)) |
| Sch 1 | | *Never in force* (repealed) |
| Sch 2 | | *Not yet in force* |
| Sch 3 | | 12 Nov 2009 (s 61(1)) |
| Sch 4 | | 12 Jan 2010 (for the purposes of making regulations) (SI 2010/45) |
| | | 1 Apr 2010 (otherwise) (SI 2010/45) |
| Sch 5 | | *Not yet in force* |

**Welfare Reform Act 2009 (c 24)**—*contd*

| | | |
|---|---|---|
| Sch 6 | para 1 | 19 Sep 2016 (SI 2016/913) |
| | paras 2–4 | *Not yet in force* |
| | paras 5–9 | 28 May 2012 (SI 2012/1256) |
| | paras 10, 11, 12(1)–(3) | *Not yet in force* |
| | para 12(4) | 28 May 2012 (SI 2012/1256) |
| | para 13 | *Not yet in force* |
| | para 14 | 28 May 2012 (SI 2012/1256) |
| | paras 15, 16 | *Not yet in force* |
| | para 17 | 19 Sep 2016 (SI 2016/913) |
| | paras 18, 19 | *Not yet in force* |
| | para 20 | 28 May 2012 (SI 2012/1256) |
| | paras 21–26 | *Not yet in force* |
| Sch 7 | Pt 1 | *Not yet in force* |
| | Pt 2 | 12 Jan 2010 (s 61(2)), repeals and revocations of or in— |

     Social Security Contributions and Benefits Act 1992, ss 20, 63, 82, 90, 114, Sch 4;

     Jobseekers Act 1995, Sch 2, para 24;

     Welfare Reform and Pensions Act 1999;

     Tax Credits Act 2002;

     Regulatory Reform (Carer's Allowance) Order 2002, SI 2002/1457;

     Civil Partnership Act 2004;

     Child Benefit Act 2005

*Not yet in force*, repeals and revocations of or in—

     Social Security Contributions and Benefits Act 1992, ss 88, 89, 91, 92;

     Social Security (Incapacity for Work) Act 1994;

     Jobseekers Act 1995, Sch 2, para 27;

     Pensions Act 2004 (PPF Payments and FAS Payments) (Consequential Provisions) Order 2006, SI 2006/343;

     Pensions Act 2007;

     Welfare Reform Act 2007

Pt 3    22 Mar 2010 (SI 2010/293)[1], repeals of or in—

     Social Security Administration Act 1992, s 170(5), para (af) of definitions "the relevant enactments" and "the relevant Northern Ireland enactments";

     Social Security Act 1998, Sch 3;

     Child Support, Pensions and Social Security Act 2000;

     Criminal Justice and Court Services Act 2000;

     Social Security Fraud Act 2001, ss 8, 12;

     Criminal Justice Act 2003;

     Welfare Reform Act 2007, Sch 3, para 20;

     Criminal Justice and Immigration Act 2008

1 Apr 2010 (SI 2010/293), repeals of or in—

     Social Security Fraud Act 2001, ss 7, 13;

     State Pension Credit Act 2002;

     Welfare Reform Act 2007, Sch 3, para 23

*Not yet in force*, repeals and revocations of or in—

     Social Security Administration Act 1992 (except as noted above);

     Jobseekers Act 1995;

     Employment Rights Act 1996;

     Social Security Act 1998, Schs 2, 7;

     Welfare Reform and Pensions Act 1999;

     Scotland Act 1998 (Transfer of Functions to Scottish Ministers etc) Order 2000, SI 2000/1563;

     Employment Act 2002;

     Civil Partnership Act 2004;

     Welfare Reform Act 2007, Sch 3, para 12;

**Welfare Reform Act 2009 (c 24)**—*contd*

Transfer of Tribunal Functions Order 2008, SI 2008/2833

Pts 4, 5         *Not yet in force*

[1] In the case of a person who immediately before 22 Mar 2010 is subject to a restriction under section 62 or 63 of the Child Support, Pensions and Social Security Act 2000, the day appointed for the coming into force of this provision is the first day of the first benefit week to commence for that person on or after 22 Mar 2010

[2] For a transitory provision, see SI 2010/293, art 3

# 2010 Acts

## Academies Act 2010 (c 32)

*RA:* 27 Jul 2010

*Commencement provisions:* s 19; Academies Act 2010 (Commencement and Transitional Provisions) Order 2010, SI 2010/1937, as amended by SI 2010/3037; Academies Act 2010 (Commencement No 2) Order 2011, SI 2011/1149

| | | |
|---|---|---|
| 1 | | 29 Jul 2010 (SI 2010/1937) |
| 2 | (1)–(4) | 29 Jul 2010 (SI 2010/1937) |
| | (5), (6) | 1 Sep 2010 (SI 2010/1937) |
| 3–6 | | 29 Jul 2010 (SI 2010/1937)[1] |
| 7 | | 1 Sep 2010 (SI 2010/1937) |
| 8–11 | | 29 Jul 2010 (SI 2010/1937) |
| 12 | (1)–(3) | 29 Jul 2010 (SI 2010/1937) |
| | (4) | 1 Aug 2011 (SI 2011/1149) |
| 13 | | See Sch 1 below |
| 14 | | See Sch 2 below |
| 15–20 | | 27 Jul 2010 (s 19(1)) |
| Sch 1 | | 29 Jul 2010 (SI 2010/1937) |
| Sch 2 | paras 1–9 | 29 Jul 2010 (SI 2010/1937) |
| | para 10 | 1 Sep 2010 (in relation to the proprietor of an Academy opening on or after 1 Sep 2010) (SI 2010/1937) |
| | | 1 Jan 2011 (otherwise) (SI 2010/1937) |
| | paras 11–26 | 29 Jul 2010 (SI 2010/1937) |

[1] For transitional provisions, see SI 2010/1937, arts 5, 6

## Alcohol etc (Scotland) Act 2010 (asp 18)

*RA:* 15 Dec 2010

*Commencement provisions:* s 18(1), (2); Alcohol etc (Scotland) Act 2010 (Commencement) Order 2011, SSI 2011/149

| | | |
|---|---|---|
| 1 | | *Not yet in force* |
| 2–8 | | 1 Oct 2011 (SSI 2011/149) |
| 9 | | 1 Oct 2011 (in respect of licensing policy statements or supplementary policy statements published on or after 1 Oct 2011) (SSI 2011/149) |
| 10 | | 1 Oct 2011 (SSI 2011/149) |
| 11 | (1) | 1 Oct 2011 (SSI 2011/149) |
| | (2)(a) | 1 Oct 2011 (in respect of licensing policy statements or supplementary policy statements published on or after 1 Oct 2011) (SSI 2011/149) |
| | (2)(b) | 1 Oct 2011 (SSI 2011/149) |
| | (3) | 1 Oct 2011 (in respect of licensing policy statements or supplementary policy statements published on or after 1 Oct 2011) (SSI 2011/149) |

**Alcohol etc (Scotland) Act 2010 (asp 18)**—*contd*

|  | (4) | 1 Oct 2011 (in respect of premises licence applications received on or after 1 Oct 2011) (SSI 2011/149) |
| --- | --- | --- |
|  | (5)–(7) | 1 Oct 2011 (SSI 2011/149) |
| 12 |  | 1 Apr 2012 (SSI 2011/149) |
| 13–16 |  | 1 Oct 2011 (SSI 2011/149) |
| 17, 18 |  | 15 Dec 2010 (RA) |

**Anti-Slavery Day Act 2010 (c 14)**

*RA:* 8 Apr 2010

Whole Act in force 8 Apr 2010 (RA)

**Appropriation Act 2010 (c 5)**

*RA:* 18 Mar 2010

Whole Act in force 18 Mar 2010 (RA)

**Appropriation (No 2) Act 2010 (c 12)**

*RA:* 8 Apr 2010

Whole Act in force 8 Apr 2010 (RA)

**Appropriation (No 3) Act 2010 (c 30)**

*RA:* 27 Jul 2010

Whole Act in force 27 Jul 2010 (RA)

**Arbitration (Scotland) Act 2010 (asp 1)**

*RA:* 5 Jan 2010

*Commencement provisions:* s 35; Arbitration (Scotland) Act 2010 (Commencement No 1 and Transitional Provisions) Order 2010, SSI 2010/195[1]

| 1 | 7 Jun 2010 (except for the purposes of "statutory arbitration", as defined by s 16 of this Act) (SSI 2010/195) |
| --- | --- |
|  | *Not yet in force* (exception noted above) |
| 2 | 5 Jan 2010 (s 35(1)) |
| 3–6 | 7 Jun 2010 (except for the purposes of "statutory arbitration", as defined by s 16 of this Act) (SSI 2010/195) |
|  | *Not yet in force* (exception noted above) |
| 7 | See Sch 1 below |
| 8–16 | 7 Jun 2010 (except for the purposes of "statutory arbitration", as defined by s 16 of this Act) (SSI 2010/195) |
|  | *Not yet in force* (exception noted above) |
| 17 | 7 Jun 2010 (SSI 2010/195) |
| 18–28 | 7 Jun 2010 (except for the purposes of "statutory arbitration", as defined by s 16 of this Act) (SSI 2010/195) |
|  | *Not yet in force* (exception noted above) |
| 29 | See Sch 2 below |
| 30 | 7 Jun 2010 (except for the purposes of "statutory arbitration", as defined by s 16 of this Act) (SSI 2010/195) |
|  | *Not yet in force* (exception noted above) |
| 31–35 | 5 Jan 2010 (s 35(1)) |

## Arbitration (Scotland) Act 2010 (asp 1)—*contd*

| | |
|---|---|
| 36 | 7 Jun 2010 (except for the purposes of "statutory arbitration", as defined by s 16 of this Act) (SSI 2010/195) |
| | *Not yet in force* (exception noted above) |
| 37 | 5 Jan 2010 (s 35(1)) |
| Schs 1, 2 | 7 Jun 2010 (except for the purposes of "statutory arbitration", as defined by s 16 of this Act) (SSI 2010/195) |
| | *Not yet in force* (exception noted above) |

[1] For transitional provisions and savings, see SSI 2010/195, arts 3–6

## Bribery Act 2010 (c 23)

*RA:* 8 Apr 2010

*Commencement provisions:* s 19; Bribery Act 2010 (Commencement) Order 2011, SI 2011/1418

| | | |
|---|---|---|
| 1–15 | | 1 Jul 2011 (SI 2011/1418) |
| 16 | | 8 Apr 2010 (s 19(2)) |
| 17 | (1)–(3) | 1 Jul 2011 (SI 2011/1418) |
| | (4)–(10) | 8 Apr 2010 (s 19(2)) |
| 18 | | 8 Apr 2010 (s 19(2)) |
| 19 | (1)–(4) | 8 Apr 2010 (s 19(2)) |
| | (5)–(7) | 1 Jul 2011 (SI 2011/1418) |
| 20 | | 8 Apr 2010 (s 19(2)) |
| Schs 1, 2 | | 1 Jul 2011 (SI 2011/1418) |

## Budget (Scotland) Act 2010 (asp 4)

*RA:* 10 Mar 2010

Whole Act in force 10 Mar 2010 (RA)

## Carers Strategies (Wales) Measure 2010 (nawm 5)

*Passed by the National Assembly for Wales:* 21 Sep 2010

*Approved by Her Majesty in Council:* 11 Nov 2010

*Commencement provisions:* s 11; Carers Strategies (Wales) Measure 2010 (Commencement) Order 2011, SI 2011/2842

| | | |
|---|---|---|
| 1 | | 24 Nov 2011 (SI 2011/2842) |
| 2 | (1) | 24 Nov 2011 (SI 2011/2842) |
| | (2) | 1 Jan 2012 (SI 2011/2842) |
| | (3)–(5) | 24 Nov 2011 (SI 2011/2842) |
| 3 | (1), (2) | 24 Nov 2011 (SI 2011/2842) |
| | (3) | 1 Jan 2012 (SI 2011/2842) |
| 4, 5 | | 24 Nov 2011 (SI 2011/2842) |
| 6 | (1)–(3) | 1 Jan 2012 (SI 2011/2842) |
| | (4) | 24 Nov 2011 (SI 2011/2842) |
| 7 | | 1 Jan 2012 (SI 2011/2842) |
| 8 | | 24 Nov 2011 (SI 2011/2842) |
| 9 | | 1 Jan 2012 (SI 2011/2842) |
| 10–12 | | 24 Nov 2011 (SI 2011/2842) |

## Child Poverty Act 2010 (c 9)

*RA:* 25 Mar 2010

*Commencement provisions:* s 31

| | |
|---|---|
| 1–18 | 25 Mar 2010 (s 31(1)) |
| 19–26 | 25 May 2010 (s 31(2)) |
| 27–32 | 25 Mar 2010 (s 31(1)) |
| Schs 1, 2 | 25 Mar 2010 (s 31(1)) |

## Children and Families (Wales) Measure 2010 (nawm 1)

*Passed by the National Assembly for Wales:* 10 Nov 2009

*Approved by Her Majesty in Council:* 10 Feb 2010

*Commencement provisions:* s 75; Children and Families (Wales) Measure 2010 (Commencement) Order 2010, SI 2010/1699; Children and Families (Wales) Measure 2010 (Commencement No 2, Savings and Transitional Provisions) Order 2010, SI 2010/2582, as amended by SI 2011/577; Children and Families (Wales) Measure 2010 (Commencement No 3 and Savings Provision) Order 2010, SI 2010/2994; Children and Families (Wales) Measure 2010 (Commencement No 4) Order 2012, SI 2012/191; Children and Families (Wales) Measure 2010 (Commencement No 5) Order 2012, SI 2012/2453; Children and Families (Wales) Measure 2010 (Commencement No 6) Order 2013, SI 2013/18; Children and Families (Wales) Measure 2010 (Commencement No 7) Order 2013, SI 2013/1830; Children and Families (Wales) Measure 2010 (Commencement No 8) Order 2014, SI 2014/373; Children and Families (Wales) Measure 2010 (Commencement No 9) Order 2014, SI 2014/1606

| | | |
|---|---|---|
| 1 | | 10 Apr 2010 (s 75(1)) |
| 2 | | 10 Apr 2010 (in so far as it applies to the Welsh Ministers) (s 75(1)) |
| | | 10 Jan 2011 (in so far as it applies to the Welsh authorities) (SI 2010/2994) |
| 3 | | 10 Apr 2010 (s 75(1)) |
| 4 | | 10 Jan 2011 (SI 2010/2994)[3] |
| 5, 6 | | 10 Jan 2011 (SI 2010/2994) |
| 7–10 | | *Not yet in force* |
| 11 | (1), (2) | 1 Nov 2012 (SI 2012/2453) |
| | (3), (4) | 1 Jul 2014 (SI 2014/1606) |
| | (5), (6) | 1 Nov 2012 (SI 2012/2453) |
| 12 | | 31 Jan 2012 (SI 2012/191) |
| 13–16 | | *Not yet in force* |
| 17, 18 | | 10 Jan 2011 (SI 2010/2994) |
| 19–56 | | 1 Apr 2011 (SI 2010/2582)[2] |
| 57 | | 1 Sep 2010 (in relation to specified local authority areas[1]) (SI 2010/1699) |
| | | 28 Feb 2012 (in relation to specified local authority areas[4]) (SI 2012/191) |
| | | 31 Mar 2012 (in relation to specified local authority areas[5]) (SI 2012/191) |
| | | 1 Feb 2013 (in relation to specified local authority areas[6]) (SI 2013/18) |
| | | 19 Jul 2013 (in relation to specified local authority areas[7]) (SI 2013/1830) |
| | | 28 Feb 2014 (in relation to specified local authority areas[8]) (SI 2014/373) |
| 58 | (1) | 1 Sep 2010 (in relation to specified local authority areas[1]) (SI 2010/1699) |
| | | 28 Feb 2012 (in relation to specified local authority areas[4]) (SI 2012/191) |
| | | 31 Mar 2012 (in relation to specified local authority areas[5]) (SI 2012/191) |

**Children and Families (Wales) Measure 2010 (nawm 1)**—*contd*

|  |  |  |
|---|---|---|
|  | 1 Feb 2013 (in relation to specified local authority areas[6]) (SI 2013/18) |
|  | 19 Jul 2013 (in relation to specified local authority areas[7]) (SI 2013/1830) |
|  | 28 Feb 2014 (in relation to specified local authority areas[8]) (SI 2014/373) |
| (2) | 1 Sep 2010 (in relation to specified local authority areas[1]) (SI 2010/1699) |
|  | 27 Jan 2012 (otherwise) (SI 2012/191) |
| (3)–(5), (6)(a) | 1 Sep 2010 (in relation to specified local authority areas[1]) (SI 2010/1699) |
|  | 28 Feb 2012 (in relation to specified local authority areas[4]) (SI 2012/191) |
|  | 31 Mar 2012 (in relation to specified local authority areas[5]) (SI 2012/191) |
|  | 1 Feb 2013 (in relation to specified local authority areas[6]) (SI 2013/18) |
|  | 19 Jul 2013 (in relation to specified local authority areas[7]) (SI 2013/1830) |
|  | 28 Feb 2014 (in relation to specified local authority areas[8]) (SI 2014/373) |
| (6)(b)–(d) | *Not yet in force* |
| (7)–(9) | 1 Sep 2010 (in relation to specified local authority areas[1]) (SI 2010/1699) |
|  | 28 Feb 2012 (in relation to specified local authority areas[4]) (SI 2012/191) |
|  | 31 Mar 2012 (in relation to specified local authority areas[5]) (SI 2012/191) |
|  | 1 Feb 2013 (in relation to specified local authority areas[6]) (SI 2013/18) |
|  | 19 Jul 2013 (in relation to specified local authority areas[7]) (SI 2013/1830) |
|  | 28 Feb 2014 (in relation to specified local authority areas[8]) (SI 2014/373) |
| (10) | 1 Sep 2010 (in relation to specified local authority areas[1]) (SI 2010/1699) |
|  | 28 Feb 2012 (in relation to specified local authority areas[4]) (SI 2012/191) |
|  | 31 Mar 2012 (in relation to specified local authority areas[5]) (SI 2012/191) |
|  | 1 Feb 2013 (in relation to specified local authority areas[6]) (SI 2013/18) |
|  | 19 Jul 2013 (otherwise) (SI 2013/1830) |
| (11)–(14) | 1 Sep 2010 (in relation to specified local authority areas[1]) (SI 2010/1699) |
|  | 28 Feb 2012 (in relation to specified local authority areas[4]) (SI 2012/191) |
|  | 31 Mar 2012 (in relation to specified local authority areas[5]) (SI 2012/191) |
|  | 1 Feb 2013 (in relation to specified local authority areas[6]) (SI 2013/18) |
|  | 19 Jul 2013 (in relation to specified local authority areas[7]) (SI 2013/1830) |
|  | 28 Feb 2014 (in relation to specified local authority areas[8]) (SI 2014/373) |
| 59 | (1) | 1 Sep 2010 (in relation to specified local authority areas[1]) (SI 2010/1699) |
|  | 28 Feb 2012 (in relation to specified local authority areas[4]) (SI 2012/191) |

**Children and Families (Wales) Measure 2010 (nawm 1)**—*contd*

|   |   |   |
|---|---|---|
|   |   | 31 Mar 2012 (in relation to specified local authority areas[5]) (SI 2012/191) |
|   |   | 1 Feb 2013 (in relation to specified local authority areas[6]) (SI 2013/18) |
|   |   | 19 Jul 2013 (in relation to specified local authority areas[7]) (SI 2013/1830) |
|   |   | 28 Feb 2014 (in relation to specified local authority areas[8]) (SI 2014/373) |
|   | (2) | 1 Sep 2010 (in relation to specified local authority areas[1]) (SI 2010/1699) |
|   |   | 28 Feb 2012 (in relation to specified local authority areas[4]) (SI 2012/191) |
|   |   | 31 Mar 2012 (in relation to specified local authority areas[5]) (SI 2012/191) |
|   |   | 1 Feb 2013 (in relation to specified local authority areas[6]) (SI 2013/18) |
|   |   | 19 Jul 2013 (otherwise) (SI 2013/1830) |
|   | (3) | 1 Sep 2010 (in relation to specified local authority areas[1]) (SI 2010/1699) |
|   |   | 28 Feb 2012 (in relation to specified local authority areas[4]) (SI 2012/191) |
|   |   | 31 Mar 2012 (in relation to specified local authority areas[5]) (SI 2012/191) |
|   |   | 1 Feb 2013 (in relation to specified local authority areas[6]) (SI 2013/18) |
|   |   | 19 Jul 2013 (in relation to specified local authority areas[7]) (SI 2013/1830) |
|   |   | 28 Feb 2014 (in relation to specified local authority areas[8]) (SI 2014/373) |
| 60 | (1) | 1 Sep 2010 (in relation to specified local authority areas[1]) (SI 2010/1699) |
|   |   | 27 Jan 2012 (otherwise) (SI 2012/191) |
|   | (2) | 1 Sep 2010 (in relation to specified local authority areas[1]) (SI 2010/1699) |
|   |   | 28 Feb 2012 (in relation to specified local authority areas[4]) (SI 2012/191) |
|   |   | 31 Mar 2012 (in relation to specified local authority areas[5]) (SI 2012/191) |
|   |   | 1 Feb 2013 (in relation to specified local authority areas[6]) (SI 2013/18) |
|   |   | 19 Jul 2013 (in relation to specified local authority areas[7]) (SI 2013/1830) |
|   |   | 28 Feb 2014 (in relation to specified local authority areas[8]) (SI 2014/373) |
| 61 |   | 1 Sep 2010 (in relation to specified local authority areas[1]) (SI 2010/1699) |
|   |   | 28 Feb 2012 (in relation to specified local authority areas[4]) (SI 2012/191) |
|   |   | 31 Mar 2012 (in relation to specified local authority areas[5]) (SI 2012/191) |
|   |   | 1 Feb 2013 (in relation to specified local authority areas[6]) (SI 2013/18) |
|   |   | 19 Jul 2013 (in relation to specified local authority areas[7]) (SI 2013/1830) |
|   |   | 28 Feb 2014 (in relation to specified local authority areas[8]) (SI 2014/373) |
| 62 | (1) | 1 Sep 2010 (in relation to specified local authority areas[1]) (SI 2010/1699) |
|   |   | 28 Feb 2012 (in relation to specified local authority areas[4]) (SI 2012/191) |

**Children and Families (Wales) Measure 2010 (nawm 1)**—*contd*

|  |  |  |
|---|---|---|
|  |  | 31 Mar 2012 (in relation to specified local authority areas[5]) (SI 2012/191) |
|  |  | 1 Feb 2013 (in relation to specified local authority areas[6]) (SI 2013/18) |
|  |  | 19 Jul 2013 (in relation to specified local authority areas[7]) (SI 2013/1830) |
|  |  | 28 Feb 2014 (in relation to specified local authority areas[8]) (SI 2014/373) |
|  | (2) | 1 Sep 2010 (in relation to specified local authority areas[1]) (SI 2010/1699) |
|  |  | 27 Jan 2012 (otherwise) (SI 2012/191) |
| 63 |  | 1 Sep 2010 (in relation to specified local authority areas[1]) (SI 2010/1699) |
|  |  | 27 Jan 2012 (otherwise) (SI 2012/191) |
| 64, 65 |  | 1 Sep 2010 (in relation to specified local authority areas[1]) (SI 2010/1699) |
|  |  | 28 Feb 2012 (in relation to specified local authority areas[4]) (SI 2012/191) |
|  |  | 31 Mar 2012 (in relation to specified local authority areas[5]) (SI 2012/191) |
|  |  | 1 Feb 2013 (in relation to specified local authority areas[6]) (SI 2013/18) |
|  |  | 19 Jul 2013 (in relation to specified local authority areas[7]) (SI 2013/1830) |
|  |  | 28 Feb 2014 (in relation to specified local authority areas[8]) (SI 2014/373) |
| 66–69 |  | *Not yet in force* |
| 70 |  | 30 Jun 2014 (SI 2014/1606) |
| 71 |  | *Not yet in force* |
| 72 |  | See Sch 1 below |
| 73 |  | See Sch 2 below |
| 74–76 |  | 10 Apr 2010 (s 75(1)) |
| Sch 1 | paras 1–18 | 1 Apr 2011 (SI 2010/2582)[2] |
|  | paras 19, 20 | 10 Feb 2010 (s 75(2)) |
|  | paras 21–28 | 1 Apr 2011 (SI 2010/2582)[2] |
| Sch 2 |  | 1 Apr 2011 (SI 2010/2582)[2], repeals of or in— Children Act 1989; Education Act 2002; Childcare Act 2006 *Not yet in force*, repeals of or in— Education Act 2005; Education and Inspections Act 2006; Education and Skills Act 2008 |

[1] The specified local authority areas are: Merthyr Tydfil; Newport; Rhondda Cynon Taff; and Wrexham

[2] For transitional provisions and savings, see SI 2010/2582, arts 3, 4, Schs 2, 3

[3] For a saving, see SI 2010/2994, art 3

[4] The specified local authority areas are: Cardiff; and Vale of Glamorgan

[5] The specified local authority areas are: Carmarthen; Ceredigion; Pembrokeshire; and Powys

[6] The specified local authority areas are: Neath Port Talbot; Bridgend; and Swansea

[7] The specified local authority areas are: Blaenau Gwent; Caerphilly; Flintshire; Monmouthshire; and Torfaen

[8] The specified local authority areas are: Anglesey; Conwy; Denbighshire; and Gwynedd

## Children, Schools and Families Act 2010 (c 26)

*RA:* 8 Apr 2010

*Commencement provisions*: s 29; Children, Schools and Families Act 2010 (Commencement No 1) Order 2010, SI 2010/1817; Children, Schools and Families Act 2010 (Commencement No 2) Order 2011, SI 2011/1100; Children, Schools and Families Act 2010 (Commencement No 3) Order 2013, SI 2013/668; Children, Schools and Families Act 2010 (Commencement No 4) Order 2013, SI 2013/1573

| | | |
|---|---|---|
| 1, 2 | | 1 Sep 2010 (SI 2010/1817) |
| 3 | | 1 Sep 2011 (SI 2011/1100) |
| 4 | (1) | *Not yet in force* |
| | (2)–(4) | 1 Apr 2011 (SI 2010/1817) |
| 5, 6 | | 19 Jul 2010 (SI 2010/1817) |
| 7 | | *Not yet in force* |
| 8 | | 15 Apr 2013 (SI 2013/668) |
| 9 | | *Not yet in force* |
| 10 | | 3 Jul 2013 (SI 2013/1573) |
| 11–18 | | *Never in force (repealed)* |
| 19 | (1) | See Sch 1 below |
| | (2)–(6) | *Never in force (repealed)* |
| 20–22 | | *Never in force (repealed)* |
| 23 | | 8 Jun 2010 (s 29(2)) |
| 24 | | 8 Apr 2010 (s 29(1)) |
| 25 | | See Schs 3, 4 below |
| 26–30 | | 8 Apr 2010 (s 29(1)) |
| Schs 1, 2 | | *Never in force (repealed)* |
| Sch 3 | para 1 | *Not yet in force* |
| | para 2 | 19 Jul 2010 (SI 2010/1817) |
| | paras 3–14 | *Never in force (repealed)* |
| Sch 4 | Pt 1 | *Not yet in force* |
| | Pt 2 | *Never in force (repealed)* |

## Church of England (Miscellaneous Provisions) Measure 2010 (No 1)

*RA:* 18 Mar 2010

Provisions of this Measure were brought into force on the following dates by instruments made by the Archbishops of Canterbury and York under s 13(2), and dated 10 Jun 2010

| | | |
|---|---|---|
| 1 | | See Sch 1 below |
| 2 | | 1 Sep 2010 |
| 3, 4 | | 1 Jul 2010 |
| 5–7 | | 1 Sep 2010 |
| 8 | | *Never in force (repealed)* |
| 9 | | 1 Jul 2010 |
| 10 | (1) | 1 Jul 2010 |
| | (2) | 1 Sep 2010 |
| | (3) | 1 Jul 2010 |
| 11 | | 1 Sep 2010 |
| 12 | (1)–(3) | 1 Sep 2010 |
| | (4) | See Sch 2 below |
| 13 | | 1 Jul 2010 |
| Schs 1, 2 | | 1 Sep 2010 |

## Cluster Munitions (Prohibitions) Act 2010 (c 11)

*RA:* 25 Mar 2010

*Commencement provisions*: s 34(1)

**Cluster Munitions (Prohibitions) Act 2010 (c 11)**—*contd*
Whole Act in force 25 Mar 2010 (s 34(1))

---

**Consolidated Fund Act 2010 (c 39)**

*RA:* 21 Dec 2010

Whole Act in force 21 Dec 2010 (RA)

---

**Constitutional Reform and Governance Act 2010 (c 25)**

*RA:* 8 Apr 2010

*Commencement provisions*: s 52(2), (3); Constitutional Reform and Governance Act 2010 (Commencement No 1) Order 2010, SI 2010/1277; Constitutional Reform and Governance Act 2010 (Commencement No 2 and Transitional Provisions) Order 2010, SI 2010/1931; Constitutional Reform and Governance Act 2010 (Commencement No 3) Order 2010, SI 2010/2703; Constitutional Reform and Governance Act 2010 (Commencement No 4 and Saving Provision) Order 2011, SI 2011/46; Constitutional Reform and Governance Act 2010 (Commencement No 5) Order 2011, SI 2011/1274; Constitutional Reform and Governance Act 2010 (Commencement No 6, Specified Day and Transitional Provision) Order 2011, SI 2011/2485; Constitutional Reform and Governance Act 2010 (Commencement No 7) Order 2012, SI 2012/3001; Constitutional Reform and Governance Act 2010 (Commencement No 8 and Saving Provision) Order 2013, SI 2013/2826; Constitutional Reform and Governance Act 2010 (Commencement No 9) Order 2014, SI 2014/3245

| | | |
|---|---|---|
| 1–25 | | 11 Nov 2010 (SI 2010/2703) |
| 26 | | 19 Apr 2010 (SI 2010/1277) |
| 27 | | 7 May 2010 (SI 2010/1277) |
| 28 | (1)–(3) | 7 May 2010 (SI 2010/1277) |
| | (4) | 27 Jul 2010 (SI 2010/1931)[1] |
| 29 | | 24 May 2011 (SI 2011/1274) |
| 30 | | 7 May 2010 (SI 2010/1277) |
| 31 | (1)–(5) | 27 Jul 2010 (SI 2010/1931) |
| | (6) | 7 May 2010 (SI 2010/1277) |
| 32 | | 7 May 2010 (SI 2010/1277) |
| 33, 34 | | 27 Jul 2010 (SI 2010/1931)[1] |
| 35 | | 27 Jul 2010 (SI 2010/1931) |
| 36, 37 | | 7 May 2010 (SI 2010/1277) |
| 38 | | See Sch 5 below |
| 39 | | 24 May 2011 (SI 2011/1274) |
| 40 | | See Sch 6 below |
| 41, 42 | | 8 Apr 2010 (s 52(3)) |
| 43, 44 | | 11 Nov 2010 (SI 2010/2703) |
| 45 | (1) | 1 Jan 2013 (except for certain purposes)[4] (SI 2012/3001) |
| | | 1 Jan 2015 (exception noted above) (SI 2014/3245) |
| | (2)–(5) | 30 Nov 2012 (SI 2012/3001) |
| 46 | (1) | See Sch 7 below |
| | (2)–(5) | 30 Nov 2012 (SI 2012/3001) |
| 47–52 | | 8 Apr 2010 (s 52(3)) |
| Schs 1, 2 | | 11 Nov 2010 (SI 2010/2703) |
| Sch 3 | | 19 Apr 2010 (SI 2010/1277) |
| Sch 4 | | 27 Jul 2010 (SI 2010/1931)[1] |
| Sch 5 | para 1 | 19 Apr 2010 (SI 2010/1277) |
| | para 2(a) | 7 May 2010 (SI 2010/1277) |
| | para 2(b) | 19 Apr 2010 (SI 2010/1277) |
| | para 3 | 7 May 2010 (SI 2010/1277) |
| | para 4(1), (2)(a) | 19 Apr 2010 (SI 2010/1277) |
| | para 4(2)(b) | 7 May 2010 (SI 2010/1277) |
| | para 4(3) | 27 Jul 2010 (SI 2010/1931) |

**Constitutional Reform and Governance Act 2010 (c 25)**—*contd*

| | | |
|---|---|---|
| | para 5(1) | 19 Apr 2010 (SI 2010/1277) |
| | para 5(2) | 7 May 2010 (SI 2010/1277) |
| | para 5(3) | 19 Apr 2010 (SI 2010/1277) |
| | para 6 | 7 May 2010 (SI 2010/1277) |
| | para 7(1) | 19 Apr 2010 SI 2010/1277) |
| | para 7(2) | 7 May 2010 (SI 2010/1277) |
| | para 7(3)(a) | 24 May 2011 (SI 2011/1274) |
| | para 7(3)(b) | 27 Jul 2010 (SI 2010/1931) |
| | para 7(3)(c) | 7 May 2010 (SI 2010/1277) |
| | para 7(4)(a) | 24 May 2011 (SI 2011/1274) |
| | para 7(4)(b) | 27 Jul 2010 (SI 2010/1931) |
| | para 7(4)(c) | 7 May 2010 (SI 2010/1277) |
| | para 7(4)(d) | 19 Apr 2010 (in so far as substitutes Parliamentary Standards Act 2009, Sch 1, para 18(2)(e)) (SI 2010/1277) |
| | | 27 Jul 2010 (in so far as substitutes para 18(2)(c), (d), (f) of that Schedule) (SI 2010/1931) |
| | para 7(5) | 27 Jul 2010 (SI 2010/1931) |
| | paras 8–12 | 24 May 2011 (SI 2011/1274) |
| Sch 6 | paras 1–11 | 24 Oct 2011 (SI 2011/2485) |
| | para 12 | 24 Oct 2011 (SI 2011/2485)[3] |
| | paras 13–34 | 24 Oct 2011 (SI 2011/2485) |
| | para 35(1), (2) | 24 Oct 2011 (SI 2011/2485) |
| | para 35(3) | 1 Nov 2013 (SI 2013/2826) |
| | paras 36, 37 | 24 Oct 2011 (SI 2011/2485) |
| | paras 38–41 | 1 Nov 2013 (SI 2013/2826) |
| | paras 42–46 | 24 Oct 2011 (SI 2011/2485) |
| | para 47(1) | 24 Oct 2011 (SI 2011/2485) |
| | para 47(2) | 24 Oct 2011 (except so far as inserts words ", 4 and 6" and "or 4" into Parliamentary Standards Act 2009, Sch 1, para 18(3)(a)) (SI 2011/2485) |
| | | 1 Nov 2013 (exception noted above) (SI 2013/2826) |
| | paras 47(3), 48–50 | 24 Oct 2011 (SI 2011/2485) |
| Sch 7 | paras 1–3 | 19 Jan 2011 (SI 2011/46)[2] |
| | paras 4, 5(1), (2)(a) | 1 Jan 2013 (SI 2012/3001) |
| | para 5(2)(b) | 19 Jan 2011 (in so far as omits reference "37(1)(a)" from Freedom of Information Act 2000, s 63(1)) (SI 2011/46)[2] |
| | | 1 Jan 2013 (otherwise) (SI 2012/3001) |
| | para 5(3) | 1 Jan 2013 (SI 2012/3001) |
| | para 5(4) | 19 Jan 2011 (in so far as inserts Freedom of Information Act 2000, s 63(2E), (2F)) (SI 2011/46)[2] |
| | | 1 Jan 2013 (in so far as inserts sub-ss (2A)–(2D) of that section) (SI 2012/3001) |
| | para 6 | 19 Jan 2011 (except so far as inserts Freedom of Information Act 2000, s 80A(5), (6)(b) and reference to s 63(2A)–(2D) in s 80A(6)(c)) (SI 2011/46)[2] |
| | | *Never in force* (exception noted above) (repealed) |

[1]   For transitional provisions, see SI 2010/1931, arts 4, 5

[2]   For savings, see SI 2011/46, art 4

[3]   For transitional provisions, see SI 2011/2485, art 4

[4]   The certain purposes are transfers in accordance with the Public Records Act 1958, s 3(4) of records of a description set out in SI 2012/3001, art 3(2), Schedule

## Control of Dogs (Scotland) Act 2010 (asp 9)

*RA:* 26 May 2010

*Commencement provisions:* s 18(2)

| | |
|---|---|
| 1–17 | 26 Feb 2011 (s 18(2)) |
| 18 | 26 May 2010 (RA) |
| Schs 1, 2 | 26 Feb 2011 (s 18(2)) |

## Co-operative and Community Benefit Societies and Credit Unions Act 2010 (c 7)

*RA:* 18 Mar 2010

*Commencement provisions:* s 8(2), (3); Co-operative and Community Benefit Societies and Credit Unions Act 2010 (Commencement No 1) Order 2013, SI 2013/2936; Co-operative and Community Benefit Societies and Credit Unions Act 2010 (Commencement No 2) Order 2014, SI 2014/183

| | |
|---|---|
| 1 | 1 Aug 2014 (SI 2014/183) |
| 2 | *Never in force* (repealed) |
| 3 | 6 Apr 2014 (SI 2014/183) |
| 4–7 | 1 Dec 2013 (SI 2013/2936) |
| 8 | 18 Mar 2010 (s 8(2)) |

## Corporation Tax Act 2010 (c 4)

*RA:* 3 Mar 2010

*Commencement provisions:* s 1184

| | | |
|---|---|---|
| 1–1177 | | 1 Apr 2010 (s 1184(1)) |
| 1178, 1179 | | 3 Mar 2010 (s 1184(2)(a), (b)) |
| 1180 | (1) | 1 Apr 2010 (s 1184(1)) |
| | (2)–(4) | 3 Mar 2010 (s 1184(2)(c)) |
| 1181, 1182 | | 1 Apr 2010 (s 1184(1)) |
| 1183–1185 | | 3 Mar 2010 (s 1184(2)(d)–(f)) |
| Schs 1–4 | | 1 Apr 2010 (s 1184(1)) |

## Crime and Security Act 2010 (c 17)

*RA:* 8 Apr 2010

*Commencement provisions:* ss 33, 59; Crime and Security Act 2010 (Commencement No 1) Order 2010, SI 2010/2989; Crime and Security Act 2010 (Commencement No 2) Order 2011, SI 2011/144; Crime and Security Act 2010 (Commencement No 3) Order 2011, SI 2011/414; Crime and Security Act 2010 (Domestic Violence: Pilot Schemes) Order 2011, SI 2011/1440; Crime and Security Act 2010 (Domestic Violence: Pilot Schemes) Order (No 2) 2011, SI 2011/2279; Crime and Security Act 2010 (Commencement No 4) Order 2011, SI 2011/3016; Crime and Security Act 2010 (Commencement No 5) Order 2012, SI 2012/584; Crime and Security Act 2010 (Commencement No 6) Order 2012, SI 2012/1615; Crime and Security Act 2010 (Commencement No 7) Order 2014, SI 2014/478; Crime and Security Act 2010 (Commencement No 8) Order 2021, SI 2021/621; Crime and Security Act 2010 (Commencement No 1) (Northern Ireland) Order 2021, SR 2021/135

| | | |
|---|---|---|
| 1–5 | | 7 Mar 2011 (SI 2011/414) |
| 6 | (1) | 7 Mar 2011 (SI 2011/414) |
| | (2) | 7 Mar 2011 (in so far as inserts Police and Criminal Evidence Act 1984, Sch 2A (except paras 4 and 12)) (SI 2011/414) |
| | | *Not yet in force* (exceptions noted above) |
| | (3), (4) | 7 Mar 2011 (SI 2011/414) |
| 7 | | 7 Mar 2011 (SI 2011/414) |
| 8–23 | | *Not yet in force* |

**Crime and Security Act 2010 (c 17)**—*contd*

| | | |
|---|---|---|
| 13 | | 1 Jun 2021 (for the purposes of Police and Criminal Evidence (Northern Ireland) Order 1989, SI 1989/1341 (NI 12), art 53A(2)(l), (n), (r) in so far as relate to Counter-Terrorism and Border Security Act 2019, Sch 3, paras 44, 45, Terrorism Act 2000, Sch 8, paras 20D, 20G, Counter-Terrorism Act 2008, s 18E, Terrorism Prevention and Investigation Measures Act 2011, Sch 6, para 10) (SI 2021/621) |
| | | 1 Jun 2021 (in so far as relates to Counter-Terrorism and Border Security Act 2019, Sch 3, paras 44, 45, Terrorism Act 2000, Sch 8, paras 20D, 20G, Terrorism Prevention and Investigation Measures Act 2011, Sch 6, para 10) (NI) (SR 2021/135) |
| | | *Not yet in force* (otherwise) |
| 14–23 | | *Not yet in force* (repealed) |
| 24–30 | | 30 Jun 2012 (in the police areas of Greater Manchester, West Mercia and Wiltshire only) (SI 2012/1615)[1] |
| | | 8 Mar 2014 (otherwise) (SI 2014/478) |
| 31 | | 8 Mar 2014 (SI 2014/478) |
| 32 | | *Not yet in force* |
| 33 | | 8 Apr 2010 (s 59(2)(a)) |
| 34–36 | | 9 Jan 2012 (SI 2011/3016) |
| 37, 38 | | 31 Jan 2011 (SI 2010/2989) |
| 39 | | 9 Jan 2012 (SI 2011/3016) |
| 40, 41 | | *Never in force* (repealed) |
| 42 | (1)–(7) | *Not yet in force* (sub-s (3) repealed) |
| | (8) | See Sch 1 below |
| 43, 44 | | *Not yet in force* (s 44 repealed) |
| 45 | | 26 Mar 2012 (SI 2012/584) |
| 46 | | 10 Feb 2011 (SI 2011/144) |
| 47–54 | | 8 Apr 2010 (s 59(2)(b)) |
| 55, 56 | | *Never in force* (repealed) |
| 57–60 | | 8 Apr 2010 (s 59(2)(c)) |
| Sch 1 | | *Not yet in force* (paras 3(5), 7 repealed) |
| Sch 2 | | 8 Apr 2010 (s 59(2)(b)) |

---

[1]  These provisions were previously brought into force for limited pilot periods in these police areas (or parts thereof) by SI 2011/1440 and SI 2011/2279

---

## Criminal Justice and Licensing (Scotland) Act 2010 (asp 13)

*RA:* 6 Aug 2010

*Commencement provisions:* s 206(1); Criminal Justice and Licensing (Scotland) Act 2010 (Commencement No 1) Order 2010, SSI 2010/297; Criminal Justice and Licensing (Scotland) Act 2010 (Commencement No 2) Order 2010, SSI 2010/339; Protection of Vulnerable Groups (Scotland) Act 2007 (Commencement No 4) and the Criminal Justice and Licensing (Scotland) Act 2010 (Commencement No 3) Order 2010, SSI 2010/344; Sexual Offences (Scotland) Act 2009 (Commencement No 1) and the Criminal Justice and Licensing (Scotland) Act 2010 (Commencement No 4) Order 2010, SSI 2010/357; Criminal Justice and Licensing (Scotland) Act 2010 (Commencement No 5) Order 2010, SSI 2010/385; Criminal Justice and Licensing (Scotland) Act 2010 (Commencement No 6, Transitional and Savings Provisions) Order 2010, SSI 2010/413; Protection of Vulnerable Groups (Scotland) Act 2007 (Commencement No 5, Savings, Transitional and Consequential Provisions) and the Criminal Justice and Licensing (Scotland) Act 2010 (Commencement No 7, Savings and Transitional Provisions) Order 2011, SSI 2011/157; Criminal Justice and Licensing (Scotland) Act 2010 (Commencement No 8, Transitional and Savings Provisions) Order 2011, SSI 2011/178; Criminal Justice and Licensing (Scotland) Act 2010 (Commencement No 9, Transitional and Savings Provisions) Order 2011, SSI 2011/354, as amended by SSI 2011/366; Criminal Justice and Licensing (Scotland) Act 2010 (Commencement No 10 and Saving Provisions) Order 2012, SSI 2012/160; Criminal Justice and Licensing (Scotland) Act 2010 (Commencement No 11 and Saving Provision) Order 2013, SSI 2013/214; Criminal Justice and Licensing (Scotland) Act 2010 (Commencement No 12) Order 2015, SSI 2015/177; Criminal Justice and Licensing

**Criminal Justice and Licensing (Scotland) Act 2010 (asp 13)**—*contd*
(Scotland) Act 2010 (Commencement No 13) and the Courts Reform (Scotland) Act 2014 (Commencement No 4) Order 2015, SSI 2015/336; Criminal Justice and Licensing (Scotland) Act 2010 (Commencement No 14 and Saving Provision) Order 2017, SSI 2017/445; Criminal Justice and Licensing (Scotland) Act 2010 (Commencement No 15 and Saving Provision) and the Air Weapons and Licensing (Scotland) Act 2015 (Commencement No 8) Order 2018, SSI 2018/102; Criminal Justice and Licensing (Scotland) Act 2010 (Commencement No16) Order 2021, SSI 2021/355

| | | |
|---|---|---|
| 1 | (1) | 7 May 2015 (SSI 2015/177) |
| | (2) | See Sch 1 below |
| 2–13 | | 19 Oct 2015 (SSI 2015/336) |
| 14 | (1) | 1 Feb 2011 (except so far as inserts Criminal Procedure (Scotland) Act 1995, s 227M) (SSI 2010/413)[2] |
| | | 1 Apr 2011 (exception noted above) (SSI 2010/413)[2] |
| | (2) | See Sch 2 below |
| 15 | | 28 Mar 2011 (for all purposes where the misconduct complained of occurred on or after that date) (SSI 2011/178) |
| 16 | | 13 Dec 2010 (in respect of offences committed on or after that date) (SSI 2010/413) |
| 17 | | 1 Feb 2011 (in respect of offences committed on or after that date) (SSI 2010/413) |
| 18 | (1)–(8) | *Not yet in force* |
| | (9) | See Sch 3 below |
| 19 | | 28 Mar 2011 (SSI 2011/178) |
| 20 | | 1 Feb 2011 (SSI 2010/413)[2] |
| 21 | | 1 Feb 2011 (in respect of offences committed on or after that date) (SSI 2010/413) |
| 22 | | 28 Mar 2011 (in respect of offences committed on or after that date) (SSI 2011/178) |
| 23 | | 13 Dec 2010 (in respect of offences committed on or after that date) (SSI 2010/413) |
| 24 | (1)–(3) | 28 Mar 2011 (SSI 2011/178) |
| | (4), (5) | 28 Mar 2011 (in respect of offences committed on or after that date) (SSI 2011/178) |
| 25, 26 | | 13 Dec 2010 (in respect of offences committed on or after that date) (SSI 2010/413) |
| 27 | | 28 Mar 2011 (SSI 2011/178) |
| 28 | | 13 Dec 2010 (SSI 2010/413) |
| 29 | | 13 Dec 2010 (in respect of offences committed on or after that date) (SSI 2010/413) |
| 30, 31 | | 13 Dec 2010 (SSI 2010/413) |
| 32, 33 | | 28 Mar 2011 (SSI 2011/178) |
| 34 | | 13 Dec 2010 (SSI 2010/413) |
| 35 | (1) | See sub-ss (2)–(4) below |
| | (2), (3) | 28 Mar 2011 (in respect of offences committed on or after that date) (SSI 2011/178) |
| | (4) | 28 Mar 2011 (SSI 2011/178) |
| 36 | (1) | See sub-ss (2)–(4) below |
| | (2), (3) | 28 Mar 2011 (SSI 2011/178) |
| | (4) | 28 Mar 2011 (in respect of offences committed on or after that date) (SSI 2011/178) |
| 37 | | 13 Dec 2010 (in respect of offences committed on or after that date) (SSI 2010/413) |
| 38 | | 6 Oct 2010 (SSI 2010/339) |
| 39 | | 13 Dec 2010 (SSI 2010/413) |
| 40 | | 13 Dec 2010 (SSI 2010/413)[2] |
| 41 | | 13 Dec 2010 (SSI 2010/413) |
| 42 | (1) | 28 Mar 2011 (in respect of offences committed on or after that date) (SSI 2011/178) |
| | (2), (3) | 28 Mar 2011 (SSI 2011/178) |

**Criminal Justice and Licensing (Scotland) Act 2010 (asp 13)**—*contd*

| | | |
|---|---|---|
| 43, 44 | | 1 Dec 2010 (SSI 2010/357) |
| 45 | | 13 Dec 2010 (in respect of offences committed on or after that date) (SSI 2010/413) |
| 46 | | 28 Mar 2011 (in respect of offences committed on or after that date) (SSI 2011/178) |
| 47 | | 28 Mar 2011 (SSI 2011/178) |
| 48 | | 28 Mar 2011 (in respect of offences committed on or after that date) (SSI 2011/178) |
| 49 | | 28 Mar 2011 (SSI 2011/178) |
| 50 | | 28 Mar 2011 (in respect of acts done by a person in Scotland on or after that date which would amount to conspiracy to commit an offence) (SSI 2011/178) |
| 51, 52 | | 28 Mar 2011 (SSI 2011/178) |
| 53 | | 28 Mar 2011 (in respect of offences committed on or after that date) (SSI 2011/178) |
| 54 | | 28 Mar 2011 (in respect of criminal proceedings in which (a) the first appearance of the accused, or (b) the recording of a plea of not guilty against an accused charged on summary complaint, is on or after that date) (SSI 2011/178) |
| 55 | | 28 Mar 2011 (in respect of any breach of undertaking committed on or after that date) (SSI 2011/178) |
| 56 | | 13 Dec 2010 (SSI 2010/413) |
| 57 | | 28 Mar 2011 (in respect of any applications under the Criminal Procedure (Scotland) Act 1995, s 30(2) received on or after that date) (SSI 2011/178) |
| 58 | | 28 Mar 2011 (for all purposes where the court grants bail to a person on or after that date) (SSI 2011/178) |
| 59 | | 13 Dec 2010 (SSI 2010/413) |
| 60 | | 13 Dec 2010 (SSI 2010/413)[2] |
| 61 | | 28 Mar 2011 (SSI 2011/178) |
| 62 | | 28 Mar 2011 (in respect of any breach of bail committed on or after that date) (SSI 2011/178) |
| 63 | | 1 Dec 2010 (SSI 2010/357) |
| 64 | | 13 Dec 2010 (SSI 2010/413) |
| 65–68 | | 28 Mar 2011 (for all proceedings commenced on or after that date)[4] (SSI 2011/178) |
| 69 | | 28 Mar 2011 (in respect of criminal proceedings commenced on or after that date, with proceedings taken to have commenced when a report of the case has been received by the procurator fiscal) (SSI 2011/178) |
| 70 | | 28 Mar 2011 (in respect of offences committed on or after that date) (SSI 2011/178) |
| 71 | (1) | See Sch 4 below |
| | (2)–(5) | 13 Dec 2010 (SSI 2010/413) |
| 72 | | 28 Mar 2011 (SSI 2011/178) |
| 73, 74 | | 28 Mar 2011 (in respect of any trial which commences on or after that date, with a trial taken to have commenced in solemn proceedings when the oath is administered to the jury and in summary proceedings when the first witness is sworn) (SSI 2011/178) |
| 75 | | 28 Mar 2011 (SSI 2011/178) |
| 76 | | 28 Mar 2011 (in respect of any trial which commences on or after that date, with a trial taken to have commenced in solemn proceedings when the oath is administered to the jury and in summary proceedings when the first witness is sworn) (SSI 2011/178) |
| 77 | (1) | See sub-ss (2), (3) below |
| | (2)(a) | 28 Mar 2011 (SSI 2011/178) |
| | (2)(b), (c) | 1 Aug 2011 (SSI 2011/178) |
| | (3) | 28 Mar 2011 (SSI 2011/178)[5] |

**Criminal Justice and Licensing (Scotland) Act 2010 (asp 13)**—*contd*

| | | |
|---|---|---|
| 78, 79 | | 28 Mar 2011 (SSI 2011/178)[5] |
| 80 | | 13 Dec 2010 (so far as inserts Criminal Procedure (Scotland) Act 1995 s 18E(6), (7), (10)) (SSI 2010/413) |
| | | 15 Apr 2011 (otherwise) (SSI 2011/178)[5] |
| 81 | | 28 Mar 2011 (SSI 2011/178)[5] |
| 82 | | 1 Aug 2011 (SSI 2011/178)[5] |
| 83 | | 5 Nov 2010 (SSI 2010/385)[1] |
| 84 | | 28 Mar 2011 (SSI 2011/178) |
| 85 | | 6 Jun 2011 (in respect of criminal proceedings in which the first appearance of the accused or the recording of a plea of not guilty against an accused charged on summary complaint is on or after that date) (SSI 2011/178) |
| 86 | | 28 Mar 2011 (for all proceedings commenced on or after that date)[4] (SSI 2011/178) |
| 87, 88 | | 28 Mar 2011 (in respect of criminal proceedings commenced on or after that date, with proceedings taken to have commenced when a report of the case has been received by the procurator fiscal) (SSI 2011/178) |
| 89, 90 | | 28 Mar 2011 (SSI 2011/178) |
| 91 | | 28 Mar 2011 (in respect of criminal proceedings commenced on or after that date, with proceedings taken to have commenced when a report of the case has been received by the procurator fiscal) (SSI 2011/178) |
| 92 | | *Not yet in force* |
| 93 | | 13 Dec 2010 (SSI 2010/413) |
| 94–96 | | 10 Jan 2011 (SSI 2010/413) |
| 97 | | 6 Oct 2010 (SSI 2010/339) |
| 98 | | 8 Nov 2021 (SSI 2021/355) |
| 99 | | 13 Dec 2010 (SSI 2010/413)[2] |
| 100 | | 1 Nov 2011 (SSI 2011/354) |
| 101 | | 13 Dec 2010 (SSI 2010/413) |
| 102 | (1) | See sub-ss (2)–(6) below |
| | (2) | 28 Mar 2011 (for the purpose of commencing the amendments to the Sexual Offences Act 2003, s 85 to enable regulations to be made thereunder) (SSI 2011/178) |
| | | 8 Jul 2013 (otherwise) (SSI 2013/214)[8] |
| | (3)–(6) | 28 Mar 2011 (SSI 2011/178) |
| 103 | | 1 Nov 2011 (SSI 2011/354) |
| 104, 105 | | 13 Dec 2010 (SSI 2010/413) |
| 106, 107 | | 28 Mar 2011 (SSI 2011/178) |
| 108 | (1) | See sub-ss (2)–(4) below |
| | (2), (3) | 28 Feb 2011 (SSI 2011/157)[3] |
| | (4) | 12 Oct 2010 (SSI 2010/344) |
| 109 | (1), (2) | 1 Nov 2011 (SSI 2011/354) |
| | (3) | 1 Nov 2011 (for all purposes in respect of offences committed on or after that date) (SSI 2011/354) |
| | (4) | 1 Nov 2011 (SSI 2011/354) |
| 110 | (1) | 1 Nov 2011 (SSI 2011/354) |
| | (2) | 1 Nov 2011 (for all purposes in respect of offences committed under the Prisons (Scotland) Act 1989, s 41D, on or after that date) (SSI 2011/354) |
| | (3)–(5) | 1 Nov 2011 (SSI 2011/354) |
| 111, 112 | | 13 Dec 2010 (SSI 2010/413) |
| 113 | | 13 Dec 2010 (SSI 2010/413)[2] |
| 114 | | 13 Dec 2010 (SSI 2010/413) |
| 115 | | 28 Mar 2011 (in respect of offences committed on or after that date) (SSI 2011/178) |
| 116 | | 6 Jun 2011 (SSI 2011/178) |

**Criminal Justice and Licensing (Scotland) Act 2010 (asp 13)**—*contd*

| | | |
|---|---|---|
| 117, 118 | | 6 Jun 2011 (in respect of criminal proceedings in which the first appearance of the accused is on or after that date) (SSI 2011/178) |
| 119, 120 | | 6 Jun 2011 (in respect of criminal proceedings in which the recording of a plea of not guilty against an accused charged on summary complaint is on or after that date) (SSI 2011/178) |
| 121 | | 6 Jun 2011 (in respect of criminal proceedings in which the first appearance of the accused or the recording of a plea of not guilty against an accused charged on summary complaint is on or after that date) (SSI 2011/178) |
| 122 | | 6 Jun 2011 (in respect of criminal proceedings in which the first appearance of the accused is on or after that date) (SSI 2011/178) |
| 123 | (1), (2) | 6 Jun 2011 (in respect of criminal proceedings in which the first appearance of the accused or the recording of a plea of not guilty against an accused charged on summary complaint is on or after that date) (SSI 2011/178) |
| | (3), (4) | 6 Jun 2011 (in respect of criminal proceedings in which the first appearance of the accused is on or after that date) (SSI 2011/178) |
| | (5), (6) | 6 Jun 2011 (in respect of criminal proceedings in which the first appearance of the accused or the recording of a plea of not guilty against an accused charged on summary complaint is on or after that date) (SSI 2011/178) |
| 124 | | 6 Jun 2011 (in respect of criminal proceedings in which the first appearance of the accused is on or after that date) (SSI 2011/178) |
| 125, 126 | | 6 Jun 2011 (in respect of criminal proceedings in which the recording of a plea of not guilty against an accused charged on summary complaint is on or after that date) (SSI 2011/178) |
| 127–131 | | 6 Jun 2011 (in respect of criminal proceedings in which the first appearance of the accused or the recording of a plea of not guilty against an accused charged on summary complaint is on or after that date) (SSI 2011/178) |
| 132–135 | | 6 Jun 2011 (in respect of appellate proceedings arising out of earlier proceedings) (SSI 2011/178) |
| 136 | | 6 Jun 2011 (in respect of appellate proceedings, as concluded, which arose in respect of earlier proceedings) (SSI 2011/178) |
| 137 | | 6 Jun 2011 (in respect of criminal proceedings in which the first appearance of the accused or the recording of a plea of not guilty against an accused charged on summary complaint is on or after that date) (SSI 2011/178) |
| 138 | | 6 Jun 2011 (in respect of appellate proceedings, in respect of which this section makes provision, arising out of proceedings in which the first appearance of the accused is, or the recording of a plea of not guilty against an accused charged on summary complaint is, on or after that date) (SSI 2011/178) |
| 139, 140 | | 6 Jun 2011 (in respect of appellate proceedings arising out of earlier proceedings) (SSI 2011/178) |
| 141–149 | | 6 Jun 2011 (in respect of (a) criminal proceedings in which the first appearance of the accused or the recording of a plea of not guilty against an accused charged on summary complaint is on or after that date, and (b) appellate proceedings arising out of such criminal proceedings) (SSI 2011/178) |
| 150–165 | | 6 Jun 2011 (SSI 2011/178) |
| 166 | | 6 Jun 2011 (in respect of (a) criminal proceedings in which the first appearance of the accused or the recording of a plea of not guilty against an accused charged on summary complaint is on or after that date, and (b) appellate proceedings arising out of such criminal proceedings) (SSI 2011/178) |
| 167 | | 6 Jun 2011 (SSI 2011/178) |

**Criminal Justice and Licensing (Scotland) Act 2010 (asp 13)**—*contd*

| | | |
|---|---|---|
| 168–171 | | 25 Jun 2012 (SSI 2012/160)[7] |
| 172 | (1)–(3), (4)(a) | 6 Jun 2011 (in respect of licence applications under the Civic Government (Scotland) Act 1982, Sch 1, para (1) made to a licensing authority on or after that date) (SSI 2011/178) |
| | (4)(b) | *Not yet in force* |
| | (5), (6) | 6 Jun 2011 (in respect of licence applications under the Civic Government (Scotland) Act 1982, Sch 1, para (1) made to a licensing authority on or after that date) (SSI 2011/178) |
| 173 | | 13 Dec 2010 (SSI 2010/413) |
| 174 | | 1 Nov 2011 (SSI 2011/354)[6] |
| 175 | | 6 Jun 2011 (in respect of applications for a street trader's licence under the Civic Government (Scotland) Act 1982, Sch 1, para (1) made to a licensing authority on or after that date) (SSI 2011/178) |
| 176 | | 1 Apr 2012 (SSI 2011/178) |
| 177 | | 1 Oct 2012 (SSI 2011/178)[5] |
| 178 | (1) | See sub-ss (2), (3) below |
| | (2) | 28 Feb 2011 (in respect of applications for the grant or renewal of licences under the Civic Government (Scotland) Act 1982, Sch 1, para 1 made on or after that date) (SSI 2010/413) |
| | (3)(a)–(d) | 28 Feb 2011 (in respect of applications for the grant or renewal of licences under the Civic Government (Scotland) Act 1982, Sch 2, para 6 made on or after that date) (SSI 2010/413) |
| | (3)(e) | 16 Aug 2010 (only in respect of applications for the grant or renewal of licences under the Civic Government (Scotland) Act 1982, Sch 2, para 6 made to the local authority on or after that date) (SSI 2010/297) |
| | (3)(f)–(h) | 28 Feb 2011 (in respect of applications for the grant or renewal of licences under the Civic Government (Scotland) Act 1982, Sch 2, para 6 made on or after that date) (SSI 2010/413) |
| 179 | | 30 Mar 2018 (SSI 2017/445)[9] |
| 180, 181 | | 13 Dec 2010 (in respect of premises licence applications made to a Licensing Board on or after that date) (SSI 2010/413) |
| 182 | | 28 Feb 2011 (in respect of premises licence review proposals made by a Licensing Board under the Licensing (Scotland) Act 2005, s 37(1) and all premises licence applications made to a Licensing Board on or after that date) (SSI 2010/413) |
| 183 | | 13 Dec 2010 (in respect of premises licence applications made to a Licensing Board on or after that date) (SSI 2010/413) |
| 184 | (1) | 13 Dec 2010 (SSI 2010/413) |
| | (2) | 13 Dec 2010 (so far as inserts Licensing (Scotland) Act 2005, s 40A(1)(a), (2) (except words "or an interested party"), (3)–(5)) (SSI 2010/413) |
| | | 29 Jun 2018 (otherwise) (SSI 2018/102) |
| | (3)(a)(i) | 13 Dec 2010 (SSI 2010/413) |
| | (3)(a)(ii) | 13 Dec 2010 (so far as inserts Licensing (Scotland) Act 2005 s 48(1)(c)(i)) (SSI 2010/413) |
| | | 29 Jun 2018 (otherwise) (SSI 2018/102) |
| | (3)(b) | 13 Dec 2010 (SSI 2010/413) |
| | (4), (5) | 29 Jun 2018 (SSI 2018/102) |
| 185 | | 13 Dec 2010 (SSI 2010/413)[2] |
| 186 | | 28 Mar 2011 (in respect of premises licence applications under the Licensing (Scotland) Act 2005, s 20 made to a Licensing Board on or after that date) (SSI 2011/178) |
| 187 | | 13 Dec 2010 (in respect of premises licence applications or an application under the Licensing (Scotland) Act 2005, s 47(2) made to a Licensing Board on or after that date) (SSI 2010/413) |
| 188 | (1) | 13 Dec 2010 (SSI 2010/413) |
| | (2) | 28 Mar 2011 (in respect of offences committed on or after that date) (SSI 2011/178) |

**Criminal Justice and Licensing (Scotland) Act 2010 (asp 13)**—*contd*

| | | |
|---|---|---|
| | (3) | 13 Dec 2010 (in respect of offences committed on or after that date) (SSI 2010/413) |
| 189 | | 1 Oct 2011 (in respect of applications for an occasional licence made under the Licensing (Scotland) Act 2005, s 56 to a Licensing Board on or after that date) (SSI 2011/178) |
| 190, 191 | | 1 Oct 2011 (in respect of extended hours applications under the Licensing (Scotland) Act 2005, s 68 made to a Licensing Board on or after that date) (SSI 2011/178) |
| 192 | (1) | See sub-ss (2)–(4) below |
| | (2) | 13 Dec 2010 (in respect of applications for a personal licence under the Licensing (Scotland) Act 2005, s 72(1) made to a Licensing Board on or after that date) (SSI 2010/413) |
| | (3) | 13 Dec 2010 (in respect of all personal licences granted following an application made to a Licensing Board on or after that date) (SSI 2010/413) |
| | (4) | 13 Dec 2010 (in respect of applications for a replacement personal licence received by a Licensing Board on or after that date) (SSI 2010/413) |
| 193 | | 13 Dec 2010 (SSI 2010/413) |
| 194 | | 13 Dec 2010 (in respect of decisions that may be appealed under the Licensing (Scotland) Act 2005, s 131(1), Sch 5 made by a Licensing Board on or after that date) (SSI 2010/413) |
| 195 | (1) | See sub-ss (2), (3) below |
| | (2) | 13 Dec 2010 (in respect of offences committed on or after that date) (SSI 2010/413) |
| | (3) | 13 Dec 2010 (so far as inserts Licensing (Scotland) Act 2005, ss 141A, 141B(1)(a), (2) (except the words "or, as the case may be, the interested party"), (3) (except the words "or an interested party" and "as the case may be, the interested party"), (4) (except the words "or the interested party"), (5) (in respect of offences committed on or after that date) (SSI 2010/413)) |
| | | 1 Nov 2011 (otherwise, in respect of offences committed on or after that date) (SSI 2011/354) |
| 196 | | 13 Dec 2010 (in respect of offences committed on or after that date) (SSI 2010/413) |
| 197 | | 29 Jun 2018 (SSI 2018/102)[10] |
| 198 | | See Sch 6 below |
| 199 | | 13 Dec 2010 (SSI 2010/413) |
| 200 | | *Not yet in force* |
| 201, 202 | | 6 Aug 2010 (RA) |
| 203 | | See Sch 7 below |
| 204–206 | | 6 Aug 2010 (RA) |
| Sch 1 | para 1 | *Not yet in force* |
| | para 2 | 7 May 2015 (for the purpose of enabling the Scottish Ministers to make regulations prescribing the procedure by which a person may be nominated or otherwise selected as suitable for appointment, as a member of the Scottish Sentencing Council) (SSI 2015/177) |
| | | 19 Oct 2015 (otherwise) (SSI 2015/336) |
| | paras 3–14 | *Not yet in force* |
| Sch 2 | paras 1–37 | 1 Feb 2011 (SSI 2010/413)[2] |
| | para 38 | In force on the day the Welfare Reform Act 2009, s 25(2) comes into force (SSI 2010/413) |
| | paras 39–53 | 1 Feb 2011 (SSI 2010/413)[2] |
| Sch 3 | | *Not yet in force* |
| Sch 4 | paras 1–11 | 13 Dec 2010 (in respect of offences committed on or after that date) (SSI 2010/413) |
| | para 12 | *Not yet in force* |

**Criminal Justice and Licensing (Scotland) Act 2010 (asp 13)**—*contd*

|  |  |  |
|---|---|---|
|  | para 13 | 13 Dec 2010 (in respect of offences committed on or after that date) (SSI 2010/413) |
| Sch 5 |  | 28 Mar 2011 (SSI 2011/178) |
| Sch 6 | para 1 | 13 Dec 2010 (SSI 2010/413) |
|  | para 2 | 1 Nov 2011 (SSI 2011/354)[6] |
|  | paras 3, 4 | 13 Dec 2010 (SSI 2010/413) |
|  | para 5 | 13 Dec 2010 (in respect of applications for a premises licence under Licensing (Scotland) Act 2005, s 20 made to a Licensing Board on or after that date) (SSI 2010/413) |
|  | para 6(1), (2) | 13 Dec 2010 (SSI 2010/413) |
|  | para 6(3) | 13 Dec 2010 (in respect of applications for a premises licence under Licensing (Scotland) Act 2005, s 20 made to a Licensing Board on or after that date) (SSI 2010/413) |
|  | para 7 | 13 Dec 2010 (in respect of applications for the transfer of a premises licence made to a Licensing Board on or after that date) (SSI 2010/413) |
|  | para 8 | 13 Dec 2010 (in respect of any notice of conviction given by a Licensing Board to the appropriate chief constable under the Licensing (Scotland) Act 2005, s 44(2) on or after that date) (SSI 2010/413) |
|  | paras 9, 10 | 1 Nov 2011 (SSI 2011/354) |
|  | para 11 | 13 Dec 2010 (in respect of any notice given by a Licensing Board to the appropriate chief constable under the Licensing (Scotland) Act 2005, s 69(1) on or after that date) (SSI 2010/413) |
|  | para 12 | 13 Dec 2010 (in respect of any notice given by a Licensing Board to the appropriate chief constable under the Licensing (Scotland) Act 2005, s 73(1) in respect of an application for a personal licence made on or after that date) (SSI 2010/413) |
|  | paras 13–15 | 13 Dec 2010 (in respect of applications for a personal licence under the Licensing (Scotland) Act 2005, s 72 made on or after that date) (SSI 2010/413) |
|  | para 16 | 13 Dec 2010 (SSI 2010/413) |
|  | para 17 | 1 Nov 2011 (SSI 2011/354)[6] |
|  | para 18 | 13 Dec 2010 (in respect of applications for occasional licences made to a Licensing Board on or after that date) (SSI 2010/413) |
| Sch 7 | paras 1–3 | 28 Mar 2011 (SSI 2011/178) |
|  | paras 4, 5 | 13 Dec 2010 (SSI 2010/413) |
|  | para 6 | 28 Mar 2011 (SSI 2011/178) |
|  | para 7 | 1 Nov 2011 (SSI 2011/354) |
|  | para 8 | 25 Jun 2012 (SSI 2012/160) |
|  | paras 9, 10 | 1 Nov 2011 (SSI 2011/354) |
|  | paras 11, 12 | 28 Mar 2011 (SSI 2011/178) |
|  | para 13 | 13 Dec 2010 (SSI 2010/413) |
|  | paras 14, 15 | 28 Mar 2011 (SSI 2011/178) |
|  | para 16 | 25 Jun 2012 (SSI 2012/160) |
|  | paras 17–23 | 28 Mar 2011 (SSI 2011/178) |
|  | para 24 | 28 Mar 2011 (in respect of offences committed on or after that date) (SSI 2011/178) |
|  | para 25 | 28 Mar 2011 (SSI 2011/178) |
|  | para 26 | *Not yet in force* |
|  | paras 27–31 | 28 Mar 2011 (SSI 2011/178) |
|  | para 32 | 25 Jun 2012 (SSI 2012/160) |
|  | para 33 | 1 Aug 2011 (SSI 2011/178) |
|  | paras 34–36 | 28 Mar 2011 (SSI 2011/178) |
|  | paras 37–43 | 25 Jun 2012 (SSI 2012/160) |
|  | paras 44, 45 | 28 Mar 2011 (SSI 2011/178) |
|  | para 46 | 25 Jun 2012 (SSI 2012/160) |
|  | para 47 | 28 Mar 2011 (SSI 2011/178) |

**Criminal Justice and Licensing (Scotland) Act 2010 (asp 13)**—*contd*

| | |
|---|---|
| para 48 | 10 Jan 2011 (SSI 2010/413) |
| para 49 | 13 Dec 2010 (SSI 2010/413) |
| para 50 | 28 Mar 2011 (SSI 2011/178) |
| para 51 | 25 Jun 2012 (SSI 2012/160) |
| paras 52–56 | 28 Mar 2011 (SSI 2011/178) |
| paras 57, 58 | 25 Jun 2012 (SSI 2012/160) |
| paras 59–61 | 28 Mar 2011 (SSI 2011/178) |
| para 62 | 25 Jun 2012 (SSI 2012/160) |
| paras 63–65 | 28 Mar 2011 (SSI 2011/178) |
| para 66 | 25 Jun 2012 (SSI 2012/160) |
| paras 67–69 | 28 Mar 2011 (SSI 2011/178) |
| para 70 | *Not yet in force* |
| para 71 | 25 Jun 2012 (SSI 2012/160) |
| para 72 | 28 Mar 2011 (SSI 2011/178) |
| para 73 | 25 Jun 2012 (SSI 2012/160) |
| para 74 | 28 Mar 2011 (SSI 2011/178) |
| paras 75, 76 | 25 Jun 2012 (SSI 2012/160) |
| paras 77–83 | 28 Mar 2011 (SSI 2011/178) |
| paras 84, 85 | 25 Jun 2012 (SSI 2012/160) |
| para 86 | 13 Dec 2010 (SSI 2010/413) |
| para 87 | 25 Jun 2012 (SSI 2012/160) |

[1]  For transitional provisions and savings, see SSI 2010/385, arts 3, 4

[2]  For transitional provisions and savings, see SSI 2010/413, arts 3–8

[3]  For transitional provisions and savings, see SSI 2011/157, art 3

[4]  Proceedings are taken to have commenced—

(a)  in summary proceedings, on the date of the first calling of the case; and

(b)  in solemn cases, on the date on whichever of the following first occurs:

(i)  the grant of a warrant to arrest and commit;

(ii)  the intimation of a person; or

(iii)  the service of an indictment

[5]  For transitional provisions and savings, see SSI 2011/178, arts 4–10

[6]  For transitional provisions and savings, see SSI 2011/354, arts 3, 5

[7]  For savings, see SSI 2012/160, art 4

[8]  For savings, see SSI 2013/214, art 3

[9]  For a saving, see SSI 2017/445, art 3

[10]  For a saving, see SSI 2018/102, art 4

---

**Criminal Procedure (Legal Assistance, Detention and Appeals) (Scotland) Act 2010 (asp 15)**

*RA:* 29 Oct 2010

*Commencement provisions:* s 9

Whole Act in force 30 Oct 2010 (s 9)

---

**Crofting Reform (Scotland) Act 2010 (asp 14)**

*RA:* 6 Aug 2010

*Commencement provisions:* s 57(2), (3); Crofting Reform (Scotland) Act 2010 (Commencement, Saving and Transitory Provisions) Order 2010, SSI 2010/437; Crofting Reform (Scotland) Act 2010

**Crofting Reform (Scotland) Act 2010 (asp 14)**—*contd*
(Commencement No 2, Transitory, Transitional and Saving Provisions) Order 2011, SSI 2011/334;
Crofting Reform (Scotland) Act 2010 (Commencement No 3, Transitory, Transitional and Saving
Provisions) Order 2012, SSI 2012/288

| | | |
|---|---|---|
| 1 | (1), (2) | 1 Apr 2012 (SSI 2011/334)[2] |
| | (3) | See Sch 1 below |
| | (4) | 1 Apr 2012 (SSI 2011/334)[2] |
| 2 | (1) | 1 Oct 2011 (SSI 2011/334)[2] |
| | (2) | 1 Oct 2011 (in so far as inserts Crofters (Scotland) Act 1993, s 2A) (SSI 2011/334)[2] |
| | | 1 Apr 2012 (otherwise) (SSI 2011/334)[2] |
| 3 | | 30 Oct 2012 (SSI 2012/288) |
| 4 | (1) | 30 Oct 2012 (for the purpose of enabling the Scottish Ministers to exercise powers to make orders or regulations) (SSI 2012/288) |
| | | 30 Nov 2013 (otherwise) (SSI 2012/288)[3] |
| | (2), (3) | 30 Oct 2012 (for the purpose of enabling the Scottish Ministers to exercise powers to make orders or regulations) (SSI 2012/288) |
| | | 30 Nov 2012 (otherwise) (SSI 2012/288) |
| | (4)–(9) | 30 Oct 2012 (for the purpose of enabling the Scottish Ministers to exercise powers to make orders or regulations) (SSI 2012/288) |
| | | 30 Nov 2013 (otherwise) (SSI 2012/288) |
| | (10) | 30 Oct 2012 (for the purpose of enabling the Scottish Ministers to exercise powers to make orders or regulations) (SSI 2012/288) |
| | | 30 Nov 2012 (otherwise) (SSI 2012/288) |
| | (11) | 30 Oct 2012 (for the purpose of enabling the Scottish Ministers to exercise powers to make orders or regulations) (SSI 2012/288)[3] |
| | | 30 Nov 2012 (otherwise) (SSI 2012/288) |
| 5 | | 30 Oct 2012 (for the purpose of enabling the Scottish Ministers to exercise powers to make orders or regulations) (SSI 2012/288)[3] |
| | | 30 Nov 2012 (otherwise) (SSI 2012/288) |
| 6 | (1) | 30 Nov 2013 (SSI 2012/288) |
| | (2) | 30 Nov 2012 (SSI 2012/288) |
| 7 | (1) | 30 Nov 2012 (SSI 2012/288) |
| | (2) | 30 Nov 2013 (SSI 2012/288) |
| | (3) | 30 Nov 2012 (SSI 2012/288)[3] |
| | (4)–(8) | 30 Nov 2012 (SSI 2012/288) |
| 8, 9 | | 30 Nov 2012 (SSI 2012/288)[3] |
| 10 | (1), (2) | 30 Nov 2012 (SSI 2012/288)[3] |
| | (3)–(8) | 30 Nov 2013 (SSI 2012/288) |
| 11 | | 30 Oct 2012 (for the purpose of enabling the Scottish Ministers to exercise powers to make orders) (SSI 2012/288) |
| | | 30 Nov 2012 (otherwise) (SSI 2012/288) |
| 12 | (1), (2)(a) | 30 Oct 2012 (for the purpose of enabling the Scottish Ministers to exercise powers to make orders) (SSI 2012/288) |
| | | 30 Nov 2012 (otherwise) (SSI 2012/288) |
| | (2)(b) | 30 Oct 2012 (for the purpose of enabling the Scottish Ministers to exercise powers to make orders) (SSI 2012/288) |
| | | 30 Nov 2013 (otherwise) (SSI 2012/288) |
| | (3)–(10) | 30 Oct 2012 (for the purpose of enabling the Scottish Ministers to exercise powers to make orders) (SSI 2012/288)[3] |
| | | 30 Nov 2012 (otherwise) (SSI 2012/288) |
| 13 | | 30 Nov 2012 (SSI 2012/288) |
| 14 | (1), (2) | 30 Nov 2012 (SSI 2012/288) |
| | (3) | 30 Nov 2013 (otherwise) (SSI 2012/288) |
| | (4)–(7) | 30 Nov 2012 (SSI 2012/288) |
| 15, 16 | | 30 Nov 2012 (SSI 2012/288) |
| 17 | | 30 Nov 2012 (SSI 2012/288)[3] |
| 18 | | 30 Nov 2012 (SSI 2012/288) |
| 19 | | 30 Oct 2012 (SSI 2012/288) |
| 20 | | 30 Nov 2012 (SSI 2012/288) |

**Crofting Reform (Scotland) Act 2010 (asp 14)**—*contd*

| | | |
|---|---|---|
| 21 | (1), (2) | 30 Nov 2012 (SSI 2012/288) |
| | (3) | 30 Nov 2013 (SSI 2012/288) |
| | (4), (5) | 30 Nov 2012 (SSI 2012/288) |
| 22 | | 30 Nov 2012 (SSI 2012/288) |
| 23 | | 30 Nov 2013 (SSI 2012/288)[3] |
| 24 | (1)(a) | 30 Nov 2013 (SSI 2012/288)[3] |
| | (1)(b) | 30 Nov 2012 (SSI 2012/288)[3] |
| | (2), (3) | 30 Nov 2012 (SSI 2012/288) |
| | (4) | 30 Nov 2013 (SSI 2012/288) |
| 25 | | 30 Oct 2012 (for the purpose of enabling the Scottish Ministers to exercise powers to make orders or regulations) (SSI 2012/288) |
| | | 30 Nov 2012 (otherwise) (SSI 2012/288) |
| 26 | (1)(a) | 30 Nov 2013 (SSI 2012/288) |
| | (1)(b) | 30 Nov 2012 (SSI 2012/288) |
| | (2) | 30 Nov 2013 (SSI 2012/288) |
| | (3)–(14) | 30 Nov 2012 (SSI 2012/288)[3] |
| 27 | | 30 Nov 2013 (SSI 2012/288)[3] |
| 28 | | See Sch 3 below |
| 29 | (1)–(3) | 30 Nov 2013 (SSI 2012/288)[3] |
| | (4)–(6) | 30 Nov 2012 (SSI 2012/288) |
| 30, 31 | | 30 Nov 2012 (SSI 2012/288) |
| 32 | (1)–(11) | 30 Oct 2012 (for the purpose of enabling the Scottish Ministers to exercise powers to make orders) (SSI 2012/288) |
| | | 30 Nov 2012 (otherwise) (SSI 2012/288) |
| | (12) | 30 Oct 2012 (for the purpose of the application of ss 11, 12, 19 of this Act to land held runrig, but in the case of ss 11, 12 only for the purpose of enabling the Scottish Ministers to exercise powers to make orders) (SSI 2012/288) |
| | | 30 Nov 2012 (otherwise) (SSI 2012/288) |
| | (13)–(16) | 30 Oct 2012 (for the purpose of enabling the Scottish Ministers to exercise powers to make orders) (SSI 2012/288) |
| | | 30 Nov 2012 (otherwise) (SSI 2012/288) |
| 33 | | 1 Oct 2011 (SSI 2011/334)[2] |
| 34 | | 22 Dec 2010 (in so far as inserts Crofters (Scotland) Act 1993, s 19B for the purpose of enabling the Scottish Ministers to make a scheme or regulations under s 42, 46 or 46A of that Act) (SSI 2010/437)[1] |
| | | 1 Oct 2011 (in so far as inserts Crofters (Scotland) Act 1993, ss 19B (for all remaining purposes), 19C, 19D(1), (2), (6)–(8)) (SSI 2011/334)[2] |
| | | 30 Nov 2012 (in so far as inserts Crofters (Scotland) Act 1993, s 19D(4), (5)) (SSI 2012/288)[3] |
| | | 30 Nov 2013 (in so far as inserts s 19D(3) thereof) (SSI 2012/288)[3] |
| 35 | | 1 Oct 2011 (SSI 2011/334)[2] |
| 36 | | 1 Apr 2012 (SSI 2011/334)[2] |
| 37 | | 1 Oct 2011 (in so far as inserts Crofters (Scotland) Act 1993, ss 26A–26F, 26G(1), (2), (5)–(7), 26H, 26J(1)–(4), (7), (8), (11) and (12), 26K(1)–(8)) (SSI 2011/334)[2] |
| | | 30 Nov 2012 (in so far as inserts Crofters (Scotland) Act 1993, ss 26G(3), (4), 26J(6), (10), 26K(9)) (SSI 2012/288)[3] |
| | | 30 Nov 2013 (in so far as inserts s 26J(5), (9) thereof) (SSI 2012/288)[3] |
| 38 | | 1 Apr 2012 (SSI 2011/334)[2] |
| 39 | | 22 Dec 2010 (for the purpose of enabling the Scottish Ministers to make a scheme or regulations under the Crofters (Scotland) Act 1993, s 42, 46 or 46A) (SSI 2010/437)[1] |
| | | 1 Oct 2011 (in so far as inserts Crofters (Scotland) Act 1993, ss 29A(1), (4)–(6), (9), (10) and 29B) (SSI 2011/334)[2] |
| | | 30 Nov 2012 (in so far as inserts Crofters (Scotland) Act 1993, s 29A(3), (8)) (SSI 2012/288)[3] |

**Crofting Reform (Scotland) Act 2010 (asp 14)**—*contd*

| | | |
|---|---|---|
| | | 30 Nov 2013 (otherwise) (SSI 2012/288)[3] |
| 40, 41 | | 1 Jul 2011 (SSI 2010/437)[1] |
| 42–45 | | 1 Oct 2011 (SSI 2011/334)[2] |
| 46 | | 1 Oct 2011 (in so far as repeals Crofters (Scotland) Act 1993, s 4, and replaces it with s 4(1), (2), (4), (7)) (SSI 2011/334)[2] |
| | | 30 Nov 2012 (in so far as inserts Crofters (Scotland) Act 1993, s 4(5), (6)) (SSI 2012/288)[3] |
| | | 30 Nov 2013 (otherwise) (SSI 2012/288)[3] |
| 47 | | 1 Oct 2011 (in so far as repeals Crofters (Scotland) Act 1993, s 51, and replaces it with s 51(1)–(3)) (SSI 2011/334)[2] |
| | | 30 Nov 2012 (otherwise) (SSI 2012/288) |
| 48 | (1)–(6) | 1 Oct 2011 (SSI 2011/334)[2] |
| | (7) | 1 Oct 2011 (in so far as repeals Crofters (Scotland) Act 1993, ss 58A(7)–(10) and replaces them with sub-ss (7)(a)–(f), (h)) (SSI 2011/334)[2] |
| | | 1 Apr 2012 (otherwise) (SSI 2011/334)[2] |
| | (8)–(12) | 1 Oct 2011 (SSI 2011/334)[2] |
| 49 | (1)–(3) | 1 Oct 2011 (SSI 2011/334)[2] |
| | (4) | 1 Oct 2011 (in so far as repeals Crofters (Scotland) Act 1993, s 10(2B)–(4D) and replaces them with sub-ss (3), (4A), (4C)(a)) (SSI 2011/334)[2] |
| | | 30 Nov 2012 (otherwise) (SSI 2012/288) |
| | (5), (6) | 1 Oct 2011 (SSI 2011/334)[2] |
| | (7), (8) | 30 Nov 2012 (otherwise) (SSI 2012/288) |
| 50 | (1) | 1 Feb 2011 (SSI 2010/437)[1] |
| | (2) | 1 Oct 2011 (SSI 2011/334)[2] |
| 51 | | 22 Dec 2010 (SSI 2010/437)[1] |
| 52 | | 30 Oct 2012 (SS1 2012/288) |
| 53, 54 | | 6 Aug 2010 (RA) |
| 55 | | See Sch 4 below |
| 56 | | 22 Dec 2010 (SSI 2010/437)[1] |
| 57 | | 6 Aug 2010 (RA) |
| Sch 1 | | 1 Oct 2011 (in so far as repeals Crofters (Scotland) Act 1993, Sch 1, and replaces it with paras 1, 2, 7, 10, 12–17 and 20 of the substituted Sch 1) (SSI 2011/334)[2] |
| | | 1 Apr 2012 (otherwise) (SSI 2011/334)[2] |
| Sch 2 | Table 1 | 30 Nov 2013 (SSI 2012/288) |
| | Table 2 | 30 Nov 2012 (SSI 2012/288) |
| Sch 3 | paras 1–3 | 30 Nov 2012 (SSI 2012/288) |
| | paras 4, 5 | 30 Oct 2012 (for the purpose of enabling the Scottish Ministers to exercise powers to make orders) (SSI 2012/288) |
| | | 30 Nov 2012 (otherwise) (SSI 2012/288) |
| | paras 6–11 | 30 Nov 2012 (otherwise) (SSI 2012/288) |
| | para 12 | 30 Oct 2012 (SSI 2012/288) |
| | paras 13, 14 | 30 Nov 2012 (otherwise) (SSI 2012/288) |
| Sch 4 | para 1 | 22 Dec 2010 (SSI 2010/437)[1] |
| | para 2 | 1 Oct 2011 (SSI 2011/334)[2] |
| | para 3(1) | 1 Oct 2011 (SSI 2011/334)[2] |
| | para 3(2) | 1 Apr 2012 (SSI 2011/334)[2] |
| | para 3(3) | 1 Oct 2011 (SSI 2011/334)[2] |
| | para 3(4) | 22 Dec 2010 (SSI 2010/437)[1] |
| | para 3(5)(a) | 30 Nov 2012 (in so far as inserts Crofters (Scotland) Act 1993, s 4A(2B)) (SSI 2012/288)[3] |
| | | 30 Nov 2013 (otherwise) (SSI 2012/288)[3] |
| | para 3(5)(b), (6), (7) | 1 Oct 2011 (SSI 2011/334)[2] |
| | para 3(8)(a) | 1 Oct 2011 (in so far as inserts Crofters (Scotland) Act 1993, s 8(1A)) (SSI 2011/334)[2] |
| | | 30 Nov 2013 (in so far as inserts s 8(1B) thereof) (SSI 2012/288)[3] |
| | para 3(8)(b) | 1 Oct 2011 (SSI 2011/334)[2] |

**Crofting Reform (Scotland) Act 2010 (asp 14)**—*contd*

| | |
|---|---|
| para 3(8)(c), (d) | 30 Nov 2012 (SSI 2012/288)[3] |
| para 3(9)(a) | 30 Nov 2013 (SSI 2012/288)[3] |
| para 3(9)(b) | 1 Oct 2011 (SSI 2011/334)[2] |
| para 3(9)(c) | 30 Nov 2012 (SSI 2012/288)[3] |
| para 3(10)(a) | 1 Oct 2011 (SSI 2011/334)[2] |
| para 3(10)(b) | 30 Nov 2012 (SSI 2012/288)[3] |
| para 3(10)(c)–(e) | 1 Oct 2011 (SSI 2011/334)[2] |
| para 3(11)(a) | 30 Nov 2012 (for the purpose of inserting the Crofters (Scotland) Act 1993, s 20(1ZB), (1ZC)) (SSI 2012/288) |
| | 30 Nov 2013 (otherwise) (SSI 2012/288)[3] |
| para 3(11)(b)–(d) | 30 Nov 2012 (SSI 2012/288)[3] |
| para 3(12)(a) | 30 Nov 2012 (for the purpose of inserting the Crofters (Scotland) Act 1993, s 21A(1B), (1C)) (SSI 2012/288) |
| | 30 Nov 2013 (otherwise) (SSI 2012/288)[3] |
| para 3(12)(b) | 30 Nov 2012 (SSI 2012/288) |
| para 3(13) | 1 Oct 2011 (SSI 2011/334)[2] |
| para 3(14)(a) | 30 Nov 2012 (for the purpose of inserting the Crofters (Scotland) Act 1993, s 23(3ZB)) (SSI 2012/288)[3] |
| | 30 Nov 2013 (otherwise) (SSI 2012/288)[3] |
| para 3(14)(b) | 1 Oct 2011 (SSI 2011/334)[2] |
| para 3(14)(c)(i) | 30 Nov 2013 (SSI 2012/288) |
| para 3(14)(c)(ii)–(iv) | 1 Oct 2011 (SSI 2011/334)[2] |
| para 3(14)(d) | 30 Nov 2012 (for the purpose of inserting the Crofters (Scotland) Act 1993, s 23(5ZE)) (SSI 2012/288) |
| | 30 Nov 2013 (otherwise) (SSI 2012/288)[3] |
| para 3(14)(e) | 30 Nov 2012 (for the purpose of inserting the Crofters (Scotland) Act 1993, s 23(5E)) (SSI 2012/288) |
| | 30 Nov 2013 (otherwise) (SSI 2012/288)[3] |
| para 3(14)(f)–(i) | 1 Oct 2011 (SSI 2011/334)[2] |
| para 3(15)(a) | 1 Oct 2011 (SSI 2011/334)[2] |
| para 3(15)(b) | 30 Nov 2013 (SSI 2012/288)[3] |
| para 3(15)(c) | 30 Nov 2012 (for the purpose of inserting the Crofters (Scotland) Act 1993, s 24(3C)) (SSI 2012/288)[3] |
| | 30 Nov 2013 (otherwise) (SSI 2012/288)[3] |
| para 3(16)(a) | 30 Nov 2012 (SSI 2012/288)[3] |
| para 3(16)(b) | 30 Nov 2012 (for the purpose of inserting the Crofters (Scotland) Act 1993, s 24(4ZC), (4ZD)) (SSI 2012/288) |
| | 30 Nov 2013 (otherwise) (SSI 2012/288)[3] |
| para 3(17)–(22) | 1 Oct 2011 (SSI 2011/334)[2] |
| para 3(23) | 30 Nov 2013 (SSI 2012/288)[3] |
| para 3(24), (25) | 1 Oct 2011 (SSI 2011/334)[2] |
| para 3(26)–(28) | 22 Dec 2010 (SSI 2010/437)[1] |
| para 3(29), (30) | 1 Oct 2011 (SSI 2011/334)[2] |
| para 3(31)(a), (b) | 30 Nov 2012 (SSI 2012/288) |
| para 3(31)(c) | 30 Nov 2012 (for the purpose of inserting the Crofters (Scotland) Act 1993, s 52(5B)–(5D)) (SSI 2012/288)[3] |
| | 30 Nov 2013 (otherwise) (SSI 2012/288)[3] |
| para 3(31)(d)–(h) | 30 Nov 2012 (SSI 2012/288)[3] |
| para 3(31)(i) | 30 Nov 2013 (SSI 2012/288) |
| para 3(32)(a) | 30 Nov 2012 (SSI 2012/288) |
| para 3(32)(b)–(d) | 1 Oct 2011 (SSI 2011/334)[2] |
| para 3(33) | 30 Nov 2012 (SSI 2012/288) |
| para 3(34), (35) | 1 Oct 2011 (SSI 2011/334)[2] |
| para 3(36)(a) | 22 Dec 2010 (SSI 2010/437)[1] |
| para 3(36)(b) | 1 Apr 2012 (SSI 2011/334)[2] |
| para 3(36)(c) | 30 Nov 2012 (SSI 2012/288) |
| para 3(36)(d) | 1 Oct 2011 (in so far as inserts definition "cultivate") (SSI 2011/334)[2] |

**Crofting Reform (Scotland) Act 2010 (asp 14)**—*contd*

|  |  |  |
|---|---|---|
|  | 30 Nov 2012 (in so far as inserts definition "date of registration") (SSI 2012/288) |
| para 3(36)(e) | 30 Nov 2012 (for the purpose of inserting definition "first registration" in the Crofters (Scotland) Act 1993, s 6(1)) (SSI 2012/288) |
| para 3(36)(f), (g) | 30 Nov 2013 (SSI 2012/288) |
| para 3(36)(h) | 1 Oct 2011 (SSI 2011/334)[2] |
| para 3(36)(i) | 22 Dec 2010 (SSI 2010/437)[1] |
| para 3(36)(j) | 1 Oct 2011 (in so far as inserts definition "purposeful use") (SSI 2011/334)[2] |
|  | 30 Nov 2012 (in so far as inserts definitions "registered", "unregistered" and "registration schedule") (SSI 2012/288) |
| para 3(37) | 1 Oct 2011 (SSI 2011/334)[2] |
| para 4 | 1 Apr 2012 (SSI 2011/334)[2] |

[1]   For transitional provisions and savings, see SSI 2010/437, arts 4, 5

[2]   For transitional provisions and savings, see SSI 2011/334, arts 4–8

[3]   For transitional provisions and savings, see SSI 2012/288, art 4, Sch 2

---

**Crown Benefices (Parish Representatives) Measure 2010 (No 3)**

*RA:* 18 Mar 2010

*Commencement provisions:* s 2(2)

This Measure was brought into force on 1 Jan 2011 by an instrument made by the Archbishops of Canterbury and York and dated 23 Nov 2010 (made under s 2(2))

---

**Debt Relief (Developing Countries) Act 2010 (c 22)**

*RA:* 8 Apr 2010

*Commencement provisions:* s 10(1)

Whole Act in force 8 Jun 2010 (s 10(1))

---

**Digital Economy Act 2010 (c 24)**

*RA:* 8 Apr 2010

*Commencement provisions:* ss 28(8), 47; Digital Economy Act 2010 (Appointed Day No 1) Order 2011, SI 2011/1170; Digital Economy Act 2010 (Appointed Day No 2) Order 2012, SI 2012/1164; Digital Economy Act 2010 (Appointed Day No 3) Order 2012, SI 2012/1766; Digital Economy Act 2010 (Appointed Day No 4) Order 2014, SI 2014/1659

|  |  |  |
|---|---|---|
| 1–4 |  | 8 Jun 2010 (s 47(1)) |
| 5–7 |  | 8 Apr 2010 (s 47(2)(a)) |
| 8–14 |  | 8 Jun 2010 (s 47(1)) |
| 15 |  | 8 Apr 2010 (s 47(2)(a)) |
| 16 | (1) | 8 Apr 2010 (s 47(2)(a)) |
|  | (2), (3) | 8 Jun 2010 (s 47(1)) |
| 17, 18 |  | 8 Jun 2010 (s 47(1)) |
| 19–21 |  | *Not yet in force* |
| 22–27 |  | 8 Jun 2010 (s 47(1)) |
| 28 | (1)–(7) | *Not yet in force* |
|  | (8)–(11) | 8 Jun 2010 (s 47(1)) |
| 29 |  | 22 Jun 2011 (SI 2011/1170) |
| 30–32 |  | 8 Apr 2010 (s 47(2)(b)) |
| 33–39 |  | 8 Jun 2010 (s 47(1)) |

**Digital Economy Act 2010 (c 24)**—*contd*

| | | |
|---|---|---|
| 40 | (1) | 8 Jun 2010 (s 47(1)) |
| | (2), (3) | 30 Jul 2012 (SI 2012/1766) |
| | (4) | 8 Jun 2010 (s 47(1)) |
| | (5), (6) | 30 Jul 2012 (SI 2012/1766) |
| | (7) | 8 Jun 2010 (s 47(1)) |
| 41 | (1) | 1 May 2012 (SI 2012/1164) |
| | (2) | See Sch 1 below |
| 42 | | 8 Jun 2010 (s 47(1)) |
| 43 | | 30 Jun 2014 (SI 2014/1659) |
| 44 | | 8 Jun 2010 (s 47(1)) |
| 45 | | See Sch 2 below |
| 46–48 | | 8 Apr 2010 (s 47(2)(c)) |
| Sch 1 | para 1 | 8 Jun 2010 (s 47(1)) |
| | paras 2–4 | 1 May 2012 (SI 2012/1164) |
| | para 5 | 8 Jun 2010 (s 47(1)) |
| | paras 6–9 | 1 May 2012 (SI 2012/1164) |
| | para 10(1) | 8 Jun 2010 (s 47(1)) |
| | para 10(2) | 1 May 2012 (SI 2012/1164) |
| | para 10(3), (4) | 8 Jun 2010 (s 47(1)) |
| | paras 11, 12 | 8 Jun 2010 (s 47(1)) |
| Sch 2 | | 8 Jun 2010 (s 47(1)), repeals of or in— |
| | | Video Recordings Act 1984, s 8; |
| | | Broadcasting Act 1990, ss 14, 106; |
| | | Communications Act 2003, ss 224, 314 |
| | | 22 Jun 2011 (SI 2011/1170), repeals of or in— |
| | | Broadcasting Act 1990, ss 183A, 184 |
| | | 1 May 2012 (SI 2012/1164), repeals of or in— |
| | | Video Recordings Act 1984, ss 4, 22 |
| | | 30 Jul 2012 (SI 2012/1766), repeals of or in— |
| | | Video Recordings Act 1984, s 2 |
| | | 30 Jun 2014 (SI 2014/1659), repeals of or in— |
| | | Public Lending Right Act 1979, s 5 |
| | | *Not yet in force*, repeals of or in— |
| | | Communications Act 2003, ss 218, 221, Sch 15 |

**Energy Act 2010 (c 27)**

*RA*: 8 Apr 2010

*Commencement provisions*: s 38; Energy Act 2010 (Commencement) Order 2012, SI 2012/1841

| | | |
|---|---|---|
| 1–17 | | 8 Jun 2010 (s 38(3)) |
| 18–23 | | 16 Jul 2012 (SI 2012/1841) |
| 24–29 | | 8 Jun 2010 (s 38(3)) |
| 30–34 | | 8 Apr 2010 (s 38(1)) |
| 35 | | See Schedule below |
| 36–39 | | 8 Apr 2010 (s 38(1)) |
| Schedule | paras 1–4 | 8 Apr 2010 (s 38(1)) |
| | para 5 | See paras 6–10 below |
| | para 6 | 8 Jun 2010 (s 38(3)) |
| | paras 7, 8 | 16 Jul 2012 (SI 2012/1841) |
| | paras 9–16 | 8 Jun 2010 (s 38(3)) |

**Equality Act 2010 (c 15)**

*RA*: 8 Apr 2010

*Commencement provisions*: s 216; Equality Act (Commencement No 1) Order 2010, SI 2010/1736; Equality Act 2010 (Commencement No 2) Order 2010, SI 2010/1966; Equality Act 2010 (Commencement

**Equality Act 2010 (c 15)**—*contd*

No 3) Order 2010, SI 2010/2191; Equality Act 2010 (Commencement No 4, Savings, Consequential, Transitional, Transitory and Incidental Provisions and Revocation) Order 2010, SI 2010/2317[2], as amended by SI 2010/2337; Equality Act 2010 (Commencement No 5) Order 2011, SI 2011/96; Equality Act 2010 (Commencement No 6) Order 2011, SI 2011/1066; Equality Act 2010 (Commencement No 7) Order 2011, SI 2011/1636; Equality Act 2010 (Commencement No 8) Order 2011, SI 2011/2646; Equality Act 2010 (Commencement No 9) Order 2012, SI 2012/1569; Equality Act 2010 (Commencement No 10) Order 2012, SI 2012/2184; Equality Act 2010 (Commencement No 11) Order 2016, SI 2016/839; Equality Act 2010 (Commencement No 12) Order 2017, SI 2017/107; Equality Act 2010 (Commencement No 13) (Scotland) Order 2017, SSI 2017/403; Equality Act 2010 (Commencement No 14) (Wales) Order 2019, SI 2019/1469; Equality Act 2010 (Commencement No 15) (Wales) Order 2021, SI 2021/298; Equality Act 2010 (Commencement No 16) (Wales and Scotland) Order 2021, SI 2021/1322

| | | |
|---|---|---|
| 1 | (1), (2) | 1 Apr 2018 (S) (SSI 2017/403) |
| | | 31 Mar 2021 (W) (so far as applies to a relevant authority) |
| | | *Not yet in force* (E) (W, otherwise) |
| | (3)(a)–(g) | 1 Apr 2018 (S) (SSI 2017/403) |
| | | 31 Mar 2021 (W) (so far as applies to a relevant authority) |
| | | *Not yet in force* (E) (W, otherwise) |
| | (3)(h)–(j) | *Never in force* (repealed) |
| | (3)(k) | 1 Apr 2018 (S) (SSI 2017/403) |
| | | 31 Mar 2021 (W) (so far as applies to a relevant authority) |
| | | *Not yet in force* (E) (W, otherwise) |
| | (4), (5) | *Never in force* (repealed) |
| | (6) | 1 Apr 2018 (S) (SSI 2017/403) |
| | | 31 Mar 2021 (W) (so far as applies to a relevant authority) |
| | | *Not yet in force* (E) (W, otherwise) |
| 2 | | 1 Apr 2018 (so far as confers a power on the Scottish Ministers) (SSI 2017/403) |
| | | 22 Nov 2019 (so far as confers a power on the Welsh Ministers) (SI 2019/1469) |
| | | *Not yet in force* (otherwise) |
| 3 | | 1 Apr 2018 (S) (SSI 2017/403) |
| | | 31 Mar 2021 (W) (for the purposes of s 1 so far as applies to a relevant authority) (SI 2021/298) |
| | | *Not yet in force* (E) (W, otherwise) |
| 4, 5 | | 1 Oct 2010 (SI 2010/2317) |
| 6 | (1)–(4) | 1 Oct 2010 (SI 2010/2317) |
| | (5) | 6 Jul 2010 (for the purpose of enabling subordinate legislation or guidance to be made) (SI 2010/1736) |
| | | 1 Oct 2010 (otherwise) (SI 2010/2317)[2] |
| | (6) | See Sch 1 below |
| 7–13 | | 1 Oct 2010 (SI 2010/2317) |
| 14 | | *Not yet in force* |
| 15–21 | | 1 Oct 2010 (SI 2010/2317) |
| 22 | | 6 Jul 2010 (for the purpose of enabling subordinate legislation or guidance to be made) (SI 2010/1736) |
| | | 1 Oct 2010 (otherwise) (SI 2010/2317) |
| 23–27 | | 1 Oct 2010 (SI 2010/2317)[2] |
| 28–30 | | 1 Oct 2010 (except in so far as they relate to the protected characteristic of age) (SI 2010/2317)[2] |
| | | 1 Oct 2012 (exception noted above) (SI 2012/1569) |
| 31 | (1)–(8) | 1 Oct 2010 (except in so far as they relate to the protected characteristic of age) (SI 2010/2317) |
| | | 1 Oct 2012 (exception noted above) (SI 2012/1569) |
| | (9) | See Sch 2 below |
| | (10) | See Sch 3 below |
| 32–35 | | 1 Oct 2010 (SI 2010/2317) |
| 36 | (1)(a)–(c) | 1 Oct 2010 (SI 2010/2317) |
| | (1)(d) | *Not yet in force* |

**Equality Act 2010 (c 15)**—*contd*

| | | |
|---|---|---|
| | (2)–(4) | 1 Oct 2010 (SI 2010/2317) |
| | (5), (6) | *Not yet in force* |
| | (7), (8) | 1 Oct 2010 (SI 2010/2317) |
| 37 | | 11 Jul 2011 (SI 2011/1636) |
| 38 | (1)–(7) | 1 Oct 2010 (SI 2010/2317) |
| | (8) | See Sch 4 below |
| | (9) | See Sch 5 below |
| 39–60 | | 1 Oct 2010 (SI 2010/2317) |
| 61 | (1)–(7) | 1 Oct 2010 (SI 2010/2317) |
| | (8), (9) | 6 Jul 2010 (for the purpose of enabling subordinate legislation or guidance to be made) (SI 2010/1736) |
| | | 1 Oct 2010 (otherwise) (SI 2010/2317) |
| | (10), (11) | 1 Oct 2010 (SI 2010/2317) |
| 62–77 | | 1 Oct 2010 (SI 2010/2317) |
| 78 | | 22 Aug 2016 (SI 2016/839) |
| 79 | | 1 Oct 2010 (SI 2010/2317) |
| 80 | (1)–(7) | 1 Oct 2010 (SI 2010/2317) |
| | (8) | See Sch 7 below |
| 81, 82 | | 6 Jul 2010 (for the purpose of enabling subordinate legislation or guidance to be made) (SI 2010/1736) |
| | | 1 Oct 2010 (otherwise) (SI 2010/2317) |
| 83 | (1)–(9) | 1 Oct 2010 (SI 2010/2317) |
| | (10) | See Sch 8 below |
| | (11) | See Sch 9 below |
| 84–93 | | 1 Oct 2010 (SI 2010/2317) |
| 94 | (1)–(11) | 1 Oct 2010 (SI 2010/2317) |
| | (12) | See Sch 12 below |
| 95 | | 1 Oct 2010 (SI 2010/2317) |
| 96 | (1)–(8) | 1 Oct 2010 (SI 2010/2317) |
| | (9)(a) | 1 Oct 2010 (SI 2010/2317) |
| | (9)(b) | 3 Sep 2010 (for the purpose of enabling regulations to be made) (SI 2010/2191) |
| | | 1 Oct 2010 (otherwise) (SI 2010/2317) |
| | (10), (11) | 6 Jul 2010 (for the purpose of enabling subordinate legislation or guidance to be made) (SI 2010/1736) |
| | | 1 Oct 2010 (otherwise) (SI 2010/2317) |
| 97 | | 6 Jul 2010 (for the purpose of enabling subordinate legislation or guidance to be made) (SI 2010/1736) |
| | | 1 Oct 2010 (otherwise) (SI 2010/2317) |
| 98 | | See Sch 13 below |
| 99 | | See Sch 14 below |
| 100–105 | | 1 Oct 2010 (except in so far as they apply to the protected characteristic of age) (SI 2010/2317) |
| | | 1 Oct 2012 (exception noted above) (SI 2012/1569) |
| 106 | | *Not yet in force* |
| 107 | (1)–(7) | 1 Oct 2010 (except in so far as applies to the protected characteristic of age) (SI 2010/2317) |
| | | 1 Oct 2012 (exception noted above) (SI 2012/1569) |
| | (8) | See Sch 15 below |
| | (9) | See Sch 16 below |
| 108–115 | | 1 Oct 2010 (SI 2010/2317)[2] |
| 116 | (1)(a), (b) | 1 Oct 2010 (SI 2010/2317)[2] |
| | (1)(c) | 1 Oct 2010 (in so far as relates to, and for the purposes of, making rules under Sch 17, Pt 3) (SI 2010/2317)[2] |
| | | 18 Mar 2011 (otherwise) (SI 2010/2317) |
| | (2) | 1 Oct 2010 (SI 2010/2317)[2] |
| | (3) | See Sch 17 below |
| 117 | (1)–(4) | 6 Jul 2010 (for the purpose of enabling subordinate legislation or guidance to be made) (SI 2010/1736) |

**Equality Act 2010 (c 15)**—*contd*

| | | |
|---|---|---|
| | | 1 Oct 2010 (otherwise) (SI 2010/2317)[2] |
| | (5)–(7) | 1 Oct 2010 (SI 2010/2317)[2] |
| 118–135 | | 1 Oct 2010 (SI 2010/2317)[2] |
| 136 | (1)–(5) | 1 Oct 2010 (SI 2010/2317)[2] |
| | (6)(a)–(e) | 1 Oct 2010 (SI 2010/2317)[2] |
| | (6)(f) | 18 Mar 2011 (SI 2010/2317)[2] |
| 137 | | 1 Oct 2010 (SI 2010/2317)[2] |
| 138 | (1), (2) | 6 Jul 2010 (for the purpose of enabling subordinate legislation or guidance to be made) (SI 2010/1736) |
| | | 1 Oct 2010 (otherwise) (SI 2010/2317)[2] |
| | (3), (4) | 1 Oct 2010 (SI 2010/2317)[2] |
| | (5)–(7) | 6 Jul 2010 (for the purpose of enabling subordinate legislation or guidance to be made) (SI 2010/1736) |
| | | 1 Oct 2010 (otherwise) (SI 2010/2317)[2] |
| | (8) | 1 Oct 2010 (SI 2010/2317)[2] |
| 139–146 | | 1 Oct 2010 (SI 2010/2317)[2] |
| 147 | (1)–(3) | 1 Oct 2010 (SI 2010/2317) |
| | (4) | 6 Jul 2010 (for the purpose of enabling subordinate legislation or guidance to be made) (SI 2010/1736) |
| | | 1 Oct 2010 (otherwise) (SI 2010/2317) |
| | (5)–(9) | 1 Oct 2010 (SI 2010/2317) |
| 148 | | 1 Oct 2010 (SI 2010/2317) |
| 149 | | 5 Apr 2011 (SI 2011/1066) |
| 150 | | 18 Jan 2011 (for the purposes of ss 151–155, 157, Sch 19) (SI 2011/96) |
| | | 5 Apr 2011 (otherwise) (SI 2011/1066) |
| 151–155 | | 18 Jan 2011 (SI 2011/96) |
| 156 | | 5 Apr 2011 (SI 2011/1066) |
| 157 | | 18 Jan 2011 (SI 2011/96) |
| 158 | | 1 Oct 2010 (SI 2010/2317) |
| 159 | (1), (2) | 6 Apr 2011 (SI 2011/96) |
| | (3) | 1 Oct 2010 (for the purposes of s 158(4)) (SI 2010/2317) |
| | | 6 Apr 2011 (otherwise) (SI 2011/96) |
| | (4)–(6) | 6 Apr 2011 (SI 2011/96) |
| 160 | | *Not yet in force* |
| 161 | | 1 Oct 2010 (in so far as confers power to make regulations) (SI 2010/2317) |
| | | *Not yet in force* (otherwise) |
| 162–164 | | *Not yet in force* |
| 165 | | 1 Oct 2010 (in so far as relates to, and for the purposes of, the issue of exemption certificates under s 166) (SI 2010/2317) |
| | | 6 Apr 2017 (otherwise) (SI 2017/107) |
| 166 | | 1 Oct 2010 (SI 2010/2317) |
| 167 | (1)–(5) | 1 Oct 2010 (in so far as relates to, and for the purposes of, the issue of exemption certificates under s 166) (SI 2010/2317) |
| | | 6 Apr 2017 (otherwise) (SI 2017/107) |
| | (6) | 1 Oct 2010 (SI 2010/2317) |
| | (7) | 1 Oct 2010 (in so far as relates to, and for the purposes of, the issue of exemption certificates under s 166) (SI 2010/2317) |
| | | 6 Apr 2017 (otherwise) (SI 2017/107) |
| 168–185 | | 1 Oct 2010 (SI 2010/2317) |
| 186 | (1) | See Sch 20 below |
| | (2) | 8 Apr 2010 (s 216(1)(a)) |
| 187, 188 | | 1 Oct 2010 (SI 2010/2317) |
| 189 | | See Sch 21 below |
| 190 | | 1 Oct 2010 (SI 2010/2317) |
| 191 | | See Sch 22 below |
| 192–195 | | 1 Oct 2010 (SI 2010/2317) |
| 196 | | See Sch 23 below |

**Equality Act 2010 (c 15)**—*contd*

| | | |
|---|---|---|
| 197 | | 19 Jun 2012 (SI 2012/1569) |
| 198–201 | | *Not yet in force* |
| 202 | (1) | See sub-ss (2)–(4) below |
| | (2) | 5 Dec 2011 (SI 2011/2646) |
| | (3) | 11 Jul 2011 (SI 2011/1636) |
| | (4) | 11 Jul 2011 (in so far as inserts Civil Partnership Act 2004 s 6A(3B), (3C)) (SI 2011/1636) |
| | | 5 Dec 2011 (otherwise) (SI 2011/2646) |
| 203–205 | | 8 Apr 2010 (s 216(1)(b)) |
| 206 | | See Sch 25 below |
| 207–210 | | 8 Apr 2010 (s 216(1)(b)) |
| 211 | (1) | See Sch 26 below |
| | (2) | See Sch 27 below |
| 212–218 | | 8 Apr 2010 (s 216(1)(b)) |
| Sch 1 | paras 1–5 | 6 Jul 2010 (for the purpose of enabling subordinate legislation or guidance to be made) (SI 2010/1736) |
| | | 1 Oct 2010 (otherwise) (SI 2010/2317) |
| | para 6 | 1 Oct 2010 (SI 2010/2317) |
| | paras 7, 8 | 6 Jul 2010 (for the purpose of enabling subordinate legislation or guidance to be made) (SI 2010/1736) |
| | | 1 Oct 2010 (otherwise) (SI 2010/2317) |
| | para 9 | 1 Oct 2010 (SI 2010/2317) |
| | paras 10, 11 | 6 Jul 2010 (for the purpose of enabling subordinate legislation or guidance to be made) (SI 2010/1736) |
| | | 1 Oct 2010 (otherwise) (SI 2010/2317) |
| | para 12 | 1 Oct 2010 (SI 2010/2317) |
| | paras 13–16 | 6 Jul 2010 (for the purpose of enabling subordinate legislation or guidance to be made) (SI 2010/1736) |
| | | 1 Oct 2010 (otherwise) (SI 2010/2317) |
| Sch 2 | para 1 | 1 Oct 2010 (except in so far as they relate to the protected characteristic of age) (SI 2010/2317)[2] |
| | | 1 Sep 2012 (exception noted above) (SI 2012/2184) |
| | para 2 | 1 Oct 2010 (except in so far as relates to the protected characteristic of age, and except in so far as relates to the third requirement in specified cases[3]) (SI 2010/2317) |
| | | 1 Sep 2012 (exceptions noted above) (SI 2012/2184) |
| | paras 3, 4 | 1 Oct 2010 (except in so far as they relate to the protected characteristic of age) (SI 2010/2317)[2] |
| | | 1 Sep 2012 (exception noted above) (SI 2012/2184) |
| Sch 3 | | 1 Oct 2010 (except in so far as they relate to the protected characteristic of age) (SI 2010/2317)[2] |
| | | 1 Oct 2012 (exception noted above) (SI 2012/1569) |
| Sch 4 | paras 1–4 | 1 Oct 2010 (SI 2010/2317) |
| | paras 5–7 | *Not yet in force* |
| | para 8 | 1 Oct 2010 (except in so far as relates to para 5(4)(c)) (SI 2010/2317) |
| | | *Not yet in force* (exception noted above) |
| | para 9 | 6 Jul 2010 (for the purpose of enabling subordinate legislation or guidance to be made) (SI 2010/1736) |
| | | 1 Oct 2010 (otherwise) (SI 2010/2317) |
| Schs 5, 6 | | 1 Oct 2010 (SI 2010/2317) |
| Sch 7 | paras 1–3 | 1 Oct 2010 (SI 2010/2317) |
| | paras 4–6 | 6 Jul 2010 (for the purpose of enabling subordinate legislation or guidance to be made) (SI 2010/1736) |
| | | 1 Oct 2010 (otherwise) (SI 2010/2317) |
| Sch 8 | | 1 Oct 2010 (SI 2010/2317) |
| Sch 9 | paras 1–15 | 1 Oct 2010 (SI 2010/2317) (para 8 repealed) |
| | para 16 | 6 Jul 2010 (for the purpose of enabling subordinate legislation or guidance to be made) (SI 2010/1736) |
| | | 1 Oct 2010 (otherwise) (SI 2010/2317) |

**Equality Act 2010 (c 15)**—*contd*

| | | |
|---|---|---|
| | paras 17–20 | 1 Oct 2010 (SI 2010/2317) |
| Schs 10, 11 | | 1 Oct 2010 (SI 2010/2317) |
| Sch 12 | paras 1–4 | 1 Oct 2010 (SI 2010/2317) |
| | para 5 | 6 Jul 2010 (for the purpose of enabling subordinate legislation or guidance to be made) (SI 2010/1736) |
| | | 1 Oct 2010 (otherwise) (SI 2010/2317) |
| | paras 6, 7 | 1 Oct 2010 (SI 2010/2317) |
| Sch 13 | para 1 | 1 Oct 2010 (SI 2010/2317) |
| | para 2 | 1 Oct 2010 (except in so far as it relates to the third requirement) (SI 2010/2317) |
| | | 1 Sep 2012 (exception noted above) (SI 2012/2184) |
| | paras 3, 4 | 1 Oct 2010 (SI 2010/2317) |
| | para 5 | 1 Oct 2010 (except in so far as relates to the third requirement in a case where A is the governing body of a maintained school) (SI 2010/2317) |
| | | 1 Sep 2012 (exception noted above) (SI 2012/2184) |
| | paras 6–9 | 1 Oct 2010 (SI 2010/2317) |
| Schs 14, 15 | | 1 Oct 2010 (SI 2010/2317) |
| Sch 16 | | 1 Oct 2010 (except in so far as applies to the protected characteristic of age) (SI 2010/2317) |
| | | 1 Oct 2012 (exception noted above) (SI 2012/1569) |
| Sch 17 | para 1 | 6 Jul 2010 (for the purpose of enabling subordinate legislation or guidance to be made) (SI 2010/1736) |
| | | 1 Oct 2010 (otherwise) (SI 2010/2317)[2] |
| | paras 2–5 | 1 Oct 2010 (SI 2010/2317)[2] |
| | para 6(1)–(7) | 6 Jul 2010 (for the purpose of enabling subordinate legislation or guidance to be made) (SI 2010/1736) |
| | | 1 Oct 2010 (otherwise) (SI 2010/2317)[2] |
| | para 6(8), (9) | 1 Oct 2010 (SI 2010/2317)[2] |
| | paras 7–12 | 1 Oct 2010 (in so far as they confer or relate to the power to make rules under para 10) (SI 2010/2317) |
| | | 18 Mar 2011 (otherwise) (SI 2010/2317)[2] |
| | paras 13, 14 | 1 Oct 2010 (SI 2010/2317)[2] |
| Sch 18 | | 5 Apr 2011 (SI 2011/1066) |
| Sch 19 | | 18 Jan 2011 (SI 2011/96) |
| Sch 20 | | *Never in force* (repealed) |
| Sch 21 | paras 1–5 | 1 Oct 2010 (SI 2010/2317) |
| | para 6 | 6 Jul 2010 (for the purpose of enabling subordinate legislation or guidance to be made) (SI 2010/1736) |
| | | 1 Oct 2010 (otherwise) (SI 2010/2317) |
| | para 7 | 1 Oct 2010 (SI 2010/2317) |
| Schs 22, 23 | | 1 Oct 2010 (except in so far as they apply to the protected characteristic of age in Pts 3, 7 of this Act) (SI 2010/2317) |
| | | 1 Oct 2012 (exception noted above) (SI 2012/1569) |
| Sch 24 | | 8 Apr 2010 (s 216(1)(b)) |
| Sch 25 | | 1 Oct 2010 (SI 2010/2317) |
| Sch 26 | paras 1–8 | 1 Oct 2010 (SI 2010/2317) |
| | paras 9–12 | 5 Apr 2011 (SI 2011/1066) |
| | paras 13–60 | 1 Oct 2010 (SI 2010/2317)[2] |
| | para 61 | See paras 62–85 below |
| | para 62–64 | 1 Oct 2010 (SI 2010/2317) |
| | para 65(1)–(3) | 6 Jul 2010 (SI 2010/1736)[1] |
| | para 65(4) | 1 Oct 2010 (SI 2010/2317) |
| | para 65(5) | 6 Jul 2010 (SI 2010/1736)[1] |
| | para 65(6) | 5 Apr 2011 (SI 2011/1066) |
| | paras 66–72 | 1 Oct 2010 (SI 2010/2317)[2] |
| | paras 73, 74 | 5 Apr 2011 (SI 2011/1066) |
| | para 75 | 1 Oct 2010 (SI 2010/2317) |

**Equality Act 2010 (c 15)**—*contd*

|  |  |  |
|---|---|---|
| | para 76 | 1 Oct 2010 (except in so far as relates to the Equality Act 2006, s 34(2)(a), (b), as substituted by sub-para (3)(b)) (SI 2010/2317)[2] |
| | | 5 Apr 2011 (in so far as relates to the Equality Act 2006, s 34(2)(b), as substituted by sub-para (3)(b)) (SI 2011/1066) |
| | | 20 Nov 2021 (in so far as relates to s 34(2)(a) of that Act) (W), (S) (SI 2021/1322) |
| | | *Not yet in force* (in so far as relates to s 34(2)(a) of that Act) (E) |
| | paras 77–81 | 1 Oct 2010 (SI 2010/2317) |
| | para 82 | 1 Oct 2010 (except in so far as relates to the Equality Act 2006, ss 84, 85) (SI 2010/2317) |
| | | 5 Apr 2011 (exception noted above) (SI 2011/1066) |
| | paras 83–107 | 1 Oct 2010 (SI 2010/2317) |
| Sch 27 | Pt 1 | 1 Oct 2010 (SI 2010/2317)[2], repeals of or in— |

Sex Disqualification Removal Act 1919;
Equal Pay Act 1970;
Sex Discrimination Act 1975 (except ss 76A–76C, and s 81 so far as relates thereto);
Race Relations Act 1976 (except ss 71–71B, Sch 1A);
Estate Agents Act 1979, s 5(3);
Further Education Act 1985, s 4;
Sex Discrimination Act 1986;
Employment Act 1989;
Local Government and Housing Act 1989;
Social Security Act 1989;
Enterprise and New Towns (Scotland) Act 1990;
Contracts (Applicable Law) Act 1990;
Further and Higher Education Act 1992;
Trade Union and Labour Relations (Consolidation) Act 1992;
Trade Union Reform and Employment Rights Act 1993;
Race Relations (Remedies) Act 1994;
Disability Discrimination Act 1995 (except ss 49A–49D);
Pensions Act 1995;
Employment Tribunals Act 1996;
Employment Rights Act 1996;
Armed Forces Act 1996;
Education Act 1996;
Employment Rights (Dispute Resolution) Act 1998;
School Standards and Framework Act 1998;
Learning and Skills Act 2000;
Race Relations (Amendment) Act 2000;
Standards in Scotland's Schools etc Act 2000;
Special Educational Needs and Disability Act 2001;
Sex Discrimination (Election Candidates) Act 2002;
Employment Act 2002;
Education Act 2002;
Private Hire Vehicles (Carriage of Guide Dogs etc) Act 2002;
Nationality, Immigration and Asylum Act 2002;
Gender Recognition Act 2004;
Civil Partnership Act 2004;
Higher Education Act 2004;
Education (Additional Support for Learning) (Scotland) Act 2004;
Disability Discrimination Act 2005;
Serious Organised Crime and Police Act 2005;
Education Act 2005;
Charities and Trustee Investment (Scotland) Act 2005;
Equality Act 2006 (except ss 84, 85);
Education and Inspections Act 2006, Schs 1, 3;

**Equality Act 2010 (c 15)**—*contd*

                    Legal Services Act 2007;
                    Greater London Authority Act 2007;
                    Regulatory Enforcement and Sanctions Act 2008;
                    Education and Skills Act 2008;
                    Apprenticeships, Skills, Children and Learning Act 2009
                 5 Apr 2011 (SI 2011/1066), repeals of or in—
                    Sex Discrimination Act 1975, ss 76A–76C (and s 81 in so far as
                        relates to those sections);
                    Race Relations Act 1976, ss 71–71B, Sch 1A;
                    Local Government Act 1988 (note that SI 2010/2317,
                        art 2(15)(f)(iii) refers to a repeal of s 17(8) of the 1988 Act;
                        however it is thought that this should be a reference to s 17(9)
                        thereof);
                    Disability Discrimination Act 1995, ss 49A–49D;
                    Greater London Authority Act 1999, s 404;
                    Equality Act 2006, ss 84, 85
                    *Not yet in force,* repeals of or in—
                    Local Transport Act 2008, ss 55, 56

|          |    |                                |
|----------|----|--------------------------------|
|          | Pt 2 | 1 Oct 2010 (SI 2010/2317)    |
| Sch 28   |    | 8 Apr 2010 (s 216(1)(b))       |

[1]  For a saving, see SI 2010/1736, art 3(2)

[2]  For savings, consequential, transitional, transitory and incidental provisions, see SI 2010/2317, arts 4–22, Schs 1–7

[3]  The specified cases are—

(i) a local authority in England or Wales exercising functions under the Education Acts, or

(ii) an education authority exercising functions under an enactment specified in Sch 3, para 10(2) of this Act

---

**Equitable Life (Payments) Act 2010 (c 34)**

*RA:* 16 Dec 2010

Whole Act in force 16 Dec 2010 (RA)

---

**Finance Act 2010 (c 13)**

*Budget Day:* 24 Mar 2010

*RA:* 8 Apr 2010

The commencement details of Finance Acts are not set out, as the dates from which their provisions take effect are usually stated clearly and unambiguously in the text of the Act, and charging provisions will normally state for which year or years of assessment they are to have effect.

---

**Finance (No 2) Act 2010 (c 31)**

*Budget Day:* 22 Jun 2010

*RA:* 27 Jul 2010

The commencement details of Finance Acts are not set out, as the dates from which their provisions take effect are usually stated clearly and unambiguously in the text of the Act, and charging provisions will normally state for which year or years of assessment they are to have effect.

---

## Finance (No 3) Act 2010 (c 33)

*RA:* 16 Dec 2010

The commencement details of Finance Acts are not set out, as the dates from which their provisions take
    effect are usually stated clearly and unambiguously in the text of the Act, and charging provisions will
    normally state for which year or years of assessment they are to have effect.

## Financial Services Act 2010 (c 28)

*RA:* 8 Apr 2010

*Commencement provisions:* s 26; Financial Services Act 2010 (Commencement No 1 and Transitional
    Provision) Order 2010, SI 2010/2480

| | | |
|---|---|---|
| 1 | | 8 Apr 2010 (s 26(1)(a)) |
| 2 | (1) | 8 Apr 2010 (s 26(1)(b)) |
| | (2)–(4) | 12 Oct 2010 (SI 2010/2480) |
| | (5) | 8 Apr 2010 (s 26(1)(b)) |
| | (6) | See Sch 1 below |
| | (7), (8) | 8 Apr 2010 (s 26(1)(b)) |
| 3 | (1) | 8 Apr 2010 (s 26(1)(c)) |
| | (2), (3) | 8 Jun 2010 (s 26(2)(a)) |
| | (4) | 8 Apr 2010 (s 26(1)(c)) |
| | (5) | 8 Jun 2010 (s 26(2)(a)) |
| 4, 5 | | 8 Apr 2010 (s 26(1)(d)) |
| 6–12 | | 8 Jun 2010 (s 26(2)(b)) |
| 13, 14 | | 12 Oct 2010 (SI 2010/2480)[1] |
| 15 | | *Not yet in force* |
| 16 | | 8 Apr 2010 (s 26(1)(e)) |
| 17 | | 12 Oct 2010 (SI 2010/2480) |
| 18 | | 8 Jun 2010 (s 26(2)(c)) |
| 19–23 | | 8 Apr 2010 (s 26(1)(f)) |
| 24 | (1), (2) | See Sch 2 below |
| | (3)–(5) | 8 Apr 2010 (s 26(1)(g)) |
| 25 | | 8 Apr 2010 (s 26(1)(h)) |
| 26 | | 8 Apr 2010 (s 26(1)(i)) |
| 27 | | 8 Apr 2010 (s 26(1)(j)) |
| Sch 1 | | 8 Apr 2010 (except so far as it relates to the Financial Services and Markets Act 2000, Sch 1A, paras 13, 15, 16) (s 26(1)(k)) |
| | | 1 Apr 2011 (otherwise) (SI 2010/2480) |
| Sch 2 | paras 1–6 | 8 Apr 2010 (s 26(1)(l)) |
| | paras 7–10 | 8 Jun 2010 (s 26(2)(e)) |
| | para 11 | 8 Apr 2010 (s 26(1)(l)) |
| | para 12 | 8 Jun 2010 (s 26(2)(e)) |
| | para 13 | 8 Apr 2010 (s 26(1)(l)) |
| | paras 14, 15 | 8 Jun 2010 (s 26(2)(e)) |
| | para 16(1), (2) | 8 Apr 2010 (s 26(1)(l)) |
| | paras 16(3), 17–20 | 8 Jun 2010 (s 26(2)(e)) |
| | para 21 | 12 Oct 2010 (SI 2010/2480) |
| | para 22 | 8 Apr 2010 (s 26(1)(l)) |
| | para 23 | 12 Oct 2010 (SI 2010/2480) |
| | para 24(1), (2) | 8 Apr 2010 (s 26(1)(l)) |
| | para 24(3) | 12 Oct 2010 (SI 2010/2480) |
| | para 25 | 8 Apr 2010 (s 26(1)(l)) |
| | para 26 | 8 Jun 2010 (s 26(2)(e)) |
| | paras 27, 28 | 8 Apr 2010 (s 26(1)(l)) |
| | para 29 | 8 Jun 2010 (s 26(2)(e)) |
| | paras 30–32, 33(1) | 8 Apr 2010 (s 26(1)(l)) |
| | para 33(2) | 12 Oct 2010 (SI 2010/2480) |
| | para 33(3) | 8 Apr 2010 (s 26(1)(l)) |

**Financial Services Act 2010 (c 28)**—*contd*

| | | |
|---|---|---|
| para 33(4) | 8 Jun 2010 (s 26(2)(e)) | |
| paras 34, 35 | 8 Apr 2010 (s 26(1)(l)) | |
| para 36 | *Not yet in force* | |
| paras 37–45 | 8 Apr 2010 (s 26(1)(l)) | |
| paras 46, 47 | 8 Jun 2010 (s 26(2)(e)) | |
| para 48 | 8 Apr 2010 (s 26(1)(l)) | |

¹ For a transitional provision, see SI 2010/2480, art 4

---

**Fiscal Responsibility Act 2010 (c 3)**

*RA:* 10 Feb 2010

Whole Act in force 10 Feb 2010 (RA)

---

**Flood and Water Management Act 2010 (c 29)**

*RA:* 8 Apr 2010

*Commencement provisions*: s 49(3); Flood and Water Management Act 2010 (Commencement No 1 and Transitional Provisions) Order 2010, SI 2010/2169; Flood and Water Management Act 2010 (Commencement No 2) Order 2011, SI 2011/95; Flood and Water Management Act 2010 (Commencement No 3 and Transitional Provisions) Order 2011, SI 2011/694, as amended by SI 2013/755; Flood and Water Management Act 2010 (Commencement No 1 and Transitional Provisions) (England) Order 2011, SI 2011/1770; Flood and Water Management Act 2010 (Commencement No 4 and Transitional Provisions) Order 2011, SI 2011/2204; Flood and Water Management Act 2010 (Commencement No 5 and Transitional Provisions) Order 2011, SI 2011/2856; Flood and Water Management Act 2010 (Commencement No 6 and Transitional Provisions) Order 2012, SI 2012/879; Flood and Water Management Act 2010 (Commencement No 7) Order 2012, SI 2012/2000; Flood and Water Management Act 2010 (Commencement No 8 and Transitional Provisions) Order 2012, SI 2012/2048; Flood and Water Management Act 2010 (Commencement No 2, Transitional and Savings Provisions) (England) Order 2013, SI 2013/1590; Flood and Water Management Act 2010 (Commencement No 9) Order 2014, SI 2014/3155; Flood and Water Management Act 2010 (Commencement No 1 and Transitional Provisions) (Wales) Order 2016, SI 2016/79; Flood and Water Management Act 2010 (Commencement No 2) (Wales) Order 2018, SI 2018/557

| | | |
|---|---|---|
| 1–3 | | 1 Sep 2010 (in so far as required for the exercise of the power in s 4(2)(f)) (SI 2010/2169) |
| | | 1 Oct 2010 (otherwise) (SI 2010/2169) |
| 4 | | 1 Sep 2010 (in so far as provides power for the Minister to make an order under sub-s (2)(f)) (SI 2010/2169) |
| | | 1 Oct 2010 (otherwise) (SI 2010/2169) |
| 5 | | 1 Oct 2010 (SI 2010/2169) |
| 6 | | 1 Sep 2010 (in so far as required for the exercise of the power in s 4(2)(f)) (SI 2010/2169) |
| | | 1 Oct 2010 (otherwise) (SI 2010/2169) |
| 7–10 | | 1 Oct 2010 (SI 2010/2169) |
| 11 | | 19 Jul 2011 (E) (SI 2011/1770) |
| | | 1 Nov 2011 (W) (SI 2011/2204) |
| 12 | | 1 Nov 2011 (SI 2011/2204) |
| 13 | | 1 Oct 2010 (SI 2010/2169) |
| 14 | | 6 Apr 2011 (SI 2011/694) |
| 15 | | 18 Jan 2011 (so far as provides power for the Minister, as defined in sub-s (10), to make regulations under sub-s (8)) (SI 2011/95) |
| | | 6 Apr 2011 (W) (otherwise) (SI 2011/694) |
| | | *Not yet in force* (E) (otherwise) |
| 16 | | 1 Oct 2010 (SI 2010/2169) |
| 17 | (1) | 1 Apr 2011 (SI 2011/694) |

**Flood and Water Management Act 2010 (c 29)**—*contd*

|       |         |                                                                                                                           |
|-------|---------|---------------------------------------------------------------------------------------------------------------------------|
|       | (2), (3) | 1 Oct 2010 (in so far as they provide power for the Secretary of State to make regulations under the Local Government Finance Act 1988, s 74 for the purpose of this section) (SI 2010/2169) |
|       |         | 1 Apr 2011 (otherwise) (SI 2011/694)                                                                                      |
|       | (4)     | 1 Apr 2011 (SI 2011/694)                                                                                                  |
| 18    |         | 19 Jul 2011 (E) (SI 2011/1770)                                                                                            |
|       |         | 1 Nov 2011 (W) (SI 2011/2204)                                                                                             |
| 19    |         | 6 Apr 2011 (SI 2011/694)                                                                                                  |
| 20    |         | 1 Oct 2010 (SI 2010/2169)                                                                                                 |
| 21    |         | 6 Apr 2011 (SI 2011/694)                                                                                                  |
| 22    | (1)(a)  | 1 Apr 2011 (SI 2011/694)                                                                                                  |
|       | (1)(b)  | 1 Oct 2010 (in so far as it defines an "English Committee") (SI 2010/2169)                                                |
|       |         | 1 Apr 2011 (otherwise) (SI 2011/694)                                                                                      |
|       | (1)(c)  | 1 Oct 2010 (in so far as it defines a "Welsh Committee") (SI 2010/2169)                                                   |
|       |         | 1 Apr 2011 (otherwise) (SI 2011/694)                                                                                      |
|       | (2)     | 1 Oct 2010 (SI 2010/2169)                                                                                                 |
| 23    |         | 1 Apr 2011 (SI 2011/694)                                                                                                  |
| 24    |         | 1 Oct 2010 (SI 2010/2169)                                                                                                 |
| 25    |         | 1 Apr 2011 (SI 2011/694)                                                                                                  |
| 26    |         | 1 Oct 2010 (SI 2010/2169)                                                                                                 |
| 27    |         | 1 Oct 2011 (SI 2011/2204)                                                                                                 |
| 28, 29 |        | 1 Oct 2010 (SI 2010/2169)                                                                                                 |
| 30    |         | See Sch 1 below                                                                                                          |
| 31    |         | See Sch 2 below                                                                                                          |
| 32    |         | See Sch 3 below                                                                                                          |
| 33    |         | See Sch 4 below                                                                                                          |
| 34    |         | See Sch 5 below                                                                                                          |
| 35    |         | 1 Oct 2010 (in so far as it relates to water or sewerage undertakers whose areas are wholly or mainly in England) (SI 2010/2169) |
|       |         | *Not yet in force* (otherwise)                                                                                            |
| 36    |         | 1 Sep 2010 (in so far as provides power for the Minister to make an order under the Water Industry Act 1991, s 76A(2)) (SI 2010/2169)[1] |
|       |         | 1 Oct 2010 (otherwise) (SI 2010/2169)                                                                                     |
| 37    |         | 6 Apr 2011 (SI 2011/694)                                                                                                  |
| 38    |         | 18 Jan 2011 (so far as provides power for the Minister, as defined in sub-s (10), to make regulations under sub-s (8)) (SI 2011/95) |
|       |         | 1 Dec 2011 (otherwise) (SI 2011/2856)[5]                                                                                  |
| 39    |         | 18 Jan 2011 (so far as provides power for the Minister, as defined in sub-s (14), to make regulations under sub-s (12)) (SI 2011/95) |
|       |         | 1 Dec 2011 (otherwise) (SI 2011/2856)[5]                                                                                  |
| 40, 41 |        | 1 Oct 2010 (SI 2010/2169)                                                                                                 |
| 42    |         | 1 Oct 2010 (in so far as provides power for the Minister to make regulations under the Water Industry Act 1991, s 106B(5), (6)) (SI 2010/2169) |
|       |         | 1 Oct 2012 (in so far as it relates to water or sewerage undertakers whose areas are wholly or mainly in Wales) (SI 2012/2048)[7] |
|       |         | *Not yet in force* (otherwise)                                                                                            |
| 43    |         | 1 Oct 2010 (in so far as it relates to water or sewerage undertakers whose areas are wholly or mainly in England) (SI 2010/2169) |
|       |         | *Not yet in force* (otherwise)                                                                                            |
| 44    |         | 1 Oct 2011 (SI 2011/2204)                                                                                                 |
| 45    |         | 1 Oct 2010 (in so far as provides power for the Minister to make regulations under the Water Industry Act 1991, s 144C(4), (5)) (SI 2010/2169) |
|       |         | 1 Jan 2015 (in relation to an undertaker whose area is wholly or mainly in Wales) (SI 2014/3155)                          |

**Flood and Water Management Act 2010 (c 29)**—*contd*

|  |  |  |
|---|---|---|
|  |  | *Not yet in force* (otherwise) |
| 46, 47 |  | 1 Oct 2010 (SI 2010/2169) |
| 48, 49 |  | 1 Apr 2010 (s 49(3)(k)) |
| Sch 1 | paras 1–14 | 1 Aug 2012 (SI 2012/2000) |
|  | paras 15, 16 | 6 Apr 2011 (in so far as they provide power for the Minister, as defined by para 17, to make regulations) (SI 2011/694) |
|  |  | 1 Aug 2012 (otherwise) (SI 2012/2000) |
|  | para 17 | 6 Apr 2011 (SI 2011/694) |
| Sch 2 | paras 1–24 | 19 Jul 2011 (E) (SI 2011/1770)[3] |
|  |  | 1 Oct 2011 (W) (SI 2011/2204)[4] |
|  | para 25 | 1 Oct 2010 (SI 2010/2169) |
|  | paras 26, 27 | 6 Apr 2012 (SI 2012/879) |
|  | para 28 | 1 Oct 2010 (SI 2010/2169) |
|  | para 29 | 19 Jul 2011 (E) (SI 2011/1770) |
|  |  | 1 Oct 2011 (W) (SI 2011/2204) |
|  | para 30 | 19 Jul 2011 (E) (SI 2011/1770)[3] |
|  |  | 1 Oct 2011 (W) (SI 2011/2204)[4] |
|  | para 31 | 6 Apr 2012 (SI 2012/879) |
|  | paras 32(1)–(3) | 6 Apr 2012 (SI 2012/879)[6] |
|  | para 32(4) | *Not yet in force* |
|  | paras 32(5)–(7), 33, 34 | 6 Apr 2012 (SI 2012/879)[6] |
|  | paras 35, 36 | 19 Jul 2011 (E) (SI 2011/1770) |
|  |  | 1 Oct 2011 (W) (SI 2011/2204) |
|  | para 37 | 6 Apr 2011 (SI 2011/694) |
|  | paras 38, 39 | 19 Jul 2011 (E) (SI 2011/1770) |
|  |  | 1 Oct 2011 (W) (SI 2011/2204) |
|  | paras 40, 41 | 1 Apr 2011 (SI 2011/694) |
|  | para 42 | *Not yet in force* |
|  | para 43 | 1 Apr 2011 (SI 2011/694) |
|  | para 44 | 1 Apr 2011 (SI 2011/694)[2] |
|  | paras 45–47 | 19 Jul 2011 (E) (SI 2011/1770) |
|  |  | 1 Oct 2011 (W) (SI 2011/2204) |
|  | para 48 | 1 Apr 2011 (SI 2011/694) |
|  | para 49 | 19 Jul 2011 (E) (SI 2011/1770) |
|  |  | 1 Oct 2011 (W) (SI 2011/2204) |
|  | paras 50–52 | 1 Apr 2011 (SI 2011/694) |
|  | para 53 | 1 Apr 2011 (SI 2011/694)[2] |
|  | para 54 | 1 Oct 2010 (in so far as provides power for the Minister to make regulations under the Local Government Act 2000, s 21F) (SI 2010/2169) |
|  |  | 6 Apr 2011 (otherwise) (SI 2011/694) |
| Sch 3 |  | 2 May 2018 (W) (for the purposes of making subordinate legislation) (SI 2018/557) |
|  |  | 7 Jan 2019 (W) (otherwise) (SI 2018/557) |
|  |  | *Not yet in force* (E) |
| Sch 4 | para 1 | 1 Oct 2011 (SI 2011/2204) |
|  | para 2 | 1 Oct 2011 (in so far as provides power for the Minister to make regulations or orders under the Reservoirs Act 1975) (SI 2011/2204) |
|  |  | 30 Jul 2013 (E) (otherwise) (SI 2013/1590)[8] |
|  |  | 1 Apr 2016 (W) (otherwise) (SI 2016/79) |
|  | para 3 | 30 Jul 2013 (E) (SI 2013/1590) |
|  |  | 1 Apr 2016 (W) (SI 2016/79) |
|  | para 4 | 1 Oct 2011 (in so far as provides power for the Minister to make regulations or orders under the Reservoirs Act 1975) (SI 2011/2204) |
|  |  | 30 Jul 2013 (E) (otherwise) (SI 2013/1590) |
|  |  | 1 Apr 2016 (W) (otherwise) (SI 2016/79) |

**See Halsbury's Statutes Citator for amendments to these Acts** 2113

Flood and Water Management Act 2010 (c 29)—*contd*

| | |
|---|---|
| paras 5, 6 | 30 Jul 2013 (E) (SI 2013/1590) |
| | 1 Apr 2016 (W) (SI 2016/79) |
| para 7 | 1 Oct 2011 (in so far as provides power for the Minister to make regulations or orders under the Reservoirs Act 1975) (SI 2011/2204) |
| | 30 Jul 2013 (E) (otherwise) (SI 2013/1590) |
| | 1 Apr 2016 (W) (otherwise) (SI 2016/79) |
| paras 8, 9 | 30 Jul 2013 (E) (SI 2013/1590) |
| | 1 Apr 2016 (W) (SI 2016/79) |
| para 10 | 1 Oct 2011 (in so far as provides power for the Minister to make regulations or orders under the Reservoirs Act 1975) (SI 2011/2204) |
| | 30 Jul 2013 (E) (otherwise) (SI 2013/1590)[8] |
| | 1 Apr 2016 (W) (otherwise) (SI 2016/79) |
| para 11 | 30 Jul 2013 (E) (SI 2013/1590) |
| | 1 Apr 2016 (W) (SI 2016/79) |
| para 12 | 1 Oct 2011 (in so far as provides power for the Minister to make regulations or orders under the Reservoirs Act 1975) (SI 2011/2204) |
| | 30 Jul 2013 (E) (otherwise) (SI 2013/1590) |
| | 1 Apr 2016 (W) (otherwise) (SI 2016/79)[9] |
| paras 13, 14 | 30 Jul 2013 (E) (SI 2013/1590)[8] |
| | 1 Apr 2016 (W) (SI 2016/79) |
| paras 15–19 | 30 Jul 2013 (E) (SI 2013/1590)[8] |
| | 1 Apr 2016 (W) (SI 2016/79)[9] |
| paras 20, 21 | 30 Jul 2013 (E) (SI 2013/1590)[8] |
| | 1 Apr 2016 (W) (SI 2016/79) |
| para 22 | 1 Oct 2011 (in so far as amends power for the Minister to make regulations or rules under the Reservoirs Act 1975) (SI 2011/2204) |
| | 30 Jul 2013 (E) (otherwise) (SI 2013/1590) |
| | 1 Apr 2016 (W) (otherwise) (SI 2016/79) |
| paras 23, 24 | 30 Jul 2013 (E) (SI 2013/1590) |
| | 1 Apr 2016 (W) (SI 2016/79) |
| para 25 | 1 Oct 2011 (in so far as provides power for the Minister to make regulations or orders under the Reservoirs Act 1975) (SI 2011/2204) |
| | 30 Jul 2013 (E) (otherwise) (SI 2013/1590)[8] |
| | 1 Apr 2016 (W) (otherwise) (SI 2016/79) |
| para 26 | 30 Jul 2013 (E) (SI 2013/1590) |
| | 1 Apr 2016 (W) (SI 2016/79) |
| para 27 | 1 Oct 2011 (in so far as provides power for the Minister to make regulations or orders under the Reservoirs Act 1975) (SI 2011/2204) |
| | 30 Jul 2013 (E) (otherwise) (SI 2013/1590) |
| | 1 Apr 2016 (W) (otherwise) (SI 2016/79) |
| paras 28, 29 | 30 Jul 2013 (E) (SI 2013/1590) |
| | 1 Apr 2016 (W) (SI 2016/79) |
| para 30 | 1 Oct 2011 (in so far as provides power for the Minister to make regulations or orders under the Reservoirs Act 1975) (SI 2011/2204) |
| | *Not yet in force* (otherwise) |
| para 31 | 1 Oct 2011 (in so far as amends power for the Minister to make regulations or rules under the Reservoirs Act 1975) (SI 2011/2204) |
| | *Not yet in force* (otherwise) |
| para 32 | 1 Oct 2011 (in so far as provides power for the Minister to make regulations or orders under the Reservoirs Act 1975) (SI 2011/2204) |
| | *Not yet in force* (otherwise) |

**Flood and Water Management Act 2010 (c 29)**—*contd*

|  |  |  |
|---|---|---|
| | para 33 | 1 Oct 2011 (in so far as provides power for the Minister to make regulations or orders under the Reservoirs Act 1975) (SI 2011/2204) |
| | | 30 Jul 2013 (E) (otherwise) (SI 2013/1590) |
| | | 1 Apr 2016 (W) (otherwise) (SI 2016/79) |
| | paras 34–36 | 30 Jul 2013 (E) (SI 2013/1590) |
| | | 1 Apr 2016 (W) (SI 2016/79) |
| | para 37 | 1 Oct 2011 (in so far as provides power for the Minister to make regulations or orders under the Reservoirs Act 1975) (SI 2011/2204) |
| | | *Not yet in force* (otherwise) |
| | paras 38–40 | 1 Oct 2011 (SI 2011/2204) |
| | para 41 | 30 Jul 2013 (E) (SI 2013/1590) |
| | | 1 Apr 2016 (W) (SI 2016/79) |
| | paras 42, 43 | 1 Oct 2011 (SI 2011/2204) |
| Sch 5 | paras 1, 2 | 1 Apr 2011 (SI 2011/694)[2] |
| | para 3 | 1 Oct 2010 (in so far as provides power for the Secretary of State to make regulations under the Water Industry Act 1991, s 23(2E)) (SI 2010/2169) |
| | | *Not yet in force* (otherwise) |
| | para 4 | 1 Apr 2011 (SI 2011/694) |
| | para 5 | 1 Oct 2010 (in so far as provides power for the Secretary of State to amend the Water Industry Act 1991, Sch 2) (SI 2010/2169) |
| | | *Not yet in force* (otherwise) |
| | para 6 | 1 Oct 2010 (in so far as provides power for the Secretary of State to make regulations under the Water Industry Act 1991, s 23(3A)) (SI 2010/2169) |
| | | *Not yet in force* (otherwise) |
| | para 7 | 1 Apr 2011 (SI 2011/694) |

[1]    For transitional provisions, see SI 2010/2169, art 5

[2]    For transitional provisions, see SI 2011/694, art 5

[3]    For transitional provisions, see SI 2011/1770, art 4

[4]    For transitional provisions, see SI 2011/2204, art 5

[5]    For transitional provisions, see SI 2011/2856, art 4

[6]    For transitional provisions, see SI 2012/879, art 4

[7]    For transitional provisions, see SI 2012/2048, art 3

[8]    For transitional and savings provisions, see SI 2013/1590, art 4

[9]    For transitional and savings provisions, see SI 2016/79, art 3

---

**Home Owner and Debtor Protection (Scotland) Act 2010 (asp 6)**

*RA:* 18 Mar 2010

*Commencement provisions:* s 17(2)–(4); Home Owner and Debtor Protection (Scotland) Act 2010 (Commencement) Order 2010, SSI 2010/314

|  |  |  |
|---|---|---|
| 1–6 | | 30 Sep 2010 (SSI 2010/314) |
| 7 | | 3 Oct 2010 (SSI 2010/314) |
| 8 | | 30 Sep 2010 (SSI 2010/314) |
| 9 | (1) | 15 Nov 2010 (SSI 2010/314) |
| | (2) | 7 Sep 2010 (in so far as it inserts Bankruptcy (Scotland) Act 1985, s 5B(5)) (SSI 2010/314) |
| | | 15 Nov 2010 (otherwise) (SSI 2010/314) |
| | (3) | 15 Nov 2010 (SSI 2010/314) |
| 10 | | 15 Nov 2010 (SSI 2010/314) |

**Home Owner and Debtor Protection (Scotland) Act 2010 (asp 6)**—*contd*

| | | |
|---|---|---|
| 11 | | 7 Sep 2010 (in so far as it inserts Bankruptcy (Scotland) Act 1985, s 40(3B)) (SSI 2010/314) |
| | | 15 Nov 2010 (otherwise) (SSI 2010/314) |
| 12 | | 15 Nov 2010 (SSI 2010/314) |
| 13 | | 7 Sep 2010 (SSI 2010/314) |
| 14–17 | | 18 Mar 2010 (s 17(2)) |

**Housing (Scotland) Act 2010 (asp 17)**

*RA:* 9 Dec 2010

*Commencement provisions:* s 166; Housing (Scotland) Act 2010 (Commencement No 1) Order 2010, SSI 2010/444; Housing (Scotland) Act 2010 (Commencement No 2, Transitional, Transitory and Saving Provisions) Order 2011, SSI 2011/96; Housing (Scotland) Act 2010 (Commencement No 3) Order 2011, SSI 2011/181; Housing (Scotland) Act 2010 (Commencement No 4) Order 2011, SSI 2011/339; Housing (Scotland) Act 2010 (Commencement No 5) Order 2012, SSI 2012/19; Housing (Scotland) Act 2010 (Commencement No 6, Transitional and Savings Provisions) Order 2012, SSI 2012/39[2], as amended by SSI 2012/91; Housing (Scotland) Act 2010 (Commencement No 7 and Transitional Provision) Order 2012, SSI 2012/91; Housing (Scotland) Act 2010 (Commencement No 8 and Saving Provision) Order 2012, SSI 2012/283

| | | |
|---|---|---|
| 1, 2 | | 1 Apr 2011 (SSI 2011/96) |
| 3 | (1) | 1 Apr 2012 (SSI 2012/39) |
| | (2) | 1 Apr 2011 (SSI 2011/96) |
| 4 | | 1 Apr 2011 (for the purpose of requiring preparation of the Regulator's statement) (SSI 2011/96) |
| | | 1 Apr 2012 (otherwise) (SSI 2012/39) |
| 5 | (1)(a) | 1 Apr 2011 (SSI 2011/96) |
| | (1)(b) | 1 Apr 2012 (SSI 2012/39) |
| | (2), (3) | 1 Apr 2011 (SSI 2011/96) |
| 6 | (1) | 1 Apr 2012 (SSI 2012/39) |
| | (2) | 1 Apr 2011 (SSI 2011/96) |
| 7–12 | | 1 Apr 2011 (SSI 2011/96) |
| 13, 14 | | 1 Apr 2012 (SSI 2012/39) |
| 15–17 | | 1 Apr 2011 (SSI 2011/96) |
| 18 | (1), (2) | 1 Apr 2011 (SSI 2011/96) |
| | (3) | 1 Apr 2012 (SSI 2012/39) |
| 19 | | 1 Apr 2011 (SSI 2011/96) |
| 20–23 | | 1 Apr 2012 (SSI 2012/39) |
| 24 | | 1 Apr 2011 (for the purpose of enabling the Scottish Ministers to make provision by order) (SSI 2011/96) |
| | | 1 Apr 2012 (otherwise) (SSI 2012/39) |
| 25, 26 | | 1 Apr 2011 (for the purpose of enabling consultation by the Regulator) (SSI 2011/96) |
| | | 1 Apr 2012 (otherwise) (SSI 2012/39) |
| 27 | | 1 Apr 2012 (SSI 2012/39) |
| 28 | | 1 Apr 2011 (for the purpose of enabling consultation by the Regulator) (SSI 2011/96) |
| | | 1 Apr 2012 (otherwise) (SSI 2012/39) |
| 29, 30 | | 1 Apr 2012 (SSI 2012/39) |
| 31–33 | | 1 Apr 2011 (SSI 2011/96) |
| 34 | | 1 Apr 2012 (SSI 2012/39) |
| 35, 36 | | 1 Apr 2011 (for the purpose of enabling consultation by the Regulator) (SSI 2011/96) |
| | | 1 Apr 2012 (otherwise) (SSI 2012/39) |
| 37, 38 | | 1 Apr 2012 (SSI 2012/39) |
| 39 | | 1 Apr 2011 (SSI 2011/96) |
| 40–45 | | 1 Apr 2012 (SSI 2012/39) |
| 46 | (1) | 1 Apr 2012 (SSI 2012/39) |
| | (2) | 1 Apr 2011 (SSI 2011/96) |

**Housing (Scotland) Act 2010 (asp 17)**—*contd*

| | | |
|---|---|---|
| | (3), (4) | 1 Apr 2012 (SSI 2012/39) |
| 47 | (1) | 1 Apr 2012 (SSI 2012/39) |
| | (2) | 1 Apr 2011 (SSI 2011/96) |
| 48, 49 | | 1 Apr 2012 (SSI 2012/39) |
| 50, 51 | | 1 Apr 2011 (for the purpose of enabling consultation by the Regulator) (SSI 2011/96) |
| | | 1 Apr 2012 (otherwise) (SSI 2012/39) |
| 52, 53 | | 1 Apr 2012 (SSI 2012/39) |
| 54 | | 1 Apr 2011 (for the purpose of enabling consultation by the Regulator) (SSI 2011/96) |
| | | 1 Apr 2012 (otherwise) (SSI 2012/39) |
| 55–67 | | 1 Apr 2012 (SSI 2012/39) |
| 68 | | 1 Apr 2011 (for the purpose of enabling consultation by the Regulator) (SSI 2011/96) |
| | | 1 Apr 2012 (otherwise) (SSI 2012/39) |
| 69–72 | | 1 Apr 2012 (SSI 2012/39) |
| 73 | (1), (2) | 1 Apr 2012 (SSI 2012/39) |
| | (3) | 1 Apr 2011 (for the purpose of enabling consultation by the Regulator) (SSI 2011/96) |
| | | 1 Apr 2012 (otherwise) (SSI 2012/39) |
| | (4) | 1 Apr 2012 (SSI 2012/39) |
| 74–107 | | 1 Apr 2012 (SSI 2012/39) |
| 108 | (1), (2) | 1 Apr 2012 (SSI 2012/39) |
| | (3) | 1 Apr 2011 (for the purpose of enabling consultation by the Regulator) (SSI 2011/96) |
| | | 1 Apr 2012 (otherwise) (SSI 2012/39) |
| | (4) | 1 Apr 2012 (SSI 2012/39) |
| 109 | (1)–(3) | 1 Apr 2012 (SSI 2012/39) |
| | (4) | 1 Apr 2011 (for the purpose of enabling consultation by the Regulator) (SSI 2011/96) |
| | | 1 Apr 2012 (otherwise) (SSI 2012/39) |
| 110 | | 1 Apr 2012 (for the purpose of applying to a proposed disposal of land other than a disposal by way of granting security over the land or any interest in it) (SSI 2012/39) |
| | | *Not yet in force* (otherwise) |
| 111–137 | | 1 Apr 2012 (SSI 2012/39) |
| 138–141 | | 1 Mar 2011 (SSI 2011/96)[1] |
| 142 | | 30 Jun 2011 (SSI 2011/96) |
| 143 | | 3 Jan 2011 (for the purpose of enabling regulations prescribing a form of notice under the Housing (Scotland) Act 1987, s 61F(2)(d) to be made) (SSI 2010/444) |
| | | 1 Mar 2011 (otherwise) (SSI 2011/96)[1] |
| 144 | | 1 Mar 2011 (SSI 2011/96)[1] |
| 145, 146 | | 1 Apr 2013 (SSI 2012/283)[4] |
| 147 | | *Not yet in force* |
| 148–151 | | 1 Mar 2011 (SSI 2011/96) |
| 152 | (1), (2) | 1 Mar 2011 (SSI 2011/96) |
| | (3) | 4 Apr 2011 (SSI 2011/96) |
| 153 | (a) | 20 Mar 2011 (for the purpose of enabling consultation by the Scottish Ministers in terms of the Housing (Scotland) Act 2001, s 16(5B)) (SSI 2011/181) |
| | | 22 Feb 2012 (for the purposes of enabling the Scottish Ministers to make provision by order in terms of s 16(5A)(c) of that Act and to issue guidance in terms of s 16(5A)(d) thereof) (SSI 2012/19) |
| | | 1 Aug 2012 (otherwise) (SSI 2012/91) |
| | (b) | 22 Feb 2012 (SSI 2012/19) |
| 154 | | 1 Mar 2011 (SSI 2011/96) |

**Housing (Scotland) Act 2010 (asp 17)**—*contd*

| | | |
|---|---|---|
| 155 | (a), (b) | 22 Feb 2012 (for the purposes of enabling the Scottish Ministers to make regulations in terms of the Housing (Scotland) Act 2001, s 14(2A)(b), to issue guidance in terms of s 14A(8) thereof and to make provision by order in terms of s 14A(9) thereof) (SSI 2012/19) |
| | | 1 Aug 2012 (otherwise) (SSI 2012/91)[3] |
| | (c) | 22 Feb 2012 (SSI 2012/19) |
| 156 | | 1 Mar 2011 (SSI 2011/96) |
| 157 | | 7 Oct 2011 (SSI 2011/339) |
| 158 | | 7 Oct 2011 (only for the purpose of enabling construction by the Scottish Ministers in terms of the Housing (Scotland) Act 1987, s 32B(7)) (SSI 2011/339) |
| | | 1 Jun 2013 (otherwise) (SSI 2012/283) |
| 159, 160 | | 1 Apr 2012 (SSI 2012/39) |
| 161 | | 9 Dec 2010 (s 166(1)) |
| 162 | | See Sch 2 below |
| 163 | | 9 Dec 2010 (s 166(1)) |
| 164 | | 1 Mar 2011 (SSI 2011/96) |
| 165–167 | | 9 Dec 2010 (s 166(1)) |
| Sch 1 | | 1 Apr 2012 (SSI 2012/39) |
| Sch 2 | para 1 | 1 Apr 2012 (SSI 2012/39) |
| | para 2 | 1 Mar 2011 (SSI 2011/96) |
| | paras 3–5 | 1 Apr 2012 (SSI 2012/39) |
| | para 6 | 1 Apr 2011 (SSI 2011/96) |
| | para 7 | 1 Apr 2012 (SSI 2012/39) |
| | paras 8–10 | 1 Apr 2011 (SSI 2011/96) |
| | paras 11–15 | 1 Apr 2012 (SSI 2012/39) |

[1]   For transitional, transitory and saving provisions, see SSI 2011/96, arts 3–6

[2]   For transitional, transitory and saving provisions, see SSI 2012/39, art 3, Sch 2

[3]   For a transitional provision, see SSI 2012/91, art 3

[4]   For a saving, see SSI 2012/283, art 4

---

**Identity Documents Act 2010 (c 40)**

*RA:* 21 Dec 2010

*Commencement provisions:* s 14(1), (2)

| | |
|---|---|
| 1 | 21 Jan 2011 (s 14(2)) |
| 2, 3 | 21 Dec 2010 (s 14(1)) |
| 4–13 | 21 Jan 2011 (s 14(2)) |
| 14 | 21 Dec 2010 (s 14(1)) |
| Schedule | 21 Jan 2011 (s 14(2)) |

---

**Interpretation and Legislative Reform (Scotland) Act 2010 (asp 10)**

*RA:* 3 Jun 2010

*Commencement provisions:* s 58; Interpretation and Legislative Reform (Scotland) Act 2010 (Commencement) Order 2011, SSI 2011/4, as revoked by SSI 2011/17; Interpretation and Legislative Reform (Scotland) Act 2010 (Commencement No 2 and Transitional Provisions) Order 2011, SSI 2011/17

| | | |
|---|---|---|
| 1–26 | | 4 Jun 2010 (s 58(2)) |
| 27 | (1), (2)(a) | 26 Jan 2011 (in relation to subordinate legislation made under this Act) (SSI 2011/17) |
| | | 6 Apr 2011 (otherwise) (SSI 2011/17)[1] |
| | (2)(b)–(f) | 6 Apr 2011 (SSI 2011/17)[1] |

**Interpretation and Legislative Reform (Scotland) Act 2010 (asp 10)**—*contd*

|  |  |  |
|---|---|---|
| | (3) | 26 Jan 2011 (in relation to subordinate legislation made under this Act) (SSI 2011/17) |
| | | 6 Apr 2011 (otherwise) (SSI 2011/17)[1] |
| | (4)–(6) | 6 Apr 2011 (SSI 2011/17)[1] |
| 28–32 | | 26 Jan 2011 (in relation to subordinate legislation made under this Act) (SSI 2011/17) |
| | | 6 Apr 2011 (otherwise) (SSI 2011/17)[1] |
| 33–36 | | 6 Apr 2011 (SSI 2011/17)[1] |
| 37 | | 26 Jan 2011 (in relation to subordinate legislation made under this Act) (SSI 2011/17) |
| | | 6 Apr 2011 (otherwise) (SSI 2011/17)[1] |
| 38–47 | | 4 Jun 2010 (s 58(2)) |
| 48–54 | | 6 Apr 2011 (SSI 2011/17)[1] |
| 55 | (1), (2) | 4 Jun 2010 (s 58(2)) |
| | (3) | 6 Apr 2011 (SSI 2011/17)[1] |
| | (4), (5) | 4 Jun 2010 (s 58(2)) |
| 56–58 | | 4 Jun 2010 (s 58(2)) |
| Sch 1 | | 4 Jun 2010 (s 58(2)) |
| Schs 2–4 | | 6 Apr 2011 (SSI 2011/17)[1] |

[1]    For a transitional provision, see SSI 2011/17, art 5

---

**Legal Services (Scotland) Act 2010 (asp 16)**

*RA:* 9 Nov 2010

*Commencement provisions:* s 150(1)–(4); Legal Services (Scotland) Act 2010 (Commencement No 1 and Saving Provision) Order 2011, SSI 2011/180[1]; Legal Services (Scotland) Act 2010 (Commencement No 2 and Transitional Provisions) Order 2012, SSI 2012/152[2]

|  |  |  |
|---|---|---|
| 1–9 | | 1 Apr 2011 (SSI 2011/180) |
| 10 | (1) | 1 Apr 2011 (SSI 2011/180) |
| | (2)–(6) | 1 Apr 2011 (for the purpose of making regulations) (SSI 2011/180) |
| | | 2 Jul 2012 (otherwise) (SSI 2012/152) |
| 11 | | 2 Jul 2012 (SSI 2012/152) |
| 12–16 | | 1 Apr 2011 (SSI 2011/180) |
| 17 | | 2 Jul 2012 (SSI 2012/152) |
| 18–30 | | 1 Apr 2011 (SSI 2011/180) |
| 31 | | 1 Apr 2011 (in so far as relates to s 21(3) above, and for the purpose of making regulations) (SSI 2011/180) |
| | | 2 Jul 2012 (otherwise) (SSI 2012/152) |
| 32–37 | | 2 Jul 2012 (SSI 2012/152) |
| 38 | (1), (2) | 1 Apr 2011 (for the purpose of making regulations) (SSI 2011/180) |
| | | 2 Jul 2012 (otherwise) (SSI 2012/152) |
| | (3) | See Schs 1–6 below |
| | (4)–(8) | 1 Apr 2011 (for the purpose of making regulations) (SSI 2011/180) |
| | | 2 Jul 2012 (otherwise) (SSI 2012/152) |
| 39 | (1) | 2 Jul 2012 (SSI 2012/152) |
| | (2) | See Sch 7 below |
| | (3), (4) | 2 Jul 2012 (SSI 2012/152) |
| 40, 41 | | 2 Jul 2012 (SSI 2012/152) |
| 42 | | 1 Apr 2011 (SSI 2011/180) |
| 43 | | 1 Apr 2011 (for the purpose of making regulations) (SSI 2011/180) |
| | | 2 Jul 2012 (otherwise) (SSI 2012/152) |
| 44, 45 | | 1 Apr 2011 (SSI 2011/180) |
| 46 | | 2 Jul 2012 (SSI 2012/152) |
| 47 | | 1 Apr 2011 (SSI 2011/180) |
| 48, 49 | | 1 Apr 2011 (for the purpose of making regulations) (SSI 2011/180) |
| | | 2 Jul 2012 (otherwise) (SSI 2012/152) |

**Legal Services (Scotland) Act 2010 (asp 16)**—*contd*

| | | |
|---|---|---|
| 50 | | 2 Jul 2012 (SSI 2012/152) |
| 51–53 | | 1 Apr 2011 (for the purpose of making regulations) (SSI 2011/180) |
| | | 2 Jul 2012 (otherwise) (SSI 2012/152) |
| 54 | | 2 Jul 2012 (SSI 2012/152) |
| 55–57 | | 1 Apr 2011 (in so far as they relate to ss 14, 18 above) (SSI 2011/180) |
| | | 2 Jul 2012 (otherwise) (SSI 2012/152) |
| 58 | | 2 Jul 2012 (SSI 2012/152) |
| 59 | | 1 Apr 2011 (SSI 2011/180) |
| 60, 61 | | 2 Jul 2012 (SSI 2012/152) |
| 62, 63 | | 1 Apr 2011 (in so far as they relate to s 14 above) (SSI 2011/180) |
| | | 2 Jul 2012 (otherwise) (SSI 2012/152) |
| 64 | | 2 Jul 2012 (SSI 2012/152) |
| 65 | | 1 Apr 2011 (in so far as it relates to s 18 above) (SSI 2011/180) |
| | | 2 Jul 2012 (otherwise) (SSI 2012/152) |
| 66 | | 2 Jul 2012 (SSI 2012/152) |
| 67 | (1) | See Sch 8 below |
| | (2)–(5) | 1 Apr 2011 (for the purpose of making regulations) (SSI 2011/180) |
| | | 2 Jul 2012 (otherwise) (SSI 2012/152) |
| | (6), (7) | 1 Apr 2011 (SSI 2011/180) |
| 68, 69 | | 2 Jul 2012 (SSI 2012/152) |
| 70 | | 1 Apr 2011 (for the purpose of making regulations) (SSI 2011/180) |
| | | 2 Jul 2012 (otherwise) (SSI 2012/152) |
| 71–75 | | 2 Jul 2012 (SSI 2012/152) |
| 76 | | 1 Apr 2011 (SSI 2011/180) |
| 77 | | 2 Jul 2012 (SSI 2012/152) |
| 78 | | 1 Apr 2011 (SSI 2011/180) |
| 79 | | 1 Apr 2011 (for the purpose of making regulations) (SSI 2011/180) |
| | | 2 Jul 2012 (otherwise) (SSI 2012/152) |
| 80 | | 2 Jul 2012 (SSI 2012/152)[2] |
| 81 | | 1 Apr 2011 (for the purpose of making regulations) (SSI 2011/180) |
| | | 2 Jul 2012 (otherwise) (SSI 2012/152) |
| 82 | | 2 Jul 2012 (SSI 2012/152) |
| 83, 84 | | 1 Apr 2011 (for the purpose of making regulations) (SSI 2011/180) |
| | | 2 Jul 2012 (otherwise) (SSI 2012/152) |
| 85–89 | | 2 Jul 2012 (SSI 2012/152) |
| 90 | | *Not yet in force* |
| 91–93 | | 1 Apr 2011 (for the purpose of making regulations) (SSI 2011/180) |
| | | *Not yet in force* (otherwise) |
| 94 | | *Not yet in force* |
| 95 | | 1 Apr 2011 (for the purpose of making regulations) (SSI 2011/180) |
| | | *Not yet in force* (otherwise) |
| 96–99 | | *Not yet in force* |
| 100 | | 1 Apr 2011 (for the purpose of making regulations) (SSI 2011/180) |
| | | *Not yet in force* (otherwise) |
| 101 | | *Not yet in force* |
| 102–104 | | 1 Apr 2011 (for the purpose of making regulations) (SSI 2011/180) |
| | | *Not yet in force* (otherwise) |
| 105 | | *Not yet in force* |
| 106 | | 1 Apr 2011 (for the purpose of making regulations) (SSI 2011/180) |
| | | *Not yet in force* (otherwise) |
| 107–110 | | *Not yet in force* |
| 111, 112 | | 1 Apr 2011 (for the purpose of making regulations) (SSI 2011/180) |
| | | *Not yet in force* (otherwise) |
| 113 | | *Not yet in force* |
| 114 | | 1 Apr 2011 (for the purpose of making regulations) (SSI 2011/180) |
| | | *Not yet in force* (otherwise) |
| 115–118 | | *Not yet in force* |
| 119 | | 1 Apr 2011 (SSI 2011/180) |

**Legal Services (Scotland) Act 2010 (asp 16)**—*contd*

| | | |
|---|---|---|
| 120–122 | | 1 Jun 2011 (SSI 2011/180) |
| 123, 124 | | 2 Jul 2012 (SSI 2012/152) |
| 125 | | 1 Apr 2011 (SSI 2011/180) |
| 126, 127 | | 1 Sep 2011 (SSI 2011/180) |
| 128 | (1)(a)(i) | 2 Jul 2012 (SSI 2012/152) |
| | (1)(a)(ii) | 1 Apr 2011 (SSI 2011/180) |
| | (1)(a)(iii) | 2 Jul 2012 (SSI 2012/152) |
| | (1)(b)(i) | 1 Apr 2011 (SSI 2011/180) |
| | (1)(b)(ii), (c), (d) | 2 Jul 2012 (SSI 2012/152) |
| | (2), (3) | 1 Apr 2011 (SSI 2011/180) |
| 129 | (1)(a)(i), (ii) | 1 Apr 2011 (SSI 2011/180) |
| | (1)(a)(iii), (b)–(g) | 2 Jul 2012 (SSI 2012/152) |
| | (2) | 1 Apr 2011 (SSI 2011/180) |
| | (3) | 2 Jul 2012 (SSI 2012/152) |
| 130, 131 | | 1 Apr 2011 (SSI 2011/180) |
| 132 | | 30 Jun 2011 (SSI 2011/180) |
| 133 | | 1 Apr 2011 (for the purpose of making regulations) (SSI 2011/180) |
| | | 1 Jun 2011 (otherwise) (SSI 2011/180) |
| 134–139 | | 1 May 2011 (SSI 2011/180) |
| 140 | | 1 May 2011 (SSI 2011/180)[1] |
| 141–145 | | 1 Apr 2011 (SSI 2011/180) |
| 146–150 | | 10 Nov 2010 (s 150(1)) |
| Schs 1–6 | | 1 Apr 2011 (for the purpose of making regulations) (SSI 2011/180) |
| | | 2 Jul 2012 (otherwise) (SSI 2012/152) |
| Sch 7 | | 2 Jul 2012 (SSI 2012/152) |
| Sch 8 | paras 1–3 | 1 Apr 2011 (for the purpose of making regulations) (SSI 2011/180) |
| | | 2 Jul 2012 (otherwise) (SSI 2012/152) |
| | para 4 | 1 Apr 2011 (in so far as relates to s 14 above, and for the purpose of making regulations) (SSI 2011/180) |
| | | 2 Jul 2012 (otherwise) (SSI 2012/152) |
| | paras 5, 6 | 1 Apr 2011 (for the purpose of making regulations) (SSI 2011/180) |
| | | 2 Jul 2012 (otherwise) (SSI 2012/152) |
| Sch 9 | | 10 Nov 2010 (s 150(1)) |

[1] For savings, see SSI 2011/180, art 8

[2] For transitional provisions, see SSI 2012/152, arts 3, 4

---

**Loans to Ireland Act 2010 (c 41)**

*RA:* 21 Dec 2010

*Commencement provisions:* s 3(2)

Whole Act in force 21 Dec 2010 (s 3(2))

---

**Local Government Act 2010 (c 35)**

*RA:* 16 Dec 2010

*Commencement provisions:* s 2(2)

Whole Act in force 16 Dec 2010 (s 2(2))

---

**Marine (Scotland) Act 2010 (asp 5)**

*RA:* 10 Mar 2010

*Commencement provisions:* s 168(1); Marine (Scotland) Act 2010 (Commencement No 1) Order 2010, SSI 2010/230; Marine (Scotland) Act 2010 (Commencement No 2 and Transitional Provisions)

**Marine (Scotland) Act 2010 (asp 5)**—*contd*
Order 2011, SSI 2011/58; Marine (Scotland) Act 2010 (Commencement No 3 and Consequential Provisions) Order 2013, SSI 2013/276

| | | |
|---|---|---|
| 1, 2 | | 10 Mar 2010 (s 168(1)) |
| 3–18 | | 1 Jul 2010 (SSI 2010/230) |
| 19 | | 10 Mar 2010 (s 168(1)) |
| 20–63 | | 6 Apr 2011 (SSI 2011/58) |
| 64–66 | | 10 Mar 2010 (s 168(1)) |
| 67–105 | | 1 Jul 2010 (SSI 2010/230) |
| 106 | | 10 Mar 2010 (s 168(1)) |
| 107–109 | | 31 Jan 2011 (SSI 2010/230) |
| 110–112 | | 1 Sep 2010 (SSI 2010/230) |
| 113 | | 31 Jan 2011 (SSI 2010/230) |
| 114–116 | | 1 Sep 2010 (SSI 2010/230) |
| 117–119 | | 31 Jan 2011 (SSI 2010/230) |
| 120 | | 1 Sep 2010 (SSI 2010/230) |
| 121 | | 31 Jan 2011 (SSI 2010/230) |
| 122–125 | | 1 Sep 2010 (SSI 2010/230) |
| 126, 127 | | 31 Jan 2011 (SSI 2010/230) |
| 128 | (1)–(3) | 31 Jan 2011 (SSI 2010/230) |
| | (4) | 1 Sep 2010 (SSI 2010/230) |
| 129, 130 | | 31 Jan 2011 (SSI 2010/230) |
| 131 | (1)–(3) | 6 Apr 2011 (SSI 2011/58) |
| | (4) | 1 Jul 2010 (SSI 2010/230) |
| 132 | | 1 Jul 2010 (SSI 2010/230) |
| 133 | | 10 Mar 2010 (s 168(1)) |
| 134–149 | | 1 Jul 2010 (SSI 2010/230) |
| 150 | | 6 Apr 2011 (SSI 2011/58) |
| 151–156 | | 1 Jul 2010 (SSI 2010/230) |
| 157 | | 10 Mar 2010 (s 168(1)) |
| 158–160 | | 24 Feb 2011 (SSI 2011/58) |
| 161 | | 24 Feb 2011 (SSI 2011/58)[1] |
| 162–164 | | 1 Jul 2010 (SSI 2010/230) |
| 165, 166 | | 10 Mar 2010 (s 168(1)) |
| 167 | | See Sch 4 below |
| 168 | | 10 Mar 2010 (s 168(1)) |
| Sch 1 | | 1 Jul 2010 (SSI 2010/230) |
| Sch 2 | | 6 Apr 2011 (SSI 2011/58) |
| Sch 3 | | 1 Jul 2010 (SSI 2010/230) |
| Sch 4 | paras 1–3 | 6 Apr 2011 (SSI 2011/58) |
| | para 4 | 1 Nov 2013 (SSI 2013/276) |
| | paras 5–9 | 1 Sep 2010 (SSI 2010/230) |
| | para 10 | 24 Feb 2011 (SSI 2011/58)[1] |
| | paras 11–13 | 24 Feb 2011 (SSI 2011/58) |
| Sch 5 | | 10 Mar 2010 (s 168(1)) |

[1] For transitional provisions, see SSI 2011/58, arts 4, 5

---

**Marriage (Wales) Act 2010 (c 6)**

*RA:* 18 Mar 2010

Whole Act in force 18 Mar 2010 (RA)

---

**Mental Health (Wales) Measure 2010 (nawm 7)**

*Passed by the National Assembly for Wales:* 2 Nov 2010

*Approved by Her Majesty in Council:* 15 Dec 2010

*Commencement provisions:* s 55; Mental Health (Wales) Measure 2010 (Commencement No 1 and Transitional Provision) Order 2011, SI 2011/3046; Mental Health (Wales) Measure 2010

**Mental Health (Wales) Measure 2010 (nawm 7)**—*contd*
(Commencement No 2) Order 2012, SI 2012/1397; Mental Health (Wales) Measure 2010 (Commencement No 3) Order 2012, SI 2012/2411

| | |
|---|---|
| 1, 2 | 8 May 2012 (SI 2011/3046) |
| 3 | 1 Oct 2012 (SI 2012/2411) |
| 4, 5 | 8 May 2012 (SI 2011/3046) |
| 6 | 1 Oct 2012 (SI 2012/2411) |
| 7 | 15 Feb 2011 (to the extent that power to make regulations or an order is conferred) (s 55(1)) |
| | 1 Oct 2012 (otherwise) (SI 2012/2411) |
| 8–10 | 1 Oct 2012 (SI 2012/2411) |
| 11 | 15 Feb 2011 (to the extent that power to make regulations or an order is conferred) (s 55(1)) |
| | 8 May 2012 (otherwise) (SI 2011/3046) |
| 12–14 | 6 Jun 2012 (SI 2012/1397) |
| 15, 16 | 15 Feb 2011 (to the extent that power to make regulations or an order is conferred) (s 55(1)) |
| | 6 Jun 2012 (otherwise) (SI 2012/1397) |
| 17 | 6 Jun 2012 (except in so far as relates to Pt 1 of this Measure) (SI 2012/1397) |
| | 1 Oct 2012 (exception noted above) (SI 2012/2411) |
| 18 | 15 Feb 2011 (to the extent that power to make regulations or an order is conferred) (s 55(1)) |
| | 6 Jun 2012 (otherwise, except in so far as relates to Pt 1 of this Measure) (SI 2012/1397) |
| | 1 Oct 2012 (exception noted above) (SI 2012/2411) |
| 19–22 | 6 Jun 2012 (SI 2012/1397) |
| 23 | 15 Feb 2011 (to the extent that power to make regulations or an order is conferred) (s 55(1)) |
| | 6 Jun 2012 (otherwise) (SI 2012/1397) |
| 24, 25 | 6 Jun 2012 (SI 2012/1397) |
| 26 | 15 Feb 2011 (to the extent that power to make regulations or an order is conferred) (s 55(1)) |
| | 6 Jun 2012 (otherwise) (SI 2012/1397) |
| 27, 28 | 6 Jun 2012 (SI 2012/1397) |
| 29 | 15 Feb 2011 (to the extent that power to make regulations or an order is conferred) (s 55(1)) |
| | 6 Jun 2012 (otherwise) (SI 2012/1397) |
| 30 | 6 Jun 2012 (SI 2012/1397) |
| 31 | 3 Jan 2012 (except in so far as it relates to Welsh qualifying informal patients) (SI 2011/3046) |
| | 2 Apr 2012 (otherwise) (SI 2011/3046) |
| 32 | 15 Feb 2011 (to the extent that power to make regulations or an order is conferred) (s 55(1)) |
| | 3 Jan 2012 (otherwise) (SI 2011/3046) |
| 33 | 15 Feb 2011 (to the extent that power to make regulations or an order is conferred) (s 55(1)) |
| | 2 Apr 2012 (otherwise) (SI 2011/3046) |
| 34 | 15 Feb 2011 (to the extent that power to make regulations or an order is conferred) (s 55(1)) |
| | 3 Jan 2012 (except in so far as it relates to Welsh qualifying informal patients) (SI 2011/3046) |
| | 2 Apr 2012 (otherwise) (SI 2011/3046) |
| 35 | 15 Feb 2011 (to the extent that power to make regulations or an order is conferred) (s 55(1)) |
| | 3 Jan 2012 (otherwise) (SI 2011/3046) |
| 36 | 15 Feb 2011 (to the extent that power to make regulations or an order is conferred) (s 55(1)) |
| | 2 Apr 2012 (otherwise) (SI 2011/3046) |

**Mental Health (Wales) Measure 2010 (nawm 7)**—*contd*

| | | |
|---|---|---|
| 37 | | 15 Feb 2011 (to the extent that power to make regulations or an order is conferred) (s 55(1)) |
| | | 3 Jan 2012 (otherwise) (SI 2011/3046) |
| 38 | | 15 Feb 2011 (to the extent that power to make regulations or an order is conferred) (s 55(1)) |
| | | 2 Apr 2012 (otherwise) (SI 2011/3046) |
| 39, 40 | | 3 Jan 2012 (except in so far as they relate to Welsh qualifying informal patients) (SI 2011/3046) |
| | | 2 Apr 2012 (otherwise) (SI 2011/3046) |
| 41, 42 | | 6 Jun 2012 (in so far as relate to Pts 2 and 3 of this Measure) (SI 2012/1397) |
| | | 1 Oct 2012 (otherwise) (SI 2012/2411) |
| 43 | | 8 May 2012 (in so far as it relates to ss 1, 2, 4, 5, 11 of this Measure) (SI 2011/3046) |
| | | 6 Jun 2012 (in so far as relates to Pts 2 and 3 of this Measure) (SI 2012/1397) |
| | | 1 Oct 2012 (otherwise) (SI 2012/2411) |
| 44 | | 3 Jan 2012 (otherwise) (SI 2011/3046) |
| 45 | | 15 Feb 2011 (to the extent that power to make regulations or an order is conferred) (s 55(1)) |
| | | 8 May 2012 (otherwise) (SI 2011/3046) |
| 46 | | 15 Feb 2011 (to the extent that power to make regulations or an order is conferred) (s 55(1)) |
| | | 6 Jun 2012 (otherwise) (SI 2012/1397) |
| 47 | | 15 Feb 2011 (to the extent that power to make regulations or an order is conferred) (s 55(1)) |
| | | 6 Jun 2012 (in so far as relates to Pt 2 of this Measure) (SI 2012/1397) |
| | | 1 Oct 2012 (otherwise) (SI 2012/2411) |
| 48 | | 1 Oct 2012 (SI 2012/2411) |
| 49–52 | | 15 Feb 2011 (s 55(1)) |
| 53 | (1) | See Sch 1 below |
| | (2)–(4) | 15 Feb 2011 (s 55(1)) |
| 54 | | See Sch 2 below |
| 55, 56 | | 15 Feb 2011 (s 55(1)) |
| Schs 1, 2 | | 3 Jan 2012 (except in so far as they relate to Welsh qualifying informal patients) (SI 2011/3046)[1] |
| | | 2 Apr 2012 (otherwise) (SI 2011/3046)[1] |

[1]   For a transitional provision, see SI 2011/3046, art 5

---

**Mortgage Repossessions (Protection of Tenants Etc) Act 2010 (c 19)**

*RA:* 8 Apr 2010

*Commencement provisions:* s 4(1), (2); Mortgage Repossessions (Protection of Tenants etc) Act 2010 (Commencement) Order 2010, SI 2010/1705

| | |
|---|---|
| 1–3 | 30 Jun 2010 (for the purpose of making regulations) (SI 2010/1705) |
| | 1 Oct 2010 (otherwise) (SI 2010/1705) |
| 4 | 8 Apr 2010 (s 4(1)) |

---

## National Assembly for Wales (Remuneration) Measure 2010 (nawm 4)

*Passed by the National Assembly for Wales:* 26 May 2010

*Approved by Her Majesty in Council:* 21 Jul 2010

*Commencement provisions:* s 20(2), (3)

| | |
|---|---|
| 1 | 22 Jul 2010 (s 20(2)) |
| 2, 3 | 24 Sep 2010 (the day after that on which Statutory notice made under s 20(4) of this Act was laid before the Assembly) |
| 4–9 | 22 Jul 2010 (s 20(2)) |
| 10, 11 | 24 Sep 2010 (the day after that on which Statutory notice made under s 20(4) of this Act was laid before the Assembly) |
| 12 | 22 Jul 2010 (s 20(2)) |
| 13–15 | 24 Sep 2010 (the day after that on which Statutory notice made under s 20(4) of this Act was laid before the Assembly) |
| 16 | See Sch 3 below |
| 17, 18 | 22 Jul 2010 (s 20(2)) |
| 19 | 24 Sep 2010 (the day after that on which Statutory notice made under s 20(4) of this Act was laid before the Assembly) |
| 20 | 22 Jul 2010 (s 20(2)) |
| Schs 1, 2 | 22 Jul 2010 (s 20(2)) |
| Sch 3 | 24 Sep 2010 (the day after that on which Statutory notice made under s 20(4) of this Act was laid before the Assembly) |

## Northern Ireland Assembly Members Act 2010 (c 16)

*RA:* 8 Apr 2010

*Commencement provisions:* s 3(2), (3); Northern Ireland Assembly Members Act 2010 (Commencement) Order 2010, SI 2010/1726

| | |
|---|---|
| 1, 2 | 5 Jul 2010 (SI 2010/1726) |
| 3 | 8 Apr 2010 (s 3(2)) |

## Personal Care at Home Act 2010 (c 18)

*RA:* 8 Apr 2010

*Commencement provisions:* s 2(3)

| | |
|---|---|
| 1, 2 | *Not yet in force* |

## Playing Fields (Community Involvement in Disposal Decisions) (Wales) Measure 2010 (nawm 6)

*Passed by the National Assembly for Wales:* 6 Oct 2010

*Approved by Her Majesty in Council:* 15 Dec 2010

Whole Measure in force 15 Dec 2010 (s 5(2))

## Public Services Reform (Scotland) Act 2010 (asp 8)

*RA:* 28 Apr 2010

*Commencement provisions:* s 134(2), (7); Public Services Reform (Scotland) Act 2010 (Commencement No 1) Order 2010, SSI 2010/221; Public Services Reform (Scotland) Act 2010 (Commencement No 2) Order 2010, SSI 2010/321; Public Services Reform (Scotland) Act 2010 (Commencement No 3) Order 2011, SSI 2011/30; Public Services Reform (Scotland) Act 2010 (Commencement No 4) Order 2011, SSI 2011/122; Public Services Reform (Scotland) Act 2010 (Commencement

**Public Services Reform (Scotland) Act 2010 (asp 8)**—*contd*
No 5) Order 2011, SSI 2011/278; Public Services Reform (Scotland) Act 2010 (Commencement No 6) Order 2012, SSI 2012/218; Public Services Reform (Scotland) Act 2010 (Commencement No 7) Order 2016, SSI 2016/22

| | | |
|---|---|---|
| 1 | (1)–(4) | 1 Aug 2010 (SSI 2010/221) |
| | (5) | See Sch 1 below |
| 2 | | 1 Aug 2010 (SSI 2010/221) |
| 3 | | 15 Aug 2011 (SSI 2011/278) |
| 4–12 | | 1 Aug 2010 (SSI 2010/221) |
| 13 | | See Sch 4 below |
| 14 | | 1 Aug 2010 (SSI 2010/221) |
| 15 | (1) | See Sch 5 below |
| | (2)–(9) | 1 Aug 2010 (SSI 2010/221) |
| 16–28 | | 1 Aug 2010 (SSI 2010/221) |
| 29 | | See Sch 7 below |
| 30 | | 1 Aug 2010 (SSI 2010/221) |
| 31–35 | | 1 Oct 2010 (SSI 2010/321) |
| 36 | (1) | 1 Jul 2010 (SSI 2010/221) |
| | (2) | See Sch 9 below |
| 37–42 | | 1 Jul 2010 (SSI 2010/221) |
| 43 | | See Sch 10 below |
| 44 | (1)–(3) | 1 Oct 2010 (for the purpose of making subordinate legislation) (SSI 2010/321) |
| | | 1 Apr 2011 (otherwise) (SSI 2011/122) |
| | (4) | See Sch 11 below |
| 45, 46 | | 1 Oct 2010 (for the purpose of making subordinate legislation) (SSI 2010/321) |
| | | 1 Apr 2011 (otherwise) (SSI 2011/122) |
| 47–102 | | 1 Oct 2010 (for the purpose of making subordinate legislation) (SSI 2010/321) |
| | | 1 Apr 2011 (otherwise) (SSI 2011/122) |
| 103 | | 28 Apr 2010 (s 134(2)) |
| 104, 105 | | 1 Oct 2010 (for the purpose of making subordinate legislation) (SSI 2010/321) |
| | | 1 Apr 2011 (otherwise) (SSI 2011/122) |
| 106 | | See Sch 14 below |
| 107 | | See Sch 15 below |
| 108 | | 1 Aug 2010 (for the purpose of making appointments) (SSI 2010/221) |
| | | 1 Oct 2010 (for the purpose of making subordinate legislation) (SSI 2010/321) |
| | | 1 Apr 2011 (otherwise, except in relation to Healthcare Improvement Scotland's functions relating to independent clinics, independent medical agencies and independent ambulance services) (SSI 2011/122) |
| | | 1 Apr 2016 (otherwise, except insofar as inserts National Health Service (Scotland) Act 1978, s 10Z9(1)(a) and except in relation to Healthcare Improvement Scotland's functions relating to independent medical agencies and independent ambulance services) (SSI 2016/22) |
| | | 1 Apr 2017 (otherwise, except in relation to Healthcare Improvement Scotland's functions relating to independent medical agencies and independent ambulance services) (SSI 2016/22) |
| | | *Not yet in force* (exceptions noted above) |
| 109 | | 28 Apr 2010 (s 134(2)) |
| 110 | (1) | See Sch 16 below |
| | (2) | See Sch 17 below |
| 111 | (1)–(14) | 1 Aug 2010 (for the purpose of making appointments) (SSI 2010/221) |

**Public Services Reform (Scotland) Act 2010 (asp 8)**—*contd*

| | | |
|---|---|---|
| | | 1 Oct 2010 (for the purpose of making subordinate legislation) (SSI 2010/321) |
| | | 1 Apr 2011 (otherwise) (SSI 2011/122) |
| | (15) | See Sch 18 below |
| 112–114 | | 1 Oct 2010 (SSI 2010/321) |
| 115–117 | | 1 Oct 2010 (for the purpose of making subordinate legislation) (SSI 2010/321) |
| | | 1 Apr 2011 (otherwise) (SSI 2011/122) |
| 118 | | 1 Oct 2010 (SSI 2010/321) |
| 119–124 | | 1 Aug 2010 (SSI 2010/221) |
| 125 | | 1 Oct 2010 (for the purpose of making subordinate legislation) (SSI 2010/321) |
| | | 1 Nov 2012 (otherwise) (SSI 2012/218) |
| 126–129 | | 1 Aug 2010 (SSI 2010/221) |
| 130, 131 | | 15 Aug 2011 (SSI 2011/278) |
| 132–134 | | 28 Apr 2010 (s 134(2)) |
| Sch 1 | | 1 Aug 2010 (SSI 2010/221) |
| Schs 2, 3 | | 15 Aug 2011 (SSI 2011/278) |
| Sch 4 | para 1 | See paras 2–8 below |
| | paras 2, 3 | 31 Jan 2011 (SSI 2011/30) |
| | paras 4–7 | 1 Apr 2011 (SSI 2011/30) |
| | para 8 | 31 Jan 2011 (SSI 2011/30) |
| | para 9 | See paras 10–32 below |
| | paras 10–13 | 31 Jan 2011 (SSI 2011/30) |
| | para 14 | 1 Apr 2011 (SSI 2011/30) |
| | para 15 | 31 Jan 2011 (SSI 2011/30) |
| | paras 16–19 | 1 Apr 2011 (SSI 2011/30) |
| | paras 20–33 | 31 Jan 2011 (SSI 2011/30) |
| Schs 5–7 | | 1 Aug 2010 (SSI 2010/221) |
| Sch 8 | | 1 Oct 2010 (SSI 2010/321) |
| Schs 9, 10 | | 1 Jul 2010 (SSI 2010/221) |
| Sch 11 | (1)–(14) | 1 Aug 2010 (for the purpose of making appointments) (SSI 2010/221) |
| | | 1 Oct 2010 (for the purpose of making subordinate legislation) (SSI 2010/321) |
| | | 1 Apr 2011 (otherwise) (SSI 2011/122) |
| | (15) | 1 Oct 2010 (for the purpose of making subordinate legislation) (SSI 2010/321) |
| | | 1 Apr 2011 (otherwise) (SSI 2011/122) |
| Sch 12 | | 1 Oct 2010 (for the purpose of making subordinate legislation) (SSI 2010/321) |
| | | 1 Apr 2011 (otherwise) (SSI 2011/122) |
| Sch 13 | | 1 Oct 2010 (SSI 2010/321) |
| Sch 14 | paras 1–34 | 1 Oct 2010 (for the purpose of making subordinate legislation) (SSI 2010/321) |
| | | 1 Apr 2011 (otherwise) (SSI 2011/122) |
| | para 35(a) | *Never in force* (repealed) |
| | paras 35(b), (c), 36, 37 | 1 Oct 2010 (for the purpose of making subordinate legislation) (SSI 2010/321) |
| | | 1 Apr 2011 (otherwise) (SSI 2011/122) |
| Sch 15 | | 1 Aug 2010 (SSI 2010/221) |
| Sch 16 | | 1 Aug 2010 (for the purpose of making appointments) (SSI 2010/221) |
| | | 1 Oct 2010 (for the purpose of making subordinate legislation) (SSI 2010/321) |
| | | 1 Apr 2011 (otherwise) (SSI 2011/122) |
| Sch 17 | | 1 Oct 2010 (for the purpose of making subordinate legislation) (SSI 2010/321) |
| | | 1 Apr 2011 (otherwise) (SSI 2011/122) |

**Public Services Reform (Scotland) Act 2010 (asp 8)**—*contd*

| | |
|---|---|
| Sch 18 | 1 Aug 2010 (for the purpose of making appointments) (SSI 2010/221) |
| | 1 Oct 2010 (for the purpose of making subordinate legislation) (SSI 2010/321) |
| | 1 Apr 2011 (otherwise) (SSI 2011/122) |
| Schs 19, 20 | 1 Oct 2010 (for the purpose of making subordinate legislation) (SSI 2010/321) |
| | *Not yet in force* (otherwise) |

---

**Red Meat Industry (Wales) Measure 2010 (nawm 3)**

*Passed by the National Assembly for Wales:* 10 Mar 2010

*Approved by Her Majesty in Council:* 11 May 2010

*Commencement provisions*: s 18; Red Meat Industry (Wales) Measure (Commencement, Transitional and Saving Provisions) Order 2011, SI 2011/2802[1]

| | | |
|---|---|---|
| 1–3 | | 1 Apr 2012 (SI 2011/2802) |
| 4 | (1), (2) | 1 Apr 2012 (SI 2011/2802) |
| | (3) | 28 Nov 2011 (SI 2011/2802) |
| | (4)–(6) | 1 Apr 2012 (SI 2011/2802) |
| 5 | (1)–(3) | 1 Apr 2012 (SI 2011/2802) |
| | (4) | 28 Nov 2011 (SI 2011/2802) |
| | (5) | 1 Apr 2012 (SI 2011/2802) |
| 6–16 | | 1 Apr 2012 (SI 2011/2802) |
| 17–19 | | 11 Jul 2010 (s 18(1)) |
| Schs 1, 2 | | 1 Apr 2012 (SI 2011/2802) |

[1] For transitional provisions and savings, see SI 2011/2802, arts 3, 4

---

**Savings Accounts and Health in Pregnancy Grant Act 2010 (c 36)**

*RA:* 16 Dec 2010

*Commencement provisions*: s 4(2), (3)

| | |
|---|---|
| 1 | 16 Dec 2010 (s 4(3)) |
| 2 | 16 Feb 2011 (s 4(2)) |
| 3, 4 | 16 Dec 2010 (s 4(3)) |

---

**Schools (Consultation) (Scotland) Act 2010 (asp 2)**

*RA:* 5 Jan 2010

*Commencement provisions*: s 22(1)–(4); Schools (Consultation) (Scotland) Act 2010 (Commencement) Order 2010, SSI 2010/70

| | |
|---|---|
| 1–18 | 5 Apr 2010 (SSI 2010/70) |
| 19–22 | 6 Jan 2010 (s 22(1)) |
| Schs 1–3 | 5 Apr 2010 (SSI 2010/70) |

---

**Scottish Parliamentary Commissions and Commissioners etc Act 2010 (asp 11)**

*RA:* 19 Jul 2010

*Commencement provisions*: s 31

| | | |
|---|---|---|
| 1–28 | | 1 Apr 2011 (s 31(5)) |
| 29 | (1) | 1 Apr 2011 (s 31(5)) |
| | (2) | See Sch 2 below |

## Scottish Parliamentary Commissions and Commissioners etc Act 2010 (asp 11)—*contd*

| | | |
|---|---|---|
| | (3) | See Sch 3 below |
| | (4)–(11) | 1 Apr 2011 (s 31(5)) |
| 30 | | 19 Jul 2010 (s 31(2)) |
| 31 | (1)–(5) | 19 Jul 2010 (s 31(2)) |
| | (6) | See Sch 7 below |
| Sch 1 | | 1 Apr 2011 (s 31(5)) |
| Sch 2 | paras 1–13 | 1 Apr 2011 (s 31(5)) |
| | para 14 | 1 Aug 2010 (to the extent that it inserts Ethical Standards in Public Life etc (Scotland) Act 2000, Sch 1, para 10C) (s 31(3)) |
| | | 1 Apr 2011 (otherwise) (s 31(5)) |
| | paras 15–17 | 1 Apr 2011 (s 31(5)) |
| Sch 3 | paras 1–19 | 1 Apr 2011 (s 31(5)) |
| | para 20 | 1 Oct 2010 (s 31(4)) |
| | para 21 | 1 Apr 2011 (s 31(5)) |
| Schs 4–7 | | 1 Apr 2011 (s 31(5)) |

## Social Care Charges (Wales) Measure 2010 (nawm 2)

*Passed by the National Assembly for Wales:* 19 Jan 2010

*Approved by Her Majesty in Council:* 17 Mar 2010

*Commencement provisions:* s 18; Social Care Charges (Wales) Measure 2010 (Commencement) Order 2011, SI 2011/849

| | |
|---|---|
| 1–16 | 18 Mar 2011 (SI 2011/849) |
| 17–19 | 17 May 2010 (s 18(2)) |

## Sunbeds (Regulation) Act 2010 (c 20)

*RA:* 8 Apr 2010

*Commencement provisions:* s 14(2)

Whole Act in force 8 Apr 2011 (s 14(2))

## Superannuation Act 2010 (c 37)

*RA:* 16 Dec 2010

*Commencement provisions:* s 4(2), (3)

| | |
|---|---|
| 1 | 16 Dec 2010 (s 4(2)) |
| 2 | 16 Feb 2011 (s 4(3)) |
| 3, 4 | 16 Dec 2010 (s 4(2)) |

## Sustainable Communities Act 2007 (Amendment) Act 2010 (c 21)

*RA:* 8 Apr 2010

*Commencement provisions:* s 3(2)

Whole Act in force 8 Jun 2010 (s 3(2))

## Taxation (International and Other Provisions) Act 2010 (c 8)

*RA:* 18 Mar 2010

*Commencement provisions:* s 381

| | | |
|---|---|---|
| 1–371 | | 1 Apr 2010 (s 381(1)) |
| 372, 373 | | 18 Mar 2010 (s 381(2)(a), (b)) |
| 374 | | See Sch 8 below |
| 375, 376 | | 18 Mar 2010 (s 381(2)(e), (f)) |
| 377 | (1) | 1 Apr 2010 (s 381(1)) |
| | (2), (3) | 18 Mar 2010 (s 381(2)(g)) |
| 380–382 | | 18 Mar 2010 (s 381(2)(h)–(j)) |
| Schs 1–7 | | 1 Apr 2010 (s 381(1)) |
| Sch 8 | paras 1–316 | 1 Apr 2010 (s 381(1)) |
| | paras 317–319 | 18 Mar 2010 (s 381(2)(c)) |
| | paras 320–325 | 1 Apr 2010 (s 381(1)) |
| | paras 326–328 | 18 Mar 2010 (s 381(2)(c)) |
| | paras 329–332 | 1 Apr 2010 (s 381(1)) |
| Schs 9–11 | | 1 Apr 2010 (s 381(1)) |

## Terrorist Asset-Freezing etc Act 2010 (c 38)

*RA:* 16 Dec 2010

*Commencement provisions:* s 55; Terrorist Asset-Freezing etc Act 2010 (Commencement) Order 2011, SI 2011/2835

| | | |
|---|---|---|
| 1–50 | | 17 Dec 2010 (s 55(1)) |
| 51 | | 31 Mar 2012 (SI 2011/2835) |
| 52 | (1) | See Sch 1 below |
| | (2) | See Sch 2 below |
| 53–56 | | 16 Dec 2010 (s 55(4)) |
| Sch 1 | Pt 1 | 17 Dec 2010 (s 55(1)) |
| | Pt 2 | 17 Dec 2010 (except so far as relating to s 51 above) (s 55(1), (2)) |
| | | 31 Mar 2012 (otherwise) (SI 2011/2835) |
| Sch 2 | Pt 1 | 17 Dec 2010 (s 55(1)) |
| | Pt 2 | 17 Dec 2010 (except so far as relating to s 51 above) (s 55(1), (2)) |
| | | 31 Mar 2012 (otherwise) (SI 2011/2835) |

## Terrorist Asset-Freezing (Temporary Provisions) Act 2010 (c 2)

*RA:* 10 Feb 2010

Whole Act in force 10 Feb 2010 (RA)

## Third Parties (Rights against Insurers) Act 2010 (c 10)

*RA:* 25 Mar 2010

*Commencement provisions:* s 21(2); Third Parties (Rights Against Insurers) Act 2010 (Commencement) Order 2016, SI 2016/550

| | | |
|---|---|---|
| 1–10 | | 1 Aug 2016 (SI 2016/550) |
| 11 | | See Sch 1 below |
| 12–19 | | 1 Aug 2016 (SI 2016/550) (s 19 substituted) |
| 20 | (1) | See Sch 2 below |
| | (2) | See Sch 3 below |
| | (3) | See Sch 4 below |
| 21 | | 25 Mar 2010 (RA) |
| Schs 1–4 | | 1 Aug 2016 (SI 2016/550) |

### Tobacco and Primary Medical Services (Scotland) Act 2010 (asp 3)

*RA:* 3 Mar 2010

*Commencement provisions:* s 43(2), (3); Tobacco and Primary Medical Services (Scotland) Act 2010 (Commencement No 1, Consequential and Saving Provisions) Order 2010, SSI 2010/345, as amended by SSI 2013/106; Tobacco and Primary Medical Services (Scotland) Act 2010 (Commencement No 2) Order 2010, SSI 2010/372; Tobacco and Primary Medical Services (Scotland) Act 2010 (Commencement No 3) Order 2013, SSI 2013/38; Tobacco and Primary Medical Services (Scotland) Act 2010 (Incidental Provision and Commencement No 4) Order 2013, SSI 2013/106

| | | |
|---|---|---|
| 1–3 | | 26 Feb 2013 (for the purpose of enabling the Scottish Ministers to make regulations under ss 1(2)(c), (3)(b), (4), 2, 3(1), (2), (5)) (SSI 2013/38) |
| | | 29 Apr 2013 (otherwise, but only for the purposes of "large shops", as defined by SSI 2013/38, art 1(2)) (SSI 2013/38) |
| | | 6 Apr 2015 (otherwise) (SSI 2013/38) |
| 4 | | 24 Oct 2010 (for the purpose of prescribing under sub-s (4)(c)) (SSI 2010/345) (SSI 2010/345) |
| | | 1 Apr 2011 (otherwise) (SSI 2010/345)[2] |
| 5–7 | | 1 Apr 2011 (SSI 2010/345) |
| 8 | | 24 Oct 2010 (for the purpose of prescribing under sub-s (5)) (SSI 2010/345) |
| | | 1 Apr 2011 (otherwise) (SSI 2010/345) |
| 9 | | 29 Apr 2013 (SSI 2013/106) |
| 10 | | 1 Apr 2011 (SSI 2010/345) |
| 11 | | 24 Oct 2010 (for the purpose of prescribing under sub-s (2)(d)) (SSI 2010/345) |
| | | 1 Apr 2011 (otherwise) (SSI 2010/345) |
| 12–14 | | 1 Apr 2011 (SSI 2010/345) |
| 15–18 | | 1 Oct 2011 (SSI 2010/345) |
| 19 | | 24 Oct 2010 (for the purpose of prescribing under sub-s (5)) (SSI 2010/345) |
| | | 1 Oct 2011 (otherwise) (SSI 2010/345) |
| 20–23 | | 1 Oct 2011 (SSI 2010/345) |
| 24 | | 24 Oct 2010 (SSI 2010/345) |
| 25, 26 | | 1 Apr 2011 (SSI 2010/345) |
| 27 | (1)–(3) | 1 Apr 2011 (SSI 2010/345) |
| | (4) | See Sch 1 below |
| 28–36 | | 1 Apr 2011 (SSI 2010/345) |
| 37 | | 22 Dec 2010 (SSI 2010/372) |
| 38 | | 8 Nov 2010 (for the purpose of enabling the Scottish Ministers to make regulations under the inserted National Health Service (Scotland) Act 1978, s 17CA(1), (5)–(7)) (SSI 2010/372) |
| | | 22 Dec 2010 (otherwise) (SSI 2010/372) |
| 39 | | 8 Nov 2010 (for the purpose of enabling the Scottish Ministers to make regulations under the substituted National Health Service (Scotland) Act 1978, s 17L(1), (5)–(7)) (SSI 2010/372) |
| | | 22 Dec 2010 (otherwise) (SSI 2010/372) |
| 40–43 | | 3 Mar 2010 (s 43(2)) |
| Sch 1 | | 24 Oct 2010 (for the purpose of prescribing under paras 3, 4) (SSI 2010/345) |
| | | 1 Apr 2011 (otherwise) (SSI 2010/345) |
| Sch 2 | | 3 Mar 2010 (s 43(2))[1] |

[1]   But note that the Tobacco and Primary Medical Services (Scotland) Act 2010 (Ancillary Provisions) Order 2010, SSI 2010/77, art 2 provides that the amendments made by the paragraphs of this Schedule shall not take effect until the coming into force for all purposes of specified sections above:

paras 1, 2(a) (as they relate to the Children and Young Persons (Protection from Tobacco) Act 1991, s 2), 2(c), 5: s 4; para 2(a) (as it relates to s 4 of the 1991 Act): s 9; para 2(b): s 26; paras 3, 4: s 1; paras 6, 7: s 38

**Tobacco and Primary Medical Services (Scotland) Act 2010 (asp 3)**—*contd*
2    For a saving, see SSI 2010/345, art 4

**Ure Elder Fund Transfer and Dissolution Act 2010 (asp 7)**

*RA:* 9 Apr 2010

*Commencement provisions:* s 4(2)

Whole Act in force 9 Jun 2010 (s 4(2))

**Vacancies in Suffragan Sees and Other Ecclesiastical Offices Measure 2010 (No 2)**

*RA:* 18 Mar 2010

*Commencement provisions:* s 4(2)

Provisions of this Measure were brought into force on the following dates by instruments made by the Archbishops of Canterbury and York, and dated 17 May 2010, 10 Jun 2010 and 23 Nov 2010

| | |
|---|---|
| 1 | 1 Jun 2010 |
| 2 | 1 Jan 2011 |
| 3 | 1 Jun 2010 |
| 4 | 11 Jun 2010 |

**Video Recordings Act 2010 (c 1)**

*RA:* 21 Jan 2010

Whole Act in force 21 Jan 2010 (s 2(2))

**Waste (Wales) Measure 2010 (nawm 8)**

*Passed by the National Assembly for Wales:* 2 Nov 2010

*Approved by Her Majesty in Council:* 15 Dec 2010

*Commencement provisions:* s 21; Waste (Wales) Measure 2010 (Commencement) Order 2011, SI 2011/476

| | |
|---|---|
| 1, 2 | 15 Feb 2011 (s 21(2)) |
| 3 | 4 Mar 2011 (SI 2011/476) |
| 4–22 | 15 Feb 2011 (s 21(2)) |
| Schedule | 15 Feb 2011 (s 21(2)) |

**William Simpson's Home (Transfer of Property etc) (Scotland) Act 2010 (asp 12)**

*RA:* 27 Jul 2010

Whole Act in force 27 Sep 2010 (except s 5, which comes into force on the day of royal assent) (s 5(2))

# 2011 Acts

## Appropriation Act 2011 (c 2)

*RA*: 16 Mar 2011

Whole Act in force 16 Mar 2011 (RA)

---

## Armed Forces Act 2011 (c 18)

*RA*: 3 Nov 2011

*Commencement provisions*: s 32; Armed Forces Act 2011 (Commencement No 1, Transitional and Transitory Provisions) Order 2012, SI 2012/669; Armed Forces Act 2011 (Commencement No 2) Order 2012, SI 2012/2921; Armed Forces Act 2011 (Commencement No 3) Order 2013, SI 2013/784; Armed Forces Act 2011 (Commencement No 4) Order 2013, SI 2013/2501; Armed Forces Act 2011 (Commencement No 5) Order 2014, SI 2014/1444; Armed Forces Act 2011 (Commencement No 6) Order 2016, SI 2016/1232

| | | |
|---|---|---|
| 1 | | 3 Nov 2011 (s 32(1)) |
| 2, 3 | | 2 Apr 2012 (SI 2012/669) |
| 4 | | 4 Jun 2014 (SI 2014/1444) |
| 5 | | 2 Apr 2012 (SI 2012/669) |
| 6 | | 8 Mar 2012 (SI 2012/669) |
| 7 | | 14 Dec 2012 (SI 2012/2921) |
| 8 | | 8 Mar 2012 (SI 2012/669) |
| 9 | | 1 Nov 2013 (SI 2013/2501) |
| 10 | | 8 Mar 2012 (for the purpose only of conferring power to make regulations under Armed Forces Act 2006, s 20A) (SI 2012/669) |
| | | 1 Nov 2013 (otherwise) (SI 2013/2501) |
| 11 | (1) | 8 Mar 2012 (for the purpose only of conferring powers to make regulations under Armed Forces Act 2006, ss 93A(5), 93F(4) and to issue a code of practice under s 93C(3) of that Act) (SI 2012/669) |
| | | 1 Nov 2013 (otherwise) (SI 2013/2501) |
| | (2) | 1 Nov 2013 (SI 2013/2501) |
| 12, 13 | | 2 Apr 2012 (SI 2012/669)[1] |
| 14 | | 2 Apr 2012 (SI 2012/669) |
| 15 | | 2 Apr 2012 (SI 2012/669)[1] |
| 16 | (1) | 1 Nov 2013 (SI 2013/2501) |
| | (2) | 8 Mar 2012 (SI 2012/669) |
| 17 | (1) | 8 Mar 2012 (for the purpose only of conferring power to make rules under Armed Forces Act 2006, s 232F) (SI 2012/669) |
| | | *Never in force* (otherwise) (repealed) |
| | (2) | *Never in force* (repealed) |
| 18–20 | | 2 Apr 2012 (SI 2012/669) |
| 21 | | 23 Dec 2016 (SI 2016/1232) |
| 22 | | 14 Dec 2012 (SI 2012/2921) |
| 23 | (1) | 8 Mar 2012 (SI 2012/669) |
| | (2) | *Not yet in force* |

**Armed Forces Act 2011 (c 18)**—*contd*

| | | |
|---|---|---|
| 24 | | 8 Mar 2012 (SI 2012/669) |
| 25 | | 6 Apr 2013 (SI 2013/784) |
| 26 | | See Sch 2 below |
| 27 | | 2 Apr 2012 (SI 2012/669) |
| 28 | | 3 Jan 2012 (s 32(2)) |
| 29 | | See Sch 3 below |
| 30 | (1) | See Sch 4 below |
| | (2) | See Sch 5 below |
| 31–34 | | 3 Nov 2011 (s 32(1)) |
| Sch 1 | | 2 Apr 2012 (SI 2012/669)[1] |
| Sch 2 | | 2 Apr 2012 (SI 2012/669) |
| Sch 3 | paras 1–22 | 2 Apr 2012 (SI 2012/669)[1] |
| | para 23 | 8 Mar 2012 (SI 2012/669) |
| | para 24 | 2 Apr 2012 (SI 2012/669) |
| Sch 4 | paras 1, 2 | 2 Apr 2012 (SI 2012/669) |
| | para 3(1), (2) | 1 Nov 2013 (SI 2013/2501) |
| | para 3(3) | *Never in force* (repealed) |
| | para 3(4) | 1 Nov 2013 (SI 2013/2501) |
| | para 4 | 1 Nov 2013 (SI 2013/2501) |
| | paras 5–7 | 14 Dec 2012 (SI 2012/2921) |
| | para 8 | 1 Nov 2013 (SI 2013/2501) |
| | para 9 | 2 Apr 2012 (SI 2012/669) |
| | paras 10–13 | 1 Nov 2013 (SI 2013/2501) |
| | paras 14, 15 | 8 Mar 2012 (SI 2012/669) |
| Sch 5 | | 8 Mar 2012 (SI 2012/669), repeals of or in— |

Military Lands Act 1900

2 Apr 2012 (SI 2012/669) repeals of or in—
   Naval Medical Compassionate Fund Act 1915;
   Defence (Transfer of Functions) (No 1) Order 1964
      (SI 1964/488);
   Juries Act 1974;
   Reserve Forces Act 1996;
   Courts Act 2003;
   Civil Partnership Act 2004;
   Armed Forces Act 2006, ss 125, 164(3), 194(6), 293, 305(5),
      375(5), 380(9);
   Criminal Justice and Immigration Act 2008;
   Naval Medical Compassionate Fund Order 2008 (SI 2008/3129);
   Coroners and Justice Act 2009;
   Armed Forces (Court Martial) Rules 2009 (SI 2009/2041)
14 Dec 2012 (SI 2012/2921), repeal of—
   Armed Forces Act 2006, s 336(3)
1 Nov 2013 (SI 2013/2501), repeals of or in—
   Armed Forces Act 2006, ss 305(2)(b), 306–308
*Not yet in force*, repeals of or in—
   Court Martial Appeals Act 1968;
   Armed Forces Act 2006, Sch 8, para 50

---

[1]   For transitional and transitory provisions and savings, see SI 2012/669, arts 5–13

**Budget Responsibility and National Audit Act 2011 (c 4)**

*RA:* 22 Mar 2011

*Commencement provisions*: s 29; Budget Responsibility and National Audit Act 2011 (Commencement
   No 1) Order 2011, SI 2011/892; Budget Responsibility and National Audit Act 2011
   (Commencement No 2) Order 2011, SI 2011/2576

| | |
|---|---|
| 1, 2 | 23 Mar 2011 (SI 2011/892) |

**Budget Responsibility and National Audit Act 2011 (c 4)**—*contd*

| | | |
|---|---|---|
| 3–9 | | 4 Apr 2011 (SI 2011/892) |
| 10 | | 23 Mar 2011 (SI 2011/892) |
| 11, 12 | | 1 Apr 2012 (SI 2011/2576) |
| 13 | | 1 Jan 2012 (SI 2011/2576)[1] |
| 14–16 | | 1 Apr 2012 (SI 2011/2576) |
| 17 | | 1 Jan 2012 (for the purpose of Sch 3, para 10(2)) (SI 2011/2576)[1] |
| | | 1 Apr 2012 (otherwise) (SI 2011/2576) |
| 18 | | 1 Apr 2012 (SI 2011/2576) |
| 19 | | 1 Nov 2011 (SI 2011/2576) |
| 20 | (1), (2) | 1 Nov 2011 (SI 2011/2576) |
| | (3) | See Sch 2 below |
| 21 | | 1 Apr 2012 (SI 2011/2576) |
| 22 | | See Sch 3 below |
| 23 | | 1 Jan 2012 (for the purpose of authorising NAO's expenditure for the first financial year) (SI 2011/2576)[1] |
| | | 1 Apr 2012 (otherwise) (SI 2011/2576) |
| 24 | | 1 Apr 2012 (SI 2011/2576) |
| 25 | | 1 Nov 2011 (SI 2011/2576) |
| 26 | (1) | See Sch 4 below |
| | (2) | See Sch 5 below |
| 27 | | See Sch 6 below |
| 28–31 | | 22 Mar 2011 (s 29(1)) |
| Sch 1 | | 4 Apr 2011 (SI 2011/892) |
| Sch 2 | paras 1, 2(1) | 1 Nov 2011 (for the purpose of appointing the non-executive members of NAO) (SI 2011/2576) |
| | | 1 Jan 2012 (otherwise) (SI 2011/2576)[1] |
| | para 2(2) | 1 Jan 2012 (SI 2011/2576)[1] |
| | paras 3–10 | 1 Nov 2011 (SI 2011/2576) |
| | paras 11–28 | 1 Jan 2012 (SI 2011/2576)[1] |
| Sch 3 | para 1 | 1 Jan 2012 (SI 2011/2576)[1] |
| | para 2(1) | 1 Jan 2012 (for the purposes of approving the provision of services under para 3(1), and determining the maximum amount of resources that the Comptroller and Auditor General may require for the function of providing those services) (SI 2011/2576)[1] |
| | | 1 Apr 2012 (otherwise) (SI 2011/2576) |
| | para 2(2) | 1 Apr 2012 (SI 2011/2576) |
| | para 2(3), (4) | 1 Jan 2012 (for the purposes of approving the provision of services under para 3(1), and determining the maximum amount of resources that the Comptroller and Auditor General may require for the function of providing those services) (SI 2011/2576)[1] |
| | | 1 Apr 2012 (otherwise) (SI 2011/2576) |
| | paras 3–5 | 1 Apr 2012 (SI 2011/2576) |
| | para 6(1), (2) | 1 Jan 2012 (SI 2011/2576)[1] |
| | paras 6(3), (4), 7 | 1 Apr 2012 (SI 2011/2576) |
| | para 8(1)–(3) | 1 Jan 2012 (for the purpose of preparing a scheme for charging audit fees) (SI 2011/2576)[1] |
| | | 1 Apr 2012 (otherwise) (SI 2011/2576) |
| | paras 8(4)–(8), 9 | 1 Apr 2012 (SI 2011/2576) |
| | paras 10–12 | 1 Jan 2012 (SI 2011/2576)[1] |
| | para 13 | 1 Apr 2012 (SI 2011/2576) |
| Sch 4 | para 1 | 1 Jan 2012 (SI 2011/2576)[1] |
| | paras 2–4 | 1 Apr 2012 (SI 2011/2576) |
| | para 5 | 1 Jan 2012 (SI 2011/2576) |
| | paras 6–8 | 1 Apr 2012 (SI 2011/2576) |
| | para 9 | 1 Jan 2012 (SI 2011/2576)[1] |
| Sch 5 | | 1 Apr 2012 (SI 2011/2576)[1] |

**Budget Responsibility and National Audit Act 2011 (c 4)**—*contd*
Sch 6                                    22 May 2011 (s 29(2))

[1]   For transitional provisions and savings, see SI 2011/2576, arts 4, 6

---

**Budget (Scotland) Act 2011 (asp 4)**

*RA:* 16 Mar 2011

Whole Act in force 16 Mar 2010 (RA)

---

**Care of Cathedrals Measure 2011 (No 1)**

*RA:* 24 May 2011

*Commencement provisions*: s 34(2)

This Measure was brought into force on 1 Sep 2011 by an instrument made by the Archbishops of Canterbury and York and dated 12 Jul 2011 (made under s 34(2))

---

**Certification of Death (Scotland) Act 2011 (asp 11)**

*RA:* 20 Apr 2011

*Commencement provisions*: s 32(2)–(4); Certification of Death (Scotland) Act 2011 (Commencement No 1) Order 2013, SSI 2013/159; Certification of Death (Scotland) Act 2011 (Commencement No 2) Order 2015, SSI 2015/115

| | | |
|---|---|---|
| 1 | (1), (2) | 8 Jun 2013 (for the purpose of allowing medical reviewers and senior medical reviewers to exercise functions under ss 20 and 21) (SSI 2013/159) |
| | | 13 May 2015 (otherwise) (SSI 2015/115) |
| | (3) | See Sch 1 below |
| 2, 3 | | 13 May 2015 (SSI 2015/115) |
| 4 | (1)–(7) | 13 May 2015 (SSI 2015/115) |
| | (8) | 25 Mar 2015 (for the purpose of enabling regulations to be made) (SSI 2015/115) |
| | | 13 May 2015 (otherwise) (SSI 2015/115) |
| 5–17 | | 13 May 2015 (SSI 2015/115) |
| 18 | (1)–(3) | 13 May 2015 (SSI 2015/115) |
| | (4) | 25 Mar 2015 (for the purpose of enabling regulations to be made) (SSI 2015/115) |
| | | 13 May 2015 (otherwise) (SSI 2015/115) |
| 19 | (1)–(3) | 13 May 2015 (SSI 2015/115) |
| | (4) | 25 Mar 2015 (for the purpose of enabling regulations to be made) (SSI 2015/115) |
| | | 13 May 2015 (otherwise) (SSI 2015/115) |
| 20 | | 8 Jun 2013 (SSI 2013/159) |
| 21, 22 | | 8 Jun 2013 (for the purposes of s 20) (SSI 2013/159) |
| | | 13 May 2015 (otherwise) (SSI 2015/115) |
| 23, 24 | | 13 May 2015 (SSI 2015/115) |
| 25 | | 25 Mar 2015 (for the purpose of enabling regulations to be made under the Registration of Births, Deaths and Marriages (Scotland) Act 1965, s 27A(2)) (SSI 2015/115) |
| | | 13 May 2015 (otherwise) (SSI 2015/115) |
| 26, 27 | | 8 Jun 2013 (SSI 2013/159) |
| 28, 29 | | 21 Apr 2011 (s 32(2)) |
| 30 | | See Sch 2 below |
| 31 | | 8 Jun 2013 (SSI 2013/159) |
| 32 | | 21 Apr 2011 (s 32(2)) |

**Certification of Death (Scotland) Act 2011 (asp 11)**—*contd*

| | |
|---|---|
| Sch 1 | 8 Jun 2013 (SSI 2013/159) |
| Sch 2 | 13 May 2015 (SSI 2015/115) |

**Charities Act 2011 (c 25)**

*RA:* 14 Dec 2011

Whole Act in force 14 Mar 2012 (s 355) (commencement orders have been made under Sch 9 to this Act which do not affect its initial commencement)

**Children's Hearings (Scotland) Act 2011 (asp 1)**

*RA:* 6 Jan 2011

*Commencement provisions*: s 206(2), (3); Children's Hearings (Scotland) Act 2011 (Commencement No 1) Order 2011, SSI 2011/8; Children's Hearings (Scotland) Act 2011 (Commencement No 2) Order 2011, SSI 2011/111; Children's Hearings (Scotland) Act 2011 (Commencement No 3) Order 2012, SSI 2012/1; Children's Hearings (Scotland) Act 2011 (Commencement No 4) Order 2012, SSI 2012/23; Children's Hearings (Scotland) Act 2011 (Commencement No 5) Order 2012, SSI 2012/246; Children's Hearings (Scotland) Act 2011 (Commencement No 6) Order 2012, SSI 2012/252; Children's Hearings (Scotland) Act 2011 (Commencement No 7) Order 2013, SSI 2013/98; Children's Hearings (Scotland) Act 2011 (Commencement No 8) Order 2013, SSI 2013/190; Children's Hearings (Scotland) Act 2011 (Commencement No 9) Order 2013, SSI 2013/195; Children's Hearings (Scotland) Act 2011 (Commencement No 10) Order 2020, SSI 2020/243

| | | |
|---|---|---|
| 1 | | 19 Jan 2011 (SSI 2011/8) |
| 2 | | 18 Apr 2011 (SSI 2011/111) |
| 3 | | See Sch 1 below |
| 4 | (1), (2) | 24 Jun 2013 (SSI 2013/195) |
| | (3) | See Sch 2 below |
| 5 | | 24 Jun 2013 (SSI 2013/195) |
| 6 | | 31 Mar 2013 (SSI 2013/98) |
| 7–9 | | 24 Jun 2013 (SSI 2013/195) |
| 10–13 | | 18 Apr 2011 (SSI 2011/111) |
| 14, 15 | | 24 Jun 2013 (SSI 2013/195) |
| 16 | | See Sch 3 below |
| 17–23 | | 24 Jun 2013 (SSI 2013/195) |
| 24 | | See Sch 4 below |
| 25–31 | | 24 Jun 2013 (SSI 2013/195) |
| 32 | | 13 Feb 2012 (SSI 2012/23) |
| 33–121 | | 24 Jun 2013 (SSI 2013/195) |
| 122 | (1)–(3) | 21 Nov 2020 (SSI 2020/243) |
| | (4)–(7) | 7 Sep 2020 (SSI 2020/243) |
| 123–186 | | 24 Jun 2013 (SSI 2013/195) |
| 187, 188 | | *Not yet in force* |
| 189, 190 | | 24 Jun 2013 (SSI 2013/195) |
| 191 | | 31 Jan 2012 (in so far as inserts Legal Aid (Scotland) Act 1986, ss 28B(2), 28M(7) (only in respect of applying s 25A(5) and (6) of that Act for the purposes of enabling the Scottish Legal Aid Board to determine the form of the application for entry on the register of solicitors and firms eligible to provide children's legal assistance under section 28M, to specify the documents which are to accompany the application and to invite and consider comments on its draft proposals), 28N) (SSI 2012/1) |
| | | 26 Mar 2012 (in so far as inserts s 28M(1), (2), (7) (for remaining purposes), (8), 28S of that Act) (SSI 2012/1) |
| | | 24 Jun 2013 (otherwise) (SSI 2013/195) |
| 192 | | 24 Jun 2013 (SSI 2013/195) |
| 193–202 | | 6 Jan 2011 (s 206(2)) |

**Children's Hearings (Scotland) Act 2011 (asp 1)**—*contd*

| | | |
|---|---|---|
| 203 | (1) | See Sch 5 below |
| | (2) | See Sch 6 below |
| 204–206 | | 6 Jan 2011 (s 206(2)) |
| Sch 1 | paras 1–7 | 18 Apr 2011 (SSI 2011/111) |
| | para 8(1)–(6) | 18 Apr 2011 (SSI 2011/111) |
| | para 8(7) | 19 Jan 2011 (SSI 2011/8) |
| | para 8(8)–(10) | 18 Apr 2011 (SSI 2011/111) |
| | para 9 | 18 Apr 2011 (SSI 2011/111) |
| | para 10(1) | 19 Sep 2012 (SSI 2012/246) |
| | para 10(2)(a) | 19 Sep 2012 (SSI 2012/252) |
| | para 10(2)(b) | 31 Mar 2013 (SSI 2013/98) |
| | para 10(3) | 19 Sep 2012 (SSI 2012/246) |
| | para 10(4), (5) | 31 Mar 2013 (SSI 2013/98) |
| | para 10(6) | 19 Sep 2012 (SSI 2012/246) |
| | para 10(7)–(9) | 31 Mar 2013 (SSI 2013/98) |
| | para 11 | 18 Apr 2011 (SSI 2011/111) |
| | para 12(1)–(3) | 19 Sep 2012 (SSI 2012/246) |
| | para 12(4)–(6) | 31 Mar 2013 (SSI 2013/98) |
| | paras 12(7), 13(1)–(4) | 19 Sep 2012 (SSI 2012/246) |
| | para 13(5), (6) | 24 Jun 2013 (SSI 2013/195) |
| | para 13(7) | 19 Sep 2012 (SSI 2012/246) |
| | para 14(1) | 31 Mar 2013 (SSI 2013/98) |
| | para 14(2) | 19 Sep 2012 (SSI 2012/246) |
| | para 14(3)–(5) | 31 Mar 2013 (SSI 2013/98) |
| | para 14(6)–(8) | 19 Sep 2012 (SSI 2012/246) |
| | para 15(1)–(5) | 18 Apr 2011 (SSI 2011/111) |
| | para 15(6) | 24 Jun 2013 (SSI 2013/195) |
| | para 16 | 18 Apr 2011 (SSI 2011/111) |
| | para 17(1) | 18 Apr 2011 (SSI 2011/111) |
| | para 17(2) | 31 Mar 2013 (SSI 2013/98) |
| | paras 18–25 | 18 Apr 2011 (SSI 2011/111) |
| Sch 2 | para 1(1) | 19 Sep 2012 (SSI 2012/246) |
| | para 1(2)–(6) | 31 Mar 2013 (SSI 2013/98) |
| | para 2 | 24 Jun 2013 (SSI 2013/195) |
| | para 3 | 31 Mar 2013 (SSI 2013/98) |
| | para 4 | 19 Sep 2012 (SSI 2012/246) |
| Schs 3, 4 | | 24 Jun 2013 (SSI 2013/195) |
| Sch 5 | para 1(1)–(7) | 24 Jun 2013 (SSI 2013/195) |
| | para 1(8)(a), (b) | 31 Jan 2012 (SSI 2012/1) |
| | paras 1(8)(c), (9), 2(1)–(7) | 24 Jun 2013 (SSI 2013/195) |
| | para 2(8) | 12 Jun 2013 (to enable the Scottish Ministers to make regulations under Children (Scotland) Act 1995, s 75 but only where such regulations will come into force on or after the date on which s 152 of this Act comes into force) (SSI 2013/190) |
| | | 24 Jun 2013 (otherwise) (SSI 2013/195) |
| | para 2(9) | 24 Jun 2013 (SSI 2013/195) |
| | para 2(10) | 24 Jun 2013 (except in so far as amendment of definition "children's hearing" in Children (Scotland) Act 1995, s 93(1) has effect in relation to s 44 thereof) (SSI 2013/195) |
| | | *Not yet in force* (exception noted above) |
| | paras 2(11), 3 | 24 Jun 2013 (SSI 2013/195) |
| Sch 6 | | 24 Jun 2013 (except repeals of or in Rehabilitation of Offenders Act 1974; Children (Scotland) Act 1995, s 44 and reference to "44" in s 105(8) thereof) (SSI 2013/195) |
| | | *Not yet in force* (exceptions noted above) |

## Coinage (Measurement) Act 2011 (c 17)

*RA:* 3 Nov 2011

Whole Act in force 3 Jan 2012 (RA)

---

## Damages (Scotland) Act 2011 (asp 7)

*RA:* 7 Apr 2011

*Commencement provisions:* s 19(3), (4); Damages (Scotland) Act 2011 (Commencement, Transitional Provisions and Savings) Order 2011, SSI 2011/268

| | |
|---|---|
| 1–17 | 7 Jul 2011 (SSI 2011/268)[1] |
| 18, 19 | 7 Apr 2011 (RA) |
| Schs 1, 2 | 7 Jul 2011 (SSI 2011/268) |

[1]    For transitional provisions and savings, see SSI 2011/268, art 4

---

## Domestic Abuse (Scotland) Act 2011 (asp 13)

*RA:* 20 Apr 2011

*Commencement provisions:* s 5(2)

| | |
|---|---|
| 1–3 | 21 Jul 2011 (s 5(2)) |
| 4, 5 | 20 Apr 2011 (RA) |

---

## Domestic Fire Safety (Wales) Measure 2011 (nawm 3)

*Passed by the National Assembly for Wales:* 16 Feb 2011

*Approved by Her Majesty in Council:* 7 Apr 2011

*Commencement provisions:* s 9(2), (3); Domestic Fire Safety (Wales) Measure 2011 (Commencement No 1) Order 2013, SI 2013/2727

| 1 | (1)–(3) | 30 Apr 2014 (in so far as relates to care homes, children's homes, halls of residence and rooms for residential purposes except in relation to certain types of building) (SI 2013/2727)[1] |
|---|---|---|
| | | 1 Jan 2016 (in so far as relates to dwelling-houses and flats except in relation to certain types of building) (SI 2013/2727)[1] |
| | | *Not yet in force* (exception noted above) |
| | (4) | 8 Apr 2011 (for the purpose of enabling matters to be prescribed under para (c)) (s 9(2)(a)) |
| | | 30 Apr 2014 (in so far as relates to care homes, children's homes, halls of residence and rooms for residential purposes except in relation to certain types of building) (SI 2013/2727)[1] |
| | | 1 Jan 2016 (in so far as relates to dwelling-houses and flats except in relation to certain types of building) (SI 2013/2727)[1] |
| | | *Not yet in force* (exception noted above) |
| | (5) | 30 Apr 2014 (in so far as relates to care homes, children's homes, halls of residence and rooms for residential purposes except in relation to certain types of building) (SI 2013/2727)[1] |
| | | 1 Jan 2016 (in so far as relates to dwelling-houses and flats except in relation to certain types of building) (SI 2013/2727)[1] |
| | | *Not yet in force* (exception noted above) |
| 2 | (1) | *Not yet in force* |
| | (2) | See Sch 1 below |
| | (3) | See Sch 2 below |
| 3 | (1), (2) | 8 Apr 2011 (for the purpose of enabling matters to be prescribed) (s 9(2)(a)) |

**Domestic Fire Safety (Wales) Measure 2011 (nawm 3)**—*contd*

|  | | *Not yet in force* (otherwise) |
|---|---|---|
| | (3)–(8) | *Not yet in force* |
| 4, 5 | | *Not yet in force* |
| 6–9 | | 8 Apr 2011 (s 9(2)(b), (c)) |
| Schs 1, 2 | | *Not yet in force* |

[1]     The certain types of building are those which are: (a) listed in accordance with the Planning (Listed Buildings and Conservation Areas) Act 1990, s 1; (b) in a conservation area designated in accordance with s 69 of the 1990 Act; (c) included in the schedule of monuments maintained under the Ancient Monuments and Archaeological Areas Act 1979, s 1; (d) excepted energy buildings (as defined in the Welsh Ministers (Transfer of Functions) (No 2) Order 2009, SI 2009/3019); or (e) temporary buildings, that is to say, buildings with a planned time of use of two years or less

---

**Double Jeopardy (Scotland) Act 2011 (asp 16)**

*RA:* 27 Apr 2011

*Commencement provisions:* s 17(3); Double Jeopardy (Scotland) Act 2011 (Commencement and Transitional Provisions) Order 2011, SSI 2011/365

| 1–16 | 28 Nov 2011 (SSI 2011/365)[1] |
|---|---|
| 17 | 27 Apr 2011 (RA) |
| Schedule | 28 Nov 2011 (SSI 2011/365)[1] |

[1]     For transitional provisions, see SSI 2011/365, arts 4, 5

---

**Ecclesiastical Fees (Amendment) Measure 2011 (No 2)**

*RA:* 24 May 2011

Provisions of this Measure were brought into force on the following dates by instruments made by the Archbishops of Canterbury and York under s 6(2), and dated 7 Jun 2011 and 29 Sep 2011

| 1, 2 | | 1 Jul 2011 |
|---|---|---|
| 3 | | 1 Oct 2011 |
| 4 | | 1 Jul 2011 |
| 5 | (1) | 1 Oct 2011 |
| | (2), (3) | 1 Jul 2011 |
| 6 | | 1 Jul 2011 |
| Schs 1, 2 | | 1 Jul 2011 |

---

**Education Act 2011 (c 21)**

*RA:* 15 Nov 2011

*Commencement provisions:* s 82; Education Act 2011 (Commencement No 1) Order 2011, SI 2011/2750; Education Act 2011 (Commencement No 2) Order 2012, SI 2012/84; Education Act 2011 (Commencement No 3 and Transitional and Savings Provisions) Order 2012, SI 2012/924; Education Act 2011 (Commencement No 4 and Transitional and Savings Provisions) Order 2012, SI 2012/1087, as amended by SI 2018/809; Education Act 2011 (Commencement No 5) Order 2012, SI 2012/2213

| 1 | (1) | See sub-ss (2), (3) below |
|---|---|---|
| | (2) | 1 Sep 2012 (for the purpose of making regulations under the Childcare Act 2006, s 7) (SI 2012/1087) |
| | | 1 Sep 2013 (otherwise) (SI 2012/2213) |
| | (3), (4) | 1 Sep 2012 (SI 2012/1087) |
| 2, 3 | | 1 Apr 2012 (SI 2012/924) |
| 4 | | 1 Sep 2012 (SI 2012/1087)[3] |
| 5 | | 15 Jan 2012 (SI 2012/84) |
| 6 | | 15 Jan 2012 (s 82(2)) |

**Education Act 2011 (c 21)**—*contd*

| | | |
|---|---|---|
| 7–10 | | 1 Apr 2012 (SI 2012/924) |
| 11, 12 | | 1 Apr 2012 (SI 2012/924) |
| 13 | | 1 Oct 2012 (SI 2012/2213) |
| 14–17 | | 1 Apr 2012 (SI 2012/924) |
| 18–20 | | 1 Feb 2012 (SI 2012/84) |
| 21 | | See Sch 7 below |
| 22 | | 1 Feb 2012 (SI 2012/84) |
| 23, 24 | | 1 May 2012 (SI 2012/924) |
| 25 | | 1 Apr 2012 (SI 2012/924) |
| 26 | (1) | See Sch 8 below |
| | (2), (3) | 1 Apr 2012 (SI 2012/924) |
| 27 | | See Sch 9 below |
| 28 | (1)–(4) | 1 Sep 2012 (SI 2012/1087) |
| | (5) | 1 Feb 2012 (SI 2012/84) |
| | (6) | 1 Sep 2012 (SI 2012/1087) |
| 29 | (1), (2) | 1 Feb 2012 (for the purposes of making regulations under the Education Act 1997, s 46) (SI 2012/84) |
| | | 1 Sep 2012 (otherwise) (SI 2012/1087) |
| | (3)–(7) | 1 Sep 2012 (SI 2012/1087) |
| | (8) | 1 Feb 2012 (for the purposes of making regulations under the Education Act 1997, s 46) (SI 2012/84) |
| | | 1 Sep 2012 (otherwise) (SI 2012/1087) |
| | (9) | 1 Sep 2012 (SI 2012/1087) |
| 30, 31 | | 15 Jan 2012 (s 82(2)) |
| 32 | | 1 Feb 2012 (SI 2012/84) |
| 33 | | 15 Nov 2011 (RA) |
| 34–36 | | 1 Feb 2012 (SI 2012/84) |
| 37 | | See Sch 11 below |
| 38 | | 1 Sep 2012 (SI 2012/1087) |
| 39 | | 1 Sep 2012 (SI 2012/1087)[3] |
| 40 | (1)–(3) | 15 Nov 2011 (RA) |
| | (4) | 1 Feb 2012 (SI 2012/84) |
| | (5)–(9) | 15 Nov 2011 (RA) |
| 41 | | 15 Nov 2011 (RA) |
| 42 | (1)–(7) | 15 Nov 2011 (RA) |
| | (8) | 1 Feb 2012 (SI 2012/84) |
| | (9)–(11) | 15 Nov 2011 (RA) |
| 43 | | 1 Feb 2012 (SI 2012/84) |
| 44 | | 17 Nov 2011 (SI 2011/2750) |
| 45 | | 1 Aug 2012 (SI 2012/1087)[3] |
| 46 | | 1 Feb 2012 (SI 2012/84) |
| 47, 48 | | 15 Jan 2012 (s 82(2)) |
| 49 | | See Sch 12 below |
| 50 | | 1 Sep 2012 (but not in respect of any funding period before 1 Apr 2013) (SI 2012/1087) |
| 51 | | 15 Jan 2012 (SI 2012/84) |
| 52 | | 1 Feb 2012 (SI 2012/84) |
| 53 | | 1 Feb 2012 (for the purposes of applying for and making Academy orders in respect of alternative provision Academies under the Academies Act 2010, ss 3, 4) (SI 2012/84) |
| | | 1 Apr 2012 (otherwise) (SI 2012/924) |
| 54 | (1) | See Sch 13 below |
| | (2), (3) | 1 Apr 2012 (SI 2012/924) |
| 55, 56 | | 1 Feb 2012 (SI 2012/84) |
| 57 | | 1 Apr 2012 (SI 2012/924) |
| 58 | | 15 Nov 2011 (RA) |
| 59, 60 | | 1 Feb 2012 (SI 2012/84) |
| 61 | | 15 Jan 2012 (s 82(2)) |
| 62–65 | | 1 Feb 2012 (SI 2012/84) |

**Education Act 2011 (c 21)**—*contd*

| | | |
|---|---|---|
| 66–68 | | 1 Apr 2012 (SI 2012/924) |
| 69, 70 | | 1 Sep 2012 (SI 2012/1087) |
| 71, 72 | | 1 Apr 2012 (SI 2012/924) |
| 73 | (1) | See sub-ss (2), (3) below |
| | (2)(a), (b) | 1 Aug 2012 (SI 2012/1087) |
| | (2)(c) | 1 Aug 2012 (in so far as relates to the Apprenticeships, Skills, Learning and Children Act 2009, s 88(2A), as inserted by sub-s (2)(b)) (SI 2012/1087) |
| | | 1 Aug 2013 (otherwise) (SI 2012/2213) |
| | (3) | 1 Apr 2012 (SI 2012/924) |
| 74 | | 1 Feb 2012 (SI 2012/84) |
| 75–83 | | 15 Nov 2011 (RA) |
| Sch 1 | | 1 Sep 2012 (SI 2012/1087)[3] |
| Schs 2, 3 | | 1 Apr 2012 (SI 2012/924) |
| Sch 4 | | 1 Oct 2012 (SI 2012/2213) |
| Schs 5, 6 | | 1 Apr 2012 (SI 2012/924) |
| Sch 7 | | 1 Apr 2012 (SI 2012/924)[2] |
| Sch 8 | paras 1–10 | 1 Apr 2012 (SI 2012/924) |
| | para 11 | See paras 12–15 below |
| | paras 12–14 | 1 Apr 2012 (SI 2012/924) |
| | para 15 | 15 Jan 2012 (SI 2012/84) |
| | paras 16–21 | 1 Apr 2012 (SI 2012/924) |
| | para 22 | See paras 23–26 below |
| | paras 23–25 | 1 Apr 2012 (SI 2012/924) |
| | para 26 | 15 Jan 2012 (in so far as repeals Apprenticeships, Skills, Children and Learning Act 2009, Sch 12, para 37) (SI 2012/84) |
| | | 1 Apr 2012 (otherwise) (SI 2012/924) |
| Sch 9 | | 1 Apr 2012 (SI 2012/924) |
| Sch 10 | | 1 Feb 2012 (SI 2012/84) |
| Sch 11 | para 1 | See paras 2–10 below |
| | para 2 | 1 Feb 2012 (so far as it relates to a new school that is not a pupil referral unit or a maintained nursery school) (SI 2012/84)[1] |
| | | 1 Sep 2012 (in so far as relates to a new school that is a pupil referral unit) (SI 2012/2213) |
| | | *Not yet in force* (otherwise) |
| | paras 3–11 | 1 Feb 2012 (SI 2012/84)[1] |
| Sch 12 | | 1 Apr 2012 (SI 2012/924)[2] |
| Sch 13 | paras 1–16, 17(1) | 1 Apr 2012 (SI 2012/924) |
| | para 17(2) | *Not yet in force* |
| | paras 17(3), 18–20 | 1 Apr 2012 (SI 2012/924) |
| Schs 14, 15 | | 1 Feb 2012 (SI 2012/84) |
| Schs 16, 17 | | 1 Apr 2012 (SI 2012/924) |
| Sch 18 | | 1 Sep 2012 (SI 2012/1087) |

[1]   For transitional provisions and savings, see SI 2012/84, art 4

[2]   For transitional provisions and savings, see SI 2012/924, arts 4–7

[3]   For transitional provisions and savings, see SI 2012/1087, arts 4–6

**Education (Wales) Measure 2011 (nawm 7)**

*Passed by the National Assembly for Wales:* 29 Mar 2011

*Approved by Her Majesty in Council:* 10 May 2011

*Commencement provisions:* s 33; Education (Wales) Measure 2011 (Commencement No 1) Order 2012, SI 2012/2656; Education (Wales) Measure 2011 (Commencement No 2) Order 2013, SI 2013/2090; Education (Wales) Measure 2011 (Commencement No 3) Order 2014, SI 2014/1066

| | |
|---|---|
| 1–9 | 16 Nov 2012 (SI 2012/2656) |

**Education (Wales) Measure 2011 (nawm 7)**—*contd*

| | |
|---|---|
| 10–15 | 28 Apr 2014 (SI 2014/1066) |
| 16 | *Never in force* (repealed) |
| 17–19 | 28 Apr 2014 (SI 2014/1066) |
| 20 | *Never in force* (repealed) |
| 21 | 28 Apr 2014 (SI 2014/1066) |
| 22–25 | 22 Aug 2013 (SI 2013/2090) |
| 26–34 | 10 Jul 2011 (s 33(1)) |

---

## Energy Act 2011 (c 16)

*RA:* 18 Oct 2011

*Commencement provisions:* s 121; Energy Act 2011 (Commencement No 1 and Saving) Order 2012, SI 2012/873; Energy Act 2011 (Commencement No 1) (Scotland) Order 2012, SSI 2012/191; Energy Act 2011 (Commencement No 2) Order 2013, SI 2013/125; Energy Act 2011 (Commencement No 3) Order 2015, SI 2015/880; Energy Act 2011 (Commencement No 2) (Scotland) Order 2019, SSI 2019/181

| | | |
|---|---|---|
| 1, 2 | | 21 Mar 2012 (in so far as necessary for the purposes of interpreting ss 1–41 and of enabling the exercise of any power thereunder to make an order or regulations or to issue a code of practice) (SI 2012/873) |
| | | 28 Jan 2013 (otherwise) (SI 2013/125) |
| 3 | | 21 Mar 2012 (SI 2012/873) |
| 4, 5 | | 21 Mar 2012 (in so far as necessary for the purposes of interpreting ss 1–41 and of enabling the exercise of any power thereunder to make an order or regulations or to issue a code of practice) (SI 2012/873) |
| | | 28 Jan 2013 (otherwise) (SI 2013/125) |
| 6 | | 21 Mar 2012 (SI 2012/873) |
| 7–9 | | 21 Mar 2012 (in so far as necessary for the purposes of interpreting ss 1–41 and of enabling the exercise of any power thereunder to make an order or regulations or to issue a code of practice) (SI 2012/873) |
| | | 28 Jan 2013 (otherwise) (SI 2013/125) |
| 10 | | 22 Jun 2012 (SSI 2012/191) |
| 11 | | 21 Mar 2012 (in so far as necessary for the purposes of interpreting ss 1–41 and of enabling the exercise of any power thereunder to make an order or regulations or to issue a code of practice) (SI 2012/873) |
| | | 28 Jan 2013 (otherwise) (SI 2013/125) |
| 12, 13 | | 21 Mar 2012 (in so far as necessary for the purposes of interpreting ss 1–41 and of enabling the exercise of any power thereunder to make an order or regulations or to issue a code of practice) (SI 2012/873) |
| | | 28 Jan 2013 (otherwise) (SI 2013/125) |
| 14 | (1)–(5) | 21 Mar 2012 (in so far as necessary for the purposes of interpreting ss 1–41 and of enabling the exercise of any power thereunder to make an order or regulations or to issue a code of practice) (SI 2012/873) |
| | | 28 Jan 2013 (otherwise) (SI 2013/125) |
| | (6)–(8) | 22 Jun 2012 (SSI 2012/191) |
| | (9) | 21 Mar 2012 (in so far as necessary for the purposes of interpreting ss 1–41 and of enabling the exercise of any power thereunder to make an order or regulations or to issue a code of practice) (SI 2012/873) |
| | | 28 Jan 2013 (otherwise) (SI 2013/125) |
| 15 | (1)–(3) | 21 Mar 2012 (SI 2012/873) |
| | (4) | 22 Jun 2012 (SSI 2012/191) |
| | (5) | 21 Mar 2012 (SI 2012/873) |
| 16–22 | | 21 Mar 2012 (SI 2012/873) |

**Energy Act 2011 (c 16)**—*contd*

| | | |
|---|---|---|
| 23–28 | | 28 Jan 2013 (SI 2013/125) |
| 29 | | 21 Mar 2012 (in so far as necessary for the purposes of interpreting ss 1–41 and of enabling the exercise of any power thereunder to make an order or regulations or to issue a code of practice) (SI 2012/873) |
| | | 28 Jan 2013 (otherwise) (SI 2013/125) |
| 30–34 | | 21 Mar 2012 (SI 2012/873) |
| 35 | (1)–(5) | 21 Mar 2012 (SI 2012/873) |
| | (6) | 22 Jun 2012 (SSI 2012/191) |
| | (7) | 21 Mar 2012 (SI 2012/873) |
| 36 | | 21 Mar 2012 (SI 2012/873) |
| 37 | | 18 Oct 2011 (s 121(4)(a)) |
| 38–41 | | 21 Mar 2012 (SI 2012/873) |
| 42–44 | | 26 Mar 2015 (SI 2015/880) |
| 45 | (1)–(4), (5)(a), (b) | 26 Mar 2015 (SI 2015/880) |
| | (5)(c) | *Not yet in force* |
| | (5)(d)–(f) | 26 Mar 2015 (SI 2015/880) |
| | (6)(a)–(c) | 26 Mar 2015 (SI 2015/880) |
| | (6)(d) | *Not yet in force* |
| | (7) | 26 Mar 2015 (as if the reference to "(c)" therein were omitted) (SI 2015/880) |
| | | *Not yet in force* (otherwise) |
| | (8) | 26 Mar 2015 (SI 2015/880) |
| 46, 47 | | 26 Mar 2015 (SI 2015/880) |
| 48 | (1)–(3) | 26 Mar 2015 (SI 2015/880) |
| | (4)–(6) | *Not yet in force* |
| | (7)(a) | 26 Mar 2015 (SI 2015/880) |
| | (7)(b) | *Not yet in force* |
| | (8) | 26 Mar 2015 (SI 2015/880) |
| 49, 50 | | 26 Mar 2015 (SI 2015/880) |
| 51 | (1)–(3), (4)(a), (b) | 26 Mar 2015 (SI 2015/880) |
| | (4)(c) | *Not yet in force* |
| | (4)(d)–(f) | 26 Mar 2015 (SI 2015/880) |
| | (5)(a)–(c) | 26 Mar 2015 (SI 2015/880) |
| | (5)(d) | *Not yet in force* |
| | (6) | 26 Mar 2015 (as if the reference to "(c)" therein were omitted) (SI 2015/880) |
| | | *Not yet in force* (otherwise) |
| | (7) | 26 Mar 2015 (SI 2015/880) |
| 52, 53 | | 26 Mar 2015 (SI 2015/880) |
| 54–65 | | 1 Jul 2019 (SSI 2019/181) |
| 66–74 | | 18 Dec 2011 (s 121(3)(a)–(c)) |
| 75 | | 22 Jun 2012 (SSI 2012/191) |
| 76–80 | | 18 Dec 2011 (s 121(3)(d), (e)) |
| 81 | | 18 Oct 2011 (s 121(4)(b)) |
| 82–92 | | 21 Mar 2012 (SI 2012/873)[1] |
| 93–103 | | 18 Dec 2011 (s 121(3)(f), (g)) |
| 104 | (1), (2) | 18 Oct 2011 (s 121(4)(c)) |
| | (3) | 18 Dec 2011 (s 121(3)(h)) |
| 105–107 | | 18 Dec 2011 (s 121(3)(i)–(k)) |
| 108 | | 21 Mar 2012 (SI 2012/873) |
| 109–110 | | *Not yet in force* |
| 111–114 | | 18 Dec 2011 (s 121(3)(l)–(n)) |
| 115, 116 | | 26 Mar 2015 (SI 2015/880) |
| 117 | | *Not yet in force* |
| 118 | | 21 Mar 2012 (SI 2012/873) |
| 119–122 | | 18 Oct 2011 (s 121(4)(d)) |
| Sch 1 | paras 1, 2 | 18 Dec 2011 (s 121(5)(a)) |
| | para 3 | 6 Apr 2014 (s 121(5)(c)) |

**Energy Act 2011 (c 16)**—*contd*

|  |  |
|---|---|
| para 4 | 1 Jan 2013 (s 121(5)(b)) |
| paras 5, 6 | 6 Apr 2014 (s 121(5)(c)) |
| paras 7, 8(1), (2)(a) | 18 Dec 2011 (s 121(5)(a)) |
| para 8(2)(b) | 1 Jan 2013 (s 121(5)(b)) |
| para 8(3)(a) | 18 Dec 2011 (s 121(5)(a)) |
| para 8(3)(b) | 1 Jan 2013 (s 121(5)(b)) |
| para 8(4) | 18 Dec 2011 (s 121(5)(a)) |
| para 8(5) | 1 Jan 2013 (s 121(5)(b)) |
| para 9 | 18 Dec 2011 (s 121(5)(a)) |
| Sch 2 | 21 Mar 2012 (SI 2012/873)[1] |

[1]    For transitional provisions and savings, see SI 2012/873, art 4

---

## Estates of Deceased Persons (Forfeiture Rule and Law of Succession) Act 2011 (c 7)

*RA:* 12 Jul 2011

*Commencement provisions:* s 4(2), (3); Estates of Deceased Persons (Forfeiture Rule and Law of Succession) Act 2011 (Commencement) Order 2011, SI 2011/2913

|  |  |
|---|---|
| 1–3 | 1 Feb 2012 (SI 2011/2913) |
| 4 | 12 Jul 2011 (RA) |

---

## European Union Act 2011 (c 12)

*RA:* 19 Jul 2011

*Commencement provisions:* s 21; European Union Act 2011 (Commencement No 1) Order 2011, SI 2011/1984; European Union Act 2011 (Commencement No 2) Order 2011, SI 2011/1985

|  |  |
|---|---|
| 1–14 | 19 Aug 2011 (SI 2011/1984) |
| 15 | 19 Jul 2011 (s 21(1)(a)) |
| 16, 17 | 19 Sep 2011 (SI 2011/1985) |
| 18–22 | 19 Jul 2011 (s 21(1)(b)) |
| Sch 1 | 19 Aug 2011 (SI 2011/1984) |
| Sch 2 | 19 Sep 2011 (SI 2011/1985) |

---

## Finance Act 2011 (c 11)

*Budget Day:* 23 Mar 2011

*RA:* 19 Jul 2011

The commencement details of Finance Acts are not set out, as the dates from which their provisions take effect are usually stated clearly and unambiguously in the text of the Act, and charging provisions will normally state for which year or years of assessment they are to have effect.

---

## Fixed-term Parliaments Act 2011 (c 14)

*RA:* 15 Sep 2011

*Commencement provisions:* s 7(2)

Whole Act in force 15 Sep 2011 (s 7(2))

---

## Forced Marriage etc (Protection and Jurisdiction) (Scotland) Act 2011 (asp 15)

*RA:* 27 Apr 2011

*Commencement provisions:* s 19(2); Forced Marriage etc (Protection and Jurisdiction) (Scotland) Act 2011 (Commencement) Order 2011, SSI 2011/352

| | |
|---|---|
| 1–18 | 28 Nov 2011 (SSI 2011/352) |
| 19 | 27 Apr 2011 (RA) |

## Forth Crossing Act 2011 (asp 2)

*RA:* 20 Jan 2011

*Commencement provisions:* s 80; Forth Crossing Act 2011 (Commencement) Order 2011, SSI 2011/38

| | |
|---|---|
| 1–20 | 18 Mar 2011 (SSI 2011/38) |
| 21–56 | 3 Feb 2011 (SSI 2011/38) |
| 57–71 | 18 Mar 2011 (SSI 2011/38) |
| 72–76 | 3 Feb 2011 (SSI 2011/38) |
| 77 | 20 Jan 2011 (s 80(1)) |
| 78 | 3 Feb 2011 (SSI 2011/38) |
| 79–81 | 20 Jan 2011 (s 80(1)) |
| Schs 1–8 | 18 Mar 2011 (SSI 2011/38) |
| Schs 9, 10 | 3 Feb 2011 (SSI 2011/38) |
| Sch 11 | 18 Mar 2011 (SSI 2011/38) |

## Historic Environment (Amendment) (Scotland) Act 2011 (asp 3)

*RA:* 23 Feb 2011

*Commencement provisions:* s 33(2), (3); Historic Environment (Amendment) (Scotland) Act 2011 (Commencement No 1) Order 2011, SSI 2011/174; Historic Environment (Amendment) (Scotland) Act 2011 (Commencement No 2) Order 2011, SSI 2011/372

| | |
|---|---|
| 1 | 30 Jun 2011 (SSI 2011/174) |
| 2–4 | 1 Dec 2011 (SSI 2011/372) |
| 5 | 30 Jun 2011 (SSI 2011/174) |
| 6 | 30 Jun 2011 (for the purpose of enabling regulations to be made) (SSI 2011/174) |
| | 1 Dec 2011 (otherwise) (SSI 2011/372) |
| 7–9 | 30 Jun 2011 (SSI 2011/174) |
| 10 | 1 Dec 2011 (SSI 2011/372) |
| 11–13 | 30 Jun 2011 (SSI 2011/174) |
| 14 | 1 Dec 2011 (SSI 2011/372) |
| 15 | 30 Jun 2011 (for the purpose of enabling regulations to be made) (SSI 2011/174) |
| | 1 Dec 2011 (otherwise) (SSI 2011/372) |
| 16–19 | 1 Dec 2011 (SSI 2011/372) |
| 20 | 30 Jun 2011 (for the purpose of enabling regulations to be made) (SSI 2011/174) |
| | 1 Dec 2011 (otherwise) (SSI 2011/372) |
| 21, 22 | 1 Dec 2011 (SSI 2011/372) |
| 23, 24 | 30 Jun 2011 (for the purpose of enabling regulations to be made) (SSI 2011/174) |
| | 1 Dec 2011 (otherwise) (SSI 2011/372) |
| 25 | 1 Dec 2011 (SSI 2011/372) |
| 26 | 30 Jun 2011 (for the purpose of enabling regulations to be made) (SSI 2011/174) |
| | 1 Dec 2011 (otherwise) (SSI 2011/372) |
| 27 | 30 Jun 2011 (SSI 2011/174) |
| 28 | 1 Dec 2011 (SSI 2011/372) |

**Historic Environment (Amendment) (Scotland) Act 2011 (asp 3)**—*contd*

| | | |
|---|---|---|
| 29 | (1) | 30 Jun 2011 (SSI 2011/174) |
| | (2) | *Not yet in force* |
| 30 | | *Not yet in force* |
| 31–33 | | 23 Feb 2011 (s 33(2)) |

**Housing (Wales) Measure 2011 (nawm 5)**

*Passed by the National Assembly for Wales:* 22 Mar 2011

*Approved by Her Majesty in Council:* 10 May 2011

*Commencement provisions:* s 90; Housing (Wales) Measure 2011 (Commencement No 1) Order 2011, SI 2011/2475; Housing (Wales) Measure 2011 (Commencement No 2) Order 2012, SI 2012/2091

| | | |
|---|---|---|
| 1–34 | | 3 Sep 2012 (SI 2012/2091) |
| 35 | | 18 Oct 2011 (for the purpose of consultation on setting standards of performance under Housing Act 1996, s 33A) (SI 2011/2475) |
| | | 2 Dec 2011 (otherwise) (SI 2011/2475) |
| 36 | | 18 Oct 2011 (for the purpose of consultation on the issue of guidance on standards of performance under Housing Act 1996, s 33B) (SI 2011/2475) |
| | | 2 Dec 2011 (otherwise) (SI 2011/2475) |
| 37 | | 18 Oct 2011 (SI 2011/2475) |
| 38 | | 2 Dec 2011 (SI 2011/2475) |
| 39–41 | | 18 Oct 2011 (SI 2011/2475) |
| 42 | | 2 Dec 2011 (SI 2011/2475) |
| 43–51 | | 18 Oct 2011 (SI 2011/2475) |
| 52 | | 18 Oct 2011 (except in so far as relates to standards applicable under the Housing Act 1996, s 33A) (SI 2011/2475) |
| | | 2 Dec 2011 (exception noted above) (SI 2011/2475) |
| 53–56 | | 18 Oct 2011 (SI 2011/2475) |
| 57 | | 18 Oct 2011 (except in so far as relates to standards applicable under the Housing Act 1996, s 33A) (SI 2011/2475) |
| | | 2 Dec 2011 (exception noted above) (SI 2011/2475) |
| 58–63 | | 18 Oct 2011 (SI 2011/2475) |
| 64 | | 18 Oct 2011 (except in so far as relates to standards applicable under the Housing Act 1996, s 33A) (SI 2011/2475) |
| | | 2 Dec 2011 (exception noted above) (SI 2011/2475) |
| 65–71 | | 18 Oct 2011 (SI 2011/2475) |
| 72 | | 18 Oct 2011 (except in so far as relates to standards applicable under the Housing Act 1996, s 33A) (SI 2011/2475) |
| | | 2 Dec 2011 (exception noted above) (SI 2011/2475) |
| 73–75 | | 18 Oct 2011 (SI 2011/2475) |
| 76 | | 18 Oct 2011 (except in so far as relates to standards applicable under the Housing Act 1996, s 33A) (SI 2011/2475) |
| | | 2 Dec 2011 (exception noted above) (SI 2011/2475) |
| 77–87 | | 18 Oct 2011 (SI 2011/2475) |
| 88 | | See Schedule below |
| 89–91 | | 10 Jul 2011 (s 90(1)) |
| Schedule | paras 1–3 | 18 Oct 2011 (SI 2011/2475) |
| | paras 4–8 | 2 Dec 2011 (SI 2011/2475) |
| | paras 9–20 | 18 Oct 2011 (SI 2011/2475) |

**Local Electoral Administration (Scotland) Act 2011 (asp 10)**

*RA:* 20 Apr 2011

*Commencement provisions:* s 21; Local Electoral Administration (Scotland) Act 2011 (Commencement) Order 2011, SSI 2011/277

**Local Electoral Administration (Scotland) Act 2011 (asp 10)**—*contd*

| | |
|---|---|
| 1–19 | 29 Jun 2011 (SSI 2011/277) |
| 20–22 | 20 Apr 2011 (RA) |

---

**Local Government (Wales) Measure 2011 (nawm 4)**

*Passed by the National Assembly for Wales:* 15 Mar 2011

*Approved by Her Majesty in Council:* 10 May 2011

*Commencement provisions:* s 178; Local Government (Wales) Measure 2011 (Commencement No 1) Order 2011, SI 2011/2011; Local Government (Wales) Measure 2011 (Commencement No 2 and Saving Provisions) Order 2012, SI 2012/1187; Local Government (Wales) Measure 2011 (Commencement No 3) Order 2014, SI 2014/453

| | | |
|---|---|---|
| 1–3 | | 31 Aug 2011 (SI 2011/2011) |
| 4 | | 28 Feb 2014 (sub-s (8) repealed) (SI 2014/453) |
| 5–33 | | 30 Apr 2012 (SI 2012/1187) |
| 34–54 | | 10 Jul 2011 (s 178(2)(a)) |
| 55 | | 10 Jul 2011 (s 178(2)(b)) |
| 56, 57 | | 30 Apr 2012 (SI 2012/1187) |
| 58 | | 11 May 2011 (s 178(1)(a)) |
| 59, 60 | | *Not yet in force* |
| 61–75 | | 30 Apr 2012 (SI 2012/1187) |
| 76 | | 10 Jul 2011 (s 178(2)(b)) |
| 77 | | 11 May 2011 (s 178(1)(a)) |
| 78 | | 30 Apr 2012 (SI 2012/1187) |
| 79, 80 | | 11 May 2011 (s 178(1)(a)) |
| 81–99 | | 30 Apr 2012 (SI 2012/1187) |
| 100–140 | | 10 Jul 2011 (s 178(2)(c)) |
| 141 | | 31 Aug 2011 (SI 2011/2011) |
| 142, 143 | | 31 Aug 2011 (in so far as they relate to a report under s 146) (SI 2011/2011) |
| | | 30 Apr 2012 (otherwise) (SI 2012/1187) |
| 144 | | 31 Aug 2011 (SI 2011/2011) |
| 145 | | 31 Aug 2011 (in so far as it relates to a report under s 146) (SI 2011/2011) |
| | | 30 Apr 2012 (otherwise) (SI 2012/1187) |
| 146 | | 31 Aug 2011 (SI 2011/2011) |
| 147 | | 30 Apr 2012 (SI 2012/1187) |
| 148–152 | | 31 Aug 2011 (in so far as they relate to a report under s 146) (SI 2011/2011) |
| | | 30 Apr 2012 (otherwise) (SI 2012/1187) |
| 153 | | 30 Apr 2012 (SI 2012/1187) |
| 154 | | 31 Aug 2011 (in so far as it relates to a report under s 146) (SI 2011/2011) |
| | | 30 Apr 2012 (otherwise) (SI 2012/1187) |
| 155 | (1) | 30 Apr 2012 (SI 2012/1187) |
| | (2)–(4) | 31 Aug 2011 (in so far as they relate to a report under s 146) (SI 2011/2011) |
| | | 30 Apr 2012 (otherwise) (SI 2012/1187) |
| | (5) | 28 Feb 2014 (SI 2014/453) |
| 156, 157 | | 31 Aug 2011 (in so far as they relate to a report under s 146) (SI 2011/2011) |
| | | 30 Apr 2012 (otherwise) (SI 2012/1187) |
| 158 | | 31 Aug 2011 (SI 2011/2011) |
| 159 | | 11 May 2011 (s 178(1)(a)) |
| 160 | | See Sch 3 below |
| 161–171 | | 31 Aug 2011 (SI 2011/2011) |
| 172–175 | | 11 May 2011 (s 178(1)(b)) |
| 176 | (1) | 30 Apr 2012 (SI 2012/1187) |

**Local Government (Wales) Measure 2011 (nawm 4)**—*contd*

|  | (2) | See Sch 4 below |
|---|---|---|
|  | (3) | *Not yet in force* |
| 177–179 |  | 11 May 2011 (s 178(1)(b)) |
| Sch 1 |  | 10 Jul 2011 (s 178(2)(a)) |
| Sch 2 |  | 31 Aug 2011 (SI 2011/2011) |
| Sch 3 |  | 30 Apr 2012 (SI 2012/1187) |
| Sch 4 | Pt A | 30 Apr 2012 (SI 2012/1187) |
|  | Pts B, C | 10 Jul 2011 (s 178(2)(d)) |
|  | Pt D | 30 Apr 2012 (SI 2012/1187) |
|  | Pt E | 11 May 2011 (s 178(1)(c))[1] |
|  | Pt F | 30 Apr 2012 (SI 2012/1187)[2] |

[1]    S 178(1)(c) purports to bring Sch 4, Pt E into force on 11 May 2011. However, it is thought that this is a drafting error; s 100 of the Measure (which makes an identical repeal) comes into force on 10 Jul 2011 and it is thought that Sch 4, Pt E should have been brought into force on this latter date

[2]    For savings, see SI 2012/1187, art 3

---

## Localism Act 2011 (c 20)

*RA:* 15 Nov 2011

*Commencement provisions*: s 240; Localism Act 2011 (Commencement No 1 and Transitional Provisions) Order 2011, SI 2011/2896; Localism Act 2011 (Commencement No 2 and Transitional and Saving Provision) Order 2012, SI 2012/57; Localism Act 2011 (Commencement No 1) (Wales) Order 2012, SI 2012/193; Localism Act 2011 (Commencement No 3) Order 2012, SI 2012/411; Localism Act 2011 (Commencement No 4 and Transitional, Transitory and Saving Provisions) Order 2012, SI 2012/628, as amended by SI 2012/2029; Localism Act 2011 (Commencement No 2 and Saving Provision) (Wales) Order 2012, SI 2012/887; Localism Act 2011 (Commencement No 5 and Transitional, Savings and Transitory Provisions) Order 2012, SI 2012/1008; Localism Act 2011 (Commencement No 6 and Transitional, Savings and Transitory Provisions) Order 2012, SI 2012/1463, as amended by SI 2012/1714; Localism Act 2011 (Commencement No 7 and Transitional, Saving and Transitory Provisions) Order 2012, SI 2012/2029, as amended by SI 2013/797; Localism Act 2011 (Commencement No 1) (England) Order 2012, SI 2012/2420; Localism Act 2011 (Commencement No 2 and Transitional Provisions) (England) Order 2012, SI 2012/2599; Localism Act 2011 (Commencement No 8 and Transitional, Transitory and Savings Provisions) Order 2012, SI 2012/2913; Localism Act 2011 (Commencement No 2 and Transitional Provisions) Order 2013, SI 2013/722; Localism Act 2011 (Commencement No 9) Order 2013, SI 2013/797; Localism Act 2011 (Commencement No 3) Order 2013, SI 2013/2931

| 1 | (1)–(6) | 18 Feb 2012 (SI 2012/411) |
|---|---|---|
|  | (7) | See Sch 1 below |
| 2–7 |  | 18 Feb 2012 (SI 2012/411) |
| 8 | (1) | 18 Feb 2012 (SI 2012/411) |
|  | (2) | 3 Dec 2011 (SI 2011/2896) |
| 9 | (1) | 18 Feb 2012 (except in so far as inserts Fire and Rescue Services Act 2004, ss 5A, 5B (in so far as they relate to fire and rescue authorities in Wales), ss 5C, 5D (in so far as they relate to the power of the Welsh Ministers to make orders) and ss 5F–5L) (SI 2012/411) |
|  |  | 1 Apr 2012 (exceptions noted above) (SI 2012/887) |
|  | (2) | 18 Feb 2012 (except in so far as relates to fire and rescue authorities in Wales) (SI 2012/411) |
|  |  | 1 Apr 2012 (exception noted above) (SI 2012/887) |
|  | (3) | 1 Apr 2012 (SI 2012/887) |
|  | (4), (5) | 18 Feb 2012 (SI 2012/411) |
|  | (6), (7)(a) | 1 Apr 2012 (SI 2012/887) |
|  | (7)(b) | 18 Feb 2012 (except in so far as inserts Fire and Rescue Services Act 2004, s 62(1A)(a), (d) and s 62(1A)(b) (in so far as relates to power of the Welsh ministers to make orders)) (SI 2012/411) |
|  |  | 1 Apr 2012 (exception noted above) (SI 2012/887) |

**Localism Act 2011 (c 20)**—*contd*

| | | |
|---|---|---|
| | (7)(c) | 1 Apr 2012 (SI 2012/887) |
| | (8) | 18 Feb 2012 (SI 2012/411) |
| 10 | (1)–(3) | 18 Feb 2012 (except in so far as relate to fire and rescue authorities in Wales) (SI 2012/411) |
| | | 1 Apr 2012 (exception noted above) (SI 2012/887) |
| | (4) | 1 Apr 2012 (SI 2012/887) |
| | (5) | 18 Feb 2012 (except in so far as relates to fire and rescue authorities in Wales) (SI 2012/411) |
| | | 1 Apr 2012 (exception noted above) (SI 2012/887) |
| 11–14 | | 18 Feb 2012 (SI 2012/411) |
| 15 | | 3 Dec 2011 (SI 2011/2896) |
| 16–18 | | 15 Jan 2012 (SI 2012/57) |
| 19 | | 3 Dec 2011 (SI 2011/2896) |
| 20 | | 3 Dec 2011 (for the purposes of enabling the Secretary of State to make an order under s 15) (SI 2011/2896) |
| | | 15 Jan 2012 (otherwise) (SI 2012/57) |
| 21 | | See Sch 2 below |
| 22 | | See Sch 3 below |
| 23 | | 15 Nov 2011 (s 240(5)(a)) |
| 24 | | 15 Jan 2012 (SI 2012/57)[2] |
| 25 | | 15 Jan 2012 (s 240(1)(a)) |
| 26 | | See Sch 4 below |
| 27 | (1)–(5) | 7 Jun 2012 (in so far as they enable a relevant authority to adopt a code of conduct which will take effect on or after 1 Jul 2012) (SI 2012/1463) |
| | | 1 Jul 2012 (otherwise) (SI 2012/1463) |
| | (6)(a)–(j) | 7 Jun 2012 (in so far as they enable a relevant authority to adopt a code of conduct which will take effect on or after 1 Jul 2012) (SI 2012/1463) |
| | | 1 Jul 2012 (otherwise) (SI 2012/1463) |
| | (6)(k) | *Never in force* (repealed) |
| | (6)(l)–(p) | 7 Jun 2012 (in so far as they enable a relevant authority to adopt a code of conduct which will take effect on or after 1 Jul 2012) (SI 2012/1463) |
| | | 1 Jul 2012 (otherwise) (SI 2012/1463) |
| | (7)–(10) | 7 Jun 2012 (in so far as they enable a relevant authority to adopt a code of conduct which will take effect on or after 1 Jul 2012) (SI 2012/1463) |
| | | 1 Jul 2012 (otherwise) (SI 2012/1463) |
| 28 | | 7 Jun 2012 (in so far as enables a relevant authority to make arrangements under which allegations can be investigated on or after 1 Jul 2012) (SI 2012/1463)[6] |
| | | 1 Jul 2012 (otherwise) (SI 2012/1463)[6] |
| 29 | | 7 Jun 2012 (in so far as enables a monitoring officer of a relevant authority to prepare a register of interests which will take effect on or after 1 Jul 2012) (SI 2012/1463) |
| | | 1 Jul 2012 (otherwise) (SI 2012/1463) |
| 30 | | 31 Jan 2012 (in so far as confers power on the Secretary of State to make regulations) (SI 2012/57) |
| | | 1 Jul 2012 (otherwise) (SI 2012/1463) |
| 31 | (1)–(9) | 1 Jul 2012 (SI 2012/1463) |
| | (10) | 7 Jun 2012 (in so far as enables a relevant authority to make standing orders that will take effect on or after 1 Jul 2012) (SI 2012/1463) |
| | | 1 Jul 2012 (otherwise) (SI 2012/1463) |
| | (11) | 1 Jul 2012 (SI 2012/1463) |
| 32 | | 1 Jul 2012 (SI 2012/1463) |
| 33 | | 7 Jun 2012 (in so far as enables a relevant authority to grant a dispensation that will take effect on or after 1 Jul 2012) (SI 2012/1463) |

**Localism Act 2011 (c 20)**—*contd*

|  |  |  |
|---|---|---|
|  |  | 1 Jul 2012 (otherwise) (SI 2012/1463) |
| 34 |  | 1 Jul 2012 (SI 2012/1463) |
| 35 |  | 7 Jun 2012 (SI 2012/1463) |
| 36 | (a) | 15 Jan 2012 (SI 2012/57) |
|  | (b) | 22 Nov 2012 (SI 2012/2913) |
| 37 |  | 15 Nov 2011 (s 240(5)(c)) |
| 38–43 |  | 15 Jan 2012 (E) (s 240(1)(b)) |
|  |  | 31 Jan 2012 (W) (SI 2012/193) |
| 44, 45 |  | 15 Jan 2012 (s 240(1)(c), (d)) |
| 46 |  | 1 Apr 2012 (SI 2012/628; SI 2012/887) |
| 47 |  | 15 Jan 2012 (s 240(1)(e)) |
| 48–57 |  | 31 May 2012 (SI 2012/1008) |
| 58–67 |  | *Not yet in force* |
| 68 |  | 15 Jan 2012 (E) (SI 2012/57) |
|  |  | *Not yet in force* (W) |
| 69 | (1)–(7) | 15 Jan 2012 (E) (in so far as necessary to enable a billing authority to make decisions and determinations under Local Government Finance Act 1988, s 47 (as amended by s 69(1)–(7), prior to 1 Apr 2012 but which apply to chargeable days on or after 1 Apr 2012)) (SI 2012/57) |
|  |  | 31 Jan 2012 (W) (SI 2012/193) |
|  |  | 1 Apr 2012 (E) (otherwise) (SI 2012/628)[3] |
|  | (8) | 3 Dec 2011 (SI 2011/2896) |
| 70 |  | 15 Jan 2012 (SI 2012/57)[2] |
| 71 |  | 15 Jan 2012 (s 240(1)(f)) |
| 72 | (1) | See Sch 5 below |
|  | (2) | See Sch 6 below |
| 73–75 |  | 3 Dec 2011 (SI 2011/2896) |
| 76 |  | 3 Dec 2011 (SI 2011/2896)[1] |
| 77, 78 |  | 3 Dec 2011 (SI 2011/2896) |
| 79 |  | See Sch 7 below |
| 80 |  | 15 Jan 2012 (s 240(1)(g)) |
| 81–85 |  | 15 Nov 2011 (so far as they confer power on the Secretary of State to make regulations) (s 240(5)(d)) |
|  |  | 27 Jun 2012 (otherwise) (SI 2012/1463) |
| 86 |  | 15 Nov 2011 (s 240(5)(e)) |
| 87–102 |  | 15 Nov 2011 (so far as they confer power on the Secretary of State, or the Welsh Ministers, to make regulations or orders) (s 240(5)(f)) |
|  |  | 21 Sep 2012 (E) (otherwise) (SI 2012/2420) |
|  |  | *Not yet in force* (W) (otherwise) |
| 103, 104 |  | 15 Nov 2011 (s 240(5)(g)) |
| 105–108 |  | 15 Nov 2011 (so far as they confer power on the Secretary of State, or the Welsh Ministers, to make regulations or orders) (s 240(5)(f)) |
|  |  | 21 Sep 2012 (E) (otherwise) (SI 2012/2420) |
|  |  | *Not yet in force* (W) (otherwise) |
| 109 | (1)(a) | *Not yet in force* |
|  | (1)(b) | 15 Nov 2011 (s 240(5)(h)) |
|  | (2)–(6) | 15 Nov 2011 (s 240(5)(h)) |
|  | (7) | See Sch 8 below |
| 110 |  | 15 Nov 2011 (s 240(5)(i)) |
| 111–113 |  | 15 Jan 2012 (s 240(1)(h)) |
| 114 |  | 16 Nov 2011 (s 240(6)) |
| 115 |  | 15 Jan 2012 (SI 2012/57) |
| 116 | (1) | See Sch 9 below |
|  | (2) | See Sch 10 below |
|  | (3) | See Sch 11 below |
| 117–120 |  | 15 Nov 2011 (s 240(5)(k)) |

**Localism Act 2011 (c 20)**—*contd*

| | | |
|---|---|---|
| 121 | | See Sch 12 below |
| 122 | | 15 Nov 2011 (in so far as inserts Town and Country Planning Act 1990, ss 61W–61Y, 62(7), (8), to the extent that those provisions require or authorise the making of provision in a development order) (s 240(5)(l)) |
| | | 17 Dec 2013 (otherwise) (SI 2013/2931) |
| 123 | | 6 Apr 2012 (SI 2012/628)[3] |
| 124 | (1) | 6 Apr 2012 (SI 2012/628)[3] |
| | (2) | 15 Jan 2012 (in so far as amendments made thereby to Town and Country Planning Act 1990 confer power on the Secretary of State to prescribe matters by, or make provision in, a development order) (SI 2012/57) |
| | | 6 Apr 2012 (otherwise) (SI 2012/628)[3] |
| | (3) | 6 Apr 2012 (SI 2012/628)[3] |
| 125–127 | | 6 Apr 2012 (SI 2012/628) |
| 128 | (1) | 1 Apr 2012 (SI 2012/628) |
| | (2) | See Sch 13 below |
| | (3)–(6) | 1 Apr 2012 (SI 2012/628) |
| 129 | | 15 Jan 2012 (in so far as confers power on the Secretary of State to give directions) (SI 2012/57) |
| | | 1 Apr 2012 (otherwise) (SI 2012/628) |
| 130–137 | | 1 Apr 2012 (SI 2012/628) |
| 138 | (1)–(4) | 1 Apr 2012 (SI 2012/628) |
| | (5) | 15 Jan 2012 (in so far as amendments made thereby to Planning Act 2008 confer power on the Secretary of State to make regulations) (SI 2012/57) |
| | | 1 Apr 2012 (otherwise) (SI 2012/628) |
| | (6)–(10) | 1 Apr 2012 (SI 2012/628) |
| 139–141 | | 1 Apr 2012 (SI 2012/628) |
| 142 | (1), (2) | 1 Apr 2012 (SI 2012/628) |
| | (3) | 15 Jan 2012 (in so far as amendments made thereby to Planning Act 2008 confer power on the Secretary of State to make regulations) (SI 2012/57) |
| | | 1 Apr 2012 (otherwise) (SI 2012/628) |
| | (4) | 1 Apr 2012 (SI 2012/628) |
| 143 | | 15 Jan 2012 (s 240(1)(i)) |
| 144 | | 15 Nov 2011 (s 240(5)(m)) |
| 145 | | 15 Jan 2012 (in so far as enables local housing authorities to draft and consult on allocation schemes under Housing Act 1996, s 166A (as inserted by s 147 of this Act)) (SI 2012/57) |
| | | 18 Jun 2012 (otherwise) (SI 2012/1463) |
| 146 | | 15 Jan 2012 (in so far as confers power on the Secretary of State to make regulations and enable local housing authorities to draft and consult on allocation schemes under Housing Act 1996, s 166A) (as inserted by s 147 of this Act) (SI 2012/57) |
| | | 18 Jun 2012 (otherwise) (SI 2012/1463) |
| 147 | (1) | 15 Jan 2012 (SI 2012/57) |
| | (2)–(5) | 15 Jan 2012 (in so far as confer power on the Secretary of State to make regulations and enable local housing authorities to draft and consult on allocation schemes under Housing Act 1996, s 166A) (SI 2012/57)[2] |
| | | 18 Jun 2012 (otherwise) (SI 2012/1463) |
| | (6) | 15 Jan 2012 (SI 2012/57)[3] |
| | (7) | 18 Jun 2012 (SI 2012/1463) |
| 148, 149 | | 9 Nov 2012 (E) (SI 2012/2599)[8] |
| | | *Not yet in force* (W) |
| 150 | (1), (2) | 15 Jan 2012 (SI 2012/57) |
| | (3) | 15 Jan 2013 (SI 2012/1008) |
| | (4)–(8) | 15 Jan 2012 (SI 2012/57) |
| 151, 152 | | 15 Jan 2012 (SI 2012/57)[2] |

**Localism Act 2011 (c 20)**—*contd*

| | | |
|---|---|---|
| 153 | | 15 Jan 2012 (in so far as inserts Homelessness Act 2002, s 3(7A)(a), (c)) (SI 2012/57)[2] |
| | | 7 Jun 2012 (in so far as inserts s 3(7A)(b) thereof) (SI 2012/1463) |
| 154 | | 15 Jan 2012 (in so far as amendments made to Housing Act 1985 thereby confer power on the Secretary of State to make regulations) (SI 2012/57) |
| | | 1 Apr 2012 (otherwise) (SI 2012/628) |
| 155–157 | | 1 Apr 2012 (SI 2012/628) |
| 158 | | 15 Jan 2012 (in so far as confers power on the Secretary of State to make regulations) (SI 2012/57) |
| | | 1 Apr 2012 (otherwise) (SI 2012/628) |
| 159–161 | | 1 Apr 2012 (SI 2012/628) |
| 162 | (1), (2), (3)(a) | 1 Apr 2012 (SI 2012/628)[3] |
| | (3)(b), (c) | 1 Apr 2012 (W) (SI 2012/887)[4] |
| | (4), (5) | 1 Apr 2012 (SI 2012/628)[3] |
| 163, 164 | | 1 Apr 2012 (SI 2012/628) |
| 165 | | 15 Jan 2012 (in so far as amendments made to Housing and Regeneration Act 2008 confer power on the Secretary of State to make regulations) (SI 2012/57) |
| | | 1 Apr 2012 (otherwise) (SI 2012/628) |
| 166 | | 1 Apr 2012 (SI 2012/628)[3] |
| 167 | | See Sch 15 below |
| 168–175 | | 15 Nov 2011 (s 240(5)(n)) |
| 176 | | 15 Jan 2012 (SI 2012/57) |
| 177 | | 15 Jan 2012 (s 240(1)(j)) |
| 178 | | See Sch 16 below |
| 179 | | See Sch 17 below |
| 180 | (1) | 1 Apr 2013 (E) (in so far as inserts Housing Act 1996, Sch 2, paras 7A–7C) (SI 2013/722)[10] |
| | | *Not yet in force* (otherwise) |
| | (2), (3) | 1 Apr 2013 (E) (SI 2013/722) |
| | | *Not yet in force* (W) |
| | (4), (5) | *Not yet in force* |
| 181, 182 | | 1 Apr 2013 (SI 2013/722) |
| 183 | | 15 Jan 2012 (s 240(1)(k)) |
| 184 | | 6 Apr 2012 (SI 2012/628)[3] |
| 185 | | 1 Apr 2012 (SI 2012/628)[3] |
| 186 | | 15 Jan 2012 (in so far as relates to the provisions of s 187 commenced by SI 2012/57) (SI 2012/57) |
| | | 1 Apr 2012 (otherwise) (SI 2012/628) |
| 187 | (1), (2) | 15 Jan 2012 (SI 2012/57) |
| | (3), (4) | 15 Jan 2012 (in so far as insert Greater London Authority Act 1999, ss 333ZA–333ZD, and s 333E (in so far as required for the interpretation of those sections)) (SI 2012/57) |
| | | 1 Apr 2012 (otherwise) (SI 2012/628) |
| 188 | | 3 May 2012 (SI 2012/1008) |
| 189 | | 1 Apr 2012 (SI 2012/628) |
| 190 | | 15 Jan 2012 (SI 2012/57) |
| 191 | (1) | 31 Mar 2012 (SI 2012/628) |
| | (2)–(5) | 15 Jan 2012 (SI 2012/57) |
| 192 | | 3 May 2012 (SI 2012/1008)[5] |
| 193, 194 | | 15 Jan 2012 (SI 2012/57) |
| 195 | (1) | See Sch 19 below |
| | (2) | See Sch 20 below |
| 196 | | 15 Jan 2012 (s 240(1)(l)) |
| 197 | (1), (2), (3)(a)–(d) | 15 Jan 2012 (s 240(1)(l)) |
| | (3)(e), (f) | 15 Jan 2012 (SI 2012/57) |
| | (4) | 15 Jan 2012 (s 240(1)(l)) |
| | (5) | 15 Jan 2012 (SI 2012/57) |

**Localism Act 2011 (c 20)**—*contd*

|  |  |  |
|---|---|---|
|  | (6), (7) | 15 Jan 2012 (s 240(1)(l)) |
| 198 | (1)–(5) | 15 Jan 2012 (s 240(1)(l)) |
|  | (6) | See Sch 21 below |
| 199–221 |  | 15 Jan 2012 (s 240(1)(l)) |
| 222 |  | See Sch 22 below |
| 223, 224 |  | 15 Jan 2012 (SI 2012/57) |
| 225 | (1) | 3 May 2012 (SI 2012/1008)[5] |
|  | (2) | See Sch 23 below |
| 226–228 |  | 3 May 2012 (SI 2012/1008) |
| 229 |  | 3 May 2012 (SI 2012/1008)[5] |
| 230 |  | 15 Jan 2012 (SI 2012/57) |
| 231 |  | 3 May 2012 (SI 2012/1008) |
| 232 |  | 6 Apr 2012 (SI 2012/628)[3] |
| 233 |  | See Sch 24 below |
| 234–236 |  | 15 Nov 2011 (s 240(5)(p)) |
| 237 |  | See Sch 25 below |
| 238–241 |  | 15 Nov 2011 (s 240(5)(p)) |
| Sch 1 |  | 4 Apr 2012 (SI 2012/1008)[5] |
| Sch 2 |  | 3 Dec 2011 (in so far as enables the Secretary of State to make regulations or orders under the Local Government Act 2000, Pt 1A and Sch A1) (SI 2011/2896) |

Sch 2 *(contd)*

15 Jan 2012 (SI 2012/57)[2]—

(a) in so far as inserts Local Government Act 2000, ss 9B, 9C (in so far as they enable a local authority to change to a permitted form of governance, including executive arrangements, under ss 9K–9OA, and enable any person to take any step under or for the purposes of regulations made under s 9MC or 9MG of that Act)

(b) in so far as inserts ss 9K–9OA of that Act

(c) in so far as inserts s 9R of that Act (in so far as required for the interpretation of ss 9B, 9C and ss 9K–9OA and regulations and orders made under Part 1A thereof)

9 Mar 2012 (SI 2012/628)—

(a) in so far as inserts Local Government Act 2000, s 9GB (in so far as it relates to Sch A1, paras 1–5)

(b) in so far as inserts ss 9H–9HE of that Act

(c) in so far as inserts s 9R of that Act (in so far as required for the interpretation of ss 9H–9HE)

(d) in so far as inserts Sch A1, paras 1–5 of that Act

4 May 2012 (otherwise) (SI 2012/1008)

| Sch 3 | paras 1–9 | 4 May 2012 (SI 2012/1008) |
|---|---|---|
|  | paras 10, 11 | 15 Jan 2012 (SI 2012/57)— |

(a) in so far as they enable a local authority to change to a permitted form of governance, including executive arrangements, under Local Government Act 2000, ss 9K–9OA

(b) in so far as they enable any person to take any step under or for the purposes of regulations made under ss 9MC or 9MG of that Act

4 May 2012 (otherwise) (SI 2012/1008)

|  | paras 12–29 | 4 May 2012 (SI 2012/1008) |
|---|---|---|
|  | paras 30–32 | 15 Jan 2012 (SI 2012/57) |
|  | paras 33, 34 | 4 May 2012 (SI 2012/1008) |
|  | paras 35–38 | 15 Jan 2012 (SI 2012/57) |
|  | para 39 | 4 May 2012 (SI 2012/1008) |
|  | paras 40–53 | 15 Jan 2012 (SI 2012/57) |
|  | paras 54, 55 | 4 May 2012 (SI 2012/1008) |
|  | paras 56, 57 | 9 Mar 2012 (SI 2012/628) |
|  | paras 58–65 | 4 May 2012 (SI 2012/1008) |
|  | paras 66, 67 | 15 Jan 2012 (SI 2012/57) |
|  | para 68(1), (2)(a) | 4 May 2012 (SI 2012/1008) |

**Localism Act 2011 (c 20)**—*contd*

| | | |
|---|---|---|
| | para 68(2)(b) | 9 Mar 2012 (in so far as the definition of "local authority" applies in relation to the Local Government Act 2000, ss 39–44, Sch 1, paras 1, 6) (SI 2012/628) |
| | | 4 May 2012 (otherwise) (SI 2012/1008) |
| | para 68(2)(c), (3) | 9 Mar 2012 (SI 2012/628) |
| | paras 68(4)–(6), 69 | 4 May 2012 (SI 2012/1008) |
| | para 70 | 3 Dec 2011 (SI 2011/2896) |
| | paras 71–81 | 4 May 2012 (SI 2012/1008) |
| Sch 4 | paras 1–3 | 1 Apr 2012 (SI 2012/628) |
| | para 4 | 1 Jul 2012 (except in so far as repeals and amendments made thereby apply in relation to a police authority) (SI 2012/1463)[6] |
| | | 22 Nov 2012 (exception noted above) (SI 2012/2913) |
| | paras 5, 6 | 31 Jan 2012 (SI 2012/57) |
| | paras 7–9, 10(1), (2) | 1 Jul 2012 (except in so far as repeals and amendments made thereby apply in relation to a police authority) (SI 2012/1463)[6] |
| | | 22 Nov 2012 (exception noted above) (SI 2012/2913)[9] |
| | para 10(3)(a) | 31 Jan 2012 (SI 2012/57) |
| | paras 10(3)(b), 11, 12(1), (2) | 1 Jul 2012 (except in so far as repeals and amendments made thereby apply in relation to a police authority) (SI 2012/1463)[6] |
| | | 22 Nov 2012 (exception noted above) (SI 2012/2913)[9] |
| | para 12(3) | 31 Jan 2012 (in so far as repeals Local Government Act 2000, s 53(7), (9)) (SI 2012/57) |
| | | 1 Jul 2012 (in so far as repeals s 53(3)–(6), (8), (10) thereof) (except in so far as repeals made thereby apply in relation to a police authority) (SI 2012/1463)[6] |
| | | 22 Nov 2012 (exception noted above) (SI 2012/2913)[9] |
| | para 12(4), (5) | 1 Jul 2012 (except in so far as repeals and amendments made thereby apply in relation to a police authority) (SI 2012/1463)[6] |
| | | 22 Nov 2012 (exception noted above) (SI 2012/2913)[9] |
| | para 13(1), (2) | 7 Jun 2012 (in so far as repeals provisions which enable regulations to enable a standards committee of a relevant authority to suspend or partially suspend a person from being a member or co-opted member of the authority) (SI 2012/1463)[6] |
| | | 1 Jul 2012 (otherwise, except in so far as repeals and amendments made thereby apply in relation to a police authority) (SI 2012/1463)[6] |
| | | 22 Nov 2012 (exception noted above) (SI 2012/2913)[9] |
| | para 13(3) | 1 Jul 2012 (except in so far as amendments made thereby apply in relation to a police authority) (SI 2012/1463)[6] |
| | | 22 Nov 2012 (exception noted above) (SI 2012/2913)[9] |
| | para 13(4) | 31 Jan 2012 (SI 2012/57) |
| | paras 13(5), 14–16 | 1 Jul 2012 (except in so far as repeals and amendments made thereby apply in relation to a police authority) (SI 2012/1463)[6] |
| | | 22 Nov 2012 (exception noted above) (SI 2012/2913)[9] |
| | para 17 | 31 Jan 2012 (in so far as repeals Local Government Act 2000, s 57(3)–(5)) (SI 2012/57)[2] |
| | | 1 Apr 2012 (otherwise) (SI 2012/628) |
| | para 18 | 31 Jan 2012 (in so far as repeals Local Government Act 2000, s 57A(2)(b) (apart from word "or" at the end), (5), (6)) (SI 2012/57)[2] |
| | | 1 Jul 2012 (in so far as repeals the remainder of s 57A thereof) (except in so far as repeal made thereby applies in relation to a police authority) (SI 2012/1463)[6] |
| | | 22 Nov 2012 (exception noted above) (SI 2012/2913)[9] |
| | para 19 | 31 Jan 2012 (in so far as repeals Local Government Act 2000, s 57B(4)(b) (words "or (b)"), (6)) (SI 2012/57)[2] |
| | | 1 Jul 2012 (in so far as repeals the remainder of s 57B thereof) (except in so far as repeal made thereby applies in relation to a police authority) (SI 2012/1463)[6] |
| | | 22 Nov 2012 (exception noted above) (SI 2012/2913)[9] |

**Localism Act 2011 (c 20)**—*contd*

| | |
|---|---|
| para 20 | 31 Jan 2012 (in so far as repeals Local Government Act 2000, s 57C(6)) (SI 2012/57)[2] |
| | 1 Jul 2012 (in so far as repeals the remainder of s 57C thereof) (except in so far as repeal made thereby applies in relation to a police authority) (SI 2012/1463)[6] |
| | 22 Nov 2012 (exception noted above) (SI 2012/2913)[9] |
| paras 21–30 | 31 Jan 2012 (SI 2012/57)[2] |
| para 31 | 7 Jun 2012 (in so far as repeals provisions which enable regulations to enable a standards committee of a relevant authority to suspend or partially suspend a person from being a member or co-opted member of the authority) (SI 2012/1463)[6] |
| | 1 Jul 2012 (except in so far as repeals and amendments made thereby apply in relation to a police authority) (SI 2012/1463)[6] |
| | 22 Nov 2012 (exception noted above) (SI 2012/2913)[9] |
| para 32 | 1 Jul 2012 (except in so far as repeal made thereby applies in relation to a police authority) (SI 2012/1463)[6] |
| | 22 Nov 2012 (exception noted above) (SI 2012/2913)[9] |
| paras 33, 34 | 31 Jan 2012 (SI 2012/57) |
| para 35 | 31 Jan 2012 (in so far as repeals Local Government Act 2000, s 67(1), (1A) and words "the Standards Board for England or" in s 67(2), (2A)) (SI 2012/57)[2] |
| | 1 Jul 2012 (in so far as repeals the remainder of s 67 thereof) (except in so far as repeal made thereby applies in relation to a police authority) (SI 2012/1463)[6] |
| | 22 Nov 2012 (exception noted above) (SI 2012/2913)[9] |
| paras 36–42, 43(1)–(5) | 1 Jul 2012 (except in so far as repeals and amendments made thereby apply in relation to a police authority) (SI 2012/1463)[6] |
| | 22 Nov 2012 (exception noted above) (SI 2012/2913)[9] |
| para 43(6) | 31 Jan 2012 (SI 2012/57) |
| paras 43(7)–(10), 44 | 1 Jul 2012 (except in so far as repeals and amendments made thereby apply in relation to a police authority) (SI 2012/1463)[6] |
| | 22 Nov 2012 (exception noted above) (SI 2012/2913)[9] |
| para 45 | 31 Jan 2012 (in so far as repeals Local Government Act 2000, s 78B(1)(a)) (SI 2012/57) |
| | 1 Jul 2012 (in so far as repeals the remainder of s 67 thereof) (except in so far as repeals and amendments made thereby apply in relation to a police authority) (SI 2012/1463)[6] |
| | 22 Nov 2012 (exception noted above) (SI 2012/2913)[9] |
| para 46 | 1 Jul 2012 (except in so far as repeals and amendments made thereby apply in relation to a police authority) (SI 2012/1463)[6] |
| | 22 Nov 2012 (exception noted above) (SI 2012/2913)[9] |
| para 47 | 31 Jan 2012 (in so far as repeals Local Government Act 2000, s 80(3) (in so far as it requires a relevant authority in England to prepare a report), (5) (in relation to relevant authorities in England), (6)(a)) (SI 2012/57) |
| | 1 Jul 2012 (otherwise, except in so far as repeals and amendments made thereby apply in relation to a police authority) (SI 2012/1463)[6] |
| | 22 Nov 2012 (exception noted above) (SI 2012/2913)[9] |
| para 48(1), (2) | 1 Jul 2012 (except in so far as repeals and amendments made thereby apply in relation to a police authority) (SI 2012/1463)[6] |
| | 22 Nov 2012 (exception noted above) (SI 2012/2913)[9] |
| para 48(3)(a) | 31 Jan 2012 (SI 2012/57) |
| paras 48(3)(b), (4), 49, 50 | 1 Jul 2012 (except in so far as repeals and amendments made thereby apply in relation to a police authority) (SI 2012/1463)[6] |
| | 22 Nov 2012 (exception noted above) (SI 2012/2913)[9] |
| para 51 | 1 Jul 2012 (except in so far as repeals and amendments made thereby apply in relation to a police authority) (SI 2012/1463)[6] |
| | 22 Nov 2012 (exception noted above) (SI 2012/2913)[9] |

**Localism Act 2011 (c 20)**—*contd*

|  |  |  |
|---|---|---|
| | para 52 | 1 Jul 2012 (except in so far as repeals and amendments made thereby apply in relation to a police authority) (SI 2012/1463)[6] |
| | | 22 Nov 2012 (exception noted above) (SI 2012/2913)[9] |
| | para 53 | 31 Jan 2012 (in so far as it repeals Local Government Act 2000, Sch 4 paras 2(1)(b)–(e), 3, 4) (SI 2012/57)[2] |
| | | 1 Apr 2012 (otherwise) (SI 2012/628)[3] |
| | para 54 | 1 Apr 2012 (SI 2012/628) |
| | paras 55, 56 | 1 Jul 2012 (except in so far as repeals and amendments made thereby apply in relation to a police authority) (SI 2012/1463)[6] |
| | | 22 Nov 2012 (exception noted above) (SI 2012/2913) |
| | paras 57, 58 | 15 Nov 2011 (s 240(5)(b)) |
| | paras 59–61 | 1 Jul 2012 (except in so far as repeals and amendments made thereby apply in relation to a police authority) (SI 2012/1463)[6] |
| | | 22 Nov 2012 (exception noted above) (SI 2012/2913) |
| Sch 5 | | 3 Dec 2011 (SI 2011/2896)[1] |
| Schs 6, 7 | | 3 Dec 2011 (SI 2011/2896) |
| Sch 8 | para 1 | 15 Nov 2011 (s 240(5)(h)) |
| | paras 2–12 | *Not yet in force* |
| | para 13(1) | 15 Nov 2011 (s 240(5)(h)) |
| | paras 13(2), 14–17 | *Not yet in force* |
| | paras 18, 19 | 15 Nov 2011 (s 240(5)(h)) |
| | para 20 | *Not yet in force* |
| Sch 9 | | 15 Nov 2011 (in so far as confers power on the Secretary of State to make regulations or publish documents setting standards) (s 240(5)(j)) |
| | | 6 Apr 2012 (except for the purpose of the holding of a referendum under Town and Country Planning Act 1990, Sch 4B, paras 14, 15) (SI 2012/628)[3] |
| | | 3 Aug 2012 (except for the purpose of holding a business referendum and its corresponding residential referendum under Sch 4B, paras 14, 15 of the 1990 Act in a neighbourhood area which has been designated as a business area under s 61H thereof) (SI 2012/2029)[7] |
| | | 6 Apr 2013 (exception noted above) (SI 2013/797) |
| Schs 10, 11 | | 15 Nov 2011 (in so far as confers power on the Secretary of State to make regulations or publish documents setting standards) (s 240(5)(j)) |
| | | 15 Jan 2012 (in so far as amendments made to Town and Country Planning Act 1990 confer power on the Secretary of State to prescribe matters by, or make provision in, a development order) (SI 2012/57) |
| | | 6 Apr 2012 (except for the purpose of the holding of a referendum under Town and Country Planning Act 1990, Sch 4B, paras 14, 15) (SI 2012/628)[3] |
| | | 3 Aug 2012 (except for the purpose of holding a business referendum and its corresponding residential referendum under Sch 4B, paras 14, 15 of the 1990 Act in a neighbourhood area which has been designated as a business area under s 61H thereof) (SI 2012/2029)[7] |
| | | 6 Apr 2013 (exception noted above) (SI 2013/797) |
| Sch 12 | paras 1–21 | 15 Nov 2011 (in so far as they confer power on the Secretary of State to make regulations or publish documents setting standards) (s 240(5)(j)) |
| | | 15 Jan 2012 (in so far as the amendments made to Town and Country Planning Act 1990 confer power on the Secretary of State to prescribe matters by, or make provision in, a development order) (SI 2012/57) |
| | | 6 Apr 2012 (except for the purpose of the holding of a referendum under Town and Country Planning Act 1990, Sch 4B, paras 14, 15) (SI 2012/628)[3] |

**Localism Act 2011 (c 20)**—*contd*

| | | |
|---|---|---|
| | | 3 Aug 2012 (except for the purpose of holding a business referendum and its corresponding residential referendum under Sch 4B, paras 14, 15 of the 1990 Act in a neighbourhood area which has been designated as a business area under s 61H thereof) (SI 2012/2029)[7] |
| | | 6 Apr 2013 (exception noted above) (SI 2013/797) |
| | para 22 | 15 Nov 2011 (in so far as confers power on the Secretary of State to make regulations or publish documents setting standards) (s 240(5)(j)) |
| | | 15 Jan 2012 (otherwise) (SI 2012/57) |
| | para 23 | 15 Nov 2011 (in so far as confers power on the Secretary of State to make regulations or publish documents setting standards) (s 240(5)(j)) |
| | | 15 Jan 2012 (in so far as the amendments made to Town and Country Planning Act 1990 confer power on the Secretary of State to prescribe matters by, or make provision in, a development order) (SI 2012/57)[2] |
| | | 6 Apr 2012 (except for the purpose of the holding of a referendum under Town and Country Planning Act 1990, Sch 4B, paras 14, 15) (SI 2012/628)[3] |
| | | 3 Aug 2012 (except for the purpose of holding a business referendum and its corresponding residential referendum under Sch 4B, paras 14, 15 of the 1990 Act in a neighbourhood area which has been designated as a business area under s 61H thereof) (SI 2012/2029)[7] |
| | | 6 Apr 2013 (exception noted above) (SI 2013/797) |
| | paras 24–31 | 15 Nov 2011 (in so far as they confer power on the Secretary of State to make regulations or publish documents setting standards) (s 240(5)(j)) |
| | | 6 Apr 2012 (except for the purpose of the holding of a referendum under Town and Country Planning Act 1990, Sch 4B, paras 14, 15) (SI 2012/628)[3] |
| | | 3 Aug 2012 (except for the purpose of holding a business referendum and its corresponding residential referendum under Sch 4B, paras 14, 15 of the 1990 Act in a neighbourhood area which has been designated as a business area under s 61H thereof) (SI 2012/2029)[7] |
| | | 6 Apr 2013 (exception noted above) (SI 2013/797) |
| Sch 13 | paras 1, 2 | 1 Apr 2012 (SI 2012/628) |
| | para 3 | 15 Jan 2012 (in so far as amendments made thereby to Planning Act 2008 confer power on the Secretary of State to make regulations or rules) (SI 2012/57) |
| | | 1 Apr 2012 (otherwise) (SI 2012/628) |
| | paras 4–9 | 1 Apr 2012 (SI 2012/628) |
| | para 10 | 15 Jan 2012 (in so far as amendments made thereby to Planning Act 2008 confer power on the Secretary of State to make regulations or rules) (SI 2012/57) |
| | | 1 Apr 2012 (otherwise) (SI 2012/628) |
| | paras 11–41 | 1 Apr 2012 (SI 2012/628) |
| | para 42 | 15 Jan 2012 (in so far as amendments made thereby to Planning Act 2008 confer power on the Secretary of State to make regulations or rules) (SI 2012/57) |
| | | 1 Apr 2012 (otherwise) (SI 2012/628) |
| | paras 43–79 | 1 Apr 2012 (SI 2012/628) |
| Sch 14 | | 4 Apr 2012 (SI 2012/1008) |
| Sch 15 | | 1 Oct 2013 (SI 2013/797) |
| Sch 16 | para 1 | 15 Jan 2012 (SI 2012/57) |
| | paras 2–25 | 1 Apr 2012 (SI 2012/628) |
| | para 26 | 15 Jan 2012 (in so far as it inserts Housing and Regeneration Act 2008, ss 92B(1), 92C–92I) (SI 2012/57) |
| | | 1 Apr 2012 (otherwise) (SI 2012/628) |

**Localism Act 2011 (c 20)**—*contd*

| | | |
|---|---|---|
| | paras 27–52 | 1 Apr 2012 (SI 2012/628) |
| | para 53(1)–(5) | 1 Apr 2012 (SI 2012/628) |
| | para 53(6) | 15 Jan 2012 (SI 2012/57) |
| | para 54 | 15 Jan 2012 (SI 2012/57) |
| | paras 55–70 | 1 Apr 2012 (SI 2012/628) |
| Sch 17 | | 1 Apr 2012 (SI 2012/628)[3] |
| Sch 18 | | 15 Jan 2012 (s 240(1)(k)) |
| Sch 19 | paras 1, 2 | 1 Apr 2012 (SI 2012/628) |
| | para 3 | 15 Jan 2012 (SI 2012/57) |
| | paras 4–64 | 1 Apr 2012 (SI 2012/628) |
| Sch 20 | | 31 Mar 2012 (SI 2012/628) |
| Schs 21, 22 | | 15 Jan 2012 (s 240(1)(l)) |
| Sch 23 | | 3 May 2012 (SI 2012/1008)[5] |
| Sch 24 | | 15 Nov 2011 (in so far as confers power on the Treasury to make regulations or orders) (s 240(5)(o)) |
| | | 30 Mar 2012 (E) (W) (otherwise) (SI 2012/628) |
| | | *Not yet in force* (S) (NI) (otherwise) |
| Sch 25 | Pt 1 | 4 Apr 2012 (SI 2012/1008) |
| | Pt 2 | 18 Feb 2012 (SI 2012/411) repeals of— |
| | | Fire and Rescue Services Act 2004, ss 5, 19 (except in so far as they relate to fire and rescue authorities in Wales) |
| | | 1 Apr 2012 (otherwise) (SI 2012/887) |
| | Pt 3 | 18 Feb 2012 (SI 2012/411) |
| | Pt 4 | 15 Jan 2012 (SI 2012/57)[2], repeals of or in— |
| | | Local Government Act 2000, ss 33ZA, 33A–33C, 33E–33O, 34(3), 35(3), 36(3), 45(9), 47(4), (6)(b); |
| | | Local Government and Public Involvement in Health Act 2007, ss 33, 34, 38, 40, 62, 64, 65, 69 |
| | | 9 Mar 2012 (SI 2012/628), repeals of or in— |
| | | Local Government Act 2000, s 39 |
| | | 4 May 2012 (SI 2012/1008), repeals of or in— |
| | | Local Government Act 1972; |
| | | Local Government Act 2000, ss 11, 13, 14, 18, 19, 21, 21ZA, 21A, 21C–21F, 22, 22A, 31, 32, 33D, 44A–44H, 48, 106, Sch 1; |
| | | Local Government Act 2003; |
| | | National Health Service Act 2006; |
| | | Police and Justice Act 2006; |
| | | Local Government and Public Involvement in Health Act 2007, ss 63, 67, 70, 121, 124, 127, 236, Sch 3; |
| | | Local Democracy, Economic Development and Construction Act 2009; |
| | | Flood and Water Management Act 2010; |
| | | Local Education Authorities and Children's Services Authorities (Integration of Functions) Order 2010 (SI 2010/1158); |
| | | Local Government (Wales) Measure 2011 |
| | Pt 5 | 31 Jan 2012 (in so far as relates to repeals effected by provisions of Sch 4 brought into force by SI 2012/57, art 5(2)) (SI 2012/57)[2] |
| | | 1 Jul 2012 (otherwise) (except in so far as repeals and amendments made thereby apply in relation to a police authority) (SI 2012/1463)[6] |
| | | 22 Nov 2012 (exception noted above) (SI 2012/2913)[9] |
| | Pt 6 | 15 Jan 2012 (s 240(1)(m)) |
| | Pt 7 | 1 Apr 2012 (SI 2012/628; SI 2012/887) |
| | Pt 8 | 15 Jan 2012 (s 240(1)(m)) |
| | Pt 9 | 15 Jan 2012 (SI 2012/57) |
| | Pt 10 | 1 Apr 2012 (E) (SI 2012/628)[3] |
| | | 1 Apr 2012 (W) (SI 2012/887) |
| | Pts 11–13 | 15 Jan 2012 (SI 2012/57)[2] |

**Localism Act 2011 (c 20)**—*contd*

| | |
|---|---|
| Pt 14 | 15 Jan 2012 (s 240(1)(m)) |
| Pt 15 | 15 Nov 2011 (s 240(5)(q)) |
| Pt 16 | *Not yet in force* |
| Pt 17 | 15 Jan 2012 (s 240(1)(m)) |
| Pts 18, 19 | 6 Apr 2012 (SI 2012/628) |
| Pts 20, 21 | 1 Apr 2012 (SI 2012/628) |
| Pt 22 | *Not yet in force* |
| Pt 23 | 3 Aug 2012 (SI 2012/2029) |
| Pt 24 | *Not yet in force* |
| Pt 25 | 15 Jan 2012 (SI 2012/57) |
| Pts 26, 27 | 1 Apr 2012 (SI 2012/628)[3] |
| Pt 28 | *Not yet in force* |
| Pt 29 | 15 Jan 2012 (s 240(1)(m)) |
| Pt 30 | 6 Apr 2012 (SI 2012/628) |
| Pt 31 | 1 Apr 2012 (except in so far as repeals Housing and Regeneration Act 2008, Sch 8, paras 73(2), (3), 74(a)) (SI 2012/628) |
| | 7 Jun 2012 (exception noted above) (SI 2012/1463) |
| Pt 32 | 31 Mar 2012 (SI 2012/628) |
| Pt 33 | 3 May 2012 (SI 2012/1008) |
| Pt 34 | 6 Apr 2012 (SI 2012/628)[3] |

[1] For transitional provisions, see SI 2011/2896, art 3

[2] For transitional provisions and savings, see SI 2012/57, arts 6–11

[3] For transitional, transitory and saving provisions, see SI 2012/628, arts 9–20

[4] For a saving provision, see SI 2012/887, art 4

[5] For transitional, transitory and savings provisions, see SI 2012/1008, arts 7–12

[6] For transitional, transitory and savings provisions, see SI 2012/1463, arts 6, 7

[7] For transitional, transitory and savings provisions, see SI 2012/2029, art 5

[8] For transitional provisions, see SI 2012/2599, art 3

[9] For transitional, transitory and savings provisions, see SI 2012/2913, arts 3–6

[10] For transitional provisions, see SI 2013/722, art 3

---

**London Olympic Games and Paralympic Games (Amendment) Act 2011 (c 22)**

*RA:* 14 Dec 2011

*Commencement provisions:* s 112(3)

| | |
|---|---|
| 1–9 | 14 Feb 2012 (s 10(1)) |
| 10 | 14 Dec 2011 (RA) |

---

**Mission and Pastoral Measure 2011 (No 3)**

*RA:* 24 May 2011

This Measure was brought into force on 1 Jul 2012 by an instrument made by the Archbishops of Canterbury and York and dated 2 May 2012 (made under s 112(3))

---

**National Insurance Contributions Act 2011 (c 3)**

*RA:* 22 Mar 2011

*Commencement provisions:* s 13

| | |
|---|---|
| 1–3 | 6 Apr 2011 (s 13(1)) |
| 4–15 | 22 Mar 2011 (s 13(2)) |

## Parliamentary Voting System and Constituencies Act 2011 (c 1)

*RA:* 16 Feb 2011

*Commencement provisions:* ss 8(1), 19

| | | |
|---|---|---|
| 1–8 | | 16 Feb 2011 (s 19(2)) |
| 9 | | *Never in force* (repealed) |
| 10–15 | | 16 Feb 2011 (s 19(2)) |
| 16 | | See Sch 12 below |
| 17–20 | | 16 Feb 2011 (s 19(2)) |
| Schs 1–9 | | 16 Feb 2011 (s 19(2)) |
| Sch 10 | | *Never in force* (repealed) |
| Sch 11 | | 16 Feb 2011 (s 19(2)) |
| Sch 12 | Pt 1 | *Never in force* (repealed) |
| | Pt 2 | 16 Feb 2011 (s 19(2)) |

## Patient Rights (Scotland) Act 2011 (asp 5)

*RA:* 31 Mar 2011

*Commencement provisions:* s 26; Patient Rights (Scotland) Act 2011 (Commencement) Order 2012, SSI 2012/35

| | |
|---|---|
| 1–7 | 1 Apr 2012 (SSI 2012/35) |
| 8–13 | 1 Oct 2012 (SSI 2012/35) |
| 14–21 | 1 Apr 2012 (SSI 2012/35) |
| 22 | 31 Mar 2011 (RA) |
| 23 | 1 Apr 2012 (SSI 2012/35) |
| 24–26 | 31 Mar 2011 (RA) |
| Schedule | 1 Apr 2012 (SSI 2012/35) |

## Pensions Act 2011 (c 19)

*RA:* 3 Nov 2011

*Commencement provisions:* s 38; Pensions Act 2011 (Commencement No 1) Order 2011, SI 2011/3034; Pensions Act 2011 (Commencement No 2) Order 2012, SI 2012/682; Pensions Act 2011 (Commencement No 3) Order 2012, SI 2012/1681; Pensions Act 2011 (Commencement No 4) Order 2013, SI 2013/585; Pensions Act 2011 (Commencement No 5) Order 2014, SI 2014/1683; Pensions Act 2011 (Commencement No 6) Order 2015, SI 2015/676

| | | |
|---|---|---|
| 1 | | 3 Jan 2012 (s 38(3)(a)) |
| 2 | (1)–(4) | 6 Apr 2012 (SI 2011/3034) |
| | (5) | 6 Apr 2012 (in so far as repeals Social Security Contributions and Benefits Act 1992, Sch 5, paras 5A(2)(b), (3)(a), 6(2)(b), (3)(c), (4)(b), 6A(2)(b), 7(1)) (SI 2011/3034) |
| | | *Never in force* (otherwise) (repealed) |
| | (6) | See Sch 2 below |
| | (7) | 6 Apr 2012 (in so far as sub-s (5) comes into force on that date) (SI 2011/3034) |
| | | *Never in force* (otherwise) (repealed) |
| | (8) | 6 Apr 2012 (in so far as Sch 2 comes into force on that date) (SI 2011/3034) |
| | | *Never in force* (otherwise) (repealed) |
| | (9), (10) | 6 Apr 2012 (SI 2011/3034) |
| 3 | | See Sch 3 below |
| 4 | | 3 Nov 2011 (in so far as modifies a power to make an order or regulations or confers any such power, for the purposes of the exercise of that power) (s 38(1)) |
| | | 30 Jun 2012 (otherwise) (SI 2012/1681) |
| 5 | | 30 Jun 2012 (SI 2012/1681) |

**Pensions Act 2011 (c 19)**—*contd*

| | |
|---|---|
| 6 | 3 Nov 2011 (in so far as modifies a power to make an order or regulations or confers any such power, for the purposes of the exercise of that power) (s 38(1)) |
| | 30 Jun 2012 (otherwise) (SI 2012/1681) |
| 7 | 3 Nov 2011 (in so far as modifies a power to make an order or regulations or confers any such power, for the purposes of the exercise of that power) (s 38(1)) |
| | 1 Apr 2015 (otherwise) (SI 2015/676) |
| 8 | 3 Nov 2011 (in so far as modifies a power to make an order or regulations or confers any such power, for the purposes of the exercise of that power) (s 38(1)) |
| | 3 Jan 2012 (otherwise) (SI 2011/3034) |
| 9 | 3 Nov 2011 (in so far as modifies a power to make an order or regulations or confers any such power, for the purposes of the exercise of that power) (s 38(1)) |
| | 6 Mar 2012 (otherwise) (SI 2012/682) |
| 10 | 3 Nov 2011 (in so far as modifies a power to make an order or regulations or confers any such power, for the purposes of the exercise of that power) (s 38(1)) |
| | *Never in force* (otherwise) (repealed) |
| 11 | 3 Nov 2011 (in so far as modifies a power to make an order or regulations or confers any such power, for the purposes of the exercise of that power) (s 38(1)) |
| | 30 Jun 2012 (otherwise) (SI 2012/1681) |
| 12, 13 | 3 Nov 2011 (in so far as modifies a power to make an order or regulations or confers any such power, for the purposes of the exercise of that power) (s 38(1)) |
| | 6 Mar 2012 (otherwise) (SI 2012/682) |
| 14, 15 | 3 Nov 2011 (in so far as modifies a power to make an order or regulations or confers any such power, for the purposes of the exercise of that power) (s 38(1)) |
| | 30 Jun 2012 (otherwise) (SI 2012/1681) |
| 16, 17 | 30 Jun 2012 (SI 2012/1681) |
| 18 | 3 Nov 2011 (in so far as modifies a power to make an order or regulations or confers any such power, for the purposes of the exercise of that power) (s 38(1)) |
| | *Never in force* (otherwise) (repealed) |
| 19 | 3 Jan 2012 (SI 2011/3034) |
| 20 | 1 Jan 2012 (SI 2011/3034) |
| 21 | 3 Jan 2012 (SI 2011/3034) |
| 22 | See Sch 4 below |
| 23, 24 | 3 Jan 2012 (SI 2011/3034) |
| 25 | 3 Jan 2012 (s 38(3)(b)) |
| 26 | 3 Jan 2012 (SI 2011/3034) |
| 27, 28 | 3 Jan 2012 (s 38(3)(c), (d)) |
| 29 | 24 Jul 2014 (SI 2014/1683) |
| 30–33 | 3 Nov 2011 (s 38(2)(a)) |
| 34, 35 | 3 Jan 2012 (SI 2011/3034) |
| 36 | 30 Jun 2012 (SI 2012/1681) |
| 37–39 | 3 Nov 2011 (s 38(2)(b)–(d)) |
| Sch 1 | 3 Jan 2012 (s 38(3)(a)) |
| Sch 2 | para 1 | See paras 2, 3 below |
| | para 2 | *Never in force* (repealed) |
| | para 3(1) | See sub-paras (2)–(8) below |
| | para 3(2)–(6) | *Never in force* (repealed) |
| | para 3(7), (8) | 6 Apr 2012 (SI 2011/3034) |
| | para 4(a) | 6 Apr 2012 (SI 2011/3034) |
| | para 4(b), (c) | *Never in force* (repealed) |
| | para 4(d) | 6 Apr 2012 (SI 2011/3034) |
| Sch 3 | | *Never in force* (repealed) |

**Pensions Act 2011 (c 19)**—*contd*

| | | |
|---|---|---|
| Sch 4 | para 1 | See paras 2–16 below |
| | paras 2–16 | 23 Jul 2012 (SI 2012/1681) |
| | paras 17–20 | 3 Jan 2012 (SI 2011/3034) |
| | paras 21–36 | 13 Mar 2013 (SI 2013/585) |
| | para 37 | 3 Jan 2012 (SI 2011/3034) |
| Sch 5 | | 3 Jan 2012 (SI 2011/3034) |

**Police (Detention and Bail) Act 2011 (c 9)**

*RA:* 12 Jul 2011

Whole Act in force 12 Jul 2011 (RA)

**Police Reform and Social Responsibility Act 2011 (c 13)**

*RA:* 15 Sep 2011

*Commencement provisions:* s 157; Police Reform and Social Responsibility Act 2011 (Commencement No 1) Order 2011, SI 2011/2515; Police Reform and Social Responsibility Act 2011 (Commencement No 2) Order 2011, SI 2011/2834; Police Reform and Social Responsibility Act 2011 (Commencement No 3 and Transitional Provisions) Order 2011, SI 2011/3019, as amended by SI 2012/75, SI 2012/2892; Police Reform and Social Responsibility Act 2011 (Commencement No 4) Order 2012, SI 2012/896; Police Reform and Social Responsibility Act 2011 (Commencement No 5) Order 2012, SI 2012/1129; Police Reform and Social Responsibility Act 2011 (Commencement No 6) Order 2012, SI 2012/2670; Police Reform and Social Responsibility Act 2011 (Commencement No 7 and Transitional Provisions and Commencement No 3 and Transitional Provisions (Amendment)) Order 2012, SI 2012/2892

| | | |
|---|---|---|
| 1 | (1)–(9) | 22 Nov 2012 (SI 2012/2892)[2] |
| | (10) | See Sch 1 below |
| 2 | (1)–(6) | 22 Nov 2012 (SI 2012/2892) |
| | (7) | See Sch 2 below |
| | (8) | 22 Nov 2012 (SI 2012/2892) |
| 3, 4 | | 16 Jan 2012 (SI 2011/3019)[1] |
| 5 | | 22 Nov 2012 (SI 2012/2892) |
| 6 | | 16 Jan 2012 (SI 2011/3019) |
| 7 | (1)–(5) | 16 Jan 2012 (SI 2011/3019) |
| | (6)(a) | 22 Nov 2012 (SI 2012/2892) |
| | (6)(b)–(d), (7) | 16 Jan 2012 (SI 2011/3019) |
| 8 | (1), (2) | 22 Nov 2012 (SI 2012/2892) |
| | (3)–(6) | 16 Jan 2012 (SI 2011/3019) |
| | (7)(a) | 22 Nov 2012 (SI 2012/2892) |
| | (7)(b)–(d) | 16 Jan 2012 (SI 2011/3019) |
| 9, 10 | | 16 Jan 2012 (in the metropolitan police district only) (SI 2011/3019) |
| | | 22 Nov 2012 (otherwise) (SI 2012/2892) |
| 11 | (1), (2) | 15 Dec 2011 (SI 2011/3019) |
| | (3)–(5) | 16 Jan 2012 (in the metropolitan police district only) (SI 2011/3019) |
| | | 22 Nov 2012 (otherwise) (SI 2012/2892) |
| 12–16 | | 16 Jan 2012 (in the metropolitan police district only) (SI 2011/3019) |
| | | 22 Nov 2012 (otherwise) (SI 2012/2892) |
| 17 | (1)–(3) | 16 Jan 2012 (in the metropolitan police district only) (SI 2011/3019) |
| | | 22 Nov 2012 (otherwise) (SI 2012/2892) |
| | (4)–(7) | 15 Dec 2011 (to the extent that they allow the Secretary of State to make a financial code of practice, to revise the code and to lay the code or revision of the code before Parliament) (SI 2011/3019) |

**Police Reform and Social Responsibility Act 2011 (c 13)**—*contd*

|   |   |   |
|---|---|---|
|   |   | 16 Jan 2012 (otherwise, in the metropolitan police district only) (SI 2011/3019) |
|   |   | 22 Nov 2012 (otherwise) (SI 2012/2892) |
|   | (8) | 16 Jan 2012 (in the metropolitan police district only) (SI 2011/3019) |
|   |   | 22 Nov 2012 (otherwise) (SI 2012/2892) |
| 18 |   | 22 Nov 2012 (SI 2012/2892) |
| 19, 20 |   | 16 Jan 2012 (SI 2011/3019)[1] |
| 21 |   | 16 Jan 2012 (in the metropolitan police district only) (SI 2011/3019) |
|   |   | 22 Nov 2012 (otherwise) (SI 2012/2892) |
| 22 |   | 22 Nov 2012 (SI 2012/2892) |
| 23 |   | 16 Jan 2012 (SI 2011/3019) |
| 24 | (1) | 16 Jan 2012 (SI 2011/3019) |
|   | (2)–(6) | 22 Nov 2012 (SI 2012/2892) |
|   | (7) | 16 Jan 2012 (SI 2011/3019) |
|   | (8) | 22 Nov 2012 (SI 2012/2892) |
|   | (9) | 16 Jan 2012 (SI 2011/3019) |
| 25 | (1)–(3) | 16 Jan 2012 (SI 2011/3019) |
|   | (4)(a) | 22 Nov 2012 (SI 2012/2892) |
|   | (4)(b), (5) | 16 Jan 2012 (SI 2011/3019) |
|   | (6)–(11) | 22 Nov 2012 (SI 2012/2892) |
| 26 | (1)–(3) | 22 Nov 2012 (SI 2012/2892) |
|   | (4) | See Sch 5 below |
| 27 | (1), (2) | 16 Jan 2012 (SI 2011/3019) |
|   | (3), (4) | 22 Nov 2012 (SI 2012/2892) |
| 28 | (1) | 25 Apr 2012 (SI 2012/1129) |
|   | (2)–(9) | 22 Nov 2012 (SI 2012/2892) |
|   | (10) | See Sch 6 below |
|   | (11) | 22 Nov 2012 (SI 2012/2892) |
| 29 |   | 22 Nov 2012 (SI 2012/2892)[2] |
| 30 |   | 22 Nov 2012 (SI 2012/2892) |
| 31 |   | 31 Oct 2011 (SI 2011/2515) |
| 32 |   | 16 Jan 2012 (SI 2011/3019) |
| 33 | (1)–(4) | 16 Jan 2012 (SI 2011/3019) |
|   | (5) | 16 Jan 2012 (SI 2011/3019)[1] |
|   | (6)–(10) | 16 Jan 2012 (SI 2011/3019) |
| 34, 35 |   | 16 Jan 2012 (SI 2011/3019) |
| 36, 37 |   | 16 Jan 2012 (in the metropolitan police district only) (SI 2011/3019) |
|   |   | 22 Nov 2012 (otherwise) (SI 2012/2892) |
| 38 | (1)–(4) | 22 Nov 2012 (SI 2012/2892) |
|   | (5) | See Sch 8 below |
|   | (6), (7) | 22 Nov 2012 (SI 2012/2892) |
| 39–41 |   | 22 Nov 2012 (SI 2012/2892) |
| 42–49 |   | 16 Jan 2012 (SI 2011/3019) |
| 50–57 |   | 25 Apr 2012 (SI 2012/1129) |
| 58 |   | 15 Sep 2011 (s 157(3)(a)) |
| 59–73 |   | 25 Apr 2012 (SI 2012/1129) |
| 74 |   | See Sch 10 below |
| 75–77 |   | 25 Apr 2012 (SI 2012/1129) |
| 78 |   | 15 Nov 2011 (SI 2011/2515) |
| 79 | (1) | 31 Oct 2011 (SI 2011/2515) |
|   | (2) | 16 Jan 2012 (in the metropolitan police district only) (SI 2011/3019) |
|   |   | 22 Nov 2012 (otherwise) (SI 2012/2892) |
|   | (3)–(6) | 31 Oct 2011 (SI 2011/2515) |
| 80 |   | 15 Nov 2011 (SI 2011/2515) |
| 81 | (a) | 22 Nov 2012 (SI 2012/2892) |

**Police Reform and Social Responsibility Act 2011 (c 13)**—*contd*

|          | (b), (c)   | 16 Jan 2012 (SI 2011/3019)[1] |
|----------|------------|-------------------------------|
| 82       | (1)        | 15 Dec 2011 (SI 2011/3019) |
|          | (2)–(11)   | 16 Jan 2012 (SI 2011/3019)[1] |
|          | (12)       | 15 Dec 2011 (SI 2011/3019) |
| 83       | (1), (2)   | 16 Jan 2012 (SI 2011/3019) |
|          | (3)        | 22 Nov 2012 (SI 2012/2892) |
|          | (4)–(7)    | 16 Jan 2012 (SI 2011/3019) |
| 84–87    |            | 16 Jan 2012 (SI 2011/3019) |
| 88       |            | See Sch 11 below |
| 89–94    |            | 16 Jan 2012 (SI 2011/3019) |
| 95       |            | See Sch 14 below |
| 96       |            | 16 Jan 2012 (in the metropolitan police district only) (SI 2011/3019) |
|          |            | 22 Nov 2012 (otherwise) (SI 2012/2892) |
| 97       | (1), (2)   | 16 Jan 2012 (SI 2011/3019) |
|          | (3)        | 22 Nov 2012 (SI 2012/2892) |
|          | (4), (5)   | 16 Jan 2012 (SI 2011/3019) |
| 98       |            | See Sch 15 below |
| 99       |            | See Sch 16 below |
| 100, 101 |            | 16 Jan 2012 (SI 2011/3019) |
| 102      | (1)        | 16 Jan 2012 (SI 2011/3019) |
|          | (2), (3)   | 22 Nov 2012 (SI 2012/2892) |
|          | (4)–(6)    | 16 Jan 2012 (SI 2011/3019)[1] |
| 103, 104 |            | 25 Apr 2012 (SI 2012/1129) |
| 105      | (1)        | See sub-ss (2)–(9) below |
|          | (2)        | 25 Apr 2012 (SI 2012/1129) |
|          | (3)        | 22 Mar 2012 (for the purposes of making regulations under the Licensing Act 2003, s 17(5)(aa)) (SI 2012/896) |
|          |            | 25 Apr 2012 (otherwise) (SI 2012/1129) |
|          | (4)–(11)   | 25 Apr 2012 (SI 2012/1129) |
| 106      | (1)        | See sub-ss (2)–(6) below |
|          | (2)        | 22 Mar 2012 (for the purposes of making regulations under the Licensing Act 2003, s 51(1), (3)) (SI 2012/896) |
|          |            | 25 Apr 2012 (otherwise) (SI 2012/1129) |
|          | (3)        | 25 Apr 2012 (SI 2012/1129) |
|          | (4)        | 22 Mar 2012 (for the purposes of making regulations under the Licensing Act 2003, s 53A(3)(c), (e)) (SI 2012/896) |
|          |            | 25 Apr 2012 (otherwise) (SI 2012/1129) |
|          | (5)        | 25 Apr 2012 (SI 2012/1129) |
|          | (6)        | 22 Mar 2012 (for the purposes of making regulations under the Licensing Act 2003, s 167(4), (10), (14)) (SI 2012/896) |
|          |            | 25 Apr 2012 (otherwise) (SI 2012/1129) |
|          | (7)        | 25 Apr 2012 (SI 2012/1129) |
| 107      | (1)        | See sub-ss (2)–(7) below |
|          | (2)        | 25 Apr 2012 (SI 2012/1129) |
|          | (3)        | 22 Mar 2012 (for the purposes of making regulations under the Licensing Act 2003, s 71(6)) (SI 2012/896) |
|          |            | 25 Apr 2012 (otherwise) (SI 2012/1129) |
|          | (4)–(9)    | 25 Apr 2012 (SI 2012/1129) |
| 108      | (1)        | See sub-ss (2)–(4) below |
|          | (2)        | 25 Apr 2012 (SI 2012/1129) |
|          | (3)        | 22 Mar 2012 (for the purposes of making regulations under the Licensing Act 2003, s 87(3)(b), (c)) (SI 2012/896) |
|          |            | 25 Apr 2012 (otherwise) (SI 2012/1129) |
|          | (4), (5)   | 25 Apr 2012 (SI 2012/1129) |
| 109–112  |            | 25 Apr 2012 (SI 2012/1129) |
| 113      | (1)        | See sub-ss (2)–(5) below |
|          | (2)        | 25 Apr 2012 (SI 2012/1129) |

**Police Reform and Social Responsibility Act 2011 (c 13)**—*contd*

| | | |
|---|---|---|
| | (3) | 22 Mar 2012 (for the purposes of making regulations under the Licensing Act 2003, s 106A) (SI 2012/896) |
| | | 25 Apr 2012 (otherwise) (SI 2012/1129) |
| | (4)–(6) | 25 Apr 2012 (SI 2012/1129) |
| 114 | (1) | See sub-ss (2)–(12) below |
| | (2)–(6) | 25 Apr 2012 (SI 2012/1129) |
| | (7) | 22 Mar 2012 (for the purposes of making regulations under the Licensing Act 2003, s 104A) (SI 2012/896) |
| | | 25 Apr 2012 (otherwise) (SI 2012/1129) |
| | (8)–(13) | 25 Apr 2012 (SI 2012/1129) |
| 115 | (1) | See sub-ss (2), (3) below |
| | (2) | 22 Mar 2012 (for the purposes of making regulations under the Licensing Act 2003, s 100(1), (5)(b)) (SI 2012/896) |
| | | 25 Apr 2012 (otherwise) (SI 2012/1129) |
| | (3), (4) | 25 Apr 2012 (SI 2012/1129) |
| 116, 117 | | 25 Apr 2012 (SI 2012/1129) |
| 118 | (1) | See sub-ss (2), (3) below |
| | (2) | 25 Apr 2012 (SI 2012/1129) |
| | (3) | 22 Mar 2012 (for the purposes of making regulations under the Licensing Act 2003, s 169A(2)(a), (4)) (SI 2012/896) |
| | | 25 Apr 2012 (otherwise) (SI 2012/1129) |
| | (4), (5) | 25 Apr 2012 (SI 2012/1129) |
| 119 | | 31 Oct 2012 (SI 2012/2670) |
| 120 | | 25 Apr 2012 (SI 2012/1129) |
| 121 | | *Not yet in force* |
| 122–124 | | 25 Apr 2012 (SI 2012/1129) |
| 125–140 | | 31 Oct 2012 (SI 2012/2670) |
| 141 | (1) | 19 Dec 2011 (in so far as repeals Serious Organised Crime and Police Act 2005, s 137) (SI 2011/2834) |
| | | 30 Mar 2012 (otherwise) (SI 2011/2834) |
| | (2) | 30 Mar 2012 (SI 2011/2834) |
| 142–149 | | 19 Dec 2011 (SI 2011/2834) |
| 150 | (1) | 19 Dec 2011 (SI 2011/2834) |
| | (2) | 19 Dec 2011 (E) (SI 2011/2834) |
| | | *Not yet in force* (W) |
| | (3) | 19 Dec 2011 (SI 2011/2834) |
| 151 | | See Sch 17 below |
| 152 | | 15 Nov 2011 (SI 2011/2515) |
| 153–158 | | 15 Sep 2011 (s 157(3)(b), (c)) |
| Sch 1 | | 22 Nov 2012 (SI 2012/2892)[2] |
| Sch 2 | paras 1–3 | 22 Nov 2012 (SI 2012/2892) |
| | para 4(1) | 22 Nov 2012 (SI 2012/2892)[2] |
| | para 4(2), (3) | 22 Nov 2012 (SI 2012/2892) |
| | para 5(1) | 22 Nov 2012 (SI 2012/2892)[2] |
| | para 5(2), (3) | 22 Nov 2012 (SI 2012/2892) |
| | para 6–9 | 22 Nov 2012 (SI 2012/2892) |
| Schs 3, 4 | | 16 Jan 2012 (SI 2011/3019) |
| Sch 5 | | 22 Nov 2012 (SI 2012/2892) |
| Sch 6 | | 25 Apr 2012 (SI 2012/1129) |
| Sch 7 | | 31 Oct 2011 (SI 2011/2515) |
| Sch 8 | | 22 Nov 2012 (SI 2012/2892) |
| Sch 9 | | 25 Apr 2012 (SI 2012/1129) |
| Sch 10 | paras 1–11 | 25 Apr 2012 (SI 2012/1129) |
| | para 12 | *Not yet in force* |
| | paras 13, 14 | 25 Apr 2012 (SI 2012/1129) |
| Sch 11 | paras 1, 2(1) | 16 Jan 2012 (SI 2011/3019) |
| | para 2(2) | 22 Nov 2012 (SI 2012/2892) |
| | para 2(3)–(8) | 16 Jan 2012 (SI 2011/3019) |
| | para 3 | 16 Jan 2012 (SI 2011/3019) |

**Police Reform and Social Responsibility Act 2011 (c 13)**—*contd*

|  |  |  |
|---|---|---|
|  | para 4 | 22 Nov 2012 (SI 2012/2892) |
|  | para 5 | 16 Jan 2012 (SI 2011/3019) |
| Schs 12, 13 |  | 16 Jan 2012 (SI 2011/3019) |
| Sch 14 | paras 1–3 | 15 Nov 2011 (SI 2011/2515) |
|  | para 4 | 16 Jan 2012 (in the metropolitan police district only) (SI 2011/3019)[1] |
|  |  | 22 Nov 2012 (otherwise) (SI 2012/2892)[2] |
|  | paras 5, 6 | 22 Nov 2012 (SI 2012/2892)[2] |
|  | paras 7, 8(1)–(3) | 16 Jan 2012 (in the metropolitan police district only) (SI 2011/3019) |
|  |  | 22 Nov 2012 (otherwise) (SI 2012/2892)[2] |
|  | paras 8(4)–(6), 9–32 | 22 Nov 2012 (SI 2012/2892)[2] |
| Sch 15 | paras 1–23 | 16 Jan 2012 (in the metropolitan police district only) (SI 2011/3019) |
|  |  | 22 Nov 2012 (otherwise) (SI 2012/2892) |
|  | para 24 | 31 Oct 2011 (SI 2011/2515) |
|  | para 25 | 16 Jan 2012 (in the metropolitan police district only) (SI 2011/3019) |
|  |  | 22 Nov 2012 (otherwise) (SI 2012/2892) |
| Sch 16 | para 1 | 16 Jan 2012 (SI 2011/3019) |
|  | para 2 | 22 Nov 2012 (SI 2012/2892) |
|  | paras 3, 4, 5(a) | 22 Nov 2012 (SI 2012/2892)[2] |
|  | para 5(b) | 22 Nov 2012 (SI 2012/2892) |
|  | paras 6, 7 | 16 Jan 2012 (SI 2011/3019) |
|  | paras 8–12 | 22 Nov 2012 (SI 2012/2892) |
|  | paras 13, 14 | 16 Jan 2012 (SI 2011/3019) |
|  | para 15 | 22 Nov 2012 (SI 2012/2892) |
|  | para 16 | 16 Jan 2012 (SI 2011/3019) |
|  | para 17 | 22 Nov 2012 (SI 2012/2892) |
|  | para 18(1), (2) | 16 Jan 2012 (SI 2011/3019) |
|  | paras 18(3), (4), 19–21 | 22 Nov 2012 (SI 2012/2892) |
|  | paras 22–30, 31(1) | 16 Jan 2012 (SI 2011/3019) |
|  | para 31(2) | 22 Nov 2012 (SI 2012/2892) |
|  | paras 31(3), (4), 32–34, 35(1) | 16 Jan 2012 (SI 2011/3019) |
|  | para 35(2) | 22 Nov 2012 (SI 2012/2892) |
|  | para 35(3) | 16 Jan 2012 (SI 2011/3019) |
|  | para 35(4), (5) | 22 Nov 2012 (SI 2012/2892) |
|  | para 36(1), (2) | 16 Jan 2012 (SI 2011/3019) |
|  | para 36(3) | 22 Nov 2012 (SI 2012/2892) |
|  | paras 37–55 | 16 Jan 2012 (SI 2011/3019) |
|  | para 56 | 22 Nov 2012 (SI 2012/2892) |
|  | paras 57–73 | 16 Jan 2012 (SI 2011/3019) |
|  | paras 74–78 | 22 Nov 2012 (SI 2012/2892) |
|  | paras 79–84, 85(1), (2) | 16 Jan 2012 (SI 2011/3019) |
|  | para 85(3) | 22 Nov 2012 (SI 2012/2892) |
|  | paras 86–93 | 16 Jan 2012 (SI 2011/3019) |
|  | para 94 | 22 Nov 2012 (SI 2012/2892) |
|  | paras 95–100 | 16 Jan 2012 (SI 2011/3019) |
|  | para 101 | 22 Nov 2012 (SI 2012/2892) |
|  | paras 102–104 | 16 Jan 2012 (SI 2011/3019) |
|  | paras 105, 106 | 22 Nov 2012 (SI 2012/2892) |
|  | paras 107–133 | 16 Jan 2012 (SI 2011/3019) |
|  | paras 134, 135 | 22 Nov 2012 (SI 2012/2892) |
|  | paras 136–142 | 16 Jan 2012 (SI 2011/3019) |
|  | paras 143, 144 | 22 Nov 2012 (SI 2012/2892) |

**Police Reform and Social Responsibility Act 2011 (c 13)**—*contd*

| | |
|---|---|
| paras 145–157 | 16 Jan 2012 (SI 2011/3019) |
| para 158 | 22 Nov 2012 (SI 2012/2892) |
| paras 159–167 | 16 Jan 2012 (SI 2011/3019) |
| para 168 | 22 Nov 2012 (SI 2012/2892) |
| paras 169–174 | 16 Jan 2012 (SI 2011/3019) |
| para 175 | 22 Nov 2012 (SI 2012/2892) |
| paras 176, 177 | 16 Jan 2012 (SI 2011/3019) |
| para 178 | 22 Nov 2012 (SI 2012/2892) |
| paras 179, 180 | 16 Jan 2012 (SI 2011/3019) |
| para 181 | 22 Nov 2012 (SI 2012/2892) |
| para 182 | 16 Jan 2012 (SI 2011/3019) |
| paras 183–185 | 22 Nov 2012 (SI 2012/2892) |
| para 186 | 16 Jan 2012 (SI 2011/3019) |
| para 187 | 22 Nov 2012 (SI 2012/2892) |
| paras 188–190 | 16 Jan 2012 (SI 2011/3019) |
| para 191 | 22 Nov 2012 (SI 2012/2892) |
| paras 192–203 | 16 Jan 2012 (SI 2011/3019) |
| paras 204, 205 | 22 Nov 2012 (SI 2012/2892) |
| para 206(1), (2) | 16 Jan 2012 (SI 2011/3019) |
| para 206(3) | 22 Nov 2012 (SI 2012/2892) |
| paras 207–211 | 16 Jan 2012 (SI 2011/3019) |
| paras 212–216 | 22 Nov 2012 (SI 2012/2892) |
| paras 217, 218 | 16 Jan 2012 (SI 2011/3019) |
| paras 219, 220 | 22 Nov 2012 (SI 2012/2892) |
| paras 221–227 | 16 Jan 2012 (SI 2011/3019) |
| paras 228, 229 | 22 Nov 2012 (SI 2012/2892) |
| paras 230–233, 234(1), (2) | 16 Jan 2012 (SI 2011/3019) |
| para 234(3) | 22 Nov 2012 (SI 2012/2892) |
| paras 235–241, 242(1) | 16 Jan 2012 (SI 2011/3019) |
| para 242(2) | 22 Nov 2012 (SI 2012/2892) |
| para 242(3) | 16 Jan 2012 (SI 2011/3019) |
| paras 243–247 | 22 Nov 2012 (SI 2012/2892) |
| paras 248, 249 | 16 Jan 2012 (SI 2011/3019) |
| paras 250–252 | 22 Nov 2012 (SI 2012/2892) |
| paras 253–256, 257(1) | 16 Jan 2012 (SI 2011/3019) |
| para 257(2)–(4) | 22 Nov 2012 (SI 2012/2892) |
| para 257(5) | 16 Jan 2012 (SI 2011/3019) |
| paras 258–269 | 22 Nov 2012 (SI 2012/2892) |
| paras 270–290, 291(a), (b) | 16 Jan 2012 (SI 2011/3019) |
| para 291(c) | 22 Nov 2012 (SI 2012/2892) |
| paras 292–315 | 16 Jan 2012 (SI 2011/3019) |
| paras 316–321 | 22 Nov 2012 (SI 2012/2892) |
| paras 322–325 | 16 Jan 2012 (SI 2011/3019) |
| paras 326, 327 | 22 Nov 2012 (SI 2012/2892) |
| paras 328–335 | 16 Jan 2012 (SI 2011/3019) |
| paras 336–339 | 22 Nov 2012 (SI 2012/2892) |
| para 340 | 16 Jan 2012 (SI 2011/3019) |
| paras 341–343 | 22 Nov 2012 (SI 2012/2892) |
| paras 344–350 | 16 Jan 2012 (SI 2011/3019) |
| paras 351–353 | 22 Nov 2012 (SI 2012/2892) |
| paras 354–358 | 16 Jan 2012 (SI 2011/3019) |
| para 359 | 22 Nov 2012 (SI 2012/2892) |
| paras 360–368 | 16 Jan 2012 (SI 2011/3019) |
| para 369 | 22 Nov 2012 (SI 2012/2892) |
| paras 370–374 | 16 Jan 2012 (SI 2011/3019) |

**Police Reform and Social Responsibility Act 2011 (c 13)**—*contd*

|  | paras 375, 376 | 22 Nov 2012 (SI 2012/2892) |
|---|---|---|
|  | paras 377–380 | 16 Jan 2012 (SI 2011/3019) |
|  | para 381 | 22 Nov 2012 (SI 2012/2892) |
|  | paras 382, 383 | 16 Jan 2012 (SI 2011/3019) |
| Sch 17 |  | 15 Nov 2011 (SI 2011/2515) |

[1]  For transitional and transitory provisions and savings, see SI 2011/3019, arts 4–9

[2]  For transitional and transitory provisions and savings, see SI 2012/2892, arts 3–7

**Postal Services Act 2011 (c 5)**

*RA:* 13 Jun 2011

*Commencement provisions*: s 93(2)–(4); Postal Services Act 2011 (Commencement No 1 and Transitional Provisions) Order 2011, SI 2011/2329[1]; Postal Services Act 2011 (Commencement No 2) Order 2011, SI 2011/3044; Postal Services Act 2011 (Commencement No 3 and Saving Provisions) Order 2012, SI 2012/1095

| 1 |  | 20 Dec 2011 (SI 2011/3044) |
|---|---|---|
| 2–42 |  | 1 Oct 2011 (SI 2011/2329) |
| 43 |  | 13 Jun 2011 (s 93(2)(a)) |
| 44–63 |  | 1 Oct 2011 (SI 2011/2329) |
| 64 | (1) | 1 Oct 2011 (SI 2011/2329) |
|  | (2)–(6) | 15 Sep 2011 (SI 2011/2329) |
| 65 |  | 1 Oct 2011 (SI 2011/2329) |
| 66 |  | 13 Jun 2011 (s 93(2)(b)) |
| 67–88 |  | 1 Oct 2011 (SI 2011/2329) |
| 89, 90 |  | 13 Jun 2011 (s 93(2)(c)) |
| 91 | (1), (2) | See Sch 12 below |
|  | (3), (4) | 13 Jun 2011 (s 93(2)(d)) |
| 92 |  | 13 Jun 2011 (s 93(2)(e)) |
| 93 |  | 13 Jun 2011 (s 93(2)(f)) |
| Schs 1–3 |  | 1 Oct 2011 (SI 2011/2329) |
| Sch 4 |  | 13 Jun 2011 (s 93(2)(a)) |
| Schs 5–8 |  | 1 Oct 2011 (SI 2011/2329) |
| Sch 9 |  | 13 Jun 2011 (s 93(2)(b)) |
| Schs 10, 11 |  | 1 Oct 2011 (SI 2011/2329) |
| Sch 12 | paras 1–37 | 1 Oct 2011 (SI 2011/2329) |
|  | paras 38–41 | 23 Apr 2012 (SI 2012/1095)[2] |
|  | paras 42–146 | 1 Oct 2011 (SI 2011/2329) |
|  | para 147 | 23 Apr 2012 (SI 2012/1095)[2] |
|  | paras 148–191 | 1 Oct 2011 (SI 2011/2329) |

[1]  For transitional provisions, see SI 2011/2329, arts 4, 5

[2]  For saving provisions, see SI 2012/1095, arts 3(2), 4–6

**Private Rented Housing (Scotland) Act 2011 (asp 14)**

*RA:* 20 Apr 2011

*Commencement provisions*: s 41(2)–(4); Private Rented Housing (Scotland) Act 2011 (Commencement No 1 and Saving Provision) Order 2011, SSI 2011/270[1]; Private Rented Housing (Scotland) Act 2011 (Commencement No 2 and Transitional Provision) Order 2012, SSI 2012/2; Private Rented Housing (Scotland) Act 2011 (Commencement No 3) Order 2012, SSI 2012/150; Private Rented Housing (Scotland) Act 2011 (Commencement No 4) Order 2012, SSI 2012/267; Private Rented Housing (Scotland) Act 2011 (Commencement No 5 and Transitional Provision) Order 2013, SSI 2013/19;

**Private Rented Housing (Scotland) Act 2011 (asp 14)**—*contd*
Private Rented Housing (Scotland) Act 2011 (Commencement No 6 and Savings Provisions) Order 2013, SSI 2013/82; Private Rented Housing (Scotland) Act 2011 (Commencement No 7) Order 2015, SSI 2015/326

| | | |
|---|---|---|
| 1 | | 1 Jul 2012 (SSI 2012/150) |
| 2 | | 31 Aug 2011 (SSI 2011/270) |
| 3 | | 1 Apr 2013 (SSI 2013/82) |
| 4 | (a) | 31 Aug 2011 (for the purpose of enabling the Scottish Ministers to prescribe matters by regulations) (SSI 2011/270) |
| | | 1 Jul 2012 (otherwise) (SSI 2012/150) |
| | (b) | 31 Aug 2011 (SSI 2011/270) |
| 5 | | 1 Apr 2013 (SSI 2013/82) |
| 6 | | 1 Jun 2013 (SSI 2013/82)[4] |
| 7 | | 31 Aug 2011 (SSI 2011/270)[1] |
| 8 | | 1 Apr 2013 (SSI 2013/82)[4] |
| 9 | | 1 Apr 2013 (SSI 2013/82) |
| 10 | | 31 Aug 2011 (SSI 2011/270) |
| 11 | | 1 Apr 2013 (SSI 2013/82) |
| 12 | | See Schedule below |
| 13 | (1) | 31 Aug 2011 (SSI 2011/270) |
| | (2) | 31 Jan 2012 (SSI 2012/2)[2] |
| | (3) | 31 Aug 2011 (SSI 2011/270) |
| | (4) | 31 Jan 2012 (SSI 2012/2)[2] |
| | (5) | 31 Jan 2012 (SSI 2012/2) |
| | (6) | 31 Aug 2011 (SSI 2011/270) |
| 14–16 | | 31 Aug 2011 (SSI 2011/270) |
| 17 | | 31 Jan 2012 (for the purpose of enabling the Scottish Ministers to make orders) (SSI 2012/2) |
| | | *Not yet in force* (otherwise) |
| 18 | | *Not yet in force* |
| 19 | | 31 Jan 2012 (for the purpose of enabling the Scottish Ministers to make orders) (SSI 2012/2) |
| | | *Not yet in force* (otherwise) |
| 20–28 | | *Not yet in force* |
| 29 | | 31 Jan 2012 (for the purpose of requiring the Scottish Ministers to consult before issuing any guidance) (SSI 2012/2) |
| | | *Not yet in force* (otherwise) |
| 30, 31 | | *Not yet in force* |
| 32 | (1) | 30 Nov 2012 (SSI 2012/267) |
| | (2) | 31 Jan 2012 (for the purpose of enabling the Scottish Ministers to make regulations) (SSI 2012/2) |
| | | 30 Nov 2012 (otherwise) (SSI 2012/267) |
| | (3), (4) | 30 Nov 2012 (SSI 2012/267) |
| 33 | | 31 Aug 2011 (for the purpose of enabling the Scottish Ministers to prescribe matters by regulations) (SSI 2011/270) |
| | | 1 May 2013 (otherwise) (SSI 2013/19)[3] |
| 34 | | 31 Aug 2011 (SSI 2011/270) |
| 35 | (1) | 22 Sep 2015 (SSI 2015/326) |
| | (2) | 1 Dec 2015 (SSI 2015/326) |
| | (3) | *Never in force* (repealed) |
| | (4) | 22 Sep 2015 (in so far as enables the Scottish Ministers to make regulations under Housing (Scotland) Act 2006, ss 28B(1), 28C(11)) (SSI 2015/326) |
| | | 1 Dec 2015 (otherwise) (SSI 2015/326) |
| | (5)–(7) | 1 Dec 2015 (SSI 2015/326) |
| | (8) | 22 Sep 2015 (SSI 2015/326) |
| 36, 37 | | 31 Aug 2011 (SSI 2011/270) |
| 38–41 | | 21 Apr 2011 (s 41(2)) |
| Schedule | | 1 Apr 2013 (SSI 2013/82) |

**Private Rented Housing (Scotland) Act 2011 (asp 14)**—*contd*

[1] For a saving, see SSI 2011/270, art 3

[2] For a transitional provision, see SSI 2012/2, art 3

[3] For a transitional provision, see SSI 2013/19, art 3

[4] For savings provisions, see SSI 2013/82, art 3

---

**Property Factors (Scotland) Act 2011 (asp 8)**

*RA:* 7 Apr 2011

*Commencement provisions:* s 33(2), (3); Property Factors (Scotland) Act 2011 (Commencement No 1) Order 2011, SSI 2011/328; Property Factors (Scotland) Act 2011 (Commencement No 2 and Transitional) Order 2012, SSI 2012/149[1]

| | | |
|---|---|---|
| 1 | (1) | 1 Jul 2012 (SSI 2012/149) |
| | (2) | 1 Oct 2012 (s 33(2)) |
| | (3) | 23 Sep 2011 (SSI 2011/328) |
| 2 | | 23 Sep 2011 (SSI 2011/328) |
| 3 | | 23 Sep 2011 (for the purpose of enabling determinations of fees and regulations to be made) (SSI 2011/328) |
| | | 1 Jul 2012 (otherwise) (SSI 2012/149) |
| 4–6 | | 1 Jul 2012 (SSI 2012/149) |
| 7 | | 23 Sep 2011 (for the purpose of enabling determinations of fees and regulations to be made) (SSI 2011/328) |
| | | 1 Jul 2012 (otherwise) (SSI 2012/149) |
| 8, 9 | | 1 Jul 2012 (SSI 2012/149) |
| 10 | (1)–(4) | 1 Jul 2012 (SSI 2012/149) |
| | (5) | 23 Sep 2011 (SSI 2011/328) |
| 11 | | 1 Jul 2012 (SSI 2012/149) |
| 12 | | 1 Oct 2012 (s 33(2)) |
| 13 | | 23 Sep 2011 (for the purpose of enabling orders to be made) (SSI 2011/328) |
| | | 1 Jul 2012 (otherwise) (SSI 2012/149) |
| 14, 15 | | 23 Sep 2011 (SSI 2011/328) |
| 16 | | 1 Jul 2012 (SSI 2012/149) |
| 17–24 | | 1 Oct 2012 (s 33(2)) |
| 25, 26 | | 23 Sep 2011 (SSI 2011/328) |
| 27 | | 1 Oct 2012 (s 33(2)) |
| 28–33 | | 8 Apr 2011 (s 33(3)) |

[1] For transitional provisions, see SSI 2012/149, art 3

---

**Public Bodies Act 2011 (c 24)**

*RA:* 14 Dec 2011

*Commencement provisions:* s 38; Public Bodies Act 2011 (Commencement No 1) Order 2011, SI 2011/3043; Public Bodies Act 2011 (Commencement No 2) Order 2012, SI 2012/1662

| | | |
|---|---|---|
| 1–9 | | 14 Feb 2012 (s 38(1)) |
| 10, 11 | | 14 Dec 2011 (s 38(2)) |
| 12–29 | | 14 Feb 2012 (s 38(1)) |
| 30 | (1), (2) | 1 Jul 2012 (at 00:02 hours) (SI 2012/1662) |
| | (3) | See Sch 6 below |
| | (4)–(8) | 1 Jul 2012 (SI 2012/1662) |
| | (9)–(11) | 16 Dec 2011 (SI 2011/3043) |
| 31–34 | | 14 Feb 2012 (s 38(1)) |
| 35–39 | | 14 Dec 2011 (s 38(2)) |
| Schs 1–5 | | 14 Feb 2012 (s 38(1)) |

**Public Bodies Act 2011 (c 24)**—*contd*

Sch 6                                    1 Jul 2012 (at 00:02 hours) (except repeals of Regional
                                         Development Agencies Act 1998, ss 14, 15, 17 and London
                                         Olympic Games and Paralympic Games Act 2006, s 36(3)(c))
                                         (SI 2012/1662)
                                         *Not yet in force* (exception noted above)

---

**Public Records (Scotland) Act 2011 (asp 12)**

*RA:* 20 Apr 2011

*Commencement provisions*: s 16; Public Records (Scotland) Act 2011 (Commencement No 1) Order 2012,
    SSI 2012/21, as amended by SSI 2012/42; Public Records (Scotland) Act 2011 (Commencement
    No 2) Order 2012, SSI 2012/247

| | | |
|---|---|---|
| 1 | (1)–(3) | 1 Jan 2013 (SSI 2012/247) |
| | (4)–(6) | 24 Feb 2012 (SSI 2012/21) |
| | (7)–(9) | 1 Jan 2013 (SSI 2012/247) |
| 2 | (1) | See Schedule below |
| | (2)–(8) | 24 Feb 2012 (SSI 2012/21) |
| 3 | | 24 Feb 2012 (SSI 2012/21) |
| 4–7 | | 1 Jan 2013 (SSI 2012/247) |
| 8 | (1), (2) | 24 Feb 2012 (SSI 2012/21) |
| | (3)–(6) | 1 Jan 2013 (SSI 2012/247) |
| 9–12 | | 1 Jan 2013 (SSI 2012/247) |
| 13 | | 24 Feb 2012 (SSI 2012/21) |
| 14, 15 | | 1 Jan 2013 (SSI 2012/247) |
| 16, 17 | | 21 Apr 2011 (s 16(2)) |
| Schedule | | 24 Feb 2012 (SSI 2012/21) |

---

**Reservoirs (Scotland) Act 2011 (asp 9)**

*RA:* 12 Apr 2011

*Commencement provisions:* s 116(1); Reservoirs (Scotland) Act 2011 (Commencement No 1) Order 2014,
    SSI 2014/348; Reservoirs (Scotland) Act 2011 (Commencement No 2) Order 2015, SSI 2015/43;
    Reservoirs (Scotland) Act 2011 (Commencement No 3) Order 2015, SSI 2015/63; Reservoirs
    (Scotland) Act 2011 (Commencement No 4) Order 2015, SSI 2015/314; Reservoirs (Scotland)
    Act 2011 (Commencement No 5 and Transitional Provision) Order 2016, SSI 2016/42

| | | |
|---|---|---|
| 1–3 | | 12 Apr 2011 (s 116(1)) |
| 4 | | 1 Apr 2015 (SSI 2015/63) |
| 5 | (1) | 1 Apr 2015 (for the purpose of para (o) only) (SSI 2015/63) |
| | | 1 Apr 2016 (otherwise) (SSI 2016/42)[1] |
| | (2)–(4) | 1 Apr 2015 (SSI 2015/63) |
| 6 | | 1 Jan 2015 (SSI 2014/348) |
| 7 | | 12 Apr 2011 (s 116(1)) |
| 8 | | 1 Apr 2016 (SSI 2016/42)[1] |
| 9 | | 1 Apr 2015 (SSI 2015/63) |
| 10 | (1) | 1 Apr 2015 (in so far as it applies in relation to a Reservoirs Act 1975 reservoir) (SSI 2015/63) |
| | | 1 Apr 2016 (otherwise) (SSI 2016/42)[1] |
| | (2) | 1 Jan 2015 (SSI 2014/348) |
| 11 | (1), (2) | 1 Apr 2015 (SSI 2015/63) |
| | (3) | 1 Jan 2015 (SSI 2014/348) |
| 12 | | 1 Jan 2015 (for the purpose of making orders) (SSI 2014/348) |
| | | *Not yet in force* (otherwise) |
| 13 | | 1 Apr 2015 (in so far as it applies in relation to a Reservoirs Act 1975 reservoir) (SSI 2015/63) |
| | | 1 Apr 2016 (otherwise) (SSI 2016/42)[1] |
| 14 | | 1 Jan 2015 (SSI 2014/348) |

**Reservoirs (Scotland) Act 2011 (asp 9)**—*contd*

| | | |
|---|---|---|
| 15 | (1)–(3) | 1 Apr 2015 (in so far as it applies in relation to a Reservoirs Act 1975 reservoir) (SSI 2015/63) |
| | | 1 Apr 2016 (otherwise) (SSI 2016/42)[1] |
| | (4) | 1 Jan 2015 (SSI 2014/348) |
| 16 | | 1 Apr 2015 (SSI 2015/63) |
| 17 | | 1 Apr 2015 (except in relation to the requirements of s 12(1)) (SSI 2015/63) |
| | | *Not yet in force* (exception noted above) |
| 18–21 | | 1 Oct 2015 (SSI 2015/314) |
| 22 | (1)–(3) | 1 Oct 2015 (SSI 2015/314) |
| | (4) | 1 Jan 2015 (SSI 2014/348) |
| 23 | (1)–(7) | 1 Oct 2015 (SSI 2015/314) |
| | (8) | 1 Jan 2015 (SSI 2014/348) |
| 24 | (1)–(6) | 1 Oct 2015 (SSI 2015/314) |
| | (7) | 1 Jan 2015 (SSI 2014/348) |
| 25 | | 1 Jan 2015 (SSI 2014/348) |
| 26 | (1) | 1 Oct 2015 (SSI 2015/314) |
| | (2) | 1 Apr 2016 (SSI 2016/42)[1] |
| 27 | (a) | 1 Jan 2015 (for the purpose of making orders) (SSI 2014/348) |
| | | 20 Feb 2015 (otherwise) (SSI 2015/43) |
| | (b) | 1 Apr 2015 (SSI 2015/63) |
| 28 | (1)–(6) | 1 Apr 2015 (SSI 2015/63) |
| | (7), (8) | 1 Jan 2015 (SSI 2014/348) |
| 29 | | 1 Apr 2015 (SSI 2015/63) |
| 30 | (1) | 1 Apr 2015 (SSI 2015/63) |
| | (2) | 1 Jan 2015 (SSI 2014/348) |
| 31 | (1)(a) | 20 Feb 2015 (SSI 2015/43) |
| | (1)(b) | 1 Jan 2015 (SSI 2014/348) |
| | (1)(c)–(g) | 1 Apr 2015 (SSI 2015/63) |
| | (2) | 1 Jan 2015 (SSI 2014/348) |
| 32 | (1)–(3), (4)(a) | 1 Apr 2016 (SSI 2016/42)[1] |
| | (4)(b) | 1 Jan 2015 (for the purpose of making regulations) (SSI 2014/348) |
| | | 1 Apr 2016 (otherwise) (SSI 2016/42)[1] |
| | (5)–(7) | 1 Apr 2016 (SSI 2016/42)[1] |
| 33, 34 | | 1 Apr 2016 (SSI 2016/42)[1] |
| 35 | (1)(a)–(c) | 1 Apr 2016 (SSI 2016/42)[1] |
| | (1)(d) | 1 Jan 2015 (for the purpose of making regulations) (SSI 2014/348) |
| | | 1 Apr 2016 (otherwise) (SSI 2016/42)[1] |
| | (2) | 1 Apr 2016 (SSI 2016/42)[1] |
| 36, 37 | | 1 Apr 2016 (SSI 2016/42)[1] |
| 38 | (1), (2), (3)(a), (b) | 1 Apr 2016 (SSI 2016/42)[1] |
| | (3)(c) | 1 Jan 2015 (for the purpose of making regulations) (SSI 2014/348) |
| | | 1 Apr 2016 (otherwise) (SSI 2016/42)[1] |
| | (4) | 1 Apr 2016 (SSI 2016/42)[1] |
| 39–43 | | 1 Apr 2016 (SSI 2016/42)[1] |
| 44 | (1), (2) | 1 Apr 2016 (SSI 2016/42)[1] |
| | (3)–(5) | *Not yet in force* |
| | (6) | 1 Apr 2016 (SSI 2016/42)[1] |
| 45–50 | | 1 Apr 2016 (SSI 2016/42)[1] |
| 51 | (1)(a)–(d) | 1 Apr 2016 (SSI 2016/42)[1] |
| | (1)(e) | 1 Jan 2015 (for the purpose of making regulations) (SSI 2014/348) |
| | | 1 Apr 2016 (otherwise) (SSI 2016/42)[1] |
| | (2) | 1 Jan 2015 (SSI 2014/348) |
| | (3)–(6) | 1 Apr 2016 (SSI 2016/42)[1] |
| 52, 53 | | 1 Apr 2016 (SSI 2016/42)[1] |
| 54, 55 | | 1 Jan 2015 (SSI 2014/348) |
| 56 | (1), (2) | 1 Apr 2016 (SSI 2016/42)[1] |
| | (3) | 1 Jan 2015 (for the purpose of making regulations) (SSI 2014/348) |
| | | 1 Apr 2016 (otherwise) (SSI 2016/42)[1] |

**Reservoirs (Scotland) Act 2011 (asp 9)**—*contd*

| | | |
|---|---|---|
| | (4) | 1 Apr 2016 (SSI 2016/42)[1] |
| 57 | (1) | *Not yet in force* |
| | (2), (3) | 1 Jan 2015 (for the purpose of making orders) (SSI 2014/348) |
| | | *Not yet in force* (otherwise) |
| | (4)–(6) | 1 Apr 2016 (SSI 2016/42)[1] |
| 58 | | 1 Apr 2016 (except in so far as applies in relation to the requirements of s 57(1)) (SSI 2016/42)[1] |
| | | *Not yet in force* (otherwise) |
| 59–63 | | 1 Apr 2016 (SSI 2016/42)[1] |
| 64 | (1) | 1 Jan 2015 (SSI 2014/348) |
| | (2) | 1 Apr 2016 (SSI 2016/42)[1] |
| 65–68 | | 1 Apr 2016 (SSI 2016/42)[1] |
| 69 | (1)–(6) | 1 Apr 2016 (SSI 2016/42)[1] |
| | (7), (8) | 1 Jan 2015 (SSI 2014/348) |
| 70–72 | | 1 Apr 2016 (SSI 2016/42)[1] |
| 73–76 | | 1 Jan 2015 (SSI 2014/348) |
| 77 | | 1 Apr 2016 (SSI 2016/42)[1] |
| 78–81 | | *Never in force* (repealed) |
| 82–88 | | 1 Jan 2015 (SSI 2014/348) |
| 89 | | 1 Jan 2015 (except in so far as applies in pursuance of s 69) (SSI 2014/348) |
| | | 1 Apr 2016 (exception noted above) (SSI 2016/42)[1] |
| 90 | | 1 Jan 2015 (SSI 2014/348) |
| 91 | (1), (2)(a) | 1 Apr 2015 (SSI 2015/63) |
| | (2)(b) | 1 Oct 2015 (SSI 2015/314) |
| | (2)(c)–(l) | 1 Apr 2016 (SSI 2016/42)[1] |
| 92 | | 1 Apr 2015 (SSI 2015/63) |
| 93 | (1) | 1 Apr 2016 (SSI 2016/42)[1] |
| | (2)–(5) | 1 Apr 2015 (SSI 2015/63) |
| 94 | | 1 Apr 2015 (SSI 2015/63) |
| 95 | (1)–(3) | 1 Apr 2015 (SSI 2015/63) |
| | (4) | 1 Apr 2016 (SSI 2016/42)[1] |
| 96 | | 1 Apr 2015 (SSI 2015/63) |
| 97 | | 1 Apr 2016 (SSI 2016/42)[1] |
| 98 | (1) | 1 Apr 2015 (SSI 2015/63) |
| | (2)(a) | 1 Apr 2016 (SSI 2016/42)[1] |
| | (2)(b) | 1 Apr 2015 (SSI 2015/63) |
| 99 | (1)(a) | 1 Apr 2016 (SSI 2016/42)[1] |
| | (1)(b), (2) | 1 Apr 2015 (SSI 2015/63) |
| | (3) | *Not yet in force* |
| 100 | | *Not yet in force* |
| 101 | | 1 Apr 2016 (SSI 2016/42)[1] |
| 102 | | 1 Jan 2015 (SSI 2014/348) |
| 103 | | 1 Apr 2016 (SSI 2016/42)[1] |
| 104, 105 | | 1 Jan 2015 (SSI 2014/348) |
| 106 | | 1 Apr 2015 (SSI 2015/63) |
| 107 | | 1 Jan 2015 (SSI 2014/348) |
| 108 | | 1 Apr 2015 (SSI 2015/63) |
| 109 | | 1 Jan 2015 (SSI 2014/348) |
| 110 | (1) | 1 Apr 2015 (SSI 2015/63) |
| | (2) | 1 Jan 2015 (SSI 2014/348) |
| | (3)–(9) | 1 Apr 2015 (SSI 2015/63) |
| 111 | | 1 Apr 2015 (SSI 2015/63) |
| 112 | (1)–(4) | 1 Apr 2016 (SSI 2016/42) |
| | (5) | 1 Jan 2015 (SSI 2014/348) |
| 113 | | 1 Jan 2015 (SSI 2014/348) |
| 114–116 | | 12 Apr 2011 (s 116(1)) |
| Schedule | | 12 Apr 2011 (s 116(1)) |

**Reservoirs (Scotland) Act 2011 (asp 9)**—*contd*
1    For a transitional provision, see SSI 2016/42, art 3

---

**Rights of Children and Young Persons (Wales) Measure 2011 (nawm 2)**

*Passed by the National Assembly for Wales:* 18 Jan 2011

*Approved by Her Majesty in Council:* 16 Mar 2011

Whole Measure in force 16 May 2011 (s 11)

---

**Safety on Learner Transport (Wales) Measure 2011 (nawm 6)**

*Passed by the National Assembly for Wales:* 22 Mar 2011

*Approved by Her Majesty in Council:* 10 May 2011

*Commencement provisions:* s 16

| | |
|---|---|
| 1 | 1 Oct 2014 (s 16(1)) |
| 2–17 | 10 Jul 2011 (s 16(2)) |
| Schedule | 10 Jul 2011 (s 16(2)) |

---

**Sovereign Grant Act 2011 (c 15)**

*RA:* 18 Oct 2011

*Commencement provisions:* s 15(1)

Whole Act in force 1 Apr 2012 (s 15(1))

---

**Sports Grounds Safety Authority Act 2011 (c 6)**

*RA:* 12 Jul 2011

*Commencement provisions:* s 8; Sports Grounds Safety Authority Act 2011 (Commencement) Order 2011, SI 2011/2597

| | | |
|---|---|---|
| 1 | (1) | 1 Nov 2011 (SI 2011/2597) |
| | (2) | See Sch 1 below |
| | (3) | 1 Nov 2011 (SI 2011/2597) |
| 2–5 | | 1 Nov 2011 (SI 2011/2597) |
| 6 | (1) | See Sch 2 below |
| | (2) | See Sch 3 below |
| 7–9 | | 12 Jul 2011 (s 8(3)) |
| Schs 1–3 | | 1 Nov 2011 (SI 2011/2597) |

---

**Supply and Appropriation (Main Estimates) Act 2011 (c 10)**

*RA:* 19 Jul 2011

Whole Act in force 19 Jul 2011 (RA)

---

**Terrorism Prevention and Investigatory Measures Act 2011 (c 23)**

*RA:* 14 Dec 2011

*Commencement provisions:* s 31(2)

Whole Act in force 15 Dec 2011 (s 31(2))

---

**Welsh Language (Wales) Measure 2011 (nawm 1)**

*Passed by the National Assembly for Wales:* 7 Dec 2010

*Approved by Her Majesty in Council:* 9 Feb 2011

*Commencement provisions:* s 156; Welsh Language (Wales) Measure 2011 (Commencement No 1) Order 2011, SI 2011/1586; Welsh Language (Wales) Measure 2011 (Commencement No 2) Order 2012, SI 2012/46; Welsh Language (Wales) Measure 2011 (Commencement No 3) Order 2012, SI 2012/223; Welsh Language (Wales) Measure 2011 (Commencement No 4) Order 2012, SI 2012/969; Welsh Language (Wales) Measure 2011 (Commencement No 5) Order 2012, SI 2012/1096; Welsh Language (Wales) Measure 2011 (Commencement No 6) Order 2012, SI 2012/1423; Welsh Language (Wales) Measure 2011 (Commencement No 7) Order 2013, SI 2013/3140; Welsh Language (Wales) Measure 2011 (Commencement No 8) Order 2015, SI 2015/985; Welsh Language (Wales) Measure 2011 (Commencement No 9) Order 2015, SI 2015/1217; Welsh Language (Wales) Measure 2011 (Commencement No 10) Order 2015, SI 2015/1413

| | | |
|---|---|---|
| 1 | | 9 Feb 2011 (s 156(1)(a)) |
| 2 | (1) | 1 Apr 2012 (SI 2012/969) |
| | (2), (3) | See Sch 1 below |
| | (4) | 1 Apr 2012 (SI 2012/969) |
| 3 | | 1 Apr 2012 (SI 2012/969) |
| 4 | | 1 Jun 2012 (SI 2012/1423) |
| 5, 6 | | 1 Apr 2012 (SI 2012/969) |
| 7 | (1) | 1 Apr 2012 (SI 2012/969) |
| | (2) | 1 Apr 2012 (except in so far as relates to Pt 5 of this Measure) (SI 2012/969) |
| | | 7 Jul 2015 (exception noted above) (SI 2015/1413) |
| | (3)(a) | 1 Apr 2012 (SI 2012/969) |
| | (3)(b), (4) | 7 Jul 2015 (SI 2015/1413) |
| | (5) | 1 Apr 2012 (SI 2012/969) |
| | (6) | 1 Apr 2012 (except in so far as relates to Pt 5 of this Measure) (SI 2012/969) |
| | | 7 Jul 2015 (exception noted above) (SI 2015/1413) |
| | (7) | 1 Apr 2012 (SI 2012/969) |
| | (8) | 7 Jul 2015 (SI 2015/1413) |
| | (9) | See Sch 2 below |
| | (10) | 7 Jul 2015 (SI 2015/1413) |
| 8–10 | | 1 Apr 2012 (SI 2012/969) |
| 11 | | 1 Jun 2012 (SI 2012/1423) |
| 12–15 | | 1 Apr 2012 (SI 2012/969) |
| 16 | (1) | 1 Apr 2012 (SI 2012/969) |
| | (2)(a), (b) | 7 Jul 2015 (SI 2015/1413) |
| | (2)(c), (3) | 1 Apr 2012 (SI 2012/969) |
| 17–19 | | 1 Apr 2012 (SI 2012/969) |
| 20 | | 7 Jul 2015 (SI 2015/1413) |
| 21 | (1)–(9) | 7 Jul 2015 (SI 2015/1413) |
| | (10) | See Sch 3 below |
| 22 | (1), (2)(a) | 17 Apr 2012 (SI 2012/1096) |
| | (2)(b)–(d) | 7 Jul 2015 (SI 2015/1413) |
| | (2)(e)–(h), (3)–(8) | 17 Apr 2012 (SI 2012/1096) |
| | (9) | 17 Apr 2012 (except definition "standards enforcement investigation") (SI 2012/1096) |
| | | 7 Jul 2015 (exception noted above) (SI 2015/1413) |
| | (10), (11) | 17 Apr 2012 (SI 2012/1096) |
| 23 | (1) | 10 Jan 2012 (in so far as relates to Sch 4, paras 1, 5, 10 and 11 of this Measure) (SI 2012/46) |
| | | 1 Apr 2012 (otherwise) (SI 2012/969) |
| | (2), (3) | 1 Apr 2012 (SI 2012/969) |
| | (4) | See Sch 4 below |
| 24 | | 17 Apr 2012 (SI 2012/1096) |

**Welsh Language (Wales) Measure 2011 (nawm 1)**—*contd*

| | | |
|---|---|---|
| 25 | | 7 Jul 2015 (SI 2015/1413) |
| 26–43 | | 1 Apr 2012 (SI 2012/969) |
| 44 | | 17 Apr 2012 (SI 2012/1096) |
| 45–60 | | 7 Jul 2015 (SI 2015/1413) |
| 61–68 | | 1 Apr 2012 (SI 2012/969) |
| 69 | | 7 Jul 2015 (SI 2015/1413) |
| 70 | | 1 Apr 2012 (SI 2012/969) |
| 71 | (1)–(3) | 7 Jul 2015 (SI 2015/1413) |
| | (4) | See Sch 10 below |
| 72–107 | | 7 Jul 2015 (SI 2015/1413) |
| 108 | | 25 Mar 2015 (SI 2015/985) |
| 109, 110 | | 7 Jul 2015 (SI 2015/1413) |
| 111–119 | | 1 Apr 2012 (SI 2012/969) |
| 120 | (1) | 30 Apr 2015 (SI 2015/1217) |
| | (2), (3) | 7 Jan 2014 (SI 2013/3140) |
| | (4) | See Sch 11 below |
| 121, 122 | | 30 Apr 2015 (SI 2015/1217) |
| 123–125 | | 7 Jan 2014 (SI 2013/3140) |
| 126 | | 30 Apr 2015 (SI 2015/1217) |
| 127, 128 | | 7 Jan 2014 (SI 2013/3140) |
| 129, 130 | | 30 Apr 2015 (SI 2015/1217) |
| 131 | | 7 Jan 2014 (SI 2013/3140) |
| 132 | | 30 Apr 2015 (SI 2015/1217) |
| 133 | | 7 Jan 2014 (SI 2013/3140) |
| 134–137 | | 1 Apr 2012 (SI 2012/969) |
| 138, 139 | | 28 Jun 2011 (SI 2011/1586)[1] |
| 140 | (1)(a), (b) | 1 Apr 2012 (SI 2012/969) |
| | (1)(c) | 7 Jul 2015 (SI 2015/1413) |
| | (1)(d), (e) | 1 Apr 2012 (except in so far as referring to investigations under Pt 5 of this Measure) (SI 2012/969) |
| | | 7 Jul 2015 (exception noted above) (SI 2015/1413) |
| | (2) | 1 Apr 2012 (SI 2012/969) |
| 141 | | 1 Apr 2012 (except in so far as relates to definition "claimant", para (a) and definition "investigation", para (b)) (SI 2012/969) |
| | | 7 Jul 2015 (exceptions noted above) (SI 2015/1413) |
| 142, 143 | | 1 Apr 2012 (SI 2012/969) |
| 144 | (1) | 1 Jun 2012 (in so far as relates to those functions conferred upon the Commissioner by Welsh Language Act 1993, s 3) (SI 2012/1423) |
| | | 7 Jul 2015 (SI 2015/1413) |
| | (2) | 7 Jul 2015 (SI 2015/1413) |
| | (3)(a) | 1 Jun 2012 (for the purpose of repealing Welsh Language Act 1993, s 3(2)(a), (3) and (4)) (SI 2012/1423) |
| | | 6 Jul 2015 (for the purpose of repealing Welsh Language Act 1993, s 3(1), (2)(b), (c)) (S) (NI) (SI 2015/1413) |
| | | 7 Jul 2015 (for the purpose of repealing Welsh Language Act 1993, s 3(1), (2)(b), (c)) (E) (W) (SI 2015/1413) |
| | (3)(b) | 1 Apr 2012 (SI 2012/969) |
| 145 | (1) | *Not yet in force* |
| | (2) | 6 Jul 2015 (S) (NI) (SI 2015/1413) |
| | | *Not yet in force* (E) (W) |
| 146 | | See Sch 12 below |
| 147 | | 1 Apr 2012 (SI 2012/969) |
| 148, 149 | | 5 Feb 2012 (SI 2012/223) |
| 150–157 | | 9 Feb 2011 (s 156(1)(b)) |
| Sch 1 | paras 1, 2 | 1 Apr 2012 (SI 2012/969) |
| | para 3 | 28 Jun 2011 (SI 2011/1586) |
| | paras 4–6 | 1 Apr 2012 (SI 2012/969) |
| | paras 7, 8 | 28 Jun 2011 (SI 2011/1586) |

**Welsh Language (Wales) Measure 2011 (nawm 1)**—*contd*

|  |  |  |
|---|---|---|
|  | paras 9–12 | 1 Apr 2012 (SI 2012/969) |
|  | para 13 | 28 Jun 2011 (SI 2011/1586) |
|  | paras 14–20 | 1 Apr 2012 (SI 2012/969) |
|  | para 21 | 28 Jun 2011 (SI 2011/1586) |
| Sch 2 | paras 1–7, 8(1) | 1 Apr 2012 (SI 2012/969) |
|  | para 8(2)(a) | 7 Jul 2015 (SI 2015/1413) |
|  | para 8(2)(b), (3)–(8) | 1 Apr 2012 (SI 2012/969) |
| Sch 3 |  | 7 Jul 2015 (SI 2015/1413) |
| Sch 4 | para 1 | 10 Jan 2012 (SI 2012/46) |
|  | paras 2–4 | 1 Apr 2012 (SI 2012/969) |
|  | para 5 | 10 Jan 2012 (SI 2012/46) |
|  | paras 6–9 | 1 Apr 2012 (SI 2012/969) |
|  | paras 10, 11 | 10 Jan 2012 (SI 2012/46) |
| Schs 5–9 |  | 1 Apr 2012 (SI 2012/969) |
| Sch 10 |  | 7 Jul 2015 (SI 2015/1413) |
| Sch 11 | paras 1–8 | 7 Jan 2014 (SI 2013/3140) |
|  | para 9 | 1 Apr 2012 (SI 2012/969) |
|  | paras 10–17 | 7 Jan 2014 (SI 2013/3140) |
|  | para 18 | 1 Apr 2012 (SI 2012/969) |
| Sch 12 | paras 1, 2 | 28 Jun 2011 (SI 2011/1586) |
|  | paras 3–5 | 1 Apr 2012 (SI 2012/969) |
|  | para 6 | 28 Jun 2011 (SI 2011/1586) |

[1]   Note that SI 2012/969 purports to bring these sections into force on 1 Apr 2012 to the extent that they are not already in force

---

## Wildlife and Natural Environment (Scotland) Act 2011 (asp 6)

*RA:* 7 Apr 2011

*Commencement provisions:* s 43(1), (2); Wildlife and Natural Environment (Scotland) Act 2011 (Commencement No 1) Order 2011, SSI 2011/279, as amended by SSI 2011/287; Wildlife and Natural Environment (Scotland) Act 2011 (Commencement No 2) Order 2011, SSI 2011/433, as amended by SSI 2011/437, SSI 2012/281; Wildlife and Natural Environment (Scotland) Act 2011 (Commencement No 3) Order 2012, SSI 2012/116; Wildlife and Natural Environment (Scotland) Act 2011 (Commencement No 4, Savings and Transitional Provisions) Order 2012, SSI 2012/175

|  |  |  |
|---|---|---|
| 1 |  | 7 Apr 2011 (RA) |
| 2, 3 |  | 29 Jun 2011 (SSI 2011/279) |
| 4 |  | 1 Jan 2012 (SSI 2011/433) |
| 5 |  | 29 Jun 2011 (SSI 2011/279) |
| 6 | (1) | 1 Jan 2012 (SSI 2011/433) |
|  | (2) | 29 Jun 2011 (in so far as necessary to introduce the Wildlife and Countryside Act 1981, Sch 5A) (SSI 2011/279) |
|  |  | 1 Jan 2012 (otherwise) (SSI 2011/433) |
|  | (3), (4) | 1 Jan 2012 (SSI 2011/433) |
|  | (5) | 29 Jun 2011 (SSI 2011/279) |
| 7 |  | 29 Jun 2011 (SSI 2011/279) |
| 8 |  | 29 Jun 2011 (in so far as it relates to the Wildlife and Countryside Act 1981, s 11G) (SSI 2011/279) |
|  |  | 1 Jan 2012 (otherwise) (SSI 2011/433) |
| 9 |  | 29 Jun 2011 (in so far as it relates to the Wildlife and Countryside Act 1981, ss 11G(1), 11I(1)) (SSI 2011/279) |
|  |  | 1 Jan 2012 (otherwise) (SSI 2011/433) |
| 10 |  | 29 Jun 2011 (SSI 2011/279) |
| 11 |  | 1 Jan 2012 (SSI 2011/433) |
| 12 |  | 29 Jun 2011 (except to the extent that it relates to an offence under the Wildlife and Countryside Act 1981, s 10A(1)) (SSI 2011/279) |

**Wildlife and Natural Environment (Scotland) Act 2011 (asp 6)**—*contd*

| | | |
|---|---|---|
| | | 1 Jan 2012 (exception noted above) (SSI 2011/433) |
| 13 | (1), (2) | 1 Jan 2012 (SSI 2011/433) |
| | (3) | 1 Jan 2012 (in so far as is necessary to enable the Scottish Ministers to make provision by order under the Wildlife and Countryside Act 1981, ss 11A(8) and 11E(1)(f) and in so far as inserts ss 11B, 11C and 11F into that Act) (SSI 2011/433) |
| | | 22 Nov 2012 (in so far as inserts s 11A(4), (9) into Wildlife and Countryside Act 1981) (SSI 2012/433) |
| | | 1 Apr 2013 (otherwise) (SSI 2011/433) |
| | (4) | 1 Jan 2012 (SSI 2011/433) |
| | (5) | 22 Nov 2012 (SSI 2012/433) |
| 14 | (1) | See sub-ss (2)–(5) below |
| | (2)(a) | 1 May 2012 (in so far as is necessary to enable the Scottish Ministers to make provision by order under the Wildlife and Countryside Act 1981, s 14(1)(a)(ii), (2B)–(2D)) (SSI 2012/116) |
| | | 2 Jul 2012 (otherwise) (SSI 2012/175)[1] |
| | (2)(b), (c) | 2 Jul 2012 (SSI 2012/175) |
| | (3) | 1 May 2012 (in so far as is necessary to enable the Scottish Ministers to make provision by order under the Wildlife and Countryside Act 1981, s 14ZC(1), (2)) (SSI 2012/116) |
| | | 2 Jul 2012 (otherwise) (SSI 2012/175) |
| | (4) | 2 Jul 2012 (SSI 2012/175) |
| | (5) | 1 May 2012 (in so far as is necessary to enable the Scottish Ministers to make provision by order under the Wildlife and Countryside Act 1981, s 14B(1)–(4)) (SSI 2012/116) |
| | | 2 Jul 2012 (otherwise) (SSI 2012/175) |
| 15 | | 1 Jan 2012 (SSI 2011/433) |
| 16 | | 2 Jul 2012 (SSI 2012/175) |
| 17 | (1)–(5), (6)(a), (b)(i) | 2 Jul 2012 (SSI 2012/175) |
| | (6)(b)(ii), (iii) | 1 May 2012 (in so far as they insert reference to the Wildlife and Countryside Act 1981, ss 14, 14ZC, 14B) (SSI 2012/116) |
| | | 2 Jul 2012 (in so far as they insert reference to s 14A of that Act) (SSI 2012/175) |
| | (6)(c) | 1 May 2012 (in so far as relates to orders under the Wildlife and Countryside Act 1981, ss 14, 14ZC) (SSI 2012/116) |
| | | 2 Jul 2012 (in so far as relates to orders under s 14A of that Act) (SSI 2012/175) |
| | (7), (8) | 2 Jul 2012 (SSI 2012/175) |
| 18, 19 | | 29 Jun 2011 (SSI 2011/279) |
| 20 | | 2 Jan 2012 (SSI 2011/433) |
| 21 | | 1 Jan 2012 (SSI 2011/433) |
| 22 | | 2 Jul 2012 (SSI 2012/175) |
| 23, 24 | | 1 Jan 2012 (SSI 2011/433) |
| 25 | | See Schedule below |
| 26–28 | | 1 Jan 2012 (SSI 2011/433) |
| 29 | | 1 Apr 2012 (SSI 2011/433) |
| 30–32 | | 1 Jan 2012 (SSI 2011/433) |
| 33 | | 29 Jun 2011 (SSI 2011/279) |
| 34 | | 1 Aug 2011 (SSI 2011/279) |
| 35, 36 | | 1 Jan 2012 (SSI 2011/433) |
| 37–40 | | 29 Jun 2011 (SSI 2011/279) |
| 41 | | 1 Jan 2012 (SSI 2011/433) |
| 42, 43 | | 7 Apr 2011 (RA) |
| Schedule | Pt 1 | 29 Jun 2011 (SSI 2011/279) |
| | Pt 2 | 29 Jun 2011 (SSI 2011/279), repeals of or in— |
| | | Game (Scotland) Act 1772; |
| | | Night Poaching Act 1828; |
| | | Game Act 1831; |
| | | Game (Scotland) Act 1832; |

**Wildlife and Natural Environment (Scotland) Act 2011 (asp 6)**—*contd*

|  |  |
|---|---|
|  | Night Poaching Act 1844; |
|  | Hares (Scotland) Act 1848; |
|  | Game Licences Act 1860; |
|  | Poaching Prevention Act 1862; |
|  | Game Laws Amendment (Scotland) Act 1877; |
|  | Ground Game Act 1880; |
|  | Customs and Inland Revenue Act 1883; |
|  | Hares Preservation Act 1892; |
|  | Finance Act 1924; |
|  | Finance Act 1937; |
|  | Agriculture (Scotland) Act 1948; |
|  | Local Government (Scotland) Act 1966; |
|  | Game Act 1970; |
|  | Marine (Scotland) Act 2010 |
|  | 2 Jul 2012 (SSI 2012/175)[1], repeals of or in— |
|  | Destructive Imported Animals Act 1932; |
|  | Import of Live Fish (Scotland) Act 1978; |
|  | Deer (Scotland) Act 1996; |
|  | Protection of Wild Mammals (Scotland) Act 2002 |

[1]   For savings and transitional provisions, see SSI 2012/175, art 3

---

**Wreck Removal Convention Act 2011 (c 8)**

*RA:* 12 Jul 2011

*Commencement provisions:* s 2(2); Wreck Removal Convention Act 2011 (Commencement) Order 2015, SI 2015/133

| 1 | (1) | See sub-ss (2)–(5) below |
|---|---|---|
|  | (2) | 5 Feb 2015 (in so far as inserts Merchant Shipping Act 1995, ss 255A, 255J, 255N, 255R, for the purpose of enabling the Secretary of State to issue wreck removal insurance certificates in accordance with section 255N of the 1995 Act, to make regulations under s 302 of the 1995 Act prescribing the fees to be charged in respect of the issue of such certificates and to describe by order the UK's Convention area) (SI 2015/133) |
|  |  | 14 Apr 2015 (otherwise) (SI 2015/133) |
|  | (3) | 14 Apr 2015 (SI 2015/133) |
|  | (4) | See Schedule below |
|  | (5) | 14 Apr 2015 (SI 2015/133) |
| 2 |  | 14 Apr 2015 (SI 2015/133) |
| Schedule |  | 5 Feb 2015 (for the purpose of enabling the Secretary of State to issue wreck removal insurance certificates in accordance with section 255N of the 1995 Act, to make regulations under s 302 of the 1995 Act prescribing the fees to be charged in respect of the issue of such certificates and to describe by order the UK's Convention area) (SI 2015/133) |
|  |  | 14 Apr 2015 (otherwise) (SI 2015/133) |

---

# 2012 Acts

## Agricultural Holdings (Amendment) (Scotland) Act 2012 (asp 6)

*RA:* 12 Jul 2012

*Commencement provisions:* s 5

| | |
|---|---|
| 1–4 | 12 Sep 2012 (s 5(2)) |
| 5, 6 | 13 Jul 2012 (s 5(1)) |

## Alcohol (Minimum Pricing) (Scotland) Act 2012 (asp 4)

*RA:* 29 Jun 2012

*Commencement provisions:* s 5; Alcohol (Minimum Pricing) (Scotland) Act 2012 (Commencement) Order 2017, SSI 2017/402; Alcohol (Minimum Pricing) (Scotland) Act 2012 (Commencement No 2) Order 2018, SSI 2018/88

| | |
|---|---|
| 1 | 6 Dec 2017 (so far as necessary for the purpose of enabling the Scottish Ministers to make orders under Licensing (Scotland) Act 2005, Sch 3, para 6A, Sch 4, para 5A) (SSI 2017/402) |
| | 1 May 2018 (otherwise) (SSI 2018/88) |
| 2–4 | 1 May 2018 (SSI 2018/88) |
| 5, 6 | 29 Jun 2012 (s 5(1)) |

## Budget (Scotland) Act 2012 (asp 2)

*RA:* 14 Mar 2012

*Commencement provisions:* s 10

Whole Act in force 15 Mar 2012 (s 10)

## Church of England Marriage (Amendment) Measure 2012 (No 1)

*RA:* 19 Dec 2012

*Commencement provisions:* s 3(2)

Provisions of this Measure were brought into force on 1 Jun 2013 by an instrument made by the Archbishops of Canterbury and York, and dated 21 May 2013 (made under s 3(2))

| | |
|---|---|
| 1 | 1 Jun 2013 |
| 2, 3 | 19 Dec 2012 (s 3(2)) |

## Civil Aviation Act 2012 (c 19)

*RA:* 19 Dec 2012

*Commencement provisions:* s 110; Civil Aviation Act 2012 (Commencement No 1, Transitional, Transitory and Saving Provisions) Order 2013, SI 2013/589; Civil Aviation Act 2012 (Commencement No 2) Order 2014, SI 2014/262

**Civil Aviation Act 2012 (c 19)**—*contd*

| | | |
|---|---|---|
| 1–75 | | 6 Apr 2013 (SI 2013/589) |
| 76 | (1) | 6 Apr 2013 (repeal of Airports Act 1986, ss 37(2)–(7), (9), (10), 38, 40A, 40B, 41(1), 53) (SI 2013/589)[1] |
| | | 1 Apr 2014 (repeal of Airports Act 1986, ss 36, 37(1), (8), 39, 40, 41(2)–(7), 42–52, 54–56) (SI 2013/589)[1] |
| | (2) | 6 Apr 2013 (SI 2013/589) |
| | (3) | See Sch 8 below |
| | (4) | See Sch 9 below |
| | (5) | See Sch 10 below |
| 77 | | 6 Apr 2013 (SI 2013/589) |
| 78 | (1)–(5) | 1 Apr 2014 (SI 2014/262) |
| | (6) | See Sch 11 below |
| 79–81 | | 1 Apr 2014 (SI 2014/262) |
| 82 | (1)–(3) | 11 Mar 2014 (SI 2014/262) |
| | (4) | See Sch 12 below |
| 83–93 | | 19 Feb 2013 (s 110(3)(a)) |
| 94 | | 19 Feb 2013 (s 110(3)(b)) |
| 95–99 | | 19 Feb 2013 (s 110(3)(c)) |
| 100 | | 6 Apr 2013 (SI 2013/589) |
| 101 | | 19 Feb 2013 (s 110(3)(d)) |
| 102 | | 1 Apr 2014 (SI 2013/589) |
| 103, 104 | | 6 Apr 2013 (SI 2013/589) |
| 105–107 | | 19 Feb 2013 (s 110(3)(e)) |
| 108–113 | | 19 Dec 2012 (s 110(2)(b)) |
| Schs 1–8 | | 6 Apr 2013 (SI 2013/589) |
| Sch 9 | para 1 | 1 Apr 2014 (SI 2013/589) |
| | para 2 | 6 Apr 2013 (SI 2013/589) |
| | para 3(1) | See sub-paras (2), (3) below |
| | para 3(2)(a) | 1 Apr 2014 (SI 2013/589) |
| | para 3(2)(b) | 6 Apr 2013 (SI 2013/589) |
| | para 3(3)(a) | 1 Apr 2014 (SI 2013/589) |
| | para 3(3)(b) | 6 Apr 2013 (SI 2013/589) |
| | para 4 | 1 Apr 2014 (SI 2013/589) |
| | paras 5–8 | 6 Apr 2013 (SI 2013/589) |
| | para 9 | 1 Apr 2014 (SI 2013/589) |
| | paras 10–13, 14(1) | 6 Apr 2013 (SI 2013/589) |
| | para 14(2)(a) | 1 Apr 2014 (SI 2013/589) |
| | para 14(2)(b) | 6 Apr 2013 (SI 2013/589) |
| | para 14(3)(a) | 1 Apr 2014 (SI 2013/589) |
| | para 14(3)(b) | 6 Apr 2013 (SI 2013/589) |
| | paras 15, 16 | 6 Apr 2013 (SI 2013/589) |
| | para 17 | 6 Apr 2013 (in so far as repeals Enterprise Act 2002, Sch 9, paras 11(2), (4), 12, Sch 25, para 33(3)–(6); Serious Crime Act 2007, Sch 6, para 26) (SI 2013/589) |
| | | 1 Apr 2014 (otherwise) (SI 2013/589) |
| Sch 10 | para 1 | 19 Dec 2012 (s 110(2)(a)) |
| | paras 2–6 | 6 Apr 2013 (SI 2013/589) |
| | para 7 | 19 Dec 2012 (s 110(2)(a)) |
| | paras 8–18 | 6 Apr 2013 (SI 2013/589) |
| Sch 11 | | 1 Apr 2014 (SI 2014/262) |
| Sch 12 | | 11 Mar 2014 (SI 2014/262) |
| Sch 13 | | 19 Feb 2013 (s 110(3)(a)) |
| Sch 14 | | 19 Feb 2013 (s 110(3)(c)) |

[1] For transitional provisions and transitory modifications, see SI 2013/589, arts 3, 4, 6

## Consumer Insurance (Disclosure and Representations) Act 2012 (c 6)

*RA:* 8 Mar 2012

*Commencement provisions:* s 12; Consumer Insurance (Disclosure and Representations) Act 2012 (Commencement) Order 2013, SI 2013/450

| | |
|---|---|
| 1 | 8 Mar 2012 (s 12(2)) |
| 2–11 | 6 Apr 2013 (SI 2013/450) |
| 12 | 8 Mar 2012 (s 12(2)) |
| Schs 1, 2 | 6 Apr 2013 (SI 2013/450) |

## Criminal Cases (Punishment and Review) (Scotland) Act 2012 (asp 7)

*RA:* 26 Jul 2012

*Commencement provisions:* s 5; Criminal Cases (Punishment and Review) (Scotland) Act 2012 (Commencement, Transitional and Savings) Order 2012, SSI 2012/249

| | |
|---|---|
| 1–4 | 24 Sep 2012 (SSI 2012/249)[1] |
| 5, 6 | 27 Jul 2012 (s 5(1)) |

[1] For a transitional and savings provision, see SSI 2012/249, art 4

## Domestic Violence, Crime and Victims (Amendment) Act 2012 (c 4)

*RA:* 8 Mar 2012

*Commencement provisions:* Domestic Violence, Crime and Victims (Amendment) Act 2012 (Commencement) Order 2012, SI 2012/1432

Whole Act in force 2 Jul 2012 (SI 2012/1432)

## European Union (Approval of Treaty Amendment Decision) Act 2012 (c 15)

*RA:* 31 Oct 2012

*Commencement provisions:* s 2(2)

Whole Act in force 31 Oct 2012 (s 2(2))

## Finance Act 2012 (c 14)

*Budget Day:* 21 Mar 2012

*RA:* 17 Jul 2012

The commencement details of Finance Acts are not set out, as the dates from which their provisions take effect are usually stated clearly and unambiguously in the text of the Act, and charging provisions will normally state for which year or years of assessment they are to have effect.

## Financial Services Act 2012 (c 21)

*RA:* 19 Dec 2012

*Commencement provisions:* s 122; Financial Services Act 2012 (Commencement No 1) Order 2013, SI 2013/113; Financial Services Act 2012 (Commencement No 2) Order 2013, SI 2013/423; Financial Services Act 2012 (Commencement No 3) Order 2013, SI 2013/651; Financial Services Act 2012 (Commencement No 4) Order 2014, SI 2014/1447; Financial Services Act 2012 (Commencement No 5) Order 2014, SI 2014/1847; Financial Services Act 2012 (Commencement No 6) Order 2014, SI 2014/3323

**Financial Services Act 2012 (c 21)**—*contd*

| | | |
|---|---|---|
| 1 | | 19 Feb 2013 (for the purposes of making appointments) (SI 2013/113) |
| | | 1 Apr 2013 (otherwise) (SI 2013/423) |
| 2, 3 | | 1 Apr 2013 (SI 2013/423) |
| 4 | (1) | 24 Jan 2013 (in so far as inserts Bank of England Act 1998, ss 9I(2), 9L and 9N for the purposes of making orders or regulations, and in so far as inserts s 9ZA of that Act for all purposes) (SI 2013/113) |
| | | 19 Feb 2013 (in so far as inserts s 9B of that Act, for the purposes of making appointments) (SI 2013/113) |
| | | 1 Apr 2013 (otherwise) (SI 2013/423) |
| | (2) | See Sch 1, Pt 1 below |
| | (3) | See Sch 1, Pt 2 below |
| | (4) | 1 Apr 2013 (SI 2013/423) |
| 5 | | See Sch 2 below |
| 6 | (1) | 24 Jan 2013 (SI 2013/113) in so far as substitutes the following provisions of the Financial Services and Markets Act 2000— |
| | | ss 1A(2), (6), 1F–1I, 2A(1), (2), (6), 2F–2J, 3A–3D, 3R; |
| | | ss 1B–1E, 2B, 2C, in so far as they are relevant to other provisions of this Act which are in force; |
| | | s 1L, for the purposes of making orders or regulations; |
| | | ss 3E, 3F, in so far as they relate to the preparation of memoranda |
| | | 19 Feb 2013 (in so far as substitutes ss 1M–1Q, 2L, 2M of that Act, for the purposes of making appointments) (SI 2013/113) |
| | | 1 Apr 2013 (otherwise) (SI 2013/423) |
| | (2) | See Sch 3 below |
| 7–9 | | 24 Jan 2013 (SI 2013/113) |
| 10 | | 1 Apr 2013 (SI 2013/423) |
| 11 | (1) | 1 Apr 2013 (SI 2013/423) |
| | (2) | 24 Jan 2013 (SI 2013/113), in so far as substitutes the following provisions of the Financial Services and Markets Act 2000— |
| | | s 55C, for the purposes of making orders or regulations; |
| | | s 55U, in so far as it relates to the giving of directions or the imposition of requirements |
| | | 1 Apr 2013 (otherwise) (SI 2013/423) |
| | (3) | 1 Apr 2013 (SI 2013/423) |
| 12 | | See Sch 4 below |
| 13 | | 1 Apr 2013 (SI 2013/423) |
| 14 | | 24 Jan 2013 (for the purposes of making arrangements under the Financial Services and Markets Act 2000, s 59B, the issue of statements of principle under s 64 of that Act, and the making of rules) (SI 2013/113) |
| | | 1 Apr 2013 (otherwise) (SI 2013/423) |
| 15 | | See Sch 5 below |
| 16 | | 24 Jan 2013 (for the purpose of the making of rules) (SI 2013/113) |
| | | 1 Apr 2013 (otherwise) (SI 2013/423) |
| 17 | | 19 Mar 2013 (for the purpose of the making of rules) (SI 2013/651) |
| | | 1 Apr 2013 (otherwise) (SI 2013/423) |
| 18 | | 24 Jan 2013 (for the purpose of the preparation and issue of a statement of policy under the Financial Services and Markets Act 2000, s 88C) (SI 2013/113) |
| | | 19 Mar 2013 (for the purpose of the making of rules) (SI 2013/651) |
| | | 1 Apr 2013 (otherwise) (SI 2013/423) |
| 19 | | 24 Jan 2013 (for the purpose of the preparation and issue of a statement of policy under the Financial Services and Markets Act 2000, s 89S, and for the purpose of the making of rules) (SI 2013/113) |
| | | 1 Apr 2013 (otherwise) (SI 2013/423) |

**Financial Services Act 2012 (c 21)**—*contd*

| | | |
|---|---|---|
| 20–23 | | 1 Apr 2013 (SI 2013/423) |
| 24 | | 24 Jan 2013 (SI 2013/113), for the purposes of— |

    the giving of directions under the Financial Services and Markets Act 2000, s 138A;

    the issue of a statement of policy under s 138N of that Act;

    the giving of guidance under s 139A of that Act;

    the determination of a procedure and the issue of a statement of procedure under s 395 of that Act in relation to the procedure to be followed in relation to the giving of supervisory notices in accordance with s 137S(5) or (8)(a) of that Act; and

    the making of rules

    1 Apr 2013 (otherwise) (SI 2013/423)

| | | |
|---|---|---|
| 25, 26 | | 1 Apr 2013 (SI 2013/423) |
| 27 | | 24 Jan 2013 (for the purposes of making orders, regulations or rules, and for the purpose of the preparation and issue of statements of policy under the Financial Services and Markets Act 2000, ss 192H and 192N) (SI 2013/113) |
| | | 1 Apr 2013 (otherwise) (SI 2013/423) |
| 28 | | 1 Apr 2013 (SI 2013/423) |
| 29 | (1) | 24 Jan 2013 (for the purposes of making orders or regulations) (SI 2013/113) |
| | | 1 Apr 2013 (otherwise) (SI 2013/423) |
| | (2) | See Sch 7 below |
| 30 | | 24 Jan 2013 (for the purposes of making orders or regulations) (SI 2013/113) |
| | | 1 Apr 2013 (otherwise) (SI 2013/423) |
| 31, 32 | | 1 Apr 2013 (SI 2013/423) |
| 33 | | 24 Jan 2013 (for the purposes of making orders or regulations, and for the purpose of the preparation and issue of a statement under the Financial Services and Markets Act 2000, s 312J) (SI 2013/113) |
| | | 1 Apr 2013 (otherwise) (SI 2013/423) |
| 34 | | 1 Apr 2013 (SI 2013/423) |
| 35 | | See Sch 8 below |
| 36 | | 1 Apr 2013 (SI 2013/423) |
| 37 | (1) | See Sch 9 below |
| | (2) | 1 Apr 2013 (SI 2013/423) |
| 38 | (1) | See Sch 10 below |
| | (2) | 24 Jan 2013 (for the purposes of the making of rules) (SI 2013/113) |
| | | 1 Apr 2013 (otherwise) (SI 2013/423) |
| 39 | | See Sch 11 below |
| 40 | | 24 Jan 2013 (for the purpose of inserting the Financial Services and Markets Act 2000, s 314A) (SI 2013/113) |
| | | 1 Apr 2013 (otherwise) (SI 2013/423) |
| 41 | | See Sch 12 below |
| 42 | | See Sch 13 below |
| 43 | | 24 Jan 2013 (in so far as inserts Financial Services and Markets Act 2000, s 234C for the purposes of making orders or regulations, and for the purpose of the power to give guidance of the kind specified by s 234G of that Act) (SI 2013/113) |
| | | 1 Apr 2013 (otherwise) (SI 2013/423) |
| 44 | | See Sch 14 below |
| 45 | | See Sch 15 below |
| 46 | | See Sch 16 below |
| 47 | | 1 Apr 2013 (SI 2013/423) |
| 48 | (1)(a)–(c) | 1 Apr 2013 (SI 2013/423) |
| | (1)(d) | 24 Jan 2013 (SI 2013/113) |
| | (1)(e)–(i) | 1 Apr 2013 (SI 2013/423) |
| | (1)(j) | 24 Jan 2013 (SI 2013/113) |

**See Halsbury's Statutes Citator for amendments to these Acts**      2185

**Financial Services Act 2012 (c 21)**—*contd*

| | | |
|---|---|---|
| | (1)(k)–(m) | 1 Apr 2013 (SI 2013/423) |
| | (1)(n) | 24 Jan 2013 (SI 2013/113) |
| | (1)(o)–(t) | 1 Apr 2013 (SI 2013/423) |
| | (2), (3) | 24 Jan 2013 (SI 2013/113) |
| 49–52 | | 24 Jan 2013 (SI 2013/113) |
| 53–56 | | 1 Apr 2013 (SI 2013/423) |
| 57 | | 24 Jan 2013 (SI 2013/113) |
| 58–63 | | 1 Apr 2013 (SI 2013/423) |
| 64 | | 24 Jan 2013 (SI 2013/113) |
| 65, 66 | | 24 Jan 2013 (for the purpose of the preparation of a memorandum) (SI 2013/113) |
| | | 1 Apr 2013 (otherwise) (SI 2013/423) |
| 67 | | 24 Jan 2013 (SI 2013/113) |
| 68–79 | | 1 Apr 2013 (SI 2013/423) |
| 80 | | 24 Jan 2013 (for the purpose of the power to prepare and issue a statement of policy) (SI 2013/113) |
| | | 1 Apr 2013 (otherwise) (SI 2013/423) |
| 81, 82 | | 1 Apr 2013 (SI 2013/423) |
| 83 | | 24 Jan 2013 (SI 2013/113) |
| 84–87 | | 24 Jan 2013 (for the purpose of making the complaints scheme) (SI 2013/113) |
| | | 1 Apr 2013 (otherwise) (SI 2013/423) |
| 88–92 | | 1 Apr 2013 (SI 2013/423) |
| 93, 94 | | 24 Jan 2013 (SI 2013/113) |
| 95 | | 1 Apr 2013 (SI 2013/423) |
| 96 | (1), (2) | 1 Jan 2015 (SI 2014/3323) |
| | (3), (4) | *Not yet in force* |
| | (5), (6) | 1 Jan 2015 (SI 2014/3323) |
| 97 | | 1 Apr 2013 (SI 2013/423) |
| 98, 99 | | 1 Jan 2015 (SI 2014/3323) |
| 100 | (1) | 5 Jun 2014 (for the purposes of making orders or regulations) (SI 2014/1447) |
| | | 1 Aug 2014 (otherwise) (SI 2014/1847) |
| | (2)–(4) | 1 Aug 2014 (SI 2014/1847) |
| | (5) | 5 Jun 2014 (for the purposes of making orders or regulations so far as inserts Banking Act 2009, ss 81C(2), for the purpose of enabling the power conferred by section 47 of the Act to be exercised in relation to group companies, and 81D) (SI 2014/1447) |
| | | 1 Aug 2014 (otherwise) (SI 2014/1847) |
| | (6), (7) | 5 Jun 2014 (for the purposes of making orders or regulations) (SI 2014/1447) |
| | | 1 Aug 2014 (otherwise) (SI 2014/1847) |
| 101 | (1) | 5 Jun 2014 (for the purposes of making orders or regulations) (SI 2014/1447) |
| | | 1 Aug 2014 (otherwise) (SI 2014/1847) |
| | (2)–(4) | 1 Aug 2014 (SI 2014/1847) |
| | (5) | 5 Jun 2014 (for the purposes of making orders or regulations so far as inserts Banking Act 2009, s 89A(1), for the purpose of enabling the powers conferred by ss 47, 60 and 81D(1) of the Act to be exercised in relation to investment firms and companies in the same group as an investment firm which are group companies) (SI 2014/1447) |
| | | 1 Aug 2014 (otherwise) (SI 2014/1847) |
| | (6) | 1 Aug 2014 (SI 2014/1847) |
| | (7)–(9) | 5 Jun 2014 (for the purposes of making orders or regulations) (SI 2014/1447) |
| | | 1 Aug 2014 (otherwise) (SI 2014/1847) |
| | (10) | 1 Aug 2014 (SI 2014/1847) |

**Financial Services Act 2012 (c 21)**—*contd*

| | | |
|---|---|---|
| 102 | (1) | 5 Jun 2014 (for the purposes of making orders or regulations) (SI 2014/1447) |
| | | 1 Aug 2014 (otherwise) (SI 2014/1847) |
| | (2)–(5) | 1 Aug 2014 (SI 2014/1847) |
| | (6) | 5 Jun 2014 (for the purposes of making orders or regulations so far as inserts Banking Act 2009, ss 89B(1), for the purpose of enabling the powers conferred by sections 47, 48 and 81D(1) of the Act to be exercised in relation to recognised central counterparties and companies in the same group as a recognised central counterparty which are group companies, and 89G) (SI 2014/1447) |
| | | 1 Aug 2014 (otherwise) (SI 2014/1847) |
| | (7), (8) | 1 Aug 2014 (SI 2014/1847) |
| 103–107 | | 1 Apr 2013 (SI 2013/423) |
| 108 | | 19 Feb 2013 (s 122(2)) |
| 109 | | 19 Dec 2012 (s 122(1)) |
| 110 | | 24 Jan 2013 (for the purposes of making orders or regulations) (SI 2013/113) |
| | | 1 Apr 2013 (otherwise) (SI 2013/423) |
| 111 | | 1 Apr 2013 (SI 2013/423) |
| 112 | | 24 Jan 2013 (for the purposes of making orders or regulations) (SI 2013/113) |
| | | 1 Apr 2013 (otherwise) (SI 2013/423) |
| 113 | | 19 Feb 2013 (s 122(2)) |
| 114 | (1) | See Sch 18 below |
| | (2) | See Sch 19 below |
| 115–118 | | 19 Dec 2012 (s 122(1)) |
| 119 | (1) | See Sch 20 below |
| | (2) | See Sch 21 below |
| | (3)–(6) | 19 Dec 2012 (s 122(1)) |
| 120–123 | | 19 Dec 2012 (s 122(1)) |
| Sch 1 | Pt 1 | 19 Feb 2013 (for the purposes of making appointments) (SI 2013/113) |
| | | 1 Apr 2013 (otherwise) (SI 2013/423) |
| | Pt 2 | 1 Apr 2013 (SI 2013/423) |
| Sch 2 | | 19 Feb 2013 (for the purposes of making appointments) (SI 2013/113) |
| | | 1 Apr 2013 (otherwise) (SI 2013/423) |
| Sch 3 | | 24 Jan 2013 (SI 2013/113), in so far as substitutes the following provisions of the Financial Services and Markets Act 2000— |
| | | Sch 1ZA, para 20, for the purposes of making orders or regulations; |
| | | Sch 1ZA (all provisions which relate to the preparation of a scheme under para 21 thereof or to the making of rules); |
| | | Sch 1ZB, except paras 2, 3 and 8 thereof |
| | | 19 Feb 2013 (in so far as substitutes Sch 1ZA, paras 2, 3 of that Act, for the purposes of making appointments) (SI 2013/113) |
| | | 1 Apr 2013 (otherwise) (SI 2013/423) |
| Sch 4 | paras 1–6 | 27 Feb 2013 (for the purposes of making orders or regulations) (SI 2013/423) |
| | | 1 Apr 2013 (otherwise) (SI 2013/423) |
| | para 7 | 24 Jan 2013 (for the purposes of making orders or regulations) (SI 2013/113) |
| | | 1 Apr 2013 (otherwise) (SI 2013/423) |
| | paras 8–16 | 27 Feb 2013 (for the purposes of making orders or regulations) (SI 2013/423) |
| | | 1 Apr 2013 (otherwise) (SI 2013/423) |
| | para 17 | 24 Jan 2013 (in so far as it relates to the making of arrangements) (SI 2013/113) |
| | | 1 Apr 2013 (otherwise) (SI 2013/423) |

**Financial Services Act 2012 (c 21)**—*contd*

| | | |
|---|---|---|
| | paras 18–23 | 27 Feb 2013 (for the purposes of making orders or regulations) (SI 2013/423) |
| | | 1 Apr 2013 (otherwise) (SI 2013/423) |
| | para 24 | 24 Jan 2013 (for the purposes of making orders or regulations) (SI 2013/113) |
| | | 1 Apr 2013 (otherwise) (SI 2013/423) |
| | para 25 | 27 Feb 2013 (for the purposes of making orders or regulations) (SI 2013/423) |
| | | 1 Apr 2013 (otherwise) (SI 2013/423) |
| | para 26(1)–(3) | 27 Feb 2013 (for the purposes of making orders or regulations) (SI 2013/423) |
| | | 1 Apr 2013 (otherwise) (SI 2013/423) |
| | para 26(4) | 24 Jan 2013 (in so far as it relates to the giving of directions or the imposition of requirements) (SI 2013/113) |
| | | 1 Apr 2013 (otherwise) (SI 2013/423) |
| | paras 26(5) | 27 Feb 2013 (for the purposes of making orders or regulations) (SI 2013/423) |
| | | 1 Apr 2013 (otherwise) (SI 2013/423) |
| | paras 27–43 | 27 Feb 2013 (for the purposes of making orders or regulations) (SI 2013/423) |
| | | 1 Apr 2013 (otherwise) (SI 2013/423) |
| Sch 5 | paras 1–3 | 1 Apr 2013 (SI 2013/423) |
| | para 4 | 24 Jan 2013 (in so far as it relates to the giving of directions or the imposition of requirements) (SI 2013/113) |
| | | 1 Apr 2013 (otherwise) (SI 2013/423) |
| | paras 5–9 | 1 Apr 2013 (SI 2013/423) |
| | paras 10–13 | 24 Jan 2013 (in so far as they relate to the preparation and issue of a statement of policy, a statement of principle or a code of practice) (SI 2013/113) |
| | | 1 Apr 2013 (otherwise) (SI 2013/423) |
| | para 14 | 24 Jan 2013 (for the purposes of making orders or regulations) (SI 2013/113) |
| | | 1 Apr 2013 (otherwise) (SI 2013/423) |
| | paras 15, 16 | 1 Apr 2013 (SI 2013/423) |
| | paras 17, 18 | 24 Jan 2013 (in so far as they relate to the preparation and issue of a statement of policy, a statement of principle or a code of practice) (SI 2013/113) |
| | | 1 Apr 2013 (otherwise) (SI 2013/423) |
| Sch 6 | | 1 Apr 2013 (SI 2013/423) |
| Sch 7 | | 24 Jan 2013 (in so far as it relates to the preparation of a memorandum, the making of orders, regulations or rules, or the preparation and issue of a statement of policy) (SI 2013/113) |
| | | 1 Apr 2013 (otherwise) (SI 2013/423) |
| Sch 8 | paras 1–10 | 24 Jan 2013 (for the purpose of the making of rules) (SI 2013/113) |
| | | 1 Apr 2013 (otherwise) (SI 2013/423) |
| | para 11 | 24 Jan 2013 (for the purposes of making orders, regulations or rules) (SI 2013/113) |
| | | 1 Apr 2013 (otherwise) (SI 2013/423) |
| | paras 12, 13 | 24 Jan 2013 (for the purpose of the making of rules) (SI 2013/113) |
| | | 1 Apr 2013 (otherwise) (SI 2013/423) |
| | paras 14, 15 | 24 Jan 2013 (for the purposes of making orders, regulations or rules) (SI 2013/113) |
| | | 1 Apr 2013 (otherwise) (SI 2013/423) |
| | paras 16–39 | 24 Jan 2013 (for the purpose of the making of rules) (SI 2013/113) |
| | | 1 Apr 2013 (otherwise) (SI 2013/423) |
| Sch 9 | paras 1–9 | 1 Apr 2013 (SI 2013/423) |
| | para 10 | 24 Jan 2013 (for the purposes of making orders or regulations) (SI 2013/113) |
| | | 1 Apr 2013 (otherwise) (SI 2013/423) |

**Financial Services Act 2012 (c 21)**—*contd*

| | | |
|---|---|---|
| | paras 11–16 | 1 Apr 2013 (SI 2013/423) |
| | paras 17, 18 | 24 Jan 2013 (in so far as they relate to the preparation and issue of a statement of policy) (SI 2013/113) |
| | | 1 Apr 2013 (otherwise) (SI 2013/423) |
| | para 19 | 24 Jan 2013 (for the purposes of making orders or regulations) (SI 2013/113) |
| | | 1 Apr 2013 (otherwise) (SI 2013/423) |
| | para 20 | 1 Apr 2013 (SI 2013/423) |
| | para 21 | 24 Jan 2013 (for the purposes of making orders or regulations) (SI 2013/113) |
| | | 1 Apr 2013 (otherwise) (SI 2013/423) |
| | para 22 | 1 Apr 2013 (SI 2013/423) |
| | para 23 | 24 Jan 2013 (for the purposes of making orders or regulations) (SI 2013/113) |
| | | 1 Apr 2013 (otherwise) (SI 2013/423) |
| | paras 24–33 | 1 Apr 2013 (SI 2013/423) |
| | paras 34, 35 | 24 Jan 2013 (in so far as they relate to the determination of a procedure and the issue of a statement of the procedure) (SI 2013/113) |
| | | 1 Apr 2013 (otherwise) (SI 2013/423) |
| | paras 36–41 | 1 Apr 2013 (SI 2013/423) |
| Sch 10 | paras 1, 2 | 24 Jan 2013 (for the purpose of the making of rules) (SI 2013/113) |
| | | 1 Apr 2013 (otherwise) (SI 2013/423) |
| | para 3 | 24 Jan 2013 (for the purposes of making orders, regulations or rules) (SI 2013/113) |
| | | 1 Apr 2013 (otherwise) (SI 2013/423) |
| | paras 4–6 | 24 Jan 2013 (for the purpose of the making of rules) (SI 2013/113) |
| | | 1 Apr 2013 (otherwise) (SI 2013/423) |
| | para 7 | 24 Jan 2013 (for the purposes of the preparation of memoranda under the Financial Services and Markets Act 2000, s 217A) (SI 2013/113) |
| | | 1 Apr 2013 (otherwise) (SI 2013/423) |
| | paras 8–15 | 24 Jan 2013 (for the purpose of the making of rules) (SI 2013/113) |
| | | 1 Apr 2013 (otherwise) (SI 2013/423) |
| Sch 11 | | 24 Jan 2013 (for the purposes of the preparation of a memorandum under the Financial Services and Markets Act 2000, Sch 17, para 3A, and the making of rules) (SI 2013/113) |
| | | 19 Mar 2013 (in so far as para 28 of this Sch relates to the fixing of standard terms) (SI 2013/651) |
| | | 1 Apr 2013 (otherwise) (SI 2013/423) |
| Sch 12 | paras 1–4 | 1 Apr 2013 (SI 2013/423) |
| | paras 5, 6 | 24 Jan 2013 (for the purpose of the making of rules) (SI 2013/113) |
| | | 1 Apr 2013 (otherwise) (SI 2013/423) |
| | para 7 | 1 Apr 2013 (SI 2013/423) |
| | para 8 | 24 Jan 2013 (for the purposes of making orders or regulations) (SI 2013/113) |
| | | 1 Apr 2013 (otherwise) (SI 2013/423) |
| | para 9 | 24 Jan 2013 (in so far as it relates to the preparation of a statement of policy) (SI 2013/113) |
| | | 1 Apr 2013 (otherwise) (SI 2013/423) |
| | paras 10–25 | 1 Apr 2013 (SI 2013/423) |
| Sch 13 | para 1 | 1 Apr 2013 (SI 2013/423) |
| | para 2 | 24 Jan 2013 (in so far as relates to the issue of a code of practice under the Financial Services and Markets Act 2000, s 339A) (SI 2013/113) |
| | | 1 Apr 2013 (otherwise) (SI 2013/423) |
| | paras 3–6 | 1 Apr 2013 (SI 2013/423) |
| | para 7 | 24 Jan 2013 (in so far as relates to the preparation and issue of a statement of policy under the Financial Services and Markets Act 2000, s 345D) (SI 2013/113) |

**Financial Services Act 2012 (c 21)**—*contd*

|  |  |  |
|---|---|---|
|  |  | 1 Apr 2013 (otherwise) (SI 2013/423) |
|  | para 8 | 1 Apr 2013 (SI 2013/423) |
| Sch 14 |  | 1 Apr 2013 (SI 2013/423) |
| Sch 15 | paras 1–6 | 24 Jan 2013 (for the purpose of the making of rules) (SI 2013/113) |
|  |  | 1 Apr 2013 (otherwise) (SI 2013/423) |
|  | para 7 | 24 Jan 2013 (for the purposes of the preparation of a memorandum under the Financial Services and Markets Act 2000, Sch 1A, para 6A) (SI 2013/113) |
|  |  | 1 Apr 2013 (otherwise) (SI 2013/423) |
|  | paras 8–16 | 24 Jan 2013 (for the purpose of the making of rules) (SI 2013/113) |
|  |  | 1 Apr 2013 (otherwise) (SI 2013/423) |
| Schs 16, 17 |  | 1 Apr 2013 (SI 2013/423) |
| Sch 18 | paras 1–4 | 1 Apr 2013 (SI 2013/423) |
|  | para 5 | 24 Jan 2013 (for the purposes of making orders or regulations) (SI 2013/113) |
|  |  | 1 Apr 2013 (otherwise) (SI 2013/423) |
|  | paras 6–9 | 1 Apr 2013 (SI 2013/423) |
|  | para 10 | 24 Jan 2013 (in so far as relates to the preparation and issue of a statement of policy under the Financial Services and Markets Act 2000, s 345D, as applied by s 249(2) of that Act) (SI 2013/113) |
|  |  | 1 Apr 2013 (otherwise) (SI 2013/423) |
|  | paras 11–144 | 1 Apr 2013 (SI 2013/423) |
| Sch 19 |  | 1 Apr 2013 (SI 2013/423) |
| Schs 20, 21 |  | 24 Jan 2013 (SI 2013/113) |

**Health and Social Care Act 2012 (c 7)**

*RA:* 27 Mar 2012

*Commencement provisions:* s 306; Health and Social Care Act 2012 (Commencement No 1 and Transitory Provision) Order 2012, SI 2012/1319; Health and Social Care Act 2012 (Commencement No 2 and Transitional, Savings and Transitory Provisions) Order 2012, SI 2012/1831, as amended by SI 2012/2657; Health and Social Care Act 2012 (Commencement No 3, Transitional, Savings and Transitory Provisions and Amendment) Order 2012, SI 2012/2657; Health and Social Care Act 2012 (Commencement No 4, Transitional, Savings and Transitory Provisions) Order 2013, SI 2013/160; Health and Social Care Act 2012 (Commencement No 5, Transitional, Savings and Transitory Provisions) Order 2013, SI 2013/671; Health and Social Care Act 2012 (Commencement No 6) Order 2013, SI 2013/2896; Health and Social Care Act 2012 (Commencement No 7 and Transitory Provision) Order 2014, SI 2014/39; Health and Social Care Act 2012 (Commencement No 8) Order 2014, SI 2014/1454; Health and Social Care Act 2012 (Commencement No 9) Order 2015, SI 2015/409; Health and Social Care Act 2012 (Commencement No 10) Order 2016, SI 2016/81; Health and Social Care Act 2012 (Commencement No 11 and Saving Provision) Order 2018, SI 2018/617

|  |  |
|---|---|
| 1 | 27 Mar 2012 (so far as is necessary for enabling the exercise on or after that date of any power to make an order or regulations or to give directions that is conferred by these provisions or an amendment made by them) (s 306(1)(d)) |
|  | 1 Oct 2012 (in so far as substitutes National Health Service Act 2006, s 1(1) and in so far as relates to the Board's duty under s 1H(2) and (3)(b) thereof) (SI 2012/1831) |
|  | 1 Apr 2013 (otherwise) (SI 2013/160) |
| 2–7 | 27 Mar 2012 (so far as is necessary for enabling the exercise on or after that date of any power to make an order or regulations or to give directions that is conferred by these provisions or an amendment made by them) (s 306(1)(d)) |
|  | 1 Apr 2013 (otherwise) (SI 2013/160) |

**Health and Social Care Act 2012 (c 7)**—*contd*

| | | |
|---|---|---|
| 8 | | 27 Mar 2012 (so far as is necessary for enabling the exercise on or after that date of any power to make an order or regulations or to give directions that is conferred by these provisions or an amendment made by them) (s 306(1)(d)) |
| | | 1 Jun 2012 (otherwise) (SI 2012/1319) |
| 9 | (1) | 27 Mar 2012 (so far as is necessary for enabling the exercise on or after that date of any power to make an order or regulations or to give directions that is conferred by this provision or an amendment made by it) (s 306(1)(d)) |
| | | 1 Oct 2012 (in so far as inserts National Health Service Act 2006, s 1H(1), (2), (3)(b) and (4)) (SI 2012/1831)[2] |
| | | 1 Feb 2013 (in so far as inserts National Health Service Act 2006, s 1H(3)(a)) (SI 2012/2657) |
| | | 1 Apr 2013 (in so far as inserts s 1H(5) of that Act) (SI 2013/160)[4] |
| | (2) | See Sch 1 below |
| 10 | | 27 Mar 2012 (so far as is necessary for enabling the exercise on or after that date of any power to make an order or regulations or to give directions that is conferred by these provisions or an amendment made by them) (s 306(1)(d)) |
| | | 1 Oct 2012 (in so far as inserts National Health Service Act 2006, s 1I(1)) (SI 2012/1831) |
| | | 1 Feb 2013 (in so far as inserts National Health Service Act 2006, s 1I(2), in so far as the function conferred thereby relates to the provision of services for the purposes of the health service in England on or after 1 Apr 2013) (SI 2012/2657) |
| | | 1 Apr 2013 (otherwise) (SI 2013/160)[4] |
| 11, 12 | | 27 Mar 2012 (so far as is necessary for enabling the exercise on or after that date of any power to make an order or regulations or to give directions that is conferred by these provisions or an amendment made by them) (s 306(1)(d)) |
| | | 1 Apr 2013 (otherwise) (SI 2013/160)[4] |
| 13 | (1) | See sub-ss (2)–(7) below |
| | (2)–(5) | 27 Mar 2012 (so far as is necessary for enabling the exercise on or after that date of any power to make an order or regulations or to give directions that is conferred by these provisions or an amendment made by them) (s 306(1)(d)) |
| | | 1 Feb 2013 (in so far as they relate to the provision of services for the purposes of the health service in England on or after 1 Apr 2013) (SI 2012/2657) |
| | | 1 Apr 2013 (otherwise) (SI 2013/160)[4] |
| | (6), (7) | 27 Mar 2012 (so far as is necessary for enabling the exercise on or after that date of any power to make an order or regulations or to give directions that is conferred by these provisions or an amendment made by them) (s 306(1)(d)) |
| | | 1 Apr 2013 (otherwise) (SI 2013/160)[4] |
| | (8) | 27 Mar 2012 (so far as is necessary for enabling the exercise on or after that date of any power to make an order or regulations or to give directions that is conferred by these provisions or an amendment made by them) (s 306(1)(d)) |
| | | 1 Feb 2013 (otherwise) (SI 2012/2657) |
| 14 | | 27 Mar 2012 (so far as is necessary for enabling the exercise on or after that date of any power to make an order or regulations or to give directions that is conferred by these provisions or an amendment made by them) (s 306(1)(d)) |
| | | 1 Feb 2013 (in so far as relates to the provision of services for the purposes of the health service in England on or after 1 Apr 2013) (SI 2012/2657) |
| | | 1 Apr 2013 (otherwise) (SI 2013/160)[4] |

**Health and Social Care Act 2012 (c 7)**—*contd*

| | | |
|---|---|---|
| 15 | | 27 Mar 2012 (so far as is necessary for enabling the exercise on or after that date of any power to make an order or regulations or to give directions that is conferred by these provisions or an amendment made by them) (s 306(1)(d)) |
| | | 1 Feb 2013 (otherwise) (SI 2012/2657) |
| 16 | | 27 Mar 2012 (so far as is necessary for enabling the exercise on or after that date of any power to make an order or regulations or to give directions that is conferred by these provisions or an amendment made by them) (s 306(1)(d)) |
| | | 1 Apr 2013 (otherwise) (SI 2013/160) |
| 17 | (1) | 27 Mar 2012 (so far as is necessary for enabling the exercise on or after that date of any power to make an order or regulations or to give directions that is conferred by these provisions or an amendment made by them) (s 306(1)(d)) |
| | | 1 Apr 2013 (otherwise) (SI 2013/160) |
| | (2) | See sub-ss (3)–(13) below |
| | (3)–(9) | 27 Mar 2012 (so far as is necessary for enabling the exercise on or after that date of any power to make an order or regulations or to give directions that is conferred by these provisions or an amendment made by them) (s 306(1)(d)) |
| | | 1 Apr 2013 (otherwise) (SI 2013/160) |
| | (10) | 27 Mar 2012 (so far as is necessary for enabling the exercise on or after that date of any power to make an order or regulations or to give directions that is conferred by these provisions or an amendment made by them) (s 306(1)(d)) |
| | | 1 Feb 2013 (in so far as relates to the provision of services for the purposes of the health service in England on or after 1 Apr 2013) (SI 2012/2657) |
| | | 1 Apr 2013 (otherwise) (SI 2013/160) |
| | (11), (12) | 27 Mar 2012 (so far as is necessary for enabling the exercise on or after that date of any power to make an order or regulations or to give directions that is conferred by these provisions or an amendment made by them) (s 306(1)(d)) |
| | | 1 Apr 2013 (otherwise) (SI 2013/160) |
| | (13) | 27 Mar 2012 (so far as is necessary for enabling the exercise on or after that date of any power to make an order or regulations or to give directions that is conferred by these provisions or an amendment made by them) (s 306(1)(d)) |
| | | 1 Oct 2012 (in so far as confers powers on the Board) (SI 2012/1831) |
| | | 1 Apr 2013 (otherwise) (SI 2013/160) |
| 18, 19 | | 27 Mar 2012 (so far as is necessary for enabling the exercise on or after that date of any power to make an order or regulations or to give directions that is conferred by these provisions or an amendment made by them) (s 306(1)(d)) |
| | | 1 Apr 2013 (otherwise) (SI 2013/160)[4] |
| 20 | | 27 Mar 2012 (so far as is necessary for enabling the exercise on or after that date of any power to make an order or regulations or to give directions that is conferred by these provisions or an amendment made by them) (s 306(1)(d)) |
| | | 1 Feb 2013 (otherwise) (SI 2012/2657) |
| 21 | | 27 Mar 2012 (so far as is necessary for enabling the exercise on or after that date of any power to make an order or regulations or to give directions that is conferred by these provisions or an amendment made by them) (s 306(1)(d)) |
| | | 1 Oct 2012 (otherwise) (SI 2012/1831) |
| 22 | | 27 Mar 2012 (so far as is necessary for enabling the exercise on or after that date of any power to make an order or regulations or to give directions that is conferred by these provisions or an amendment made by them) (s 306(1)(d)) |
| | | 1 Oct 2012 (SI 2012/1831), for the purpose of— |

**Health and Social Care Act 2012 (c 7)**—*contd*

(a) enabling the Secretary of State to arrange for the Board or a clinical commissioning group to exercise public health functions of the Secretary of State on or after the date on which this section comes fully into force; and

(b) enabling the Board to arrange for a clinical commissioning group to exercise public health functions under National Health Service Act 2006, s 7A(4) on or after the date on which this section comes fully into force

1 Apr 2013 (otherwise) (SI 2013/160)[4]

23     27 Mar 2012 (so far as is necessary for enabling the exercise on or after that date of any power to make an order or regulations or to give directions that is conferred by these provisions or an amendment made by them) (s 306(1)(d))

1 Oct 2012 (SI 2012/1831)[2], in so far as inserts the following provisions of the National Health Service Act 2006—

ss 13A–13D, 13E(1)–(3), (4)(a), 13F–13J, 13K(1), 13L, 13N, 13P, 13R;

s 13T (for the purpose only of the first business plan of the Board for the financial year ending 31 Mar 2014 and subsequent financial years);

s 13U (except sub-s (2)(c));

ss 13W, 13Y, 13Z–13Z3; and

s 13Z4 (except in so far as definition "health services" relates to s 13Q)

1 Feb 2013 (in so far as inserts National Health Service Act 2006, ss 13O, 13Q) (SI 2012/2657)

1 Apr 2013 (otherwise) (SI 2013/160)[4]

24     27 Mar 2012 (so far as is necessary for enabling the exercise on or after that date of any power to make an order or regulations or to give directions that is conferred by these provisions or an amendment made by them) (s 306(1)(d))

1 Oct 2012 (in so far as inserts National Health Service Act 2006, s 223B(2) and (3)) (SI 2012/1831)

1 Apr 2013 (otherwise) (SI 2013/160)[4]

25     (1)     27 Mar 2012 (so far as is necessary for enabling the exercise on or after that date of any power to make an order or regulations or to give directions that is conferred by this provision or an amendment made by it) (s 306(1)(d))

1 Oct 2012 (except in so far as inserts National Health Service Act 2006, s 14I) (SI 2012/1831)[2]

1 Apr 2013 (exception noted above) (SI 2013/160)[4]

(2)     See Sch 2 below

26     27 Mar 2012 (so far as is necessary for enabling the exercise on or after that date of any power to make an order or regulations or to give directions that is conferred by these provisions or an amendment made by them) (s 306(1)(d))

1 Oct 2012 (SI 2012/1831)[2], in so far as inserts the following provisions of the National Health Service Act 2006—

ss 14P–14R, 14T–14Y, 14Z1;

s 14Z3(1), (2), (6), (7) (except in so far as sub-s (7) relates to s 14Z9);

ss 14Z4(1), 14Z5(2) and 14Z7(7) (for the purpose of Sch 6, para 11(2) only);

s 14Z7(7) (in so far as relates to s 14Z8);

ss 14Z8, 14Z10;

ss 14Z11 and 14Z12 (for the purpose only of a clinical commissioning group preparing a plan for the financial year ending 31 Mar 2014, and subsequent financial years); and

ss 14Z13(1), (2), (8)(a), (b), 14Z17–14Z20, 14Z21(1)–(10), (14), 14Z22–14Z24(1) (except in so far as definition "health services" in s 14Z24(1) relates to s 14Z2)

**Health and Social Care Act 2012 (c 7)**—*contd*

|  |  |  |
|---|---|---|
|  |  | 1 Feb 2013 (in so far as inserts National Health Service Act 2006, ss 14Z2, 14Z7(1), (6), (7)) (SI 2012/2657) |
|  |  | 1 Apr 2013 (otherwise) (SI 2013/160)[4] |
| 27 |  | 27 Mar 2012 (so far as is necessary for enabling the exercise on or after that date of any power to make an order or regulations or to give directions that is conferred by these provisions or an amendment made by them) (s 306(1)(d)) |
|  |  | 1 Oct 2012 (SI 2012/1831), in so far as inserts the following provisions of the National Health Service Act 2006— |
|  |  | s 223G(3) (for the purpose only of notifying a clinical commissioning group of its allotment for the financial year ending 31 Mar 2014 and subsequent financial years), s 223G(4) and (5) (in relation to any such allotment); |
|  |  | s 223I(2), (3), (6) (and s 223I(1) in so far as relates thereto) |
|  |  | 1 Apr 2013 (otherwise) (SI 2013/160)[4] |
| 28–34 |  | 27 Mar 2012 (so far as is necessary for enabling the exercise on or after that date of any power to make an order or regulations or to give directions that is conferred by these provisions or an amendment made by them) (s 306(1)(d)) |
|  |  | 1 Apr 2013 (otherwise) (SI 2013/160)[4] |
| 35 | (1)–(5) | 27 Mar 2012 (so far as is necessary for enabling the exercise on or after that date of any power to make an order or regulations or to give directions that is conferred by these provisions or an amendment made by them) (s 306(1)(d)) |
|  |  | 1 Apr 2013 (otherwise) (E) (SI 2013/160) |
|  |  | *Not yet in force* (otherwise) (W) (SI 2013/160) |
|  | (6) | 27 Mar 2012 (so far as is necessary for enabling the exercise on or after that date of any power to make an order or regulations or to give directions that is conferred by these provisions or an amendment made by them) (s 306(1)(d)) |
|  |  | *Not yet in force* (otherwise) |
|  | (7)–(14) | 27 Mar 2012 (so far as is necessary for enabling the exercise on or after that date of any power to make an order or regulations or to give directions that is conferred by these provisions or an amendment made by them) (s 306(1)(d)) |
|  |  | 1 Apr 2013 (otherwise) (E) (SI 2013/160) |
|  |  | *Not yet in force* (otherwise) (W) (SI 2013/160) |
| 36, 37 |  | 27 Mar 2012 (so far as is necessary for enabling the exercise on or after that date of any power to make an order or regulations or to give directions that is conferred by these provisions or an amendment made by them) (s 306(1)(d)) |
|  |  | 1 Apr 2013 (otherwise) (E) (SI 2013/160) |
|  |  | *Not yet in force* (otherwise) (W) (SI 2013/160) |
| 38 |  | 27 Mar 2012 (so far as is necessary for enabling the exercise on or after that date of any power to make an order or regulations or to give directions that is conferred by these provisions or an amendment made by them) (s 306(1)(d)) |
|  |  | 1 Apr 2013 (otherwise) (SI 2013/160)[4] |
| 39 |  | 27 Mar 2012 (so far as is necessary for enabling the exercise on or after that date of any power to make an order or regulations or to give directions that is conferred by these provisions or an amendment made by them) (s 306(1)(d)) |
|  |  | 1 Jul 2012 (otherwise) (SI 2012/1319) |
| 40 | (1)–(4) | 27 Mar 2012 (so far as is necessary for enabling the exercise on or after that date of any power to make an order or regulations or to give directions that is conferred by these provisions or an amendment made by them) (s 306(1)(d)) |
|  |  | 1 Feb 2013 (in so far as they relate to the provision of after-care services for the purposes of the health service in England on or after 1 Apr 2013) (SI 2012/2657) |
|  |  | 1 Apr 2013 (otherwise) (SI 2013/160)[4] |

**Health and Social Care Act 2012 (c 7)**—*contd*

| | | |
|---|---|---|
| (5)–(7) | | 27 Mar 2012 (so far as is necessary for enabling the exercise on or after that date of any power to make an order or regulations or to give directions that is conferred by these provisions or an amendment made by them) (s 306(1)(d)) |
| | | 1 Apr 2013 (otherwise) (SI 2013/160) |
| (8) | | 27 Mar 2012 (so far as is necessary for enabling the exercise on or after that date of any power to make an order or regulations or to give directions that is conferred by these provisions or an amendment made by them) (s 306(1)(d)) |
| | | 1 Feb 2013 (in so far as relates to the provision of after-care services for the purposes of the health service in England on or after 1 Apr 2013) (SI 2012/2657) |
| | | 1 Apr 2013 (otherwise) (SI 2013/160)[4] |
| 41 | | 27 Mar 2012 (so far as is necessary for enabling the exercise on or after that date of any power to make an order or regulations or to give directions that is conferred by these provisions or an amendment made by them) (s 306(1)(d)) |
| | | 1 Apr 2013 (otherwise) (SI 2013/160) |
| 42 | | 27 Mar 2012 (so far as is necessary for enabling the exercise on or after that date of any power to make an order or regulations or to give directions that is conferred by these provisions or an amendment made by them) (s 306(1)(d)) |
| | | 1 Jul 2012 (otherwise) (SI 2012/1319) |
| 43 | | 27 Mar 2012 (so far as is necessary for enabling the exercise on or after that date of any power to make an order or regulations or to give directions that is conferred by these provisions or an amendment made by them) (s 306(1)(d)) |
| | | 1 Apr 2013 (otherwise) (SI 2013/160)[4] |
| 44 | | 27 Mar 2012 (so far as is necessary for enabling the exercise on or after that date of any power to make an order or regulations or to give directions that is conferred by these provisions or an amendment made by them) (s 306(1)(d)) |
| | | 1 Jul 2012 (otherwise) (SI 2012/1319) |
| 45–50 | | 27 Mar 2012 (so far as is necessary for enabling the exercise on or after that date of any power to make an order or regulations or to give directions that is conferred by these provisions or an amendment made by them) (s 306(1)(d)) |
| | | 1 Apr 2013 (otherwise) (SI 2013/160)[4] |
| 51 | (1) | 27 Mar 2012 (so far as is necessary for enabling the exercise on or after that date of any power to make an order or regulations or to give directions that is conferred by this provision or an amendment made by it) (s 306(1)(d)) |
| | | 1 Apr 2013 (otherwise) (SI 2013/160)[4] |
| | (2) | See Sch 3 below |
| 52–54 | | 27 Mar 2012 (so far as is necessary for enabling the exercise on or after that date of any power to make an order or regulations or to give directions that is conferred by these provisions or an amendment made by them) (s 306(1)(d)) |
| | | 1 Apr 2013 (otherwise) (SI 2013/160)[4] |
| 55 | (1) | See Sch 4 below |
| | (2) | See Sch 5 below |
| | (3) | See Sch 6 below |
| 56 | (1)–(3) | 27 Mar 2012 (so far as is necessary for enabling the exercise on or after that date of any power to make an order or regulations or to give directions that is conferred by these provisions or an amendment made by them) (s 306(1)(d)) |
| | | 1 Apr 2013 (otherwise) (SI 2013/160)[4] |
| | (4) | See Sch 7 below |

**Health and Social Care Act 2012 (c 7)**—*contd*

| | | |
|---|---|---|
| 57, 58 | | 27 Mar 2012 (so far as is necessary for enabling the exercise on or after that date of any power to make an order or regulations or to give directions that is conferred by these provisions or an amendment made by them) (s 306(1)(d)) |
| | | 1 Apr 2013 (otherwise) (SI 2013/160) |
| 59 | | 27 Mar 2012 (so far as is necessary for enabling the exercise on or after that date of any power to make an order or regulations or to give directions that is conferred by these provisions or an amendment made by them) (s 306(1)(d)) |
| | | 1 Jul 2012 (otherwise) (SI 2012/1319) |
| 60 | | 27 Mar 2012 (so far as is necessary for enabling the exercise on or after that date of any power to make an order or regulations or to give directions that is conferred by these provisions or an amendment made by them) (s 306(1)(d)) |
| | | 1 Apr 2013 (otherwise) (SI 2013/160)[4] |
| 61 | (1) | 27 Mar 2012 (so far as is necessary for enabling the exercise on or after that date of any power to make an order or regulations or to give directions that is conferred by this provision or an amendment made by it) (s 306(1)(d)) |
| | | 1 Jul 2012 (otherwise) (SI 2012/1319) |
| | (2) | See Sch 8 below |
| 62 | (1)–(5), (6)(a) | 27 Mar 2012 (so far as is necessary for enabling the exercise on or after that date of any power to make an order or regulations or to give directions that is conferred by these provisions or an amendment made by them) (s 306(1)(d)) |
| | | 1 Nov 2012 (except in so far as they relate to Monitor's functions under National Health Service Act 2006, Pt 2, Chapter 5) (SI 2012/2657) |
| | | 1 Apr 2013 (exception noted above) (SI 2013/160) |
| | (6)(b) | 27 Mar 2012 (so far as is necessary for enabling the exercise on or after that date of any power to make an order or regulations or to give directions that is conferred by these provisions or an amendment made by them) (s 306(1)(d)) |
| | | 1 Apr 2013 (otherwise) (SI 2013/160) |
| | (7)–(11) | 27 Mar 2012 (so far as is necessary for enabling the exercise on or after that date of any power to make an order or regulations or to give directions that is conferred by these provisions or an amendment made by them) (s 306(1)(d)) |
| | | 1 Nov 2012 (except in so far as they relate to Monitor's functions under National Health Service Act 2006, Pt 2, Chapter 5) (SI 2012/2657) |
| | | 1 Apr 2013 (exception noted above) (SI 2013/160) |
| 63 | | 27 Mar 2012 (so far as is necessary for enabling the exercise on or after that date of any power to make an order or regulations or to give directions that is conferred by these provisions or an amendment made by them) (s 306(1)(d)) |
| | | 1 Nov 2012 (otherwise) (SI 2012/2657) |
| 64 | (1) | See sub-ss (2)–(6) below |
| | (2) | 27 Mar 2012 (so far as is necessary for enabling the exercise on or after that date of any power to make an order or regulations or to give directions that is conferred by these provisions or an amendment made by them) (s 306(1)(d)) |
| | | 1 Nov 2012 (otherwise) (SI 2012/2657) |
| | (3)–(5) | 27 Mar 2012 (so far as is necessary for enabling the exercise on or after that date of any power to make an order or regulations or to give directions that is conferred by these provisions or an amendment made by them) (s 306(1)(d)) |
| | | 1 Jun 2012 (so far as relating to s 8 of this Act) (SI 2012/1319) |
| | | 1 Jul 2012 (otherwise) (SI 2012/1319) |

**Health and Social Care Act 2012 (c 7)**—*contd*

| | | |
|---|---|---|
| | (6) | 27 Mar 2012 (so far as is necessary for enabling the exercise on or after that date of any power to make an order or regulations or to give directions that is conferred by these provisions or an amendment made by them) (s 306(1)(d)) |
| | | 1 Nov 2012 (otherwise) (SI 2012/2657) |
| 65 | | 27 Mar 2012 (so far as is necessary for enabling the exercise on or after that date of any power to make an order or regulations or to give directions that is conferred by these provisions or an amendment made by them) (s 306(1)(d)) |
| | | *Not yet in force* (otherwise) |
| 66 | | 27 Mar 2012 (so far as is necessary for enabling the exercise on or after that date of any power to make an order or regulations or to give directions that is conferred by these provisions or an amendment made by them) (s 306(1)(d)) |
| | | 1 Nov 2012 (except in so far as relates to Monitor's functions under National Health Service Act 2006, Pt 2, Chapter 5) (SI 2012/2657) |
| | | 1 Apr 2013 (exception noted above) (SI 2013/671) |
| 67 | (1) | 27 Mar 2012 (so far as is necessary for enabling the exercise on or after that date of any power to make an order or regulations or to give directions that is conferred by these provisions or an amendment made by them) (s 306(1)(d)) |
| | | 1 Nov 2012 (otherwise) (SI 2012/2657) |
| | (2)(a) | 27 Mar 2012 (so far as is necessary for enabling the exercise on or after that date of any power to make an order or regulations or to give directions that is conferred by these provisions or an amendment made by them) (s 306(1)(d)) |
| | | 1 Nov 2012 (otherwise) (SI 2012/2657)[3] |
| | (2)(b) | 27 Mar 2012 (so far as is necessary for enabling the exercise on or after that date of any power to make an order or regulations or to give directions that is conferred by these provisions or an amendment made by them) (s 306(1)(d)) |
| | | 1 Nov 2012 (otherwise) (SI 2012/2657) |
| | (3) | 27 Mar 2012 (so far as is necessary for enabling the exercise on or after that date of any power to make an order or regulations or to give directions that is conferred by these provisions or an amendment made by them) (s 306(1)(d)) |
| | | 1 Apr 2013 (otherwise) (SI 2013/671) |
| | (4)–(9) | 27 Mar 2012 (so far as is necessary for enabling the exercise on or after that date of any power to make an order or regulations or to give directions that is conferred by these provisions or an amendment made by them) (s 306(1)(d)) |
| | | 1 Nov 2012 (otherwise) (SI 2012/2657) |
| 68 | (1)–(3) | 27 Mar 2012 (so far as is necessary for enabling the exercise on or after that date of any power to make an order or regulations or to give directions that is conferred by these provisions or an amendment made by them) (s 306(1)(d)) |
| | | 1 Nov 2012 (except in so far as relate to Monitor's functions under National Health Service Act 2006, Pt 2, Chapter 5) (SI 2012/2657) |
| | | 1 Apr 2013 (exception noted above) (SI 2013/671) |
| | (4)–(8) | 27 Mar 2012 (so far as is necessary for enabling the exercise on or after that date of any power to make an order or regulations or to give directions that is conferred by these provisions or an amendment made by them) (s 306(1)(d)) |
| | | 1 Apr 2013 (otherwise) (SI 2013/671) |
| 69 | | 27 Mar 2012 (so far as is necessary for enabling the exercise on or after that date of any power to make an order or regulations or to give directions that is conferred by these provisions or an amendment made by them) (s 306(1)(d)) |
| | | 1 Apr 2013 (otherwise) (SI 2013/671) |

**Health and Social Care Act 2012 (c 7)**—*contd*

| | | |
|---|---|---|
| 70 | | 27 Mar 2012 (so far as is necessary for enabling the exercise on or after that date of any power to make an order or regulations or to give directions that is conferred by these provisions or an amendment made by them) (s 306(1)(d)) |
| | | 1 Nov 2012 (otherwise) (SI 2012/2657) |
| 71 | | 27 Mar 2012 (so far as is necessary for enabling the exercise on or after that date of any power to make an order or regulations or to give directions that is conferred by these provisions or an amendment made by them) (s 306(1)(d)) |
| | | 1 Nov 2012 (otherwise) (SI 2012/2657)[3] |
| 72, 73 | | 27 Mar 2012 (so far as is necessary for enabling the exercise on or after that date of any power to make an order or regulations or to give directions that is conferred by these provisions or an amendment made by them) (s 306(1)(d)) |
| | | 1 Apr 2013 (otherwise) (SI 2013/160) |
| 74 | (1)–(6) | 27 Mar 2012 (so far as is necessary for enabling the exercise on or after that date of any power to make an order or regulations or to give directions that is conferred by these provisions or an amendment made by them) (s 306(1)(d)) |
| | | 1 Apr 2013 (otherwise) (SI 2013/160) |
| | (7) | 27 Mar 2012 (so far as is necessary for enabling the exercise on or after that date of any power to make an order or regulations or to give directions that is conferred by these provisions or an amendment made by them) (s 306(1)(d)) |
| | | 1 Apr 2013 (otherwise) (SI 2013/671) |
| 75, 76 | | 27 Mar 2012 (so far as is necessary for enabling the exercise on or after that date of any power to make an order or regulations or to give directions that is conferred by these provisions or an amendment made by them) (s 306(1)(d)) |
| | | 1 Apr 2013 (otherwise) (SI 2013/160)[4] |
| 77 | (1)–(4) | 27 Mar 2012 (so far as is necessary for enabling the exercise on or after that date of any power to make an order or regulations or to give directions that is conferred by these provisions or an amendment made by them) (s 306(1)(d)) |
| | | 1 Apr 2013 (otherwise) (SI 2013/160) |
| | (5) | See Sch 9 below |
| 78 | (1) | 27 Mar 2012 (so far as is necessary for enabling the exercise on or after that date of any power to make an order or regulations or to give directions that is conferred by these provisions or an amendment made by them) (s 306(1)(d)) |
| | | 1 Feb 2013 (otherwise) (SI 2012/2657)[3] |
| | (2)–(5) | 27 Mar 2012 (so far as is necessary for enabling the exercise on or after that date of any power to make an order or regulations or to give directions that is conferred by these provisions or an amendment made by them) (s 306(1)(d)) |
| | | 1 Feb 2013 (otherwise) (SI 2012/2657) |
| 79 | | 27 Mar 2012 (so far as is necessary for enabling the exercise on or after that date of any power to make an order or regulations or to give directions that is conferred by these provisions or an amendment made by them) (s 306(1)(d)) |
| | | 1 Jul 2012 (otherwise) (SI 2012/1319) |
| 80 | | 27 Mar 2012 (so far as is necessary for enabling the exercise on or after that date of any power to make an order or regulations or to give directions that is conferred by these provisions or an amendment made by them) (s 306(1)(d)) |
| | | 1 Apr 2013 (otherwise) (SI 2013/160) |
| 81 | | 27 Mar 2012 (so far as is necessary for enabling the exercise on or after that date of any power to make an order or regulations or to give directions that is conferred by these provisions or an amendment made by them) (s 306(1)(d)) |

**Health and Social Care Act 2012 (c 7)**—*contd*

|  |  | 1 Apr 2013 (in so far as relates to NHS foundation trusts) (SI 2013/671) |
|---|---|---|
|  |  | 1 Apr 2014 (otherwise) (SI 2014/39) |
| 82 |  | 27 Mar 2012 (so far as is necessary for enabling the exercise on or after that date of any power to make an order or regulations or to give directions that is conferred by these provisions or an amendment made by them) (s 306(1)(d)) |
|  |  | 1 Apr 2013 (otherwise) (SI 2013/671) |
| 83, 84 |  | 27 Mar 2012 (so far as is necessary for enabling the exercise on or after that date of any power to make an order or regulations or to give directions that is conferred by these provisions or an amendment made by them) (s 306(1)(d)) |
|  |  | 1 Apr 2014 (otherwise) (SI 2014/39) |
| 85, 86 |  | 27 Mar 2012 (so far as is necessary for enabling the exercise on or after that date of any power to make an order or regulations or to give directions that is conferred by these provisions or an amendment made by them) (s 306(1)(d)) |
|  |  | 1 Apr 2013 (in so far as they relate to licences for NHS foundation trusts) (SI 2013/671) |
|  |  | 1 Jan 2014 (otherwise) (SI 2013/2896) |
| 87 |  | 27 Mar 2012 (so far as is necessary for enabling the exercise on or after that date of any power to make an order or regulations or to give directions that is conferred by these provisions or an amendment made by them) (s 306(1)(d)) |
|  |  | 1 Apr 2013 (in so far as they relate to licences for NHS foundation trusts) (SI 2013/671) |
|  |  | 1 Apr 2014 (otherwise) (SI 2014/39) |
| 88, 89 |  | 27 Mar 2012 (so far as is necessary for enabling the exercise on or after that date of any power to make an order or regulations or to give directions that is conferred by these provisions or an amendment made by them) (s 306(1)(d)) |
|  |  | 1 Apr 2013 (otherwise) (SI 2013/671)[5] |
| 90 | (1)(a) | 27 Mar 2012 (so far as is necessary for enabling the exercise on or after that date of any power to make an order or regulations or to give directions that is conferred by these provisions or an amendment made by them) (s 306(1)(d)) |
|  |  | 1 Apr 2014 (otherwise) (SI 2014/39) |
|  | (1)(b), (2), (3) | 27 Mar 2012 (so far as is necessary for enabling the exercise on or after that date of any power to make an order or regulations or to give directions that is conferred by these provisions or an amendment made by them) (s 306(1)(d)) |
|  |  | 1 Apr 2013 (otherwise) (SI 2013/671)[5] |
| 91 | (1)(a) | 27 Mar 2012 (so far as is necessary for enabling the exercise on or after that date of any power to make an order or regulations or to give directions that is conferred by these provisions or an amendment made by them) (s 306(1)(d)) |
|  |  | 1 Apr 2014 (otherwise) (SI 2014/39) |
|  | (1)(b), (2)–(4) | 27 Mar 2012 (so far as is necessary for enabling the exercise on or after that date of any power to make an order or regulations or to give directions that is conferred by these provisions or an amendment made by them) (s 306(1)(d)) |
|  |  | 1 Apr 2013 (otherwise) (SI 2013/671)[5] |
| 92 | (1)(a) | 27 Mar 2012 (so far as is necessary for enabling the exercise on or after that date of any power to make an order or regulations or to give directions that is conferred by these provisions or an amendment made by them) (s 306(1)(d)) |
|  |  | 1 Apr 2014 (otherwise) (SI 2014/39) |
|  | (1)(b), (2), (3) | 27 Mar 2012 (so far as is necessary for enabling the exercise on or after that date of any power to make an order or regulations or to give directions that is conferred by these provisions or an amendment made by them) (s 306(1)(d)) |

**Health and Social Care Act 2012 (c 7)**—*contd*

|  |  | 1 Apr 2013 (otherwise) (SI 2013/671)[5] |
| 93 |  | 27 Mar 2012 (so far as is necessary for enabling the exercise on or after that date of any power to make an order or regulations or to give directions that is conferred by these provisions or an amendment made by them) (s 306(1)(d)) |
|  |  | 1 Apr 2013 (otherwise) (SI 2013/671)[5] |
| 94 | (1)–(6) | 27 Mar 2012 (so far as is necessary for enabling the exercise on or after that date of any power to make an order or regulations or to give directions that is conferred by these provisions or an amendment made by them) (s 306(1)(d)) |
|  |  | 1 Nov 2012 (in so far as relate to the preparation of, and consultation on, draft standard conditions under s 94(7) of this Act, and publication of those conditions under s 94(9)) (SI 2012/2657) |
|  |  | 1 Apr 2013 (otherwise) (SI 2013/671) |
|  | (7)–(10) | 27 Mar 2012 (so far as is necessary for enabling the exercise on or after that date of any power to make an order or regulations or to give directions that is conferred by these provisions or an amendment made by them) (s 306(1)(d)) |
|  |  | 1 Nov 2012 (otherwise) (SI 2012/2657) |
|  | (11)(a) | 27 Mar 2012 (so far as is necessary for enabling the exercise on or after that date of any power to make an order or regulations or to give directions that is conferred by these provisions or an amendment made by them) (s 306(1)(d)) |
|  |  | 1 Apr 2013 (otherwise) (SI 2013/671) |
|  | (11)(b), (c) | 27 Mar 2012 (so far as is necessary for enabling the exercise on or after that date of any power to make an order or regulations or to give directions that is conferred by these provisions or an amendment made by them) (s 306(1)(d)) |
|  |  | 1 Nov 2012 (otherwise) (SI 2012/2657) |
| 95 | (1)(a) | 27 Mar 2012 (so far as is necessary for enabling the exercise on or after that date of any power to make an order or regulations or to give directions that is conferred by these provisions or an amendment made by them) (s 306(1)(d)) |
|  |  | 1 Nov 2012 (for the purpose of enabling Monitor to take steps under this section to enable it to include a special condition in the licence of an NHS foundation trust from the date upon which s 81(1) comes into force in relation to NHS foundation trusts) (SI 2012/2657)[3] |
|  |  | 1 Apr 2013 (otherwise) (SI 2013/671) |
|  | (1)(b) | 27 Mar 2012 (so far as is necessary for enabling the exercise on or after that date of any power to make an order or regulations or to give directions that is conferred by these provisions or an amendment made by them) (s 306(1)(d)) |
|  |  | 1 Nov 2012 (for the purpose of enabling Monitor to take steps under this section to enable it to include a special condition in the licence of an NHS foundation trust from the date upon which s 81(1) comes into force in relation to NHS foundation trusts) (SI 2012/2657)[3] |
|  |  | 1 Jul 2013 (otherwise) (SI 2013/671) |
|  | (2)–(5) | 27 Mar 2012 (so far as is necessary for enabling the exercise on or after that date of any power to make an order or regulations or to give directions that is conferred by these provisions or an amendment made by them) (s 306(1)(d)) |
|  |  | 1 Nov 2012 (for the purpose of enabling Monitor to take steps under this section to enable it to include a special condition in the licence of an NHS foundation trust from the date upon which s 81(1) comes into force in relation to NHS foundation trusts) (SI 2012/2657)[3] |
|  |  | 1 Apr 2013 (otherwise) (SI 2013/671)[5] |

**Health and Social Care Act 2012 (c 7)**—*contd*

| | | |
|---|---|---|
| | (6) | 27 Mar 2012 (so far as is necessary for enabling the exercise on or after that date of any power to make an order or regulations or to give directions that is conferred by these provisions or an amendment made by them) (s 306(1)(d)) |
| | | 1 Nov 2012 (for the purpose of enabling Monitor to take steps under this section to enable it to include a special condition in the licence of an NHS foundation trust from the date upon which s 81(1) comes into force in relation to NHS foundation trusts) (SI 2012/2657)[3] |
| | | 1 Jul 2013 (otherwise) (SI 2013/671) |
| 96 | | 27 Mar 2012 (so far as is necessary for enabling the exercise on or after that date of any power to make an order or regulations or to give directions that is conferred by these provisions or an amendment made by them) (s 306(1)(d)) |
| | | 1 Nov 2012 (in so far as relates to functions under sub-s (1)(a), (b), but note that sub-s (2)(a) is brought into force only for the purpose of regulating the price payable for the provision of healthcare services for the purpose of the NHS in accordance with the national tariff to be published by Monitor under s 116(1)) (SI 2012/2657) |
| | | 1 Jul 2013 (sub-s (1)(c) only) (SI 2013/671) |
| | | 1 Apr 2014 (otherwise) (SI 2014/39) |
| 97 | | 27 Mar 2012 (so far as is necessary for enabling the exercise on or after that date of any power to make an order or regulations or to give directions that is conferred by these provisions or an amendment made by them) (s 306(1)(d)) |
| | | 1 Nov 2012 (in so far as relates to the preparation of, and consultation on, draft standard conditions under s 94(7) of this Act and publication of those conditions under s 94(9), and to special conditions under s 95) (SI 2012/2657) |
| | | 1 Apr 2013 (otherwise) (SI 2013/671) |
| 98 | (1), (2) | 27 Mar 2012 (so far as is necessary for enabling the exercise on or after that date of any power to make an order or regulations or to give directions that is conferred by these provisions or an amendment made by them) (s 306(1)(d)) |
| | | 1 Nov 2012 (in so far as they relate to the preparation of, and consultation on, draft standard conditions under s 94(7) of this Act, and publication of those conditions under s 94(9), and to special conditions under s 95) (SI 2012/2657) |
| | | 1 Apr 2013 (otherwise) (SI 2013/671) |
| | (3) | 27 Mar 2012 (so far as is necessary for enabling the exercise on or after that date of any power to make an order or regulations or to give directions that is conferred by these provisions or an amendment made by them) (s 306(1)(d)) |
| | | 1 Apr 2013 (otherwise) (SI 2013/671) |
| | (4) | 27 Mar 2012 (so far as is necessary for enabling the exercise on or after that date of any power to make an order or regulations or to give directions that is conferred by these provisions or an amendment made by them) (s 306(1)(d)) |
| | | 1 Nov 2012 (otherwise) (SI 2012/2657)[3] |
| | (5), (6) | 27 Mar 2012 (so far as is necessary for enabling the exercise on or after that date of any power to make an order or regulations or to give directions that is conferred by these provisions or an amendment made by them) (s 306(1)(d)) |
| | | 1 Apr 2013 (otherwise) (SI 2013/671) |
| | (7) | 27 Mar 2012 (so far as is necessary for enabling the exercise on or after that date of any power to make an order or regulations or to give directions that is conferred by these provisions or an amendment made by them) (s 306(1)(d)) |
| | | 1 Nov 2012 (otherwise) (SI 2012/2657) |

**Health and Social Care Act 2012 (c 7)**—*contd*

| | | |
|---|---|---|
| 99 | | 27 Mar 2012 (so far as is necessary for enabling the exercise on or after that date of any power to make an order or regulations or to give directions that is conferred by these provisions or an amendment made by them) (s 306(1)(d)) |
| | | 1 Apr 2013 (otherwise) (SI 2013/671) |
| 100 | | 27 Mar 2012 (so far as is necessary for enabling the exercise on or after that date of any power to make an order or regulations or to give directions that is conferred by these provisions or an amendment made by them) (s 306(1)(d)) |
| | | 1 Jul 2013 (otherwise) (SI 2013/671) |
| 101 | (1), (2) | 27 Mar 2012 (so far as is necessary for enabling the exercise on or after that date of any power to make an order or regulations or to give directions that is conferred by these provisions or an amendment made by them) (s 306(1)(d)) |
| | | 1 Nov 2012 (except in so far as they relate to licence holders and the inclusion or modification of a special condition in their licence) (SI 2012/2657)[3] |
| | | 1 Jul 2013 (exception noted above) (SI 2013/671) |
| | (3), (4) | 27 Mar 2012 (so far as is necessary for enabling the exercise on or after that date of any power to make an order or regulations or to give directions that is conferred by these provisions or an amendment made by them) (s 306(1)(d)) |
| | | 1 Jul 2013 (otherwise) (SI 2013/671) |
| | (5) | 27 Mar 2012 (so far as is necessary for enabling the exercise on or after that date of any power to make an order or regulations or to give directions that is conferred by these provisions or an amendment made by them) (s 306(1)(d)) |
| | | 1 Nov 2012 (in so far as relates to references under sub-s (2)) (SI 2012/2657)[3] |
| | | 1 Jul 2013 (otherwise) (SI 2013/671) |
| | (6) | 27 Mar 2012 (so far as is necessary for enabling the exercise on or after that date of any power to make an order or regulations or to give directions that is conferred by these provisions or an amendment made by them) (s 306(1)(d)) |
| | | 1 Nov 2012 (in so far as relates to references under sub-s (2)) (SI 2012/2657) |
| | | 1 Jul 2013 (otherwise) (SI 2013/671) |
| | (7) | 27 Mar 2012 (so far as is necessary for enabling the exercise on or after that date of any power to make an order or regulations or to give directions that is conferred by these provisions or an amendment made by them) (s 306(1)(d)) |
| | | 1 Jul 2013 (otherwise) (SI 2013/671) |
| | (8) | 27 Mar 2012 (so far as is necessary for enabling the exercise on or after that date of any power to make an order or regulations or to give directions that is conferred by these provisions or an amendment made by them) (s 306(1)(d)) |
| | | 1 Nov 2012 (otherwise) (SI 2012/2657) |
| 102 | | 27 Mar 2012 (so far as is necessary for enabling the exercise on or after that date of any power to make an order or regulations or to give directions that is conferred by these provisions or an amendment made by them) (s 306(1)(d)) |
| | | 1 Apr 2013 (otherwise) (SI 2013/671) |
| 103 | (1), (2) | 27 Mar 2012 (so far as is necessary for enabling the exercise on or after that date of any power to make an order or regulations or to give directions that is conferred by these provisions or an amendment made by them) (s 306(1)(d)) |
| | | 1 Nov 2012 (in so far as they relate to the preparation of, and consultation on, draft standard conditions under s 94(7) of this Act, and publication of those conditions under s 94(9)) |
| | | 1 Apr 2013 (otherwise, except in so far as relates to Monitor's functions under s 100 and 101(7)) (SI 2013/671) |

**Health and Social Care Act 2012 (c 7)**—*contd*

|  |  |  |
|---|---|---|
|  |  | 1 Jul 2013 (exception noted above) (SI 2013/671) |
|  | (3) | 27 Mar 2012 (so far as is necessary for enabling the exercise on or after that date of any power to make an order or regulations or to give directions that is conferred by these provisions or an amendment made by them) (s 306(1)(d)) |
|  |  | 1 Apr 2013 (otherwise, except in so far as relates to Monitor's functions under s 100 and 101(7)) (SI 2013/671) |
|  |  | 1 Jul 2013 (exception noted above) (SI 2013/671) |
| 104 | (1) | 27 Mar 2012 (so far as is necessary for enabling the exercise on or after that date of any power to make an order or regulations or to give directions that is conferred by these provisions or an amendment made by them) (s 306(1)(d)) |
|  |  | 1 Nov 2012 (otherwise) (SI 2012/2657) |
|  | (2)(a) | 27 Mar 2012 (so far as is necessary for enabling the exercise on or after that date of any power to make an order or regulations or to give directions that is conferred by these provisions or an amendment made by them) (s 306(1)(d)) |
|  |  | 1 Nov 2012 (otherwise) (SI 2012/2657)[3] |
|  | (2)(b) | 27 Mar 2012 (so far as is necessary for enabling the exercise on or after that date of any power to make an order or regulations or to give directions that is conferred by these provisions or an amendment made by them) (s 306(1)(d)) |
|  |  | 1 Apr 2013 (otherwise) (SI 2013/671) |
|  | (2)(c), (d) | 27 Mar 2012 (so far as is necessary for enabling the exercise on or after that date of any power to make an order or regulations or to give directions that is conferred by these provisions or an amendment made by them) (s 306(1)(d)) |
|  |  | 1 Apr 2014 (otherwise) (SI 2014/39) |
|  | (2)(e) | 27 Mar 2012 (so far as is necessary for enabling the exercise on or after that date of any power to make an order or regulations or to give directions that is conferred by these provisions or an amendment made by them) (s 306(1)(d)) |
|  |  | 1 Apr 2013 (otherwise) (SI 2013/160)[4] |
|  | (2)(f), (3), (4)(a) | 27 Mar 2012 (so far as is necessary for enabling the exercise on or after that date of any power to make an order or regulations or to give directions that is conferred by these provisions or an amendment made by them) (s 306(1)(d)) |
|  |  | 1 Nov 2012 (otherwise) (SI 2012/2657) |
|  | (4)(b) | 27 Mar 2012 (so far as is necessary for enabling the exercise on or after that date of any power to make an order or regulations or to give directions that is conferred by these provisions or an amendment made by them) (s 306(1)(d)) |
|  |  | 1 Apr 2013 (in so far as refers to Chapter 4 of Pt 3 of this Act) (SI 2013/160) |
|  |  | 1 Dec 2013 (in so far as relates to Monitor's functions under s 144(3)(b) of this Act) (SI 2013/2896) |
|  |  | 1 Apr 2014 (so far as relates to Monitor's functions under section 144(6) of the Act in respect of a review published pursuant to section 144(3)(b)) (SI 2014/39) |
|  |  | *Not yet in force* (otherwise) |
|  | (4)(c) | 27 Mar 2012 (so far as is necessary for enabling the exercise on or after that date of any power to make an order or regulations or to give directions that is conferred by these provisions or an amendment made by them) (s 306(1)(d)) |
|  |  | 1 Apr 2013 (otherwise) (SI 2013/671) |
|  | (4)(d) | 27 Mar 2012 (so far as is necessary for enabling the exercise on or after that date of any power to make an order or regulations or to give directions that is conferred by these provisions or an amendment made by them) (s 306(1)(d)) |
|  |  | 1 Nov 2012 (otherwise) (SI 2012/2657) |

**Health and Social Care Act 2012 (c 7)**—*contd*

| | | |
|---|---|---|
| 105 | (1)(a) | 27 Mar 2012 (so far as is necessary for enabling the exercise on or after that date of any power to make an order or regulations or to give directions that is conferred by these provisions or an amendment made by them) (s 306(1)(d)) |
| | | 1 Apr 2014 (otherwise) (SI 2014/39) |
| | (1)(b), (c) | 27 Mar 2012 (so far as is necessary for enabling the exercise on or after that date of any power to make an order or regulations or to give directions that is conferred by these provisions or an amendment made by them) (s 306(1)(d)) |
| | | 1 Apr 2013 (otherwise) (SI 2013/671) |
| | (2)(a) | 27 Mar 2012 (so far as is necessary for enabling the exercise on or after that date of any power to make an order or regulations or to give directions that is conferred by these provisions or an amendment made by them) (s 306(1)(d)) |
| | | 1 Jul 2013 (otherwise) (SI 2013/671) |
| | (2)(b), (c), (3) | 27 Mar 2012 (so far as is necessary for enabling the exercise on or after that date of any power to make an order or regulations or to give directions that is conferred by these provisions or an amendment made by them) (s 306(1)(d)) |
| | | 1 Apr 2013 (otherwise) (SI 2013/671) |
| | (4), (5) | 27 Mar 2012 (so far as is necessary for enabling the exercise on or after that date of any power to make an order or regulations or to give directions that is conferred by these provisions or an amendment made by them) (s 306(1)(d)) |
| | | 1 Jul 2013 (otherwise) (SI 2013/671) |
| 106 | | 27 Mar 2012 (so far as is necessary for enabling the exercise on or after that date of any power to make an order or regulations or to give directions that is conferred by these provisions or an amendment made by them) (s 306(1)(d)) |
| | | 1 Apr 2013 (otherwise, except sub-s (1)(a)) (SI 2013/671) |
| | | 1 Apr 2014 (exception noted above) (SI 2014/39) |
| 107 | | See Sch 11 below |
| 108 | (1)–(4) | 27 Mar 2012 (so far as is necessary for enabling the exercise on or after that date of any power to make an order or regulations or to give directions that is conferred by these provisions or an amendment made by them) (s 306(1)(d)) |
| | | 1 Nov 2012 (for the purposes of enabling Monitor to prepare and consult on the first draft guidance under this section) (SI 2012/2657) |
| | | 1 Apr 2013 (otherwise) (SI 2013/671) |
| | (5) | 27 Mar 2012 (so far as is necessary for enabling the exercise on or after that date of any power to make an order or regulations or to give directions that is conferred by these provisions or an amendment made by them) (s 306(1)(d)) |
| | | 1 Apr 2013 (otherwise) (SI 2013/671) |
| 109–114 | | 27 Mar 2012 (so far as is necessary for enabling the exercise on or after that date of any power to make an order or regulations or to give directions that is conferred by these provisions or an amendment made by them) (s 306(1)(d)) |
| | | 1 Apr 2013 (otherwise) (SI 2013/671) |
| 115 | | 27 Mar 2012 (so far as is necessary for enabling the exercise on or after that date of any power to make an order or regulations or to give directions that is conferred by these provisions or an amendment made by them) (s 306(1)(d)) |
| | | 1 Apr 2014 (otherwise) (SI 2014/39) |
| 116 | | 27 Mar 2012 (so far as is necessary for enabling the exercise on or after that date of any power to make an order or regulations or to give directions that is conferred by these provisions or an amendment made by them) (s 306(1)(d)) |
| | | 1 Apr 2013 (for the purpose of undertaking consultation under ss 118, 119 hereof) (SI 2013/160) |

**Health and Social Care Act 2012 (c 7)**—*contd*

|  |  |  |
|---|---|---|
|  |  | 1 Dec 2013 (otherwise) (SI 2013/2896) |
| 117 | (1)–(3) | 27 Mar 2012 (so far as is necessary for enabling the exercise on or after that date of any power to make an order or regulations or to give directions that is conferred by these provisions or an amendment made by them) (s 306(1)(d)) |
|  |  | 1 Apr 2013 (in so far as relate to the national tariff published by Monitor under s 116, and only in so far as relate to consultation on a proposal for the national tariff pursuant to ss 118, 119 hereof) (SI 2013/160) |
|  |  | 1 Dec 2013 (otherwise) (SI 2013/2896) |
|  | (4), (5) | 27 Mar 2012 (so far as is necessary for enabling the exercise on or after that date of any power to make an order or regulations or to give directions that is conferred by these provisions or an amendment made by them) (s 306(1)(d)) |
|  |  | 1 Apr 2014 (otherwise) (SI 2014/39) |
| 118, 119 |  | 1 Apr 2013 (in so far as relate to the national tariff published by Monitor under s 116 hereof) (SI 2013/160) |
|  |  | 1 Apr 2014 (otherwise) (SI 2014/39) |
| 120–123 |  | 27 Mar 2012 (so far as is necessary for enabling the exercise on or after that date of any power to make an order or regulations or to give directions that is conferred by these provisions or an amendment made by them) (s 306(1)(d)) |
|  |  | 1 Sep 2013 (in so far as they relate to consultation under ss 118, 119 in relation to a tariff published by Monitor under s 116) (SI 2013/671) |
|  |  | 1 Apr 2014 (otherwise) (SI 2014/39) |
| 124, 125 |  | 27 Mar 2012 (so far as is necessary for enabling the exercise on or after that date of any power to make an order or regulations or to give directions that is conferred by these provisions or an amendment made by them) (s 306(1)(d)) |
|  |  | 1 Mar 2014 (otherwise) (SI 2014/39)[8] |
| 126 |  | 27 Mar 2012 (so far as is necessary for enabling the exercise on or after that date of any power to make an order or regulations or to give directions that is conferred by these provisions or an amendment made by them) (s 306(1)(d)) |
|  |  | 1 Mar 2014 (otherwise) (SI 2014/39) |
| 127 |  | 27 Mar 2012 (so far as is necessary for enabling the exercise on or after that date of any power to make an order or regulations or to give directions that is conferred by these provisions or an amendment made by them) (s 306(1)(d)) |
|  |  | 1 Dec 2013 (otherwise) (SI 2013/2896) |
| 128–143 |  | 27 Mar 2012 (so far as is necessary for enabling the exercise on or after that date of any power to make an order or regulations or to give directions that is conferred by these provisions or an amendment made by them) (s 306(1)(d)) |
|  |  | *Not yet in force* (otherwise) |
| 144 | (1), (2), (3)(a) | 27 Mar 2012 (so far as is necessary for enabling the exercise on or after that date of any power to make an order or regulations or to give directions that is conferred by these provisions or an amendment made by them) (s 306(1)(d)) |
|  |  | *Not yet in force* (otherwise) |
|  | (3)(b) | 27 Mar 2012 (so far as is necessary for enabling the exercise on or after that date of any power to make an order or regulations or to give directions that is conferred by these provisions or an amendment made by them) (s 306(1)(d)) |
|  |  | 1 Nov 2012 (otherwise) (SI 2012/2657) |
|  | (3)(c), (4), (5) | 27 Mar 2012 (so far as is necessary for enabling the exercise on or after that date of any power to make an order or regulations or to give directions that is conferred by these provisions or an amendment made by them) (s 306(1)(d)) |
|  |  | *Not yet in force* (otherwise) |

**Health and Social Care Act 2012 (c 7)**—*contd*

| | (6) | 27 Mar 2012 (so far as is necessary for enabling the exercise on or after that date of any power to make an order or regulations or to give directions that is conferred by these provisions or an amendment made by them) (s 306(1)(d)) |
|---|---|---|
| | | 1 Nov 2012 (otherwise) (SI 2012/2657) |
| 145, 146 | | 27 Mar 2012 (so far as is necessary for enabling the exercise on or after that date of any power to make an order or regulations or to give directions that is conferred by these provisions or an amendment made by them) (s 306(1)(d)) |
| | | *Not yet in force* (otherwise) |
| 147 | | 27 Mar 2012 (so far as is necessary for enabling the exercise on or after that date of any power to make an order or regulations or to give directions that is conferred by these provisions or an amendment made by them) (s 306(1)(d)) |
| | | 1 Oct 2012 (in so far as National Health Service Act 2006, ss 6E, 13A, 75 are in force) (SI 2012/1831) |
| | | 1 Apr 2013 (otherwise) (SI 2013/160)[4] |
| 148 | (1)–(5) | 27 Mar 2012 (so far as is necessary for enabling the exercise on or after that date of any power to make an order or regulations or to give directions that is conferred by these provisions or an amendment made by them) (s 306(1)(d)) |
| | | 1 Nov 2012 (otherwise) (SI 2012/2657) |
| | (6)(a) | 27 Mar 2012 (so far as is necessary for enabling the exercise on or after that date of any power to make an order or regulations or to give directions that is conferred by these provisions or an amendment made by them) (s 306(1)(d)) |
| | | 1 Apr 2013 (otherwise) (SI 2013/671) |
| | (6)(b), (7)–(9) | 27 Mar 2012 (so far as is necessary for enabling the exercise on or after that date of any power to make an order or regulations or to give directions that is conferred by these provisions or an amendment made by them) (s 306(1)(d)) |
| | | 1 Nov 2012 (otherwise) (SI 2012/2657) |
| 149 | | 27 Mar 2012 (so far as is necessary for enabling the exercise on or after that date of any power to make an order or regulations or to give directions that is conferred by these provisions or an amendment made by them) (s 306(1)(d)) |
| | | 1 Nov 2012 (otherwise) (SI 2012/2657) |
| 150 | (1) | 27 Mar 2012 (so far as is necessary for enabling the exercise on or after that date of any power to make an order or regulations or to give directions that is conferred by these provisions or an amendment made by them) (s 306(1)(d)) |
| | | 1 Nov 2012 (otherwise) (SI 2012/2657) |
| | (2) | 27 Mar 2012 (so far as is necessary for enabling the exercise on or after that date of any power to make an order or regulations or to give directions that is conferred by these provisions or an amendment made by them) (s 306(1)(d)) |
| | | *Not yet in force* (otherwise) |
| | (3) | 27 Mar 2012 (so far as is necessary for enabling the exercise on or after that date of any power to make an order or regulations or to give directions that is conferred by these provisions or an amendment made by them) (s 306(1)(d)) |
| | | 1 Nov 2012 (otherwise) (SI 2012/2657) |
| | (4) | 27 Mar 2012 (so far as is necessary for enabling the exercise on or after that date of any power to make an order or regulations or to give directions that is conferred by these provisions or an amendment made by them) (s 306(1)(d)) |
| | | *Not yet in force* (otherwise) |
| | (5) | See Sch 13 below |

**Health and Social Care Act 2012 (c 7)**—*contd*

| | | |
|---|---|---|
| 151 | (1) | 27 Mar 2012 (so far as is necessary for enabling the exercise on or after that date of any power to make an order or regulations or to give directions that is conferred by these provisions or an amendment made by them) (s 306(1)(d)) |
| | | 1 Oct 2012 (otherwise) (SI 2012/1831) |
| | (2)–(6) | 27 Mar 2012 (so far as is necessary for enabling the exercise on or after that date of any power to make an order or regulations or to give directions that is conferred by these provisions or an amendment made by them) (s 306(1)(d)) |
| | | 1 Apr 2013 (otherwise) (SI 2013/160) |
| | (7) | 27 Mar 2012 (so far as is necessary for enabling the exercise on or after that date of any power to make an order or regulations or to give directions that is conferred by these provisions or an amendment made by them) (s 306(1)(d)) |
| | | *Not yet in force* (otherwise) |
| | (8) | 27 Mar 2012 (so far as is necessary for enabling the exercise on or after that date of any power to make an order or regulations or to give directions that is conferred by these provisions or an amendment made by them) (s 306(1)(d)) |
| | | 1 Apr 2013 (otherwise) (SI 2013/160) |
| | (9) | 27 Mar 2012 (so far as is necessary for enabling the exercise on or after that date of any power to make an order or regulations or to give directions that is conferred by these provisions or an amendment made by them) (s 306(1)(d)) |
| | | 1 Oct 2012 (otherwise) (SI 2012/1831) |
| 152, 153 | | 27 Mar 2012 (so far as is necessary for enabling the exercise on or after that date of any power to make an order or regulations or to give directions that is conferred by these provisions or an amendment made by them) (s 306(1)(d)) |
| | | 1 Apr 2013 (otherwise) (SI 2013/160) |
| 154 | | 27 Mar 2012 (so far as is necessary for enabling the exercise on or after that date of any power to make an order or regulations or to give directions that is conferred by these provisions or an amendment made by them) (s 306(1)(d)) |
| | | 1 Oct 2012 (otherwise) (SI 2012/1831) |
| 155 | | 27 Mar 2012 (so far as is necessary for enabling the exercise on or after that date of any power to make an order or regulations or to give directions that is conferred by these provisions or an amendment made by them) (s 306(1)(d)) |
| | | *Not yet in force* (otherwise) (sub-s (2) repealed) |
| 156 | (1), (2) | 27 Mar 2012 (so far as is necessary for enabling the exercise on or after that date of any power to make an order or regulations or to give directions that is conferred by these provisions or an amendment made by them) (s 306(1)(d)) |
| | | 1 Nov 2012 (otherwise) (SI 2012/2657) |
| | (3), (4) | 27 Mar 2012 (so far as is necessary for enabling the exercise on or after that date of any power to make an order or regulations or to give directions that is conferred by these provisions or an amendment made by them) (s 306(1)(d)) |
| | | *Not yet in force* (otherwise) |
| | (5), (6) | 27 Mar 2012 (so far as is necessary for enabling the exercise on or after that date of any power to make an order or regulations or to give directions that is conferred by these provisions or an amendment made by them) (s 306(1)(d)) |
| | | 1 Apr 2013 (otherwise) (SI 2013/671) |
| 157 | | 27 Mar 2012 (so far as is necessary for enabling the exercise on or after that date of any power to make an order or regulations or to give directions that is conferred by these provisions or an amendment made by them) (s 306(1)(d)) |
| | | 1 Apr 2013 (otherwise) (SI 2013/160) |

**See Halsbury's Statutes Citator for amendments to these Acts**

**Health and Social Care Act 2012 (c 7)**—*contd*

158      27 Mar 2012 (so far as is necessary for enabling the exercise on or after that date of any power to make an order or regulations or to give directions that is conferred by these provisions or an amendment made by them) (s 306(1)(d))

1 Oct 2012 (otherwise) (SI 2012/1831)

159      27 Mar 2012 (so far as is necessary for enabling the exercise on or after that date of any power to make an order or regulations or to give directions that is conferred by these provisions or an amendment made by them) (s 306(1)(d))

1 Apr 2013 (otherwise, except sub-s (4)) (SI 2013/671)

*Not yet in force* (exception noted above)

160      27 Mar 2012 (so far as is necessary for enabling the exercise on or after that date of any power to make an order or regulations or to give directions that is conferred by these provisions or an amendment made by them) (s 306(1)(d))

1 Jul 2012 (otherwise) (SI 2012/1319)

161, 162      27 Mar 2012 (so far as is necessary for enabling the exercise on or after that date of any power to make an order or regulations or to give directions that is conferred by these provisions or an amendment made by them) (s 306(1)(d))

1 Apr 2013 (otherwise) (SI 2013/160)

163    (1)      27 Mar 2012 (so far as is necessary for enabling the exercise on or after that date of any power to make an order or regulations or to give directions that is conferred by these provisions or an amendment made by them) (s 306(1)(d))

1 Apr 2013 (for the purpose of the first report of the Secretary of State for the financial year ending 31 Mar 2014 and subsequent financial years) (SI 2013/160)

*Not yet in force* (otherwise)

   (2)      27 Mar 2012 (so far as is necessary for enabling the exercise on or after that date of any power to make an order or regulations or to give directions that is conferred by these provisions or an amendment made by them) (s 306(1)(d))

1 Apr 2013 (otherwise) (SI 2013/671)

   (3)–(6)      27 Mar 2012 (so far as is necessary for enabling the exercise on or after that date of any power to make an order or regulations or to give directions that is conferred by these provisions or an amendment made by them) (s 306(1)(d))

1 Apr 2013 (otherwise) (SI 2013/160)

   (7)–(9)      27 Mar 2012 (so far as is necessary for enabling the exercise on or after that date of any power to make an order or regulations or to give directions that is conferred by these provisions or an amendment made by them) (s 306(1)(d))

1 Apr 2013 (otherwise) (SI 2013/671)

164    (1)–(3)      27 Mar 2012 (so far as is necessary for enabling the exercise on or after that date of any power to make an order or regulations or to give directions that is conferred by these provisions or an amendment made by them) (s 306(1)(d))

1 Oct 2012 (otherwise) (SI 2012/1831)

   (4), (5)      27 Mar 2012 (so far as is necessary for enabling the exercise on or after that date of any power to make an order or regulations or to give directions that is conferred by these provisions or an amendment made by them) (s 306(1)(d))

1 Apr 2013 (otherwise) (SI 2013/671)

   (6)      27 Mar 2012 (so far as is necessary for enabling the exercise on or after that date of any power to make an order or regulations or to give directions that is conferred by these provisions or an amendment made by them) (s 306(1)(d))

1 Oct 2012 (otherwise) (SI 2012/1831)

**Health and Social Care Act 2012 (c 7)**—*contd*

| | | |
|---|---|---|
| 165 | | 27 Mar 2012 (so far as is necessary for enabling the exercise on or after that date of any power to make an order or regulations or to give directions that is conferred by these provisions or an amendment made by them) (s 306(1)(d)) |
| | | 1 Oct 2012 (otherwise) (SI 2012/1831) |
| 166 | | 27 Mar 2012 (so far as is necessary for enabling the exercise on or after that date of any power to make an order or regulations or to give directions that is conferred by these provisions or an amendment made by them) (s 306(1)(d)) |
| | | 1 Nov 2012 (otherwise) (SI 2012/2657)[3] |
| 167 | | 27 Mar 2012 (so far as is necessary for enabling the exercise on or after that date of any power to make an order or regulations or to give directions that is conferred by these provisions or an amendment made by them) (s 306(1)(d)) |
| | | 1 Apr 2013 (otherwise) (SI 2013/160) |
| 168–171 | | 27 Mar 2012 (so far as is necessary for enabling the exercise on or after that date of any power to make an order or regulations or to give directions that is conferred by these provisions or an amendment made by them) (s 306(1)(d)) |
| | | 1 Apr 2013 (otherwise) (SI 2013/671) |
| 172 | (1)–(3) | 27 Mar 2012 (so far as is necessary for enabling the exercise on or after that date of any power to make an order or regulations or to give directions that is conferred by these provisions or an amendment made by them) (s 306(1)(d)) |
| | | 1 Apr 2013 (otherwise) (SI 2013/671) |
| | (4) | 27 Mar 2012 (so far as is necessary for enabling the exercise on or after that date of any power to make an order or regulations or to give directions that is conferred by these provisions or an amendment made by them) (s 306(1)(d)) |
| | | 1 Apr 2013 (immediately before the coming into force of s 173 for remaining purposes) (otherwise) (SI 2013/671) |
| | (5)(a) | 27 Mar 2012 (so far as is necessary for enabling the exercise on or after that date of any power to make an order or regulations or to give directions that is conferred by these provisions or an amendment made by them) (s 306(1)(d)) |
| | | 1 Apr 2013 (otherwise) (SI 2013/671) |
| | (5)(b) | 27 Mar 2012 (so far as is necessary for enabling the exercise on or after that date of any power to make an order or regulations or to give directions that is conferred by these provisions or an amendment made by them) (s 306(1)(d)) |
| | | 1 Apr 2013 (immediately before the coming into force of s 173 for remaining purposes) (otherwise) (SI 2013/671) |
| | (6)–(12) | 27 Mar 2012 (so far as is necessary for enabling the exercise on or after that date of any power to make an order or regulations or to give directions that is conferred by these provisions or an amendment made by them) (s 306(1)(d)) |
| | | 1 Apr 2013 (otherwise) (SI 2013/671) |
| 173 | (1) | 27 Mar 2012 (so far as is necessary for enabling the exercise on or after that date of any power to make an order or regulations or to give directions that is conferred by these provisions or an amendment made by them) (s 306(1)(d)) |
| | | 1 Nov 2012 (otherwise) (SI 2012/2657) |
| | (2) | 27 Mar 2012 (so far as is necessary for enabling the exercise on or after that date of any power to make an order or regulations or to give directions that is conferred by these provisions or an amendment made by them) (s 306(1)(d)) |
| | | 1 Apr 2013 (otherwise) (SI 2013/671) |
| | (3)–(8) | 27 Mar 2012 (so far as is necessary for enabling the exercise on or after that date of any power to make an order or regulations or to give directions that is conferred by these provisions or an amendment made by them) (s 306(1)(d)) |

**Health and Social Care Act 2012 (c 7)**—*contd*

|  |  |  |
|---|---|---|
|  |  | 1 Nov 2012 (otherwise) (SI 2012/2657) |
| 174–178 |  | 27 Mar 2012 (so far as is necessary for enabling the exercise on or after that date of any power to make an order or regulations or to give directions that is conferred by these provisions or an amendment made by them) (s 306(1)(d)) |
|  |  | 1 Nov 2012 (otherwise) (SI 2012/2657) |
| 179 | (1)–(5) | 27 Mar 2012 (so far as is necessary for enabling the exercise on or after that date of any power to make an order or regulations or to give directions that is conferred by these provisions or an amendment made by them) (s 306(1)(d)) |
|  |  | *Repealed* (*never in force otherwise*) |
|  | (6) | See Sch 14 below |
| 180 |  | 27 Mar 2012 (so far as is necessary for enabling the exercise on or after that date of any power to make an order or regulations or to give directions that is conferred by these provisions or an amendment made by them) (s 306(1)(d)) |
|  |  | *Not yet in force* (otherwise) |
| 181 | (1)–(3) | 27 Mar 2012 (so far as is necessary for enabling the exercise on or after that date of any power to make an order or regulations or to give directions that is conferred by these provisions or an amendment made by them) (s 306(1)(d)) |
|  |  | 1 Oct 2012 (otherwise) (SI 2012/1831) |
|  | (4) | 27 Mar 2012 (so far as is necessary for enabling the exercise on or after that date of any power to make an order or regulations or to give directions that is conferred by these provisions or an amendment made by them) (s 306(1)(d)) |
|  |  | 1 Oct 2012 (otherwise) (except in so far as inserts Health and Social Care Act 2008, ss 45A(2), (4), (and 45A(1) in so far as relates thereto), 45C(2)(b), (4)) (SI 2012/1831)[2] |
|  |  | 1 Apr 2013 (exceptions noted above) (SI 2012/1831) (SI 2013/160) |
|  | (5) | 27 Mar 2012 (so far as is necessary for enabling the exercise on or after that date of any power to make an order or regulations or to give directions that is conferred by these provisions or an amendment made by them) (s 306(1)(d)) |
|  |  | 1 Oct 2012 (otherwise) (except in so far as relates to a function under provisions inserted by sub-s (4)) (SI 2012/1831) |
|  |  | 1 Apr 2013 (exception noted above) (SI 2012/1831) (SI 2013/160) |
|  | (6)–(14) | 27 Mar 2012 (so far as is necessary for enabling the exercise on or after that date of any power to make an order or regulations or to give directions that is conferred by these provisions or an amendment made by them) (s 306(1)(d)) |
|  |  | 1 Oct 2012 (otherwise) (SI 2012/1831) |
| 182–189 |  | 27 Mar 2012 (so far as is necessary for enabling the exercise on or after that date of any power to make an order or regulations or to give directions that is conferred by these provisions or an amendment made by them) (s 306(1)(d)) |
|  |  | 1 Apr 2013 (otherwise) (SI 2013/160) |
| 190 | (1)–(8) | 27 Mar 2012 (so far as is necessary for enabling the exercise on or after that date of any power to make an order or regulations or to give directions that is conferred by these provisions or an amendment made by them) (s 306(1)(d)) |
|  |  | 1 Apr 2013 (otherwise) (SI 2013/160)[4] |
|  | (9) | 27 Mar 2012 (so far as is necessary for enabling the exercise on or after that date of any power to make an order or regulations or to give directions that is conferred by these provisions or an amendment made by them) (s 306(1)(d)) |
|  |  | *Not yet in force* (otherwise) |

**Health and Social Care Act 2012 (c 7)**—*contd*

| | (10) | 27 Mar 2012 (so far as is necessary for enabling the exercise on or after that date of any power to make an order or regulations or to give directions that is conferred by these provisions or an amendment made by them) (s 306(1)(d)) |
| | | 1 Apr 2013 (otherwise) (SI 2013/160)[4] |
| 191–200 | | 27 Mar 2012 (so far as is necessary for enabling the exercise on or after that date of any power to make an order or regulations or to give directions that is conferred by these provisions or an amendment made by them) (s 306(1)(d)) |
| | | 1 Apr 2013 (otherwise) (SI 2013/160)[4] |
| 201 | | 27 Mar 2012 (so far as is necessary for enabling the exercise on or after that date of any power to make an order or regulations or to give directions that is conferred by these provisions or an amendment made by them) (s 306(1)(d)) |
| | | 1 Jul 2012 (otherwise) (SI 2012/1319) |
| 202–206 | | 27 Mar 2012 (so far as is necessary for enabling the exercise on or after that date of any power to make an order or regulations or to give directions that is conferred by these provisions or an amendment made by them) (s 306(1)(d)) |
| | | 1 Apr 2013 (otherwise) (SI 2013/160)[4] |
| 207 | (1)–(7) | 27 Mar 2012 (so far as is necessary for enabling the exercise on or after that date of any power to make an order or regulations or to give directions that is conferred by these provisions or an amendment made by them) (s 306(1)(d)) |
| | | 1 Apr 2013 (otherwise) (SI 2013/160)[4] |
| | (8) | 27 Mar 2012 (so far as is necessary for enabling the exercise on or after that date of any power to make an order or regulations or to give directions that is conferred by these provisions or an amendment made by them) (s 306(1)(d)) |
| | | 1 Jul 2012 (otherwise) (SI 2012/1319) |
| | (9) | 27 Mar 2012 (so far as is necessary for enabling the exercise on or after that date of any power to make an order or regulations or to give directions that is conferred by these provisions or an amendment made by them) (s 306(1)(d)) |
| | | 1 Apr 2013 (otherwise) (SI 2013/160) |
| | (10) | 27 Mar 2012 (so far as is necessary for enabling the exercise on or after that date of any power to make an order or regulations or to give directions that is conferred by these provisions or an amendment made by them) (s 306(1)(d)) |
| | | 1 Jul 2012 (otherwise) (SI 2012/1319) |
| | (11), (12) | 27 Mar 2012 (so far as is necessary for enabling the exercise on or after that date of any power to make an order or regulations or to give directions that is conferred by these provisions or an amendment made by them) (s 306(1)(d)) |
| | | 1 Apr 2013 (otherwise) (SI 2013/160) |
| 208 | | 27 Mar 2012 (so far as is necessary for enabling the exercise on or after that date of any power to make an order or regulations or to give directions that is conferred by these provisions or an amendment made by them) (s 306(1)(d)) |
| | | *Not yet in force* (otherwise) |
| 209–211 | | 27 Mar 2012 (so far as is necessary for enabling the exercise on or after that date of any power to make an order or regulations or to give directions that is conferred by these provisions or an amendment made by them) (s 306(1)(d)) |
| | | 1 Aug 2012 (otherwise) (SI 2012/1319) |
| 212 | (1) | 27 Mar 2012 (so far as is necessary for enabling the exercise on or after that date of any power to make an order or regulations or to give directions that is conferred by these provisions or an amendment made by them) (s 306(1)(d)) |
| | | 1 Oct 2012 (otherwise) (SI 2012/1831) |

**See Halsbury's Statutes Citator for amendments to these Acts**

**Health and Social Care Act 2012 (c 7)**—*contd*

| | | |
|---|---|---|
| | (2), (3) | 27 Mar 2012 (so far as is necessary for enabling the exercise on or after that date of any power to make an order or regulations or to give directions that is conferred by these provisions or an amendment made by them) (s 306(1)(d)) |
| | | 1 Aug 2012 (otherwise) (SI 2012/1319) |
| 213–218 | | 27 Mar 2012 (so far as is necessary for enabling the exercise on or after that date of any power to make an order or regulations or to give directions that is conferred by these provisions or an amendment made by them) (s 306(1)(d)) |
| | | 1 Aug 2012 (otherwise) (SI 2012/1319) |
| 219 | | 27 Mar 2012 (s 306(1)(a)) |
| 220 | | 27 Mar 2012 (so far as is necessary for enabling the exercise on or after that date of any power to make an order or regulations or to give directions that is conferred by this provision or an amendment made by it) (s 306(1)(d)) |
| | | 1 Aug 2012 (otherwise) (SI 2012/1319) |
| 221 | (1), (2) | 27 Mar 2012 (so far as is necessary for enabling the exercise on or after that date of any power to make an order or regulations or to give directions that is conferred by these provisions or an amendment made by them) (s 306(1)(d)) |
| | | 1 Aug 2012 (otherwise) (SI 2012/1319) |
| | (3) | 27 Mar 2012 (s 306(1)(b)) |
| 222 | | 27 Mar 2012 (so far as is necessary for enabling the exercise on or after that date of any power to make an order or regulations or to give directions that is conferred by this provision or an amendment made by it) (s 306(1)(d)) |
| | | 1 Dec 2012 (otherwise) (SI 2012/2657) |
| 223 | (1), (2) | 27 Mar 2012 (so far as is necessary for enabling the exercise on or after that date of any power to make an order or regulations or to give directions that is conferred by these provisions or an amendment made by them) (s 306(1)(d)) |
| | | 1 Aug 2012 (otherwise) (SI 2012/1319) |
| | (3) | 27 Mar 2012 (so far as is necessary for enabling the exercise on or after that date of any power to make an order or regulations or to give directions that is conferred by this provision or an amendment made by it) (s 306(1)(d)) |
| | | 1 Oct 2012 (otherwise) (SI 2012/1831)[2] |
| | (4) | 27 Mar 2012 (so far as is necessary for enabling the exercise on or after that date of any power to make an order or regulations or to give directions that is conferred by this provision or an amendment made by it) (s 306(1)(d)) |
| | | 1 Feb 2016 (otherwise) (SI 2016/81) |
| | (5) | 27 Mar 2012 (so far as is necessary for enabling the exercise on or after that date of any power to make an order or regulations or to give directions that is conferred by this provision or an amendment made by it) (s 306(1)(d)) |
| | | 1 Aug 2012 (otherwise) (SI 2012/1319) |
| | (6) | 27 Mar 2012 (so far as is necessary for enabling the exercise on or after that date of any power to make an order or regulations or to give directions that is conferred by this provision or an amendment made by it) (s 306(1)(d)) |
| | | 1 Oct 2012 (otherwise) (SI 2012/1831) |
| | (7), (8) | 27 Mar 2012 (so far as is necessary for enabling the exercise on or after that date of any power to make an order or regulations or to give directions that is conferred by these provisions or an amendment made by them) (s 306(1)(d)) |
| | | 4 Jun 2018 (otherwise) (SI 2018/617) |
| | (9), (10) | 27 Mar 2012 (so far as is necessary for enabling the exercise on or after that date of any power to make an order or regulations or to give directions that is conferred by these provisions or an amendment made by them) (s 306(1)(d)) |

**Health and Social Care Act 2012 (c 7)**—*contd*

| | | |
|---|---|---|
| | | 1 Aug 2012 (otherwise) (SI 2012/1319) |
| | (11)–(13) | 27 Mar 2012 (so far as is necessary for enabling the exercise on or after that date of any power to make an order or regulations or to give directions that is conferred by this provision or an amendment made by it) (s 306(1)(d)) |
| | | 4 Jun 2018 (otherwise) (SI 2018/617) |
| | (14) | 27 Mar 2012 (so far as is necessary for enabling the exercise on or after that date of any power to make an order or regulations or to give directions that is conferred by this provision or an amendment made by it) (s 306(1)(d)) |
| | | 1 Aug 2012 (otherwise) (SI 2012/1319) |
| 224, 225 | | 27 Mar 2012 (so far as is necessary for enabling the exercise on or after that date of any power to make an order or regulations or to give directions that is conferred by these provisions or an amendment made by them) (s 306(1)(d)) |
| | | 16 Mar 2015 (otherwise) (SI 2015/409) |
| 226 | (1) | See sub-ss (2)–(8) below |
| | (2)(a) | 27 Mar 2012 (so far as is necessary for enabling the exercise on or after that date of any power to make an order or regulations or to give directions that is conferred by this provision or an amendment made by it) (s 306(1)(d)) |
| | | 9 Jun 2014 (otherwise) (SI 2014/1454) |
| | (2)(b) | 27 Mar 2012 (so far as is necessary for enabling the exercise on or after that date of any power to make an order or regulations or to give directions that is conferred by this provision or an amendment made by it) (s 306(1)(d)) |
| | | 1 Dec 2012 (otherwise) (SI 2012/2657) |
| | (3), (4) | 27 Mar 2012 (so far as is necessary for enabling the exercise on or after that date of any power to make an order or regulations or to give directions that is conferred by these provisions or an amendment made by them) (s 306(1)(d)) |
| | | 4 Jun 2018 (otherwise) (SI 2018/617)[9] |
| | (5) | 27 Mar 2012 (so far as is necessary for enabling the exercise on or after that date of any power to make an order or regulations or to give directions that is conferred by this provision or an amendment made by it) (s 306(1)(d)) |
| | | 1 Dec 2012 (otherwise) (SI 2012/2657) |
| | (6)–(9) | 27 Mar 2012 (so far as is necessary for enabling the exercise on or after that date of any power to make an order or regulations or to give directions that is conferred by these provisions or an amendment made by them) (s 306(1)(d)) |
| | | 4 Jun 2018 (otherwise) (SI 2018/617)[9] |
| 227 | | 27 Mar 2012 (so far as is necessary for enabling the exercise on or after that date of any power to make an order or regulations or to give directions that is conferred by this provision or an amendment made by it) (s 306(1)(d)) |
| | | 1 Jul 2012 (otherwise) (SI 2012/1319)[1] |
| 228, 229 | | 27 Mar 2012 (so far as is necessary for enabling the exercise on or after that date of any power to make an order or regulations or to give directions that is conferred by these provisions or an amendment made by them) (s 306(1)(d)) |
| | | 1 Dec 2012 (otherwise) (SI 2012/2657) |
| 230 | (1) | See Sch 15, Pts 1–3 below |
| | (2)–(6) | 27 Mar 2012 (so far as is necessary for enabling the exercise on or after that date of any power to make an order or regulations or to give directions that is conferred by these provisions or an amendment made by them) (s 306(1)(d)) |
| | | 1 Aug 2012 (otherwise) (SI 2012/1319) |

**Health and Social Care Act 2012 (c 7)**—*contd*

| | | |
|---|---|---|
| 231 | | 27 Mar 2012 (so far as is necessary for enabling the exercise on or after that date of any power to make an order or regulations or to give directions that is conferred by this provision or an amendment made by it) (s 306(1)(d)) |
| | | 1 Jul 2012 (otherwise) (SI 2012/1319) |
| 232 | (1) | 27 Mar 2012 (so far as is necessary for enabling the exercise on or after that date of any power to make an order or regulations or to give directions that is conferred by this provision or an amendment made by it) (s 306(1)(d)) |
| | | 1 Apr 2013 (SI 2013/160)[4] |
| | (2) | See Sch 16 below |
| 233–248 | | 27 Mar 2012 (so far as is necessary for enabling the exercise on or after that date of any power to make an order or regulations or to give directions that is conferred by these provisions or an amendment made by them) (s 306(1)(d)) |
| | | 1 Apr 2013 (otherwise) (SI 2013/160)[4] |
| 249 | (1) | See Sch 17 below |
| | (2)–(9) | 27 Mar 2012 (so far as is necessary for enabling the exercise on or after that date of any power to make an order or regulations or to give directions that is conferred by these provisions or an amendment made by them) (s 306(1)(d)) |
| | | 1 Apr 2013 (otherwise) (SI 2013/160)[4] |
| 250, 251 | | 27 Mar 2012 (so far as is necessary for enabling the exercise on or after that date of any power to make an order or regulations or to give directions that is conferred by these provisions or an amendment made by them) (s 306(1)(d)) |
| | | 1 Apr 2013 (otherwise) (SI 2013/160)[4] |
| 252 | (1) | 27 Mar 2012 (so far as is necessary for enabling the exercise on or after that date of any power to make an order or regulations or to give directions that is conferred by this provision or an amendment made by it) (s 306(1)(d)) |
| | | 1 Apr 2013 (otherwise) (SI 2013/160)[4] |
| | (2) | See Sch 18 below |
| 253–264 | | 27 Mar 2012 (so far as is necessary for enabling the exercise on or after that date of any power to make an order or regulations or to give directions that is conferred by these provisions or an amendment made by them) (s 306(1)(d)) |
| | | 1 Apr 2013 (otherwise) (SI 2013/160)[4] |
| 265 | (1)–(6) | 27 Mar 2012 (so far as is necessary for enabling the exercise on or after that date of any power to make an order or regulations or to give directions that is conferred by these provisions or an amendment made by them) (s 306(1)(d)) |
| | | 1 Apr 2013 (otherwise) (SI 2013/160)[4] |
| 266–276 | | 27 Mar 2012 (so far as is necessary for enabling the exercise on or after that date of any power to make an order or regulations or to give directions that is conferred by these provisions or an amendment made by them) (s 306(1)(d)) |
| | | 1 Apr 2013 (otherwise) (SI 2013/160)[4] |
| 277 | | See Sch 19 below |
| 278 | | 27 Mar 2012 (so far as is necessary for enabling the exercise on or after that date of any power to make an order or regulations or to give directions that is conferred by these provisions or an amendment made by them) (s 306(1)(d)) |
| | | 1 Jul 2012 (otherwise) (SI 2012/1319) |
| 279 | (1), (2) | 27 Mar 2012 (so far as is necessary for enabling the exercise on or after that date of any power to make an order or regulations or to give directions that is conferred by these provisions or an amendment made by them) (s 306(1)(d)) |
| | | 31 Oct 2012 (otherwise) (SI 2012/1831) |
| | (3) | See Sch 20, Pt 2 below |

**Health and Social Care Act 2012 (c 7)**—*contd*

| | | |
|---|---|---|
| 280 | (1)–(7) | 27 Mar 2012 (so far as is necessary for enabling the exercise on or after that date of any power to make an order or regulations or to give directions that is conferred by these provisions or an amendment made by them) (s 306(1)(d)) |
| | | 1 Apr 2013 (otherwise) (SI 2013/160) |
| | (8) | See Sch 20, Pt 3 below |
| 281 | | 27 Mar 2012 (so far as is necessary for enabling the exercise on or after that date of any power to make an order or regulations or to give directions that is conferred by these provisions or an amendment made by them) (s 306(1)(d)) |
| | | 1 Oct 2012 (otherwise) (SI 2012/1831) |
| 282 | | 27 Mar 2012 (so far as is necessary for enabling the exercise on or after that date of any power to make an order or regulations or to give directions that is conferred by these provisions or an amendment made by them) (s 306(1)(d)) |
| | | 1 Apr 2013 (otherwise) (SI 2013/160)[4] |
| 283 | | 27 Mar 2012 (so far as is necessary for enabling the exercise on or after that date of any power to make an order or regulations or to give directions that is conferred by these provisions or an amendment made by them) (s 306(1)(d)) |
| | | 1 Jul 2012 (otherwise) (SI 2012/1319) |
| 284–287 | | 27 Mar 2012 (so far as is necessary for enabling the exercise on or after that date of any power to make an order or regulations or to give directions that is conferred by these provisions or an amendment made by them) (s 306(1)(d)) |
| | | 1 Apr 2013 (otherwise) (SI 2013/160)[4] |
| 288 | (1), (2)(a) | 27 Mar 2012 (so far as is necessary for enabling the exercise on or after that date of any power to make an order or regulations or to give directions that is conferred by these provisions or an amendment made by them) (s 306(1)(d)) |
| | | 1 Jul 2012 (otherwise) (SI 2012/1319) |
| | (2)(b), (c) | 27 Mar 2012 (so far as is necessary for enabling the exercise on or after that date of any power to make an order or regulations or to give directions that is conferred by these provisions or an amendment made by them) (s 306(1)(d)) |
| | | 1 Apr 2014 (otherwise) (SI 2014/39) |
| | (3) | 27 Mar 2012 (so far as is necessary for enabling the exercise on or after that date of any power to make an order or regulations or to give directions that is conferred by these provisions or an amendment made by them) (s 306(1)(d)) |
| | | 1 Apr 2013 (otherwise) (SI 2013/160) |
| | (4) | 27 Mar 2012 (so far as is necessary for enabling the exercise on or after that date of any power to make an order or regulations or to give directions that is conferred by these provisions or an amendment made by them) (s 306(1)(d)) |
| | | 1 Apr 2014 (otherwise) (SI 2014/39) |
| 289 | (1) | See sub-ss (2)–(6) below |
| | (2) | 27 Mar 2012 (so far as is necessary for enabling the exercise on or after that date of any power to make an order or regulations or to give directions that is conferred by these provisions or an amendment made by them) (s 306(1)(d)) |
| | | 1 Jul 2012 (otherwise) (SI 2012/1319) |
| | (3) | 27 Mar 2012 (so far as is necessary for enabling the exercise on or after that date of any power to make an order or regulations or to give directions that is conferred by these provisions or an amendment made by them) (s 306(1)(d)) |
| | | 1 Jul 2012 (so far as omits the Health and Social Care Act 2008, s 70(2) and in so far as substitutes the new s 70(2)(a) thereof) (SI 2012/1319) |
| | | 1 Apr 2014 (otherwise) (SI 2014/39) |

**Health and Social Care Act 2012 (c 7)**—*contd*

|  |  |  |
|---|---|---|
| | (4)(a) | 27 Mar 2012 (so far as is necessary for enabling the exercise on or after that date of any power to make an order or regulations or to give directions that is conferred by these provisions or an amendment made by them) (s 306(1)(d)) |
| | | 1 Jul 2012 (otherwise) (SI 2012/1319) |
| | (4)(b), (5) | 27 Mar 2012 (so far as is necessary for enabling the exercise on or after that date of any power to make an order or regulations or to give directions that is conferred by these provisions or an amendment made by them) (s 306(1)(d)) |
| | | 1 Apr 2013 (otherwise) (SI 2013/671) |
| | (6) | 27 Mar 2012 (so far as is necessary for enabling the exercise on or after that date of any power to make an order or regulations or to give directions that is conferred by these provisions or an amendment made by them) (s 306(1)(d)) |
| | | 1 Jul 2012 (otherwise) (SI 2012/1319) |
| 290 | (1), (2), (3)(a) | 27 Mar 2012 (so far as is necessary for enabling the exercise on or after that date of any power to make an order or regulations or to give directions that is conferred by these provisions or an amendment made by them) (s 306(1)(d)) |
| | | 1 Oct 2012 (otherwise) (SI 2012/1831) |
| | (3)(b), (c) | 27 Mar 2012 (so far as is necessary for enabling the exercise on or after that date of any power to make an order or regulations or to give directions that is conferred by these provisions or an amendment made by them) (s 306(1)(d)) |
| | | 1 Apr 2013 (otherwise) (SI 2013/160)[4] |
| | (3)(d), (4)–(8) | 27 Mar 2012 (so far as is necessary for enabling the exercise on or after that date of any power to make an order or regulations or to give directions that is conferred by these provisions or an amendment made by them) (s 306(1)(d)) |
| | | 1 Oct 2012 (otherwise) (SI 2012/1831) |
| 291 | | 27 Mar 2012 (so far as is necessary for enabling the exercise on or after that date of any power to make an order or regulations or to give directions that is conferred by these provisions or an amendment made by them) (s 306(1)(d)) |
| | | 1 Oct 2012 (otherwise) (SI 2012/1831) |
| 292, 293 | | 27 Mar 2012 (so far as is necessary for enabling the exercise on or after that date of any power to make an order or regulations or to give directions that is conferred by these provisions or an amendment made by them) (s 306(1)(d)) |
| | | 1 Apr 2013 (otherwise) (SI 2013/160) |
| 294 | | 27 Mar 2012 (so far as is necessary for enabling the exercise on or after that date of any power to make an order or regulations or to give directions that is conferred by these provisions or an amendment made by them) (s 306(1)(d)) |
| | | 1 Oct 2012 (otherwise) (SI 2012/1831) |
| 295, 296 | | 27 Mar 2012 (so far as is necessary for enabling the exercise on or after that date of any power to make an order or regulations or to give directions that is conferred by these provisions or an amendment made by them) (s 306(1)(d)) |
| | | 1 Oct 2012 (in so far as necessary to enable the Board to prepare itself to exercise functions under these sections on or after the date on which s 9(1) comes fully into force) (SI 2012/1831) |
| | | 1 Apr 2013 (otherwise) (SI 2013/160)[4] |
| 297 | | See Sch 21 below |
| 298 | | 27 Mar 2012 (so far as is necessary for enabling the exercise on or after that date of any power to make an order or regulations or to give directions that is conferred by these provisions or an amendment made by them) (s 306(1)(d)) |
| | | 1 Oct 2012 (otherwise) (SI 2012/1831) |

**Health and Social Care Act 2012 (c 7)**—*contd*

| | | |
|---|---|---|
| 299 | | 27 Mar 2012 (so far as is necessary for enabling the exercise on or after that date of any power to make an order or regulations or to give directions that is conferred by these provisions or an amendment made by them) (s 306(1)(d)) |
| | | 1 Jun 2012 (otherwise) (SI 2012/1319) |
| 300 | (1) | 27 Mar 2012 (so far as is necessary for enabling the exercise on or after that date of any power to make an order or regulations or to give directions that is conferred by these provisions or an amendment made by them) (s 306(1)(d)) |
| | | 1 Jul 2012 (except in so far as relates to the National Health Service Commissioning Board, a clinical commissioning group, any person with whom the Secretary of State has made, or has decided to make, an agreement under the Mental Health Act 1983, s 12ZA(1), the National Institute for Health and Care Excellence, and the Health and Social Care Information Centre) (SI 2012/1319) |
| | | 1 Oct 2012 (in so far as relates to the Board and a clinical commissioning group) (SI 2012/1831) |
| | | 1 Apr 2013 (otherwise) (SI 2013/160) |
| | (2) | See Sch 22 below |
| | (3) | See Sch 23 below |
| | (4)–(9) | 27 Mar 2012 (so far as is necessary for enabling the exercise on or after that date of any power to make an order or regulations or to give directions that is conferred by these provisions or an amendment made by them) (s 306(1)(d)) |
| | | 1 Jul 2012 (except in so far as they relate to the National Health Service Commissioning Board, a clinical commissioning group, any person with whom the Secretary of State has made, or has decided to make, an agreement under the Mental Health Act 1983, s 12ZA(1), the National Institute for Health and Care Excellence, and the Health and Social Care Information Centre) (SI 2012/1319) |
| | | 1 Oct 2012 (in so far as relates to the Board and a clinical commissioning group) (SI 2012/1831) |
| | | 1 Apr 2013 (otherwise) (SI 2013/160) |
| 301, 302 | | 27 Mar 2012 (so far as is necessary for enabling the exercise on or after that date of any power to make an order or regulations or to give directions that is conferred by these provisions or an amendment made by them) (s 306(1)(d)) |
| | | 1 Jul 2012 (except in so far as they relate to the National Health Service Commissioning Board, a clinical commissioning group, any person with whom the Secretary of State has made, or has decided to make, an agreement under the Mental Health Act 1983, s 12ZA(1), the National Institute for Health and Care Excellence, and the Health and Social Care Information Centre) (SI 2012/1319) |
| | | 1 Oct 2012 (in so far as they relate to the Board and a clinical commissioning group) (SI 2012/1831) |
| | | 1 Apr 2013 (otherwise) (SI 2013/160) |
| 303–309 | | 27 Mar 2012 (s 306(1)(c)) |
| Sch 1 | | 27 Mar 2012 (so far as is necessary for enabling the exercise on or after that date of any power to make an order or regulations or to give directions that is conferred by these provisions or an amendment made by them) (s 306(1)(d)) |
| | | 1 Oct 2012 (except in so far as inserts National Health Service Act 2006, Sch A1, para 17) (SI 2012/1831)[2] |
| | | 1 Apr 2013 (exception noted above) (SI 2013/160)[4] |
| Sch 2 | | 27 Mar 2012 (so far as is necessary for enabling the exercise on or after that date of any power to make an order or regulations or to give directions that is conferred by these provisions or an amendment made by them) (s 306(1)(d)) |

**Health and Social Care Act 2012 (c 7)**—*contd*

|  |  |  |
|---|---|---|
|  |  | 1 Oct 2012 (in so far as inserts National Health Service Act 2006, Sch 1A, paras 1–10, 12(1)–(3), (4)(a), para 12(4)(b) (except in so far as relates to employees of the group or groups), para 12(9)(a)(i), (iv), (b), para 12(9)(a)(iii) (in so far as relates to paras 17(1), (2), (9), 19)) (SI 2012/1831)[2] |
|  |  | 1 Apr 2013 (otherwise) (SI 2013/160)[4] |
| Sch 3 |  | 27 Mar 2012 (so far as is necessary for enabling the exercise on or after that date of any power to make an order or regulations or to give directions that is conferred by these provisions or an amendment made by them) (s 306(1)(d)) |
|  |  | 1 Apr 2013 (otherwise) (SI 2013/160)[4] |
| Sch 4 | para 1 | 27 Mar 2012 (so far as is necessary for enabling the exercise on or after that date of any power to make an order or regulations or to give directions that is conferred by these provisions or an amendment made by them) (s 306(1)(d)) |
|  |  | 1 Oct 2012 (in so far as relates to the Board and a clinical commissioning group) (SI 2012/1831)[2] |
|  |  | 1 Apr 2013 (otherwise) (SI 2013/160)[4] |
|  | para 2(1) | See sub-paras (2)–(4) below |
|  | para 2(2) | 27 Mar 2012 (so far as is necessary for enabling the exercise on or after that date of any power to make an order or regulations or to give directions that is conferred by these provisions or an amendment made by them) (s 306(1)(d)) |
|  |  | 1 Apr 2013 (otherwise) (SI 2013/160)[4] |
|  | para 2(3) | 27 Mar 2012 (so far as is necessary for enabling the exercise on or after that date of any power to make an order or regulations or to give directions that is conferred by these provisions or an amendment made by them) (s 306(1)(d)) |
|  |  | 1 Feb 2013 (otherwise) (SI 2012/2657) |
|  | para 2(4) | 27 Mar 2012 (so far as is necessary for enabling the exercise on or after that date of any power to make an order or regulations or to give directions that is conferred by these provisions or an amendment made by them) (s 306(1)(d)) |
|  |  | 1 Apr 2013 (otherwise) (SI 2013/160)[4] |
|  | paras 3–5 | 27 Mar 2012 (so far as is necessary for enabling the exercise on or after that date of any power to make an order or regulations or to give directions that is conferred by these provisions or an amendment made by them) (s 306(1)(d)) |
|  |  | 1 Apr 2013 (otherwise) (SI 2013/160)[4] |
|  | para 6(1) | 27 Mar 2012 (so far as is necessary for enabling the exercise on or after that date of any power to make an order or regulations or to give directions that is conferred by these provisions or an amendment made by them) (s 306(1)(d)) |
|  |  | 1 Apr 2013 (otherwise) (SI 2013/160)[4] |
|  | para 6(2)(a) | 27 Mar 2012 (so far as is necessary for enabling the exercise on or after that date of any power to make an order or regulations or to give directions that is conferred by these provisions or an amendment made by them) (s 306(1)(d)) |
|  |  | 1 Oct 2012 (otherwise) (SI 2012/1831) |
|  | para 6(2)(b), (c) | 27 Mar 2012 (so far as is necessary for enabling the exercise on or after that date of any power to make an order or regulations or to give directions that is conferred by these provisions or an amendment made by them) (s 306(1)(d)) |
|  |  | 1 Apr 2013 (otherwise) (SI 2013/160)[4] |
|  | para 7(a) | 27 Mar 2012 (so far as is necessary for enabling the exercise on or after that date of any power to make an order or regulations or to give directions that is conferred by these provisions or an amendment made by them) (s 306(1)(d)) |
|  |  | 1 Oct 2012 (otherwise) (SI 2012/1831) |

**Health and Social Care Act 2012 (c 7)**—*contd*

| | |
|---|---|
| paras 7(b), (c), 8 | 27 Mar 2012 (so far as is necessary for enabling the exercise on or after that date of any power to make an order or regulations or to give directions that is conferred by these provisions or an amendment made by them) (s 306(1)(d)) |
| | 1 Apr 2013 (otherwise) (SI 2013/160)[4] |
| para 9 | 27 Mar 2012 (so far as is necessary for enabling the exercise on or after that date of any power to make an order or regulations or to give directions that is conferred by these provisions or an amendment made by them) (s 306(1)(d)) |
| | 1 Feb 2012 (in so far as relates to commissioning arrangements that are to take effect on or after 1 Apr 2013) (SI 2012/2657) |
| | 1 Apr 2013 (otherwise) (SI 2013/160)[4] |
| paras 10–12 | 27 Mar 2012 (so far as is necessary for enabling the exercise on or after that date of any power to make an order or regulations or to give directions that is conferred by these provisions or an amendment made by them) (s 306(1)(d)) |
| | 1 Apr 2013 (otherwise) (SI 2013/160)[4] |
| para 13 | 27 Mar 2012 (so far as is necessary for enabling the exercise on or after that date of any power to make an order or regulations or to give directions that is conferred by these provisions or an amendment made by them) (s 306(1)(d)) |
| | 1 Oct 2012 (otherwise) (SI 2012/1831) |
| paras 14–17 | 27 Mar 2012 (so far as is necessary for enabling the exercise on or after that date of any power to make an order or regulations or to give directions that is conferred by these provisions or an amendment made by them) (s 306(1)(d)) |
| | 1 Apr 2013 (otherwise) (SI 2013/160)[4] |
| para 18(1) | See sub-paras (2)–(6) below |
| para 18(2)(a) | 27 Mar 2012 (so far as is necessary for enabling the exercise on or after that date of any power to make an order or regulations or to give directions that is conferred by these provisions or an amendment made by them) (s 306(1)(d)) |
| | 1 Oct 2012 (otherwise) (SI 2012/1831) |
| para 18(2)(b), (c) | 27 Mar 2012 (so far as is necessary for enabling the exercise on or after that date of any power to make an order or regulations or to give directions that is conferred by these provisions or an amendment made by them) (s 306(1)(d)) |
| | 1 Apr 2013 (otherwise) (SI 2013/160)[4] |
| para 18(2)(d), (e), (3), (4)(a) | 27 Mar 2012 (so far as is necessary for enabling the exercise on or after that date of any power to make an order or regulations or to give directions that is conferred by these provisions or an amendment made by them) (s 306(1)(d)) |
| | 1 Oct 2012 (otherwise) (SI 2012/1831) |
| para 18(4)(b), (c), (5) | 27 Mar 2012 (so far as is necessary for enabling the exercise on or after that date of any power to make an order or regulations or to give directions that is conferred by these provisions or an amendment made by them) (s 306(1)(d)) |
| | 1 Apr 2013 (otherwise) (SI 2013/160)[4] |
| para 18(6)(a) | 27 Mar 2012 (so far as is necessary for enabling the exercise on or after that date of any power to make an order or regulations or to give directions that is conferred by these provisions or an amendment made by them) (s 306(1)(d)) |
| | 1 Oct 2012 (otherwise) (SI 2012/1831) |
| para 18(6)(b), (c), 19–103 | 27 Mar 2012 (so far as is necessary for enabling the exercise on or after that date of any power to make an order or regulations or to give directions that is conferred by these provisions or an amendment made by them) (s 306(1)(d)) |
| | 1 Apr 2013 (otherwise) (SI 2013/160)[4] |
| para 104(1) | See sub-paras (2)–(4) below |

**Health and Social Care Act 2012 (c 7)**—*contd*

| | |
|---|---|
| para 104(2), (3)(a) | 27 Mar 2012 (so far as is necessary for enabling the exercise on or after that date of any power to make an order or regulations or to give directions that is conferred by these provisions or an amendment made by them) (s 306(1)(d)) |
| | 1 Oct 2012 (otherwise) (SI 2012/1831) |
| paras 104(3)(b), (c), (4), 105–108 | 27 Mar 2012 (so far as is necessary for enabling the exercise on or after that date of any power to make an order or regulations or to give directions that is conferred by these provisions or an amendment made by them) (s 306(1)(d)) |
| | 1 Apr 2013 (otherwise) (SI 2013/160)[4] |
| para 109(a) | 27 Mar 2012 (so far as is necessary for enabling the exercise on or after that date of any power to make an order or regulations or to give directions that is conferred by these provisions or an amendment made by them) (s 306(1)(d)) |
| | 1 Oct 2012 (otherwise) (SI 2012/1831) |
| para 109(b) | 27 Mar 2012 (so far as is necessary for enabling the exercise on or after that date of any power to make an order or regulations or to give directions that is conferred by these provisions or an amendment made by them) (s 306(1)(d)) |
| | 1 Apr 2013 (otherwise) (SI 2013/160)[4] |
| para 110(1) | See sub-paras (2), (3) below |
| para 110(2)(a) | 27 Mar 2012 (so far as is necessary for enabling the exercise on or after that date of any power to make an order or regulations or to give directions that is conferred by these provisions or an amendment made by them) (s 306(1)(d)) |
| | 1 Oct 2012 (otherwise) (SI 2012/1831) |
| para 110(2)(b) | 27 Mar 2012 (so far as is necessary for enabling the exercise on or after that date of any power to make an order or regulations or to give directions that is conferred by these provisions or an amendment made by them) (s 306(1)(d)) |
| | 1 Apr 2013 (otherwise) (SI 2013/160)[4] |
| para 110(3)(a) | 27 Mar 2012 (so far as is necessary for enabling the exercise on or after that date of any power to make an order or regulations or to give directions that is conferred by these provisions or an amendment made by them) (s 306(1)(d)) |
| | 1 Oct 2012 (otherwise) (SI 2012/1831) |
| para 110(3)(b) | 27 Mar 2012 (so far as is necessary for enabling the exercise on or after that date of any power to make an order or regulations or to give directions that is conferred by these provisions or an amendment made by them) (s 306(1)(d)) |
| | 1 Apr 2013 (otherwise) (SI 2013/160)[4] |
| para 111(1) | See sub-paras (2)–(4) below |
| para 111(2) | 27 Mar 2012 (so far as is necessary for enabling the exercise on or after that date of any power to make an order or regulations or to give directions that is conferred by these provisions or an amendment made by them) (s 306(1)(d)) |
| | 1 Apr 2013 (otherwise) (SI 2013/160)[4] |
| para 111(3)(a) | 27 Mar 2012 (so far as is necessary for enabling the exercise on or after that date of any power to make an order or regulations or to give directions that is conferred by these provisions or an amendment made by them) (s 306(1)(d)) |
| | 1 Oct 2012 (otherwise) (SI 2012/1831) |
| para 111(3)(b) | 27 Mar 2012 (so far as is necessary for enabling the exercise on or after that date of any power to make an order or regulations or to give directions that is conferred by these provisions or an amendment made by them) (s 306(1)(d)) |
| | 1 Apr 2013 (otherwise) (SI 2013/160)[4] |
| para 111(4)(a) | 27 Mar 2012 (so far as is necessary for enabling the exercise on or after that date of any power to make an order or regulations or to give directions that is conferred by these provisions or an amendment made by them) (s 306(1)(d)) |

**Health and Social Care Act 2012 (c 7)**—*contd*

|  |  |
|---|---|
|  | 1 Oct 2012 (otherwise) (SI 2012/1831) |
| para 111(4)(b) | 27 Mar 2012 (so far as is necessary for enabling the exercise on or after that date of any power to make an order or regulations or to give directions that is conferred by these provisions or an amendment made by them) (s 306(1)(d)) |
|  | 1 Apr 2013 (otherwise) (SI 2013/160)[4] |
| para 111(4)(c) | 27 Mar 2012 (so far as is necessary for enabling the exercise on or after that date of any power to make an order or regulations or to give directions that is conferred by these provisions or an amendment made by them) (s 306(1)(d)) |
|  | 1 Oct 2012 (otherwise) (SI 2012/1831) |
| para 112 | 27 Mar 2012 (so far as is necessary for enabling the exercise on or after that date of any power to make an order or regulations or to give directions that is conferred by these provisions or an amendment made by them) (s 306(1)(d)) |
|  | 1 Jul 2012 (otherwise) (SI 2012/1319)[7] |
| para 113(a) | 27 Mar 2012 (so far as is necessary for enabling the exercise on or after that date of any power to make an order or regulations or to give directions that is conferred by these provisions or an amendment made by them) (s 306(1)(d)) |
|  | 1 Oct 2012 (in so far as inserts National Health Service Act 2006, s 217(1)(ea)) (SI 2012/1831) |
|  | 1 Apr 2013 (in so far as inserts s 217(1)(eb) thereof) (SI 2013/160)[4] |
| paras 113(b), (c), 114 | 27 Mar 2012 (so far as is necessary for enabling the exercise on or after that date of any power to make an order or regulations or to give directions that is conferred by these provisions or an amendment made by them) (s 306(1)(d)) |
|  | 1 Apr 2013 (otherwise) (SI 2013/160)[4] |
| para 115 | 27 Mar 2012 (so far as is necessary for enabling the exercise on or after that date of any power to make an order or regulations or to give directions that is conferred by these provisions or an amendment made by them) (s 306(1)(d)) |
|  | 1 Jul 2012 (otherwise) (SI 2012/1319)[7] |
| para 116 | 27 Mar 2012 (so far as is necessary for enabling the exercise on or after that date of any power to make an order or regulations or to give directions that is conferred by these provisions or an amendment made by them) (s 306(1)(d)) |
|  | 1 Apr 2013 (otherwise) (SI 2013/160)[4] |
| para 117(1) | 27 Mar 2012 (so far as is necessary for enabling the exercise on or after that date of any power to make an order or regulations or to give directions that is conferred by these provisions or an amendment made by them) (s 306(1)(d)) |
|  | 1 Oct 2012 (otherwise) (SI 2012/1831) |
| paras 117(2), 118–124 | 27 Mar 2012 (so far as is necessary for enabling the exercise on or after that date of any power to make an order or regulations or to give directions that is conferred by these provisions or an amendment made by them) (s 306(1)(d)) |
|  | 1 Apr 2013 (otherwise) (SI 2013/160)[4] |
| para 125(1)–(3) | 27 Mar 2012 (so far as is necessary for enabling the exercise on or after that date of any power to make an order or regulations or to give directions that is conferred by these provisions or an amendment made by them) (s 306(1)(d)) |
|  | 1 Apr 2013 (otherwise) (SI 2013/160)[4] |
| para 125(4)–(6) | 27 Mar 2012 (so far as is necessary for enabling the exercise on or after that date of any power to make an order or regulations or to give directions that is conferred by these provisions or an amendment made by them) (s 306(1)(d)) |
|  | 1 Oct 2012 (otherwise) (SI 2012/1831)[2] |

**Health and Social Care Act 2012 (c 7)**—*contd*

|  |  |  |
|---|---|---|
| | paras 126–136 | 27 Mar 2012 (so far as is necessary for enabling the exercise on or after that date of any power to make an order or regulations or to give directions that is conferred by these provisions or an amendment made by them) (s 306(1)(d)) |
| | | 1 Apr 2013 (otherwise) (SI 2013/160)[4] |
| | para 137 | 27 Mar 2012 (so far as is necessary for enabling the exercise on or after that date of any power to make an order or regulations or to give directions that is conferred by these provisions or an amendment made by them) (s 306(1)(d)) |
| | | 1 Oct 2012 (otherwise) (SI 2012/1831)[2] |
| | para 138(1) | 27 Mar 2012 (so far as is necessary for enabling the exercise on or after that date of any power to make an order or regulations or to give directions that is conferred by these provisions or an amendment made by them) (s 306(1)(d)) |
| | | 1 Apr 2013 (otherwise) (SI 2013/160)[4] |
| | para 138(2)(a) | 27 Mar 2012 (so far as is necessary for enabling the exercise on or after that date of any power to make an order or regulations or to give directions that is conferred by these provisions or an amendment made by them) (s 306(1)(d)) |
| | | 1 Oct 2012 (otherwise) (SI 2012/1831) |
| | para 138(2)(b) | 27 Mar 2012 (so far as is necessary for enabling the exercise on or after that date of any power to make an order or regulations or to give directions that is conferred by these provisions or an amendment made by them) (s 306(1)(d)) |
| | | 1 Apr 2013 (otherwise) (SI 2013/160)[4] |
| | para 138(2)(c) | 27 Mar 2012 (so far as is necessary for enabling the exercise on or after that date of any power to make an order or regulations or to give directions that is conferred by these provisions or an amendment made by them) (s 306(1)(d)) |
| | | 1 Oct 2012 (otherwise) (SI 2012/1831)[2] |
| | para 138(3) | 27 Mar 2012 (so far as is necessary for enabling the exercise on or after that date of any power to make an order or regulations or to give directions that is conferred by these provisions or an amendment made by them) (s 306(1)(d)) |
| | | 1 Apr 2013 (otherwise) (SI 2013/160)[4] |
| | para 138(4), (5) | 27 Mar 2012 (so far as is necessary for enabling the exercise on or after that date of any power to make an order or regulations or to give directions that is conferred by these provisions or an amendment made by them) (s 306(1)(d)) |
| | | 1 Oct 2012 (otherwise) (SI 2012/1831) |
| | para 139(1) | See sub-paras (2)–(5) below |
| | para 139(2) | 27 Mar 2012 (so far as is necessary for enabling the exercise on or after that date of any power to make an order or regulations or to give directions that is conferred by these provisions or an amendment made by them) (s 306(1)(d)) |
| | | 1 Oct 2012 (otherwise) (SI 2012/1831) |
| | para 139(3)–(5) | 27 Mar 2012 (so far as is necessary for enabling the exercise on or after that date of any power to make an order or regulations or to give directions that is conferred by these provisions or an amendment made by them) (s 306(1)(d)) |
| | | 1 Apr 2013 (otherwise) (SI 2013/160)[4] |
| Sch 5 | paras 1–4 | 27 Mar 2012 (so far as is necessary for enabling the exercise on or after that date of any power to make an order or regulations or to give directions that is conferred by these provisions or an amendment made by them) (s 306(1)(d)) |
| | | 1 Apr 2013 (otherwise) (SI 2013/160)[4] |
| | para 5(a) | 27 Mar 2012 (so far as is necessary for enabling the exercise on or after that date of any power to make an order or regulations or to give directions that is conferred by these provisions or an amendment made by them) (s 306(1)(d)) |
| | | 1 Oct 2012 (otherwise) (SI 2012/1831) |

**Health and Social Care Act 2012 (c 7)**—*contd*

| | |
|---|---|
| para 5(b) | 27 Mar 2012 (so far as is necessary for enabling the exercise on or after that date of any power to make an order or regulations or to give directions that is conferred by these provisions or an amendment made by them) (s 306(1)(d)) |
| | 1 Apr 2013 (otherwise) (SI 2013/160)[4] |
| para 5(c) | 27 Mar 2012 (so far as is necessary for enabling the exercise on or after that date of any power to make an order or regulations or to give directions that is conferred by these provisions or an amendment made by them) (s 306(1)(d)) |
| | 1 Oct 2012 (otherwise) (SI 2012/1831) |
| para 5(d) | 27 Mar 2012 (so far as is necessary for enabling the exercise on or after that date of any power to make an order or regulations or to give directions that is conferred by these provisions or an amendment made by them) (s 306(1)(d)) |
| | 1 Apr 2013 (otherwise) (SI 2013/160)[4] |
| para 6 | 27 Mar 2012 (so far as is necessary for enabling the exercise on or after that date of any power to make an order or regulations or to give directions that is conferred by these provisions or an amendment made by them) (s 306(1)(d)) |
| | 1 Oct 2012 (otherwise) (SI 2012/1831)[2] |
| para 7(a) | 27 Mar 2012 (so far as is necessary for enabling the exercise on or after that date of any power to make an order or regulations or to give directions that is conferred by these provisions or an amendment made by them) (s 306(1)(d)) |
| | 1 Apr 2013 (otherwise) (SI 2013/160)[4] |
| para 7(b) | 27 Mar 2012 (so far as is necessary for enabling the exercise on or after that date of any power to make an order or regulations or to give directions that is conferred by these provisions or an amendment made by them) (s 306(1)(d)) |
| | 1 Oct 2012 (otherwise) (SI 2012/1831) |
| para 7(c) | 27 Mar 2012 (so far as is necessary for enabling the exercise on or after that date of any power to make an order or regulations or to give directions that is conferred by these provisions or an amendment made by them) (s 306(1)(d)) |
| | 1 Apr 2013 (otherwise) (SI 2013/160)[4] |
| para 8(a)(i) | 27 Mar 2012 (so far as is necessary for enabling the exercise on or after that date of any power to make an order or regulations or to give directions that is conferred by these provisions or an amendment made by them) (s 306(1)(d)) |
| | 1 Oct 2012 (except in so far as inserts reference to "a local authority") (SI 2012/1831) |
| | 1 Apr 2013 (exception noted above) (SI 2012/1831) (SI 2013/160)[4] |
| para 8(a)(ii), (iii) | 27 Mar 2012 (so far as is necessary for enabling the exercise on or after that date of any power to make an order or regulations or to give directions that is conferred by these provisions or an amendment made by them) (s 306(1)(d)) |
| | 1 Apr 2013 (otherwise) (SI 2013/160)[4] |
| para 8(b)(i) | 27 Mar 2012 (so far as is necessary for enabling the exercise on or after that date of any power to make an order or regulations or to give directions that is conferred by these provisions or an amendment made by them) (s 306(1)(d)) |
| | 1 Oct 2012 (except in so far as inserts reference to "a local authority") (SI 2012/1831) |
| | 1 Apr 2013 (exception noted above) (SI 2012/1831) (SI 2013/160)[4] |
| paras 8(b)(ii), (iii), 9 | 27 Mar 2012 (so far as is necessary for enabling the exercise on or after that date of any power to make an order or regulations or to give directions that is conferred by these provisions or an amendment made by them) (s 306(1)(d)) |
| | 1 Apr 2013 (otherwise) (SI 2013/160)[4] |

**Health and Social Care Act 2012 (c 7)**—*contd*

| | |
|---|---|
| para 10(a)(i) | 27 Mar 2012 (so far as is necessary for enabling the exercise on or after that date of any power to make an order or regulations or to give directions that is conferred by these provisions or an amendment made by them) (s 306(1)(d)) |
| | 1 Oct 2012 (otherwise) (SI 2012/1831) |
| para 10(a)(ii), (iii) | 27 Mar 2012 (so far as is necessary for enabling the exercise on or after that date of any power to make an order or regulations or to give directions that is conferred by these provisions or an amendment made by them) (s 306(1)(d)) |
| | 1 Apr 2013 (otherwise) (SI 2013/160)[4] |
| para 10(b)(i) | 27 Mar 2012 (so far as is necessary for enabling the exercise on or after that date of any power to make an order or regulations or to give directions that is conferred by these provisions or an amendment made by them) (s 306(1)(d)) |
| | 1 Oct 2012 (otherwise) (SI 2012/1831) |
| para 10(b)(ii), (iii) | 27 Mar 2012 (so far as is necessary for enabling the exercise on or after that date of any power to make an order or regulations or to give directions that is conferred by these provisions or an amendment made by them) (s 306(1)(d)) |
| | 1 Apr 2013 (otherwise) (SI 2013/160)[4] |
| para 11 | See paras 12, 13 below |
| para 12(1) | See sub-paras (2)–(5) below |
| para 12(2)(a) | 27 Mar 2012 (so far as is necessary for enabling the exercise on or after that date of any power to make an order or regulations or to give directions that is conferred by these provisions or an amendment made by them) (s 306(1)(d)) |
| | 1 Oct 2012 (otherwise) (SI 2012/1831) |
| paras 12(2)(b), (c), (3)–(5), 13 | 27 Mar 2012 (so far as is necessary for enabling the exercise on or after that date of any power to make an order or regulations or to give directions that is conferred by these provisions or an amendment made by them) (s 306(1)(d)) |
| | 1 Apr 2013 (otherwise) (SI 2013/160)[4] |
| para 14(a) | 27 Mar 2012 (so far as is necessary for enabling the exercise on or after that date of any power to make an order or regulations or to give directions that is conferred by these provisions or an amendment made by them) (s 306(1)(d)) |
| | 1 Oct 2012 (otherwise) (SI 2012/1831) |
| paras 14(b), 15–19, 20(a), (b) | 27 Mar 2012 (so far as is necessary for enabling the exercise on or after that date of any power to make an order or regulations or to give directions that is conferred by these provisions or an amendment made by them) (s 306(1)(d)) |
| | 1 Apr 2013 (otherwise) (SI 2013/160)[4] |
| para 20(c) | 27 Mar 2012 (so far as is necessary for enabling the exercise on or after that date of any power to make an order or regulations or to give directions that is conferred by these provisions or an amendment made by them) (s 306(1)(d)) |
| | 1 Oct 2012 (otherwise) (SI 2012/1831) |
| para 21 | See paras 22, 23 below |
| para 22(a) | 27 Mar 2012 (so far as is necessary for enabling the exercise on or after that date of any power to make an order or regulations or to give directions that is conferred by these provisions or an amendment made by them) (s 306(1)(d)) |
| | 1 Oct 2012 (otherwise) (SI 2012/1831) |
| paras 22(b), 23(a) | 27 Mar 2012 (so far as is necessary for enabling the exercise on or after that date of any power to make an order or regulations or to give directions that is conferred by these provisions or an amendment made by them) (s 306(1)(d)) |
| | 1 Apr 2013 (otherwise) (SI 2013/160)[4] |

**Health and Social Care Act 2012 (c 7)**—*contd*

| | |
|---|---|
| para 23(b) | 27 Mar 2012 (so far as is necessary for enabling the exercise on or after that date of any power to make an order or regulations or to give directions that is conferred by these provisions or an amendment made by them) (s 306(1)(d)) |
| | 1 Oct 2012 (otherwise) (SI 2012/1831) |
| paras 24–29 | 27 Mar 2012 (so far as is necessary for enabling the exercise on or after that date of any power to make an order or regulations or to give directions that is conferred by these provisions or an amendment made by them) (s 306(1)(d)) |
| | 1 Apr 2013 (otherwise) (SI 2013/160)⁴ |
| para 30 | 27 Mar 2012 (so far as is necessary for enabling the exercise on or after that date of any power to make an order or regulations or to give directions that is conferred by these provisions or an amendment made by them) (s 306(1)(d)) |
| | 1 Apr 2013 (otherwise) (SI 2013/160)⁴ |
| paras 31, 32 | 27 Mar 2012 (so far as is necessary for enabling the exercise on or after that date of any power to make an order or regulations or to give directions that is conferred by these provisions or an amendment made by them) (s 306(1)(d)) |
| | 1 Apr 2013 (otherwise) (SI 2013/160)⁴ |
| paras 33–37 | 27 Mar 2012 (so far as is necessary for enabling the exercise on or after that date of any power to make an order or regulations or to give directions that is conferred by these provisions or an amendment made by them) (s 306(1)(d)) |
| | 1 Apr 2013 (otherwise) (SI 2013/160) |
| paras 38–43 | 27 Mar 2012 (so far as is necessary for enabling the exercise on or after that date of any power to make an order or regulations or to give directions that is conferred by these provisions or an amendment made by them) (s 306(1)(d)) |
| | 1 Apr 2013 (otherwise) (SI 2013/160)⁴ |
| para 44(a) | 27 Mar 2012 (so far as is necessary for enabling the exercise on or after that date of any power to make an order or regulations or to give directions that is conferred by these provisions or an amendment made by them) (s 306(1)(d)) |
| | 1 Oct 2012 (otherwise) (SI 2012/1831) |
| paras 44(b), 45–48 | 27 Mar 2012 (so far as is necessary for enabling the exercise on or after that date of any power to make an order or regulations or to give directions that is conferred by these provisions or an amendment made by them) (s 306(1)(d)) |
| | 1 Apr 2013 (otherwise) (SI 2013/160)⁴ |
| para 49 | 27 Mar 2012 (so far as is necessary for enabling the exercise on or after that date of any power to make an order or regulations or to give directions that is conferred by these provisions or an amendment made by them) (s 306(1)(d)) |
| | 1 Apr 2013 (otherwise) (SI 2013/160)⁴ |
| paras 50–54 | 27 Mar 2012 (so far as is necessary for enabling the exercise on or after that date of any power to make an order or regulations or to give directions that is conferred by these provisions or an amendment made by them) (s 306(1)(d)) |
| | 1 Apr 2013 (otherwise) (SI 2013/160)⁴ |
| para 55 | 27 Mar 2012 (so far as is necessary for enabling the exercise on or after that date of any power to make an order or regulations or to give directions that is conferred by these provisions or an amendment made by them) (s 306(1)(d)) |
| | 1 Apr 2013 (otherwise) (SI 2013/160)⁴ |
| paras 56–62 | 27 Mar 2012 (so far as is necessary for enabling the exercise on or after that date of any power to make an order or regulations or to give directions that is conferred by these provisions or an amendment made by them) (s 306(1)(d)) |
| | 1 Apr 2013 (otherwise) (SI 2013/160)⁴ |

**Health and Social Care Act 2012 (c 7)**—*contd*

| | |
|---|---|
| para 63 | 27 Mar 2012 (so far as is necessary for enabling the exercise on or after that date of any power to make an order or regulations or to give directions that is conferred by these provisions or an amendment made by them) (s 306(1)(d)) |
| | 1 Apr 2013 (otherwise) (SI 2013/160)[4] |
| paras 64–66 | 27 Mar 2012 (so far as is necessary for enabling the exercise on or after that date of any power to make an order or regulations or to give directions that is conferred by these provisions or an amendment made by them) (s 306(1)(d)) |
| | 1 Apr 2013 (otherwise) (SI 2013/160)[4] |
| para 67 | See paras 68–70 below |
| para 68(a), (b) | 27 Mar 2012 (so far as is necessary for enabling the exercise on or after that date of any power to make an order or regulations or to give directions that is conferred by these provisions or an amendment made by them) (s 306(1)(d)) |
| | 1 Apr 2013 (otherwise) (SI 2013/160) |
| para 68(c) | 27 Mar 2012 (so far as is necessary for enabling the exercise on or after that date of any power to make an order or regulations or to give directions that is conferred by these provisions or an amendment made by them) (s 306(1)(d)) |
| | 1 Oct 2012 (otherwise) (SI 2012/1831) |
| paras 69–71 | 27 Mar 2012 (so far as is necessary for enabling the exercise on or after that date of any power to make an order or regulations or to give directions that is conferred by these provisions or an amendment made by them) (s 306(1)(d)) |
| | 1 Apr 2013 (otherwise) (SI 2013/160)[4] |
| para 72 | See paras 73–75 below |
| para 73 | 27 Mar 2012 (so far as is necessary for enabling the exercise on or after that date of any power to make an order or regulations or to give directions that is conferred by these provisions or an amendment made by them) (s 306(1)(d)) |
| | 1 Apr 2013 (otherwise) (SI 2013/160)[4] |
| para 74(a) | 27 Mar 2012 (so far as is necessary for enabling the exercise on or after that date of any power to make an order or regulations or to give directions that is conferred by these provisions or an amendment made by them) (s 306(1)(d)) |
| | 1 Oct 2012 (otherwise) (SI 2012/1831) |
| para 74(b) | 27 Mar 2012 (so far as is necessary for enabling the exercise on or after that date of any power to make an order or regulations or to give directions that is conferred by these provisions or an amendment made by them) (s 306(1)(d)) |
| | 1 Apr 2013 (otherwise) (SI 2013/160)[4] |
| para 75(a) | 27 Mar 2012 (so far as is necessary for enabling the exercise on or after that date of any power to make an order or regulations or to give directions that is conferred by these provisions or an amendment made by them) (s 306(1)(d)) |
| | 1 Oct 2012 (otherwise) (SI 2012/1831) |
| para 75(b)–(e) | 27 Mar 2012 (so far as is necessary for enabling the exercise on or after that date of any power to make an order or regulations or to give directions that is conferred by these provisions or an amendment made by them) (s 306(1)(d)) |
| | 1 Apr 2013 (otherwise) (SI 2013/160)[4] |
| para 76(a) | 27 Mar 2012 (so far as is necessary for enabling the exercise on or after that date of any power to make an order or regulations or to give directions that is conferred by these provisions or an amendment made by them) (s 306(1)(d)) |
| | 1 Oct 2012 (otherwise) (SI 2012/1831) |
| paras 76(b), (c), 77–95 | 27 Mar 2012 (so far as is necessary for enabling the exercise on or after that date of any power to make an order or regulations or to give directions that is conferred by these provisions or an amendment made by them) (s 306(1)(d)) |

**Health and Social Care Act 2012 (c 7)**—*contd*

| | |
|---|---|
| | 1 Apr 2013 (otherwise) (SI 2013/160)[4] |
| para 96 | 27 Mar 2012 (so far as is necessary for enabling the exercise on or after that date of any power to make an order or regulations or to give directions that is conferred by these provisions or an amendment made by them) (s 306(1)(d)) |
| | 1 Oct 2012 (otherwise) (SI 2012/1831)[2] |
| paras 97, 98, 99(a) | 27 Mar 2012 (so far as is necessary for enabling the exercise on or after that date of any power to make an order or regulations or to give directions that is conferred by these provisions or an amendment made by them) (s 306(1)(d)) |
| | 1 Apr 2013 (otherwise) (SI 2013/160)[4] |
| para 99(b) | 27 Mar 2012 (so far as is necessary for enabling the exercise on or after that date of any power to make an order or regulations or to give directions that is conferred by these provisions or an amendment made by them) (s 306(1)(d)) |
| | 1 Oct 2012 (otherwise) (SI 2012/1831) |
| para 99(c) | 27 Mar 2012 (so far as is necessary for enabling the exercise on or after that date of any power to make an order or regulations or to give directions that is conferred by these provisions or an amendment made by them) (s 306(1)(d)) |
| | 1 Apr 2013 (otherwise) (SI 2013/160)[4] |
| para 100(a) | 27 Mar 2012 (so far as is necessary for enabling the exercise on or after that date of any power to make an order or regulations or to give directions that is conferred by these provisions or an amendment made by them) (s 306(1)(d)) |
| | 1 Oct 2012 (otherwise) (SI 2012/1831) |
| paras 100(b), (c), 101–146 | 27 Mar 2012 (so far as is necessary for enabling the exercise on or after that date of any power to make an order or regulations or to give directions that is conferred by these provisions or an amendment made by them) (s 306(1)(d)) |
| | 1 Apr 2013 (otherwise) (SI 2013/160)[4] |
| para 147(a), (b)(i) | 27 Mar 2012 (so far as is necessary for enabling the exercise on or after that date of any power to make an order or regulations or to give directions that is conferred by these provisions or an amendment made by them) (s 306(1)(d)) |
| | 1 Oct 2012 (otherwise) (SI 2012/1831) |
| paras 147(b)(ii), (iii), 148–153 | 27 Mar 2012 (so far as is necessary for enabling the exercise on or after that date of any power to make an order or regulations or to give directions that is conferred by these provisions or an amendment made by them) (s 306(1)(d)) |
| | 1 Apr 2013 (otherwise) (SI 2013/160)[4] |
| para 154 | See paras 155–167 below |
| para 155, 156 | 27 Mar 2012 (so far as is necessary for enabling the exercise on or after that date of any power to make an order or regulations or to give directions that is conferred by these provisions or an amendment made by them) (s 306(1)(d)) |
| | 1 Apr 2013 (otherwise) (SI 2013/160[4]) |
| para 157(a) | 27 Mar 2012 (so far as is necessary for enabling the exercise on or after that date of any power to make an order or regulations or to give directions that is conferred by these provisions or an amendment made by them) (s 306(1)(d)) |
| | 1 Apr 2013 (otherwise) (SI 2013/160)[4] |
| para 157(b), (c) | 27 Mar 2012 (so far as is necessary for enabling the exercise on or after that date of any power to make an order or regulations or to give directions that is conferred by these provisions or an amendment made by them) (s 306(1)(d)) |
| | *Never in force* (otherwise) (repealed) |
| para 158 | 27 Mar 2012 (so far as is necessary for enabling the exercise on or after that date of any power to make an order or regulations or to give directions that is conferred by these provisions or an amendment made by them) (s 306(1)(d)) |

**Health and Social Care Act 2012 (c 7)**—*contd*

| | |
|---|---|
| | 1 Apr 2013 (otherwise) (SI 2013/160)[4] |
| para 159(a) | 27 Mar 2012 (so far as is necessary for enabling the exercise on or after that date of any power to make an order or regulations or to give directions that is conferred by these provisions or an amendment made by them) (s 306(1)(d)) |
| | 1 Apr 2013 (otherwise) (SI 2013/160)[4] |
| para 159(b) | 27 Mar 2012 (so far as is necessary for enabling the exercise on or after that date of any power to make an order or regulations or to give directions that is conferred by these provisions or an amendment made by them) (s 306(1)(d)) |
| | *Never in force* (otherwise) (repealed) |
| paras 160–162 | 27 Mar 2012 (so far as is necessary for enabling the exercise on or after that date of any power to make an order or regulations or to give directions that is conferred by these provisions or an amendment made by them) (s 306(1)(d)) |
| | 1 Apr 2013 (otherwise) (SI 2013/160)[4] |
| paras 163, 164 | 27 Mar 2012 (so far as is necessary for enabling the exercise on or after that date of any power to make an order or regulations or to give directions that is conferred by these provisions or an amendment made by them) (s 306(1)(d)) |
| | *Never in force* (otherwise) (repealed) |
| paras 165–172 | 27 Mar 2012 (so far as is necessary for enabling the exercise on or after that date of any power to make an order or regulations or to give directions that is conferred by these provisions or an amendment made by them) (s 306(1)(d)) |
| | 1 Apr 2013 (otherwise) (SI 2013/160)[4] |
| para 173 | See paras 174–179 below |
| para 174 | 27 Mar 2012 (so far as is necessary for enabling the exercise on or after that date of any power to make an order or regulations or to give directions that is conferred by these provisions or an amendment made by them) (s 306(1)(d)) |
| | 1 Apr 2013 (otherwise) (SI 2013/160)[4] |
| para 175(1) | See sub-paras (2)–(6) below |
| para 175(2), (3)(a), (b) | 27 Mar 2012 (so far as is necessary for enabling the exercise on or after that date of any power to make an order or regulations or to give directions that is conferred by these provisions or an amendment made by them) (s 306(1)(d)) |
| | 1 Apr 2013 (otherwise) (SI 2013/160)[4] |
| para 175(3)(c) | 27 Mar 2012 (so far as is necessary for enabling the exercise on or after that date of any power to make an order or regulations or to give directions that is conferred by these provisions or an amendment made by them) (s 306(1)(d)) |
| | 1 Oct 2012 (in so far as inserts Health Act 2009, s 2(2)(ca), (cb)) (SI 2012/1831) |
| | 1 Apr 2013 (in so far as inserts s 2(2)(cc) thereof) (SI 2013/160)[4] |
| paras 175(4)–(6), 176–179 | 27 Mar 2012 (so far as is necessary for enabling the exercise on or after that date of any power to make an order or regulations or to give directions that is conferred by these provisions or an amendment made by them) (s 306(1)(d)) |
| | 1 Apr 2013 (otherwise) (SI 2013/160)[4] |
| para 180 | See paras 181, 182 below |
| para 181 | 27 Mar 2012 (so far as is necessary for enabling the exercise on or after that date of any power to make an order or regulations or to give directions that is conferred by these provisions or an amendment made by them) (s 306(1)(d)) |
| | 1 Apr 2013 (otherwise) (SI 2013/160)[4] |
| para 182(a) | 27 Mar 2012 (so far as is necessary for enabling the exercise on or after that date of any power to make an order or regulations or to give directions that is conferred by these provisions or an amendment made by them) (s 306(1)(d)) |
| | 1 Oct 2012 (otherwise) (SI 2012/1831) |

**Health and Social Care Act 2012 (c 7)**—*contd*

| | | |
|---|---|---|
| | paras 182(b)–(d), 183 | 27 Mar 2012 (so far as is necessary for enabling the exercise on or after that date of any power to make an order or regulations or to give directions that is conferred by these provisions or an amendment made by them) (s 306(1)(d)) |
| | | 1 Apr 2013 (otherwise) (SI 2013/160)[4] |
| | para 184(a), (b) | 27 Mar 2012 (so far as is necessary for enabling the exercise on or after that date of any power to make an order or regulations or to give directions that is conferred by these provisions or an amendment made by them) (s 306(1)(d)) |
| | | 1 Apr 2013 (otherwise) (SI 2013/160)[4] |
| | para 184(c) | 27 Mar 2012 (so far as is necessary for enabling the exercise on or after that date of any power to make an order or regulations or to give directions that is conferred by these provisions or an amendment made by them) (s 306(1)(d)) |
| | | 1 Oct 2012 (otherwise) (SI 2012/1831) |
| | para 184(d) | 27 Mar 2012 (so far as is necessary for enabling the exercise on or after that date of any power to make an order or regulations or to give directions that is conferred by these provisions or an amendment made by them) (s 306(1)(d)) |
| | | 1 Apr 2013 (otherwise) (SI 2013/160)[4] |
| Sch 6 | para 1(1)–(3) | 27 Mar 2012 (so far as is necessary for enabling the exercise on or after that date of any power to make an order or regulations or to give directions that is conferred by these provisions or an amendment made by them) (s 306(1)(d)) |
| | | 1 Oct 2012 (otherwise) (SI 2012/1831) |
| | para 1(4) | 27 Mar 2012 (so far as is necessary for enabling the exercise on or after that date of any power to make an order or regulations or to give directions that is conferred by these provisions or an amendment made by them) (s 306(1)(d)) |
| | | 1 Jul 2012 (in so far as relates to para 2(1)) (SI 2012/1319) |
| | | 1 Oct 2012 (otherwise) (SI 2012/1831) |
| | para 1(5) | 27 Mar 2012 (so far as is necessary for enabling the exercise on or after that date of any power to make an order or regulations or to give directions that is conferred by these provisions or an amendment made by them) (s 306(1)(d)) |
| | | 1 Oct 2012 (otherwise) (SI 2012/1831) |
| | para 2(1) | 27 Mar 2012 (so far as is necessary for enabling the exercise on or after that date of any power to make an order or regulations or to give directions that is conferred by these provisions or an amendment made by them) (s 306(1)(d)) |
| | | 1 Jul 2012 (otherwise) (SI 2012/1319) |
| | para 2(2) | 27 Mar 2012 (so far as is necessary for enabling the exercise on or after that date of any power to make an order or regulations or to give directions that is conferred by these provisions or an amendment made by them) (s 306(1)(d)) |
| | | 1 Oct 2012 (otherwise) (SI 2012/1831) |
| | paras 3–13 | 27 Mar 2012 (so far as is necessary for enabling the exercise on or after that date of any power to make an order or regulations or to give directions that is conferred by these provisions or an amendment made by them) (s 306(1)(d)) |
| | | 1 Oct 2012 (otherwise) (SI 2012/1831) |
| Sch 7 | | 27 Mar 2012 (so far as is necessary for enabling the exercise on or after that date of any power to make an order or regulations or to give directions that is conferred by these provisions or an amendment made by them) (s 306(1)(d)) |
| | | 1 Apr 2013 (otherwise) (SI 2013/160)[4] |
| Sch 8 | | 27 Mar 2012 (so far as is necessary for enabling the exercise on or after that date of any power to make an order or regulations or to give directions that is conferred by these provisions or an amendment made by them) (s 306(1)(d)) |
| | | 1 Nov 2012 (otherwise) (SI 2012/2657)[3] |

**Health and Social Care Act 2012 (c 7)**—*contd*

| | | |
|---|---|---|
| Sch 9 | | 27 Mar 2012 (so far as is necessary for enabling the exercise on or after that date of any power to make an order or regulations or to give directions that is conferred by these provisions or an amendment made by them) (s 306(1)(d)) |
| | | 1 Apr 2013 (otherwise) (SI 2013/160) |
| Sch 10 | | 27 Mar 2012 (so far as is necessary for enabling the exercise on or after that date of any power to make an order or regulations or to give directions that is conferred by these provisions or an amendment made by them) (s 306(1)(d)) |
| | | 1 Nov 2012 (otherwise) (SI 2012/2657) |
| Sch 11 | paras 1, 2(1), (2), (3)(a), (b) | 27 Mar 2012 (so far as is necessary for enabling the exercise on or after that date of any power to make an order or regulations or to give directions that is conferred by these provisions or an amendment made by them) (s 306(1)(d)) |
| | | 1 Apr 2013 (otherwise) (SI 2013/671) |
| | para 2(3)(c) | 27 Mar 2012 (so far as is necessary for enabling the exercise on or after that date of any power to make an order or regulations or to give directions that is conferred by these provisions or an amendment made by them) (s 306(1)(d)) |
| | | 1 Jul 2013 (otherwise) (SI 2013/671) |
| | para 2(3)(d), (e) | 27 Mar 2012 (so far as is necessary for enabling the exercise on or after that date of any power to make an order or regulations or to give directions that is conferred by these provisions or an amendment made by them) (s 306(1)(d)) |
| | | 1 Apr 2013 (otherwise) (SI 2013/671) |
| | para 2(4), (5) | 27 Mar 2012 (so far as is necessary for enabling the exercise on or after that date of any power to make an order or regulations or to give directions that is conferred by these provisions or an amendment made by them) (s 306(1)(d)) |
| | | 1 Jul 2013 (otherwise) (SI 2013/671) |
| | para 3(1), (2)(a), (b) | 27 Mar 2012 (so far as is necessary for enabling the exercise on or after that date of any power to make an order or regulations or to give directions that is conferred by these provisions or an amendment made by them) (s 306(1)(d)) |
| | | 1 Apr 2013 (otherwise) (SI 2013/671) |
| | para 3(2)(c) | 27 Mar 2012 (so far as is necessary for enabling the exercise on or after that date of any power to make an order or regulations or to give directions that is conferred by these provisions or an amendment made by them) (s 306(1)(d)) |
| | | 1 Jul 2013 (otherwise) (SI 2013/671) |
| | paras 3(2)(d), (e), (3), (4), 4(a) | 27 Mar 2012 (so far as is necessary for enabling the exercise on or after that date of any power to make an order or regulations or to give directions that is conferred by these provisions or an amendment made by them) (s 306(1)(d)) |
| | | 1 Apr 2013 (otherwise) (SI 2013/671) |
| | para 4(b) | 27 Mar 2012 (so far as is necessary for enabling the exercise on or after that date of any power to make an order or regulations or to give directions that is conferred by these provisions or an amendment made by them) (s 306(1)(d)) |
| | | 1 Jul 2013 (otherwise) (SI 2013/671) |
| | paras 4(c), 5, 6, 7(1) | 27 Mar 2012 (so far as is necessary for enabling the exercise on or after that date of any power to make an order or regulations or to give directions that is conferred by these provisions or an amendment made by them) (s 306(1)(d)) |
| | | 1 Apr 2013 (otherwise) (SI 2013/671) |
| | para 7(2)(a) | 27 Mar 2012 (so far as is necessary for enabling the exercise on or after that date of any power to make an order or regulations or to give directions that is conferred by these provisions or an amendment made by them) (s 306(1)(d)) |
| | | 1 Jul 2013 (otherwise) (SI 2013/671) |

**Health and Social Care Act 2012 (c 7)**—*contd*

| | |
|---|---|
| para 7(2)(b) | 27 Mar 2012 (so far as is necessary for enabling the exercise on or after that date of any power to make an order or regulations or to give directions that is conferred by these provisions or an amendment made by them) (s 306(1)(d)) |
| | 1 Apr 2013 (otherwise) (SI 2013/671) |
| para 8(a) | 27 Mar 2012 (so far as is necessary for enabling the exercise on or after that date of any power to make an order or regulations or to give directions that is conferred by these provisions or an amendment made by them) (s 306(1)(d)) |
| | 1 Jul 2013 (otherwise) (SI 2013/671) |
| para 8(b) | 27 Mar 2012 (so far as is necessary for enabling the exercise on or after that date of any power to make an order or regulations or to give directions that is conferred by these provisions or an amendment made by them) (s 306(1)(d)) |
| | 1 Apr 2013 (otherwise) (SI 2013/671) |
| paras 9–14 | 27 Mar 2012 (so far as is necessary for enabling the exercise on or after that date of any power to make an order or regulations or to give directions that is conferred by these provisions or an amendment made by them) (s 306(1)(d)) |
| | 1 Apr 2013 (otherwise) (SI 2013/671) |
| Sch 12 | 27 Mar 2012 (so far as is necessary for enabling the exercise on or after that date of any power to make an order or regulations or to give directions that is conferred by these provisions or an amendment made by them) (s 306(1)(d)) |
| | 1 Sep 2013 (in so far as relates to consultation under ss 118, 119 in relation to a tariff published by Monitor under s 116) (SI 2013/671) |
| | 1 Apr 2014 (otherwise) (SI 2014/39) |
| Sch 13 paras 1–7 | 27 Mar 2012 (so far as is necessary for enabling the exercise on or after that date of any power to make an order or regulations or to give directions that is conferred by these provisions or an amendment made by them) (s 306(1)(d)) |
| | 1 Jul 2012 (otherwise) (SI 2012/1319) |
| para 8 | See paras 9–12 below |
| para 9(1) | 27 Mar 2012 (so far as is necessary for enabling the exercise on or after that date of any power to make an order or regulations or to give directions that is conferred by these provisions or an amendment made by them) (s 306(1)(d)) |
| | 1 Jul 2012 (so far as repeals National Health Service Act 2006, s 31(1)) (SI 2012/1319) |
| | 1 Nov 2012 (otherwise) (SI 2012/2657) |
| para 9(2) | 27 Mar 2012 (so far as is necessary for enabling the exercise on or after that date of any power to make an order or regulations or to give directions that is conferred by these provisions or an amendment made by them) (s 306(1)(d)) |
| | 1 Nov 2012 (otherwise) (SI 2012/2657) |
| para 10 | 27 Mar 2012 (so far as is necessary for enabling the exercise on or after that date of any power to make an order or regulations or to give directions that is conferred by these provisions or an amendment made by them) (s 306(1)(d)) |
| | 1 Nov 2012 (otherwise) (SI 2012/2657)[3] |
| paras 11–13 | 27 Mar 2012 (so far as is necessary for enabling the exercise on or after that date of any power to make an order or regulations or to give directions that is conferred by these provisions or an amendment made by them) (s 306(1)(d)) |
| | 1 Jul 2012 (otherwise) (SI 2012/1319) |
| paras 14–17 | 27 Mar 2012 (so far as is necessary for enabling the exercise on or after that date of any power to make an order or regulations or to give directions that is conferred by these provisions or an amendment made by them) (s 306(1)(d)) |
| | 1 Apr 2013 (otherwise) (SI 2013/160) |

**Health and Social Care Act 2012 (c 7)**—*contd*

| | | |
|---|---|---|
| | paras 18, 19 | 27 Mar 2012 (so far as is necessary for enabling the exercise on or after that date of any power to make an order or regulations or to give directions that is conferred by these provisions or an amendment made by them) (s 306(1)(d)) |
| | | 1 Jul 2012 (otherwise) (SI 2012/1319) |
| Sch 14 | | 27 Mar 2012 (so far as is necessary for enabling the exercise on or after that date of any power to make an order or regulations or to give directions that is conferred by these provisions or an amendment made by them) (s 306(1)(d)) |
| | | *Repealed (never in force otherwise)* |
| Sch 15 | Pts 1, 2 | 27 Mar 2012 (so far as is necessary for enabling the exercise on or after that date of any power to make an order or regulations or to give directions that is conferred by these provisions or an amendment made by them) (s 306(1)(d)) |
| | | 1 Aug 2012 (otherwise) (SI 2012/1319) |
| | Pt 3 | 27 Mar 2012 (so far as is necessary for enabling the exercise on or after that date of any power to make an order or regulations or to give directions that is conferred by these provisions or an amendment made by them) (s 306(1)(d)) |
| | | 1 Dec 2012 (otherwise) (SI 2012/2657) |
| | Pt 4 | 27 Mar 2012 (so far as is necessary for enabling the exercise on or after that date of any power to make an order or regulations or to give directions that is conferred by these provisions or an amendment made by them) (s 306(1)(d)) |
| | | 1 Jul 2012 (otherwise) (SI 2012/1319) |
| Sch 16 | | 27 Mar 2012 (so far as is necessary for enabling the exercise on or after that date of any power to make an order or regulations or to give directions that is conferred by these provisions or an amendment made by them) (s 306(1)(d)) |
| | | 1 Apr 2013 (otherwise) (SI 2013/160)[4] |
| Sch 17 | | 27 Mar 2012 (so far as is necessary for enabling the exercise on or after that date of any power to make an order or regulations or to give directions that is conferred by these provisions or an amendment made by them) (s 306(1)(d)) |
| | | 1 Apr 2013 (otherwise) (SI 2013/160) |
| Sch 18 | | 27 Mar 2012 (so far as is necessary for enabling the exercise on or after that date of any power to make an order or regulations or to give directions that is conferred by these provisions or an amendment made by them) (s 306(1)(d)) |
| | | 1 Apr 2013 (otherwise) (SI 2013/160)[4] |
| Sch 19 | | 27 Mar 2012 (so far as is necessary for enabling the exercise on or after that date of any power to make an order or regulations or to give directions that is conferred by these provisions or an amendment made by them) (s 306(1)(d)) |
| | | 1 Apr 2013 (otherwise) (SI 2013/160)[4] |
| Sch 20 | Pt 1 | 27 Mar 2012 (so far as is necessary for enabling the exercise on or after that date of any power to make an order or regulations or to give directions that is conferred by these provisions or an amendment made by them) (s 306(1)(d)) |
| | | 1 Jul 2012 (otherwise) (SI 2012/1319) |
| | Pt 2 | 27 Mar 2012 (so far as is necessary for enabling the exercise on or after that date of any power to make an order or regulations or to give directions that is conferred by these provisions or an amendment made by them) (s 306(1)(d)) |
| | | 31 Oct 2012 (otherwise) (SI 2012/1831) |
| | Pt 3 | 27 Mar 2012 (so far as is necessary for enabling the exercise on or after that date of any power to make an order or regulations or to give directions that is conferred by these provisions or an amendment made by them) (s 306(1)(d)) |
| | | 1 Apr 2013 (otherwise) (SI 2013/160) |
| Sch 21 | para 1 | See paras 2–4 below |

**Health and Social Care Act 2012 (c 7)**—*contd*

| | |
|---|---|
| para 2(1) | 27 Mar 2012 (so far as is necessary for enabling the exercise on or after that date of any power to make an order or regulations or to give directions that is conferred by these provisions or an amendment made by them) (s 306(1)(d)) |
| | *Not yet in force* (otherwise) |
| para 2(2) | 27 Mar 2012 (so far as is necessary for enabling the exercise on or after that date of any power to make an order or regulations or to give directions that is conferred by these provisions or an amendment made by them) (s 306(1)(d)) |
| | 1 Apr 2013 (otherwise) (SI 2013/160)[4] |
| para 2(3)(a)–(c) | 27 Mar 2012 (so far as is necessary for enabling the exercise on or after that date of any power to make an order or regulations or to give directions that is conferred by these provisions or an amendment made by them) (s 306(1)(d)) |
| | 1 Feb 2013 (otherwise) (SI 2012/2657) |
| para 2(3)(d) | 27 Mar 2012 (so far as is necessary for enabling the exercise on or after that date of any power to make an order or regulations or to give directions that is conferred by these provisions or an amendment made by them) (s 306(1)(d)) |
| | 1 Apr 2013 (otherwise) (SI 2013/160)[4] |
| para 2(3)(e) | 27 Mar 2012 (so far as is necessary for enabling the exercise on or after that date of any power to make an order or regulations or to give directions that is conferred by these provisions or an amendment made by them) (s 306(1)(d)) |
| | 1 Feb 2013 (otherwise) (SI 2012/2657) |
| para 2(3)(f) | 27 Mar 2012 (so far as is necessary for enabling the exercise on or after that date of any power to make an order or regulations or to give directions that is conferred by these provisions or an amendment made by them) (s 306(1)(d)) |
| | *Not yet in force* (otherwise) |
| para 2(3)(g) | 27 Mar 2012 (so far as is necessary for enabling the exercise on or after that date of any power to make an order or regulations or to give directions that is conferred by these provisions or an amendment made by them) (s 306(1)(d)) |
| | 1 Apr 2013 (otherwise) (SI 2013/160)[4] |
| para 2(3)(h) | 27 Mar 2012 (so far as is necessary for enabling the exercise on or after that date of any power to make an order or regulations or to give directions that is conferred by these provisions or an amendment made by them) (s 306(1)(d)) |
| | 1 Feb 2013 (otherwise) (SI 2012/2657) |
| paras 2(3)(i), (j), (4), 3, 4(a) | 27 Mar 2012 (so far as is necessary for enabling the exercise on or after that date of any power to make an order or regulations or to give directions that is conferred by these provisions or an amendment made by them) (s 306(1)(d)) |
| | 1 Apr 2013 (otherwise) (SI 2013/160)[4] |
| para 4(b) | 27 Mar 2012 (so far as is necessary for enabling the exercise on or after that date of any power to make an order or regulations or to give directions that is conferred by these provisions or an amendment made by them) (s 306(1)(d)) |
| | *Not yet in force* (otherwise) |
| para 4(c) | 27 Mar 2012 (so far as is necessary for enabling the exercise on or after that date of any power to make an order or regulations or to give directions that is conferred by these provisions or an amendment made by them) (s 306(1)(d)) |
| | 1 Apr 2013 (otherwise) (SI 2013/160)[4] |
| para 5 | See paras 6–11 below |
| para 6 | 27 Mar 2012 (so far as is necessary for enabling the exercise on or after that date of any power to make an order or regulations or to give directions that is conferred by these provisions or an amendment made by them) (s 306(1)(d)) |
| | 1 Feb 2013 (otherwise) (SI 2012/2657) |

**Health and Social Care Act 2012 (c 7)**—*contd*

| | |
|---|---|
| para 7 | 27 Mar 2012 (so far as is necessary for enabling the exercise on or after that date of any power to make an order or regulations or to give directions that is conferred by these provisions or an amendment made by them) (s 306(1)(d)) |
| | 1 Apr 2013 (otherwise) (SI 2013/160)[4] |
| paras 8–10 | 27 Mar 2012 (so far as is necessary for enabling the exercise on or after that date of any power to make an order or regulations or to give directions that is conferred by these provisions or an amendment made by them) (s 306(1)(d)) |
| | *Not yet in force* (otherwise) |
| para 11 | 27 Mar 2012 (so far as is necessary for enabling the exercise on or after that date of any power to make an order or regulations or to give directions that is conferred by these provisions or an amendment made by them) (s 306(1)(d)) |
| | 1 Apr 2013 (otherwise) (SI 2013/160)[4] |
| para 12 | See paras 13–42 below |
| para 13(a), (b) | 27 Mar 2012 (so far as is necessary for enabling the exercise on or after that date of any power to make an order or regulations or to give directions that is conferred by these provisions or an amendment made by them) (s 306(1)(d)) |
| | 1 Apr 2013 (otherwise) (SI 2013/160)[4] |
| para 13(c)–(f) | 27 Mar 2012 (so far as is necessary for enabling the exercise on or after that date of any power to make an order or regulations or to give directions that is conferred by these provisions or an amendment made by them) (s 306(1)(d)) |
| | 1 Feb 2013 (otherwise) (SI 2012/2657) |
| paras 14–17 | 27 Mar 2012 (so far as is necessary for enabling the exercise on or after that date of any power to make an order or regulations or to give directions that is conferred by these provisions or an amendment made by them) (s 306(1)(d)) |
| | 1 Apr 2013 (otherwise) (SI 2013/160)[4] |
| paras 18–21 | 27 Mar 2012 (so far as is necessary for enabling the exercise on or after that date of any power to make an order or regulations or to give directions that is conferred by these provisions or an amendment made by them) (s 306(1)(d)) |
| | 1 Feb 2013 (otherwise) (SI 2012/2657) |
| paras 22–32 | 27 Mar 2012 (so far as is necessary for enabling the exercise on or after that date of any power to make an order or regulations or to give directions that is conferred by these provisions or an amendment made by them) (s 306(1)(d)) |
| | 1 Apr 2013 (otherwise) (SI 2013/160)[4] |
| para 33 | 27 Mar 2012 (so far as is necessary for enabling the exercise on or after that date of any power to make an order or regulations or to give directions that is conferred by these provisions or an amendment made by them) (s 306(1)(d)) |
| | 1 Feb 2013 (otherwise) (SI 2012/2657) |
| paras 34–37 | 27 Mar 2012 (so far as is necessary for enabling the exercise on or after that date of any power to make an order or regulations or to give directions that is conferred by these provisions or an amendment made by them) (s 306(1)(d)) |
| | 1 Apr 2013 (otherwise) (SI 2013/160)[4] |
| para 38(1)(a) | 27 Mar 2012 (so far as is necessary for enabling the exercise on or after that date of any power to make an order or regulations or to give directions that is conferred by these provisions or an amendment made by them) (s 306(1)(d)) |
| | 1 Feb 2013 (otherwise) (SI 2012/2657) |
| para 38(1)(b) | 27 Mar 2012 (so far as is necessary for enabling the exercise on or after that date of any power to make an order or regulations or to give directions that is conferred by these provisions or an amendment made by them) (s 306(1)(d)) |
| | 1 Feb 2013 (otherwise) (SI 2012/2657)[3] |

**Health and Social Care Act 2012 (c 7)**—*contd*

| | |
|---|---|
| para 38(1)(c), (d) | 27 Mar 2012 (so far as is necessary for enabling the exercise on or after that date of any power to make an order or regulations or to give directions that is conferred by these provisions or an amendment made by them) (s 306(1)(d)) |
| | 1 Apr 2013 (otherwise) (SI 2013/160) |
| para 38(2) | 27 Mar 2012 (so far as is necessary for enabling the exercise on or after that date of any power to make an order or regulations or to give directions that is conferred by these provisions or an amendment made by them) (s 306(1)(d)) |
| | 1 Feb 2013 (otherwise) (SI 2012/2657)[3] |
| paras 39–42 | 27 Mar 2012 (so far as is necessary for enabling the exercise on or after that date of any power to make an order or regulations or to give directions that is conferred by these provisions or an amendment made by them) (s 306(1)(d)) |
| | 1 Apr 2013 (otherwise) (SI 2013/160)[4] |
| para 43(1) | See sub-paras (2), (3) below |
| para 43(2)(a)(i), (ii) | 27 Mar 2012 (so far as is necessary for enabling the exercise on or after that date of any power to make an order or regulations or to give directions that is conferred by these provisions or an amendment made by them) (s 306(1)(d)) |
| | 1 Apr 2013 (otherwise) (SI 2013/160)[4] |
| para 43(2)(a)(iii) | 27 Mar 2012 (so far as is necessary for enabling the exercise on or after that date of any power to make an order or regulations or to give directions that is conferred by these provisions or an amendment made by them) (s 306(1)(d)) |
| | Not yet in force (otherwise) |
| para 43(2)(b) | 27 Mar 2012 (so far as is necessary for enabling the exercise on or after that date of any power to make an order or regulations or to give directions that is conferred by these provisions or an amendment made by them) (s 306(1)(d)) |
| | 1 Feb 2013 (except in so far as inserts SI 1991/194, art 8(2)(gf)) (SI 2012/2657) |
| | Not yet in force (exception noted above) |
| para 43(2)(c)–(e) | 27 Mar 2012 (so far as is necessary for enabling the exercise on or after that date of any power to make an order or regulations or to give directions that is conferred by these provisions or an amendment made by them) (s 306(1)(d)) |
| | 1 Feb 2013 (otherwise) (SI 2012/2657)[3] |
| para 43(2)(f) | 27 Mar 2012 (so far as is necessary for enabling the exercise on or after that date of any power to make an order or regulations or to give directions that is conferred by these provisions or an amendment made by them) (s 306(1)(d)) |
| | 1 Apr 2013 (otherwise) (SI 2013/160)[4] |
| para 43(3) | 27 Mar 2012 (so far as is necessary for enabling the exercise on or after that date of any power to make an order or regulations or to give directions that is conferred by these provisions or an amendment made by them) (s 306(1)(d)) |
| | 1 Feb 2013 (otherwise) (SI 2012/2657)[3] |
| Schs 22, 23 | 27 Mar 2012 (so far as is necessary for enabling the exercise on or after that date of any power to make an order or regulations or to give directions that is conferred by these provisions or an amendment made by them) (s 306(1)(d)) |
| | 1 Jul 2012 (except in so far as they relate to the National Health Service Commissioning Board, a clinical commissioning group, any person with whom the Secretary of State has made, or has decided to make, an agreement under the Mental Health Act 1983, s 12ZA(1), the National Institute for Health and Care Excellence, and the Health and Social Care Information Centre) (SI 2012/1319) |
| | 1 Oct 2012 (in so far as relate to the Board and a clinical commissioning group) (SI 2012/1831) |

**Health and Social Care Act 2012 (c 7)**—*contd*
                                        1 Apr 2013 (otherwise) (SI 2013/160)[4]

[1]   For a transitory modification, see SI 2012/1319, art 3

[2]   For transitional, savings and transitory provisions, see SI 2012/1831, arts 3–14

[3]   For transitional, savings and transitory provisions, see SI 2012/2657, arts 3–14

[4]   For transitional, savings and transitory provisions, see SI 2013/160, arts 3–10, Schedule

[5]   For transitional, savings and transitory provisions, see SI 2013/671, arts 3–5

[6]   Note that SI 2012/2657 purports to bring s 230(2)–(4), (6) into force on 1 Dec 2012

[7]   Note that SI 2012/1831 purports to bring Sch 4, paras 112, 115 into force for remaining purposes on 1 Oct 2012

[8]   For transitory modifications, see SI 2014/39, art 3

[9]   For a saving provision, see SI 2018/617, art 3

---

**Infrastructure (Financial Assistance) Act 2012 (c 16)**

*RA:* 31 Oct 2012

Whole Act in force 31 Oct 2012 (s 4(2))

---

**Land Registration etc (Scotland) Act 2012 (asp 5)**

*RA:* 10 Jul 2012

*Commencement provisions*: s 123; Land Registration etc (Scotland) Act 2012 (Commencement No 1) Order 2012, SSI 2012/265; Land Registration etc (Scotland) Act 2012 (Commencement No 2 and Transitional Provisions) Order 2014, SSI 2014/41; Land Registration etc (Scotland) Act 2012 (Designated Day) Order 2014, SSI 2014/127; Land Registration etc. (Scotland) Act 2012 (Commencement No 3) Order 2021, SSI 2021/472

| | | |
|---|---|---|
| 1–19 | | 8 Dec 2014 (SSI 2014/127) |
| 20 | | See Sch 1 below |
| 21–51 | | 8 Dec 2014 (SSI 2014/127) |
| 52 | (1), (2) | 8 Dec 2014 (SSI 2014/127) |
| | (3) | See Sch 2 below |
| 53 | (1)–(3) | 8 Dec 2014 (SSI 2014/127) |
| | (4) | 1 Nov 2012 (SSI 2012/265) |
| | (5) | 8 Dec 2014 (SSI 2014/127) |
| 54–63 | | 8 Dec 2014 (SSI 2014/127) |
| 64 | | 1 Nov 2012 (SSI 2012/265) |
| 65–95 | | 8 Dec 2014 (SSI 2014/127) |
| 96 | (1) | See sub-ss (2)–(4) below |
| | (2)(a)(i) | The day designated by the Scottish Ministers by order under s 122 (except for the purposes of any will, testamentary trust disposition and settlement or codicil) (SSI 2014/41) |
| | | *Not yet in force* (exceptions noted above) |
| | (2)(a)(ii), (iii) | 11 May 2014 (except for the purposes of any will, testamentary trust disposition and settlement or codicil) (SSI 2014/41)[1] |
| | | *Not yet in force* (exceptions noted above) |
| | (2)(a)(iv), (b)(i) | The day designated by the Scottish Ministers by order under s 122 (except for the purposes of any will, testamentary trust disposition and settlement or codicil) (SSI 2014/41) |
| | | *Not yet in force* (exceptions noted above) |
| | (2)(b)(ii), (iii) | 11 May 2014 (except for the purposes of any will, testamentary trust disposition and settlement or codicil) (SSI 2014/41)[1] |
| | | *Not yet in force* (exceptions noted above) |

**Land Registration etc (Scotland) Act 2012 (asp 5)**—*contd*

| | | |
|---|---|---|
| | (2)(c) | The day designated by the Scottish Ministers by order under s 122 (except for the purposes of any will, testamentary trust disposition and settlement or codicil) (SSI 2014/41) |
| | | *Not yet in force* (exceptions noted above) |
| | (3), (4) | 11 May 2014 (except for the purposes of any will, testamentary trust disposition and settlement or codicil) (SSI 2014/41)[1] |
| | | *Not yet in force* (exceptions noted above) |
| 97 | | 22 Mar 2014 (for the purpose of making regulations) (SSI 2014/41) |
| | | 11 May 2014 (otherwise) (except for the purposes of (a) any will, testamentary trust disposition and settlement or codicil and (b) inserting Requirements of Writing (Scotland) Act 1995, section 9G(6)) (SSI 2014/41)[1] |
| | | 1 Apr 2022 (for the purpose of inserting Requirements of Writing (Scotland) Act 1995, section 9G(6)) (SSI 2021/472) |
| | | *Not yet in force* (exceptions noted above) |
| 98 | | See Sch 3 below |
| 99, 100 | | 22 Mar 2014 (SSI 2014/41) |
| 101–106 | | 8 Dec 2014 (SSI 2014/127) |
| 107–110 | | 1 Nov 2012 (SSI 2012/265) |
| 111, 112 | | 8 Dec 2014 (SSI 2014/127) |
| 113 | | 11 Jul 2012 (s 123(1)(a)) |
| 114 | (1) | 11 Jul 2012 (s 123(1)(b)) |
| | (2) | 8 Dec 2014 (SSI 2014/127) |
| 115 | | 8 Dec 2014 (SSI 2014/127) |
| 116 | | 11 Jul 2012 (s 123(1)(c)) |
| 117 | | 11 Jul 2012 (s 123(1)(d)) |
| 118 | | See Sch 4 below |
| 119 | | See Sch 5 below |
| 120, 121 | | 8 Dec 2014 (SSI 2014/127) |
| 122 | | 11 Jul 2012 (s 123(1)(e)) |
| 123 | | 11 Jul 2012 (s 123(1)(f)) |
| 124 | | 11 Jul 2012 (s 123(1)(g)) |
| Schs 1, 2 | | 8 Dec 2014 (SSI 2014/127) |
| Sch 3 | para 1 | See paras 2–27 below |
| | para 2 | The day designated by the Scottish Ministers by order under s 122 (except for the purposes of any will, testamentary trust disposition and settlement or codicil) (SSI 2014/41) |
| | | *Not yet in force* (exceptions noted above) |
| | paras 3, 4 | 11 May 2014 (except for the purposes of any will, testamentary trust disposition and settlement or codicil) (SSI 2014/41)[1] |
| | | *Not yet in force* (exceptions noted above) |
| | para 5 | The day designated by the Scottish Ministers by order under s 122 (except for the purposes of any will, testamentary trust disposition and settlement or codicil) (SSI 2014/41) |
| | | *Not yet in force* (exceptions noted above) |
| | para 6 | 11 May 2014 (except for the purposes of any will, testamentary trust disposition and settlement or codicil) (SSI 2014/41)[1] |
| | | *Not yet in force* (exceptions noted above) |
| | para 7 | The day designated by the Scottish Ministers by order under s 122 (except for the purposes of any will, testamentary trust disposition and settlement or codicil) (SSI 2014/41) |
| | | *Not yet in force* (exceptions noted above) |
| | paras 8–10 | 11 May 2014 (except for the purposes of any will, testamentary trust disposition and settlement or codicil) (SSI 2014/41)[1] |
| | | *Not yet in force* (exceptions noted above) |
| | para 11(a) | The day designated by the Scottish Ministers by order under s 122 (except for the purposes of any will, testamentary trust disposition and settlement or codicil) (SSI 2014/41) |
| | | *Not yet in force* (exceptions noted above) |

## Land Registration etc (Scotland) Act 2012 (asp 5)—*contd*

| | |
|---|---|
| para 11(b)–(g) | 11 May 2014 (except for the purposes of any will, testamentary trust disposition and settlement or codicil) (SSI 2014/41)[1] |
| | *Not yet in force* (exceptions noted above) |
| paras 12–17 | The day designated by the Scottish Ministers by order under s 122 (except for the purposes of any will, testamentary trust disposition and settlement or codicil) (SSI 2014/41) |
| | *Not yet in force* (exceptions noted above) |
| para 18 | 11 May 2014 (except for the purposes of any will, testamentary trust disposition and settlement or codicil) (SSI 2014/41)[1] |
| | *Not yet in force* (exceptions noted above) |
| para 19(a)(i) | The day designated by the Scottish Ministers by order under s 122 (except for the purposes of any will, testamentary trust disposition and settlement or codicil) (SSI 2014/41) |
| | *Not yet in force* (exceptions noted above) |
| para 19(a)(ii) | 11 May 2014 (except for the purposes of any will, testamentary trust disposition and settlement or codicil) (SSI 2014/41)[1] |
| | *Not yet in force* (exceptions noted above) |
| para 19(a)(iii)–(vi) | The day designated by the Scottish Ministers by order under s 122 (except for the purposes of any will, testamentary trust disposition and settlement or codicil) (SSI 2014/41) |
| | *Not yet in force* (exceptions noted above) |
| para 19(a)(vii) | 11 May 2014 (except for the purposes of any will, testamentary trust disposition and settlement or codicil) (SSI 2014/41)[1] |
| | *Not yet in force* (exceptions noted above) |
| para 19(a)(viii), (ix) | The day designated by the Scottish Ministers by order under s 122 (except for the purposes of any will, testamentary trust disposition and settlement or codicil) (SSI 2014/41) |
| | *Not yet in force* (exceptions noted above) |
| paras 19(b), 20–22 | 11 May 2014 (except for the purposes of any will, testamentary trust disposition and settlement or codicil) (SSI 2014/41)[1] |
| | *Not yet in force* (exceptions noted above) |
| paras 23–26 | The day designated by the Scottish Ministers by order under s 122 (except for the purposes of any will, testamentary trust disposition and settlement or codicil) (SSI 2014/41) |
| | *Not yet in force* (exceptions noted above) |
| para 27 | 11 May 2014 (except for the purposes of any will, testamentary trust disposition and settlement or codicil) (SSI 2014/41)[1] |
| | *Not yet in force* (exceptions noted above) |
| Schs 4, 5 | 8 Dec 2014 (SSI 2014/127) |

[1] For transitional provisions, see SSI 2014/41, art 3

---

## Legal Aid, Sentencing and Punishment of Offenders Act 2012 (c 10)

*RA:* 1 May 2012

*Commencement provisions:* ss 77(1), 151; Legal Aid, Sentencing and Punishment of Offenders Act 2012 (Commencement No 1) Order 2012, SI 2012/1956; Legal Aid, Sentencing and Punishment of Offenders Act 2012 (Commencement No 2 and Specification of Commencement Date) Order 2012, SI 2012/2412; Legal Aid, Sentencing and Punishment of Offenders Act 2012 (Commencement No 3 and Saving Provision) Order 2012, SI 2012/2770; Legal Aid, Sentencing and Punishment of Offenders Act 2012 (Commencement No 4 and Saving Provisions) Order 2012, SI 2012/2906; Legal Aid, Sentencing and Punishment of Offenders Act 2012 (Commencement No 5 and Saving Provision) Order 2013, SI 2013/77; Legal Aid, Sentencing and Punishment of Offenders Act 2012 (Commencement No 6) Order 2013, SI 2013/453; Legal Aid, Sentencing and Punishment of Offenders Act 2012 (Commencement No 7) Order 2013, SI 2013/773; Legal Aid, Sentencing and Punishment of Offenders Act 2012 (Commencement No 8) Order 2013, SI 2013/1127; Legal Aid, Sentencing and Punishment of Offenders Act 2012 (Commencement No 9, Saving Provision and Specification of Commencement Date) Order 2014, SI 2014/423; Legal Aid, Sentencing and Punishment of Offenders Act 2012 (Commencement No 10) Order 2014, SI 2014/1291; Legal Aid,

**Legal Aid, Sentencing and Punishment of Offenders Act 2012 (c 10)**—*contd*
Sentencing and Punishment of Offenders Act 2012 (Alcohol Abstinence and Monitoring Requirements) Piloting Order 2014, SI 2014/1777; Legal Aid, Sentencing and Punishment of Offenders Act 2012 (Commencement No 11) Order 2015, SI 2015/504; Legal Aid, Sentencing and Punishment of Offenders Act 2012 (Commencement No 12) Order 2016, SI 2016/345; Legal Aid, Sentencing and Punishment of Offenders Act 2012 (Alcohol Abstinence and Monitoring Requirements) Piloting Order 2017, SI 2017/525; Legal Aid, Sentencing and Punishment of Offenders Act 2012 (Commencement No 13) Order 2018, SI 2018/1287; Legal Aid, Sentencing and Punishment of Offenders Act 2012 (Commencement No 14) Order 2020, SI 2020/478

| | | |
|---|---|---|
| 1–18 | | 1 Apr 2013 (SI 2013/453) |
| 19 | (1)–(3) | 1 Apr 2013 (SI 2013/453) |
| | (4) | *Not yet in force* |
| | (5), (6) | 1 Apr 2013 (SI 2013/453) |
| 20–37 | | 1 Apr 2013 (SI 2013/453) |
| 38 | (1) | 1 Apr 2013 (SI 2013/453) |
| | (2) | See Sch 4 below |
| | (3)–(6) | 1 Apr 2013 (SI 2013/453) |
| 39–43 | | 1 Apr 2013 (SI 2013/453) |
| 44 | | 19 Jan 2013 (for the purpose only of exercising any power to make orders, regulations or rules of court) (SI 2013/77)[3] |
| | | 1 Apr 2013 (otherwise) (SI 2013/77)[3] |
| | | 6 Apr 2016 (in relation to proceedings in England and Wales brought by: a person acting in the capacity of a liquidator of a company which is being wound up in England and Wales or Scotland under Insolvency Act 1986, Pt IV or V, or a trustee of a bankrupt's estate under Pt IX thereof; a person acting in the capacity of administrator appointed pursuant to Pt II thereof; a company which is being wound up in England and Wales or Scotland under Pt IV or V thereof; a company which has entered administration under Pt II thereof) (SI 2016/345) |
| | | 6 Apr 2019 (in relation to publication and privacy proceedings) (SI 2018/1287) |
| | | *Not yet in force* (otherwise) |
| 45 | (1) | See sub-ss (2)–(11) below |
| | (2)–(7) | 19 Jan 2013 (for the purpose only of exercising any power to make orders, regulations or rules of court) (SI 2013/77) |
| | | 1 Apr 2013 (otherwise) (SI 2013/77) |
| | (8) | 1 Oct 2012 (SI 2012/2412) |
| | (9)–(13) | 19 Jan 2013 (for the purpose only of exercising any power to make orders, regulations or rules of court) (SI 2013/77) |
| | | 1 Apr 2013 (otherwise) (SI 2013/77) |
| 46 | | 19 Jan 2013 (for the purpose only of exercising any power to make orders, regulations or rules of court) (SI 2013/77)[3] |
| | | 1 Apr 2013 (otherwise) (SI 2013/77)[3] |
| | | 6 Apr 2016 (in relation to proceedings in England and Wales brought by: a person acting in the capacity of a liquidator of a company which is being wound up in England and Wales or Scotland under Insolvency Act 1986, Pt IV or V, or a trustee of a bankrupt's estate under Pt IX thereof; a person acting in the capacity of administrator appointed pursuant to Pt II thereof; a company which is being wound up in England and Wales or Scotland under Pt IV or V thereof; a company which has entered administration under Pt II thereof) (SI 2016/345) |
| 47 | | 1 Apr 2013 (SI 2013/77) |
| 48 | | 19 Jan 2013 (SI 2013/77) |
| 49–54 | | 1 Apr 2013 (SI 2013/773) |
| 55 | | 1 Oct 2012 (SI 2012/2412) |
| 56, 57 | | 1 Apr 2013 (SI 2013/453) |
| 58 | | 4 Mar 2013 (SI 2013/453) |
| 59 | | 1 Apr 2013 (SI 2013/453) |
| 60 | | 4 Mar 2013 (SI 2013/453) |

**Legal Aid, Sentencing and Punishment of Offenders Act 2012 (c 10)**—*contd*

| | | |
|---|---|---|
| 61 | | 1 Oct 2012 (SI 2012/2412) |
| 62 | (1) | See Sch 7 below |
| | (2) | See Sch 8 below |
| 63, 64 | | 3 Dec 2012 (SI 2012/2906) |
| 65, 66 | | 3 Dec 2012 (SI 2012/2906)[2] |
| 67 | (1) | 3 Dec 2012 (SI 2012/2906)[2] |
| | (2)(a) | *Never in force* (repealed) |
| | (2)(b), (3), (4) | 3 Dec 2012 (SI 2012/2906)[2] |
| | (5)(a) | *Never in force* (repealed) |
| | (5)(b), (6), (7) | 3 Dec 2012 (SI 2012/2906)[2] |
| 68 | | 3 Dec 2012 (SI 2012/2906) |
| 69 | | 3 Dec 2012 (SI 2012/2906)[2] |
| 70 | | 3 Dec 2012 (SI 2012/2906) |
| 71, 72 | | 3 Dec 2012 (SI 2012/2906)[2] |
| 73–75 | | 3 Dec 2012 (SI 2012/2906) |
| 76 | | 19 May 2020 (SI 2020/478) |
| 77 | | 1 May 2012 (s 151(2)(a)) |
| 78 | (1), (2) | 3 Dec 2012 (SI 2012/2906) |
| | (3) | 3 Dec 2012 (so far as relates to foreign travel prohibition requirements) (SI 2012/2906) |
| | | *Not yet in force* (so far as relates to alcohol abstinence and monitoring requirements) |
| | (4)–(10) | 3 Dec 2012 (SI 2012/2906) |
| 79, 80 | | 3 Dec 2012 (SI 2012/2906) |
| 81 | | 3 Dec 2012 (SI 2012/2906)[2] |
| 82 | | 3 Dec 2012 (SI 2012/2906) |
| 83, 84 | | 3 Dec 2012 (SI 2012/2906)[2] |
| 85 | (1), (2) | 12 Mar 2015 (SI 2015/504) |
| | (3) | 28 May 2014 (SI 2014/1291) |
| | (4) | 12 Mar 2015 (SI 2015/504) |
| | (5)–(13) | 28 May 2014 (SI 2014/1291) |
| | (14) | *Not yet in force* |
| | (15)–(17) | 28 May 2014 (SI 2014/1291) |
| 86, 87 | | 28 May 2014 (SI 2014/1291) |
| 88 | | 8 Apr 2013 (SI 2013/453) |
| 89, 90 | | 3 Dec 2012 (SI 2012/2906) |
| 91–107 | | 3 Dec 2012 (SI 2012/2906)[2] |
| 108–118 | | 3 Dec 2012 (SI 2012/2906) |
| 119 | | 1 May 2012 (s 151(2)(b)) |
| 120–122 | | 3 Dec 2012 (SI 2012/2906) |
| 123 | | 3 Dec 2012 (SI 2012/2906)[2] |
| 124–128 | | 3 Dec 2012 (SI 2012/2906) |
| 129 | | *Not yet in force* |
| 130, 131 | | 3 Dec 2012 (SI 2012/2906) |
| 132–138 | | 8 Apr 2013 (SI 2013/453) |
| 139 | (1)–(4), (5)(a) | 10 Mar 2014 (SI 2014/423)[4] |
| | (5)(b) | 10 Mar 2014 (SI 2014/423) |
| | (6), (7) | 10 Mar 2014 (SI 2014/423)[4] |
| 140 | | 1 Oct 2012 (SI 2012/2412) |
| 141 | (1)–(6) | 10 Mar 2014 (SI 2014/423)[4] |
| | (7)–(9) | 1 Oct 2012 (SI 2012/2412) |
| | (10) | See Sch 25 below |
| | (11) | 10 Mar 2014 (SI 2014/423)[4] |
| | (12) | 1 Oct 2012 (SI 2012/2412) |
| 142 | (1), (2) | 3 Dec 2012 (SI 2012/2770) |
| | (3) | See Sch 26 below |
| 143 | (1)–(6) | 3 Dec 2012 (SI 2012/2770) |
| | (7) | See Sch 27 below |
| 144 | | 1 Sep 2012 (SI 2012/1956) |

## Legal Aid, Sentencing and Punishment of Offenders Act 2012 (c 10)—*contd*

| | | |
|---|---|---|
| 145 | | 3 Dec 2012 (SI 2012/2770)[1] |
| 146, 147 | | 3 Dec 2012 (SI 2012/2770) |
| 148 | | 14 May 2013 (SI 2013/1127) |
| 149–154 | | 1 May 2012 (s 151(2)(c)) |
| Schs 1–3 | | 1 Apr 2013 (SI 2013/453) |
| Sch 4 | | 4 Mar 2013 (SI 2013/453) |
| Schs 5, 6 | | 1 Apr 2013 (SI 2013/453) |
| Schs 7, 8 | | 1 Oct 2012 (SI 2012/2412) |
| Schs 9–11 | | 3 Dec 2012 (SI 2012/2906) |
| Sch 12 | | 3 Dec 2012 (SI 2012/2906)[2] |
| Schs 13–21 | | 3 Dec 2012 (SI 2012/2906) |
| Sch 22 | | 3 Dec 2012 (SI 2012/2906)[2] |
| Schs 23, 24 | | 8 Apr 2013 (SI 2013/453) |
| Sch 25 | paras 1–3 | 10 Mar 2014 (SI 2014/423)[4] |
| | para 4 | *Not yet in force* |
| | paras 5–17 | 10 Mar 2014 (SI 2014/423)[4] |
| | Pt 2 | 10 Mar 2014 (SI 2014/423)[4] |
| Sch 26 | paras 1–18 | 3 Dec 2012 (SI 2012/2770) |
| | para 19 | *Never in force* (repealed) |
| | paras 20–31 | 3 Dec 2012 (SI 2012/2770) |
| Sch 27 | | 3 Dec 2012 (SI 2012/2770) |

[1]    For a saving provision, see SI 2012/2770, art 3

[2]    For a saving provision, see SI 2012/2906, arts 3–7

[3]    For saving provisions, see SI 2013/77, art 4

[4]    For saving and commencement of transitional provisions under s 141, see SI 2014/423, arts 3, 4

## Live Music Act 2012 (c 2)

*RA:* 8 Mar 2012

*Commencement provisions:* s 4; Live Music Act 2012 (Commencement) Order 2012, SI 2012/2115

| | |
|---|---|
| 1–4 | 1 Oct 2012 (SI 2012/2115) |

## Local Government Byelaws (Wales) Act 2012 (anaw 2)

*RA:* 29 Nov 2012

*Commencement provisions:* s 22; Local Government Byelaws (Wales) Act 2012 (Commencement No 1) Order 2014, SI 2014/2121; Local Government Byelaws (Wales) Act 2012 (Commencement No 2, Transitional Provisions and Savings) Order 2015, SI 2015/1025; Local Government Byelaws (Wales) Act 2012 (Commencement No 3) Order 2018, SI 2018/550

| | | |
|---|---|---|
| 1 | | 31 Mar 2015 (SI 2015/1025) |
| 2 | | 31 Mar 2015 (SI 2015/1025)[1] |
| 3 | | 31 Mar 2015 (SI 2015/1025) |
| 4 | | 31 Mar 2015 (SI 2015/1025)[1] |
| 5 | | 31 Mar 2015 (SI 2015/1025) |
| 6–8 | | 31 Mar 2015 (SI 2015/1025)[1] |
| 9 | | 15 Aug 2014 (SI 2014/2121) |
| 10, 11 | | 31 Mar 2015 (SI 2015/1025) |
| 12 | (1)–(12) | 31 Mar 2015 (SI 2015/1025) |
| | (13) | 15 Aug 2014 (SI 2014/2121) |
| 13 | (1), (2) | 31 Mar 2015 (SI 2015/1025) |
| | (3), (4) | 15 Aug 2014 (SI 2014/2121) |
| | (5) | 31 Mar 2015 (SI 2015/1025) |
| 14, 15 | | 31 Mar 2015 (SI 2015/1025) |

**Local Government Byelaws (Wales) Act 2012 (anaw 2)**—*contd*

| | | |
|---|---|---|
| 16 | | 15 Aug 2014 (SI 2014/2121) |
| 17 | | 31 Mar 2015 (SI 2015/1025) |
| 18 | (1) | 30 Nov 2012 (s 22(1)(a)) |
| | (2) | 31 Mar 2015 (SI 2015/1025) |
| 19 | | 31 Mar 2015 (SI 2015/1025) |
| 20 | | See Sch 2 below |
| 21 | | 30 Nov 2012 (s 22(1)(b)) |
| 22 | | 30 Nov 2012 (s 22(1)(c)) |
| 23 | | 30 Nov 2012 (s 22(1)(d)) |
| Sch 1 | | 31 Mar 2015 (SI 2015/1025)[1] |
| Sch 2 | paras 1–8 | 31 Mar 2015 (SI 2015/1025)[1] |
| | para 9(1)–(3) | 31 Mar 2015 (SI 2015/1025)[1] |
| | para 9(4) | 8 May 2018 (SI 2018/550) |
| | para 9(5) | 31 Mar 2015 (SI 2015/1025)[1] |
| | paras 10–18 | 31 Mar 2015 (SI 2015/1025)[1] |

[1]    For transitional provisions and savings, see SI 2015/1025, art 3

---

**Local Government Finance Act 2012 (c 17)**

*RA:* 31 Oct 2012

| | |
|---|---|
| 1–12 | 31 Oct 2012 (RA) |
| 13 | *Not yet in force* |
| 14–22 | 31 Oct 2012 (RA) |
| Schs 1–4 | 31 Oct 2012 (RA) |

---

**Local Government Finance (Unoccupied Properties etc) (Scotland) Act 2012 (asp 11)**

*RA:* 5 Dec 2012

*Commencement provisions:* s 5

| | |
|---|---|
| 1–3 | 5 Dec 2012 (s 5(1)) |
| 4 | 1 Apr 2013 (s 5(2)) |
| 6 | 5 Dec 2012 (s 5(1)) |

---

**Long Leases (Scotland) Act 2012 (asp 9)**

*RA:* 7 Aug 2012

*Commencement provisions:* s 83; Long Leases (Scotland) Act 2012 (Commencement No 1) Order 2013, SSI 2013/322

| | | |
|---|---|---|
| 1–7 | | 28 Nov 2013 (SSI 2013/322) |
| 8 | (1) | 21 Feb 2014 (SSI 2013/322) |
| | (2) | 28 Nov 2013 (for the purposes of making regulations) (SSI 2013/322) |
| | | 21 Feb 2014 (otherwise) (SSI 2013/322) |
| 9 | | 21 Feb 2014 (SSI 2013/322) |
| 10–12 | | 28 Nov 2013 (SSI 2013/322) |
| 13 | | 21 Feb 2014 (SSI 2013/322) |
| 14 | (1), (2) | 21 Feb 2014 (SSI 2013/322) |
| | (3)(a) | 28 Nov 2013 (for the purposes of making regulations) (SSI 2013/322) |
| | | 21 Feb 2014 (otherwise) (SSI 2013/322) |
| | (3)(b)–(h), (4)–(6) | 21 Feb 2014 (SSI 2013/322) |
| 15, 16 | | 21 Feb 2014 (SSI 2013/322) |

**Long Leases (Scotland) Act 2012 (asp 9)**—*contd*

| | | |
|---|---|---|
| 17 | (1)–(3) | 21 Feb 2014 (SSI 2013/322) |
| | (4)(a) | 28 Nov 2013 (for the purposes of making regulations) (SSI 2013/322) |
| | | 21 Feb 2014 (otherwise) (SSI 2013/322) |
| | (4)(b)–(f), (5)–(7) | 21 Feb 2014 (SSI 2013/322) |
| 18–22 | | 21 Feb 2014 (SSI 2013/322) |
| 23 | (1), (2) | 21 Feb 2014 (SSI 2013/322) |
| | (3)(a) | 28 Nov 2013 (for the purposes of making regulations) (SSI 2013/322) |
| | | 21 Feb 2014 (otherwise) (SSI 2013/322) |
| | (3)(b)–(e), (4)–(12) | 21 Feb 2014 (SSI 2013/322) |
| 24 | (1) | 21 Feb 2014 (SSI 2013/322) |
| | (2)(a) | 28 Nov 2013 (for the purposes of making regulations) (SSI 2013/322) |
| | | 21 Feb 2014 (otherwise) (SSI 2013/322) |
| | (2)(b)–(g), (3)–(5) | 21 Feb 2014 (SSI 2013/322) |
| 25 | (1) | 21 Feb 2014 (SSI 2013/322) |
| | (2)(a) | 28 Nov 2013 (for the purposes of making regulations) (SSI 2013/322) |
| | | 21 Feb 2014 (otherwise) (SSI 2013/322) |
| | (2)(b)–(f), (3)–(5) | 21 Feb 2014 (SSI 2013/322) |
| 26 | (1) | 21 Feb 2014 (SSI 2013/322) |
| | (2)(a) | 28 Nov 2013 (for the purposes of making regulations) (SSI 2013/322) |
| | | 21 Feb 2014 (otherwise) (SSI 2013/322) |
| | (2)(b)–(g), (3)–(6) | 21 Feb 2014 (SSI 2013/322) |
| 27 | (1), (2) | 21 Feb 2014 (SSI 2013/322) |
| | (3)(a) | 28 Nov 2013 (for the purposes of making regulations) (SSI 2013/322) |
| | | 21 Feb 2014 (otherwise) (SSI 2013/322) |
| | (3)(b)–(f), (4)–(7) | 21 Feb 2014 (SSI 2013/322) |
| 28 | (1), (2) | 21 Feb 2014 (SSI 2013/322) |
| | (3)(a) | 28 Nov 2013 (for the purposes of making regulations) (SSI 2013/322) |
| | | 21 Feb 2014 (otherwise) (SSI 2013/322) |
| | (3)(b)–(d), (4)–(6) | 21 Feb 2014 (SSI 2013/322) |
| 29–36 | | 28 Nov 2013 (SSI 2013/322) |
| 37–44 | | 21 Feb 2014 (SSI 2013/322) |
| 45–55 | | 28 Nov 2013 (SSI 2013/322) |
| 56 | (1), (2) | 21 Feb 2014 (SSI 2013/322) |
| | (3)(a) | 28 Nov 2013 (for the purposes of making regulations) (SSI 2013/322) |
| | | 21 Feb 2014 (otherwise) (SSI 2013/322) |
| | (3)(b) | 21 Feb 2014 (SSI 2013/322) |
| | (3)(c) | 28 Nov 2013 (for the purposes of making regulations) (SSI 2013/322) |
| | | 21 Feb 2014 (otherwise) (SSI 2013/322) |
| | (4) | 21 Feb 2014 (SSI 2013/322) |
| 57–62 | | 28 Nov 2013 (SSI 2013/322) |
| 63 | (a) | 21 Feb 2014 (SSI 2013/322) |
| | (b) | 28 Nov 2013 (for the purposes of making regulations) (SSI 2013/322) |
| | | 21 Feb 2014 (otherwise) (SSI 2013/322) |
| 64 | (1) | 21 Feb 2014 (SSI 2013/322) |
| | (2)(a) | 28 Nov 2013 (for the purposes of making regulations) (SSI 2013/322) |
| | | 21 Feb 2014 (otherwise) (SSI 2013/322) |
| | (2)(b), (c), (3) | 21 Feb 2014 (SSI 2013/322) |
| 65, 66 | | 28 Nov 2013 (SSI 2013/322) |
| 67 | (1)(a) | 21 Feb 2014 (SSI 2013/322) |

**Long Leases (Scotland) Act 2012 (asp 9)**—*contd*

|  |  |  |
|---|---|---|
|  | (1)(b) | 28 Nov 2013 (for the purposes of making regulations) (SSI 2013/322) |
|  |  | 21 Feb 2014 (otherwise) (SSI 2013/322) |
|  | (2)–(4) | 21 Feb 2014 (SSI 2013/322) |
| 68 |  | 28 Nov 2013 (SSI 2013/322) |
| 69 |  | 21 Feb 2014 (SSI 2013/322) |
| 70–72 |  | 28 Nov 2013 (SSI 2013/322) |
| 73 |  | 28 Sep 2015 (SSI 2013/322) |
| 74–76 |  | 28 Nov 2013 (SSI 2013/322) |
| 77 |  | 21 Feb 2014 (SSI 2013/322) |
| 78 | (1)–(4) | 6 Mar 2014 (SSI 2013/322) |
|  | (5), (6) | 28 Nov 2013 (SSI 2013/322) |
| 79 |  | See Schedule below |
| 80 |  | 28 Nov 2013 (SSI 2013/322) |
| 81–84 |  | 7 Aug 2012 (s 83(1)) |
| Schedule | paras 1, 2, 3(1) | 21 Feb 2014 (SSI 2013/322) |
|  | para 3(1) | See sub-paras (2)–(6) below |
|  | para 3(2)–(4) | 28 Nov 2013 (SSI 2013/322) |
|  | para 3(5), (6) | 21 Feb 2014 (SSI 2013/322) |

**Mental Health (Approval Functions) Act 2012 (c 18)**

*RA:* 31 Oct 2012

*Commencement provisions:* s 2(1)

Whole Act in force 31 Oct 2012 (s 2(1))

**National Assembly for Wales (Official Languages) Act 2012 (anaw 1)**

*RA:* 12 Nov 2012

*Commencement provisions:* s 3(b)

Whole Act in force 12 Nov 2012 (s 3(b))

**National Library of Scotland Act 2012 (asp 3)**

*RA:* 21 Jun 2012

*Commencement provisions*: s 12; National Library of Scotland Act 2012 (Commencement) Order 2013, SSI 2013/1

|  |  |  |
|---|---|---|
| 1–9 |  | 1 Feb 2013 (SSI 2013/1) |
| 10 | (1) | See Sch 2 below |
|  | (2)–(4) | 1 Feb 2013 (SSI 2013/1) |
|  | (5) | See Sch 3 below |
| 11–13 |  | 22 Jun 2012 (s 12(1)) |
| Sch 1 |  | 1 Feb 2013 (SSI 2013/1) |
| Sch 2 | Pt 1 | 21 Aug 2012 (s 12(2)) |
|  | Pt 2 | 1 Feb 2013 (SSI 2013/1) |
| Sch 3 |  | 1 Feb 2013 (SSI 2013/1) |

**Offensive Behaviour at Football and Threatening Communications (Scotland) Act 2012 (asp 1)**

*RA:* 19 Jan 2012

*Commencement provisions*: s 12; Offensive Behaviour at Football and Threatening Communications (Scotland) Act 2012 (Commencement) Order 2012, SSI 2012/20

**Offensive Behaviour at Football and Threatening Communications (Scotland) Act 2012 (asp 1)**—*contd*

| | |
|---|---|
| 1–11 | 1 Mar 2012 (SSI 2012/20) |
| 12, 13 | 19 Jan 2012 (s 12(1)) |

---

**Police and Fire Reform (Scotland) Act 2012 (asp 8)**

*RA:* 7 Aug 2012

*Commencement provisions:* s 129; Police and Fire Reform (Scotland) Act 2012 (Commencement No 1, Transitional, Transitory and Saving Provisions) Order 2012, SSI 2012/253; Police and Fire Reform (Scotland) Act 2012 (Commencement No 2, Transitory and Transitional Provisions and Appointed Day) Order 2012, SSI 2012/333; Police and Fire Reform (Scotland) Act 2012 (Commencement No 3 and Transitory Provision) Order 2013, SSI 2013/47; Police and Fire Reform (Scotland) Act 2012 (Commencement No 4, Transitory and Transitional Provisions) Order 2013, SSI 2013/51

| | | |
|---|---|---|
| 1 | | 8 Aug 2012 (s 129(1)(a)) |
| 2 | (1)(a) | 1 Apr 2013 (SSI 2013/51) |
| | (1)(b) | 1 Jan 2013 (SSI 2012/333) |
| | (1)(c) | 8 Aug 2012 (s 129(1)(a)) |
| | (1)(d), (e) | 1 Apr 2013 (SSI 2013/51) |
| | (2), (3) | 8 Aug 2012 (s 129(1)(a)) |
| 3 | (1)(a), (b) | 1 Apr 2013 (SSI 2013/51) |
| | (1)(c) | 1 Jan 2013 (SSI 2012/333)[2] |
| | (2) | 1 Jan 2013 (SSI 2012/333) |
| 4 | | 8 Aug 2012 (s 129(1)(a)) |
| 5 | | 1 Oct 2012 (SSI 2012/253) |
| 6 | | 1 Apr 2013 (SSI 2013/51) |
| 7 | | 8 Aug 2012 (s 129(1)(a)) |
| 8–10 | | 1 Apr 2013 (SSI 2013/51) |
| 11 | (1)–(4) | 1 Oct 2012 (SSI 2012/253) |
| | (5)–(7) | 1 Apr 2013 (SSI 2013/51) |
| 12–14 | | 1 Apr 2013 (SSI 2013/51) |
| 15 | (1) | 1 Oct 2012 (for the purpose of making regulations under s 15(3)) (SSI 2012/253) |
| | | 1 Apr 2013 (otherwise) (SSI 2013/51) |
| | (2) | 1 Apr 2013 (SSI 2013/51) |
| | (3), (4) | 1 Oct 2012 (SSI 2012/253) |
| | (5)–(7) | 1 Apr 2013 (SSI 2013/51) |
| 16 | | 1 Apr 2013 (SSI 2013/51) |
| 17 | (1), (2)(a), (b) | 1 Apr 2013 (SSI 2013/51) |
| | (2)(c) | 1 Oct 2012 (for the purpose of being involved in the preparation of the strategic police plan) (SSI 2012/253) |
| | | 1 Apr 2013 (otherwise) (SSI 2013/51) |
| | (2)(d) | 1 Oct 2012 (SSI 2012/253) |
| | (2)(e)–(g), (3)–(6) | 1 Apr 2013 (SSI 2013/51) |
| 18–23 | | 1 Apr 2013 (SSI 2013/51) |
| 24 | (1), (2)(a) | 1 Oct 2012 (SSI 2012/253) |
| | (2)(b) | 1 Apr 2013 (SSI 2013/51) |
| | (3)–(5) | 1 Oct 2012 (SSI 2012/253) |
| 25 | | 1 Apr 2013 (SSI 2013/51) |
| 26, 27 | | 1 Oct 2012 (SSI 2012/253) |
| 28–31 | | 1 Apr 2013 (SSI 2013/51) |
| 32, 33 | | 1 Oct 2012 (SSI 2012/253) |
| 34 | (1)–(4) | 1 Oct 2012 (SSI 2012/253) |
| | (5) | 1 Oct 2012 (SSI 2012/253)[1] |
| | (6), (7) | 1 Oct 2012 (SSI 2012/253) |
| | (8), (9) | 1 Apr 2013 (SSI 2013/51) |
| 35 | (1) | 1 Oct 2012 (but does not apply in respect of any yearly period which begins before 1 Apr 2013) (SSI 2012/253) |
| | (2)–(4) | 1 Oct 2012 (SSI 2012/253) |

**Police and Fire Reform (Scotland) Act 2012 (asp 8)**—*contd*

| | | |
|---|---|---|
| 36 | | 1 Oct 2012 (SSI 2012/253) |
| 37, 38 | | 8 Aug 2012 (s 129(1)(a)) |
| 39 | | 1 Apr 2013 (SSI 2013/51)[4] |
| 40 | (1) | 8 Aug 2012 (s 129(1)(a)) |
| | (2) | 1 Apr 2013 (SSI 2013/51) |
| | (3), (4) | 8 Aug 2012 (s 129(1)(a)) |
| 41 | | 1 Oct 2012 (SSI 2012/253) |
| 42 | (1)(a) | 1 Apr 2013 (SSI 2013/51) |
| | (1)(b), (2)–(7) | 1 Oct 2012 (SSI 2012/253)[1] |
| 43 | | 1 Oct 2012 (SSI 2012/253) |
| 44–47 | | 1 Apr 2013 (SSI 2013/51) |
| 48–55 | | 1 Oct 2012 (SSI 2012/253) |
| 56 | (1), (2) | 1 Apr 2013 (SSI 2013/51) |
| | (3) | 1 Oct 2012 (SSI 2012/253) |
| 57–63 | | 1 Apr 2013 (SSI 2013/51) |
| 64 | | 1 Oct 2012 (SSI 2012/253) |
| 65 | | 1 Apr 2013 (SSI 2013/51) |
| 66 | | 1 Oct 2012 (SSI 2012/253)[1] |
| 67–73 | | 1 Apr 2013 (SSI 2013/51) |
| 74 | (1), (2)(a) | 1 Apr 2013 (SSI 2013/51) |
| | (2)(b) | 1 Jan 2013 (SSI 2012/333)[2] |
| 75 | (1) | 1 Jan 2013 (SSI 2012/333)[2] |
| | (2) | 1 Apr 2013 (SSI 2013/51) |
| | (3), (4) | 1 Jan 2013 (SSI 2012/333)[2] |
| 76, 77 | | 1 Jan 2013 (SSI 2012/333)[2] |
| 78 | | 1 Apr 2013 (SSI 2013/51) |
| 79, 80 | | 1 Jan 2013 (SSI 2012/333)[2] |
| 81 | (1)(a) | 1 Apr 2013 (SSI 2013/51) |
| | (1)(b), (2), (3) | 1 Jan 2013 (SSI 2012/333)[2] |
| 82, 83 | | 1 Apr 2013 (SSI 2013/51) |
| 84 | (1), (2)(a) | 8 Aug 2012 (s 129(1)(a)) |
| | (2)(b), (c) | 1 Apr 2013 (SSI 2013/51) |
| | (3)–(9) | 1 Apr 2013 (SSI 2013/51) |
| | (10) | 8 Aug 2012 (s 129(1)(a)) |
| 85 | | 1 Jan 2013 (SSI 2012/333)[2] |
| 86 | | 1 Apr 2013 (SSI 2013/51) |
| 87 | | 1 Oct 2012 (for the purpose of making orders under s 87(1)(b), (3)(b)) (SSI 2012/253) |
| | | 1 Apr 2013 (otherwise) (SSI 2013/51) |
| 88, 89 | | 8 Aug 2012 (s 129(1)(a)) |
| 90–97 | | 1 Apr 2013 (SSI 2013/51) |
| 98 | (1)–(3) | 1 Oct 2012 (SSI 2012/253) |
| | (4) | See Sch 4 below |
| | (5) | 1 Oct 2012 (SSI 2012/253) |
| 99 | | 8 Aug 2012 (s 129(1)(a)) |
| 100 | | 1 Jan 2013 (SSI 2012/333) |
| 101 | (1) | 8 Aug 2012 (in so far as inserts Fire (Scotland) Act 2005, s 1A(1), (3)) (s 129(1)(b)) |
| | | 1 Apr 2013 (in so far as inserts s 1A(2) thereof) (SSI 2013/51) |
| | (2) | 8 Aug 2012 (s 129(1)(b)) |
| 102–112 | | 1 Apr 2013 (SSI 2013/51) |
| 113 | | 8 Aug 2012 (s 129(1)(b)) |
| 114 | | 1 Oct 2012 (for the purpose of inserting Fire (Scotland) Act 2005, s 41A) (SSI 2012/253)[1] |
| | | 1 Apr 2013 (for the purposes of inserting ss 41B, 41C thereof) (SSI 2013/51) |
| 115, 116 | | 1 Apr 2013 (SSI 2013/51) |
| 117 | | 8 Aug 2012 (s 129(1)(b)) |
| 118 | | 1 Oct 2012 (SSI 2012/253) |

**Police and Fire Reform (Scotland) Act 2012 (asp 8)**—*contd*

| | | |
|---|---|---|
| 119 | | 1 Jan 2013 (for the purpose of inserting Fire (Scotland) Act 2005, ss 43B(1), (3)(b), (4)–(7), 43C(1)–(3), 43E, 43F(1), (3), (4), 43G) (SSI 2012/333)[2] |
| | | 1 Apr 2013 (for the purpose of inserting ss 43A, 43B(2), (3)(a), (c), 43C(4), (5), 43D, 43F(2) thereof) (SSI 2013/51) |
| 120 | | 1 Apr 2013 (SSI 2013/51) |
| 121 | | 1 Oct 2012 (SSI 2012/253) |
| 122 | (1), (2) | 1 Oct 2012 (SSI 2012/253) |
| | (3), (4) | 8 Aug 2012 (s 129(1)(b)) |
| 123 | | 8 Aug 2012 (s 129(1)(b)) |
| 124–127 | | 8 Aug 2012 (s 129(1)(c)) |
| 128 | (1) | See Sch 7 below |
| | (2) | See Sch 8 below |
| 129, 130 | | 8 Aug 2012 (s 129(1)(c)) |
| Sch 1 | | 8 Aug 2012 (s 129(1)(a)) |
| Sch 2 | | 1 Apr 2013 (SSI 2013/51) |
| Sch 3 | | 1 Oct 2012 (SSI 2012/253) |
| Sch 4 | | 8 Aug 2012 (s 129(1)(a)) |
| Schs 5, 6 | | 1 Oct 2012 (SSI 2012/253) |
| Sch 7 | paras 1–12 | 1 Apr 2013 (SSI 2013/51) |
| | para 13(1), (2) | 1 Apr 2013 (SSI 2013/51) |
| | para 13(3) | 1 Jan 2013 (SSI 2012/333) |
| | para 13(4), (5) | 1 Apr 2013 (SSI 2013/51) |
| | paras 14–32 | 1 Apr 2013 (SSI 2013/51) |
| | para 33(1)–(14) | 1 Apr 2013 (SSI 2013/51) |
| | para 33(15) | 15 Feb 2013 (SSI 2013/47)[3] |
| | para 33(16), (17) | 1 Apr 2013 (SSI 2013/51) |
| | paras 34–60 | 1 Apr 2013 (SSI 2013/51)[4] |
| | paras 61, 62 | 1 Oct 2012 (SSI 2012/253) |
| | para 63(a) | 1 Apr 2013 (SSI 2013/51) |
| | para 63(b) | 1 Oct 2012 (SSI 2012/253) |
| | para 64 | 1 Apr 2013 (SSI 2013/51) |
| | para 65 | 1 Oct 2012 (SSI 2012/253) |
| | paras 66, 67, 68(1)–(14) | 1 Apr 2013 (SSI 2013/51) |
| | para 68(15), (16) | 1 Oct 2012 (SSI 2012/253)[1] |
| | paras 68(17)–(27), 69–71 | 1 Apr 2013 (SSI 2013/51) |
| | para 72(1), (2) | 1 Oct 2012 (SSI 2012/253) |
| | para 72(3)(a) | 1 Apr 2013 (SSI 2013/51) |
| | para 72(3)(b) | 1 Oct 2012 (SSI 2012/253) |
| | paras 72(4), 73–75 | 1 Apr 2013 (SSI 2013/51) |
| Sch 8 | | 1 Apr 2013 (SSI 2013/51) |

[1]  For transitional, transitory and savings provisions, see SSI 2012/253, arts 3–8

[2]  For transitional and transitory provisions, see SSI 2012/333, art 3, Sch 2, paras 2, 3

[3]  For a transitory provision, see SSI 2013/47, art 3

[4]  For transitional and transitory provisions, see SSI 2013/51, arts 3, 4

**Police (Complaints and Conduct) Act 2012 (c 22)**

*RA:* 19 Dec 2012

*Commencement provisions:* s 3(3)

Whole Act in force 19 Dec 2012 (s 3(3))

## Prisons (Interference with Wireless Telegraphy) Act 2012 (c 20)

*RA:* 19 Dec 2012

*Commencement provisions:* s 5(3); Prisons (Interference with Wireless Telegraphy) Act 2012 (Commencement) (England and Wales) Order 2013, SI 2013/2460; Prisons (Interference with Wireless Telegraphy) Act 2012 (Commencement) (Scotland) Order 2014, SSI 2014/34

| | |
|---|---|
| 1–4 | 21 Oct 2013 (E) (W) (SI 2013/2460) |
| | 3 Mar 2014 (S) (SSI 2014/34) |
| 5 | 19 Dec 2012 (RA) |

## Protection of Freedoms Act 2012 (c 9)

*RA:* 1 May 2012

*Commencement provisions:* s 120; Protection of Freedoms Act 2012 (Commencement No 1) Order 2012, SI 2012/1205; Protection of Freedoms Act 2012 (Commencement No 2) Order 2012, SI 2012/2075; Protection of Freedoms Act 2012 (Commencement No 3) Order 2012, SI 2012/2234, as amended by SI 2012/3006; Protection of Freedoms Act 2012 (Commencement No 4) Order 2012, SI 2012/2521; Protection of Freedoms Act 2012 (Commencement No 1) (Wales) Order 2012, SI 2012/2499; Protection of Freedoms Act 2012 (Commencement No 5 and Saving and Transitional Provision) Order 2013, SI 2013/470; Protection of Freedoms Act 2012 (Commencement No 6) Order 2013, SI 2013/1180; Protection of Freedoms Act 2012 (Commencement No 2) (Wales) Order 2013, SI 2013/1566; Protection of Freedoms Act 2012 (Commencement No 7) Order 2013, SI 2013/1814; Protection of Freedoms Act 2012 (Commencement No 8) Order 2013, SI 2013/1906; Protection of Freedoms Act 2012 (Commencement No 9) Order 2013, SI 2013/2104; Protection of Freedoms Act 2012 (Commencement No 10) Order 2014, SI 2014/3315; Protection of Freedoms Act 2012 (Commencement No 11) Order 2015, SI 2015/587

| | | |
|---|---|---|
| 1–12 | | 31 Oct 2013 (SI 2013/1814) |
| 13 | | 31 Oct 2013 (in so far as inserts Police and Criminal Evidence Act 1984, s 63Q(2)) (SI 2013/1814) |
| | | 31 Jan 2014 (otherwise) (SI 2013/1814) |
| 14 | | 31 Oct 2013 (except for the purpose of applying Police and Criminal Evidence Act 1984, s 63R to samples which are, or may become, disclosable under the Criminal Procedure and Investigations Act 1996 or under a code of practice prepared under s 23 thereof and in operation by virtue of an order under s 25 thereof) (SI 2013/1814) |
| | | *Not yet in force* (exception noted above) |
| 15–18 | | 31 Oct 2013 (SI 2013/1814) |
| 19 | | See Sch 1 below |
| 20 | (1) | 1 Oct 2012 (SI 2012/2234) |
| | (2)–(9) | 31 Oct 2013 (SI 2013/1814) |
| | (10), (11) | 1 Oct 2012 (SI 2012/2234) |
| 21 | | 31 Oct 2013 (SI 2013/1814) |
| 22 | | 1 Oct 2012 (SI 2012/2234) |
| 23–25 | | 31 Oct 2013 (SI 2013/1814) |
| 26–28 | | 1 Sep 2013 (in so far as relate to schools and further education institutions) (W) (SI 2013/1566) |
| | | 1 Sep 2013 (E) (SI 2013/2104) |
| 29–36 | | 1 Jul 2012 (SI 2012/1205) |
| 37, 38 | | 1 Nov 2012 (SI 2012/2075)[2] |
| 39 | (1) | 1 Jul 2012 (except in so far as confers functions on the Welsh Ministers) (SI 2012/1205) |
| | | *Not yet in force* (exception noted above) |
| | (2) | See Sch 2 below |
| 40, 41 | | 1 Jul 2012 (except in so far as they confer functions on the Welsh Ministers) (SI 2012/1205) |
| | | *Not yet in force* (exception noted above) |
| 42 | | 1 Jul 2012 (SI 2012/1205) |

**Protection of Freedoms Act 2012 (c 9)**—*contd*

| | | |
|---|---|---|
| 43–46 | | 1 Jul 2012 (except in so far as they confer functions on the Welsh Ministers) (SI 2012/1205) |
| | | *Not yet in force* (exception noted above) |
| 47–52 | | 1 Jul 2012 (SI 2012/1205) |
| 53 | | See Sch 3 below |
| 54, 55 | | 1 Oct 2012 (SI 2012/2075) |
| 56 | | See Sch 4 below |
| 57–60 | | 10 Jul 2012 (SI 2012/1205) |
| 61 | (1) | 10 Jul 2012 (SI 2012/1205) |
| | (2) | See Sch 5 below |
| 62 | | 9 May 2012 (SI 2012/1205) |
| 63 | | See Sch 6 below |
| 64 | | 10 Sep 2012, immediately after the coming into force of the Safeguarding Vulnerable Groups (Miscellaneous Amendments) Order 2012, SI 2012/2157 (SI 2012/2234)[3] |
| 65 | | 10 Sep 2012, immediately after the coming into force of the Safeguarding Vulnerable Groups (Miscellaneous Amendments) Order 2012, SI 2012/2157 (SI 2012/2234) |
| 66, 67 | | 10 Sep 2012, immediately after the coming into force of the Safeguarding Vulnerable Groups (Miscellaneous Amendments) Order 2012, SI 2012/2157 (SI 2012/2234)[3] |
| 68–71 | | 10 Sep 2012, immediately after the coming into force of the Safeguarding Vulnerable Groups (Miscellaneous Amendments) Order 2012, SI 2012/2157 (SI 2012/2234) |
| 72 | (1)–(3) | *Not yet in force* |
| | (4)–(6) | 10 Sep 2012, immediately after the coming into force of the Safeguarding Vulnerable Groups (Miscellaneous Amendments) Order 2012, SI 2012/2157 (SI 2012/2234) |
| 73, 74 | | *Not yet in force* |
| 75 | (1), (2) | 10 Sep 2012, immediately after the coming into force of the Safeguarding Vulnerable Groups (Miscellaneous Amendments) Order 2012, SI 2012/2157 (SI 2012/2234) |
| | (3) | 10 Sep 2012, immediately after the coming into force of the Safeguarding Vulnerable Groups (Miscellaneous Amendments) Order 2012, SI 2012/2157 (in so far as substitutes Safeguarding Vulnerable Groups Act 2006, s 43(3)–(5), (5D)–(5H)) (SI 2012/2234) |
| | | *Not yet in force* (in so far as substitutes sub-ss (1), (2), (5A)–(5C) thereof) |
| | (4)–(6) | 10 Sep 2012, immediately after the coming into force of the Safeguarding Vulnerable Groups (Miscellaneous Amendments) Order 2012, SI 2012/2157 (SI 2012/2234) |
| 76 | (1), (2) | 10 Sep 2012, immediately after the coming into force of the Safeguarding Vulnerable Groups (Miscellaneous Amendments) Order 2012, SI 2012/2157 (SI 2012/2234) |
| | (3)(a)–(e) | *Not yet in force* |
| | (3)(f) | 10 Sep 2012, immediately after the coming into force of the Safeguarding Vulnerable Groups (Miscellaneous Amendments) Order 2012, SI 2012/2157 (SI 2012/2234) |
| | (4)(a)–(e) | *Not yet in force* |
| | (4)(f), (5) | 10 Sep 2012, immediately after the coming into force of the Safeguarding Vulnerable Groups (Miscellaneous Amendments) Order 2012, SI 2012/2157 (SI 2012/2234) |
| 77 | | 10 Sep 2012, immediately after the coming into force of the Safeguarding Vulnerable Groups (Miscellaneous Amendments) Order 2012, SI 2012/2157 (SI 2012/2234) |
| 78 | | See Sch 7 below |
| 79 | (1) | 10 Sep 2012, immediately after the coming into force of the Safeguarding Vulnerable Groups (Miscellaneous Amendments) Order 2012, SI 2012/2157 (SI 2012/2234) |
| | (2)(a) | 17 Jun 2013 (SI 2013/1180) |

**Protection of Freedoms Act 2012 (c 9)**—*contd*

| | | |
|---|---|---|
| | (2)(b) | 10 Sep 2012, immediately after the coming into force of the Safeguarding Vulnerable Groups (Miscellaneous Amendments) Order 2012, SI 2012/2157 (in so far as repeals Police Act 1997, s 113B(5), 113B(6)(b)) (SI 2012/2234) |
| | | 17 Jun 2013 (in so far as repeals s 113B(6)(a) thereof) (SI 2013/1180) |
| | (3) | 10 Sep 2012, immediately after the coming into force of the Safeguarding Vulnerable Groups (Miscellaneous Amendments) Order 2012, SI 2012/2157 (in so far as it inserts Police Act 1997, s 120AC) (SI 2012/2234) |
| | | 17 Jun 2013 (in so far as inserts s 120AD thereof) (SI 2013/1180) |
| 80 | | 10 Sep 2012, immediately after the coming into force of the Safeguarding Vulnerable Groups (Miscellaneous Amendments) Order 2012, SI 2012/2157 (SI 2012/2234)[3] |
| 81, 82 | | 10 Sep 2012, immediately after the coming into force of the Safeguarding Vulnerable Groups (Miscellaneous Amendments) Order 2012, SI 2012/2157 (SI 2012/2234) |
| 83 | | 17 Jun 2013 (SI 2013/1180) |
| 84 | | 10 Sep 2012, immediately after the coming into force of the Safeguarding Vulnerable Groups (Miscellaneous Amendments) Order 2012, SI 2012/2157 (SI 2012/2234) |
| 85 | | 1 Jul 2012 (SI 2012/1205) |
| 86 | | 10 Sep 2012, immediately after the coming into force of the Safeguarding Vulnerable Groups (Miscellaneous Amendments) Order 2012, SI 2012/2157 (SI 2012/2234) |
| 87 | (1), (2) | 15 Oct 2012 (SI 2012/2521) |
| | (3) | See Sch 8 below |
| 88–91 | | 1 May 2012 (s 120(5)(a)) |
| 92–101 | | 1 Oct 2012 (SI 2012/2234) |
| 102 | | 31 Jul 2013 (for the purpose of inserting Freedom of Information Act 2000, s 11B) (SI 2013/1906) |
| | | 1 Sep 2013 (otherwise) (SI 2013/1906) |
| 103 | | 1 Sep 2013 (SI 2013/1906) |
| 104 | | 1 Jul 2012 (SI 2012/1205) |
| 105 | | 16 Mar 2015 (SI 2015/587) |
| 106–108 | | 1 Sep 2013 (SI 2013/1906) |
| 109, 110 | | 6 Apr 2013 (SI 2013/470)[4] |
| 111, 112 | | 25 Nov 2012 (SI 2012/2075) |
| 113 | | 1 May 2012 (s 120(5)(b)) |
| 114 | | 1 Oct 2012 (SI 2012/2234) |
| 115 | (1) | See Sch 9 below |
| | (2) | See Sch 10 below |
| | (3)–(7) | 1 May 2012 (s 120(5)(c)) |
| 116–121 | | 1 May 2012 (s 120(5)(c)) |
| Sch 1 | para 1(1)–(3) | 31 Oct 2013 (SI 2013/1814) |
| | para 1(4) | 31 Oct 2013 (except (i) for the purpose of inserting Terrorism Act 2000, Sch 8, para 20F(1) and (ii) for the purpose of applying Terrorism Act 2000, Sch 8, para 20G to samples which are, or may become, disclosable under the Criminal Procedure and Investigations Act 1996 or under a code of practice prepared under s 23 thereof and in operation by virtue of an order under s 25 thereof) (SI 2013/1814) |
| | | 31 Jan 2014 (for the purpose of inserting Terrorism Act 2000, Sch 8, para 20F(1)) (SI 2013/1814) |
| | | *Not yet in force* (otherwise) |
| | para 1(5)–(8) | 31 Oct 2013 (SI 2013/1814) |
| | paras 2–6 | 31 Oct 2013 (SI 2013/1814) |
| | para 7 | *Not yet in force* |
| | para 8 | 16 Dec 2014 (SI 2014/3315) |
| Sch 2 | | 1 Jul 2012 (s 120(4)(a)) |

**Protection of Freedoms Act 2012 (c 9)**—*contd*

| | | |
|---|---|---|
| Sch 3 | | *Not yet in force* |
| Sch 4 | | 1 Oct 2012 (E) (SI 2012/2075) |
| | | 1 Oct 2012 (W) (SI 2012/2499) |
| Schs 5, 6 | | 10 Jul 2012 (SI 2012/1205) |
| Sch 7 | paras 1, 2, 3(1) | 10 Sep 2012, immediately after the coming into force of the Safeguarding Vulnerable Groups (Miscellaneous Amendments) Order 2012, SI 2012/2157 (SI 2012/2234) |
| | para 3(2) | 10 Aug 2012 (for the purposes of making regulations) (SI 2012/2075) |
| | | 10 Sep 2012, immediately after the coming into force of the Safeguarding Vulnerable Groups (Miscellaneous Amendments) Order 2012, SI 2012/2157 (otherwise) (SI 2012/2234) |
| | para 3(3)–(7) | 10 Sep 2012, immediately after the coming into force of the Safeguarding Vulnerable Groups (Miscellaneous Amendments) Order 2012, SI 2012/2157 (SI 2012/2234) |
| | para 4 | 10 Sep 2012, immediately after the coming into force of the Safeguarding Vulnerable Groups (Miscellaneous Amendments) Order 2012, SI 2012/2157 (SI 2012/2234)[3] |
| | paras 5–8 | 10 Sep 2012, immediately after the coming into force of the Safeguarding Vulnerable Groups (Miscellaneous Amendments) Order 2012, SI 2012/2157 (SI 2012/2234) |
| | para 9(1)–(3) | *Not yet in force* |
| | para 9(4)–(6) | 10 Sep 2012, immediately after the coming into force of the Safeguarding Vulnerable Groups (Miscellaneous Amendments) Order 2012, SI 2012/2157 (SI 2012/2234) |
| | paras 10, 11 | *Not yet in force* |
| | para 12(1) | 10 Sep 2012, immediately after the coming into force of the Safeguarding Vulnerable Groups (Miscellaneous Amendments) Order 2012, SI 2012/2157 (SI 2012/2234) |
| | para 12(2) | 10 Sep 2012, immediately after the coming into force of the Safeguarding Vulnerable Groups (Miscellaneous Amendments) Order 2012, SI 2012/2157 (in so far as substitutes Safeguarding Vulnerable Groups (Northern Ireland) Order 2007, SI 2007/1351, art 45(3)–(5), (5D)–(5H)) (SI 2012/2234) |
| | | *Not yet in force* (in so far as substitutes art 45(1), (2), (5A)–(5C) thereof) |
| | para 12(3), (4) | 10 Sep 2012, immediately after the coming into force of the Safeguarding Vulnerable Groups (Miscellaneous Amendments) Order 2012, SI 2012/2157 (SI 2012/2234) |
| | para 13(1), (2) | 10 Sep 2012, immediately after the coming into force of the Safeguarding Vulnerable Groups (Miscellaneous Amendments) Order 2012, SI 2012/2157 (SI 2012/2234) |
| | para 13(3)(a)–(f) | *Not yet in force* |
| | para 13(3)(g) | 10 Sep 2012, immediately after the coming into force of the Safeguarding Vulnerable Groups (Miscellaneous Amendments) Order 2012, SI 2012/2157 (SI 2012/2234) |
| | para 13(4)(a)–(f) | *Not yet in force* |
| | para 13(4)(g), (5) | 10 Sep 2012, immediately after the coming into force of the Safeguarding Vulnerable Groups (Miscellaneous Amendments) Order 2012, SI 2012/2157 (SI 2012/2234) |
| | para 14(1)–(3) | 10 Sep 2012, immediately after the coming into force of the Safeguarding Vulnerable Groups (Miscellaneous Amendments) Order 2012, SI 2012/2157 (SI 2012/2234) |
| | para 14(4) | 10 Aug 2012 (for the purposes of making regulations) (SI 2012/2075) |
| | | 10 Sep 2012, immediately after the coming into force of the Safeguarding Vulnerable Groups (Miscellaneous Amendments) Order 2012, SI 2012/2157 (otherwise) (SI 2012/2234) |
| | para 14(5), (6) | 10 Sep 2012, immediately after the coming into force of the Safeguarding Vulnerable Groups (Miscellaneous Amendments) Order 2012, SI 2012/2157 (SI 2012/2234) |

**Protection of Freedoms Act 2012 (c 9)**—*contd*

| | | |
|---|---|---|
| Sch 8 | paras 1–11 | 15 Oct 2012 (SI 2012/2521) |
| | para 12 | 1 Dec 2012 (SI 2012/2521) |
| | paras 13–20 | 15 Oct 2012 (SI 2012/2521) |
| Sch 9 | Pt 1 | 1 Sep 2013 (SI 2013/2104) |
| | Pt 2 | 1 Jul 2012 (SI 2012/1205) |
| | Pt 3 | 1 Nov 2012 (except para 15, in so far as it inserts words "or 32A" into the Regulation of Investigatory Powers Act 2000, s 77A in each place they occur) (SI 2012/2075) |
| | | *Not yet in force* (exception noted above) |
| | Pt 4 | 1 Oct 2012 (SI 2012/2075) |
| | Pt 5 | 10 Jul 2012 (SI 2012/1205) |
| | Pt 6, paras 35–67 | 10 Sep 2012, immediately after the coming into force of the Safeguarding Vulnerable Groups (Miscellaneous Amendments) Order 2012, SI 2012/2157 (SI 2012/2234) |
| | Pt 6, para 68 (1)–(3), (4)(a) | 10 Sep 2012, immediately after the coming into force of the Safeguarding Vulnerable Groups (Miscellaneous Amendments) Order 2012, SI 2012/2157 (SI 2012/2234) |
| | Pt 6, para 68 (4)(b) | *Not yet in force* |
| | Pt 6, paras 68 (4)(c)–(g), 69–103 | 10 Sep 2012, immediately after the coming into force of the Safeguarding Vulnerable Groups (Miscellaneous Amendments) Order 2012, SI 2012/2157 (SI 2012/2234) |
| | Pt 7, paras 104–107 | 10 Sep 2012, immediately after the coming into force of the Safeguarding Vulnerable Groups (Miscellaneous Amendments) Order 2012, SI 2012/2157 (SI 2012/2234) |
| | Pt 7, para 108 | 17 Jun 2013 (SI 2013/1180) |
| | Pt 7, para 109(1) | See sub-paras (2)–(4) below |
| | Pt 7, para 109 (2)(a) | 17 Jun 2013 (SI 2013/1180) |
| | Pt 7, para 109 (2)(b) | 10 Sep 2012, immediately after the coming into force of the Safeguarding Vulnerable Groups (Miscellaneous Amendments) Order 2012, SI 2012/2157 (SI 2012/2234) |
| | Pt 7, para 109(3) | 17 Jun 2013 (SI 2013/1180) |
| | Pt 7, para 109(4) | 10 Sep 2012, immediately after the coming into force of the Safeguarding Vulnerable Groups (Miscellaneous Amendments) Order 2012, SI 2012/2157 (SI 2012/2234) |
| | Pt 7, para 110(1) | See sub-paras (2)–(6) below |
| | Pt 7, para 110(2) | 17 Jun 2013 (SI 2013/1180) |
| | Pt 7, para 110(3) | 10 Sep 2012, immediately after the coming into force of the Safeguarding Vulnerable Groups (Miscellaneous Amendments) Order 2012, SI 2012/2157 (SI 2012/2234) |
| | Pt 7, para 110 (4)–(6) | 17 Jun 2013 (SI 2013/1180) |
| | Pt 7, para 111(1) | See sub-paras (2)–(6) below |
| | Pt 7, para 111 (2), (3) | 10 Sep 2012, immediately after the coming into force of the Safeguarding Vulnerable Groups (Miscellaneous Amendments) Order 2012, SI 2012/2157 (SI 2012/2234) |
| | Pt 7, para 111(4) | 17 Jun 2013 (SI 2013/1180) |
| | Pt 7, para 111 (5), (6) | 10 Sep 2012, immediately after the coming into force of the Safeguarding Vulnerable Groups (Miscellaneous Amendments) Order 2012, SI 2012/2157 (SI 2012/2234) |
| | Pt 7, para 112 | 10 Sep 2012, immediately after the coming into force of the Safeguarding Vulnerable Groups (Miscellaneous Amendments) Order 2012, SI 2012/2157 (SI 2012/2234) |
| | Pt 7, para 113 | 17 Jun 2013 (SI 2013/1180) |
| | Pt 7, para 114 | *Not yet in force* |
| | Pt 7, para 115 | 10 Sep 2012, immediately after the coming into force of the Safeguarding Vulnerable Groups (Miscellaneous Amendments) Order 2012, SI 2012/2157 (SI 2012/2234) |
| | Pt 7, para 116(1) | See sub-paras (2), (3) below |

**Protection of Freedoms Act 2012 (c 9)**—*contd*

|  |  |  |
|---|---|---|
|  | Pt 7, para 116(2) | *Not yet in force* |
|  | Pt 7, para 116(3) | 10 Sep 2012, immediately after the coming into force of the Safeguarding Vulnerable Groups (Miscellaneous Amendments) Order 2012, SI 2012/2157 (SI 2012/2234) |
|  | Pt 7, para 117 | 10 Sep 2012, immediately after the coming into force of the Safeguarding Vulnerable Groups (Miscellaneous Amendments) Order 2012, SI 2012/2157 (SI 2012/2234) |
|  | Pt 7, para 118 | 10 Sep 2012, immediately after the coming into force of the Safeguarding Vulnerable Groups (Miscellaneous Amendments) Order 2012, SI 2012/2157 (in so far as insertion of Police Act 1997, s 126(1) has effect in relation to definition "certificate", para (c)) (SI 2012/2234) |
|  |  | 17 Jun 2013 (otherwise) (SI 2013/1180) |
|  | Pt 7, paras 119–128 | 17 Jun 2013 (SI 2013/1180) |
|  | Pt 7, para 129 | 10 Sep 2012, immediately after the coming into force of the Safeguarding Vulnerable Groups (Miscellaneous Amendments) Order 2012, SI 2012/2157 (SI 2012/2234) |
|  | Pt 8 | 15 Oct 2012 (SI 2012/2521) |
|  | Pt 9 | 1 Oct 2012 (SI 2012/2234) |
|  | Pt 10 | 6 Apr 2013 (SI 2013/470)[4] |
|  | Pt 11 | 25 Nov 2012 (SI 2012/2075) |
|  | Pt 12 | 1 May 2012 (s 120(5)(b)) |
| Sch 10 | Pt 1 | 1 Sep 2013 (SI 2013/2104) |
|  | Pt 2 | 1 Jul 2012 (s 120(4)(b))[1] |
|  | Pt 3 | 1 Oct 2012 (SI 2012/2075) |
|  | Pt 4 | 10 Jul 2012 (SI 2012/1205) |
|  | Pt 5 | 10 Sep 2012, immediately after the coming into force of the Safeguarding Vulnerable Groups (Miscellaneous Amendments) Order 2012, SI 2012/2157 (SI 2012/2234), repeals of or in— |
|  |  | Police Act 1997; |
|  |  | Safeguarding Vulnerable Groups Act 2006; |
|  |  | Safeguarding Vulnerable Groups (Northern Ireland) Order 2007 (SI 2007/1351); |
|  |  | Health and Social Care Act 2008; |
|  |  | Education and Skills Act 2008; |
|  |  | Offender Management Act 2007 (Consequential Amendments) Order 2008 (SI 2008/912); |
|  |  | Apprenticeships, Skills, Children and Learning Act 2009; |
|  |  | Health Act 2009; |
|  |  | Policing and Crime Act 2009; |
|  |  | Police Act 1997 (Criminal Records) (Electronic Communications) Order 2009 (SI 2009/203); |
|  |  | Health Care and Associated Professions (Miscellaneous Amendments and Practitioner Psychologists) Order 2009 (SI 2009/1182); |
|  |  | Safeguarding Vulnerable Groups Act 2006 (Regulated Activity, Miscellaneous and Transitional Provisions and Commencement No 5) Order 2009 (SI 2009/2610), art 26, Pt 8, arts 28, 30(a); |
|  |  | Safeguarding Vulnerable Groups (Regulated Activity, Transitional Provisions and Commencement No 4) Order (Northern Ireland) 2009 (SR 2009/304); |
|  |  | Safeguarding Vulnerable Groups (Miscellaneous Provisions) Order (Northern Ireland) 2009 (SR 2009/305); |
|  |  | Health and Social Care Act 2008 (Consequential Amendments No 2) Order 2010 (SI 2010/813); |
|  |  | Safeguarding Vulnerable Groups Act 2006 (Controlled Activity and Miscellaneous Provisions) Regulations 2010 (SI 2010/1146); |

**Protection of Freedoms Act 2012 (c 9)**—*contd*

|  | Safeguarding Vulnerable Groups Act 2006 (Regulated Activity, Devolution and Miscellaneous Provisions) Order 2010 (SI 2010/1154); |
|  | Local Education Authorities and Children's Services Authorities (Integration of Functions) Order 2010 (SI 2010/1158); |
|  | Safeguarding Vulnerable Groups (Regulated Activity, Devolution Alignment and Miscellaneous Provisions) Order (Northern Ireland) 2010 (SR 2010/30) |
|  | *Not yet in force*, repeal of or in— |
|  | Safeguarding Vulnerable Groups Act 2006 (Regulated Activity, Miscellaneous and Transitional Provisions and Commencement No 5) Order 2009, SI 2009/2610, art 29 |
| Pt 6 | 10 Sep 2012, immediately after the coming into force of the Safeguarding Vulnerable Groups (Miscellaneous Amendments) Order 2012, SI 2012/2157 (SI 2012/2234), repeals of or in— |
|  | Police Act 1997, ss 113B(4), (5), (6)(b), (9), 119B, 120, 124; |
|  | Safeguarding Vulnerable Groups Act 2006; |
|  | Policing and Crime Act 2009 |
|  | 17 Jun 2013 (SI 2013/1180), repeals of or in— |
|  | Police Act 1997, ss 113A(4), 113B(6)(a), 122(3A)(a), 124A(1)(c) |
| Pt 7 | 1 Jul 2012 (SI 2012/1205), repeals of or in— |
|  | Freedom of Information Act 2000, s 80A; |
|  | Constitutional Reform and Governance Act 2010, Sch 7, para 6 |
|  | *Not yet in force*, repeal in— |
|  | Freedom of Information Act 2000, s 6 |
| Pt 8 | 16 Mar 2015, repeals of or in— |
|  | Data Protection Act 1998, Sch 5, para 2(4), (5); |
|  | Freedom of Information Act 2000, s 18(5)–(7) |
|  | *Not yet in force* (otherwise) |
| Pt 9 | 6 Apr 2013 (SI 2013/470) |
| Pt 10 | 1 May 2012 (s 120(5)(b)) |
| Pt 11 | *Not yet in force* |

[1]     SI 2012/1205 also brings this Part of this Schedule into force on the same date

[2]     For transitional provisions, see SI 2012/2075, art 6

[3]     For transitional provisions, see SI 2012/2234, arts 4–16

[4]     For savings and transitional provisions, see SI 2013/470, arts 3–8

---

**Public Services (Social Value) Act 2012 (c 3)**

*RA:* 8 Mar 2012

*Commencement provisions*: s 4; Public Services (Social Value) Act 2012 (Commencement) Order 2012, SI 2012/3173

| 1, 2 | 31 Jan 2013 (SI 2012/3173) |
| 3, 4 | 8 Mar 2012 (s 4(2)) |

---

**Scotland Act 2012 (c 11)**

*RA:* 1 May 2012

*Commencement provisions*: s 44; Scotland Act 2012 (Commencement No 1) Order 2012, SI 2012/1710; Scotland Act 2012 (Commencement No 2) Order 2012, SI 2012/2516; Scotland Act 2012 (Commencement No 3) Order 2013, SI 2013/6; Scotland Act 2012 (Commencement No 4) Order 2014, SI 2014/3250; Scotland Act 2012 (Commencement No 5) Order 2015, SI 2015/682

| 1 | 1 Jul 2015 (SI 2015/682) |
| 2 | *Not yet in force* |

## Scotland Act 2012 (c 11)—*contd*

| | | |
|---|---|---|
| 3 | | 1 Jul 2015 (SI 2015/682) |
| 4, 5 | | 3 Jul 2012 (SI 2012/1710) |
| 6 | | 15 Oct 2012 (SI 2012/1710) |
| 7 | | 3 Jul 2012 (SI 2012/1710) |
| 8 | | 31 Oct 2012 (SI 2012/2516) |
| 9, 10 | | 3 Jul 2012 (SI 2012/1710) |
| 11 | | 1 Jul 2012 (s 44(2)(a)) |
| 12 | | 3 Jul 2012 (SI 2012/1710) |
| 13 | | 31 Oct 2012 (SI 2012/2516) |
| 14–16 | | 3 Jul 2012 (SI 2012/1710) |
| 17 | | 31 Oct 2012 (SI 2012/2516) |
| 18 | | 1 Aug 2013 (SI 2012/2516) |
| 19 | | 31 Oct 2012 (SI 2012/2516) |
| 20–22 | | 3 Jul 2012 (SI 2012/1710) |
| 23, 24 | | 1 Jul 2012 (s 44(2)(b)) |
| 25 | (1)–(6) | 1 Jul 2012 (s 44(2)(b)) |
| | (7) | See Sch 2 below |
| 26–31 | | 1 Jul 2012 (s 44(2)(b)) |
| 32 | | 12 Dec 2014 (SI 2014/3250) |
| 33 | | 1 Jul 2012 (s 44(2)(b)) |
| 34–38 | | 22 Apr 2013 (SI 2013/6) |
| 39 | | 31 Oct 2012 (SI 2012/2516) |
| 40–45 | | 1 May 2012 (s 44(1)) |
| Sch 1 | | 31 Oct 2012 (SI 2012/2516) |
| Sch 2 | | *Not yet in force* (para 1(2)(a), (b), (4) repealed) |
| Schs 3, 4 | | 1 Jul 2012 (s 44(2)(b)) |

## Small Charitable Donations Act 2012 (c 23)

*RA:* 19 Dec 2012

*Commencement provisions:* s 21(1)–(3)

| | | |
|---|---|---|
| 1, 2 | | 6 Apr 2013 (s 21(1)) |
| 3 | (1) | See Schedule below |
| | (2), (3) | 6 Apr 2013 (s 21(1)) |
| 4 | | 6 Apr 2013 (s 21(1)) |
| 5 | | 19 Dec 2012 (for the purposes of making regulations or orders) (s 21(2)) |
| | | 6 Apr 2013 (otherwise) (s 21(1)) |
| 6 | | 6 Apr 2013 (s 21(1)) |
| 7, 8 | | 19 Dec 2012 (for the purposes of making regulations or orders) (s 21(2)) |
| | | 6 Apr 2013 (otherwise) (s 21(1)) |
| 9, 10 | | 6 Apr 2013 (s 21(1)) |
| 11 | | 19 Dec 2012 (for the purposes of making regulations or orders) (s 21(2)) |
| | | 6 Apr 2013 (otherwise) (s 21(1)) |
| 12, 13 | | 6 Apr 2013 (s 21(1)) |
| 14 | | 19 Dec 2012 (for the purposes of making regulations or orders) (s 21(2)) |
| | | 6 Apr 2013 (otherwise) (s 21(1)) |
| 15 | | 6 Apr 2013 (s 21(1)) |
| 16–22 | | 19 Dec 2012 (s 21(3)) |
| Schedule | | 6 Apr 2013 (s 21(1)) |

## Sunday Trading (London Olympic Games and Paralympic Games) Act 2012 (c 12)

*RA:* 1 May 2012

Whole Act in force 1 May 2012 (RA)

## Supply and Appropriation (Anticipation and Adjustments) Act 2012 (c 1)

*RA:* 8 Mar 2012

Whole Act in force 8 Mar 2012 (RA)

## Supply and Appropriation (Main Estimates) Act 2012 (c 13)

*RA:* 17 Jul 2012

Whole Act in force 17 Jul 2012 (RA)

## Water Industry (Financial Assistance) Act 2012 (c 8)

*RA:* 1 May 2012

*Commencement provisions:* s 3(2), (3)

| | |
|---|---|
| 1, 2 | 1 Jul 2012 (s 3(2)) |
| 3 | 1 May 2012 (s 3(3)) |

## Welfare Reform Act 2012 (c 5)

*RA:* 8 Mar 2012

*Commencement provisions:* s 150; Welfare Reform Act 2012 (Commencement No 1) Order 2012, SI 2012/863; Welfare Reform Act 2012 (Commencement No 2) Order 2012, SI 2012/1246, as amended by SI 2012/1440, SI 2012/2530; Welfare Reform Act 2012 (Commencement No 3, Savings Provision) Order 2012, SI 2012/1651; Welfare Reform Act 2012 (Commencement No 4) Order 2012, SI 2012/2530; Welfare Reform Act 2012 (Commencement No 5) Order 2012, SI 2012/2946; Welfare Reform Act 2012 (Commencement No 6 and Savings Provisions) Order 2012, SI 2012/3090; Welfare Reform Act 2012 (Commencement No 7) Order 2013, SI 2013/178; Welfare Reform Act 2012 (Commencement No 8 and Savings and Transitional Provisions) Order 2013, SI 2013/358, as amended by SI 2013/983; Welfare Reform Act 2012 (Commencement No 9 and Transitional and Transitory Provisions and Commencement No 8 and Savings and Transitional Provisions (Amendment)) Order 2013, SI 2013/983, as amended by SI 2013/1511, SI 2014/1452, SI 2014/1661, SI 2014/2321, SI 2014/3067, SI 2014/3094, SI 2015/32, SI 2015/1537, SI 2017/483, SI 2018/138, SI 2019/167 (itself amended by SI 2022/302), SI 2022/302, as modified by SI 2014/1452, SI 2014/1661, SI 2014/1923; Welfare Reform Act 2012 (Commencement No 10) Order 2013, SI 2013/1250; Welfare Reform Act 2012 (Commencement No 11 and Transitional and Transitory Provisions and Commencement No 9 and Transitional and Transitory Provisions (Amendment)) Order 2013, SI 2013/1511, as amended by SI 2014/1661, SI 2015/32, as modified by SI 2014/1452, SI 2014/1923, SI 2017/57, SI 2018/138; Welfare Reform Act (Commencement No 12) Order 2013, SI 2013/2534; Welfare Reform Act 2012 (Commencement No 13 and Transitional and Transitory Provisions) Order 2013, SI 2013/2657, as amended by SI 2014/1661, SI 2015/32, as modified by SI 2014/1452, SI 2014/1661, SI 2014/1923, SI 2016/596 (itself amended by SI 2016/963), SI 2017/57, SI 2018/138; Welfare Reform Act 2012 (Commencement No 14 and Transitional and Transitory Provisions) Order 2013, SI 2013/2846, as amended by SI 2014/1661, SI 2015/32, as modified by SI 2014/1452, SI 2014/1661, SI 2014/1923, SI 2016/596 (itself amended by SI 2016/963); Child Maintenance and Other Payments Act 2008 (Commencement No 12 and Savings Provisions) and the Welfare Reform Act 2012 (Commencement No 15) Order 2013, SI 2013/2947; Welfare Reform Act 2012 (Commencement No 16 and Transitional and Transitory Provisions) Order 2014, SI 2014/209, as amended by SI 2014/1661, SI 2015/32, as modified by SI 2014/1452, SI 2014/1661, SI 2014/1923, SI 2016/596 (itself amended by SI 2016/963), SI 2017/57; Welfare Reform Act 2012 (Commencement No 17 and Transitional and Transitory Provisions) Order 2014, SI 2014/1583, as amended by SI 2014/1661, SI 2014/3067, SI 2015/32, as modified by SI 2014/1923, SI 2017/664, SI 2017/952, SI 2018/38, SI 2018/532, SI 2018/881; Child Maintenance and Other Payments Act 2008 (Commencement No 14 and Transitional Provisions) and the Welfare Reform Act 2012 (Commencement No 18 and Transitional and Savings Provisions) Order 2014, SI 2014/1635; Welfare Reform Act 2012 (Commencement No 19 and Transitional and Transitory Provisions and Commencement No 9 and Transitional and Transitory Provisions (Amendment)) Order 2014, SI 2014/2321, as amended by SI 2015/32, as modified by SI 2016/596

**Welfare Reform Act 2012 (c 5)**—*contd*

(itself amended by SI 2016/963), SI 2016/963, SI 2017/584 SI 2017/664, SI 2017/952, SI 2018/38, SI 2018/532, SI 2018/881; Welfare Reform Act 2012 (Commencement No 20 and Transitional and Transitory Provisions and Commencement No 9 and Transitional and Transitory Provisions (Amendment)) Order 2014, SI 2014/3094; Welfare Reform Act 2012 (Commencement No 21 and Transitional and Transitory Provisions) Order 2015, SI 2015/33, as amended by SI 2017/483, SI 2018/138, SI 2019/37 (itself amended by SI 2020/655), SI 2019/167 (itself amended by SI 2022/302); Welfare Reform Act 2012 (Commencement No 22 and Transitional and Transitory Provisions) Order 2015, SI 2015/101, as modified by SI 2016/596 (itself amended by SI 2016/963), SI 2016/963, SI 2017/57, SI 2017/584 SI 2017/664, SI 2017/952, SI 2018/138, SI 2018/532, SI 2018/881; Welfare Reform Act 2012 (Commencement No 23 and Transitional and Transitory Provisions) Order 2015, SI 2015/634, as amended by SI 2015/740, SI 2018/138, SI 2019/37 (itself amended by SI 2020/655), SI 2019/167 (itself amended by SI 2022/302), as modified by SI 2016/596 (itself amended by SI 2016/963), SI 2016/963, SI 2017/57, SI 2017/584 SI 2017/664, SI 2017/952, SI 2018/138, SI 2018/532, SI 2018/881; Welfare Reform Act 2012 (Commencement No 24 and Transitional and Transitory Provisions and Commencement No 9 and Transitional and Transitory Provisions (Amendment)) Order 2015, SI 2015/1537, as modified by SI 2016/596 (itself amended by SI 2016/963), SI 2016/963, SI 2017/57, SI 2017/584 SI 2017/664, SI 2017/952, SI 2018/138, 2018/532, SI 2018/881; Welfare Reform Act 2012 (Commencement No 25 and Transitional and Transitory Provisions) Order 2015, SI 2015/1930; Welfare Reform Act 2012 (Commencement No 26 and Transitional and Transitory Provisions and Commencement No 22, 23 and 24 and Transitional and Transitory Provisions (Modification)) Order 2016, SI 2016/33; Welfare Reform Act 2012 (Commencement No 27 and Transitional and Transitory Provisions and Commencement No 22, 23 and 24 and Transitional and Transitory Provisions (Modification)) Order 2016, SI 2016/407; Welfare Reform Act 2012 (Commencement No 28) Order 2016, SI 2016/511; Welfare Reform Act 2012 (Commencement No 29 and Commencement No 17, 19, 22, 23 and 24 and Transitional and Transitory Provisions (Modification)) Order 2017, SI 2017/664; Welfare Reform Act 2012 (Commencement No 30 and Transitory Provisions) Order 2018, SI 2018/145, as amended by SI 2019/655; Welfare Reform Act 2012 (Commencement No 31 and Savings and Transitional Provisions and Commencement No. 21 and 23 and Transitional and Transitory Provisions (Amendment)) Order 2019, SI 2019/37, as amended by SI 2019/935, SI 2020/655; Welfare Reform Act 2012 (Commencement No 32 and Savings and Transitional Provisions) Order 2019, SI 2019/167, as amended by SI 2022/302; Welfare Reform Act 2012 (Commencement No 33) Order 2019, SI 2019/1135; Welfare Reform Act 2012 (Commencement No 34 and Commencement No. 9, 21, 23, 31 and 32 and Transitional and Transitory Provisions (Amendment)) Order 2022, SI 2022/302

| | | |
|---|---|---|
| 1 | | In force in accordance with SI 2013/983, SI 2013/1511, SI 2013/2657, SI 2013/2846, SI 2014/209, SI 2014/1583, SI 2014/2321, SI 2014/3094, SI 2015/33, SI 2015/101, SI 2015/634, SI 2015/1537, SI 2015/1930, SI 2016/33, SI 2016/407, SI 2016/963, SI 2017/664 for certain claims and awards defined therein[5] |
| | | 30 Mar 2022 (otherwise) (SI 2022/302) |
| 2 | (1) | In force in accordance with SI 2013/983, SI 2013/1511, SI 2013/2657, SI 2013/2846, SI 2014/209, SI 2014/1583, SI 2014/2321, SI 2014/3094, SI 2015/33, SI 2015/101, SI 2015/634, SI 2015/1537, SI 2015/1930, SI 2016/33, SI 2016/407, SI 2016/963, SI 2017/664 for certain claims and awards defined therein[5] |
| | | 30 Mar 2022 (otherwise) (SI 2022/302) |
| | (2) | 25 Feb 2013 (SI 2013/358) |
| 3 | | In force in accordance with SI 2013/983, SI 2013/1511, SI 2013/2657, SI 2013/2846, SI 2014/209, SI 2014/1583, SI 2014/2321, SI 2014/3094, SI 2015/33, SI 2015/101, SI 2015/634, SI 2015/1537, SI 2015/1930, SI 2016/33, SI 2016/407, SI 2016/963, SI 2017/664 for certain claims and awards defined therein[5] |
| | | 30 Mar 2022 (otherwise) (SI 2022/302) |

**Welfare Reform Act 2012 (c 5)**—*contd*

| | | |
|---|---|---|
| 4 | (1) | In force in accordance with SI 2013/983, SI 2013/1511, SI 2013/2657, SI 2013/2846, SI 2014/209, SI 2014/1583, SI 2014/2321, SI 2014/3094, SI 2015/33, SI 2015/101, SI 2015/634, SI 2015/1537, SI 2015/1930, SI 2016/33, SI 2016/407, SI 2016/963, SI 2017/664 for certain claims and awards defined therein[5] |
| | | 30 Mar 2022 (otherwise) (SI 2022/302) |
| | (2), (3) | 25 Feb 2013 (SI 2013/358) |
| | (4) | In force in accordance with SI 2013/983, SI 2013/1511, SI 2013/2657, SI 2013/2846, SI 2014/209, SI 2014/1583, SI 2014/2321, SI 2014/3094, SI 2015/33, SI 2015/101, SI 2015/634, SI 2015/1537, SI 2015/1930, SI 2016/33, SI 2016/407, SI 2016/963, SI 2017/664 for certain claims and awards defined therein[5] |
| | | 30 Mar 2022 (otherwise) (SI 2022/302) |
| | (5)–(7) | 25 Feb 2013 (SI 2013/358) |
| 5 | | 25 Feb 2013 (for the purpose of making regulations) (SI 2013/358) In force in accordance with SI 2013/983, SI 2013/1511, SI 2013/2657, SI 2013/2846, SI 2014/209, SI 2014/1583, SI 2014/2321, SI 2014/3094, SI 2015/33, SI 2015/101, SI 2015/634, SI 2015/1537, SI 2015/1930, SI 2016/33, SI 2016/407, SI 2016/963, SI 2017/664 for certain claims and awards defined therein[5] |
| | | 30 Mar 2022 (otherwise) (SI 2022/302) |
| 6 | (1)(a) | 25 Feb 2013 (for the purpose of making regulations) (SI 2013/358) In force in accordance with SI 2013/983, SI 2013/1511, SI 2013/2657, SI 2013/2846, SI 2014/209, SI 2014/1583, SI 2014/2321, SI 2014/3094, SI 2015/33, SI 2015/101, SI 2015/634, SI 2015/1537, SI 2015/1930, SI 2016/33, SI 2016/407, SI 2016/963, SI 2017/664 for certain claims and awards defined therein[5] |
| | | 30 Mar 2022 (otherwise) (SI 2022/302) |
| | (1)(b), (c), (2) | In force in accordance with SI 2013/983, SI 2013/1511, SI 2013/2657, SI 2013/2846, SI 2014/209, SI 2014/1583, SI 2014/2321, SI 2014/3094, SI 2015/33, SI 2015/101, SI 2015/634, SI 2015/1537, SI 2015/1930, SI 2016/33, SI 2016/407, SI 2016/963, SI 2017/664 for certain claims and awards defined therein[5] |
| | | 30 Mar 2022 (otherwise) (SI 2022/302) |
| | (3) | 25 Feb 2013 (for the purpose of making regulations) (SI 2013/358) In force in accordance with SI 2013/983, SI 2013/1511, SI 2013/2657, SI 2013/2846, SI 2014/209, SI 2014/1583, SI 2014/2321, SI 2014/3094, SI 2015/33, SI 2015/101, SI 2015/634, SI 2015/1537, SI 2015/1930, SI 2016/33, SI 2016/407, SI 2016/963, SI 2017/664 for certain claims and awards defined therein[5] |
| | | 30 Mar 2022 (otherwise) (SI 2022/302) |
| 7 | (1) | In force in accordance with SI 2013/983, SI 2013/1511, SI 2013/2657, SI 2013/2846, SI 2014/209, SI 2014/1583, SI 2014/2321, SI 2014/3094, SI 2015/33, SI 2015/101, SI 2015/634, SI 2015/1537, SI 2015/1930, SI 2016/33, SI 2016/407, SI 2016/963, SI 2017/664 for certain claims and awards defined therein[5] |
| | | 30 Mar 2022 (otherwise) (SI 2022/302) |
| | (2), (3) | 25 Feb 2013 (SI 2013/358) |
| | (4) | In force in accordance with SI 2013/983, SI 2013/1511, SI 2013/2657, SI 2013/2846, SI 2014/209, SI 2014/1583, SI 2014/2321, SI 2014/3094, SI 2015/33, SI 2015/101, SI 2015/634, SI 2015/1537, SI 2015/1930, SI 2016/33, SI 2016/407, SI 2016/963, SI 2017/664 for certain claims and awards defined therein[5] |

**Welfare Reform Act 2012 (c 5)**—*contd*

|   |   |   |
|---|---|---|
| | | 30 Mar 2022 (otherwise) (SI 2022/302) |
| 8 | (1), (2) | In force in accordance with SI 2013/983, SI 2013/1511, SI 2013/2657, SI 2013/2846, SI 2014/209, SI 2014/1583, SI 2014/2321, SI 2015/33, SI 2015/101, SI 2015/634, SI 2015/1537, SI 2015/1930, SI 2016/33, SI 2016/407, SI 2016/963, SI 2017/664 for certain claims and awards defined therein[5] |
| | | 30 Mar 2022 (otherwise) (SI 2022/302) |
| | (3) | 25 Feb 2013 (for the purpose of making regulations) (SI 2013/358) |
| | | In force in accordance with SI 2013/983, SI 2013/1511, SI 2013/2657, SI 2013/2846, SI 2014/209, SI 2014/1583, SI 2014/2321, SI 2014/3094, SI 2015/33, SI 2015/101, SI 2015/634, SI 2015/1537, SI 2015/1930, SI 2016/33, SI 2016/407, SI 2016/963, SI 2017/664 for certain claims and awards defined therein[5] |
| | | 30 Mar 2022 (otherwise) (SI 2022/302) |
| | (4) | In force in accordance with SI 2013/983, SI 2013/1511, SI 2013/2657, SI 2013/2846, SI 2014/209, SI 2014/1583, SI 2014/2321, SI 2015/33, SI 2015/101, SI 2015/634, SI 2015/1537, SI 2015/1930, SI 2016/33, SI 2016/407, SI 2016/963, SI 2017/664 for certain claims and awards defined therein[5] |
| | | 30 Mar 2022 (otherwise) (SI 2022/302) |
| 9 | (1) | In force in accordance with SI 2013/983, SI 2013/1511, SI 2013/2657, SI 2013/2846, SI 2014/209, SI 2014/1583, SI 2014/2321, SI 2014/3094, SI 2015/33, SI 2015/101, SI 2015/634, SI 2015/1537, SI 2015/1930, SI 2016/33, SI 2016/407, SI 2016/963, SI 2017/664 for certain claims and awards defined therein[5] |
| | | 30 Mar 2022 (otherwise) (SI 2022/302) |
| | (2), (3) | 25 Feb 2013 (SI 2013/358) |
| 10 | (1) | In force in accordance with SI 2013/983, SI 2013/1511, SI 2013/2657, SI 2013/2846, SI 2014/209, SI 2014/1583, SI 2014/2321, SI 2014/3094, SI 2015/33, SI 2015/101, SI 2015/634, SI 2015/1537, SI 2015/1930, SI 2016/33, SI 2016/407, SI 2016/963, SI 2017/664 for certain claims and awards defined therein[5] |
| | | 30 Mar 2022 (otherwise) (SI 2022/302) |
| | (2)–(5) | 25 Feb 2013 (SI 2013/358) |
| 11 | (1), (2) | In force in accordance with SI 2013/983, SI 2013/1511, SI 2013/2657, SI 2013/2846, SI 2014/209, SI 2014/1583, SI 2014/2321, SI 2014/3094, SI 2015/33, SI 2015/101, SI 2015/634, SI 2015/1537, SI 2015/1930, SI 2016/33, SI 2016/407, SI 2016/963, SI 2017/664 for certain claims and awards defined therein[5] |
| | | 30 Mar 2022 (otherwise) (SI 2022/302) |
| | (3)–(5) | 25 Feb 2013 (SI 2013/358) |
| 12 | (1) | 25 Feb 2013 (for the purpose of making regulations) (SI 2013/358) |
| | | In force in accordance with SI 2013/983, SI 2013/1511, SI 2013/2657, SI 2013/2846, SI 2014/209, SI 2014/1583, SI 2014/2321, SI 2014/3094, SI 2015/33, SI 2015/101, SI 2015/634, SI 2015/1537, SI 2015/1930, SI 2016/33, SI 2016/407, SI 2016/963, SI 2017/664 for certain claims and awards defined therein[5] |
| | | 30 Mar 2022 (otherwise) (SI 2022/302) |
| | (2) | In force in accordance with SI 2013/983, SI 2013/1511, SI 2013/2657, SI 2013/2846, SI 2014/209, SI 2014/1583, SI 2014/2321, SI 2014/3094, SI 2015/33, SI 2015/101, SI 2015/634, SI 2015/1537, SI 2015/1930, SI 2016/33, SI 2016/407, SI 2016/963, SI 2017/664 for certain claims and awards defined therein[5] |

**Welfare Reform Act 2012 (c 5)**—*contd*

|  |  |  |
|---|---|---|
|  |  | 30 Mar 2022 (otherwise) (SI 2022/302) |
|  | (3), (4) | 25 Feb 2013 (SI 2013/358) |
| 13 |  | In force in accordance with SI 2013/983, SI 2013/1511, SI 2013/2657, SI 2013/2846, SI 2014/209, SI 2014/1583, SI 2014/2321, SI 2014/3094, SI 2015/33, SI 2015/101, SI 2015/634, SI 2015/1537, SI 2015/1930, SI 2016/33, SI 2016/407, SI 2016/963, SI 2017/664 for certain claims and awards defined therein[5] |
|  |  | 30 Mar 2022 (otherwise) (SI 2022/302) |
| 14 | (1)–(4) | In force in accordance with SI 2013/983, SI 2013/1511, SI 2013/2657, SI 2013/2846, SI 2014/209, SI 2014/1583, SI 2014/2321, SI 2014/3094, SI 2015/33, SI 2015/101, SI 2015/634, SI 2015/1537, SI 2015/1930, SI 2016/33, SI 2016/407, SI 2016/963, SI 2017/664 for certain claims and awards defined therein[5] |
|  |  | 30 Mar 2022 (otherwise) (SI 2022/302) |
|  | (5) | 25 Feb 2013 (for the purpose of making regulations) (SI 2013/358) |
|  |  | In force in accordance with SI 2013/983, SI 2013/1511, SI 2013/2657, SI 2013/2846, SI 2014/209, SI 2014/1583, SI 2014/2321, SI 2014/3094, SI 2015/33, SI 2015/101, SI 2015/634, SI 2015/1537, SI 2015/1930, SI 2016/33, SI 2016/407, SI 2016/963, SI 2017/664 for certain claims and awards defined therein[5] |
|  |  | 30 Mar 2022 (otherwise) (SI 2022/302) |
| 15 | (1) | In force in accordance with SI 2013/983, SI 2013/1511, SI 2013/2657, SI 2013/2846, SI 2014/209, SI 2014/1583, SI 2014/2321, SI 2014/3094, SI 2015/33, SI 2015/101, SI 2015/634, SI 2015/1537, SI 2015/1930, SI 2016/33, SI 2016/407, SI 2016/963, SI 2017/664 for certain claims and awards defined therein[5] |
|  |  | 30 Mar 2022 (otherwise) (SI 2022/302) |
|  | (2), (3) | 25 Feb 2013 (SI 2013/358) |
|  | (4) | In force in accordance with SI 2013/983, SI 2013/1511, SI 2013/2657, SI 2013/2846, SI 2014/209, SI 2014/1583, SI 2014/2321, SI 2014/3094, SI 2015/33, SI 2015/101, SI 2015/634, SI 2015/1537, SI 2015/1930, SI 2016/33, SI 2016/407, SI 2016/963, SI 2017/664 for certain claims and awards defined therein[5] |
|  |  | 30 Mar 2022 (otherwise) (SI 2022/302) |
| 16 |  | In force in accordance with SI 2013/983, SI 2013/1511, SI 2013/2657, SI 2013/2846, SI 2014/209, SI 2014/1583, SI 2014/2321, SI 2014/3094, SI 2015/33, SI 2015/101, SI 2015/634, SI 2015/1537, SI 2015/1930, SI 2016/33, SI 2016/407, SI 2016/963, SI 2017/664 for certain claims and awards defined therein[5] |
|  |  | 30 Mar 2022 (otherwise) (SI 2022/302) |
| 17 | (1), (2), (3)(a)–(e) | In force in accordance with SI 2013/983, SI 2013/1511, SI 2013/2657, SI 2013/2846, SI 2014/209, SI 2014/1583, SI 2014/2321, SI 2014/3094, SI 2015/33, SI 2015/101, SI 2015/634, SI 2015/1537, SI 2015/1930, SI 2016/33, SI 2016/407, SI 2016/963, SI 2017/664 for certain claims and awards defined therein[5] |
|  |  | 30 Mar 2022 (otherwise) (SI 2022/302) |
|  | (3)(f) | 25 Feb 2013 (SI 2013/358) |
|  | (4), (5) | 25 Feb 2013 (for the purpose of making regulations) (SI 2013/358) |
|  |  | In force in accordance with SI 2013/983, SI 2013/1511, SI 2013/2657, SI 2013/2846, SI 2014/209, SI 2014/1583, SI 2014/2321, SI 2014/3094, SI 2015/33, SI 2015/101, SI 2015/634, SI 2015/1537, SI 2015/1930, SI 2016/33, SI 2016/407, SI 2016/963, SI 2017/664 for certain claims and awards defined therein[5] |

**Welfare Reform Act 2012 (c 5)**—*contd*

|  |  |  |
|---|---|---|
|  |  | 30 Mar 2022 (otherwise) (SI 2022/302) |
| 18 | (1), (2) | In force in accordance with SI 2013/983, SI 2013/1511, SI 2013/2657, SI 2013/2846, SI 2014/209, SI 2014/1583, SI 2014/2321, SI 2014/3094, SI 2015/33, SI 2015/101, SI 2015/634, SI 2015/1537, SI 2015/1930, SI 2016/33, SI 2016/407, SI 2016/963, SI 2017/664 for certain claims and awards defined therein[5] |
|  |  | 30 Mar 2022 (otherwise) (SI 2022/302) |
|  | (3) | 25 Feb 2013 (for the purpose of making regulations) (SI 2013/358) |
|  |  | In force in accordance with SI 2013/983, SI 2013/1511, SI 2013/2657, SI 2013/2846, SI 2014/209, SI 2014/1583, SI 2014/2321, SI 2014/3094, SI 2015/33, SI 2015/101, SI 2015/634, SI 2015/1537, SI 2015/1930, SI 2016/33, SI 2016/407, SI 2016/963, SI 2017/664 for certain claims and awards defined therein[5] |
|  |  | 30 Mar 2022 (otherwise) (SI 2022/302) |
|  | (4) | In force in accordance with SI 2013/983, SI 2013/1511, SI 2013/2657, SI 2013/2846, SI 2014/209, SI 2014/1583, SI 2014/2321, SI 2014/3094, SI 2015/33, SI 2015/101, SI 2015/634, SI 2015/1537, SI 2015/1930, SI 2016/33, SI 2016/407, SI 2016/963, SI 2017/664 for certain claims and awards defined therein[5] |
|  |  | 30 Mar 2022 (otherwise) (SI 2022/302) |
|  | (5) | 25 Feb 2013 (for the purpose of making regulations) (SI 2013/358) |
|  |  | In force in accordance with SI 2013/983, SI 2013/1511, SI 2013/2657, SI 2013/2846, SI 2014/209, SI 2014/1583, SI 2014/2321, SI 2014/3094, SI 2015/33, SI 2015/101, SI 2015/634, SI 2015/1537, SI 2015/1930, SI 2016/33, SI 2016/407, SI 2016/963, SI 2017/664 for certain claims and awards defined therein[5] |
|  |  | 30 Mar 2022 (otherwise) (SI 2022/302) |
| 19 | (1), (2)(a)–(c) | In force in accordance with SI 2013/983, SI 2013/1511, SI 2013/2657, SI 2013/2846, SI 2014/209, SI 2014/1583, SI 2014/2321, SI 2014/3094, SI 2015/33, SI 2015/101, SI 2015/634, SI 2015/1537, SI 2015/1930, SI 2016/33, SI 2016/407, SI 2016/963, SI 2017/664 for certain claims and awards defined therein[5] |
|  |  | 30 Mar 2022 (otherwise) (SI 2022/302) |
|  | (2)(d), (3), (4) | 25 Feb 2013 (SI 2013/358) |
|  | (5), (6) | In force in accordance with SI 2013/983, SI 2013/1511, SI 2013/2657, SI 2013/2846, SI 2014/209, SI 2014/1583, SI 2014/2321, SI 2014/3094, SI 2015/33, SI 2015/101, SI 2015/634, SI 2015/1537, SI 2015/1930, SI 2016/33, SI 2016/407, SI 2016/963, SI 2017/664 for certain claims and awards defined therein[5] |
|  |  | 30 Mar 2022 (otherwise) (SI 2022/302) |
| 20 | (1) | 25 Feb 2013 (for the purpose of making regulations) (SI 2013/358) |
|  |  | In force in accordance with SI 2013/983, SI 2013/1511, SI 2013/2657, SI 2013/2846, SI 2014/209, SI 2014/1583, SI 2014/2321, SI 2014/3094, SI 2015/33, SI 2015/101, SI 2015/634, SI 2015/1537, SI 2015/1930, SI 2016/33, SI 2016/407, SI 2016/963, SI 2017/664 for certain claims and awards defined therein[5] |
|  |  | 30 Mar 2022 (otherwise) (SI 2022/302) |
|  | (2), (3) | In force in accordance with SI 2013/983, SI 2013/1511, SI 2013/2657, SI 2013/2846, SI 2014/209, SI 2014/1583, SI 2014/2321, SI 2014/3094, SI 2015/33, SI 2015/101, SI 2015/634, SI 2015/1537, SI 2015/1930, SI 2016/33, SI 2016/407, SI 2016/963, SI 2017/664 for certain claims and awards defined therein[5] |
|  |  | 30 Mar 2022 (otherwise) (SI 2022/302) |

**Welfare Reform Act 2012 (c 5)**—*contd*

| | | |
|---|---|---|
| 21 | | In force in accordance with SI 2013/983, SI 2013/1511, SI 2013/2657, SI 2013/2846, SI 2014/209, SI 2014/1583, SI 2014/2321, SI 2014/3094, SI 2015/33, SI 2015/101, SI 2015/634, SI 2015/1537, SI 2015/1930, SI 2016/33, SI 2016/407, SI 2016/963, SI 2017/664 for certain claims and awards defined therein[5] |
| | | 30 Mar 2022 (otherwise) (SI 2022/302) |
| 22 | (1) | In force in accordance with SI 2013/983, SI 2013/1511, SI 2013/2657, SI 2013/2846, SI 2014/209, SI 2014/1583, SI 2014/2321, SI 2014/3094, SI 2015/33, SI 2015/101, SI 2015/634, SI 2015/1537, SI 2015/1930, SI 2016/33, SI 2016/407, SI 2016/963, SI 2017/664 for certain claims and awards defined therein[5] |
| | | 30 Mar 2022 (otherwise) (SI 2022/302) |
| | (2) | 25 Feb 2013 (for the purpose of making regulations) (SI 2013/358) |
| | | In force in accordance with SI 2013/983, SI 2013/1511, SI 2013/2657, SI 2013/2846, SI 2014/209, SI 2014/1583, SI 2014/2321, SI 2014/3094, SI 2015/33, SI 2015/101, SI 2015/634, SI 2015/1537, SI 2015/1930, SI 2016/33, SI 2016/407, SI 2016/963, SI 2017/664 for certain claims and awards defined therein[5] |
| | | 30 Mar 2022 (otherwise) (SI 2022/302) |
| | (3) | In force in accordance with SI 2013/983, SI 2013/1511, SI 2013/2657, SI 2013/2846, SI 2014/209, SI 2014/1583, SI 2321, SI 2014/3094, SI 2015/33, SI 2015/101, SI 2015/634, SI 2015/1537, SI 2015/1930, SI 2016/33, SI 2016/407, SI 2016/963, SI 2017/664 for certain claims and awards defined therein[5] |
| | | 30 Mar 2022 (otherwise) (SI 2022/302) |
| 23 | | In force in accordance with SI 2013/983, SI 2013/1511, SI 2013/2657, SI 2013/2846, SI 2014/209, SI 2014/1583, SI 2014/2321, SI 2014/3094, SI 2015/33, SI 2015/101, SI 2015/634, SI 2015/1537, SI 2015/1930, SI 2016/33, SI 2016/407, SI 2016/963, SI 2017/664 for certain claims and awards defined therein[5] |
| | | 30 Mar 2022 (otherwise) (SI 2022/302) |
| 24 | (1) | 25 Feb 2013 (SI 2013/358) |
| | (2)–(4) | In force in accordance with SI 2013/983, SI 2013/1511, SI 2013/2657, SI 2013/2846, SI 2014/209, SI 2014/1583, SI 2014/2321, SI 2014/3094, SI 2015/33, SI 2015/101, SI 2015/634, SI 2015/1537, SI 2015/1930, SI 2016/33, SI 2016/407, SI 2016/963, SI 2017/664 for certain claims and awards defined therein[5] |
| | | 30 Mar 2022 (otherwise) (SI 2022/302) |
| | (5), (6) | 25 Feb 2013 (SI 2013/358) |
| 25 | | 25 Feb 2013 (SI 2013/358) |
| 26 | (1) | In force in accordance with SI 2013/983, SI 2013/1511, SI 2013/2657, SI 2013/2846, SI 2014/209, SI 2014/1583, SI 2014/2321, SI 2014/3094, SI 2015/33, SI 2015/101, SI 2015/634, SI 2015/1537, SI 2015/1930, SI 2016/33, SI 2016/407, SI 2016/963, SI 2017/664 for certain claims and awards defined therein[5] |
| | | 30 Mar 2022 (otherwise) (SI 2022/302) |
| | (2)(a) | 25 Feb 2013 (for the purpose of making regulations) (SI 2013/358) |
| | | In force in accordance with SI 2013/983, SI 2013/1511, SI 2013/2657, SI 2013/2846, SI 2014/209, SI 2014/1583, SI 2014/2321, SI 2014/3094, SI 2015/33, SI 2015/101, SI 2015/634, SI 2015/1537, SI 2015/1930, SI 2016/33, SI 2016/407, SI 2016/963, SI 2017/664 for certain claims and awards defined therein[5] |
| | | 30 Mar 2022 (otherwise) (SI 2022/302) |

**Welfare Reform Act 2012 (c 5)**—*contd*

| | | |
|---|---|---|
| | (2)(b)–(d), (3)–(5) | In force in accordance with SI 2013/983, SI 2013/1511, SI 2013/2657, SI 2013/2846, SI 2014/209, SI 2014/1583, SI 2014/2321, SI 2014/3094, SI 2015/33, SI 2015/101, SI 2015/634, SI 2015/1537, SI 2015/1930, SI 2016/33, SI 2016/407, SI 2016/963, SI 2017/664 for certain claims and awards defined therein[5] |
| | | 30 Mar 2022 (otherwise) (SI 2022/302) |
| | (6)–(8) | 25 Feb 2013 (SI 2013/358) |
| 27 | (1)–(3) | In force in accordance with SI 2013/983, SI 2013/1511, SI 2013/2657, SI 2013/2846, SI 2014/209, SI 2014/1583, SI 2014/2321, SI 2014/3094, SI 2015/33, SI 2015/101, SI 2015/634, SI 2015/1537, SI 2015/1930, SI 2016/33, SI 2016/407, SI 2016/963, SI 2017/664 for certain claims and awards defined therein[5] |
| | | 30 Mar 2022 (otherwise) (SI 2022/302) |
| | (4), (5) | 25 Feb 2013 (SI 2013/358) |
| | (6)–(8) | In force in accordance with SI 2013/983, SI 2013/1511, SI 2013/2657, SI 2013/2846, SI 2014/209, SI 2014/1583, SI 2014/2321, SI 2014/3094, SI 2015/33, SI 2015/101, SI 2015/634, SI 2015/1537, SI 2015/1930, SI 2016/33, SI 2016/407, SI 2016/963, SI 2017/664 for certain claims and awards defined therein[5] |
| | | 30 Mar 2022 (otherwise) (SI 2022/302) |
| | (9) | 25 Feb 2013 (SI 2013/358) |
| 28 | | 25 Feb 2013 (SI 2013/358) |
| 29 | | 29 Apr 2013 (SI 2013/983) |
| 30 | | See Sch 1 below |
| 31 | | See Sch 2 below |
| 32 | | 25 Feb 2013 (SI 2013/358) |
| 33 | (1)(a), (b) | In force in accordance with SI 2013/983, SI 2013/1511, SI 2013/2657, SI 2013/2846, SI 2014/209, SI 2014/1583, SI 2014/2321, SI 2014/3094, SI 2015/33, SI 2015/101, SI 2015/634, SI 2015/1537, SI 2015/1930, SI 2016/33, SI 2016/407, SI 2016/963, SI 2017/664 for certain claims and awards defined therein[5] |
| | | *Not yet in force* (otherwise) |
| | (1)(c), (d) | *Not yet in force* |
| | (1)(e) | 1 Apr 2013 (SI 2013/358) |
| | (1)(f) | 1 Feb 2019 (SI 2019/167)[9] |
| | (2) | In force in accordance with SI 2013/983, SI 2013/1511, SI 2013/2657, SI 2013/2846, SI 2014/209, SI 2014/1583, SI 2014/2321, SI 2015/32, SI 2015/33, SI 2015/101, SI 2015/634, SI 2015/1537, SI 2015/1930, SI 2016/33, SI 2016/407, SI 2016/963, SI 2017/664 for certain claims and awards defined therein[5] |
| | | *Not yet in force* (otherwise) |
| | (3) | See Sch 3 below |
| 34 | | See Sch 4 below |
| 35 | | See Sch 5 below |
| 36 | | See Sch 6 below |
| 37 | (1), (2) | 29 Apr 2013 (SI 2013/983) |
| | (3)–(7) | 25 Feb 2013 (SI 2013/358) |
| | (8), (9) | 29 Apr 2013 (SI 2013/983) |
| 38 | | 29 Apr 2013 (SI 2013/983) |
| 39 | (1), (2) | 29 Apr 2013 (SI 2013/983) |
| | (3)(a) | 25 Feb 2013 (SI 2013/358) |
| | (3)(b), (c) | 29 Apr 2013 (SI 2013/983) |
| 40 | | 25 Feb 2013 (SI 2013/358) |
| 41 | | 15 Sep 2014 (SI 2014/2321) |
| 42, 43 | | 25 Feb 2013 (SI 2013/358) |

**Welfare Reform Act 2012 (c 5)**—*contd*

| | | |
|---|---|---|
| 44 | (1) | See sub-ss (2)–(5) below |
| | (2) | In relation to a particular case, the day on which the amending provisions (as listed in SI 2013/983, art 4(1)) come into force, under any secondary legislation, in relation to that case (SI 2013/983) |
| | | *Not yet in force* (otherwise) |
| | (3), (4) | *Not yet in force* (repealed in part) |
| | (5) | 10 Jun 2012 (SI 2012/1246) |
| 45 | | 8 Oct 2012 (SI 2012/2530) |
| 46 | (1) | 10 Jun 2012 (for the purpose of exercising any power to make regulations under the Jobseekers Act 1995, ss 19–19B) (SI 2012/1246) |
| | | 22 Oct 2012 (in so far as substitutes Jobseekers Act 1995, ss 19–19B, for remaining purposes) (SI 2012/2530) |
| | | *Not yet in force* (in so far as substitutes s 19C thereof, for remaining purposes) (repealed in part) |
| | (2) | 10 Jun 2012 (SI 2012/1246) |
| | (3) | 10 Jun 2012 (for the purpose of exercising any power to make regulations) (SI 2012/1246) |
| | | 22 Oct 2012 (otherwise) (SI 2012/2530) |
| | (4) | 22 Oct 2012 (SI 2012/2530) |
| 47 | | 20 Mar 2012 (SI 2012/863) |
| 48 | | See Sch 7 below |
| 49 | (1) | See sub-ss (2)–(6) below |
| | (2) | In relation to a particular case, the day on which the amending provisions (as listed in SI 2013/983, art 4(1)) come into force, under any secondary legislation, in relation to that case (SI 2013/983) |
| | | *Not yet in force* (otherwise) |
| | (3) | 25 Feb 2013 (for the purpose of making regulations) (SI 2013/358) |
| | | In relation to a particular case, the day on which the amending provisions (as listed in SI 2013/983, art 4(1)) come into force, under any secondary legislation, in relation to that case (SI 2013/983) |
| | | *Not yet in force* (otherwise) |
| | (4), (5) | In relation to a particular case, the day on which the amending provisions (as listed in SI 2013/983, art 4(1)) come into force, under any secondary legislation, in relation to that case (SI 2013/983) |
| | | *Not yet in force* (otherwise) |
| | (6) | 25 Feb 2013 (SI 2013/358) |
| 50 | | 8 May 2012 (s 150(2)(a)) |
| 51 | (1)–(3) | 1 May 2012 (SI 2012/863) |
| | (4) | 20 Mar 2012 (for the purpose of exercising the power to make regulations) (SI 2012/863) |
| | | 1 May 2012 (otherwise) (SI 2012/863) |
| 52, 53 | | 1 May 2012 (SI 2012/863) |
| 54 | (1) | See sub-ss (2)–(6) below |
| | (2) | In relation to a particular case, the day on which the amending provisions (as listed in SI 2013/983, art 4(1)) come into force, under any secondary legislation, in relation to that case (SI 2013/983) |
| | | *Not yet in force* (otherwise) |
| | (3)–(5) | *Not yet in force* (repealed in part) |
| | (6) | 25 Feb 2013 (SI 2013/358) |
| | (7) | *Not yet in force* |
| 55 | | 3 Dec 2012 (SI 2012/2530) |
| 56 | | 26 Nov 2012 (SI 2012/2530) |
| 57 | (1) | See sub-ss (2)–(9) below |
| | (2) | 25 Feb 2013 (for the purpose of making regulations) (SI 2013/358) |

**Welfare Reform Act 2012 (c 5)**—*contd*

|  |  |  |
|---|---|---|
|  |  | In relation to a particular case, the day on which the amending provisions (as listed in SI 2013/983, art 4(1)) come into force, under any secondary legislation, in relation to that case (SI 2013/983) |
|  |  | *Not yet in force* (otherwise) |
|  | (3) | *Not yet in force* |
|  | (4), (5) | In relation to a particular case, the day on which the amending provisions (as listed in SI 2013/983, art 4(1)) come into force, under any secondary legislation, in relation to that case (SI 2013/983) |
|  |  | *Not yet in force* (otherwise) |
|  | (6) | 25 Feb 2013 (SI 2013/358) |
|  | (7), (8) | *Not yet in force* |
|  | (9) | In relation to a particular case, the day on which the amending provisions (as listed in SI 2013/983, art 4(1)) come into force, under any secondary legislation, in relation to that case (SI 2013/983) |
|  |  | *Not yet in force* (otherwise) |
| 58 | (1), (2) | 20 Mar 2012 (SI 2012/863) |
|  | (3) | *Not yet in force* (repealed in part) |
| 59 |  | *Not yet in force* (repealed in part) |
| 60 |  | 8 May 2012 (s 150(2)(b)) |
| 61–63 |  | *Not yet in force* (s 63(6), (7) repealed) |
| 64 |  | 30 Oct 2012 (for the purpose of exercising any power to make regulations) (SI 2012/2530) |
|  |  | 5 Dec 2012 (otherwise) (SI 2012/2530) |
| 65 |  | 5 Dec 2012 (SI 2012/2530) |
| 66 |  | 30 Oct 2012 (for the purpose of exercising any power to make regulations) (SI 2012/2530) |
|  |  | 31 Oct 2013 (otherwise) (SI 2013/2534) |
| 67, 68 |  | 5 Dec 2012 (SI 2012/2530) |
| 69 |  | 27 Nov 2012 (for the purpose of exercising any power to make regulations) (SI 2012/2946) |
|  |  | 1 Jan 2013 (otherwise) (SI 2012/2946) |
| 70 | (1) | 1 Apr 2013 (SI 2012/3090)[2] |
|  | (2) | 1 Aug 2013 (SI 2012/3090) |
|  | (3)–(9) | 1 Apr 2013 (SI 2012/3090) |
|  | (10) | See Sch 8 below |
| 71, 72 |  | 8 May 2012 (s 150(2)(c)) |
| 73 |  | 1 Apr 2013 (SI 2012/3090) |
| 74, 75 |  | *Not yet in force* |
| 76 |  | 8 Mar 2012 (s 150(1)(a)) |
| 77 | (1), (2) | 8 Apr 2013 (in relation to a person whose only or principal residence is, on the date on which that person makes a claim for personal independence payment, located in one of the specified postcode areas)[4] (SI 2013/358) |
|  |  | 10 Jun 2013 (in relation to a person other than a person referred to above) (SI 2013/1250) |
|  | (3) | 25 Feb 2013 (for the purpose of making regulations) (SI 2013/358) |
|  |  | 8 Apr 2013 (in relation to a person whose only or principal residence is, on the date on which that person makes a claim for personal independence payment, located in one of the specified postcode areas)[4] (SI 2013/358) |
|  |  | 10 Jun 2013 (in relation to a person other than a person referred to above) (SI 2013/1250) |
| 78 | (1), (2) | 8 Apr 2013 (in relation to a person whose only or principal residence is, on the date on which that person makes a claim for personal independence payment, located in one of the specified postcode areas)[4] (SI 2013/358) |

**Welfare Reform Act 2012 (c 5)**—*contd*

|  |  |  |
|---|---|---|
|  |  | 10 Jun 2013 (in relation to a person other than a person referred to above) (SI 2013/1250) |
|  | (3), (4) | 25 Feb 2013 (SI 2013/358) |
|  | (5), (6) | 8 Apr 2013 (in relation to a person whose only or principal residence is, on the date on which that person makes a claim for personal independence payment, located in one of the specified postcode areas)[4] (SI 2013/358) |
|  |  | 10 Jun 2013 (in relation to a person other than a person referred to above) (SI 2013/1250) |
| 79 | (1), (2) | 8 Apr 2013 (in relation to a person whose only or principal residence is, on the date on which that person makes a claim for personal independence payment, located in one of the specified postcode areas)[4] (SI 2013/358) |
|  |  | 10 Jun 2013 (in relation to a person other than a person referred to above) (SI 2013/1250) |
|  | (3), (4) | 25 Feb 2013 (SI 2013/358) |
|  | (5), (6) | 8 Apr 2013 (in relation to a person whose only or principal residence is, on the date on which that person makes a claim for personal independence payment, located in one of the specified postcode areas)[4] (SI 2013/358) |
|  |  | 10 Jun 2013 (in relation to a person other than a person referred to above) (SI 2013/1250) |
|  | (7) | 25 Feb 2013 (SI 2013/358) |
| 80, 81 |  | 25 Feb 2013 (SI 2013/358) |
| 82 |  | 8 Apr 2013 (in relation to a person whose only or principal residence is, on the date on which that person makes a claim for personal independence payment, located in one of the specified postcode areas)[4] (SI 2013/358) |
|  |  | 10 Jun 2013 (in relation to a person other than a person referred to above) (SI 2013/1250) |
| 83 | (1), (2) | 8 Apr 2013 (in relation to a person whose only or principal residence is, on the date on which that person makes a claim for personal independence payment, located in one of the specified postcode areas)[4] (SI 2013/358) |
|  |  | 10 Jun 2013 (in relation to a person other than a person referred to above) (SI 2013/1250) |
|  | (3) | 25 Feb 2013 (for the purpose of making regulations) (SI 2013/358) |
|  |  | 8 Apr 2013 (in relation to a person whose only or principal residence is, on the date on which that person makes a claim for personal independence payment, located in one of the specified postcode areas)[4] (SI 2013/358) |
|  |  | 10 Jun 2013 (in relation to a person other than a person referred to above) (SI 2013/1250) |
| 84 |  | 8 Apr 2013 (in relation to a person whose only or principal residence is, on the date on which that person makes a claim for personal independence payment, located in one of the specified postcode areas)[4] (SI 2013/358) |
|  |  | 10 Jun 2013 (in relation to a person other than a person referred to above) (SI 2013/1250) |
| 85, 86 |  | 25 Feb 2013 (SI 2013/358) |
| 87 |  | 25 Feb 2013 (for the purpose of making regulations) (SI 2013/358) |
|  |  | 8 Apr 2013 (in relation to a person whose only or principal residence is, on the date on which that person makes a claim for personal independence payment, located in one of the specified postcode areas)[4] (SI 2013/358) |
|  |  | 10 Jun 2013 (in relation to a person other than a person referred to above) (SI 2013/1250) |
| 88, 89 |  | 8 Apr 2013 (in relation to a person whose only or principal residence is, on the date on which that person makes a claim for personal independence payment, located in one of the specified postcode areas)[4] (SI 2013/358) |

**Welfare Reform Act 2012 (c 5)**—*contd*

|  |  |  |
|---|---|---|
|  |  | 10 Jun 2013 (in relation to a person other than a person referred to above) (SI 2013/1250) |
| 90 |  | *Not yet in force* |
| 91 |  | See Sch 9 below |
| 92 |  | 25 Feb 2013 (SI 2013/358) |
| 93 | (1) | 25 Feb 2013 (SI 2013/358) |
|  | (2) | See Sch 10 below |
| 94 |  | 25 Feb 2013 (SI 2013/358) |
| 95 |  | 25 Feb 2013 (for the purpose of making regulations) (SI 2013/358) |
|  |  | 8 Apr 2013 (in relation to a person whose only or principal residence is, on the date on which that person makes a claim for personal independence payment, located in one of the specified postcode areas)[4] (SI 2013/358) |
|  |  | 10 Jun 2013 (in relation to a person other than a person referred to above) (SI 2013/1250) |
| 96 |  | 27 Nov 2012 (for the purpose of exercising any power to make regulations) (SI 2012/2946) |
|  |  | 15 Apr 2013 (otherwise) (SI 2012/2946) |
| 97 | (1)–(4) | 27 Nov 2012 (SI 2012/2946) |
|  | (5), (6) | 15 Apr 2013 (SI 2012/2946) |
| 98–100 |  | 25 Feb 2013 (SI 2013/358) |
| 101 | (1) | 25 Feb 2013 (for the purpose of making regulations) (SI 2013/358) |
|  |  | *Not yet in force* (otherwise) |
|  | (2) | 1 Apr 2013 (SI 2013/358) |
| 102 | (1) | See sub-ss (2)–(5) below |
|  | (2)–(5) | 25 Feb 2013 (SI 2013/358) |
|  | (6) | See Sch 11 below |
|  | (7)–(9) | *Not yet in force* |
| 103 | (1) | See Sch 12 below |
|  | (2) | 8 Mar 2012 (s 150(1)(b)) |
| 104 |  | 25 Feb 2013 (SI 2013/358) |
| 105 | (1) | 1 Jul 2012 (in so far as inserts Social Security Administration Act 1992, s 71ZC(1), for the purpose of prescribing the benefits from which deductions may be made in order to recover the penalties, and s 71ZD) (SI 2012/1246) |
|  |  | 1 Oct 2012 (in so far as inserts ss 71ZC(1) and 71ZE of that Act, for the purpose of enabling recovery of the penalties to take place by those methods) (SI 2012/1246) |
|  |  | 29 Apr 2013 (otherwise, except in so far as inserts s 71ZB(1)(d) of that Act) (SI 2013/358)[3] |
|  |  | *Not yet in force* (exception noted above) |
|  | (2) | *Not yet in force* |
|  | (3) | 29 Apr 2013 (SI 2013/358) |
|  | (4) | 1 Oct 2012 (SI 2012/1246) |
|  | (5), (6) | 29 Apr 2013 (SI 2013/358) |
|  | (7) | 29 Apr 2013 (in so far as inserts Social Security Act 1998, Sch 3, para 6B) (SI 2013/358) |
|  |  | *Not yet in force* (otherwise) |
| 106 |  | 1 Jul 2012 (SI 2012/1246) |
| 107 |  | 8 May 2012 (s 150(2)(d)) |
| 108 |  | 8 Mar 2012 (s 150(1)(c)) |
| 109 |  | 8 Mar 2012 (s 150(1)(d)) |
| 110 |  | 17 Jun 2013 (for the purpose of making regulations) (SI 2013/1250) |
|  |  | 1 Oct 2013 (otherwise) (SI 2013/1250) |
| 111 |  | 8 May 2012 (s 150(2)(e)) |
| 112 | (1) | See sub-ss (2)–(6) below |
|  | (2) | 20 Apr 2016 (for the purpose of making regulations under Social Security Administration Act 1992, s 116ZA(8)) (SI 2016/511) |
|  |  | 24 May 2016 (otherwise) (SI 2016/511) |

**Welfare Reform Act 2012 (c 5)**—*contd*

| | | |
|---|---|---|
| | (3)–(6) | 24 May 2016 (SI 2016/511) |
| 113–115 | | 8 May 2012 (SI 2012/863) |
| 116 | (1) | 10 May 2012 (for the purpose of prescribing amounts under the Social Security Administration Act 1992, s 115C(2) or 115D(1), (2)) (SI 2012/1246) |
| | | 1 Oct 2012 (otherwise) (SI 2012/1246) |
| | (2) | 10 May 2012 (SI 2012/1246) |
| 117 | (1) | See sub-ss (2), (3) below |
| | (2) | 1 Apr 2013 (SI 2013/358) |
| | (3) | 6 Apr 2013 (SI 2013/358) |
| 118 | (1) | See sub-ss (2)–(8) below |
| | (2) | See sub-ss (3)–(6) below |
| | (3), (4) | 1 Apr 2013 (SI 2013/358) |
| | (5) | 25 Feb 2013 (for the purpose of making regulations) (SI 2013/358) |
| | | 1 Apr 2013 (otherwise) (SI 2013/358) |
| | (6), (7), (8)(a) | 1 Apr 2013 (SI 2013/358) |
| | (8)(b) | 25 Feb 2013 (for the purpose of making regulations) (SI 2013/358) |
| | | 1 Apr 2013 (otherwise) (SI 2013/358) |
| | (8)(c) | 1 Apr 2013 (SI 2013/358) |
| 119 | | 1 Apr 2013 (SI 2013/358) |
| 120 | (1) | See sub-ss (2)–(5) below |
| | (2) | 1 Feb 2013 (for the purpose of making regulations and orders) (SI 2013/178) |
| | | 6 Apr 2013 (otherwise) (SI 2013/178) |
| | (3) | 6 Apr 2013 (SI 2013/178) |
| | (4) | 1 Feb 2013 (SI 2013/178) |
| | (5) | 6 Apr 2013 (SI 2013/178) |
| 121 | | *Not yet in force* |
| 122, 123 | | 6 Jun 2012 (SI 2012/1246) |
| 124 | | *Not yet in force* |
| 125 | | 6 Jun 2012 (SI 2012/1246) |
| 126 | | 8 Mar 2012 (s 150(1)(e)) |
| 127 | | 8 May 2012 (s 150(2)(f) |
| 128, 129 | | 20 Mar 2012 (SI 2012/863) |
| 130, 131 | | 20 Mar 2012 (for the purpose of exercising any power to make regulations) (SI 2012/863) |
| | | 8 May 2012 (otherwise) (SI 2012/863) |
| 132 | (1)–(7) | 8 May 2012 (SI 2012/863) |
| | (8) | 20 Mar 2012 (SI 2012/863) |
| | (9) | 8 May 2012 (SI 2012/863) |
| 133 | (1)–(4) | 20 Mar 2012 (SI 2012/863) |
| | (5) | *Not yet in force* |
| | (6) | 2 Jul 2012 (SI 2012/1651)[1] |
| 134 | | 8 May 2012 (s 150(2)(g)) |
| 135 | | 8 May 2012 (s 150(2)(h)) |
| 136 | | 25 Nov 2013 (SI 2013/2947) |
| 137 | | 30 Jun 2014 (SI 2014/1635)[6] |
| 138 | | *Not yet in force* |
| 139 | | 4 Feb 2014 (SI 2014/209) |
| 140, 141 | | 25 Nov 2013 (SI 2013/2947) |
| 142 | | 8 May 2012 (s 150(2)(i)) |
| 143, 144 | | 8 May 2012 (SI 2012/863) |
| 145 | | See Sch 13 below |
| 146 | | 8 May 2012 (SI 2012/863) |
| 147 | | See Sch 14 below |
| 148–151 | | 8 Mar 2012 (s 150(1)(f)) |
| Sch 1 | para 1 | 25 Feb 2013 (SI 2013/358) |
| | para 2 | *Not yet in force* |
| | paras 3–5 | 25 Feb 2013 (SI 2013/358) |

**Welfare Reform Act 2012 (c 5)**—*contd*

|         | para 6 | *Not yet in force* |
|---------|--------|---------------------|
|         | para 7 | 25 Feb 2013 (SI 2013/358) |
|         | para 8 | *Not yet in force* |
| Sch 2   | para 1 | 29 Apr 2013 (SI 2013/983) |
|         | para 2 | 25 Feb 2013 (for the purpose of making regulations) (SI 2013/358) |
|         |        | 29 Apr 2013 (otherwise) (SI 2013/983) |
|         | para 3 | See paras 4–31 below |
|         | para 4 | 25 Feb 2013 (for the purpose of making regulations) (SI 2013/358) |
|         |        | 29 Apr 2013 (otherwise) (SI 2013/983) |
|         | paras 5–7 | 25 Feb 2013 (SI 2013/358) |
|         | para 8 | 29 Apr 2013 (SI 2013/983) |
|         | para 9 | 29 Apr 2013 (SI 2013/358) |
|         | paras 10–22 | 29 Apr 2013 (SI 2013/983) |
|         | para 23 | 25 Feb 2013 (for the purpose of making regulations) (SI 2013/358) |
|         |        | 29 Apr 2013 (otherwise) (SI 2013/983) |
|         | para 24 | *Not yet in force* |
|         | para 25 | 29 Apr 2013 (SI 2013/983) |
|         | para 26 | 25 Feb 2013 (SI 2013/358) |
|         | paras 27–30 | 29 Apr 2013 (SI 2013/983) |
|         | para 31 | 25 Feb 2013 (for the purpose of making regulations) (SI 2013/358) |
|         |        | 29 Apr 2013 (otherwise) (SI 2013/983) |
|         | paras 32–34 | 25 Feb 2013 (for the purpose of making regulations) (SI 2013/358) |
|         |        | 29 Apr 2013 (otherwise) (SI 2013/983) |
|         | para 35 | 29 Apr 2013 (SI 2013/983) |
|         | para 36 | 25 Feb 2013 (SI 2013/358) |
|         | paras 37–42 | 29 Apr 2013 (SI 2013/983) |
|         | para 43 | See paras 44–51 below |
|         | para 44 | 29 Apr 2013 (SI 2013/983) |
|         | para 45 | 25 Feb 2013 (for the purpose of making regulations) (SI 2013/358) |
|         |        | 29 Apr 2013 (otherwise) (SI 2013/983) |
|         | para 46 | 25 Feb 2013 (SI 2013/358) |
|         | para 47 | 25 Feb 2013 (for the purpose of making regulations) (SI 2013/358) |
|         |        | 29 Apr 2013 (otherwise) (SI 2013/983) |
|         | para 48 | 25 Feb 2013 (SI 2013/358) |
|         | para 49 | 25 Feb 2013 (for the purpose of making regulations) (SI 2013/358) |
|         |        | 29 Apr 2013 (otherwise) (SI 2013/983) |
|         | para 50(1) | See sub-paras (2), (3) below |
|         | para 50(2) | 29 Apr 2013 (SI 2013/983) |
|         | para 50(3) | *Not yet in force* |
|         | para 51 | 1 Apr 2013 (SI 2013/358) |
|         | paras 52–54 | 29 Apr 2013 (SI 2013/983) |
|         | para 55 | 25 Feb 2013 (for the purpose of making regulations) (SI 2013/358) |
|         |        | 29 Apr 2013 (otherwise) (SI 2013/983) |
|         | para 56 | See paras 57–63 below |
|         | para 57 | 1 Apr 2013 (SI 2013/358) |
|         | para 58(1) | See sub-paras (2)–(4) below |
|         | para 58(2) | 1 Apr 2013 (SI 2013/358) |
|         | para 58(3) | 25 Feb 2013 (SI 2013/358) |
|         | para 58(4) | *Not yet in force* |
|         | para 59(1) | See sub-paras (2)–(4) below |
|         | para 59(2) | 1 Apr 2013 (SI 2013/358) |
|         | para 59(3) | 25 Feb 2013 (SI 2013/358) |
|         | para 59(4) | *Not yet in force* |
|         | para 60 | *Not yet in force* |
|         | para 61(1) | See sub-paras (2)–(5) below |
|         | para 61(2)–(4) | 25 Feb 2013 (SI 2013/358) |
|         | para 61(5) | *Not yet in force* |
|         | para 62 | 1 Apr 2013 (SI 2013/358) |
|         | para 63(1) | See sub-paras (2), (3) below |

**Welfare Reform Act 2012 (c 5)**—*contd*

|  |  |  |
|---|---|---|
|  | para 63(2) | 25 Feb 2013 (SI 2013/358) |
|  | para 63(3) | *Not yet in force* |
|  | para 64 | 15 May 2019 (SI 2019/37)[8] |
|  | para 65 | 29 Apr 2013 (SI 2013/983) |
| Sch 3 | paras 1–3 | *Not yet in force* |
|  | para 4 | See paras 5–8 below |
|  | para 5 | 1 Apr 2013 (in so far as relates to the abolition of council tax benefit) (SI 2013/358) |
|  |  | *Not yet in force (otherwise)* |
|  | paras 6–14 | *Not yet in force* |
|  | paras 15–18 | 1 Apr 2013 (in so far as relate to the abolition of council tax benefit) (SI 2013/358) |
|  |  | *Not yet in force (otherwise)* |
|  | paras 19–21 | *Not yet in force* |
|  | paras 22–26 | In force in accordance with SI 2013/983, SI 2013/1511, SI 2013/2657, SI 2013/2846, SI 2014/209, SI 2014/1583, SI 2014/2321, SI 2015/32, SI 2015/33, SI 2015/101, SI 2015/634, SI 2015/1537, SI 2015/1930, SI 2016/33, SI 2016/407, SI 2016/963, SI 2017/664 for certain claims and awards defined therein[5] |
|  |  | *Not yet in force (otherwise)* |
|  | paras 27–29 | *Not yet in force* |
| Sch 4 |  | *Not yet in force* |
| Sch 5 | para 1 | 29 Apr 2013 (SI 2013/983) |
|  | paras 2, 3 | 25 Feb 2013 (SI 2013/358) |
|  | paras 4–6 | *Not yet in force* |
| Sch 6 | para 1(1) | 25 Feb 2013 (SI 2013/358) |
|  | para 1(2)(a) | 18 Jul 2019 (SI 2019/1135) |
|  | para 1(2)(b) | 25 Feb 2013 (SI 2013/358) |
|  | para 1(3), (2) | 18 Jul 2019 (SI 2019/1135) |
|  | para 3(1)(a)–(c) | 25 Feb 2013 (SI 2013/358) |
|  | para 3(1)(d), (e), (2) | 18 Jul 2019 (SI 2019/1135) |
|  | para 4(1)(a) | 25 Feb 2013 (SI 2013/358) |
|  | para 4(1)(b), (2), (3) | 18 Jul 2019 (SI 2019/1135) |
|  | para 5(1) | 25 Feb 2013 (SI 2013/358) |
|  | para 5(2)(a), (b) | 18 Jul 2019 (SI 2019/1135) |
|  | para 5(2)(c), (d), (3)(a) | 25 Feb 2013 (SI 2013/358) |
|  | para 5(3)(b), (c), (4) | 18 Jul 2019 (SI 2019/1135) |
|  | para 6 | 25 Feb 2013 (SI 2013/358) |
|  | para 7 | 18 Jul 2019 (SI 2019/1135) |
| Sch 7 | para 1 | See paras 2–10 below |
|  | paras 2, 3 | 22 Oct 2012 (SI 2012/2530) |
|  | para 4 | *Not yet in force (repealed in part)* |
|  | paras 5–9 | 22 Oct 2012 (SI 2012/2530) |
|  | para 10(1) | See sub-paras (2), (3) below |
|  | para 10(2) | *Not yet in force (repealed in part)* |
|  | para 10(3) | 22 Oct 2012 (SI 2012/2530) |
|  | para 11 | *Not yet in force (repealed in part)* |
|  | para 12 | 22 Oct 2012 (SI 2012/2530) |
|  | paras 13–15 | *Not yet in force (para 14 repealed in part)* |
|  | para 16(1) | See sub-paras (2), (3) below |
|  | para 16(2)(a), (b) | *Not yet in force (repealed in part)* |
|  | para 16(2)(c) | 22 Oct 2012 (SI 2012/2530) |
|  | para 16(3) | *Not yet in force (repealed in part)* |
| Sch 8 | para 1 | See paras 2–4 below |
|  | paras 2, 3 | 1 Apr 2013 (SI 2012/3090) |

**Welfare Reform Act 2012 (c 5)**—*contd*

| | | |
|---|---|---|
| | para 4 | 1 Aug 2013 (SI 2012/3090) |
| Sch 9 | paras 1–3 | 8 Apr 2013 (in relation to a person whose only or principal residence is, on the date on which that person makes a claim for personal independence payment, located in one of the specified postcode areas)[4] (SI 2013/358) |
| | | 10 Jun 2013 (in relation to a person other than a person referred to above) (SI 2013/1250) |
| | para 4 | *Not yet in force* |
| | paras 5, 6 | 8 Apr 2013 (in relation to a person whose only or principal residence is, on the date on which that person makes a claim for personal independence payment, located in one of the specified postcode areas)[4] (SI 2013/358) |
| | | 10 Jun 2013 (in relation to a person other than a person referred to above) (SI 2013/1250) |
| | para 7 | See paras 8–33 below |
| | para 8 | 8 Apr 2013 (in relation to a person whose only or principal residence is, on the date on which that person makes a claim for personal independence payment, located in one of the specified postcode areas)[4] (SI 2013/358) |
| | | 10 Jun 2013 (in relation to a person other than a person referred to above) (SI 2013/1250) |
| | para 9 | 25 Feb 2013 (SI 2013/358) |
| | paras 10–25 | 8 Apr 2013 (in relation to a person whose only or principal residence is, on the date on which that person makes a claim for personal independence payment, located in one of the specified postcode areas)[4] (SI 2013/358) |
| | | 10 Jun 2013 (in relation to a person other than a person referred to above) (SI 2013/1250) |
| | para 26 | 25 Feb 2013 (SI 2013/358) |
| | paras 27–31 | 8 Apr 2013 (in relation to a person whose only or principal residence is, on the date on which that person makes a claim for personal independence payment, located in one of the specified postcode areas)[4] (SI 2013/358) |
| | | 10 Jun 2013 (in relation to a person other than a person referred to above) (SI 2013/1250) |
| | para 32 | 25 Feb 2013 (for the purpose of making regulations) (SI 2013/358) |
| | | 8 Apr 2013 (in relation to a person whose only or principal residence is, on the date on which that person makes a claim for personal independence payment, located in one of the specified postcode areas)[4] (SI 2013/358) |
| | | 10 Jun 2013 (in relation to a person other than a person referred to above) (SI 2013/1250) |
| | para 33 | 8 Apr 2013 (in relation to a person whose only or principal residence is, on the date on which that person makes a claim for personal independence payment, located in one of the specified postcode areas)[4] (SI 2013/358) |
| | | 10 Jun 2013 (in relation to a person other than a person referred to above) (SI 2013/1250) |
| | para 34 | See paras 35, 36 below |
| | paras 35, 36 | 8 Apr 2013 (in relation to a person whose only or principal residence is, on the date on which that person makes a claim for personal independence payment, located in one of the specified postcode areas)[4] (SI 2013/358) |
| | | 10 Jun 2013 (in relation to a person other than a person referred to above) (SI 2013/1250) |
| | para 37 | See paras 38–43 below |
| | para 38 | 8 Apr 2013 (in relation to a person whose only or principal residence is, on the date on which that person makes a claim for personal independence payment, located in one of the specified postcode areas)[4] (SI 2013/358) |

**Welfare Reform Act 2012 (c 5)**—*contd*

|  |  |  |
|---|---|---|
|  |  | 10 Jun 2013 (in relation to a person other than a person referred to above) (SI 2013/1250) |
|  | para 39 | 25 Feb 2013 (for the purpose of making regulations) (SI 2013/358) |
|  |  | 8 Apr 2013 (in relation to a person whose only or principal residence is, on the date on which that person makes a claim for personal independence payment, located in one of the specified postcode areas)[4] (SI 2013/358) |
|  |  | 10 Jun 2013 (in relation to a person other than a person referred to above) (SI 2013/1250) |
|  | para 40 | 25 Feb 2013 (SI 2013/358) |
|  | para 41 | 25 Feb 2013 (for the purpose of making regulations) (SI 2013/358) |
|  |  | 8 Apr 2013 (in relation to a person whose only or principal residence is, on the date on which that person makes a claim for personal independence payment, located in one of the specified postcode areas)[4] (SI 2013/358) |
|  |  | 10 Jun 2013 (in relation to a person other than a person referred to above) (SI 2013/1250) |
|  | para 42 | 25 Feb 2013 (SI 2013/358) |
|  | paras 43–50 | 8 Apr 2013 (in relation to a person whose only or principal residence is, on the date on which that person makes a claim for personal independence payment, located in one of the specified postcode areas)[4] (SI 2013/358) |
|  |  | 10 Jun 2013 (in relation to a person other than a person referred to above) (SI 2013/1250) |
| Sch 10 |  | 25 Feb 2013 (SI 2013/358) |
| Sch 11 | paras 1–11 | 25 Feb 2013 (for the purpose of making regulations) (SI 2013/358) |
|  |  | 29 Apr 2013 (otherwise) (SI 2013/983) |
|  | paras 12–14 | *Not yet in force* (repealed in part) |
|  | paras 15–18 | 25 Feb 2013 (for the purpose of making regulations) (SI 2013/358) |
|  |  | 29 Apr 2013 (otherwise) (SI 2013/983) |
| Sch 12 |  | 3 Nov 2008 (s 103(2)) |
| Sch 13 |  | 8 May 2012 (s 150(2)(j)) |
| Sch 14 | Pt 1 | 1 Apr 2013 (in so far as relates to the abolition of council tax benefit) (SI 2013/358)[3], repeals of or in— |

Local Government Finance Act 1992, Sch 9;

Social Security Administration Act 1992, ss 6, 7, 110A–110AA, 111, 115A, 115B, 116, 116A, 121DA, 122C–122E, 128A, 138–140G, 176, 182A, 182B, 189, 191 (definitions "billing authority" and "council tax benefit scheme"), Sch 4;

Social Security Contributions and Benefits Act 1992, ss 123–137, 175(6);

Jobseekers Act 1995, s 28;

Social Security Administration (Fraud) Act 1997;

Audit Commission Act 1998, ss 38, 39, 50, Sch 1;

Scotland Act 1998;

Social Security Act 1998, ss 34, 79;

Immigration and Asylum Act 1999, s 115(1)(e), (j), (k);

Local Government Act 1999, ss 13A, 29;

Welfare Reform and Pensions Act 1999, ss 57, 58;

Child Support, Pensions and Social Security Act 2000, s 68, Schs 6, 7;

Social Security Fraud Act 2001, ss 1, 2, 6, 6B, 7, 9, 14;

Pensions Act 2004;

Public Audit (Wales) Act 2004;

Local Government and Public Involvement in Health Act 2007;

Welfare Reform Act 2007, ss 30–34, 37–39, 41–48, Sch 5;

Welfare Reform Act 2009, ss 35, 36;

Welfare Reform Act 2012, s 130

31 Mar 2022 (so far as relates to repeals in Education Act 1996, s 512ZB(4) (SI 2018/45)[7]

**Welfare Reform Act 2012 (c 5)**—*contd*

    1 Feb 2019 (so far as relates to repeal of Tax Credits Act 2002, Pt 1 (but not Sch 1 or 3)) (SI 2019/167)[9]

    In accordance with SI 2013/983, SI 2013/1511, SI 2013/2657, SI 2013/2846, SI 2014/209, SI 2014/1583, SI 2014/2321, SI 2015/32, SI 2015/33, SI 2015/101, SI 2015/634, SI 2015/1537, SI 2015/1930, SI 2016/33, SI 2016/407, SI 2016/963, SI 2017/664 for certain claims and awards defined therein[5], repeals of or in—

    Jobseekers Act 1995, ss 1, 2(3C), 3–5, 13, 15–17, 17A, 23, 26, 35 (except definition "income-based conditions"), 38, Sch 1;

    Welfare Reform and Pensions Act 1999, Sch 7, Sch 8, para 29(2);

    State Pension Credit Act 2002, Sch 2, paras 36–38;

    Income Tax (Earnings and Payments) Act 2003, Sch 6, paras 228–230;

    Civil Partnership Act 2004, Sch 24, paras 118–122;

    Welfare Reform Act 2007, ss 1 (except sub-s (3)(e)), 1A, 1B, 2–6, 23, 24 (except definition "income support"), 26, 27, Sch 1, Pt 1 heading, Pt 2, Sch 2;

    Welfare Reform Act 2009, Sch 7, Pt 3, entry relating to the Civil Partnership Act 2004

    *Not yet in force* (otherwise)

| | |
|---|---|
| Pt 2 | 8 May 2012 (s 150(2)(k)) |
| Pt 3 | 22 Oct 2012 (except repeals of or in Jobseekers Act 1995, ss 20(4), (6), 35(1)) (SI 2012/2530) |

    *Not yet in force* (exceptions noted above)

| | |
|---|---|
| Pts 4, 5 | In relation to a particular case, the day on which the amending provisions (as listed in SI 2013/983, art 4(1)) come into force, under any secondary legislation, in relation to that case (SI 2013/983) |

    *Not yet in force* (otherwise)

| | |
|---|---|
| Pt 6 | 8 May 2012 (s 150(2)(b)) |
| Pt 7 | *Not yet in force* |
| Pt 8 | 1 Apr 2013 (SI 2012/3090)[2], repeals of or in— |

    Social Security Administration Act 1992, ss 12, 168;

    Social Security Contributions and Benefits Act 1992, ss 138–140;

    Social Security Act 1998, ss 8–10, 36, 38

    1 Aug 2013 (SI 2012/3090), repeals of or in—

    Parliamentary Commissioner Act 1967;

    Superannuation Act 1972;

    House of Commons Disqualification Act 1975;

    Social Security Administration Act 1992, Sch 4, Pt 1;

    Social Security Act 1998, s 37;

    Freedom of Information Act 2000

    *Not yet in force,* repeals of or in—

    Social Security Administration Act 1992, ss 71ZA, 78;

    Jobseekers Act 1995;

    Social Security Act 1998, ss 70, 71, 75, Sch 7;

    Civil Partnership Act 2004;

    Welfare Reform Act 2007;

    Welfare Reform Act 2012

| | |
|---|---|
| Pts 9, 10 | *Not yet in force* |
| Pt 11 | 1 Apr 2013 (SI 2013/358), repeals of or in— |

    Social Security Administration Act 1992, ss 7(2)(a), 71(7), (8)

    29 Apr 2013 (SI 2013/358), repeals of or in—

    Social Security Administration Act 1992, s 71(10A), (10B), (11)(aa), (ac)[3]

| | |
|---|---|
| Pt 12 | *Not yet in force* |
| Pt 13 | 8 May 2012 (s 150(2)(f)) |

**Welfare Reform Act 2012 (c 5)**—*contd*
              Pt 14                    8 May 2012 (SI 2012/863)

1   For savings, see SI 2012/1651, art 3

2   For savings, see SI 2012/3090, art 3

3   For savings and transitional provisions, see SI 2013/358, arts 5(3A), (6), (7), 9, 10

4   For the specified postcodes, see SI 2013/358, art 7(1), Sch 3

5   For savings, transitional and transitory provisions, see SI 2013/983, SI 2013/1511, SI 2013/2657, SI 2013/2846, SI 2014/209, SI 2014/1583, all as modified or amended in relation to certain claims and awards (see SI 2013/1511, SI 2014/1452, SI 2014/1661, SI 2014/1923, SI 2014/2321, SI 2014/2321, SI 2014/3067, SI 2014/3094 and SI 2015/32), SI 2015/33, SI 2015/101, SI 2015/634, SI 2015/1537, SI 2015/1930, SI 2016/33, SI 2016/407, SI 2016/596 (itself amended by SI 2016/963), SI 2016/963, SI 2017/57, SI 2017/483, SI 2017/584, SI 2017/664, SI 2017/952, SI 2022/302)

6   For savings and transitional provisions, see SI 2014/1635, art 5

7   For transitory provisions, see SI 2018/145, art 3

8   For savings, see SI 2019/37, art 4

9   For savings, see SI 2019/167, art 3

---

**Welfare Reform (Further Provision) (Scotland) Act 2012 (asp 10)**

*RA:* 7 Aug 2012

*Commencement provisions:* s 6

Whole Act in force 8 Aug 2012 (s 6)

---

# 2013 Acts

## Active Travel (Wales) Act 2013 (anaw 7)

*RA*: 4 Nov 2013

*Commencement provisions*: s 14; Active Travel (Wales) Act 2013 (Commencement) Order 2014, SI 2014/2589

| | |
|---|---|
| 1, 2 | 5 Nov 2013 (s 14(2)) |
| 3–11 | 25 Sep 2014 (SI 2014/2589) |
| 12–15 | 5 Nov 2013 (s 14(2)) |

## Antarctic Act 2013 (c 15)

*RA*: 26 Mar 2013

*Commencement provisions*: s 18(3), (4)

| | |
|---|---|
| 1–3 | *Not yet in force* |
| 4 | See Schedule below |
| 5–13 | *Not yet in force* |
| 14–16 | 26 May 2013 (s 18(4)(a)) |
| 17, 18 | 26 Mar 2013 (s 18(4)(b)) |
| Schedule | *Not yet in force* |

## Aquaculture and Fisheries (Scotland) Act 2013 (asp 7)

*RA*: 18 Jun 2013

*Commencement provisions*: s 66; Aquaculture and Fisheries (Scotland) Act 2013 (Commencement and Transitional Provisions) Order 2013, SSI 2013/249

| | |
|---|---|
| 1–3 | 16 Sep 2013 (SSI 2013/249) |
| 4 | 19 Jun 2013 (s 66(1)) |
| 5–21 | 16 Sep 2013 (SSI 2013/249) |
| 22 | 19 Jun 2013 (s 66(1)) |
| 23–48 | 16 Sep 2013 (SSI 2013/249) |
| 49 | 16 Sep 2013 (SSI 2013/249)[1] |
| 50–52 | 16 Sep 2013 (SSI 2013/249) |
| 53 | 19 Jun 2013 (s 66(1)) |
| 54, 55 | 16 Sep 2013 (SSI 2013/249) |
| 56 | 16 Sep 2013 (SSI 2013/249)[1] |
| 57–61 | 16 Sep 2013 (SSI 2013/249) |
| 62–67 | 19 Jun 2013 (s 66(1)) |
| Schs 1, 2 | 16 Sep 2013 (SSI 2013/249) |

[1]   For transitional provisions, see SSI 2013/249, arts 3, 4

## Budget (Scotland) Act 2013 (asp 4)

*RA:* 13 Mar 2013

*Commencement provisions:* s 10

Whole Act in force 14 Mar 2013 (s 10)

## City of London (Various Powers) Act 2013 (c vii)

*RA:* 18 Dec 2013

Whole Act in force 18 Dec 2013 (RA)

## Clergy Discipline (Amendment) Measure 2013 (No 2)

*RA:* 26 Mar 2013

*Commencement provisions:* s 10(2)

Provisions of this Measure were brought into force on the following dates by instruments made by the Archbishops of Canterbury and York, and dated 31 May 2013 and 27 Jan 2014 (made under s 10(2))

| | | |
|---|---|---|
| 1–8 | | 1 Feb 2014 |
| 9 | (1) | See Schedule below |
| | (2)–(8) | 1 Feb 2014 |
| 10 | | 26 Mar 2013 (s 10(2)) |
| Schedule | paras 1–9 | 1 Feb 2014 |
| | para 10 | 1 Jul 2013 |
| | paras 11–18 | 1 Feb 2014 |

## Crime and Courts Act 2013 (c 22)

*RA:* 25 Apr 2013

*Commencement provisions:* s 61(2)–(11); Crime and Courts Act 2013 (Commencement No 1 and Transitional and Saving Provision) Order 2013, SI 2013/1042; Crime and Courts Act 2013 (Commencement No 2 and Saving Provision) Order 2013, SI 2013/1682; Crime and Courts Act 2013 (Commencement No 3) Order 2013, SI 2013/1725, as amended by SI 2013/2200; Crime and Courts Act 2013 (Commencement No 4) Order 2013, SI 2013/2200; Crime and Courts Act 2013 (Commencement No 5) Order 2013, SI 2013/2349; Crime and Courts Act 2013 (Commencement No 6) Order 2013, SI 2013/2981; Crime and Courts Act 2013 (Commencement No 7 and Saving and Consequential Provisions) Order 2013, SI 2013/3176; Crime and Courts Act 2013 (Commencement No 8) Order 2014, SI 2014/258; Crime and Courts Act 2013 (Commencement No 9) Order 2014, SI 2014/830; Crime and Courts Act 2013 (Commencement No 10 and Transitional Provisions) Order 2014, SI 2014/954; Crime and Courts Act 2013 (Commencement No 11) Order 2014, SI 2014/3098; Crime and Courts Act 2013 (Commencement No 1) (England and Wales) Order 2014, SI 2014/3268; Crime and Courts Act 2013 (Commencement No 12) Order 2015, SI 2015/813; Crime and Courts Act 2013 (Commencement No 13 and Savings) Order 2015, SI 2015/964; Crime and Courts Act 2013 (Commencement No 14) Order 2015, SI 2015/1837; Crime and Courts Act 2013 (Commencement No 15, Transitional and Savings Provisions) Order 2016, SI 2016/962, as amended by SI 2017/976; Crime and Courts Act 2013 (Commencement No 16 and Savings) Order 2017, SI 2017/4; Crime and Courts Act 2013 (Commencement No 17 Transitional and Savings Provisions) Order 2017, SI 2017/236, as amended by SI 2018/357; Crime and Courts Act 2013 (Commencement No 1) (Scotland) Order 2018, SI 2018/161; Crime and Courts Act 2013 (Commencement No 1) (Northern Ireland) Order 2018, SI 2018/162; Crime and Courts Act 2013 (Commencement No 18) Order 2018, SI 2018/1423; Crime and Courts Act 2013 (Commencement No 19) Order 2021, SI 2021/1018

| | | |
|---|---|---|
| 1 | (1), (2) | 27 May 2013 (SI 2013/1042) |
| | (3)–(11) | 7 Oct 2013 (SI 2013/1682) |
| | (12) | See Sch 1 below |
| 2 | | 7 Oct 2013 (SI 2013/1682) |

**Crime and Courts Act 2013 (c 22)**—*contd*

| | | |
|---|---|---|
| 3 | | 27 May 2013 (SI 2013/1042) |
| 4 | (1) | 7 Oct 2013 (SI 2013/1682) |
| | (2)–(9) | 27 May 2013 (SI 2013/1042) |
| | (10) | See Sch 2 below |
| 5 | (1)–(9) | 7 Oct 2013 (SI 2013/1682) |
| | (10) | See Sch 3 below |
| | (11), (12) | 7 Oct 2013 (SI 2013/1682) |
| 6 | (1) | 7 Oct 2013 (SI 2013/1682) |
| | (2) | 27 May 2013 (SI 2013/1042) |
| | (3), (4) | 7 Oct 2013 (SI 2013/1682) |
| 7 | | 7 Oct 2013 (SI 2013/1682) |
| 8 | (1)–(5) | 7 Oct 2013 (SI 2013/1682) |
| | (6) | See Sch 4 below |
| 9 | (1)–(3) | 7 Oct 2013 (SI 2013/1682) |
| | (4) | See Sch 5 below |
| | (5)–(8) | 7 Oct 2013 (SI 2013/1682) |
| 10 | | 7 Oct 2013 (SI 2013/1682) |
| 11 | (1)–(5) | 7 Oct 2013 (SI 2013/1682) |
| | (6) | 8 May 2013 (to the extent that it allows the Secretary of State to make regulations conferring functions on the Independent Police Complaints Commission in relation to the exercise of functions by the Director General and other National Crime Agency officers) (SI 2013/1042) |
| | | 7 Oct 2013 (otherwise) (SI 2013/1682) |
| | (7), (8) | 7 Oct 2013 (SI 2013/1682) |
| | (9) | See Sch 6 below |
| 12, 13 | | 7 Oct 2013 (SI 2013/1682) |
| 14 | | 8 May 2013 (SI 2013/1042) |
| 15 | (1), (2) | 7 Oct 2013 (SI 2013/1682) |
| | (3) | See Sch 8 below |
| 16 | | 8 May 2013 (SI 2013/1042) |
| 17 | (1)–(3) | 22 Apr 2014 (SI 2014/954)[5] |
| | (4) | 4 Sep 2013 (SI 2013/2200) |
| | (5) | See Sch 9 below |
| | (6) | See Schs 10, 11 below |
| 18 | (1)–(4) | 1 Jun 2015 (SI 2015/813) |
| | (5) | See Sch 12 below |
| | (6) | 1 Jun 2015 (SI 2015/813) |
| 19 | | 26 Apr 2013 (s 61(5)) |
| 20 | | See Sch 13 below |
| 21 | (1)–(3) | 1 Oct 2013 (SI 2013/2200) |
| | (4) | See Sch 14 below |
| 22 | | 1 Nov 2013 (SI 2013/2200)[3] |
| 23 | | 15 Jul 2013 (SI 2013/1725) |
| 24 | | 7 Jan 2014 (SI 2013/3176)[4] |
| 25 | (1)–(3) | 6 Apr 2014 (SI 2014/830) |
| | (4) | 15 Jul 2013 (for the purpose of making regulations) (SI 2013/1725) |
| | | 6 Apr 2014 (otherwise) (SI 2014/830) |
| | (5) | 15 Jul 2013 (SI 2013/1725) |
| | (6), (7) | 6 Apr 2014 (SI 2014/830) |
| | (8) | 15 Jul 2013 (SI 2013/1725) |
| | (9) | 6 Apr 2014 (SI 2014/830) |
| 26 | (1) | *Not yet in force* |
| | (2) | 25 Jun 2013 (s 61(6)) |
| | (3)–(8) | *Not yet in force* |
| 27 | | 11 Dec 2013 (SI 2013/2981) |
| 28 | | 22 Apr 2014 (SI 2014/954)[5] |
| 29 | | 15 Jul 2013 (SI 2013/1725) |
| 30 | | 1 Oct 2013 (SI 2013/2200) |

**Crime and Courts Act 2013 (c 22)**—*contd*

| | | |
|---|---|---|
| 31 | | 25 Jun 2013 (s 61(6)) |
| 32 | | 15 Jul 2013 (SI 2013/1725) |
| 33 | | 25 Jun 2013 (s 61(6)) |
| 34–39 | | In force at the end of the period of one year beginning with the day on which a body is established by Royal Charter with the purpose of carrying on activities relating to the recognition of independent regulators of relevant publishers (as defined by s 41) (s 61(7)) |
| 40 | | *Not yet in force* |
| 41 | (1)–(4) | 3 Nov 2015 (for the purposes of ss 34–39) (SI 2015/1837) |
| | | *Not yet in force* (otherwise) |
| | (5)–(7) | See Sch 15 below |
| 42 | | 3 Nov 2015 (for the purposes of ss 34–39, 41) (SI 2015/1837) |
| | | *Not yet in force* (otherwise) |
| 43 | | 25 Apr 2013 (s 61(11)(b)) |
| 44 | | See Sch 16 below |
| 45 | | See Sch 17 below |
| 46 | (1) | See sub-ss (2)–(7) below |
| | (2)–(4) | 1 Jun 2015 (SI 2015/813) |
| | (5) | 20 Mar 2015 (for the purpose of exercising the power to prescribe by regulations) (SI 2015/813) |
| | | 1 Jun 2015 (otherwise) (SI 2015/813) |
| | (6), (7) | 20 Mar 2015 (SI 2015/813) |
| 47 | | 20 Mar 2015 (SI 2015/813) |
| 48 | (1)–(5) | 25 Apr 2013 (s 61(11)(c)) |
| | (6) | See Sch 18 below |
| | (7), (8) | 25 Apr 2013 (s 61(11)(c)) |
| 49 | | See Sch 19 below |
| 50 | | See Sch 20 below |
| 51 | | 8 May 2013 (SI 2013/1042) |
| 52–54 | | 25 Jun 2013 (SI 2013/1042)[1] |
| 55 | (1), (2) | 25 Jun 2013 (SI 2013/1042) |
| | (3) | See sub-ss (4), (5) below |
| | (4) | 22 Nov 2014 (SI 2014/3098) |
| | (5)–(13) | 25 Jun 2013 (SI 2013/1042) |
| | (14) | See Sch 21 below |
| 56 | (1)–(6) | 2 Mar 2015 (E) (W) (SI 2014/3268) |
| | | 1 Mar 2018 (S) (SI 2018/161) |
| | | 1 Mar 2018 (NI) (SI 2018/162) |
| | (7) | See Sch 22 below |
| 57 | | 1 Feb 2014 (SI 2013/2981) |
| 58 | (1), (2) | 25 Apr 2013 (s 61(11)(e)) |
| | (3) | See Sch 23 below |
| | (4)–(13) | 25 Apr 2013 (s 61(11)(e)) |
| 59, 60 | | 25 Apr 2013 (s 61(11)(e)) |
| 61 | (1)–(17) | 25 Apr 2013 (s 61(11)(e)) |
| | (18) | See Sch 24 below |
| | (19) | See Sch 25 below |
| | (20)–(23) | 25 Apr 2013 (s 61(11)(e)) |
| Sch 1 | paras 1–6 | 7 Oct 2013 (SI 2013/1682) |
| | para 7 | 27 May 2013 (SI 2013/1042) |
| | paras 8–15 | 7 Oct 2013 (SI 2013/1682) |
| Sch 2 | para 1 | 27 May 2013 (SI 2013/1042) |
| | paras 2, 3 | 7 Oct 2013 (SI 2013/1682) |
| | paras 4, 5 | 27 May 2013 (SI 2013/1042) |
| | paras 6–8 | 7 Oct 2013 (SI 2013/1682) |
| Sch 3 | paras 1–33 | 7 Oct 2013 (SI 2013/1682) |
| | para 34 | 8 May 2013 (SI 2013/1042) |
| | paras 35, 36 | 7 Oct 2013 (SI 2013/1682) |

**Crime and Courts Act 2013 (c 22)**—*contd*

| | | |
|---|---|---|
| Sch 4 | para 1 | 8 May 2013 (SI 2013/1042) |
| | paras 2–5 | 7 Oct 2013 (SI 2013/1682) |
| Sch 5 | paras 1–3 | 7 Oct 2013 (SI 2013/1682) |
| | para 4 | 27 May 2013 (SI 2013/1042) |
| | para 5 | 8 May 2013 (SI 2013/1042) |
| | paras 6–26 | 7 Oct 2013 (SI 2013/1682) |
| | paras 27–30 | 8 May 2013 (SI 2013/1042) |
| Sch 6 | paras 1–4, 5(1)–(4) | 7 Oct 2013 (SI 2013/1682) |
| | para 5(5), (6) | 8 May 2013 (SI 2013/1042) |
| | paras 6–19 | 7 Oct 2013 (SI 2013/1682) |
| Sch 7 | | 7 Oct 2013 (SI 2013/1682) |
| Sch 8 | paras 1–5 | 8 May 2013 (SI 2013/1042) |
| | paras 6–10 | 7 Oct 2013 (SI 2013/1682) |
| | para 11 | *Not yet in force* |
| | para 12 | 7 Oct 2013 (SI 2013/1682) |
| | para 13 | 8 May 2013 (SI 2013/1042) (SI 2013/1682 also purports to bring this para into force on 7 Oct 2013) |
| | paras 14–100 | 7 Oct 2013 (SI 2013/1682) |
| | paras 101–103 | 27 May 2013 (SI 2013/1042) |
| | paras 104–190 | 7 Oct 2013 (SI 2013/1682) |
| Sch 9 | paras 1–20 | 22 Apr 2014 (SI 2014/954)[5] |
| | para 21(1), (2) | 1 Oct 2013 (SI 2013/1725) |
| | para 21(3) | 22 Apr 2014 (SI 2014/954)[5] |
| | paras 22–26 | 22 Apr 2014 (SI 2014/954)[5] |
| | para 27 | 1 Oct 2013 (SI 2013/1725) |
| | paras 28, 29 | 22 Apr 2014 (SI 2014/954)[5] |
| | para 30 | 1 Oct 2013 (SI 2013/1725) |
| | paras 31–141 | 22 Apr 2014 (SI 2014/954)[5] |
| Schs 10, 11 | | 22 Apr 2014 (SI 2014/954)[5] |
| Sch 12 | | 1 Jun 2015 (SI 2015/813) |
| Sch 13 | Pt 1 | 1 Oct 2013 (SI 2013/2200) |
| | Pt 2 | 15 Jul 2013 (SI 2013/1725) |
| | Pt 3 | 4 Sep 2013 (SI 2013/2200) |
| | Pt 4 | 1 Oct 2013 (except in so far as entry in para 41(4) thereof referring to Justice of the Peace appointed under Courts Act 2003, s 10(1) relates to Constitutional Reform Act 2005, ss 85–97, 99, and except in so far as para 49(6)(a) applies to the Deputy Chief Coroner) (SI 2013/2200) |
| | | *Not yet in force* (exceptions noted above) |
| | Pt 5 | 25 Apr 2013 (s 61(11)(a)) |
| | Pts 6, 7 | 15 Jul 2013 (SI 2013/1725) |
| Sch 14 | | 1 Oct 2013 (SI 2013/2200) |
| Sch 15 | | 3 Nov 2015 (for the purposes of ss 34–39) (SI 2015/1837) |
| | | *Not yet in force* (otherwise) |
| Sch 16 | paras 1–10 | 11 Dec 2013 (SI 2013/2981) |
| | paras 11–21 | 17 Oct 2016 (in relation to specified local justice areas)[7] (ceases to be in force on 30 Jun 2018, see SI 2016/962, art 3) (SI 2016/962)[8] |
| | | 13 Mar 2017 (in relation to specified local justice areas)[10] (ceases to be in force on 12 Mar 2018, see SI 2017/236, art 3) (SI 2017/236)[11] |
| | | 1 Apr 2019 (otherwise) (SI 2019/1423) |
| | paras 22–30 | 11 Dec 2013 (SI 2013/2981) |
| | paras 31–36 | 11 Dec 2013 (so far as extending to the United Kingdom) (SI 2013/2981) |
| | | *Not yet in force* (otherwise) |
| | para 37 | *Not yet in force* |
| | para 38 | 11 Dec 2013 (so far as extending to the United Kingdom) (SI 2013/2981) |
| | | *Not yet in force* (otherwise) |

**Crime and Courts Act 2013 (c 22)**—*contd*

| | | |
|---|---|---|
| Sch 17 | | 24 Feb 2014 (SI 2014/258) |
| Sch 18 | Pt 1 | 1 Jun 2015 (SI 2015/964) |
| | Pt 2 | 25 Apr 2013 (s 61(11)(d)) |
| Sch 19 | paras 1–13 | 1 Jun 2015 (E) (W) (S)[6] (SI 2015/964) |
| | | 1 Feb 2017 (NI)[9] (SI 2017/4) |
| | paras 14–23 | 1 Jun 2015 (SI 2015/964)[6] |
| | para 24 | See paras 25–28 below |
| | para 25 | 1 Jun 2015 (E) (W) (S) (SI 2015/964) |
| | | 1 Feb 2017 (NI) (SI 2017/4) |
| | para 26 | 22 Nov 2014 (in so far as inserts Proceeds of Crime Act 2002, ss 375A(5), (10), (11), in so far as is necessary for the purpose of making rules of court) (SI 2014/3098) |
| | | 1 Jun 2015 (otherwise) (E) (W) (S) (SI 2015/964) |
| | | 1 Feb 2017 (otherwise) (NI) (SI 2017/4) |
| | para 27 | 1 Jun 2015 (E) (W) (S) (SI 2015/964) |
| | | 1 Feb 2017 (NI) (SI 2017/4) |
| | para 28 | 22 Nov 2014 (in so far as inserts Proceeds of Crime Act 2002, ss 408A(5), (10), (11), in so far as is necessary for the purpose of making rules of court) (SI 2014/3098) |
| | | 1 Jun 2015 (otherwise) (SI 2015/964) |
| | paras 29, 30 | 1 Jun 2015 (E) (W) (S) (SI 2015/964) |
| | | 1 Feb 2017 (NI) (SI 2017/4) |
| Sch 20 | paras 1–9 | 18 Sep 2013 (for the purposes of paras 3 and 6 in so far as they insert ss 19F(2), 83E(2) in to the Extradition Act 2003, for the purposes of making orders) (SI 2013/2349) |
| | | 14 Oct 2013 (E) (W) (NI) (otherwise) (SI 2013/2349) |
| | | 17 Sep 2021 (S) (otherwise) (SI 2021/1018) |
| | paras 10–15 | 29 Jul 2013 (E) (W) (SI 2013/1682) |
| | | 14 Oct 2013 (NI) (SI 2013/2349) |
| | | 17 Sep 2021 (S) (SI 2021/1018) |
| | paras 16–29 | 29 Jul 2013 (SI 2013/1682)[2] |
| Sch 21 | paras 1–13 | 25 Jun 2013 (SI 2013/1042) |
| | para 14 | See paras 15–38 below |
| | paras 15–18 | 22 Nov 2014 (SI 2014/3098) |
| | para 19 | 25 Jun 2013 (SI 2013/1042) |
| | paras 20–29 | 22 Nov 2014 (SI 2014/3098) |
| | paras 30–50 | 25 Jun 2013 (SI 2013/1042) |
| Sch 22 | | 2 Mar 2015 (E) (W) (SI 2014/3268) |
| | | 1 Mar 2018 (S) (SI 2018/161) |
| | | 1 Mar 2018 (NI) (SI 2018/162) |
| Sch 23 | | *Not yet in force* |
| Schs 24, 25 | | 25 Apr 2013 (s 61(11)(f)) |

[1]    For transitional and saving provisions, see SI 2013/1042, art 5

[2]    For saving provisions, see SI 2013/1682, art 4

[3]    This provision was previously brought into force on 1 Oct 2013 by SI 2013/1725, art 3(b), which was repealed by SI 2013/2200, art 6

[4]    For saving provisions, see SI 2013/3176, art 3

[5]    For a transitional provision, see SI 2014/954, art 3

[6]    For saving provisions, see SI 2015/964, art 3

[7]    The specified local justice areas are:

    (a)   Birmingham and Solihull,

    (b)   Black Country,

    (c)   Central and South West Staffordshire,

    (d)   Coventry and Warwickshire,

**Crime and Courts Act 2013 (c 22)**—*contd*

   (e)   Leicestershire and Rutland,

   (f)   North Staffordshire,

   (g)   Nottinghamshire, and

   (h)   South East Staffordshire

[8]   For transitional and saving provisions, see SI 2016/962, art 4(1), (2)

[9]   For saving provisions, see SI 2017/4, art 3

[10]   The specified local justice areas are:

   (a)   East London, and

   (b)   North London

[11]   For transitional and saving provisions, see SI 2017/236, art 3

**Crofting (Amendment) (Scotland) Act 2013 (asp 10)**

*RA*: 31 Jul 2013

*Commencement provisions*: s 6

Whole Act in force 31 Jul 2013 (s 6)

**Defamation Act 2013 (c 26)**

*RA*: 25 Apr 2013

*Commencement provisions*: s 17(4)–(6); Defamation Act 2013 (Commencement) (Scotland) Order 2013, SSI 2013/339; Defamation Act 2013 (Commencement) (England and Wales) Order 2013, SI 2013/3027

| | | |
|---|---|---|
| 1–14 | | 1 Jan 2014 (SI 2013/3027) |
| 6 | | 1 Jan 2014 (S) (SSI 2013/339) |
| | | 1 Jan 2014 (E) (W) (SI 2013/3027) |
| 7 | (1)–(8) | 1 Jan 2014 (SI 2013/3027) |
| | (9) | 1 Jan 2014 (S) (SSI 2013/339) |
| | | 1 Jan 2014 (E) (W) (SI 2013/3027) |
| | (10), (11) | 1 Jan 2014 (SI 2013/3027) |
| 8–14 | | 1 Jan 2014 (SI 2013/3027) |
| 15 | | 25 Apr 2013 (s 17(6)) |
| 16 | (1)–(3) | 1 Jan 2014 (SI 2013/3027) |
| | (4)–(8) | 25 Apr 2013 (s 17(6)) |
| 17 | | 25 Apr 2013 (s 17(6)) |

**Diocese in Europe Measure 2013 (No 1)**

*RA*: 26 Mar 2013

*Commencement provisions*: s 3(2)

Provisions of this Measure were brought into force on the following dates by an instrument made by the Archbishops of Canterbury and York, and dated 10 Jun 2013 (made under s 3(2))

| | |
|---|---|
| 1 | 1 Jan 2014 |
| 2 | 1 Jul 2013 |
| 3 | 26 Mar 2013 (RA) |

## Disabled Persons' Parking Badges Act 2013 (c 4)

*RA:* 31 Jan 2013

*Commencement provisions*: s 7(2); Disabled Persons' Parking Badges Act 2013 (Commencement) Order 2013, SI 2013/2202

1–7                                         8 Oct 2013 (SI 2013/2202)

---

## Electoral Registration and Administration Act 2013 (c 6)

*RA:* 31 Jan 2013

*Commencement provisions*: s 27; Electoral Registration and Administration Act 2013 (Commencement No 1) Order 2013, SI 2013/219; Electoral Registration and Administration Act 2013 (Commencement No 2) Order 2013, SI 2013/702; Electoral Registration and Administration Act 2013 (Commencement No 3) Order 2013, SI 2013/969; Electoral Registration and Administration Act 2013 (Commencement No 4 and Consequential Provision) Order 2014, SI 2014/336; Electoral Registration and Administration Act 2013 (Commencement No 5 and Transitory Provisions) Order 2014, SI 2014/414; Electoral Registration and Administration Act 2013 (Commencement No 1) (Northern Ireland) Order 2014, SI 2014/2439

| | | |
|---|---|---|
| 1 | (1) | 10 Jun 2014 (E) (W) (SI 2014/414) |
| | | 19 Sep 2014 (S) (SI 2014/414) |
| | | 15 Sep 2014 (NI) (SI 2014/2439) |
| | (2) | See Sch 1 below |
| | (3)–(5) | 10 Jun 2014 (E) (W) (SI 2014/414) |
| | | 19 Sep 2014 (S) (SI 2014/414) |
| | | 15 Sep 2014 (NI) (SI 2014/2439) |
| 2 | (1)–(5) | 10 Jun 2014 (E) (W) (SI 2014/414) |
| | | 19 Sep 2014 (S) (SI 2014/414) |
| | | 15 Sep 2014 (NI) (SI 2014/2439) |
| | (6) | See Sch 2 below |
| 3 | | 10 Jun 2014 (E) (W) (SI 2014/414) |
| | | 19 Sep 2014 (S) (SI 2014/414) |
| 4 | | 10 Jun 2014 (E) (W) (SI 2014/414) |
| | | 19 Sep 2014 (S) (SI 2014/414) |
| | | 15 Sep 2014 (NI) (SI 2014/2439) |
| 5 | (1) | 10 Jun 2014 (E) (W) (SI 2014/414) |
| | | 19 Sep 2014 (S) (SI 2014/414) |
| | | 15 Sep 2014 (NI) (SI 2014/2439) |
| | (2) | See Sch 3 below |
| 6 | | 23 Apr 2013 (SI 2013/969) |
| 7–9 | | 10 Jun 2014 (E) (W) (SI 2014/414) |
| | | 19 Sep 2014 (S) (SI 2014/414) |
| | | 15 Sep 2014 (NI) (SI 2014/2439) |
| 10 | | 2 Apr 2013 (SI 2013/702) |
| 11 | | 25 Mar 2013 (SI 2013/702) |
| 12 | | 10 Jun 2014 (E) (W) (SI 2014/414) |
| | | 19 Sep 2014 (S) (SI 2014/414) |
| | | 15 Sep 2014 (NI) (SI 2014/2439) |
| 13 | (1) | See Sch 4 below |
| | (2) | See Sch 5 below |
| | (3), (4) | 26 Feb 2014 (SI 2014/414) |
| 14 | | 6 Apr 2014 (SI 2014/414)[1] |
| 15 | | 2 Apr 2013 (SI 2013/702) |
| 16 | | 6 Apr 2014 (SI 2014/414)[1] |
| 17 | | 2 Apr 2013 (SI 2013/702) |
| 18 | | 6 Apr 2014 (SI 2014/414)[1] |
| 19 | | 22 May 2014 (SI 2014/336) |
| 20, 21 | | 6 Apr 2014 (SI 2014/414)[1] |
| 22, 23 | | 2 Apr 2013 (SI 2013/702) |

**Electoral Registration and Administration Act 2013 (c 6)**—*contd*

| | | |
|---|---|---|
| 24–28 | | 31 Jan 2013 (s 27(3)) |
| Sch 1 | | 10 Jun 2014 (E) (W) (SI 2014/414) |
| | | 19 Sep 2014 (S) (SI 2014/414) |
| | | 15 Sep 2014 (NI) (SI 2014/2439) |
| Sch 2 | | 5 Feb 2013 (SI 2013/219) |
| Sch 3 | | 10 Jun 2014 (E) (W) (SI 2014/414) |
| | | 19 Sep 2014 (S) (SI 2014/414) |
| | | 15 Sep 2014 (NI) (SI 2014/2439) |
| Sch 4 | paras 1–8 | 10 Jun 2014 (E) (W) (SI 2014/414) |
| | | 19 Sep 2014 (S) (SI 2014/414) |
| | para 9(1)–(3), (4)(a) | 10 Jun 2014 (E) (W) (SI 2014/414) |
| | | 19 Sep 2014 (S) (SI 2014/414) |
| | | 15 Sep 2014 (NI) (SI 2014/2439) |
| | para 9(4)(b) | *Never in force* (repealed) |
| | para 9(5)–(9) | 10 Jun 2014 (E) (W) (SI 2014/414) |
| | | 19 Sep 2014 (S) (SI 2014/414) |
| | | 15 Sep 2014 (NI) (SI 2014/2439) |
| | para 10(1)–(4) | 10 Jun 2014 (E) (W) (SI 2014/414) |
| | | 19 Sep 2014 (S) (SI 2014/414) |
| | | 15 Sep 2014 (NI) (SI 2014/2439) |
| | para 10(5) | *Never in force* (repealed) |
| | paras 10(6)–(12), 11–22 | 10 Jun 2014 (E) (W) (SI 2014/414) |
| | | 19 Sep 2014 (S) (SI 2014/414) |
| | para 23 | 10 Jun 2014 (E) (W) (SI 2014/414) |
| | | 19 Sep 2014 (S) (SI 2014/414) |
| | | 15 Sep 2014 (NI) (except repeal of Electoral Administration Act 2006, Sch 1, paras 5, 6(2)) (SI 2014/2439) |
| | | *Not yet in force* (exception noted above) |
| | para 24 | 10 Jun 2014 (E) (W) (SI 2014/414) |
| | | 19 Sep 2014 (S) (SI 2014/414) |
| | | 15 Sep 2014 (NI) (SI 2014/2439) |
| Sch 5 | paras 1–3 | 10 Jun 2014 (E) (W) (SI 2014/414) |
| | | 19 Sep 2014 (S) (SI 2014/414) |
| | | 15 Sep 2014 (NI) (SI 2014/2439) |
| | para 4(1)–(3) | 10 Jun 2014 (E) (W) (SI 2014/414) |
| | | 19 Sep 2014 (S) (SI 2014/414) |
| | | 15 Sep 2014 (NI) (SI 2014/2439) |
| | para 4(4) | 5 Feb 2013 (SI 2013/219) |
| | para 4(5) | 10 Jun 2014 (E) (W) (SI 2014/414) |
| | | 19 Sep 2014 (S) (SI 2014/414) |
| | | 15 Sep 2014 (NI) (SI 2014/2439) |
| | paras 5–8 | 10 Jun 2014 (E) (W) (SI 2014/414) |
| | | 19 Sep 2014 (S) (SI 2014/414) |
| | | 15 Sep 2014 (NI) (SI 2014/2439) |
| | para 9(1) | 5 Feb 2013 (SI 2013/219) |
| | para 9(2)–(4) | 10 Jun 2014 (E) (W) (SI 2014/414) |
| | | 19 Sep 2014 (S) (SI 2014/414) |
| | | 15 Sep 2014 (NI) (SI 2014/2439) |
| | para 9(5)–(7) | 5 Feb 2013 (SI 2013/219) |
| | paras 10–27 | 10 Jun 2014 (E) (W) (SI 2014/414) |
| | | 19 Sep 2014 (S) (SI 2014/414) |
| | | 15 Sep 2014 (NI) (SI 2014/2439) |
| | para 28 | 31 Mar 2013 (s 27(2)) |
| | paras 29, 30 | 10 Jun 2014 (E) (W) (SI 2014/414) |
| | | 19 Sep 2014 (S) (SI 2014/414) |
| | | 15 Sep 2014 (NI) (SI 2014/2439) |

**Electoral Registration and Administration Act 2013 (c 6)**—*contd*
1  For transitory provision, see SI 2014/414, art 4

**Energy Act 2013 (c 32)**

*RA:* 18 Dec 2013

*Commencement provisions:* s 156; Energy Act 2013 (Commencement No 1) Order 2014, SI 2014/251; Energy Act 2013 (Commencement No 2) Order 2015, SI 2015/614; Energy Act 2013 (Commencement No 3) Order 2015, SI 2015/817

| | | |
|---|---|---|
| 1–4 | | 18 Dec 2013 (s 156(3)(a)) |
| 5 | | 18 Dec 2013 (s 156(3)(b)) |
| 6 | | 18 Dec 2013 (s 156(3)(c)) |
| 7 | (1)–(7) | 18 Dec 2013 (s 156(3)(c)) |
| | (8) | See Sch 1 below |
| | (9), (10) | 18 Dec 2013 (s 156(3)(c)) |
| 8–26 | | 18 Dec 2013 (s 156(3)(c)) |
| 27–43 | | 18 Dec 2013 (s 156(3)(d)) |
| 44 | | See Sch 2 below |
| 45, 46 | | 18 Feb 2014 (s 156(2)(a)) |
| 47 | (1)–(7) | 18 Feb 2014 (s 156(2)(a)) |
| | (8) | See Sch 3 below |
| | (9)–(11) | 18 Feb 2014 (s 156(2)(a)) |
| 48 | | 18 Feb 2014 (s 156(2)(a)) |
| 49–54 | | 18 Feb 2014 (s 156(2)(b)) |
| 55 | | 18 Dec 2013 (s 156(3)(f)) |
| 56 | | 18 Feb 2014 (s 156(2)(c)) |
| 57 | (1)–(6)(a) | 18 Feb 2014 (s 156(2)(d)) |
| | (6)(b) | See Sch 4 below |
| | (7), (8) | 18 Feb 2014 (s 156(2)(d)) |
| 58, 59 | | 18 Feb 2014 (s 156(2)(d)) |
| 60 | (1) | 18 Feb 2014 (s 156(2)(d)) |
| | (2) | See Sch 5 below |
| | (3)–(5) | 18 Feb 2014 (s 156(2)(d)) |
| 61, 62 | | 18 Feb 2014 (s 156(2)(d)) |
| 63–66 | | 18 Dec 2013 (s 156(3)(g)) |
| 67–69 | | 1 Apr 2014 (SI 2014/251) |
| 70 | (1), (2) | 1 Apr 2014 (SI 2014/251) |
| | (3) | 18 Feb 2014 (SI 2014/251) |
| 71 | | 10 Mar 2014 (SI 2014/251) |
| 72, 73 | | 1 Apr 2014 (SI 2014/251) |
| 74 | (1) | 1 Apr 2014 (SI 2014/251) |
| | (2) | See Sch 6 below |
| | (3)–(11) | 1 Apr 2014 (SI 2014/251) |
| 75, 76 | | 1 Apr 2014 (SI 2014/251) |
| 77 | (1), (2) | 10 Mar 2014 (SI 2014/251) |
| | (3) | See Sch 7 below |
| 78–82 | | 1 Apr 2014 (SI 2014/251) |
| 83 | | See Sch 8 below |
| 84–89 | | 1 Apr 2014 (SI 2014/251) |
| 90 | (1)–(4) | 10 Mar 2014 (SI 2014/251) |
| | (5) | 1 Apr 2014 (SI 2014/251) |
| 91, 92 | | 1 Apr 2014 (SI 2014/251) |
| 93 | (1) | 1 Apr 2014 (SI 2014/251) |
| | (2)–(5) | 10 Mar 2014 (SI 2014/251) |
| | (6) | 1 Apr 2014 (SI 2014/251) |
| 94–99 | | 1 Apr 2014 (SI 2014/251) |
| 100 | | See Sch 9 below |
| 101–105 | | 1 Apr 2014 (SI 2014/251) |

**Energy Act 2013 (c 32)**—*contd*

| | | |
|---|---|---|
| 106 | (1) | See Sch 10 below |
| | (2) | 1 Apr 2014 (SI 2014/251) |
| 107, 108 | | 1 Apr 2014 (SI 2014/251) |
| 109, 110 | | 10 Mar 2014 (SI 2014/251) |
| 111, 112 | | 1 Apr 2014 (SI 2014/251) |
| 113 | | 18 Dec 2013 (s 156(3)(h)) |
| 114 | (1) | 18 Dec 2013 (s 156(3)(i)) |
| | (2)–(5) | 1 Apr 2014 (SI 2014/251) |
| 115 | | See Sch 11 below |
| 116 | (1) | See Sch 12 below |
| | (2) | 18 Dec 2013 (s 156(3)(k)) |
| | (3), (4) | 1 Apr 2014 (SI 2014/251) |
| 117 | | 1 Apr 2014 (SI 2014/251) |
| 118 | | 18 Dec 2013 (s 156(3)(l)) |
| 119–128 | | 30 Apr 2015 (SI 2015/817) |
| 129 | (1), (2) | 30 Apr 2015 (SI 2015/817) |
| | (3) | See Sch 13 below |
| | (4), (5) | 30 Apr 2015 (SI 2015/817) |
| 130 | | 30 Apr 2015 (SI 2015/817) |
| 131–137 | | 18 Feb 2014 (s 156(2)(e)) |
| 138 | (1) | *Not yet in force* |
| | (2), (3) | 18 Feb 2014 (s 156(2)(e)) |
| | (4), (5) | *Not yet in force* |
| 139–142 | | 18 Feb 2014 (s 156(2)(f)) |
| 143 | | 18 Feb 2014 (s 156(2)(g)) |
| 144 | | See Sch 14 below |
| 145 | | 18 Feb 2014 (s 156(2)(i)) |
| 146 | | 18 Feb 2014 (s 156(2)(j)) |
| 147 | | 18 Feb 2014 (s 156(2)(k)) |
| 148 | | 18 Feb 2014 (SI 2014/251) |
| 149 | | 18 Feb 2014 (s 156(2)(l)) |
| 150 | | 11 Mar 2015 (SI 2015/614) |
| 151 | | 18 Dec 2013 (s 156(3)(m)) |
| 152–157 | | 18 Dec 2013 (s 156(3)(n)) |
| Sch 1 | | 18 Dec 2013 (s 156(3)(c)) |
| Sch 2 | | 18 Dec 2013 (s 156(3)(e)) |
| Sch 3 | | 18 Feb 2014 (s 156(2)(a)) |
| Schs 4, 5 | | 18 Feb 2014 (s 156(2)(d)) |
| Sch 6 | | 1 Apr 2014 (SI 2014/251) |
| Sch 7 | | 10 Mar 2014 (SI 2014/251) |
| Schs 8–10 | | 1 Apr 2014 (SI 2014/251) |
| Sch 11 | | 18 Dec 2013 (s 156(3)(j)) |
| Sch 12 | paras 1–14 | 1 Apr 2014 (SI 2014/251) |
| | para 15(1)–(12) | 1 Apr 2014 (SI 2014/251) |
| | para 15(13) | 10 Mar 2014 (SI 2014/251) |
| | paras 16–53 | 1 Apr 2014 (SI 2014/251) |
| | paras 54–56 | 10 Mar 2014 (SI 2014/251) |
| | paras 57–71 | 1 Apr 2014 (SI 2014/251) |
| | para 72 | 10 Mar 2014 (SI 2014/251) |
| | para 73 | 1 Apr 2014 (SI 2014/251) |
| | para 74 | *Not yet in force* |
| | para 75 | 10 Mar 2014 (SI 2014/251) |
| | paras 76–89 | 1 Apr 2014 (SI 2014/251) |
| | para 90 | 10 Mar 2014 (SI 2014/251) |
| | paras 91–101 | 1 Apr 2014 (SI 2014/251) |
| | para 102 | 10 Mar 2014 (SI 2014/251) |
| | para 103 | 1 Apr 2014 (SI 2014/251) |
| Sch 13 | | 30 Apr 2015 (SI 2015/817) |
| Sch 14 | | 18 Feb 2014 (s 156(2)(h)) |

**Enterprise and Regulatory Reform Act 2013 (c 24)**

*RA:* 25 Apr 2013

*Commencement provisions:* s 103; Enterprise and Regulatory Reform Act 2013 (Commencement No 1, Transitional Provisions and Savings) Order 2013, SI 2013/1455, as amended by SI 2013/2271, SI 2014/2481; Enterprise and Regulatory Reform Act 2013 (Commencement No 2) Order 2013, SI 2013/1648; Enterprise and Regulatory Reform Act 2013 (Commencement No 3, Transitional Provisions and Savings) Order 2013, SI 2013/2227; Enterprise and Regulatory Reform Act 2013 (Commencement No 4 and Saving Provision) Order 2013, SI 2013/2979, as amended by SI 2014/824, SI 2014/2481; Enterprise and Regulatory Reform Act 2013 (Commencement No 5, Transitional Provisions and Savings) Order 2014, SI 2014/253; Enterprise and Regulatory Reform Act 2013 (Commencement No 6, Transitional Provisions and Savings) Order 2014, SI 2014/416; Enterprise and Regulatory Reform Act 2013 (Commencement No 7 and Amendment) Order 2014, SI 2014/2481; Enterprise and Regulatory Reform Act 2013 (Commencement No 8 and Saving Provisions) Order 2015, SI 2015/641 (revoked); Enterprise and Regulatory Reform Act 2013 (Commencement No 9 and Saving Provisions) Order 2016, SI 2016/191; Enterprise and Regulatory Reform Act 2013 (Commencement No 10 and Saving Provisions) Order 2016, SI 2016/593

| | | |
|---|---|---|
| 1–6 | | 25 Apr 2013 (so far as is necessary for enabling the exercise of any power (arising under or by virtue hereof) to make provision by regulations, rules or orders made by statutory instrument) (s 103(1)(i)) |
| | | 25 Jun 2013 (otherwise) (s 103(2)(a)) |
| 7 | (1) | 25 Apr 2013 (so far as is necessary for enabling the exercise of any power (arising under or by virtue hereof) to make provision by regulations, rules or orders made by statutory instrument) (s 103(1)(i)) |
| | | 6 Apr 2014 (otherwise) (SI 2014/253)[5] |
| | (2) | See Sch 1 below |
| 8 | | See Sch 2 below |
| 9 | | 25 Apr 2013 (so far as is necessary for enabling the exercise of any power (arising under or by virtue hereof) to make provision by regulations, rules or orders made by statutory instrument) (s 103(1)(i)) |
| | | 6 Apr 2014 (otherwise) (SI 2014/253) |
| 10 | | 25 Apr 2013 (s 103(1)(a)) |
| 11 | | 25 Apr 2013 (so far as is necessary for enabling the exercise of any power (arising under or by virtue hereof) to make provision by regulations, rules or orders made by statutory instrument) (s 103(1)(i)) |
| | | *Not yet in force* (otherwise) |
| 12, 13 | | 25 Apr 2013 (so far as is necessary for enabling the exercise of any power (arising under or by virtue hereof) to make provision by regulations, rules or orders made by statutory instrument) (s 103(1)(i)) |
| | | 25 Jun 2013 (otherwise) (s 103(2)(b)) |
| 14 | | 25 Apr 2013 (so far as is necessary for enabling the exercise of any power (arising under or by virtue hereof) to make provision by regulations, rules or orders made by statutory instrument) (s 103(1)(i)) |
| | | 29 Jul 2013 (otherwise) (SI 2013/1648) |
| 15 | | 25 Apr 2013 (so far as is necessary for enabling the exercise of any power (arising under or by virtue hereof) to make provision by regulations, rules or orders made by statutory instrument) (s 103(1)(i)) |
| | | 25 Jun 2013 (otherwise) (s 103(2)(b))[2] |
| 16 | (1) | 25 Apr 2013 (so far as is necessary for enabling the exercise of any power (arising under or by virtue hereof) to make provision by regulations, rules or orders made by statutory instrument) (s 103(1)(i)) |
| | | 6 Apr 2014 (otherwise) (SI 2014/253) |
| | (2) | See Sch 3 below |

**Enterprise and Regulatory Reform Act 2013 (c 24)**—*contd*

| | | |
|---|---|---|
| 17, 18 | | 25 Apr 2013 (so far as is necessary for enabling the exercise of any power (arising under or by virtue hereof) to make provision by regulations, rules or orders made by statutory instrument) (s 103(1)(i)) |
| | | 25 Jun 2013 (otherwise) (s 103(2)(b)) |
| 19 | | 25 Apr 2013 (so far as is necessary for enabling the exercise of any power (arising under or by virtue hereof) to make provision by regulations, rules or orders made by statutory instrument) (s 103(1)(i)) |
| | | 25 Jun 2013 (otherwise) (SI 2013/1455) |
| 20–22 | | 25 Apr 2013 (so far as is necessary for enabling the exercise of any power (arising under or by virtue hereof) to make provision by regulations, rules or orders made by statutory instrument) (s 103(1)(i)) |
| | | 25 Jun 2013 (otherwise) (s 103(2)(b)) |
| 23 | | 25 Apr 2013 (so far as is necessary for enabling the exercise of any power (arising under or by virtue hereof) to make provision by regulations, rules or orders made by statutory instrument) (s 103(1)(i)) |
| | | 29 Jul 2013 (otherwise) (SI 2013/1648) |
| 24 | | 25 Apr 2013 (s 103(1)(b)) |
| 25 | (1), (2) | 25 Apr 2013 (so far as is necessary for enabling the exercise of any power (arising under or by virtue hereof) to make provision by regulations, rules or orders made by statutory instrument) (s 103(1)(i)) |
| | | 1 Oct 2013 (otherwise) (SI 2013/2227) |
| | (3) | 25 Apr 2013 (so far as is necessary for enabling the exercise of any power (arising under or by virtue hereof) to make provision by regulations, rules or orders made by statutory instrument) (s 103(1)(i)) |
| | | 1 Apr 2014 (otherwise) (SI 2014/416)[6] |
| | (4) | See Sch 4 below |
| 26 | (1) | 25 Apr 2013 (so far as is necessary for enabling the exercise of any power (arising under or by virtue hereof) to make provision by regulations, rules or orders made by statutory instrument) (s 103(1)(i))[3] |
| | | 1 Apr 2014 (otherwise) (SI 2014/416)[6] |
| | (2) | 25 Apr 2013 (so far as is necessary for enabling the exercise of any power (arising under or by virtue hereof) to make provision by regulations, rules or orders made by statutory instrument) (s 103(1)(i)) |
| | | 1 Apr 2014 (otherwise) (SI 2014/416)[6] |
| | (3) | See Sch 5 below |
| | (4) | See Sch 6 below |
| 27 | | 25 Apr 2013 (so far as is necessary for enabling the exercise of any power (arising under or by virtue hereof) to make provision by regulations, rules or orders made by statutory instrument) (s 103(1)(i)) |
| | | 1 Oct 2013 (otherwise) (SI 2013/2227) |
| 28 | | 25 Apr 2013 (s 103(1)(c)) |
| 29 | | 25 Apr 2013 (so far as is necessary for enabling the exercise of any power (arising under or by virtue hereof) to make provision by regulations, rules or orders made by statutory instrument) (s 103(1)(i)) |
| | | 1 Apr 2014 (otherwise) (SI 2014/416)[6] |
| 30 | (1)–(9) | 25 Apr 2013 (so far as is necessary for enabling the exercise of any power (arising under or by virtue hereof) to make provision by regulations, rules or orders made by statutory instrument) (s 103(1)(i)) |
| | | 1 Apr 2014 (otherwise) (SI 2014/416)[6] |
| | (10) | See Sch 7 below |

**Enterprise and Regulatory Reform Act 2013 (c 24)**—*contd*

| | | |
|---|---|---|
| 31 | | 25 Apr 2013 (so far as is necessary for enabling the exercise of any power (arising under or by virtue hereof) to make provision by regulations, rules or orders made by statutory instrument) (s 103(1)(i)) |
| | | 1 Apr 2014 (otherwise) (SI 2014/416)[6] |
| 32 | (1) | 25 Apr 2013 (so far as is necessary for enabling the exercise of any power (arising under or by virtue hereof) to make provision by regulations, rules or orders made by statutory instrument) (s 103(1)(i)) |
| | | 1 Apr 2014 (otherwise) (SI 2014/416)[6] |
| | (2) | See Sch 8 below |
| 33 | | 25 Apr 2013 (so far as is necessary for enabling the exercise of any power (arising under or by virtue hereof) to make provision by regulations, rules or orders made by statutory instrument) (s 103(1)(i)) |
| | | 1 Apr 2014 (otherwise) (SI 2014/416)[6] |
| 34 | (1)–(3) | 25 Apr 2013 (so far as is necessary for enabling the exercise of any power (arising under or by virtue hereof) to make provision by regulations, rules or orders made by statutory instrument) (s 103(1)(i)) |
| | | 1 Apr 2014 (otherwise) (SI 2014/416)[6] |
| | (4) | See Sch 9 below |
| 35 | (1)–(9) | 25 Apr 2013 (so far as is necessary for enabling the exercise of any power (arising under or by virtue hereof) to make provision by regulations, rules or orders made by statutory instrument) (s 103(1)(i)) |
| | | 1 Apr 2014 (otherwise) (SI 2014/416)[6] |
| | (10) | See Sch 10 below |
| 36 | (1)–(7) | 25 Apr 2013 (so far as is necessary for enabling the exercise of any power (arising under or by virtue hereof) to make provision by regulations, rules or orders made by statutory instrument) (s 103(1)(i)) |
| | | 1 Apr 2014 (otherwise) (SI 2014/416)[6] |
| | (8) | See Sch 11 below |
| 37 | | 25 Apr 2013 (so far as is necessary for enabling the exercise of any power (arising under or by virtue hereof) to make provision by regulations, rules or orders made by statutory instrument) (s 103(1)(i)) |
| | | 1 Apr 2014 (otherwise) (SI 2014/416)[6] |
| 38 | | See Sch 12 below |
| 39, 40 | | 25 Apr 2013 (so far as is necessary for enabling the exercise of any power (arising under or by virtue hereof) to make provision by regulations, rules or orders made by statutory instrument) (s 103(1)(i)) |
| | | 1 Apr 2014 (otherwise) (SI 2014/416)[6] |
| 41 | | See Sch 13 below |
| 42–50 | | 25 Apr 2013 (so far as is necessary for enabling the exercise of any power (arising under or by virtue hereof) to make provision by regulations, rules or orders made by statutory instrument) (s 103(1)(i)) |
| | | 1 Apr 2014 (otherwise) (SI 2014/416)[6] |
| 51 | (1)–(4) | 25 Apr 2013 (so far as is necessary for enabling the exercise of any power (arising under or by virtue hereof) to make provision by regulations, rules or orders made by statutory instrument) (s 103(1)(i)) |
| | | 1 Apr 2014 (otherwise) (SI 2014/416)[6] |
| | (5) | See Sch 14 below |
| 52, 53 | | 25 Apr 2013 (s 103(1)(d)) |

**Enterprise and Regulatory Reform Act 2013 (c 24)**—*contd*

| | | |
|---|---|---|
| 54–56 | | 25 Apr 2013 (so far as is necessary for enabling the exercise of any power (arising under or by virtue hereof) to make provision by regulations, rules or orders made by statutory instrument) (s 103(1)(i)) |
| | | 1 Apr 2014 (otherwise) (SI 2014/416)⁶ |
| 57 | | See Sch 15 below |
| 58 | | 25 Apr 2013 (so far as is necessary for enabling the exercise of any power (arising under or by virtue hereof) to make provision by regulations, rules or orders made by statutory instrument) (s 103(1)(i)) |
| | | 1 Apr 2014 (otherwise) (SI 2014/416)⁶ |
| 59 | | 25 Apr 2013 (s 103(1)(e)) |
| 60 | (1)–(4) | 25 Apr 2013 (so far as is necessary for enabling the exercise of any power (arising under or by virtue hereof) to make provision by regulations, rules or orders made by statutory instrument) (s 103(1)(i)) |
| | | 6 Apr 2014 (otherwise) (SI 2014/416) |
| | (5) | See Sch 16 below |
| 61 | | 25 Apr 2013 (so far as is necessary for enabling the exercise of any power (arising under or by virtue hereof) to make provision by regulations, rules or orders made by statutory instrument) (s 103(1)(i)) |
| | | 6 Apr 2014 (otherwise) (SI 2014/416) |
| 62 | | 25 Apr 2013 (so far as is necessary for enabling the exercise of any power (arising under or by virtue hereof) to make provision by regulations, rules or orders made by statutory instrument) (s 103(1)(i)) |
| | | 25 Jun 2013 (otherwise) (s 103(2)(c)) |
| 63 | | See Sch 17 below |
| 64 | | 25 Apr 2013 (so far as is necessary for enabling the exercise of any power (arising under or by virtue hereof) to make provision by regulations, rules or orders made by statutory instrument) (s 103(1)(i)) |
| | | 25 Jun 2013 (otherwise) (s 103(2)(d)) |
| 65 | | 25 Apr 2013 (so far as is necessary for enabling the exercise of any power (arising under or by virtue hereof) to make provision by regulations, rules or orders made by statutory instrument) (s 103(1)(i)) |
| | | 1 Oct 2013 (otherwise) (SI 2013/2227)³ |
| 66 | | 25 Apr 2013 (so far as is necessary for enabling the exercise of any power (arising under or by virtue hereof) to make provision by regulations, rules or orders made by statutory instrument) (s 103(1)(i)) |
| | | 6 Apr 2014 (otherwise) (SI 2014/416) |
| 67 | | 25 Apr 2013 (so far as is necessary for enabling the exercise of any power (arising under or by virtue hereof) to make provision by regulations, rules or orders made by statutory instrument) (s 103(1)(i)) |
| | | 1 Oct 2013 (otherwise) (SI 2013/2227) |
| 68 | (1), (2) | 25 Apr 2013 (so far as is necessary for enabling the exercise of any power (arising under or by virtue hereof) to make provision by regulations, rules or orders made by statutory instrument) (s 103(1)(i)) |
| | | 1 Oct 2013 (otherwise) (SI 2013/2227) |
| | (3)–(6) | 25 Apr 2013 (so far as is necessary for enabling the exercise of any power (arising under or by virtue hereof) to make provision by regulations, rules or orders made by statutory instrument) (s 103(1)(i)) |
| | | 1 Oct 2013 (otherwise) (SI 2013/2227)³ |

**Enterprise and Regulatory Reform Act 2013 (c 24)**—*contd*

| | | |
|---|---|---|
| | (7) | 25 Apr 2013 (so far as is necessary for enabling the exercise of any power (arising under or by virtue hereof) to make provision by regulations, rules or orders made by statutory instrument) (s 103(1)(i)) |
| | | 1 Oct 2013 (otherwise) (SI 2013/2227) |
| | (8), (9) | 25 Apr 2013 (so far as is necessary for enabling the exercise of any power (arising under or by virtue hereof) to make provision by regulations, rules or orders made by statutory instrument) (s 103(1)(i)) |
| | | 1 Oct 2013 (otherwise) (SI 2013/2227)[3] |
| 69, 70 | | 25 Apr 2013 (so far as is necessary for enabling the exercise of any power (arising under or by virtue hereof) to make provision by regulations, rules or orders made by statutory instrument) (s 103(1)(i)) |
| | | 1 Oct 2013 (otherwise) (SI 2013/2227) |
| 71 | (1) | 25 Apr 2013 (so far as is necessary for enabling the exercise of any power (arising under or by virtue hereof) to make provision by regulations, rules or orders made by statutory instrument) (s 103(1)(i)) |
| | | 6 Apr 2016 (otherwise) (SI 2016/191)[7] |
| | (2) | See Sch 18 below |
| | (3) | See Sch 19 below |
| 72 | (1) | 25 Apr 2013 (so far as is necessary for enabling the exercise of any power (arising under or by virtue hereof) to make provision by regulations, rules or orders made by statutory instrument) (s 103(1)(i)) |
| | | 25 Jun 2013 (otherwise) (SI 2013/1455) |
| | (2), (3) | 25 Apr 2013 (so far as is necessary for enabling the exercise of any power (arising under or by virtue hereof) to make provision by regulations, rules or orders made by statutory instrument) (s 103(1)(i)) |
| | | 16 Dec 2013 (otherwise) (SI 2013/2979) |
| | (4) | See Sch 20 below |
| 73 | | See Sch 21 below |
| 74 | | 25 Apr 2013 (so far as is necessary for enabling the exercise of any power (arising under or by virtue hereof) to make provision by regulations, rules or orders made by statutory instrument) (s 103(1)(i)) |
| | | 28 Jul 2016 (otherwise) (SI 2016/593)[8] |
| 75–78 | | 25 Apr 2013 (s 103(1)(f)) |
| 79–82 | | 25 Apr 2013 (so far as is necessary for enabling the exercise of any power (arising under or by virtue hereof) to make provision by regulations, rules or orders made by statutory instrument) (s 103(1)(i)) |
| | | 1 Oct 2013 (otherwise) (SI 2013/2227) |
| 83–89 | | 25 Apr 2013 (so far as is necessary for enabling the exercise of any power (arising under or by virtue hereof) to make provision by regulations, rules or orders made by statutory instrument) (s 103(1)(i)) |
| | | *Not yet in force* (otherwise) |
| 90 | (1)–(6) | 25 Apr 2013 (so far as is necessary for enabling the exercise of any power (arising under or by virtue hereof) to make provision by regulations, rules or orders made by statutory instrument) (s 103(1)(i)) |
| | | *Not yet in force* (otherwise) |
| | (7) | 25 Apr 2013 (so far as is necessary for enabling the exercise of any power (arising under or by virtue hereof) to make provision by regulations, rules or orders made by statutory instrument) (s 103(1)(i)) |
| | | 1 Oct 2013 (otherwise) (SI 2013/2227) |

**Enterprise and Regulatory Reform Act 2013 (c 24)**—*contd*

|  |  |  |
|---|---|---|
| (8) | | 25 Apr 2013 (so far as is necessary for enabling the exercise of any power (arising under or by virtue hereof) to make provision by regulations, rules or orders made by statutory instrument) (s 103(1)(i))<br>*Not yet in force* (otherwise) |
| 91 | | 25 Apr 2013 (so far as is necessary for enabling the exercise of any power (arising under or by virtue hereof) to make provision by regulations, rules or orders made by statutory instrument) (s 103(1)(i))<br>*Not yet in force* (otherwise) |
| 92–96 | | 25 Apr 2013 (s 103(1)(g)) |
| 97 | | 25 Apr 2013 (so far as is necessary for enabling the exercise of any power (arising under or by virtue hereof) to make provision by regulations, rules or orders made by statutory instrument) (s 103(1)(i))<br>25 Jun 2013 (otherwise) (s 103(2)(e)) |
| 98–104 | | 25 Apr 2013 (s 103(1)(h)) |
| Sch 1 | para 1 | 25 Apr 2013 (so far as is necessary for enabling the exercise of any power (arising under or by virtue hereof) to make provision by regulations, rules or orders made by statutory instrument) (s 103(1)(i))<br>6 Apr 2014 (otherwise) (SI 2014/253)[5] |
| | paras 2, 3 | 25 Apr 2013 (so far as is necessary for enabling the exercise of any power (arising under or by virtue hereof) to make provision by regulations, rules or orders made by statutory instrument) (s 103(1)(i))<br>6 Mar 2014 (otherwise) (SI 2014/253) |
| | paras 4–13 | 25 Apr 2013 (so far as is necessary for enabling the exercise of any power (arising under or by virtue hereof) to make provision by regulations, rules or orders made by statutory instrument) (s 103(1)(i))<br>6 Apr 2014 (otherwise) (SI 2014/253)[5] |
| Schs 2, 3 | | 25 Apr 2013 (so far as is necessary for enabling the exercise of any power (arising under or by virtue hereof) to make provision by regulations, rules or orders made by statutory instrument) (s 103(1)(i))<br>6 Apr 2014 (otherwise) (SI 2014/253) |
| Sch 4 | para 1(1)(a) | 25 Apr 2013 (so far as is necessary for enabling the exercise of any power (arising under or by virtue hereof) to make provision by regulations, rules or orders made by statutory instrument) (s 103(1)(i))<br>1 Oct 2013 (otherwise) (SI 2013/2227) |
| | para 1(1)(b) | 25 Apr 2013 (so far as is necessary for enabling the exercise of any power (arising under or by virtue hereof) to make provision by regulations, rules or orders made by statutory instrument) (s 103(1)(i))<br>1 Oct 2013 (otherwise) (SI 2013/2227)[3] |
| | para 1(2)–(7) | 25 Apr 2013 (so far as is necessary for enabling the exercise of any power (arising under or by virtue hereof) to make provision by regulations, rules or orders made by statutory instrument) (s 103(1)(i))<br>1 Oct 2013 (otherwise) (SI 2013/2227) |
| | paras 2–18 | 25 Apr 2013 (so far as is necessary for enabling the exercise of any power (arising under or by virtue hereof) to make provision by regulations, rules or orders made by statutory instrument) (s 103(1)(i))<br>1 Oct 2013 (otherwise) (SI 2013/2227) |
| | para 19 | 25 Apr 2013 (so far as is necessary for enabling the exercise of any power (arising under or by virtue hereof) to make provision by regulations, rules or orders made by statutory instrument) (s 103(1)(i)) |

**Enterprise and Regulatory Reform Act 2013 (c 24)**—*contd*

1 Apr 2014 (otherwise) (SI 2014/416)[6]

paras 20–28     25 Apr 2013 (so far as is necessary for enabling the exercise of any power (arising under or by virtue hereof) to make provision by regulations, rules or orders made by statutory instrument) (s 103(1)(i))

1 Oct 2013 (otherwise) (SI 2013/2227)

para 29(1)      25 Apr 2013 (so far as is necessary for enabling the exercise of any power (arising under or by virtue hereof) to make provision by regulations, rules or orders made by statutory instrument) (s 103(1)(i))

1 Oct 2013 (otherwise) (SI 2013/2227)

para 29(2), (3)   25 Apr 2013 (so far as is necessary for enabling the exercise of any power (arising under or by virtue hereof) to make provision by regulations, rules or orders made by statutory instrument) (s 103(1)(i))

1 Apr 2014 (otherwise) (SI 2014/416)[6]

para 30         25 Apr 2013 (so far as is necessary for enabling the exercise of any power (arising under or by virtue hereof) to make provision by regulations, rules or orders made by statutory instrument) (s 103(1)(i))

1 Apr 2014 (otherwise) (SI 2014/416)[6]

paras 31, 32    25 Apr 2013 (so far as is necessary for enabling the exercise of any power (arising under or by virtue hereof) to make provision by regulations, rules or orders made by statutory instrument) (s 103(1)(i))

1 Oct 2013 (otherwise) (SI 2013/2227)

para 33         25 Apr 2013 (so far as is necessary for enabling the exercise of any power (arising under or by virtue hereof) to make provision by regulations, rules or orders made by statutory instrument) (s 103(1)(i))

1 Apr 2014 (otherwise) (SI 2014/416)[6]

paras 34, 35    25 Apr 2013 (so far as is necessary for enabling the exercise of any power (arising under or by virtue hereof) to make provision by regulations, rules or orders made by statutory instrument) (s 103(1)(i))

1 Oct 2013 (otherwise) (SI 2013/2227)

paras 36–50     25 Apr 2013 (so far as is necessary for enabling the exercise of any power (arising under or by virtue hereof) to make provision by regulations, rules or orders made by statutory instrument) (s 103(1)(i))

1 Apr 2014 (otherwise) (SI 2014/416)[6]

para 51         1 Oct 2013 (for the purposes of making and publishing rules of procedure) (SI 2013/2227)

1 Apr 2014 (otherwise) (SI 2014/416)[6]

para 52         1 Oct 2013 (for the purposes of preparing and issuing guidance) (SI 2013/2227)

1 Apr 2014 (otherwise) (SI 2014/416)[6]

para 53         1 Oct 2013 (for the purposes of making and publishing rules of procedure) (SI 2013/2227)

1 Apr 2014 (otherwise) (SI 2014/416)[6]

paras 54–58     25 Apr 2013 (so far as is necessary for enabling the exercise of any power (arising under or by virtue hereof) to make provision by regulations, rules or orders made by statutory instrument) (s 103(1)(i))

1 Apr 2014 (otherwise) (SI 2014/416)[6]

paras 59, 60    25 Apr 2013 (so far as is necessary for enabling the exercise of any power (arising under or by virtue hereof) to make provision by regulations, rules or orders made by statutory instrument) (s 103(1)(i))

1 Oct 2013 (otherwise) (SI 2013/2227)

**Enterprise and Regulatory Reform Act 2013 (c 24)**—*contd*

| | | |
|---|---|---|
| | para 61(1)–(4) | 25 Apr 2013 (so far as is necessary for enabling the exercise of any power (arising under or by virtue hereof) to make provision by regulations, rules or orders made by statutory instrument) (s 103(1)(i)) |
| | | 1 Oct 2013 (otherwise) (SI 2013/2227) |
| | para 61(5) | 25 Apr 2013 (so far as is necessary for enabling the exercise of any power (arising under or by virtue hereof) to make provision by regulations, rules or orders made by statutory instrument) (s 103(1)(i)) |
| | | 1 Apr 2014 (otherwise) (SI 2014/416)[6] |
| | paras 62–65 | 25 Apr 2013 (so far as is necessary for enabling the exercise of any power (arising under or by virtue hereof) to make provision by regulations, rules or orders made by statutory instrument) (s 103(1)(i)) |
| | | 1 Oct 2013 (otherwise) (SI 2013/2227) |
| Schs 5–13 | | 25 Apr 2013 (so far as is necessary for enabling the exercise of any power (arising under or by virtue hereof) to make provision by regulations, rules or orders made by statutory instrument) (s 103(1)(i)) |
| | | 1 Apr 2014 (otherwise) (SI 2014/416)[6] |
| Sch 14 | paras 1–19 | 25 Apr 2013 (so far as is necessary for enabling the exercise of any power (arising under or by virtue hereof) to make provision by regulations, rules or orders made by statutory instrument) (s 103(1)(i)) |
| | | 1 Apr 2014 (otherwise) (SI 2014/416)[6] |
| | paras 20–22 | 25 Apr 2013 (so far as is necessary for enabling the exercise of any power (arising under or by virtue hereof) to make provision by regulations, rules or orders made by statutory instrument) (s 103(1)(i)) |
| | | *Not yet in force* (otherwise) |
| | paras 23–29 | 25 Apr 2013 (so far as is necessary for enabling the exercise of any power (arising under or by virtue hereof) to make provision by regulations, rules or orders made by statutory instrument) (s 103(1)(i)) |
| | | 1 Apr 2014 (otherwise) (SI 2014/416) |
| Sch 15 | | 25 Apr 2013 (so far as is necessary for enabling the exercise of any power (arising under or by virtue hereof) to make provision by regulations, rules or orders made by statutory instrument) (s 103(1)(i)) |
| | | 1 Apr 2014 (otherwise) (SI 2014/416)[6] |
| Sch 16 | | 25 Apr 2013 (so far as is necessary for enabling the exercise of any power (arising under or by virtue hereof) to make provision by regulations, rules or orders made by statutory instrument) (s 103(1)(i)) |
| | | 6 Apr 2014 (otherwise) (SI 2014/416) |
| Sch 17 | paras 1–6 | 25 Apr 2013 (so far as is necessary for enabling the exercise of any power (arising under or by virtue hereof) to make provision by regulations, rules or orders made by statutory instrument) (s 103(1)(i)) |
| | | 1 Oct 2013 (otherwise) (SI 2013/2227) |
| | paras 7, 8 | 25 Apr 2013 (so far as is necessary for enabling the exercise of any power (arising under or by virtue hereof) to make provision by regulations, rules or orders made by statutory instrument) (s 103(1)(i)) |
| | | 25 Jun 2013 (otherwise) (s 103(2)(f)) |
| | para 9 | 25 Apr 2013 (so far as is necessary for enabling the exercise of any power (arising under or by virtue hereof) to make provision by regulations, rules or orders made by statutory instrument) (s 103(1)(i)) |
| | | 25 Jun 2013 (otherwise) (SI 2013/1455) |

**Enterprise and Regulatory Reform Act 2013 (c 24)**—*contd*

|  |  |  |
|---|---|---|
| | para 10 | 25 Apr 2013 (so far as is necessary for enabling the exercise of any power (arising under or by virtue hereof) to make provision by regulations, rules or orders made by statutory instrument) (s 103(1)(i)) |
| | | 1 Oct 2013 (otherwise) (SI 2013/2227) |
| | para 11 | 25 Apr 2013 (so far as is necessary for enabling the exercise of any power (arising under or by virtue hereof) to make provision by regulations, rules or orders made by statutory instrument) (s 103(1)(i)) |
| | | 6 Apr 2014 (otherwise) (SI 2014/416) |
| | paras 12, 13 | 25 Apr 2013 (so far as is necessary for enabling the exercise of any power (arising under or by virtue hereof) to make provision by regulations, rules or orders made by statutory instrument) (s 103(1)(i)) |
| | | 1 Oct 2013 (otherwise) (SI 2013/2227) |
| | paras 14–19 | 25 Apr 2013 (so far as is necessary for enabling the exercise of any power (arising under or by virtue hereof) to make provision by regulations, rules or orders made by statutory instrument) (s 103(1)(i)) |
| | | 6 Apr 2014 (otherwise) (SI 2014/416) |
| | para 20 | 25 Apr 2013 (so far as is necessary for enabling the exercise of any power (arising under or by virtue hereof) to make provision by regulations, rules or orders made by statutory instrument) (s 103(1)(i)) |
| | | 25 Jun 2013 (otherwise) (SI 2013/1455) |
| Schs 18, 19 | | 25 Apr 2013 (so far as is necessary for enabling the exercise of any power (arising under or by virtue hereof) to make provision by regulations, rules or orders made by statutory instrument) (s 103(1)(i)) |
| | | 6 Apr 2016 (otherwise) (SI 2016/191)[7] |
| Sch 20 | para 1 | 25 Apr 2013 (so far as is necessary for enabling the exercise of any power (arising under or by virtue hereof) to make provision by regulations, rules or orders made by statutory instrument) (s 103(1)(i)) |
| | | 1 Oct 2013 (otherwise) (SI 2013/1455)[1] |
| | para 2 | 25 Apr 2013 (so far as is necessary for enabling the exercise of any power (arising under or by virtue hereof) to make provision by regulations, rules or orders made by statutory instrument) (s 103(1)(i)) |

25 Jun 2013 (SI 2013/1455)[1], repeals of or in—
Agricultural Wages Act 1948, ss 1, 2(4), 3, 6(8), 7(1), 16, Sch 1, paras 1–7, Sch 4;
Public Records Act 1958;
Agriculture Act 1967;
Parliamentary Commissioner Act 1967;
Employment Protection Act 1975, s 97(1), Sch 9, Pt 1, Pt 2, para 6, Sch 17, para 12;
House of Commons Disqualification Act 1975;
Northern Ireland Assembly Disqualification Act 1975;
Social Security (Consequential Provisions) Act 1975;
Social Security Pensions Act 1975;
Agriculture (Miscellaneous Provisions) Act 1976;
Social Security (Consequential Provisions) Act 1992;
National Minimum Wage Act 1998, Sch 2, para 2;
Freedom of Information Act 2000;
Public Contracts Regulations 2006 (SI 2006/5)
1 Oct 2013 (E) (SI 2013/1455)[1], repeals of or in—
Agricultural Wages Act 1948, ss 3A, 4, 6(1)–(7), 7(3), 8, 9(1), 10–12, 15A, 17(1), (1A), 17A;
Agriculture (Miscellaneous Provisions) Act 1968;

**Enterprise and Regulatory Reform Act 2013 (c 24)**—*contd*

Employment Protection Act 1975 (so far as not already repealed);

Employment Rights Act 1996;

National Minimum Wage Act 1998 (so far as not already repealed);

National Minimum Wage Regulations 1999 (SI 1999/584);

Criminal Justice Act 2003;

Employment Relations Act 2004;

Employment Act 2008

16 Dec 2013 (E) (SI 2013/2979), repeals of or in—

Agricultural Wages Act 1948, ss 2(1), 9(2), 15[4];

Agricultural Wages Committees Regulations 1949, reg 16 (SI 1949/1885);

Agricultural Wages Committees (Wages Structure) Regulations 1971 (SI 1971/844);

16 Dec 2013 (SI 2013/2979), repeals of or in—

Agricultural Wages Act 1948, ss 2(1), 18, 19, Sch 2 (in so far as relates to counties in England);

Agricultural Wages Committees Regulations 1949, reg 3 (SI 1949/1885);

Agricultural Wages Committees (Areas) Order 1974 (SI 1974/515);

Agricultural Wages Committees (New Combinations of Counties) Order (SI 1981/179);

Agricultural Wages Committee (Cleveland, Durham, Northumberland and Tyne andWear) Order 1989 (SI 1989/1173);

Agricultural Wages Committees (Areas) (England) Order 1995 (SI 1995/3186)

31 Mar 2014 (E) (SI 2013/2979), repeals of or in—

Agricultural Wages Act 1948, Sch 1

15 Sep 2014 (SI 2014/2481), repeals of or in—

Public Contracts (Scotland) Regulations 2012 (SSI 2012/88)

31 Dec 2014 (E) (SI 2013/2979), repeals of or in—

Agricultural Wages Act 1948, ss 13, 14

*Not yet in force* (otherwise)

| | | |
|---|---|---|
| Sch 21 | Pts 1, 2 | 25 Apr 2013 (so far as is necessary for enabling the exercise of any power (arising under or by virtue hereof) to make provision by regulations, rules or orders made by statutory instrument) (s 103(1)(i)) |
| | | 25 Jun 2013 (otherwise) (s 103(2)(g)) |
| | Pt 3 | 25 Apr 2013 (so far as is necessary for enabling the exercise of any power (arising under or by virtue hereof) to make provision by regulations, rules or orders made by statutory instrument) (s 103(1)(i)) |
| | | 1 Oct 2013 (otherwise) (SI 2013/2227)[3] |
| Sch 22 | | 25 Apr 2013 (s 103(1)(f)) |

[1]    For transitional and savings provisions, see SI 2013/1455, art 4, Sch 3, as amended by SI 2013/2271, art 2(b)–(d)

[2]    SI 2013/1648, art 2(b) also purports to bring s 15(10) into force on 29 Jul 2013

[3]    For transitional and savings provisions, see SI 2013/2227, arts 3–6

[4]    For a saving provision, see SI 2013/2979, art 4

[5]    For transitional and saving provisions, see SI 2014/253, art 4

[6]    For transitional and saving provisions, see SI 2014/416, art 2(2), Schedule

[7]    For saving provisions, see SI 2016/191, arts 3, 4

**Enterprise and Regulatory Reform Act 2013 (c 24)**—*contd*
8    For saving provisions, see SI 2016/593, arts 4, 5

---

**European Union (Approvals) Act 2013 (c 9)**

*RA:* 28 Feb 2013

*Commencement provisions:* s 3(2)

Whole Act in force 28 Feb 2013 (s 3(2))

---

**European Union (Croatian Accession and Irish Protocol) Act 2013 (c 5)**

*RA:* 31 Jan 2013

Whole Act in force 31 Jan 2013 (s 6(2))

---

**Finance Act 2013 (c 29)**

*Budget Day:* 20 Mar 2013

*RA:* 17 Jul 2013

The commencement details of Finance Acts are not set out, as the dates from which their provisions take effect are usually stated clearly and unambiguously in the text of the Act, and charging provisions will normally state for which year or years of assessment they are to have effect.

---

**Financial Services (Banking Reform) Act 2013 (c 33)**

*RA:* 18 Dec 2013

*Commencement provisions:* s 148(1)–(6); Financial Services (Banking Reform) Act 2013 (Commencement No 1) Order 2014, SI 2014/377; Financial Services (Banking Reform) Act 2013 (Commencement No 2) Order 2014, SI 2014/772; Financial Services (Banking Reform) Act 2013 (Commencement No 3) Order 2014, SI 2014/785; Financial Services (Banking Reform) Act 2013 (Commencement No 4) Order 2014, SI 2014/823; Financial Services (Banking Reform) Act 2013 (Commencement No 5) Order 2014, SI 2014/1819; Financial Services (Banking Reform) Act 2013 (Commencement No 6) Order 2014, SI 2014/2458; Financial Services (Banking Reform) Act 2013 (Commencement No 7) Order 2014, SI 2014/3160; Financial Services (Banking Reform) Act 2013 (Commencement (No 8) and Consequential Provisions) Order 2015, SI 2015/428; Financial Services (Banking Reform) Act 2013 (Commencement No 9) Order 2015, SI 2015/490, as amended by SI 2015/2055; Financial Services (Banking Reform) Act 2013 (Commencement No 9) (Amendment) Order 2015, SI 2015/2055; Financial Services (Banking Reform) Act 2013 (Commencement No 10) Order 2016, SI 2016/512; Financial Services (Banking Reform) Act 2013 (Commencement No 11) Order 2016, SI 2016/568; Financial Services (Banking Reform) Act 2013 (Commencement No 1) (England and Wales) Order 2018, SI 2018/848; Financial Services (Banking Reform) Act 2013 (Commencement No 12) Order 2018, SI 2018/1306

| | | |
|---|---|---|
| 1–3 | | 1 Jan 2019 (SI 2018/1306) |
| 4 | (1) | 1 Mar 2014 (in so far as inserts Financial Services and Markets Act 2000, ss 142A–142F, 142I, 142W–142Z, 142Z1 for the purpose of making orders and regulations) (SI 2014/377) |
| | | 21 Apr 2016 (in so far as inserts Financial Services and Markets Act 2000, s 142H) (SI 2016/512) |
| | | 1 Jan 2019 (in so far as inserts ss 142A–142F, 142I, 142W–142Z, 142Z1 of the 2000 Act for remaining purposes and in so far as inserts ss 142G, 142J–142V of that Act) (SI 2018/1306) |
| | (2)–(7) | 1 Jan 2019 (SI 2018/1306) |
| 5 | | 1 Jan 2019 (SI 2018/1306) |
| 6 | | See Sch 1 below |
| 7–12 | | 1 Jan 2019 (SI 2018/1306) |

**Financial Services (Banking Reform) Act 2013 (c 33)**—*contd*

| | | |
|---|---|---|
| 13 | | 31 Dec 2014 (SI 2014/3160) |
| 14, 15 | | 1 Mar 2014 (SI 2014/377) |
| 16 | | 1 Apr 2014 (SI 2014/377) |
| 17 | (1) | See Sch 2 below |
| | (2)–(5) | 1 Mar 2014 (SI 2014/377) |
| 18 | | 25 Jul 2014 (for the purpose of making rules) (SI 2014/1819) |
| | | 7 Mar 2016 (otherwise) (SI 2015/490) |
| 19 | | 25 Jul 2014 (SI 2014/1819) |
| 20 | | 25 Jul 2014 (for the purpose of giving directions or imposing requirements) (SI 2014/1819) |
| | | 7 Mar 2016 (otherwise) (SI 2015/490) |
| 21–26 | | 7 Mar 2016 (SI 2015/490) |
| 27, 28 | | 25 Jul 2014 (SI 2014/1819) |
| 29 | | 25 Jul 2014 (for the purpose of making rules) (SI 2014/1819) |
| | | 7 Mar 2016 (for the purpose of inserting Financial Services and Markets Act 2000, s 63F) (SI 2015/490) |
| | | 7 Mar 2017 (otherwise) (SI 2015/490) |
| 30 | (1), (2) | 25 Jul 2014 (for the purpose of making rules) (SI 2014/1819) |
| | | 7 Mar 2016 (otherwise) (SI 2015/490) |
| | (3) | 25 Jul 2014 (for the purpose of making rules) (SI 2014/1819) |
| | | 7 Mar 2016 (so far as inserts Financial Services and Markets Act 2000, ss 64A, 64B(1)–(4), (6), (7)) (SI 2015/490)[1] |
| | | *Not yet in force* (otherwise) |
| 31 | | 25 Jul 2014 (for the purpose of making rules) (SI 2014/1819) |
| | | 7 Mar 2016 (otherwise) (SI 2015/490) |
| 32 | (1) | 7 Mar 2016 (SI 2015/490) |
| | (2) | 7 Mar 2016 (so far as inserts Financial Services and Markets Act 2000, ss 66A(1), 66B(1) so far as they apply to Conditions A and B; ss 66A(2)–(4), (8), (9), 66B(2)–(4), (8), (9)) (SI 2015/490)[1] |
| | | 10 May 2016 (otherwise) (SI 2016/568) |
| 33 | | 25 Jul 2014 (SI 2014/1819) |
| 34 | | 7 Mar 2016 (SI 2015/490) |
| 35 | | See Sch 3 below |
| 36–38 | | 7 Mar 2016 (SI 2015/490) |
| 39 | | 1 Mar 2014 (SI 2014/377) |
| 40 | (1)–(4) | 1 Mar 2014 (SI 2014/377) |
| | (5) | See Sch 4 below |
| 41–58 | | 1 Mar 2014 (SI 2014/377) |
| 59 | | 1 Apr 2014 (SI 2014/823) |
| 60 | (1)–(3) | 1 Apr 2014 (SI 2014/823) |
| | (4)–(6) | 1 Apr 2015 (SI 2014/2458) |
| | (7) | 1 Apr 2014 (SI 2014/823) |
| 61 | | 1 Nov 2014 (for the purpose of enabling the Payment Systems Regulator to carry out functions under the Competition Act 1998, s 52) (SI 2014/2458) |
| | | 1 Apr 2015 (otherwise) (SI 2014/2458) |
| 62 | | 1 Apr 2015 (SI 2014/2458) |
| 63–66 | | 1 Apr 2014 (SI 2014/823) |
| 67 | (1) | 1 Apr 2015 (SI 2014/2458) |
| | (2) | 1 Nov 2014 (for the purpose of enabling the Payment Systems Regulator to carry out functions under the Competition Act 1998, s 52) (SI 2014/2458) |
| | | 1 Apr 2015 (otherwise) (SI 2014/2458) |
| | (3)–(5) | 1 Apr 2014 (SI 2014/823) |
| 68–78 | | 1 Mar 2014 (SI 2014/377) |
| 79 | (1)–(7) | 1 Mar 2014 (SI 2014/377) |
| | (8) | See Sch 5 below |
| 80–110 | | 1 Mar 2014 (SI 2014/377) |

**Financial Services (Banking Reform) Act 2013 (c 33)**—*contd*

| | | |
|---|---|---|
| 111–120 | | 13 Jul 2018 (E) (W) (SI 2018/848) |
| | | *Not yet in force* (S) (NI) |
| 121 | (1) | See Sch 6 below |
| | (2) | See Sch 7 below |
| | (3) | 1 Mar 2014 (for the purpose of making rules) (SI 2014/377) |
| | | 13 Jul 2018 (otherwise) (E) (W) (SI 2018/848) |
| | | *Not yet in force* (otherwise) (S) (NI) |
| 122–128 | | 13 Jul 2018 (E) (W) (SI 2018/848) |
| | | *Not yet in force* (S) (NI) |
| 129 | | See Sch 8 below |
| 130 | | 1 Mar 2014 (SI 2014/377) |
| 131 | | 18 Feb 2014 (s 148(2)) |
| 132 | | 1 Mar 2014 (SI 2014/377) |
| 133 | (1) | 31 Dec 2014 (in so far as inserts Financial Services and Markets Act 2000, s 192JB) (SI 2014/3160) |
| | | 21 Apr 2016 (in so far as inserts Financial Services and Markets Act 2000, s 192JA) (SI 2016/512) |
| | | 1 Jan 2019 (otherwise) (SI 2018/1306) |
| | (2)(a) | 31 Dec 2014 (SI 2014/3160) |
| | (2)(b) | 1 Jan 2019 (SI 2018/1306) |
| 134–137 | | 1 Mar 2014 (SI 2014/377) |
| 138 | | See Sch 9 below |
| 139 | | 21 Mar 2014 (SI 2014/772) |
| 140 | (1)–(3) | 21 Mar 2014 (SI 2014/772) |
| | (4)–(6) | 21 Mar 2014 (SI 2014/785) |
| 141 | | See Sch 10 below |
| 142–148 | | 18 Dec 2013 (s 148(1)) |
| Sch 1 | | 1 Mar 2014 (SI 2014/377) |
| Sch 2 | paras 1–3 | 31 Dec 2014 (SI 2014/3160) |
| | para 4 | 1 Mar 2014 (in so far as inserts Banking Act 2009, s 48P for the purpose of making orders) (SI 2014/377) |
| | | 31 Dec 2014 (in so far as inserts s 48P of the 2009 Act for remaining purposes and in so far as inserts ss 48B–48O, 48Q–48W of that Act) (SI 2014/3160) |
| | para 5 | 31 Dec 2014 (SI 2014/3160) |
| | para 6(1)–(7) | 31 Dec 2014 (SI 2014/3160) |
| | para 6(8) | 1 Mar 2014 (so far as inserts Banking Act 2009, ss 60A and 60B for the purpose of making regulations) (SI 2014/377) |
| | | 31 Dec 2014 (otherwise) (SI 2014/3160) |
| | para 6(9), (10) | 31 Dec 2014 (SI 2014/3160) |
| | paras 7–33 | 31 Dec 2014 (SI 2014/3160) |
| Sch 3 | para 1 | 7 Mar 2016 (SI 2015/490) |
| | para 2 | 25 Jul 2014 (in so far as relates to the making of rules) (SI 2014/1819) |
| | | 7 Mar 2016 (otherwise) (SI 2015/490) |
| | paras 3–6 | 7 Mar 2016 (SI 2015/490) |
| | paras 7–9 | 25 Jul 2014 (SI 2014/1819) |
| | paras 10–15, 16(a) | 7 Mar 2016 (SI 2015/490) |
| | para 16(b)(i) | 25 Jul 2014 (SI 2014/1819) |
| | paras 16(b)(ii), 17(a) | 7 Mar 2016 (SI 2015/490) |
| | para 17(b)(i) | 25 Jul 2014 (SI 2014/1819) |
| | paras 17(b)(ii), 18, 19(1), (2)(a) | 7 Mar 2016 (SI 2015/490) |
| | para 19(2)(b)(i) | 25 Jul 2014 (SI 2014/1819) |
| | para 19(2)(b)(ii), (3)(a) | 7 Mar 2016 (SI 2015/490) |
| | para 19(3)(b)(i) | 25 Jul 2014 (SI 2014/1819) |
| | para 19(3)(b)(ii) | 7 Mar 2016 (SI 2015/490) |

## Financial Services (Banking Reform) Act 2013 (c 33)—*contd*

| | | |
|---|---|---|
| Schs 4, 5 | | 1 Mar 2014 (SI 2014/377) |
| Sch 6 | paras 1–5 | 13 Jul 2018 (E) (W) (SI 2018/848) |
| | | *Not yet in force* (S) (NI) |
| | para 6 | 1 Mar 2014 (for the purpose of making orders) (SI 2014/377) |
| | | 13 Jul 2018 (otherwise) (E) (W) (SI 2018/848) |
| | | *Not yet in force* (otherwise) (S) (NI) |
| Sch 7 | | 13 Jul 2018 (E) (W) (SI 2018/848) |
| | | *Not yet in force* (S) (NI) |
| Sch 8 | paras 1, 2 | 1 Apr 2015 (SI 2014/2458) |
| | para 3 | 1 Nov 2014 (so far as inserts Financial Services Act 2000, 243J, 234M, for the purpose of enabling the Financial Conduct Authority to carry out functions under the Competition Act 1998, s 52, and ss 243N, 234O of the 2000 Act) (SI 2014/2458) |
| | | 1 Apr 2015 (otherwise) (SI 2014/2458) |
| | paras 4, 5 | 1 Nov 2014 (SI 2014/2458) |
| | para 6 | 1 Apr 2015 (SI 2014/2458) |
| | para 7 | 1 Nov 2014 (SI 2014/2458) |
| | para 8 | 1 Apr 2015 (SI 2014/2458) |
| | para 9 | 1 Nov 2014 (for the purpose of enabling the Financial Conduct Authority to carry out functions under the Competition Act 1998, s 52) (SI 2014/2458) |
| | | 1 Apr 2015 (otherwise) (SI 2014/2458) |
| | paras 10–12 | 1 Apr 2015 (SI 2014/2458) |
| Sch 9 | paras 1–3 | 18 Feb 2014 (s 148(2)) |
| | para 4 | 26 Mar 2015 (SI 2015/428) |
| | paras 5–18 | 18 Feb 2014 (s 148(2)) |
| Sch 10 | paras 1, 2 | 1 Mar 2014 (SI 2014/377) |
| | para 3 | 1 Apr 2014 (SI 2014/377) |
| | paras 4–9 | 1 Mar 2014 (SI 2014/377) |
| | para 10 | 1 Mar 2014 (for the purpose of making orders) (SI 2014/377) |
| | | 1 Jun 2014 (otherwise) (SI 2014/377) |

[1]   As amended by SI 2015/2055, art 2

## Food Hygiene Rating (Wales) Act 2013 (anaw 2)

*RA*: 4 Mar 2013

*Commencement provisions*: s 27; Food Hygiene Rating (Wales) Act 2013 (Commencement No 1) Order 2013, SI 2013/2617; Food Hygiene Rating (Wales) Act 2013 (Commencement No 2) Order 2014, SI 2014/3089

| | | |
|---|---|---|
| 1 | | 28 Nov 2013 (SI 2013/2617) |
| 2 | (1)–(4), (5)(a) | 28 Nov 2013 (SI 2013/2617) |
| | (5)(b) | 28 Nov 2014 (SI 2014/3089) |
| | (6) | 28 Nov 2013 (SI 2013/2617) |
| 3 | (1) | 28 Nov 2013 (SI 2013/2617) |
| | (2) | 28 Oct 2013 (for the purpose of making regulations) (SI 2013/2617) |
| | | 28 Nov 2013 (for remaining purposes) (SI 2013/2617) |
| | (3)(a), (b) | 28 Nov 2013 (SI 2013/2617) |
| | (3)(c), (d) | 28 Oct 2013 (for the purpose of making regulations) (SI 2013/2617) |
| | | 28 Nov 2013 (for remaining purposes) (SI 2013/2617) |
| | (4) | 28 Nov 2013 (SI 2013/2617) |
| | (5) | 28 Oct 2013 (for the purpose of making regulations) (SI 2013/2617) |
| | | 28 Nov 2013 (for remaining purposes) (SI 2013/2617) |

**Food Hygiene Rating (Wales) Act 2013 (anaw 2)**—*contd*

| | | |
|---|---|---|
| 4 | | 28 Nov 2013 (SI 2013/2617) |
| 5 | (1)–(3) | 28 Nov 2013 (SI 2013/2617) |
| | (4) | 28 Oct 2013 (for the purpose of making regulations) (SI 2013/2617) |
| | | 28 Nov 2013 (for remaining purposes) (SI 2013/2617) |
| | (5)–(9), (10)(a)–(c) | 28 Nov 2013 (SI 2013/2617) |
| | (10)(d) | 28 Oct 2013 (for the purpose of making regulations) (SI 2013/2617) |
| | | 28 Nov 2013 (for remaining purposes) (SI 2013/2617) |
| | (11), (12) | 28 Nov 2013 (SI 2013/2617) |
| 6 | (1) | 28 Nov 2013 (SI 2013/2617) |
| | (2), (3) | 28 Oct 2013 (for the purpose of making regulations) (SI 2013/2617) |
| | | 28 Nov 2013 (for remaining purposes) (SI 2013/2617) |
| | (4) | 28 Nov 2013 (SI 2013/2617) |
| 7 | (1), (2) | 28 Nov 2013 (SI 2013/2617) |
| | (3), (4) | 28 Oct 2013 (for the purpose of making regulations) (SI 2013/2617) |
| | | 28 Nov 2013 (for remaining purposes) (SI 2013/2617) |
| | (5), (6) | 28 Nov 2013 (SI 2013/2617) |
| 8–11 | | 28 Nov 2013 (SI 2013/2617) |
| 12 | (1) | 28 Nov 2013 (SI 2013/2617) |
| | (2) | 28 Oct 2013 (for the purpose of making regulations) (SI 2013/2617) |
| | | 28 Nov 2013 (for remaining purposes) (SI 2013/2617) |
| | (3)–(8), (9)(a)–(c) | 28 Nov 2013 (SI 2013/2617) |
| | (9)(d) | 28 Oct 2013 (for the purpose of making regulations) (SI 2013/2617) |
| | | 28 Nov 2013 (for remaining purposes) (SI 2013/2617) |
| | (10), (11) | 28 Nov 2013 (SI 2013/2617) |
| 13, 14 | | 28 Nov 2013 (SI 2013/2617) |
| 15 | (1) | 28 Oct 2013 (for the purpose of making regulations) (SI 2013/2617) |
| | | 28 Nov 2013 (for remaining purposes) (SI 2013/2617) |
| | (2)–(5) | 28 Nov 2013 (SI 2013/2617) |
| 16–20 | | 28 Nov 2013 (SI 2013/2617) |
| 21 | (1), (2) | 28 Nov 2013 (SI 2013/2617) |
| | (3) | See Schedule below |
| 22–26 | | 28 Nov 2013 (SI 2013/2617) |
| 27 | | 4 May 2013 (s 27(1)) |
| 28 | | 28 Nov 2013 (SI 2013/2617) |
| Schedule | | 28 Nov 2013 (SI 2013/2617) |

---

**Forth Road Bridge Act 2013 (asp 8)**

*RA:* 28 Jun 2013

*Commencement provisions*: s 7; Forth Road Bridge Act 2013 (Commencement) Order 2015, SSI 2015/190

| | |
|---|---|
| 1–5 | 1 Jun 2015 (SI 2015/190) |
| 6–8 | 29 Jun 2013 (s 7(2)) |
| Schedule | 1 Jun 2015 (SI 2015/190) |

---

**Freedom of Information (Amendment) (Scotland) Act 2013 (asp 2)**

*RA:* 19 Feb 2013

*Commencement provisions*: s 7; Freedom of Information (Amendment) (Scotland) Act 2013 (Commencement and Transitional Provision) Order 2013, SSI 2013/136

**Freedom of Information (Amendment) (Scotland) Act 2013 (asp 2)**—*contd*

| | |
|---|---|
| 1–5 | 31 May 2013 (SSI 2013/136)[1] |
| 6–8 | 20 Feb 2013 (s 7(1)) |

[1] For transitional and savings provisions, see SSI 2013/136, art 3

---

## Groceries Code Adjudicator Act 2013 (c 19)

*RA:* 25 Apr 2013

*Commencement provisions*: s 25; Groceries Code Adjudicator Act 2013 (Commencement) Order 2013, SI 2013/1236

| | |
|---|---|
| 1–21 | 25 Jun 2013 (SI 2013/1236) |
| 22–26 | 25 Apr 2013 (s 25(2)) |
| Schs 1, 2 | 25 Jun 2013 (SI 2013/1236) |

---

## Growth and Infrastructure Act 2013 (c 27)

*RA:* 25 Apr 2013

*Commencement provisions*: s 35; Growth and Infrastructure (Commencement No 1 and Transitional and Saving Provisions) Order 2013, SI 2013/1124; Growth and Infrastructure Act 2013 (Commencement No 2 and Transitional and Saving Provisions) Order 2013, SI 2013/1488; Growth and Infrastructure Act 2013 (Commencement No 3 and Savings) Order 2013, SI 2013/1766; Growth and Infrastructure Act 2013 (Commencement No 4) Order 2013, SI 2013/2143; Growth and Infrastructure Act 2013 (Commencement) (Scotland) Order 2013, SSI 2013/303; Growth and Infrastructure Act 2013 (Commencement No 5 and Transitional and Saving Provisions) Order 2013, SI 2013/2878; Growth and Infrastructure Act 2013 (Commencement No 6) Order 2014, SI 2014/1531

| | | |
|---|---|---|
| 1 | (1) | 25 Apr 2013 (in so far as inserts Town and Country Planning Act 1990, s 62B) (s 35(2)) |
| | | 9 May 2013 (to the extent that Town and Country Planning Act 1990, ss 62A, 62C inserted thereby enable the Secretary of State to make regulations or orders) (E) (SI 2013/1124) |
| | | 1 Oct 2013 (otherwise, except in relation to s 62A(3) and (4) of the 1990 Act) (SI 2013/2143) |
| | | 1 Oct 2014 (exception noted above) (SI 2014/1531) |
| | (2) | See Sch 1 below |
| 2 | (1)–(6) | 1 Oct 2013 (SI 2013/2143) |
| | (7) | 25 Jun 2013 (SI 2013/1488) |
| 3 | | 25 Jun 2013 (SI 2013/1488)[2] |
| 4 | | 25 Apr 2013 (s 35(2)) |
| 5 | | 9 Dec 2013 (SI 2013/2878)[4] |
| 6 | | 25 Jun 2013 (SI 2013/1488) |
| 7 | | 25 Apr 2013 (s 35(2)) |
| 8 | | 25 Jun 2013 (E) (SI 2013/1124) |
| | | *Not yet in force* (otherwise) |
| 9 | | 25 Apr 2013 (s 35(2)) |
| 10 | (1) | See Sch 3 below |
| | (2)–(6) | 25 Jun 2013 (SI 2013/1488) |
| 11, 12 | | 25 Jun 2013 (s 35(3)) |
| 13 | | 25 Jun 2013 (for the purpose of making regulations) (SI 2013/1488) |
| | | 1 Oct 2013 (otherwise) (SI 2013/1766)[3] |
| 14 | | 1 Oct 2013 (SI 2013/1488)[2] |
| 15 | | 25 Jun 2013 (for the purpose of making regulations) (SI 2013/1488) |
| | | 1 Oct 2013 (otherwise) (SI 2013/1766) |
| 16 | | 25 Apr 2013 (s 35(2)) |
| 17, 18 | | 25 Jun 2013 (s 35(3)) |

**Growth and Infrastructure Act 2013 (c 27)**—*contd*

| | | |
|---|---|---|
| 19 | | 25 Apr 2013 (s 35(2)) |
| 20 | | 19 Jun 2013 (for the purpose of enabling the Secretary of State or the Scottish Ministers to make regulations) (SI 2013/1488) |
| | | 31 Jul 2013 (otherwise) (E) (W) (SI 2013/1488) |
| | | 1 Dec 2013 (otherwise) (S) (SI 2013/1488) |
| 21 | (1)–(3) | 31 Jul 2013 (SI 2013/1488) |
| | (4)–(6) | 1 Dec 2013 (SSI 2013/303) |
| 22 | | 25 Jun 2013 (SI 2013/1124) |
| 23, 24 | | 25 Jun 2013 (SI 2013/1124)[1] |
| 25 | (1)–(6) | 25 Jun 2013 (in so far as they relate to an order which is subject to the provisions of the Statutory Orders (Special Procedure) Act 1945 by virtue of Planning Act 2008, ss 130, 131 or 132) (SI 2013/1124)[1] |
| | | 25 Jun 2013 (otherwise) (SI 2013/1488)[2] |
| | (7)–(9) | 25 Jun 2013 (SI 2013/1488)[2] |
| | (10) | 25 Jun 2013 (in so far as relates to an order which is subject to the provisions of the Statutory Orders (Special Procedure) Act 1945 by virtue of Planning Act 2008, ss 130, 131 or 132) (SI 2013/1124)[1] |
| | | 25 Jun 2013 (otherwise) (SI 2013/1488)[2] |
| 26 | | 25 Apr 2013 (s 35(2)) |
| 27 | | 25 Jun 2013 (SI 2013/1124)[1] |
| 28 | | 1 Oct 2013 (SI 2013/2143) |
| 29, 30 | | 25 Jun 2013 (s 35(3)) |
| 31 | | 1 Sep 2013 (SI 2013/1766) |
| 32, 33 | | 25 Apr 2013 (s 35(2)) |
| 34 | | *Not yet in force* |
| 35, 36 | | 25 Apr 2013 (s 35(2)) |
| Sch 1 | | 9 May 2013 (to the extent that the provisions inserted thereby into the Town and Country Planning Act 1990 enable the Secretary of State to make regulations or orders) (E) (SI 2013/1124) |
| | | 1 Oct 2013 (otherwise, except in relation to s 62A(3) and (4) of the 1990 Act) (SI 2013/2143) |
| | | 1 Oct 2014 (exception noted above) (SI 2014/1531) |
| Sch 2 | | 25 Apr 2013 (s 35(2)) |
| Sch 3 | | 25 Jun 2013 (SI 2013/1488) |
| Sch 4 | | 25 Apr 2013 (s 35(2)) |

[1]   For transitional and saving provisions, see SI 2013/1124, arts 5–8, 10, 11

[2]   For transitional and saving provisions, see SI 2013/1488, art 8

[3]   For savings, see SI 2013/1766, art 4

[4]   For transitional and saving provisions, see SI 2013/2878, art 3

---

**HGV Road User Levy Act 2013 (c 7)**

*RA:* 28 Feb 2013

*Commencement provisions:* s 21; HGV Road User Levy Act 2013 (Commencement No 1) Order 2014, SI 2014/175; HGV Road User Levy Act 2013 (Commencement No 2) Order 2014, SI 2014/797

| | |
|---|---|
| 1–10 | 1 Apr 2014 (SI 2014/797) |
| 11 | 30 Jan 2014 (for the purposes of the exercise of powers under Road Traffic Offenders Act 1988, ss 20(3), 53, 90A(2)(b) and 90B(2)) (SI 2014/175) |
| | 1 Apr 2014 (otherwise) (SI 2014/797) |
| 12 | See Sch 2 below |
| 13 | 30 Jan 2014 (for the purposes of the exercise of powers under Road Traffic Offenders Act 1988, ss 20(3), 53, 90A(2)(b) and 90B(2)) (SI 2014/175) |

## HGV Road User Levy Act 2013 (c 7)—*contd*

|         |                                    |
|---------|------------------------------------|
|         | 1 Apr 2014 (otherwise) (SI 2014/797) |
| 14–16   | 1 Apr 2014 (SI 2014/797)           |
| 17–22   | 28 Feb 2013 (s 21(3))              |
| Schs 1, 2 | 1 Apr 2014 (SI 2014/797)          |

## High Hedges (Scotland) Act 2013 (asp 6)

*RA*: 2 May 2013

*Commencement provisions*: s 38; High Hedges (Scotland) Act 2013 (Commencement) Order 2014, SSI 2014/54

|         |                            |
|---------|----------------------------|
| 1–33    | 1 Apr 2014 (SSI 2014/54)   |
| 34      | 3 May 2013 (s 38(1))       |
| 35      | 1 Apr 2014 (SSI 2014/54)   |
| 36      | 3 May 2013 (s 38(1))       |
| 37      | 1 Apr 2014 (SSI 2014/54)   |
| 38, 39  | 3 May 2013 (s 38(1))       |

## High Speed Rail (Preparation) Act 2013 (c 31)

*RA*: 21 Nov 2013

*Commencement provisions*: s 3(2)

Whole Act in force 21 Nov 2013 (s 3(2))

## Human Transplantation (Wales) Act 2013 (anaw 5)

*RA*: 10 Sep 2013

*Commencement provisions*: s 21; Human Transplantation (Wales) Act 2013 (Commencement) Order 2015, SI 2015/1679

|         |                     |                                                        |
|---------|---------------------|--------------------------------------------------------|
| 1, 2    |                     | 10 Sep 2013 (s 21(4)(a), (b))                          |
| 3–6     |                     | 1 Dec 2015 (SI 2015/1679)                              |
| 7–9     |                     | 12 Sep 2015 (for the purpose of making regulations) (SI 2015/1679) |
|         |                     | 1 Dec 2015 (otherwise) (SI 2015/1679)                  |
| 10–13   |                     | 1 Dec 2015 (SI 2015/1679)                              |
| 14      | (1), (2), (3)(a)    | 1 Dec 2015 (SI 2015/1679)                              |
|         | (3)(b)              | Not yet in force                                       |
| 15      | (1)–(3), (4)(a)–(d) | 12 Sep 2015 (SI 2015/1679)                             |
|         | (4)(e)              | Not yet in force                                       |
|         | (5)                 | 12 Sep 2015 (SI 2015/1679)                             |
| 16–19   |                     | 1 Dec 2015 (SI 2015/1679)                              |
| 20      |                     | 12 Sep 2015 (SI 2015/1679)                             |
| 21, 22  |                     | 10 Sep 2013 (s 21(4)(c), (d))                          |

## Jobseekers (Back to Work Schemes) Act 2013 (c 17)

*RA*: 26 Mar 2013

Whole Act in force 26 Mar 2013 (RA)

## Justice and Security Act 2013 (c 18)

*RA:* 25 Apr 2013

*Commencement provisions:* s 20(1), (2); Justice and Security Act 2013 (Commencement, Transitional and Saving Provisions) Order 2013, SI 2013/1482

| | | |
|---|---|---|
| 1–18 | | 25 Jun 2013 (SI 2013/1482)[1] |
| 19 | (1) | See Schs 2, 3 below |
| | (2) | 25 Apr 2013 (s 20(2)(c)) |
| 20 | | 25 Apr 2013 (s 20(2)(d)) |
| Schs 1, 2 | | 25 Jun 2013 (SI 2013/1482)[1] |
| Sch 3 | paras 1–3 | 25 Jun 2013 (SI 2013/1482)[1] |
| | para 4 | 25 Apr 2013 (s 20(2)(b)) |
| | para 5 | 25 Jun 2013 (SI 2013/1482)[1] |

[1]   For transitional and saving provisions, see SI 2013/1482, arts 3, 4

---

## Land and Buildings Transaction Tax (Scotland) Act 2013 (asp 11)

*RA:* 31 Jul 2013

*Commencement provisions:* s 70; Land and Buildings Transaction Tax (Scotland) Act 2013 (Commencement No 1) Order 2014, SI 2014/279; Land and Buildings Transaction Tax (Scotland) Act 2013 (Commencement No 2) Order 2015, SSI 2015/108

| | | |
|---|---|---|
| 1–15 | | 1 Apr 2015 (SSI 2015/108) |
| 16 | | See Sch 1 below |
| 17 | (1) | See Sch 2 below |
| | (2) | 1 Apr 2015 (SSI 2015/108) |
| 18–23 | | 1 Apr 2015 (SSI 2015/108) |
| 24 | | 7 Nov 2014 (SSI 2014/279) |
| 25, 26 | | 1 Apr 2015 (SSI 2015/108) |
| 27 | (1) | See Schs 3–16 below |
| | (2) | 1 Apr 2015 (SSI 2015/108) |
| | (3), (4) | 7 Nov 2014 (SSI 2014/279) |
| 28–41 | | 1 Apr 2015 (SSI 2015/108) |
| 42 | | 7 Nov 2014 (SSI 2014/279) |
| 43–48 | | 1 Apr 2015 (SSI 2015/108) |
| 49 | (1) | See Sch 17 below |
| | (2) | 1 Apr 2015 (SSI 2015/108) |
| 50 | (1) | See Sch 18 below |
| | (2) | 1 Apr 2015 (SSI 2015/108) |
| 51 | | 1 Apr 2015 (SSI 2015/108) |
| 52 | (1) | See Sch 19 below |
| | (2) | 1 Apr 2015 (SSI 2015/108) |
| 53 | | 7 Nov 2014 (SSI 2014/279) |
| 54, 55 | | 31 Jul 2013 (s 70(1)) |
| 56–58 | | 1 Apr 2015 (SSI 2015/108) |
| 59 | | 7 Nov 2014 (for the purpose of making orders) (SSI 2014/279) |
| | | 1 Apr 2015 (otherwise) (SSI 2015/108) |
| 60–65 | | 1 Apr 2015 (SSI 2015/108) |
| 66 | | See Sch 20 below |
| 67–71 | | 31 Jul 2013 (s 70(1)) |
| Schs 1–4 | | 1 Apr 2015 (SSI 2015/108) |
| Sch 5 | paras 1–11 | 1 Apr 2015 (SSI 2015/108) |
| | para 12 | 7 Nov 2014 (for the purpose of making orders) (SSI 2014/279) |
| | | 1 Apr 2015 (otherwise) (SSI 2015/108) |
| | paras 13–30 | 1 Apr 2015 (SSI 2015/108) |
| Schs 6–10 | | 1 Apr 2015 (SSI 2015/108) |
| Sch 11 | paras 1–5 | 1 Apr 2015 (SSI 2015/108) |

**Land and Buildings Transaction Tax (Scotland) Act 2013 (asp 11)**—*contd*

|  |  |  |
|---|---|---|
|  | para 6 | 7 Nov 2014 (for the purpose of making orders) (SSI 2014/279) |
|  |  | 1 Apr 2015 (otherwise) (SSI 2015/108) |
|  | paras 7–42 | 1 Apr 2015 (SSI 2015/108) |
| Sch 12 |  | 1 Apr 2015 (SSI 2015/108) |
| Sch 13 | paras 1–14 | 1 Apr 2015 (SSI 2015/108) |
|  | para 15 | 7 Nov 2014 (for the purpose of making orders) (SSI 2014/279) |
|  |  | 1 Apr 2015 (otherwise) (SSI 2015/108) |
|  | paras 16, 17 | 1 Apr 2015 (SSI 2015/108) |
| Schs 14–18 |  | 1 Apr 2015 (SSI 2015/108) |
| Sch 19 | paras 1, 2 | 1 Apr 2015 (SSI 2015/108) |
|  | para 3 | 7 Nov 2014 (SSI 2014/279) |
|  | paras 4–30 | 1 Apr 2015 (SSI 2015/108) |
| Sch 20 |  | 1 Apr 2015 (SSI 2015/108) |

---

## Local Government (Democracy) (Wales) Act 2013 (anaw 4)

*RA:* 30 Jul 2013

*Commencement provisions:* s 75; Local Government (Democracy) (Wales) Act 2013 (Commencement No 1) Order 2014, SI 2014/380; Local Government (Democracy) (Wales) Act 2013 (Commencement No 2) Order 2015, SI 2015/1182

|  |  |  |
|---|---|---|
| 1 |  | 30 Jul 2013 (s 75(1)(a)) |
| 2–20 |  | 30 Sep 2013 (s 75(2)(a)) |
| 21–49 |  | 30 Sep 2013 (s 75(2)(b)) |
| 50 |  | 30 Sep 2013 (s 75(2)(c)) |
| 51–54 |  | 30 Sep 2013 (s 75(2)(d)) |
| 55–58 |  | 1 May 2015 (SI 2015/1182) |
| 59–62 |  | 30 Sep 2013 (s 75(2)(d)) |
| 63 |  | 1 Apr 2014 (SI 2014/380) |
| 64–67 |  | 30 Sep 2013 (s 75(2)(d)) |
| 68, 69 |  | 1 May 2015 (SI 2015/1182) |
| 70 |  | 30 Jul 2013 (s 75(1)(b)) |
| 71 |  | 30 Jul 2013 (s 75(1)(c)) |
| 72 | (1) | 30 Jul 2013 (s 75(1)(d)) |
|  | (2) | See Sch 3 below |
| 73 | (1) | See Sch 1 below |
|  | (2) | See Sch 2 below |
| 74 |  | 30 Sep 2013 (s 75(2)(d)) |
| 75 |  | 30 Jul 2013 (s 75(1)(e)) |
| 76 |  | 30 Jul 2013 (s 75(1)(f)) |
| Schs 1, 2 |  | 30 Sep 2013 (s 75(2)(d)) |
| Sch 3 |  | 30 Jul 2013 (s 75(1)(d)) |

---

## London Local Authorities and Transport for London Act 2013 (c v)

*RA:* 18 Dec 2013

*Commencement provisions:* s 1(2), (3)

|  |  |  |
|---|---|---|
| 1–3 |  | 18 Feb 2014 (s 1(2)) |
| 4 | (1)–(12) | Not yet in force |
|  | (13) | 18 Feb 2014 (s 1(2)) |
|  | (14), (15) | Not yet in force |
| 5 |  | Not yet in force |
| 6 |  | 18 Feb 2014 (s 1(2)) |
| 7–14 |  | Not yet in force |
| 15–20 |  | 18 Feb 2014 (s 1(2)) |

## Marine Navigation Act 2013 (c 23)

*RA:* 25 Apr 2013

*Commencement provisions:* s 13; Marine Navigation Act 2013 (Commencement) Order 2013, SI 2013/1489; Marine Navigation Act 2013 (Commencement) (Wales) Order 2013, SI 2013/2006; Marine Navigation Act 2013 (Commencement) (Scotland) Order 2013, SSI 2013/254

| | | |
|---|---|---|
| 1–4 | | 1 Oct 2013 (E) (W) (SI 2013/1489) |
| | | 1 Oct 2013 (S) (SSI 2013/254) |
| 5, 6 | | 1 Oct 2013 (except in relation to Scotland, and to fishery harbours in Wales) (SI 2013/1489) |
| | | 1 Oct 2013 (in relation to fishery harbours in Wales) (SI 2013/2006) |
| | | 1 Oct 2013 (S) (SSI 2013/254) |
| 7–11 | | 26 Jun 2013 (SI 2013/1489) |
| 12–14 | | 25 Apr 2013 (RA) |

## Marriage (Same Sex Couples) Act 2013 (c 30)

*RA:* 17 Jul 2013

*Commencement provisions:* s 21(2), (3); Marriage (Same Sex Couples) Act 2013 (Commencement No 1) Order 2013, SI 2013/2789; Marriage (Same Sex Couples) Act 2013 (Commencement No 2 and Transitional Provision) Order 2014, SI 2014/93; Marriage (Same Sex Couples) Act 2013 (Commencement No 3) Order 2014, SI 2014/1662; Marriage (Same Sex Couples) Act 2013 (Commencement No 4) Order 2014, SI 2014/3169

| | | |
|---|---|---|
| 1–3 | | 13 Mar 2014 (SI 2014/93) |
| 4 | (1) | 31 Oct 2013 (for the purpose of exercising any power to make subordinate legislation) (SI 2013/2789) |
| | | 13 Mar 2014 (otherwise) (SI 2014/93) |
| | (2) | See Sch 1 below |
| 5 | | 13 Mar 2014 (SI 2014/93) |
| 6 | | 21 Jan 2014 (to the extent that it confers or relates to the power to make subordinate legislation, for the purpose of exercising such a power) (SI 2014/93) |
| | | 3 Jun 2014 (otherwise) (SI 2014/93) |
| 7, 8 | | 13 Mar 2014 (SI 2014/93) |
| 9 | (1)–(5) | 30 Jun 2014 (for the purpose of exercising any power to make subordinate legislation) (SI 2014/1662) |
| | | 10 Dec 2014 (otherwise) (SI 2014/3169) |
| | (6) | 10 Dec 2014 (SI 2014/3169) |
| | (7) | 30 Jun 2014 (for the purpose of exercising any power to make subordinate legislation) (SI 2014/1662) |
| | | 10 Dec 2014 (otherwise) (SI 2014/3169) |
| 10 | (1), (2) | 13 Mar 2014 (SI 2014/93)[1] |
| | (3) | See Sch 2 below |
| 11 | (1), (2) | 13 Mar 2014 (SI 2014/93) |
| | (3) | See Sch 3 below |
| | (4) | See Sch 4 below |
| | (5)–(7) | 13 Mar 2014 (SI 2014/93) |
| 12 | | See Sch 5 below |
| 13 | (1) | See Sch 6 below |
| | (2) | 3 Jun 2014 (SI 2014/93) |
| 14 | | 31 Oct 2013 (SI 2013/2789) |
| 15, 16 | | 17 Jul 2013 (s 21(2)) |
| 17 | (1)–(3) | 31 Oct 2013 (SI 2013/2789) |
| | (4) | See Sch 7 below |
| 18–20 | | 31 Oct 2013 (SI 2013/2789) |
| 21 | | 17 Jul 2013 (s 21(2)) |

**Marriage (Same Sex Couples) Act 2013 (c 30)**—*contd*

| | | |
|---|---|---|
| Sch 1 | | 31 Oct 2013 (for the purpose of exercising any power to make subordinate legislation) (SI 2013/2789) |
| | | 13 Mar 2014 (otherwise) (SI 2014/93) |
| Sch 2 | para 1 | 31 Oct 2013 (SI 2013/2789) |
| | para 2(1) | 13 Mar 2014 (SI 2014/93) |
| | para 2(2) | 31 Oct 2013 (SI 2013/2789) |
| | paras 3, 4 | 13 Mar 2014 (SI 2014/93) |
| | para 5 | *Not yet in force* |
| Sch 3 | | 13 Mar 2014 (SI 2014/93) |
| Sch 4 | paras 1–4 | 13 Mar 2014 (SI 2014/93) |
| | para 5 | 31 Oct 2013 (for the purpose of exercising any power to make subordinate legislation) (SI 2013/2789) |
| | | 13 Mar 2014 (otherwise) (SI 2014/93) |
| | paras 6, 7 | 13 Mar 2014 (SI 2014/93) |
| | para 8 | 31 Oct 2013 (for the purpose of exercising any power to make subordinate legislation) (SI 2013/2789) |
| | | 13 Mar 2014 (otherwise) (SI 2014/93) |
| | paras 9, 10 | 13 Mar 2014 (SI 2014/93) |
| | paras 11–13 | 13 Mar 2014 (except in so far as relate to a case where a spouse is, or was at the time of her death, a woman by virtue of a full gender recognition certificate having been issued under the Gender Recognition Act 2004 and the marriage subsisted before the time when that certificate was issued) (SI 2014/93) |
| | | 10 Dec 2014 (exception noted above) (SI 2014/3169) |
| | para 14 | 31 Oct 2013 (for the purpose of exercising any power to make subordinate legislation) (SI 2013/2789) |
| | | 13 Mar 2014 (except in so far as relates to a case where a spouse is, or was at the time of her death, a woman by virtue of a full gender recognition certificate having been issued under the Gender Recognition Act 2004 and the marriage subsisted before the time when that certificate was issued) (SI 2014/93) |
| | | 10 Dec 2014 (exception noted above) (SI 2014/3169) |
| | paras 15, 16 | 10 Dec 2014 (SI 2014/3169) |
| | para 17 | 13 Mar 2014 (except in so far as relates to a relevant gender change case for the purposes of Equality Act 2010) (SI 2014/93) |
| | | *Not yet in force* (exception noted above) |
| | para 18 | 13 Mar 2014 (except in so far as it relates to a relevant gender change case for the purposes of Pension Schemes Act 1993) (SI 2014/93) |
| | | 30 Jun 2014 (in so far as relates to para 23 below) (SI 2014/1662) |
| | | 10 Dec 2014 (exception noted above) (SI 2014/3169) |
| | para 19 | 13 Mar 2014 (SI 2014/93) |
| | paras 20–22 | 13 Mar 2014 (except in so far as relate to a relevant gender change case for the purposes of Pension Schemes Act 1993) (SI 2014/93) |
| | | 10 Dec 2014 (exception noted above) (SI 2014/3169) |
| | para 23 | 30 Jun 2014 (SI 2014/1662) |
| | paras 24–26 | 13 Mar 2014 (SI 2014/93) |
| | para 27(1), (2) | 13 Mar 2014 (SI 2014/93) |
| | para 27(3), (4) | 31 Oct 2013 (SI 2013/2789) |
| Sch 5 | para 1 | 30 Jun 2014 (for the purpose of exercising any power to make subordinate legislation) (SI 2014/1662) |
| | | 10 Dec 2014 (otherwise) (SI 2014/3169) |
| | paras 2–8 | 10 Dec 2014 (SI 2014/3169) |
| | para 9 | 30 Jun 2014 (for the purpose of exercising any power to make subordinate legislation) (SI 2014/1662) |
| | | 10 Dec 2014 (otherwise) (SI 2014/3169) |
| | paras 10–18 | 10 Dec 2014 (SI 2014/3169) |

**Marriage (Same Sex Couples) Act 2013 (c 30)**—*contd*

|  |  |  |
|---|---|---|
|  | para 19 | 30 Jun 2014 (for the purpose of exercising any power to make subordinate legislation) (SI 2014/1662) |
|  |  | 10 Dec 2014 (otherwise) (SI 2014/3169) |
|  | para 20 | 10 Dec 2014 (SI 2014/3169) |
| Sch 6 | paras 1, 2 | 21 Jan 2014 (to the extent that they confer or relate to the power to make subordinate legislation, for the purpose of exercising such a power) (SI 2014/93) |
|  |  | 3 Jun 2014 (otherwise) (SI 2014/93) |
|  | para 3 | 3 Jun 2014 (SI 2014/93) |
|  | para 4 | 21 Jan 2014 (to the extent that it confers or relates to the power to make subordinate legislation, for the purpose of exercising such a power) (SI 2014/93) |
|  |  | 3 Jun 2014 (otherwise) (SI 2014/93) |
|  | para 5 | 3 Jun 2014 (SI 2014/93) |
|  | paras 6–10 | 21 Jan 2014 (to the extent that they confer or relate to the power to make subordinate legislation, for the purpose of exercising such a power) (SI 2014/93) |
|  |  | 3 Jun 2014 (otherwise) (SI 2014/93) |
|  | para 11 | 3 Jun 2014 (SI 2014/93) |
|  | paras 12–15 | 21 Jan 2014 (to the extent that they confer or relate to the power to make subordinate legislation, for the purpose of exercising such a power) (SI 2014/93) |
|  |  | 3 Jun 2014 (otherwise) (SI 2014/93) |
| Sch 7 | paras 1–20 | 13 Mar 2014 (SI 2014/93) |
|  | para 21 | 3 Jun 2014 (SI 2014/93) |
|  | para 22–28 | 13 Mar 2014 (SI 2014/93) |
|  | paras 29, 30 | 10 Dec 2014 (SI 2014/3169) |
|  | paras 31–33 | 13 Mar 2014 (SI 2014/93) |
|  | para 34 | 10 Dec 2014 (SI 2014/3169) |
|  | paras 35–45 | 13 Mar 2014 (SI 2014/93) |

[1]    For transitional provision, see SI 2014/93, art 4

---

**Mental Health (Discrimination) Act 2013 (c 8)**

*RA:* 28 Feb 2013

*Commencement provisions:* s 4(1), (2); Mental Health (Discrimination) Act 2013 (Commencement) Order 2013, SI 2013/1694

|  |  |
|---|---|
| 1 | 28 Apr 2013 (s 4(1)) |
| 2 | 15 Jul 2013 (SI 2013/1694) |
| 3 | 28 Apr 2013 (s 4(1)) |
| 4 | 28 Feb 2013 (RA) |
| Schedule | 28 Apr 2013 (s 4(1)) |

---

**Mobile Homes Act 2013 (c 14)**

*RA:* 26 Mar 2013

*Commencement provisions:* s 15(1)–(4); Mobile Homes Act 2013 (Commencement and Saving Provision) (England) Order 2014, SI 2014/816; Mobile Homes Act 2013 (Commencement No 2) (England) Order 2020, SI 2020/565

|  |  |
|---|---|
| 1–7 | 1 Apr 2014 (s 15(1))[1] |
| 8 | 15 Jun 2020 (SI 2020/565) |
| 9–12 | 26 May 2013 (s 15(3)) |
| 13, 14 | 1 Apr 2014 (E) (SI 2014/816)[1] |
|  | *Not yet in force* (W) |

**Mobile Homes Act 2013 (c 14)**—*contd*

| | | |
|---|---|---|
| 15 | | 26 May 2013 (s 15(3)) |

[1]    For savings and transitional provisions, see SI 2014/816, arts 3–5

---

## Mobile Homes (Wales) Act 2013 (anaw 6)

*RA:* 4 Nov 2013

*Commencement provisions*: s 64; Mobile Homes (Wales) Act 2013 (Commencement, Transitional and Saving Provisions) Order 2014, SI 2014/11

| | | |
|---|---|---|
| 1 | | 1 Oct 2014 (SI 2014/11) |
| 2 | (1)(a) | See Sch 1 below |
| | (1)(b) | 1 Oct 2014 (SI 2014/11) |
| | (2)–(5) | 1 Oct 2014 (SI 2014/11) |
| 3–49 | | 1 Oct 2014 (SI 2014/11) |
| 50 | | See Sch 2 below |
| 51 | | 1 Oct 2014 (SI 2014/11) |
| 52 | | 7 Jan 2014 (for the purposes of making regulations) (SI 2014/11) |
| | | 1 Oct 2014 (otherwise) (SI 2014/11) |
| 53–56 | | 1 Oct 2014 (SI 2014/11) |
| 57 | | See Sch 3 below |
| 58 | | See Schs 4, 5 below |
| 59–65 | | 5 Nov 2013 (s 64(1)) |
| Sch 1 | | 1 Oct 2014 (SI 2014/11) |
| Sch 2 | paras 1–8 | 1 Oct 2014 (SI 2014/11) |
| | paras 9–13 | 7 Jan 2014 (for the purposes of making regulations) (SI 2014/11) |
| | | 1 Oct 2014 (otherwise) (SI 2014/11)[2] |
| | paras 14–22 | 1 Oct 2014 (SI 2014/11) |
| | para 23 | 7 Jan 2014 (for the purposes of making regulations) (SI 2014/11) |
| | | 1 Oct 2014 (otherwise) (SI 2014/11) |
| | paras 24–58 | 1 Oct 2014 (SI 2014/11) |
| Sch 3 | | 1 Oct 2014 (SI 2014/11) |
| Schs 4, 5 | | 5 Nov 2013 (s 64(1))[1] |

[1]    For a transitional provision, see SI 2014/11, art 3(2)

[2]    For saving provisions, see SI 2014/11, art 4

---

## National Trust for Scotland (Governance etc) Act 2013 (asp 9)

*RA:* 28 Jun 2013

*Commencement provisions:* s 7

Whole Act in force 29 Jun 2013 (s 7)

---

## Partnerships (Prosecution) (Scotland) Act 2013 (c 21)

*RA:* 25 Apr 2013

*Commencement provisions:* s 8(2)

Whole Act in force 26 Apr 2013 (s 8(2))

---

## Post-16 Education (Scotland) Act 2013 (asp 12)

*RA:* 7 Aug 2013

*Commencement provisions:* s 23; Post-16 Education (Scotland) Act 2013 (Commencement No 1) Order 2013, SSI 2013/281; Post-16 Education (Scotland) Act 2013 (Commencement No 2) Order 2013, SSI 2013/348; Post-16 Education (Scotland) Act 2013 (Commencement No 3 and Transitory and Savings Provisions) Order 2014, SSI 2014/21; Post-16 Education (Scotland) Act 2013 (Commencement No 4 and Transitory Provisions) Order 2014, SSI 2014/79; Post-16 Education (Scotland) Act 2013 (Commencement No 5) Order 2014, SSI 2014/144; Post-16 Education (Scotland) Act 2013 (Commencement No 6) Order 2015, SSI 2015/82

| | | |
|---|---|---|
| 1 | | 10 Oct 2013 (SSI 2013/281) |
| 2–4 | | 3 Mar 2014 (SSI 2014/21) |
| 5 | (1) | 13 Jan 2014 (SSI 2013/348) |
| | (2) | 3 Mar 2014 (SSI 2014/21) |
| 6 | (1) | 3 Mar 2014 (SSI 2014/21)[1] |
| | (2) | 10 Oct 2013 (SSI 2013/281) |
| 7 | | 3 Mar 2014 (SSI 2014/21)[1] |
| 8 | (1), (2) | 3 Mar 2014 (for the purposes of (a) the amendments to Further and Higher Education (Scotland) Act 2005, s 35(1) in relation to definitions "regional board" and "regional strategic body" and (b) allowing the Scottish Ministers to make an order under section 7B(2) thereof) (SSI 2014/21) |
| | | 1 May 2014 (for the purpose of inserting the Regional Board for Glasgow Colleges into the Further and Higher Education (Scotland) Act 2005, Sch 2A, Pt 1) (SSI 2014/79) |
| | | 1 Aug 2014 (for the purpose of inserting the University of the Highlands and Islands into the Further and Higher Education (Scotland) Act 2005, Sch 2A, Pt 2) (SSI 2014/144) |
| | | 31 Mar 2015 (otherwise) (SSI 2015/82) |
| | (3) | 3 Mar 2014 (SSI 2014/21) |
| 9 | (1) | 3 Mar 2014 (SSI 2014/21) |
| | (2) | 1 May 2014 (for the purpose of inserting the Further and Higher Education (Scotland) Act 2005, s 12A) (SSI 2014/79) |
| | | 1 Aug 2014 (otherwise) (SSI 2014/79) |
| 10 | | 1 Aug 2014 (SSI 2014/79) |
| 11 | (1) | 31 Mar 2015 (SSI 2015/82) |
| | (2) | 1 Aug 2014 (SSI 2014/79)[2] |
| 12 | | 1 May 2014 (SSI 2014/79) |
| 13 | | 10 Oct 2013 (in so far as inserts Further and Higher Education (Scotland) Act 2005, s 23R(1), (2) for the purpose of allowing the Scottish Ministers to make arrangements) (SSI 2013/281) |
| | | 3 Mar 2014 (otherwise) (SSI 2014/21) |
| 14–17 | | 3 Mar 2014 (SSI 2014/21) |
| 18 | | 13 Jan 2014 (SSI 2013/348) |
| 19 | | 3 Mar 2014 (for all purposes other than imposing a duty under Further and Higher Education (Scotland) Act 2005, s 26A(1) on any regional strategic body) (SSI 2014/21) |
| | | 1 May 2014 (exception noted above) (SSI 2014/79) |
| 20 | | 13 Jan 2014 (SSI 2013/348) |
| 21 | | See Schedule below |
| 22–24 | | 8 Aug 2013 (s 23(1)) |
| Schedule | para 1 | 3 Mar 2014 (SSI 2014/21) |
| | para 2(1) | 13 Jan 2014 (SSI 2013/348) |
| | para 2(2)(a) | 3 Mar 2014 (SSI 2014/21) |
| | para 2(2)(b) | 13 Jan 2014 (for the purpose of inserting Further and Higher Education (Scotland) Act 1992, s 3(7)(a), (c)–(i)) (SSI 2013/348) |
| | | 3 Mar 2014 (otherwise) (SSI 2014/21) |
| | para 2(3) | 3 Mar 2014 (SSI 2014/21) |
| | para 2(4)(a) | 1 May 2014 (SSI 2014/79) |

**Post-16 Education (Scotland) Act 2013 (asp 12)**—*contd*

| | |
|---|---|
| para 2(4)(b) | 3 Mar 2014 (SSI 2014/21) |
| para 2(5), (6), (7)(a)–(c) | 3 Mar 2014 (SSI 2014/21) |
| para 2(7)(d) | 10 Oct 2013 (repeal of the Further and Higher Education (Scotland) Act 1992, Sch 2, para 6) (SSI 2013/281) |
| | 3 Mar 2014 (repeal of the Further and Higher Education (Scotland) Act 1992, Sch 2, paras 7–10) (SSI 2014/21) |
| para 2(7)(e)–(h) | 3 Mar 2014 (SSI 2014/21) |
| para 3 | 10 Oct 2013 (SSI 2013/281) |
| para 4 | 1 May 2014 (SSI 2014/79) |
| para 5 | 3 Mar 2014 (SSI 2014/21) |
| para 6 | 1 May 2014 (SSI 2014/79) |
| para 7 | 3 Mar 2014 (for the purpose of inserting "The chairing member of the board of management of a college of further education which is designated as a regional college by order under section 7A of Further and Higher Education (Scotland) Act 2005" into Public Appointments and Public Bodies etc (Scotland) Act 2003, Sch 2) (SSI 2014/21) |
| | 1 May 2014 (otherwise) (SSI 2014/79) |
| para 8(1) | 13 Jan 2014 (SSI 2013/348) |
| para 8(2)–(4) | 3 Mar 2014 (SSI 2014/21) |
| para 8(5)(a)(i) | 10 Oct 2013 (SSI 2013/281) |
| para 8(5)(a)(ii) | 3 Mar 2014 (SSI 2014/21) |
| para 8(5)(a) (iii)–(iv), (b), (c) | 1 May 2014 (SSI 2014/79) |
| para 8(6) | 3 Mar 2014 (for the purpose of inserting Further and Higher Education (Scotland) Act 2005, s 7D(1) to (6)) (SSI 2014/21)[1] |
| | 31 Mar 2015 (otherwise) (SSI 2015/82) |
| para 8(7)(a)(i) | 1 May 2014 (SSI 2014/79) |
| para 8(7)(a)(ii), (b), (c) | 3 Mar 2014 (SSI 2014/21) |
| para 8(7)(d) | 1 May 2014 (SSI 2014/79) |
| para 8(7)(e)–(j), (8)–(10) | 3 Mar 2014 (SSI 2014/21) |
| para 8(11) | 1 May 2014 (SSI 2014/79) |
| para 8(12)–(17) | 3 Mar 2014 (SSI 2014/21) |
| para 8(18) | 3 Mar 2014 (for the purpose of inserting Further and Higher Education (Scotland) Act 2005, s 25A(1), (2)(b)(i)) (SSI 2014/21) |
| | 1 May 2014 (otherwise) (SSI 2014/79) |
| para 8(19), (20)(a) | 3 Mar 2014 (SSI 2014/21) |
| para 8(20)(b) | 1 May 2014 (SSI 2014/79) |
| para 8(21) | 3 Mar 2014 (SSI 2014/21) |
| para 8(22)(a), (b) | 10 Oct 2013 (SSI 2013/281) |
| para 8(22)(c) | 10 Oct 2013 (in so far as inserts Further and Higher Education (Scotland) Act 2005, s 34(4)(ba)) (SSI 2013/281) |
| | 3 Mar 2014 (in so far as inserts Further and Higher Education (Scotland) Act 2005, s 34(4)(bb)–(be)) (SSI 2014/21) |
| | 1 May 2014 (otherwise) (SSI 2014/79) |
| para 8(22)(d) | 1 May 2014 (SSI 2014/79) |
| para 8(23)(a)(i) | 13 Jan 2014 (SSI 2013/348) |
| para 8(23)(a)(ii) | 3 Mar 2014 (SSI 2014/21) |
| para 8(23)(a)(iii) | 13 Jan 2014 (for the purpose of inserting Further and Higher Education (Scotland) Act 2005, s 35, definition "higher education institution") (SSI 2013/348) |
| | 3 Mar 2014 (otherwise) (SSI 2014/21) |
| para 8(23)(a)(iv) | 13 Jan 2014 (for the purpose of inserting Further and Higher Education (Scotland) Act 2005, s 35, definitions "recognised" and "regional college") (SSI 2013/348) |
| | 3 Mar 2014 (otherwise) (SSI 2014/21) |

**Post–16 Education (Scotland) Act 2013 (asp 12)**—*contd*

|  | para 8(23)(b), (c) | 3 Mar 2014 (SSI 2014/21) |
|---|---|---|
|  | para 8(24) | 3 Mar 2014 (SSI 2014/21) |
|  | para 9 | 1 Aug 2014 (SSI 2014/79) |

[1]  For transitory saving provisions, see SSI 2014/21, art 5

[2]  For a transitory modification, see SSI 2014/79, art 3

---

## Presumption of Death Act 2013 (c 13)

*RA:* 26 Mar 2013

*Commencement provisions*: s 22; Presumption of Death Act 2013 (Commencement and Transitional and Saving Provision) Order 2014, SI 2014/1810

| 1–8 |  | 1 Oct 2014 (SI 2014/1810) |
|---|---|---|
| 9 |  | 26 Mar 2013 (so far as it confers a power to make rules) (s 22(1)(a)) |
|  |  | 1 Oct 2014 (otherwise) (SI 2014/1810) |
| 10–14 |  | 1 Oct 2014 (SI 2014/1810) |
| 15 | (1)–(3) | 1 Oct 2014 (SI 2014/1810) |
|  | (4) | See Sch 1 below |
| 16 | (1), (2) | 1 Oct 2014 (SI 2014/1810) |
|  | (3) | See Sch 2 below |
|  | (4) | 1 Oct 2014 (SI 2014/1810) |
| 17–21 |  | 26 Mar 2013 (s 22(1)(c)) |
| 22 |  | 26 Mar 2013 (s 22(1)(d)) |
| 23, 24 |  | 26 Mar 2013 (s 22(1)(e)) |
| Sch 1 |  | 26 Mar 2013 (so far as it confers a power to make regulations) (s 22(1)(a)) |
|  |  | 1 Oct 2014 (otherwise) (SI 2014/1810) |
| Sch 2 |  | 1 Oct 2014 (SI 2014/1810) |

---

## Prevention of Social Housing Fraud Act 2013 (c 3)

*RA:* 31 Jan 2013

*Commencement provisions*: s 12(3)–(5); Prevention of Social Housing Fraud Act 2013 (Commencement) (England) Order 2013, SI 2013/2622; Prevention of Social Housing Fraud Act 2013 (Commencement) (Wales) Order 2013, SI 2013/2861

| 1–9 | 15 Oct 2013 (E) (SI 2013/2622) |
|---|---|
|  | 5 Nov 2013 (W) (SI 2013/2861) |
| 10 | See Schedule below |
| 11 | 15 Oct 2013 (E) (SI 2013/2622) |
|  | 5 Nov 2013 (W) (SI 2013/2861) |
| 12 | 31 Jan 2013 (RA) |
| Schedule | 15 Oct 2013 (E) (SI 2013/2622) |
|  | 5 Nov 2013 (W) (SI 2013/2861) |

---

## Prisons (Property) Act 2013 (c 11)

*RA:* 28 Feb 2013

*Commencement provisions*: s 2(2), (3); Prisons (Property) Act 2013 (Commencement) Order 2015, SI 2015/771

| 1 | 26 Mar 2015 (SI 2015/771) |
|---|---|
| 2 | 28 Feb 2013 (s 2(3)) |

---

## Public Audit (Wales) Act 2013 (anaw 3)

*RA:* 29 Apr 2013

*Commencement provisions:* s 35; Public Audit (Wales) Act 2013 (Commencement, Consequential Amendments, Transitional and Saving Provisions) (Wales) Order 2013, SI 2013/1466

| | | |
|---|---|---|
| 1 | | 4 Jul 2013 (SI 2013/1466) |
| 2–7 | | 1 Apr 2014 (SI 2013/1466) |
| 8 | | 4 Jul 2013 (in so far as is necessary to prepare the code of practice, code of audit practice, annual plan and estimate of income and expenditure for financial year 2014–2015) (SI 2013/1466) |
| | | 1 Apr 2014 (otherwise) (SI 2013/1466) |
| 9 | | 1 Apr 2014 (SI 2013/1466) |
| 10 | | 4 Jul 2013 (SI 2013/1466) |
| 11 | | 1 Apr 2014 (SI 2013/1466) |
| 12 | | 4 Jul 2013 (SI 2013/1466) |
| 13 | (1) | 4 Jul 2013 (except in respect of provisions relating to employee members) (SI 2013/1466) |
| | | 1 Apr 2014 (exception noted above) (SI 2013/1466) |
| | (2) | See Sch 1 below |
| 14, 15 | | 4 Jul 2013 (SI 2013/1466) |
| 16 | (1) | 4 Jul 2013 (SI 2013/1466) |
| | (2) | See Sch 2 below |
| 17 | (1) | 1 Apr 2014 (SI 2013/1466) |
| | (2), (3) | 4 Jul 2013 (in so far as is necessary to prepare the code of practice, annual plan and estimate of income and expenditure for financial year 2014–2015) (SI 2013/1466) |
| | | 1 Apr 2014 (otherwise) (SI 2013/1466) |
| 18 | | 4 Jul 2013 (in so far as is necessary to prepare the delegation scheme) (SI 2013/1466) |
| | | 1 Apr 2014 (otherwise) (SI 2013/1466) |
| 19 | | 1 Apr 2014 (SI 2013/1466) |
| 20 | | 4 Jul 2013 (only in so far as relates to the financial year 2014–2015) (SI 2013/1466) |
| | | 1 Apr 2014 (otherwise) (SI 2013/1466) |
| 21–23 | | 1 Apr 2014 (SI 2013/1466) |
| 24–28 | | 4 Jul 2013 (SI 2013/1466) |
| 29 | (1), (2) | 4 Jul 2013 (SI 2013/1466) |
| | (3)(a) | 1 Apr 2014 (SI 2013/1466) |
| | (3)(b), (c) | 4 Jul 2013 (SI 2013/1466) |
| | (3)(d), (e) | 1 Apr 2014 (SI 2013/1466) |
| | (4) | 4 Jul 2013 (SI 2013/1466) |
| 30 | | 29 Apr 2013 (s 35(1)(a)) |
| 31, 32 | | 4 Jul 2013 (SI 2013/1466) |
| 33 | (1) | See Sch 3 below |
| | (2)–(4) | 4 Jul 2013 (SI 2013/1466) |
| 34 | | See Sch 4 below |
| 35, 36 | | 29 Apr 2013 (s 35(1)(b), (c)) |
| Sch 1 | paras 1–3 | 4 Jul 2013 (except in respect of provisions relating to the employee members) (SI 2013/1466) |
| | | 1 Apr 2014 (exception noted above) (SI 2013/1466) |
| | paras 4–13 | 4 Jul 2013 (SI 2013/1466) |
| | paras 14–25 | 1 Apr 2014 (SI 2013/1466) |
| | para 26 | 4 Jul 2013 (except in respect of provisions relating to the employee members) (SI 2013/1466) |
| | | 1 Apr 2014 (exception noted above) (SI 2013/1466) |
| | paras 27, 28, 29(1) | 4 Jul 2013 (SI 2013/1466) |
| | para 29(2), (3) | 1 Apr 2014 (SI 2013/1466) |
| | paras 30, 31 | 4 Jul 2013 (SI 2013/1466) |
| | para 32 | 4 Jul 2013 (except in relation to employee members and employees) (SI 2013/1466) |

**Public Audit (Wales) Act 2013 (anaw 3)**—*contd*

|  |  |  |
|---|---|---|
|  |  | 1 Apr 2014 (exception noted above) (SI 2013/1466) |
|  | paras 33–36 | 1 Apr 2014 (SI 2013/1466) |
| Sch 2 | paras 1, 2 | 4 Jul 2013 (SI 2013/1466) |
|  | paras 3, 4 | 1 Apr 2014 (SI 2013/1466) |
|  | paras 5–14 | 4 Jul 2013 (SI 2013/1466) |
| Sch 3 | paras 1–3 | 1 Apr 2014 (SI 2013/1466) |
|  | para 4 | 4 Jul 2013 (SI 2013/1466) |
|  | paras 5–12 | 1 Apr 2014 (SI 2013/1466) |
|  | para 13 | 4 Jul 2013 (SI 2013/1466) |
| Sch 4 | paras 1–78 | 1 Apr 2014 (SI 2013/1466) |
|  | para 79(1) | See sub-paras (2)–(6) below |
|  | para 79(2) | 4 Jul 2013 (in so far as relates to Government of Wales Act 2006, Sch 8, para 12) (SI 2013/1466) |
|  |  | 1 Apr 2014 (otherwise) (SI 2013/1466)[1] |
|  | paras 79(3)–(6) | 1 Apr 2014 (SI 2013/1466) |
|  | paras 80–92 | 1 Apr 2014 (SI 2013/1466) |

[1]  For saving provisions, see SI 2013/1466, art 5

---

**Public Service Pensions Act 2013 (c 25)**

*RA:* 25 Apr 2013

*Commencement provisions*: s 41; Public Service Pensions Act 2013 (Commencement No 1) Order 2013, SI 2013/1518; Public Service Pensions Act 2013 (Commencement No 2 and Transitional Provisions) Order 2013, SI 2013/2818; Public Service Pensions Act 2013 (Commencement No 3) Order 2014, SI 2014/433; Public Service Pensions Act 2013 (Commencement No 4) Order 2014, SI 2014/839; Public Service Pensions Act 2013 (Commencement No 5) Order 2014, SI 2014/1912, as amended by SI 2015/4; Public Service Pensions Act 2013 (Commencement No 6, Saving Provision and Amendment) Order 2015, SI 2015/4

|  |  |  |
|---|---|---|
| 1–3 |  | 28 Feb 2014 (SI 2014/433) |
| 4–7 |  | 28 Feb 2014 (for the purpose of making scheme regulations to establish schemes for the payment of pensions and other benefits to or in respect of teachers) (SI 2014/433) |
|  |  | 1 Apr 2014 (except for the purpose of making scheme regulations to establish schemes for the payment of pensions and other benefits to or in respect of local government workers in England and Wales or in respect of fire and rescue workers) (SI 2014/839) |
|  |  | 1 Apr 2015 (except for the purpose of making scheme regulations to establish schemes for the payment of pensions and other benefits to or in respect of local government workers in England and Wales) (SI 2014/1912) |
|  |  | 1 Apr 2015 (for the purpose of making scheme regulations to establish schemes for the payment of pensions and other benefits to or in respect of local government workers in England and Wales) (SI 2015/4) |
| 8 |  | 28 Feb 2014 (SI 2014/433) |
| 9 | (1)–(3) | 28 Feb 2014 (SI 2014/433) |
|  | (4)(a) | 1 Apr 2015 (for the purposes of an order in respect of scheme regulations to establish schemes for the payment of pensions and other benefits to or in respect of local government workers in England and Wales) (SI 2014/839) |
|  |  | 1 Apr 2016 (otherwise) (SI 2014/839) |
|  | (4)(b), (5), (6) | 28 Feb 2014 (SI 2014/433) |
| 10 |  | 25 Jun 2013 (for the purposes of the report under s 36) (SI 2013/1518) |

**Public Service Pensions Act 2013 (c 25)**—*contd*

28 Feb 2014 (for the purpose of making scheme regulations to establish schemes for the payment of pensions and other benefits to or in respect of teachers) (SI 2014/433)

1 Apr 2014 (except for the purposes of any requirements relating to transitional councillor members in connection with their membership of schemes for the payment of pensions and other benefits to or in respect of local government workers in England and Wales) (SI 2014/839)

*Not yet in force* (exception noted above)

11      (1)      1 Apr 2015 (except for the purpose of making scheme regulations to establish schemes for the payment of pensions and other benefits to or in respect of local government workers in England and Wales) (SI 2014/1912)

1 Apr 2015 (for the purpose of making scheme regulations to establish schemes for the payment of pensions and other benefits to or in respect of local government workers in England and Wales) (SI 2015/4)

(2)–(4)      1 Dec 2013 (for the purposes of making Treasury directions under sub-s (2)) (SI 2013/2818)

1 Apr 2015 (except for the purpose of making scheme regulations to establish schemes for the payment of pensions and other benefits to or in respect of local government workers in England and Wales) (SI 2014/1912)

1 Apr 2015 (for the purpose of making scheme regulations to establish schemes for the payment of pensions and other benefits to or in respect of local government workers in England and Wales) (SI 2015/4)

(5)      1 Apr 2015 (except for the purpose of making scheme regulations to establish schemes for the payment of pensions and other benefits to or in respect of local government workers in England and Wales) (SI 2014/1912)

1 Apr 2015 (for the purpose of making scheme regulations to establish schemes for the payment of pensions and other benefits to or in respect of local government workers in England and Wales) (SI 2015/4)

12      (1)      1 Apr 2015 (except for the purpose of making scheme regulations to establish schemes for the payment of pensions and other benefits to or in respect of local government workers) (SI 2014/1912)

1 Apr 2015 (for the purpose of making scheme regulations to establish schemes for the payment of pensions and other benefits to or in respect of local government workers in England and Wales) (SI 2015/4)

1 Apr 2016 (otherwise) (SI 2015/4)

(2)–(5)      1 Dec 2013 (for the purposes of making Treasury directions or regulations under s 11(3), (5)) (SI 2013/2818)

28 Feb 2014 (for the purpose of making Treasury directions under s 12(3) and Treasury regulations under s 12(5)) (SI 2014/433)

1 Apr 2015 (except for the purpose of making scheme regulations to establish schemes for the payment of pensions and other benefits to or in respect of local government workers) (SI 2014/1912)

1 Apr 2015 (for the purpose of making scheme regulations to establish schemes for the payment of pensions and other benefits to or in respect of local government workers in England and Wales) (SI 2015/4)

1 Apr 2016 (otherwise) (SI 2015/4)

(6), (7)      1 Apr 2015 (except for the purpose of making scheme regulations to establish schemes for the payment of pensions and other benefits to or in respect of local government workers) (SI 2014/1912)

**Public Service Pensions Act 2013 (c 25)**—*contd*

|  |  |  |
|---|---|---|
|  |  | 1 Apr 2015 (for the purpose of making scheme regulations to establish schemes for the payment of pensions and other benefits to or in respect of local government workers in England and Wales) (SI 2015/4) |
|  |  | 1 Apr 2016 (otherwise) (SI 2015/4) |
|  | (8), (9) | 1 Dec 2013 (for the purposes of making Treasury directions or regulations under s 11(3), (5)) (SI 2013/2818) |
|  |  | 28 Feb 2014 (for the purpose of making Treasury directions under s 12(3) and Treasury regulations under s 12(5)) (SI 2014/433) |
|  |  | 1 Apr 2015 (except for the purpose of making scheme regulations to establish schemes for the payment of pensions and other benefits to or in respect of local government workers) (SI 2014/1912) |
|  |  | 1 Apr 2015 (for the purpose of making scheme regulations to establish schemes for the payment of pensions and other benefits to or in respect of local government workers in England and Wales) (SI 2015/4) |
|  |  | 1 Apr 2016 (otherwise) (SI 2015/4) |
| 13 |  | 2 Apr 2014 (SI 2014/839) |
| 14 | (1) | 28 Feb 2014 (SI 2014/433) |
|  | (2), (3) | 1 Nov 2013 (for the purpose of making Treasury directions) (SI 2013/2818) |
|  |  | 28 Feb 2014 (otherwise) (SI 2014/433) |
|  | (4), (5) | 28 Feb 2014 (SI 2014/433) |
|  | (6) | 1 Nov 2013 (for the purpose of making Treasury directions) (SI 2013/2818) |
|  |  | 28 Feb 2014 (otherwise) (SI 2014/433) |
| 15 |  | 1 Apr 2015 (SI 2015/4) |
| 16 |  | 1 Nov 2013 (for the purpose of making regulations) (SI 2013/2818) |
|  |  | 1 Apr 2015 (otherwise) (SI 2015/4) |
| 17 | (1) | See Sch 4 below |
|  | (2)–(5) | 1 Nov 2013 (SI 2013/2818) |
| 18 | (1) | 28 Feb 2014 (for the purpose of making scheme regulations to establish schemes for the payment of pensions and other benefits to or in respect of teachers) (SI 2014/433) |
|  |  | *Not yet in force* (otherwise) |
|  | (2) | See Sch 5 below |
|  | (3)–(10) | 28 Feb 2014 (for the purpose of making scheme regulations to establish schemes for the payment of pensions and other benefits to or in respect of teachers) (SI 2014/433) |
|  |  | *Not yet in force* (otherwise) |
| 19 | (1) | See Sch 6 below |
|  | (2)–(4) | 28 Feb 2014 (SI 2014/433) |
| 20 |  | See Sch 7 below |
| 21 |  | 1 Nov 2013 (SI 2013/2818) |
| 22 |  | 28 Feb 2014 (SI 2014/433) |
| 23 |  | 1 Nov 2013 (SI 2013/2818) |
| 24–26 |  | 28 Feb 2014 (SI 2014/433) |
| 27 |  | See Sch 8 below |
| 28 |  | 1 Apr 2014 (SI 2014/839) |
| 29 |  | See Sch 9 below |
| 30 |  | 1 Apr 2015 (SI 2015/4) |
| 31 | (1) | See Sch 10 below |
|  | (2)–(14) | 1 Apr 2015 (SI 2015/4) |
| 32 |  | 1 Apr 2015 (SI 2015/4) |
| 33 |  | See Sch 11 below |
| 34 |  | 31 Jul 2014 (SI 2014/1912) |
| 35 |  | 1 Nov 2013 (SI 2013/2818) |
| 36 |  | 25 Jun 2013 (SI 2013/1518) |

**Public Service Pensions Act 2013 (c 25)**—*contd*

| | | |
|---|---|---|
| 37–42 | | 25 Apr 2013 (s 41(1)(c))[1] |
| Sch 1–3 | | 28 Feb 2014 (SI 2014/433) |
| Sch 4 | para 1 | 1 Nov 2013 (SI 2013/2818) |
| | paras 2–13 | 1 Apr 2015 (SI 2015/4)[2] |
| | paras 14–16 | 1 Nov 2013 (SI 2013/2818) |
| | para 17 | 1 Apr 2015 (SI 2015/4)[2] |
| | para 18 | 1 Nov 2013 (SI 2013/2818) |
| | paras 19–21 | 1 Apr 2015 (SI 2015/4)[2] |
| | para 22 | 1 Nov 2013 (SI 2013/2818) |
| Sch 5 | | 28 Feb 2014 (for the purpose of making scheme regulations to establish schemes for the payment of pensions and other benefits to or in respect of teachers) (SI 2014/433) |
| | | *Not yet in force* (otherwise) |
| Schs 6, 7 | | 28 Feb 2014 (SI 2014/433) |
| Sch 8 | paras 1–3 | 1 Apr 2014 (SI 2014/839) |
| | paras 4, 5 | 28 Feb 2014 (SI 2014/433) |
| | paras 6–17 | 1 Apr 2014 (SI 2014/839) |
| | paras 18–20 | 1 Apr 2014 (except for the purposes of any requirements relating to transitional councillor members in connection with their membership of schemes for the payment of pensions and other benefits to or in respect of local government workers in England and Wales) (SI 2014/839) |
| | | *Not yet in force* (exception noted above) |
| | para 21 | 1 Feb 2014 (SI 2013/2818) |
| | paras 22–31 | 1 Apr 2014 (SI 2014/839) |
| Sch 9 | | 25 Apr 2013 (s 41(1)(a)) |
| Sch 10 | | 1 Apr 2015 (SI 2015/4) |
| Sch 11 | | 25 Apr 2013 (s 41(1)(b)) |

[1]  SI 2014/433, art 2(2)(l) also purports to bring s 37 into force on 28 Feb 2014

[2]  For a saving, see SI 2015/4, art 4(2)

---

**School Standards and Organisation (Wales) Act 2013 (anaw 1)**

*RA:* 4 Mar 2013

*Commencement provisions:* s 100; School Standards and Organisation (Wales) Act 2013 (Commencement No 1) Order 2013, SI 2013/1000; School Standards and Organisation (Wales) Act 2013 (Commencement No 2, Savings and Transitional Provisions) Order 2013, SI 2013/1800; School Standards and Organisation (Wales) Act 2013 (Commencement No 3) Order 2013, SI 2013/3024; School Standards and Organisation (Wales) Act 2013 (Commencement No 4 and Savings Provisions) Order 2014, SI 2014/178

| | |
|---|---|
| 1 | 5 Mar 2013 (s 100(1)) |
| 2–17 | 20 Feb 2014 (SI 2014/178)[2] |
| 18 | See Sch 1 below |
| 19–31 | 20 Feb 2014 (SI 2014/178)[2] |
| 32–37 | 4 May 2013 (s 100(3)) |
| 38, 39 | 26 Apr 2013 (in so far as relating to the laying of the School Organisation Code) (SI 2013/1000) |
| | 19 Jul 2013 (otherwise) (SI 2013/1800) |
| 40–56 | 1 Oct 2013 (SI 2013/1800)[1] |
| 57–77 | 1 Oct 2013 (SI 2013/1800) |
| 78–83 | 1 Oct 2013 (SI 2013/1800)[1] |
| 84–87 | 3 Dec 2013 (SI 2013/3024) |
| 88–90 | 1 Apr 2013 (s 100(2)) |
| 91 | 4 May 2013 (s 100(3)) |
| 92, 93 | 1 Apr 2013 (s 100(2)) |
| 94, 95 | 4 May 2013 (s 100(3)) |

**School Standards and Organisation (Wales) Act 2013 (anaw 1)**—*contd*

| | | |
|---|---|---|
| 96 | | 20 Feb 2014 (SI 2014/178)[2] |
| 97, 98 | | 26 Apr 2013 (in so far as relating to the laying of the School Organisation Code) (SI 2013/1000) |
| | | 4 May 2013 (otherwise) (SI 2013/1000) |
| 99 | | See Sch 5 below |
| 100, 101 | | 5 Mar 2013 (s 100(1)) |
| Sch 1 | | 20 Feb 2014 (SI 2014/178)[2] |
| Schs 2, 3 | | 1 Oct 2013 (SI 2013/1800) |
| Sch 4 | paras 1–7 | 1 Oct 2013 (SI 2013/1800) |
| | para 8 | *Not yet in force* |
| | paras 9–39 | 1 Oct 2013 (SI 2013/1800) |
| Sch 5 | paras 1–13 | 20 Feb 2014 (SI 2014/178)[2] |
| | paras 14–18 | 1 Oct 2013 (SI 2013/1800) |
| | para 19 | 1 Oct 2013 (SI 2013/1800)[1] |
| | paras 20–30 | 1 Oct 2013 (SI 2013/1800) |
| | para 31 | 4 May 2013 (s 100(3)) |
| | para 32 | 20 Feb 2014 (SI 2014/178)[2] |
| | paras 33, 34(1) | 4 May 2013 (s 100(3)) |
| | para 34(2) | 20 Feb 2014 (SI 2014/178)[2] |
| | para 34(3) | 4 May 2013 (s 100(3)) |
| | paras 35, 36 | 4 May 2013 (s 100(3)) |

[1]   For transitional and saving provisions, see SI 2013/1800, arts 4, 5

[2]   For saving provisions, see SI 2014/178, art 3

---

**Scottish Civil Justice Council and Criminal Legal Assistance Act 2013 (asp 3)**

*RA:* 5 Mar 2013

*Commencement provisions*: s 25; Scottish Civil Justice Council and Criminal Legal Assistance Act 2013 (Commencement No 1, Transitional and Transitory Provisions) Order 2013, SSI 2013/124; Scottish Civil Justice Council and Criminal Legal Assistance Act 2013 (Commencement Order No 2) Order 2013, SSI 2013/262, as amended by SSI 2013/271

| | | |
|---|---|---|
| 1–16 | | 28 May 2013 (SSI 2013/124)[1] |
| 17 | | 11 Oct 2013 (SSI 2013/262) |
| 18 | (1) | 11 Oct 2013 (SSI 2013/262) |
| | (2) | *Not yet in force* |
| 19 | | 11 Oct 2013 (SSI 2013/262) |
| 20, 21 | | *Not yet in force* |
| 22, 23 | | 11 Oct 2013 (SSI 2013/262) |
| 24–26 | | 6 Mar 2013 (s 25(1)) |

[1]   For transitional and transitory provisions, see SSI 2013/124, art 3

---

**Scottish Independence Referendum Act 2013 (asp 14)**

*RA:* 17 Dec 2013

*Commencement provisions:* s 36

Whole Act in force 18 Dec 2013 (s 36)

---

**Scottish Independence Referendum (Franchise) Act 2013 (asp 13)**

*RA:* 7 Aug 2013

*Commencement provisions:* s 13(1)

**Scottish Independence Referendum (Franchise) Act 2013 (asp 13)**—*contd*
Whole Act in force 8 Aug 2013 (s 13(1))

---

**Scrap Metal Dealers Act 2013 (c 10)**

*RA:* 28 Feb 2013

*Commencement provisions:* s 23(2), (3); Scrap Metal Dealers Act 2013 (Commencement and Transitional
   Provisions) Order 2013, SI 2013/1966

| | | |
|---|---|---|
| 1 | (1), (2) | 1 Oct 2013 (SI 2013/1966)[1] |
| | (3) | 1 Dec 2013 (SI 2013/1966) |
| 2 | | 1 Oct 2013 (SI 2013/1966) |
| 3 | (1)–(7) | 1 Oct 2013 (SI 2013/1966) |
| | (8) | 1 Oct 2013 (SI 2013/1966)[1] |
| | (9) | 1 Oct 2013 (SI 2013/1966) |
| 4 | | 1 Oct 2013 (SI 2013/1966) |
| 5 | | See Sch 1 below |
| 6 | | 1 Oct 2013 (SI 2013/1966) |
| 7 | (1)–(3) | 1 Oct 2013 (SI 2013/1966)[1] |
| | (4), (5) | 1 Oct 2013 (SI 2013/1966) |
| 8 | (1)–(8) | 1 Oct 2013 (SI 2013/1966) |
| | (9), (10) | 1 Dec 2013 (SI 2013/1966) |
| | (11) | 1 Oct 2013 (SI 2013/1966) |
| 9 | | See Sch 2 below |
| 10 | (1)–(4) | 1 Oct 2013 (SI 2013/1966)[1] |
| | (5) | 1 Dec 2013 (SI 2013/1966)[1] |
| 11 | (1)–(3) | 1 Oct 2013 (SI 2013/1966) |
| | (4)–(7) | 1 Dec 2013 (SI 2013/1966) |
| 12–14 | | 1 Oct 2013 (SI 2013/1966) |
| 15 | (1)–(3) | 1 Oct 2013 (SI 2013/1966) |
| | (4)–(6) | 1 Dec 2013 (SI 2013/1966) |
| 16–19 | | 1 Oct 2013 (SI 2013/1966) |
| 20 | | 28 Feb 2013 (RA) |
| 21, 22 | | 1 Oct 2013 (SI 2013/1966) |
| 23 | | 28 Feb 2013 (RA) |
| Sch 1 | paras 1, 2 | 1 Oct 2013 (SI 2013/1966) |
| | para 3(1)–(4) | 1 Oct 2013 (SI 2013/1966) |
| | para 3(5), (6) | 1 Dec 2013 (SI 2013/1966) |
| | para 4 | 1 Oct 2013 (SI 2013/1966) |
| | para 5 | 1 Dec 2013 (SI 2013/1966) |
| | para 6 | 1 Sep 2013 (SI 2013/1966) |
| | paras 7, 8 | 1 Oct 2013 (SI 2013/1966) |
| | para 9 | 1 Oct 2013 (SI 2013/1966)[1] |
| Sch 2 | | 1 Dec 2013 (SI 2013/1966) |

[1]   For transitional provisions, see SI 2013/1966, art 5

---

**Social Care (Self-directed Support) (Scotland) Act 2013 (asp 1)**

*RA:* 10 Jan 2013

*Commencement provisions:* s 28; Social Care (Self-directed Support) (Scotland) Act 2013 (Commencement,
   Transitional and Saving Provisions) Order 2014, SSI 2014/32

| | |
|---|---|
| 1–14 | 1 Apr 2014 (SSI 2014/32)[1] |
| 15 | 11 Jan 2013 (s 28(1)) |
| 16, 17 | 1 Apr 2014 (SSI 2014/32) |
| 18 | 17 Feb 2014 (SSI 2014/32) |
| 19–21 | 1 Apr 2014 (SSI 2014/32) |

**Social Care (Self-directed Support) (Scotland) Act 2013 (asp 1)**—*contd*

| | |
|---|---|
| 22 | 11 Jan 2013 (s 28(1)) |
| 23 | 1 Apr 2014 (SSI 2014/32) |
| 24 | 11 Jan 2013 (s 28(1)) |
| 25 | 1 Apr 2014 (SSI 2014/32)[2] |
| 26–29 | 11 Jan 2013 (s 28(1)) |

[1]   For transitional provisions, see SSI 2014/32, art 4

[2]   For a transitional provision, see SSI 2014/32, art 5

---

**Statute Law (Repeals) Act 2013 (c 2)**

*RA:* 31 Jan 2013

*Commencement provisions:* s 3(2)

Whole Act in force 31 Jan 2013 (s 3(2))

---

**Succession to the Crown Act 2013 (c 20)**

*RA:* 25 Apr 2013

*Commencement provisions:* s 5(1)–(3); Succession to the Crown Act 2013 (Commencement) Order 2015, SI 2015/894

| | | |
|---|---|---|
| 1–3 | | 26 Mar 2015 (SI 2015/894) |
| 4 | (1) | See Schedule below |
| | (2), (3) | 26 Mar 2015 (SI 2015/894) |
| 5 | | 25 Apr 2013 (s 5(1)) |
| Schedule | | 26 Mar 2015 (SI 2015/894) |

---

**Supply and Appropriation (Anticipation and Adjustments) Act 2013 (c 12)**

*RA:* 26 Mar 2013

Whole Act in force 26 Mar 2013 (RA)

---

**Supply and Appropriation (Main Estimates) Act 2013 (c 28)**

*RA:* 17 Jul 2013

Whole Act in force 17 Jul 2013 (RA)

---

**Trusts (Capital and Income) Act 2013 (c 1)**

*RA:* 31 Jan 2013

*Commencement provisions:* s 5(3), (4); Trusts (Capital and Income) Act 2013 (Commencement No 1) Order 2013, SI 2013/676; Trusts (Capital and Income) Act 2013 (Commencement No 2) Order 2013, SI 2013/2461

| | |
|---|---|
| 1–3 | 1 Oct 2013 (SI 2013/676) |
| 4 | 6 Apr 2013 (for the purpose of exercising the power to make regulations in accordance with the Charities Act 2011, s 104B, as inserted by this section) (SI 2013/676) |
| | 1 Jan 2014 (otherwise) (SI 2013/2461) |
| 5, 6 | 31 Jan 2013 (s 5(3)) |

---

## Water Resources (Scotland) Act 2013 (asp 5)

*RA:* 9 Apr 2013

*Commencement provisions*: s 56; Water Resources (Scotland) Act 2013 (Commencement No 1) Order 2013, SSI 2013/163; Water Resources (Scotland) Act 2013 (Commencement No 2) Order 2013, SSI 2013/342; Water Resources (Scotland) Act 2013 (Commencement No 3) Order 2016, SSI 2016/14; Water Resources (Scotland) Act 2013 (Commencement No 4) Order 2016, SSI 2016/327

| | | |
|---|---|---|
| 1–4 | | 10 Jun 2013 (SSI 2013/163) |
| 5–9 | | 10 Jun 2013 (for the purpose of making subordinate legislation) (SSI 2013/163) |
| | | *Not yet in force* (otherwise) |
| 10 | (1) | *Not yet in force* |
| | (2), (3) | 10 Jun 2013 (for the purpose of making subordinate legislation) (SSI 2013/163) |
| | | *Not yet in force* (otherwise) |
| 11, 12 | | *Not yet in force* |
| 13 | | 10 Jun 2013 (for the purpose of making subordinate legislation) (SSI 2013/163) |
| | | *Not yet in force* (otherwise) |
| 14 | | *Not yet in force* |
| 15 | (1)(a), (b) | *Not yet in force* |
| | (1)(c) | 10 Jun 2013 (for the purpose of making subordinate legislation) (SSI 2013/163) |
| | | *Not yet in force* (otherwise) |
| | (2) | *Not yet in force* |
| 16 | | *Not yet in force* |
| 17 | | 10 Jun 2013 (SSI 2013/163) |
| 18, 19 | | *Not yet in force* |
| 20 | | 10 Jun 2013 (SSI 2013/163) |
| 21 | | 10 Jun 2013 (for the purpose of making subordinate legislation) (SSI 2013/163) |
| | | *Not yet in force* (otherwise) |
| 22 | | 10 Jun 2013 (SSI 2013/163) |
| 23–27 | | 21 Dec 2013 (SSI 2013/342) |
| 28 | | 10 Jun 2013 (for the purpose of making subordinate legislation) (SSI 2013/163) |
| | | 21 Dec 2013 (otherwise) (SSI 2013/342) |
| 29 | | 10 Jun 2013 (for the purpose of making subordinate legislation) (SSI 2013/163) |
| | | *Not yet in force* (otherwise) |
| 30 | | 10 Jun 2013 (for the purpose of making subordinate legislation) (SSI 2013/163) |
| | | 21 Dec 2013 (otherwise) (SSI 2013/342) |
| 31 | | 21 Dec 2013 (SSI 2013/342) |
| 32 | | 10 Jun 2013 (for the purpose of making a scheme) (SSI 2013/163) |
| | | 1 Apr 2016 (otherwise) (SSI 2016/14) |
| 33 | | 10 Jun 2013 (for the purpose of making subordinate legislation) (SSI 2013/163) |
| | | 1 Jan 2017 (otherwise) (SSI 2016/327) |
| 34 | | 10 Jun 2013 (for the purpose of making subordinate legislation) (SSI 2013/163) |
| | | 21 Dec 2013 (otherwise) (SSI 2013/342) |
| 35, 36 | | 21 Dec 2013 (SSI 2013/342) |
| 37 | | 10 Jun 2013 (for the purpose of making subordinate legislation) (SSI 2013/163) |
| | | 21 Dec 2013 (otherwise) (SSI 2013/342) |
| 38–51 | | 10 Jun 2013 (SSI 2013/163) |
| 52 | | 10 Apr 2013 (s 56(1)) |
| 53 | | See Sch 4 below |

**Water Resources (Scotland) Act 2013 (asp 5)**—*contd*

| | |
|---|---|
| 54–57 | 10 Apr 2013 (s 56(1)) |
| Schs 1, 2 | 10 Jun 2013 (SSI 2013/163) |
| Sch 3 | 10 Apr 2013 (s 56(1)) |
| Sch 4 | 10 Jun 2013 (SSI 2013/163) |

---

**Welfare Benefits Up-rating Act 2013 (c 16)**

*RA*: 26 Mar 2013

*Commencement provisions*: s 3(3), (4); Welfare Benefits Up-rating Act 2013 (Commencement) Order 2013, SI 2013/2317

| | |
|---|---|
| 1, 2 | 1 Oct 2013 (SI 2013/2317) |
| 3 | 26 Mar 2013 (s 3(3)) |
| Schedule | 1 Oct 2013 (SI 2013/2317) |

---

# 2014 Acts

## Agricultural Sector (Wales) Act 2014 (anaw 6)

*RA:* 30 Jul 2014

*Commencement provisions:* s 19

Whole Act in force 30 Jul 2014 (s 19)

---

## Anti-social Behaviour, Crime and Policing Act 2014 (c 12)

*RA:* 13 Mar 2014

*Commencement provisions:* s 185; Anti-social Behaviour, Crime and Policing Act 2014 (Commencement No 1) Order 2014, SI 2014/630; Anti-social Behaviour, Crime and Policing Act 2014 (Commencement No 2, Transitional and Transitory Provisions) Order 2014, SI 2014/949; Anti-social Behaviour, Crime and Policing Act 2014 (Commencement No 3) Order 2014, SI 2014/1226; Anti-social Behaviour, Crime and Policing Act 2014 (Commencement No 1 and Transitory Provisions) (Wales) Order 2014, SI 2014/1241; Anti-social Behaviour, Crime and Policing Act 2014 (Commencement No 4 and Transitional Provisions) Order 2014, SI 2014/1916; Anti-social Behaviour, Crime and Policing Act 2014 (Commencement No 5) Order 2014, SI 2014/2125; Anti-social Behaviour, Crime and Policing Act 2014 (Commencement) (Scotland) Order 2014, SSI 2014/221 (S); Anti-social Behaviour, Crime and Policing Act 2014 (Commencement No 6) Order 2014, SI 2014/2454; Anti-social Behaviour, Crime and Policing Act 2014 (Commencement No 7, Saving and Transitional Provisions) Order 2014, SI 2014/2590, as amended by SI 2014/2754; Anti-social Behaviour, Crime and Policing Act 2014 (Commencement No 2 and Transitional Provisions) (Wales) Order 2014, SI 2014/2830; Anti-social Behaviour, Crime and Policing Act 2014 (Commencement No 8, Saving and Transitional Provisions) Order 2015, SI 2015/373; Anti-social Behaviour, Crime and Policing Act 2014 (Commencement No 9 and Transitional Provisions) Order 2015, SI 2015/987; Anti-social Behaviour, Crime and Policing Act 2014 (Commencement No 10) Order 2017, SI 2017/1018; Anti-social Behaviour, Crime and Policing Act 2014 (Commencement No 11) Order 2021, SI 2021/532; Anti-social Behaviour, Crime and Policing Act 2014 (Commencement No 12) Order 2021, SI 2021/1006

| | | |
|---|---|---|
| 1–10 | | 23 Mar 2015 (SI 2015/373) |
| 11 | | See Sch 1 below |
| 12 | | See Sch 2 below |
| 13–21 | | 23 Mar 2015 (SI 2015/373) |
| 22–93 | | 20 Oct 2014 (SI 2014/2590) |
| 94 | (1) | 20 Oct 2014 (E) (SI 2014/2590)[3] |
| | | 21 Oct 2014 (W) (SI 2014/2830)[5] |
| | (2) | See Sch 3 below |
| 95 | | 20 Oct 2014 (E) (SI 2014/2590) |
| | | 21 Oct 2014 (W) (SI 2014/2830) |
| 96 | | 17 Sep 2014 (or the purpose of making regulations under Housing Act 1985, s 85ZA(7)) (SI 2014/2454) |
| | | 20 Oct 2014 (otherwise) (E) (SI 2014/2590) |
| | | 21 Oct 2014 (otherwise) (W) (SI 2014/2830) |
| 97 | | 20 Oct 2014 (E) (SI 2014/2590)[3] |
| | | 21 Oct 2014 (W) (SI 2014/2830)[5] |
| 98 | | 13 May 2014 (SI 2014/949, SI 2014/1241) |

**Anti-social Behaviour, Crime and Policing Act 2014 (c 12)**—*contd*

| | | |
|---|---|---|
| 99 | | 13 May 2014 (SI 2014/949) |
| 100 | (1) | 13 May 2014 (SI 2014/949, SI 2014/1241) |
| | (2), (3) | 20 Oct 2014 (E) (SI 2014/2590) |
| | | 21 Oct 2014 (W) (SI 2014/2830) |
| 101 | | 13 May 2014 (SI 2014/949) |
| 102 | | 20 Oct 2014 (SI 2014/2590)[4] |
| 103 | | 20 Oct 2014 (SI 2014/2590) |
| 104 | (1) | 20 Oct 2014 (SI 2014/2590) |
| | (2)(a) | 13 May 2014 (for the purpose of making arrangements about the carrying out of ASB case reviews by relevant bodies) (SI 2014/949) |
| | | 20 Oct 2014 (otherwise) (SI 2014/2590) |
| | (2)(b) | 20 Oct 2014 (SI 2014/2590) |
| | (3) | 13 May 2014 (for the purpose of making arrangements about the carrying out of ASB case reviews by relevant bodies) (SI 2014/949) |
| | | 20 Oct 2014 (otherwise) (SI 2014/2590) |
| | (4) | 20 Oct 2014 (SI 2014/2590) |
| | (5) | 13 May 2014 (for the purpose of making arrangements about the carrying out of ASB case reviews by relevant bodies) (SI 2014/949)[1] |
| | | 20 Oct 2014 (otherwise) (SI 2014/2590) |
| | (6)–(12) | 20 Oct 2014 (SI 2014/2590) |
| | (13) | See Sch 4 below |
| 105–107 | | 13 May 2014 (SI 2014/949)[1] |
| 108–111 | | 14 Jul 2014 (SI 2014/949) |
| 112 | | 13 May 2014 (SI 2014/949) |
| 113 | (1) | See Sch 5 below |
| | (2) | 8 Mar 2015 (SI 2015/373) |
| 114 | | 8 Mar 2015 (SI 2015/373) |
| 115 | (1) | See Sch 6 below |
| | (2) | 8 Mar 2015 (SI 2015/373) |
| 116–118 | | 1 Sep 2014 (SI 2014/2125) |
| 119 | | 13 May 2014 (SI 2014/949) |
| 120, 121 | | 16 Jun 2014 (SI 2014/949)[1] |
| 122 | | 30 Sep 2014 (SSI 2014/221) |
| 123–130 | | 13 May 2014 (SI 2014/949) |
| 131 | | 1 Sep 2014 (E) (W) (NI) (SI 2014/2125) |
| 132 | (1) | 1 Sep 2014 (SI 2014/2125) |
| | (2) | See Sch 7 below |
| | (3) | 1 Sep 2014 (SI 2014/2125) |
| 133 | (1), (2) | 1 Sep 2014 (SI 2014/2125) |
| | (3) | 1 Sep 2014 (E) (W) (SI 2014/2125) |
| | (4) | 1 Sep 2014 (SI 2014/2125) |
| | (5) | 1 Sep 2014 (E) (W) (NI) (SI 2014/2125) |
| 134 | | 1 Sep 2014 (SI 2014/2125) |
| 135 | | 8 Apr 2015 (SI 2015/373)[6] |
| 136 | | 1 Oct 2014 (SI 2014/2454) |
| 137 | | 8 Apr 2015 (SI 2015/373) |
| 138, 139 | | 1 Oct 2014 (SI 2014/2454) |
| 140 | | 21 Jul 2014 (SI 2014/1916) |
| 141, 142 | | 13 May 2014 (SI 2014/949) |
| 143 | | 20 Mar 2014 (SI 2014/630) |
| 144–146 | | 13 May 2014 (SI 2014/949) |
| 147 | | See Sch 8 below |
| 148 | | See Sch 9 below |
| 149 | | 2 Jun 2014 (SI 2014/1226) |
| 150 | | 13 Mar 2014 (s 185(2)(a)) |
| 151 | | 13 May 2014 (s 185(2)(b)) |

**Anti-social Behaviour, Crime and Policing Act 2014 (c 12)**—*contd*

| | | |
|---|---|---|
| 152 | | See Sch 10 below |
| 153 | | 13 May 2014 (SI 2014/949) |
| 154 | | 25 Oct 2017 (SI 2017/1018) |
| 155–159 | | 21 Jul 2014 (SI 2014/1916) |
| 160 | | 15 Apr 2015 (SI 2015/987)[7] |
| 161, 162 | | 21 Jul 2014 (SI 2014/1916) |
| 163, 164 | | 21 Jul 2014 (SI 2014/1916)[2] |
| 165–167 | | 21 Jul 2014 (SI 2014/1916) |
| 168 | | 1 May 2021 (SI 2021/532) |
| 169–173 | | 21 Jul 2014 (SI 2014/1916) |
| 174 | | 6 Oct 2014 (SI 2014/2454) |
| 175 | | 13 Mar 2014 (s 185(2)(a)) |
| 176 | | 13 May 2014 (SI 2014/949) |
| 177 | | 13 May 2014 (s 185(2)(b)) |
| 178 | | 13 May 2014 (SI 2014/949) |
| 179 | | 1 Jun 2014 (SI 2014/949) |
| 180 | | 13 Mar 2014 (s 185(2)(a)) |
| 181 | (1) | See Sch 11 below |
| | (2) | 13 Mar 2014 (s 185(2)(a)) |
| | (3) | *Not yet in force* |
| | (4) | 13 Mar 2014 (s 185(2)(a)) |
| 182–186 | | 13 Mar 2014 (s 185(2)(a)) |
| Schs 1, 2 | | 23 Mar 2015 (SI 2015/373) |
| Sch 3 | | 20 Oct 2014 (E) (SI 2014/2590) |
| | | 21 Oct 2014 (W) (SI 2014/2830) |
| Sch 4 | paras 1–5 | 13 May 2014 (SI 2014/949) |
| | paras 6, 7 | 20 Oct 2014 (SI 2014/2590) |
| | paras 8, 9 | 13 May 2014 (SI 2014/949) |
| Schs 5, 6 | | 8 Mar 2015 (SI 2015/373) |
| Sch 7 | | 23 Mar 2015 (SI 2015/373) |
| Sch 8 | | 14 Mar 2014 (SI 2014/630) |
| Sch 9 | para 1(1) | See paras 1(2), (3) below |
| | para 1(2) | 31 Jul 2014 (SI 2014/1916) |
| | para 1(3) | 13 May 2014 (to the extent that it inserts Terrorism Act 2000, Sch 7, para 1A(1)–(3)) (SI 2014/949) |
| | | 31 Jul 2014 (otherwise) (SI 2014/1916) |
| | paras 2–6 | 31 Jul 2014 (SI 2014/1916) |
| | para 7(1) | See paras 7(2), (3) below |
| | para 7(2) | 1 Apr 2015 (SI 2014/1916) |
| | para 7(3) | 13 May 2014 (to the extent that it inserts Terrorism Act 2000, Sch 8, para 20K(8), (9)) (SI 2014/949) |
| | | 1 Apr 2015 (otherwise) (SI 2014/1916) |
| | para 8 | 13 May 2014 (SI 2014/949) |
| Sch 10 | | 13 May 2014 (SI 2014/949) |
| Sch 11 | para 1 | 23 Mar 2015 (SI 2015/373) |
| | para 2 | 20 Oct 2014 (E) (SI 2014/2590) |
| | | 21 Oct 2014 (W) (SI 2014/2830) |
| | paras 3–5 | 20 Oct 2014 (SI 2014/2590) |
| | para 6 | 23 Mar 2015 (SI 2015/373) |
| | para 7–10 | 20 Oct 2014 (E) (SI 2014/2590) |
| | | 21 Oct 2014 (W) (SI 2014/2830) |
| | para 11 | 23 Mar 2015 (SI 2015/373) |
| | para 12 | 13 May 2014 (SI 2014/949, SI 2014/1241) |
| | paras 13, 14 | 20 Oct 2014 (E) (SI 2014/2590) |
| | | 21 Oct 2014 (W) (SI 2014/2830) |
| | para 15(1)–(3) | 13 May 2014 (SI 2014/949) |
| | para 15(4)(a) | 20 Oct 2014 (E) (SI 2014/2590) |
| | | 21 Oct 2014 (W) (SI 2014/2830) |
| | para 15(4)(b) | 20 Oct 2014 (E) (SI 2014/2590) |

**Anti-social Behaviour, Crime and Policing Act 2014 (c 12)**—*contd*

| | |
|---|---|
| | *Not yet in force* (W) |
| para 15(4)(c) | 20 Oct 2014 (E) (SI 2014/2590) |
| | 21 Oct 2014 (W) (SI 2014/2830) |
| para 15(5)–(7) | 13 May 2014 (SI 2014/949) |
| para 16 | 20 Oct 2014 (E) (SI 2014/2590) |
| | 21 Oct 2014 (W) (SI 2014/2830) |
| para 17 | 23 Mar 2015 (SI 2015/373) |
| paras 18, 19 | 20 Oct 2014 (E) (SI 2014/2590) |
| | 21 Oct 2014 (W) (SI 2014/2830) |
| para 20 | 13 May 2014 (SI 2014/949, SI 2014/1241) |
| para 21 | 20 Oct 2014 (SI 2014/2590) |
| paras 22, 23 | 23 Mar 2015 (SI 2015/373) |
| para 24(a) | 20 Oct 2014 (SI 2014/2590), following repeals in Crime and Disorder Act 1998— |
| | s 1(1A), reference to "1C, 1CA"; |
| | s 1A(2)(a), reference to "1CA"; |
| | ss 1C, 1CA, 1D(1)(c), (d), (6); |
| | s 1D(2), in so far as relates to a case falling within sub-s (1)(c) or (d); |
| | s 1D(4)(c), in so far as relates to a case falling within sub-s (1)(c) or (d); |
| | ss 1I(1)(b), 1J(1)(c), 1K(2) |
| | 23 Mar 2015 (otherwise) (SI 2015/373) |
| para 24(b), (c) | 23 Mar 2015 (SI 2015/373) |
| paras 25, 26 | 20 Oct 2014 (SI 2014/2590)[3] |
| paras 27–29 | 23 Mar 2015 (SI 2015/373) |
| para 30 | 20 Oct 2014 (SI 2014/2590) |
| para 31 | 23 Mar 2015 (SI 2015/373) |
| paras 32–43 | 20 Oct 2014 (SI 2014/2590, SI 2014/2754) |
| para 44 | 20 Oct 2014 (in so far as relates to the repeal of Violent Crime Reduction Act 2006, ss 6–8, 9(1)(b), (9) and 9(7)(b) and 10(1), in so far as relate to an order made under s 6 thereof) (SI 2014/2754) |
| | 23 Mar 2015 (otherwise) (SI 2015/373) |
| para 45 | 20 Oct 2014 (SI 2014/2590, SI 2014/2754) |
| para 46 | 23 Mar 2015 (SI 2015/373) |
| para 47(1)–(3) | 13 May 2014 (SI 2014/949) |
| para 47(4) | 20 Oct 2014 (E) (SI 2014/2590) |
| | *Not yet in force* (W) |
| para 47(5)–(7) | 13 May 2014 (SI 2014/949) |
| paras 48 | 20 Oct 2014 (E) (SI 2014/2590) |
| | *Not yet in force* (W) |
| para 49(1), (2) | 23 Mar 2015 (SI 2015/373) |
| para 49(3) | *Not yet in force* |
| para 50 | 20 Oct 2014 (SI 2014/2590), repeals of or in— |
| | Anti-social Behaviour Act 2003, ss 14(3), 56(1); |
| | Criminal Justice Act 2003, Sch 26, para 59; |
| | Licensing Act 2003; |
| | Clean Neighbourhoods and Environment Act 2005; |
| | Drugs Act 2005, Sch 1, para 7; |
| | Serious Organised Crime and Police Act 2005, Sch 7, para 36; |
| | Violent Crime Reduction Act 2006, ss 8(7), 26; |
| | Criminal Justice and Immigration Act 2008, s 118, Sch 20; |
| | Policing and Crime Act 2009; |
| | Localism Act 2011; |
| | Police Reform and Social Responsibility Act 2011 |
| | 23 Mar 2015 (otherwise) (SI 2015/373) |
| paras 51–82 | 8 Mar 2015 (SI 2015/373) |
| para 83 | 1 Sep 2014 (SI 2014/2125) |

**Anti-social Behaviour, Crime and Policing Act 2014 (c 12)**—*contd*

| | |
|---|---|
| paras 84–86 | 13 May 2014 (SI 2014/949) |
| para 87 | 1 Sep 2014 (SI 2014/2125) |
| para 88 | 13 May 2014 (SI 2014/949) |
| para 89 | 1 Sep 2014 (SI 2014/2125) |
| para 90 | *Not yet in force* |
| para 91 | 1 Sep 2014 (SI 2014/2125) |
| para 92 | 13 May 2014 (to the extent that it inserts entry "The College of Policing" into the Freedom of Information Act 2000, Sch 1, Pt 6) (SI 2014/949) |
| | 1 Sep 2014 (otherwise) (SI 2014/2125) |
| para 93 | 1 Oct 2014 (SI 2014/2454) |
| para 94 | 8 Apr 2015 (SI 2015/373)[6] |
| para 95(1) | See sub-paras (2)–(9) below |
| para 95(2) | 1 Oct 2014 (SI 2014/2454) |
| para 95(3)–(6) | 8 Apr 2015 (SI 2015/373) |
| para 95(7)–(9) | 1 Oct 2014 (SI 2014/2454) |
| para 96 | 13 May 2014 (SI 2014/949) |
| paras 97, 98 | 20 Mar 2014 (SI 2014/630) |
| paras 99, 100 | 13 May 2014 (SI 2014/949) |
| para 101 | *Not yet in force* |
| para 102 | 13 May 2014 (SI 2014/949), repeals of or in— |
| | Greater London Authority Act 1999; |
| | Police Reform Act 2002; |
| | Police Reform and Social Responsibility Act 2011, s 24(2)(a), Sch 16, paras 30(3), 35(3) |
| | 1 Sep 2014 (SI 2014/2125), repeals of or in— |
| | Police Act 1996; |
| | Police (Northern Ireland) Act 1998; |
| | Freedom of Information Act 2000; |
| | Police (Northern Ireland) Act 2000; |
| | Northern Ireland Act 1998 (Devolution of Policing and Justice Functions) the Order 2010, SI 2010/976; |
| | Police Reform and Social Responsibility Act 2011, Sch 16, para 38 |
| | *Not yet in force* (otherwise) |
| paras 103–105 | 21 Jul 2014 (SI 2014/1916) |
| paras 106, 107 | 15 Apr 2015 (SI 2015/987)[7] |
| paras 108–110 | 21 Jul 2014 (SI 2014/1916) |
| paras 111–112 | 15 Apr 2015 (SI 2015/987)[7] |
| para 113(1), (2) | 15 Apr 2015 (SI 2015/987)[7] |
| para 113(3)–(6) | 15 Apr 2015 (E) (W) (NI) (SI 2015/987)[7] |
| | 17 Sep 2021 (S) (SI 2021/1006) |
| para 114 | 15 Apr 2015 (SI 2015/987)[7] |
| paras 115–121 | 21 Jul 2014 (SI 2014/1916) |
| para 122 | *Not yet in force* |
| paras 123, 124 | 21 Jul 2014 (SI 2014/1916) |
| paras 125, 126 | 13 May 2014 (SI 2014/949) |

[1] For transitional and transitory provisions, see SI 2014/949, arts 7–10

[2] For transitional provisions, see SI 2014/1916, arts 5, 6

[3] For saving and transitional provisions, see SI 2014/2590, arts 4, 5

[4] For a transitional provision, see SI 2014/2754, art 5

[5] For transitional provisions, see SI 2014/2830, art 3

[6] For saving and transitional provisions, see SI 2015/373, arts 6, 7

[7] For transitional provisions, see SI 2015/987, art 4

## Bankruptcy and Debt Advice (Scotland) Act 2014 (asp 11)

*RA:* 29 Apr 2014

*Commencement provisions:* s 57; Bankruptcy and Debt Advice (Scotland) Act 2014 (Commencement No 1 and Saving) Order 2014, SSI 2014/172; Bankruptcy and Debt Advice (Scotland) Act 2014 (Commencement No 2, Savings and Transitionals) Order 2014, SSI 2014/261

| | | |
|---|---|---|
| 1 | (1) | 1 Apr 2015 (SSI 2014/261)[2] |
| | (2) | 30 Jun 2014 (for the purpose of making regulations, orders or rules of court) (SSI 2014/172) |
| | | 1 Apr 2015 (otherwise) (SSI 2014/261)[2] |
| 2 | | 30 Jun 2014 (for the purpose of making regulations, orders or rules of court) (SSI 2014/172) |
| | | 1 Apr 2015 (otherwise) (SSI 2014/261)[2] |
| 3 | | 30 Jun 2014 (SSI 2014/172) |
| 4 | | 30 Jun 2014 (for the purpose of making regulations, orders or rules of court) (SSI 2014/172) |
| | | 1 Apr 2015 (otherwise) (SSI 2014/261)[2] |
| 5 | (1) | 30 Jun 2014 (for the purpose of making regulations, orders or rules of court) (SSI 2014/172) |
| | | 1 Apr 2015 (otherwise) (SSI 2014/261)[2] |
| | (2) | See Sch 1 below |
| 6 | | 1 Apr 2015 (SSI 2014/261)[2] |
| 7 | | 30 Jun 2014 (for the purpose of making regulations, orders or rules of court) (SSI 2014/172) |
| | | 1 Apr 2015 (otherwise) (SSI 2014/261)[2] |
| 8 | | 1 Apr 2015 (SSI 2014/261)[2] |
| 9 | (1) | 30 Jun 2014 (for the purpose of making regulations, orders or rules of court) (SSI 2014/172) |
| | | 1 Apr 2015 (otherwise) (SSI 2014/261)[2] |
| | (2) | 1 Apr 2015 (SSI 2014/261)[2] |
| 10–16 | | 1 Apr 2015 (SSI 2014/261)[2] |
| 17 | | 30 Jun 2014 (for the purpose of making regulations, orders or rules of court) (SSI 2014/172) |
| | | 1 Apr 2015 (otherwise) (SSI 2014/261)[2] |
| 18 | | 1 Apr 2015 (SSI 2014/261)[2] |
| 19 | | 30 Jun 2014 (for the purpose of making regulations, orders or rules of court) (SSI 2014/172) |
| | | 1 Apr 2015 (otherwise) (SSI 2014/261)[2] |
| 20 | | 1 Apr 2015 (SSI 2014/261)[2] |
| 21, 22 | | 30 Jun 2014 (for the purpose of making regulations, orders or rules of court) (SSI 2014/172) |
| | | 1 Apr 2015 (otherwise) (SSI 2014/261)[2] |
| 23 | (1) | 30 Jun 2014 (for the purpose of making regulations, orders or rules of court) (SSI 2014/172) |
| | | 1 Apr 2015 (otherwise) (SSI 2014/261)[2] |
| | (2) | 1 Apr 2015 (SSI 2014/261)[2] |
| | (3) | 30 Jun 2014 (for the purpose of making regulations, orders or rules of court) (SSI 2014/172) |
| | | 1 Apr 2015 (otherwise) (SSI 2014/261)[2] |
| | (4) | See Sch 2 below |
| 24–26 | | 1 Apr 2015 (SSI 2014/261)[2] |
| 27 | | 1 Apr 2015 (except for the purpose of inserting Bankruptcy (Scotland) Act 1985, s 17G(7)) (SSI 2014/261)[2] |
| | | *Not yet in force* (exception noted above) |
| 28–35 | | 1 Apr 2015 (SSI 2014/261)[2] |
| 36 | | 30 Jun 2014 (SSI 2014/172) |
| 37–43 | | 1 Apr 2015 (SSI 2014/261)[2] |
| 44 | | 30 Jun 2014 (SSI 2014/172) |
| 45 | | 1 Apr 2015 (SSI 2014/261)[2] |
| 46 | | 30 Jun 2014 (for the purpose of making regulations, orders or rules of court) (SSI 2014/172) |

**Bankruptcy and Debt Advice (Scotland) Act 2014 (asp 11)**—*contd*

| | | |
|---|---|---|
| 47 | | 1 Apr 2015 (otherwise) (SSI 2014/261)[2] |
| 48 | | 30 Jun 2014 (for the purpose of making regulations, orders or rules of court) (SSI 2014/172) |
| | | 1 Apr 2015 (otherwise) (SSI 2014/261)[2] |
| 53 | (1) | See sub-ss (1)–(4) below |
| | (2) | 30 Jun 2014 (for the purpose of making regulations, orders or rules of court) (SSI 2014/172)[1] |
| | | 1 Apr 2015 (otherwise) (SSI 2014/261)[2] |
| | (3) | 30 Jun 2014 (SSI 2014/172)[1] |
| | (4) | 30 Jun 2014 (for the purpose of making regulations, orders or rules of court) (SSI 2014/172)[1] |
| | | 1 Apr 2015 (otherwise) (SSI 2014/261)[2] |
| 54, 55 | | 30 Apr 2014 (s 57(1)) |
| 56 | (1) | See Sch 3 below |
| | (2) | See Sch 4 below |
| 57, 58 | | 30 Apr 2014 (s 57(1)) |
| Sch 1 | | 30 Jun 2014 (for the purpose of making regulations, orders or rules of court) (SSI 2014/172) |
| Sch 2 | | 1 Apr 2015 (SSI 2014/261)[2] |
| Sch 3 | para 1 | 30 Jun 2014 (SSI 2014/172) |
| | para 2 | See paras 3–37 below |
| | paras 3–33 | 1 Apr 2015 (SSI 2014/261)[2] |
| | para 34 | 30 Jun 2014 (SSI 2014/172) |
| | para 35(a)–(g) | 1 Apr 2015 (SSI 2014/261)[2] |
| | para 35(h) | 30 Jun 2014 (SSI 2014/172) |
| | paras 36, 37 | 1 Apr 2015 (SSI 2014/261)[2] |
| | para 38 | 30 Jun 2014 (SSI 2014/172)[1] |
| | paras 39–41 | 1 Apr 2015 (SSI 2014/261)[2] |
| Sch 4 | | 30 Jun 2014 (SSI 2014/172), repeals of or in— |
| | | Bankruptcy (Scotland) Act 1985, ss 5B(5)(d), 72(1), Sch 5, para 5(2)(aa); |
| | | Home Owner and Debtor Protection (Scotland) Act 2010 |
| | | 1 Apr 2015 (otherwise) (SSI 2014/261)[2] |

[1]  For a saving, see SSI 2014/172, art 3

[2]  For savings and transitional arrangements, see SSI 2014/261, arts 4–12

## Bishops and Priests (Consecration and Ordination of Women) Measure 2014 (No 2)

*RA:* 23 Oct 2014

*Commencement provisions:* s 4(2)

This Measure was brought into force by the following instruments made under s 4(2) by the Archbishops of Canterbury and York:

Bishops and Priests (Consecration and Ordination of Women) Measure 2014 (Appointed Day No 1) Instrument 2014, 2014 No 4, dated 14 Nov 2014

Bishops and Priests (Consecration and Ordination of Women) Measure 2014 (Appointed Day No 2) Instrument 2014, 2014 No 5, dated 17 Nov 2017

| | |
|---|---|
| 1(1) | 14 Nov 2014 (2014 No 4) |
| 1(2), (3) | 17 Nov 2014 (2014 No 5) |
| 2 | 17 Nov 2014 (2014 No 5) |
| 3 | See Schedule below |
| 4 | 14 Nov 2014 (2014 No 4) |
| Schedule | 17 Nov 2014 (2014 No 5) |

## Budget (Scotland) Act 2014 (asp 6)

*RA:* 12 Mar 2014

*Commencement provisions:* s 10

Whole Act in force 13 Mar 2014 (s 10)

---

## Buildings (Recovery of Expenses) (Scotland) Act 2014 (asp 13)

*RA:* 24 Jul 2014

*Commencement provisions:* s 3

| | |
|---|---|
| 1, 2 | 24 Jan 2015 (s 3(2)) |
| 3, 4 | 25 Jul 2014 (s 3(1)) |

---

## Burrell Collection (Lending and Borrowing) (Scotland) Act 2014 (asp 4)

*RA:* 25 Feb 2014

*Commencement provisions:* s 4

| | | |
|---|---|---|
| 1 | (1) | *Not yet in force* |
| | (2)(a) | 26 Feb 2014 (s 4(1)) |
| | (2)(b), (3) | *Not yet in force* |
| 2 | | *Not yet in force* |
| 3–5 | | 26 Feb 2014 (s 4(1)) |

---

## Care Act 2014 (c 23)

*RA:* 14 May 2014

*Commencement provisions:* s 127; Care Act 2014 (Commencement No 1) Order 2014, SI 2014/1714; Care Act 2014 (Commencement No 2) Order 2014, SI 2014/2473; Care Act 2014 (Commencement No 3) Order 2014, SI 2014/3186; Care Act 2014 (Commencement No 4) Order 2015, SI 2015/993; Care Act 2014 (Commencement No 5) Order 2016, SI 2016/464

| | | |
|---|---|---|
| 1 | | 1 Apr 2015 (SI 2015/993) |
| 2 | (1), (2) | 1 Apr 2015 (SI 2015/993) |
| | (3), (4) | 1 Oct 2014 (in so far as is necessary for enabling the exercise of any power to make regulations or amendments) (SI 2014/2473) |
| | | 1 Apr 2015 (otherwise) (SI 2015/993) |
| 3–11 | | 1 Apr 2015 (SI 2015/993) |
| 12 | (1), (2) | 1 Oct 2014 (in so far as is necessary for enabling the exercise of any power to make regulations or amendments) (SI 2014/2473) |
| | | 1 Apr 2015 (otherwise) (SI 2015/993) |
| | (3)–(11) | 1 Apr 2015 (SI 2015/993) |
| 13 | (1)–(6) | 1 Apr 2015 (SI 2015/993) |
| | (7), (8) | 1 Oct 2014 (in so far as is necessary for enabling the exercise of any power to make regulations or amendments) (SI 2014/2473) |
| | | 1 Apr 2015 (otherwise) (SI 2015/993) |
| 14 | (1) | 1 Apr 2015 (SI 2015/993) |
| | (2) | *Not yet in force* |
| | (3), (4) | 1 Apr 2015 (SI 2015/993) |
| | (5)–(8) | 1 Oct 2014 (in so far as is necessary for enabling the exercise of any power to make regulations or amendments) (SI 2014/2473) |
| | | 1 Apr 2015 (otherwise) (SI 2015/993) |
| 15, 16 | | *Not yet in force* |
| 17 | (1) | 1 Apr 2015 (SI 2015/993) |
| | (2) | *Not yet in force* |
| | (3)–(6) | 1 Apr 2015 (SI 2015/993) |

**Care Act 2014 (c 23)**—*contd*

|  |  |  |
|---|---|---|
| | (7) | 1 Oct 2014 (in so far as is necessary for enabling the exercise of any power to make regulations or amendments) (SI 2014/2473) |
| | | 1 Apr 2015 (otherwise) (SI 2015/993) |
| | (8) | 1 Oct 2014 (in so far as is necessary for enabling the exercise of the power to make regulations) (SI 2014/2473)[1] |
| | | 1 Apr 2015 (otherwise) (SI 2015/993) |
| | (9)–(13) | 1 Oct 2014 (in so far as is necessary for enabling the exercise of any power to make regulations or amendments) (SI 2014/2473) |
| | | 1 Apr 2015 (otherwise) (SI 2015/993) |
| 18 | (1)(a) | 1 Apr 2015 (except in so far as it imposes any duty on a local authority to meet an adult's needs for care and support by the provision of accommodation in a care home in a case where Condition 2 in section 18(3) is met) (SI 2015/993)[2] |
| | | *Not yet in force* (exception noted above) |
| | (1)(b) | *Not yet in force* |
| | (1)(c), (2)–(4) | 1 Apr 2015 (except in so far as it imposes any duty on a local authority to meet an adult's needs for care and support by the provision of accommodation in a care home in a case where Condition 2 in section 18(3) is met) (SI 2015/993) |
| | | *Not yet in force* (exception noted above) |
| | (5) | *Not yet in force* |
| | (6), (7) | 1 Apr 2015 (except in so far as it imposes any duty on a local authority to meet an adult's needs for care and support by the provision of accommodation in a care home in a case where Condition 2 in section 18(3) is met) (SI 2015/993) |
| | | *Not yet in force* (exception noted above) |
| 19–21 | | 1 Apr 2015 (SI 2015/993) |
| 22 | (1)–(3) | 1 Apr 2015 (SI 2015/993) |
| | (4)(a) | 1 Oct 2014 (in so far as is necessary for enabling the exercise of any power to make regulations or amendments) (SI 2014/2473) |
| | | 1 Apr 2015 (otherwise) (SI 2015/993) |
| | (4)(b), (5) | 1 Apr 2015 (SI 2015/993) |
| | (6) | 1 Oct 2014 (in so far as is necessary for enabling the exercise of any power to make regulations or amendments) (SI 2014/2473) |
| | | 1 Apr 2015 (otherwise) (SI 2015/993) |
| | (7)–(10) | 1 Apr 2015 (SI 2015/993) |
| 23 | (1)(a) | 1 Apr 2015 (SI 2015/993) |
| | (1)(b) | 1 Oct 2014 (in so far as is necessary for enabling the exercise of any power to make regulations or amendments) (SI 2014/2473) |
| | | 1 Apr 2015 (otherwise) (SI 2015/993) |
| | (2), (3) | 1 Apr 2015 (SI 2015/993) |
| 24 | (1), (2) | 1 Apr 2015 (SI 2015/993) |
| | (3) | *Not yet in force* |
| 25 | | 1 Apr 2015 (SI 2015/993) |
| 26 | (1) | 1 Apr 2015 (SI 2015/993) |
| | (2) | *Not yet in force* |
| | (3) | 1 Apr 2015 (SI 2015/993) |
| | (4) | 1 Oct 2014 (in so far as is necessary for enabling the exercise of any power to make regulations or amendments) (SI 2014/2473) |
| | | 1 Apr 2015 (otherwise) (SI 2015/993) |
| 27 | | 1 Apr 2015 (SI 2015/993) |
| 28, 29 | | *Not yet in force* |
| 30 | | 1 Oct 2014 (in so far as is necessary for enabling the exercise of any power to make regulations or amendments) (SI 2014/2473) |
| | | 1 Apr 2015 (otherwise) (SI 2015/993) |
| 31, 32 | | 1 Apr 2015 (SI 2015/993) |
| 33 | (1), (2) | 1 Oct 2014 (in so far as is necessary for enabling the exercise of any power to make regulations or amendments) (SI 2014/2473) |
| | | 1 Apr 2015 (otherwise) (SI 2015/993) |
| | (3)–(5) | 1 Apr 2015 (SI 2015/993) |

**Care Act 2014 (c 23)**—*contd*

| | | |
|---|---|---|
| 34 | (1), (2) | 1 Oct 2014 (in so far as is necessary for enabling the exercise of any power to make regulations or amendments) (SI 2014/2473) |
| | | 1 Apr 2015 (otherwise) (SI 2015/993) |
| | (3) | 1 Apr 2015 (SI 2015/993) |
| | (4)–(8) | 1 Oct 2014 (in so far as is necessary for enabling the exercise of any power to make regulations or amendments) (SI 2014/2473) |
| | | 1 Apr 2015 (otherwise) (SI 2015/993) |
| 35 | | 1 Oct 2014 (in so far as is necessary for enabling the exercise of any power to make regulations or amendments) (SI 2014/2473) |
| | | 1 Apr 2015 (otherwise) (SI 2015/993) |
| 36 | | *Not yet in force* |
| 37 | (1) | 1 Apr 2015 (SI 2015/993) |
| | (2) | *Not yet in force* |
| | (3), (4)(a) | 1 Apr 2015 (SI 2015/993) |
| | (4)(b) | 1 Apr 2015 (SI 2015/993)[2] |
| | (5)(a) | 1 Apr 2015 (SI 2015/993) |
| | (5)(b)–(d) | *Not yet in force* |
| | (5)(e), (f), (6)–(13) | 1 Apr 2015 (SI 2015/993) |
| | (14) | 1 Apr 2015 (SI 2015/993)[2] |
| | (15) | 1 Apr 2015 (SI 2015/993) |
| 38 | (1)(a) | 1 Apr 2015 (SI 2015/993)[2] |
| | (1)(b) | *Not yet in force* |
| | (2)–(7) | 1 Apr 2015 (SI 2015/993) |
| | (8) | 1 Oct 2014 (in so far as is necessary for enabling the exercise of any power to make regulations or amendments) (SI 2014/2473) |
| | | 1 Apr 2015 (otherwise) (SI 2015/993) |
| 39 | (1) | 1 Oct 2014 (in so far as is necessary for enabling the exercise of any power to make regulations or amendments) (SI 2014/2473) |
| | | 1 Apr 2015 (otherwise) (SI 2015/993) |
| | (2) | 1 Apr 2015 (SI 2015/993) |
| | (3) | 1 Oct 2014 (in so far as is necessary for enabling the exercise of any power to make regulations or amendments) (SI 2014/2473) |
| | | 1 Apr 2015 (otherwise) (SI 2015/993) |
| | (4)(a) | 1 Apr 2015 (SI 2015/993) |
| | (4)(b) | 1 Apr 2015 (SI 2015/993)[2] |
| | (5)–(7) | 1 Apr 2015 (SI 2015/993) |
| | (8) | See Sch 1 below |
| 40 | (1)–(3) | 1 Apr 2015 (SI 2015/993) |
| | (4) | 1 Oct 2014 (in so far as is necessary for enabling the exercise of any power to make regulations or amendments) (SI 2014/2473) |
| | | 1 Apr 2015 (otherwise) (SI 2015/993) |
| 41, 42 | | 1 Apr 2015 (SI 2015/993) |
| 43 | (1)–(4) | 1 Apr 2015 (SI 2015/993) |
| | (5) | See Sch 2 below |
| | (6) | 1 Apr 2015 (SI 2015/993) |
| 44–49 | | 1 Apr 2015 (SI 2015/993) |
| 50 | | 6 Apr 2016 (SI 2016/464) |
| 51 | | 1 Apr 2015 (SI 2015/993) |
| 52 | (1)–(11) | 1 Apr 2015 (in so far as relates to ss 48, 49, 51) (SI 2015/993) |
| | | 6 Apr 2016 (otherwise) (SI 2016/464) |
| | (12) | 1 Oct 2014 (in so far as is necessary for enabling the exercise of any power to make regulations or amendments) (SI 2014/2473) |
| | | 1 Apr 2015 (otherwise, in so far as relates to ss 48, 49, 51) (SI 2015/993) |
| | | 6 Apr 2016 (otherwise) (SI 2016/464) |
| | (13) | 6 Apr 2016 (otherwise) (SI 2016/464) (SI 2015/993) |
| | | 6 Apr 2016 (otherwise) (SI 2016/464) |
| | (14) | *Not yet in force* |

**Care Act 2014 (c 23)**—*contd*

| | | |
|---|---|---|
| 53 | (1), (2) | 1 Oct 2014 (in so far as is necessary for enabling the exercise of any power to make regulations or amendments) (SI 2014/2473) |
| | | 6 Apr 2015 (otherwise) (SI 2015/993) |
| | (3)–(6) | 6 Apr 2015 (SI 2015/993) |
| | (7) | 1 Oct 2014 (in so far as is necessary for enabling the exercise of any power to make regulations or amendments) (SI 2014/2473) |
| | | 6 Apr 2015 (otherwise) (SI 2015/993) |
| 54 | | 6 Apr 2015 (SI 2015/993) |
| 55 | (1)–(4) | 6 Apr 2015 (SI 2015/993) |
| | (5) | 1 Oct 2014 (in so far as is necessary for enabling the exercise of any power to make regulations or amendments) (SI 2014/2473) |
| | | 6 Apr 2015 (otherwise) (SI 2015/993) |
| | (6), (7) | 6 Apr 2015 (SI 2015/993) |
| 56, 57 | | 6 Apr 2015 (SI 2015/993) |
| 58–61 | | 1 Apr 2015 (SI 2015/993) |
| 62 | (1) | 1 Apr 2015 (SI 2015/993) |
| | (2) | 1 Oct 2014 (in so far as is necessary for enabling the exercise of any power to make regulations or amendments) (SI 2014/2473) |
| | | 1 Apr 2015 (otherwise) (SI 2015/993) |
| | (3), (4) | 1 Apr 2015 (SI 2015/993) |
| 63, 64 | | 1 Apr 2015 (SI 2015/993) |
| 65 | (1) | 1 Oct 2014 (in so far as is necessary for enabling the exercise of any power to make regulations or amendments) (SI 2014/2473) |
| | | 1 Apr 2015 (otherwise) (SI 2015/993) |
| | (2)–(7) | 1 Apr 2015 (SI 2015/993) |
| 66 | | 1 Apr 2015 (SI 2015/993) |
| 67 | (1)–(6) | 1 Apr 2015 (SI 2015/993) |
| | (7) | 1 Oct 2014 (in so far as is necessary for enabling the exercise of any power to make regulations or amendments) (SI 2014/2473) |
| | | 1 Apr 2015 (otherwise) (SI 2015/993) |
| | (8), (9) | 1 Apr 2015 (SI 2015/993) |
| 68–70 | | 1 Apr 2015 (SI 2015/993) |
| 71, 72 | | *Not yet in force* |
| 73 | | 1 Apr 2015 (SI 2015/993) |
| 74 | | See Sch 3 below |
| 75 | (1)–(5) | 1 Apr 2015 (SI 2015/993)[2] |
| | (6) | 1 Oct 2014 (in so far as is necessary for enabling the exercise of any power to make regulations or amendments) (SI 2014/2473) |
| | | 1 Apr 2015 (otherwise) (SI 2015/993)[2] |
| | (7) | See Sch 4, Pt 1 below |
| | (8) | 6 Apr 2016 (SI 2016/464) |
| | (9) | See Sch 4, Pt 2 below |
| | (10), (11) | 6 Apr 2016 (SI 2016/464) |
| | (12), (13) | 1 Apr 2015 (SI 2015/993)[2] |
| 76 | | 1 Apr 2015 (SI 2015/993) |
| 77 | (1) | 1 Apr 2015 (SI 2015/993) |
| | (2) | 1 Oct 2014 (in so far as is necessary for enabling the exercise of any power to make regulations or amendments) (SI 2014/2473) |
| | | 1 Apr 2015 (otherwise) (SI 2015/993) |
| | (3)–(5) | 1 Apr 2015 (SI 2015/993) |
| 78, 79 | | 1 Apr 2015 (SI 2015/993) |
| 80 | (1) | 1 Oct 2014 (in so far as is necessary for enabling the exercise of any power to make regulations or amendments) (SI 2014/2473) |
| | | 1 Apr 2015 (in so far as relates to provisions commenced by SI 2015/993) (SI 2015/993) |
| | | *Not yet in force* (otherwise) |
| | (2), (3) | 1 Apr 2015 (in so far as relates to provisions commenced by SI 2015/993) (SI 2015/993) |
| | | *Not yet in force* (otherwise) |

**See Halsbury's Statutes Citator for amendments to these Acts**

**Care Act 2014 (c 23)**—*contd*

| | | |
|---|---|---|
| 81 | | 7 Jul 2014 (in so far as necessary to enable the making of regulations) (SI 2014/1714) |
| | | 15 Jul 2014 (otherwise) (SI 2014/1714) |
| 82, 83 | | 1 Apr 2015 (SI 2015/993) |
| 84, 85 | | 15 Jul 2014 (SI 2014/1714) |
| 86–90 | | 1 Oct 2014 (SI 2014/2473) |
| 91 | (1) | See sub-ss (2)–(9) below |
| | (2) | 7 Jul 2014 (in so far as necessary to enable the making of regulations) (SI 2014/1714) |
| | | 1 Oct 2014 (otherwise) (SI 2014/1714) |
| | (3)–(9) | 1 Oct 2014 (SI 2014/1714) |
| 92 | (1) | 15 Jul 2014 (in so far as necessary to enable the making of regulations) (SI 2014/1714) |
| | | 1 Apr 2015 (otherwise) (SI 2015/993) |
| | (2) | 1 Apr 2015 (SI 2015/993) |
| | (3)–(6) | 15 Jul 2014 (in so far as necessary to enable the making of regulations) (SI 2014/1714) |
| | | 1 Apr 2015 (otherwise) (SI 2015/993) |
| | (7)–(9) | 1 Apr 2015 (SI 2015/993) |
| 93–94 | | 1 Apr 2015 (SI 2015/993) |
| 95 | | 1 Oct 2014 (SI 2014/2473) |
| 96 | (1) | 1 Apr 2015 (SI 2014/3186) |
| | (2) | See Sch 5 below |
| | (3) | 1 Apr 2015 (SI 2014/3186) |
| | (4) | 1 Oct 2014 (in so far as is necessary for enabling the exercise of any power to make regulations or orders or to give directions) (SI 2014/2473) |
| | | 1 Apr 2015 (otherwise) (SI 2014/3186) |
| 97 | (1)–(6) | 1 Apr 2015 (SI 2014/3186) |
| | (7) | 1 Oct 2014 (SI 2014/2473) |
| | (8), (9) | 1 Apr 2015 (SI 2014/3186) |
| 98 | | 1 Apr 2015 (SI 2014/3186) |
| 99–103 | | 1 Apr 2015 (SI 2014/3186) |
| 104 | (1), (2), (3)(a) | 1 Apr 2015 (SI 2014/3186) |
| | (3)(b) | 1 Oct 2014 (in so far as is necessary for enabling the exercise of any power to make regulations or orders or to give directions) (SI 2014/2473) |
| | | 1 Apr 2015 (otherwise) (SI 2014/3186) |
| | (3)(c) | 1 Apr 2015 (SI 2014/3186) |
| | (4) | 1 Oct 2014 (in so far as is necessary for enabling the exercise of any power to make regulations or orders or to give directions) (SI 2014/2473) |
| | | 1 Apr 2015 (otherwise) (SI 2014/3186) |
| | (5)–(12) | 1 Apr 2015 (SI 2014/3186) |
| | (13)(a) | 1 Oct 2014 (in so far as is necessary for enabling the exercise of any power to make regulations or orders or to give directions) (SI 2014/2473) |
| | | 1 Apr 2015 (otherwise) (SI 2014/3186) |
| | (13)(b), (c) | 1 Apr 2015 (SI 2014/3186) |
| | (14) | See Sch 6 below |
| 105 | (1) | 1 Oct 2014 (in so far as is necessary for enabling the exercise of any power to make regulations or orders or to give directions) (SI 2014/2473) |
| | | 1 Apr 2015 (otherwise) (SI 2014/3186) |
| | (2), (3) | 1 Apr 2015 (SI 2014/3186) |
| | (4) | 1 Oct 2014 (in so far as is necessary for enabling the exercise of any power to make regulations or orders or to give directions) (SI 2014/2473) |
| | | 1 Apr 2015 (otherwise) (SI 2014/3186) |
| 106–108 | | 1 Apr 2015 (SI 2014/3186) |

**Care Act 2014 (c 23)**—*contd*

| | | |
|---|---|---|
| 109 | (1) | 1 Jan 2015 (SI 2014/2473) |
| | (2) | See Sch 7 below |
| | (3) | *Not yet in force* |
| | (4) | 1 Oct 2014 (SI 2014/2473) |
| 110–112 | | 1 Jan 2015 (SI 2014/2473) |
| 113 | (1)–(3) | 1 Jan 2015 (SI 2014/2473) |
| | (4) | See Sch 8 below |
| 114–117 | | 1 Jan 2015 (SI 2014/2473) |
| 118 | | 1 Oct 2014 (SI 2014/2473) |
| 119 | | 1 Oct 2014 (in so far as is necessary for enabling the exercise of any power to make regulations or orders or to give directions, in so far as it relates to Health Education England) (SI 2014/2473) |
| | | 1 Jan 2015 (in so far as it relates to Health Research Authority) (SI 2014/2473) |
| | | 1 Apr 2015 (otherwise) (SI 2014/3186) |
| 120 | | 15 Jul 2014 (SI 2014/1714) |
| 121 | | 1 Oct 2014 (SI 2014/2473) |
| 122 | (1) | See sub-ss (2)–(4) below |
| | (2), (3) | 15 Jul 2014 (SI 2014/1714) |
| | (4) | 1 Jan 2015 (SI 2014/2473) |
| 123–129 | | 14 May 2014 (s 127(2)) |
| Sch 1 | para 1(1)–(5) | 1 Apr 2015 (SI 2015/993) |
| | para 1(6), (7) | 1 Oct 2014 (in so far as is necessary for enabling the exercise of any power to make regulations or amendments) (SI 2014/2473) |
| | | 1 Apr 2015 (otherwise) (SI 2015/993) |
| | para 2(1) | 1 Apr 2015 (SI 2015/993) |
| | para 2(2)–(8) | 6 Apr 2016 (SI 2016/464) |
| | para 2(9), (10) | 1 Oct 2014 (in so far as is necessary for enabling the exercise of any power to make regulations or amendments) (SI 2014/2473) |
| | | 1 Apr 2015 (otherwise) (SI 2015/993) |
| | para 3(1)–(3) | 1 Apr 2015 (SI 2015/993) |
| | para 3(4) | 1 Oct 2014 (SI 2014/2473) |
| | paras 3(5) | 1 Apr 2015 (SI 2015/993) |
| | para 4(1)–(4) | 1 Apr 2015 (SI 2015/993) |
| | para 4(5), (6) | 1 Oct 2014 (in so far as is necessary for enabling the exercise of any power to make regulations or amendments) (SI 2014/2473) |
| | | 1 Apr 2015 (otherwise) (SI 2015/993) |
| | para 5(1)–(8) | 1 Apr 2015 (SI 2015/993) |
| | para 5(9)–(11) | 1 Oct 2014 (in so far as is necessary for enabling the exercise of any power to make regulations or amendments) (SI 2014/2473) |
| | | 1 Apr 2015 (otherwise) (SI 2015/993) |
| | paras 6–8 | 1 Apr 2015 (SI 2015/993) |
| | paras 9, 10 | *Not yet in force* |
| | para 11 | 1 Oct 2014 (in so far as is necessary for enabling the exercise of any power to make regulations or amendments) (SI 2014/2473) |
| | | 1 Apr 2015 (otherwise) (SI 2015/993) |
| | para 12 | 1 Apr 2015 (SI 2015/993) |
| | para 13 | 6 Apr 2016 (SI 2016/464) |
| | para 14(1), (2) | 1 Apr 2015 (SI 2015/993) |
| | para 14(3) | 1 Apr 2015 (in so far as relates to para 2(1)) (SI 2015/993) |
| | | *Not yet in force* (otherwise) |
| | para 14(4) | *Not yet in force* |
| | para 14(5)–(7) | 1 Apr 2015 (SI 2015/993) |
| Sch 2 | | 1 Apr 2015 (SI 2015/993) |
| Sch 3 | para 1 | 1 Apr 2015 (SI 2015/993) |
| | para 2(1)–(4) | 1 Apr 2015 (SI 2015/993) |
| | para 2(5)(a) | 1 Apr 2015 (SI 2015/993) |

**Care Act 2014 (c 23)**—*contd*

| | | |
|---|---|---|
| | para 2(5)(b) | 1 Oct 2014 (in so far as is necessary for enabling the exercise of any power to make regulations or amendments) (SI 2014/2473) |
| | | 1 Apr 2015 (otherwise) (SI 2015/993) |
| | para 2(6) | 1 Apr 2015 (SI 2015/993) |
| | paras 3, 4(1)–(5) | 1 Apr 2015 (SI 2015/993) |
| | para 4(6) | 1 Oct 2014 (in so far as is necessary for enabling the exercise of any power to make regulations or amendments) (SI 2014/2473) |
| | | 1 Apr 2015 (otherwise) (SI 2015/993) |
| | para 4(7) | 1 Apr 2015 (SI 2015/993) |
| | para 5 | 1 Apr 2015 (SI 2015/993) |
| | para 6 | 1 Oct 2014 (in so far as is necessary for enabling the exercise of any power to make regulations or amendments) (SI 2014/2473) |
| | | 1 Apr 2015 (otherwise) (SI 2015/993) |
| | para 7 | 1 Apr 2015 (SI 2015/993) |
| | para 8 | 1 Oct 2014 (in so far as is necessary for enabling the exercise of any power to make regulations or amendments) (SI 2014/2473) |
| | | 1 Apr 2015 (otherwise) (SI 2015/993) |
| Sch 4 | Pt 1, para 1(1)–(9) | 1 Apr 2015 (SI 2015/993)[2] |
| | Pt 1, para 1(10), (11) | 1 Oct 2014 (in so far as is necessary for enabling the exercise of any power to make regulations or amendments) (SI 2014/2473) |
| | | 1 Apr 2015 (otherwise) (SI 2015/993) |
| | Pt 2 | 6 Apr 2016 (SI 2016/464) |
| Sch 5 | para 1 | *Not yet in force* |
| | para 2(1), (2) | 1 Oct 2014 (in so far as is necessary for enabling the exercise of any power to make regulations or amendments) (SI 2014/2473) |
| | | 1 Apr 2015 (otherwise) (SI 2014/3186) |
| | para 2(3) | 1 Apr 2015 (SI 2014/3186) |
| | paras 3–24 | 1 Apr 2015 (SI 2014/3186) |
| | paras 25, 26 | 1 Oct 2014 (in so far as is necessary for enabling the exercise of any power to make regulations or amendments) (SI 2014/2473) |
| | | 1 Apr 2015 (otherwise) (SI 2014/3186) |
| | paras 27–35 | 1 Apr 2015 (SI 2014/3186) |
| Sch 6 | paras 1, 2(1)–(7) | 1 Apr 2015 (SI 2014/3186) |
| | para 2(8) | 1 Oct 2014 (in so far as is necessary for enabling the exercise of any power to make regulations or amendments) (SI 2014/2473) |
| | | 1 Apr 2015 (otherwise) (SI 2014/3186) |
| | para 2(9), (10) | 1 Apr 2015 (SI 2014/3186) |
| | paras 3, 4 | 1 Apr 2015 (SI 2014/3186) |
| Sch 7 | paras 1–8 | 1 Jan 2015 (SI 2014/2473) |
| | para 9 | 15 Jul 2014 (in so far as necessary to enable the making of regulations) (SI 2014/1714) |
| | | 1 Jan 2015 (otherwise) (SI 2014/2473) |
| | paras 10–27 | 1 Jan 2015 (SI 2014/2473) |
| Sch 8 | | 1 Jan 2015 (SI 2014/2473) |

[1]   For a transitory modification, see SI 2014/2473, art 7(2)

[2]   For transitory modifications, see SI 2015/993, arts 5–7

---

**Childcare Payments Act 2014 (c 28)**

*RA:* 17 Dec 2014

*Commencement provisions*: s 75; Childcare Payments Act 2014 (Commencement No 1) Regulations 2016, SI 2016/763; Childcare Payments Act 2014 (Commencement No 2) Regulations 2016, SI 2016/1083; Childcare Payments Act 2014 (Commencement No 3 and Transitional Provisions) Regulations 2017, SI 2017/578; Childcare Payments Act 2014 (Commencement No 4) Regulations 2017, SI 2017/750; Childcare Payments Act 2014 (Commencement No 5) Regulations 2017, SI 2017/1116; Childcare Payments Act 2014 (Commencement No 6) Regulations 2018, SI 2018/27

**Childcare Payments Act 2014 (c 28)**—*contd*

| | |
|---|---|
| 1 | 14 Nov 2016 (for the purpose of "the trial") (SI 2016/1083)[1] |
| | 21 Apr 2017 (in respect of (a) a child born on or after 1 Sep 2013 and any sibling; and (b) a disabled child and any sibling) (SI 2017/578) |
| | 16 May 2017 (in respect of those recruited to participate in "the trial") (SI 2017/578)[1] |
| | 14 Jul 2017 (in respect of a child born on or after 1 Apr 2013 and before 1 Sep 2013, and any sibling) (SI 2017/750) |
| | 24 Nov 2017 (in respect of a child born on or after 24 Nov and before 1 Apr 2013 and any sibling) (SI 2017/1116) |
| | 15 Jan 2018 (in respect of a child born on or after 15 Jan 2009 and before 24 Nov 2011) (SI 2018/27) |
| | 14 Feb 2018 (otherwise) (SI 2018/27) |
| 2 | 14 Nov 2016 (for the purpose of "the trial") (SI 2016/1083)[1] |
| | 21 Apr 2017 (otherwise) (SI 2017/578) |
| 3 | 14 Nov 2016 (for the purpose of "the trial") (SI 2016/1083)[1, 2] |
| | 21 Apr 2017 (in respect of (a) a child born on or after 1 Sep 2013 and any sibling; and (b) a disabled child and any sibling) (SI 2017/578) |
| | 16 May 2017 (in respect of those recruited to participate in "the trial") (SI 2017/578)[1] |
| | 14 Jul 2017 (in respect of a child born on or after 1 Apr 2013 and before 1 Sep 2013, and any sibling) (SI 2017/750) |
| | 24 Nov 2017 (in respect of a child born on or after 24 Nov and before 1 Apr 2013 and any sibling) (SI 2017/1116) |
| | 15 Jan 2018 (in respect of a child born on or after 15 Jan 2009 and before 24 Nov 2011) (SI 2018/27) |
| | 14 Feb 2018 (otherwise) (SI 2018/27) |
| 4 | 14 Nov 2016 (for the purpose of "the trial") (SI 2016/1083)[1] |
| | 21 Apr 2017 (in respect of (a) a child born on or after 1 Sep 2013 and any sibling; and (b) a disabled child and any sibling) (SI 2017/578) |
| | 16 May 2017 (in respect of those recruited to participate in "the trial") (SI 2017/578)[1] |
| | 14 Jul 2017 (in respect of a child born on or after 1 Apr 2013 and before 1 Sep 2013, and any sibling) (SI 2017/750) |
| | 24 Nov 2017 (in respect of a child born on or after 24 Nov and before 1 Apr 2013 and any sibling) (SI 2017/1116) |
| | 15 Jan 2018 (in respect of a child born on or after 15 Jan 2009 and before 24 Nov 2011) (SI 2018/27) |
| | 14 Feb 2018 (otherwise) (SI 2018/27) |
| 5 | 14 Nov 2016 (for the purpose of "the trial") (SI 2016/1083)[1] |
| | 21 Apr 2017 (otherwise) (SI 2017/578) |
| 6–11 | 14 Nov 2016 (for the purpose of "the trial") (SI 2016/1083)[1] |
| | 21 Apr 2017 (in respect of (a) a child born on or after 1 Sep 2013 and any sibling; and (b) a disabled child and any sibling) (SI 2017/578) |
| | 16 May 2017 (in respect of those recruited to participate in "the trial") (SI 2017/578)[1] |
| | 14 Jul 2017 (in respect of a child born on or after 1 Apr 2013 and before 1 Sep 2013, and any sibling) (SI 2017/750) |
| | 24 Nov 2017 (in respect of a child born on or after 24 Nov and before 1 Apr 2013 and any sibling) (SI 2017/1116) |
| | 15 Jan 2018 (in respect of a child born on or after 15 Jan 2009 and before 24 Nov 2011) (SI 2018/27) |
| | 14 Feb 2018 (otherwise) (SI 2018/27) |
| 12 | 21 Apr 2017 (in respect of (a) a child born on or after 1 Sep 2013 and any sibling; and (b) a disabled child and any sibling) (SI 2017/578)[3] |

**Childcare Payments Act 2014 (c 28)**—*contd*

|  |  |
|---|---|
|  | 16 May 2017 (in respect of those recruited to participate in "the trial") (SI 2017/578)[1] |
|  | 14 Jul 2017 (in respect of a child born on or after 1 Apr 2013 and before 1 Sep 2013, and any sibling) (SI 2017/750) |
|  | 24 Nov 2017 (in respect of a child born on or after 24 Nov and before 1 Apr 2013 and any sibling) (SI 2017/1116) |
|  | 15 Jan 2018 (in respect of a child born on or after 15 Jan 2009 and before 24 Nov 2011) (SI 2018/27) |
|  | 14 Feb 2018 (otherwise) (SI 2018/27) |
| 13–15 | 14 Nov 2016 (for the purpose of "the trial") (SI 2016/1083)[1] |
|  | 21 Apr 2017 (in respect of (a) a child born on or after 1 Sep 2013 and any sibling; and (b) a disabled child and any sibling) (SI 2017/578) |
|  | 16 May 2017 (in respect of those recruited to participate in "the trial") (SI 2017/578)[1] |
|  | 14 Jul 2017 (in respect of a child born on or after 1 Apr 2013 and before 1 Sep 2013, and any sibling) (SI 2017/750) |
|  | 24 Nov 2017 (in respect of a child born on or after 24 Nov and before 1 Apr 2013 and any sibling) (SI 2017/1116) |
|  | 15 Jan 2018 (in respect of a child born on or after 15 Jan 2009 and before 24 Nov 2011) (SI 2018/27) |
|  | 14 Feb 2018 (otherwise) (SI 2018/27) |
| 16 | 14 Nov 2016 (for the purpose of "the trial") (SI 2016/1083)[1] |
|  | 21 Apr 2017 (otherwise) (SI 2017/578) |
| 17–25 | 14 Nov 2016 (for the purpose of "the trial") (SI 2016/1083)[1] |
|  | 21 Apr 2017 (in respect of (a) a child born on or after 1 Sep 2013 and any sibling; and (b) a disabled child and any sibling) (SI 2017/578) |
|  | 16 May 2017 (in respect of those recruited to participate in "the trial") (SI 2017/578)[1] |
|  | 14 Jul 2017 (in respect of a child born on or after 1 Apr 2013 and before 1 Sep 2013, and any sibling) (SI 2017/750) |
|  | 24 Nov 2017 (in respect of a child born on or after 24 Nov and before 1 Apr 2013 and any sibling) (SI 2017/1116) |
|  | 15 Jan 2018 (in respect of a child born on or after 15 Jan 2009 and before 24 Nov 2011) (SI 2018/27) |
|  | 14 Feb 2018 (otherwise) (SI 2018/27) |
| 26–29 | 20 Jul 2016 (SI 2016/763) |
| 30 | 14 Nov 2016 (for the purpose of "the trial") (SI 2016/1083)[1] |
|  | 21 Apr 2017 (otherwise) (SI 2017/578)[3] |
| 31 | 21 Apr 2017 (SI 2017/578) |
| 32–38 | 14 Nov 2016 (for the purpose of "the trial") (SI 2016/1083)[1] |
|  | 21 Apr 2017 (otherwise) (SI 2017/578) |
| 39 | 21 Apr 2017 (SI 2017/578) |
| 40–42 | 14 Nov 2016 (for the purpose of "the trial") (SI 2016/1083)[1] |
|  | 21 Apr 2017 (otherwise) (SI 2017/578) |
| 43 | 20 Jul 2016 (SI 2016/763) |
| 44–46 | 14 Nov 2016 (for the purpose of "the trial") (SI 2016/1083)[1] |
|  | 21 Apr 2017 (otherwise) (SI 2017/578) |
| 47 | 20 Jul 2016 (in respect of penalties under s 43) (SI 2016/763) |
|  | 14 Nov 2016 (for the purpose of "the trial") (SI 2016/1083)[1] |
|  | 21 Apr 2017 (otherwise) (SI 2017/578) |
| 48–61 | 14 Nov 2016 (for the purpose of "the trial") (SI 2016/1083)[1] |
|  | 21 Apr 2017 (otherwise) (SI 2017/578) |
| 62 | 14 Nov 2016 (for the purpose of "the trial") (SI 2016/1083)[1] |
|  | 21 Apr 2017 (in respect of (a) a child born on or after 1 Sep 2013 and any sibling; and (b) a disabled child and any sibling) (SI 2017/578) |
|  | 16 May 2017 (in respect of those recruited to participate in "the trial") (SI 2017/578)[1] |

**Childcare Payments Act 2014 (c 28)**—*contd*

|  |  |  |
|---|---|---|
|  |  | 14 Jul 2017 (in respect of a child born on or after 1 Apr 2013 and before 1 Sep 2013, and any sibling) (SI 2017/750) |
|  |  | 24 Nov 2017 (in respect of a child born on or after 24 Nov and before 1 Apr 2013 and any sibling) (SI 2017/1116) |
|  |  | 15 Jan 2018 (in respect of a child born on or after 15 Jan 2009 and before 24 Nov 2011) (SI 2018/27) |
|  |  | 14 Feb 2018 (otherwise) (SI 2018/27) |
| 63, 64 |  | 21 Apr 2017 (SI 2017/578)[3] |
| 65 |  | 17 Dec 2014 (s 75(1)) |
| 66, 67 |  | 14 Nov 2016 (for the purpose of "the trial") (SI 2016/1083)[1] |
|  |  | 21 Apr 2017 (otherwise) (SI 2017/578) |
| 68–72 |  | 17 Dec 2014 (s 75(1)) |
| 73 | (1) | 17 Dec 2014 (s 75(1)) |
|  | (2)–(4) | 14 Nov 2016 (for the purpose of "the trial") (SI 2016/1083)[1] |
|  |  | 21 Apr 2017 (in respect of (a) a child born on or after 1 Sep 2013 and any sibling; and (b) a disabled child and any sibling) (SI 2017/578)[3] |
|  |  | 16 May 2017 (in respect of those recruited to participate in "the trial") (SI 2017/578)[1] |
|  |  | 14 Jul 2017 (in respect of a child born on or after 1 Apr 2013 and before 1 Sep 2013, and any sibling) (SI 2017/750) |
|  |  | 24 Nov 2017 (in respect of a child born on or after 24 Nov and before 1 Apr 2013 and any sibling) (SI 2017/1116) |
|  |  | 15 Jan 2018 (in respect of a child born on or after 15 Jan 2009 and before 24 Nov 2011) (SI 2018/27) |
|  |  | 14 Feb 2018 (otherwise) (SI 2018/27) |
| 74, 75 |  | 17 Dec 2014 (s 75(1)) |

[1]  "The trial" is defined in SI 2016/1083, reg 1(2)

[2]  S 3 of the Act comes into force on 14 Nov 2016 for the purposes of "the trial" (as defined in SI 2016/1083, reg 1(2)) with the modifications set out in reg 3 of those regulations

[3]  For transitional provisions, see SI 2017/578, regs 5–8

---

**Children and Families Act 2014 (c 6)**

*RA:* 13 Mar 2014

*Commencement provisions:* s 139; Children and Families Act 2014 (Commencement No 1) Order 2014, SI 2014/793; Children and Families Act 2014 (Commencement No 2) Order 2014, SI 2014/889, as amended by SI 2014/1134; Children and Families Act 2014 (Commencement No 3, Transitional Provisions and Savings) Order 2014, SI 2014/1640; Children and Families Act 2014 (Commencement No 4) Order 2014, SI 2014/2609; Children and Families Act 2014 (Commencement No 5 and Transitional Provision) Order 2014, SI 2014/2749; Children and Families Act 2014 (Commencement No 6) Order 2015, SI 2015/375; Children and Families Act 2014 (Commencement) (Wales) Order 2015, SI 2015/1808

| 1 |  | 25 Jul 2014 (E) (SI 2014/889) |
|---|---|---|
|  |  | 19 Oct 2015 (W) (SI 2015/1808) |
| 2, 3 |  | 25 Jul 2014 (SI 2014/889) |
| 4 |  | 13 May 2014 (SI 2014/889) |
| 5 |  | *Not yet in force* |
| 6 |  | 25 Jul 2014 (SI 2014/889) |
| 7 | (1)–(7) | 13 May 2014 (SI 2014/889) |
|  | (8) | See Sch 1 below |
| 8 |  | 25 Jul 2014 (SI 2014/889) |
| 9 |  | 22 Apr 2014 (SI 2014/889) |
| 10 |  | 22 Apr 2014 (SI 2014/793) |
| 11 |  | 22 Oct 2014 (SI 2014/2749)[3] |
| 12 | (1)–(3) | 22 Apr 2014 (SI 2014/889) |

**Children and Families Act 2014 (c 6)**—*contd*

| | | |
|---|---|---|
| | (4) | See Sch 2 below |
| 13 | | 22 Apr 2014 (SI 2014/793) |
| 14 | | 22 Apr 2014 (SI 2014/889) |
| 15 | (1) | 22 Apr 2014 (SI 2014/889) |
| | (2) | *Not yet in force* |
| | (3) | 22 Apr 2014 (SI 2014/889) |
| 16 | | 22 Apr 2014 (SI 2014/889) |
| 17 | | 22 Apr 2014 (SI 2014/793) |
| 18 | | 13 May 2014 (s 139(4)) |
| 19–29 | | 1 Sep 2014 (SI 2014/889) |
| 30, 31 | | 1 Apr 2014 (for the purposes of making orders or regulations) (SI 2014/889) |
| | | 1 Sep 2014 (otherwise) (SI 2014/889) |
| 32, 33 | | 1 Sep 2014 (SI 2014/889) |
| 34 | | 1 Apr 2014 (for the purposes of making orders or regulations) (SI 2014/889) |
| | | 1 Sep 2014 (otherwise) (SI 2014/889) |
| 35 | | 1 Sep 2014 (SI 2014/889) |
| 36, 37 | | 1 Apr 2014 (for the purposes of making orders or regulations) (SI 2014/889) |
| | | 1 Sep 2014 (otherwise) (SI 2014/889) |
| 38–40 | | 1 Sep 2014 (SI 2014/889) |
| 41 | | 1 Apr 2014 (for the purposes of making orders or regulations) (SI 2014/889) |
| | | 1 Sep 2014 (otherwise) (SI 2014/889) |
| 42, 43 | | 1 Sep 2014 (SI 2014/889) |
| 44–47 | | 1 Apr 2014 (for the purposes of making orders or regulations) (SI 2014/889) |
| | | 1 Sep 2014 (otherwise) (SI 2014/889) |
| 48 | | 1 Sep 2014 (SI 2014/889) |
| 49 | | 1 Apr 2014 (for the purposes of making orders or regulations) (SI 2014/889) |
| | | 1 Sep 2014 (otherwise) (SI 2014/889) |
| 50 | | 1 Sep 2014 (SI 2014/889) |
| 51, 52 | | 1 Apr 2014 (for the purposes of making orders or regulations) (SI 2014/889) |
| | | 1 Sep 2014 (otherwise) (SI 2014/889) |
| 53–55 | | 1 Sep 2014 (SI 2014/889) |
| 56 | | 1 Apr 2014 (for the purposes of making orders or regulations) (SI 2014/889) |
| | | 1 Sep 2014 (otherwise) (SI 2014/889) |
| 57–66 | | 1 Sep 2014 (SI 2014/889) |
| 67 | | 1 Apr 2014 (for the purposes of making orders or regulations) (SI 2014/889) |
| | | 1 Sep 2014 (otherwise) (SI 2014/889) |
| 68 | | 1 Sep 2014 (SI 2014/889) |
| 69 | | 1 Apr 2014 (for the purposes of making orders or regulations) (SI 2014/889) |
| | | 1 Sep 2014 (otherwise) (SI 2014/889) |
| 70 | (1) | 1 Sep 2014 (except the words "Subject to this section and sections 71 to 75,") (SI 2014/889) |
| | | 1 Apr 2015 (exception noted above) (SI 2015/375) |
| | (2)–(7) | 1 Apr 2015 (SI 2015/375) |
| 71–75 | | 1 Apr 2015 (SI 2015/375) |
| 76, 77 | | 1 Sep 2014 (SI 2014/889) |
| 78 | | 1 May 2014 (SI 2014/1134)[1] |
| 79 | | 1 Sep 2014 (SI 2014/889) |
| 80 | | 1 Apr 2014 (for the purposes of making orders or regulations) (SI 2014/889) |
| | | 1 Sep 2014 (otherwise) (SI 2014/889) |

**Children and Families Act 2014 (c 6)**—*contd*

| | | |
|---|---|---|
| 81 | | 1 Sep 2014 (SI 2014/889) |
| 82 | | See Sch 3 below |
| 83 | | 1 Sep 2014 (SI 2014/889) |
| 84 | | See Sch 4 below |
| 85–89 | | 13 May 2014 (SI 2014/889) |
| 90 | | 13 May 2014 (s 139(4)) |
| 91–95 | | 1 Oct 2014 (for the purposes of making orders or regulations) (SI 2014/2609) |
| | | 1 Oct 2015 (otherwise) (SI 2015/375) |
| 96, 97 | | 1 Apr 2015 (SI 2015/375) |
| 98, 99 | | 13 May 2014 (SI 2014/889) |
| 100 | | 1 Sep 2014 (SI 2014/889) |
| 101–104 | | 13 May 2014 (s 139(4)) |
| 105 | | 1 Apr 2015 (SI 2015/375) |
| 106 | | 1 Sep 2014 (SI 2014/889) |
| 107–116 | | 1 Apr 2014 (s 139(5)) |
| 117–122 | | 30 Jun 2014 (SI 2014/1640)[2] |
| 123 | (1), (2) | 30 Jun 2014 (SI 2014/1640)[2] |
| | (3), (4) | *Not yet in force* |
| 124, 125 | | 5 Apr 2015 (SI 2014/1640)[2] |
| 126 | (1) | See Sch 7 below |
| | (2)–(4) | *Not yet in force* |
| 127 | (1) | 1 Oct 2014 (SI 2014/1640)[2] |
| | (2)(a), (b) | 30 Jun 2014 (SI 2014/1640)[2] |
| | (2)(c) | 1 Oct 2014 (SI 2014/1640)[2] |
| 128 | (1) | 5 Apr 2015 (SI 2014/1640)[2] |
| | (2)(a)–(c) | 30 Jun 2014 (SI 2014/1640)[2] |
| | (2)(d), (e) | 5 Apr 2015 (SI 2014/1640)[2] |
| 129 | (1) | 1 Oct 2014 (in so far as inserts Employment Rights Act 1996, s 47C(5)(a), (b), (6), (7)) (SI 2014/1640)[2] |
| | | 5 Apr 2015 (otherwise) (SI 2014/1640)[2] |
| | (2), (3) | 1 Oct 2014 (SI 2014/1640)[2] |
| 130 | | 1 Oct 2014 (SI 2014/1640)[2] |
| 131–134 | | 30 Jun 2014 (SI 2014/1640)[2] |
| 135–140 | | 13 Mar 2014 (s 139(1)) |
| Sch 1 | | 13 May 2014 (SI 2014/889) |
| Sch 2 | | 22 Apr 2014 (SI 2014/889) |
| Sch 3 | paras 1–54 | 1 Sep 2014 (SI 2014/889) |
| | paras 55–58 | 1 Apr 2015 (SI 2015/375) |
| | paras 59–96 | 1 Sep 2014 (SI 2014/889) |
| Sch 4 | | 1 Apr 2014 (for the purposes of making orders or regulations) (SI 2014/889) |
| | | 1 Sep 2014 (otherwise) (SI 2014/889) |
| Schs 5, 6 | | 1 Apr 2014 (s 139(5)) |
| Sch 7 | para 1 | 30 Jun 2014 (SI 2014/1640)[2] |
| | para 2(1) | 30 Jun 2014 (SI 2014/1640)[2] |
| | para 2(2) | 5 Apr 2015 (SI 2014/1640)[2] |
| | para 2(3)(a) | 1 Dec 2014 (in so far as relates to Social Security Act 1989, Sch 5, inserted para 5A(7B)) (SI 2014/1640)[2] |
| | | *Not yet in force* (otherwise) |
| | para 2(3)(b), (c) | 5 Apr 2015 (SI 2014/1640)[2] |
| | para 2(4) | 30 Jun 2014 (SI 2014/1640)[2] |
| | para 2(5) | 1 Dec 2014 (in so far as inserts Social Security Act 1989, Sch 5, para 5A(7B)) (SI 2014/1640)[2] |
| | | 5 Apr 2015 (otherwise) (SI 2014/1640)[2] |
| | para 2(6) | 5 Apr 2015 (SI 2014/1640)[2] |
| | para 3 | 1 Dec 2014 (in so far as relates to Social Security Act 1989, Sch 5, inserted para 5A(8)) (SI 2014/1640)[2] |
| | | 5 Apr 2015 (otherwise) (SI 2014/1640)[2] |

**See Halsbury's Statutes Citator for amendments to these Acts**

**Children and Families Act 2014 (c 6)**—*contd*

| | |
|---|---|
| paras 4, 5(1) | 1 Dec 2014 (SI 2014/1640)[2] |
| para 5(2)(a) | 5 Apr 2015 (SI 2014/1640)[2] |
| para 5(2)(b) | 1 Dec 2014 (SI 2014/1640)[2] |
| para 5(3)(a) | 5 Apr 2015 (SI 2014/1640)[2] |
| para 5(3)(b) | 1 Dec 2014 (SI 2014/1640)[2] |
| para 5(4)(a) | 5 Apr 2015 (SI 2014/1640)[2] |
| para 5(4)(b) | 1 Dec 2014 (SI 2014/1640)[2] |
| para 5(5)(a) | 5 Apr 2015 (SI 2014/1640)[2] |
| para 5(5)(b) | 1 Dec 2014 (SI 2014/1640)[2] |
| para 5(6) | 15 Mar 2015 (the date on which Northern Ireland legislation containing provision corresponding to Social Security Contributions and Benefits Act 1992, Pt 12ZC came into force) |
| para 6 | 1 Dec 2014 (SI 2014/1640)[2] |
| para 7(a) | 5 Apr 2015 (SI 2014/1640)[2] |
| para 7(b) | 1 Dec 2014 (SI 2014/1640)[2] |
| para 8(a) | 5 Apr 2015 (SI 2014/1640)[2] |
| para 8(b), (c) | 1 Dec 2014 (SI 2014/1640)[2] |
| para 9(a) | 5 Apr 2015 (SI 2014/1640)[2] |
| para 9(b) | 30 Jun 2014 (SI 2014/1640)[2] |
| paras 10–22 | 5 Apr 2015 (SI 2014/1640)[2] |
| para 23 | 30 Jun 2014 (SI 2014/1640)[2] |
| para 24(a) | 5 Apr 2015 (SI 2014/1640)[2] |
| para 24(b) | 30 Jun 2014 (SI 2014/1640)[2] |
| para 25(a) | 5 Apr 2015 (SI 2014/1640)[2] |
| para 25(b) | 1 Dec 2014 (SI 2014/1640)[2] |
| paras 26, 27(a) | 5 Apr 2015 (SI 2014/1640)[2] |
| para 27(b) | 1 Dec 2014 (SI 2014/1640)[2] |
| para 28(1) | 1 Dec 2014 (SI 2014/1640)[2] |
| para 28(2)(a), (b) | 5 Apr 2015 (SI 2014/1640)[2] |
| para 28(2)(c) | 1 Dec 2014 (SI 2014/1640)[2] |
| para 28(3)(a) | 5 Apr 2015 (SI 2014/1640)[2] |
| para 28(3)(b) | 1 Dec 2014 (SI 2014/1640)[2] |
| para 29 | 30 Jun 2014 (SI 2014/1640)[2] |
| para 30(a) | 5 Apr 2015 (SI 2014/1640)[2] |
| para 30(b) | 1 Dec 2014 (SI 2014/1640)[2] |
| para 31(a) | 30 Jun 2014 (SI 2014/1640)[2] |
| paras 31(b), 32, 33 | 5 Apr 2015 (SI 2014/1640)[2] |
| para 34(1) | 30 Jun 2014 (SI 2014/1640)[2] |
| para 34(2), (3)(a), (b) | 5 Apr 2015 (SI 2014/1640)[2] |
| para 34(3)(c), (d) | 30 Jun 2014 (SI 2014/1640)[2] |
| para 34(4), (5)(a), (b) | 5 Apr 2015 (SI 2014/1640)[2] |
| para 34(5)(c) | 30 Jun 2014 (SI 2014/1640)[2] |
| para 34(5)(d), (6), (7) | 5 Apr 2015 (SI 2014/1640)[2] |
| paras 35, 36 | 5 Apr 2015 (SI 2014/1640)[2] |
| para 37(1), (2)(a) | 1 Dec 2014 (SI 2014/1640)[2] |
| para 37(2)(b), (3)(a) | 5 Apr 2015 (SI 2014/1640)[2] |
| para 37(3)(b) | 1 Dec 2014 (SI 2014/1640)[2] |
| para 38(1), (2)(a) | 1 Dec 2014 (SI 2014/1640)[2] |
| para 38(2)(b), (3)(a) | 5 Apr 2015 (SI 2014/1640)[2] |
| para 38(3)(b) | 1 Dec 2014 (SI 2014/1640)[2] |
| para 39(a) | 30 Jun 2014 (SI 2014/1640)[2] |
| para 39(b) | 5 Apr 2015 (SI 2014/1640)[2] |

**Children and Families Act 2014 (c 6)**—*contd*

| | |
|---|---|
| para 40 | 1 Dec 2014 (SI 2014/1640)[2] |
| para 41 | 30 Jun 2014 (SI 2014/1640)[2] |
| para 42(a) | 5 Apr 2015 (SI 2014/1640)[2] |
| para 42(b), (c) | 30 Jun 2014 (SI 2014/1640)[2] |
| para 43 | 5 Apr 2015 (SI 2014/1640)[2] |
| para 44 | 1 Dec 2014 (SI 2014/1640)[2] |
| para 45(1) | 1 Dec 2014 (SI 2014/1640)[2] |
| para 45(2)(a) | 5 Apr 2015 (SI 2014/1640)[2] |
| para 45(2)(b), (c) | 1 Dec 2014 (SI 2014/1640)[2] |
| para 45(2)(d) | 5 Apr 2015 (SI 2014/1640)[2] |
| para 45(2)(e) | 1 Dec 2014 (SI 2014/1640)[2] |
| para 45(2)(f) | 5 Apr 2015 (SI 2014/1640)[2] |
| para 45(2)(g) | 1 Dec 2014 (SI 2014/1640)[2] |
| para 45(3)(a) | 5 Apr 2015 (SI 2014/1640)[2] |
| para 45(3)(b) | 1 Dec 2014 (SI 2014/1640)[2] |
| para 46(a) | 5 Apr 2015 (SI 2014/1640)[2] |
| para 46(b) | 1 Dec 2014 (SI 2014/1640)[2] |
| para 47(1) | 30 Jun 2014 (SI 2014/1640)[2] |
| para 47(2)(a) | 5 Apr 2015 (SI 2014/1640)[2] |
| para 47(2)(b) | 30 Jun 2014 (SI 2014/1640)[2] |
| para 47(3)(a) | 5 Apr 2015 (SI 2014/1640)[2] |
| para 47(3)(b) | 30 Jun 2014 (SI 2014/1640)[2] |
| para 48(1) | 30 Jun 2014 (SI 2014/1640)[2] |
| para 48(2) | 15 Mar 2015 (the date on which Northern Ireland legislation containing provision corresponding to Social Security Contributions and Benefits Act 1992, Pt 12ZC came into force) |
| para 49 | 1 Dec 2014 (SI 2014/1640)[2] |
| para 50 | 30 Jun 2014 (SI 2014/1640)[2] |
| para 51(1) | 30 Jun 2014 (SI 2014/1640)[2] |
| para 51(2)(a) | 5 Apr 2015 (SI 2014/1640)[2] |
| para 51(2)(b) | 30 Jun 2014 (SI 2014/1640)[2] |
| para 51(3)(a)(i) | 5 Apr 2015 (SI 2014/1640)[2] |
| para 51(3)(a)(ii) | 30 Jun 2014 (SI 2014/1640)[2] |
| para 51(3)(b)(i) | 5 Apr 2015 (SI 2014/1640)[2] |
| para 51(3)(b)(ii) | 30 Jun 2014 (SI 2014/1640)[2] |
| para 51(4)(a) | 5 Apr 2015 (SI 2014/1640)[2] |
| para 51(4)(b), (c) | 30 Jun 2014 (SI 2014/1640)[2] |
| para 52(1) | 30 Jun 2014 (SI 2014/1640)[2] |
| para 52(2)(a) | 5 Apr 2015 (SI 2014/1640)[2] |
| para 52(2)(b) | 30 Jun 2014 (SI 2014/1640)[2] |
| para 52(3)(a)(i) | 5 Apr 2015 (SI 2014/1640)[2] |
| para 52(3)(a)(ii) | 30 Jun 2014 (SI 2014/1640)[2] |
| para 52(3)(b)(i) | 5 Apr 2015 (SI 2014/1640)[2] |
| para 52(3)(b)(ii) | 30 Jun 2014 (SI 2014/1640)[2] |
| para 52(3)(c)(i) | 5 Apr 2015 (SI 2014/1640)[2] |
| para 52(3)(c)(ii) | 30 Jun 2014 (SI 2014/1640)[2] |
| para 53(1) | 30 Jun 2014 (SI 2014/1640)[2] |
| para 53(2)(a) | 5 Apr 2015 (SI 2014/1640)[2] |
| para 53(2)(b) | 30 Jun 2014 (SI 2014/1640)[2] |
| para 53(3)(a) | 5 Apr 2015 (SI 2014/1640)[2] |
| para 53(3)(b) | 30 Jun 2014 (SI 2014/1640)[2] |
| para 54(a) | 5 Apr 2015 (SI 2014/1640)[2] |
| para 54(b) | 1 Dec 2014 (SI 2014/1640)[2] |
| para 55(1) | 1 Dec 2014 (SI 2014/1640)[2] |
| para 55(2) | 5 Apr 2015 (SI 2014/1640)[2] |
| para 55(3) | 1 Dec 2014 (SI 2014/1640)[2] |
| para 55(4) | 5 Apr 2015 (SI 2014/1640)[2] |
| para 55(5) | 1 Dec 2014 (SI 2014/1640)[2] |

**Children and Families Act 2014 (c 6)**—*contd*

| | |
|---|---|
| para 55(6) | 5 Apr 2015 (SI 2014/1640)[2] |
| para 56(a) | 5 Apr 2015 (SI 2014/1640)[2] |
| para 56(b) | 1 Dec 2014 (SI 2014/1640)[2] |
| para 57(1) | 1 Dec 2014 (SI 2014/1640)[2] |
| para 57(2)(a) | 5 Apr 2015 (SI 2014/1640)[2] |
| para 57(2)(b) | 1 Dec 2014 (SI 2014/1640)[2] |
| para 57(3)(a) | 5 Apr 2015 (SI 2014/1640)[2] |
| para 57(3)(b) | 1 Dec 2014 (SI 2014/1640)[2] |
| para 58(a), (b) | 5 Apr 2015 (SI 2014/1640)[2] |
| para 58(c), (d) | 1 Dec 2014 (SI 2014/1640)[2] |
| para 59(a) | 5 Apr 2015 (SI 2014/1640)[2] |
| para 59(b), (c) | 15 Mar 2015 (the date on which Northern Ireland legislation containing provision corresponding to Social Security Contributions and Benefits Act 1992, Pt 12ZC came into force) |
| para 60(1) | 1 Dec 2014 (SI 2014/1640)[2] |
| para 60(2)(a), (b) | 5 Apr 2015 (SI 2014/1640)[2] |
| para 60(2)(c) | 1 Dec 2014 (SI 2014/1640)[2] |
| para 60(3)(a), (b) | 5 Apr 2015 (SI 2014/1640)[2] |
| para 60(3)(c) | 1 Dec 2014 (SI 2014/1640)[2] |
| para 60(4) | 15 Mar 2015 (the date on which Northern Ireland legislation containing provision corresponding to Social Security Contributions and Benefits Act 1992, Pt 12ZC came into force) |
| para 61 | 1 Dec 2014 (SI 2014/1640)[2] |
| para 62(1) | 1 Dec 2014 (SI 2014/1640)[2] |
| para 62(2), (3) | 5 Apr 2015 (SI 2014/1640)[2] |
| para 62(4) | 1 Dec 2014 (SI 2014/1640)[2] |
| para 62(5)(a), (b) | 5 Apr 2015 (SI 2014/1640)[2] |
| paras 62(5)(c), 63 | 1 Dec 2014 (SI 2014/1640)[2] |
| para 64(1) | 1 Dec 2014 (SI 2014/1640)[2] |
| para 64(2), (3) | 5 Apr 2015 (SI 2014/1640)[2] |
| para 64(4) | 1 Dec 2014 (SI 2014/1640)[2] |
| para 64(5) | *Not yet in force* |
| paras 65–67 | 5 Apr 2015 (SI 2014/1640)[2] |
| para 68 | 5 Apr 2015 (in so far as relates to Work and Families Act 2006, Sch 1 paras 1(4), 11, 17, 19, 22, 38(3)) (SI 2014/1640)[2] |
| | 15 Mar 2015 (the date on which Northern Ireland legislation containing provision corresponding to Social Security Contributions and Benefits Act 1992, Pt 12ZC came into force) |
| paras 69–72 | 1 Dec 2014 (SI 2014/1640)[2] |
| para 73(1)–(3) | 30 Jun 2014 (SI 2014/1640)[2] |
| para 73(4) | 5 Apr 2015 (SI 2014/1640)[2] |
| para 74(a) | 5 Apr 2015 (SI 2014/1640)[2] |
| para 74(b) | 1 Dec 2014 (SI 2014/1640)[2] |
| para 75 | 5 Apr 2015 (SI 2014/1640)[2] |

[1]   This provision was previously brought into force on 13 May 2014 by SI 2014/889, art 5(c), which was repealed by SI 2014/1134, art 2(3)

[2]   For savings and transitional provisions, see SI 2014/1640, arts 9–19

[3]   For a transitional provision, see SI 2014/2749, art 4

---

**Children and Young People (Scotland) Act 2014 (asp 8)**

*RA:* 27 Mar 2014

*Commencement provisions*: s 102; Children and Young People (Scotland) Act 2014 (Commencement No 1 and Transitory Provisions) Order 2014, SSI 2014/131; Children and Young People (Scotland) Act 2014

**Children and Young People (Scotland) Act 2014 (asp 8)**—*contd*
(Commencement No 2, Transitional and Transitory Provisions) Order 2014, SI 2014/165; Children and Young People (Scotland) Act 2014 (Commencement No 3) Order 2014, SSI 2014/251; Children and Young People (Scotland) Act 2014 (Commencement No 4) Order 2014, SSI 2014/314; Children and Young People (Scotland) Act 2014 (Commencement No 5 and Saving Provision) Order 2014, SI 2014/353; Children and Young People (Scotland) Act 2014 (Commencement No 6) Order 2014, SSI 2014/365; Children and Young People (Scotland) Act 2014 (Commencement No 7) Order 2014, SSI 2015/61; Children and Young People (Scotland) Act 2014 (Commencement No 8 and Saving Provision) Order 2015, SSI 2015/104; Children and Young People (Scotland) Act 2014 (Commencement No 9 and Saving Provision) Order 2015, SSI 2015/317; Children and Young People (Scotland) Act 2014 (Commencement No 10 and Saving Provision) Order 2015, SSI 2015/406; Children and Young People (Scotland) Act 2014 (Commencement No 11) Order 2016, SSI 2016/60, as amended by SSI 2016/233; Children and Young People (Scotland) Act 2014 (Commencement No 12 and Saving Provision) Order 2016, SSI 2016/254

| | |
|---|---|
| 1 | 15 Jun 2015 (SSI 2015/61) |
| 2, 3 | 1 Apr 2017 (SSI 2016/254) |
| 4 | 15 Jun 2015 (SSI 2015/61) |
| 5 | 7 Aug 2017 (SSI 2016/254)[7] |
| 6 | 7 Aug 2017 (SSI 2016/254) |
| 7 | 7 Oct 2016 (SSI 2016/254) |
| 8 | 30 Sep 2015 (in so far as necessary to enable the Scottish Ministers to make orders under s 8(2)(a)) (SSI 2015/317) |
| | 7 Oct 2016 (otherwise) (SSI 2016/254) |
| 9–18 | 7 Oct 2016 (SSI 2016/254) |
| 19 | 5 Jan 2016 (so far as necessary to enable the Scottish Ministers to make orders under sub-s (3)(b)) (SSI 2015/406) |
| | *Not yet in force* (otherwise) |
| 20–29 | 31 Aug 2016 (SSI 2016/60) |
| 30 | 5 Jan 2016 (so far as necessary to enable the Scottish Ministers to make orders under sub-s (1)) (SSI 2015/406) |
| | *Not yet in force* (otherwise) |
| 31 | 5 Jan 2016 (so far as necessary to enable the Scottish Ministers to make orders under sub-s (2)) (SSI 2015/406) |
| | *Not yet in force* (otherwise) |
| 32 | *Not yet in force* |
| 33 | 5 Jan 2016 (so far as necessary to enable the Scottish Ministers to make orders under sub-s (6)) (SSI 2015/406) |
| | *Not yet in force* (otherwise) |
| 34 | 5 Jan 2016 (so far as necessary to enable the Scottish Ministers to make orders under sub-s (4)) (SSI 2015/406) |
| | *Not yet in force* (otherwise) |
| 35 | 5 Jan 2016 (so far as necessary to enable the Scottish Ministers to make orders under sub-ss (6), (8)) (SSI 2015/406) |
| | *Not yet in force* (otherwise) |
| 36 | *Not yet in force* |
| 37 | 5 Jan 2016 (so far as necessary to enable the Scottish Ministers to make orders under sub-s (7)) (SSI 2015/406) |
| | *Not yet in force* (otherwise) |
| 38 | *Not yet in force* |
| 39 | 5 Jan 2016 (so far as necessary to enable the Scottish Ministers to make orders under sub-ss (2), (6)) (SSI 2015/406) |
| | *Not yet in force* (otherwise) |
| 40–42 | *Not yet in force* |
| 43 | 5 Jan 2016 (so far as necessary to enable the Scottish Ministers to make orders under sub-s (1)) (SSI 2015/406) |
| | *Not yet in force* (otherwise) |
| 44 | 5 Jan 2016 (so far as necessary to enable the Scottish Ministers to make orders under sub-s (2)) (SSI 2015/406) |
| | *Not yet in force* (otherwise) |
| 45 | *Not yet in force* |
| 46 | 28 Jun 2014 (SSI 2014/131) |

**Children and Young People (Scotland) Act 2014 (asp 8)**—*contd*

| | | |
|---|---|---|
| 47 | (1) | 1 Aug 2014 (SSI 2014/131) |
| | (2)–(5) | 28 Mar 2014 (s 102(2)) |
| | (6) | 1 Aug 2014 (SSI 2014/131) |
| 48–55 | | 1 Aug 2014 (SSI 2014/131)[1] |
| 56 | | 1 Apr 2015 (SSI 2015/61) |
| 57 | | 1 Aug 2014 (so far as necessary to enable Scottish Ministers to make an order under s 57(2)(b) of this Act) (SSI 2014/131) |
| | | 1 Apr 2015 (otherwise) (SSI 2015/61) |
| 58–65 | | 1 Apr 2015 (SSI 2015/61) |
| 66 | | 1 Aug 2014 (so far as necessary to enable Scottish Ministers to make orders under the Children (Scotland) Act 1995, ss 29(1)(b), (8), 30(2)(b)(ii)) (SSI 2014/131) |
| | | 1 Apr 2015 (otherwise) (SSI 2015/61) |
| 67 | (1) | 1 Aug 2014 (so far as necessary to enable Scottish Ministers to make orders under the Children (Scotland) Act 1995, ss 26A(2)(b), (6), (9), (11)(a)) (SSI 2014/131) |
| | | 1 Apr 2015 (otherwise) (SSI 2015/61) |
| | (2) | 1 Apr 2015 (SSI 2015/61) |
| 68 | | 1 Aug 2014 (so far as necessary to enable Scottish Ministers to make orders under s 68(1), (3)(b) of this Act) (SSI 2014/131)[2] |
| | | 31 Aug 2016 (otherwise) (SSI 2016/60) |
| 69, 70 | | 1 Aug 2014 (SSI 2014/131) |
| 71 | | 1 Aug 2014 (so far as necessary to enable Scottish Ministers to make orders under s 71(1), (2), (5)(b) and for the purposes of s 47(3)(b) of this Act) (SSI 2014/131)[2] |
| | | 1 Apr 2016 (otherwise) (SSI 2016/406) |
| 72 | | 1 Aug 2014 (SSI 2014/131) |
| 73 | | 1 Aug 2014 (so far as necessary to enable Scottish Ministers to make orders under ss 71(1), (2), 73(3) of this Act) (SSI 2014/131)[2] |
| | | 1 Apr 2016 (otherwise) (SSI 2016/406) |
| 74 | | 1 Aug 2014 (SSI 2014/131) |
| 75 | | 30 Sep 2015 (in so far as necessary to enable the Scottish Ministers to make regulations under Adoption and Children (Scotland) Act 2007, s 13A(2)) (SSI 2015/317) |
| | | 1 Apr 2016 (otherwise) (SSI 2016/406) |
| 76–80 | | 1 Aug 2014 (SSI 2014/165)[3] |
| 81 | (1)(a)–(c) | 1 Aug 2014 (SSI 2014/165) |
| | (1)(d), (2), (3)(a) | 30 Mar 2015 (SSI 2015/104)[4] |
| | (3)(b) | 1 Aug 2014 (SSI 2014/165) |
| | (4) | 1 Aug 2014 (for the purpose of commencing Schools (Consultation) (Scotland) Act 2010, s 17B(3)) (SSI 2014/165) |
| | | 1 Aug 2014 (in so far as is necessary to enable Scottish Ministers to make regulations under Schools (Consultation) (Scotland) Act 2010, s 17B(5)) (SSI 2014/165) |
| | | 6 Oct 2014 (for the purpose of commencing Schools (Consultation) (Scotland) Act 2010, s 17A(6) only in so far as is necessary to enable Scottish Ministers to make regulations under Schools (Consultation) (Scotland) Act 2010, Sch 2A, paras 1(9), 2(5)) (SSI 2014/251) |
| | | 9 Jan 2015 (for the purpose of commencing Schools (Consultation) (Scotland) Act 2010, s 17A(5)) (SSI 2014/353) |
| | | 9 Jan 2015 (for the purpose of commencing Schools (Consultation) (Scotland) Act 2010, s 17A(6), in so far as not already in force) (SSI 2014/365) |
| | (5) | 1 Aug 2014 (in so far as is necessary to enable Scottish Ministers to make regulations under Schools (Consultation) (Scotland) Act 2010, Sch 2A, paras 1(9), 2(5)) (SSI 2014/165) |
| | | 9 Jan 2015 (otherwise) (SSI 2014/353) |
| | (6) | 30 Mar 2015 (SSI 2015/104) |

**Children and Young People (Scotland) Act 2014 (asp 8)**—*contd*

|  |  |  |
|---|---|---|
| | (7) | 9 Jan 2015 (SSI 2014/353) |
| | (8)(a) | 30 Mar 2015 (SSI 2015/104) |
| | (8)(b) | 1 Aug 2014 (in so far as is necessary to enable Scottish Ministers to make regulations under Schools (Consultation) (Scotland) Act 2010, s 17B(5), Sch 2A, paras 1(9), 2(5)) |
| | | *Not yet in force* (otherwise) |
| | (9) | 6 Oct 2014 (in so far as is necessary to enable Scottish Ministers to make regulations under Schools (Consultation) (Scotland) Act 2010, Sch 2A, paras 1(9), 2(5)) (SSI 2014/251) |
| | | 9 Jan 2015 (otherwise) (SSI 2014/365) |
| | (10)–(12) | 9 Jan 2015 (SSI 2014/353) |
| | (11)(b) | 30 Mar 2015 (SSI 2015/104) |
| | (12) | 9 Jan 2015 (SSI 2014/353) |
| 82–90 | | 9 Jan 2015 (SSI 2014/353) |
| 91 | | 1 Aug 2014 (so far as necessary to enable Scottish Ministers to make regulations under the Criminal Procedure (Scotland) Act 1995, s 44A(5), (6)) (SSI 2014/131) |
| | | 1 Feb 2016 (otherwise) (SSI 2015/406)[6] |
| 92 | | 28 Nov 2016 (SSI 2016/254) |
| 93 | (1)–(5) | 5 Jan 2015 (SSI 2014/314) |
| | (6) | 1 Aug 2014 (so far as necessary to enable Scottish Ministers to make regulations under the Education (Scotland) Act 1980, s 53(3)(c)) (SSI 2014/131) |
| | | *Not yet in force* (otherwise) |
| 94 | | 1 Aug 2014 (SSI 2014/131) |
| 95 | | 31 Aug 2016 (SSI 2016/60) |
| 96 | | 1 Aug 2014 (for the purpose of s 49 of this Act) (SSI 2014/131) |
| | | 1 Apr 2015 (for the purpose of ss 58(1)(a), (d), 60(1) of this Act) (SSI 2015/61) |
| | | 5 Jan 2016 (otherwise) (SSI 2015/406) |
| 97 | | 1 Aug 2014 (SSI 2014/131) |
| 98 | | See Sch 5 below |
| 99–103 | | 28 Mar 2014 (s 102(1)) |
| Sch 1 | | 1 Apr 2017 (SSI 2016/254) |
| Schs 2, 3 | | *Not yet in force* |
| Sch 4 | | 1 Apr 2015 (SSI 2015/61) |
| Sch 5 | para 1 | 1 Aug 2014 (SSI 2014/131) |
| | para 2(1) | 28 Jun 2014 (SSI 2014/131) |
| | para 2(2) | 1 Aug 2014 (SSI 2014/131) |
| | para 2(3) | 5 Jan 2015 (SSI 2014/314) |
| | para 2(4)(a) | 5 Jan 2015 (SSI 2014/314) |
| | para 2(4)(b) | 1 Aug 2014 (so far as necessary to enable Scottish Ministers to make regulations under the Education (Scotland) Act 1980, s 53B(1A)) (SSI 2014/131) |
| | | 5 Jan 2015 (otherwise) (SSI 2014/314) |
| | para 2(5)(a) | 5 Jan 2015 (SSI 2014/314) |
| | para 2(5)(b) | 1 Aug 2014 (so far as necessary to enable Scottish Ministers to make regulations under the Education (Scotland) Act 1980, s 53(3)(c)) (SSI 2014/131) |
| | | *Not yet in force* (otherwise) |
| | para 2(6) | 28 Jun 2014 (SSI 2014/131) |
| | para 3(1), (2) | 26 Jan 2015 (SSI 2014/353) |
| | para 3(3) | 28 Nov 2016 (SSI 2016/254) |
| | para 4(1) | 30 Sep 2015 (SSI 2015/317) |
| | para 4(2), (3) | 1 Apr 2017 (SSI 2016/254) |
| | para 4(4) | 30 Sep 2015 (SSI 2015/317)[5] |
| | para 5(1), (2) | 30 Sep 2015 (SSI 2015/317) |
| | para 5(3) | 1 Apr 2017 (SSI 2016/254) |
| | para 6 | 1 Aug 2014 (SSI 2014/131) |
| | para 7 | 28 Jun 2014 (SSI 2014/131) |

**Children and Young People (Scotland) Act 2014 (asp 8)**—*contd*

| | | |
|---|---|---|
| | para 8 | 1 Apr 2015 (SSI 2015/61) |
| | para 9 | 1 Apr 2017 (SSI 2016/254) |
| | para 10 | 1 Aug 2014 (SSI 2014/131) |
| | para 11(1) | See sub-paras (2)–(6) below |
| | para 11(2)–(4) | 1 Apr 2017 (SSI 2016/254) |
| | para 11(5), (6) | 30 Sep 2015 (in so far as necessary to enable the Scottish Ministers to make regulations under Adoption and Children (Scotland) Act 2007, s 13A(2)) (SSI 2015/317) |
| | | 1 Apr 2016 (otherwise) (SSI 2016/406) |
| | para 12(1)–(9) | 26 Jan 2015 (SSI 2014/353) |
| | para 12(10) | 30 Sep 2015 (SSI 2015/317) |

[1]   For a transitional provision, see SSI 2014/131, art 3

[2]   For a transitional provision, see SSI 2014/131, art 4

[3]   For a transitional provision, see SSI 2014/165, art 3

[4]   For a saving, see SSI 2015/104, art 3

[5]   For a saving, see SSI 2015/317, art 3

[6]   For a saving, see SSI 2015/406, art 3

[7]   For a saving, see SSI 2016/254, art 4

---

**Church of England (Miscellaneous Provisions) Measure 2014 (No 1)**

*RA:* 14 May 2014

*Commencement provisions:* s 21(2), (7); Church of England (Miscellaneous Provisions) Measure 2014 (Appointed Day No 1) Order 2014, SI 2014/1369; Church of England (Miscellaneous Provisions) Measure 2014 (Appointed Day No 2 and Transitional and Saving Provisions) Order 2014, SI 2014/2077

| | | |
|---|---|---|
| 1 | | 19 May 2014 (SI 2014/1369) |
| 2 | | 30 Jul 2014 (SI 2014/2077)[1] |
| 3–6 | | 19 May 2014 (SI 2014/1369) |
| 7 | | 30 Jul 2014 (SI 2014/2077)[1] |
| 8–11 | | 19 May 2014 (SI 2014/1369) |
| 12 | | 30 Jul 2014 (SI 2014/2077)[1] |
| 13 | | 19 May 2014 (SI 2014/1369) |
| 14 | (1)–(4) | 19 May 2014 (SI 2014/1369) |
| | (5) | See Sch 1 below |
| 15–19 | | 19 May 2014 (SI 2014/1369) |
| 20 | | See Sch 2 below |
| 21 | | 14 May 2014 (s 21(2)) |
| Sch 1 | | 19 May 2014 (SI 2014/1369) |
| Sch 2 | paras 1–4 | 19 May 2014 (SI 2014/1369) |
| | para 5(1), (2) | 19 May 2014 (SI 2014/1369) |
| | para 5(3), (4) | See Sch 3 below |
| | para 5(5) | 19 May 2014 (SI 2014/1369) |
| | para 6 | 19 May 2014 (SI 2014/1369) |
| | para 7 | 30 Jul 2014 (SI 2014/2077) |
| | para 8 | 19 May 2014 (SI 2014/1369) |
| | para 9 | 30 Jul 2014 (SI 2014/2077)[1] |
| | paras 10–18 | 19 May 2014 (SI 2014/1369) |
| | para 19(1)–(3) | 19 May 2014 (SI 2014/1369) |
| | para 19(4), (5) | 30 Jul 2014 (SI 2014/2077)[1] |
| | para 19(6)–(11) | 19 May 2014 (SI 2014/1369) |
| | para 19(12) | 30 Jul 2014 (SI 2014/2077)[1] |
| | para 20 | 19 May 2014 (SI 2014/1369) |

**Church of England (Miscellaneous Provisions) Measure 2014 (No 1)**—*contd*
Sch 3                    19 May 2014 (SI 2014/1369)

¹    For transitional provisions, see SI 2014/2077, art 3, Schedule

---

**Citizenship (Armed Forces) Act 2014 (c 8)**

*RA:* 13 Mar 2014

*Commencement provisions:* s 2(2)

Whole Act in force 13 May 2014 (s 2(2))

---

**City of Edinburgh Council (Leith Links and Surplus Fire Fund) Act 2014 (asp 7)**

*RA:* 27 Mar 2014

*Commencement provisions:* s 7

| | |
|---|---|
| 1, 2 | 28 Mar 2014 (s 7(1)) |
| 3, 4 | 2 Apr 2014 (s 7(2)) |
| 5 | 3 Apr 2014 (s 7(3)) |
| 6–8 | 28 Mar 2014 (s 7(1)) |

---

**City of Edinburgh Council (Portobello Park) Act 2014 (asp 15)**

*RA:* 1 Aug 2014

*Commencement provisions:* s 5

Whole Act in force 2 Aug 2014 (s 5)

---

**Control of Horses (Wales) Act 2014 (anaw 3)**

*RA:* 27 Jan 2014

*Commencement provisions:* s 10(1)

Whole Act in force 28 Jan 2014 (s 10(1))

---

**Co-operative and Community Benefit Societies Act 2014 (c 14)**

*RA:* 14 May 2014

*Commencement provisions:* s 154

Whole Act in force 1 Aug 2014 (s 154)

---

**Courts Reform (Scotland) Act 2014 (asp 18)**

*RA:* 10 Nov 2014

*Commencement provisions:* s 138; Courts Reform (Scotland) Act 2014 (Commencement No 1) Order 2015, SSI 2015/12; Courts Reform (Scotland) Act 2014 (Commencement No 2, Transitional and Saving Provisions) Order 2015, SI 2015/77; Courts Reform (Scotland) Act 2014 (Commencement No 3, Transitional and Saving Provisions) Order 2015, SSI 2015/247; Criminal Justice and Licensing (Scotland) Act 2010 (Commencement No 13) and the Courts Reform (Scotland) Act 2014 (Commencement No 4) Order 2015, SSI 2015/336; Courts Reform (Scotland) Act 2014 (Commencement No 5, Transitional and Saving Provisions) Order 2015, SSI 2015/378; Courts

**Courts Reform (Scotland) Act 2014 (asp 18)**—*contd*
Reform (Scotland) Act 2014 (Commencement No 6 and Transitional Provisions) Order 2016, SSI 2016/13; Courts Reform (Scotland) Act 2014 (Commencement No 7, Transitional and Saving Provisions) Order 2016, SSI 2016/291

| | | |
|---|---|---|
| 1–4 | | 1 Apr 2015 (SSI 2015/77) |
| 5 | | 1 Apr 2015 (for the purpose of making appointments) (SSI 2015/77) |
| | | 22 Sep 2015 (otherwise) (SSI 2015/247) |
| 6–9 | | 1 Apr 2015 (SSI 2015/77) |
| 10 | | 1 Apr 2015 (for the purpose of making appointments) (SSI 2015/77) |
| | | 22 Sep 2015 (otherwise) (SSI 2015/247) |
| 11–15 | | 1 Apr 2015 (SSI 2015/77) |
| 16 | (1)–(11) | 1 Apr 2015 (SSI 2015/77)[1] |
| | (12), (13) | 1 Apr 2016 (SSI 2016/13)[4] |
| 17–20 | | 1 Apr 2015 (SSI 2015/77) |
| 21 | | 1 Apr 2015 (SSI 2015/77)[1] |
| 22 | | 1 Apr 2015 (SSI 2015/77) |
| 23 | (1)–(4) | 1 Apr 2015 (SSI 2015/77) |
| | (5) | 12 Mar 2015 (SSI 2015/77) |
| | (6) | 1 Apr 2015 (SSI 2015/77) |
| 24, 25 | | 1 Apr 2015 (SSI 2015/77) |
| 26 | | *Not yet in force* |
| 27–38 | | 1 Apr 2015 (SSI 2015/77) |
| 39 | | 1 Apr 2015 (for the purpose of making provision by act of sederunt) (SSI 2015/77) |
| | | 22 Sep 2015 (otherwise) (SSI 2015/247)[2] |
| 40–43 | | 1 Apr 2015 (SSI 2015/77) |
| 44 | (1) | See Sch 1 below |
| | (2), (3) | 22 Sep 2015 (SSI 2015/247) |
| 45 | | 22 Sep 2015 (SSI 2015/247) |
| 46 | | 1 Apr 2015 (for the purpose of enabling appointments under ss 49–51, 53, 54, 59, 60) (SSI 2015/77) |
| | | 22 Sep 2015 (otherwise) (SSI 2015/247) |
| 47, 48 | | 22 Sep 2015 (for the purposes of the Sheriff Appeal Court's criminal competence and jurisdiction) (SSI 2015/247) |
| | | 1 Jan 2016 (otherwise) (SSI 2015/378) |
| 49, 50 | | 1 Apr 2015 (SSI 2015/77) |
| 51 | | 1 Apr 2015 (SSI 2015/77)[1] |
| 52 | | 1 Apr 2015 (SSI 2015/77) |
| 53 | | See Sch 2 below |
| 54–56 | | 1 Apr 2015 (SSI 2015/77) |
| 57 | (1), (2) | 22 Sep 2015 (SSI 2015/247) |
| | (3)–(5) | 1 Apr 2015 (SSI 2015/77) |
| 58 | | 22 Sep 2015 (SSI 2015/247) |
| 59–62 | | 1 Apr 2015 (SSI 2015/77) |
| 63–68 | | 22 Sep 2015 (SSI 2015/247) |
| 69–71 | | 22 Sep 2015 (SSI 2015/247)[2] |
| 72 | | 1 Apr 2015 (for the purpose of making provision by act of sederunt) (SSI 2015/77) |
| | | 28 Nov 2016 (for the purposes of a relevant claim) (SSI 2016/291) |
| | | *Not yet in force* (otherwise) |
| 73 | | 28 Nov 2016 (for the purposes of a relevant claim) (SSI 2016/291) |
| | | *Not yet in force* (otherwise) |
| 74 | | *Not yet in force* |
| 75, 76 | | 1 Apr 2015 (SSI 2015/77) |
| 77, 78 | | 28 Nov 2016 (for the purposes of a relevant claim) (SSI 2016/291) |
| | | *Not yet in force* (otherwise) |
| 79 | | 22 Sep 2015 (SSI 2015/247)[2] |
| 80 | | 28 Nov 2016 (for the purposes of a relevant claim) (SSI 2016/291) |

**Courts Reform (Scotland) Act 2014 (asp 18)**—*contd*

|  |  |  |
|---|---|---|
|  |  | *Not yet in force* (otherwise) |
| 81 |  | 1 Apr 2015 (for the purpose of enabling an order to be made) (SSI 2015/77) |
|  |  | 28 Nov 2016 (for the purposes of a relevant claim) (SSI 2016/291) |
|  |  | *Not yet in force* (otherwise) |
| 82 |  | 28 Nov 2016 (for the purposes of a relevant claim) (SSI 2016/291) |
|  |  | *Not yet in force* (otherwise) |
| 83 |  | *Not yet in force* |
| 84, 85 |  | 28 Nov 2016 (SSI 2016/291) |
| 86 |  | 1 Apr 2015 (for the purpose of enabling an order to be made) (SSI 2015/77) |
|  |  | 28 Nov 2016 (otherwise) (SSI 2016/291) |
| 87, 88 |  | 1 Apr 2015 (SSI 2015/77) |
| 89 |  | 22 Sep 2015 (SSI 2015/247)² |
| 90, 91 |  | 1 Apr 2015 (SSI 2015/77) |
| 92 |  | 22 Sep 2015 (SSI 2015/247)² |
| 93 |  | 22 Sep 2015 (SSI 2015/247)² |
| 94 |  | 22 Sep 2015 (SSI 2015/247) |
| 95 |  | 28 Nov 2016 (SSI 2016/291) |
| 96 |  | 28 Nov 2016 (for the purposes of a relevant claim) (SSI 2016/291) |
|  |  | *Not yet in force* (otherwise) |
| 97 |  | 28 Nov 2016 (SSI 2016/291) |
| 98 |  | 1 Apr 2015 (SSI 2015/77) |
| 99 |  | 22 Sep 2015 (SSI 2015/247) |
| 100, 101 |  | 28 Nov 2016 (SSI 2016/291) |
| 102 |  | 1 Apr 2015 (for the purpose of enabling regulations to be made) (SSI 2015/77) |
|  |  | 28 Nov 2016 (otherwise) (SSI 2016/291) |
| 103–107 |  | 1 Apr 2015 (for the purpose of enabling an order to be made) (SSI 2015/77) |
|  |  | *Not yet in force* (otherwise) |
| 108 |  | 22 Sep 2015 (SSI 2015/247) |
| 109–114 |  | 1 Jan 2016 (SSI 2015/378) |
| 115 |  | 1 Apr 2015 (for the purpose of enabling an order to be made) (SSI 2015/77) |
| 116 |  | 1 Jan 2016 (SSI 2015/378) |
| 117 |  | 22 Sep 2015 (SSI 2015/247)² |
| 118 | (1), (2) | 22 Sep 2015 (SSI 2015/247)² |
|  | (3) | See Sch 3 below |
| 119 |  | 1 Apr 2015 (for the purpose of enabling the making of an act of adjournal in reliance upon Criminal Procedure (Scotland) Act 1995, s 194ZF(1)(c)(ii)) (SSI 2015/77) |
|  |  | 22 Sep 2015 (otherwise) (SSI 2015/247) |
| 120, 121 |  | 22 Sep 2015 (SSI 2015/247) |
| 122 |  | 22 Sep 2015 (SSI 2015/247)² |
| 123 |  | 1 Apr 2015 (SSI 2015/77) |
| 124 |  | 1 Apr 2016 (SSI 2016/13)⁴ |
| 125 |  | 1 Apr 2015 (SSI 2015/77) |
| 126 |  | 1 Apr 2016 (SSI 2016/13)⁴ |
| 127 |  | 1 Apr 2015 (SSI 2015/77) |
| 128, 129 |  | 1 Apr 2016 (SSI 2016/13)⁴ |
| 130 | (1), (2) | 2 Feb 2015 (for the purpose of enabling the Scottish Ministers to make regulations under the Judiciary and Courts (Scotland) Act 2008, s 72(2), Sch 3, para 3(2), (3) prescribing the procedure by which a person may be nominated, or otherwise selected for appointment, as a member of the Scottish Courts and Tribunals Service and permitting the nomination of a member in accordance with such regulations) (SSI 2015/12) |
|  |  | 1 Apr 2015 (otherwise) (SSI 2015/77) |
|  | (3) | See Sch 4 below |

**Courts Reform (Scotland) Act 2014 (asp 18)**—*contd*

| | | |
|---|---|---|
| 131 | | 1 Apr 2015 (SSI 2015/77) |
| 132 | | See Sch 5 below |
| 133 | | 11 Nov 2014 (s 138(1)) |
| 134 | (1) | 11 Nov 2014 (s 138(1)) |
| | (2) | 1 Apr 2015 (SSI 2015/77) |
| | (3) | 11 Nov 2014 (s 138(1)) |
| 135–139 | | 11 Nov 2014 (s 138(1)) |
| Sch 1 | paras 1–11 | 22 Sep 2015 (SSI 2015/247) |
| | para 12 | 22 Sep 2015 (SSI 2015/247)[2] |
| Sch 2 | | 1 Apr 2015 (for the purpose of enabling appointments to be made under para 2(1)) (SSI 2015/77) |
| | | 22 Sep 2015 (otherwise) (SSI 2015/247) |
| Sch 3 | paras 1–9 | 22 Sep 2015 (SSI 2015/247) |
| | para 10(1)–(3) | 22 Sep 2015 (SSI 2015/247) |
| | para 10(4), (5) | *Not yet in force* |
| | para 10(6), (7) | 22 Sep 2015 (SSI 2015/247) |
| | para 10(8) | *Not yet in force* |
| | paras 11–21 | 22 Sep 2015 (SSI 2015/247) |
| | para 22 | *Not yet in force* |
| | paras 23, 24 | 22 Sep 2015 (SSI 2015/247) |
| | para 25 | *Not yet in force* |
| | para 26 | 22 Sep 2015 (SSI 2015/247) |
| Sch 4 | para 1(1), (2) | 2 Feb 2015 (for the purpose of enabling the Scottish Ministers to make regulations under the Judiciary and Courts (Scotland) Act 2008, s 72(2), Sch 3, para 3(2), (3) prescribing the procedure by which a person may be nominated, or otherwise selected for appointment, as a member of the Scottish Courts and Tribunals Service and permitting the nomination of a member in accordance with such regulations) (SSI 2015/12) |
| | | 1 Apr 2015 (otherwise) (SSI 2015/77) |
| | para 1(3)–(5) | 1 Apr 2015 (SSI 2015/77) |
| | para 1(6) | 2 Feb 2015 (for the purpose of enabling the Scottish Ministers to make regulations under the Judiciary and Courts (Scotland) Act 2008, s 72(2), Sch 3, para 3(2), (3) prescribing the procedure by which a person may be nominated, or otherwise selected for appointment, as a member of the Scottish Courts and Tribunals Service and permitting the nomination of a member in accordance with such regulations) (SSI 2015/12) |
| | | 1 Apr 2015 (otherwise) (SSI 2015/77) |
| | para 1(7) | 1 Apr 2015 (SSI 2015/77) |
| | para 1(8), (9) | 2 Feb 2015 (for the purpose of enabling the Scottish Ministers to make regulations under the Judiciary and Courts (Scotland) Act 2008, s 72(2), Sch 3, para 3(2), (3) prescribing the procedure by which a person may be nominated, or otherwise selected for appointment, as a member of the Scottish Courts and Tribunals Service and permitting the nomination of a member in accordance with such regulations) (SSI 2015/12) |
| | | 1 Apr 2015 (otherwise) (SSI 2015/77) |
| | para 1(10)–(12) | 1 Apr 2015 (SSI 2015/77) |
| | para 2 | 1 Apr 2015 (SSI 2015/77) |
| | para 3(1)–(4) | 2 Feb 2015 (for the purpose of enabling the Scottish Ministers to make regulations under the Judiciary and Courts (Scotland) Act 2008, s 72(2), Sch 3, para 3(2), (3) prescribing the procedure by which a person may be nominated, or otherwise selected for appointment, as a member of the Scottish Courts and Tribunals Service and permitting the nomination of a member in accordance with such regulations) (SSI 2015/12) |
| | | 1 Apr 2015 (otherwise) (SSI 2015/77) |
| | para 3(5) | 1 Apr 2015 (SSI 2015/77) |

**Courts Reform (Scotland) Act 2014 (asp 18)**—*contd*

| | | |
|---|---|---|
| | para 3(6) | 2 Feb 2015 (for the purpose of enabling the Scottish Ministers to make regulations under the Judiciary and Courts (Scotland) Act 2008, s 72(2), Sch 3, para 3(2), (3) prescribing the procedure by which a person may be nominated, or otherwise selected for appointment, as a member of the Scottish Courts and Tribunals Service and permitting the nomination of a member in accordance with such regulations) (SSI 2015/12) |
| | | 1 Apr 2015 (otherwise) (SSI 2015/77) |
| | paras 4–9 | 1 Apr 2015 (SSI 2015/77) |
| Sch 5 | paras 1, 2 | 1 Apr 2015 (SSI 2015/77) |
| | para 3 | 1 Apr 2015 (SSI 2015/77)[1] |
| | para 4(a) | 1 Apr 2015 (for the purpose of repealing Sheriff Courts (Scotland) Act 1907, ss 4–6) (SSI 2015/77) |
| | | 22 Sep 2015 (for the purpose of repealing Sheriff Courts (Scotland) Act 1907, s 7) (SSI 2015/247)[2] |
| | para 4(b), (c) | 1 Apr 2015 (SSI 2015/77) |
| | para 4(d) | *Not yet in force* |
| | para 4(e) | 1 Jan 2016 (SSI 2015/378)[3] |
| | para 4(f) | 1 Apr 2015 (for the purpose of repealing Sheriff Courts (Scotland) Act 1907, s 40) (SSI 2015/77)[1] |
| | | *Not yet in force* (otherwise) |
| | para 4(g), (h) | *Not yet in force* |
| | para 5 | 1 Apr 2015 (SSI 2015/77) |
| | para 6(1), (2) | 1 Apr 2015 (for the purpose of repealing Sheriff Courts (Scotland) Act 1971, except ss 31, 35, 36(2), (3), 36A, 36B, 37, 38, 45 thereof) (SSI 2015/77)[1] |
| | | 22 Sep 2015 (for the purpose of repealing Sheriff Courts (Scotland) Act 1971, ss 31, 37(1)(b), (2A), (2D) (SSI 2015/247) |
| | | 28 Nov 2016 (for the purpose of repealing Sheriff Courts (Scotland) Act 1971, ss 35(2)–(4), 36A, 36B, 37(2B) and words "other than a small claim" in s 38(b) thereof) (SSI 2016/291)[5] |
| | | *Not yet in force* (otherwise) |
| | para 6(3), (4) | *Not yet in force* |
| | para 7 | 1 Apr 2015 (SSI 2015/77) |
| | para 8 | 22 Sep 2015 (SSI 2015/247) |
| | paras 9–11 | 1 Apr 2015 (SSI 2015/77) |
| | para 12(1) | 1 Apr 2015 (SSI 2015/77) |
| | para 12(2), (3) | 1 Jan 2016 (SSI 2015/378) |
| | para 12(4) | 1 Apr 2015 (SSI 2015/77) |
| | para 13 | 1 Jan 2016 (SSI 2015/378) |
| | para 14(1)–(3) | 22 Sep 2015 (SSI 2015/247) |
| | para 14(4) | 1 Jan 2016 (SSI 2015/378) |
| | para 15 | 22 Sep 2015 (SSI 2015/247) |
| | para 16 | 1 Apr 2015 (SSI 2015/77) |
| | para 17 | 19 Oct 2015 (SSI 2015/336) |
| | para 18 | 1 Apr 2015 (SSI 2015/77) |
| | para 19 | 22 Sep 2015 (SSI 2015/247) |
| | paras 20–22 | *Not yet in force* |
| | para 23 | 28 Nov 2016 (SSI 2016/291) |
| | para 24 | 22 Sep 2015 (SSI 2015/247) |
| | para 25 | 22 Sep 2015 (SSI 2015/247)[2] |
| | para 26 | 1 Apr 2015 (SSI 2015/77)[1] |
| | para 27 | 28 Nov 2016 (SSI 2016/291)[5] |
| | para 28 | 1 Apr 2015 (SSI 2015/77)[1] |
| | para 29 | 1 Apr 2015 (SSI 2015/77) |
| | para 30(1), (2) | 1 Apr 2015 (SSI 2015/77) |
| | para 30(3) | 1 Apr 2015 (SSI 2015/77)[1] |
| | para 30(4) | 1 Apr 2015 (SSI 2015/77) |
| | para 31 | 1 Apr 2015 (SSI 2015/77) |
| | para 32(1) | 22 Sep 2015 (SSI 2015/247) |

**Courts Reform (Scotland) Act 2014 (asp 18)**—*contd*

| | | |
|---|---|---|
| para 32(2) | 22 Sep 2015 (SSI 2015/247)[2] | |
| para 32(3) | 1 Jan 2016 (SSI 2015/378) | |
| para 32(4) | 22 Sep 2015 (SSI 2015/247) | |
| para 33 | 22 Sep 2015 (SSI 2015/247) | |
| para 34 | 1 Apr 2015 (SSI 2015/77) | |
| para 35 | 1 Apr 2016 (SSI 2016/13)[4] | |
| paras 36–38 | 1 Apr 2015 (SSI 2015/77) | |
| paras 39–41 | 1 Apr 2016 (SSI 2016/13)[4] | |
| paras 42–45 | 1 Apr 2015 (SSI 2015/77) | |

[1]   For transitional and saving provisions, see SSI 2015/77, arts 3–7

[2]   For transitional and saving provisions, see SSI 2015/247, arts 3–12

[3]   For transitional and saving provisions, see SSI 2015/378, arts 3, 4

[4]   For transitional provisions, see SSI 2016/13, art 3

[5]   For transitional provisions, see SSI 2016/291, arts 3, 4

---

**Data Retention and Investigatory Powers Act 2014 (c 27)**

*RA:* 17 Jul 2014

*Commencement provisions:* s 8(1), (2); Data Retention and Investigatory Powers Act 2014 (Commencement) Order 2015, SI 2015/929

| | | |
|---|---|---|
| 1 | (1)–(5) | 17 Jul 2014 (s 8(1)) |
| | (6) | 13 Apr 2015 (SI 2015/929) |
| | (7) | 17 Jul 2014 (s 8(1)) |
| 2–8 | | 17 Jul 2014 (s 8(1)) |

---

**Deep Sea Mining Act 2014 (c 15)**

*RA:* 14 May 2014

*Commencement provisions:* s 2(3)

Whole Act in force 14 Jul 2014 (s 2(3))

---

**Defence Reform Act 2014 (c 20)**

*RA:* 14 May 2014

*Commencement provisions:* s 50; Defence Reform Act 2014 (Commencement No 1) Order 2014, SI 2014/1751; Defence Reform Act 2014 (Commencement No 2) Order 2014, SI 2014/2370; Defence Reform Act 2014 (Commencement No 3) Order 2014, SI 2014/3162; Defence Reform Act 2014 (Commencement No 4) Order 2015, SI 2015/791

| | | |
|---|---|---|
| 1–3 | | *Not yet in force* |
| 4 | | See Sch 1 below |
| 5, 6 | | *Not yet in force* |
| 7 | | See Sch 2 below |
| 8, 9 | | *Not yet in force* |
| 10 | (1)–(4) | *Not yet in force* |
| | (5) | See Sch 3 below |
| | (6) | *Not yet in force* |
| 11, 12 | | *Not yet in force* |
| 13 | (1), (2) | 14 Jul 2014 (SI 2014/1751) |
| | (3) | See Sch 4 below |

**Defence Reform Act 2014 (c 20)**—*contd*

| | | |
|---|---|---|
| 14–18 | | 14 Jul 2014 (so far as necessary for the purpose of enabling the drafting of single source contract regulations and statutory guidance) (SI 2014/1751) |
| | | 5 Dec 2014 (otherwise) (SI 2014/3162) |
| 19 | (1) | 14 Jul 2014 (SI 2014/1751) |
| | (2), (3) | 5 Dec 2014 (SI 2014/3162) |
| | (4) | 14 Jul 2014 (SI 2014/1751) |
| | (5), (6) | 5 Dec 2014 (SI 2014/3162) |
| 20, 21 | | 14 Jul 2014 (so far as necessary for the purpose of enabling the drafting of single source contract regulations and statutory guidance) (SI 2014/1751) |
| | | 5 Dec 2014 (otherwise) (SI 2014/3162) |
| 22 | | 5 Dec 2014 (SI 2014/3162) |
| 23–25 | | 14 Jul 2014 (so far as necessary for the purpose of enabling the drafting of single source contract regulations and statutory guidance) (SI 2014/1751) |
| | | 5 Dec 2014 (otherwise) (SI 2014/3162) |
| 26 | | 5 Dec 2014 (SI 2014/3162) |
| 27–33 | | 14 Jul 2014 (so far as necessary for the purpose of enabling the drafting of single source contract regulations and statutory guidance) (SI 2014/1751) |
| | | 5 Dec 2014 (otherwise) (SI 2014/3162) |
| 34 | | 5 Dec 2014 (SI 2014/3162) |
| 35 | | 14 Jul 2014 (so far as necessary for the purpose of enabling the drafting of single source contract regulations and statutory guidance) (SI 2014/1751) |
| | | 5 Dec 2014 (otherwise) (SI 2014/3162) |
| 36 | | 5 Dec 2014 (SI 2014/3162) |
| 37 | | 14 Jul 2014 (SI 2014/1751) |
| 38 | | See Sch 5 below |
| 39 | | 5 Dec 2014 (SI 2014/3162) |
| 40–42 | | 14 Jul 2014 (SI 2014/1751) |
| 43 | | 14 Jul 2014 (so far as necessary for the purpose of enabling the drafting of single source contract regulations and statutory guidance) (SI 2014/1751) |
| | | 5 Dec 2014 (otherwise) (SI 2014/3162) |
| 44, 45 | | 1 Oct 2014 (SI 2014/2370) |
| 46 | | 5 Sep 2014 (SI 2014/2370) |
| 47, 48 | | 1 Oct 2014 (SI 2014/2370) |
| 49–51 | | 14 May 2014 (s 50(9)) |
| Schs 1–3 | | *Not yet in force* |
| Sch 4 | paras 1–9 | 14 Jul 2014 (SI 2014/1751) |
| | para 10(1) | 14 Jul 2014 (SI 2014/1751) |
| | para 10(2)–(6) | 5 Dec 2014 (SI 2014/3162) |
| | para 10(7) | 14 Jul 2014 (SI 2014/1751) |
| | paras 11–18 | 14 Jul 2014 (SI 2014/1751) |
| | para 19(a) | 14 Jul 2014 (SI 2014/1751) |
| | para 19(b) | 31 Mar 2015 (SI 2015/791) |
| | para 20(a) | 14 Jul 2014 (SI 2014/1751) |
| | para 20(b) | 31 Mar 2015 (SI 2015/791) |
| | para 21(a) | 14 Jul 2014 (SI 2014/1751) |
| | para 21(b) | 31 Mar 2015 (SI 2015/791) |
| Sch 5 | para 1(1)(a), (b) | 5 Dec 2014 (SI 2014/3162) |
| | para 1(1)(c) | 14 Jul 2014 (so far as necessary for the purpose of enabling the drafting of single source contract regulations and statutory guidance) (SI 2014/1751) |
| | | 5 Dec 2014 (otherwise) (SI 2014/3162) |
| | para 1(2) | 5 Dec 2014 (SI 2014/3162) |
| | para 2(1)–(4) | 5 Dec 2014 (SI 2014/3162) |
| | para 2(5) | *Not yet in force* |

**Defence Reform Act 2014 (c 20)**—*contd*

| | | |
|---|---|---|
| | paras 3–5 | 5 Dec 2014 (SI 2014/3162) |
| | para 6(1)–(3) | 5 Dec 2014 (SI 2014/3162) |
| | para 6(4) | *Not yet in force* |
| | para 6(5), (6) | 5 Dec 2014 (SI 2014/3162) |
| Sch 6 | | 1 Oct 2014 (SI 2014/2370) |
| Sch 7 | | 5 Sep 2014 (SI 2014/2370) |

**Disabled Persons' Parking Badges (Scotland) Act 2014 (asp 17)**

*RA:* 24 Sep 2014

*Commencement provisions:* s 7; Disabled Persons' Parking Badges (Scotland) Act 2014 (Commencement) Order 2015, SSI 2015/8

| | |
|---|---|
| 1–5 | 30 Mar 2015 (SSI 2015/8) |
| 6–8 | 25 Sep 2014 (s 7(1)) |

**Education (Wales) Act 2014 (anaw 5)**

*RA:* 12 May 2014

*Commencement provisions:* s 50; Education (Wales) Act 2014 (Commencement No 1) Order 2014, SI 2014/1605; Education (Wales) Act 2014 (Commencement No 2) Order 2014, SI 2014/2162; Education (Wales) Act 2014 (Commencement No 3 and Saving and Transitional Provisions) Order 2015, SI 2015/29; Education (Wales) Act 2014 (Commencement No 4) Order 2015, SI 2015/1688

| | | |
|---|---|---|
| 1 | | 12 May 2014 (s 50(1)(a)) |
| 2 | (1) | 16 Jan 2015 (for the purpose of making orders or regulations) (SI 2015/29) |
| | | 1 Apr 2015 (otherwise) (SI 2015/29) |
| | (2) | See Sch 1 below |
| 3, 4 | | 1 Apr 2015 (SI 2015/29) |
| 5 | | 16 Jan 2015 (SI 2015/29) |
| 6–8 | | 1 Apr 2015 (SI 2015/29) |
| 9 | (1) | 16 Jan 2015 (for the purpose of making orders or regulations) (SI 2015/29) |
| | | 1 Apr 2015 (otherwise) (SI 2015/29) |
| | (2) | 1 Apr 2015 (SI 2015/29) |
| | (3) | See Sch 2 below |
| | (4), (5) | 1 Apr 2015 (SI 2015/29) |
| 10 | | 16 Jan 2015 (SI 2015/29) |
| 11 | | 1 Apr 2015 (SI 2015/29) |
| 12, 13 | | 16 Jan 2015 (SI 2015/29) |
| 14 | | 16 Jan 2015 (in so far as applies to school teachers) (SI 2015/29) |
| | | 1 Jan 2016 (otherwise) (SI 2015/1688) |
| 15 | | 16 Jan 2015 (SI 2015/29) |
| 16 | | 1 Jan 2016 (SI 2015/1688) |
| 17 | | 16 Jan 2015 (SI 2015/29) |
| 18 | | 16 Jan 2015 (for the purpose of making regulations under s 17) (SI 2015/29) |
| | | 1 Apr 2015 (otherwise) (SI 2015/29) |
| 19 | | 16 Jan 2015 (for the purpose of making regulations) (SI 2015/29) |
| | | 1 Apr 2015 (otherwise) (SI 2015/29) |
| 20 | | 1 Apr 2015 (SI 2015/29) |
| 21 | | 16 Jan 2015 (SI 2015/29) |
| 22 | | 1 Apr 2015 (SI 2015/29) |
| 23 | | *Not yet in force* |
| 24 | | 16 Jan 2015 (for the purpose of making regulations) (SI 2015/29) |
| | | 1 Apr 2015 (otherwise) (SI 2015/29) |

**Education (Wales) Act 2014 (anaw 5)**—*contd*

| | | |
|---|---|---|
| 25–28 | | 16 Jan 2015 (SI 2015/29) |
| 29–31 | | 16 Jan 2015 (for the purpose of making regulations) (SI 2015/29) |
| | | 1 Apr 2015 (otherwise) (SI 2015/29) |
| 32 | | 1 Apr 2015 (SI 2015/29) |
| 33 | | 16 Jan 2015 (SI 2015/29) |
| 34 | | 1 Apr 2015 (SI 2015/29) |
| 35–37 | | 16 Jan 2015 (SI 2015/29) |
| 38–40 | | 1 Apr 2015 (SI 2015/29) |
| 41 | | 16 Jan 2015 (SI 2015/29) |
| 42 | | 12 May 2014 (in so far as necessary for regulations to be made under the Education Act 2002, s 32A(6) or 32B(4)) (s 50(2)) |
| | | 14 Jul 2014 (otherwise) (SI 2014/1605) |
| 43 | | 1 Sep 2014 (SI 2014/1605) |
| 44 | | 14 Jul 2014 (SI 2014/1605) |
| 45–47 | | 12 May 2014 (s 50(1)(b)–(d)) |
| 48 | | See Sch 3 below |
| 49–51 | | 12 May 2014 (s 50(1)(e)–(g)) |
| Sch 1 | paras 1, 2 | 1 Apr 2015 (SI 2015/29) |
| | para 3(1)–(3), (4)(a) | 18 Aug 2014 (SI 2014/2162) |
| | para 3(4)(b) | 1 Apr 2015 (SI 2015/29) |
| | paras 4–7 | 18 Aug 2014 (SI 2014/2162) |
| | para 8 | 1 Apr 2015 (SI 2015/29) |
| | para 9(1)–(3) | 18 Aug 2014 (SI 2014/2162) |
| | para 9(4)–(8) | 1 Apr 2015 (SI 2015/29) |
| | paras 10, 11 | 1 Apr 2015 (SI 2015/29) |
| | para 12 | 18 Aug 2014 (SI 2014/2162) |
| | paras 13–22 | 1 Apr 2015 (SI 2015/29) |
| Sch 2 | para 1 | 16 Jan 2015 (for the purpose of rows 1 and 3 of the table) (SI 2015/29) |
| | | 1 Jan 2016 (otherwise) (SI 2015/1688) |
| | para 2 | 1 Apr 2015 (SI 2015/29) |
| | para 3 | 16 Jan 2015 (SI 2015/29) |
| Sch 3 | para 1(1), (2) | 14 Jul 2014 (SI 2014/1605) |
| | para 1(3) | *Not yet in force* |
| | para 1(4), (5) | 1 Apr 2015 (SI 2015/29) |
| | para 1(6) | 14 Jul 2014 (SI 2014/1605) |
| | para 2 | 12 Jul 2014 (s 50(3)) |
| | para 3 | 1 Apr 2015 (except repeal of Education Act 2002, s 131(7)) (SI 2015/29)[1] |
| | | *Not yet in force* (exception noted above) |
| Sch 4 | | 12 May 2014 (s 50(1)(a)) |

[1]   For savings and transitional provisions, see SI 2015/29, art 4

---

**European Union (Approvals) Act 2014 (c 3)**

*RA:* 30 Jan 2014

*Commencement provisions:* s 2(2)

Whole Act in force 30 Jan 2014 (s 2(2))

---

**Finance Act 2014 (c 26)**

*Budget Day:* 19 Mar 2014

*RA:* 17 Jul 2014

The commencement details of Finance Acts are not set out, as the dates from which their provisions take effect are usually stated clearly and unambiguously in the text of the Act, and charging provisions will normally state for which year or years of assessment they are to have effect.

---

## Further and Higher Education (Governance and Information) (Wales) Act 2014 (anaw 1)

*RA:* 27 Jan 2014

*Commencement provisions:* s 11; Further and Higher Education (Governance and Information) (Wales) Act 2014 (Commencement) Order 2014, SI 2014/1706

| | | |
|---|---|---|
| 1 | | 1 Sep 2014 (SI 2014/1706) |
| 2 | (1) | 1 Sep 2014 (SI 2014/1706) |
| | (2) | See Sch 1 below |
| | (3) | 1 Sep 2014 (SI 2014/1706) |
| 3 | | 1 Aug 2014 (for the purpose of making regulations) (SI 2014/1706) |
| | | 1 Sep 2014 (otherwise) (SI 2014/1706) |
| 4–7 | | 1 Sep 2014 (SI 2014/1706) |
| 8 | | See Sch 2 below |
| 9 | | 27 Jan 2014 (s 11(1)) |
| 10 | | 1 Sep 2014 (SI 2014/1706) |
| 11, 12 | | 27 Jan 2014 (s 11(1)) |
| Schs 1, 2 | | 1 Sep 2014 (SI 2014/1706) |

## Gambling (Licensing and Advertising) Act 2014 (c 17)

*RA:* 14 May 2014

*Commencement provisions:* s 6(4)–(6); Gambling (Licensing and Advertising) Act 2014 (Commencement No 1) Order 2014, SI 2014/2444, as amended by SI 2014/2646; Gambling (Licensing and Advertising) Act 2014 (Commencement No 2) Order 2017, SI 2017/20

| | | |
|---|---|---|
| 1 | (1)–(3) | 1 Nov 2014 (except in relation to remote gambling which is or relates to a MiFID financial instrument or which relates to a factor to which a MiFID financial instrument relates[1]) (SI 2014/2444, SI 2014/2646) |
| | | *Not yet in force* (exception noted above) |
| | (4)–(7) | 14 May 2014 (s 6(4)) |
| 2 | | 31 Jan 2017 (SI 2017/20) |
| 3–5 | | 1 Nov 2014 (SI 2014/2444, SI 2014/2646) |
| 6 | | 14 May 2014 (s 6(4)) |

[1]   "MiFID financial instrument" means a financial instrument listed in Section C of Annex I to the Directive 2004/39/EC of the European Parliament and of the Council of 21 Apr 2004 on markets in financial instruments (OJ L 145, 30.04.2004)

## Historic Environment Scotland Act 2014 (asp 19)

*RA:* 14 May 2014

*Commencement provisions:* s 31; Historic Environment Scotland Act 2014 (Commencement No 1) Order 2014, SSI 2014/368; Historic Environment Scotland Act 2014 (Commencement No 2) Order 2015, SSI 2015/31; Historic Environment Scotland Act 2014 (Commencement No 3) Order 2015, SSI 2015/196

| | |
|---|---|
| 1 | See Sch 1 below |
| 2 | 27 Feb 2015 (for the purpose of enabling Historic Environment Scotland to exercise any function conferred on it under or by virtue of ss 9, 12, 13, 19, Sch 5) (SSI 2015/31) |
| | 1 Oct 2015 (otherwise) (SSI 2015/196) |
| 3–8 | 1 Oct 2015 (SSI 2015/196) |
| 9 | 27 Feb 2015 (SSI 2015/31) |
| 10, 11 | 1 Oct 2015 (SSI 2015/196) |
| 12–14 | 27 Feb 2015 (SSI 2015/31) |

**Historic Environment Scotland Act 2014 (asp 19)**—*contd*

| | | |
|---|---|---|
| 15 | | See Sch 2 below |
| 16 | | See Sch 3 below |
| 17 | | See Sch 4 below |
| 18 | | *Not yet in force* |
| 19 | | See Sch 5 below |
| 20–24 | | 1 Oct 2015 (SSI 2015/196) |
| 25–27 | | 10 Dec 2014 (s 31(1)) |
| 28 | | See Sch 6 below |
| 29–32 | | 10 Dec 2014 (s 31(1)) |
| Sch 1 | | 19 Jan 2015 (only for the purposes of certain appointments)[1] (SSI 2014/368) |
| | | 27 Feb 2015 (for the purpose of enabling Historic Environment Scotland to exercise any function conferred on it under or by virtue of ss 9, 12, 13, 19, Sch 5) (SSI 2015/31) |
| | | 1 Oct 2015 (otherwise) (SSI 2015/196) |
| Schs 2, 3 | | 27 Feb 2015 (for the purpose of making regulations or giving directions) (SSI 2015/31) |
| | | 1 Oct 2015 (otherwise) (SSI 2015/196) |
| Sch 4 | | 1 Oct 2015 (SSI 2015/196) |
| Sch 5 | | 27 Feb 2015 (SSI 2015/31) |
| Sch 6 | para 1(a) | 1 Oct 2015 (SSI 2015/196) |
| | paras 1(b), 2(a) | 27 Feb 2015 (SSI 2015/31) |
| | para 2(b) | 1 Oct 2015 (SSI 2015/196) |
| | para 3(a) | 27 Feb 2015 (SSI 2015/31) |
| | para 3(b) | 1 Oct 2015 (SSI 2015/196) |
| | para 4(a) | 27 Feb 2015 (SSI 2015/31) |
| | para 4(b) | 1 Oct 2015 (SSI 2015/196) |
| | para 5(a)(i) | 27 Feb 2015 (SSI 2015/31) |
| | para 5(a)(ii) | 1 Oct 2015 (SSI 2015/196) |
| | para 5(b)(i) | 27 Feb 2015 (SSI 2015/31) |
| | para 5(b)(ii) | 1 Oct 2015 (SSI 2015/196) |
| | para 6(a) | 27 Feb 2015 (SSI 2015/31) |
| | para 6(b) | 1 Oct 2015 (SSI 2015/196) |

[1] For the certain appointments, see SSI 2014/368, art 2

---

**House of Lords Reform Act 2014 (c 24)**

*RA:* 14 May 2014

*Commencement provisions:* s 7(2), (3)

| | |
|---|---|
| 1, 2 | 14 Aug 2014 (s 7(2)) |
| 3–7 | 14 May 2014 (s 7(3)) |

---

**Housing (Scotland) Act 2014 (asp 14)**

*RA:* 1 Aug 2014

*Commencement provisions:* s 104; Housing (Scotland) Act 2014 (Commencement No 1, Transitional and Saving Provisions) Order 2014, SSI 2014/264; Housing (Scotland) Act 2014 (Commencement No 2) Order 2015, SSI 2015/122; Housing (Scotland) Act 2014 (Commencement No 3 and Transitional Provision) Order 2015, SSI 2015/272; Housing (Scotland) Act 2014 (Commencement No 4 and Amendment) Order 2015, SSI 2015/349; Housing (Scotland) Act 2014 (Commencement No 5 and Consequential Provision) Order 2015, SSI 2015/430; Housing (Scotland) Act 2014 (Commencement No 6 and Transitional Provision) Order 2016, SSI 2016/412, as amended by SSI 2017/330; Housing (Scotland) Act 2014 (Commencement No 7, Amendment and Saving Provision) Order 2017, SSI 2017/330; Housing (Scotland) Act 2014 (Commencement No. 8, Savings, Transitional and Supplemental Provisions) Order 2018, SSI 2018/153

**See Halsbury's Statutes Citator for amendments to these Acts** 2359

**Housing (Scotland) Act 2014 (asp 14)**—*contd*

| | | |
|---|---|---|
| 1 | (1) | 1 Aug 2016 (SSI 2014/264)[1] |
| | (2) | 20 Nov 2014 (SSI 2014/264) |
| | (3) | 20 Nov 2014 (for the purpose of repealing Housing (Scotland) Act 2010, s 147) (SSI 2014/264) |
| | | 1 Jul 2017 (otherwise) (SSI 2014/264) |
| 2 | | 20 Nov 2014 (SSI 2014/264)[1] |
| 3 | | 1 May 2019 (SSI 2018/153) |
| 4 | (1) | 1 May 2019 (SSI 2018/153) |
| | (2) | 20 Nov 2014 (for the purpose of enabling consultation by the Scottish Ministers under Housing (Scotland) Act 1987, s 21(3B)) (SSI 2014/264) |
| | | 1 May 2019 (otherwise) (SSI 2018/153) |
| | (3) | 1 May 2019 (SSI 2018/153) |
| 5 | | 1 May 2019 (SSI 2018/153) |
| 6 | (1) | 1 May 2019 (SSI 2018/153) |
| | (2) | 20 Nov 2014 (for the purpose of enabling consultation by the Scottish Ministers under Housing (Scotland) Act 1987, s 20B(4)) (SSI 2014/264) |
| | | 1 May 2019 (otherwise) (SSI 2018/153) |
| | (3)–(11) | 1 May 2019 (SSI 2018/153) |
| 7 | (1)(a) | 1 May 2019 (SSI 2018/153) |
| | (1)(b) | 20 Nov 2014 (SSI 2014/264) |
| | (2), (3), (4)(a) | 1 May 2019 (SSI 2018/153) |
| | (4)(b) | 1 May 2019 (SSI 2018/153)[5] |
| | (5) | 1 May 2019 (SSI 2018/153) |
| 8 | | 1 May 2019 (SSI 2018/153) |
| 9 | (1), (2) | 1 May 2019 (SSI 2018/153)[5] |
| | (2), (3) | 1 May 2019 (SSI 2018/153) |
| 10 | | 1 May 2019 (SSI 2018/153)[5] |
| 11 | (a), (b) | 1 May 2019 (SSI 2018/153)[5] |
| | (c) | 1 May 2019 (SSI 2018/153) |
| | (d)–(f) | 1 May 2019 (SSI 2018/153)[5] |
| 12 | | 1 Nov 2019 (SSI 2018/153)[5] |
| 13 | | 1 Nov 2019 (SSI 2018/153) |
| 14 | (1) | 20 Nov 2014 (SSI 2014/264) |
| | (2) | 1 May 2019 (SSI 2018/153) |
| 15 | | 1 May 2019 (SSI 2018/153) |
| 16 | (1), (2) | 1 Dec 2017 (SSI 2017/330)[4] |
| | (3) | See Sch 1, Pt 1 below |
| 17 | (1)–(4) | *Not yet in force* |
| | (5) | See Sch 1, Pt 2 below |
| 18 | (1) | *Not yet in force* |
| | (2) | See Sch 1, Pt 3 below |
| 19 | (1)–(3) | *Not yet in force* |
| | (4) | See Sch 1, Pt 4 below |
| 20 | | 20 Nov 2014 (SSI 2014/264) |
| 21 | | *Not yet in force* |
| 22 | | 1 Dec 2015 (SSI 2015/272) |
| 23 | (1) | 20 Nov 2014 (SSI 2014/264) |
| | (2) | 1 Dec 2015 (SSI 2015/272)[2] |
| 24 | | 20 Nov 2014 (SSI 2014/264) |
| 25 | (1)(a) | 1 Dec 2015 (for the purpose of Dumfries and Galloway Council, Dundee City Council and Glasgow City Council making applications under section 22(1A) of the Housing (Scotland) Act 2006, s 22(1A)) (SSI 2015/349) |

**Housing (Scotland) Act 2014 (asp 14)**—*contd*

|  |  |  |
|---|---|---|
|  |  | 1 Apr 2016 (for the purpose of Aberdeen City Council, Aberdeenshire Council, City of Edinburgh Council, Comhairle nan Eilean Siar, East Ayrshire Council, East Dunbartonshire Council, East Lothian Council, Highland Council, Moray Council, North Ayrshire Council, North Lanarkshire Council, Orkney Islands Council, Renfrewshire Council, Shetland Islands Council and West Lothian Council making applications under section 22(1A) of the Housing (Scotland) Act 2006, s 22(1A)) (SSI 2015/349) |
|  |  | 1 Jun 2016 (all remaining purposes) (SSI 2015/349) |
|  | (1)(b)–(e) | 1 Dec 2015 (SSI 2015/349) |
|  | (2)–(11) | 1 Dec 2015 (SSI 2015/349) |
| 26 | (1)–(6) | 1 Dec 2015 (SSI 2015/272) |
| 26 | (7) | 20 Nov 2014 (SSI 2014/264) |
| 27 |  | 1 Dec 2015 (SSI 2015/272) |
| 28 |  | 20 Nov 2014 (SSI 2014/264) |
| 29 | (1) | 31 Jan 2018 (SSI 2016/412) |
|  | (2)(a) | 31 Jan 2018 (SSI 2016/412) |
|  | (2)(b) | 2 Feb 2016 (for the purpose of making regulations) (SSI 2015/430) |
|  |  | 31 Jan 2018 (otherwise) (SSI 2016/412) |
|  | (3) | 31 Jan 2018 (SSI 2016/412) |
| 30 | (1) | 31 Jan 2018 (SSI 2016/412) |
|  | (2)(a)–(e) | 31 Jan 2018 (SSI 2016/412) |
|  | (2)(f) | 2 Feb 2016 (for the purpose of making regulations) (SSI 2015/430) |
|  |  | 31 Jan 2018 (otherwise) (SSI 2016/412) |
|  | (3) | 31 Jan 2018 (SSI 2016/412) |
| 31 |  | 31 Jan 2018 (SSI 2016/412) |
| 32 | (1) | 31 Jan 2018 (SSI 2016/412) |
|  | (2)(a), (b) | 31 Jan 2018 (SSI 2016/412) |
|  | (2)(c) | 2 Feb 2016 (for the purpose of making regulations) (SSI 2015/430) |
|  |  | 31 Jan 2018 (otherwise) (SSI 2016/412) |
|  | (3)–(10) | 31 Jan 2018 (SSI 2016/412) |
| 33–43 |  | 31 Jan 2018 (SSI 2016/412) |
| 44 |  | 2 Oct 2018 (SSI 2016/412)[3] |
| 45 |  | 31 Jan 2018 (SSI 2016/412) |
| 46 |  | 20 Nov 2014 (SSI 2014/264) |
| 47–51 |  | 31 Jan 2018 (SSI 2016/412) |
| 52 | (1) | 31 Jan 2018 (SSI 2016/412) |
|  | (2) | 2 Feb 2016 (SSI 2015/430) |
|  | (3) | 31 Jan 2018 (SSI 2016/412) |
| 53–60 |  | 31 Jan 2018 (SSI 2016/412) |
| 61 |  | 20 Nov 2014 (SSI 2014/264) |
| 62 |  | 20 Nov 2014 (definitions "house", "landlord" and "tenant") (SSI 2014/264) |
|  |  | 31 Jan 2018 (otherwise) (SSI 2016/412) |
| 63 |  | 1 May 2017 (SSI 2016/412) |
| 64 |  | 20 Nov 2014 (in so far as is necessary to enable the Scottish Ministers to make regulations under Caravan Sites and Control of Development Act 1960, s 32C(4)) (SSI 2014/264) |
|  |  | 1 May 2017 (otherwise) (SSI 2016/412) |
| 65 |  | 20 Nov 2014 (in so far as is necessary to enable the Scottish Ministers to make regulations under Caravan Sites and Control of Development Act 1960, s 32F(3)) (SSI 2014/264) |
|  |  | 1 May 2017 (otherwise) (SSI 2016/412) |
| 66–69 |  | 1 May 2017 (SSI 2016/412) |
| 70 |  | 20 Nov 2014 (SSI 2014/264) |
| 71–76 |  | 1 May 2017 (SSI 2016/412) |
| 77 |  | 20 Nov 2014 (in so far as is necessary to enable the Scottish Ministers to make regulations under Caravan Sites and Control of Development Act 1960, s 32Y(5)) (SSI 2014/264) |

**Housing (Scotland) Act 2014 (asp 14)**—*contd*

|  |  |  |
|---|---|---|
|  |  | 1 May 2017 (otherwise) (SSI 2016/412) |
| 78–81 |  | 1 May 2017 (SSI 2016/412) |
| 82 |  | 20 Nov 2014 (SSI 2014/264) |
| 83, 84 |  | 1 May 2017 (SSI 2016/412) |
| 85 | (1), (2) | 1 Apr 2015 (SSI 2015/122) |
|  | (3), (4) | 20 Nov 2014 (SSI 2014/264) |
| 86 | (1) | 13 Nov 2014 (in so far as is necessary to enable the Scottish Ministers to make an order under Title Conditions (Scotland) Act 2003, s 10A(3B)(a)) (SSI 2014/264) |
|  |  | 16 Dec 2014 (otherwise) (SSI 2014/264) |
|  | (2) | 13 Nov 2014 (in so far as is necessary to enable the Scottish Ministers to make an order under Tenements (Scotland) Act 2004, s 13(3B)(a)) (SI 2014/264) |
|  |  | 16 Dec 2014 (otherwise) (SSI 2014/264) |
| 87, 88 |  | 1 Apr 2015 (SSI 2015/122) |
| 89 |  | 13 Jul 2015 (SSI 2015/272) |
| 90–92 |  | 1 Apr 2015 (SSI 2015/122) |
| 93 |  | 1 Oct 2014 (s 104(2)) |
| 94–96 |  | 20 Nov 2014 (SSI 2014/264) |
| 97 |  | 20 Nov 2014 (for the purpose of enabling consultation by the Regulator under Housing (Scotland) Act 2010, s 67(4B)(b)) (SSI 2014/264) |
|  |  | 31 Aug 2015 (otherwise) (SSI 2015/272) |
| 98 |  | 20 Nov 2014 (SSI 2014/264)[1] |
| 99 |  | 30 Jul 2018 (SSI 2018/153) |
| 100–102 |  | 1 Aug 2014 (s 104(1)) |
| 103 |  | See Sch 2 below |
| 104, 105 |  | 1 Aug 2014 (s 104(1)) |
| Sch 1 | paras 1–6 | 1 Dec 2017 (SSI 2017/330) |
|  | para 7 | 1 Dec 2017 (for the purpose of proceedings in relation to a regulated tenancy (within the meaning of Rent (Scotland) Act 1984, s 8) and an assured tenancy (within the meaning of Housing (Scotland) Act 1988, s 12)) (SSI 2017/330) |
|  |  | *Not yet in force* (otherwise) |
|  | para 8 | 1 Dec 2017 (SSI 2017/330) |
|  | para 9 | *Not yet in force* |
|  | paras 10–60 | 1 Dec 2017 (SSI 2017/330) |
| Sch 2 | paras 1, 2 | 1 Aug 2016 (SSI 2014/264)[1] |
|  | para 3 | 20 Nov 2014 (SSI 2014/264)[1] |
|  | para 4(1)–(4) | 20 Nov 2014 (SSI 2014/264) |
|  | para 4(5), (6) | *Not yet in force* |
|  | para 4(7), (8) | 1 Aug 2016 (SSI 2014/264)[1] |
|  | para 4(9)(a) | *Not yet in force* |
|  | para 4(9)(b) | 20 Nov 2014 (SSI 2014/264) |
|  | para 5(1) | 20 Nov 2014 (SSI 2014/264) |
|  | para 5(2) | *Not yet in force* |
|  | para 5(3) | 20 Nov 2014 (SSI 2014/264) |
|  | paras 6–9 | *Not yet in force* |
|  | para 9 | 1 Aug 2016 (SSI 2014/264)[1] |
|  | para 10(1) | 20 Nov 2014 (SSI 2014/264) |
|  | para 10(2) | *Not yet in force* |
|  | para 10(3), (4) | 1 Aug 2016 (SSI 2014/264)[1] |
|  | para 10(5)(a) | 20 Nov 2014 (SSI 2014/264) |
|  | para 10(5)(b) | 1 Aug 2016 (SSI 2014/264)[1] |
|  | para 10(5)(c) | *Not yet in force* |
|  | para 11 | *Not yet in force* |
|  | paras 12, 13 | 20 Nov 2014 (SSI 2014/264) |
|  | paras 14–16 | 1 Aug 2016 (SSI 2014/264)[1] |
|  | paras 17, 18(1), (2) | 20 Nov 2014 (SSI 2014/264) |

## Housing (Scotland) Act 2014 (asp 14)—*contd*

| | | |
|---|---|---|
| para 18(3) | 1 Aug 2016 (SSI 2014/264)[1] | |
| para 18(4), (5) | 20 Nov 2014 (SSI 2014/264) | |
| para 18(6), (7)(a) | 1 Aug 2016 (SSI 2014/264)[1] | |
| para 18 (7)(b) | 20 Nov 2014 (SSI 2014/264) | |
| para 19 | 1 Aug 2016 (SSI 2014/264)[1] | |

[1]  For transitional and saving provisions, see SSI 2014/264, arts 3–6

[2]  For transitional provisions, see SSI 2015/272, art 3

[3]  For transitional provisions, see SSI 2015/412, art 3

[4]  For savings, see SSI 2017/330, art 3

[5]  For transitional and saving provisions, see SSI 2018/153, arts 3–6

## Housing (Wales) Act 2014 (anaw 7)

*RA:* 18 Sep 2014

*Commencement provisions:* s 145; Housing (Wales) Act 2014 (Commencement No 1) Order 2014, SI 2014/3127; Housing (Wales) Act 2014 (Commencement No 2) Order 2015, SI 2015/380; Housing (Wales) Act 2014 (Commencement No 3 and Transitory, Transitional and Saving Provisions) Order 2015, SI 2015/1272; Housing (Wales) Act 2014 (Commencement No 4) Order 2015, SI 2015/1826; Housing (Wales) Act 2014 (Commencement No 5) Order 2015, SI 2015/2046; Housing (Wales) Act 2014 (Commencement No 6) Order 2016, SI 2016/266; Housing (Wales) Act 2014 (Commencement No 7) Order 2016, SI 2016/1009 (revoked by SI 2016/1066); Housing (Wales) Act 2014 (Commencement No 8) Order 2016, SI 2016/1066; Housing (Wales) Act 2014 (Commencement No 9) Order 2019, SI 2019/553; Housing (Wales) Act 2014 (Commencement No 10) Order 2019, SI 2019/1479

| | | |
|---|---|---|
| 1 | (1)–(5) | 23 Nov 2015 (SI 2015/1826) |
| | (6) | See Sch 1 below |
| | (7)–(12) | 23 Nov 2015 (SI 2015/1826) |
| 2, 3 | | 1 Dec 2014 (for the purposes of making orders, regulations and directions) (SI 2014/3127) |
| | | 23 Nov 2015 (otherwise) (SI 2015/1826) |
| 4 | | 23 Nov 2016 (SI 2016/1066) |
| 5–8 | | 1 Dec 2014 (for the purposes of making orders, regulations and directions) (SI 2014/3127) |
| | | 23 Nov 2016 (otherwise) (SI 2016/1066) |
| 9 | | 23 Nov 2016 (SI 2016/1066) |
| 10 | | 1 Dec 2014 (for the purposes of making orders, regulations and directions) (SI 2014/3127) |
| | | 23 Nov 2016 (otherwise) (SI 2016/1066) |
| 11 | | 23 Nov 2016 (SI 2016/1066) |
| 12 | | 1 Dec 2014 (for the purposes of making orders, regulations and directions) (SI 2014/3127) |
| | | 23 Nov 2016 (otherwise) (SI 2016/1066) |
| 13 | | 23 Nov 2016 (SI 2016/1066) |
| 14–16 | | 1 Dec 2014 (for the purposes of making orders, regulations and directions) (SI 2014/3127) |
| | | 23 Nov 2015 (otherwise) (SI 2015/1826) |
| 17, 18 | | 23 Nov 2015 (SI 2015/1826) |
| 19 | | 1 Dec 2014 (for the purposes of making orders, regulations and directions) (SI 2014/3127) |
| | | 23 Nov 2015 (otherwise) (SI 2015/1826) |
| 20 | | 1 Dec 2014 (for the purposes of making orders, regulations and directions and for the purposes of giving, revising or revoking statutory guidance and issuing, amending or withdrawing a code of practice) (SI 2014/3127) |
| | | 23 Nov 2015 (otherwise) (SI 2015/1826) |

**Housing (Wales) Act 2014 (anaw 7)**—*contd*

| | | |
|---|---|---|
| 21 | | 1 Dec 2014 (for the purposes of making orders, regulations and directions) (SI 2014/3127) |
| | | 23 Nov 2015 (otherwise) (SI 2015/1826) |
| 22 | | 23 Nov 2015 (SI 2015/1826) |
| 23 | | 1 Dec 2014 (for the purposes of making orders, regulations and directions) (SI 2014/3127) |
| | | 23 Nov 2015 (otherwise) (SI 2015/1826) |
| 24–27 | | 23 Nov 2015 (SI 2015/1826) |
| 28 | | 23 Nov 2016 (SI 2016/1066) |
| 29 | | 1 Dec 2014 (for the purposes of making orders, regulations and directions) (SI 2014/3127) |
| | | 23 Nov 2016 (otherwise) (SI 2016/1066) |
| 30–33 | | 23 Nov 2016 (SI 2016/1066) |
| 34 | | 1 Dec 2014 (for the purposes of making orders, regulations and directions) (SI 2014/3127) |
| | | 23 Nov 2016 (otherwise) (SI 2016/1066) |
| 35 | | 23 Nov 2016 (SI 2016/1066) |
| 36–39 | | 23 Nov 2015 (SI 2015/1826) |
| 40, 41 | | 1 Dec 2014 (for the purposes of giving, revising or revoking statutory guidance and issuing, amending or withdrawing a code of practice) (SI 2014/3127) |
| | | 23 Nov 2016 (otherwise) (SI 2016/1066) |
| 42 | | 1 Dec 2014 (for the purposes of making orders, regulations and directions) (SI 2014/3127) |
| | | 23 Nov 2016 (otherwise) (SI 2016/1066) |
| 43, 44 | | 23 Nov 2016 (SI 2016/1066) |
| 45 | | 23 Nov 2015 (SI 2015/1826) |
| 46 | | 1 Dec 2014 (for the purposes of making orders, regulations and directions) (SI 2014/3127) |
| | | 23 Nov 2016 (otherwise) (SI 2016/1066) |
| 47, 48 | | 23 Nov 2015 (SI 2015/1826) |
| 49 | | 1 Dec 2014 (for the purposes of making orders, regulations and directions) (SI 2014/3127) |
| | | 23 Nov 2015 (otherwise) (SI 2015/1826) |
| 50 | | 1 Dec 2014 (for the purposes of making orders, regulations and directions) (SI 2014/3127) |
| | | 27 Apr 2015 (otherwise) (SI 2015/1272) |
| 51–56 | | 27 Apr 2015 (SI 2015/1272) |
| 57 | | 1 Dec 2014 (for the purposes of making orders, regulations and directions) (SI 2014/3127) |
| | | 27 Apr 2015 (otherwise) (SI 2015/1272) |
| 58 | | 27 Apr 2015 (SI 2015/1272) |
| 59 | | 1 Dec 2014 (for the purposes of making orders, regulations and directions) (SI 2014/3127) |
| | | 27 Apr 2015 (otherwise) (SI 2015/1272) |
| 60 | | 27 Apr 2015 (SI 2015/1272) |
| 61 | | See Sch 2 below |
| 62, 63 | | 27 Apr 2015 (SI 2015/1272) |
| 64 | | 1 Dec 2014 (for the purposes of giving, revising or revoking statutory guidance and issuing, amending or withdrawing a code of practice) (SI 2014/3127) |
| | | 27 Apr 2015 (otherwise) (SI 2015/1272) |
| 65–71 | | 27 Apr 2015 (SI 2015/1272) |
| 72 | | 1 Dec 2014 (for the purposes of making orders, regulations and directions) (SI 2014/3127) |
| | | 27 Apr 2015 (otherwise) (SI 2015/1272) |
| 73, 74 | | 27 Apr 2015 (SI 2015/1272) |
| 75 | (1), (2) | 27 Apr 2015 (SI 2015/1272)[1] |
| | (3) | 2 Dec 2019 (SI 2019/1479) |
| | (4) | 27 Apr 2015 (SI 2015/1272) |

**Housing (Wales) Act 2014 (anaw 7)**—*contd*

| | | |
|---|---|---|
| 76, 77 | | 27 Apr 2015 (SI 2015/1272) |
| 78 | | 1 Dec 2014 (for the purposes of making orders, regulations and directions) (SI 2014/3127) |
| | | 27 Apr 2015 (for the purpose of enabling a local housing authority to make a decision and to publish a notice of that decision) (SI 2015/1272)[1] |
| | | 1 Jul 2015 (otherwise) (SI 2015/1272) |
| 79 | | 27 Apr 2015 (SI 2015/1272) |
| 80, 81 | | 1 Dec 2014 (for the purposes of making orders, regulations and directions) (SI 2014/3127) |
| | | 27 Apr 2015 (otherwise) (SI 2015/1272) |
| 82–85 | | 27 Apr 2015 (SI 2015/1272) |
| 86 | | 1 Dec 2014 (for the purposes of making orders, regulations and directions) (SI 2014/3127) |
| | | 27 Apr 2015 (otherwise) (SI 2015/1272) |
| 87–94 | | 27 Apr 2015 (SI 2015/1272) |
| 95 | | 1 Dec 2014 (for the purposes of making orders, regulations and directions) (SI 2014/3127) |
| | | 27 Apr 2015 (otherwise) (SI 2015/1272) |
| 96, 97 | | 27 Apr 2015 (SI 2015/1272) |
| 98 | | 1 Dec 2014 (for the purposes of giving, revising or revoking statutory guidance and issuing, amending or withdrawing a code of practice) (SI 2014/3127) |
| | | 27 Apr 2015 (otherwise) (SI 2015/1272) |
| 99 | | 1 Dec 2014 (for the purposes of making orders, regulations and directions) (SI 2014/3127) |
| | | 27 Apr 2015 (otherwise) (SI 2015/1272) |
| 100 | | See Sch 3, Pt 1 below |
| 101, 102 | | 25 Feb 2015 (SI 2015/380) |
| 103, 104 | | 16 Mar 2016 (SI 2016/266) |
| 105 | | 25 Feb 2015 (SI 2015/380) |
| 106 | | 1 Dec 2014 (for the purposes of giving, revising or revoking statutory guidance and issuing, amending or withdrawing a code of practice) (SI 2014/3127) |
| | | 25 Feb 2015 (otherwise) (SI 2015/380) |
| 107–109 | | 25 Feb 2015 (SI 2015/380) |
| 110 | | See Sch 3, Pt 2 below |
| 111–128 | | 1 Dec 2014 (SI 2014/3127) |
| 129 | | *Not yet in force* |
| 130 | | See Sch 3, Pt 3 below |
| 131 | (1)–(3), (4)(a), (b) | 20 Mar 2019 (SI 2019/553) |
| | (4)(c) | 1 Dec 2014 (SI 2014/3127) |
| 132–136 | | 18 Nov 2014 (s 145(2)) |
| 137 | | 1 Dec 2014 (SI 2014/3127) |
| 138 | | *Not yet in force* |
| 139 | (1) | 16 Dec 2015 (SI 2015/2046) |
| | (2) | 16 Dec 2015 (except for the purpose of the Local Government Finance Act 1992, s 12A(12)) (SI 2015/2046) |
| | | 1 Apr 2016 (for the purpose of the Local Government Finance Act 1992, s 12A(12)) (SI 2015/2046) |
| | (3) | See Sch 3, Pt 4 below |
| 140 | | 1 Dec 2014 (SI 2014/3127) |
| 141 | | See Sch 3, Pt 5 below |
| 142, 143 | | 18 Sep 2014 (s 145(1)) |
| 144 | | 1 Dec 2014 (SI 2014/3127) |
| 145, 146 | | 18 Sep 2014 (s 145(1)) |
| Sch 1 | | 23 Nov 2015 (SI 2015/1826) |
| Sch 2 | para 1 | 1 Dec 2014 (for the purposes of making orders, regulations and directions) (SI 2014/3127) |
| | | 27 Apr 2015 (otherwise) (SI 2015/1272)[1] |

**See Halsbury's Statutes Citator for amendments to these Acts**

**Housing (Wales) Act 2014 (anaw 7)**—*contd*

|  |  |  |
|---|---|---|
|  | paras 2, 3 | 27 Apr 2015 (SI 2015/1272)[1] |
| Sch 3 | Pt 1 | 27 Apr 2015 (SI 2015/1272)[1] |
|  | Pt 2 | 25 Feb 2015 (SI 2015/380) |
|  | Pt 3 | 1 Dec 2014 (SI 2014/3127) |
|  | Pt 4 | 16 Dec 2015 (SI 2015/2046) |
|  | Pt 5 | 1 Dec 2014 (SI 2014/3127) |

[1]　For transitory, transitional and saving provisions, see SI 2015/1272, arts 4–8

---

**Immigration Act 2014 (c 22)**

*RA:* 14 May 2014

*Commencement provisions:* s 75; Immigration Act 2014 (Commencement No 1, Transitory and Saving Provisions) Order 2014, SI 2014/1820, as amended by SI 2014/2771; Immigration Act 2014 (Commencement No 2) Order 2014, SI 2014/1943; Immigration Act 2014 (Commencement No 3, Transitional and Saving Provisions) Order 2014, SI 2014/2771, as amended by SI 2015/371; Immigration Act 2014 (Commencement No 4, Transitional and Saving Provisions and Amendment) Order 2015, SI 2015/371; Immigration Act 2014 (Commencement No 5) Order 2015, SI 2015/874; Immigration Act 2014 (Commencement No 6) Order 2016, SI 2016/11; Immigration Act 2014 (Commencement No 7) Order 2021, SI 2021/771

|  |  |  |
|---|---|---|
| 1 |  | 20 Oct 2014 (SI 2014/2771)[2] |
| 2, 3 |  | 28 Jul 2014 (SI 2014/1820) |
| 4 |  | See Sch 1 below |
| 5, 6 |  | 28 Jul 2014 (SI 2014/1820) |
| 7 | (1), (2) | 28 Jul 2014 (SI 2014/1820) |
|  | (3), (4) | 20 Oct 2014 (SI 2014/2771) |
|  | (5) | 28 Jul 2014 (SI 2014/1820) |
|  | (6) | 20 Oct 2014 (SI 2014/2771) |
| 8–11 |  | 28 Jul 2014 (SI 2014/1820) |
| 12 | (1)–(3) | 28 Jul 2014 (SI 2014/1820) |
|  | (4) | See Sch 2 below |
| 13, 14 |  | 28 Jul 2014 (SI 2014/1820) |
| 15 |  | 20 Oct 2014 (SI 2014/2771)[2] |
| 16 |  | 20 Oct 2014 (SI 2014/2771) |
| 17 | (1) | 28 Jul 2014 (SI 2014/1820) |
|  | (2) | 20 Oct 2014 (SI 2014/2771)[2] |
|  | (3) | 28 Jul 2014 (SI 2014/1820)[1] |
| 18 |  | 6 Apr 2015 (SI 2015/371) |
| 19 |  | 28 Jul 2014 (SI 2014/1820) |
| 20–31 |  | 1 Dec 2014 (in respect of premises located in the areas of the relevant local authorities) (SI 2014/2771)[3] |
|  |  | 1 Feb 2016 (in respect of premises located in England) (SI 2016/11) |
|  |  | *Not yet in force* (otherwise) |
| 32–37 |  | 1 Dec 2014 (SI 2014/2771) |
| 38 |  | 20 Oct 2014 (SI 2014/2771) |
| 39 |  | 6 Apr 2015 (SI 2015/874) |
| 40 |  | 12 Dec 2014 (SI 2014/1943) |
| 41–43 |  | 14 Jul 2014 (SI 2014/1820) |
| 44, 45 |  | 28 Jul 2014 (SI 2014/1820)[1] |
| 46, 47 |  | 14 Jul 2014 (SI 2014/1820) |
| 48 |  | 1 Mar 2015 (SI 2015/371) |
| 49–51 |  | 20 Oct 2014 (for the purpose of making regulations) (SI 2014/2771) |
|  |  | 1 Mar 2015 (otherwise) (SI 2015/371) |
| 52 |  | See Sch 4 below |

**Immigration Act 2014 (c 22)**—*contd*

| | | |
|---|---|---|
| 53 | | 20 Oct 2014 (for the purpose of making regulations) (SI 2014/2771) |
| | | 1 Mar 2015 (otherwise) (SI 2015/371) |
| 54 | (1) | 20 Oct 2014 (for the purpose of making regulations) (SI 2014/2771) |
| | | 1 Mar 2015 (otherwise) (SI 2015/371) |
| | (2) | 20 Oct 2014 (for the purpose of making regulations) (SI 2014/2771) |
| | | *Not yet in force* (otherwise) |
| | (3) | See Sch 5 below |
| | (4)–(7) | 20 Oct 2014 (for the purpose of making regulations) (SI 2014/2771) |
| | (8) | 20 Oct 2014 (for the purpose of making regulations) (SI 2014/2771) |
| | | 1 Mar 2015 (otherwise) (SI 2015/371) |
| 55 | | 1 Mar 2015 (SI 2015/371) |
| 56 | | 14 Jul 2014 (s 75(2)) |
| 57 | | 2 Mar 2015 (SI 2015/371)[4] |
| 58 | | 1 Mar 2015 (SI 2015/371)[4] |
| 59 | | See Sch 6 below |
| 60, 61 | | 20 Oct 2014 (SI 2014/2771) |
| 62 | | 14 Jul 2014 (s 75(2)) |
| 63 | | See Sch 7 below |
| 64 | | 28 Jul 2014 (SI 2014/1820) |
| 65 | | 6 Apr 2015 (SI 2015/371) |
| 66 | | 28 Jul 2014 (SI 2014/1820) |
| 67 | | See Sch 8 below |
| 68, 69 | | 15 Dec 2014 (SI 2014/2771) |
| 70, 71 | | 28 Jul 2014 (SI 2014/1820) |
| 72 | | 14 May 2014 (s 75(1)) |
| 73 | (1) | 14 May 2014 (s 75(1)) |
| | (2) | 14 May 2014 (s 75(1))[1] |
| | (3)–(5) | 14 May 2014 (s 75(1)) |
| | (6) | See Sch 9 below |
| 74–77 | | 14 May 2014 (s 75(1)) |
| Schs 1, 2 | | 28 Jul 2014 (SI 2014/1820) |
| Sch 3 | | 1 Dec 2014 (in respect of premises located in the areas of the relevant local authorities) (SI 2014/2771)[3] |
| | | 1 Feb 2016 (in respect of premises located in England) (SI 2016/11) |
| | | *Not yet in force* (otherwise) |
| Sch 4 | para 1 | 20 Oct 2014 (for the purpose of making regulations) (SI 2014/2771) |
| | | 1 Mar 2015 (otherwise) (SI 2015/371) |
| | paras 2, 3 | 1 Mar 2015 (SI 2015/371) |
| | para 4 | 20 Oct 2014 (for the purpose of making regulations) (SI 2014/2771) |
| | | 1 Mar 2015 (otherwise) (SI 2015/371) |
| | paras 5, 6 | 1 Mar 2015 (SI 2015/371) |
| | paras 7, 8 | 20 Oct 2014 (for the purpose of making regulations) (SI 2014/2771) |
| | | 1 Mar 2015 (otherwise) (SI 2015/371) |
| | para 9 | 1 Mar 2015 (SI 2015/371) |
| | para 10 | 20 Oct 2014 (for the purpose of making regulations) (SI 2014/2771) |
| | | 1 Mar 2015 (otherwise) (SI 2015/371) |
| | paras 11–14 | 1 Mar 2015 (SI 2015/371) |
| | para 15 | 20 Oct 2014 (for the purpose of making regulations) (SI 2014/2771) |
| | | 1 Mar 2015 (otherwise) (SI 2015/371) |

**Immigration Act 2014 (c 22)**—*contd*

| | | |
|---|---|---|
| | para 16 | 1 Mar 2015 (SI 2015/371) |
| | paras 17, 18 | 20 Oct 2014 (for the purpose of making regulations) (SI 2014/2771) |
| | | 1 Mar 2015 (otherwise) (SI 2015/371) |
| | para 19 | 1 Mar 2015 (SI 2015/371) |
| | paras 20, 21 | 20 Oct 2014 (for the purpose of making regulations) (SI 2014/2771) |
| | | 1 Mar 2015 (otherwise) (SI 2015/371) |
| | para 22 | 1 Mar 2015 (SI 2015/371) |
| | paras 23, 24 | 20 Oct 2014 (for the purpose of making regulations) (SI 2014/2771) |
| | | 1 Mar 2015 (otherwise) (SI 2015/371) |
| | paras 25, 26 | 1 Mar 2015 (SI 2015/371) |
| | paras 27, 28 | 20 Oct 2014 (for the purpose of making regulations) (SI 2014/2771) |
| | | 1 Mar 2015 (otherwise) (SI 2015/371) |
| | para 29 | 1 Mar 2015 (SI 2015/371) |
| Sch 5 | | 20 Oct 2014 (SI 2014/2771) |
| Sch 6 | | 14 Jul 2014 (s 75(2)) |
| Sch 7 | para 1 | See paras 1–8 below |
| | para 2 | 17 Nov 2014 (SI 2014/2771) |
| | para 3 | 20 Oct 2014 (SI 2014/2771) |
| | paras 4, 5 | 17 Nov 2014 (SI 2014/2771) |
| | para 6 | 28 Jul 2014 (SI 2014/1820) |
| | paras 7, 8 | 17 Nov 2014 (SI 2014/2771) |
| Sch 8 | | 28 Jul 2014 (SI 2014/1820) |
| Sch 9 | para 1 | 20 Oct 2014 (SI 2014/2771)[2] |
| | para 2 | 28 Jul 2014 (SI 2014/1820) |
| | paras 3–7 | 20 Oct 2014 (SI 2014/2771)[2] |
| | para 8 | 28 Jul 2014 (SI 2014/1820) |
| | para 9 | 20 Oct 2014 (SI 2014/2771)[2] |
| | para 10(1) | 28 Jul 2014 (SI 2014/1820) |
| | para 10(2) | 20 Oct 2014 (SI 2014/2771)[2] |
| | para 10(3) | 28 Jul 2014 (SI 2014/1820) |
| | paras 11–16 | 28 Jul 2014 (SI 2014/1820) |
| | paras 17, 18 | 1 Jul 2021 (SI 2021/771) |
| | para 19 | 1 Mar 2015 (SI 2015/371) |
| | paras 20–25 | 20 Oct 2014 (SI 2014/2771)[2] |
| | para 26(1) | 20 Oct 2014 (SI 2014/2771)[2] |
| | para 26(2), (3) | *Not yet in force* |
| | para 26(4) | 20 Oct 2014 (SI 2014/2771)[2] |
| | para 26(5) | *Not yet in force* |
| | paras 27–29 | 20 Oct 2014 (SI 2014/2771)[2] |
| | para 30 | See paras 31–55 below |
| | para 31 | 20 Oct 2014 (SI 2014/2771)[2] |
| | para 32 | 28 Jul 2014 (SI 2014/1820) |
| | paras 33–60 | 20 Oct 2014 (SI 2014/2771)[2] |
| | para 61 | 28 Jul 2014 (SI 2014/1820) |
| | paras 62–65 | 14 Jul 2014 (SI 2014/1820) |
| | para 66 | 1 Mar 2015 (SI 2015/371) |
| | paras 67–69 | 17 Nov 2014 (SI 2014/2771) |
| | paras 70, 71 | 6 Apr 2015 (SI 2015/874) |
| | para 72 | 28 Jul 2014 (SI 2014/1820) |
| | paras 73–76 | 15 Dec 2014 (SI 2014/2771) |

[1]  For transitory and saving provisions, see SI 2014/1820, art 4

[2]  For transitional and saving provisions, see SI 2014/2771, arts 9–11

[3]  The relevant local authorities are—

**Immigration Act 2014 (c 22)**—*contd*

   (a)   Birmingham City Council;

   (b)   Dudley Metropolitan Borough Council;

   (c)   Sandwell Metropolitan Borough Council;

   (d)   Walsall Metropolitan Borough Council; and

   (e)   Wolverhampton City Council

[4]   For transitional and savings provisions, see SI 2015/371, arts 5, 6

---

**Inheritance and Trustees' Powers Act 2014 (c 16)**

*RA:* 14 May 2014

*Commencement provisions:* s 12(2), (3); Inheritance and Trustees' Powers Act 2014 (Commencement) Order 2014, SI 2014/2039

| | | |
|---|---|---|
| 1–11 | | 1 Oct 2014 (SI 2014/2039) |
| 12 | | 14 May 2014 (s 12(2)) |
| Schs 1–4 | | 1 Oct 2014 (SI 2014/2039) |

---

**Intellectual Property Act 2014 (c 18)**

*RA:* 14 May 2014

*Commencement provisions:* s 24(1), (2); Intellectual Property Act 2014 (Commencement No 1) Order 2014, SI 2014/1715; Intellectual Property Act 2014 (Commencement No 2) Order 2014, SI 2014/2069; Intellectual Property Act 2014 (Commencement No 3 and Transitional Provisions) Order 2014, SI 2014/2330; Intellectual Property Act 2014 (Commencement No 4) Order 2015; SI 2015/165; Intellectual Property Act 2014 (Commencement No 5 and Saving Provisions) Order 2016, SI 2016/1139

| | | |
|---|---|---|
| 1–5 | | 1 Oct 2014 (SI 2014/2330) |
| 6 | (1) | 1 Oct 2014 (SI 2014/2330)[1] |
| | (2) | 1 Oct 2014 (SI 2014/2330) |
| 7, 8 | | 1 Oct 2014 (SI 2014/2330) |
| 9 | (1) | 1 Oct 2014 (SI 2014/2330) |
| | (2)–(6) | *Not yet in force* |
| 10 | (1) | 1 Oct 2014 (SI 2014/2330) |
| | (2) | 15 Jul 2014 (for the purposes of appointing the appointed person under the Registered Designs Act 1949, ss 27A(1)(a), 27B) (SI 2014/1715) |
| | | 6 Apr 2015 (otherwise) (SI 2015/165) |
| | (3)–(11) | 6 Apr 2015 (SI 2015/165) |
| 11–14 | | 1 Oct 2014 (SI 2014/2330) |
| 15 | | 1 Oct 2014 (SI 2014/2330)[1] |
| 16 | (1)–(3) | 1 Oct 2014 (SI 2014/2330) |
| | (4) | 1 Oct 2014 (SI 2014/2330)[1] |
| 17 | | 1 Oct 2014 (SI 2014/2330) |
| 18 | | 1 Oct 2014 (SI 2014/2330)[1] |
| 19 | | See Schedule below |
| 20, 21 | | 1 Oct 2014 (SI 2014/2330) |
| 22 | | 1 Dec 2016 (for the purpose of making Orders in Council) (SI 2016/1139)[2] |
| | | 6 Apr 2017 (otherwise) (SI 2016/1139)[2] |
| 23 | | 1 Aug 2014 (SI 2014/2069) |
| 24 | | 14 May 2014 (s 24(1)) |
| Schedule | paras 1–5 | 1 Oct 2014 (SI 2014/2330) |
| | para 6 | 1 Oct 2014 (SI 2014/2330)[1] |

[1]   For transitional provisions, see SI 2014/2330, arts 4–8

**Intellectual Property Act 2014 (c 18)**—*contd*
2   For savings, see SI 2016/1139, art 4

---

**International Development (Gender Equality) Act 2014 (c 9)**

*RA:* 13 Mar 2014

*Commencement provisions:* s 3(2)

Whole Act in force 13 May 2014 (s 3(2))

---

**Landfill Tax (Scotland) Act 2014 (asp 2)**

*RA:* 21 Jan 2014

*Commencement provisions:* s 43; Landfill Tax (Scotland) Act 2014 (Commencement No 1) Order 2014, SSI 2014/277; Landfill Tax (Scotland) Act 2014 (Commencement No 2) Order 2015, SSI 2015/17; Landfill Tax (Scotland) Act 2014 (Commencement No 3 and Transitional Provisions) Order 2015, SSI 2015/109

| | |
|---|---|
| 1 | 1 Apr 2015 (SSI 2015/109) |
| 5, 6 | 7 Nov 2014 (for the purpose of making orders) (SSI 2014/277) |
| | 1 Apr 2015 (otherwise) (SSI 2015/109) |
| 7–10 | 1 Apr 2015 (SSI 2015/109) |
| 11 | 7 Nov 2014 (SSI 2014/277) |
| 12 | 1 Apr 2015 (SSI 2015/109) |
| 13 | 7 Nov 2014 (for the purpose of making orders and setting criteria under sub-s (7)(a)) (SSI 2014/277) |
| | 1 Apr 2015 (otherwise) (SSI 2015/109) |
| 14 | 7 Nov 2014 (for the purpose of making orders) (SSI 2014/277) |
| | 1 Apr 2015 (otherwise) (SSI 2015/109) |
| 15 | 7 Nov 2014 (for the purpose of making regulations) (SSI 2014/277) |
| | 1 Apr 2015 (otherwise) (SSI 2015/109) |
| 16 | 1 Apr 2015 (SSI 2015/109) |
| 17 | 7 Nov 2014 (for the purpose of making regulations) (SSI 2014/277) |
| | 1 Apr 2015 (otherwise) (SSI 2015/109) |
| 18–20 | 7 Nov 2014 (SSI 2014/277) |
| 21 | 1 Apr 2015 (SSI 2015/109) |
| 22, 23 | 7 Nov 2014 (SSI 2014/277) |
| 24 | 1 Apr 2015 (SSI 2015/109) |
| 25 | 7 Nov 2014 (SSI 2014/277) |
| 26–29 | 1 Apr 2015 (SSI 2015/109) |
| 30 | 7 Nov 2014 (SSI 2014/277) |
| 31–33 | 1 Apr 2015 (SSI 2015/109) |
| 34, 35 | 21 Jan 2014 (s 43(1)) |
| 36 | 1 Apr 2015 (SSI 2015/109) |
| 37 | 7 Nov 2014 (for the purpose of making regulations) (SSI 2014/277) |
| | 16 Feb 2015 (otherwise) (SSI 2015/17) |
| 38 | 16 Feb 2015 (SSI 2015/17) |
| 39 | 1 Apr 2015 (SSI 2015/109) |
| 40–44 | 21 Jan 2014 (s 43(1)) |

---

**Leasehold Reform (Amendment) Act 2014 (c 10)**

*RA:* 13 Mar 2014

*Commencement provisions:* s 2(2)

**Leasehold Reform (Amendment) Act 2014 (c 10)**—*contd*
Whole Act in force 13 May 2014 (s 2(2))

---

## Local Audit and Accountability Act 2014 (c 2)

*RA:* 30 Jan 2014

*Commencement provisions:* s 49; Local Audit and Accountability Act 2014 (Commencement No 1) Order 2014, SI 2014/900; Local Audit and Accountability Act 2014 (Commencement No 2) Order 2014, SI 2014/940; Local Audit and Accountability Act 2014 (Commencement No 3) Order 2014, SI 2014/1596; Local Audit and Accountability Act 2014 (Commencement No 4) Order 2014, SI 2014/3319; Local Audit and Accountability Act 2014 (Commencement No 5) Order 2015, SI 2015/179; Local Audit and Accountability Act 2014 (Commencement No 6) Order 2015, SI 2015/223; Local Audit and Accountability Act 2014 (Commencement No 7, Transitional Provisions and Savings) Order 2015, SI 2015/841, as amended by SI 2016/675, SI 2018/1369, SI 2020/1565

| | | |
|---|---|---|
| 1 | (1), (2) | 1 Apr 2015 (SI 2015/841)[2] |
| | (3) | See Sch 1 below |
| | (4), (5) | 1 Apr 2015 (SI 2015/841)[2] |
| 2 | (1), (2) | See Sch 2 below |
| | (3)–(6) | 16 Dec 2014 (for the purpose of enabling the Secretary of State to make regulations or an order) (SI 2014/3319) |
| | | 1 Apr 2015 (otherwise) (SI 2015/841)[2] |
| 3 | (1)–(4) | 1 Apr 2015 (SI 2015/841)[2] |
| | (5)–(7) | 4 Apr 2014 (for the purpose of enabling the Secretary of State to make regulations) (SI 2014/900) |
| | | 1 Apr 2015 (otherwise) (SI 2015/841)[2] |
| | (8), (9) | 1 Apr 2015 (SI 2015/841)[2] |
| 4 | (1)(a) | 1 Apr 2015 (SI 2015/841)[2] |
| | (1)(b) | 16 Dec 2014 (for the purpose of the definition of "local auditor" so far as relating to s 18 and Sch 5 and the audit of accounts for financial years commencing on or after 1 Apr 2017) (SI 2014/3319) |
| | | 1 Apr 2015 (otherwise) (SI 2015/841)[2] |
| | (2)–(5) | 1 Apr 2015 (SI 2015/841)[2] |
| 5 | | 4 Apr 2014 (for the purpose of enabling the Secretary of State to make regulations) (SI 2014/900) |
| | | 18 Jun 2014 (in so far as relate to the amendments made by s 38) (SI 2014/1596) |
| | | 16 Dec 2014 (otherwise) (SI 2014/3319) |
| 6 | | 4 Apr 2014 (for the purpose of enabling the Secretary of State to make regulations) (SI 2014/900) |
| | | 18 Jun 2014 (in so far as relate to the amendments made by s 38) (SI 2014/1596) |
| | | 1 Apr 2015 (otherwise) (SI 2015/841)[2] |
| 7 | (1)–(7) | 1 Apr 2015 (SI 2015/841)[2] |
| | (8) | See Sch 3 below |
| 8 | | 1 Apr 2015 (SI 2015/841)[2] |
| 9 | (1), (2) | 1 Apr 2015 (SI 2015/841)[2] |
| | (3) | See Sch 4 below |
| 10 | | 4 Apr 2014 (for the purpose of enabling the Secretary of State to make regulations) (SI 2014/900) |
| | | 1 Apr 2015 (otherwise) (SI 2015/841)[2] |
| 11–13 | | 1 Apr 2015 (SI 2015/841)[2] |
| 14 | | 4 Apr 2014 (for the purpose of enabling the Secretary of State to make regulations) (SI 2014/900) |
| | | 1 Apr 2015 (otherwise) (SI 2015/841)[2] |
| 15 | | 1 Apr 2015 (SI 2015/841)[2] |
| 16 | | 4 Apr 2014 (for the purpose of enabling the Secretary of State to make regulations) (SI 2014/900) |

**Local Audit and Accountability Act 2014 (c 2)**—*contd*

|  |  |  |
|---|---|---|
|  |  | 1 Apr 2015 (otherwise) (SI 2015/841)[2] |
| 17 |  | 4 Apr 2014 (for the purpose of enabling the Secretary of State to make regulations) (SI 2014/900) |
|  |  | 16 Dec 2014 (otherwise) (SI 2014/3319) |
| 18 | (1) | See Sch 5 below |
|  | (2) | 4 Apr 2014 (for the purpose of enabling the Secretary of State to make regulations) (SI 2014/900) |
|  |  | 16 Dec 2014 (otherwise) (SI 2014/3319) |
| 19 |  | See Sch 6 below |
| 20–23 |  | 1 Apr 2015 (SI 2015/841)[2] |
| 24 |  | See Sch 7 below |
| 25–28 |  | 1 Apr 2015 (SI 2015/841)[2] |
| 29 |  | See Sch 8 below |
| 30, 31 |  | 1 Apr 2015 (SI 2015/841)[2] |
| 32 |  | 4 Apr 2014 (for the purpose of enabling the Secretary of State to make regulations) (SI 2014/900) |
|  |  | 1 Apr 2015 (otherwise) (SI 2015/841)[2] |
| 33 |  | See Sch 9 below |
| 34 |  | See Sch 10 below |
| 35 |  | 4 Apr 2014 (SI 2014/900) |
| 36 |  | See Sch 11 below |
| 37 |  | 1 Apr 2015 (SI 2015/841)[2] |
| 38 |  | 4 Apr 2014 (for the purpose of enabling the Secretary of State to make regulations under Local Government, Planning and Land Act 1980, s 3 in relation to authorities within s 2(1A) thereof) (SI 2014/900) |
|  |  | 18 Jun 2014 (otherwise) (SI 2014/1596) |
| 39, 40 |  | 30 Mar 2014 (s 49(2)) |
| 41 |  | 30 Jan 2014 (s 49(3)) |
| 42 |  | 4 Apr 2014 (for the purpose of enabling the Secretary of State to exercise the power to make regulations under Local Government Act 1972, Sch 12, para 18(8)) (SI 2014/900) |
|  |  | *Not yet in force* (otherwise) |
| 43 |  | 30 Jan 2014 (s 49(4)(a)) |
| 44 |  | 30 Jan 2014 (s 49(4)(b)) |
| 45 |  | See Sch 12 below |
| 46 |  | 30 Jan 2014 (s 49(4)(c)) |
| 47 |  | See Sch 13 below |
| 48 |  | 30 Jan 2014 (s 49(4)(d)) |
| 49 |  | 30 Jan 2014 (s 49(4)(e)) |
| 50 |  | 30 Jan 2014 (s 49(4)(f)) |
| Sch 1 |  | 1 Apr 2015 (SI 2015/841)[2] |
| Sch 2 |  | 4 Apr 2014 (in so far as relates to ss 3(5)–(7), 5, 6, 7(8), 9(3), 10, 14, 16–18, 24, 32, 34–36, 38, 42, 45, Sch 3, para 4, Sch 4, paras 2(9), 3–5, 8(3), Sch 5, Sch 7, para 5, Schs 10, 11, Sch 12, paras 2(1), (5), 31(1), (5), 44(1), (4), 46(1), (5), 69(1), (3), (4), 88(1), (3)) (SI 2014/900) |
|  |  | 16 Dec 2014 (in so far as relates to ss 2, 4(1)(b), 17, 18, Sch 5, Sch 6, para 9, Sch 13, paras 1–5, 11) (SI 2014/3319) |
|  |  | 1 Apr 2015 (otherwise) (SI 2015/841)[2] |
| Sch 3 | paras 1–3 | 1 Apr 2015 (SI 2015/841)[2] |
|  | para 4 | 4 Apr 2014 (for the purpose of enabling the Secretary of State to make regulations) (SI 2014/900) |
|  |  | 1 Apr 2015 (otherwise) (SI 2015/841)[2] |
| Sch 4 | paras 1, 2(1)–(8) | 1 Apr 2015 (SI 2015/841)[2] |
|  | paras 2(9), 3–5 | 4 Apr 2014 (for the purpose of enabling the Secretary of State to make regulations) (SI 2014/900) |
|  |  | 1 Apr 2015 (otherwise) (SI 2015/841)[2] |
|  | paras 6, 7, 8(1), (2) | 1 Apr 2015 (SI 2015/841)[2] |

**Local Audit and Accountability Act 2014 (c 2)**—*contd*

| | | |
|---|---|---|
| | para 8(3) | 4 Apr 2014 (for the purpose of enabling the Secretary of State to make regulations) (SI 2014/900) |
| | | 1 Apr 2015 (otherwise) (SI 2015/841)[2] |
| | para 8(4) | 1 Apr 2015 (SI 2015/841)[2] |
| Sch 5 | | 4 Apr 2014 (for the purpose of enabling the Secretary of State to exercise any power to make regulations or orders under Companies Act 2006, ss 1214, 1219, 1239, 1252, 1253, Sch 10, para 13) (SI 2014/900) |
| | | 16 Dec 2014 (otherwise) (SI 2014/3319) |
| Sch 6 | paras 1–8 | 9 Apr 2014 (in so far as enables a code of audit practice to come into force on or after 1 Apr 2015) (SI 2014/940) |
| | | 1 Apr 2015 (otherwise) (SI 2015/841)[2] |
| | para 9 | 16 Dec 2014 (for the purpose of enabling the Comptroller and Auditor General to issue guidance) (SI 2014/3319) |
| | | 1 Apr 2015 (otherwise) (SI 2015/841)[2] |
| | para 10, 11 | 9 Apr 2014 (in so far as enables a code of audit practice to come into force on or after 1 Apr 2015) (SI 2014/940) |
| | | 1 Apr 2015 (otherwise) (SI 2015/841)[2] |
| Sch 7 | paras 1–4 | 1 Apr 2015 (SI 2015/841)[2] |
| | para 5 | 4 Apr 2014 (for the purpose of enabling the Secretary of State to make regulations) (SI 2014/900) |
| | | 1 Apr 2015 (otherwise) (SI 2015/841)[2] |
| | paras 6–10 | 1 Apr 2015 (SI 2015/841)[2] |
| Schs 8, 9 | | 1 Apr 2015 (SI 2015/841)[2] |
| Sch 10 | | 4 Apr 2014 (SI 2014/900) |
| Sch 11 | | 4 Apr 2014 (in so far as applies to information relating to a particular body or person that is obtained by an inspector or an assistant inspector, or a person acting on behalf of an inspector or an assistant inspector, under Local Government Act 1999, Pt 1, or in the course of an inspection thereunder) (SI 2014/900) |
| | | 1 Apr 2015 (otherwise) (SI 2015/841)[2] |
| Sch 12 | para 1 | 1 Apr 2015 (SI 2015/841)[2] |
| | para 2(1) | See sub-paras (2)–(5) below |
| | para 2(2)–(4) | 1 Apr 2015 (SI 2015/841)[2] |
| | para 2(5) | 4 Apr 2014 (SI 2014/900) |
| | paras 3–30 | 1 Apr 2015 (SI 2015/841)[2] |
| | para 31(1) | See sub-paras (2)–(5) below |
| | para 31(2)–(4) | 1 Apr 2015 (SI 2015/841)[2] |
| | para 31(5) | 4 Apr 2014 (SI 2014/900) |
| | paras 32–36 | 1 Apr 2015 (SI 2015/841)[2] |
| | para 37 | 12 Feb 2015 (for the purpose of the Secretary of State making regulations under the Greater London Authority Act 1999, s 32) SI 2015/223 |
| | | 1 Apr 2015 (otherwise) (SI 2015/841)[2] |
| | paras 38–42 | 1 Apr 2015 (SI 2015/841)[2] |
| | para 43(1) | 12 Feb 2015 (for the purpose of the Secretary of State making regulations under s 32) SI 2015/223 |
| | | 1 Apr 2015 (otherwise) (SI 2015/841)[2] |
| | para 43(2), (3) | 1 Apr 2015 (SI 2015/841)[2] |
| | para 43(4) | 12 Feb 2015 (for the purpose of the Secretary of State making regulations under the Greater London Authority Act 1999, s 32) SI 2015/223 |
| | | 1 Apr 2015 (otherwise) (SI 2015/841)[2] |
| | para 44(1) | See sub-paras (2)–(4) below |
| | para 44(2), (3) | 1 Apr 2015 (SI 2015/841)[2] |
| | para 44(4) | 4 Apr 2014 (SI 2014/900) |
| | para 45 | 1 Apr 2018 (SI 2015/841)[2] |
| | para 46(1) | See sub-paras (2)–(5) below |
| | para 46(2)–(4) | 1 Apr 2015 (SI 2015/841)[2] |

**Local Audit and Accountability Act 2014 (c 2)**—*contd*

|  |  |  |
|---|---|---|
| | para 46(5) | 4 Apr 2014 (SI 2014/900) |
| | paras 47, 48 | 1 Apr 2015 (SI 2015/841)[2] |
| | para 49 | See paras 50–54 below |
| | para 50(1) | 10 Feb 2015 (for the purpose of the Secretary of State making regulations under the Local Government Act 2003, s 21) (SI 2015/179)[1] |
| | | 1 Apr 2015 (otherwise) (SI 2015/841)[2] |
| | para 50(2) | 1 Apr 2015 (SI 2015/841)[2] |
| | para 50(3) | 10 Feb 2015 (for the purpose of the Secretary of State making regulations under the Local Government Act 2003, s 21) (SI 2015/179)[1] |
| | | 1 Apr 2015 (otherwise) (SI 2015/841)[2] |
| | paras 51, 52 | 10 Feb 2015 (for the purpose of the Secretary of State making regulations under the Local Government Act 2003, s 21) (SI 2015/179)[1] |
| | | 1 Apr 2015 (otherwise) (SI 2015/841)[2] |
| | paras 53–68 | 1 Apr 2015 (SI 2015/841)[2] |
| | para 69(1) | See sub-paras (2)–(4) below |
| | para 69(2) | 1 Apr 2015 (SI 2015/841)[2] |
| | para 69(3), (4) | 4 Apr 2014 (SI 2014/900) |
| | paras 70–87 | 1 Apr 2015 (SI 2015/841)[2] |
| | para 88(1) | See sub-paras (2), (3) below |
| | para 88(2) | 1 Apr 2015 (SI 2015/841)[2] |
| | para 88(3) | 4 Apr 2014 (SI 2014/900) |
| | paras 89–117 | 1 Apr 2015 (SI 2015/841)[2] |
| | paras 118–122 | 1 Apr 2017 (SI 2015/841)[2] |
| | para 123 | 1 Apr 2015 (SI 2015/841)[2] |
| Sch 13 | paras 1–5 | 16 Dec 2014 (SI 2014/3319) |
| | paras 6–10 | 1 Apr 2015 (SI 2015/841)[2] |
| | para 11 | 16 Dec 2014 (SI 2014/3319) |
| | paras 12, 13 | 1 Apr 2015 (SI 2015/841)[2] |

[1]  For transitory provisions, see SI 2015/179, art 3

[2]  For transitional provisions and savings, see SI 2015/841, arts 5–8

---

**Marriage and Civil Partnership (Scotland) Act 2014 (asp 5)**

*RA:* 12 Mar 2014

*Commencement provisions:* s 36; Marriage and Civil Partnership (Scotland) Act 2014 (Commencement No 1) Order 2014, SSI 2014/121; Marriage and Civil Partnership (Scotland) Act 2014 (Commencement No 2 and Saving Provisions) Order 2014, SSI 2014/212, as amended by SSI 2014/218; Marriage and Civil Partnership (Scotland) Act 2014 (Commencement No 3, Saving, Transitional Provision and Revocation) Order 2014, SSI 2014/287; Marriage and Civil Partnership (Scotland) Act 2014 (Commencement No 4 and Savings Provisions) Order 2015, SSI 2015/14

|  |  |  |
|---|---|---|
| 1–3 | | 16 Dec 2014 (SSI 2014/287) |
| 4 | (1)–(7) | 16 Dec 2014 (SSI 2014/287) |
| | (8)–(10) | 1 Sep 2014 (SSI 2014/212) |
| | (11)–(15) | 16 Dec 2014 (SSI 2014/287) |
| 5 | | 16 Dec 2014 (SSI 2014/287) |
| 6 | | See Sch 1 below |
| 7 | | 21 May 2014 (SSI 2014/121) |
| 8 | | 16 Dec 2014 (SSI 2014/287) |
| 9, 10 | | 1 Sep 2014 (SSI 2014/1212) |
| 11 | (1)–(4) | 16 Dec 2014 (SSI 2014/287) |
| | (5), (6) | 1 Sep 2014 (SSI 2014/212) |
| | (7)–(9) | 16 Dec 2014 (SSI 2014/287) |
| 12 | (1) | See sub-ss (2)–(4) below |

**Marriage and Civil Partnership (Scotland) Act 2014 (asp 5)**—*contd*

|  |  |  |
|---|---|---|
| | (2)(a) | 1 Sep 2014 (for the purpose of making regulations under Marriage (Scotland) Act 1977, s 8(1)(a)(ii)) (SSI 2014/212)[1] |
| | | 16 Dec 2014 (otherwise) (SSI 2014/287)[2] |
| | (2)(b) | 1 Sep 2014 (for the purpose of making regulations under Marriage (Scotland) Act 1977, s 8(1B)(a)(i), (1E)) (SSI 2014/212)[1] |
| | | 16 Dec 2014 (for the purpose of inserting Marriage (Scotland) Act 1977, s 8(1A)(a), (1B), (1C)(a) for remaining purposes) (SSI 2014/287)[2] |
| | | *Not yet in force* (otherwise) |
| | (2)(c) | 16 Dec 2014 (SSI 2014/287)[2] |
| | (3), (4) | 16 Dec 2014 (SSI 2014/287)[2] |
| 13 | (1) | See sub-ss (2)–(5) below |
| | (2)(a)–(c) | 16 Dec 2014 (SSI 2014/287)[2] |
| | (2)(d) | *Not yet in force* |
| | (2)(e) | 1 Sep 2014 (for the purpose of making regulations under Marriage (Scotland) Act 1977, s 9(2A)) (SSI 2014/212) |
| | | *Not yet in force* (otherwise) |
| | (2)(f)–(l) | 16 Dec 2014 (SSI 2014/287)[2] |
| | (3)–(5) | 16 Dec 2014 (SSI 2014/287)[2] |
| 14 | (1) | See sub-ss (2), (3) below |
| | (2)(a) | 16 Dec 2014 (SSI 2014/287)[2] |
| | (2)(b) | 1 Sep 2014 (for the purpose of making regulations under Marriage (Scotland) Act 1977, s 12(1D)) (SSI 2014/212) |
| | | 16 Dec 2014 (for the purpose of inserting the Marriage (Scotland) Act 1977, s 12(1B), (1C)) (SSI 2014/287)[2] |
| | | *Not yet in force* (otherwise) |
| | (3) | 16 Dec 2014 (SSI 2014/287)[2] |
| 15, 16 | | 16 Dec 2014 (SSI 2014/287) |
| 17 | | 1 Sep 2014 (SSI 2014/212) |
| 18 | (1) | 1 Mar 2015 (SS1 2015/14) |
| | (2)(a) | 1 Sep 2014 (SSI 2014/212) |
| | (2)(b) | 1 Mar 2015 (SS1 2015/14)[3] |
| | (3), (4) | 1 Mar 2015 (SS1 2015/14) |
| 19, 20 | | 21 May 2014 (SSI 2014/121) |
| 21 | | 1 Sep 2014 (SSI 2014/212) |
| 22, 23 | | 21 May 2014 (SSI 2014/121) |
| 24 | (1) | See sub-ss (2)–(22) below |
| | (2)–(7)(a) | 16 Dec 2014 (SSI 2014/287) |
| | (7)(b) | 1 Mar 2015 (SS1 2015/14)[3] |
| | (7)(c)–(8)(b)(i) | 16 Dec 2014 (SSI 2014/287) |
| | (8)(b)(ii) | 1 Mar 2015 (SS1 2015/14)[3] |
| | (8)(b)(iii)–(12)(a) | 16 Dec 2014 (SSI 2014/287) |
| | (12)(b)(i) | 1 Mar 2015 (SS1 2015/14)[3] |
| | (12)(b)(ii), (c) | 16 Dec 2014 (SSI 2014/287) |
| | (13) | 1 Sep 2014 (for the purpose of making regulations under Civil Partnership Act 2004, ss 94A(1)(a)(i), (5), 94B(3), 94E(4)) (SSI 2014/212) |
| | | 16 Dec 2014 (otherwise) (SSI 2014/287) |
| | (14) | 16 Dec 2014 (SSI 2014/287) |
| | (15) | 1 Sep 2014 (for the purpose of prescribing forms of notice referred to in Civil Partnership Act 2004, s 95ZA(1), (2)) (SSI 2014/212) |
| | | 16 Dec 2014 (otherwise) (SSI 2014/287) |
| | (16), (17) | 16 Dec 2014 (SSI 2014/287) |
| | (18)(a) | 1 Mar 2015 (SS1 2015/14)[3] |
| | (18)(b)–(22) | 16 Dec 2014 (SSI 2014/287) |
| 25 | | 1 Sep 2014 (SSI 2014/212) |
| 26 | | 16 Dec 2014 (SSI 2014/287)[2] |
| 27 | | 21 May 2014 (SSI 2014/121) |
| 28 | | 1 Sep 2014 (SSI 2014/212)[1] |

**Marriage and Civil Partnership (Scotland) Act 2014 (asp 5)**—*contd*

| | | |
|---|---|---|
| 29 | | See Sch 2 below |
| 30 | | 1 Sep 2014 (SSI 2014/212) |
| 31 | | 16 Dec 2014 (SSI 2014/287) |
| 32 | | 21 May 2014 (SSI 2014/121) |
| 33 | | 1 Sep 2014 (SSI 2014/212) |
| 34–37 | | 13 Mar 2014 (s 36(1)) |
| Sch 1 | para 1(1) | See sub-paras (2)–(4) below |
| | para 1(2), (3) | 16 Dec 2014 (SSI 2014/287) |
| | para 1(4) | 1 Sep 2014 (for the purpose of making regulations under Domicile and Matrimonial Proceedings Act 1973, Sch 1B, para 2) (SSI 2014/212) |
| | | 16 Dec 2014 (otherwise) (SSI 2014/287) |
| | para 2 | 16 Dec 2014 (SSI 2014/287) |
| Sch 2 | para 1 | See paras 2–19 below |
| | paras 2–6 | 16 Dec 2014 (SSI 2014/287) |
| | para 7 | 1 Sep 2014 (for the purpose of making an order under Gender Recognition Act 2004, s 5D) (SSI 2014/212) |
| | | 16 Dec 2014 (otherwise) (SSI 2014/287) |
| | para 8 | 16 Dec 2014 (SSI 2014/287) |
| | para 9(1), (2)(a) | 16 Dec 2014 (SSI 2014/287) |
| | para 9(2)(b) | 1 Sep 2014 (for the purpose of making regulations under Gender Recognition Act 2004, Sch 3, para 20A(1)) (SSI 2014/212) |
| | | 16 Dec 2014 (otherwise) (SSI 2014/287) |
| | paras 10–14 | 16 Dec 2014 (SSI 2014/287) |
| | para 15 | 1 Sep 2014 (for the purpose of making an order under Gender Recognition Act 2004, s 3C(5)(b)(ii)) (SSI 2014/212) |
| | | 16 Dec 2014 (otherwise) (SSI 2014/287) |
| | para 16 | 16 Dec 2014 (otherwise) (SSI 2014/287) |
| | para 17 | 1 Sep 2014 (for the purpose of making an order under Gender Recognition Act 2004, s 3D(6)(b)) (SSI 2014/212) |
| | | 16 Dec 2014 (otherwise) (SSI 2014/287) |
| | paras 18, 19 | 16 Dec 2014 (otherwise) (SSI 2014/287) |

[1]   For savings, see SSI 2014/212, art 3

[2]   For transitional and saving provisions, see SSI 2014/287, arts 3, 4

[3]   For savings, see SSI 2015/14, art 3

---

**Mesothelioma Act 2014 (c 1)**

*RA*: 30 Jan 2014

*Commencement provisions*: s 19; Mesothelioma Act 2014 (Commencement No 1) Order 2014, SI 2014/459

| | |
|---|---|
| 1–6 | 31 Mar 2014 (SI 2014/459) |
| 7 | 4 Mar 2014 (SI 2014/459) |
| 8–10 | 31 Mar 2014 (SI 2014/459) |
| 11 | See Sch 1 below |
| 12 | See Sch 2 below |
| 13 | 1 Sep 2014 (SI 2014/459) |
| 14 | 31 Mar 2014 (SI 2014/459) |
| 15, 16 | *Not yet in force* |
| 17, 18 | 31 Mar 2014 (SI 2014/459) |
| 19–21 | 30 Jan 2014 (s 19(2)) |
| Schs 1, 2 | 31 Mar 2014 (SI 2014/459) |

---

**National Health Service Finance (Wales) Act 2014 (anaw 2)**

*RA*: 27 Jun 2014

*Commencement provisions*: s 3(2)

**National Health Service Finance (Wales) Act 2014 (anaw 2)**—*contd*
Whole Act in force 1 Apr 2014 (s 3(2))

**National Insurance Contributions Act 2014 (c 7)**

*RA:* 13 Mar 2014

*Commencement provisions:* ss 8, 9(11), (12), 13(7), 15(4), 18(7)

| | | |
|---|---|---|
| 1–7 | | 6 Apr 2014 (s 8) |
| 8 | | 13 Mar 2014 (RA) |
| 9 | (1) | See sub-ss (2)–(5) below |
| | (2) | 6 Apr 2015 (s 9(12)) |
| | (3) | 13 May 2014 (in so far as confers on the Treasury power to make regulations) (s 9(11)(a)) |
| | | 6 Apr 2015 (otherwise) (s 9(12)) |
| | (4) | 6 Apr 2015 (s 9(12)) |
| | (5) | 13 May 2014 (s 9(11)(b)) |
| | (6) | See sub-ss (7)–(10) below |
| | (7) | 6 Apr 2015 (s 9(12)) |
| | (8) | 13 May 2014 (in so far as confers on the Treasury power to make regulations) (s 9(11)(a)) |
| | | 6 Apr 2015 (otherwise) (s 9(12)) |
| | (9) | 6 Apr 2015 (s 9(12)) |
| | (10) | 13 May 2014 (s 9(11)(b)) |
| | (11), (12) | 13 Mar 2014 (RA) |
| 10–12 | | 13 Mar 2014 (RA) |
| 13 | | 13 May 2014 (s 13(7)) |
| 14 | | 13 Mar 2014 (RA) |
| 15 | | 13 May 2014 (s 15(4)) |
| 16, 17 | | 13 Mar 2014 (RA) |
| 18 | | 13 May 2014 (s 18(7)) |
| 19–21 | | 13 Mar 2014 (RA) |
| Sch 1 | | 6 Apr 2014 (s 8) |
| Sch 2 | | 13 May 2014 (s 15(4)) |

**Northern Ireland (Miscellaneous Provisions) Act 2014 (c 13)**

*RA:* 13 Mar 2014

*Commencement provisions:* s 28; Northern Ireland (Miscellaneous Provisions) Act 2014 (Commencement No 1) Order 2014, SI 2014/2613

| | | |
|---|---|---|
| 1 | (1), (2) | 13 Mar 2014 (s 28(1)(a)(i)) |
| | (3) | 13 Mar 2014 (for the purpose of prescribing requirements) (s 28(1)(a)(ii)) |
| | | *Not yet in force* (otherwise) |
| 2 | (1) | 13 Mar 2014 (s 28(1)(b)(i)) |
| | (2) | 13 Mar 2014 (for the purpose of prescribing requirements) (s 28(1)(b)(ii)) |
| | | *Not yet in force* (otherwise) |
| | (3) | 13 Mar 2014 (s 28(1)(b)(iii)) |
| 3–5 | | 30 Mar 2016 (s 28(6)) |
| 6 | | 13 May 2014 (s 28(4)) |
| 7 | | 13 Mar 2014 (s 28(1)(c)) |
| 8, 9 | | 27 Sep 2014 (SI 2014/2613) |
| 10–13 | | 13 May 2014 (s 28(4)) |
| 14–16 | | 1 Oct 2014 (SI 2014/2613) |
| 17 | | 13 May 2014 (s 28(4)) |
| 18 | (1), (2) | 13 May 2014 (s 28(4)) |

**Northern Ireland (Miscellaneous Provisions) Act 2014 (c 13)**—*contd*

|          | (3)                        | 10 Jun 2014 (E) (W) (in force immediately after Electoral Registration and Administration Act 2013, Sch 4, para 6 comes into force) (s 28(5)) |
|          |                            | 19 Sep 2014 (S) (in force immediately after Electoral Registration and Administration Act 2013, Sch 4, para 6 comes into force) (s 28(5)) |
|          | (4)                        | 13 May 2014 (s 28(4)) |
| 19       |                            | 13 Mar 2014 (s 28(1)(d)) |
| 20       | (1), (2)(a), (b)           | 13 Mar 2014 (s 28(1)(e)) |
|          | (2)(c)(i)                  | In force immediately after the Electoral Registration and Administration Act 2013, Sch 4, para 10 comes fully into force (s 28(2)) |
|          | (2)(c)(ii), (d), (e), (3)–(7) | 13 Mar 2014 (s 28(1)(e)) |
| 21       |                            | 13 May 2014 (s 28(4)) |
| 22       |                            | 13 Mar 2014 (s 28(1)(f)) |
| 23       |                            | 13 Mar 2014 (s 28(1)(g)) |
| 24       |                            | In force immediately after Protection of Freedoms Act 2012, Sch 1, para 8(1) comes into force (s 28(3)) |
| 25       |                            | 13 May 2014 (s 28(4)) |
| 26–29    |                            | 13 Mar 2014 (s 28(1)(i)) |
| Schedule |                            | 13 May 2014 (s 28(4)) |

**Offender Rehabilitation Act 2014 (c 11)**

*RA:* 13 Mar 2014

*Commencement provisions:* s 22; Offender Rehabilitation Act 2014 (Commencement No 1) Order 2014, SI 2014/1287; Offender Rehabilitation Act 2014 (Commencement No 2) Order 2015, SI 2015/40

| 1     |            | 1 Feb 2015 (SI 2015/40) |
| 2     | (1)–(3)    | 1 Feb 2015 (SI 2015/40) |
|       | (4)        | See Sch 1 below |
| 3     | (1)        | 1 Feb 2015 (SI 2015/40) |
|       | (2)        | See Sch 2 below |
| 4–6   |            | 1 Feb 2015 (SI 2015/40) |
| 7     | (1)        | See Sch 3 below |
|       | (2)        | 1 Feb 2015 (SI 2015/40) |
| 8, 9  |            | 1 Feb 2015 (SI 2015/40) |
| 10    |            | 1 Jun 2014 (SI 2014/1287) |
| 11–13 |            | 1 Feb 2015 (SI 2015/40) |
| 14    | (1)        | 1 Jun 2014 (SI 2014/1287) |
|       | (2)        | See Sch 4 below |
| 15    | (1)–(4)    | 1 Feb 2015 (SI 2015/40) |
|       | (5)        | See Sch 5 below |
| 16, 17|            | 1 Feb 2015 (SI 2015/40) |
| 18    | (1)–(4)    | 1 Feb 2015 (SI 2015/40) |
|       | (5)        | 1 Feb 2015 (except in so far as substitutes Criminal Justice Act 2003, Sch 8, para 16(3)) (SI 2015/40) |
|       |            | *Not yet in force* (exception noted above) |
|       | (6), (7)   | 1 Feb 2015 (SI 2015/40) |
|       | (8)        | 1 Feb 2015 (except in so far as substitutes Criminal Justice Act 2003, Sch 12, para 14(3)) (SI 2015/40) |
|       |            | *Not yet in force* (exception noted above) |
|       | (9)–(12)   | 1 Feb 2015 (SI 2015/40) |
| 19    |            | See Sch 6 below |
| 20    |            | 13 Mar 2014 (s 22(2)) |
| 21    | (1)        | See Sch 7 below |
|       | (2)–(4)    | 13 Mar 2014 (s 22(2)) |
| 22–24 |            | 13 Mar 2014 (s 22(2)) |

**Offender Rehabilitation Act 2014 (c 11)**—*contd*

| | | |
|---|---|---|
| Schs 1–3 | | 1 Feb 2015 (SI 2015/40) |
| Sch 4 | | 1 Jun 2014 (SI 2014/1287) |
| Sch 5 | | 1 Feb 2015 (SI 2015/40) |
| Sch 6 | paras 1–3 | 1 Feb 2015 (SI 2015/40) |
| | paras 4–7 | 1 Jun 2014 (SI 2014/1287) |
| | paras 8–11 | 1 Feb 2015 (SI 2015/40) |
| Sch 7 | | 1 Feb 2015 (SI 2015/40) |

---

**Pensions Act 2014 (c 19)**

*RA:* 14 May 2014

*Commencement provisions*: s 56; Pensions Act 2014 (Commencement No 1) Order 2014, SI 2014/1965; Pensions Act 2014 (Commencement No 2) Order 2014, SI 2014/2377; Pensions Act 2014 (Commencement No 3) Order 2014, SI 2014/2727; Pensions Act 2014 (Commencement No 4) Order 2015, SI 2015/134; Pensions Act 2014 (Commencement No 5) Order 2015, SI 2015/1475; Pensions Act 2014 (Commencement No 6) Order 2015, SI 2015/1670; Pensions Act 2014 (Commencement No 7) and (Savings) (Amendment) Order 2015, SI 2015/2058; Pensions Act 2014 (Commencement No 8) Order 2016, SI 2016/203; Pensions Act 2014 (Commencement No 9) and the Welfare Reform and Work Act 2016 (Commencement No 4) Regulations 2017, SI 2017/111; Pensions Act 2014 (Commencement No 10) Order 2017, SI 2017/297; Pensions Act 2014 (Commencement No 11) and the Pension Schemes Act 2015 (Commencement No 2) Regulations 2017, SI 2017/916

| | | |
|---|---|---|
| 1 | | 6 Apr 2016 (s 56(4))[1] |
| 2 | (1), (2) | 6 Apr 2016 (s 56(4))[1] |
| | (3) | 5 Feb 2015 (for the purpose of making regulations) (SI 2015/134) |
| | | 6 Apr 2016 (s 56(4))[1] (otherwise) |
| | (4)–(7) | 6 Apr 2016 (s 56(4))[1] |
| 3 | (1) | 23 Feb 2016 (SI 2016/203) |
| | (2), (3) | 6 Apr 2016 (s 56(4))[1] |
| 4 | (1) | 6 Apr 2016 (s 56(4))[1] |
| | (2) | 5 Feb 2015 (for the purpose of making regulations) (SI 2015/134) |
| | | 6 Apr 2016 (s 56(4))[1] (otherwise) |
| | (3)–(7) | 6 Apr 2016 (s 56(4))[1] |
| 5 | (1) | See Sch 1 below |
| | (2) | See Sch 2 below |
| | (3), (4) | 6 Apr 2016 (s 56(4))[1] |
| 6 | | 6 Apr 2016 (s 56(4))[1] |
| 7 | (1)(a), (b) | 6 Apr 2016 (s 56(4))[1] |
| | (1)(c) | See Sch 3 below |
| | (2) | 6 Apr 2016 (s 56(4))[1] |
| | (3) | See Sch 4 below |
| | (4)–(6) | 6 Apr 2016 (s 56(4))[1] |
| 8 | (1), (2) | 6 Apr 2016 (s 56(4))[1] |
| | (3) | 5 Feb 2015 (for the purpose of making regulations) (SI 2015/134) |
| | | 6 Apr 2016 (s 56(4))[1] (otherwise) |
| | (4)–(6) | 6 Apr 2016 (s 56(4))[1] |
| | (7), (8) | 5 Feb 2015 (for the purpose of making regulations) (SI 2015/134) |
| | | 6 Apr 2016 (s 56(4))[1] (otherwise) |
| | (9) | 6 Apr 2016 (s 56(4))[1] |
| 9 | (1)(a)–(c) | 6 Apr 2016 (s 56(4))[1] |
| | (1)(d) | See Sch 5 below |
| | (1)(e) | 6 Apr 2016 (s 56(4))[1] |
| 10 | | 23 Feb 2016 (SI 2016/203) |
| 11, 12 | | 6 Apr 2016 (s 56(4))[1] |
| 13 | (1) | 6 Apr 2016 (s 56(4))[1] |
| | (2) | See Sch 8 below |
| | (3) | See Sch 9 below |
| | (4)–(6) | 6 Apr 2016 (s 56(4))[1] |

**Pensions Act 2014 (c 19)**—*contd*

| | | |
|---|---|---|
| 14 | (1) | 6 Apr 2016 (s 56(4))[1] |
| | (2) | See Sch 10 below |
| | (3), (4) | 6 Apr 2016 (s 56(4))[1] |
| 15 | | See Sch 11 below |
| 16 | (1) | 5 Feb 2015 (for the purpose of making regulations) (SI 2015/134) |
| | | 6 Apr 2016 (s 56(4))[1] (otherwise) |
| | (2)–(5) | 6 Apr 2016 (s 56(4))[1] |
| | (6) | 5 Feb 2015 (for the purpose of making regulations) (SI 2015/134) |
| | | 6 Apr 2016 (s 56(4))[1] (otherwise) |
| 17 | (1)–(3) | 6 Apr 2016 (s 56(4))[1] |
| | (4), (5) | 5 Feb 2015 (for the purpose of making regulations) (SI 2015/134) |
| | | 6 Apr 2016 (s 56(4))[1] (otherwise) |
| | (6)–(9) | 6 Apr 2016 (s 56(4))[1] |
| 18 | (1) | 5 Feb 2015 (for the purpose of making regulations) (SI 2015/134) |
| | | 6 Apr 2016 (s 56(4))[1] (otherwise) |
| | (2)–(4) | 23 Feb 2016 (SI 2016/203) |
| | (5) | 6 Apr 2016 (s 56(4))[1] |
| 19 | (1) | 5 Feb 2015 (for the purpose of making regulations) (SI 2015/134) |
| | | 6 Apr 2016 (s 56(4))[1] (otherwise) |
| | (2) | 6 Apr 2016 (s 56(4))[1] |
| | (3) | 5 Feb 2015 (for the purpose of making regulations) (SI 2015/134) |
| | | 6 Apr 2016 (s 56(4))[1] (otherwise) |
| 20 | | 23 Feb 2016 (SI 2016/203) |
| 21 | | 6 Apr 2016 (s 56(4))[1] |
| 22 | (1) | 5 Feb 2015 (for the purpose of making regulations) (SI 2015/134) |
| | | 6 Apr 2016 (s 56(4))[1] (otherwise) |
| | (2) | 6 Apr 2016 (s 56(4))[1] |
| 23 | | See Sch 12 below |
| 24 | (1) | See Sch 13 below |
| | (2)–(5) | 23 Feb 2015 (SI 2015/134) |
| | (6) | See Sch 14 below |
| | (7)–(9) | 23 Feb 2015 (SI 2015/134) |
| 25 | | See Sch 15 below |
| 26, 27 | | 14 Jul 2014 (s 56(3)(a)) |
| 28 | (1), (2) | 6 Apr 2016 (SI 2015/1475) |
| | (3) | 7 Jul 2015 (SI 2015/1475) |
| 29 | | 14 May 2014 (s 56(2)(a)) |
| 30 | | 8 Mar 2017 (for the purpose of making regulations) (SI 2017/297) |
| | | 6 Apr 2017 (otherwise) (SI 2017/297) |
| 31 | (1)–(4) | 8 Mar 2017 (for the purpose of making regulations) (SI 2017/297) |
| | | 6 Apr 2017 (otherwise) (SI 2017/297) |
| | (5) | See Sch 16 below |
| 32 | | 8 Mar 2017 (for the purpose of making regulations) (SI 2017/297) |
| | | 6 Apr 2017 (otherwise) (SI 2017/297) |
| 33 | | See Sch 17 below |
| 34, 35 | | 14 Jul 2014 (s 56(3)(b)) |
| 36 | | 1 Oct 2015 (SI 2015/134) |
| 37, 38 | | 11 Sep 2014 (SI 2014/2377) |
| 39 | | 12 Sep 2014 (SI 2014/2377) |
| 40 | | 11 Sep 2014 (SI 2014/2377) |
| 41 | | 14 Jul 2014 (s 56(3)(c)) |
| 42 | | 11 Sep 2014 (SI 2014/2377) |
| 43 | | See Sch 18 below |
| 44 | (1) | 18 Sep 2017 (except in relation to a scheme which falls within Occupational Pension Schemes (Scheme Administration) Regulations 1996, SI 1997/1715, reg 1(2), definition "relevant scheme", paras (a)–(e)) (SI 2017/916) |
| | | *Not yet in force* (exception noted above) |
| | (2) | 18 Sep 2017 (SI 2017/916) |

**Pensions Act 2014 (c 19)**—*contd*

| | | |
|---|---|---|
| 45 | | 11 Sep 2014 (SI 2014/2377) |
| 46 | (1)–(5) | 11 Sep 2014 (SI 2014/2377) |
| | (6) | See Sch 19 below |
| 47, 48 | | 14 Jul 2014 (s 56(3)(d)) |
| 49 | | 11 Sep 2014 (SI 2014/2377) |
| 50 | | See Sch 20 below |
| 51 | | 14 May 2014 (s 56(2)(b)) |
| 52 | | 23 Jul 2014 (SI 2014/1965) |
| 53–57 | | 14 May 2014 (s 56(2)(c)) |
| Schs 1–7 | | 6 Apr 2016 (s 56(4))[1] |
| Sch 8 | paras 1–3 | 6 Apr 2016 (s 56(4))[1] |
| | para 4 | 5 Feb 2015 (for the purpose of making regulations) (SI 2015/134) |
| | | 6 Apr 2016 (s 56(4))[1] (otherwise) |
| Sch 9 | | 6 Apr 2016 (s 56(4))[1] |
| Sch 10 | paras 1–3 | 6 Apr 2016 (s 56(4))[1] |
| | para 4 | 5 Feb 2015 (for the purpose of making regulations) (SI 2015/134) |
| | | 6 Apr 2016 (s 56(4))[1] (otherwise) |
| Sch 11 | paras 1–10 | 6 Apr 2016 (s 56(4))[1] |
| | para 11 | 5 Feb 2015 (for the purpose of making regulations) (SI 2015/134) |
| | | 6 Apr 2016 (s 56(4))[1] (otherwise) |
| | paras 12–16 | 6 Apr 2016 (s 56(4))[1] |
| Sch 12 | paras 1–24 | 6 Apr 2016 (s 56(4))[1] |
| | para 25 | 7 Jul 2015 (SI 2015/1475) |
| | paras 26–89 | 6 Apr 2016 (s 56(4))[1] |
| | para 90 | 7 Jul 2015 (SI 2015/1475) |
| | para 96 | 1 Oct 2014 (SI 2014/2377) |
| | para 97(a) | 6 Apr 2016 (s 56(4))[1] |
| | para 97(b) | 1 Oct 2014 (SI 2014/2377) |
| Sch 13 | paras 1–23 | 6 Apr 2016 (s 56(4))[1] |
| | paras 24, 25 | 7 Jul 2015 (for the purpose of making regulations) (SI 2015/1475) |
| | | 6 Apr 2016 (otherwise) (s 56(4))[1] |
| | paras 26–30(1) | 6 Apr 2016 (s 56(4))[1] |
| | para 30(2) | 14 Jul 2014 (s 56(3)(e)) |
| | paras 31–83 | 6 Apr 2016 (s 56(4))[1] |
| Sch 14 | | 23 Feb 2015 (SI 2015/134) |
| Sch 15 | paras 1, 2 | 12 Oct 2015 (SI 2015/1475) |
| | para 3 | 1 Oct 2014 (for the purposes of making regulations) (SI 2014/2377) |
| | | 12 Oct 2015 (otherwise) (SI 2015/1475) |
| | paras 4–6 | 12 Oct 2015 (SI 2015/1475) |
| | para 7 | 1 Oct 2014 (for the purposes of making regulations) (SI 2014/2377) |
| | | 12 Oct 2015 (otherwise) (SI 2015/1475) |
| | paras 8–10 | 12 Oct 2015 (SI 2015/1475) |
| | para 11 | 13 Oct 2014 (SI 2014/2727) |
| | paras 12–14 | 12 Oct 2015 (SI 2015/1475) |
| | paras 15, 16 | 12 Oct 2015 (SI 2015/1670) |
| | para 17 | 1 Oct 2014 (for the purposes of making regulations) (SI 2014/2377) |
| | | 12 Oct 2015 (otherwise) (SI 2015/1670) |
| | paras 18, 19 | 12 Oct 2015 (SI 2015/1670) |
| | para 20 | 13 Oct 2014 (SI 2014/2727) |
| | paras 21, 22 | 12 Oct 2015 (SI 2015/1670) |
| Sch 16 | paras 1–19 | 6 Apr 2017 (except in relation to specified persons[2]) (SI 2017/297) |
| | | *Not yet in force* (exception noted above) |
| | para 20 | 8 Feb 2017 (SI 2017/111) |
| | paras 21–32 | 6 Apr 2017 (except in relation to specified persons[2]) (SI 2017/297) |
| | | *Not yet in force* (exception noted above) |
| | para 33 | 8 Feb 2017 (SI 2017/111) |

**Pensions Act 2014 (c 19)**—*contd*

| | paras 34–48 | 6 Apr 2017 (except in relation to specified persons[2]) (SI 2017/297) |
| | | *Not yet in force* (exception noted above) |
| Sch 17 | paras 1–14 | *Not yet in force* |
| | para 15(1) | 11 Sep 2014 (for the purposes only of Sch 18, para 4(1)) (SI 2014/2377) |
| | | *Not yet in force* (otherwise) |
| | para 15(2) | *Not yet in force* |
| | paras 16–21 | *Not yet in force* |
| Schs 18, 19 | | 11 Sep 2014 (SI 2014/2377) |
| Sch 20 | paras 1–5 | 6 Apr 2017 (SI 2017/297) |
| | para 6(1), (2) | 6 Apr 2017 (SI 2017/297) |
| | para 6(3) | 8 Mar 2017 (SI 2017/297) |
| | para 6(4) | 6 Apr 2017 (SI 2017/297) |
| | paras 7–21 | 6 Apr 2017 (SI 2017/297) |
| | para 22 | 8 Mar 2017 (SI 2017/297) |

[1]   In so far as not brought into force before this date by order under s 56(1)

[2]   See further SI 2017297, arts 4, 5

---

**Procurement Reform (Scotland) Act 2014 (asp 12)**

*RA:* 17 Jun 2014

*Commencement provisions*: s 45; Procurement Reform (Scotland) Act 2014 (Commencement No 1) Order 2015, SSI 2015/331; Procurement Reform (Scotland) Act 2014 (Commencement No 2) Order 2015, SSI 2015/411; Procurement Reform (Scotland) Act 2014 (Commencement No 3 and Transitional Provisions) Order 2016, SSI 2016/30

| | | |
|---|---|---|
| 1 | (1)(a) | See Schedule below |
| | (1)(b), (2), (3) | 28 Sep 2015 (SSI 2015/331) |
| 2 | | 28 Sep 2015 (SSI 2015/331) |
| 3–7 | | 18 Apr 2016 (SSI 2016/30) |
| 8 | (1) | 18 Apr 2016 (SSI 2016/30) |
| | (2), (3) | 1 Jun 2016 (SSI 2016/30) |
| | (4), (5) | 18 Apr 2016 (SSI 2016/30) |
| 9 | | 1 Jun 2016 (SSI 2016/30) |
| 10 | | 11 Jan 2016 (SSI 2015/411) |
| 11, 12 | | 18 Apr 2016 (SSI 2016/30) |
| 13 | | 11 Jan 2016 (SSI 2015/411) |
| 14 | | 18 Apr 2016 (SSI 2016/30) |
| 15 | (1)–(4) | 18 Apr 2016 (SSI 2016/30)[1] |
| | (5)(a), (b)(i), (ii) | 18 Apr 2016 (SSI 2016/30)[1] |
| | (5)(b)(iii) | 28 Sep 2015 (for the purpose only of the definition "living wage") (SSI 2015/331) |
| | | 18 Apr 2016 (otherwise) (SSI 2016/30)[1] |
| | (5)(b)(iv), (v), (c)–(e) | 18 Apr 2016 (SSI 2016/30)[1] |
| | (6) | 18 Apr 2016 (SSI 2016/30)[1] |
| | (7) | 28 Sep 2015 (SSI 2015/331) |
| 16–19 | | 18 Apr 2016 (SSI 2016/30) |
| 20 | | 11 Jan 2016 (SSI 2015/411) |
| 21–23 | | 18 Apr 2016 (SSI 2016/30) |
| 24, 25 | | 1 Jun 2016 (SSI 2016/30) |
| 26 | | 11 Jan 2016 (SSI 2015/411) |
| 27, 28 | | 18 Apr 2016 (SSI 2016/30) |
| 29 | | 28 Sep 2015 (SSI 2015/331) |
| 30–40 | | 18 Apr 2016 (SSI 2016/30) |
| 41–46 | | 17 Jun 2014 |

**Procurement Reform (Scotland) Act 2014 (asp 12)**—*contd*
Schedule                          28 Sep 2015 (SSI 2015/331)

---

[1]    For a transitional provision, see SSI 2016/30, art 3

---

**Public Bodies (Joint Working) (Scotland) Act 2014 (asp 9)**

*RA:* 1 Apr 2014

*Commencement provisions*: s 72; Public Bodies (Joint Working) (Scotland) Act 2014 (Commencement No 1) Order 2014, SSI 2014/202; Public Bodies (Joint Working) (Scotland) Act 2014 (Commencement No 2) Order 2014, SSI 2014/231, as amended by SSI 2015/44

| | | |
|---|---|---|
| 1 | (1), (2) | 22 Sep 2014 (SSI 2014/231) |
| | (3), (4) | 2 Apr 2014 (s 72(1)) |
| | (5) | See Schedule below |
| | (6)–(16) | 2 Apr 2014 (s 72(1)) |
| 2–4 | | 22 Sep 2014 (SSI 2014/231) |
| 5 | | 2 Apr 2014 (s 72(1)) |
| 6–48 | | 22 Sep 2014 (SSI 2014/231) |
| 49 | | 2 Apr 2014 (s 72(1)) |
| 50–52 | | 22 Sep 2014 (SSI 2014/231) |
| 53 | | 2 Apr 2014 (s 72(1)) |
| 54–63 | | 22 Sep 2014 (SSI 2014/231) |
| 64 | | 25 Jul 2014 (SSI 2014/202) |
| 65 | | 25 Feb 2015 (SSI 2014/231) |
| 66, 67 | | 22 Sep 2014 (SSI 2014/231) |
| 68–70 | | 2 Apr 2014 (s 72(1)) |
| 71 | (1)–(4) | 1 Apr 2015 (SSI 2014/231) |
| | (5) | 22 Sep 2014 (SSI 2014/231) |
| | (6) | 1 Apr 2015 (SSI 2014/231) |
| | (7) | 22 Sep 2014 (SSI 2014/231) |
| 72, 73 | | 2 Apr 2014 (s 72(1)) |
| Schedule | | 2 Apr 2014 (s 72(1)) |

---

**Regulatory Reform (Scotland) Act 2014 (asp 3)**

*RA:* 19 Feb 2014

*Commencement provisions*: s 61; Regulatory Reform (Scotland) Act 2014 (Commencement No 1 and Transitional Provision) Order 2014, SSI 2014/160; Regulatory Reform (Scotland) Act 2014 (Commencement No 2 and Transitional Provision) Order 2015, SSI 2015/52

| | | |
|---|---|---|
| 1–17 | | 30 Jun 2014 (SSI 2014/160) |
| 18 | | See Sch 2 below |
| 19–53 | | 30 Jun 2014 (SSI 2014/160) |
| 54 | | 26 Feb 2015 (SSI 2015/52)[2] |
| 55 | | 30 Jun 2014 (SSI 2014/160) |
| 56 | | 30 Jun 2014 (SSI 2014/160)[1] |
| 57 | | See Sch 3 below |
| 58–62 | | 20 Feb 2014 (s 61(1)) |
| Schs 1, 2 | | 30 Jun 2014 (SSI 2014/160) |
| Sch 3 | para 1 | *Not yet in force* |
| | paras 2–5 | 30 Jun 2014 (SSI 2014/160) |
| | para 6 | 1 Oct 2015 (SSI 2015/52) |
| | para 7 | 30 Jun 2014 (SSI 2014/160) |
| | para 8(1), (2) | 30 Jun 2014 (SSI 2014/160) |
| | para 8(3)–(10) | *Not yet in force* |
| | para 9 | 30 Jun 2014 (SSI 2014/160) |
| | para 10 | *Not yet in force* |

**Regulatory Reform (Scotland) Act 2014 (asp 3)**—*contd*

| | | |
|---|---|---|
| para 11(1)–(3) | 30 Jun 2014 (SSI 2014/160) | |
| para 11(4) | 1 Apr 2015 (SSI 2014/160) | |
| paras 12–23 | 30 Jun 2014 (SSI 2014/160) | |
| para 24 | *Not yet in force* | |
| paras 25–44 | 30 Jun 2014 (SSI 2014/160) | |

[1]   For transitional provisions, see SSI 2014/160, art 3

[2]   For transitional provisions, see SSI 2015/52, art 3

## Revenue Scotland and Tax Powers Act 2014 (asp 16)

*RA:* 24 Sep 2014

*Commencement provisions*: s 260; Revenue Scotland and Tax Powers Act 2014 (Commencement No 1) Order 2014, SSI 2014/278; Revenue Scotland and Tax Powers Act 2014 (Commencement No 2) Order 2014, SSI 2014/370; Revenue Scotland and Tax Powers Act 2014 (Commencement No 3) Order 2015, SSI 2015/18; Revenue Scotland and Tax Powers Act 2014 (Commencement No 4) Order 2015, SSI 2015/110

| | | |
|---|---|---|
| 1 | | 1 Jan 2015 (SSI 2014/370) |
| 2 | (1), (2) | 1 Apr 2015 (SSI 2015/110) |
| | (3) | See Sch 1 below |
| 3–10 | | 1 Jan 2015 (SSI 2014/370) |
| 11 | | 7 Nov 2014 (for the purpose of making orders) (SSI 2014/278) |
| | | 1 Jan 2015 (otherwise) (SSI 2014/370) |
| 12–19 | | 1 Jan 2015 (SSI 2014/370) |
| 20, 21 | | 1 Apr 2015 (SSI 2015/110) |
| 22 | | 24 Feb 2015 (SSI 2015/18) |
| 23–25 | | 1 Apr 2015 (SSI 2015/110) |
| 26 | (1)–(3) | 1 Apr 2015 (SSI 2015/110) |
| | (4) | See Sch 2 below |
| 27–31 | | 1 Apr 2015 (SSI 2015/110) |
| 32, 33 | | 7 Nov 2014 (SSI 2014/278) |
| 34–38 | | 1 Apr 2015 (SSI 2015/110) |
| 39 | (1) | 7 Nov 2014 (for the purpose of making regulations) (SSI 2014/278) |
| | | 1 Apr 2015 (otherwise) (SSI 2015/110) |
| | (2) | 1 Apr 2015 (SSI 2015/110) |
| 40 | | 1 Apr 2015 (SSI 2015/110) |
| 41 | | The day on which the Courts Reform (Scotland) Act 2014, s 89 comes into force (SSI 2015/110) |
| 42–44 | | 1 Apr 2015 (SSI 2015/110) |
| 45 | (1) | 1 Apr 2015 (SSI 2015/110) |
| | (2) | 7 Nov 2014 (for the purpose of making tribunal rules) (SSI 2014/278) |
| | | 1 Apr 2015 (otherwise) (SSI 2015/110) |
| 46–48 | | 7 Nov 2014 (for the purpose of making tribunal rules) (SSI 2014/278) |
| | | 1 Apr 2015 (otherwise) (SSI 2015/110) |
| 49 | | 1 Apr 2015 (SSI 2015/110) |
| 50–56 | | 7 Nov 2014 (SSI 2014/278) |
| 57–73 | | 1 Apr 2015 (SSI 2015/110) |
| 74 | | 7 Nov 2014 (for the purpose of making regulations) (SSI 2014/278) |
| | | 1 Apr 2015 (otherwise) (SSI 2015/110) |
| 75–80 | | 1 Apr 2015 (SSI 2015/110) |
| 81 | | 7 Nov 2014 (SSI 2014/278) |
| 82–91 | | 1 Apr 2015 (SSI 2015/110) |

**Revenue Scotland and Tax Powers Act 2014 (asp 16)**—*contd*

| | | |
|---|---|---|
| 92 | | 7 Nov 2014 (for the purpose of making tribunal rules) (SSI 2014/278) |
| | | 1 Apr 2015 (otherwise) (SSI 2015/110) |
| 93 | | 1 Apr 2015 (SSI 2015/110) |
| 94 | | 7 Nov 2014 (for the purpose of making tribunal rules) (SSI 2014/278) |
| | | 1 Apr 2015 (otherwise) (SSI 2015/110) |
| 95–110 | | 1 Apr 2015 (SSI 2015/110) |
| 111 | | 7 Nov 2014 (for the purpose of making regulations) (SSI 2014/278) |
| | | 1 Apr 2015 (otherwise) (SSI 2015/110) |
| 112, 113 | | 1 Apr 2015 (SSI 2015/110) |
| 114 | | See Sch 3 below |
| 115–137 | | 1 Apr 2015 (SSI 2015/110) |
| 138 | | 7 Nov 2014 (for the purpose of making regulations) (SSI 2014/278) |
| | | 1 Apr 2015 (otherwise) (SSI 2015/110) |
| 139–141 | | 1 Apr 2015 (SSI 2015/110) |
| 142 | | 7 Nov 2014 (for the purpose of making orders) (SSI 2014/278) |
| | | 1 Apr 2015 (otherwise) (SSI 2015/110) |
| 143–157 | | 1 Apr 2015 (SSI 2015/110) |
| 158 | | 16 Feb 2015 (SSI 2015/18) |
| 159–208 | | 1 Apr 2015 (SSI 2015/110) |
| 209–212 | | 16 Feb 2015 (SSI 2015/18) |
| 213 | (1)–(4) | 16 Feb 2015 (SSI 2015/18) |
| | (5) | 1 Apr 2015 (SSI 2015/110) |
| 214 | | 16 Feb 2015 (for the purposes of Revenue Scotland's functions) (SSI 2015/18) |
| | | 1 Apr 2015 (otherwise) (SSI 2015/110) |
| 215 | | 16 Feb 2015 (SSI 2015/18) |
| 216 | | 1 Apr 2015 (SSI 2015/110) |
| 217 | | 7 Nov 2014 (for the purpose of making regulations) (SSI 2014/278) |
| | | 1 Apr 2015 (otherwise) (SSI 2015/110) |
| 218, 219 | | 1 Apr 2015 (SSI 2015/110) |
| 220 | | 7 Nov 2014 (for the purpose of making regulations) (SSI 2014/278) |
| | | 1 Apr 2015 (otherwise) (SSI 2015/110) |
| 221 | | 1 Apr 2015 (SSI 2015/110) |
| 222 | | 7 Nov 2014 (SSI 2014/278) |
| 223–232 | | 1 Apr 2015 (SSI 2015/110) |
| 233 | | 16 Feb 2015 (for the purposes of reviews in relation to Landfill Tax (Scotland) Act 2014, ss 37(3), 38, or Pt 2 of the Scottish Landfill Tax (Administration) Regulations 2015, SSI 2015/3) (SSI 2015/18) |
| | | 1 Apr 2015 (otherwise) (SSI 2015/110) |
| 234 | (1)–(4)(a) | 16 Feb 2015 (for the purposes of reviews in relation to Landfill Tax (Scotland) Act 2014, ss 37(3), 38, or Pt 2 of the Scottish Landfill Tax (Administration) Regulations 2015, SSI 2015/3) (SSI 2015/18) |
| | | 1 Apr 2015 (otherwise) (SSI 2015/110) |
| | (4)(b) | 1 Apr 2015 (SSI 2015/110) |
| | (5), (6) | 16 Feb 2015 (for the purposes of reviews in relation to Landfill Tax (Scotland) Act 2014, ss 37(3), 38, or Pt 2 of the Scottish Landfill Tax (Administration) Regulations 2015, SSI 2015/3) (SSI 2015/18) |
| | | 1 Apr 2015 (otherwise) (SSI 2015/110) |

**See Halsbury's Statutes Citator for amendments to these Acts**

**Revenue Scotland and Tax Powers Act 2014 (asp 16)**—*contd*

| | | |
|---|---|---|
| 235–240 | | 16 Feb 2015 (for the purposes of reviews in relation to Landfill Tax (Scotland) Act 2014, ss 37(3), 38, or Pt 2 of the Scottish Landfill Tax (Administration) Regulations 2015, SSI 2015/3) (SSI 2015/18) |
| | | 1 Apr 2015 (otherwise) (SSI 2015/110) |
| 241–244 | | 1 Apr 2015 (SSI 2015/110) |
| 245 | | 7 Nov 2014 (for the purpose of making regulations) (SSI 2014/278) |
| | | 1 Apr 2015 (otherwise) (SSI 2015/110) |
| 246–248 | | 1 Apr 2015 (SSI 2015/110) |
| 249 | | 7 Nov 2014 (for the purpose of making tribunal rules) (SSI 2014/278) |
| | | 1 Apr 2015 (otherwise) (SSI 2015/110) |
| 250 | | 16 Feb 2015 (for the purposes of reviews in relation to Landfill Tax (Scotland) Act 2014, ss 37(3), 38, or Pt 2 of the Scottish Landfill Tax (Administration) Regulations 2015, SSI 2015/3) (SSI 2015/18) |
| | | 1 Apr 2015 (otherwise) (SSI 2015/110) |
| 251 | | 1 Jan 2015 (SSI 2014/370) |
| 252 | | 1 Apr 2015 (SSI 2015/110) |
| 253 | | See Sch 5 below |
| 254, 255 | | 25 Sep 2014 (s 7(1)) |
| 256 | | See Sch 4 below |
| 257–261 | | 25 Sep 2014 (s 7(1)) |
| Sch 1 | | 1 Jan 2015 (SSI 2014/370) |
| Sch 2 | para 1 | 24 Feb 2015 (for the purpose of appointing the first President of the Scottish Tax Tribunals) (SSI 2015/18) |
| | | 1 Apr 2015 (otherwise) (SSI 2015/110) |
| | para 2(1), (2) | 1 Apr 2015 (SSI 2015/110) |
| | para 2(3) | 7 Nov 2014 (for the purpose of making regulations or rules) (SSI 2014/278) |
| | | 1 Apr 2015 (otherwise) (SSI 2015/110) |
| | paras 3–6 | 1 Apr 2015 (SSI 2015/110) |
| | para 7 | 24 Feb 2015 (for the purpose of appointing the first President of the Scottish Tax Tribunals) (SSI 2015/18) |
| | | 1 Apr 2015 (otherwise) (SSI 2015/110) |
| | para 8 | 1 Apr 2015 (SSI 2015/110) |
| | para 9 | 7 Nov 2014 (for the purpose of making regulations or rules) (SSI 2014/278) |
| | | 1 Apr 2015 (otherwise) (SSI 2015/110) |
| | para 10(1) | 1 Apr 2015 (SSI 2015/110) |
| | para 10(2) | 24 Feb 2015 (for the purpose of appointing the first President of the Scottish Tax Tribunals) (SSI 2015/18) |
| | | 1 Apr 2015 (otherwise) (SSI 2015/110) |
| | paras 11–15 | 1 Apr 2015 (SSI 2015/110) |
| | paras 16, 17 | 24 Feb 2015 (for the purpose of appointing the first President of the Scottish Tax Tribunals) (SSI 2015/18) |
| | paras 18–21 | 1 Apr 2015 (SSI 2015/110) |
| | para 22 | 7 Nov 2014 (for the purpose of making regulations or rules) (SSI 2014/278) |
| | | 1 Apr 2015 (otherwise) (SSI 2015/110) |
| | para 23 | 1 Jan 2015 (SSI 2014/370) |
| | paras 24–31 | 1 Apr 2015 (SSI 2015/110) |
| | para 32 | 7 Nov 2014 (for the purpose of making regulations or rules) (SSI 2014/278) |
| | | 1 Apr 2015 (otherwise) (SSI 2015/110) |
| | paras 33–43 | 1 Apr 2015 (SSI 2015/110) |
| Sch 3 | paras 1, 2 | 1 Apr 2015 (SSI 2015/110) |
| | para 3 | 7 Nov 2014 (for the purpose of making regulations or tribunal rules) (SSI 2014/278) |

**Revenue Scotland and Tax Powers Act 2014 (asp 16)**—*contd*

|       |                    |                                                                                             |
|-------|--------------------|---------------------------------------------------------------------------------------------|
|       |                    | 1 Apr 2015 (otherwise) (SSI 2015/110)                                                       |
|       | paras 4–14         | 1 Apr 2015 (SSI 2015/110)                                                                   |
|       | para 15            | 7 Nov 2014 (for the purpose of making regulations or tribunal rules) (SSI 2014/278)         |
|       |                    | 1 Apr 2015 (otherwise) (SSI 2015/110)                                                       |
|       | paras 16, 17       | 1 Apr 2015 (SSI 2015/110)                                                                   |
| Sch 4 | para 1             | 1 Apr 2015 (SSI 2015/110)                                                                   |
|       | paras 2–8          | 1 Jan 2015 (SSI 2014/370)                                                                   |
|       | para 9(1)          | 7 Nov 2014 (SSI 2014/278)                                                                   |
|       | para 9(2)–(5)      | 1 Apr 2015 (SSI 2015/110)                                                                   |
|       | para 9(6)          | 7 Nov 2014 (SSI 2014/278)                                                                   |
|       | para 9(7)          | 1 Apr 2015 (SSI 2015/110)                                                                   |
|       | para 9(8), (9)     | 7 Nov 2014 (SSI 2014/278)                                                                   |
|       | para 9(10)–(12)    | 1 Apr 2015 (SSI 2015/110)                                                                   |
|       | para 9(13)         | 1 Jan 2015 (SSI 2014/370)                                                                   |
|       | para 9(14)         | 1 Apr 2015 (SSI 2015/110)                                                                   |
|       | para 9(15), (16)(a)| 7 Nov 2014 (SSI 2014/278)                                                                   |
|       | para 9(16)(b)      | 1 Apr 2015 (SSI 2015/110)                                                                   |
|       | para 9(16)(c)      | 7 Nov 2014 (SSI 2014/278)                                                                   |
|       | para 9(17)         | 1 Jan 2015 (SSI 2014/370)                                                                   |
|       | para 9(18), (19)   | 7 Nov 2014 (SSI 2014/278)                                                                   |
|       | para 9(20), (21)(a)| 1 Apr 2015 (SSI 2015/110)                                                                   |
|       | para 9(21)(b), (c) | 1 Jan 2015 (SSI 2014/370)                                                                   |
|       | para 9(21)(d)      | 1 Apr 2015 (SSI 2015/110)                                                                   |
|       | para 9(22)(a)(i)   | 7 Nov 2014 (SSI 2014/278)                                                                   |
|       | para 9(22)(a)(ii), (b)| 1 Apr 2015 (SSI 2015/110)                                                                |
|       | para 9(23)         | 1 Apr 2015 (SSI 2015/110)                                                                   |
|       | para 10(1)–(8)     | 7 Nov 2014 (SSI 2014/278)                                                                   |
|       | para 10(9), (10)   | 1 Apr 2015 (SSI 2015/110)                                                                   |
|       | para 10(11), (12)  | 7 Nov 2014 (SSI 2014/278)                                                                   |
|       | para 10(13), (14)) | 1 Apr 2015 (SSI 2015/110)                                                                   |
|       | para 10(15)        | 1 Jan 2015 (SSI 2014/370)                                                                   |
|       | para 10(16)        | 1 Apr 2015 (SSI 2015/110)                                                                   |
|       | para 10(17), (18)(a)| 7 Nov 2014 (SSI 2014/278)                                                                  |
|       | para 10(18)(b)     | 1 Apr 2015 (SSI 2015/110)                                                                   |
|       | para 10(19)        | 1 Jan 2015 (SSI 2014/370)                                                                   |
|       | para 11            | 1 Apr 2015 (SSI 2015/110)                                                                   |
|       | para 12            | 1 Jan 2015 (SSI 2014/370)                                                                   |
| Sch 5 |                    | 1 Apr 2015 (SSI 2015/110)                                                                   |

**Social Services and Well-being (Wales) Act 2014 (anaw 4)**

*RA:* 1 May 2014

*Commencement provisions:* s 199; Social Services and Well-being (Wales) Act 2014 (Commencement No 1) Order 2014, SI 2014/2718; Social Services and Well-being (Wales) Act 2014 (Commencement No 2) Order 2015, SI 2015/1744; Social Services and Well-being (Wales) Act 2014 (Commencement No 3, Savings and Transitional Provisions) Order 2016, SI 2016/412

|          |     |                                  |
|----------|-----|----------------------------------|
| 1–4      |     | 2 May 2014 (s 199(1))            |
| 5–84     |     | 6 Apr 2016 (SI 2016/412)[1]      |
| 85       |     | See Sch 1 below                  |
| 86–131   |     | 6 Apr 2016 (SI 2016/412)[1]      |
| 132, 133 |     | 21 Oct 2015 (SI 2015/1744)       |
| 134–142  |     | 6 Apr 2016 (SI 2016/412)[1]      |
| 143      | (1) | See Sch 2 below                  |
|          | (2) | 6 Apr 2016 (SI 2016/412)[1]      |
| 144–169  |     | 6 Apr 2016 (SI 2016/412)[1]      |
| 170      |     | 1 Nov 2014 (SI 2014/2718)        |

**Social Services and Well-being (Wales) Act 2014 (anaw 4)**—*contd*

| | |
|---|---|
| 171–178 | 6 Apr 2016 (SI 2016/412)[1] |
| 179 | See Sch 3 below |
| 180 | 1 Nov 2014 (SI 2014/2718) |
| 181–195 | 6 Apr 2016 (SI 2016/412)[1] |
| 196–200 | 2 May 2014 (s 199(1)) |
| Schs 1, 2 | 6 Apr 2016 (SI 2016/412)[1] |
| Sch 3 | 1 Nov 2014 (SI 2014/2718) |

[1]   For transitional provisions and savings, see SI 2016/412, art 3, Schs 1, 2

---

**Supply and Appropriation (Anticipation and Adjustments) Act 2014 (c 5)**

*RA:* 13 Mar 2014

Whole Act in force 13 Mar 2014 (RA)

---

**Supply and Appropriation (Main Estimates) Act 2014 (c 25)**

*RA:* 17 Jul 2014

Whole Act in force 17 Jul 2014 (RA)

---

**Taxation of Pensions Act 2014 (c 30)**

*RA:* 17 Dec 2014

Whole Act in force 17 Dec 2014 (RA) (amendments have effect either from RA or from 6 Apr 2015)

---

**Transparency of Lobbying, Non-Party Campaigning and Trade Union Administration Act 2014 (c 4)**

*RA:* 30 Jan 2014

*Commencement provisions*: s 45, Transparency of Lobbying, Non-Party Campaigning and Trade Union Administration Act 2014 (Commencement and Transitional Provision No 1) Order 2014, SI 2014/1236; Transparency of Lobbying, Non-Party Campaigning and Trade Union Administration Act 2014 (Commencement No 2 and Transitional Provision) Order 2015, SI 2015/717; Transparency of Lobbying, Non-Party Campaigning and Trade Union Administration Act 2014 (Commencement No 3) Order 2015, SI 2015/954

| | | |
|---|---|---|
| 1 | | 1 Apr 2015 (SI 2015/954) |
| 2 | (1) | 23 May 2014 (SI 2014/1236) |
| | (2) | See Sch 1 below |
| | (3), (4) | 23 May 2014 (SI 2014/1236) |
| | (5) | 30 Jan 2014 (for the purpose of exercising the power to make regulations) (s 45(3)(a)) |
| | | 23 May 2014 (otherwise) (SI 2014/1236) |
| | (6) | 23 May 2014 (SI 2014/1236) |
| 3 | (1) | 23 May 2014 (SI 2014/1236) |
| | (2) | See Sch 2 below |
| 4, 5 | | 30 Jan 2014 (in so far as confer a power to make regulations, for the purpose of exercising that power) (s 45(3)(a)) |
| | | 1 Apr 2015 (otherwise) (SI 2015/954) |
| 6–8 | | 1 Apr 2015 (SI 2015/954) |
| 9 | | 30 Jan 2014 (in so far as confers a power to make regulations, for the purpose of exercising that power) (s 45(3)(a)) |
| | | 1 Apr 2015 (otherwise) (SI 2015/954) |
| 10 | | 1 Apr 2015 (SI 2015/954) |

**Transparency of Lobbying, Non–Party Campaigning and Trade Union Administration Act 2014 (c 4)**—*contd*

| | | |
|---|---|---|
| 11 | | 30 Jan 2014 (in so far as confers a power to make regulations, for the purpose of exercising that power) (s 45(3)(a)) |
| | | 1 Apr 2015 (otherwise) (SI 2015/954) |
| 12–15 | | 1 Apr 2015 (SI 2015/954) |
| 16, 17 | | 30 Jan 2014 (in so far as confers a power to make regulations, for the purpose of exercising that power) (s 45(3)(a)) |
| | | 1 Apr 2015 (otherwise) (SI 2015/954) |
| 18, 19 | | 1 Apr 2015 (SI 2015/954) |
| 20 | | 30 Jan 2014 (in so far as confers a power to make regulations, for the purpose of exercising that power) (s 45(3)(a)) |
| | | 1 Apr 2015 (otherwise) (SI 2015/954) |
| 21 | | 23 May 2014 (SI 2014/1236) |
| 22, 23 | | 30 Jan 2014 (in so far as confers a power to make regulations, for the purpose of exercising that power) (s 45(3)(a)) |
| | | 1 Apr 2015 (otherwise) (SI 2015/954) |
| 24 | | 30 Jan 2014 (in so far as confers a power to make regulations, for the purpose of exercising that power) (s 45(3)(a)) |
| | | 23 May 2014 (otherwise) (SI 2014/1236) |
| 25 | | 23 May 2014 (SI 2014/1236) |
| 26 | (1)–(10) | 30 Jan 2014 (s 45(3)(b))[1] |
| | (11), (12) | 23 May 2014 (SI 2014/1236) |
| | (13) | 30 Jan 2014 (s 45(3)(b))[1] |
| | (14) | See Sch 3 below |
| 27–30 | | 30 Jan 2014 (s 45(3)(b))[1] |
| 31, 32 | | 23 May 2014 (SI 2014/1236) |
| 33 | (1)–(6) | 30 Jan 2014 (s 45(3)(b))[1] |
| | (7) | See Sch 4 below |
| | (8)–(13) | 30 Jan 2014 (s 45(3)(b))[1] |
| 34, 35 | | 30 Jan 2014 (s 45(3)(b))[1] |
| 36, 37 | | 1 Jul 2014 (SI 2014/1236)[2] |
| 38 | | 23 May 2014 (SI 2014/1236) |
| 39 | | 30 Jan 2014 (s 45(3)(b))[1] |
| 40 | | 6 Apr 2015 (SI 2015/717) |
| 41 | | 30 Jan 2014 (for the purposes of the exercise of the power to make subordinate legislation conferred by Trade Union and Labour Relations (Consolidation) Act 1992, s 24ZB(3)) (s 45(3)(c)) |
| | | 6 Apr 2015 (otherwise) (SI 2015/717) |
| 42, 43 | | 1 Jun 2016 (SI 2015/717) |
| 44–49 | | 30 Jan 2014 (s 45(3)(d)) |
| Schs 1, 2 | | 23 May 2014 (SI 2014/1236) |
| Schs 3, 4 | | 30 Jan 2014 (s 45(3)(b)) |

[1]  For transitional provisions, see ss 45(4), 46

[2]  For transitional provision, see SI 2014/1236, art 3

---

**Tribunals (Scotland) Act 2014 (asp 10)**

*RA:* 15 Apr 2014

*Commencement provisions:* s 83; Tribunals (Scotland) Act 2014 (Commencement No 1) Order 2014, SSI 2014/183; Tribunals (Scotland) Act 2014 (Commencement No 2) Order 2015, SSI 2015/116; Tribunals (Scotland) Act 2014 (Commencement No 3) Order 2015, SSI 2015/422

| | | |
|---|---|---|
| 1–3 | | 1 Apr 2015 (SSI 2015/116) |
| 4 | (1)–(3) | 14 Jul 2014 (SSI 2014/183) |
| | (4) | 1 Apr 2015 (SSI 2015/116) |
| | (5) | 14 Jul 2014 (for the purpose of assigning a person to office under s 4(2)) (SSI 2014/183) |

**Tribunals (Scotland) Act 2014 (asp 10)**—*contd*

|  |  |  |
|---|---|---|
|  |  | 1 Apr 2015 (otherwise) (SSI 2015/116) |
| 5–76 |  | 1 Apr 2015 (SSI 2015/116) |
| 77 | (1) | *Never in force* (repealed) |
|  | (2) | 1 Apr 2015 (SSI 2015/116) |
|  | (3)–(5) | *Never in force* (repealed) |
| 78–81 |  | 1 Apr 2015 (SSI 2015/116) |
| 82–84 |  | 16 Apr 2014 (s 83(1)) |
| Schs 1–8 |  | 1 Apr 2015 (SSI 2015/116) |
| Sch 9 | paras 1–12 | 1 Apr 2015 (SSI 2015/116) |
|  | para 13(1) | See sub-paras (2)–(10) below |
|  | para 13(2)(a) | *Not yet in force* |
|  | para 13(2)(b)(i) | 8 Jan 2016 (SSI 2015/422) |
|  | para 13(2)(b)(ii) | *Not yet in force* |
|  | para 13(3)–(10) | *Not yet in force* |
| Sch 10 |  | 1 Apr 2015 (SSI 2015/116) |

---

## Victims and Witnesses (Scotland) Act 2014 (asp 1)

*RA:* 17 Jan 2014

*Commencement provisions*: s 34; Victims and Witnesses (Scotland) Act 2014 (Commencement No 2 and Transitional Provision) Order 2014, SSI 2014/210; Victims and Witnesses (Scotland) Act 2014 (Commencement No 3 and Transitional Provision) Order 2014, SI 2014/359; Victims and Witnesses (Scotland) Act 2014 (Commencement No 4 and Transitional Provisions) Order 2015, SSI 2015/200; Victims and Witnesses (Scotland) Act 2014 (Commencement No. 5) Order 2019, SSI 2019/283; Victims and Witnesses (Scotland) Act 2014 (Commencement No 6) Order 2020, SSI 2020/237; Victims and Witnesses (Scotland) Act 2014 (Commencement No 7 and Transitional Provisions) Order 2020, SSI 2020/405; Victims and Witnesses (Scotland) Act 2014 (Commencement No 8) Order 2021, SSI 2021/39; Victims and Witnesses (Scotland) Act 2014 (Commencement No 9) Order 2022, SSI 2022/22

|  |  |  |
|---|---|---|
| 1 |  | 30 Jan 2015 (SSI 2014/359) |
| 2 |  | 13 Aug 2014 (for the purpose of making an order under s 2(6)) (SSI 2014/210) |
|  |  | 30 Jan 2015 (otherwise) (SSI 2014/359)[2] |
| 3 |  | 30 Jan 2015 (SSI 2014/359) |
| 4 |  | 1 Jul 2015 (SSI 2015/200) |
| 5 |  | 24 Feb 2021 (SSI 2021/39) |
| 6 | (1)–(6) | 13 Aug 2014 (for the purpose of making an order under s 6(2)(b)) (SSI 2014/210) |
|  |  | 30 Jan 2015 (otherwise) (SSI 2014/359) |
|  | (7)(a)–(c) | 13 Aug 2014 (for the purpose of making an order under s 6(2)(b)) (SSI 2014/210) |
|  |  | 30 Jan 2015 (in relation to decisions taken on or after that date) (SSI 2014/359) |
|  |  | *Not yet in force* (otherwise) |
|  | (7)(d)–(j) | 13 Aug 2014 (for the purpose of making an order under s 6(2)(b)) (SSI 2014/210) |
|  |  | 30 Jan 2015 (in relation to all criminal proceedings except those which have been concluded before that date) (SSI 2014/359) |
|  |  | *Not yet in force* (exception noted above) |
|  | (8), (9) | 13 Aug 2014 (for the purpose of making an order under s 6(2)(b)) (SSI 2014/210) |
|  |  | 30 Jan 2015 (otherwise) (SSI 2014/359) |
| 7 |  | 1 Sep 2015 (SSI 2015/200)[3] |
| 8 |  | 13 Aug 2014 (SSI 2014/210) |
| 9 |  | 1 Apr 2022 (SSI 2022/22) |
| 10–14 |  | 1 Sep 2015 (SSI 2015/200)[3] |
| 15 |  | 1 Sep 2015 (SSI 2015/200) |
| 16–18 |  | 1 Sep 2015 (SSI 2015/200)[3] |

**Victims and Witnesses (Scotland) Act 2014 (asp 1)**—*contd*

| | | |
|---|---|---|
| 19 | | 1 Sep 2015 (SSI 2015/200) |
| 20 | | 1 Sep 2015 (SSI 2015/200)[3] |
| 21 | | 1 Sep 2015 (SSI 2015/200) |
| 22 | | 1 Sep 2015 (SSI 2015/200)[3] |
| 23 | (1) | See sub-ss (2)–(7) below[1] |
| | (2) | 13 Aug 2014 (for the purposes of criminal proceedings commenced on or after 13 Aug 2014) (SSI 2014/210)[1] |
| | | 10 Feb 2021 (otherwise) (SSI 2020/405) |
| | (3), (4) | 13 Aug 2014 (for the purposes of criminal proceedings commenced on or after 13 Aug 2014 and for the purposes of Criminal Justice (Scotland) Act 2003, s 16(5)(b)(i), (6)) (SSI 2014/210)[1] |
| | | 10 Feb 2021 (otherwise) (SSI 2020/405) |
| | (5), (6) | 13 Aug 2014 (for the purposes of criminal proceedings commenced on or after 13 Aug 2014) (SSI 2014/210)[1] |
| | | 10 Feb 2021 (otherwise) (SSI 2020/405) |
| | (7) | 10 Feb 2021 (SSI 2020/405) |
| | (8) | See sub-ss (9)–(13) below |
| | (9)–(13) | 13 Aug 2014 (SSI 2014/210)[1] |
| | (14) | 10 Feb 2021 (SSI 2020/405) |
| 24 | | *Not yet in force* |
| 25 | | 25 Aug 2020 (for the purpose of enabling an order to be made under Criminal Procedure (Scotland) Act 253B(5) or (6) (SSI 2020/237) |
| | | 10 Feb 2021 (SSI 2020/405)[4] |
| 26 | | 13 Aug 2014 (in so far as inserts Criminal Procedure (Scotland) Act 1995, ss 253F, 253G but only for the purposes of making regulations under s 253F, and an order and regulations under s 253G) (SSI 2014/210) |
| | | 25 Nov 2019 (so far as not already in force, only in so far as inserts Criminal Procedure (Scotland) Act 1995, ss 253F, 253G (except sub-ss (4)(a), (b) thereof), 253H, 253J) (SSI 2019283) |
| | | *Not yet in force* (otherwise) |
| 27–29 | | 13 Aug 2014 (SSI 2014/210)[1] |
| 30 | | 18 Jan 2014 (in so far as it inserts Mental Health (Care and Treatment) (Scotland) Act 2003, s 4ZA) (s 34(1)) |
| | | *Not yet in force* (in so far as it inserts Mental Health (Care and Treatment) (Scotland) Act 2003, ss 4ZB–4ZD) |
| 31 | (1) | 18 Jan 2014 (s 34(1)) |
| | (2) | 18 Jan 2014 (in so far as it inserts Mental Health (Care and Treatment) (Scotland) Act 2003, Sch 1A, paras 1, 2, 5) (s 34(1)) |
| | | *Not yet in force* (in so far as it inserts Mental Health (Care and Treatment) (Scotland) Act 2003, Sch 1A, paras 3, 4, 6–14) |
| | (3) | 18 Jan 2014 (s 34(1)) |
| 32–35 | | 18 Jan 2014 (s 34(1)) |

[1]   For transitional provisions, see SSI 2014/210, art 3

[2]   For a transitional provision, see SSI 2014/359, art 3

[3]   For transitional provisions, see SSI 2015/200, arts 3–5

[4]   For transitional provisions, see SSI 2020/405, art 3

---

## Wales Act 2014 (c 29)

*RA:* 17 Dec 2014

*Commencement provisions:* s 29; Wales Act 2014 (Commencement No 1) Order 2016, SI 2016/1264; Wales Act 2014 (Commencement No 2) Order 2018, SI 2018/892

| | | |
|---|---|---|
| 1–5 | | 17 Feb 2015 (s 29(2)(a)) |
| 6, 7 | | 17 Feb 2015 (s 29(2)(b), (3)) |

**Wales Act 2014 (c 29)**—*contd*

| | | |
|---|---|---|
| 8, 9 | | 24 Jul 2018 (SI 2018/892) |
| 10 | | *Not yet in force* |
| 11 | (1)–(4) | 17 Feb 2015 (s 29(2)(b), (3)) |
| | (5), (6), (7)(a) | 24 Jul 2018 (SI 2018/892) |
| | (7)(b) | 17 Feb 2015 (s 29(2)(b), (3)) |
| | (8)(a) | 24 Jul 2018 (SI 2018/892) |
| | (8)(b) | 17 Feb 2015 (s 29(2)(b), (3)) |
| 12–19 | | 17 Feb 2015 (s 29(2)(b), (3)) |
| 20 | | 1 Jan 2017 (SI 2016/1264) |
| 21 | | *Not yet in force* |
| 22, 23 | | 17 Feb 2015 (s 29(2)(b), (3)) |
| 24 | | *Not yet in force* |
| 25 | | 17 Feb 2015 (s 29(2)(c)) |
| 26–30 | | 17 Dec 2014 (s 29(1)) |
| Schs 1, 2 | | 17 Feb 2015 (s 29(2)(b), (3)) |

**Water Act 2014 (c 21)**

*RA:* 14 May 2014

*Commencement provisions:* s 94; Water Act 2014 (Commencement No 1) Order 2014, SI 2014/1823; Water Act 2014 (Commencement No 2 and Transitional Provisions) Order 2014, SI 2014/3320; Water Act 2014 (Commencement No 3 and Transitional Provisions) Order 2015, SI 2015/773; Water Act 2014 (Commencement No 4 and Transitional Provisions) Order 2015, SI 2015/1469; Water Act 2014 (Commencement No 1 and Transitional Provision) (Wales) Order 2015, SI 2015/1786; Water Act 2014 (Commencement No 1) (Scotland) Order 2015, SSI 2015/360; Water Act 2014 (Commencement No 5 and Transitional Provisions) Order 2015, SI 2015/1938; Water Act 2014 (Commencement No 2) (Scotland) Order 2016, SSI 2016/48; Water Act 2014 (Commencement No 6, Transitional Provisions and Savings) Order 2016, SI 2016/465, as amended by SI 2017/462; Water Act 2014 (Commencement No 7 and Transitional Provisions) Order 2016, SI 2016/1007; Water Act 2014 (Commencement No 8 and Transitional Provisions) Order 2017, SI 2017/58; Water Act 2014 (Commencement No 9 and Transitional Provisions) Order 2017, SI 2017/462, as amended by SI 2017/926; Water Act 2014 (Commencement No 10) Order 2017, SI 2017/1288, as amended by SI 2019/706; Water Act 2014 (Commencement No 11) Order 2018, SI 2018/397

| | | |
|---|---|---|
| 1 | (1) | 1 Jan 2016 (so far as substitutes Water Industry Act 1991, s 17A(2)–(6)) (SI 2015/1938)[5] |
| | | 1 Apr 2016 (so far as substitutes Water Industry Act 1991, s 17A(1) (but only in relation to the grant of a water supply licence with a retail authorisation or a restricted retail authorisation), s 17A(7), and inserts s 17AA(3)–(5)) (SI 2016/465)[6] |
| | | 1 Nov 2016 (otherwise) (SI 2016/1007)[7] |
| | (2) | See Sch 1 below |
| | (3) | See Sch 2 below |
| 2 | | 1 Apr 2017 (SI 2017/462) |
| 3 | | 14 Jul 2014 (s 94(2)(a)) |
| 4 | (1) | 1 Jan 2016 (so far as inserts Water Industry Act 1991, s 17BA(2)–(5)) (SI 2015/1938) |
| | | 1 Apr 2016 (so far as inserts Water Industry Act 1991, s 17BA(1) (but only in relation to the grant of a sewerage licence with a retail authorisation), ss 17BA(7), 17BB(2)–(4)) (SI 2016/465)[6] |
| | | *Not yet in force* (otherwise) |
| | (2) | See Sch 3 below |
| | (3) | See Sch 4 below |
| 5 | | *Not yet in force* |
| 6 | (1) | See sub-s (2) below |
| | (2) | 18 Dec 2015 (in so far as inserts Water Industry Act 1991, s 17FA) (SI 2015/1938) |
| | | 1 Apr 2016 (otherwise) (SI 2016/465)[6] |

**Water Act 2014 (c 21)**—*contd*

| | | |
|---|---|---|
| 7 | (1), (2) | 20 Nov 2015 (in so far as inserts Water Services etc (Scotland) Act 2005, Sch 2, para 1A) (SSI 2015/360) |
| | | 1 Apr 2016 (otherwise) (SSI 2016/48) |
| | (3), (4) | 20 Nov 2015 (SSI 2015/360) |
| 8 | (1) | 6 Apr 2015 (in so far as inserts Water Industry Act 1991, s 40J) (SI 2015/773)[2] |
| | | 1 Nov 2016 (in so far as inserts Water Industry Act 1991, s 40E (for the purpose of s 40I thereof) and s 40I) (SI 2016/1007) |
| | | 1 Apr 2018 (in relation to bulk supply agreements to which all parties are a water undertaker whose area is wholly or mainly in England, or a person who would, if the person's application for an appointment or variation is determined in accordance with the application, be such a water undertaker) (SI 2018/397) |
| | | 1 Apr 2019 (otherwise) (SI 2017/1288) |
| | (2) | 6 Apr 2015 (in so far as relates to Water Industry Act 1991, s 40J) (SI 2015/773) |
| | | 1 Apr 2018 (in relation to bulk supply agreements to which all parties are a water undertaker whose area is wholly or mainly in England, or a person who would, if the person's application for an appointment or variation is determined in accordance with the application, be such a water undertaker) (SI 2018/397) |
| | | 1 Apr 2019 (otherwise) (SI 2017/1288) |
| 9 | (1) | 1 Nov 2016 (in so far as substitutes Water Industry Act 1991, s 110A and inserts ss 110B, 110J thereof) (SI 2016/1007) |
| | | 1 Apr 2018 (in relation to main connection agreements under which any main connection into a sewerage system, or each such connection, is or would be a main connection into the sewerage system of a sewerage undertaker whose area is wholly or mainly in England for the benefit of another such undertaker) (SI 2018/397) |
| | | 1 Apr 2019 (otherwise) (W) (SI 2017/1288) |
| | (2), (3) | 1 Nov 2016 (in so far as relate to Water Industry Act 1991, ss 110B, 110J) (SI 2016/1007) |
| | | 1 Apr 2018 (in relation to main connection agreements under which any main connection into a sewerage system, or each such connection, is or would be a main connection into the sewerage system of a sewerage undertaker whose area is wholly or mainly in England for the benefit of another such undertaker) (SI 2018/397) |
| | | 1 Apr 2019 (otherwise) (W) (SI 2017/1288) |
| 10 | (1) | See sub-ss (2)–(4) below |
| | (2) | 1 Oct 2017 (E) (SI 2017/462)[9] |
| | | *Not yet in force* (W) |
| | (3) | 18 Dec 2015 (in so far as inserts Water Industry Act 1991, ss 51CD–51CG) (SI 2015/1938) |
| | | 1 Apr 2017 (in so far as substitutes Water Industry Act 1991, s 51B(6), so far as it confers power on the Secretary of State to make regulations or make provision in relation to the exercise of that power, and inserts s 51CB thereof) (SI 2017/462) |
| | | 1 Oct 2017 (otherwise) (E) (SI 2017/462)[9] |
| | | *Not yet in force* (otherwise) (W) |
| | (4) | 1 Oct 2017 (E) (SI 2017/462) |
| | | *Not yet in force* (W) |
| 11 | (1) | See sub-ss (2)–(5) below |
| | (2) | 1 Oct 2017 (E) (SI 2017/462)[9] |
| | | *Not yet in force* (W) |
| | (3) | 18 Dec 2015 (in so far as inserts Water Industry Act 1991, ss 105ZF–105ZI) (SI 2015/1938) |

**Water Act 2014 (c 21)**—*contd*

|  |  |  |
|---|---|---|
|  |  | 1 Apr 2017 (in so far as inserts Water Industry Act 1991, s 105ZD) (SI 2017/462) |
|  |  | 1 Oct 2017 (otherwise) (E) (SI 2017/462)[9] |
|  |  | *Not yet in force* (W) |
|  | (4), (5) | 1 Oct 2017 (E) (SI 2017/462) |
|  |  | *Not yet in force* (W) |
| 12 |  | *Not yet in force* |
| 13 |  | 14 Jul 2014 (s 94(2)(b)) |
| 14 | (1) | 18 Dec 2015 (SI 2015/1938) |
|  | (2) | 6 Apr 2015 (in so far as inserts Water Industry Act 1991, s 33C) (SI 2015/773) |
|  |  | 18 Dec 2015 (otherwise) (SI 2015/1938) |
|  | (3) | 18 Dec 2015 (SI 2015/1938) |
| 15 |  | 14 Jul 2014 (s 94(2)(c)) |
| 16 | (1) | 1 Nov 2015 (SI 2015/1469) |
|  | (2) | 15 Jul 2015 (in so far as inserts Water Industry Act 1991, s 143C, except sub-s (8) thereof) (SI 2015/1469)[3] |
|  |  | 1 Nov 2015 (otherwise) (SI 2015/1469)[3] |
| 17 |  | 6 Apr 2015 (in so far as inserts Water Industry Act 1991, s 144ZD) (SI 2015/773) |
|  |  | 15 Jul 2015 (in so far as inserts Water Industry Act 1991, s 144ZB, except sub-s (3)(e) thereof in so far as relates to sewerage licences and sub-s (8) thereof) (SI 2015/1469)[3] |
|  |  | 1 Apr 2016 (otherwise) (E) (SI 2016/465)[6] |
|  |  | 15 Dec 2017 (otherwise) (W) (SI 2017/1288) |
| 18–20 |  | 1 Apr 2018 (SI 2017/462)[9] |
| 21 |  | 14 Jul 2014 (s 94(2)(d)) |
| 22 |  | 14 Jul 2014 (in so far as relating to water or sewerage undertakers whose areas are wholly or mainly in England) (s 94(2)(e)) |
|  |  | 18 Dec 2015 (otherwise) (SI 2015/1938) |
| 23 |  | 1 Jan 2015 (E) (except in so far as it relates to sewerage licensees in Water Industry Act 1991, s 2(3)(ba)(ii)) (SI 2014/3320)[1] |
|  |  | 6 Apr 2015 (W) (except in so far as it relates to sewerage licensees in Water Industry Act 1991, s 2(3)(ba)(ii)) (SI 205/773)[2] |
|  |  | 1 Apr 2016 (exception noted above) (SI 2016/465)[6] |
| 24 |  | 6 Apr 2015 (SI 2015/773)[2] |
| 25 | (1), (2) | 1 Apr 2016 (SI 2016/465)[6] |
|  | (3) | 14 Jul 2014 (s 94(2)(f)) |
|  | (4) | 1 Apr 2016 (SI 2016/465)[6] |
| 26–28 |  | 14 Jul 2014 (s 94(2)(g)) |
| 29 | (1) | 1 Nov 2016 (SI 2016/1007) |
|  | (2) | See sub-ss (3)–(6) below |
|  | (3), (4) | 1 Nov 2016 (SI 2016/1007) |
|  | (5) | 1 Jan 2015 (except in so far as it relates to Water Industry Act 1991, s 38A(2A)) (SI 2014/3320) |
|  |  | 1 Nov 2016 (exception noted above) (SI 2016/1007) |
|  | (6) | 1 Nov 2016 (SI 2016/1007) |
|  | (7) | 15 Jul 2015 (SI 2015/1469)[3] |
| 30 | (1) | 1 Nov 2016 (SI 2016/1007) |
|  | (2) | See sub-ss (3)–(6) below |
|  | (3), (4) | 1 Nov 2016 (SI 2016/1007) |
|  | (5) | 1 Jan 2015 (except in so far as it relates to Water Industry Act 1991, s 95A(2A)) (SI 2014/3320) |
|  |  | 1 Nov 2016 (exception noted above) (SI 2016/1007) |
|  | (6) | 1 Nov 2016 (SI 2016/1007) |
|  | (7) | 15 Jul 2015 (SI 2015/1469)[3] |
| 31 |  | 1 Apr 2017 (SI 2017/462) |
| 32 |  | 6 Mar 2017 (in so far as inserts Water Industry Act 1991, s 110K) (SI 2017/58)[8] |
|  |  | 1 Apr 2017 (otherwise) (SI 2017/462) |

**Water Act 2014 (c 21)**—*contd*

| | | |
|---|---|---|
| 33 | | 14 Jul 2014 (s 94(2)(h)) |
| 34 | (1) | See sub-ss (2), (3) below |
| | (2) | 14 Jul 2014 (s 94(2)(i)) |
| | (3) | 1 Sep 2016 (in so far as inserts Water Industry Act 1991, s 195(3D)(b), (d)) (SI 2016/465)[6] |
| | | *Not yet in force* (otherwise) |
| 35, 36 | | 14 Jul 2014 (s 94(2)(j)) |
| 37 | | 1 Apr 2016 (SI 2016/465)[6] |
| 38 | | 1 Jan 2015 (E) (except in so far as it relates to sewerage licensees in Water Industry Act 1991, s 144ZE(9)(e)) (SI 2014/3320)[1] |
| | | 6 Apr 2015 (W) (except in so far as it relates to sewerage licensees in Water Industry Act 1991, s 144ZE(9)(e)) (SI 2015/773)[2] |
| | | 1 Apr 2016 (exception noted above) (E) (SI 2016/465)[6] |
| | | 15 Dec 2017 (exception noted above) (W) (SI 2017/1288) |
| 39 | | *Not yet in force* |
| 40 | (1) | 14 Jul 2014 (SI 2014/1823) |
| | (2)(a) | *Not yet in force* |
| | (2)(b) | 1 Nov 2016 (SI 2016/1007) |
| 41 | | 1 Nov 2015 (W) (SI 2015/1786)[4] |
| | | *Not yet in force* (E) |
| 42–49 | | 6 Apr 2015 (SI 2015/773) |
| 50 | | *Not yet in force* |
| 51, 52 | | 6 Apr 2015 (SI 2015/773) |
| 53 | | 6 Apr 2015 (SI 2015/773)[2] |
| 54 | | *Not yet in force* |
| 55 | | 1 Jan 2015 (SI 2014/3320) |
| 56 | | See Sch 7 below |
| 57, 58 | | 14 Jul 2014 (s 94(2)(k), (l)) |
| 59 | | 1 Oct 2014 (SI 2014/1823) |
| 60–63 | | 14 Jul 2014 (s 94(2)(m)–(o)) |
| 64–68 | | 1 Jan 2015 (SI 2014/3320) |
| 69 | | 14 May 2014 (in so far as relating to the power to disclose information under sub-s (1)(a)) (s 94(1)(1)) |
| | | 1 Jan 2015 (otherwise) (SI 2014/3320) |
| 70–81 | | *Not yet in force* |
| 82 | (1)–(5) | 1 Jan 2015 (SI 2014/3320) |
| | (6) | *Not yet in force* |
| | (7) | 1 Jan 2015 (in so far as it relates to sub-s (5) above) (SI 2014/3320) |
| | | *Not yet in force* (otherwise) |
| | (8) | *Not yet in force* |
| 83, 84 | | 1 Jan 2015 (SI 2014/3320) |
| 85–89 | | 14 Jul 2014 (s 94(2)(p)–(r)) |
| 90–95 | | 14 May 2014 (s 94(1)(b)–(f)) |
| Sch 1 | | 1 Jan 2016 (SI 2015/1938) |
| Sch 2 | para 1 | 1 Apr 2017 (so far as substitutes Water Industry Act 1991, ss 66A, 66AA, 66C) (SI 2017/462)[9] |
| | | *Not yet in force* (otherwise) |
| | para 2 | 1 Apr 2017 (except so far as relates to Water Industry Act 1991, s 66CA(1)(c), (2), (3)) (SI 2017/462) |
| | | *Not yet in force* (exception noted above) |
| | para 3 | 1 Apr 2017 (SI 2017/462)[9] |
| | para 4 | 1 Sep 2015 (in so far as inserts Water Industry Act 1991, s 66DB, except sub-ss (1)(b), (3), (12) thereof) (SI 2015/773)[2] |
| | | 1 Sep 2015 (in so far as inserts Water Industry Act 1991, s 66DB(3)) (SI 2015/1469)[3] |
| | | 1 Apr 2016 (in so far as inserts Water Industry Act 1991, s 66DB(1)(b)) (SI 2016/465)[6] |
| | | 30 Mar 2017 (otherwise) (SI 2017/462) |

**Water Act 2014 (c 21)**—*contd*

|  |  |  |
|---|---|---|
| | para 5 | 1 Sep 2015 (in so far as inserts Water Industry Act 1991, s 66EB, except sub-s (8) thereof) (SI 2015/1469)[3] |
| | | 1 Sep 2016 (in so far as substitutes Water Industry Act 1991, s 66E, in relation to rules about charges that may be imposed by a water undertaker under a s 66D agreement where a water supply licensee with a retail authorisation or a restricted retail authorisation is a party to that agreement) (SI 2016/465)[6] |
| | | 1 Sep 2016 (in so far as inserts Water Industry Act 1991, ss 66EA, 66EB(8), 66EC, 66ED) (SI 2016/465)[6] |
| | | 1 Apr 2017 (otherwise) (SI 2017/462) |
| | paras 6–8 | 1 Apr 2017 (SI 2017/462) |
| | para 9(1) | See sub-paras 9(2)–(5) below |
| | para 9(2), (3) | 1 Apr 2016 (SI 2016/465)[6] |
| | para 9(4), (5) | 1 Apr 2017 (SI 2017/462) |
| Sch 3 | | 1 Jan 2016 (SI 2015/1938) |
| Sch 4 | | 1 Sep 2015 (in so far as inserts Water Industry Act 1991, s 117G, except sub-ss (2)(e), (7) thereof) (SI 2015/773) |
| | | 1 Sep 2015 (in so far as inserts Water Industry Act 1991, s 117K, except sub-ss (2)(e), (8) thereof) (SI 2015/1469) |
| | | 1 Apr 2016 (in so far as inserts Water Industry Act 1991, ss 117G(2)(e), 117P(4), 117R, 117S) (SI 2016/465)[6] |
| | | 1 Sep 2016 (in so far as inserts Water Industry Act 1991, ss 117I (so far as relates to rules about charges that may be imposed by a sewerage undertaker under a s 117E agreement where a sewerage licensee with a retail authorisation is a party to that agreement), 117J, 117K(2)(e), (8), 117L) (SI 2016/465)[6] |
| | | 30 Mar 2017 (in so far as inserts Water Industry Act 1991, ss 117F, 117G (so far as not already in force), 117H) (SI 2017/462) |
| | | 1 Apr 2017 (in so far as inserts Water Industry Act 1991, ss 117A, 117B, 117E, so far as it relates to ss 117A, 117B, s 117M, 117P, so far as not already in force) (SI 2017/462) |
| | | *Not yet in force* (otherwise) |
| Sch 5 | | *Not yet in force* |
| Sch 6 | | 1 Apr 2016 (SI 2016/465)[6] |
| Sch 7 | para 1 | 1 Apr 2016 (SI 2016/465)[6] |
| | para 2 | See paras 3–123 below |
| | para 3(1) | See sub-paras 3(2)–(8) below |
| | para 3(2) | 1 Nov 2016 (SI 2016/1007) |
| | para 3(3) | 1 Apr 2016 (SI 2016/465)[6] |
| | para 3(4), (5) | 1 Apr 2017 (SI 2017/462) |
| | para 3(6), (7) | 1 Apr 2016 (SI 2016/465)[6] |
| | para 3(8) | 1 Jul 2015 (so far as relates to Water Industry Act 1991, ss 39ZA, 39D, 40J, 96ZA, 143C, 144ZB, 144ZD–144ZF and Water Act 2014, ss 42–47, 49, 51–53) (SI 2015/1469) |
| | | 1 Sep 2015 (in so far as relates to Water Industry Act 1991, ss 66DB, 66EB, 117G, 117K) (SI 2015/1469) |
| | | 1 Nov 2015 (in so far as relates to Water Industry Act 1991, ss 143B, 143D, 143E) (SI 2015/1469) |
| | | 18 Dec 2015 (in so far as relates to Water Industry Act 1991, ss 51CD–51CG, 105ZF–105ZI) (SI 2015/1938) |
| | | 1 Apr 2016 (in so far as relates to Water Industry Act 1991, ss 117R, 117S, 144ZA, 144ZC) (SI 2016/465)[6] |
| | | 1 Sep 2016 (in so far as relates to Water Industry Act 1991, ss 66E, 66EA, 66EC, 66ED, 117I, 117J, 117L) (SI 2016/465)[6] |
| | | 1 Nov 2016 (in so far as relates to Water Industry Act 1991, ss 38ZA, 40I, 95ZA, 110J) (SI 2016/1007) |
| | | 1 Apr 2017 (otherwise) (SI 2017/462) |
| | paras 4–6 | 1 Apr 2016 (SI 2016/465)[6] |
| | para 7 | 1 Nov 2016 (SI 2016/1007) |
| | para 8 | 14 Jul 2014 (s 94(2)(s)) |

**Water Act 2014 (c 21)**—*contd*

| | |
|---|---|
| para 9 | 1 Apr 2016 (SI 2016/465)[6] |
| para 10(1) | See sub-paras (2)–(4) below |
| para 10(2), (3) | 1 Apr 2017 (SI 2017/462) |
| para 10(4) | 1 Apr 2016 (SI 2016/465)[6] |
| para 11 | 1 Jan 2016 (SI 2015/1938) |
| para 12(1) | See sub-paras (2)–(11) below |
| para 12(2) | 1 Jan 2016 (SI 2015/1938) |
| para 12(3) | 1 Apr 2016 (SI 2016/465)[6] |
| para 12(4)–(11) | 1 Apr 2017 (SI 2017/462) |
| para 13 | 1 Jan 2016 (SI 2015/1938) |
| para 14 | 1 Apr 2016 (SI 2016/465)[6] |
| para 15(1) | See sub-para (2)–(5) below |
| para 15(2) | 1 Apr 2016 (SI 2016/465)[6] |
| para 15(3) | 1 Jan 2016 (SI 2015/1938) |
| para 15(4)(a) | 1 Jan 2016 (SI 2015/1938) |
| para 15(4)(b) | 1 Apr 2016 (SI 2016/465)[6] |
| para 15(4)(c), (d) | 1 Jan 2016 (SI 2015/1938) |
| para 15(5) | 1 Jan 2016 (SI 2015/1938) |
| paras 16–18 | 1 Jan 2016 (SI 2015/1938) |
| paras 19–34 | 1 Apr 2016 (SI 2016/465)[6] |
| para 35(1) | See sub-paras (2)–(10) below |
| para 35(2) | 1 Apr 2017 (except as it relates to qualifying sewerage licensees) (SI 2017/462) |
| | *Not yet in force* (exception noted above) |
| para 35(3) | 1 Apr 2017 (SI 2017/462) |
| para 35(4)–(6) | *Not yet in force* |
| para 35(7) | 1 Apr 2017 (so far as substitutes Water Industry Act 1991, s 23(4)(b)(i)) (SI 2017/462) |
| | *Not yet in force* (otherwise) |
| para 35(8), (9) | 1 Apr 2017 (SI 2017/462) |
| para 35(10) | *Not yet in force* |
| paras 36–38 | 1 Apr 2017 (except as they relate to qualifying sewerage licensees) (SI 2017/462) |
| | *Not yet in force* (exception noted above) |
| paras 39–53 | 1 Apr 2016 (SI 2016/465)[6] |
| paras 54–57 | 1 Apr 2018 (so far as they relate to a water undertaker whose area is wholly or mainly in England) (SI 2017/462) |
| | *Not yet in force* (otherwise) |
| paras 58–61 | 1 Apr 2017 (SI 2017/462) |
| paras 62, 63 | 1 Apr 2016 (SI 2016/465)[6] |
| para 64 | 6 Mar 2017 (SI 2017/58)[8] |
| paras 65–72 | 1 Apr 2016 (SI 2016/465)[6] |
| para 73 | 1 Apr 2017 (SI 2017/462) |
| para 74(1) | See sub-paras (2), (3) below |
| para 74(2) | 1 Apr 2016 (SI 2016/465)[6] |
| para 74(3) | 1 Apr 2017 (SI 2017/462) |
| paras 75–84 | 1 Apr 2016 (SI 2016/465)[6] |
| para 85 | 1 Apr 2017 (SI 2017/462) |
| para 86 | 1 Apr 2016 (SI 2016/465)[6] |
| paras 87, 88 | 1 Apr 2018 (so far as they relate to a sewerage undertaker whose area is wholly or mainly in England) (SI 2017/462)[9] |
| | *Not yet in force* (otherwise) |
| para 89(a) | 1 Apr 2018 (SI 2017/462) |
| para 89(b) | 1 Apr 2018 (so far as it relates to a sewerage undertaker whose area is wholly or mainly in England) (SI 2017/462)[9] |
| | *Not yet in force* (otherwise) |
| para 90 | 1 Apr 2017 (so far as relates to a retail authorisation) (SI 2017/462) |
| | *Not yet in force* (otherwise) |
| para 91 | *Not yet in force* |

**Water Act 2014 (c 21)**—*contd*

| | |
|---|---|
| para 92 | 1 Oct 2017 (so far as it relates to a sewerage undertaker whose area is wholly or mainly in England) (SI 2017/462)[9] |
| | *Not yet in force* (otherwise) |
| para 93 | 1 Apr 2017 (so far as relates to a retail authorisation) (SI 2017/462) |
| | *Not yet in force* (otherwise) |
| para 94 | *Not yet in force* |
| para 95 | 1 Oct 2017 (so far as it relates to a sewerage undertaker whose area is wholly or mainly in England) (SI 2017/462) |
| | *Not yet in force* (otherwise) |
| para 96 | 1 Apr 2017 (SI 2017/462) |
| para 97 | 1 Jan 2015 (SI 2014/3320) |
| para 98(1) | See sub-paras (2)–(4) below |
| para 98(2) | 1 Oct 2017 (so far as it relates to a sewerage undertaker whose area is wholly or mainly in England) (SI 2017/462) |
| | *Not yet in force* (otherwise) |
| para 98(3), (4) | 1 Apr 2017 (SI 2017/462) |
| para 99 | 1 Apr 2016 (SI 2016/465)[6] |
| para 100 | 1 Apr 2017 (SI 2017/462) |
| paras 101–103 | 1 Apr 2016 (SI 2016/465)[6] |
| para 104 | *Not yet in force* |
| para 105(1) | See sub-paras 105(2)–(4) below |
| para 105(2)(a) | 1 Apr 2016 (SI 2016/465)[6] |
| para 105(2)(b), (3), (4) | 1 Apr 2017 (SI 2017/462) |
| para 106 | *Not yet in force* |
| para 107 | 14 Jul 2014 (s 94(2)(t)) |
| para 108(1) | See sub-paras 108(2)–(7) below |
| para 108(2), (3) | 1 Apr 2016 (SI 2016/465)[6] |
| para 108(4)(a)–(c) | 1 Apr 2016 (SI 2016/465)[6] |
| para 108(4)(d) | 1 Apr 2017 (SI 2017/462) |
| para 108(5)–(7) | 1 Apr 2016 (SI 2016/465)[6] |
| paras 109, 110 | 1 Apr 2016 (SI 2016/465)[6] |
| para 111 | 1 Apr 2017 (SI 2017/462) |
| para 112(1) | See sub-paras 112(2), (3) below |
| para 112(2) | 1 Apr 2017 (SI 2017/462) |
| para 112(3) | 1 Apr 2016 (SI 2016/465)[6] |
| paras 113, 114 | 1 Apr 2016 (SI 2016/465)[6] |
| para 115(a) | 1 Apr 2017 (SI 2017/462) |
| para 115(b) | 1 Apr 2016 (SI 2016/465)[6] |
| para 115(c) | 1 Apr 2017 (SI 2017/462) |
| paras 116, 117 | 1 Apr 2016 (SI 2016/465)[6] |
| para 118 | 1 Apr 2017 (SI 2017/462) |
| para 119(1) | See sub-paras (2)–(4) below |
| para 119(2), (3) | *Not yet in force* |
| para 119(4) | 1 Nov 2016 (SI 2016/1007) |
| para 120(1) | See sub-paras (2), (3) below |
| para 120(2)(a) | 1 Apr 2016 (SI 2016/465)[6] |
| para 120(2)(b) | 1 Jan 2015 (SI 2014/3320) |
| para 120(2)(c)–(f) | 1 Apr 2016 (SI 2016/465)[6] |
| para 120(3) | 1 Jan 2015 (in so far as it relates to Water Industry Act 1991, ss 8, 86ZA) (SI 2014/3320) |
| | 1 Nov 2016 (in so far as relates to Water Industry Act 1991, ss 17AA, 66DB) (SI 2016/1007) |
| | 1 Apr 2017 (in so far as relates to Water Industry Act 1991, ss 51CA, 51CB) (SI 2017/462) |
| | *Not yet in force* (otherwise) |
| paras 121, 122 | 1 Apr 2016 (SI 2016/465)[6] |
| para 123 | 1 Apr 2017 (SI 2017/462) |
| paras 124–127 | 1 Apr 2016 (SI 2016/465)[6] |

**Water Act 2014 (c 21)**—*contd*

|  |  |  |
|---|---|---|
| paras 128–130 | 1 Apr 2017 (SI 2017/462) |
| para 131 | See paras 132–134 below |
| para 132 | *Not yet in force* |
| paras 133, 134 | 1 Apr 2016 (SI 2016/465)[6] |
| para 135 | 1 Apr 2016 (SI 2016/465)[6] |
| paras 136–142 | 1 Apr 2017 (SI 2017/462) |
| para 143 | See paras 144–147 below |
| para 144 | 1 Apr 2016 (SI 2016/465)[6] |
| paras 145, 146 | *Not yet in force* |
| para 147 | 18 Dec 2015 (SI 2015/1938) |
| Sch 8 | 14 Jul 2014 (s 94(2)(n)) |
| Sch 9 | 14 Jul 2014 (SI 2014/1823) |
| Sch 10 | 14 Jul 2014 (s 94(2)(r)) |
| Schs 11, 12 | 14 May 2014 (s 94(1)(c), (e)) |

[1] For transitional provisions, see SI 2014/3320, art 3

[2] For transitional provisions, see SI 2015/773, arts 4–6

[3] For transitional provisions, see SI 2015/1469, art 5

[4] For a transitional provision, see SI 2015/1786, art 3

[5] For transitional provisions, see SI 2015/1938, art 4

[6] For transitional and saving provisions, see SI 2016/465, art 4, Sch 2

[7] For transitional and saving provisions, see SI 2016/1007, arts 3, 4

[8] For transitional provisions, see SI 2017/58, art 3

[9] For transitional provisions, see SI 2017/462, arts 6–15

# 2015 Acts

## Air Weapons and Licensing (Scotland) Act 2015 (asp 10)

*RA:* 4 Aug 2015

*Commencement provisions*: s 88; Air Weapons and Licensing (Scotland) Act 2015 (Commencement No 1) Order 2015, SSI 2015/382; Air Weapons and Licensing (Scotland) Act 2015 (Commencement No 2 and Transitional Provisions) Order 2016, SSI 2016/85; Air Weapons and Licensing (Scotland) Act 2015 (Commencement No 3 and Transitional Provisions) Order 2016, SSI 2016/130; Air Weapons and Licensing (Scotland) Act 2015 (Commencement No 4, Transitional and Saving Provisions) Order 2016, SSI 2016/132; Air Weapons and Licensing (Scotland) Act 2015 (Commencement No 5 and Saving Provisions) Order 2016, SSI 2016/307; Air Weapons and Licensing (Scotland) Act 2015 (Commencement No 6 and Saving Provisions) Order 2017, SSI 2017/119; Air Weapons and Licensing (Scotland) Act 2015 (Commencement No 7) Order 2017, SSI 2017/424; Criminal Justice and Licensing (Scotland) Act 2010 (Commencement No 15 and Saving Provision) and the Air Weapons and Licensing (Scotland) Act 2015 (Commencement No 8) Order 2018, SSI 2018/102; Air Weapons and Licensing (Scotland) Act 2015 (Commencement No 9 and Transitional Provisions) Order 2019, SSI 2019/99

| | | |
|---|---|---|
| 1 | | 1 Dec 2015 (SSI 2015/382) |
| 2 | (1), (2) | 31 Dec 2016 (SSI 2016/130)[2] |
| | (3) | See Sch 1 below |
| | (4) | 1 Dec 2015 (SSI 2015/382) |
| 3–5 | | 1 Jul 2016 (for the purpose of enabling advance applications for the grant of an air weapon certificate to be made, registered and determined and enabling such certificates to be granted (and, if required, to be subsequently varied or revoked) before 31 Dec 2016) (SSI 2016/130)[2] |
| | | 31 Dec 2016 (otherwise) (SSI 2016/130)[2] |
| 6 | (1)–(3) | 1 Jul 2016 (for the purpose of enabling advance applications for the grant of an air weapon certificate to be made, registered and determined and enabling such certificates to be granted (and, if required, to be subsequently varied or revoked) before 31 Dec 2016) (SSI 2016/130)[2] |
| | | 31 Dec 2016 (otherwise) (SSI 2016/130)[2] |
| | (4), (5) | 31 Dec 2016 (SSI 2016/130)[2] |
| 7 | | 1 Jul 2016 (for the purpose of enabling advance applications for the grant of an air weapon certificate to be made, registered and determined and enabling such certificates to be granted (and, if required, to be subsequently varied or revoked) before 31 Dec 2016) (SSI 2016/130)[2] |
| | | 31 Dec 2016 (otherwise) (SSI 2016/130)[2] |
| 8 | (1) | 1 Jul 2016 (for the purpose of enabling advance applications for the grant of an air weapon certificate to be made, registered and determined and enabling such certificates to be granted (and, if required, to be subsequently varied or revoked) before 31 Dec 2016) (SSI 2016/130)[2] |
| | | 31 Dec 2016 (otherwise) (SSI 2016/130)[2] |
| | (2), (3) | 31 Dec 2016 (SSI 2016/130)[2] |

**Air Weapons and Licensing (Scotland) Act 2015 (asp 10)**—*contd*

| | | |
|---|---|---|
| 9 | (1), (2) | 1 Jul 2016 (for the purpose of enabling advance applications for the grant of an air weapon certificate to be made, registered and determined and enabling such certificates to be granted (and, if required, to be subsequently varied or revoked) before 31 Dec 2016) (SSI 2016/130)[2] |
| | | 31 Dec 2016 (otherwise) (SSI 2016/130)[2] |
| | (3), (4) | 31 Dec 2016 (SSI 2016/130)[2] |
| 10 | | 1 Jul 2016 (for the purpose of enabling advance applications for the grant of an air weapon certificate to be made, registered and determined and enabling such certificates to be granted (and, if required, to be subsequently varied or revoked) before 31 Dec 2016) (SSI 2016/130)[2] |
| | | 31 Dec 2016 (otherwise) (SSI 2016/130)[2] |
| 11 | (1)–(4) | 1 Jul 2016 (for the purpose of enabling advance applications for the grant of an air weapon certificate to be made, registered and determined and enabling such certificates to be granted (and, if required, to be subsequently varied or revoked) before 31 Dec 2016) (SSI 2016/130)[2] |
| | | 31 Dec 2016 (otherwise) (SSI 2016/130)[2] |
| | (5), (6) | 31 Dec 2016 (SSI 2016/130)[2] |
| | (7) | 1 Jul 2016 (for the purpose of enabling advance applications for the grant of an air weapon certificate to be made, registered and determined and enabling such certificates to be granted (and, if required, to be subsequently varied or revoked) before 31 Dec 2016) (SSI 2016/130)[2] |
| | | 31 Dec 2016 (otherwise) (SSI 2016/130)[2] |
| 12–14 | | 1 Jul 2016 (for the purpose of enabling advance applications for the grant of a police permit, visitor permit or event permit to be made and determined and enabling such permits to be granted (and, if required, to be subsequently varied or revoked) before 31 Dec 2016) (SSI 2016/130)[2] |
| | | 31 Dec 2016 (otherwise) (SSI 2016/130)[2] |
| 15 | (1)–(3) | 1 Jul 2016 (for the purpose of enabling advance applications for the grant of a police permit, visitor permit or event permit to be made and determined and enabling such permits to be granted (and, if required, to be subsequently varied or revoked) before 31 Dec 2016) (SSI 2016/130)[2] |
| | | 31 Dec 2016 (otherwise) (SSI 2016/130)[2] |
| | (4), (5) | 31 Dec 2016 (SSI 2016/130)[2] |
| 16 | (1)–(5) | 1 Jul 2016 (for the purpose of enabling advance applications for the grant of a police permit, visitor permit or event permit to be made and determined and enabling such permits to be granted (and, if required, to be subsequently varied or revoked) before 31 Dec 2016) (SSI 2016/130)[2] |
| | | 31 Dec 2016 (otherwise) (SSI 2016/130)[2] |
| | (6), (7) | 31 Dec 2016 (SSI 2016/130)[2] |
| | (8) | 1 Jul 2016 (for the purpose of enabling advance applications for the grant of a police permit, visitor permit or event permit to be made and determined and enabling such permits to be granted (and, if required, to be subsequently varied or revoked) before 31 Dec 2016) (SSI 2016/130)[2] |
| | | 31 Dec 2016 (otherwise) (SSI 2016/130)[2] |
| 17 | (1), (2) | 1 Jul 2016 (for the purpose of enabling advance applications for the grant of a police permit, visitor permit or event permit to be made and determined and enabling such permits to be granted (and, if required, to be subsequently varied or revoked) before 31 Dec 2016) (SSI 2016/130)[2] |
| | | 31 Dec 2016 (otherwise) (SSI 2016/130)[2] |
| | (3)–(5) | 31 Dec 2016 (SSI 2016/130)[2] |

**Air Weapons and Licensing (Scotland) Act 2015 (asp 10)**—*contd*

| | | |
|---|---|---|
| | (6), (7) | 1 Jul 2016 (for the purpose of enabling advance applications for the grant of a police permit, visitor permit or event permit to be made and determined and enabling such permits to be granted (and, if required, to be subsequently varied or revoked) before 31 Dec 2016) (SSI 2016/130)[2] |
| | | 31 Dec 2016 (otherwise) (SSI 2016/130)[2] |
| 18–22 | | 1 Jul 2016 (SSI 2016/130)[2] |
| 23–27 | | 31 Dec 2016 (SSI 2016/130)[2] |
| 28 | | 1 Jul 2016 (SSI 2016/130)[2] |
| 29, 30 | | 31 Dec 2016 (SSI 2016/130)[2] |
| 31 | (1) | 1 Jul 2016 (SSI 2016/130)[2] |
| | (2) | 31 Dec 2016 (SSI 2016/130)[2] |
| | (3) | 1 Jul 2016 (SSI 2016/130)[2] |
| 32, 33 | | 1 Jul 2016 (SSI 2016/130)[2] |
| 34 | (1) | 1 Jul 2016 (SSI 2016/130)[2] |
| | (2)(a)–(m) | 1 Jul 2016 (SSI 2016/130)[2] |
| | (2)(n) | 31 Dec 2016 (SSI 2016/130)[2] |
| | (3)–(8) | 1 Jul 2016 (SSI 2016/130)[2] |
| 35 | (1), (2) | 1 Dec 2015 (SSI 2015/382) |
| | (3) | 1 Jul 2016 (SSI 2016/130)[2] |
| | (4) | 1 Dec 2015 (SSI 2015/382) |
| 36 | | 1 Dec 2015 (SSI 2015/382) |
| 37 | | 1 Jul 2016 (SSI 2016/130)[2] |
| 38 | | 31 Dec 2016 (SSI 2016/130)[2] |
| 39 | (1) | 1 Jul 2016 (SSI 2016/130)[2] |
| | (2), (3) | 1 Dec 2015 (SSI 2015/382) |
| | (4)–(10) | 31 Dec 2016 (SSI 2016/130)[2] |
| 40 | | 1 Dec 2015 (SSI 2015/382) |
| 41 | | 15 May 2017 (SSI 2017/119) |
| 42 | | 30 Sep 2016 (SSI 2016/132)[2] |
| 43–48 | | 15 May 2017 (SSI 2017/119)[4] |
| 49 | | *Not yet in force* |
| 50, 51 | | 15 May 2017 (SSI 2017/119)[4] |
| 52 | | *Not yet in force* |
| 5, 54 | | 15 May 2017 (SSI 2017/119) |
| 55 | | 30 Sep 2016 (SSI 2016/132)[2] |
| 56 | | 1 Dec 2015 (for the purpose of making regulations under Licensing (Scotland) Act 2005, ss 9A(6), 9B(5)) (SSI 2015/382) |
| | | 15 May 2017 (for the purpose of inserting Licensing (Scotland) Act 2005, s 9B and amending s 146 thereof) (SSI 2017/119) |
| | | 20 Dec 2017 (otherwise) (SSI 2017/424) |
| 57, 58 | | 15 May 2017 (SSI 2017/119) |
| 59 | | 29 Jun 2018 (SSI 2018/102) |
| 60 | (1), (2) | 5 Aug 2015 (s 88(1)) |
| | (3)–(5) | 15 May 2017 (SSI 2017/119) |
| 61 | | *Not yet in force* |
| 62 | | 15 May 2017 (SSI 2017/119) |
| 63 | | 1 May 2017 (SSI 2016/307) |
| 64 | | 1 Nov 2016 (SSI 2016/307) |
| 65 | (1), (2) | 1 Dec 2015 (SSI 2015/382) |
| | (3) | *Not yet in force* |
| | (4), (5) | 1 Dec 2015 (SSI 2015/382) |
| 66, 67 | | 1 Sep 2016 (SSI 2016/85)[1] |
| 68, 69 | | 1 Sep 2016 (SSI 2016/85) |
| 70 | (1) | 1 Dec 2015 (SSI 2015/382) |
| | (2) | 1 Sep 2016 (SSI 2016/85) |
| | (3) | 1 Dec 2015 (SSI 2015/382) |
| | (4) | 1 Sep 2016 (SSI 2016/85) |
| 71 | | 1 Nov 2016 (SSI 2016/307) |

**Air Weapons and Licensing (Scotland) Act 2015 (asp 10)**—*contd*

| | | |
|---|---|---|
| 72 | | 16 Mar 2016 (for the purpose of enabling applications for metal dealer licences or itinerant metal dealer licences to be made, considered and determined in accordance with the provisions of Civic Government (Scotland) Act 1982 by the licensing authority or any other person or appealed to and decided by the Courts before 1 Sep 2016; and for enabling such licences to be granted and for the provisions of the 1982 Act to apply to any such licence so far as the notification of changes, alteration of circumstances or the variation or suspension of the licences are concerned, which arise before 1 Sep 2016) (SSI 2016/85)[1] |
| | | 1 Sep 2016 (otherwise) (SSI 2016/85)[1] |
| 73 | | 1 Dec 2015 (SSI 2015/382) |
| 74 | (1) | 26 Apr 2019 (SSI 2019/99)[5] |
| | (2)–(6) | 27 Jan 2021 (SSI 2019/99)[5] |
| 75 | | 1 Nov 2016 (SSI 2016/307)[3] |
| 76 | (1) | 1 Dec 2015 (SSI 2015/382) |
| | (2) | 26 Apr 2019 (SSI 2019/99) |
| | (3) | 1 Dec 2015 (SSI 2015/382) |
| | (4) | 26 Apr 2019 (SSI 2019/99)[5] |
| 77 | | 1 May 2017 (SSI 2016/307)[3] |
| 78 | | 1 Nov 2016 (SSI 2016/307)[3] |
| 79 | | 1 Dec 2015 (SSI 2015/382) |
| 80 | (1), (2) | 1 Dec 2015 (SSI 2015/382) |
| | (3) | 1 Nov 2016 (SSI 2016/307) |
| 81 | | 1 Nov 2016 (SSI 2016/307) |
| 82 | | 1 May 2017 (SSI 2016/307) |
| 83 | | 1 Nov 2016 (SSI 2016/307) |
| 84–86 | | 5 Aug 2015 (s 88(1)) |
| 87 | | See Sch 2 below |
| 88, 89 | | 5 Aug 2015 (s 88(1)) |
| Sch 1 | | 31 Dec 2016 (SSI 2016/130)[2] |
| Sch 2 | paras 1–3 | 31 Dec 2016 (SSI 2016/130) |
| | para 4(1) | 15 May 2017 (SSI 2017/119) |
| | para 4(2) | *Not yet in force* |
| | para 4(3) | 15 May 2017 (SSI 2017/119) |
| | para 4(4) | *Not yet in force* |
| | para 4(5) | 15 May 2017 (SSI 2017/119) |
| | para 4(6) | *Not yet in force* |
| | para 4(7) | 15 May 2017 (SSI 2017/119) |
| | para 5 | 20 Dec 2017 (SSI 2017/424) |

[1] For transitional provisions, see SSI 2016/85, arts 3–6

[2] For transitional and saving provisions, see SSI 2016/132, arts 3, 4

[3] For saving provisions, see SSI 2016/307, arts 3–5

[4] For saving provisions, see SSI 2017/119, arts 3–5

[5] For transitional provisions, see SSI 2019/99, art 3

**Armed Forces (Service Complaints and Financial Assistance) Act 2015 (c 19)**

*RA:* 26 Mar 2015

*Commencement provisions*: s 7; Armed Forces (Service Complaints and Financial Assistance) Act 2015 (Commencement) Regulations 2015, SI 2015/1957

| | |
|---|---|
| 1–3 | 1 Jan 2016 (SI 2015/1957) |
| 4–8 | 26 Mar 2015 (s 7(3)) |
| Schedule | 1 Jan 2016 (SI 2015/1957) |

## British Sign Language (Scotland) Act 2015 (asp 11)

*RA:* 22 Oct 2015

*Commencement provisions:* s 8

Whole Act in force 23 Oct 2015 (s 8)

---

## Budget (Scotland) Act 2015 (asp 2)

*RA:* 11 Mar 2015

*Commencement provisions:* s 10

Whole Act in force 12 Mar 2015 (s 10)

---

## Care of Churches and Ecclesiastical Jurisdiction (Amendment) Measure 2015 (No 1)

*RA:* 12 Feb 2015

*Commencement provisions:* s 11(2); Care of Churches and Ecclesiastical Jurisdiction (Amendment) Measure 2015 (Commencement, Transitional and Saving Provisions) Order 2015, SI 2015/593

| | |
|---|---|
| 1–10 | 1 Apr 2015 (SI 2015/593)[1] |
| 11 | 12 Feb 2015 (s 11(2)) |

[1]   For transitional and saving provisions, see SI 2015/593, art 3, Schedule

---

## Church of England (Pensions) (Amendment) Measure 2015 (No 3)

*RA:* 12 Feb 2015

*Commencement provisions:* s 2(4)

Whole Measure in force 12 Feb 2015 (s 2(4))

---

## Community Charge Debt (Scotland) Act 2015 (asp 3)

*RA:* 25 Mar 2015

*Commencement provisions:* s 3

Whole Act in force 25 Mar 2015 (s 3)

---

## Community Empowerment (Scotland) Act 2015 (asp 6)

*RA:* 24 Jul 2015

*Commencement provisions:* s 145; Community Empowerment (Scotland) Act 2015 (Commencement No 1) Order 2015, SSI 2015/344; Community Empowerment (Scotland) Act 2015 (Commencement No 2) Order 2015, SSI 2015/358; Community Empowerment (Scotland) Act 2015 (Commencement No 3 and Savings) Order 2015, SSI 2015/399; Community Empowerment (Scotland) Act 2015 (Commencement No 4 and Transitory Provision) Order 2016, SI 2016/363; Community Empowerment (Scotland) Act 2015 (Commencement No 5) Order 2016, SSI 2016/394; Community Empowerment (Scotland) Act 2015 (Commencement No 6) Order 2016, SI 2016/410; Community Empowerment (Scotland) Act 2015 (Commencement No 7) Order 2017, SSI 2017/40; Community Empowerment (Scotland) Act 2015 (Commencement No 8) Order 2017, SSI 2017/192; Community Empowerment (Scotland) Act 2015 (Commencement No 9) Order 2017, SSI 2017/420; Community Empowerment (Scotland) Act 2015 (Commencement No 10, Saving, Transitional and Transitory Provisions) Order 2017, SSI 2017/458; Community Empowerment (Scotland) Act 2015

**Community Empowerment (Scotland) Act 2015 (asp 6)**—*contd*
(Commencement No. 11) Order 2018, SSI 2018/139; Community Empowerment (Scotland) Act 2015 (Commencement No 12 and Saving Provision) Order 2020, SSI 2020/448

| | | |
|---|---|---|
| 1–3 | | 15 Apr 2016 (SSI 2015/399) |
| 4–8 | | 20 Dec 2016 (SSI 2016/363) |
| 9 | (1) | 20 Dec 2016 (SSI 2016/363) |
| | (2) | 13 Nov 2015 (for the purpose of making regulations) (SSI 2015/358) |
| | | 20 Dec 2016 (otherwise) (SSI 2016/363) |
| | (3), (4) | 20 Dec 2016 (SSI 2016/363) |
| | (5), (6) | 13 Nov 2015 (for the purpose of making regulations) (SSI 2015/358) |
| | | 20 Dec 2016 (otherwise) (SSI 2016/363) |
| | (7) | 20 Dec 2016 (SSI 2016/363) |
| 10–14 | | 20 Dec 2016 (SSI 2016/363) |
| 15 | | 13 Nov 2015 (for the purpose of issuing guidance for the purposes of Pt 2) (SSI 2015/358) |
| | | 20 Dec 2016 (otherwise) (SSI 2016/363) |
| 16, 17 | | 20 Dec 2016 (SSI 2016/363) |
| 18 | | 13 Nov 2015 (SSI 2015/358) |
| 19 | | 22 Jan 2017 (SSI 2016/363) |
| 20 | (1) | 1 Apr 2017 (SSI 2017/40) |
| | (2), (3) | 13 Nov 2015 (for the purpose of making orders) (SSI 2015/358) |
| | | 1 Apr 2017 (otherwise) (SSI 2017/40) |
| | (4) | 1 Apr 2017 (SSI 2017/40) |
| 21 | (1) | 1 Apr 2017 (SSI 2017/40) |
| | (2)–(4) | 13 Nov 2015 (for the purpose of making orders) (SSI 2015/358) |
| | | 1 Apr 2017 (otherwise) (SSI 2017/40) |
| | (5)–(7) | 1 Apr 2017 (SSI 2017/40) |
| | (8), (9) | 13 Nov 2015 (for the purpose of making orders) (SSI 2015/358) |
| | | 1 Apr 2017 (otherwise) (SSI 2017/40) |
| 22 | | 1 Apr 2017 (SSI 2017/40) |
| 23 | | 13 Nov 2015 (SSI 2015/358) |
| 24 | (1)–(6) | 1 Apr 2017 (SSI 2017/40) |
| | (7)(a) | 13 Nov 2015 (for the purpose of making regulations) (SSI 2015/358) |
| | | 1 Apr 2017 (otherwise) (SSI 2017/40) |
| | (7)(b), (8) | 1 Apr 2017 (SSI 2017/40) |
| 25 | | 1 Apr 2017 (SSI 2017/40) |
| 26 | (1)–(5) | 1 Apr 2017 (SSI 2017/40) |
| | (6) | 13 Nov 2015 (for the purpose of making regulations) (SSI 2015/358) |
| | | 1 Apr 2017 (otherwise) (SSI 2017/40) |
| | (7) | 1 Apr 2017 (SSI 2017/40) |
| 27, 28 | | 1 Apr 2017 (SSI 2017/40) |
| 29 | (1), (2) | 1 Apr 2017 (SSI 2017/40) |
| | (3) | 13 Nov 2015 (for the purpose of making regulations) (SSI 2015/358) |
| | | 1 Apr 2017 (otherwise) (SSI 2017/40) |
| 30 | | *Not yet in force* |
| 31 | (1)–(5) | 1 Apr 2017 (SSI 2017/40) |
| | (6) | 13 Nov 2015 (for the purpose of making regulations) (SSI 2015/358) |
| | | 1 Apr 2017 (otherwise) (SSI 2017/40) |
| 32, 33 | | 1 Apr 2017 (SSI 2017/40) |
| 34 | | 13 Nov 2015 (for the purpose of issuing guidance for the purposes of Pt 3) (SSI 2015/358) |
| | | 1 Apr 2017 (otherwise) (SSI 2017/40) |
| 35 | | 13 Nov 2015 (SSI 2015/358) |
| 36 | | 15 Apr 2016 (SSI 2015/399)[1] |

**Community Empowerment (Scotland) Act 2015 (asp 6)**—*contd*

| | | |
|---|---|---|
| 37 | (1) | 13 Nov 2015 (for the purpose of making regulations under Land Reform (Scotland) Act 2003, s 34(5)(a)) (SSI 2015/358) |
| | | 15 Apr 2016 (otherwise) (SSI 2015/399) |
| | (2), (3) | 15 Apr 2016 (SSI 2015/399) |
| | (4) | 13 Nov 2016 (for the purpose of making regulations under Land Reform (Scotland) Act 2003, s 34(5)(a)) (SSI 2015/358) |
| | | 15 Apr 2016 (otherwise) (SSI 2015/399) |
| | (5), (6) | 15 Apr 2016 (SSI 2015/399) |
| | (7), (8) | 13 Nov 2015 (for the purpose of making regulations under Land Reform (Scotland) Act 2003, s 34(5)(a)) (SSI 2015/358) |
| | | 15 Apr 2016 (otherwise) (SSI 2015/399) |
| 38, 39 | | 15 Apr 2016 (SSI 2015/399) |
| 40 | | 13 Nov 2015 (for the purpose of making regulations under Land Reform (Scotland) Act 2003, s 37(4)(b), (4A)) (SSI 2015/358) |
| | | 15 Apr 2016 (otherwise) (SSI 2015/399) |
| 41 | | 15 Apr 2016 (SSI 2015/399) |
| 42 | (1), (2) | 13 Nov 2015 (for the purpose of making regulations under Land Reform (Scotland) Act 2003, s 39(7)(c)) (SSI 2015/358) |
| | | 15 Apr 2016 (otherwise) (SSI 2015/399) |
| | (3) | 15 Apr 2016 (SSI 2015/399) |
| | (4) | 13 Nov 2015 (for the purpose of making regulations under Land Reform (Scotland) Act 2003, s 39(7)(c)) (SSI 2015/358) |
| | | 15 Apr 2016 (otherwise) (SSI 2015/399) |
| | (5)–(8) | 15 Apr 2016 (SSI 2015/399) |
| | (9) | 13 Nov 2015 (for the purpose of making regulations under Land Reform (Scotland) Act 2003, s 39(7)(c)) (SSI 2015/358) |
| | | 15 Apr 2016 (otherwise) (SSI 2015/399) |
| 43 | | 15 Apr 2016 (SSI 2015/399) |
| 44 | | 13 Nov 2015 (for the purpose of making regulations under Land Reform (Scotland) Act 2003, s 41(3)(b)) (SSI 2015/358) |
| | | 15 Apr 2016 (otherwise) (SSI 2015/399) |
| 45–48 | | 15 Apr 2016 (SSI 2015/399) |
| 49 | | 13 Nov 2015 (for the purpose of making regulations under Land Reform (Scotland) Act 2003, s 51A(2)(b), (6)) (SSI 2015/358) |
| | | 15 Apr 2016 (otherwise) (SSI 2015/399) |
| 50 | | 13 Nov 2015 (for the purpose of making regulations under Land Reform (Scotland) Act 2003, s 51B(2)(b), (3), (4)) (SSI 2015/358) |
| | | 15 Apr 2016 (otherwise) (SSI 2015/399) |
| 51 | | 15 Apr 2016 (SSI 2015/399) |
| 52 | | 13 Nov 2015 (for the purpose of making regulations under Land Reform (Scotland) Act 2003, s 52(7)) (SSI 2015/358) |
| | | 15 Apr 2016 (otherwise) (SSI 2015/399) |
| 53–61 | | 15 Apr 2016 (SSI 2015/399) |
| 62 | | 16 Dec 2016 (for the purpose of making regulations under Land Reform (Scotland) Act 2003, s 71(A1)(b), (4A), (4B), (5)(a)(iv)) (SSI 2016/394) |
| | | 24 Feb 2021 (otherwise) (SSI 2020/448)[4] |
| 63 | | 16 Dec 2016 (for the purpose of making orders under Land Reform (Scotland) Act 2003, s 72(4), (5)) (SSI 2016/394) |
| | | *Not yet in force* (otherwise) |
| 64 | | 16 Dec 2016 (for the purpose of making regulations under Land Reform (Scotland) Act 2003, s 73(5), (5AA), (11)) (SSI 2016/394) |
| | | *Not yet in force* (otherwise) |
| 65 | | *Not yet in force* |
| 66 | | 16 Dec 2016 (for the purpose of making regulations under Land Reform (Scotland) Act 2003, s 75(6), (7)) (SSI 2016/394) |
| | | *Not yet in force* (otherwise) |
| 67–69 | | *Not yet in force* |

**Community Empowerment (Scotland) Act 2015 (asp 6)**—*contd*

| | | |
|---|---|---|
| 70 | | 16 Dec 2016 (for the purpose of making orders under Land Reform (Scotland) Act 2003, s 89(4)) (SSI 2016/394) |
| | | *Not yet in force* (otherwise) |
| 71–73 | | *Not yet in force* |
| 74 | | 30 Jun 2017 (for the purpose of making regulations under Land Reform (Scotland) Act 2003, ss 97C(4)–(6), 97D(1), (7)–(9), 97F(9), (10), 97G(5), (12), 97H(6), 97J(2)–(4), (7), (8), 97M(1), (2), 97N(1)–(4), 97U(6) and orders under ss 97E(4), (5), 97T(4) of the 2003 Act) (SSI 2017/192) |
| | | 27 Jun 2018 (otherwise) (SSI 2018/139) |
| 75 | | 15 Apr 2016 (for the purpose of inserting Land Reform (Scotland) Act 2003, s 97ZI so far as relating to Pt 2 of that Act) (SSI 2015/399) |
| | | 27 Jun 2018 (so far as it relates to Pt 3A of the Land Reform (Scotland) Act 2003) (SSI 2018/139) |
| | | *Not yet in force* (otherwise) |
| 76 | | 13 Nov 2015 (SSI 2015/358) |
| 77 | (1) | 22 Jan 2017 (SSI 2016/363) |
| | (2), (3) | 13 Nov 2015 (for the purpose of making orders) (SSI 2015/358) |
| | | 22 Jan 2017 (otherwise) (SSI 2016/363) |
| 78 | (1) | 22 Jan 2017 (SSI 2016/363) |
| | (2)–(4) | 13 Nov 2015 (for the purpose of making orders) (SSI 2015/358) |
| | | 22 Jan 2017 (otherwise) (SSI 2016/363) |
| | (5)–(7) | 22 Jan 2017 (SSI 2016/363) |
| 79, 80 | | 22 Jan 2017 (SSI 2016/363) |
| 81 | | 13 Nov 2015 (SSI 2015/358) |
| 82 | (1)–(7) | 22 Jan 2017 (SSI 2016/363) |
| | (8)(a) | 13 Nov 2015 (for the purpose of making regulations) (SSI 2015/358) |
| | | 22 Jan 2017 (otherwise) (SSI 2016/363) |
| | (8)(b), (9) | 22 Jan 2017 (SSI 2016/363) |
| 83 | (1)–(9) | 22 Jan 2017 (SSI 2016/363) |
| | (10) | 13 Nov 2015 (for the purpose of making regulations) (SSI 2015/358) |
| | | 22 Jan 2017 (otherwise) (SSI 2016/363) |
| 84 | | 22 Jan 2017 (SSI 2016/363) |
| 85 | (1), (2) | 22 Jan 2017 (SSI 2016/363) |
| | (3), (4) | 13 Nov 2015 (for the purpose of making regulations) (SSI 2015/358) |
| | | 22 Jan 2017 (otherwise) (SSI 2016/363) |
| | (5)–(9) | 22 Jan 2017 (SSI 2016/363) |
| | (10) | 13 Nov 2015 (for the purpose of making regulations) (SSI 2015/358) |
| | | 22 Jan 2017 (otherwise) (SSI 2016/363) |
| 86 | (1), (2) | 22 Jan 2017 (SSI 2016/363) |
| | (3), (4) | 13 Nov 2015 (for the purpose of making regulations) (SSI 2015/358) |
| | | 22 Jan 2017 (otherwise) (SSI 2016/363) |
| | (5), (6), (7)(a) | 22 Jan 2017 (SSI 2016/363) |
| | (7)(b)(i) | 13 Nov 2015 (for the purpose of making regulations) (SSI 2015/358) |
| | | 22 Jan 2017 (otherwise) (SSI 2016/363) |
| | (7)(b)(ii), (8) | 22 Jan 2017 (SSI 2016/363) |
| | (9) | 13 Nov 2015 (for the purpose of making regulations) (SSI 2015/358) |
| | | 22 Jan 2017 (otherwise) (SSI 2016/363) |
| | (10) | 22 Jan 2017 (SSI 2016/363) |
| 87 | (1), (2) | 22 Jan 2017 (SSI 2016/363) |
| | (3), (4) | 13 Nov 2015 (for the purpose of making regulations) (SSI 2015/358) |

**Community Empowerment (Scotland) Act 2015 (asp 6)**—*contd*

| | | |
|---|---|---|
| | | 22 Jan 2017 (otherwise) (SSI 2016/363) |
| | (5)–(8) | 22 Jan 2017 (SSI 2016/363) |
| | (9) | 13 Nov 2015 (for the purpose of making regulations) (SSI 2015/358) |
| | | 22 Jan 2017 (otherwise) (SSI 2016/363) |
| 88 | (1), (2) | 22 Jan 2017 (SSI 2016/363) |
| | (3) | 13 Nov 2015 (for the purpose of making regulations) (SSI 2015/358) |
| | | 22 Jan 2017 (otherwise) (SSI 2016/363) |
| | (4) | 22 Jan 2017 (SSI 2016/363) |
| 89 | (1) | 22 Jan 2017 (SSI 2016/363) |
| | (2)–(4) | 13 Nov 2015 (for the purpose of making orders) (SSI 2015/358) |
| | | 22 Jan 2017 (otherwise) (SSI 2016/363) |
| 90 | (1)–(11) | 22 Jan 2017 (SSI 2016/363) |
| | (12)–(14) | 13 Nov 2015 (for the purpose of making regulations) (SSI 2015/358) |
| | | 22 Jan 2017 (otherwise) (SSI 2016/363) |
| 91–93 | | 22 Jan 2017 (SSI 2016/363) |
| 94 | (1)–(3) | 22 Jan 2017 (SSI 2016/363) |
| | (4)–(6) | 13 Nov 2015 (for the purposes of making regulations and issuing guidance for the purposes of that section) (SSI 2015/358) |
| | | 22 Jan 2017 (otherwise) (SSI 2016/363) |
| | (7) | 22 Jan 2017 (SSI 2016/363) |
| 95 | | 22 Jan 2017 (SSI 2016/363)[2] |
| 96 | | 13 Nov 2015 (for the purpose of issuing guidance for the purposes of Pt 5) (SSI 2015/358) |
| | | 22 Jan 2017 (otherwise) (SSI 2016/363) |
| 97 | | 13 Nov 2015 (SSI 2015/358) |
| 98 | | 22 Jan 2017 (SSI 2016/363) |
| 99–101 | | *Not yet in force* |
| 102 | | 27 Jun 2018 (SSI 2018/139) |
| 103 | | 13 Nov 2015 (SSI 2015/358) |
| 104 | | 27 Jun 2018 (SSI 2018/139) |
| 105, 106 | | 13 Nov 2015 (SSI 2015/358) |
| 107–132 | | 1 Apr 2018 (SSI 2017/458)[3] |
| 133 | (1)–(3) | *Not yet in force* |
| | (4)–(6) | 15 Dec 2017 (only for the purpose of making regulations) (SSI 2017/420) |
| | | 1 Apr 2018 (otherwise) (SSI 2017/458) |
| | (7) | 1 Apr 2018 (SSI 2017/458) |
| 134 | (1)–(3) | 1 Apr 2018 (SSI 2017/458) |
| | (4)–(6) | 15 Dec 2017 (only for the purpose of making regulations) (SSI 2017/420) |
| | | 1 Apr 2018 (otherwise) (SSI 2017/458) |
| | (7) | 1 Apr 2018 (SSI 2017/458) |
| 135 | (1), (2) | 1 Apr 2018 (SSI 2017/458) |
| | (3)–(5) | 15 Dec 2017 (only for the purpose of making regulations) (SSI 2017/420) |
| | | 1 Apr 2018 (otherwise) (SSI 2017/458) |
| | (6) | 1 Apr 2018 (SSI 2017/458) |
| 137 | | 13 Nov 2015 (for the purpose of issuing guidance under sub-s (1) thereof) (SSI 2015/358) |
| | | 1 Apr 2018 (otherwise) (SSI 2017/458) |
| 138 | | 1 Apr 2018 (SSI 2017/458) |
| 139 | (1)–(5) | 13 Nov 2015 (for the purpose of making regulations) (SSI 2015/358) |
| | | *Not yet in force* (otherwise) |
| | (6) | *Not yet in force* |
| | (7) | 13 Nov 2015 (for the purpose of making regulations) (SSI 2015/358) |

**Community Empowerment (Scotland) Act 2015 (asp 6)**—*contd*

|  |  |  |
|---|---|---|
|  |  | *Not yet in force* (otherwise) |
|  | (8) | *Not yet in force* |
| 140 |  | 31 Oct 2015 (SSI 2015/344) |
| 141–143 |  | 25 Jul 2015 (s 145(1)) |
| 144 | (1) | See Sch 4 below |
|  | (2) | See Sch 5 below |
| 145, 146 |  | 25 Jul 2015 (s 145(1)) |
| Sch 1 |  | 20 Dec 2016 (SSI 2016/363) |
| Sch 2 |  | 1 Apr 2017 (SSI 2017/40) |
| Sch 3 |  | 22 Jan 2017 (SSI 2016/363) |
| Sch 4 | paras 1–4, 5(a) | 1 Apr 2018 (SSI 2017/458)[3] |
|  | para 5(b), (c) | 20 Dec 2016 (SSI 2016/410) |
|  | paras 6, 7 | 20 Dec 2016 (SSI 2016/410) |
|  | para 8(1) | See sub-paras (2)–(6) below |
|  | para 8(2)(a)–(c) | 15 Apr 2016 (SSI 2015/399) |
|  | para 8(2)(d) | 13 Nov 2015 (for the purpose of making regulations under Land Reform (Scotland) Act 2003, s 37(18)) (SSI 2015/358) |
|  |  | 15 Apr 2016 (otherwise) (SSI 2015/399) |
|  | para 8(2)(e) | 15 Apr 2016 (SSI 2015/399) |
|  | para 8(3) | 15 Apr 2016 (SSI 2015/399) |
|  | para 8(4)(a) | 13 Nov 2015 (for the purpose of making regulations under Land Reform (Scotland) Act 2003, s 52(3)) (SSI 2015/358) |
|  |  | 15 Apr 2016 (otherwise) (SSI 2015/399) |
|  | para 8(4)(b)–(5), (6) | 15 Apr 2016 (SSI 2015/399) |
|  | paras 9–12 | 20 Dec 2016 (SSI 2016/410) |
| Sch 5 |  | 15 Apr 2016 (in so far as relates to repeals in or of Land Reform (Scotland) Act 2003) (SSI 2015/399) |
|  |  | 20 Dec 2016 (in so far as relates to repeals in or of Local Government in Scotland Act 2003) (SSI 2016/410) |
|  |  | 1 Apr 2018 (SSI 2017/458), so far as relates to repeals in or of— |
|  |  | Allotments (Scotland) Act 1892[3]; |
|  |  | Land Settlement (Scotland) Act 1919[3]; |
|  |  | Allotments (Scotland) Act 1922[3]; |
|  |  | Agricultural Land (Utilisation) Act 1931; |
|  |  | Acquisition of Land (Authorisation Procedure) (Scotland) Act 1947; |
|  |  | Allotments (Scotland) Act 1950[3]; |
|  |  | Emergency Laws (Miscellaneous Provisions) Act 1953; |
|  |  | Opencast Coal Act 1958[3]; |
|  |  | Town and Country Planning (Scotland) Act 1959; |
|  |  | Local Government (Scotland) Act 1973[3]; |
|  |  | Local Government etc. (Scotland) Act 1994 |
|  |  | *Not yet in force* (otherwise) |

[1]   For savings, see SSI 2015/399, art 3

[2]   For a transitional provision, see SSI 2016/363, art 4

[3]   For transitional provisions and savings, see SSI 2017/458, arts 3–21

[4]   For savings, see SSI 2020/448, reg 3

---

**Consumer Rights Act 2015 (c 15)**

*RA*: 26 Mar 2015

*Commencement provisions*: s 100; Consumer Rights Act 2015 (Commencement) (England) Order 2015, SI 2015/965; Consumer Rights Act 2015 (Commencement No 1) Order 2015, SI 2015/1333; Consumer Rights Act 2015 (Commencement No 2 and Transitional Provision) (England) Order 2015, SI 2015/1575; Consumer Rights Act 2015 (Commencement No 2) Order 2015, SI 2015/1584;

**Consumer Rights Act 2015 (c 15)**—*contd*
Consumer Rights Act 2015 (Commencement No 1 and Transitional Provision) (Wales) Order 2015,
SI 2015/1605; Consumer Rights Act 2015 (Commencement No 3, Transitional Provisions, Savings
and Consequential Amendments) Order 2015, SI 2015/1630, as amended by SI 2016/484; Consumer
Rights Act 2015 (Commencement No 2) (Wales) Order 2015, SI 2015/1831, as revoked by
SI 2015/1904; Consumer Rights Act 2015 (Commencement No 3) (Wales) Order 2015,
SI 2015/1904; Consumer Rights Act 2015 (Commencement No 3, Transitional Provisions, Savings
and Consequential Amendments) (Amendment) Order 2016, SI 2016/484

| | | |
|---|---|---|
| 1–47 | | 1 Oct 2015 (SI 2015/1630)[3] |
| 48 | (1)–(4) | 1 Oct 2015 (except for the purpose of a contract to supply a consumer transport service) (SI 2015/1630)[3] |
| | | 1 Oct 2016 (for the purpose of a contract to supply a consumer transport service) (SI 2015/1630) |
| | (5)–(8) | 26 Mar 2015 (s 100(2)) |
| 49–59 | | 1 Oct 2015 (except for the purpose of a contract to supply a consumer transport service) (SI 2015/1630)[3] |
| | | 1 Oct 2016 (for the purpose of a contract to supply a consumer transport service) (SI 2015/1630)[3] |
| 60 | | See Sch 1 below |
| 61, 62 | | 1 Oct 2015 (SI 2015/1630)[3] |
| 63 | (1), (2) | See Sch 2 below |
| | (3)–(7) | 1 Oct 2015 (SI 2015/1630)[3] |
| 64–69 | | 1 Oct 2015 (SI 2015/1630)[3] |
| 70 | (1) | See Sch 3 below |
| | (2) | 1 Oct 2015 (SI 2015/1630)[3] |
| 71–74 | | 1 Oct 2015 (SI 2015/1630)[3] |
| 75 | | See Sch 4 below |
| 76 | | 1 Oct 2015 (SI 2015/1630)[3] |
| 77 | (1) | See Sch 5 below |
| | (2) | See Sch 6 below |
| 78 | | 1 Oct 2015 (SI 2015/1630) |
| 79 | | See Sch 7 below |
| 80 | | 1 Oct 2015 (SI 2015/1630)[3] |
| 81 | | See Sch 8 below |
| 82 | | 27 May 2015 (SI 2015/1333) |
| 83–86 | | 26 Mar 2015 (in so far as they confer power to make regulations) (s 100(2)) |
| | | 27 May 2015 (E) (otherwise) (SI 2015/965) |
| | | 23 Nov 2015 (W) (otherwise) (SI 2015/1904) |
| 87 | (1)–(7) | 26 Mar 2015 (in so far as they confer power to make regulations) (s 100(2)) |
| | | 27 May 2015 (E) (otherwise) (SI 2015/965) |
| | | 23 Nov 2015 (W) (otherwise) (SI 2015/1904) |
| | (8) | See Sch 9 below |
| | (9)–(12) | 26 Mar 2015 (in so far as they confer power to make regulations) (s 100(2)) |
| | | 27 May 2015 (E) (otherwise) (SI 2015/965) |
| | | 23 Nov 2015 (W) (otherwise) (SI 2015/1904) |
| 88 | (1)–(4) | 27 May 2015 (E) (SI 2015/965) |
| | | 23 Nov 2015 (W) (otherwise) (SI 2015/1904) |
| | (5)–(11) | 26 Mar 2015 (s 100(2)) |
| 89 | | 1 Sep 2015 (E) (SI 2015/1575)[1] |
| | | 1 Sep 2015 (W) (SI 2015/1605)[2] |
| 90–95 | | 26 May 2015 (s 100(4)) |
| 96–101 | | 26 Mar 2015 (s 100(2)) |
| Schs 1–3 | | 1 Oct 2015 (SI 2015/1630) |
| Sch 4 | para 1 | 1 Oct 2015 (SI 2015/1630)[3] |
| | paras 2–6 | 1 Oct 2015 (except for the purpose of a contract to supply a consumer transport service) (SI 2015/1630)[3] |

**Consumer Rights Act 2015 (c 15)**—*contd*

|  |  |  |
|---|---|---|
|  |  | 1 Oct 2016 (for the purpose of a contract to supply a consumer transport service) (SI 2015/1630)[3] |
|  | paras 7–9 | 1 Oct 2015 (SI 2015/1630)[3] |
|  | paras 10–17 | 1 Oct 2015 (except for the purpose of a contract to supply a consumer transport service) (SI 2015/1630)[3] |
|  |  | 1 Oct 2016 (for the purpose of a contract to supply a consumer transport service) (SI 2015/1630)[3] |
|  | paras 18–20 | 1 Oct 2015 (SI 2015/1630)[3] |
|  | paras 21–27 | 1 Oct 2015 (except for the purpose of a contract to supply a consumer transport service) (otherwise) (SI 2015/1630)[3] |
|  |  | 1 Oct 2016 (for the purpose of a contract to supply a consumer transport service) (SI 2015/1630)[3] |
|  | paras 28–39 | 1 Oct 2015 (SI 2015/1630)[3] |
| Sch 5 | paras 1–11 | 27 May 2015 (in so far as they relate to Pt 3, Chapter 3) (SI 2015/965) |
|  |  | 27 May 2015 (in so far as they relate to Pt 3, Chapter 5) (SI 2015/1333) |
|  |  | 1 Oct 2015 (otherwise) (SI 2015/1630) |
|  | para 12 | 26 Mar 2015 (s 100(2)) |
|  | paras 13–46 | 27 May 2015 (in so far as they relate to Pt 3, Chapter 3) (SI 2015/965) |
|  |  | 27 May 2015 (in so far as they relate to Pt 3, Chapter 5) (SI 2015/1333) |
|  |  | 1 Oct 2015 (otherwise) (SI 2015/1630) |
| Schs 6, 7 |  | 1 Oct 2015 (SI 2015/1630) |
| Sch 8 | paras 1–11 | 1 Oct 2015 (SI 2015/1630) |
|  | para 12 | 3 Aug 2015 (for the purpose of making regulations or guidance) (SI 2015/1584) |
|  |  | 1 Oct 2015 (otherwise) (SI 2015/1630) |
|  | paras 13–17 | 1 Oct 2015 (SI 2015/1630) |
|  | para 18 | 3 Aug 2015 (for the purpose of making regulations or guidance) (SI 2015/1584) |
|  |  | 1 Oct 2015 (otherwise) (SI 2015/1630) |
|  | para 19 | 1 Oct 2015 (SI 2015/1630) |
|  | paras 20–22 | 3 Aug 2015 (for the purpose of making regulations or guidance) (SI 2015/1584) |
|  |  | 1 Oct 2015 (otherwise) (SI 2015/1630) |
|  | paras 23–27 | 1 Oct 2015 (SI 2015/1630) |
|  | paras 28–35 | 3 Aug 2015 (for the purpose of making regulations or guidance) (SI 2015/1584) |
|  |  | 1 Oct 2015 (otherwise) (SI 2015/1630) |
|  | paras 36, 37 | 1 Oct 2015 (SI 2015/1630) |
| Sch 9 |  | 27 May 2015 (E) (SI 2015/965) |
|  |  | 23 Nov 2015 (W) (otherwise) (SI 2015/1904) |
| Sch 10 |  | 26 May 2015 (s 100(4)) |

[1]   For transitional provisions, see SI 2015/1575, art 3

[2]   For transitional provisions, see SI 2015/1605, art 3

[3]   For transitional and savings provisions, see SI 2015/1630, arts 6–8

**Control of Horses Act 2015 (c 23)**

*RA:* 26 Mar 2015

*Commencement provisions:* s 5(1)

Whole Act in force 26 May 2015 (s 5(1))

## Counter-Terrorism and Security Act 2015 (c 6)

*RA:* 12 Feb 2015

*Commencement provisions:* s 52; Counter-Terrorism and Security Act 2015 (Commencement No 1) Regulations 2015, SI 2015/956; Counter-Terrorism and Security Act 2015 (Commencement No 2) Regulations 2015, SI 2015/1698; Counter-Terrorism and Security Act 2015 (Commencement No 3) Regulations 2015, SI 2015/1729

| | | |
|---|---|---|
| 1 | | 13 Feb 2015 (s 52(1)) |
| 2–20 | | 12 Feb 2015 (s 52(5)) |
| 21 | | 13 Apr 2015 (SI 2015/956) |
| 22 | (1)–(9) | 12 Feb 2015 (s 52(5)) |
| | (10) | 31 Mar 2015 (SI 2015/956) |
| 23, 24 | | 12 Feb 2015 (s 52(5)) |
| 25 | | See Sch 5 below |
| 26 | | 1 Jul 2015 (except in respect of any specified authority to which s 31 of this Act is expressed to apply) (SI 2015/956) |
| | | 18 Sep 2015 (exception noted above) (SI 2015/1698) |
| 27–29 | | 12 Feb 2015 (s 52(5)) |
| 30 | | 1 Jul 2015 (SI 2015/956) |
| 31 | (1) | 12 Feb 2015 (s 52(5)) |
| | (2) | 1 Jul 2015 (SI 2015/956) |
| | (3) | 12 Feb 2015 (s 52(5)) |
| | (4) | 1 Jul 2015 (SI 2015/956) |
| | (5) | 12 Feb 2015 (s 52(5)) |
| 32–34 | | 1 Jul 2015 (SI 2015/956) |
| 35 | | 12 Feb 2015 (s 52(5)) |
| 36–38 | | 12 Apr 2015 (s 52(2)(a)) |
| 39 | | 12 Feb 2015 (s 52(5)) |
| 40 | | 12 Apr 2015 (s 52(2)(a)) |
| 41–43 | | 12 Feb 2015 (s 52(5)) |
| 44–46 | | 12 Apr 2015 (s 52(2)(b)) |
| 47–53 | | 12 Feb 2015 (s 52(5)) |
| Sch 1 | | 13 Feb 2015 (s 52(1)) |
| Schs 2–4 | | 12 Feb 2015 (s 52(5)) |
| Sch 5 | paras 1–11 | 12 Feb 2015 (s 52(5)) |
| | paras 12–14 | 1 Oct 2015 (SI 2015/1729) |
| Schs 6–8 | | 12 Feb 2015 (s 52(5)) |

## Criminal Justice and Courts Act 2015 (c 2)

*RA:* 12 Feb 2015

*Commencement provisions:* s 95; Criminal Justice and Courts Act 2015 (Commencement No 1, Saving and Transitional Provisions) Order 2015, SI 2015/778; Criminal Justice and Courts Act 2015 (Commencement No 2) Order 2015, SI 2015/1463; Criminal Justice and Courts Act 2015 (Commencement No 3 and Transitional Provisions) Order 2015, SI 2015/1778; Criminal Justice and Courts Act 2015 (Commencement No 4 and Transitional Provisions) Order 2016, SI 2016/717; Criminal Justice and Courts Act 2015 (Commencement No 5) Order 2016, SI 2016/896; Criminal Justice and Courts Act 2015 (Commencement No 6) Order 2017, SI 2017/189; Criminal Justice and Courts Act 2015 (Commencement No 7 and Transitional Provision) Order 2018, SI 2018/732; Criminal Justice and Courts Act 2015 (Commencement No 8) Order 2022, SI 2022/716

| | | |
|---|---|---|
| 1–5 | | 13 Apr 2015 (SI 2015/778) |
| 6 | | See Sch 1 below |
| 7 | (1)–(3) | 13 Apr 2015 (SI 2015/778) |
| | (4) | See Sch 2 below |
| | (5) | 13 Apr 2015 (SI 2015/778) |
| 8 | (1), (2) | *Not yet in force* |
| | (3) | See Sch 3 below |
| 9, 10 | | *Not yet in force* |

**Criminal Justice and Courts Act 2015 (c 2)**—*contd*

| | | |
|---|---|---|
| 11 | (1) | *Not yet in force* |
| | (2), (3) | 29 Jun 2022 (SI 2022/716) |
| | (4) | *Not yet in force* |
| | (5) | 29 Jun 2022 (SI 2022/716) |
| 12–27 | | 13 Apr 2015 (SI 2015/778) |
| 28 | (1)–(7) | 17 Jul 2015 (SI 2015/1463) |
| | (8) | See Sch 5 below |
| 29 | (1)–(3) | 13 Apr 2015 (SI 2015/778) |
| | (4) | See Sch 6 below |
| | (5) | 13 Apr 2015 (SI 2015/778) |
| 30 | | 13 Apr 2015 (SI 2015/778) |
| 31 | (1)–(4) | 1 Aug 2017 (SI 2017/189)[4] |
| | (5) | 23 Feb 2017 (or the purposes of making regulations to specify an agreement made between the United Kingdom and the Republic of Ireland) (SI 2017/189) |
| | | 1 Aug 2017 (SI 2017/189)[4] |
| | (6) | See Sch 7 below |
| 32 | | 13 Apr 2015 (SI 2015/778) |
| 33 | (1)–(9) | 13 Apr 2015 (SI 2015/778) |
| | (10) | See Sch 8 below |
| | (11), (12) | 13 Apr 2015 (SI 2015/778) |
| 34–36 | | 13 Apr 2015 (SI 2015/778) |
| 37 | | 13 Apr 2015 (SI 2015/778)[1] |
| 38 | (1), (2) | 20 Mar 2015 (except in relation to the power to which s 95(9) of this Act applies) (SI 2015/778) |
| | | *Not yet in force* (exception noted above) |
| | (3) | See Sch 9 below |
| 39 | | See Sch 10 below |
| 40, 41 | | 13 Apr 2015 (SI 2015/778) |
| 42 | | 26 Oct 2015 (SI 2015/1778) |
| 43–49 | | 13 Apr 2015 (SI 2015/778) |
| 50 | | See Sch 9 below |
| 51 | | 13 Apr 2015 (SI 2015/778) |
| 52 | | 12 Apr 2015 (s 95(2)) |
| 53 | | 13 Apr 2015 (SI 2015/778) |
| 54 | (1), (2) | 13 Apr 2015 (SI 2015/778) |
| | (3) | See Sch 12 below |
| | (4) | 13 Apr 2015 (SI 2015/778) |
| 55–61 | | 13 Apr 2015 (SI 2015/778) |
| 62 | | 12 Feb 2015 (s 95(3)) |
| 63 | | 13 Apr 2015 (SI 2015/778)[1] |
| 64, 65 | | 8 Aug 2016 (SI 2016/717)[3] |
| 66 | | 28 Jun 2018 (SI 2018/732)[5] |
| 67 | | 13 Apr 2015 (SI 2015/778) |
| 68 | | See sub-ss (2), (3) below |
| | (2) | 1 Dec 2016 (SI 2016/896) |
| | (3) | 9 Sep 2016 (SI 2016/896) |
| 69–73 | | 13 Apr 2015 (SI 2015/778) |
| 74 | | 13 Apr 2015 (SI 2015/778)[1] |
| 75 | | See Sch 13 below |
| 76 | | See Sch 14 below |
| 77–79 | | 13 Apr 2015 (SI 2015/778)[1] |
| 80 | | See Sch 15 below |
| 81–83 | | 13 Apr 2015 (SI 2015/778) |
| 84 | (1)–(3) | 13 Apr 2015 (SI 2015/778) |
| | (4)–(6) | 8 Aug 2016 (SI 2016/717)[3] |
| 85, 86 | | *Not yet in force* |
| 87 | | 13 Apr 2015 (SI 2015/778)[1] |
| 88–90 | | 8 Aug 2016 (SI 2016/717)[3] |

**Criminal Justice and Courts Act 2015 (c 2)**—*contd*

| | | |
|---|---|---|
| 91 | | See Sch 16 below |
| 92 | | 13 Apr 2015 (SI 2015/778) |
| 93, 94 | | *Not yet in force* |
| 95 | | 12 Feb 2015 (RA) |
| 96–98 | | *Not yet in force* |
| Schs 1, 2 | | 13 Apr 2015 (SI 2015/778) |
| Sch 3 | | *Not yet in force* |
| Sch 4 | | 13 Apr 2015 (SI 2015/778) |
| Sch 5 | | 17 Jul 2015 (SI 2015/1463) |
| Sch 6 | | 13 Apr 2015 (SI 2015/778) |
| Sch 7 | paras 1–13 | 1 Aug 2017 (SI 2017/189)[4] |
| | para 14 | 23 Feb 2017 (SI 2017/189) |
| | paras 15–22 | 1 Aug 2017 (SI 2017/189)[4] |
| | paras 23–25 | 12 Feb 2015 (s 95(4)) |
| | paras 26, 27 | 1 Aug 2017 (SI 2017/189)[4] |
| Sch 8 | | 13 Apr 2015 (SI 2015/778) |
| Schs 9, 10 | | 20 Mar 2015 (SI 2015/778) |
| Schs 11–15 | | 13 Apr 2015 (SI 2015/778)[1] |
| Sch 16 | | 26 Oct 2015 (SI 2015/1778)[2] |

[1]   For transitional provisions, see SI 2015/778, art 4, Sch 2

[2]   For transitional provisions, see SI 2015/1778, art 4

[3]   For transitional provisions, see SI 2016/717, arts 4, 5

[4]   See the London Gazetter, 4 Aug 2017

[5]   For transitional provisions, see SI 2018/732

---

**Deregulation Act 2015 (c 20)**

*RA:* 26 Mar 2015

*Commencement provisions:* s 115; Deregulation Act 2015 (Commencement No 1 and Transitional and Saving Provisions) Order 2015, SI 2015/994, as amended by SI 2015/1405; Deregulation Act 2015 (Commencement No 2 and Transitional Provisions) Order 2015, SI 2015/1402; Deregulation Act 2015 (Commencement No 3 and Transitional and Saving Provisions) Order 2015, SI 2015/1732; Deregulation Act 2015 (Commencement No 4) Order 2015, SI 2015/2074; Deregulation Act 2015 (Commencement No 5) Order 2016, SI 2016/206; Deregulation Act 2015 (Commencement No 6 and Savings Provision) Order 2016, SI 2016/1016; Deregulation Act 2015 (Commencement No. 7) Order 2017, SI 2017/273; Deregulation Act 2015 (Commencement No 8) Order 2017, SI 2017/331; Deregulation Act 2015 (Commencement No 1) (Wales) Order 2018, SI 2018/883

| | | |
|---|---|---|
| 1 | | 26 Mar 2015 (in so far as necessary for enabling the exercise of any power to make provision by order or regulations) (s 115(2)) |
| | | 1 Oct 2015 (otherwise) (SI 2015/1732) |
| 2 | | 1 Oct 2015 (SI 2015/994)[1] |
| 3 | | See Sch 1 below |
| 4, 5 | | 26 May 2015 (SI 2015/994) |
| 6, 7 | | 1 Oct 2015 (SI 2015/994)[1] |
| 8 | | See Sch 2 below |
| 9 | (1)–(4) | 30 Jun 2015 (SI 2015/994) |
| | (5) | See Sch 3 below |
| 10–12 | | 1 Oct 2015 (SI 2015/994) |
| 13 | | See Sch 4 below |
| 14 | | 26 May 2015 (SI 2015/994) |
| 15 | | 1 Oct 2015 (SI 2015/1732) |
| 16 | | 26 May 2015 (s 115(3)) |
| 17 | | 1 Oct 2015 (SI 2015/1732) |
| 18 | (1)–(4) | 1 Oct 2015 (SI 2015/1732)[3] |
| | (5) | See Sch 5 below |

**Deregulation Act 2015 (c 20)**—*contd*

| | | |
|---|---|---|
| 19 | | See Sch 6 below |
| 20–25 | | *Not yet in force* |
| 26 | | See Sch 7 below |
| 27–29 | | 26 May 2015 (s 115(3)) |
| 30–32 | | 26 Mar 2015 (s 115(1)) |
| 33–36 | | 1 Oct 2015 (SI 2015/994) |
| 37 | | 1 Jul 2015 (SI 2015/994) |
| 38, 39 | | 1 Jul 2015 (so far as necessary for enabling the exercise on or after that day of any power to make provision by regulations made by statutory instrument) (SI 2015/994) |
| | | 1 Oct 2015 (otherwise) (SI 2015/994) |
| 40, 41 | | 1 Oct 2015 (SI 2015/994) |
| 42 | | 26 Mar 2015 (s 115(1)) |
| 43 | | *Not yet in force* |
| 44, 45 | | 26 May 2015 (SI 2015/994) |
| 46, 47 | | 26 Mar 2015 (s 115(1)) |
| 48 | | 1 Apr 2015 (SI 2015/994) |
| 49 | (1) | 1 Oct 2015 (SI 2015/994) |
| | (2) | See Sch 8 below |
| 50 | (1)–(5) | 26 May 2015 (s 115(3)) |
| | (6) | See Sch 9 below |
| 51 | | See Sch 10 below |
| 52 | | See Sch 11 below |
| 53 | | 26 Mar 2015 (in so far as necessary for enabling the exercise of any power to make provision by order or regulations) (s 115(2)) |
| | | 1 Apr 2015 (otherwise) (SI 2015/994) |
| 54–57 | | 26 May 2015 (s 115(3)) |
| 58 | (1)–(5) | 26 Mar 2015 (in so far as necessary for enabling the exercise of any power to make provision by order or regulations) (s 115(2)) |
| | | 15 Jun 2015 (otherwise) (SI 2015/994) |
| | (6) | See Sch 12 below |
| 59 | | See Sch 13 below |
| 60, 61 | | 26 May 2015 (s 115(3)) |
| 62, 63 | | 26 Mar 2015 (in so far as necessary for enabling the exercise of any power to make provision by order or regulations) (s 115(2)) |
| | | 6 Apr 2015 (otherwise) (SI 2015/994) |
| 64 | (1), (2) | 26 May 2015 (s 115(3)) |
| | (3) | See Sch 14 below |
| 65 | | See Sch 15 below |
| 66 | (1)–(4) | 1 Oct 2015 (SI 2015/1732) |
| | (5) | See Sch 16 below |
| 67 | (1) | *Not yet in force* |
| | (2) | See Sch 17 below |
| | (3)–(12) | *Not yet in force* |
| 68 | | 26 May 2015 (SI 2015/994) |
| 69 | | 1 Apr 2015 (SI 2015/994) |
| 70 | | 26 May 2015 (SI 2015/994) |
| 71 | | 1 Oct 2015 (SI 2015/1732) |
| 72 | | 26 May 2015 (SI 2015/994) |
| 73–75 | | 10 Mar 2017 (SI 2017/273) |
| 76 | | 6 Apr 2015 (SI 2015/994) |
| 77, 78 | | 26 May 2015 (SI 2015/994) |
| 79 | | 26 May 2015 (s 115(3)) |
| 80–82 | | 26 May 2015 (SI 2015/994) |
| 83, 84 | | 26 May 2015 (s 115(3)) |
| 85 | | 26 Mar 2015 (s 115(1)) |
| 86, 87 | | 29 Jun 2015 (SI 2015/1402) |
| 88 | | See Sch 19 below |
| 89 | | See Sch 20 below |

**Deregulation Act 2015 (c 20)**—*contd*

| | | |
|---|---|---|
| 90 | | See Sch 21 below |
| 91 | | 2 Mar 2016 (SI 2016/206) |
| 92 | | *Not yet in force* |
| 93 | | 26 May 2015 (SI 2015/994) |
| 94, 95 | | 1 Jan 2016 (SI 2015/1732) |
| 96 | | 26 May 2015 (SI 2015/994) |
| 97–102 | | 26 May 2015 (s 115(3)) |
| 103 | (1), (2) | 26 May 2015 (s 115(3)) |
| | (3) | See Sch 22 below |
| 104–106 | | 26 May 2015 (s 115(3)) |
| 107 | | See Sch 23 below |
| 108 | | 29 Mar 2017 (SI 2017/331) |
| 109 | | 26 Mar 2015 (s 115(1)) |
| 110 | (1), (2) | 26 Mar 2015 (s 115(1)) |
| | (3) | 29 Mar 2017 (SI 2017/331) |
| | (4)–(8) | 26 Mar 2015 (s 115(1)) |
| 111–116 | | 26 Mar 2015 (s 115(1)) |
| Sch 1 | paras 1–4 | 26 Mar 2015 (in so far as necessary for enabling the exercise of any power to make provision by order or regulations) (s 115(2)) |
| | | 26 May 2015 (otherwise) (SI 2015/994)[1] |
| | paras 5–23 | 26 May 2015 (SI 2015/994)[1] |
| | paras 24–27 | 21 Sep 2018 (SI 2018/883) |
| | para 28 | 26 Mar 2015 (in so far as necessary for enabling the exercise of any power to make provision by order or regulations) (s 115(2)) |
| | | *Not yet in force* (otherwise) |
| Sch 2 | paras 1–15 | 26 Mar 2015 (in so far as necessary for enabling the exercise of any power to make provision by order or regulations) (s 115(2)) |
| | | *Not yet in force* (otherwise) |
| | paras 16–30 | 26 Mar 2015 (in so far as necessary for enabling the exercise of any power to make provision by order or regulations) (s 115(2)) |
| | | 8 Jun 2015 (otherwise) (SI 2015/994)[1] |
| | para 31 | 26 Mar 2015 (in so far as necessary for enabling the exercise of any power to make provision by order or regulations) (s 115(2)) |
| | | *Not yet in force* (otherwise) |
| | paras 32, 33 | 26 Mar 2015 (in so far as necessary for enabling the exercise of any power to make provision by order or regulations) (s 115(2)) |
| | | 8 Jun 2015 (otherwise) (SI 2015/994)[1] |
| Sch 3 | paras 1–3 | 30 Jun 2015 (SI 2015/994) |
| | paras 4, 5 | 30 Jun 2015 (SI 2015/994)[1] |
| | paras 6, 7 | 30 Jun 2015 (SI 2015/994) |
| Sch 4 | | 26 Mar 2015 (in so far as necessary for enabling the exercise of any power to make provision by order or regulations) (s 115(2)) |
| | | 26 May 2015 (otherwise) (s 115(3)) |
| Sch 5 | | 1 Oct 2015 (SI 2015/1732)[3] |
| Sch 6 | paras 1–4 | 1 Oct 2015 (SI 2015/1732) |
| | para 5 | 26 May 2015 (s 115(3)) |
| | paras 6–11 | 1 Oct 2015 (SI 2015/1732)[3] |
| | para 12 | 29 Mar 2017 (SI 2017/331) |
| | para 13(1) | 6 Apr 2017 (SI 2016/1016) |
| | para 13(2) | *Not yet in force* |
| | para 14 | 6 Apr 2017 (SI 2016/1016) |
| | para 15 | 6 Apr 2017 (SI 2016/1016)[4] |
| | paras 16–23 | 1 Oct 2015 (SI 2015/1732) |
| | paras 24–30 | 26 May 2015 (s 115(3)) |
| Sch 7 | | *Not yet in force* |
| Sch 8 | | 26 Mar 2015 (in so far as necessary for enabling the exercise of any power to make provision by order or regulations) (s 115(2)) |
| | | 1 Oct 2015 (otherwise) (SI 2015/994) |
| Sch 9 | | 26 May 2015 (s 115(3)) |

**Deregulation Act 2015 (c 20)**—*contd*

| | | |
|---|---|---|
| Sch 10 | paras 1–3 | 26 May 2015 (s 115(3)) |
| | paras 4–12 | 26 Mar 2015 (in so far as necessary for enabling the exercise of any power to make provision by order or regulations) (s 115(2)) |
| | | 30 Jun 2015 (otherwise) (SI 2015/994) |
| | paras 13–22 | *Not yet in force* |
| | paras 23, 24 | 26 May 2015 (s 115(3)) |
| | paras 25–27 | 26 Mar 2015 (in so far as necessary for enabling the exercise of any power to make provision by order or regulations) (s 115(2)) |
| | | 8 Jun 2015 (otherwise) (SI 2015/994)[1] |
| | paras 28–31 | 1 Oct 2015 (SI 2015/994) |
| Sch 11 | paras 1–16 | 10 Apr 2015 (SI 2015/994) |
| | paras 17–19 | 26 May 2015 (s 115(3)) |
| Sch 12 | | 26 Mar 2015 (in so far as necessary for enabling the exercise of any power to make provision by order or regulations) (s 115(2)) |
| | | 15 Jun 2015 (otherwise) (SI 2015/994) |
| Sch 13 | paras 1–3 | 26 May 2015 (s 115(3)) |
| | paras 4–6 | 26 May 2015 (SI 2015/994) |
| | paras 7, 8 | 26 May 2015 (s 115(3)) |
| | paras 9–15 | 1 Oct 2015 (SI 2015/1732) |
| Schs 14, 15 | | 26 May 2015 (s 115(3)) |
| Sch 16 | para 1 | *Not yet in force* |
| | para 2 | 1 Jan 2016 (SI 2015/2074) |
| | para 3 | *Not yet in force* |
| | paras 4, 5 | 1 Jan 2016 (SI 2015/1732) |
| | para 6 | *Not yet in force* |
| Sch 17 | | *Not yet in force* |
| Sch 18 | | 1 Apr 2015 (SI 2015/994) |
| Sch 19 | | 29 Jun 2015 (SI 2015/1402) |
| Sch 20 | para 1 | See paras 2–10 below |
| | para 2 | 29 Jun 2015 (SI 2015/1402)[2] |
| | para 3(1) | See sub-paras (2)–(5) below |
| | para 3(2), (3) | 29 Jun 2015 (SI 2015/1402)[2] |
| | para 3(4), (5) | 29 Jun 2015 (SI 2015/1402) |
| | paras 4–10 | 29 Jun 2015 (SI 2015/1402) |
| Sch 21 | | 26 Mar 2015 (in so far as necessary for enabling the exercise of any power to make provision by order or regulations) (s 115(2)) |
| | | 20 Apr 2015 (for the purposes of enabling applications for licences under Poisons Act 1972, s 4A, to be made, considered and determined, and of enabling such licenses to be issued, before 26 May 2015) (SI 2015/994) |
| | | 26 May 2015 (otherwise) (SI 2015/994) |
| Sch 22 | | 26 May 2015 (s 115(3)) |
| Sch 23 | paras 1–34 | 26 May 2015 (s 115(3)) |
| | paras 35, 36 | *Never in force* (repealed) |
| | paras 37–40 | 26 May 2015 (s 115(3)) |
| | para 41 | *Never in force* (repealed) |
| | paras 42–46 | 26 May 2015 (s 115(3)) |

[1]   For transitional provisions and savings, see SI 2015/994, arts 12, 13, Schedule

[2]   For transitional provisions, see SI 2015/1402, art 3

[3]   For transitional provisions and savings, see SI 2015/1732, arts 4–7

[4]   For savings, see SI 2016/1016, art 3

## Ecclesiastical Property Measure 2015 (No 2)

*RA:* 12 Feb 2015

*Commencement provisions*: s 3(2); Ecclesiastical Property Measure 2015 (Commencement) Order 2015, SI 2015/1468

**Ecclesiastical Property Measure 2015 (No 2)**—*contd*

| | |
|---|---|
| 1, 2 | 1 Jul 2015 (SI 2015/1468) |
| 3 | 12 Feb 2015 (s 3(2)) |

## European Union (Approvals) Act 2015 (c 37)

*RA:* 17 Dec 2015

*Commencement provisions:* s 2(2)

Whole Act in force 17 Dec 2015 (s 2(2))

## European Union (Finance) Act 2015 (c 32)

*RA:* 21 Jul 2015

*Commencement provisions:* s 2(3)

Whole Act in force 21 Sep 2015 (s 2(3))

## European Union Referendum Act 2015 (c 36)

*RA:* 17 Dec 2015

*Commencement provisions:* s 13(1), (2); European Union Referendum Act 2015 (Commencement) Regulations 2016, SI 2016/69

| | |
|---|---|
| 1–8 | 1 Feb 2016 (SI 2016/69) |
| 9–14 | 17 Dec 2015 (s 13(1)) |
| Schs 1–3 | 1 Feb 2016 (SI 2016/69) |

## Finance Act 2015 (c 26)

*Budget Day:* 18 Mar 2015

*RA:* 26 Mar 2015

The commencement details of Finance Acts are not set out, as the dates from which their provisions take effect are usually stated clearly and unambiguously in the text of the Act, and charging provisions will normally state for which year or years of assessment they are to have effect.

## Finance Act (No 2) 2015 (c 26)

*Budget Day:* 8 Jul 2015

*RA:* 18 Nov 2015

The commencement details of Finance Acts are not set out, as the dates from which their provisions take effect are usually stated clearly and unambiguously in the text of the Act, and charging provisions will normally state for which year or years of assessment they are to have effect.

## Food (Scotland) Act 2015 (asp 1)

*RA:* 13 Jan 2015

*Commencement provisions:* s 63; Food (Scotland) Act 2015 (Commencement) Order 2015, SSI 2015/99

| | |
|---|---|
| 1–59 | 1 Apr 2015 (SSI 2015/99) |
| 60–64 | 14 Jan 2015 (s 63(1)) |
| Schedule | 1 Apr 2015 (SSI 2015/99) |

## Harbours (Scotland) Act 2015 (asp 13)

*RA:* 2 Dec 2015

*Commencement provisions:* s 3

Whole Act in force 3 Dec 2015 (s 3)

---

## Health and Social Care (Safety and Quality) Act 2015 (c 28)

*RA:* 26 Mar 2015

*Commencement provisions:* s 6(4), (5); Health and Social Care (Safety and Quality) Act 2015 (Commencement No 1 and Transitory Provision) Regulations 2015, SI 2015/1438; Health and Social Care (Safety and Quality) Act 2015 (Commencement No 2) Regulations 2016, SI 2016/906

| | |
|---|---|
| 1 | 1 Oct 2015 (SI 2015/1438) |
| 2 | 25 Jun 2015 (SI 2015/1438) |
| 3 | 1 Oct 2015 (SI 2015/1438) |
| 4 | 25 Jun 2015 (SI 2015/1438)[1] |
| 5 | 26 Sep 2016 (SI 2016/906) |
| 6 | 26 Mar 2015 (RA) |
| Schedule | 26 Sep 2016 (SI 2016/906) |

[1]  For transitory modifications, see SI 2015/1438, art 4

---

## Health Service Commissioner for England (Complaint Handling) Act 2015 (c 29)

*RA:* 26 Mar 2015

*Commencement provisions:* s 2(1)

Whole Act in force 26 May 2015 (s 2(1))

---

## Higher Education (Wales) Act 2015 (anaw 1)

*RA:* 12 Mar 2015

*Commencement provisions:* s 59; Higher Education (Wales) Act 2015 (Commencement No 1 and Saving Provision) Order 2015, SI 2015/1327; Higher Education (Wales) Act 2015 (Commencement No 2) Order 2016, SI 2016/110; Higher Education (Wales) Act 2015 (Commencement No 3) Order 2017, SI 2017/239

| | | |
|---|---|---|
| 1 | | 12 Mar 2015 (s 59(1)) |
| 2 | (1)–(3) | 1 Jan 2016 (SI 2015/1327) |
| | (4) | 20 May 2015 (for the purpose of making regulations) (SI 2015/1327) |
| | | 1 Jan 2016 (otherwise) (SI 2015/1327) |
| 3 | (1)–(3) | 1 Sep 2015 (SI 2015/1327) |
| | (4) | 20 May 2015 (for the purpose of making regulations) (SI 2015/1327) |
| | | 1 Sep 2015 (otherwise) (SI 2015/1327) |
| 4 | (1), (2) | 1 Jan 2016 (SI 2015/1327) |
| | (3), (4) | 20 May 2015 (for the purpose of making regulations) (SI 2015/1327) |
| | | 1 Jan 2016 (otherwise) (SI 2015/1327) |
| | (5) | 1 Jan 2016 (SI 2015/1327) |
| 5 | (1), (2)(a) | 1 Jan 2016 (SI 2015/1327) |
| | (2)(b) | 20 May 2015 (for the purpose of making regulations) (SI 2015/1327) |
| | | 1 Jan 2016 (otherwise) (SI 2015/1327) |
| | (2)(c) | 1 Jan 2016 (SI 2015/1327) |

**Higher Education (Wales) Act 2015 (anaw 1)**—*contd*

| | | |
|---|---|---|
| | (3) | 20 May 2015 (for the purpose of making regulations) (SI 2015/1327) |
| | | 1 Jan 2016 (otherwise) (SI 2015/1327) |
| | (4) | 1 Jan 2016 (SI 2015/1327) |
| | (5)–(9) | 20 May 2015 (for the purpose of making regulations) (SI 2015/1327) |
| | | 1 Jan 2016 (otherwise) (SI 2015/1327) |
| 6 | (1) | 20 May 2015 (for the purpose of making regulations) (SI 2015/1327) |
| | | 1 Jan 2016 (otherwise) (SI 2015/1327) |
| | (2) | 1 Jan 2016 (SI 2015/1327) |
| | (3)–(6) | 20 May 2015 (for the purpose of making regulations) (SI 2015/1327) |
| | | 1 Jan 2016 (otherwise) (SI 2015/1327) |
| | (7) | 25 May 2015 (SI 2015/1327) |
| 7 | (1), (2) | 1 Jan 2016 (SI 2015/1327) |
| | (3) | 20 May 2015 (for the purpose of making regulations) (SI 2015/1327) |
| | | 1 Jan 2016 (otherwise) (SI 2015/1327) |
| | (4) | 1 Jan 2016 (SI 2015/1327) |
| | (5) | 25 May 2015 (SI 2015/1327) |
| | (6)–(8) | 1 Jan 2016 (SI 2015/1327) |
| 8, 9 | | 20 May 2015 (for the purpose of making regulations) (SI 2015/1327) |
| 10 | | 1 Sep 2015 (SI 2015/1327) |
| 11 | (1)–(4) | 1 Sep 2015 (SI 2015/1327) |
| | (5) | 20 May 2015 (for the purpose of making regulations) (SI 2015/1327) |
| | | 1 Sep 2015 (otherwise) (SI 2015/1327) |
| | (6) | 1 Sep 2015 (SI 2015/1327) |
| 12 | | 1 Sep 2015 (SI 2015/1327) |
| 13 | | 1 Aug 2017 (SI 2017/239) |
| 14 | | 1 Sep 2015 (SI 2015/1327) |
| 15 | (1)(a) | 1 Sep 2015 (SI 2015/1327) |
| | (1)(b)–(d), (2) | 1 Aug 2017 (SI 2017/239) |
| 16 | | 1 Sep 2015 (SI 2015/1327) |
| 17 | (1)–(3) | 1 Sep 2015 (SI 2015/1327) |
| | (4)(a) | 20 May 2015 (for the purpose of making regulations) (SI 2015/1327) |
| | | 1 Sep 2015 (otherwise) (SI 2015/1327) |
| | (4)(b) | 1 Sep 2015 (SI 2015/1327) |
| 18–25 | | 1 Sep 2015 (SI 2015/1327) |
| 26 | | 1 Aug 2017 (SI 2017/239) |
| 27 | (1) | 25 May 2015 (in so far as it relates to the preparation of a code) (SI 2015/1327) |
| | | 1 Sep 2016 (otherwise) (SI 2016/110) |
| | (2), (3) | 25 May 2015 (SI 2015/1327) |
| | (4) | 1 Aug 2017 (SI 2017/239) |
| | (5), (6) | 1 Sep 2016 (SI 2016/110) |
| | (7), (8) | 25 May 2015 (SI 2015/1327) |
| | (9) | 1 Sep 2015 (SI 2015/1327) |
| 28, 29 | | 1 Sep 2015 (SI 2015/1327) |
| 30 | | 1 Sep 2016 (SI 2016/110) |
| 31–36 | | 1 Aug 2017 (SI 2017/239) |
| 37 | (1)–(6) | 1 Aug 2017 (SI 2017/239) |
| | (7) | 20 May 2015 (for the purpose of making regulations) (SI 2015/1327) |
| | (8), (9) | 1 Aug 2017 (SI 2017/239) |
| 38 | (1) | 1 Aug 2016 (SI 2016/110) |

**Higher Education (Wales) Act 2015 (anaw 1)**—*contd*

|  |  |  |
|---|---|---|
|  | (2) | 20 May 2015 (for the purpose of making regulations) (SI 2015/1327) |
|  | (3) | 3 Feb 2016 (SI 2016/110) |
| 39 | (1)–(3) | 1 Aug 2017 (SI 2017/239) |
|  | (4) | 20 May 2015 (for the purpose of making regulations) (SI 2015/1327) |
|  | (5) | 1 Aug 2017 (SI 2017/239) |
| 40 | (1) | 1 Aug 2016 (SI 2016/110) |
|  | (2) | 20 May 2015 (for the purpose of making regulations) (SI 2015/1327) |
|  |  | 1 Aug 2016 (otherwise) (SI 2016/110) |
| 41 | (1)(a) | 1 Jan 2016 (SI 2015/1327) |
|  | (1)(b) | 1 Sep 2015 (SI 2015/1327) |
|  | (1)(c) | 1 Aug 2017 (SI 2017/239) |
|  | (1)(d) | 1 Sep 2015 (SI 2015/1327) |
|  | (1)(e)–(g) | 1 Aug 2017 (SI 2017/239) |
|  | (2) | 1 Sep 2015 (SI 2015/1327) |
| 42 | (1) | 1 Sep 2015 (SI 2015/1327) |
|  | (2)(a)–(c) | 1 Sep 2015 (SI 2015/1327) |
|  | (2)(d) | 20 May 2015 (for the purpose of making regulations) (SI 2015/1327) |
|  |  | 1 Sep 2015 (otherwise) (SI 2015/1327) |
|  | (3), (4) | 1 Sep 2015 (SI 2015/1327) |
| 43 |  | 20 May 2015 (for the purpose of making regulations) (SI 2015/1327) |
|  |  | 1 Sep 2015 (otherwise) (SI 2015/1327) |
| 44 | (1), (2) | 1 Sep 2015 (SI 2015/1327) |
|  | (3), (4) | 20 May 2015 (for the purpose of making regulations) (SI 2015/1327) |
|  |  | 1 Sep 2015 (otherwise) (SI 2015/1327) |
| 45, 46 |  | 1 Sep 2015 (SI 2015/1327) |
| 47–49 |  | 25 May 2015 (SI 2015/1327) |
| 50 |  | 1 Aug 2017 (SI 2017/239) |
| 51 | (1)(a) | 1 Sep 2015 (SI 2015/1327) |
|  | (1)(b)–(d) | 1 Aug 2017 (SI 2017/239) |
|  | (1)(e) | 1 Sep 2015 (SI 2015/1327) |
|  | (1)(f) | 1 Aug 2017 (SI 2017/239) |
|  | (2) | 1 Sep 2015 (SI 2015/1327) |
| 52 | (1) | 25 May 2015 (in so far as relates to the preparation of a statement) (SI 2015/1327) |
|  |  | 1 Sep 2015 (in so far as it relates to the publication of a statement in connection with sub-ss (5)(a), (5)(c), (5)(d)) (SI 2015/1327) |
|  |  | 3 Feb 2016 (otherwise) (SI 2016/110) |
|  | (2), (3) | 1 Sep 2015 (SI 2015/1327) |
|  | (4) | 20 May 2015 (for the purpose of making regulations) (SI 2015/1327) |
|  | (5) | 25 May 2015 (SI 2015/1327) |
| 53 |  | 1 Sep 2015 (SI 2015/1327) |
| 54 | (1) | 1 Sep 2015 (SI 2015/1327) |
|  | (2) | 1 Aug 2017 (SI 2017/239) |
|  | (3), (4) | 25 May 2015 (SI 2015/1327) |
| 55–57 |  | 12 Mar 2015 (s 59(1)) |
| 58 | (1), (2) | See Schedule below |
|  | (3), (4) | 12 Mar 2015 (s 59(1)) |
| 59, 60 |  | 12 Mar 2015 (s 59(1)) |
| Schedule | para 1 | See paras 2–4 below |
|  | para 2 | 1 Sep 2015 (SI 2015/1327) |
|  | paras 3–6 | 1 Aug 2017 (SI 2017/239) |
|  | paras 7–10 | 1 Sep 2015 (SI 2015/1327) |

## Higher Education (Wales) Act 2015 (anaw 1)—*contd*

| | | |
|---|---|---|
| paras 11, 12 | 1 Sep 2015 (SI 2015/1327)[1] | |
| para 13 | 1 Sep 2015 (SI 2015/1327) | |
| para 14 | 1 Sep 2015 (SI 2015/1327)[1] | |
| para 15 | 1 Sep 2015 (SI 2015/1327)[1] | |
| para 16 | 1 Sep 2015 (SI 2015/1327)[1] | |
| paras 17, 18 | 1 Sep 2015 (SI 2015/1327) | |
| para 19 | 1 Sep 2015 (SI 2015/1327)[1] | |
| paras 20–26 | 1 Sep 2015 (SI 2015/1327) | |
| para 27 | 1 Aug 2015 (SI 2015/1327) | |
| para 28(a)–(f) | 20 May 2015 (for the purpose of making regulations) (SI 2015/1327) | |
| | 1 Aug 2015 (otherwise) (SI 2015/1327) | |
| para 28(g) | 20 May 2015 (for the purpose of making regulations) (SI 2015/1327) | |
| para 29 | 1 Aug 2015 (SI 2015/1327) | |
| para 30 | 20 May 2015 (for the purpose of making regulations) (SI 2015/1327) | |
| para 31 | 1 Sep 2015 (SI 2015/1327) | |

[1]   For savings, see SI 2015/1327, arts 7–9

## House of Commons Commission Act 2015 (c 24)

*RA:* 26 Mar 2015

*Commencement provisions:* s 3

| | |
|---|---|
| 1 | 26 Mar 2015 (for the purpose of making appointment) (s 3(2)) |
| | 10 Jul 2015 (otherwise) (s 3(3)) |
| 2 | 10 Jul 2015 (s 3(3)) |
| 3 | 26 Mar 2015 (s 3(1)) |
| Schedule | 26 Mar 2015 (for the purpose of making appointment) (s 3(2)) |
| | 10 Jul 2015 (otherwise) (s 3(3)) |

## House of Lords (Expulsion and Suspension) Act 2015 (c 14)

*RA:* 26 Mar 2015

*Commencement provisions:* s 4(2)

| | |
|---|---|
| 1–3 | 26 Jun 2015 (s 4(2)) |
| 4 | 26 Mar 2015 (RA) |

## Human Trafficking and Exploitation (Scotland) Act 2015 (asp 12)

*RA:* 4 Nov 2015

*Commencement provisions:* s 45; Human Trafficking and Exploitation (Scotland) Act 2015 (Commencement No 1 and Transitory Provisions) Regulations 2016, SSI 2016/128; Human Trafficking and Exploitation (Scotland) Act 2015 (Commencement No 2 and Transitional Provisions) Regulations 2016, SSI 2016/385; Human Trafficking and Exploitation (Scotland) Act 2015 (Commencement No 3 and Transitional Provisions) Regulations 2017, SSI 2017/140; Human Trafficking and Exploitation (Scotland) Act 2015 (Commencement No 4) Regulations 2018, SSI 2018/9

| | |
|---|---|
| 1–8 | 31 May 2016 (SSI 2016/128) |
| 9 | 31 May 2016 (for the purpose of making regulations under sub-ss (2)(b)(i), (8)) (SSI 2016/128) |
| | 1 Apr 2018 (otherwise) (SSI 2018/9) |
| 10 | 31 May 2016 (SSI 2016/128) |

**Human Trafficking and Exploitation (Scotland) Act 2015 (asp 12)**—*contd*

| | | |
|---|---|---|
| 11 | | 31 May 2016 (for the purpose of making regulations under sub-ss (7), (8)) (SSI 2016/128) |
| | | *Not yet in force* (otherwise) |
| 12 | | 31 May 2016 (for the purpose of making regulations under sub-s (5)) (SSI 2016/128) |
| | | 31 Jan 2018 (otherwise) (SSI 2018/9) |
| 13–15 | | 31 May 2016 (SSI 2016/128) |
| 16 | | 29 Jun 2017 (SSI 2017/140) |
| 17–25 | | 30 Jun 2017 (SSI 2017/140) |
| 26–31 | | 31 Oct 2017 (SSI 2017/140) |
| 32, 33 | | 31 May 2016 (SSI 2016/128) |
| 34 | (1) | 31 May 2016 (SSI 2016/128) |
| | (2)–(6) | 30 Jun 2017 (SSI 2017/140)[3] |
| 35–37 | | 31 May 2016 (SSI 2016/128) |
| 38 | | 31 May 2016 (for the purpose of making regulations under sub-ss (3), (4)) (SSI 2016/128) |
| | | *Not yet in force* (otherwise) |
| 39 | | 31 May 2016 (SSI 2016/128) |
| 40–42 | | 5 Nov 2015 (s 45(1)) |
| 43 | | See the Schedule below |
| 44–46 | | 5 Nov 2015 (s 45(1)) |
| Schedule | para 1 | 31 May 2016 (SSI 2016/128) |
| | para 2 | 17 Dec 2016 (SSI 2016/385)[2] |
| | para 3 | 31 May 2016 (SSI 2016/128)[1] |
| | paras 4, 5 | 17 Dec 2016 (SSI 2016/385)[2] |
| | para 6 | 31 May 2016 (SSI 2016/128) |

[1]   For transitory provisions, see SSI 2016/128, reg 3

[2]   For transitional provisions, see SSI 2016/385

[3]   For transitional provisions, see SSI 2017/140, art 3

---

**Infrastructure Act 2015 (c 7)**

*RA:* 12 Feb 2015

*Commencement provisions*: s 57; Infrastructure Act 2015 (Commencement No 1) Regulations 2015, SI 2015/481; Infrastructure Act 2015 (Commencement No 2 and Transitional Provisions) Regulations 2015, SI 2015/758; Infrastructure Act 2015 (Commencement) (Wales) Regulations 2015, SI 2015/990; Infrastructure Act 2015 (Commencement No 3) Regulations 2015, SI 2015/1543; Infrastructure Act 2015 (Commencement No 4) Regulations 2015, SI 2015/1576; Infrastructure Act (Commencement No 5) Regulations 2016, SI 2016/455; Infrastructure Act 2015 (Commencement No 6 and Savings) Regulations 2017, SI 2017/108; Infrastructure Act 2015 (Commencement No 7) Regulations 2017, SI 2017/315

| | | |
|---|---|---|
| 1 | (1)–(5) | 12 Feb 2015 (in so far as they confer power to make regulations) (s 57(1)(a)) |
| | | 5 Mar 2015 (otherwise) (SI 2015/481) |
| | (6) | See Sch 1 below |
| 2 | | 12 Feb 2015 (in so far as it confers power to make regulations) (s 57(1)(a)) |
| | | 5 Mar 2015 (otherwise) (SI 2015/481) |
| 3 | (1)–(7) | 12 Feb 2015 (in so far as they confer power to make regulations) (s 57(1)(a)) |
| | | 5 Mar 2015 (otherwise) (SI 2015/481) |
| | (8) | See Sch 2 below |
| 4–14 | | 12 Feb 2015 (in so far as they confer power to make regulations) (s 57(1)(a)) |
| | | 5 Mar 2015 (otherwise) (SI 2015/481) |

**Infrastructure Act 2015 (c 7)**—*contd*

| | | |
|---|---|---|
| 15 | (1), (2) | 12 Feb 2015 (in so far as they confer power to make regulations) (s 57(1)(a)) |
| | | 5 Mar 2015 (otherwise) (SI 2015/481) |
| | (3) | See Sch 3 below |
| | (4) | 12 Feb 2015 (in so far as it confers power to make regulations) (s 57(1)(a)) |
| | | 5 Mar 2015 (otherwise) (SI 2015/481) |
| 16–20 | | 12 Feb 2015 (in so far as they confer power to make regulations) (s 57(1)(a)) |
| | | 5 Mar 2015 (otherwise) (SI 2015/481) |
| 21 | | 31 Jul 2015 (SI 2015/1543) |
| 22 | | 12 Apr 2015 (s 57(3)) |
| 23 | | 12 Apr 2015 (E) (SI 2015/481) |
| | | 12 Apr 2015 (W) (SI 2015/990) |
| 24, 25 | | 5 Mar 2015 (E) (SI 2015/481) |
| | | 12 Apr 2015 (W) (SI 2015/990) |
| 26 | | 12 Apr 2015 (SI 2015/758)[1] |
| 27 | | 5 Apr 2017 (SI 2017/315) |
| 28 | | 12 Feb 2015 (in so far as it confers power to make regulations) (s 57(5)(b)(i)) |
| | | 14 Jul 2015 (otherwise) (SI 2015/758)[1] |
| 29 | | 12 Feb 2015 (s 57(5)(c)) |
| 30 | | 12 Feb 2015 (in so far as it confers power to make provision by regulations or by development order) (s 57(5)(d)(i)) |
| | | *Not yet in force* (otherwise) |
| 31, 32 | | 12 Apr 2015 (s 57(5)(e)) |
| 33 | | 12 Feb 2015 (s 57(5)(c)) |
| 34–36 | | 12 Apr 2015 (s 57(5)(e)) |
| 37 | | *Not yet in force* |
| 38, 39 | | 1 Jun 2016 (s 57(7)(a)) |
| 40 | | 12 Apr 2015 (s 57(7)(b)) |
| 41, 42 | | 12 Apr 2015 (SI 2015/481) |
| 43–49 | | 12 Apr 2015 (s 57(7)(b)) |
| 50 | | 30 Jul 2015 (in so far as inserts Petroleum Act 1998, s 4B(4)–(7)) (SI 2015/1576) |
| | | 6 Apr 2016 (otherwise) (SI 2016/455) |
| 51 | | 12 Feb 2015 (s 57(7)(d)) |
| 52 | | 6 Apr 2017 (SI 2017/108) |
| 53 | | 12 Feb 2015 (s 57(7)(d)) |
| 54 | | 12 Apr 2015 (s 57(8)) |
| 55–58 | | 12 Feb 2015 (s 57(9)) |
| Schs 1–3 | | 12 Feb 2015 (in so far as they confer power to make regulations) (s 57(1)(a)) |
| | | 5 Mar 2015 (otherwise) (SI 2015/481) |
| Sch 4 | | 12 Feb 2015 (in so far as it confers power to make provision by regulations or by development order) (s 57(5)(d)) |
| | | *Not yet in force* (otherwise) |
| Sch 5 | | 12 Apr 2015 (s 57(5)(e)) |
| Sch 6 | | 1 Jun 2016 (s 57(7)(a)) |
| Sch 7 | | 12 Apr 2015 (SI 2015/481) |

[1]  For transitional provisions, see SI 2015/758, reg 4

[2]  For savings, see SI 2017/108, reg 2

**Insurance Act 2015 (c 4)**

*RA:* 12 Feb 2015

*Commencement provisions:* s 23(2), (3)

| | |
|---|---|
| 1–18 | 12 Aug 2016 (s 23(2)) |
| 19 | 12 Apr 2015 (s 23(3)(a)) |
| 20 | 1 Aug 2016 (s 23(3)(b)) |
| 21, 22 | 12 Aug 2016 (s 23(2)) |
| 23 | 12 Feb 2015 (s 23(4)) |
| Sch 1 | 12 Aug 2016 (s 23(2)) |
| Sch 2 | 1 Aug 2016 (s 23(3)(b)) |

**International Development (Official Development Assistance Target) Act 2015 (c 12)**

*RA:* 26 Mar 2015

*Commencement provisions:* s 6(2)

Whole Act in force 1 Jun 2015 (s 6(2))

**Legal Writings (Counterparts and Delivery) (Scotland) Act 2015 (asp 4)**

*RA:* 1 Apr 2015

*Commencement provisions:* s 6; Legal Writings (Counterparts and Delivery) (Scotland) Act 2015 (Commencement) Order 2015, SSI 2015/242

| | |
|---|---|
| 1–4 | 1 Jul 2015 (SSI 2015/242) |
| 5–7 | 2 Apr 2015 (s 6(1)) |

**Local Government (Religious etc Observances) Act 2015 (c 27)**

*RA:* 26 Mar 2015

*Commencement provisions:* s 3(2)

Whole Act in force 26 May 2015 (s 3(2))

**Local Government (Review of Decisions) Act 2015 (c 22)**

*RA:* 26 Mar 2015

*Commencement provisions:* s 4(2)

Whole Act in force 26 May 2015 (s 4(2))

**Local Government (Wales) Act 2015 (c 35)**

*RA:* 25 Nov 2015

*Commencement provisions:* s 46

| | |
|---|---|
| 1–24 | 26 Nov 2016 (s 46(2)) |
| 25–28 | 25 Jan 2016 (s 46(1)) |
| 29–36 | 26 Nov 2016 (s 46(2)) |
| 37–43 | 25 Jan 2016 (s 46(1)) |
| 44–47 | 26 Nov 2016 (s 46(2)) |

## Lords Spiritual (Women) Act 2015 (c 18)

*RA*: 26 Mar 2015

*Commencement provisions*: s 2

Whole Act in force 18 May 2015 (s 2(1))

---

## Mental Health (Scotland) Act 2015 (asp 9)

*RA*: 4 Aug 2015

*Commencement provisions*: s 61; Mental Health (Scotland) Act 2015 (Commencement No 1, Transitional and Saving Provisions) Order 2015, SSI 2015/361; Mental Health (Scotland) Act 2015 (Commencement No 2) Order 2015, SSI 2015/417; Mental Health (Scotland) Act 2015 (Commencement No 3) Order 2017, SSI 2017/126; Mental Health (Scotland) Act 2015 (Commencement No 4 and Transitional and Savings Provisions) Order 2017, SSI 2017/197; Mental Health (Scotland) Act 2015 (Commencement No 5 and Transitional Provisions) Order 2017, SSI 2017/234

| 1 | | Not yet in force |
|---|---|---|
| 2 | | 30 Jun 2017 (SSI 2017/197)[2] |
| 3 | | 30 Jun 2017 (SSI 2017/197) |
| 4, 5 | | 30 Jun 2017 (SSI 2017/197)[2] |
| 6 | | 30 Jun 2017 (SSI 2017/197) |
| 7, 8 | | 30 Jun 2017 (SSI 2017/197)[2] |
| 9 | | 30 Jun 2017 (SSI 2017/197) |
| 10 | | 30 Jun 2017 (SSI 2017/197)[2] |
| 11–13 | | 30 Jun 2017 (SSI 2017/197) |
| 14, 15 | | 16 Nov 2015 (SSI 2015/361)[1] |
| 16 | | 16 Nov 2015 (SSI 2015/361) |
| 17 | | 5 Aug 2015 (s 61(1)) |
| 18 | | 16 Nov 2015 (SSI 2015/361) |
| 19–22 | | 30 Jun 2017 (SSI 2017/197)[2] |
| 23 | (1), (2) | 5 May 2017 (so far as is necessary to enable the Scottish Ministers to make regulations under s 250(2A) of the Mental Health (Care and Treatment) (Scotland) Act 2003) (SSI 2017/126) |
| | | 30 Jun 2017 (so far as not already in force except in so far as the amendment made to the Mental Health (Care and Treatment) (Scotland) Act 2003, s 250 by s 23(2)(b) of has effect in relation to s 257A(7), (8) of the 2003 Act) (SSI 2017/197)[2] |
| | | Not yet in force (exception noted above) |
| | (3) | 30 Jun 2017 (SSI 2017/197)[2] |
| 24–28 | | 30 Jun 2017 (SSI 2017/197) |
| 29 | | 5 May 2017 (so far as is necessary to enable the Scottish Ministers to make regulations under s 291A(2) of the Mental Health (Care and Treatment) (Scotland) Act 2003) (SSI 2017/126) |
| | | 30 Jun 2017 (otherwise) (SSI 2017/197) |
| 30, 31 | | 30 Jun 2017 (SSI 2017/197) |
| 32 | | 5 May 2017 (So far as is necessary to enable the Scottish Ministers to make regulations under ss 289(1)(3), 290(1)(4), 309A(1)(5) of the Mental Health (Care and Treatment) (Scotland) Act 2003) (SSI 2017/126) |
| | | 30 Jun 2017 (otherwise) (SSI 2017/197) |
| 33 | | 5 May 2017 (so far as is necessary to enable the Scottish Ministers to make regulations under ss 309(1)(6), (2ZA)(7), 310(1) as read with s 310(3A)(8) of the Mental Health (Care and Treatment) (Scotland) Act 2003) (SSI 2017/126) |
| | | 30 Jun 2017 (otherwise) (SSI 2017/197) |
| 34 | | 30 Jun 2017 (SSI 2017/197) |
| 35, 36 | | 30 Jun 2017 (SSI 2017/197)[2] |
| 37 | | 24 Dec 2015 (SSI 2015/417) |
| 38, 39 | | 30 Jun 2017 (SSI 2017/197) |

**Mental Health (Scotland) Act 2015 (asp 9)**—*contd*

| | |
|---|---|
| 40–44 | 30 Jun 2017 (SSI 2017/197)[2] |
| 45–48 | 30 Jun 2017 (SSI 2017/197) |
| 49, 50 | 30 Jun 2017 (SSI 2017/197)[2] |
| 51 | 30 Jun 2017 (SSI 2017/197) |
| 52 | 30 Jun 2017 (SSI 2017/197)[2] |
| 53 | 30 Jun 2017 (SSI 2017/197) |
| 54 | 5 May 2017 (so far as is necessary to enable the Scottish Ministers to make regulations under s 16(4)(b), (c) of the Criminal Justice (Scotland) Act 2003) (SSI 2017/126) |
| | 15 Sep 2017 (for the purpose only of enabling any person who is entitled to receive information under Criminal Justice (Scotland) Act 2003, s16(1) to intimate a wish to receive the information that is required to be given by virtue of the amendments made to that section by s 54 of this Act) (SSI 2017/234)[3] |
| | 30 Sep 2017 (otherwise) (SSI 2017/234)[3] |
| 55 | 15 Sep 2017 (for the purpose only of enabling persons who are entitled by virtue of Criminal Justice (Scotland) Act 2003, s 16A(1)(c) to ask to be given information about O under section 16 A(1) of the 2003 Act) (SSI 2017/234)[3] |
| | 30 Sep 2017 (otherwise) (SSI 2017/234)[3] |
| 56 | 15 Sep 2017 (for the purpose only of enabling a person who is to be given information under Criminal Justice (Scotland) Act 2003, ss 16, 16A to intimate under s17B of that Act a wish to be afforded an opportunity to make representations under that section; and under s 17D of that Act a wish to receive information under that section) (SSI 2017/234) |
| | 30 Sep 2017 (otherwise) (SSI 2017/234) |
| 57 | 15 Sep 2017 (SSI 2017/234) |
| 58 | 5 May 2017 (so far as is necessary to enable the Scottish Ministers to make regulations under s 16(4)(b), (c) of the Criminal Justice (Scotland) Act 2003) (SSI 2017/126) |
| | 15 Sep 2017 (otherwise) (SSI 2017/234) |
| 59, 60 | 30 Sep 2017 (SSI 2017/234) |
| 61, 62 | 5 Aug 2015 (s 61(1)) |

[1] For transitional and saving provisions, see SSI 2015/361, arts 3–6

[1] For transitional and saving provisions, see SSI 2017/197, arts 3–25

[3] For transitional provisions, see SSI 2017/234, arts 3–8

---

**Modern Slavery Act 2015 (c 30)**

*RA:* 26 Mar 2015

*Commencement provisions:* s 61; Modern Slavery Act 2015 (Commencement No 1, Saving and Transitional Provisions) Regulations 2015, SI 2015/1476; Modern Slavery Act 2015 (Commencement No 2) Regulations 2015, SI 2015/1690; Modern Slavery Act 2015 (Commencement No 3 and Transitional Provision) Regulations 2015, SI 2015/1816; Modern Slavery Act 2015 (Commencement No 4) Regulations 2016, SI 2016/243; Modern Slavery Act 2015 (Commencement No 5) Regulations 2016, SI 2016/740

| | | |
|---|---|---|
| 1–6 | | 31 Jul 2015 (SI 2015/1476) |
| 7 | (1), (2) | 31 Jul 2015 (SI 2015/1476) |
| | (3) | 31 Jul 2015 (SI 2015/1476)[1] |
| 8–34 | | 31 Jul 2015 (SI 2015/1476) |
| 35–37 | | 8 Aug 2016 (SI 2016/740) |
| 38 | | *Not yet in force* |
| 39 | | 8 Aug 2016 (SI 2016/740) |
| 40–45 | | 31 Jul 2015 (SI 2015/1476) |

**Modern Slavery Act 2015 (c 30)**—*contd*

| | | |
|---|---|---|
| 46 | | 31 Jul 2015 (SI 2015/1476)[1] |
| 47 | | 31 Jul 2015 (SI 2015/1476) |
| 48 | (1)–(6) | *Not yet in force* |
| | (7) | 26 May 2015 (s 61(2)) |
| 49 | | 15 Oct 2015 (SI 2015/1690) |
| 50 | | *Not yet in force* |
| 51 | | 15 Oct 2015 (SI 2015/1690) |
| 52 | | 1 Nov 2015 (SI 2015/1690) |
| 53 | | 15 Oct 2015 (SI 2015/1690) |
| 54 | | 29 Oct 2015 (SI 2015/1816)[2] |
| 55, 56 | | 26 Mar 2015 (s 61(3)) |
| 57 | (1) | See Sch 5 below |
| | (2), (3) | 26 Mar 2015 (s 61(3)) |
| 58–62 | | 26 Mar 2015 (s 61(3)) |
| Sch 1 | | 31 Jul 2015 (SI 2015/1476) |
| Sch 2 | | 8 Aug 2016 (in so far as relates to powers exercisable under ss 35–37) (SI 2016/740) |
| | | *Not yet in force* (otherwise) |
| Schs 3, 4 | | 31 Jul 2015 (SI 2015/1476) |
| Sch 5 | paras 1, 2 | 31 Jul 2015 (SI 2015/1476)[1] |
| | para 3, 4 | 31 Jul 2015 (SI 2015/1476) |
| | para 5(1)–(3) | 31 Jul 2015 (SI 2015/1476) |
| | para 5(4) | 31 Jul 2015 (SI 2015/1476)[1] |
| | para 6(1) | 31 Jul 2015 (SI 2015/1476) |
| | para 6(2), (3) | 31 Jul 2015 (SI 2015/1476)[1] |
| | para 6(4)(a) | 31 Jul 2015 (SI 2015/1476)[1] |
| | para 6(4)(b) | 31 Jul 2015 (SI 2015/1476) |
| | para 7 | 31 Jul 2015 (SI 2015/1476) |
| | paras 8, 9 | 31 Jul 2015 (SI 2015/1476)[1] |
| | para 10 | 31 Jul 2015 (SI 2015/1476) |
| | para 11 | 17 Mar 2016 (SI 2016/243) |
| | paras 12–14 | 31 Jul 2015 (SI 2015/1476) |
| | para 15 | 17 Mar 2016 (SI 2016/243) |
| | paras 16–19 | 31 Jul 2015 (SI 2015/1476) |
| | para 20 | *Never in force* (repealed) |
| | paras 21–26 | 31 Jul 2015 (SI 2015/1476) |
| | para 27(1), (2) | 31 Jul 2015 (SI 2015/1476) |
| | para 27(3) | 17 Mar 2016 (SI 2016/243) |

[1] For transitional and saving provisions, see SI 2015/1476, arts 3–8

[2] For a transitional provision, see SI 2015/1816, reg 3

---

**Mutuals' Deferred Shares Act 2015 (c 13)**

*RA*: 26 Mar 2015

*Commencement provisions*: s 4(2)

| | |
|---|---|
| 1–3 | *Not yet in force* |
| 4 | 26 Mar 2015 (RA) |

---

**National Insurance Contributions Act 2015 (c 5)**

*RA*: 12 Feb 2015

*Commencement provisions*: ss 1(11), 5(7), 6(7), Sch 2, Pt 4

| | | |
|---|---|---|
| 1 | (1)–(3) | 6 Apr 2016 (s 1(11)(b)) |

**National Insurance Contributions Act 2015 (c 5)**—*contd*

|         |          |                                                                                 |
|---------|----------|---------------------------------------------------------------------------------|
|         | (4)      | 12 Apr 2015 (for the purpose of making regulations under the Social Security Contributions and Benefits Act 1992, s 9B) (s 1(11)(a)) |
|         |          | 6 Apr 2016 (s 1(11)(b)) (otherwise)                                             |
|         | (5)–(8)  | 6 Apr 2016 (s 1(11)(b))                                                         |
|         | (9)      | 12 Apr 2015 (for the purpose of making regulations under the Social Security Contributions and Benefits (Northern Ireland) Act 1992, s 9B) (s 1(11)(a)) |
|         |          | 6 Apr 2016 (s 1(11)(b)) (otherwise)                                            |
|         | (10)     | 6 Apr 2016 (s 1(11)(b))                                                         |
|         | (11)     | 12 Feb 2015 (RA)                                                                |
| 2, 3    |          | 12 Feb 2015 (RA)                                                                |
| 4       |          | See Sch 2 below                                                                 |
| 5       |          | 12 Apr 2015 (s 5(7))                                                            |
| 6       | (1)      | 6 Apr 2014 (for the purpose of inserting SI 1978/1689, reg 5A(1)–(5), (6)(a), (7)) (s 6(7)(a)) |
|         |          | 12 Feb 2015 (for the purpose of inserting SI 1978/1689, reg 5A(6)(b)) (s 6(7)(b)) |
|         | (2)      | 6 Apr 2014 (for the purpose of inserting SR 1978/401, reg 5A(1)–(5), (6)(a), (7)) (s 6(7)(a)) |
|         |          | 12 Feb 2015 (for the purpose of inserting SR 1978/401, reg 5A(6)(b)) (s 6(7)(b)) |
|         | (3)–(11) | 12 Feb 2015 (RA)                                                                |
| 7–9     |          | 12 Feb 2015 (RA)                                                                |
| Sch 1   |          | 12 Feb 2015 (RA)                                                                |
| Sch 2   | Pt 1     | 12 Apr 2015 (Sch 2, Pt 4, para 33(1))                                          |
|         | Pt 2     | 12 Feb 2015 (for the purpose of making regulations under Finance Act 2015, Pt 5) (Sch 2, Pt 4, para 33(2)(a)) |
|         |          | 12 Apr 2015 (Sch 2, Pt 4, para 33(2)(b)) (otherwise)                          |
|         | Pt 3     | 12 Apr 2015 (Sch 2, Pt 4, para 33(1))                                          |
|         | Pt 4     | 12 Feb 2015 (RA)                                                                |

**National Insurance Contributions (Rate Ceilings) Act 2015 (c 35)**

*RA:* 17 Dec 2015

*Commencement provisions:* s 5(2)

Whole Act in force 17 Dec 2015 (s 5(2))

**Northern Ireland (Welfare Reform) Act 2015 (c 34)**

*RA:* 25 Nov 2015

*Commencement provisions:* s 3(2)

Whole Act in force 25 Nov 2015 (s 34(2))

**Pension Schemes Act 2015 (c 8)**

*RA:* 3 Mar 2015

*Commencement provisions:* s 89; Pension Schemes Act 2015 (Commencement No 1) Regulations 2015, SI 2015/1851; Pensions Act 2014 (Commencement No 11) and the Pension Schemes Act 2015 (Commencement No 2) Regulations 2017, SI 2017/916

|       |          |                                   |
|-------|----------|-----------------------------------|
| 1–37  |          | *Not yet in force*                |
| 38    | (1)      | 18 Sep 2017 (SI 2017/916)         |
|       | (2), (3) | *Not yet in force*                |
|       | (4)      | 18 Sep 2017 (SI 2017/916)         |

**Pension Schemes Act 2015 (c 8)**—*contd*

|  |  |  |
|---|---|---|
| | (5)–(7) | *Not yet in force* |
| 39 | | *Not yet in force* |
| 40 | | See Sch 1 below |
| 41–45 | | *Not yet in force* |
| 46 | | See Sch 2 below |
| 47 | | 3 Mar 2015 (s 89(1)(a)) |
| 48–76 | | 3 Mar 2015 (in so far as necessary for enabling the exercise of any |
| | | power to make provision by regulations) (s 89(1)(b)) |
| | | 6 Apr 2015 (otherwise) (s 89(3)(b)) |
| 77 | | 16 Nov 2015 (SI 2015/1851) |
| 78, 79 | | 3 Mar 2015 (s 89(1)(c)) |
| 80 | | 3 Mar 2015 (s 89(1)(d)) |
| 81 | | 16 Nov 2015 (SI 2015/1851) |
| 82 | | 1 Apr 2015 (s 89(2)) |
| 83–90 | | 3 Mar 2015 (s 89(1)(e)) |
| Sch 1 | | *Not yet in force* |
| Sch 2 | paras 1–23 | *Not yet in force* |
| | para 24 | 6 Apr 2015 (s 89(3)(a)) |
| | paras 25–29 | *Not yet in force* |
| | para 30 | 6 Apr 2015 (s 89(3)(a)) |
| | paras 31, 32 | *Not yet in force* |
| | para 33 | 6 Apr 2015 (s 89(3)(a)) |
| | paras 34, 35 | *Not yet in force* |
| | para 36 | 6 Apr 2015 (s 89(3)(a)) |
| | paras 37–51 | *Not yet in force* |
| Sch 3 | | 3 Mar 2015 (s 89(1)(a)) |
| Sch 4 | | 3 Mar 2015 (in so far as necessary for enabling the exercise of any |
| | | power to make provision by regulations) (s 89(1)(b)) |
| | | 6 Apr 2015 (otherwise) (s 89(3)(b)) |
| Sch 5 | | 3 Mar 2015 (s 89(1)(c)) |

**Planning (Wales) Act 2015 (anaw 4)**

*RA:* 6 Jul 2015

*Commencement provisions*: s 58; Planning (Wales) Act 2015 (Commencement No 1) Order 2015, SI 2015/1736; Planning (Wales) Act 2015 (Commencement No 2 and Transitional and Saving Provisions) Order 2015, SI 2015/1987; Planning (Wales) Act 2015 (Commencement No 3 and Transitional Provisions) Order 2016, SI 2016/52; Planning (Wales) Act 2015 (Commencement No 4 and Transitional Provisions) Order 2017, SI 2017/546; Planning (Wales) Act 2015 (Commencement No 5 and Transitional Provisions) Order 2018, SI 2018/1022; Planning (Wales) Act 2015 (Commencement No 6) Order 2020, SI 2020/1216; Planning (Wales) Act 2015 (Commencement No 7) Order 2021, SI 2021/7

|  |  |  |
|---|---|---|
| 1 | | 6 Jul 2015 (s 58(1)) |
| 2 | | 1 Apr 2016 (SI 2015/1987)[1] |
| 3 | | 4 Jan 2016 (so far as it substitutes the Planning and Compulsory |
| | | Purchase Act 2004, ss 60–60B) (SI 2015/1987)[1] |
| | | 4 Dec 2020 (otherwise) (SI 2020/1216) |
| 4 | (1) | 6 Sep 2015 (so far as is necessary for enabling the Welsh Ministers |
| | | to make regulations or orders under the enactment(s) amended |
| | | by this section) (s 58(2)) |
| | | 5 Oct 2015 (otherwise) (SI 2015/1736) |
| | (2) | See Sch 1 below |
| 5 | | 7 Jan 2021 (SI 2021/7) |
| 6 | | 6 Sep 2015 (so far as is necessary for enabling the Welsh Ministers |
| | | to make regulations or orders under the enactment(s) amended |
| | | by this section) (s 58(2)) |
| | | 7 Jan 2021 (SI 2021/7) (otherwise) |
| 7 | | 4 Dec 2020 (SI 2020/1216) |

**Planning (Wales) Act 2015 (anaw 4)**—*contd*

| | | |
|---|---|---|
| 8 | | 6 Sep 2015 (so far as is necessary for enabling the Welsh Ministers to make regulations or orders under the enactment(s) amended by this section) (s 58(2)) |
| | | 4 Dec 2020 (otherwise) (SI 2020/1216) |
| 9, 10 | | 4 Dec 2020 (SI 2020/1216) |
| 11, 12 | | 4 Jan 2016 (SI 2015/1987)[1] |
| 13, 14 | | 6 Sep 2015 (so far as is necessary for enabling the Welsh Ministers to make regulations or orders under the enactment(s) amended by this section) (s 58(2)) |
| | | 4 Jan 2016 (otherwise) (SI 2015/1987) |
| 15 | (1), (2) | 16 Mar 2016 (SI 2015/1987) |
| | (3) | 1 Apr 2016 (SI 2015/1987) |
| 16 | | See Sch 2 below |
| 17 | | 1 Mar 2016 (SI 2016/52)[2] |
| 18 | | 6 Sep 2015 (so far as is necessary for enabling the Welsh Ministers to make regulations or orders under the enactment(s) amended by this section) (s 58(2)) |
| | | 1 Mar 2016 (otherwise) (SI 2016/52) |
| 19 | | 6 Sep 2015 (so far as is necessary for enabling the Welsh Ministers to make regulations or orders under the enactment(s) amended by this section) (s 58(2)) |
| | | 1 Mar 2016 (otherwise) (SI 2016/52)[2] |
| 20 | | 6 Sep 2015 (so far as is necessary for enabling the Welsh Ministers to make regulations or orders under the enactment(s) amended by this section) (s 58(2)) |
| | | 1 Mar 2016 (otherwise) (SI 2016/52) |
| 21 | | 1 Mar 2016 (SI 2016/52) |
| 22 | | 6 Sep 2015 (so far as is necessary for enabling the Welsh Ministers to make regulations or orders under the enactment(s) amended by this section) (s 58(2)) |
| | | 1 Mar 2016 (otherwise) (SI 2016/52) |
| 23 | | 6 Sep 2015 (so far as is necessary for enabling the Welsh Ministers to make regulations or orders under the enactment(s) amended by this section) (s 58(2)) |
| | | *Not yet in force* (otherwise) |
| 24, 25 | | 1 Mar 2016 (in so far as relate to developments of national significance and secondary consents) (SI 2016/52) |
| | | *Not yet in force* (otherwise) |
| 26 | (1) | 1 Mar 2016 (in so far as relates to developments of national significance and secondary consents) (SI 2016/52) |
| | | *Not yet in force* (otherwise) |
| | (2) | See Sch 3 below |
| 27 | | See Sch 4 below |
| 28, 29 | | 16 Mar 2016 (SI 2016/52)[2] |
| 30 | | 16 Mar 2016 (SI 2016/52) |
| 31 | | 4 Jan 2016 (SI 2015/1987) |
| 32 | | 16 Mar 2016 (SI 2016/52)[2] |
| 33, 34 | | 1 Mar 2016 (in so far as relate to developments of national significance and secondary consents) (SI 2016/52)[2] |
| | | 16 Mar 2016 (otherwise) (SI 2016/52)[2] |
| 35, 36 | | 16 Mar 2016 (SI 2016/52)[2] |
| 37, 38 | | 16 Mar 2016 (SI 2016/52) |
| 39 | | 6 Sep 2015 (so far as is necessary for enabling the Welsh Ministers to make regulations or orders under the enactment(s) amended by this section) (s 58(2)) |
| | | 5 May 2017 (so far as not already in force) (SI 2017/546) |
| 40 | | 16 Mar 2016 (SI 2015/1987) |
| 41 | | 6 Sep 2015 (so far as is necessary for enabling the Welsh Ministers to make regulations or orders under the enactment(s) amended by this section) (s 58(2)) |

**Planning (Wales) Act 2015 (anaw 4)**—*contd*

|  |  |  |
|---|---|---|
|  |  | 16 Mar 2016 (otherwise) (SI 2015/1987) |
| 42 |  | 16 Mar 2016 (SI 2015/1987) |
| 43 |  | 16 Mar 2016 (SI 2016/52) |
| 44–46 |  | 16 Mar 2016 (SI 2016/52)[2] |
| 47 |  | 6 Sep 2015 (so far as is necessary for enabling the Welsh Ministers to make regulations or orders under the enactment(s) amended by this section) (s 58(2)) |
|  |  | 5 May 2017 (so far as not already in force) (SI 2017/546)[3] |
| 48 |  | 6 Sep 2015 (so far as is necessary for enabling the Welsh Ministers to make regulations or orders under the enactment(s) amended by this section) (s 58(2)) |
|  |  | 5 May 2017 (so far as not already in force) (SI 2017/546)[4] |
| 49 |  | 6 Sep 2015 (so far as is necessary for enabling the Welsh Ministers to make regulations or orders under the enactment(s) amended by this section) (s 58(2)) |
|  |  | 1 Mar 2016 (otherwise) (SI 2016/52)[2] |
| 50 |  | 6 Sep 2015 (so far as is necessary for enabling the Welsh Ministers to make regulations or orders under the enactment(s) amended by this section) (s 58(2)) |
|  |  | 1 Mar 2016 (in so far as relates to developments of national significance and secondary consents) (SI 2016/52) |
|  |  | 5 May 2017 (so far as not already in force) (SI 2017/546) |
| 51 |  | See Sch 5 below |
| 52 |  | 22 Oct 2018 (SI 2018/1022) |
| 53 | (1), (2) | 22 Oct 2018 (SI 2018/1022)[5] |
|  | (3) | See Sch 6 below |
| 54 |  | 10 Apr 2017 (SI 2017/546) |
| 55 |  | 6 Sep 2015 (s 58(2)) |
| 56–59 |  | 6 Jul 2015 (s 58(1)) |
| Sch 1 | Pt 1 | 6 Sep 2015 (so far as is necessary for enabling the Welsh Ministers to make regulations or orders under the enactment(s) amended by this section) (s 58(2)) |
|  |  | 5 Oct 2015 (otherwise) (SI 2015/1736) |
|  | Pt 2 | 6 Sep 2015 (so far as is necessary for enabling the Welsh Ministers to make regulations or orders under the enactment(s) amended by this section) (s 58(2)) |
|  | Pt 2, paras 2–5 | 7 Jan 2021 (otherwise) (SI 2021/7) |
|  | Pt 2, para 6 | *Not yet in force* (otherwise) |
|  | Pt 2, paras 7–9 | 7 Jan 2021 (otherwise) (SI 2021/7) |
| Sch 2 | para 1–9 | 7 Jan 2021 (otherwise) (SI 2021/7) |
|  | para 10(1)–(6) | 7 Jan 2021 (otherwise) (SI 2021/7) |
|  | para 11–14 | 7 Jan 2021 (otherwise) (SI 2021/7) |
|  | para 15 | 4 Dec 2020 (SI 2020/1216) |
|  | paras 16–22 | 7 Jan 2021 (otherwise) (SI 2021/7) |
|  | paras 23–27 | 4 Dec 2020 (SI 2020/1216) |
|  | para 28 | Never in force (repealed) |
|  | para 29 | 4 Dec 2020 (SI 2020/1216) |
|  | paras 30–32 | 7 Jan 2021 (otherwise) (SI 2021/7) |
|  | para 33 | 4 Dec 2020 (SI 2020/1216) |
|  | para 34(1) | See sub-paras (2), (3) below |
|  | para 34(2) | 7 Jan 2021 (otherwise) (SI 2021/7) |
|  | para 34(3)(a) | 4 Dec 2020 (SI 2020/1216) |
|  | para 34(3)(b) | 7 Jan 2021 (otherwise) (SI 2021/7) |
|  | paras 35, 36 | 4 Dec 2020 (SI 2020/1216) |
| Schs 3, 4 |  | 6 Sep 2015 (so far as is necessary for enabling the Welsh Ministers to make regulations or orders under the enactment(s) amended by this section) (s 58(2)) |
|  |  | 1 Mar 2016 (in so far as relate to developments of national significance and secondary consents) (SI 2016/52) |
|  |  | *Not yet in force* (otherwise) |

**Planning (Wales) Act 2015 (anaw 4)**—*contd*

| | | |
|---|---|---|
| Sch 5 | paras 1–14 | 1 Mar 2016 (SI 2016/52)[2] |
| | para 15 | 5 May 2017 (SI 2017/546) |
| | para 16(1) | See sub-paras (2), (3) below |
| | para 16(2) | 1 Mar 2016 (SI 2016/52)[2] |
| | para 16(3) | 5 May 2017 (SI 2017/546) |
| | para 17 | 5 May 2017 (SI 2017/546) |
| | para 18 | 1 Mar 2016 (in so far as relates to Town and Country Planning Act 1990, Sch 8, para 5(4)) (SI 2016/52)[2] |
| | | 5 May 2017 (so far as not already in force) (SI 2017/546) |
| | para 19 | See paras 20–22 below |
| | para 20 | 1 Mar 2016 (SI 2016/52)[2] |
| | para 21(1) | See sub-paras (2), (3) below |
| | para 21(2)(a), (b) | 1 Mar 2016 (SI 2016/52)[2] |
| | para 21(2)(c), (d), (3) | 5 May 2017 (SI 2017/546) |
| | para 22 | 1 Mar 2016 (SI 2016/52)[2] |
| | para 23 | See paras 24–26 below |
| | para 24 | 1 Mar 2016 (SI 2016/52)[2] |
| | para 25(1), (2)(a), (b) | 1 Mar 2016 (SI 2016/52) |
| | para 25(2)(c), (d), (3) | 5 May 2017 (SI 2017/546) |
| | para 26 | 1 Mar 2016 (SI 2016/52)[2] |
| | para 27 | 5 May 2017 (SI 2017/546) |
| Sch 6 | | 6 Sep 2015 (so far as is necessary for enabling the Welsh Ministers to make regulations or orders under the enactment(s) amended by this section) (s 58(2)) |
| | | 22 Oct 2018 (otherwise) (SI 2018/1022)[5] |
| Sch 7 | | 6 Sep 2015 (s 58(2)) |

[1] For transitional and saving provisions, see SI 2015/1987, arts 6, 7

[2] For transitional and saving provisions, see SI 2016/52, arts 6–17

[3] For transitional provisions, see SI 2017/546, art 4

[4] For transitional provisions, see SI 2017/546, art 5

[5] For transitional provisions, see SI 2018/1022, art 3

---

**Prisoners (Control of Release) (Scotland) Act 2015 (asp 8)**

*RA:* 4 Aug 2015

*Commencement provisions*: s 3; Prisoners (Control of Release) (Scotland) Act 2015 (Commencement) Order 2015, SSI 2015/409

| | |
|---|---|
| 1, 2 | 1 Feb 2016 (SSI 2015/409) |
| 3, 4 | 5 Aug 2015 (s 3(1)) |

---

**Qualifications Wales Act 2015 (anaw 5)**

*RA:* 5 Aug 2015

*Commencement provisions*: s 60; Qualifications Wales Act 2015 (Commencement No 1) Order 2015, SI 2015/1591; Qualifications Wales Act 2015 (Commencement No 2 and Transitional and Saving Provisions) Order 2015, SI 2015/1687

| | | |
|---|---|---|
| 1 | | 5 Aug 2015 (s 60(1)(a)) |
| 2 | (1) | 6 Aug 2015 (SI 2015/1591) |
| | (2) | See Sch 1 below |
| | (3) | 5 Aug 2015 (s 60(1)(b)) |

**Qualifications Wales Act 2015 (anaw 5)**—*contd*

| | | |
|---|---|---|
| 3, 4 | | 21 Sep 2015 (SI 2015/1687) |
| 5 | | 21 Sep 2015 (SI 2015/1687)[1] |
| 6, 7 | | 21 Sep 2015 (SI 2015/1687) |
| 8 | | 21 Sep 2015 (SI 2015/1687)[1] |
| 9, 10 | | 21 Sep 2015 (SI 2015/1687) |
| 11 | (1) | 21 Sep 2015 (SI 2015/1687) |
| | (2) | See Sch 3 below |
| 12–18 | | 21 Sep 2015 (SI 2015/1687) |
| 19 | | 21 Sep 2015 (SI 2015/1687)[1] |
| 20, 21 | | 21 Sep 2015 (SI 2015/1687) |
| 22 | (1), (2) | 21 Sep 2015 (SI 2015/1687) |
| | (3) | 21 Sep 2015 (SI 2015/1687)[1] |
| | (4)–(7) | 21 Sep 2015 (SI 2015/1687) |
| 23 | (1) | 21 Sep 2015 (SI 2015/1687) |
| | (2) | 21 Sep 2015 (SI 2015/1687)[1] |
| 24–28 | | 21 Sep 2015 (SI 2015/1687) |
| 29 | | 21 Sep 2015 (SI 2015/1687)[1] |
| 30–47 | | 21 Sep 2015 (SI 2015/1687) |
| 48 | | 21 Sep 2015 (SI 2015/1687)[1] |
| 49–54 | | 21 Sep 2015 (SI 2015/1687) |
| 55–57 | | 5 Aug 2015 (s 60(1)(c)) |
| 58 | | See Sch 4 below |
| 59–62 | | 5 Aug 2015 (s 60(1)(d)–(f)) |
| Sch 1 | paras 1–35 | 6 Aug 2015 (SI 2015/1591) |
| | para 36 | 21 Sep 2015 (SI 2015/1687) |
| | para 37 | 6 Aug 2015 (SI 2015/1591) |
| | paras 38–40 | 21 Sep 2015 (SI 2015/1687) |
| Sch 2 | | 5 Aug 2015 (s 60(1)(g)) |
| Sch 3 | para 1 | 21 Sep 2015 (SI 2015/1687) |
| | para 2(1) | 21 Sep 2015 (SI 2015/1687)[1] |
| | para 2(2)–(6) | 21 Sep 2015 (SI 2015/1687) |
| | paras 3–16 | 21 Sep 2015 (SI 2015/1687) |
| | para 17 | 21 Sep 2015 (SI 2015/1687)[1] |
| | paras 18–23 | 21 Sep 2015 (SI 2015/1687) |
| Sch 4 | para 1 | 21 Sep 2015 (SI 2015/1687) |
| | para 2(1) | See sub-paras (2)–(4) below |
| | para 2(2), (3)(a) | 21 Sep 2015 (SI 2015/1687)[1] |
| | para 2(3)(b), (c), (4) | 21 Sep 2015 (SI 2015/1687) |
| | paras 3–11 | 21 Sep 2015 (SI 2015/1687) |

[1]  For transitional and saving provisions, see SI 2015/1687, arts 3–13

---

**Recall of MPs Act 2015 (c 24)**

*RA: 26 Mar 2015*

*Commencement provisions*: s 24; Recall of MPs Act 2015 (Commencement) Regulations 2016, SI 2016/290

| | | |
|---|---|---|
| 1–5 | | 4 Mar 2016 (SI 2016/290) |
| 6 | (1), (2) | 4 Mar 2016 (SI 2016/290) |
| | (3) | See Sch 1 below |
| 7 | | 4 Mar 2016 (SI 2016/290) |
| 8 | | 26 Mar 2015 (so far as relates to the making of regulations under s 18)) (s 24(2)) |
| | | 4 Mar 2016 (otherwise) (SI 2016/290) |
| 9 | (1)–(4) | 4 Mar 2016 (SI 2016/290) |
| | (5), (6) | 26 Mar 2015 (s 24(1)) |
| 10 | (1)–(5) | 4 Mar 2016 (SI 2016/290) |
| | (6) | See Sch 2 below |

**Recall of MPs Act 2015 (c 24)**—*contd*

| | | |
|---|---|---|
| 11–15 | | 4 Mar 2016 (SI 2016/290) |
| 16 | (1) | See Sch 3 below |
| | (2) | See Sch 4 below |
| | (3) | See Sch 5 below |
| | (4), (5) | 26 Mar 2015 (s 24(1)) |
| 17, 18 | | 26 Mar 2015 (s 24(1)) |
| 19 | | 4 Mar 2016 (SI 2016/290) |
| 20 | | See Sch 6 below |
| 21–25 | | 26 Mar 2015 (s 24(1)) |
| Sch 1 | paras 1, 2 | 4 Mar 2016 (SI 2016/290) |
| | para 3 | 26 Mar 2015 (for the purpose of making regulations) (s 24(2)) |
| | | 4 Mar 2016 (otherwise) (SI 2016/290) |
| | para 4 | 4 Mar 2016 (SI 2016/290) |
| Sch 2 | para 1 | See paras 2–9 below |
| | paras 2–6 | 4 Mar 2016 (SI 2016/290) |
| | para 7 | 26 Mar 2015 (for the purpose of making regulations under Representation of the People Act 1983, s 13BC) (s 24(2)) |
| | | 4 Mar 2016 (otherwise) (SI 2016/290) |
| | paras 8, 9 | 4 Mar 2016 (SI 2016/290) |
| Sch 3 | paras 1–15 | 4 Mar 2016 (SI 2016/290) |
| | para 16 | 26 Mar 2015 (s 24(2)) |
| | paras 17–22 | 4 Mar 2016 (SI 2016/290) |
| | paras 23, 24 | 26 Mar 2015 (s 24(2)) |
| | paras 25, 26 | 4 Mar 2016 (SI 2016/290) |
| Sch 4 | paras 1, 2 | 4 Mar 2016 (SI 2016/290) |
| | para 3(1)–(3) | 4 Mar 2016 (SI 2016/290) |
| | para 3(4)–(6) | 26 Mar 2015 (s 24(2)) |
| | para 3(7) | 4 Mar 2016 (SI 2016/290) |
| | paras 4–7 | 4 Mar 2016 (SI 2016/290) |
| | para 8 | 26 Mar 2015 (s 24(2)) |
| | paras 9–22 | 4 Mar 2016 (SI 2016/290) |
| Sch 5 | para 1 | 26 Mar 2015 (for the purpose of making regulations) (s 24(2)) |
| | | 4 Mar 2016 (otherwise) (SI 2016/290) |
| | para 2 | 4 Mar 2016 (SI 2016/290) |
| | paras 3, 4 | 26 Mar 2015 (for the purpose of making regulations) (s 24(2)) |
| | | 4 Mar 2016 (otherwise) (SI 2016/290) |
| | paras 5–8 | 4 Mar 2016 (SI 2016/290) |
| | para 9 | 26 Mar 2015 (for the purpose of making regulations) (s 24(2)) |
| | | 4 Mar 2016 (otherwise) (SI 2016/290) |
| | para 10 | 4 Mar 2016 (SI 2016/290) |
| Sch 6 | para 1 | 4 Mar 2016 (SI 2016/290) |
| | para 2 | See paras 3–7 below |
| | para 3(1) | See sub-paras (2)–(9) below |
| | para 3(2)–(5) | 4 Mar 2016 (SI 2016/290) |
| | para 3(6) | 26 Mar 2015 (s 24(2)) |
| | para 3(7)–(9) | 4 Mar 2016 (SI 2016/290) |
| | paras 4–9 | 4 Mar 2016 (SI 2016/290) |

**Scottish Elections (Reduction of Voting Age) Act 2015 (asp 7)**

*RA:* 24 Jul 2015

*Commencement provisions:* s 21

Whole Act in force 25 Jul 2015 (s 21)

## Self-build and Custom Housebuilding Act 2015 (c 17)

*RA:* 26 Mar 2015

*Commencement provisions*: s 6; Self-build and Custom Housebuilding Act 2015 (Commencement) Regulations 2016, SI 2016/113

| | |
|---|---|
| 1–5 | 1 Apr 2016 (SI 2016/113) |
| 6 | 26 Mar 2015 (s 6(2)) |
| Schedule | 1 Apr 2016 (SI 2016/113) |

## Serious Crime Act 2015 (c 3)

*RA:* 3 Mar 2015

*Commencement provisions*: s 88; Serious Crime Act 2015 (Commencement No 1) Regulations 2015, SI 2015/820; Serious Crime (2015 Act) (Commencement) Regulations (Northern Ireland) 2015, SR 2015/190; Serious Crime Act 2015 (Commencement No 2) Regulations 2015, SI 2015/1428; Serious Crime Act 2015 (Commencement No 3) Regulations 2015, SI 2015/1809; Serious Crime Act 2015 (Commencement No 4) Regulations 2015, SI 2015/1976; Serious Crime Act 2015 (Commencement No 1 and Saving Provision) (Scotland) Regulations 2016, SSI 2016/11; Serious Crime Act 2015 (Commencement No 5 and Transitional Provisions and Savings) Regulations 2016, SI 2016/148; Serious Crime Act 2015 (Commencement No 6) Regulations 2017, SI 2017/451; Serious Crime Act 2015 (Commencement No 7) Regulations 2017, SI 2017/511; Serious Crime Act 2015 (Commencement No 2) (Scotland) Regulations 2019, SSI 2019/281; Serious Crime Act 2015 (Commencement No 3) (Scotland) Regulations 2020, SSI 2020/407

| | | |
|---|---|---|
| 1–12 | | 1 Jun 2015 (SI 2015/820) |
| 13 | | 1 Mar 2016 (SI 2016/148) |
| | | 1 Jun 2015 (SI 2015/820) |
| 15 | | 25 Nov 2019 (only in so far as relates to the victim surcharge and not in so far as relates to restitution orders) (SSI 2019/281) |
| | | 10 Feb 2021 (otherwise) (SSI 2020/407) |
| 16–18 | | 1 Mar 2016 (SSI 2016/11) |
| 19 | | 1 Mar 2016 (SSI 2016/11)[1] |
| 20–22 | | 1 Mar 2016 (SSI 2016/11) |
| 23 | | 1 Mar 2016 (SI 2016/148) |
| 24–36 | | 1 Jun 2015 (NI) (SR 2015/190) |
| | | *Not yet in force* (otherwise) |
| 37 | | 1 Jun 2015 (SI 2015/820) |
| 38 | (1), (2) | 1 Mar 2016 (SI 2016/148) |
| | (3) | 1 Mar 2016 (SSI 2016/11) |
| 39, 40 | | 1 Jun 2015 (SI 2015/820) |
| 41–45 | | 3 May 2015 (SI 2015/820) |
| 46 | | 1 Mar 2016 (SI 2016/148) |
| 47–49 | | 3 May 2015 (SI 2015/820) |
| 50 | (1)(a) | 3 May 2015 (SI 2015/820) |
| | (1)(b) | 1 Mar 2016 (SI 2016/148) |
| | (1)(c) | 3 May 2015 (SI 2015/820) |
| | (2) | 3 May 2015 (SI 2015/820) |
| 51 | | 1 Jun 2015 (SI 2015/820) |
| 52–66 | | 3 May 2015 (SI 2015/820) |
| 67 | | 3 Apr 2017 (SI 2017/451) |
| 68, 69 | | 3 May 2015 (SI 2015/820) |
| 70–72 | | 3 May 2015 (s 88(4)) |
| 73 | | 17 Jul 2015 (SI 2015/1428) |
| 74, 75 | | 31 Oct 2015 (SI 2015/1809) |
| 76, 77 | | 29 Dec 2015 (SI 2015/1976) |
| 78 | | 1 Jun 2015 (SI 2015/820) |
| 79 | | 10 Nov 2015 (SI 2015/1809) |
| 80–83 | | 3 Mar 2015 (s 88(5)) |
| 84 | | 3 May 2015 (SI 2015/820) |

**Serious Crime Act 2015 (c 3)**—*contd*

| | | |
|---|---|---|
| 85 | (1) | See Sch 4 below |
| | (2)–(7) | 3 Mar 2015 (s 88(5)) |
| 86–89 | | 3 Mar 2015 (s 88(5)) |
| Sch 1 | para 1 | See paras 2–31 below |
| | para 2 | 1 Mar 2016 (SI 2016/148)[2] |
| | paras 3–16 | 1 Mar 2016 (SI 2016/148) |
| | para 17 | 1 Mar 2016 (SI 2016/148)[2] |
| | paras 18–31 | 1 Mar 2016 (SI 2016/148) |
| Schs 2, 3 | | 3 May 2015 (SI 2015/820) |
| Sch 4 | paras 1, 2 | 3 May 2015 (SI 2015/820) |
| | para 3 | 1 Jun 2015 (SI 2015/820) |
| | para 4 | 1 Jun 2015 (NI) (SR 2015/190) |
| | para 5 | 17 Jul 2015 (SI 2015/1428) |
| | para 6 | 1 Jun 2015 (SI 2015/820) |
| | paras 7–12 | 3 May 2015 (SI 2015/820) |
| | para 13 | 17 Jul 2015 (SI 2015/1428) |
| | paras 14, 15 | 1 Mar 2016 (SI 2016/148) |
| | para 16 | 1 Mar 2016 (SSI 2016/11) |
| | para 17 | 17 Jul 2015 (SI 2015/1428) |
| | para 18 | 3 May 2015 (SI 2015/820) |
| | paras 19–34 | 1 Jun 2015 (SI 2015/820) |
| | para 35 | 1 Mar 2016 (SSI 2016/11) |
| | paras 36–41 | 25 Nov 2019 (only in so far as relates to the victim surcharge and not in so far as relates to restitution orders) (SSI 2019/281) |
| | | 10 Feb 2021 (otherwise) (SSI 2020/407) |
| | para 42 | 1 Mar 2016 (SSI 2016/11)[1] |
| | para 43 | 1 Mar 2016 (SSI 2016/11) |
| | para 44 | 25 Nov 2019 (only in so far as relates to the victim surcharge and not in so far as relates to restitution orders) (SSI 2019/281) |
| | | *Not yet in force* (otherwise) |
| | para 45 | 1 Mar 2016 (SSI 2016/11)[1] |
| | paras 46–51 | 1 Jun 2015 (NI) (SR 2015/190) |
| | paras 52–54 | 1 Jun 2015 (SI 2015/820) |
| | para 55 | 1 Mar 2016 (SI 2016/148) |
| | paras 56, 57 | 1 Jun 2015 (SI 2015/820) |
| | para 58 | 3 May 2015 (SI 2015/820) |
| | para 59 | 1 Jun 2015 (SI 2015/820) |
| | para 60 | 31 Oct 2015 (SI 2015/1809) |
| | para 61 | 1 Jun 2015 (SI 2015/820) |
| | para 62 | 3 May 2015 (SI 2015/820) |
| | para 63 | 3 Apr 2017 (SI 2017/511) |
| | paras 64, 65 | 3 May 2015 (SI 2015/820) |
| | para 66(1) | 3 May 2015 (SI 2015/820) |
| | para 66(2) | 3 Apr 2017 (SI 2017/511) |
| | para 66(3) | 3 May 2015 (SI 2015/820) |
| | para 66(4) | 3 May 2015 (NI) (SR 2015/190) |
| | | *Not yet in force* (otherwise) |
| | para 67 | 1 Jun 2015 (SI 2015/820) |
| | para 68(1) | 3 May 2015 (SI 2015/820) |
| | para 68(2) | 3 Apr 2017 (SI 2017/511) |
| | para 68(3)–(5) | 3 May 2015 (SI 2015/820) |
| | para 69 | 3 May 2015 (SI 2015/820) |
| | para 70(1) | 3 May 2015 (SI 2015/820) |
| | para 70(2) | 3 Apr 2017 (SI 2017/511) |
| | para 70(3), (4) | 3 May 2015 (SI 2015/820) |
| | para 71 | 1 Mar 2016 (SI 2016/148) |
| | para 72 | 3 May 2015 (SI 2015/820) |
| | para 73(1) | 3 May 2015 (SI 2015/820) |
| | para 73(2)–(4) | 1 Mar 2016 (SI 2016/148) |

**Serious Crime Act 2015 (c 3)**—*contd*

|                |                              |
|----------------|------------------------------|
| para 73(5)     | 3 May 2015 (SI 2015/820)     |
| para 74        | 3 Mar 2015 (s 88(5))         |
| paras 75–82    | 3 May 2015 (SI 2015/820)     |
| paras 83–86    | 1 Jun 2015 (SI 2015/820)     |
| para 87(1)     | 1 Jun 2015 (SI 2015/820)     |
| para 87(2)     | 17 Jul 2015 (SI 2015/1428)   |
| para 87(3), (4)| 1 Jun 2015 (SI 2015/820)     |
| para 88        | 17 Jul 2015 (SI 2015/1428)   |
| para 89        | 1 Jun 2015 (SI 2015/820)     |
| para 90        | 3 May 2015 (SI 2015/820)     |

[1]   For a saving, see SSI 2016/11, art 3

[2]   For transitional provisions and savings, see SI 2015/148, arts 4, 5

---

**Small Business, Enterprise and Employment Act 2015 (c 26)**

*RA:* 26 Mar 2015

*Commencement provisions:* s 164; Small Business, Enterprise and Employment Act 2015 (Commencement No 1) Regulations 2015, SI 2015/1329; Small Business, Enterprise and Employment Act 2015 (Commencement No 2 and Transitional Provisions) Regulations 2015, SI 2015/1689; Small Business, Enterprise and Employment Act 2015 (Commencement No 1) (Wales) Regulations 2015, SI 2015/1710; Small Business, Enterprise and Employment Act 2015 (Commencement No 3) Regulations 2015, SI 2015/2029; Small Business, Enterprise and Employment Act 2015 (Commencement No 4, Transitional and Savings Provisions) Regulations 2016, SI 2016/321; Small Business, Enterprise and Employment Act 2015 (Commencement No 5 and Saving Provision) Regulations 2016, SI 2016/532; Small Business, Enterprise and Employment Act 2015 (Commencement No 6 and Transitional and Savings Provisions) Regulations 2016, SI 2016/1020, as amended by SI 2017/363; Small Business, Enterprise and Employment Act 2015 (Commencement No 7, Consequential, Transitional and Savings Provisions) Regulations 2019, SI 2019/816

|          |          |                                                                                   |
|----------|----------|-----------------------------------------------------------------------------------|
| 1–3      |          | 26 May 2015 (s 164(3))                                                            |
| 4–7      |          | 26 Mar 2015 (s 164(2))                                                            |
| 8–12     |          | 26 May 2015 (s 164(3))                                                            |
| 13       |          | 26 Mar 2015 (for the purpose of enabling the making of regulations under Bills of Exchange Act 1882, Pt 4A) (s 164(4)) |
|          |          | 31 Jul 2016 (otherwise)                                                           |
| 14–16    |          | 26 May 2015 (s 164(3))                                                            |
| 17       |          | 1 Oct 2016 (SI 2016/321)                                                          |
| 18       |          | 26 May 2015 (SI 2015/1329)                                                        |
| 19       | (1)      | 26 May 2015 (SI 2015/1329)                                                        |
|          | (2)      | 1 Oct 2016 (SI 2016/321)                                                          |
|          | (3), (4) | 26 May 2015 (SI 2015/1329)                                                        |
| 20       |          | 1 Oct 2015 (SI 2015/1689)                                                         |
| 21–27    |          | 26 May 2015 (s 164(3))                                                            |
| 28–32    |          | 1 Jul 2015 (SI 2015/1329)                                                         |
| 33       | (1)–(3)  | *Not yet in force*                                                               |
|          | (4)      | 26 May 2015 (SI 2015/1329)                                                        |
|          | (5)      | *Not yet in force*                                                               |
|          | (6), (7) | 26 May 2015 (SI 2015/1329)                                                        |
| 34       |          | 26 May 2015 (SI 2015/1329)                                                        |
| 35, 36   |          | 1 Oct 2015 (E) (SI 2015/1689)                                                     |
|          |          | 1 Oct 2015 (W) (SI 2015/1710)                                                     |
| 37       |          | 26 May 2015 (s 164(3))                                                            |
| 38       |          | 1 Jan 2016 (for the purposes of enabling the exercise of any power to make provision by regulations, rules or order made by statutory instrument) (SI 2015/2029) |
|          |          | 1 Jun 2016 (otherwise) (SI 2016/532)[5]                                           |
| 39       |          | 26 Mar 2015 (s 164(2))                                                            |

**Small Business, Enterprise and Employment Act 2015 (c 26)**—*contd*

| | | |
|---|---|---|
| 40 | | 26 May 2015 (s 164(3)) |
| 41 | (1) | 2 May 2016 (SI 2016/532) |
| | (2)–(4) | See Sch 1 below |
| 42–44 | | 26 May 2015 (s 164(3)) |
| 45 | | 6 Apr 2016 (for the purposes of enabling the exercise of any power to make provision by regulations, rules or order made by statutory instrument or to prepare and issue guidance) (SI 2016/321)[3] |
| | | 21 Jul 2016 (otherwise) (SI 2016/532)[4] |
| 46 | | 21 Jul 2016 (SI 2016/532)[4] |
| 47 | | 6 Apr 2016 (for the purposes of enabling the exercise of any power to make provision by regulations, rules or order made by statutory instrument or to prepare and issue guidance) (SI 2016/321)[3] |
| | | 21 Jul 2016 (otherwise) (SI 2016/532)[4] |
| 48–50 | | 21 Jul 2016 (SI 2016/532)[4] |
| 51 | | 6 Apr 2016 (for the purposes of enabling the exercise of any power to make provision by regulations, rules or order made by statutory instrument or to prepare and issue guidance) (SI 2016/321)[3] |
| | | 21 Jul 2016 (otherwise) (SI 2016/532)[4] |
| 52–57 | | 21 Jul 2016 (SI 2016/532)[4] |
| 58 | | 6 Apr 2016 (for the purposes of enabling the exercise of any power to make provision by regulations, rules or order made by statutory instrument or to prepare and issue guidance) (SI 2016/321)[3] |
| | | 21 Jul 2016 (otherwise) (SI 2016/532)[4] |
| 59–62 | | 21 Jul 2016 (SI 2016/532)[4] |
| 63–65 | | 2 May 2016 (SI 2016/532) |
| 66, 67 | | 21 Jul 2016 (SI 2016/532)[4] |
| 68–73 | | 26 May 2015 (s 164(3)) |
| 74 | | 26 Mar 2015 (s 164(2)) |
| 75 | | 26 May 2015 (s 164(3)) |
| 76 | | 1 Jan 2016 (SI 2015/1329) |
| 77 | | See Sch 2 below |
| 78–80 | | 26 May 2015 (s 164(3)) |
| 81 | | See Sch 3 below |
| 82 | | 6 Apr 2016 (SI 2015/2029) |
| 83–86 | | 26 May 2015 (s 164(3)) |
| 87, 88 | | *Not yet in force* |
| 89–91 | | 26 May 2015 (s 164(3)) |
| 92 | | 1 May 2016 (for the purpose of enabling the registrar to impose the requirements referred to in s 853F(6) of the Companies Act 2006) (SI 2016/321) |
| | | 30 Jun 2016 (otherwise) (SI 2016/321)[3] |
| 93 | (1), (2) | 30 Jun 2016 (SI 2016/321)[3] |
| | (3) | 1 Jan 2016 (for the purposes of enabling the exercise of any power to make provision by regulations, rules or order made by statutory instrument) (SI 2015/2029) |
| | | 30 Jun 2016 (otherwise) (SI 2016/321)[3] |
| | (4)–(7) | 30 Jun 2016 (SI 2016/321)[3] |
| 94 | | See Sch 5 below |
| 95 | | 26 May 2015 (s 164(3)) |
| 96 | | 26 May 2015 (for the purposes of enabling the exercise of any power to make provision by regulations, rules or order made by statutory instrument or to prepare and issue guidance) (SI 2015/1329) |
| | | 10 Oct 2015 (otherwise, except in so far as inserts Companies Act 2006, ss 1087A(3)(b), (4)(a), (b), (5)–(7), 1087B(4)) (SI 2015/1689) |

**Small Business, Enterprise and Employment Act 2015 (c 26)**—*contd*

|  |  |
|---|---|
|  | 30 Jun 2016 (exception noted above) (SI 2016/321)[3] |
| 97 | See Sch 6 below |
| 98 | 30 Jun 2016 (SI 2016/321)[3] |
| 99 | 26 May 2015 (s 164(3)) |
| 100, 101 | 10 Oct 2015 (SI 2015/1689) |
| 102 | 6 Apr 2016 (SI 2016/321)[3] |
| 103 | 10 Oct 2015 (SI 2015/1689) |
| 104 | 26 May 2015 (for the purposes of enabling the exercise of any power to make provision by regulations, rules or order made by statutory instrument or to prepare and issue guidance) (SI 2015/1329) |
|  | 1 Oct 2015 (otherwise) (SI 2015/1689) |
| 105, 106 | 26 May 2015 (for the purposes of enabling the exercise of any power to make provision by regulations, rules or order made by statutory instrument or to prepare and issue guidance) (SI 2015/1329) |
|  | 1 Oct 2015 (otherwise) (SI 2015/1689)[2] |
| 107 | 26 May 2015 (for the purposes of enabling the exercise of any power to make provision by regulations, rules or order made by statutory instrument or to prepare and issue guidance) (SI 2015/1329) |
|  | 6 Apr 2016 (otherwise) (SI 2016/321)[3] |
| 108, 109 | 26 May 2015 (for the purposes of enabling the exercise of any power to make provision by regulations, rules or order made by statutory instrument or to prepare and issue guidance) (SI 2015/1329) |
|  | 1 Oct 2015 (otherwise) (SI 2015/1689) |
| 110 | 26 May 2015 (for the purposes of enabling the exercise of any power to make provision by regulations, rules or order made by statutory instrument or to prepare and issue guidance) (SI 2015/1329) |
|  | 1 Oct 2015 (otherwise) (SI 2015/1689)[2] |
| 111 | See Sch 7 below |
| 112 | See Sch 8 below |
| 113–119 | 1 Oct 2015 (SI 2015/1689)[2] |
| 120, 121 | 26 May 2015 (s 164(3)) |
| 122 | 26 May 2015 (for the purposes of enabling the exercise of any power to make provision by regulations, rules or order made by statutory instrument or to prepare and issue guidance) (SI 2015/1329) |
|  | 6 Apr 2017 (E) (W) (otherwise) (SI 2016/1020)[6] |
|  | 6 Apr 2019 (S) (SI 2019/816)[7] |
|  | *Not yet in force* (otherwise) (NI) |
| 123 | 26 May 2015 (for the purposes of enabling the exercise of any power to make provision by regulations, rules or order made by statutory instrument or to prepare and issue guidance) (SI 2015/1329) |
|  | 6 Apr 2017 (E) (W) (otherwise) (SI 2016/1020)[6] |
|  | *Not yet in force* (otherwise) (S) (NI) |
| 124 | 26 May 2015 (for the purposes of enabling the exercise of any power to make provision by regulations, rules or order made by statutory instrument or to prepare and issue guidance) (SI 2015/1329) |
|  | 6 Apr 2017 (E) (W) (otherwise) (SI 2016/1020)[6] |
|  | 6 Apr 2019 (S) (SI 2019/816)[7] |
|  | *Not yet in force* (otherwise) (NI) |
| 125 | 26 May 2015 (for the purposes of enabling the exercise of any power to make provision by regulations, rules or order made by statutory instrument or to prepare and issue guidance) (SI 2015/1329) |

**Small Business, Enterprise and Employment Act 2015 (c 26)**—*contd*

| | | |
|---|---|---|
| | | 6 Apr 2017 (E) (W) (otherwise) (SI 2016/1020)[6] |
| | | *Not yet in force* (otherwise) (S) (NI) |
| 126 | | See Sch 9 below |
| 127–132 | | 26 May 2015 (s 164(3)) |
| 133 | (1) | 6 Apr 2017 (SI 2016/1020)[6] |
| | (2) | See Sch 10 below |
| 134–136 | | 26 May 2015 (s 164(3)) |
| 137–143 | | 1 Oct 2015 (immediately after Deregulation Act 2015, s 17 came into force) |
| 144 | | See Sch 11 below |
| 145, 146 | | 1 Oct 2015 (immediately after Deregulation Act 2015, s 17 came into force) |
| 147 | | *Not yet in force* |
| 148 | | 1 Jan 2016 (SI 2015/2029) |
| 149 | | 26 May 2015 (SI 2015/1329) |
| 150 | | 6 Apr 2016 (SI 2016/321)[3] |
| 151 | | 26 Mar 2015 (s 164(2)) |
| 152, 153 | | 26 May 2015 (SI 2015/1329) |
| 154–157 | | 1 Jan 2016 (SI 2015/2029) |
| 158 | | 26 May 2015 (s 164(3))[1] |
| 159–165 | | 26 Mar 2015 (s 164(2)) |
| Sch 1 | Pt 1 | 2 May 2016 (SI 2016/532) |
| | Pt 2 | 21 Jul 2016 (SI 2016/532)[4] |
| | Pt 3 | 2 May 2016 (SI 2016/532) |
| Sch 2 | paras 1–15 | 1 Jan 2016 (SI 2015/1329) |
| | para 16(a) | 15 Jun 2015 (SI 2015/1329) |
| | para 16(b)–(e) | 1 Jan 2016 (SI 2015/1329) |
| | para 17 | 15 Jun 2015 (SI 2015/1329) |
| | paras 18–20 | 1 Jan 2016 (SI 2015/1329) |
| Sch 3 | Pt 1, paras 1, 2 | 26 May 2015 (for the purposes of enabling the exercise of any power to make provision by regulations, rules or order made by statutory instrument or to prepare and issue guidance) (SI 2015/1329) |
| | | 6 Apr 2016 (for the purpose of inserting Companies Act 2006, ss 790A–790L, 790M(1)–(8), (9)(a), (b), (10)–(14), 790N–790V, 790ZF, 790ZG, Schs 1A, 1B, so far as not already in force) (SI 2015/2029) |
| | | 30 Jun 2016 (for the purpose of inserting Companies Act 2006, ss 790M(9)(c), 790W–790ZE, so far as not already in force) (SI 2015/2029) |
| | Pt 2, para 3 | 26 May 2015 (for the purposes of enabling the exercise of any power to make provision by regulations, rules or order made by statutory instrument or to prepare and issue guidance) (SI 2015/1329) |
| | | 6 Apr 2016 (otherwise) (SI 2015/2029) |
| | Pt 2, paras 4, 5 | 26 May 2015 (for the purposes of enabling the exercise of any power to make provision by regulations, rules or order made by statutory instrument or to prepare and issue guidance) (SI 2015/1329) |
| | | 30 Jun 2016 (otherwise) (SI 2015/2029) |
| | Pt 2, para 6 | 26 May 2015 (for the purposes of enabling the exercise of any power to make provision by regulations, rules or order made by statutory instrument or to prepare and issue guidance) (SI 2015/1329) |
| | | 6 Apr 2016 (otherwise) (SI 2015/2029) |
| | Pt 2, para 7 | 26 May 2015 (for the purposes of enabling the exercise of any power to make provision by regulations, rules or order made by statutory instrument or to prepare and issue guidance) (SI 2015/1329) |
| | | 30 Jun 2016 (otherwise) (SI 2015/2029) |

**Small Business, Enterprise and Employment Act 2015 (c 26)**—*contd*

| | | |
|---|---|---|
| | Pt 2, paras 8–11 | 26 May 2015 (for the purposes of enabling the exercise of any power to make provision by regulations, rules or order made by statutory instrument or to prepare and issue guidance) (SI 2015/1329) |
| | | 6 Apr 2016 (otherwise) (SI 2015/2029) |
| Sch 4 | | 26 May 2015 (s 164(3)) |
| Schs 5, 6 | | 30 Jun 2016 (SI 2016/321)[3] |
| Sch 7 | | 26 May 2015 (for the purposes of enabling the exercise of any power to make provision by regulations, rules or order made by statutory instrument or to prepare and issue guidance) (SI 2015/1329) |
| | | 1 Oct 2015 (otherwise) (SI 2015/1689) |
| Sch 8 | paras 1, 2 | 1 Oct 2015 (SI 2015/1689) |
| | para 3 | 1 Oct 2015 (SI 2015/1689)[2] |
| | para 4 | 1 Oct 2015 (SI 2015/1689) |
| | para 5 | 6 Apr 2016 (SI 2016/321)[3] |
| | para 6 | 1 Oct 2015 (SI 2015/1689) |
| | paras 7, 8 | 1 Oct 2015 (SI 2015/1689)[2] |
| | paras 9, 10 | 1 Oct 2015 (SI 2015/1689) |
| Sch 9 | paras 1–59 | 26 May 2015 (for the purposes of enabling the exercise of any power to make provision by regulations, rules or order made by statutory instrument or to prepare and issue guidance) (SI 2015/1329) |
| | | 6 Apr 2017 (E) (W) (otherwise) (SI 2016/1020)[6] |
| | | 6 Apr 2019 (S) (otherwise) (SI 2019/816)[7] |
| | | *Not yet in force* (NI) (otherwise) |
| | paras 60–88 | 26 May 2015 (for the purposes of enabling the exercise of any power to make provision by regulations, rules or order made by statutory instrument or to prepare and issue guidance) (SI 2015/1329) |
| | | 6 Apr 2017 (E) (W) (otherwise) (SI 2016/1020)[6] |
| | | *Not yet in force* (S) (NI) (otherwise) |
| Sch 10 | | 6 Apr 2017 (E) (W) (SI 2016/1020)[6] |
| Sch 11 | | 1 Oct 2015 (immediately after Deregulation Act 2015, s 17 came into force) |

[1]  Note that SI 2015/1329 also purports to bring that section into force on 26 May 2015

[2]  For transitional provisions, see SI 2015/1689, reg 5, Schedule

[3]  For transitional provisions and savings, see SI 2016/321, reg 8, Schedule

[4]  That, is the day on which the Pubs Code etc Regulations 2016 were made, see SI 2016/532, reg 3

[5]  For a saving, see SI 2016/532, reg 4(2)

[6]  For transitional provisions and savings, see SI 2016/1020, reg 5

[7]  For transitional provisions and savings, see SI 2019/816, reg 5

---

**Social Action, Responsibility and Heroism Act 2015 (c 3)**

*RA:* 12 Feb 2015

*Commencement provisions*: s 5; Social Action, Responsibility and Heroism Act 2015 (Commencement and Transitional Provision) Regulations 2015, SI 2015/808

| | |
|---|---|
| 1–4 | 13 Apr 2015 (SI 2015/808)[1] |
| 5 | 12 Feb 2015 (s 5(4)) |

[1]  For a transitional provision, see SI 2015/808, reg 3

---

**Specialist Printing Equipment and Materials (Offences) Act 2015 (c 16)**

*RA*: 26 Mar 2015

*Commencement provisions*: s 5(3)

Whole Act in force 26 May 2015 (s 5(3))

---

**Stamp Duty Land Tax Act 2015 (c 1)**

*RA*: 12 Feb 2015

Whole Act in force 12 Feb 2015 (RA)

---

**Supply and Appropriation (Anticipation and Adjustments) Act 2015 (c 10)**

*RA*: 26 Mar 2015

Whole Act in force 26 Mar 2015 (RA)

---

**Supply and Appropriation (Main Estimates) Act 2015 (c 31)**

*RA*: 21 Jul 2015

Whole Act in force 21 Jul 2015 (RA)

---

**Violence against Women, Domestic Abuse and Sexual Violence (Wales) Act 2015 (anaw 3)**

*RA*: 29 Apr 2015

*Commencement provisions*: s 25; Violence against Women, Domestic Abuse and Sexual Violence (Wales) Act 2015 (Commencement No 1) Order 2015, SI 2015/1680; Violence against Women, Domestic Abuse and Sexual Violence (Wales) Act 2015 (Commencement No 2) Order 2015, SI 2015/2019

| | |
|---|---|
| 1 | 29 Apr 2015 (s 25(1)) |
| 2–4 | 5 Oct 2015 (SI 2015/1680) |
| 5–8 | 4 Jan 2016 (SI 2015/2019) |
| 9 | 5 Oct 2015 (SI 2015/1680) |
| 10 | 29 Jun 2015 (s 25(2)) |
| 11, 12 | 5 Oct 2015 (SI 2015/1680) |
| 13 | 4 Jan 2016 (SI 2015/2019) |
| 14–21 | 29 Jun 2015 (s 25(2)) |
| 22, 23 | 5 Oct 2015 (SI 2015/1680) |
| 24–26 | 29 Apr 2015 (s 25(1)) |

---

**Welfare Funds (Scotland) Act 2015 (asp 5)**

*RA*: 8 Apr 2015

*Commencement provisions*: s 14; Welfare Funds (Scotland) Act 2015 (Commencement) Order 2015, SSI 2015/428

| | | |
|---|---|---|
| 1, 2 | | 1 Apr 2016 (SSI 2015/428) |
| 3 | (1), (2) | 1 Apr 2016 (SSI 2015/428) |
| | (3), (4) | 1 Feb 2016 (SSI 2015/428) |
| 4 | | 1 Feb 2016 (SSI 2015/428) |
| 5 | | 1 Apr 2016 (SSI 2015/428) |
| 6 | | 1 Feb 2016 (SSI 2015/428) |
| 7–13 | | 1 Apr 2016 (SSI 2015/428) |

**Welfare Funds (Scotland) Act 2015 (asp 5)**—*contd*
14, 15                                                 9 Apr 2015 (s 14(1))

---

**Well-being of Future Generations (Wales) Act 2015 (anaw 2)**

*RA:* 29 Apr 2015

*Commencement provisions:* s 56; Well-being of Future Generations (Wales) Act 2015 (Commencement)
Order 2015, SI 2015/1785; Well-being of Future Generations (Wales) Act 2015 (Commencement
No 2) Order 2016, SI 2016/86

| | | |
|---|---|---|
| 1 | | 16 Oct 2015 (SI 2015/1785) |
| 2–5 | | 1 Apr 2016 (SI 2016/86) |
| 6 | | 16 Oct 2015 (SI 2015/1785) |
| 7–9 | | 1 Apr 2016 (SI 2016/86) |
| 10 | | 16 Oct 2015 (SI 2015/1785) |
| 11–13 | | 1 Apr 2016 (SI 2016/86) |
| 14 | | 16 Oct 2015 (SI 2015/1785) |
| 15, 16 | | 1 Apr 2016 (SI 2016/86) |
| 17 | | 16 Oct 2015 (SI 2015/1785) |
| 18–21 | | 1 Feb 2016 (SI 2016/86) |
| 22 | (1) | 1 Feb 2016 (SI 2016/86) |
| | (2), (3) | 16 Oct 2015 (SI 2015/1785) |
| | (4) | 1 Feb 2016 (SI 2016/86) |
| 23 | | 30 Apr 2015 (in so far as enables the exercise of any power to make regulations) (s 56(1)(b)) |
| | | 1 Feb 2016 (otherwise) (SI 2016/86) |
| 24, 25 | | 1 Feb 2016 (SI 2016/86) |
| 26–28 | | 16 Oct 2015 (SI 2015/1785) |
| 29–32 | | 1 Apr 2016 (SI 2016/86) |
| 33 | | 30 Apr 2015 (in so far as enables the exercise of any power to make regulations) (s 56(1)(b)) |
| | | 1 Apr 2016 (otherwise) (SI 2016/86) |
| 34–36 | | 1 Apr 2016 (SI 2016/86) |
| 37, 38 | | 30 Apr 2015 (in so far as enables the exercise of any power to make regulations) (s 56(1)(b)) |
| | | 1 Apr 2016 (otherwise) (SI 2016/86) |
| 39 | | 1 Apr 2016 (SI 2016/86) |
| 40 | (1)–(6) | 30 Apr 2015 (in so far as enables the exercise of any power to make regulations) (s 56(1)(b)) |
| | | 1 Apr 2016 (otherwise) (SI 2016/86) |
| | (7), (8) | 30 Apr 2015 (in so far as enables the exercise of any power to make regulations) (s 56(1)(b)) |
| | | 16 Oct 2015 (otherwise) (SI 2015/1785) |
| 41–49 | | 1 Apr 2016 (SI 2016/86) |
| 50 | | 30 Apr 2015 (in so far as enables the exercise of any power to make regulations) (s 56(1)(b)) |
| | | 1 Apr 2016 (otherwise) (SI 2016/86) |
| 51 | | 16 Oct 2015 (SI 2015/1785) |
| 52 | | 30 Apr 2015 (in so far as enables the exercise of any power to make regulations) (s 56(1)(b)) |
| | | 16 Oct 2015 (otherwise) (SI 2015/1785) |
| 53–57 | | 30 Apr 2015 (s 56(1)(a)) |
| Sch 1 | | 1 Apr 2016 (SI 2016/86) |
| Sch 2 | | 30 Apr 2015 (in so far as enables the exercise of any power to make regulations) (s 56(1)(b)) |
| | | 16 Oct 2015 (otherwise) (SI 2015/1785) |
| Schs 3, 4 | | 1 Apr 2016 (SI 2016/86) |

# 2016 Acts

## Abusive Behaviour and Sexual Harm (Scotland) Act 2016 (asp 22)

*RA:* 28 Apr 2016

*Commencement provisions:* s 45; Abusive Behaviour and Sexual Harm (Scotland) Act 2016 (Commencement No 1 and Transitional Provision) Regulations 2017, SSI 2017/93; Abusive Behaviour and Sexual Harm (Scotland) Act 2016 (Commencement No 2) Regulations 2017, SSI 2017/183

| | | |
|---|---|---|
| 1 | | 24 Apr 2017 (SSI 2017/93)[1] |
| 2, 3 | | 3 Jul 2017 (SSI 2017/183) |
| 4 | | See Sch 1 below |
| 5, 6 | | 24 Apr 2017 (SSI 2017/93)[1] |
| 7–9 | | 24 Apr 2017 (SSI 2017/93) |
| 10–40 | | *Not yet in force* |
| 41 | | 24 Apr 2017 (SSI 2017/93) |
| 42 | | 29 Apr 2016 (s 45(1)) |
| 43 | | See Sch 2 below |
| 44–46 | | 29 Apr 2016 (s 45(1)) |
| Sch 1 | | 3 Jul 2017 (SSI 2017/183) |
| Sch 2 | paras 1–5 | *Not yet in force* |
| | para 6 | 24 Apr 2017 (SSI 2017/93) |
| | paras 7–10 | *Not yet in force* |

[1]  For transitional provisions, see SSI 2017/93, regs 3–5

## Access to Medical Treatments (Innovation) Act 2016 (c 9)

*RA:* 23 Mar 2016

*Commencement provisions:* s 4(2)–(4)

| | |
|---|---|
| 1–3 | *Not yet in force* |
| 4 | 23 Mar 2016 (s 4(4)) |

## Apologies (Scotland) Act 2016 (asp 5)

*RA:* 23 Feb 2016

*Commencement provisions:* s 5; Apologies (Scotland) Act 2016 (Commencement and Transitory Provision) Regulations 2016, SSI 2016/256, as amended by SSI 2016/395

| | | |
|---|---|---|
| 1 | | 19 Jun 2017 (SSI 2016/256) |
| 2 | (1) | 19 Jun 2017 (SSI 2016/256)[1] |
| | (2), (3) | 19 Jun 2017 (SSI 2016/256) |
| | (4)–(6) | 22 Sep 2016 (SSI 2016/256) |
| 3, 4 | | 19 Jun 2017 (SSI 2016/256) |
| 5, 6 | | 24 Feb 2016 (s 5(1)) |

**Apologies (Scotland) Act 2016 (asp 5)**—*contd*
[1]   For a transitory provision, see SSI 2016/256, art 3

---

**Armed Forces Act 2016 (c 21)**

*RA:* 12 May 2016

*Commencement provisions:* s 19(1)–(3); Armed Forces Act 2016 (Commencement No 1) Regulations 2017, SI 2017/1131; Armed Forces Act 2016 (Commencement No 2) Regulations 2018, SI 2018/876; Armed Forces Act 2016 (Commencement No 3) Regulations 2019, SI 2019/961

| | | |
|---|---|---|
| 1 | | 12 May 2016 (s 19(2)(a)) |
| 2 | | 19 Jul 2018 (for the purpose of conferring power to make regulations under Armed Forces Act 2006, s 93AA(2)–(4)) (SI 2018/876) |
| | | 1 Jan 2019 (otherwise) (SI 2018/876) |
| 3–5 | | 22 May 2019 (for the purpose only of conferring power to make Pt 5 regulations in connection with the coming into force of ss 3–5) (SI 2019/961)[1] |
| | | 1 Jul 2019 (otherwise) (SI 2019/961)[1] |
| 6 | | 1 Jul 2019 (SI 2019/961) |
| 7–12 | | *Not yet in force* |
| 13 | (1)–(3) | 12 May 2016 (s 19(2)(b)) |
| | (4) | See Schedule below |
| 14 | | 12 Jul 2016 (s 19(3)(a)) |
| 15 | | 21 Nov 2017 (SI 2017/1131) |
| 16, 17 | | 12 Jul 2016 (s 19(3)(b)) |
| 18–22 | | 12 May 2016 (s 19(2)(c)) |
| Schedule | | 12 May 2016 (s 19(2)(b)) |

[1]   For transitional provisions, see SI 2019/961, reg 3

---

**Bank of England and Financial Services Act 2016 (c14)**

*RA:* 4 May 2016

*Commencement provisions:* s 41; Bank of England and Financial Services Act 2016 (Commencement No 1) Regulations 2016, SI 2016/569; Bank of England and Financial Services Act 2016 (Commencement No 2) Regulations 2016, SI 2016/579; Bank of England and Financial Services Act 2016 (Commencement No 3) Regulations 2016, SI 2016/627; Bank of England and Financial Services Act 2016 (Commencement No 4 and Saving Provision) Regulations 2017, SI 2017/43; Bank of England and Financial Services Act 2016 (Commencement No 5 and Transitional Provisions) Regulations 2018, SI 2018/990; Bank of England and Financial Services Act 2016 (Commencement No 6 and Transitional Provisions) Regulations 2019, SI 2019/1136, as amended by SI 2020/929, SI 2020/929

| | | |
|---|---|---|
| 1 | (1), (2) | 6 Jul 2016 (SI 2016/627) |
| | (3) | 6 Jul 2016 (for the purpose of inserting Bank of England Act 1998, 1A, except sub-s (3) thereof) (SI 2016/627) |
| | | 1 Mar 2017 (exception noted above) (SI 2017/43) |
| 2–10 | | 6 Jul 2016 (SI 2016/627) |
| 11 | | 6 Jul 2016 (for the purpose of inserting Bank of England Act 1998, ss 7D, 7E, 7G, 7H) (SI 2016/627) |
| | | 1 Mar 2017 (otherwise) (SI 2017/43) |
| 12 | | 1 Mar 2017 (SI 2017/43) |
| 13 | (1), (2) | 1 Mar 2017 (SI 2017/43) |
| | (3) | See Sch 1 below |
| 14, 15 | | 1 Mar 2017 (SI 2017/43) |
| 16 | | See Sch 2 below |
| 17 | | See Sch 3 below |
| 18–20 | | 6 Jul 2016 (SI 2016/627) |

**Bank of England and Financial Services Act 2016 (c14)**—*contd*

| | | |
|---|---|---|
| 21 | | See Sch 4 below |
| 22–24 | | 6 Jul 2016 (SI 2016/627) |
| 25 | (1) | See sub-ss (2), (3) below |
| | (2)(a)–(d) | 6 Jul 2016 (SI 2016/627) |
| | (2)(e)–(g) | 10 May 2016 (SI 2016/569) |
| | (2)(h) | 6 Jul 2016 (SI 2016/627) |
| | (3)(a)–(d) | 6 Jul 2016 (SI 2016/627) |
| | (3)(e)–(g) | 10 May 2016 (SI 2016/569) |
| | (3)(h) | 6 Jul 2016 (SI 2016/627) |
| 26–29 | | 6 Jul 2016 (SI 2016/627) |
| 30 | | *Not yet in force* |
| 31 | | 4 May 2016 (s 41(1)(a)) |
| 32 | | 13 May 2016 (SI 2016/579) |
| 33–36 | | 6 Jul 2016 (SI 2016/627) |
| 37 | | 4 May 2016 (s 41(1)(b)) |
| 38 | | 6 Jul 2016 (SI 2016/627) |
| 39–42 | | 4 May 2016 (s 41(1)(c)) |
| Sch 1 | | 1 Mar 2017 (SI 2017/43) |
| Sch 2 | para 1 | 6 Jul 2016 (SI 2016/627) |
| | paras 2–4 | 1 Mar 2017 (SI 2017/43) |
| | paras 5–7 | 6 Jul 2016 (SI 2016/627) |
| | para 8(1), (2)(a), (b) | 6 Jul 2016 (SI 2016/627) |
| | para 8(2)(c) | 1 Mar 2017 (SI 2017/43) |
| | para 8(3)(a) | 6 Jul 2016 (SI 2016/627) |
| | para 8(3)(b), (4), (5)(a)(i) | 1 Mar 2017 (SI 2017/43) |
| | para 8(5)(a)(ii) | 6 Jul 2016 (SI 2016/627) |
| | para 8(5)(b), (c) | 1 Mar 2017 (SI 2017/43) |
| | para 8(6) | 6 Jul 2016 (SI 2016/627) |
| | para 9(1), (2) | 6 Jul 2016 (SI 2016/627) |
| | para 9(3) | 1 Mar 2017 (SI 2017/43) |
| | para 9(4) | 6 Jul 2016 (SI 2016/627) |
| | para 9(5) | 1 Mar 2017 (SI 2017/43) |
| | para 10 | 1 Mar 2017 (SI 2017/43) |
| | para 11 | 6 Jul 2016 (SI 2016/627) |
| | paras 12–14 | 1 Mar 2017 (SI 2017/43) |
| | paras 15–18 | 6 Jul 2016 (SI 2016/627) |
| | para 19 | 1 Mar 2017 (SI 2017/43) |
| | para 20(1), (2) | 6 Jul 2016 (SI 2016/627) |
| | para 20(3) | 1 Mar 2017 (SI 2017/43) |
| | para 20(4)–(7) | 6 Jul 2016 (SI 2016/627) |
| | para 21(1), (2) | 6 Jul 2016 (SI 2016/627) |
| | para 21(3) | 1 Mar 2017 (SI 2017/43) |
| | para 21(4)–(7) | 6 Jul 2016 (SI 2016/627) |
| | paras 22–31 | 1 Mar 2017 (SI 2017/43) |
| | para 32 | 6 Jul 2016 (SI 2016/627) |
| | paras 33–49 | 1 Mar 2017 (SI 2017/43) |
| | para 50(1)–(5) | 1 Mar 2017 (SI 2017/43) |
| | para 50(6) | 1 Mar 2017 (SI 2017/43)[1] |
| | para 50(7) | 1 Mar 2017 (SI 2017/43) |
| | paras 51–67 | 1 Mar 2017 (SI 2017/43) |
| | para 68 | 6 Jul 2016 (except repeals of Financial Services Act 2012, s 2(3); Financial Services (Banking Reform) Act 2013, Sch 3, para 17) (SI 2016/627) |
| | | 1 Mar 2017 (in so far as not already in force) (SI 2017/43) |
| Sch 3 | para 1 | See paras 2–12 below |
| | paras 2–5 | 1 Mar 2017 (SI 2017/43) |
| | para 6 | 6 Jul 2016 (SI 2016/627) |

**Bank of England and Financial Services Act 2016 (c14)**—*contd*

| | paras 7–12 | 1 Mar 2017 (SI 2017/43) |

Sch 4    paras 1–10    13 Sep 2018 (in relation to insurers, for the purpose of making rules, giving directions, imposing requirements and making statements of policy by the appropriate regulator) (SI 2018/990)[2]

10 Dec 2018 (in relation to insurers, otherwise) (SI 2018/990)[2]

18 Jul 2019 (for the purpose of the making of rules, the giving of directions, the imposition of requirements and the issuing of statements of policy by the FCA) (SI 2019/1136)[3]

9 Aug 2019 (for remaining purposes in relation to authorised persons who are not solo-regulated firms) (SI 2019/1136)[3]

7 Dec 2020 (for remaining purposes in relation to benchmark firms, except in relation to the employee certification provisions) (SI 2019/1136)[3]

31 Mar 2021 (for the purpose of employee certification provisions for remaining purposes in relation to solo-regulated firms other than benchmark firms) (SI 2019/1136)[3]

31 Mar 2021 (for remaining purposes in relation to solo-regulated firms other than benchmark firms, except in relation to the employee certification provisions) (SI 2019/1136)[3]

7 Dec 2021 (for the purpose of employee certification provisions for remaining purposes in relation to benchmark firms) (SI 2019/1136)[3]

para 11    13 Sep 2018 (in relation to insurers, for the purpose of making rules, giving directions, imposing requirements and making statements of policy by the appropriate regulator) (SI 2018/990)[2]

10 Dec 2019 (in relation to insurers, otherwise) (SI 2018/990)[2]

18 Jul 2019 (for the purpose of the making of rules, the giving of directions, the imposition of requirements and the issuing of statements of policy by the FCA) (SI 2019/1136)[3]

9 Aug 2019 (for remaining purposes in relation to authorised persons who are not solo-regulated firms) (SI 2019/1136)[3]

9 Dec 2019 (for remaining purposes in relation to solo-regulated firms other than benchmark firms, except in relation to the employee certification provisions) (SI 2019/1136)[3]

7 Dec 2020 (for remaining purposes in relation to benchmark firms, except in relation to the employee certification provisions) (SI 2019/1136)[3]

31 Mar 2021 (for the purpose of employee certification provisions for remaining purposes in relation to solo-regulated firms other than benchmark firms) (SI 2019/1136)[3]

31 Mar 2021 (for remaining purposes in relation to solo-regulated firms other than benchmark firms, except in relation to the employee certification provisions) (SI 2019/1136)[3]

7 Dec 2021 (for the purpose of employee certification provisions for remaining purposes in relation to benchmark firms) (SI 2019/1136)[3]

paras 12–22    13 Sep 2018 (in relation to insurers, for the purpose of making rules, giving directions, imposing requirements and making statements of policy by the appropriate regulator) (SI 2018/990)[2]

10 Dec 2018 (in relation to insurers, otherwise) (SI 2018/990)[2]

18 Jul 2019 (for the purpose of the making of rules, the giving of directions, the imposition of requirements and the issuing of statements of policy by the FCA) (SI 2019/1136)[3]

9 Aug 2019 (for remaining purposes in relation to authorised persons who are not solo-regulated firms) (SI 2019/1136)[3]

9 Dec 2019 (for remaining purposes in relation to solo-regulated firms other than benchmark firms, except in relation to the employee certification provisions) (SI 2019/1136)[3]

## Bank of England and Financial Services Act 2016 (c14)—*contd*

7 Dec 2020 (for remaining purposes in relation to benchmark firms, except in relation to the employee certification provisions) (SI 2019/1136)[3]

31 Mar 2021 (for the purpose of employee certification provisions for remaining purposes in relation to solo-regulated firms other than benchmark firms) (SI 2019/1136)[3]

31 Mar 2021 (for remaining purposes in relation to solo-regulated firms other than benchmark firms, except in relation to the employee certification provisions) (SI 2019/1136)[3]

7 Dec 2021 (for the purpose of employee certification provisions for remaining purposes in relation to benchmark firms) (SI 2019/1136)[3]

[1]   For saving provisions, see SI 2017/43, reg 3

[2]   For transitional provisions, see SI 2018/990, regs 3–6

[3]   For transitional provisions, see SI 2019/1136, regs 3–7, as amended by SI 2020/929, reg 2(1), (3)

## Bankruptcy (Scotland) Act 2016 (asp 21)

*RA:* 28 Apr 2016

*Commencement provisions*: s 237; Bankruptcy (Scotland) Act 2016 (Commencement) Regulations 2016, SSI 2016/294

| | |
|---|---|
| 1–224 | 30 Nov 2016 (SSI 2016/294) |
| 225, 226 | 29 Apr 2016 (s 237(1)) |
| 227 | 30 Nov 2016 (SSI 2016/294) |
| 228–230 | 29 Apr 2016 (s 237(1)) |
| 231–236 | 30 Nov 2016 (SSI 2016/294) |
| 237, 238 | 29 Apr 2016 (s 237(1)) |
| Schs 1–9 | 30 Nov 2016 (SSI 2016/294) |

## Budget (Scotland) Act 2016 (asp 12)

*RA:* 30 Mar 2016

*Commencement provisions*: s 10

Whole Act in force 31 Mar 2016 (s 10)

## Burial and Cremation (Scotland) Act 2016 (asp 20)

*RA:* 28 Apr 2016

*Commencement provisions*: s 112; Burial and Cremation (Scotland) Act 2016 (Commencement No 1, Transitory and Transitional Provisions) Regulations 2016, SSI 2016/417; Burial and Cremation (Scotland) Act 2016 (Commencement No 2) Regulations 2018, SSI 2018/157; Burial and Cremation (Scotland) Act 2016 (Commencement No 3, Transitional, Saving and Transitory Provisions) Regulations 2018, SSI 2018/380; Burial and Cremation (Scotland) Act 2016 (Commencement No 4) Regulations 2021, SSI 2021/126

| | |
|---|---|
| 1–7 | 15 Dec 2016 (SSI 2016/417) |
| 8–16 | *Not yet in force* |
| 17 | 15 Dec 2016 (SSI 2016/417) |
| 18, 19 | *Not yet in force* |
| 20 | 15 Dec 2016 (SSI 2016/417) |
| 21–44 | *Not yet in force* |
| 45–47 | 4 Apr 2019 (SSI 2018/380) |
| 48–50 | 4 Apr 2019 (SSI 2018/380)[1] |

**Burial and Cremation (Scotland) Act 2016 (asp 20)**—*contd*

| | | |
|---|---|---|
| 51 | | 4 Apr 2019 (SSI 2018/380) |
| 52–55 | | 4 Apr 2019 (SSI 2018/380)[1] |
| 56 | | 4 Apr 2019 (SSI 2018/380) |
| 57 | | 4 Apr 2019 (SSI 2018/380)[1] |
| 58 | | 4 Apr 2019 (SSI 2018/380) |
| 59 | | 4 Apr 2019 (SSI 2018/380)[1] |
| 60 | | 4 Apr 2019 (SSI 2018/380) |
| 61, 62 | | *Not yet in force* |
| 63 | | 4 Apr 2019 (SSI 2018/380) |
| 64 | | *Not yet in force* |
| 65–88 | | 4 Apr 2019 (SSI 2018/380) |
| 89 | (1)(a) | 15 Dec 2016 (SSI 2016/417) |
| | (1)(b) | 4 Apr 2019 (SSI 2018/380)[1] |
| | (1)(c) | 15 Dec 2016 (SSI 2016/417) |
| | (2)–(6) | 15 Dec 2016 (SSI 2016/417) |
| 90–92 | | *Not yet in force* |
| 93 | | 15 Dec 2016 (so far as applies to an appointment made under s 89(1)(a) or (c)) (SSI 2016/417) |
| | | 4 Apr 2019 (otherwise) (SSI 2018/380) |
| 94–96 | | *Not yet in force* |
| 97 | | 24 Mar 2021 (SSI 2021/126) |
| 98 | | 1 Jun 2018 (SSI 2018/157) |
| 99 | | 4 Apr 2019 (SSI 2018/380) |
| 100 | | 29 Apr 2016 (s 112(1)) |
| 101 | | 15 Dec 2016 (SSI 2016/417) |
| 102 | | *Not yet in force* |
| 103 | | 4 Apr 2019 (SSI 2018/380) |
| 104 | (1) | 15 Dec 2016 (so far as applies to s 6) (SSI 2016/417) |
| | | 4 Apr 2019 (otherwise) (SSI 2018/380) |
| | (2)–(6) | 4 Apr 2019 (SSI 2018/380) |
| 105 | | *Not yet in force* |
| 106–108 | | 29 Apr 2016 (s 112(1)) |
| 109 | | See Sch 1 below |
| 110 | | See Sch 2 below |
| 111 | | 4 Apr 2019 (SSI 2018/380) |
| 112, 113 | | 29 Apr 2016 (s 112(1)) |
| Sch 1 | | 4 Apr 2019 (SSI 2018/380) |
| Sch 2 | | 15 Dec 2016 (SSI 2016/417) repeals of— |
| | | Burial Grounds (Scotland) Act 1855; |
| | | Scottish Board of Health Act 1919; |
| | | Church of Scotland (Property and Endowments) Act 1925; |
| | | Acquisition of Land (Authorisation Procedure) (Scotland) Act 1947; |
| | | Local Government etc. (Scotland) Act 1994 |
| | | 4 Apr 2019 (otherwise) (SSI 2018/380) |

[1]  For transitory, transitional and saving provisions, see SSI 2018/380, regs 3–8

**Carers (Scotland) Act 2016 (asp 9)**

*RA:* 9 Mar 2016

*Commencement provisions:* s 45; Carers (Scotland) Act 2016 (Commencement No 1) Regulations 2017, SSI 2017/94; Carers (Scotland) Act 2016 (Commencement No 2 and Savings Provision) Regulations 2017, SSI 2017/152; Carers (Scotland) Act 2016 (Commencement No 3) Regulations 2018, SSI 2018/25

| | | |
|---|---|---|
| 1 | (1), (2) | 1 Oct 2017 (SSI 2017/152) |

**Carers (Scotland) Act 2016 (asp 9)**—*contd*

| | | |
|---|---|---|
| | (3)(a) | 31 May 2017 (for the purpose of enabling regulations to be made) (SSI 2017/152) |
| | | 1 Oct 2017 (otherwise) (SSI 2017/152) |
| | (3)(b), (4) | 1 Oct 2017 (SSI 2017/152) |
| 2–5 | | 1 Oct 2017 (SSI 2017/152) |
| 6, 7 | | *Not yet in force* |
| 8 | | 9 Feb 2018 (SSI 2018/25) |
| 9 | | *Not yet in force* |
| 10 | | 31 May 2017 (SSI 2017/152) |
| 11–13 | | *Not yet in force* |
| 14 | | 9 Feb 2018 (SSI 2018/25) |
| 15 | | *Not yet in force* |
| 16 | | 31 May 2017 (SSI 2017/152) |
| 17–20 | | *Not yet in force* |
| 21 | | 1 Oct 2017 (SSI 2017/152) |
| 22 | (1) | 1 Oct 2017 (SSI 2017/152) |
| | (2) | 31 May 2017 (for the purpose of enabling regulations to be made) (SSI 2017/152) |
| | | 1 Oct 2017 (otherwise) (SSI 2017/152) |
| | (3) | 31 May 2017 (for the purpose of enabling regulations to be made) (SSI 2017/152) |
| | | *Not yet in force (otherwise)* |
| | (4)–(7) | *Not yet in force* |
| 23, 24 | | *Not yet in force* |
| 25 | (1) | *Not yet in force* |
| | (2)(a) | 31 May 2017 (for the purpose of enabling regulations to be made) (SSI 2017/152) |
| | | *Not yet in force (otherwise)* |
| | (2)(b) | *Not yet in force* |
| | (3)–(5) | *Not yet in force* |
| 26 | | 31 May 2017 (SSI 2017/152) |
| 27–34 | | *Not yet in force* |
| 35 | (1)–(3) | *Not yet in force* |
| | (4) | 31 May 2017 (for the purpose of enabling regulations to be made) (SSI 2017/152) |
| | | *Not yet in force (otherwise)* |
| 36 | | *Not yet in force* |
| 37 | | 1 Oct 2017 (SSI 2017/152) |
| 38–40 | | *Not yet in force* |
| 41–43 | | 10 Mar 2016 (s 45(1)) |
| 44 | | See Schedule below |
| 45, 46 | | 10 Mar 2016 (s 45(1)) |
| Schedule | paras 1–5 | *Not yet in force* |
| | para 6(1) | See para 6(2) below |
| | para 6(2)(a), (b) | *Not yet in force* |
| | para 6(2)(c) | 24 Apr 2017 (SSI 2017/94) |

---

## Charities (Protection and Social Investment) Act 2016 (c 4)

*RA:* 16 Mar 2016

*Commencement provisions*: s 17(3), (4); Charities (Protection and Social Investment) Act 2016 (Commencement No 1 and Transitional Provision) Regulations 2016, SI 2016/815; Charities (Protection and Social Investment) Act 2016 (Commencement No 2 and Transitional Provision) Regulations 2018, SI 2018/47

| | |
|---|---|
| 1 | 1 Nov 2016 (SI 2016/815) |
| 2 | 31 Jul 2016 (except to the extent that sub-s (2) thereof inserts ", a failure to remedy any breach specified in a warning under section 75A," into Charities Act 2011, 76(1)(a)) (SI 2016/815) |

**Charities (Protection and Social Investment) Act 2016 (c 4)**—*contd*

|  |  |  |
|---|---|---|
|  |  | 1 Nov 2016 (exception noted above) (SI 2016/815) |
| 3–8 |  | 31 Jul 2016 (SI 2016/815) |
| 9 | (1)–(3), (4)(a) | 1 Feb 2018 (for the purpose only of making an application to the Commission for a waiver under s 181(2), permitting the Commission to consider such an application, and bringing an appeal in respect of a decision of the Commission relating to such an application) (SI 2018/47)[2] |
|  |  | 1 Aug 2018 (otherwise) (SI 2018/47)[2] |
|  | (4)(b) | 31 Jul 2016 (SI 2016/815) |
|  | (5)–(21) | 1 Feb 2018 (for the purpose only of making an application to the Commission for a waiver under s 181(2), permitting the Commission to consider such an application, and bringing an appeal in respect of a decision of the Commission relating to such an application) (SI 2018/47)[2] |
|  |  | 1 Aug 2018 (otherwise) (SI 2018/47)[2] |
| 10 |  | 1 Oct 2016 (SI 2016/815) |
| 11 | (1)–(4) | 1 Aug 2018 (SI 2018/47) |
|  | (5) | 31 Jul 2016 (only to the extent required to bring Charities Act 2011, s 182(1C) into force) (SI 2016/815) |
|  |  | 1 Oct 2016 (otherwise) (SI 2016/815) |
| 12 |  | 1 Aug 2018 (SI 2018/47) |
| 13 |  | 1 Nov 2016 (SI 2016/815)[1] |
| 14, 15 |  | 31 Jul 2016 (SI 2016/815) |
| 16, 17 |  | 16 Mar 2016 (s 17(3)) |

[1]    For a transitional provision, see SI 2016/815, reg 5

[2]    For a transitional provision, see SI 2018/47, reg 4

---

**Childcare Act 2016 (c 5)**

*RA:* 16 Mar 2016

*Commencement provisions:* s 7; Childcare Act 2016 (Commencement No 1) Regulations 2016, SI 2016/1055; Childcare Act 2016 (Commencement No 2) Regulations 2017, SI 2017/785

|  |  |  |
|---|---|---|
| 1 | (1) | 1 Sep 2017 (SI 2017/785) |
|  | (2)–(4) | 3 Nov 2016 (SI 2016/1055) |
|  | (5) | 16 Mar 2016 (s 7(1)) |
|  | (6) | 1 Sep 2017 (SI 2017/785) |
|  | (7)–(9) | 3 Nov 2016 (SI 2016/1055) |
| 2–5 |  | 3 Nov 2016 (SI 2016/1055) |
| 6–8 |  | 16 Mar 2016 (s 7(1)) |

---

**Cities and Local Government Devolution Act 2016 (c 1)**

*RA:* 28 Jan 2016

*Commencement provisions:* s 25

|  |  |  |
|---|---|---|
| 1 |  | 28 Mar 2016 (s 25(2)(b)) |
| 2 | (1) | 28 Jan 2016 (for the purpose of making orders) (s 25(2)(a)) |
|  |  | 28 Mar 2016 (otherwise) (s 25(2)(b)) |
|  | (2) | See Sch 1 below |
| 3 |  | 28 Mar 2016 (s 25(2)(b)) |
| 4 | (1) | 28 Jan 2016 (for the purpose of making orders) (s 25(2)(a)) |
|  |  | 28 Mar 2016 (otherwise) (s 25(2)(b)) |
|  | (2) | See Sch 2 below |
| 5 |  | 28 Jan 2016 (for the purpose of making orders) (s 25(2)(a)) |
|  |  | 28 Mar 2016 (otherwise) (s 25(2)(b)) |

**Cities and Local Government Devolution Act 2016 (c 1)**—*contd*

| | | |
|---|---|---|
| 6 | | 28 Mar 2016 (s 25(2)(b)) |
| 7 | | 28 Jan 2016 (for the purpose of making orders) (s 25(2)(a)) |
| | | 28 Mar 2016 (otherwise) (s 25(2)(b)) |
| 8 | (1) | 28 Mar 2016 (s 25(2)(b)) |
| | (2) | See Sch 3 below |
| 9 | | 28 Jan 2016 (for the purpose of making regulations) (s 25(2)(a)) |
| | | 28 Mar 2016 (otherwise) (s 25(2)(b)) |
| 10 | | 28 Jan 2016 (for the purpose of making orders) (s 25(2)(a)) |
| | | 28 Mar 2016 (otherwise) (s 25(2)(b)) |
| 11–13 | | 28 Mar 2016 (s 25(2)(b)) |
| 14 | | 28 Jan 2016 (for the purpose of making orders) (s 25(2)(a)) |
| | | 28 Mar 2016 (otherwise) (s 25(2)(b)) |
| 15–17 | | 28 Jan 2016 (for the purpose of making regulations) (s 25(2)(a)) |
| | | 28 Mar 2016 (otherwise) (s 25(2)(b)) |
| 18 | | 28 Mar 2016 (s 25(2)(b)) |
| 19 | | See Sch 4 below |
| 20 | | 28 Mar 2016 (s 25(2)(b)) |
| 21, 22 | | 28 Jan 2016 (for the purpose of making regulations) (s 25(2)(a)) |
| | | 28 Mar 2016 (otherwise) (s 25(2)(b)) |
| 23 | (1) | See Sch 5 below |
| | (2)–(5) | 28 Jan 2016 (for the purpose of making regulations) (s 25(2)(a)) |
| | | 28 Mar 2016 (otherwise) (s 25(2)(b)) |
| 24–26 | | 28 Jan 2016 (s 25(1)) |
| Schs 1–3 | | 28 Jan 2016 (for the purpose of making orders) (s 25(2)(a)) |
| | | 28 Mar 2016 (otherwise) (s 25(2)(b)) |
| Sch 4 | | 28 Jan 2016 (for the purpose of making regulations) (s 25(2)(a)) |
| | | 28 Mar 2016 (otherwise) (s 25(2)(b)) |
| Sch 5 | | 28 Mar 2016 (s 25(2)(b)) |

**Community Justice (Scotland) Act 2016 (asp 10)**

*RA:* 21 Mar 2016

*Commencement provisions:* s 41; Community Justice (Scotland) Act 2016 (Commencement No 1 and Transitional Provision) Regulations 2016, SSI 2016/262; Community Justice (Scotland) Act 2016 (Commencement No 2, Transitional and Saving Provisions) Regulations 2017, SSI 2017/33

| | | |
|---|---|---|
| 1, 2 | | 22 Mar 2016 (s 41(1)) |
| 3 | (1) | 1 Oct 2016 (SSI 2016/262) |
| | (2) | See Sch 1 below |
| 4–6 | | 1 Apr 2017 (SSI 2017/33) |
| 7 | | 1 Oct 2016 (SSI 2016/262) |
| 8 | | 1 Apr 2017 (SSI 2017/33) |
| 9, 10 | | 1 Oct 2016 (SSI 2016/262) |
| 11 | | 1 Apr 2017 (SSI 2017/33)[1] |
| 12 | | 1 Oct 2016 (SSI 2016/262) |
| 13 | (1) | 22 Mar 2016 (s 41(1)) |
| | (2)–(4) | 1 Oct 2016 (SSI 2016/262) |
| 14 | (1)–(6) | 22 Mar 2016 (s 41(1)) |
| | (7) | 1 Oct 2016 (SSI 2016/262) |
| 15 | | 22 Mar 2016 (s 41(1)) |
| 16 | | 1 Apr 2017 (SSI 2017/33) |
| 17 | | 22 Mar 2016 (s 41(1)) |
| 18 | | 1 Apr 2017 (SSI 2017/33) |
| 19–24 | | 1 Oct 2016 (SSI 2016/262) |
| 25–35 | | 1 Apr 2017 (SSI 2017/33) |
| 36 | | 31 Mar 2017 (SSI 2017/33) |
| 37 | | 22 Mar 2016 (s 41(1)) |
| 38 | | See Sch 2 below |

**Community Justice (Scotland) Act 2016 (asp 10)**—*contd*

| | | |
|---|---|---|
| 39–42 | | 22 Mar 2016 (s 41(1)) |
| Sch 1 | paras 1–13 | 1 Oct 2016 (for the purpose of establishing Community Justice Scotland and making appointments under Sch 1; and for the purpose of enabling Community Justice Scotland to exercise any function conferred on it under or by virtue of ss 10, 12 and 19 to 21 of the Act) (SSI 2016/262) |
| | | 1 Apr 2017 (otherwise) (SSI 2017/33) |
| | para 14 | 1 Apr 2017 (SSI 2017/33) |
| Sch 2 | para 1 | 31 Mar 2017 (SSI 2017/33) |
| | para 2 | 1 Apr 2017 (SSI 2017/33) |
| | paras 3–6 | 31 Mar 2017 (SSI 2017/33)[1] |

[1]    For transitional and saving provisions, see SSI 2017/33, regs 3–5

---

**Criminal Cases Review Commission (Information) Act 2016 (c 17)**

*RA:* 12 May 2016

*Commencement provisions:* s 2(2)

Whole Act in force 12 Jul 2016 (s 2(2))

---

**Criminal Justice (Scotland) Act 2016 (asp 1)**

*RA:* 13 Jan 2016

*Commencement provisions:* s 117; Criminal Justice (Scotland) Act 2016 (Commencement No 1 and Saving Provision) Order 2016, SSI 2016/95; Criminal Justice (Scotland) Act 2016 (Commencement No 2) Order 2016, SSI 2016/199; Criminal Justice (Scotland) Act 2016 (Commencement No 3 and Saving Provision) Order 2016, SSI 2016/426; Criminal Justice (Scotland) Act 2016 (Commencement No 4, Transitional, Transitory and Saving Provisions) Order 2017, SSI 2017/99; Criminal Justice (Scotland) Act 2016 (Commencement No 5, Transitional and Saving Provisions) Order 2017, SSI 2017/345; Criminal Justice (Scotland) Act 2016 (Commencement No 6 and Transitional Provision) Order 2019, SSI 2019/363

| | | |
|---|---|---|
| 1 | | 25 Jan 2018 (SSI 2017/345)[4] |
| 2 | | 25 Jan 2018 (SSI 2017/345) |
| 3–41 | | 25 Jan 2018 (SSI 2017/345)[4] |
| 42 | | 10 Jan 2020 (SSI 2019/363)[5] |
| 43, 44 | | 25 Jan 2018 (SSI 2017/345)[4] |
| 45–53 | | 25 Jan 2018 (SSI 2017/345) |
| 54, 55 | | 25 Jan 2018 (SSI 2017/345)[4] |
| 56–59 | | 25 Jan 2018 (SSI 2017/345) |
| 60–64 | | 17 Jan 2017 (SSI 2016/426) |
| 65–69 | | 11 May 2017 (SSI 2017/99) |
| 70 | | *Not yet in force* |
| 71 | | 14 Jan 2016 (s 117(1)(a)) |
| 72 | | 11 May 2017 (SSI 2017/99) |
| 73–77 | | 14 Jan 2016 (s 117(1)(a)) |
| 78 | | 17 Jan 2017 (SSI 2016/426)[2] |
| 79 | | 29 May 2017 (for the purposes of any indictment served on an accused on or after that day) (SSI 2017/99)[3] |
| | | *Not yet in force* (otherwise) |
| 80 | | 29 May 2017 (for the purposes of any indictment served on an accused on or after that day) (SSI 2017/99) |
| | | *Not yet in force* (otherwise) |
| 81 | (1), (2) | 29 May 2017 (for the purposes of any indictment served on an accused on or after that day) (SSI 2017/99) |
| | | *Not yet in force* (otherwise) |
| | (3), (4) | 31 Jul 2017 (SSI 2017/99)[3] |

**Criminal Justice (Scotland) Act 2016 (asp 1)**—*contd*

| | | |
|---|---|---|
| | (5) | 29 May 2017 (for the purposes of any indictment served on an accused on or after that day) (SSI 2017/99) |
| | | *Not yet in force* (otherwise) |
| | (6), (7) | 28 Aug 2017 (SSI 2017/99) |
| 82, 83 | | 17 Jan 2017 (SSI 2016/426) |
| 84 | | 10 Mar 2016 (SSI 2016/95)[1] |
| 85, 86 | | *Not yet in force* |
| 87–96 | | 17 Jan 2017 (SSI 2016/426) |
| 97 | | 25 Jan 2018 (SSI 2017/345) |
| 98–101 | | 17 Jan 2017 (SSI 2016/426) |
| 102, 103 | | 10 Jan 2020 (SSI 2019/363) |
| 104–106 | | 17 Jan 2017 (SSI 2016/426) |
| 107, 108 | | *Not yet in force* |
| 109 | | 25 Jan 2018 (SSI 2017/345)[4] |
| 110 | (1) | 25 Jan 2018 (SSI 2017/345) |
| | (2)(a) | 17 Jan 2017 (SSI 2016/426) |
| | (2)(b) | 25 Jan 2018 (SSI 2017/345)[4] |
| 111 | (1) | 17 Jan 2017 (SSI 2016/426) |
| | (2), (3) | *Not yet in force* |
| 112 | | 1 Jul 2016 (SSI 2016/199) |
| 113, 114 | | *Not yet in force* |
| 115–118 | | 14 Jan 2016 (s 117(1)(b)) |
| Schs 1, 2 | | 25 Jan 2018 (SSI 2017/345) |
| Sch 3 | | *Not yet in force* |

[1]    For a saving, see SSI 2016/95, art 3

[2]    For a saving, see SSI 2016/426, art 3

[3]    For transitional, transitory and saving provisions, see SSI 2017/99, arts 3–6

[4]    For transitional and saving provisions, see SSI 2017/345, arts 4–10

[5]    For transitional provisions, see SSI 2019/363, art 4

---

**Diocesan Stipends Funds (Amendment) Measure 2016 (No 2)**

*RA:* 16 Mar 2016

*Commencement provisions:* s 2(2)

Whole Measure in force 16 May 2016 (s 2(2))

---

**Driving Instructors (Registration) Act 2016 (c 16)**

*RA:* 12 May 2016

*Commencement provisions:* s 7(1)–(3)

| | |
|---|---|
| 1–4 | *Not yet in force* |
| 5–7 | 12 May 2016 (s 7(3)(b)) |

---

**Education and Adoption Act 2016 (c 6)**

*RA:* 16 Mar 2016

*Commencement provisions:* s 19; Education and Adoption Act 2016 (Commencement, Transitional Provisions and Savings) Regulations 2016, SI 2016/466; Education and Adoption Act 2016 (Commencement No 2) Regulations 2016, SI 2016/866; Education and Adoption Act 2016 (Commencement No 3) Regulations 2017, SI 2017/6; Education and Adoption Act 2016 (Commencement No 4) Regulations 2018, SI 2018/300

**See Halsbury's Statutes Citator for amendments to these Acts**    2457

**Education and Adoption Act 2016 (c 6)**—*contd*

| | | |
|---|---|---|
| 1 | | 5 Sep 2016 (for the purpose of making regulations) (SI 2016/866) |
| | | 11 Jan 2017 (otherwise) (SI 2017/6) |
| 2–14 | | 18 Apr 2016 (SI 2016/466)[1] |
| 15 | | 7 Mar 2018 (SI 2018/300) |
| 16 | (a), (b) | 11 Jan 2017 (in so far as repeals provisions of Apprenticeship, Skills, Children and Learning Act 2009 and Education Act 2011) (SI 2017/6) |
| | | *Not yet in force* (otherwise) |
| | (c) | 11 Jan 2017 (in so far as repeals provisions of Apprenticeship, Skills, Children and Learning Act 2009 and Education Act 2011) (SI 2017/6) |
| | | 7 Mar 2018 (otherwise) (SI 2018/300) |
| 17–20 | | 16 Mar 2016 (s 19(1)) |

[1]  For transitional provisions and savings, see SI 2016/466, regs 4, 5

---

**Education (Scotland) Act 2016 (asp 8)**

*RA:* 8 Mar 2016

*Commencement provisions*: s 33; Education (Scotland) Act 2016 (Commencement No 1) Regulations 2016, SSI 2016/192; Education (Scotland) Act 2016 (Commencement No 2) Regulations 2016, SSI 2016/386; Education (Scotland) Act 2016 (Commencement No 3) Regulations 2017, SSI 2017/164, as amended by SSI 2017/352; Education (Scotland) Act 2016 (Commencement No. 4) Regulations 2017, SSI 2017/354; Education (Scotland) Act 2016 (Commencement No 5 and Savings Provision) Regulations 2018, SSI 2018/36

| | | |
|---|---|---|
| 1 | | 1 Aug 2016 (for the purpose of inserting Standards in Scotland's Schools etc. Act 2000, s 3A) (SSI 2016/192) |
| | | 1 Aug 2017 (for the purpose of inserting Standards in Scotland's Schools etc. Act 2000, s 3B) (SSI 2017/64) |
| 2 | (1) | See sub-ss (2)–(4) below |
| | (2) | 1 Aug 2016 (for the purpose of inserting Standards in Scotland's Schools etc. Act 2000, s 3C) (SSI 2016/192) |
| | | 1 Aug 2017 (for the purpose of inserting Standards in Scotland's Schools etc. Act 2000, s 3D) (SSI 2017/64) |
| | (3) | 1 Aug 2016 (for the purpose of repealing Standards in Scotland's Schools etc. Act 2000, s 4) (SSI 2016/192) |
| | | 1 Aug 2017 (for the purpose of repealing Standards in Scotland's Schools etc. Act 2000, s 5) (SSI 2017/64) |
| | (4)(a) | 1 Aug 2016 (for the purpose of repealing definition "national priorities in education" in Standards in Scotland's Schools etc. Act 2000, s 58(1)) (SSI 2016/192) |
| | | 1 Aug 2017 (for the purpose of repealing definition "annual statement of education improvement objectives" in Standards in Scotland's Schools etc. Act 2000, s 58(1)) (SSI 2017/164) |
| | (4)(b) | 1 Aug 2016 (SSI 2016/192) |
| 3 | (1) | See sub-ss (2)–(7) below |
| | (2) | 1 Aug 2016 (so far as necessary to enable the Scottish Ministers to make regulations under Standards in Scotland's Schools etc. Act 2000, ss 3E(2), 3F(4)) (SSI 2016/192) |
| | | 1 Dec 2016 (for the purpose of inserting Standards in Scotland's Schools etc. Act 2000, s 3E for remaining purposes, and s 3G thereof) (SSI 2016/192) |
| | | 17 Aug 2017 (for the purpose of inserting Standards in Scotland's Schools etc. Act 2000, s 3F for remaining purposes, and ss 3H, 3I thereof) (SSI 2017/164) |
| | (3)–(7) | 1 Aug 2017 (SSI 2017/164) |
| 4 | | 1 Aug 2016 (SSI 2016/192) |
| 5–6 | | 1 Aug 2017 (SSI 2017/164) |

**Education (Scotland) Act 2016 (asp 8)**—*contd*

| | | |
|---|---|---|
| 7 | | 1 Aug 2016 (so far as necessary to enable the Scottish Ministers to make regulations under s 7(5)) (SSI 2016/192) |
| | | 1 Feb 2017 (otherwise) (SSI 2016/386) |
| 8–15 | | 1 Feb 2017 (SSI 2016/386) |
| 16, 17 | | 15 Jul 2016 (SSI 2016/192) |
| 18 | | 1 Feb 2017 (SSI 2016/386) |
| 19 | | See Schedule below |
| 20 | | 1 Jan 2017 (SSI 2016/386) |
| 21 | (1), (2) | 1 Aug 2016 (for the purpose of inserting Education (Scotland) Act 1980, s 2ZA(11) (SSI 2016/192) |
| | | *Not yet in force* (otherwise) |
| | (3) | *Not yet in force* |
| 22 | (1), (2) | 1 Apr 2018 (SSI 2018/36)[1] |
| | (3) | *Not yet in force* |
| | (4)–(6) | 1 Apr 2018 (SSI 2018/36) |
| 23 | | *Not yet in force* |
| 24 | | 1 Jan 2017 (so far as is necessary to enable the Scottish Ministers to make regulations under Education (Scotland) Act 1980, s 70(5), (6) and for the purpose of consulting under s 70(7) thereof) (SSI 2016/386) |
| | | 10 Jan 2018(otherwise) (SSI 2017/164) |
| 25 | | *Not yet in force* |
| 26, 27 | | 1 Jan 2017 (SSI 2016/386) |
| 28 | (1) | 1 Jan 2017 (SSI 2016/386) |
| | (2) | *Not yet in force* |
| | (3) | 10 Jan 2018 (SSI 2017/354) |
| 29, 30 | | 1 Aug 2016 (SSI 2016/192) |
| 31–34 | | 9 Mar 2016 (s 33(1)) |
| Schedule | paras 1–14 | 10 Jan 2018 (SSI 2017/354) |
| | para 15 | 1 Aug 2017 (SSI 2017/164) |
| | paras 16–19 | 10 Jan 2018 (SSI 2017/354) |
| | para 20 | 1 Jan 2017 (so far as is necessary to enable the Scottish Ministers to make regulations under Education (Additional Support for Learning) (Scotland) Act 2004, s 27A(1) and for the purpose of consulting under s 27A(1A) thereof) (SSI 2016/386) |
| | | 10 Jan 2018 (otherwise) (SSI 2017/354) |
| | paras 21–25 | 10 Jan 2018 (SSI 2017/354) |

[1]  For savings, see SSI 2018/36, reg 3

---

**Energy Act 2016 (c 20)**

*RA:* 12 May 2016

*Commencement provisions*: s 84; Energy Act 2016 (Commencement No 1 and Savings Provisions) Regulations 2016, SI 2016/602, as amended by SI 2016/710; Energy Act 2016 (Commencement No 2 and Transitional Provisions) Regulations 2016, SI 2016/920; Energy Act 2016 (Commencement No 3) Regulations 2016, SI 2016/1198; Energy Act 2016 (Commencement No 4 and Transitory Provision) Regulations 2017, SI 2017/942

| | | |
|---|---|---|
| 1 | (1)–(3) | 12 Jul 2016 (SI 2016/602) |
| | (4) | 24 May 2016 (SI 2016/602) |
| 2 | (1) | See Sch 1 below |
| | (2)–(6) | 24 May 2016 (SI 2016/602) |
| 3–5 | | 12 Jul 2016 (SI 2016/602) |
| 6–12 | | 1 Oct 2016 (SI 2016/920) |
| 13, 14 | | 12 Jul 2016 (SI 2016/602) |
| 15–29 | | 1 Oct 2016 (SI 2016/920) |
| 30 | | 21 Oct 2017 (SI 2017/942) |
| 31 | | 21 Oct 2017 (SI 2017/942)[2] |

**Energy Act 2016 (c 20)**—*contd*

| | | |
|---|---|---|
| 32, 33 | | 21 Oct 2017 (SI 2017/942) |
| 34 | (1)(a) | 19 Dec 2016 (SI 2016/1198) |
| | (1)(b) | 21 Oct 2017 (SI 2017/942) |
| | (2)–(6) | 19 Dec 2016 (SI 2016/1198) |
| 35 | | 21 Oct 2017 (SI 2017/942) |
| 36 | | 19 Dec 2016 (insofar as applies to a decision of the OGA to give a notice under section 34(1)(a)) (SI 2016/1198) |
| | | 21 Oct 2017 (otherwise) (SI 2017/942) |
| 37–65 | | 1 Oct 2016 (SI 2016/920) |
| 66 | (1), (2) | 1 Oct 2016 (SI 2016/920) |
| | (3), (4) | 24 May 2016 (SI 2016/602) |
| | (5)–(7) | 1 Oct 2016 (SI 2016/920) |
| 67–71 | | 1 Oct 2016 (SI 2016/920) |
| 72 | | See Sch 2 below |
| 73–75 | | 1 Oct 2016 (SI 2016/920) |
| 76, 77 | | 12 Jul 2016 (s 84(2)) |
| 78 | | 12 Jul 2016 (SI 2016/602)[1] |
| 79–85 | | 12 May 2016 (s 84(1)) |
| Schs 1, 2 | | 1 Oct 2016 (SI 2016/920) |

[1]   For savings, see SI 2016/602, reg 4

[2]   For a transitory provision, see SI 2017/942, reg 3

---

**Enterprise Act 2016 (c 12)**

*RA:* 4 May 2016

*Commencement provisions*: s 44; Enterprise Act 2016 (Commencement No 1) Regulations 2016, SI 2016/695; Enterprise Act 2016 (Commencement No 2) Regulations 2017, SI 2017/70; Enterprise Act 2016 (Commencement No 3) Regulations 2017, SI 2017/346; Enterprise Act 2016 (Commencement No 4 and Appointed Start Date) Regulations 2017, SI 2017/473; Enterprise Act 2016 (Commencement No 5) Regulations 2017, SI 2017/842

| | | |
|---|---|---|
| 1 | (1) | 6 Apr 2017 (SI 2017/473) |
| | (2) | 1 Oct 2017 (SI 2017/473) |
| | (3) | See Sch 1 below |
| 2–13 | | 4 May 2016 (in so far as confers power to make regulations) (s 44(1)(a)) |
| | | 1 Oct 2017 (otherwise) (SI 2017/473) |
| 14 | (1)–(3) | 4 May 2016 (for the purpose of enabling the exercise of the power to make regulations under Small Business, Enterprise and Employment Act 2015, s 22(9)) (s 44(1)(b)) |
| | | 4 Jul 2016 (otherwise) (s 44(2)(a)) |
| | (4) | See Sch 2 below |
| | (5)–(9) | 4 May 2016 (for the purpose of enabling the exercise of the power to make regulations under Small Business, Enterprise and Employment Act 2015, s 22(9)) (s 44(1)(b)) |
| | | 4 Jul 2016 (otherwise) (s 44(2)(a)) |
| 15, 16 | | *Not yet in force* |
| 17 | | 1 Oct 2016 (SI 2016/695) |
| 18 | | 4 Jul 2016 (s 44(2)(b)) |
| 19 | | 1 Oct 2016 (SI 2016/695) |
| 20 | (1) | 4 May 2016 (for the purpose of enabling the exercise of any power to make regulations under any provision of Regulatory Enforcement and Sanctions Act 2008 inserted by s 20 of or Sch 3 to this Act) (s 44(1)(c)) |
| | | 1 Oct 2017 (otherwise) (SI 2017/473) |
| | (2) | See Sch 3 below |
| 21 | | 1 Oct 2016 (SI 2016/695) |

**Enterprise Act 2016 (c 12)**—*contd*

| | | |
|---|---|---|
| 22 | | See Sch 4 below |
| 23 | | 1 Apr 2017 (SI 2017/346) |
| 24 | | 4 Jul 2016 (s 44(2)(c)) |
| 25 | | 1 Apr 2017 (SI 2017/346) |
| 26, 27 | | 4 Jul 2016 (SI 2016/695) |
| 28–30 | | 4 May 2017 (s 44(3)) |
| 31 | | 4 Jul 2016 (s 44(2)(d)) |
| 32 | | 4 Jul 2016 (s 44(2)(e)) |
| 33 | | See Sch 5 below |
| 34, 35 | | 4 Jul 2016 (s 44(2)(f)) |
| 36 | | 1 Feb 2017 (SI 2017/70) |
| 37 | | 18 Aug 2017 (SI 2017/842) |
| 38 | | 4 May 2016 (s 44(1)(e)) |
| 39, 40 | | 21 Jul 2016 (the day after the day on which the Pubs Code etc Regulations 2016, SI 2016/790, were made) (SI 2016/695) |
| 41 | (1) | 1 Feb 2017 (SI 2017/70) |
| | (2) | See Sch 6 below |
| 42–46 | | 4 May 2016 (s 44(1)(g)) |
| Sch 1 | | 4 May 2016 (in so far as confers power to make regulations) (s 44(1)(a)) |
| | | 6 Apr 2017 (otherwise) (SI 2017/473) |
| Sch 2 | para 1 | 4 Jul 2016 (s 44(2)(g)) |
| | para 2 | 4 May 2016 (s 44(1)(f)) |
| | paras 3–5 | 4 Jul 2016 (s 44(2)(g)) |
| Sch 3 | | 4 May 2016 (for the purpose of enabling the exercise of any power to make regulations under any provision of Regulatory Enforcement and Sanctions Act 2008 inserted by s 20 of or Sch 3 to this Act) (s 44(1)(c)) |
| | | 1 Oct 2017 (otherwise) (SI 2017/473) |
| Sch 4 | | 1 Apr 2017 (SI 2017/346) |
| Sch 5 | | 4 May 2016 (for the purpose of enabling the exercise of any power to make regulations under any provision of Employment Rights Act 1996 inserted by Sch 5) (s 44(1)(d)) |
| | | *Not yet in force* (otherwise) |
| Sch 6 | paras 1–4 | 1 Feb 2017 (SI 2017/70) |
| | para 5 | *Not yet in force* |

## Environment (Wales) Act 2016 (anaw 3)

*RA:* 21 Mar 2016

*Commencement provisions*: s 88; Environment (Wales) Act 2016 (Commencement No 1) Order 2017, SI 2017/152; Environment (Wales) Act 2016 (Commencement No 2) Order 2017, SI 2017/504; Environment (Wales) Act 2016 (Commencement No 3) Order 2017, SI 2017/714

| | | |
|---|---|---|
| 1–26 | | 21 May 2016 (s 88(2)(a)) |
| 27 | (1) | 21 May 2016 (s 88(2)(a)) |
| | (2) | See Sch 2, Pt 1 below |
| 28–53 | | 21 May 2016 (s 88(2)(b)) |
| 54–60 | | *Not yet in force* |
| 61 | | See Sch 1 below |
| 62, 63 | | *Not yet in force* |
| 64 | | See Sch 2, Pt 2 below |
| 65–69 | | *Not yet in force* |
| 70 | | See Sch 2, Pt 3 below |
| 71–75 | | 21 May 2016 (s 88(2)(c)) |
| 76 | | 1 Apr 2016 (SI 2017/504) |
| 77–79 | | 24 Feb 2017 (for the purpose of making regulations) (SI 2017/152) |
| | | 1 Apr 2016 (otherwise) (SI 2017/504) |
| 80 | | 1 Apr 2016 (SI 2017/504) |

**Environment (Wales) Act 2016 (anaw 3)**—*contd*

| | | |
|---|---|---|
| 81 | (1), (2) | 14 Jul 2017 (SI 2017/714) |
| | (3) | See Sch 2, Pt 4 below |
| 82 | | 21 May 2016 (s 88(2)(d)) |
| 83 | | *Not yet in force* |
| 84, 85 | | 21 May 2016 (s 88(2)(e), (f)) |
| 86 | | See Sch 2, Pt 5 below |
| 87–89 | | 21 Mar 2016 (s 88(1)) |
| Sch 1 | | *Not yet in force* |
| Sch 2 | Pt 1 | 21 May 2016 (s 88(2)(a)) |
| | Pts 2, 3 | *Not yet in force* |
| | Pt 4 | 14 Jul 2017 (SI 2017/714) |
| | Pt 5 | 21 May 2016 (s 88(2)(g)) |

---

**Finance Act 2016 (c 24)**

*Budget Day:* 16 Mar 2016

*RA:* 15 Sep 2016

The commencement details of Finance Acts are not set out, as the dates from which their provisions take effect are usually stated clearly and unambiguously in the text of the Act, and charging provisions will normally state for which year or years of assessment they are to have effect.

---

**Health (Tobacco, Nicotine etc and Care) (Scotland) Act 2016 (asp 14)**

*RA:* 6 Apr 2016

*Commencement provisions:* s 36; Health (Tobacco, Nicotine etc. and Care) (Scotland) Act 2016 (Commencement No 1) Regulations 2017, SSI 2017/12; Health (Tobacco, Nicotine etc. and Care) (Scotland) Act 2016 (Commencement No 2) Regulations 2017, SSI 2017/294; Health (Tobacco, Nicotine etc. and Care) (Scotland) Act 2016 (Commencement No 3) Regulations 2018, SSI 2018/26; Health (Tobacco, Nicotine etc. and Care) (Scotland) Act 2016 (Commencement No 4) Regulations 2018, SI 2018/56; Health (Tobacco, Nicotine etc. and Care) (Scotland) Act 2016 (Commencement No 5) Regulations 2022, SSI 2022/43

| | | |
|---|---|---|
| 1 | | 6 Feb 2017 (SSI 2017/12) |
| 2 | | 6 Feb 2017 (so far as is necessary to enable the Scottish Ministers to make regulations under Tobacco and Primary Medical Services (Scotland) Act 2010s 4A(4)(c)) (SSI 2017/12) |
| | | 1 Apr 2017 (otherwise) (SSI 2017/12) |
| 3 | | 1 Apr 2017 (SSI 2017/12) |
| 4 | | 6 Feb 2017 (so far as is necessary to enable the Scottish Ministers to make regulations under Tobacco and Primary Medical Services (Scotland) Act 2010s 4C(5)) (SSI 2017/12) |
| | | 1 Apr 2017 (otherwise) (SSI 2017/12) |
| 5–7 | | 1 Apr 2017 (SSI 2017/12) |
| 8 | | 6 Feb 2017 (so far as is necessary to enable the Scottish Ministers to make regulations under Tobacco and Primary Medical Services (Scotland) Act 2010s 11(2)(d)) (SSI 2017/12) |
| | | 1 Apr 2017 (otherwise) (SSI 2017/12) |
| 9 | (1) | 6 Feb 2017 (so far as is necessary to enable the Scottish Ministers to make regulations under Tobacco and Primary Medical Services (Scotland) Act 2010s 11(2)(d)) (SSI 2017/12) |
| | | 1 Apr 2017 (otherwise) (SSI 2017/12) |
| | (2)–(4) | 1 Apr 2017 (SSI 2017/12) |
| 10 | | 6 Feb 2017 (so far as is necessary to enable the Scottish Ministers to make regulations under Tobacco and Primary Medical Services (Scotland) Act 2010s 19(5)) (SSI 2017/12) |
| | | 1 Oct 2017 (otherwise) (SSI 2017/12) |
| 11 | | 1 Oct 2017 (SSI 2017/12) |

**Health (Tobacco, Nicotine etc and Care) (Scotland) Act 2016 (asp 14)**—*contd*

| | | |
|---|---|---|
| 12 | | 1 Apr 2017 (SSI 2017/12) |
| 13 | | 6 Feb 2017 (SSI 2017/12) |
| 14 | | 1 Apr 2017 (SSI 2017/12) |
| 15 | (1), (2) | 1 Apr 2017 (SSI 2017/12) |
| | (3)–(8) | 1 Oct 2017 (SSI 2017/12) |
| | (9)–(11) | 1 Apr 2017 (SSI 2017/12) |
| 16 | | 6 Feb 2017 (SSI 2017/12) |
| 17–19 | | *Not yet in force* |
| 20 | | 2 Mar 2022 (so far as is s is necessary to enable the Scottish Ministers to lay and make regulations under Smoking, Health and Social Care (Scotland) Act 2005, ss 4C(4), 4D(2), (4), (5), Sch 1, para 4(1) (SI 2022/43) |
| | | 5 Sep 2022 (otherwise) (SI 2022/43) |
| 21–23 | | 1 Oct 2017 (for the purpose of making regulations) (SSI 2017/294) |
| | | 1 Apr 2018 (otherwise) (SI 2018/56) |
| 24 | | 1 Apr 2018 (SI 2018/56) |
| 25 | (1) | 1 Oct 2017 (for the purpose of making regulations) (SSI 2017/294) |
| | | 1 Apr 2018 (otherwise) (SI 2018/56) |
| | (2) | 1 Apr 2018 (SI 2018/56) |
| 26–32 | | 1 Oct 2017 (SSI 2017/294) |
| 33 | | 19 Mar 2018 (SSI 2018/26) |
| 34–37 | | 7 Apr 2016 (s 36(1)) |

## Higher Education Governance (Scotland) Act 2016 (asp 15)

*RA:* 13 Apr 2016

*Commencement provisions:* s 26; Higher Education Governance (Scotland) Act 2016 (Commencement, Transitory, Transitional and Savings Provisions) Regulations 2016, SSI 2016/382

| | | |
|---|---|---|
| 1, 2 | | 30 Dec 2016 (SSI 2016/382) |
| 3–9 | | 30 Jun 2017 (SSI 2016/382)[1] |
| 10 | | 30 Dec 2016 (SSI 2016/382)[1] |
| 11–14 | | 30 Dec 2016 (SSI 2016/382) |
| 15 | | 30 Dec 2016 (SSI 2016/382)[1] |
| 16–25 | | 30 Dec 2016 (SSI 2016/382) |
| 26, 27 | | 14 Apr 2016 (s 26(1)) |
| Schedule | para 1 | 30 Dec 2016 (SSI 2016/382) |
| | para 2 | 30 Dec 2016 (SSI 2016/382)[1] |
| | para 3 | 30 Dec 2016 (SSI 2016/382) |

[1]   For transitory provisions, see SSI 2016/382

## Historic Environment (Wales) Act 2016 (anaw 4)

*RA:* 21 Mar 2016

*Commencement provisions:* s 41; Historic Environment (Wales) Act 2016 (Commencement No 1 and Transitional Provisions) Order 2017, SI 2017/633; Historic Environment (Wales) Act 2016 (Commencement No 2) Order 2021, SI 2021/1059

| | | |
|---|---|---|
| 1 | | 21 Mar 2016 (s 41(1)(a)) |
| 2 | | 21 Mar 2016 (s 41(1)(b)) |
| 3 | (1), (2) | 21 Mar 2016 (for the purpose of making regulations under the Ancient Monuments and Archaeological Areas Act 1979) (s 41(1)(c)) |
| | | 31 May 2017 (otherwise) (SI 2017/633)[1] |
| | (3) | See Sch 1 below |
| 4 | | 31 May 2017 (SI 2017/633)[1] |

**Historic Environment (Wales) Act 2016 (anaw 4)**—*contd*

| | | |
|---|---|---|
| 5 | | 21 Mar 2016 (for the purpose of making regulations under the Ancient Monuments and Archaeological Areas Act 1979) (s 41(1)(c)) |
| | | 31 May 2017 (otherwise) (SI 2017/633) |
| 6–9 | | 21 May 2016 (s 41(2)) |
| 10 | | *Not yet in force* |
| 11 | | 21 Mar 2016 (for the purpose of making regulations under the Ancient Monuments and Archaeological Areas Act 1979) (s 41(1)(c)) |
| | | 1Jan 2022 (otherwise) (SI 2021/1059) |
| 12–17 | | 21 May 2016 (s 41(2)) |
| 18 | | 1 Feb 2022 (SI 2021/1059) |
| 19–22 | | 21 May 2016 (s 41(2)) |
| 23 | | 21 Mar 2016 (s 41(1)(d)) |
| 24 | (1)–(3) | 21 Mar 2016 (for the purpose of making regulations under the Planning (Listed Buildings and Conservation Areas) Act 1990) (s 41(1)(e)) |
| | | 31 May 2017 (otherwise) (SI 2017/633)[1] |
| | (4) | See Sch 2 below |
| 25, 26 | | 31 May 2017 (SI 2017/633)[1] |
| 27 | | 21 May 2016 (s 41(2)) |
| 28 | | 21 Mar 2016 (for the purpose of making regulations under the Planning (Listed Buildings and Conservation Areas) Act 1990) (s 41(1)(e)) |
| | | 1Jan 2022 (otherwise) (SI 2021/1059) |
| 29 | | 21 May 2016 (s 41(2)) |
| 30 | (1)–(5) | 21 May 2016 (s 41(2)) |
| | (6) | 4 May 2017 (so far as confers power to make orders under the Planning (Listed Buildings and Conservation Areas) Act 1990) (SI 2017/633)[1] |
| | | 31 May 2017 (otherwise) (SI 2017/633)[1] |
| 31 | | *Not yet in force* |
| 32, 33 | | 21 May 2016 (s 41(2)) |
| 34 | | 8 May 2017 (SI 2017/633) |
| 35–37 | | 31 May 2017 (SI 2017/633) |
| 38, 39 | | *Not yet in force* |
| 40–42 | | 21 Mar 2016 (s 41(1)(e)) |
| Sch 1 | | 21 Mar 2016 (for the purpose of making regulations under the Ancient Monuments and Archaeological Areas Act 1979) (s 41(1)(c)) |
| | | 31 May 2017 (otherwise) (SI 2017/633) |
| Sch 2 | | 21 Mar 2016 (for the purpose of making regulations under the Planning (Listed Buildings and Conservation Areas) Act 1990) (s 41(1)(e)) |
| | | 31 May 2017 (otherwise) (SI 2017/633) |

[1]    For transitional provisions, see SI 2017/633, art 6

---

**House of Commons Members' Fund Act 2016 (c 18)**

*RA:* 12 May 2016

*Commencement provisions:* s 10

Whole Act in force 12 Aug 2016 (s 10)

---

## Housing and Planning Act 2016 (c 22)

*RA:* 12 May 2016

*Commencement provisions:* s 216; Housing and Planning Act 2016 (Commencement No 1) Regulations 2016, SI 2016/609; Housing and Planning Act 2016 (Commencement No 2, Transitional Provisions and Savings) Regulations 2016, SI 2016/733; Housing and Planning Act 2016 (Commencement No 3) Regulations 2016, SI 2016/956; Housing and Planning Act 2016 (Commencement No 4 and Transitional Provisions) Regulations 2017, SI 2017/75; Housing and Planning Act 2016 (Commencement No 5, Transitional Provisions and Savings) Regulations 2017, SI 2017/281; Housing and Planning Act 2016 (Commencement No 6) Regulations 2017, SI 2017/1052; Housing and Planning Act 2016 (Commencement No 7 and Transitional Provisions) Regulations 2018, SI 2018/251; Housing and Planning Act 2016 (Commencement No 8) Regulations 2018, SI 2018/393; Housing and Planning Act 2016 (Commencement No 9 and Transitional and Saving Provisions) Regulations 2018, SI 2018/805; Housing and Planning Act 2016 (Commencement No 10 and Transitional Provision) Regulations 2019, SI 2019/427; Housing and Planning Act 2016 (Commencement No 11) Regulations 2019, SI 2019/1359

| | | |
|---|---|---|
| 1–8 | | *Not yet in force* |
| 9–11 | | 31 Oct 2016 (SI 2016/733) |
| 12 | | 13 Jul 2016 (SI 2016/733) |
| 13 | | 6 Apr 2018 (SI 2018/393) |
| 14 | (1), (2) | 6 Apr 2018 (SI 2018/393) |
| | (3), (4) | 3 Nov 2017 (for the purpose only of making regulations to specify the description of an offence that is a banning order offence) (SI 2017/1052) |
| | | 6 Apr 2018 (otherwise) (SI 2018/393) |
| 15–22 | | 6 Apr 2018 (SI 2018/393) |
| 23 | (1)–(6) | 6 Apr 2018 (SI 2018/393) |
| | (7) | See Sch 1 below |
| | (8) | 3 Nov 2017 (SI 2017/1052) |
| | (9), (10) | 6 Apr 2018 (SI 2018/393) |
| 24 | | 6 Apr 2018 (SI 2018/393) |
| 25 | | See Sch 2 below |
| 26 | | See Sch 3 below |
| 27–32 | | 6 Apr 2018 (SI 2018/393) |
| 33 | | 3 Nov 2017 (SI 2017/1052) |
| 34–39 | | 6 Apr 2018 (SI 2018/393) |
| 40, 41 | | 6 Apr 2017 (for the purpose only of conferring power on the First-tier Tribunal to make a rent repayment order where a landlord has committed an offence mentioned in rows 1 to 6 of the table in s 40(3)) (SI 2017/281)[4] |
| | | 6 Apr 2018 (otherwise) (SI 2018/393) |
| 42 | | 6 Apr 2017 (for the purpose only of conferring power on the First-tier Tribunal to make a rent repayment order where a landlord has committed an offence mentioned in rows 1 to 6 of the table in s 40(3)) (SI 2017/281) |
| | | 6 Apr 2018 (otherwise) (SI 2018/393) |
| 43 | | 6 Apr 2017 (for the purpose only of conferring power on the First-tier Tribunal to make a rent repayment order where a landlord has committed an offence mentioned in rows 1 to 6 of the table in s 40(3)) (SI 2017/281)[4] |
| | | 6 Apr 2018 (otherwise) (SI 2018/393) |
| 44–46 | | 6 Apr 2017 (for the purpose only of conferring power on the First-tier Tribunal to make a rent repayment order where a landlord has committed an offence mentioned in rows 1 to 6 of the table in s 40(3)) (SI 2017/281) |
| | | 6 Apr 2018 (otherwise) (SI 2018/393) |
| 47 | (1), (2) | 6 Apr 2017 (SI 2017/281) |
| | (3) | 10 Mar 2017 (SI 2017/281) |

**Housing and Planning Act 2016 (c 22)**—*contd*

| | | |
|---|---|---|
| 48 | | 6 Apr 2017 (for the purpose only of requiring a local housing authority to consider applying for a rent repayment order where a landlord has committed an offence mentioned in rows 1 to 6 of the table in s 40(3)) (SI 2017/281)[4] |
| | | 6 Apr 2018 (otherwise) (SI 2018/393) |
| 49–56 | | 6 Apr 2017 (SI 2017/281) |
| 57–63 | | *Not yet in force* |
| 64, 65 | | 26 May 2016 (SI 2016/609) |
| 66 | | 13 Jul 2016 (SI 2016/733) |
| 67, 68 | | 26 May 2016 (SI 2016/609) |
| 69–79 | | 12 May 2016 (s 216(1)(b)) |
| 80–91 | | 1 Oct 2016 (SI 2016/956) |
| 92 | | See Sch 4 below |
| 93, 94 | | 3 Feb 2017 (SI 2017/75) |
| 95–101 | | 5 Jul 2018 (SI 2018/805) |
| 102 | (1) | See Sch 5 below |
| | (2)–(6) | 3 Feb 2017 (SI 2017/75) |
| 103–114 | | 5 Jul 2018 (SI 2018/805) |
| 115 | | See Sch 6 below |
| 116, 117 | | 5 Jul 2018 (SI 2018/805) |
| 118 | | See Sch 7 below |
| 119 | | *Not yet in force* |
| 120 | | See Sch 8 below |
| 121 | | *Not yet in force* |
| 122, 123 | | 25 Oct 2019 (SI 2019/1359) |
| 124 | | 12 Jul 2016 (s 216(2)(a)) |
| 125 | | *Not yet in force* |
| 126 | | See Sch 9 below |
| 127 | | *Not yet in force* |
| 128, 129 | | 6 Apr 2017 (SI 2017/281) |
| 130 | | 12 Jul 2016 (s 216(2)(b)) |
| 131 | | 6 Apr 2017 (SI 2017/281)[4] |
| 132 | | 1 Oct 2016 (SI 2016/733) |
| 133–135 | | 19 Mar 2018 (SI 2018/251) |
| 136 | | See Sch 10 below |
| 137 | | 12 May 2016 (s 216(1)(c)) |
| 138 | | *Not yet in force* |
| 139, 140 | | 12 May 2016 (s 216(1)(d)) |
| 141, 142 | | 1 Oct 2016 (SI 2016/733) |
| 143, 144 | | 13 Jul 2016 (SI 2016/733) |
| 145 | (1)–(4) | 1 Oct 2016 (SI 2016/733) |
| | (5) | 26 May 2016 (SI 2016/609) |
| 146 | | 1 Oct 2016 (SI 2016/733) |
| 147 | (1) | 1 Oct 2016 (SI 2016/733) |
| | (2) | See Sch 11 below |
| | (3) | 1 Oct 2016 (SI 2016/733) |
| 148 | | 1 Oct 2016 (SI 2016/733) |
| 149 | | 12 May 2016 (s 216(1)(d)) |
| 150 | (1)–(3) | 12 Jul 2016 (s 216(2)(c)) |
| | (4) | 13 Jul 2016 (SI 2016/733) |
| | (5) | See Sch 12 below |
| 151 | | 12 May 2016 (s 216(1)(d)) |
| 152 | (1) | 12 May 2016 (s 216(1)(d)) |
| | (2)–(4) | 13 Jul 2016 (SI 2016/733) |
| 153 | | 12 Jul 2016 (s 216(2)(c)) |
| 154 | | 13 Jul 2016 (SI 2016/733) |
| 155 | | *Not yet in force*[1] |
| 156 | | 1 Oct 2016 (SI 2016/733) |
| 157 | | 12 May 2016 (s 216(1)(d)) |

**Housing and Planning Act 2016 (c 22)**—*contd*

| | | |
|---|---|---|
| 158 | (1) | *Not yet in force* |
| | (2) | See Sch 13 below |
| | (3) | *Not yet in force* |
| 159 | | *Not yet in force* |
| 160 | | 6 Apr 2017 (SI 2017/281)[4] |
| 161–168 | | 12 May 2016 (s 216(1)(e)) |
| 169, 170 | | 13 Jul 2016 (SI 2016/733) |
| 171 | | 1 Oct 2016 (SI 2016/733) |
| 172–178 | | 13 Jul 2016 (SI 2016/733) |
| 179 | | See Sch 14 below |
| 180 | | 6 Apr 2018 (SI 2018/251)[5] |
| 181 | | 6 Apr 2018 (except in relation to a compulsory purchase order for which the confirming authority is the Welsh Ministers) (SI 2018/251)[5] |
| | | 6 Apr 2019 (exception noted above) (SI 2019/427)[7] |
| 182 | | 13 Jul 2016 (SI 2016/733)[2] |
| 183 | | See Sch 15 below |
| 184–189 | | 3 Feb 2017 (SI 2017/75)[3] |
| 190 | | See Sch 16 below |
| 191 | | 3 Feb 2017 (SI 2017/75)[3] |
| 192–195 | | 6 Apr 2018 (SI 2018/251)[5] |
| 196 | (1), (2)(a) | 6 Apr 2018 (SI 2018/251) |
| | (2)(b) | *Not yet in force* |
| | (3) | 6 Apr 2017 (for the purpose only of making regulations under Land Compensation Act 1973, s 52B(4)) (SI 2017/281) |
| | | *Not yet in force* (otherwise) |
| 197, 198 | | 6 Apr 2018 (SI 2018/251)[5] |
| 199 | (1) | See Sch 17 below |
| | (2) | See Sch 18 below |
| 200 | | 3 Feb 2017 (SI 2017/75) |
| 201, 202 | | 13 Jul 2016 (SI 2016/733)[2] |
| 203–205 | | 13 Jul 2016 (SI 2016/733) |
| 206 | | See Sch 19 below |
| 207–209 | | *Not yet in force* |
| 210 | (1) | See Sch 20 below |
| | (2)–(9) | *Not yet in force* |
| 211 | | *Not yet in force* |
| 212–217 | | 12 May 2016 (s 216(1)(a)) |
| Schs 1, 2 | | 6 Apr 2018 (SI 2018/393) |
| Sch 3 | paras 1–4 | 6 Apr 2018 (SI 2018/393) |
| | para 5(1), (2) | 6 Apr 2018 (SI 2018/393) |
| | para 5(3) | 3 Nov 2017 (SI 2017/1052) |
| | paras 6–8 | 6 Apr 2018 (SI 2018/393) |
| | para 9 | 3 Nov 2017 (SI 2017/1052) |
| | paras 10–12 | 6 Apr 2018 (SI 2018/393) |
| Sch 4 | paras 1–14 | 6 Apr 2017 (SI 2017/75) |
| | para 15 | 6 Apr 2017 (SI 2017/75)[3] |
| | paras 16–32 | 6 Apr 2017 (SI 2017/75) |
| | para 33 | 6 Apr 2017 (SI 2017/75)[3] |
| | paras 34–38 | 6 Apr 2017 (SI 2017/75) |
| Sch 5 | | 5 Jul 2018 (SI 2018/805) |
| Sch 6 | paras 1, 2 | 5 Jul 2018 (SI 2018/805) |
| | paras 3, 4 | 5 Jul 2018 (SI 2018/805)[6] |
| | paras 5–8 | 5 Jul 2018 (SI 2018/805) |
| | para 9 | 5 Jul 2018 (SI 2018/805)[6] |
| | para 10 | 5 Jul 2018 (SI 2018/805) |
| Schs 7, 8 | | *Not yet in force* |
| Sch 9 | paras 1–6 | 6 Apr 2017 (SI 2017/281) |

**Housing and Planning Act 2016 (c 22)**—*contd*

| | | |
|---|---|---|
| | para 7 | 10 Mar 2017 (for the purpose of making regulations under Housing Act 2004, s 249A(7)) (SI 2017/281) |
| | | 6 Apr 2017 (otherwise) (SI 2017/281) |
| | para 8 | 6 Apr 2017 (SI 2017/281) |
| Sch 10 | | 12 May 2016 (s 216(1)(c)) |
| Sch 11 | | 1 Oct 2016 (SI 2016/733) |
| Sch 12 | paras 1–26 | 13 Jul 2016 (SI 2016/733) |
| | para 27 | *Not yet in force* |
| | paras 28–44 | 13 Jul 2016 (SI 2016/733) |
| Sch 13 | | *Not yet in force* |
| Sch 14 | | 13 Jul 2016 (SI 2016/733)[2] |
| Sch 15 | para 1 | 1 Oct 2016 (for the purpose of exercising the power to prescribe by regulations the statement referred to in s 15(4)(e) and in para 6(4)(e) of Sch 1 to the Acquisition of Land Act 1981 and the form referred to in s 15(4)(f) and in para 6(4)(f) of Sch 1 to that Act) (SI 2016/956) |
| | | 3 Feb 2017 (otherwise, except in relation to a compulsory purchase order which is made by, or for which the confirming authority is, the Welsh Ministers) (SI 2017/75)[3] |
| | | 6 Apr 2017 (exception noted above) (SI 2017/281)[4] |
| | para 2(1), (2) | 1 Oct 2016 (for the purpose of exercising the power to prescribe by regulations the statement referred to in s 15(4)(e) of the Acquisition of Land Act 1981 and the form referred to in s 15(4)(f) of that Act) (SI 2016/956)[3] |
| | | 3 Feb 2017 (otherwise, except in relation to a compulsory purchase order which is made by, or for which the confirming authority is, the Welsh Ministers) (SI 2017/75)[3] |
| | | 6 Apr 2017 (exception noted above) (SI 2017/281)[4] |
| | para 2(3) | 3 Feb 2017 (except in relation to a compulsory purchase order which is made by, or for which the confirming authority is, the Welsh Ministers) (SI 2017/75)[3] |
| | | 6 Apr 2017 (exception noted above) (SI 2017/281)[4] |
| | para 3(1), (2) | 1 Oct 2016 (for the purpose of exercising the power to prescribe by regulations the statement referred to in para 6(4)(e) of Sch 1 to the Acquisition of Land Act 1981 and the form referred to in para 6(4)(f) of Sch 1 to that Act) (SI 2016/956)[3] |
| | | 3 Feb 2017 (otherwise, except in relation to a compulsory purchase order which is made by, or for which the confirming authority is, the Welsh Ministers) (SI 2017/75)[3] |
| | | 6 Apr 2017 (exception noted above) (SI 2017/281)[4] |
| | para 3(3) | 3 Feb 2017 (except in relation to a compulsory purchase order which is made by, or for which the confirming authority is, the Welsh Ministers) (SI 2017/75)[3] |
| | | 6 Apr 2017 (exception noted above) (SI 2017/281)[4] |
| | paras 4–7 | 3 Feb 2017 (except in relation to a compulsory purchase order, or any other order which authorises the compulsory purchase of land, which is made by, or for which the confirming authority is, the Welsh Ministers) (SI 2017/75)[3] |
| | | 6 Apr 2017 (exception noted above) (SI 2017/281) |
| | para 8 | 1 Oct 2016 (SI 2016/956) |
| Sch 16 | | 13 Jul 2016 (SI 2016/733) |
| Sch 17 | paras 1–3 | 3 Feb 2017 (SI 2017/75)[3] |
| | para 4 | 3 Feb 2017 (SI 2017/75) |
| | paras 5–8 | 3 Feb 2017 (SI 2017/75)[3] |
| | paras 9–11 | 3 Feb 2017 (SI 2017/75) |
| Sch 18 | paras 1–9 | 3 Feb 2017 (SI 2017/75)[3] |
| | para 10 | *Not yet in force* |
| Sch 19 | | 13 Jul 2016 (SI 2016/733)[2] |
| Sch 20 | | *Not yet in force* |

## Housing and Planning Act 2016 (c 22)—*contd*

[1] For the purposes of the reference to "a report of the kind mentioned in section 75ZA(1)" in the Town and Country Planning Act 1990, s 75ZB(1)(a) (as inserted by s 156 of this Act), s 155 (which inserts s 75ZA of the 1990 Act) is treated as if it were in force; see SI 2016/733, reg 4(2)

[2] For saving and transitional provisions, see SI 2016/733, regs 6–10

[3] For transitional provisions, see SI 2017/75, regs 5–7

[4] For saving and transitional provisions, see SI 2017/281, regs 5–8

[5] For transitional provisions, see SI 2018/251, regs 5, 6

[6] For transitional and saving provisions, see SI 2018/805, regs 4, 5

[7] For transitional provisions, see SI 2019/427, reg 4

## Immigration Act 2016 (c 19)

*RA:* 12 May 2016

*Commencement provisions*: s 94; Immigration Act 2016 (Commencement No 1) Regulations 2016, SI 2016/603; Immigration Act 2016 (Commencement No 2 and Transitional Provisions) Regulations 2016, SI 2016/1037; Immigration Act 2016 (Commencement No 3 and Transitional Provision) Regulations 2017, SI 2017/380; Immigration Act 2016 (Commencement No 4) Regulations 2017, SI 2017/799; Immigration Act 2016 (Commencement No 5) Regulations 2017, SI 2017/929; Immigration Act 2016 (Commencement No 6) Regulations 2017, SI 2017/1210; Immigration Act 2016 (Commencement No 7 and Transitional Provisions) Regulations 2017, SI 2017/1241, as amended by SI 2018/31; Immigration Act 2016 (Commencement and Transitional Provisions No 1) (England and Wales) Regulations 2021, SI 2021/939; Immigration Act 2016 (Commencement No 1 and Transitional Provisions) (Scotland and Northern Ireland) Regulations 2022, SI 2022/863

| | | |
|---|---|---|
| 1–5 | | 12 Jul 2016 (SI 2016/603) |
| 6 | (1)–(3) | 12 Jul 2016 (SI 2016/603) |
| | (4) | See Sch 1 below |
| | (5), (6) | 12 Jul 2016 (SI 2016/603) |
| 7–10 | | 12 Jul 2016 (SI 2016/603) |
| 11 | (1) | See Sch 2 below |
| | (2) | 12 Jul 2016 (SI 2016/603) |
| 12, 13 | | 12 Jul 2016 (SI 2016/603) |
| 14–24 | | 25 Nov 2016 (SI 2016/1037) |
| 25 | | 12 Jul 2016 (SI 2016/603) |
| 26–30 | | 25 Nov 2016 (SI 2016/1037) |
| 31 | | See Sch 3 below |
| 32–35 | | 12 Jul 2016 (SI 2016/603) |
| 36 | (1) | See Sch 4 below |
| | (2)–(5) | 6 Apr 2017 (SI 2017/380) |
| 37 | | See Sch 5 below |
| 38 | | See Sch 6 below |
| 39, 40 | | 1 Nov 2016 (for the purpose of making subordinate legislation) (SI 2016/1037) |
| | | 1 Dec 2016 (otherwise) (SI 2016/1037) |
| 41 | | 1 Dec 2016 (SI 2016/1037) |
| 42 | | *Not yet in force* |
| 43 | | 31 Jul 2017 (in the police areas of Kent and West Yorkshire) (SI 2017/799) |
| | | *Not yet in force* (otherwise) |
| 44 | | *Not yet in force* |
| 45 | (1) | See Sch 7 below |
| | (2), (3) | 1 Nov 2016 (for the purpose of making subordinate legislation) (SI 2016/1037) |
| | | 30 Oct 2017 (otherwise) (SI 2017/929) |
| 46–53 | | 12 Jul 2016 (SI 2016/603) |
| 54 | | See Sch 8 below |

**Immigration Act 2016 (c 19)**—*contd*

| | | |
|---|---|---|
| 55 | (1)–(12) | 12 Jul 2016 (SI 2016/603) |
| | (13) | See Sch 9 below |
| 56–60 | | 12 Jul 2016 (SI 2016/603) |
| 61 | (1), (2) | See Sch 10 below |
| | (3)–(5) | 12 May 2016 (s 94(3)) |
| | (6) | 15 Jan 2018 (on the coming into force of the repeal of the Immigration Act 1971, Sch 2, paras 22, 29, by Sch 10, para 20 below) |
| 62–65 | | 1 Dec 2016 (SI 2016/1037) |
| 66 | | See Sch 11 below |
| 67 | | 31 May 2016 (SI 2016/603) |
| 68 | | See Sch 12 below |
| 69–72 | | 31 May 2016 (SI 2016/603) |
| 73 | | 1 Jan 2018 (SI 2017/1210) |
| 74 | (1) | *Not yet in force* |
| | (2) | See Sch 13 below |
| 75 | | See Sch 14 below |
| 76 | | 12 Jul 2016 (SI 2016/603) |
| 77–84 | | 21 Nov 2016 (SI 2016/1037) |
| 85 | | 12 Jul 2016 (s 94(4)) |
| 86–88 | | 12 Jul 2016 (SI 2016/603) |
| 89 | | See Sch 15 below |
| 90–96 | | 12 May 2016 (s 94(5)) |
| Schs 1–3 | | 12 Jul 2016 (SI 2016/603) |
| Sch 4 | para 1 | 6 Apr 2017 (SI 2017/380)[2] |
| | paras 2–36 | 6 Apr 2017 (SI 2017/380) |
| Schs 5, 6 | | 1 Dec 2016 (SI 2016/1037)[1] |
| Sch 7 | | 1 Nov 2016 (for the purpose of making subordinate legislation) (SI 2016/1037) |
| | | 30 Oct 2017 (otherwise) (SI 2017/929) |
| Sch 8 | | 1 Dec 2016 (SI 2016/1037) |
| Sch 9 | | 12 Jul 2016 (SI 2016/603) |
| Sch 10 | para 1 | 15 Jan 2018 (SI 2017/1241)[3] |
| | para 2(1) | 15 Jan 2018 (SI 2017/1241)[3] |
| | para 2(2), (3) | 31 Aug 2021 (E), (W) (SI 2021/939) |
| | | 31 Aug 2022 (S), (NI) (SI 2022/863) |
| | para 2(4) | 15 Jan 2018 (SI 2017/1241)[3] |
| | para 2(5)–(10) | 31 Aug 2021 (E), (W) (SI 2021/939) |
| | | 31 Aug 2022 (S), (NI) (SI 2022/863) |
| | para 2(11) | 15 Jan 2018 (SI 2017/1241)[3] |
| | paras 3–6 | 15 Jan 2018 (SI 2017/1241)[3] |
| | paras 7, 8 | 31 Aug 2021 (E), (W) (SI 2021/939) |
| | | 31 Aug 2022 (S), (NI) (SI 2022/863)[4] |
| | paras 9–24 | 15 Jan 2018 (SI 2017/1241)[3] |
| | para 25 | 15 Jan 2018 (except in so far as it applies, in a modified form, to paras 2(2), (3), (5)–(10), 7, 8, 26–43 above) (SI 2017/1241)[3] |
| | | 31 Aug 2021 (E), (W) (exception noted above) (SI 2021/939) |
| | | 31 Aug 2022 (S), (NI) (exception noted above) (SI 2022/863) |
| | paras 26–43 | 15 Jan 2018 (SI 2017/1241)[3] |
| Sch 11 | para 1 | 15 Jan 2018 (to the extent that it repeals Immigration Act 1999, s 4(1)) (SI 2017/1241) |
| | | *Not yet in force* (exception noted above) |
| | paras 2–45 | *Not yet in force* |
| | para 46 | 15 Jan 2018 (so far as it relates to the repeal of the Immigration Act 1999, s 4(1)) (SI 2017/1241) |
| | | *Not yet in force* (exception noted above) |
| | paras 47, 48 | *Not yet in force* |
| Schs 12, 13 | | *Not yet in force* |
| Sch 14 | | 31 May 2016 (SI 2016/603) |

**Immigration Act 2016 (c 19)**—*contd*

Sch 15                                          12 Jul 2016 (SI 2016/603)

¹    For transitional provisions, see SI 2016/1037, regs 6, 7

²    For transitional provisions, see SI 2017/380, reg 3

³    For transitional provisions, see SI 2017/1241, reg 3, Schedule

⁴    For transitional provisions, see SI 2022/863, reg 3, Schedule

---

## Inquiries into Fatal Accidents and Sudden Deaths etc (Scotland) Act 2016 (asp 2)

*RA:* 14 Jan 2016

*Commencement provisions:* s 42; Inquiries into Fatal Accidents and Sudden Deaths etc. (Scotland) Act 2016 (Commencement No 1 and Transitional Provision) Regulations 2016, SSI 2016/196; Inquiries into Fatal Accidents and Sudden Deaths etc. (Scotland) Act 2016 (Commencement No 2, Transitional and Transitory Provision) Regulations 2016, SSI 2016/370; Inquiries into Fatal Accidents and Sudden Deaths etc. (Scotland) Act 2016 (Commencement No 3, Transitional and Saving Provisions) Regulations 2017, SSI 2017/155

| | | |
|---|---|---|
| 1–7 | | 15 Jun 2017 (SSI 2017/155) |
| 8 | (1) | 1 Sep 2016 (SSI 2016/196) |
| | (2) | 1 Sep 2016 (SSI 2016/196)¹ |
| | (3)–(5) | 1 Sep 2016 (SSI 2016/196) |
| 9–11 | | 15 Jun 2017 (SSI 2017/155) |
| 12 | | 1 Sep 2016 (SSI 2016/196) |
| 13, 14 | | 1 Dec 2016 (SSI 2016/370)² |
| 15 | | 15 Jun 2017 (SSI 2017/155) |
| 16 | (1)–(3) | 15 Jun 2017 (SSI 2017/155) |
| | (4) | 1 Sep 2016 (SSI 2016/196) |
| 17 | | 15 Jun 2017 (SSI 2017/155) |
| 18 | | 1 Sep 2016 (SSI 2016/196) |
| 19–26 | | 15 Jun 2017 (SSI 2017/155) |
| 27 | (1)–(3) | 15 Jun 2017 (SSI 2017/155) |
| | (4) | 1 Sep 2016 (SSI 2016/196) |
| | (5), (6) | 15 Jun 2017 (SSI 2017/155) |
| 28–35 | | 15 Jun 2017 (SSI 2017/155) |
| 36 | (1)–(5) | 1 Sep 2016 (SSI 2016/196) |
| | (6) | See Sch 1 below |
| 37, 38 | | 15 Jun 2017 (SSI 2017/155) |
| 39 | (1) | 15 Jun 2017 (SSI 2017/155)³ |
| | (2) | See Sch 2 below |
| 40–43 | | 15 Jan 2016 (s 42(1)) |
| Sch 1 | | 15 Jan 2016 (s 42(1)) |
| Sch 2 | paras 1–15 | 15 Jun 2017 (SSI 2017/155)³ |
| | para 16 | 1 Sep 2016 (SSI 2016/196) |

¹    For a transitional provision, see SSI 2016/196, reg 3

²    For transitional and transitory provisions, see SSI 2016/370, reg 3

³    For transitional provisions, see SSI 2017/155, reg 4

---

## Interests of Members of the Scottish Parliament (Amendment) Act 2016 (asp 4)

*RA:* 21 Jan 2016

*Commencement provisions:* ss 16–18

| | |
|---|---|
| 1 | See ss 2–14 below |
| 2 | 5 May 2016 (s 16(3)) |

**Interests of Members of the Scottish Parliament (Amendment) Act 2016 (asp 4)**—*contd*

| | | |
|---|---|---|
| 3–5 | | 5 May 2016 (s 16(2))[1] |
| 6 | (1), (2) | 5 May 2016 (s 16(2))[1] |
| | (3) | 5 May 2016 (s 16(3)) |
| 7 | | 5 May 2016 (s 16(2))[1] |
| 8 | | 22 Jan 2016 (s 16(4)) |
| 9–12 | | 5 May 2016 (s 16(3)) |
| 13, 14 | | 5 May 2016 (s 16(2))[1] |
| 15–19 | | 22 Jan 2016 (s 16(4)) |

[1]    For alternative commencement dates where specified conditions are met, see s 17 of the Act

---

**Investigatory Powers Act 2016 (c 25)**

*RA*: 29 Nov 2016

*Commencement provisions*: s 272; Investigatory Powers Act 2016 (Commencement No 1 and Transitional Provisions) Regulations 2016, SI 2016/1233; Investigatory Powers Act 2016 (Commencement No 2 and Transitory Provision) Regulations 2017, SI 2017/137, as amended by SI 2017/143; Investigatory Powers Act 2016 (Commencement No 3 and Transitory, Transitional and Saving Provisions) Regulations 2017, SI 2017/859; Investigatory Powers Act 2016 (Commencement No 4 and Transitional and Saving Provisions) Regulations 2018, SI 2018/341, as amended by SI 2018/652; Investigatory Powers Act 2016 (Commencement No 5 and Transitional and Saving Provisions) Regulations 2018, SI 2018/652, as amended by SI 2018/940; Investigatory Powers Act 2016 (Commencement No 6) Regulations 2018, SI 2018/817; Investigatory Powers Act 2016 (Commencement No 7 and Transitional and Saving Provisions) Regulations 2018, SI 2018/873; Investigatory Powers Act 2016 (Commencement No 8 and Transitional and Saving Provisions) Regulations 2018, SI 2018/940; Investigatory Powers Act 2016 (Commencement No 9) Regulations 2018, SI 2018/1246; Investigatory Powers Act 2016 (Commencement No 10 and Transitional Provision) Regulations 2018, SI 2018/1379; Investigatory Powers Act 2016 (Commencement No 11) Regulations 2019, SI 2019/174; Investigatory Powers Act 2016 (Commencement No 12) Regulations 2020, SI 2020/766

| | |
|---|---|
| 1 | 13 Feb 2017 (SI 2017/137) |
| 2 | 30 Dec 2016 (in so far as it applies to Pt 4) (SI 2016/1233) |
| | 12 Mar 2018 (so far as it applies to decisions relating to notices under s 252 or 253) (SI 2018/341) |
| | 31 May 2018 (so far as applies to decisions relating to warrants under Pt 2 or 5 or Pt 6, Chapters 1, 3, except decisions regarding whether to approve the use of criteria under s 153 or 194) (SI 2018/652) |
| | 27 Jun 2018 (so far as it applies to decisions regarding whether to approve the use of criteria under s 153 or 194) (SI 2018/652) |
| | 25 Jul 2018 (so far as applies to decisions relating to Pt 6, Chapter 2, Pt 7, except decisions whether to approve the use of criteria under s 222, to give an authorisation under s 219(3)(b) and to approve a decision to give an authorisation under s 219(3)(b)) (SI 2018/873) |
| | 22 Aug 2018 (so far as applies to decisions whether to approve the use of criteria under s 222, to give an authorisation under s 219(3)(b)) (SI 2018/873) |
| | 5 Feb 2019 (otherwise) (SI 2019/174) |
| 3 | 27 Jun 2018 (SI 2018/652) |
| 4–6 | 31 May 2018 (SI 2018/652) |
| 7, 8 | 27 Jun 2018 (SI 2018/652) |
| 9 | 27 Jun 2018 (so far as applies to requests other than requests made by or on behalf of the Director General of the National Crime Agency; the Commissioner of Police of the Metropolis; the Chief Constable of the Police Service of Northern Ireland; the chief constable of the Police Service of Scotland; or the Commissioners for Her Majesty's Revenue and Customs) (SI 2018/652) |

**Investigatory Powers Act 2016 (c 25)**—*contd*

|  |  |  |
|---|---|---|
|  |  | 26 Sep 2018 (otherwise) (2018/940) |
| 10 | (1), (2) | 27 Jun 2018 (so far as applies to requests other than requests made by or on behalf of the Director General of the National Crime Agency; the Commissioner of Police of the Metropolis; the Chief Constable of the Police Service of Northern Ireland; the chief constable of the Police Service of Scotland; or the Commissioners for Her Majesty's Revenue and Customs) (SI 2018/652) |
|  |  | 26 Sep 2018 (otherwise) (2018/940) |
|  | (3) | 31 May 2018 (for the purpose of the definitions of "EU mutual assistance instrument" and "international mutual assistance agreement" in s 60(1)) (SI 2018/652) |
|  |  | 27 Jun 2018 (otherwise) (SI 2018/652) |
| 11 |  | 5 Feb 2019 (SI 2019/174) |
| 12 |  | 22 Jul 2020 (SI 2020/766) |
| 13 |  | 8 Aug 2018 (SI 2018/652)⁴ |
| 14 |  | 16 Jan 2019 (SI 2018/1246) |
| 15 | (1), (2) | 31 May 2018 (SI 2018/652) |
|  | (3) | 31 May 2018 (SI 2018/652)⁴ |
|  | (4), (5) | 31 May 2018 (SI 2018/652) |
|  | (6) | 1 Sep 2017 (definition of "related systems data" for the purpose of the definition of "related systems data" in s 229(9)) (SI 2017/859) |
|  |  | 31 May 2018 (otherwise) (SI 2018/652) |
|  | (7) | 31 May 2018 (SI 2018/652) |
| 16 | (1)–(3) | 31 May 2018 (SI 2018/652) |
|  | (4)–(6) | 1 Sep 2017 (for the purpose of the definition of "secondary data" in s 229(9)) (SI 2017/859) |
|  |  | 31 May 2018 (otherwise) (SI 2018/652) |
|  | (7) | 31 May 2018 (SI 2018/652) |
| 17 |  | 31 May 2018 (SI 2018/652) |
| 18 | (1)(a) | 31 May 2018 (SI 2018/652) |
|  | (1)(b)–(f) | 30 Aug 2018 (SI 2018/940) |
|  | (1)(g) | 31 May 2018 (SI 2018/652) |
|  | (1)(h) | 30 Aug 2018 (SI 2018/940) |
|  | (2), (3) | 31 May 2018 (SI 2018/652) |
| 19 | (1)–(3) | 31 May 2018 (for the purpose of the Secretary of State deciding to issue a warrant but not for the purpose of the issuing of a warrant) (SI 2018/652)⁴ |
|  |  | 27 Jun 2018 (otherwise) (SI 2018/652)⁴ |
|  | (4), (5) | 31 May 2018 (SI 2018/652)⁴ |
| 20 |  | 31 May 2018 (SI 2018/652) |
| 21 | (1)–(3) | 31 May 2018 (for the purpose of the Scottish Ministers deciding to issue a warrant but not for the purpose of the issuing of a warrant) (SI 2018/652)⁴ |
|  |  | 30 Aug 2018 (otherwise) (SI 2018/940)⁶ |
|  | (4)–(6) | 31 May 2018 (SI 2018/652) |
| 22, 23 |  | 31 May 2018 (SI 2018/652) |
| 24, 25 |  | 27 Jun 2018 (SI 2018/652) |
| 26–31 |  | 31 May 2018 (SI 2018/652) |
| 32–34 |  | 27 Jun 2018 (SI 2018/652) |
| 35 | (1)–(5) | 27 Jun 2018 (SI 2018/652) |
|  | (6)(a) | 27 Jun 2018 (SI 2018/652) |
|  | (6)(b)–(d) | 26 Sep 2018 (2018/940) |
|  | (6)(e) | 27 Jun 2018 (SI 2018/652) |
|  | (7) | 27 Jun 2018 (SI 2018/652) |
| 36–39 |  | 27 Jun 2018 (SI 2018/652) |
| 40 | (1)–(3) | 31 May 2018 (SI 2018/652) |
|  | (4)–(7) | 27 Jun 2018 (SI 2018/652) |
|  | (8) | 31 May 2018 (SI 2018/652) |

**Investigatory Powers Act 2016 (c 25)**—*contd*

| | | |
|---|---|---|
| 41–52 | | 27 Jun 2018 (SI 2018/652) |
| 53, 54 | | 31 May 2018 (SI 2018/652) |
| 55–57 | | 27 Jun 2018 (SI 2018/652)[4] |
| 58 | (1), (2) | 27 Jun 2018 (SI 2018/652) |
| | (3) | 26 Sep 2018 (2018/940) |
| | (4)–(9) | 27 Jun 2018 (SI 2018/652) |
| 59 | | 27 Jun 2018 (SI 2018/652) |
| 60 | (1) | 13 Feb 2017 (for the purpose of the definition of "police force" in section 229(9)) (SI 2017/137) |
| | | 31 May 2018 (otherwise) (SI 2018/652) |
| | (2), (3) | 31 May 2018 (SI 2018/652) |
| 61 | (1)–(6) | 5 Feb 2019 (SI 2019/174) |
| | (7) | 30 Dec 2016 (for the purpose of the operation of ss 87, 94) (SI 2016/1233) |
| | | 5 Feb 2019 (otherwise) (SI 2019/174) |
| | (8), (9) | *Not yet in force* |
| 62–86 | | 5 Feb 2019 (SI 2019/174) |
| 87 | (1)(a) | 30 Dec 2016 (SI 2016/1233) |
| | (1)(b) | 1 Nov 2018 (SI 2018/873) |
| | (2)–(11) | 30 Dec 2016 (SI 2016/1233) |
| 88 | | 30 Dec 2016 (SI 2016/1233) |
| 89 | | 1 Nov 2018 (SI 2018/873) |
| 90 | (1)–(12) | 1 Nov 2018 (SI 2018/873) |
| | (13) | 30 Dec 2016 (SI 2016/1233) |
| 91 | | 1 Nov 2018 (SI 2018/873) |
| 92, 93 | | 30 Dec 2016 (SI 2016/1233) |
| 94 | (1)–(3) | 30 Dec 2016 (SI 2016/1233) |
| | (4)(a) | 30 Dec 2016 (SI 2016/1233) |
| | (4)(b) | 1 Nov 2018 (SI 2018/873) |
| | (5) | 30 Dec 2016 (SI 2016/1233) |
| | (6) | 1 Nov 2018 (SI 2018/873) |
| | (7) | 30 Dec 2016 (SI 2016/1233) |
| | (8) | 30 Dec 2016 (except in so far as it applies to s 94(4)(b)) (SI 2016/1233) |
| | | 1 Nov 2018 (otherwise) (SI 2018/873) |
| | (9) | 30 Dec 2016 (so far as it applies to s 90(13)) (SI 2016/1233) |
| | | 1 Nov 2018 (otherwise) (SI 2018/873) |
| | (10) | 1 Nov 2018 (SI 2018/873) |
| | (11) | 30 Dec 2016 (so far as it applies to s 90(13)) (SI 2016/1233) |
| | | 1 Nov 2018 (otherwise) (SI 2018/873) |
| | (12) | 1 Nov 2018 (SI 2018/873) |
| | (13)–(16) | 30 Dec 2016 (SI 2016/1233) |
| 95 | | 30 Dec 2016 (SI 2016/1233) |
| 96 | | 1 Nov 2018 (SI 2018/873) |
| 97, 98 | | 30 Dec 2016 (SI 2016/1233) |
| 99–101 | | 31 May 2018 (SI 2018/652) |
| 102 | (1)–(3) | 31 May 2018 (for the purpose of the Secretary of State deciding to issue a warrant but not for the purpose of the issuing of a warrant) (SI 2018/652)[4] |
| | | 27 Jun 2018 (otherwise) (SI 2018/652) |
| | (4) | 31 May 2018 (for the purpose of the Secretary of State deciding to issue a warrant but not for the purpose of the issuing of a warrant and only if the Secretary of State considers that the only grounds for considering the warrant to be necessary is for the purpose of preventing or detecting serious crime) (SI 2018/652)[4] |
| | | 27 Jun 2018 (to the extent it applies if the Secretary of State considers that the only ground for considering the warrant to be necessary is for the purpose of preventing or detecting serious crime) (SI 2018/652)[4] |

**Investigatory Powers Act 2016 (c 25)**—*contd*

|  |  |  |
|---|---|---|
|  |  | *Not yet in force* (otherwise) |
|  | (5)–(9) | 31 May 2018 (SI 2018/652)[4] |
| 103 | (1), (2) | 31 May 2018 (for the purpose of the Scottish Ministers deciding to issue a warrant but not for the purpose of the issuing of a warrant) (SI 2018/652)[4] |
|  |  | 27 Jun 2018 (otherwise) (SI 2018/652)[4] |
|  | (3), (4) | 31 May 2018 (SI 2018/652) |
| 104 | (1) | 31 May 2018 (for the purpose of the Secretary of State deciding to issue a warrant but not for the purpose of the issuing of a warrant) (SI 2018/652) |
|  |  | 27 Jun 2018 (otherwise) (SI 2018/652) |
|  | (2), (3) | 31 May 2018 (SI 2018/652) |
| 105 |  | 31 May 2018 (SI 2018/652) |
| 106 | (1) | 28 Nov 2018 (or the purpose of the law enforcement chief deciding to issue a warrant but not for the purpose of the issuing of a warrant) (SI 2018/1246) |
|  |  | 5 Dec 2018 (otherwise) (SI 2018/1246) |
|  | (2) | 28 Nov 2018 (SI 2018/1246) |
|  | (3), (4) | 28 Nov 2018 (for the purpose of the law enforcement chief, or appropriate delegate, deciding to issue a warrant but not for the purpose of the issuing of a warrant) (SI 2018/1246) |
|  |  | 5 Dec 2018 (otherwise) (SI 2018/1246) |
|  | (5)–(14) | 28 Nov 2018 (SI 2018/1246) |
| 107 |  | 28 Nov 2018 (SI 2018/1246) |
| 108 |  | 31 May 2018 (so far as relating to decisions to issue warrants under any of ss 102–104) (SI 2018/652) |
|  |  | 28 Nov 2018 (otherwise) (SI 2018/1246) |
| 109, 110 |  | 27 Jun 2018 (SI 2018/652) |
| 111 | (1)–(3) | 31 May 2018 (SI 2018/652) |
|  | (4)–(7) | 28 Nov 2018 (SI 2018/1246) |
|  | (8) | 31 May 2018 (SI 2018/652) |
| 112 |  | 31 May 2018 (SI 2018/652)[4] |
| 113, 114 |  | 31 May 2018 (SI 2018/652) |
| 115 |  | 31 May 2018 (so far as relating to warrants under any of ss 102–104) (SI 2018/652) |
|  |  | 28 Nov 2018 (otherwise) (SI 2018/1246) |
| 116 |  | 27 Jun 2018 (SI 2018/652) |
| 117 |  | 27 Jun 2018 (so far as relating to warrants under any of ss 102–104) (SI 2018/652) |
|  |  | 5 Dec 2018 (otherwise) (SI 2018/1246) |
| 118–122 |  | 27 Jun 2018 (SI 2018/652) |
| 123–124 |  | 5 Dec 2018 (SI 2018/1246) |
| 125 |  | 27 Jun 2018 (so far as relating to warrants under any of ss 102–104) (SI 2018/652) |
|  |  | 5 Dec 2018 (otherwise) (SI 2018/1246) |
| 126, 127 |  | 27 Jun 2018 (SI 2018/652) |
| 128 | (1) | 27 Jun 2018 (SI 2018/652) |
|  | (2)–(4) | 5 Dec 2018 (SI 2018/1246) |
|  | (5)–(7) | 27 Jun 2018 (SI 2018/652) |
| 129 |  | 31 May 2018 (so far as relating to warrants under any of ss 102–104) (SI 2018/652)[4] |
|  |  | 28 Nov 2018 (otherwise) (SI 2018/1246) |
| 130 |  | 31 May 2018 (SI 2018/652)[4] |
| 131 |  | 27 Jun 2018 (SI 2018/652)[4] |
| 132–134 |  | 27 Jun 2018 (SI 2018/652) |
| 135–137 |  | 31 May 2018 (SI 2018/652) |
| 138 |  | 31 May 2018 (for the purpose of the Secretary of State deciding to issue a bulk interception warrant but not for the purpose of the issuing of such a warrant) (SI 2018/652)[4] |

**Investigatory Powers Act 2016 (c 25)**—*contd*

| | | |
|---|---|---|
| | | 27 Jun 2018 (otherwise) (SI 2018/652)[4] |
| 139–142 | | 31 May 2018 (SI 2018/652) |
| 143–149 | | 27 Jun 2018 (SI 2018/652) |
| 150 | | 31 May 2018 (SI 2018/652)[4] |
| 151 | | 31 May 2018 (SI 2018/652) |
| 152 | | 27 Jun 2018 (SI 2018/652) |
| 153, 154 | | 27 Jun 2018 (SI 2018/652)[4] |
| 155, 156 | | 27 Jun 2018 (SI 2018/652) |
| 157 | | 31 May 2018 (SI 2018/652) |
| 158 | | 25 Jul 2018 (or the purpose of the Secretary of State deciding to issue a bulk acquisition warrant, but not for the purpose of the issuing of such a warrant) (SI 2018/873) |
| | | 22 Aug 2018 (otherwise) (SI 2018/873)[5] |
| 159–161 | | 25 Jul 2018 (SI 2018/873) |
| 162–170 | | 22 Aug 2018 (SI 2018/873) |
| 171, 172 | | 25 Jul 2018 (SI 2018/873) |
| 173, 174 | | 22 Aug 2018 (SI 2018/873) |
| 175 | | 25 Jul 2018 (SI 2018/873) |
| 176, 177 | | 31 May 2018 (SI 2018/652) |
| 178 | | 31 May 2018 (for the purpose of the Secretary of State deciding to issue a bulk equipment interference warrant but not for the purpose of the issuing of such a warrant) (SI 2018/652) |
| | | 27 Jun 2018 (otherwise) (SI 2018/652) |
| 179 | | 31 May 2018 (SI 2018/652) |
| 180, 181 | | 27 Jun 2018 (SI 2018/652) |
| 182, 183 | | 31 May 2018 (SI 2018/652) |
| 184–190 | | 27 Jun 2018 (SI 2018/652) |
| 191, 192 | | 31 May 2018 (SI 2018/652) |
| 193 | | 27 Jun 2018 (SI 2018/652)[4] |
| 194–197 | | 27 Jun 2018 (SI 2018/652) |
| 198 | | 31 May 2018 (SI 2018/652) |
| 199 | | 1 Sep 2017 (for the purpose of the definition of "bulk personal dataset" in s 229(9)) (SI 2017/859) |
| | | 25 Jul 2018 (otherwise) (SI 2018/873) |
| 200 | (1), (2) | 22 Aug 2018 (SI 2018/873)[5] |
| | (3) | 25 Jul 2018 (SI 2018/873) |
| | (4) | 22 Aug 2018 (SI 2018/873) |
| 201 | | 22 Aug 2018 (SI 2018/873)[5] |
| 202, 203 | | 25 Jul 2018 (SI 2018/873) |
| 204 | | 25 Jul 2018 (for the purpose of an application for a class BPD warrant and the Secretary of State deciding to issue such a warrant, but not for the purpose of the issuing of such a warrant) (SI 2018/873)[5] |
| | | 22 Aug 2018 (otherwise) (SI 2018/873)[5] |
| 205 | | 25 Jul 2018 (for the purpose of an application for a specific BPD warrant and the Secretary of State deciding to issue such a warrant, but not for the purpose of the issuing of such a warrant) (SI 2018/873)[5] |
| | | 22 Aug 2018 (otherwise) (SI 2018/873) |
| 206–208 | | 25 Jul 2018 (SI 2018/873) |
| 209, 210 | | 22 Aug 2018 (SI 2018/873) |
| 211, 212 | | 25 Jul 2018 (SI 2018/873) |
| 213–219 | | 22 Aug 2018 (SI 2018/873) |
| 220 | | 22 Aug 2018 (SI 2018/873)[5] |
| 221 | | 25 Jul 2018 (SI 2018/873)[5] |
| 222–224 | | 22 Aug 2018 (SI 2018/873) |
| 225 | | 25 Jul 2018 (for the purpose of the Secretary of State deciding to give a direction and a Judicial Commissioner giving approval, but not for the purpose of the giving of such a direction) (SI 2018/873)[5] |

**Investigatory Powers Act 2016 (c 25)**—*contd*

|  |  |  |
|---|---|---|
| | | 22 Aug 2018 (otherwise) (SI 2018/873)[5] |
| 226 | | 25 Jul 2018 (SI 2018/873) |
| 227, 228 | | 29 Jan 2017 (s 272(3)) |
| 229 | (1)(a)–(c) | 1 Sep 2017 (2017/859)[2] |
| | (1)(d) | 12 Mar 2018 (so far as relates to the exercise of statutory functions relating to equipment interference which are exercised in relation to a notice under s 253) (SI 2018/341) |
| | | 27 Jun 2018 (otherwise) (SI 2018/652) |
| | (2)(a)–(c) | 1 Sep 2017 (2017/859)[2] |
| | (2)(d) | 27 Jun 2018 (SI 2018/652) |
| | (3)(a)–(c) | 1 Sep 2017 (2017/859) |
| | (3)(d)–(i) | 12 Mar 2018 (so far as relates to sub-s (3)(b)) (SI 2018/341) |
| | | 5 Feb 2019 (otherwise) (SI 2019/174) |
| | (3)(j) | 1 Sep 2017 (2017/859) |
| | (4), (5) | 1 Sep 2017 (2017/859)[2] |
| | (6), (7) | 13 Feb 2017 (SI 2017/137) |
| | (8)(a) | 1 Sep 2017 (2017/859)[2] |
| | (8)(b), (c) | 27 Jun 2018 (SI 2018/652) |
| | (8)(d)(i) | 1 Sep 2017 (so far as it applies to deciding whether to approve the grant or renewal of an authorisation) (2017/859) |
| | | 5 Feb 2019 (otherwise) (SI 2019/174) |
| | (8)(d)(ii) | 1 Sep 2017 (2017/859) |
| | (8)(e)(i) | 12 Mar 2018 (so far as applies to the giving or varying of a notice under s 253 or 254) (SI 2018/341) |
| | | 1 Nov 2018 (otherwise) (SI 2018/873) |
| | (8)(e)(ii) | 12 Mar 2018 (so far as applies to the giving of a notice under s 257(9)(b)) (SI 2018/341) |
| | | 1 Nov 2018 (otherwise) (SI 2018/873) |
| | (8)(f) | 12 Mar 2018 (so far as applies to participating in a review under s 257) (SI 2018/341) |
| | | 1 Nov 2018 (otherwise) (SI 2018/873) |
| | (8)(g)–(i) | 22 Aug 2018 (SI 2018/873) |
| | (8)(j)–(m) | 1 Sep 2017 (2017/859) |
| | (9) | 13 Feb 2017 (the definition of "police force") (SI 2017/137) |
| | | 1 Sep 2017 (the definitions of "bulk personal datasets", "judicial authority", "related systems data", "relevant Minister" and "secondary data") (2017/859) |
| | | 27 Jun 2018 (otherwise) (SI 2018/652) |
| 230 | | 13 Feb 2017 (SI 2017/137) |
| 231 | (1)–(8) | 27 Jun 2018 (SI 2018/652) |
| | (9)(a) | 27 Jun 2018 (to the extent that it applies to an error by an intelligence service or the Ministry of Defence relating to interception or equipment interference) (SI 2018/652) |
| | | 22 Aug 2018 (to the extent that it applies to an error relating to Pt 6, Chapter 2 or Pt 7) (SI 2018/873) |
| | | 26 Sep 2018 (to the extent that it applies to an error by a public authority relating to interception, so far as not already in force for that purpose) (2018/940) |
| | | 1 Nov 2018 (to the extent it applies to an error relating to Pt 4 of the 2016 Act) (SI 2018/873) |
| | | 5 Dec 2018 (to the extent that it applies to an error by a public authority relating to equipment interference, so far as not already in force for that purpose) (SI 2018/1246) |
| | | 5 Feb 2019 (to the extent it applies to an error relating to Pt 3 of this Act) (SI 2019/174) |
| | | *Not yet in force* (otherwise) |
| | (9)(b) | 27 Jun 2018 (to the extent that it applies to an error by a public authority exercising any function conferred by this Act) (SI 2018/652) |

**Investigatory Powers Act 2016 (c 25)**—*contd*

|   |   |   |
|---|---|---|
| | | 5 Feb 2019 (to the extent it applies to an error relating to Pt 3 of this Act) (SI 2019/174) |
| | | *Not yet in force* (otherwise) |
| 232 | | 13 Feb 2017 (SI 2017/137) |
| 233 | (1) | 13 Feb 2017 (so far as it relates to functions exercisable by virtue of any other Part of the Act) (SI 2017/137) |
| | | 1 Sep 2017 (otherwise) (SI 2017/859) |
| | (2)–(6) | 1 Sep 2017 (2017/859) |
| 234 | (1) | 13 Feb 2017 (SI 2017/137) |
| | (2)(a)–(c) | 1 Sep 2017 (2017/859) |
| | (2)(d) | 27 Jun 2018 (SI 2018/652) |
| | (2)(e) | 27 Jun 2018 (to the extent it applies to information about the operational purposes specified during the year in warrants issued under Pt 6, Chapter 1 or 3) (SI 2018/652) |
| | | 22 Aug 2018 (otherwise) (SI 2018/873) |
| | (2)(f) | 1 Sep 2017 (2017/859) |
| | (2)(g)–(i) | 13 Feb 2017 (SI 2017/137) |
| | (3)–(9) | 13 Feb 2017 (SI 2017/137) |
| | (10), (11) | 1 Sep 2017 (2017/859) |
| 235 | (1)–(4) | 13 Feb 2017 (SI 2017/137) |
| | (5) | 1 Sep 2017 (2017/859) |
| | (6) | 27 Jun 2018 (SI 2018/652) |
| | (7) | 13 Feb 2017 (SI 2017/137) |
| 236 | | 1 Sep 2017 (2017/859) |
| 237 | | 13 Feb 2017 (SI 2017/137) |
| 238 | (1)–(5), (6)(a) | 13 Feb 2017 (SI 2017/137) |
| | (6)(b), (c) | 25 Jul 2018 (SI 2018/873) |
| | (7) | 13 Feb 2017 (SI 2017/137) |
| 239 | | 13 Feb 2017 (SI 2017/137) |
| 240 | | 1 Sep 2017 (2017/859)[2] |
| 241 | | 13 Feb 2017 (SI 2017/137) |
| 242 | | 31 Dec 2018 (SI 2018/1379)[7] |
| 243 | (1)(a) | 22 Jul 2020 (SI 2020/766) |
| | (1)(b) | 27 Jun 2018 (SI 2018/652) |
| | (1)(c) | 12 Mar 2018 (so far as repeals Regulation of Investigatory Powers Act 2000, s 65(5)(c) and inserts sub-s (5)(czb), (czc), (czi), (czj), (czl)(iii) thereof, and sub-s (5)(czm) so far as it applies to conduct falling within paras (czb) and (czi)) (SI 2018/341) |
| | | 27 Jun 2018 (so far as inserts Regulation of Investigatory Powers Act 2000, s 65(5)(czd), (cze), (czk) and (czl)(i) thereof so far as it applies to any failure to cancel a warrant under Pt 2, 5, or Pt 6, Chapter 1 or 3 of this Act) (SI 2018/652) |
| | | 22 Aug 2018 (so far as inserts Regulation of Investigatory Powers Act 2000, s 65(5)(c) so far as it applies to conduct of a kind which may be permitted or required by a warrant under Pt 6, Chapter 2 of the 2016 Act, s 65(cza) so far as it applies to the issue, modifications, renewal or service of a warrant under Pt 6, Chapter 2 of the 2016 Act, s 65(5)(czf)–(czh), s 65(5)(czl)(i) so far as it applies to any failure to cancel a warrant under Pt 6, Chapter 2 or Pt 7 of the 2016 Act, s 65(5)(czl)(iv) and s 65(5)(czm) for all remaining purposes) (SI 2018/873) |
| | | 5 Feb 2019 (so far as inserts Regulation of Investigatory Powers Act 2000, s 65(5)(cza), (czl)(i), (ii), so far as not already in force) (SI 2019/174) |
| | | 22 Jul 2020 (otherwise) (SI 2020/766) |
| | (1)(d), (e) | 5 Dec 2018 (SI 2018/1246) |
| | (1)(f) | 27 Jun 2018 (SI 2018/652) |
| | (1)(g) | 30 Aug 2018 (SI 2018/940) |

**Investigatory Powers Act 2016 (c 25)**—*contd*

| | | |
|---|---|---|
| (1)(h) | 12 Mar 2018 (so far as inserts Regulation of Investigatory Powers Act 2000, s 65(7ZB) so far as applies to conduct which is, or purports to be, conduct falling within s 65(5)(czc), (czj), (czl)(iii) thereof) (SI 2018/341) | |
| | 22 Aug 2018 (so far as inserts Regulation of Investigatory Powers Act 2000, s 65(7ZB) so far as it applies to conduct which is or purports to be conduct falling within s 65(5)(cza) of the 2000 Act so far as it applies to the issue, modification, renewal or service of a warrant under Pt 6, Chapter 2 of the 2016 Act, s 65(5)(czf), (czg) or (czh), (czl)(i) for all remaining purposes and (5)(czl)(iv)) (SI 2018/873) | |
| | 5 Feb 2019 (so far as inserts Regulation of Investigatory Powers Act 2000, s 65(7ZB) in so far as it applies to conduct which is, or purports to be, conduct falling within s 65(5)(cza), (czl)(i), (ii) (SI 2019/174) | |
| | 22 Jul 2020 (otherwise) (SI 2020/766) | |
| (1)(i) | 12 Mar 2018 (so far as repeals Regulation of Investigatory Powers Act 2000, s 65(8)(a), (b) and inserts sub-s (8)(bc) thereof) (SI 2018/341)[3] | |
| | 27 Jun 2018 (so far as inserts Regulation of Investigatory Powers Act 2000, s 65(8)(a) so far as applies to a warrant under Pt 2 or 5 or Pt 6, Chapter 1 or 3 of this Act) (SI 2018/652) | |
| | 22 Aug 2018 (so far as inserts Regulation of Investigatory Powers Act 2000, s 65(8)(a) for all remaining purposes and s 65(8)(bb)) (SI 2018/873) | |
| | 1 Nov 2018 (so far as inserts Regulation of Investigatory Powers Act 2000, s 65(8)(ba)) (SI 2018/873) | |
| | 5 Feb 2019 (otherwise) (SI 2019/174) | |
| (1)(j) | 27 Jun 2018 (SI 2018/652) | |
| (2)(a) | 12 Mar 2018 (so far as inserts Regulation of Investigatory Powers Act 2000, s 67(7)(aza) so far as it relates to an order quashing or cancelling a retention notice under Pt 4 of that Act) (SI 2018/341) | |
| | 22 Aug 2018 (so far as inserts Regulation of Investigatory Powers Act 2000, s 67(7)(azb)) (SI 2018/873) | |
| | 5 Feb 2019 (otherwise) (SI 2019/174) | |
| (2)(b) | 5 Feb 2019 (so far as repeals the reference to Regulation of Investigatory Powers Act 2000, s 23A) (SI 2019/174) | |
| | 22 Jul 2020 (otherwise) (SI 2020/766) | |
| (2)(c) | 5 Feb 2019 (SI 2019/174) | |
| (3), (4) | 12 Mar 2018 (SI 2018/341) | |
| (5)(a) | 27 Jun 2018 (SI 2018/652) | |
| (5)(b), (c) | 12 Mar 2018 (SI 2018/341) | |
| (5)(d), (e) | 22 Aug 2018 (SI 2018/873) | |
| (5)(f) | 27 Jun 2018 (SI 2018/652) | |
| (6) | 12 Mar 2018 (SI 2018/341) | |
| 244 | 30 Dec 2016 (SI 2016/1233) | |
| 245 | 12 Mar 2018 (SI 2018/341) | |
| 246, 247 | 13 Feb 2017 (SI 2017/137) | |
| 248 | See Sch 8 below | |
| 249 | 30 Dec 2016 (for the purposes of the payment of a contribution in respect of costs incurred, or likely to be incurred, in complying with Pt 4 and the purposes of para 3 of Sch 9) (SI 2016/1233) | |
| | 12 Mar 2018 (or the purposes of the payment of a contribution in respect of costs incurred, or likely to be incurred, in complying with a notice under s 252 or 253) (SI 2018/341) | |
| | 27 Jun 2018 (otherwise) (SI 2018/652) | |
| 250, 251 | 13 Feb 2017 (SI 2017/137) | |
| 252 | 12 Mar 2018 (SI 2018/341) | |
| 253 | (1), (2) | 12 Mar 2018 (SI 2018/341) |

**Investigatory Powers Act 2016 (c 25)**—*contd*

| | | |
|---|---|---|
| | (3)–(6) | 13 Feb 2017 (SI 2017/137)[1] |
| | (7)–(9) | 12 Mar 2018 (SI 2018/341) |
| 254–258 | | 12 Mar 2018 (SI 2018/341) |
| 259 | | 27 Jun 2018 (SI 2018/652) |
| 260–269 | | 29 Nov 2016 (s 272(2)) |
| 270 | (1) | See Sch 9 below |
| | (2) | 29 Nov 2016 (s 272(2)) |
| 271 | (1) | See Sch 10 below |
| | (2)–(4) | 29 Nov 2016 (s 272(2)) |
| 272 | | 29 Nov 2016 (s 272(2)) |
| Sch 1 | | 27 Jun 2018 (SI 2018/652) |
| Sch 2 | | 22 Jul 2020 (SI 2020/766) |
| Sch 3 | | 27 Jun 2018 (SI 2018/652) |
| Schs 4, 5 | | 5 Feb 2019 (SI 2019/174) |
| Sch 6 | | 28 Nov 2018 (SI 2018/1246) |
| Sch 7 | | 13 Feb 2017 (SI 2017/137) |
| Sch 8 | paras 1, 2 | 31 May 2018 (for the purpose of the Secretary of State or Scottish Ministers deciding to issue a combined warrant but not for the purpose of the issuing of such a warrant) (SI 2018/652) |
| | | 6 Jul 2018 (otherwise) (SI 2018/817) |
| | para 3 | 30 Aug 2018 (for the purpose of the Secretary of State or the Scottish Ministers deciding to issue a combined warrant but not for the purpose of the issuing of such a warrant) (SI 2018/940) |
| | | 26 Sep 2018 (otherwise) (SI 2018/940) |
| | para 4 | 31 May 2018 (for the purpose of the Secretary of State or Scottish Ministers deciding to issue a combined warrant but not for the purpose of the issuing of such a warrant) (SI 2018/652) |
| | | 6 Jul 2018 (otherwise) (SI 2018/817) |
| | paras 5–7 | 30 Aug 2018 (for the purpose of the Secretary of State or the Scottish Ministers deciding to issue a combined warrant but not for the purpose of the issuing of such a warrant) (SI 2018/940) |
| | | 26 Sep 2018 (otherwise) (SI 2018/940) |
| | paras 8–10 | 31 May 2018 (for the purpose of the Secretary of State or Scottish Ministers deciding to issue a combined warrant but not for the purpose of the issuing of such a warrant) (SI 2018/652) |
| | | 6 Jul 2018 (otherwise) (SI 2018/817) |
| | paras 11, 12 | 28 Nov 2018 (for the purpose of the law enforcement chief deciding to issue a warrant but not for the purpose of the issuing of a warrant) (SI 2018/1246) |
| | | 5 Dec 2018 (otherwise) (SI 2018/1246) |
| | paras 13, 14 | 31 May 2018 (for the purpose of the Secretary of State or Scottish Ministers deciding to issue a combined warrant but not for the purpose of the issuing of such a warrant) (SI 2018/652) |
| | | 6 Jul 2018 (otherwise) (SI 2018/817) |
| | para 15 | 31 May 2018 (SI 2018/652) |
| | para 16(1) | 31 May 2018 (for the purpose of the Secretary of State or Scottish Ministers deciding to issue a combined warrant but not for the purpose of the issuing of such a warrant) (SI 2018/652) |
| | | 27 Jun 2018 (otherwise) (SI 2018/652) |
| | para 16(2) | 31 May 2018 (SI 2018/652) |
| | paras 17–19 | 31 May 2018 (SI 2018/652) |
| | para 20(1) | 31 May 2018 (for the purpose of the matters in para 20(1)(a)–(e)) |
| | | 27 Jun 2018 (otherwise) (SI 2018/652) |
| | para 20(2) | 31 May 2018 (for the purpose of the matters in para 20(2)(a), (b)) |
| | | 27 Jun 2018 (otherwise) (SI 2018/652) |
| | para 20(3) | 31 May 2018 (SI 2018/652) |
| | para 21(1) | 31 May 2018 (so far as relating to the issue of a combined warrant under Sch 8, Pt 1) (SI 2018/652) |

**Investigatory Powers Act 2016 (c 25)**—*contd*

| | | |
|---|---|---|
| | | 27 Jun 2018 (otherwise) (SI 2018/652) |
| | para 21(2) | 31 May 2018 (for the purpose of the matters in para 21(2)(a)–(c)) (SI 2018/652) |
| | | 27 Jun 2018 (otherwise) (SI 2018/652) |
| | para 21(3) | 31 May 2018 (SI 2018/652) |
| | para 22(1) | 31 May 2018 (so far as relating to the issue of a combined warrant under Sch 8, Pt 2) (SI 2018/652) |
| | | 27 Jun 2018 (otherwise) (SI 2018/652) |
| | para 22(2), (3) | 31 May 2018 (SI 2018/652) |
| | para 23(1) | 31 May 2018 (so far as relating to the issue of a combined warrant under Sch 8, Pt 3) (SI 2018/652) |
| | | 27 Jun 2018 (otherwise) (SI 2018/652) |
| | para 23(2) | 31 May 2018 (SI 2018/652) |
| | para 24 | 26 Sep 2018 (SI 2018/940) |
| | para 25 | 27 Jun 2018 (SI 2018/652) |
| | para 26 | 26 Sep 2018 (SI 2018/940) |
| | paras 27–32 | 27 Jun 2018 (SI 2018/652) |
| | para 33 | 31 May 2018 (SI 2018/652) |
| Sch 9 | para 1 | 27 Jun 2018 (SI 2018/652) |
| | para 2 | 5 Feb 2019 (SI 2019/174) |
| | paras 3–5 | 30 Dec 2016 (SI 2016/1233) |
| | para 6 | 25 Jul 2018 (SI 2018/873) |
| | para 7 | 30 Aug 2018 (SI 2018/940) |
| | paras 8, 9 | 30 Dec 2016 (SI 2016/1233) |
| | para 10 | 27 Jun 2018 (SI 2018/652) |
| Sch 10 | Pt 1, paras 1–4 | 27 Jun 2018 (SI 2018/652) |
| | Pt 1, para 5 | 27 Dec 2018 (SI 2018/940) |
| | Pt 1, para 6(1), (2) | 5 Feb 2019 (SI 2019/174) |
| | Pt 1, para 6(3) | 27 Dec 2018 (SI 2018/940) |
| | Pt 1, para 6(4) | 27 Jun 2018 (for the purposes of the references to interception in Regulation of Investigatory Powers Act 2000, ss 21(1), 26(4)(b), 48(4), 65(5)(b)) (SI 2018/652) |
| | | 22 Jul 2020 (except in so far as relates to protected information (as defined by the Regulation of Investigatory Powers Act 2000) which has come into the possession of a person in the circumstances specified in s 49(1)(b) of that Act by means of the exercise of any power conferred by an authorisation under Chapter 1 of Part 1 of that Act) (SI 2020/766) |
| | | *Not yet in force* (otherwise) |
| | Pt 1, para 6(5) | 27 Jun 2018 (for the purposes of the references to postal services in Regulation of Investigatory Powers Act 2000, ss 48(4), 65(4), (5), 67(3)) (SI 2018/652) |
| | | 22 Jul 2020 (except in so far as relates to protected information (as defined by the Regulation of Investigatory Powers Act 2000) which has come into the possession of a person in the circumstances specified in s 49(1)(b) of that Act by means of the exercise of any power conferred by an authorisation under Chapter 1 of Part 1 of that Act) (SI 2020/766) |
| | | *Not yet in force* (otherwise) |
| | Pt 1, para 6(6), (7) | 27 Dec 2018 (SI 2018/940) |
| | Pt 1, paras 7–35 | 27 Jun 2018 (SI 2018/652) |
| | Pt 2, paras 36 | 27 Dec 2018 (SI 2018/940) |
| | Pt 2, para 37 | 27 Jun 2018 (SI 2018/652) |
| | Pt 2, para 38 | 27 Dec 2018 (SI 2018/940) |
| | Pt 2, para 39 | 27 Jun 2018 (SI 2018/652) |
| | Pt 2, para 40 | 27 Dec 2018 (SI 2018/940) |
| | Pt 2, paras 41–44 | 27 Jun 2018 (SI 2018/652) |
| | Pt 2, para 45 | 12 Mar 2018 (so far as repeals Regulation of Investigatory Powers Act 2000, ss 12, 13, 14(2)(c)) (SI 2018/341)[3] |

**Investigatory Powers Act 2016 (c 25)**—*contd*

|  |  |
|--|--|
|  | 27 Jun 2018 (so far as repeals Regulation of Investigatory Powers Act 2000, ss 1(1)–(4), except for the purpose of requests by or on behalf of the Director General of the National Crime Agency; the Commissioner of Police of the Metropolis; the Chief Constable of the Police Service of Northern Ireland; the chief constable of the Police Service of Scotland; or the Commissioners for Her Majesty's Revenue and Customs, (5)–(8), 3, 4, 17–19) (SI 2018/652) |
|  | 8 Aug 2018 (so far as repeals Regulation of Investigatory Powers Act 2000, ss 6(2)(a)–(c), (i), (3), to the extent it applies to an application for the issue of an interception warrant made on behalf of a person specified in sub-ss (2)(a)–(c) or (i), 9(1)(b), to the extent it applies to warrants issued on an application made by or on behalf of the head of an intelligence service or the Chief of Defence Intelligence) (SI 2018/652) |
|  | 26 Sep 2018 (so far as repeals Regulation of Investigatory Powers Act 2000, s 1, so far as not already repealed) (SI 2018/940)[6] |
|  | 7 Nov 2018 (so far as repeals Regulation of Investigatory Powers Act 2000, s 6, so far as not already repealed, s 7, s 9(1)(b) and the word "but" at the end of para (a), (2), (5)) (SI 2018/940)[6] |
|  | 27 Dec 2018 (otherwise) (SI 2018/940)[6] |
| Pt 2, para 46 | 30 Aug 2018 (SI 2018/940) |
| Pt 2, para 47 | 27 Dec 2018 (SI 2018/940) |
| Pt 2, para 48 | 12 Mar 2018 (SI 2018/341) |
| Pt 2, para 49 | 27 Dec 2018 (SI 2018/940) |
| Pt 2, paras 50–52 | 27 Jun 2018 (SI 2018/652) |
| Pt 3, paras 53 | 5 Feb 2019 (SI 2019/174) |
| Pt 3, para 54 | 22 Jul 2020 (SI 2020/766) |
| Pt 3, para 55 | 5 Feb 2019 (in so far as the protected information referred to in Regulation of Investigatory Powers Act 2000, s 49 came into the possession of the person referred to in that section by means of the exercise of any power conferred by an authorisation under Pt 3 of this Act, or in pursuance of an authorisation under the said Pt 3 or as the result of the issue of a warrant under Pt 6, Chapter 2 of this Act) (SI 2019/174) |
|  | *Not yet in force* (otherwise) |
| Pt 3, paras 56–60 | 22 Jul 2020 (SI 2020/766) |
| Pt 3, para 61 | 5 Feb 2019 (SI 2019/174) |
| Pt 4, para 62 | 1 Nov 2018 (SI 2018/873) |
| Pt 4, para 63 | 30 Dec 2016 (SI 2016/1233) |
| Pt 4, paras 64, 65 | 27 Jun 2018 (SI 2018/652) |
| Pt 5, para 66 | 5 Dec 2018 (SI 2018/1246) |
| Pt 5, para 67 | 1 Sep 2017 (SI 2017/859) |
| Pt 5, para 68 | 5 Dec 2018 (SI 2018/1246) |
| Pt 5, para 69 | 1 Sep 2017 (SI 2017/859) |
| Pt 5, para 70 | 5 Dec 2018 (SI 2018/1246) |
| Pt 6, paras 71–98 | 1 Sep 2017 (SI 2017/859) |
| Pt 7, para 99 | 12 Mar 2018 (except to the extent that a direction under Telecommunications Act 1984, s 94 may impose requirements relating to the acquisition of communications data in bulk) (SI 2018/341)[3] |
|  | 22 Aug 2018 (exception noted above) (SI 2018/873)[5] |
| Pt 7, para 100 | 12 Mar 2018 (SI 2018/341) |
| Pt 7, para 101 (1), (2) | 27 Jun 2018 (SI 2018/652) |
| Pt 7, para 101(3) | 5 Feb 2019 (SI 2019/174) |
| Pt 8 | 30 Dec 2016 (repeals relating to Counter-Terrorism and Security Act 2015, ss 21, 52(3)(a)) (SI 2016/1233) |
|  | 22 Aug 2018 (repeal relating to Communications Act 2003, Sch 17, para 70) (SI 2018/873) |

**Investigatory Powers Act 2016 (c 25)**—*contd*

30 Aug 2018 (SI 2018/940), repeals of or in—

Scotland Act 1998 (Cross-Border Public Authorities) (Adaptation of Functions etc.) Order 1999, SI 1999/1747, Sch 6, para 2(2), (5);

Regulation of Investigatory Powers Act 2000, Sch 4, paras 7(2), 8(1), (10), (11), 9;

Insolvency Act 2000, Sch 4, para 22(2);

Scotland Act 1998 (Transfer of Functions to the Scottish Ministers etc.) (No 2) Order 2000, SI 2000/3253, Sch 3, paras 9–12;

Insolvency Act 2000 (Company Directors Disqualification Undertakings) Order 2004, SI 2004/1941, Schedule, para 10;

Constitutional Reform Act 2005, Sch 17, paras 27, 30(2)(a), (b);

Inquires Act 2005, Sch 2, paras 20, 21;

Wireless Telegraphy Act 2006, Sch 7, paras 22, 23;

National Health Service (Consequential Provisions) Act 2006, Sch 1, para 208;

Armed Forces Act 2006, Sch 16, para 169;

Counter-Terrorism Act 2008, ss 69, 74;

Tribunals, Courts and Enforcement Act 2007, Sch 16, para 11(2);

Serious Crime Act 2007, Sch 12, para 3;

Policing and Crime Act 2009, s 100;

Companies Act 2006 (Consequential Amendments, Transitional Provisions and Savings) Order 2009, SI 2009/1941, Sch 1, para 169;

Terrorist Asset-Freezing etc. Act 2010, s 28(2), (3);

Police Reform and Social Responsibility Act 2011, Sch 16, para 222;

Terrorism Prevention and Investigation Measures Act 2011, Sch 7, para 4;

Regulation of Investigatory Powers (Monetary Penalty Notices and Consents for Interceptions) Regulations 2011, SI 2011/1340, regs 2(1), (4), 3;

Health and Social Care Act 2012, Sch 5, para 98;

Protection of Freedoms Act 2012, Sch 9, paras 10, 11;

Justice and Security Act 2013, ss 5, 16, Sch 2, paras 4, 11;

Crime and Courts Act 2013, Sch 8, paras 59, 78, Sch 9, para 125, Sch 21, para 4;

Police and Fire Reform (Scotland) Act 2012 (Consequential Provisions and Modifications) Order 2013, SI 2013/602, Sch 2, para 33(20), (22)(c);

Anti-social Behaviour, Crime and Policing Act 2014, s 150;

Data Retention and Investigatory Powers Act 2014, s 6;

Counter-Terrorism and Security Act 2015, s 15(3), Sch 8, para 2

7 Nov 2018 (repeal of Serious Crime Act 2007, Sch 12, para 6) (SI 2018/940)

27 Dec 2018 (SI 2018/940), repeals of or in—

Anti-terrorism, Crime and Security Act 2001, s 116(3);

Terrorism Act 2006, s 32;

Regulation of Investigatory Powers (Monetary Penalty Notices and Consents for Interceptions) Regulations 2011, so far as not already revoked

22 Jul 2020 (SI 2020/766), repeals of or in—

Serious Crime Act 2015, ss 83, 86(12), Sch 4, para 18

Serious Crime Act 2007, Sch 12, paras 7, 8;

Police, Public Order and Criminal Justice (Scotland) Act 2006 (Consequential Provisions and Modifications) Order 2007, SI 2007/1098, Schedule, para 4(5);

Policing and Crime Act 2009, s 7, Sch 7, paras 13, 14;

**Investigatory Powers Act 2016 (c 25)**—*contd*

Protection of Freedoms Act 2012, s 37, Sch 9, paras 7, 8,
16(b)(i);
Crime and Courts Act 2013, Schedule, para 81;
Police and Fire Reform (Scotland) Act 2012 (Consequential
Provisions and Modifications) Order 2013, SI 2013/602, Sch 2,
para 33(5)–(8)

*Not yet in force* (otherwise)

1   For a transitory provision, see SI 2017/137, reg 3

2   For transitory and saving provisions, see SI 2017/859, regs 3–11

3   For transitional and saving provisions, see SI 2018/341, regs 3–7

4   For transitional and saving provisions, see SI 2018/652, regs 15–27

5   For transitional and saving provisions, see SI 2018/873, regs 5–10

6   For transitional and saving provisions, see SI 2018/940, regs 6–8

7   For a transitional provision, see SI 2018/1379, reg 3

---

**Land and Buildings Transaction Tax (Amendment) Act 2016 (asp 11)**

*RA:* 24 Mar 2016

*Commencement provisions:* s 5

| | |
|---|---|
| 1–3 | 25 Mar 2016 (s 5(1)) |
| 4–6 | 1 Apr 2016 (s 5(2)) |

---

**Land Reform (Scotland) Act 2016 (asp 18)**

*RA:* 22 Apr 2016

*Commencement provisions:* s 130; Land Reform (Scotland) Act 2016 (Commencement No 1 and Transitional Provision) Regulations 2016, SSI 2016/193; Land Reform (Scotland) Act 2016 (Commencement No 2 and Transitory Provisions) Regulations 2016, SSI 2016/250; Land Reform (Scotland) Act 2016 (Commencement No 4, Transitional and Saving Provisions) Regulations 2016, SSI 2016/372; Land Reform (Scotland) Act 2016 (Commencement No 5 and Transitory Provisions) Regulations 2017, SSI 2017/20; Land Reform (Scotland) Act 2016 (Commencement No 6, Transitory and Saving Provisions) Regulations 2017, SSI 2017/299, as amended by SSI 2017/370; Land Reform (Scotland) Act 2016 (Commencement No 7) Regulations 2018, SSI 2018/99; Land Reform (Scotland) Act 2016 (Commencement No 8 and Saving Provision) Regulations 2018, SSI 2018/138; Land Reform (Scotland) Act 2016 (Commencement No. 9) Regulations 2019, SSI 2019/420; Land Reform (Scotland) Act 2016 (Commencement No 10) Regulations 2020, SSI 2020/20; Land Reform (Scotland) Act 2016 (Commencement No 11) Regulations 2020, SSI 2020/383; Land Reform (Scotland) Act 2016 (Commencement No 12) Regulations 2020, SSI 2020/428

| | | |
|---|---|---|
| 1, 2 | | 1 Oct 2016 (SSI 2016/193) |
| 3 | | 1 Oct 2017 (SSI 2016/193) |
| 4 | (1)–(5) | 1 Nov 2016 (SSI 2016/250) |
| | (6)–(8) | 1 Apr 2017 (SSI 2016/250) |
| 5 | | 1 Nov 2016 (SSI 2016/250) |
| 6 | | 1 Apr 2017 (SSI 2016/250)[2] |
| 7 | | 1 Nov 2016 (SSI 2016/250)[2] |
| 8, 9 | | 1 Apr 2017 (SSI 2016/250) |
| 10, 11 | | 1 Nov 2016 (SSI 2016/250) |
| 12 | (1), (2), (3)(a) | 1 Nov 2016 (SSI 2016/250) |
| | (3)(b) | 1 Nov 2016 (for the purpose of a tenancy under Agricultural Holdings (Scotland) Act 2003, s 4 or 5) (SSI 2016/250) |
| | | *Not yet in force* (otherwise) |
| | (4), (5) | 1 Nov 2016 (SSI 2016/250) |
| 13 | | 1 Nov 2016 (SSI 2016/250) |

**Land Reform (Scotland) Act 2016 (asp 18)**—*contd*

| | | |
|---|---|---|
| 14 | | 1 Nov 2016 (SSI 2016/250)[2] |
| 15, 16 | | 1 Nov 2016 (SSI 2016/250) |
| 17 | | 1 Nov 2016 (SSI 2016/250)[2] |
| 18 | | 1 Nov 2016 (SSI 2016/250) |
| 19, 20 | | 1 Nov 2016 (SSI 2016/250)[2] |
| 21 | (1), (2) | 1 Nov 2016 (SSI 2016/250) |
| | (3) | 1 Apr 2017 (SSI 2016/250) |
| 22 | (1), (2) | 1 Apr 2017 (SSI 2016/250)[2] |
| | (3)(a)(i) | *Not yet in force* |
| | (3)(a)(ii), (iii), (b), (4), (5) | 1 Apr 2017 (SSI 2016/250)[2] |
| 23 | | 1 Apr 2017 (SSI 2016/250) |
| 24 | | 1 Apr 2017 (SSI 2016/250)[2] |
| 25, 26 | | 1 Apr 2017 (SSI 2016/250) |
| 27 | (1), (2)(a)–(f) | 1 Apr 2017 (SSI 2016/250) |
| | (2)(g) | *Not yet in force* |
| | (2)(h), (i), (3)–(9) | 1 Apr 2017 (SSI 2016/250) |
| 28–38 | | 1 Apr 2017 (SSI 2016/250) |
| 39 | | 17 May 2018 (for the purpose of consultation in accordance with s 41(1), (2)) (SSI 2018/138)[6] |
| | | 16 Dec 2020 (otherwise) (SSI 2020/383) |
| 40 | | 17 May 2018 (for the purpose of consultation in accordance with s 41(1), (2)) (SSI 2018/138)[6] |
| | | 10 Jan 2020 (otherwise) (SSI 2019/420) |
| 41 | | 17 May 2018 (SSI 2018/138)[6] |
| 42 | | 17 May 2018 (for the purpose of consultation in accordance with s 41(1), (2)) (SSI 2018/138)[6] |
| | | 10 Jan 2020 (otherwise) (SSI 2019/420) |
| 43 | | *Not yet in force* |
| 44 | | 1 Nov 2016 (SSI 2016/250) |
| 45–51 | | 26 Apr 2020 (SSI 2020/20) |
| 52 | (1) | 23 Apr 2018 (for the purpose of making regulations under sub-s (10)(b)) (SSI 2018/99) |
| | | 27 Jun 2018 (otherwise) (SSI 2018/138)[6] |
| | (2)–(9) | 23 Apr 2018 (for the purpose of making regulations under sub-s (10)(b)) (SSI 2018/99) |
| | | 26 Apr 2020 (otherwise) (SSI 2020/20) |
| | (10)–(13) | 23 Apr 2018 (for the purpose of making regulations under sub-s (10)(b)) (SSI 2018/99) |
| | | 27 Jun 2018 (otherwise) (SSI 2018/138)[6] |
| 53 | | 27 Jun 2018 (SSI 2018/138)[6] |
| 54–73 | | 26 Apr 2020 (SSI 2020/20) |
| 74–76 | | 28 Jun 2016 (SSI 2016/193)[1] |
| 77–82 | | 28 Jun 2016 (SSI 2016/193) |
| 83, 84 | | 31 Dec 2016 (SSI 2016/372)[3] |
| 85–91 | | 30 Nov 2017 (SSI 2017/299)[5] |
| 92–104 | | *Not yet in force* |
| 105 | | 30 Nov 2017 (SSI 2017/299) |
| 106, 107 | | *Not yet in force* |
| 108 | | 30 Nov 2017 (SSI 2017/299)[5] |
| 109 | | *Not yet in force* |
| 110, 111 | | 28 Feb 2021 (SSI 2020/428) |
| 112–114 | | 13 Jun 2017 (SSI 2017/20)[4] |
| 115–118 | | 13 Jun 2017 (SSI 2017/20) |
| 119–124 | | *Not yet in force* |
| 125–127 | | 23 Apr 2016 (s 130(1)) |
| 128 | | 16 Dec 2020 (SSI 2020/383) |
| 129 | (1) | 27 Jun 2018 (SSI 2018/138)[6] |
| | (2) | See Sch 2 below |

**Land Reform (Scotland) Act 2016 (asp 18)**—*contd*

| | | |
|---|---|---|
| 130, 131 | | 23 Apr 2016 (s 130(1)) |
| Sch 1 | | 27 Jun 2018 (SSI 2018/138)[6] |
| Sch 2 | paras 1–6 | 30 Nov 2017 (SSI 2017/299) |
| | para 7(1) | See sub-paras 2–30 below |
| | para 7(2)–(16)(a) | 30 Nov 2017 (SSI 2017/299)[5] |
| | para 7(16)(b) | *Not yet in force* |
| | para 7(17)–(28) | 30 Nov 2017 (SSI 2017/299)[5] |
| | para 7(29) | *Not yet in force* |
| | para 7(30)(a) | 30 Nov 2017 (SSI 2017/299) |
| | para 7(30)(b) | *Not yet in force* |
| | paras 8, 9 | 30 Nov 2017 (SSI 2017/299)[5] |
| | paras 10–19 | *Not yet in force* |

[1]   For transitional provisions, see SSI 2016/193, reg 3

[2]   For transitory provisions, see SSI 2016/250, regs 3, 4

[3]   For transitional and saving provisions, see SSI 2016/372, regs 3, 4

[4]   For transitory provisions, see SSI 2017/20, regs 3–5

[5]   For savings and transitory provisions, see SSI 2017/299, regs 3–14

[6]   For a saving provision, see SSI 2018/138, reg 4

---

**Lobbying (Scotland) Act 2016 (asp 16)**

*RA:* 14 Apr 2016

*Commencement provisions:* s 52; Lobbying (Scotland) Act 2016 (Commencement No 1) Regulations 2017, SSI 2017/201; Lobbying (Scotland) Act 2016 (Commencement No 2) Regulations 2018, SSI 2018/73

| | | |
|---|---|---|
| 1–14 | | 12 Mar 2018 (SSI 2018/73) |
| 15 | | 6 Sep 2017 (SSI 2017/201) |
| 16–19 | | 12 Mar 2018 (SSI 2018/73) |
| 20 | | 6 Sep 2017 (SSI 2017/201) |
| 21–30 | | 12 Mar 2018 (SSI 2018/73) |
| 31 | | 6 Sep 2017 (SSI 2017/201) |
| 32–40 | | 12 Mar 2018 (SSI 2018/73) |
| 41 | | 6 Sep 2017 (SSI 2017/201) |
| 42 | | 12 Mar 2018 (SSI 2018/73) |
| 43–45 | | 6 Sep 2017 (SSI 2017/201) |
| 46 | | 12 Mar 2018 (SSI 2018/73) |
| 47, 48 | | 15 Apr 2016 (s 52(1)) |
| 49 | (1) | 6 Sep 2017 (SSI 2017/201) |
| | (2) | 12 Mar 2018 (SSI 2018/73) |
| | (3) | 6 Sep 2017 (SSI 2017/201) |
| | (4) | 12 Mar 2018 (SSI 2018/73) |
| 50 | | 12 Mar 2018 (SSI 2018/73) |
| 51–53 | | 15 Apr 2016 (s 52(1)) |
| Schedule | | 12 Mar 2018 (SSI 2018/73) |

---

**National Galleries of Scotland Act 2016 (asp 6)**

*RA:* 23 Feb 2016

*Commencement provisions:* s 4

Whole Act in force 24 Feb 2016 (s 4)

---

## NHS (Charitable Trusts Etc) Act 2016 (c 10)

*RA:* 23 Mar 2016

*Commencement provisions:* s 5; NHS (Charitable Trusts Etc) Act 2016 (Commencement) Regulations 2021, SI 2021/712

| | | |
|---|---|---|
| 1 | (1)–(8) | 17 Jun 2021 (SI 2021/712) |
| | (9) | See Sch 1 below |
| 2 | | 17 Jun 2021 (SI 2021/712) |
| 3 | (1)–(11) | 23 May 2016 (s 5(3)) |
| | (12) | See Sch 2 below |
| 4–6 | | 23 Mar 2016 (s 5(4)) |
| Sch 1 | paras 1–3, 4(a), (b)(i) | 17 Jun 2021 (SI 2021/712) |
| | para 4(b)(ii) | *Not yet in force* |
| | para 4(c) | 17 Jun 2021 (SI 2021/712) |
| | paras 5–13 | 17 Jun 2021 (SI 2021/712) |
| | para 14 | *Not yet in force* |
| | paras 15–17, 18(a)–(e) | 17 Jun 2021 (SI 2021/712) |
| | para 18(f) | *Not yet in force* |
| | para 18(g) | 17 Jun 2021 (SI 2021/712) |
| | para 18(h) | *Not yet in force* |
| | para 18(i), (j) | 17 Jun 2021 (SI 2021/712) |
| | para 19 | *Not yet in force* |
| Sch 2 | | 23 May 2016 (s 5(3)) |

## Northern Ireland (Stormont Agreement and Implementation Plan) Act 2016 (c 13)

*RA:* 4 May 2016

*Commencement provisions:* s 11(2)–(4); Northern Ireland (Stormont Agreement and Implementation Plan) Act 2016 (Commencement) Regulations 2016, SI 2016/1258

| | |
|---|---|
| 1–5 | *Not yet in force*[1] |
| 6–8 | 4 May 2016 (s 11(2)) |
| 9 | 4 Jul 2016 (s 11(3)) |
| 10, 11 | 4 May 2016 (s 11(2)) |
| Schs 1, 2 | 4 May 2016 (s 11(2)) |

[1] By the Northern Ireland (Stormont Agreement and Implementation Plan) Act 2016 (Commencement) Regulations 2016, SI 2016/1258, reg 2, ss 1–5 of this Act come into force on the day on which the agreement relating to paramilitary activity (as defined in s 4(1) of the Act) enters into force

## Nurse Staffing Levels (Wales) Act 2016 (anaw 5)

*RA:* 21 Mar 2016

*Commencement provisions:* s 2; Nurse Staffing Levels (Wales) Act 2016 (Commencement) Order 2016, SI 2016/829; Nurse Staffing Levels (Wales) Act 2016 (Commencement No 2) Order 2021, SI 2021/61

| | | |
|---|---|---|
| 1 | (1) | 3 Aug 2016 (in so far as it inserts National Health Service (Wales) Act 2006, s 25D) (SI 2016/829) |
| | | 6 Apr 2017 (in so far as it inserts National Health Service (Wales) Act 2006, s 25A) (SI 2016/829) |
| | | 6 Apr 2018 (in so far as it inserts National Health Service (Wales) Act 2006, ss 25B, 25C, 25E) (SI 2016/829) |
| | (2), (3) | 21 Jan 2021 (SI 2021/61) |
| 2, 3 | | 21 Mar 2016 (s 2(1)) |

## Private Housing (Tenancies) (Scotland) Act 2016 (asp 19)

*RA:* 22 Apr 2016

*Commencement provisions:* s 79; Private Housing (Tenancies) (Scotland) Act 2016 (Commencement No 1) Regulations 2016, SSI 2016/298; Private Housing (Tenancies) (Scotland) Act 2016 (Commencement No 2 and Saving Provision) Regulations 2017, SSI 2017/293, revoked by SSI 2017/346; Private Housing (Tenancies) (Scotland) Act 2016 (Commencement No 3, Amendment, Saving Provision and Revocation) Regulations 2017, SSI 2017/346

| | | |
|---|---|---|
| 1–6 | | 1 Dec 2017 (SSI 2017/346) |
| 7 | | 31 Oct 2016 (for the purpose of making regulations) (SSI 2016/298) |
| | | 1 Dec 2017 (otherwise) (SSI 2017/346) |
| 8 | | 31 Oct 2016 (SSI 2016/298) |
| 9, 10 | | 1 Dec 2017 (SSI 2017/346) |
| 11, 12 | | 31 Oct 2016 (SSI 2016/298) |
| 13–16 | | 1 Dec 2017 (SSI 2017/346) |
| 17 | (1), (2) | 1 Dec 2017 (SSI 2017/346) |
| | (3) | 31 Oct 2016 (for the purpose of making regulations) (SSI 2016/298) |
| | | 1 Dec 2017 (otherwise) (SSI 2017/346) |
| 18–21 | | 1 Dec 2017 (SSI 2017/346) |
| 22 | (1) | 1 Dec 2017 (SSI 2017/346) |
| | (2) | 31 Oct 2016 (for the purpose of making regulations) (SSI 2016/298) |
| | | 1 Dec 2017 (otherwise) (SSI 2017/346) |
| | (3)–(6) | 1 Dec 2017 (SSI 2017/346) |
| 23 | | 1 Dec 2017 (SSI 2017/346) |
| 24 | (1), (2) | 1 Dec 2017 (SSI 2017/346) |
| | (3), (4) | 31 Oct 2016 (for the purpose of making regulations) (SSI 2016/298) |
| | | 1 Dec 2017 (otherwise) (SSI 2017/346) |
| 25–33 | | 1 Dec 2017 (SSI 2017/346) |
| 34 | (1) | 1 Dec 2017 (SSI 2017/346) |
| | (2) | 31 Oct 2016 (SSI 2016/298) |
| 35–42 | | 1 Dec 2017 (SSI 2017/346) |
| 43 | (1) | 31 Oct 2016 (for the purpose of making regulations) (SSI 2016/298) |
| | | 1 Dec 2017 (otherwise) (SSI 2017/346) |
| | (2)–(6) | 1 Dec 2017 (SSI 2017/346) |
| 44–60 | | 1 Dec 2017 (SSI 2017/346) |
| 61 | (1), (2) | 1 Dec 2017 (SSI 2017/346) |
| | (3) | 31 Oct 2016 (for the purpose of making regulations) (SSI 2016/298) |
| | | 1 Dec 2017 (otherwise) (SSI 2017/346) |
| | (4) | 1 Dec 2017 (SSI 2017/346) |
| 62 | (1) | 31 Oct 2016 (for the purpose of making regulations) (SSI 2016/298) |
| | | 1 Dec 2017 (otherwise) (SSI 2017/346) |
| | (2)–(5) | 1 Dec 2017 (SSI 2017/346) |
| 63–73 | | 1 Dec 2017 (SSI 2017/346) |
| 74 | | See Sch 4 below |
| 75 | | 1 Dec 2017 (SSI 2017/346)[1] |
| 76–80 | | 23 Apr 2016 (s 79(1)) |
| Sch 1 | | 1 Dec 2017 (SSI 2017/346) |
| Sch 2 | | 31 Oct 2016 (SSI 2016/298) |
| Sch 3 | | 1 Dec 2017 (SSI 2017/346) |
| Sch 4 | paras 1–4 | 1 Dec 2017 (SSI 2017/346) |
| | para 5 | *Not yet in force* |
| | paras 6–11 | 1 Dec 2017 (SSI 2017/346) |
| Sch 5 | para 1 | 1 Dec 2017 (SSI 2017/346) |

### Private Housing (Tenancies) (Scotland) Act 2016 (asp 19)—*contd*

| | | |
|---|---|---|
| para 2 | 1 Dec 2017 (SSI 2017/346)[1] |
| paras 3–5 | 1 Dec 2017 (SSI 2017/346) |

[1]   For a saving provision, see SSI 2017/346, reg 6

---

### Psychoactive Substances Act 2016 (c 2)

*RA:* 28 Jan 2016

*Commencement provisions:* s 63; Psychoactive Substances Act 2016 (Commencement) Regulations 2016, SI 2016/553

| | | |
|---|---|---|
| 1, 2 | | 26 May 2016 (SI 2016/553) |
| 3 | | 28 Jan 2016 (for the purpose of making regulations) (s 63(1)(b)) |
| | | 26 May 2016 (otherwise) (SI 2016/553) |
| 4–10 | | 26 May 2016 (SI 2016/553) |
| 11 | | 28 Jan 2016 (for the purpose of making regulations) (s 63(1)(b)) |
| | | 26 May 2016 (otherwise) (SI 2016/553) |
| 12–39 | | 26 May 2016 (SI 2016/553) |
| 40 | (1)–(6) | 26 May 2016 (SI 2016/553) |
| | (7) | See Sch 3 below |
| | (8) | 26 May 2016 (SI 2016/553) |
| 41–56 | | 26 May 2016 (SI 2016/553) |
| 57 | | See Sch 4 below |
| 58 | | 26 May 2016 (SI 2016/553) |
| 59 | | 28 Jan 2016 (s 63(1)(a)) |
| 60 | | See Sch 5 below |
| 61–63 | | 28 Jan 2016 (s 63(1)(a)) |
| Schs 1–5 | | 26 May 2016 (SI 2016/553) |

---

### Regulation and Inspection of Social Care (Wales) Act 2016 (anaw 2)

*RA:* 18 Jan 2016

*Commencement provisions:* s 188; Regulation and Inspection of Social Care (Wales) Act 2016 (Commencement No 1) Order 2016, SI 2016/467; Regulation and Inspection of Social Care (Wales) Act 2016 (Commencement No 2) Order 2016, SI 2016/713; Regulation and Inspection of Social Care (Wales) Act 2016 (Commencement No 3, Savings and Transitional Provisions) Order 2017, SI 2017/309; Regulation and Inspection of Social Care (Wales) Act 2016 (Commencement No 4) Order 2017, SI 2017/846; Regulation and Inspection of Social Care (Wales) Act 2016 (Commencement No 5, Savings, Transitory and Transitional Provisions) Order 2017, SI 2017/1326; Regulation and Inspection of Social Care (Wales) Act 2016 (Commencement No 6, Savings and Transitional Provisions) Order 2019, SI 2019/864; Regulation and Inspection of Social Care (Wales) Act 2016 (Commencement No 7) Order 2021, SI 2021/181

| | | |
|---|---|---|
| 1 | | 2 Apr 2018 (SI 2017/1326) |
| 2 | (1)(a)–(c) | 2 Apr 2018 (SI 2017/1326) |
| | (1)(d)–(g) | 29 Apr 2019 (SI 2019/964) |
| | (1)(h), (i) | 2 Apr 2018 (SI 2017/1326) |
| | (2) | See Sch 1 below |
| | (3), (4) | 2 Apr 2018 (SI 2017/1326) |
| 3, 4 | | 2 Apr 2018 (SI 2017/1326) |
| 5 | | 2 Apr 2018 (SI 2017/1326)[2] |
| 6 | | 1 Feb 2018 (so far as applies to a person who wants to provide one of the services specified in s 2(1)(a)–(c), (h)) (SI 2017/1326) |
| | | 29 Apr 2019 (so far as applies to a person who wants to provide one of the services specified in s 2(1)(d)–(g)) (SI 2019/864)[3] |
| | | 23 Feb 2021 (to the extent that it applies to a person who wants to provide a service specified in regulations made under s 2(1)(i)) (SI 2021/181) |

**Regulation and Inspection of Social Care (Wales) Act 2016 (anaw 2)**—*contd*

| | | |
|---|---|---|
| | | *Not yet in force* (otherwise)[2] |
| 7 | | 2 Apr 2018 (SI 2017/1326)[2] |
| 8–55 | | 2 Apr 2018 (SI 2017/1326) |
| 56 | (1) | 4 Sep 2017 (in so far as inserts Social Services and Well-being (Wales) Act 2014, s 144A) (SI 2017/846) |
| | | 29 Apr 2019 (in so far as inserts Social Services and Well-being (Wales) Act 2014, s 144C) (SI 2019/964) |
| | | 23 Feb 2021 (in so far as inserts Social Services and Well-being (Wales) Act 2014, s 144B, except sub-s (2)(a)(ii) thereof) (SI 2021/181) |
| | | *Not yet in force* (otherwise) |
| | (2) | 4 Sep 2017 (SI 2017/846) |
| 57 | | 29 Apr 2019 (SI 2019/864)[3] |
| 58 | | 2 Apr 2018 (SI 2017/1326) |
| 59–63 | | *Not yet in force* |
| 64 | | 2 Apr 2018 (SI 2017/1326) |
| 65, 66 | | 3 Apr 2017 (SI 2017/309)[1] |
| 67, 68 | | 11 Jul 2016 (for the purpose of the effective discharge by Social Care Wales of its duty to consult under section 75(2)) (SI 2016/713) |
| | | 3 Apr 2017 (otherwise) (SI 2017/309)[1] |
| 69–72 | | 3 Apr 2017 (SI 2017/309)[1] |
| 73 | (1), (2) | 11 Jul 2016 (for the purpose of the effective discharge by Social Care Wales of its duty to consult under section 75(2)) (SI 2016/713) |
| | | 3 Apr 2017 (otherwise) (SI 2017/309)[1] |
| | (3)–(6) | 3 Apr 2017 (SI 2017/309)[1] |
| 74 | | 3 Apr 2017 (SI 2017/309) |
| 75 | | 11 Jul 2016 (for the purpose of the effective discharge by Social Care Wales of its duty to consult under sub-s (2)) (SI 2016/713) |
| | | 3 Apr 2017 (otherwise) (SI 2017/309)[1] |
| 76–185 | | 3 Apr 2017 (SI 2017/309)[1] |
| 186–190 | | 19 Jan 2016 (s 188(2)) |
| Sch 1 | paras 1–3 | 2 Apr 2018 (SI 2017/1326)[2] |
| | paras 4–7 | 29 Apr 2019 (SI 2019/964) |
| | para 8 | 2 Apr 2018 (SI 2017/1326) |
| | para 9 | 29 Apr 2019 (SI 2019/964) |
| Sch 2 | | 3 Apr 2017 (SI 2017/309)[1] |
| Sch 3 | paras 1–3 | 2 Apr 2018 (SI 2017/1326)[2] |
| | para 4(a), (b) | 2 Apr 2018 (SI 2017/1326)[2] |
| | para 4(c) | 29 Apr 2019 (SI 2019/864)[3] |
| | para 4(d) | 2 Apr 2018 (SI 2017/1326)[2] |
| | para 4(e), (f) | 29 Apr 2019 (SI 2019/864)[3] |
| | para 4(g)–(i) | 2 Apr 2018 (SI 2017/1326)[2] |
| | para 5 | 29 Apr 2019 (SI 2019/864)[3] |
| | paras 6–11 | 2 Apr 2018 (SI 2017/1326)[2] |
| | paras 12–15 | 29 Apr 2019 (SI 2019/864)[3] |
| | para 16 | 2 Apr 2018 (SI 2017/1326)[2] |
| | paras 17–24 | 29 Apr 2019 (SI 2019/864)[3] |
| | paras 25–27 | 2 Apr 2018 (SI 2017/1326)[2] |
| | para 28(a) | 2 Apr 2018 (SI 2017/1326)[2] |
| | para 28(b), (c) | 29 Apr 2019 (SI 2019/864)[3] |
| | para 29 | 2 Apr 2018 (SI 2017/1326)[2] |
| | para 30 | 23 Feb 2021 (SI 2021/181) |
| | paras 31–36 | 2 Apr 2018 (SI 2017/1326)[2] |
| | paras 37–58 | 3 Apr 2017 (SI 2017/309)[1] |
| | paras 59–65 | 6 Apr 2016 (SI 2016/467) |

### Regulation and Inspection of Social Care (Wales) Act 2016 (anaw 2)—*contd*

1 For savings and transitional provisions, see SI 2017/309, art 3, Schedule

2 For savings, transitory and transitional provisions, see SI 2017/1326, arts 3–15

3 For transitional provisions and savings, see SI 2019/864, arts 3–13

### Renting Homes (Wales) Act 2016 (anaw 1)

*RA:* 18 Jan 2016

*Commencement provisions:* s 257; Renting Homes (Wales) Act 2016 (Commencement No 1) Order 2016, SI 2016/813; Renting Homes (Wales) Act 2016 (Commencement No 2 and Consequential Amendments) Order 2022, SI 2022/906

| | | |
|---|---|---|
| 1–22 | | 1 Dec 2022 (SI 2022/906) |
| 23 | | 5 Aug 2016 (for the purpose of making regulations) (SI 2016/813) |
| | | 1 Dec 2022 (otherwise) (SI 2022/906) |
| 24–28 | | 1 Dec 2022 (SI 2022/906) |
| 29 | | 5 Aug 2016 (for the purpose of making regulations) (SI 2016/813) |
| | | 1 Dec 2022 (otherwise) (SI 2022/906) |
| 30, 31 | | 1 Dec 2022 (SI 2022/906) |
| 32 | (1)–(3) | 1 Dec 2022 (SI 2022/906) |
| | (4) | 5 Aug 2016 (for the purpose of making regulations) (SI 2016/813) |
| | | 1 Dec 2022 (otherwise) (SI 2022/906) |
| 33–44 | | 1 Dec 2022 (SI 2022/906) |
| 45 | (1), (2) | 1 Dec 2022 (SI 2022/906) |
| | (3) | 5 Aug 2016 (for the purpose of making regulations) (SI 2016/813) |
| | | 1 Dec 2022 (otherwise) (SI 2022/906) |
| | (4) | 1 Dec 2022 (SI 2022/906) |
| 46–93 | | 1 Dec 2022 (SI 2022/906) |
| 94 | | 5 Aug 2016 (for the purpose of making regulations) (SI 2016/813) |
| | | 1 Dec 2022 (otherwise) (SI 2022/906) |
| 95–111 | | 1 Dec 2022 (SI 2022/906) |
| 112 | | 5 Aug 2016 (for the purpose of making regulations) (SI 2016/813) |
| | | 1 Dec 2022 (otherwise) (SI 2022/906) |
| 113–115 | | 1 Dec 2022 (SI 2022/906) |
| 116 | (1)–(3) | 1 Dec 2022 (SI 2022/906) |
| | (4) | 5 Aug 2016 (for the purpose of issuing guidance) (SI 2016/813) |
| | | 1 Dec 2022 (otherwise) (SI 2022/906) |
| | (5), (6) | 1 Dec 2022 (SI 2022/906) |
| 117–130 | | 1 Dec 2022 (SI 2022/906) |
| 131 | | 5 Aug 2016 (for the purpose of making regulations) (SI 2016/813) |
| | | 1 Dec 2022 (otherwise) (SI 2022/906) |
| 132–145 | | 1 Dec 2022 (SI 2022/906) |
| 146 | (1) | 5 Aug 2016 (for the purpose of issuing guidance) (SI 2016/813) |
| | | 1 Dec 2022 (otherwise) (SI 2022/906) |
| | (2) | 1 Dec 2022 (SI 2022/906) |
| 147–202 | | 1 Dec 2022 (SI 2022/906) |
| 203 | (1)–(4) | 1 Dec 2022 (SI 2022/906) |
| | (5), (6) | 5 Aug 2016 (for the purpose of making regulations) (SI 2016/813) |
| | | 1 Dec 2022 (otherwise) (SI 2022/906) |
| 204–220 | | 1 Dec 2022 (SI 2022/906) |
| 221 | | 5 Aug 2016 (for the purpose of making regulations) (SI 2016/813) |
| | | 1 Dec 2022 (otherwise) (SI 2022/906) |
| 222–235 | | 1 Dec 2022 (SI 2022/906) |
| 236 | (1), (2) | 1 Dec 2022 (SI 2022/906) |
| | (3), (4) | 5 Aug 2016 (for the purpose of making regulations) (SI 2016/813) |
| | | 1 Dec 2022 (otherwise) (SI 2022/906) |
| | (5)–(7) | 1 Dec 2022 (SI 2022/906) |
| 237–242 | | 1 Dec 2022 (SI 2022/906) |

**Renting Homes (Wales) Act 2016 (anaw 1)**—*contd*

| | | |
|---|---|---|
| 243–258 | | 19 Jan 2016 (s 257(1)) |
| Sch 1 | | 1 Dec 2022 (SI 2022/906) |
| Sch 2 | paras 1–14 | 1 Dec 2022 (SI 2022/906) |
| | para 15(1)–(9) | 1 Dec 2022 (SI 2022/906) |
| | para 15(10) | 5 Aug 2016 (for the purpose of making regulations) (SI 2016/813) |
| | | 1 Dec 2022 (otherwise) (SI 2022/906) |
| | para 16 | 1 Dec 2022 (SI 2022/906) |
| | para 17 | 5 Aug 2016 (SI 2016/813) |
| Sch 3 | paras 1–9 | 1 Dec 2022 (SI 2022/906) |
| | para 10(1) | 1 Dec 2022 (SI 2022/906) |
| | para 10(2) | 5 Aug 2016 (for the purpose of making regulations) (SI 2016/813) |
| | | 1 Dec 2022 (otherwise) (SI 2022/906) |
| | para 10(3) | 1 Dec 2022 (SI 2022/906) |
| | paras 11–14 | 1 Dec 2022 (SI 2022/906) |
| | para 15(1), (2) | 1 Dec 2022 (SI 2022/906) |
| | para 15(3), (4) | 5 Aug 2016 (for the purpose of making regulations) (SI 2016/813) |
| | | 1 Dec 2022 (otherwise) (SI 2022/906) |
| | paras 16, 17 | 1 Dec 2022 (SI 2022/906) |
| Sch 4 | paras 1–3 | 1 Dec 2022 (SI 2022/906) |
| | para 4(1)–(6) | 1 Dec 2022 (SI 2022/906) |
| | para 4(7), (8) | 5 Aug 2016 (for the purpose of making regulations) (SI 2016/813) |
| | | 1 Dec 2022 (otherwise) (SI 2022/906) |
| | paras 5–9 | 1 Dec 2022 (SI 2022/906) |
| Sch 5 | para 1(1)–(5) | 1 Dec 2022 (SI 2022/906) |
| | para 1(6) | 5 Aug 2016 (for the purpose of making regulations) (SI 2016/813) |
| | | 1 Dec 2022 (otherwise) (SI 2022/906) |
| | paras 2–5 | 1 Dec 2022 (SI 2022/906) |
| Sch 6 | | 1 Dec 2022 (SI 2022/906) |
| Sch 7 | paras 1–4 | 1 Dec 2022 (SI 2022/906) |
| | para 5(1)–(6) | 1 Dec 2022 (SI 2022/906) |
| | para 5(7), (8) | 5 Aug 2016 (for the purpose of making regulations) (SI 2016/813) |
| | | 1 Dec 2022 (otherwise) (SI 2022/906) |
| | paras 6–8 | 1 Dec 2022 (SI 2022/906) |
| Schs 8–11 | | 1 Dec 2022 (SI 2022/906) |
| Sch 12 | paras 1–14 | 1 Dec 2022 (SI 2022/906) |
| | para 15(1) | 1 Dec 2022 (SI 2022/906) |
| | para 15(2) | 5 Aug 2016 (for the purpose of making regulations) (SI 2016/813) |
| | | 1 Dec 2022 (otherwise) (SI 2022/906) |
| | para 15(3) | 1 Dec 2022 (SI 2022/906) |
| | paras 16–32 | 1 Dec 2022 (SI 2022/906) |
| | para 33 | 5 Aug 2016 (for the purpose of making regulations) (SI 2016/813) |
| | | 1 Dec 2022 (otherwise) (SI 2022/906) |

---

**Riot Compensation Act 2016 (c 8)**

*RA:* 23 Mar 2016

*Commencement provisions*: s 12(1), (2); Riot Compensation Act 2016 (Commencement) Regulations 2017, SI 2017/379

| | |
|---|---|
| 1–10 | 6 Apr 2017 (SI 2017/379) |
| 11, 12 | 23 Mar 2016 (s 12(2)) |
| Schedule | 6 Apr 2017 (SI 2017/379) |

---

**Safeguarding and Clergy Discipline Measure 2016 (No 1)**

*RA:* 16 Mar 2016

*Commencement provisions*: s 12(2)–(5); Safeguarding and Clergy Discipline Measure 2016 (Commencement No 1) Order 2016, SI 2016/552; Safeguarding and Clergy Discipline Measure 2016 (Commencement No 2) Order 2016, SI 2016/938; Safeguarding and Clergy Discipline Measure 2016 (Commencement No 3) Order 2016, SI 2016/1213

**Safeguarding and Clergy Discipline Measure 2016 (No 1)**—*contd*

| | |
|---|---|
| 1–3 | 1 Jan 2017 (SI 2016/1213) |
| 4 | 16 May 2016 (SI 2016/552) |
| 5, 6 | 1 Oct 2016 (SI 2016/938) |
| 7, 8 | 1 Jan 2017 (SI 2016/1213) |
| 9 | 16 May 2016 (SI 2016/552) |
| 10 | 1 Jan 2017 (SI 2016/1213) |
| 11 | 16 May 2016 (SI 2016/552) |
| 12 | 23 Mar 2016 (s 12(2)) |

**Scotland Act 2016 (c 11)**

*RA:* 23 Mar 16

*Commencement provisions*: s 72; Scotland Act 2016 (Commencement No 1) Regulations 2016, SI 2016/759; Scotland Act 2016 (Commencement No 2) Regulations 2016, SI 2016/1161; Scotland Act 2016 (Commencement No 3) Regulations 2016, SI 2016/1178; Scotland Act 2016 (Commencement No 4, Transitional and Savings) Regulations 2017, SI 2017/300; Scotland Act 2016 (Commencement No 5) Regulations 2017, SI 2017/455, as amended by SI 2022/409; Scotland Act 2016 (Commencement No 6) Regulations 2017, SI 2017/608; Scotland Act 2016 (Commencement No 7) Regulations 2017, SI 2017/1157; Scotland Act 2016 (Commencement No 8) Regulations 2018, SI 2018/163; Scotland Act 2016 (Commencement No 9) Regulations 2018, SI 2018/1364

| | | |
|---|---|---|
| 1 | | 23 Mar 2016 (s 72(1)(a)) |
| 2 | | 23 May 2016 (s 72(7)) |
| 3–12 | | 18 May 2017 (SI 2017/608) |
| 13 | | 30 Nov 2016 (SI 2016/1161) |
| 14, 15 | | *Not yet in force* |
| 16 | | 23 May 2016 (s 72(3)) |
| 17 | (1), (2) | 23 May 2016 (s 72(3)) |
| | (3)–(6) | *Not yet in force* |
| | (7) | 23 May 2016 (s 72(3)) |
| 18 | (1), (2) | 23 May 2016 (s 72(3)) |
| | (3) | *Not yet in force* |
| | (4) | See Sch 1 below |
| 19 | | 23 May 2016 (s 72(3)) |
| 20, 21 | | 1 Apr 2017 (SI 2016/1178) |
| 22 | (1) | See sub-ss (2)–(4) below |
| | (2) | 17 May 2017 (SI 2017/455) |
| | (3) | 5 Sep 2016 (SI 2016/759) |
| | (4) | 17 May 2017 (SI 2017/455) |
| 23 | (1) | See sub-ss (2)–(5) below |
| | (2) | 17 May 2017 (SI 2017/455) |
| | (3) | 5 Sep 2016 (SI 2016/759) |
| | (4) | 17 May 2017 (SI 2017/455) |
| | (5) | 1 Apr 2023 (SI 2017/455) |
| 24 | | 5 Sep 2016 (SI 2016/759) |
| 25 | | 1 Apr 2017 (SI 2016/759) |
| 26 | | 5 Sep 2016 (SI 2016/759) |
| 27 | | 8 Feb 2019 (SI 2018/1364) |
| 28–35 | | 5 Sep 2016 (SI 2016/759) |
| 36 | (1) | 23 Mar 2016 (s 72(1)(b)) |
| | (2)–(4) | *Not yet in force*[1] |
| | (5), (6) | 23 Mar 2016 (s 72(1)(b)) |
| | (7), (8) | *Not yet in force*[1] |
| | (9)–(12) | 23 Mar 2016 (s 72(1)(b)) |
| | (13)–(15) | *Not yet in force*[1] |
| 37–43 | | 23 May 2016 (s 72(7)) |
| 44 | (1) | 23 May 2016 (s 72(7)) |
| | (2) | See Sch 2 below |
| 45, 46 | | 23 May 2016 (s 72(7)) |

## Scotland Act 2016 (c 11)—*contd*

| | |
|---|---|
| 47, 48 | 9 Feb 2018 (SI 2018/163) |
| 49 | 29 Nov 2017 (SI 2017/1157) |
| 50–57 | 23 May 2016 (s 72(7)) |
| 58 | 1 Dec 2017 (for the purpose of making regulations to come into force not earlier than 1 Apr 2018) (SI 2017/1157) |
| | 1 Apr 2018 (otherwise) (SI 2017/1157) |
| 59, 60 | 1 Dec 2017 (for the purpose of making regulations to come into force not earlier than 1 Oct 2018) (SI 2017/1157) |
| | 1 Oct 2018 (otherwise) (SI 2017/1157) |
| 61 | 23 May 2016 (s 72(7)) |
| 62 | 1 Apr 2017 (SI 2017/300)[2] |
| 63, 64 | 23 May 2016 (s 72(7)) |
| 65 | 18 Aug 2016 (SI 2016/759) |
| 66 | 23 May 2016 (s 72(7)) |
| 67 | 1 Apr 2017 (SI 2016/1178) |
| 68–73 | 23 Mar 2016 (s 72(1)(c)) |
| Sch 1 | *Not yet in force* |
| Sch 2 | 23 May 2016 (s 72(7)) |

[1]     These provisions come into force on the date specified under the Scotland Act 1998, s 90B(20)

[2]     For transitional and saving provisions, see SI 2017/300, regs 4–6

## Scottish Elections (Dates) Act 2016 (asp 13)

*RA:* 30 Mar 2016

*Commencement provisions:* s 3

Whole Act in force 31 Mar 2016 (s 3)

## Scottish Fiscal Commission Act 2016 (asp 17)

*RA:* 14 Apr 2016

*Commencement provisions:* s 31; Scottish Fiscal Commission Act 2016 (Commencement and Transitory Provision) Regulations 2016, SSI 2016/326

| | |
|---|---|
| 1–7 | 1 Apr 2017 (SSI 2016/326) |
| 8 | 9 Nov 2016 (SSI 2016/326)[1] |
| 9–31 | 1 Apr 2017 (SSI 2016/326) |
| 30–32 | 15 Apr 2016 (s 31(1)) |

[1]     For a transitory provision, see SSI 2016/326, reg 3

## Smoking Prohibition (Children in Motor Vehicles) (Scotland) Act 2016 (asp 3)

*RA:* 21 Jan 2016

*Commencement provisions:* s 6

| | | |
|---|---|---|
| 1–3 | | *Not yet in force* |
| 4–7 | | 22 Jan 2016 (s 6(1)) |
| Schedule | paras 1–10 | *Not yet in force* |
| | paras 11, 12 | 22 Jan 2016 (s 6(1)) |

## Succession (Scotland) Act 2016 (asp 7)

*RA:* 3 Mar 2016

*Commencement provisions*: s 31; Succession (Scotland) Act 2016 (Commencement, Transitional and Saving
   Provisions) Regulations 2016, SSI 2016/210

| | | |
|---|---|---|
| 1–4 | | 1 Nov 2016 (SSI 2016/210) |
| 5, 6 | | 1 Nov 2016 (SSI 2016/210)[1] |
| 7 | | 1 Nov 2016 (SSI 2016/210) |
| 8 | | 1 Nov 2016 (SSI 2016/210)[1] |
| 9–17 | | 1 Nov 2016 (SSI 2016/210) |
| 18–22 | | 4 Mar 2016 (s 31(1)) |
| 23–24 | | 1 Nov 2016 (SSI 2016/210) |
| 25 | | 1 Nov 2016 (SSI 2016/210)[1] |
| 26–28 | | 1 Nov 2016 (SSI 2016/210) |
| 29 | (1) | 1 Nov 2016 (SSI 2016/210)[1] |
| | (2) | See Schedule below |
| 30–32 | | 4 Mar 2016 (s 31(1)) |
| Schedule | para 1(1)–(4) | 1 Nov 2016 (SSI 2016/210) |
| | para 1(5)(a), (b) | 1 Nov 2016 (SSI 2016/210)[1] |
| | para 1(5)(c) | 1 Nov 2016 (SSI 2016/210) |
| | para 2 | 1 Nov 2016 (SSI 2016/210)[1] |
| | paras 3, 4 | 1 Nov 2016 (SSI 2016/210) |

[1]   For transitional provisions and savings, see SSI 2016/210, reg 3

---

## Supply and Appropriation (Anticipation and Adjustments) Act 2016 (c 3)

*RA:* 16 Mar 2016

Whole Act in force 16 Mar 2016 (RA)

---

## Supply and Appropriation (Main Estimates) Act 2016 (c 23)

*RA:* 20 Jul 2016

Whole Act in force 20 Jul 2016 (RA)

---

## Tax Collection and Management (Wales) Act 2016 (anaw 6)

*RA:* 25 Apr 2016

*Commencement provisions*: s 194; Tax Collection and Management (Wales) Act 2016 (Commencement No 1)
   Order 2017, SI 2017/954; Tax Collection and Management (Wales) Act 2016 (Commencement No 2)
   Order 2018, SI 2018/33

| | | |
|---|---|---|
| 1 | | 26 Apr 2016 (s 194(1)(a)) |
| 2–20 | | 18 Oct 2017 (SI 2017/954) |
| 21 | (1) | 18 Oct 2017 (SI 2017/954) |
| | (2) | 1 Apr 2018 (SI 2018/33) |
| 22, 23 | | 18 Oct 2017 (SI 2017/954) |
| 24 | | 1 Apr 2018 (SI 2018/33) |
| 25, 26 | | 25 Jan 2018 (SI 2018/33) |
| 27 | | 18 Oct 2017 (SI 2017/954) |
| 28 | | 1 Apr 2018 (SI 2018/33) |
| 29 | | 18 Oct 2017 (SI 2017/954) |
| 30–32 | | 1 Apr 2018 (SI 2018/33) |
| 33–35 | | 18 Oct 2017 (SI 2017/954) |
| 36 | | 1 Apr 2018 (SI 2018/33) |

**Tax Collection and Management (Wales) Act 2016 (anaw 6)**—*contd*

| | | |
|---|---|---|
| 37 | | 26 Apr 2016 (s 194(1)(b)) |
| 38–65 | | 1 Apr 2018 (SI 2018/33) |
| 66 | | 18 Oct 2017 (SI 2017/954) |
| 67, 68 | | 1 Apr 2018 (SI 2018/33) |
| 69 | (1), (2) | 1 Apr 2018 (SI 2018/33) |
| | (3), (4) | 18 Oct 2017 (SI 2017/954) |
| | (5) | 1 Apr 2018 (SI 2018/33) |
| 70–81 | | 1 Apr 2018 (SI 2018/33) |
| 82 | | 26 Apr 2016 (s 194(1)(b)) |
| 83–100 | | 25 Jan 2018 (SI 2018/33) |
| 101 | (1), (2) | 25 Jan 2018 (SI 2018/33) |
| | (3), (4) | 18 Oct 2017 (SI 2017/954) |
| 102–116 | | 25 Jan 2018 (SI 2018/33) |
| 117 | | 26 Apr 2016 (s 194(1)(b)) |
| 118–145 | | 1 Apr 2018 (SI 2018/33) |
| 146–155 | | 25 Jan 2018 (SI 2018/33) |
| 156–159 | | 1 Apr 2018 (SI 2018/33) |
| 160–162 | | 25 Jan 2018 (SI 2018/33) |
| 163 | | 18 Oct 2017 (SI 2017/954) |
| 164–166 | | 25 Jan 2018 (SI 2018/33) |
| 167 | | 18 Oct 2017 (SI 2017/954) |
| 168–170 | | 25 Jan 2018 (SI 2018/33) |
| 171 | | 26 Apr 2016 (s 194(1)(b)) |
| 172–187 | | 25 Jan 2018 (SI 2018/33) |
| 188–195 | | 26 Apr 2016 (s 194(1)(c)) |

**Trade Union Act 2016 (c 15)**

*RA:* 4 May 2016

*Commencement provisions*: s 25; Trade Union Act 2016 (Commencement No 1) Regulations 2016, SI 2016/1051; Trade Union Act 2016 (Commencement No 2) Regulations 2016, SI 2016/1170; Trade Union Act 2016 (Commencement No 3 and Transitional) Regulations 2017, SI 2017/139; Trade Union Act 2016 (Commencement No 4 and Transitional) Regulations 2021, SI 2021/1373

| | | |
|---|---|---|
| 1 | | 3 Nov 2016 (SI 2016/1051) |
| 2 | | 1 Mar 2017 (SI 2017/139) |
| 3 | | 5 Dec 2016 (for the purpose of enabling the exercise of the power to make regulations under Trade Union and Labour Relations (Consolidation) Act 1992, s 226(2D)) (SI 2016/1170) |
| | | 1 Mar 2017 (otherwise) (SI 2017/139) |
| 4 | | 3 Nov 2016 (SI 2016/1051) |
| 5–9 | | 1 Mar 2017 (SI 2017/139) |
| 10 | | 1 Mar 2017 (SI 2017/139)[1] |
| 11 | | 5 Dec 2016 (for the purpose of enabling the exercise the power to make regulations under sub-ss (6)–(8)) (SI 2016/1170) |
| | | 1 Mar 2017 (otherwise) (SI 2017/139) |
| 12, 13 | | 1 Mar 2017 (SI 2017/139) |
| 14 | | *Not yet in force* |
| 15 | | 1 Mar 2017 (for the purpose of making regulations under Trade Union and Labour Relations (Consolidation) Act 1992, s 116B) (SI 2017/139) |
| | | *Not yet in force (otherwise)* |
| 16 | | 1 Apr 2022 (SI 2021/1373) |
| 17 | (1) | 8 Dec 2021 (for the purpose of enabling the exercise of the power to make regulations under Trade Union and Labour Relations (Consolidation) Act 1992, s 256D, Sch A4, paras 6–8, in so far as relates to the insertion of s 256C of the 1992 Act) (SI 2021/1373)[2] |
| | | 1 Apr 2022 (otherwise) (SI 2021/1373)[2] |

**Trade Union Act 2016 (c 15)**—*contd*

| | | |
|---|---|---|
| | (2) | See Sch 1 below |
| | (3) | See Sch 2 below |
| 18 | | 1 Mar 2017 (SI 2017/139) |
| 19 | (1) | 8 Dec 2021 (for the purpose of enabling the exercise of the power to make regulations under Trade Union and Labour Relations (Consolidation) Act 1992, s 256D, Sch A4, paras 6–8) (SI 2021/1373) |
| | | 1 Apr 2022 (otherwise) (SI 2021/1373) |
| | (2) | See Sch 3 below |
| | (3) | 1 Apr 2022 (SI 2021/1373) |
| | (4) | 1 Apr 2022 (SI 2021/1373)[2] |
| 20 | | 8 Dec 2021 (SI 2021/1373) |
| 21 | | 1 Apr 2022 (SI 2021/1373)[2] |
| 22 | | See Sch 4 below |
| 23–26 | | 4 May 2016 (s 25(1)) |
| Sch 1 | | 8 Dec 2021 (for the purpose of enabling the exercise of the power to make regulations under Trade Union and Labour Relations (Consolidation) Act 1992, s 256D, Sch A4, paras 6–8, in so far as relates to the insertion of Sch A3, para 5(1) to the 1992 Act) (SI 2021/1373)[2] |
| | | 1 Apr 2022 (otherwise) (SI 2021/1373)[2] |
| Sch 2 | paras 1–6 | 1 Apr 2022 (SI 2021/1373)[2] |
| | para 7(1) | See sub-paras (2)–(5) below |
| | para 7(2) | 1 Apr 2022 (SI 2021/1373)[2] |
| | para 7(3) | 8 Dec 2021 (for the purpose of enabling the exercise of the power to make regulations under Trade Union and Labour Relations (Consolidation) Act 1992, s 256D, Sch A4, paras 6–8, in so far as relates to the amendment of s 82(2A) of the 1992 Act) (SI 2021/1373)[2] |
| | | 1 Apr 2022 (otherwise) (SI 2021/1373)[2] |
| | para 7(4), (5) | 1 Apr 2022 (SI 2021/1373)[2] |
| | para 8 | 1 Apr 2022 (SI 2021/1373)[2] |
| Sch 3 | | 8 Dec 2021 (for the purpose of enabling the exercise of the power to make regulations under Trade Union and Labour Relations (Consolidation) Act 1992, s 256D, Sch A4, paras 6–8) (SI 2021/1373) |
| | | 1 Apr 2022 (otherwise) (SI 2021/1373) |
| Sch 4 | paras 1–3 | 1 Apr 2022 (SI 2021/1373) |
| | para 4 | 1 Mar 2017 (SI 2017/139) |
| | paras 5–11 | 1 Mar 2017 (SI 2017/139)[1] |
| | paras 12–14 | 1 Mar 2017 (SI 2017/139) |
| | paras 15, 16 | 1 Apr 2022 (SI 2021/1373) |
| | paras 17–20, 21(a) | 1 Mar 2017 (SI 2017/139) |
| | para 21(b) | 1 Apr 2022 (SI 2021/1373) |
| | para 21(c) | 1 Mar 2017 (SI 2017/139) |

[1]   For transitional provisions, see SI 2017/139, regs 3, 4

[2]   For transitional provisions, see SI 2021/1373, regs 5–16

---

**Transport for London Act 2016 (c i)**

*RA:* 4 May 2016

*Commencement provisions:* s 1

| | |
|---|---|
| 1–3 | 4 Jul 2016 (s 1(1)) |
| 4 | *Not yet in force* |
| 5–7 | 4 Jul 2016 (s 1(1)) |
| Schedule | *Not yet in force* |

---

**See Halsbury's Statutes Citator for amendments to these Acts**

**Welfare Reform and Work Act 2016 (c 7)**

*RA:* 16 Mar 2016

*Commencement provisions:* s 36; Welfare Reform and Work Act 2016 (Commencement No 1)
Regulations 2016, SI 2016/394; Welfare Reform and Work Act 2016 (Commencement No 2)
Regulations 2016, SI 2016/610; Welfare Reform and Work Act 2016 (Commencement No 3)
Regulations 2016, SI 2016/910; Pensions Act 2014 (Commencement No 9) and the Welfare Reform
and Work Act 2016 (Commencement No 4) Regulations 2017, SI 2017/111; Welfare Reform and
Work Act 2016 (Commencement No 5) Regulations 2017, SI 2017/802; Welfare Reform and Work
Act 2016 (Commencement No 6 and Transitional Provision) Regulations 2018, SI 2018/438

| | | |
|---|---|---|
| 1, 2 | | 16 May 2016 (s 36(2)(a), (b)) |
| 3 | | 16 May 2016 (SI 2016/394) |
| 4–7 | | 16 May 2016 (s 36(2)(c), (d)) |
| 8 | | 16 Mar 2016 (for the purpose of making regulations) (s 36(3)(a)) |
| | | 7 Nov 2016 (otherwise) (SI 2016/910)[1] |
| 9 | (1)–(5) | 16 Mar 2016 (for the purpose of making regulations) (s 36(3)(a)) |
| | | 7 Nov 2016 (otherwise) (SI 2016/910) |
| | (6), (7) | 16 Mar 2016 (s 36(1)(a)) |
| 10 | | 9 Jun 2016 (SI 2016/610) |
| 11, 12 | | 16 Mar 2016 (s 36(1)(b)) |
| 13 | | 16 Mar 2016 (for the purpose of making regulations) (s 36(4)(a)) |
| | | 6 Apr 2017 (otherwise) (s 36(4)(b)) |
| 14 | (1)–(5) | 6 Apr 2017 (SI 2017/111) |
| | (6)–(8) | 8 Feb 2017 (SI 2017/111) |
| 15 | (1)–(3) | 3 Apr 2017 (SI 2017/111) |
| | (4)–(7) | 8 Feb 2017 (SI 2017/111) |
| 16–19 | | 3 Apr 2017 (SI 2017/111) |
| 20 | (1) | 6 Apr 2018 (SI 2018/438)[2] |
| | (2)–(7) | 27 Jul 2017 (SI 2017/802) |
| | (8), (9) | 6 Apr 2018 (SI 2018/438)[2] |
| | (10) | 27 Jul 2017 (SI 2017/802) |
| | (11) | 6 Apr 2018 (SI 2018/438)[2] |
| 21 | | 3 Apr 2017 (SI 2017/111) |
| 22 | | 30 May 2016 (SI 2016/394) |
| 23 | (1), (2) | 16 Mar 2016 (for the purpose of making regulations) (s 36(5)(a)) |
| | | 1 Apr 2016 (otherwise) (SI 2016/394) |
| | (3), (4) | 16 Mar 2016 (s 36(1)(c)) |
| | (5)–(9) | 16 Mar 2016 (for the purpose of making regulations) (s 36(5)(a)) |
| | | 1 Apr 2016 (SI 2016/394) |
| 24 | | 16 Mar 2016 (for the purpose of making regulations) (s 36(5)(a)) |
| | | 1 Apr 2016 (otherwise) (SI 2016/394) |
| 25 | | 16 Mar 2016 (s 36(1)(d)) |
| 26 | | See Sch 2 below |
| 27–32 | | 16 Mar 2016 (for the purpose of making regulations) (s 36(5)(a)) |
| | | 1 Apr 2016 (otherwise) (SI 2016/394) |
| 33 | (1), (2) | 16 Mar 2016 (for the purpose of making regulations) (s 36(5)(a)) |
| | | 1 Apr 2016 (otherwise) (SI 2016/394) |
| | (3)(a) | 16 Mar 2016 (for the purpose of making regulations) (s 36(5)(a)) |
| | | 1 Apr 2016 (otherwise) (SI 2016/394) |
| | (3)(b), (c) | 16 Mar 2016 (for the purpose of making regulations) (s 36(3)(a)) |
| | | *Not yet in force* (otherwise) |
| | (4)–(9) | 16 Mar 2016 (for the purpose of making regulations) (s 36(5)(a)) |
| | | 1 Apr 2016 (otherwise) (SI 2016/394) |
| 34–37 | | 16 Mar 2016 (s 36(1)(f)) |
| Sch 1 | | 16 Mar 2016 (s 36(1)(a)) |
| Sch 2 | paras 1–5 | 16 Mar 2016 (for the purpose of making regulations) (s 36(5)(a)) |
| | | 1 Apr 2016 (otherwise) (SI 2016/394) |
| | paras 6 | 16 Mar 2016 (s 36(1)(e)) |
| | para 7 | 16 Mar 2016 (for the purpose of making regulations) (s 36(5)(a)) |
| | | 1 Apr 2016 (otherwise) (SI 2016/394) |

**Welfare Reform and Work Act 2016 (c 7)**—*contd*

| | |
|---|---|
| para 8(1) | 16 Mar 2016 (for the purpose of making regulations) (s 36(5)(a)) |
| | 18 Mar 2016 (otherwise) (SI 2016/394) |
| para 8(2) | 16 Mar 2016 (for the purpose of making regulations) (s 36(5)(a)) |
| | 1 Apr 2016 (otherwise) (SI 2016/394) |
| para 9 | 16 Mar 2016 (s 36(1)(e)) |

[1] For savings, see SI 2016/910, reg 2(2)

[2] For transitional provisions, see SI 2018/438, reg 2(2), (3)

# 2017 Acts

## Air Departure Tax (Scotland) Act 2017 (asp 2)

*RA:* 25 Jul 2017

*Commencement provisions:* s 48

| | |
|---|---|
| 1–41 | *Not yet in force* |
| 42–44 | 25 Jul 2017 (s 48(1)) |
| 45 | *Not yet in force* |
| 46–49 | 25 Jul 2017 (s 48(1)) |
| Schs 1–3 | *Not yet in force* |

## Air Travel Organisers' Licensing Act 2017 (c 33)

*RA:* 16 Nov 2017

*Commencement provisions:* s 4; Air Travel Organisers' Licensing Act 2017 (Commencement) Regulations 2018, SI 2018/669

| | |
|---|---|
| 1, 2 | 16 Nov 2017 (s 4(2)) |
| 3 | 1 Jul 2018 (SI 2018/669) |
| 4 | 16 Nov 2017 (s 4(2)) |

## Broadcasting (Radio Multiplex Services) Act 2017 (c 12)

*RA:* 27 Apr 2017

*Commencement provisions:* s 2(3), (4)

| | |
|---|---|
| 1 | 27 Jun 2017 (s 2(3)) |
| 2 | 27 Apr 2017 (s 2(4)) |

## Budget (Scotland) Act 2017 (asp 1)

*RA:* 31 Mar 2017

*Commencement provisions:* s 10

Whole Act in force 1 Apr 2017 (s 10)

## Bus Services Act 2017 (c 21)

*RA:* 27 Apr 2017

*Commencement provisions:* s 26; Bus Services Act 2017 (Commencement) Regulations 2018, SI 2018/758

| | |
|---|---|
| 1–16 | 27 Apr 2017 (for the purposes of making regulations or orders) (s 26(3)(a)) |
| | 27 Jun 2017 (otherwise) (s 26(3)(b)) |
| 17 | 26 Jun 2018 (SI 2018/758) |

**Bus Services Act 2017 (c 21)**—*contd*

| | |
|---|---|
| 18–22 | 27 Apr 2017 (for the purposes of making regulations or orders) (s 26(3)(a)) |
| | 27 Jun 2017 (otherwise) (s 26(3)(b)) |
| 23–27 | 27 Apr 2017 (s 26(1)) |
| Schs 1–4 | 27 Apr 2017 (for the purposes of making regulations or orders) (s 26(3)(a)) |
| | 27 Jun 2017 (otherwise) (s 26(3)(b)) |

---

**Child Poverty (Scotland) Act 2017 (asp 6)**

*RA:* 18 Dec 2017

*Commencement provisions*: s 16

| | |
|---|---|
| 1–7 | 18 Feb 2018 (s 6(3)) |
| 8 | 1 Jul 2019 (s 6(2)) |
| 9–13 | 18 Feb 2018 (s 6(3)) |
| 14 | 19 Dec 2017 (s 6(1)) |
| 15 | 18 Feb 2018 (s 6(3)) |
| 16, 17 | 19 Dec 2017 (s 6(1)) |
| Schedule | 1 Jul 2019 (s 6(2)) |

---

**Children and Social Work Act 2017 (c 16)**

*RA:* 27 Apr 2017

*Commencement provisions*: s 70; Children and Social Work Act 2017 (Commencement No 1) Regulations 2017, SI 2017/918; Children and Social Work Act 2017 (Commencement No 2) Regulations 2017, SI 2017/1217; Children and Social Work Act 2017 (Commencement No 3) Regulations 2018, SI 2018/346; Children and Social Work Act 2017 (Commencement No 4 and Transitional and Saving Provisions) Regulations 2018, SI 2018/497; Children and Social Work Act 2017 (Commencement No 5) Regulations 2018, SI 2018/945; Children and Social Work Act 2017 (Commencement No 6 and Saving Provision) Regulations 2019, SI 2019/1436

| | |
|---|---|
| 1–3 | 1 Apr 2018 (SI 2018/346) |
| 4–7 | 1 Sep 2018 (SI 2018/497) |
| 8, 9 | 31 Oct 2017 (SI 2017/918) |
| 10 | See Sch 1 below |
| 11 | 1 Apr 2018 (SI 2018/346) |
| 12 | 29 Jun 2018 (SI 2018/497) |
| 13 | 19 Mar 2018 (so far as inserts Children Act 2004, s 16B(1), (6)) (SI 2018/346) |
| | 29 Jun 2018 (otherwise) (SI 2018/497) |
| 14, 15 | 29 Jun 2018 (SI 2018/497) |
| 16 | 19 Mar 2018 (so far as inserts Children Act 2004, s 16E(3)) (SI 2018/346) |
| | 29 Jun 2018 (otherwise) (SI 2018/497) |
| 17 | 19 Mar 2018 (so far as inserts Children Act 2004, s 16F(6)) (SI 2018/346) |
| | 29 Jun 2018 (otherwise) (SI 2018/497) |
| 18 | 19 Mar 2018 (so far as inserts Children Act 2004, s 16G(5), (6)) (SI 2018/346) |
| | 29 Jun 2018 (otherwise) (SI 2018/497)[1] |
| 19–28 | 29 Jun 2018 (SI 2018/497) |
| 29 | 19 Mar 2018 (SI 2018/346) |
| 30 | 29 Sep 2020 (SI 2018/497)[1, 2] |
| 31 | 29 Jun 2018 (SI 2018/497)[1] |
| 32 | *Not yet in force* |
| 33 | 31 Oct 2017 (SI 2017/918) |
| 34, 35 | 1 Apr 2018 (SI 2018/346) |

**Children and Social Work Act 2017 (c 16)**—*contd*

| | | |
|---|---|---|
| 36 | (1), (2) | 1 Apr 2018 (SI 2018/346) |
| | (3) | See Sch 3 below |
| | (4), (5) | 1 Apr 2018 (SI 2018/346) |
| 37 | | 2 Dec 2019 (SI 2019/1436) |
| 38 | | 1 Apr 2018 (SI 2018/346) |
| 39 | (1) | 2 Dec 2019 (SI 2019/1436)[3] |
| | (2)–(4) | 1 Apr 2018 (SI 2018/346) |
| 40 | | 1 Apr 2018 (SI 2018/346) |
| 41 | (1), (2) | 2 Dec 2019 (SI 2019/1436) |
| | (3), (4) | 1 Apr 2018 (SI 2018/346) |
| | (5) | 2 Dec 2019 (SI 2019/1436) |
| 42 | | 31 Oct 2017 (SI 2017/918) |
| 43 | (1) | 2 Dec 2019 (SI 2019/1436) |
| | (2)–(6) | 1 Apr 2018 (SI 2018/346) |
| 44 | (1) | 2 Dec 2019 (SI 2019/1436) |
| | (2)–(5) | 1 Apr 2018 (SI 2018/346) |
| 45 | | 1 Apr 2018 (SI 2018/346) |
| 46, 47 | | 2 Dec 2019 (SI 2019/1436) |
| 48, 49 | | 1 Apr 2018 (SI 2018/346) |
| 50 | (1) | 1 Apr 2018 (SI 2018/346) |
| | (2) | 2 Dec 2019 (SI 2019/1436) |
| | (3)–(7) | 1 Apr 2018 (SI 2018/346) |
| 51 | | 1 Apr 2018 (SI 2018/346) |
| 52 | (1) | 2 Dec 2019 (SI 2019/1436) |
| | (2) | 1 Apr 2018 (SI 2018/346) |
| 53 | (1) | 1 Apr 2018 (SI 2018/346) |
| | (2) | 2 Dec 2019 (SI 2019/1436) |
| 54 | | 2 Dec 2019 (SI 2019/1436) |
| 55 | (1) | 2 Dec 2019 (SI 2019/1436) |
| | (2), (3) | 1 Apr 2018 (SI 2018/346) |
| 56 | | See Sch 4 below |
| 57 | | 1 Apr 2018 (SI 2018/346) |
| 58 | | 15 Jan 2018 (SI 2017/1217) |
| 59, 60 | | 1 Apr 2018 (SI 2018/346) |
| 61–64 | | 2 Dec 2019 (SI 2019/1436) |
| 65–71 | | 27 Apr 2017 (s 70(1)(b)) |
| Sch 1 | | 27 Apr 2017 (s 70(1)(a)) |
| Sch 2 | paras 1–6 | 1 Apr 2018 (SI 2018/346) |
| | paras 7–9 | 1 Sep 2018 (SI 2018/497)[1] |
| Sch 3 | paras 1–12 | 1 Apr 2018 (SI 2018/346) |
| | paras 13–20 | 1 Sep 2018 (SI 2018/945) |
| | paras 21–24 | 1 Apr 2018 (SI 2018/346) |
| Sch 4 | para 1 | See paras 2–16 below |
| | paras 2, 3 | 2 Dec 2019 (SI 2019/1436) |
| | para 4 | 15 Jan 2018 (so far as inserts National Health Service Reform and Health Care Professions Act 2002, s 25AA(12)) (SI 2017/1217) |
| | | 1 Apr 2018 (otherwise) (SI 2018/346) |
| | paras 5–14 | 2 Dec 2019 (SI 2019/1436) |
| | para 15(1) | See paras 15(2), (3) below |
| | para 15(2) | 1 Apr 2018 (for the purpose of making regulations) (SI 2018/346) |
| | | 2 Dec 2019 (otherwise) (SI 2019/1436) |
| | para 15(3) | 2 Dec 2019 (SI 2019/1436) |
| | para 16 | 1 Apr 2018 (SI 2018/346) |
| Sch 5 | | 2 Dec 2019 (SI 2019/1436) |

[1]    For transitional and saving provisions, see SI 2018/497, regs 5–11

[2]    By SI 2018/497, reg 8, for the purpose of giving effect to the Children Act 2004, ss 16E–16g, s 30 comes into force in a local authority area on its implementation date and comes fully into force on 29 Sep 2020

**Children and Social Work Act 2017 (c 16)**—*contd*
3   For savings, see SI 2019/1436, reg 3

---

**Commonwealth Development Corporation Act 2017 (c 5)**

*RA:* 23 Feb 2017

*Commencement provisions:* s 2(3)

Whole Act in force 23 Feb 2017  (s 2(3))

---

**Contract (Third Party Rights) (Scotland) Act 2017 (asp 5)**

*RA:* 30 Oct 2017

*Commencement provisions:* s 13; Contract (Third Party Rights) (Scotland) Act 2017 (Commencement) Regulations 2018, SSI 2018/8

| | |
|---|---|
| 1–11 | 26 Feb 2018 |
| 12–14 | 31 Oct 2017 (s 13(1)) |

---

**Criminal Finances Act 2017 (c 22)**

*RA:* 27 Apr 2017

*Commencement provisions:* s 58; Criminal Finances Act 2017 (Commencement No 1) Regulations 2017, SI 2017/739; Criminal Finances Act 2017 (Commencement No 2 and Transitional Provisions) Regulations 2017, SI 2017/991; Criminal Finances Act 2017 (Commencement No 3) Regulations 2017, SI 2017/1028; Criminal Finances Act 2017 (Commencement) (Scotland) Regulations 2017, SI 2017/456; Criminal Finances Act 2017 (Commencement No 4) Regulations 2018, SI 2018/78; Criminal Finances (2017 Act) (Commencement) Regulations (Northern Ireland) 2021, SR 2021/167; Criminal Finances Act 2017 (Commencement No. 5) Regulations 2021, SI 2021/724

| | |
|---|---|
| 1–3 | 31 Jan 2018 (E) (W) (SI 2018/78) |
| | 28 Jun 2021 (NI) (SI 2021/724) |
| 4–6 | 31 Jan 2018 (SI 2018/78) |
| 7 | 31 Jan 2018 (E) (W) (SI 2018/78) |
| | 28 Jun 2021 (NI) (SI 2021/724) |
| 8 | 31 Jan 2018 (SI 2018/78) |
| 9 | 27 Jun 2017 (s 58(4)(a)) |
| 10 | 31 Oct 2017 (E) (W) (SI 2017/991)[1] |
| | 28 Jun 2021 (NI) (SI 2021/724) |
| 11 | 31 Oct 2017 (so far as applies to relevant undertakings within Proceeds of Crime Act 2002, s 339ZG(5)(b)) (SI 2017/991)[1] |
| | 31 Oct 2017 (so far as applies to relevant undertakings within Proceeds of Crime Act 2002, s 339ZG(5)(a)) (SI 2017/1028) |
| | *Not yet in force* (otherwise) |
| 12 | 27 Apr 2017 (so far as necessary for enabling the exercise of any power to make provision by subordinate legislation) (s 58(6)) |
| | 31 Oct 2017 (otherwise) (SI 2017/991)[1] |
| 13 | 31 Jan 2018 (E) (W) (SI 2018/78) |
| | 28 Jun 2021 (NI) (SI 2021/724) |
| 14 | 16 Apr 2018 (E) (W) (SI 2018/78) |
| | 28 Jun 2021 (NI) (SI 2021/724) |
| 15 | 31 Oct 2017 (so far as inserts Proceeds of Crime Act 2002, ss 303G–303H) (SI 2017/991) |
| | 30 Jan 2018 (so far as inserts Proceeds of Crime Act 2002, s 303E(4)) (E) (W) (S) (SI 2018/78) |
| | 16 Apr 2018 (otherwise) (E) (W) (S) (SI 2018/78) |
| | 28 Jun 2021 (otherwise) (NI) (SI 2021/724) |

**Criminal Finances Act 2017 (c 22)**—*contd*

| | | |
|---|---|---|
| 16 | | 30 Jan 2018 (so far as inserts Proceeds of Crime Act 2002, ss 303Z2(4), 303Z10) (E) (W) (S) (SI 2018/78) |
| | | 31 Jan 2018 (otherwise) (E) (W) (S) (SI 2018/78) |
| | | 28 Jun 2021 (otherwise) (NI) (SI 2021/724) |
| 17 | | See Sch 1 below |
| 18 | | 27 Jun 2017 (s 58(4)) |
| 19, 20 | | 31 Jan 2018 (E) (W) (S) (SI 2018/78) |
| | | 28 Jun 2021 (NI) (SI 2021/724) |
| 21 | (1)–(4) | 31 Jan 2018 (E) (W) (S) (SI 2018/78) |
| | | 28 Jun 2021 (NI) (SI 2021/724) |
| | (5) | 30 Jan 2018 (E) (W) (S) (SI 2018/78) |
| | | 28 Jun 2021 (NI) (SI 2021/724) |
| | (6)–(11) | 31 Jan 2018 (E) (W) (S) (SI 2018/78) |
| | | 28 Jun 2021 (NI) (SI 2021/724) |
| 22 | | 31 Jan 2018 (except so far as inserts Proceeds of Crime Act 2002, s 356A(3)(b), (4)(b)) (E) (W) (SI 2018/78) |
| | | 28 Jun 2021 (exception noted above)) (SI 2021/724) |
| 23 | | 31 Jan 2018 (except so far as inserts Proceeds of Crime Act 2002, s 453B(3)(b), (4)(b)) (E) (W) (SI 2018/78) |
| | | 28 Jun 2021 (exception noted above) (SI 2021/724) |
| 24 | | 31 Jan 2018 (E) (W) (S) (SI 2018/78) |
| | | 28 Jun 2021 (NI) (SI 2021/724) |
| 25 | | 31 Jan 2018 (except so far as inserts Proceeds of Crime Act 2002, s 453C(2)(c)) (E) (W) (S) (SI 2018/78) |
| | | 28 Jun 2021 (exception noted above) (SI 2021/724) |
| 26 | | 31 Jan 2018 (SI 2018/78) |
| 27 | | 28 Jun 2021 (SR 2021/167) |
| 28 | | 27 Apr 2017 (so far as necessary for enabling the exercise of any power to make provision by subordinate legislation) (s 58(6)) |
| | | 31 Jan 2018 (otherwise) (SSI 2017/456) |
| 29 | | 31 Jan 2018 (SI 2018/78) |
| 30 | | 31 Jan 2018 (SSI 2017/456) |
| 31 | (1) | See sub-ss (2)–(4) below |
| | (2) | 31 Jan 2018 (SI 2018/78) |
| | (3) | 28 Jun 2021 (SR 2021/167) |
| | (4) | 31 Jan 2018 (E) (W) (S) (SI 2018/78) |
| | | 28 Jun 2021 (NI) (SI 2021/724) |
| 32 | (1) | 31 Jan 2018 (E) (W) (S) (SI 2018/78) |
| | | 28 Jun 2021 (NI) (SI 2021/724) |
| | (2), (3) | 31 Jan 2018 (SI 2018/78) |
| | (4) | 31 Jan 2018 (SSI 2017/456) |
| | (5), (6) | 28 Jun 2021 (SR 2021/167) |
| | (7) | 31 Jan 2018 (E) (W) (S) (SI 2018/78) |
| | | 28 Jun 2021 (NI) (SI 2021/724) |
| 33 | | 31 Jan 2018 (E) (W) (S) (SI 2018/78) |
| | | 28 Jun 2021 (NI) (SI 2021/724) |
| 34 | (1) | See sub-ss (2)–(10) below |
| | (2) | 31 Jan 2018 (SI 2018/78) |
| | (3) | 31 Jan 2018 (SSI 2017/456) |
| | (4) | 28 Jun 2021 (SR 2021/167) |
| | (5)–(11) | 31 Jan 2018 (SI 2018/78) |
| 35 | | See Sch 2 below |
| 36 | | 31 Oct 2017 (so far as applies to a relevant undertaking within Terrorism Act 2000, s 21CF(6)(b)) (SI 2017/991) |
| | | 31 Oct 2017 (so far as applies to a relevant undertaking within Terrorism Act 2000, s 21CF(6)(a)) (SI 2017/1028) |
| | | *Not yet in force* (otherwise) |
| 37 | | 27 Apr 2017 (so far as necessary for enabling the exercise of any power to make provision by subordinate legislation) (s 58(6)) |

**Criminal Finances Act 2017 (c 22)**—*contd*

| | | |
|---|---|---|
| | | 31 Oct 2017 (otherwise) (SI 2017/991) |
| 38 | (1)–(3) | 31 Jan 2018 (SSI 2017/456) |
| | (4) | 30 Jan 2018 (so far as inserts Anti-terrorism, Crime and Security Act 2001, Sch 1, para 5A(10)) (SI 2018/78) |
| | | 31 Jan 2018 (otherwise) (SSI 2017/456) |
| | (5)–(7) | 31 Jan 2018 (otherwise) (SSI 2017/456) |
| 39 | | See Sch 3 below |
| 40 | | See Sch 4 below |
| 41, 42 | | 27 Jun 2017 (s 58(4)) |
| 43 | | 27 Apr 2017 (so far as necessary for enabling the exercise of any power to make provision by subordinate legislation) (s 58(6)) |
| | | 31 Oct 2017 (otherwise) (SI 2017/991) |
| 44–46 | | 30 Sep 2017 (SI 2017/739) |
| 47 | | 27 Apr 2017 (so far as necessary for enabling the exercise of any power to make provision by subordinate legislation) (s 58(6)) |
| | | 17 Jul 2017 (otherwise) (SI 2017/739) |
| 48–52 | | 30 Sep 2017 (SI 2017/739) |
| 53 | | See Sch 5 below |
| 54–59 | | 27 Apr 2017 (s 58(6)) |
| Sch 1 | para 1 | See paras 2–26 below |
| | para 2 | 31 Jan 2018 (in so far as inserts references to Proceeds of Crime Act 2002, Pt 2) (E) (W) (S) (SI 2018/78) |
| | | *Not yet in force* (otherwise) |
| | | 28 Jun 2021 (NI) (SI 2021/724) |
| | paras 3–5 | 31 Jan 2018 (SI 2018/78) |
| | para 6 | 31 Oct 2017 (SI 2017/991) |
| | paras 7–10 | 28 Jun 2021 (SI 2021/724) |
| | paras 11–13 | 31 Jan 2018 (E) (W) (S) (SI 2018/78) |
| | | 28 Jun 2021 (NI) (SI 2021/724) |
| | para 14 | 31 Oct 2017 (SI 2017/991) |
| | paras 15–23 | 31 Jan 2018 (E) (W) (S) (SI 2018/78) |
| | | 28 Jun 2021 (NI) (SI 2021/724) |
| | para 24 | 31 Oct 2017 (SI 2017/991) |
| | paras 25, 26 | 31 Jan 2018 (E) (W) (S) (SI 2018/78) |
| | | 28 Jun 2021 (NI) (SI 2021/724) |
| Sch 2 | | 31 Jan 2018 (SI 2018/78) |
| Sch 3 | para 1 | See paras 2, 3 below |
| | para 2 | 27 Apr 2017 (so far as necessary for enabling the exercise of any power to make provision by subordinate legislation) (s 58(6)) |
| | | 30 Jan 2018 (so far as inserts Anti-terrorism, Crime and Security Act 2001, Sch 1, para 10G(9)) (SI 2018/78) |
| | | 31 Jan 2018 (otherwise) (SI 2018/78) |
| | para 3 | 27 Apr 2017 (so far as necessary for enabling the exercise of any power to make provision by subordinate legislation) (s 58(6)) |
| | | 31 Jan 2018 (otherwise) (SI 2018/78) |
| Sch 4 | para 1 | See paras 2, 3 below |
| | para 2 | 27 Apr 2017 (so far as necessary for enabling the exercise of any power to make provision by subordinate legislation) (s 58(6)) |
| | | 30 Jan 2018 (so far as inserts Anti-terrorism, Crime and Security Act 2001, Sch 1, para 10X) (SI 2018/78) |
| | | 31 Jan 2018 (otherwise) (SI 2018/78) |
| | para 3 | 27 Apr 2017 (so far as necessary for enabling the exercise of any power to make provision by subordinate legislation) (s 58(6)) |
| | | 31 Jan 2018 (otherwise) (SI 2018/78) |
| Sch 5 | paras 1, 2 | 31 Jan 2018 (SI 2018/78) |
| | para 3 | 27 Apr 2017 (so far as necessary for enabling the exercise of any power to make provision by subordinate legislation) (s 58(6)) |
| | | 31 Jan 2018 (otherwise, except as provided below) (E) (W) (S) (SI 2018/78) |

**Criminal Finances Act 2017 (c 22)**—*contd*

|  |  |
|---|---|
|  | 16 Apr 2018 (so far as relates to provisions within Proceeds of Crime Act 2002, Pt 5, Chapter 3A or to detained property investigations, as defined in s 341(3B) of the 2002 Act) (E) (W) (S) (SI 2018/78) |
|  | 28 Jun 2021 (otherwise) (NI) (SI 2021/724) |
| para 4 | 31 Jan 2018 (E) (W) (S) (SI 2018/78) |
|  | 28 Jun 2021 (NI) (SI 2021/724) |
| para 5 | 28 Jun 2021 (SI 2021/724) |
| paras 6–8 | 31 Oct 2017 (SI 2017/991) |
| para 9 | See paras 10–13 below |
| para 10 | 31 Oct 2017 (SI 2017/991) |
| para 11 | 27 Apr 2017 (so far as necessary for enabling the exercise of any power to make provision by subordinate legislation) (s 58(6)) |
|  | 31 Oct 2017 (otherwise) (SI 2017/991) |
| para 12 | 31 Oct 2017 (SI 2017/991) |
| para 13 | 27 Apr 2017 (so far as necessary for enabling the exercise of any power to make provision by subordinate legislation) (s 58(6)) |
|  | 31 Oct 2017 (for the purpose of issuing a code of practice under Terrorism Act 2000, Sch 14, para 6) (SI 2017/991) |
|  | 31 Jan 2018 (otherwise) (SI 2018/78) |
| paras 14–16 | 31 Jan 2018 (SI 2018/78) |
| para 17 | See paras 18–88 below |
| para 18 | 31 Jan 2018 (E) (W) (S) (SI 2018/78) |
|  | 28 Jun 2021 (NI) (SI 2021/724) |
| para 19(1) | See sub-paras (2), (3) below |
| para 19(2) | 31 Jan 2018 (E) (W) (S) (SI 2018/78) |
|  | 28 Jun 2021 (NI) (SI 2021/724) |
| para 19(3) | 28 Jun 2021 (NI) (SI 2021/724) |
|  | *Not yet in force* (E) (W) (S) |
| para 20(a) | 31 Jan 2018 (so far as relates to provisions within Proceeds of Crime Act 2002, Pt 5, Chapter 3B) (SI 2018/78) |
|  | 16 Apr 2018 (otherwise) (SI 2018/78) |
| para 20(b) | 16 Apr 2018 (SI 2018/78) |
| para 20(c), (d) | 31 Jan 2018 (so far as relates to provisions within Proceeds of Crime Act 2002, Pt 5, Chapter 3B) (SI 2018/78) |
|  | 16 Apr 2018 (otherwise) (SI 2018/78) |
| para 21 | 31 Jan 2018 (E) (W) (S) (SI 2018/78) |
|  | *Not yet in force* (NI) |
| para 22 | 31 Jan 2018 (except as provided below) (E) (W) (S) (SI 2018/78) |
|  | 16 Apr 2018 (so far as relates to provisions within Proceeds of Crime Act 2002, Pt 5, Chapter 3A or to detained property investigations, as defined in s 341(3B) of the 2002 Act) (E) (W) (S) (SI 2018/78) |
|  | *Not yet in force* (NI) |
| para 23(a) | 31 Jan 2018 (so far as relates to provisions within Proceeds of Crime Act 2002, Pt 5, Chapter 3B) (SI 2018/78) |
|  | 16 Apr 2018 (otherwise) (SI 2018/78) |
| para 23(b) | 16 Apr 2018 (SI 2018/78) |
| para 23(c), (d) | 31 Jan 2018 (so far as relates to provisions within Proceeds of Crime Act 2002, Pt 5, Chapter 3B) (SI 2018/78) |
|  | 16 Apr 2018 (otherwise) (SI 2018/78) |
| para 24 | 31 Jan 2018 (except as provided below) (E) (W) (S) (SI 2018/78) |
|  | 16 Apr 2018 (so far as relates to provisions within Proceeds of Crime Act 2002, Pt 5, Chapter 3A or to detained property investigations, as defined in s 341(3B) of the 2002 Act) (E) (W) (S) (SI 2018/78) |
|  | *Not yet in force* (NI) |
| para 25 | 31 Jan 2018 (except as provided below) (SI 2018/78) |
|  | 16 Apr 2018 (so far as relates to provisions within Proceeds of Crime Act 2002, Pt 5, Chapter 3A) (SI 2018/78) |

**Criminal Finances Act 2017 (c 22)**—*contd*

| | |
|---|---|
| para 26 | 28 Jun 2021 (SI 2021/724) |
| para 27 | 31 Jan 2018 (except as provided below) (SI 2018/78) |
| | 16 Apr 2018 (so far as relates to provisions within Proceeds of Crime Act 2002, Pt 5, Chapter 3A) (SI 2018/78) |
| paras 28, 29 | 31 Jan 2018 (E) (W) (S) (SI 2018/78) |
| | 28 Jun 2021 (NI) (SI 2021/724) |
| para 30 | 31 Jan 2018 (except as provided below) (E) (W) (S) (SI 2018/78) |
| | 16 Apr 2018 (so far as relates to provisions within Proceeds of Crime Act 2002, Pt 5, Chapter 3A or to detained property investigations, as defined in s 341(3B) of the 2002 Act) (E) (W) (S) (SI 2018/78) |
| | 28 Jun 2021 (NI) (SI 2021/724) |
| para 31 | 31 Jan 2018 (E) (W) (S) (SI 2018/78) |
| | 28 Jun 2021 (NI) (SI 2021/724) |
| para 32 | 31 Jan 2018 (except as provided below) (E) (W) (S) (SI 2018/78) |
| | 16 Apr 2018 (so far as relates to provisions within Proceeds of Crime Act 2002, Pt 5, Chapter 3A or to detained property investigations, as defined in s 341(3B) of the 2002 Act) (E) (W) (S) (SI 2018/78) |
| | 28 Jun 2021 (NI) (SI 2021/724) |
| para 33 | 31 Jan 2018 (E) (W) (S) (SI 2018/78) |
| | 28 Jun 2021 (NI) (SI 2021/724) |
| para 34 | 31 Jan 2018 (except as provided below) (E) (W) (S) (SI 2018/78) |
| | 16 Apr 2018 (so far as relates to provisions within Proceeds of Crime Act 2002, Pt 5, Chapter 3A or to detained property investigations, as defined in s 341(3B) of the 2002 Act) (E) (W) (S) (SI 2018/78) |
| | 28 Jun 2021 (NI) (SI 2021/724) |
| para 35 | 31 Jan 2018 (so far as relates to provisions within Proceeds of Crime Act 2002, Pt 5, Chapter 3B) (E) (W) (S) (SI 2018/78) |
| | 16 Apr 2018 (otherwise) (E) (W) (S) (SI 2018/78) |
| | 28 Jun 2021 (NI) (SI 2021/724) |
| para 36 | 31 Jan 2018 (except as provided below) (E) (W) (S) (SI 2018/78) |
| | 16 Apr 2018 (so far as relates to provisions within Proceeds of Crime Act 2002, Pt 5, Chapter 3A or to detained property investigations, as defined in s 341(3B) of the 2002 Act) (E) (W) (S) (SI 2018/78) |
| | 28 Jun 2021 (NI) (SI 2021/724) |
| para 37 | 31 Oct 2017 (E) (W) (S) (SI 2021/991) |
| | 31 Oct 2017 (except in so far as relates to Proceeds of Crime Act 2002, s 333D(1)(aa), (1A)) (NI) (SI 2021/991) |
| | 28 Jun 2021 (exception noted above) (NI) (SI 2021/724) |
| para 38 | 31 Oct 2017 (SI 2017/991) |
| para 39 | 31 Jan 2018 (so far as relates to provisions within Proceeds of Crime Act 2002, Pt 5, Chapter 3B) (E) (W) (S) (SI 2018/78) |
| | 16 Apr 2018 (otherwise) (E) (W) (S) (SI 2018/78) |
| | 28 Jun 2021 (NI) (SI 2021/724) |
| paras 40–45 | 31 Jan 2018 (except as provided below) (E) (W) (S) (SI 2018/78) |
| | 16 Apr 2018 (so far as relates to provisions within Proceeds of Crime Act 2002, Pt 5, Chapter 3A or to detained property investigations, as defined in s 341(3B) of the 2002 Act) (E) (W) (S) (SI 2018/78) |
| | 28 Jun 2021 (NI) (SI 2021/724) |
| para 46 | 27 Apr 2017 (so far as necessary for enabling the exercise of any power to make provision by subordinate legislation) (s 58(6)) |
| | 31 Jan 2018 (otherwise) (E) (W) (S) (SI 2018/78) |
| | 28 Jun 2021 (otherwise) (NI) (SI 2021/724) |
| paras 47, 48 | 31 Jan 2018 (except as provided below) (E) (W) (S) (SI 2018/78) |

**Criminal Finances Act 2017 (c 22)**—*contd*

|  |  |
|---|---|
|  | 16 Apr 2018 (so far as relates to provisions within Proceeds of Crime Act 2002, Pt 5, Chapter 3A or to detained property investigations, as defined in s 341(3B) of the 2002 Act) (E) (W) (S) (SI 2018/78) |
|  | 28 Jun 2021 (NI) (SI 2021/724) |
| para 49 | 30 Jan 2018 (E) (W) (S) (SI 2018/78) |
|  | 28 Jun 2021 (NI) (SI 2021/724) |
| para 50 | 31 Jan 2018 (E) (W) (S) (SI 2018/78) |
|  | 28 Jun 2021 (NI) (SI 2021/724) |
| paras 51, 52 | 31 Jan 2018 (except as provided below) (E) (W) (S) (SI 2018/78) |
|  | 16 Apr 2018 (so far as relates to provisions within Proceeds of Crime Act 2002, Pt 5, Chapter 3A or to detained property investigations, as defined in s 341(3B) of the 2002 Act) (E) (W) (S) (SI 2018/78) |
|  | 28 Jun 2021 (NI) (SI 2021/724) |
| para 53 | 27 Apr 2017 (so far as necessary for enabling the exercise of any power to make provision by subordinate legislation) (s 58(6)) |
|  | 31 Jan 2018 (otherwise) (E) (W) (S) (SI 2018/78) |
|  | 28 Jun 2021 (otherwise) (NI) (SI 2021/724) |
| para 54 | 31 Jan 2018 (except as provided below) (E) (W) (S) (SI 2018/78) |
|  | 16 Apr 2018 (so far as relates to provisions within Proceeds of Crime Act 2002, Pt 5, Chapter 3A or to detained property investigations, as defined in s 341(3B) of the 2002 Act) (E) (W) (S) (SI 2018/78) |
|  | 28 Jun 2021 (NI) (SI 2021/724) |
| para 55 | 27 Apr 2017 (so far as necessary for enabling the exercise of any power to make provision by subordinate legislation) (s 58(6)) |
|  | 31 Jan 2018 (otherwise) (E) (W) (S) (SI 2018/78) |
|  | 28 Jun 2021 (otherwise) (NI) (SI 2021/724) |
| paras 56, 57 | 31 Jan 2018 (except as provided below) (E) (W) (S) (SI 2018/78) |
|  | 16 Apr 2018 (so far as relates to provisions within Proceeds of Crime Act 2002, Pt 5, Chapter 3A or to detained property investigations, as defined in s 341(3B) of the 2002 Act) (E) (W) (S) (SI 2018/78) |
|  | 28 Jun 2021 (NI) (SI 2021/724) |
| para 58 | 27 Apr 2017 (so far as necessary for enabling the exercise of any power to make provision by subordinate legislation) (s 58(6)) |
|  | 31 Oct 2017 (otherwise) (SI 2017/991) |
|  | 28 Jun 2021 (otherwise) (NI) (SI 2021/724) |
| paras 59–62 | 31 Jan 2018 (except as provided below) (E) (W) (S) (SI 2018/78) |
|  | 16 Apr 2018 (so far as relates to provisions within Proceeds of Crime Act 2002, Pt 5, Chapter 3A or to detained property investigations, as defined in s 341(3B) of the 2002 Act) (E) (W) (S) (SI 2018/78) |
|  | 28 Jun 2021 (NI) (SI 2021/724) |
| para 63 | 27 Apr 2017 (so far as necessary for enabling the exercise of any power to make provision by subordinate legislation) (s 58(6)) |
|  | 31 Jan 2018 (otherwise, except as provided below) (E) (W) (S) (SI 2018/78) |
|  | 16 Apr 2018 (so far as relates to provisions within Proceeds of Crime Act 2002, Pt 5, Chapter 3A or to detained property investigations, as defined in s 341(3B) of the 2002 Act) (E) (W) (S) (SI 2018/78) |
|  | 28 Jun 2021 (otherwise) (NI) (SI 2021/724) |
| paras 64–72 | 31 Jan 2018 (except as provided below) (E) (W) (S) (SI 2018/78) |
|  | 16 Apr 2018 (so far as relates to provisions within Proceeds of Crime Act 2002, Pt 5, Chapter 3A or to detained property investigations, as defined in s 341(3B) of the 2002 Act) (E) (W) (S) (SI 2018/78) |
|  | 28 Jun 2021 (NI) (SI 2021/724) |

**See Halsbury's Statutes Citator for amendments to these Acts**          2509

**Criminal Finances Act 2017 (c 22)**—*contd*

| | |
|---|---|
| para 73 | 31 Jan 2018 (E) (W) (S) (SI 2018/78) |
| | 28 Jun 2021 (NI) (SI 2021/724) |
| para 74 | 27 Apr 2017 (so far as necessary for enabling the exercise of any power to make provision by subordinate legislation) (s 58(6)) |
| | 31 Jan 2018 (otherwise) (E) (W) (S) (SI 2018/78) |
| | 28 Jun 2021 (otherwise) (NI) (SI 2021/724) |
| paras 75–82 | 31 Jan 2018 (E) (W) (S) (SI 2018/78) |
| | 28 Jun 2021 (NI) (SI 2021/724) |
| para 83 | 27 Apr 2017 (so far as necessary for enabling the exercise of any power to make provision by subordinate legislation) (s 58(6)) |
| | 31 Oct 2017 (otherwise) (SI 2017/991) |
| para 84 | 31 Jan 2018 (E) (W) (S) (SI 2018/78) |
| | 28 Jun 2021 (NI) (SI 2021/724) |
| para 85 | 31 Jan 2018 (except as provided below) (E) (W) (S) (SI 2018/78) |
| | 16 Apr 2018 (so far as relates to provisions within Proceeds of Crime Act 2002, Pt 5, Chapter 3A or to detained property investigations, as defined in s 341(3B) of the 2002 Act) (E) (W) (S) (SI 2018/78) |
| | 28 Jun 2021 (NI) (SI 2021/724) |
| para 86 | 16 Apr 2018 (E) (W) (S) (SI 2018/78) |
| | 28 Jun 2021 (NI) (SI 2021/724) |
| para 87(1), (2) | 27 Apr 2017 (so far as necessary for enabling the exercise of any power to make provision by subordinate legislation) (s 58(6)) |
| | 31 Jan 2018 (otherwise, except as provided below) (E) (W) (S) (SI 2018/78) |
| | 16 Apr 2018 (so far as relates to provisions within Proceeds of Crime Act 2002, Pt 5, Chapter 3A or to detained property investigations, as defined in s 341(3B) of the 2002 Act) (E) (W) (S) (SI 2018/78) |
| | 28 Jun 2021 (otherwise) (NI) (SI 2021/724) |
| para 87(3)–(6) | 27 Apr 2017 (so far as necessary for enabling the exercise of any power to make provision by subordinate legislation) (s 58(6)) |
| | 31 Oct 2017 (so far as relate to Proceeds of Crime Act 2002, ss 303G(5), 303H(4)) (SI 2017/991) |
| | 16 Apr 2018 (otherwise) (E) (W) (S) (SI 2018/78) |
| | 28 Jun 2021 (otherwise) (NI) (SI 2021/724) |
| para 87(7)–(11) | 27 Apr 2017 (so far as necessary for enabling the exercise of any power to make provision by subordinate legislation) (s 58(6)) |
| | 31 Jan 2018 (otherwise, except as provided below) (E) (W) (S) (SI 2018/78) |
| | 16 Apr 2018 (so far as relates to provisions within Proceeds of Crime Act 2002, Pt 5, Chapter 3A or to detained property investigations, as defined in s 341(3B) of the 2002 Act) (E) (W) (S) (SI 2018/78) |
| | 28 Jun 2021 (otherwise) (NI) (SI 2021/724) |
| para 88 | 31 Jan 2018 (E) (W) (S) (SI 2018/78) |
| | 28 Jun 2021 (NI) (SI 2021/724) |
| para 89 | 27 Apr 2017 (so far as necessary for enabling the exercise of any power to make provision by subordinate legislation) (s 58(6)) |
| | 31 Oct 2017 (otherwise) (SI 2017/991) |
| para 90 | See paras 91–93 below |
| para 91 | 31 Oct 2017 (far as necessary for enabling an Act of Sederunt to be made under Bankruptcy and Diligence etc. (Scotland) Act 2007, s 215, in relation to a decree of removing or warrant for ejection granted under Proceeds of Crime Act 2002, s 266(8ZA)) (SI 2017/991) |
| | 31 Jan 2018 (otherwise) (SI 2018/78) |
| para 92 | 27 Apr 2017 (so far as necessary for enabling the exercise of any power to make provision by subordinate legislation) (s 58(6)) |
| | 31 Jan 2018 (otherwise) (SI 2018/78) |

**Criminal Finances Act 2017 (c 22)**—*contd*
        para 93            31 Jan 2018 (SI 2018/78)

[1]   For transitional provisions, see SI 2017/991, reg 3

---

**Cultural Property (Armed Conflicts) Act 2017 (c 6)**

*RA:* 23 Feb 2017

*Commencement provisions:* s 32; Cultural Property (Armed Conflicts) Act 2017 (Commencement) Regulations 2017, SI 2017/1087

| | |
|---|---|
| 1–28 | 12 Dec 2017 (SI 2017/1087) |
| 29–33 | 23 Feb 2017 (s 32(1)) |
| Schs 1–4 | 12 Dec 2017 (SI 2017/1087) |

---

**Digital Economy Act 2017 (c 30)**

*RA:* 27 Apr 2017

*Commencement provisions:* s 118; Digital Economy Act 2017 (Commencement No 1) Regulations 2017, SI 2017/765; Digital Economy Act 2017 (Commencement No 2) Regulations 2017, SI 2017/1136; Digital Economy Act 2017 (Commencement No 3) Regulations 2017, SI 2017/1286; Digital Economy Act 2017 (Commencement No 1) (England and Wales) Regulations 2018, SI 2018/342; Digital Economy Act 2017 (Commencement No 4) Regulations 2018, SI 2018/382; Digital Economy Act 2017 (Commencement No 5) Regulations 2018, SI 2018/624; Digital Economy Act 2017 (Commencement No 6) Regulations 2018, SI 2018/690; Digital Economy Act 2017 (Commencement No 7) Regulations 2020, SI 2020/70; Digital Economy Act 2017 (Commencement No 1) (Northern Ireland) Regulations 2021, SI 2021/680; Digital Economy Act 2017 (Commencement No 8) Regulations 2021, SI 2021/1170

| | | |
|---|---|---|
| 1–3 | | 27 Jun 2017 (s 118(2)) |
| 4 | | 28 Dec 2017 (SI 2017/1286) |
| 5, 6 | | 31 Jul 2017 (SI 2017/765) |
| 7 | | 27 Jun 2017 (s 118(2)) |
| 8 | | 31 Jul 2017 (SI 2017/765) |
| 9–13 | | 27 Jun 2017 (s 118(2)) |
| 14 | | 31 Jul 2017 (for the purpose of making regulations) (SI 2017/765) |
| | | *Not yet in force* (otherwise) |
| 15 | | 31 Jul 2017 (for the purpose of making regulations and so far as relates to ss 21(5), 25, 27 of the Act) (SI 2017/765) |
| | | *Not yet in force* (otherwise) |
| 16, 17 | | 31 Jul 2017 (SI 2017/765) |
| 18–20 | | *Not yet in force* |
| 21 | (1)–(4) | *Not yet in force* |
| | (5) | 31 Jul 2017 (so far as relates to s 27 of the Act) (SI 2017/765) |
| | | *Not yet in force* (otherwise) |
| | (6) | *Not yet in force* |
| 22 | | 31 Jul 2017 (so far as relates to ss 15, 21(5), 25 of the Act) (SI 2017/765) |
| | | *Not yet in force* (otherwise) |
| 23, 24 | | *Not yet in force* |
| 25 | | 31 Jul 2017 (SI 2017/765) |
| 26 | (1) | *Not yet in force* |
| | (2) | 31 Jul 2017 (SI 2017/765) |
| 27 | | 31 Jul 2017 (SI 2017/765) |
| 28, 29 | | *Not yet in force* |
| 30 | (1), (2) | 31 Jul 2017 (so far as relates to ss 14–17, 21(5), 22, 25, 26(2), 27 of the Act) (SI 2017/765) |
| | | *Not yet in force* (otherwise) |
| | (3) | *Not yet in force* |

**Digital Economy Act 2017** (c 30)—*contd*

| | |
|---|---|
| 31 | 30 Jun 2018 (SI 2018/690) (E) (W) (S) |
| | 30 Jun 2021 (SI 2021/680) (NI) |
| 32, 33 | 1 Oct 2017 (SI 2017/765) |
| 34 | 31 Jul 2017 (SI 2017/765) |
| 35 | 1 Oct 2017 (for the purpose of making regulations and in relation to England and Wales (except so far as it relates to the disclosure of information to or by a water or sewerage undertaker for an area which is wholly or mainly in Wales) and Scotland only) (SI 2017/765) |
| | 9 Mar 2018 (for the purposes of making regulations in relation to the disclosure of information to or by a water or sewerage undertaker for an area which is wholly or mainly in Wales) (SI 2018/342) |
| | 1 Apr 2018 (so far as relates to the disclosure of information to or by a water or sewerage undertaker for an area which is wholly or mainly in Wales) (SI 2018/342) |
| | 1 May 2018 (otherwise) (E) (W) (S) (SI 2018/382) |
| | *Not yet in force* (otherwise) (NI) |
| 36 | 1 Oct 2017 (for the purpose of making regulations) (SI 2017/765) |
| | 1 May 2018 (otherwise) (SI 2018/382) |
| 37 | 1 May 2018 (SI 2018/382) |
| 38 | 9 Mar 2018 (for the purposes of making regulations in relation to the disclosure of information to or by a water or sewerage undertaker for an area which is wholly or mainly in Wales) (SI 2018/342) |
| | 1 Apr 2018 (so far as relates to the disclosure of information to or by a water or sewerage undertaker for an area which is wholly or mainly in Wales) (SI 2018/342) |
| | 1 May 2018 (otherwise) (SI 2018/382) |
| 39 | 1 Apr 2018 (so far as relates to the disclosure of information to or by a water or sewerage undertaker for an area which is wholly or mainly in Wales) (SI 2018/342) |
| | 1 May 2018 (otherwise) (SI 2018/382) |
| 40–42 | 1 Apr 2018 (so far as relates to the disclosure of information to or by a water or sewerage undertaker for an area which is wholly or mainly in Wales) (SI 2018/342) |
| | 1 May 2018 (otherwise) (E) (W) (S) (SI 2018/382) |
| | *Not yet in force* (otherwise) (NI) |
| 43 | 1 Oct 2017 (so far as it relates to the disclosure of information to or by a water or sewerage undertaker for an area which is wholly or mainly in Wales, and in relation to England and Wales and Scotland only) (SI 2017/765) |
| | 1 Apr 2018 (so far as relates to the disclosure of information to or by a water or sewerage undertaker for an area which is wholly or mainly in Wales) (SI 2018/342) |
| | *Not yet in force* (otherwise) |
| 44 | 1 Oct 2017 (for the purpose of making regulations and in relation to England and Wales (except so far as it relates to the disclosure of information to or by a water or sewerage undertaker for an area which is wholly or mainly in Wales) and Scotland only) (SI 2017/765) |
| | 9 Mar 2018 (for the purposes of making regulations in relation to the disclosure of information to or by a water or sewerage undertaker for an area which is wholly or mainly in Wales) (SI 2018/342) |
| | 1 Apr 2018 (so far as relates to the disclosure of information to or by a water or sewerage undertaker for an area which is wholly or mainly in Wales) (SI 2018/342) |
| | 1 May 2018 (otherwise) (E) (W) (S) (SI 2018/382) |
| | *Not yet in force* (otherwise) (NI) |

**Digital Economy Act 2017 (c 30)**—*contd*

| | |
|---|---|
| 45 | 1 Apr 2018 (so far as relates to the disclosure of information to or by a water or sewerage undertaker for an area which is wholly or mainly in Wales) (SI 2018/342) |
| | 1 May 2018 (otherwise) (E) (W) (S) (SI 2018/382) |
| | *Not yet in force* (otherwise) (NI) |
| 46 | 31 Jul 2017 (only for the purpose of issuing the code of practice under Registration Service Act 1953, s 19AC) (SI 2017/765) |
| | 1 May 2018 (otherwise) (E) (W) (S) (SI 2018/382) |
| | *Not yet in force* (otherwise) (NI) |
| 47 | 31 Jul 2017 (only for the purpose of issuing the code of practice under Registration Service Act 1953, s 19AC) (SI 2017/765) |
| | 1 May 2018 (otherwise) (E) (W) (S) (SI 2018/382) |
| | *Not yet in force* (otherwise) (NI) |
| 48 | 1 Oct 2017 (E) (W) (S) (for the purpose of making regulations) (SI 2017/765) |
| | 1 May 2018 (otherwise) (E) (W) (S) (SI 2018/382) |
| | *Not yet in force* (otherwise) (NI) |
| 49–51 | 1 May 2018 (E) (W) (S) (SI 2018/382) |
| | *Not yet in force* (NI) |
| 52 | 1 Oct 2017 (E) (W) (S) (SI 2017/765) |
| | *Not yet in force* (NI) |
| 53 | 1 May 2018 (E) (W) (S) (SI 2018/382) |
| | *Not yet in force* (NI) |
| 54 | 1 Oct 2017 (E) (W) (S) (for the purpose of making regulations) (SI 2017/765) |
| | 1 May 2018 (otherwise) (E) (W) (S) (SI 2018/382) |
| | *Not yet in force* (NI) |
| 55 | 1 May 2018 (E) (W) (S) (SI 2018/382) |
| | *Not yet in force* (NI) |
| 56 | 1 Oct 2017 (E) (W) (S) (for the purpose of making regulations) (SI 2017/765) |
| | 1 May 2018 (otherwise) (E) (W) (S) (SI 2018/382) |
| | *Not yet in force* (NI) |
| 57–61 | 1 Oct 2017 (E) (W) (S) (SI 2017/765) |
| | *Not yet in force* (NI) |
| 62 | 1 Oct 2017 (E) (W) (S) (for the purpose of making regulations) (SI 2017/765) |
| | 1 May 2018 (otherwise) (E) (W) (S) (SI 2018/382) |
| | *Not yet in force* (NI) |
| 63 | 1 Oct 2017 (E) (W) (S) (SI 2017/765) |
| | *Not yet in force* (NI) |
| 64–69 | 1 Apr 2018 (so far as relates to the disclosure of information by the Welsh Revenue Authority) (SI 2018/342) |
| | 1 May 2018 (otherwise) (SI 2018/382) |
| 70 | 1 Oct 2017 (E) (W) (S) (except so far as it relates to the disclosure of information by the Welsh Revenue Authority) (SI 2017/765) |
| | 1 Apr 2018 (E) (W) (so far as relates to the disclosure of information by the Welsh Revenue Authority) (SI 2018/342) |
| | 1 May 2018 (otherwise) (E) (W) (S) (SI 2018/382) |
| | 1 May 2018 (NI) (SI 2018/382) |
| 71–73 | 1 Apr 2018 (so far as relates to the disclosure of information by the Welsh Revenue Authority) (SI 2018/342) |
| | 1 May 2018 (otherwise) (SI 2018/382) |
| 74 | 31 Jul 2017 (SI 2017/765) |
| 75 | 1 Apr 2018 (so far as relates to the disclosure of information by the Welsh Revenue Authority) (SI 2018/342) |
| | *Not yet in force* (otherwise) |
| 76–78 | 31 Jul 2017 (SI 2017/765) |
| 79    (1), (2) | 31 Jul 2017 (E) (W) (S) (SI 2017/765) |
| | 1 May 2018 (NI) (SI 2018/382) |

**Digital Economy Act 2017 (c 30)**—*contd*

| | | |
|---|---|---|
| | (3) | 1 May 2018 (SI 2018/382) |
| | (4)–(6) | 31 Jul 2017 (E) (W) (S) (SI 2017/765) |
| | | 1 May 2018 (NI) (SI 2018/382) |
| 80 | | 1 Oct 2017 (E) (W) (S) (only for the purposes of preparing and publishing the statement under Statistics and Registration Service Act 2007, s 45E, and the code of practice under s 45G thereof) (SI 2017/765) |
| | | 1 May 2018 (otherwise) (E) (W) (S) (SI 2018/382) |
| | | 1 May 2018 (NI) (SI 2018/382) |
| 81 | | 31 Jul 2017 (E) (W) (S) (SI 2017/765) |
| | | 1 May 2018 (NI) (SI 2018/382) |
| 82–86 | | 27 Jun 2017 (s 118(2)) |
| 87 | | 31 Jul 2017 (SI 2017/765) |
| 88 | | 27 Apr 2017 (s 118(1)) |
| 89 | | 1 Jun 2020 (s 118(3)) |
| 90, 91 | | 27 Jun 2017 (s 118(2)) |
| 92 | | 31 Jul 2017 (SI 2017/765) |
| 93 | (1), (2) | 31 Jul 2017 (SI 2017/765) |
| | (3) | *Not yet in force* |
| | (4)–(8) | 31 Jul 2017 (SI 2017/765) |
| 94 | | *Not yet in force* |
| 95 | | 31 Jul 2017 (SI 2017/765) |
| 96, 97 | | 27 Jun 2017 (s 118(2)) |
| 98 | | 31 Jul 2017 (SI 2017/765) |
| 99 | | 29 Oct 2021 (SI 2021/1170) |
| 100, 101 | | 31 Jul 2017 (SI 2017/765) |
| 102 | | 1 Oct 2018 (SI 2017/765) |
| 103 | | 27 Jun 2017 (s 118(2)) |
| 104 | | 31 Jul 2017 (SI 2017/765) |
| 105 | | 6 Apr 2018 (E) (W) (S) (SI 2018/382) |
| | | *Not yet in force* (NI) |
| 106 | | 31 Jul 2017 (E) (W) (S) (SI 2017/765) |
| | | *Not yet in force* (NI) |
| 107 | | 27 Jun 2017 (s 118(2)) |
| 108–110 | | 31 Jul 2017 (SI 2017/765) |
| 111 | (1)–(7) | *Not yet in force* |
| | (8), (9) | 25 May 2018 (SI 2018/624) |
| 112 | | 27 Apr 2017 (s 118(1)) |
| 113 | | 27 Jun 2017 (s 118(2)) |
| 114 | | 1 Aug 2020 (SI 2020/70) |
| 115–120 | | 27 Apr 2017 (s 118(1)) |
| Sch 1 | | 31 Jul 2017 (only for the purpose of making regulations under Communications Act 2003, Sch 3A, para 95) (SI 2017/765) |
| | | 22 Nov 2017 (only in relation to Communications Act 2003, Sch 3A, para 106) (SI 2017/1136) |
| | | 28 Dec 2017 (otherwise) (SI 2017/1286) |
| Sch 2 | | 28 Dec 2017 (SI 2017/1286) |
| Sch 3 | paras 1–46 | 28 Dec 2017 (SI 2017/1286) |
| | para 47 | 31 Jul 2017 (SI 2017/765) |
| | paras 48–57 | 28 Dec 2017 (SI 2017/1286) |
| Sch 4 | | 1 Apr 2018 (so far as relates to the disclosure of information to or by a water or sewerage undertaker for an area which is wholly or mainly in Wales) (SI 2018/342) |
| | | 1 May 2018 (otherwise) (E) (W) (S) (SI 2018/382) |
| | | *Not yet in force* (NI) |
| Sch 5 | | 1 May 2018 (SI 2018/382) |
| Sch 6 | | 1 Apr 2018 (so far as relates to the disclosure of information to or by a water or sewerage undertaker for an area which is wholly or mainly in Wales) (SI 2018/342) |

**Digital Economy Act 2017 (c 30)**—*contd*

|  | 1 May 2018 (otherwise) (SI 2018/382) |
| Schs 7, 8 | 1 May 2018 (E) (W) (S) (SI 2018/382) |
|  | *Not yet in force* (NI) |
| Sch 9 | 27 Jun 2017 (s 118(2)) |

---

**European Union (Approvals) Act 2017 (c 35)**

*RA:* 7 Dec 2017

*Commencement provisions:* s 2(2)

Whole Act in force 7 Dec 2017 (s 2(2))

---

**European Union (Notification of Withdrawal) Act 2017 (c 9)**

*RA:* 16 Mar 2017

Whole Act in force 16 Mar 2017 (RA)

---

**Farriers (Registration) Act 2017 (c 28)**

*RA:* 27 Apr 2017

*Commencement provisions:* s 3(2), (3); Farriers (Registration) Act 2017 (Commencement) Regulations 2017, SI 2017/921

| 1, 2 | 15 Sep 2017 (SI 2017/921) |
| 3 | 27 Apr 2017 (s 3(3)) |
| Schedule | 15 Sep 2017 (SI 2017/921) |

---

**Finance Act 2017 (c 10)**

*Budget Day:* 8 Mar 2017

*RA:* 27 Apr 2017

The commencement details of Finance Acts are not set out, as the dates from which their provisions take effect are usually stated clearly and unambiguously in the text of the Act, and charging provisions will normally state for which year or years of assessment they are to have effect.

---

**Finance (No 2) Act 2017 (c 32)**

*RA:* 16 Nov 2017

The commencement details of Finance Acts are not set out, as the dates from which their provisions take effect are usually stated clearly and unambiguously in the text of the Act, and charging provisions will normally state for which year or years of assessment they are to have effect.

---

**Guardianship (Missing Persons) Act 2017 (c 28)**

*RA:* 27 Apr 2017

*Commencement provisions:* s 25(2), (3); Guardianship (Missing Persons) Act 2017 (Commencement) Regulations 2019, SI 2019/1032

| 1–15 |  | 31 Jul 2019 (SI 2019/1032) |
| 16 | (1)–(4) | 31 Jul 2019 (SI 2019/1032) |
|  | (5)–(7) | 27 Apr 2017 (s 25(2)(a)) |

## Guardianship (Missing Persons) Act 2017 (c 28)—*contd*

| | | |
|---|---|---|
| 17 | | 27 Apr 2017 (so far as confers power to make regulations) (s 25(2)(b)) |
| | | 31 Jul 2019 (otherwise) (SI 2019/1032) |
| 18 | (1)–(5) | 31 Jul 2019 (SI 2019/1032) |
| | (6)–(8) | 27 Apr 2017 (s 25(2)(c)) |
| 19–21 | | 31 Jul 2019 (SI 2019/1032) |
| 22, 23 | | 19 Jun 2019 (SI 2019/1032) |
| 24, 25 | | 27 Apr 2017 (s 25(2)(d)) |
| Schedule | | 31 Jul 2019 (SI 2019/1032) |

## Health Service Medical Supplies (Costs) Act 2017 (c 23)

*RA:* 27 Apr 2017

*Commencement provisions:* s 12; Health Service Medical Supplies (Costs) Act 2017 (Commencement No 1 and Saving Provision) Regulations 2017, SI 2017/809

| | | |
|---|---|---|
| 1 | | 7 Aug 2017 (SI 2017/809) |
| 2 | | *Not yet in force* |
| 3–8 | | 7 Aug 2017 (SI 2017/809) |
| 9 | | *Not yet in force* |
| 10 | (1)–(5) | 7 Aug 2017 (SI 2017/809) |
| | (6) | 7 Aug 2017 (SI 2017/809)[1] |
| | (7)–(18) | 7 Aug 2017 (SI 2017/809) |
| | (19) | *Not yet in force* |
| 11–13 | | 27 Apr 2017 (s 12(1)) |

[1] For savings, see SI 2017/809, reg 3

## High Speed Rail (London–West Midlands) Act 2017 (c 7)

*RA:* 23 Feb 2017

*Commencement provisions:* s 70(1)–(3); High Speed Rail (London–West Midlands) Act 2017 (Commencement) Regulations 2017, SI 2017/209

| | |
|---|---|
| 1–10 | 23 Feb 2017 (s 70(1)) |
| 11 | 24 Feb 2017 (SI 2017/209) |
| 12–70 | 23 Feb 2017 (s 70(1)) |
| Schs 1–13 | 23 Feb 2017 (s 70(1)) |
| Sch 14 | 24 Feb 2017 (SI 2017/209) |
| Schs 15–33 | 23 Feb 2017 (s 70(1)) |

## Higher Education and Research Act 2017 (c 29)

*RA:* 27 Apr 2017

*Commencement provisions:* s 124; Higher Education and Research Act 2017 (Commencement No 1) Regulations 2017, SI 2017/788; Higher Education and Research Act 2017 (Commencement No 2) Regulations 2017, SI 2017/1146; Higher Education and Research Act 2017 (Commencement No 3) Regulations 2018, SI 2018/241; Higher Education and Research Act 2017 (Commencement No 1) (Wales) Regulations 2018, SI 2018/415; Higher Education and Research Act 2017 (Commencement No 4) Regulations 2018, SI 2018/1054; Higher Education and Research Act 2017 (Commencement No 5) Regulations 2018, SI 2018/1226; Higher Education and Research Act 2017 (Commencement No 6) Regulations 2020, SI 2020/321

| | | |
|---|---|---|
| 1 | | 1 Jan 2018 (SI 2017/788) |
| 2 | | 1 Jan 2018 (SI 2017/1146) |
| 3 | (1) | 1 Jan 2018 (in so far as defines "the register") (SI 2017/1146) |
| | | 1 Apr 2018 (otherwise) (SI 2018/241) |

**Higher Education and Research Act 2017 (c 29)**—*contd*

| | | |
|---|---|---|
| | (2)–(6) | 1 Apr 2018 (SI 2018/241) |
| | (7) | 1 Jan 2018 (only in so far as necessary for the definition of "the ongoing registration conditions" in s 3(8), for the purposes of s 85(3)) (SI 2017/1146) |
| | | 1 Apr 2018 (otherwise) (SI 2018/241) |
| | (8) | 1 Jan 2018 (SI 2017/1146) |
| | (9) | 1 Apr 2018 (SI 2018/241) |
| | (10) | 1 Jan 2018 (SI 2017/1146) |
| 4–12 | | 1 Apr 2018 (SI 2018/241) |
| 13 | (1)(a) | 1 Jan 2018 (only in so far as necessary for the purposes of the designation of a body under Sch 4, Pt 1 and allowing the OfS to make arrangements under para 7 of that Sch) (SI 2017/1146) |
| | | 1 Apr 2018 (otherwise) (SI 2018/241) |
| | (1)(b)–(f) | 1 Apr 2018 (SI 2018/241) |
| | (2), (3) | 1 Jan 2018 (only in so far as necessary for the purposes of the designation of a body under Sch 4, Pt 1 and allowing the OfS to make arrangements under para 7 of that Sch) (SI 2017/1146) |
| | | 1 Apr 2018 (otherwise) (SI 2018/241) |
| | (4), (5) | 1 Apr 2018 (SI 2018/241) |
| 14 | | 1 Apr 2018 (SI 2018/241) |
| 15 | | 1 Aug 2019 (SI 2018/1226) |
| 16, 17 | | 1 Apr 2018 (SI 2018/241) |
| 18 | | 1 Apr 2018 (except so far as refers to s 15) (SI 2018/241) |
| | | 1 Aug 2019 (exception noted above) (SI 2018/1226) |
| 19, 20 | | 1 Apr 2018 (SI 2018/241) |
| 21 | | 1 Aug 2019 (SI 2018/1226) |
| 22 | | 1 Apr 2018 (SI 2018/241) |
| 23 | | 1 Jan 2018 (only in so far as necessary for the purposes of the designation of a body under Sch 4, Pt 1 and allowing the OfS to make arrangements under para 7 of that Sch) (SI 2017/1146) |
| | | 1 Apr 2018 (otherwise) (SI 2018/241) |
| 24 | | 1 Apr 2018 (SI 2018/241) |
| 25–27 | | 1 Jan 2018 (SI 2017/1146) |
| 28 | | 1 Apr 2018 (SI 2018/241) |
| 29 | (1) | 1 Apr 2018 (SI 2018/241) |
| | (2) | 1 Jan 2018 (only in so far as necessary for the definition of an "access and participation plan" for the purposes of s 29(4)) (SI 2017/1146) |
| | | 1 Apr 2018 (otherwise) (SI 2018/241) |
| | (3) | 1 Apr 2018 (SI 2018/241) |
| | (4) | 1 Jan 2018 (SI 2017/1146) |
| | (5)–(7) | 1 Apr 2018 (SI 2018/241) |
| 30–32 | | 1 Jan 2018 (only in so far as necessary for the definition of an "access and participation plan" for the purposes of s 29(4)) (SI 2017/1146) |
| | | 1 Apr 2018 (otherwise) (SI 2018/241) |
| 33–35 | | 1 Apr 2018 (SI 2018/241) |
| 36 | | 1 Jan 2018 (only in so far as it relates to the functions of the OfS under s 29(4)) (SI 2017/1146) |
| | | 1 Apr 2018 (otherwise) (SI 2018/241) |
| 37 | | 1 Apr 2018 (SI 2018/241) |
| 38 | | 1 Aug 2019 (SI 2018/1226) |
| 39–41 | | 1 Jan 2019 (SI 2018/1226) |
| 42 | (1) | 1 Jan 2018 (only in so far as necessary for the purposes of the designation of a body under Sch 4, Pt 1 and allowing the OfS to make arrangements under para 7 of that Sch) (SI 2017/1146) |

**See Halsbury's Statutes Citator for amendments to these Acts** 2517

**Higher Education and Research Act 2017 (c 29)**—*contd*

|  |  |  |
|---|---|---|
|  |  | 1 Apr 2018 (otherwise) (SI 2018/241) |
|  | (2) | 1 Apr 2018 (SI 2018/241) |
|  | (3) | 1 Jan 2018 (only in so far as necessary for the purposes of the designation of a body under Sch 4, Pt 1 and allowing the OfS to make arrangements under para 7 of that Sch) (SI 2017/1146) |
|  |  | 1 Apr 2018 (otherwise) (SI 2018/241) |
|  | (4)–(13) | 1 Apr 2018 (SI 2018/241) |
| 43 |  | 1 Apr 2018 (SI 2018/241) |
| 44 | (1)–(4) | 1 Apr 2018 (SI 2018/241) |
|  | (5) | 1 Jan 2018 (only in so far as necessary for the purposes of the designation of a body under Sch 4, Pt 1 and allowing the OfS to make arrangements under para 7 of that Sch) (SI 2017/1146) |
|  |  | 1 Apr 2018 (otherwise) (SI 2018/241) |
|  | (6)–(8) | 1 Apr 2018 (SI 2018/241) |
| 45 | (1) | 1 Jan 2018 (only in so far as necessary for the purposes of the designation of a body under Sch 4, Pt 1 and allowing the OfS to make arrangements under para 7 of that Sch) (SI 2017/1146) |
|  |  | 1 Apr 2018 (otherwise) (SI 2018/241) |
|  | (2)–(6) | 1 Apr 2018 (SI 2018/241) |
|  | (7) | 1 Jan 2018 (only in so far as necessary for the purposes of the designation of a body under Sch 4, Pt 1 and allowing the OfS to make arrangements under para 7 of that Sch) (SI 2017/1146) |
|  |  | 1 Apr 2018 (otherwise) (SI 2018/241) |
|  | (8)–(13) | 1 Apr 2018 (SI 2018/241) |
| 46 |  | 1 Jan 2018 (only in so far as necessary for the purposes of the designation of a body under Sch 4, Pt 1 and allowing the OfS to make arrangements under para 7 of that Sch) (SI 2017/1146) |
|  |  | 1 Apr 2018 (otherwise) (SI 2018/241) |
| 47–49 |  | 1 Apr 2018 (SI 2018/241) |
| 50, 51 |  | 1 Aug 2019 (SI 2018/1226) |
| 52 |  | *Not yet in force* |
| 53–55 |  | 1 Apr 2018 (SI 2018/241) |
| 56, 57 |  | 1 Apr 2019 (SI 2018/1226) |
| 58–61 |  | 1 Apr 2018 (SI 2018/241) |
| 62 | (1)–(4) | 1 Jan 2018 (SI 2017/1146) |
|  | (5) | 1 Jan 2019 (SI 2018/1226) |
| 63 |  | 1 Jan 2018 (SI 2017/1146) |
| 64, 65 |  | 1 Jan 2018 (only in so far as necessary for the purposes of the designation of a body under Sch 6, Pt 1) (SI 2017/1146) |
|  |  | 1 Apr 2018 (otherwise) (SI 2018/241) |
| 66 | (1) | 1 Jan 2018 (only in so far as necessary for the purposes of the designation of a body under Sch 6, Pt 1) (SI 2017/1146) |
|  |  | 1 Apr 2018 (otherwise) (SI 2018/241) |
|  | (2)(a) | 1 Jan 2018 (SI 2017/1146) |
|  | (2)(b), (3)–(8) | 1 Apr 2018 (SI 2018/241) |
| 67–69 |  | 1 Aug 2019 (SI 2018/1226) |
| 70 |  | 1 Jan 2019 (SI 2018/1226) |
| 71 |  | 1 Aug 2019 (SI 2018/1226) |
| 72 |  | 1 Jan 2019 (except to the extent it refers to anything in s 71) (SI 2018/1226) |
|  |  | 1 Aug 2019 (exception noted above) (SI 2018/1226) |
| 73 |  | 1 Aug 2019 (SI 2018/1226) |
| 74 |  | 1 Jan 2019 (SI 2018/1226) |
| 75 |  | 1 Jan 2018 (SI 2017/1146) |
| 76 |  | 1 Apr 2018 (SI 2018/241) |

**Higher Education and Research Act 2017 (c 29)**—*contd*

| | | |
|---|---|---|
| 77, 78 | | 1 Jan 2018 (SI 2017/1146) |
| 79–82 | | 1 Apr 2018 (SI 2018/241) |
| 83 | | 1 Jan 2018 (SI 2017/1146) |
| 84 | | 1 Apr 2018 (SI 2018/241) |
| 85 | (1)–(3) | 1 Jan 2018 (SI 2017/1146) |
| | (4), (5) | 1 Apr 2018 (SI 2018/241) |
| 86, 87 | | *Not yet in force* |
| 88 | | 1 Apr 2018 (E) (SI 2018/241) |
| | | 1 Apr 2018 (W) (SI 2018/415) |
| 89 | (1), (2)(a)–(h)(i) | 1 Apr 2018 (SI 2018/241) |
| | (2)(h)(ii) | 1 Apr 2018 (E) (SI 2018/241) |
| | | 1 Apr 2018 (W) (SI 2018/415) |
| | (2)(i), (j), (3) | 1 Apr 2018 (SI 2018/241) |
| | (4) | 1 Apr 2018 (E) (SI 2018/241) |
| | | 1 Apr 2018 (W) (SI 2018/415) |
| | (5)–(7) | 1 Apr 2018 (SI 2018/241) |
| 90 | | 1 Aug 2019 (SI 2018/1226) |
| 91–108 | | 30 Mar 2018 (SI 2018/241) |
| 109 | (1)(a)–(d) | 31 Oct 2018 (SI 2018/1054) |
| | (1)(e) | *Not yet in force* |
| | (1)(f) | 31 Oct 2018 (SI 2018/1054) |
| | (1)(g) | 30 Mar 2020 (SI 2020/321) |
| | (1)(h) | 31 Oct 2018 (SI 2018/1054) |
| | (2) | 31 Oct 2018 (to the extent it applies to any research council which ceases to exist by virtue of s 109(1) except paras (e), (g)) (SI 2018/1054) |
| | | 30 Mar 2020 (to the extent it applies to the Science and Technology Facilities Council which ceases to exist by virtue of s 109(1)(g) (SI 2020/321) |
| | | *Not yet in force (otherwise)* |
| | (3), (4) | 30 Mar 2018 (SI 2018/241) |
| 110 | | 27 Jun 2017 (s 124(4)) |
| 111 | | 30 Mar 2018 (SI 2018/241) |
| 112–114 | | 1 Apr 2018 (SI 2018/241) |
| 115–117 | | 27 Apr 2017 (s 124(1)) |
| 118 | | 1 Jan 2018 (SI 2017/1146) |
| 119–121 | | 27 Apr 2017 (s 124(1)) |
| 122 | (1) | See Sch 11 below |
| | (2) | See Sch 12 below |
| 123–125 | | 27 Apr 2017 (s 124(1)) |
| Sch 1 | | 1 Jan 2018 (SI 2017/788) |
| Sch 2 | | 1 Apr 2018 (SI 2018/241) |
| Sch 3 | | 1 Aug 2019 (SI 2018/1226) |
| Sch 4 | paras 1–5 | 1 Jan 2018 (SI 2017/1146) |
| | para 6 | 1 Apr 2018 (SI 2018/241) |
| | para 7 | 1 Jan 2018 (SI 2017/1146) |
| | paras 8–11 | 1 Apr 2018 (SI 2018/241) |
| | para 12 | 1 Jan 2018 (SI 2017/1146) |
| Sch 5 | | 1 Apr 2018 (SI 2018/241) |
| Sch 6 | paras 1–5 | 1 Jan 2018 (SI 2017/1146) |
| | paras 6–10 | 1 Jan 2019 (SI 2018/1226) |
| | para 11 | 1 Jan 2018 (SI 2017/1146) |
| Schs 7, 8 | | 1 Aug 2019 (SI 2018/1226) |
| Sch 9 | | 30 Mar 2018 (SI 2018/241) |
| Sch 10 | | 1 Jan 2018 (SI 2017/1146) |
| Sch 11 | paras 1–4 | 1 Apr 2018 (SI 2018/241) |
| | para 5 | 1 Aug 2019 (SI 2018/1226) |
| | para 6 | 1 Apr 2018 (SI 2018/241) |
| | paras 7–9 | 1 Aug 2019 (SI 2018/1226) |

**Higher Education and Research Act 2017 (c 29)**—*contd*

| | | |
|---|---|---|
| | para 10 | 1 Apr 2018 (SI 2018/241) |
| | para 11 | 1 Aug 2019 (SI 2018/1226) |
| | paras 12–28 | 1 Apr 2018 (SI 2018/241) |
| | para 29(1) | 1 Apr 2018 (SI 2018/241) |
| | para 29(2), (3) | 1 Aug 2019 (SI 2018/1226) |
| | para 29(4) | 1 Apr 2018 (SI 2018/241) |
| | paras 30–35 | 1 Apr 2018 (SI 2018/241) |
| Sch 12 | paras 1, 2 | 1 Apr 2018 (SI 2018/241) |
| | para 3 | 31 Oct 2018 (except the entry for the Medical Research Council) (SI 2018/1054) |
| | | *Not yet in force* (exception noted above) |
| | para 4(1) | See sub-paras (2)–(5) below |
| | para 4(2)(a) | 31 Oct 2018 (except to the extent it applies to either or both of the Medical Research Council or the Science and Technology Facilities Council) (SI 2018/1054) |
| | | 30 Mar 2020 (to the extent it applies to the Science and Technology Facilities Council) (SI 2020/321) |
| | | *Not yet in force* (exception noted above) |
| | para 4(2)(b) | 31 Oct 2018 (except to the extent it applies to either or both of the Medical Research Council or the Science and Technology Facilities Council) (SI 2018/1054) |
| | | *Not yet in force* (exception noted above) |
| | para 4(2)(c) | 31 Oct 2018 (except to the extent it applies to either or both of the Medical Research Council or the Science and Technology Facilities Council) (SI 2018/1054) |
| | | 30 Mar 2020 (exception noted above) (SI 2020/321) |
| | para 4(3)–(5) | 31 Oct 2018 (except to the extent it applies to either or both of the Medical Research Council or the Science and Technology Facilities Council) (SI 2018/1054) |
| | | *Not yet in force* (exception noted above) |
| | para 5 | 31 Oct 2018 (except to the extent it applies to the Medical Research Council and the Science and Technology Facilities Council) (SI 2018/1054) |
| | | 30 Mar 2020 (to the extent it applies to the Science and Technology Facilities Council) (SI 2012/321) |
| | | *Not yet in force* (exception noted above) |
| | paras 6, 7 | 1 Apr 2018 (SI 2018/241) |
| | para 8 | *Not yet in force* |
| | paras 9, 10 | 1 Apr 2018 (SI 2018/241) |
| | para 11 | 31 Oct 2018 (except the entries for the Chair or Chief Executive of the Science and Technology Facilities Council and the Chairman, Deputy Chairman or Chief Executive of the Medical Research Council) (SI 2018/1054) |
| | | 30 Mar 2020 (entry for the Chair or Chief Executive of the Science and Technology Facilities Council) (SI 2020/321) |
| | | *Not yet in force* (exception noted above) |
| | para 12 | 31 Oct 2018 (except to the extent it applies to the Medical Research Council and the Science and Technology Facilities Council) (SI 2018/1054) |
| | | 30 Mar 2020 (the Chair or Chief Executive of the Science and Technology Facilities Council) (SI 2020/321) |
| | | *Not yet in force* (exception noted above) |
| | paras 13–15 | 1 Apr 2018 (SI 2018/241) |
| | para 16(1)–(4) | 1 Apr 2018 (SI 2018/241) |
| | para 16(5), (6) | 31 Oct 2018 (SI 2018/1054) |
| | para 17 | 31 Oct 2018 (SI 2018/1054) |
| | para 18 | 1 Apr 2018 (SI 2018/241) |
| | para 19 | 31 Oct 2018 (SI 2018/1054) |
| | paras 20–23 | 1 Apr 2018 (SI 2018/241) |
| | para 24(1)–(3) | 1 Apr 2018 (SI 2018/241) |

## Higher Education and Research Act 2017 (c 29)—*contd*

|  |  |  |
|---|---|---|
| para 24(4)(a) | 31 Oct 2018 (SI 2018/1054) |
| para 24(4)(b), (c) | 1 Apr 2018 (SI 2018/241) |
| paras 25–29 | 1 Apr 2018 (SI 2018/241) |

## Homelessness Reduction Act 2017 (c 13)

*RA*: 27 Apr 2017

*Commencement provisions*: s 13(2), (3); Homelessness Reduction Act 2017 (Commencement and Transitional and Savings Provisions) Regulations 2018, SI 2018/167

| | | |
|---|---|---|
| 1 | | 3 Apr 2018 (SI 2018/167)[1] |
| 2, 3 | | 3 Apr 2018 (SI 2018/167) |
| 4, 5 | | 3 Apr 2018 (SI 2018/167)[1] |
| 6 | | 3 Apr 2018 (SI 2018/167) |
| 7 | (1) | 12 Feb 2018 (only in so far as is necessary for enabling the exercise of the power to make regulations conferred by Housing Act 1996, s 193B(7)) (SI 2018/167) |
| | | 3 Apr 2018 (otherwise) (SI 2018/167) |
| | (2) | 3 Apr 2018 (SI 2018/167) |
| 8 | | 3 Apr 2018 (SI 2018/167) |
| 9 | (1), (2) | 12 Feb 2018 (only in so far as is necessary for enabling the exercise of the power to make regulations under Housing Act 1996, s 203(1) as to the procedure to be followed in relation to reviews under s 202(1)(ba)–(bc), (h) thereof) (SI 2018/167)[1] |
| | | 3 Apr 2018 (otherwise) (SI 2018/167)[1] |
| | (3) | 3 Apr 2018 (SI 2018/167)[1] |
| 10 | | 12 Feb 2018 (only in so far as is necessary for enabling the exercise of the power to make regulations conferred by Housing Act 1996, s 213B(4)) (SI 2018/167) |
| | | 3 Apr 2018 (otherwise) (SI 2018/167) |
| 11, 12 | | 3 Apr 2018 (SI 2018/167) |
| 13 | | 27 Apr 2017 (s 13(2)) |

[1]   For transitional and savings provisions, see SI 2018/167, reg 4

## Intellectual Property (Unjustified Threats) Act 2017 (c 14)

*RA*: 27 Apr 2017

*Commencement provisions*: s 8; Intellectual Property (Unjustified Threats) Act 2017 (Commencement and Transitional Provisions) Regulations 2017, SI 2017/771

| | | |
|---|---|---|
| 1 | (1), (2) | 1 Oct 2017 (SI 2017/771)[2] |
| | (3) | *Not yet in force*[1] |
| | (4)–(7) | 1 Oct 2017 (SI 2017/771)[2] |
| | (8) | *Not yet in force*[1] |
| 2–6 | | 1 Oct 2017 (SI 2017/771)[2] |
| 7 | (1)–(3) | 27 Apr 2017 (s 8(1)) |
| | (4) | 1 Oct 2017 (SI 2017/771)[2] |
| 8 | | 27 Apr 2017 (s 8(1)) |

[1]   S 1(3), (8) come into force on the date of entry into force of the Agreement on a Unified Patent Court signed at Brussels on 19 Feb 2013

[2]   For transitional provisions, see SI 2017/771, reg 3

## Land Transaction Tax and Anti-avoidance of Devolved Taxes (Wales) Act 2017 (anaw 1)

*RA:* 24 May 2017

*Commencement provisions:* s 81; Land Transaction Tax and Anti-avoidance of Devolved Taxes (Wales) Act 2017 (Commencement No 1) Order 2017, SI 2017/953; Land Transaction Tax and Antiavoidance of Devolved Taxes (Wales) Act 2017 (Commencement No 2) Order 2018, SI 2018/34

| | | |
|---|---|---|
| 1–8 | | 1 Apr 2018 (SI 2018/34) |
| 9 | (1)–(5) | 1 Apr 2018 (SI 2018/34) |
| | (6) | 18 Oct 2017 (SI 2017/953) |
| | (7)–(9) | 1 Apr 2018 (SI 2018/34) |
| 10–23 | | 1 Apr 2018 (SI 2018/34) |
| 24 | | 18 Oct 2017 (for the purpose of making regulations) (SI 2017/953) |
| | | 1 Apr 2018 (otherwise) (SI 2018/34) |
| 25 | | 18 Oct 2017 (SI 2017/953) |
| 26–29 | | 1 Apr 2018 (SI 2018/34) |
| 30 | (1) | See Schs 9–22 below |
| | (2)–(6) | 1 Apr 2018 (SI 2018/34) |
| 31 | | 1 Apr 2018 (SI 2018/34) |
| 32 | (1) | 1 Apr 2018 (SI 2018/34) |
| | (2) | See Sch 6 below |
| 33–64 | | 1 Apr 2018 (SI 2018/34) |
| 65 | (1)–(4) | 1 Apr 2018 (SI 2018/34) |
| | (5), (6) | 18 Oct 2017 (SI 2017/953) |
| | (7)(a) | 1 Apr 2018 (SI 2018/34) |
| | (7)(b) | 18 Oct 2017 (SI 2017/953) |
| 66, 67 | | 1 Apr 2018 (SI 2018/34) |
| 68–75 | | 25 May 2017 (s 81(1)) |
| 76 | | See Sch 23 below |
| 77 | | 1 Apr 2018 (SI 2018/34) |
| 78–82 | | 25 May 2017 (s 81(1)) |
| Schs 1–5 | | 1 Apr 2018 (SI 2018/34) |
| Sch 6 | paras 1–27 | 1 Apr 2018 (SI 2018/34) |
| | para 28 | 18 Oct 2017 (SI 2017/953) |
| | paras 29–35 | 1 Apr 2018 (SI 2018/34) |
| | para 36(1)(a) | 1 Apr 2018 (SI 2018/34) |
| | para 36(1)(b) | 18 Oct 2017 (for the purpose of making regulations) (SI 2017/953) |
| | | 1 Apr 2018 (otherwise) (SI 2018/34) |
| | para 36(2) | 1 Apr 2018 (SI 2018/34) |
| | para 37 | 1 Apr 2018 (SI 2018/34) |
| Schs 7–10 | | 1 Apr 2018 (SI 2018/34) |
| Sch 11 | para 1 | 1 Apr 2018 (SI 2018/34) |
| | para 2 | 18 Oct 2017 (SI 2017/953) |
| | paras 3–8 | 1 Apr 2018 (SI 2018/34) |
| | para 9(1) | 18 Oct 2017 (for the purpose of making regulations) (SI 2017/953) |
| | | 1 Apr 2018 (otherwise) (SI 2018/34) |
| | para 9(2) | 1 Apr 2018 (SI 2018/34) |
| | para 10–15 | 1 Apr 2018 (SI 2018/34) |
| | para 16 | 18 Oct 2017 (for the purpose of making regulations) (SI 2017/953) |
| | | 1 Apr 2018 (otherwise) (SI 2018/34) |
| | para 17 | 1 Apr 2018 (SI 2018/34) |
| | para 18(1)–(3) | 1 Apr 2018 (SI 2018/34) |
| | para 18(4)(a) | 18 Oct 2017 (for the purpose of making regulations) (SI 2017/953) |
| | | 1 Apr 2018 (otherwise) (SI 2018/34) |
| | para 18(4)(b) | 1 Apr 2018 (SI 2018/34) |
| | para 18(5) | 18 Oct 2017 (SI 2017/953) |
| | para 18(6) | 1 Apr 2018 (SI 2018/34) |
| | para 19 | 1 Apr 2018 (SI 2018/34) |
| Schs 12–22 | | 1 Apr 2018 (SI 2018/34) |

**Land Transaction Tax and Anti-avoidance of Devolved Taxes (Wales) Act 2017 (anaw 1)**—*contd*

| | | |
|---|---|---|
| Sch 23 | paras 1–7 | 1 Apr 2018 (SI 2018/34) |
| | para 8 | 18 Oct 2017 (SI 2017/953) |
| | paras 9–34 | 1 Apr 2018 (SI 2018/34) |
| | paras 35–38 | 25 Jan 2018 (SI 2018/34) |
| | paras 39–55 | 1 Apr 2018 (SI 2018/34) |
| | paras 56–59 | 25 Jan 2018 (SI 2018/34) |
| | para 60 | 1 Apr 2018 (SI 2018/34) |
| | para 61 | 25 Jan 2018 (SI 2018/34) |
| | paras 62, 63 | 1 Apr 2018 (SI 2018/34) |
| | para 64 | 25 Jan 2018 (SI 2018/34) |
| | paras 65–67 | 1 Apr 2018 (SI 2018/34) |
| | paras 68–70 | 25 Jan 2018 (SI 2018/34) |
| | para 71 | 1 Apr 2018 (SI 2018/34) |

## Landfill Disposals Tax (Wales) Act 2017 (anaw 3)

*RA:* 7 Sep 2017

*Commencement provisions:* s 97; Landfill Disposals Tax (Wales) Act 2017 (Commencement No 1) Order 2017, SI 2017/955; Landfill Disposals Tax (Wales) Act 2017 (Commencement No 2) Order 2018, SI 2018/35

| | | |
|---|---|---|
| 1 | | 8 Sep 2017 (s 97(1)) |
| 2–7 | | 1 Apr 2018 (SI 2018/35) |
| 8 | (1)–(3) | 1 Apr 2018 (SI 2018/35) |
| | (4) | 25 Jan 2018 (SI 2018/35) |
| | (5), (6) | 1 Apr 2018 (SI 2018/35) |
| 9–13 | | 1 Apr 2018 (SI 2018/35) |
| 14 | (1), (2) | 1 Apr 2018 (SI 2018/35) |
| | (3) | 18 Oct 2017 (for the purpose of making regulations) (SI 2017/955) |
| | | 1 Apr 2018 (otherwise) (SI 2018/35) |
| | (4), (5) | 1 Apr 2018 (SI 2018/35) |
| | (6) | 18 Oct 2017 (for the purpose of making regulations) (SI 2017/955) |
| | | 1 Apr 2018 (otherwise) (SI 2018/35) |
| | (7), (8) | 1 Apr 2018 (SI 2018/35) |
| 15, 16 | | 1 Apr 2018 (SI 2018/35) |
| 17 | | 18 Oct 2017 (SI 2017/955) |
| 18–19 | | 1 Apr 2018 (SI 2018/35) |
| 20 | (1), (2) | 1 Apr 2018 (SI 2018/35) |
| | (3)–(6) | 25 Jan 2018 (SI 2018/35) |
| | (7), (8) | 1 Apr 2018 (SI 2018/35) |
| 21 | (1)–(5) | 25 Jan 2018 (SI 2018/35) |
| | (6) | 1 Apr 2018 (SI 2018/35) |
| | (7) | 25 Jan 2018 (SI 2018/35) |
| | (8) | 1 Apr 2018 (SI 2018/35) |
| 22, 23 | | 1 Apr 2018 (SI 2018/35) |
| 24–26 | | 25 Jan 2018 (SI 2018/35) |
| 27, 28 | | 1 Apr 2018 (SI 2018/35) |
| 29 | (1) | 1 Apr 2018 (SI 2018/35) |
| | (2), (3) | 25 Jan 2018 (SI 2018/35) |
| 30, 31 | | 25 Jan 2018 (SI 2018/35) |
| 32 | | 1 Apr 2018 (SI 2018/35) |
| 33 | | 18 Oct 2017 (SI 2017/955) |
| 34 | | 25 Jan 2018 (SI 2018/35) |
| 35 | (1) | 1 Apr 2018 (SI 2018/35) |
| | (2)–(5) | 25 Jan 2018 (SI 2018/35) |
| 36 | | 25 Jan 2018 (SI 2018/35) |
| 37 | (1)–(4) | 1 Apr 2018 (SI 2018/35) |

**Landfill Disposals Tax (Wales) Act 2017 (anaw 3)**—*contd*

|  |  |  |
|---|---|---|
|  | (5), (6) | 25 Jan 2018 (SI 2018/35) |
| 38 |  | 25 Jan 2018 (SI 2018/35) |
| 39 | (1)–(4) | 1 Apr 2018 (SI 2018/35) |
|  | (5)–(8) | 25 Jan 2018 (SI 2018/35) |
| 40 |  | 25 Jan 2018 (SI 2018/35) |
| 41 | (1)–(8) | 1 Apr 2018 (SI 2018/35) |
|  | (9) | 18 Oct 2017 (SI 2017/955) |
| 42 |  | 1 Apr 2018 (SI 2018/35) |
| 43 | (1) | 1 Apr 2018 (SI 2018/35) |
|  | (2) | 25 Jan 2018 (SI 2018/35) |
|  | (3) | 1 Apr 2018 (SI 2018/35) |
| 44, 45 |  | 1 Apr 2018 (SI 2018/35) |
| 46 | (1)–(3) | 1 Apr 2018 (SI 2018/35) |
|  | (4) | 18 Oct 2017 (for the purpose of making regulations) (SI 2017/955) |
|  |  | 1 Apr 2018 (otherwise) (SI 2018/35) |
|  | (5) | 1 Apr 2018 (SI 2018/35) |
| 47–53 |  | 1 Apr 2018 (SI 2018/35) |
| 54 |  | 18 Oct 2017 (SI 2017/955) |
| 55 |  | 25 Jan 2018 (SI 2018/35) |
| 56 |  | 1 Apr 2018 (SI 2018/35) |
| 57 | (1), (2) | 1 Apr 2018 (SI 2018/35) |
|  | (3) | 25 Jan 2018 (SI 2018/35) |
|  | (4)–(6) | 1 Apr 2018 (SI 2018/35) |
| 58, 59 |  | 25 Jan 2018 (SI 2018/35) |
| 60 |  | 8 Nov 2017 (SI 2017/955) |
| 61–65 |  | 1 Apr 2018 (SI 2018/35) |
| 66, 67 |  | 25 Jan 2018 (SI 2018/35) |
| 68, 69 |  | 1 Apr 2018 (SI 2018/35) |
| 70–72 |  | 25 Jan 2018 (SI 2018/35) |
| 73–76 |  | 1 Apr 2018 (SI 2018/35) |
| 77–84 |  | 25 Jan 2018 (SI 2018/35) |
| 85 |  | 1 Apr 2018 (SI 2018/35) |
| 86 |  | 25 Jan 2018 (SI 2018/35) |
| 87 |  | 18 Oct 2017 (SI 2017/955) |
| 88, 89 |  | 1 Apr 2018 (SI 2018/35) |
| 90 |  | 25 Jan 2018 (SI 2018/35) |
| 91 |  | 18 Oct 2017 (SI 2017/955) |
| 92 |  | 8 Nov 2017 (SI 2017/955) |
| 93–98 |  | 8 Sep 2017 (s 97(1)) |
| Sch 1 |  | 1 Apr 2018 (SI 2018/35) |
| Sch 2 |  | 25 Jan 2018 (SI 2018/35) |
| Sch 3 |  | 1 Apr 2018 (SI 2018/35) |
| Sch 4 | paras 1–3 | 1 Apr 2018 (SI 2018/35) |
|  | paras 4–8 | 25 Jan 2018 (SI 2018/35) |
|  | paras 9–15 | 1 Apr 2018 (SI 2018/35) |
|  | para 16 | 25 Jan 2018 (SI 2018/35) |
|  | para 17 | 1 Apr 2018 (SI 2018/35) |
|  | paras 18–20 | 25 Jan 2018 (SI 2018/35) |

**Limitation (Childhood Abuse) (Scotland) Act 2017 (asp 3)**

*RA:* 28 Jul 2017

*Commencement provisions:* s 2; Limitation (Childhood Abuse) (Scotland) Act 2017 (Commencement) Regulations 2017, SSI 2017/279

|  |  |
|---|---|
| 1 | 4 Oct 2017 (SSI 2017/279) |
| 2, 3 | 29 Jul 2017 (s 2(1)) |

## Local Audit (Public Access to Documents) Act 2017 (c 25)

*RA:* 27 Apr 2017

Whole Act in force 27 Jun 2017 (s 2(1))

## Merchant Shipping (Homosexual Conduct) Act 2017 (c 26)

*RA:* 27 Apr 2017

Whole Act in force 27 Apr 2017 (RA)

## National Citizen Service Act 2017 (c 15)

*RA:* 27 Apr 2017

*Commencement provisions*: s 14; National Citizen Service Act 2017 (Commencement No 1) Regulations 2017, SI 2017/1228; National Citizen Service Act 2017 (Commencement No 2) Regulations 2018, SI 2018/1239

| | | |
|---|---|---|
| 1 | | 27 Apr 2017 (s 14(1)) |
| 2 | | See Sch 1 below |
| 3–9 | | 1 Dec 2018 (SI 2018/1239) |
| 10 | | 27 Apr 2017 (s 14(1)) |
| 11 | | See Sch 2 below |
| 12–15 | | 27 Apr 2017 (s 14(1)) |
| Sch 1 | | 13 Dec 2017 (SI 2017/1228) |
| Sch 2 | para 1 | 13 Dec 2017 (SI 2017/1228) |
| | paras 2–4 | 1 Dec 2018 (SI 2018/1239) |

## Neighbourhood Planning Act 2017 (c 20)

*RA:* 27 Apr 2017

*Commencement provisions*: s 46; Neighbourhood Planning Act 2017 (Commencement No 1) Regulations 2017, SI 2017/767; Neighbourhood Planning Act 2017 (Commencement No 2) Regulations 2017, SI 2017/936; Neighbourhood Planning Act 2017 (Commencement No 3) Regulations 2018, SI 2018/38; Neighbourhood Planning Act 2017 (Commencement No 4 and Transitional Provisions) Regulations 2018, SI 2018/252; Neighbourhood Planning Act 2017 (Commencement No 5) Regulations 2018, SI 2018/567; Neighbourhood Planning Act 2017(Commencement No 6) Regulations 2019, SI 2019/1081

| | | |
|---|---|---|
| 1 | | 19 Jul 2017 (SI 2017/767) |
| 2 | | 27 Apr 2017 (for the purposes only of enabling the Secretary of State to make provision by development order under Town and Country Planning Act 1990, Sch 1, para 8(6)) (s 46(3)(a)) |
| | | 31 Jan 2018 (otherwise) (SI 2018/38) |
| 3 | | 19 Jul 2017 (SI 2017/767) |
| 4 | | 27 Apr 2017 (in so far as confers power on the Secretary of State to make regulations) (s 46(3)(b)) |
| | | 31 Jan 2018 (otherwise) (SI 2018/38) |
| 5 | | 31 Jan 2018 (otherwise) (SI 2018/38) |
| 6 | | 31 Jul 2018 (otherwise) (SI 2018/38) |
| 7 | | *Not yet in force* |
| 8 | (1) | 16 Jan 2018 (SI 2018/38) |
| | (2) | 4 Jul 2019 (SI 2019/1081) |
| | (3) | 16 Jan 2018 (SI 2018/38) |
| 9 | | 27 Apr 2017 (in so far as confers power on the Secretary of State to make regulations) (s 46(3)(b)) |
| | | 16 Jan 2018 (otherwise) (SI 2018/38) |
| 10 | | 16 Jan 2018 (SI 2018/38) |

**Neighbourhood Planning Act 2017 (c 20)**—*contd*

| | | |
|---|---|---|
| 11 | | 19 Jul 2017 (SI 2017/767) |
| 12 | | 27 Apr 2017 (in so far as confer power on the Secretary of State to make regulations) (s 46(3)(b)) |
| | | 19 Jul 2017 (otherwise) (SI 2017/767) |
| 13 | (1) | See sub-ss (2), (3) below |
| | (2) | 31 Jul 2018 (SI 2018/38)[2] |
| | (3) | 27 Apr 2017 (s 46(3)(b)) |
| 14 | (1) | 19 Jul 2017 (for the purpose only of making regulations under Town and Country Planning Act 1990, s 100ZA) (SI 2017/767) |
| | | 1 Oct 2018 (for the purpose only of commencing s 100ZA(4)–(13) of the Town and Country Planning Act 1990) (SI 2018/567) |
| | | *Not yet in force* (otherwise) |
| | (2) | 19 Jul 2017 (for the purpose only of making regulations under Town and Country Planning Act 1990, s 100ZA) (SI 2017/767) |
| | | *Not yet in force* (otherwise) |
| | (3) | 19 Jul 2017 (for the purpose only of making regulations under Town and Country Planning Act 1990, s 100ZA) (SI 2017/767) |
| | | 1 Oct 2018 (for the purpose only of commencing s 100ZA(4)–(13) of the Town and Country Planning Act 1990) (SI 2018/567) |
| | | *Not yet in force* (otherwise) |
| | (4) | See Sch 3 below |
| | | *Not yet in force* (otherwise) |
| 15 | | 27 Apr 2017 (s 46(3)(c)) |
| 16 | | 19 Jul 2017 (SI 2017/767) |
| 17 | | 27 Apr 2017 (s 46(3)(d)) |
| 18–25 | | *Not yet in force* |
| 26 | (1)–(7), (8)(a) | *Not yet in force* |
| | (8)(b) | 22 Sep 2017 (SI 2017/936)[1] |
| 27, 28 | | *Not yet in force* |
| 29, 30 | | 19 Jul 2017 (SI 2017/767) |
| 31 | | *Not yet in force* |
| 32 | | 22 Sep 2017 (SI 2017/936)[1] |
| 33, 34 | | 22 Sep 2017 (SI 2017/936) |
| 35 | | 22 Sep 2017 (SI 2017/936)[1] |
| 36 | | 22 Sep 2017 (SI 2017/936) |
| 37 | | 19 Jul 2017 (SI 2017/767) |
| 38 | | 6 Apr 2018 (SI 2018/252)[3] |
| 39–40 | | *Not yet in force* |
| 41 | | 19 Jul 2017 (SI 2017/767) |
| 42 | | 27 Apr 2017 (s 46(3)(e)) |
| 43–47 | | 27 Apr 2017 (s 46(3)(f)) |
| Sch 1 | | 27 Apr 2017 (in so far as confers power on the Secretary of State to make regulations) (s 46(3)(b)) |
| | | 31 Jan 2018 (otherwise) (SI 2018/38) |
| Sch 2 | | 16 Jan 2018 (SI 2018/38) |
| Sch 3 | para 1 | 1 Oct 2018 (SI 2018/567) |
| | para 2 | *Not yet in force* |
| | paras 3–5 | 1 Oct 2018 (SI 2018/567) |
| | paras 6, 7 | *Not yet in force* |
| | para 8 | 1 Oct 2018 (SI 2018/567) |

---

[1]  For transitional provisions, see SI 2017/936, regs 4, 5

[2]  For transitional provisions, see SI 2018/38, reg 5

[3]  For transitional provisions, see SI 2018/252, reg 4

---

**Northern Ireland Budget Act 2017 (c 34)**

*RA:* 16 Nov 2017

Whole Act in force 16 Nov 2017 (RA)

---

**Northern Ireland (Ministerial Appointments and Regional Rates) Act 2017 (c 24)**

*RA:* 27 Apr 2017

Whole Act in force 27 Apr 2017 (RA)

---

**Parking Places (Variation of Charges) Act 2017 (c 25)**

*RA:* 27 Apr 2017

Whole Act in force 27 Jun 2017 (s 3(1))

---

**Pension Schemes Act 2017 (c 17)**

*RA:* 27 Apr 2017

*Commencement provisions:* s 44; Pension Schemes Act 2017 (Commencement No 1) Regulations 2018, SI 2018/62; Pension Schemes Act 2017 (Commencement No 2) Regulations 2018, SI 2018/965

| | |
|---|---|
| 1, 2 | 27 Apr 2017 (as they apply to existing Master Trust schemes within the meaning of Sch 2) (s 44(1)(a)) |
| | 5 Sep 2018 (for the purpose of making regulations) (SI 2018/965) |
| | 1 Oct 2018 (otherwise) (SI 2018/965) |
| 3–16 | 5 Sep 2018 (for the purpose of making regulations) (SI 2018/965) |
| | 1 Oct 2018 (otherwise) (SI 2018/965) |
| 17, 18 | 27 Apr 2017 (as they apply to existing Master Trust schemes within the meaning of Sch 2) (s 44(1)(a)) |
| | 5 Sep 2018 (for the purpose of making regulations) (SI 2018/965) |
| | 1 Oct 2018 (otherwise) (SI 2018/965) |
| 19 | 5 Sep 2018 (for the purpose of making regulations) (SI 2018/965) |
| | 1 Oct 2018 (otherwise) (SI 2018/965) |
| 20–22 | 27 Apr 2017 (as they apply to existing Master Trust schemes within the meaning of Sch 2) (s 44(1)(a)) |
| | 5 Sep 2018 (for the purpose of making regulations) (SI 2018/965) |
| | 1 Oct 2018 (otherwise) (SI 2018/965) |
| 23, 24 | 5 Sep 2018 (for the purpose of making regulations) (SI 2018/965) |
| | 1 Oct 2018 (otherwise) (SI 2018/965) |
| 25 | 27 Apr 2017 (as it applies to existing Master Trust schemes within the meaning of Sch 2) (s 44(1)(a)) |
| | 5 Sep 2018 (for the purpose of making regulations) (SI 2018/965) |
| | 1 Oct 2018 (otherwise) (SI 2018/965) |
| 26–30 | 5 Sep 2018 (for the purpose of making regulations) (SI 2018/965) |
| | 1 Oct 2018 (otherwise) (SI 2018/965) |
| 31 | See Sch 1 below |
| 32 | 5 Sep 2018 (for the purpose of making regulations) (SI 2018/965) |
| | 1 Oct 2018 (otherwise) (SI 2018/965) |
| 33 | 27 Apr 2017 (as it applies to existing Master Trust schemes within the meaning of Sch 2) (s 44(1)(a)) |
| | 5 Sep 2018 (for the purpose of making regulations) (SI 2018/965) |
| | 1 Oct 2018 (otherwise) (SI 2018/965) |
| 34–36 | 5 Sep 2018 (for the purpose of making regulations) (SI 2018/965) |
| | 1 Oct 2018 (otherwise) (SI 2018/965) |
| 37 | See Sch 2 below |
| 38 | See Sch 3 below |

**Pension Schemes Act 2017 (c 17)**—*contd*

| | | |
|---|---|---|
| 39 | | 27 Apr 2017 (as it applies to existing Master Trust schemes within the meaning of Sch 2) (s 44(1)(a)) |
| | | 5 Sep 2018 (for the purpose of making regulations) (SI 2018/965) |
| | | 1 Oct 2018 (otherwise) (SI 2018/965) |
| 40 | | 5 Sep 2018 (for the purpose of making regulations) (SI 2018/965) |
| | | 1 Oct 2018 (otherwise) (SI 2018/965) |
| 41 | | 27 Apr 2017 (s 44(1)(d)) |
| 42–46 | | 27 Apr 2017 (s 44(1)(e)) |
| Sch 1 | | 5 Sep 2018 (for the purpose of making regulations) (SI 2018/965) |
| | | 1 Oct 2018 (otherwise) (SI 2018/965) |
| Sch 2 | paras 1–7 | 27 Apr 2017 (s 44(1)(b)) |
| | paras 8–15 | 5 Sep 2018 (for the purpose of making regulations) (SI 2018/965) |
| | | 1 Oct 2018 (otherwise) (SI 2018/965) |
| Sch 3 | paras 1–4 | 27 Apr 2017 (s 44(1)(c)) |
| | para 5 | See paras 6–13 below |
| | paras 6, 7 | 5 Sep 2018 (for the purpose of making regulations) (SI 2018/965) |
| | | 1 Oct 2018 (otherwise) (SI 2018/965) |
| | para 8 | 27 Apr 2017 (as it applies to existing Master Trust schemes within the meaning of Sch 2) (s 44(1)(a)) |
| | | 5 Sep 2018 (for the purpose of making regulations) (SI 2018/965) |
| | | 1 Oct 2018 (otherwise) (SI 2018/965) |
| | para 9 | 1 Feb 2018 (SI 2018/62) |
| | paras 10, 11 | 5 Sep 2018 (for the purpose of making regulations) (SI 2018/965) |
| | | 1 Oct 2018 (otherwise) (SI 2018/965) |
| | para 12 | 27 Apr 2017 (s 44(1)(c)) |
| | paras 13, 14 | 5 Sep 2018 (for the purpose of making regulations) (SI 2018/965) |
| | | 1 Oct 2018 (otherwise) (SI 2018/965) |

**Policing and Crime Act 2017 (c 3)**

*RA:* 31 Jan 2017

*Commencement provisions*: s 183; Policing and Crime Act 2017 (Commencement No 1 and Transitional Provisions) Regulations 2017, SI 2017/399; Policing and Crime Act 2017 (Commencement No 2) Regulations 2017, SI 2017/482; Policing and Crime Act 2017 (Commencement No 3 and Transitional and Saving Provisions) Regulations 2017, SI 2017/726; Policing and Crime Act 2017 (Commencement No 4 and Saving Provisions) Regulations 2017, SI 2017/1017; Policing and Crime Act 2017 (Commencement No 5 and Transitional Provisions) Regulations 2017, SI 2017/1139, as amended by SI 2017/1162; Policing and Crime Act 2017 (Commencement No 6 and Transitional Provisions) Regulations 2017, SI 2017/1249; Policing and Crime Act 2017 (Commencement No 7) Regulations 2018, SI 2018/227; Policing and Crime Act 2017 (Commencement No 1) Order (Northern Ireland) 2018, SR 2018/34; Policing and Crime Act 2017 (Commencement No. 8) Regulations 2018, SI 2018/456; Policing and Crime Act 2017 (Commencement No 2) Order (Northern Ireland) 2018, SR 2018/128; Policing and Crime Act 2017 (Commencement No 9 and Transitional Provision) Regulations 2019, SI 2019/1141; Policing and Crime Act 2017 (Commencement No 10 and Transitional and Saving Provisions) Regulations 2020, SI 2020/5; Policing and Crime Act 2017 (Commencement No 11 and Transitional Provisions) Regulations 2021, SI 2021/282, as amended by SI 2021/945

| | | |
|---|---|---|
| 1–7 | | 31 Jan 2017 (so far as necessary for enabling the exercise of any power to make provision by subordinate legislation or to issue codes of practice or guidance) (s 183(5)(e)) |
| | | 3 Apr 2017 (otherwise) (SI 2017/399) |
| 8 | | 31 Jan 2017 (so far as necessary for enabling the exercise of any power to make provision by subordinate legislation or to issue codes of practice or guidance) (s 183(5)(e)) |
| | | 17 Jul 2017 (otherwise) (SI 2017/726) |
| 9 | (1), (2) | 31 Jan 2017 (so far as necessary for enabling the exercise of any power to make provision by subordinate legislation or to issue codes of practice or guidance) (s 183(5)(e)) |

**Policing and Crime Act 2017 (c 3)**—*contd*

| | | |
|---|---|---|
| | | 1 Apr 2018 (otherwise) (SI 2018/227) |
| | (3) | See Sch 2 below |
| 10 | | 31 Jan 2017 (so far as necessary for enabling the exercise of any power to make provision by subordinate legislation or to issue codes of practice or guidance) (s 183(5)(e)) |
| | | 10 Mar 2018 (otherwise) (SI 2018/227) |
| 11 | (1)–(7) | 31 Jan 2017 (so far as necessary for enabling the exercise of any power to make provision by subordinate legislation or to issue codes of practice or guidance) (s 183(5)(e)) |
| | | 17 Jul 2017 (otherwise) (SI 2017/726)[2] |
| | (8) | 31 Jan 2017 (so far as necessary for enabling the exercise of any power to make provision by subordinate legislation or to issue codes of practice or guidance) (s 183(5)(e)) |
| | | *Not yet in force* (otherwise) |
| 12 | | 31 Jan 2017 (so far as necessary for enabling the exercise of any power to make provision by subordinate legislation or to issue codes of practice or guidance) (s 183(5)(e)) |
| | | 17 Jul 2017 (otherwise) (SI 2017/726) |
| 13–19 | | 31 Jan 2017 (so far as necessary for enabling the exercise of any power to make provision by subordinate legislation or to issue codes of practice or guidance) (s 183(5)(e)) |
| | | 1 Feb 2020 (otherwise) (SI 2020/5)[7] |
| 20 | | 31 Jan 2017 (so far as necessary for enabling the exercise of any power to make provision by subordinate legislation or to issue codes of practice or guidance) (s 183(5)(e)) |
| | | *Not yet in force* (otherwise) |
| 21–23 | | 31 Jan 2017 (so far as necessary for enabling the exercise of any power to make provision by subordinate legislation or to issue codes of practice or guidance) (s 183(5)(e)) |
| | | 1 Feb 2020 (otherwise) (SI 2020/5)[7] |
| 24 | | 31 Jan 2017 (so far as necessary for enabling the exercise of any power to make provision by subordinate legislation or to issue codes of practice or guidance) (s 183(5)(e)) |
| | | 18 Jul 2019 (otherwise) (SI 2019/1141) |
| 25–27 | | 31 Jan 2017 (so far as necessary for enabling the exercise of any power to make provision by subordinate legislation or to issue codes of practice or guidance) (s 183(5)(e)) |
| | | 16 Apr 2018 (SI 2018/456) |
| 28 | | 31 Jan 2017 (so far as necessary for enabling the exercise of any power to make provision by subordinate legislation or to issue codes of practice or guidance) (s 183(5)(e)) |
| | | *Not yet in force* (otherwise) |
| 29 | (1)–(7) | 31 Jan 2017 (so far as necessary for enabling the exercise of any power to make provision by subordinate legislation or to issue codes of practice or guidance) (s 183(5)(e)) |
| | | 15 Dec 2017 (otherwise) (SI 2017/1139) |
| | (8) | See Sch 7 below |
| 30 | | 31 Jan 2017 (so far as necessary for enabling the exercise of any power to make provision by subordinate legislation or to issue codes of practice or guidance) (s 183(5)(e)) |
| | | 15 Dec 2017 (otherwise) (SI 2017/1139) |
| 31 | | 31 Jan 2017 (so far as necessary for enabling the exercise of any power to make provision by subordinate legislation or to issue codes of practice or guidance) (s 183(5)(e)) |
| | | 1 Feb 2020 (otherwise) (SI 2020/5)[7] |
| 32 | | 31 Jan 2017 (so far as necessary for enabling the exercise of any power to make provision by subordinate legislation or to issue codes of practice or guidance) (s 183(5)(e)) |
| | | 3 Apr 2017 (otherwise) (SI 2017/399) |

**See Halsbury's Statutes Citator for amendments to these Acts**

**Policing and Crime Act 2017 (c 3)**—*contd*

| | | |
|---|---|---|
| 33 | (1) | 31 Jan 2017 (so far as necessary for enabling the exercise of any power to make provision by subordinate legislation or to issue codes of practice or guidance) (s 183(5)(e)) |
| | | 8 Jan 2018 (otherwise) (SI 2017/1249)[5] |
| | (2) | See sub-ss (3)–(8) below |
| | (3), (4) | 31 Jan 2017 (so far as necessary for enabling the exercise of any power to make provision by subordinate legislation or to issue codes of practice or guidance) (s 183(5)(e)) |
| | | 8 Jan 2018 (otherwise) (SI 2017/1249)[5] |
| | (5), (6) | 31 Jan 2017 (so far as necessary for enabling the exercise of any power to make provision by subordinate legislation or to issue codes of practice or guidance) (s 183(5)(e)) |
| | | 3 Apr 2017 (for the purpose of appointing the Director General and non-executive members) (SI 2017/399) |
| | | 8 Jan 2018 (otherwise) (SI 2017/1249)[5] |
| | (7), (8) | 31 Jan 2017 (so far as necessary for enabling the exercise of any power to make provision by subordinate legislation or to issue codes of practice or guidance) (s 183(5)(e)) |
| | | 8 Jan 2018 (otherwise) (SI 2017/1249)[5] |
| | (9) | See Sch 9 below |
| 34 | (1), (2) | 31 Jan 2017 (so far as necessary for enabling the exercise of any power to make provision by subordinate legislation or to issue codes of practice or guidance) (s 183(5)(e)) |
| | | 8 Jan 2018 (otherwise) (SI 2017/1249)[5] |
| | (3) | 31 Jan 2017 (so far as necessary for enabling the exercise of any power to make provision by subordinate legislation or to issue codes of practice or guidance) (s 183(5)(e)) |
| | | *Not yet in force* (otherwise) |
| | (4)–(6) | 31 Jan 2017 (so far as necessary for enabling the exercise of any power to make provision by subordinate legislation or to issue codes of practice or guidance) (s 183(5)(e)) |
| | | 8 Jan 2018 (otherwise) (SI 2017/1249)[5] |
| 35 | | 31 Jan 2017 (so far as necessary for enabling the exercise of any power to make provision by subordinate legislation or to issue codes of practice or guidance) (s 183(5)(e)) |
| | | 8 Jan 2018 (otherwise) (SI 2017/1249)[5] |
| 36 | | 31 Jan 2017 (so far as necessary for enabling the exercise of any power to make provision by subordinate legislation or to issue codes of practice or guidance) (s 183(5)(e)) |
| | | 2 May 2017 (otherwise) (SI 2017/399) |
| 37 | (1) | 31 Jan 2017 (so far as necessary for enabling the exercise of any power to make provision by subordinate legislation or to issue codes of practice or guidance) (s 183(5)(e)) |
| | | 2 May 2017 (otherwise) (SI 2017/399) |
| | (2) | 31 Jan 2017 (so far as necessary for enabling the exercise of any power to make provision by subordinate legislation or to issue codes of practice or guidance) (s 183(5)(e)) |
| | | 2 May 2017 (otherwise) (SI 2017/399)[1] |
| | (3)–(5) | 31 Jan 2017 (so far as necessary for enabling the exercise of any power to make provision by subordinate legislation or to issue codes of practice or guidance) (s 183(5)(e)) |
| | | 2 May 2017 (otherwise) (SI 2017/399) |
| | (6) | 31 Jan 2017 (so far as necessary for enabling the exercise of any power to make provision by subordinate legislation or to issue codes of practice or guidance) (s 183(5)(e)) |
| | | 2 May 2017 (otherwise) (SI 2017/399)[1] |
| 38 | | 31 Jan 2017 (so far as necessary for enabling the exercise of any power to make provision by subordinate legislation or to issue codes of practice or guidance) (s 183(5)(e)) |
| | | 15 Dec 2017 (otherwise) (SI 2017/1139)[4] |

**Policing and Crime Act 2017 (c 3)**—*contd*

| | |
|---|---|
| 39–44 | 31 Jan 2017 (so far as necessary for enabling the exercise of any power to make provision by subordinate legislation or to issue codes of practice or guidance) (s 183(5)(e)) |
| | 15 Dec 2017 (otherwise) (SI 2017/1139) |
| 45 | See Sch 12 below |
| 46 | 31 Jan 2017 (so far as necessary for enabling the exercise of any power to make provision by subordinate legislation or to issue codes of practice or guidance) (s 183(5)(e)) |
| | 1 Dec 2018 (otherwise) (SI 2017/1139) |
| 47, 48 | 31 Jan 2017 (so far as necessary for enabling the exercise of any power to make provision by subordinate legislation or to issue codes of practice or guidance) (s 183(5)(e)) |
| | *Not yet in force* (otherwise) |
| 49, 50 | 31 Jan 2017 (so far as necessary for enabling the exercise of any power to make provision by subordinate legislation or to issue codes of practice or guidance) (s 183(5)(e)) |
| | 3 Apr 2017 (otherwise) (SI 2017/399) |
| 51 | See Sch 14 below |
| 52–58 | 31 Jan 2017 (so far as necessary for enabling the exercise of any power to make provision by subordinate legislation or to issue codes of practice or guidance) (s 183(5)(e)) |
| | 3 Apr 2017 (otherwise) (SI 2017/399)[1] |
| 59 | 31 Jan 2017 (so far as necessary for enabling the exercise of any power to make provision by subordinate legislation or to issue codes of practice or guidance) (s 183(5)(e)) |
| | 3 Apr 2017 (otherwise) (SI 2017/399) |
| 60 | 31 Jan 2017 (so far as necessary for enabling the exercise of any power to make provision by subordinate legislation or to issue codes of practice or guidance) (s 183(5)(e)) |
| | 3 Apr 2017 (otherwise) (SI 2017/399)[1] |
| 61 | 31 Jan 2017 (so far as necessary for enabling the exercise of any power to make provision by subordinate legislation or to issue codes of practice or guidance) (s 183(5)(e)) |
| | 3 Apr 2017 (otherwise) (SI 2017/399) |
| 62–65 | 31 Jan 2017 (so far as necessary for enabling the exercise of any power to make provision by subordinate legislation or to issue codes of practice or guidance) (s 183(5)(e)) |
| | 3 Apr 2017 (otherwise) (SI 2017/399)[1] |
| 66–69 | 31 Jan 2017 (so far as necessary for enabling the exercise of any power to make provision by subordinate legislation or to issue codes of practice or guidance) (s 183(5)(e)) |
| | 3 Apr 2017 (otherwise) (SI 2017/399) |
| 70 | 31 Jan 2017 (so far as necessary for enabling the exercise of any power to make provision by subordinate legislation or to issue codes of practice or guidance) (s 183(5)(e)) |
| | 3 Apr 2017 (otherwise) (SI 2017/399)[1] |
| 71–75 | 31 Jan 2017 (so far as necessary for enabling the exercise of any power to make provision by subordinate legislation or to issue codes of practice or guidance) (s 183(5)(e)) |
| | 3 Apr 2017 (otherwise) (SI 2017/399) |
| 76 | 31 Mar 2017 (s 183(6)(a)) |
| 77–79 | 31 Jan 2017 (so far as necessary for enabling the exercise of any power to make provision by subordinate legislation or to issue codes of practice or guidance) (s 183(5)(e)) |
| | 3 Apr 2017 (otherwise) (SI 2017/399) |
| 80–82 | 31 Jan 2017 (so far as necessary for enabling the exercise of any power to make provision by subordinate legislation or to issue codes of practice or guidance) (s 183(5)(e)) |
| | 11 Dec 2017 (otherwise) (SI 2017/1017) |

**Policing and Crime Act 2017 (c 3)**—*contd*

| | |
|---|---|
| 83 | 31 Jan 2017 (so far as necessary for enabling the exercise of any power to make provision by subordinate legislation or to issue codes of practice or guidance) (s 183(5)(e)) |
| | 11 Dec 2017 (otherwise) (SI 2017/1017)[3] |
| 84–106 | 31 Jan 2017 (so far as necessary for enabling the exercise of any power to make provision by subordinate legislation or to issue codes of practice or guidance) (s 183(5)(e)) |
| | 10 Mar 2018 (otherwise) (SI 2018/227) |
| 107–115 | 31 Jan 2017 (so far as necessary for enabling the exercise of any power to make provision by subordinate legislation or to issue codes of practice or guidance) (s 183(5)(e)) |
| | 1 Mar 2018 (otherwise) (SR 2018/34) |
| 116–119 | 31 Jan 2017 (so far as necessary for enabling the exercise of any power to make provision by subordinate legislation or to issue codes of practice or guidance) (s 183(5)(e)) |
| | 10 Mar 2018 (otherwise) (SI 2018/227) |
| 120–122 | 31 Jan 2017 (so far as necessary for enabling the exercise of any power to make provision by subordinate legislation or to issue codes of practice or guidance) (s 183(5)(e)) |
| | 3 Apr 2017 (otherwise) (SI 2017/399) |
| 123 | 31 Jan 2017 (so far as necessary for enabling the exercise of any power to make provision by subordinate legislation or to issue codes of practice or guidance) (s 183(5)(e)) |
| | 1 Apr 2018 (otherwise) (SI 2018/227) |
| 124 | 31 Jan 2017 (s 183(5)(a)) |
| 125 | 31 Jan 2017 (so far as necessary for enabling the exercise of any power to make provision by subordinate legislation or to issue codes of practice or guidance) (s 183(5)(e)) |
| | 2 May 2017 (otherwise) (SI 2017/399) |
| 126 | 31 Jan 2017 (so far as necessary for enabling the exercise of any power to make provision by subordinate legislation or to issue codes of practice or guidance) (s 183(5)(e)) |
| | 22 Mar 2021 (otherwise) (SI 2021/282)[8] |
| 127–130 | 31 Jan 2017 (so far as necessary for enabling the exercise of any power to make provision by subordinate legislation or to issue codes of practice or guidance) (s 183(5)(e)) |
| | 2 May 2017 (otherwise) (SI 2017/399) |
| 131 | 31 Jan 2017 (so far as necessary for enabling the exercise of any power to make provision by subordinate legislation or to issue codes of practice or guidance) (s 183(5)(e)) |
| | 17 Apr 2018 (otherwise) (SI 2018/456) |
| 132 | 31 Jan 2017 (so far as necessary for enabling the exercise of any power to make provision by subordinate legislation or to issue codes of practice or guidance) (s 183(5)(e)) |
| | 18 Jul 2019 (otherwise) (SI 2019/1141)[6] |
| 133, 134 | 31 Jan 2017 (so far as necessary for enabling the exercise of any power to make provision by subordinate legislation or to issue codes of practice or guidance) (s 183(5)(e)) |
| | 3 Apr 2017 (otherwise) (SI 2017/399) |
| 135–140 | 31 Jan 2017 (so far as necessary for enabling the exercise of any power to make provision by subordinate legislation or to issue codes of practice or guidance) (s 183(5)(e)) |
| | 6 Apr 2017 (otherwise) (SI 2017/399) |
| 141 | 31 Jan 2017 (so far as necessary for enabling the exercise of any power to make provision by subordinate legislation or to issue codes of practice or guidance) (s 183(5)(e)) |
| | 6 Apr 2018 (otherwise) (SI 2018/456) |
| 142 | 31 Jan 2017 (so far as necessary for enabling the exercise of any power to make provision by subordinate legislation or to issue codes of practice or guidance) (s 183(5)(e)) |
| | *Not yet in force* (otherwise) |

**Policing and Crime Act 2017 (c 3)**—*contd*

| | |
|---|---|
| 143–156 | 31 Jan 2017 (so far as necessary for enabling the exercise of any power to make provision by subordinate legislation or to issue codes of practice or guidance) (s 183(5)(e)) |
| | 1 Apr 2017 (otherwise) (SI 2017/482) |
| 157 | 31 Mar 2017 (s 183(6)(b)) |
| 158 | 31 Mar 2017 (s 183(6)(c)) |
| 159–161 | 31 Jan 2017 (so far as necessary for enabling the exercise of any power to make provision by subordinate legislation or to issue codes of practice or guidance) (s 183(5)(e)) |
| | *Not yet in force* (otherwise) |
| 162 | 31 Jan 2017 (so far as necessary for enabling the exercise of any power to make provision by subordinate legislation or to issue codes of practice or guidance) (s 183(5)(e)) |
| | 13 Nov 2017 (otherwise) (SI 2017/1017) |
| 163 | 31 Jan 2017 (so far as necessary for enabling the exercise of any power to make provision by subordinate legislation or to issue codes of practice or guidance) (s 183(5)(e)) |
| | 3 Apr 2017 (otherwise) (SI 2017/399) |
| 164–165 | 31 Jan 2017 (s 183(5)(b)) |
| 166 | 31 Jan 2017 (so far as necessary for enabling the exercise of any power to make provision by subordinate legislation or to issue codes of practice or guidance) (s 183(5)(e)) |
| | *Not yet in force* (otherwise) |
| 167 | 31 Jan 2017 (s 183(5)(b)) |
| 168–172 | 31 Jan 2017 (so far as necessary for enabling the exercise of any power to make provision by subordinate legislation or to issue codes of practice or guidance) (s 183(5)(e)) |
| | 28 Jun 2018 (otherwise) (SR 2018/128) |
| 173, 174 | 31 Mar 2017 (s 183(6)(d)) |
| 175 | 31 Jan 2017 (so far as necessary for enabling the exercise of any power to make provision by subordinate legislation or to issue codes of practice or guidance) (s 183(5)(e)) |
| | 3 Apr 2017 (otherwise) (SI 2017/399) |
| 176 | 31 Mar 2017 (s 183(6)(e)) |
| 177, 178 | 31 Jan 2017 (so far as necessary for enabling the exercise of any power to make provision by subordinate legislation or to issue codes of practice or guidance) (s 183(5)(e)) |
| | 3 Apr 2017 (otherwise) (SI 2017/399) |
| 179 | 31 Jan 2017 (s 183(5)(c)) |
| 180–184 | 31 Jan 2017 (s 183(5)(d)) |
| Sch 1 | 31 Jan 2017 (so far as necessary for enabling the exercise of any power to make provision by subordinate legislation or to issue codes of practice or guidance) (s 183(5)(e)) |
| | 3 Apr 2017 (otherwise) (SI 2017/399) |
| Sch 2   para 1 | See paras 2–17 below |
| para 2 | 31 Jan 2017 (so far as necessary for enabling the exercise of any power to make provision by subordinate legislation or to issue codes of practice or guidance) (s 183(5)(e)) |
| | 1 Mar 2018 (otherwise) (SI 2018/227) |
| paras 3, 4 | 31 Jan 2017 (so far as necessary for enabling the exercise of any power to make provision by subordinate legislation or to issue codes of practice or guidance) (s 183(5)(e)) |
| | 1 Apr 2018 (otherwise) (SI 2018/227) |
| para 5 | 31 Jan 2017 (so far as necessary for enabling the exercise of any power to make provision by subordinate legislation or to issue codes of practice or guidance) (s 183(5)(e)) |
| | 1 Mar 2018 (otherwise) (SI 2018/227) |
| para 6 | 31 Jan 2017 (so far as necessary for enabling the exercise of any power to make provision by subordinate legislation or to issue codes of practice or guidance) (s 183(5)(e)) |

**Policing and Crime Act 2017 (c 3)**—*contd*

|  |  |
|---|---|
|  | 1 Apr 2018 (otherwise) (SI 2018/227) |
| paras 7–9 | 31 Jan 2017 (so far as necessary for enabling the exercise of any power to make provision by subordinate legislation or to issue codes of practice or guidance) (s 183(5)(e)) |
|  | 1 Mar 2018 (otherwise) (SI 2018/227) |
| para 10 | 31 Jan 2017 (so far as necessary for enabling the exercise of any power to make provision by subordinate legislation or to issue codes of practice or guidance) (s 183(5)(e)) |
|  | 10 Mar 2018 (in so far as inserts Greater London Authority Act 1999, ss 327A(1)–(3), (7), (8), 327B–327D, 327F, 327H(1), (2)(b), (3)–(12), (13)(b)) (SI 2018/227) |
|  | 22 Mar 2018 (in so far as inserts Greater London Authority Act 1999, s 327A(4) in respect of the functions of the London Fire Commissioner in relation to the firefighters' pension scheme and the firefighters' compensation scheme as they apply to a person who holds office as the London Fire Commissioner) (SI 2017/227) |
|  | 1 Apr 2018 (otherwise) (SI 2018/227) |
| paras 11–13 | 31 Jan 2017 (so far as necessary for enabling the exercise of any power to make provision by subordinate legislation or to issue codes of practice or guidance) (s 183(5)(e)) |
|  | 1 Apr 2018 (otherwise) (SI 2018/227) |
| para 14 | 31 Jan 2017 (so far as necessary for enabling the exercise of any power to make provision by subordinate legislation or to issue codes of practice or guidance) (s 183(5)(e)) |
|  | 1 Mar 2018 (otherwise) (SI 2018/227) |
| para 15 | 31 Jan 2017 (so far as necessary for enabling the exercise of any power to make provision by subordinate legislation or to issue codes of practice or guidance) (s 183(5)(e)) |
|  | 10 Mar 2018 (so far as inserts Greater London Authority Act 1999, Sch 27A, paras 1–3) (SI 2018/227) |
|  | 1 Apr 2018 (otherwise) (SI 2018/227) |
| paras 16–34 | 31 Jan 2017 (so far as necessary for enabling the exercise of any power to make provision by subordinate legislation or to issue codes of practice or guidance) (s 183(5)(e)) |
|  | 1 Apr 2018 (otherwise) (SI 2018/227) |
| para 35 | 31 Jan 2017 (so far as necessary for enabling the exercise of any power to make provision by subordinate legislation or to issue codes of practice or guidance) (s 183(5)(e)) |
|  | 22 Mar 2018 (for the purpose of the appointment of a Deputy London Fire Commissioner) (SI 2018/227) |
|  | 1 Apr 2018 (otherwise) (SI 2018/227) |
| paras 36–42 | 31 Jan 2017 (so far as necessary for enabling the exercise of any power to make provision by subordinate legislation or to issue codes of practice or guidance) (s 183(5)(e)) |
|  | 1 Apr 2018 (otherwise) (SI 2018/227) |
| para 43(1) | 31 Jan 2017 (so far as necessary for enabling the exercise of any power to make provision by subordinate legislation or to issue codes of practice or guidance) (s 183(5)(e)) |
|  | 22 Mar 2018 (for the purpose of the appointment of a Deputy London Fire Commissioner) (SI 2018/227) |
|  | 1 Apr 2018 (otherwise) (SI 2018/227) |
| para 43(2)(a) | 31 Jan 2017 (so far as necessary for enabling the exercise of any power to make provision by subordinate legislation or to issue codes of practice or guidance) (s 183(5)(e)) |
|  | 1 Apr 2018 (otherwise) (SI 2018/227) |
| para 43(2)(b) | 31 Jan 2017 (so far as necessary for enabling the exercise of any power to make provision by subordinate legislation or to issue codes of practice or guidance) (s 183(5)(e)) |
|  | 22 Mar 2018 (for the purpose of the appointment of a Deputy London Fire Commissioner) (SI 2018/227) |

**Policing and Crime Act 2017 (c 3)**—*contd*

|  |  |
|---|---|
|  | 1 Apr 2018 (otherwise) (SI 2018/227) |
| para 43(3), (4) | 31 Jan 2017 (so far as necessary for enabling the exercise of any power to make provision by subordinate legislation or to issue codes of practice or guidance) (s 183(5)(e)) |
|  | 1 Apr 2018 (otherwise) (SI 2018/227) |
| paras 44–84 | 31 Jan 2017 (so far as necessary for enabling the exercise of any power to make provision by subordinate legislation or to issue codes of practice or guidance) (s 183(5)(e)) |
|  | 1 Apr 2018 (otherwise) (SI 2018/227) |
| para 85 | 31 Jan 2017 (so far as necessary for enabling the exercise of any power to make provision by subordinate legislation or to issue codes of practice or guidance) (s 183(5)(e)) |
|  | 22 Mar 2018 (for the purpose of the appointment of a Deputy London Fire Commissioner) (SI 2018/227) |
|  | 1 Apr 2018 (otherwise) (SI 2018/227) |
| para 86 | 31 Jan 2017 (so far as necessary for enabling the exercise of any power to make provision by subordinate legislation or to issue codes of practice or guidance) (s 183(5)(e)) |
|  | *Not yet in force* (otherwise) |
| paras 87, 88 | 31 Jan 2017 (so far as necessary for enabling the exercise of any power to make provision by subordinate legislation or to issue codes of practice or guidance) (s 183(5)(e)) |
|  | 1 Apr 2018 (otherwise) (SI 2018/227) |
| para 89(1) | 31 Jan 2017 (so far as necessary for enabling the exercise of any power to make provision by subordinate legislation or to issue codes of practice or guidance) (s 183(5)(e)) |
|  | 22 Mar 2018 (for the purpose of the appointment of a Deputy London Fire Commissioner) (SI 2018/227) |
| para 89(2) | 31 Jan 2017 (so far as necessary for enabling the exercise of any power to make provision by subordinate legislation or to issue codes of practice or guidance) (s 183(5)(e)) |
|  | 1 Apr 2018 (otherwise) (SI 2018/227) |
| para 89(3) | 31 Jan 2017 (so far as necessary for enabling the exercise of any power to make provision by subordinate legislation or to issue codes of practice or guidance) (s 183(5)(e)) |
|  | 22 Mar 2018 (for the purpose of the appointment of a Deputy London Fire Commissioner and in so far as inserts Local Government and Housing Act 1989, s 21(1C)) (SI 2018/227) |
|  | 1 Apr 2018 (except so far as inserts Local Government and Housing Act 1989, s 21(1D)) (SI 2018/227) |
|  | *Not yet in force* (exception noted above) |
| paras 90–123 | 31 Jan 2017 (so far as necessary for enabling the exercise of any power to make provision by subordinate legislation or to issue codes of practice or guidance) (s 183(5)(e)) |
|  | 1 Apr 2018 (otherwise) (SI 2018/227) |
| Sch 3 | 31 Jan 2017 (so far as necessary for enabling the exercise of any power to make provision by subordinate legislation or to issue codes of practice or guidance) (s 183(5)(e)) |
|  | 17 Jul 2017 (otherwise) (SI 2017/726) |
| Schs 4, 5 | 31 Jan 2017 (so far as necessary for enabling the exercise of any power to make provision by subordinate legislation or to issue codes of practice or guidance) (s 183(5)(e)) |
|  | 1 Feb 2020 (otherwise) (SI 2020/5)[7] |
| Sch 6 | 31 Jan 2017 (so far as necessary for enabling the exercise of any power to make provision by subordinate legislation or to issue codes of practice or guidance) (s 183(5)(e)) |
|  | *Not yet in force* (otherwise) |
| Sch 7 paras 1–5 | 31 Jan 2017 (so far as necessary for enabling the exercise of any power to make provision by subordinate legislation or to issue codes of practice or guidance) (s 183(5)(e)) |
|  | 15 Dec 2017 (otherwise) (SI 2017/1139) |

**See Halsbury's Statutes Citator for amendments to these Acts** 2535

**Policing and Crime Act 2017 (c 3)**—*contd*

| | | |
|---|---|---|
| | paras 6–14 | 31 Jan 2017 (so far as necessary for enabling the exercise of any power to make provision by subordinate legislation or to issue codes of practice or guidance) (s 183(5)(e)) |
| | | 1 Feb 2020 (otherwise) (SI 2020/5)[7] |
| Sch 8 | | 31 Jan 2017 (so far as necessary for enabling the exercise of any power to make provision by subordinate legislation or to issue codes of practice or guidance) (s 183(5)(e)) |
| | | 15 Dec 2017 (otherwise) (SI 2017/1139) |
| Sch 9 | para 1 | See paras 2–14 below |
| | para 2 | 31 Jan 2017 (so far as necessary for enabling the exercise of any power to make provision by subordinate legislation or to issue codes of practice or guidance) (s 183(5)(e)) |
| | | 3 Apr 2017 (for the purpose of making appointments and the removal of persons from office) (SI 2017/399)[5] |
| | | 8 Jan 2018 (otherwise) (SI 2017/1249)[5] |
| | para 3 | 31 Jan 2017 (so far as necessary for enabling the exercise of any power to make provision by subordinate legislation or to issue codes of practice or guidance) (s 183(5)(e)) |
| | | 3 Apr 2017 (in so far as inserts Police Reform Act 2002, Sch 2, para 1A(1)) (SI 2017/399) |
| | | 8 Jan 2018 (otherwise) (SI 2017/1249)[5] |
| | para 4 | 31 Jan 2017 (so far as necessary for enabling the exercise of any power to make provision by subordinate legislation or to issue codes of practice or guidance) (s 183(5)(e)) |
| | | 3 Apr 2017 (for the purpose of making appointments and the removal of persons from office) (SI 2017/399) |
| | | 8 Jan 2018 (otherwise) (SI 2017/1249)[5] |
| | paras 5–8 | 31 Jan 2017 (so far as necessary for enabling the exercise of any power to make provision by subordinate legislation or to issue codes of practice or guidance) (s 183(5)(e)) |
| | | 8 Jan 2018 (otherwise) (SI 2017/1249)[5] |
| | para 9 | 31 Jan 2017 (so far as necessary for enabling the exercise of any power to make provision by subordinate legislation or to issue codes of practice or guidance) (s 183(5)(e)) |
| | | 17 Jul 2017 (for the purpose of making remuneration or other payments to the Director General and non-executive member) (SI 2017/726)[2] |
| | | 8 Jan 2018 (otherwise) (SI 2017/1249)[5] |
| | paras 10–74 | 31 Jan 2017 (so far as necessary for enabling the exercise of any power to make provision by subordinate legislation or to issue codes of practice or guidance) (s 183(5)(e)) |
| | | 8 Jan 2018 (otherwise) (SI 2017/1249)[5] |
| Schs 10, 11 | | 31 Jan 2017 (so far as necessary for enabling the exercise of any power to make provision by subordinate legislation or to issue codes of practice or guidance) (s 183(5)(e)) |
| | | 15 Dec 2017 (otherwise) (SI 2017/1139) |
| Sch 12 | Pts 1, 2 | 31 Jan 2017 (so far as necessary for enabling the exercise of any power to make provision by subordinate legislation or to issue codes of practice or guidance) (s 183(5)(e)) |
| | | 15 Dec 2017 (otherwise) (SI 2017/1139) |
| | Pt 3 | 3 Apr 2017 (SI 2017/399) |
| Sch 13 | | 31 Jan 2017 (so far as necessary for enabling the exercise of any power to make provision by subordinate legislation or to issue codes of practice or guidance) (s 183(5)(e)) |
| | | 1 Dec 2018 (otherwise) (SI 2017/1139) |
| Sch 14 | | 31 Jan 2017 (so far as necessary for enabling the exercise of any power to make provision by subordinate legislation or to issue codes of practice or guidance) (s 183(5)(e)) |
| | | 3 Apr 2017 (except for reference in para 7(e) to Police Reform Act 2002, s 45(3)(f)) (SI 2017/399) |
| | | *Not yet in force* (exception noted above) |

**Policing and Crime Act 2017 (c 3)**—*contd*

| | |
|---|---|
| Schs 15–17 | 31 Jan 2017 (so far as necessary for enabling the exercise of any power to make provision by subordinate legislation or to issue codes of practice or guidance) (s 183(5)(e)) |
| | 10 Mar 2018 (otherwise) (SI 2018/227) |
| Sch 18 | 31 Jan 2017 (so far as necessary for enabling the exercise of any power to make provision by subordinate legislation or to issue codes of practice or guidance) (s 183(5)(e)) |
| | *Not yet in force* |
| Sch 19 | 31 Mar 2017 (s 183(6)(b)) |

[1] For transitional provisions, see SI 2017/399, regs 5–7

[2] For transitional and saving provisions, see SI 2017/725, regs 3, 4

[3] For savings, see SI 2017/1017, reg 4

[4] For a transitional provision, see SI 2017/1139, reg 4

[5] For a transitional provision, see SI 2017/1249, reg 3

[6] S 132(3), (5) are treated as though they are not in force in relation to an application made before 1 Oct 2019 for an approval under the Firearms (Amendment) Act 1988, s 15, or a licence under the Schedule to that Act

[7] For transitional and saving provisions, see SI 2020/5, reg 3

[8] For transitional provisions, see SI 2021/282, regs 3, 4

---

**Preventing and Combating Violence Against Women and Domestic Violence (Ratification of Convention) Act 2017 (c 18)**

*RA:* 27 Apr 2017

Whole Act in force 27 Jun 2017 (s 3(2))

---

**Public Health (Wales) Act 2017 (anaw 2)**

*RA:* 3 Jul 2017

*Commencement provisions*: s 126; Public Health (Wales) Act 2017 (Commencement) Order 2017, SI 2017/949, as amended by SI 2017/967; Public Health (Wales) Act 2017 (Commencement No 2) Order 2018, SI 2018/1; Public Health (Wales) Act 2017 (Commencement No 3) Order 2018, SI 2018/605; Public Health (Wales) Act 2017 (Commencement No 4) Order 2019, SI 2019/829; Public Health (Wales) Act 2017 (Commencement No 5) Order 2020, SI 2020/1048; Public Health (Wales) Act 2017 (Commencement No 6) Order 2021, SI 2021/202

| | |
|---|---|
| 1 | 3 Jul 2017 (s 126(1)(a)) |
| 2, 3 | 4 Oct 2017 (SI 2017/949) |
| 4, 5 | 1 Mar 2021 (SI 2021/202) |
| 6 | 29 Sep 2020 (for the purpose of making regulations) |
| | 1 Mar 2021 (otherwise) (SI 2021/202) |
| 7–9 | 1 Mar 2021 (SI 2021/202) |
| 10, 11 | 29 Sep 2020 (for the purpose of making regulations) |
| | 1 Mar 2021 (otherwise) (SI 2021/202) |
| 12–14 | 1 Mar 2021 (SI 2021/202) |
| 15, 16 | 29 Sep 2020 (SI 2020/1048) |
| 17, 18 | 29 Sep 2020 (for the purpose of making regulations) |
| | 1 Mar 2021 (otherwise) (SI 2021/202) |
| 19–26 | 1 Mar 2021 (SI 2021/202) |
| 27, 28 | 29 Sep 2020 (for the purpose of making regulations) |
| | 1 Mar 2021 (otherwise) (SI 2021/202) |
| 29 | 1 Mar 2021 (SI 2021/202) |
| 30–93 | *Not yet in force* |

**Public Health (Wales) Act 2017 (anaw 2)**—*contd*

| | |
|---|---|
| 94 | 1 Feb 2018 (for the purpose of Pt 5) (SI 2018/1) |
| | *Not yet in force (otherwise)* |
| 95–107 | 1 Feb 2018 (SI 2018/1) |
| 108–110 | *Not yet in force* |
| 111, 112 | 1 Apr 2019 (SI 2019/829) |
| 113–118 | 31 May 2018 (SI 2018/605) |
| 119 | 4 Oct 2017 (SI 2017/949) |
| 120–127 | 3 Jul 2017 (s 126(1)) |
| Sch 1 | 29 Sep 2020 (for the purpose of making regulations) |
| | 1 Mar 2021 (otherwise) (SI 2021/202) |
| Sch 2 | 1 Mar 2021 (SI 2021/202) |
| Sch 3 | *Not yet in force* |
| Sch 4 | 31 May 2018 (SI 2018/605) |

**Railway Policing (Scotland) Act 2017 (asp 4)**

*RA:* 1 Aug 2017

*Commencement provisions:* s 8

| | |
|---|---|
| 1–6 | *Not yet in force* |
| 7–9 | 2 Aug 2017 (s 8(1)) |

**Savings (Government Contributions) Act 2017 (c 2)**

*RA:* 16 Jan 2017

*Commencement provisions:* s 6(2)–(4)

| | | |
|---|---|---|
| 1 | | 17 Jan 2017 (s 6(2)) |
| 2 | (1), (2) | *Not yet in force* |
| | (3) | See Sch 2 below |
| 3–6 | | 17 Jan 2017 (s 6(2)) |
| Schs 1, 2 | | 17 Jan 2017 (s 6(2)) |

**Seat Belts on School Transport (Scotland) Act 2017 (asp 7)**

*RA:* 18 Dec 2017

*Commencement provisions:* s 6; Seat Belts on School Transport (Scotland) Act 2017 (Commencement) Regulations 2018, SSI 2018/195

| | |
|---|---|
| 1 | 1 Aug 2018 (otherwise) (SSI 2018/195) |
| | 1 Aug 2021 (in respect of arrangements to provide a home-to-school transport service for pupils for whom secondary education is provided where the service is provided under a contract entered into by or on behalf of a school authority before 18 Dec 2017 and the contract as constituted before that date does not require that the motor vehicle used to provide the service has a seat belt fitted to each passenger seat) (SSI 2018/195) |
| 2, 3 | 19 Dec 2017 (s 6(1)) |
| 4, 5 | 1 Aug 2018 (otherwise) (SSI 2018/195) |
| | 1 Aug 2021 (in respect of arrangements to provide a home-to-school transport service for pupils for whom secondary education is provided where the service is provided under a contract entered into by or on behalf of a school authority before 18 Dec 2017 and the contract as constituted before that date does not require that the motor vehicle used to provide the service has a seat belt fitted to each passenger seat) (SSI 2018/195) |

**Seat Belts on School Transport (Scotland) Act 2017 (asp 7)**—*contd*

| | |
|---|---|
| 6, 7 | 19 Dec 2017 (s 6(1)) |

**Small Charitable Donations and Childcare Payments Act 2017 (c 1)**

*RA:* 16 Jan 2017

*Commencement provisions:* s 7

| | |
|---|---|
| 1 | 6 Apr 2017 (s 7(1), (2))[1] |
| 2–4 | 6 Apr 2017 (s 7(1), (2)) |
| 5 | 16 Mar 2017 (s 7(3)) |
| 6–9 | 16 Jan 2017 (s 7(4)) |

[1]   For transitional and saving provisions, see the Small Charitable Donations and Childcare Payments Act 2017, s 8

**Supply and Appropriation (Anticipation and Adjustments) Act 2017 (c 8)**

*RA:* 16 Mar 2017

Whole Act in force 16 Mar 2017 (RA)

**Supply and Appropriation (Main Estimates) Act 2017 (c 31)**

*RA:* 19 Jul 2017

Whole Act in force 19 Jul 2017 (RA)

**Technical and Further Education Act 2017 (c 19)**

*RA:* 27 Apr 2017

*Commencement provisions:* s 47; Technical and Further Education Act 2017 (Commencement No 1 and Transitional Provision) Regulations 2017, SI 2017/844; Technical and Further Education Act 2017 (Commencement No 2 and Transitional Provision) Regulations 2017, SI 2017/1055; Technical and Further Education Act 2017 (Commencement No 3) Regulations 2018, SI 2018/140; Technical and Further Education Act 2017 (Commencement No 4) Regulations 2018, SI 2018/1161; Technical and Further Education Act 2017 (Commencement No 5) Regulations 2019, SI 2019/61

| | | |
|---|---|---|
| 1 | (1)–(4) | 31 Jan 2019 (SI 2019/61) |
| | (5) | See Sch 1 below |
| 2 | | 2 Jan 2018 (SI 2017/1055) |
| 3–39 | | 31 Jan 2019 (SI 2018/1161) |
| 40 | | 12 Nov 2018 (SI 2018/1161) |
| 41 | | 2 Jan 2018 (SI 2017/1055) |
| 42–48 | | 27 Apr 2017 (s 47(1)) |
| Sch 1 | para 1 | See paras 2–32 below |
| | para 2(1) | See para 2(2), (3) below |
| | para 2(2) | 8 Nov 2017 (SI 2017/1055) |
| | para 2(3) | 31 Jan 2019 (SI 2019/61) |
| | para 3(1) | See para 3(2), (3) below |
| | para 3(2) | 9 Feb 2018 (SI 2018/140) |
| | para 3(3) | 31 Jan 2019 (SI 2019/61)[1] |
| | paras 4–6 | 31 Jan 2019 (SI 2019/61) |
| | para 7 | 8 Nov 2017 (SI 2017/1055)[2] |
| | paras 8–10 | 8 Nov 2017 (SI 2017/1055) |
| | para 11 | 8 Nov 2017 (SI 2017/1055)[2] |
| | para 12 | 8 Nov 2017 (SI 2017/1055) |
| | paras 13, 14 | 16 Aug 2017 (SI 2017/844)[1] |

**Technical and Further Education Act 2017 (c 19)**—*contd*

| | | |
|---|---|---|
| | paras 15, 16 | 31 Jan 2019 (SI 2019/61) |
| | paras 17–20 | 8 Nov 2017 (SI 2017/1055) |
| | para 21 | 31 Jan 2019 (SI 2019/61) |
| | para 22 | 8 Nov 2017 (SI 2017/1055) |
| | paras 23, 24 | 31 Jan 2019 (SI 2019/61) |
| | paras 25, 26 | 2 Jan 2018 (SI 2017/1055) |
| | para 27 | 2 Jan 2018 (SI 2017/1055)[2] |
| | para 28 | 2 Jan 2018 (SI 2017/1055) |
| | paras 29, 30 | 31 Jan 2019 (SI 2019/61) |
| | para 31 | 2 Jan 2018 (SI 2017/1055) |
| | para 32 | 8 Nov 2017 (for the purposes of those provisions referred to within that paragraph which are already in force) (SI 2017/1055)[2] |
| | | 31 Jan 2019 (otherwise) (SI 2019/61) |
| | paras 33, 34 | 8 Nov 2017 (SI 2017/1055) |
| | para 35 | 27 Apr 2017 (s 47(1)) |
| Schs 2–4 | | 31 Jan 2019 (SI 2018/1161) |

[1]   For transitional provisions, see SI 2017/844, reg 3

[2]   For transitional provisions, see SI 2017/1055, reg 4

---

**Trade Union (Wales) Act 2017 (anaw 4)**

*RA:* 7 Sep 2017

*Commencement provisions*: s 3; Trade Union (Wales) Act 2017 (Commencement) Order 2017, SI 2017/903

| | |
|---|---|
| 1, 2 | 13 Sep 2017 (SI 2017/903) |
| 3, 4 | 8 Sep 2017 (s 3) |

---

**Wales Act 2017 (c 4)**

*RA:* 31 Jan 2017

*Commencement provisions*: s 71; Wales Act 2017 (Commencement No 1) Regulations 2017, SI 2017/351; Wales Act 2017 (Commencement No 2) Regulations 2017, SI 2017/893; Wales Act (Commencement No 3) Regulations 2017, SI 2017/1069; Wales Act 2017 (Commencement No 4) Regulations 2017, SI 2017/1179

| | |
|---|---|
| 1, 2 | 31 Mar 2017 (s 71(2)(a)) |
| 3–8 | 1 Apr 2018 (SI 2017/1179) |
| 9, 10 | 31 Mar 2017 (so far as relating to a provision of a Bill that would change the name of the Assembly or confer power to do so) (s 71(2)(c)) |
| | 1 Apr 2018 (otherwise) (SI 2017/1179) |
| 11–13 | 1 Apr 2018 (SI 2017/1179) |
| 14, 15 | 31 Mar 2017 (s 71(2)(b)) |
| 16 | 31 Mar 2017 (so far as relating to a provision of a Bill that would change the name of the Assembly or confer power to do so) (s 71(2)(c)) |
| | *Not yet in force* (otherwise) |
| 17, 18 | 31 Mar 2017 (s 71(2)(d)) |
| 19–20 | 1 Apr 2018 (SI 2017/1179) |
| 21 | 7 Jan 2018 (SI 2017/893) |
| 22 | 1 Apr 2018 (SI 2017/1179) |
| 23 | 1 Oct 2018 (SI 2017/1179) |
| 24 | 6 Mar 2018 (SI 2017/1069) |
| 25 | 1 Oct 2018 (SI 2017/1179) |
| 26–38 | 1 Apr 2018 (SI 2017/1179) |

**Wales Act 2017 (c 4)**—*contd*

| | | |
|---|---|---|
| 39 | (1)–(3) | 1 Apr 2018 (for the purpose of Sch 1 to this Act) (SI 2017/1179) |
| | | 1 Apr 2019 (otherwise) (SI 2017/1179) |
| | (4) | 31 Mar 2017 (for the purposes of s 43) (s 71(2)(e)) |
| | | 1 Apr 2018 (for the purpose of Sch 1 to this Act) (SI 2017/1179) |
| | | 1 Apr 2019 (otherwise) (SI 2017/1179) |
| | (5) | 1 Apr 2018 (for the purpose of Sch 1 to this Act) (SI 2017/1179) |
| | | 1 Apr 2019 (otherwise) (SI 2017/1179) |
| | (6) | 31 Mar 2017 (for the purposes of s 43) (s 71(2)(e)) |
| | | 1 Apr 2018 (for the purpose of Sch 1 to this Act) (SI 2017/1179) |
| | | 1 Apr 2019 (otherwise) (SI 2017/1179) |
| | (7)–(13) | 1 Apr 2018 (for the purpose of Sch 1 to this Act) (SI 2017/1179) |
| | | 1 Apr 2019 (otherwise) (SI 2017/1179) |
| 40, 41 | | 1 Apr 2019 (SI 2017/1179) |
| 42 | (1)–(3) | 1 Apr 2019 (SI 2017/1179) |
| | (4) | 31 Mar 2017 (for the purposes of s 43) (s 71(2)(e)) |
| | | 1 Apr 2019 (otherwise) (SI 2017/1179) |
| 43 | | 31 Mar 2017 (s 71(2)(e)) |
| 44–47 | | 1 Apr 2018 (SI 2017/1179) |
| 48 | (1) | *Not yet in force* |
| | (2) | 31 Mar 2017 (s 71(2)(f)) |
| 49 | | 7 Jan 2018 (SI 2017/893) |
| 50, 51 | | 31 Mar 2017 (s 71(2)(g)) |
| 52–58 | | 1 Apr 2018 (SI 2017/1179) |
| 59–64 | | 9 Jul 2017 (SI 2017/351)[1] |
| 65–68 | | 1 Apr 2018 (SI 2017/1179) |
| 69 | (1) | See Sch 6 below |
| | (2)–(8) | 31 Jan 2017 (s 71(1)) |
| 70–72 | | 31 Jan 2017 (s 71(1)) |
| Schs 1–4 | | 1 Apr 2018 (SI 2017/1179) |
| Sch 5 | | 9 Jul 2017 (SI 2017/351)[1] |
| Sch 6 | paras 1–14 | 1 Apr 2018 (SI 2017/1179) |
| | paras 15–32 | 1 Oct 2018 (SI 2017/1179) |
| | paras 33–46 | 1 Apr 2018 (SI 2017/1179) |
| | paras 47–51 | 1 Apr 2019 (SI 2017/1179) |
| | para 52 | 1 Apr 2018 (SI 2017/1179) |
| | para 53 | 9 Jul 2017 (SI 2017/351)[1] |
| | paras 54–57 | 1 Apr 2018 (SI 2017/1179) |
| | para 58 | 9 Jul 2017 (SI 2017/351)[1] |
| | paras 59–60 | 1 Apr 2018 (SI 2017/1179) |
| | para 61 | 1 Apr 2019 (SI 2017/1179) |
| | para 62 | 9 Jul 2017 (SI 2017/351)[1] |
| | paras 63–67 | 1 Apr 2018 (SI 2017/1179) |
| | para 68 | 9 Jul 2017 (SI 2017/351)[1] |
| | paras 69–76 | 1 Apr 2018 (SI 2017/1179) |
| | para 77, 78 | 1 Apr 2019 (SI 2017/1179) |
| | paras 79, 80 | 1 Apr 2018 (SI 2017/1179) |
| | para 81 | 1 Apr 2019 (SI 2017/1179) |
| | para 82–91 | 1 Apr 2018 (SI 2017/1179) |
| | para 92 | 9 Jul 2017 (SI 2017/351)[1] |
| | para 93 | 1 Apr 2018 (SI 2017/1179) |
| | para 94 | 9 Jul 2017 (SI 2017/351)[1] |
| | paras 95–113 | 1 Apr 2018 (SI 2017/1179) |
| Sch 7 | | 31 Jan 2017 (s 71(1)) |

---

[1]   Or on the first day on which regulations made under Sch 5, para 7(1) come into force, if later; see SI 2017/351, reg 2(1)

# 2018 Acts

## Abolition of the Right to Buy and Associated Rights (Wales) Act 2018 (anaw 1)

*RA*: 24 Jan 2018

*Commencement provisions*: s 11; Abolition of the Right to Buy and Associated Rights (Wales) Act 2018 (Commencement and Saving Provisions) Order 2018, SI 2018/100

| | |
|---|---|
| 1 | 24 Jan 2018 (s 11(1)) |
| 2–5 | 24 Mar 2018 (s 11(2)) |
| 6, 7 | 26 Jan 2019 (SI 2018/100)[1] |
| 8–12 | 24 Jan 2018 (s 11(1)) |
| Sch 1 | 26 Jan 2019 (SI 2018/100)[1] |

[1]    For savings, see SI 2018/100, art 3

---

## Additional Learning Needs and Education Tribunal (Wales) Act 2018 (anaw 2)

*RA*: 24 Jan 2018

*Commencement provisions*: s 100; Additional Learning Needs and Education Tribunal (Wales) Act 2018 (Commencement No 1) Order 2020, SI 2020/1182; Additional Learning Needs and Education Tribunal (Wales) Act 2018 (Commencement No 2) Order 2021, SI 2021/373, as amended by SI 2021/735; Additional Learning Needs and Education Tribunal (Wales) Act 2018 (Commencement No 3 and Transitional and Saving Provisions) Order 2021, SI 2021/381, as amended by SI 2021/516 (both revoked by SI 2021/938), SI 2021/735; Additional Learning Needs and Education Tribunal (Wales) Act 2018 (Commencement No 4 and Transitional and Saving Provisions) Order 2021, SI 2021/383, as amended by SI 2021/516 (both revoked by SI 2021/938), SI 2021/735; Additional Learning Needs and Education Tribunal (Wales) Act 2018 (Commencement No 5 and Transitional and Saving Provisions) Order 2021, SI 2021/1243, as amended by SI 2021/1428, SI 2022/663; Additional Learning Needs and Education Tribunal (Wales) Act 2018 (Commencement No 6 and Transitional and Saving Provisions) Order 2021, SI 2021/1244, as amended by SI 2021/1428, SI 2022/663; Additional Learning Needs and Education Tribunal (Wales) Act 2018 (Commencement No 7) Order 2021, SI 2021/1245; Additional Learning Needs and Education Tribunal (Wales) Act 2018 (Commencement No 8 and Transitional and Saving Provisions) Order 2022, SI 2022/891; Additional Learning Needs and Education Tribunal (Wales) Act 2018 (Commencement No 9 and Transitional and Saving Provisions) Order 2022, SI 2022/892; Additional Learning Needs and Education Tribunal (Wales) Act 2018 (Commencement No 10) Order 2022, SI 2022/893; Additional Learning Needs and Education Tribunal (Wales) Act 2018 (Commencement No 11) Order 2022, SI 2022/894; Additional Learning Needs and Education Tribunal (Wales) Act 2018 (Commencement No 12) Order 2022, SI 2022/895; Additional Learning Needs and Education Tribunal (Wales) Act 2018 (Commencement No 13 and Transitional and Saving Provisions) Order 2022, SI 2022/896; Additional Learning Needs and Education Tribunal (Wales) Act 2018 (Commencement No 14 and Transitional and Saving Provisions) Order 2022, SI 2022/897; Additional Learning Needs and Education Tribunal (Wales) Act 2018 (Commencement No 15) Order 2022, SI 2022/898

| | |
|---|---|
| 1 | 25 Jan 2018 (s 100(1)) |
| 2, 3 | 1 Sep 2021 (except in relation to specified persons[1]) (SI 2021/373) |
| | 1 Jan 2022 (in relation to a child who has identified special educational needs) (SI 2021/1243)[2, 3]; (SI 2021/1244)[4, 5] |
| | 1 Jan 2022 (except in relation to specified persons[6]) (SI 2021/1245) |

**Additional Learning Needs and Education Tribunal (Wales) Act 2018 (anaw 2)**—*contd*

1 Sep 2022 (in relation to a child to whom a local authority is maintaining a statement of special educational needs under Education Act 1996, s 324 or 331) (SI 2022/891)

1 Sep 2022 (in relation to a child to whom there is a matter ongoing on 1 Sep 2022) (SI 2022/892)

1 Sep 2022 (in relation to a child who has identified special educational needs)[9] (SI 2022/894)

1 Sep 2022 (except in relation to specified persons)[10] (SI 2022/895)

1 Sep 2022 (in relation to a child who has identified special educational needs)[11] (SI 2022/896)

1 Sep 2022 (in relation to a child who has identified special educational needs)[13] (SI 2022/897)

1 Sep 2022 (in relation to specified persons)[15] (SI 2022/898)

1 Sep 2025 (in relation to a person who is over compulsory school age on 1 Sep 2022) (SI 2022/893)

*Not yet in force* (otherwise)

4     2 Nov 2020 (for the purpose of issuing or revising the code under s 4) (SI 2020/1182)

1 Sep 2021 (except in relation to specified persons[1]) (SI 2021/373)

1 Jan 2022 (in relation to a child who has identified special educational needs) (SI 2021/1243)[2, 3]; (SI 2021/1244)[4, 5]

1 Jan 2022 (except in relation to specified persons[6]) (SI 2021/1245)

1 Sep 2022 (in relation to a child to whom a local authority is maintaining a statement of special educational needs under Education Act 1996, s 324 or 331) (SI 2022/891)

1 Sep 2022 (in relation to a child to whom there is a matter ongoing on 1 Sep 2022) (SI 2022/892)

1 Sep 2022 (in relation to a child who has identified special educational needs)[9] (SI 2022/894)

1 Sep 2022 (except in relation to specified persons)[10] (SI 2022/895)

1 Sep 2022 (in relation to a child who has identified special educational needs)[11] (SI 2022/896)

1 Sep 2022 (in relation to a child who has identified special educational needs)[13] (SI 2022/897)

1 Sep 2022 (in relation to specified persons)[15] (SI 2022/898)

1 Sep 2025 (in relation to a person who is over compulsory school age on 1 Sep 2022) (SI 2022/893)

*Not yet in force* (otherwise)

5     2 Nov 2020 (SI 2020/1182)
6     1 Sep 2021 (except in relation to specified persons[1]) (SI 2021/373)

1 Jan 2022 (in relation to a child who has identified special educational needs) (SI 2021/1243)[2, 3]; (SI 2021/1244)[4, 5]

1 Jan 2022 (except in relation to specified persons[6]) (SI 2021/1245)

1 Sep 2022 (in relation to a child to whom a local authority is maintaining a statement of special educational needs under Education Act 1996, s 324 or 331) (SI 2022/891)

1 Sep 2022 (in relation to a child to whom there is a matter ongoing on 1 Sep 2022) (SI 2022/892)

1 Sep 2022 (in relation to a child who has identified special educational needs)[9] (SI 2022/894)

1 Sep 2022 (except in relation to specified persons)[10] (SI 2022/895)

1 Sep 2022 (in relation to a child who has identified special educational needs)[11] (SI 2022/896)

1 Sep 2022 (in relation to a child who has identified special educational needs)[13] (SI 2022/897)

1 Sep 2022 (in relation to specified persons)[15] (SI 2022/898)

1 Sep 2025 (in relation to a person who is over compulsory school age on 1 Sep 2022) (SI 2022/893)

*Not yet in force* (otherwise)

**Additional Learning Needs and Education Tribunal (Wales) Act 2018 (anaw 2)**—*contd*

| | |
|---|---|
| 7, 8 | 2 Nov 2020 (for the purpose of issuing or revising the code under s 4) (SI 2020/1182) |
| | 1 Sep 2021 (except in relation to specified persons[1]) (SI 2021/373) |
| | 1 Jan 2022 (in relation to a child who has identified special educational needs) (SI 2021/1243)[2, 3]; (SI 2021/1244)[4, 5] |
| | 1 Jan 2022 (except in relation to specified persons[6]) (SI 2021/1245) |
| | 1 Sep 2022 (in relation to a child to whom a local authority is maintaining a statement of special educational needs under Education Act 1996, s 324 or 331) (SI 2022/891) |
| | 1 Sep 2022 (in relation to a child to whom there is a matter ongoing on 1 Sep 2022) (SI 2022/892) |
| | 1 Sep 2022 (in relation to a child who has identified special educational needs)[9] (SI 2022/894) |
| | 1 Sep 2022 (except in relation to specified persons[10]) (SI 2022/895) |
| | 1 Sep 2022 (in relation to a child who has identified special educational needs)[11] (SI 2022/896) |
| | 1 Sep 2022 (in relation to a child who has identified special educational needs)[13] (SI 2022/897) |
| | 1 Sep 2022 (in relation to specified persons)[15] (SI 2022/898) |
| | 1 Sep 2025 (in relation to a person who is over compulsory school age on 1 Sep 2022) (SI 2022/893) |
| | *Not yet in force* (otherwise) |
| 9–14 | 1 Sep 2021 (except in relation to specified persons[1]) (SI 2021/373) |
| | 1 Jan 2022 (in relation to a child who has identified special educational needs) (SI 2021/1243)[2, 3]; (SI 2021/1244)[4, 5] |
| | 1 Jan 2022 (except in relation to specified persons[6]) (SI 2021/1245) |
| | 1 Sep 2022 (in relation to a child to whom a local authority is maintaining a statement of special educational needs under Education Act 1996, s 324 or 331) (SI 2022/891) |
| | 1 Sep 2022 (in relation to a child to whom there is a matter ongoing on 1 Sep 2022) (SI 2022/892) |
| | 1 Sep 2022 (in relation to a child who has identified special educational needs)[9] (SI 2022/894) |
| | 1 Sep 2022 (except in relation to specified persons[10]) (SI 2022/895) |
| | 1 Sep 2022 (in relation to a child who has identified special educational needs)[11] (SI 2022/896) |
| | 1 Sep 2022 (in relation to a child who has identified special educational needs)[13] (SI 2022/897) |
| | 1 Sep 2022 (in relation to specified persons)[15] (SI 2022/898) |
| | 1 Sep 2025 (in relation to a person who is over compulsory school age on 1 Sep 2022) (SI 2022/893) |
| | *Not yet in force* (otherwise) |
| 15 | 2 Nov 2020 (SI 2020/1182) |
| 16 | 2 Nov 2020 (for the purpose of making regulations) (SI 2020/1182) |
| | 1 Sep 2021 (otherwise) (SI 2021/373) |
| 17–20 | 1 Sep 2021 (except in relation to specified persons[1]) (SI 2021/373) |
| | 1 Jan 2022 (in relation to a child who has identified special educational needs) (SI 2021/1243)[2, 3]; (SI 2021/1244)[4, 5] |
| | 1 Jan 2022 (except in relation to specified persons[6]) (SI 2021/1245) |
| | 1 Sep 2022 (in relation to a child to whom a local authority is maintaining a statement of special educational needs under Education Act 1996, s 324 or 331) (SI 2022/891) |
| | 1 Sep 2022 (in relation to a child to whom there is a matter ongoing on 1 Sep 2022) (SI 2022/892) |
| | 1 Sep 2022 (in relation to a child who has identified special educational needs)[9] (SI 2022/894) |
| | 1 Sep 2022 (except in relation to specified persons[10]) (SI 2022/895) |

**Additional Learning Needs and Education Tribunal (Wales) Act 2018 (anaw 2)**—*contd*

|    |    |
|----|----|
|    | 1 Sep 2022 (in relation to a child who has identified special educational needs)[11] (SI 2022/896) |
|    | 1 Sep 2022 (in relation to a child who has identified special educational needs)[13] (SI 2022/897) |
|    | 1 Sep 2022 (in relation to specified persons)[15] (SI 2022/898) |
|    | 1 Sep 2025 (in relation to a person who is over compulsory school age on 1 Sep 2022) (SI 2022/893) |
|    | *Not yet in force* (otherwise) |
| 21 | 1 Sep 2021 (except in relation to specified persons[1]) (SI 2021/373) |
|    | 2 Nov 2020 (for the purpose of making regulations) (SI 2020/1182) |
|    | 1 Jan 2022 (in relation to a child who has identified special educational needs) (SI 2021/1243)[2, 3]; (SI 2021/1244)[4, 5] |
|    | 1 Jan 2022 (except in relation to specified persons[6]) (SI 2021/1245) |
|    | 1 Sep 2022 (in relation to a child to whom a local authority is maintaining a statement of special educational needs under Education Act 1996, s 324 or 331) (SI 2022/891) |
|    | 1 Sep 2022 (in relation to a child to whom there is a matter ongoing on 1 Sep 2022) (SI 2022/892) |
|    | 1 Sep 2022 (in relation to a child who has identified special educational needs)[9] (SI 2022/894) |
|    | 1 Sep 2022 (except in relation to specified persons)[10] (SI 2022/895) |
|    | 1 Sep 2022 (in relation to a child who has identified special educational needs)[11] (SI 2022/896) |
|    | 1 Sep 2022 (in relation to a child who has identified special educational needs)[13] (SI 2022/897) |
|    | 1 Sep 2022 (in relation to specified persons)[15] (SI 2022/898) |
|    | 1 Sep 2025 (in relation to a person who is over compulsory school age on 1 Sep 2022) (SI 2022/893) |
|    | *Not yet in force* (otherwise) |
| 22–31 | 1 Sep 2021 (except in relation to specified persons[1]) (SI 2021/373) |
|    | 1 Jan 2022 (in relation to a child who has identified special educational needs) (SI 2021/1243)[2, 3]; (SI 2021/1244)[4, 5] |
|    | 1 Jan 2022 (except in relation to specified persons[6]) (SI 2021/1245) |
|    | 1 Sep 2022 (in relation to a child to whom a local authority is maintaining a statement of special educational needs under Education Act 1996, s 324 or 331) (SI 2022/891) |
|    | 1 Sep 2022 (in relation to a child to whom there is a matter ongoing on 1 Sep 2022) (SI 2022/892) |
|    | 1 Sep 2022 (in relation to a child who has identified special educational needs)[9] (SI 2022/894) |
|    | 1 Sep 2022 (except in relation to specified persons)[10] (SI 2022/895) |
|    | 1 Sep 2022 (in relation to a child who has identified special educational needs)[11] (SI 2022/896) |
|    | 1 Sep 2022 (in relation to a child who has identified special educational needs)[13] (SI 2022/897) |
|    | 1 Sep 2022 (in relation to specified persons)[15] (SI 2022/898) |
|    | 1 Sep 2025 (in relation to a person who is over compulsory school age on 1 Sep 2022) (SI 2022/893) |
|    | *Not yet in force* (otherwise) |
| 32 | 2 Nov 2020 (for the purpose of making regulations) (SI 2020/1182) |
|    | 1 Sep 2021 (except in relation to specified persons[1]) (SI 2021/373) |
|    | 1 Jan 2022 (in relation to a child who has identified special educational needs) (SI 2021/1243)[2, 3]; SI 2021/1244[4, 5] |
|    | 1 Jan 2022 (except in relation to specified persons[6]) (SI 2021/1245) |
|    | 1 Sep 2022 (in relation to a child to whom a local authority is maintaining a statement of special educational needs under Education Act 1996, s 324 or 331) (SI 2022/891) |

**Additional Learning Needs and Education Tribunal (Wales) Act 2018 (anaw 2)**—*contd*

|  |  |
|---|---|
|  | 1 Sep 2022 (in relation to a child to whom there is a matter ongoing on 1 Sep 2022) (SI 2022/892) |
|  | 1 Sep 2022 (in relation to a child who has identified special educational needs)[9] (SI 2022/894) |
|  | 1 Sep 2022 (except in relation to specified persons)[10] (SI 2022/895) |
|  | 1 Sep 2022 (in relation to a child who has identified special educational needs)[11] (SI 2022/896) |
|  | 1 Sep 2022 (in relation to a child who has identified special educational needs)[13] (SI 2022/897) |
|  | 1 Sep 2022 (in relation to specified persons)[15] (SI 2022/898) |
|  | 1 Sep 2025 (in relation to a person who is over compulsory school age on 1 Sep 2022) (SI 2022/893) |
|  | *Not yet in force* (otherwise) |
| 33–35 | 1 Sep 2021 (except in relation to specified persons[1]) (SI 2021/373) |
|  | 1 Jan 2022 (in relation to a child who has identified special educational needs) (SI 2021/1243)[2, 3]; (SI 2021/1244)[4, 5] |
|  | 1 Jan 2022 (except in relation to specified persons[6]) (SI 2021/1245) |
|  | 1 Sep 2022 (in relation to a child to whom a local authority is maintaining a statement of special educational needs under Education Act 1996, s 324 or 331) (SI 2022/891) |
|  | 1 Sep 2022 (in relation to a child to whom there is a matter ongoing on 1 Sep 2022) (SI 2022/892) |
|  | 1 Sep 2022 (in relation to a child who has identified special educational needs)[9] (SI 2022/894) |
|  | 1 Sep 2022 (except in relation to specified persons)[10] (SI 2022/895) |
|  | 1 Sep 2022 (in relation to a child who has identified special educational needs)[11] (SI 2022/896) |
|  | 1 Sep 2022 (in relation to a child who has identified special educational needs)[13] (SI 2022/897) |
|  | 1 Sep 2025 (in relation to a person who is over compulsory school age on 1 Sep 2022) (SI 2022/893) |
|  | 1 Sep 2022 (in relation to specified persons)[15] (SI 2022/898) |
|  | *Not yet in force* (otherwise) |
| 36 | 2 Nov 2020 (for the purpose of making regulations) (SI 2020/1182) |
|  | 1 Sep 2021 (except in relation to specified persons[1]) (SI 2021/373) |
|  | 1 Jan 2022 (in relation to a child who has identified special educational needs) (SI 2021/1243)[2, 3]; (SI 2021/1244)[4, 5] |
|  | 1 Jan 2022 (except in relation to specified persons[6]) (SI 2021/1245) |
|  | 1 Sep 2022 (in relation to a child to whom a local authority is maintaining a statement of special educational needs under Education Act 1996, s 324 or 331) (SI 2022/891) |
|  | 1 Sep 2022 (in relation to a child to whom there is a matter ongoing on 1 Sep 2022) (SI 2022/892) |
|  | 1 Sep 2022 (in relation to a child who has identified special educational needs)[9] (SI 2022/894) |
|  | 1 Sep 2022 (except in relation to specified persons)[10] (SI 2022/895) |
|  | 1 Sep 2022 (in relation to a child who has identified special educational needs)[11] (SI 2022/896) |
|  | 1 Sep 2022 (in relation to a child who has identified special educational needs)[13] (SI 2022/897) |
|  | 1 Sep 2022 (in relation to specified persons)[15] (SI 2022/898) |
|  | 1 Sep 2025 (in relation to a person who is over compulsory school age on 1 Sep 2022) (SI 2022/893) |
|  | *Not yet in force* (otherwise) |
| 37 | 2 Nov 2020 (SI 2020/1182) |
| 38 | 1 Sep 2021 (except in relation to specified persons[1]) (SI 2021/373) |
|  | 1 Jan 2022 (in relation to a child who has identified special educational needs) (SI 2021/1243)[2, 3]; (SI 2021/1244)[4, 5] |

**Additional Learning Needs and Education Tribunal (Wales) Act 2018 (anaw 2)**—*contd*

1 Jan 2022 (except in relation to specified persons[6]) (SI 2021/1245)

1 Sep 2022 (in relation to a child to whom a local authority is maintaining a statement of special educational needs under Education Act 1996, s 324 or 331) (SI 2022/891)

1 Sep 2022 (in relation to a child to whom there is a matter ongoing on 1 Sep 2022) (SI 2022/892)

1 Sep 2022 (in relation to a child who has identified special educational needs)[9] (SI 2022/894)

1 Sep 2022 (except in relation to specified persons[10]) (SI 2022/895)

1 Sep 2022 (in relation to a child who has identified special educational needs)[11] (SI 2022/896)

1 Sep 2022 (in relation to a child who has identified special educational needs)[13] (SI 2022/897)

1 Sep 2022 (in relation to specified persons[15]) (SI 2022/898)

1 Sep 2025 (in relation to a person who is over compulsory school age on 1 Sep 2022) (SI 2022/893)

*Not yet in force* (otherwise)

| | |
|---|---|
| 39 | 2 Nov 2020 (SI 2020/1182) |
| 40–44 | 1 Sep 2021 (in relation to a child who on 1 Sep 2021 is not over compulsory school age and except in relation to specified persons[1]) (SI 2021/373) |

1 Jan 2022 (in relation to a child who has identified special educational needs) (SI 2021/1243)[2, 3]; (SI 2021/1244)[4, 5]

1 Jan 2022 (except in relation to specified persons[6]) (SI 2021/1245)

1 Sep 2022 (in relation to a child to whom a local authority is maintaining a statement of special educational needs under Education Act 1996, s 324 or 331) (SI 2022/891)

1 Sep 2022 (in relation to a child to whom there is a matter ongoing on 1 Sep 2022) (SI 2022/892)

1 Sep 2022 (in relation to a child who has identified special educational needs)[9] (SI 2022/894)

1 Sep 2022 (except in relation to specified persons[10]) (SI 2022/895)

1 Sep 2022 (in relation to a child who has identified special educational needs)[11] (SI 2022/896)

1 Sep 2022 (in relation to a child who has identified special educational needs)[13] (SI 2022/897)

1 Sep 2022 (in relation to specified persons[15]) (SI 2022/898)

1 Sep 2025 (in relation to a person who is over compulsory school age on 1 Sep 2022) (SI 2022/893)

*Not yet in force* (otherwise)

| | |
|---|---|
| 45, 46 | 2 Nov 2020 (SI 2020/1182) |
| 47 | 2 Nov 2020 (for the purpose of issuing or revising the code under s 4) (SI 2020/1182) |

1 Sep 2021 (except in relation to specified persons[1]) (SI 2021/373)

1 Jan 2022 (in relation to a child who has identified special educational needs) (SI 2021/1243)[2, 3]; (SI 2021/1244)[4, 5]

1 Jan 2022 (except in relation to specified persons[6]) (SI 2021/1245)

1 Sep 2022 (in relation to a child to whom a local authority is maintaining a statement of special educational needs under Education Act 1996, s 324 or 331) (SI 2022/891)

1 Sep 2022 (in relation to a child to whom there is a matter ongoing on 1 Sep 2022) (SI 2022/892)

1 Sep 2022 (in relation to a child who has identified special educational needs)[9] (SI 2022/894)

1 Sep 2022 (except in relation to specified persons[10]) (SI 2022/895)

1 Sep 2022 (in relation to a child who has identified special educational needs)[11] (SI 2022/896)

1 Sep 2022 (in relation to a child who has identified special educational needs)[13] (SI 2022/897)

**Additional Learning Needs and Education Tribunal (Wales) Act 2018 (anaw 2)**—*contd*

|  |  |  |
|---|---|---|
|  |  | 1 Sep 2022 (in relation to specified persons)[15] (SI 2022/898) |
|  |  | 1 Sep 2025 (in relation to a person who is over compulsory school age on 1 Sep 2022) (SI 2022/893) |
|  |  | *Not yet in force* (otherwise) |
| 48, 49 |  | 1 Sep 2021 (except in relation to specified persons[1]) (SI 2021/373) |
|  |  | 1 Jan 2022 (in relation to a child who has identified special educational needs) (SI 2021/1243)[2, 3]; (SI 2021/1244)[4, 5] |
|  |  | 1 Jan 2022 (except in relation to specified persons[6]) (SI 2021/1245) |
|  |  | 1 Sep 2022 (in relation to a child to whom a local authority is maintaining a statement of special educational needs under Education Act 1996, s 324 or 331) (SI 2022/891) |
|  |  | 1 Sep 2022 (in relation to a child to whom there is a matter ongoing on 1 Sep 2022) (SI 2022/892) |
|  |  | 1 Sep 2022 (in relation to a child who has identified special educational needs)[9] (SI 2022/894) |
|  |  | 1 Sep 2022 (except in relation to specified persons)[10] (SI 2022/895) |
|  |  | 1 Sep 2022 (in relation to a child who has identified special educational needs)[11] (SI 2022/896) |
|  |  | 1 Sep 2022 (in relation to a child who has identified special educational needs)[13] (SI 2022/897) |
|  |  | 1 Sep 2022 (in relation to specified persons)[15] (SI 2022/898) |
|  |  | 1 Sep 2025 (in relation to a person who is over compulsory school age on 1 Sep 2022) (SI 2022/893) |
|  |  | *Not yet in force* (otherwise) |
| 50 | (1) | See sub-ss (2)–(5) below |
|  | (2), (3) | 1 Sep 2021 (SI 2021/373) |
|  | (4), (5) | 1 Sep 2021 (except in relation to specified persons[1]) (SI 2021/373) |
|  |  | 1 Jan 2022 (in relation to a child who has identified special educational needs) (SI 2021/1243)[2, 3]; (SI 2021/1244)[4, 5] |
|  |  | 1 Jan 2022 (except in relation to specified persons[6]) (SI 2021/1245) |
|  |  | 1 Sep 2022 (in relation to a child to whom a local authority is maintaining a statement of special educational needs under Education Act 1996, s 324 or 331) (SI 2022/891) |
|  |  | 1 Sep 2022 (in relation to a child to whom there is a matter ongoing on 1 Sep 2022) (SI 2022/892) |
|  |  | 1 Sep 2022 (in relation to a child who has identified special educational needs)[9] (SI 2022/894) |
|  |  | 1 Sep 2022 (except in relation to specified persons)[10] (SI 2022/895) |
|  |  | 1 Sep 2022 (in relation to a child who has identified special educational needs)[11] (SI 2022/896) |
|  |  | 1 Sep 2022 (in relation to a child who has identified special educational needs)[13] (SI 2022/897) |
|  |  | 1 Sep 2022 (in relation to specified persons)[15] (SI 2022/898) |
|  |  | 1 Sep 2025 (in relation to a person who is over compulsory school age on 1 Sep 2022) (SI 2022/893) |
|  |  | *Not yet in force* (otherwise) |
| 51–53 |  | 1 Sep 2021 (except in relation to specified persons[1]) (SI 2021/373) |
|  |  | 1 Jan 2022 (in relation to a child who has identified special educational needs) (SI 2021/1243)[2, 3]; (SI 2021/1244)[4, 5] |
|  |  | 1 Jan 2022 (except in relation to specified persons[6]) (SI 2021/1245) |
|  |  | 1 Sep 2022 (in relation to a child to whom a local authority is maintaining a statement of special educational needs under Education Act 1996, s 324 or 331) (SI 2022/891) |
|  |  | 1 Sep 2022 (in relation to a child to whom there is a matter ongoing on 1 Sep 2022) (SI 2022/892) |
|  |  | 1 Sep 2022 (in relation to a child who has identified special educational needs)[9] (SI 2022/894) |
|  |  | 1 Sep 2022 (except in relation to specified persons)[10] (SI 2022/895) |

**Additional Learning Needs and Education Tribunal (Wales) Act 2018 (anaw 2)**—*contd*

|  |  |  |
|---|---|---|
|  |  | 1 Sep 2022 (in relation to a child who has identified special educational needs)[11] (SI 2022/896) |
|  |  | 1 Sep 2022 (in relation to a child who has identified special educational needs)[13] (SI 2022/897) |
|  |  | 1 Sep 2022 (in relation to specified persons)[15] (SI 2022/898) |
|  |  | 1 Sep 2025 (in relation to a person who is over compulsory school age on 1 Sep 2022) (SI 2022/893) |
|  |  | *Not yet in force* (otherwise) |
| 54 |  | 2 Nov 2020 (for the purpose of making regulations) (SI 2020/1182) |
|  |  | 1 Sep 2021 (otherwise) (SI 2021/373) |
| 55 |  | 1 Sep 2021 (except in relation to specified persons[1]) (SI 2021/373) |
|  |  | 1 Jan 2022 (in relation to a child who has identified special educational needs) (SI 2021/1243)[2, 3]; (SI 2021/1244)[4, 5] |
|  |  | 1 Jan 2022 (except in relation to specified persons[6]) (SI 2021/1245) |
|  |  | 1 Sep 2022 (in relation to a child to whom a local authority is maintaining a statement of special educational needs under Education Act 1996, s 324 or 331) (SI 2022/891) |
|  |  | 1 Sep 2022 (in relation to a child to whom there is a matter ongoing on 1 Sep 2022) (SI 2022/892) |
|  |  | 1 Sep 2022 (in relation to a child who has identified special educational needs)[9] (SI 2022/894) |
|  |  | 1 Sep 2022 (except in relation to specified persons)[10] (SI 2022/895) |
|  |  | 1 Sep 2022 (in relation to a child who has identified special educational needs)[11] (SI 2022/896) |
|  |  | 1 Sep 2022 (in relation to a child who has identified special educational needs)[13] (SI 2022/897) |
|  |  | 1 Sep 2022 (in relation to specified persons)[15] (SI 2022/898) |
|  |  | 1 Sep 2025 (in relation to a person who is over compulsory school age on 1 Sep 2022) (SI 2022/893) |
|  |  | *Not yet in force* (otherwise) |
| 56 | (1) | 2 Nov 2020 (for the purpose of making regulations) (SI 2020/1182) |
|  |  | 4 Jan 2021 (otherwise) (SI 2020/1182) |
|  | (2), (3) | 2 Nov 2020 (for the purpose of making regulations) (SI 2020/1182) |
|  |  | 1 Sep 2021 (otherwise) (SI 2021/373) |
|  | (4)–(6) | 2 Nov 2020 (for the purpose of making regulations) (SI 2020/1182) |
|  |  | 4 Jan 2021 (otherwise) (SI 2020/1182) |
| 57, 58 |  | 1 Sep 2021 (SI 2021/373) |
| 59 |  | 1 Sep 2021 (except in relation to specified persons[1]) (SI 2021/373) |
|  |  | 1 Jan 2022 (in relation to a child who has identified special educational needs) (SI 2021/1243)[2, 3]; (SI 2021/1244)[4, 5] |
|  |  | 1 Jan 2022 (except in relation to specified persons[6]) (SI 2021/1245) |
|  |  | 1 Sep 2022 (in relation to a child to whom a local authority is maintaining a statement of special educational needs under Education Act 1996, s 324 or 331) (SI 2022/891) |
|  |  | 1 Sep 2022 (in relation to a child to whom there is a matter ongoing on 1 Sep 2022) (SI 2022/892) |
|  |  | 1 Sep 2022 (in relation to a child who has identified special educational needs)[9] (SI 2022/894) |
|  |  | 1 Sep 2022 (except in relation to specified persons)[10] (SI 2022/895) |
|  |  | 1 Sep 2022 (in relation to a child who has identified special educational needs)[11] (SI 2022/896) |
|  |  | 1 Sep 2022 (in relation to a child who has identified special educational needs)[13] (SI 2022/897) |
|  |  | 1 Sep 2022 (in relation to specified persons)[15] (SI 2022/898) |

**Additional Learning Needs and Education Tribunal (Wales) Act 2018 (anaw 2)**—*contd*

|  |  |
|---|---|
|  | 1 Sep 2025 (in relation to a person who is over compulsory school age on 1 Sep 2022) (SI 2022/893) |
|  | *Not yet in force* (otherwise) |
| 60 | 2 Nov 2020 (for the purpose of making regulations) (SI 2020/1182) |
|  | 4 Jan 2021 (otherwise) (SI 2020/1182) |
| 61, 62 | 4 Jan 2021 (SI 2020/1182) |
| 63, 64 | 1 Sep 2021 (except in relation to specified persons[1]) (SI 2021/373) |
|  | 1 Jan 2022 (in relation to a child who has identified special educational needs) (SI 2021/1243)[2, 3]; (SI 2021/1244)[4, 5] |
|  | 1 Jan 2022 (except in relation to specified persons[6]) (SI 2021/1245) |
|  | 1 Sep 2022 (in relation to a child to whom a local authority is maintaining a statement of special educational needs under Education Act 1996, s 324 or 331) (SI 2022/891) |
|  | 1 Sep 2022 (in relation to a child to whom there is a matter ongoing on 1 Sep 2022) (SI 2022/892) |
|  | 1 Sep 2022 (in relation to a child who has identified special educational needs)[9] (SI 2022/894) |
|  | 1 Sep 2022 (except in relation to specified persons[10]) (SI 2022/895) |
|  | 1 Sep 2022 (in relation to a child who has identified special educational needs)[11] (SI 2022/896) |
|  | 1 Sep 2022 (in relation to a child who has identified special educational needs)[13] (SI 2022/897) |
|  | 1 Sep 2022 (in relation to specified persons[15]) (SI 2022/898) |
|  | 1 Sep 2025 (in relation to a person who is over compulsory school age on 1 Sep 2022) (SI 2022/893) |
|  | *Not yet in force* (otherwise) |
| 65 | 2 Nov 2020 (for the purpose of making regulations) (SI 2020/1182) |
|  | 1 Sep 2021 (except in relation to specified persons[1]) (SI 2021/373) |
|  | 1 Jan 2022 (in relation to a child who has identified special educational needs) (SI 2021/1243)[2, 3]; (SI 2021/1244)[4, 5] |
|  | 1 Jan 2022 (except in relation to specified persons[6]) (SI 2021/1245) |
|  | 1 Sep 2022 (in relation to a child to whom a local authority is maintaining a statement of special educational needs under Education Act 1996, s 324 or 331) (SI 2022/891) |
|  | 1 Sep 2022 (in relation to a child to whom there is a matter ongoing on 1 Sep 2022) (SI 2022/892) |
|  | 1 Sep 2022 (in relation to a child who has identified special educational needs)[9] (SI 2022/894) |
|  | 1 Sep 2022 (except in relation to specified persons[10]) (SI 2022/895) |
|  | 1 Sep 2022 (in relation to a child who has identified special educational needs)[11] (SI 2022/896) |
|  | 1 Sep 2022 (in relation to a child who has identified special educational needs)[13] (SI 2022/897) |
|  | 1 Sep 2022 (in relation to specified persons[15]) (SI 2022/898) |
|  | 1 Sep 2025 (in relation to a person who is over compulsory school age on 1 Sep 2022) (SI 2022/893) |
|  | *Not yet in force* (otherwise) |
| 66 | 1 Sep 2021 (except in relation to specified persons[1]) (SI 2021/373) |
|  | 1 Jan 2022 (in relation to a child who has identified special educational needs) (SI 2021/1243)[2, 3]; (SI 2021/1244)[4, 5] |
|  | 1 Jan 2022 (except in relation to specified persons[6]) (SI 2021/1245) |
|  | 1 Sep 2022 (in relation to a child to whom a local authority is maintaining a statement of special educational needs under Education Act 1996, s 324 or 331) (SI 2022/891) |
|  | 1 Sep 2022 (in relation to a child to whom there is a matter ongoing on 1 Sep 2022) (SI 2022/892) |

**Additional Learning Needs and Education Tribunal (Wales) Act 2018 (anaw 2)**—*contd*

| | |
|---|---|
| | 1 Sep 2022 (in relation to a child who has identified special educational needs)[9] (SI 2022/894) |
| | 1 Sep 2022 (except in relation to specified persons)[10] (SI 2022/895) |
| | 1 Sep 2022 (in relation to a child who has identified special educational needs)[11] (SI 2022/896) |
| | 1 Sep 2022 (in relation to a child who has identified special educational needs)[13] (SI 2022/897) |
| | 1 Sep 2022 (in relation to specified persons)[15] (SI 2022/898) |
| | 1 Sep 2025 (in relation to a person who is over compulsory school age on 1 Sep 2022) (SI 2022/893) |
| | *Not yet in force* (otherwise) |
| 67 | 2 Nov 2020 (SI 2020/1182) |
| 68, 69 | 1 Sep 2021 (except in relation to specified persons[1]) (SI 2021/373) |
| | 1 Jan 2022 (in relation to a child who has identified special educational needs) (SI 2021/1243)[2, 3]; (SI 2021/1244)[4, 5] |
| | 1 Jan 2022 (except in relation to specified persons[6]) (SI 2021/1245) |
| | 1 Sep 2022 (in relation to a child to whom a local authority is maintaining a statement of special educational needs under Education Act 1996, s 324 or 331) (SI 2022/891) |
| | 1 Sep 2022 (in relation to a child to whom there is a matter ongoing on 1 Sep 2022) (SI 2022/892) |
| | 1 Sep 2022 (in relation to a child who has identified special educational needs)[9] (SI 2022/894) |
| | 1 Sep 2022 (except in relation to specified persons)[10] (SI 2022/895) |
| | 1 Sep 2022 (in relation to a child who has identified special educational needs)[11] (SI 2022/896) |
| | 1 Sep 2022 (in relation to a child who has identified special educational needs)[13] (SI 2022/897) |
| | 1 Sep 2022 (in relation to specified persons)[15] (SI 2022/898) |
| | 1 Sep 2025 (in relation to a person who is over compulsory school age on 1 Sep 2022) (SI 2022/893) |
| | *Not yet in force* (otherwise) |
| 70–73 | 1 Sep 2021 (SI 2021/373) |
| 74 | 2 Nov 2020 (SI 2020/1182) |
| 75–77 | 2 Nov 2020 (for the purpose of making regulations) (SI 2020/1182) |
| | 1 Sep 2021 (otherwise) (SI 2021/373) |
| 78–81 | 1 Sep 2021 (SI 2021/373) |
| 82 | 2 Nov 2020 (SI 2020/1182) |
| 83 | 2 Nov 2020 (for the purpose of making regulations) (SI 2020/1182) |
| | 1 Sep 2021 (otherwise) (SI 2021/373) |
| 84 | 1 Sep 2021 (SI 2021/373) |
| 85 | 2 Nov 2020 (for the purpose of making regulations) (SI 2020/1182) |
| | 1 Sep 2021 (otherwise) (SI 2021/373) |
| 86–90 | 1 Sep 2021 (SI 2021/373) |
| 91, 92 | 2 Nov 2020 (for the purpose of making regulations) (SI 2020/1182) |
| | 1 Sep 2021 (otherwise) (SI 2021/373) |
| 93, 94 | 1 Sep 2021 (SI 2021/373) |
| 95 | 2 Nov 2020 (for the purpose of making regulations) (SI 2020/1182) |
| | 1 Sep 2021 (otherwise) (SI 2021/373) |
| 96 | See Sch 1 below |
| 97–101 | 25 Jan 2018 (s 100(1)) |
| Schedule     para 1 | 1 Sep 2021 (except in relation to specified persons[1]) (SI 2021/373) |
| | 1 Jan 2022 (in relation to a child who has identified special educational needs) (SI 2021/1243)[2, 3]; (SI 2021/1244)[4, 5] |

**Additional Learning Needs and Education Tribunal (Wales) Act 2018 (anaw 2)**—*contd*

|  |  |
|---|---|
|  | 1 Jan 2022 (except in relation to specified persons[6]) (SI 2021/1245) |
|  | 1 Sep 2022 (in relation to a child to whom a local authority is maintaining a statement of special educational needs under Education Act 1996, s 324 or 331) (SI 2022/891) |
|  | 1 Sep 2022 (in relation to a child to whom there is a matter ongoing on 1 Sep 2022) (SI 2022/892) |
|  | 1 Sep 2022 (in relation to a child who has identified special educational needs)[9] (SI 2022/894) |
|  | 1 Sep 2022 (except in relation to specified persons[10]) (SI 2022/895) |
|  | 1 Sep 2022 (in relation to a child who has identified special educational needs)[11] (SI 2022/896) |
|  | 1 Sep 2022 (in relation to a child who has identified special educational needs)[13] (SI 2022/897) |
|  | 1 Sep 2022 (in relation to specified persons)[15] (SI 2022/898) |
|  | 1 Sep 2025 (in relation to a person who is over compulsory school age on 1 Sep 2022) (SI 2022/893) |
|  | *Not yet in force* (otherwise) |
| para 2(1) | See sub-paras (2), (3) below |
| para 2(2)(a) | *Not yet in force* |
| para 2(2)(b) | 1 Sep 2021 (SI 2021/373) |
| para 2(3) | 1 Sep 2021 (SI 2021/373) |
| para 3 | 1 Sep 2021 (SI 2021/373) |
| para 4(1) | See sub-paras (2)–(34) below |
| para 4(2)–(8) | 1 Sep 2021 (except in relation to specified persons[1]) (SI 2021/373) |
|  | 1 Jan 2022 (in relation to a child who has identified special educational needs) (SI 2021/1243)[2, 3]; (SI 2021/1244)[4, 5] |
|  | 1 Jan 2022 (except in relation to specified persons[6]) (SI 2021/1245) |
|  | 1 Sep 2022 (in relation to a child to whom a local authority is maintaining a statement of special educational needs under Education Act 1996, s 324 or 331) (SI 2022/891) |
|  | 1 Sep 2022 (in relation to a child to whom there is a matter ongoing on 1 Sep 2022) (SI 2022/892) |
|  | 1 Sep 2022 (in relation to a child who has identified special educational needs)[9] (SI 2022/894) |
|  | 1 Sep 2022 (except in relation to specified persons[10]) (SI 2022/895) |
|  | 1 Sep 2022 (in relation to a child who has identified special educational needs)[11] (SI 2022/896) |
|  | 1 Sep 2022 (in relation to a child who has identified special educational needs)[13] (SI 2022/897) |
|  | 1 Sep 2022 (in relation to specified persons)[15] (SI 2022/898) |
|  | 1 Sep 2025 (in relation to a person who is over compulsory school age on 1 Sep 2022) (SI 2022/893) |
|  | *Not yet in force* (otherwise) |
| para 4(9) | 1 Sep 2021 (except in relation to specified persons[1]) (SI 2021/373) |
|  | 1 Sep 2021 (in so far as repeals Education Act 1996, ss 333(1ZA), 333(2)–(6), 334, 335) (SI 2021/373) |
|  | 1 Jan 2022 (in relation to a child who has identified special educational needs) (SI 2021/1243)[2, 3]; (SI 2021/1244)[4, 5] |
|  | 1 Jan 2022 (except in relation to specified persons[6]) (SI 2021/1245) |
|  | 1 Sep 2022 (in relation to a child to whom a local authority is maintaining a statement of special educational needs under Education Act 1996, s 324 or 331) (SI 2022/891)[7] |
|  | 1 Sep 2022 (in relation to a child to whom there is a matter ongoing on 1 Sep 2022) (SI 2022/892)[8] |
|  | 1 Sep 2022 (in relation to a child who has identified special educational needs)[9] (SI 2022/894) |
|  | 1 Sep 2022 (except in relation to specified persons[10]) (SI 2022/895) |
|  | 1 Sep 2022 (in relation to a child who has identified special educational needs)[11] (SI 2022/896)[12] |

**Additional Learning Needs and Education Tribunal (Wales) Act 2018 (anaw 2)**—*contd*

|  |  |
|---|---|
|  | 1 Sep 2022 (in relation to a child who has identified special educational needs)[13] (SI 2022/897)[14] |
|  | 1 Sep 2022 (in relation to specified persons)[15] (SI 2022/898) |
|  | 1 Sep 2025 (in relation to a person who is over compulsory school age on 1 Sep 2022) (SI 2022/893) |
|  | *Not yet in force (otherwise)* |
| para 4(10) | 1 Sep 2021 (except in relation to specified persons[1]) (SI 2021/373) |
|  | 1 Jan 2022 (in relation to a child who has identified special educational needs) (SI 2021/1243)[2, 3]; (SI 2021/1244)[4, 5] |
|  | 1 Jan 2022 (except in relation to specified persons[6]) (SI 2021/1245) |
|  | 1 Sep 2022 (in relation to a child to whom a local authority is maintaining a statement of special educational needs under Education Act 1996, s 324 or 331) (SI 2022/891) |
|  | 1 Sep 2022 (in relation to a child to whom there is a matter ongoing on 1 Sep 2022) (SI 2022/892) |
|  | 1 Sep 2022 (in relation to a child who has identified special educational needs)[9] (SI 2022/894) |
|  | 1 Sep 2022 (except in relation to specified persons)[10] (SI 2022/895) |
|  | 1 Sep 2022 (in relation to a child who has identified special educational needs)[11] (SI 2022/896) |
|  | 1 Sep 2022 (in relation to a child who has identified special educational needs)[13] (SI 2022/897) |
|  | 1 Sep 2022 (in relation to specified persons)[15] (SI 2022/898) |
|  | 1 Sep 2025 (in relation to a person who is over compulsory school age on 1 Sep 2022) (SI 2022/893) |
|  | *Not yet in force (otherwise)* |
| para 4(11) | *Not yet in force* |
| para 4(12) | 1 Sep 2021 (SI 2021/373) |
| para 4(13)–(18) | 1 Sep 2021 (except in relation to specified persons[1]) (SI 2021/373) |
|  | 1 Jan 2022 (in relation to a child who has identified special educational needs) (SI 2021/1243)[2, 3]; (SI 2021/1244)[4, 5] |
|  | 1 Jan 2022 (except in relation to specified persons[6]) (SI 2021/1245) |
|  | 1 Sep 2022 (in relation to a child to whom a local authority is maintaining a statement of special educational needs under Education Act 1996, s 324 or 331) (SI 2022/891) |
|  | 1 Sep 2022 (in relation to a child to whom there is a matter ongoing on 1 Sep 2022) (SI 2022/892) |
|  | 1 Sep 2022 (in relation to a child who has identified special educational needs)[9] (SI 2022/894) |
|  | 1 Sep 2022 (except in relation to specified persons)[10] (SI 2022/895) |
|  | 1 Sep 2022 (in relation to a child who has identified special educational needs)[11] (SI 2022/896) |
|  | 1 Sep 2022 (in relation to a child who has identified special educational needs)[13] (SI 2022/897) |
|  | 1 Sep 2022 (in relation to specified persons)[15] (SI 2022/898) |
|  | 1 Sep 2025 (in relation to a person who is over compulsory school age on 1 Sep 2022) (SI 2022/893) |
|  | *Not yet in force (otherwise)* |
| para 4(19)(a) | 1 Sep 2021 (SI 2021/373) |
| para 4(19)(b) | 1 Sep 2021 (except in relation to specified persons[1]) (SI 2021/373) |
|  | 1 Jan 2022 (in relation to a child who has identified special educational needs) (SI 2021/1243)[2, 3]; (SI 2021/1244)[4, 5] |
|  | 1 Jan 2022 (except in relation to specified persons[6]) (SI 2021/1245) |
|  | 1 Sep 2022 (in relation to a child to whom a local authority is maintaining a statement of special educational needs under Education Act 1996, s 324 or 331) (SI 2022/891) |
|  | 1 Sep 2022 (in relation to a child to whom there is a matter ongoing on 1 Sep 2022) (SI 2022/892) |

**Additional Learning Needs and Education Tribunal (Wales) Act 2018 (anaw 2)**—*contd*

|  |  |
|---|---|
|  | 1 Sep 2022 (in relation to a child who has identified special educational needs)[9] (SI 2022/894) |
|  | 1 Sep 2022 (except in relation to specified persons)[10] (SI 2022/895) |
|  | 1 Sep 2022 (in relation to a child who has identified special educational needs)[11] (SI 2022/896) |
|  | 1 Sep 2022 (in relation to a child who has identified special educational needs)[13] (SI 2022/897) |
|  | 1 Sep 2022 (in relation to specified persons)[15] (SI 2022/898) |
|  | 1 Sep 2025 (in relation to a person who is over compulsory school age on 1 Sep 2022) (SI 2022/893) |
|  | *Not yet in force* (otherwise) |
| para 4(20), (21) | 1 Sep 2021 (except in relation to specified persons[1]) (SI 2021/373) |
|  | 1 Jan 2022 (in relation to a child who has identified special educational needs) (SI 2021/1243)[2, 3]; (SI 2021/1244)[4, 5] |
|  | 1 Jan 2022 (except in relation to specified persons[6]) (SI 2021/1245) |
|  | 1 Sep 2022 (in relation to a child to whom a local authority is maintaining a statement of special educational needs under Education Act 1996, s 324 or 331) (SI 2022/891) |
|  | 1 Sep 2022 (in relation to a child to whom there is a matter ongoing on 1 Sep 2022) (SI 2022/892) |
|  | 1 Sep 2022 (in relation to a child who has identified special educational needs)[9] (SI 2022/894) |
|  | 1 Sep 2022 (except in relation to specified persons)[10] (SI 2022/895) |
|  | 1 Sep 2022 (in relation to a child who has identified special educational needs)[11] (SI 2022/896) |
|  | 1 Sep 2022 (in relation to a child who has identified special educational needs)[13] (SI 2022/897) |
|  | 1 Sep 2022 (in relation to specified persons)[15] (SI 2022/898) |
|  | 1 Sep 2025 (in relation to a person who is over compulsory school age on 1 Sep 2022) (SI 2022/893) |
|  | *Not yet in force* (otherwise) |
| para 4(22) | 1 Sep 2021 (SI 2021/373) |
| para 4(23)–(29) | 1 Sep 2021 (except in relation to specified persons[1]) (SI 2021/373) |
|  | 1 Jan 2022 (in relation to a child who has identified special educational needs) (SI 2021/1243)[2, 3]; (SI 2021/1244)[4, 5] |
|  | 1 Jan 2022 (except in relation to specified persons[6]) (SI 2021/1245) |
|  | 1 Sep 2022 (in relation to a child to whom a local authority is maintaining a statement of special educational needs under Education Act 1996, s 324 or 331) (SI 2022/891) |
|  | 1 Sep 2022 (in relation to a child to whom there is a matter ongoing on 1 Sep 2022) (SI 2022/892) |
|  | 1 Sep 2022 (in relation to a child who has identified special educational needs)[9] (SI 2022/894) |
|  | 1 Sep 2022 (except in relation to specified persons)[10] (SI 2022/895) |
|  | 1 Sep 2022 (in relation to a child who has identified special educational needs)[11] (SI 2022/896) |
|  | 1 Sep 2022 (in relation to a child who has identified special educational needs)[13] (SI 2022/897) |
|  | 1 Sep 2022 (in relation to specified persons)[15] (SI 2022/898) |
|  | 1 Sep 2025 (in relation to a person who is over compulsory school age on 1 Sep 2022) (SI 2022/893) |
|  | *Not yet in force* (otherwise) |
| para 4(30)(a)(i) | *Not yet in force* |
| para 4(30)(a)(ii) | 1 Sep 2021 (SI 2021/373) |
| para 4(30)(b) | 1 Sep 2021 (SI 2021/373) |
| para 4(30)(c) | *Not yet in force* |
| para 4(31) | 1 Sep 2021 (SI 2021/373) |
| para 4(32)(a)(i), (ii) | 1 Sep 2021 (except in relation to specified persons[1]) (SI 2021/373) |

**Additional Learning Needs and Education Tribunal (Wales) Act 2018 (anaw 2)**—*contd*

|  |  |
|---|---|
|  | 1 Jan 2022 (in relation to a child who has identified special educational needs) (SI 2021/1243)[2, 3]; (SI 2021/1244)[4, 5] |
|  | 1 Jan 2022 (except in relation to specified persons[6]) (SI 2021/1245) |
|  | 1 Sep 2022 (in relation to a child to whom a local authority is maintaining a statement of special educational needs under Education Act 1996, s 324 or 331) (SI 2022/891) |
|  | 1 Sep 2022 (in relation to a child to whom there is a matter ongoing on 1 Sep 2022) (SI 2022/892) |
|  | 1 Sep 2022 (in relation to a child who has identified special educational needs)[9] (SI 2022/894) |
|  | 1 Sep 2022 (except in relation to specified persons)[10] (SI 2022/895) |
|  | 1 Sep 2022 (in relation to a child who has identified special educational needs)[11] (SI 2022/896) |
|  | 1 Sep 2022 (in relation to a child who has identified special educational needs)[13] (SI 2022/897) |
|  | 1 Sep 2022 (in relation to specified persons)[15] (SI 2022/898) |
|  | 1 Sep 2025 (in relation to a person who is over compulsory school age on 1 Sep 2022) (SI 2022/893) |
|  | *Not yet in force* (otherwise) |
| para 4(32)(a)(iii) | 1 Sep 2021 (SI 2021/373) |
| para 4(32)(b) | 1 Sep 2021 (except in relation to specified persons[1]) (SI 2021/373) |
|  | 1 Jan 2022 (in relation to a child who has identified special educational needs) (SI 2021/1243)[2, 3]; (SI 2021/1244)[4, 5] |
|  | 1 Jan 2022 (except in relation to specified persons[6]) (SI 2021/1245) |
|  | 1 Sep 2022 (in relation to a child to whom a local authority is maintaining a statement of special educational needs under Education Act 1996, s 324 or 331) (SI 2022/891) |
|  | 1 Sep 2022 (in relation to a child to whom there is a matter ongoing on 1 Sep 2022) (SI 2022/892) |
|  | 1 Sep 2022 (in relation to a child who has identified special educational needs)[9] (SI 2022/894) |
|  | 1 Sep 2022 (except in relation to specified persons)[10] (SI 2022/895) |
|  | 1 Sep 2022 (in relation to a child who has identified special educational needs)[11] (SI 2022/896) |
|  | 1 Sep 2022 (in relation to a child who has identified special educational needs)[13] (SI 2022/897) |
|  | 1 Sep 2022 (in relation to specified persons)[15] (SI 2022/898) |
|  | 1 Sep 2025 (in relation to a person who is over compulsory school age on 1 Sep 2022) (SI 2022/893) |
|  | *Not yet in force* (otherwise) |
| para 4(33)(a) | 1 Sep 2021 (SI 2021/373) |
| para 4(33)(b) | 1 Sep 2021 (in so far as repeals Education Act 1996, s 580, entries relating to "the appropriate national authority (in Chapter 2 of Part 4)", "the chairman's panel", "the lay panel", "the President", "the Tribunal") (SI 2021/373) |
|  | *Not yet in force* (otherwise) |
| para 4(33)(c) | *Not yet in force* |
| para 4(33)(d), (e) | 1 Sep 2021 (SI 2021/373) |
| para 4(33)(f) | *Not yet in force* |
| para 4(33)(g) | 1 Sep 2021 (SI 2021/373) |
| para 4(34) | *Not yet in force* |
| para 5 | 24 Mar 2018 (s 100(2)) |
| para 6(a)–(c) | *Not yet in force* |
| para 6(d)(i)–(iv) | *Not yet in force* |
| para 6(d)(v) | 1 Sep 2021 (SI 2021/373) |
| para 6(d)(vi) | *Not yet in force* |
| para 6(e) | *Not yet in force* |
| para 6(f), (g) | 1 Sep 2021 (SI 2021/373) |
| para 6(h), (i) | *Not yet in force* |

**Additional Learning Needs and Education Tribunal (Wales) Act 2018 (anaw 2)**—*contd*

| | |
|---|---|
| para 6(j)(i) | 1 Sep 2021 (SI 2021/373) |
| para 6(j)(ii), (k) | *Not yet in force* |
| para 6(l)(i) | 1 Sep 2021 (SI 2021/373) |
| para 6(l)(ii) | *Not yet in force* |
| para 6(l)(iii) | 1 Sep 2021 (SI 2021/373) |
| para 6(m) | *Not yet in force* |
| para 6(n)(i) | *Not yet in force* |
| para 6(n)(ii) | 1 Sep 2021 (in so far as repeals Apprenticeships, Skills, Children and |
| | Learning Act 2009, Sch 2, para 11) (SI 2021/373) |
| | *Not yet in force* (otherwise) |
| para 6(o)–(s) | *Not yet in force* |
| para 6(t) | 1 Sep 2021 (SI 2021/373) |
| paras 7, 8 | 1 Sep 2021 (except in relation to specified persons[1]) (SI 2021/373) |
| | 1 Jan 2022 (in relation to a child who has identified special educational needs) (SI 2021/1243)[2, 3]; (SI 2021/1244)[4, 5] |
| | 1 Jan 2022 (except in relation to specified persons[6]) (SI 2021/1245) |
| | 1 Sep 2022 (in relation to a child to whom a local authority is maintaining a statement of special educational needs under Education Act 1996, s 324 or 331) (SI 2022/891) |
| | 1 Sep 2022 (in relation to a child to whom there is a matter ongoing on 1 Sep 2022) (SI 2022/892) |
| | 1 Sep 2022 (in relation to a child who has identified special educational needs)[9] (SI 2022/894) |
| | 1 Sep 2022 (except in relation to specified persons)[10] (SI 2022/895) |
| | 1 Sep 2022 (in relation to a child who has identified special educational needs)[11] (SI 2022/896) |
| | 1 Sep 2022 (in relation to a child who has identified special educational needs)[13] (SI 2022/897) |
| | 1 Sep 2022 (in relation to specified persons)[15] (SI 2022/898) |
| | 1 Sep 2025 (in relation to a person who is over compulsory school age on 1 Sep 2022) (SI 2022/893) |
| | *Not yet in force* (otherwise) |
| paras 9, 10 | 1 Sep 2021 (SI 2021/373) |
| para 11(a) | 1 Sep 2021 (except in relation to specified persons[1]) (SI 2021/373) |
| | 1 Jan 2022 (in relation to a child who has identified special educational needs) (SI 2021/1243)[2, 3]; (SI 2021/1244)[4, 5] |
| | 1 Jan 2022 (except in relation to specified persons[6]) (SI 2021/1245) |
| | 1 Sep 2022 (in relation to a child to whom a local authority is maintaining a statement of special educational needs under Education Act 1996, s 324 or 331) (SI 2022/891) |
| | 1 Sep 2022 (in relation to a child to whom there is a matter ongoing on 1 Sep 2022) (SI 2022/892) |
| | 1 Sep 2022 (in relation to a child who has identified special educational needs)[9] (SI 2022/894) |
| | 1 Sep 2022 (except in relation to specified persons)[10] (SI 2022/895) |
| | 1 Sep 2022 (in relation to a child who has identified special educational needs)[11] (SI 2022/896) |
| | 1 Sep 2022 (in relation to a child who has identified special educational needs)[13] (SI 2022/897) |
| | 1 Sep 2022 (in relation to specified persons)[15] (SI 2022/898) |
| | 1 Sep 2025 (in relation to a person who is over compulsory school age on 1 Sep 2022) (SI 2022/893) |
| | *Not yet in force* (otherwise) |
| para 11(b) | 1 Sep 2021 (SI 2021/373) |
| para 12(a) | 1 Sep 2021 (except in relation to specified persons[1]) (SI 2021/373) |
| | 1 Jan 2022 (in relation to a child who has identified special educational needs) (SI 2021/1243)[2, 3]; (SI 2021/1244)[4, 5] |
| | 1 Jan 2022 (except in relation to specified persons[6]) (SI 2021/1245) |

**Additional Learning Needs and Education Tribunal (Wales) Act 2018 (anaw 2)**—*contd*

|   |   |
|---|---|
|   | 1 Sep 2022 (in relation to a child to whom a local authority is maintaining a statement of special educational needs under Education Act 1996, s 324 or 331) (SI 2022/891) |
|   | 1 Sep 2022 (in relation to a child to whom there is a matter ongoing on 1 Sep 2022) (SI 2022/892) |
|   | 1 Sep 2022 (in relation to a child who has identified special educational needs)[9] (SI 2022/894) |
|   | 1 Sep 2022 (except in relation to specified persons)[10] (SI 2022/895) |
|   | 1 Sep 2022 (in relation to a child who has identified special educational needs)[11] (SI 2022/896) |
|   | 1 Sep 2022 (in relation to a child who has identified special educational needs)[13] (SI 2022/897) |
|   | 1 Sep 2022 (in relation to specified persons)[15] (SI 2022/898) |
|   | 1 Sep 2025 (in relation to a person who is over compulsory school age on 1 Sep 2022) (SI 2022/893) |
|   | *Not yet in force* (otherwise) |
| para 12(b) | 1 Sep 2021 (SI 2021/373) |
| para 13 | 1 Sep 2021 (SI 2021/373) |
| para 14(1) | See sub-paras (2)–(4) below |
| para 14(2), (3) | 1 Sep 2021 (except in relation to specified persons[1]) (SI 2021/373) |
|   | 1 Jan 2022 (in relation to a child who has identified special educational needs) (SI 2021/1243)[2, 3]; (SI 2021/1244)[4, 5] |
|   | 1 Jan 2022 (except in relation to specified persons[6]) (SI 2021/1245) |
|   | 1 Sep 2022 (in relation to a child to whom a local authority is maintaining a statement of special educational needs under Education Act 1996, s 324 or 331) (SI 2022/891) |
|   | 1 Sep 2022 (in relation to a child to whom there is a matter ongoing on 1 Sep 2022) (SI 2022/892) |
|   | 1 Sep 2022 (in relation to a child who has identified special educational needs)[9] (SI 2022/894) |
|   | 1 Sep 2022 (except in relation to specified persons)[10] (SI 2022/895) |
|   | 1 Sep 2022 (in relation to a child who has identified special educational needs)[11] (SI 2022/896) |
|   | 1 Sep 2022 (in relation to a child who has identified special educational needs)[13] (SI 2022/897) |
|   | 1 Sep 2022 (in relation to specified persons)[15] (SI 2022/898) |
|   | 1 Sep 2025 (in relation to a person who is over compulsory school age on 1 Sep 2022) (SI 2022/893) |
|   | *Not yet in force* (otherwise) |
| para 14(4) | 1 Sep 2021 (SI 2021/373) |
| para 15(1) | See sub-paras (2)–(5) below |
| para 15(2) | *Not yet in force* |
| para 15(3), (4) | 1 Sep 2021 (SI 2021/373) |
| para 15(5) | *Not yet in force* |
| para 16 | *Not yet in force* |
| paras 17, 18 | 1 Sep 2021 (SI 2021/373) |
| para 19(1) | See sub-paras (2)–(6) below |
| para 19(2), (3) | 1 Sep 2021 (SI 2021/373) |
| para 19(4) | 2 Nov 2020 (for the purpose of making regulations) (SI 2020/1182) |
|   | 1 Sep 2021 (otherwise) (SI 2021/373) |
| para 19(5)(a)–(d) | 1 Sep 2021 (SI 2021/373) |
| para 19(5)(e)(i) | 1 Sep 2021 (SI 2021/373) |
| para 19(5)(e)(ii) | 1 Sep 2021 (except in relation to specified persons[1]) (SI 2021/373) |
|   | 1 Jan 2022 (in relation to a child who has identified special educational needs) (SI 2021/1243)[2, 3]; (SI 2021/1244)[4, 5] |
|   | 1 Jan 2022 (except in relation to specified persons[6]) (SI 2021/1245) |

**Additional Learning Needs and Education Tribunal (Wales) Act 2018 (anaw 2)**—*contd*

|  |  |
|---|---|
|  | 1 Sep 2022 (in relation to a child to whom a local authority is maintaining a statement of special educational needs under Education Act 1996, s 324 or 331) (SI 2022/891) |
|  | 1 Sep 2022 (in relation to a child to whom there is a matter ongoing on 1 Sep 2022) (SI 2022/892) |
|  | 1 Sep 2022 (in relation to a child who has identified special educational needs)[9] (SI 2022/894) |
|  | 1 Sep 2022 (except in relation to specified persons)[10] (SI 2022/895) |
|  | 1 Sep 2022 (in relation to a child who has identified special educational needs)[11] (SI 2022/896) |
|  | 1 Sep 2022 (in relation to a child who has identified special educational needs)[13] (SI 2022/897) |
|  | 1 Sep 2022 (in relation to specified persons)[15] (SI 2022/898) |
|  | 1 Sep 2025 (in relation to a person who is over compulsory school age on 1 Sep 2022) (SI 2022/893) |
|  | *Not yet in force* (otherwise) |
| para 19(5)(f) | 1 Sep 2021 (SI 2021/373) |
| para 19(5)(g), (h) | 2 Nov 2020 (for the purpose of making regulations) (SI 2020/1182) |
|  | 1 Sep 2021 (otherwise) (SI 2021/373) |
| para 19(6) | 1 Sep 2021 (SI 2021/373) |
| para 20 | 1 Sep 2021 (SI 2021/373) |
| para 21(1) | See sub-para (2) below |
| para 21(2)(a)(i) | 1 Sep 2021 (except in relation to specified persons[1]) (SI 2021/373) |
|  | 1 Jan 2022 (in relation to a child who has identified special educational needs) (SI 2021/1243)[2, 3]; (SI 2021/1244)[4, 5] |
|  | 1 Jan 2022 (except in relation to specified persons[6]) (SI 2021/1245) |
|  | 1 Sep 2022 (in relation to a child to whom a local authority is maintaining a statement of special educational needs under Education Act 1996, s 324 or 331) (SI 2022/891) |
|  | 1 Sep 2022 (in relation to a child to whom there is a matter ongoing on 1 Sep 2022) (SI 2022/892) |
|  | 1 Sep 2022 (in relation to a child who has identified special educational needs)[9] (SI 2022/894) |
|  | 1 Sep 2022 (except in relation to specified persons)[10] (SI 2022/895) |
|  | 1 Sep 2022 (in relation to a child who has identified special educational needs)[11] (SI 2022/896) |
|  | 1 Sep 2022 (in relation to a child who has identified special educational needs)[13] (SI 2022/897) |
|  | 1 Sep 2022 (in relation to specified persons)[15] (SI 2022/898) |
|  | 1 Sep 2025 (in relation to a person who is over compulsory school age on 1 Sep 2022) (SI 2022/893) |
|  | *Not yet in force* (otherwise) |
| para 21(2)(a)(ii) | *Not yet in force* |
| para 21(2)(b)(i) | 1 Sep 2021 (SI 2021/373) |
| para 21(2)(b)(ii) | 1 Sep 2021 (except in relation to specified persons[1]) (SI 2021/373) |
|  | 1 Jan 2022 (in relation to a child who has identified special educational needs) (SI 2021/1243)[2, 3]; (SI 2021/1244)[4, 5] |
|  | 1 Jan 2022 (except in relation to specified persons[6]) (SI 2021/1245) |
|  | 1 Sep 2022 (in relation to a child to whom a local authority is maintaining a statement of special educational needs under Education Act 1996, s 324 or 331) (SI 2022/891) |
|  | 1 Sep 2022 (in relation to a child to whom there is a matter ongoing on 1 Sep 2022) (SI 2022/892) |
|  | 1 Sep 2022 (in relation to a child who has identified special educational needs)[9] (SI 2022/894) |
|  | 1 Sep 2022 (except in relation to specified persons)[10] (SI 2022/895) |
|  | 1 Sep 2022 (in relation to a child who has identified special educational needs)[11] (SI 2022/896) |

**See Halsbury's Statutes Citator for amendments to these Acts** 2559

**Additional Learning Needs and Education Tribunal (Wales) Act 2018 (anaw 2)**—*contd*

|  |  |
|---|---|
|  | 1 Sep 2022 (in relation to a child who has identified special educational needs)[13] (SI 2022/897) |
|  | 1 Sep 2022 (in relation to specified persons)[15] (SI 2022/898) |
|  | 1 Sep 2025 (in relation to a person who is over compulsory school age on 1 Sep 2022) (SI 2022/893) |
|  | *Not yet in force* (otherwise) |
| para 22 | 1 Sep 2021 (except in relation to specified persons[1]) (SI 2021/373) |
|  | 1 Jan 2022 (in relation to a child who has identified special educational needs) (SI 2021/1243)[2, 3]; (SI 2021/1244)[4, 5] |
|  | 1 Jan 2022 (except in relation to specified persons[6]) (SI 2021/1245) |
|  | 1 Sep 2022 (in relation to a child to whom a local authority is maintaining a statement of special educational needs under Education Act 1996, s 324 or 331) (SI 2022/891) |
|  | 1 Sep 2022 (in relation to a child to whom there is a matter ongoing on 1 Sep 2022) (SI 2022/892) |
|  | 1 Sep 2022 (in relation to a child who has identified special educational needs)[9] (SI 2022/894) |
|  | 1 Sep 2022 (except in relation to specified persons)[10] (SI 2022/895) |
|  | 1 Sep 2022 (in relation to a child who has identified special educational needs)[11] (SI 2022/896) |
|  | 1 Sep 2022 (in relation to a child who has identified special educational needs)[13] (SI 2022/897) |
|  | 1 Sep 2022 (in relation to specified persons)[15] (SI 2022/898) |
|  | 1 Sep 2025 (in relation to a person who is over compulsory school age on 1 Sep 2022) (SI 2022/893) |
|  | *Not yet in force* (otherwise) |
| para 23(1) | See sub-paras (2)–(6) |
| para 23(2) | *Not yet in force* |
| para 23(3)(a)–(c) | 1 Sep 2021 (SI 2021/373) |
| para 23(3)(d) | *Not yet in force* |
| para 23(4) | 1 Sep 2021 (except in relation to specified persons[1]) (SI 2021/373) |
|  | 1 Jan 2022 (in relation to a child who has identified special educational needs) (SI 2021/1243)[2, 3]; (SI 2021/1244)[4, 5] |
|  | 1 Jan 2022 (except in relation to specified persons[6]) (SI 2021/1245) |
|  | 1 Sep 2022 (in relation to a child to whom a local authority is maintaining a statement of special educational needs under Education Act 1996, s 324 or 331) (SI 2022/891) |
|  | 1 Sep 2022 (in relation to a child to whom there is a matter ongoing on 1 Sep 2022) (SI 2022/892) |
|  | 1 Sep 2022 (in relation to a child who has identified special educational needs)[9] (SI 2022/894) |
|  | 1 Sep 2022 (except in relation to specified persons)[10] (SI 2022/895) |
|  | 1 Sep 2022 (in relation to a child who has identified special educational needs)[11] (SI 2022/896) |
|  | 1 Sep 2022 (in relation to a child who has identified special educational needs)[13] (SI 2022/897) |
|  | 1 Sep 2022 (in relation to specified persons)[15] (SI 2022/898) |
|  | 1 Sep 2025 (in relation to a person who is over compulsory school age on 1 Sep 2022) (SI 2022/893) |
|  | *Not yet in force* (otherwise) |
| para 23(5) | 1 Sep 2021 (SI 2021/373) |
| para 23(6) | *Not yet in force* |
| para 24(1) | See sub-paras (2)–(6) below |
| para 24(2) | 1 Sep 2021 (SI 2021/373) |
| para 24(3) | 1 Sep 2021 (except in relation to specified persons[1]) (SI 2021/373) |
|  | 1 Jan 2022 (in relation to a child who has identified special educational needs) (SI 2021/1243)[2, 3]; (SI 2021/1244)[4, 5] |
|  | 1 Jan 2022 (except in relation to specified persons[6]) (SI 2021/1245) |

**Additional Learning Needs and Education Tribunal (Wales) Act 2018 (anaw 2)**—*contd*

|  |  |
|---|---|
|  | 1 Sep 2022 (in relation to a child to whom there is a matter ongoing on 1 Sep 2022) (SI 2022/892) |
|  | 1 Sep 2022 (in relation to a child who has identified special educational needs)[9] (SI 2022/894) |
|  | 1 Sep 2022 (except in relation to specified persons)[10] (SI 2022/895) |
|  | 1 Sep 2022 (in relation to a child who has identified special educational needs)[11] (SI 2022/896) |
|  | 1 Sep 2022 (in relation to a child who has identified special educational needs)[13] (SI 2022/897) |
|  | 1 Sep 2022 (in relation to specified persons)[15] (SI 2022/898) |
|  | 1 Sep 2025 (in relation to a person who is over compulsory school age on 1 Sep 2022) (SI 2022/893) |
|  | *Not yet in force* (otherwise) |
| para 24(4) | 22 Jun 2021 (SI 2021/373) |
| para 24(5) | 1 Sep 2021 (SI 2021/373) |
| para 24(6)(a) | 1 Sep 2021 (except in relation to specified persons[1]) (SI 2021/373) |
|  | 1 Jan 2022 (in relation to a child who has identified special educational needs) (SI 2021/1243)[2, 3]; (SI 2021/1244)[4, 5] |
|  | 1 Jan 2022 (except in relation to specified persons[6]) (SI 2021/1245) |
|  | 1 Sep 2022 (in relation to a child to whom a local authority is maintaining a statement of special educational needs under Education Act 1996, s 324 or 331) (SI 2022/891) |
|  | 1 Sep 2022 (in relation to a child to whom there is a matter ongoing on 1 Sep 2022) (SI 2022/892) |
|  | 1 Sep 2022 (in relation to a child who has identified special educational needs)[9] (SI 2022/894) |
|  | 1 Sep 2022 (except in relation to specified persons)[10] (SI 2022/895) |
|  | 1 Sep 2022 (in relation to a child who has identified special educational needs)[11] (SI 2022/896) |
|  | 1 Sep 2022 (in relation to a child who has identified special educational needs)[13] (SI 2022/897) |
|  | 1 Sep 2022 (in relation to specified persons)[15] (SI 2022/898) |
|  | 1 Sep 2025 (in relation to a person who is over compulsory school age on 1 Sep 2022) (SI 2022/893) |
|  | *Not yet in force* (otherwise) |
| para 24(6)(b), (c) | 1 Sep 2021 (SI 2021/373) |

[1] For the specified persons, see SI 2021/373, arts 4, 7

[2] For the meaning of identified special educational needs, see SI 2021/1243, art 2

[3] For transitional provisions and savings, see SI 2021/1243, arts 4–23

[4] For the meaning of identified special educational needs, see SI 2021/1243, art 2

[5] For transitional provisions and savings, see SI 2021/1244, arts 4–21

[6] For the specified persons, see SI 2021/1245, art 4

[7] For savings, see SI 2022/891, art 4

[8] For savings, see SI 2022/892, art 4

[9] For the meaning of identified special educational needs, see SI 2022/894, art 2

[10] For the specified persons, see SI 2022/895, art 4

[11] For the meaning of identified special educational needs, see SI 2022/896, art 2

[12] For savings, see SI 2022/896, art 4

[13] For the meaning of identified special educational needs, see SI 2022/897, art 2

[14] For savings, see SI 2022/897, art 4

[15] For the meaning of identified special educational needs, see SI 2022/898, art 3

## Armed Forces (Flexible Working) Act 2018 (c 2)

*RA:* 8 Feb 2018

*Commencement provisions:* s 3(2)–(4); Armed Forces (Flexible Working) Act 2018 (Commencement) Regulations 2018, SI 2018/799

| | |
|---|---|
| 1, 2 | 30 Jun 2018 (SI 2018/799) |
| 3 | 8 Feb 2018 (s 3(2)) |

## Assaults on Emergency Workers (Offences) Act 2018 (c 23)

*RA:* 13 Sep 2018

*Commencement provisions:* s 4(2)

Whole Act in force 13 Nov 2018 (s 4(2))

## Automated and Electric Vehicles Act 2018 (c 18)

*RA:* 19 Jul 2018

*Commencement provisions:* s 21; Automated and Electric Vehicles Act 2018 (Commencement No 1) Regulations 2021, SI 2021/396; Automated and Electric Vehicles Act 2018 (Commencement No 2) Regulations 2022, SI 2022/587

| | | |
|---|---|---|
| 1–10 | | 21 Apr 2021 (SI 2021/396) |
| 11 | | 27 May 2022 (SI 2022/587) |
| 12 | | *Not yet in force* |
| 13–19 | | 21 Apr 2021 (SI 2021/396) |
| 20 | (1) | 21 Apr 2021 (SI 2021/396) |
| | (2)–(7) | 19 Jul 2018 (s 21(2)) |
| 21–23 | | 19 Jul 2018 (s 21(2)) |
| Schedule | | 21 Apr 2021 (SI 2021/396) |

## Budget (Scotland) Act 2018 (asp 6)

*RA:* 28 Mar 2018

*Commencement provisions:* s 10

Whole Act in force 29 Mar 2018 (s 10)

## Church of England (Miscellaneous Provisions) Measure 2018 (No 7)

*RA:* 20 Dec 2018

*Commencement provisions:* s 17(2)–(6); Church of England (Miscellaneous Provisions) Measure 2018 (Commencement) Order 2019, SI 2019/67

| | | |
|---|---|---|
| 1 | | 1 Mar 2019 (SI 2019/67) |
| 2 | | 20 Dec 2018 (s 17(2)) |
| 3 | | 1 Mar 2019 (SI 2019/67) |
| 4 | (1)–(7) | 1 May 2019 (SI 2019/67) |
| | (8) | 1 Mar 2019 (SI 2019/67) |
| 5 | | 1 Mar 2019 (SI 2019/67) |
| 6 | (1) | 1 Mar 2019 (SI 2019/67) |
| | (2), (3) | 20 Dec 2018 (s 17(2)) |
| | (4)–(6) | 1 Mar 2019 (SI 2019/67) |
| | (7), (8) | 20 Dec 2018 (s 17(2)) |
| | (9)–(11) | 1 Mar 2019 (SI 2019/67) |
| | (12) | 20 Dec 2018 (s 17(2)) |

**Church of England (Miscellaneous Provisions) Measure 2018 (No 7)**—*contd*

|        |            |                              |
|--------|------------|------------------------------|
|        | (13)–(15)  | 1 Mar 2019 (SI 2019/67)      |
| 7      |            | 1 Mar 2019 (SI 2019/67)      |
| 8      | (1)        | 1 Mar 2019 (SI 2019/67)      |
|        | (2)        | 1 May 2019 (SI 2019/67)      |
|        | (3), (4)   | 1 Mar 2019 (SI 2019/67)      |
|        | (5), (6)   | 20 Dec 2018 (s 17(2))        |
| 9      | (1), (2)   | 20 Dec 2018 (s 17(2))        |
|        | (3)        | 1 Mar 2019 (SI 2019/67)      |
|        | (4)        | 20 Dec 2018 (s 17(2))        |
| 10     | (1), (2)   | 20 Dec 2018 (s 17(2))        |
|        | (3), (4)   | 1 Mar 2019 (SI 2019/67)      |
| 11     | (1)–(7)    | 1 Mar 2019 (SI 2019/67)      |
|        | (8), (9)   | 20 Dec 2018 (s 17(2))        |
| 12–16  |            | 1 Mar 2019 (SI 2019/67)      |
| 17     |            | 20 Dec 2018 (s 17(2))        |
| Schedule | para 1   | 20 Dec 2018 (s 17(2))        |
|        | paras 2–6  | 1 Mar 2019 (SI 2019/67)      |
|        | para 7     | 20 Dec 2018 (s 17(2))        |

**Church of England Pensions Measure 2018 (No 9)**

*RA:* 20 Dec 2018

*Commencement provisions*: s 61; Church of England Pensions Measure 2018 (Commencement and Savings) Order 2019, SI 2019/98

|         |                                      |
|---------|--------------------------------------|
| 1–60    | 1 Mar 2019 (SI 2019/98)              |
| 61–63   | 20 Dec 2018 (s 61(1))                |
| Schs 1–4| 1 Mar 2019 (SI 2019/98)              |
| Sch 5   | 1 Mar 2019 (SI 2019/98)[1]           |

[1]  For savings, see SI 2019/98, art 3

**Church Property Measure 2018 (No 8)**

*RA:* 20 Dec 2018

*Commencement provisions*: s 53; Church Property Measure 2018 (Commencement) Order 2019, SI 2019/97

|         |          |                              |
|---------|----------|------------------------------|
| 1–11    |          | 1 Mar 2019 (SI 2019/97)      |
| 12      | (1)–(4)  | 1 Mar 2019 (SI 2019/97)      |
|         | (5)      | *Not yet in force*           |
| 13–35   |          | 1 Mar 2019 (SI 2019/97)      |
| 36      | (1)      | 1 Mar 2019 (SI 2019/97)      |
|         | (2)      | *Not yet in force*           |
|         | (3), (4) | 1 Mar 2019 (SI 2019/97)      |
| 37–52   |          | 1 Mar 2019 (SI 2019/97)      |
| 53–55   |          | 20 Dec 2018 (s 53(1))        |
| Schs 1–3|          | 1 Mar 2019 (SI 2019/97)      |

**Civil Liability Act 2018 (c 29)**

*RA:* 20 Dec 2018

*Commencement provisions*: s 14; Civil Liability Act 2018 (Commencement No 1 and Transitional Provision) Regulations 2021, SI 2021/195

|      |                                                                      |
|------|----------------------------------------------------------------------|
| 1, 2 | 31 May 2021 (SI 2021/195)[1]                                         |
| 3    | 25 Feb 2021 (for the purpose only of exercising any power to make regulations) (SI 2021/195)[1] |

**See Halsbury's Statutes Citator for amendments to these Acts**          2563

**Civil Liability Act 2018 (c 29)**—*contd*

| | | |
|---|---|---|
| | | 31 May 2021 (otherwise) (SI 2021/195)[1] |
| 4 | | 31 May 2021 (SI 2021/195)[1] |
| 5, 6 | | 25 Feb 2021 (for the purpose only of exercising any power to make regulations) (SI 2021/195)[1] |
| | | 31 May 2021 (otherwise) (SI 2021/195)[1] |
| 7 | | 31 May 2021 (SI 2021/195)[1] |
| 8, 9 | | 25 Feb 2021 (for the purpose only of exercising any power to make regulations) (SI 2021/195)[1] |
| | | 31 May 2021 (otherwise) (SI 2021/195) |
| 10–15 | | 20 Dec 2018 (s 14(2)) |

[1]  For transitional provisions, see SI 2021/195, reg 4

---

**Civil Litigation (Expenses and Group Proceedings) (Scotland) Act 2018 (asp 10)**

*RA:* 5 Jun 2018

*Commencement provisions*: s 27; Civil Litigation (Expenses and Group Proceedings) (Scotland) Act 2018 (Commencement No 1, Transitional and Saving Provisions) Regulations 2018, SSI 2018/368; Civil Litigation (Expenses and Group Proceedings) (Scotland) Act 2018 (Commencement No 2 and Transitional Provision) Regulations 2020, SSI 2020/23; Civil Litigation (Expenses and Group Proceedings) (Scotland) Act 2018 (Commencement No 3) Regulations 2020, SSI 2020/167; Civil Litigation (Expenses and Group Proceedings) (Scotland) Act 2018 (Commencement No 4 and Transitional Provision) Regulations 2021, SSI 2021/125

| | | |
|---|---|---|
| 1–3 | | 23 Apr 2020 (SI 2020/23)[2] |
| 4 | (1), (2) | 30 Jan 2019 (SSI 2018/368) |
| | (3)–(5) | 23 Apr 2020 (SI 2020/23)[2] |
| 5 | | 30 Jan 2019 (SSI 2018/368) |
| 6 | (1)–(7) | 23 Apr 2020 (SI 2020/23)[2] |
| | (8) | 30 Jan 2019 (SSI 2018/368) |
| | (9), (10) | 23 Apr 2020 (SI 2020/23)[2] |
| 7 | (1), (2) | 23 Apr 2020 (SI 2020/23)[2] |
| | (3), (4) | 30 Jan 2019 (SSI 2018/368) |
| 8 | | 30 Jun 2021 (SSI 2021/125)[3] |
| 9–11 | | *Not yet in force* |
| 12 | (1) | 30 Jan 2019 (SSI 2018/368) |
| | (2) | 30 Jun 2021 (SSI 2021/125)[3] |
| | (3), (4) | 30 Jan 2019 (SSI 2018/368) |
| 13 | | 30 Jun 2021 (SSI 2021/125)[3] |
| 14 | (1)–(4) | 30 Jan 2019 (SSI 2018/368) |
| | (5) | 30 Jan 2019 (SSI 2018/368)[1] |
| | (6), (7) | 30 Jan 2019 (SSI 2018/368) |
| 15 | | 30 Jan 2019 (SSI 2018/368)[1] |
| 16–18 | | 30 Jan 2019 (SSI 2018/368) |
| 19 | | 30 Jan 2019 (SSI 2018/368)[1] |
| 20 | (1)–(6) | 31 Jul 2020 (SSI 2020/167) |
| | (7), (8) | 30 Jan 2019 (SSI 2018/368) |
| | (9), (10) | 31 Jul 2020 (SSI 2020/167) |
| 21, 22 | | 30 Jan 2019 (SSI 2018/368) |
| 23 | | 6 Aug 2018 (s 27(2)) |
| 24–28 | | 6 Jun 2018 (s 27(1)) |
| Schedule | | 30 Jan 2019 (SSI 2018/368)[1] |

[1]  For transitional and saving provisions, see SSI 2018/368, reg s 3–6

[2]  For transitional provisions, see SSI 2020/23, reg 4

[3]  For transitional provisions, see SSI 2021/125, reg 3

---

## Courts and Tribunals (Judiciary and Functions of Staff) Act 2018 (c 33)

*RA:* 20 Dec 2018

*Commencement provisions:* s 4; Courts and Tribunals (Judiciary and Functions of Staff) Act 2018 (Commencement) Regulations 2020, SI 2020/24

| | | |
|---|---|---|
| 1, 2 | | 20 Feb 2019 (s 4(2)) |
| 3 | | 10 Jan 2020 (for the purpose of making regulations) (SI 2020/24) |
| | | 6 Apr 2020 (otherwise) (SI 2020/24) |
| 4 | | 20 Dec 2018 (s 4(5)) |
| Schedule | paras 1–11 | 6 Apr 2020 (SI 2020/24) |
| | para 12 | See paras 13–15 below |
| | para 13 | 6 Apr 2020 (SI 2020/24) |
| | paras 14, 15 | 10 Jan 2020 (for the purpose of making regulations under Matrimonial and Family Proceedings Act 1984, s 31O(2)(b)) (SI 2020/24) |
| | | 6 Apr 2020 (otherwise) (SI 2020/24) |
| | paras 16–24 | 6 Apr 2020 (SI 2020/24) |
| | para 25 | See paras 26–36 below |
| | para 26 | 10 Jan 2020 (for the purpose of making regulations under Courts Act 2003, s 28(3)(b)) (SI 2020/24) |
| | | 6 Apr 2020 (otherwise) (SI 2020/24) |
| | paras 27–31 | 6 Apr 2020 (SI 2020/24) |
| | para 32 | 10 Jan 2020 (for the purpose of making regulations under Courts Act 2003, s 67B(1), 67F(4)) (SI 2020/24) |
| | | 6 Apr 2020 (otherwise) (SI 2020/24) |
| | paras 33–35 | 6 Apr 2020 (SI 2020/24) |
| | para 36 | 10 Jan 2020 (for the purpose of making regulations under Courts Act 2003, s 67B(1), 67F(4)) (SI 2020/24) |
| | | 6 Apr 2020 (otherwise) (SI 2020/24) |
| | paras 37, 38 | 6 Apr 2020 (SI 2020/24) |
| | para 39 | See paras 40–45 below |
| | para 40 | 6 Apr 2020 (SI 2020/24) |
| | paras 41–45 | 10 Jan 2020 (for the purpose of making regulations under Tribunals, Courts and Enforcement Act 2007, s 29D(4)) (SI 2020/24) |
| | | 6 Apr 2020 (otherwise) (SI 2020/24) |

## Data Protection Act 2018 (c 12)

*RA:* 23 May 2018

*Commencement provisions:* s 212; Data Protection Act 2018 (Commencement No 1 and Transitional and Saving Provisions) Regulations 2018, SI 2018/625; Data Protection Act 2018 (Commencement No 2) Regulations 2019, SI 2019/1188; Data Protection Act 2018 (Commencement No 3) Regulations 2019, SI 2019/1434

| | |
|---|---|
| 1 | 23 May 2018 (s 212(2)) |
| 2 | 23 May 2018 (so far as confers power to make regulations or Tribunal Procedure Rules or is otherwise necessary for enabling the exercise of such a power on or after 23 May 2018) (s 212(2)) |
| | 25 May 2018 (otherwise) (SI 2018/625) |
| 3 | 23 May 2018 (s 212(2)) |
| 4–92 | 23 May 2018 (so far as confers power to make regulations or Tribunal Procedure Rules or is otherwise necessary for enabling the exercise of such a power on or after 23 May 2018) (s 212(2)) |
| | 25 May 2018 (otherwise) (SI 2018/625) |

**See Halsbury's Statutes Citator for amendments to these Acts**          2565

**Data Protection Act 2018 (c 12)**—*contd*

| | |
|---|---|
| 93 | 23 May 2018 (so far as confers power to make regulations or Tribunal Procedure Rules or is otherwise necessary for enabling the exercise of such a power on or after 23 May 2018) (s 212(2)) |
| | 16 Sep 2019 (otherwise) (SI 2019/1188) |
| 94–101 | 23 May 2018 (so far as confers power to make regulations or Tribunal Procedure Rules or is otherwise necessary for enabling the exercise of such a power on or after 23 May 2018) (s 212(2)) |
| | 25 May 2018 (otherwise) (SI 2018/625) |
| 102–105 | 23 May 2018 (so far as confers power to make regulations or Tribunal Procedure Rules or is otherwise necessary for enabling the exercise of such a power on or after 23 May 2018) (s 212(2)) |
| | 16 Sep 2019 (otherwise) (SI 2019/1188) |
| 106, 107 | 23 May 2018 (so far as confers power to make regulations or Tribunal Procedure Rules or is otherwise necessary for enabling the exercise of such a power on or after 23 May 2018) (s 212(2)) |
| | 25 May 2018 (otherwise) (SI 2018/625) |
| 108 | 23 May 2018 (so far as confers power to make regulations or Tribunal Procedure Rules or is otherwise necessary for enabling the exercise of such a power on or after 23 May 2018) (s 212(2)) |
| | 16 Sep 2019 (otherwise) (SI 2019/1188) |
| 109–122 | 23 May 2018 (so far as confers power to make regulations or Tribunal Procedure Rules or is otherwise necessary for enabling the exercise of such a power on or after 23 May 2018) (s 212(2)) |
| | 25 May 2018 (otherwise) (SI 2018/625) |
| 123 | 23 May 2018 (so far as confers power to make regulations or Tribunal Procedure Rules or is otherwise necessary for enabling the exercise of such a power on or after 23 May 2018) (s 212(2)) |
| | 23 Jul 2018 (otherwise) (SI 2018/625) |
| 124 | 23 Jul 2018 (s 212(3)) |
| 125–127 | 23 Jul 2018 (so far as relate to a code prepared under s 124) (s 212(3)) |
| | 23 Jul 2018 (so far as relate to a code prepared under s 123) (SI 2018/625) |
| | *Not yet in force* (otherwise) |
| 128–141 | 23 May 2018 (so far as confers power to make regulations or Tribunal Procedure Rules or is otherwise necessary for enabling the exercise of such a power on or after 23 May 2018) (s 212(2)) |
| | 25 May 2018 (otherwise) (SI 2018/625) |
| 142 | 23 May 2018 (so far as confers power to make regulations or Tribunal Procedure Rules or is otherwise necessary for enabling the exercise of such a power on or after 23 May 2018) (s 212(2)) |
| | 25 May 2018 (otherwise) (SI 2018/625)[1] |
| 143–145 | 23 May 2018 (so far as confers power to make regulations or Tribunal Procedure Rules or is otherwise necessary for enabling the exercise of such a power on or after 23 May 2018) (s 212(2)) |
| | 25 May 2018 (otherwise) (SI 2018/625) |
| 146 | 23 May 2018 (so far as confers power to make regulations or Tribunal Procedure Rules or is otherwise necessary for enabling the exercise of such a power on or after 23 May 2018) (s 212(2)) |
| | 25 May 2018 (otherwise) (SI 2018/625)[1] |

**Data Protection Act 2018 (c 12)**—*contd*

| | |
|---|---|
| 147, 148 | 23 May 2018 (so far as confers power to make regulations or Tribunal Procedure Rules or is otherwise necessary for enabling the exercise of such a power on or after 23 May 2018) (s 212(2)) |
| | 25 May 2018 (otherwise) (SI 2018/625) |
| 149 | 23 May 2018 (so far as confers power to make regulations or Tribunal Procedure Rules or is otherwise necessary for enabling the exercise of such a power on or after 23 May 2018) (s 212(2)) |
| | 25 May 2018 (otherwise) (SI 2018/625)[1] |
| 150–154 | 23 May 2018 (so far as confers power to make regulations or Tribunal Procedure Rules or is otherwise necessary for enabling the exercise of such a power on or after 23 May 2018) (s 212(2)) |
| | 25 May 2018 (otherwise) (SI 2018/625) |
| 155 | 23 May 2018 (so far as confers power to make regulations or Tribunal Procedure Rules or is otherwise necessary for enabling the exercise of such a power on or after 23 May 2018) (s 212(2)) |
| | 25 May 2018 (otherwise) (SI 2018/625)[1] |
| 156–161 | 23 May 2018 (so far as confers power to make regulations or Tribunal Procedure Rules or is otherwise necessary for enabling the exercise of such a power on or after 23 May 2018) (s 212(2)) |
| | 25 May 2018 (otherwise) (SI 2018/625) |
| 162 | 23 May 2018 (so far as confers power to make regulations or Tribunal Procedure Rules or is otherwise necessary for enabling the exercise of such a power on or after 23 May 2018) (s 212(2)) |
| | 25 May 2018 (otherwise) (SI 2018/625)[1] |
| 163–176 | 23 May 2018 (so far as confers power to make regulations or Tribunal Procedure Rules or is otherwise necessary for enabling the exercise of such a power on or after 23 May 2018) (s 212(2)) |
| | 25 May 2018 (otherwise) (SI 2018/625) |
| 177–179 | 23 Jul 2018 (s 212(3)) |
| 180, 181 | 23 May 2018 (so far as confers power to make regulations or Tribunal Procedure Rules or is otherwise necessary for enabling the exercise of such a power on or after 23 May 2018) (s 212(2)) |
| | 25 May 2018 (otherwise) (SI 2018/625) |
| 182 | 23 May 2018 (s 212(2)) |
| 183–187 | 23 May 2018 (so far as confers power to make regulations or Tribunal Procedure Rules or is otherwise necessary for enabling the exercise of such a power on or after 23 May 2018) (s 212(2)) |
| | 25 May 2018 (otherwise) (SI 2018/625) |
| 188–195 | 23 May 2018 (so far as confers power to make regulations or Tribunal Procedure Rules or is otherwise necessary for enabling the exercise of such a power on or after 23 May 2018) (s 212(2)) |
| | 23 Jul 2018 (otherwise) (SI 2018/625) |
| 196–203 | 23 May 2018 (so far as confers power to make regulations or Tribunal Procedure Rules or is otherwise necessary for enabling the exercise of such a power on or after 23 May 2018) (s 212(2)) |
| | 25 May 2018 (otherwise) (SI 2018/625) |
| 204–206 | 23 May 2018 (s 212(2)) |

**Data Protection Act 2018 (c 12)**—*contd*

| | | |
|---|---|---|
| 207, 208 | | 23 May 2018 (so far as confers power to make regulations or Tribunal Procedure Rules or is otherwise necessary for enabling the exercise of such a power on or after 23 May 2018) (s 212(2)) |
| | | 25 May 2018 (otherwise) (SI 2018/625) |
| 209, 210 | | 23 May 2018 (s 212(2)) |
| 211 | | 23 May 2018 (so far as confers power to make regulations or Tribunal Procedure Rules or is otherwise necessary for enabling the exercise of such a power on or after 23 May 2018) (s 212(2)) |
| | | 25 May 2018 (otherwise) (SI 2018/625) |
| 212 | | 23 May 2018 (s 212(2)) |
| 213 | (1) | 23 May 2018 (so far as confers power to make regulations or Tribunal Procedure Rules or is otherwise necessary for enabling the exercise of such a power on or after 23 May 2018) (s 212(2)) |
| | | 25 May 2018 (otherwise) (SI 2018/625) |
| | (2) | 23 May 2018 (s 212(2)) |
| | (3) | 23 May 2018 (so far as confers power to make regulations or Tribunal Procedure Rules or is otherwise necessary for enabling the exercise of such a power on or after 23 May 2018) (s 212(2)) |
| | | 25 May 2018 (otherwise) (SI 2018/625) |
| 214, 215 | | 23 May 2018 (s 212(2)) |
| Schs 1–5 | | 23 May 2018 (so far as confers power to make regulations or Tribunal Procedure Rules or is otherwise necessary for enabling the exercise of such a power on or after 23 May 2018) (s 212(2)) |
| | | 25 May 2018 (otherwise) (SI 2018/625) |
| Sch 6 | paras 1–61 | 23 May 2018 (so far as confers power to make regulations or Tribunal Procedure Rules or is otherwise necessary for enabling the exercise of such a power on or after 23 May 2018) (s 212(2)) |
| | | 25 May 2018 (otherwise) (SI 2018/625) |
| | para 62 | 23 May 2018 (so far as confers power to make regulations or Tribunal Procedure Rules or is otherwise necessary for enabling the exercise of such a power on or after 23 May 2018) (s 212(2)) |
| | | *Not yet in force* (otherwise) |
| | paras 63–75 | 23 May 2018 (so far as confers power to make regulations or Tribunal Procedure Rules or is otherwise necessary for enabling the exercise of such a power on or after 23 May 2018) (s 212(2)) |
| | | 25 May 2018 (otherwise) (SI 2018/625) |
| Schs 7–14 | | 23 May 2018 (so far as confers power to make regulations or Tribunal Procedure Rules or is otherwise necessary for enabling the exercise of such a power on or after 23 May 2018) (s 212(2)) |
| | | 25 May 2018 (otherwise) (SI 2018/625) |
| Sch 15 | | 23 May 2018 (so far as confers power to make regulations or Tribunal Procedure Rules or is otherwise necessary for enabling the exercise of such a power on or after 23 May 2018) (s 212(2)) |
| | | 25 May 2018 (otherwise) (SI 2018/625)[1] |
| Sch 16 | | 23 May 2018 (so far as confers power to make regulations or Tribunal Procedure Rules or is otherwise necessary for enabling the exercise of such a power on or after 23 May 2018) (s 212(2)) |
| | | 25 May 2018 (otherwise) (SI 2018/625) |
| Sch 17 | | 23 Jul 2018 (s 212(3)) |

**Data Protection Act 2018 (c 12)**—*contd*

| | | |
|---|---|---|
| Sch 18 | | 23 May 2018 (so far as confers power to make regulations or Tribunal Procedure Rules or is otherwise necessary for enabling the exercise of such a power on or after 23 May 2018) (s 212(2)) |
| | | 25 May 2018 (otherwise) (SI 2018/625) |
| Sch 19 | paras 1–75 | 23 May 2018 (so far as confers power to make regulations or Tribunal Procedure Rules or is otherwise necessary for enabling the exercise of such a power on or after 23 May 2018) (s 212(2)) |
| | | 25 May 2018 (otherwise) (SI 2018/625) |
| | para 76 | 23 May 2018 (so far as confers power to make regulations or Tribunal Procedure Rules or is otherwise necessary for enabling the exercise of such a power on or after 23 May 2018) (s 212(2)) |
| | | *Not yet in force* (otherwise) |
| | paras 77–200 | 23 May 2018 (so far as confers power to make regulations or Tribunal Procedure Rules or is otherwise necessary for enabling the exercise of such a power on or after 23 May 2018) (s 212(2)) |
| | | 25 May 2018 (otherwise) (SI 2018/625) |
| | para 201 | 23 May 2018 (so far as confers power to make regulations or Tribunal Procedure Rules or is otherwise necessary for enabling the exercise of such a power on or after 23 May 2018) (s 212(2)) |
| | | *Not yet in force* (otherwise) |
| | paras 202–210 | 23 May 2018 (so far as confers power to make regulations or Tribunal Procedure Rules or is otherwise necessary for enabling the exercise of such a power on or after 23 May 2018) (s 212(2)) |
| | | 25 May 2018 (otherwise) (SI 2018/625) |
| | para 211 | 23 May 2018 (so far as confers power to make regulations or Tribunal Procedure Rules or is otherwise necessary for enabling the exercise of such a power on or after 23 May 2018) (s 212(2)) |
| | | 2 Dec 2019 (otherwise) (SI 2019/1434) |
| | para 212–226 | 23 May 2018 (so far as confers power to make regulations or Tribunal Procedure Rules or is otherwise necessary for enabling the exercise of such a power on or after 23 May 2018) (s 212(2)) |
| | | 25 May 2018 (otherwise) (SI 2018/625) |
| | para 227 | 23 May 2018 (so far as confers power to make regulations or Tribunal Procedure Rules or is otherwise necessary for enabling the exercise of such a power on or after 23 May 2018) (s 212(2)) |
| | | 2 Dec 2019 (otherwise) (SI 2019/1434) |
| | paras 228–405 | 23 May 2018 (so far as confers power to make regulations or Tribunal Procedure Rules or is otherwise necessary for enabling the exercise of such a power on or after 23 May 2018) (s 212(2)) |
| | | 25 May 2018 (otherwise) (SI 2018/625) |
| | para 406 | 23 May 2018 (so far as confers power to make regulations or Tribunal Procedure Rules or is otherwise necessary for enabling the exercise of such a power on or after 23 May 2018) (s 212(2)) |
| | | 25 May 2018 (otherwise) (SI 2018/625)[1] |
| | paras 407–434 | 23 May 2018 (so far as confers power to make regulations or Tribunal Procedure Rules or is otherwise necessary for enabling the exercise of such a power on or after 23 May 2018) (s 212(2)) |
| | | 25 May 2018 (otherwise) (SI 2018/625) |

**See Halsbury's Statutes Citator for amendments to these Acts**

### Data Protection Act 2018 (c 12)—*contd*

| | |
|---|---|
| Sch 20 | 23 May 2018 (so far as confers power to make regulations or Tribunal Procedure Rules or is otherwise necessary for enabling the exercise of such a power on or after 23 May 2018) (s 212(2)) |
| | 25 May 2018 (otherwise) (SI 2018/625) |

[1]    For transitional provisions, see SI 2018/625, reg 4

---

### Domestic Abuse (Scotland) Act 2018 (asp 5)

*RA:* 9 Mar 2018

*Commencement provisions:* s 15; Domestic Abuse (Scotland) Act 2018 (Commencement and Transitional Provision) Regulations 2018, SSI 2018/387

| | |
|---|---|
| 1–11 | 1 Apr 2019 (SSI 2018/387)[1] |
| 12 | 1 Apr 2019 (SSI 2018/387) |
| 13 | 10 Mar 2018 (s 15(1)(a)) |
| 14 | 1 Apr 2019 (SSI 2018/387)[1] |
| 15, 16 | 10 Mar 2018 (s 15(1)(a)) |
| Schedule | 1 Apr 2019 (SSI 2018/387)[1] |

[1]    For transitional provisions, see SSI 2018/387

---

### Domestic Gas and Electricity (Tariff Cap) Act 2018 (c 21)

*RA:* 19 Jul 2018

*Commencement provisions:* s 13(1)

Whole Act in force 19 Jul 2018 (s 13(2))

---

### Ecclesiastical Jurisdiction and Care of Churches Measure 2018 (No 3)

*RA:* 10 May 2018

*Commencement provisions:* s 99; Ecclesiastical Jurisdiction and Care of Churches Measure 2018 (Commencement and Transitional Provision) Order 2018, SI 2018/720

| | | |
|---|---|---|
| 1–98 | | 1 Sep 2018 (SI 2018/720) |
| 99–101 | | 10 May 2018 (s 99(1)) |
| Sch 1 | paras 1–19 | 1 Sep 2018 (SI 2018/720) |
| | para 20 | 1 Sep 2018 (SI 2018/720)[1] |
| | paras 21–29 | 1 Sep 2018 (SI 2018/720) |
| | para 30 | 1 Sep 2018 (SI 2018/720)[1] |
| Schs 2–5 | | 1 Sep 2018 (SI 2018/720) |

[1]    For transitional provisions, see SI 2018/720, art 3

---

### Ecumenical Relations Measure 2018 (No 6)

*RA:* 20 Dec 2018

*Commencement provisions:* s 4(2)–(5); Ecumenical Relations Measure 2018 (Commencement) Order 2019, SI 2019/99

| | |
|---|---|
| 1–3 | 1 Feb 2019 (SI 2019/99) |
| 4 | 20 Dec 2018 (s 4(2)) |

---

### Edinburgh Bakers' Widows' Fund Act 2018 (asp 1)

*RA:* 12 Jan 2018

*Commencement provisions:* s 5

| | |
|---|---|
| 1 | 13 Jan 2018 (s 5(1)) |
| 2 | 13 Feb 2018 (s 5(2)) |
| 3 | 14 Feb 2018 (s 5(3)) |
| 4–6 | 13 Jan 2018 (s 5(1)) |

### European Union (Withdrawal) Act 2018 (c 16)

*RA:* 26 Jun 2018

*Commencement provisions:* s 25; European Union (Withdrawal) Act 2018 (Commencement and Transitional Provisions) Regulations 2018, SI 2018/808, as amended by SI 2020/74; European Union (Withdrawal) Act 2018 (Commencement No 2) Regulations 2019, SI 2019/399; European Union (Withdrawal) Act 2018 (Commencement No 3) Regulations 2019, SI 2019/1077; European Union (Withdrawal) Act 2018 (Commencement No 4) Regulations 2019, SI 2019/1198; European Union (Withdrawal) Act 2018 (Commencement No 5, Transitional Provisions and Amendment) Regulations 2020, SI 2020/74; European Union (Withdrawal) Act 2018 and European Union (Withdrawal Agreement) Act 2020 (Commencement, Transitional and Savings Provisions) Regulations 2020, SI 2020/1622

| | | |
|---|---|---|
| 1 | | 11 Aug 2019 (SI 2019/1198) |
| 2–4 | | IP completion day (as defined by European Union (Withdrawal Agreement) Act 2020, s 39(1)–(5)) (SI 2020/1622)[2] |
| 5 | (1)–(5) | IP completion day (as defined by European Union (Withdrawal Agreement) Act 2020, s 39(1)–(5)) (SI 2020/1622)[2] |
| | (6) | See Sch 1 below |
| 6 | (1)–(6) | IP completion day (as defined by European Union (Withdrawal Agreement) Act 2020, s 39(1)–(5)) (SI 2020/1622)[2] |
| | (7) | 4 Jul 2018 (SI 2018/808) |
| 7 | (1) | In force as from exit day (as defined by European Union (Withdrawal) Act 2018, s 20(1)–(5)) (SI 2020/74) |
| | (2)–(5) | IP completion day (as defined by European Union (Withdrawal Agreement) Act 2020, s 39(1)–(5)) (SI 2020/1622)[2] |
| | (6) | In force as from exit day (as defined by European Union (Withdrawal) Act 2018, s 20(1)–(5)) (SI 2020/74) |
| 8–10 | | 26 Jun 2018 (s 25(1)(a)) |
| 11 | | See Sch 2 below |
| 12 | (1) | IP completion day (as defined by European Union (Withdrawal Agreement) Act 2020, s 39(1)–(5)) (SI 2020/1622)[2] |
| | (2) | 26 Jun 2018 (for the purposes of making regulations under the Scotland Act 1998, s 30A) (s 25(2)(a)) |
| | | IP completion day (as defined by European Union (Withdrawal Agreement) Act 2020, s 39(1)–(5)) (otherwise) (SI 2020/1622)[2] |
| | (3) | IP completion day (as defined by European Union (Withdrawal Agreement) Act 2020, s 39(1)–(5)) (SI 2020/1622)[2] |
| | (4) | 26 Jun 2018 (for the purposes of making regulations under the Government of Wales Act 2006, s 109A) (s 25(2)(b)) |
| | | IP completion day (as defined by European Union (Withdrawal Agreement) Act 2020, s 39(1)–(5)) (otherwise) (SI 2020/1622)[2] |
| | (5) | IP completion day (as defined by European Union (Withdrawal Agreement) Act 2020, s 39(1)–(5)) (SI 2020/1622)[2] |
| | (6) | 26 Jun 2018 (for the purposes of making regulations under the Northern Ireland Act 1998, s 6A) (s 25(2)(c)) |
| | | IP completion day (as defined by European Union (Withdrawal Agreement) Act 2020, s 39(1)–(5)) (otherwise) (SI 2020/1622)[2] |
| | (7), (8) | See Sch 3 below |
| | (9)–(11) | 4 Jul 2018 (SI 2018/808) |
| | (12) | See Sch 3 below |

**European Union (Withdrawal) Act 2018 (c 16)**—*contd*

| | | |
|---|---|---|
| | (13) | 4 Jul 2018 (SI 2018/808) |
| 13 | | 26 Jun 2018 (s 25(1)(c)) |
| 14 | (1) | See Sch 4 below |
| | (2)–(4) | 26 Jun 2018 (s 25(1)(c)) |
| 15 | | See Sch 5 below |
| 16–18 | | 26 Jun 2018 (s 25(1)(d)) |
| 19 | | 4 Jul 2018 (SI 2018/808) |
| 20, 21 | | 26 Jun 2018 (s 25(1)(e)) |
| 22 | | See Sch 7 below |
| 23 | (1)–(4) | 26 Jun 2018 (s 25(1)(f)) |
| | (5) | See Sch 8, Pts 1, 2 below |
| | (6) | 26 Jun 2018 (s 25(1)(f)) |
| | (7) | See Sch 8, Pts 3, 4 below |
| | (8) | See Sch 9 below |
| 24 | | 26 Jun 2018 (s 25(1)(h)) |
| 25 | | 26 Jun 2018 (s 25(1)(i)) |
| Sch 1 | para 1(1), (2)(a) | IP completion day (as defined by European Union (Withdrawal Agreement) Act 2020, s 39(1)–(5)) (SI 2020/1622)[2] |
| | para 1(2)(b) | 4 Jul 2018 (for the purpose of making regulations) (SI 2018/808) |
| | | IP completion day (as defined by European Union (Withdrawal Agreement) Act 2020, s 39(1)–(5)) (otherwise) (SI 2020/1622)[2] |
| | para 1(3) | 4 Jul 2018 (SI 2018/808) |
| | paras 2–5 | IP completion day (as defined by European Union (Withdrawal Agreement) Act 2020, s 39(1)–(5)) (SI 2020/1622)[2] |
| Sch 2 | | 26 Jun 2018 (s 25(1)(a)) |
| Sch 3 | para 1(a) | IP completion day (as defined by European Union (Withdrawal Agreement) Act 2020, s 39(1)–(5)) (SI 2020/1622)[2] |
| | para 1(b) | 26 Jun 2018 (for the purposes of making regulations under the Scotland Act 1998, s 57(4)) (s 25(3)(a)) |
| | | IP completion day (as defined by European Union (Withdrawal Agreement) Act 2020, s 39(1)–(5)) (otherwise) (SI 2020/1622)[2] |
| | para 2 | 26 Jun 2018 (for the purposes of making regulations under the Government of Wales Act 2006, s 80(8)) (s 25(3)(b)) |
| | | IP completion day (as defined by European Union (Withdrawal Agreement) Act 2020, s 39(1)–(5)) (otherwise) (SI 2020/1622)[2] |
| | para 3(a) | IP completion day (as defined by European Union (Withdrawal Agreement) Act 2020, s 39(1)–(5)) (SI 2020/1622)[2] |
| | para 3(b) | 26 Jun 2018 (for the purposes of making regulations under the Northern Ireland Act 1998, s 24(3)) (s 25(3)(c)) |
| | | IP completion day (as defined by European Union (Withdrawal Agreement) Act 2020, s 39(1)–(5)) (otherwise) (SI 2020/1622)[2] |
| | paras 4, 5 | 26 Jun 2018 (s 25(1)(b)) |
| | paras 6–20, 21(1), (2)(a) | IP completion day (as defined by European Union (Withdrawal Agreement) Act 2020, s 39(1)–(5)) (SI 2020/1622)[2] |
| | para 21(2)(b) | 26 Jun 2018 (s 25(1)(b)) |
| | paras 21(3), 22, 23, 24(1) | IP completion day (as defined by European Union (Withdrawal Agreement) Act 2020, s 39(1)–(5)) (SI 2020/1622)[2] |
| | para 24(2) | 26 Jun 2018 (for the purposes of making regulations under the Scotland Act 1998, s 30A) (s 25(3)(d)) |
| | | IP completion day (as defined by European Union (Withdrawal Agreement) Act 2020, s 39(1)–(5)) (otherwise) (SI 2020/1622)[2] |
| | para 24(3) | 26 Jun 2018 (for the purposes of making regulations under the Scotland Act 1998, s 57(4)) (s 25(3)(e)) |
| | | IP completion day (as defined by European Union (Withdrawal Agreement) Act 2020, s 39(1)–(5)) (otherwise) (SI 2020/1622)[2] |
| | para 25 | 26 Jun 2018 (for the purposes of making regulations under the Scotland Act 1998, ss 30A, 57(4)) (s 25(3)(f)) |
| | | IP completion day (as defined by European Union (Withdrawal Agreement) Act 2020, s 39(1)–(5)) (otherwise) (SI 2020/1622)[2] |

**European Union (Withdrawal) Act 2018 (c 16)**—*contd*

| | | |
|---|---|---|
| | paras 26–42 | IP completion day (as defined by European Union (Withdrawal Agreement) Act 2020, s 39(1)–(5)) (SI 2020/1622)[2] |
| | para 43 | 26 Jun 2018 (for the purposes of making regulations under the Government of Wales Act 2006, ss 80(8), 109A) (s 25(3)(g)) |
| | | IP completion day (as defined by European Union (Withdrawal Agreement) Act 2020, s 39(1)–(5)) (otherwise) (SI 2020/1622)[2] |
| | paras 44–47, 48(a) | IP completion day (as defined by European Union (Withdrawal Agreement) Act 2020, s 39(1)–(5)) (SI 2020/1622)[2] |
| | para 48(b) | 26 Jun 2018 (s 25(1)(b)) |
| | paras 49, 50, 51(1), (2)(a), (b) | IP completion day (as defined by European Union (Withdrawal Agreement) Act 2020, s 39(1)–(5)) (SI 2020/1622)[2] |
| | para 51(2)(c), (d) | 26 Jun 2018 (s 25(1)(b)) |
| | para 51(3) | IP completion day (as defined by European Union (Withdrawal Agreement) Act 2020, s 39(1)–(5)) (SI 2020/1622)[2] |
| | para 51(4) | 26 Jun 2018 (s 25(1)(b)) |
| | paras 52–56 | IP completion day (as defined by European Union (Withdrawal Agreement) Act 2020, s 39(1)–(5)) (SI 2020/1622)[2] |
| | paras 57, 58 | 26 Jun 2018 (for the purposes of making regulations under the Northern Ireland Act 1998, ss 6A, 24(3)) (s 25(3)(h)) |
| | | IP completion day (as defined by European Union (Withdrawal Agreement) Act 2020, s 39(1)–(5)) (otherwise) (SI 2020/1622)[2] |
| | paras 59–62 | IP completion day (as defined by European Union (Withdrawal Agreement) Act 2020, s 39(1)–(5)) (SI 2020/1622)[2] |
| Sch 4 | | 26 Jun 2018 (s 25(1)(c)) |
| Sch 5 | para 1 | 3 Jul 2019 (SI 2019/1077) |
| | para 2 | 4 Jul 2018 (SI 2018/808) |
| | para 3 | IP completion day (as defined by European Union (Withdrawal Agreement) Act 2020, s 39(1)–(5)) (SI 2020/1622)[2] |
| | para 4 | 4 Jul 2018 (SI 2018/808) |
| Schs 6, 7 | | 26 Jun 2018 (s 25(1)(e)) |
| Sch 8 | paras 1–6 | IP completion day (as defined by European Union (Withdrawal Agreement) Act 2020, s 39(1)–(5)) (SI 2020/1622)[2] |
| | paras 7, 8 | In force as from exit day (as defined by European Union (Withdrawal) Act 2018, s 20(1)–(5)) (SI 2020/74) |
| | para 9 | IP completion day (as defined by European Union (Withdrawal Agreement) Act 2020, s 39(1)–(5)) (SI 2020/1622)[2] |
| | paras 10–12 | In force as from exit day (as defined by European Union (Withdrawal) Act 2018, s 20(1)–(5)) (SI 2020/74) |
| | paras 13–17 | IP completion day (as defined by European Union (Withdrawal Agreement) Act 2020, s 39(1)–(5)) (SI 2020/1622)[2] |
| | para 18 | 4 Jul 2018 (SI 2018/808) |
| | para 19 | IP completion day (as defined by European Union (Withdrawal Agreement) Act 2020, s 39(1)–(5)) (SI 2020/1622)[2] |
| | para 20 | 4 Jul 2018 (SI 2018/808) |
| | para 21 | IP completion day (as defined by European Union (Withdrawal Agreement) Act 2020, s 39(1)–(5)) (SI 2020/1622)[2] |
| | para 22(a)–(c) | IP completion day (as defined by European Union (Withdrawal Agreement) Act 2020, s 39(1)–(5)) (SI 2020/1622)[2] |
| | para 22(d) | 4 Jul 2018 (for the purpose of the term "enactment" in Interpretation Act 1978, ss 15–17) (SI 2018/808) |
| | | IP completion day (as defined by European Union (Withdrawal Agreement) Act 2020, s 39(1)–(5)) (otherwise) (SI 2020/1622)[2] |
| | para 22(e) | 4 Jul 2018 (so far as relates to definitions "exit day and related expressions", "retained EU law", "retained direct minor EU legislation", "retained direct principal EU legislation", "retained direct EU legislation" and "retained EU obligation") (SI 2018/808) |
| | | IP completion day (as defined by European Union (Withdrawal Agreement) Act 2020, s 39(1)–(5)) (otherwise) (SI 2020/1622)[2] |

**European Union (Withdrawal) Act 2018 (c 16)**—*contd*

| | |
|---|---|
| paras 23–30 | IP completion day (as defined by European Union (Withdrawal Agreement) Act 2020, s 39(1)–(5)) (SI 2020/1622)[2] |
| paras 31–34 | 4 Jul 2018 (SI 2018/808) |
| para 35 | IP completion day (as defined by European Union (Withdrawal Agreement) Act 2020, s 39(1)–(5)) (SI 2020/1622)[2] |
| para 36 | 4 Jul 2018 (SI 2018/808)[1] |
| paras 37–39 | IP completion day (as defined by European Union (Withdrawal Agreement) Act 2020, s 39(1)–(5)) (SI 2020/1622)[2] |
| para 40 | 4 Jul 2018 (SI 2018/808) |
| para 41(1), (2) | IP completion day (as defined by European Union (Withdrawal Agreement) Act 2020, s 39(1)–(5)) (SI 2020/1622)[2] |
| para 41(3)–(9) | 1 Mar 2019 (SI 2019/399) |
| para 41(10) | 26 Jun 2018 (s 25(1)(g)) |
| para 42 | IP completion day (as defined by European Union (Withdrawal Agreement) Act 2020, s 39(1)–(5)) (SI 2020/1622)[2] |
| paras 43, 44 | 26 Jun 2018 (s 25(1)(g)) |
| para 45 | IP completion day (as defined by European Union (Withdrawal Agreement) Act 2020, s 39(1)–(5)) (SI 2020/1622)[2] |
| Sch 9 | 4 Jul 2018 (SI 2018/808), so far as relates to repeals of or in— |
| | European Parliamentary Elections Act 2002, s 1A, Sch 1A; |
| | European Union (Amendment) Act 2008, ss 4, 5[1]; |
| | European Union Act 2011, ss 1–13, 14(1), 15(1), Sch 1[1]; |
| | European Union (Approval of Treaty Amendment Decision) Act 2012; |
| | European Union (Approvals) Act 2013; |
| | European Union (Approvals) Act 2014; |
| | Serious Crime Act 2005, ss 82, 88(5)(c); |
| | European Union (Finance) Act 2015, s 1(1); |
| | European Union (Approvals) Act 2015 |
| | In force as from IP completion day, as defined by European Union (Withdrawal Agreement) Act 2020, s 39(1)–(5) (repeal of remainder of European Union Act 2011) (SI 2018/808) |
| | 31 Dec 2020 (SI 2020/1622[2]), so far as relates to repeals of or in— |
| | European Parliamentary Elections Act 2002 (in so far as not already repealed); |
| | European Parliament (Representation) Act 2003 |
| | IP completion day (as defined by European Union (Withdrawal Agreement) Act 2020, s 39(1)–(5)) (SI 2020/1622[2]), so far as relates to repeals of or in— |
| | European Union (Amendment) Act 2008 (in so far as not already repealed); |
| | European Union (Finance) Act 2015 (in so far as not already repealed) |
| | *Not yet in force* (otherwise) |

[1]   For transitional provisions, see SI 2018/808, regs 5–8

[2]   For transitional and saving provisions, see SI 2020/1622, regs 6–22

**Finance Act 2018 (c 3)**

*RA:* 15 Mar 2018

The commencement details of Finance Acts are not set out, as the dates from which their provisions take effect are usually stated clearly and unambiguously in the text of the Act, and charging provisions will normally state for which year or years of assessment they are to have effect.

**Financial Guidance and Claims Act 2018 (c 10)**

*RA:* 10 May 2018

*Commencement provisions*: s 37; Financial Guidance and Claims Act 2018 (Commencement No 1 and Transitional Provision) Regulations 2018, SI 2018/987; Financial Guidance and Claims Act 2018 (Commencement No 2) Regulations 2018, SI 2018/1003; Financial Guidance and Claims Act 2018 (Commencement No 3 and Transitory Provisions (Modification)) Regulations 2018, SI 2018/1029; Financial Guidance and Claims Act 2018 (Commencement No 4) Regulations 2018, SI 2018/1045; Financial Guidance and Claims Act 2018 (Commencement No 5) Regulations 2018, SI 2018/1330; Financial Guidance and Claims Act 2018 (Commencement No 6) Regulations 2019, SI 2019/743; Financial Guidance and Claims Act 2018 (Commencement No 7) (Dissolution of the Consumer Financial Education Body) Regulations 2021, SI 2021/433; Financial Guidance and Claims Act 2018 (Commencement No 8) Regulations 2021, SI 2021/764; Financial Guidance and Claims Act 2018 (Commencement No 1) Order (Northern Ireland) 2022, SR 2022/107; Financial Guidance and Claims Act 2018 (Commencement No 9) Regulations 2022, SI 2022/509; Financial Guidance and Claims Act 2018 (Commencement No 2) Order (Northern Ireland) 2022, SR 2022/175

| | | |
|---|---|---|
| 1 | (1)–(5) | 1 Oct 2018 (SI 2018/1029) |
| | (6) | 6 Apr 2021 (SI 2021/433) |
| | (7) | 1 Oct 2018 (SI 2018/1029) |
| 2 | | 1 Oct 2018 (SI 2018/1029) |
| 3 | (1)(a)–(c) | 1 Oct 2018 (for the purposes of ss 3(2)(a), (3), 8(1), 9(1), 17(1)–(3)) (SI 2018/1029) |
| | | 1 Jan 2019 (otherwise) (SI 2018/1330) |
| | (1)(d), (e) | 1 Oct 2018 (for the purposes of ss 3(2)(a), (3), 8(1), 17(1)–(3)) (SI 2018/1029) |
| | | 1 Jan 2019 (otherwise) (SI 2018/1330) |
| | (2), (3) | 1 Oct 2018 (SI 2018/1029) |
| | (4)–(6) | 1 Oct 2018 (for the purposes of ss 3(2)(a), (3), 8(1), 9(1), 17(1)–(3)) (SI 2018/1029) |
| | | 1 Jan 2019 (otherwise) (SI 2018/1330) |
| | (7) | 1 Oct 2018 (for the purposes of ss 3(2)(a), (3), 8(1), 17(1)–(3)) (SI 2018/1029) |
| | | 1 Jan 2019 (otherwise) (SI 2018/1330) |
| | (8) | 1 Jan 2019 (SI 2018/1330) |
| | (9) | 1 Oct 2018 (for the purposes of ss 3(2)(a), (3), 8(1), 17(1)–(3)) (SI 2018/1029) |
| | | 1 Jan 2019 (otherwise) (SI 2018/1330) |
| | (10) | 1 Jan 2019 (SI 2018/1330) |
| 4, 5 | | 1 Jan 2019 (SI 2018/1330) |
| 6–9 | | 1 Oct 2018 (SI 2018/1029) |
| 10 | | 1 Jan 2019 (SI 2018/1330) |
| 11 | (1) | 10 May 2018 (s 37(1)) |
| | (2) | 1 Oct 2018 (SI 2018/1029) |
| | (3) | 10 May 2018 (s 37(1)) |
| 12, 13 | | 10 May 2018 (s 37(1)) |
| 14 | | 1 Oct 2018 (SI 2018/1003) |
| 15, 16 | | 1 Oct 2018 (SI 2018/1029) |
| 17 | (1)–(3) | 1 Oct 2018 (SI 2018/1029) |
| | (4), (5) | 1 Jan 2019 (SI 2018/1330) |
| | (6)(a) | 1 Oct 2018 (SI 2018/1029) |
| | (6)(b) | 1 Jan 2019 (SI 2018/1330) |
| | (7), (8) | 1 Oct 2018 (SI 2018/1029) |
| 18 | (1) | See sub-ss (2)–(7) below |
| | (2) | 5 Jul 2021 (for the purpose of making rules) (SI 2021/764) |
| | | 1 Jun 2022 (otherwise) (SI 2022/509) |
| | (3)–(6) | 5 Jul 2021 (SI 2021/764) |
| | (7) | 1 Jan 2019 (SI 2018/1330) |
| 19 | (1) | See sub-ss (2)–(9) below |
| | (2), (3) | 5 Jul 2021 (for the purpose of making regulations) (SI 2021/764) |
| | | 1 Jun 2022 (otherwise) (SI 2022/509) |

**Financial Guidance and Claims Act 2018 (c 10)**—*contd*

|  |  |  |
|---|---|---|
|  | (4) | 5 Jul 2021 (SI 2021/764) |
|  | (5) | *Not yet in force* |
|  | (6) | See sub-ss (7)–(9) below |
|  | (7), (8) | 15 Mar 2022 (for the purpose only of making regulations) (SR 2022/107) |
|  |  | 1 Jun 2022 (otherwise) (SR 2022/175) |
|  | (9) | 15 Mar 2022 (SR 2022/107) |
| 20 |  | 1 Jan 2019 (SI 2018/1003) |
| 21 |  | 10 May 2018 (s 37(1)) |
| 22 |  | 10 Jul 2018 (s 37(4)) |
| 23, 24 |  | 1 Oct 2018 (SI 2018/1029) |
| 25 |  | See Sch 3 below |
| 26 |  | 1 Oct 2018 (SI 2018/1029) |
| 27 | (1)–(14) | 6 Oct 2018 (SI 2018/1045) |
|  | (15) | 10 May 2018 (s 37(1)) |
| 28 |  | 29 Mar 2019 (SI 2019/743) |
| 29–32 |  | 10 Jul 2018 (s 37(4)) |
| 33, 34 |  | 29 Mar 2019 (SI 2019/743) |
| 35 |  | 8 Sep 2018[1] |
| 36–38 |  | 10 May 2018 (s 37(1)) |
| Schs 1, 2 |  | 1 Oct 2018 (SI 2018/1029) |
| Sch 3 | paras 1–4 | 1 Oct 2018 (SI 2018/1029) |
|  | para 5 | 10 May 2018 (s 37(1)) |
|  | para 6 | 1 Oct 2018 (SI 2018/1029) |
|  | para 7 | 1 Jan 2019 (SI 2018/1330) |
|  | para 8 | 6 Apr 2021 (SI 2021/433) |
|  | paras 9, 10 | 1 Jan 2019 (SI 2018/1330) |
|  | para 11 | 1 Oct 2018 (SI 2018/1029)[2] |
|  | para 12 | 6 Apr 2021 (SI 2021/433) |
|  | para 13(a) | 10 May 2018 (s 37(1)) |
|  | para 13(b) | 1 Jan 2019 (SI 2018/1330) |
|  | para 13(c) | 1 Oct 2018 (SI 2018/1029) |
|  | para 13(d) | 1 Jan 2019 (SI 2018/1330) |
|  | para 14(1), (2)(a) | 10 May 2018 (s 37(1)) |
|  | para 14(2)(b) | 1 Jan 2019 (SI 2018/1330) |
|  | para 14(2)(c) | 1 Oct 2018 (SI 2018/1029) |
|  | para 14(2)(d) | 1 Jan 2019 (SI 2018/1330) |
|  | para 14(3)(a) | 10 May 2018 (s 37(1)) |
|  | para 14(3)(b) | 1 Jan 2019 (SI 2018/1330) |
|  | para 14(3)(c) | 1 Oct 2018 (SI 2018/1029) |
|  | para 14(3)(d) | 1 Jan 2019 (SI 2018/1330) |
|  | para 15 | 6 Apr 2021 (SI 2021/433) |
|  | paras 16–20 | 1 Jan 2019 (SI 2018/1330) |
|  | para 21(1) | 10 May 2018 (s 37(1)) |
|  | para 21(2)(a) | 1 Jan 2019 (SI 2018/1330) |
|  | para 21(2)(b) | 1 Oct 2018 (SI 2018/1029)[2] |
|  | para 21(2)(c) | 1 Jan 2019 (SI 2018/1330) |
|  | para 21(3)(a) | 1 Jan 2019 (SI 2018/1330) |
|  | para 21(3)(b) | 1 Oct 2018 (SI 2018/1029)[2] |
|  | para 21(4) | 1 Jan 2019 (SI 2018/1330) |
|  | para 21(5)(a)(i) | 10 May 2018 (s 37(1)) |
|  | para 21(5)(a)(ii) | 1 Oct 2018 (SI 2018/1029) |
|  | para 21(5)(a)(iii) | 1 Jan 2019 (SI 2018/1330) |
|  | para 21(5)(b)(i), (ii) | 1 Jan 2019 (SI 2018/1330) |
|  | para 21(5)(b)(iii) | 10 May 2018 (s 37(1)) |
|  | para 21(5)(b)(iv) | 1 Oct 2018 (SI 2018/1029) |
|  | para 22 | 6 Apr 2021 (SI 2021/433) |
|  | paras 23, 24 | 1 Oct 2018 (SI 2018/1029) |
|  | paras 25–27 | 6 Apr 2021 (SI 2021/433) |

**Financial Guidance and Claims Act 2018 (c 10)**—*contd*

|  |  |  |
|---|---|---|
| | para 28 | 1 Oct 2018 (SI 2018/1029) |
| | para 29 | 6 Apr 2021 (SI 2021/433) |
| | para 30(a) | 1 Oct 2018 (SI 2018/1029) |
| | para 30(b) | 1 Jan 2019 (SI 2018/1330) |
| | para 30(c) | 1 Oct 2018 (SI 2018/1029)[2] |
| | paras 31, 32 | 1 Jan 2019 (SI 2018/1330) |
| Sch 4 | | 6 Oct 2018 (SI 2018/1045) |
| Sch 5 | | 10 May 2018 (s 37(1)) |

[1]   For transitional provisions, see SI 2018/987, reg 4

[2]   For transitory modifications, see SI 2018/1029, reg 4, Schedule

**Forestry and Land Management (Scotland) Act 2018 (asp 8)**

*RA:* 1 May 2018

*Commencement provisions*: s 85; Forestry and Land Management (Scotland) Act 2018 (Commencement, Transitional and Saving Provisions) Regulations 2019, SSI 2019/47

|  |  |
|---|---|
| 1–75 | 1 Apr 2019 (SSI 2019/47)[1] |
| 76–78 | 2 May 2018 (s 85(1)) |
| 79–81 | 1 Apr 2019 (SSI 2019/47)[1] |
| 82–86 | 2 May 2018 (s 85(1)) |
| Schs 1–3 | 1 Apr 2019 (SSI 2019/47)[1] |

[1]   For transitional and saving provisions, see SSI 2019/47, regs 3–22

**Gender Representation on Public Boards (Scotland) Act 2018 (asp 4)**

*RA:* 9 Mar 2018

*Commencement provisions*: s 13; Gender Representation on Public Boards (Scotland) Act 2018 (Commencement No 1) Regulations 2018, SSI 2018/340; Gender Representation on Public Boards (Scotland) Act 2018 (Commencement No 2) Regulations 2020, SSI 2020/119

|  |  |
|---|---|
| 1 | 29 May 2020 (SSI 2020/119) |
| 2 | 1 Dec 2018 (SSI 2018340) |
| 3–6 | 29 May 2020 (SSI 2020/119) |
| 7, 8 | 1 Dec 2018 (SSI 2018340) |
| 9–11 | *Not yet in force* |
| 12 | 1 Dec 2018 (SSI 2018340) |
| 13, 14 | 10 Mar 2018 (s 13(1)) |
| Sch 1 | 1 Dec 2018 (SSI 2018340) |
| Sch 2 | *Not yet in force* |

**Haulage Permits and Trailer Registration Act 2018 (c 19)**

*RA:* 19 Jul 2018

*Commencement provisions*: s 27; Haulage Permits and Trailer Registration Act 2018 (Commencement) Regulations 2018, SI 2018/1343

|  |  |
|---|---|
| 1–5 | 19 Jul 2018 (s 27(1)) |
| 6–8 | 1 Jan 2019 (SI 2018/1343) |
| 9–28 | 19 Jul 2018 (s 27(1)) |
| Schedule | 19 Jul 2018 (s 27(1)) |

## Health and Social Care (National Data Guardian) Act 2018 (c 31)

*RA:* 20 Dec 2018

*Commencement provisions*: s 5; Health and Social Care (National Data Guardian) Act 2018 (Commencement) Regulations 2019, SI 2019/580

| | |
|---|---|
| 1–6 | 1 Apr 2019 (SI 2019/580) |
| 3 | See Sch 2 below |
| 4–6 | 1 Apr 2019 (SI 2019/580) |
| Schs 1, 2 | 1 Apr 2019 (SI 2019/580) |

## Historical Sexual Offences (Pardons and Disregards) (Scotland) Act 2018 (asp 14)

*RA:* 11 Jul 2018

*Commencement provisions*: s 17; Historical Sexual Offences (Pardons and Disregards) (Scotland) Act 2018 (Commencement) Regulations 2019, SSI 2019/205

| | |
|---|---|
| 1–14 | 15 Oct 2019 (SSI 2019/205) |
| 15–18 | 20 Jul 2018 (s 17(1)) |

## Homes (Fitness for Human Habitation) Act 2018 (c 34)

*RA:* 20 Dec 2018

*Commencement provisions*: s 2(2)

Whole Act in force 20 Mar 2019 (s 2(2))

## Housing (Amendment) (Scotland) Act 2018 (asp 13)

*RA:* 6 Jul 2018

*Commencement provisions*: s 11; Housing (Amendment) (Scotland) Act 2018 (Commencement and Savings Provisions) Regulations, SSI 2018/253

| | |
|---|---|
| 1 | 8 Mar 2019 (SSI 2018/253) |
| 2, 3 | 8 Mar 2019 (SSI 2018/253)[1] |
| 4 | 8 Mar 2019 (SSI 2018/253) |
| 5, 6 | 8 Mar 2019 (SSI 2018/253)[1] |
| 7 | 8 Mar 2019 (SSI 2018/253) |
| 8–10 | 6 Sep 2018 (SSI 2018/253) |
| 11, 12 | 7 Jul 2018 (s 11(1)) |

[1]  For savings, see SSI 2018/253, regs 3–8

## Islands (Scotland) Act 2018 (asp 12)

*RA:* 6 Jul 2018

*Commencement provisions*: s 31; Islands (Scotland) Act 2018 (Commencement) Regulations 2018, SSI 2018/282; Islands (Scotland) Act 2018 (Commencement No 2) Regulations 2019, SSI 2019/134; Islands (Scotland) Act 2018 (Commencement No 3) Regulations 2020, SSI 2020/346

| | | |
|---|---|---|
| 1, 2 | | 7 Jul 2018 (s 31(1)) |
| 3–6 | | 4 Oct 2018 (SSI 2018/282) |
| 7–10 | | 23 Dec 2020 (SSI 2020/346) |
| 11 | (1) | 23 Dec 2020 (SSI 2020/346) |
| | (2) | 18 Apr 2019 (SSI 2019/134) |
| 12–14 | | 23 Dec 2020 (SSI 2020/346) |
| 15–21 | | 4 Oct 2018 (SSI 2018/282) |

**Islands (Scotland) Act 2018 (asp 12)**—*contd*

| | |
|---|---|
| 22–26 | *Not yet in force* |
| 27–29 | 4 Oct 2018 (SSI 2018/282) |
| 30–32 | 7 Jul 2018 (s 31(1)) |
| Schedule | *Not yet in force* |

## Ivory Act 2018 (c 30)

*RA*: 20 Dec 2018

*Commencement provisions*: s 43; Ivory Act 2018 (Commencement No 1) Regulations 2022, SI 2022/93; Ivory Act 2018 (Commencement No 2 and Transitional Provision) Regulations 2022, SI 2022/288

| | | |
|---|---|---|
| 1 | | 1 Feb 2022 (for the purpose of exercising any power to make regulations) (SI 2022/93) |
| | | 6 Jun 2022 (otherwise) (SI 2022/288)[1] |
| 2–10 | | 1 Feb 2022 (for the purpose of exercising any power to make regulations) (SI 2022/93) |
| | | 24 Feb 2022 (otherwise) (SI 2022/93) |
| 11 | | 24 Feb 2022 (SI 2022/93) |
| 12 | | 15 Mar 2022 (or the purpose of exercising any power to make regulations, or to prepare and publish guidance under Sch 1, para 21) (SI 2022/288) |
| | | 6 Jun 2022 (otherwise) (SI 2022/288) |
| 13 | | See Sch 1 below |
| 14–36 | | 6 Jun 2022 (SI 2022/288) |
| 37 | (1) | 1 Feb 2022 (for the purpose of exercising any power to make regulations) (SI 2022/93) |
| | | 24 Feb 2022 (otherwise) (SI 2022/93) |
| | (2)–(6) | *Not yet in force* |
| | (7), (8) | 1 Feb 2022 (for the purpose of exercising any power to make regulations) (SI 2022/93) |
| | | 24 Feb 2022 (otherwise) (SI 2022/93) |
| 38, 39 | | 1 Feb 2022 (for the purpose of exercising any power to make regulations) (SI 2022/93) |
| | | 24 Feb 2022 (otherwise) (SI 2022/93) |
| 40, 41 | | 24 Feb 2022 (SI 2022/93) |
| 42–44 | | 1 Feb 2022 (for the purpose of exercising any power to make regulations) (SI 2022/93) |
| | | 24 Feb 2022 (otherwise) (SI 2022/93) |
| Sch 1 | paras 1–3 | 15 Mar 2022 (or the purpose of exercising any power to make regulations, or to prepare and publish guidance under Sch 1, para 21) (SI 2022/288) |
| | | 6 Jun 2022 (otherwise) (SI 2022/288) |
| | para 4 | 6 Jun 2022 (SI 2022/288) |
| | paras 5–8 | 15 Mar 2022 (or the purpose of exercising any power to make regulations, or to prepare and publish guidance under Sch 1, para 21) (SI 2022/288) |
| | | 6 Jun 2022 (otherwise) (SI 2022/288) |
| | para 9 | 6 Jun 2022 (SI 2022/288) |
| | para 10 | 15 Mar 2022 (or the purpose of exercising any power to make regulations, or to prepare and publish guidance under Sch 1, para 21) (SI 2022/288) |
| | | 6 Jun 2022 (otherwise) (SI 2022/288) |
| | paras 11–13 | *Not yet in force* |
| | paras 14–18 | 15 Mar 2022 (or the purpose of exercising any power to make regulations, or to prepare and publish guidance under Sch 1, para 21) (SI 2022/288) |
| | | 6 Jun 2022 (otherwise) (SI 2022/288) |
| | paras 19, 20 | 6 Jun 2022 (SI 2022/288) |

**Ivory Act 2018 (c 30)**—*contd*

| | |
|---|---|
| paras 21, 22 | 15 Mar 2022 (or the purpose of exercising any power to make regulations, or to prepare and publish guidance under Sch 1, para 21) (SI 2022/288) |
| | 6 Jun 2022 (otherwise) (SI 2022/288) |
| paras 23, 24 | 6 Jun 2022 (SI 2022/288) |
| para 25 | 15 Mar 2022 (or the purpose of exercising any power to make regulations, or to prepare and publish guidance under Sch 1, para 21) (SI 2022/288) |
| | 6 Jun 2022 (otherwise) (SI 2022/288) |
| Sch 2 | 6 Jun 2022 (SI 2022/288) |

[1]  For transitional provisions see SI 2022/288, reg 5

---

**Land and Buildings Transaction Tax (Relief from Additional Amount) (Scotland) Act 2018 (asp 11)**

*RA:* 22 Jun 2018

*Commencement provisions*: s 2

Whole Act in force 23 Jun 2018 (s 2)

---

**Laser Misuse (Vehicles) Act 2018 (c 9)**

*RA:* 10 May 2018

*Commencement provisions*: s 4

| | |
|---|---|
| 1 | 10 Jul 2018 (E) (W) (S) (s 4(3)) |
| | *Not in force* (NI) |
| 2 | 10 Jul 2018 (s 4(5)) |
| 3, 4 | 10 May 2018 (s 4(2)) |

---

**Law Derived from the European Union (Wales) Act 2018 (anaw 3)**

*RA:* 6 Jun 2018

*Commencement provisions*: s 21

Whole Act in force 7 Jun 2018 (s 21)

---

**Legislative Reform Measure 2018 (No 5)**

*RA:* 10 May 2018

*Commencement provisions:* s 11

Whole Measure in force 10 May 2018 (s 11(2))

---

**Mental Health Units (Use of Force) Act 2018 (c 27)**

*RA:* 1 Nov 2018

*Commencement provisions:* s 17(2)–(4); Mental Health Units (Use of Force) Act 2018 Commencement (No 1) Regulations 2019, SI 2019/1373; Mental Health Units (Use of Force) Act 2018 (Commencement No 2) Regulations 2021, SI 2021/1372; Mental Health Units (Use of Force) Act 2018 (Commencement No 3) Regulations 2022, SI 2022/909

| | |
|---|---|
| 1–6 | 31 Mar 2022 (SI 2021/1372) |
| 7, 8 | *Not yet in force* |

**Mental Health Units (Use of Force) Act 2018 (c 27)**—*contd*

| | | |
|---|---|---|
| 9, 10 | | 31 Mar 2022 (SI 2021/1372) |
| 11 | (1), (2) | 31 Mar 2022 (SI 2021/1372) |
| | (3) | 28 Oct 2019 (SI 2019/1373) |
| | (4)–(6) | 31 Mar 2022 (SI 2021/1372) |
| 12 | | 18 Aug 2022 (SI 2022/909) |
| 13 | | 31 Mar 2022 (SI 2021/1372) |
| 14 | | *Not yet in force* |
| 15 | | 31 Mar 2022 (SI 2021/1372) |
| 16, 17 | | 1 Nov 2018 (s 17(2)) |

**Mission and Pastoral etc (Amendment) Measure 2018 (No 4)**

*RA:* 10 May 2018

*Commencement provisions:* s 14; Mission and Pastoral etc (Amendment) Measure 2018 (Commencement No 1 and Transitional Provisions) Order 2018, SI 2018/722; Mission and Pastoral etc (Amendment) Measure 2018 (Commencement No 2) Order 2018, SI 2018/1032; Mission and Pastoral etc. (Amendment) Measure 2018 (Commencement No 3) Order 2019, SI 2019/66

| | | |
|---|---|---|
| 1, 2 | | 1 Oct 2018 (SI 2018/722) |
| 3 | (1), (2) | 1 Oct 2018 (SI 2018/722) |
| | (3), (4) | 1 Oct 2018 (SI 2018/722)[1] |
| | (5)(a) | 1 Oct 2018 (SI 2018/1032) |
| | (5)(b), (c) | 1 Mar 2019 (SI 2019/66) |
| | (6) | 1 Mar 2019 (SI 2019/66) |
| | (7) | 1 Oct 2018 (SI 2018/722) |
| | (8) | 1 Oct 2018 (SI 2018/722)[1] |
| | (9), (10) | 1 Mar 2019 (SI 2019/66) |
| | (11) | 1 Oct 2018 (SI 2018/722) |
| 4 | (1) | 1 Mar 2019 (SI 2019/66) |
| | (2), (3) | 1 Oct 2018 (SI 2018/722) |
| | (4) | 1 Oct 2018 (so far as inserts Mission and Pastoral Measure 2011, s 26(7)) (SI 2018/722) |
| | | 1 Mar 2019 (so far as inserts Mission and Pastoral Measure 2011, s 26(5), (6)) (SI 2019/66) |
| 5 | | 1 Oct 2018 (SI 2018/722)[1] |
| 6 | | 1 Jul 2018 (SI 2018/722)[1] |
| 7 | | 1 Oct 2018 (SI 2018/722) |
| 8 | | 1 Jul 2018 (SI 2018/722) |
| 9 | | 1 Oct 2018 (SI 2018/722) |
| 10 | | 1 Jul 2018 (SI 2018/722) |
| 11 | | 1 Jul 2018 (SI 2018/722)[1] |
| 12 | | 1 Jul 2018 (SI 2018/722) |
| 13 | | *Never in force* (repealed) |
| 14 | | 10 May 2018 (s 14(2)) |
| Schedule | | 1 Jul 2018 (SI 2018/722)[1] |

[1]   For transitional provisions, see SI 2018/722, art 4, Schedule

**Non-Domestic Rating (Nursery Grounds) Act 2018 (c 26)**

*RA:* 1 Nov 2018

Whole Act in force 1 Nov 2018 (RA)

## Northern Ireland Assembly Members (Pay) Act 2018 (c 7)

*RA:* 28 Mar 2018

*Commencement provisions*: s 2(2)

Whole Act in force 28 Mar 2018  (s 2(2))

---

## Northern Ireland Budget Act 2018 (c 20)

*RA:* 19 Jul 2018

Whole Act in force 19 Jul 2018 (RA)

---

## Northern Ireland Budget (Anticipation and Adjustments) Act 2018 (c 8)

*RA:* 28 Mar 2018

Whole Act in force 28 Mar 2018 (RA)

---

## Northern Ireland (Executive Formation and Exercise of Functions) Act 2018 (c 28)

*RA:* 1 Nov 2018

*Commencement provisions*: s 10

Whole Act in force 1 Nov 2018 (RA)

---

## Northern Ireland (Regional Rates and Energy) Act 2018 (c 6)

*RA:* 28 Mar 2018

*Commencement provisions*: s 3(2), (3)

| | |
|---|---|
| 1 | 28 Mar 2018 (s 3(2)) |
| 2 | 1 Apr 2018 (s 3(3)) |
| 3 | 28 Mar 2018 (s 3(2)) |
| Schedule | 1 Apr 2018 (s 3(3)) |

---

## Nuclear Safeguards Act 2018 (c 15)

*RA:* 26 Jun 2018

*Commencement provisions*: s 6; Nuclear Safeguards Act 2018 (Commencement No 1) Regulations 2018, SI 2018/1079; Nuclear Safeguards Act 2018 (Commencement No 2) Regulations 2020, SI 2020/1547

| | | |
|---|---|---|
| 1(1) | | 31 Dec 2020 at 11.00 pm (IP completion day) (SI 2020/1547) |
| 1(2)–(4) | | 26 Oct 2018 (SI 2018/1079) |
| 1(5) | | See Schedule below |
| 2 | | 26 Oct 2018 (SI 2018/1079) |
| 3 | | 26 Jun 2018 (s 6(1)) |
| 4 | | 26 Oct 2018 (SI 2018/1079) |
| 5–7 | | 26 Jun 2018 (s 6(1)) |
| Schedule | para 1 | 26 Oct 2018 (SI 2018/1079) |
| | para 2 | 31 Dec 2020 at 11.00 pm (IP completion day) (SI 2020/1547) |
| | para 3 | 26 Oct 2018 (SI 2018/1079) |
| | para 4 | 31 Dec 2020 at 11.00 pm (IP completion day) (SI 2020/1547) |
| | para 5 | 26 Oct 2018 (SI 2018/1079) |
| | paras 6–8 | 31 Dec 2020 at 11.00 pm (IP completion day) (SI 2020/1547) |
| | paras 9, 10 | 26 Oct 2018 (SI 2018/1079) |
| | paras 11, 12 | 31 Dec 2020 at 11.00 pm (IP completion day) (SI 2020/1547) |

**Nuclear Safeguards Act 2018 (c 15)**—*contd*
para 13                    26 Oct 2018 (SI 2018/1079)

**Offensive Behaviour at Football and Threatening Communications (Repeal) (Scotland) Act 2018 (asp 7)**

*RA:* 19 Apr 2018

*Commencement provisions:* s 6

Whole Act in force 20 Apr 2018 (s 6)

**Parental Bereavement (Leave and Pay) Act 2018 (c 24)**

*RA:* 13 Sep 2018

*Commencement provisions:* s 2(2), (3); Parental Bereavement (Leave and Pay) Act 2018 (Commencement) Regulations 2020, SI 2020/45

| | |
|---|---|
| 1 | 18 Jan 2020 (SI 2020/45) |
| 2 | 13 Sep 2018 (s 2(3)) |
| Schedule | 18 Jan 2020 (SI 2020/45) |

**Pensions (Pre-consolidation) Measure 2018 (No 2)**

*RA:* 10 May 2018

*Commencement provisions:* s 2; Pensions (Pre-consolidation) Measure 2018 (Commencement) Order 2018, SI 2018/716

| | |
|---|---|
| 1 | Not yet in force[1] |
| 2 | 10 May 2018 (s 2(2)) |
| Schedule | Not yet in force[1] |

[1]  S 1 and the Schedule to this Measure come into force immediately before the commencement of the Measure resulting from the draft Church of England Pensions Measure given First Consideration by the General Synod on 9 Feb 2018; see SI 2018/716

**Prescription (Scotland) Act 2018 (asp 15)**

*RA:* 18 Dec 2018

*Commencement provisions:* s 17; Prescription (Scotland) Act 2018 (Commencement, Saving and Transitional Provisions) Regulations 2022, SSI 2022/78

| | |
|---|---|
| 1–4 | 28 Feb 2025 (SSI 2022/78)[1] |
| 5 | 1 Jun 2022 (SSI 2022/78) |
| 6–12 | 28 Feb 2025 (SSI 2022/78)[1] |
| 13 | 1 Jun 2022 (SSI 2022/78) |
| 15 | 19 Dec 2018 (s 17(1)) |
| 16 | 28 Feb 2025 (SSI 2022/78)[1] |
| 17, 18 | 19 Dec 2018 (s 17(1)) |

[1]  For transitional provisions and savings see SSI 2022/78, regs 3, 4

## Prisons (Interference with Wireless Telegraphy) Act 2018 (c 32)

*RA:* 20 Dec 2018

*Commencement provisions:* s 2

| | |
|---|---|
| 1, 2 | *Not yet in force* |
| Sch 1 | *Not yet in force* |

## Public Health (Minimum Price for Alcohol) (Wales) Act 2018 (anaw 5)

*RA:* 9 Aug 2018

*Commencement provisions:* s 28; Public Health (Minimum Price for Alcohol) (Wales) Act 2018 (Commencement No 1) Order 2019, SI 2019/1336; Public Health (Minimum Price for Alcohol) (Wales) Act 2018 (Commencement No 2) Order 2020, SI 2020/175

| | |
|---|---|
| 1 | 14 Oct 2019 (for the purpose of making regulations) (SI 2019/1336) |
| | 2 Mar 2020 (otherwise) (SI 2020/175) |
| 2–25 | 2 Mar 2020 (SI 2020/175) |
| 26–30 | 10 Aug 2018 (s 28(1)) |
| Sch 1 | 2 Mar 2020 (SI 2020/175) |

## Rating (Property in Common Occupation) and Council Tax (Empty Dwellings) Act 2018 (c 25)

*RA:* 1 Nov 2018

Whole Act in force 1 Nov 2018 (RA)

## Regulation of Registered Social Landlords (Wales) Act 2018 (anaw 4)

*RA:* 13 Jun 2018

*Commencement provisions:* s 19; Regulation of Registered Social Landlords (Wales) Act 2018 (Commencement and Transitional Provision) Order 2018, SI 2018/777

| | |
|---|---|
| 1, 2 | 15 Jun 2018 (SI 2018/777) |
| 3–14 | 15 Aug 2018 (SI 2018/777) |
| 15 | 15 Aug 2018 (SI 2018/777)[1] |
| 16, 17 | 15 Aug 2018 (SI 2018/777) |
| 18 | 15 Jun 2018 (SI 2018/777) |
| 19, 20 | 14 Jun 2018 (s 19(1)) |
| Schs 1, 2 | 15 Aug 2018 (SI 2018/777) |

[1]  For a transitional provision, see SI 2018/777, art 4

## Sanctions and Anti-Money Laundering Act 2018 (c 13)

*RA:* 23 May 2018

*Commencement provisions:* s 64; Sanctions and Anti-Money Laundering Act 2018 (Commencement No 1) Regulations 2018, SI 2018/1213; Sanctions and Anti-Money Laundering Act 2018 (Commencement No 2) Regulations 2020, SI 2020/1535; Sanctions and Anti-Money Laundering Act 2018 (Commencement No 3) Regulations 2021, SI 2021/628

| | |
|---|---|
| 1–31 | 22 Nov 2018 (SI 2018/1213) |
| 32 | 23 May 2018 (s 64(1)) |
| 33–48 | 22 Nov 2018 (SI 2018/1213) |
| 49 | In force as from IP completion day (as defined by European Union (Withdrawal Agreement) Act 2020, s 39(1)–(5)) (SI 2020/1535) |

## Sanctions and Anti-Money Laundering Act 2018 (c 13)—*contd*

| | | |
|---|---|---|
| 50 | | 23 May 2018 (s 64(1)) |
| 51 | | 15 Dec 2020 (SI 2020/1535) |
| 52–56 | | 23 May 2018 (s 64(1)) |
| 57, 58 | | 22 Nov 2018 (SI 2018/1213) |
| 59 | (1)–(3) | In force as from IP completion day (as defined by European Union (Withdrawal Agreement) Act 2020, s 39(1)–(5)) (SI 2020/1535) |
| | (4), (5) | See Sch 3 below |
| 60–65 | | 23 May 2018 (s 64(1)) |
| Sch 1 | | 22 Nov 2018 (SI 2018/1213) |
| Sch 2 | | In force as from IP completion day (as defined by European Union (Withdrawal Agreement) Act 2020, s 39(1)–(5)) (SI 2020/1535) |
| Sch 3 | paras 1–7 | 22 Nov 2018 (SI 2018/1213) |
| | para 8(1)–(3) | 22 Nov 2018 (SI 2018/1213) |
| | para 8(4) | 27 May 2021 (SI 2021/628) |
| | para 9 | In force as from IP completion day (as defined by European Union (Withdrawal Agreement) Act 2020, s 39(1)–(5)) (except revocations in the Electronic Money Regulations 2011, SI 2011/99 and the Payment Services Regulations 2017, SI 2017/752) (SI 2020/1535) |
| | | *Not yet in force (exceptions noted above)* |
| | para 10 | In force as from IP completion day (as defined by European Union (Withdrawal Agreement) Act 2020, s 39(1)–(5)) (SI 2020/1535) |

## Secure Tenancies (Victims of Domestic Abuse) Act 2018 (c 11)

*RA:* 10 May 2018

*Commencement provisions:* s 2

| | |
|---|---|
| 1 | *Not yet in force* |
| 2 | 10 May 2018 (s 2(3)) |

## Smart Meters Act 2018 (c 14)

*RA:* 23 May 2018

*Commencement provisions:* s 14(2)–(5)

| | |
|---|---|
| 1 | 23 May 2018 (s 14(2)) |
| 2–10 | 23 Jul 2018 (s 14(5)) |
| 11–13 | *Not yet in force* |
| 14 | 23 May 2018 (s 14(2)) |

## Social Security (Scotland) Act 2018 (asp 9)

*RA:* 1 Jun 2018

*Commencement provisions:* s 99; Social Security (Scotland) Act 2018 (Commencement No 1) Regulations 2018, SSI 2018/250; Social Security (Scotland) Act 2018 (Commencement No 2, Transitory and Saving Provision) Regulations 2018, SI 2018/298, as amended by SSI 2019/406; Social Security (Scotland) Act 2018 (Commencement No 3) Regulations 2018, SSI 2018/357; Social Security (Scotland) Act 2018 (Commencement No 4 and Saving Provision) Regulations 2018, SSI 2018/393, as amended by SSI 2019/406; Social Security (Scotland) Act 2018 (Commencement No 5, Revocation and Saving Provision) Regulations 2019, SSI 2019/269; Social Security (Scotland) Act 2018 (Commencement No 6) Regulations 2020, SSI 2020/75; Social Security (Scotland) Act 2018 (Commencement No 7) Regulations 2020, SSI 2020/127; Social Security (Scotland) Act 2018 (Commencement No 8) Regulations 2020, SSI 2020/295; Social Security (Scotland) Act 2018 (Commencement No 9) Regulations 2021, SSI 2021/474

| | |
|---|---|
| 1–9 | 22 Oct 2018 (SSI 2018/298) |
| 10 | 30 Jun 2020 (SSI 2020/75) |

**Social Security (Scotland) Act 2018 (asp 9)**—*contd*

| | |
|---|---|
| 11 | 27 Mar 2020 (SSI 2020/75) |
| 12–14 | 17 Jan 2022 (SSI 2021/474) |
| 15–19 | 22 Oct 2018 (SSI 2018/298) |
| 20 | 22 Oct 2018 (SSI 2018/298)[2] |
| 21, 22 | 21 Jan 2019 (SSI 2018/393)[3] |
| 23–27 | 22 Oct 2018 (SSI 2018/298) |
| 28 | 14 Oct 2019 (SSI 2019/269) |
| 29 | *Not yet in force* |
| 30 | 1 Sep 2020 (SSI 2020/127) |
| 31 | 8 Oct 2020 (SSI 2020/295) |
| 32 | 10 Dec 2018 (SSI 2018/357) |
| 33 | *Not yet in force* |
| 34 | 11 Sep 2019 (SSI 2019/269) |
| 35 | *Not yet in force* |
| 36 | 8 Oct 2020 (SSI 2020/295) |
| 37–54 | 22 Oct 2018 (SSI 2018/298) |
| 55 | 17 Jan 2022 (SSI 2021/474) |
| 56–59 | 22 Oct 2018 (SSI 2018/298) |
| 60 | 17 Jan 2022 (SSI 2021/474) |
| 61–69 | 22 Oct 2018 (SSI 2018/298) |
| 70 | 11 Sep 2019 (SSI 2019/269) |
| 71–75 | 22 Oct 2018 (SSI 2018/298) |
| 76 | 3 Sep 2018 (so far as necessary for the purpose of enabling the Scottish Ministers to consult publicly on a draft code of practice as required under s 76(3) and to publish a code of practice) (SSI 2018/250)[1] |
| | 22 Oct 2018 (otherwise) (SSI 2018/298) |
| 77, 78 | 30 Oct 2019 (SSI 2019/269)[4] |
| 79, 80 | 1 May 2020 (SSI 2020/127) |
| 81–85 | 3 Sep 2018 (SSI 2018/250)[1] |
| 86 | *Not yet in force* |
| 87 | 22 Oct 2018 (otherwise) (SSI 2018/298)[2] |
| 88–90 | *Not yet in force* |
| 91 | 1 Apr 2020 (to enable the Scottish Ministers to consult in accordance with sub-s (4)) (SSI 2020/75) |
| | *Not yet in force* (otherwise) |
| 92–94 | *Not yet in force* |
| 95–100 | 2 Jun 2018 (s 99(1)) |
| Sch 1 | 21 Jan 2019 (SSI 2018/393)[3] |
| Sch 2 | 14 Oct 2019 (SSI 2019/269) |
| Sch 3 | *Not yet in force* |
| Sch 4 | 1 Sep 2020 (SSI 2020/127) |
| Sch 5 | 8 Oct 2020 (SSI 2020/295) |
| Sch 6 | 10 Dec 2018 (SSI 2018/357) |
| Sch 7 | *Not yet in force* |
| Sch 8 | 11 Sep 2019 (SSI 2019/269) |
| Sch 9 | *Not yet in force* |
| Sch 10 | 8 Oct 2020 (SSI 2020/295) |

[1]   For savings, see SSI 2018/250, reg 3

[2]   For transitory and saving provisions, see SSI 2018/298, reg 3

[3]   For savings, see SSI 2018/393, reg 3

[4]   For savings, see SSI 2019/269, reg 6

## Space Industry Act 2018 (c 5)

*RA:* 15 Mar 2018

*Commencement provisions:* s 70; Space Industry Act 2018 (Commencement No 1) Regulations 2018, SI 2018/1224; Space Industry Act 2018 (Commencement No 2, Transitional and Savings Provisions) Regulations 2021, SI 2021/817, as amended by SI 2021/874

| | | |
|---|---|---|
| 1 | (1), (2) | 29 Jul 2021 (SI 2021/817)[1] |
| | (3) | 29 Jul 2021 (except in so far as it relates to an activity of procuring the launch of a space object where he activity is carried out in the United Kingdom by persons to whom the Outer Space Act 1986 applies by virtue of section 2 of that Act, and the launch of the space object is to be carried out outside the United Kingdom) (SI 2021/817)[1] |
| | | *Not yet in force* (otherwise) |
| | (4) | 29 Jul 2021 (except in so far as definition "space activity" relates to an activity of procuring the launch of a space object where he activity is carried out in the United Kingdom by persons to whom the Outer Space Act 1986 applies by virtue of section 2 of that Act, and he launch of the space object is to be carried out outside the United Kingdom) (SI 2021/817)[1] |
| | | *Not yet in force* (otherwise) |
| | (5) | 26 Nov 2018 (SI 2018/1224) |
| | (6) | 29 Jul 2021 (SI 2021/817)[1] |
| 2 | (1)–(3) | 29 Jul 2021 (SI 2021/817)[1] |
| | (4)–(7) | 26 Nov 2018 (SI 2018/1224) |
| 3 | (1) | 29 Jul 2021 (except in so far as this definition relates to an activity of procuring the launch of a space object where the activity is carried out in the United Kingdom by persons to whom the Outer Space Act 1986 applies by virtue of section 2 of that Act, and the launch of the space object is to be carried out outside the United Kingdom) (SI 2021/817)[1] |
| | | *Not yet in force* (otherwise) |
| | (2), (3) | 26 Nov 2018 (SI 2018/1224) |
| | (4) | 29 Jul 2021 (SI 2021/817)[1] |
| | (5) | 26 Nov 2018 (SI 2018/1224) |
| | (6), (7) | 29 Jul 2021 (SI 2021/817)[1] |
| 4 | (1) | 29 Jul 2021 (SI 2021/817)[1] |
| | (2)–(4) | 26 Nov 2018 (SI 2018/1224) |
| 5 | (1), (2) | 26 Nov 2018 (SI 2018/1224) |
| | (3) | 29 Jul 2021 (SI 2021/817)[1] |
| 6 | | 26 Nov 2018 (SI 2018/1224) |
| 7 | (1) | 29 Jul 2021 (SI 2021/817)[1] |
| | (2) | 26 Nov 2018 (SI 2018/1224) |
| | (3) | 29 Jul 2021 (SI 2021/817)[1] |
| | (4)–(7) | 26 Nov 2018 (SI 2018/1224) |
| | (8), (9) | 29 Jul 2021 (SI 2021/817)[1] |
| 8 | (1)–(3) | 29 Jul 2021 (except in so far as it relates to the licensing of spaceflight activities involving an orbital launch vehicle with human occupants and hypersonic or other point to point transport) (SI 2021/817)[1] |
| | | *Not yet in force* (otherwise) |
| | (4) | 29 Jul 2021 (SI 2021/817)[1] |
| | (5)–(7) | 26 Nov 2018 (SI 2018/1224) |
| 9 | (1) | 29 Jul 2021 (SI 2021/817)[1] |
| | (2), (3) | 26 Nov 2018 (for the purpose only of prescribing the matters mentioned in those provisions) (SI 2018/1224) |
| | | 29 Jul 2021 (otherwise) (SI 2021/817)[1] |
| | (4) | 29 Jul 2021 (SI 2021/817)[1] |
| | (5)–(7) | 26 Nov 2018 (SI 2018/1224) |
| | (8) | 29 Jul 2021 (SI 2021/817)[1] |

**Space Industry Act 2018 (c 5)**—*contd*

| | | |
|---|---|---|
| | (9) | 26 Nov 2018 (SI 2018/1224) |
| 10 | | 26 Nov 2018 (for the purpose only of prescribing the criteria or requirements mentioned in paragraph (b)) (SI 2018/1224) |
| | | 29 Jul 2021 (otherwise) (SI 2021/817)[1] |
| 11 | (1), (2) | 29 Jul 2021 (SI 2021/817)[1] |
| | (3), (4) | 26 Nov 2018 (SI 2018/1224) |
| | (5) | 29 Jul 2021 (SI 2021/817)[1] |
| | (6) | 26 Nov 2018 (SI 2018/1224) |
| 12 | | 29 Jul 2021 (SI 2021/817)[1] |
| 13 | (1), (2) | 29 Jul 2021 (SI 2021/817)[1] |
| | (3) | 26 Nov 2018 (SI 2018/1224) |
| | (4)–(6) | 29 Jul 2021 (SI 2021/817)[1] |
| | (7) | 26 Nov 2018 (SI 2018/1224) |
| | (8) | 29 Jul 2021 (SI 2021/817)[1] |
| 14 | (1)–(3) | 29 Jul 2021 (SI 2021/817)[1] |
| | (4) | 26 Nov 2018 (SI 2018/1224) |
| 15 | | 29 Jul 2021 (SI 2021/817)[1] |
| 16 | (1)–(3) | 26 Nov 2018 (SI 2018/1224) |
| | (4), (5) | 29 Jul 2021 (SI 2021/817)[1] |
| | (6), (7) | 26 Nov 2018 (SI 2018/1224) |
| | (8) | 29 Jul 2021 (SI 2021/817)[1] |
| 17 | (1) | 26 Nov 2018 (for the purpose only of prescribing the matters mentioned in that provision (SI 2018/1224) |
| | | 29 Jul 2021 (otherwise) (SI 2021/817)[1] |
| | (2) | 26 Nov 2018 (only for the purpose of defining the term "consent form") (SI 2018/1224) |
| | | 29 Jul 2021 (otherwise) (SI 2021/817)[1] |
| | (3) | 26 Nov 2018 (SI 2018/1224) |
| | (4) | 29 Jul 2021 (SI 2021/817)[1] |
| 18 | (1)–(3) | 26 Nov 2018 (SI 2018/1224) |
| | (4) | 26 Nov 2018 (for the purpose only of enabling criteria to be specified in training regulations) (SI 2018/1224) |
| | | 29 Jul 2021 (otherwise) (SI 2021/817)[1] |
| | (5) | 26 Nov 2018 (SI 2018/1224) |
| | (6)–(8) | 29 Jul 2021 (SI 2021/817)[1] |
| 19, 20 | | 26 Nov 2018 (SI 2018/1224) |
| 21 | (1) | 29 Jul 2021 (SI 2021/817)[1] |
| | (2) | 26 Nov 2018 (for the purpose only of prescribing the body or person mentioned in sub-s (2)(c)) (SI 2018/1224) |
| | | 29 Jul 2021 (otherwise) (SI 2021/817)[1] |
| | (3)–(5) | 29 Jul 2021 (SI 2021/817)[1] |
| | (6) | 26 Nov 2018 (SI 2018/1224) |
| 22 | | 29 Jul 2021 (SI 2021/817)[1] |
| 23 | (1)–(3) | 26 Nov 2018 (SI 2018/1224) |
| | (4)–(7) | 29 Jul 2021 (SI 2021/817)[1] |
| 24, 25 | | 29 Jul 2021 (SI 2021/817)[1] |
| 26 | (1), (2) | 29 Jul 2021 (SI 2021/817)[1] |
| | (3) | 26 Nov 2018 (SI 2018/1224) |
| | (4) | 29 Jul 2021 (SI 2021/817)[1] |
| 27–33 | | 29 Jul 2021 (SI 2021/817)[1] |
| 34 | (1), (2) | 29 Jul 2021 (SI 2021/817)[1] |
| | (3) | 26 Nov 2018 (for the purpose only of prescribing the matters mentioned in sub-s (3)(a)) (SI 2018/1224) |
| | | 29 Jul 2021 (otherwise) (SI 2021/817)[1] |
| | (4) | 29 Jul 2021 (SI 2021/817)[1] |
| | (5), (6) | 26 Nov 2018 (SI 2018/1224) |
| 35 | (1)(a) | 29 Jul 2021 (SI 2021/817)[1] |
| | (1)(b) | 26 Nov 2018 (for the purpose only of prescribing the matters mentioned in sub-s (1)(b)) (SI 2018/1224) |

**Space Industry Act 2018 (c 5)**—*contd*

| | | |
|---|---|---|
| | | 29 Jul 2021 (otherwise) (SI 2021/817)[1] |
| | (1)(c) | 29 Jul 2021 (SI 2021/817)[1] |
| | (2)–(4) | 29 Jul 2021 (SI 2021/817)[1] |
| | (5) | 26 Nov 2018 (SI 2018/1224) |
| 36 | (1), (2) | 29 Jul 2021 (SI 2021/817)[1] |
| | (3) | 26 Nov 2018 (for the purpose only of prescribing the cases or circumstances mentioned in sub-s (3)(a)) (SI 2018/1224) |
| | | 29 Jul 2021 (otherwise) (SI 2021/817)[1] |
| | (4) | 29 Jul 2021 (SI 2021/817)[1] |
| 37 | | 29 Jul 2021 (SI 2021/817)[1] |
| 38 | (1), (2) | 26 Nov 2018 (SI 2018/1224) |
| | (3) | 29 Jul 2021 (SI 2021/817)[1] |
| | (4) | 26 Nov 2018 (for the purpose only of making regulations under s 38(2)) (SI 2018/1224) |
| | | 29 Jul 2021 (otherwise) (SI 2021/817)[1] |
| | (5)–(7) | 29 Jul 2021 (SI 2021/817)[1] |
| | (8) | 26 Nov 2018 (SI 2018/1224) |
| | (9), (10) | 29 Jul 2021 (SI 2021/817)[1] |
| 39–51 | | 29 Jul 2021 (SI 2021/817)[1] |
| 52 | | 26 Nov 2018 (SI 2018/1224) |
| 53 | | 29 Jul 2021 (SI 2021/817)[1] |
| 54 | | 26 Nov 2018 (SI 2018/1224) |
| 55 | | 29 Jul 2021 (SI 2021/817)[1] |
| 56 | (1)–(3) | 29 Jul 2021 (SI 2021/817)[1] |
| | (4) | 26 Nov 2018 (SI 2018/1224) |
| 57, 58 | | 29 Jul 2021 (SI 2021/817)[1] |
| 59 | | 26 Nov 2018 (SI 2018/1224) |
| 60 | | See Sch 10 below |
| 61 | | 29 Jul 2021 (SI 2021/817)[1] |
| 62 | | See Sch 11 below |
| 63, 64 | | 29 Jul 2021 (SI 2021/817)[1] |
| 65 | | 26 Nov 2018 (SI 2018/1224) |
| 66 | (1) | 26 Nov 2018 (for the purpose only of prescribing the person mentioned in that provision) (SI 2018/1224) |
| | | 29 Jul 2021 (otherwise) (SI 2021/817)[1] |
| | (2) | 29 Jul 2021 (SI 2021/817)[1] |
| | (3), (4) | 26 Nov 2018 (for the purpose only of prescribing the person mentioned in that provision) (SI 2018/1224) |
| | | 29 Jul 2021 (otherwise) (SI 2021/817)[1] |
| | (5) | 29 Jul 2021 (SI 2021/817)[1] |
| 67 | (1) | See Sch 12 below |
| | (2)–(4) | 26 Nov 2018 (SI 2018/1224) |
| 68–72 | | 15 Mar 2018 (s 70(1)) |
| Sch 1 | | 29 Jul 2021 (SI 2021/817)[1] |
| Schs 2, 3 | | 26 Nov 2018 (SI 2018/1224) |
| Sch 4 | | 29 Jul 2021 (SI 2021/817)[1] |
| Sch 5 | | 26 Nov 2018 (SI 2018/1224) |
| Schs 6–9 | | 29 Jul 2021 (SI 2021/817)[1] |
| Sch 10 | para 1 | 26 Nov 2018 (SI 2018/1224) |
| | paras 2, 3 | 29 Jul 2021 (SI 2021/817) |
| | para 4 | 26 Nov 2018 (for the purpose only of prescribing decisions against which an appeal lies or persons by whom an appeal may be brought) (SI 2018/1224) |
| | | 29 Jul 2021 (otherwise) (SI 2021/817)[1] |
| | para 5(1), (2) | 29 Jul 2021 (SI 2021/817)[1] |
| | para 5(3) | 26 Nov 2018 (for the purpose only of prescribing the period within which an application for permission to appeal must be made) (SI 2018/1224) |
| | | 29 Jul 2021 (otherwise) (SI 2021/817)[1] |

**Space Industry Act 2018 (c 5)**—*contd*

|  |  |  |
|---|---|---|
|  | paras 6–9 | 29 Jul 2021 (SI 2021/817)[1] |
|  | para 10 | 26 Nov 2018 (SI 2018/1224) |
|  | para 11 | 26 Nov 2018 (for the purpose only of prescribing the period within which an appeal must be determined) (SI 2018/1224) |
|  |  | 29 Jul 2021 (otherwise) (SI 2021/817)[1] |
|  | para 12(1) | 29 Jul 2021 (SI 2021/817)[1] |
|  | para 12(2), (3) | 26 Nov 2018 (for the purpose only of prescribing the period within which representations must be made) (SI 2018/1224) |
|  |  | 29 Jul 2021 (otherwise) (SI 2021/817)[1] |
|  | para 12(4), (5) | 29 Jul 2021 (SI 2021/817)[1] |
|  | para 13(1) | 29 Jul 2021 (SI 2021/817)[1] |
|  | para 13(2) | 26 Nov 2018 (SI 2018/1224) |
|  | para 13(3), (4) | 29 Jul 2021 (SI 2021/817)[1] |
|  | para 14 | 29 Jul 2021 (SI 2021/817)[1] |
|  | para 15 | 26 Nov 2018 (SI 2018/1224) |
|  | para 16(1)–(3) | 26 Nov 2018 (SI 2018/1224) |
|  | para 16(4) | 29 Jul 2021 (SI 2021/817)[1] |
| Sch 11 | para 1 | 26 Nov 2018 (SI 2018/1224) |
|  | para 2(1) | 26 Nov 2018 (SI 2018/1224) |
|  | para 2(2), (3) | 29 Jul 2021 (SI 2021/817)[1] |
|  | para 3(1) | 26 Nov 2018 (SI 2018/1224) |
|  | para 3(2) | 29 Jul 2021 (SI 2021/817)[1] |
|  | para 3(3) | 26 Nov 2018 (SI 2018/1224) |
|  | para 4 | 29 Jul 2021 (SI 2021/817)[1] |
|  | para 5(1)–(3) | 26 Nov 2018 (SI 2018/1224) |
|  | para 5(4) | 29 Jul 2021 (SI 2021/817)[1] |
|  | paras 6, 7 | 29 Jul 2021 (SI 2021/817)[1] |
| Sch 12 | paras 1–7 | 29 Jul 2021 (SI 2021/817)[1] |
|  | para 8 | 26 Nov 2018 (SI 2018/1224) |
|  | para 9 | *Not yet in force* |
|  | para 10 | 26 Nov 2018 (SI 2018/1224) |
|  | paras 11–33 | 29 Jul 2021 (SI 2021/817)[1] |

[1]    For transitional provisions and savings see SI 2021/817, reg 3

---

**Statute Law (Repeals) Measure 2018 (No 1)**

*RA:* 10 May 2018

*Commencement provisions:* s 2

|  |  |
|---|---|
| 1 | 1 Jul 2018 (SI 2018/718) |
| 2 | 10 May 2018 |
| Schedule | 1 Jul 2018 (SI 2018/718) |

---

**Supply and Appropriation (Anticipation and Adjustments) Act 2018 (c 4)**

*RA:* 15 Mar 2018

Whole Act in force 15 Mar 2018 (RA)

---

**Supply and Appropriation (Main Estimates) Act 2018 (c 17)**

*RA:* 19 Jul 2018

Whole Act in force 19 Jul (RA)

---

## Taxation (Cross-border Trade) Act 2018 (c 22)

*RA:* 13 Sep 2018

*Commencement provisions:* s 57; Taxation (Cross-border Trade) Act 2018 (Appointed day No 1) (EU Exit) Regulations 2018, SI 2018/1362; Taxation (Cross-border Trade) Act 2018 (Appointed Day No 2) (EU Exit) Regulations 2019, SI 2019/69; Taxation (Cross-border Trade) Act 2018 (Appointed day No 3) and the Value Added Tax (Postal Packets and Amendment) (EU Exit) Regulations 2018 (Appointed day) (EU Exit) Regulations 2019, SI 2019/104; Taxation (Cross-border Trade) Act 2018 (Appointed Days No 4 and Transitional Provisions) (Modification) (EU Exit) Regulations 2019, SI 2019/429; Taxation (Cross-border Trade) Act 2018 (Appointed Day No 5 and Miscellaneous Commencements) (EU Exit) Regulations 2019, SI 2019/819; Taxation (Cross-border Trade) Act 2018 (Appointed Day No 7 and Transitory Provisions) (EU Exit) Regulations 2020, SI 2020/97; Finance Act 2016, Section 126 (Appointed Day), the Taxation (Cross-border Trade) Act 2018 (Appointed Day No 8, Transition and Saving Provisions) and the Taxation (Post transition Period) Act 2020 (Appointed Day No. 1) (EU Exit) Regulations 2020, SI 2020/1642

| | | |
|---|---|---|
| 1–9 | | 13 Sep 2018 (so far as making provision for anything to be done by regulations or public notice) (s 57(1)(a)) |
| | | 31 Dec 2020 at 11.00pm (IP completion day) (otherwise) (SI 2020/1642)[4] |
| 10 | | 23 Jan 2019 (SI 2019/69) |
| 11, 12 | | 13 Sep 2018 (so far as making provision for anything to be done by regulations or public notice) (s 57(1)(a)) |
| | | 31 Dec 2020 at 11.00pm (IP completion day) (otherwise) (SI 2020/1642)[4] |
| 13 | | 4 Mar 2019 (SI 2019/429)[2] |
| 14 | | 13 Sep 2018 (so far as making provision for anything to be done by regulations or public notice) (s 57(1)(a)) |
| | | 31 Dec 2020 at 11.00pm (IP completion day) (otherwise) (SI 2020/1642)[4] |
| 15 | | 23 Jan 2019 (SI 2019/69) |
| 16–38 | | 13 Sep 2018 (so far as making provision for anything to be done by regulations or public notice) (s 57(1)(a)) |
| | | 31 Dec 2020 at 11.00pm (IP completion day) (otherwise) (SI 2020/1642)[4] |
| 39, 40 | | 13 Sep 2018 (s 57(1)(b)) |
| 41 | (1), (2)(a) | 31 Dec 2020 at 11.00pm (IP completion day) (SI 2020/1642) |
| | (2)(b) | 28 Jan 2019 (only to the extent that it relates to, and for the purpose of, the interpretation of the definition of "import VAT" in the Value Added Tax (Postal Packets and Amendment) (EU Exit) Regulations 2018, SI 2018/1376) (SI 2019/104) |
| | | 31 Dec 2020 at 11.00pm (IP completion day) (otherwise) (SI 2020/1642)[4] |
| | (3) | 31 Dec 2020 at 11.00pm (IP completion day) (SI 2020/1642) |
| 42, 43 | | 31 Dec 2020 at 11.00pm (IP completion day) (otherwise) (SI 2020/1642)[4] |
| 44–46 | | 13 Sep 2018 (s 57(1)(c)) |
| 47 | | 31 Dec 2020 at 11.00pm (IP completion day) (SI 2020/1642)[4] |
| 48, 49 | | 13 Sep 2018 (s 57(1)(c)) |
| 50 | | 31 Dec 2020 at 11.00pm (IP completion day) (SI 2020/1642)[4] |
| 51–53 | | 13 Sep 2018 (s 57(1)(d)) |
| 54–58 | | 13 Sep 2018 (s 57(1)(e)) |
| Schs 1, 2 | | 13 Sep 2018 (so far as making provision for anything to be done by regulations or public notice) (s 57(1)(a)) |
| | | 31 Dec 2020 at 11.00pm (IP completion day) (otherwise) (SI 2020/1642)[4] |
| Sch 3 | | 23 Jan 2019 (SI 2019/69) |
| Sch 4 | paras 1–21 | 4 Mar 2019 (SI 2019/429)[2] |
| | para 22 | 30 Jan 2020 (SI 2020/97)[3] |
| | paras 23–29 | 4 Mar 2019 (SI 2019/429)[2] |
| | para 30 | 31 Dec 2020 at 11.00pm (IP completion day) (SI 2020/1642)[4] |
| | paras 31, 32 | 4 Mar 2019 (SI 2019/429)[2] |

**See Halsbury's Statutes Citator for amendments to these Acts**

**Taxation (Cross-border Trade) Act 2018 (c 22)**—*contd*

| | | |
|---|---|---|
| Sch 5 | paras 1–21 | 4 Mar 2019 (SI 2019/429)[2] |
| | para 22 | 30 Jan 2020 (SI 2020/97)[3] |
| | paras 23–28 | 4 Mar 2019 (SI 2019/429)[2] |
| | para 29 | 31 Dec 2020 at 11.00pm (IP completion day) (SI 2020/1642)[4] |
| | paras 30, 31 | 4 Mar 2019 (SI 2019/429)[2] |
| Sch 6 | | 13 Sep 2018 (so far as making provision for anything to be done by regulations or public notice) (s 57(1)(a)) |
| | | 31 Dec 2020 at 11.00pm (IP completion day) (otherwise) (SI 2020/1642)[4] |
| Sch 7 | para 1 | 13 Sep 2018 (so far as making provision for anything to be done by regulations or public notice, except so far as relating to EU trade duties) (s 57(1)(a), (2)(d))[1, 2] |
| | | 31 Dec 2020 at 11.00pm (IP completion day) (otherwise) (SI 2020/1642)[4] |
| | paras 2–15 | 13 Sep 2018 (so far as making provision for anything to be done by regulations or public notice) (s 57(1)(a)) |
| | | 31 Dec 2020 at 11.00pm (IP completion day) (otherwise) (SI 2020/1642)[4] |
| | para 16(1) | See paras 16(2)–(6) below |
| | para 16(2)(a) | 13 Sep 2018 (so far as making provision for anything to be done by regulations or public notice) (s 57(1)(a)) |
| | | 8 Apr 2019 (otherwise) (SI 2019/819) |
| | para 16(2)(b) | 13 Sep 2018 (so far as making provision for anything to be done by regulations or public notice) (s 57(1)(a)) |
| | | 31 Dec 2020 at 11.00pm (IP completion day) (otherwise) (SI 2020/1642)[4] |
| | para 16(3) | 13 Sep 2018 (so far as making provision for anything to be done by regulations or public notice) (s 57(1)(a)) |
| | | 8 Apr 2019 (otherwise) (SI 2019/819) |
| | para 16(4)–(6) | 13 Sep 2018 (so far as making provision for anything to be done by regulations or public notice) (s 57(1)(a)) |
| | | 31 Dec 2020 at 11.00pm (IP completion day) (otherwise) (SI 2020/1642)[4] |
| | paras 17–89 | 13 Sep 2018 (so far as making provision for anything to be done by regulations or public notice) (s 57(1)(a)) |
| | | 31 Dec 2020 at 11.00pm (IP completion day) (otherwise) (SI 2020/1642)[4] |
| | para 90 | 13 Sep 2018 (so far as making provision for anything to be done by regulations or public notice) (s 57(1)(a)) |
| | | *Not yet in force* (otherwise) |
| | paras 91–157 | 13 Sep 2018 (so far as making provision for anything to be done by regulations or public notice) (s 57(1)(a)) |
| | | 31 Dec 2020 at 11.00pm (IP completion day) (otherwise) (SI 2020/1642)[4] |
| Sch 8 | para 1 | See paras 2–99 below |
| | paras 2–13 | 31 Dec 2020 at 11.00pm (otherwise) (SI 2020/1642)[4] |
| | para 14 | 16 Dec 2018 (SI 2018/1362) |
| | paras 15–132 | 31 Dec 2020 at 11.00pm (otherwise) (SI 2020/1642)[4] |
| Sch 9 | | 31 Dec 2020 at 11.00pm (otherwise) (SI 2020/1642)[4] |

[1]    Sch 7, para 1 comes into force, so far as relates to EU trade duties, immediately after the coming into force of the European Union (Withdrawal) Act 2018, s 3

[2]    For transitional provisions, see SI 2019/429, regs 4–9, Schedule

[3]    For transitory provisions, see SI 2020/97, reg 4, Schedule

[4]    For transitional provisions, see SI 2020/1642, regs 5–6

**Telecommunications Infrastructure (Relief from Non-Domestic Rates) Act 2018 (c 1)**

*RA:* 8 Feb 2018

Whole Act in force 8 Feb 2018

---

**Wild Animals in Travelling Circuses (Scotland) Act 2018 (asp 3)**

*RA:* 24 Jan 2018

*Commencement provisions:* s 9; Wild Animals in Travelling Circuses (Scotland) Act 2018 (Commencement) Regulations 2018, SSI 2018/149

| | |
|---|---|
| 1–8 | 28 May 2018 (SSI 2018/149) |
| 9, 10 | 25 Jan 2018 (s 9(1)) |
| Schs 1, 2 | 28 May 2018 (SSI 2018/149) |

---

**Writers to the Signet Dependants' Annuity Fund Amendment (Scotland) Act 2018 (asp 2)**

*RA:* 18 Jan 2018

*Commencement provisions:* s 2

Whole Act in force 19 Jan 2018 (s 2)

# 2019 Acts

## Age of Criminal Responsibility (Scotland) Act 2019 (asp 7)

*RA*: 11 Jun 2019

*Commencement provisions*: s 84; Age of Criminal Responsibility (Scotland) Act 2019 (Commencement No 1 and Transitory Provision) Regulations 2019, SSI 2019/349; Age of Criminal Responsibility (Scotland) Act 2019 (Commencement No 2) Regulations 2020, SSI 2020/74; Age of Criminal Responsibility (Scotland) Act 2019 (Commencement No 3) Regulations 2020, SI 2020/369; Age of Criminal Responsibility (Scotland) Act 2019 (Commencement No 4) Regulations 2021, SSI 2021/449

| | | |
|---|---|---|
| 1, 2 | | 17 Dec 2021 (SSI 2021/449) |
| 3 | | 29 Nov 2019 (SSI 2019/349)[1] |
| 4–21 | | 30 Nov 2020 (SSI 2020/369) |
| 22–24 | | 31 Mar 2020 (SSI 2020/74) |
| 25, 26 | | 30 Nov 2020 (SSI 2020/369) |
| 27 | | 29 Nov 2019 (SSI 2019/349) |
| 28 | | 17 Dec 2021 (SSI 2021/449) |
| 29–32 | | 31 Mar 2020 (SSI 2020/74) |
| 33 | (1)–(3) | 17 Dec 2021 (SSI 2021/449) |
| | (4) | 31 Mar 2020 (SSI 2020/74) |
| 34–55 | | 17 Dec 2021 (SSI 2021/449) |
| 56 | (1), (2) | 17 Dec 2021 (SSI 2021/449) |
| | (3), (4) | 31 Mar 2020 (SSI 2020/74) |
| | (5) | 17 Dec 2021 (SSI 2021/449) |
| 57 | | 31 Mar 2020 (SSI 2020/74) |
| 58, 59 | | 17 Dec 2021 (SSI 2021/449) |
| 60 | (1)–(5) | 17 Dec 2021 (SSI 2021/449) |
| | (6) | 31 Mar 2020 (SSI 2020/74) |
| 61–64 | | 17 Dec 2021 (SSI 2021/449) |
| 65 | (1), (2)(a) | 17 Dec 2021 (SSI 2021/449) |
| | (2)(b)(i), (ii) | 17 Dec 2021 (SSI 2021/449) |
| | (2)(b)(iii) | 31 Mar 2020 (SSI 2020/74) |
| | (3) | 31 Mar 2020 (SSI 2020/74) |
| 66 | (1)–(8) | 17 Dec 2021 (SSI 2021/449) |
| | (9) | 31 Mar 2020 (SSI 2020/74) |
| | (10) | 17 Dec 2021 (SSI 2021/449) |
| 67–72 | | 17 Dec 2021 (SSI 2021/449) |
| 73 | | 31 Mar 2020 (SSI 2020/74) |
| 74–79 | | 17 Dec 2021 (SSI 2021/449) |
| 80–83 | | 31 Mar 2020 (SSI 2020/74) |
| 84, 85 | | 12 Jun 2019 (s 84(1)) |

[1]  For transitory provisions, see SSI 2019/349, reg 3

---

## Animal Welfare (Service Animals) Act 2019 (c 15)

*RA*: 8 Apr 2019

*Commencement provisions*: s 2(2)

---

**Animal Welfare (Service Animals) Act 2019 (c 15)**—*contd*
Whole Act in force 8 Jun 2019 (s 2(2))

---

**Census (Amendment) (Scotland) Act 2019 (asp 12)**

*RA:* 18 Jul 2019

*Commencement provisions:* s 2

| | |
|---|---|
| 1 | 18 Sep 2019 (s 2(2)) |
| 2, 3 | 19 Jul 2019 (s 2(1)) |

---

**Census (Return Particulars and Removal of Penalties) Act 2019 (c 28)**

*RA:* 8 Oct 2019

*Commencement provisions:* s 3(4)

Whole Act in force 8 Oct 2019 (s 3(4))

---

**Childcare Funding (Wales) Act 2019 (anaw 1)**

*RA:* 30 Jan 2019

*Commencement provisions:* s 13

| | |
|---|---|
| 1–12 | *Not yet in force* |
| 13, 14 | 31 Jan 2019 (s 13(1)) |

---

**Children Act 1989 (Amendment) (Female Genital Mutilation) Act 2019 (c 10)**

*RA:* 15 Mar 2019

*Commencement provisions:* s 2(2)

Whole Act in force 15 Mar 2019 (s 2(2))

---

**Children (Equal Protection from Assault) (Scotland) Act 2019 (asp 16)**

*RA:* 7 Nov 2019

*Commencement provisions:* s 4

| | | |
|---|---|---|
| 1 | | *Not yet in force* |
| 2 | | 8 Nov 2019 (s 4(1)) |
| 3 | (1), (2) | *Not yet in force* |
| | (3), (4) | 8 Nov 2019 (s 4(1)) |
| 4, 5 | | 8 Nov 2019 (s 4(1)) |

---

**Church Representation and Ministers Measure 2019 (No 1)**

*RA:* 4 Jul 2019

*Commencement provisions:* s 3(2)–(5); Church Representation and Ministers Measure 2019 (Commencement) Order 2019, SI 2019/1460

| | |
|---|---|
| 1, 2 | 1 Jan 2020 (SI 2019/1460) |
| 3 | 4 Jul 2019 (s 3(2)) |
| Schs 1–3 | 1 Jan 2020 (SI 2019/1460) |

---

## Civil Partnerships, Marriages and Deaths (Registration etc) Act 2019 (c 12)

*RA:* 26 Mar 2019

*Commencement provisions*: s 6(3)

Whole Act in force 26 May 2019 (s 6(3))

---

## Climate Change (Emissions Reduction Targets) (Scotland) Act 2019 (asp 15)

*RA:* 31 Oct 2019

*Commencement provisions*: s 32; Climate Change (Emissions Reduction Targets) (Scotland) Act 2019 (Commencement) Regulations 2020, SSI 2020/66

| | |
|---|---|
| 1–29 | 23 Mar 2020 (SSI 2020/66) |
| 30–33 | 1 Nov 2019 (s 32(1)) |
| Schedule | 23 Mar 2020 (SSI 2020/66) |

---

## Counter-Terrorism and Border Security Act 2019 (c 3)

*RA:* 12 Feb 2019

*Commencement provisions*: s 27; Counter-Terrorism and Border Security Act 2019 (Commencement No 1) Regulations 2020, SI 2020/792; Counter-Terrorism and Border Security Act 2019 (Commencement No 1) (Northern Ireland) Regulations 2021, SI 2021/622

| | | |
|---|---|---|
| 1–15 | | 12 Apr 2019 (s 27(3)) |
| 16–18 | | 13 Aug 2020 (SI 2020/792) |
| 19 | | See Sch 2 below |
| 20 | | 12 Apr 2019 (s 27(3)) |
| 21 | | 12 Feb 2019 (s 27(1)) |
| 22 | | See Sch 3 below |
| 23 | (1) | See Sch 4 below |
| | (2)–(7) | 12 Feb 2019 (s 27(1)) |
| 24, 25 | | 12 Apr 2019 (s 27(3)) |
| 26–28 | | 12 Feb 2019 (s 27(1)) |
| Sch 1 | | 12 Apr 2019 (s 27(3)) |
| Sch 2 | paras 1–4 | 13 Aug 2020 (SI 2020/792) |
| | para 5 | *Not yet in force* |
| | paras 6–17 | 13 Aug 2020 (SI 2020/792) |
| | paras 18–20 | *Not yet in force* |
| Sch 3 | paras 1–43 | 12 Feb 2019 (so far as necessary for enabling the exercise of any power under Sch 3 to make regulations or issue codes of practice) (s 27(1)) |
| | | 13 Aug 2020 (otherwise) (SI 2020/792) |
| | paras 44, 45 | 12 Feb 2019 (so far as necessary for enabling the exercise of any power under Sch 3 to make regulations or issue codes of practice) (s 27(1)) |
| | | 13 Aug 2020 (otherwise) (E) (W) (S) (SI 2020/792) |
| | | 1 Jun 2021 (otherwise) (NI) (SI 2021/622) |
| | paras 46–64 | 12 Feb 2019 (so far as necessary for enabling the exercise of any power under Sch 3 to make regulations or issue codes of practice) (s 27(1)) |
| | | 13 Aug 2020 (otherwise) (SI 2020/792) |
| Sch 4 | paras 1–16 | 12 Apr 2019 (s 27(3)) |
| | paras 17, 18 | 13 Aug 2020 (otherwise) (SI 2020/792) |
| | para 19 | 12 Feb 2019 (s 27(1)) |
| | para 20(1) | See para 20(2)–(9) below |
| | para 20(2)–(8) | 13 Aug 2020 (SI 2020/792) |
| | para 20(9) | *Not yet in force* |
| | paras 21–26 | 13 Aug 2020 (SI 2020/792) |

**Counter-Terrorism and Border Security Act 2019 (c 3)**—*contd*

| | | |
|---|---|---|
| | para 27 | 12 Apr 2019 (s 27(3)) |
| | paras 28–33 | 13 Aug 2020 (SI 2020/792) |
| | paras 34–51 | 12 Apr 2019 (s 27(3)) |

**Crime (Overseas Production Orders) Act 2019 (c 5)**

*RA:* 12 Feb 2019

*Commencement provisions*: s 20; Crime (Overseas Production Orders) Act 2019 (Commencement No 1) Regulations 2019, SI 2019/1318; Crime (Overseas Production Orders) Act 2019 (Commencement No 2) (Northern Ireland) Regulations 2021, SI 2021/146

| | | |
|---|---|---|
| 1 | (1)–(4) | 9 Oct 2019 (E) (W) (S) (SI 2019/1318) |
| | | 9 Oct 2019 (NI) (but only to the extent they apply, by virtue of s 15(2), in relation to an application under s 15(1) and an overseas production order made under that section and for the purpose of making rules of court under section 11(1) which make provision as to the practice and procedure to be followed in connection with proceedings relating to an overseas production order made under section 15(1) of the 2019 Act) |
| | | 22 Feb 2021 (otherwise) (NI) |
| | (5), (6) | 9 Oct 2019 (SI 2019/1318) |
| | (7) | 9 Oct 2019 (E) (W) (S) (SI 2019/1318) |
| | | 9 Oct 2019 (NI) (but only to the extent they apply, by virtue of s 15(2), in relation to an application under s 15(1) and an overseas production order made under that section and for the purpose of making rules of court under section 11(1) which make provision as to the practice and procedure to be followed in connection with proceedings relating to an overseas production order made under section 15(1) of the 2019 Act) |
| | | 22 Feb 2021 (otherwise) (NI) |
| 2–14 | | 9 Oct 2019 (E) (W) (S) (SI 2019/1318) |
| | | 9 Oct 2019 (NI) (but only to the extent they apply, by virtue of s 15(2), in relation to an application under s 15(1) and an overseas production order made under that section and for the purpose of making rules of court under section 11(1) which make provision as to the practice and procedure to be followed in connection with proceedings relating to an overseas production order made under section 15(1) of the 2019 Act) |
| | | 22 Feb 2021 (otherwise) (NI) |
| 15, 16 | | 9 Oct 2019 (SI 2019/1318) |
| 17–21 | | 12 Feb 2019 (s 20(3)) |

**Damages (Investment Returns and Periodical Payments) (Scotland) Act 2019 (asp 4)**

*RA:* 24 Apr 2019

*Commencement provisions*: s 9; Damages (Investment Returns and Periodical Payments) (Scotland) Act 2019 (Commencement No 1) Regulations 2019, SSI 2019/197

| | |
|---|---|
| 1, 2 | 1 Jul 2019 (SSI 2019/197) |
| 3–7 | *Not yet in force* |
| 8–10 | 25 Apr 2019 (s 9(1)) |
| Schedule | 1 Jul 2019 (SSI 2019/197) |

**Early Parliamentary General Election Act 2019(c 29)**

*RA:* 31 Oct 2019

*Commencement provisions*: s 2(1)

**Early Parliamentary General Election Act 2019(c 29)**—*contd*
Whole Act in force 31 Oct 2019 (s 2(1))

---

**European Union (Withdrawal) Act 2019 (c 16)**

*RA:* 8 Apr 2019

*Commencement provisions:* s 3(2)

| | |
|---|---|
| 1–3 | 8 Apr 2019 (s 3(2)) |

---

**European Union (Withdrawal) (No 2) Act 2019 (c 26)**

*RA:* 10 Sep 2019

*Commencement provisions:* s 5(5)

Whole Act in force 10 Sep 2019 (s 5(5))

---

**Finance Act 2019 (c 1)**

*RA:* 12 Feb 2019

The commencement details of Finance Acts are not set out, as the dates from which their provisions take effect are usually stated clearly and unambiguously in the text of the Act, and charging provisions will normally state for which year or years of assessment they are to have effect.

---

**Fuel Poverty (Targets, Definition and Strategy) (Scotland) Act 2019 (asp 10)**

*RA:* 18 Jul 2019

*Commencement provisions:* s 20; Fuel Poverty (Targets, Definition and Strategy) (Scotland) Act 2019 (Commencement No 1) Regulations 2019, SSI 2019/277; Fuel Poverty (Targets, Definition and Strategy) (Scotland) Act 2019 (Commencement No 2) Regulations 2021, SSI 2021/332

| | | |
|---|---|---|
| 1–6 | | 19 Sep 2019 (SSI 2019/277) |
| 7 | (1), (2)(a)–(f) | 19 Sep 2019 (SSI 2019/277) |
| | (2)(g) | 11 Oct 2021 (SSI 2021/332) |
| | (3)–(5) | 19 Sep 2019 (SSI 2019/277) |
| 8–17 | | 19 Sep 2019 (SSI 2019/277) |
| 18 | (1), (2) | 19 Sep 2019 (SSI 2019/277) |
| | (3), (4) | *Not yet in force* |
| 19–21 | | 19 Jul 2019 (s 20(1)) |

---

**Health and Care (Staffing) (Scotland) Act 2019 (asp 6)**

*RA:* 6 Jun 2019

*Commencement provisions:* s 15

| | |
|---|---|
| 1–13 | *Not yet in force* |
| 14–16 | 7 Jun 2019 (s 15(1)) |

---

**Healthcare (European Economic Area and Switzerland Arrangements) Act 2019 (c 14)**

*RA:* 26 Mar 2019

*Commencement provisions:* s 8(2)

**Healthcare (European Economic Area and Switzerland Arrangements) Act 2019 (c 14)**—*contd*
Whole Act in force 26 Mar 2019 (s 8(2))

---

**Historical Institutional Abuse (Northern Ireland) Act 2019 (c 31)**

*RA:* 5 Nov 2019

*Commencement provisions:* s 33

| | |
|---|---|
| 1–30 | *Not yet in force* |
| 31–34 | 5 Nov 2019 (33(1)) |
| Schs 1, 2 | *Not yet in force* |

---

**Holocaust (Return of Cultural Objects) (Amendment) Act 2019 (c 20)**

*RA:* 4 Jul 2019

*Commencement provisions:* s 2(2)

Whole Act in force 4 Jul 2019 (s 2(2))

---

**Human Tissue (Authorisation) (Scotland) Act 2019 (asp 11)**

*RA:* 18 Jul 2019

*Commencement provisions:* s 29; Human Tissue (Authorisation) (Scotland) Act 2019 (Commencement No 1) Regulations 2019, SSI 2019/305; Human Tissue (Authorisation) (Scotland) Act 2019 (Commencement No 2) Regulations 2021, SSI 2021/108

| | |
|---|---|
| 1 | 1 Oct 2019 (SSI 2019/305) |
| 2–6 | 26 Mar 2021 (SSI 2021/108) |
| 7 | 1 Oct 2019 (only so far as is necessary to enable the Scottish Ministers to consult under Human Tissue (Scotland) Act 2006, s 6D(6) and make regulations under s 6D(5) thereof) (SSI 2019/305) |
| | 26 Mar 2021 (otherwise) (SSI 2021/108) |
| 8–22 | 26 Mar 2021 (SSI 2021/108) |
| 23 | 1 Oct 2019 (only so far as is necessary to enable the Scottish Ministers to consult under Human Tissue (Scotland) Act 2006, ss 16B(4), 16C(4), and make regulations under ss 16B(1) 16C(1) thereof) (SSI 2019/305) |
| | 26 Mar 2021 (otherwise) (SSI 2021/108) |
| 24 | 26 Mar 2021 (SSI 2021/108) |
| 25, 26 | 18 Jul 2019 (s 29(1)) |
| 27, 28 | 26 Mar 2021 (SSI 2021/108) |
| 29, 30 | 18 Jul 2019 (s 29(1)) |

---

**Hutchesons' Hospital Transfer and Dissolution (Scotland) Act 2019 (asp 5)**

*RA:* 31 May 2019

*Commencement provisions:* s 4

Whole Act in force 28 Jun 2019 (s 4)

---

## Kew Gardens (Leases) Act 2019 (c 25)

*RA:* 10 Sep 2019

*Commencement provisions*: s 2(2)

Whole Act in force 10 Nov 2019 (s 2(2))

---

## Legislation (Wales) Act 2019 (anaw 4)

*RA:* 10 Sep 2019

*Commencement provisions*: s 44; Legislation (Wales) Act 2019 (Commencement) Order 2019, SI 2019/1333

| | | |
|---|---|---|
| 1, 2 | | 11 Sep 2019 (s 44(1)) |
| 3–5 | | 11 Sep 2019 (so far as apply to this Act) (s 44(1)) |
| | | 1 Jan 2020 (otherwise) (SI 2019/1333) |
| 6 | (1) | 11 Sep 2019 (so far as apply to this Act) (s 44(1)) |
| | | 1 Jan 2020 (otherwise) (SI 2019/1333) |
| | (2), (3) | 11 Sep 2019 (s 44(1)) |
| 7–37 | | 11 Sep 2019 (so far as apply to this Act) (s 44(1)) |
| | | 1 Jan 2020 (otherwise) (SI 2019/1333) |
| 38–45 | | 11 Sep 2019 (s 44(1)) |
| Sch 1 | | 11 Sep 2019 (so far as apply to this Act) (s 44(1)) |
| | | 1 Jan 2020 (otherwise) (SI 2019/1333) |
| Sch 2 | | 11 Sep 2019 (s 44(1)) |

---

## Management of Offenders (Scotland) Act 2019 (asp 14)

*RA:* 30 Jul 2019

*Commencement provisions*: s 63; Management of Offenders (Scotland) Act 2019 (Commencement No 1, Saving and Transitional Provisions) Regulations 2019, SSI 2019/309; Management of Offenders (Scotland) Act 2019 (Commencement No 2) Regulations 2019, SSI 2019/413; Management of Offenders (Scotland) Act 2019 (Commencement No. 3 and Transitory Provision) Regulations 2019, SSI 2019/417; Management of Offenders (Scotland) Act 2019 (Commencement No 4 and Saving Provision) Regulations 2020, SSI 2020/245; Management of Offenders (Scotland) Act 2019 (Commencement No 5 and Saving Provisions) Regulations 2020, SSI 2020/283; Management of Offenders (Scotland) Act 2019 (Commencement No 6 and Saving Provisions) Regulations 2022, SSI 2022/94

| | | |
|---|---|---|
| 1 | | 17 May 2022 (for the purpose of the disposals listed at s 3(2)(b)–(d), (g), (h)) (SSI 2022/94)[5] |
| | | *Not yet in force* (otherwise) |
| 2 | | 17 May 2022 (SSI 2022/94) |
| 3, 4 | | 1 Oct 2020 (SSI 2020/283) |
| 5–7 | | 17 May 2022 (SSI 2022/94) |
| 8, 9 | | 1 Oct 2020 (SSI 2020/283) |
| 10–14 | | 17 May 2022 (SSI 2022/94) |
| 15 | | 1 Oct 2020 (SSI 2020/283) |
| 16 | | See Sch 1 below |
| 17–31 | | 30 Nov 2020 (SSI 2020/245)[3] |
| 32 | | 21 Dec 2019 (SSI 2019/413) |
| 33–38 | | 30 Nov 2020 (SSI 2020/245)[3] |
| 39 | | 21 Dec 2019 (SSI 2019/413) |
| 40–42 | | 1 Oct 2020 (SSI 2020/283) |
| 43 | | 1 Oct 2020 (SSI 2020/283)[4] |
| 44 | | 31 Dec 2019 (SSI 2019/417)[2] |
| 45–47 | | 1 Oct 2020 (SSI 2020/283) |
| 48, 49 | | *Not yet in force* |
| 50 | (1) | 11 Oct 2019 (SSI 2019/309) |
| | (2) | 11 Oct 2019 (SSI 2019/309)[1] |

**Management of Offenders (Scotland) Act 2019 (asp 14)**—*contd*

|  |  |  |
|---|---|---|
|  | (3) | 1 Oct 2020 (SSI 2020/283)[4] |
|  | (4) | 11 Oct 2019 (SSI 2019/309) |
| 51 |  | *Not yet in force* |
| 52 |  | 1 Oct 2020 (SSI 2020/283) |
| 53 | (1) | 11 Oct 2019 (SSI 2019/309) |
|  | (2) | 1 Oct 2020 (SSI 2020/283) |
|  | (3)(a) | 11 Oct 2019 (SSI 2019/309) |
|  | (3)(b) | 1 Oct 2020 (SSI 2020/283)[4] |
| 54 |  | 1 Oct 2020 (SSI 2020/283) |
| 55–57 |  | 11 Oct 2019 (SSI 2019/309) |
| 58 |  | *Not yet in force* |
| 59 |  | 11 Oct 2019 (SSI 2019/309)[1] |
| 60, 61 |  | 11 Oct 2019 (SSI 2019/309) |
| 62–64 |  | 31 Jul 2019 (s 63(1)) |
| Sch 1 | para 1 | 11 Oct 2019 (SSI 2019/309) |
|  | para 2 | 17 May 2022 (SSI 2022/94)[5] |
|  | paras 3–5 | 11 Oct 2019 (SSI 2019/309) |
|  | paras 6–9 | 17 May 2022 (SSI 2022/94)[5] |
|  | para 10 | 17 May 2022 (SSI 2022/94) |
| Sch 2 |  | 30 Nov 2020 (SSI 2020/245)[3] |

[1]  For transitional and saving provisions, see SSI 2019/309, regs, 3, 4

[2]  For a transitory provision, see SSI 2019/417, reg 3

[3]  For savings, see SSI 2020/245, reg 3

[4]  For savings, see SSI 2020/283, regs 3–5

[5]  For savings, see SSI 2022/94, reg 3

---

**Mental Capacity (Amendment) Act 2019 (c 18)**

*RA:* 16 May 2019

*Commencement provisions:* s 6(2)–(7)

|  |  |  |
|---|---|---|
| 1 | (1)–(3) | *Not yet in force* |
|  | (4) | See Sch 1 below |
| 2–4 |  | *Not yet in force* |
| 5 | (1)–(5) | 16 May 2019 (s 6(2)) |
|  | (6) | See Sch 2 below |
| Sch 1 |  | 16 May 2019 (for the purpose only of enabling the exercise of any power to make regulations) (s 6(2)) |
|  |  | *Not yet in force* (otherwise) |
| Sch 2 |  | *Not yet in force* |

---

**National Insurance Contributions (Termination Awards and Sporting Testimonials) Act 2019 (c 23)**

*RA:* 24 Jul 2019

*Commencement provisions:* s 5(2)–(4); National Insurance Contributions (Termination Awards and Sporting Testimonials) Act 2019 (Commencement and Transitional Provisions) Regulations 2020, SI 2020/285

|  |  |
|---|---|
| 1, 2 | 6 Apr 2020 (except in relation to termination awards received on or after 6th Apr 2020 in respect of employment which was terminated before 6th Apr 2020; or termination awards which are received in instalments where the first instalment of the termination award was received before 6th Apr 2020 (SI 2020/285) |
|  | *Not yet in force* (exception noted above) |

**National Insurance Contributions (Termination Awards and Sporting Testimonials) Act 2019 (c 23)**—*contd*

3, 4                                        6 Apr 2020 (except in relation to sporting testimonials which take
                                            place on or after 6th Apr 2020 but which were announced
                                            before 6th Apr 2020) (SI 2020/285)
                                            *Not yet in force* (exception noted above)
5                                          24 Jul 2019 (s 4(2))

**Non-Domestic Rating (Preparation for Digital Services) Act 2019 (c 19)**

*RA:* 4 Jul 2019

Whole Act in force 4 Jul 2019 (RA)

**Northern Ireland Budget Act 2019 (c 30)**

*RA:* 31 Oct 2019

Whole Act in force 31 Oct 2019 (RA)

**Northern Ireland Budget (Anticipation and Adjustments) Act 2019 (c 11)**

*RA:* 15 Mar 2019

Whole Act in force 15 Mar 2019 (RA)

**Northern Ireland (Executive Formation etc) Act 2019 (c 22)**

*RA:* 24 Jul 2019

*Commencement provisions*: s 13(3), (4)

1–7                                        24 Jul 2019 (s 13(3))
8–12                                       22 Oct 2019 (s 13(4))[1]
13                                         24 Jul 2019 (s 13(3))

[1]   Ss 8–12 do not come into force at all if an Executive in Northern Ireland is formed on or before
      21 Oct 2019

**Northern Ireland (Regional Rates and Energy) Act 2019 (c 13)**

*RA:* 26 Mar 2019

*Commencement provisions*: s 6

1                                          26 Mar 2019 (s 6(1))
2, 3                                       1 Apr 2019 (s 6(2))
4, 5                                       26 May 2019 (s 6(3))
6, 7                                       26 Mar 2019 (s 6(1))
Schedule                                   1 Apr 2019 (s 6(2))

**Offensive Weapons Act 2019 (c 17)**

*RA:* 16 May 2019

*Commencement provisions*: s 70; Offensive Weapons Act 2019 (Commencement No 1) (Scotland)
     Regulations 2020, SSI 2020/410; Offensive Weapons Act 2019 (Commencement No 1) (England and
     Wales) Regulations 2020, SI 2020/1480; Offensive Weapons Act 2019 (Commencement No 2)
     (England and Wales) Regulations 2021, SI 2021/762, as amended by SI 2022/828; Offensive Weapons

**Offensive Weapons Act 2019 (c 17)**—*contd*
   Act 2019 (Commencement No 1) Regulations 2021, SI 2021/819; Offensive Weapons Act 2019
   (Commencement No 2 and Saving Provision) Regulations 2022, SI 2022/418; Offensive Weapons
   Act 2019 (Commencement No 2) (Scotland) Regulations 2022, SSI 2022/150; Offensive Weapons
   Act 2019 (Commencement No 1) Order (Northern Ireland) 2022, SI 2022/235

| | | |
|---|---|---|
| 1–4 | | 6 Apr 2022 (E), (W), (S) (SI 2022/418)[2] |
| | | *Not yet in force* (NI) |
| 5 | | 1 Jan 2021 (SSI 2020/410) |
| 6 | | 6 Apr 2022 (E), (W) (SI 2022/418)[2] |
| | | 28 Jun 2022 (S) (SSI 2022/150) |
| | | 6 Oct 2022 (NI) (SR 2022/235) |
| 7 | | 1 Jan 2021 (SSI 2020/410) |
| 8, 9 | | Repealed *(never in force)* |
| 10 | | 6 Apr 2022 (SI 2022/418)[2] |
| 11 | | 1 Jan 2021 (SSI 2020/410) |
| 12 | | *Not yet in force* |
| 13 | (1) | Repealed *(never in force)* |
| | (2), (3) | *Not yet in force* |
| | (4) | Repealed *(never in force)* |
| | (5) | 1 Jan 2021 (SSI 2020/410) |
| | (6), (7) | Repealed *(never in force)* |
| 14 | (1)–(6) | 5 Jul 2021 (in relation to the metropolitan police district for the period beginning with 5 Jul 2021 and ending with 31 Mar 2023) (SI 2021/762) |
| | | *Not yet in force* (otherwise) |
| | (7), (8) | 5 Jul 2021 (so far as relate to a knife crime prevention order or interim knife crime protection order applied for or made in the metropolitan police district for the period beginning with 5 Jul 2021 and ending with 31 Mar 2023) (E) (W) (SI 2021/762) |
| | | *Not yet in force* (otherwise) |
| | (9), (10) | 5 Jul 2021 (in relation to the metropolitan police district for the period beginning with 5 Jul 2021 and ending with 31 Mar 2023) (SI 2021/762) |
| | | *Not yet in force* (otherwise) |
| 15, 16 | | 5 Jul 2021 (in relation to the metropolitan police district for the period beginning with 5 Jul 2021 and ending with 31 Mar 2023) (SI 2021/762) |
| | | *Not yet in force* (otherwise) |
| 17 | (1)–(3) | 5 Jul 2021 (in relation to the metropolitan police district for the period beginning with 5 Jul 2021 and ending with 31 Mar 2023) (SI 2021/762) |
| | | *Not yet in force* (otherwise) |
| | (4)–(6) | 5 Jul 2021 (so far as relate to a knife crime prevention order or interim knife crime protection order applied for or made in the metropolitan police district for the period beginning with 5 Jul 2021 and ending with 31 Mar 2023) |
| | | *Not yet in force* (otherwise) |
| 18 | (1)–(5) | 5 Jul 2021 (in relation to the metropolitan police district for the period beginning with 5 Jul 2021 and ending with 31 Mar 2023) (SI 2021/762) |
| | | *Not yet in force* (otherwise) |
| | (6), (7) | 5 Jul 2021 (so far as relate to a knife crime prevention order or interim knife crime protection order applied for or made in the metropolitan police district for the period beginning with 5 Jul 2021 and ending with 31 Mar 2023) (E) (W) (SI 2021/762) |
| | | *Not yet in force* (otherwise) |
| | (8) | 5 Jul 2021 (in relation to the metropolitan police district for the period beginning with 5 Jul 2021 and ending with 31 Mar 2023) (SI 2021/762) |
| | | *Not yet in force* (otherwise) |

**Offensive Weapons Act 2019 (c 17)**—*contd*

| | | |
|---|---|---|
| 19 | (1)–(4) | 5 Jul 2021 (in relation to the metropolitan police district for the period beginning with 5 Jul 2021 and ending with 31 Mar 2023) (SI 2021/762) |
| | | *Not yet in force* (otherwise) |
| | (5), (6) | 5 Jul 2021 (so far as relate to a knife crime prevention order or interim knife crime protection order applied for or made in the metropolitan police district for the period beginning with 5 Jul 2021 and ending with 31 Mar 2023) (E) (W) (SI 2021/762) |
| | | *Not yet in force* (otherwise) |
| | (7)–(11) | 5 Jul 2021 (in relation to the metropolitan police district for the period beginning with 5 Jul 2021 and ending with 31 Mar 2023) (SI 2021/762) |
| | | *Not yet in force* (otherwise) |
| 20 | | 5 Jul 2021 (in relation to the metropolitan police district for the period beginning with 5 Jul 2021 and ending with 31 Mar 2023) (SI 2021/762) |
| | | *Not yet in force* (otherwise) |
| 21–25 | | 5 Jul 2021 (so far as relate to a knife crime prevention order or interim knife crime protection order applied for or made in the metropolitan police district for the period beginning with 5 Jul 2021 and ending with 31 Mar 2023) (E) (W) (SI 2021/762)[1] |
| | | *Not yet in force* (otherwise) |
| 26–28 | | 5 Jul 2021 (in relation to the metropolitan police district for the period beginning with 5 Jul 2021 and ending with 31 Mar 2023) (SI 2021/762)[1] |
| | | *Not yet in force* (otherwise) |
| 29 | | 5 Jul 2021 (so far as relate to a knife crime prevention order or interim knife crime protection order applied for or made in the metropolitan police district for the period beginning with 5 Jul 2021 and ending with 31 Mar 2023) (E) (W) (SI 2021/762)[1] |
| | | *Not yet in force* (otherwise) |
| 30, 31 | | 16 May 2019 (s 70(5)) |
| 32 | | 5 Jul 2021 (in relation to the metropolitan police district for the period beginning with 5 Jul 2021 and ending with 31 Mar 2023) (SI 2021/762)[1] |
| | | *Not yet in force* (otherwise) |
| 33 | | 5 Jul 2021 (so far as relate to a knife crime prevention order or interim knife crime protection order applied for or made in the metropolitan police district for the period beginning with 5 Jul 2021 and ending with 31 Mar 2023) (E) (W) (SI 2021/762)[1] |
| | | *Not yet in force* (otherwise) |
| 34 | (1) | 1 Jan 2021 (S) (SSI 2020/410) |
| | | 6 Apr 2022 (E) (W) (SI 2022/418)[2] |
| | (2) | *Not yet in force* |
| 35 | | 6 Apr 2022 (SI 2022/418)[2] |
| 36 | | 1 Jan 2021 (SSI 2020/410) |
| 37 | | *Not yet in force* |
| 38–42 | | 6 Apr 2022 (E) (W) (SI 2022/418)[2] |
| | | 28 Jun 2022 (S) (SSI 2022/150) |
| | | *Not yet in force* (NI) |
| 43 | (1) | 14 Jul 2021 (SI 2021/819) |
| | (2) | *Not yet in force* |
| 44 | (1) | See sub-ss (2)–(4) below |
| | (2), (3) | 14 Jul 2021 (E) (W) (SI 2021/819) |
| | | *Not yet in force* (S) |
| | (4) | 10 Dec 2020 (for the purpose of inserting Restriction of Offensive Weapons Act 1959, s 1(3)(a) and (6)–(8) in so far as they apply to sub-s (3) of that section) (SI 2020/1480) |
| | | 14 Jul 2021 (otherwise) (SI 2021/819) |
| | (5)–(7) | *Not yet in force* |

**Offensive Weapons Act 2019 (c 17)**—*contd*

| | | |
|---|---|---|
| 45 | | 6 Apr 2022 (E) (W) (SI 2022/418)[2] |
| | | *Not yet in force* (NI) |
| 46 | (1) | See sub-ss (2)–(19) below |
| | (2)–(7) | 14 Jul 2021 (E) (W) (SI 2021/819) |
| | | *Not yet in force* (S), (NI) |
| | (8)–(11) | 14 Jul 2021 (E) (W) (SI 2021/819) |
| | | *Not yet in force* (NI) |
| | (12)–(14) | *Not yet in force* |
| | (15) | 1 Jan 2021 (S) (SSI 2020/410) |
| | | 14 Jul 2021 (E) (W) (SI 2021/819) |
| | | *Not yet in force* (NI) |
| | (16)–(19) | *Not yet in force* |
| 47 | (1) | See sub-ss (2)–(14) below |
| | (2) | *Not yet in force* |
| | (3)–(10) | 14 Jul 2021 (E) (W) (SI 2021/819) |
| | | *Not yet in force* (NI) |
| | (11) | See sub-ss (12)–(14) below |
| | (12) | 28 Jun 2022 (SSI 2022/150) |
| | (13) | *Not yet in force* |
| | (14) | 28 Jun 2022 (in so far as relates to sub-s (12)) (SSI 2022/150) |
| | | *Not yet in force* (otherwise) |
| 48, 49 | | 16 May 2019 (except so far as confer functions on the Department of Justice in Northern Ireland or the Chief Constable of the Police Service of Northern Ireland) (s 70(5)) |
| | | *Not yet in force* (exception noted above) |
| 50–53 | | 6 Apr 2022 (2022/418)[2] |
| 54 | (1) | 16 May 2019 (s 70(5)) |
| | (2) | 16 May 2019 (so far as has effect of prohibiting the purchase or acquisition of a weapon of a kind referred to in that subsection, or the manufacture, sale or transfer, or purchase or acquisition for sale or transfer, of such a weapon) (S 70(5)) |
| | | 14 Jul 2021 (otherwise) (SI 2021/819) |
| | (3) | 16 May 2019 (so far as has effect of prohibiting the purchase or acquisition of a device of a kind referred to in that subsection, or the manufacture, sale or transfer, or purchase or acquisition for sale or transfer, of such a device) (s 70(5)) |
| | | 14 Jul 2021 (otherwise) (SI 2021/819) |
| | (4) | 16 May 2019 (so far as has effect of prohibiting the manufacture, sale or transfer, or purchase or acquisition for sale or transfer, of a device of a kind referred to in that subsection) (s 70(5)) |
| | | 14 Jul 2021 (otherwise) (SI 2021/819) |
| | (5) | 16 May 2019 (s 70(5)) |
| | (6) | 14 Jul 2021 (S) (SI 2021/819) |
| | | Repealed *(never in force)* (E) (W) |
| | (7)(a) | 16 May 2019 (s 70(5)) |
| | (7)(b), (c) | 14 Jul 2021 (SI 2021/819) |
| | (8) | 14 Jul 2021 (SI 2021/819) |
| 55 | (1) | 16 May 2019 (s 70(5)) |
| | (2) | 16 May 2019 (so far as it has the effect of prohibiting the purchase or acquisition, or manufacture, sale or transfer, of a weapon of a kind referred to in that subsection) (s 70(5)) |
| | | 14 Jul 2021 (otherwise) (SI 2021/819) |
| | (3) | 16 May 2019 (so far as it has the effect of prohibiting the purchase or acquisition, or manufacture, sale or transfer, of a device of a kind referred to in that subsection) (s 70(5)) |
| | | 14 Jul 2021 (otherwise) (SI 2021/819) |
| | (4), (5) | 14 Jul 2021 (SI 2021/819) |
| | (6)(a) | 16 May 2019 (s 70(5)) |
| | (6)(b), (c) | 14 Jul 2021 (SI 2021/819) |
| | (7) | 14 Jul 2021 (SI 2021/819) |

**Offensive Weapons Act 2019 (c 17)**—*contd*

| | | |
|---|---|---|
| 56 | | 14 Jul 2021 (SI 2021/819) |
| 57–61 | | 16 May 2019 (s 70(5)) |
| 62 | | *Not yet in force* |
| 63 | | 16 May 2019 (s 70(5)) |
| 64 | (1)–(4) | 6 Apr 2022 (E), (W) (SI 2022/418)[2] |
| | | *Not yet in force* (S) |
| | (5) | 6 Apr 2022 (2022/418) |
| 65 | | 6 Apr 2022 (2022/418) |
| 66 | (1) | 1 Jan 2021 (so far as it confers functions on the Scottish Ministers) (SSI 2020/410) |
| | | 6 Apr 2022 (otherwise) (2022/418) |
| | (2), (3) | *Not yet in force* |
| | (4)–(10) | 6 Apr 2022 (except so far as confer functions on the Scottish Ministers or the Department of Justice in Northern Ireland) (2022/418) |
| | | *Not yet in force* (exception noted above) |
| 67 | | 6 Apr 2022 (2022/418) |
| 68–71 | | 16 May 2019 (s 70(5)) |
| Sch 1 | | 6 Apr 2022 (E), (W), (S) (SI 2022/418)[2] |
| | | *Not yet in force* (NI) |
| Sch 2 | paras 1–6 | 14 Jul 2021 (SI 2021/819) |
| | paras 7, 8 | Repealed *(never in force)* |
| | para 9 | 14 Jul 2021 (SI 2021/819) |
| | para 10 | Repealed *(never in force)* |
| | para 11 | 14 Jul 2021 (SI 2021/819) |
| | para 12 | Repealed *(never in force)* |
| | para 13 | 14 Jul 2021 (SI 2021/819) |

[1]  For savings, see SI 2021/762, reg 4

[2]  For savings, see SI 2022/418, reg 3

## Organ Donation (Deemed Consent) Act 2019 (c 7)

*RA:* 15 Mar 2019

*Commencement provisions*: s 3(2), (3); Organ Donation (Deemed Consent) Act 2019 (Commencement No 1) Regulations 2019, SI 2019/1262; Organ Donation (Deemed Consent) Act 2019 (Commencement No 2) Regulations 2020, SI 2020/86; Organ Donation (Deemed Consent) Act 2019 (Commencement No 3) Regulations 2020, SI 2020/520

| | | |
|---|---|---|
| 1 | (1) | See sub-ss (2)–(5) below |
| | (2), (3) | 20 May 2020 (SI 2020/520) |
| | (4) | 6 Feb 2020 (SI 2020/86) |
| | (5) | 1 Oct 2019 (for the purpose of making regulations) (SI 2019/1262) |
| | | 20 May 2020 (otherwise) (SI 2020/520) |
| 2 | (1) | See sub-ss (2)–(7) below |
| | (2)–(4) | 20 May 2020 (SI 2020/520) |
| | (5)–(7) | 1 Oct 2019 (SI 2019/1262) |
| 3 | | 15 Mar 2019 (s 3(1)) |

## Parking (Code of Practice) Act 2019 (c 8)

*RA:* 15 Mar 2019

*Commencement provisions*: s 12(1), (2)

| | |
|---|---|
| 1–8 | *Not yet in force* |
| 9 | 15 Mar 2019 (s 12(1)) |
| 10, 11 | *Not yet in force* |

**Parking (Code of Practice) Act 2019 (c 8)**—*contd*
12                                          15 Mar 2019 (s 12(1))

**Parliamentary Buildings (Restoration and Renewal) Act 2019 (c 27)**

*RA:* 8 Oct 2019

*Commencement provisions:* s 14

| | |
|---|---|
| 1–12 | *Not yet in force* |
| 13–15 | 10 Mar 2020 (s 14(2))[1] |
| Schs 1–4 | *Not yet in force* |

[1]    The Leader of the House of Commons may by regulations made by statutory instrument appoint a day, falling before 10 Mar 2020; see s 14(3), (4)

**Planning (Scotland) Act 2019 (asp 13)**

*RA:* 25 Jul 2019

*Commencement provisions:* s 63; Planning (Scotland) Act 2019 (Commencement No 1) Regulations 2019, SSI 2019/314; Planning (Scotland) Act 2019 (Commencement No 2, Saving and Transitional Provisions) Regulations 2019, SSI 2019/377, as amended by SSI 2019/411; Planning (Scotland) Act 2019 (Commencement No 3) Regulations 2019, SSI 2019/385; Planning (Scotland) Act 2019 (Commencement No 4 and Transitional Provision) Regulations 2020, SSI 2020/67; Planning (Scotland) Act 2019 (Commencement No 5 and Saving, Transitional and Consequential Provisions) Regulations 2020, SSI 2020/294; Planning (Scotland) Act 2019 (Commencement No 6 and Transitional Provision) Regulations 2021, SSI 2021/101, as amended by SSI 2021/291, SSI 2022/67; Planning (Scotland) Act 2019 (Commencement No 7) Regulations 2021, SSI 2021/244; Planning (Scotland) Act 2019 (Commencement No 8) Regulations 2021, SSI 2021/480; Planning (Scotland) Act 2019 (Commencement No 9 and Saving and Transitional Provisions) Regulations 2022, SSI 2022/275

| | | |
|---|---|---|
| 1, 2 | | 8 Nov 2019 (SSI 2019/314) |
| 3 | | 8 Nov 2019 (for the purpose of making regulations under Town and Country Planning (Scotland) Act 1997, s 3G(5)) (SSI 2019/314) |
| | | *Not yet in force (otherwise)* |
| 4 | | *Not yet in force* |
| 5 | | 8 Nov 2019 (for the purpose of issuing, varying, publishing and revoking guidance under Town and Country Planning (Scotland) Act 1997, s 4ZE) (SSI 2019/314) |
| | | *Not yet in force (otherwise)* |
| 6 | | *Not yet in force* |
| 7 | | 8 Nov 2019 (for the purpose of making regulations under Town and Country Planning (Scotland) Act 1997, ss 16B, 16D, 18, 19, 20A, and issuing, varying, publishing and revoking guidance under s 16C thereof) (SSI 2019/314) |
| | | *Not yet in force (otherwise)* |
| 8, 9 | | *Not yet in force* |
| 10 | | 8 Nov 2019 (SSI 2019/314) |
| 11 | | 8 Nov 2019 (for the purpose of making regulations under Town and Country Planning (Scotland) Act 1997, s 21(7)) (SSI 2019/314) |
| | | *Not yet in force (otherwise)* |
| 12, 13 | | *Not yet in force* |
| 14 | (1) | See sub-ss (2)–(7) below |
| | (2) | *Not yet in force* |
| | (3) | 22 Jan 2022 (SSI 2021/480) |
| | (4)–(6) | *Not yet in force* |

**Planning (Scotland) Act 2019 (asp 13)**—*contd*

| | | |
|---|---|---|
| | (7) | 8 Nov 2019 (for the purpose of making regulations under Town and Country Planning (Scotland) Act 1997, Sch 19) (SSI 2019/314) |
| | | 22 Jan 2022 (otherwise) (SSI 2021/480) |
| 15, 16 | | *Not yet in force* |
| 17 | | 18 May 2020 (otherwise) (for the purpose of making regulations under Town and Country Planning (Scotland) Act 1997, s 26B(5)) (SSI 2020/67)[2] |
| | | 1 Apr 2021 (otherwise) (SSI 2021/101) |
| 18 | (1), (2) | 1 Dec 2020 (SSI 2019/385) |
| | (3) | 1 Oct 2022 (SSI 2021/101)[4] |
| | (4) | 1 Dec 2020 (SSI 2019/385) |
| 19 | | *Not yet in force* |
| 20 | | 1 Dec 2020 (SSI 2019/385) |
| 21 | | *Not yet in force* |
| 22 | | 1 Oct 2022 (SSI 2022/275)[5] |
| 23 | | 1 Mar 2020 (SSI 2019/377)[1] |
| 24 | | 1 Dec 2020 (SSI 2019/385) |
| 25 | | 20 Dec 2019 (SSI 2019/377)[1] |
| 26 | | 1 Dec 2019 (for the purpose of making regulations under Town and Country Planning (Scotland) Act 1997 s 41B(4)) (SSI 2019/385) |
| | | 18 May 2020 (otherwise) (for the purpose of making regulations under Town and Country Planning (Scotland) Act 1997, s 26B(5)) (SSI 2020/67)[2] |
| | | *Not yet in force* (otherwise) |
| 27 | | 1 Mar 2020 (SSI 2019/385) |
| 28 | | *Not yet in force* |
| 29 | | 1 Dec 2020 (SSI 2019/385) |
| 30 | | 1 Mar 2020 (SSI 2019/385) |
| 31 | | *Not yet in force* |
| 32, 33 | | 1 Oct 2022 (SSI 2022/275)[5] |
| 34 | | 18 Nov 2020 (SSI 2020/294)[3] |
| 35, 36 | | *Not yet in force* |
| 37 | | 18 Nov 2020 (SSI 2020/294) |
| 38 | | 1 Oct 2022 (SSI 2022/275)[2] |
| 39 | | *Not yet in force* |
| 40 | | 17 Jul 2021 (SSI 2021/244) |
| 41 | | 1 Dec 2020 (SSI 2019/385) |
| 42 | | 20 Dec 2019 (SSI 2019/377)[1] |
| 43–46 | | *Not yet in force* |
| 47–49 | | 1 Dec 2020 (SSI 2019/385) |
| 50 | | *Not yet in force* |
| 51–53 | | 1 Dec 2020 (SSI 2019/385) |
| 54–57 | | *Not yet in force* |
| 58–64 | | 26 Jul 2019 (s 63(1)) |
| Sch 1 | | *Not yet in force* |
| Sch 2 | paras 1–5 | *Not yet in force* |
| | para 6 | 1 Oct 2022 (SSI 2022/275)[5] |
| | paras 7, 8 | *Not yet in force* |
| | para 9 | 8 Nov 2019 (for the purpose of making regulations under Town and Country Planning (Scotland) Act 1997, s 3G(5)(b)) (SSI 2019/314) |
| | | 1 Dec 2019 (for the purpose of making regulations under Town and Country Planning (Scotland) Act 1997, ss 41B(4), 251B(2)) (SSI 2019/314) |
| | | 18 May 2020 (otherwise) (for the purpose of making regulations under Town and Country Planning (Scotland) Act 1997, s 26B(5)) (SSI 2020/67)[2] |

**Planning (Scotland) Act 2019 (asp 13)**—*contd*

*Not yet in force* (otherwise)

¹   For saving and transitional provisions, see SSI 2019/377, regs 4–11

²   For transitional provisions, see SSI 2020/67, reg 3

³   For transitional provisions and savings, see SSI 2020/294, reg 3

⁴   For transitional provisions, see SSI 2021/101, reg 4

⁵   For saving and transitional provisions, see SSI 2022/275, reg 3

---

**Pow of Inchaffray Drainage Commission (Scotland) Act 2019 (asp 2)**

*RA:* 17 Jan 2019

*Commencement provisions:* s 28

| | |
|---|---|
| 1 | 18 Jan 2019 (s 28(1)) |
| 2 | 18 Apr 2019 (s 28(2)) |
| 3–29 | 18 Jan 2019 (s 28(1)) |
| Schs 1–7 | 18 Jan 2019 (s 28(1)) |

---

**Public Services Ombudsman (Wales) Act 2019 (anaw 3)**

*RA:* 22 May 2019

*Commencement provisions:* s 77; Public Services Ombudsman (Wales) Act 2019 (Commencement) Regulations 2019, SI 2019/1096

| | |
|---|---|
| 1–76 | 23 Jul 2019 (SI 2019/1096) |
| 77–82 | 22 May 2019 (s 77(2)) |
| Schs 1–5 | 23 Jul 2019 (SI 2019/1096) |

---

**Renting Homes (Fees etc) (Wales) Act (anaw 2)**

*RA:* 15 May 2019

*Commencement provisions:* s 30; Renting Homes (Fees etc) (Wales) Act 2019 (Commencement No 1) Order 2019, SI 2019/1150

| | |
|---|---|
| 1–19 | 1 Sep 2019 (SI 2019/1150) |
| 20 | *Not yet in force* |
| 21–29 | 1 Sep 2019 (SI 2019/1150) |
| 30, 31 | 16 May 2019 (s 30(1)) |
| Schs 1, 2 | 1 Sep 2019 (SI 2019/1150) |
| Sch 3 | *Not yet in force* |

---

**Scottish Crown Estate Act 2019 (asp 1)**

*RA:* 15 Jan 2019

*Commencement provisions:* s 46; Scottish Crown Estate Act 2019 (Commencement No 1) Regulations 2019, SSI 2019/170; Scottish Crown Estate Act 2019 (Commencement No 2 and Saving Provisions) Regulations 2020, SSI 2020/77; Scottish Crown Estate Act 2019 (Commencement No 3) Regulations 2021, SSI 2021/308

| | | |
|---|---|---|
| 1 | | 1 Apr 2020 (SSI 2020/77)¹ |
| 2 | | 1 Jun 2019 (SSI 2019/170) |
| 3–6 | | 27 Sep 2021 (SSI 2021/308) |
| 7–14 | | 1 Apr 2020 (SSI 2020/77)¹ |
| 15 | | 1 Apr 2020 (SSI 2020/77)¹ |
| 16 | (1) | 1 Apr 2020 (SSI 2020/77)¹ |

**Scottish Crown Estate Act 2019 (asp 1)**—*contd*

| | | |
|---|---|---|
| | (2), (3) | 27 Sep 2021 (SSI 2021/308) |
| | (4) | 1 Apr 2020 (SSI 2020/77)[1] |
| 17–19 | | 1 Apr 2020 (SSI 2020/77)[1] |
| 20 | | 27 Sep 2021 (SSI 2021/308) |
| 21 | | 1 Apr 2020 (SSI 2020/77)[1] |
| 22, 23 | | 1 Jun 2019 (SSI 2019/170) |
| 24–26 | | 27 Sep 2021 (SSI 2021/308) |
| 27 | (1)–(3) | 1 Apr 2020 (SSI 2020/77)[1] |
| | (4), (5)(a) | 27 Sep 2021 (SSI 2021/308) |
| | (5)(b) | 1 Apr 2020 (SSI 2020/77)[1] |
| 28 | | 1 Apr 2020 (SSI 2020/77)[1] |
| 29 | (1)–(5) | 1 Apr 2020 (SSI 2020/77)[1] |
| | (6) | 27 Sep 2021 (SSI 2021/308) |
| 30 | (1)–(3) | 1 Apr 2020 (SSI 2020/77)[1] |
| | (4) | 27 Sep 2021 (SSI 2021/308) |
| | (5) | 1 Apr 2020 (SSI 2020/77)[1] |
| 31–33 | | 27 Sep 2021 (SSI 2021/308) |
| 34 | (1) | 1 Apr 2020 (SSI 2020/77)[1] |
| | (2) | 27 Sep 2021 (SSI 2021/308) |
| | (3), (4) | 1 Apr 2020 (SSI 2020/77)[1] |
| | (5) | 27 Sep 2021 (SSI 2021/308) |
| 35 | (1)(a) | 1 Apr 2020 (SSI 2020/77)[1] |
| | (1)(b) | 27 Sep 2021 (SSI 2021/308) |
| | (2) | 1 Apr 2020 (SSI 2020/77)[1] |
| 36 | | 27 Sep 2021 (SSI 2021/308) |
| 37, 38 | | 1 Jun 2019 (SSI 2019/170) |
| 39 | | 27 Sep 2021 (SSI 2021/308) |
| 40, 41 | | 1 Jun 2019 (SSI 2019/170) |
| 42, 43 | | 16 Jan 2019 (s 46(1)) |
| 44 | | *Not yet in force* |
| 45–47 | | 16 Jan 2019 (s 46(1)) |
| Schs 1, 2 | | 1 Apr 2020 (SSI 2020/77)[1] |

[1]    For savings, see SSI 2020/77, regs 3, 4

---

**South of Scotland Enterprise Act 2019 (asp 9)**

*RA:* 12 Jul 2019

*Commencement provisions:* s 24; South of Scotland Enterprise Act 2019 (Commencement and Transitional Provision) Regulations 2019, SSI 2019/308, as amended by SSI 2020/85

| | | |
|---|---|---|
| 1–7 | | 1 Apr 2020 (SSI 2019/308) |
| 8 | | 1 Apr 2020 (SSI 2019/308)[1] |
| 9–19 | | 1 Apr 2020 (SSI 2019/308) |
| 20 | (1) | 1 Jun 2020 (SSI 2019/308) |
| | (2) | 1 Apr 2020 (SSI 2019/308) |
| 21 | | 1 Apr 2020 (SSI 2019/308) |
| 22–25 | | 13 Jul 2019 (s 24(1)) |
| Schs 1, 2 | | 1 Apr 2020 (SSI 2019/308) |

[1]    For transitional provision, see SSI 2019/308, reg 4

---

**Stalking Protection Act 2019 (c 9)**

*RA:* 15 Mar 2019

*Commencement provisions:* s 15(2), (3); Stalking Protection Act 2019 (Commencement) Regulations 2020, SI 2020/26

**Stalking Protection Act 2019 (c 9)**—*contd*

| | | |
|---|---|---|
| 1–14 | | 20 Jan 2020 (SI 2020/26) |
| 15 | | 15 Mar 2019 (s 15(2)) |

**Supply and Appropriation (Anticipation and Adjustments) Act 2019 (c 6)**

*RA:* 15 Mar 2019

Whole Act in force 15 Mar 2019 (RA)

**Tenant Fees Act 2019 (c 4)**

*RA:* 12 Feb 2019

*Commencement provisions*: s 34; Tenant Fees Act 2019 (Commencement No 1) Regulations 2019, SI 2019/260; Tenant Fees Act 2019 (Commencement No 2) Regulations 2019, SI 2019/428; Tenant Fees Act 2019 (Commencement No 3) Regulations 2019, SI 2019/857

| | | |
|---|---|---|
| 1, 2 | | 1 Jun 2019 (SI 2019/857) |
| 3 | (1) | 1 Jun 2019 (SI 2019/857) |
| | (2)–(7) | 12 Feb 2019 (s 34(3)) |
| 4–8 | | 1 Jun 2019 (SI 2019/857) |
| 9 | | 12 Feb 2019 (s 34(3)) |
| 10–20 | | 1 Jun 2019 (SI 2019/857) |
| 21 | (1) | 1 Apr 2019 (SI 2019/428) |
| | (2) | 1 Jun 2019 (SI 2019/857) |
| | (3) | 1 Apr 2019 (SI 2019/428) |
| 22 | | 14 Feb 2019 (SI 2019/260) |
| 23 | | 1 Apr 2019 (SI 2019/428) |
| 24 | (1)–(3) | 15 Apr 2019 (SI 2019/857) |
| | (4), (5) | 12 Feb 2019 (s 34(3)) |
| | (6) | 15 Apr 2019 (SI 2019/857) |
| 25 | | 15 Apr 2019 (SI 2019/857) |
| 26 | | 15 Apr 2019 (so far as applies to the relevant letting agency legislation as defined in s 24(6) of the Act excluding para (a) of that definition) (SI 2019/857) |
| | | 1 Jun 2019 (otherwise) (SI 2019/857) |
| 27 | | 1 Jun 2019 (SI 2019/857) |
| 28 | (1) | 12 Feb 2019 (s 34(3)) |
| | (2) | 1 Jun 2019 (SI 2019/857) |
| 29 | | 15 Apr 2019 (SI 2019/857) |
| 30 | (1)–(11) | 1 Jun 2019 (SI 2019/857) |
| | (12) | 12 Feb 2019 (s 34(3)) |
| 31 | | 12 Feb 2019 (s 34(3)) |
| 32 | | 1 Jun 2019 (SI 2019/857) |
| 33–35 | | 12 Feb 2019 (s 34(3)) |
| Schs 1–3 | | 1 Jun 2019 (SI 2019/857) |

**Transport (Scotland) Act 2019 (asp 17)**

*RA:* 15 Nov 2019

*Commencement provisions*: s 130; Transport (Scotland) Act 2019 (Commencement No 1) Regulations 2019, SSI 2019/428; Transport (Scotland) Act 2019 (Commencement No 2) Regulations 2020, SSI 2020/69; Transport (Scotland) Act 2019 (Commencement No 3) Regulations 2020, SI 2020/429; Transport (Scotland) Act 2019 (Commencement No 4) Regulations 2021, SSI 2021/428; Transport (Scotland) Act 2019 (Commencement No. 5) Regulations 2022, SSI 2022/204

| | | |
|---|---|---|
| 1–5 | | 15 Jan 2020 (SSI 2019/428) |
| 6–24 | | 14 Jan 2021 (SSI 2020/429) |
| 25 | | 15 Jan 2020 (SSI 2019/428) |

## Transport (Scotland) Act 2019 (asp 17)—*contd*

| | | |
|---|---|---|
| 26–33 | | 14 Jan 2021 (SSI 2020/429) |
| 34 | | 24 Jun 2022 (SSI 2022/204) |
| 35–42 | | *Not yet in force* |
| 43 | | 10 Jan 2022 (SSI 2021/428) |
| 44–48 | | *Not yet in force* |
| 49 | | 14 Jan 2021 (SSI 2020/429) |
| 50 | | *Not yet in force* |
| 51 | | 10 Jan 2022 (SSI 2021/428) |
| 52 | | 14 Jan 2021 (SSI 2020/429) |
| 53 | | 14 Jan 2021 (SSI 2020/429) |
| 54–66 | | *Not yet in force* |
| 67, 68 | | 14 Jan 2021 (SSI 2020/429) |
| 69 | | *Not yet in force* |
| 70–89 | | 10 Jan 2022 (SSI 2021/428) |
| 90–108 | | *Not yet in force* |
| 109 | | 14 Jan 2021 (SSI 2020/429) |
| 110–112 | | *Not yet in force* |
| 113–115 | | 14 Jan 2021 (SSI 2020/429) |
| 116–121 | | *Not yet in force* |
| 122 | (1)(a) | 19 Mar 2020 (SSI 2020/68) |
| | (1)(b) | 1 Apr 2020 (SSI 2020/68) |
| | (2), (3) | 19 Mar 2020 (SSI 2020/68) |
| 123 | | 10 Jan 2022 (SSI 2021/428) |
| 124–126 | | *Not yet in force* |
| 127 | | 10 Jan 2022 (SSI 2021/428) |
| 128–131 | | 16 Nov 2019 (s 130(1)) |
| Schedule | paras 1, 2 | *Not yet in force* |
| | para 3(1) | See sub-paras (2)–(9) |
| | para 3(2)–(5) | *Not yet in force* |
| | para 3(6)(a)(i)–(iv) | *Not yet in force* |
| | para 3(6)(a)(v)(A) | 24 Jun 2022 (SSI 2022/204) |
| | para 3(6)(a)(v)(B) | *Not yet in force* |
| | para 3(6)(a)(vi)–(viii) | *Not yet in force* |
| | (b), (7)–(9) | |
| | para 4 | *Not yet in force* |
| | para 5 | 10 Jan 2022 (SSI 2021/428) |
| | para 6(1) | See sub-paras (2)–(10) below |
| | para 6(2) | 10 Jan 2022 (SSI 2021/428) |
| | para 6(3)–(5) | *Not yet in force* |
| | para 6(6)–(8) | 10 Jan 2022 (SSI 2021/428) |
| | para 6(9), (10) | *Not yet in force* |
| | para 7(1) | See sub-paras (2)–(4) below |
| | para 7(2) | *Not yet in force* |
| | para 7(3) | 10 Jan 2022 (SSI 2021/428) |
| | para 7(4) | *Not yet in force* |

## Voyeurism (Offences) Act 2019 (c 2)

*RA:* 12 Feb 2019

*Commencement provisions*: s 2(2)

Whole Act in force 12 Apr 2019 (s 2(2))

## Vulnerable Witnesses (Criminal Evidence) (Scotland) Act 2019 (asp 8)

*RA:* 13 Jun 2019

*Commencement provisions*: s 12; Vulnerable Witnesses (Criminal Evidence) (Scotland) Act 2019 (Commencement No 1 and Transitional Provisions) Regulations 2019, SSI 2019/392

**Vulnerable Witnesses (Criminal Evidence) (Scotland) Act 2019 (asp 8)**—*contd*

| | | |
|---|---|---|
| 1 | | 20 Jan 2020 (for the purpose of hearings in proceedings in High Court of Judiciary) (SSI 2019/392)[1] |
| | | *Not yet in force* (otherwise) |
| 2 | | 20 Jan 2020 (SSI 2019/392) |
| 3 | | *Not yet in force* |
| 4 | | 20 Jan 2020 (for the purpose of hearings in proceedings in High Court of Judiciary) (SSI 2019/392) |
| | | *Not yet in force* (otherwise) |
| 5 | | 20 Jan 2020 (SSI 2019/392)[1] |
| 6 | | *Not yet in force* |
| 7–9 | | 20 Jan 2020 (SSI 2019/392) |
| 10 | (1)–(3) | 20 Jan 2020 (SSI 2019/392) |
| | (4) | *Not yet in force* |
| 11–13 | | 14 Jun 2019 (s 12(1)) |

[1]   For transitional provisions, see SSI 2019/392, regs 3, 4

---

**Wild Animals in Circuses Act 2019 (c 24)**

*RA:* 24 Jul 2019

*Commencement provisions*: s 4(2)

Whole Act in force 20 Jan 2019 (s 4(2))

---

# 2020 Acts

## Agriculture Act 2020 (c 21)

*RA:* 11 Nov 2020

*Commencement provisions*: s 57; Agriculture Act 2020 (Commencement No 1) (Wales) Regulations 2020,
SI 2020/1648; Agriculture Act 2020 (Commencement No 1) Regulations 2020, SI 2020/1650;
Agriculture Act 2020 (Commencement No 1 and Transitional Provision) (England) Regulations 2021,
SI 2021/597; Agriculture (2020 Act) (Commencement No 1) Regulations (Northern Ireland) 2022,
SR 2022/147

| | |
|---|---|
| 1–16 | 11 Nov 2020 (so far as confers a power to make regulations or modifies legislation so as to confer a power to make regulations or a power to make an order by statutory instrument, or so far as they, or a modification of legislation they make, affects the exercise of such a power) (s 57(1)(b), (c)) |
| | 11 Jan 2020 (otherwise) (s 57(6)) |
| 17, 18 | 11 Nov 2020 (s 57(1)(a)) |
| 19 | 11 Nov 2020 (so far as confers a power to make regulations or modifies legislation so as to confer a power to make regulations or a power to make an order by statutory instrument, or so far as they, or a modification of legislation they make, affects the exercise of such a power) (s 57(1)(b), (c)) |
| | 11 Jan 2020 (otherwise) (s 57(6)) |
| 20, 21 | 11 Nov 2020 (so far as confers a power to make regulations or modifies legislation so as to confer a power to make regulations or a power to make an order by statutory instrument, or so far as they, or a modification of legislation they make, affects the exercise of such a power) (s 57(1)(b), (c)) |
| | 1 Jan 2021 (otherwise) (SI 2020/1650) |
| 22–29 | 11 Nov 2020 (so far as confers a power to make regulations or modifies legislation so as to confer a power to make regulations or a power to make an order by statutory instrument, or so far as they, or a modification of legislation they make, affects the exercise of such a power) (s 57(1)(b), (c)) |
| | 11 Jan 2020 (otherwise) (s 57(6)) |
| 30, 31 | 11 Nov 2020 (so far as confers a power to make regulations or modifies legislation so as to confer a power to make regulations or a power to make an order by statutory instrument, or so far as they, or a modification of legislation they make, affects the exercise of such a power) (s 57(1)(b), (c)) |
| | *Not yet in force* (otherwise) |
| 32, 33 | 11 Nov 2020 (so far as confers a power to make regulations or modifies legislation so as to confer a power to make regulations or a power to make an order by statutory instrument, or so far as they, or a modification of legislation they make, affects the exercise of such a power) (s 57(1)(b), (c)) |
| | 11 Jan 2020 (otherwise) (s 57(6)) |

Agriculture Act 2020 (c 21)—*contd*

| | | |
|---|---|---|
| 34 | (1), (2) | 11 Nov 2020 (so far as confers a power to make regulations or modifies legislation so as to confer a power to make regulations or a power to make an order by statutory instrument, or so far as they, or a modification of legislation they make, affects the exercise of such a power) (s 57(1)(b), (c)) |
| | | 11 Jan 2020 (otherwise) (s 57(6)) |
| | (3), (4) | 11 Nov 2020 (so far as confers a power to make regulations or modifies legislation so as to confer a power to make regulations or a power to make an order by statutory instrument, or so far as they, or a modification of legislation they make, affects the exercise of such a power) (s 57(1)(b), (c)) |
| | | *Not yet in force* (otherwise) |
| 35 | | 11 Nov 2020 (so far as confers a power to make regulations or modifies legislation so as to confer a power to make regulations or a power to make an order by statutory instrument, or so far as they, or a modification of legislation they make, affects the exercise of such a power) (s 57(1)(b), (c)) |
| | | 11 Jan 2020 (otherwise) (s 57(6)) |
| 36 | | See Sch 3 below |
| 37–45 | | 11 Nov 2020 (so far as confers a power to make regulations or modifies legislation so as to confer a power to make regulations or a power to make an order by statutory instrument, or so far as they, or a modification of legislation they make, affects the exercise of such a power) (s 57(1)(b), (c)) |
| | | 11 Jan 2020 (otherwise) (s 57(6)) |
| 46 | | See Sch 5 below |
| 47, 48 | | 11 Nov 2020 (so far as confers a power to make regulations or modifies legislation so as to confer a power to make regulations or a power to make an order by statutory instrument, or so far as they, or a modification of legislation they make, affects the exercise of such a power) (s 57(1)(b), (c)) |
| | | 11 Jan 2020 (otherwise) (s 57(6)) |
| 49–51 | | 11 Nov 2020 (s 57(1)(d)) |
| 52 | | See Sch 7 below |
| 53–58 | | 11 Nov 2020 (s 57(1)(d)) |
| Schs 1, 2 | | 11 Nov 2020 (so far as confers a power to make regulations or modifies legislation so as to confer a power to make regulations or a power to make an order by statutory instrument, or so far as they, or a modification of legislation they make, affects the exercise of such a power) (s 57(1)(b), (c)) |
| | | *Not yet in force* (otherwise) |
| Sch 3 | 1–9 | 11 Nov 2020 (so far as confers a power to make regulations or modifies legislation so as to confer a power to make regulations or a power to make an order by statutory instrument, or so far as they, or a modification of legislation they make, affects the exercise of such a power) (s 57(1)(b), (c)) |
| | | 11 Jan 2020 (otherwise) (s 57(6)) |
| | para 10–16 | 11 Nov 2020 (so far as confers a power to make regulations or modifies legislation so as to confer a power to make regulations or a power to make an order by statutory instrument, or so far as they, or a modification of legislation they make, affects the exercise of such a power) (s 57(1)(b), (c)) |
| | | 1 Sep 2024 (otherwise) (SI 2021/597)[1] |
| | para 17 | 11 Nov 2020 (so far as confers a power to make regulations or modifies legislation so as to confer a power to make regulations or a power to make an order by statutory instrument, or so far as they, or a modification of legislation they make, affects the exercise of such a power) (s 57(1)(b), (c)) |
| | | 11 Jan 2020 (otherwise) (s 57(6)) |

**Agriculture Act 2020 (c 21)**—*contd*

| | | |
|---|---|---|
| | para 18 | 11 Nov 2020 (so far as confers a power to make regulations or modifies legislation so as to confer a power to make regulations or a power to make an order by statutory instrument, or so far as they, or a modification of legislation they make, affects the exercise of such a power) (s 57(1)(b), (c)) |
| | | 1 Sep 2024 (otherwise) (SI 2021/597)[1] |
| | para 19–29 | 11 Nov 2020 (so far as confers a power to make regulations or modifies legislation so as to confer a power to make regulations or a power to make an order by statutory instrument, or so far as they, or a modification of legislation they make, affects the exercise of such a power) (s 57(1)(b), (c)) |
| | | 11 Jan 2020 (otherwise) (s 57(6)) |
| Sch 4 | | 11 Nov 2020 (so far as confers a power to make regulations or modifies legislation so as to confer a power to make regulations or a power to make an order by statutory instrument, or so far as they, or a modification of legislation they make, affects the exercise of such a power) (s 57(1)(b), (c)) |
| | | 11 Jan 2020 (otherwise) (s 57(6)) |
| Sch 5 | paras 1–6 | 11 Nov 2020 (so far as confers a power to make regulations or modifies legislation so as to confer a power to make regulations or a power to make an order by statutory instrument, or so far as they, or a modification of legislation they make, affects the exercise of such a power) (s 57(1)(b), (c)) |
| | | 11 Jan 2020 (otherwise) (s 57(6)) |
| | paras 7, 8 | 11 Nov 2020 (so far as confers a power to make regulations or modifies legislation so as to confer a power to make regulations or a power to make an order by statutory instrument, or so far as they, or a modification of legislation they make, affects the exercise of such a power) (s 57(1)(b), (c)) |
| | | 1 Jan 2021 (otherwise) (SI 2020/1648) |
| | para 9 | 11 Nov 2020 (so far as confers a power to make regulations or modifies legislation so as to confer a power to make regulations or a power to make an order by statutory instrument, or so far as they, or a modification of legislation they make, affects the exercise of such a power) (s 57(1)(b), (c)) |
| | | *Not yet in force* (otherwise) |
| | paras 10–19 | 11 Nov 2020 (so far as confers a power to make regulations or modifies legislation so as to confer a power to make regulations or a power to make an order by statutory instrument, or so far as they, or a modification of legislation they make, affects the exercise of such a power) (s 57(1)(b), (c)) |
| | | 11 Jan 2020 (otherwise) (s 57(6)) |
| Sch 6 | paras 1–7 | 11 Nov 2020 (so far as confers a power to make regulations or modifies legislation so as to confer a power to make regulations or a power to make an order by statutory instrument, or so far as they, or a modification of legislation they make, affects the exercise of such a power) (s 57(1)(b), (c)) |
| | | 11 Jan 2020 (otherwise) (s 57(6)) |
| | para 8 | 11 Nov 2020 (so far as confers a power to make regulations or modifies legislation so as to confer a power to make regulations or a power to make an order by statutory instrument, or so far as they, or a modification of legislation they make, affects the exercise of such a power) (s 57(1)(b), (c)) |
| | | 28 Mar 2022 (otherwise) (SR 2022/147) |
| | para 9 | 11 Nov 2020 (so far as confers a power to make regulations or modifies legislation so as to confer a power to make regulations or a power to make an order by statutory instrument, or so far as they, or a modification of legislation they make, affects the exercise of such a power) (s 57(1)(b), (c)) |
| | | *Not yet in force* (otherwise) |

**See Halsbury's Statutes Citator for amendments to these Acts**

**Agriculture Act 2020 (c 21)**—*contd*

| | | |
|---|---|---|
| | paras 10–19 | 11 Nov 2020 (so far as confers a power to make regulations or modifies legislation so as to confer a power to make regulations or a power to make an order by statutory instrument, or so far as they, or a modification of legislation they make, affects the exercise of such a power) (s 57(1)(b), (c)) |
| | | 11 Jan 2020 (otherwise) (s 57(6)) |
| Sch 7 | | 11 Nov 2020 (so far as confers a power to make regulations or modifies legislation so as to confer a power to make regulations or a power to make an order by statutory instrument, or so far as they, or a modification of legislation they make, affects the exercise of such a power) (s 57(1)(b), (c)) |
| | | *Not yet in force* (otherwise) |

[1]   For transitional provisions, see SI 2021/597, reg 3

---

**Agriculture (Retained EU Law and Data) (Scotland) Act 2020 (asp 17)**

*RA:* 1 Oct 2020

*Commencement provisions*: s 26; Agriculture (Retained EU Law and Data) (Scotland) Act 2020 (Commencement No 1) Regulations 2020, SSI 2020/315; Agriculture (Retained EU Law and Data) (Scotland) Act 2020 (Commencement No 2) Regulations 2020, SSI 2020/373

| | |
|---|---|
| 1–4 | 5 Nov 2020 (SSI 2020/315) |
| 5 | 2 Oct 2020 (s 26(1)) |
| 6–12 | 1 Jan 2021 (SSI 2020/373) |
| 13–20 | 1 Dec 2020 (SSI 2020/373) |
| 21–27 | 2 Oct 2020 (s 26(1)) |
| Schedule | 1 Jan 2021 (SSI 2020/373) |

---

**Animals and Wildlife (Penalties, Protections and Powers) (Scotland) Act 2020 (asp 14)**

*RA:* 21 Jul 2020

*Commencement provisions*: s 22; Animals and Wildlife (Penalties, Protections and Powers) (Scotland) Act 2020 (Commencement No 1 and Transitional Provision) Regulations 2020, SSI 2020/379; Animals and Wildlife (Penalties, Protections and Powers) (Scotland) Act 2020 (Commencement No 2) Regulations 2021, SSI 2021/42; Animals and Wildlife (Penalties, Protections and Powers) (Scotland) Act 2020 (Commencement No 3 and Transitional Provision) Regulations 2021, SSI 2021/303

| | | |
|---|---|---|
| 1 | | 30 Nov 2020 (SSI 2020/379)[1] |
| 2, 3 | | 30 Nov 2020 (SSI 2020/379) |
| 4, 5 | | 30 Sep 2021 (SSI 2021/303) |
| 6 | | 30 Nov 2020 (SSI 2020/379) |
| 7–12 | | 30 Nov 2020 (SSI 2020/379)[1] |
| 13 | | 30 Nov 2020 (SSI 2020/379) |
| 14 | (1) | 30 Nov 2020 (SSI 2020/379) |
| | (2)–(6) | 1 Feb 2021 (SSI 2020/379) |
| | (7) | 30 Nov 2020 (SSI 2020/379)[1] |
| 15, 16 | | 30 Nov 2020 (SSI 2020/379) |
| 17 | | 22 Jul 2020 (s 22(1)) |
| 18 | | 1 Mar 2021 (SSI 2021/42) |
| 19, 20 | | 30 Sep 2021 (SSI 2021/303) |
| 21 | | 30 Sep 2021 (SSI 2021/303)[2] |
| 22, 23 | | 22 Jul 2020 (s 22(1)) |

[1]   For transitional provisions, see SSI 2020/379, reg 3

[2]   For transitional provisions, see SSI 2021/303, reg 3

---

## Birmingham Commonwealth Games Act 2020 (c 10)

*RA:* 25 Jun 2020

*Commencement provisions*: s 33

| | |
|---|---|
| 1, 2 | 25 Jun 2020 (s 33(1)(a)) |
| 3–7 | 25 Aug 2020 (s 33(2)) |
| 8 | 25 Jun 2020 (s 33(1)(b)) |
| 9–12 | 25 Aug 2020 (s 33(2)) |
| 13 | 25 Jun 2020 (in so far as confers power to make regulations) (s 33(1)(d)) |
| | 25 Aug 2020 (otherwise) (s 33(2)) |
| 14 | 25 Aug 2020 (s 33(2)) |
| 15, 16 | 25 Jun 2020 (in so far as confers power to make regulations) (s 33(1)(d)) |
| | 25 Aug 2020 (otherwise) (s 33(2)) |
| 17, 18 | 25 Aug 2020 (s 33(2)) |
| 19 | 25 Jun 2020 (in so far as confers power to make regulations) (s 33(1)(d)) |
| | 25 Aug 2020 (otherwise) (s 33(2)) |
| 20–26 | 25 Aug 2020 (s 33(2)) |
| 27 | 25 Jun 2020 (in so far as confers power to make regulations) (s 33(1)(d)) |
| | 25 Aug 2020 (otherwise) (s 33(2)) |
| 28, 29 | 25 Aug 2020 (s 33(2)) |
| 30–34 | 25 Jun 2020 (s 33(1)(c)) |
| Schs 1–3 | 25 Aug 2020 (s 33(2)) |

## Budget (Scotland) Act 2020 (asp 5)

*RA:* 18 Mar 2020

*Commencement provisions*: s 10

Whole Act in force 18 Mar 2020 (s 10)

## Business and Planning Act 2020 (c 16)

*RA:* 22 Jul 2020

*Commencement provisions*: s 25

| | |
|---|---|
| 1–11 | 22 Jul 2020 (s 25(1)) |
| 12 | 4 May 2020 (s 25(2)(a)) |
| 13–15 | 22 Jul 2020 (s 25(1)) |
| 16 | 28 Jul 2020 (s 25(3)(a)) |
| 17–19 | 19 Aug 2020 (s 25(3)(b)) |
| 20–22 | 22 Jul 2020 (s 25(3)(c)) |
| 23–27 | 22 Jul 2020 (s 25(4)) |

## Channel Islands Measure 2020 (No 2)

*RA:* 22 Jul 2020

*Commencement provisions*: s 5(1)–(3)

| | |
|---|---|
| 1 | 22 Jul 2020 (s 5(1)) |
| 2 | *Not yet in force* |
| 3 | 22 Jul 2020 (s 5(1)) |
| 4 | *Not yet in force* |
| 5 | 22 Jul 2020 (s 5(1)) |

**Children (Abolition of Defence of Reasonable Punishment) (Wales) Act 2020 (anaw 3)**

*RA:* 20 Mar 2020

*Commencement provisions:* s 5

| | | |
|---|---|---|
| 1 | | 21 Mar 2022 (s 5(2)) |
| 2–6 | | 21 Mar 2020 (s 5(1)) |

**Children (Scotland) Act 2020 (asp 16)**

*RA:* 1 Oct 2020

*Commencement provisions:* s 34; Children (Scotland) Act 2020 (Commencement No 1 and Saving Provisions) Regulations 2020, SSI 2020/412; Children (Scotland) Act 2020 (Commencement No 2) Regulations 2021, SSI 2021/339

| | | |
|---|---|---|
| 1–6 | | *Not yet in force* |
| 7 | (1), (2) | *Not yet in force* |
| | (3), (4) | 25 Oct 2021 (SSI 2021/339) |
| 8 | | *Not yet in force* |
| 9 | | 25 Oct 2021 (SSI 2021/339) |
| 10 | (1) | See sub-ss (2), (3) below |
| | (2) | *Not yet in force* |
| | (3) | 25 Oct 2021 (SSI 2021/339) |
| 11, 12 | | *Not yet in force* |
| 13, 14 | | 26 Jul 2021 (SSI 2020/412) |
| 15 | | 17 Jan 2021 (SSI 2020/412)[1] |
| 16 | | *Not yet in force* |
| 17 | (1) | See sub-ss (2), (3) below |
| | (2) | *Not yet in force* |
| | (3) | 25 Oct 2021 (SSI 2021/339) |
| 18–22 | | *Not yet in force* |
| 23, 24 | | 17 Jan 2021 (SSI 2020/412) |
| 25, 26 | | 26 Jul 2021 (SSI 2020/412) |
| 27–31 | | *Not yet in force* |
| 32–35 | | 2 Oct 2020 (s 34(1)) |

[1]   For a saving, see SSI 2020/412, reg 3

**Church of England (Miscellaneous Provisions) Measure 2020 (No 1)**

*RA:* 16 Mar 2020

*Commencement provisions:* s 16(2)–(5); Church of England (Miscellaneous Provisions) Measure 2020 Commencement (No. 1) Order 2020, SI 2020/835; Church of England (Miscellaneous Provisions) Measure 2020 (Commencement No 2) Order 2021, SI 2021/545

| | | |
|---|---|---|
| 1 | (1)–(3) | 1 Sep 2020 (SI 2020/835) |
| | (4), (5) | 14 Jul 2021 (SI 2021/545) |
| 2–7 | | 1 Sep 2020 (SI 2020/835) |
| 8 | | *Not yet in force* |
| 9–11 | | 1 Sep 2020 (SI 2020/835) |
| 12–16 | | 16 Mar 2020 (s 16(2)) |
| Schedule | | 1 Sep 2020 (SI 2020/835) |

## Civil Partnership (Scotland) Act 2020 (asp 15)

*RA:* 28 Jul 2020

*Commencement provisions*: s 16; Civil Partnership (Scotland) Act 2020 (Commencement No 1 and Interim Recognition of Different Sex Relationships) Regulations 2020, SSI 2020/414; Civil Partnership (Scotland) Act 2020 (Commencement No 2) Regulations 2020, SSI 2020/457; Civil Partnership (Scotland) Act 2020 (Commencement No 3, Saving and Transitional Provision) Regulations 2021, SSI 2021/23; Civil Partnership (Scotland) Act 2020 (Commencement No 4, Saving and Transitional Provision) Regulations 2021, SSI 2021/351

| | | |
|---|---|---|
| 1 | | 1 Feb 2021 (for the purposes of s 3 of this Act and the Civil Partnership Act 2004, s 1(3)(a), Pt 3, Chapter 5, Pt 5, Chapter 3) (SSI 2020/414) |
| | | 1 Jun 2021 (otherwise) (SSI 2021/23)[1] |
| 2 | (1) | See sub-ss (2)–(6) below |
| | (2), (3)(a)–(e) | 1 Feb 2021 (for the purposes of s 3 of this Act and the Civil Partnership Act 2004, s 1(3)(a), Pt 3, Chapter 5, Pt 5, Chapter 3) (SSI 2020/414) |
| | | 1 Jun 2021 (otherwise) (SSI 2021/23)[1] |
| | (3)(f) | 1 Feb 2021 (for the purposes of s 3 of this Act and the Civil Partnership Act 2004, s 1(3)(a), Pt 3, Chapter 5, Pt 5, Chapter 3) (SSI 2020/414) |
| | (3)(f) | 18 Jan 2021 (for the purpose of making regulations under Civil Partnership Act 2004, ss 213(7), 215(3B)) (SSI 2020/457) |
| | | 1 Jun 2021 (otherwise) (SSI 2021/23)[1] |
| | (4)(a) | 1 Feb 2021 (for the purposes of s 3 of this Act and the Civil Partnership Act 2004, s 1(3)(a), Pt 3, Chapter 5, Pt 5, Chapter 3) (SSI 2020/414) |
| | | 1 Jun 2021 (otherwise) (SSI 2021/23)[1] |
| | (4)(b) | 18 Jan 2021 (for the purpose of making regulations under Civil Partnership Act 2004, ss 213(7), 215(3B)) (SSI 2020/457) |
| | | 1 Feb 2021 (for the purposes of s 3 of this Act and the Civil Partnership Act 2004, s 1(3)(a), Pt 3, Chapter 5, Pt 5, Chapter 3) (SSI 2020/414) |
| | | 1 Jun 2021 (otherwise) (SSI 2021/23)[1] |
| | (4)(c), (5), (6) | 1 Feb 2021 (for the purposes of s 3 of this Act and the Civil Partnership Act 2004, s 1(3)(a), Pt 3, Chapter 5, Pt 5, Chapter 3) (SSI 2020/414) |
| | | 1 Jun 2021 (otherwise) (SSI 2021/23)[1] |
| 3 | | 1 Feb 2021 (SSI 2020/414) |
| 4–6 | | 1 Jun 2021 (SSI 2021/23)[1] |
| 7 | (1) | See sub-s (2) below |
| | (2)(a) | 1 Jun 2021 (SSI 2021/23)[1] |
| | (2)(b) | 18 Jan 2021 (for the purpose of making regulations under Civil Partnership Act 2004, s 94A(2A)(a)(i)) (SSI 2020/457) |
| | | 1 Jun 2021 (for the purpose of inserting and bringing into force for all remaining purposes Civil Partnership Act 2004, s 94A(2A), (2B)(a)) (SSI 2021/23) |
| | | *Not yet in force* (otherwise) |
| | (2)(c)–(d) | 1 Jun 2021 (SSI 2021/23)[1] |
| | (2)(e) | *Not yet in force* |
| | (2)(f) | 18 Jan 2021 (for the purpose of making regulations under Civil Partnership Act 2004, s 94A(2A)(a)(i)) (SSI 2020/457) |
| | | 1 Jun 2021 (otherwise) (SSI 2021/23)[1] |
| 8, 9 | | 1 Jun 2021 (SSI 2021/23)[1] |
| 10 | | 30 Nov 2021 (SSI 2021/351)[2] |
| 11 | | 1 Feb 2021 (for the purpose of enabling the Scottish Ministers to make regulations under Civil Partnership Act 2004, s 121A(7)) (SSI 2020/414) |
| | | 1 Jun 2021 (otherwise) (SSI 2021/23)[1] |
| 12 | | 1 Jun 2021 (SSI 2021/23)[1] |
| 13 | | *Not yet in force* |

**Civil Partnership (Scotland) Act 2020 (asp 15)**—*contd*

| | | |
|---|---|---|
| 14 | | See Sch 2 below |
| 15–17 | | 29 Jul 2020 (s 16(1))) |
| Sch 1 | | 1 Feb 2021 (for the purposes of s 3 of this Act and the Civil Partnership Act 2004, s 1(3)(a), Pt 3, Chapter 5, Pt 5, Chapter 3) (SSI 2020/414) |
| | | 1 Jun 2021 (otherwise) (SSI 2021/23)[1] |
| Sch 2 | paras 1–4 | 1 Jun 2021 (SSI 2021/23)[1] |
| | para 5(1) | 18 Jan 2021 (for the purpose of modifying the power to make regulations under Civil Partnership Act 2004, Sch 3, para 20A(1)) (SSI 2020/457) |
| | | 30 Nov 2021 (otherwise) (SSI 2021/351)[2] |
| | para 5(2)–(19)(a) | 1 Jun 2021 (SSI 2021/23)[1] |
| | para 5(19)(b) | 18 Jan 2021 (for the purpose of modifying the power to make regulations under Civil Partnership Act 2004, Sch 3, para 20A(1)) (SSI 2020/457) |
| | | 30 Nov 2021 (otherwise) (SSI 2021/351)[2] |
| | para 6(1) | See sub-paras (2)–(5) below |
| | para 6(2) | 30 Nov 2021 (SSI 2021/351)[2] |
| | para 6(3)–(5) | 1 Jun 2021 (SSI 2021/23)[1] |
| | para 7 | 30 Nov 2021 (SSI 2021/351)[2] |

[1]    For transitional provisions and savings, see SSI 2021/23, regs 2–4

[2]    For transitional provisions and savings, see SSI 2021/351, regs 3

**Consumer Scotland Act 2020 (asp 11)**

*RA:* 9 Jun 2020

*Commencement provisions*: s 29; Consumer Scotland Act 2020 (Commencement) Regulations 2021, SSI 2021/464

| | |
|---|---|
| 1–24 | 1 Apr 2022 (SSI 2021/464) |
| 25–27 | 10 Jun 2020 (s 29(1)) |
| 28 | 1 Apr 2022 (SSI 2021/464) |
| 29, 30 | 10 Jun 2020 (s 29(1)) |
| Schs 1, 2 | 1 Apr 2022 (SSI 2021/464) |

**Contingencies Fund Act 2020 (c 6)**

*RA:* 25 Mar 2020

Whole Act in force 25 Mar 2020 (RA)

**Coronavirus Act 2020 (c 7)**

*RA:* 25 Mar 2020

*Commencement provisions*: s 87; Coronavirus Act 2020 (Commencement No 1) Regulations 2020, SI 2020/361; Coronavirus Act 2020 (Commencement No 1) (Wales) Regulations 2020, SI 2020/366; Coronavirus Act 2020 (Commencement No 2) Regulations 2020, SI 2020/388; Coronavirus Act 2020 (Commencement No 1) Order (Northern Ireland) 2020, SR 2020/58; Coronavirus Act 2020 (Commencement No 1) (Scotland) Regulations 2020, SSI 2020/121

| | | |
|---|---|---|
| 1–7 | | 25 Mar 2020 (s 87(1)) |
| 8, 9 | | *Not yet in force* |
| 10 | (1) | See Sch 8 below |
| | (2) | See Sch 9 below |
| | (3) | See Sch 10 below |
| | (4) | See Sch 11 below |

**Coronavirus Act 2020 (c 7)**—*contd*

| | | |
|---|---|---|
| 11–14 | | 25 Mar 2020 (s 87(1)) |
| 15 | | See Sch 12 below |
| 16, 17 | | 5 Apr 2020 (SSI 2020/121) |
| 18, 19 | | 26 Mar 2020 (SI 2020/361) |
| 20 | | 25 Mar 2020 (s 87(1)) |
| 21 | | 26 Mar 2020 (SI 2020/361) |
| 22–24 | | 25 Mar 2020 (s 87(1)) |
| 25–29 | | *Not yet in force* |
| 30–102 | | 25 Mar 2020 (s 87(1)) |
| Schs 1–6 | | 25 Mar 2020 (s 87(1)) |
| Sch 7 | | *Not yet in force* |
| Sch 8 | paras 1, 2 | 27 Mar 2020 (W) (SI 2020/366) |
| | | *Not yet in force* (E) |
| | paras 3–10 | *Not yet in force* |
| | paras 11–13 | 27 Mar 2020 (SI 2020/366) |
| | paras 14–19 | *Not yet in force* |
| Sch 9 | | *Not yet in force* |
| Sch 10 | | 2 Apr 2020 (SR 2020/58) |
| Sch 11 | paras 1–10 | 2 Apr 2020 (SR 2020/58) |
| | paras 11–18 | *Not yet in force* |
| | para 19 | 2 Apr 2020 (SR 2020/58) |
| | para 20 | 2 Apr 2020 (insofar as it refers to paras 5 and 9) (SR 2020/58) |
| | | *Not yet in force* (otherwise) |
| | para 21 | *Not yet in force* |
| | para 22 | 2 Apr 2020 (SR 2020/58) |
| Sch 12 | paras 1–18 | 31 Mar 2020 (SI 2020/388) |
| | paras 19–35 | 1 Apr 2020 (SI 2020/366) |
| Sch 13 | | 26 Mar 2020 (SI 2020/361) |
| Sch 14 | | 25 Mar 2020 (s 87(1)) |
| Sch 15 | | *Not yet in force* |
| Schs 16–29 | | 25 Mar 2020 (s 87(1)) |

**Coronavirus (Scotland) Act 2020 (asp 7)**

*RA:* 6 Apr 2020

*Commencement provisions:* s 17

| | | |
|---|---|---|
| 1–3 | | 7 Apr 2020 (s 17(1)) |
| 4 | | See Sch 3 below |
| 5–18 | | 7 Apr 2020 (s 17(1)) |
| Schs 1, 2 | | 7 Apr 2020 (s 17(1)) |
| Sch 3 | paras 1–10 | 7 Apr 2020 (s 17(1)) |
| | para 11(1) | *Not yet in force* |
| | para 11(2), (3) | 7 Apr 2020 (s 17(1)) |
| Schs 4–7 | | 7 Apr 2020 (s 17(1)) |

**Coronavirus (Scotland) (No 2) Act 2020 (asp 10)**

*RA:* 26 May 2020

*Commencement provisions:* s 16(1)

Whole Act in force 27 May 2020 (s 16)

## Corporate Insolvency and Governance Act 2020 (c 12)

*RA*: 25 Jun 2020

*Commencement provisions*: s 49

| | | |
|---|---|---|
| 1–50 | | 26 Jun 2020 (s 49(1)) |
| Schs 1, 2 | | 26 Jun 2020 (s 49(1)) |
| Sch 3 | paras 1–50 | 26 Jun 2020 (s 49(1)) |
| | para 51 | *Not yet in force* |
| | paras 52–55 | 26 Jun 2020 (s 49(1)) |
| Schs 4–14 | | 26 Jun 2020 (s 49(1)) |

## Direct Payments to Farmers (Legislative Continuity) Act 2020 (c 2)

*RA*: 30 Jan 2020

*Commencement provisions*: s 9(2), (3)

| | |
|---|---|
| 1–4 | 30 Jan 2020 (s 9(1)) |
| 5 | In force as from exit day (as defined by European Union (Withdrawal) Act 2018, s 20(1)–(5)) (s 9(2)) |
| 6–9 | 30 Jan 2020 (s 9(1)) |
| Schs 1, 2 | 30 Jan 2020 (s 9(1)) |

## Disclosure (Scotland) Act 2020 (asp 13)

*RA*: 14 Jul 2020

*Commencement provisions*: s 97; Disclosure (Scotland) Act 2020 (Commencement No 1 and Transitory Provision) Regulations 2021, SSI 2021/380

| | | |
|---|---|---|
| 1–62 | | *Not yet in force* |
| 63 | | 10 Dec 2021 (only insofar as necessary to enable the Scottish Ministers to consult the chief constable in accordance with sub-s (4)) (SSI 2021/380) |
| | | *Not yet in force* (otherwise) |
| 64–68 | | *Not yet in force* |
| 69 | | 10 Dec 2021 (only insofar as necessary to bring into force the definitions of "chief constable" and "police force") (SSI 2021/380) |
| | | *Not yet in force* (otherwise) |
| 70–77 | | *Not yet in force* |
| 78 | | 10 Dec 2021 (SSI 2021/380)[1] |
| 79–82 | | *Not yet in force* |
| 83–85 | | 10 Dec 2021 (SSI 2021/380)[1] |
| 86 | | *Not yet in force* |
| 87 | | 10 Dec 2021 (SSI 2021/380) |
| 88 | (1), (2) | 10 Dec 2021 (SSI 2021/380) |
| | (3) | *Not yet in force* |
| 89 | | 10 Dec 2021 (only insofar as necessary to enable the Scottish Ministers to consult the chief constable in accordance with Protection of Vulnerable Groups (Scotland) Act 2007, s 84A(3)) (SSI 2021/380) |
| | | *Not yet in force* (otherwise) |
| 90 | | 10 Dec 2021 (SSI 2021/380) |
| 91, 92 | | 15 Jul 2020 (s 97(1)) |
| 93 | | See Sch 5 below |
| 94–98 | | 15 Jul 2020 (s 97(1)) |
| Schs 1–4 | | *Not yet in force* |
| Sch 5 | paras 1–11 | *Not yet in force* |
| | para 12 | 10 Dec 2021 (SSI 2021/380) |

## Disclosure (Scotland) Act 2020 (asp 13)—*contd*

| | | |
|---|---|---|
| para 13 | | *Not yet in force* |

[1] For transitory provisions see SSI 2021/380, regs 3, 4

## Divorce, Dissolution and Separation Act 2020 (c 11)

*RA:* 25 Jun 2020

*Commencement provisions*: 8(1)–(3); Divorce, Dissolution and Separation Act 2020 (Commencement) Regulations 2022, SI 2022/283

| | | |
|---|---|---|
| 1 | | 25 Jun 2020 (in so far as confers power to make provision by Family Procedure Rules) (s 8(3)(a)) |
| | | 6 Apr 2022 (otherwise) (SI 2022/283) |
| 2 | | 6 Apr 2022 (SI 2022/283) |
| 3 | | 25 Jun 2020 (in so far as confers power to make provision by Family Procedure Rules) (s 8(3)(b)) |
| | | 6 Apr 2022 (otherwise) (SI 2022/283) |
| 4, 5 | | 6 Apr 2022 (SI 2022/283) |
| 6 | (1) | See Schedule below |
| | (2)–(7) | 25 Jun 2020 (s 8(2)) |
| 7–9 | | 25 Jun 2020 (s 8(2)) |
| Schedule | | 6 Apr 2022 (SI 2022/283) |

## European Union (Future Relationship) Act 2020 (c 29)

*RA:* 31 Dec 2020

*Commencement provisions*: s 40(6), (7); European Union (Future Relationship) Act 2020 (Commencement No 1) Regulations 2020, SI 2020/1662

| | | |
|---|---|---|
| 1–5 | | IP completion day (as defined by European Union (Withdrawal Agreement) Act 2020, s 39(1)–(5)) (SI 2020/1662) |
| 6 | (1) | 31 Dec 2020 (for the purposes of the Secretary of State giving a direction as provided for in the definition of "designated UK authority") (s 40(6)(a)) |
| | | IP completion day (as defined by European Union (Withdrawal Agreement) Act 2020, s 39(1)–(5)) (otherwise) (SI 2020/1662) |
| | (2)–(4) | IP completion day (as defined by European Union (Withdrawal Agreement) Act 2020, s 39(1)–(5)) (SI 2020/1662) |
| 7 | | See Sch 2 below |
| 8 | | *Not yet in force* |
| 9 | | See Sch 3 below |
| 10–20 | | IP completion day (as defined by European Union (Withdrawal Agreement) Act 2020, s 39(1)–(5)) (SI 2020/1662) |
| 21 | | 1 Mar 2021 (SI 2020/1662) |
| 22–26 | | IP completion day (as defined by European Union (Withdrawal Agreement) Act 2020, s 39(1)–(5)) (SI 2020/1662) |
| 27 | | 1 Mar 2021 (SI 2020/1662) |
| 28, 29 | | IP completion day (as defined by European Union (Withdrawal Agreement) Act 2020, s 39(1)–(5)) (SI 2020/1662) |
| 30–33 | | 31 Dec 2020 (s 40(6)(d)) |
| 34 | | 1 Mar 2021 (SI 2020/1662) |
| 35–38 | | 31 Dec 2020 (s 40(6)(e)) |
| 39 | (1), (2) | 31 Dec 2020 (s 40(6)(f)) |
| | (3) | See Sch 6 below |
| | (4) | 31 Dec 2020 (s 40(6)(f)) |
| | (5) | See Sch 6 below |
| 40 | | 31 Dec 2020 (s 40(6)(h)) |

## European Union (Future Relationship) Act 2020 (c 29)—*contd*

| | | |
|---|---|---|
| Sch 1 | | IP completion day (as defined by European Union (Withdrawal Agreement) Act 2020, s 39(1)–(5)) (SI 2020/1662) |
| Sch 2 | paras 1–3 | IP completion day (as defined by European Union (Withdrawal Agreement) Act 2020, s 39(1)–(5)) (SI 2020/1662) |
| | para 4 | 31 Dec 2020 (for the purposes of the Secretary of State giving a direction under the Passenger Name Record Data and Miscellaneous Amendments Regulations 2018, SI 2018/598, reg 4A(1), and any other provision of that Schedule so far as necessary for those purposes) (s 40(6)(b) |
| | | IP completion day (as defined by European Union (Withdrawal Agreement) Act 2020, s 39(1)–(5)) (otherwise) (SI 2020/1662) |
| | paras 5–13 | IP completion day (as defined by European Union (Withdrawal Agreement) Act 2020, s 39(1)–(5)) (SI 2020/1662) |
| | para 14 | *Not yet in force* |
| | paras 15–18 | IP completion day (as defined by European Union (Withdrawal Agreement) Act 2020, s 39(1)–(5)) (SI 2020/1662) |
| Sch 3 | para 1 | IP completion day (as defined by European Union (Withdrawal Agreement) Act 2020, s 39(1)–(5)) (SI 2020/1662) |
| | para 2(1)–(5) | 31 Dec 2020 (s 40(6)(c)) |
| | (6) | IP completion day (as defined by European Union (Withdrawal Agreement) Act 2020, s 39(1)–(5)) (SI 2020/1662) |
| | paras 3–7 | IP completion day (as defined by European Union (Withdrawal Agreement) Act 2020, s 39(1)–(5)) (SI 2020/1662) |
| Sch 4 | | IP completion day (as defined by European Union (Withdrawal Agreement) Act 2020, s 39(1)–(5)) (SI 2020/1662) |
| Sch 5 | | 31 Dec 2020 (s 40(6)(e)) |
| Sch 6 | 1–3 | IP completion day (as defined by European Union (Withdrawal Agreement) Act 2020, s 39(1)–(5)) (SI 2020/1662) |
| | 4 | 31 Dec 2020 (s 40(6)(g)) |
| | 5–10 | IP completion day (as defined by European Union (Withdrawal Agreement) Act 2020, s 39(1)–(5)) (SI 2020/1662) |
| | 11–13 | 31 Dec 2020 (s 40(6)(g)) |

## European Union (Withdrawal Agreement) Act 2020 (c 1)

*RA:* 23 Jan 2020

*Commencement provisions*: s 42; European Union (Withdrawal Agreement) Act 2020 (Commencement No 1) Regulations 2020, SI 2020/75; European Union (Withdrawal Agreement) Act 2020 (Commencement No 2) Regulations 2020, SI 2020/317; European Union (Withdrawal Agreement) Act 2020 (Commencement No 3) Regulations 2020, SI 2020/518; European Union (Withdrawal) Act 2018 and European Union (Withdrawal Agreement) Act 2020 (Commencement, Transitional and Savings Provisions) Regulations 2020, SI 2020/1622

| | | |
|---|---|---|
| 1, 2 | | In force as from exit day (as defined by European Union (Withdrawal) Act 2018, s 20(1)–(5)) (SI 2020/75) |
| 3, 4 | | 23 Jan 2020 (s 42(6)(a)) |
| 5, 6 | | In force as from exit day (as defined by European Union (Withdrawal) Act 2018, s 20(1)–(5)) (SI 2020/75) |
| 7–9 | | 19 May 2020 (SI 2020/518) |
| 10 | | In force as from exit day (as defined by European Union (Withdrawal) Act 2018, s 20(1)–(5)) (SI 2020/75) |
| 11 | | 23 Jan 2020 (s 42(6)(b)) |
| 12, 13 | | 19 May 2020 (SI 2020/518) |
| 14 | (1)–(6) | 19 May 2020 (SI 2020/518) |
| | (7) | See Sch 1 below |
| 15 | (1), (2) | In force as from exit day (as defined by European Union (Withdrawal) Act 2018, s 20(1)–(5)) (SI 2020/75) |
| | (3) | See Sch 2 below |
| 16, 17 | | 23 Jan 2020 (s 42(6)(b)) |

**European Union (Withdrawal Agreement) Act 2020 (c 1)**—*contd*

| | | |
|---|---|---|
| 18, 19 | | 19 May 2020 (SI 2020/518) |
| 20 | | 23 Jan 2020 (s 42(6)(c)) |
| 21, 22 | | 19 May 2020 (SI 2020/518) |
| 23 | | See Sch 3 below |
| 24 | | IP completion day (as defined by European Union (Withdrawal Agreement) Act 2020, s 39(1)–(5)) (SI 2020/1622)[1] |
| 25 | (1)–(3) | IP completion day (as defined by European Union (Withdrawal Agreement) Act 2020, s 39(1)–(5)) (SI 2020/1622)[1] |
| | (4)(a) | IP completion day (as defined by European Union (Withdrawal Agreement) Act 2020, s 39(1)–(5)) (SI 2020/1622)[1] |
| | (4)(b) | In force as from exit day (as defined by European Union (Withdrawal) Act 2018, s 20(1)–(5)), for the purposes of s 5(6) of, and Sch 1 to, the 2018 Act in so far as they are in force on exit day (SI 2020/75) |
| | | IP completion day (as defined by European Union (Withdrawal Agreement) Act 2020, s 39(1)–(5)) (otherwise) (SI 2020/1622)[1] |
| | (5) | IP completion day (as defined by European Union (Withdrawal Agreement) Act 2020, s 39(1)–(5)) (SI 2020/1622)[1] |
| | (6)(a) | In force as from exit day (as defined by European Union (Withdrawal) Act 2018, s 20(1)–(5)), for the purposes of s 5(6) of, and Sch 1 to, the 2018 Act in so far as they are in force on exit day (SI 2020/75) |
| | | IP completion day (as defined by European Union (Withdrawal Agreement) Act 2020, s 39(1)–(5)) (otherwise) (SI 2020/1622)[1] |
| | (6)(b) | IP completion day (as defined by European Union (Withdrawal Agreement) Act 2020, s 39(1)–(5)) (SI 2020/1622)[1] |
| 26 | (1)(a) | In force as from exit day (as defined by European Union (Withdrawal) Act 2018, s 20(1)–(5)), in so far it relates to s 6(7) of the 2018 Act (SI 2020/75) |
| | | IP completion day (as defined by European Union (Withdrawal Agreement) Act 2020, s 39(1)–(5)) (otherwise) (SI 2020/1622)[1] |
| | (1)(b), (c) | IP completion day (as defined by European Union (Withdrawal Agreement) Act 2020, s 39(1)–(5)) (SI 2020/1622)[1] |
| | (1)(d) | 19 May 2020 (SI 2020/518) |
| | (1)(e) | IP completion day (as defined by European Union (Withdrawal Agreement) Act 2020, s 39(1)–(5)) (SI 2020/1622)[1] |
| | (2) | In force as from exit day (as defined by European Union (Withdrawal) Act 2018, s 20(1)–(5)) (SI 2020/75) |
| 27 | | In force as from exit day (as defined by European Union (Withdrawal) Act 2018, s 20(1)–(5)) (SI 2020/75) |
| 28 | | 19 May 2020 (SI 2020/518) |
| 29 | | 23 Jan 2020 (s 42(6)(c)) |
| 30 | | IP completion day (as defined by European Union (Withdrawal Agreement) Act 2020, s 39(1)–(5)) (SI 2020/1622)[1] |
| 31–40 | | 23 Jan 2020 (s 42(6)(c)) |
| 41 | (1)–(3) | 23 Jan 2020 (s 42(6)(d)) |
| | (4) | See Sch 5, Pts 1, 2 below |
| | (5) | 23 Jan 2020 (s 42(6)(d)) |
| | (6) | See Sch 5, Pt 3 below |
| 42 | | 23 Jan 2020 (s 42(6)(f)) |
| Sch 1 | | 19 May 2020 (SI 2020/518) |
| Sch 2 | paras 1–13 | In force as from exit day (as defined by European Union (Withdrawal) Act 2018, s 20(1)–(5)) (SI 2020/75) |
| | paras 14–17 | 18 Mar 2020 (SI 2020/317) |
| | paras 18, 19 | In force as from exit day (as defined by European Union (Withdrawal) Act 2018, s 20(1)–(5)) (SI 2020/75) |
| | paras 20, 21 | 18 Mar 2020 (SI 2020/317) |
| | para 22(1), (2) | IP completion day (as defined by European Union (Withdrawal Agreement) Act 2020, s 39(1)–(5)) (SI 2020/1622)[1] |
| | para 22(3) | 18 Mar 2020 (definition "Part 2") (SI 2020/317) |

**European Union (Withdrawal Agreement) Act 2020 (c 1)**—*contd*

|  |  |  |
|---|---|---|
|  |  | IP completion day (as defined by European Union (Withdrawal Agreement) Act 2020, s 39(1)–(5)) (otherwise) (SI 2020/1622)[1] |
|  | paras 23–31 | IP completion day (as defined by European Union (Withdrawal Agreement) Act 2020, s 39(1)–(5)) (SI 2020/1622)[1] |
|  | para 32 | 18 Mar 2020 (SI 2020/317) |
|  | para 33 | IP completion day (as defined by European Union (Withdrawal Agreement) Act 2020, s 39(1)–(5)) (SI 2020/1622)[1] |
|  | para 34 | In force as from exit day (as defined by European Union (Withdrawal) Act 2018, s 20(1)–(5)) (SI 2020/75) |
|  | paras 35–40 | IP completion day (as defined by European Union (Withdrawal Agreement) Act 2020, s 39(1)–(5)) (SI 2020/1622)[1] |
|  | para 41 | In force as from exit day (as defined by European Union (Withdrawal) Act 2018, s 20(1)–(5)) (SI 2020/75) |
| Sch 3 | paras 1–4 | IP completion day (as defined by European Union (Withdrawal Agreement) Act 2020, s 39(1)–(5)) (SI 2020/1622)[1] |
|  | para 5 | 23 Mar 2020 (SI 2020/317) |
|  | paras 6, 7 | IP completion day (as defined by European Union (Withdrawal Agreement) Act 2020, s 39(1)–(5)) (SI 2020/1622)[1] |
| Sch 4 |  | 23 Jan 2020 (s 42(6)(c)) |
| Sch 5 | para 1(1), (2) | In force as from immediately before exit day (as defined by European Union (Withdrawal) Act 2018, s 20(1)–(5)) (SI 2020/75) |
|  | para 1(3)–(6) | 23 Jan 2020 (s 42(6)(e)(i)) |
|  | para 2 | 23 Jan 2020 (s 42(6)(e)(i)) |
|  | para 3(1) | In force as from exit day (as defined by European Union (Withdrawal) Act 2018, s 20(1)–(5)) (SI 2020/75) |
|  | para 3(2)–(8) | 23 Jan 2020 (s 42(6)(e)(ii)) |
|  | para 4 | 23 Jan 2020 (s 42(6)(e)(iii)) |
|  | para 5 | 23 Jan 2020 (s 42(6)(e)(iv)) |
|  | para 6 | IP completion day (as defined by European Union (Withdrawal Agreement) Act 2020, s 39(1)–(5)) (SI 2020/1622)[1] |
|  | para 7(a), (b) | 23 Jan 2020 (s 42(6)(e)(iv)) |
|  | para 7(c) | In force as from exit day (as defined by European Union (Withdrawal) Act 2018, s 20(1)–(5)) (SI 2020/75) |
|  | para 8 | 23 Jan 2020 (s 42(6)(e)(v)) |
|  | paras 9, 10 | IP completion day (as defined by European Union (Withdrawal Agreement) Act 2020, s 39(1)–(5)) (SI 2020/1622)[1] |
|  | para 11 | In force as from exit day (as defined by European Union (Withdrawal) Act 2018, s 20(1)–(5)) (SI 2020/75) |
|  | para 12(a), (b) | 23 Jan 2020 (s 42(6)(e)(v)) |
|  | para 12(c) | In force as from exit day (as defined by European Union (Withdrawal) Act 2018, s 20(1)–(5)) (SI 2020/75) |
|  | para 12(d) | IP completion day (as defined by European Union (Withdrawal Agreement) Act 2020, s 39(1)–(5)) (SI 2020/1622)[1] |
|  | paras 13–16 | IP completion day (as defined by European Union (Withdrawal Agreement) Act 2020, s 39(1)–(5)) (SI 2020/1622)[1] |
|  | para 17 | 23 Jan 2020 (s 42(6)(e)(vi)) |
|  | para 18 | In force as from exit day (as defined by European Union (Withdrawal) Act 2018, s 20(1)–(5)), for the purposes of making regulations under Scotland Act 1998, s 30A (SI 2020/75) |
|  |  | IP completion day (as defined by European Union (Withdrawal Agreement) Act 2020, s 39(1)–(5)) (otherwise) (SI 2020/1622)[1] |
|  | para 19 | In force as from exit day (as defined by European Union (Withdrawal) Act 2018, s 20(1)–(5)), for the purposes of making regulations under Scotland Act 1998, s 57(4) (SI 2020/75) |
|  |  | *Not yet in force* (otherwise) |
|  | para 20 | 23 Jan 2020 (s 42(6)(e)(vi)) |

**European Union (Withdrawal Agreement) Act 2020 (c 1)**—*contd*

| | |
|---|---|
| para 21 | IP completion day (as defined by European Union (Withdrawal Agreement) Act 2020, s 39(1)–(5)) (SI 2020/1622)[1] |
| para 22 | 23 Jan 2020 (s 42(6)(e)(vi)) |
| para 23 | In force as from exit day (as defined by European Union (Withdrawal) Act 2018, s 20(1)–(5)), for the purposes of making regulations under Northern Ireland Act 1998, s 6A (SI 2020/75) |
| | IP completion day (as defined by European Union (Withdrawal Agreement) Act 2020, s 39(1)–(5)) (otherwise) (SI 2020/1622)[1] |
| para 24 | 23 Jan 2020 (s 42(6)(e)(vi)) |
| para 25 | In force as from exit day (as defined by European Union (Withdrawal) Act 2018, s 20(1)–(5)), for the purposes of making regulations under Northern Ireland Act 1998, s 24(3) (SI 2020/75) |
| | IP completion day (as defined by European Union (Withdrawal Agreement) Act 2020, s 39(1)–(5)) (otherwise) (SI 2020/1622)[1] |
| para 26 | IP completion day (as defined by European Union (Withdrawal Agreement) Act 2020, s 39(1)–(5)) (SI 2020/1622)[1] |
| para 27 | 23 Jan 2020 (s 42(6)(e)(vi)) |
| para 28 | In force as from exit day (as defined by European Union (Withdrawal) Act 2018, s 20(1)–(5)), for the purposes of making regulations under Government of Wales Act 2006, s 80(8) (SI 2020/75) |
| | IP completion day (as defined by European Union (Withdrawal Agreement) Act 2020, s 39(1)–(5)) (otherwise) (SI 2020/1622)[1] |
| para 29 | In force as from exit day (as defined by European Union (Withdrawal) Act 2018, s 20(1)–(5)), for the purposes of making regulations under Government of Wales Act 2006, s 109A (SI 2020/75) |
| | IP completion day (as defined by European Union (Withdrawal Agreement) Act 2020, s 39(1)–(5)) (otherwise) (SI 2020/1622)[1] |
| para 30 | IP completion day (as defined by European Union (Withdrawal Agreement) Act 2020, s 39(1)–(5)) (SI 2020/1622)[1] |
| para 31 | 23 Jan 2020 (s 42(6)(e)(vi)) |
| para 32 | 23 Jan 2020 (s 42(6)(e)(vii)) |
| para 33 | In force as from exit day (as defined by European Union (Withdrawal) Act 2018, s 20(1)–(5)) (SI 2020/75) |
| para 34 | IP completion day (as defined by European Union (Withdrawal Agreement) Act 2020, s 39(1)–(5)) (SI 2020/1622)[1] |
| para 35 | In force as from exit day (as defined by European Union (Withdrawal) Act 2018, s 20(1)–(5)) (SI 2020/75) |
| para 36(a), (b) | 23 Jan 2020 (s 42(6)(e)(vii)) |
| para 36(c) | In force as from exit day (as defined by European Union (Withdrawal) Act 2018, s 20(1)–(5)) (SI 2020/75) |
| para 36(d) | IP completion day (as defined by European Union (Withdrawal Agreement) Act 2020, s 39(1)–(5)) (SI 2020/1622)[1] |
| para 37(a) | IP completion day (as defined by European Union (Withdrawal Agreement) Act 2020, s 39(1)–(5)) (SI 2020/1622)[1] |
| para 37(b), (c) | 23 Jan 2020 (s 42(6)(e)(vii)) |
| para 37(d) | In force as from exit day (as defined by European Union (Withdrawal) Act 2018, s 20(1)–(5)) (SI 2020/75) |
| para 37(e), (f) | IP completion day (as defined by European Union (Withdrawal Agreement) Act 2020, s 39(1)–(5)) (SI 2020/1622)[1] |
| para 38 | 23 Jan 2020 (s 42(6)(e)(viii)) |
| para 39 | IP completion day (as defined by European Union (Withdrawal Agreement) Act 2020, s 39(1)–(5)) (SI 2020/1622)[1] |
| para 40(1), (2) | In force as from exit day (as defined by European Union (Withdrawal) Act 2018, s 20(1)–(5)) (SI 2020/75) |
| para 40(3), (4) | IP completion day (as defined by European Union (Withdrawal Agreement) Act 2020, s 39(1)–(5)) (SI 2020/1622)[1] |

**European Union (Withdrawal Agreement) Act 2020 (c 1)**—*contd*

| | |
|---|---|
| para 40(5) | In force as from exit day (as defined by European Union (Withdrawal) Act 2018, s 20(1)–(5)) (SI 2020/75) |
| para 41(1) | 23 Jan 2020 (s 42(6)(e)(viii)) |
| para 41(2) | IP completion day (as defined by European Union (Withdrawal Agreement) Act 2020, s 39(1)–(5)) (SI 2020/1622)[1] |
| para 41(3)(a) | 23 Jan 2020 (s 42(6)(e)(viii)) |
| para 41(3)(b) | IP completion day (as defined by European Union (Withdrawal Agreement) Act 2020, s 39(1)–(5)) (SI 2020/1622)[1] |
| para 42 | 23 Jan 2020 (s 42(6)(e)(viii)) |
| para 43 | In force as from exit day (as defined by European Union (Withdrawal) Act 2018, s 20(1)–(5)) (SI 2020/75) |
| para 44(1), (2)(a) | 23 Jan 2020 (s 42(6)(e)(viii)) |
| para 44(2)(b), (c) | In force as from exit day (as defined by European Union (Withdrawal) Act 2018, s 20(1)–(5)) (SI 2020/75) |
| para 44(2)(d), (e) | 23 Jan 2020 (s 42(6)(e)(viii)) |
| para 44(2)(f)–(h) | In force as from exit day (as defined by European Union (Withdrawal) Act 2018, s 20(1)–(5)) (SI 2020/75) |
| para 44(3) | 23 Jan 2020 (s 42(6)(e)(viii)) |
| para 44(4) | In force as from exit day (as defined by European Union (Withdrawal) Act 2018, s 20(1)–(5)) (SI 2020/75) |
| paras 45, 46 | In force as from exit day (as defined by European Union (Withdrawal) Act 2018, s 20(1)–(5)) (SI 2020/75) |
| para 47(1), (2) | 23 Jan 2020 (s 42(6)(e)(viii)) |
| para 47(3) | In force as from exit day (as defined by European Union (Withdrawal) Act 2018, s 20(1)–(5)) (SI 2020/75) |
| para 47(4) | 23 Jan 2020 (s 42(6)(e)(viii)) |
| para 47(5) | In force as from exit day (as defined by European Union (Withdrawal) Act 2018, s 20(1)–(5)) (SI 2020/75) |
| para 47(6) | 23 Jan 2020 (s 42(6)(e)(viii)) |
| para 48(1), (2) | In force as from exit day (as defined by European Union (Withdrawal) Act 2018, s 20(1)–(5)) (SI 2020/75) |
| para 48(3) | IP completion day (as defined by European Union (Withdrawal Agreement) Act 2020, s 39(1)–(5)) (SI 2020/1622)[1] |
| paras 48(4), 49 | In force as from exit day (as defined by European Union (Withdrawal) Act 2018, s 20(1)–(5)) (SI 2020/75) |
| para 50 | 23 Jan 2020 (s 42(6)(e)(viii)) |
| para 51 | 23 Jan 2020 (for the purpose of making regulations under the European Union (Withdrawal) Act 2018, s 8A or Sch 2, Pt 1A) (s 42(6)(e)(ix)) |
| | In force as from exit day (as defined by European Union (Withdrawal) Act 2018, s 20(1)–(5)), for the purposes of making regulations under s 1A(3)(a)(ii) of the 2018 Act (SI 2020/75) |
| | 19 May 2020 (otherwise) (SI 2020/518) |
| para 52(1) | 23 Jan 2020 (s 42(6)(e)(x)) |
| para 52(2) | 19 May 2020 (SI 2020/518) |
| para 52(3)–(7) | 23 Jan 2020 (s 42(6)(e)(x)) |
| para 53(1)–(4) | 23 Jan 2020 (s 42(6)(e)(x)) |
| para 53(5) | In force as from exit day (as defined by European Union (Withdrawal) Act 2018, s 20(1)–(5)) (SI 2020/75) |
| para 53(6), (7)(a) | 23 Jan 2020 (s 42(6)(e)(x)) |
| para 53(7)(b) | In force as from exit day (as defined by European Union (Withdrawal) Act 2018, s 20(1)–(5)) (SI 2020/75) |
| para 53(8)(a) | 23 Jan 2020 (s 42(6)(e)(x)) |
| para 53(8)(b) | In force as from exit day (as defined by European Union (Withdrawal) Act 2018, s 20(1)–(5)) (SI 2020/75) |
| para 53(9)–(13) | 23 Jan 2020 (s 42(6)(e)(x)) |
| para 54(1) | In force as from exit day (as defined by European Union (Withdrawal) Act 2018, s 20(1)–(5)) (SI 2020/75) |

**European Union (Withdrawal Agreement) Act 2020 (c 1)**—*contd*

| | | |
|---|---|---|
| para 54(2), (3) | IP completion day (as defined by European Union (Withdrawal Agreement) Act 2020, s 39(1)–(5)) (SI 2020/1622)[1] |
| para 54(4), (5) | In force as from exit day (as defined by European Union (Withdrawal) Act 2018, s 20(1)–(5)) (SI 2020/75) |
| para 54(6) | IP completion day (as defined by European Union (Withdrawal Agreement) Act 2020, s 39(1)–(5)) (SI 2020/1622)[1] |
| para 54(7) | In force as from exit day (as defined by European Union (Withdrawal) Act 2018, s 20(1)–(5)) (SI 2020/75) |
| para 54(8)–(11) | IP completion day (as defined by European Union (Withdrawal Agreement) Act 2020, s 39(1)–(5)) (SI 2020/1622)[1] |
| para 55(1), (2) | In force as from exit day (as defined by European Union (Withdrawal) Act 2018, s 20(1)–(5)) (SI 2020/75) |
| para 55(3) | IP completion day (as defined by European Union (Withdrawal Agreement) Act 2020, s 39(1)–(5)) (SI 2020/1622)[1] |
| para 56(1) | See sub-paras (2)–(8) below |
| para 56(2)–(5) | IP completion day (as defined by European Union (Withdrawal Agreement) Act 2020, s 39(1)–(5)) (SI 2020/1622)[1] |
| para 56(6)(a) | 19 May 2020 (SI 2020/518) |
| para 56(6)(b)–(d) | 23 Jan 2020 (s 42(6)(e)(xi)) |
| para 56(7)(a) | In force as from exit day (as defined by European Union (Withdrawal) Act 2018, s 20(1)–(5)), in so far as it amends Sch 8, para 41(3)–(9) of the 2018 Act) (SI 2020/75) |
| | IP completion day (as defined by European Union (Withdrawal Agreement) Act 2020, s 39(1)–(5)) (otherwise) (SI 2020/1622)[1] |
| para 56(7)(b) | 23 Jan 2020 (for the purpose of making regulations under the European Union (Withdrawal) Act 2018, s 8A or Sch 2, Pt 1A) (s 42(6)(e)(ix)) |
| | 19 May 2020 (except so far as relates to the making of regulations under the European Union (Withdrawal) Act 2018, Sch 2, Pt 1) (SI 2020/518) |
| | IP completion day (as defined by European Union (Withdrawal Agreement) Act 2020, s 39(1)–(5)) (otherwise) (SI 2020/1622)[1] |
| para 56(8) | IP completion day (as defined by European Union (Withdrawal Agreement) Act 2020, s 39(1)–(5)) (SI 2020/1622)[1] |
| para 57 | 31 Dec 2020 (SI 2020/1622)[1] |
| paras 58–63 | In force as from exit day (as defined by European Union (Withdrawal) Act 2018, s 20(1)–(5)) (SI 2020/75) |
| para 64 | 19 May 2020 (SI 2020/518) |
| paras 65–68 | 23 Jan 2020 (s 42(6)(e)(xii)) |

---

[1]   For transitional and saving provision, see SI 2020/1622, regs 20, 21

---

**Extradition (Provisional Arrest) Act 2020 (c 18)**

*RA:* 22 Oct 2020

*Commencement provisions*: s 2(4); Extradition (Provisional Arrest) Act 2020 (Commencement No 1) Regulations 2020, SI 2020/1652

| | | |
|---|---|---|
| 1 | | IP completion day (as defined by European Union (Withdrawal Agreement) Act 2020, s 39(1)–(5)) (SI 2020/1652) |
| 2 | | 22 Oct 2020 (s 2(3)) |
| Schedule | paras 1–3 | IP completion day (as defined by European Union (Withdrawal Agreement) Act 2020, s 39(1)–(5)) (SI 2020/1652) |
| | para 4 | Immediately before IP completion day (as defined by European Union (Withdrawal Agreement) Act 2020, s 39(1)–(5)) (in so far as applies to Norway and Iceland) (SI 2020/1652) |
| | | *Not yet in force* (otherwise) |
| | paras 5–31 | IP completion day (as defined by European Union (Withdrawal Agreement) Act 2020, s 39(1)–(5)) (SI 2020/1652) |

### Female Genital Mutilation (Protection and Guidance) (Scotland) Act 2020 (asp 9)

*RA:* 24 Apr 2020

*Commencement provisions:* s 11

| | |
|---|---|
| 1 | 25 Apr 2020 (in so far as inserts Prohibition of Female Genital Mutilation (Scotland) Act 2005, s 5R(4)(b)(ii), for the purpose only of making regulations) (s 11(1)(a)) |
| | *Not yet in force* (otherwise) |
| 2–9 | *Not yet in force* |
| 10–12 | 25 Apr 2020 (s 11(1)(b)–(d)) |

### Finance Act 2020 (c 14)

*RA:* 22 Jul 2020

The commencement details of Finance Acts are not set out, as the dates from which their provisions take effect are usually stated clearly and unambiguously in the text of the Act, and charging provisions will normally state for which year or years of assessment they are to have effect.

### Fisheries Act 2020 (c 22)

*RA:* 23 Nov 2020

*Commencement provisions:* s 54

| | |
|---|---|
| 1–11 | 23 Nov 2020 (s 54(1)(a)) |
| 12, 13 | IP completion day (as defined by European Union (Withdrawal Agreement) Act 2020, s 39(1)–(5)) (s 54(3)(a)) |
| 14–22 | IP completion day (as defined by European Union (Withdrawal Agreement) Act 2020, s 39(1)–(5)) (s 54(3)(b)) |
| 23, 24 | 23 Nov 2020 (s 54(1)(b)) |
| 25 | IP completion day (as defined by European Union (Withdrawal Agreement) Act 2020, s 39(1)–(5)) (s 54(3)(c)) |
| 26 | 23 Nov 2020 (s 54(1)(b)) |
| 27 | IP completion day (as defined by European Union (Withdrawal Agreement) Act 2020, s 39(1)–(5)) or, if later, 23 Jan 2021 (s 54(4)(a)) |
| 28–32 | IP completion day (as defined by European Union (Withdrawal Agreement) Act 2020, s 39(1)–(5)) or, if later, 23 Jan 2021 (s 54(4)(b)) |
| 33 | 23 Nov 2020 (s 54(1)(c)) |
| 34 | IP completion day (as defined by European Union (Withdrawal Agreement) Act 2020, s 39(1)–(5)) or, if later, 23 Jan 2021 (s 54(4)(c)) |
| 35 | IP completion day (as defined by European Union (Withdrawal Agreement) Act 2020, s 39(1)–(5)) (s 54(3)(d)) |
| 36–42 | 23 Nov 2020 (s 54(1)(d)) |
| 43 | 23 Nov 2020 (s 54(1)(e)) |
| 44 | IP completion day (as defined by European Union (Withdrawal Agreement) Act 2020, s 39(1)–(5)) (s 54(3)(e)) |
| 45, 46 | 23 Jan 2021 (s 54(2)) |
| 47 | 1 Mar 2021 (s 54(5)) |
| 48 | See Sch 10 below |
| 49 | IP completion day (as defined by European Union (Withdrawal Agreement) Act 2020, s 39(1)–(5)) (s 54(3)(f)) |
| 50–55 | 23 Nov 2020 (s 54(1)(g)) |
| Sch 1 | 23 Nov 2020 (s 54(1)(a)) |
| Sch 2 | IP completion day (as defined by European Union (Withdrawal Agreement) Act 2020, s 39(1)–(5)) (s 54(3)(a)) |

**Fisheries Act 2020 (c 22)**—*contd*

| | | |
|---|---|---|
| Schs 3, 4 | | IP completion day (as defined by European Union (Withdrawal Agreement) Act 2020, s 39(1)–(5)) (s 54(3)(b)) |
| Sch 5 | | IP completion day (as defined by European Union (Withdrawal Agreement) Act 2020, s 39(1)–(5)) or, if later, 23 Jan 2021 (s 54(4)(a)) |
| Sch 6 | | 23 Nov 2020 (s 54(1)(c)) |
| Sch 7 | | IP completion day (as defined by European Union (Withdrawal Agreement) Act 2020, s 39(1)–(5)) or, if later, 23 Jan 2021 (s 54(4)(c)) |
| Sch 8 | | 23 Nov 2020 (s 54(1)(d)) |
| Sch 9 | | 1 Mar 2021 (s 54(5)) |
| Sch 10 | paras 1–5 | 23 Nov 2020 (s 54(1)(f)) |
| | paras 6–32 | IP completion day (as defined by European Union (Withdrawal Agreement) Act 2020, s 39(1)–(5)) or, if later, 23 Jan 2021 (s 54(4)(d)) |
| Sch 11 | | IP completion day (as defined by European Union (Withdrawal Agreement) Act 2020, s 39(1)–(5)) (s 54(3)(f)) |

---

## General Synod (Remote Meetings) (Temporary Standing Orders) Measure 2020 (No 2)

*RA:* 4 Nov 2020

*Commencement provisions*: s 5(2)

Whole Act in force 4 Nov 2020 (s 5(2))

---

## Health and Social Care (Quality and Engagement) (Wales) Act 2020 (asc 1)

*RA:* 1 Jun 2020

*Commencement provisions*: s 29; Health and Social Care (Quality and Engagement) (Wales) Act 2020 (Commencement No 1) Order 2022, SI 2022/208; Health and Social Care (Quality and Engagement) (Wales) Act 2020 (Commencement No 2) Order 2022, SI 2022/996

| | | |
|---|---|---|
| 1–11 | | *Not yet in force* |
| 12 | | 1 Apr 2022 (SI 2022/208) |
| 13–18 | | *Not yet in force* |
| 19 | (1), (2) | 1 Apr 2022 (SI 2022/208) |
| | (3), (4) | *Not yet in force* |
| | (5) | 1 Apr 2022 (SI 2022/208) |
| 20 | | *Not yet in force* |
| 21, 22 | | 1 Apr 2022 (SI 2022/208) |
| 23 | | *Not yet in force* |
| 24 | | 8 Mar 2022 (SI 2022/208) |
| 25 | | *Not yet in force* |
| 26 | | 8 Mar 2022 (SI 2022/208) |
| 29, 30 | | 2 Jun 2020 (s 29(1)) |
| Sch 1 | paras 1–5 | 1 Apr 2022 (SI 2022/208) |
| | paras 6–8 | *Not yet in force* |
| | paras 9–21 | 1 Apr 2022 (SI 2022/208) |
| | para 22 | 1 Oct 2022 (SI 2022/996) |
| | paras 23–25 | 1 Apr 2022 (SI 2022/208) |
| Schs 2, 3 | | *Not yet in force* |

## Immigration and Social Security Co-ordination (EU Withdrawal) Act 2020 (c 20)

*RA:* 11 Nov 2020

*Commencement provisions*: s 9; Immigration and Social Security Co-ordination (EU Withdrawal) Act 2020 (Commencement) Regulations 2020, SI 2020/1279

| | | |
|---|---|---|
| 1 | | In force as from IP completion day (as defined by European Union (Withdrawal Agreement) Act 2020, s 39(1)–(5)) (SI 2020/1279) |
| 2 | | In force as from immediately before IP completion day (as defined by European Union (Withdrawal Agreement) Act 2020, s 39(1)–(5)) (SI 2020/1279) |
| 3 | (1) | 12 Jan 2021 (SI 2020/1279) |
| | (2) | 11 Jan 2021 (so far as relates to s 3(4)) (s 9(2)(b)) |
| | | 12 Jan 2021 (otherwise) (SI 2020/1279) |
| | (3) | 12 Jan 2021 (SI 2020/1279) |
| | (4) | 11 Jan 2021 (s 9(2)(a)) |
| | (5) | 12 Jan 2021 (SI 2020/1279) |
| | (6) | 11 Jan 2021 (so far as relates to s 3(4)) (s 9(2)(b)) |
| | | 12 Jan 2021 (otherwise) (SI 2020/1279) |
| 4 | | In force as from IP completion day (as defined by European Union (Withdrawal Agreement) Act 2020, s 39(1)–(5)) (SI 2020/1279) |
| 5, 6 | | 14 Nov 2020 (SI 2020/1279) |
| 7–10 | | 11 Nov 2020 (s 9(6)) |
| Sch 1 | | In force as from IP completion day (as defined by European Union (Withdrawal Agreement) Act 2020, s 39(1)–(5)) (SI 2020/1279) |
| Schs 2, 3 | | 14 Nov 2020 (SI 2020/1279) |

## National Health Service (Indemnities) (Wales) Act 2020 (anaw 2)

*RA:* 26 Feb 2020

*Commencement provisions*: s 2(2)

Whole Act in force 27 Feb 2020 (s 2(2))

## NHS Funding Act 2020 (c 5)

*RA:* 16 Mar 2020

*Commencement provisions*: s 2(2)

Whole Act in force 16 Mar 2020 (s 2(2))

## Non-Domestic Rates (Scotland) Act 2020 (asp 4)

*RA:* 11 Mar 2020

*Commencement provisions*: s 44; Non-Domestic Rates (Scotland) Act 2020 (Commencement No 1 and Transitional Provision) Regulations 2020, SSI 2020/107; Non-Domestic Rates (Scotland) Act 2020 (Commencement No 2, Transitional and Saving Provisions) Regulations 2020, SSI 2020/327, as amended by SSI 2021/120, SSI 2022/23; Non-Domestic Rates (Scotland) Act 2020 (Commencement No. 2, Transitional and Saving Provisions (Amendment) and Commencement No 3 and Saving Provision) Regulations 2022, SSI 2022/23

| | | |
|---|---|---|
| 1 | | *Not yet in force* |
| 2 | (a) | *Not yet in force* |
| | (b) | 5 Nov 2020 (SSI 2020/327) |

## Non-Domestic Rates (Scotland) Act 2020 (asp 4)—*contd*

| | | |
|---|---|---|
| 3 | | 5 Nov 2020 (so far as necessary to allow the Scottish Ministers to make regulations under Local Government (Scotland) Act 1975, s 2A(7), lay draft regulations under s 2A(7)(b) thereof, and to consult on proposals for regulations under s 2A(7) thereof) (SSI 2020/327) |
| | | 1 Apr 2021 (otherwise) (SSI 2020/327) |
| 4 | | 1 Apr 2022 (SSI 2020/327) |
| 5 | | 1 Apr 2023 (SSI 2020/327) |
| 6–9 | | 5 Nov 2020 (SSI 2020/327) |
| 10 | | 5 Nov 2020 (so far as necessary to allow the Scottish Ministers to make regulations under Local Government (Scotland) Act 1975, ss 3ZA(7), 3ZB(7), lay draft regulations under ss 3ZA(7)(e), 3ZB(7)(d) thereof, and to consult on proposals for regulations under ss 3ZA(7)(e), 3ZB(7)(d) thereof) (SSI 2020/327) |
| | | 1 Jan 2023 (otherwise) (SSI 2020/327) |
| 11 | | 1 Jan 2023 (SSI 2020/327) |
| 12 | | 1 Jan 2023 (SSI 2020/327)[2] |
| 13 | | 2 Apr 2020 (SSI 2020/107)[1] |
| 14–16 | | 5 Nov 2020 (SSI 2020/327) |
| 17 | | 1 Apr 2022 (SSI 2020/327) |
| 18 | | 5 Nov 2020 (SSI 2020/327) |
| 19 | | 1 Apr 2023 (SSI 2022/23) |
| 20 | | 1 Apr 2021 (SSI 2020/327) |
| 21 | | 1 Apr 2021 (SSI 2020/327)[2] |
| 22–25 | | 5 Nov 2020 (SSI 2020/327) |
| 26 | (1)–(4) | 12 Mar 2020 (s 44(1)(b)) |
| | (5) | 1 Apr 2021 (SSI 2020/327)[2] |
| 27 | | 1 Apr 2021 (SSI 2020/327) |
| 28 | | 1 Apr 2021 (SSI 2020/327)[2] |
| 29 | (1)(a) | 12 Mar 2020 (s 44(1)(c)) |
| | (1)(b) | 1 Apr 2021 (SSI 2020/327) |
| | (2) | 1 Apr 2021 (SSI 2020/327) |
| | (3) | 12 Mar 2020 (in so far as relates to s 29(1)(d)) (s 44(1)(a)) |
| | | *Not yet in force* (otherwise) |
| 30 | (1)–(7) | 12 Mar 2020 (s 44(1)(e)) |
| | (8)–(11) | 5 Nov 2020 (SSI 2020/327) |
| | (12)–(14) | 12 Mar 2020 (s 44(1)(e)) |
| 31 | | 12 Mar 2020 (s 44(1)(f)) |
| 32 | | 5 Nov 2020 (SSI 2020/327) |
| 33 | | 1 Apr 2021 (SSI 2020/327) |
| 34 | (1)–(4) | 1 Apr 2021 (SSI 2020/327) |
| | (5)–(8) | 5 Nov 2020 (SSI 2020/327) |
| 35–41 | | 1 Apr 2021 (SSI 2020/327) |
| 42 | | 12 Mar 2020 (s 44(1)(g)) |
| 43 | | 12 Mar 2020 (s 44(1)(h)) |
| 44 | | 12 Mar 2020 (s 44(1)(i)) |
| 45 | | 12 Mar 2020 (s 44(1)(j)) |

[1]  For transitional provisions, see SSI 2020/107, reg 3

[2]  For transitional and saving provisions, see SSI 2020/327, regs 3–6

## Parliamentary Constituencies Act 2020 (c 25)

*RA:* 14 Dec 2020

*Commencement provisions:* s 14(2)

Whole Act in force 14 Dec 2020 (s 14(2))

## Prisoners (Disclosure of Information About Victims) Act 2020 (c 19)

*RA:* 4 Nov 2020

*Commencement provisions:* s 3(2)–(4); Prisoners (Disclosure of Information About Victims) Act 2020 (Commencement) Regulations 2020, SI 2020/1537

| | |
|---|---|
| 1, 2 | 4 Jan 2021 (SI 2020/1537) |
| 3 | 4 Nov 2020 (s 3(4)) |

## Private International Law (Implementation of Agreements) Act 2020 (c 24)

*RA:* 14 Dec 2020

*Commencement provisions:* s 4(3), (4)

| | | |
|---|---|---|
| 1 | | IP completion day (as defined by European Union (Withdrawal Agreement) Act 2020, s 39(1)–(5)) (s 4(3)) |
| 2 | | 14 Dec 2020 (s 4(4)) |
| 3 | (1) | IP completion day (as defined by European Union (Withdrawal Agreement) Act 2020, s 39(1)–(5)) (s 4(3)) |
| | (2), (3) | 14 Dec 2020 (s 4(4)) |
| 4 | | 14 Dec 2020 (s 4(4)) |
| Schs 1–5 | | IP completion day (as defined by European Union (Withdrawal Agreement) Act 2020, s 39(1)–(5)) (s 4(3)) |
| Sch 6 | | 14 Dec 2020 (s 4(4)) |

## Referendums (Scotland) Act 2020 (asp 2)

*RA:* 29 Jan 2020

*Commencement provisions:* s 41

Whole Act in force 30 Jan 2020 (s 41)

## Scottish Biometrics Commissioner Act 2020 (asp 8)

*RA:* 20 Apr 2020

*Commencement provisions:* s 40; Scottish Biometrics Commissioner Act 2020 (Commencement) Regulations 2020, SSI 2020/250

| | |
|---|---|
| 1–36 | 1 Dec 2020 (SSI 2020/250) |
| 37, 38 | 21 Apr 2020 (s 40(1)) |
| 39 | 1 Dec 2020 (SSI 2020/250) |
| 40, 41 | 21 Apr 2020 (s 40(1)) |
| Schs 1, 2 | 1 Dec 2020 (SSI 2020/250) |

## Scottish Elections (Franchise and Representation) Act 2020 (asp 6)

*RA:* 1 Apr 2020

*Commencement provisions:* s 12; Scottish Elections (Franchise and Representation) Act 2020 (Commencement) Regulations 2020, SSI 2020/162

| | |
|---|---|
| 1–4 | 3 Aug 2020 (SSI 2020/162) |
| 5–13 | 2 Apr 2020 (s 12(1)) |
| Schedule | 2 Apr 2020 (s 12(1)) |

## Scottish Elections (Reform) Act 2020 (asp 12)

*RA:* 8 Jul 2020

*Commencement provisions:* s 35; Scottish Elections (Reform) Act 2020 (Commencement No 1) Regulations 2020, SSI 2020/278; Scottish Elections (Reform) Act 2020 (Commencement No 2 and Saving Provision) Regulations 2021, SSI 2021/124; Scottish Elections (Reform) Act 2020 (Commencement No 3 and Transitional Provision) Regulations 2021, SSI 2021/311

| | |
|---|---|
| 1 | 1 Oct 2020 (SSI 2020/278) |
| 2 | 14 May 2021 (SSI 2021/124) |
| 3 | 1 Oct 2020 (SSI 2020/278) |
| 4 | 14 May 2021 (SSI 2021/124) |
| 5 | 29 Sep 2021 (SSI 2021/311)[2] |
| 6–9 | 1 Oct 2020 (SSI 2020/278) |
| 10 | 29 Sep 2021 (SSI 2021/311)[2] |
| 11 | 1 Oct 2020 (SSI 2020/278) |
| 12 | 29 Sep 2021 (SSI 2021/311)[2] |
| 13–19 | 1 Oct 2020 (SSI 2020/278) |
| 20, 21 | 29 Sep 2021 (SSI 2021/311)[2] |
| 22–27 | 1 Oct 2020 (SSI 2020/278) |
| 28–30 | 14 May 2021 (SSI 2021/124) |
| 31 | 14 May 2021 (SSI 2021/124)[1] |
| 32, 33 | 14 May 2021 (SSI 2021/124) |
| 34–36 | 9 Jul 2020 (s 35(1)) |
| Schedule | 14 May 2021 (SSI 2021/124) |

[1]   For savings, see SSI 2021/124, reg 3

[2]   For a transitional provision, see SSI 2021/311, reg 3

## Scottish National Investment Bank Act 2020 (asp 3)

*RA:* 25 Feb 2020

*Commencement provisions:* s 35; Scottish National Investment Bank Act 2020 (Commencement) Regulations 2020, SSI 2020/272

| | |
|---|---|
| 1–33 | 16 Sep 2020 (SSI 2020/272) |
| 34–36 | 26 Feb 2020 (s 35(1)) |
| Schedule | 16 Sep 2020 (SSI 2020/272) |

## Senedd and Elections (Wales) Act 2020 (anaw 1)

*RA:* 15 Jan 2020

*Commencement provisions:* s 42; Senedd and Elections (Wales) Act 2020 (Commencement) Order 2020, SI 2020/1052

| | |
|---|---|
| 1 | 15 Jan 2020 (s 42(1)) |
| 2–9 | 6 May 2020 (s 42(2)) |
| 10, 11 | 15 Jan 2020 (s 42(1)) |
| 12–26 | 1 Jun 2020 (s 42(3)) |
| 27 | 15 Jan 2020 (s 42(1)) |
| 28 | 1 Oct 2020 (SI 2020/1052) |
| 29–35 | 15 Jan 2020 (s 42(1))[1] |
| 36 | *Not yet in force*[2] |
| 37–43 | 15 Jan 2020 (s 42(1)) |
| Sch 1 | 6 May 2020 (s 42(2)) |
| Sch 2 | 1 Oct 2020 (SI 2020/1052) |
| Sch 3 | 15 Jan 2020 (s 42(1))[1] |

**Senedd and Elections (Wales) Act 2020 (anaw 1)**—*contd*
[1]    With effect for the purposes of a Senedd election at which the poll is held on or after 5 Apr 2021

[2]    S 36 comes into force on the day of the first Senedd election at which the poll is held on or after 5 Apr 2021

---

## Sentencing Act 2020 (c 17)

*RA:* 22 Oct 2020

*Commencement provisions*: ss 416–418 (note, amendments to ss 417, 418 have been incorporated into the table below; see further footnotes 1–3); Sentencing Act 2020 (Commencement No 1) Regulations 2020, SI 2020/1236; Sentencing Act 2020 (Commencement No 1) (England and Wales) Regulations 2022, SI 2022/415; Criminal Justice Act 2003 (Commencement No 33) and Sentencing Act 2020 (Commencement No 2) Regulations 2022, SI 2022/500

| | | |
|---|---|---|
| 1–420 | | 1 Dec 2020 (SI 2020/1236) |
| Schs 1–21 | | 1 Dec 2020 (SI 2020/1236) |
| Sch 22 | paras 1–10 | *Not yet in force* |
| | para 11 | *Not yet in force* (comes into force at the same time as para 1) (s 417(5)) |
| | paras 12–20 | *Not yet in force* |
| | paras 21, 22 | *Not yet in force* (come into force at the same time as para 13) (s 417(6)) |
| | para 23 | *Not yet in force* |
| | para 24 | 2 May 2022 (for the purposes only of offences which are triable either way) (SI 2022/500) |
| | | *Not yet in force* (otherwise) |
| | paras 25–27 | *Not yet in force* |
| | para 28 | *Not yet in force* (comes into force 2 years after para 27) (s 417(7)) |
| | paras 29–35 | *Not yet in force* |
| | paras 36–38B[1] | *Not yet in force* (come into force at the same time as the Criminal Justice and Courts Services Act 2000, s 61) (s 417(3)) |
| | para 39 | *Not yet in force* |
| | paras 40, 40A[5], 41 | *Not yet in force* (come into force at the same time as the Criminal Justice and Courts Services Act 2000, s 61) (s 417(3)) |
| | paras 42–44 | *Not yet in force* |
| | paras 45, 46 | *Not yet in force* (come into force at the same time as the Criminal Justice and Courts Services Act 2000, s 61) (s 417(3)) |
| | para 47(a) | *Not yet in force* |
| | para 47(b) | *Not yet in force* (comes into force at the same time as the Criminal Justice and Courts Services Act 2000, s 61) (s 417(3)) |
| | paras 48–50 | *Not yet in force* |
| | paras 51, 51A, 52[1] | *Not yet in force* (come into force at the same time as the Criminal Justice and Courts Services Act 2000, s 61) (s 417(3)) |
| | para 53 | *Not yet in force* (so far as relating to ss 264, 265, 266–268C, 273, 274, 274A comes into force at the same time as the Criminal Justice and Courts Services Act 2000, s 61) (s 417(3))[1, 5] |
| | | *Not yet in force* (otherwise) |
| | paras 54–64 | *Not yet in force* (come into force at the same time as the Criminal Justice and Courts Services Act 2000, s 61) (s 417(3)) |
| | para 65 | *Not yet in force* (comes into force at the same time as para 44) (s 417(2)) |
| | para 66, 67 | *Not yet in force* |
| | para 68 | *Not yet in force* (comes into force at the same time as para 44) (s 417(2)) |
| | paras 68A, 69, 70[1] | *Not yet in force* (come into force at the same time as the Criminal Justice and Courts Services Act 2000, s 61) (s 417(3)) |
| | para 71 | *Not yet in force* |
| | paras 72–75 | *Not yet in force* (come into force at the same time as the Criminal Justice and Courts Services Act 2000, s 61) (s 417(3)) |

**Sentencing Act 2020 (c 17)**—*contd*

| | | |
|---|---|---|
| | para 76 | *Not yet in force* |
| | paras 77, 78 | *Not yet in force* (come into force at the same time as the Criminal Justice and Courts Services Act 2000, s 61) (s 417(3)) |
| | paras 79, 80 | *Not yet in force* |
| | paras 81–83 | 6 Apr 2022 (SI 2022/415) |
| | para 84 | *Not yet in force* |
| | para 85 | *Repealed (never in force)* |
| | paras 86–97 | 31 Dec 2020 at 11.00 pm (IP completion day) (s 417(9)) |
| | paras 98–100 | *Not yet in force* |
| | paras 101, 102 | *Not yet in force* (come into force at the same time as the Criminal Justice and Courts Services Act 2000, s 61) (s 417(3)(g)) |
| Schs 23–25 | | 1 Dec 2020 (SI 2020/1236) |
| Sch 26 | para 1 | See paras 2–25 below |
| | para 2(a) | *Not yet in force* (comes into force at the same time as the Criminal Justice and Courts Services Act 2000, s 61) (s 418(2)) |
| | para 2(b) | *Not yet in force* (comes into force at the same time as Sch 22, para 24) (s 418(4)) |
| | para 3(a) | *Not yet in force* (comes into force at the same time as the Criminal Justice and Courts Services Act 2000, s 61) (s 418(2)) |
| | para 3(b) | *Not yet in force* (comes into force at the same time as Sch 22, para 24) (s 418(4)) |
| | para 4(a) | *Not yet in force* (comes into force at the same time as the Criminal Justice and Courts Services Act 2000, s 61) (s 418(2)) |
| | para 4(b) | *Not yet in force* (comes into force at the same time as Sch 22, para 24) (s 418(4)) |
| | para 5(a) | *Not yet in force* (comes into force at the same time as the Criminal Justice and Courts Services Act 2000, s 61) (s 418(2)) |
| | para 5(b) | *Not yet in force* (comes into force at the same time as Sch 22, para 24) (s 418(4)) |
| | paras 6–11 | *Not yet in force* (come into force at the same time as the Criminal Justice and Courts Services Act 2000, s 61) (s 418(2)) |
| | para 12(1)(a)–(d) | *Not yet in force* (come into force at the same time as the Criminal Justice and Courts Services Act 2000, s 61) (s 418(2)) |
| | para 12(1)(da), (db) | 31 Dec 2020 (s 418(4A))[2] |
| | para 12(1)(dc)–(f)[3] | *Not yet in force* (come into force at the same time as the Criminal Justice and Courts Services Act 2000, s 61) (s 418(2)) |
| | para 12(2)(a) | *Not yet in force* (comes into force at the same time as the Criminal Justice and Courts Services Act 2000, s 61) (s 418(2)) |
| | para 12(2)(b) | 31 Dec 2020 (s 418(4A))[2] |
| | para 13 | *Not yet in force* (comes into force at the same time as the Criminal Justice and Courts Services Act 2000, s 61) (s 418(2)) |
| | para 13A | *Not yet in force* (comes into force at the same time as the Criminal Justice and Courts Services Act 2000, s 61) (s 418(2A))[4] |
| | para 14(a) | *Not yet in force* (comes into force at the same time as the Criminal Justice and Courts Services Act 2000, s 61) (s 418(2)) |
| | para 14(aa), (ab) | 31 Dec 2020 (s 418(4A))[2] |
| | para 14(b)–(d) | *Not yet in force* (come into force at the same time as the Criminal Justice and Courts Services Act 2000, s 61) (s 418(2)) |
| | para 15 | *Not yet in force* (comes into force at the same time as the Criminal Justice and Courts Services Act 2000, s 61) (s 418(2)) |
| | paras 15A, 15B | 31 Dec 2020 (s 418(4A))[2] |
| | paras 16–20 | *Not yet in force* (come into force at the same time as the Criminal Justice and Courts Services Act 2000, s 61) (s 418(2)) |
| | para 20A | *Not yet in force* (come into force at the same time as the Criminal Justice and Courts Services Act 2000, s 61) (s 418(2A))[4] |
| | paras 21–23 | *Not yet in force* (come into force at the same time as the Criminal Justice and Courts Services Act 2000, s 61) (s 418(2)) |
| | para 24(a), (b) | *Not yet in force* (come into force at the same time as Sch 22, para 24) (s 418(4)) |

**Sentencing Act 2020 (c 17)**—*contd*

| | | |
|---|---|---|
| | para 24(c) | *Not yet in force* (comes into force at the same time as the Criminal Justice and Courts Services Act 2000, s 61) (s 418(2)) |
| | para 24A | *Not yet in force* (comes into force at the same time as the Criminal Justice and Courts Services Act 2000, s 61) (s 418(2A))[4] |
| | para 25 | *Not yet in force* (comes into force at the same time as the Criminal Justice Act 2003, s 281(5)) (s 418(5)) |
| | para 26 | 31 Dec 2020 (s 418(4A))[2] |
| Sch 27 | | 1 Dec 2020 (SI 2020/1236) |
| Sch 28 | | 1 Dec 2020 (except repeal relating to the Powers of Criminal Courts (Sentencing) Act 2000, s 159 as it applies to process issued under Sch 5 to that Act) (SI 2020/1236) |
| | | *Not yet in force* (exception noted above comes into force at the same time as the repeal of that Schedule by the Criminal Justice and Immigration Act 2008, s 6(1)) (s 416(9)) |
| Sch 29 | | 1 Dec 2020 (SI 2020/1236) |

[1]  Entry adjusted to take account of amendments to s 417(3) made by the Counter-Terrorism and Sentencing Act 2021, s 46, Sch 13, paras 11, 26

[2]  S 418(4A) was inserted by the Taking Account of Convictions (EU Exit) (Amendment) Regulations 2020, SI 2020/1520, reg 4(1), (3)

[3]  Entry adjusted to take account of an amendment to s 418(2) by the Taking Account of Convictions (EU Exit) (Amendment) Regulations 2020, SI 2020/1520, reg 4(1), (2)

[4]  S 418(2A) is prospectively inserted by the Counter-Terrorism and Sentencing Act 2021, s 46, Sch 13, para 43(1), (5), as from a day to be appointed under s 50(3)(j) thereof; and Sch 26, paras 13A, 20A, 24A are prospectively inserted by the Counter-Terrorism and Sentencing Act 2021, s 46, Sch 13, para 43(1), (7), as from a day to be appointed under s 50(3)(j) thereof

[5]  Entry adjusted to take account of amendments to s 417(3) by the Police, Crime, Sentencing and Courts Act 2022, ss 3(1), (14), 140(4)(a)

---

**Sentencing (Pre-consolidation Amendments) Act 2020 (c 9)**

*RA:* 8 Jun 2020

*Commencement provisions:* s 5(1)–(3)

| | |
|---|---|
| 1–5 | 8 Jun 2020 (in so far as necessary to enable regulations to be made under ss 1, 2 of this Act) (s 5(1)) |
| | Immediately before 1 Dec 2020 (otherwise) (by virtue of s 5(3) and SI 2020/1236) |
| Sch 1 | 8 Jun 2020 (in so far as necessary to enable regulations to be made under ss 1, 2 of this Act) (s 5(1)) |
| | Immediately before 1 Dec 2020 (otherwise) (by virtue of s 5(3) and SI 2020/1236) |
| Sch 2 | Immediately before 1 Dec 2020 (by virtue of s 5(3) and SI 2020/1236) |

---

**Social Security Administration and Tribunal Membership (Scotland) Act 2020 (asp 18)**

*RA:* 10 Nov 2020

*Commencement provisions:* s 18; Social Security Administration and Tribunal Membership (Scotland) Act 2020 (Commencement No 1) Regulations 2020, SSI 2020/422; Social Security Administration and Tribunal Membership (Scotland) Act 2020 (Commencement No 2) Regulations 2021, SI 2021/232; Social Security Administration and Tribunal Membership (Scotland) Act 2020 (Commencement No 3) Regulations 2021, SSI 2021/338; Social Security Administration and Tribunal Membership (Scotland) Act 2020 (Commencement No 4) Regulations 2021, SSI 2021/352; Social Security Administration and Tribunal Membership (Scotland) Act 2020 (Commencement No 5

**Social Security Administration and Tribunal Membership (Scotland) Act 2020 (asp 18)**—*contd*

and Transitional Provisions) Regulations 2021, SSI 2021/442; Social Security Administration and Tribunal Membership (Scotland) Act 2020 (Commencement No 6) Regulations 2022, SSI 2022/146

| | | |
|---|---|---|
| 1 | | 11 Nov 2020 (s 18(1)) |
| 2 | (1)–(3) | 24 Jan 2022 (SSI 2021/442)[1] |
| | (4) | 23 Dec 2020 (for the purpose of inserting Social Security (Scotland) Act 2018, s 85B(1)–(11) in order to allow appointments to be made by the Scottish Ministers in connection with the determination of an individual's entitlement to assistance under regulations made under s 79 of the 2018 Act in circumstances where the condition in s 85B(3)(b) is met) (SSI 2020/422) |
| | | 24 Jan 2022 (otherwise) (SSI 2021/442)[1] |
| | (5) | 26 Jul 2021 (SSI 2021/232) |
| | (6)–(8) | *Not yet in force* |
| | | *Not yet in force* (otherwise) |
| 3 | | 26 Jul 2021 (SSI 2021/232) |
| 4–6 | | 11 Nov 2020 (s 18(1)) |
| 7 | | 11 Oct 2021 (SSI 2021/338) |
| 8 | | 20 Oct 2021 (SSI 2021/352) |
| 9–13 | | 26 Jul 2021 (SSI 2021/232) |
| 14 | | 11 Nov 2020 (s 18(1)) |
| 15, 16 | | 13 May 2022 (SSI 2022/146) |
| 17–19 | | 11 Nov 2020 (s 18(1)) |

[1]   For transitional provisions see SSI 2021/442, reg 3.

**Social Security (Up-rating of Benefits) Act 2020 (c 23)**

*RA:* 23 Nov 2020

*Commencement provisions:* s 2(2)

Whole Act in force 23 Nov 2020 (s 2(2))

**Stamp Duty Land Tax (Temporary Relief) Act 2020 (c 15)**

*RA:* 22 Jul 2020

Whole Act in force 22 Jul 2020

**Supply and Appropriation (Anticipation and Adjustments) Act 2020 (c 4)**

*RA:* 16 Mar 2020

Whole Act in force 16 Mar 2020 (RA)

**Supply and Appropriation (Main Estimates) Act 2020 (c 13)**

*RA:* 22 Jul 2020

Whole Act in force 22 Jul 2020 (RA)

## Taxation (Post-transition Period) Act 2020 (c 26)

*RA:* 17 Dec 2020

*Commencement provisions:* s 11; Finance Act 2016, Section 126 (Appointed Day), the Taxation (Cross-border Trade) Act 2018 (Appointed Day No 8, Transition and Saving Provisions) and the Taxation (Post transition Period) Act 2020 (Appointed Day No 1) (EU Exit) Regulations 2020, SI 2020/1642

| | | |
|---|---|---|
| 1–5 | | 17 Dec 2020 (so far as making provision for anything to be done by regulations or order) (s 11(1)) |
| | | 31 Dec 2020, at 11.00pm (IP completion day) (otherwise) (SI 2020/1642) |
| 6 | | 1 Jan 2021 (s 11(2)) |
| 7, 8 | | 17 Dec 2020 (so far as making provision for anything to be done by regulations or order) (s 11(1)) |
| | | 31 Dec 2020, at 11.00pm (IP completion day) (otherwise) (SI 2020/1642) |
| 9–12 | | 17 Dec 2020 (s 11(1)) |
| Sch 1 | | 17 Dec 2020 (so far as making provision for anything to be done by regulations or order) (s 11(1)) |
| | | 31 Dec 2020, at 11.00pm (IP completion day) (otherwise) (SI 2020/1642) |
| Sch 2 | paras 1–6 | 17 Dec 2020 (so far as making provision for anything to be done by regulations or order) (s 11(1)) |
| | | 31 Dec 2020, at 11.00pm (IP completion day) (otherwise) (SI 2020/1642) |
| | para 7(1), (2) | 17 Dec 2020 (so far as making provision for anything to be done by regulations or order) (s 11(1)) |
| | | 31 Dec 2020, at 11.00pm (IP completion day) (otherwise) (SI 2020/1642) |
| | para 7(3) | 17 Dec 2020 (so far as making provision for anything to be done by regulations or order) (s 11(1)) |
| | | *Not yet in force* (otherwise) |
| | para 7(4)–(6) | 17 Dec 2020 (so far as making provision for anything to be done by regulations or order) (s 11(1)) |
| | | 31 Dec 2020, at 11.00pm (IP completion day) (otherwise) (SI 2020/1642) |
| | paras 8–13 | 17 Dec 2020 (so far as making provision for anything to be done by regulations or order) (s 11(1)) |
| | | 31 Dec 2020, at 11.00pm (IP completion day) (otherwise) (SI 2020/1642) |
| Sch 3 | | 17 Dec 2020 (so far as making provision for anything to be done by regulations or order) (s 11(1)) |
| | | 31 Dec 2020, at 11.00pm (IP completion day) (otherwise) (SI 2020/1642) |
| Sch 4 | | 17 Dec 2020 (s 11(1)) |

## Terrorist Offenders (Restriction of Early Release) Act 2020 (c 3)

*RA:* 26 Feb 2020

*Commencement provisions:* s 10(4)

Whole Act in force 26 Feb 2020 (s 10(4))

## Trade (Disclosure of Information) Act 2020 (c 28)

*RA:* 17 Dec 2020

*Commencement provisions:* s 6(2)

**Trade (Disclosure of Information) Act 2020 (c 28)**—*contd*

Whole Act in force 17 Dec 2020 (s 6(2))

---

**UEFA European Championship (Scotland) Act 2020 (asp 1)**

*RA:* 23 Jan 2020

*Commencement provisions:* s 35; UEFA European Championship (Scotland) Act 2020 (Commencement No 1) Regulations 2020, SSI 2020/49; UEFA European Championship (Scotland) Act 2020 (Commencement No 2) Regulations 2020, SSI 2020/189

| | |
|---|---|
| 1 | 9 Mar 2020 (SSI 2020/49) |
| 2–4 | 10 Jul 2020 (SSI 2020/189) |
| 5–8 | 9 Mar 2020 (SSI 2020/49) |
| 9–11 | 24 Mar 2020 (s 35(2)) |
| 12–14 | 9 Mar 2020 (SSI 2020/49) |
| 15–25 | 24 Mar 2020 (s 35(2)) |
| 26 | 9 Mar 2020 (SSI 2020/49) |
| 27, 28 | 24 Mar 2020 (s 35(2)) |
| 29 | 9 Mar 2020 (SSI 2020/49) |
| 30, 31 | 24 Mar 2020 (s 35(2)) |
| 32–37 | 24 Jan 2020 (s 35(1)) |

---

**United Kingdom Internal Market Act 2020 (c 27)**

*RA:* 17 Dec 2020

*Commencement provisions:* s 59(2)–(4); United Kingdom Internal Market Act 2020 (Commencement No 1) Regulations 2020, SI 2020/1621; United Kingdom Internal Market Act 2020 (Commencement No 2) Regulations 2021, SI 2021/706; United Kingdom Internal Market Act 2020 (Commencement No 3) Regulations 2021, SI 2021/1062

| | | |
|---|---|---|
| 1–29 | | IP completion day (as defined by European Union (Withdrawal Agreement) Act 2020, s 39(1)–(5)) (SI 2020/1621) |
| 30 | (1)–(9) | 20 Sep 2021 (SI 2021/1062) |
| | (10) | IP completion day (as defined by European Union (Withdrawal Agreement) Act 2020, s 39(1)–(5)) (SI 2020/1621) |
| 31 | | 20 Sep 2021 (SI 2021/1062) |
| 32 | | IP completion day (as defined by European Union (Withdrawal Agreement) Act 2020, s 39(1)–(5)) (SI 2020/1621) |
| 33–38 | | 20 Sep 2021 (SI 2021/1062) |
| 39 | | IP completion day (as defined by European Union (Withdrawal Agreement) Act 2020, s 39(1)–(5)) (SI 2020/1621) |
| 40 | | 20 Sep 2021 (SI 2021/1062) |
| 41–43 | | 14 Jun 2021 (SI 2021/706) |
| 44, 45 | | 20 Sep 2021 (SI 2021/1062) |
| 46–58 | | IP completion day (as defined by European Union (Withdrawal Agreement) Act 2020, s 39(1)–(5)) (SI 2020/1621) |
| 59 | | 17 Dec 2020 (s 59(2)) |
| Schs 1–3 | | IP completion day (as defined by European Union (Withdrawal Agreement) Act 2020, s 39(1)–(5)) (SI 2020/1621) |

---

**Wild Animals and Circuses (Wales) Act 2020 (asc 2)**

*RA:* 7 Sep 2020

*Commencement provisions:* s 12

Whole Act in force 1 Dec 2020 (s 12)

---

**Windrush Compensation Scheme (Expenditure) Act 2020 (c 8)**

*RA:* 8 Jun 2020

*Commencement provisions*: s 2(2)

Whole Act in force 8 Jun 2020 (s 2(2))

# 2021 Acts

## Air Traffic Management and Unmanned Aircraft Act 2021 (c 12)

*RA:* 29 Apr 2021

*Commencement provisions:* s 21; Air Traffic Management and Unmanned Aircraft Act 2021 (Commencement No 1) Regulations 2021, SI 2021/748; Air Traffic Management and Unmanned Aircraft Act 2021 (Commencement No 2) Regulations 2022, SI 2022/119

| | | |
|---|---|---|
| 1–6 | | 18 Feb 2022 (SI 2022/119) |
| 7 | (1) | See Sch 1 below |
| | (2) | See Sch 2 below |
| 8 | | 18 Feb 2022 (SI 2022/119) |
| 9–11 | | 29 Jun 2021 (SI 2021/748) |
| 12 | | 29 Apr 2021 (s 21(1)) |
| 13 | | 29 Apr 2021 (for the purpose of making regulations) (s 21(1)) |
| | | 29 Jun 2021 (otherwise) (SI 2021/748) |
| 14 | | 29 Apr 2021 (for the purpose of making regulations) (s 21(1)) |
| | | 29 Jun 2021 (otherwise) (s 21(2)) |
| 15 | | 29 Apr 2021 (for the purpose of making regulations) (s 21(1)) |
| | | 29 Jun 2021 (otherwise) (SI 2021/748) |
| 16–22 | | 29 Apr 2021 (s 21(1)) |
| Sch 1 | | 18 Feb 2022 (SI 2022/119) |
| Sch 2 | | 29 Apr 2021 (for the purpose of making regulations) (s 21(1)) |
| | | 18 Feb 2022 (otherwise) (SI 2022/119) |
| Schs 3–7 | | 29 Jun 2021 (SI 2021/748) |
| Sch 8 | | 29 Apr 2021 (for the purpose of making regulations) (s 21(1)) |
| | | 29 Jun 2021 (otherwise) (SI 2021/748) |
| Sch 9 | | 29 Apr 2021 (for the purpose of making regulations) (s 21(1)) |
| | | 29 Jun 2021 (otherwise) (s 21(2)) |
| Sch 10 | | 29 Apr 2021 (for the purpose of making regulations) (s 21(1)) |
| | | 29 Jun 2021 (otherwise) (SI 2021/748) |
| Sch 11 | | 29 Apr 2021 (s 21(1)) |

## Animal Welfare (Sentencing) Act 2021 (c 21)

*RA:* 29 Apr 2021

*Commencement provisions:* s 2(2)

Whole Act in force 29 Jun 2021 (s 2(2))

## Armed Forces Act 2021 (c 35)

*RA:* 15 Dec 2021

*Commencement provisions:* s 24; Armed Forces Act 2021 (Commencement No1) Regulations 2022, SI 2022/471; Armed Forces Act 2021 (Commencement No 2) Regulations 2022, SI 2022/625

| | |
|---|---|
| 1 | 15 Dec 2021 (s 24(2)(a)) |

**Armed Forces Act 2021 (c 35)**—*contd*

| | | |
|---|---|---|
| 2 | | 1 May 2022 (for the purpose only of conferring power to make subordinate legislation) (SI 2022/471) |
| | | *Not yet in force* (otherwise) |
| 3 | | 1 May 2022 (SI 2022/471) |
| 4–6 | | 1 May 2022 (for the purpose only of conferring power to make subordinate legislation) (SI 2022/471) |
| | | *Not yet in force* (otherwise) |
| 7 | | 1 May 2022 (in so far as inserts Armed Forces Act 2006, s 320A) (SI 2022/471) |
| | | *Not yet in force* (otherwise) |
| 8 | | 1 May 2022 (for the purpose only of conferring power to make subordinate legislation or issue guidance) (SI 2022/471) |
| | | *Not yet in force* (otherwise) |
| 9 | | 1 May 2022 (for the purpose only of conferring power to make subordinate legislation) (SI 2022/471) |
| | | *Not yet in force* (otherwise) |
| 10 | | 1 May 2022 (for the purpose only of conferring power to make subordinate legislation) (SI 2022/471) |
| | | 15 Jun 2022 (otherwise) (SI 2022/625) |
| 11 | | *Not yet in force* |
| 12 | | 1 May 2022 (for the purpose only of conferring power to make subordinate legislation) (SI 2022/471) |
| | | *Not yet in force* (otherwise) |
| 13 | | 1 May 2022 (SI 2022/471)[1] |
| 14–16 | | 1 May 2022 (for the purpose only of conferring power to make subordinate legislation) (SI 2022/471) |
| | | *Not yet in force* (otherwise) |
| 17 | (1)–(4) | *Not yet in force* |
| | (5) | 15 Dec 2021 (s 24(2)(a)) |
| 18 | | 1 May 2022 (SI 2022/471) |
| 19 | | 15 Feb 2022 (s 24(3)) |
| 20 | | 15 Dec 2021 (s 24(2)(a)) |
| 21 | | 1 May 2022 (for the purpose only of conferring power to make subordinate legislation) (SI 2022/471) |
| | | *Not yet in force* (otherwise) |
| 22 | (1) | See sub-ss (2), (3) below |
| | (2) | 15 Feb 2022 (s 24(3)) |
| | (3) | 15 Dec 2021 (s 24(2)(a)) |
| 23–27 | | 15 Dec 2021 (s 24(2)(b)) |
| Schs 1, 2 | | 1 May 2022 (for the purpose only of conferring power to make subordinate legislation) (SI 2022/471) |
| | | *Not yet in force* (otherwise) |
| Sch 3 | | 1 May 2022 (for the purpose only of conferring power to make subordinate legislation) (SI 2022/471) |
| | | 15 Jun 2022 (otherwise) (SI 2022/625) |
| Sch 4 | | *Not yet in force* |
| Schs 5, 6 | | 1 May 2022 (for the purpose only of conferring power to make subordinate legislation) (SI 2022/471) |
| | | *Not yet in force* (otherwise) |

[1]  For transitional provisions see SI 2022/471, reg 5

---

**Botulinum Toxin and Cosmetic Fillers (Children) Act 2021 (c 19)**

*RA*: 29 Apr 2021

*Commencement provisions*: s 6(3), (4); Botulinum Toxin and Cosmetic Fillers (Children) Act 2021 (Commencement) Regulations 2021, SI 2021/1004

| | |
|---|---|
| 1–4 | 1 Oct 2021 (SI 2021/1004) |

**Botulinum Toxin and Cosmetic Fillers (Children) Act 2021 (c 19)**—*contd*

5, 6                       29 Apr 2021 (s 6(4))

---

**British Library Board (Power to Borrow) Act 2021 (c 15)**

*RA:* 29 Apr 2021

*Commencement provisions:* s 2(2)

Whole Act in force 29 Jun 2021 (s 2(2))

---

**Budget (Scotland) Act 2021 (asp 8)**

*RA:* 29 Mar 2021

*Commencement provisions:* s 10

Whole Act in force 30 Mar 2021 (s 10)

---

**Carer's Allowance Supplement (Scotland) Act 2021 (asp 20)**

*RA:* 15 Nov 2021

*Commencement provisions:* s 3

| | |
|---|---|
| 1 | 16 Nov 2021 (s 3(1)) |
| 2 | *Not yet in force* |
| 3, 4 | 16 Nov 2021 (s 3(1)) |

---

**Cathedrals Measure 2021 (No 2)**

*RA:* 29 Apr 2021

*Commencement provisions:* s 53

| | | |
|---|---|---|
| 1–30 | | *Not yet in force* |
| 31 | (1), (2) | 29 Apr 2021 (s 54(1)) |
| | (3) | *Not yet in force* |
| | (4)–(7) | 29 Apr 2021 (s 54(1)) |
| 32 | | 29 Apr 2021 (s 54(1)) |
| 33 | (1) | 29 Apr 2021 (s 54(1)) |
| | (2) | *Not yet in force* |
| | (3) | 29 Apr 2021 (s 54(1)) |
| 34 | (1)–(3) | 29 Apr 2021 (s 54(1)) |
| | (4), (5) | *Not yet in force* |
| 35–44 | | *Not yet in force* |
| 45 | | 29 Apr 2021 (for the purposes of ss 31–34, 46–48, 51(1), 52–54, Sch 4, paras 6, 7, 9(1), (2)) (s 54(1)) |
| | | *Not yet in force (otherwise)* |
| 46–48 | | 29 Apr 2021 (s 54(1)) |
| 49 | | *Not yet in force* |
| 50 | (1) | See Sch 4 below |
| 51 | (1) | 29 Apr 2021 (so far as relates to Cathedrals Measure 1999, Pt 3) (s 54(1)) |
| | | *Not yet in force (otherwise)* |
| | (2), (3) | *Not yet in force* |
| 52–54 | | 29 Apr 2021 (s 54(1)) |
| Schs 1–3 | | *Not yet in force* |
| Sch 4 | paras 1–5 | *Not yet in force* |
| | paras 6, 7 | 29 Apr 2021 (s 54(1)) |
| | para 8 | *Not yet in force* |

**Cathedrals Measure 2021 (No 2)**—*contd*

| | | |
|---|---|---|
| para 9(1), (2) | 29 Apr 2021 (s 54(1)) | |
| para 9(3) | *Not yet in force* | |
| para 9(4) | 29 Apr 2021 (s 54(1)) | |
| paras 10–45 | *Not yet in force* | |

**Compensation (London Capital & Finance plc and Fraud Compensation Fund) Act 2021 (c 29)**

*RA:* 20 Oct 2021

Whole Act in force 20 Oct 2021 (RA)

**Contingencies Fund Act 2021 (c 9)**

*RA:* 15 Mar 2021

Whole Act in force 15 Mar 2021 (RA)

**Coronavirus (Extension and Expiry) (Scotland) Act 2021 (asp 19)**

*RA:* 4 Aug 2021

*Commencement provisions:* s 11

| | | |
|---|---|---|
| 1–7 | | 5 Aug 2021 (s 11(2)) |
| 8 | (1) | 30 Sep 2021 (s 11(1)) |
| | (2) | 5 Aug 2021 (s 11(2)) |
| | (3)–(5) | 30 Sep 2021 (s 11(1)) |
| | (6) | 5 Aug 2021 (s 11(2)) |
| | (7), (8) | 30 Sep 2021 (s 11(1)) |
| | (9), (10) | 5 Aug 2021 (s 11(2)) |
| | (11), (12) | 30 Sep 2021 (s 11(1)) |
| 9–12 | | 5 Aug 2021 (s 11(2)) |
| Schedule | | 5 Aug 2021 (s 11(2)) |

**Counter-Terrorism and Sentencing Act 2021 (c 11)**

*RA:* 29 Apr 2021

*Commencement provisions:* s 50

| | |
|---|---|
| 1 | 29 Jun 2021 (exception noted below) (s 50(2)) |
| | *Not yet in force* (as it has effect for the purposes of the Sentencing Code, s 69 as applied by Armed Forces Act 2006, s 238) |
| 2 | 29 Jun 2021 (s 50(2)) |
| 3 | 30 Apr 2021 (s 50(1)) |
| 4–10 | 29 Jun 2021 (s 50(2)) |
| 11 | 29 Jun 2021 (exception noted below) (s 50(2)) |
| | *Not yet in force* (as it has effect for the purposes of the Sentencing Code, s 323 as applied by Armed Forces Act 2006, s 261A) |
| 12–14 | 29 Jun 2021 (s 50(2)) |
| 15 | 29 Jun 2021 (exception noted below) (s 50(2)) |
| | *Not yet in force* (as it has effect for the purposes of the Sentencing Code, Sch 18 as applied by Armed Forces Act 2006, ss 219A, 221A) |
| 16 | 29 Jun 2021 (exception noted below) (s 50(2)) |
| | *Not yet in force* (as it has effect for the purposes of the Sentencing Code, s 256 as applied by Armed Forces Act 2006, s 221A) |
| 17, 18 | 29 Jun 2021 (exception noted below) (s 50(2)) |

**Counter-Terrorism and Sentencing Act 2021 (c 11)**—*contd*

|  |  |  |
|---|---|---|
|  |  | *Not yet in force* (as they have effect for the purposes of the Sentencing Code, ss 268, 281 as applied by Armed Forces Act 2006, s 219A) |
| 19 |  | 29 Jun 2021 (s 50(2)) |
| 20 |  | 29 Jun 2021 (s 50(2)) |
| 21 |  | 30 Apr 2021 (exception noted below) (s 50(1)) |
|  |  | *Not yet in force* (as it has effect for the purposes of the Sentencing Code, Sch 13 as applied by Armed Forces Act 2006, s 224A) |
| 22–24 |  | 30 Apr 2021 (s 50(1)) |
| 25 |  | See Sch 8 below |
| 26–29 |  | 29 Jun 2021 (s 50(2)) |
| 30 |  | 30 Apr 2021 (s 50(1)) |
| 31–44 |  | 29 Jun 2021 (s 50(2)) |
| 45 |  | 30 Apr 2021 (s 50(1)) |
| 46 |  | See Sch 13 below |
| 47–51 |  | 30 Apr 2021 (s 50(1)) |
| Sch 1 |  | 29 Jun 2021 (exception noted below) (s 50(2)) |
|  |  | *Not yet in force* (as it has effect for the purposes of the Sentencing Code, s 69 as applied by Armed Forces Act 2006, s 238) |
| Sch 2 |  | 29 Jun 2021 (s 50(2)) |
| Sch 3 |  | 30 Apr 2021 (s 50(1)) |
| Sch 4 |  | 29 Jun 2021 (s 50(2)) |
| Sch 5 |  | 29 Jun 2021 (s 50(2)) |
| Sch 6 |  | 30 Apr 2021 (exception noted below) (s 50(1)) |
|  |  | *Not yet in force* (as it has effect for the purposes of the Sentencing Code, Sch 13 as applied by Armed Forces Act 2006, s 224A) |
| Sch 7 |  | 30 Apr 2021 (s 50(1)) |
| Sch 8 |  | *Not yet in force* |
| Schs 9–12 |  | 29 Jun 2021 (s 50(2)) |
| Sch 13 | paras 1–5 | 29 Jun 2021 (s 50(2)) |
|  | para 6(3)(a) | 29 Jun 2021 (exception noted below) (s 50(2)) |
|  |  | *Not yet in force* (as it has effect for the purposes of the Sentencing Code, s 69 as applied by Armed Forces Act 2006, s 238) |
|  | para 6(3)(b) | 29 Jun 2021 (s 50(2)) |
|  | para 6(4) | 29 Jun 2021 (exception noted below) (s 50(2)) |
|  |  | *Not yet in force* (as it has effect for the purposes of the Sentencing Code, s 69 as applied by Armed Forces Act 2006, s 238) |
|  | para 6(5) | 29 Jun 2021 (s 50(2)) |
|  | paras 7–11 | 29 Jun 2021 (s 50(2)) |
|  | para 12 | 30 Apr 2021 (exception noted below) (s 50(1)) |
|  |  | *Not yet in force* (as it has effect for the purposes of the Sentencing Code, Sch 13 as applied by Armed Forces Act 2006, s 224A) |
|  | paras 13–32 | 30 Apr 2021 (s 50(1)) |
|  | paras 33–43 | *Not yet in force* |
|  | para 44 | 30 Apr 2021 (s 50(1)) |
|  | para 45(1)–(3) | 30 Apr 2021 (s 50(1)) |
|  | para 45(4) | 29 Jun 2021 (s 50(2)) |
|  | para 45(5), (6) | 30 Apr 2021 (s 50(1)) |
|  | para 46 | 29 Jun 2021 (s 50(2)) |
|  | paras 47–51 | 30 Apr 2021 (s 50(1)) |
|  | para 52(1)–(6) | 30 Apr 2021 (s 50(1)) |
|  | para 52(7)(a) | 29 Jun 2021 (s 50(2)) |
|  | para 52(7)(b)–(d) | 30 Apr 2021 (s 50(1)) |
|  | para 52(8)–(17) | 30 Apr 2021 (s 50(1)) |
|  | para 53(1)–(3) | 30 Apr 2021 (s 50(1)) |
|  | para 53(4) | 29 Jun 2021 (s 50(2)) |
|  | paras 54–60 | 30 Apr 2021 (s 50(1)) |
|  | paras 61–66 | 29 Jun 2021 (s 50(2)) |
|  | paras 67–76 | 30 Apr 2021 (s 50(1)) |

**See Halsbury's Statutes Citator for amendments to these Acts**                2649

## Covert Human Intelligence Sources (Criminal Conduct) Act 2021 (c 4)

*RA:* 1 Mar 2021

*Commencement provisions*: s 9; Covert Human Intelligence Sources (Criminal Conduct) Act 2021 (Commencement and Transitional Provisions) Regulations 2021, SI 2021/605

| | | |
|---|---|---|
| 1 | (1)–(3) | 10 Aug 2021 (for the purposes of criminal conduct authorisations granted by a person holding an office, rank or position with any intelligence service) (SI 2021/605) |
| | | 15 Sep 2021 (for the purposes of criminal conduct authorisations granted by a person holding an office, rank or position with any police force) (SI 2021/605) |
| | | 30 Sep 2021 (otherwise) (SI 2021/605) |
| | (4) | 10 Aug 2021 (for the purposes of criminal conduct authorisations granted by a person holding an office, rank or position with any intelligence service) (SI 2021/605)[1] |
| | | 15 Sep 2021 (for the purposes of criminal conduct authorisations granted by a person holding an office, rank or position with any police force) (SI 2021/605)[1] |
| | | 30 Sep 2021 (otherwise) (SI 2021/605)[1] |
| | (5) | 10 Aug 2021 (for the purposes of criminal conduct authorisations granted by a person holding an office, rank or position with any intelligence service) (SI 2021/605) |
| | | 15 Sep 2021 (for the purposes of criminal conduct authorisations granted by a person holding an office, rank or position with any police force) (SI 2021/605) |
| | | 30 Sep 2021 (otherwise) (SI 2021/605) |
| 2–8 | | 10 Aug 2021 (for the purposes of criminal conduct authorisations granted by a person holding an office, rank or position with any intelligence service) (SI 2021/605) |
| | | 15 Sep 2021 (for the purposes of criminal conduct authorisations granted by a person holding an office, rank or position with any police force) (SI 2021/605) |
| | | 30 Sep 2021 (otherwise) (SI 2021/605) |
| 9, 10 | | 1 Mar 2021 (s 9(1)) |
| Schedule | | 10 Aug 2021 (for the purposes of criminal conduct authorisations granted by a person holding an office, rank or position with any intelligence service) (SI 2021/605) |
| | | 15 Sep 2021 (for the purposes of criminal conduct authorisations granted by a person holding an office, rank or position with any police force) (SI 2021/605) |
| | | 30 Sep 2021 (otherwise) (SI 2021/605) |

[1] For transitional provisions, see SI 2021/605, reg 3

## Critical Benchmarks (References and Administrators' Liability) Act 2021 (c 33)

*RA:* 15 Dec 2021

*Commencement provisions*: s 4(3)

Whole Act in force 15 Dec 2021 (s 4(3))

## Curriculum and Assessment (Wales) Act 2021 (asc 4)

*RA:* 29 Apr 2021

*Commencement provisions*: s 84; Curriculum and Assessment (Wales) Act 2021 (Commencement No 1) Order 2021, SI 2021/1069; Curriculum and Assessment (Wales) Act 2021 (Commencement No 2) Order 2022, SI 2022/12; Curriculum and Assessment (Wales) Act 2021 (Commencement No 3 and Transitional Provision) Order 2022, SI 2022/652

**Curriculum and Assessment (Wales) Act 2021 (asc 4)**—*contd*

| | | |
|---|---|---|
| 1–5 | | 29 Sep 2021 (SI 2021/1069) |
| 6, 7 | | 29 Sep 2021 (for the purpose only of issuing or revising a code) (SI 2021/1069) |
| | | 1 Sep 2022 (otherwise) (SI 2022/652) |
| 8 | | 23 Nov 2021 (for the purpose only of issuing or revising a code) (SI 2021/1069) |
| | | 1 Sep 2022 (otherwise) (SI 2022/652) |
| 9–23 | | 1 Sep 2022 (in respect of a child pr pupil who is provided with nursery education, in a reception year, in years 1 to 6, and in year 7 in those maintained schools and pupil referral units set out in SI 2022/652, Schedule) (SI 2022/652)[3] |
| | | 1 Sep 2023 (in respect of a child or pupil in year 7 for all other settings not listed in SI 2022/652, Schedule) (SI 2022/652)[3] |
| | | 1 Sep 2024 (in respect of a child or pupil in year 9) (SI 2022/652)[3] |
| | | 1 Sep 2025 (in respect of a child or pupil in year 10) (SI 2022/652)[3] |
| | | 1 Sep 2026 (otherwise) (SI 2022/652)[3] |
| 24 | (1)–(4) | 1 Sep 2022 (in respect of a child pr pupil who is provided with nursery education, in a reception year, in years 1 to 6, and in year 7 in those maintained schools and pupil referral units set out in SI 2022/652, Schedule) (SI 2022/652)[3] |
| | | 1 Sep 2023 (in respect of a child or pupil in year 7 for all other settings not listed in SI 2022/652, Schedule) (SI 2022/652)[3] |
| | | 1 Sep 2024 (in respect of a child or pupil in year 9) (SI 2022/652)[3] |
| | | 1 Sep 2025 (in respect of a child or pupil in year 10) (SI 2022/652)[3] |
| | | 1 Sep 2026 (otherwise) (SI 2022/652)[3] |
| | (5) | 1 Sep 2025 (in respect of a child or pupil in year 10) (SI 2022/652)[3] |
| | | 1 Sep 2026 (otherwise) (SI 2022/652)[3] |
| 25–29 | | 1 Sep 2022 (in respect of a child pr pupil who is provided with nursery education, in a reception year, in years 1 to 6, and in year 7 in those maintained schools and pupil referral units set out in SI 2022/652, Schedule) (SI 2022/652)[3] |
| | | 1 Sep 2023 (in respect of a child or pupil in year 7 for all other settings not listed in SI 2022/652, Schedule) (SI 2022/652)[3] |
| | | 1 Sep 2024 (in respect of a child or pupil in year 9) (SI 2022/652)[3] |
| | | 1 Sep 2025 (in respect of a child or pupil in year 10) (SI 2022/652)[3] |
| | | 1 Sep 2026 (otherwise) (SI 2022/652)[3] |
| 30–33 | | 1 Sep 2025 (in respect of a child or pupil in year 10) (SI 2022/652)[3] |
| | | 1 Sep 2026 (otherwise) (SI 2022/652)[3] |
| 34–41 | | 1 Sep 2022 (in respect of a child pr pupil who is provided with nursery education, in a reception year, in years 1 to 6, and in year 7 in those maintained schools and pupil referral units set out in SI 2022/652, Schedule) (SI 2022/652)[3] |
| | | 1 Sep 2023 (in respect of a child or pupil in year 7 for all other settings not listed in SI 2022/652, Schedule) (SI 2022/652)[3] |
| | | 1 Sep 2024 (in respect of a child or pupil in year 9) (SI 2022/652)[3] |
| | | 1 Sep 2025 (in respect of a child or pupil in year 10) (SI 2022/652)[3] |
| | | 1 Sep 2026 (otherwise) (SI 2022/652)[3] |
| 42, 43 | | 14 Jun 2022 (for the purpose of making regulations) (SI 2022/652)[3] |
| | | 1 Sep 2022 (otherwise) (SI 2022/652)[3] |
| 44–55 | | 1 Sep 2022 (in respect of a child pr pupil who is provided with nursery education, in a reception year, in years 1 to 6, and in year 7 in those maintained schools and pupil referral units set out in SI 2022/652, Schedule) (SI 2022/652) |

**See Halsbury's Statutes Citator for amendments to these Acts** 2651

**Curriculum and Assessment (Wales) Act 2021 (asc 4)**—*contd*

|  |  |  |
|---|---|---|
|  |  | 1 Sep 2023 (in respect of a child or pupil in year 7 for all other settings not listed in SI 2022/652, Schedule) (SI 2022/652) |
|  |  | 1 Sep 2024 (in respect of a child or pupil in year 9) (SI 2022/652) |
|  |  | 1 Sep 2025 (in respect of a child or pupil in year 10) (SI 2022/652) |
|  |  | 1 Sep 2026 (otherwise) (SI 2022/652) |
| 56 | (1) | 11 Jan 2022 (for the purpose of making regulations under s 56) (SI 2022/12) |
|  |  | 1 Sep 2022 (otherwise) (SI 2022/12)[2] |
|  | (2)–(6) | 1 Sep 2022 (SI 2022/12)[2] |
| 57 | (1) | 11 Jan 2022 (for the purpose of issuing a direction under s 57) (SI 2022/12) |
|  |  | 1 Sep 2022 (otherwise) (SI 2022/12)[2] |
|  | (2), (3) | 1 Sep 2022 (SI 2022/12)[1] |
| 58–62 |  | 1 Sep 2026 (SI 2022/652) |
| 63–67 |  | 1 Sep 2022 (SI 2022/652) |
| 68 |  | 1 Sep 2024 (in respect of a child or pupil in year 9 (SI 2022/652) |
|  |  | 1 Sep 2026 (otherwise) (SI 2022/652) |
| 69 |  | 14 Jun 2022 (for the purpose of making regulations) (SI 2022/652) |
|  |  | 1 Sep 2022 (otherwise) (SI 2022/652) |
| 70, 71 |  | 1 Sep 2022 (SI 2022/652) |
| 72–85 |  | 30 Apr 2021 (s 84(1)) |
| Sch 1 |  | 1 Sep 2022 (in respect of a child pr pupil who is provided with nursery education, in a reception year, in years 1 to 6, and in year 7 in those maintained schools and pupil referral units set out in SI 2022/652, Schedule) (SI 2022/652) |
|  |  | 1 Sep 2023 (in respect of a child or pupil in year 7 for all other settings not listed in SI 2022/652, Schedule) (SI 2022/652) |
|  |  | 1 Sep 2024 (in respect of a child or pupil in year 9) (SI 2022/652) |
|  |  | 1 Sep 2025 (in respect of a child or pupil in year 10) (SI 2022/652) |
|  |  | 1 Sep 2026 (otherwise) (SI 2022/652) |
| Sch 2 |  | 30 Apr 2021 (s 84(1))[1] |

[1] For transitional provisions and savings, see SI 2022/111,reg 3

[2] Note that SI 2022/652 also purports to bring these provisions into force on 1 September 2022

[3] For transitional provisions, see SI 222/652, reg 2

---

**Defamation and Malicious Publication (Scotland) Act 2021 (asp 10)**

*RA:* 21 Apr 2021

*Commencement provisions*: s 39; Defamation and Malicious Publication (Scotland) Act 2021 (Commencement and Transitional Provision) Regulations 2022, SSI 2022/154

|  |  |
|---|---|
| 1 | 8 Aug 2022 (SSI 2022/154) |
| 2, 3 | 8 Aug 2022 (SSI 2022/154)[1] |
| 4–32 | 8 Aug 2022 (SSI 2022/154) |
| 33 | 8 Aug 2022 (SSI 2022/154)[1] |
| 34, 35 | 8 Aug 2022 (SSI 2022/154) |
| 36–40 | 22 Apr 2021 (s 39(1)) |

---

**Diocesan Boards of Education Measure 2021 (No 1)**

*RA:* 29 Apr 2021

*Commencement provisions*: s 24(2)–(6)

|  |  |
|---|---|
| 1, 2 | 29 Jun 2021 (s 24(3)) |

**Diocesan Boards of Education Measure 2021 (No 1)**—*contd*

| | | |
|---|---|---|
| 3 | (1)–(9) | 29 Jun 2021 (s 24(3)) |
| | (10) | *Not yet in force* |
| 4–21 | | 29 Jun 2021 (s 24(3)) |
| 22 | | 29 Apr 2021 (s 24(2)) |
| 23 | | 29 Jun 2021 (s 24(3)) |
| 24 | | 29 Apr 2021 (s 24(2)) |
| Sch 1 | | 29 Jun 2021 (s 24(3)) |
| Sch 2 | | *Not yet in force* |

---

**Dogs (Protection of Livestock) (Amendment) (Scotland) Act 2021 (asp 18)**

*RA*: 5 May 2021

*Commencement provisions*: s 7

| | |
|---|---|
| 1–6 | 6 Nov 2021 (s 7(2)) |
| 7, 8 | 6 May 2021 (s 7(1)) |

---

**Domestic Abuse Act 2021 (c 17)**

*RA*: 29 Apr 2021

*Commencement provisions*: s 90; Domestic Abuse Act 2021 (Commencement) (Scotland) Regulations 2021, SSI 2021/239; Domestic Abuse Act 2021 (Commencement No 1 and Saving Provisions) Regulations 2021, SI 2021/797; Domestic Abuse Act 2021 (Commencement No 2) Regulations 2021, SI 2021/1038; Domestic Abuse Act 2021 (Commencement No 3) Regulations 2022, SI 2022/73; Domestic Abuse Act 2021 (Commencement No 1) Order (Northern Ireland) 2022, SR 2022/52; Domestic Abuse Act 2021 (Commencement No 4) Regulations 2022, SI 2022/553; Domestic Abuse Act 2021 (Commencement No 5 and Transitional Provision) Regulations 2022, SI 2022/840

| | |
|---|---|
| 1 | 29 Apr 2021 (in so far as confers power to make regulations under or by virtue of this Act) (s 90(1)) |
| | 5 Jul 2021 (only for the purposes of ss 75, 76, 83, 177, 179, 189 of this Act, Housing Act 1996, s 198 and Homelessness (Priority Need for Accommodation) (England) Order 2002, SI 2002/2051) (SI 2021/797) |
| | 1 Oct 2021 (otherwise) (SI 2021/1038) |
| 2 | 29 Apr 2021 (in so far as confers power to make regulations under or by virtue of this Act) (s 90(1)) |
| | 1 Oct 2021 (otherwise) (SI 2021/1038) |
| 3 | 29 Apr 2021 (in so far as confers power to make regulations under or by virtue of this Act) (s 90(1)) |
| | 1 Oct 2021 (only for the purposes of s 63 and Pt 4 of the Act) (SI 2021/1038) |
| | 1 Nov 2021 (only for the purposes of s 79 of the Act) (SI 2021/1038) |
| | 31 Jan 2022 (otherwise) (SI 2022/73) |
| 4–21 | 29 Apr 2021 (in so far as confers power to make regulations under or by virtue of this Act) (s 90(1)) |
| | 1 Nov 2021 (otherwise) (SI 2021/1038) |
| 22–56 | 29 Apr 2021 (in so far as confers power to make regulations under or by virtue of this Act) (s 90(1)) |
| | *Not yet in force* (otherwise) |
| 57–61 | 29 Apr 2021 (in so far as confers power to make regulations under or by virtue of this Act) (s 90(1)) |
| | 1 Oct 2021 (otherwise) (SI 2021/1038) |
| 62 | 29 Apr 2021 (in so far as confers power to make regulations under or by virtue of this Act) (s 90(1)) |

**Domestic Abuse Act 2021 (c 17)**—*contd*

|  | 19 May 2022 (except for enabling a special measures direction to include the provision for which Youth Justice and Criminal Evidence Act 1999, ss 27, 28 provide) (SI 2022/553) |
|--|--|
|  | *Not yet in force* (exception noted above) |
| 63 | 29 Apr 2021 (in so far as confers power to make regulations under or by virtue of this Act) (s 90(1)) |
|  | 1 Oct 2021 (otherwise) (SI 2021/1038) |
| 64 | 29 Apr 2021 (in so far as confers power to make regulations under or by virtue of this Act) (s 90(1)) |
|  | 14 Jun 2022 (otherwise) (SI 2022/553) |
| 65, 66 | 29 Apr 2021 (in so far as confers power to make regulations under or by virtue of this Act) (s 90(1)) |
|  | 21 Jul 2022 (otherwise) (SI 2022/840)[3] |
| 67 | 29 Apr 2021 (in so far as confers power to make regulations under or by virtue of this Act) (s 90(1)) |
|  | 19 May 2022 (otherwise) (SI 2022/553) |
| 68 | 29 Apr 2021 (in so far as confers power to make regulations under or by virtue of this Act) (s 90(1)) |
|  | *Not yet in force* (otherwise) |
| 69 | 29 Jun 2021 (s 90(2)) |
| 70 | 29 Apr 2021 (in so far as confers power to make regulations under or by virtue of this Act) (s 90(1)) |
|  | 7 Jun 2022 (otherwise) (SI 2022/553) |
| 71 | 29 Apr 2021 (s 90(1)) |
| 72 | 29 Jun 2021 (s 90(2)) |
| 73 | 29 Apr 2021 (in so far as confers power to make regulations under or by virtue of this Act) (s 90(1)) |
|  | 21 Feb 2022 (SR 2022/52) |
| 74 | See Sch 3 below |
| 75 | 29 Apr 2021 (s 90(1)) |
| 76 | 29 Apr 2021 (in so far as confers power to make regulations under or by virtue of this Act) (s 90(1)) |
|  | 5 Jul 2021 (in relation to specified areas[1] and until 5 Jul 2024) (SI 2021/797) |
|  | *Not yet in force* (otherwise) |
| 77 | 29 Apr 2021 (in so far as confers power to make regulations under or by virtue of this Act) (s 90(1)) |
|  | *Not yet in force* (otherwise) |
| 78 | 29 Apr 2021 (in so far as confers power to make regulations under or by virtue of this Act) (s 90(1)) |
|  | 5 Jul 2021 (otherwise) (SI 2021/797)[2] |
| 79 | 29 Apr 2021 (in so far as confers power to make regulations under or by virtue of this Act) (s 90(1)) |
|  | 1 Nov 2021 (otherwise) (SI 2021/1038) |
| 80 | 1 Oct 2021 (s 90(5)) |
| 81 | 29 Apr 2021 (s 90(1)) |
| 82 | 29 Apr 2021 (in so far as confers power to make regulations under or by virtue of this Act) (s 90(1)) |
|  | *Not yet in force* (otherwise) |
| 83 | 29 Apr 2021 (s 90(1)) |
| 84 | 29 Apr 2021 (in so far as confers power to make regulations under or by virtue of this Act) (s 90(1)) |
|  | 1 Nov 2021 (otherwise) (SI 2021/1038) |
| 85–91 | 29 Apr 2021 (s 90(1)) |
| Sch 1 | 29 Apr 2021 (in so far as confers power to make regulations under or by virtue of this Act) (s 90(1)) |
|  | *Not yet in force* (otherwise) |
| Sch 2 | 29 Apr 2021 (in so far as confers power to make regulations under or by virtue of this Act) (s 90(1)) |
|  | 7 Jun 2022 (otherwise) (SI 2022/553) |

**Domestic Abuse Act 2021 (c 17)**—*contd*

| | | |
|---|---|---|
| Sch 3 | paras 1–3 | 29 Jun 2021 (s 90(2)) |
| | paras 4–6 | 29 Jun 2021 (SSI 2021/239) |
| | paras 7, 8 | 21 Feb 2022 (SI 2022/52) |

[1]  The specified areas are the following police areas:

a) Cheshire;

b) Cleveland;

c) Cumbria;

d) Durham;

e) Greater Manchester;

f) Humberside;

g) Lancashire;

h) Lincolnshire;

i) Merseyside;

j) Northumbria;

k) North Yorkshire;

l) South Yorkshire; and

m) West Yorkshire

[2]  For savings, see SI 2021/797, reg 4

[3]  For transitional provisions, see SI 2022/840, reg 3

---

**Domestic Abuse (Protection) (Scotland) Act 2021 (asp 16)**

*RA:* 5 May 2021

*Commencement provisions*: s 24

| | |
|---|---|
| 1–20 | *Not yet in force* |
| 21 | 6 May 2021 (s 24(1)) |
| 22 | *Not yet in force* |
| 23–25 | 6 May 2021 (s 24(1)) |

---

**Education and Training (Welfare of Children) Act 2021 (c 16)**

*RA:* 29 Apr 2021

*Commencement provisions*: s 3(2)

Whole Act in force 29 Jun 2021 (s 3(2))

---

**Education (Guidance about Costs of School Uniforms) Act 2021 (c 20)**

*RA:* 29 Apr 2021

*Commencement provisions*: s 2(2)

Whole Act in force 29 Jun 2021 (s 2(2))

---

**Environment Act 2021 (c 30)**

*RA:* 9 Nov 2021

*Commencement provisions:* s 147; Environment Act 2021 (Commencement No 1) Regulations 2021, SI 2021/1274; Environment Act 2021 (Commencement No 2 and Saving Provision) Regulations 2022, SI 2022/48; Environment (2021 Act) (Commencement and Saving Provision) Order (Northern Ireland) 2022, SR 2022/54; Environment Act 2021 (Commencement No 1 and Saving Provision) (Wales) Regulations 2022, SI 2022/223; Environment Act 2021 (Commencement No 3) Regulations 2022, SI 2022/518; Environment Act 2021 (Commencement No 4) Regulations 2022, SI 2022/988

| | | |
|---|---|---|
| 1–16 | | 24 Jan 2022 (SI 2022/48) |
| 17, 18 | | 10 May 2022 (SI 2022/518) |
| 19 | (1)–(4) | *Not yet in force* |
| | (5), (6) | 10 May 2022 (SI 2022/518) |
| 20 | | 10 May 2022 (SI 2022/518) |
| 21 | | 1 Apr 2022 (SI 2022/48) |
| 22–24 | | 17 Nov 2021 (SI 2021/1274) |
| 25 | | 24 Jan 2022 (SI 2022/48) |
| 26 | | 17 Nov 2021 (SI 2021/1274) |
| 27–43 | | 24 Jan 2022 (SI 2022/48) |
| 44–47 | | 17 Nov 2021 (SI 2021/1274) |
| 48 | | *Not yet in force* |
| 49 | | 28 Feb 2022 (SR 2022/54) |
| 50 | | 24 Jan 2022 (SI 2022/48)[1] (E) |
| | | 28 Feb 2022 (SR 2022/54) (NI) |
| | | 7 Mar 2022 (SI 2022/223) (W)[2] |
| | | *Not yet in force* (S) |
| 51 | | 9 Jan 2022 (E), (W), (S) (s 147(2)(a)) |
| | | 28 Feb 2022 (SR 2022/54) (NI) |
| 52 | | 9 Jan 2022 (E), (W), (S) (s 147(2)(b)) |
| | | 28 Feb 2022 (SR 2022/54) (NI) |
| 53 | | 9 Jan 2022 (E), (W), (S) (s 147(2)(c)) |
| | | 28 Feb 2022 (SR 2022/54) (NI) |
| 54 | | 9 Jan 2022 (E), (W) (s 147(2)(d)) |
| | | 28 Feb 2022 (SR 2022/54) (NI) |
| | | *Not yet in force* (S) |
| 55 | | 9 Jan 2022 (E), (W) (s 147(2)(e)) |
| | | *Not yet in force* (S), (NI) |
| 56 | | 9 Jan 2022 (E), (W) (s 147(2)(f)) |
| | | 28 Feb 2022 (SR 2022/54) (NI) |
| | | *Not yet in force* (S) |
| 57 | | *Not yet in force* |
| 58 | | 9 Jan 2022 (s 147(2)(g)) |
| 59 | | 28 Feb 2022 (SR 2022/54) (NI) |
| 60 | | 24 Jan 2022 (SI 2022/48) (E) |
| | | 7 Mar 2022 (SI 2022/223) (W) |
| 61 | | 28 Feb 2022 (SR 2022/54) (NI) |
| 62 | | 24 Jan 2022 (SI 2022/48) |
| 63 | | 9 Nov 2021 (s 147(a)) |
| 64 | | 24 Jan 2022 (in so far as relates to the Environment Agency) (SI 2022/48) |
| | | 7 Mar 2022 (in so far as relates to the Natural Resources Body for Wales) (SI 2022/223) |
| | | *Not yet in force* (otherwise) |
| 65 | | 28 Feb 2022 (SR 2022/54) (NI) |
| 66 | | 9 Jan 2022 (s 147(2)(h)) |
| 67 | | 28 Feb 2022 (SR 2022/54) (NI) |
| 68, 69 | | *Not yet in force* |
| 70 | | 9 Jan 2022 (s 147(2)(i)) |
| 71 | | 28 Feb 2022 (SR 2022/54) (NI) |

**Environment Act 2021 (c 30)**—*contd*

| | |
|---|---|
| 72, 73 | 1 May 2022 (SI 2022/48) |
| 74–79 | *Not yet in force* |
| 80 | 9 Jan 2022 (s 147(2)(j)) |
| 81–83 | *Not yet in force* |
| 84 | 9 Jan 2022 (s 147(2)(j)) |
| 85 | 10 May 2022 (so far as relating to undertakers whose areas are wholly or mainly in England and licensees using the systems of such undertakers(SI 2022/518) |
| | *Not yet in office* (otherwise) |
| 86 | 24 Jan 2022 (SI 2022/48) |
| 87 | 10 May 2022 (so far as relating to undertakers whose areas are wholly or mainly in England and licensees using the systems of such undertakers) (SI 2022/518) |
| | *Not yet in office* (otherwise) |
| 88 | 9 Jan 2022 (s 147(2)(k)) |
| 89 | 9 Jan 2022 (except so far as relating to legislation within s 89(2)(d)–(f) and any regulations modifying that legislation made under or by virtue of European Union (Withdrawal) Act 2018 (s 147(2)(l)) |
| | 28 Feb 2022 (exception noted above) (SR 2022/54) (NI) |
| | *Not yet in force* (exception noted above) |
| 90 | 9 Jan 2022 (s 147(2)(m)) |
| 91 | 28 Feb 2022 (SR 2022/54) (NI) |
| 92, 93 | 9 Jan 2022 (s 147(2)(m)) |
| 94 | 29 Sep 2022 (SI 2022/988) |
| 95 | *Not yet in force* |
| 96 | 29 Sep 2022 (so far as relates to internal drainage districts which are wholly or mainly in England) (SI 2022/988) |
| | *Not yet in force* (otherwise) |
| 97 | 9 Jan 2022 (s 147(2)(n)) |
| 98–103 | *Not yet in force* |
| 104–108 | 24 Jan 2022 (SI 2022/48) |
| 109 | 30 Sep 2022 (SI 2022/518) |
| 110 | 24 Jan 2022 (SI 2022/48) |
| 111 | 30 Sep 2022 (SI 2022/518) |
| 112, 113 | 24 Jan 2022 (SI 2022/48) |
| 114, 115 | *Not yet in force* |
| 116 | 30 Sep 2022 (for the purpose of making regulations) (SI 2022/518) |
| | *Not yet in office* (otherwise) |
| 117–139 | 30 Sep 2022 (SI 2022/48) |
| 140 | See Sch 21 below |
| 141–149 | 9 Nov 2021 (s 147(a)) |
| Sch 1 | 17 Nov 2021 (SI 2021/1274) |
| Schs 2, 3 | *Not yet in force* |
| Sch 4 | 24 Jan 2022 (SI 2022/48) (E) |
| | 28 Feb 2022 (SR 2022/54) (NI) |
| | 7 Mar 2022 (SI 2022/223) (W) |
| | *Not yet in force* (S) |
| Sch 5 | 9 Jan 2022 (E), (W), (S) (s 147(2)(a)) |
| | 28 Feb 2022 (SR 2022/54) (NI) |
| Sch 6 | 9 Jan 2022 (E), (W), (S) (s 147(2)(b)) |
| | 28 Feb 2022 (SR 2022/54) (NI) |
| Sch 7 | 9 Jan 2022 (E), (W), (S) (s 147(2)(c)) |
| | 28 Feb 2022 (SR 2022/54) (NI) |
| Sch 8 | 9 Jan 2022 (E), (W) (s 147(2)(d)) |
| | 28 Feb 2022 (SR 2022/54) (NI) |
| | *Not yet in force* (S) |
| Sch 9 | 9 Jan 2022 (E), (W) (s 147(2)(e)) |
| | *Not yet in force* (S), (NI) |

**Environment Act 2021 (c 30)**—*contd*

| | | |
|---|---|---|
| Sch 10 | | 9 Jan 2022 (s 147(2)(h)) |
| Sch 11 | | 1 May 2022 (SI 2022/48) |
| Sch 12 | paras 1–8 | 1 May 2022 (SI 2022/48) |
| | paras 9–11 | *Not yet in force* |
| | paras 12–25 | 1 May 2022 (SI 2022/48) |
| | para 26 | *Not yet in force* |
| Sch 13 | | 24 Jan 2022 (SI 2022/48) |
| Schs 14–16 | | *Not yet in force* |
| Sch 17 | | 30 Sep 2022 (for the purpose of making regulations) (SI 2022/518) |
| | | *Not yet in office* (otherwise) |
| Schs 18–20 | | 30 Sep 2022 (SI 2022/48) |
| Sch 21 | | 9 Nov 2022 (except so far as relating to powers of a Northern Ireland department to make regulations under para 2) (s 147(1)(b)) |
| | | 28 Feb 2022 (exception noted above) (SR 2022/54) |

[1]   For savings see SI 2022/48, reg 6

[2]   For savings see SI 2022/223, reg 3

---

**Finance Act 2021 (c 22)**

*RA*: 10 Jun 2021

The commencement details of Finance Acts are not set out, as the dates from which their provisions take effect are usually stated clearly and unambiguously in the text of the Act, and charging provisions will normally state for which year or years of assessment they are to have effect.

---

**Financial Services Act 2021 (c 22)**

*RA*: 29 Apr 2021

*Commencement provisions*: s 49; Financial Services Act 2021 (Commencement No 1) Regulations 2021, SI 2021/671, as amended by SI 2021/1163; Financial Services Act 2021 (Commencement No 2) Regulations 2021, SI 2021/739; Financial Services Act 2021 (Commencement No 3) Regulations 2021, SI 2021/1173; Financial Services Act 2021 (Commencement No 4) Regulations 2022, SI 2022/163

| | | |
|---|---|---|
| 1 | | 1 Jan 2022 (SI 2021/671) |
| 2 | | 1 Jul 2021 (SI 2021/671) |
| 3–5 | | 9 Jun 2021 (SI 2021/671) |
| 6 | | *Not yet in force* |
| 7 | | 26 Jun 2021 (SI 201/671) |
| 8–21 | | 1 Jul 2021 (SI 2021/739) |
| 22, 23 | | *Not yet in force* |
| 24 | | 23 Feb 2022 (SI 2022/163) |
| 25 | (1)–(3) | 23 Feb 2022 (SI 2022/163) |
| | (4)(a) | 1 Jan 2023 (SI 2022/163) |
| | (4)(b)–(d) | 23 Feb 2022 (SI 2022/163) |
| | (5)–(8) | 23 Feb 2022 (SI 2022/163) |
| 26 | | 23 Feb 2022 (SI 2022/163) |
| 27–29 | | 1 Jul 2021 (SI 2021/739) |
| 30 | | 29 Jun 2021 (s 49(2)(a)) |
| 31 | | 1 Nov 2021 (SI 2021/1173) |
| 32 | | 29 Jun 2021 (s 49(2)(b)) |
| 33 | | 29 Apr 2021 (s 49(1)(a)) |
| 34 | | 1 Jul 2021 (SI 2021/739) |
| 35 | | 29 Jun 2021 (s 49(2)(c)) |
| 36 | | 29 Apr 2021 (s 49(1)(b)) |
| 37–40 | | 1 Jul 2021 (SI 2021/739) |

## Financial Services Act 2021 (c 22)—*contd*

| | | |
|---|---|---|
| 41 | | 29 Apr 2021 (s 49(1)(c)) |
| 42 | | 29 Jun 2021 (s 49(2)(d)) |
| 43 | | 1 Jul 2021 (SI 2021/739) |
| 44 | | 29 Jun 2021 (s 49(2)(e)) |
| 45–50 | | 29 Apr 2021 (s 49(1)(d)–(h)) |
| Sch 1 | | 1 Jan 2022 (SI 2021/671) |
| Sch 2 | | 1 Jul 2021 (SI 2021/671) |
| Sch 3 | | 9 Jun 2021 (SI 2021/671) |
| Sch 4 | paras 1–11 | 1 Jan 2022 (SI 2021/671) |
| | para 12 | 26 Jun 2021 (SI 2021/671) |
| | para 13 | 1 Jan 2022 (SI 2021/671) |
| Sch 5 | | 1 Jul 2021 (SI 2021/739) |
| Schs 6–8 | | *Not yet in force* |
| Sch 9 | | 23 Feb 2022 (SI 2022/163) |
| Schs 10, 11 | | 1 Jul 2021 (SI 2021/739) |
| Sch 12 | paras 1–9 | 29 Apr 2021 (s 49(1)(a)) |
| | paras 10–21 | 29 Apr 2021 (except in so far as extending to Northern Ireland) (s 49(1)(a)) |
| | | 28 Jun 2021 (exception noted above) (SI 2021/739) |

## Fire Safety Act 2021 (c 24)

*RA:* 29 Apr 2021

*Commencement provisions:* s 4(2)–(6); Fire Safety Act 2021 (Commencement) (Wales) Regulations 2021, SI 2021/1092; Fire Safety Act 2021 (Commencement) (England) Regulations 2022, SI 2022/544

| | |
|---|---|
| 1 | 1 Oct 2021 (W) (SI 2021/1092) |
| | 16 May 200 (E) (SI 2022/544) |
| 2 | 29 Jun 2021 (s 4(4)) |
| 3 | *Not yet in force* |
| 4 | 29 Apr 2021 (s 4(6)) |

## Forensic Medical Services (Victims of Sexual Offences) (Scotland) Act 2021 (asp 3)

*RA:* 20 Jan 2021

*Commencement provisions:* s 20; Forensic Medical Services (Victims of Sexual Offences) (Scotland) Act 2021 Commencement Regulations 2022, SSI 2022/24

| | |
|---|---|
| 1–16 | 1 Apr 2022 (SSI 2022/24) |
| 17–21 | 21 Jan 2021 (s 20(1)) |
| Schedule | 1 Apr 2022 (SSI 2022/24) |

## Forensic Science Regulator Act 2021 (c 14)

*RA:* 29 Apr 2021

*Commencement provisions:* s 13(4)–(6); Forensic Science Regulator Act 2021 (Commencement No 1 and Transitional Provision) Regulations 2022, SI 2022/856

| | |
|---|---|
| 1–4 | 25 Jul 2022 (SI 2022/856) |
| 5 | 25 Jul 2022 (SI 2022/856)[1] |
| 6–8 | *Not yet in force* |
| 9, 10 | 25 Jul 2022 (SI 2022/856) |
| 11 | 29 Apr 2021 (s 13(6)) |
| 12 | 25 Jul 2022 (SI 2022/856) |
| 13 | 29 Apr 2021 (s 13(6)) |
| Schedule | 25 Jul 2022 (SI 2022/856) |

**Forensic Science Regulator Act 2021 (c 14)**—*contd*
1   For transitional provisions, see SI 2022/856, reg 3

---

**Hate Crime and Public Order (Scotland) Act 2021 (asp 14)**

*RA:* 23 Apr 2021

*Commencement provisions:* s 21

| | |
|---|---|
| 1–16 | *Not yet in force* |
| 17 | 24 Apr 2021 (s 21(1)) |
| 18–20 | *Not yet in force* |
| 21, 22 | 24 Apr 2021 (s 21(1)) |
| Schs 1, 2 | *Not yet in force* |

---

**Health and Social Care Levy Act (c 29)**

*RA:* 20 Oct 2021

Whole Act in force 20 Oct 2021 (RA)

---

**Heat Networks (Scotland) Act 2021 (asp 9)**

*RA:* 30 Mar 2021

*Commencement provisions:* s 102

| | |
|---|---|
| 1–96 | *Not yet in force* |
| 97–103 | 31 Mar 2021 (s 102(1)) |

---

**High Speed Rail (West Midlands – Crewe) Act 2021 (c 2)**

*RA:* 11 Feb 2021

*Commencement provisions:* s 64(1)

Whole Act in force 11 Feb 2021 (s 64(1))

---

**Local Government and Elections (Wales) Act 2021 (asc 1)**

*RA:* 20 Jan 2021

*Commencement provisions:* s 175; Local Government and Elections (Wales) Act 2021 (Commencement No 1 and Saving Provision) Order 2021, SI 2021/231 (as amended by SI 2021/1249); Local Government and Elections (Wales) Act 2021 (Commencement No 2 and Saving Provisions) Order 2021, SI 2021/297; Local Government and Elections (Wales) Act 2021 (Commencement No 3 and Transitional Provision) Order 2021, SI 2021/354; Local Government and Elections (Wales) Act 2021 (Commencement No 4 and Transitional Provision and Amendment of Commencement Order No 1) Order 2021, SI 2021/1249; Local Government and Elections (Wales) Act 2021 (Commencement No 5 and Transitional Provision) Order 2022, SI 2022/98

| | | |
|---|---|---|
| 1 | | 20 Mar 2021 (s 175(3)) |
| 2 | (1) | 20 Mar 2021 (s 175(3))[1] |
| | (2) | 5 May 2022 (s 175(5)) |
| | (3) | 20 Mar 2021 (s 175(3))[1] |
| 3, 4 | | 20 Mar 2021 (s 175(3)) |
| 5–12 | | 6 May 2022 (s 175(6)) |
| 13–17 | | 20 Mar 2021 (s 175(3)) |
| 18 | | *Not yet in force* |
| 19–21 | | 17 Nov 2021 (SI 2021/1249)[5] |
| 22 | | 20 Mar 2021 (s 175(3))[1] |

**Local Government and Elections (Wales) Act 2021 (asc 1)**—*contd*

| | | |
|---|---|---|
| 23 | | 20 Mar 2021 (s 175(3)) |
| 24–27 | | 1 Nov 2021 (SI 2021/231) |
| 28 | | 4 Mar 2021 (SI 2021/231) |
| 29 | | 1 Nov 2021 (SI 2021/231) |
| 30 | (1), (2) | 5 May 2022 (SI 2021/231) |
| | (3) | 4 Mar 2021 (SI 2021/231) |
| | (4)–(6) | 5 May 2022 (SI 2021/231) |
| 31–34 | | 5 May 2022 (SI 2021/231) |
| 35 | | 4 Mar 2021 (SI 2021/231) |
| 36, 37 | | 5 May 2022 (SI 2021/231) |
| 38 | | 20 Mar 2021 (s 175(3)) |
| 39–45 | | 5 May 2022 (SI 2021/231) |
| 46 | (1)(a) | 5 May 2022 (SI 2021/231) |
| | (1)(b), (c) | 4 Mar 2021 (for the purpose of making regulations) (SI 2021/231) |
| | | 5 May 2022 (otherwise) (SI 2021/231) |
| | (2)(a) | 5 May 2022 (SI 2021/231) |
| | (2)(b) | 4 Mar 2021 (for the purpose of making regulations) (SI 2021/231) |
| | | 5 May 2022 (otherwise) (SI 2021/231) |
| | (3), (4) | 4 Mar 2021 (SI 2021/231) |
| | (5)–(7) | 5 May 2022 (SI 2021/231) |
| | (8)–(10) | 4 Mar 2021 (SI 2021/231) |
| 47 | (1)–(7) | 1 May 2021 (SI 2021/354)[4] |
| | (8) | 4 Mar 2021 (SI 2021/231) |
| | (9) | 1 May 2021 (SI 2021/354)[4] |
| 48 | | 5 May 2022 (SI 2021/231) |
| 49 | | See Sch 4 below |
| 50, 51 | | 21 Jan 2021 (s 175(1)) |
| 52 | | 1 Apr 2022 (SI 2021/231) |
| 53 | | 20 Mar 2021 (s 175(3)) |
| 54 | | 5 May 2022 (SI 2021/231) |
| 55 | | 20 Mar 2021 (s 175(3)) |
| 56–58 | | 5 May 2022 (SI 2021/231) |
| 59 | | 4 Mar 2021 (SI 2021/231) |
| 60 | | 20 Mar 2021 (s 175(3)) |
| 61 | | 21 Jan 2021 (s 175(1)) |
| 62, 63 | | 5 May 2022 (SI 2021/231) |
| 64 | | 5 May 2022 (SI 2022/98)[6] |
| 65–67 | | 5 May 2022 (SI 2021/231) |
| 68–88 | | 21 Jan 2021 (s 175(1)) |
| 89–91 | | 1 Apr 2021 (SI 2021/297) |
| 92, 93 | | 5 May 2022 (SI 2021/297) |
| 94 | | 20 Mar 2021 (s 175(3)) |
| 95–112 | | 1 Apr 2021 (SI 2021/297) |
| 113 | | 1 Apr 2021 (SI 2021/297)[3] |
| 114, 115 | | 1 Apr 2021 (SI 2021/297) |
| 116–118 | | 5 May 2022 (SI 2021/297) |
| 119, 120 | | 1 Apr 2021 (SI 2021/297) |
| 121–128 | | 21 Jan 2021 (s 175(1)) |
| 129–135 | | 1 Apr 2021 (SI 2021/297) |
| 136, 137 | | 21 Jan 2021 (s 175(1)) |
| 138 | (1)(a) | 21 Jan 2021 (s 175(1)) |
| | (1)(b) | 1 Apr 2021 (SI 2021/297) |
| | (2) | 21 Jan 2021 (s 175(1)) |
| | (3) | 1 Apr 2021 (SI 2021/297) |
| | (4)–(6) | 21 Jan 2021 (s 175(1)) |
| 139 | (1) | 21 Jan 2021 (s 175(1)) |
| | (2) | 1 Apr 2021 (SI 2021/297) |
| | (3) | 21 Jan 2021 (except words "or (2)") (s 175(1)) |
| | | 1 Apr 2021 (exception noted above) (SI 2021/297) |

**See Halsbury's Statutes Citator for amendments to these Acts**

**Local Government and Elections (Wales) Act 2021 (asc 1)**—*contd*

| | | |
|---|---|---|
| 140 | (1)(a) | 21 Jan 2021 (except words "to another principal council ("council B") or") (s 175(1)) |
| | | 1 Apr 2021 (exception noted above) (SI 2021/297) |
| | (1)(b), (c) | 21 Jan 2021 (s 175(1)) |
| | (2) | 1 Apr 2021 (SI 2021/297) |
| 141 | (1)(a) | 21 Jan 2021 (except words "to another principal council ("council B") or") (s 175(1)) |
| | | 1 Apr 2021 (exception noted above) (SI 2021/297) |
| | (1)(b), (c) | 21 Jan 2021 (s 175(1)) |
| | (2)(a) | 21 Jan 2021 (except words "or restructuring regulations" and "(including council B)") (s 175(1)) |
| | | 1 Apr 2021 (exception noted above) (SI 2021/297) |
| | (2)(b) | 21 Jan 2021 (s 175(1)) |
| | (2)(c) | 21 Jan 2021 (except words "if a new principal area containing all or part of council A's area is to be constituted,") (s 175(1)) |
| | | 1 Apr 2021 (exception noted above) (SI 2021/297) |
| | (3) | 1 Apr 2021 (SI 2021/297) |
| 142 | (1)(a) | 21 Jan 2021 (except words "or restructuring regulations") (s 175(1)) |
| | | 1 Apr 2021 (exception noted above) (SI 2021/297) |
| | (1)(b), (2)–(5) | 21 Jan 2021 (s 175(1)) |
| 143, 144 | | 21 Jan 2021 (s 175(1)) |
| 145 | (1)–(7)(a) | 21 Jan 2021 (s 175(1)) |
| | (7)(b) | 1 Apr 2021 (SI 2021/297) |
| 146 | | 21 Jan 2021 (s 175(1)) |
| 147 | (1) | 21 Jan 2021 (except words "and restructuring regulations") (s 175(1)) |
| | | 1 Apr 2021 (exception noted above) (SI 2021/297) |
| | (2) | 21 Jan 2021 (except words "or particular restructuring regulations") (s 175(1)) |
| | | 1 Apr 2021 (exception noted above) (SI 2021/297) |
| | (3) | 21 Jan 2021 (s 175(1)) |
| | (4) | 21 Jan 2021 (except words "or particular restructuring regulations") (s 175(1)) |
| | | 1 Apr 2021 (exception noted above) (SI 2021/297) |
| | (5) | 21 Jan 2021 (except words "or restructuring councils") (s 175(1)) |
| | | 1 Apr 2021 (exception noted above) (SI 2021/297) |
| | (6) | 21 Jan 2021 (except words "or restructuring regulations" and "or restructuring councils") (s 175(1)) |
| | | 1 Apr 2021 (exception noted above) (SI 2021/297) |
| | (7), (8) | 21 Jan 2021 (except words ", restructuring regulations") (s 175(1)) |
| | | 1 Apr 2021 (exception noted above) (SI 2021/297) |
| | (9) | 21 Jan 2021 (s 175(1)) |
| | (10) | 21 Jan 2021 (except words "or restructuring regulations" and ", restructuring regulations") (s 175(1)) |
| | | 1 Apr 2021 (exception noted above) (SI 2021/297) |
| 148 | | 1 Apr 2021 (SI 2021/297) |
| 149 | | 21 Jan 2021 (except definitions "abolition request", "council under consideration" and "restructuring council" and definition "shadow council", para (b) and definition "transfer date", para (b)) (s 175(1)) |
| | | 1 Apr 2021 (exception noted above) (SI 2021/297) |
| 150 | (1)(a) | 1 Apr 2021 (SI 2021/297) |
| | (1)(b)(i) | 21 Jan 2021 (s 175(1)) |
| | (1)(b)(ii) | 1 Apr 2021 (SI 2021/297) |
| | (1)(b)(iii) | 21 Jan 2021 (s 175(1)) |
| | (1)(b)(iv), (v) | 1 Apr 2021 (SI 2021/297) |
| | (1)(b)(vi) | 21 Jan 2021 (s 175(1)) |
| | (2)(a) | 21 Jan 2021 (s 175(1)) |
| | (2)(b), (c) | 1 Apr 2021 (SI 2021/297) |
| | (2)(d), (3) | 21 Jan 2021 (s 175(1)) |

**Local Government and Elections (Wales) Act 2021 (asc 1)**—*contd*

| | | |
|---|---|---|
| 151 | | 1 Apr 2021 (s 175(4)) |
| 152 | | 20 Mar 2021 (s 175(3)) |
| 153 | | 1 Apr 2021 (s 175(4)) |
| 154–156 | | 20 Mar 2021 (s 175(3)) |
| 157 | | 1 Apr 2021 (s 175(4)) |
| 158 | | 20 Mar 2021 (s 175(3)) |
| 159 | (1)–(4)(a) | 21 Jan 2021 (s 175(1)) |
| | (4)(b)(c) | 1 Apr 2021 (SI 2021/297) |
| | (5) | 21 Jan 2021 (except Table 2, entry relating to the Auditor General for Wales' functions under Chapter 1 of Part 6 and in the entry relating to the Welsh Ministers' functions under this Act, the words from ", Chapter 1" to "areas)") (s 175(1)) |
| | | 1 Apr 2021 (exception noted above) (SI 2021/297) |
| | (6)–(10) | 21 Jan 2021 (s 175(1)) |
| 160 | | 21 Jan 2021 (s 175(1)) |
| 161 | (1) | 4 Mar 2021 (SI 2021/231) |
| | (2), (3) | 5 May 2022 (SI 2021/231) |
| 162 | | 5 May 2022 (SI 2021/231) |
| 163, 164 | | 1 Apr 2021 (SI 2021/231) |
| 165 | | 20 Mar 2021 (s 175(3)) |
| 166 | (1), (2)(a), (b)(ii) | 20 Mar 2021 (s 175(3)) |
| | (2)(b)(iii) | 21 Jan 2021 (s 175(1)) |
| | (2)(b)(iv) | 20 Mar 2021 (s 175(3)) |
| | (2)(c) | 21 Jan 2021 (s 175(1)) |
| | (3)(a) | 20 Mar 2021 (s 175(3)) |
| | (3)(b) | 21 Jan 2021 (s 175(1)) |
| | (4) | 20 Mar 2021 (s 175(3)) |
| 167 | | 20 Mar 2021 (s 175(3)) |
| 168 | (1)(a)–(f) | *Not yet in force* |
| | (1)(g)(i) | 20 Mar 2021 (s 175(3)) |
| | (1)(g)(ii) | *Not yet in force* |
| | (2) | 20 Mar 2021 (s 175(3)) |
| | (3) | *Not yet in force* |
| 169 | | 1 Apr 2021 (SI 2021/297)[3] |
| 170 | | *Not yet in force* |
| 171–176 | | 21 Jan 2021 (s 175(1)) |
| Sch 1 | para 1(1), (2) | 21 Jan 2021 (s 175(1)) |
| | para 1(3) | 21 Jan 2021 (except words "11(3) or") (s 175(1)) |
| | | 6 May 2022 (exception noted above) (s 175(6)) |
| | para 2(1) | 21 Jan 2021 (s 175(1)) |
| | para 2(2) | 6 May 2022 (s 175(6)) |
| | para 2(3) | 21 Jan 2021 (s 175(1)) |
| | para 2(4), (5) | 1 Apr 2021 (SI 2021/297) |
| | para 4(1)–(3) | 21 Jan 2021 (except words "11 or") (s 175(1)) |
| | | 6 May 2022 (exception noted above) (s 175(6)) |
| | para 4(4), (5) | 21 Jan 2021 (s 175(1)) |
| | para 4(6) | 21 Jan 2021 (except words "11 or") (s 175(1)) |
| | | 6 May 2022 (exception noted above) (s 175(6)) |
| | para 4(7) | 21 Jan 2021 (s 175(1)) |
| | para 5 | 21 Jan 2021 (s 175(1)) |
| | para 6(1) | 21 Jan 2021 (s 175(1)) |
| | para 6(2)(a) | 6 May 2022 (s 175(6)) |
| | para 6(2)(b) | 21 Jan 2021 (except words "or the restructuring councils") (s 175(1)) |
| | | 1 Apr 2021 (exception noted above) (SI 2021/297) |
| | para 6(2)(c), (d) | 21 Jan 2021 (s 175(1)) |
| | paras 7–11 | 21 Jan 2021 (s 175(1)) |
| | para 12(1)(a) | 6 May 2022 (s 175(6)) |
| | para 12(1)(b) | 21 Jan 2021 (s 175(1)) |

**Local Government and Elections (Wales) Act 2021 (asc 1)**—*contd*

| | | |
|---|---|---|
| | para 12(2) | 6 May 2022 (s 175(6)) |
| | para 12(3) | 21 Jan 2021 (s 175(1)) |
| | para 12(4)(a) | 6 May 2022 (s 175(6)) |
| | paras 12(4)(b) | 21 Jan 2021 (s 175(1)) |
| | paras 13, 14 | 21 Jan 2021 (s 175(1)) |
| Sch 2 | para 1(1), (2) | 20 Mar 2021 (s 175(3)) |
| | para 1(3)–(5) | 17 Nov 2021 (SI 2021/1249)[5] |
| | para 1(6) | 20 Mar 2021 (s 175(3)) |
| | para 1(7) | 17 Nov 2021 (SI 2021/1249)[5] |
| | para 1(8) | 20 Mar 2021 (s 175(3)) |
| | para 1(9) | 17 Nov 2021 (SI 2021/1249)[5] |
| | para 2(1) | 20 Mar 2021 (s 175(3)) |
| | para 2(2) | 21 Jan 2021 (s 175(1)) |
| | para 2(3)–(8) | 20 Mar 2021 (s 175(3)) |
| | para 2(9), (10) | 6 May 2022 (s 175(6)) |
| | para 2(11) | 20 Mar 2021 (s 175(3)) |
| | para 2(12) | 20 Mar 2021 (s 175(3))[1] |
| | para 2(13)–(18)(a) | 20 Mar 2021 (s 175(3)) |
| | para 2(18)(b) | 6 May 2022 (s 175(6)) |
| | paras 3, 4 | 20 Mar 2021 (s 175(3)) |
| | para 5 | 17 Nov 2021 (SI 2021/1249)[5] |
| | paras 6, 7 | 20 Mar 2021 (s 175(3)) |
| | para 8(1), (2), (3)(a) | 20 Mar 2021 (s 175(3)) |
| | para 8(3)(b) | 20 Mar 2021 (s 175(3))[1] |
| | paras 9–12 | 20 Mar 2021 (s 175(3)) |
| | para 13 | 17 Nov 2021 (SI 2021/1249)[5] |
| | para 14 | 20 Mar 2021 (s 175(3)) |
| | para 15 | 20 Mar 2021 (s 175(3))[1] |
| | para 16(1) | 20 Mar 2021 (s 175(3)) |
| | para 16(2) | *Not yet in force* |
| | para 16(3) | 21 Jan 2021 (s 175(1)) |
| | para 16(4) | 20 Mar 2021 (s 175(3)) |
| | paras 17, 18 | 20 Mar 2021 (s 175(3)) |
| | para 19 | 20 Mar 2021 (s 175(3))[1] |
| Sch 3 | paras 1–8 | 1 Nov 2021 (SI 2021/231) |
| | paras 9–15 | 5 May 2022 (SI 2021/231)[2] |
| Sch 4 | paras 1–16 | 1 May 2021 (SI 2021/354)[4] |
| | para 17(1)–(3) | 1 May 2021 (SI 2021/354)[4] |
| | para 17(4) | 21 Jan 2021 (s 175(1)) |
| | paras 18–23 | 1 May 2021 (SI 2021/354)[4] |
| Sch 5 | | 5 May 2022 (SI 2021/231) |
| Sch 6 | paras 1–3 | 5 May 2022 (SI 2021/231) |
| | para 4 | *Not yet in force* |
| | para 5 | 5 May 2022 (SI 2021/231) |
| | para 6(1)–(4) | 5 May 2022 (SI 2021/231) |
| | para 6(5) | *Not yet in force* |
| Sch 7 | | 5 May 2022 (SI 2021/231) |
| Sch 8 | | 5 May 2022 (SI 2022/98)[6] |
| Sch 9 | | 21 Jan 2021 (s 175(1)) |
| Sch 10 | | 1 Apr 2021 (SI 2021/297) |
| Sch 11 | paras 1–3 | 21 Jan 2021 (s 175(1)) |
| | para 4 | 1 Apr 2021 (SI 2021/297) |
| | paras 5, 6 | 21 Jan 2021 (s 175(1)) |
| | para 7(1), (2) | 21 Jan 2021 (s 175(1)) |
| | para 7(3)(a) | 21 Jan 2021 (except words "or by virtue of paragraph 4") (s 175(1)) |
| | | 1 Apr 2021 (exception noted above) (SI 2021/297) |
| | para 7(3)(b) | 21 Jan 2021 (s 175(1)) |
| | para 7(3)(c) | 1 Apr 2021 (SI 2021/297) |

**Local Government and Elections (Wales) Act 2021 (asc 1)**—*contd*

|  | para 7(4) | 21 Jan 2021 (s 175(1)) |
|---|---|---|
| Sch 12 | para 1(1) | 21 Jan 2021 (except words "or after giving notice as described in section 129(6)") (s 175(1)) |
|  |  | 1 Apr 2021 (exception noted above) (SI 2021/297) |
|  | paras 2–6 | 21 Jan 2021 (s 175(1)) |
|  | para 7(1)–(5) | 21 Jan 2021 (s 175(1)) |
|  | para 7(6) | 21 Jan 2021 (except definition "the relevant date", para (b)) (s 175(1)) |
|  |  | 1 Apr 2021 (exception noted above) (SI 2021/297) |
|  | paras 8, 9 | 21 Jan 2021 (s 175(1)) |
| Sch 13 |  | 5 May 2022 (SI 2021/231) |
| Sch 14 |  | 20 Mar 2021 (s 175(3)) |

[1] For transitional provisions, see the Local Government and Elections (Wales) Act 2021, s 3

[2] For savings, see SI 2021/231, art 7

[3] For savings, see SI 2021/297, arts 4–9

[4] For transitional provisions, see SI 2021/354, art 3

[5] For transitional provisions, see SI 2021/1249, art 4

[6] For transitional provisions, see SI 2022/98, art 3

---

**Medicines and Medical Devices Act 2021 (c 3)**

*RA:* 11 Feb 2021

*Commencement provisions:* s 50; Medicines and Medical Devices Act 2021 (Commencement No 1 and Transitional and Savings Provision) Regulations 2021, SI 2021/610

| 1 |  | 11 Apr 2021 (s 50(2)) |
|---|---|---|
| 2 |  | 11 Feb 2021 (s 50(1)) |
| 3–5 |  | 11 Apr 2021 (s 50(2)) |
| 6, 7 |  | 11 Feb 2021 (s 50(1)) |
| 8 |  | 11 Apr 2021 (s 50(2)) |
| 9 |  | 11 Feb 2021 (s 50(1)) |
| 10–14 |  | 11 Apr 2021 (s 50(2)) |
| 15 |  | 11 Feb 2021 (s 50(1)) |
| 16 |  | 11 Apr 2021 (s 50(2)) |
| 17, 18 |  | 11 Feb 2021 (s 50(1)) |
| 19, 20 |  | 11 Apr 2021 (s 50(2)) |
| 21–30 |  | 26 May 2021 (SI 2021/610) |
| 31 |  | *Not yet in force* |
| 32–40 |  | 26 May 2021 (SI 2021/610) |
| 41 | (1)–(8) | 26 May 2021 (SI 2021/610)[1] |
|  | (9) | *Not yet in force* |
| 42–52 |  | 11 Feb 2021 (s 50(1)) |
| Sch 1 |  | 11 Apr 2021 (s 50(2)) |
| Schs 2, 3 |  | *Not yet in force* |

[1] For transitional and saving provisions, see SI 2021/610, reg 3

---

**Ministerial and other Maternity Allowances Act 2021 (c 5)**

*RA:* 1 Mar 2021

*Commencement provisions:* s 7(2)

Whole Act in force 1 Mar 2021 (s 7(2))

---

## National Security and Investment Act 2021 (c 25)

*RA:* 29 Apr 2021

*Commencement provisions:* s 66(2)–(4); National Security and Investment Act 2021 (Commencement No 1 and Transitional Provision) Regulations 2021, SI 2021/788; National Security and Investment Act 2021 (Commencement No 2 and Transitional and Saving Provision) Regulations 2021, SI 2021/1465

| | | |
|---|---|---|
| 1, 2 | | 4 Jan 2022 (SI 2021/1465)[2] |
| 3,4 | | 1 Jul 2021 (SI 2021/788) |
| 5 | | 4 Jan 2022 (SI 2021/1465)[2] |
| 6 | (1) | 29 Apr 2021 (s 66(2)) |
| | (2)–(8) | 1 Jul 2021 (SI 2021/788) |
| 7–10 | | 4 Jan 2022 (SI 2021/1465)[2] |
| 11 | (1), (2) | 4 Jan 2022 (SI 2021/1465)[2] |
| | (3) | 29 Apr 2021 (s 66(2)) |
| 12–13 | | 4 Jan 2022 (SI 2021/1465)[2] |
| 14 | (1)–(3) | 4 Jan 2022 (SI 2021/1465)[2] |
| | (4) | 29 Apr 2021 (s 66(2)) |
| | (5)–(10) | 4 Jan 2022 (SI 2021/1465)[2] |
| 15 | | 4 Jan 2022 (SI 2021/1465)[2] |
| 16 | (1), (2) | 4 Jan 2022 (SI 2021/1465)[2] |
| | (3) | 29 Apr 2021 (s 66(2)) |
| | (4)–(9) | 4 Jan 2022 (SI 2021/1465)[2] |
| 17 | | 4 Jan 2022 (SI 2021/1465)[2] |
| 18 | (1)–(3) | 4 Jan 2022 (SI 2021/1465)[2] |
| | (4) | 29 Apr 2021 (s 66(2)) |
| | (5)–(10) | 4 Jan 2022 (SI 2021/1465)[2] |
| 19–35 | | 4 Jan 2022 (SI 2021/1465)[2] |
| 36 | (1)–(4) | 4 Jan 2022 (SI 2021/1465)[2] |
| | (5) | 29 Apr 2021 (s 66(2)) |
| 37–40 | | 4 Jan 2022 (SI 2021/1465)[2] |
| 41 | (1)–(7) | 4 Jan 2022 (SI 2021/1465)[2] |
| | (8) | 29 Apr 2021 (s 66(2)) |
| | (9) | 1 Jul 2021 (SI 2021/788) |
| 42–52 | | 4 Jan 2022 (SI 2021/1465)[2] |
| 53 | (1) | 29 Apr 2021 (s 66(2)) |
| | (2), (3) | 1 Jul 2021 (SI 2021/788) |
| 54–58 | | 4 Jan 2022 (SI 2021/1465)[2] |
| 59 | | 1 Jul 2021 (SI 2021/788)[1] |
| 60, 61 | | 4 Jan 2022 (SI 2021/1465)[2] |
| 62–66 | | 29 Apr 2021 (s 66(2)) |
| Schs 1, 2 | | 4 Jan 2022 (SI 2021/1465)[2] |

[1]  For transitional provisions see SI 2021/788, reg 3

[2]  For transitional and saving provisions see SI 2021/1465, regs 4, 5

## Non-Domestic Rating (Lists) Act 2021 (c 8)

*RA:* 15 Mar 2021

Whole Act in force 15 Mar 2021 (RA)

## Non-Domestic Rating (Public Lavatories) Act 2021 (c 13)

*RA:* 29 Apr 2021

Whole Act in force 29 Apr 2021 (RA)

## Overseas Operations (Service Personnel and Veterans) Act 2021 (c 23)

*RA:* 29 Apr 2021

*Commencement provisions:* s 14; Overseas Operations (Service Personnel and Veterans) Act 2021 (Commencement) Regulations 2021, SI 2021/678

| | |
|---|---|
| 1–11 | 30 Jun 2021 (SI 2021/678) |
| 12–15 | 29 Apr 2021 (s 14(1)) |
| Schs 1–4 | 30 Jun 2021 (SI 2021/678) |

## Pension Schemes Act 2021 (c 1)

*RA:* 11 Feb 2021

*Commencement provisions:* s 131; Pension Schemes Act 2021 (Commencement No 1) Regulations 2021, SI 2021/620; Pension Schemes Act 2021 (Commencement No 2) Regulations 2021, SI 2021/752; Pension Schemes Act 2021 (Commencement No 3 and Transitional and Saving Provisions) Regulations 2021, SI 2021/950; Pension Schemes Act 2021 (Commencement No 1) Order (Northern Ireland) 2021, SR 2021/240; Pension Schemes Act 2021 (Commencement No 2 and Transitional and Saving Provisions) Order (Northern Ireland) 2021, SR 2021/271; Pension Schemes Act 2021 (Commencement No 4) Regulations 2021, SI 2021/1236; Pension Schemes Act 2021 (Commencement No 3) Order (Northern Ireland) 2021, SR 2021/300; Pension Schemes Act 2021 (Commencement No 5) Regulations 2021, SI 2021/1394; Pension Schemes Act 2021 (Commencement No 4) Order (Northern Ireland) 2022, SR 2022/173; Pension Schemes Act 2021 (Commencement No 6 and Transitional Provision) Regulations 2022, SI 2022/721; Pension Schemes Act 2021 (Commencement No 5 and Transitional Provision) Order (Northern Ireland) 2022, SR 2022/197; Pension Schemes Act 2021 (Commencement No 7 and Transitory Provision) Regulations 2022, SI 2022/1044

| | | |
|---|---|---|
| 1, 2 | | 11 Feb 2021 (so far as confer power to make regulations or is otherwise necessary for enabling the exercise of such a power on or after 11 Feb 2021) (s 131(3)(a)) |
| | | 1 Aug 2022 (otherwise) (SI 2022/721) |
| 3 | | 11 Feb 2021 (so far as confer power to make regulations or is otherwise necessary for enabling the exercise of such a power on or after 11 Feb 2021) (s 131(3)(a)) |
| | | 1 Aug 2022 (otherwise) (SI 2022/721)[3] |
| 4–51 | | 11 Feb 2021 (so far as confer power to make regulations or is otherwise necessary for enabling the exercise of such a power on or after 11 Feb 2021) (s 131(3)(a)) |
| | | 1 August 2022 (otherwise) (SI 2022/721) |
| 52, 53 | | 11 Feb 2021 (so far as confer power to make regulations or is otherwise necessary for enabling the exercise of such a power on or after 11 Feb 2021) (s 131(3)(a)) |
| | | 1 Aug 2022 (otherwise) (SR 2022/197) |
| 54 | | 11 Feb 2021 (so far as confer power to make regulations or is otherwise necessary for enabling the exercise of such a power on or after 11 Feb 2021) (s 131(3)(a)) |
| | | 1 Aug 2022 (otherwise) (SR 2022/197)[4] |
| 55–102 | | 11 Feb 2021 (so far as confer power to make regulations or is otherwise necessary for enabling the exercise of such a power on or after 11 Feb 2021) (s 131(3)(a)) |
| | | 1 Aug 2022 (otherwise) (SR 2022/197) |
| 103 | (1)–(3) | 1 Oct 2021 (SI 2021/950)[1] |
| | (4) | 31 May 2021 (for the purpose of making regulations) (SI 2021/620) |
| | | 1 Oct 2021 (otherwise) (SI 2021/950)[1] |
| 104 | (1) | See sub-ss (2)–(4) below |
| | (2) | *Not yet in force* |
| | (3), (4) | 1 Oct 2021 (SI 2021/950)[1] |
| 105–108 | | 1 Oct 2021 (SI 2021/950)[1] |
| 109 | | *Not yet in force* |

**Pension Schemes Act 2021 (c 1)**—*contd*

| | | |
|---|---|---|
| 110 | (1) | 1 Oct 2021 (SI 2021/950)[1] |
| | (2) | 31 May 2021 (for the purpose of making regulations) (SI 2021/620) |
| | | 1 Oct 2021 (otherwise) (SI 2021/950)[1] |
| | (3), (4) | 1 Oct 2021 (SI 2021/950)[1] |
| 111 | (1) | See sub-paras (2)–(7) below |
| | (2)(a) | 1 Oct 2021 (except so far as inserts Pensions Act 2004, s 73(2)(da) (SI 2021/950) |
| | | 1 Aug 2022 (otherwise) (SI 2022/721) |
| | (2)(b) | 29 Jun 2022 (insofar as it adds to the provisions coming within Pensions Act 2004, s 73(2)(e) provisions in force in Northern Ireland corresponding to provisions contained in or made by virtue of Pensions Schemes Act 2017) (SI 2022/721) |
| | | 1 Aug 2022 (otherwise) (SI 2022/721) |
| | (3)–(7) | 1 Oct 2021 (SI 2021/950) |
| 112 | | 31 May 2021 (for the purpose of making regulations) (SI 2021/620) |
| | | 1 Oct 2021 (otherwise) (SI 2021/950)[1] |
| 113 | | 1 Oct 2021 (except so far as inserts Pensions Act 2004, s 80A(2)(a)(iv), (c)(vi)) (SI 2021/950)[1] |
| | | 1 Aug 2022 (so far as inserts Pensions Act 2004, s 80A(2)(c)(vi)) (SI 2022/721) |
| | | *Not yet in force* (exception noted above) |
| 114 | | 1 Oct 2021 (SI 2021/950)[1] |
| 115 | | 1 Oct 2021 (SI 2021/950)[1] |
| 116 | | See Sch 7 below |
| 117 | | See Sch 8 below |
| 118, 119 | | 11 Feb 2021 (so far as confer power to make regulations or is otherwise necessary for enabling the exercise of such a power on or after 11 Feb 2021) (s 131(3)(a)) |
| | | 14 Oct 2022 (otherwise) (SI 2022/1044) |
| 120 | | 11 Feb 2021 (so far as confer power to make regulations or is otherwise necessary for enabling the exercise of such a power on or after 11 Feb 2021) (s 131(3)(a)) |
| | | *Not yet in force* (otherwise) |
| 121 | | 11 Feb 2021 (so far as confer power to make regulations or is otherwise necessary for enabling the exercise of such a power on or after 11 Feb 2021) (s 131(3)(a)) |
| | | 14 Oct 2022 (otherwise) (SI 2022/1044) |
| 122 | | 11 Feb 2021 (so far as confer power to make regulations or is otherwise necessary for enabling the exercise of such a power on or after 11 Feb 2021) (s 131(3)(a)) |
| | | 14 Oct 2022 (so far as inserts e Financial Guidance and Claims Act 2018, s 4A(2)–(6)) (SI 2022/1044)[5] |
| | | *Not yet in force* (otherwise) |
| 123 | | *Not yet in force* |
| 124 | | 31 May 2021 (SI 2021/620) |
| 125 | (1) | 30 Nov 2021 (SI 2021/1236) |
| | (2) | 31 May 2021 (for the purpose of making regulations) (SI 2021/620) |
| | | 30 Nov 2021 (otherwise) (SI 2021/1236) |
| | (3)–(5) | 30 Nov 2021 (SI 2021/1236) |
| | (6) | 31 May 2021 (for the purpose of making regulations) (SI 2021/620) |
| | | 30 Nov 2021 (otherwise) (SI 2021/1236) |
| | (7), (8) | 30 Nov 2021 (SI 2021/1236) |
| 126 | | 31 May 2021 (SI 2021/620) |
| 127 | (1) | *Not yet in force* |
| | (2) | 31 Aug 2021 (for the purpose of making regulations) (SI 2021/950) |

**Pension Schemes Act 2021 (c 1)**—*contd*

|  |  |  |
|---|---|---|
|  |  | 1 Oct 2021 (otherwise) (SI 2021/950)[1] |
|  | (3), (4) | 1 Oct 2021 (SI 2021/950) |
| 128 | (a), (b) | 1 Aug 2022 (SI 2022/721) |
|  | (c) | 1 Aug 2022 (except in so far as repeals Pension Schemes Act 2015, s 44) (SI 2022/721) |
|  |  | *Not yet in force* (exception noted above) |
|  | (d), (e) | 1 Aug 2022 (SI 2022/721) |
| 129 |  | See Sch 11 below |
| 130–132 |  | 11 Feb 2021 (s 131(3)(d)–(e)) |
| Schs 1, 2 |  | 11 Feb 2021 (so far as confer power to make regulations or is otherwise necessary for enabling the exercise of such a power on or after 11 Feb 2021) (s 131(3)(a)) |
|  |  | 1 Aug 2022 (otherwise) (SI 2022/721) |
| Sch 3 | paras 1–10 | 11 Feb 2021 (so far as confer power to make regulations or is otherwise necessary for enabling the exercise of such a power on or after 11 Feb 2021) (s 131(3)(a)) |
|  |  | 1 Aug 2022 (otherwise) (SI 2022/721) |
|  | para 11 | See paras 12–21 below |
|  | para 12 | 11 Feb 2021 (so far as confer power to make regulations or is otherwise necessary for enabling the exercise of such a power on or after 11 Feb 2021) (s 131(3)(a)) |
|  |  | 1 Aug 2022 (otherwise) (SI 2022/721) |
|  | para 13 | 11 Feb 2021 (so far as confer power to make regulations or is otherwise necessary for enabling the exercise of such a power on or after 11 Feb 2021) (s 131(3)(a)) |
|  |  | 13 Dec 2021 (otherwise) (SI 2021/1394) |
|  | paras 14–18 | 11 Feb 2021 (so far as confer power to make regulations or is otherwise necessary for enabling the exercise of such a power on or after 11 Feb 2021) (s 131(3)(a)) |
|  |  | *Not yet in force* (otherwise) |
|  | para 19 | 11 Feb 2021 (so far as confer power to make regulations or is otherwise necessary for enabling the exercise of such a power on or after 11 Feb 2021) (s 131(3)(a)) |
|  |  | *Not yet in force* (otherwise) |
|  | paras 20–22 | 11 Feb 2021 (so far as confer power to make regulations or is otherwise necessary for enabling the exercise of such a power on or after 11 Feb 2021) (s 131(3)(a)) |
|  |  | 1 Aug 2022 (otherwise) (SI 2022/721) |
|  | paras 23–25 | 11 Feb 2021 (so far as confer power to make regulations or is otherwise necessary for enabling the exercise of such a power on or after 11 Feb 2021) (s 131(3)(a)) |
|  |  | 13 Dec 2021 (otherwise) (SI 2021/1394) |
| Schs 4, 5 |  | 11 Feb 2021 (so far as confer power to make regulations or is otherwise necessary for enabling the exercise of such a power on or after 11 Feb 2021) (s 131(3)(a)) |
|  |  | 1 Aug 2022 (otherwise) (SR 2022/197) |
| Sch 6 | paras 1–10 | 11 Feb 2021 (so far as confer power to make regulations or is otherwise necessary for enabling the exercise of such a power on or after 11 Feb 2021) (s 131(3)(a)) |
|  |  | 1 Aug 2022 (otherwise) (SR 2022/197) |
|  | para 11 | See paras 12–22 below |
|  | paras 12, 13 | 11 Feb 2021 (so far as confer power to make regulations or is otherwise necessary for enabling the exercise of such a power on or after 11 Feb 2021) (s 131(3)(a)) |
|  |  | 1 Aug 2022 (otherwise) (SR 2022/197) |
|  | para 14 | 11 Feb 2021 (so far as confer power to make regulations or is otherwise necessary for enabling the exercise of such a power on or after 11 Feb 2021) (s 131(3)(a)) |
|  |  | 29 Apr 2022 (otherwise) (SR 2022/173) |

**See Halsbury's Statutes Citator for amendments to these Acts**

**Pension Schemes Act 2021 (c 1)**—*contd*

|  |  |  |
|--|--|--|
| | paras 15–19 | 11 Feb 2021 (so far as confer power to make regulations or is otherwise necessary for enabling the exercise of such a power on or after 11 Feb 2021) (s 131(3)(a)) |
| | | 1 Aug 2022 (otherwise) (SR 2022/197) |
| | para 20 | 11 Feb 2021 (so far as confer power to make regulations or is otherwise necessary for enabling the exercise of such a power on or after 11 Feb 2021) (s 131(3)(a)) |
| | | *Not yet in force* (otherwise) |
| | paras 21, 22 | 11 Feb 2021 (so far as confer power to make regulations or is otherwise necessary for enabling the exercise of such a power on or after 11 Feb 2021) (s 131(3)(a)) |
| | | 1 Aug 2022 (otherwise) (SR 2022/197) |
| | paras 23–25 | 11 Feb 2021 (so far as confer power to make regulations or is otherwise necessary for enabling the exercise of such a power on or after 11 Feb 2021) (s 131(3)(a)) |
| | | 29 Apr 2022 (otherwise) (SR 2022/173) |
| Sch 7 | para 1 | 1 Oct 2021 (SI 2021/950) |
| | para 2 | See paras 3–14 below |
| | paras 3–6 | 1 Oct 2021 (SI 2021/950) |
| | para 7 | 1 Oct 2021 (except for the reference in the amendment made by para 7(3) to Pension Schemes Act 2021, Pt 1) (SI 2021/950) |
| | | 1 Aug 2022 (exception noted above) (SI 2022/721) |
| | para 8(a) | 31 May 2021 (SI 2021/620) |
| | para 8(b) | 1 Oct 2021 (SI 2021/950) |
| | paras 9–11 | 1 Oct 2021 (SI 2021/950) |
| | para 12(1) | See sub-paras (2)–(3) below |
| | para 12(2) | 25 Jun 2021 (SI 2021/752) |
| | para 12(3) | 1 Oct 2021 (SI 2021/950) |
| | paras 13–20 | 29 Jun 2022 (SI 2022/721) |
| Sch 8 | para 1 | See paras 2–14 below |
| | para 2(1), (2) | 1 Oct 2021 (SR 2021/271)[2] |
| | para 2(3) | 1 Sep 2021 (for the purpose of authorising the making of regulations) (SR 2021/240) |
| | | 1 Oct 2021 (otherwise) (SR 2021/271)[2] |
| | para 3(1) | See sub-paras (2)–(4) below |
| | para 3(2) | 1 Oct 2021 (SR 2021/271)[2] |
| | para 3(3), (4) | *Not yet in force* |
| | paras 4–7 | 1 Oct 2021 (SR 2021/271)[2] |
| | para 8(1) | 1 Sep 2021 (for the purpose of authorising the making of regulations) (SR 2021/240) |
| | | *Not yet in force* (otherwise) |
| | para 8(2) | *Not yet in force* |
| | para 9(1) | 1 Sep 2021 (for the purpose of authorising the making of regulations) (SR 2021/240) |
| | | 1 Oct 2021 (otherwise) (SR 2021/271)[2] |
| | para 9(2), (3) | 1 Oct 2021 (SR 2021/271)[2] |
| | para 10(1) | See sub-paras (2)–(7) |
| | para 10(2)(a) | 1 Aug 2022 (SR 2022/197) |
| | para 10(2)(b)(i) | 1 Oct 2021 (SR 2021/271)[2] |
| | para 10(2)(b)(ii) | 1 Aug 2022 (SR 2022/197) |
| | para 10(3)–(7) | 1 Oct 2021 (SR 2021/271)[2] |
| | para 11 | 1 Sep 2021 (for the purpose of authorising the making of regulations) (SR 2021/240) |
| | | 1 Oct 2021 (otherwise) (SR 2021/271)[2] |
| | para 12 | 1 Oct 2021 (except so far as inserts Pensions (Northern Ireland) Order 2005, SI 2005/255, art 75A(2)(a)(iv), (c)(v)) (SR 2021/271)[2] |
| | | 1 Aug 2022 (so far as inserts Pensions (Northern Ireland) Order 2005, SI 2005/255, art 75A(2)(c)(v)) (SR 2022/197) |
| | | *Not yet in force* (exception noted above) |

**Pension Schemes Act 2021 (c 1)**—*contd*

| | | |
|---|---|---|
| | paras 13–15 | 1 Oct 2021 (SR 2021/271)[2] |
| | para 16 | See paras 17–28 below |
| | paras 17–20 | 1 Oct 2021 (SR 2021/271)[2] |
| | para 21 | 1 Oct 2021 (except for the reference in the amendment made by paragraph 21(3) to Part 2 of the Pension Schemes Act 2021) (SR 2021/271)[2] |
| | | 1 Aug 2022 (exception noted above) (SR 2022/197) |
| | para 22(a) | 1 Sep 2021 (SR 2021/240) |
| | para 22(b) | 1 Oct 2021 (SR 2021/271)[2] |
| | paras 23–25 | 1 Oct 2021 (SR 2021/271)[2] |
| | para 26(1) | See sub-paras (2), (3) below |
| | para 26(2) | 1 Sep 2021 (SR 2021/240) |
| | para 26(3) | 1 Oct 2021 (SR 2021/271)[2] |
| | paras 27–31 | 28 Jul 2022 (SR 2022/197) |
| Sch 9 | | 11 Feb 2021 (so far as confer power to make regulations or is otherwise necessary for enabling the exercise of such a power on or after 11 Feb 2021) (s 131(3)(a)) |
| | | *Not yet in force* (otherwise) |
| Sch 10 | | 11 Feb 2021 (so far as confers power to make regulations or is otherwise necessary for enabling the exercise of such a power on or after 11 Feb 2021) (s 131(3)(b)) |
| | | *Not yet in force* (otherwise) |
| Sch 11 | paras 1–11 | 11 Feb 2021 (so far as confers power to make regulations or is otherwise necessary for enabling the exercise of such a power on or after 11 Feb 2021) (s 131(3)(c)) |
| | | *Not yet in force* (otherwise) |
| | para 12 | 1 Sep 2021 (SR 2021/240) |
| | para 13(1) | See sub-paras (2)–(8) below |
| | para 13(2)–(5) | 30 Nov 2021 (SR 2021/300) |
| | para 13(6) | 1 Sep 2021 (for the purpose of authorising the making of regulations) (SR 2021/240) |
| | | 30 Nov 2021 (otherwise) (SR 2021/300) |
| | para 14 | 1 Sep 2021 (SR 2021/240) |
| | para 15(1) | *Not yet in force* |
| | para 15(2) | 29 Sep 2021 (for the purpose only of authorising the making of regulations) (SR 2021/271)[2] |
| | | 1 Oct 2021 (otherwise) (SR 2021/271)[2] |
| | para 15(3) | 1 Oct 2021 (SR 2021/271)[2] |
| | para 16(a), (b) | 1 Aug 2022 (SR 2022/197) |
| | para 16(c) | 1 Aug 2022 (except in so far as repeals Pension Schemes (Northern Ireland) Act 2016, s 44) (SR 2022/197) |
| | | *Not yet in force* (exception noted above) |
| | para 16(d), (e) | 1 Aug 2022 (SR 2022/197) |

[1]   For transitional and saving provisions, see SI 2021/950, regs 3–10

[2]   For transitional and saving provisions, see SR 2021/271, regs 3–10

[3]   For transitional provisions, see SI 2022/721, reg 4

[4]   For transitional provisions, see SR 2022/197, art 4

[5]   For transitory modifications, see SI 2022/1044, reg 3

## Period Products (Free Provision) (Scotland) Act 2021 (asp 1)

*RA*: 12 Jan 2021

*Commencement provisions*: s 11; Period Products (Free Provision) (Scotland) Act 2021 (Commencement No 1) Regulations 2021, SSI 2021/104; Period Products (Free Provision) (Scotland) Act 2021 (Commencement No 2) Regulations 2022, SSI 2022/208

**Period Products (Free Provision) (Scotland) Act 2021 (asp 1)**—*contd*

| | |
|---|---|
| 1–4 | 15 Aug 2022 (SSI 2022/208) |
| 5–7 | 18 Mar 2021 (SSI 2021/104) |
| 8 | 15 Aug 2022 (SSI 2022/208) |
| 9–12 | 13 Jan 2021 (s 11(1)) |

**Pre-release Access to Official Statistics (Scotland) Act 2021 (asp 11)**

*RA*: 21 Apr 2021

*Commencement provisions*: s 4

Whole Act in force 22 Apr 2021 (s 4)

**Prisons (Substance Testing) Act 2021 (c 18)**

*RA*: 29 Apr 2021

*Commencement provisions*: s 3(2); Prisons (Substance Testing) Act 2021 (Commencement) Regulations 2021, SI 2021/1280

| | |
|---|---|
| 1, 2 | 8 Dec 2021 (SI 2021/1280) |
| 3 | 29 Apr 2021 (RA) |

**Protection of Workers (Retail and Age-restricted Goods and Services) (Scotland) Act 2021 (asp 6)**

*RA*: 24 Feb 2021

*Commencement provisions*: s 6

| | | |
|---|---|---|
| 1–3 | | 24 Aug 2021 (s 6(2)) |
| 4 | (1), (2) | 25 Feb 2021 (s 6(1)) |
| | (3) | 24 Aug 2021 (s 6(2)) |
| 5 | | 25 Feb 2021 (s 6(1)) |
| 6 | | 24 Aug 2021 (s 6(2)) |
| (7) | | 25 Feb 2021 (s 6(1)) |

**Rating (Coronavirus) and Directors Disqualification (Dissolved Companies) Act 2021 (c 34)**

*RA*: 15 Dec 2021

*Commencement provisions*: s 4(4), (5)

| | |
|---|---|
| 1 | 15 Dec 2021 (s 4(4)(a)) |
| 2 | 15 Dec 2021 (the purposes of the exercise by the Secretary of State or the official receiver of powers under Company Directors Disqualification Act 1986, s 7(4)) (s 4(4)(b)) |
| | 15 Feb 2022 (otherwise) (s 4(5)) |
| 3 | 15 Dec 2021 (for the purposes of the exercise by the Department or the official receiver of powers under Company Directors Disqualification (Northern Ireland) Order 2002, SI 2002/3150 (NI 4), art 10(5A)) (s 4(4)(c)) |
| | 15 Feb 2022 (otherwise) (s 4(5)) |
| 4 | 15 Dec 2021 (s 4(4)(d)) |

## Redress for Survivors (Historical Child Abuse in Care) (Scotland) Act 2021 (asp 15)

*RA:* 23 Apr 2021

*Commencement provisions*: s 109; Redress for Survivors (Historical Child Abuse in Care) (Scotland) Act 2021 (Commencement No 1) Regulations 2021, SSI 2021/234; Redress for Survivors (Historical Child Abuse in Care) (Scotland) Act 2021 (Commencement No 2) Regulations 2021, SSI 2021/419

| | | |
|---|---|---|
| 1–6 | | 28 Jun 2021 (SSI 2021/234) |
| 7 | | 7 Dec 2021 (SSI 2021/419) |
| 8 | | 28 Jun 2021 (SSI 2021/234) |
| 9 | | 7 Dec 2021 (SSI 2021/419) |
| 10–17 | | 28 Jun 2021 (SSI 2021/234) |
| 18–22 | | 7 Dec 2021 (SSI 2021/419) |
| 23 | | 28 Jun 2021 (SSI 2021/234) |
| 24–46 | | 7 Dec 2021 (SSI 2021/419) |
| 47 | | 28 Jun 2021 (SSI 2021/234) |
| 48–77 | | 7 Dec 2021 (SSI 2021/419) |
| 78 | | 28 Jun 2021 (SSI 2021/234) |
| 79–86 | | 7 Dec 2021 (SSI 2021/419) |
| 87 | | 28 Jun 2021 (SSI 2021/234) |
| 88 | | 7 Dec 2021 (SSI 2021/419) |
| 89–91 | | 28 Jun 2021 (SSI 2021/234) |
| 92, 93 | | 7 Dec 2021 (SSI 2021/419) |
| 94 | (1), (2) | 7 Dec 2021 (SSI 2021/419) |
| | (3)–(6) | 28 Jun 2021 (SSI 2021/234) |
| 95 | (1)–(4) | 7 Dec 2021 (SSI 2021/419) |
| | (5) | 28 Jun 2021 (SSI 2021/234) |
| 96, 97 | | 7 Dec 2021 (SSI 2021/419) |
| 98 | | 28 Jun 2021 (SSI 2021/234) |
| 99–101 | | 7 Dec 2021 (SSI 2021/419) |
| 102, 103 | | 28 Jun 2021 (SSI 2021/234) |
| 105 | | 24 Apr 2021 (s 109(1)) |
| 106 | | 28 Jun 2021 (SSI 2021/234) |
| 107–110 | | 24 Apr 2021 (s 109(1)) |
| Schs 1, 2 | | 28 Jun 2021 (SSI 2021/234) |

## Renting Homes (Amendment) (Wales) Act 2021 (asc 3)

*RA:* 7 Apr 2021

*Commencement provisions*: s 19; Renting Homes (Amendment) (Wales) Act 2021 (Commencement) Order 2022, SI 2022/904

| | | |
|---|---|---|
| 1–14 | | 8 Jun 2021 (s 19(3)) |
| 15 | | 8 Apr 2021 (19(1)) |
| 16 | | 8 Jun 2021 (s 19(3)) |
| 17 | | 8 Apr 2021 (19(1)) |
| 18 | | 8 Jun 2021 (s 19(3)) |
| 19, 20 | | 8 Apr 2021 (19(1)) |
| Schs 1–5 | | 8 Jun 2021 (s 19(3)) |
| Sch 6 | paras 1–27 | 8 Jun 2021 (s 19(3)) |
| | para 28 | 1 Dec 2022 (SI 2022/904) |

## Safeguarding (Code of Practice) Measure 2021 (No 3)

*RA: 20 Oct 2021*

*Commencement provisions*: s 3(2)–(6); Safeguarding (Code of Practice) Measure 2021 (Commencement and Transitional Provision) Order 2022, SI 2022/118

| | |
|---|---|
| 1, 2 | 1 Mar 2022 (SI 2022/118)[1] |

**See Halsbury's Statutes Citator for amendments to these Acts** 2673

**Safeguarding (Code of Practice) Measure 2021 (No 3)**—*contd*

3                              20 Oct 2021 (s 3(2))

[1]   For transitional provisions see SI 2022/118, art 3

---

## Scottish General Election (Coronavirus) Act 2021 (asp 5)

*RA:* 29 Jan 2021

*Commencement provisions*: s 15

Whole Act in force 30 Jan 2021 (s 15)

---

## Scottish Parliament (Assistance for Political Parties) Act 2021 (asp 7)

*RA:* 22 Mar 2021

*Commencement provisions*: s 4

Whole Act in force 22 May 2021 (s 4)

---

## Scottish Parliamentary Standards (Sexual Harassment and Complaints Process) Act 2021 (asp 12)

*RA:* 21 Apr 2021

*Commencement provisions*: s 4

1–3                            21 Oct 2021 (s 4(2))
4, 5                           22 Apr 2021 (s 4(1))

---

## Social Security (Up-rating of Benefits) Act 2021 (c 32)

*RA:* 17 Nov 2021

*Commencement provisions*: s 2

Whole Act in force 17 Nov 2021 (s 2)

---

## Solicitors in the Supreme Courts of Scotland (Amendment) Act 2021 (asp 2)

*RA:* 20 Jan 2021

*Commencement provisions*: s 5

Whole Act in force 20 Feb 2021 (s 5)

---

## Supply and Appropriation (Anticipation and Adjustments) Act 2021 (c 6)

*RA:* 15 Mar 2021

Whole Act in force 15 Mar 2021 (RA)

---

## Telecommunications Infrastructure (Leasehold Property) Act 2021 (c 7)

*RA:* 15 Mar 2021

*Commencement provisions:* s 3(3)–(7)

| | |
|---|---|
| 1, 2 | 15 Mar 2021 (so far as necessary for enabling the exercise, on or after that day of any power to make regulations under Communications Act 2003, Sch 3A, Pt 4A) (s 3(3)(b)) |
| | *Not yet in force* (otherwise) |
| 3 | 15 Mar 2021 (s 3(3)(a)) |
| Schedule | 15 Mar 2021 (so far as necessary for enabling the exercise, on or after that day of any power to make regulations under Communications Act 2003, Sch 3A, Pt 4A) (s 3(3)(b)) |
| | *Not yet in force* (otherwise) |

## Telecommunications (Security) Act 2021 (c 31)

*RA:* 17 Nov 2021

*Commencement provisions:* s 28; Telecommunications (Security) Act 2021 (Commencement) Regulations 2022, SI 2022/931

| | | |
|---|---|---|
| 1, 2 | | 17 Nov 2021 (so far as confer power to make regulations) (s 28(1)(a)) |
| | | 1 Oct 2022 (otherwise) (SI 2022/931) |
| 3 | | 17 Nov 2021 (so far as confers power to issue codes of practice) (s 28(1)(b)) |
| | | 1 Oct 2022 (otherwise) (SI 2022/931) |
| 4–13 | | 1 Oct 2022 (SI 2022/931) |
| 14–23 | | 17 Nov 2021 (s 28(1)(c)) |
| 24 | | 17 Nov 2021 (so far as relates to s 18) (s 28(1)(d)) |
| | | 1 Oct 2022 (otherwise) (SI 2022/931) |
| 25 | (1) | 17 Nov 2021 (s 28(1)(e)) |
| | (2) | 1 Oct 2022 (otherwise) (SI 2022/931) |
| | (3) | 17 Nov 2021 (s 28(1)(e)) |
| 26 | | 17 Nov 2021 (s 28(1)(f)) |
| 27 | | 17 Nov 2021 (s 28(1)(g)) |
| 28 | | 17 Nov 2021 (s 28(1)(h)) |
| 29 | | 17 Nov 2021 (s 28(1)(i)) |

## Tied Pubs (Scotland) Act 2021 (asp 17)

*RA:* 5 May 2021

*Commencement provisions:* s 25

| | |
|---|---|
| 1, 2 | *Not yet in force* |
| 3–5 | 6 May 2021 (s 25(1)) |
| 6–19 | *Not yet in force* |
| 20–26 | 6 May 2021 (s 25(1)) |
| Schs 1, 2 | *Not yet in force* |

## Trade Act 2021 (c 10)

*RA:* 29 Apr 2021

*Commencement provisions:* s 18; Trade Act 2021 (Commencement No 1 and Expiry Provision) Regulations 2021, SI 2021/550

| | |
|---|---|
| 1, 2 | 6 May 2021 (SI 2021/550) |
| 3 | 30 Jun 2021 (SI 2021/550) |
| 4, 5 | 6 May 2021 (SI 2021/550) |

**See Halsbury's Statutes Citator for amendments to these Acts** 2675

**Trade Act 2021 (c 10)**—*contd*

| | | |
|---|---|---|
| 6 | (1), (2) | 1 Jun 2021 (SI 2021/550) |
| | (3) | 6 May 2021 (SI 2021/550) |
| 7 | | 1 Jun 2021 (SI 2021/550) |
| 8–11 | | *Not yet in force* |
| 12–15 | | 30 Jun 2021 (SI 2021/550) |
| 16–19 | | 29 Apr 2021 (s 18(1)) |
| Schs 1–3 | | 6 May 2021 (SI 2021/550) |
| Sch 4 | | 1 Jun 2021 (SI 2021/550) |
| Sch 5 | | 6 May 2021 (SI 2021/550) |
| Sch 6 | | *Not yet in force* |

## UK Withdrawal from the European Union (Continuity) (Scotland) Act 2021 (asp 4)

*RA:* 29 Jan 2021

*Commencement provisions*: s 51; UK Withdrawal from the European Union (Continuity) (Scotland) Act 2021 (Commencement No 1) Regulations 2021, SSI 2021/141; UK Withdrawal from the European Union (Continuity) (Scotland) Act 2021 (Commencement No 2) Regulations 2021, SSI 2021/304

| | |
|---|---|
| 1–13 | 29 Mar 2021 (SSI 2021/141) |
| 14 | *Not yet in force* |
| 15 | 29 Mar 2021 (for the purpose of enabling consultation by the Scottish Ministers under s 18(3)(b)) (SSI 2021/141) |
| | *Not yet in force (otherwise)* |
| 16, 17 | *Not yet in force* |
| 18 | 29 Mar 2021 (SSI 2021/141) |
| 19–46 | 1 Oct 2021 (SSI 2021/304) |
| 47 | 29 Mar 2021 (SSI 2021/141) |
| 48–53 | 30 Jan 2021 (s 51(1)) |
| Schs 1, 2 | 1 Oct 2021 (SSI 2021/304) |

## University of St. Andrews (Degrees in Medicine and Dentistry) Act 2021 (asp 13)

*RA:* 23 Apr 2021

*Commencement provisions*: s 2

Whole Act in force 23 Apr 2021 (s 2)

## Welsh Elections (Coronavirus) Act 2021 (asc 2)

*RA:* 16 Mar 2021

*Commencement provisions*: s 18

Whole Act in force 17 Mar 2021 (s 18)

# 2022 Acts

## Advanced Research and Invention Agency Act 2022 (c 4)

*RA*: 24 Feb 2022

*Commencement provisions*: s 13

| | | |
|---|---|---|
| 1–9 | | Not yet in force |
| 10–14 | | 24 Feb 2022 (s 13(2)) |
| Sch 1 | paras 1–10 | Not yet in force |
| | para 11 | 24 Feb 2022 (s 13(2)) |
| | paras 12–18 | Not yet in force |
| Schs 2, 3 | | Not yet in force |

## Animal Welfare (Sentience) Act 2022 (c 22)

*RA*: 28 Apr 2022

*Commencement provisions*: s 6(2), (3)

| | |
|---|---|
| 1–5 | Not yet in force |
| 6 | 28 Apr 2022 (s 6(3)) |

## Animals (Penalty Notices) Act 2022 (c 19)

*RA*: 28 Apr 2022

*Commencement provisions*: s 9(2), (3)

| | | |
|---|---|---|
| 1 | (1) | Not yet in force |
| | (2)–(5) | 28 Jun 2022 (s 9(1)) |
| | (6) | Not yet in force |
| 2 | (1) | Not yet in force |
| | (2), (3) | 28 Jun 2022 (s 9(1)) |
| | (4) | Not yet in force |
| 3 | | Not yet in force |
| 4 | (1), (2) | Not yet in force |
| | (3), (4) | 28 Jun 2022 (s 9(1)) |
| | (5) | Not yet in force |
| 5, 6 | | Not yet in force |
| 7–9 | | 28 Jun 2022 (s 9(1)) |

## Approved Premises (Substance Testing) Act 2022 (c 27)

*RA*: 28 Apr 2022

*Commencement provisions*: s 2(2); Approved Premises (Substance Testing) Act 2022 (Commencement) Regulations 2022, SI 2022/1013

| | |
|---|---|
| 1, 2 | 3 Oct 2022 (SI 2022/1013) |

## British Sign Language Act 2022 (c 34)

*RA:* 28 Apr 2022

*Commencement provisions:* s 4(2)–(4)

| | |
|---|---|
| 1, 2 | 28 Jun 2022 (s 4(3)) |
| 3 | *Not yet in force* |
| 4 | 28 Apr 2022 (s 4(2)) |
| Schedule | 28 Jun 2022 (s 4(3)) |

## Budget (Scotland) Act 2022 (asp 3)

*RA:* 23 Mar 2022

*Commencement provisions:* s 10

Whole Act in force 24 Mar 2022 (s 10)

## Building Safety Act 2022 (c 30)

*RA:* 28 Apr 2022

*Commencement provisions:* s 170; Building Safety Act 2022 (Commencement No 1, Transitional and Saving Provisions) Regulations 2022, SI 2022/561; Building Safety Act 2022 (Commencement No 1) (Wales) Regulations 2022, SI 2022/774; Building Safety Act 2022 (Commencement No 2) Regulations 2022, SI 2022/927

| | | |
|---|---|---|
| 1 | | 28 Apr 2022 (s 170(1)(a)) |
| 2 | (1) | 28 Apr 2022 (s 170(1)(b)) |
| | (2) | 28 Apr 2022 (for the purpose of making regulations) (s 170(2)(a)) |
| | | 28 Jun 2022 (otherwise) (SI 2022/561) |
| 3 | | 28 Apr 2022 (for the purpose of making regulations) (s 170(2)(a)) |
| | | 28 Jun 2022 (otherwise) (SI 2022/561) |
| 4–6 | | 28 Apr 2022 (for the purpose of making regulations) (s 170(2)(a)) |
| | | *Not yet in force* (otherwise) |
| 7 | | 28 Apr 2022 (s 170(1)(c)) |
| 8–16 | | 28 Apr 2022 (for the purpose of making regulations) (s 170(2)(a)) |
| | | *Not yet in force* (otherwise) |
| 17, 18 | | 28 Apr 2022 (for the purpose of making regulations) (s 170(2)(a)) |
| | | 28 Jun 2022 (otherwise) (SI 2022/561)[1] |
| 19–27 | | 28 Apr 2022 (for the purpose of making regulations) (s 170(2)(a)) |
| | | *Not yet in force* (otherwise) |
| 28 | | 28 Apr 2022 (s 170(1)(d)) |
| 29 | | 28 Apr 2022 (for the purpose of making regulations) (s 170(2)(a)) |
| | | *Not yet in force* (otherwise) |
| 30 | | 28 Apr 2022 (s 170(1)(e)) |
| 31 | | 28 Jun 2022 (so far as relates to Building Act 1984, ss 120D–120H) (SI 2022/561) |
| | | *Not yet in force* (otherwise) |
| 32–40 | | *Not yet in force* |
| 41 | | 28 Jun 2022 (E) (SI 2022/561) |
| | | *Not yet in force* (W) |
| 42–47 | | *Not yet in force* |
| 48 | | 28 Jul 2022 (E) (SI 2022/561) |
| | | 28 Jul 2022 (W) (SI 2022/774) |
| 49–54 | | *Not yet in force* |
| 55 | | See Sch 5 below |
| 56 | | *Not yet in force* |
| 57 | | 28 Jun 2022 (E) (SI 2022/561) |
| | | *Not yet in force* (W) |
| 58–60 | | *Not yet in force* |

**Building Safety Act 2022 (c 30)**—*contd*

| | | |
|---|---|---|
| 61–70 | | 28 Apr 2022 (s 170(1)(f)) |
| 71–114 | | 28 Apr 2022 (for the purpose of making regulations) (s 170(2)(a)) |
| | | *Not yet in force* (otherwise) |
| 115 | | 28 Apr 2022 (s 170(1)(g)) |
| 116–125 | | 28 Apr 2022 (s 170(3)(a)) |
| 126–129 | | 1 Sep 2022 (SI 2022/927) |
| 130, 131 | | 28 Jun 2022 (SI 2022/561) |
| 132 | | 28 May 2022 (for the purpose of making regulations) (SI 2022/561) |
| | | 28 Jun 2022 (otherwise) (SI 2022/561) |
| 133 | | *Not yet in force* |
| 134 | | 28 Jun 2022 (s 170(3)(b)) |
| 135 | | 28 Jun 2022 (s 170(3)(c)) |
| 136–145 | | *Not yet in force* |
| 146 | | 28 Jun 2022 (s 170(3)(d)) |
| 147–155 | | 28 Jun 2022 (s 170(3)(e)) |
| 156 | | *Not yet in force* |
| 157–159 | | 28 Jun 2022 (s 170(3)(f)) |
| 160 | | 1 Oct 2022 (SI 2022/561) |
| 161 | | *Not yet in force* |
| 162, 163 | | 28 Apr 2022 (s 170(1)(h)) |
| 164 | | *Not yet in force* |
| 165–171 | | 28 Apr 2022 (s 170(1)(h)) |
| Sch 1 | | 28 Apr 2022 (for the purpose of making regulations) (s 170(2)(a)) |
| | | 28 June 2022 (otherwise) (SI 2022/561) |
| Schs 2, 3 | | 28 Apr 2022 (for the purpose of making regulations) (s 170(2)(a)) |
| | | *Not yet in force* (otherwise) |
| Sch 4 | | *Not yet in force* |
| Sch 5 | para 1 | See paras 2–86 below |
| | paras 2, 3 | 28 Jun 2022 (E) (SI 2022/561) |
| | | *Not yet in force* (W) |
| | para 4(1) | See para 4(2), (3) below |
| | para 4(2) | 28 Jun 2022 (E) (SI 2022/561) |
| | | *Not yet in force* (W) |
| | para 4(3) | *Not yet in force* |
| | para 5(1) | See para 5(2)–(4) below |
| | para 5(2) | 28 Jun 2022 (E) (SI 2022/561) |
| | | *Not yet in force* (W) |
| | para 5(3), (4) | *Not yet in force* |
| | para 6 | 28 Jun 2022 (E) (SI 2022/561) |
| | | *Not yet in force* (W) |
| | paras 7, 8 | *Not yet in force* |
| | paras 9, 10 | 28 Jun 2022 (E) (SI 2022/561) |
| | | *Not yet in force* (W) |
| | para 11(1) | See para 11(2)–(4) below |
| | para 11(2), (3) | 28 Jun 2022 (E) (SI 2022/561) |
| | | *Not yet in force* (W) |
| | para 11(4) | *Not yet in force* |
| | para 12(1) | See para 12(2)–(5) below |
| | para 12(2) | 28 Jun 2022 (E) (SI 2022/561) |
| | | *Not yet in force* (W) |
| | para 12(3)–(5) | *Not yet in force* |
| | para 13(1) | See para 13(2)–(6) below |
| | para 13(2) | 28 Jun 2022 (E) (SI 2022/561) |
| | | *Not yet in force* (W) |
| | para 13(3), (4) | *Not yet in force* |
| | para 13(5), (6) | 28 Jun 2022 (E) (SI 2022/561) |
| | | *Not yet in force* (W) |
| | para 14(1) | See para 14(2)–(8) below |

**Building Safety Act 2022 (c 30)**—*contd*

| | |
|---|---|
| para 14(2) | 28 Jun 2022 (E) (SI 2022/561) |
| | *Not yet in force* (W) |
| para 14(3)(a) | *Not yet in force* |
| para 14(3)(b) | 28 Jun 2022 (E) (SI 2022/561) |
| | *Not yet in force* (W) |
| para 14(4)(a) | *Not yet in force* |
| para 14(4)(b) | 28 Jun 2022 (E) (SI 2022/561) |
| | *Not yet in force* (W) |
| para 14(5)–(8) | *Not yet in force* |
| para 15(1) | See para 15(2)–(10) below |
| para 15(2)–(5) | 28 Jun 2022 (E) (SI 2022/561) |
| | *Not yet in force* (W) |
| para 15(6)–(8) | *Not yet in force* |
| para 15(9) | 28 Jun 2022 (E) (SI 2022/561) |
| | *Not yet in force* (W) |
| para 15(10) | *Not yet in force* |
| para 16 | 28 Jun 2022 (E) (SI 2022/561) |
| | *Not yet in force* (W) |
| paras 17–21 | *Not yet in force* |
| para 22(1) | See paras (2)–(8) below |
| para 22(2)–(7) | *Not yet in force* |
| para 22(8) | 28 Jun 2022 (E) (SI 2022/561) |
| | *Not yet in force* (W) |
| paras 23–45 | *Not yet in force* |
| para 46(1) | See para 46(2), (3) below |
| para 46(2) | 28 Jun 2022 (E) (SI 2022/561) |
| | *Not yet in force* (W) |
| para 46(3) | *Not yet in force* |
| paras 47–49 | *Not yet in force* |
| paras 50, 51 | 28 Jun 2022 (E) (SI 2022/561) |
| | *Not yet in force* (W) |
| para 52 | *Not yet in force* |
| para 53 | 28 Jun 2022 (E) (SI 2022/561) |
| | *Not yet in force* (W) |
| para 54 | *Not yet in force* |
| para 55(1) | See para 55(2)–(6) below |
| para 55(2), (3) | *Not yet in force* |
| para 55(4)(a) | 28 Jun 2022 (E) (SI 2022/561) |
| | *Not yet in force* (W) |
| para 55(4)(b) | *Not yet in force* |
| para 55(5) | *Not yet in force* |
| para 55(6) | 28 Jun 2022 (E) (SI 2022/561) |
| | *Not yet in force* (W) |
| para 56 | *Not yet in force* |
| para 57(1) | See para 57(2), (3) below |
| para 57(2) | *Not yet in force* |
| para 57(3) | 28 Jun 2022 (E) (SI 2022/561) |
| | *Not yet in force* (W) |
| paras 58–66 | *Not yet in force* |
| para 67 | 28 Jun 2022 (E) (SI 2022/561) |
| | *Not yet in force* (W) |
| paras 68–70 | *Not yet in force* |
| para 71 | 28 Jun 2022 (E) (SI 2022/561) |
| | *Not yet in force* (W) |
| paras 72,73 | *Not yet in force* |
| para 74(1) | See para 74(2), (3) below |
| para 74(2) | 28 Jun 2022 (E) (SI 2022/561) |
| | *Not yet in force* (W) |
| para 74(3) | *Not yet in force* |

**Building Safety Act 2022 (c 30)**—*contd*

| | | |
|---|---|---|
| para 75 | 28 Jun 2022 (E) (SI 2022/561) | |
| | *Not yet in force* (W) | |
| para 76(1) | See para 76(2), (3) below | |
| para 76(2) | *Not yet in force* | |
| para 76(3) | 28 Jun 2022 (E) (SI 2022/561) | |
| | *Not yet in force* (W) | |
| para 77 | 28 Jun 2022 (in so far as relates to Building Act 1984, s 120B, for the purposes only of regulations under the 1984 Act other than building regulations) (E) (SI 2022/561) | |
| | *Not yet in force* (otherwise) (E) | |
| | *Not yet in force* (W) | |
| para 78 | 28 Jun 2022 (E) (SI 2022/561) | |
| | *Not yet in force* (W) | |
| paras 79, 80 | *Not yet in force* | |
| para 81(1) | 28 Jun 2022 (so far as it relates to definitions "appropriate national authority", "higher-risk building" and "the regulator") (E) (SI 2022/561) | |
| | *Not yet in force* (otherwise) (E) | |
| | *Not yet in force* (W) | |
| para 81(2) | 28 Jun 2022 (E) (so far as relates to definitions "appropriate national authority", "higher-risk building" and "the regulator") (SI 2022/561) | |
| | *Not yet in force* (otherwise) (E) | |
| | *Not yet in force* (W) | |
| para 81(3) | *Not yet in force* | |
| para 82 | 28 Jun 2022 (E) (SI 2022/561) | |
| | *Not yet in force* (W) | |
| para 83(1) | See para 83(2)–(9) below | |
| para 83(2) | 28 Jun 2022 (E) (SI 2022/561) | |
| | *Not yet in force* (W) | |
| para 83(3) | 28 Jun 2022 (so far as relates to Building Act 1984, Sch 1, para 5) (E) (SI 2022/561)[1] | |
| | *Not yet in force* (otherwise) (E) | |
| | *Not yet in force* (W) | |
| para 83(4)–(6) | *Not yet in force* | |
| para 83(7) | 28 Jun 2022 (E) (SI 2022/561) | |
| | *Not yet in force* (W) | |
| para 83(8) | *Not yet in force* | |
| para 83(9) | 28 Jun 2022 (E) (SI 2022/561) | |
| | *Not yet in force* (W) | |
| para 84(1) | See para 84(2), (3) below | |
| para 84(2) | *Not yet in force* | |
| para 84(3) | 28 Jun 2022 (E) (SI 2022/561) | |
| | *Not yet in force* (W) | |
| paras 85–90 | *Not yet in force* | |
| Sch 6 | *Not yet in force* | |
| Sch 7 | 28 Apr 2022 (for the purpose of making regulations) (s 170(2)(a)) | |
| | *Not yet in force* (otherwise) | |
| Sch 8 | 28 Jun 2022 (s 170(3)(a)) | |
| Schs 9, 10 | *Not yet in force* | |
| Sch 11 | 28 Jun 2022 (s 170(3)(d)) | |

[1]  For transitional and saving provisions see SI 2022/561, regs 6, 7

## Charities Act 2022 (c 6)

*RA*: 24 Feb 2022

*Commencement provisions*: s 41(3), (4)

| | |
|---|---|
| 1–40 | *Not yet in force* |
| 41 | 24 Feb 2022 (s 41(3)) |
| Schs 1, 2 | *Not yet in force* |

## Commercial Rent (Coronavirus) Act 2022 (c 12)

*RA*: 24 Mar 2022

*Commencement provisions*: s 31(4), (5)

| | | |
|---|---|---|
| 1–26 | | 24 Mar 2022 (s 31(4)) |
| 27 | | See Sch 3 below |
| 28–31 | | 24 Mar 2022 (s 31(4)) |
| Schs 1, 2 | | 24 Mar 2022 (s 31(4)) |
| Sch 3 | para 1 | 1 Apr 2022 (s 31(5)) |
| | paras 2–4 | 24 Mar 2022 (s 31(4)) |

## Coronavirus (Discretionary Compensation for Self-isolation) (Scotland) Act 2022 (asp 2)

*RA*: 23 Mar 2022

*Commencement provisions*: s 6

Whole Act in force 24 Mar 2022 (s 6)

## Coronavirus (Recovery and Reform) (Scotland) Act 2022 (asp 8)

*RA*: 10 Aug 2022

*Commencement provisions*: s 59; Coronavirus (Recovery and Reform) (Scotland) Act 2022 (Commencement No 1) Regulations 2022, SSI 2022/274

| | | |
|---|---|---|
| 1–3 | | 1 Sep 2022 (s 59(1)) |
| 4 | | 24 Sep 2022 (s 59(1)) |
| 5–15 | | 1 Sep 2022 (s 59(1)) |
| 16, 17 | | 1 Oct 2022 (SSI 2022/274) |
| 18–21 | | 1 Oct 2022 (s 59(1)) |
| 22 | | 1 Nov 2022 (s 59(1)) |
| 23, 24 | | 1 Oct 2022 (s 59(1)) |
| 25 | (1)–(5) | 24 Sep 2022 (s 59(2)(b)) |
| | (6), (7) | 1 Sep 2022 (for the purpose of making regulations under Registration of Births, Deaths and Marriages (Scotland) Act 1965, ss 18, 18B) (s 59(2)(a)(i)) |
| | | 24 Sep 2022 (otherwise) (s 59(2)(a)(ii)) |
| | (8) | 24 Sep 2022 (s 59(2)(b)) |
| 26 | | 24 Sep 2022 (s 59(1)) |
| 27 | (1) | 24 Sep 2022 (s 59(3)(b)) |
| | (2) | 1 Sep 2022 (for the purpose of making regulations under Registration of Births, Deaths and Marriages (Scotland) Act 1965, ss 23, 25, 28A) (s 59(3)(a)(i)) |
| | | 24 Sep 2022 (otherwise) (s 59(3)(a)(ii)) |
| | (3) | 24 Sep 2022 (s 59(3)(b)) |
| | (4) | 1 Sep 2022 (for the purpose of making regulations under Registration of Births, Deaths and Marriages (Scotland) Act 1965, ss 23, 25, 28A) (s 59(3)(a)(i)) |

### Coronavirus (Recovery and Reform) (Scotland) Act 2022 (asp 8)—*contd*

|  |  |
|---|---|
|  | 24 Sep 2022 (otherwise) (s 59(3)(a)(ii)) |
| (5) | 24 Sep 2022 (s 59(3)(b)) |
| (6) | 1 Sep 2022 (for the purpose of making regulations under Registration of Births, Deaths and Marriages (Scotland) Act 1965, ss 23, 25, 28A) (s 59(3)(a)(i)) |
|  | 24 Sep 2022 (otherwise) (s 59(3)(a)(ii)) |
| 28, 29 | *Not yet in force* |
| 30–41 | 1 Oct 2022 (s 59(1)) |
| 42 | 1 Nov 2022 (s 59(1)) |
| 43–50 | 1 Oct 2022 (s 59(1)) |
| 51 | 1 Sep 2022 (s 59(1)) |
| 52, 53 | 1 Oct 2022 (s 59(1)) |
| 54 | 1 Sep 2022 (s 59(1)) |
| 55–57 | 1 Oct 2022 (s 59(1)) |
| 58–60 | 11 Aug 2022 (s 59(1)) |
| Schedule | 1 Oct 2022 (s 59(1)) |

### Cultural Objects (Protection from Seizure) Act 2022 (c 24)

*RA*: 28 Apr 2022

*Commencement provisions*: s 2(2)

Whole Act in force 28 Jun 2022 (s 2(2))

### Dissolution and Calling of Parliament Act 2022 (c 11)

*RA*: 24 Mar 2022

*Commencement provisions*: s 6(3)

Whole Act in force 24 Mar 2022 (s 6(3))

### Dormant Assets Act 2022 (c 5)

*RA*: 24 Feb 2022

*Commencement provisions*: s 34(2), (3); Dormant Assets Act 2022 (Commencement) Regulations 2022, SI 2022/582

|  |  |
|---|---|
| 1–33 | 6 Jun 2022 (SI 2022/582) |
| 34 | 24 Feb 2022 (s 34(2)) |
| Schs 1, 2 | 6 Jun 2022 (SI 2022/582) |

### Down Syndrome Act 2022 (c 18)

*RA*: 28 Apr 2022

*Commencement provisions*: s 2(2)

|  |  |
|---|---|
| 1, 2 | *Not yet in force* |

### Economic Crime (Transparency and Enforcement) Act 2022 (c 10)

*RA*: 15 Mar 2022

*Commencement provisions*: s 69; Economic Crime (Transparency and Enforcement) Act 2022 (Commencement No 1) Regulations 2022,SI 2022/519; Economic Crime (Transparency and Enforcement) Act 2022 (Commencement No 2 and Saving Provision) Regulations 2022, SI 2022/638; Economic Crime (Transparency and Enforcement) Act 2022 (Commencement No 3)

**Economic Crime (Transparency and Enforcement) Act 2022 (c 10)**—*contd*
Regulations 2022, SI 2022/876; Economic Crime (Transparency and Enforcement) Act 2022 (Commencement No 4) Regulations 2022, SI 2022/1039

| | | |
|---|---|---|
| 1–6 | | 1 Aug 2022 (except so far as they relate to ss 7–11) (SI 2022/876) |
| | | 12 Oct 2022 (exception noted above) (SI 2022/1039) |
| 7, 8 | | 16 Jan 2023 (exception noted above) (SI 2022/1039) |
| 9 | (1)–(9) | 1 Oct 2022 (SI 2022/1039) |
| | (10)–(12) | 5 Sep 2022 (SI 2022/876) |
| 10, 11 | | 1 Oct 2022 (SI 2022/1039) |
| 12–32 | | 1 Aug 2022 (except so far as they relate to ss 7–11) (SI 2022/876) |
| | | 12 Oct 2022 (exception noted above) (SI 2022/1039) |
| 33, 34 | | 5 Sep 2022 (SI 2022/876) |
| 35–44 | | 1 Aug 2022 (except so far as they relate to ss 7–11) (SI 2022/876) |
| | | 12 Oct 2022 (exception noted above) (SI 2022/1039) |
| 45–53 | | 15 May 2022 (SI 2022/519)[1] |
| 54–56 | | 15 Jun 2022 (SI 2022/638)[2] |
| 57–70 | | 15 Mar 2022 (s 69(3)) |
| Schs 1, 2 | | 12 Oct 2022 (SI 2022/1039) |
| Schs 3–5 | | 5 Sep 2022 (SI 2022/876) |

[1]　　For savings in relation to ss 52, 53, see SI 2022/519, reg 3

[2]　　For a saving in relation to s 54, see SI 2022/638, reg 3

---

**Education (Careers Guidance in Schools) Act 2022 (c 13)**

*RA:* 31 Mar 2022

*Commencement provisions*: s 3(2), (3); Education (Careers Guidance in Schools) Act 2022 (Commencement) Regulations 2022, SI 2022/724

| | |
|---|---|
| 1, 2 | 1 September 2022 (SI 2022/724) |
| 3 | 31 Mar 2022 (s 3(3)) |

---

**Elections Act 2022 (c 37)**

*RA:* 28 Apr 2022

*Commencement provisions*: s 67; Elections Act 2022 (Commencement No 1 and Saving Provision) Regulations 2022, SI 2022/908; Elections Act 2022 (Commencement No 2) Regulations 2022, SI 2022/916

| | | |
|---|---|---|
| 1 | | See Sch 1 below |
| 2 | | See Sch 2 below |
| 3–11 | | *Not yet in force* |
| 12 | | See Sch 6 below |
| 13–15 | | *Not yet in force* |
| 16 | | 19 Aug 2022 (SI 2022/908) |
| 17 | | 19 Aug 2022 (SI 2022/908)[1] |
| 18, 19 | | 19 Aug 2022 (SI 2022/908) |
| 20–61 | | *Not yet in force* |
| 62–68 | | 28 Apr 2022 (s 67(3)) |
| Sch 1 | para 1 | See paras 2–33 below |
| | para 2 | 27 Aug 2022 (for the purposes of making regulations under Representation of the People Act 1983, ss 13BD(3), (4), (8)–(10), 13BE(3), (4), (8)–(10), (12)) (SI 2022/916) |
| | | *Not yet in force* (otherwise) |
| | para 3 | 27 Aug 2022 (for the purposes of making regulations under Representation of the People Act 1983, s 13C(3A), (4A)) (SI 2022/916) |
| | | *Not yet in force* (otherwise) |

**Elections Act 2022 (c 37)**—*contd*

|  | para 4 | *Not yet in force* |
|--|--------|-------------------|
|  | para 5 | 27 Aug 2022 (for the purposes of making regulations under Representation of the People Act 1983, s 56(1), (5)) (SI 2022/916) |
|  |  | *Not yet in force* (otherwise) |
|  | para 6 | 27 Aug 2022 (for the purposes of making regulations under Representation of the People Act 1983, s 58(2), (6)(a)) (SI 2022/916) |
|  |  | *Not yet in force* (otherwise) |
|  | paras 7–9 | *Not yet in force* |
|  | para 10 | See paras 11–33 below |
|  | para 11 | 27 Aug 2022 (for the purpose of making regulations under Representation of the People Act 1983, Sch 1, r 19B(6)) (SI 2022/916) |
|  |  | *Not yet in force* (otherwise) |
|  | paras 12–14 | *Not yet in force* |
|  | para 15(1) | See sub-paras (2)–(4) below |
|  | para 15(2) | *Not yet in force* |
|  | para 15(3) | 27 Aug 2022 (for the purpose of making regulations under Representation of the People Act 1983, Sch 1, r 29(3ZA)) (SI 2022/916) |
|  | para 15(4) | *Not yet in force* |
|  | para 16 | *Not yet in force* |
|  | para 17(1) | See sub-paras (2)–(10) below |
|  | para 17(2)–(7) | *Not yet in force* |
|  | para 17(8) | 27 Aug 2022 (SI 2022/916) |
|  | para 17(9), (10) | *Not yet in force* |
|  | paras 18–23 | *Not yet in force* |
|  | para 30 | 27 Aug 2022 (SI 2022/916) |
|  | para 31 | *Not yet in force* |
|  | para 32 | 27 Aug 2022 (so far as relates to para 30) (SI 2022/916) |
|  |  | *Not yet in force* (otherwise) |
|  | paras 33–40 | *Not yet in force* |
| Sch 2 | paras 1–11 | 27 Aug 2022 (SI 2022/916) |
|  | paras 12, 13 | *Not yet in force* |
|  | para 14(a) | *Not yet in force* |
|  | para 14(b), (c) | 27 Aug 2022 (SI 2022/916) |
| Schs 3–5 |  | *Not yet in force* |
| Sch 6 | paras 1–29 | *Not yet in force* |
|  | para 30(1) | See sub-paras (2)–(4) below |
|  | para 30(2) | 27 Aug 2022 (SI 2022/916) |
|  | para 30(3) | *Not yet in force* |
|  | para 30(4) | 27 Aug 2022 (SI 2022/916) |
|  | paras 31–48 | *Not yet in force* |
| Schs 7–12 |  | *Not yet in force* |

1    For savings, see SI 2022/908, reg 3

**Energy (Oil and Gas) Profits Levy Act 2022 (c 40)**

*RA:* 14 Jul 2022

Whole Act in force 14 July 2022 (RA)

**Finance Act 2022 (c 3)**

*RA:* 24 Feb 2022

The commencement details of Finance Acts are not set out, as the dates from which their provisions take effect are usually stated clearly and unambiguously in the text of the Act, and charging provisions will normally state for which year or years of assessment they are to have effect.

**Fireworks and Pyrotechnic Articles (Scotland) Act 2022 (asp 9)**

*RA:* 10 Aug 2022

*Commencement provisions:* s 56; Fireworks and Pyrotechnic Articles (Scotland) Act 2022 (Commencement No 1) Regulations 2022, SSI 2022/280

| | | |
|---|---|---|
| 1, 2 | | 10 Oct 2022 (SSI 2022/280) |
| 3–19 | | *Not yet in force* |
| 20 | (1)(a) | 10 Oct 2022 (SSI 2022/280) |
| | (1)(b), (c) | *Not yet in force* |
| | (2)(a) | 10 Oct 2022 (SSI 2022/280) |
| | (2)(b) | *Not yet in force* |
| | (3) | 10 Oct 2022 (SSI 2022/280) |
| 21 | | 10 Oct 2022 (SSI 2022/280) |
| 22–37 | | *Not yet in force* |
| 38 | (1) | See Sch 1 below |
| | (2), (3) | 10 Oct 2022 (SSI 2022/280) |
| 39 | | *Not yet in force* |
| 40, 41 | | 10 Oct 2022 (SSI 2022/280) |
| 42, 43 | | *Not yet in force* |
| 44–47 | | 10 Oct 2022 (SSI 2022/280) |
| 48 | (1)(a) | *Not yet in force* |
| | (1)(b) | 10 Oct 2022 (SSI 2022/280) |
| | (1)(c) | *Not yet in force* |
| | (2)–(5) | *Not yet in force* |
| | (6)–(8) | 10 Oct 2022 (SSI 2022/280) |
| 49 | | 10 Oct 2022 (SSI 2022/280) |
| 50–53 | | 11 Aug 2022 (s 56(1)) |
| 54, 55 | | 10 Oct 2022 (SSI 2022/280) |
| 56, 57 | | 11 Aug 2022 (s 56(1)) |
| Sch 1 | paras 1–8 | *Not yet in force* |
| | para 9 | 10 Oct 2022 (SSI 2022/280) |
| | paras 10–24 | *Not yet in force* |
| | para 25 | 10 Oct 2022 (SSI 2022/280) |
| | paras 26, 27 | *Not yet in force* |
| | para 28 | 10 Oct 2022 (SSI 2022/280) |
| | para 29 | *Not yet in force* |
| | para 30 | 10 Oct 2022 (SSI 2022/280) |
| Sch 2 | | *Not yet in force* |

**Glue Traps (Offences) Act 2022 (c 26)**

*RA:* 28 Apr 2022

*Commencement provisions:* s 10(2)

| | |
|---|---|
| 1–10 | *Not yet in force* |

## Good Food Nation (Scotland) Act 2022 (asp 5)

*RA*: 26 Jul 2022

*Commencement provisions*: s 28

| | |
|---|---|
| 1–24 | *Not yet in force* |
| 24, 25 | 27 Jul 2022 (s 28(1)) |
| 26 | *Not yet in force* |
| 27–29 | 27 Jul 2022 (s 28(1)) |
| Schedule | *Not yet in force* |

## Health and Care Act 2022 (c 31)

*RA*: 28 Apr 2022

*Commencement provisions*: s 186; Health and Care Act 2022 (Commencement No 1) Regulations 2022, SI 2022/515; Health and Care Act 2022 (Commencement No 2 and Transitional and Saving Provision) Regulations 2022, SI 2022/734; Health and Care Act 2022 (Commencement No 3) Regulations 2022, SI 2022/1003

| | | |
|---|---|---|
| 1 | (1) | 9 May 2022 (in so far as it is required for the purposes of interpreting the words "NHS England" in s 38 and in the National Health Service Act 2006, ss 14Z25(1), (2), (3), (5), (6)(a), (8), 14Z26, 14Z28 and Sch 1B, Pt 1) (SI 2022/515) |
| | | 1 Jul 2022 (otherwise) (SI 2022/734) |
| | (2) | See Sch 1 below |
| 2–4 | | 1 Jul 2022 (SI 2022/734) |
| 5 | | *Not yet in force* |
| 6–12 | | 1 Jul 2022 (SI 2022/734) |
| 13 | | *Not yet in force* |
| 14–18 | | 1 Jul 2022 (SI 2022/734)[1] |
| 19 | (1) | 9 May 2022 (SI 2022/515) |
| | (2) | 9 May 2022 (in so far as inserts the National Health Service Act 2006, ss 14Z25(1), (2), (3), (5), (6)(a), (8), 14Z26, 14Z28) (SI 2022/515) |
| | | 1 Jul 2022 (otherwise) (SI 2022/734) |
| | (3) | 9 May 2022 (SI 2022/515) |
| | (4) | See Sch 2 below |
| 20, 21 | | 1 Jul 2022 (SI 2022/734) |
| 22 | | See Sch 3 below |
| 23 | | *Not yet in force* |
| 24–27 | | 1 Jul 2022 (SI 2022/734) |
| 28 | | *Not yet in force* |
| 29 | | 1 Jul 2022 (SI 2022/734) |
| 30, 31 | | *Not yet in force* |
| 32–37 | | 1 Jul 2022 (SI 2022/734)[1] |
| 38 | | 9 May 2022 (SI 2022/515) |
| 39–45 | | 1 Jul 2022 (SI 2022/734) |
| 46 | | *Not yet in force* |
| 47–50 | | 1 Jul 2022 (SI 2022/734) |
| 51 | | *Not yet in force* |
| 52–76 | | 1 Jul 2022 (SI 2022/734)[1] |
| 77 | | See Sch 10 below |
| 78–80 | | *Not yet in force* |
| 81–94 | | 1 Jul 2022 (SI 2022/734)[1] |
| 95, 96 | | *Not yet in force* |
| 97 | | 1 Oct 2022 (SI 2022/1003) |
| 98 | | *Not yet in force* |
| 99 | | 31 Jul 2022 (in so far as inserts the Health and Social Care Act 2012, ss 227A(1)–(5), (7), 227B, 227C) (SI 2022/734) |

**Health and Care Act 2022 (c 31)**—*contd*

| | | |
|---|---|---|
| | | 1 Oct 2022 (in so far as inserts the Health and Social Care Act 2012, s 227A(6)) (SI 2022/1003) |
| | | *Not yet in force (otherwise)* |
| 100 | | 1 Oct 2022 (SI 2022/1003) |
| 101–108 | | 1 Jul 2022 (SI 2022/734) |
| 109–135 | | *Not yet in force* |
| 136–160 | | 1 Jul 2022 (SI 2022/734) |
| 161 | (1) | 1 Jul 2022 (SI 2022/734) |
| | (2) | *Not yet in force* |
| 162–166 | | *Not yet in force* |
| 167, 168 | | 1 Jul 2022 (SI 2022/734) |
| 169 | | *Not yet in force* |
| 170 | | 1 Jul 2022 (SI 2022/734) |
| 171 | | 1 Jul 2022 (s 186(3)) |
| 172 | | 28 Jun 2022 (s 186(4)) |
| 173, 174 | | 1 Jul 2022 (SI 2022/734) |
| 175, 176 | | 1 Oct 2022 (SI 2022/1003) |
| 177 | | 1 Nov 2022 (SI 2022/1003) |
| 178 | | 30 Aug 2022 (SI 2022/734) |
| 179 | | 28 Jul 2022 (s 186(5)) |
| 180, 181 | | 1 Jul 2022 (SI 2022/734) |
| 182–187 | | 28 Apr 2022 (s 186(1)) |
| Sch 1 | | 1 Jul 2022 (SI 2022/734) |
| Sch 2 | | 9 May 2022 (in so far as inserts the National Health Service Act 2006, Sch 1B, Pt 1) (SI 2022/515) |
| | | 1 Jul 2022 (otherwise) (SI 2022/734) |
| Sch 3 | paras 1–6 | *Not yet in force* |
| | para 7(1) | See sub-paras (2), (3) below |
| | para 7(2) | 1 Jul 2022 (SI 2022/734) |
| | para 7(3) | *Not yet in force* |
| | paras 8–10 | *Not yet in force* |
| | para 11(1) | See sub-paras (2)–(6) below |
| | para 11(2), (3) | *Not yet in force* |
| | para 11(4) | 1 Jul 2022 (SI 2022/734) |
| | para 11(5), (6) | *Not yet in force* |
| | paras 12–58 | *Not yet in force* |
| Schs 4, 5 | | 1 Jul 2022 (SI 2022/734)[1] |
| Sch 6 | | *Not yet in force* |
| Schs 7–9 | | 1 Jul 2022 (SI 2022/734) |
| Sch 10 | | 1 Jul 2022 (only in so far as required for the purposes of conducting a consultation in accordance with the Health and Social Care Act 2012, s 114C(2) including for the purposes of dealing with objections to the proposed NHS payment scheme received in accordance with s 114D of that Act) (SI 2022/734) |
| | | *Not yet in force (otherwise)* |
| Sch 11 | | *Not yet in force* |
| Sch 12 | | 1 Jul 2022 (SI 2022/734) |
| Schs 13–15 | | *Not yet in force* |
| Sch 16 | | 1 Jul 2022 (SI 2022/734) |
| Sch 17 | | 1 Jul 2022 (s 186(3)) |
| Sch 18 | | 28 Jun 2022 (s 186(4)) |
| Sch 19 | | 1 Jul 2022 (SI 2022/734) |

[1]  For transitional and saving provisions see SI 2022/734, regs 5–35

## Judicial Review and Courts Act 2022 (c 35)

*RA:* 28 Apr 2022

*Commencement provisions*: s 51; Criminal Justice Act 2003 (Commencement No 34) and Judicial Review and Courts Act 2022 (Commencement No 1) Regulations 2022, SI 2022/816

| | | |
|---|---|---|
| 1, 2 | | 14 Jul 2022 (SI 2022/816) |
| 3–10 | | *Not yet in force* |
| 11 | | 28 Apr 2022 (s 51(1)(a)) |
| 12 | | *Not yet in force* |
| 13 | (1), (2) | 14 Jul 2022 (SI 2022/816) |
| | (3) | 28 Apr 2022 (s 51(1)(b)) |
| | (4)–(11) | 14 Jul 2022 (SI 2022/816) |
| 14 | | *Not yet in force* |
| 15 | | 28 Jun 2022 (s 51(3)(a)) |
| 16 | | 28 Jun 2022 (s 51(3)(b)) |
| 17 | | *Not yet in force* |
| 18 | | See Sch 2 below |
| 19–38 | | *Not yet in force* |
| 39–43 | | 28 Jun 2022 (s 51(3)(c)) |
| 44–47 | | *Not yet in force* |
| 48 | | 28 Jun 2022 (s 51(3)(d)) |
| 49–52 | | 28 Apr 2022 (s 51(1)(d)) |
| Sch 1 | | 28 Jun 2022 (s 51(3)(b)) |
| Sch 2 | paras 1–11 | *Not yet in force* |
| | paras 12–14 | 28 Apr 2022 (s 51(1)(c)) |
| | para 15 | *Not yet in force* |
| | paras 16–21 | 14 Jul 2022 (SI 2022/816) |
| Schs 3–5 | | *Not yet in force* |

## Leasehold Reform (Ground Rent) Act 2022 (c 1)

*RA:* 8 Feb 2022

*Commencement provisions*: s 25; Leasehold Reform (Ground Rent) Act 2022 (Commencement) Regulations 2022, SI 2022/694

| | |
|---|---|
| 1 | 30 Jun 2022 (except for the purposes of leases of retirement homes) (SI 2022/694) |
| | 1 Apr 2023 (for the purposes of leases of retirement homes) (SI 2022/694) |
| 2 | 8 Feb 2022 (for the purposes of making regulations) (s 25(1)(a)) |
| | 30 Jun 2022 (except for the purposes of leases of retirement homes) (SI 2022/694) |
| | 1 Apr 2023 (for the purposes of leases of retirement homes) (SI 2022/694) |
| 3–8 | 30 Jun 2022 (except for the purposes of leases of retirement homes) (SI 2022/694) |
| | 1 Apr 2023 (for the purposes of leases of retirement homes) (SI 2022/694) |
| 9 | 8 Feb 2022 (for the purposes of making regulations) (s 25(1)(a)) |
| | 30 Jun 2022 (except for the purposes of leases of retirement homes) (SI 2022/694) |
| | 1 Apr 2023 (for the purposes of leases of retirement homes) (SI 2022/694) |
| 10–19 | 30 Jun 2022 (except for the purposes of leases of retirement homes) (SI 2022/694) |
| | 1 Apr 2023 (for the purposes of leases of retirement homes) (SI 2022/694) |
| 20–26 | 8 Feb 2022 (s 25(1)(b)) |

**Leasehold Reform (Ground Rent) Act 2022 (c 1)**—*contd*

Schedule                                       30 Jun 2022 (except for the purposes of leases of retirement
                                               homes) (SI 2022/694)
                                               1 Apr 2023 (for the purposes of leases of retirement homes)
                                               (SI 2022/694)

**Local Government (Disqualification) Act 2022 (c 17)**

*RA:* 28 Apr 2022

*Commencement provisions*: s 6(2)

Whole Act in force 28 Jun 2022 (s 6(2))

**Marriage and Civil Partnership (Minimum Age) Act 2022 (c 28)**

*RA:* 28 Apr 2022

*Commencement provisions*: s 7

1–9                                            *Not yet in force*
Schedule                                       *Not yet in force*

**Miners' Strike (Pardons) (Scotland) Act 2022 (asp 6)**

*RA:* 26 Jul 2022

*Commencement provisions*: s 6

Whole Act in force 27 Jul 2022 (s 6)

**Motor Vehicles (Compulsory Insurance) Act 2022 (c 25)**

*RA:* 28 Apr 2022

*Commencement provisions*: s 2(1)

Whole Act in force 28 Jun 2022 (s 2(1))

**National Insurance Contributions Act 2022 (c 9)**

*RA:* 15 Mar 2022

Whole Act in force 15 Mar 2022 (RA)

**National Insurance Contributions (Increase of Thresholds) Act 2022 (c 16)**

*RA:* 31 Mar 2022

Whole Act in force 31 Mar 2022 (RA)

**Nationality and Borders Act 2022 (c 36)**

*RA:* 28 Apr 2022

*Commencement provisions*: s 87; Nationality and Borders Act 2022 (Commencement No 1, Transitional and
Saving Provisions) Regulations 2022, SI 2022/590; Nationality and Borders Act 2022
(Commencement No 2) Regulations 2022, SI 2022/912; Nationality and Borders Act 2022
(Commencement No 3) Regulations 2022, SI 2022/1056

**Nationality and Borders Act 2022 (c 36)**—*contd*

| | | |
|---|---|---|
| 1, 2 | | 28 Jun 2022 (SI 2022/590) |
| 3 | | 23 Nov 2022 (SI 2022/1056) |
| 4 | | 28 Jun 2022 (except to the extent that British Nationality Act 1981, s 4K(1)(a) refers to British Nationality Act 1981, s 17H) (SI 2022/590) |
| | | 23 Nov 2022 (exception noted above) (SI 2022/1056) |
| 5–9 | | 28 Jun 2022 (SI 2022/590)[1] |
| 10 | (1) | 28 Apr 2022 (s 87(3)(a)) |
| | (2)–(5) | *Not yet in force* |
| | (6)–(8) | 28 Apr 2022 (s 87(3)(a)) |
| 11, 12 | | 28 Jun 2022 (SI 2022/590)[1] |
| 13 | (1) | 28 Jun 2022 (SI 2022/590) |
| | (2) | *Not yet in force* |
| | (3) | 28 Jun 2022 (SI 2022/590) |
| | (4)–(7) | *Not yet in force* |
| 14 | (1), (2) | 28 Apr 2022 (for the purpose of making and consulting on regulations) (s 87(4)(a)) |
| | | 28 Jun 2022 (otherwise) (SI 2022/590)[1] |
| | (3) | 28 Apr 2022 (for the purpose of making and consulting on regulations) (s 87(4)(a)) |
| | | 28 Jun 2022 (for the purposes of ss 15, 16) (SI 2022/590)[1] |
| | | *Not yet in force* (otherwise) |
| | (4) | 28 Apr 2022 (for the purpose of making and consulting on regulations) (s 87(4)(a)) |
| | | *Not yet in force* (otherwise) |
| | (5) | 28 Apr 2022 (for the purpose of making and consulting on regulations) (s 87(4)(a)) |
| | | 28 Jun 2022 (for the purposes of ss 15, 16) (SI 2022/590)[1] |
| | | *Not yet in force* (otherwise) |
| | (6), (7) | 28 Apr 2022 (for the purpose of making and consulting on regulations) (s 87(4)(a)) |
| | | 28 Jun 2022 (otherwise) (SI 2022/590)[1] |
| | (8) | 28 Apr 2022 (for the purpose of making and consulting on regulations) (s 87(4)(a)) |
| | | *Not yet in force* (otherwise) |
| 15–17 | | 28 Jun 2022 (SI 2022/590)[1] |
| 18–26 | | *Not yet in force* |
| 27 | | 28 Apr 2022 (for the purpose of making and consulting on regulations) (s 87(4)(b)) |
| | | *Not yet in force* (otherwise) |
| 28 | | 28 Jun 2022 (s 87(5)(a)) |
| 29 | | See Sch 4 below |
| 30 | (1), (2) | 28 Jun 2022 (s 87(5)(c)) |
| | (3) | 28 Jun 2022 (SI 2022/590) |
| | (4)–(6) | 28 Jun 2022 (s 87(5)(c))[1] |
| 31–36 | | 28 Jun 2022 (s 87(5)(d)) |
| 37 | | 28 Jun 2022 (SI 2022/590)[1] |
| 38 | | 28 Jun 2022 (s 87(5)(d)) |
| 39 | | 28 Jun 2022 (s 87(5)(e)) |
| 40 | | 28 Jun 2022 (except in so far as relates to insertion of Immigration Act 1971, s 24(E1) (SI 2022/590)[1] |
| | | *Not yet in force* (exception noted above) |
| 41 | | 28 Jun 2022 (SI 2022/590)[1] |
| 42 | | 28 Apr 2022 (for the purpose of making and consulting on regulations) (s 87(4)(c)) |
| | | *Not yet in force* (otherwise) |
| 43 | (1) | 28 Apr 2022 (for the purpose of making and consulting on regulations) (s 87(4)(d)) |
| | | *Not yet in force* (otherwise) |
| | (2) | See Sch 6 below |

**Nationality and Borders Act 2022 (c 36)**—*contd*

| | | |
|---|---|---|
| 44 | | 28 Jun 2022 (s 87(5)(f)) |
| 45 | | 28 Jun 2022 (SI 2022/590)[1] |
| 46 | (1)–(5) | *Not yet in force* |
| | (6) | 28 Jun 2022 (SI 2022/590) |
| | (7), (8) | *Not yet in force* |
| 47, 48 | | 28 Jun 2022 (SI 2022/590)[1] |
| 49 | (1)–(4) | 28 Jun 2022 (s 87(5)(g)) |
| | (5) | *Not yet in force* |
| 50 | | 28 Apr 2022 (for the purpose of making and consulting on regulations) (s 87(4)(e)) |
| | | *Not yet in force* (otherwise) |
| 51 | | *Not yet in force* |
| 52 | | 28 Apr 2022 (for the purpose of making and consulting on regulations) (s 87(4)(f)) |
| | | *Not yet in force* (otherwise) |
| 53 | | 28 Apr 2022 (for the purpose of making and consulting on regulations) (s 87(4)(g)) |
| | | *Not yet in force* (otherwise) |
| 54–68 | | *Not yet in force* |
| 69 | | 28 Apr 2022 (for the purpose of making and consulting on regulations) (s 87(4)(h)) |
| | | *Not yet in force* (otherwise) |
| 70, 71 | | 28 Apr 2022 (s 87(3)(b)) |
| 72 | | 28 Jun 2022 (s 87(5)(h)) |
| 73 | | 28 Apr 2022 (s 87(3)(b)) |
| 74 | | 28 Jun 2022 (s 87(5)(h)) |
| 75 | | 28 Jun 2022 (SI 2022/590) |
| 76 | | *Not yet in force* |
| 77 | | 28 Jun 2022 (SI 2022/590) |
| 78 | | 28 Jun 2022 (s 87(5)(i)) |
| 79 | | 28 Jun 2022 (SI 2022/590) |
| 80, 81 | | *Not yet in force* |
| 82 | | 28 Apr 2022 (for the purpose of making and consulting on regulations) (s 87(4)(i)) |
| | | 28 Jun 2022 (otherwise) (SI 2022/590) |
| 83–88 | | 28 Apr 2022 (s 87(3)(c)) |
| Sch 1 | paras 1, 2 | 28 Jun 2022 (SI 2022/590)[1] |
| | para 3(1)–(3), (4)(a)–(c) | 28 Jun 2022 (SI 2022/590)[1] |
| | para 3(4)(d) | *Not yet in force* |
| | para 3(5) | 28 Jun 2022 (SI 2022/590)[1] |
| | para 4 | 28 Jun 2022 (SI 2022/590)[1] |
| Schs 2, 3 | | *Not yet in force* |
| Sch 4 | paras 1–4 | 28 Jun 2022 (SI 2022/590)[1] |
| | 5–19 | 28 Jun 2022 (s 87(5)(b)) |
| Sch 5 | | 28 Apr 2022 (for the purpose of making and consulting on regulations) (s 87(4)(c)) |
| | | *Not yet in force* (otherwise) |
| Sch 6 | paras 1–3, 4(a) | *Not yet in force* |
| | para 4(b) | 24 Aug 2022 (SI 2022/912) |
| | paras 5–11 | *Not yet in force* |
| Schs 7, 8 | | 28 Jun 2022 (SI 2022/590)[1] |

[1]　For transitional provisions and savings, see SI 2022/590, reg 3, Sch 2

---

**Non-Domestic Rates (Coronavirus) (Scotland) Act 2022 (asp 7)**

*RA*: 28 Jul 2022

*Commencement provisions*: s 5

**Non-Domestic Rates (Coronavirus) (Scotland) Act 2022 (asp 7)**—*contd*
Whole Act in force 29 Jul 2022 (s 6(2))

---

**Northern Ireland (Ministers, Elections and Petitions of Concern) Act 2022 (c 2)**

*RA:* 8 Feb 2022

*Commencement provisions:* s 9

Whole Act in force 8 Feb 2022 (s 9)

---

**Nuclear Energy (Financing) Act 2022 (c 15)**

*RA:* 31 Mar 2022

*Commencement provisions:* s 44

| | |
|---|---|
| 1–5 | 31 Mar 2022 (s 44(1)) |
| 6–10 | 31 May 2022 (s 44(2)) |
| 11 | 31 Mar 2022 (s 44(1)) |
| 12 | 31 May 2022 (s 44(2)) |
| 13, 14 | 31 Mar 2022 (s 44(1)) |
| 15 | 31 May 2022 (s 44(2)) |
| 16 | 31 Mar 2022 (s 44(1)) |
| 17–30 | 31 May 2022 (s 44(2)) |
| 31–39 | 31 Mar 2022 (for the purposes of making rules under Insolvency Act 1986 Act, s 411) (s 44(1)) |
| | 31 May 2022 (otherwise) (s 44(2)) |
| 40 | 31 Mar 2022 (s 44(1)) |
| 41 | 31 Mar 2022 (s 44(1)) |
| 42 | 31 May 2022 (s 44(2)) |
| 43–45 | 31 Mar 2022 (s 44(1)) |
| Schedule | 31 May 2022 (s 44(2)) |

---

**Pension Schemes (Conversion of Guaranteed Minimum Pensions) Act 2022 (c 33)**

*RA:* 28 Apr 2022

*Commencement provisions:* s 3(4)–(6)

| | |
|---|---|
| 1 | 28 Apr 2022 (for the purposes of making regulations under the Pension Schemes Act 1993) (s 3(4)(a)) |
| | *Not yet in force* (otherwise) |
| 2 | 28 Apr 2022 (for the purposes of making regulations under the Pension Schemes (Northern Ireland) Act 1993) (s 3(4)(b)) |
| | *Not yet in force* (otherwise) |
| 3 | 28 Apr 2022 (s 3(4)(c)) |

---

**Police, Crime, Sentencing and Courts Act 2022 (c 32)**

*RA:* 28 Apr 2022

*Commencement provisions:* s 208; Police, Crime, Sentencing and Courts Act 2022 (Commencement No 1 and Transitional Provision) Regulations 2022, SI 2022/520, as amended by SI 2022/680; Police, Crime, Sentencing and Courts Act 2022 (Commencement No 2) Regulations 2022, SI 2022/704

| | |
|---|---|
| 1 | 28 Jun 2022 (SI 2022/520) |
| 2 | 28 Jun 2022 (s 208(5)(a)) |
| 3 | 28 Jun 2022 (s 208(5)(b)) |

**Police, Crime, Sentencing and Courts Act 2022 (c 32)**—*contd*

| | | |
|---|---|---|
| 4 | | 28 Apr 2022 (for the purpose of making regulations) (s 208(4)(a)) |
| | | 28 Jun 2022 (otherwise) (SI 2022/520) |
| 5–7 | | *Not yet in force* |
| 8–12 | | 28 Apr 2022 (for the purpose of making regulations) (s 208(4)(b)) |
| | | *Not yet in force (otherwise)* |
| 13 | | 28 Apr 2022 (s 208(4)(c)) |
| 14 | | 28 Apr 2022 (for the purpose of making regulations) (s 208(4)(d)) |
| | | *Not yet in force (otherwise)* |
| 15–18 | | *Not yet in force* |
| 19 | | 28 Apr 2022 (for the purpose of making regulations) (s 208(4)(e)) |
| | | *Not yet in force (otherwise)* |
| 20 | | 28 Apr 2022 (for the purpose of making regulations) (s 208(4)(f)) |
| | | *Not yet in force (otherwise)* |
| 21 | | *Not yet in force* |
| 22, 23 | | 28 Apr 2022 (s 208(4)(g)) |
| 24–26 | | 28 Apr 2022 (for the purpose of making regulations) (s 208(4)(h)) |
| | | *Not yet in force (otherwise)* |
| 27–30 | | *Not yet in force* |
| 31 | | 28 Apr 2022 (s 208(4)(i)) |
| 32 | | 28 Apr 2022 (for the purpose of issuing guidance) (s 208(4)(j)) |
| | | *Not yet in force (otherwise)* |
| 33 | | *Not yet in force* |
| 34–36 | | 28 Apr 2022 (s 208(4)(k)) |
| 37–41 | | *Not yet in force* |
| 42 | (1)–(7) | 12 May 2022 (SI 2022/520) |
| | (8)–(12) | *Not yet in force* |
| 43–45 | | *Not yet in force* |
| 46 | | 28 Jun 2022 (SI 2022/520) |
| 47 | | 28 Jun 2022 (s 208(5)(c)) |
| 48, 49 | | 28 Jun 2022 (SI 2022/520) |
| 50 | | 28 Jun 2022 (s 208(5)(c)) |
| 51 | | 28 Jun 2022 (s 208(5)(d)) |
| 52, 53 | | 28 Jun 2022 (s 208(5)(e)) |
| 54 | | 28 Jun 2022 (s 208(5)(f)) |
| 55–57 | | 28 Jun 2022 (SI 2022/520) |
| 58 | | 28 Jun 2022 (s 208(5)(g)) |
| 59 | | 28 Jun 2022 (s 208(5)(h)) |
| 60, 61 | | *Not yet in force* |
| 62–70 | | 1 Aug 2022 (SI 2022/520) |
| 71 | | 28 Apr 2022 (s 208(4)(l)) |
| 72 | | 28 Apr 2022 (s 208(4)(m)) |
| 73–79 | | 28 Jun 2022 (SI 2022/520) |
| 80 | | 12 May 2022 (SI 2022/520)[1] |
| 81 | | *Not yet in force* |
| 82 | | 28 Apr 2022 (for the purpose of making regulations) (s 208(4)(n)) |
| | | 28 Jun 2022 (otherwise) (SI 2022/520) |
| 83–88 | | 28 Jun 2022 (s 208(5)(i)) |
| 89 | | *Not yet in force* |
| 90 | | 28 Apr 2022 (for the purpose of making regulations) (s 208(4)(o)) |
| | | 28 Jun 2022 (otherwise) (SI 2022/520) |
| 91–121 | | *Not yet in force* |
| 122, 123 | | 28 Jun 2022 (s 208(5)(j)) |
| 124 | | 28 Jun 2022 (s 208(5)(k)) |
| 125–128 | | 28 Jun 2022 (s 208(5)(l)) |
| 129 | | 28 Jun 2022 (SI 2022/520) |
| 130, 131 | | 28 Jun 2022 (s 208(5)(m)) |
| 132 | | 28 Apr 2022 (s 208(4)(p)) |
| 133, 134 | | 28 Jun 2022 (SI 2022/520) |
| 135 | | 28 Jun 2022 (s 208(5)(n)) |

**Police, Crime, Sentencing and Courts Act 2022 (c 32)**—*contd*

| | | |
|---|---|---|
| 136, 137 | | 28 Jun 2022 (SI 2022/520) |
| 138 | | 28 Jun 2022 (s 208(5)(o)) |
| 139 | | *Not yet in force* |
| 140–143 | | 28 Apr 2022 (s 208(4)(q)) |
| 144–148 | | 28 Jun 2022 (s 208(5)(p)) |
| 149 | | *Not yet in force* |
| 150, 151 | | 28 Jun 2022 (s 208(5)(q)) |
| 152 | | 28 Jun 2022 (SI 2022/520) |
| 153 | | 28 Jun 2022 (s 208(5)(r)) |
| 154 | | 28 Jun 2022 (s 208(5)(s)) |
| 155, 156 | | 28 Jun 2022 (SI 2022/520) |
| 157–160 | | 28 Jun 2022 (s 208(5)(t)) |
| 161 | (1) | See Sch 17 below |
| | (2)–(9) | 28 Apr 2022 (s 208(4)(s)) |
| 162 | | 28 Jun 2022 (s 208(5)(v)) |
| 163, 164 | | 28 Apr 2022 (s 208(4)(t)) |
| 165 | | 28 Apr 2022 (for the purpose of issuing guidance and making regulations) (s 208(4)(u)) |
| | | *Not yet in force (otherwise)* |
| 166 | | 28 Apr 2022 (s 208(4)(v)) |
| 167 | (1) | 28 Jun 2022 (SI 2022/520) |
| | (2)–(4) | 28 Apr 2022 (s 208(4)(w)) |
| 168–171 | | *Not yet in force* |
| 172 | (1)–(4) | 28 Jun 2022 (SI 2022/520) |
| | (5)–(10) | *Not yet in force* |
| | (11) | 28 Jun 2022 (SI 2022/520) |
| 173–183 | | *Not yet in force* |
| 184–188 | | 28 Jun 2022 (s 208(5)(w)) |
| 189 | | 28 Apr 2022 (s 208(4)(x)) |
| 190 | | 28 Apr 2022 (for the purpose of making an order) (s 208(4)(y)) |
| | | 29 Jun 2022 (otherwise) (SI 2022/520) |
| 191 | | 28 Apr 2022 (s 208(4)(z)) |
| 192 | | 29 Jun 2022 (SI 2022/520) |
| 193–195 | | *Not yet in force* |
| 196, 197 | | 28 Jun 2022 (s 208(5)(x)) |
| 198, 199 | | 28 Apr 2022 (s 208(4)(aa)) |
| 200 | | 28 Jun 2022 (s 208(5)(y)) |
| 201 | (1) | 28 Jun 2022 (s 208(5)(z)) |
| | (2) | 28 Jun 2022 (except for the purposes of Employment Appeal Tribunal (Coronavirus) (Amendment) Rules 2020, SI 2020/415, r 2, Tribunal Procedure (Coronavirus) (Amendment) Rules 2020, SI 2020/416 and Tribunal Procedure (Amendment) Rules 2020, SI 2020/651, r 1(2)) (SI 2022/704) |
| | | *Not yet in force (otherwise)* |
| | (3) | *Not yet in force* |
| 202 | | 28 Apr 2022 (s 208(4)(ab)) |
| 203 | | 28 Apr 2022 (s 208(4)(ac)) |
| 204 | | 28 Jun 2022 (s 208(5)(aa)) |
| 205–209 | | 28 Apr 2022 (s 208(4)(ac)) |
| Schs 1, 2 | | 28 Apr 2022 (for the purpose of making regulations) (s 208(4)(b)) |
| | | *Not yet in force (otherwise)* |
| Schs 3, 4 | | *Not yet in force* |
| Sch 5 | | 28 Jun 2022 (s 208(5)(d)) |
| Sch 6 | | 28 Jun 2022 (SI 2022/520) |
| Sch 7 | | 28 Jun 2022 (SI 2022/520) |
| Sch 8 | | 28 Jun 2022 (s 208(5)(i)) |
| Schs 9–11 | | *Not yet in force* |
| Sch 12 | | 28 Jun 2022 (s 208(5)(k)) |

**Police, Crime, Sentencing and Courts Act 2022 (c 32)**—*contd*

| | | |
|---|---|---|
| Sch 13 | | 28 Jun 2022 (SI 2022/520) |
| Sch 14 | | 28 Jun 2022 (s 208(5)(r)) |
| Sch 15 | | 28 Jun 2022 (s 208(5)(s)) |
| Sch 16 | | 28 Jun 2022 (s 208(5)(t)) |
| Sch 17 | para 1 | 28 Jun 2022 (s 208(5)(u)) |
| | paras 2–14 | 28 Apr 2022 (for the purpose of making regulations) (s 208(4)(r)) |
| | | *Not yet in force* (otherwise) |
| | paras 15–17 | *Not yet in force* |
| | paras 18–23 | 28 Jun 2022 (s 208(5)(u)) |
| Sch 18 | | *Not yet in force* |
| Sch 19 | | 28 Jun 2022 (s 208(5)(w)) |
| Sch 20 | | 28 Jun 2022 (s 208(5)(y)) |
| Sch 21 | | 28 Jun 2022 (s 208(5)(aa)) |

[1]   For transitional provisions see SI 2022/520, reg 8

---

**Professional Qualifications Act 2022 (c 20)**

*RA:* 28 Apr 2022

*Commencement provisions*: s 21; Professional Qualifications Act 2022 (Commencement No 1) Regulations 2022, SI 2022/936

| | | |
|---|---|---|
| 1–4 | | 28 Apr 2022 (s 21(1)(a)) |
| 5 | (1) | *Not yet in force* |
| | (2) | 28 Apr 2022 (s 21(1)(b)) |
| 6 | | 28 Apr 2022 (s 21(1)(c)) |
| 7 | | *Not yet in force* |
| 8 | | 28 Apr 2022 (so far as confers power to make regulations) (s 21(1)(d)) |
| | | 28 Oct 2022 (otherwise) (s 21(3)) |
| 9 | | 28 Oct 2022 (SI 2022/936) |
| 10 | | 28 Apr 2022 (so far as confers power to make regulations) (s 21(1)(e)) |
| | | 28 Oct 2022 (otherwise) (SI 2022/936) |
| 11 | (1)–(3) | 28 Jul 2022 (s 21(2)) |
| | (4), (5) | *Not yet in force* |
| 12–20 | | 28 Apr 2022 (s 21(1)(f)) |
| 21 | | 28 Apr 2022 (s 21(1)(f)) |
| 22 | | 28 Apr 2022 (s 21(1)(g)) |

---

**Public Service Pensions and Judicial Offices Act 2022 (c 7)**

*RA:* 10 Mar 2022

*Commencement provisions*: s 131; Public Service Pensions and Judicial Offices (Commencement No 1 and Transitional and Saving Provision) Regulations 2022, SI 2022/1014

| | |
|---|---|
| 1–38 | 10 Mar 2022 (so far as comfers power to make subordinate legislation or give directions or otherwise relates to the exercise of a power to make subordinate legislation, or give directions) (s 131(1)) |
| | 1 Oct 2023 (in relation to a Chapter 1 scheme within s 33(2)(a), (2)(b), (3)(a), (3)(b)) (s 131(2)(a), (b)) |
| | *Not yet in force* (otherwise) |
| 39–76 | 10 Mar 2022 (so far as comfers power to make subordinate legislation or give directions or otherwise relates to the exercise of a power to make subordinate legislation, or give directions) (s 131(1)) |
| | *Not yet in force* (otherwise) |

**Public Service Pensions and Judicial Offices Act 2022 (c 7)**—*contd*

| | | |
|---|---|---|
| 77–87 | | 10 Mar 2022 (so far as comfers power to make subordinate legislation or give directions or otherwise relates to the exercise of a power to make subordinate legislation, or give directions) (s 131(1)) |
| | | 1 Oct 2023 (in relation to a local government scheme within s 86(2)(a), (2)(b), (3)(a), (3)(b)) (s 131(2)(d), (e)) |
| | | *Not yet in force* (otherwise) |
| 88–108 | | 10 Mar 2022 (so far as comfers power to make subordinate legislation or give directions or otherwise relates to the exercise of a power to make subordinate legislation, or give directions) (s 131(1)) |
| | | 1 Apr 2022 (otherwise) (s 131(f)) |
| 109. 110 | | 10 Mar 2022 (so far as comfers power to make subordinate legislation or give directions or otherwise relates to the exercise of a power to make subordinate legislation, or give directions) (s 131(1)) |
| | | 1 Apr 2022 (in so far as relate to Pt 1, Chapter 4) (s 131(f)) |
| | | 1 Oct 2023 (in so far as relate to Pt 1, Chapters 1, 3) (s 131(a), (b), (d), (e)) |
| | | *Not yet in force* (in so far as relate to Pt 1, Chapter 2) |
| 111–120 | | 10 May 2022 (s 131(3)) |
| 121 | | 10 Mar 2022 (so far as comfers power to make subordinate legislation or give directions or otherwise relates to the exercise of a power to make subordinate legislation, or give directions) (s 131(1)) |
| | | 10 Mar 2022 (s 131(4)(a)) |
| 122 | | 10 Mar 2022 (so far as comfers power to make subordinate legislation or give directions or otherwise relates to the exercise of a power to make subordinate legislation, or give directions) (s 131(1)) |
| | | 10 May 2022 (otherwise) (s 131(4)(b)) |
| 123–128 | | 10 Mar 2022 (so far as comfers power to make subordinate legislation or give directions or otherwise relates to the exercise of a power to make subordinate legislation, or give directions) (s 131(1)) |
| | | 1 Oct 2022 (otherwise) (SI 2022/1014) |
| 129–132 | | 10 Mar 2022 (s 131(5)) |
| Sch 1 | paras 1–24 | 10 Mar 2022 (so far as comfers power to make subordinate legislation or give directions or otherwise relates to the exercise of a power to make subordinate legislation, or give directions) (s 131(1)) |
| | | 10 Mar 2022 (otherwise) (s 131(4)(a)) |
| | para 25(1), (2) | 10 Mar 2022 (so far as comfers power to make subordinate legislation or give directions or otherwise relates to the exercise of a power to make subordinate legislation, or give directions) (s 131(1)) |
| | | 10 Mar 2022 (otherwise) (s 131(4)(a)) |
| | para 25(3) | 10 Mar 2022 (so far as comfers power to make subordinate legislation or give directions or otherwise relates to the exercise of a power to make subordinate legislation, or give directions) (s 131(1)) |
| | | 10 May 2022 (otherwise) (s 131(4)(b)) |
| | para 25(4) | 10 Mar 2022 (so far as comfers power to make subordinate legislation or give directions or otherwise relates to the exercise of a power to make subordinate legislation, or give directions) (s 131(1)) |
| | | 10 Mar 2022 (otherwise) (s 131(4)(a)) |
| | paras 26–50 | 10 Mar 2022 (so far as comfers power to make subordinate legislation or give directions or otherwise relates to the exercise of a power to make subordinate legislation, or give directions) (s 131(1)) |

**Public Service Pensions and Judicial Offices Act 2022 (c 7)**—*contd*

|  |  |
|---|---|
|  | 10 Mar 2022 (otherwise) (s 131(4)(a)) |
| Sch 2 | 10 Mar 2022 (so far as comfers power to make subordinate legislation or give directions or otherwise relates to the exercise of a power to make subordinate legislation, or give directions) (s 131(1)) |
|  | 10 May 2022 (otherwise) (s 131(4)(b)) |
| Sch 3 | 1 Oct 2022 (SI 2022/1014) |
| Sch 4 | 1 Oct 2022 (SI 2022/1014)[1] |

[1]    For transitional and saving provision see SI 2022/1014, reg 3

---

**Scottish Local Government Elections (Candidacy Rights of Foreign Nationals) Act 2022 (asp 4)**

*RA:* 19 Jul 2022

*Commencement provisions:* s 3

Whole Act in force 20 2022 (s 3)

---

**Skills and Post-16 Education Act 2022 (c 22)**

*RA:* 28 Apr 2022

*Commencement provisions:* s 36; Skills and Post-16 Education Act 2022 (Commencement No 1 and Transitional Provision) (England) Regulations 2022, SI 2022/965

|  |  |
|---|---|
| 1–5 | 28 Jun 2022 (s 36(2)) |
| 6 | 30 Sep 2022 (SI 2022/965) |
| 7 | 30 Sep 2022 (SI 2022/965)[1] |
| 8–13 | 30 Sep 2022 (SI 2022/965) |
| 14–17 | *Not yet in force* |
| 18 | 28 Jun 2022 (s 36(2)) |
| 19–22 | *Not yet in force* |
| 23–34 | 28 Jun 2022 (s 36(2)) |
| 35–37 | 28 Apr 2022 (s 36(1)) |

[1]    For transitional provisions see SI 2022/965, regs 4, 5

---

**Social Security (Additional Payments) Act 2022 (c 38)**

*RA:* 28 Jun 2022

*Commencement provisions:* s 11(2)

Whole Act in force 28 Jun 2022 (s 11(2))

---

**Subsidy Control Act 2022 (c 23)**

*RA:* 28 Apr 2022

*Commencement provisions:* s 91

|  |  |
|---|---|
| 1–11 | 28 Apr 2022 (s 91(1)(a)) |
| 12–69 | 28 Apr 2022 (in respect of any power to make regulations) (s 91(1)(b)) |
|  | *Not yet in force* (otherwise) |
| 70–77 | *Not yet in force* |

**Subsidy Control Act 2022 (c 23)**—*contd*

| | |
|---|---|
| 78–83 | 28 Apr 2022 (in respect of any power to make regulations) (s 91(1)(b)) |
| | *Not yet in force* (otherwise) |
| 84–92 | 28 Apr 2022 (s 91(1)(c)) |
| Schs 1, 2 | 28 Apr 2022 (s 91(1)(a)) |
| Sch 3 | 28 Apr 2022 (in respect of any power to make regulations) (s 91(1)(b)) |
| | *Not yet in force* (otherwise) |

---

**Supply and Appropriation (Anticipation and Adjustments) Act 2022 (c 8)**

*RA:* 15 Mar 2022

Whole Act in force 15 Mar 2022 (RA)

---

**Supply and Appropriation (Anticipation and Adjustments) Act 2022 (c 39)**

*RA:* 14 Jul 2022

Whole Act in force 14 July 2022 (RA)

---

**Taxis and Private Hire Vehicles (Disabled Persons) Act 2022 (c 29)**

*RA:* 28 Apr 2022

*Commencement provisions:* s 6(2)

Whole Act in force 28 Jun 2022 (s 6(2))

---

**Taxis and Private Hire Vehicles (Safeguarding and Road Safety) Act 2022 (c 14)**

*RA:* 31 Mar 2022

*Commencement provisions:* s 9

| | | |
|---|---|---|
| 1 | | 31 Mar 2022 (s 9(2)(a)) |
| 2 | | 31 Mar 2022 (for the purpose of making regulations) (s 9(2)(b)) |
| | | *Not yet in force* (otherwise) |
| 3 | | *Not yet in force* |
| 4 | | 31 May 2022 (insofar as empowering the Secretary of State to make, vary and withdraw a designation under s 4) (s 9(3)(a)) |
| | | *Not yet in force* (otherwise) |
| 5, 6 | | 31 May 2022 (s 9(3)(b)) |
| 7 | (1)–(3) | 31 Mar 2022 (s 9(2)(c)) |
| | (4) | 31 May 2022 (s 9(3)(c)) |
| 8 | | 31 Mar 2022 (s 9(2)(d)) |

---

**Transvaginal Mesh Removal (Cost Reimbursement) (Scotland) Act 2022 (asp 1)**

*RA:* 3 Mar 2022

*Commencement provisions:* s 4

| | |
|---|---|
| 1, 2 | 3 May 2022 (s 4(2)) |
| 3–5 | 4 Mar 2022 (s 4(1)) |

---